A CONCORDANCE TO THE WORKS OF JANE AUSTEN

GARLAND REFERENCE LIBRARY
OF THE HUMANITIES
(VOL. 357)

A CONCORDANCE TO THE WORKS OF JANE AUSTEN

Peter L. De Rose
S.W. McGuire

in three volumes
VOLUME II

GARLAND PUBLISHING, INC. • NEW YORK & LONDON
1982

Library of Congress Cataloging in Publication Data

De Rose, Peter L.
A concordance to the works of Jane Austen.

(Garland reference library of the humanities, v. 357)
"Text of this concordance is based on The novels of Jane Austen, edited by R.W. Chapman (5 vols., 3rd ed., 1932–34, and vol. VI, Minor works, 1954)"—Pref.
1. Austen, Jane, 1775–1817—Concordances. I. McGuire, S.W. (Sterling W.) II. Austen, Jane, 1775–1817. Works. 3rd ed. III. Title. IV. Series.
PR4036.A24 1982 823′.7 82-48283
ISBN 0-8240-9245-7

Printed on acid-free, 250-year-life paper
Manufactured in the United States of America

CONTENTS

CONCORDANCE
M–Z, NUMBERS

M---- (1)
"Yours, affectionately. "Mary m----." P IV 6 164 7
M. (6)
"And so, you really did not dance with Tom M. at all?-- W 342 19
by William, with H. M. S. Antwerp at the bottom, in MP I 16 152 2
as second lieutenant of H. M. Sloop Thrush, being made out, MP II 13 298 3
of H. M. S. Thrush, in all his glory, in another light. MP III 6 368 8
M. and a.-- E III 7 371 34
the building in which N. takes M. for better, for worse." E III 17 463 14
M. C. (1)
happier than he goes. your's affectionately, M. C." MP II 13 303 15
M. D. (3)
For the present, adieu. M. D. SS II 7 187 38
assurance of its being otherwise." M. D. SS II 7 187 40
hair which is in your possession." M. D. SS II 7 188 42
M. GARDINER (1)
Your's, very sincerely, "M. Gardiner. PP III 10 325 2
MA (1)
something like forgiveness from Ma--from your sister." SS III 8 319 23
MA'AM (98)
"Well, ma'am, what do you say to it? NA I 9 61 6
"Yes, ma'am, I thank you; we could not have had a nicer NA I 9 68 35
"I must not tell, ma'am. SS I 12 61 22
"None at all, ma'am, I thank you." SS I 13 63 9
"No, ma'am. SS I 13 63 11
"Whom do you mean, ma'am?" said he, colouring a little. SS I 13 64 17
"I am particularly sorry, ma'am," said he, addressing Lady SS I 13 64 19
"Can you, ma'am?" said almost every body. SS I 13 66 54
I always thought it such a sweet place, ma'am! (turning to SS I 19 107 24
that instrument you know, ma'am," said Elinor, SS II 1 145 17
"I thank you, ma'am, sincerely thank you," said Marianne, SS II 3 154 5
"No, ma'am, for my mistress." SS II 5 169 18
"and have you really, ma'am, talked yourself into a SS II 7 181 9
"Indeed, ma'am," said Elinor, very seriously, "you are SS II 7 182 11
"Dear ma'am, this kindness is quite unnecessary, Marianne SS II 8 195 15
"Aye, if we can but do that, ma'am," said Elinor, "we SS II 8 197 23
"Dear ma'am," replied Elinor, smiling at the difference of SS II 8 198 28
said, "they are very pretty, ma'am--an't they?" SS II 12 235 30
31
are something in Miss Morton's style of painting, ma'am?-- SS II 12 235 31
32
"No, ma'am. SS III 1 257 4
nothing, and was heard three times to say, "yes, ma'am."-- SS III 1 265 33
"I am sorry to say, ma'am, in a most unhappy rupture:-- SS III 1 268 48
"What, indeed, ma'am! SS III 1 268 50
"Thank you, ma'am," said Elinor. SS III 4 285 2
"Certainly, ma'am, I shall tell Marianne of it; but I SS III 4 286 13
"No, ma'am, not even Lucy if you please. SS III 4 286 15
"Certainly, ma'am," replied Elinor, not hearing much of SS III 4 287 23
"No, ma'am; that was not very likely." SS III 4 291 48
"My dear ma'am," said Elinor, "what can you be thinking of? SS III 4 291 52
"I suppose you know, ma'am, that Mr. Ferrars is married." SS III 11 353 22
23
"I see Mr. Ferrars myself, ma'am, this morning in Exeter, SS III 11 354 27
and inquired after you, ma'am, and the young ladies, SS III 11 354 27
"Yes, ma'am. SS III 11 354 29
"Yes, ma'am, I just see him leaning back in it, but he did SS III 11 354 31
"No, ma'am, only they two." SS III 11 354 34
"Yes, ma'am--but not to bide long. SS III 11 354 38
"No, ma'am--the horses was just coming out, but I could SS III 11 355 42
"Yes, ma'am, she said how she was very well; and to my SS III 11 355 44
"When do you write to Colonel Brandon, ma'am?" was an SS III 12 358 5
"Yes ma'am."-- W 326 5
in her head, said "please ma'am, master wants to know why W 346 21
"Are you quite sure, ma'am?--is not there a little mistake? PP I 5 19 11
"I believe, ma'am, I may safely promise you never to dance PP I 5 20 17
away, when Elizabeth called out, "dear ma'am, do not go.-- PP I 19 104 4
5
"Yes, ma'am, all." PP II 6 165 33
But really, ma'am, I think it would be very hard upon PP II 6 165 35
"And do not you think him a very handsome gentleman, ma'am? PP III 1 247 16
"Yes, ma'am, that he was indeed: and his son will be just PP III 1 249 36
my master, ma'am, he is walking towards the little copse." PP III 7 301 4
5
"It wants improvement, ma'am, beyond any thing. MP I 6 53 4
"You were imposed on, ma'am," replied Dr. Grant; "these MP I 6 54 12
"The truth is, ma'am," said Mrs. Grant, pretending to MP I 6 54 13
exclaiming, "I must say, ma'am, that Fanny is as little MP I 7 71 35
the hot park to your house, and doing it twice, ma'am?-- MP I 7 72 47
Upon my word, ma'am, it has been a very ill-managed MP I 7 73 52
"I wish Fanny had half your strength, ma'am." MP I 7 73 54
ma'am you would be glad to give her the pleasure now?" MP I 8 78 21
"I think you have done pretty well yourself, ma'am. MP I 10 105 54
"I think, ma'am," said Mrs. Norris--her eyes directed MP I 12 117 12
"Yes, ma'am, indeed"--replied the other, with a stately MP I 12 117 13
"I dare say he did, ma'am.-- MP I 12 117 14
Dear ma'am, only look at her face at this moment;--how MP I 12 117 14
Mrs. Norris continued, "it is quite delightful, ma'am, to MP I 12 118 16
And what do you say, ma'am, to the chance of another match? MP I 12 118 16
"The couple above, ma'am. MP I 12 118 17
"It is not a settled thing, ma'am, yet.-- MP I 12 118 21
"Oh! dear, ma'am--nobody suspected you----- MP I 13 126 23
"If you cannot do without me, ma'am," said Fanny in a self- MP II 5 217 4
"Suppose you take my father's opinion, ma'am." MP II 5 217 7
"As you please, ma'am, on that head; but I meant my MP II 5 217 9
"Yes, ma'am, I should not think of any thing else." MP II 5 221 33
occasion offered,--"Ah! ma'am, how much we want dear Mrs. MP II 10 277 16
You are to deal, ma'am; shall I deal for you?" MP II 11 283 6
Thomas wishes to speak with you, ma'am, in his own room." MP III 1 324 60
"No, ma'am, it is Miss Price, I am certain of its being MP III 1 325 61
"Do you, ma'am?" cried he with quickness. MP III 3 339 20
it to make out all that chequer-work'--don't you, ma'am? E II 1 157 10
Ma'am," addressing her, "do you hear what Miss Woodhouse E II 1 158 12
"Should I send it to Mrs. Goddard's, ma'am?" asked Mrs. E II 9 235 36
"No trouble in the world, ma'am," said the obliging Mrs. E II 9 235 39
"Excuse me, ma'am, but this is by no means my intention; I E II 17 300 13
"Very well, I thank you, ma'am. E III 2 322 19
I said to my mother, 'upon my word, ma'am-----.' E III 2 322 19
"Ah! ma'am, but there may be a difficulty. E III 7 370 26
"Now, ma'am," said Jane to her aunt, "shall we join Mrs. E III 7 374 52
I am very little able--have you a chair, ma'am? E III 8 378 6
say, come ma'am, do not let us think about it any more." E III 8 382 27
"What a great traveller you must have been, ma'am!" said P III 8 70 51
"Pretty well, ma'am, in the fifteen years of my marriage; P III 8 70 52
"And I do assure you, ma'am," pursued Mrs. Croft, "that P III 8 70 54
"No, ma'am,--he did not mention no particular family; but P III 12 106 15
to do very soon, I can tell you, ma'am," said Charles. P IV 2 131 12
find any thing very agreeable in him, I assure you, ma'am. P IV 2 132 16
"Why, to be sure, ma'am," said she, "it would not prevent P IV 9 208 92
only on my inclination, ma'am, the party at home (P IV 10 224 52
53
"And so, ma'am, all these things considered," said Mrs. P IV 11 230 6
"Yes, dear ma'am," said Mrs. Croft, "or an uncertain P IV 11 231 9
"I am afraid, ma'am, that it is not perfectly understood. P IV 11 239 48
49
MAAM (1)
Maam was instantly ready to attend his new acquaintance.-- W 331 11
MACBETH (1)
Neither Hamlet, nor Macbeth, nor Othello, nor Douglas, nor MP I 14 130 3
MACHINATIONS (2)
of danger to her daughter from their machinations. NA I 2 18 2
to the high-toned machinations of the prime character, the S 8 403 1
MACHINE (1)
her spirits, & go in the Machine with her if she wished it- S 12 424 1
MACHINES (2)
is animated with bathing machines and company, the Cobb P III 11 95 9
beach, & to the bathing machines--& this was therefore the S 4 384 1
MACKENZIE (1)
I have been several times in the garden with Mackenzie, P III 5 38 34
MAD (16)
must be scrupulousness run mad, that could see any thing MP I 13 128 38
trim, I thought they were mad; but Fanny can reconcile me MP II 6 235 19
My friend Mrs. Fraser is mad for such a house, and it MP III 12 416 2
For his own sake, I would not have him do so mad a thing." E II 8 225 72
"Imprudent, if you please--but not mad. E II 8 225 73
mad, to let your niece sing herself hoarse in this manner? E II 8 229 97
not the presumption to suppose--indeed I am not so mad.-- E III 4 341 36
no flight of generosity run mad, opposing all that could E III 13 431 38
Had she refused, I should have gone mad.-- E III 14 437 8
and in how bewildered, how mad a state: and I am not much E III 14 439 8
my uncle's generosity, I am mad with joy: but when I E III 14 439 8
how little I deserve to be forgiven, I am mad with anger. E III 14 439 8
I was mad enough, however, to resent.-- E III 14 441 8
She must wait a moment, or he would think her mad. E III 18 472 21
mad idea of her recognising him so soon as she did herself. P IV 7 179 28
Activity run mad!"--had just passed through Charlotte's S 9 410 1
MADAM (72)
You may guess therefore my dear madam, with what feelings LS 3 247 1
change from you my dear madam, tho@ I think you had better LS 8 254 1
My dear madam I am very glad to find that my LS 18 272 1
I think my dear madam, you would not disapprove of her as LS 18 272 2
Adieu my dear madam, Yrs &c. Cath. Vernon. LS 20 279 12
You know his eager manner, my dear madam, when his mind is LS 23 283 3
Prepare my dear madam, for the worst. LS 24 291 17
My dear madam Your letter has surprised me beyond LS 41 309 1
hitherto been very remiss, madam, in the proper attentions NA I 3 25 2
"No trouble I assure you, madam." NA I 3 26 4
with a simpering air, "have you been long in Bath, madam?" NA I 3 26 4
Were you never here before, madam?" NA I 3 26 8
That, madam, is what I wish you to say." NA I 3 27 26
My dear madam, I am not so ignorant of young ladies' ways NA I 3 27 28
"That is exactly what I should have guessed it, madam," NA I 3 28 36
"I hope I am, madam." NA I 3 28 40
"It is very pretty, madam," said he, gravely examining it; NA I 3 28 42
"But then you know, madam, muslin always turns to some NA I 3 28 45
in these words:--"I think, madam, I cannot be mistaken; it NA I 4 31 2
"And I hope, madam, that Mr. Allen will be obliged to like NA I 8 54 6
"Very agreeable, madam." NA I 8 58 26
"Dear madam," said Catherine, "they why did not you tell NA I 13 104 35
"My dear madam," said Lady Middleton, "recollect what you SS I 13 64 13
my dear madam, I have just had the SS II 7 183 13
I am, dear madam, your most obedient humble servant, John SS II 7 183 13
will be spared, as you my dear madam will easily believe." SS II 8 195 17
'My dear madam,' I always say to her, 'you must make SS II 14 251 13
speak disrespectfully of any relation of yours, madam. SS III 1 267 44
45
said to her, 'my dear madam, I do not know what you may SS III 5 299 35
which was now searched by madam with the most ingratiating SS III 8 329 63
"You may depend upon it, madam," said Miss Bingley, with PP I 9 41 5
"I am very sensible, madam, of the hardship to my fair PP I 13 65 25
"I know very well, madam," said he, "that when persons sit PP I 16 83 50
"For heaven's sake, madam, speak lower.-- PP I 18 99 66
these words, "may I hope, madam, for your interest with PP I 19 104 1
2
"Pardon me for interrupting you, madam," cried Mr. Collins; PP I 20 110 4
"My dear madam," replied he, "let us be for ever silent on PP I 20 114 32
to your family, my dear madam, by thus withdrawing my PP I 20 114 32
"My dear madam," he replied, "this invitation is PP I 22 123 5
"We are speaking of music, madam," said he, when no longer PP II 8 173 5
"I assure you, madam," he replied, "that she does not need PP II 8 173 9
"You have said quite enough, madam. PP II 11 193 29
"Be not alarmed, madam, on receiving this letter, by the PP II 12 196 4
This, madam, is a faithful narrative of every event in PP II 12 202 5
"You are all kindness, madam; but I believe we must abide PP II 14 211 11
"I beg your pardon, madam, for interrupting you, but I was PP III 7 301 1
"Dear madam," cried Mrs. Hill, in great astonishment, " PP III 7 301 3
"This is the consequence you see, madam, of marrying a PP III 11 330 11
"Yes, madam," said Mrs. Bennet, delighted to speak to a PP III 14 352 8
"Indeed, you are mistaken, madam. PP III 14 353 25
"The tree thrives well beyond a doubt, madam," replied Dr. MP I 6 54 10
"You are very kind, you are all kindness, my dear madam," MP I 8 76 5
"You can have no reason I imagine madam," said he, MP I 8 78 18
"I am convinced, madam," said Edmund, preventing Fanny, " MP I 15 141 17
do sincerely give you joy, madam, as well as Mrs. Norris, MP I 15 143 26
"Do not urge her, madam," said Edmund. MP I 15 146 54
began, 'my dear madam,' but I forget how it went on; and E I 11 96 24
"Never, madam," cried he, affronted, in his turn: never, I E I 15 131 35
No, madam, my visits to Hartfield have been for yourself E I 15 132 35
36
I have the pleasure, madam, (to Mrs. Bates,) of restoring E II 10 242 15
a very good grace, immediately exclaimed, "my dear madam! E II 18 307 24
25
"Ah! madam," cried Emma, "if other children are at all E III 8 382 24
Do not imagine, madam,' she continued, 'that I was taught E III 12 419 8
To Mrs. Weston. Windsor-July. My dear Madam, "If I E III 14 436 8
I have the honour, my dear madam, of being your husband's E III 14 437 8
my dear madam, is much beyond my power of doing justice to. E III 14 439 8
Here, my dear madam, I was obliged to leave off abruptly, E III 14 440 8
In short, my dear madam, it was a quarrel blameless on her E III 14 441 8
Now my dear madam, I will release you; but I could not E III 14 443 8
"I beg your pardon, madam, this is your seat;" and though P III 8 72 58
59
to hear her father say, "my dear madam, this must not be. P IV 4 145 1
"My dear madam, they can only raise the price of S 6 392 1
MADAME DE GENLIS' (1)
D'Ostalis, in Madame de Genlis' Adelaide and Theodore, and E III 17 461 2
MADDEN (1)
Oh! there is pathos to madden one!-- S 7 397 1
MADDISON (2)
I am not satisfied about Maddison.-- MP III 11 411 20
Maddison is a clever fellow; I do not wish to displace him- MP III 11 412 20
MADE (906)
I long to be made known to your dear little children, in LS 1 243 1
I have made him sensible of my power, & can now enjoy the LS 10 257 1
me; but having once made him doubt the justice of her LS 10 257 1
& serious conversation, & made him I may venture to say at LS 10 258 2
he accused her of having made Mr Manwaring & a young man LS 11 259 1
that no objection can be made to either, I can promise you LS 12 261 3
with all my heart that my father is made easy by it. LS 15 266 1
credit what Lady Susan has made him & wants to make me LS 17 271 7
Sir James talked a good deal, & made many civil excuses to LS 20 276 3
that some attempts were made to prejudice you against me. LS 20 277 6
7
I could have poisoned him; I made the best of it however, LS 22 280 1
I made a point also of Frederica's behaving civilly to Sir LS 22 280 1
gallant to me, very soon made the whole party understand LS 22 280 2
Do not let Frederica vernon be made unhappy by that Martin. LS 23 284 4
I know that Frederica is made wretched by Sir James' LS 23 284 4
My dear mother, every hope which but two hours ago made me LS 24 285 1
The quarrel between Lady Susan & Reginald is made up, & we LS 24 285 1
Depend upon it that you shall not be made unhappy any LS 24 287 7
I made no remarks however, for words would have been in LS 24 287 10
ever, tho' so innocently, made her unhappy on that score. LS 24 290 13
swallowed my dinner when Manwaring made his appearance. LS 29 299 2

perverted abilities had made me resolve to disallow, have LS 36 305 1
as it made the poor girl, it was impossible to detain her. LS 41 310 3
say all this, & I hope made her a little more comfortable. LS 41 310 4
Her anxiety on the subject made her press for an early LS 42 311 2
affection as made her almost turn from her with horror. LS 42 311 2
Catherine too made some purchases herself, and when all NA I 2 20 8
her protegee, Mrs. Allen made her way through the throng NA I 2 21 9
They made their appearance in the Lower Rooms; and here NA I 3 25 2
which her keen eye soon made, that the lace on Mrs. NA I 4 32 2
was--"my dearest creature, what can have made you so late? NA I 6 39 2
together; and I have made out a list of ten or twelve more NA I 6 40 8
you ever see an animal so made for speed in your life?" NA I 7 46 9
flattered her once, made her way to Mrs. Allen and Mrs. NA I 8 58 25
And what a dust you would have made, if I had not come." NA I 9 61 5
her companion immediately made the matter perfectly simple NA I 9 62 10
plain which he had before made ambiguous; and, joining to NA I 9 66 31
you would have made some droll remark or other about it." NA I 10 71 3
"Indeed you do me injustice; I would not have made so NA I 10 71 6
not an observation was made, nor an expression used by NA I 10 72 8
either which had not been made and used some thousands of NA I 10 72 8
many ladies, could they be made to understand how little NA I 10 74 22
of them in terms which made her all eagerness to know them NA I 10 80 61
Ten minutes more made it certain that a bright afternoon NA I 11 83 16
encouraged his horse, made odd noises, and drove on; and NA I 11 87 53
them, made his friend pull up, to know what was the matter. NA I 11 88 54
Allen's wavering convictions only made it more doubtful. NA I 12 91 3
To Milsom-Street she was directed; and having made herself NA I 12 91 3
to have it put off, made a point of her being denied. NA I 12 94 10
me; and, if I had not made one of the cleanest strokes NA I 12 96 20
that perhaps ever was made in this world-----I took his NA I 12 96 20
she drew away her arm, and Isabella made no opposition. NA I 13 100 13
I have been to Miss Tilney, and made your excuses." NA I 13 100 13
a promise voluntarily made only five minutes before, and NA I 13 101 25
declarations immediately made every look and sentence as NA I 13 102 26
to her mind, and made her think with pleasure that he NA I 13 102 27
her engagement, though it was made with the hero himself. NA I 14 106 1
breaking the promise I had made of reading it aloud, and NA I 14 107 9
by whomsoever it may be made--and probably with much NA I 14 109 23
"And now, Henry," said Miss Tilney, "that you have made us NA I 14 113 40
No difficulty was made on Mrs. Allen's side--and the only NA I 14 114 49
Maria" must immediately be made sharers in their felicity; NA I 15 121 27
resigned, or funded money made over, was a matter in which NA I 15 122 28
He made no answer; but after a minute's silence burst out NA I 15 122 30
their brother's engagement, made her expect to raise no NA I 15 124 48
the family to be very high, and this made it certain. NA II 1 129 1
Tilney, made but a small part of Catherine's speculation. NA II 2 138 1
castles and abbies made usually the charm of those NA II 2 141 11
He says so in this letter, says that he as good as made NA II 3 144 10
His first address made Catherine start. NA II 3 147 21
When Catherine knew this, her resolution was directly made. NA II 4 150 1
He made no reply, and was beginning to talk of something NA II 4 150 4
and cheerfulness had made her a valuable companion, and in NA II 5 154 1
on a breakfast-table--made it impossible for her to forget NA II 5 154 2
impatience at the waiters, made Catherine grow every NA II 5 156 4
men's open carriages, made her blush at the mention of NA II 5 156 5
A sudden scud of rain driving full in her face, made it NA II 5 161 25
The sight of it made her start; and, forgetting every NA II 6 163 1
2
at the door of the room made her, starting, quit her hold, NA II 6 164 3
The dimness of the light her candle emitted made her turn NA II 6 169 12
Till she had made herself mistress of its contents, NA II 6 170 12
His cruelty to such a charming woman made him odious to NA II 7 181 40
seeming length of which made her peculiarly sensible of NA II 8 187 15
by such appearances as made their dismissal impossible. NA II 8 188 18
would be more satisfactory if made without any companion. NA II 9 192 5
she could hardly tell where, made her pause and tremble. NA II 9 194 6
dread of further questions made her, for the first time in NA II 9 195 19
But now--in short, she made herself as miserable as NA II 10 199 1
Her mind made up on these several points, and her NA II 10 201 4
in performing it! this made it so particularly strange! NA II 10 201 5
She has made me miserable for ever! NA II 10 202 7
Tilney, whenever he made his application, would give his NA II 11 208 2
You must know it to be so; and the General made such a NA II 11 211 13
master of the house, and made unusually tidy on the NA II 11 213 21
before at the concert, but made wretched work of it--it NA II 12 217 2
On Henry's arrival from Woodston, she made known to him NA II 12 218 4
"And only made believe to do so for mischief's sake?" NA II 12 219 10
But, suppose he had made her very much in love with him?" NA II 12 219 12
unpardonably guilty, while Henry made himself so agreeable. NA II 12 219 16
at their own command, made her thoroughly sensible of the NA II 13 220 1
Such ease and such delights made her love the place and NA II 13 220 1
moving close to her door made her start; it seemed as if NA II 13 222 9
Eleanor made no answer; and Catherine's thoughts recurring NA II 13 224 17
made her for a short time sensible only of resentment. NA II 13 228 27
with quivering lips just made it intelligible that she NA II 13 229 31
It was there, it was on that day that the General had made NA II 14 230 2
as the letter was finished; "soon made and soon ended.-- NA II 14 236 15
her complaisance, and made her reply less rational; for NA II 14 237 20
good enough to be immediately made use of again by herself. NA II 14 237 22
cheek and brightened eye made her mother trust that this NA II 15 242 8
than his vanity and avarice had made him believe them. NA II 15 244 12
Her intimacy there had made him seriously determine on her NA II 15 245 12
their own hearts made them trust that it could not be very NA II 16 249 2
as Northanger had been made by Henry's banishment, to the NA II 16 250 5
to Northanger, and thence made him the bearer of his NA II 16 252 7
woman, he might have been made still more respectable than SS I 1 5 7
might even have been made amiable himself; for he was very SS I 1 5 7
warmed his heart and made him feel capable of generosity.-- SS I 1 5 8
could, by any alteration, be made comfortable to her. SS I 4 23 20
beyond her wishes, she made no attempt to dissuade her SS I 4 24 21
her daughter-in-law had made her resolve on remaining at SS I 5 25 3
In the mean time, till all these alterations could be made SS I 6 29 5
The friendliness of his disposition made him happy in SS I 7 33 3
and made them wish to be better acquainted with it. SS I 9 40 2
day gave greater kindness, made such an excuse unnecessary SS I 10 48 7
"He would have told me so, I doubt not, had I made any SS I 10 51 22
parties on the water were made and accomplished as often SS I 11 53 1
Such conduct made them of course most exceedingly laughed SS I 11 54 3
This of course made every body laugh; and Elinor tried to SS I 12 61 16
had been, she had actually made her own woman enquire of SS I 13 67 65
As this silence continued, every day made it appear more SS I 14 71 3
which has made every thing belonging to you so dear to me." SS I 14 74 19
that a promise had been made by Willoughby the night SS I 15 75 1
And is no allowance to be made for inadvertence, or for SS I 15 78 28
which ought to be made for him, and it is my wish to be SS I 15 79 29
But the feelings which made such composure a disgrace, SS I 16 83 1
last to whom the affair is made known, when circumstances SS I 16 84 9
Edward made no answer. SS I 17 95 50
friends, have made me what I am, an idle, helpless being. SS I 19 102 4
chambers in the temple, made a very good appearance in the SS I 19 102 4
to Mrs. Dashwood,) but you have made it so charming! SS I 19 107 24
Mr. Palmer made her no answer, and did not even raise his SS I 19 107 25
quite so fast, nor made such a long journey of it, for SS I 19 107 29
He made her no answer; and only observed, after again SS I 19 108 39
He then made his bow and departed with the rest. SS I 19 108 39
Her love made no answer; and after slightly bowing to the SS I 20 110 7
of Sir John's proposal to your mother before it was made? SS I 20 117 63
Their being her relations too made it so much the worse; SS I 21 118 2
which this politeness made on it, was spent in admiration SS I 21 120 6
years old, who had not made a noise for the last two SS I 21 121 9
generally made an amendment to all her sister's assertions. SS I 21 126 40
conduct towards others, made every shew of attention and SS I 22 127 2

Elinor made her a civil reply, and they walked on for a SS I 21 128 8
was the matter; but it made him so melancholy, not being SS I 22 134 52
its dupe, for a short time made her feel only for herself; SS II 1 139 1
His imprudence had made her miserable for a while; but it SS II 1 140 1
No one made any objection but Marianne, who, with her SS II 1 144 15
heaven that she had never made so rude a speech. SS II 1 145 16
Lucy made room for her with ready attention, and the two SS II 1 145 23
in your manner, that made me quite uncomfortable. SS II 2 146 5
and if she were to be made less happy, less comfortable by SS II 3 154 5
be with Willoughby again, made no further direct SS II 3 154 6
so happy in their lives as this intelligence made them. SS II 3 157 19
him every hour of the day, made her unfit for anything. SS II 5 169 15
He made no reply; his complexion changed and all his SS II 6 177 11
continual change of place, made her wander about the house SS II 7 180 5
a sickness at heart as made her hardly able to hold up her SS II 7 181 7
such a general tremour as made her fear it impossible to SS II 7 181 7
procured for her directly, made her more comfortable, and SS II 7 185 16
17
on your side, would have made the blow more dreadful." SS II 7 186 29
almost ridiculous, made her those acknowledgments, and SS II 8 193 7
choose for herself; and a pretty choice she has made!-- SS II 8 195 14
I made sure of its being nothing but a common love letter, SS II 8 195 16
He made no answer; and soon afterwards, by the removal of SS II 8 200 43
it had been made over some months before to another person. SS II 9 207 26
relief of one, whom he had made poor and miserable; but SS II 9 209 30
On the contrary, every friend must be made still more her SS II 9 210 32
and submissive attention, made neither objection nor SS II 10 212 1
yew arbour, would all be made over to her; and Mrs. SS II 10 216 15
She received the news with resolute composure; made no SS II 10 217 17
My cousins say they are sure I have made a conquest; but SS II 10 218 26
would not, and Miss Steele was made completely happy. SS II 10 218 29
And then I have made a little purchase within this half SS II 11 225 31
had their assiduities made them to her, that though Lucy SS II 12 230 8
Elinor could not now be made unhappy by this behaviour.- SS II 12 232 16
seemed purposely made to humble her more, only amused her. SS II 12 232 16
If she had only made me a formal curtsey, for instance, SS II 13 240 17
Their hours were therefore made over to Lady Middleton and SS II 14 246 2
An effort even yet lighter might have made her their SS II 14 247 4
One thing did disturb her; and of that she made her daily SS II 14 247 5
affecting to be so, she made no scruple of turning away SS II 14 250 11
nor too speedily made use of; and the visit to Lady SS II 14 254 26
of Lady Middleton, and made an entry into the close heart SS II 14 254 27
of them a needle book, made by some emigrant; called Lucy SS II 14 254 28
valued is so easily to be made up by something else, your SS III 1 263 28
"Oh! Elinor," she cried, "you have made me hate myself for SS III 1 264 31
Such advances towards heroism in her sister, made Elinor SS III 1 265 33
room; and as her vehemence made reserve impossible in SS III 1 269 58
Look, she made me this bow to my hat, and put in the SS III 2 272 12
together, she never made any bones of hiding in a closet, SS III 2 274 20
the approach of her own party made another more necessary. SS III 2 275 24
She had not thought her old friend could have made so SS III 3 282 15
made very light of, at least as far as regarded its size. SS III 3 283 20
that, when a man has once made up his mind to such a thing, SS III 4 285 5
The particular circumstances between them made a SS III 4 287 24
made her feel particularly uncomfortable for some minutes. SS III 4 288 26
to be on the safe side, he made his apology in form as SS III 4 288 26
"The unkindness of your own relations has made you SS III 4 289 33
Edward made no answer; but when she had turned away her SS III 4 290 39
him that he has made me a very--an exceedingly happy man." SS III 4 290 42
Elinor made what excuse she could for her. SS III 5 294 7
him off for ever, and has made all those over whom she had SS III 5 296 19
and elegance, which made her often deficient in the forms SS III 6 304 13
a kindness of heart which made Elinor really love her, SS III 7 308 3
for this unlucky illness, made every ailment more severe; SS III 7 308 4
sat up to have her bed made; and carefully administering SS III 7 310 9
Elinor made no resistance that was not easily overcome. SS III 7 311 15
of a collected mind, made every necessary arrangement with SS III 7 312 17
His opinion, however, made some little amends for his SS III 7 312 19
and in spite of herself made her think him sincere. SS III 8 319 25
But this note made me know myself better. SS III 8 326 53
the young lady was, and made her more jealous than ever. SS III 8 328 61
She read what made her wretched. SS III 8 328 61
You have made your own choice. SS III 8 329 64
inflicted--I hardly know what could have made it worse." SS III 8 330 66
My resolution was soon made, and at eight o'clock this SS III 8 331 69
Elinor made no answer. SS III 8 331 70
and luxury, had made in the mind, the character, the SS III 8 331 70
The world had made him extravagant and vain----- SS III 8 331 70
Extravagance and vanity had made him cold-hearted and SS III 8 331 70
produced by them, which made her think of him as now SS III 9 333 2
made her only fearful of betraying herself to her sister. SS III 9 333 3
to irresistible feelings, made me acquainted with his SS III 9 336 12
however, you have not yet made him equally sanguine." SS III 9 338 19
whose active good-nature made her friendly and hospitable SS III 10 341 4
But the resolution was made only to be broken. SS III 10 344 10
My illness has made me think----- SS III 10 345 28
No--my Marianne has not a heart to be made happy with such SS III 11 350 7
on his heart, and made him regret the connection which had SS III 11 351 9
It was selfishness which first made him sport with your SS III 11 351 11
when his own were engaged, made him delay the confession SS III 11 351 11
It has not made him happy. SS III 11 351 13
So, I made free to wish her joy." SS III 11 354 29
of such agitation as made her hardly know where she was. SS III 12 360 24
other claims might be made on him, it was impossible that SS III 13 363 9
made, till it has been made at least twenty times over. SS III 13 364 9
knowledge of each party made it appear to her in every SS III 13 364 10
substance made me any amends for the defect of the style." SS III 13 365 17
fond of each other, made that mutual regard inevitable and SS III 13 370 36
few days before would have made every nerve in Elinor's SS III 13 370 37
the smallest objection was made against Edward's taking SS III 14 374 4
that befell her, and made her his secret standard of SS III 14 379 19
me over, as soon as I had made tea for him; & I should be W 319 2
Emma for a moment made no answer--at last she said--"I W 319 2
Elizabeth, you had not made a point of my going to this W 319 2
made farther conversation most thoroughly undesirable.-- W 321 2
to her own family, had made her more open to disagreeable W 322 3
Among the increasing numbers of military men, one now made W 328 8
which made her think her brother Sam's a hopeless case.-- W 328 8
height--well made & plump, with an air of healthy vigour.-- W 328 9
to open a door which was never shut, made their appearance. W 329 9
observe that they had made a point of coming early for the W 329 9
had done, so happy had it made both the boy & his mother; W 331 11
Emma curtsied, the gentleman bowed--made a hasty request W 333 13
expressing himself, which made them all worth hearing, & W 335 13
the words themselves which made his Lordship think;--and W 346 21
An absence of 14 years had made all her brothers & sisters W 348 23
she had heard things which made her dread her return; & W 348 23
A pretty peice of work your Aunt Turner has made of it!-- W 351 26
good to me; & if she has made an imprudent choice, she W 352 26
Tom made no reply.-- W 357 28
& few situations made him appear to greater advantage. W 359 28
would willingly have made a confidante of Emma when they W 360 29
in the words, made some very inapplicable reply, & jumping W 360 29
dinner, preparations were made for his entertainment much W 360 30
could produce, made her thankfully turn to a book.-- W 361 31
Mr. Bennet made no answer. PP I 1 3 6
Mr. Bingley had soon made himself acquainted with all the PP I 3 10 6
Mr. Bingley intended it likewise, and sometimes made PP I 4 15 12
in Meryton, where he had made a tolerable fortune and PP I 5 18 1
his presentation at St. James's had made him courteous. PP I 5 18 1
But no sooner had he made it clear to himself and his PP I 6 23 12
he was only the man who made himself agreeable no where, PP I 6 23 12

Context	Work	Vol	Ch	Page	Line
Catherine was disconcerted, and made no answer; but Lydia,	PP	I	7	29	7
To this speech Bingley made no answer; but his sisters	PP	I	8	37	20
Darcy only smiled; and the general pause which ensued made	PP	I	9	45	35
He made no answer.	PP	I	10	47	4
She smiled, but made no answer.	PP	I	10	52	49
I have therefore made up my mind to tell you, that I do	PP	I	10	52	50
in her manner which made it difficult for her to affront	PP	I	10	52	52
Mr. Hurst also made her a slight bow, and said he was "	PP	I	11	54	2
No one made any reply.	PP	I	11	55	5
has made white soup enough I shall send round my cards."	PP	I	11	55	7
conversation instead of dancing made the order of the day."	PP	I	11	55	8
Miss Bingley made no answer; and soon afterwards got up	PP	I	11	56	10
"No"--said Darcy, "I have made no such pretension.	PP	I	11	58	28
Her sister made not the smallest objection, and the piano	PP	I	11	58	34
that morning should be mentioned, and the request made.	PP	I	12	59	1
My mind however is now made up on the subject, for having	PP	I	13	62	12
any other gentleman; she made not the smallest objection	PP	I	14	66	1
his rights as a rector, made him altogether a mixture of	PP	I	15	70	1
The next morning, however, made an alteration; for in a	PP	I	15	70	3
Philips's house, and then made their bows, in spite of	PP	I	15	73	10
As no objection was made to the young people's engagement	PP	I	16	75	1
of a rainy season, made her feel that the commonest,	PP	I	16	76	4
intended for, but circumstances have now made it eligible.	PP	I	16	79	23
pride of this Mr. Darcy has not made him just to you!--	PP	I	16	81	38
The usual inquiries as to his success were made by the	PP	I	16	83	49
This information made Elizabeth smile, as she thought of	PP	I	16	83	56
on Tuesday, could have made such a Friday, Saturday,	PP	I	17	88	15
Elizabeth made no answer, and took her place in the set,	PP	I	18	90	8
him to talk, she made some slight observation on the dance.	PP	I	18	91	8
He made no answer, and they were again silent till they	PP	I	18	93	18
Darcy made no answer, and seemed desirous of changing the	PP	I	18	92	22
interruption has made me forget what we were talking of."	PP	I	18	93	24
					25
I am most thankful that the discovery is made in time for	PP	I	18	97	57
of it he only made him a slight bow, and moved another way.	PP	I	18	98	61
gave birth to, made her perhaps almost as happy as Jane.	PP	I	18	98	63
To Elizabeth it appeared, that had her family made an	PP	I	18	101	72
Mr. Collins made his declaration in form.	PP	I	19	104	1
away with by his feelings, made Elizabeth so near laughing	PP	I	19	105	9
					10
"You forget that I have made no answer.	PP	I	19	106	12
that another offer of marriage may ever be made you.	PP	I	19	108	19
I understand that Mr. Collins has made you an offer of	PP	I	20	111	15
Mr. Collins has made an offer to Lizzy, and she will not	PP	I	20	112	25
Mr. Collins's present circumstances made it a most	PP	I	22	122	3
Her disappointment in Charlotte made her turn with fonder	PP	I	23	128	9
resolution which now made him the slave of his designing	PP	II	1	133	3
He made her an offer in this very room, and she refused	PP	II	2	140	4
correspondence with her, made her sister a slight answer,	PP	II	2	140	5
of the officers always made part of it, of which officers	PP	II	2	142	18
On being made acquainted with the present Mr. Darcy's	PP	II	2	143	20
had no pleasure in it; she made a slight, formal, apology,	PP	II	3	148	26
her grandfather's death made her mistress of this fortune."	PP	II	4	153	12
sake, she made more favourable than it really was.	PP	II	6	166	42
ashamed of his aunt's ill breeding, and made no answer.	PP	II	8	173	11
were made, seemed in danger of sinking into total silence.	PP	II	9	177	3
Elizabeth made no answer.	PP	II	9	178	11
have accepted him, or have made him happy if they had.	PP	II	9	178	15
Elizabeth made no answer, and walked on, her heart	PP	II	10	185	33
Colonel Fitzwilliam had made it clear that he had no	PP	II	11	188	2
"you could not have made me the offer of your hand in any	PP	II	11	192	25
					26
the objections which had made him prevent his friend's	PP	II	11	193	31
Lady Catherine's carriage made her feel how unequal she	PP	II	11	194	32
The five weeks which she had now passed in Kent, had made	PP	II	12	195	2
with you, I was first made acquainted, by Sir William	PP	II	12	197	5
made her too angry to have any wish of doing him justice.	PP	II	13	204	1
have made a stronger impression on his mind than on hers.	PP	II	13	209	10
of her long absence, made her at length return home; and	PP	II	13	209	12
made a point of her having two men servants go with her.--	PP	II	14	211	13
Elizabeth made no objection;--the door was then allowed to	PP	II	15	217	10
And that made the men suspect something, and then they	PP	II	16	221	17
sisterly partiality which made any admiration of Elizabeth	PP	II	17	224	2
To have his errors made public might ruin him for ever.	PP	II	17	227	24
comfort from any such expectation, she made no answer.	PP	II	17	228	30
flirt that ever made herself and her family ridiculous.	PP	II	18	231	18
There was a something in her countenance which made him	PP	II	18	234	35
					36
of her mother and Kitty made inevitable; and could she	PP	II	19	237	3
beautiful ornaments as made her quite wild; that she had a	PP	II	19	238	5
much too full of lines under the words to be made public.	PP	II	19	238	5
The introduction, however, was immediately made; and as	PP	III	1	255	59
his resentment had not made him think really ill of her.	PP	III	1	256	64
surprise in her uncle and aunt, as made every thing worse.	PP	III	2	260	2
and a positive engagement made of his meeting some of the	PP	III	2	266	18
the more necessary to be made, but perhaps not the more	PP	III	3	268	8
for jealousy had not yet made her desperate, and her	PP	III	3	269	8
Her pale face and impetuous manner made him start, and	PP	III	4	276	6
so breathless an accent as made her almost unintelligible,	PP	III	4	276	8
Darcy made no answer.	PP	III	4	278	19
and try if any thing could be made out from them.	PP	III	5	293	69
in the habit of saying; made no mention of the business	PP	III	6	299	18
Mr. Bennet made no answer, and each of them, deep in	PP	III	7	304	33
to fulfil the engagements that had been made for him.	PP	III	8	309	4
would be so short; and she made the most of the time, by	PP	III	9	318	18
The loss of her daughter made Mrs. Bennet very dull for	PP	III	11	330	9
degree of civility, which made her two daughters ashamed,	PP	III	11	335	41
Bingley replied that he did, and made his congratulations.	PP	III	11	336	50
Her mother's ungraciousness, made the sense of what they	PP	III	12	340	13
and dull to a degree, that almost made her uncivil.	PP	III	12	341	14
Elizabeth made no attempt to reason with her mother, but	PP	III	13	345	17
to her face, as made her look handsomer than ever.	PP	III	13	348	34
"He has made me so happy," said she, one evening, "by	PP	III	13	349	45
"He made a little mistake to be sure; but it is to the	PP	III	13	350	50
than usually ungracious, made no other reply to	PP	III	14	351	3
entrance, though no request of introduction had been made.	PP	III	14	351	3
Has he, has my nephew, made you an offer of marriage?"	PP	III	14	354	34
of infatuation, have made him forget what he owes to	PP	III	14	354	36
Elizabeth made no answer; and without attempting to	PP	III	14	358	74
made every body eager for another, to supply the idea.	PP	III	15	360	1
was to him, made his affection every moment more valuable.	PP	III	16	366	8
to London," said he "I made a confession to him, which I	PP	III	16	370	40
to him, which I believe I ought to have made long ago.	PP	III	16	370	40
made her here; and I was convinced of her affection."	PP	III	16	371	43
a case, but his reliance on mine, made every thing easy.	PP	III	16	371	45
feelings had made her equally avoid the name of his friend.	PP	III	17	374	19
but he was going to be made unhappy, and that it should be	PP	III	17	375	28
And so, Darcy did every thing; made up the match, gave the	PP	III	17	377	39
she followed her, and made the important communication.	PP	III	17	377	42
when you had once made a beginning; but what could set you	PP	III	18	380	1
what made you so unwilling to come to the point at last.	PP	III	18	381	7
What made you so shy of me, when you first called, and	PP	III	18	381	7
to make the confession to him which I have since made."	PP	III	18	382	16
Nor was her respect for him, though it made her more quiet,	PP	III	18	384	27
She could hardly have made a more untoward choice.	MP	I	1	3	1
to supply their wants, made her eager to regain the	MP	I	1	4	2
Sir Thomas no longer made any objection, and a more	MP	I	1	8	9
Poor Mr. Norris's indifferent state of health made it an	MP	I	1	9	10
Lady Bertram made no opposition.	MP	I	1	10	13
distinction proper to be made between the girls as they	MP	I	1	10	17
which had at first made grievous inroads on the	MP	I	2	17	21
he made her some very pretty presents, and laughed at her.	MP	I	2	17	22
of his profession, as made her gradually admit that the	MP	I	2	21	34
leaving Eton for Oxford made no change in his kind	MP	I	2	21	34
corrected her judgment; he made reading useful by talking	MP	I	2	22	35
this circumstance had made the arrangement somewhat easier	MP	I	3	23	2
2dly, that his father had made a most tiresome piece of	MP	I	3	24	4
for a friend, of which she made a very particular point;--	MP	I	3	28	38
on being the first person made acquainted with any fatal	MP	I	4	34	2
both being alive and well, made it necessary to lay by her	MP	I	4	34	2
and the charge was made over to her sister, who desired	MP	I	4	35	5
made up his mind, the whole business was soon completed.	MP	I	4	37	8
and no other attempt made at secrecy, than Mrs. Norris's	MP	I	4	39	12
with pretty furniture, and made a choice collection of	MP	I	4	41	15
more be made to his person than to his situation in life.	MP	I	4	42	18
good, and he was so well made, that one soon forgot he was	MP	I	5	44	2
Miss Bertram's engagement made him in equity the property	MP	I	5	44	2
temper which ought to have made him judge and feel better,	MP	I	5	45	3
Her choice is made."	MP	I	5	45	11
thing which Miss Crawford's habits made her likely to feel.	MP	I	5	47	27
races, and schemes were made for a large party to them,	MP	I	5	48	29
I made my bow in form, and as Mrs. Sneyd was surrounded by	MP	I	5	51	40
side all the way home, and made myself as agreeable as I	MP	I	5	51	40
I would have every thing done in the best style, and made	MP	I	6	53	9
We did a vast deal in that way at the parsonage; we made	MP	I	6	54	9
you what improvements we made; and a great deal more would	MP	I	6	54	9
on the garden wall, and made the plantation to shut out	MP	I	6	54	9
a stream, which, I dare say, might be made a good deal of.	MP	I	6	56	26
in the world, has made me consider improvements in hand as	MP	I	6	57	31
"I was astonished to find what a piece of work was made of	MP	I	6	58	37
of my own, could have made me so remiss; but now I could	MP	I	6	62	58
Lady Bertram made no objection, and every one concerned in	MP	I	6	62	59
She made me almost laugh; but I cannot rate so very highly	MP	I	7	64	10
Miss Crawford made her first essay with great credit to	MP	I	7	66	15
rather small, strongly made, she seemed formed for a	MP	I	7	66	15
At first Miss Crawford and her companion made the circuit	MP	I	7	67	16
feelings created, made it easier to swallow than to speak.	MP	I	7	74	57
occasioned, made her hardly know how to support herself.	MP	I	7	74	59
losses both of health and pleasure would be soon made good.	MP	I	8	75	1
placid manner of refusal made Mrs. Rushworth still think	MP	I	8	76	2
successful; and Edmund made his appearance just in time to	MP	I	8	77	7
Why is not use to be made of my mother's chaise?	MP	I	8	77	9
family were not to be made in the carriage of the family."	MP	I	8	77	9
Mr. Rushworth has made it since he succeeded to the estate.	MP	I	8	82	34
Bertram's feelings, and made it a point of honour to	MP	I	8	82	35
No objection was made, but for some time there seemed no	MP	I	9	90	36
up to practise as a duty, made it impossible for her to	MP	I	9	91	36
part of her education, made her miserable under it.	MP	I	9	91	36
Fanny made the first interruption by saying, "I wonder	MP	I	9	94	57
for the first time, made him a little forgetful of Fanny.	MP	I	9	94	59
exit; and though she made the best of the story, he was	MP	I	10	101	33
"If I made any difficulty about fetching the key, there	MP	I	10	102	45
with whom she had made a most satisfactory acquaintance,	MP	I	10	103	50
from the housekeeper, and made abundance of civil speeches	MP	I	10	104	52
Miss Bertram had made up her mind to something different,	MP	I	10	105	52
preferring an income ready made, to the trouble of working	MP	I	11	110	23
It is a great defect of temper, made worse by a very	MP	I	11	111	29
think more would have been made unhappy by him as a sailor	MP	I	11	111	30
his own will to consult, made it perfectly clear that he	MP	I	12	114	2
both on their guard, and made even Julia admit in her	MP	I	12	114	3
made some important communications to her usual confidant.	MP	I	12	115	5
a man, before he has quite made up his own mind, will	MP	I	12	116	10
to be close at his elbow, made so instantaneous a change	MP	I	12	119	22
each other as they may be made to do in five minutes, by	MP	I	13	125	14
difficulties, and having made the necessity of an	MP	I	14	130	1
The first use she made of her solitude was to take up the	MP	I	14	137	23
direct him, but upon being made to understand the	MP	I	15	138	1
so forth, which will be made, of course, I can see nothing	MP	I	15	140	12
table, while his sister made her way to Lady Bertram, and	MP	I	15	143	26
Every allowance will be made for you.	MP	I	15	146	52
proof of affection which made her tears delightful--and	MP	I	16	152	2
three transparencies, made in a rage for transparencies,	MP	I	16	152	2
unsteadiness; and his happiness under it made her wretched.	MP	I	17	159	6
Julia made no communication, and Fanny took no liberties.	MP	I	17	163	20
little short of a declaration of love be made by the lady.	MP	I	18	167	12
mind; and about noon she made her escape with her work to	MP	I	18	168	14
up from the parsonage, made no change in her wish of	MP	I	18	168	14
My dear Miss Price, I beg your pardon, but I have made my	MP	I	18	168	15
There--very good school-room chairs, not made for a	MP	I	18	169	21
Her pleasant manners and cheerful conformity made her	MP	I	18	171	28
Julia's looks were an evidence of the fact that made it	MP	II	1	175	1
altogether was such as made her reproach herself for	MP	II	1	178	7
after such a separation, made him communicative and chatty	MP	II	1	178	8
deal of carpet work and made many yards of fringe; and she	MP	II	1	179	9
so blind an interest as made him not only totally	MP	II	1	184	27
"If I had not been active," said she, "and made a point of	MP	II	2	188	3
coachman's sponges, and made five of the under-servants	MP	II	2	190	9
the same table, which made Mr. Yates think it wiser to let	MP	II	2	191	10
for the last time, he had made his parting bow, and she	MP	II	2	193	18
Sir Thomas's return made a striking change in the ways of	MP	II	3	196	1
Anybody but myself would have made something more of it,	MP	II	3	197	8
delight--for she had made the match--she had done every	MP	II	3	203	30
Their departure made another material change at Mansfield,	MP	II	3	204	33
of Edmund, such a memento made her particularly awake to	MP	II	4	207	10
Such a match as Miss Bertram has made is a public blessing,	MP	II	4	210	21
Crawford's side as she made some laughing answer, was	MP	II	4	214	46
Park, striking three, made her feel that she had really	MP	II	4	214	46
of astonishment which made it impossible for her to speak.	MP	II	5	221	35
With a significant smile, which made Fanny quite hate him,	MP	II	5	224	49
Henry Crawford had quite made up his mind by the next	MP	II	6	229	1
It was but the day before, that Crawford had made himself	MP	II	6	232	13
temper, made it as natural for him to express as to feel.	MP	II	6	234	17
of exertion, of endurance, made his own habits of selfish	MP	II	6	236	22
manner not to be resisted, made over to his use entirely	MP	II	6	237	23
I think the house and premises may be made comfortable,	MP	II	7	242	24
expression of his hope, made a hasty finish of her	MP	II	7	242	25
Every body gets made but me."	MP	II	7	250	54
sure he will do every thing in his power to get you made.	MP	II	7	250	55
William's desire of seeing Fanny dance, made more than a	MP	II	8	252	1
best judgment and taste, made every thing easy by her	MP	II	8	257	15
consciousness of looking well, made her look still better.	MP	II	10	272	4
happy, and she was soon made still happier; for in	MP	II	10	272	4
it was delightful to see the effort so successfully made.	MP	II	10	273	6
there was a smile--which made her blush and feel wretched.	MP	II	10	274	8
But it was not to be avoided; he made her feel that she	MP	II	10	278	20
But still his attentions made no part of her satisfaction.	MP	II	10	278	20
had made in that room, and all that part of the house.	MP	II	11	283	6
lamenting the change it made in the prospect of Julia's	MP	II	11	284	10
wretchedness; and she made her way to the park, through	MP	II	11	287	17
My mind is entirely made up.	MP	II	12	291	4
I have (I flatter myself) made no inconsiderable progress	MP	II	12	292	6
You chose to consult the Admiral, before you made up your	MP	II	12	292	8
He is made.	MP	II	13	298	2
H. M. Sloop Thrush, being made out, was spreading general	MP	II	13	298	3
He had previously made her the happiest of human beings,	MP	II	13	302	10
made up the note; "you cannot think I have any such object.	MP	II	13	307	33
to a degree that made either speaking or looking up quite	MP	III	1	313	15
But now, when he has made his overtures so properly, and	MP	III	1	315	18
It would have made no difference to you, I suppose,	MP	III	1	323	54
more warmth than delicacy, made her affection appear of	MP	III	2	326	2
Her diffidence, gratitude, and softness, made every	MP	III	2	327	6
a nervous agitation which made nothing clear to her but	MP	III	2	329	10
it made her feel a sort of credit in calling her niece.	MP	III	2	332	22
questions which being made--though with the vivacity of	MP	III	3	340	24

Context	Work	Vol	Ch	Page	Line
urn, and cake-bearers, made its appearance, and delivered	MP	III	3	344	43
Her heart is made for love and kindness, not for	MP	III	4	352	42
Miss Crawford made us laugh by her plans of encouragement	MP	III	4	354	46
What a difference it might have made.	MP	III	4	354	48
You and Miss Crawford have made me too nice."	MP	III	4	355	54
Her habits of ready submission, on the contrary, made her	MP	III	5	357	5
knowledge of the world made her judgment very generally	MP	III	5	361	16
She had made a sure push at Fanny's feelings here.	MP	III	5	364	27
Besides, there was gratitude towards her, for having made	MP	III	5	365	33
still remaining which made the prospect of it most	MP	III	6	367	4
made, to shew his happiness and describe his uniform.	MP	III	6	368	7
a year or two, and sees others made commanders before him?	MP	III	6	368	8
So reasoned Edmund, till his father made him the confident	MP	III	6	368	8
he absolutely made up his mind, he consulted his son.	MP	III	6	368	9
when her uncle first made her the offer of visiting the	MP	III	6	369	11
It made the substance of one other confidential discourse	MP	III	6	373	26
involved Mr. Crawford, made no part of their conversation.	MP	III	7	375	3
as they passed along, and made no stop any where, till	MP	III	7	376	5
brother bestowed;--but he made no objection to her kissing	MP	III	7	377	8
I jumped up, and made but two steps to the platform.	MP	III	7	380	20
have scarcely an enquiry made after Mansfield!	MP	III	7	382	29
She might have made just as good a woman of consequence as	MP	III	8	390	5
The usual plea of increasing engagements was made in	MP	III	9	393	1
made her as able as she was willing to be generous.	MP	III	9	396	7
It was made, however, at last; a silver knife was bought	MP	III	9	396	7
that where nature had made no little difference,	MP	III	11	408	2
circumstances should have made so much, and that her	MP	III	11	408	2
But Sunday made her a very creditable and tolerably	MP	III	11	408	2
them, and made one in the family party on the ramparts.	MP	III	11	408	3
It made her uncomfortable for a time--but yet there were	MP	III	11	409	5
of charms for Fanny, as made her gradually almost careless	MP	III	11	409	6
to a degree that made it impossible for her to say much,	MP	III	11	411	19
akin to envy, as made her hate herself for having them.	MP	III	11	413	31
made her a most attentive, profitable, thankful pupil.	MP	III	12	418	7
That a girl so capable of being made, every thing good,	MP	III	12	419	9
did see her, I should have made no complaint, but from the	MP	III	13	421	2
her tenderness of heart made her feel that she could not	MP	III	13	428	13
Delicacy to her parents made her careful not to betray	MP	III	14	431	8
I looked upon him as the sort of person to be made a fuss	MP	III	14	433	13
together, would have made her (as she felt), incapable of	MP	III	14	435	15
him, made it instantly plain to her, what she had to do.	MP	III	14	436	15
instead of cheering, made her still more melancholy; for	MP	III	15	439	9
strength of feeling, made her think it scarcely possible	MP	III	15	442	21
state of his own mind made him find relief only in motion.	MP	III	15	445	29
It made her melancholy again; and the knowledge of what	MP	III	15	447	36
softened, so devoted, as made it for a few moments	MP	III	16	454	18
by a man who had long ago made his indifference clear.	MP	III	16	454	18
She would have fixed him, she would have made him happy	MP	III	16	455	21
made it natural to her to treat the subject as she did.	MP	III	16	456	25
how delightful nature had made her, and how excellent she	MP	III	16	459	31
his unjustifiable theatre, made an impression on his mind	MP	III	17	462	4
were made known to him only in their sad result.	MP	III	17	464	10
severity and restraint--made her hastily resolve on	MP	III	17	466	18
party; his staying was made of flattering consequence, and	MP	III	17	467	20
He might have made her childhood happier; but it had been	MP	III	17	472	30
Her more fearless disposition and happier nerves made	MP	III	17	472	31
her father awoke, and made it necessary to be cheerful.	E	I	1	7	10
immediately afterwards walked in and made it unnecessary.	E	I	1	9	20
"and a very considerable one--that I made the match myself.	E	I	1	11	39
I made the match, you know, four years ago; and to have it	E	I	1	11	39
from Farmer Mitchell's, I made up my mind on the subject.	E	I	1	12	41
made a lucky guess; and that is all that can be said."	E	I	1	12	42
heart and sweet temper made him think every thing due to	E	I	2	15	3
He had made his fortune, bought his house, and obtained	E	I	2	17	6
man had made Highbury feel a sort of pride in him too.	E	I	2	17	7
and large dinner-parties made him unfit for any	E	I	3	20	1
of three such women made her feel that every evening so	E	I	3	22	6
being very unwholesome made him rather sorry to see any	E	I	3	24	12
care for their health made him grieve that they would eat.	E	I	3	24	12
they talked together, soon made her quick eye sufficiently	E	I	4	31	27
and I dare say she may have made out a very good list now.	E	I	5	37	7
intimacy being made a matter of much discussion among you.	E	I	5	40	24
"Mrs. John Knightley is easily alarmed, and might be made	E	I	5	40	26
Knightley soon afterwards made to "what does weston think	E	I	5	41	31
required," said he; "you have made her graceful and easy.	E	I	6	42	2
almost immediately made; and she had no scruples which	E	I	6	44	19
She had always wanted to do everything, and had made more	E	I	6	44	19
of sitting for his picture made him so nervous, that I	E	I	6	45	21
I should have made a good likeness of her, if she would	E	I	6	45	21
and when I had really made a very good likeness of it-- (	E	I	6	45	21
It was made a great favour of; and altogether it was more	E	I	6	46	21
made him discern a likeness almost before it was possible.	E	I	6	47	26
"You have made her too tall, Emma," said Mr. Knightley.	E	I	6	48	33
mind ought to be quite made up--one should not be	E	I	7	52	20
and really almost made up my mind--to refuse Mr. Martin.	E	I	7	53	22
					23
who had previously made up his mind to walk out, was	E	I	8	57	2
Even your satisfaction I made sure of.	E	I	8	61	38
Emma made no answer, and tried to look cheerfully	E	I	8	65	50
judgment in general, which made her dislike having it so	E	I	8	65	50
Emma's side to talk of the weather, but he made no answer.	E	I	8	65	50
of hot-pressed paper, made up by her friend, and	E	I	9	69	3
to soften and heal.-- made her quite sorry to	E	I	9	70	7
Where would be the use of his bringing us a charade made	E	I	9	73	18
If I had studied a twelvemonth, I could never have made	E	I	9	76	28
consciousness of having made a push--of having thrown a	E	I	9	81	78
Woodhouse's party could be made up in the evening without	E	I	9	81	78
his dining with him--had made such a point of it, that he	E	I	9	81	78
impression of the scene as made her say to Harriet, as	E	I	10	86	24
					25
The lane made a slight bend; and when that bend was passed,	E	I	10	87	29
					30
Harriet into the house, made her again find something very	E	I	10	89	36
compliment could have made her regardless of that greatest	E	I	11	93	5
when John Knightley made his appearance, and "how d'ye do,	E	I	12	99	14
and the little party made two natural divisions; on one	E	I	12	100	15
How they were all to be conveyed, he would have made a	E	I	13	108	3
venturing; but as he has made up his mind, and does not	E	I	13	110	9
Mr. Woodhouse had so completely made up his mind to the	E	I	13	112	24
Emma's project of forgetting Mr. Elton for a while, made	E	I	14	118	4
made it some effort with her to preserve her good manners.	E	I	14	118	4
Mr. Weston, at dinner, he made use of the very first	E	I	14	119	6
					7
Poor little creatures, how unhappy she would have made	E	I	14	122	17
Angry as she was, the thought of the moment made her	E	I	15	129	24
You have made yourself too clear.	E	I	15	130	30
She had taken up the idea, she supposed, and made every	E	I	16	134	3
made it impossible for Emma to be ever perfectly at ease.	E	I	16	139	20
sight of Harriet's tears made her think that she should	E	I	17	141	6
that no dignity could have made it more respectable in	E	I	17	142	9
such a progress might be made towards a state of composure	E	I	17	142	11
If Mr. Elton, on his return, made his own indifference as	E	I	17	143	13
sight of him would have made; and ending with reflections	E	I	18	145	5
he has not the power of coming, if he made a point of it.	E	I	18	145	8
a man, there would be no opposition made to his going."	E	I	18	146	16
perhaps there might be some made to his coming back again.	E	I	18	147	17
and the declaration --made, of course, as a man of sense	E	I	18	147	18
degree of vexation, which made Emma immediately talk of	E	I	18	150	36
But now she made the sudden resolution of not passing	E	II	1	155	3
she would pore over it till she had made out every word.	E	II	1	157	10
talker! --and she was made such a fuss with by every body!-	E	II	2	166	11
charitable feelings, as made her look around in walking	E	II	2	168	14
I was glad you made her play so much, for having no	E	II	3	170	2
to arrive which had made him alter his plan, and travel	E	II	5	190	23
The word home made his father look on him with fresh	E	II	5	191	26
confessed his wish to be made acquainted with the whole	E	II	6	196	2
pleasant a companion he made himself--how much she saw to	E	II	7	205	2
liberal allowances were made for the little excesses of	E	II	7	206	4
But she had made up her mind how to meet this presumption	E	II	7	207	7
were at Hartfield, which made their presence so acceptable;	E	II	7	208	8
since the new approach was made; but still I have no doubt	E	II	7	210	14
such a present had been made; and there were enough ready	E	II	8	215	15
Miss Woodhouse made the proper acquiescence; and finding	E	II	8	216	17
"I rather wonder that it was never made before."	E	II	8	216	22
If I had been there, I think I should have made some	E	II	8	218	36
to say, however, that you might not have made discoveries."	E	II	8	218	37
Miss Bates and her niece, made his way directly to the	E	II	8	220	47
for going; that they made a point of visiting no fresh	E	II	8	221	48
"I have made a most wretched discovery," said he, after a	E	II	8	221	51
having his approbation, I made my way directly to Miss	E	II	8	223	63
In short, I have made a match between Mr. Knightley and	E	II	8	224	65
and the suddenness of it made it very delightful, and she	E	II	8	230	100
Coles--worthy people, who deserved to be made happy!--	E	II	9	231	1
to her penetration which made it difficult for her to be	E	II	9	231	2
twice, and Mr. Woodhouse made us promise to have them done	E	II	9	238	51
she wished I had made him believe we had a great many left.	E	II	9	238	51
is to hear a tune again which has made one happy!--	E	II	10	242	19
when a beginning is made--when the felicities of rapid	E	II	11	247	1
in to see what it could be made to hold--and then in	E	II	11	247	2
It made him so very unhappy, indeed, that it could not be	E	II	11	248	10
was now endeavoured to be made out quite enough for ten.	E	II	11	249	12
This made a difficulty.	E	II	11	254	44
and music, tea and supper, made themselves; or were left	E	II	11	255	59
This Emma felt was aimed at her; and it made her quite	E	II	12	258	4
It made her animated--open hearted--she voluntarily said;--	E	II	12	258	4
					5
have ended, if his father had not made his appearance?	E	II	12	261	34
followed; and the necessity of exertion made him composed.	E	II	12	261	34
joined to all the rest, made her think that she must be a	E	II	12	262	38
to a degree, which made her aunt declare, that had the	E	II	12	263	42
to do otherwise, as my own mind is quite made up.	E	II	13	265	4
and admiration which made her at first shake her head over	E	II	13	265	5
really loved extremely, made her wretched for a while, and	E	II	13	268	13
look and manner could do, made Emma feel that she had	E	II	13	269	15
pay her respects; and she made a point of Harriet's going	E	II	14	270	2
When the visit was returned, Emma made up her mind.	E	II	14	272	16
Emma made as slight a reply as she could; but it was fully	E	II	14	273	20
with the help of a boarder, just made a shift to live!--	E	II	14	275	33
thing; but my resources made me quite independent.	E	II	14	276	36
I made the best excuses I could for not having been able	E	II	14	280	54
of alarm and delicacy made her irresolute what else to say.	E	II	15	287	24
Dinner-parties and evening-parties were made for him and	E	II	16	290	1
Her Bath habits made evening-parties perfectly natural to	E	II	16	290	3
no unwillingness, and only made the usual stipulation of	E	II	16	291	4
done his duty, and made every fair lady welcome and easy.	E	II	16	295	28
must be some arrangement made, there must indeed.	E	II	16	295	34
were farther talked of, and the usual observations made.	E	II	16	297	44
She could have made an inquiry or two, as to the	E	II	16	298	59
"I have not even made any inquiry; I do not wish to make	E	II	17	299	5
myself, and should be sorry to have any made by my friends.	E	II	17	300	13
when Mr. Weston made his appearance among them.	E	II	17	302	23
Weston and Emma, to be made happy;--from them he would	E	II	17	304	30
When he was here before, we made the best of it; but there	E	II	18	309	30
Your description of Mrs. Churchill made me think of them	E	II	18	310	34
of spirits which would have made her prefer being silent.	E	II	18	311	36
half year has made a great difference in your way of life."	E	II	18	311	44
open-heartedness would have made him a higher character.--	E	III	2	320	4
General benevolence, but not general friendship, made a	E	III	2	320	4
I made her take her shawl--for the evenings are not warm--	E	III	2	322	19
their rubbers were made up,--so young as he looked!--	E	III	2	325	32
Tea was made down stairs, biscuits and baked apples and	E	III	2	329	45
A few minutes made Emma acquainted with the whole.	E	III	3	333	4
made the best of her way by a short cut back to Highbury.	E	III	3	333	5
on such a return of it as made her absolutely powerless--	E	III	3	333	5
a ground-work of anticipation as her mind had already made.	E	III	3	335	9
the beginning was already made, and could not but hope	E	III	4	340	28
no fortune, might be proved to have made Harriet's.--	E	III	4	340	28
Emma was not thinking of it at the moment, which made the	E	III	4	340	28
and of the use to be made of their barouche-landau; and	E	III	5	343	1
The quietness of the game made it particularly eligible	E	III	5	347	20
He saw that Emma had soon made it out, and found it highly	E	III	5	348	22
what this word might be, made him seize every possible	E	III	5	348	23
Her face was averted from those who had made the attack,	E	III	5	349	23
I could very ill be spared--but such a point had been made	E	III	6	364	55
and, at last, made himself talk nonsense very agreeably.	E	III	6	364	59
He made no answer; merely looked, and bowed in submission;	E	III	7	373	45
					46
go away; and that was what made us keep you waiting--and	E	III	8	379	8
dreadful gratitude, Emma made the direct inquiry of-- "	E	III	8	380	11
					12
as you say, she had made up her mind to close with nothing	E	III	8	380	15
He took her hand;--whether she had not herself made the	E	III	9	386	7
He had long made up his mind to Jane Fairfax's going out	E	III	9	387	9
fever to a degree, which made him doubt the possibility of	E	III	9	389	16
hint the wish, Miss Bates made it appear that she had	E	III	9	390	18
denied--and Mrs. Cole had made such a point--and Mrs.	E	III	9	390	18
indeed--to a degree that made him appear quite a different	E	III	10	399	57
behaviour as her own, which made her so angry with him.	E	III	11	402	1
Mr. Churchill had made a point of it, as a token of	E	III	11	403	2
that was the service which made me begin to feel how	E	III	11	406	24
A mind like her's, once opening to suspicion, made rapid	E	III	11	407	32
that she should not be made unhappy by any coldness now,)	E	III	11	408	33
the many bitter feelings, made the utmost exertion	E	III	11	411	40
					41
young man who would have made her happy and respectable in	E	III	11	413	49
A little curiosity Emma had; and she made the most of it	E	III	12	417	5
thousand inquietudes, and made her captious and irritable	E	III	12	419	12
greatly feared had been made a subject of material	E	III	12	421	17
day, which only made such cruel sights the longer visible.	E	III	12	421	18
She made her plan; she would speak of something totally	E	III	13	429	26
					27
points to consider, as made her feel, that even her	E	III	14	434	4
had not made him ill. "your's ever, "A. W. "	E	III	14	436	7
My dear Madam, "if I made myself intelligible	E	III	14	436	8
which might have made every previous caution useless?--	E	III	14	441	8
her again speedily; but I made excuses for her, and was	E	III	14	442	8
me till I reached Highbury, and saw how ill I had made her.	E	III	14	443	8
After this, he made some progress without any pause.	E	III	15	446	19
right, he made a fuller pause to say, "this is very bad.--	E	III	15	446	20
Goddard's, or in London, made perhaps an unreasonable	E	III	16	452	5
poor Miss Bates had before made so happily intelligible.--	E	III	16	452	8
had not checked her, and made it expedient to compress all	E	III	16	453	10
Mr. Elton made his appearance.	E	III	16	457	35
tone of great ill usage,) which made it so much the worse.	E	III	16	457	40
which she immediately made use of, to say, "it is well,	E	III	16	459	45
					46
Mrs. Weston's friends were all made happy by her safety;	E	III	17	461	1
you; but, as you made no objection, I never did it again."	E	III	17	462	12
little inferior to the pain of having made Harriet unhappy.	E	III	17	463	15
Hartfield, had, indeed, made a melancholy change: but she	E	III	17	466	29
No more exploring parties to Donwell made for her.	E	III	17	469	36
She made him, by her acceptance, as happy even as he is	E	III	18	472	20
Her mind was in a state of flutter and wonder, which made	E	III	18	475	37
I hope time has not made you less willing to pardon.	E	III	18	476	47

could the valet of any new made Lord be more delighted P III 1 4 5
youthful infatuation which made her Lady Elliot, had never P III 1 4 6
that of a youngest sister, made the book an evil; and more P III 1 7 12
acre been alienable, it would have made no difference. P III 1 10 20
She drew up plans of economy, she made exact calculations, P III 2 12 3
and the first outline of this important change made out. P III 2 13 8
Kellynch-Hall; and who had made herself so acceptable to P III 2 15 15
Many a noble fortune has been made during the war. P III 3 17 1
made up my mind as to the privileges to be annexed to it. P III 3 18 8
deputation, certainly, but made no great point of it;-- P III 3 22 23
family, which made him peculiarly desirable as a tenant. P III 3 22 24
his brother, who being made commander in consequence of P III 4 26 1
from what she had been made to think at nineteen.-- P III 4 29 8
now, by successive captures, have made a handsome fortune. P III 4 29 8
resenting the suspicion, might yet be made observant by it. P III 5 35 17
Accordingly their removal was made together, and Anne was P III 5 36 19
"Yes, I made the best of it; I always do; but I was very P III 5 37 24
I have made no enquiries, because I concluded you must P III 5 39 36
such a present was not made, he always contended for his P III 6 43 5
A beloved home made over to others; all the precious rooms P III 6 47 16
Admiral sat by Mary, and made himself very agreeable by P III 6 48 17
at sea as her husband, made her seem to have lived some P III 6 48 18
year for such visits to be made on foot, the coach was P III 6 50 26
be affronted, when Louisa made all right by saying, that P III 6 50 26
men or ships, that it had made scarcely any impression at P III 6 51 31
Captain Wentworth made a very early return to Mr. P III 7 53 2
"A strong mind, with sweetness of manner," made the first P III 7 62 40
How fast I made money in her.-- P III 8 67 23
Her feelings made her speak low; and Captain Wentworth, P III 8 67 25
Musgrove had most readily made room for him;--they were P III 8 68 29
have made it credible that they were not decided rivals. P III 8 71 57
They had each had money, but their marriages had made a P III 9 74 5
Musgroves, as made them pleased to improve their cousins.-- P III 9 74 6
had not made less than twenty thousand pounds by the war. P III 9 75 10
If he should ever be made a baronet! P III 9 75 11
have made, she has no right to throw herself away. P III 9 75 13
him by some one without, made his determined appearance P III 9 79 28
Her sensations on the discovery made her perfectly P III 9 80 34
paths across the fields made many separations necessary, P III 10 84 7
What Anne first heard was, "and so, I made her go. P III 10 87 22
23
When I have made up my mind, I have made it. P III 10 87 23
And Henrietta seemed entirely to have made up hers to call P III 10 87 23
towards her which all these things made apparent. P III 10 91 42
of calmer praise, such as made Anne suspect that her P III 10 92 47
happiness it presented, made it to her a something more, P III 11 98 17
He drew, he varnished, he carpentered, he glued; he made P III 11 99 18
The word curricle made Charles Musgrove jump up, that he P III 12 105 9
he came home from the Cape,--just made into the Grappler. P III 12 108 28
The hardness of the pavement for her feet, made him less P III 12 109 32
without sufferings which made her worse than helpless! P III 12 114 59
ladies. when the plan was made known to Mary, however, P III 12 115 65
Charles was listened to, made but a mortifying reception P III 12 115 68
made the road appear but half as long as on the day before. P III 12 117 73
He made it his business to go to Lyme, and his account was P IV 1 122 4
A few days had made a change indeed! P IV 1 123 6
Scenes had passed in Uppercross, which made it precious. P IV 1 123 8
"We have made very few changes either!" continued the P IV 1 127 28
we have made have been all very much for the better. P IV 1 127 28
so very useful, had made really an agreeable fortnight. P IV 2 130 3
on Tuesday night, he made a very awkward sort of excuse; " P IV 2 130 5
visit; and Mr. Musgrove made a point of paying his P IV 2 134 29
and the ceaseless clink of pattens, she made no complaint. P IV 2 135 33
which made a material difference in the discredit of it. P IV 3 139 8
Allowances, large allowances, she knew, must be made for P IV 3 140 11
Lady Russell listened, and looked, and made only this P IV 4 147 7
liking to the cause, which made him enter warmly into her P IV 4 148 10
in her legs, had made her for the present a cripple. P IV 5 152 4
that part of mankind which made her think worse of the P IV 5 156 12
She made no reply. P IV 5 158 20
Elliot; and Mr. Elliot had made a point of leaving Colonel P IV 5 158 21
Anne heard her, and made no violent exclamations. P IV 5 159 22
No, it was not regret which made Anne's heart beat in P IV 6 167 21
wait, for the Admiral had made up his mind not to begin, P IV 6 170 30
He is only a commander, it is true, made last summer, and P IV 6 171 37
Mrs. Smith made no reply; but when she was leaving her, P IV 7 180 35
an idea which made her yet more anxious to be encouraging. P IV 8 190 49
to be made acquainted with Mr. Elliot's real character. P IV 9 199 53
Anne's astonished air, and exclamation of wonder, made her P IV 9 199 54
55
I wish nature had made such hearts as yours more common, " P IV 9 203 72
"They are gone back to Kellynch, and almost made me swear " P IV 9 203 72
efforts he made towards a reconciliation with my father. P IV 9 205 83
Christmas, Colonel Wallis made him acquainted with the P IV 9 206 90
assured that he could have made no attempt of that nature, P IV 9 210 99
he might not yet have made the offer, and I could no more P IV 9 211 101
induced to marry him, as made her shudder at the idea of P IV 9 211 102
bear to be left, and had made herself so unhappy about it P IV 10 216 19
happiness, which made her full of regard and interest for P IV 10 220 31
and embarrassed her, and made her regret that she had said P IV 10 222 36
seen them off, and then made a face at them, and abused P IV 10 223 40
41
When she reached the White Hart, and made her way to the P IV 11 229 2
The revolution which one instant had made in Anne, was P IV 11 237 41
That evening seemed to be made up of exquisite moments. P IV 11 244 71
Sir Walter made no objection, and Elizabeth did nothing P IV 12 248 1
made a baronet, she would not change situations with Anne. P IV 12 250 5
Well sir--I dare say it is as you say, & I have made an S 1 367 1
ungrateful that it can hardly be made to yeild a Cabbage.-- S 1 369 1
which Sanditon could be made to supply by the gratitude of S 2 374 1
parish of Sanditon, with manor & mansion house made a part. S 3 375 1
she was said to have made this boast to a friend "that S 3 375 1
You will not think I have made a bad exchange, when we S 4 380 1
two ladies whose arrival made an alteration necessary, S 6 390 1
the same ill-luck which made him derive only false S 8 404 1
Arthur made no difficulties--our plan was arranged S 9 409 1
She was not made acquainted with the others till the S 10 413 1
on the mantelpeice,--& made a great many odd faces & S 10 413 1
great deal Stouter--broad made & Lusty--and with no other S 10 413 1
in the reports of each made that matter quite certain. S 10 419 1
had been asking for; & she made the acquaintance for Sir S 11 422 1
many an eye upwards, & made many a Gazer gaze again.-- S 11 422 1

MADEIRA (2)
brought a glass of Madeira to Fanny, and obliged her to MP I 7 74 57
Another slice of cold meat, another draught of Madeira and E III 6 365 65

MADNESS (8)
of his own; it would be madness to marry upon that, though SS II 2 147 7
No, that is madness indeed, absolute madness!" MP I 11 109 21
Harriet Smith refuse Robert Martin? madness, if it is so; E I 8 60 34
"It seems like madness! E III 4 337 6
I met one as I came--madness in such weather!--absolute E III 6 364 55
as I came--madness in such weather!--absolute madness!" E III 6 364 55
What blindness, what madness, had led her on! E III 11 408 33
the pride, the folly, the madness of resentment, which had P IV 11 242 63

MAGDALEN BRIDGE (1)
to meet him on Magdalen Bridge, as he was driving into NA I 7 46 11

MAGISTRATE (2)
she was a most active magistrate in her own parish, the PP II 7 169 4
As a magistrate, he had generally some point of law to E I 12 100 16

MAGISTRATES (1)
The magistrates, and overseers, and churchwardens, are E III 16 455 23

MAGNANIMITY (1)
In that point, however, I undervalued my own magnanimity, SS III 8 323 40

MAGNIFICENCE (1)
in its way, of equal magnificence, exhibiting a collection NA II 8 182 2

MAGNIFICENT (8)
the remains of magnificent furniture, though now for many NA I 11 88 54
into a room magnificent both in size and furniture--the NA II 8 182 2
But neither the business alleged, nor the magnificent NA II 8 187 16
"What magnificent orders would travel from this family to SS I 17 92 25
the powerful protection of a very magnificent concerto----- SS II 2 149 24
25
drew several plans for magnificent cottages;--and from SS III 14 376 11
"We were too magnificent," said he. E II 11 249 13
detailing her magnificent intentions, from the procuring E II 15 288 39

MAGNIFIED (2)
sinned against his character, or magnified his cruelty. NA II 15 247 14
imputed fault was so magnified by fancy, that she never E II 2 167 12

MAGNITUDE (3)
means of equal magnitude you last night laid to my charge. PP II 12 196 5
of such magnitude as must, if possible, be prevented. MP I 16 154 8
this sin of the first magnitude, who could try to gloss it MP III 15 441 19

MAHOGANY (4)
a bright Bath stove, mahogany wardrobes and neatly-painted NA II 9 193 6
shining floors, solid mahogany, rich damask, marble, MP I 9 84 3
than the profusion of mahogany, and the crimson velvet MP I 9 85 6
his face the colour of mahogany, rough and rugged to the P III 3 19 16

MAID (39)
and her maid declared she looked quite as she should do. NA I 2 20 8
in it, and his daughter's maid had so crowded it with NA II 5 155 4
This ill-timed intruder was Miss Tilney's maid, sent by NA II 6 164 3
The treachery, or the folly, of my cousin's maid betrayed SS II 9 206 24
But whether she would do for a lady's maid, I am sure I SS III 4 287 22
early to bed; her maid, who was one of the principal SS III 7 310 9
as she had rung up the maid to take her place by her SS III 7 311 14
Jennings's maid with her sister, she hurried down stairs. SS III 7 316 30
in the gossip of her maid for the loss of her two young SS III 10 341 5
care of Margaret and the maid, returned to Elinor, who, SS III 11 353 25
You will find Mrs Edwards' maid very willing to help you, W 315 1
prepared, & the neat upper maid was lighting the candles--" W 336 14
to bring her without her maid, & I am as particular as W 350 24
from their apprehension of Charlotte's dying an old maid. PP I 22 122 3
Jane will be quite an old maid soon, I declare. PP II 16 221 17
of gentleness and commiseration, "let me call your maid. PP III 4 276 9
impossible, so I told my maid to speak for one directly; MP I 6 58 37
I shall get the dairy maid to set them under the first MP I 10 106 57
removed herself, her maid, her footman, and her chariot, MP II 3 202 28
the housekeeper, and her maid was rather hurried in making MP II 8 254 9
maid to assist her; too late of course to be of any use. MP II 9 271 41
jellies to nurse a sick maid, there was peace and good MP II 11 283 4
of the house, pushed the maid aside, and while William was MP III 7 377 7
or sending your aunt's maid for you, without involving the MP III 11 410 16
and of her having an upper maid who had lived five-and- E I 4 27 4
And it always ended in "Kitty, a fair but frozen maid." E I 9 70 5
Kitty, a fair but frozen maid, kindled a flame I yet E I 9 78 54
Kitty, a fair but frozen maid. E I 9 79 56
"But then, to be an old maid at last, like Miss Bates!" " E I 10 84 16
"But still, you will be an old maid! and that's so E I 10 85 18
"Never mind, Harriet, I shall not be a poor old maid; and E I 10 85 19
disagreeable, old maid! the proper sport of boys and girls; E I 10 85 19
The hair was curled, and the maid sent away, and Emma sat E I 16 134 1
to eat; that her own maid should sit up for her; and that E II 7 211 22
to be done in a hurry; the maid looked frightened and E III 8 378 4
Was not it Mrs. Speed, as usual, or the maid? P IV 9 197 39
maid servants, were now seen issueing from the house)-- S 1 370 1
for a situation little better than a nursery maid.-- S 3 379 1
chilly & tender, had a maid of her own, was to have the S 11 421 1

MAID'S (1)
in the very moment of the maid's going away, she eagerly NA II 7 172 1

MAID-SERVANT (3)
The moment they stopt, a trollopy-looking maid-servant, MP III 7 377 7
The maid-servant of Mrs. Rushworth, senior, threatened MP III 16 450 9
there had been only a maid-servant to wait, and at first, P IV 2 129 3

MAID-SERVANTS (1)
her ignorance, and the maid-servants sneered at her MP I 2 14 8

MAIDEN (1)
father kept, and what had been her mother's maiden name?-- PP II 6 163 15

MAIDS (8)
servants to three; two maids and a man, with whom they SS I 5 26 5
The man and one of the maids were sent off immediately SS I 5 26 6
a little bigger--with two maids and two men; and I believe SS III 1 260 7
Two maids and two men indeed!--as I talked of t'other day.- SS III 2 277 28
enough to call one of the maids, who, with Mrs. Dashwood's SS III 11 353 25
them, but Eliz. & the maids cd never do anything right--& W 360 30
The maids do their work very well, and I think we shall be MP I 15 141 22
on by mistresses and maids, being also obliged on MP II 4 206 3

MAIDS' (1)
the children away in the maids' room, or swinging a cot P III 12 113 56

MAIL (2)
should go up by the mail from Northampton the following MP II 9 266 21
You will see me early, by the mail. your's, &c." MP III 15 443 23

MAILS (1)
mails;--it was at her tongue's end--but she abstained. E II 16 298 59

MAIN (7)
agree with you in the main as to the propriety of doing MP I 1 6 6
satisfaction in the main among their new acquaintance. MP I 3 31 59
and there was no introducing the main point before her. MP III 10 403 15
As for the main subject of the letter--there was nothing MP III 13 424 4
broad, though irregular, main street of the place; and, as E I 10 83 2
side of the lane, leaving them together in the main road. E I 10 88 33
And Sir Edw: is a very steady man in the main, & has got S 7 400 1

MAIN-MAST (1)
Antwerp at the bottom, in letters as tall as the main-mast. MP I 16 152 2

MAINLY (2)
and advice, Lady Elliot mainly relied for the best help P III 1 5 6
even when the event is mainly anti-prosperous to the high- S 8 403 1

MAINTAIN (9)
within its view, maintain so elevated an air, look so NA II 9 190 2
not know who is to maintain you when your father is dead.-- PP I 20 113 28
I will maintain--that we shall be doing no harm." MP I 13 126 23
Emma spared no exertions to maintain this happier flow of E I 1 9 20
a poorer man than at first, and with a child to maintain. E I 2 16 4
Harriet did think him all perfection, and maintain the non- E I 17 142 12
He has a wife and family to maintain, and is not to be E II 1 162 31
the subject could still maintain itself, by the natural E III 15 444 1
or sense enough to maintain himself in the situation in P IV 12 248 1

MAINTAINED (17)
a celebrated writer has maintained, that no young lady can NA I 3 29 52
James, who was now in constant attendance, maintained a NA I 10 71 8
But for this strange kind of secrecy maintained by them SS I 14 71 4
that it could not be maintained if their correspondence SS I 16 84 6
"A family cannot well be maintained on a smaller. SS I 17 91 14
could not have been maintained; but not a syllable escaped SS II 8 193 6
Mr. Palmer maintained the common, but unfatherly opinion SS II 14 248 5
far from him as she could, and maintained a strict silence. SS III 12 359 13
interest, & perhaps maintained little complaisance, but W 359 28
humility of behaviour is at the same time maintained. PP I 18 97 60
61
and has since maintained herself by letting lodgings. PP III 10 322 2
elevation which he had maintained before, and they were MP I 17 158 1
her imagination it maintained its ground, and Henry and E III 3 336 13
voluntarily formed and maintained--or to deserve to be E III 11 408 33
and the secrecy she had maintained, as to any such design E III 14 442 8
him; but, as Charles maintained to the last, Captain P IV 2 133 25

themselves, but still maintained that as a family P IV 4 150 15
MAINTAINING (9)
the keenest enjoyment, maintaining at the same time the PP I 14 68 12
The difficulty was in maintaining the conviction quite so MP II 13 306 26
to show his liberty, and his resolution of maintaining it. E III 2 327 34
been a happier woman in maintaining the engagement, than P III 4 29 8
the idea of merit in maintaining her own way, bore down P III 11 94 7
for them; Miss Elliot maintaining that Mrs. Clay had a P IV 7 174 3
and half jesting, maintaining the scheme for the play; and P IV 10 224 50
as perfection itself, maintaining the loveliest medium of P IV 11 241 61
to be trusted;--and he maintaining that he only eat enough S 10 417 1
MAINTENANCE (9)
farther than their maintenance for six months at Norland. SS I 5 27 6
for her comfortable maintenance, and I learnt from my SS II 9 207 26
be to the future maintenance of the eight already in being. MP I 1 5 2
of being at any expense whatever in her maintenance. MP I 1 8 9
What can you want but a decent maintenance? MP II 4 213 40
from any allusion that might endanger its maintenance. E III 9 388 14
her the comfortable maintenance which had ever been her's, E III 19 481 3
for the best help and maintenance of the good principles P III 1 5 6
at Bath;--but the maintenance, education & fitting out of S 2 373 1
MAKE (888)
Sir James did make proposals to me for Frederica--but LS 2 245 1
She will make good connections there, as the girls are all LS 2 246 1
a circumstance which is not likely to make us any amends. LS 3 246 1
his heart, & make him really confide in her sincerity. LS 3 247 1
has now written, I cannot make up my mind, till I better LS 3 247 1
who is therefore well qualified to make the communication. LS 4 248 1
is too often used I believe to make black appear white. LS 6 251 1
might for a time make her wish for retirement. LS 6 252 2
I am sure of Sir James at any time, & could make him renew LS 7 253 1
measure, merely propose to make it her own choice by LS 7 253 2
in the space of a fortnight to make my brother like her. LS 8 255 1
be to any one, I should make a point of not bestowing my LS 10 258 2
afford me amusement, & to make many of those hours pass LS 10 258 3
My years & increasing infirmities make me very desirous my LS 12 261 3
goodness of my own, will make me indifferent; but her LS 12 261 3
could render probable, and must in the end make wretched. LS 12 261 3
of a matter which we foresaw would make him so uneasy. LS 13 262 1
I know not why she should chuse to make herself & her LS 14 263 1
of being able to make a worthy man completely miserable. LS 14 264 4
I have sent Charles to town to make matters up if he can, LS 16 268 1
I trust I shall be able to make my story as good as her's. LS 16 268 2
seem to have the sort of temper to make severity necessary. LS 17 270 4
has made him & wants to make me beleive, that it was LS 17 271 7
I want to make him sensible of all this, for we know power LS 18 272 2
when alone with me, to make it clear that if properly LS 18 273 3
As for Reginald, I beleive he does not know what to make LS 20 278 9
angry it will make mama, but I must run the risk. LS 21 279 1
only on compassion, must make them both, in my eyes, I LS 22 280 1
you must make it your business to see justice done her. LS 23 284 4
She has no right to make you unhappy, & she shall not do LS 24 287 7
but her good--but Frederica will not make a friend of her. LS 24 287 9
Lady Susan therefore does not always know what will make LS 24 287 9
Sir James is certainly under par--(his boyish manners make LS 24 288 11
that it was my object to make my own child miserable, & LS 24 289 12
She shall have all the retribution in my power to make; if LS 24 290 13
be hastened; & I make it my particular request that I may LS 25 293 3
young man--& I must make myself amends for the LS 25 293 4
in spite of Mr Johnson, to make opportunities of seeing me. LS 26 295 3
last fit of the gout to make me detest Mr Johnson; but now LS 29 298 1
make me, even with you, the most miserable of beings. LS 30 300 3
Depend upon it, I can make my own story with Reginald. LS 30 300 4
I hope nothing will make it inconvenient to Mr Vernon, & LS 33 303 1
before, but this happy meeting will make us young again. LS 40 309 1
enquiry till she could make it personally in town, ceased LS 40 309 1
shall make but a poor figure in your journal to-morrow." LS 42 311 1
make me dance with him, and distressed me by his nonsense." NA I 3 26 20
friend, they proceeded to make inquiries and give NA I 3 26 22
to read, I feel as if nobody could make me miserable. NA I 4 32 2
I make it a rule never to mind what they say. NA I 6 41 19
treat them with spirit, and make them keep their distance." NA I 6 42 26
If we make haste, we shall pass by them presently, and I NA I 6 42 26
defy any man in England to make my horse go less than ten NA I 6 43 41
written by that woman they make such a fuss about, she who NA I 7 45 7
too much good-nature to make any opposition, and the NA I 7 49 38
It would make us the talk of the place, if we were not to NA I 8 52 2
I have a thousand things to say to you; but make haste and NA I 8 57 21
Make haste, my dear creature, and come to us. NA I 9 62 7
of the woman; the woman to make the home agreeable to the NA I 10 75 23
Yet, though longing to make her acquainted with her NA I 10 77 35
"Make haste! make haste!" as he threw open the door--" put NA I 10 81 61
"Make yourself easy, there is no danger of that, for I NA I 11 84 18
of rudeness in return it might justly make her amenable. NA I 11 86 46
been quite wild to speak to you, and make my apologies. NA I 12 92 3
She was very much vexed, and meant to make her apology as NA I 12 93 5
He replied by asking her to make room for him, and talking NA I 12 94 10
I could not make you understand it without a table;-- NA I 12 95 15
would make it impossible for her to accompany them now. NA I 12 96 20
ridiculous, quite absurd to make any further objection. NA I 13 97 1
He should make a point of inquiring into the matter." NA I 13 100 19
city of Bath, as unworthy to make part of a landscape. NA I 13 103 27
He laughed, and added, "come, shall I make you understand NA I 14 111 29
other, you may as well make Miss Morland understand NA I 14 112 36
"I shall be most happy to make her better acquainted with NA I 14 113 40
all speed to Fullerton, to make known his situation and NA I 14 113 41
his honour was pledged to make every thing easy; and by NA I 15 119 14
seemed to be his only care to entertain and make me happy." NA I 15 122 28
"Nay, since you make such a point of it, I can refuse you NA II 1 130 8
"you would be so good--it would make me very happy if-----" NA II 1 130 13
"I was just beginning to make the request, sir, as you NA II 2 139 4
I am almost ashamed to make the request, though its NA II 2 139 6
us with a visit, you will make us happy beyond expression. NA II 2 139 7
our side to make Northanger Abbey not wholly disagreeable." NA II 2 139 7
Many were the inquiries she was eager to make of Miss NA II 2 139 7
make him understand what I mean, in the properest way. NA II 2 141 13
The compliment of John Thorpe's affection did not make NA II 3 145 13
of her situation, and make her aware of this double NA II 3 148 29
and entreating him to make known her prior engagement. NA II 4 150 1
Absence will in time make him comfortable again; but he NA II 4 150 1
he loves; it is the woman only who can make it a torment." NA II 4 150 4
her uneasiness, or make her quit them in apprehension. NA II 4 151 12
would make as little alteration as possible in her dress. NA II 4 153 31
it would be simple not to make use of them; but, upon his NA II 5 162 28
But she would not make up her fire; that would seem NA II 6 166 7
Mrs. Allen used to take pains, year after year, to make me NA II 6 167 10
"Woodston will make but a sombre appearance to-day." NA II 7 174 7
But though I may not exactly make converts of you young NA II 7 175 13
"But perhaps it might be more agreeable to her to make NA II 7 176 15
health in vain, was too polite to make further opposition. NA II 7 176 17
gratifying, he should make no apology for leading her on. NA II 7 179 29
to make her feel secure at least of life for the present. NA II 8 184 4
need of my being played off to make her secure of Tilney. NA II 9 192 4
make her distress known to them was another consideration. NA II 10 202 7
has happened that would make it very dreadful for me to be NA II 10 203 9
three terriers, was ready to receive and make much of them. NA II 10 204 17
a thousand apologies to make for not answering them sooner. NA II 11 212 17
NA II 12 216 1
2
make her character better known to me than mine is to her. NA II 12 218 4
Why should he pay her such attentions as to make her NA II 12 218 6
as would make their meeting materially painful. NA II 13 222 8
His unlooked-for return was enough in itself to make NA II 13 223 13
pain of being urged, as to make her friend comfortable; NA II 13 228 27
new friends you make I hope will be better worth keeping." NA II 14 236 15
happen within that time to make a meeting dreadful to her. NA II 14 236 18
of reason and the dictate of conscience could make it. NA II 15 247 15
"Catherine would make a sad heedless young house-keeper to NA II 16 249 1
were not refined enough to make any parading stipulation; NA II 16 249 2
to do every thing in his power to make them comfortable. SS I 1 5 6
It would be enough to make them completely easy. SS I 1 5 8
terms, to assist them, and make their situation more SS I 2 9 6
husband, very gravely, "that would make a great difference. SS I 2 9 8
A hundred a year would make them all perfectly comfortable. SS I 2 10 16
and his manners required intimacy to make them pleasing. SS I 3 15 6
They wanted him to make a fine figure in the world in some SS I 3 15 6
day to make on the difference between him and his sister. SS I 3 16 7
greater certainty of it to make Marianne's conviction of SS I 4 21 11
behaved to him so as to make his home comfortable at SS I 4 22 18
by his sister, to make her uneasy; and at the same time, (SS I 4 23 19
time, (which was still more common,) to make her uncivil. SS I 4 23 19
our family, but we will make ourselves tolerably SS I 6 29 4
and garret above, will make it a very snug little cottage. SS I 6 29 4
shy before company as he could make noise enough at home. SS I 6 31 9
could want to make her mind as captivating as her person. SS I 7 33 3
She was perfectly disposed to make every allowance for the SS I 7 35 9
is not old enough to make his friends yet apprehensive of SS I 8 37 8
enough to love, to make him a desirable companion to her. SS I 8 38 11
and he then departed, to make himself still more SS I 9 42 10
will make conquests enough, I day say, one way or other. SS I 9 45 31
32
early the next morning to make his personal inquiries. SS I 10 46 1
and Marianne, will make amends for the regard of Lady SS I 10 50 18
They afforded her no companion that could make amends for SS I 11 54 6
saying-- "does your sister make no distinction in her SS I 11 56 14
15
Seven years would be insufficient to make some people SS I 12 59 4
such as to make further entreaty on his side impossible. SS I 12 59 6
"It must be something extraordinary that could make SS I 13 63 6
make it one of the pleasantest summer-rooms in England." SS I 13 69 76
sum may remain, when I make up my accounts in the spring, SS I 14 72 10
Extend it a little farther, and it will make me happy. SS I 14 74 19
when circumstances make the revealment of it eligible. SS I 16 84 9
Greatness will not make me so." SS I 17 91 7
directly before her, as to make a ring, with a plait of SS I 18 98 10
door and the window, as to make it hardly possible to SS I 19 105 13
to him! for he is forced to make every body like him." SS I 20 113 33
will make Miss Dashwood believe you think of nothing else." SS I 21 124 31
having been so lucky as to make a conquest of a very smart SS I 21 125 34
of probabilities to make it natural that Lucy should be SS II 1 142 7
And we will make the dear little love some amends for her SS II 1 144 11
to know whether you can make your party without me, or I SS II 1 144 12
would make you overlook every thing else I am sure." SS II 2 146 5
side, that though it would make us miserable for a time, SS II 2 149 30
Elinor thought it wisest to make no answer to this, lest SS II 2 150 35
said on either side, to make them dislike each other less SS II 2 151 41
that she could not make them choose their own dinners at SS II 4 160 2
Elinor now began to make the tea, and Marianne was obliged SS II 4 163 19
likewise some purchases to make themselves; and Marianne, SS II 4 164 23
Elinor, persuaded that he had some communication to make SS II 5 172 40
three or four days, to make Elinor regret what she had SS II 6 175 1
by saying, "poor Elinor! how unhappy I make you!" SS II 7 185 16
17
which her sister could not make or return for herself. SS II 8 193 7
thing was due to her which might make her at all less so. SS II 8 193 7
turn off his servants, and make a thorough reform at once? SS II 8 194 10
in it, make it unfit to become the public conversation. SS II 8 196 19
be supposed that it could make any impression on you)--a SS II 9 205 22
neither prevail on him to make the offer himself, nor SS II 10 216 15
nor commission her to make it for him, began, at the end SS II 10 216 15
and she hardly knew how to make a very gracious return to SS II 10 217 20
her self-command to make it appear that she did not. SS II 10 217 22
which make her unfit for company or conversation." SS II 10 219 38
to make a very creditable appearance in Mr. Gray's shop. SS II 11 221 7
make your situation pleasant, might be reasonably expected. SS II 11 222 11
of your fortune may make him hang back; his friends may SS II 11 223 24
on my part, to make him pleased with you and your family. SS II 11 224 24
to make over for ever; but Mrs. Ferrars has a noble spirit. SS II 11 224 28
But, in consequence of it, we have been obliged to make SS II 11 225 35
The old walnut trees are all come down to make room for it. SS II 11 226 39
Having now said enough to make his poverty clear, and to SS II 11 226 41
however, was enough to make her interested in the SS II 12 230 6
Don't let them make you unhappy." SS II 12 236 40
She had found in her every thing that could tend to make a SS II 13 238 1
very much blind her, as to make the attention which seemed SS II 13 238 2
To this, Elinor had no answer to make, and did not attempt SS II 13 239 10
Elinor tried to make a civil answer, though doubting her SS II 13 240 14
though his sex might make it rare; for his heart had not SS II 13 241 21
air, seemed determined to make no contribution to the SS II 13 241 22
This would almost make amends for every thing!" SS II 13 242 24
This remark was not calculated to make Edward or Elinor SS II 13 242 27
and however it may make against his interest or pleasure. SS II 13 243 40
into the value and make of her gown, the colour of her SS II 14 249 8
and she dared to say would make a great many conquests." SS II 14 249 8
'My dear madam,' I always say to her, 'you must make SS II 14 251 13
that another year would make the invitation needless, by SS II 14 253 25
This was enough to make Lucy really and reasonably happy. SS II 14 254 26
Lucy, to be sure they will make no difficulty about it;' SS III 1 258 7
that she thought to make a match between Edward and some SS III 1 258 7
than any body how to make the most of everything; and I SS III 1 259 7
hundred a-year, she would make as good an appearance with SS III 1 259 7
give such an answer, and make such observations, as the SS III 1 260 8
her good opinion,--and to make Marianne, by a resemblance SS III 1 261 11
knowing that it would make you and my mother most unhappy SS III 1 263 29
that could make me less desire the connection.-- SS III 1 264 29
Is this the only return I can make you?-- SS III 1 264 31
injured, no reparation could be too much for her to make. SS III 1 265 32
All that Mrs. Ferrars could say to make him put an end to SS III 1 266 38
matters grew desperate, to make it twelve hundred; and in SS III 1 266 38
I do not know; for we of course can make no inquiry." SS III 1 268 48
But I don't think mine would be, to make one son SS III 1 269 54
Miss Dashwood, do you think people make love when any body SS III 2 274 18
friendship for me will make you pleased to hear such a SS III 2 277 29
30
lately, therefore will make no more apologies, but proceed SS III 2 277 29
30
ennui, to provoke him to make that offer, which might give SS III 3 280 9
I believe, did not make more than 2001. per annum, and SS III 3 282 19
that she would not on any account make farther opposition. SS III 3 283 20
"This little rectory can do no more than make Mr. Ferrars SS III 3 284 23
housekeeper told me, could make up fifteen beds!--and to SS III 4 292 55
and make it comfortable for them, before Lucy goes to it." SS III 4 292 55
good-humour could do, to make them feel themselves welcome. SS III 6 304 13
his real favourite, to make her suspect it herself. SS III 6 305 16
to raise her spirits, and make her believe, as she then SS III 7 308 4
"I mean"--said he, with serious energy--"if I can, to make SS III 8 319 23
means in my power, to make myself pleasing to her, without SS III 8 320 29
affluence, lost every thing that could make it a blessing." SS III 8 321 32
that could make my conduct most hateful. SS III 8 327 55
broke it thus: "well, let me make haste and be gone. SS III 8 327 56
57
letter will only make them think me a blackguard one.' SS III 8 328 63
to make requisite, was kept off by irritation of spirits. SS III 9 334 5
to be an advantage, as to make his character and SS III 9 338 20
is exactly the very one to make your sister happy. SS III 9 338 20

not been long enough to make her recovery slow; and with SS III 10 340 1
designs,--but what must it make me appear to myself?-- SS III 10 345 20
He would have had a wife of whose temper he could make no SS III 11 351 13
Edward, and can make no inquiries on so prohibited a SS III 11 353 21
when they come back, they'd make sure to come and see you." SS III 11 354 27
be able to speak--and to make them understand that she SS III 12 358 9
and as my mother did not make my home in every respect SS III 13 362 5
that I could make no comparisons, and see no defects. SS III 13 362 5
by his family--it was beyond her comprehension to make out. SS III 13 364 10
at a loss with herself to make out; for at Oxford, where SS III 13 364 13
has put it in his power to make his own choice; and she SS III 13 366 18
and till I began to make comparisons between yourself and SS III 13 368 28
of each other seemed to make their happiness certain--and SS III 13 369 32
of her mother's language, to make it cheerful. SS III 13 369 35
on purpose we suppose to make a shew with, and poor Nancy SS III 13 370 37
I can make no submission--I am grown neither humble nor SS III 13 372 41
I know of no submission that is proper for me to make." SS III 13 372 41
and therefore, to make it easier to him, as he declared a SS III 13 372 45
greater willingness to make mean concessions by word of SS III 13 372 45
had brought her up, was to make her first public W 315 1
And since then, she has been trying to make some match at W 317 2
at home; to be able to make an immediate friend of each."-- W 318 2
fair a chance as we have all had, to make your fortune.-- W 320 2
of such delicacy should make any part of the scanty W 321 2
all weathers, to make a likeness to him very flattering." W 324 3
"Elderly ladies should be careful how they make a second W 326 6
& expression to make that beauty improve on acquaintance.-- W 328 9
began to make civil enquiries after her family.-- W 334 13
But I shall now endeavour to make myself amends for the W 335 13
the only objection she could make to Mr Howard.-- W 335 13
make his pupil's manners as unexceptionable as his own.-- W 335 13
in her bar to make fresh negus for the happy dancers above. W 336 14
leave to ring the bell & make enquiries, when the light W 338 17
an invalid.-- they would make me sit near the fire, & as W 344 20
from the bottom to the top, & would make me take his arm.-- W 344 20
presuming to make it, than have seen him at Stanton.-- W 347 22
of the house, she could make no change without a bustle.-- W 348 23
have not been able to make Croydon agreable this autumn."-- W 350 24
I don't find she is likely to make anything of it. W 351 24
How the devil came he to make such a will?"-- W 352 26
"I do not mean to make you cry.--said robt rather softened- W 352 26
her dress--"I would not make you wait, said she, so I put W 353 26
"Indeed you ought to make some alteration in your dress W 353 26
to make such nonsense easy) began to admire her gown.-- W 353 26
He says his head won't bear whist--but perhaps if we make W 354 28
You know what a sad visitor I make.-- W 356 28
You would be astonished to hear the noise we make there.-- W 358 28
wit himself, cd sometimes make use of the wit of an absent W 359 28
was hardly such as to make reflection very soothing. W 361 31
insufficient to make his wife understand his character. PP I 1 5 34
Mrs. Bennet deigned not to make any reply; but unable to PP I 2 6 7
I know, and read great books, and make extracts." PP I 2 7 18
"I do not know how you will ever make him amends for his PP I 2 8 26
every body's character and make it still better, and say PP I 4 14 9
Jane should therefore make the most of every half hour in PP I 6 22 6
This is not quite enough to make her understand his PP I 6 22 7
"You make me laugh, Charlotte; but it is not sound. PP I 6 23 11
was not disposed to make any; and Elizabeth at that PP I 6 26 37
38
Well, Jane, make haste and tell us; make haste, my love." PP I 7 30 15
"If we make haste," said Lydia, as they walked along, " PP I 7 32 40
Mr. Bingley's, she could not make a very favourable answer. PP I 8 35 1
not wish to see your sister make such an exhibition." PP I 8 36 7
Bingley, "it would not make them one jot less agreeable." PP I 8 37 18
"But I would really advise you to make your purchase in PP I 8 38 35
was sure he would make her an offer before we came away. PP I 9 44 31
A regard for the requester would often make one readily PP I 10 50 37
to make them every possible amends,--but of this hereafter. PP I 13 63 12
and if he is disposed to make them any amends, I shall not PP I 13 63 14
in what way he can mean to make us the atonement he thinks PP I 13 63 15
"I cannot make him out.-- PP I 13 64 17
before, to make up her pool of quadrille in the evening. PP I 14 66 1
wanted only regimentals to make him completely charming. PP I 15 72 8
and their aunt promised to make her husband call on Mr. PP I 15 74 11
mere trifle, and begged she would not make herself uneasy. PP I 16 83 49
in such circumstances as to make five shillings any object. PP I 16 83 50
Mr. Collins might never make the offer, and till he did, PP I 17 88 14
which he directly afterwards approached to make.-- PP I 18 89 3
week, she was soon able to make a voluntary transition to PP I 18 90 4
her fancy for Wickham to make her appear unpleasant in the PP I 18 90 8
I talked about the dance, and you ought to make some kind PP I 18 91 9
"I am trying to make it out." PP I 18 93 38
to make inquiries on the same subject of Bingley. PP I 18 95 48
been so fortunate as to make a most important discovery. PP I 18 96 56
It was necessary to make this circumstance a matter of PP I 18 99 63
In the first place, he must make such an agreement for PP I 18 101 71
make a point of remaining close to her the whole evening. PP I 18 102 73
him how happy he would make them, by eating a family PP I 18 103 76
feelings of diffidence to make it distressing to himself PP I 19 104 1
up high, but able to make a small income go a good way. PP I 19 105 10
To fortune I am perfectly indifferent, and shall make no PP I 19 106 10
You could not make me happy, and I am convinced that I am PP I 19 107 14
am the last woman in the world who would make you so.- PP I 19 107 14
Elizabeth would make no reply, and immediately and in PP I 19 109 22
know her own interest; but I will make her know it." PP I 20 110 3
You must come and make Lizzy marry Mr. Collins, for she PP I 20 111 7
make haste he will change his mind and not have her." PP I 20 111 7
"your representation of all this, might make me quite easy. PP I 21 119 21
name the day that was to make him the happiest of men; and PP I 22 121 2
from any charm that could make a woman wish for its PP I 22 122 2
and his wife should make their appearance at St. James's. PP I 22 122 3
Longbourn only in time to make an apology for his absence PP I 23 129 15
I should be forced to make way for her, and live to see PP I 23 130 17
You do not make allowance enough for difference of PP II 1 135 12
to do wrong, or to make others unhappy, there may be error, PP II 1 136 17
By supposing such an affection, you make every body acting PP II 1 137 24
affectionate mother who will always make the most of it." PP II 1 138 29
would be fixed that was to make him the happiest of men. PP II 2 139 1
other was plain enough to make her a little uneasy; and PP II 2 142 18
which the want of fortune would make so very imprudent. PP II 3 144 2
think only of what will make me happy, your affection, and PP II 3 148 26
would make him abundantly regret what he had thrown away. PP II 3 149 27
His present pursuit could not make him forget that PP II 4 151 3
were not of a kind to make her think him less agreeable. PP II 4 152 4
wishing to make her feel what she had lost in refusing him. PP II 5 155 4
"Oh, my dear Eliza! pray make haste and come into the PP II 5 158 11
12
Make haste, and come down this moment." PP II 5 158 12
She will make him a very proper wife." PP II 5 158 18
make yourself uneasy, my dear cousin, about your apparel. PP II 6 160 5
6
but just courage enough to make a very low bow, and take PP II 6 162 11
such as to make her visitors forget their inferior rank. PP II 6 162 11
honour of assisting Mrs. Jenkinson to make up her party. PP II 6 166 41
Where there is fortune to make the expence of travelling PP II 9 179 22
Mrs. Collins knew not what to make of him. PP II 9 180 29
"Our habits of expence make us too dependant, and there PP II 10 183 14
To interrupt a silence which might make him fancy her PP II 10 184 16
17
And pray what sort of guardians do you make? PP II 10 184 19
Your superior knowledge of your sister must make the PP II 12 197 5
If your abhorrence of me should make my assertions PP II 12 203 5
must make him entirely blameless throughout the whole. PP II 13 205 3
such reflections as must make her unfit for conversation. PP II 13 209 12
near the lodges, to make them his parting obeisance, was PP II 14 210 1
make her very desirous of having them all to dine with her. PP II 14 210 1
now so much affected as to make it almost impossible for PP II 14 213 19
we see of the world, must make Hunsford extremely dull to PP II 15 215 2
she had received, must make her feel the obliged. PP II 15 215 3
as I get home, and see if I can make it up any better." PP II 16 219 3
"You never will be able to make both of them good for any PP II 17 225 10
them; just enough to make one good sort of man; and of PP II 17 225 10
I want to be told whether I ought, or ought not to make PP II 17 226 21
Mr. Darcy has not authorised me to make his communication PP II 17 226 23
We must not make him desperate." PP II 17 227 24
But I make no doubt, they often talk of it between PP II 17 228 35
In vain did Elizabeth attempt to make her reasonable, and PP II 18 230 14
to make her reasonable, and Jane to make her resigned. PP II 18 230 14
as such a step must make her were it known, she could not PP II 18 230 14
hand, said in reply, "do not make yourself uneasy, my love. PP II 18 231 19
20
such happy promise as to make Elizabeth hope, that by the PP II 19 238 6
to compose her own, and to make herself agreeable to all; PP III 2 262 7
enquiries to make after all their Hertfordshire friends. PP III 2 264 12
lay awake two whole hours, endeavouring to make them out. PP III 2 265 16
believed her partial, to make her betray a sensibility PP III 3 269 10
I am afraid you will not be able to make it out, but I PP III 4 274 3
Many circumstances might make it more eligible for them to PP III 4 275 5
It was, on the contrary, exactly calculated to make her PP III 4 278 19
good humour, that could make him for her sake, forego PP III 5 283 8
I, thought it necessary to make our knowledge public; for PP III 5 285 16
go to my brother, and make him come home with me to PP III 5 288 37
and if they are not married already, make them marry. PP III 5 288 38
their separate apartments, to make their appearance before. PP III 5 289 41
in amazement, but was too much oppressed to make reply. PP III 5 289 44
not like it, for it will make the surprise the greater, PP III 5 291 60
Pray make my excuses to Pratt, for not keeping my PP III 5 291 60
might be remarked, he meant to make enquiries at Clapham. PP III 5 293 69
his fare, he determined to make enquiries there, and hoped PP III 5 293 69
said, believed enough to make her former assurance of her PP III 6 295 4
Who is to fight Wickham, and make him marry her, if he PP III 6 298 14
"Well, well," said he, "do not make yourself unhappy. PP III 6 300 32
which I have ventured to make on your side, I hope it will PP III 7 302 14
If such goodness does not make her miserable now, she will PP III 7 305 36
as may in time make their past imprudence forgotten." PP III 7 305 37
whether he would not wish them to make it known to her. PP III 7 305 39
all have a bowl of punch, to make merry at her wedding." PP III 7 307 49
of the moment, been led to make Mr. Darcy acquainted with PP III 8 311 11
been so well known, as to make it impossible for any young PP III 10 321 2
Darcy's next step was to make your uncle acquainted with PP III 10 323 2
"It must make you better satisfied that your other four PP III 11 330 11
Elizabeth did not know what to make of it. PP III 11 332 18
That will make thirteen with ourselves, so there will be PP III 11 333 26
wonder how he came to make such an awkward business of it. PP III 11 336 49
he meant to make any stay in the country at present. PP III 11 337 52
of happiness could not make Jane or herself amends, for PP III 11 337 54
give pleasure either, or make either appear to advantage. PP III 12 340 12
the room, as to make him play as unsuccessfully as herself. PP III 12 342 26
seeing him there again the next day, to make his proposals. PP III 12 343 29
in indifference, do not make me your confidante." PP III 12 343 37
crying out, "my dear Jane, make haste and hurry down. PP III 13 344 6
7
Make haste, make haste. PP III 13 344 7
Her younger sisters soon began to make interest with her PP III 13 349 41
was determined to make no effort for conversation with a PP III 14 353 20
this place, that I might make my sentiments known to you." PP III 14 353 26
can have no reason to suppose he will make an offer to me." PP III 14 354 41
to his cousin, why is not he to make another choice? PP III 14 355 44
"That will make your ladyship's situation at present more PP III 14 356 49
"I will make no promise of the kind." PP III 14 356 59
promise, make their marriage at all more probable? PP III 14 357 61
accept his hand, make him wish to bestow it on his cousin? PP III 14 357 61
all his friends, and make him the contempt of the world." PP III 14 358 69
once to be as happy, as dignity unblemished could make him. PP III 15 361 3
For what do we live, but to make sport for our neighbours, PP III 15 364 22
your pointed dislike, make it so delightfully absurd! PP III 15 364 24
Elizabeth had never been more at a loss to make her PP III 15 364 25
to which he alluded, as to make her receive with gratitude PP III 16 366 8
"I was certainly very far from expecting them to make so PP III 16 368 15
"Did it," said he, "did it soon make you think better of PP III 16 368 18
I can remember some expressions which might justly make PP III 16 368 20
I told him of all that had occurred to make my former PP III 16 371 40
But will they make you happy?" PP III 17 376 31
But make a virtue of it by all means. PP III 18 381 7
which ought to make her happy, for she loves to be of use. PP III 18 381 15
if I could, whether I might ever hope to make you love me. PP III 18 382 16
to make the confession to him which I have since made." PP III 18 382 16
her more quiet, at all likely to make her more elegant. PP III 18 384 27
so happy an effect as to make her a sensible, amiable, PP III 19 385 1
that Darcy might yet be prevailed on to make his fortune. PP III 19 386 6
years, or at least to make it very wonderful to Sir Thomas, MP I 1 4 2
would be enough to make either of the dear sweet-tempered MP I 1 7 6
engaged in, and that to make it really serviceable to Mrs. MP I 1 7 7
poor sister to-morrow, and make the proposal; and, as soon MP I 1 7 8
to make her remember that she is not a Miss Bertram. MP I 1 10 17
did Lady Bertram smile and make her sit on the sofa with MP I 2 13 4
a good deal; but we must make allowances for such a child-- MP I 2 13 5
they could do no more than make her a generous present of MP I 2 14 7
and friends, who all love you, and wish to make you happy. MP I 2 15 11
Would it make you happy to write to William?" MP I 2 16 13
nor did her aunt Norris's voice make her start very much. MP I 2 17 21
sometimes of a nature to make a third very useful, MP I 2 17 21
make allowance for your cousin, and pity her deficiency. MP I 2 19 27
of her feelings, trying to make her good qualities MP I 2 21 34
It can make very little difference to you, whether you are MP I 3 25 16
If I can but make both ends meet, that's all I ask for." MP I 3 29 48
if the Antigua estate is to make such poor returns." MP I 3 30 54
as she took early care to make him, as well as Lady MP I 3 30 57
confidence to make him go without fears for their conduct. MP I 3 32 62
fears, and trying to make Edmund participate them whenever MP I 4 34 2
or the economy of his aunt, to make it appear unimportant. MP I 4 36 7
and accomplishments, the best adapted to make him happy. MP I 4 39 10
"I have thought of something to make it quite complete. MP I 4 42 19
accomplished girl, who will make you very happy." MP I 4 42 19
calculation is wrong, we make a second better; we find MP I 5 46 23
dearest Mary, who make much of a little, are more taken in MP I 5 46 23
acquiescence, and tried to make out something MP I 6 55 17
Does not it make you think of Cowper? MP I 6 56 20
make the fortune, and there be discretion in spending it. MP I 6 60 51
go?-- why should not we make a little party? here are many MP I 6 62 58
by her early progress, to make her unwilling to dismount. MP I 7 66 15
It was a sound which did not make her cheerful; she MP I 7 67 16
into the park, and make towards the spot where she stood. MP I 7 68 17
hearing, "I am come to make my own apologies for keeping MP I 7 68 18
she would ride well," said Julia; "she has the make for it. MP I 7 69 24
Mrs. Norris trying to make up her mind as to whether Miss MP I 8 77 8
"You do not make me of any use. MP I 9 94 59
"Your attentiveness and consideration make me more MP I 9 95 70
nice old gardener would make me take; but if it is in your MP I 10 105 55
serenity of nature could make it; but when Mrs. Norris MP I 10 106 58
no reason why a man should make a worse clergyman for MP I 11 109 17
the trouble of being agreeable, which make men clergymen. MP I 11 110 23
It must make him think, and I have no doubt that he MP I 11 112 30
want to make a table for Mrs. Rushworth, you know.-- MP I 12 119 23

accept again; but I was determined to make no difficulties. MP I 13 122 2
materially; but I was resolved to make no difficulties. MP I 13 122 2
sorry to withdraw; and to make you amends, Yates, I think MP I 13 123 5
so much leisure as to make almost any novelty a certain MP I 13 123 6
We must rather adopt Mr. Crawford's views, and make the MP I 13 124 9
seemed so decided, as to make Edmund quite uncomfortable. MP I 13 124 13
he was mistaken in supposing she would wish to make any. MP I 13 129 40
and his power, seemed to make allies unnecessary; and MP I 14 130 3
I do not wish to make objections, I shall be happy to be MP I 14 131 3
From this moment I make no difficulties. MP I 14 131 5
It could make no difference in the play; and as for MP I 14 134 14
"it will be impossible to make any thing of it fit for MP I 14 134 15
pacify her, and make her overlook the previous affront? MP I 14 135 18
by the remonstrance which Edmund would certainly make. MP I 14 137 23
Mr. Yates, who was trying to make himself agreeable to MP I 15 142 24
I only puzzle them, and oblige them to make civil speeches. MP I 15 144 36
be sorry to make the character ridiculous by bad acting. MP I 15 145 41
and a mob cap, and we must make you a few wrinkles, and a MP I 15 146 52
ashamed of you, Fanny, to make such a difficulty of MP I 15 146 53
most anxiously trying to make it out to be feasible,--but MP I 15 148 58
at the time, to make the remembrance when she was alone MP I 16 150 1
talk to him seriously, and make him know his own mind; and MP I 17 162 18
or principle enough to make them merciful or just, to give MP I 17 162 19
his parts together, and make him more ready to regret that MP I 18 164 1
in her power, trying to make an artificial memory for him, MP I 18 166 4
credit, and make it a very suffering exhibition to herself. MP I 18 170 24
to it, and finally would make him hear the whole history MP II 1 184 25
partial good as to make his judgment in it very doubtful. MP II 2 187 1
in that case, he should make a point of returning to MP II 2 192 11
Dr. and Mrs. Grant would enliven us, and make our evenings MP II 3 196 2
Mrs. Rushworth was quite ready to retire, and make way for MP II 3 202 28
sufficiently friends to make each of them exceedingly glad MP II 3 203 32
variety, but that does not make it less amazing, that the MP II 4 209 16
These are something like grievances, and make me think the MP II 4 212 31
that his mother would make any difficulty of sparing her, MP II 4 215 47
on my account; so you must make up your mind to what may MP II 5 221 34
will ever want him to make two-and-forty speeches to her"-- MP II 5 224 53
patience in trying to make it possible for him to learn MP II 5 224 53
to make money--how to turn a good income into a better. MP II 5 226 61
He will have a very pretty income to make ducks and drakes MP II 5 226 61
"Bertram," said Henry Crawford, "I shall make a point of MP II 5 227 65
No, my plan it to make Fanny Price in love with me." MP II 6 229 3
said, "I do not quite know what to make of Miss Fanny. MP II 6 230 7
happiness could be said to make her happy, before the MP II 6 233 17
been obliged to give up, and make the best of his way back. MP II 7 240 13
You must make you a new garden at what is not the back of MP II 7 242 23
receive such an air as to make its owner be set down as MP II 7 244 27
You must think of that; you must try to make up your mind MP II 7 249 53
you can make on the subject, to your entire satisfaction. MP II 7 250 61
quiescent and contented, and had no objections to make. MP II 8 253 6
a serious character as to make the ball, which would be MP II 8 254 10
she love him well enough to make them no longer essential? MP II 8 255 11
tried to make every thing agreeable by her encouragement. MP II 8 257 15
given her consent, proceeded to make the selection. MP II 8 258 17
He gave it to me, and with the necklace I make over to you MP II 8 259 19
Its being a gift of my brother's need not make the MP II 8 259 22
Fanny dared not make any further opposition; and with MP II 8 260 23
will, upon consideration, make that sacrifice rather than MP II 9 263 16
and natural delicacy as to make the few slight differences, MP II 9 263 16
that if William could make up his mind to leave Mansfield MP II 9 265 21
people invited, was not to make her first appearance, and MP II 9 266 22
William, determined to make this last day a day of MP II 9 267 22
Fanny, not liking to complain, found it easiest to make no MP II 9 268 27
I am now persuaded she is the very one to make you happy. MP II 12 294 19
I will make her very happy, Mary, happier than she has MP II 12 295 20
thing in the world to make Fanny Price happy, or of MP II 12 296 30
Henry was most happy to make it more intelligible, by MP II 13 300 7
no want of delicacy on his part could make a trifle to her. MP II 13 301 7
him about William as to make her feel as if nothing had MP II 13 303 12
keep himself, which would make a vast difference to his MP II 13 304 19
it would make some difference in her presents too. MP II 13 304 19
the lover of Fanny, make decided proposals for her, and MP III 1 314 16
(I have no accusation to make on that head,) I never MP III 1 316 29
make him happy, and that I should be miserable myself." MP III 1 320 43
And, Fanny, (turning back again for a moment) I shall make MP III 1 322 48
be able in time to make those feelings what he wished. MP III 2 326 1
totally dissimilar, as to make mutual affection MP III 2 327 5
She must do her duty, and trust that time might make her MP III 2 331 17
were as exactly fitted to make them blessed in each other, MP III 3 335 6
Meanwhile, he saw enough of Fanny's embarrassment to make MP III 3 335 6
not to see it, as to make it clear that the voice was MP III 3 339 21
it might be as well to make one more effort for the young MP III 4 345 2
that the man who means to make you love him (you having MP III 4 347 21
not in the smallest degree make against the probability of MP III 4 348 23
He will make you happy, Fanny, I know he will make you MP III 4 351 32
he will make you happy; but you will make him every thing." MP III 4 351 32
which I ventured to make for you to your friend and Mrs. MP III 4 353 46
to make the idea first familiar, and then agreeable to her. MP III 5 356 1
well; she does not seem to know how to make the best of it. MP III 5 361 16
But this I will say, that his fault, the liking to make MP III 5 363 24
call on Mrs. Grant and make her amends for my being gone." MP III 5 364 32
be allowed to make her absence three) must do her good. MP III 6 370 12
you will teach Betsey, and make the boys love and mind you. MP III 6 372 20
He too had a sacrifice to make to Mansfield Park, as well MP III 6 373 25
reservation of enough to make the little cottage MP III 7 375 2
more than once tried to make his father think of Fanny, MP III 7 380 23
and change his dress, and make the necessary preparations MP III 7 381 24
to, but to run about and make a noise; and both boys had MP III 7 381 25
she had not yet heard all the noise they could make. MP III 7 381 26
"to hurry sally and help make the toast, and spread the MP III 7 383 32
noticed her, but to make her the object of a coarse joke. MP III 8 389 3
servants, without skill to make them better, and whether MP III 8 389 4
She might scruple to make use of the words, but she must MP III 8 390 6
As for any society in Portsmouth, that could at all make MP III 9 395 3
to make her better bear with its excesses to the others. MP III 9 396 5
it would not be unbecoming in her to make such a present. MP III 9 396 7
having so struggled as to make the purchase necessary for MP III 9 397 7
a somebody that would make Everingham and all about it, a MP III 10 404 15
enough inured to, for her often to make a tolerable meal. MP III 10 407 23
I must make him know that I will not be tricked on the MP III 11 411 20
for such a house, and it would not make me miserable. MP III 12 416 2
I should like the scheme, and we would make a little MP III 12 416 3
must not be allowed to wear her out, and make her useless. MP III 12 418 6
God grant that her influence do not make him cease to be MP III 13 424 4
at a time when she could make no advantage of it, and will MP III 13 425 6
which I make no doubt will give you much concern." MP III 13 425 7
8

far pronounced safe, as to make his mother perfectly easy; MP III 14 429 1
her, and tried at once to make her feel the blessing of MP III 14 432 10
made a fuss with, and to make a fuss himself in any MP III 14 433 13
Now do not make yourself uneasy with any queer fancies, MP III 14 435 14
have preceded them, or at least should make any impression. MP III 15 438 4
Mr. Price cared too little about the report, to make her MP III 15 440 17
had read so often as to make every line her own, was in MP III 15 441 19
distance every pain, and make her incapable of suitably MP III 15 443 24
any thing could occur to make me suffer more, but that she MP III 16 457 30
which such a disappointment must make on his mind. MP III 16 460 31
and happy as all this must make her, she would still have MP III 17 461 2
in his presence, as to make their real disposition unknown MP III 17 463 7
him so like hatred, as to make them for a while each MP III 17 464 10
such circumstances as to make any better end, the effect MP III 17 464 12
of such irritation, as to make her every where tormenting. MP III 17 466 16
for a mind unused to make any sacrifice to right; he MP III 17 467 20
get the better of it, and make Mrs. Rushworth Maria MP III 17 467 20
of prudence to stop him or make his progress slow; no MP III 17 471 28
No happiness of son or niece could make her wish the MP III 17 472 31
and I am sure she will make a very good servant; she is a E I 1 9 19
dear, I wish you would not make matches and foretel things, E I 1 12 40
Pray do not make any more matches." E I 1 12 40
"I promise you to make none for myself, papa; but I must, E I 1 12 41
"But, my dear, pray do not make any more matches, they are E I 1 13 45
to make his merit and prospects a kind of common concern. E I 2 17 7
circumstances, which would make the approaching season no E I 2 18 11
week in which Emma could not make up a card-table for him. E I 3 20 1
superiority to make atonement to herself, or frighten E I 3 21 4
the endeavour to make a small income go as far as possible. E I 3 21 4
was sure whenever he married he would make a good husband. E I 4 28 6
Mr. Martin, I imagine, has his fortune entirely to make-- E I 4 30 20
The misfortune of your birth ought to make you E I 4 30 22
of mind, or tend at all to make a girl adapt herself E I 5 39 15
one really wrong; she will make so lasting blunder; where E I 5 40 22
return to Hartfield, to make a regular visit of some days. E I 8 57 1
"My dear sir, do not make a stranger of me." E I 8 57 4
"Well, well, means to make her an offer then. E I 8 59 27
It was most convenient to Emma not to make a direct reply E I 8 63 43
reason you have, is almost enough to make me think so too. E I 8 64 45
to yourself; but as you make no secret of your love of E I 8 66 51
Highbury, but not at all likely to make an imprudent match. E I 8 66 53
Harriet's staying away so long was beginning to make her E I 8 67 56
Mr. Knightley did not make the allowance for the influence E I 8 67 57
"I cannot make a question, or listen to a question about E I 9 74 23
he seemed then about to make his bow, when taking the E I 9 81 79
80

smilingly said, "you must make my apologies to your friend; E I 9 82 81
82

How trifling they make every thing else appear!-- I feel E I 10 87 25
having some alteration to make in the lacing of her half- E I 10 88 33
and endeavouring to make every thing appear to advantage. E I 10 89 38
conversation, she hoped to make it practicable for him to E I 10 89 38
She was then obliged to be finished and make her E I 10 89 38
She thought it was time to make up. E I 12 98 2
My dear Isabella, I have not heard you make one inquiry E I 12 101 23
You make the best of it--but after you have been a week at E I 12 103 38
Why does he make it any business of his, to wonder at what E I 12 106 60
he was not able to make more than a simple question on E I 13 108 3
well know what answer to make; which was exactly the case; E I 13 110 10
"You do quite right," said she;--"we will make your E I 13 110 11
How very comfortable they make it;--impossible to feel E I 13 115 37
Another hour or two's snow can hardly make the road E I 15 126 10
a word, lest it should make Mr. Woodhouse uncomfortable, E I 15 126 11
return only were wanted to make every thing go well: for E I 15 132 38
sources, was such as to make them scarcely secondary to E I 16 136 9
not two years ago, to make his way as he could, without E I 16 136 9
The distressing explanation she had to make to Harriet, E I 16 137 12
particularly amiable as to make it shocking to disappoint E I 16 138 15
They must encounter each other, and make the best of it. E I 17 143 14
What has Mr. Frank Churchill done, to make you suppose him E I 18 145 9
always find me ready to make to your convenience; but I E I 18 146 16
as a man of sense would make it, in a proper manner--would E I 18 147 18
first attempt on their side to make him slight his father. E I 18 148 22
body's character, and make every body's talents conduce to E I 18 150 32
he may make all appear like fools compared with himself! E I 18 150 32
supposed it could make him unjust to the merit of another. E I 18 150 37
My mother often wonders that I can make it out so well. E II 1 157 10
it to make out all that chequer-work'--don't you, ma'am? E II 1 157 10
sure she would contrive to make it out herself, if she had E II 1 157 10
Cole, we shall hardly know how to make enough of her now." E II 1 158 14
much as a week, which must make it very strange to be in E II 1 159 20
I always make a point of reading Jane's letters through to E II 1 162 31
I fancied at first; and I make so light of it now to her, E II 1 162 31
and before he could make any reply, Mr. Woodhouse, whose E II 3 171 16
17

Oh! Miss Woodhouse, do talk to me and make me comfortable E II 3 179 52
difference did this make in the evils of the connection? E II 3 179 53
She exerted herself; and did try to make her comfortable, E II 3 180 54
certain was enough to make Emma consider it so, and E II 5 188 8
Emma was directly sure that he knew how to make himself E II 5 191 26
always the last to make his way in conversation; "then E II 5 194 45
If he were deficient there, nothing should make amends for E II 6 196 2
could make amends for the want of the fine glow of health. E II 6 199 10
of public fame would not make me amends for the loss of E II 6 200 16
that Enscombe could not make him happy, and that whenever E II 6 204 43
Something occurred while they were at Hartfield, to make E II 7 206 5
"You will make my excuses, my dear, as civilly as possible. E II 7 209 14
beauty of her dress, to make the two ladies all the amends E II 8 213 6
as any reason for their not meaning to make the present. E II 8 215 14
perhaps may never make any thing of it; and there is poor E II 8 215 16
my suspicions, though you make so noble a profession of E II 8 217 32
and the sort; and could make out from his answers that, as E II 8 221 48
"I often feel concerned," said she, "that I dare not make E II 8 228 89
You could make it into two parcels, Mrs. Ford, could not E II 9 235 36
Miss Fairfax in trying to make her instrument stand E II 10 240 5
for her, and trying to make her help or advise him in his E II 10 240 6
I wish I could conjecture how soon I shall make this rivet E II 10 242 15
couple are not enough to make it worth while to stand up. E II 11 248 7
8

representations were necessary to make it acceptable. E II 11 251 25
However, this does make a difference; and, perhaps, when E II 11 252 32
One thing was wanting to make the prospect of the ball E II 12 257 1
Pray make my excuses and adieus to her." E II 13 266 5
to, without being able to make their opinions the same. E II 13 267 9
Harriet, is the strongest reproach you can make me. E II 13 268 10
of pride or propriety, to make her resolve on not being E II 14 270 2
Their propriety, simplicity, and elegance, would make them E II 14 278 47
young lady, and no doubt will make him a very good wife. E II 14 279 54
It is encouraging people to marry if you make so much of E II 14 280 57
in a style which could not make the addition of Jane E II 15 283 9
up such a dinner, as could make me regret having asked E II 15 283 9
Harriet must be asked to make the eighth:--but this E II 16 291 5
whom she really wanted to make the eighth, Jane Fairfax.-- E II 16 291 5
though he certainly would make them nine, yet he always E II 16 292 8
Mrs. Elton, as elegant as lace and pearls could make her, E II 16 292 10
growing older should make me indifferent about letters." E II 16 293 17
18

"I have not even made any inquiry; I do not wish to make E II 17 299 5
no means my intention; I make no inquiry myself, and E II 17 300 13
and soon moved away to make the rest of his friends happy E II 17 304 29
in her character which make it difficult for me to speak E II 18 309 33
harm nobody, and only make himself a little helpless and E II 18 309 33
do all in my power to make them happy, which will be E II 18 311 39
an hour, and hurrying away to make other calls in Highbury. E III 1 316 4
and London was enough to make the whole difference of E III 1 317 10
It was almost enough to make her think of marrying. E III 2 325 31
so much brother and sister as to make it at all improper." E III 2 331 62
work to make them peculiarly interesting to each other?-- E III 3 335 9
illnesses for her, she could make no figure in a message. E III 3 336 12
confession to make--and then, you know, it will be over." E III 4 337 1
2

up, "you make me more ashamed of myself than I can bear. E III 4 338 13
evening, he wanted to make a memorandum in his pocket-book; E III 4 339 18
Why do you make a doubt of it?" E III 5 350 33
down out of doors to eat would inevitably make him ill. E III 6 356 29
He was not hungry; it would only make him hotter." E III 6 364 57
water, will make you nearly on a par with the rest of us." E III 6 365 65

And Mr. Weston tried, in vain, to make them harmonize E III 7 367 1
I must make myself very disagreeable, or she would not E III 7 371 28
"And make her like myself." E III 7 373 47
Hazel eyes excepted, two years more might make her all E III 7 373 51
is every thing in the world that can make her happy in it. E III 8 382 23
the mere proposal of going out seemed to make her worse.-- E III 9 390 18
It may make many things intelligible and excusable which E III 10 398 53
Let us make the best of it--and, indeed, almost every E III 10 400 65
"that I must often have contributed to make her unhappy." E III 12 419 11
'I did not make the allowances,' said she, 'which I ought E III 12 419 12
"I cannot make speeches, emma:"--he soon resumed; and in a E III 13 430 37
unnecessary pain; how to make her any possible atonement; E III 14 435 4
to me, I was led on to make more than an allowable use of E III 14 438 8
enough to make the rest of my letter what it ought to be.-- E III 14 440 8
away determined that she should make the first advances.-- E III 14 441 8
This letter must make its way to Emma's feelings. E III 15 444 1
could be competent to make--the confession of her E III 16 452 6
you and I should make, if we could be shaken together. E III 16 456 33
I long to make apologies, excuses, to urge something for E III 16 459 47
such a time, and follow up the beginning she was to make.-- E III 17 465 28
She must not make it a more decided subject of misery to E III 17 465 28
Woodhouse, so as to make such an arrangement desirable!-- E III 17 467 31
Time, you may be very sure, will make one or the other of E III 18 471 16
"It is not that such a circumstance would now make me E III 18 471 17
now tell me every thing; make this intelligible to me. E III 18 471 19
I never was more surprised--but it does not make me E III 18 471 19
Your friend Harriet will make a much longer history when E III 18 472 20
which only woman's language can make interesting.-- E III 18 472 20
were in such a crowd, as to make Miss Smith rather uneasy." E III 18 472 20
circumstance would not now make you unhappy; but I am E III 18 472 21
22

to attach her to life, and make it no matter of P III 1 4 6
enough to dissuade him from it, and make Bath preferred. P III 2 14 10
and are as likely to make desirable tenants as any set of P III 3 17 4
established usages which make every thing plain and easy P III 3 18 9
10

By the report which he hastened over to Kellynch to make, P III 3 21 18
himself to him in order to make particular inquiries, and P III 3 21 18
behaviour;--not likely to make the smallest difficulty P III 3 22 23
and, at the same time, can never make a baronet look small. P III 3 24 36
so soon, and wanted to make it possible for her to stay P III 5 33 6
herself from trying to make it perceptible to her sister. P III 5 34 12
make a degrading match; but he might be rendered unhappy. P III 5 35 14
she had determined to make her own absence from home begin P III 5 36 19
trying to understand, and make him understand, which of P III 5 38 34
conversation, or grace, to make the past, as they were P III 6 43 5
And on Mrs. Musgrove's side, it was,--"I make a rule of P III 6 45 9
such near neighbours, and make those hints broadest which P III 6 46 11
gloom of the evening, to make enquiries; and Mr. Musgrove, P III 7 54 5
mother's property, her own feelings generally make it so." P III 7 56 11
You can make little Charles do any thing; he always minds P III 7 57 16
in no such state as could make it inconvenient, Captain P III 7 59 24
Mary had no feelings to make her respect her sister's in a P III 7 60 32
they composed, and consequently must make her happier. P III 7 61 35
here I am, Sophia, quite ready to make a foolish match. P III 7 61 38
39

who has had no society among women to make him nice?" P III 7 62 39
"I had no more discoveries to make, than you would have as P III 8 65 16
all one's sacrifices, to make the accommodations on board, P III 8 68 35
he had sat down to try to make out an air which he wished P III 8 72 58
I do not think any young woman has a right to make a P III 9 76 13
into his hands, he will make a different sort of place of P III 9 76 15
Either of them would, in all probability, make him an P III 9 77 18
engaging a curate; should make his curacy quite as good as P III 9 78 19
and the Miss Musgroves to make over her little patient to P III 9 80 34
You make the most of it, I know," cried Louisa, "but if it P III 10 85 9
could not endure to make a third in a one horse chaise. P III 10 90 38
too, long enough, one would think, to make up his mind. P III 10 92 44
We sailors, Miss Elliot, cannot afford to make long P III 10 92 44
environs of Lyme, to make him wish to know it better. P III 11 95 9
low rock among the sands make it the happiest spot for P III 11 95 9
and visited again, to make the worth of Lyme understood. P III 11 95 9
acquaintance, which would make it cheerful for her,--and I P III 12 102 2
been on such terms as to make the power of attempting an P III 12 106 18
the last, proceeded to make the proper adieus to the Cobb. P III 12 108 30
There was too much wind to make the high part of the new P III 12 109 32
with his own horror to make him immoveable; and in another P III 12 109 34
the windows, was enough to make the sound of Lady P IV 1 123 8
be talked of, she must make enquiries, she must regret the P IV 1 124 12
formal visit here, he will make his way over to Kellynch P IV 2 131 12
enquiries to make, before the talk must be all their own. P IV 3 137 3
But this was not all which they had to make them happy. P IV 3 138 6
He hoped she might make some amends for the many very P IV 3 141 13
is necessary in manners to make him quite the thing, are P IV 3 144 20
Will it make you happy? P IV 4 150 17
affairs, no health to make all the rest supportable. P IV 5 154 8
which, as a companion, make her infinitely superior to P IV 5 155 9
I mean to make my profit of Mrs. Wallis, however. P IV 5 156 13
by a bad cold, was glad to make use of the relationship P IV 5 157 14
questions enough asked, to make it understood what this P IV 5 157 14
"February 1st, ----. "my dear Anne, "I make no apology P IV 6 162 7
therefore be able to make my letter as long "as I like. P IV 6 164 8
letter to make you and Mrs. Croft particularly uneasy. P IV 6 172 42
manner of writing to make you suppose he thinks himself P IV 6 172 46
It began to rain, not much, but enough to make shelter P IV 7 174 2
women, and quite enough to make it very desirable for Miss P IV 7 174 2
and a talking, which must make all the little crowd in the P IV 7 176 10
"I wish you would make use of it, if you are determined to P IV 7 177 14
to stand near her, and make enquiries in return, in spite P IV 8 181 1
animate her features, and make her rejoice to talk of it. P IV 9 192 5
to make it an object to yourself, of course it is done." P IV 9 195 24
"She could not make a very long history, I think, of one P IV 9 197 41
"Nay," said Anne, "I have no particular enquiry to make P IV 9 200 58
had one object in view--to make his fortune, and by a P IV 9 200 59
He was determined to make it by marriage. P IV 9 200 59
not large, would be enough to make her comparatively rich. P IV 9 210 98
Make a civil message. P IV 10 215 16
at her time of life, who make themselves up so little. P IV 10 215 16
I cannot make her attend to the value of the property. P IV 10 218 22
You will be too late, if you do not make haste. P IV 10 222 38
it, and not omitting to make it known, that however P IV 10 224 50
by Henrietta, eager to make use of the present leisure for P IV 10 225 61
which were to make it the most completely elegant of its P IV 10 227 69
make the best of it, as many others have done before them. P IV 11 230 6
I am not sorry, indeed, to make it over to another. P IV 11 232 15
feeling, "if I could but make you comprehend what a man P IV 11 234 31
of conversation would make the present hour a blessing P IV 11 240 59
Was it not enough to make the fool of me which I appeared? P IV 11 244 72
This is a recollection which ought to make me forgive P IV 11 247 84
no vanity flattered, to make him really happy on the P IV 12 248 2
His profession was all that could ever make her friends P IV 12 252 12
pressing them to make use of his house for both purposes.-- S 1 367 1
the price of provisions & make the poor good for nothing-- S 1 368 1
manner calculated to make the strangers easy--and as Mrs P- S 1 370 1
what returns it will make her in a year or two. S 3 376 1
whom her 2d husband had hoped to make a good bargain for.-- S 3 376 1
a little parasol, which will make her as proud as can be. S 4 381 1
He pretends to advise me to make a Hospital of it. S 4 382 1
in this letter & make us laugh for half an hour together I S 5 387 1
We wanted just to see you & make sure of your being really S 6 391 1
I make no apologies for my heroine's vanity.-- S 7 395 1
Sir Edw: has no Payments to make me. S 7 400 1
about the fair, to make fine speeches to every pretty girl, S 8 405 2
with cautious assiduity to make an impression on her heart, S 8 405 2
come, & meant to get into lodgings & make some stay."-- S 9 407 1
& indolent, as wealth & a hot climate are apt to make us. S 9 409 1
you hardly know what to make of me.-- I see by your looks, S 9 410 1
at Sanditon, intending to make some stay, & without S 10 412 1
he began even to make a sort of apology for having a fire. S 10 415 1
messages enough to make everything appear what it was not. S 11 420 1
could not for some time make out what sort of carriage it S 12 425 1

MAKE-BELIEVE (1)

treated them with the make-believe of decent affection, SS III 14 375 10

MAKES (80)

acquainted with me, & makes very gracious mention of my LS 3 247 1
of the world which makes conversation easy, & talks very LS 6 251 1
Frederica makes me very unhappy. LS 24 289 12
It makes me miserable--but Mr Johnson vows that if I LS 38 306 1
an hour in harness; that makes it exactly twenty-five." NA I 7 45 7
that quiz of a hat, it makes you look like an old witch? NA I 7 49 43
attachment now; his coming back to Bath makes it too plain. NA I 10 70 1
reward in the affection it makes every body feel for you. NA II 1 136 46
It is not the want of more money that makes me just at NA II 1 136 48
The worst of it is that its weight makes it difficult to NA II 6 165 4
over before Captain Tilney makes his engagement known, or NA II 10 202 7
a few hours sooner or later, you know, makes no difference. NA II 13 226 24
"Your promise makes me easy. SS I 14 74 19
"Such weather makes every thing and every body disgusting. SS I 20 110 8
It makes one detest all one's acquaintance. SS I 20 111 8
he who he will, comes and makes love to a pretty girl, and SS II 8 194 10
He makes a monstrous deal of money, and they keep their SS III 2 275 25
good friends, as our near relationship now makes proper. SS III 13 365 14
Penelope makes light of her conduct, but I think such W 316 2
as it makes me nervous to be much alone." W 351 25
Ld Osborne enjoys it famously--he makes the best dealer W 358 28
"I know you do; and it is that which makes the wonder. PP I 4 14 9
it is a subject which always makes a lady energetic." PP I 6 24 19
brotherly affection, makes him a very kind and careful PP I 16 82 41
It makes me very nervous and poorly, to be thwarted so in PP II 2 140 4
Your profusion makes me saving; and if you lament over him PP II 17 225 13
He simpers, and smirks, and makes love to us all. PP III 11 330 8
"Yes--that is what makes it amusing. PP III 15 364 24
is little enough, and makes it more surprising that the MP I 6 55 17
prospect amazingly which makes me think that repton, or MP I 6 55 17
herself, "he is a well bred man; he makes the best of it." MP I 6 56 27
a correspondent, makes her think you too severe upon us." MP I 6 59 45
those of the aunt; and it makes one more sensible of the MP I 7 64 9
makes a blunder, is out of humour with his excellent wife. MP I 11 111 28
But then he is your cousin, which makes all the difference. MP I 18 168 19
"She always makes tea, you know, when my sister is not MP II 5 219 21
appear above themselves, makes me think it right to give MP II 5 221 32
her such a soft skin and makes her so much taller, and MP II 6 230 8
assure you it makes none in my willingness to part with it. MP II 8 259 22
her brother's gift makes no difference, for as she was not MP II 9 263 14
of her former companions makes her seem, gives to her MP II 9 269 31
makes thirty-one;--four in hand and eight in crib.-- MP II 11 283 6
on, that sweetness which makes so essential a part of MP II 12 294 16
Your kindness to William makes me more obliged to you than MP II 13 302 8
and you know it makes very little difference to Sir Thomas. MP II 13 305 25
can judge, matrimony makes no part of his plans or thought. MP III 1 317 34
I will explain to you instantly all that makes me urge you MP III 3 342 36
teeth, and how you do your hair, and who makes your shoes. MP III 5 360 16
for her judgment, which makes one feel there is attachment; MP III 5 361 16
What a difference a vowel makes!--if his rents were but MP III 9 394 1
He makes me write, but I do not know what else is to be MP III 12 415 2
"Which makes his good manners the more valuable. E I 4 33 36
Harriet's features are very delicate, which makes a E I 6 44 15
her shoulders--and it makes one think she must catch cold." E I 6 48 36
Who makes you their confidant?" E I 8 59 23
The name makes me think of poor Isabella; for she was very E I 9 79 56
which makes celibacy contemptible to a generous public! E I 10 85 19
his being a disengaged and social man makes it all easy. E I 11 94 15
as he finds them, and makes enjoyment of them somehow or E I 11 96 26
It makes me envious and miserable;--I who have never seen E I 12 101 23
"Yes; and every delay makes one more apprehensive of other E I 14 122 21
natural, that while she makes no sacrifice for the comfort E I 14 123 24
she really eats nothing--makes such a shocking breakfast, E II 9 237 46
Patty makes an excellent apple-dumpling. E II 9 237 46
one solicitude generally makes way for another, Emma, E II 12 257 2
Every consideration of the subject, in short, makes me E II 13 265 4
It is tenderness of heart which makes my dear father so E II 13 269 16
which makes the difference, it is not age, but situation. E II 16 294 22
see him again, which makes this day's news doubly welcome. E II 18 308 27
The difference which Randalls, Randalls alone makes in E II 18 312 46
is singularity which often makes the worst part of our P III 2 12 4
How low it makes me!" P III 6 48 16
assure you--but my sister makes nothing of it--she would P III 10 84 8
that being by the sea, always makes him feel young again. P III 12 102 2
to have something that makes one know one's species better. P IV 5 155 9
You did not use to like cards; but time makes many changes. P IV 10 225 59
A thing of this kind soon makes a stir in a lonely place S 1 370 1
often makes me laugh at them all in spite of myself.-- S 5 385 1
I have Miss Clara with me now, which makes a great S 7 401 1
And she makes every body mean about her.-- S 7 402 1

MAKING (199)

delicious gratification of making a whole family miserable. LS 4 248 1
an insolent spirit, in making a person pre-determined to LS 7 254 3
I scolded him for making love to Maria Manwaring; he LS 9 257 1
took this opportunity of making downright love to him; I LS 22 282 6
& the rest of his family, by making her marry Sir James. LS 26 295 1
of a generous mind making light of the obligation; and Mrs. NA I 8 55 10
clearer insights, in making those things plain which he NA I 9 66 31
as when I had the honour of making the inquiry before?" NA I 10 78 41
looking morning; the sun making only a few efforts to NA I 11 82 1
She was right; in a few minutes he appeared, and, making NA I 12 93 5
of her dancing, and making her one of the most graceful NA I 13 103 28
injuring my dear Morland, making him sit down upon an NA II 1 135 45
ancient building still making a part of the present NA II 2 141 13
And as to making me an offer, or any thing like it, there NA II 3 144 11
quietly--without making any disturbance, without parading NA II 5 157 5
desire of making use of the present smiling weather.-- NA II 7 177 17
of making her next attempt on the forbidden door alone. NA II 9 192 5
making Miss Morland's time at Northanger pass pleasantly. NA II 11 209 5
I think I can answer for the young ladies making allowance NA II 11 210 6
Catherine walked on to her chamber, making up her mind as NA II 13 222 8
or 'making a conquest,' are the most odious of all. SS I 9 45 30
was enough to prevent her making any inquiry of Marianne. SS I 14 71 4
they were making themselves agreeable to Lady Middleton. SS I 21 120 6
their unreserve, by making the Miss Steeles acquainted SS I 21 125 34
very capable of making a woman sincerely attached to him." SS I 22 130 28
was due to you after my making such particular inquiries SS I 22 132 42
I cannot bear the thoughts of making him so miserable, as SS I 22 133 44
than in making a fillagree basket for a spoilt child. SS II 1 144 14
at seeing them in London, making the usual inquiries about SS II 4 162 11
obliged to assist in making a whist-table for the others. SS II 4 166 31
wish of going away, and making over her cards to a friend, SS II 6 178 16
naming Mr. Willoughby, or making the slightest allusion to SS II 8 195 17
ranging over the town and making what acquaintance they SS II 9 209 28
and additions which were making to the Norland estate, and SS II 12 233 18
Elinor was prevented from making any reply to this civil SS II 13 240 18
I have no notion of people's making such a to-do about SS III 1 259 7
No time was to be lost in undeceiving her, in making her SS III 1 260 10
sang-froid, and go away without making her any reply!-- SS III 3 282 15
the Colonel been really making her an offer of his hand. SS III 3 283 20

You are making a most disgraceful connection, and such a SS III 5 300 37
than her friend's, in making very light of the SS III 7 310 8
of making myself contemptible and wretched for ever. SS III 8 321 34
of Elinor, was making considerable improvements; and after SS III 14 374 6
take the right turning, & making only one blunder, in W 322 2
of whom was continually making opportunities of addressing W 331 11
"It is making it too much of a fatigue I think, to stay so W 340 19
for two or three nights, without making a peice of work. W 351 25
I can tell you, to be making new acquaintance every day; PP I 2 8 26
once, as if the credit of making it rain were all her own. PP I 7 31 29
high she declined it, and making her sister the excuse, PP I 8 37 21
either making some inquiry, or looking at his page. PP I 11 54 4
alterations he had been making, and had even vouchsafed to PP I 14 66 1
which has prevented her making that progress in many PP I 11 67 7
in the game, too eager in making bets and exclaiming after PP I 16 76 8
as may ensure his <u>making</u> friends--whether he may be PP I 18 92 20
She looked at his <u>two</u> sisters, and saw them making signs PP I 18 100 68
cannot be excused from making as comfortable as possible. PP I 18 101 71
a moment's consideration making her also sensible that it PP I 19 104 7
In making me the offer, you must have satisfied the PP I 19 107 16
of making one in the croud, but of that I despair. PP I 21 117 11
But Elizabeth had now recollected herself, and making a PP I 22 125 16
The strangeness of Mr. Collins's making two offers of PP I 22 125 18
joined by Jane, and by making a variety of remarks on the PP I 23 126 4
to name an early day for making him the happiest of men. PP I 23 128 10
instead of making any answer, she went on as before. PP I 23 130 19
sorry to be the means of making any of you unhappy; but PP II 3 145 7
could there be for making love to a girl whom he did not PP II 4 153 13
of it; and after making his bow as the carriage turned PP II 7 170 7
"I have been making the tour of the park," he replied, "as PP II 10 183 4
good humour, that on his making some enquiry as to the PP II 18 233 26
of her friends, and bent on making her known to his sister. PP III 2 265 16
from a determination of making him speak, she continued, " PP III 3 271 16
17
After making every possible enquiry on that side London, PP III 4 275 5
of the opportunity of making many enquiries, which Jane PP III 5 289 45
making his fortune by marriage, in some other country. PP III 10 323 2
"How should you have liked making sermons?" PP III 10 328 27
"I think you are in very great danger of making him as PP III 12 339 9
where Miss Bennet was making tea, and Elizabeth pouring PP III 12 341 16
a considerable time, without making any impression on them. PP III 13 345 11
saw no occasion for making it a general concern, when PP III 16 365 2
or lessen the comfort of making a yearly addition to an MP I 1 8 9
of what they are, without making them think too lowly of MP I 1 10 17
moment, making artificial flowers or wasting gold paper. MP I 2 14 7
she must say, that to be making such a purchase in his MP I 4 36 7
and he began with no object but of making them like him. MP I 5 44 3
Rushworth, who was now making his appearance at Mansfield, MP I 6 52 1
there certainly <u>is</u> impropriety in making them public." MP I 7 63 7
that Edmund should be making himself useful, and proving MP I 7 67 16
Fanny, feeling all this to be wrong, could not help making MP I 10 99 21
must be with the doctor," making a sly face as he spoke MP I 12 119 22
the greater our credit in making any thing of it. MP I 14 131 5
will have more credit in making something of it; and if MP I 14 134 14
I <u>am</u> of some use I hope in preventing waste and making the MP I 15 141 22
I see but Dick Jackson making up to the servants' hall MP I 15 141 22
among you am I to have the pleasure of making love to?" MP I 15 143 27
smallness of the one making the use of the other so MP I 16 151 1
It is an evil--but I am certainly making it less than it MP I 16 156 27
in making them was spoken of with a glow of admiration. MP I 17 159 6
As to his ever making any thing <u>tolerable</u> of them, nobody MP I 18 166 4
had an opportunity of making his <u>passage</u> thither in a MP II 1 178 8
and easy Mr. Yates, making his bow and apology to Sir MP II 1 182 22
in his own house, making part of a ridiculous exhibition MP II 1 183 23
Price, without making a small hole in Fanny Price's heart. MP II 6 229 5
I do desire that you will not be making her really unhappy; MP II 6 230 8
her sister, that after making up the whist table there MP II 7 239 4
was rather hurried in making up a new dress for her; Sir MP II 8 254 9
the scruples which were making Fanny start back at first MP II 8 258 15
necklace round her and making her see how well it looked. MP II 8 258 17
in, was making use of your inkstand to explain my errand. MP II 9 261 2
wondered at if, after making all these good resolutions on MP II 9 265 19
she found for herself, in making up card-tables, giving MP II 10 277 16
of this room by way of making you perfectly comfortable.-- MP III 1 312 10
he felt the necessity of making his own wife and sister-in- MP III 2 332 19
the havock he might be making in young ladies' affections. MP III 5 363 22
and nothing at all with any idea of making her happy. MP III 6 368 9
always for the best; and making light of his own MP III 7 378 11
immediately set about making it, as if pleased to have the MP III 7 383 33
suggest the expediency of making friends, and of MP III 8 390 8
Their sister soon despaired of making the smallest MP III 8 391 8
interest at least--which was making his manner perfect. MP III 10 399 5
seen before; he had begun making acquaintance with MP III 10 404 15
I will not be prevented, however, from making my own MP III 13 420 2
got into the way of making and keeping correspondents, and MP III 13 425 6
for doing so, and for making his pleasure conduce to yours. MP III 14 435 14
remarks, and evidently making Mr. Rushworth uneasy. MP III 16 450 8
But if, which I rather imagine, your making the match, as E I 1 12 42
by the Churchills, as making such an amazing match, was E I 2 16 4
There will be very little merit in making a good wife to E I 5 38 12
refuse; but there is no making children of three or four E I 6 45 21
concerned at the idea of making him unhappy, and thought E I 7 55 35
making so much of her) as in a line of society above him. E I 8 59 27
We shall only be making each other more angry. E I 8 65 48
mental provision she was making for the evening of life, E I 9 69 3
months old, who was now making her first visit to E I 12 98 2
resolution enough to refrain from making any answer at all. E I 13-113 27
Churchill and Miss Smith making their party quite complete. E I 14 119 8
him as before, and on his making Harriet his very first E I 15 124 2
Something new for your coachman and horses to be making E I 15 126 8
and Mr. Elton actually making violent love to her: E I 15 129 24
thought you judged ill in making your visits so frequent. E I 15 131 34
It was adventuring too far, assuming too much, making E I 16 137 10
and making use of Mrs. Weston's arguments against herself. E I 18 145 5
Mr. Frank Churchill to be making such a speech as that to E I 18 147 17
seeming very rude, of making her escape from Jane E II 1 158 13
inherited from her father making independence impossible. E II 2 164 5
could be sure of their making it into steaks, nicely fried, E II 3 171 16
17
where a young woman was making up a gown for her, she E II 3 177 52
been acting a part, or making a parade of insincere E II 6 197 4
quickly as possible, and making no other comment than that E II 7 205 1
either that, after making his proposals to her friend, he E II 8 217 32
I have been making discoveries and forming plans, just E II 8 222 59
for I thought it would be making her comfortable at once. E II 8 223 63
--every day making me less fit to bear any other place. E II 12 260 21
"I do not find myself making any use of the word <u>sacrifice</u>, E II 13 264 2
negatives, is there any allusion to making a sacrifice. E II 13 264 2
custom on such occasions, making the circle of his guests, E II 16 294 24
25
possible to prevent their making two distinct parties;-- E II 17 299 1
But I would not wish you to take the trouble of making any E II 17 300 9
form home confers, was making himself agreeable among the E II 17 303 24
Mrs. Churchill's making incredible exertions to avoid it. E II 18 306 12
About half a mile beyond Highbury, making a sudden turn, E III 3 333 5
And so then, in my nonsense, I could not help making a E III 4 338 12
to Emma, and Emma herself making him over to Harriet, Mr. E III 5 343 2
and the river making a close and handsome curve around it. E III 6 360 38
grew talkative and gay, making her his first object. E III 7 367 3
I am making a conundrum. E III 7 371 29
having taken no leave, making no acknowledgement, parting E III 7 376 62
aware of it, had been making up her mind the whole day." E III 8 381 20
How could he tell that he might not be making me in love E III 10 396 44
A few minutes were sufficient for making her acquainted E III 11 407 32
yet dread making the story known to Colonel Campbell.'" E III 12 419 8
in," she said, "was that of making her <u>unreasonable</u>. E III 12 419 12
it was with any view of making a match <u>for her</u>, hereafter, E III 17 461 1
The good was all to myself, by making you an object of the E III 17 462 7
you, he is so far from making flourishes, that any other E III 17 464 19
persevered in seeking it, making allowance for the modest P III 1 7 14
advantage of renting it; making it appear as if they P III 3 23 34
no time to be lost in making every dependant arrangement. P III 5 33 5
which he was continually making severe remarks upon, in P III 5 34 12
I have been making a duplicate of the catalogue of my P III 5 38 34
go; and it ended in his making a bold public declaration, P III 7 55 7
half a mile distant, making himself agreeable to others! P III 7 58 20
or that she would be the making of me; and I never had two P III 8 65 16
much less calculated for making matters easy--Charles P III 9 79 25
noise he was studiously making with the child, that he P III 9 80 34
Other opportunities of making her observations could not P III 10 82 1
behind her, as if making their way back, along the rough, P III 10 87 22
done a good deed in making that poor fellow talk so much. P III 12 107 24
A new sort of way this, for a young fellow to be making P IV 1 126 22
Her making a fourth, when they sat down to dinner, was P IV 3 137 2
It had increased her comforts by making her feel herself P IV 5 154 9
she put me in the way of making these little thread-cases, P IV 5 155 9
Anne was the nearest to him, and making yet a little P IV 8 181 1
on Captain Wentworth's making a distant bow, she P IV 8 181 2
officious, to be giving bad impressions, making mischief. P IV 9 198 53
strenuous opposer of Sir Walter's making a second match. P IV 9 208 92
Mr. Elliot, and be making some struggles to become truly P IV 12 249 3
caressed at last into making her the wife of Sir William. P IV 12 250 8
get out;--and while making that home extremely comfortable, S 2 374 1

MAKING-UP (1)
Making-up would not do. E I 12 98 2

MALADY (3)
The malady itself, one from which she had often suffered, NA II 9 196 25
anxious to lose no time in attacking so dreadful a malady. NA II 15 241 7
from the nature of her malady, and feeling herself SS III 7 308 4

MALE (3)
in default of heirs male, on a distant relation; and their PP I 7 28 1
the male part of Mr. Cox's family, the lawyer of Highbury. E II 8 214 13
any individual among their male acquaintance, who had been P III 7 54 4

MALEVOLENCE (2)
however upright, can escape the malevolence of slander. LS 14 264 3
and laudable pride which resists such malevolence." SS II 7 189 51

MALEVOLENT (1)
must have heard some malevolent misrepresentation of her, NA II 1 132 16

MALICE (5)
more than merely malice against herself; and might be SS II 14 254 27
her passion--her malice--at all events it must be appeased. SS III 8 328 61
go off with a flourish of malice against him in her SS III 13 366 21
but your own wilful ignorance and the malice of Mr. Darcy." PP I 18 95 48
But we must stem the tide of malice, and pour into the PP III 5 289 42

MALICIOUS (3)
than by his subsequent malicious overthrow of it; that in NA II 16 251 6
of descending to such malicious revenge, such injustice, PP I 16 80 33
unless by some cruel and malicious arrangement at the war- PP II 19 238 6

MALIGNANT (1)
them be cheated of their malignant triumph, my dear sister, SS II 7 189 51

MALL (3)
"In a stationer's shop in Pall Mall, where I had business. SS II 8 199 37
said she, "but now he is lodging at no.--, Pall Mall. SS III 2 275 22
broad walk in front, aspiring to be the Mall of the place. S 4 384 1

MALT (1)
Perry tells me that Mr. Cole never touches malt liquor. E II 7 210 20

MAMA (38)
"It is Mr. De Courcy, said she, colouring violently, Mama LS 20 275 1
love with Frederica, & with full encouragement from mama. LS 20 276 2
angry it will make mama, but I must run the risk. LS 21 279 1
misery I have been in, & mama had ordered me never to LS 24 286 5
Mama will never forgive me, & I shall be worse off than LS 24 286 7
"Oh! mama, how shall we do without her?" SS I 3 17 16
And besides all this, I am afraid, mama, he has no real SS I 3 17 18
Oh! mama, how spiritless, how tame was Edward's manner in SS I 3 17 18
"Nay, mama, if he is not to be animated by Cowper!--but we SS I 3 18 20
Mama, the more I know of the world, the more am I SS I 3 18 20
"But at least, mama, you cannot deny the absurdity of the SS I 8 37 4
"Mama, you are not doing me justice. SS I 8 37 8
Soon after this, upon Elinor's leaving the room, "mama," SS I 8 38 14
expence would be a trifle; mama she was sure would never SS I 12 58 3
any other creature in the world, except yourself and mama. SS I 12 59 4
Last night after tea, when you and mama went out of the SS I 12 60 13
Only think, mama, how it is improved since I was here last! SS I 19 107 24
Do but look, mama, how sweet! SS I 19 108 36
Mama saw him here once before;--but I was with my uncle at SS I 20 114 44
cottage, I hear, and mama sends me word they are very SS I 20 115 50
Mama says <u>he</u> was in love with your sister too.-- SS I 20 115 56
But mama did not think the match good enough for me, SS I 20 116 62
"Oh! no; but if mama had not objected to it, I dare say he SS I 20 117 64
you think he said when he heard of your coming with mama? SS II 4 164 22
mama, and Edward, may have been so barbarous to bely me. SS II 7 189 50
I must go and comfort mama. SS II 7 190 60
with feverish wildness, cried out-- "is mama coming?--" SS III 7 310 10
11
still talking wildly of mama, her alarm increased so SS III 7 311 14
through her tears, "tell mama," withdrew from her sister SS III 10 348 34
sister, that they & their mama all lived with his uncle at W 331 11
Mama said I should be asleep before ten.-- W 332 12
"But you may come to Wickstead & see mama, & she can take W 332 12
"But you forget, mama," said Elizabeth, "that we shall PP I 2 6 4
"Mama," cried Lydia, "my aunt says that Colonel Forster PP I 7 30 13
"Indeed, mama, you are mistaken," said Elizabeth, blushing PP I 9 43 24
him with, "do you know, mama, that my uncle Philips talks PP I 14 68 13
14
& joy between papa & mama & their children; while S 4 384 1
eagerly called out, "T'is uncle Sidney mama, it is indeed." S 12 425 1

MAMA'S (2)
& not the spirit of mama's commands, but if <u>you</u> do not LS 21 279 1
are coarser featured than any mama's children ever were. E I 6 45 21

MAMMA (26)
If I could but have papa and mamma, and the rest of them NA I 10 79 56
Mamma says, I am never within." NA II 7 174 9
"Oh! as to <u>that</u>, papa and mamma were in no hurry at all. NA II 13 221 2
Mamma would like to go too of all things! PP II 16 220 6
mamma, do the people here abouts know I am married to-day? PP III 9 316 8
"Well, mamma," said she, when they were all returned to PP III 9 317 11
What a pity it is, mamma, we did not all go." PP III 9 317 11
You were not by, when I told mamma, and the others, all PP III 9 318 22
"There is a gentleman with him, mamma," said Kitty; "who PP III 11 333 32
did, she very innocently said, "what is the matter mamma? PP III 13 345 11
"You are sorry to leave mamma, my dear little Fanny," said MP I 2 15 11
"Dear mamma, only think, my cousin cannot put the map of MP I 2 18 23
to me) your papa and mamma are so good as to bring her up MP I 2 19 29
friend in the "mamma" who had certainly shewn no MP III 6 371 17
"I was up stairs, mamma, moving my things;" said Susan, in MP III 7 379 18
But mamma kept it from her, and was always letting Betsey MP III 7 386 42
get it for her own, though mamma had <u>promised</u> her that MP III 7 386 42
Susan have my knife, mamma, when I am dead and buried.'-- MP III 7 386 44
"Henry is a fine boy, but John is very like his mamma. E I 9 80 72
be always putting herself forward to take place of mamma. P III 6 46 10
Nobody doubts her right to have precedence of mamma, but P III 6 46 10
It is not that mamma cares about it the least in the world, P III 6 46 10
I am come on to give you notice, that papa and mamma are P III 6 50 27

mamma; she is thinking so much of poor Richard! P III 6 50 27
"My brother," whispered one of the girls; "mamma is P III 8 67 26
deal better; and papa and mamma always think it was her P III 10 89 33
MAMMA'S (3)
of papa and mamma's approbation, was eagerly given.-- NA II 2 140 8
unluckily it came into mamma's head, when they were gone, P III 6 50 27
in reply to papa and mamma's farther pressing invitations, P III 7 54 4
MAMMAS (1)
But papas and mammas, and brothers and intimate friends NA I 10 79 57
MAN (911)
house, "I like this man; pray heaven no harm come of it!" LS 2 244 1
with all his faults is a man to whom that great word " LS 2 245 1
her attentions to a young man previously attached to Mr LS 4 248 1
Charles is very rich I am sure; when a man has once got LS 5 250 2
a handsome young man, who promises me some amusement. LS 7 254 3
with the attentions of any man inclined to flirt with her. LS 8 255 1
produced on the heart of man by such loveliness & such LS 8 255 2
to see a young man of Reginald's sense duped by her at all. LS 8 256 4
I hear the young man well spoken of, & tho' no one can LS 9 256 1
affection on a man who had dared to think so meanly of me. LS 10 258 2
made Mr Manwaring & a young man engaged to Miss Manwaring LS 11 259 1
gaining the admiration of a man whom she must imagine to LS 12 261 4
Lady Susan, to a young man of his age & high expectations. LS 13 262 1
attention, & as he is a man of fortune, it was easy to see LS 14 264 4
of being able to make a worthy man completely miserable. LS 14 264 4
her being ridiculed & despised by every man who sees her. LS 19 274 2
In the breakfast room we found Lady Susan & a young man of LS 20 275 2
he appears both to Mr. Vernon & me a very weak young man. LS 20 276 2
Sir James is a young man of an amiable disposition, & LS 20 276 5
some years hence on a man, which in connection & character LS 20 277 5
The folly of the young man, and the confusion of Frederica LS 20 278 9
I shall ever despise the man who can be gratified by the LS 22 282 6
the protection of a young man with whom she had scarcely LS 22 282 6
"I knew that he was not absolutely the man she would have LS 24 289 12
of a man whose passions were so violent and resentful. LS 25 292 1
save that ill-fated young man--& I must make myself amends LS 25 293 4
Silly woman, to expect constancy from so charming a man! LS 26 296 5
you guilty in marrying a man of his age!--just old enough LS 29 298 1
If the old man would die, I might not hesitate; but a LS 29 299 3
to exist between you & the man, whose family you robbed of LS 36 305 1
and a very respectable man, though his name was Richard-- NA I 1 13 1
at their door--not one young man whose origin was unknown. NA I 1 16 10
the choice of a sensible, intelligent man, like Mr. Allen. NA I 2 20 8
gentlemanlike young man as a partner;--his name was Tilney. NA I 3 25 2
by a queer, half-witted man, who would make me dance with NA I 3 26 22
"I danced with a very agreeable young man, introduced by NA I 3 27 26
an intimacy with a young man of his own college, of the NA I 4 33 5
he must be a charming young man; and was equally sure that NA I 5 36 2
of England, or of the man who collects and publishes in a NA I 5 37 4
yesterday, I saw a young man looking at you so earnestly-- NA I 6 41 16
to ask you what is your favourite complexion in a man. NA I 6 42 28
"One was a very good-looking young man." NA I 6 43 37
He was a stout young man of middling height, who, with a NA I 7 45 5
eleven; and I defy any man in England to make my horse go NA I 7 45 7
It was built for a Christchurch man, a friend of mine, a NA I 7 46 11
'Oh! d----,' said I, 'I am your man; what do you ask?' NA I 7 46 11
to that of a self-assured man, especially where the beauty NA I 7 48 32
And old man playing at see-saw! NA I 7 49 40
"I dare say he does; and I do not know any man who is a NA I 7 51 51
fix the attention of every man near her, and without NA I 8 56 11
silence, she added, "he is a very agreeable young man." NA I 8 58 32
that there is not a more agreeable young man in the world." NA I 8 58 33
adding in explanation, "old Allen, the man you are with." NA I 9 63 10
He is a very temperate man, and you could not fancy him in NA I 9 63 19
Why you do not suppose a man is overset by a bottle? NA I 9 63 20
You would hardly meet with a man who goes beyond his four NA I 9 64 24
Oh, curse it! the carriage is safe enough, if a man knows NA I 9 65 30
young man Mrs. Hughes says, and likely to do very well." NA I 9 69 50
My mother says he is the most delightful young man in the NA I 10 70 1
might have warned her, for man only can be aware of the NA I 10 73 22
be aware of the insensibility of man towards a new gown. NA I 10 73 22
how little the heart of man is affected by what is costly NA I 10 74 22
No man will admire her the more, no woman will like her NA I 10 74 22
A good figure of a man; well put together.-- NA I 10 76 28
You will allow, that in both, man has the advantage of NA I 10 77 33
it is an engagement between man and woman, formed for the NA I 10 77 33
In marriage, the man is supposed to provide for the NA I 10 77 35
agreeable to the man; he is to purvey, and she is to smile. NA I 10 77 35
He was a very handsome man, of a commanding aspect, past NA I 10 80 59
You are talking of the man you danced with last night, are NA I 11 85 35
heard Tilney hallooing to a man who was just passing by on NA I 11 86 46
The man believed Miss Tilney to be at home, but was not NA I 12 91 3
like every military man, had a very large acquaintance. NA I 12 95 17
young man, unless circumstances are particularly untoward. NA I 14 111 29
I will prove myself a man, no less by the generosity of my NA I 14 112 36
altogether a very charming man, did not admit of a doubt, NA II 1 129 1
I believe he is a very gentleman-like man. NA II 1 130 9
handsome young man, whom she had never seen before, and NA II 1 131 15
I hate a florid complexion and dark eyes in a man. NA II 1 135 41
for I am sure he must be an excellent good hearted man. NA II 1 135 44
I always heard he was a most excellent man; and you know, NA II 1 136 46
more, for I am sure he must be a most liberal-minded man." NA II 1 136 46
of one man more than another--he is not the person." NA II 3 145 13
No man is offended by another man's admiration of the NA II 4 151 12
A woman in love with one man cannot flirt with another." NA II 4 151 15
a thoughtless young man; he has had about a week's NA II 4 152 26
though so charming a man, seemed always a check upon his NA II 5 156 4
it expedient to give every young man some employment. NA II 7 176 15
as any private man in the county, has his profession." NA II 7 176 15
"He is a happy man!" said the General, with a look of very NA II 7 179 26
on which an humble man might have looked with pride.-- NA II 8 182 2
of thinking well of a man so kindly disposed towards NA II 8 185 5
Unhappy man!-- NA II 8 187 13
her, a very respectable man, and one in whom she had NA II 9 196 25
such a footing; where every man is surrounded by a NA II 9 197 29
man had reason to believe himself loved, I was that man. NA II 10 202 7
Frederick will not be the first man who has chosen a wife NA II 10 205 24
an engagement voluntarily entered into with another man! NA II 10 205 30
He is a deceased man--defunct in understanding. NA II 10 206 31
Now she has really got the man she likes, she may be NA II 10 206 33
Your kind offices will set all right:--he is the only man NA II 12 216 2
I rejoice to say, that the young man whom, of all others, NA II 12 216 2
upon me; but he is the last man whose word I would take. NA II 12 217 2
And all this by such a man as General Tilney, so polite, NA II 13 226 25
he must be a very strange man," grew enough for all their NA II 14 234 10
man all his life, for the foolishness of his first choice." NA II 14 237 19
Very unfriendly, certainly; and he must be a very odd man;- NA II 14 237 21
Such an agreeable, worthy man as he seemed to be! NA II 14 238 26
Mrs. Morland, you ever saw a better-bred man in your life. NA II 14 238 26
she beheld was a young man whom she had never seen before. NA II 15 241 7
Thorpe, most happy to be on speaking terms with a man of NA II 15 244 12
to believe his father a man of substance and credit, NA II 15 246 12
the young man on whom the Fullerton estate must devolve. NA II 15 247 13
of his daughter with a man of fortune and consequence, NA II 16 250 4
home of her choice and the man of her choice, is an event NA II 16 250 5
to a precision the most charming young man in the world. NA II 16 251 5
the most charming young man in the world is instantly NA II 16 251 5
The late owner of this estate was a single man, who lived SS I 1 3 1
The son, a steady respectable young man, was amply SS I 1 3 2
He was not an ill-disposed young man, unless to be rather SS I 1 5 7
between the children of any man by different marriages; SS I 2 8 3
and pleasing young man, who was introduced to their SS I 3 15 4
was the eldest son of a man who had died very rich; and SS I 3 15 5
But yet--he is not the kind of young man--there is a SS I 3 17 18
expect in the man who could seriously attach my sister. SS I 3 17 18
I could not be happy with a man whose taste did not in SS I 3 17 18
that I shall never see a man whom I can really love. SS I 3 18 20
to three; two maids and a man, with whom they were SS I 5 26 5
The man and one of the maids were sent off immediately SS I 5 26 6
upon his purse, which a man of any consequence in the SS I 5 27 6
Sir John Middleton was a good looking man about forty. SS I 6 30 6
enough to allow that a man of five and thirty might well SS I 7 35 9
her power over such a young man; and this kind of SS I 8 36 1
Mrs. Dashwood, who could not think a man five years SS I 8 37 3
When is a man to be safe from such wit, if age and SS I 8 37 4
and twenty could feel for a man of thirty-five any thing SS I 8 38 11
"And what sort of a young man is he?" SS I 9 43 16
man, and one whose acquaintance will not be ineligible." SS I 9 44 24
"That is what I like; that is what a young man ought to be. SS I 9 45 28
'setting one's cap at a man,' or 'making a conquest,' are SS I 9 45 30
a delight, that any young man of five and twenty must have SS I 10 47 3
Willoughby was a young man of good abilities, quick SS I 10 48 7
a half, of ever seeing a man who could satisfy her ideas SS I 10 49 10
She saw it with concern; for what could a silent man of SS I 10 50 12
man, and she regarded him with respect and compassion. SS I 10 50 12
"Brandon is just the kind of man," said Willoughby one day, SS I 10 50 14
"My protege, as you call him, is a sensible man; and sense SS I 10 51 20
Yes, Marianne, even in a man between thirty and forty. SS I 10 51 20
I consider him, on the contrary, as a very respectable man, SS I 10 51 25
I can only pronounce him to be a sensible man, well-bred, SS I 10 51 27
and a far less agreeable man might have been pleasing. SS I 11 55 7
from a man so little, or at least so lately known to her. SS I 12 58 3
give the name of the young man who was Elinor's particular SS I 12 61 15
there was such a man once, and his name begins with an F." SS I 12 62 26
Poor man! SS I 14 70 2
for he is a very prudent man, and to be sure must have SS I 14 70 2
Is nothing due to the man whom we have all so much reason SS I 15 79 28
Is he not a man of honour and feeling? SS I 15 81 42
one; it was a man on horseback riding towards them. SS I 16 86 16
Indeed a man could not very well be in love with either of SS I 17 90 1
"you would be a happier man if you had any profession to SS I 19 102 3
and honourable, and a young man of eighteen is not in SS I 19 103 4
Her husband was a grave looking young man of five or six SS I 19 106 22
common for any sensible man to be lastingly hurt by it.-- SS I 20 112 28
He seems an excellent man; and I think him uncommonly SS I 20 115 55
He is such a charming man, that it is quite a pity he SS I 20 115 56
Mr. Palmer is just the kind of man I like." SS I 20 117 64
Benevolent, philanthropic man! SS I 21 119 3
cried the elder sister, "what a charming man he is!" SS I 21 122 15
a prodigious smart young man, quite a beau, clerk to Mr. SS I 21 123 28
Miss Steele; "Mr. Ferrars is the happy man, is he? SS I 21 126 39
very agreeable young man to be sure; I know him very well." SS I 21 126 39
as to the name of the man on who all my happiness depends." SS I 22 131 30
on the perfections of a man, of whose whole heart she felt SS II 1 141 4
With almost every other man in the world, it would be an SS II 2 147 7
induce a woman to keep a man to an engagement, of which SS II 2 151 41
Sir John was delighted; for to a man, whose prevailing SS II 3 157 19
particularly hurt that a man so partial to her sister SS II 4 162 8
Ah! poor man! he has been dead these eight years and SS II 4 163 18
The man replied that none had. SS II 4 165 27
a daughter so young, a man so little known, to be carried SS II 4 165 29
her abhorrence of the man, and so bitter were her feelings SS II 7 184 15
life, with an unprincipled man, as a deliverance the most SS II 7 184 15
he is not the only young man in the world worth having; SS II 8 192 3
Well, it is the oddest thing to me, that a man should use SS II 8 194 8
very well, Biddy Henshawe; she married a very wealthy man. SS II 8 194 10
Well, it don't signify talking, but when a young man, be SS II 8 194 10
to think--in short, that a man, whom I knew to be engaged-- SS II 8 199 35
it served to identify the man still more:--as soon as the SS II 8 199 37
as might have become a man in the bloom of youth, of hope SS II 8 200 43
"A man who has nothing to do with his own time has no SS II 9 204 16
I knew him to be a very good sort of man, and I thought SS II 9 209 28
but not a quick-sighted man, could really, I believe, give SS II 9 209 28
No, he had already done that, which no man who can feel SS II 9 209 30
but to a man and a soldier, she presumed not to censure it. SS II 9 211 39
"A man of whom he had always had such reason to think well! SS II 10 214 9
indeed! and the doctor is a single man, I warrant you." SS II 10 218 25
talking--but it won't do-- the doctor is the man, I see." SS II 10 218 27
Is he a man of fortune?" SS II 11 223 16
He seems a most gentlemanlike man; and I think, Elinor, I SS II 11 223 18
Colonel Brandon must be the man; and no civility shall be SS II 11 224 24
A man must pay for his convenience; and it has cost me a SS II 11 225 31
I question whether Marianne now, will marry a man worth SS II 11 227 50
Jennings was the widow of a man who had got all his money SS II 11 228 53
as a man of taste, will, I dare say, be pleased with them. SS II 12 234 27
was as well fitted to mix in the world as any other man. SS II 14 250 12
Mr. Edward Ferrars, the very young man I used to joke with SS III 1 258 7
of attaching a sensible man, that she could not be SS III 1 261 13
able to be silent, "he has acted like an honest man! SS III 1 267 43
engagement with a young man under her uncle's care, the SS III 1 267 45
"Poor young man!--and what is to become of him?" SS III 1 268 49
The interest of two thousand pounds--how can a man live on SS III 1 268 50
"Poor young man!" cried Mrs. Jennings, "I am sure he SS III 1 268 51
"Can any thing be more galling to the spirit of a man," SS III 1 269 56
He is not a young man with whom one can be intimately SS III 3 282 19
as to that, when a man has once made up his mind to such a SS III 4 285 5
Mr. Ferrars is to be the man. SS III 4 286 17
"Colonel Brandon is so delicate a man, that he rather SS III 4 287 19
Brandon seems a man of great worth and respectability. SS III 4 290 36
37
He is undoubtedly a sensible man, and in his manners SS III 4 290 37
him that he has made me a very--an exceedingly happy man." SS III 4 290 42
"Well, my dear," she cried, "I sent you up the young man. SS III 4 291 47
of repair; but to hear a man apologising, as I thought, SS III 4 292 55
Now indeed it would be too late to sell it, but a man of SS III 5 295 12
Colonel Brandon may be, Edward is a very lucky man!-- SS III 5 295 16
Is there a man on earth who could have done it?-- SS III 8 321 34
the happiness, of a man who, to every advantage of person SS III 8 331 70
for that worthless young man!--and without selfishness-- SS III 9 336 14
said Elinor, "as an excellent man, is well established." SS III 9 337 15
is not to be wasted for ever on such a man as Willoughby.-- SS III 9 337 18
"Happy with a man of libertine practices!-- SS III 11 350 7
has not a heart to be made happy with such a man!-- SS III 11 350 7
figure of a man on horseback drew her eyes to the window. SS III 12 358 8
to her, to be fettered to a man for whom she had not the SS III 13 367 22
that other, a man who had suffered no less than herself SS III 14 378 15
"A young man of very good fortune, quite independant, & W 315 1
much attached to a young man of the name of Purvis a W 316 2
I shall never love any man as I loved Purvis. W 316 2
I should not refuse a man because he was not Purvis--. W 317 2
To be so bent on marriage--to pursue a man merely for the W 318 2
think of nothing worse) than marry a man I did not like."-- W 318 2
I should not like marrying a disagreable man any more than W 318 2
like any good humoured man with a comfortable income.-- W 318 2
"A young man must think of somebody. said eliz:--& why W 321 2
The door will be opened by a man in livery with a powder'd W 322 2
Mr Sam Watson is a very good sort of young man, & I dare W 324 3
were accosted by a young man in a morning dress & boots, W 327 7
who was certainly a genteel, good looking young man.-- W 329 9
Ld Osborne was a very fine young man; but there was an air W 329 10
Mr Howard was an agreable-looking man, a little more than W 330 10
"Aye--that is just like him. & yet this is the man, she W 342 19
"I should like to know the man you do think agreable." W 343 19
ways of a man, when he is bent upon pleasing her.--" W 343 19

Context	Work	Vol.	Ch.	Page	Line
It struck me as very becoming in so young a man, but I am	W			344	20
to nothing, the smartest & most fashionable man of the two.	W			347	22
wd not have had to talk to such a great man for the world.	W			347	22
Robert was carelessly kind, as became a prosperous man & a	W			349	24
had been reckoned an extraordinary sensible, clever man.--	W			352	26
pounds, there was a young man who wd have thought of her."	W			353	26
They were the steps of a man.	W			355	28
ten minutes--which to a man whose heart had been long	W			359	28
far as to say--"the young man who was here last night my	W			360	29
& silence; &, being a man of sense and education, was if	W			361	30
It is a truth universally acknowledged, that a single man	PP	I	1	3	1
However little known the feelings or views of such a man	PP	I	1	3	2
is taken by a young man of large fortune from the north of	PP	I	1	3	10
A single man of large fortune; four or five thousand a	PP	I	1	3	14
One cannot know what a man really is by the end of a	PP	I	2	7	16
sisters, the husband of the eldest, and another young man.	PP	I	3	10	4
The gentlemen pronounced him to be a fine figure of a man,	PP	I	3	10	5
He was the proudest, most disagreeable man in the world,	PP	I	3	11	6
a most disagreeable, horrid man, not at all worth pleasing.	PP	I	3	13	20
I quite detest the man."	PP	I	3	13	20
"He is just what a young man ought to be," said she, "	PP	I	4	14	2
a young man ought likewise to be, if he possibly can.	PP	I	4	14	3
Hurst, who had married a man of more fashion than fortune,	PP	I	4	15	13
man that it would be quite a misfortune to be liked by him.	PP	I	5	19	10
One cannot wonder that so very fine a young man, with	PP	I	5	20	18
"But if a woman is partial to a man, and does not	PP	I	6	22	5
her he was only the man who made himself agreeable no	PP	I	6	23	12
sat, he was an indolent man, who lived only to eat, drink,	PP	I	8	35	2
What an agreeable man Sir William is, Mr. Bingley--is not	PP	I	9	44	27
so much the man of fashion! so genteel and so easy!--	PP	I	9	44	27
on chance as that of any man I know; and if, as you were	PP	I	10	49	29
of admiration to so great a man; and yet that he should	PP	I	10	51	46
Pray do not talk of that odious man.	PP	I	13	61	7
daughters, in favour of a man whom nobody cared anything	PP	I	13	62	8
"He seems to be a most conscientious and polite young man,	PP	I	13	63	13
Can he be a sensible man, sir?"	PP	I	13	64	17
pleasure from the society of a man in any other colour.	PP	I	13	64	20
He was a tall, heavy looking young man of five and twenty.	PP	I	13	64	21
Mr. Collins was not a sensible man, and the deficiency of	PP	I	15	70	1
daughters married; and the man whom she could not bear to	PP	I	15	71	5
was soon caught by a young man, whom they had never seen	PP	I	15	72	8
it should be; for the young man wanted only regimentals to	PP	I	15	72	8
Mr. Wickham was the happy man towards whom almost every	PP	I	16	76	4
a man of very large property in Derbyshire, I understand."	PP	I	16	77	9
"that he or that any man should not be estimated beyond	PP	I	16	78	16
on my slight acquaintance, to be an ill-tempered man."	PP	I	16	78	17
I have been a disappointed man, and my spirits will not	PP	I	16	79	23
A man of honour could not have doubted the intention, but	PP	I	16	79	27
it was given to another man; and no less certain is it,	PP	I	16	79	27
She could have added, "a young man too, like you, whose	PP	I	16	80	36
believe, truly amiable, be in friendship with such a man?	PP	I	16	82	44
					45
"He is a sweet tempered, amiable, charming man.	PP	I	16	82	47
very different man from what he is to the less prosperous.	PP	I	16	82	48
of a young man of such amiable appearance as Wickham.--	PP	I	17	85	1
No man of common humanity, no man who had any value for	PP	I	17	85	4
this kind, given by a young man of character, to	PP	I	17	87	13
To find a man agreeable whom one is determined to hate!--	PP	I	18	90	7
in the eyes of a man of ten times his consequence.	PP	I	18	90	8
and I find that the young man forgot to tell you, among	PP	I	18	94	45
Mr. Wickham is by no means a respectable young man.	PP	I	18	95	50
It vexed her to see him expose himself to such a man.	PP	I	18	98	61
His being such a charming young man, and so rich, and	PP	I	18	99	63
could I think well of the man who should omit an occasion	PP	I	18	101	71
that he was a remarkably clever, good kind of young man.	PP	I	18	101	71
children; and though the man and the match were quite good	PP	I	18	103	77
reject the addresses of the man whom they secretly mean to	PP	I	19	107	13
of your sex to reject a man on the first application, and	PP	I	19	108	16
					17
of elegance which consists in tormenting a respectable man.	PP	I	19	108	20
a very desirable wife to a man in my situation, who	PP	I	20	110	4
peculiar duty of a young man who has been so fortunate as	PP	I	20	114	32
the best, in accepting a man whose sisters and friends are	PP	I	21	119	23
influence a young man so totally independent of every one.	PP	I	21	120	28
He may live in my memory as the most amiable man of my	PP	II	1	134	7
narrow-minded, silly man; you know he is, as well as I do;	PP	II	1	135	13
We must not expect a lively young man to be always so	PP	II	1	136	14
young ladies in the country. let Wickham be your man.	PP	II	1	138	27
"Thank you, sir, but a less agreeable man would satisfy me.	PP	II	1	138	28
Mr. Gardiner was a sensible, gentlemanlike man, greatly	PP	II	2	139	2
in believing that a man who lived by trade, and within	PP	II	2	139	2
A young man, such as you describe Mr. Bingley, so easily	PP	II	2	140	6
will persuade a young man of independent fortune to think	PP	II	2	140	7
with regard to this young man will influence her.	PP	II	2	141	12
is a most interesting young man; and if he had the fortune	PP	II	3	144	2
But he is, beyond all comparison, the most agreeable man I	PP	II	3	144	7
"A man in distressed circumstances has not time for all	PP	II	4	153	15
I should be sorry, you know, to think ill of a young man	PP	II	4	153	18
I am going to-morrow where I shall find a man who has not	PP	II	4	154	19
and ease of a well-bred man, and talked very pleasantly;	PP	II	7	171	10
"Shall we ask him why a man of sense and education, and	PP	II	8	175	22
He was beyond comparison the pleasantest man; he certainly	PP	II	9	181	31
Their brother is a pleasant gentleman-like man--he is a	PP	II	10	184	22
him the kind of young man to get into a scrape of that	PP	II	10	185	28
tempt me to accept the man, who has been the means of	PP	II	11	190	10
felt that you were the last man in the world whom I could	PP	II	11	193	28
of my father, a young man who had scarcely any other	PP	II	12	196	5
Mr. Wickham is the son of a very respectable man, who had	PP	II	12	199	5
the observation of a young man of nearly the same age with	PP	II	12	200	5
the persuasion of the young man, who, on meeting him	PP	II	13	205	4
such an amiable man as Mr. Bingley, was incomprehensible.	PP	II	13	208	6
of man; and of late it has been shifting about pretty much.	PP	II	17	225	10
a man without now and then stumbling on something witty."	PP	II	17	226	17
prefer him to every other man, that all her good sense,	PP	II	17	227	26
Well, he is a very undeserving young man--and I do not	PP	II	17	228	27
Colonel Forster is a sensible man, and will keep her out	PP	II	18	232	20
a very gentlemanlike man, asked her how she had liked him.	PP	II	18	233	27
This is not the sort of happiness which a man would in	PP	II	19	236	1
That he was not a good-tempered man, had been her firmest	PP	III	1	248	31
"His father was an excellent man," said Mrs. Gardiner.	PP	III	1	249	35
a disgraceful light might it not strike so vain a man!	PP	III	1	252	54
talking to the man about them, that he advanced but little.	PP	III	1	254	57
It was acknowledged, however, that he was a liberal man,	PP	III	2	265	14
Such a change in a man of so much pride, excited not only	PP	III	2	266	16
forward the idea of a man to whom she believed her partial,	PP	III	3	269	10
hopes, and said he feared W. was not a man to be trusted.	PP	III	4	275	5
How is such a man to be worked on?	PP	III	4	277	16
It appears to me so very unlikely, that any young man	PP	III	5	282	1
what manner he spoke of the man, who had behaved with such	PP	III	5	284	14
is but one man in the world I love, and he is an angel.	PP	III	5	291	60
All Meryton seemed striving to blacken the man, who, but	PP	III	6	294	4
Every body declared that he was the wickedest young man in	PP	III	6	294	4
Yet he is such a man!"	PP	III	7	304	26
"I mean, that no man in his senses, would marry Lydia on	PP	III	7	304	29
Generous, good man, I am afraid he has distressed himself.	PP	III	7	304	30
of the nearest kind with the man whom he so justly scorned.	PP	III	8	311	12
She began now to comprehend that he was exactly the man,	PP	III	8	312	15
no limits in future to the impudence of an impudent man.	PP	III	9	316	5
Is not he a charming man?	PP	III	9	317	11
young man to resist an opportunity of having a companion.	PP	III	9	318	19
was called away upon business to that horrid man Mr. Stone.	PP	III	9	319	25
and finally bribe, the man whom he always most wished to	PP	III	10	326	3

Context	Work	Vol.	Ch.	Page	Line
thought, "that this poor man cannot come to a house, which	PP	III	11	332	19
"La!" replied Kitty, "it looks just like that man that	PP	III	11	334	34
That tall, proud man."	PP	III	11	334	34
To Jane, he could be only a man whose proposals she had	PP	III	11	334	36
could be good enough for a man, on whom she had such	PP	III	11	338	60
Teazing, teazing, man!	PP	III	12	339	4
"A man who has once been refused!	PP	III	12	341	19
and sensible young man, without having a wish beyond it.	PP	III	12	343	32
stronger desire of generally pleasing than any other man."	PP	III	12	343	32
Oh! he is the handsomest young man that ever was seen!"	PP	III	13	349	41
If there were but such another man for you!"	PP	III	13	350	53
Some-where about the grounds, walking with a young man,	PP	III	14	352	8
"Mr. Darcy, you see, is the man!	PP	III	15	363	18
Could he, or the lucases, have pitched on any man, within	PP	III	15	363	18
Had they fixed on any other man it would have been nothing;	PP	III	15	364	24
as warmly as a man violently in love can be supposed to do.	PP	III	16	366	8
be forced to have that disagreeable man all to yourself.	PP	III	17	375	25
					26
would be enough to overcome her abhorrence of the man.	PP	III	17	375	27
Are you out of your senses, to be accepting this man?	PP	III	17	376	29
We all know him to be a proud, unpleasant sort of man; but	PP	III	17	376	33
He is the kind of man, indeed, to whom I should never dare	PP	III	17	376	35
Such a charming man!--so handsome! so tall!--	PP	III	17	378	43
"A man who had felt less, might."	PP	III	18	381	12
of merriment which a young man of seventeen will always	MP	I	2	17	22
on proving to be a hearty man of forty-five, seemed likely	MP	I	3	24	5
the introduction of a young man who had recently succeeded	MP	I	4	38	9
He was a heavy young man, with not more than common sense;	MP	I	4	38	10
appeared precisely the young man to deserve and attach her.	MP	I	4	39	10
company, "if this man had not twelve thousand a year, he	MP	I	4	40	13
Admiral Crawford was a man of vicious conduct, who chose,	MP	I	4	41	15
a young man and woman of very prepossessing appearance.	MP	I	4	41	17
He was, in fact, the most agreeable young man the sisters	MP	I	5	44	2
"There could be no harm in her liking an agreeable man--	MP	I	5	44	3
good sort of young man, and it is a great match for her."	MP	I	5	45	13
an indolent, stay-at-home man; and Mr. Crawford's being	MP	I	5	47	26
he was the sort of young man to be generally liked, his	MP	I	5	47	28
mother, and an agreeable man himself--with the advantage	MP	I	5	48	28
He could hardly ever get out, poor man, to enjoy any thing,	MP	I	6	54	9
herself, "he is a well bred man; he makes the best of it."	MP	I	6	56	27
the hands of a professional man, Mr. Rushworth was very	MP	I	6	61	58
that without his being a man of the world or an elder	MP	I	7	65	13
right is the steward's house; he is a very respectable man.	MP	I	8	82	34
If the man who holds it is so, it is by the neglect of his	MP	I	9	92	45
in the weight of a woman's arm from that of a man!	MP	I	9	94	59
At Oxford I have been a good deal used to have a man lean	MP	I	9	94	59
a man of the world not to see with the eyes of the world.	MP	I	10	98	8
"I am afraid I am not quite so much the man of the world	MP	I	10	98	10
Nobody can call such an under-sized man handsome.	MP	I	10	102	43
and I see no reason why a man should make a worse	MP	I	11	109	17
"But the motives of a man who takes orders with the	MP	I	11	109	20
"Shall I ask you how the church is to be filled, if a man	MP	I	11	109	22
A man--a sensible man like Dr. Grant, cannot be in the	MP	I	11	112	30
than to be the wife of a man whose amiableness depends	MP	I	11	112	31
"I think the man who could often quarrel with Fanny," said	MP	I	11	112	32
it often happens, that a man, before he has quite made up	MP	I	12	116	10
steady young man, so I hope Miss Julia will be very happy."	MP	I	12	118	20
A little man, with a weak voice, always hoarse after the	MP	I	13	122	2
is to the family, employing the man all the year round!"	MP	I	15	142	22
solemn lecturer; and the man who chooses the profession	MP	I	15	145	41
him a very fine young man, and advised Fanny to get his	MP	I	15	147	57
is as gentlemanlike a man as you will see any where, so I	MP	I	15	148	58
A quiet-looking young man.	MP	I	15	148	59
Charles Maddox was to be the man.--	MP	I	15	148	60
the help of a young man very slightly known to any of us.	MP	I	16	153	8
"No man can like being driven into the appearance of such	MP	I	16	154	12
A man might represent the county with such an estate; a	MP	I	17	161	13
a man might escape a profession and represent the county."	MP	I	17	161	13
She did not like him as a man, but she must admit him to	MP	I	18	165	3
little, mean-looking man, set up for a fine actor, is very	MP	I	18	165	3
so truly feminine, as to be no very good picture of a man.	MP	I	18	169	22
young man, who appeared likely to knock him down backwards.	MP	II	1	182	22
the acquaintance of a young man whom he felt sure of	MP	II	1	183	23
"Mr. Crawford was a most pleasant gentleman-like man;--his	MP	II	1	186	30
feet eight, or he will be expecting a well-looking man."	MP	II	1	186	31
a well-judging steady young man, with better notions than	MP	II	1	186	35
of amiable modest young man who wants a great deal of	MP	II	2	188	3
He was not a man to be endured but for his children's sake,	MP	II	2	191	10
the introduction of the man she loved to her father.	MP	II	2	192	11
She must admire him as a fine looking man, with most	MP	II	3	199	13
was an inferior young man, as ignorant in business as in	MP	II	3	200	19
affection, and contempt of the man she was to marry.	MP	II	3	202	26
his fair bride are at Brighton, I understand--happy man!"	MP	II	5	224	49
sorry to see you trying at it, than almost any other man."	MP	II	5	227	66
of a fortnight) of such a man as Crawford, in spite of	MP	II	6	231	11
years ago, but a young man of an open, pleasant	MP	II	6	233	16
recitor, to know the young man by his histories; and he	MP	II	6	236	21
it was as well to be a man of fortune at once with horses	MP	II	6	236	23
But I told a man mending a hedge that it was Thornton	MP	II	7	241	17
man of education, taste, modern manners, good connections.	MP	II	7	244	27
their relations, and Mr. Rushworth is a most amiable man.	MP	II	7	245	32
occasional residence of a man of independent fortune--was	MP	II	7	248	47
No other man would have thought of it.	MP	II	10	274	9
chair of each young man might exercise her tender	MP	II	11	282	2
he was the finest young man in the room; somebody had	MP	II	11	283	4
He is a very--a very pleasing young man himself, and I	MP	II	11	287	22
it never pardonable in a young man of independent fortune.	MP	II	12	292	9
every prejudice of such a man as the Admiral, for she is	MP	II	12	293	10
worth in the judgment of man that though he sometimes	MP	II	12	294	16
What could be more encouraging to a man who had her love	MP	II	12	294	16
as might warrant any man in the fullest dependence on her	MP	II	12	294	16
The Admiral has his faults, but he is a very good man, and	MP	II	12	296	28
it is that can attach me, that can attach a man of sense.	MP	II	12	297	33
My uncle, who is the very best man in the world, has	MP	II	13	299	5
How could she have excited serious attachment in a man,	MP	II	13	305	26
meaning; in any other man at least, she would have said	MP	II	13	306	26
Here is a young man wishing to pay his addresses to you,	MP	III	1	315	27
and would have every young man, with a sufficient income,	MP	III	1	317	34
She had hoped that to a man like her uncle, so discerning,	MP	III	1	318	38
Here is a young man of sense, of character, of temper, of	MP	III	1	319	39
being addressed by a man of half Mr. Crawford's estate, or	MP	III	1	319	39
from the personal intreaty of the young man himself.	MP	III	1	320	44
and felt, as a good man must feel, how wretched, and how	MP	III	1	324	58
Love such as his, in a man like himself, must with	MP	III	2	327	4
tone, and spirit of a man of talent too, that he sought	MP	III	2	328	6
intreaty from a young man like Crawford could not have	MP	III	2	329	11
He is a most extraordinary young man, and whatever be the	MP	III	2	330	14
To know Fanny to be sought in marriage by a man of fortune,	MP	III	2	332	22
were married to a man of such good estate as Mr. Crawford.	MP	III	2	333	26
No man of any brain can open at a good part of one of his	MP	III	3	338	13
of his hearers, is a man whom one could not (in his public	MP	III	3	341	28
I should like to be such a man."	MP	III	3	341	28
more effort for the young man before he left Mansfield,	MP	III	4	345	2
I am aware, more aware than Crawford can be, that the man	MP	III	4	347	21
with such encouragement, a man like Crawford, lively, and	MP	III	4	350	30
You will supply the rest; and a most fortunate man he is	MP	III	4	351	32
That you could refuse such a man as Henry Crawford, seems	MP	III	4	352	44
set down as certain, that a man must be acceptable to	MP	III	4	353	45
Good-humoured, unaffected girls, will not do for a man who	MP	III	4	355	54
jilted a very nice young man in the blues, for the sake of	MP	III	5	361	16
"I cannot think well of a man who sports with any woman's	MP	III	5	363	23
If any man ever loved a woman for ever, I think Henry will	MP	III	5	363	24

Context	Reference	Line
opinions of the man she loved and respected, as her own.--	MP III 6 367	6
should be so cold towards a man whom he must consider as	MP III 7 375	3
her the addresses of the man she did not love, and	MP III 7 376	4
adverse passion of the man she did, was cruelly mortifying.	MP III 7 376	4
a very well behaved young man, who came to call for his	MP III 7 384	36
She felt that she had never seen so agreeable a man in her	MP III 10 400	7
by a clever, agreeable man, than have him driven away by	MP III 10 402	11
father was a very different man, a very different Mr.	MP III 10 402	12
father, and a sensible man;--his loud tones did very well	MP III 10 402	12
Such a man could come from no place, no society, without	MP III 10 404	15
The mischief such a man does on an estate, both as to the	MP III 11 412	20
be simple to be duped by a man who has no right of	MP III 11 412	20
honest man, to whom I have given half a promise already.--	MP III 11 412	20
The value of a man like Henry on such an occasion, is what	MP III 12 417	3
To have such a fine young man cut off in the flower of his	MP III 14 434	13
Poor young man!--	MP III 14 434	13
A little flogging for man and woman too, would be the best	MP III 15 440	13
A woman married only six months ago, a man professing	MP III 15 441	20
How a man who had once loved, could desert you!	MP III 15 446	34
by a man who had long ago made his indifference clear.	MP III 16 454	18
I was like a man stunned.	MP III 16 455	21
we may fairly consider a man of sense like Henry Crawford,	MP III 17 468	22
Mr. Weston was a man of unexceptionable character, easy	E I 1 6	6
body, he was a much older man in ways than in years; and	E I 1 7	8
He was a nervous man, easily depressed; fond of every body	E I 1 7	10
pleasant, excellent man, that he thoroughly deserves a	E I 1 8	12
Mr. Knightley, a sensible man about seven or eight-and-	E I 1 9	21
"A straight-forward, open-hearted man, like weston, and a	E I 1 13	44
"Mr. Elton is a very pretty young man to be sure, and a	E I 1 14	47
a very good young man, and I have a great regard for him.	E I 1 14	47
Depend upon it, a man of six or seven-and-twenty can take	E I 1 14	48
a poorer man than at first, and with a child to maintain.	E I 2 16	4
He had never been an unhappy man; his own temper had	E I 2 17	6
man had made Highbury feel a sort of pride in him too.	E I 2 17	7
idea of the young man; and such a pleasing attention was	E I 2 18	10
Mr. Perry was an intelligent, gentlemanlike man, whose	E I 2 19	14
and by Mr. Elton, a young man living alone without liking	E I 3 20	2
or other, was a single man; that there was no young Mrs.	E I 4 27	5
"Mr. Martin, I suppose, is not a man of information beyond	E I 4 29	9
The next question was: "what sort of looking man is Mr.	E I 4 29	10
		11
"I have no doubt of his being a very respectable young man.	E I 4 29	16
They have no in-doors man--else they do not want for any	E I 4 30	21
The young man had been the first admirer, but she trusted	E I 4 31	26
like a sensible young man, but his person had no other	E I 4 31	27
But Mr. Knightley is so very fine a man!"	E I 4 33	33
But Mr. Weston is almost an old man.	E I 4 33	35
else--which is just as it should be, for a thriving man.	E I 4 34	40
thrive and be a very rich man in time--and his being	E I 4 34	40
allow it; but if any young man were to set about copying	E I 4 34	42
On the contrary, I think a young man might be very safely	E I 4 34	42
respectable young man, with any deficiency of useful	E I 4 35	44
And he was really a very pleasing young man, a young man	E I 4 35	45
a companion; and perhaps no man can be a good judge of the	E I 5 36	6
merit in making a good wife to such a man as Mr. Weston."	E I 5 38	12
I hope, with all my heart, the young man may be a weston	E I 5 38	15
But I have no idea that she has yet ever seen a man she	E I 5 41	29
being a remarkably handsome man, with most agreeable	E I 6 42	1
Yes, good man!--thought Emma--but what has all that to do	E I 6 43	15
"This man is almost too gallant to be in love," thought	E I 6 49	44
He is an excellent young man, and will suit Harriet	E I 6 49	44
"Upon my word," she cried, "the young man is determined	E I 7 50	2
I can hardly imagine the young man whom I saw talking with	E I 7 51	5
No doubt he is a sensible man, and I suppose may have a	E I 7 51	5
accept a man or not, she certainly ought to refuse him.	E I 7 52	18
		19
him the most agreeable man you have ever been in company	E I 7 53	21
how the young man could have the assurance to ask it.	E I 7 54	29
Martin a very amiable young man, and have a great opinion	E I 7 54	30
A woman is not to marry a man merely because she is asked,	E I 7 54	31
Emma believed if the young man had come in her way at that	E I 7 55	35
a most unexceptionable quarter:--Robert Martin is the man.	E I 8 59	25
He is an excellent young man, both as son and brother.	E I 8 59	27
thinking me the best friend and counsellor man ever had.	E I 8 59	27
a man that a woman should ever refuse an offer of marriage.	E I 8 60	33
A man always imagines a woman to be ready for anybody who	E I 8 60	33
"Nonsense! a man does not imagine any such thing.	E I 8 60	34
Mr. Martin is a very respectable young man, but I cannot	E I 8 61	37
But I could not reason so to a man in love, and was	E I 8 61	38
for the sake of marrying a man whom I could never admit as	E I 8 62	39
And as to conceit, he is the farthest from it of any man I	E I 8 63	42
is exactly what every man delights in--what at once	E I 8 64	46
with nothing less than a man of consequence and large	E I 8 64	47
elton is the man, I think it will be all labour in vain."	E I 8 66	51
Elton is a very good sort of man, and a very respectable	E I 8 66	53
He knows that he is a very handsome young man, and a great	E I 8 66	53
He felt the disappointment of the young man, and was	E I 8 66	55
Another view of man, my second brings, behold him there,	E I 9 71	14
A man must be very much in love indeed, to describe her so.	E I 9 72	15
Another view of man, my second brings; behold him there,	E I 9 73	18
And he, the very handsomest man that ever was, and a man	E I 9 75	26
married, here is a man whose amiable character gives every	E I 9 75	27
and very clever man; rising in his profession, domestic,	E I 11 92	5
He was not an ill-tempered man, not so often unreasonably	E I 11 92	5
his being a disengaged and social man makes it all easy.	E I 11 94	15
of the man may very likely strike us with equal force.	E I 11 95	18
be a more feeling heart nor a better man in existence.--	E I 11 95	19
"Where is the young man?" said John Knightley.	E I 11 95	20
"I have no doubt of his being a most amiable young man.	E I 11 96	25
Mr. Weston is rather an easy, cheerful tempered man, than	E I 11 96	26
tempered man, than a man of strong feelings; he takes	E I 11 96	26
"A man cannot be more so," was his short, full answer.	E I 12 99	12
I suppose there is not a man in such practice any where.	E I 12 101	25
But then, there is not so clever a man any where."	E I 12 101	25
amiable, pleasing young man undoubtedly, and very much in	E I 13 111	13
saw a man more intent on being agreeable than Mr. Elton.	E I 13 111	15
		16
Where a man does his best with only moderate powers, he	E I 13 111	17
"A man," said he, "must have a very good opinion of	E I 13 113	26
of nature, which tells man, in every thing given to his	E I 13 113	26
can it be possible for this man to be beginning to	E I 14 118	4
of that poor young man without the greatest compassion.	E I 14 121	17
those views on the young man, of which her own imagination	E I 14 122	18
"If I had not persuaded Harriet into liking the man, I	E I 16 134	2
might warrant a man of ordinary observation and delicacy,	E I 16 136	9
poor Harriet into being very much attached to this man.	E I 16 137	11
The affection of such a man as Mr. Elton would have been	E I 17 141	8
on seeing the young man had been so much more sober: but a	E I 18 144	2
could wish, that a young man, brought up by those who are	E I 18 145	10
A man at his age--what is he?--three or four-and-twenty--	E I 18 145	10
"It is not to be conceived that a man of three or four-and-	E I 18 146	12
"There is one thing, Emma, which a man can always do, if	E I 18 146	16
A man who felt rightly would say at once, simply and	E I 18 146	16
a man, there would be no opposition made to his going."	E I 18 146	16
Such language for a young man entirely dependent, to use!--	E I 18 147	17
"Depend upon it, Emma, a sensible man would find no	E I 18 147	18
--made, of course, as a man of sense would make it, in a	E I 18 147	18
what an amiable young man may be likely to feel in	E I 18 148	21
"Your amiable young man is a very weak young man, if this	E I 18 148	22
I can allow for the fears of the child, but not of the man.	E I 18 148	22
I have not the least idea of his being a weak young man: I	E I 18 148	23
No, Emma, your amiable young man can be amiable only in	E I 18 149	26
his merits as any other man; but I hear of none, except	E I 18 149	28
of his company --the great man--the practised politician,	E I 18 150	32
To take a dislike to a young man, only because he appeared	E I 18 150	37
He is a most amiable, charming young man, I believe.	E II 1 160	20
He is a most charming young man.	E II 1 160	23
and most deserving young man; and farther, had been	E II 2 163	4
He was a married man, with only one living child, a girl,	E II 2 163	4
of Mr. Dixon, a young man, rich and agreeable, almost as	E II 2 165	7
Highbury afforded no young man worthy of giving her	E II 2 168	14
"She believed he was reckoned a very fine young man."	E II 2 169	17
"Did he appear a sensible young man; a young man of	E II 2 169	17
starting on this appeal; "is he--is he a tall man?"	E II 3 174	37
He is the very best young man--but, my dear Jane, if you	E II 3 174	39
And Mr. Dixon seems a very charming young man, quite	E II 3 175	39
is a most worthy young man--but'---- in short, I do not	E II 3 176	44
Mr. Elton returned, a very happy man.	E II 4 181	3
and was just the happy man he ought to be; talking only of	E II 4 182	5
without delay, and unattended by any alarming young man.	E II 5 186	3
some time; the man believed they were gone to Hartfield.	E II 5 187	5
such a <u>very</u> fine young man; you have only had <u>my</u> account	E II 5 189	13
<u>very</u> good looking young man; height, air, address, all	E II 5 190	22
<u>in</u> it," said the young man, "though there are not many	E II 5 190	25
morning," said the young man; "another day would do as	E II 5 194	39
		40
He argued like a young man very much bent on dancing; and	E II 6 198	5
Col. Campbell is a very agreeable man, and Mrs. Campbell a	E II 6 201	20
thought to play well:--a man, a very musical man, and in	E II 6 201	28
man, a very musical man, and in love with another woman--	E II 6 201	28
That I thought, in a man of known musical talent, was some	E II 6 201	28
He was not exactly what she had expected; less of the man	E II 6 203	42
not such a house as a man was to be pitied for having.	E II 6 204	42
could not think any man to be pitied for having that house.	E II 6 204	42
The man must be a blockhead who wanted more.	E II 6 204	42
he would be the best man in the world if he were left to	E II 7 205	2
of such a handsome young man--one who smiled so often and	E II 7 206	4
Mr. Knightley, he is <u>not</u> a trifling, silly young man.	E II 8 212	3
a young man who had more retirement at home than he liked.	E II 8 221	49
I know no man more likely than Mr. Knightley to do the	E II 8 223	64
He is not a gallant man, but he is a very humane one; and	E II 8 223	64
Busy as he was, however, the young man was yet able to	E II 10 240	2
That young man (speaking lower) is very thoughtless.	E II 11 249	11
Do not tell his father, but that young man is not quite	E II 11 249	11
The loss of the ball--the loss of the young man--and all	E II 12 259	10
young man--and all that the young man might be feeling!--	E II 12 259	10
time to go;" and the young man, though he might and did	E II 12 261	35
to be quite the sort of man--I do not altogether build	E II 13 265	4
I mention no names; but happy the man who changes Emma for	E II 13 269	16
wedding-visits, and a man had need be all grace to acquit	E II 14 271	5
of bashfulness, but the man had only his own good sense to	E II 14 271	5
Decidedly, I think, a very gentleman-like man."	E II 14 279	50
She has not the open temper which a man would wish for in	E II 15 288	36
The kind-hearted, polite old man might then sit down and	E II 16 295	28
The man who fetches our letters every morning (one of our	E II 16 295	34
"Oh! when a gallant young man, like Mr. Frank Churchill,"	E II 16 298	55
That a man who might have spent his evening quietly at	E II 17 302	23
A man who had been in motion since eight o'clock in the	E II 17 303	23
Such a man, to quit the tranquillity and independence of	E II 17 303	23
He is generally thought a fine young man, but do not	E II 18 309	30
What were nine miles to a young man?--	E III 1 317	10
favourite and intimate of a man who had so many intimates	E III 2 319	4
not general friendship, made a man what he ought to be.--	E III 2 320	4
She could fancy such a man.	E III 2 320	4
she begin, that the young man himself, though by no means	E III 2 321	14
"A very fine young man indeed, Mr. Weston.	E III 2 321	15
I think him a very handsome young man, and his manners are	E III 2 321	15
A fine young man certainly is Frank Churchill.	E III 2 324	21
boasted himself an engaged man, which his father looked	E III 2 325	31
rather an old married man, and that my dancing days are	E III 2 327	36
extremely obliging--and if I were not an old married man.--	E III 2 327	37
any man of sense and taste to such a woman as Mrs. Elton.	E III 2 331	55
Such an adventure as this,--a fine young man and a lovely	E III 3 334	9
for the child of such a man, for she hardly knew what	E III 3 336	12
This gallant young man, who seemed to love without feeling,	E III 5 348	23
I should not like a man who is so soon discomposed by a	E III 6 364	58
be something for a young man so much in want of a change.	E III 6 365	67
An old married man--quite good for nothing.	E III 7 372	38
How many a man has committed himself on a short	E III 7 372	40
years; and now, poor old man, he is bed-ridden, and very	E III 8 383	29
you know, being head man at the crown, ostler, and every	E III 8 383	29
guidable man, to be persuaded into any thing by his nephew.	E III 9 388	13
So unlike what a man should be!--	E III 10 397	48
a man should display in every transaction of his life."	E III 10 397	48
Mr. Knightley is the last man in the world, who would	E III 11 411	40
		41
Was it a new circumstance for a man of first-rate	E III 11 413	48
the unexceptionable young man who would have made her	E III 11 413	49
the chosen of such a man till actually assured of it!--	E III 11 414	50
He is a disgrace to the name of man.--	E III 13 426	16
"He is a most fortunate man!" returned Mr. Knightley, with	E III 13 428	23
when, if a man chooses a wife, he generally chooses ill.	E III 13 428	23
What years of felicity that man, in all human calculation,	E III 13 428	23
A man would always wish to give a woman a better home than	E III 13 428	23
He is a fortunate man indeed!"	E III 13 428	23
him in the breast of that man whom he was so cordially	E III 14 434	3
and could say at last, poor man! with a deep sigh, that he	E III 14 443	8
Ah! that was the act of a very, very young man, one too	E III 15 446	18
What a letter the man writes!"	E III 15 447	26
Charming young man!--that is--so very friendly; I mean	E III 16 455	20
"He writes like a sensible man," replied Emma, when she	E III 17 464	20
Poor man!--it was at first a considerable shock to him,	E III 17 466	29
As far as the man is concerned, you could not wish your	E III 18 472	22
against any young man who told her he loved her."	E III 18 473	25
to know what a man is talking of?-- what do you deserve?"	E III 18 474	28
He is a man whom I cannot presume to praise."	E III 18 478	59
able to accept another man from unbiassed inclination, it	E III 19 481	1
father's side; the young man was treated liberally; it was	E III 19 482	4
with any good tempered man; but with him, and in the home	E III 19 482	4
an affection in such a man;--or, if not quite the luckiest,	E III 19 482	4
of all her turkies--evidently by the ingenuity of man.	E III 19 483	10
in Somersetshire, was a man who, for his own amusement,	P III 1 3	1
his youth; and, at fifty-four, was still a very fine man.	P III 1 4	5
He was at that time a very young man, just engaged in the	P III 1 8	15
after taking the young man so publicly by the hand: "for	P III 1 8	16
who had liked the man for himself, and still more for	P III 1 8	17
of sensible people, by his acting like a man of principle.	P III 2 12	4
there is still more due to the character of an honest man."	P III 2 12	4
"He would be a very lucky man, Shepherd," replied Sir	P III 3 17	2
sooner than any other man; I have observed it all my life.	P III 3 19	16
A man is in greater danger in the navy of being insulted	P III 3 19	16
for the place as a man who knew it only by description,	P III 3 21	18
hale, hearty, well-looking man, a little weather-beaten,	P III 3 22	23
He was a married man, and without children; the very state	P III 3 22	24
of his neighbours; farmer's man breaking into his orchard--	P III 3 23	28
Mr. Wentworth was the very man.	P III 3 23	32
He was, at that time, a remarkably fine young man, with a	P III 4 26	1
an engagement with a young man, who had nothing but	P III 4 26	3
her name, by the young man, who not long afterwards found	P III 4 28	7
was the eldest son of a man, whose landed property and	P III 4 28	7
being tempted, by some man of talents and independence, to	P III 4 29	7
being a sensible man, and, moreover, a single man at the	P III 4 30	10
and, moreover, a single man at the time, she had a fond	P III 4 30	10
as to say, that, if his own man might have had the	P III 5 32	4

that this must be the very man, and her head is quite full P III 6 50 27
Clifton;--a very fine young man; but they could not say P III 6 52 33
Nursing does not belong to a man, it is not his province. P III 7 56 11
and a few compliments to the navy, and I am a lost man. P III 7 62 39
I was the last man who commanded her.-- P III 8 64 9
If a man has not a wife, he soon wants to be afloat again." P III 8 65 14
that she too had been one of the best friends man ever had. P III 8 66 22
nothing superior to the accommodations of a man of war. P III 8 69 37
a man you of war; I speak, you know, of the higher rates. P III 8 70 54
amiable, pleasing young man, between whom and Henrietta P III 9 73 4
Charles "had never seen a pleasanter man in his life; and P III 9 75 10
a man to distinguish himself as any officer in the navy. P III 9 75 10
with that property, he will never be a contemptible man. P III 9 76 15
very alarming, when such a man as Captain Wentworth was to P III 9 77 19
If I loved a man, as she loves the Admiral, I would be P III 10 85 9
him as an excellent young man and an officer, whom he had P III 11 96 12
Captain Wentworth believed it impossible for man to be P III 11 96 12
I am; younger in feeling, if not in fact; younger as a man. P III 11 97 13
Captain Harville was a tall, dark man, with a sensible, P III 11 97 14
the three, and, compared with either of them, a little man. P III 11 97 14
He was evidently a young man of considerable taste in P III 11 100 23
and resignation to a young man whom she had never seen P III 11 101 26
a young lady as of a young man,--though here it was good P III 12 103 3
active, respectable young man, as a resident curate, and P III 12 103 3
which seemed to say, "that man is struck with you,--and P III 12 104 6
Both master and man being in mourning, assisted the idea. P III 12 104 7
apologies, that he was a man of exceedingly good manners. P III 12 104 7
half a glance at Anne; "it is they very man we passed." P III 12 105 10
pleased contempt, that the man who at twenty-three had P IV 1 125 13
A very good man, and very much the gentleman I am sure-- P IV 1 127 28
he must be rather a dressy man for his time of life.-- P IV 1 127 28
is very well, I believe, but he is a very odd young man. P IV 2 130 5
cottage for such a heart-broken man as Captain Benwick." P IV 2 130 5
He is not at all a well-bred young man. P IV 2 132 16
"He is a man," said Lady Russell, "whom I have no wish to P IV 2 133 23
to Mary, of his being "a man whom she had no wish to see." P IV 2 135 35
such as becomes a man of consequence; and both he and P IV 3 137 1
a highly respectable man, perfectly the gentleman, (and P IV 3 139 8
(and not an ill-looking man, Sir Walter added) who was P IV 3 139 8
A sensible man! and he had looked like a very sensible man, P IV 3 140 11
very sensible man, why should it be an object to him? P IV 3 140 11
by the effect which a man of decent appearance produced. P IV 3 142 13
It was the same, the very same man, with no difference but P IV 3 142 18
There could be no doubt of his being a sensible man. P IV 3 143 19
adopted, when quite a young man, on the principle of its P IV 3 144 19
"The notions of a young man of one or two and twenty," P IV 3 144 20
picture to herself a more agreeable or estimable man. P IV 4 146 6
with the liberality of a man of fortune, without display; P IV 4 146 6
was said to have married a man of fortune, and this was P IV 5 152 3
highly rated by a sensible man, without many of those P IV 5 159 21
"Mr. Elliot is an exceedingly agreeable man, and in many P IV 5 159 24
were still adverse to any man save one; her judgment, on a P IV 5 160 26
That he was a sensible man, an agreeable man,--that he P IV 5 160 27
and as a man of principle,--this was all clear enough. P IV 5 160 27
man, grown old enough to appreciate a fair character? P IV 5 161 27
She could not imagine a man more exactly what he ought to P IV 5 161 30
allowed to prefer another man, there was nothing in the P IV 6 167 21
"I thought Captain Benwick a very pleasing young man," P IV 6 171 36
his letter does not breathe the spirit of an ill-used man." P IV 6 172 42
"No, no; Frederick is not a man to whine and complain; he P IV 6 172 45
If the girl likes another man better, it is very fit she P IV 6 172 45
There was no difference between him and the man who had P IV 7 177 16
What a very good-looking man!" P IV 7 177 19
he is the most agreeable man she ever was in company with." P IV 7 177 20
He is a clever man, a reading man--and I confess that I do P IV 8 182 10
A man like him, in his situation! P IV 8 183 10
A man does not recover from such a devotion of the heart P IV 8 183 10
"A well-looking man," said Sir Walter, "a very well- P IV 8 188 38
man," said Sir Walter, "a very well-looking man." P IV 8 188 38
"A very fine young man indeed!" said Lady Dalrymple. P IV 8 188 39
It is a thing of course among us, that every man is P IV 9 195 30
Where could you expect a more gentlemanlike, agreeable man? P IV 9 196 30
But I have not known him long; and he is not a man, I P IV 9 196 33
curiosity to know what Mr. Elliot was as a very young man. P IV 9 198 51
Mr. Elliot is a man without heart or conscience; a P IV 9 199 53
It seemed to announce a different sort of man." P IV 9 200 56
When one lives in the world, a man or woman's marrying for P IV 9 201 64
now, as a young man he had not the smallest value for it. P IV 9 202 66
But it shews you the man. P IV 9 204 75
of blood and connexion, he is a completely altered man. P IV 9 206 90
You can imagine what an artful man would do; and with this P IV 9 207 90
artificial, worldly man, who has never had any better P IV 9 208 93
Mr. Smith to have been a man of warm feelings, easy temper, P IV 9 209 95
he had become a prudent man) and beginning to be rich, P IV 9 209 95
Poor man! P IV 10 213 4
she; "but I do believe him to be an excellent young man." P IV 10 218 25
every man to have the same objects and pleasures as myself. P IV 10 218 26
importance of a man of such an air and appearance as his. P IV 10 226 64
Man is more robust than woman, but he is not longer-lived; P IV 11 233 23
No man and woman would, probably. P IV 11 234 27
make you comprehend what a man suffers when he takes a P IV 11 234 31
If I could explain to you all this, and all that a man can P IV 11 235 31
"Dare not say that man forgets sooner than woman, that " P IV 11 237 42
he, "that I was considered by Harville an engaged man! P IV 11 242 65
that you had refused one man at least, of better P IV 11 244 70
In marrying a man indifferent to me, all risk would P IV 11 244 73
the ease which your engagement to another man would give. P IV 11 245 76
the man who was securing the happiness of her other child. P IV 12 249 4
richer man than either Captain Benwick or Charles Hayter.-- P IV 12 249 5
to bestow on him which a man of sense could value. P IV 12 251 10
and exertion of a fearless man and a determined friend, P IV 12 251 11
hale, gentlemanlike man, of middle age, the proprietor of S 1 364 1
here ever since I was born, man & boy 57 years, I think I S 1 366 1
by nature, & promising to be the most chosen by man."-- S 1 368 1
to establish some medical man at Sanditon, which the S 2 371 1
He was convinced that the advantage of a medical man at S 2 372 1
wife in the world for a man of strong understanding, but S 2 372 1
Her first husband had been a Mr Hollis, a man of S 3 375 1
He had been an elderly man when she married him;--her own S 3 375 1
her brother was a poor man for his rank in society. S 3 377 1
do not want the imagination of a man to operate upon. S 3 378 1
I have given it up you know to the man who occupies the S 4 380 1
In ours, it is Sidney; who is a very clever young man,-- S 4 382 1
Such a young man as Sidney, with his neat equipage & S 4 382 1
you the most experienced man in his line settled at S 5 386 1
place, to get a medical man there, I will undertake the S 5 387 1
& there a solitary elderly man might be seen, who was S 6 389 1
Ten fees, one after another, did the man take who sent him S 6 394 1
she cd not but think him a man of feeling--till he began S 7 396 1
That man who can read them unmoved must have the nerves of S 7 396 1
Heaven defend me from meeting such a man un-armed."-- S 7 397 1
If ever there was a man who felt, it was Burns.-- S 7 397 1
The man who cannot do justice to the attributes of woman S 7 397 1
of the affections of a man of his description. S 7 397 1
feeling in the breast of man, are perhaps incompatible S 7 398 1
be a fair judge of what a man may be propelled to say, S 7 398 1
honourable man, quite the gentleman of ancient family.-- S 7 398 1
And poor young man, he needs it bad enough;--for though I S 7 400 1
He is a very fine young man;--particularly elegant in his S 7 400 1
And Sir Edw: is a very steady man in the main, & has got S 7 400 1
such fire in the soul of man as leads him--(though at the S 8 403 1
of the most anti-puerile man, to be conversant with."-- S 8 404 1
He felt that he was formed to be a dangerous man--quite in S 8 405 2
I got that man a hare from one of Sidney's friends--and he S 9 412 1
very puny, delicate-looking man, the smallest very S 10 413 1
captivate some man of much better fortune than their own.-- S 11 421 1
And then,--there is the family of the poor man who was S 12 424 1
man at their back--and a great thickness of air, in aid--. S 12 427 1

MAN'S (45)
could prevent a young man's being in love if he chose it. LS 10 258 2
at her allowing of such a man's attentions to her daughter. LS 20 278 9
the world in it but an old man's playing at see-saw and NA I 7 49 42
No man is offended by another man's admiration of the NA II 4 151 12
ideas of what a young man's address ought to be, was no SS I 3 16 13
And so, you like this man's sisters too, do you? PP I 4 15 9
the compliment of such a man's affection, and though her PP II 11 189 6
My father was not only fond of this young man's society, PP II 12 200 5
from some of the young man's intimates in the regiment, PP III 6 295 6
I know it all; that the young man's marrying her, was a PP III 14 357 62
foliage of summer, was enough to catch any man's heart. MP I 7 65 13
arise from a young man's being received in this manner-- MP I 16 154 14
There was no want of respect in the young man's address; MP II 7 246 37
very fine speech of that man's--what's his name, Fanny?-- MP III 3 336 9
felt the possibility of a man's not being approved, not MP III 4 353 45
the young man's inclination for paying them were over. MP III 5 356 3
misery in another man's family, as he had known himself. MP III 17 465 13
The possibility of the young man's coming to Mrs. E I 8 67 56
Man's boasted power and freedom, all are flown; Lord of E I 9 71 14
Man's boasted power and freedom, all are flown. E I 9 73 18
and always right in any man's eyes as I am in my father's." E I 10 84 15
five dull hours in another man's house, with nothing to E I 13 113 26
man's not having it in his power to do as much as that. E I 14 122 22
comprehend a young man's being being under such restraint, E I 14 122 22
than would suit your notions of man's perfection. E I 18 148 23
The young man's conduct, and his sister's, seemed the E II 3 179 53
I could not excuse a man's having more music than love -- E II 6 202 31
is more like a young woman's scheme than an elderly man's. E II 8 217 29
And for a wife--a sensible man's wife--it is invaluable. E II 13 269 16
"Perhaps she might; but it is not every man's fate to E II 14 271 14
half-a-mile to another man's house, for the sake of being E II 17 302 23
spend some quiet interval in the young man's company. E III 2 319 2
young man's spirits now rose to a pitch almost unpleasant. E III 7 374 54
One man's style must not be the rule of another's. E III 15 445 7
I cannot comprehend a man's wishing to give a woman any E III 15 446 18
secondly, as it cuts up a man's youth and vigour most P III 3 19 16
seldom leaves a man's looks to the natural effect of time. P III 3 20 17
One man's ways may be as good as another's, but we all P IV 1 127 26
within; it must be nature, man's nature, which has done P IV 11 233 21
"No, no, it is not man's nature. P IV 11 233 22
I will not allow it to be more man's nature than woman's P IV 11 233 22
sacrificed, for the young man's sake, the possibility of P IV 12 250 8
enough to separate a man's poetry entirely from his S 7 397 1
steps, so far as man's determined pursuit of woman in S 8 404 1
The young man's attentions were instantly lost. S 10 416 1

MAN-SERVANT (2)
Their man-servant had been sent one morning to Exeter on SS III 11 353 22
23
He keeps a man-servant, does he?-- PP II 14 212 15

MANAGE (20)
for she could now manage them with perfect ease. NA II 7 173 4
of your advice how to manage in such an uncomfortable SS I 22 128 9
well manage before the carriage stopped at Longbourn house. PP I 16 84 59
a little difficult to manage, and if she has the true PP II 10 184 19
I knew how it would be--I knew he would manage every thing. PP III 7 306 44
"Mary, how shall we manage him?" MP I 5 46 15
Now I can manage the other parcel and the basket very well. MP I 10 106 55
Manage your own concerns, Edmund, and I'll take care of MP I 13 127 27
in my life--you must manage as well as you can, and not be MP II 5 221 34
two persons' cards to manage as well as his own--for MP II 7 240 8
And my friend does not manage him well: she does not seem MP III 5 361 16
to have her older head to manage for them; and she could MP III 6 372 21
trunk, which he would manage all his own way; and lastly MP III 7 379 19
did her sister Bertram manage about her servants? MP III 7 385 38
Taylor, may be safely left to manage their own concerns. E I 1 13 44
You do not know what it is to have tempers to manage." E I 18 146 11
manage; and he is extremely fond of his brother's children. E II 8 225 74
say, "I think you could manage this without effort; the E II 8 229 95
till she is in being, I will manage such matters myself." E III 6 355 17
"I could manage them very well, if it were not for Mary's P III 6 44 6

MANAGED (8)
'my dear ferrars, do tell me how it is to be managed. SS II 14 252 18
She managed the recital, as she hoped, with address; SS III 10 347 33
Are not you curious to hear how it was managed?" PP III 9 318 22
him to hope that between them it would be easily managed. MP I 1 11 18
could not conceive how they would have managed without her. MP III 8 390 7
I managed it extremely well." E III 16 454 15
You see how it was all managed. S 9 408 1
appearing however--Mrs Charles Dupuis managed it all.--" S 9 412 1

MANAGEMENT (12)
occurring in the management of this inner lock as of the NA II 6 169 11
utmost of your single management do to stop the ruin which SS III 11 350 9
of advice, as to the management of them all; told her how PP II 6 163 15
had for many years the management of all the Pemberley PP II 12 199 5
"A great deal of good management, depend upon it. PP II 17 228 33
by proper attention and management, less irritable, less PP III 19 385 4
evidently directing her management of the bridle, he had MP I 7 67 16
a saving, by her good management, of full three quarters MP I 14 130 1
was at all equal to the management of a high-fed hunter in MP II 6 237 23
causes, the want of management of the voice, of proper MP III 3 339 22
run away from your own management; but to-day you are got E III 7 369 11
As to the management of their children, his theory was P III 6 44 6

MANAGER (6)
the active, contriving manager, uniting at once a desire SS III 12 357 3
Charlotte is an excellent manager, I dare say. PP II 17 228 31
retrench where I can, and learn to be a better manager. MP I 3 29 50
theatre at Mansfield, and ask you to be our manager." MP I 13 123 5
a little more justice, Mr. Manager, if you please. MP I 14 134 13
She was a manager by necessity, without any of Mrs. MP III 8 390 5

MANAGING (2)
yet got quite the right way of managing their daughters. MP I 5 50 36
you cannot put your sister in the way of managing them. P III 6 44 8

MANCHESTER-STREET (1)
full eighteen to Manchester-Street--was a serious obstacle. E III 1 318 10

MANIA (1)
herself, she just recovering from her mania for Mr. Elton. E III 3 335 10

MANIFOLD (1)
that in spite of your manifold attractions, it is by no PP I 19 108 19

MANKIND (5)
a girl of her age, bid fairer to be the sport of mankind. LS 19 274 2
only could convince her, a better knowledge of mankind. SS III 1 261 13
race of mankind, as was here collected in one individual. PP II 17 224 9
the first importance to mankind, individually or MP I 9 92 45
led among that part of mankind which made her think worse P IV 5 156 12

MANLY (6)
His manly beauty and more than common gracefulness were SS I 9 43 11
all manly dresses a shooting-jacket was the most becoming. SS I 9 43 11
to other people, and their manly unstudied simplicity is SS III 9 338 22
That is the true manly style; that is a complete brother's MP I 6 59 43
were grateful, animated, manly; his expressions were those MP III 10 402 12
given him a more growing, manly, open look, in no respect P III 7 61 34

MANNER (410)
One is apt I beleive to connect assurance of manner with LS 6 251 1
is absolutely sweet, & her voice & manner winningly mild. LS 6 251 1
that her friends' manner of living did not suit her LS 6 252 2

MANNER / MANNER

Grace & manner after all are of the greatest importance. LS 7 253 1
opposed to the immediate influence of intellect and manner. LS 10 257 1
to observe his altered manner in consequence of my LS 10 257 2
He has told me so in a warmth of manner which spoke his LS 11 259 1
is an openness in his manner that must be highly LS 18 272 1
not yet quite resolved on the manner of bringing it about. LS 19 275 4
convinced of it, from the manner in which he spoke of her. LS 22 282 6
You know his eager manner, my dear madam, when his mind is LS 23 283 3
not in his nature to refuse, when urged in such a manner?" LS 24 290 12
triumph of her look & manner since Sir James has been LS 25 293 4
Mr Johnson has hit on the most effectual manner of LS 28 297 1
Her manner, to be sure, was very kind & proper--& Mr LS 41 310 3
be able to judge, in what manner her actions will NA I 2 19 7
She had neither beauty, genius, accomplishment, nor manner. NA I 2 20 8
and pleasantry in his manner which interested, though it NA I 3 25 2
either the matter or manner would not disgust a young NA I 5 38 4
The very easy manner in which he then told her that he had NA I 8 55 10
they went in the quietest manner imaginable, without a NA I 9 62 10
the peculiarly judicious manner in which he had then held NA I 9 62 10
go on in the same quiet manner, without shewing the NA I 9 62 10
they walked in that manner for some time, till Catherine NA I 10 71 8
in a consequential manner, whether she had seen him NA I 12 95 18
manner; addressing her by the most endearing names. NA I 13 98 2
in a most uncomfortable manner to poor Catherine; some NA I 13 99 9
His manner might sometimes surprize, but his meaning must NA I 14 114 49
"Perhaps," said Miss Tilney in an embarrassed manner, "you NA II 2 139 4
urge his suit, and say all manner of pretty things to you. NA II 3 144 10
the whole of their conversation her manner had been odd. NA II 3 148 28
by Miss Tilney in such a manner as convinced her that the NA II 5 162 27
in an agitated manner, "that, if your brother should be NA II 10 204 15
conduct by the manner in which her proposal might be taken. NA II 13 220 1
The kindness, the earnestness of Eleanor's manner in NA II 13 221 6
cheeks were pale, and her manner greatly agitated. NA II 13 223 9
The manner in which it was done so grossly uncivil; NA II 13 226 25
for to return in such a manner to Fullerton was almost to NA II 14 231 5
lived in so respectable a manner, as to engage the general SS I 1 3 1
to make a fine figure in the world in some manner or other. SS I 3 15 6
even that quietness of manner which militated against all SS I 3 16 13
Oh! mama, how spiritless, how tame was Edward's manner in SS I 3 17 18
adapted by resemblance of manner to be his friend, than SS I 7 34 6
relating its cause, in a manner so frank and so grateful, SS I 9 42 9
mere calmness of manner with which sense had nothing to do. SS I 11 55 6
of the sentence, in his manner of pronouncing it, and in SS I 12 59 7
and saying in an angry manner to Margaret, "remember that SS I 12 61 17
18

by than dispose of it in a manner so painful to you. SS I 14 72 10
with a faint smile, "it is folly to linger in this manner. SS I 15 76 16
looks, his manner, his attentive and affectionate respect? SS I 15 80 36
and towards us have behaved in the friendliest manner. SS I 16 88 40
"Reserved!--how, in what manner? SS I 17 95 48
the reservedness of his manner towards her contradicted SS I 18 96 1
the quiet archness of his manner, and, after a moment's SS I 18 100 28
29

manner in which it was spoken, Elinor replied that she was. SS I 21 123 22
The manner in which Miss Steele had spoken of Edward, SS I 21 126 41
said with a calmness of manner, which tolerably well SS I 22 130 17
18

in your manner, that made me quite uncomfortable. SS II 2 146 5
by it in look, voice, and manner, restored to all her SS II 3 158 20
This, and the manner in which it was said, immediately SS II 4 162 13
to be carried on in so doubtful, so mysterious a manner! SS II 4 165 29
in the strongest manner to her mother the necessity of SS II 4 165 30
They had not remained in this manner long, before Elinor SS II 6 176 3
inquired in a hurried manner after Mrs. Dashwood, and SS II 6 176 7
Had you seen his look, his manner, had you heard his voice SS II 7 189 46
were at tea, and by his manner of looking round the room SS II 8 198 30
a strong sensibility, and the graces of a polished manner. SS II 9 201 4
In this manner they had continued about a quarter of an SS II 9 203 11
Elinor, startled by his manner, looked at him anxiously, SS II 9 211 36
37

and most afflicting manner, by constantly placing SS II 10 213 3
on the puppyism of his manner in deciding on all the SS II 11 221 4
him, with a look and manner that were almost easy, and SS II 13 241 20
in the handsomest manner, for she loitered away several SS II 13 241 23
"They had already spent a week in this manner in Conduit- SS II 14 253 22
It was told me,--it was in a manner forced on my by the SS III 1 263 29
but what he did say, was in the most determined manner. SS III 1 267 42
more comfortable manner, than any other plan could do, and SS III 3 280 6
intruded on you in such a manner; though at the same time, SS III 4 288 27
"I only mean, that I suppose from your manner of speaking, SS III 5 296 28
self-complacency of his manner while enjoying so unfair a SS III 5 298 32
The openness and heartiness of her manner, more than SS III 6 304 13
manner, "I shall never see her, if she goes by London." SS III 7 311 13
The steadiness of his manner, and the intelligence of his SS III 8 318 21
22

coming here in this manner, and forcing yourself upon my SS III 8 318 21
22

was acting in this manner, trying to engage her regard, SS III 8 320 32
I could not bear to leave the country in a manner that SS III 8 324 42
had of her;--the last manner in which she appeared to me. SS III 8 327 55
affectionate, and lively manner which it was no merit to SS III 9 333 2
In the whole of her subsequent manner, she traced the SS III 10 342 7
his countenance and his manner, it is probable that her SS III 11 349 2
In an hurried manner, he replied in the affirmative. SS III 12 359 14
it occurred, in what manner he expressed himself, and how SS III 13 361 3
sense, in disposition and manner of thinking, would SS III 13 370 36
in the manner pointed out by their brother and sister. SS III 13 371 40
in the manner in which Mr E. took up the subject.-- W 324 3
to be at hand, in a manner which convinced her of Mrs E.'s W 331 11
by the coldness of her manner that she did it unwillingly. W 334 13
& in a very impressive manner; & at the same time without W 343 20
Her manner had been neither sententious nor sarcastic, but W 346 21
occasion of shew, her manner was all affection & her voice W 349 23
such a proposition--& the manner in which it was spoken, W 349 24
It was then disclosed in the following manner. PP I 2 6 1
see you standing about by yourself in this stupid manner. PP I 3 11 8
The manner in which they spoke of the Meryton assembly was PP I 4 16 15
a uniform cheerfulness of manner, which would guard her PP I 6 21 1
air and conceited manner, which would have injured a PP I 6 25 24
many evenings in this manner--in such society; and indeed PP I 6 27 47
entertain herself in this manner, and as his composure PP I 6 27 54
I can collect by your manner of talking, you must be two PP I 7 29 5
6

something in her air and manner of walking, the tone of PP I 8 39 50
on in the wild manner that you are suffered to do at home." PP I 9 42 14
"Yes, indeed." cried Mrs. Bennet, offended by his manner PP I 9 43 19
and archness in her manner which made it difficult for her PP I 10 52 52
carried on in a different manner; but there is something PP I 11 55 8
be a little softened by his manner of expressing himself." PP I 13 62 9
than usual solemnity of manner, and with a most important PP I 14 66 1
great humility of manner, but it was now a good deal PP I 15 70 1
and the agreeable manner in which he immediately fell into PP I 16 76 4
manner how long Mr. Darcy had been staying there. PP I 16 77 8
with his family in a particular manner from my infancy." PP I 16 77 10
might, the very cold manner of our meeting yesterday.-- PP I 16 77 12
"to treat in such a manner, the godson, the friend, the PP I 16 80 36
together, as I think you said, in the closest manner!" PP I 16 80 36
from her authoritative manner, and the rest from the pride PP I 16 84 58
favourite in such a manner,--one, whom his father had PP I 17 85 4
At length Darcy spoke, and in a constrained manner said, PP I 18 92 19
20

a manner which he is likely to suffer from all his life." PP I 18 92 21

Wickham has treated Mr. Darcy in a most infamous manner. PP I 18 94 45
a display; her voice was weak, and her manner affected.-- PP I 18 100 68
it in a very orderly manner, with all the observances PP I 19 104 1
be uttered in such a manner as must be decisive, and whose PP I 19 109 22
Though her manner varied however, her determination never PP I 20 112 23
your family, and if my manner has been at all PP I 20 114 32
avoid her but by stiffness of manner and resentful silence. PP I 21 115 1
with it in what ever manner he thought best; but her PP II 1 133 3
her manner, would allow Jane to deceive herself no longer. PP II 3 147 25
yet it should seem by her manner of talking, as if she PP II 3 148 26
detest his very name, and wish him all manner of evil. PP II 3 150 29
to be admired; and in his manner of bidding her adieu, PP II 4 151 3
quality, who has neither manner nor sense to recommend him. PP II 4 154 19
Such formidable accounts of her ladyship, and her manner PP II 6 161 7
was performed in a proper manner, without any of those PP II 6 161 10
Her air was not conciliating, nor was her manner of PP II 6 162 11
manner which Elizabeth wondered lady Catherine could bear. PP II 6 163 14
subject in so decisive a manner as proved that she was not PP II 6 163 15
in the masterly manner which I see so many women's do. PP II 8 175 25
at her earnestly, and the manner in which he immediately PP II 10 184 20
and direct in what manner that friend was to be happy." PP II 10 185 36
In an hurried manner he immediately began an enquiry after PP II 11 189 3
agitated manner, and thus began, "in vain have I struggled. PP II 11 189 3
4

you, had you behaved in a more gentleman-like manner." PP II 11 192 23
24

it, and the unfeeling manner in which he had mentioned Mr. PP II 11 193 31
I first began to think of him in a very different manner. PP II 12 200 5
advancement in the best manner that his profession might PP II 12 200 5
I know not in what manner, under what form of falsehood he PP II 12 202 5
His countenance, voice, and manner, had established him at PP II 13 206 4
air and manner, not often united with great sensibility. PP II 13 208 9
not have appeared with propriety in a different manner.-- PP II 14 212 13
Our plain manner of living, our small rooms, and few PP II 15 215 2
his sentiments in a manner so little suited to recommend PP II 17 224 2
such an openness and gentleness in his manner." PP II 17 225 14
Bingley may tell in a much more agreeable manner himself. PP II 17 227 25
unguarded and imprudent manner; nay, which has already PP II 18 231 16
some enquiry as to the manner in which her time had passed PP II 18 233 26
Amazed at the alteration in his manner since they last PP III 1 252 52
in his mind; in what manner he thought of her, and whether, PP III 1 253 55
Whilst wandering on in this slow manner, they were again PP III 1 254 57
too great for her to know in what manner she acceded to it. PP III 1 256 64
in as guarded a manner as she could, that by what she had PP III 1 258 75
the embarrassment of her manner as she spoke, joined to PP III 2 260 1
to know, whether any of his were directed in a like manner. PP III 2 262 8
but there was a look and a manner which gave them meaning. PP III 2 263 9
and acrimony of her manner in rejecting him, and all the PP III 2 265 16
or any peculiarity of manner, where their two selves only PP III 2 265 16
After sitting in this manner a quarter of an hour, without PP III 3 268 5
to us in a manner most creditable to his heart. PP III 4 275 5
Her pale face and impetuous manner made him start, and PP III 4 276 6
her companion, who, in a manner, which though it spoke PP III 4 278 20
manner, and to adopt any opinions that came in her way. PP III 5 283 10
Longbourn, heard in what manner he spoke of the man, who PP III 5 284 14
talking with her in this manner till dinner was on table, PP III 5 288 39
have spent ten minutes of every day in a rational manner." PP III 6 300 30
and live in so rational a manner, as may in time make PP III 7 305 37
tell me in an honourable manner, I shall certainly be PP III 9 320 34
I talked to her repeatedly in the most serious manner, PP III 10 325 2
how formal and cold was their manner, whenever they did. PP III 12 340 13
voice and manner plainly shewed how really happy he was. PP III 13 348 34
began in the following manner:-- "you can be at no loss, PP III 14 353 22
23

I am only resolved to act in that manner, which will, in PP III 14 358 68
In this manner Lady Catherine talked on, till they were at PP III 14 358 72
73

its being in some manner connected with the letter he held. PP III 15 361 8
Never had his wit been directed in a manner so little PP III 15 363 19
'had you behaved in a more gentleman-like manner.' PP III 16 367 14
After walking several miles in a leisurely manner, and too PP III 16 370 35
Elizabeth could not help smiling at his easy manner of PP III 16 371 41
it was certain that her manner would be equally ill PP III 17 375 27
Their manner of living, even when the restoration of peace PP III 19 387 8
at her lively, sportive manner of talking to her brother. PP III 19 387 11
for a child one had in a manner taken into one's own hands; MP I 1 6 6
distressing vulgarity of manner; but these are not MP I 1 10 14
by her quiet passive manner, when she was found one MP I 2 15 9
ways, and to catch the best manner of conforming to them. MP I 2 17 21
manner repressed all the flow of their spirits before him. MP I 2 19 30
them becoming in person, manner, and accomplishments, MP I 2 20 33
he, in his most dignified manner; "I blush for the MP I 3 23 3
"I can say nothing for her manner to you as a child; but MP I 3 26 25
had already arranged the manner of breaking it to all the MP I 4 34 2
brilliant acquirements, a manner naturally easy, and MP I 4 34 4
The soup would be sent round in a most spiritless manner, MP I 6 52 1
You see the house in the most surprising manner. MP I 6 53 2
manner of Miss Crawford, nothing sharp, or loud, or coarse. MP I 7 64 11
Four fine mornings successively were spent in this manner, MP I 7 70 30
Lady Bertram constantly declined it; but her placid manner MP I 8 76 2
How would Mr. Crawford like, in what manner would he MP I 9 84 1
own way--to choose their own time and manner of devotion. MP I 9 87 15
"Nothing could be more obliging than your manner, I am MP I 10 102 46
manner as he does, without being the better for it himself. MP I 11 112 30
time to say in a pleasant manner, "I fancy Miss Price has MP I 11 112 33
days passed away in this manner, Edmund began almost to MP I 14 130 1
Pleasantly, courteously it was spoken; but the manner was MP I 14 133 12
not ask him," replied Tom, in a cold determined manner. MP I 15 144 35
"It is not fair to urge her in this manner.-- MP I 15 146 54
observed in a sarcastic manner, and with a glance, first MP I 15 148 60
To be called into notice in such a manner, to hear that it MP I 16 150 1
admitted among us in this manner, is highly objectionable, MP I 16 153 8
being received in this manner--domesticated among us-- MP I 16 154 14
to her," said Fanny, trying for greater warmth of manner. MP I 16 155 23
He has a fine dignified manner, which suits the head of MP I 17 162 16
rest, was evident by the manner in which she claimed it: " MP I 18 166 6
so maternal in her manner, so completely maternal in her MP I 18 169 21
spirit of Edmund's manner, had once closed the page and MP I 18 170 24
His manner seemed changed; his voice was quick from the MP II 1 178 7
alarm; but she was vexed by the manner of his return. MP II 1 179 10
of the acquaintance as with the manner of its commencement. MP II 1 183 23
poor, is precisely what I have no manner of concern with. MP II 4 213 41
seemed a consciousness of manner on Miss Crawford's side MP II 4 214 46
from Edmund's manner that he did mean to go with her.-- MP II 4 215 47
Miss Crawford is in a manner at home, at the parsonage, MP II 5 221 32
me more than the easy manner with which every body settles MP II 5 226 62
And then--her air, her manner, her tout ensemble is so MP II 6 230 5
by all that talent, manner, attention, and flattery can do, MP II 6 231 11
cordiality, and in a manner not to be resisted, made over MP II 6 237 23
for the time his measured manner needed; and very little MP II 7 240 10
which his character and manner commanded, and from not MP II 7 248 47
she had worn it in that manner once, would it be allowable MP II 8 254 8
in a much more cordial manner than before, and proposed MP II 8 257 15
visit; and in the kindest manner she now urged Fanny's MP II 8 258 15
in a very agitated manner, "thanks are out of the question. MP II 9 261 5
I have been pained by her manner this morning, and cannot MP II 9 268 31
than manner; it appears as if the mind itself was tainted." MP II 9 269 33
was a pointedness in his manner of asking her, which she MP II 10 274 8
or ostentation in his manner--and sometimes, when he MP II 10 278 20
pained him by her manner of speaking of the profession to MP II 10 279 21
of manner and goodness of heart were the exhaustless theme. MP II 12 294 16
invite her in the kindest manner to his own house, and to MP II 12 295 22

in his voice and manner in addressing her, very different MP II 13 304 16
against their being serious, but his words and manner. MP II 13 305 26
I begged him never to talk to me in that manner again.-- MP III 1 315 19
There was comfort too in his words, as well as his manner, MP III 1 321 47
and generous manner; and has confirmed me in a most MP III 1 321 47
Not to excite suspicion by her look or manner was now an MP III 1 322 50
knew her own meaning, but was no judge of her own manner. MP III 2 327 6
Her manner was incurably gentle, and she was not aware how MP III 2 327 6
The effect of the whole was a manner so pitying and MP III 2 328 7
You will see him with the rest of us, in the same manner, MP III 2 331 16
however, and forbearing manner, were sensibly felt; and MP III 2 331 17
a clear manner, and good delivery, have been attended to! MP III 3 339 23
own as to the properest manner in which particular MP III 3 340 24
makes me urge you in this manner, all that gives me an MP III 3 342 36
very much pleased by her manner of speaking of it MP III 4 351 35
36
and sweet peculiarity of manner, that spirit and MP III 4 351 36
A very, very kind embrace, and some agitation of manner, MP III 5 364 31
way, though with no advantage of manner in receiving her. MP III 7 377 9
But manner Fanny did not want. MP III 7 377 9
and Rebecca, about the manner of carrying up his sister's MP III 7 379 19
That her manner was wrong, however, at times very wrong-- MP III 9 396 6
interest at least--which was making his manner perfect. MP III 10 399 5
She could not have a doubt of the manner in which Mr. MP III 10 402 11
opinion) in a singular manner, had Mr. Price been allowed MP III 10 403 14
It was her manner, however, rather than any unfrequency of MP III 13 421 2
myself for a too harsh construction of a playful manner. MP III 13 421 2
voice still faltered, his manner showed the wish of self- MP III 15 444 29
nothing--of the tranquil manner in which the daughters MP III 15 445 31
He called it a bad thing, done in the worst manner, and at MP III 16 452 13
the subject in a manner which he owned had shocked him. MP III 16 454 18
That the manner in which she treated the dreadful crime MP III 16 457 30
not to say)--but the manner in which she spoke of the MP III 16 457 30
I do, in a very pretty manner; and when you have had her E I 1 9 19
Mr. Knightley had a cheerful manner which always did him E I 1 9 21
All manner of solemn nonsense was talked on the subject, E I 1 12 41
Harriet was not insensible of manner; she had voluntarily E I 4 32 27
Mr. Martin looked as if he did not know what manner was. E I 4 32 27
awkward look and abrupt manner--and the uncouthness of a E I 4 33 32
Compare their manner of carrying themselves; of walking; E I 4 33 34
commanding sort of manner--though it suits him very well; E I 4 34 42
improvement of Harriet's manner, since her introduction at E I 6 42 1
She was not less pleased another day with the manner in E I 6 43 8
Did not you observe her manner of answering me? E I 6 44 17
With a little reserve of manner, Emma continued: "you mean E I 7 52 14
15
to her, for the clownish manner which might be offending E I 7 54 33
sweetness of temper and manner, a very humble opinion of E I 8 63 44
His appearance is so much against him, and his manner so E I 8 65 48
in education and manner has any chance with Harriet." E I 8 65 48
Harriet's cheerful look and manner established her's; she E I 8 68 58
his manner, Emma was immediately convinced must be his own. E I 9 71 10
"I thought he meant to try his skill, by his manner of E I 9 76 29
to receive her assistance in the most comfortable manner. E I 10 89 38
deal of sentiment in his manner of naming Harriet at E I 13 111 14
which, in words and manner, was assuming to himself the E I 15 125 6
not speak either to me, or of Harriet, in such a manner. E I 15 130 26
27
be addressing me in this manner--this is an unsteadiness E I 15 130 30
He was too angry to say another word; her manner too E I 15 132 37
him much credit for the manner in which it was announced. E I 17 140 3
make it, in a proper manner--would do him more good, raise E I 18 147 18
If he would act in this sort of manner, on principle, E I 18 147 18
not often deficient either in manner or comprehension. E II 3 170 5
the loin to be dressed directly in any manner they like." E II 3 172 18
brought on a more interesting subject, and a warmer manner. E II 5 186 4
innocent, and answer in a manner that appropriated nothing. E II 5 189 14
was a well-bred ease of manner, and a readiness to talk, E II 5 190 22
His manner had no air of study or exaggeration. E II 5 191 26
pleasing than his whole manner to her--nothing could more E II 6 196 2
cautiousness of word and manner, such a dread of giving a E II 6 203 41
She was particularly struck by his manner of considering E II 6 203 42
in the manner of it--so much consideration for her father. E II 7 208 9
not have distinguished how I came, by my look or manner." E II 8 213 9
sweetness and the artless manner, but could most heartily E II 8 219 44
they were conveyed hither?--the manner of their coming?" E II 8 223 61
mad, to let your niece sing herself hoarse in this manner? E II 8 229 97
is, in the most obliging manner in the world, fastening in E II 9 236 46
I never shall forget his manner. E II 9 238 51
And I am sure, by his manner, it was no compliment. E II 9 238 51
"Well," said he in a deliberating manner, "for five E II 10 244 43
in what possible manner they could be disposed of. E II 11 248 9
on what she had said, and trying to understand the manner. E II 12 261 32
and in a more determined manner said, "it was something to E II 12 261 32
33
warm simplicity of her manner; and all the probabilities E II 13 266 6
every thing that look and manner could do, made Emma feel E II 13 269 15
an affectionate, open manner, will beat all the clearness E II 13 269 16
feature, nor air, nor voice, nor manner, were elegant. E II 14 270 4
both of mind and manner; and that face to face Mrs. Elton E II 15 286 23
was thoughtful--and in a manner which shewed him not E II 15 287 33
34
in how gentlemanlike a manner, with what natural grace, he E III 2 326 32
From Harriet's manner of speaking of the circumstance E III 3 332 1
There was a seriousness in Harriet's manner which prepared E III 4 337 3
it of all things," was not plainer in words than manner. E III 6 354 9
Under that peculiar sort of dry, blunt manner, I know you E III 6 356 28
Miss Bates, deceived by the mock ceremony of her manner, E III 7 371 27
I would not quarrel with you for any liberties of manner. E III 7 375 61
volubility as before--less ease of look and manner. E III 8 378 7
Mr. Knightley immediately got up, and in a manner E III 9 385 1
2
write; and he spoke in a manner which seemed to promise me E III 10 398 53
on the subject in a manner to prove, that he now only E III 10 400 69
by the now encouraging manner of such a judge, and such a E III 11 408 34
manner towards her; a manner of kindness and sweetness!-- E III 11 409 35
was pained by the manner in which they had been received. E III 13 424 1
by the depressed manner in which he still spoke--"I should E III 13 429 32
The manner, perhaps, may have as little to recommend them. E III 13 430 37
which her countenance or manner could ever have wanted.-- E III 16 453 8
for you to feel that it was done in a disagreeable manner. E III 17 462 7
already beginning, and in the most gradual, natural manner. E III 19 482 5
its being offered in any manner; forbad the slightest hint P III 2 15 14
tenderness of manner, be continually advising her in vain. P III 4 27 5
an agreeable manner might not gradually reconcile one to." P III 5 35 15
shortly; "an agreeable manner may set off handsome P III 5 35 16
You wrote in the cheerfullest manner, and said you were P III 5 38 32
And he had promised it in so pleasant a manner, as if he P III 7 54 4
Mary knew, from Charles's manner of speaking, that he was P III 7 55 9
and the sincerity of her manner being soon sufficient to P III 7 58 20
"A strong mind, with sweetness of manner," made the first P III 7 62 40
but for him, as to the manner of living on board, daily P III 8 64 4
at that time, and had all manner of imaginary complaints P III 8 71 54
to her relief--the manner--the silence in which it had P III 9 80 34
There was no triumph, no pitiful triumph in his manner. P III 10 82 1
When people come in this manner on purpose to ask us, how P III 10 83 5
short, her look and manner declared, that go she would not. P III 10 86 17
her in his manner, which must give her extreme agitation. P III 10 89 34
Anne was amused by Henrietta's manner of being grateful, P III 12 103 5
(completely a gentleman in manner; admired her exceedingly. P III 12 104 6
helpless; and in this manner, Anne walking by her side, P III 12 111 49
between them; and in this manner, under these P III 12 116 70
In general, his voice and manner were studiously calm. P III 12 116 70
from his manner that you will have him calling here soon. P IV 2 131 12
that she would very soon see no deficiency in his manner." P IV 2 132 17
difference in their manner of doing it could not be unfelt. P IV 3 144 22
which, in a more rational manner, neither Lady Russell nor P IV 4 149 12
There was no superiority of manner, accomplishment, or P IV 4 150 14
for that soft sort of manner does not do him justice." P IV 6 171 37
in Captain Wentworth's manner of writing to make you P IV 6 172 46
The character of his manner was embarrassment. P IV 7 175 7
again to Anne, and by manner, rather than words, was P IV 7 176 10
and look and manner of the privileged relation and friend. P IV 7 177 16
and still more his manner and look, had been such as she P IV 8 185 21
Your person, your disposition, accomplishments, manner-- P IV 8 187 32
and Miss Carteret, in a manner not to be refused, to sit P IV 8 189 46
Will not this manner of speaking of him, Mrs. Smith, P IV 9 196 33
wonder, made her pause, and in a calmer manner she added, P IV 9 199 54
55
such in situation and manner, as to give a general idea P IV 9 206 88
witnessed; and of the manner in which it had been received, P IV 10 226 65
it had been received, a manner of doubtful meaning, of P IV 10 226 65
easy kindness of manner which denoted the feelings of an P IV 11 231 12
"I should have thought," said Anne, "that my manner to P IV 11 245 75
"No, no! your manner might be only the ease which your P IV 11 245 76
In a most friendly manner Mr Heywood here interposed, S 1 367 1
& in an unaffected manner calculated to make the strangers S 1 370 1
kindest & most unpretending manner, to both husband & wife. S 2 370 1
countenance--& tho' her manner was rather downright & S 6 391 1
Sir Edwd was much her superior in air & manner;--certainly S 7 394 1
her sister in person or manner--tho' more thin & worn by S 10 413 1
There was nothing dubious in her manner of declining it, S 10 415 1

MANNERS (251)

as she has not even manners to recommend her, & according LS 4 248 2
woman of fashion, but her manners are not such as can LS 5 249 1
If her manners have so great an influence on my resentful LS 6 251 2
& delicacy of her manners; but when he has mentioned her LS 8 255 2
or more obliging manners, when acting without restraint. LS 18 273 3
Sir James is certainly under par--(his boyish manners make LS 24 288 11
"Frederica never does justice to herself; her manners are LS 24 288 11
between his person & manners, & those of Reginald, to the LS 29 299 2
the same restrained manners, the same timid look in the LS 42 311 3
of any kind--her manners just removed from the awkwardness NA I 2 18 1
gaiety of Miss Thorpe's manners, and her frequent NA I 4 33 7
and manners, and increased her anxiety to know more of him. NA I 5 35 2
These manners did not please Catherine; but he was James's NA I 7 50 44
Her manners shewed good sense and good breeding; they were NA I 8 56 11
by James, that his manners would recommend him to all her NA I 9 66 32
been no insolence in the manners of either of brother or NA II 1 131 14
His taste and manners were beyond a doubt decidedly NA II 1 131 15
her change of manners was so trifling that, had it gone no NA II 4 149 1
Miss Tilney's manners and Henry's smiles soon did away NA II 5 154 2
in the laws of the land, and the manners of the age. NA II 10 200 3
Her youth, civil manners and liberal pay, procured her all NA II 14 232 6
His pleasing manners and good sense were self-evident NA II 16 249 1
He was not handsome, and his manners required intimacy to SS I 3 15 6
Her manners were attaching and soon banished his reserve. SS I 3 16 13
and his person and manners must ornament his goodness with SS I 3 18 20
as much upon acquaintance as his manners and person. SS I 4 20 9
his manners were as friendly as the style of his letter. SS I 6 30 6
Her manners had all the elegance which her husband's SS I 6 31 8
"But what are his manners on more intimate acquaintance? SS I 9 44 18
lively spirits, and open, affectionate manners. SS I 10 48 7
His manners, though serious, were mild; and his reserve SS I 10 50 12
by the alteration in his manners this morning;--he did not SS I 15 81 43
to Willoughby, whose manners formed a contrast SS I 16 87 23
quite overcome by the captivating manners of Mrs. Dashwood. SS I 17 90 1
If I could persuade myself that my manners were perfectly SS I 17 94 44
Her manners were by no means so elegant as her sister's, SS I 19 106 22
Their dress was very smart, their manners very civil, they SS I 21 119 3
Their manners were particularly civil, and Elinor soon SS I 21 120 6
became evident in the manners of both, but especially of SS I 22 127 1
with Mrs. Jennings' manners, and invariably disgusted by SS II 3 155 6
life, acquainted with the manners and amusements of London. SS II 3 156 8
indifference towards the manners of a person, to whom she SS II 3 156 15
much sweetness to the manners of one sister, was of SS II 10 219 42
His manners to them, though calm, were perfectly kind; to SS II 11 223 14
The same manners however, which recommended Mrs. John SS II 12 229 3
Her manners gave some re-assurance to Edward, and he had SS II 13 241 21
great amendment of his manners towards them since her SS III 3 279 1
He is undoubtedly a sensible man, and in his manners SS III 4 290 37
His manners are certainly not the happiest in nature.-- SS III 5 299 35
his presence, his manners, his assistance, would lessen it. SS III 7 311 16
such a visit, and of such manners, seemed no otherwise SS III 8 318 16
17
Your sister's lovely person and interesting manners could SS III 8 319 29
And his person, his manners too, are all in his favour. SS III 9 338 20
continued, "and his manners, the Colonel's manners are not SS III 9 338 21
22
manners, the Colonel's manners are not only more pleasing SS III 9 338 21
22
"He seems to have most engaging manners!--said Emma.-- W 319 2
There was nothing in the manners of mrs or Miss Edwardes W 322 3
make his pupil's manners as unexceptionable as his own.-- W 335 13
"Perhaps she is not critically handsome, but her manners W 340 19
"His manners are of a kind to give me much more ease & W 342 19
I allow his person & air to be good--& that his manners to W 342 19
In her person there was nothing remarkable; her manners W 349 23
but his presence gave variety & secured good manners.-- W 359 28
had a pleasant countenance, and easy, unaffected manners. PP I 3 10 5
the evening, till his manners gave a disgust which turned PP I 3 10 5
I never saw such happy manners!--so much ease, with such PP I 4 14 2
Their manners are not equal to his." PP I 4 15 9
and his manners, though well bred, were not inviting. PP I 4 16 14
Miss Bennet's pleasing manners grew on the good will of PP I 6 21 1
of his asserting that her manners were not those of the PP I 6 23 12
and in their brother's manners there was something better PP I 7 33 42
Her manners were pronounced to be very bad indeed, a PP I 8 35 3
Such a countenance, such manners! and so extremely PP I 8 38 42
easy manners recommended her, had increased into assurance. PP I 9 45 36
His air was grave and stately, and his manners were very PP I 13 64 21
Bennet by admiring Mrs. Philips's manners and politeness. PP I 15 74 13
manners, and sees him only as he chuses to be seen." PP I 16 78 16
her, and that her manners were dictatorial and insolent. PP I 16 84 58
party, but his manners recommended him to every body. PP I 16 84 59
"Mr. Wickham is blessed with such happy manners as may PP I 18 92 20
and conciliatory manners towards every body, especially PP I 18 101 71
You will find her manners beyond any thing I can describe; PP I 19 106 10
She saw instantly that her cousin's manners were not PP II 5 155 3
knowledge of what the manners of the great really are, PP II 6 160 3
Colonel Fitzwilliam's manners were very much admired at PP II 8 172 1
manners, she believed he might have the best informed mind. PP II 9 180 28
excellent, her mind improved, and her manners captivating. PP II 10 186 40
with you, your manners impressing me with the fullest PP II 11 193 28
Her look and manners were open, cheerful and engaging as PP II 12 197 5
man's society, whose manners were always engaging; he had PP II 12 200 5
and repulsive as were his manners, she had never, in the PP II 13 207 6
and her mother, with manners so far from right herself, PP II 14 213 17
"His manners are very different from his cousin's." PP II 18 234 31
that either his mind or manners were in a state of PP II 18 234 35
36
Mr. Gardiner, whose manners were easy and pleasant, PP III 1 248 23
Never in her life had she seen his manners so little PP III 1 252 54
marked his intelligence, his taste, or his good manners. PP III 1 255 59

be for my sake that his manners are thus softened. PP III 1 255 60
face, and her manners were perfectly unassuming and gentle. PP III 2 261 4
that the improvement of manners which she had yesterday PP III 2 263 10
years old, and whose own manners indicated respectability, PP III 2 264 14
have been softened, his manners improved, and from his PP III 8 312 15
than herself, but his manners were always so pleasing, PP III 9 316 5
I am perfectly satisfied from what his manners now are, PP III 12 343 32
said, of my conduct, my manners, my expressions during the PP III 16 367 14
"My manners must have been in fault, but not intentionally PP III 16 369 27
"My beauty you had early withstood, and as for my manners-- PP III 18 380 3
of her youth and her manners, she retained all the claims PP III 19 387 8
carrying their obliging manners to the sacrifice of any MP I 4 35 7
air and countenance; the manners of both were lively and MP I 4 41 17
as early an intimacy as good manners would warrant. MP I 5 44 1
manners, particularly those of the eldest, were very good. MP I 5 47 27
stamp, for he had easy manners, excellent spirits, a large MP I 5 47 28
Manners as well as appearance are, generally speaking, so MP I 5 49 32
that the alteration of manners on being introduced into MP I 5 49 32
"Those who are showing the world what female manners MP I 5 50 37
easy in her manners, and as ready to talk as to listen. MP I 5 51 40
Mrs. Grant's manners are just what they ought to be. MP I 7 64 9
injury, and her good manners were severely taxed to MP I 7 70 30
Mrs. Rushworth, whose own manners were such a pattern of MP I 8 78 23
of the manners which result from their influence. MP I 9 92 45
manners of a large congregation for the rest of the week? MP I 9 92 46
And with regard to their influencing public manners, Miss MP I 9 93 49
The manners I speak of, might rather be called conduct, MP I 9 93 49
her obliging manners down to her light and graceful tread. MP I 11 112 33
before his absence; his manners being to each so animated MP I 12 115 4
"Yes, his manners to women are such as must please. MP I 12 116 8
Her pleasant manners and cheerful conformity made her MP I 18 171 28
There is nothing very striking in Mr. Rushworth's manners, MP II 2 190 6
dignified, consistent manners; but perhaps having seen him MP II 3 199 13
was entertaining, and his manners were so improved, so MP II 6 232 11
respectful manners, and such as confirmed him his friend. MP II 6 233 16
man of education, taste, modern manners, good connections. MP II 7 244 27
her to be insensible of Mr. Crawford's change of manners. MP II 8 260 24
with all the benefit of her cousins' manners before her. MP II 10 272 3
great circle, which the manners of neither Sir Thomas nor MP II 10 273 7
way before their popular manners and more diffused MP II 10 273 8
every thing else;--education and manners she owed to him. MP II 10 276 13
manners were the mirror of her own modest and elegant mind. MP II 12 294 16
the Admiral before your manners are hurt by the contagion MP II 12 295 27
whose characters and manners were less accordant; time MP II 12 296 29
not to understand his manners; if he understood me as well, MP II 13 307 31
aware of a particularity in Mr. Crawford's manners to you. MP III 1 316 29
character, of temper, of manners, and of fortune, MP III 1 319 39
be extracted from her manners; and it was so little, so MP III 3 336 7
of the spirits, in the manners, in the inclination for MP III 4 349 23
continual, is the best safeguard of manners and conduct." MP III 4 349 23
In their house I shall call to mind the conjugal manners MP III 5 361 16
and his manners coarser, than she had been prepared for. MP III 8 389 3
character of her general manners had astonished and MP III 9 395 4
Mrs. Price's manners were also at their best. MP III 10 400 6
His manners now, though not polished, were more than MP III 10 402 12
Such was his instinctive compliment to the good manners of MP III 10 402 12
that her own dress and manners did her the greatest credit. MP III 12 416 2
the manners, the amusements, the ways of Mansfield Park. MP III 12 419 8
that all her best manners, all her lately acquired MP III 15 446 35
of lively, agreeable manners, and probably of morals and MP III 16 450 8
to the understanding and manners, not the disposition; and MP III 17 463 8
her sense, and wonderfully borne with her manners before. MP III 17 465 15
whose character and manners could authorise a hope of the MP III 17 469 24
suitable age and pleasant manners; and there was some E I 1 6 6
as much pleased with her manners as her person, and quite E I 3 23 9
good society; she would form her opinions and her manners. E I 3 23 10
"Which makes his good manners the more valuable. E I 4 33 36
it is that their manners should not be bad--the more E I 4 33 36
manners are superior to Mr. Knightley's or Mr. Weston's. E I 4 34 41
42

me that his manners are softer than they used to be. E I 4 34 42
man, with most agreeable manners; and as she had no E I 6 42 1
The naivete of Miss Smith's manners--and altogether--Oh, E I 6 48 39
compare them, person and manners, there is no comparison E I 7 54 30
to whom his looks and manners have explained themselves." E I 7 56 41
"Robert Martin's manners have sense, sincerity, and good- E I 8 65 49
woman, of gentle, quiet manners, and a disposition E I 11 92 4
but with reserved manners which prevented his being E I 11 92 5
Perhaps she might have passed over more had his manners E I 11 93 5
by John, as his cooler manners rendered possible; and if E I 12 100 16
"Mr. Elton's manners are not perfect," replied Emma; "but E I 13 111 17
I think your manners to him encouraging. E I 13 112 22
made it some effort with her to preserve her good manners. E I 14 118 4
To restrain him as much as might be, by her own manners. E I 15 129 24
His manners, however, must have been unmarked, wavering, E I 16 134 3
of late, thought his manners to herself unnecessarily E I 16 134 5
been no real affection either in his language or manners. E I 16 135 7
incongruity of gentle manners and a conceited head, Emma E I 16 136 9
He may be very 'aimable', have very good manners, and be E I 18 149 26
grown and good-looking, with smooth, plausible manners." E I 18 149 28
the very appearance and manners, which for those two whole E II 2 167 12
Manners were all that could be safely judged of, under a E II 2 169 17
She believed every body found his manners pleasing." E II 2 169 17
"Elegant, agreeable manners, I was prepared for," said he; E II 5 192 30
"If you were never particularly struck by her manners E II 5 194 44
of judging of his general manners, and by inference, of E II 8 212 4
of the meaning of his manners towards herself; of guessing E II 8 212 4
assurance of his attentions, his liveliness, his manners! E II 12 262 38
As for Mr. Elton, his manners did not appear--but no, she E II 14 270 5
a hasty or a witty word from herself about his manners. E II 14 270 5
very superior, but with manners which had been formed in a E II 14 272 16
"Mrs. Weston's manners," said Emma, "were always E II 14 278 47
Her manners too--and Mr. Elton's, were unpleasant towards E II 15 281 3
in the manners of either but what is highly conciliating.-- E II 15 284 9
and yet by their manners they evidently think themselves E II 18 310 34
She liked his open manners, but a little less of open- E III 2 320 4
I think him a very handsome young man, and his manners are E III 2 321 15
cool--and, with good manners, like himself--able to draw a E III 6 364 59
mean, as to the character and manners of the family." E III 8 381 22
whether it was that his manners had in general so little E III 9 386 7
faith engaged, and with manners so very disengaged? E III 10 396 44
I could never, I confess, from your manners, assure myself E III 13 426 16
yet, perhaps, since my manners gave such an impression, I E III 13 426 17
and all the habits and manners that are important; E III 13 428 23
And here I can admit, that my manners to Miss W., in being E III 14 440 8
No judge of his own manners by you.-- E III 15 445 15
"You are very kind, but I know what my manners were to you. E III 16 459 49
with manners that were held a standard of good-breeding. P III 2 11 2
therefore, but good manners in the other; and, with regard P III 5 32 2
and assiduous pleasing manners, infinitely more dangerous P III 5 34 12
Their children had more modern minds and manners. P III 5 40 45
extremely good, their manners unembarrassed and pleasant; P III 5 40 45
Her manners were open, easy, and decided, like one who had P III 6 48 18
most agreeable; charming manners in Captain Wentworth, no P III 7 58 22
very altered manners, and of seeing Captain Wentworth. P III 9 74 4
very superior in cultivation and manners to all the rest. P III 9 74 5
Anne Elliot, deprived his manners of their usual composure: P III 9 78 22
serious, and retiring manners, and a decided taste for P III 11 97 12
Captain Wentworth in manners, was a perfect gentleman, P III 11 97 15
and gentleness of her manners, soon had their effect; and P III 11 100 23
apologies, that he was a man of exceedingly good manners. P III 12 104 7
it was to affect their manners; what was to be their sort P III 12 116 70

Admiral Croft's manners were not quite of the tone to suit P IV 1 127 23
with well-bred, elegant manners, and her character might P IV 3 140 11
by speaking, and his manners were so exactly what they P IV 3 143 18
compare them in excellence to only one person's manners. P IV 3 143 18
to what is necessary in manners to make him quite the P IV 3 144 20
Lady Russell's composed mind and polite manners were put P IV 4 146 5
His manners were an immediate recommendation; and on P IV 4 146 6
Good company requires only birth, education and manners, P IV 4 150 17
Birth and good manners are essential; but a little P IV 4 150 17
excepting bloom, and with manners as consciously right as P IV 5 153 6
good sense and agreeable manners which she had almost P IV 5 153 7
in her temper, manners, mind, a model of female excellence. P IV 5 159 21
never augur want of spirit from Captain Benwick's manners. P IV 6 171 38
I cannot help thinking Frederick's manners better than his. P IV 6 172 39
Captain Benwick's manners as the very best that could P IV 6 172 40
41

She meant to avoid any such alteration of manners as might P IV 10 214 11
blush for in the public manners of her father and sister. P IV 11 246 78
Captain Wentworth's manners had not suited her own ideas, P IV 12 249 3
that because Mr. Elliot's manners had precisely pleased P IV 12 249 3
of generally pleasant manners on either, they grew to like S 2 371 1
Mr Parker again, whose manners recommended him to every S 6 390 1
a very animated eye;--her manners resembling her brother's S 9 407 1
The manners of the parkers were always pleasant among S 12 425 1

MANOEUVRE (2)
to depart; and by a manoeuvre of Mrs. Bennet had to wait PP I 18 102 75
work on, in any little manoeuvre against common sense, MP II 4 212 30

MANOEUVRED (1)
and Mr. Elliot had manoeuvred so well, with the assistance P IV 8 186 23

MANOEUVRES (2)
Silly woman! what does she expect by such manoeuvres? LS 33 303 1
The manoeuvres of selfishness and duplicity must ever be P IV 9 207 91

MANOEUVRING (2)
from my own observation, it is a manoeuvring business. MP I 5 46 22
by manoeuvring and finessing, but by vigour and resolution. E I 18 146 16

MANOR (5)
by admitting them to a residence within his own manor. SS I 7 33 3
house and the liberty of a manor, it was doubtful to many PP I 4 15 12
and shoot as many as you please, on Mr. Bennet's manor. PP III 11 337 53
inquired about the manor;--would be glad of the deputation, P III 3 22 23
parish of Sanditon, with manor & mansion house made a part. S 3 375 1

MANORIAL (1)
mansion, and ancient manorial residence of the family, MP I 8 81 33

MANSFIELD (149)
income in the living of Mansfield, and Mr. and Mrs. Norris MP I 1 3 1
child to Mansfield; you shall have no trouble about it. MP I 1 7 8
to reside at Mansfield, and on proving to be a hearty man MP I 3 24 5
among the buildings of Mansfield parish; the white house MP I 3 28 38
every thing at Mansfield went on for some time as usual. MP I 3 31 58
write and invite him to Mansfield as soon as the squadron MP I 3 33 64
"if William does come to Mansfield, I hope you may be able MP I 3 33 64
and as Miss Lee had left Mansfield, she naturally became MP I 4 35 6
chief anxiety was lest Mansfield should not satisfy the MP I 4 41 15
before he had been at Mansfield a week, she was quite MP I 5 44 2
Mansfield shall cure you both--and without any taking in. MP I 5 47 25
a few days with them, Mansfield promised well, and there MP I 5 47 26
Mansfield, for the first time since the Crawfords' arrival. MP I 6 52 1
her being settled at Mansfield from the example of the MP I 7 66 14
She has a great desire to get as far as Mansfield common, MP I 7 69 28
comfort, and the ride to Mansfield common took place the MP I 7 70 30
The next meeting of the two Mansfield families produced MP I 8 79 28
from Antigua, which soon afterwards reached Mansfield. MP I 11 107 1
lengthened absence from Mansfield, without any thing but MP I 12 114 2
Bertram back to Mansfield, took Mr. Crawford into Norfolk. MP I 12 114 3
the social pleasures of Mansfield, he gladly returned to MP I 12 115 3
He is used to much gayer places than Mansfield." MP I 12 116 5
his introduction at Mansfield by no means desirable. MP I 13 121 1
being invited to take Mansfield in his way, whenever he MP I 13 121 1
theatre at Mansfield, and ask you to be our manager." MP I 13 123 5
at Edmund, that "the Mansfield theatricals would enliven MP I 15 148 60
deferred coming over to Mansfield till they were forward MP I 18 166 4
in the objects most intimately connected with Mansfield. MP II 1 179 8
The first day I went over Mansfield wood, and Edmund took MP II 1 181 16
I never saw Mansfield wood so full of pheasants in my life MP II 1 181 16
Crawford were mentioned in my last letters from Mansfield. MP II 1 185 29
wonted concerns of his Mansfield life, to see his steward MP II 2 190 9
He believed this very stoutly while he was in Mansfield MP II 2 191 10
a point of returning to Mansfield, at any time required by MP II 2 192 11
preparation at Mansfield, the removal of every thing MP II 2 194 21
Under his government, Mansfield was an altered place. MP II 3 196 1
for her not finding Mansfield dull as winter comes on." MP II 3 199 15
nearness of Sotherton to Mansfield must naturally hold out MP II 3 201 22
Henry Crawford's leaving Mansfield, before her feelings MP II 3 201 24
in the retirement of Mansfield for him, rejecting MP II 3 202 25
than ever; the want of it at Mansfield more sensibly felt. MP II 3 202 25
She must escape from him and Mansfield as soon as possible, MP II 3 202 25
Their departure made another material change at Mansfield, MP II 3 204 33
her having never yet heard it since its being in Mansfield. MP II 4 206 5
till I came to Mansfield, I had not imagined a country MP II 4 209 15
But we have no such people in Mansfield. MP II 4 213 33
extending his stay at Mansfield, and sending for his MP II 5 223 48
as if he had never known Mansfield in any other state. MP II 5 224 49
coming to Mansfield to hear you preach your first sermon. MP II 5 227 65
You must preach at Mansfield, you know, that Sir Thomas MP II 5 227 65
another fortnight to Mansfield, and having sent for his MP II 6 229 1
try to keep me longer at Mansfield, and feel when I go MP II 6 231 9
of her home, at Mansfield--ready to think of every member MP II 6 234 18
at some distance from Mansfield, when his horse being MP II 7 240 13
be tempted to give the young people a dance at Mansfield. MP II 8 252 2
I think of giving at Mansfield, will be for their cousins. MP II 8 252 3
Miss Crawford was soon to leave Mansfield, and on this MP II 8 255 12
was already looking forward to being at Mansfield again. MP II 8 256 12
up his mind to leave Mansfield half a day earlier than had MP II 9 265 21
her transplantation to Mansfield, he was pleased with MP II 10 276 13
Mansfield, had a very different character at the parsonage. MP II 11 285 15
a week, when her own departure from Mansfield was so near. MP II 11 286 15
or four days, she should now have been leaving Mansfield. MP II 11 287 17
he comes there will be nothing to detain me at Mansfield. MP II 11 287 22
Well, when your cousin comes back, he will find Mansfield MP II 11 288 30
That Mansfield should have done so much for--that you MP II 12 293 11
you should have found your fate in Mansfield! MP II 12 293 11
the supposed inmate of Mansfield parsonage, and replied MP II 12 295 22
object would have detained me half the time from Mansfield. MP II 13 299 5
to do, and as he returned to Mansfield on purpose to do. MP III 1 311 1
Crawford once gone from Mansfield, that every thing would MP III 1 324 59
He was returning to Mansfield with spirits ready to feed MP III 3 334 1
situation of matters at Mansfield were known to him. MP III 3 334 4
none such might occur again before his leaving Mansfield. MP III 3 343 40
young man before he left Mansfield, that all his MP III 4 345 2
quit Mansfield will for a time be arming you against him. MP III 4 348 21
Had I received any letter from Mansfield, to tell me how MP III 4 354 50
was no getting rid of it till I was in Mansfield again." MP III 4 355 52
the conjugal manners of Mansfield parsonage with respect. MP III 5 361 16
I shall be at Mansfield for ever, Fanny. MP III 5 361 16
fate as unconnected with Mansfield, as she was determined MP III 6 366 4
What might have been hard to bear at Mansfield, was to MP III 6 370 12
days more to be spent at Mansfield; and for part of one of MP III 6 372 21
since their leaving Mansfield, and in each letter there MP III 7 375 4
recollection, so much of Mansfield in every letter, that MP III 7 376 4
have scarcely an enquiry made after Mansfield! MP III 7 382 29
It did pain her to have Mansfield forgotten; the friends MP III 7 382 29
Yet she thought it would not have been so at Mansfield. MP III 7 382 29

Mansfield, had for a short time been quite afflicted.-- MP III 7 386 40
Such was the home which was to put Mansfield out of her MP III 8 391 10
On the contrary, she could think of nothing but Mansfield, MP III 8 391 10
and tranquillity of Mansfield, were brought to her MP III 8 391 10
At Mansfield, no sounds of contention, no raised voice, no MP III 8 391 11
of the recollections of Mansfield which were too apt to MP III 9 398 10
nearly four weeks from Mansfield--a point which she never MP III 10 399 2
Mansfield, and was to dine, as yesterday, with the Frasers. MP III 10 400 8
After talking a little more about Mansfield, a subject in MP III 10 401 10
as well to talk of something else, and turned to Mansfield. MP III 10 405 17
a real indulgence to her to hear or to speak of Mansfield. MP III 10 405 17
He had a great attachment to Mansfield himself; he said so; MP III 10 405 18
"Mansfield, Sotherton, Thornton Lacey," he continued, " MP III 10 405 19
than he had ever been at Mansfield; she had never seen him MP III 10 406 21
the pleasure of talking of Mansfield was so very great! MP III 10 406 21
for her being again at Mansfield, where her own happiness, MP III 11 410 7
It is only four weeks tomorrow since I left Mansfield." MP III 11 410 9
replied, "I know Mansfield, I know its way, I know its MP III 11 410 16
about your returning to Mansfield--without waiting for the MP III 11 411 16
will immediately come down, and take you back to Mansfield. MP III 11 411 16
After being nursed up at Mansfield, it was too late in the MP III 11 413 30
renewed separation from Mansfield; and she could not think MP III 11 413 31
I am returned to Mansfield in a less assured state than MP III 13 420 2
me hopes of an intercourse at all like that of Mansfield. MP III 13 420 2
resolved on doing nothing till she returns to Mansfield. MP III 13 422 2
Even now, she speaks with pleasure of being in Mansfield MP III 13 422 2
that the Grants go to Bath; they leave Mansfield on Monday. MP III 13 423 2
of Mansfield news should fall to my pen instead of her's. MP III 13 424 2
such a capital piece of Mansfield news, as the certainty MP III 13 425 6
as his physician to have a little dispatched to Mansfield. MP III 13 426 10
be able to bring him to Mansfield shortly, which Sir MP III 13 426 11
small party remaining at Mansfield, were cares to shut out MP III 13 427 12
was actually conveyed to Mansfield, and her own eyes had MP III 13 427 12
Tom's extreme impatience to be removed to Mansfield, and MP III 13 427 13
At about the week's end from his return to Mansfield, MP III 14 429 1
Such was the state of Mansfield, and so it continued, with MP III 14 430 5
and so it still was, but it must be applied to Mansfield. MP III 14 431 8
Portsmouth was Portsmouth; Mansfield was home. MP III 14 431 8
or when I return to Mansfield, I shall do so and so."-- MP III 14 431 8
They might return to Mansfield when they chose; travelling MP III 14 432 11
in town, except through Mansfield, and she was beginning MP III 14 433 12
days, transported to Mansfield, was an image of the MP III 14 435 15
concerned and for Mansfield, if the report should spread MP III 15 438 4
If the Rushworths were gone themselves to Mansfield, as MP III 15 438 4
was no intelligence from Mansfield, though it was now full MP III 15 442 22
this, and hope to find you ready to set off for Mansfield. MP III 15 442 23
When Mansfield was considered, time was precious; and the MP III 15 445 29
They were in the environs of Mansfield long before the MP III 15 446 35
to have a claim at Mansfield, and was ready to kiss and MP III 16 448 3
to any creature at Mansfield, when it was followed by MP III 16 450 9
They reached Mansfield on Thursday, and it was not till MP III 16 453 17
At this rate, you will soon reform every body at Mansfield MP III 16 458 30
It ended in Mrs. Norris's resolving to quit Mansfield, and MP III 17 465 14
Mrs. Norris's removal from Mansfield was the great MP III 17 465 15
She was regretted by no one at Mansfield. MP III 17 466 16
an occasion for leaving Mansfield, an excuse for residence MP III 17 469 23
she had acquired at Mansfield, whose character and manners MP III 17 469 24
her than any one else at Mansfield, what was there now to MP III 17 470 27
at Mansfield, with every appearance of equal permanency. MP III 17 472 31
good, the acquisition of Mansfield living by the death of MP III 17 473 32
On that event they removed to Mansfield, and the parsonage MP III 17 473 33

MANSFIELD PARK (33)
Thomas Bertram, of Mansfield Park, in the country of MP I 1 3 1
to the novelty of Mansfield Park, and the separation from MP I 2 14 6
was fixed at Mansfield Park, and learning to transfer in MP I 2 20 32
I am to leave Mansfield Park, and go to the white house, I MP I 3 25 20
Mansfield Park, and was scarcely ever seen in her offices. MP I 3 31 59
Mansfield Park, and a baronetey, did no harm to all this. MP I 5 47 28
the evening at Mansfield Park, heard the good news; and MP I 11 108 4
forth the owner of Mansfield Park, the Sir Thomas complete, MP I 12 114 2
the great clock at Mansfield Park, striking three, made MP II 4 214 46
in the letters to Mansfield Park; do you, Miss Price?-- MP II 5 224 52
of events--if Mansfield Park had had the government of the MP II 5 225 57
intimacy with the Mansfield Park family which was MP II 7 246 37
without giving up Mansfield Park; he might ride over, MP II 7 247 42
Henry Crawford was at Mansfield Park again the next MP II 13 298 1
or the theatre at Mansfield Park; but he approached her MP III 2 328 7
At Mansfield Park Mr. Crawford would always be welcome; he MP III 2 329 12
and luxuries of Mansfield Park, would bring her mind into MP III 6 369 9
But he was master at Mansfield Park. MP III 6 370 14
be spared from Mansfield Park at present; that she was a MP III 6 373 23
He too had a sacrifice to make to Mansfield Park, as well MP III 6 373 25
last evening at Mansfield Park must still be wretchedness. MP III 6 374 28
spirits, when Mansfield Park was fairly left behind, and MP III 7 375 1
the drawing-room at Mansfield Park, about sending her a MP III 7 387 45
own little attic at Mansfield Park, in that house reckoned MP III 7 387 47
say, that though Mansfield Park might have some pains, MP III 8 392 12
between them, as Mansfield Park, a description of the MP III 12 419 8
the manners, the amusements, the ways of Mansfield Park. MP III 12 419 8
"Mansfield Park. "my dear Fanny, "excuse me MP III 13 420 2
I want to know the state of things at Mansfield Park, and MP III 14 433 13
know, and be no trouble to our friends at Mansfield Park. MP III 14 435 14
they are only gone to Mansfield Park, and Julia with them. MP III 15 437 3
She was returned to Mansfield Park, she was useful, she MP III 17 461 2
the view and patronage of Mansfield Park, had long been. MP III 17 473 33

MANSFIELD-COMMON (1)
the having been to Mansfield-Common, disposed them all for MP I 7 -70 30

MANSION (7)
respectable looking mansion, which, by reminding them a SS I 9 40 2
of Lady Catherine and her mansion, with occasional PP I 16 75 3
towards one in that mansion; and she lay awake two whole PP III 2 265 16
to the capital freehold mansion, and ancient manorial MP I 8 81 33
no longer dreaded by the fair mistress of the mansion. E I 3 22 7
and labourers,--the mansion of the 'squire, with its high P III 5 36 20
parish of Sanditon, with manor & mansion house made a part. S 3 375 1

ANSION-HOUSE (8)
is almost close to the mansion-house," it is particularly SS III 4 290 38
between the parsonage and the mansion-house much greater. SS III 4 290 39
their friend at the mansion-house, from whence they could SS III 14 374 7
mansion-house was equally the wish of Edward and Elinor. SS III 14 378 13
about them, in the mansion-house; but it was different at P III 9 75 9
at the window by the sisters from the mansion-house. P III 10 83 3
spent entirely at the mansion-house, and she had the P IV 1 121 1
she could not quit the mansion-house, or look an adieu to P IV 1 123 8

ANSION-LIKE (1)
a solid walled, roomy, mansion-like looking house, such as MP II 7 243 27

ANTLE-PIECE (7)
against the mantle-piece with his back towards them. SS I 15 75 2
against the mantle-piece as if forgetting he was to go. SS16 331 75
Mr. Darcy, who was leaning against the mantle-piece with PP II 11 190 8
amongst several other miniatures, over the mantle-piece. PP III 1 247 9
else, over the mantle-piece, and by their side and pinned MP I 16 152 2
being hung over the mantle-piece of the common sitting- E I 9 69 2
The elegant little clock on the mantle-piece had struck " P IV 3 144 23

NTLEPIECE (3)
It had formerly been Charlotte's, and over the mantlepiece SS II 4 160 3
mantlepiece, the interval of waiting appeared very long. PP I 16 75 3
to hold a very honourable station over the mantlepiece. E I 6 46 23

NUFACTURE (2)
right to encourage the manufacture of his country; and for NA II 7 175 12
The manufacture was much improved since that time; he had NA II 7 175 12

NUSCRIPT (7)
many sheets of manuscript--you hasten with the precious NA II 5 160 21
She seized, with an unsteady hand, the precious manuscript, NA II 6 169 11
A could sweat stood on her forehead, the manuscript fell NA II 6 170 12
The manuscript so wonderfully found, so wonderfully NA II 6 170 12
her recollection of the manuscript; and springing from the NA II 7 172 1
She now plainly saw that she must not expect a manuscript NA II 7 172 1
To suppose that a manuscript of many generations back NA II 7 173 2

MANWARING (21)
came to Langford; and Manwaring is so uncommonly pleasing LS 2 244 1
family are at war, & Manwaring scarcely dares speak to me. LS 2 245 1
Poor Manwaring!-- LS 5 250 3
Manwaring will storm of course, but you may easily pacify LS 9 256 1
I scolded him for making love to Maria Manwaring; he LS 9 257 1
He is less polished, less insinuating than Manwaring, and LS 10 258 3
& liberal spirit of Manwaring, which impressed with the LS 16 269 3
Manwaring is indeed beyond compare superior to Reginald-- LS 16 269 3
Manwaring came to town last week, & has contrived, in LS 26 295 3
necessary for you to get Manwaring out of the way, & you LS 26 295 3
Poor Manwaring gives me such histories of his wife's LS 26 296 5
& in particular tell me what you mean to do with Manwaring. LS 28 298 2
swallowed my dinner when Manwaring made his appearance. LS 29 299 2
He must not come till Manwaring is gone. LS 29 299 2
I have not given Manwaring any hint of my intention--or LS 29 299 4
as Manwaring comes within half an hour. adeiu. S. V. LS 31 302 1
If Manwaring is now with you, he had better be gone. LS 32 303 2
Manwaring is just gone; he brought me the news of his LS 33 303 1
as handsome I think as Manwaring, & with such an open, LS 38 307 3
Manwaring is more devoted to me than ever; & were he at LS 39 308 1
& let Maria Manwaring tremble for the consequence. LS 39 308 1

MANWARING'S (2)
no one's attentions but Manwaring's, I have avoided all LS 2 244 1
she had wormed out of Manwaring's servant that he had LS 32 302 1

MANWARINGS (3)
of her visit to the Manwarings, & when I recollect on the LS 6 252 2
many of my friends are in town--among them, the Manwarings. LS 30 301 5
You have heard of course that the Manwarings are to part; LS 38 307 2

MANY (676)
am forced to recollect how many successive springs her LS 6 251 1
as every visit is so many hours deducted from the grand LS 7 252 1
me amusement, & to make many of those hours pass very LS 10 258 3
us, & I have given him as many hints of my father's LS 11 259 1
But in this case, as well as in many others, the world has LS 14 264 2
distressing her, to ask many questions as they travelled. LS 17 271 6
Sir James talked a good deal, & made many civil excuses to LS 20 276 3
the subject required; said many things over and over again, LS 20 276 3
preface informed me in so many words, that he wished to LS 22 281 4
I have many things to compass. LS 25 293 4
& my wishes, he will be laid up with the gout many weeks. LS 26 295 4
many of my friends are in town--among them, the Manwarings. LS 30 301 5
You have owed us a visit many long weeks. LS 40 309 1
and Catherine, for many years of her life, as plain as any. NA I 1 13 1
hare and many friends," as quickly as any girl in England. NA I 1 14 1
From Gray, that "many a flower is born to blush NA I 1 15 5
So far her improvement was sufficient--and in many other NA I 1 16 10
She was now seen by many young men who had not been near NA I 2 23 27
"Bath is a charming place, sir; there are so many good NA I 3 29 46
since their respective marriages, and that many years ago. NA I 4 31 2
The whole being explained, many obliging things were said NA I 4 33 6
of her new friend in many articles of tasteful attire; NA I 4 33 7
or fashion, our foes are almost as many as our readers. NA I 5 37 4
and supplying the place of many ideas by a squeeze of the NA I 8 52 1
for the comprehension of many; but it did not puzzle Mrs. NA I 8 59 34
rattle, nor to know to how many idle assertions and NA I 9 65 31
which he calmly concluded had broken the necks of many. NA I 9 66 31
to utter some few of the many thousand things which had NA I 10 70 1
It would be mortifying to the feelings of many ladies, NA I 10 74 22
through laura-place, without the exchange of many words. NA I 11 86 51
furniture, though now for many years deserted--the NA I 11 88 54
feared that, amongst the many perfections of the family, a NA I 12 92 4
if they do--for they read nearly as many as women. NA I 14 107 11
Consider how many years I have had the start of you. NA I 14 107 11
So many instances within my small circle of friends is NA I 14 109 24
Oh! Catherine, the many sleepless nights I have had on NA I 15 118 13
but we must not expect such disinterestedness in many. NA I 15 119 18
and while away the many tedious hours before the delivery NA I 15 121 26
in the world, but swore off many sentences in his praise. NA I 15 121 27
"Oh! dear, there are a great many people like me, I dare NA I 15 123 39
truth, there are not many that I know my own mind about." NA I 15 124 45
The important affair, which many words of preparation NA I 15 124 48
return, without spending many hours in the examination of NA II 1 129 1
of the other, had been for many weeks a darling wish, NA II 2 141 11
Many were the inquiries she was eager to make of Miss NA II 2 141 13
because there would be so many people in the house--and NA II 5 158 14
staircase, and along many gloomy passages, into an NA II 5 158 15
seize it--it contains many sheets of manuscript--you NA II 5 160 21
shining oak, which, after many flights and many landing- NA II 5 162 28
many landing-places, brought them upon a long wide gallery. NA II 5 162 28
attempt, she could not remain many paces from the chest. NA II 6 164 3
"It is impossible to say how many generations it has been NA II 6 165 4
family are in bed, as so many poor girls have been obliged NA II 6 167 9
But many were the tedious hours which must yet intervene. NA II 6 170 12
To suppose that a manuscript of many generations back NA II 7 173 2
is well to have as many holds upon happiness as possible. NA II 7 174 8
by the most impartial eye to have many recommendations. NA II 7 175 15
the suspicion of there being many chambers secreted. NA II 8 183 2
And yet how many were the examples to justify even the NA II 8 186 13
"I have many pamphlets to finish," said he to Catherine, " NA II 8 187 15
Not however that many instances of beings equally hardened NA II 9 190 2
Many girls might have been taken in, for never were such NA II 12 217 2
here as I hoped for many, many weeks longer, how can I NA II 13 223 13
here as I hoped for many, many weeks longer, how can I NA II 13 223 13
but she had appetite, and could not swallow many mouthfuls. NA II 13 228 27
Henry, in an agitation of mind which many solitary hours NA II 15 248 16
their property, where, for many generations, they had SS I 1 3 1
advanced age, and who for many years of his life, had a SS I 1 3 1
of having his own way, many cunning tricks, and a great SS I 1 4 3
reasonably hope to live many years, and by living SS I 1 4 4
He thought of it all day long, and for many days SS I 1 5 8
Marianne's abilities were, in many respects, quite equal SS I 1 6 12
I have not had so many opportunities of estimating the SS I 4 19 6
aware that there would be many difficulties in his way, if SS I 4 21 15
she continued, "but I hope to see many of my friends in it. SS I 5 25 2
Many were the tears shed by them in their last adieus to a SS I 5 27 8
It had not been built many years and was in good repair. SS I 6 28 2
style of life rendered many additions to the latter SS I 6 29 4
dinner was over had said many witty things on the subject SS I 7 34 5
blushes and the vanity of many a young lady by SS I 8 36 1
from Barton Park, were not many; for, in spite of Sir SS I 9 40 2
into Devonshire, that so many engagements would arise to SS I 11 53 1
loved by him as his home; many more of his hours were SS I 14 71 5
began, and in which so many happy hours have been since SS I 14 73 17
the probability of many, and hope for the justice of all. SS I 15 82 45
witticisms added pain to many a painful hour;--but one SS I 16 85 11
12
"No--nor many weeks." SS I 16 85 13
Have you forgot, Marianne, how many pleasant days we have SS I 16 88 40
"No," said Marianne in a low voice, "nor how many painful SS I 16 88 41
the village, he had seen many parts of the valley to SS I 18 96 4
Because he believes many people pretend to more admiration SS I 18 97 6
The law was allowed to be genteel enough; many young men, SS I 19 102 4
will be brought up to as many pursuits, employments, SS I 19 103 5
"I think," replied Edward, "that I may defy many months to SS I 19 103 8

MANY / MANY

soured by finding, like many others of his sex, that SS I 20 112 28
the election; and so many people come to dine with us that SS I 20 113 33
"Oh! yes, extremely well; that is, I do not believe many SS I 20 116 58
in a quietness which the room had not known for many hours. SS I 21 122 10
"And had you a great many smart beaux there? SS I 21 123 26
I suppose you have not so many in this part of the world; SS I 21 123 26
not as many genteel young men in Devonshire as Sussex?" SS I 21 123 27
I'm sure there's a vast many smart beaux in Exeter; but SS I 21 123 28
at Barton, if they had not so many as they used to have. SS I 21 123 28
and so many nods and winks, as to excite general attention. SS I 21 125 36
my behaviour in asking so many questions about Mrs. SS I 22 129 16
"Our acquaintance, however, is of many years date. SS I 22 130 24
She wanted to hear many particulars of their engagement SS II 1 141 7
We must wait, it may be for many years. SS II 2 147 7
had failed, as between many people and under many SS II 2 147 8
many people and under many circumstances it naturally SS II 2 147 8
all the tediousness of the many years of suspense in which SS II 2 148 14
They were again silent for many minutes. SS II 2 149 29
Another pause therefore of many minutes' duration, SS II 2 150 35
a great deal of joy, and many assurances of kindness and SS II 3 157 19
and disposition, and so many had been her objections SS II 4 159 1
and what he meant, before many meetings had taken place. SS II 4 159 1
Every thing was silent; this could not be borne many SS II 4 161 7
if appearances continued many days longer, as unpleasant SS II 4 165 30
This weather will keep many sportsmen in the country." SS II 5 167 2
"By many--by some of whom you know nothing, by others with SS II 5 173 44
many weeks, I believe, before this engagement is fulfilled. SS II 7 183 13
rest and food; for it was many days since she had any SS II 7 185 16
she had any appetite, and many nights since she had really SS II 7 185 16
"Many, many circumstances," said Elinor, solemnly. SS II 7 186 25
When he told me that it might be many weeks before we meet SS II 7 189 46
give him such a dressing as he has not had this many a day. SS II 8 192 3
more so perhaps than in many cases of a similar kind, for SS II 8 196 19
with many particulars of preparations and other matters. SS II 8 199 37
on its object, that after many expressions of pity, she SS II 9 202 8
though where so many hours have been spent in convincing SS II 9 204 18
Knowing all this, as I have now known it many weeks, guess SS II 9 210 32
which now, as on many occasions, though it did not give SS II 10 219 42
On ascending the stairs, the Miss Dashwoods found so many SS II 11 220 3
"Not so large, I dare say, as many people suppose. SS II 11 225 31
It will be a very fine object from many parts of the park, SS II 11 226 39
of the gentleman who for many years had had the care of SS II 12 231 9
she was not a woman of many words: for, unlike people in SS II 12 232 15
and she dared to say would make a great many conquests." SS II 14 249 8
comprehended a great many people who had real taste for SS II 14 250 10
performance, and a great many more who had none at all; SS II 14 250 10
I have many things to support me. SS III 1 263 27
a Sunday as to draw many to Kensington Gardens, though it SS III 2 271 4
Martha Sharpe and I had so many secrets together, she SS III 2 274 20
gratefully acknowledge many friends, yourself not the SS III 2 277 30
it aloud with many comments of satisfaction and praise. SS III 2 278 31
There are not many men who would act as he has done. SS III 4 285 2
she could have no share, without shedding many tears. SS III 6 302 4
to render absurd; but the many hours of each day in which SS III 7 309 7
for having trifled with so many days of illness, and SS III 7 312 18
With strong concern, and with many reproaches for not SS III 7 313 20
of this attack, to the many weeks of previous SS III 7 313 21
Elinor's heart, which had undergone many changes in the SS III 8 325 51
days, that in spite of the many, many weeks we had been SS III 8 325 53
that in spite of the many, many weeks we had been SS III 8 325 53
I have entered many a shop to avoid your sight, as the SS III 8 326 55
But the rest, which one night entirely sleepless, and many SS III 9 334 5
the probable recurrence of many past scenes of misery to SS III 10 340 2
But there are many works well worth reading, at the park; SS III 10 343 9
not only in this, but in many other circumstances, reason SS III 11 350 9
must have involved you in many certain troubles and SS III 11 350 9
For many years of her life she had had two sons; but the SS III 14 373 2
it was earned by them before many months had passed away. SS III 14 375 10
at Dawlish; for she had many relations and old SS III 14 376 11
son, might have puzzled many people to find out; and what SS III 14 377 12
perfection in woman;--and many a rising beauty would be SS III 14 379 19
"I dare say it will be a very good ball, & among so many W 315 1
as you were coming home after so many years absence."-- W 317 2
& truly enough, that "too many cooks spoil the broth".-- W 318 2
do not think there are many very disagreable men;--I think W 318 2
But I can see in a great many things that you are very W 318 2
will dispose a great many people to attend the second.-- W 323 3
of nature that she should suffer from it many years." W 326 6
of whether there were many people come yet was told by the W 327 7
hesitatingly--"yes--he is very much liked by many people.-- W 328 8
Tom Musgrave who was dancing with Miss Carr, gave her many W 331 11
themselves so many dances beforehand, Mr Edwards."-- W 337 15
The next morng brought a great many visitors. W 337 16
Many were the eyes, & various the degrees of approbation W 337 17
aunt's family been used to many of the elegancies of life, W 345 21
I was thinking of you,--as many at a greater distance are W 357 28
"But I hope you will get over it, and live to see many PP I 1 5 31
Upon my honour, I never met with so many pleasant girls in PP I 3 11 10
You have liked many a stupider person." PP I 4 14 5
manor, it was doubtful to many of those who best knew the PP I 4 15 12
think there were a great many pretty women in the room, PP I 5 19 7
often, it is never for many hours together; and as they PP I 6 22 6
it would be to pass many evenings in this manner--in such PP I 6 27 47
to the door with many cheerful prognostics of a bad day. PP I 7 31 28
a great reader, and I have pleasure in many things." PP I 8 37 24
though I have not many, I have more than I ever look into." PP I 8 38 27
he replied. "it has been the work of many generations." PP I 8 38 30
The word is applied to many a woman who deserves it no PP I 8 39 46
protesting that they knew many women who answered this PP I 8 40 55
their own; and with many men, I dare say, it succeeds. PP I 8 40 56
but as to not meeting with many people in this PP I 9 43 25
"There has been many a one, I fancy, overcome in the same PP I 9 44 32
"How many letters you must have occasion to write in the PP I 10 47 7
by her two friends with many professions of pleasure; and PP I 11 54 1
something to say to him before he had advanced many steps. PP I 11 54 2
be a great loss to me to have many such acquaintance. PP I 11 57 19
The communication excited many professions of concern; and PP I 12 59 2
Lady Catherine was reckoned proud by many people he knew, PP I 14 66 1
shaking her head, "then she is better off than many girls. PP I 14 67 6
making that progress in many accomplishments, which she PP I 11 67 7
After many pauses and many trials of other subjects, PP I 16 82 44
45

There are undoubtedly many who could not say the same, but PP I 16 83 50
"I have not seen her for many years, but I very well PP I 16 84 58
She concluded with many good wishes that Lady Lucas might PP I 18 99 63
By many significant looks and silent entreaties, did she PP I 18 100 68
Many stared.-- PP I 18 101 71
Many smiled; but no one looked more amused than Mr. Bennet PP I 18 101 71
where I assure you there are many amiable young women. PP I 19 106 10
(who, however, may live many years longer,) I could not PP I 19 106 10
same party with him for so many hours together, might be PP I 21 115 4
future period, to enjoy many returns of the delightful PP I 21 116 8
Many of my acquaintance are already there for the winter; PP I 21 117 11
of an event which will secure the happiness of so many?" PP I 21 118 14
ever excited before, how many years longer Mr. Bennet was PP I 22 122 3
With many compliments to them, and much self-gratulation PP I 23 126 1
2

without being rude, and many months were gone before she PP I 23 127 5
to inform them, with many rapturous expressions, of his PP I 23 128 10
Her many attractions were again dwelt on, and Caroline PP II 1 133 2
They may wish many things besides his happiness; they may PP II 1 136 23
occurrences had thrown on many of the Longbourn family. PP II 1 138 30
Mrs. Bennet had many grievances to relate, and much to PP II 2 139 3
They had, therefore, many acquaintance in common; and, PP II 2 142 19
to be wiser than so many of my fellow creatures if I am PP II 3 145 7
tell how many trees there were in the most distant clump. PP II 5 156 4
sight of such rooms, so many servants, and so splendid a PP II 6 160 4
She asked her at different times, how many sisters she had, PP II 6 163 15
It is wonderful how many families I have been the means of PP II 6 165 32
fish he won, and apologising if he thought he won too many. PP II 6 166 41
of the coach, and with many speeches of thankfulness on Mr. PP II 6 166 42
side, and as many bows on Sir William's, they departed. PP II 6 166 42
walk to Rosings, and not many in which his wife did not PP II 7 168 3
she could not understand that sacrifice of so many hours. PP II 7 168 3
and though there were not many of her acquaintance whom PP II 7 170 6
in the masterly manner which I see so many women's do. PP II 8 175 25
mixing with them many instructions on execution and taste. PP II 8 176 30
He has many friends, and he is at a time of life when PP II 9 178 8
The far and the near must be relative, and depend on many PP II 9 179 22
It is only that he has better means of having it than many PP II 10 183 10
many others, because he is rich, and many others are poor. PP II 10 183 10
say that I have experienced many hardships of that nature. PP II 10 183 12
and there are not many in my rank of life who can afford PP II 10 183 14
recital which I received many months ago from Mr. Wickham. PP II 11 191 17
in love with her for so many months! so much in love as to PP II 11 193 31
man, who had for many years the management of all the PP II 12 199 5
As for myself, it is many, many years since I first began PP II 12 200 5
as the idleness and vice of many years continuance. PP II 13 206 4
Many of his expressions were still fresh in her memory. PP II 13 206 5
Lady Catherine had many other questions to ask respecting PP II 14 212 16
we first came!--and yet how many things have happened!" PP II 15 217 11
"A great many indeed," said her companion with a sigh. PP II 15 217 12
She had not been many hours at home, before she found that PP II 16 223 26
At any rate, she cannot grow many degrees worse, without PP II 18 232 20
if not to himself, to many others, for it must deter him PP II 18 234 38
With the mention of Derbyshire, there were many ideas PP II 19 239 9
"A place too, with which so many of your acquaintance are PP II 19 240 13
after going over so many, she really had no pleasure in PP II 19 240 14
dwelt with energy on his many merits, as they proceeded PP III 1 249 37
In the former were many good paintings; but Elizabeth knew PP III 1 250 46
In the gallery there were many family portraits, but they PP III 1 250 47
how many people's happiness were in his guardianship!-- PP III 1 250 48
eye power to wander, were many charming views of the PP III 1 253 57
overspreading many, and occasionally part of the stream. PP III 1 253 57
of an intercourse renewed after many years discontinuance. PP III 1 259 76
circumstance itself, and many of the circumstances of the PP III 2 260 1
deal to say to her, and many enquiries to make after all PP III 2 264 12
Derbyshire, he had left many debts behind him, which Mr. PP III 2 265 15
not take place till after many a significant look and PP III 3 268 6
first knew her, for it is many months since I have PP III 3 271 18
Brighton the day before, not many hours after the express. PP III 4 274 5
Many circumstances might make it more eligible for them to PP III 4 275 5
many enquiries, which Jane was equally eager to satisfy. PP III 5 289 45
seems, of their being in love with each other, many weeks." PP III 5 290 50
a father and mother, both of whom had been dead many years. PP III 6 296 8
come; and Mrs. Bennet, for many years after Lydia's birth, PP III 8 308 3
be, rejected many as deficient in size and importance. PP III 8 310 7
was acquainted with every body, and had so many favourites. PP III 8 313 20
He has been accused of many faults at different times; but PP III 10 324 2
He smiled, looked handsome, and said many pretty things. PP III 11 330 7
It was many months since she had mentioned his name to PP III 11 331 16
17

A great many changes have happened in the neighbourhood, PP III 11 336 49
friends, though perhaps not so many as he deserves." PP III 11 337 51
and shoot as many as you please, on Mr. Bennet's manor. PP III 11 337 53
Mrs. Bennet invited him to dine with them; but, with many PP III 13 344 1
them so many previous months of suspense and vexation. PP III 13 347 28
have chosen so much more advantageously in many respects. PP III 13 349 47
for many hours, learn to think of it less than incessantly. PP III 15 360 1
before many days had passed after Lady Catherine's visit. PP III 16 365 1
so many mortifications, for the sake of discovering them." PP III 16 366 5
now, and has been many months, inexpressibly painful to me. PP III 16 367 14
Unfortunately an only son, (for many years an only child) PP III 16 369 24
but had stood the test of many months suspense, and PP III 17 376 36
Nor was it under many, many minutes, that she could PP III 17 378 42
in the establishment of so many of her children, produced PP III 19 385 1
But there certainly are not so many men of large fortune MP I 1 3 1
not grow up in this neighbourhood without many advantages. MP I 1 6 6
fixed on, when she had so many fine boys, but accepted the MP I 1 11 19
change of air might agree with many of her children. MP I 1 11 19
found her ignorant of many things with which they had been MP I 2 18 23
Once, and once only in the course of many years, had she MP I 2 21 34
Here, there are too many, whom you can hide behind; but MP I 3 27 31
A great many things were due from poor Mr. Norris as MP I 3 30 50
to convince him that the many years which have passed MP I 3 33 64
who had, for many weeks past, felt the expediency of Mr. MP I 4 39 11
I know so many who have married in the full expectation MP I 5 46 22
It would save me many a heart-ache." MP I 5 47 24
many weeks, it would bring his passion to an early proof. MP I 5 48 29
but respectable looking, and has many good rooms. MP I 6 56 26
a little party? here are many that would be interested in MP I 6 62 58
An uncle with whom she has been living so many years, and MP I 7 63 4
She was a little surprised that he could spend so many MP I 7 66 14
There were many other views to the shewn, and though the MP I 7 70 30
of rooms, all lofty, and many large, and amply furnished MP I 9 84 3
Having visited many more rooms than could be supposed to MP I 9 85 5
in it by the domestic chaplain, within the memory of many. MP I 9 86 9
house of Rushworth did many a time repair to this chapel? MP I 9 87 15
proposition which many a clearer head does not always MP I 9 89 31
the youngest, where there were many to choose before him." MP I 9 92 42
housekeeper, after a great many courtesies on the subject MP I 10 103 50
an absence not only long, but including so many dangers." MP I 11 108 7
seen by too many to leave any deficiency of information." MP I 11 110 25
or army have had a great many more people under his MP I 11 111 30
of admiration of all her many virtues, from her obliging MP I 11 112 33
preparation or spendour of many a young lady's first ball, MP I 12 117 11
If you look at them, you may see they are so many couple MP I 12 119 22
inimitable, and the duke was thought very great by many. MP I 13 122 2
Many parts of our best plays are independent of scenery." MP I 13 124 9
How many a time have we mourned over the dead body of MP I 13 126 25
There could be no harm in what had been done in so many MP I 13 128 38
families, and by so many women of the first consideration; MP I 13 128 38
There were, in fact, so many things to be attended to, so MP I 14 130 2
to be attended to, so many people to be pleased, so many MP I 14 130 2
people to be pleased, so many best characters required, MP I 14 130 2
Too many characters----- MP I 14 131 3
A few characters too many, must not frighten us. MP I 14 131 5
who taking up one of the many volumes of plays that lay on MP I 14 132 7
The many laughs we have had together would infallibly come MP I 14 133 11
be one steady head to superintend so many young ones. MP I 15 141 22
For a moment no one spoke; and then many spoke together to MP I 15 143 28
a great many of my own, before we rehearse together.-- MP I 15 149 61
a fire it was habitable in many an early spring, and late MP I 16 151 2
it escaped the notice of many of her own family likewise. MP I 17 162 19
arose, Fanny found, before many days were past, that it MP I 18 164 1
Edmund had many. MP I 18 164 1
on this point there were not many who differed from her. MP I 18 165 3
Many uncomfortable, anxious, apprehensive feelings she MP I 18 166 5
She had read, and read the scene again with many painful, MP I 18 167 13
again with many painful, many wondering emotions, and MP I 18 167 13
of carpet work and made many yards of fringe; and she MP II 1 179 9
Not that she was incommoded by many fears of Sir Thomas's MP II 1 179 10
have killed six times as many; but we respect your MP II 1 181 16
and with many awkward sensations he did his best. MP II 1 183 23

Context	Work	Vol	Ch	Page	Line
of the uneasy movements of many of his friends as they sat,	MP	II	1	184	27
That I should be cautious and quick-sighted, and feel many	MP	II	1	186	34
It was impossible for many of the others not to smile.	MP	II	1	186	35
it too much indeed for many words; and having shaken hands	MP	II	2	187	2
family, much exertion and many sacrifices to glance at in	MP	II	2	188	3
her own fire-side, and many excellent hints of distrust	MP	II	2	188	3
He had known many disagreeable fathers before, and often	MP	II	2	191	10
It was the first day for many, many weeks, in which the	MP	II	2	192	11
forwarding it; but with so many to care for, how was it	MP	II	2	194	20
away and the spirits of many others saddened, it was all	MP	II	3	196	1
It entertains me more than many other things have done--	MP	II	3	197	5
define many as accurately, did not delicacy forbid it.	MP	II	3	198	13
She went however, and they sauntered about together many	MP	II	4	208	11
to our owing her a great many gay, brilliant, happy hours.	MP	II	4	210	21
fear of being late, been many minutes seated in the	MP	II	5	222	41
the Admiral, in having for many years taken in the paper	MP	II	6	232	13
heart had been yearning to do, through many a past year.	MP	II	6	233	17
he had ridden, or his many narrow escapes from dreadful	MP	II	6	237	23
at last hazarded, after many debates and many doubts as to	MP	II	7	238	2
after many debates and many doubts as to whether it were	MP	II	7	238	2
impossible among so many dishes but that some must be cold.	MP	II	7	238	3
"My plan may not be the best possible; I had not many	MP	II	7	243	27
low single rooms, with as many roofs as windows--it is not	MP	II	7	243	27
We used to jump about together many a time, did not we?	MP	II	7	250	59
Invitations were sent with dispatch, and many a young lady	MP	II	8	254	8
had to offer her--he had many anxious feelings, many	MP	II	8	255	10
anxious feelings, many doubting hours as to the result.	MP	II	8	255	10
Such a trifle is not worth half so many words."	MP	II	8	260	22
Till she had shed many tears over this deception, Fanny	MP	II	9	264	17
her duty; but having also many of the feelings of youth	MP	II	9	265	19
would rob her of many hours of his company, she was too	MP	II	9	266	21
As for the ball so near at hand, she had too many	MP	II	9	266	22
supposed to have, by the many young ladies looking forward	MP	II	9	266	22
How many a time have we talked over her little errors!	MP	II	9	270	38
subdued; the sight of so many strangers threw her back	MP	II	10	273	7
To be placed above so many elegant young women!	MP	II	10	275	12
Norris paid her with as many smiles and courteous words as	MP	II	10	277	16
Fanny was too urgent, however, and had too many tears in	MP	II	10	280	30
So many months acquaintance!--	MP	II	11	288	22
How many Miss Owens are there?"	MP	II	11	288	24
"You cannot doubt your being missed by many," said she.	MP	II	11	289	31
the guest of neither brother nor sister many months longer.	MP	II	12	295	24
on Monday, trusting that many posts would not pass before	MP	II	13	299	5
to give her so many painful sensations on the first day of	MP	II	13	303	13
that he would have many things to buy, though to be sure	MP	II	13	305	19
in a man, who had seen so many, and been admired by so	MP	II	13	305	26
and been admired by so many, and flirted with so many,	MP	II	13	305	26
many, and flirted with so many, infinitely her superiors--	MP	II	13	305	26
Many surprises were awaiting him.	MP	III	3	334	1
and inanimate, which so many years growth have confirmed,	MP	III	4	347	21
Thomas, though I certainly did hate him for many a week.	MP	III	5	358	9
After this speech, the two girls sat many minutes silent,	MP	III	5	360	13
who has been shot at by so many; of having it in one's	MP	III	5	363	22
favours; and there are so many young men's claims to be	MP	III	5	364	29
To be in the centre of such a circle, loved by so many,	MP	III	6	370	11
a larger share than any one among so many could deserve.	MP	III	6	371	17
her own perfect consciousness, many drawbacks suppressed.	MP	III	8	388	1
Charles being at least as many years as they were his	MP	III	8	390	8
love or assist; and of Susan's temper, she had many doubts.	MP	III	8	391	9
by Susan, which after many hesitations of delicacy, she at	MP	III	9	396	7
much better knowledge, so many good notions, should have	MP	III	9	397	8
not regret it; for to her many other sources of uneasiness	MP	III	10	400	6
he have suspected how many privations, besides that of	MP	III	11	412	30
so very ill-looking as I did, at least one sees many worse.	MP	III	12	416	2
and many days to come, without producing any conclusion.	MP	III	12	417	4
all, less affluent than many of her acquaintance,	MP	III	13	421	2
find how many weeks more she is likely to be without you.	MP	III	13	423	2
occupation for the pen for many days to come, being no	MP	III	13	426	9
for what might be; and how many walks up and down stairs	MP	III	14	432	10
saved her, and how many messages she might have carried.	MP	III	14	432	10
Varnish and gilding hide many stains.	MP	III	14	434	13
illness had continued so many weeks without her being	MP	III	14	436	15
"It might be all a lie," he acknowledged; "but so many	MP	III	15	440	17
of being exquisitely happy, while so many were miserable.	MP	III	15	443	24
Lady Bertram could not give her much time, or many words,	MP	III	16	448	3
blessings, an escape from many certain evils, that she	MP	III	16	448	3
that I had been too apt to dwell on for many months past.	MP	III	16	457	30
I imagined I saw a mixture of many feelings--a great,	MP	III	16	458	30
that considering the many counteractions of opposing	MP	III	16	459	31
which threatened alloy to her many enjoyments.	E	I	1	5	4
her daily reach; and many a long October and November	E	I	1	7	9
She had many acquaintance in the place, for her father was	E	I	1	7	10
did him good; and his many inquiries after "poor Isabella"	E	I	1	9	21
in the right, when so many people said Mr. Weston would	E	I	1	11	39
visits here and given many little encouragements, and	E	I	1	13	43
and smoothed many little matters, it might not have come	E	I	1	13	43
many--perhaps with most people, unless taken moderately.	E	I	2	19	14
the seat of Mr. Knightley, comprehended many such.	E	I	3	20	1
an excellent mother and so many good neighbours and	E	I	3	21	4
and describe the many comforts and wonders of the place.	E	I	4	27	4
I have seen a great many lists of her drawing up at	E	I	5	37	7
It has been so many years my province to give advice, that	E	I	5	40	24
scruples which could stand many minutes against the	E	I	6	44	19
Her many beginnings were displayed.	E	I	6	44	19
in drawing and music than many might have done with so	E	I	6	44	19
of both; with as many other agreeable associations as Mr.	E	I	6	47	27
choosing from among many, consequently a claim to be nice.	E	I	8	63	44
with Miss Woodhouse's help, to get a great many more.	E	I	9	69	4
"So many clever riddles as there used to be when he was	E	I	9	70	5
was all that Harriet, with many tender embraces could	E	I	9	74	21
They are all remarkably clever; and they have so many	E	I	9	80	72
busy mind, with a great many independent resources; and I	E	I	10	85	21
and it was therefore many months since they had been seen	E	I	11	91	2
The bustle and joy of such an arrival, the many to be	E	I	11	92	3
that of her children, had many fears and many nerves, and	E	I	11	92	4
had many fears and many nerves, and was as fond of her own	E	I	11	92	4
"Ah! my dear, but Perry had many doubts about the sea	E	I	12	101	22
be said--much praise and many comments--undoubting	E	I	12	104	50
severe Philippics upon the many houses where it was never	E	I	12	104	50
"I know there is such an idea with many people, but indeed	E	I	12	105	55
been attributing many of his own feelings and expressions;-	E	I	12	107	62
though she could not speak of her loss without many tears.	E	I	13	109	5
She had not advanced many yards from Mrs. Goddard's door,	E	I	13	109	6
there is, I believe, in many men, especially single men,	E	I	13	111	13
are sometimes to be pleased only by a good many sacrifices.	E	I	14	120	9
having so many friends about them, revived him a little.	E	I	15	127	12
above half an inch deep in many places hardly enough to	E	I	15	127	16
Every thing that I have said or done, for many weeks past,	E	I	15	131	31
was proving himself, in many respects, the very reverse of	E	I	16	135	6
freeze, she was for many days a most honourable prisoner.	E	I	16	138	17
off from some advantages, it will secure him many others."	E	I	18	148	23
She had had many a hint from Mr. Knightley and some from	E	II	1	155	3
independent fortune, of so many thousands as would always	E	II	4	181	4
Many vain solicitudes would be prevented--many	E	II	4	182	8
The charm of an object to occupy the many vacancies of	E	II	4	183	10
man, "though there are not many houses that I should	E	II	5	190	25
about his hay, and a great many errands for Mrs. Weston at	E	II	5	193	6
and there are a great many houses; you might be very much	E	II	5	195	47
added; it had been built many years ago for a ball-room,	E	II	6	197	5
He could not be persuaded that so many good-looking houses	E	II	6	198	5
that he had heard many people say the same--but yet he	E	II	6	199	10
without ever thinking how many advantages and	E	II	6	204	43
meet this presumption so many weeks before it appeared,	E	II	7	207	7
There will be a great many people talking at once.	E	II	7	210	16
Mrs. Cole had many to agree with her; every body who spoke	E	II	8	215	15
It seemed quite a shame, especially considering how many	E	II	8	215	16
which allowed her so many alleviations of pleasure, in the	E	II	8	219	44
There she sat--and who would have guessed how many tears	E	II	8	219	44
'Nobody was ever so fortunate as herself!'--but many, many	E	II	8	223	63
herself!'--but many, many thanks,--'there was no occasion	E	II	8	223	63
with it; as you have many a time reproached me with doing.	E	II	8	226	84
The visit afforded her many pleasant recollections the	E	II	9	231	1
supply; for I have a great many more than I can ever use.	E	II	9	238	51
say that we had a great many left--it was but half a dozen	E	II	9	238	51
she wished I had made him believe we had a great many left.	E	II	9	238	51
his master had sold so many; for William, you know, thinks	E	II	9	239	51
and as long as so many sacks were sold, it did not signify	E	II	9	239	51
Quite delightful; so many friends!"	E	II	10	244	44
You said you had a great many, and now you have not one	E	II	10	245	52
Instances have been known of young people passing many,	E	II	11	247	1
young people passing many, many months successively,	E	II	11	247	1
two Miss Coxes five," had been repeated many times over.	E	II	11	248	4
it was not so good but that many of them wanted a better.	E	II	11	248	10
Do not you remember what Mr. Perry said, so many years ago,	E	II	11	252	37
We shall not be many, you know."	E	II	11	254	46
I shall have many fellow-mourners for the ball, if not for	E	II	12	262	39
I have spent so many happy months there!(with a little	E	II	14	273	19
Many counties, I believe, are called the garden of England,	E	II	14	273	25
You have many parties of that kind here, I suppose, Miss	E	II	14	274	28
Many a time has Selina said, when she has been going to	E	II	14	274	30
Many a time has she said so; and yet I am no advocate for	E	II	14	275	30
Blessed with so many resources within myself, the world	E	II	14	276	36
I hope we shall have many sweet little concerts together.	E	II	14	277	38
that a married woman has many things to call her attention.	E	II	14	277	40
lines of the poet, 'full many a flower is born to blush	E	II	15	282	5
If we set the example, many will follow it as far as they	E	II	15	283	9
equal satisfaction, and on many accounts Emma was	E	II	16	291	5
hence you may have as many concentrated objects as I have."	E	II	16	294	23
You do not know how many candidates there always are for	E	II	17	299	8
your own terms, have as many rooms as you like, and mix in	E	II	17	301	18
I always say a woman cannot have too many resources--and I	E	II	18	307	21
have so many myself as to be quite independent of society."	E	II	18	307	21
there, and encumbered with many low connections, but	E	II	18	310	34
the Tupmans, though a good many things I assure you are	E	II	18	310	34
I should like to know how many of all my numerous	E	II	18	312	50
fortune in meeting with so many of your friends at once	E	II	18	312	50
that she might not have many years of existence before her;	E	III	1	317	6
such near neighbourhood to many dear friends--for the	E	III	1	317	8
of a man who had so many intimates and confidantes, was	E	III	2	319	4
finished her speech under many minutes after her being	E	III	2	322	18
After a good many compliments to Jane on her dress and	E	III	2	324	20
How has Wright done my hair?"--with many other relative	E	III	2	324	20
she had so many hours of unusual festivity before her.--	E	III	2	325	32
It was some comfort to him that many inquiries after	E	III	3	336	12
But while so many were devoting him to Emma, and Emma	E	III	5	343	2
her letters to Enscombe, many weeks ago, with all these	E	III	5	345	13
to quit the table; but so many were also moving, that she	E	III	5	349	25
let a woman have ever so many resources, it is not	E	III	6	356	26
with many comfortable and one or two handsome rooms.--	E	III	6	358	35
Mrs. Churchill's state, however, as many were ready to	E	III	6	361	41
How many a man has committed himself on a short	E	III	7	372	40
Such another scheme, composed of so many ill-assorted	E	III	7	374	54
too --and before others, many of whom (certainly some,)	E	III	7	375	61
whom she had been so many months neglecting, was now the	E	III	9	389	16
Consider how many of my dearest friends are now in	E	III	10	393	12
for his having many, very many, good qualities; and-----"	E	III	10	397	49
to promise me many particulars that could not be given now.	E	III	10	398	53
It may bring many extenuations.	E	III	10	398	53
It may make many things intelligible and excusable which	E	III	10	398	53
by herself--very ill in many ways,--but it was not so much	E	III	11	402	1
This discovery laid many smaller matters open.	E	III	11	403	2
Much that lived in Harriet's memory, many little	E	III	11	409	35
The bitter feelings occasioned by this speech, the many	E	III	11	411	40 41
She had herself been first with him for many years past.	E	III	12	415	1
so many months," continued Mrs. Weston, "she was energetic.	E	III	12	418	6
tempted to say and do many things which may well lay me	E	III	13	426	15
Many circumstances assisted the temptation.	E	III	13	427	19
of being sent with all the many other letters of that day,	E	III	14	442	8
It is remarkable, that Emma, in the many, very many,	E	III	15	449	35
and my instrument, if I had half so many applicants.'--	E	III	16	455	23
and by dint of fancying so many errors, have been in love	E	III	17	462	7
wonder in many a family circle, with great sagacity.	E	III	17	468	35
you, in the confusion of so many subjects, mistake him?--	E	III	18	473	26
perhaps, as the blood of many a gentleman: but what a	E	III	19	482	3
What will he be doing, in fact, but what very many of our	P	III	2	12	4
which shut her out, and on many lesser occasions had	P	III	2	16	16
Many a noble fortune has been made during the war.	P	III	3	17	1
let him have taken ever so many before--hey, Shepherd?"	P	III	3	17	2
But then, is not it the same with many other professions,	P	III	3	20	17
where there was no lady, as where there were many children.	P	III	3	22	24
One wonders how the names of many of our nobility become	P	III	3	23	33
of former pain; and many a stroll and many a sigh were	P	III	4	30	10
and many a stroll and many a sigh were necessary to dispel	P	III	4	30	10
"A great many things, I assure you.	P	III	5	38	34
houses in Kellynch for many weeks, she had expected rather	P	III	6	42	1
for his father's having many other uses for his money, and	P	III	6	43	5
world, but I know it is taken notice of by many persons."	P	III	6	46	10
she was left with as many sensations of comfort, as were,	P	III	7	58	20
But they have a great many to provide for; and among the	P	III	8	65	11
him do as you and I, and a great many others, have done.	P	III	8	70	46
years of my marriage; though many women have done more.	P	III	8	70	52
now growing too infirm for many of them, should be quite	P	III	9	78	19
across the fields made many separations necessary, to keep	P	III	10	84	7
After one of the many praises of the day, which were	P	III	10	84	7 8
solemnity,--"while so many of its brethren have fallen and	P	III	10	88	26
"Mary is good-natured enough in many respects," said she; "	P	III	10	88	28
be plainer; and where many divisions were necessary, or	P	III	10	90	37
How many days was it, my dear, between the first time of	P	III	10	92	44
growth declare that many a generation must have passed	P	III	11	95	9
the heart could think capable of accommodating so many.	P	III	11	98	17
of being oppressed by the presence of so many strangers.	P	III	11	99	22
reflection, that, like many other great moralists and	P	III	11	101	26
She has cousins here, you know, and many acquaintance,	P	III	12	102	2
Many had looked on each other, and many had repeated the	P	III	12	105	13
Mr. Elliot had not, for many years, been on such terms as	P	III	12	106	18
The offence which had been given her father, many years	P	III	12	107	21
about the Cobb, and many were collected near them, to be	P	III	12	111	49
It stood the record of many sensations of pain, once	P	IV	1	123	8
Every thing was safe enough, and she smiled over the many	P	IV	1	128	32
day, there had been so many walks between their lodgings	P	IV	2	129	3
and there were a great many more people to look at in the	P	IV	2	130	3
was more than she could say for many other persons in Bath.	P	IV	2	136	36
an imprisonment of many months, and anxiously saying to	P	IV	3	137	2
their drawing-rooms had many decided advantages over all	P	IV	3	137	4
They had drawn back from many introductions, and still	P	IV	3	138	4
an interval of so many years, to be well received by them.	P	IV	3	140	11
He hoped she might make some amends for the many very	P	IV	3	141	13
still it had existed so many years that she could not	P	IV	4	147	8
the particulars of their first meeting a great many times.	P	IV	4	148	9
was swept away for many days; for the Dalrymples (in	P	IV	4	148	10
tremulously) "there are so many who forget to think	P	IV	5	156	11
by a sensible man, without many of those agreeable	P	IV	5	159	21

"Mr. Elliot is an exceedingly agreeable man, and in many P IV 5 159 24
Happily for her, they were not many. P IV 6 165 9
should not have many acquaintance in such a place as this." P IV 6 166 14
The Crofts knew quite as many people in Bath as they P IV 6 168 24
The carriage would not accommodate so many. P IV 7 176 11
There were many other men about him, many groups walking P IV 7 179 28
me to-morrow if I may not have many more visits from you." P IV 7 180 35
in their power, draw as many eyes, excite as many whispers, P IV 8 185 19
as many whispers, and disturb as many people as they could. P IV 8 185 19
I have been acquainted with you by character many years. P IV 8 187 32
He had many years ago received such a description of Miss P IV 8 187 34
with partiality of her many years ago, as the Mr. P IV 8 187 35
In re-settling themselves, there were now many changes, P IV 8 189 46
you must have so many pleasanter demands upon your time." P IV 9 194 18
for him now, with so many affairs and engagements of his P IV 9 196 32
"I think you spoke of having known Mr. Elliot many years?" P IV 9 198 45
There were many things to be taken into the account. P IV 9 198 53
here and there, while many letters and memorandums of real P IV 9 203 70
through the hands of so many, to be misconceived by folly P IV 9 205 85
Indies, which had been for many years under a sort of P IV 9 210 98
many evils, without knowing how to avert any one of them.-- P IV 10 212 1
"but he gave so many hints; so Mrs. Clay says, at least." P IV 10 213 3
possibly claim it under many years; and that, on the P IV 10 217 20
operation, and it streightens him as to many things. P IV 10 218 22
of good will which many associations contributed to form. P IV 10 220 30
You did not use to like cards; but time makes many changes. P IV 10 225 59
could not avoid hearing many undesirable particulars, such P IV 11 230 5
make the best of it, as many others have done before them. P IV 11 230 6
within our own circle; many of which circumstances (P IV 11 234 30
heaven had given them wings, by many hours sooner still! P 1 6 235 31
by so many, many years of division and estrangement. P IV 11 240 59
of ill consequence in many ways; and that I had no right P IV 11 242 65
young women followed by as many maid servants, were now S 1 370 1
account--& probably very many more--and his own sisters S 2 372 1
He wanted to secure the promise of a visit--to get as many S 2 373 1
of society--for she had many thousands a year to bequeath, S 3 376 1
no doubt we shall have many a candidate for, before the S 3 377 1
After having avoided London for many years, principally on S 3 378 1
"It seems to have as many comforts about it as Willingden," S 4 379 1
what effect it might have: many a respectable family, many S 4 382 1
many a respectable family, many a careful mother, many a S 4 382 1
many a careful mother, many a pretty daughter, might it S 4 382 1
Many thanks my dear Tom for the kindness with respect to S 5 386 1
I will not tell you how many people I have employed in the S 5 387 1
done without, & among so many pretty temptations, & with S 6 390 1
faster, & seemed to have many harassing apprehensions of S 6 392 1
Here are a great many empty houses--3 on this very terrace; S 7 402 1
We have many leisure hours, & read a great deal.-- S 8 403 1
Though he owed many of his ideas to this sort of reading, S 8 404 1
Already had he had many musings on the subject. S 8 405 2
They had charitable hearts & many amiable feelings--but a S 10 412 1
made a great many odd faces & contortions, Charlotte could S 10 413 1
she had also opened so many Treaties with cooks, S 10 414 1
provided with almost as many Teapots &c as there were S 10 416 1
or the blunders of the many engaged in the cause by the S 11 420 1
There were so many to share in the shame & the blame, that S 11 420 1
to be attributed the giddiness & false steps of many.-- S 11 421 1
many an eye upwards, & made many a Gazer gaze again.-- S 11 422 1
Denham--and that one among many miniatures in another part S 12 427 1

MAP (1)
"Dear mamma, only think, my cousin cannot put the map of MP I 2 18 23

MAPLE GROVE (31)
The very first subject after being seated was Maple Grove, E II 14 272 18
Suckling's seat"--a comparison of Hartfield to Maple Grove. E II 14 272 18
"Very like Maple Grove indeed!-- E II 14 272 18
at Maple Grove; her sister's favourite room."-- E II 14 272 18
She could really almost fancy herself at Maple Grove." E II 14 272 18
of a place I am so extremely partial to as Maple Grove. E II 14 273 19
"So extremely like Maple Grove! E II 14 273 21
The laurels at Maple Grove are in the same profusion as E II 14 273 21
I was quite a proverb for it at Maple Grove. E II 14 274 30
society, both at Maple Grove and in Bath, it would have E II 14 276 36
to every luxury at Maple Grove; but I did assure him that E II 14 277 36
Maple Grove will probably by my model more than it ought E II 15 283 9
to her, and Maple Grove had given her a taste for dinners. E II 16 290 3
a vast deal of that in the neighbourhood round Maple Grove. E II 17 299 8
Sixty-five miles farther than from Maple Grove to London. E II 18 306 10
"Aye--like Maple Grove, I dare say. E II 18 307 21
can stand more retired from the road than Maple Grove. E II 18 307 21
Maple Grove has given me a thorough disgust of people of E II 18 310 34
years a resident at Maple Grove, and whose father had it E II 18 310 34
They were never tolerated at Maple Grove. E III 2 321 15
but when she got to Maple Grove, he could recollect that E III 2 321 16
exploring party from Maple Grove to kings weston." E III 6 354 7
about Bristol--Maple Grove--cultivation-- beds when to be E III 6 358 35
acquaintance of Mrs. Suckling, a lady known at Maple Grove. E III 6 359 37
a letter to Maple Grove by one lady, to Ireland by another. E III 7 368 3
neighbourhood:--lives only four miles from Maple Grove. E III 8 380 13
Jane will be only four miles from Maple Grove." E III 8 380 13
A style of living almost equal to Maple Grove--and as to E III 8 382 23
neighbour of Maple Grove; and, by the bye, I wonder how E III 15 447 25
We never heard of such things at Maple Grove." E III 16 456 29
She knew a family near Maple Grove who had tried it, and E III 17 469 36

MAPS (1)
way of proving it, however, will be to turn to our maps. E I 12 107 61

MAR (1)
He was determined, at least, not to mar it by an imprudent P IV 9 201 59

MARAUDING (1)
will cure him of coming marauding about the house for one MP I 15 142 22

MARBLE (2)
of plain though handsome marble, and ornaments over it of NA II 5 162 26
marble, gilding and carving, each handsome in its way. MP I 9 84 3

MARCH (10)
were beautiful even in the leafless month of March. NA II 7 177 19
Gardens, though it was only the second week in March. SS III 2 271 4
It was as follows: Bartlett's Buildings, March. I hope my SS III 2 277 29
30
Cleveland about the end of March, for the Easter holidays; SS III 3 279 1
no more follow her to Croydon now than he did last March.-- W 319 2
"My father and Maria are to come to me in March," added PP II 3 146 18
March was to take Elizabeth to Hunsford. PP II 4 151 1
It was really March; but it was April in its mild air, MP III 11 409 6
she had to lose in passing March and April in a town. MP III 14 431 9
do for them in the months of January, February, and March? E II 8 217 32

MARE (13)
line, "to poultice chesnut mare,"--a farrier's bill! NA II 7 172 2
curricle, and I cannot persuade him to buy my brown mare. SS I 10 52 28
The old mare trotted heavily on, wanting no direction of W 322 2
The new mare proved a treasure; with a very little trouble, MP I 4 37 8
her delight in Edmund's mare was far beyond any former MP I 4 37 8
the offer of his own quiet mare for the purpose of her MP I 7 66 14
The mare was only to be taken down to the parsonage half MP I 7 66 14
Edmund, who had taken down the mare and presided at the MP I 7 66 15
She began to think it rather hard upon the mare to have MP I 7 68 16
if she were forgotten the poor mare should be remembered. MP I 7 68 16
"No, I do not know, not if you want the mare," was her MP I 7 69 27
be cured of wishing that he would part with his black mare. E III 6 361 41
The black mare was blameless; they were right who had E III 6 363 53

MARGARET (46)
Margaret, the other sister, was a good-humoured well- SS I 1 7 14
opinion of Marianne and Margaret an absolute old bachelor, SS I 7 34 6
hills did Marianne and Margaret one memorable morning SS I 9 40 3
Margaret, we will walk here at least two hours." SS I 9 41 5
Margaret agreed, and they pursued their way against the SS I 9 41 6
to the ground, and Margaret, unable to stop herself to SS I 9 41 7
had been left open by Margaret, he bore her directly into SS I 9 42 8
into the house, whither Margaret was just arrived, and SS I 9 42 8
Marianne's perserver, as Margaret, with more elegance than SS I 10 46 1
Margaret related something to her the next day, which SS I 12 60 8
evening with them, and Margaret, by being left some time SS I 12 60 8
"Take care, Margaret. SS I 12 60 12
great curiosity to her, Margaret answered by looking at SS I 12 61 15
She was convinced that Margaret had fixed on a person, SS I 12 61 16
in an angry manner to Margaret, "remember that whatever SS I 12 61 17
18
"I never had any conjectures about it," replied Margaret; " SS I 12 61 19
This increased the mirth of the company, and Margaret was SS I 12 61 20
"Margaret," said Marianne with great warmth, "you know SS I 12 61 25
They were interrupted by the entrance of Margaret; and SS I 15 82 45
"I wish," said Margaret, striking out a novel thought, " SS I 17 92 18
"Oh dear!" cried Margaret, "how happy I should be! SS I 17 92 21
Mrs. Dashwood and Margaret came down stairs at the same SS I 19 106 21
accepted the invitation; Margaret, with her mother's SS II 1 143 9
Margaret and I shall be as much benefited by it as SS II 3 155 8
You will find Margaret so improved when you come back SS II 3 155 8
every moment to fetch Margaret away, as her mother was SS III 9 335 6
You, my mother, and Margaret, must henceforth be all the SS III 10 347 30
Margaret returned, and the family were again all restored SS III 11 352 20
her to the care of Margaret and the maid, returned to SS III 11 353 25
were equally lost, and Margaret might think herself very SS III 11 355 45
her distress; and Margaret, understanding some part, but SS III 12 359 13
was taken from them, Margaret had reached an age highly SS III 14 380 20
her for Margaret, & poor Penelope was very wretched--. W 317 2
"Margaret is more gentle I imagine?"-- W 318 2
It is well Margaret is not by.-- W 342 19
the speedy return of Margaret, & a visit of two or three W 348 23
in her expectation of Margaret there was more than the W 348 23
Margaret was not without beauty; she had a slight, pretty W 349 23
Have you seen the one I gave Margaret?"-- W 353 26
Margaret & I have played at cribbage, most nights that we W 354 28
"Musgrave!"--ejaculated Margaret in a tender voice.-- W 355 28
or emotion towards Margaret, Emma who closely observed him, W 355 28
to Margaret which she was assiduous in providing him.-- W 356 28
He hesitated; Margaret was fair herself, & he did not W 357 28
Poor Margaret fraser will be at me for ever about your MP III 5 360 16
I wish Margaret were married, for my poor friend's sake, MP III 5 361 16

MARGARET'S (6)
Margaret's sagacity was not always displayed in a way so SS I 12 61 15
penetration, founded on Margaret's instructions, extended. SS I 18 99 15
the pleasure of Margaret's return, and talking of the dear SS III 10 343 8
Such, she feared would be Margaret's common voice, when W 351 25
eliz.'s opinions tho' Margaret's modest smiles imported W 355 28
At last however he was at liberty to hear Margaret's soft W 356 28

MARGT (16)
But Margt wd never forgive such words." W 342 19
"I wish Margt could have heard him profess his ignorance W 342 19
satisfied as you--but poor Margt is very snappish, & W 343 19
"Sweet little darling!--cried Margt--it quite broke my W 350 24
"How charming Emma is!--" whispered Margt to Mrs Robert in W 350 24
it better when she heard Margt 5 minutes afterwards say to W 351 24
"I suppose, said Margt rather quickly to Emma, you & I are W 351 25
I beleive if Margt had had a thousand or fifteen hundred W 353 26
"You may imagine, said Margt in a sort of whisper what are W 356 28
"Emma is delightful, is not she?--whispered Margt. W 357 28
"Dear me!--cried Margt why should not we play at vingt-un?- W 358 28
On finding him determined to go, Margt began to wink & nod W 359 28
Margt in the joy of her heart under circumstances, which W 360 29
As Margt would not allow a doubt to be repeated of W 360 30
T. Musgrave never came, & Margt was at no pains to conceal W 360 30
Margt had just respect enough for her Br & Sr's opinion, W 360 30

MARGT'S (2)
every interruption of Margt's perverseness, than sit with W 361 30
been used to be; but poor Margt's disagreable ways are new W 362 32

MARIA (132)
Sir James is gone, Maria highly incensed, and Mrs LS 2 245 1
I scolded him for making love to Maria Manwaring; he LS 9 257 1
To-morrow I shall fetch her from Churchill, & let Maria LS 39 308 1
Belle went with your brother, and John drove Maria." NA I 14 115 50
"Oh! yes," rejoined the other, "Maria is gone. NA I 14 115 52
Maria desired no greater pleasure than to speak of it; and NA I 15 116 1
Maria was without ceremony sent away, and Isabella, NA I 15 117 4
than either Anne or Maria: I feel that I shall be so much NA I 15 118 9
friend;--but Anne and Maria soon set her heart at ease by NA I 15 121 25
"dear Anne and dear Maria" must immediately be made NA I 15 121 27
"My father and Maria are to come to me in March," added PP II 3 146 18
Pray go to see them, with Sir William and Maria. PP II 3 149 26
Sir William Lucas, and his daughter Maria, a good humoured PP II 4 152 4
include you and my sister Maria in every invitation with PP II 5 157 7
She opened the door, and met Maria in the landing place, PP II 5 158 11
12
Elizabeth asked questions in vain; Maria would tell her PP II 5 158 13
"La! my dear," said Maria quite shocked at the mistake, " PP II 5 158 15
Maria thought speaking out of the question, and the PP II 6 163 14
a variety of questions to Maria and Elizabeth, but PP II 6 163 15
while Mrs. Collins and Maria were gone on business into PP II 9 177 1
the only right way, that Maria thought herself obliged, on PP II 14 213 20
He then handed her in, Maria followed, and the door was on PP II 15 217 8
"Good gracious!" cried Maria, after a few minutes silence, PP II 15 217 11
the lucases came to meet Maria and hear the news: and PP II 16 222 21
Lucas was enquiring of Maria across the table, after the PP II 16 222 21
Kitty wished to call upon Maria; and as Elizabeth saw no PP III 16 365 2
quite as handsome as Miss Maria, did not scruple to MP I 1 3 1
Julia Bertram was only twelve, and Maria but a year older. MP I 2 13 4
or had she quarrelled with Maria and Julia? or was she MP I 2 15 10
with Maria and Julia, and being as merry as possible. MP I 2 17 20
There was no positive ill-nature in Maria or Julia; and MP I 2 20 32
to see their dear Maria well married," she very often MP I 4 38 9
Being now in her twenty-first year, Maria Bertram was MP I 4 38 10
Maria was indeed the pride and delight of them all-- MP I 4 39 10
"Yes," added Maria, "and her spirits are as good, and she MP I 7 69 25
ladies sitting there, for Maria would scarcely raise her MP I 7 71 31
"Besides," said Maria, "I know that Mr. Crawford depends MP I 8 77 11
Mr. Crawford's," said Maria; "but the truth is, that MP I 8 77 13
"Unpleasant!" cried Maria; "Oh! dear, I believe it would MP I 8 78 15
"It seems very odd," said Maria, "that you should be MP I 8 79 24
Unhappy Maria! MP I 8 80 30
look at Mr. Rushworth and Maria, standing side by side, MP I 9 88 19
and stepping forward to Maria, said, in a voice which she MP I 9 88 20
are not ordained, Mr. Rushworth and Maria are quite ready." MP I 9 89 25
I thought Maria and Mr. Crawford were with you." MP I 10 100 24
I think I am equal to as much as Maria, even without help." MP I 10 100 26
"They desired me to stay--my cousin Maria charged me to to MP I 10 101 34
Maria was just discontented enough to say directly, "I MP I 10 105 54
"What else have you been spunging?" said Maria, half MP I 10 106 56
Maria was more to be pitied than Julia, for to her the MP I 11 107 3
Maria, with only Mr. Rushworth to attend to her, and MP I 12 115 4
she wished, and Maria by the hints of Mr. Crawford himself. MP I 12 115 4
himself in any danger from Maria; and I am not at all MP I 12 116 10
towards Mr. Rushworth and Maria, who were partners for the MP I 12 117 12
But dear Maria has such a strict sense of propriety, so MP I 12 117 14
"I believe we must be satisfied with less," said Maria. MP I 13 124 9
Maria, Julia, Henry Crawford, and Mr. Yates, were in the MP I 13 125 14
I think, with regard to Maria, whose situation is a very MP I 13 125 17
was at liberty; and Maria evidently considered her MP I 13 128 38

Maria gave Edmund a glance, which meant, "what say you now? MP I 13 129 39
was always answered for by Maria as willing to do any MP I 14 133 8
Amelia and Agatha may do for Maria and me, but here is MP I 14 133 9
She saw a glance at Maria, which confirmed the injury to MP I 14 133 12
trick; she was slighted, Maria was preferred; the smile of MP I 14 133 12
the smile of triumph which Maria was trying to suppress MP I 14 133 12
her too, by saying, "Oh! yes, Maria must be Agatha. MP I 14 133 12
Maria will be the best Agatha. MP I 14 134 12
vexed and alarmed--but Maria looked all serenity and MP I 14 135 18
on this ground Maria could not be happy but at her expense. MP I 14 135 18
would be necessary--while Maria and Henry Crawford MP I 14 136 21
that displeasure, which Maria had been half prepared for. MP I 15 138 1
was high between Tom, Maria, and Mr. Yates; and Mr. MP I 15 138 2
do for women?" said Edmund gravely, and looking at Maria. MP I 15 139 7
Maria blushed in spite of herself as she answered, "I take MP I 15 139 8
I must now, my dear Maria, tell you, that I think it MP I 15 139 11
"We see things very differently," cried Maria--"I am MP I 15 140 12
loved better to lead than Maria;--and with far more good MP I 15 140 14
"If I were to decline the part," said Maria with renewed MP I 15 141 19
I do not know the play; but, as Maria says, if there is MP I 15 141 22
Maria, wanting Henry Crawford's animating support, thought MP I 15 142 24
giving fresh courage, Tom, Maria, and Mr. Yates, soon MP I 15 142 25
was now backed by Maria and Mr. Crawford, and Mr. Yates, MP I 15 146 53
While he spoke, Maria was looking apprehensively round at MP I 15 148 59
with a glance, first at Maria, and then at Edmund, that " MP I 15 148 60
urgency that Tom and Maria were capable of; and Edmund MP I 16 150 1
The east room as it had been called, ever since Maria MP I 16 151 1
It was, indeed, a triumphant day to Mr. Bertram and Maria. MP I 17 158 1
of his preference for Maria had been forced on her, she MP I 17 160 8
But, Mary, do not fancy that Maria Bertram cares for Henry. MP I 17 162 16
Yates; and though he and Maria are very good friends, I MP I 17 162 16
there, some punishment to Maria for conduct so shameful MP I 17 162 19
Maria felt her triumph, and pursued her purpose careless MP I 17 163 19
and Julia could never see Maria distinguished by Henry MP I 17 163 19
of the feelings it excited in some speeches for Maria.-- MP I 18 165 3
Maria she also thought acted well--too well;--and after MP I 18 165 3
his former jealousy, which Maria, from increasing hopes of MP I 18 165 4
every word of it," added Maria, "for she could put Mrs. MP I 18 172 31
Maria joined them with the same intent, just then the MP II 1 176 3
"It is time to think of our visitors," said Maria, still MP II 1 182 19
bringing Mr. Rushworth's admiration of Maria to any effect. MP II 2 188 3
Maria was in a good deal of agitation. MP II 2 191 11
Sir Thomas soon appeared, and Maria saw with delight and MP II 2 192 11
was under discussion, Maria, who wanted neither pride nor MP II 2 193 17
his selfish vanity had raised in Maria and Julia Bertram. MP II 2 193 18
be odious to her; and if Maria gained him not, she was now MP II 2 194 19
give something that Rushworth and Maria had never met." MP II 3 200 19
Maria had a moment's struggle as she listened, and only a MP II 3 200 21
in good society; and if Maria could now speak so securely MP II 3 201 22
Every public place was new to Maria, and Brighton is MP II 3 203 31
novelty and pleasure as Maria, though she might not have MP II 3 204 32
Her two absent cousins, especially Maria, were much in her MP II 5 224 48
Well, I am much mistaken if his lovely Maria will ever MP II 5 224 53
to go to town with Maria; and as Sir Thomas thought it MP II 11 284 10
Maria might be very glad to see her at Sotherton now and MP II 11 285 14
Maria and Julia--and especially Maria, were so closely MP III 1 318 38
Maria is nobly married--but had Mr. Crawford sought MP III 1 319 39
treacherous admirer of Maria Bertram, had been her MP III 2 327 6
is more than I did for Maria--the next time pug has a MP III 2 333 28
attentions to my cousin Maria, which--in short, at the MP III 4 349 25
Maria was wrong, Crawford was wrong, we were all wrong MP III 4 349 26
I am shocked whenever I think that Maria could be capable MP III 4 350 28
Mrs. Norris, however, as most attached to Maria, was MP III 16 448 1
Maria was her first favourite, the dearest of all; the MP III 16 448 1
her back to town, and Maria was with these friends without MP III 16 450 8
as more pardonable than Maria as folly than vice, he could MP III 16 452 13
more the folly of--poor Maria, in sacrificing such a MP III 16 454 18
opposite treatment which Maria and Julia had been always MP III 17 463 7
Maria had destroyed her own character, and he would not by MP III 17 465 13
herself to her unfortunate Maria, and in an establishment MP III 17 465 14
That Julia escaped better than Maria was owing, in some MP III 17 466 17
always used to think herself a little inferior to Maria. MP III 17 466 17
Rushworth Maria Bertram again in her treatment of himself. MP III 17 467 20

MARIA LUCAS (2)

the two fourth with Maria Lucas, and the two fifth with PP I 3 13 16
quite frightened Maria Lucas, who had been little used to PP II 6 161 7

MARIA'S (15)

Maria's intelligence concluded with a tender effusion of NA I 15 116 2
When they ascended the steps to the hall, Maria's alarm PP II 6 161 9
Maria's astonishment, at her being so thin, and so small. PP II 6 162 12
Maria's notions on the subject were more confused and MP I 5 44 2
"That is Miss Maria's concern. MP I 10 101 32
I assure you is quite as voluntary as Maria's marrying." MP I 11 108 13
Julia did seem inclined to admit that Maria's situation MP I 13 128 38
She looked suspiciously at her sister; Maria's countenance MP I 14 135 18
it without any alarm for Maria's situation, or any MP I 17 160 8
to her eye was her cousin Maria's avoidance of him, and so MP I 18 164 2
on Maria's account, tried to understand her feelings. MP II 3 200 20
satisfaction than I gave Maria's to Mr. Rushworth." MP III 1 319 39
You will wish to hear my opinion of Maria's degree of MP III 13 423 2
with his vanity, Maria's decided attachment, and no MP III 15 441 20
Maria's guilt had induced Julia's folly. MP III 17 467 18

MARIANNE (476)

"In a few months, my dear Marianne," said she, "Elinor SS I 3 17 15
But you look grave, Marianne; do you disapprove your SS I 3 17 17
"Perhaps," said Marianne, "I may consider it with some SS I 3 17 18
In one circumstance only, my Marianne, may your destiny be SS I 3 18 21
"What a pity it is, Elinor," said Marianne, "that Edward SS I 4 19 1
Marianne was afraid of offending, and said no more on the SS I 4 19 3
"I hope, Marianne," continued Elinor, "you do not consider SS I 4 19 4
Marianne hardly knew what to say. SS I 4 19 5
Marianne was rejoiced to find her sister so easily pleased. SS I 4 20 8
What say you, Marianne?" SS I 4 20 9
She knew that what Marianne and her mother conjectured one SS I 4 21 11
Marianne here burst forth with indignation-- SS I 4 21 13
14

Marianne was astonished to find how much the imagination SS I 4 22 16
in so prosperous a state as Marianne had believed it. SS I 4 22 18
"Dear, dear Norland!" said Marianne, as she wandered alone SS I 5 27 8
Marianne was vexed at it for her sister's sake, and turned SS I 7 34 5
being in the opinion of Marianne and Margaret an absolute SS I 7 34 6
In the evening, as Marianne was discovered to be musical, SS I 7 35 8
to be charmed, and Marianne, who sang very well, at their SS I 7 35 8
for a moment, and asked Marianne to sing a particular song SS I 7 35 9
to sing a particular song which Marianne had just finished. SS I 7 35 9
Brandon was very much in love with Marianne Dashwood. SS I 8 36 1
she laughed at the Colonel, and in the cottage at Marianne. SS I 8 36 2
"A woman of seven and twenty," said Marianne, after SS I 8 38 10
"But he talked of flannel waistcoats," said Marianne; "and SS I 8 38 12
Confess, Marianne, is not there something interesting to SS I 8 38 13
the room, "mama," said Marianne, "I have an alarm on the SS I 8 38 14
one of these hills did Marianne and Margaret one memorable SS I 9 40 3
"Is there a felicity in the world," said Marianne, " SS I 9 41 5
Marianne had at first the advantage, but a false step SS I 9 41 7
within a few yards of Marianne, when her accident happened. SS I 9 42 8
gallantry raised against Marianne, received particular SS I 9 43 11
Marianne herself had seen less of his person than the rest, SS I 9 43 11
"And is that all you can say for him?" cried Marianne, SS I 9 43 18
But Marianne could no more satisfy him as to the colour of SS I 9 44 21
"Did he indeed?" cried Marianne, with sparkling eyes, "and SS I 9 45 26
"That is an expression, Sir John," said Marianne, warmly, " SS I 9 45 30
Marianne was still handsomer. SS I 10 46 2
"Well, Marianne," said Elinor, as soon as he had left them, SS I 10 47 4
"Elinor," cried Marianne, "is this fair? is this just? are SS I 10 47 5
Marianne was softened in a moment. SS I 10 48 6
To inquire after Marianne was at first his excuse; but the SS I 10 48 7
spite of all that he and Marianne could say in its support. SS I 10 49 9
Marianne began now to perceive that the desperation which SS I 10 49 10
Colonel Brandon's partiality for Marianne, which had so SS I 10 49 12
by Willoughby and Marianne, who, prejudiced against him SS I 10 50 13
"That is exactly what I think of him," cried Marianne. SS I 10 50 15
people as yourself and Marianne, will make amends for the SS I 10 50 18
Yes, Marianne, even in a man between thirty and forty. SS I 10 51 20
"That is to say," cried Marianne contemptuously, "he has SS I 10 51 21
"Add to which," cried Marianne, "that he has neither SS I 10 51 26
When Marianne was recovered, the schemes of amusement at SS I 11 53 1
the excellencies of Marianne, of marking his animated SS I 11 53 1
to suggest the propriety of some self-command to Marianne. SS I 11 53 2
But Marianne abhorred all concealment where no real SS I 11 53 2
This was the season of happiness to Marianne. SS I 11 54 5
to think only of Marianne, and in conversing with Elinor SS I 11 55 7
His eyes were fixed on Marianne, and, after a silence of SS I 11 55 8
But Marianne, in her place, would not have done so little. SS I 11 57 17
As Elinor and Marianne were walking together the next SS I 12 58 1
Marianne told her, with the greatest delight, that SS I 12 58 1
of establishment, Marianne was shortly subdued; and she SS I 12 59 5
same low voice--"but, Marianne, the horse is still yours, SS I 12 59 6
with only him and Marianne, had had opportunity for SS I 12 60 8
cried, "I have such a secret to tell you about Marianne. SS I 12 60 9
you were certain that Marianne wore his picture round her SS I 12 60 10
Marianne felt for her most sincerely; but she did more SS I 12 61 17
18

"Margaret," said Marianne with great warmth, "you know SS I 12 61 25
"Well then he is lately dead, Marianne, for I am sure SS I 12 62 26
Willoughby opened the piano-forte, and asked Marianne to SS I 12 62 27
Brandon," Marianne eagerly, "will it not be sufficient?" SS I 13 64 23
say in a low voice to Marianne, "there are some people who SS I 13 64 30
"I have no doubt of it," replied Marianne. SS I 13 65 31
To Marianne, he merely bowed and said nothing. SS I 13 66 49
"And who is Miss Williams?" asked Marianne. SS I 13 66 56
Marianne never looked happier than when she got into it. SS I 13 66 60
Willoughby, and said to Marianne, loud enough for them SS I 13 67 61
Marianne coloured, and replied very hastily, "where pray?"- SS I 13 67 62
Marianne turned away in great confusion. SS I 13 67 65
should propose, or Marianne consent, to enter the house SS I 13 68 66
it, with whom Marianne had not the smallest acquaintance. SS I 13 68 66
Marianne was quite angry with her for doubting it. SS I 13 68 67
"Yes, Marianne, but I would not go while Mrs. Smith was SS I 13 68 69
"But, my dear Marianne, as it has already exposed you to SS I 13 68 73
"If they were one day to be your own, Marianne, you would SS I 13 69 75
was enough to prevent her making any inquiry of Marianne. SS I 14 71 4
To Marianne it had all the distinguishing tenderness which SS I 14 71 5
side of Marianne, and by his favourite pointer at her feet. SS I 14 71 5
Mrs. Dashwood looked with pleasure at Marianne, whose fine SS I 14 73 16
Must it not have been so, Marianne?" speaking to her in a SS I 14 73 17
went with her; but Marianne excused herself from being of SS I 15 75 1
They were no sooner in the passage than Marianne came SS I 15 75 2
strongly partook of the emotion which overpowered Marianne. SS I 15 75 2
distress in which Marianne had quitted the room was such SS I 15 77 19
violent sorrow which Marianne was in all probability not SS I 15 77 20
suspects his regard for Marianne, disapproves of it, (SS I 15 78 26
her his engagement with Marianne, and he feels himself SS I 15 78 26
You had rather look out for misery for Marianne and guilt SS I 15 78 28
do you accuse Willoughby and Marianne of concealment? SS I 15 79 32
Has not his behaviour to Marianne and to all of us, for at SS I 15 80 36
They saw nothing of Marianne till dinner time, when she SS I 15 82 46
Marianne would have thought herself very inexcusable had SS I 16 83 1
from Willoughby came; and none seemed expected by Marianne. SS I 16 84 5
"Why do you not ask Marianne at once," said she, "whether SS I 16 84 8
was mentioned before Marianne by any of her family; Sir SS I 16 85 11
12

never finished Hamlet, Marianne; our dear Willoughby went SS I 16 85 11
12

"Months!" cried Marianne, with strong surprise. SS I 16 85 13
it produced a reply from Marianne so expressive of SS I 16 85 14
his leaving the country, Marianne was prevailed on to join SS I 16 85 15
in a moment afterwards Marianne rapturously exclaimed, "it SS I 16 86 16
17

cried out, "indeed, Marianne, I think you are mistaken. SS I 16 86 17
18

"He has, he has," cried Marianne, "I am sure he has. SS I 16 86 19
and Elinor, to screen Marianne from particularity, as she SS I 16 86 20
Marianne looked again; her heart sunk within her; and SS I 16 86 20
but especially by Marianne, who shewed more warmth of SS I 16 87 23
To Marianne, indeed, the meeting between Edward and her SS I 16 87 23
Marianne saw and listened with increasing surprise. SS I 16 87 23
Marianne asked Edward if he came directly from London. SS I 16 87 24
"And how does dear, dear Norland look?" cried Marianne. SS I 16 87 29
"Oh!" cried Marianne, "with what transporting sensations SS I 16 87 31
"How strange!" said Marianne to herself as she walked on. SS I 16 88 37
"No, not at all," answered Marianne, "we could not be more SS I 16 88 39
"Marianne," cried her sister, "how can you say so? SS I 16 88 40
Have you forgot, Marianne, how many pleasant days we have SS I 16 88 40
"No," said Marianne in a low voice, "nor how many painful SS I 16 88 41
"Strange if it would!" cried Marianne. SS I 17 91 8
"Elinor, for shame!" said Marianne; "money can only give SS I 17 91 10
thousand a-year is a very moderate income," said Marianne. SS I 17 91 14
Marianne coloured as she replied, "but most people do." SS I 17 92 17
"Oh that they would!" cried Marianne, her eyes sparkling SS I 17 92 19
Marianne looked as if she had no doubt on that point. SS I 17 92 22
be sent you--and as for Marianne, I know her greatness of SS I 17 92 25
Should not you, Marianne? SS I 17 92 25
"Marianne is as stedfast as ever, you see," said Elinor, " SS I 17 93 31
"Nay, Edward," said Marianne, "you need not reproach me. SS I 17 93 33
"But I thought it was right, Elinor," said Marianne, "to SS I 17 93 38
"No, Marianne, never. SS I 17 94 39
replied Elinor, looking expressively at Marianne. SS I 17 94 41
"Marianne has not shyness to excuse any inattention of SS I 17 94 43
"But you would still be reserved," said Marianne, "and SS I 17 94 45
Am I reserved, Marianne?" SS I 17 94 46
He joined her and Marianne in the breakfast-room the next SS I 18 96 2
others were down; and Marianne, who was always eager to SS I 18 96 2
not inquire too far, Marianne-- remember I have no SS I 18 96 4
"I am afraid it is but too true," said Marianne; "but why SS I 18 97 5
"It is very true," said Marianne, "that admiration of SS I 18 97 7
Marianne looked with amazement at Edward, with compassion SS I 18 98 9
The subject was continued no farther; and Marianne SS I 18 98 10
Marianne spoke inconsiderately what she really felt--but SS I 18 98 12
as well satisfied as Marianne; the only difference in SS I 18 98 13
was, that what Marianne considered as a free gift from her SS I 18 98 13
Marianne severely censured herself for what she had said; SS I 18 99 14
"A dance!" cried Marianne. SS I 18 99 19
Marianne was surprised and confused, yet she could not SS I 18 100 28
29

judiciously employed by Marianne, on a similar occasion, SS I 19 104 9
to Marianne, than her own had seemed faulty to her. SS I 19 104 11
"Where is Marianne? SS I 19 105 18
"Here comes Marianne," cried Sir John. SS I 19 108 34
"Why should they ask us?" said Marianne, as soon as they SS I 19 109 41
between Elinor and Marianne, "for it is so bad a day I was SS I 20 110 2
Marianne looked very grave and said nothing. SS I 20 111 11
Marianne remained perfectly silent, though her countenance SS I 20 111 16
as might remove the possibility of fear for Marianne. SS I 20 114 43
than that Elinor and Marianne should sit so composedly by, SS I 21 121 6

MARIANNE / MARIANNE

"Yet I hardly know how," cried Marianne, "unless it had	SS I 21 122 12
Marianne was silent; it was impossible for her to say what	SS I 21 122 14
had been with respect to Marianne; indeed it was rather	SS I 21 125 36
Marianne, who had never much toleration for any thing like	SS I 22 127 1
of her love, and that Marianne was internally dwelling on	SS II 1 141 4
The necessity of concealing from her mother and Marianne,	SS II 1 141 5
equally compliant, and Marianne, though always unwilling	SS II 1 143 9
No one made any objection but Marianne, who, with her	SS II 1 144 15
"Marianne can never keep long from that instrument you	SS II 1 145 17
of that address, which Marianne could never condescend to	SS II 1 145 23
The piano-forte, at which Marianne, wrapt up in her own	SS II 1 145 23
in a lower tone, though Marianne was then giving them the	SS II 2 149 24
	25
"I thank you, ma'am, sincerely thank you," said Marianne,	SS II 3 154 5
could not approve of for Marianne, and which on her own	SS II 3 154 6
Whatever Marianne was desirous of, her mother would be	SS II 3 155 6
That Marianne, fastidious as she was, thoroughly	SS II 3 155 6
how much the heart of Marianne was in it, would not hear	SS II 3 155 7
of Mrs. Jennings," said Marianne, "at least it need not	SS II 3 156 14
difficulty in persuading Marianne to behave with tolerable	SS II 3 156 15
not think it proper that Marianne should be left to the	SS II 3 156 15
of Marianne for all the comfort of her domestic hours.	SS II 3 156 15
Marianne lifted up her eyes in astonishment, and Elinor	SS II 3 157 18
ardour of youth which Marianne and her mother equally	SS II 4 159 1
beamed in the eyes of Marianne, without feeling how blank	SS II 4 159 1
might lessen her satisfaction in the happiness of Marianne.	SS II 4 159 1
In a few moments Marianne did the same.	SS II 4 160 4
"I am writing home, Marianne," said Elinor; "had not you	SS II 4 160 4
to my mother," replied Marianne hastily, and as if wishing	SS II 4 160 5
was it complete than Marianne, ringing the bell, requested	SS II 4 161 5
The tea things were brought in, and already had Marianne	SS II 4 161 7
approach, and Marianne starting up moved towards the door.	SS II 4 161 7
that he even observed Marianne as she quitted the room,	SS II 4 162 8
Elinor now began to make the tea, and Marianne was obliged	SS II 4 163 19
Marianne rose the next morning with recovered spirits and	SS II 4 164 21
to make themselves; and Marianne, though declining it at	SS II 4 164 23
entered the house than Marianne flew eagerly up stairs,	SS II 4 165 25
Marianne was of no use on these occasions, as she would	SS II 4 166 31
"That is true," cried Marianne in a cheerful voice, and	SS II 5 167 2
it, yet while she saw Marianne in spirits, she could not	SS II 5 167 7
And Marianne was in spirits; happy in the mildness of the	SS II 5 168 7
her being in town; and Marianne was all the time busy in	SS II 5 168 8
Elinor was alternately diverted and pained; but Marianne	SS II 5 168 10
day; he came to look at Marianne and talk to Elinor, who	SS II 5 168 12
which he often watched Marianne, and his spirits were	SS II 5 169 12
"Good God!" cried Marianne, "he has been here while we	SS II 5 169 14
But Marianne seemed hardly to hear her, and on Mrs.	SS II 5 169 14
"For me?" cried Marianne, stepping hastily forward.	SS II 5 169 17
But Marianne, not convinced, took it instantly up.	SS II 5 169 19
a short pause, "you have no confidence in me, Marianne."	SS II 5 169 23
come confusion; "indeed, Marianne, I have nothing to tell."	SS II 5 170 25
"Nor I," answered Marianne with energy, "our situations	SS II 5 170 26
circumstances, to press for greater openness in Marianne.	SS II 5 170 27
Marianne gave one glance round the apartment as she	SS II 5 171 30
Never had Marianne been so unwilling to dance in her life,	SS II 5 171 35
"Invited!" cried Marianne.	SS II 5 171 37
Marianne said no more, but looked exceedingly hurt.	SS II 5 171 38
fears for the health of Marianne, to procure those	SS II 5 171 38
on the morrow, that Marianne was again writing to	SS II 5 171 38
letter directly, while Marianne, too restless for	SS II 5 172 39
affection to demand from Marianne, an account of her real	SS II 5 172 39
Marianne, who had seen him from the window, and who hated	SS II 5 172 40
and for this party, Marianne, wholly dispirited, careless	SS II 6 175 1
down to Casino, and as Marianne was not in spirits for	SS II 6 175 2
to her, or to approach Marianne, though he could not but	SS II 6 176 3
Elinor turned involuntarily to Marianne, to see whether it	SS II 6 176 3
only beyond the reach of Marianne, it was beyond her wish.	SS II 6 176 6
rather to Elinor than Marianne, as if wishing to avoid her	SS II 6 176 7
"But have you not received my notes?" cried Marianne in	SS II 6 177 10
Marianne, now looking dreadfully white, and unable to	SS II 6 177 12
No, my dearest Marianne, you must wait.	SS II 6 177 14
was impossible; for Marianne continued incessantly to give	SS II 6 177 15
staircase, and telling Marianne that he was gone, urged	SS II 6 178 15
on being informed that Marianne was unwell, was too polite	SS II 6 178 16
Marianne was in a silent agony, too much oppressed even	SS II 6 178 16
between Willoughby and Marianne she could not doubt; and	SS II 6 178 17
clear; for however Marianne might still feed her own	SS II 6 178 17
As for Marianne, on the pangs which so unhappy a meeting	SS II 6 179 18
heighten the misery of Marianne in a final separation from	SS II 6 179 18
morning in January, Marianne, only half dressed, was	SS II 7 180 1
most considerate gentleness, "Marianne, may I ask?"-----	SS II 7 180 1
	2
her still more, had not Marianne entreated her, with all	SS II 7 180 5
letter was delivered to Marianne, which she eagerly caught	SS II 7 181 7
That good lady, however, saw only that Marianne had	SS II 7 181 7
her talk, as soon as Marianne disappeared, she said, "upon	SS II 7 181 7
	8
the door, she saw Marianne stretched on the bed, almost	SS II 7 182 12
lest she might wound Marianne still deeper by treating	SS II 7 184 15
Determined not to quit Marianne, though hopeless of	SS II 7 184 16
safe off, returned to Marianne, whom she found attempting	SS II 7 185 16
been, was too much for Marianne, who could only exclaim,	SS II 7 185 19
"Exert yourself, dear Marianne," she cried, "if you would	SS II 7 185 21
"I cannot, I cannot," cried Marianne; "leave me, leave me,	SS II 7 185 22
"Do you call <u>me</u> happy, Marianne?	SS II 7 185 23
"No, no, no," cried Marianne wildly, "he loves you, and	SS II 7 186 26
"You must not talk so, Marianne.	SS II 7 186 29
"Engagement!" cried Marianne, "there has been no	SS II 7 186 30
by the event, when Marianne, perceiving that she had	SS II 7 188 43
"Dearest Marianne, who but himself?	SS II 7 189 49
"No, no," cried Marianne, "misery such as mine has no	SS II 7 189 52
through the other; and Marianne, seated at the foot of the	SS II 7 190 55
	56
"No, Marianne, in no possible way."	SS II 7 190 57
Another pause ensued; Marianne was greatly agitated, and	SS II 7 190 59
"To-morrow, Marianne!"	SS II 7 190 61
of great compassion to Marianne, who turned away her face	SS II 8 192 2
Marianne, to the surprise of her sister, determined on	SS II 8 192 5
well as she could, while Marianne still remained on the	SS II 8 193 5
Their good friend saw that Marianne was unhappy, and felt	SS II 8 193 7
Marianne was to have the best place by the fire, was to be	SS II 8 193 7
continual repetition on Marianne, she could stay no longer.	SS II 8 193 7
"Dear ma'am, this kindness is quite unnecessary. Marianne	SS II 8 195 15
since though Marianne might lose much, he could gain very	SS II 8 196 21
And then rising, she went away to join Marianne, whom she	SS II 8 197 23
But I have just left Marianne in bed, and, I hope, almost	SS II 8 198 28
round the room for Marianne, Elinor immediately fancied	SS II 8 198 30
"Marianne is not well," said she.	SS II 8 198 32
From a night of more sleep than she had expected, Marianne	SS II 9 201 1
are clever and good, Marianne, with excellent abilities	SS II 9 201 4
Marianne heard enough.	SS II 9 202 7
to intreat from Marianne greater openness towards them	SS II 9 202 8
it were better for Marianne to be in London or at Barton,	SS II 9 203 9
for the future; while Marianne, who came into the drawing-	SS II 9 203 10
quarter of an hour, when Marianne, whose nerves could not	SS II 9 203 11
Marianne moved to the window----- "it is Colonel Brandon!"	SS II 9 203 13
	14
that solicitude for Marianne brought him thither, and who	SS II 9 204 17
the greatest act of friendship that can be shewn Marianne.	SS II 9 204 19
as resembling, in some measure, your sister Marianne."	SS II 9 205 22
to Marianne, from the communication of what had passed.	SS II 9 211 33
Not that Marianne appeared to distrust the truth of any	SS II 10 212 1
anxious solicitude for Marianne, and entreat she would	SS II 10 213 2
it would be better for Marianne to be anywhere, at that	SS II 10 213 3
yet, she hoped, cheat Marianne, at times, into some	SS II 10 213 3
Marianne had promised to be guided by her mother's opinion,	SS II 10 214 6
for Marianne than an immediate return into Devonshire.	SS II 10 214 7
Marianne, though without knowing it herself, reaped all	SS II 10 214 8
pitying eye with which Marianne sometimes observed him,	SS II 10 216 15
as she was desirous that Marianne should not receive the	SS II 10 217 16
"I am sorry she is not well;" for Marianne had left the	SS II 10 219 37
After some opposition, Marianne yielded to her sister's	SS II 11 220 1
Marianne was spared from the troublesome feelings of	SS II 11 221 4
that Marianne was not present, to share the provocation.	SS II 11 226 40
But, my dear Elinor, what is the matter with Marianne?--	SS II 11 227 48
I question whether Marianne <u>now</u>, will marry a man worth	SS II 11 227 50
farther assertion; and Marianne, when called on for her's,	SS II 12 234 25
Marianne could not bear this.--	SS II 12 235 34
as they were fixed on Marianne, declared that he noticed	SS II 12 236 38
In a few minutes, however, Marianne was recovered enough	SS II 12 236 42
"Poor Marianne!" said her brother to Colonel Brandon in a	SS II 12 236 43
You would not think it perhaps, but Marianne <u>was</u>	SS II 12 237 43
pretence of fetching Marianne, to leave the others by	SS II 13 241 23
all were silent; while Marianne was looking with the most	SS II 13 242 25
looked up at Marianne with no very benignant expression.	SS II 13 242 27
But Marianne, who saw his agitation, and could easily	SS II 13 243 32
Elinor was very angry, but Marianne seemed entirely	SS II 13 243 39
	40
"Going so soon!" said Marianne; "my dear Edward, this must	SS II 13 244 42
"What can bring her here so often! "said Marianne, on her	SS II 13 244 44
Marianne looked at her steadily, and said, "you know	SS II 13 244 46
that would convince Marianne; and painful as the	SS II 13 244 47
Elinor and Marianne, she did not really like them at all.	SS II 14 246 3
the whole affair between Marianne and Mr. Willoughby, she	SS II 14 247 4
of beaux before Marianne, no effect was produced, but a	SS II 14 247 4
Marianne had now been brought by degrees, so much into the	SS II 14 249 7
better judgment than Marianne herself, and was not without	SS II 14 249 8
was considered by Marianne as the greatest impertinence of	SS II 14 249 8
Colonel Brandon's wife, and Marianne as <u>their</u> visitor.	SS II 14 253 25
rest, in the absence of Marianne, she felt very well able	SS III 1 260 8
saw the necessity of preparing Marianne for its discussion.	SS III 1 260 10
opinion,--and to make Marianne, by a resemblance in their	SS III 1 261 11
might suggest a hint of what was practicable to Marianne.	SS III 1 261 12
<u>That</u> belonged rather to the hearer, for Marianne listened	SS III 1 261 12
<u>But</u> Marianne for some time would give credit to neither.	SS III 1 261 13
"Four months!"--cried Marianne again.--	SS III 1 262 22
Marianne seemed much struck.--	SS III 1 262 24
And after all, Marianne, after all that is bewitching in	SS III 1 263 27
"If such is your way of thinking," said Marianne, "if the	SS III 1 263 28
For four months, Marianne, I have had all this hanging on	SS III 1 263 29
not occur to relieve my spirits at first--no, Marianne.--	SS III 1 264 29
Marianne was quite subdued.--	SS III 1 264 30
and at her request, Marianne engaged never to speak of the	SS III 1 264 32
These were great concessions;--but where Marianne felt	SS III 1 265 32
to have invited you and Marianne to be with us, while your	SS III 1 266 36
Here Marianne, in an ecstacy of indignation, clapped her	SS III 1 267 39
"Well may you wonder, Marianne," replied her brother, "at	SS III 1 267 40
Marianne was going to retort, but she remembered her	SS III 1 267 41
Marianne sighed out her similar apprehension; and Elinor's	SS III 1 268 46
Marianne got up, and walked about the room.	SS III 1 269 55
but only Elinor and Marianne understood its true merit.	SS III 2 270 1
Elinor gloried in his integrity; and Marianne forgave all	SS III 2 270 1
positive assurances of Marianne, that belief of Edward's	SS III 2 270 1
Mrs. Jennings and Elinor were of the number; but Marianne,	SS III 2 271 4
which Marianne could not be brought to acknowledge.	SS III 3 279 1
When she told Marianne what she had done, however, her	SS III 3 279 2
far as it could be;--and Marianne found some relief in	SS III 3 280 7
the piano forte on which Marianne was playing, she could	SS III 3 281 9
Marianne had left the room before the conversation began.	SS III 4 286 12
"Certainly, ma'am, I shall tell Marianne of it; but I	SS III 4 286 13
concern which I am sure Marianne, myself, and all your	SS III 4 289 31
Marianne, not contented with absolutely refusing to go	SS III 5 294 3
however, you and Marianne were always great favourites.--	SS III 5 294 6
Why would not Marianne come?"--	SS III 5 294 6
Marianne, few as had been her hours of comfort in London,	SS III 6 301 4
Marianne entered the house with an heart swelling with	SS III 6 302 8
The morning was fine and dry, and Marianne, in her plan of	SS III 6 303 11
in their discourse, and Marianne, who had the knack of	SS III 6 304 12
from the first, believed Marianne his real favourite, to	SS III 6 305 16
and stockings--given Marianne a cold so violent, as,	SS III 6 305 17
Marianne got up the next morning at her usual time; to	SS III 7 307 1
at night, trusted, like Marianne, to the certainty and	SS III 7 307 1
of both; and when Marianne, after persisting in rising,	SS III 7 307 2
Cleveland as long as Marianne remained ill, and of	SS III 7 308 3
Poor Marianne, languid and low from the nature of her	SS III 7 308 4
Marianne was of course kept in ignorance of all these	SS III 7 309 6
in the seisure that Marianne would never get over it, and	SS III 7 309 7
mind the persuasion that he should see Marianne no more.	SS III 7 309 7
fixing on the time when Marianne would be able to travel.	SS III 7 310 8
Towards the evening, Marianne became ill again, growing	SS III 7 310 9
room, and Elinor remained alone with Marianne.	SS III 7 310 9
painful a slumber, when Marianne, suddenly awakened by	SS III 7 310 10
	11
terror, and assisting Marianne to lie down again, "but she	SS III 7 311 12
"But she must not go round by London," cried Marianne, in	SS III 7 311 13
It was lower and quicker than ever! and Marianne, still	SS III 7 311 14
so young, so lovely as Marianne, must have struck a less	SS III 7 313 20
Jennings considered that Marianne might probably be to <u>her</u>	SS III 7 313 20
fever was unabated; and Marianne only more quiet--not more	SS III 7 313 21
signs of amendment, and Marianne fixed her eyes on her	SS III 7 314 22
Marianne was in every respect materially better, and he	SS III 7 314 23
Marianne restored to life, health, friends, and to her	SS III 7 315 24
continued, and saw Marianne at six o'clock sink into a	SS III 7 315 25
At seven o'clock, leaving Marianne still sweetly asleep,	SS III 7 315 27
to take her place by Marianne; but Elinor had no sense of	SS III 7 315 27
Marianne slept through every blast, and the travellers--	SS III 7 316 28
Marianne <u>does</u>--she has <u>long</u> forgiven you."	SS III 8 319 26
My affection for Marianne, my thorough conviction of her	SS III 8 323 40
To see Marianne, I felt would be dreadful, and I even	SS III 8 323 40
To know that Marianne was in town was--in the same	SS III 8 325 50
I sent no answer to Marianne, intending by that means to	SS III 8 326 53
The next morning brought another short note from Marianne--	SS III 8 327 55
Marianne, beautiful as an angel on one side, calling me	SS III 8 327 55
"Your poor mother too!--doting on Marianne."	SS III 8 327 59
in the opinion of Marianne and her friends, in what	SS III 8 328 63
wife's words, and parted with the last relics of Marianne.	SS III 8 329 63
is no atonement to Marianne--nor can I suppose it a relief	SS III 8 329 64
he told me that Marianne Dashwood was dying of a putrid	SS III 8 330 69
Marianne to be sure is lost to me for ever.	SS III 8 332 77
for Marianne, which it was not even innocent to indulge.	SS III 9 333 2
When at last she returned to the unconscious Marianne, she	SS III 9 333 3
herself, to see Marianne was her first desire; and in two	SS III 9 334 5
of its robbing Marianne of farther sleep;--but Mrs.	SS III 9 334 5
child was at stake, and Marianne, satisfied in knowing her	SS III 9 334 5
what its effect on Marianne might be; doubted whether	SS III 9 335 5
was her uneasiness about Marianne, that she had already	SS III 9 335 6
Marianne continued to mend every day, and the brilliant	SS III 9 335 7
Marianne was restored to her from a danger in which, as	SS III 9 335 7
Colonel Brandon loves Marianne.	SS III 9 336 8
And I believe Marianne will be the most happy with him of	SS III 9 336 10
with his earnest, tender, constant, affection for Marianne.	SS III 9 336 12
which his affection for Marianne, were humanity out of the	SS III 9 337 17
and esteem him, that if Marianne can be happy with him, I	SS III 9 337 17
Marianne might at that moment be dying.	SS III 9 337 18

kind I well know to be more solidly attaching to Marianne. SS III 9 338 21
22
himself the contrary, Marianne would yet never have been SS III 9 338 22
than his affection for Marianne, or the consciousness of SS III 10 340 2
that resemblance between Marianne and Eliza already SS III 10 340 2
the actions and words of Marianne she persuaded herself to SS III 10 340 3
At the end of another day or two, Marianne growing visibly SS III 10 340 4
The day of separation and departure arrived; and Marianne, SS III 10 341 5
The Dashwoods were two days on the road, and Marianne bore SS III 10 341 6
she saw, as she assisted Marianne from the carriage, that SS III 10 342 7
sitting-room, than Marianne turned her eyes around it with SS III 10 342 7
unsettle the mind of Marianne, and ruin at least for a SS III 10 343 10
Marianne had been two or three days at home, before the SS III 10 344 11
mother's confidence; and Marianne, leaning on Elinor's arm, SS III 10 344 11
as the feebleness of Marianne in an exercise hitherto SS III 10 344 12
13
eyes turned towards it, Marianne calmly said, "there, SS III 10 344 12
13
"As for regret," said Marianne, "I have done with that, as SS III 10 344 17
or postponing it till Marianne were in stronger health;-- SS III 10 345 23
"I am not wishing him too much good," said Marianne at SS III 10 345 24
Marianne pressed her hand and replied, "you are very good.- SS III 10 347 29
30
Marianne said not a word.-- SS III 10 347 33
As soon as they entered the house, Marianne with a kiss of SS III 10 348 34
subject again, should Marianne fail to do it, she turned SS III 10 348 34
a faith unbroken--a character unblemished, to Marianne. SS III 11 349 1
were all three together, Marianne began voluntarily to SS III 11 349 3
Marianne slowly continued-- "it is a great relief to me-- SS III 11 350 5
6
No--my Marianne has not a heart to be made happy with such SS III 11 350 7
Marianne sighed, and repeated--"I wish for no change." SS III 11 350 8
"I have not a doubt of it," said Marianne; "and I have SS III 11 352 14
Marianne would not let her proceed;--and Elinor, satisfied SS III 11 352 16
17
Marianne assented most feelingly to the remark; and her SS III 11 352 18
following days, that Marianne did not continue to gain SS III 11 352 19
Marianne gave a violent start, fixed her eyes upon Elinor, SS III 11 353 24
By that time, Marianne was rather better, and her mother SS III 11 353 25
Marianne had already sent to say that she should eat SS III 11 355 45
suffering as she then had suffered for Marianne. SS III 11 355 46
She saw her mother and Marianne change colour; saw them SS III 12 358 9
Marianne had retreated as much as possible out of sight, SS III 12 359 13
She dared not look up;--but her mother and Marianne both SS III 12 360 20
"Mrs Robert Ferrars!"--was repeated by Marianne and her SS III 12 360 22
Marianne could speak her happiness only by tears. SS III 13 363 7
themselves," said Marianne, in her new character of SS III 13 372 45
and Marianne, and rather better pasturage for their cows. SS III 14 374 7
And though, perhaps, Marianne may not seem exactly the SS III 14 375 9
for her wish of bringing Marianne and Colonel Brandon SS III 14 378 13
friend; and to see Marianne settled at the mansion-house SS III 14 378 13
Marianne, by general consent, was to be the reward of all. SS III 14 378 13
Marianne Dashwood was born to an extraordinary fate. SS III 14 378 15
he deserved to be;--in Marianne he was consoled for every SS III 14 379 17
cheerfulness; and that Marianne found her own happiness in SS III 14 379 17
Marianne could never love by halves; and her whole heart SS III 14 379 17
Marianne, he might at once have been happy and rich. SS III 14 379 18
of Colonel Brandon with envy, and of Marianne with regret. SS III 14 379 18
For Marianne, however--in spite of his incivility in SS III 14 379 19
and Mrs. Jennings, when Marianne was taken from them, SS III 14 380 20
happiness of Elinor and Marianne, let it not be ranked as SS III 14 380 21

MARIANNE'S (73)
Marianne's abilities were, in many respects, quite equal SS I 1 6 12
imbibed a good deal of Marianne's romance, without having SS I 1 7 14
Marianne's conviction of their attachment agreeable to her. SS I 4 21 11
and books, with an handsome pianoforte of Marianne's. SS I 5 26 4
Marianne's pianoforte was unpacked and properly disposed SS I 6 30 5
Marianne's performance was highly applauded. SS I 7 35 9
their book, in spite of Marianne's declaration that the SS I 9 41 3
get out of doors; and Marianne's accident being related to SS I 9 43 12
Marianne's perserver, as Margaret, with more elegance than SS I 10 46 1
had ceased to be possible, by Marianne's perfect recovery. SS I 10 48 7
He was exactly formed to engage Marianne's heart, for with SS I 10 48 7
was as faultless as in Marianne's; and Elinor saw nothing SS I 10 48 9
attentions were wholly Marianne's, and a far less SS I 11 55 7
such feelings as Marianne's, which all the charms of SS I 11 56 13
that she knew before of Marianne's imprudence and want of SS I 12 58 1
"But indeed, Elinor, it is Marianne's. SS I 12 60 13
she considered what Marianne's love for him was, a quarrel SS I 15 77 19
I know Marianne's heart: I know that she dearly loves me, SS I 16 84 9
chiefly in silence, for Marianne's mind could not be SS I 16 85 15
"Nor do I think it a part of Marianne's," said Elinor; "I SS I 17 93 35
This was a subject which ensured Marianne's attention, and SS I 18 96 4
This, and Marianne's blushing, gave new suspicions to SS I 18 100 22
Marianne's countenance was more communicative. SS I 18 100 23
of others, but such of Marianne's expressions as had SS I 18 100 23
caught those words by a sudden pause in Marianne's music.-- SS II 2 148 20
Marianne's countenance sunk. SS II 3 156 10
Marianne's joy was almost a degree beyond happiness, so SS II 3 158 21
in the solicitude of Marianne's situation to have the same SS II 4 159 1
Marianne's eagerness to be gone declared her dependence on SS II 4 159 1
They were three days on their journey, and Marianne's SS II 4 160 2
Marianne's was finished in a very few minutes; in length SS II 4 161 5
Yet as she was convinced that Marianne's affection for SS II 5 174 45
the restless state of Marianne's mind not only prevented SS II 7 180 5
which at first was scarcely less violent than Marianne's. SS II 7 182 12
feelings and varying opinions on Marianne's, as before. SS II 9 201 2
and perceiving by Marianne's letter how ill she had SS II 9 203 10
Marianne's, and an indignation even greater than Elinor's. SS II 10 212 2
Bad indeed must the nature of Marianne's affliction be, SS II 10 213 2
Elinor was much more hurt by Marianne's warmth, than she SS II 12 236 38
Marianne's feelings did not stop here. SS II 12 236 39
of Edward to cease; for Marianne's joy hurried her into SS II 13 242 23
and it was to notice Marianne's altered looks, and express SS II 13 242 25
the distress of hearing Marianne's mistaken warmth, nor to SS II 13 245 47
price of every part of Marianne's dress; could have SS II 14 249 8
Marianne's feelings had then broken in, and put an end to SS III 1 262 14
At these words, Marianne's eyes expressed the astonishment, SS III 1 262 17
Marianne's indignation burst forth as soon as he quitted SS III 1 269 58
wished to do away; and Marianne's courage soon failed her, SS III 2 270 1
and Marianne's impatience to be gone increased every day. SS III 3 279 1
As Marianne's affection for her mother was sincere, it SS III 3 280 6
in the interval of Marianne's turning from one lesson to SS III 3 281 9
another lucky stop in Marianne's performance brought her SS III 3 281 9
10
restoring Marianne's peace of mind, and confirming her own. SS III 6 302 5
it dwelt on by turns in Marianne's imagination; and in the SS III 6 302 6
anxious solicitude on Marianne's feeling, in her head and SS III 6 305 16
the whole day, against Marianne's inclination, and forcing SS III 7 307 1
from the first to think Marianne's complaint more serious SS III 7 307 3
pain and delirium on Marianne's side, and in the most SS III 7 312 17
Marianne's ideas were still, at intervals, fixed SS III 7 312 18
which Marianne's disappointment had brought on. SS III 7 313 21
"Marianne's note, by assuring me that I was still as dear SS III 8 325 53
I had seen Marianne's sweet face as white as death.-- SS III 8 327 55
Willoughby's visit, Marianne's safety, and her mother's SS III 9 333 3
the conviction of Marianne's being no more, had no voice SS III 9 334 4
the knowledge of dear Marianne's unhappy prepossession for SS III 9 336 14
will do everything;-- Marianne's heart is not to be wasted SS III 9 337 18
He thinks Marianne's affection too deeply rooted for any SS III 9 338 20
Marianne's illness, though weakening in its kind, had not SS III 10 340 1
Marianne's lips quivered, and she repeated the word " SS III 11 351 10
in consequence of Marianne's illness; and in the first of SS III 11 353 21
alike distressed by Marianne's situation, knew not on SS III 11 353 24
to her Elinor;--that Marianne's affliction, because more SS III 11 356 46
all the improvement in Marianne's looks, all the kindness SS III 13 369 35

MARINERS (1)
direful deceptions, it's Mariners tempting it in sunshine S 7 396 1

MARINES (1)
fixing on a lieutenant of Marines, without education, MP I 1 3 1

MARK (19)
I am grateful for it as a mark of your friendship; but as LS 7 252 1
He meant not to be unkind however, and, as a mark of his SS I 1 4 3
and distinguished Elinor by no mark of affection. SS I 16 87 23
the remembrance of every mark of regard in look or word SS I 19 102 2
Elinor, "to shew any mark of my esteem and friendship for SS II 2 149 26
they received no mark of recognition on their entrance. SS II 5 171 30
of Lucy; for such a mark of uncommon kindness, vouchsafed SS II 14 254 27
as well as for every other mark of your regard during my PP I 22 124 10
and disdain of all restraint which mark Lydia's character. PP II 18 231 18
He protested that she should receive from him no mark of PP III 8 310 10
him any attention, or mark her deference for his opinion. PP III 17 378 46
minutes seemed to mark him the most at home of the two. MP II 1 183 23
as thinking it my duty to mark my opinion of your conduct-- MP III 1 318 39
I know he would be hurt by my failing in such a mark of E I 18 146 16
Every thing tender and charming was to mark their parting; E II 13 264 1
mark of good taste which I shall always know how to value." E III 4 342 39
Miss Musgroves, enough to mark an easy footing: the room P III 7 59 25
with no circumstance to mark them excepting the receipt of P IV 1 125 14
Mark his professions to my poor husband. P IV 9 204 75

MARKED (34)
The angry emotions which had marked every feature when we LS 25 292 2
taste which marked the reasonableness of that attachment. NA I 6 39 1
Two others, penned by the same hand, marked an expenditure NA II 7 172 2
She gave her an answer which marked her contempt, and SS I 4 23 19
so direct, as marked a perfect agreement between them. SS I 12 59 7
things he said too, which marked the turn of his feelings SS I 19 101 1
and nothing but the plan of the flower-garden marked out." SS II 11 226 37
For the rest of his character and habits, they were marked, SS III 6 304 15
the preceding evening had marked who the young lady was, SS III 8 328 61
as sufficiently marked how well she was satisfied with the PP I 18 95 48
which had marked their behaviour to their guests. PP I 18 102 75
my attentions have been too marked to be mistaken. PP I 19 105 8
continued in a voice that marked his displeasure, "to PP I 20 114 32
authoritative a tone, as marked her self-importance, and PP II 6 162 11
attentions which had marked the early part of their PP II 18 233 25
marked his intelligence, his taste, or his good manners. PP III 1 255 59
Miss Darcy, though with a diffidence which marked her PP III 2 263 11
curiosity so strongly marked as in Miss Bingley's, in PP III 3 269 8
Her nose wants character; there is nothing marked in its PP III 3 271 15
one of which was marked that it had been missent elsewhere. PP III 4 273 1
of cordiality as had marked their several meetings in PP III 4 279 23
had been generally proved to be marked out for misfortune. PP III 13 350 56
delight, which any marked or unlooked-for instance of MP II 6 234 18
There was marked coolness on her side. MP III 13 423 2
Yet there must have been some marked display of attentions MP III 15 438 6
wander from the walls marked by her father's head, to the MP III 15 439 9
being marked out for her by all their joint acquaintance. E II 7 206 2
cheerful eagerness which marked her as his peculiar object, E II 8 214 12
which this one article marked, gave her severe pain. E III 11 410 35
Instead of pushing his fortune in the line marked out for P III 1 8 15
glad to have any thing marked out as a duty, and certainly P III 5 33 9
Every thing now marked out Louisa for Captain Wentworth; P III 10 90 37
two subsequent moments, marked by returning hope or P IV 11 244 71
Nature had marked it out--had spoken in most intelligible S 1 369 1

MARKET (5)
She says there was hardly any veal to be got at market NA I 9 68 38
arrived;--& by the market clock, we have been only five & W 322 2
his residence in a small market town; and quitting them PP I 5 18 1
He was a great deal too full of the market to think of any E I 4 34 40
lived in the neighbouring market town, and Lady Russell, P III 1 10 21

MARKET-PLACE (2)
moment she was herself whisked into the market-place. NA I 11 87 53
And I ought to be at that fellow's in the market-place. P IV 11 240 58

MARKET-TOWN (1)
of a small market-town, where the family did not visit. PP III 2 265 14

MARKING (5)
of Marianne, of marking his animated admiration of her, SS I 11 53 1
with the sole view of marking my adoration of yourself. E I 15 131 31
Jane, and had now great pleasure in marking an improvement. E II 3 170 1
Birth, abilities, and education, had been equally marking E III 12 421 17
was influenced by her, in marking out the scheme of P III 2 12 3

MARKS (5)
daughter's, which equally marks her want of judgement, and LS 24 289 12
which marks the young woman of distinguished birth. PP I 14 67 7
(and let us rejoice over it) marks nothing bad at heart. PP III 4 273 3
There were the pencilled marks and memorandums on the E II 5 187 4
considered as marks of acquiescence, or proofs of defiance. E II 5 192 33

MARLBOROUGH (5)
A pint of porter with my cold beef at Marlborough was SS III 8 318 18
"At Marlborough!"--cried Elinor, more and more at a loss SS III 8 318 19
since that time, procured me a nuncheon at Marlborough." SS III 8 318 20
in very good style in Marlborough buildings, and had, at P IV 3 139 8
Mr. Elliot, and his friends in Marlborough buildings, were P IV 3 141 13

MARLBOROUGH-BUILDINGS (3)
She is only nursing Mrs. Wallis of Marlborough-Buildings-- P IV 5 156 13
She came away from Marlborough-Buildings only on Sunday; P IV 9 197 40
let me thus much into the secrets of Marlborough-Buildings. P IV 9 205 82

MARMALADE (1)
last week, some apricot marmalade had been successfully SS I 21 121 10

MARMION (1)
to ascertain whether Marmion or The Lady of the Lake were P III 11 100 23

MARQUIS OF LONGTOWN (1)
of seeing the Marquis of Longtown and General Courteney NA II 2 139 7

MARRIAGE (231)
his life was his throwing her off forever on her marriage. LS 2 245 1
and ungenerous since our marriage was first in agitation, LS 3 247 1
at the time of his marriage--& everybody ought to respect LS 5 249 1
force Frederica into a marriage from which her heart LS 7 253 2
marriage, & that she was altogether a wonderful woman. LS 8 255 2
I cannot easily resolve on anything so serious as marriage, LS 10 257 1
hardly suppose that Lady Susan's veiws extend to marriage. LS 11 259 1
In the very important concern of marriage especially, LS 12 260 1
attached you, to a marriage, which the whole of your LS 12 260 1
assurances as to marriage &c., do not set my heart at ease. LS 13 262 1
attached, would be absolutely destroyed by the marriage. LS 14 264 3
it was easy to see that her veiws extended to marriage. LS 14 264 4
given up my plan of her marriage; no, I am unalterably LS 19 275 4
for the conclusion of my marriage, or look forward with LS 29 299 2
I am still doubtful at times, as to marriage. LS 29 299 3
of so early a second marriage, must subject me to the LS 30 300 3
I consider a country-dance as an emblem of marriage. NA I 10 76 29
In marriage, the man is supposed to provide for the NA I 10 77 35
She endeavoured to believe that the delay of the marriage NA II 1 137 50
Of her unhappiness in marriage, she felt persuaded. NA II 7 180 37
positive conviction of his actually wishing their marriage. NA II 14 230 2
the first overture of a marriage between the families, NA II 15 246 12
Of a very considerable fortune, his son was, by marriage NA II 16 249 2
The means by which their early marriage was effected can NA II 16 250 4
The circumstance which chiefly availed, was the marriage NA II 16 250 4
The marriage of Eleanor Tilney, her removal from all the NA II 16 250 5
soon after Eleanor's marriage, permitted his son to return NA II 16 252 7
By a former marriage, Mr. Henry Dashwood had one son: by SS I 1 3 2
By his own marriage, likewise, which happened soon SS I 1 3 2

looked forward to their marriage as rapidly approaching. SS I 3 17 14
into the family on her marriage, and which perhaps had SS I 7 35 8
In my eyes it would be no marriage at all, but that would SS I 8 38 10
thought of their marriage had been raised, by his prospect SS I 10 49 11
She could easily conceive that marriage might not be SS I 14 71 4
begun, for their marriage must be at a very uncertain SS I 15 81 44
being tolerably happy in marriage, which sincere affection SS II 2 151 41
correspond, and their marriage is universally talked of." SS II 5 173 42
girl, and promises marriage, he has no business to fly off SS II 8 194 10
forced calmness, "Mr. Willoughby's marriage with Miss Grey. SS II 8 199 36
settled respecting his marriage with Miss Grey--it was no SS II 8 199 37
severe one--but had her marriage been happy, so young as I SS II 9 206 24
a few months after their marriage, and I was with my SS II 9 206 24
The shock which her marriage had given me," he continued, SS II 9 206 24
mind, or an happier marriage, she might have been all that SS II 9 208 28
visit at Allenham on his marriage, which Mrs. Dashwood, SS II 10 213 4
the approaching marriage, and communicating them to Elinor. SS II 10 215 11
and promoting the marriage by every possible attention. SS II 11 228 51
to tell her that his marriage with Miss Morton was SS II 12 229 4
and retarded the marriage, of Edward and herself, had he SS II 13 238 1
otherwise at last, than in the marriage of Edward and Lucy. SS III 1 260 9
Edward's marriage with Lucy was as firmly determined on, SS III 2 276 26
Mr. Ferrars's marriage as the certain consequence of the SS III 3 284 22
His marriage must still be a distant good;--at least, I am SS III 3 284 23
worded than if it had arisen from an offer of marriage. SS III 3 284 24
When the marriage takes place, I fear she must hear of it SS III 5 296 18
publishing the banns of marriage between John Smith and SS III 5 298 33
by Willoughby since his marriage, and she looked forward SS III 6 302 5
That he had cut me ever since my marriage, I had seen SS III 8 330 69
"Your sister's marriage." SS III 8 332 81
lie in promoting their marriage; and since our arrival, SS III 9 337 18
be convinced that your marriage must have involved you in SS III 11 350 9
to stop the ruin which had begun before your marriage?-- SS III 11 350 9
Lucy's marriage, the unceasing and reasonable wonder among SS III 13 364 10
No rumour of Lucy's marriage had yet reached him;--he knew SS III 13 370 35
taken to prevent the marriage; and he called on Elinor to SS III 13 371 38
her decree of consent to the marriage of Edward and Elinor. SS III 14 373 3
The first month after their marriage was spent with their SS III 14 374 7
They had in fact nothing to wish for, but the marriage of SS III 14 374 7
Elinor's marriage divided her as little from her family as SS III 14 378 13
Willoughby could not hear of her marriage without a pang; SS III 14 379 18
who, by stating his marriage with a woman of character, as SS III 14 379 18
To be so bent on marriage--to pursue a man merely for the W 318 2
Happiness in marriage is entirely a matter of chance. PP I 6 23 10
marriage, and planning his happiness in such an alliance. PP I 10 52 54
seeing them all in due time well disposed of in marriage. PP I 13 64 21
of their marriage was exceedingly agreeable to <u>her</u>. PP I 17 88 14
all the felicity which a marriage of true affection could PP I 18 98 63
that another offer of marriage may ever be made you. PP I 19 108 19
who naturally looks for happiness in the marriage state. PP I 20 110 4
that Mr. Collins has made you an offer of marriage. PP I 20 111 15
"Very well--and this offer of marriage you have refused?" PP I 20 111 15
refusing every offer of marriage in this way, you will PP I 20 113 28
of men or of matrimony, marriage had always been her PP I 22 122 3
as most people can boast on entering the marriage state." PP I 22 125 17
making two offers of marriage within three days, was PP I 22 125 18
so heartily approved his marriage, that she wished it to PP I 23 128 10
one I will not mention; the other is Charlotte's marriage. PP II 1 135 11
Two of her girls had been on the point of marriage, and PP II 2 139 3
About ten or a dozen years ago, before her marriage, she PP II 2 142 19
His marriage was now fast approaching, and she was at PP II 3 145 11
were not altered by his marriage; his formal civility was PP II 5 155 3
of a most imprudent marriage, but without mentioning names PP II 10 185 28
That she should receive an offer of marriage from Mr. PP II 11 193 31
had given rise to a general expectation of their marriage. PP II 12 197 5
My objections to the marriage were not merely those, which PP II 12 198 5
Ultimately have prevented the marriage, had it not been PP II 12 199 5
heart most cordially wish you equal felicity in marriage. PP II 15 216 6
in their marriage put an end to all real affection for her. PP II 19 236 1
of so unsuitable a marriage, nor ever been so fully aware PP II 19 236 2
Imprudent as a marriage between Mr. Wickham and our poor PP III 4 274 3
to depend upon their marriage; he shook his head when I PP III 4 275 5
without the intention of marriage, she had no difficulty PP III 4 279 24
Why must their marriage be private? PP III 5 283 8
to live with him on any other terms than marriage?" PP III 5 283 9
their proceedings, and perhaps announce the marriage. PP III 5 287 33
happiness with him in marriage, because I knew that his PP III 5 290 50
Five thousand pounds was settled by marriage articles on PP III 8 308 4
The marriage of a daughter, which had been the first PP III 8 310 7
without which her marriage would scarcely seem valid, PP III 8 310 10
sister; for since her marriage would so shortly give the PP III 8 311 11
Had Lydia's marriage been concluded on the most honourable PP III 8 311 12
But no such happy marriage could now teach the admiring PP III 8 312 16
do so," he added, "as soon as his marriage was fixed on. PP III 8 312 19
should be noticed on her marriage by her parents, urged PP III 8 314 22
his character and his marriage been exactly what they PP III 9 316 5
to secure and expedite a marriage, which, in his very PP III 10 323 2
and his situation must have been benefited by marriage. PP III 10 323 2
making his fortune by marriage, in some other country. PP III 10 323 2
"Perhaps preparing for his marriage with Miss de Bourgh," PP III 10 328 17
Has he, has my nephew, made you an offer of marriage?" PP III 14 354 34
at the moment, in their marriage, is to be prevented by a PP III 14 355 43
both did as much as you could, in planning the marriage. PP III 14 355 44
promise, make <u>their</u> marriage at all more probable? PP III 14 357 61
"No principle of <u>either</u>, would be violated by my marriage PP III 14 358 70
She had not herself forgotten to feel that the marriage of PP III 15 360 1
to prevent their marriage, it occurred to Elizabeth that PP III 15 360 2
the miseries of a marriage with <u>one</u>, whose immediate PP III 15 360 2
"After mentioning the likelihood of this marriage to her PP III 15 363 22
into a marriage which has not been properly sanctioned." PP III 15 363 22
the marriage took place, should be so generally known. PP III 15 363 22
no longer conceal from her, his share in Lydia's marriage. PP III 17 374 19
place you in the greatest danger in an unequal marriage. PP III 17 376 35
marriage, were all that was affectionate and insincere. PP III 18 383 24
suffered no revolution from the marriage of her sisters. PP III 19 386 6
from Lydia on her marriage, explained to her that, by his PP III 19 386 6
the claims to reputation which her marriage had given her. PP III 19 387 8
Miss Bingley was very deeply mortified by Darcy's marriage; PP III 19 387 10
Lady Catherine was extremely indignant on the marriage of PP III 19 388 12
such as a very imprudent marriage almost always produces. MP I 1 4 1
a duty; and as a marriage with Mr. Rushworth would give MP I 4 38 10
He only conditioned that the marriage should not take MP I 4 40 14
Crawford, the children of her mother by a second marriage. MP I 4 40 15
of them; but, as her own marriage had been soon followed MP I 4 40 15
"to what any young person says on the subject of marriage. MP I 4 43 25
"Not always in marriage, dear Mary." MP I 5 46 19
"In marriage especially. MP I 5 46 20
events; your sister's marriage, and your taking orders." MP I 11 108 8
The whole subject of it was love--a marriage of love was MP I 18 167 12
it, happy to secure a marriage which would bring him such MP II 3 201 22
hardly be more impatient for the marriage than herself. MP II 3 202 26
my uncle was so good as to give me on my cousin's marriage. MP II 5 222 43
The Admiral hated marriage, and thought it never MP II 12 292 9
I would prevent the marriage, if possible; but I know you, MP II 12 296 29
receiving a proposal of marriage at any time, which might MP III 1 319 39
were all fixed on a marriage of attachment; who was MP III 2 328 6
To know Fanny to be sought in marriage by a man of fortune, MP III 2 332 22
How could you imagine me an advocate for marriage without MP III 4 346 14
received at the end of about ten years' happy marriage." MP III 4 354 46
'When two sympathetic hearts meet in the marriage state, MP III 5 358 9
of the one, which her imprudent marriage had placed her in. MP III 8 390 5
evidently unhappy in her marriage, places her MP III 13 421 2
having early in her marriage, from the want of other MP III 13 425 6
been on the point of marriage, and Henry would have been MP III 16 455 23
now to be done, was to bring about a marriage between them. MP III 16 456 29
sin, on the chance of a marriage which, thinking as I now MP III 16 457 30
He felt that he ought not to have allowed the marriage, MP III 17 461 4
divorce; and so ended a marriage contracted under such MP III 17 464 12
especially when that marriage had taken place, which would MP III 17 467 19
happiness of son or niece could make her wish the marriage. MP III 17 472 31
of her sister's marriage, been mistress of his house from E I 1 5 2
soon followed Isabella's marriage on their being left to E I 1 6 6
But she knows how much the marriage is to Miss Taylor's E I 1 11 38
for the last four years to bring about this marriage. E I 1 12 42
to be dissuaded from the marriage, and it took place to E I 2 15 3
after a three years' marriage, he was rather a poorer man E I 2 16 4
that, even in his first marriage; but his second must shew E I 2 17 6
Now, upon his father's marriage, it was very generally E I 2 17 9
of congratulation which her marriage had already secured. E I 2 18 10
Weston's marriage her exercise had been too much confined. E I 4 26 1
Mr. Martin, and contained a direct proposal of marriage. E I 7 50 1
Yes, quite a proposal of marriage; and a very good letter, E I 7 50 1
soon have an offer of marriage, and from a most E I 8 59 25
what they all proposed doing in the event of his marriage. E I 8 59 27
a man that a woman should ever refuse an offer of marriage. E I 8 60 33
Miss Harriet Smith may not find offers of marriage flow in E I 8 64 47
Till this year, every long vacation since their marriage E I 11 91 2
coming soon after the marriage, but it ended in nothing; E I 11 95 21
since his father's marriage with Miss Taylor--that if she E I 14 119 5
The marriage of Lieut. Fairfax, of the ---- regiment of E II 2 163 2
regard however, till the marriage of Miss Campbell, who by E II 2 165 7
time of their daughter's marriage; and till she should E II 2 165 9
however, must certainly be lessened by his marriage. E II 4 182 8
"His father's marriage," he said, "had been the wisest E II 5 192 28
Though always objecting to every marriage that was E II 5 193 35
to her--on the point of marriage --would yet never ask E II 6 201 28
Elton, was disposed to pay him attention on his marriage. E II 16 290 1
Marriage, in fact, would not do for her. E III 12 416 1
as much happiness in the marriage state as he had done.-- E III 14 443 8
the answer to the communication of his intended marriage. E III 17 464 18
might not be so very bad if the marriage did take place. E III 17 467 30
plans and her own, for a marriage between Frank and Emma. E III 17 467 31
They had determined that their marriage ought to be E III 19 483 8
never yet alluded to their marriage but as a distant event. E III 19 483 8
within a month from the marriage of Mr. and Mrs. Robert E III 19 484 11
no thought of a second marriage, needs no apology to the P III 1 5 8
own birth, and see no marriage follow but that of a P III 1 7 12
The disgrace of his first marriage might, perhaps, as P III 1 8 17
after an unprosperous marriage, to her father's house, P III 2 15 15
that upon the subject of marriage they are particularly P III 5 35 14
casements; but upon the marriage of the young 'squire, it P III 5 36 20
"Pretty well, ma'am, in the fifteen years of my marriage; P III 8 70 52
The circumstances of his marriage too were found to admit P IV 3 139 8
things relative to the marriage, which made a material P IV 3 139 8
The evil of the marriage would be much diminished, if P IV 4 146 4
She was sure that he had not been happy in marriage. P IV 4 147 6
for though his marriage had not been very happy, still it P IV 4 147 8
The intimacy had been formed before our marriage. P IV 9 199 55
the circumstances of his marriage, which I never could P IV 9 200 56
and as to his marriage, I knew all about it at the time. P IV 9 200 57
He was determined to make it by marriage. P IV 9 200 59
mar it by an imprudent marriage; and I know it was his P IV 9 201 59
Elliot to him before our marriage, and happened to be P IV 9 203 70
it is to be put into the marriage articles when you and Mr. P IV 9 208 92
by Mr. Elliot's marriage) they had been as before always P IV 9 208 95
Mr. Elliot, raised by his marriage to great affluence, and P IV 9 209 95
She had previously, in the anticipation of their marriage, P IV 9 210 99
have compounded for the marriage at once, with all its P IV 10 215 13
as must prevent the marriage from being near at hand; but P IV 10 217 20
wishes, and that their marriage was likely to take place P IV 10 217 20
for the insertion of the marriage in the volume of honour. P IV 12 248 2
in themselves; and their marriage, instead of depriving P IV 12 251 11

MARRIAGES (7)

since their respective marriages, and that many years ago. NA I 4 31 2
of any man by different marriages; and why was he to ruin SS I 2 8 3
marriages, and then you can have nothing farther to ask."-- SS I 10 47 4
I am an advocate for early marriages, where there are MP III 1 317 34
and Mrs. Weston, whose marriages taking them from E III 17 466 29
They had each had money, but their marriages had made a P III 9 74 5
Anne, "should be happy in their children's marriages. P IV 10 218 23

MARRIED (223)

life, to know that you were married to Lady Susan Vernon. LS 12 261 4
another school, unless we can get her married immediately. LS 16 268 1
Lady Susan announced her being married to Sir James Martin. LS 42 312 6
such a fuss about, she who married the French emigrant." NA I 7 49 38
soon as I heard she has married an emigrant, I was sure I NA I 7 49 40
him lost to her for ever, by being married already. NA I 8 53 3
that Mr. Tilney could be married; he had not behaved, he NA I 8 53 3
had not talked, like the married men to whom she had been NA I 8 53 3
fortune; and, when she married, her father gave her twenty NA I 9 68 46
Henry and Catherine were married, the bells rang and every NA II 16 252 7
Had he married a more amiable woman, he might have been SS I 1 5 7
was very young when he married, and very fond of his wife. SS I 1 5 7
lived to see respectably married, and she had now SS I 8 36 1
see Colonel Brandon well married, ever since her SS I 8 36 1
I am sure she will be married to Mr. Willoughby very soon." SS I 12 60 9
I am sure they will be married very soon, for he has got a SS I 12 60 11
that your cousin Fanny is married?" said Mrs. Jennings, SS I 13 64 14
the altar, you would suppose they were going to be married. SS I 15 80 42
is going to be married to Mr. Willoughby of Combe Magna. SS I 20 115 50
And I am so glad your sister is going to be well married! SS I 20 116 60
"Yes, a great while; ever since my sister married.-- SS I 20 116 62
the Colonel, and we should have been married immediately." SS I 20 116 62
Miss Dashwood, before he married, as he was so rich?" SS I 21 124 28
was a beau before he he married, he is one still, for SS I 21 124 29
"Oh! dear! one never thinks of married mens' being beaux-- SS I 21 124 30
" twill be a fine thing to have her married so young to be SS I 21 125 35
that his mother might give him if he married to please her. SS II 2 147 7
one of you at least well married before I have done with SS II 3 153 2
Pray, when are they to be married?" SS II 7 181 8
me more than to hear of their being going to be married." SS II 7 182 9
He is to me married very soon--a good-for-nothing fellow! SS II 8 192 3
I remember her aunt very well, Biddy Henshawe; she married SS II 8 194 10
married, for she and Mrs. Ellison could never agree."-- SS II 8 194 12
Mind me, now, if they an't married by midsummer. SS II 8 196 22
She was married--married against her inclination to my SS II 9 205 24
fortune, to leave her card with her as soon as she married. SS II 10 215 14
they would not be married till Michaelmas, and by the end SS II 10 216 15
painful office of informing her sister that he was married. SS II 10 216 16
The Willoughbys left town as soon as they were married; SS II 10 217 18
said Elinor, with resolution, "going to be married?" SS II 11 224 27
"Her daughters are both exceedingly well married, and SS II 11 227 46
and they must wait to be married till he got a living. SS III 2 274 16
Remember that you are married. SS III 8 325 52
shall be heartily glad to hear she is well married.'-- SS III 8 326 53
She must be attached to you, or she would not have married SS III 8 329 64
She knew I had no regard for her when we married.-- SS III 8 329 65
Well, married we were, and came down to Combe Magna to be SS III 8 329 65
Had you married, you must have been always poor. SS III 11 350 9
has married a woman of a less amiable temper than yourself. SS III 11 351 13
But does it thence follow that had he married you, he SS III 11 351 13
"I suppose you know, ma'am, that Mr. Ferrars is married." SS III 11 353 22
23

"Who told you that Mr. Ferrars was married, thomas?" SS III 11 354 26

"But did she tell you she was married, thomas?" SS III 11 354 28
But he was now married, and she condemned her heart for SS III 12 357 1
That he should be married so soon, before (as she imagined) SS III 12 357 2
They were married, married in town, and now hastening down SS III 12 357 2
lately married to--to the youngest--to Miss Lucy Steele." SS III 12 360 22
23
"Yes," said he, "they were married last week, and are now SS III 12 360 25
From the moment of learning that Lucy was married to SS III 13 363 8
said Elinor, after a pause--"they are certainly married. SS III 13 366 18
before she went off to be married, on purpose we suppose SS III 13 370 37
considered too old to be married.--and who still sought SS III 14 378 15
he is married to another woman, while I am still single.-- W 316 2
There is nothing she wd not do to get married--she would W 316 2
I wish with all my heart she was well married. W 317 2
say much for you, as my aunt married again so foolishly.-- W 321 2
her in the old rooms at Bath, the year before I married--. W 325 4
the same, & for having married the only daughter of the W 348 23
Pity, you can none of you get married!-- W 353 26
"Is he married or single?" PP I 1 3 13
The business of her life was to get her daughters married; PP I 1 5 34
equally well married, I shall have nothing to wish for." PP I 3 9 2
was Mrs. Hurst, who had married a man of more fashion than PP I 4 15 13
the desire of being well married; and if I were determined PP I 6 22 7
my heart; and if she were married to him to-morrow, I PP I 6 23 10
She had a sister married to a Mr. Phillips, who had been a PP I 7 28 2
been hinted that Colonel Forster was going to be married. PP I 12 60 7
soon have two daughters married; and the man whom she PP I 15 71 5
that Jane would be soon married to Mr. Bingley.-- PP I 18 98 63
Of having another daughter married to Mr. Collins, she PP I 18 103 77
reproach shall ever pass my lips when we are married." PP I 19 106 10
of having a daughter well married; and she called at PP I 23 127 8
Next to being married, a girl likes to be crossed in love PP II 1 137 27
will have a daughter married before I have, and that PP II 2 140 4
convinced, that whether married or single, he must always PP II 4 151 3
of them were likely to be married, whether they were PP II 6 163 15
The younger ones out before the elder are married!-- PP II 6 165 34
Lord, how ashamed I should be of not being married before PP II 16 221 17
Lord! how I should like to be married before any of you; PP II 16 221 17
friend was a very young woman, and very lately married. PP II 18 230 11
generally give, had married a woman whose weak PP II 19 236 1
eligible for them to be married privately in town than to PP III 4 275 5
less expeditiously, married in London, than in Scotland." PP III 5 282 7
we know that they are not married, and have no design of PP III 5 288 37
and if they are not married already, make them marry. PP III 5 288 38
money as she chuses, to buy them, after they are married. PP III 5 288 38
a doubt, I suppose, of their being really married?" PP III 5 290 49
is, as I always hoped," cried Jane; "they are married!" PP III 7 302 14
They are not married, nor can I find there was any PP III 7 302 14
We have judged it best, that my niece should be married PP III 7 303 14
"And they are really to be married!" cried Elizabeth, as PP III 7 304 34
of Lydia's being soon married, her joy burst forth, and PP III 7 305 43
To know that her daughter would be married was enough. PP III 7 306 43
She will be married!-- PP III 7 306 44
She will be married at sixteen!-- PP III 7 306 44
In a short time, I shall have a daughter married. PP III 7 306 47
Miss Lydia is going to be married; and you shall all have PP III 7 307 49
When first Mr. Bennet had married, economy was held to be PP III 8 308 3
as soon as they were married, that he was prevailed on to PP III 8 314 22
be able to shew her married daughter in the neighbourhood, PP III 8 314 22
had no more idea of being married till I came back again! PP III 9 316 7
mamma, do the people here abouts know I am married to-day? PP III 9 316 8
now, and you must go lower, because I am a married woman." PP III 9 317 9
of being married, to Mrs. Hill and the two housemaids. PP III 9 317 10
We were married, you know, at St. Clement's, because PP III 9 318 24
I longed to know whether he would be married in his blue PP III 9 319 24
we were beyond the hour, we could not be married all day. PP III 9 319 25
She was sure they should be married some time or other, PP III 10 323 2
Mr. Darcy asked him why he had not married your sister at PP III 10 323 2
But you know married women have never much time for PP III 11 330 6
Lydia does not leave me because she is married; but only PP III 11 331 12
Miss Lucas is married and settled. and one of my own PP III 11 336 49
to have a daughter well married," continued her mother, " PP III 11 336 51
My youngest of all, is lately married, and my eldest is PP III 14 352 8
being most advantageously married, but that you, that Miss PP III 14 353 26
young couple into your house as soon as they were married. PP III 15 363 22
Three daughters married! PP III 17 378 43
You must and shall be married by a special licence. PP III 17 378 45
you believe me actually married, you cannot greatly err. PP III 18 382 21
But Miss Frances married, in the common phrase, to MP I 1 3 1
wrote to her family on the subject till actually married. MP I 1 4 1
Having married on a narrower income than she had been used MP I 1 8 9
see their dear Maria well married," she very often thought; MP I 4 38 9
company as chance to be married, my dear Mrs. Grant, there MP I 5 46 20
I know so many who have married in the full expectation MP I 5 46 22
out when her cousin was married, Miss Crawford proceeded MP I 15 147 57
generous present to her when dear Mrs. Rushworth married. MP II 10 272 3
Maria is nobly married--but had Mr. Crawford sought MP III 1 319 39
He who had married a daughter to Mr. Rushworth. MP III 2 331 17
would be advantageously married, it made her feel a sort MP III 2 332 22
I could do very well without you, if you were married to a MP III 2 333 26
whom she is wild to get married, and wants Henry to take. MP III 5 360 16
I wish Margaret were married, for my poor friend's sake, MP III 5 361 16
to be about as unhappy as most other married people. MP III 5 361 16
She is a cold-hearted, vain woman, who has married MP III 13 421 2
A woman married only six months ago, a man professing MP III 15 441 20
that way; and, when once married, and properly supported MP III 16 457 29
the happiness of the married cousins must appear as secure MP III 17- 473 32
just after they had been married long enough to begin to MP III 17 473 32
Miss Taylor married. E I 1 6 5
Mr. Woodhouse had not married early) was much increased by E I 1 7 8
Miss Taylor must be glad to have her so happily married." E I 1 11 38
for a woman neither young, handsome, rich, nor married. E I 3 21 4
was sure whenever he married he would make a good husband. E I 4 28 6
sister very well married, and it is only a linen-draper." E I 7 55 40
envy you such an opportunity as this of being married. E I 7 56 41
married to a respectable, intelligent gentleman-farmer!" E I 8 62 40
If they are anxious to see you happily married, here is a E I 9 75 27
phrase, be well married, here is the comfortable fortune, E I 9 75 27
surprized when I first heard she was going to be married." E I 9 79 60
that you should not be married, or going to be married! so E I 10 84 8
9
or going to be married! so charming as you are!"-- E I 10 84 8
9
And I am not only, not going to be married, at present, E I 10 84 11
not want: I believe few married women are half as much E I 10 84 15
missed seeing them but one entire day since they married. E I 11 94 14
As for Isabella, she has been married long enough to see E I 11 95 18
but now their daughter is married, I suppose Colonel and E I 12 104 46
them again--for till she married, last October, she was E II 1 159 20
He was a married man, with only one living child, a girl, E II 2 163 4
Mr. Elton is going to be married." E II 3 173 24
state, that he was going to be married to a Miss Hawkins. E II 3 174 32
"Mr. Elton going to be married!" said Emma, as soon as she E II 3 174 33
And as it is some months since Miss Campbell married, the E II 3 175 43
who was very well married, to a gentleman in a great way, E II 4 183 9
to an old servant who was married, and settled in Donwell. E II 5 186 2
you had not married, you would have staid at home with me." E II 7 209 10
the woman he had just married, the woman he had wanted to E II 14 271 5
He is just as superior as ever;--but being married, you E II 14 271 15
keep me in practice; for married women, you know--there is E II 14 277 38
that a married woman has many things to call her attention. E II 14 277 40
Though I think he had better not have married. E II 14 279 54
sit with us in this comfortable way, if you were married." E II 15 288 35
Upon my word, if this is what I am to expect, we married E II 18 305 6
She was nobody when he married her, barely the daughter of E II 18 310 33
feel myself rather an old married man, and that my dancing E III 2 327 36
extremely obliging--and if I were not an old married man.-- E III 2 327 37
you know, to keep any remembrances, after he was married. E III 4 340 24
Married women, you know, may be safely authorized. E III 6 354 14
"No,"--he calmly replied,--"there is but one married woman E III 6 354 15
parties--young ladies-- married women-----" E III 7 370 20
An old married man--quite good for nothing. E III 7 372 38
Frank Churchill are to be married, and that they have been E III 11 404 8
They would be married, and settled either at or near E III 12 422 20
couple engaged of the three, were the first to be married. E III 19 483 6
date of Mary's birth--"married, Dec. 16, 1810, Charles, P III 1 3 2
and Elizabeths they had married; forming altogether two P III 1 3 3
4
not come; and the next tidings were that he was married. P III 1 8 15
He was a married man, and without children; the very state P III 3 22 24
of his constancy, she had no reason to believe him married. P III 4 30 8
"Perhaps you may not have heard that he is married," added P III 6 49 21
exception even among the married couples) there could have P III 8 63 3
When he is married, if we have the good luck to live to P III 8 70 46
Wentworth--"when once married people begin to attack me P III 8 70 48
you will think very differently, when you are married.' P III 8 70 48
We do so wish that Charles had married Anne instead.-- P III 10 88 28
time; but I believe about a year before he married Mary. P III 10 89 33
at the advantage of such resident curate's being married. P III 12 103 3
Miss Hamilton had left school, had married not long P IV 5 152 3
was said to have married a man of fortune, and this was P IV 5 152 3
Nay, most likely they are married already, for I do not P IV 6 171 35
His sister married my tenant in Somersetshire,--the Croft, P IV 8 188 40
Do not forget me when you are married, that's all. P IV 9 196 32
"Not before he married, I suppose?" P IV 9 198 47
"Yes; he was not married when I knew him first." P IV 9 198 48
Mr. Elliot married then, completely for money? P IV 9 201 63
of every thing great and good in your married lives. P IV 11 235 32
It was creditable to have a sister married, and she might P IV 12 249 5
about 5 & 30--had been married,--very happily married 7 S 2 371 1
married,--very happily married 7 years--& had 4 sweet S 2 371 1
had been new when they married & fresh lined on their S 2 373 1
He had been an elderly man when she married him;--her own S 3 375 1
For the title, it was to be supposed that she had married-- S 3 376 1
good deal for a woman to say that has been married twice.-- S 7 399 1

MARRIES (6)

me that the Colonel only marries you for the sake of SS III 4 291 53
who marries him, cannot have a proper way of thinking. PP II 1 135 13
country when Mr. Martin marries, I wish you may not be E I 4 31 24
But if he marries a very ignorant, vulgar woman, certainly E I 4 31 25
either marries or dies, is sure of being kindly spoken of. E II 4 181 1
Harriet Smith marries Robert Martin." E III 18 470 12

MARRY (212)

I have more than once repented that I did not marry him LS 2 245 1
advise you by all means to marry him; his father's estate LS 9 256 1
that I am sure he would marry either of you with pleasure. LS 9 257 1
I would rather work for my bread than marry him. LS 21 279 1
He wants to marry her--her mother promotes the match--but LS 23 284 4
to take her to town, & marry her immediately to Sir James. LS 25 294 5
& the rest of his family, by making her marry Sir James. LS 26 295 1
Besides, if you take my advice, & resolve to marry de LS 26 295 3
de courcy of intending to marry you, & would speak with LS 32 303 1
have brought myself to marry Reginald; & am equally LS 39 308 0
1000
more as if she were to marry him when she got back to town, LS 41 309 1
in the world who could like them well enough to marry them. NA I 2 20 8
do not chuse to dance or marry themselves, have no NA I 10 76 29
People that marry can never part, but must go and keep NA I 10 77 32
Your brother, who might marry any body!" NA I 15 119 15
And to marry for money I think the wickedest thing in NA I 15 124 47
years before they could marry, being. however unwelcome, NA II 1 135 43
has deserted my brother, and is to marry your's! NA II 10 204 19
his happiness, to enable him to marry such a girl?-- NA II 10 205 30
Your sisters will marry, and it will be gone for ever. SS I 2 9 7
If they marry, they will be sure of doing well, and if SS I 2 10 15
way, if he were to wish to marry a woman who had not SS I 4 21 15
that both her sons should marry well, and of the danger SS I 4 23 19
nothing to do but to marry all the rest of the world. SS I 8 36 1
Had he been in a situation to act independently and marry SS I 15 81 44
inquire about him, very well; your sister is to marry him. SS I 20 114 44
If in the supposition of his seeking to marry herself, his SS II 1 140 3
it would be madness to marry upon that, though for my own SS II 2 147 7
That would be enough for us to marry upon, and we might SS II 2 149 25
marry him; guess what I must have felt for all your sakes. SS II 9 210 32
I remember Fanny used to say that she would marry sooner SS II 11 227 50
I question whether Marianne now, will marry a man worth SS II 11 227 50
Edward and Lucy should not marry; for I am sure Mrs. SS III 1 259 7
Edward will marry Lucy; he will marry a woman superior in SS III 1 263 27
or of wishing to marry Miss Morton, or anything like it. SS III 2 273 16
provided to enable him to marry;-- and she, of all people SS III 3 283 20
comfortable as a bachelor; it cannot enable him to marry. SS III 3 284 23
idea of the living's being enough to allow them to marry." SS III 4 292 56
himself, he thinks that nobody else can marry on less. SS III 4 292 57
same to Miss Morton whether she marry Edward or Robert." SS III 5 296 28
marry this young woman, I never will see him again.' SS III 5 299 35
she offered to forgive the past, if I would marry Eliza. SS III 8 323 40
It was only to ask Elinor to marry him;--and considering SS III 13 361 2
could be drawn on to marry a girl, of whose beauty she had SS III 13 364 10
would be better for her to marry you than be single." SS III 13 367 23
would still be unable to marry Miss Morton, and his SS III 13 369 33
having once intended to marry her, and Elinor, though SS III 14 377 11
"Not much indeed--but you know we must marry.-- W 317 2
I have lost Purvis, it is true but very few people marry W 317 2
think of nothing worse) than marry a man I did not like."-- W 318 2
He will never marry unless he can marry somebody very W 319 2
She had even condescended to advise him to marry as soon PP I 14 66 1
income, he intended to marry; and in seeking a PP I 15 70 2
foot-stool, that she said, 'Mr. Collins, you must marry. PP I 19 105 10
A clergyman like you must marry.-- chuse properly, chuse a PP I 19 105 10
You must come and make Lizzy marry Mr. Collins, for she PP I 20 111 7
again if you do not marry Mr. Collins, and I will never PP I 20 112 19
is in love with you, and wants him to marry Miss Darcy. PP I 21 118 18
and friends are all wishing him to marry elsewhere?" PP I 21 119 23
lately as Mr. Collins was wishing to marry you. PP I 22 125 17
Do not you know that Mr. Collins wants to marry Lizzy?" PP I 23 126 2
they may wish him to marry a girl who has all the PP II 1 136 23
hoped he might really soon marry Mr. Darcy's sister, as, PP II 3 149 27
may not have the means or inclination to marry early.-- PP II 6 165 35
just as likely to marry her, had she been his relation. PP II 8 176 29
Younger sons cannot marry where they like." PP II 10 183 12
who can afford to marry without some attention to money." PP II 10 183 14
I wonder he does not marry, to secure a lasting PP II 10 184 17
in the world whom I could ever be prevailed on to marry." PP II 11 193 28
much in love as to wish to marry her in spite of all the PP II 11 193 31
"If your master would marry, you might see more of him." PP III 1 248 27
to go there, or to marry Lydia at all, which was repeated PP III 4 274 5
of Wickham's meaning to marry her. no one but Jane, she PP III 4 279 24
that Wickham should marry a girl, whom it was impossible PP III 4 279 24
it was impossible he could marry for money; and how Lydia PP III 4 279 24
account, was persuaded of his never intending to marry her. PP III 5 283 8
Wickham will never marry a woman without some money. PP III 5 283 8
and if they are not married already, make them marry. PP III 5 288 38
"And was Denny convinced that Wickham would not marry? PP III 5 290 47
Who is to fight Wickham, and make him marry her, if he PP III 6 298 14

"Can it be possible that he will marry her?" PP III 7 303 15
"And they must marry! PP III 7 304 26
Yes, yes they must marry. PP III 7 304 27
"I mean, that no man in his senses, would marry Lydia on PP III 7 304 29
That they should marry, small as is their chance of PP III 7 304 34
would not marry Lydia, if he had not a real regard for her. PP III 7 304 35
His consenting to marry her is a proof, I will believe, PP III 7 305 37
Wickham be prevailed on to marry his daughter, it would be PP III 8 309 4
if he marry prudently, his wife may teach him. PP III 10 325 2
if I went to see him, he should marry one of my daughters. PP III 11 332 23
his mother and aunt wished him to marry Miss de Bourgh. PP III 14 355 44
Your ladyship wants Mr. Darcy to marry your daughter; but PP III 14 357 61
Oh, Lizzy! do any thing rather than marry without PP III 17 373 11
and being inclined to marry, soon fancied himself in love. MP I 4 38 10
her evident duty to marry Mr. Rushworth if she could. MP I 4 38 10
that her son should marry, and declared that of all the MP I 4 39 10
Matrimony was her object, provided she could marry well, MP I 4 42 18
Henry, you shall marry the youngest Miss Bertram, a nice, MP I 4 42 19
If you can persuade Henry to marry, you must have the MP I 4 42 21
I would have every body marry if they can do it properly; MP I 4 43 27
body should marry as soon as they can do it to advantage." MP I 4 43 27
hundred of either sex, who is not taken in when they marry. MP I 5 46 20
so far from now meaning to marry the elder, she did not MP I 12 114 2
A well-disposed young woman, who did not marry for love, MP II 3 201 22
affection, and contempt of the man she was to marry. MP II 3 202 26
He would marry Miss Crawford. MP II 9 264 17
not think him likely to marry at all--or not at present." MP II 11 289 36
No--you must be aware that I am quite determined to marry MP II 12 291 4
From my soul I do not think she would marry you without MP II 12 293 15
"I--I cannot like him, sir, well enough to marry him." MP III 1 315 26
wishing to marry at all so early is recommendatory to me. MP II 13 317 34
cousin, Mr. Bertram, is to marry early; but at present, as MP III 1 317 34
habits as much more likely to marry early than his brother. MP III 1 317 34
hopeless and how wicked it was, to marry without affection. MP III 1 324 58
trying to persuade you to marry against your inclinations. MP III 2 330 16
You cannot wish me to marry; for you would miss me, me, MP III 2 333 25
He will marry her, and be poor and miserable. MP III 13 424 4
"We must persuade Henry to marry her," said she, "and what MP III 16 456 29
She hoped to marry him, and they continued together till MP III 17 464 10
as anxious to marry Fanny, as Fanny herself could desire. MP III 17 470 26
would never marry again, may comfort me for any thing." E I 1 11 39
Every body said that Mr. Weston would never marry again. E I 1 12 41
Mr. Weston certainly would never marry again. E I 1 12 41
if Mr. Weston were to marry her,' and saying it again to E I 1 12 42
longed for--enough to marry a woman as portionless even as E I 2 16 5
Not that she wanted him to marry. E I 4 28 6
take any pains to marry him, she would probably repent it. E I 4 30 18
can afford to marry, who are not born to an independence. E I 4 30 20
Harriet, whenever he does marry;--I mean, as to being E I 4 30 22
that he might marry any body at all fit for you to notice. E I 4 30 22
Not that I think Mr. Martin would ever marry any body but E I 4 31 25
"She always declares she will never marry, which, of E I 5 41 29
A woman is not to marry a man merely because she is asked, E I 7 54 31
He is desperately in love and means to marry her." E I 8 59 25
Emma; "but is he sure that Harriet means to marry him?" E I 8 59 26
I had no hesitation in advising him to marry. E I 8 59 27
Harriet's claims to marry well are not so contemptible as E I 8 63 44
Were you, yourself, ever to marry, she is the very woman E I 8 64 46
Let her marry Robert Martin, and she is safe, respectable, E I 8 64 47
encourage her to expect to marry greatly, and teach her to E I 8 64 47
Smith is a girl who will marry somebody or other,) till E I 8 64 47
But as to my letting her marry Robert Martin, it is E I 8 65 48
Mr. Elton, who might marry any body! E I 9 74 22
enough to induce me to marry; I must find other people E I 10 84 10
11
If I were to marry, I must expect to repent it." E I 10 84 13
"I have none of the usual inducements of women to marry. E I 10 84 15
relative to every body about me, I would marry to-morrow. E I 10 84 16
if she were to marry, he was the very person to suit her E I 14 119 5
that Mr. Elton would never marry indiscreetly; and blushed E I 16 135 6
He wanted to marry well, and having the arrogance to raise E I 16 135 7
meaning (in short), to marry him!--should suppose himself E I 16 135 8
be in such a hurry to marry--and to marry strangers too-- E II 3 177 51
a hurry to marry--and to marry strangers too--and the E II 3 177 51
they meant to marry till it were proved against them. E II 5 193 35
to settle early in life, and to marry, from worthy motives. E II 6 204 43
Mr. Knightley must not marry!-- E II 8 224 66
Knightley really wished to marry, you would not have him E II 8 224 67
Mr. Knightley marry!-- E II 8 224 68
"But Mr. Knightley does not want to marry. E II 8 225 74
Why should be marry?-- E II 8 225 74
He has no occasion to marry, either to fill up his time or E II 8 225 74
No--Mr. Knightley must never marry. E II 8 228 87
either of the Coxes would be very glad to marry him." E II 9 233 21
Had she intended ever to marry him, it might have been E II 11 250 19
quit her father, never to marry, a strong attachment E II 13 264 1
the woman he had wanted to marry, and the woman whom he E II 14 271 5
he had been expected to marry, she must allow him to have E II 14 271 5
not every man's fate to marry the woman who loves him best. E II 14 271 14
It is encouraging people to marry if you make so much of E II 14 280 57
"No, my dear, I never encouraged any body to marry, but I E II 14 280 58
"Well, papa, if this is not encouragement to marry, I do E II 14 280 59
nothing to do with any encouragement to people to marry." E II 14 280 60
you have been settling that I should marry Jane Fairfax." E II 15 287 33
34
but confess, Emma, that you did want him to marry Harriet." E III 2 330 48
Harriet, whenever you marry I would advise you to do and E III 4 340 28
Harriet say in a very serious tone, "I shall never marry." E III 4 340 28
it should pass unnoticed or not, replied, "never marry!-- E III 4 341 29
30
I marry, I hope somebody will choose my wife for me. E III 7 373 45
46
arrow, that Mr. Knightley must marry no one but herself! E III 11 408 32
She would not marry, even if she were asked by Mr. E III 12 416 1
because he could not marry them both, Emma had it not. E III 13 431 38
marry him, without attacking the happiness of her father. E III 15 448 31
and Mr. Knightley meant to marry; by which means Hartfield E III 17 465 28
said she would never marry, and assured that it would be a E III 17 466 29
This friend, and Sir Walter, did not marry, whatever might P III 1 5 7
when a woman does marry again, than when she does not; but P III 1 5 8
none: Elizabeth would, one day or other, marry suitably. P III 1 6 10
marry him; and her father had always meant that she should. P III 1 7 14
It was now his object to marry. P III 7 61 38
to have him marry either would be extremely delightful. P III 9 75 9
No, no; Henrietta might do worse than marry Charles Hayter; P III 9 76 15
shocking to have Henrietta marry Charles Hayter; a very P III 9 76 16
I suppose you know he wanted to marry Anne?" P III 10 88 28
would be much diminished, if Elizabeth were also to marry. P IV 4 146 4
Louisa, we all thought, you know, was to marry Frederick. P IV 6 171 33
of being to marry Frederick, is to marry James benwick. P IV 6 171 33
"Well, she is to marry him. P IV 6 171 35
Russell that Louisa Musgrove was to marry Captain Benwick. P IV 7 178 27
I am not going to marry Mr. Elliot. P IV 9 195 28
have fancied she was to marry Mr. Elliot, where she could P IV 9 197 34
and she it was who told me you were to marry Mr. Elliot. P IV 9 197 40
is not unlikely to marry "again; he is quite fool enough. P IV 9 203 72
He truly wants to marry you. P IV 9 204 80
Elliot marry, that your father is not to marry Mrs. Clay. P IV 9 208 92
of having been induced to marry him, as made her shudder P IV 9 211 102
we thought they had better marry at once, and make the P IV 11 230 6
of their being able to marry in six months, or even in P IV 11 231 8
it into their heads to marry, they are pretty sure by P IV 12 248 1
of some years, she had been induced to marry again. S 3 375 1
will think so--for Sir Edwd must marry for money.-- S 7 400 1
compliments, but he knows he must marry for money.-- S 7 400 1
"And Miss Esther must marry somebody of fortune too--she S 7 401 1

MARRYING (104)

my brother-in-law's marrying her, this want of cordiality LS 5 249 1
of marrying Miss De Courcy, & the event has justified me. LS 5 249 1
always disliked me for marrying Mr Vernon, & that we had LS 6 251 1
take all possible pains to prevent his marrying Catherine. LS 12 260 2
present intention of marrying Lady Susan--not that he is LS 15 266 1
that I was absolutely determined on her marrying him. LS 22 280 1
Frederica had set herself violently against marrying Sir LS 24 288 11
The probability of their marrying is surely heightened. LS 24 291 17
our reconciliation, or by marrying & teizing him for ever. LS 25 293 4
well established by marrying Mr De Courcy, than to LS 26 295 1
But she was always silly; intolerably so, in marrying him LS 26 296 5
were you guilty in marrying a man of his age!--just old LS 29 298 1
in my resolution of marrying him--& tho' this was too idle LS 29 299 2
father's side of your marrying to advantage; where LS 30 300 2
ask our consent to his marrying Lady Susan, but to tell us LS 40 308 1
"a famous good thing this marrying scheme, upon my soul! NA I 15 122 30
His marrying Miss Thorpe is not probable. NA II 10 204 20
marrying her, than at any other part of the story." NA II 10 204 20
difficulties in the way of her marrying their brother. NA II 11 208 1
well resolved upon marrying Catherine himself, his vanity NA II 15 244 12
for their consent to his marrying their daughter, was, for NA II 16 249 1
being thirty-five any objection to his marrying her. SS I 8 38 9
In his marrying such a woman therefore there would be SS I 8 38 10
Brandon has not the smallest wish of marrying me." SS II 11 223 23
was no likelihood of her marrying Colonel Brandon; but it SS II 11 228 51
designs, in case of his marrying Miss Morton; told him SS III 1 266 38
a short pause, "of Robert's marrying Miss Morton." SS III 5 296 24
my circumstances by marrying a woman of fortune. SS III 8 320 32
Brandon's marrying one of you as the object most desirable. SS III 9 336 10
occur to prevent his marrying Lucy; that some resolution SS III 12 357 1
I suppose, by Robert's marrying Lucy, than she would have SS III 13 366 18
Lucy, than she would have been by your marrying her." SS III 13 366 18
to dissuade him from marrying Miss Dashwood, by every SS III 14 373 3
resolution of not marrying till every thing was ready, and SS III 14 374 6
proud of marrying privately without his mother's consent. SS III 14 376 11
his visits & soon after marrying somebody else.-- W 316 2
I should not like marrying a disagreable man any more than W 318 2
You must know that I am thinking of his marrying one of PP I 1 4 16
my hearty consent to his marrying which ever he chuses of PP I 1 4 25
lessen their chance of marrying men of any consideration PP I 8 37 19
of christening, marrying, and burying his parishioners PP I 13 64 16
daughters, as Jane's marrying so greatly must throw them PP I 18 99 63
to state my reasons for marrying--and moreover for coming PP I 19 105 8
"my reasons for marrying are, first, that I think it a PP I 19 105 9
10
Tell her that you insist upon her marrying him." PP I 20 111 12
You promised me to insist upon her marrying him." PP I 20 112 21
Last Christmas you were afraid of his marrying me, because PP II 4 153 9
her marrying Mr. Collins as the wisest thing she ever did. PP II 9 178 15
she sometimes planned her marrying Colonel Fitzwilliam. PP II 9 181 31
him prevent his friend's marrying her sister, and which PP II 11 193 31
There is no danger of Wickham's marrying Mary king. PP II 16 220 10
every chance of benefiting himself by marrying well? PP III 5 283 8
of marrying, do not let us give the matter over as lost. PP III 5 288 37
He did not repeat his persuasion of their not marrying-- PP III 5 290 48
But there was much to be talked of, in marrying her; and PP III 8 309 6
"This is the consequence you see, madam, of marrying a PP III 11 330 11
If there is no other objection to my marrying your nephew, PP III 14 355 44
"In marrying your nephew, I should not consider myself as PP III 14 356 51
I know it all; that the young man's marrying her, was a PP III 14 357 62
were excited by his marrying me, it would not give me one PP III 14 358 70
to predict their marrying with almost equal advantage. MP I 1 3 1
the expediency of Mr. Rushworth's marrying Miss Bertram. MP I 4 39 11
coax, or trick him into marrying, is inconceivable! MP I 4 42 21
I assure you is quite as voluntary as Maria's marrying." MP I 11 108 13
with her brother's marrying a little beneath him. MP II 12 292 5
estimation, your marrying early may be the saving of you. MP II 12 296 27
Crawford's marrying Edmund than it had ever been before.-- MP III 6 366 4
chance of his marrying her, than if she remain with him. MP III 16 457 29
a reasonable period from Edmund's marrying Mary. MP III 17 467 19
to his own daughter's marrying, nor could ever speak of E I 1 7 10
must have been the consequence of your marrying Mr. Martin. E I 7 53 24
Not regret her leaving Highbury for the sake of marrying a E I 8 62 39
"If I had set my heart on Mr. Elton's marrying Harriet, it E I 8 66 54
Your marrying will be equal to the match at Randalls. E I 9 75 25
but have very little intention of ever marrying at all." E I 10 84 11
to be avoided in not marrying, I shall be very well off, E I 10 85 21
resolution of never marrying, there was something in the E I 14 118 5
resolution held of never marrying)--the honour, in short, E II 7 206 2
I cannot at all consent to Mr. Knightley's marrying; and I E II 8 224 66
all day long for his great kindness in marrying Jane?-- E II 8 225 78
Mr. Knightley has any thought of marrying Jane Fairfax." E II 8 226 84
Her objections to Mr. Knightley's marrying did not in the E II 8 227 87
about Mr. Elton's marrying, Harriet, is the strongest E II 13 268 10
wish for your marrying Jane Fairfax or Jane any body. E II 15 288 35
do you say now to Mr. Knightley's marrying Jane Fairfax?" E II 15 289 41
It was almost enough to make her think of marrying. E III 2 325 31
expectation of never marrying, results from an idea that E III 4 341 35
Very lucky--marrying as they did, upon an acquaintance E III 7 372 40
express, prevented her marrying the unexceptionable young E III 11 413 49
in marrying her, than she now seemed of Mr. Knightley's.-- E III 11 414 50
Could she be secure of that, indeed, of his never marrying E III 12 416 1
of Mr. Knightley's marrying Jane Fairfax, or any body else, E III 15 449 35
This proposal of his, this plan of marrying and continuing E III 15 450 36
only means so far as your having some thoughts of marrying. E III 17 465 26
at this time for my marrying any more than at another.-- E III 17 465 27
it is not "equal to her marrying Captain Wentworth, it is P IV 6 165 8
a "million times better than marrying among the Hayters." P IV 6 165 8
acquaintance on marrying, should be your cousin; and that, P IV 9 201 59
When one lives in the world, a man or woman's marrying for P IV 9 201 64
she, "it would not prevent his marrying any body else." P IV 9 208 92
I considered your marrying him as certain, though he might P IV 9 211 101
will be the means of marrying, I hold to be very unsafe P IV 11 231 9
In marrying a man indifferent to me, all risk would P IV 11 244 73
Marrying early & having a very numerous family, their S 2 373 1

MARSH (1)

it does between a stagnant marsh, a bleak moor & the S 1 369 1

MARSHAL (1)

all that remained, was to marshal themselves, and proceed P IV 8 185 19

MARTHA SHARPE (1)

or two back, when Martha Sharpe and I had so many secrets SS III 2 274 20

MARTIN (36)

hither, except Sir James Martin, on whom I bestowed a LS 2 244 1
Sir James Martin had been drawn in by that young lady to LS 14 264 4
by the name of Sir James Martin, the very person, as you LS 20 275 2
I am very miserable about Sir James Martin, & have no LS 21 279 1
Who should come on Tuesday but Sir James Martin? LS 22 280 1
of allowing Sir James Martin to address my daughter, LS 22 281 4
Do not let Frederica vernon be made unhappy by that Martin. LS 23 284 4
One point only is gained; Sir James Martin is dismissed. LS 24 285 1
will have Sir James Martin before she leaves London again. LS 38 307 3
Lady Susan announced her being married to Sir James Martin. LS 42 312 6
They were a family of the name of Martin, whom Emma well E I 3 23 10
a most unexceptionable quarter:--Robert Martin is the man. E I 8 59 25
I never heard better sense from any one than Robert Martin. E I 8 59 27
Harriet Smith refuse Robert Martin? madness, if it is so; E I 8 60 34
or education, to any connection higher than Robert Martin? E I 8 61 38

Context	Work	Vol	Ch	Page	Line
Robert Martin would never have proceeded so far, if he had	E	I	8	63	42
Let her marry Robert Martin, and she is safe, respectable,	E	I	8	64	47
But as to my letting her marry Robert Martin, it is	E	I	8	65	48
"Robert Martin has no great loss--if he can but think so;	E	I	8	66	51
satisfied with persuading her not to accept young Martin.	E	I	16	137	11
should come in, but Elizabeth Martin and her brother!--	E	II	3	178	52
be clearer; even a Robert Martin would have been	E	II	4	183	10
without being suspected of introducing Robert Martin."--	E	III	6	361	40
Robert Martin had probably ceased to think of Harriet.--	E	III	6	361	40
Harriet Smith marries Robert Martin."	E	III	18	470	12
Mr. Knightley; "I have it from Robert Martin himself.	E	III	18	471	14
mean to say, that Harriet Smith has accepted Robert Martin.	E	III	18	471	17
Larkins; but I could quite as ill spare Robert Martin."	E	III	18	473	22
Mr. Knightley and Robert Martin was, at this moment, so	E	III	18	473	27
than to think of Robert Martin," that she was really	E	III	18	473	27
It would be a great pleasure to know Robert Martin.	E	III	18	475	41
as it was!--that Robert Martin had thoroughly supplanted	E	III	19	481	1
had always liked Robert Martin; and that his continuing to	E	III	19	481	2
acquainted with Robert Martin, who was now introduced at	E	III	19	482	4
hand bestowed on Robert Martin with so complete a	E	III	19	482	6
Robert Martin and Harriet Smith, the latest couple engaged	E	III	19	483	6

MARTIN'S (8)

Context	Work	Vol	Ch	Page	Line
her, a better fate than to be Sir James Martin's wife.	LS		20	278	11
be gratified by a Robert Martin's riding about the country	E	I	4	35	45
"Robert Martin's manners have sense, sincerity, and good-	E	I	8	65	49
Martin's calling at Mrs. Goddard's a few days afterwards.	E	II	4	184	11
judged it best for her to return Elizabeth Martin's visit.	E	II	4	185	11
However, I must say that Robert Martin's heart seemed for	E	III	18	472	20
sake, and for Robert Martin's sake, (whom I have always	E	III	18	474	34
me of pleading poor Martin's cause, which was never the	E	III	18	474	34

MARTINS (12)

Context	Work	Vol	Ch	Page	Line
Martins of Abbey-Mill-Farm, it must have been the whole.	E	I	4	27	4
But the Martins occupied her thoughts a good deal; she had	E	I	4	27	4
She was as happy as possible with the Martins in the	E	I	8	63	42
last, in order to put the Martins out of her head, was	E	II	3	180	56
place the Martins under proper subordination in her fancy.	E	II	3	180	57
As Harriet now lived, the Martins could not get at her,	E	II	3	180	58
Sometimes Mr. Elton predominated, sometimes the Martins;	E	II	4	184	11
While he staid, the Martins were forgotten; and on the	E	II	4	185	11
deal, to have had the Martins in a higher rank of life.	E	II	5	187	4
Her mind was quite sick of Mr. Elton and the Martins.	E	II	5	187	4
Another accidental meeting with the Martins was possible,	E	II	9	233	23
her engagements with the Martins, was less and less at	E	III	19	482	5

MARY (249)

Context	Work	Vol	Ch	Page	Line
Mary always has her own way."	SS	II	5	167	5
and Mary brown, he could conceive nothing more ridiculous.	SS	III	5	298	33
But Mary Edwardes is rather prim & reserved; I do not	W			321	2
to his daughter with "well Mary, I bring you good news.--	W			323	3
E. not less satisfied with Mary, paid some compliments of	W			323	3
"You are paying Miss Emma no great compliment I think Mary,	W			324	3
Mary apologized in some confusion.	W			324	3
followed her with Mary, in less than five minutes.--	W			333	13
with either of the Mr Tomlinsons, Mary?--said her mother.	W			336	14
"So, you ended with Capt. Hunter Mary, did you?" said her	W			337	15
Mary was surrounded by red coats the whole eveng.	W			337	15
Mrs E. said no more, & Mary breathed again.--	W			337	15
quite at your service, & Mary will be pleased with the	W			339	18
him no favour, & I doubt his having any interest with Mary.	W			341	19
What say you, Mary? for you are a young lady of deep	PP	I	2	7	18
Mary wished to say something very sensible, but knew not	PP	I	2	7	19
"While Mary is adjusting her ideas," he continued, "let us	PP	I	2	7	20
Mary had heard herself mentioned to Miss Bingley as the	PP	I	3	12	15
"Pride," observed Mary, who piqued herself upon the	PP	I	5	20	20
instrument by her sister Mary, who having, in consequence	PP	I	6	25	23
Mary had neither genius nor taste; and though vanity had	PP	I	6	25	24
playing half so well; and Mary, at the end of a long	PP	I	6	25	24
"I admire the activity of your benevolence," observed Mary,	PP	I	7	32	38
They found Mary, as usual, deep in the study of thorough	PP	I	12	60	7
"In point of composition," said Mary, "his letter does not	PP	I	13	64	19
every sister except Mary agreed to go with her; and Mr.	PP	I	15	71	6
And even Mary could assure her family that she had no	PP	I	17	87	10
mortification of seeing Mary, after very little entreaty,	PP	I	18	100	68
in vain; Mary would not understand them; such an	PP	I	18	100	68
at their close; for Mary, on receiving amongst the thanks	PP	I	18	100	68
his interference, lest Mary should be singing all night.	PP	I	18	100	68
He took the hint, and when Mary had finished her second	PP	I	18	100	68
					69
Mary, though pretending not to hear, was somewhat	PP	I	18	101	70
girls, and Mary might have been prevailed on to accept him.	PP	I	22	124	11
There is no danger of Wickham's marrying Mary king.	PP	II	16	220	10
"And Mary king is safe!" added Elizabeth; "safe from a	PP	II	16	220	11
"Oh! Mary," said she, " I wish you had gone with us, for	PP	II	16	222	22
To this, Mary very gravely replied, "far be it from me, my	PP	II	16	222	23
more than half a minute, and never attended to Mary at all.	PP	II	16	223	24
Mary and Kitty, thank heaven! are quite well."	PP	III	5	286	30
In the dining-room they were soon joined by Mary and Kitty,	PP	III	5	289	41
as for Mary, she was mistress enough of herself to whisper	PP	III	5	289	41
Mary, however, continued to console herself with such kind	PP	III	5	289	44
"Mary and Kitty have been very kind, and would have shared	PP	III	5	292	66
Kitty is slight and delicate, and Mary studies so much,	PP	III	5	292	66
Mary and Kitty were both with Mrs. Bennet: one	PP	III	7	305	43
was his custom, and Mary went up stairs to her instrument.	PP	III	13	344	11
Mary petitioned for the use of the library at Netherfield;	PP	III	13	349	42
in the habit of walking, Mary could never spare time, but	PP	III	16	365	1
Mary or Kitty, send them in, for I am quite at leisure."	PP	III	17	377	40
Mary was the only daughter who remained at home; and she	PP	III	19	386	5
Mary was obliged to mix more with the world, but she could	PP	III	19	386	5
She was delighted with each, but Mary was her dearest	MP	I	4	42	17
unreserved woman, Mary had not been three hours in the	MP	I	4	42	17
"My dear sister," said Mary, "if you can persuade him into	MP	I	4	42	21
You will be kinder than Mary.	MP	I	4	43	23
"Mary, how shall we manage him?"	MP	I	5	46	15
"Not always in marriage, dear Mary."	MP	I	5	46	19
observers, dearest Mary, who make much of a little, are	MP	I	5	46	23
"You are as bad as your brother, Mary; but we will cure	MP	I	5	47	25
Mary was satisfied with the parsonage as a present home,	MP	I	5	47	26
it is nothing more than, 'dear Mary, I am just arrived.	MP	I	6	59	43
for her sister; and Mary, properly pressed and persuaded,	MP	I	8	76	7
is not in love with Henry," was her observation to Mary.	MP	I	17	161	10
"I dare say she is," replied Mary, coldly.	MP	I	17	161	11
things when he comes home," said Mary, after a pause.	MP	I	17	161	15
But, Mary, do not fancy that Maria Bertram cares for Henry.	MP	I	17	162	16
"Do not flatter yourself, my dearest Mary.	MP	II	4	212	31
these little vexations, Mary, live where we may; and when	MP	II	4	213	35
to amuse myself, Mary, on the days that I do not hunt?	MP	II	6	229	1
"Moderation itself!" said Mary.	MP	II	6	231	10
let me see, Mary; Lady Bertram bids a dozen for that	MP	II	7	243	27
Did, soon afterwards, when Mary, perceiving her on a sofa	MP	II	10	276	14
and comfort to Fanny was tediousness and vexation to Mary.	MP	II	11	285	15
To Mary it was every way painful.	MP	II	11	285	15
"Sitting with them an hour and half!" exclaimed Mary.	MP	II	12	291	2
"Yes, Mary," said he, drawing her arm within his, and	MP	II	12	291	4
I am quite determined, Mary.	MP	II	12	291	4
Mary was in a state of mind to rejoice in a connection	MP	II	12	292	5
"Yes, Mary," was Henry's concluding assurance, "I am	MP	II	12	292	6
"Lucky, lucky girl!" cried Mary as soon as she could speak-	MP	II	12	292	7
No, Mary, you are quite mistaken.	MP	II	12	293	10
Mary, she is not like her cousins; but I think I shall not	MP	II	12	293	14
I will make her very happy, Mary, happier than she has	MP	II	12	295	20
"Ha!" cried Mary, "settle in Northamptonshire!	MP	II	12	295	21
Mary had only to be grateful and give general assurances;	MP	II	12	295	24
Mary refrained from saying what she felt, that there could	MP	II	12	296	29
"Had you seen her this morning, Mary," he continued, "	MP	II	12	296	31
Had you seen her so, Mary, you would not have implied the	MP	II	12	297	31
"My dearest Henry," cried Mary, stopping short, and	MP	II	12	297	32
Yes, Mary, my Fanny will feel a difference indeed, a daily,	MP	II	12	297	33
a syllable of it even to Mary; while uncertain of the	MP	II	13	300	7
moment, and saying, "have you nothing to send to Mary?	MP	II	13	306	28
the world, Mary on something of less philosophic tendency.	MP	III	5	360	13
been happier," continued Mary, presently, "than when he	MP	III	5	363	26
thinking deeply of it till Mary, who had been first	MP	III	5	364	30
The sight of Betsey brought the image of little Mary back	MP	III	7	386	40
own knife; little sister Mary had left it to her upon her	MP	III	7	386	42
Poor Mary little thought it would be such a bone of	MP	III	7	386	44
there has been no 'well, Mary, when do you write to Fanny?-	MP	III	9	393	1
himself lucky in seeing Mary for even half an hour, having	MP	III	10	400	8
say, in every letter to Mary, 'I am well.'--and I know you	MP	III	11	411	18
and being frequently with Mary and Edmund, without	MP	III	11	413	31
The loss of Mary I must consider as comprehending the loss	MP	III	13	422	2
'The loss of Mary, I must consider as comprehending the	MP	III	13	424	4
Even in the sick chamber, the fortunate Mary was not	MP	III	14	430	4
ago, but for this illness?-- yours ever, Mary."	MP	III	14	435	13
whether she ought to keep Edmund and Mary asunder or not.	MP	III	14	436	15
a reasonable period from Edmund's marrying Mary.	MP	III	17	467	19
had again a home to offer Mary; and Mary had had enough of	MP	III	17	469	24
a home to offer Mary; and Mary had had enough of her own	MP	III	17	469	24
still lived together; for Mary, though perfectly resolved	MP	III	17	469	24
a still-born son, nov. 5, 1789; mary, born nov. 20, 1791."	P	III	1	3	1
Mary had acquired a little artificial importance, by	P	III	1	5	8
rest with Elizabeth; for Mary had merely connected herself	P	III	1	6	10
Anne haggard, Mary coarse, every face in the neighbourhood	P	III	1	6	11
society, still be near Mary, and still have the pleasure	P	III	2	14	9
and her own sister, Mary, had been at school while it all	P	III	4	31	11
resident in Kellynch, and Mary fixed only three miles off,	P	III	4	31	12
Mary, often a little unwell, and always thinking a great	P	III	5	33	7
a surprise to her to find Mary alone; but being alone, her	P	III	5	36	21
Though better endowed than the elder sister, Mary had not	P	III	5	37	21
"My dear Mary, recollect what a comfortable account you	P	III	5	38	32
And one thing I have had to do, Mary, of a more trying	P	III	5	39	34
anxious supplement from Mary, of "upon my word, I shall be	P	III	6	42	1
Mary was not so repulsive and unsisterly as Elizabeth, nor	P	III	6	43	4
the superiority, for while Mary thought it a great shame	P	III	6	43	5
"I wish you could persuade Mary not to be always fancying	P	III	6	44	7
unhappy mood, thus spoke Mary;--"I do believe if Charles	P	III	6	44	7
She had this communication, moreover, from Mary.	P	III	6	45	9
I wish any body could give Mary a hint that it would be a	P	III	6	46	10
touch in the evening, from Mary, who, on having occasion	P	III	6	48	16
Mary deplored the necessity for herself.	P	III	6	48	17
while the Admiral sat by Mary, and made himself very	P	III	6	48	17
heard the Admiral say to Mary, "we are expecting a brother	P	III	6	49	23
					24
the first black idea; and Mary was quite ready to be	P	III	6	50	26
She and Mary were actually setting forward for the great	P	III	7	53	2
Mary knew, from Charles's manner of speaking, that he was	P	III	7	55	9
fears; and indeed, Mary, I cannot wonder at your husband.	P	III	7	56	11
"Are you serious?" cried Mary, her eyes brightening.	P	III	7	57	16
was so great, that Mary and Anne were not more than	P	III	7	59	24
sisters meaning to visit Mary and the child, and Captain	P	III	7	59	24
Mary, very much gratified by this attention, was delighted	P	III	7	59	25
his voice--he talked to Mary, said all that was right;	P	III	7	59	25
Mary talked, but she could not attend.	P	III	7	60	27
information from mary: "Captain Wentworth is not very	P	III	7	60	31
					32
Mary had no feelings to make her respect her sister's in a	P	III	7	60	32
to give a passage to Lady Mary Grierson and her daughters."	P	III	8	68	31
					32
Charles gave it for Louisa, Mary for Henrietta, but quite	P	III	9	75	9
"Upon my word it would," replied Mary.	P	III	9	75	11
It suited Mary best to think Henrietta the one preferred,	P	III	9	75	12
"Now you are talking nonsense, Mary," was therefore his	P	III	9	76	15
"Charles may say what he pleases," cried Mary to Anne, as	P	III	9	76	16
enabled by the entrance of Mary and the Miss Musgroves to	P	III	9	80	34
and, therefore, concluded Mary could not like to go with	P	III	10	83	4
to go with them; and when Mary immediately replied, with	P	III	10	83	4
She tried to dissuade Mary from going, but in vain; and	P	III	10	83	4
not like a long walk!" said Mary, as she went up stairs.	P	III	10	83	5
Mary exclaimed, "bless me! here is Winthrop--I declare I	P	III	10	85	15
gate, was ready to do as Mary wished; but "no," said	P	III	10	85	16
spot; Louisa returned, and Mary finding a comfortable seat	P	III	10	86	21
out of sight and sound, Mary was happy no longer; she	P	III	10	86	21
Mary sat down for a moment, but it would not do; she was	P	III	10	87	21
"Mary is good-natured enough in many respects," said she; "	P	III	10	88	28
time; but I believe about a year before he married Mary.	P	III	10	89	33
As soon as she could, she went after Mary, and having	P	III	10	89	35
She joined Charles and Mary, and was tired enough to be	P	III	10	90	37
Mary had shewn herself disobliging to him, and was now to	P	III	10	90	37
with his switch; and when Mary began to complain of it,	P	III	10	90	37
The Miss Musgroves were not at all tired, and Mary was	P	III	10	90	38
of domestic society, in leaving poor Mary for Lady Russell.	P	III	11	93	2
Mary, Anne, Henrietta, Louisa, and Captain Wentworth.	P	III	11	94	7
"Bless me!" cried Mary; "it must be our cousin;--it must	P	III	12	105	14
"There! you see!" cried Mary, in an ecstacy, "just as I	P	III	12	106	16
the second time; luckily Mary did not much attend to their	P	III	12	106	19
"Oh course," said Mary, "you will mention our seeing Mr.	P	III	12	107	20
Mary never wrote to Bath herself; all the toil of keeping	P	III	12	107	21
"She is dead! she is dead!" screamed Mary, catching hold	P	III	12	109	34
the others, tried to quiet Mary, to animate Charles, to	P	III	12	111	44
of her own insensibility. Mary, too, was growing calmer.	P	III	12	112	51
to Mary, however, there was an end of all peace in it.	P	III	12	115	65
no help for it: the change of Mary for Anne was inevitable.	P	III	12	115	65
and ill-judging claims of Mary; but so it must be, and	P	III	12	115	66
"She really left nothing for Mary to do.	P	IV	1	121	2
He and Mary had been persuaded to go early to their inn	P	IV	1	121	2
Mary had been hysterical again this morning.	P	IV	1	121	2
Though Charles and Mary had remained at Lyme much longer	P	IV	2	129	1
Mary had had her evils; but upon the whole, as was evident	P	IV	2	129	3
Charles laughed again and said, "now Mary, you know very	P	IV	2	130	6
Mary knows it is."	P	IV	2	130	6
But Mary did not give into it very graciously; whether	P	IV	2	130	7
cried Charles, "in such terms,"--Mary interrupted him.	P	IV	2	131	8
Now Mary, I declare it was so, I heard it myself, and you	P	IV	2	131	9
"And I am sure," cried Mary warmly, "it was very little to	P	IV	2	131	10
"Oh! as to being Anne's acquaintance," said Mary, "I think	P	IV	2	132	14
"There we differ, Mary," said Anne.	P	IV	2	132	17
"Yes, that he will!" exclaimed Mary, tauntingly.	P	IV	2	132	19
And when he does, Mary, you may depend upon hearing my	P	IV	2	132	20
Mary spoke with animation of their meeting with, or rather	P	IV	2	132	22
Charles and Mary also came in, of course, during their	P	IV	2	134	29
to Mary, of his being "a man whom she had no wish to see."	P	IV	2	135	35
"How is Mary looking?" said Sir Walter, in the height of	P	IV	3	142	14
occasion for remembering Mary) and Anne, smiling and	P	IV	3	143	18
She wanted to hear much more than Mary communicated.	P	IV	6	162	1
letter than usual from Mary was delivered to her, and to	P	IV	6	162	1
"Yours, affectionately, "Mary m----."	P	IV	6	164	7
Mary need not have feared her sister's being in any degree	P	IV	6	165	9
"How is Mary?" said Elizabeth; and without waiting for an	P	IV	6	165	10
the same conclusion as Mary, from the present course of	P	IV	6	167	19
it to gratify her vanity, than Mary might have allowed.	P	IV	6	167	19
"Old Lady Mary Maclean?	P	IV	9	193	10
the goodness to ring for Mary--stay, I am sure you will	P	IV	9	202	68
and Elizabeth were walking Mary into the other drawing-	P	IV	10	216	18
ostentatiously dropped by Mary, as well as of some	P	IV	10	216	18
to her husband; but Mary could not bear to be left, and	P	IV	10	216	19
Mary were included in it, by way of general convenience.	P	IV	10	217	19

Mary does not above half like Henrietta's match. P IV 10 218 22
Mary was in excellent spirits, enjoying the gaiety and the P IV 10 219 28
promised for the absent, Mary was as completely satisfied. P IV 10 220 29
Charles and Mary, to go and see her and Henrietta directly. P IV 10 220 29
of every help which Mary required, from altering her P IV 10 220 31
used by any body; which Mary, well amused as she generally P IV 10 220 31
"Anne," cried Mary, still at her window, "there is Mrs. P IV 10 222 34
Mary, resenting that she should be supposed not to know P IV 10 222 37
"Do come, Anne," cried Mary, "come and look yourself. P IV 10 222 38
To pacify Mary, and perhaps screen her own embarrassment, P IV 10 222 39
the others liked it, when Mary eagerly interrupted her by P IV 10 223 42
43
Charles and Mary still talked on in the same style; he, P IV 10 224 50
including every body!" whispered Mary very audibly. P IV 10 227 66
she immediately heard that Mary and Henrietta, too P IV 11 229 2
full sensation, Charles, Mary, and Henrietta all came in. P IV 11 238 44
Of all the family, Mary was probably the one most P IV 12 249 5
at Whitby's for little Mary at any time, or a large bonnet S 4 381 1
"Yes indeed, I am sure we do--& I will get Mary a little S 4 381 1
"Oh! my dear Mary, merely a joke of his. S 4 382 1
fashionable air,--you & I Mary, know what effect it might S 4 382 1
Look my dear Mary--look at William Heeley's windows.-- S 4 383 1
Now Mary, (smiling at his wife)--before I open it, what S 5 385 1
Mary, you will be quite sorry to hear how ill they have S 5 386 1
"Well, well--my dear Mary--I grant you, it is unfortunate S 5 388 1
what think you Miss H. of Burns lines to his Mary?-- S 7 397 1
But my dear Mary, send for the children;--I long to see S 9 407 1
Mary, my love, is not she a wonderful creature?-- S 9 409 1
You will not dislike speaking to her about it, Mary?"-- S 12 423 1
"My dear Mary, cried he, it is impossible you can be S 12 423 1
And while you are on the subject of subscriptions Mary, I S 12 424 1
he ought; --but you see Mary, how impossible it is for me S 12 424 1
"Upon second thoughts Mary, said her husband, I will not S 12 425 1
with kind notice of little Mary, & a very well-bred bow & S 12 425 1

MARY CRAWFORD (8)
Mary Crawford was remarkably pretty; Henry, though not MP I 4 41 17
Can we be wrong if Mary Crawford feels the same?" MP I 13 129 39
was evident that Mary Crawford's wishes, though politely MP I 14 130 3
dirt of a November day, most acceptable to Mary Crawford. MP II 4 205 2
her eyes from wandering between Edmund and Mary Crawford. MP II 10 273 8
to be, to give up Mary Crawford, would be to give up the MP III 13 422 2
Scarcely had he done regretting Mary Crawford, and MP III 17 470 25
all her ways, as Mary Crawford had ever been; and whether MP III 17 470 25

MARY EDWARDS (2)
"You will take notice who Mary Edwards dances with."-- W 320 2
How nice Mary Edwards looks in her new pelisse!-- W 341 19

MARY EDWARDS'S (1)
you to ask Mary Edwards's opinion if you are at all at a W 315 1

MARY'S (21)
Mary's powers were by no means fitted for such a display; PP I 18 100 68
If she could have believed Mary's future fate as MP III 6 366 4
correspondence had begun; Mary's next letter was after a MP III 9 393 1
words, after the date of Mary's birth--"married, Dec. 16, P III 1 3 2
"I cannot possibly do without Anne," was Mary's reasoning; P III 5 33 7
This invitation of Mary's removed all Lady Russell's P III 5 34 10
of Anne's side, produced nearly a cure on Mary's. P III 5 39 40
both the Miss Musgroves, at Mary's particular invitation. P III 5 41 46
"I could manage them very well, if it were not for Mary's P III 6 44 6
when listening in turn to Mary's reproach of "Charles P III 6 44 6
Mary's declaration was, "I hate sending the children to P III 6 44 8
Again; it was Mary's complaint, that Mrs. Musgrove was P III 6 45 10
miles from Kellynch: Mary's ailments lessened by having a P III 6 46 12
which began with Mary's saying, in a tone of great P III 7 57 17
18
It was Mary's hope and belief, that he had received a P III 10 82 2
When she could command Mary's attention, Anne quietly P III 12 106 18
Mary's face was clouded directly. P IV 2 130 4
This decision checked Mary's eagerness, and stopped her P IV 2 133 24
very recently, (since Mary's last letter to herself) P IV 10 217 20
on Mary's account) would not be the smallest impediment. P IV 10 224 52
53
of a Tandem, little Mary's young eyes distinguished the S 12 425 1

MARYS (1)
Charles ii., with all the Marys and Elizabeths they had P III 1 3 3
4

MASCULINE (1)
She must have too masculine & bold a temper.-- W 318 2

MASS (2)
"You decide on his imperfections so much in the mass," SS I 10 51 27
such an heterogeneous mass of hearers, on subjects limited, MP III 3 341 28

MASSY (3)
door being only secured by massy bars and a padlock, you NA II 5 159 19
to afford a glimpse of its massy walls of grey stone, NA II 5 161 24
the convent, rich in the massy walls and smoke of former NA II 8 183 3

MASTER (59)
The master of the ceremonies introduced to her a very NA I 3 25 2
the rest for a minute; but he will soon know his master. NA I 9 62 9
of his master for ever, if not his place, by her rapidity. NA I 13 103 27
He knows what he is about, and must be his own master." NA II 4 150 6
peculiarly to the master of the house, and made unusually NA II 11 213 21
hour before they were joined by the master of the house.-- W 322 3
preceded by the attentive master of the inn to open a door W 329 9
master wants to know why he be'nt to have his dinner."-- W 346 21
The master of the house heard with real sorrow that they PP I 12 59 3
He is his own master. PP I 21 117 14
about Netherfield and its master, she could not help PP II 1 134 4
5
more, and could have the advantage of a London master. PP II 8 176 27
28
But I was not then master enough of myself to know what PP II 12 202 5
her master were really absent, but had not courage for it. PP III 1 246 8
of the miniatures, "is my master--and very like him. PP III 1 247 11
to increase on this intimation of her knowing her master. PP III 1 247 13
present from my master; she comes here to-morrow with him." PP III 1 248 22
great pleasure in talking of her master and his sister. PP III 1 248 23
"Is your master much at Pemberley in the course of the PP III 1 248 24
"If your master would marry, you might see more of him." PP III 1 248 27
You are lucky in having such a master." PP III 1 249 32
commendation of her master, soon led again to the subject; PP III 1 249 37
"He is the best landlord, and the best master," said she, " PP III 1 249 38
As a brother, a landlord, a master, she considered how PP III 1 250 48
on beholding his master, must immediately have told it. PP III 1 251 52
But he is a liberal master, I suppose, and that in the eye PP III 1 258 74
She wished, she feared that the master of the house might PP III 3 268 5
to fetch his master and mistress home, instantly. PP III 4 276 8
of their journey, and brought its master back to Longbourn. PP III 6 298 15
there is an express come for master from Mr. Gardiner! PP III 7 301 3
He has been here this half hour, and master has had a PP III 7 301 4
my master, ma'am, he is walking towards the little copse." PP III 7 301 4
5
for the arrival of her master, who was coming down in a PP III 11 331 13
"If the master and mistress do not attend themselves, MP I 9 87 14
than in him who was now master of the house; and who MP I 13 123 6
he resumed his seat as master of the house at dinner, he MP II 2 190 9
made himself thoroughly master of the subject, or had in MP II 6 232 13
particulars, he was soon master of; and with such a secret MP III 3 334 3
But he was master at Mansfield Park. MP III 6 370 14
on the north, that I will be master of my own property. MP III 11 411 20
easily felt by you, who have always been your own master. E I 18 145 11
he went, and how full the master of the ceremonies' ball E II 1 156 5
they heard that neither "master nor mistress was at home;" E II 5 187 5
of that sort his master had; he had brought them all--and E II 9 239 51
all--and now his master had not one left to bake or boil. E II 9 239 51
so pleased to think his master had sold so many; for E II 9 239 51
She could not bear that her master should not be able to E II 9 239 51
any thing without the concurrence of my Lord and master. E II 16 296 36
and where the same master teaches, it is natural enough. E II 16 297 45
but the truth is, that I am waiting for my Lord and master. E III 16 455 20
21
You knew I should not stir till my Lord and master E III 16 457 36
not find his master at home, but I did not believe him.-- E III 16 458 43
He did not know what was come to his master lately, he E III 16 458 43
They came; the master of the house was not at home, but P III 6 48 17
She hoped, on turning her head, to see the master of the P III 9 79 25
Both master and man being in mourning, assisted the idea. P III 12 104 7
family; but he said his master was a very rich gentleman, P III 12 106 15
lingering and long-petted master Harry, sent to school P IV 1 121 3
summoned to attend their master--to say nothing of all the S 1 364 1

MASTER BLAKE (1)
"I am not going to dance with Master Blake sir." W 334 13

MASTER'S (8)
When the butler would have lit his master's candle, NA II 8 187 15
to shew, and the master's ability to support it. SS II 12 233 18
Nanny came in with her master's Bason of gruel, he had the W 359 28
the son of her late master's steward, who had been brought PP III 1 247 9
"I have heard much of your master's fine person," said Mrs. PP III 1 247 12
This room was my late master's favourite room, and these PP III 1 247 18
and is glad to catch at the old writing master's son." E I 8 64 47
know, thinks more of his master's profit than any thing; E II 9 239 51

MASTERLY (2)
in the masterly manner which I see so many women's do. PP II 8 175 25
of measures in that masterly style was ill-suited to his S 8 405 2

MASTERS (12)
of masters which brought on the plan of an elopement. LS 17 271 7
for the benefit of masters, but we over-ruled her there. LS 27 296 1
Not all the masters in London could compensate for the LS 27 296 1
be easy if her daughter were not with her, for masters, &c. LS 41 310 3
taken you to town every spring for the benefit of masters." PP II 6 164 24
We were always encouraged to read, and had all the masters PP II 6 165 31
with proper masters, and could want nothing more. MP I 2 20 31
feel a most melancholy difference in the change of masters. MP I 6 52 1
and courtesy, the masters of the ceremonies of life. MP I 9 93 49
full justice to, by the attendance of first-rate masters. E II 2 164 6
the carriage was not his masters own) if the road had not S 1 364 1
ladies, as wanted either masters for finishing their S 11 420 1

MAT (1)
extremely--and there was a mat to step upon--I shall never E III 2 323 19

MATCH (121)
so violently against the match, that I thought it better LS 2 245 1
gentleman's death, be very little benefited by the match. LS 10 257 1
it is my duty to oppose a match, which deep art only could LS 12 261 3
so very eligible a match for Frederica that I have always LS 20 276 5
resolved on the match, from seeing the rapid increase of LS 22 280 1
in desiring the match; & the whole business seemed most LS 22 281 3
He wants to marry her--her mother promotes the match--but LS 23 284 4
as she does, I should not have been anxious for the match." LS 24 288 11
character, to complete the match between my daughter & Sir LS 25 294 5
than now appears, of the match, which the conclusion of LS 41 310 5
is no harm done in the match going off; for it could not NA II 14 236 19
view, it was a match beyond the claims of their daughter. NA II 16 249 2
totally she disregarded her disapprobation of the match. SS I 5 25 3
It would be an excellent match, for he was rich and she SS I 8 36 1
than I do, if you have any reason to expect such a match." SS I 20 114 45
But mama did not think the match good enough for me, SS I 20 116 62
Don't we all know that it must be a match, that they were SS II 7 182 10
It will be all to one a better match for your sister. SS II 8 196 22
an account of the intended match, in a voice so little SS II 8 199 37
by the end of a week that it would not be a match at all. SS II 10 216 15
It is a match that must give universal satisfaction. SS II 11 224 24
settle on him a thousand a-year, if the match takes place. SS II 11 224 28
that she thought to make a match between Edward and some SS III 1 258 7
with all my heart, it will be a match in spite of her. SS III 1 259 7
to him the certain penury that must attend the match. SS III 1 266 38
When Edward's unhappy match takes place, depend upon it SS III 5 296 20
and dissuade him from the match; but it was too late then, SS III 5 299 37
Every body thought it would have been a match." W 316 2
And since then, she has been trying to make some match at W 317 2
I am no match for your arch sallies.--" W 350 24
of fatigue while enumerating the advantages of the match. PP I 18 99 63
and though the man and the match were quite good enough PP I 18 103 77
made it a most eligible match for their daughter, to whom PP I 22 122 3
at all reconciled to the idea of so unsuitable a match. PP I 22 125 18
might be expected from the match, the excellent character PP I 23 126 4
together; and fourthly, that the match might be broken off. PP I 23 127 5
Jane confessed herself a little surprised at the match; PP I 23 127 7
The very mention of any thing concerning the match threw PP I 23 129 16
it is a most eligible match; and be ready to believe, for PP II 1 135 12
"It seems likely to have been a desirable match for Jane," PP II 2 140 6
light, it is certainly a very good match for her." PP II 9 178 15
one of the advantages of the match," cried Elizabeth. PP II 9 179 19
worst objections to the match, made her too angry to have PP II 13 204 1
his wish of forwarding the match with Miss de Bourgh, PP II 18 235 38
So imprudent a match on both sides!-- PP III 4 273 3
of that, they only felt how imprudent a match it must be. PP III 5 290 50
to forward her sister's match, which she had feared to PP III 10 326 3
This match, to which you have the presumption to aspire, PP III 14 354 40
de Bourgh, does not look on the match with a friendly eye." PP III 15 363 17
give her consent to what she termed so disgraceful a match. PP III 15 363 22
But whether she were violently set against the match, or PP III 17 375 27
her father's incredulity, and reconcile him to the match. PP III 17 376 36
And so, Darcy did every thing; made up the match, gave the PP III 17 377 39
really rejoicing in the match, was anxious to get away PP III 18 383 26
All Huntingdon exclaimed on the greatness of the match, MP I 1 3 1
Miss Ward's match, indeed, when it came to the point, was MP I 1 3 1
Mrs. Norris was most zealous in promoting the match, by MP I 4 39 10
to look out for a suitable match for her; she had fixed on MP I 4 42 17
good sort of young man, and it is a great match for her." MP I 5 45 13
And what do you say, ma'am, to the chance of another match? MP I 12 118 16
Yes, indeed, a very pretty match. MP I 12 118 18
she had made the match--she had done every thing--and no MP II 3 203 30
Such a match as Miss Bertram has made is a public blessing, MP II 4 210 21
She would learn to match him in his indifference. MP II 5 228 69
Mary as soon as she could speak--"what a match for her! MP II 12 292 7
What an amazing match for her! MP II 12 292 7
that it would be a match at last, and that, united by MP III 3 335 6
And yet it was a most desirable match for Janet at the MP III 5 361 16
the match inconsiderately, there was no want of foresight. MP III 5 361 16
inclination for the match; and yet, though she had been so MP III 10 402 11
the dearest off all; the match had been her own contriving, MP III 16 448 1
Julia's match became a less desperate business than he had MP III 17 462 4
It was a match which Sir Thomas's wishes had even MP III 17 471 29
the match; but it was a black morning's work for her. E I 1 6 6
it had been entirely a match of affection, when he was now E I 1 7 10
"and a very considerable one--that I made the match myself. E I 1 11 39
I made the match, you know, four years ago; and to have it E I 1 11 39
I planned the match from that hour; and when such success E I 1 12 41
But if, which I rather imagine, your making the match, as E I 1 12 42
as making such an amazing match, was proved to have much E I 2 16 4
She thought it would be an excellent match; and only too E I 4 34 44
My only scruple in advising the match was on his account, E I 8 61 38
The advantage of the match I felt to be all on her side; E I 8 61 38
her partiality for Harriet, will think this a good match." E I 8 62 38
is nothing more,) a good match for my intimate friend! E I 8 62 39
Highbury, but not at all likely to make an imprudent match. E I 8 66 53

Your marrying will be equal to the match at Randalls. E I 9 75 25
She could not but suppose it to be a match that every body E I 14 119 5
his company, or opinion of the suitableness of the match. E II 2 169 16
In short, I have made a match between Mr. Knightley and E II 8 224 65
I do not want the match--I do not want to injure dear E II 8 224 67
"But the imprudence of such a match!" E II 8 224 70
so beautiful, would still never match her yellow pattern. E II 9 235 35
Harriet would have been a better match. E II 14 272 17
at ease, and incline him to be satisfied with the match. E III 10 400 65
with any view of making a match for her, hereafter, with E III 17 461 1
He saw the advantages of the match, and rejoiced in them E III 17 468 33
In general, it was a very well approved match. E III 17 468 36
"You need not be at any pains to reconcile me to the match. E III 18 473 24
a proper match for Sir Walter Elliot's eldest daughter. P III 1 8 17
make a degrading match; but he might be rendered unhappy. P III 5 35 14
Russell, that a more equal match might have greatly P III 6 43 5
here I am, Sophia, quite ready to make a foolish match. P III 7 61 38
39
"It would not be a great match for her; but if Henrietta P III 9 74 6
Oh! it would be a capital match for either of his sisters." P III 9 75 10
think him at all a fit match for Henrietta; and P III 9 75 13
A most improper match for Miss Musgrove, of Uppercross." P III 9 76 13
"It would not be a great match for Henrietta, but Charles P III 9 76 15
would be a very shocking match for Henrietta, and indeed P III 9 76 15
"Certainly not a great match for Louisa Musgrove; but a " P IV 6 165 8
it appears--I should hope it would be a very happy match. P IV 8 182 7
Where can you look for a more suitable match? P IV 9 196 30
were designing a match between the heir and the young lady; P IV 9 201 59
was impossible that such a match should have answered his P IV 9 201 59
strenuous opposer of Sir Walter's making a second match. P IV 9 208 92
Mary does not above half like Henrietta's match. P IV 10 218 22
It is a very fair match, as times go; and I have liked P IV 10 218 22
the horrible eligibilities and proprieties of the match! P IV 11 244 72
was very far from thinking it a bad match for her. P IV 12 248 2
the other of them being a match for every disorder, of the S 2 373 1
Her motives for such a match could be little understood at S 3 375 1

MATCH-MAKER (1)
"I am no match-maker, as you well know," said Lady Russell, P IV 5 159 23

MATCH-MAKING (6)
you cannot think that I shall leave off match-making." E I 1 12 41
secret of your love of match-making, it is fair to suppose E I 8 66 51
I have done with match-making indeed. E I 8 66 54
own affection in some better method than by match-making. E I 17 142 10
My dear Mrs. Weston, do not take to match-making. E II 8 225 72
You have scolded me too much for match-making, for me to E II 15 288 35

MATCHED (2)
of Isabella's having matched some fine netting-cotton, on NA II 10 201 5
and she found herself well matched in a partner. E II 8 230 100

MATCHES (7)
sums; of racing matches, in which his judgment had NA I 9 66 31
I wish you would not make matches and foretel things, for E I 1 12 40
Pray do not make any more matches." E I 1 12 40
"But, my dear, pray do not make any more matches, they are E I 1 13 45
taken place, there have been matches of greater disparity. E III 4 342 39
that there had been matches of greater disparity (those E III 11 406 18
things had happened, matches of greater disparity had E III 11 407 28

MATERIAL (57)
Lady Susan's age is itself a material objection, but her LS 12 260 2
I hope he has not had any material share in bringing on Mr. NA II 10 204 20
material passages of her letter with strong indignation. NA II 12 218 4
relaxation of anger, or any material digression of thought. NA II 14 238 22
This was so material an amendment of his late expectations, NA II 16 251 6
"That is a material consideration undoubtedly. SS I 2 13 27
its favour which was of material service in recommending SS I 6 28 2
Willoughby was not very material; but any testimony in his SS I 20 116 59
of her expecting material advantage to Marianne, from the SS II 9 211 33
any particular, any material superiority by nature, merely SS II 14 250 12
all things, the most material to her interest, and such an SS II 14 254 26
believed there was no material danger in Fanny's SS III 1 269 57
not think that any material objection;--and Mrs. Jennings SS III 3 281 9
One day's delay will not be very material; and till I have SS III 4 286 15
the moment, without any material loss of happiness to SS III 4 292 54
often by her better experience in nursing, of material use. SS III 7 308 3
allow the danger to be material, and talked of the relief SS III 7 312 19
the last day must have material weight in confirming or PP I 12 60 4
so material a step without her ladyship's concurrence." PP I 22 123 8
Mr. Wickham's society was of material service in PP II 1 138 30
but she could see it and write of it without material pain. PP II 3 149 28
objections there had material weight with Mr. Darcy, whose PP II 10 187 40
received soon afterwards material relief, from observing PP III 11 337 56
had undergone so material a change, since the period to PP III 16 366 8
was no longer any thing material to be dreaded, and the PP III 17 377 41
Kitty, to her very material advantage, spent the chief of PP III 19 385 4
paper and every other material, and you may write your MP I 2 16 13
This will be a material gain. MP I 16 155 16
With no material fault of temper, or difference of opinion, MP I 17 162 19
Their departure made another material change at Mansfield, MP II 3 204 33
they now were without material inconvenience; but his MP II 7 246 37
in her power, without material inconvenience just at that MP II 13 304 19
The intimacy thus begun between them was a material MP III 9 398 9
does me good), one very material thing I had to say from MP III 12 416 3
would have a material drawback in leaving Susan behind. MP III 12 419 9
To be at an early certainty is a material object. MP III 13 422 2
bear the removal without material inconvenience or injury. MP III 13 426 11
it would have been a material drawback, to be owing such MP III 14 435 15
but this, though most material to herself, would be poor MP III 16 452 14
her, on the very material matrimonial point of submitting E I 5 38 11
the change being so very material to Hartfield as you E I 11 94 15
"A material difference then," she replied--"and no doubt E I 12 99 7
of removal, or of effecting any material change of society. E I 17 143 14
mortifying change, and material loss to them all;--a very E II 8 228 87
any description, and no material injury accrue either to E II 11 247 1
as was the letter in the material part, its sentiments, E II 13 266 6
To Highbury in general it brought no material change. E III 5 343 1
I am thwarted in every thing material. E III 6 365 64
on one point, the one material point, I am sincerely E III 10 398 53
been made a subject of material distress to the delicacy E III 12 421 17
the feelings are not, it may not be very material.-- E III 13 431 39
Two material advantages of Bath over London had of course P III 2 14 10
by one part, and a very material part of the scheme, which P III 2 15 13
made a material difference in their degree of consequence. P III 9 74 5
which made a material difference in the discredit of it. P IV 3 139 8
time had worked a very material change in Mr. Elliot's P IV 9 206 90
and of circumventing the lady if he found it material. P IV 9 207 90

MATERIALLY (25)
Lady Susan had heard something so materially to the LS 14 264 3
as would make their meeting materially painful. NA II 13 222 8
But (with a smile) you would be materially benefited in SS I 19 102 3
that disposition is not materially altered by a change of SS II 5 170 29
but in the end may prove materially advantageous.-- SS II 11 226 42
for I assure you I no longer suffer materially myself. SS III 1 263 27
Donavan says there is nothing materially to be apprehended; SS III 1 265 36
Harris arrived, he declared his patient materially better. SS III 7 310 8
Marianne was in every respect materially better, and he SS III 7 314 23
"But it must very materially lessen their chance of PP I 8 37 19
opinion of him must be materially affected by the PP II 1 134 3
and reflected how materially the credit of both must be PP II 13 209 11
Lambton friends, that could materially lessen its weight. PP III 2 264 14
cause where her peace of mind must be materially concerned. PP III 10 326 3
the hope of her being materially better for change of air. MP I 1 11 19
and she was no longer materially afraid to appear before MP I 2 17 21
It must have injured the piece materially; but I was MP I 13 122 2
She was not so materially cast down, however, but that a E I 8 67 56
an accidental division, but it never materially varied. E III 7 367 1
I think we shall never materially disagree about the E III 14 436 7
"You are materially changed since we talked on this E III 18 474 32
It did not appear to him that Sir Walter could materially P III 2 13 7
not materially disfigured by a few, but he abominates them. P III 5 35 14
man at hand wd very materially promote the rise & S 2 372 1
man, the smallest very materially of not a robust family, S 10 413 1

MATERIALS (3)
her materials without knowing what in the world to say! MP II 13 307 30
talking of, Harville, now, if you will give me materials." P IV 11 229 2
3
Materials were all at hand, on a separate table; he went P IV 11 229 4

MATERNAL (16)
the sacred impulse of maternal affection, it was the LS 2 245 1
mothers, she is accused of wanting maternal tenderness. LS 14 265 5
Lady Susan's maternal fears were then too much awakened LS 42 312 6
When the hour of departure drew near, the maternal anxiety NA I 2 18 2
to listen to all these maternal effusions, consoling NA I 4 32 2
of politeness or maternal affection on the side of the SS I 3 14 3
She saw with maternal complacency all the impertinent SS I 21 120 6
They are descended on the maternal side, from the same PP III 14 356 50
Happy for all her maternal feelings was the day on which PP III 19 385 1
there is something so maternal in her manner, so MP I 18 169 21
so completely maternal in her voice and countenance.' MP I 18 169 21
all the rest of her maternal solicitude, alternately her MP III 8 389 4
and never was there any maternal tenderness to buy her off. MP III 9 396 5
artless, maternal gratitude, which could not be unpleasing. MP III 10 400 6
The real solicitude now awakened in the maternal bosom was MP III 13 427 13
that in spite of maternal solicitude for the immediate E I 11 92 3

MATHEMATICIAN (1)
could even a mathematician have seen what she did, have E III 3 335 9

MATILDA (1)
memoirs of the wretched Matilda may fall'--when your lamp NA II 5 160 21

MATILDA'S (1)
her to use her own fancy in the perusal of Matilda's woes. NA II 5 160 23

MATLOCK (2)
beauties of Matlock, Chatsworth, Dovedale, or the peak. PP II 19 239 7
talked of Matlock and Dove Dale with great perseverance. PP III 1 257 66

MATRIMONIAL (10)
I am suspected of matrimonial veiws in my behaviour to her. LS 14 263 1
"Pray, my dear aunt, what is the difference in matrimonial PP II 4 153 9
Nobody can think more highly of the matrimonial state than MP I 4 43 23
the most advantageous matrimonial establishment that could MP II 7 238 1
uncle too well to consult him on any matrimonial scheme. MP II 12 292 9
am thoroughly convinced, friendly to matrimonial happiness. MP III 4 349 23
This seems as if nothing were a security for matrimonial MP III 5 361 16
to the world, a matrimonial fracas in the family of Mr. R. MP III 15 440 14
on the very material matrimonial point of submitting your E I 5 38 11
defies anticipation in matrimonial affairs, giving E II 2 165 7

MATRIMONY (33)
doubt if I could resist even matrimony offered by him. LS 39 308 1
"And such is your definition of matrimony and dancing. NA I 10 77 33
I am glad you are no enemy to matrimony however. NA I 15 122 32
But thirty-five has nothing to do with matrimony." SS I 8 37 8
better not have any thing to do with matrimony together. SS I 8 37 9
like yours can have little inclination for matrimony."-- W 317 2
admiration to love, from love to matrimony in a moment. PP I 6 27 52
myself) to set the example of matrimony in his parish. PP I 19 105 9
10
Thus much for my general intention in favour of matrimony; PP I 19 106 10
Without thinking highly either of men or of matrimony, PP I 22 122 3
She had always felt that Charlotte's opinion of matrimony PP I 22 125 18
that I had two daughters on the brink of matrimony. PP III 15 362 10
was beginning to think matrimony a duty; and as a marriage MP I 4 38 10
Matrimony was her object, provided she could marry well, MP I 4 42 18
You have been in a bad school for matrimony, in Hill MP I 5 46 21
being prepared for matrimony by an hatred of home, MP II 3 202 26
in life--ordination and matrimony--events of such a MP II 8 254 10
and worldly notions of matrimony, would be forwarding any MP II 13 306 26
can judge, matrimony makes no part of his plans or thought. MP III 1 317 34
He was to be describing and recommending matrimony to me. MP III 5 358 9
marriage state, matrimony may be called a happy life.' MP III 5 358 9
would be finally wasted on her even in years of matrimony. MP III 6 367 5
judgment as to matrimony and celibacy, and say, that MP III 8 392 12
could attract him into matrimony again, and he might set MP III 17 464 12
but little removed by matrimony, being settled in London, E I 1 7 9
Matrimony, as the origin of change, was always E I 1 7 10
I do not recommend matrimony at present to Emma, though I E I 5 41 30
a greater advocate for matrimony than I am; and if it had E I 11 95 19
I have no thoughts of matrimony at present." E I 15 132 36
Happily he was not farther from approving matrimony than E II 5 193 35
I always say this is quite one of the evils of matrimony." E II 14 273 19
"But, my dear papa, you are no friend to matrimony; and E II 14 280 57
She must be allowed to be a favourer of matrimony you know, P IV 9 208 92

MATTER (208)
of a matter which we foresaw would make him so uneasy. LS 13 262 1
I instantly followed, & asked her what was the matter. LS 20 275 1
of so important a matter took from me the power of LS 20 277 6
I beleive he does not know what to make of the matter. LS 20 278 9
Instantly saw that something was the matter; his LS 23 283 3
& sat with him in his room, talking over the whole matter. LS 24 285 2
With a heart full of the matter, Mrs Vernon waited on Lady LS 42 311 2
of which either the matter or manner would not disgust a NA I 5 38 4
for you are not to know any thing at all of the matter." NA I 8 57 18
immediately made the matter perfectly simple by assuring NA I 9 62 10
some time to consider the matter as entirely decided, and NA I 9 65 27
By him the whole matter seemed entirely forgotten; and all NA I 9 66 31
five minutes, she would give up the matter as hopeless. NA I 11 83 14
them, made his friend pull up, to know what was the matter. NA I 11 88 54
"well, I have settled the matter, and now we may all go to- NA I 13 100 13
He should make a point of inquiring into the matter." NA I 13 103 27
very few notions she had entertained on the matter before. NA I 14 110 28
"Thank you; but it is quite a matter of indifference to me. NA I 14 115 54
of her friend on a matter of the utmost importance, NA I 15 116 1
it is not a little matter that puts me out of temper." NA I 15 117 3
a matter in which her disinterested spirit took no concern. NA I 15 122 28
No matter which has it, so that there is enough. NA I 15 124 47
in love with her, was a matter of lively astonishment. NA II 3 148 29
respect that Eleanor should know nothing of the matter. NA II 9 192 5
but no matter--it is your dear brother's favourite colour. NA II 12 218 2
heaven! what can be the matter?" it was quickly decided by NA II 13 222 7
actual ill-will, was a matter which they were at least as NA II 14 234 10
any thing else, it is no matter now; Catherine is safe at NA II 14 234 12
she draws, that in fact he knows nothing of the matter. SS I 3 17 18
I suppose it would be no difficult matter to widen them. SS I 6 29 4
the country was always a matter of joy to him, and in SS I 7 33 3
Willoughby's opinion in almost every matter of importance. SS I 10 47 4
day, which placed this matter in a still clearer light. SS I 12 60 8
which had been long a matter of great curiosity to her, SS I 12 61 15
"What is the matter with brandon?" said Sir John. SS I 13 63 4
"Something very melancholy must be the matter, I am sure," SS I 14 70 2
"Is any thing the matter with her?" cried Mrs. Dashwood as SS I 15 75 3
that I have never considered this matter as certain. SS I 15 80 41
youth, and urged the matter farther, but in vain; common SS I 16 85 10
and no assurance, you may find it a difficult matter." SS I 17 90 4
know much more of the matter than I do, if you have any SS I 20 114 45
Our first care has been to keep the matter secret.-- SS I 22 131 32
be better for us both, to break off the matter entirely." SS I 22 133 44
suspect what was the matter; but it made him so melancholy, SS I 22 134 52
readiness to enter on the matter again, and her calmness SS II 1 141 7
of the family, it is a matter of perfect indifference to SS II 3 157 17

and care; nor was it a matter of pleasure merely to her. SS II 3 157 19
With regard to herself, it was now a matter of unconcern SS II 3 158 20
This decided the matter at once. SS II 4 161 5
for heaven's sake tell me, what is the matter?" SS II 6 177 10
week or two, for this matter I suppose has been hanging SS II 8 195 16
But it was a matter of great consolation to her, that what SS II 10 214 7
a word of the matter; and having thus supported the SS II 10 215 14
But, my dear Elinor, what is the matter with Marianne?-- SS II 11 227 48
day, that it was become a matter of indifference to her, SS II 14 249 7
This is the way in which I always consider the matter, and SS II 14 251 13
short of the matter, by all I can learn, seems to be this. SS III 1 258 7
And not a creature knowing a syllable of the matter except SS III 1 258 7
suspected a word of the matter;--till this very morning, SS III 1 258 7
present to consider the matter, the consolation that I SS III 1 264 29
But though so much of the matter was known to them already, SS III 2 270 3
to the matter directly, and leave him to shift for himself. SS III 2 273 16
what little matter Mr. Steele and Mr. Pratt can give her.-- SS III 2 276 28
This set the matter beyond a doubt. SS III 3 281 9
for if I understand the matter right, he has been entirely SS III 3 282 17
"It is a matter of great joy to me; and I feel the SS III 4 285 2
mind is too full of the matter to care for company; and SS III 4 286 11
And how came he not to have settled that matter before SS III 5 295 12
You will not mention the matter to Fanny, however, for SS III 5 295 16
The matter itself I could not deny, and vain was every SS III 8 323 40
dreadful; and to heighten the matter, I found her alone. SS III 8 324 42
"You consider the matter," said Elinor, "exactly as a good SS III 11 350 9
But so little interest had he taken in the matter, that he SS III 13 368 31
Not a soul suspected anything of the matter, not even SS III 13 370 37
that one or two interviews would settle the matter. SS III 14 376 11
This matter was settled, & they went to dinner.-- W 324 4
chairs, it might have seemed a matter scarcely perceived.-- W 336 14
9, as he observed, was a matter of very little consequence. W 356 28
him amends for his kindness; or me either, for that matter. PP I 2 8 26
Happiness in marriage is entirely a matter of chance. PP I 6 23 10
it, I shall consider the matter as absolutely settled. PP I 6 27 53
there is not much the matter with me. PP I 7 31 30
thought no more of the matter: and their indifference PP I 8 35 1
and never open their mouths, quite mistake the matter." PP I 9 44 27
"Upon my word I cannot exactly explain the matter, Darcy PP I 10 50 33
It was necessary to make this circumstance a matter of PP I 18 99 63
This matter may be considered, therefore, as finally PP I 19 107 16
more interest than the matter had ever excited before, how PP I 22 122 3
houses, he unfolded the matter,--to an audience not merely PP I 23 126 1
2
the whole of the matter; secondly, she was very sure that PP I 23 127 5
was no longer a matter of pleasure to Mrs. Bennet. PP I 23 128 11
Mr. Bennet treated the matter differently. PP II 1 137 27
Mr. Darcy before they had known any thing of the matter. PP II 1 138 30
and then they soon found out what was the matter." PP II 16 221 17
I am sure you could not treat the matter as you do now." PP II 17 226 18
It settled the matter; and they pursued the accustomed PP III 1 253 57
Of Mr. Darcy it was now a matter of anxiety to think well; PP III 2 264 14
but as it was a matter of confidence one cannot wonder. PP III 4 275 5
"Good God! what is the matter?" cried he, with more PP III 4 276 7
"There is nothing the matter with me. PP III 4 276 10
I was to judge as your eldest sister does of the matter. PP III 5 282 1
little about it, as any father could do, in such a matter." PP III 5 283 8
of marrying, do not let us give the matter over as lost. PP III 5 288 37
did, she very innocently said, "what is the matter mamma? PP III 13 345 11
had been concerned in the matter; and, of course, I could PP III 16 366 5
"You know nothing of the matter. PP III 17 373 7
his love for you, and there will be an end of the matter." PP III 17 377 39
thinking no more of the matter: but Mrs. Norris had a MP I 1 4 1
I look to in any little matter I may ever have to bestow, MP I 1 6 6
and what was begun as a matter of prudence, soon grew into MP I 1 8 9
soon grew into a matter of choice, as an object of that MP I 1 8 9
it would be a different matter: she should then be glad to MP I 1 9 10
of such a companion, as a matter of very serious moment; MP I 1 10 14
of an excellent nature, "what can be the matter?" MP I 2 15 10
Lady Bertram soon brought the matter to a certainty, by MP I 3 28 38
39
it every where as a matter not to be talked of at present. MP I 4 39 12
sort, it will be a fresh matter of delight to me, to find MP I 4 42 21
and liveliness, to put the matter by for the present. MP I 6 57 32
matter, and had no active kindness in comparison of Edmund. MP I 7 67 16
others, to secure it, the matter was settled by Mrs. MP I 8 80 29
I am a very matter of fact, plain spoken being, and may MP I 9 94 56
it be a German play, no matter what, with a good tricking, MP I 13 124 10
"What is the matter?" asked her ladyship in the heavy tone MP I 13 126 22
No matter what, so that something is chosen. MP I 14 131 5
but the manner was lost in the matter of Julia's feelings. MP I 14 133 12
knew any thing of the matter; but when he entered the MP I 15 138 2
"I am sorry for it," was his answer--"but in this matter MP I 15 140 13
grace, and let us hear no more of the matter, I entreat." MP I 15 146 53
matter whom; the look of a gentleman is to be enough. MP I 16 155 22
Sleeping or waking, my head has been full of this matter MP I 16 156 27
obliged to yield--no matter--it was all misery now. MP I 16 157 28
but as it was not a matter which really involved her MP I 17 161 9
Fanny--and that is the long and the short of the matter. MP II 3 197 8
perhaps to urge the matter quite so far as his judgment MP II 3 201 22
engaged apart in some matter of business with Dr. Grant, MP II 5 224 49
and having thought the matter over and taken his MP II 8 252 1
evening, it had been as a matter of course that Edmund MP II 10 275 11
cannot think what is the matter with me!" said Lady MP II 11 283 5
all interference, he shall know nothing of the matter. MP II 12 293 10
so much as if it were a matter of course that she was not MP II 12 296 31
its sufficiency, began to take the matter in another point. MP II 13 305 23
without her being obliged to know any thing of the matter. MP III 1 311 3
as he considered the matter with more impartiality, and MP III 1 324 58
With him, it is entirely a matter of feeling; he claims no MP III 2 330 14
a little of the matter, and who can judge and criticize." MP III 3 340 23
But the matter does not end here. MP III 4 347 18
Mrs. Norris was left to settle the matter by herself; and MP III 6 373 23
But no matter--here's Fanny in the parlour, and why should MP III 7 378 12
deliberately, to supply matter for much reflection, and to MP III 12 417 4
I must think this matter over a little. MP III 13 423 2
so that a very little matter was enough for her; she could MP III 13 425 6
have breathed--was afterwards matter of wonder to herself. MP III 15 440 16
indeed a matter of certified guilt and public exposure. MP III 15 441 21
"And you have forgotten one matter of joy to me," said E I 1 11 39
intimacy being made a matter of much discussion among you. E I 5 40 24
"What is the matter, sir?-- E I 12 103 41
in this carriage we know nothing of the matter.-- E I 13 115 37
say, has been telling you exactly how the matter stands." E I 14 121 14
supplied them with fresh matter for thought and E I 17 141 4
but undoubtedly he could know very little of the matter. E II 5 191 28
whole village, and found matter of commendation and E II 6 196 2
taste, but I know nothing of the matter myself.-- E II 6 201 28
There was no occasion to press the matter farther. E II 8 219 43
"What is the matter?" said she. E II 8 222 55
a boy of six years old, who knows nothing of the matter?" E II 8 224 67
of the matter, and had no voice at all, roundly asserted. E II 8 227 86
the spirit of cutting the matter short, she believed it to E II 8 228 88
"What is the matter now?" E II 10 245 51
proceeded so far, one is unwilling to give the matter up. E II 11 250 18
Go and fetch Miss Bates, and let us end the matter at once. E II 11 255 55
This is a matter of mere common politeness and good- E II 14 280 60
Letters are no matter of indifference; they are generally E II 16 293 19
any thing the matter with them, while dear Emma were gone. E III 1 318 13
dwindled soon into a matter of little importance but to E III 3 336 13
Henceforward I know nothing of the matter. E III 4 342 39
"It is too much a matter of fact, but here it is.-- E III 7 371 32
But what can be the matter?-- E III 10 392 5
This, though very undesirable, would be no matter of agony E III 10 393 18
"I have escaped; and that I should escape, may be a matter E III 10 396 44
And here, instead of its being a matter of condolence, it E III 10 400 68
and every surprise must be matter of humiliation to her.-- E III 11 411 43
on this important matter--which was most probable--still, E III 12 421 17
"but as it seems a matter of justice, it shall be done." E III 15 444 5
to day; and it becomes a matter, therefore, of very E III 16 458 43
to life, and make it no matter of indifference to her when P III 1 4 6
almost all the time they were talking the matter over. P III 3 22 24
when any thing was the matter, was indisposed; and P III 5 33 7
unwell and out of spirits, was almost a matter of course. P III 5 36 21
I was very well yesterday; nothing at all the matter with P III 5 39 37
he would not think there was any thing the matter with me. P III 6 44 7
Anne will send for me if any thing is the matter." P III 7 55 8
matter; but I dare say there will be nothing to alarm you. P III 7 57 16
her sister aside, seemed to be arguing the matter warmly. P III 10 85 16
conjecture, steady and matter of fact as I may call myself. P IV 2 132 20
but her courtesies and smiles were more a matter of course. P IV 3 137 3
be very sure is a matter of perfect indifference to them." P IV 4 151 18
willing to leave the matter to its own operation; and P IV 5 160 26
protests solemnly that she knew nothing of "matter. P IV 6 165 8
the Elliots as a mere matter of form, and not in the least P IV 6 168 24
But now, the matter has taken the strangest turn of all; P IV 6 171 33
matter might add another shade of prejudice against him. P IV 7 178 27
I see you know nothing of the matter. P IV 8 186 26
She felt that something must be the matter. P IV 8 190 47
quarter, that it became a matter of course the next P IV 11 229 1
I little thought then--but no matter. P IV 11 232 15
gravely answered "I really know nothing of the matter.-- S 7 398 1
He & I often talk that matter over.-- S 7 400 1
in the reports of each made that matter quite certain. S 10 419 1

MATTER-OF-FACT (2)

Her own family were plain matter-of-fact people, who NA I 9 65 31
and will be soon followed by matter-of-fact prose." E I 9 74 23

MATTERS (67)

Could matters have been so arranged as to prevent the LS 5 249 1
I have sent Charles to town to make matters up if he can, LS 16 268 1
Artlessness will never do in love matters, & that girl is LS 19 274 3
Our prospect is most delightful; & since matters have now LS 23 283 1
Send me your opinion on all these matters, my dear Alicia, LS 25 294 7
I wish matters did not go so perversely. LS 38 307 3
and when all these matters were arranged, the important NA I 2 20 8
After chatting some time on such matters as naturally NA I 3 25 2
rest, and other family matters, now passed between them, NA I 7 51 54
"neither desires nor dares to interfere in such matters. NA I 14 112 35
you and I think pretty much alike upon most matters." NA I 15 124 44
And as to most matters, to say the truth, there are not NA I 15 124 45
Though careless enough in most matters of eating, he loved NA II 7 178 21
In revolving these matters, while she undressed, it NA II 8 188 17
disposition in such matters misunderstood by his children. NA II 11 208 1
for; and other family matters occurring to detain her, a NA II 15 241 7
He distrusts his own judgment in such matters so much, SS I 4 19 2
I do think he must have been sent for about money matters, SS I 14 70 2
or conform to their judgment in serious matters?" SS I 17 94 39
my head, for bringing matters to bear; indeed I am bound SS II 2 149 25
a little, and settle my matters; for it is a long while SS II 4 163 14
would have been ready to wait till matters came round. SS II 8 194 10
with many particulars of preparations and other matters. SS II 8 199 37
one another; but that matters should be brought so forward SS III 1 258 7
offered even, when matters grew desperate, to make it SS III 1 266 38
far beyond the necessity of regarding little matters." PP I 16 83 50
excellent judgment in all matters within the scope of your PP I 18 97 60
61
"Lizzy is only headstrong in such matters as these. PP I 20 111 5
But in matters of greater weight, I may suffer from the PP II 10 183 12
on indifferent matters till they reached the parsonage. PP II 10 186 38
and all money matters were then to receive the last finish. PP III 10 324 2
Imprudence or thoughtlessness in money matters, would be PP III 13 348 39
Young ladies have great penetration in such matters as PP III 15 362 12
proposal; and, as soon as matters are settled, I will MP I 1 7 8
At the white house, matters must be better looked after. MP I 3 30 50
I have no eye or ingenuity for such matters, but as they MP I 6 57 29
come to you to know what I am to think of public matters." MP I 12 119 22
the general little matters of the company, superintending MP I 17 163 21
in peace over domestic matters of a calmer hue; but Mr. MP II 1 184 25
With such matters to ponder over, and arrange, and re- MP II 8 256 13
and learn from him exactly how matters stand between you. MP III 2 330 14
situation of matters at Mansfield were known to him. MP III 3 334 4
Were I even careless in general on such matters, how could MP III 4 347 14
together and discussing matters of equal and never-failing MP III 10 403 15
Others had their hour; and of lesser matters, none MP III 12 419 8
I don't know what Sir Thomas may think of such matters; he MP III 15 439 13
matters, it might not have come to any thing after all. E I 1 13 43
She was a great talker upon little matters, which exactly E I 3 21 4
of all those little matters of which the daily happiness E I 14 117 1
indifferent judge of such matters in general, and very E I 17 142 11
Having arranged all these matters, looked them through, E III 3 332 3
till she is in being, I will manage such matters myself." E III 6 355 17
This discovery laid many smaller matters open. E III 11 403 2
than by saying--"those matters will take care of E III 17 467 31
"These matters are always a secret, till it is found out E III 17 468 34
should dictate its own matters of discourse; and hoped, P III 6 43 3
How was Anne to set all these matters to rights? P III 6 46 11
of attending to such matters, so unobservant and incurious P III 6 51 31
There was a very general ignorance of all naval matters P III 8 64 4
calculated for making matters easy--Charles Hayter, P III 9 79 25
as well as in other matters; and sounds are quite P IV 2 135 33
careless on all serious matters; and, though he might now P IV 5 161 27
You are safe in all wordly matters, and safe in his P IV 9 196 32
will come to care about such matters herself in time. S 6 393 1
Matters are altered with me since last summer you know--. S 7 401 1
& scrupulous on all those matters more on account of a S 9 409 1
I know how little it suits you to be pressing matters upon S 12 425 1

MATTING (1)

up--quantities of matting--my dear Jane, indeed you must. E III 2 328 45

MATURE (3)

of the most advanced reason and mature time of life. NA I 14 109 25
Elizabeth, "and if upon mature deliberation, you find that PP I 21 119 24
that Mr. Elliot, at a mature time of life, should feel it P IV 4 147 7

MATURITY (1)

with the advantage of maturity of mind, consciousness of P IV 12 248 1

MAXIM (2)

defence of your favorite maxim, that no one can ever be in SS I 17 93 29
down with the true London maxim, that every thing is to be MP I 6 58 39

MAXIMS (3)

for it is one of my maxims always to buy a good horse when NA I 10 76 28
to counteract, by her conduct, her most favourite maxims. SS III 14 378 15
I was afraid of the bias of those worldly maxims, which MP III 4 351 36

MAYORALTY (1)

knighthood by an address to the king, during the mayoralty. PP I 5 18 1

MAYST (1)

thou--whomsoever thou mayst be, into whose hands these NA II 5 160 21

MEADOW (5)

walk round two sides of a meadow, on which Henry's genius NA II 11 214 25
road; and in Dr. Grant's meadow she immediately saw the MP I 7 67 16
She could not turn her eyes from the meadow, she could not MP I 7 67 16
seeing the party in the meadow disperse, and Miss Crawford MP I 7 68 17
This long meadow bordered a lane, which their footpath, at P III 10 90 38

MEADOW-LAND (1)

In a long strip of meadow-land, where there was ample P III 10 90 37

MEADOWS (13)

The house stands among fine meadows facing the southeast, NA II 7 175 15
though only over green meadows; and she expressed her NA II 11 213 21
A saunter into other meadows, and through part of the NA II 11 214 26
and snug--with rich meadows and several neat farm houses SS I 18 97 4
led them round his two meadows, but the ladies not having PP II 5 156 5
reckoning the water meadows; so that I think, if so much MP I 6 55 17
The meadows beyond what will be the garden, as well as MP II 7 242 23
very pretty meadows they are, finely sprinkled with timber. MP II 7 242 23
through the home meadows, I cannot conceive any difficulty. E I 12 106 61
stretching down to meadows washed by a stream, of which E III 6 358 35
the Abbey-Mill Farm, with meadows in front, and the river E III 6 360 38
seen wandering about the meadows, at some distance from E III 9 391 21
in the garden, orchard & meadows which are the best S 4 379 1

MEAGERNESS (1)
her aunt Norris in the meagerness and cheerlessness of her MP II 11 282 3

MEAL (17)
laugh indulged, every meal a scene of ease and good-humour, NA II 13 220 1
As this was a favourite meal with Mrs. Jennings, it lasted SS II 7 181 7
As their quietly-sociable little meal concluded, Miss W 343 19
of the nearness of that meal, now jumped up with apologies, W 346 21
calling his next meal a dinner, was quite insupportable.-- W 359 28
very punctual, and short and pleasant had been the meal. MP II 11 282 1
of every family-meeting and every meal chiefly depended. MP II 11 284 8
where a comfortable meal, uniting dinner and supper, wound MP III 7 376 5
thing necessary for the meal; Susan looking as she put the MP III 7 383 32
enough inured to, for her often to make a tolerable meal. MP III 10 407 23
to defer her heartiest meal, till she could send her MP III 11 413 30
He had already ate, and declined staying for their meal. MP III 15 445 29
Fanny's last meal in her father's house was in character MP III 15 445 31
do all the honours of the meal, and help and recommend the E I 3 24 11
he need not eat a single meal by himself if he does not E I 9 75 26
might have obliged them to practise during the meal.-- E II 8 213 6
had a very comfortable meal, and came back all the better-- E III 6 364 59

MEALS (3)
to be careless of their meals, she had never been obliged SS III 11 355 45
two of his daily meals had, for forty years, been crowded. E III 5 347 18
furniture, I think is best observed by meals within doors. E III 6 355 21

MEAN (245)
I mean to win my sister in law's heart through her LS 5 250 2
I do not mean therefore that Frederica's acquirements LS 7 253 1
Your account of Sir James is most satisfactory, & I mean LS 10 258 4
He is only a fool--but what her mother can mean, heaven LS 23 284 4
"What is it that you mean to infer said I, by this LS 24 290 12
& in particular tell me what you mean to do with Manwaring. LS 28 298 2
What do you mean?" NA I 6 42 31
John Thorpe, who in the mean time had been giving orders NA I 7 45 5
"I suppose you mean Camilla?" NA I 7 49 39
besides, I am tired, and do not mean to dance any more." NA I 8 59 36
"What do you mean?" said Catherine, "where are you all NA I 9 61 2
"Oh! Mr. Allen, you mean. NA I 9 63 11
Fletcher and I mean to get a house in Leicestershire, NA I 10 76 28
"Not go!--my beloved creature, what do you mean?" NA I 11 85 31
"What did William mean by it? NA I 13 103 27
"Oh! no, I only mean what I have read about. NA I 14 106 4
"The nicest;--by which I suppose you mean the neatest. NA I 14 107 13
"I am sure," cried Catherine, "I did not mean to say any NA I 14 108 15
yourself--unless you mean to have her think you NA I 14 113 40
out, "good heaven!--my dear Isabella, what do you mean? NA I 15 117 7
she was very sure Miss Thorpe did not mean to dance at all. NA II 1 132 16
What do you mean?" NA II 1 132 19
"But pray tell me what you mean." NA II 1 133 25
make him understand what I mean, in the properest way. NA II 3 145 13
What one means one day, you know, one may not mean the NA II 3 146 18
But I am sure she cannot mean to torment, for she is very NA II 4 151 13
"But what can your brother mean? NA II 4 151 19
If he knows her engagement, what can he mean by his NA II 4 151 19
I thought you did not mean to come back till to-morrow." NA II 9 195 11
and mean another all the while, was most unaccountable! NA II 11 211 15
You will know, from this description, I must mean Captain NA II 12 216 2
What could all this mean but an intentional affront? NA II 13 226 25
"I would not wish to do any thing mean," he replied. SS I 2 9 12
than for them--something of the annuity kind I mean.-- SS I 2 10 16
My father certainly could mean nothing more by his request SS I 2 12 25
Mrs. John Dashwood wished it likewise; but in the mean SS I 3 16 6
In the mean time, till all these alterations could be made SS I 6 29 5
But I see what you mean. SS I 10 48 5
"Whom do you mean, ma'am?" said he, colouring a little. SS I 13 64 17
"Oh! you know who I mean." SS I 13 64 18
"What do you mean?" SS I 18 100 24
Mrs. Jennings, in the mean time, talked on as loud as she SS I 19 107 28
"They mean no less to be civil and kind to us now," said SS I 19 109 42
What the devil does Sir John mean by not having a billiard SS I 20 111 8
justice of believing that I do not mean to be impertinent." SS I 22 128 7
"Good heavens!" cried Elinor, "what do you mean? SS I 22 129 13
We cannot mean the same Mr. Ferrars." SS I 22 131 29
"We can mean no other," cried Lucy smiling. SS I 22 131 30
Dashwood, is the person I mean; you must allow that I am SS I 22 131 30
I do not mean to say that I am particularly observant or SS II 2 148 12
"You mean," answered Elinor, with forced calmness, "Mr. SS II 8 199 36
My beau, indeed! said I--I cannot think who you mean. SS II 10 218 26
"Me, brother! what do you mean?" SS II 11 223 19
Recollecting himself, however, he added, "that is, I mean SS II 11 224 24
I do not mean to complain, however; it is undoubtedly a SS II 11 225 31
way-- you know what I mean,--if I had been treated in that SS II 13 240 17
In short, I do not mean to reflect upon the behaviour of SS III 1 268 45
"I do not understand what you mean by interrupting them," SS III 2 274 17
"You mean to go to Delaford after them I suppose," said SS III 4 285 6
that, understanding you mean to take orders, he has great SS III 4 288 28
Sure you do not mean to persuade me that the Colonel only SS III 4 291 53
"Choice!--how do you mean?"-- SS III 5 296 27
"I only mean, that I suppose from your manner of speaking, SS III 5 296 28
What is it, that you mean by it?"-- SS III 8 319 22
"I mean"--said he, with serious energy--"if I can, to make SS III 8 319 23
I mean to offer some kind of explanation, some kind of SS III 8 319 23
I do not mean to justify myself, but at the same time SS III 8 322 36
understanding--I do not mean, however, to defend myself. SS III 8 322 36
"What do you mean?" SS III 8 332 80
I mean never to be later in rising than six, and from that SS III 10 343 9
I do not mean to talk to you of what my feelings have been SS III 10 344 17
mean--my brother--you mean Mrs.-- Mrs. Robert Ferrars." SS III 12 360 20
21

willingness to make mean concessions by word of mouth than SS III 13 372 45
"I do not mean to distress you, but you know every body W 352 26
"I do not mean to make you cry.--said robt rather softened- W 352 26
She was a woman of mean understanding, little information, PP I 1 5 34
"Which do you mean?" and turning round, he looked for a PP I 3 11 13
"Oh!--you mean Jane, I suppose--because he danced with her PP I 5 18 6
"Perhaps you mean what I overheard between him and Mr. PP I 5 19 7
"What does Mr. Darcy mean," said she to Charlotte, "by PP I 6 24 14
and alone, quite alone! what could she mean by it? PP I 8 36 10
My dear Charles, what do you mean?" PP I 8 39 44
But, in my opinion, it is a paltry device, a very mean art. PP I 8 40 56
"If you mean Darcy," cried her brother, "he may go to bed, PP I 11 55 7
"What could he mean? she was dying to know what could be PP I 11 56 12
"Who do you mean, my dear? PP I 13 61 2
guess in what way he can mean to make us the atonement he PP I 13 63 15
And what can he mean by apologizing for being next in the PP I 13 64 17
Not that I mean to find fault with you, for such things I PP I 13 65 24
I do not mean however to assert that we can be justified PP I 18 101 71
the man whom they secretly mean to accept, when he first PP I 19 107 13
"What do you mean, Mr. Bennet, by talking in this way? PP I 20 112 21
we have known, and in the mean while may lessen the pain PP I 21 116 8
"It is only evident that Miss Bingley does not mean he PP I 21 117 13
and not a note, not a line, did I receive in the mean time. PP II 3 148 26
arch smile, and said, "you mean to frighten me, Mr. Darcy, PP II 8 174 12
13

"I do not mean to say that a woman may not be settled too PP II 9 179 22
She supposed, if he meant any thing, he must mean an PP II 10 182 1
"What is it you mean?" PP II 10 185 25
as he was, she did not mean to be unhappy about him. PP II 11 188 2
"And we mean to treat you all," added Lydia; "but you must PP II 16 219 3
on acquaintance, I did not mean that either his mind or PP II 18 234 35
36

his behaviour, so strikingly altered,--what could it mean? PP III 1 252 54
"What do you mean, hill? PP III 7 301 2
"Money! my uncle!" cried Jane, "what do you mean, sir?" PP III 7 304 28
"I mean, that no man in his senses, would marry Lydia on PP III 7 304 29
each of them; and in the mean time, she went after dinner PP III 9 317 10
Don't think me angry, however, for I only mean to let you PP III 10 321 2
power, that I was not so mean as to resent the past; and I PP III 16 370 32
"What do you mean?" PP III 17 373 13
What can he mean by being so tiresome as to be always PP III 17 374 20
A mean opinion of her abilities was not confined to them. MP I 2 18 23
"Live with me, dear Lady Bertram, what do you mean?" MP I 3 28 40
be received; but in the mean while, as no one felt a doubt MP I 4 39 12
Mr. Crawford did not mean to be in any danger; the Miss MP I 5 44 3
When I am a wife, I mean to be just as staunch myself; and MP I 5 47 24
you mean--but I will not undertake to answer the question. MP I 5 49 31
Miss Anderson! I do not know who or what you mean. MP I 5 49 34
"You can, if I stay at home with you, as I mean to do." MP I 8 78 20
is no necessity for my going, and I mean to stay at home. MP I 8 78 21
me, or suppose I mean to call them the arbiters of good MP I 9 93 49
"Do you mean literally or figuratively? MP I 10 99 17
We mean nothing but a little amusement among ourselves, MP I 13 125 18
be some guess-work; but I mean no disparagement to Julia. MP I 14 134 14
to you, Edmund;--you mean very well, I am sure--but I MP I 15 140 14
at leisure, I mean to look in at their rehearsals too. MP I 18 167 7
8

"Have you ever happened to look at the part I mean?" MP I 18 168 19
did yet mean to stay a few days longer under his roof. MP II 2 191 10
than we used to be; I mean before my uncle went abroad. MP II 3 196 3
"I mean to be too rich to lament or to feel any thing of MP II 4 213 36
I do not mean to be poor. MP II 4 214 41
from Edmund's manner that he did mean to go with her.-- MP II 4 215 47
"and how do you think I mean to amuse myself, Mary, on the MP II 6 229 1
and principal rooms, I mean, must be on that side, where MP II 7 242 23
been no ball just at--I mean not this very week, this very MP II 9 268 29
long enough, or he might mean to recommend her as a wife MP II 10 281 34
"You cannot think I mean to hurry you," said he, in an MP II 13 307 33
silence, "that you mean to refuse Mr. Crawford?" MP III 1 315 21
she was sure he did not mean there should be any change, MP III 1 323 53
It is me, Baddeley, you mean; I am coming this moment. MP III 1 325 60
You mean me, Baddeley, I am sure; Sir Thomas wants me, not MP III 1 325 60
She found that he did mean to persevere; but how he could, MP III 2 327 5
I mean when you are settled there. MP III 3 339 19
"What did that shake of the head mean?" said he. MP III 3 342 33
What did that shake of the head mean?" MP III 3 342 33
I do not mean to press you, however. MP III 4 346 10
"I mean," she cried, sorrowfully, correcting herself, " MP III 4 347 20
had better be unlike; I mean unlike in the flow of the MP III 4 349 23
"Do you mean then that your brother knew of the necklace MP III 5 362 19
allowed himself in gallantries which did mean nothing." MP III 5 363 21
I mean about our taking you back into Northamptonshire. MP III 12 416 3
cannot be true--it must mean some other people." MP III 15 440 15
do not mean to defend Henry at your sister's expence.' MP III 16 454 18
You do not think I could mean you, or suppose Mr. E I 1 10 32
mean you, or suppose Mr. Knightley to mean you. E I 1 10 32
"I do not understand what you mean by 'success;'" said Mr. E I 1 12 42
him--but he knows you very well indeed--I mean by sight." E I 4 29 15
whenever he does marry;--I mean, as to being acquainted E I 4 30 22
However, I do not mean to set up my opinion against your's- E I 4 31 25
Emma, though I mean no slight to the state I assure you." E I 5 41 30
Do you mean with regard to this letter?" E I 7 51 7
My dear Harriet, what do you mean? E I 7 52 13
With a little reserve of manner, Emma continued: "you mean E I 7 52 14
15

"No, I do not; that is, I do not mean--what shall I do? E I 7 52 16
best do--no, no, I do not mean that--as you say, one's E I 7 52 20
I am convinced that he does not mean to throw himself away. E I 8 66 53
you, and ascertain what you do, and what you mean to do." E I 13 112 22
to Miss Smith!--what could she possibly mean!"-- E I 15 130 26
instant, suspected it to mean any thing but grateful E I 16 134 5
She was pondering, in the mean while, upon the possibility, E II 1 158 13
beauty; from Mr. Dixon I mean--I do not know that she ever E II 1 159 20
I dare say he would not mean to charge anything for E II 1 162 31
I hope you mean to take an interest in this news. E II 3 175 41
42

I mean in person--tall, and with that sort of look--and E II 3 176 44
and seemed to mean always to speak of her with respect. E II 7 205 2
I do not mean to reflect upon the good intentions of E II 8 217 32
I do not mean to say, however, that you might not have E II 8 218 37
I do not mean to set you against him, but indeed he is not E II 11 249 11
Jane looked as if she did not mean to be conquered; but E II 16 296 39
I know what you mean--but Emma's hand is the strongest." E II 16 297 46
You quite shock me; if you mean a fling at the slave-trade, E II 17 300 14
"I did not mean, I was not thinking of the slave-trade," E II 17 300 15
But I only mean to say that there are advertising offices, E II 17 301 15
She did not mean to have her own affections entangled E III 1 315 1
What do you mean?" E III 2 325 28
do not tell me-- I do not want to know what you mean.-- E III 2 325 28
"Mrs. Gilbert does not mean to dance, but there is a young E III 2 327 37
still more valuable, I mean that has been more valuable, E III 4 339 16
might have--I do not mean to say that he did not dream it-- E III 5 345 16
You know who I mean--(nodding to her husband). E III 7 372 37
I would be understood to mean, that it can be only weak, E III 7 373 44
mean, as to the character and manners of the family." E III 8 381 22
You do not mean it?" E III 10 395 34
What could he mean by such horrible indelicacy? E III 10 397 50
for him, for Frank, I mean, that he should have attached E III 10 400 65
"What news do you mean?" replied Emma, unable to guess, by E III 11 404 5
smiling; "but you do not mean to deny that there was a E III 11 405 13
cried Emma, after a moment's pause--"what do you mean?-- E III 11 405 15
Good heaven! what do you mean?-- E III 11 405 15
possible that I could be supposed to mean any other person. E III 11 405 18
"Oh, dear," cried Harriet, "now I recollect what you mean; E III 11 406 24
more, he replied, "if you mean Miss Fairfax and Frank E III 13 425 6
7

of situation--I mean, as far as regards society, and all E III 13 428 23
Even then, I was not such a fool as not to mean to be E III 14 441 8
What does this mean? E III 15 447 24
Jane's prospects--that is, I do not mean.-- E III 16 455 20
Charming young man!--that is--so very friendly; I mean E III 16 455 20
You mean the crown; you come from the meeting at the crown. E III 16 457 39
You cannot mean to say, that Harriet Smith has accepted E III 18 471 17
You cannot mean that he has even proposed to her again-- E III 18 471 17
You only mean, that he intends it." E III 18 471 17
"I mean that he has done it," answered Mr. Knightley, with E III 18 471 18
I mean of late. E III 18 477 53
"I have no conception whom you can mean, Shepherd; I P III 3 23 27
After waiting another moment-- "you mean Mr. Wentworth, I P III 3 23 29
30

of great exultation, "I mean to go with you, Charles, for P III 7 57 17
18

Wentworth said, "do you mean that she refused him?" P III 10 89 29

30
the end of it was, I found, that he did not mean to come. P IV 2 130 5
please himself, he might mean to pay his addresses to her. P IV 3 140 11
He did not mean to complain, however. P IV 3 141 12
He did not mean to say that there were no pretty women, P IV 3 141 13
I mean to make my profit of Mrs. Wallis, however. P IV 5 156 13
I only mean that if Mr. Elliot should some time hence pay P IV 5 159 23
"Does she never mean to go away? P IV 6 163 7
She did not mean, however, to derive much more from it to P IV 6 167 19
But what I mean is, that I hope there is nothing in P IV 6 172 46
Elliot; and she did not mean, what ever she might feel on P IV 8 189 44
Till it does come, you know, we women never mean to have P IV 9 195 30
And you may say, that I mean to call upon her soon. P IV 10 215 16
However, I do not mean to say they have not a right to it. P IV 10 218 22
did not mean to stir, and tried to be cool and unconcerned. P IV 10 222 37
I mean, while the woman you love lives, and lives for you. P IV 11 235 32
of the right and wrong, I mean with regard to myself; and P IV 11 246 79
80
But I mean, that I was right in submitting to her, and P IV 11 246 80
"I do not mean to take exceptions to any place in S 1 368 1
In the mean while we have the canvas Awning, which gives S 4 381 1
Stationing himself close by her, he seemed to mean to S 7 396 1
"What description do you mean?--said Charlotte. S 7 397 1
"She is thoroughly mean. S 7 402 1
But she is very, very mean.-- S 7 402 1
And she makes every body mean about her.-- S 7 402 1
are obliged to be mean in their servility to her.-- S 7 402 1
And I am mean too, in giving her my attention, with the S 7 402 1
myself--he replied--& mean to walk a great deal while I am S 10 416 1
said Mr P. (who did not mean to go with them)--I think you S 12 423 1
MEAN-LOOKING (1)
an undersized, little, mean-looking man, set up for a fine MP I 18 165 3
MEAN-SPIRITED (1)
not reflect on the mean-spirited folly from which it SS II 12 233 16
MEANEST (1)
A flirt too, in the worst and meanest degree of flirtation; PP II 18 231 18
MEANING (116)
till I better understand her real meaning in coming to us. LS 3 247 1
from our not rightly understanding each other's meaning. LS 24 287 11
mistaken in each other's meaning, I resolved to have an LS 24 290 13
could bear a doubtful meaning, & which the ill-nature of LS 35 304 1
affect farther wonder at my meaning in bidding you adeiu. LS 36 306 2
"Hey-day, Miss Morland!" said he, "what is the meaning of NA I 10 75 25
His manner might sometimes surprize, but his meaning must NA I 14 114 49
all praise that had much meaning, was supplied by the NA II 8 182 2
Miss Tilney's meaning, in her own calculation! NA II 9 193 6
of words in reply, the meaning, which one short syllable NA II 15 242 9
"How strange this is! what can be the meaning of it! SS I 8 39 18
an intimacy so decided, a meaning so direct, as marked a SS I 12 59 7
You must not confound my meaning. SS I 17 94 39
what was worn and hackneyed out of all sense and meaning." SS I 18 97 7
Edward saw enough to comprehend, not only the meaning of SS I 18 100 23
for I do not perfectly comprehend the meaning of the word. SS I 21 124 29
little sharp eyes full of meaning, "there seemed to me to SS II 2 146 5
Willoughby, what is the meaning of this? SS II 6 176 7
What can be the meaning of it? SS II 6 177 10
meaning, and conversed with her there for several minutes. SS III 3 280 9
But it was then too late, and with a countenance meaning SS III 12 359 12
"What can be the meaning of that emphatic exclamation?" PP I 2 7 18
to know what could be his meaning"--and asked Elizabeth PP I 11 56 12
What could be the meaning of it?-- PP I 15 73 8
appeared close to them, meaning to pass through the set to PP I 18 92 22
directly, and of their meaning to dine that day in PP I 21 116 8
individual, change the meaning of principle and integrity, PP II 1 135 13
"What can be the meaning of this!" said Charlotte, as soon PP II 9 179 27
civil reflection, but its meaning did not escape, nor was PP II 11 191 16
herself so far as to examine the meaning of every sentence. PP II 13 205 3
to rejoice over her words, or to distrust their meaning. PP II 18 234 35
but there was a look and a manner which gave them meaning. PP III 2 263 9
He had certainly formed such a plan, and without meaning PP III 3 270 10
a hope of Wickham's meaning to marry her. no one but Jane, PP III 4 279 24
Conjectures as to the meaning of it, rapid and wild, PP III 9 320 32
Mr. Rushworth is quite right, I think, in meaning to give MP I 6 56 26
it very awkwardly," was his reply, with a look of meaning. MP I 9 88 22
was; and so far from now meaning to marry the elder, she MP I 12 114 2
"You are not serious, Tom, in meaning to act?" said Edmund MP I 13 125 15
do any thing; when Julia, meaning like her sister to be MP I 14 133 8
cause, or explained her meaning, he had told her not to MP I 16 152 2
to catch Sir Thomas's meaning, or diffidence, or delicacy, MP II 1 184 25
Mr. Rushworth hardly knew what to do with so much meaning; MP II 1 186 35
which, to Fanny's eye, had a great deal of serious meaning. MP II 4 213 37
have the meaning, is not in your nature I am sure. MP II 9 263 16
plain as to bear but one meaning even to her, offering MP II 13 301 7
of Miss Crawford's meaning, it was evident that she meant MP II 13 304 16
to class among the common meaning; in any other man at MP II 13 306 26
"I do not catch your meaning," said Sir Thomas, sitting MP III 1 315 18
been quite certain of his meaning any thing seriously, but MP III 1 315 19
With a few words, therefore, of no particular meaning, he MP III 1 320 45
Fanny knew her own meaning, but was no judge of her own MP III 2 327 6
of satisfaction, and words of simple, pleasant meaning. MP III 3 334 2
without falling into the flow of his meaning immediately." MP III 3 338 13
enough to convey the full meaning of the protestation; and MP III 3 339 21
intreating to know her meaning; and as Edmund perceived, MP III 3 341 31
to me before had any meaning; and surely I was not to be MP III 4 353 45
then I considered it as meaning nothing, I put it down as MP III 5 362 21
Had she doubted his meaning while she listened, the glow MP III 6 374 26
eyes, meaning to screen it at the same time from Susan's. MP III 7 386 40
underhand dealing--of meaning to bias him against the MP III 10 404 15
of one half of his meaning, and encouraged him to say MP III 10 406 20
without or against her meaning--whether his importance to MP III 12 417 4
Do justice to his meaning, however I may confuse it. MP III 15 443 23
I do not consider her as meaning to wound my feelings. MP III 16 456 25
increased in number and meaning; and she particularly led E I 4 28 6
"Emma has been meaning to read more ever since she was E I 5 37 7
Part of her meaning was to conceal some favourite thoughts E I 5 41 31
Your meaning must be unequivocal; no doubts or demurs: and E I 7 51 11
But what is the meaning of this? E I 8 60 34
road to London, and not meaning to return till the morrow, E I 8 68 58
She cast her eye over it, pondered, caught the meaning, E I 9 72 15
"There is so pointed, and so particular a meaning in this E I 9 73 20
The couplet does not cease to be, nor does its meaning E I 9 77 42
and appear to affix more meaning, or even quite all the E I 9 77 47
or even quite all the meaning which may be affixed to it. E I 9 77 47
persuaded; and though not meaning to be induced by him, or E I 14 119 5
He perfectly knew his own meaning; and having warmly E I 15 130 28
"Good heaven!" cried Mr. Elton, "what can be the meaning E I 15 130 31
accepting his attentions, meaning (in short), to marry him! E I 16 135 8
understanding, and warm-hearted, well meaning relations. E II 2 163 3
an air of greatness, meaning only to shew off in higher E II 2 168 15
But she had believed them to be well meaning, worthy E II 3 179 53
be giving her refusal less meaning than she could wish. E II 7 207 6
and by inference, of the meaning of his manners towards E II 8 212 4
as any reason for their not meaning to make the present. E II 8 215 14
I am not in the least ashamed of my meaning." E II 10 243 25
and Mrs. Weston gave Emma a look of particular meaning. E II 10 244 36
things, of course, without any idea of a serious meaning. E II 15 288 35
"Harriet, I will not affect to be in doubt of your meaning. E III 4 341 34
35
to think entirely void of meaning, however he might wish E III 5 343 2
cheek which gave it a meaning not otherwise ostensible. E III 5 348 21
more equal to the covert meaning, the superior E III 5 348 23
not immediately catch her meaning; but, when it burst on E III 7 371 27
She felt your full meaning. E III 7 375 59
While he stood, as if meaning to go, but not going--her E III 9 385 5
not be deceived as to the meaning of his countenance, and E III 9 386 8
indeed--I have had no idea of their meaning any thing.-- E III 13 427 19
was a side-glance of great meaning at Jane.) E III 16 454 17
his meaning to dress directly, and dine at the other house. P III 7 55 7
Wentworth, his sisters meaning to visit Mary and the child, P III 7 59 24
poetical despondence, and meaning to have spring again, P III 10 85 13
glance, as he turned away, which Anne knew the meaning of. P III 10 86 20
pretence on the lady's side of meaning to leave them. P IV 4 145 1
She was as much convinced of his meaning to gain Anne in P IV 5 159 22
the sense, or rather the meaning of the words, for P IV 8 186 25
it is as nearly the meaning as I can give; for I do not P IV 8 186 25
of going to Mrs. Smith; meaning that it should engage her P IV 9 192 1
with my second W. again, "meaning, for the rest of my life, P IV 9 203 73
terms, I have a perfect impression of the general meaning. P IV 9 204 75
acquaintance, of her meaning to be Lady Elliot, and as P IV 9 206 88
a manner of doubtful meaning, of surprise rather than P IV 10 226 65
to his brother's, meaning after a while to return to P IV 11 243 66
period of Lady Russell's meaning to love Captain Wentworth P IV 12 251 10
Charlotte, meaning to overthrow his attempts at surprise, S 10 418 1
of meaning to be the most stylish girls in the place.-- S 11 421 1
MEANLY (5)
affection on a man who had dared to think so meanly of me. LS 10 258 2
entitled to think well of themselves, and meanly of others. PP I 4 15 11
family circle, to think meanly of all the rest of the PP III 16 369 24
think meanly of their sense and worth compared with my own. PP III 16 369 24
to his father; and while meanly exerting their power to E I 18 147 18
MEANNESS (5)
She had seen enough of her pride, her meanness, and her SS II 13 238 1
thought of;--and with a meanness, selfishness, cruelty-- SS III 8 320 32
her capable of the utmost meanness of wanton ill-nature. SS III 13 366 21
addressed, "there is meanness in all the arts which ladies PP I 8 40 57
gross ignorance, some meanness of opinions, and very MP I 1 10 14
MEANS (282)
I was by no means prepared for such an event, nor can I LS 3 246 1
He means to send for his horses immediately, & it is LS 8 254 1
& advise you by all means to marry him; his father's LS 9 256 1
to read it to me, by which means he became acquainted to LS 13 262 1
up if he can, for I do not by any means want her here. LS 16 268 1
Tho' totally without accomplishment, she is by no means so LS 18 273 3
by no means assured that such might not be the consequence. LS 22 280 1
to anyone who is the means of sending my brother home; LS 24 286 4
Frederica does not know her mother--Lady Susan means LS 24 287 9
He had heard I imagine by some means or other, that you LS 28 298 1
Not that Catherine was always stupid,--by no means; she NA I 1 14 1
along the room was by no means the way to disengage NA I 2 21 9
friends by no means so expensively dressed as herself. NA I 5 36 3
"Oh! d---- it, when one has the means of doing a kind NA I 7 47 17
waiting, did not by any means reconcile her more to her NA I 8 55 10
ten miles an hour) by no means alarmingly fast, gave NA I 9 62 10
that the drive had by no means been very pleasant and that NA I 9 69 51
"Go by all means, my dear; only put on a white gown; Miss NA I 12 91 2
to the other in her vindication, had no means of knowing. NA I 13 102 26
happiness to both destroyed, perhaps through her means. NA I 13 103 29
the woman; but she is by no means a simpleton in general." NA I 14 113 39
thing easy; and by what means their income was to be NA I 15 122 28
has by no means chosen ill in fixing on the present hour." NA II 1 134 36
I cannot bear to be the means of injuring my dear Morland, NA II 1 135 45
"Well, proceed by all means. NA II 2 139 7
What one means one day, you know, one may not mean the NA II 3 146 18
for all the world be the means of hurrying you into an NA II 3 146 20
young lady is (by whatever means) introduced into a NA II 5 158 15
It was by no means unreasonably large, and contained NA II 6 163 1
means, the lid in one moment should be thrown back. NA II 6 164 3
that it was by no means an ill-sized room; and further NA II 6 166 6
could it relate?--by what means could it have been so long NA II 6 170 12
in your sex, as a means of getting you out of doors, and NA II 7 174 8
by some secret means with those cells, might well have NA II 8 188 17
before.)--"James only means to give me good advice." NA II 10 205 23
the General by that means to form a cool and impartial NA II 11 208 2
By some means or other she must have had the misfortune to NA II 13 226 25
the house without even the means of getting home; and the NA II 13 229 31
not oppress them by any means so long; and, after a due NA II 14 234 10
beyond example; by no means respected in their own NA II 15 246 12
The means by which their early marriage was effected can NA II 16 250 4
of his pride, and by no means without its effect was the NA II 16 251 6
attractions as are by no means unusual in children of two SS I 1 4 3
by no means desirable: it takes away one's independence." SS I 2 11 21
I assure you he is by no means deficient in natural taste, SS I 4 19 2
I am by no means assured of his regard for me. SS I 4 21 15
six years old, by which means there was one subject always SS I 6 31 9
The immediate advantage to herself was by no means SS I 8 36 2
memory been equal to her means of improvement, she might SS I 11 54 6
know my sister well enough to understand what she means? SS I 17 95 49
Their means were as different as their objects, and SS I 19 104 9
Her manners were by no means so elegant as her sister's, SS I 19 106 22
The motive was too common to be wondered at; but the means SS I 20 112 28
The young ladies arrived, their appearance was by no means SS I 21 119 3
too well to be the selfish means of robbing him, perhaps, SS II 2 147 7
me, 'I advise you by all means to put an end to your SS II 2 150 32
the evening was by no means more productive of pleasure to SS II 4 166 31
believe it is--is to be a means of giving comfort;--no, I SS II 9 204 18
therefore, by all means not to shorten their visit to Mrs. SS II 10 213 3
indeed!" and by the means of this continual though gentle SS II 10 215 14
was the easiest means of atoning for his own neglect. SS II 11 228 51
were staying, by no means unworthy her notice; and as for SS II 12 229 1
adopt either of them, but by all means build a cottage.' SS II 14 252 17
resentment, "I would by no means speak disrespectfully of SS III 1 267 44
45
The continuance of their engagement, and the means that SS III 2 276 27
being given through her means, that she would not on any SS III 3 283 20
was over; "Colonel Brandon means it as a testimony of his SS III 4 289 31
I cannot help thinking, in short, that means might have SS III 5 300 37
She knew not that she had been the means of sending the SS III 7 309 6
the expectation of the others was by no means so cheerful. SS III 7 309 7
To consult with Colonel Brandon on the best means of SS III 7 311 14
I endeavoured, by every means in my power, to make myself SS III 8 320 29
I sent no answer to Marianne, intending by that means to SS III 8 326 53
actions, it may be the means-- it may put me on my guard-- SS III 8 332 77
means, now remove the guilt of his conduct towards Eliza. SS III 11 349 1
had no means of lessening but by their own conjectures. SS III 12 360 26
London, he had had no means of hearing of her but from SS III 13 364 13
be the means of spreading misery farther in the family.-- SS III 13 371 38
he was by no means inclined to be guided by it, she judged SS III 14 373 3
her only son, he was by no means her eldest; for while SS III 14 374 4
His attendance was by this means secured, and the rest SS III 14 376 11
advise you by all means not to give him any encouragement. W 315 1
but he is a great flirt & never means anything serious." W 315 1
very fond of; but he never means anything serious, & when W 317 2
Your Cloathes I would undertake to find means of sending W 320 2
I would not be the means of keeping you from being seen.-- W 320 2
her spirits were by no means insensible to the expected W 322 3
distressed, but by no means displeased, & heard an W 328 8
every woman may not have the inclination, or the means." W 345 21
once they had the inclination, the means wd soon follow."-- W 345 21
gratification was by no means unalloyed; his coming was a W 347 22
"By all means my dear creature. W 354 28
now added to his ordinary means of entertainment; he W 359 28
I would advise you be all means to accept the invitation, W 362 32
Miss Bingley was by no means unwilling to preside at his PP I 4 15 13
Bingley was by no means deficient, but Darcy was clever. PP I 4 16 14

Her performance was pleasing, though by no means capital. PP I 6 25 23
Jane was by no means better. PP I 8 35 1
to express them--by which means my letters sometimes PP I 10 48 23
"I dare say you believed it; but I am by no means PP I 10 49 29
that gentleman did by no means intend; for he would PP I 10 49 31
"By all means," cried Bingley; "let us hear all the PP I 10 50 39
"but depend upon it, he means to be severe on us, and our PP I 11 56 13
I cannot be otherwise than concerned at being the means of PP I 13 63 12
being in town; and by that means, as I told Lady Catherine PP I 14 67 9
Mr. Wickham, he was by no means the only partner who could PP I 17 86 10
"I am by no means of opinion, I assure you," said he, " PP I 17 87 13
"I would by no means suspend any pleasure of yours," he PP I 18 94 43
Mr. Wickham is by no means a respectable young man. PP I 18 95 50
Mary's powers were by no means fitted for such a display; PP I 18 100 68
I am therefore by no means discouraged by what you have PP I 19 107 13
attractions, it is by no means certain that another offer PP I 19 108 19
for him, she means (most kindly!) to put me on my guard? PP I 21 118 15
Believe her to be deceived by all means. PP I 21 119 22
being his wife, I advise you by all means to refuse him." PP I 21 119 24
Bennet, who could by no means wish for so speedy a return, PP I 22 123 6
7
her, and though by no means so clever as herself, she PP I 22 124 11
Women fancy admiration means more than it does." PP II 1 136 14
To Mrs. Gardiner, Wickham had one means of affording PP II 2 142 19
be very sorry to be the means of making any of you unhappy; PP II 3 145 7
but such of us as wished to learn, never wanted the means. PP II 6 165 31
It is wonderful how many families I have been the means of PP II 6 165 32
situated through my means; and it was but the other day, PP II 6 165 32
may not have the means or inclination to marry early.-- PP II 6 165 35
some trouble, could by no means satisfy Mr. Collins, and PP II 6 167 42
their company was by no means so acceptable as when she PP II 8 172 2
"If he means to be but little at Netherfield, it would be PP II 9 178 9
It is only that he has better means of having it than many PP II 10 183 10
the man, who has been the means of ruining, perhaps for PP II 11 190 10
principal, if not the only means of dividing them from PP II 11 191 12
"Two offences of a very different nature, and by no means PP II 12 196 5
with Rosings, the frequent means of varying the humble PP II 15 215 4
his character was by no means so faulty, nor Wickham's so PP III 1 258 75
means unpleasing, though it could not be exactly defined. PP III 2 266 16
and her attentions to Mr. Darcy were by no means over. PP III 3 269 8
What he means to do, I am sure I know not; but his PP III 4 276 5
a girl who is by no means unprotected or friendless, and PP III 5 282 1
and younger children would by that means be provided for. PP III 8 308 3
had no fear of its spreading farther, through his means. PP III 8 311 12
company, for she had by no means given up her plan of PP III 8 313 20
liberality, and he had the means of exercising it; and PP III 10 326 3
as her husband by no means entered into her scheme of PP III 11 330 2
My mother means well; but she does not know, no one can PP III 11 333 28
his own and Mrs. Bennet's means, for his coming next PP III 13 345 19
Your tempers are by no means unlike. PP III 13 348 38
was gone, Jane constantly sought the same means of relief. PP III 13 349 44
I have by no means done. PP III 14 357 62
it should be through her means, that she, his favourite PP III 17 375 28
But make a virtue of it by all means. PP III 18 381 7
to separate us, were the means of removing all my doubts. PP III 18 381 14
her into Derbyshire, had been the means of uniting them. PP III 19 388 13
as almost to preclude the means of ever hearing of each MP I 1 4 2
ten to one but she has the means of settling well, without MP I 1 6 6
"Why, you know Sir Thomas's means will be rather MP I 3 30 54
thoroughly relished the means it afforded her of mixing in MP I 4 35 5
for Fanny the immediate means of exercise, which he could MP I 4 37 8
party; and, among other means, by seeking an intimacy with MP I 4 39 10
whatever means; and hope there will be no farther delay." MP I 6 58 34
But yes, in the never of conversation which means not very MP I 9 92 44
for so doing did by no means lessen, it ended in Mr. MP I 10 98 4
not entirely without the means of seeing what clergymen MP I 11 111 28
his introduction at Mansfield by no means desirable. MP I 13 121 1
and if we can be the means of amusing that anxiety, and MP I 13 126 18
"That circumstance would by no means tempt me," he replied, MP I 15 145 41
It will be very disagreeable, and by no means what I MP I 15 149 61
But if I can be the means of restraining the publicity of MP I 16 155 16
his own mind; and if he means nothing, we will send him MP I 17 162 18
and encouraging him by all means to pay his respects to MP II 1 176 3
Mrs. Norris was by no means to be compared in happiness to MP II 1 179 10
I do not think you will find your woods by any means worse MP II 1 181 16
that moment in having the means of immediate communication, MP II 1 182 22
differing in the sort of evil, did by no means bring less. MP II 2 192 11
that he did not by any means consider Fanny as the only, MP II 4 211 25
with such limited means and indifferent connections.-- MP II 4 213 40
Be honest and poor, by all means--but I shall not envy you; MP II 4 213 40
She had by no means forgotten the past, and she thought as MP II 6 232 11
and habits, have some means of enjoyment in their power, MP II 6 235 18
With such means in his power he had a right to be listened MP II 6 236 21
In one respect it was better, as it gave him the means of MP II 6 237 23
She feared for William; by no means convinced by all that MP II 6 237 23
The house is by no means bad, and when the yard is removed, MP II 7 242 22
and Sir Thomas, by no means displeased, prolonged the MP II 7 251 63
inexperienced, with small means of choice and no MP II 8 254 8
had been beyond his means, and therefore not to wear the MP II 8 254 8
speaking low and seriously, "you know what all this means. MP II 9 268 31
would by no means go through the ring of the cross. MP II 9 270 40
advantages you and I have been the means of giving her. MP II 10 272 3
She was almost at the door, and not chusing by any means MP II 13 298 1
with her limited means, for now it would all be useful in MP II 13 304 19
The rest of your note I know means nothing; but I am so MP II 13 307 31
Fanny had by no means forgotten Mr. Crawford, when she MP III 1 311 1
marriages, where there are means in proportion, and would MP III 1 317 34
their wishes, might be their surest means of forwarding it. MP III 2 330 14
means of effecting it would be by not trying him too long. MP III 4 345 3
can be, that the man who means to make you love him (you MP III 4 347 21
means of address which she had spirits or time to attempt. MP III 8 391 8
admitting they were by no means without provocation, she MP III 8 391 9
done away, and it was the means of opening Susan's heart MP III 9 397 7
occasionally, though by no means to the extent he wished; MP III 10 403 14
I am sure he still means to impose on me if possible, and MP III 11 411 20
What may be the likeliest means? MP III 13 422 2
My father means to fetch you himself, but it will not be MP III 13 423 2
only in contriving the means for doing so, and for making MP III 14 435 14
you are,) keep away, when you have the means of returning. MP III 14 435 14
they did not by any means rank as misfortunes with her. E I 1 5 4
and he was by no means yet reconciled to his own E I 1 7 10
the match, as you call it, means only your planning it, E I 1 12 42
of his mother's, been the means of a sort of E I 2 16 4
If he means anything, it must be to please you. E I 4 34 42
She means it, I know." E I 5 36 6
never marry, which, of course, means just nothing at all. E I 5 41 29
"By all means. E I 6 47 29
He is desperately in love and means to marry her." E I 8 59 25
Emma; "but is he sure that Harriet means to marry him?" E I 8 59 26
"Well, well, means to make her an offer then. E I 8 59 27
I much think your statement by no means fair. E I 8 62 39
mortified to have been the means of promoting it, by the E I 8 66 55
It was by no means his daughter's wish that the intellects E I 9 70 7
design; and by this means the others were still able to E I 10 88 33
our missing her by any means to the extent we ourselves E I 11 94 14
I should not attempt it, if it were to be the means of E I 12 106 61
Knightley did not by any means like; he anticipated E I 13 113 25
Smith was not better, by no means better, rather worse. E I 13 114 31
that we are by no means so sure of seeing Mr. Frank E I 14 121 16
consider this visit from your son as by any means certain. E I 14 122 20
19
cannot be without the means of doing as much as that. E I 18 145 10
is not, by any means, to be compared with Miss Fairfax." E II 1 161 26
only what very limited means could command, and growing up E II 2 163 3
supplying the means of respectable subsistance hereafter. E II 2 164 5
before she was, by some means or other, discovered to have E II 4 181 2
Call upon her, by all means." E II 5 194 38
considerable increase of means--the house in town had E II 7 207 6
No, I would not be the means of giving them any pain. E II 7 210 20
we do now, it will be the means of confirming us in that E II 13 267 7
Would Jane but go, means were to be found, servants sent, E II 15 285 14
"Excuse me," said Jane earnestly, "I cannot by any means E II 16 296 37
"No, it by no means wanted strength--it was not a large E II 16 297 51
"Excuse me, ma'am, but this is by no means my intention; I E II 17 300 13
that she means to sleep only two nights on the road.-- E II 18 306 11
It was by no means her object to have it believed that her E II 18 307 17
and are by no means implicitly guided by others. E II 18 309 31
by no means moving slowly, could hardly be out of hearing. E III 2 321 14
I do not by any means engage for its being returned. E III 4 342 39
her suspicions were by no means removed, she was really E III 5 350 28
Yes, I see what she means, (turning to Mr. Knightley,) and E III 7 371 28
"By all means, if you can." E III 7 373 48
He had not left her long, by no means long enough for her E III 14 436 6
"My Emma, he means no such thing. E III 17 464 21
He only means-----" E III 17 464 21
"If I understand your brother, he only means so far as E III 17 465 26
meant to marry; by which means Hartfield would receive the E III 17 465 28
that my uncle means to give her all my aunt's jewels. E III 18 479 70
of them able to devise any means of lessening their P III 1 10 19
let my house, I have by no means made up my mind as to the P III 3 18 8
First, as being the means of bringing persons of obscure P III 3 19 16
Anne had very sincerely rejoiced in there being no means P III 6 48 17
"He certainly means to have one or other of those two P III 10 92 44
the weather was by no means bad; and, in short, Louisa, P III 11 94 7
And they were by no means tired of wondering and admiring; P III 11 96 11
from: he was by no means hopeless; he spoke cheerfully. P III 12 112 52
which he had by no means forgotten, and instantly saw, P IV 3 143 18
The folly of the means they often employ is only to be P IV 3 144 20
Sir Walter, however, would choose his own means, and at P IV 4 149 13
a little learning is by no means a dangerous thing in good P IV 4 150 17
which supply me with the means of doing a little good to P IV 5 155 9
"By all means," said she; "only tell me all about it, when P IV 7 180 34
but suffering--which was by no means the case at Lyme. P IV 8 184 16
as might give him the means of ascertaining the degree of P IV 9 207 90
was a cruel aggravation of actually streightened means. P IV 9 210 98
a time there will be the means of marrying, I hold to be P IV 11 231 9
"I must speak to you by such means as are within my reach. P IV 11 237 42
"By all means, my dear," cried Mrs. Musgrove, "go home P IV 11 238 46
He would gladly weaken, by any fair means, whatever P IV 11 243 66
perhaps--tho' I am by no means the first of my family, S 1 368 1
I shall have the means of accomplishing between you.-- S 5 386 1
being moreover by no means pleased with his extraordinary S 7 398 1
in the place, & no means of ascertaining that she should S 9 409 1
of the drops & the salts by means of one or the other. S 10 413 1
Arthur was heavy in eye as well as figure, but by no means S 10 415 1
her that Arthur was by no means so fond of being starved S 10 417 1
different from his sisters--by no means so spiritualized.-- S 10 418 1
kindness than by giving her the means of being useful.-- S 10 419 1

MEANT (160)

I meant moreover to have reminded him of our being quite LS 13 262 1
She meant I suppose to go to the Clarkes in Staffordshire, LS 16 268 1
was no explanation; I begged her to tell me what she meant. LS 20 275 1
of what her character is meant to be; that her heart was NA I 2 18 1
"Aye, that is what I meant. NA I 9 63 18
She was very much vexed, and meant to make her apology as NA I 12 94 10
seemed neither kindly meant, nor consistently supported; NA I 15 121 25
"Well then, I only meant that your attributing my NA II 1 133 28
affection, and as certainly never meant to encourage it." NA II 3 145 15
You are convinced that I never meant to deceive your NA II 3 146 17
What would be meant by such unsteady conduct, what her NA II 4 149 1
Pushed back too, as if meant to be out of sight!-- NA II 6 163 2
He meant not to be unkind however, and, as a mark of his SS I 1 4 3
I'll lay my life that he meant nothing farther; indeed, it SS I 2 12 24
"Excuse me," said she, "and be assured that I meant no SS I 4 21 15
what is meant at present to be unacknowledged to any one. SS I 16 84 9
in a low voice as if she meant to be heard by no one else, SS I 19 107 29
because it was always meant to be a great secret, and I am SS I 22 129 16
and what he meant, before many meetings had taken place. SS II 4 159 1
the simple and common expedient, of asking what he meant? SS II 5 172 40
of more than I felt, or meant to express, I shall reproach SS II 7 183 13
That I should ever have meant more you will allow to be SS II 7 183 13
Had I remained in England, perhaps--but I meant to promote SS II 9 206 24
of what was principally meant by it, provoked her SS II 12 235 34
35
a compliment, which though meant as its douceur, was SS II 14 249 8
to have been always meant to end in two days time. SS II 14 254 26
person, it is not meant--it is not fit--it is not possible SS III 1 263 27
her what he meant to do himself towards removing them.-- SS III 6 305 16
daughter, by whom she then meant in the warmth of her SS III 12 359 11
"I meant," said Elinor, taking up some work from the table, SS III 12 359 19
That Lucy had certainly meant to deceive, to go off with a SS III 13 366 21
He merely meant to persuade her to give up the engagement; SS III 14 376 11
imported that she meant to take the visit to herself.-- W 355 28
he meant to be at the next assembly with a large party. PP I 3 9 1
He only meant that there were not such a variety of people PP I 9 43 24
gone in five minutes, you meant it to be a sort of PP I 10 49 27
had a wife in view, as he meant to chuse one of the PP I 15 70 2
He meant to provide for me amply, and thought he had done PP I 16 79 25
they each, like Elizabeth, meant to dance half the evening PP I 17 86 10
It was kindly meant." PP I 18 95 47
that her daughter had meant to encourage him by protesting PP I 20 110 2
I have certainly meant well through the whole affair. PP I 20 114 32
gone on Saturday, and to Saturday he still meant to stay. PP I 21 115 2
She supposed, if he meant any thing, he must mean an PP II 10 182 1
"Is this," thought Elizabeth, "meant for me?" and she PP II 10 183 15
have no right to suppose that Bingley was the person meant. PP II 10 185 24
could be meant than those with whom she was connected. PP II 10 186 38
circumstance with what she meant to be impartiality-- PP II 13 205 3
"And yet I meant to be uncommonly clever in taking so PP II 17 225 17
to his sister, was meant to be kept as much as possible to PP II 17 226 23
livery, guessed what it meant, and imparted no small PP III 2 260 1
family, told her that he meant to be in London the very PP III 5 287 36
Elizabeth; "perhaps she meant well, but , under such a PP III 5 293 67
"He meant, I believe," replied Jane, "to go to Epsom, the PP III 5 293 69
might be remarked, he meant to make enquiries at Clapham. PP III 5 293 69
was eager in it, he meant to assist him in pursuing it. PP III 6 295 5
He meant to resign his commission immediately; and as to PP III 10 323 2
People did say, you meant to quit the place entirely at PP III 11 336 49
he meant to make any stay in the country at present. PP III 11 337 52
"Can you possibly guess, Lizzy, who is meant by this?" PP III 15 362 15
I never meant to deceive you, but my spirits might often PP III 16 369 27
I only meant to observe, that it ought not to be lightly MP I 1 7 7
Nobody meant to be unkind, but nobody put themselves out MP I 2 14 6
my sister always meant to take you when Mr. Norris died. MP I 3 25 9
Edmund asked Fanny whether she meant to ride the next day. MP I 7 69 26
It was meant and done by Mrs. Grant, with perfect good MP I 7 70 30
Fanny supposed she must have been mistaken, and meant to MP I 12 116 11
Maria gave Edmund a glance, which meant, "what say you now? MP I 13 129 39
I knew what all this meant, for the servants' dinner bell MP I 15 142 22
Sir Thomas meant to be giving Mr. Rushworth's opinion in MP II 1 186 35
shaken hands with Edmund, meant to try to lose the MP II 2 187 2
"As you please, ma'am, on that head; but I meant my MP II 5 217 9
Nor must you be fancying, that the invitation is meant as MP II 5 220 28
voice, not meant to reach far, and the subject dropped. MP II 7 246 35

Mr. Crawford meant to be in town by his uncle's MP II 9 266 21
My uncle meant it so." MP II 9 268 30
She meant to be giving her little heart a happy flutter, MP II 10 277 17
remove to London, meant something that she could not bear. MP II 11 287 17
and gallantry, which meant only to deceive for the hour; MP II 13 301 7
use of such words and offers, if they meant but to trifle? MP II 13 302 10
it was evident that she meant to compliment her on her MP II 13 304 16
said that it meant something very earnest, very pointed. MP II 13 306 26
unnecessary, it was kindly meant; and of this you may be MP III 1 313 12
And there was a half smile with the words which meant, "I MP III 1 325 61
He had concluded,--he had meant them to be far distant. MP III 3 334 1
smile, which evidently meant, "that lady will never allow MP III 3 339 20
"What was it meant to express? MP III 3 342 33
must have thought it so, supposing he had meant nothing. MP III 4 353 45
She meant to urge him to persevere in the hope of being MP III 4 354 46
Oh! you received it just as it was meant. MP III 5 362 18
could not but suppose it meant for him to hear; and to MP III 7 376 4
her mother meant to part with her when her year was up. MP III 7 385 38
How Miss Crawford really felt--how she meant to act, or MP III 12 417 4
"Her uncle, she understood, meant to fetch her; and as her MP III 14 436 15
regarding it as what was meant to be the last, last MP III 16 454 18
He had meant them to be good, but his cares had been MP III 17 463 8
I meant only myself. E I 1 10 32
said Mr. Knightley; "but I meant no reflection on any body. E I 1 11 34
times of books that she meant to read regularly through-- E I 5 37 7
How completely it meant, 'why should my picture be drawn?'" E I 6 44 17
the attitude, and as she meant to throw in a little E I 6 47 27
Could it really be meant for me?" E I 9 74 22
"I thought he meant to try his skill, by his manner of E I 9 76 29
to understand what she meant by a basin of nice smooth E I 12 104 50
No!--(in an accent meant to be insinuating)--I am sure you E I 15 131 31
reverse of what she had meant and believed him; proud, E I 16 135 6
she entered the house; but meant, having once talked him E II 1 156 6
on the news, which she had meant to give with so much E II 3 180 56
She meant to take her in the carriage, leave her at the E II 4 185 13
spoken with some anxiety, and meant only for her. E II 5 189 15
they meant to marry till it were proved against them. E II 5 193 35
and not meant to provoke; and therefore she let it pass. E II 7 206 4
She meant to be very happy, in spite of the scene being E II 8 213 5
I do not know what she meant, but she asked me if I E II 9 232 19
"She meant to be impertinently curious, just as such an E II 9 232 20
"I thought you meant to go with me. E II 9 234 29
great an attention! and I always thought you meant it." E II 9 234 34
I meant to take them over to John Saunders the first thing E II 9 236 46
The ladies here probably exchanged looks which meant, "men E II 11 253 43
own importance; that she meant to shine and be very E II 14 272 16
and condescending as Mrs. Elton meant to be considered. E II 15 284 12
What I said just now, meant nothing. E II 15 288 35
which was all that was meant--and it is very shameful.-- E II 16 291 6
said John Knightley, "I meant to imply the change of E II 16 294 23
A pleasant "thank you" seemed meant to laugh it off, but a E II 16 294 24
eyes declared that he meant to have a delightful evening. E III 2 319 3
say and know at once, all that she meant to say and know. E III 4 341 34
If meant to be immediately mixed with the others, and E III 5 348 21
"Oh!" she cried in evident embarrassment, "it all meant E III 5 350 29
looks, which I did not believe meant to be public." E III 5 350 36
in her own estimation, meant nothing, though in the E III 7 368 3
"Perhaps I intended you to say so, but I meant self- E III 7 369 11
To guess what all this meant, was impossible even for Emma. E III 10 392 7
and words that were never meant for both to hear.-- E III 10 399 61
you entirely approved and meant to encourage me in my E III 11 405 18
the gipsies--it was not Mr. Frank Churchill that I meant. E III 11 406 24
He meant to walk with her, she found. E III 13 424 1
all--she and Mr. Knightley meant to marry; by which means E III 17 465 28
supposed "she had always meant to catch Knightley if she E III 17 469 36
the future baronet, meant to marry him; and her father had P III 1 7 14
marry him; and her father had always meant that she should. P III 1 7 14
measures advised, as he meant to see finally adopted. P III 2 11 1
hints broadest which were meant for her sister's benefit. P III 6 46 11
with the child, that he meant to avoid hearing her thanks, P III 9 80 34
They meant to take a long drive this morning; perhaps we P III 10 84 8
so entirely as if he meant to be understood, that she P III 11 100 23
of what he particularly meant; and though Anne could not P IV 4 151 22
agreeable sensations which her friend meant to create. P IV 5 159 21
She had only meant to oppose the too-common idea of spirit P IV 6 172 40
41
which the Admiral meant to convey, but it would have been P IV 6 173 48
to know, was how long he meant to be in Bath; he had not P IV 7 178 26
She meant to avoid any such alteration of manners as might P IV 10 214 11
On Friday morning she meant to go very early to Lady P IV 10 215 14
he had meant to forget her, and believed it to be done. P IV 11 241 61
she had rendered, or ever meant to render, to his wife. P IV 12 251 11
This poor Sir Edward & his sister.--how far nature meant S 7 402 1
serious designs; it was clara whom he meant to seduce.-- S 8 405 2
come, & meant to get into lodgings & make some stay."-- S 9 407 1
Mrs G. meant to go to the sea, for her young people's S 9 408 1
already command, they meant to be very economical, very S 11 421 1

MEANWHILE (39)
I shall trouble you meanwhile to prevent his forming any LS 7 253 1
Her ladyship is comforting herself meanwhile by strolling LS 15 267 4
For this I shall impatiently wait; & meanwhile can safely LS 39 307 1
Having learnt enough in the meanwhile from her openhearted LS 42 311 2
John Thorpe, in the meanwhile, had walked away; and NA I 8 58 25
Catherine's silent appeal to her friend, meanwhile, was NA I 9 61 6
In the meanwhile, they proceeded on their journey without NA I 11 88 54
Isabella, in the meanwhile, had applied her handkerchief NA I 13 98 3
Catherine, meanwhile, undisturbed by presentiments of such NA II 1 131 15
Dorothy meanwhile, no less struck by your appearance, NA II 5 158 17
The General, meanwhile, though offended every morning by NA II 11 209 5
Catherine meanwhile,--the anxious, agitated, happy, NA II 15 242 8
He, meanwhile, whatever he might feel, acted with all the SS III 7 312 17
Emma in the meanwhile was not unobserved, or unadmired W 328 9
Mr. Collins, meanwhile, was meditating in solitude on what PP I 20 112 24
It was not without an effort meanwhile that she could wait PP II 15 217 17
and Mr. Gardiner meanwhile having settled his account at PP III 4 281 29
and Mrs. Bennet, in the meanwhile, was giving way to all PP III 12 339 10
The little visitor meanwhile was as unhappy as possible. MP I 2 13 4
The subject of improving grounds meanwhile was still under MP I 6 60 53
Henry Crawford, who meanwhile had taken up the play, and MP I 14 133 11
and out--but pray let me know my fate in the meanwhile. MP I 15 143 27
You in the meanwhile will be taking a trip into china, I MP I 16 156 27
Her cause meanwhile went on well. MP II 5 218 12
minutes; himself in the meanwhile observed by Sir Thomas, MP II 7 249 49
The preparations meanwhile went on, and Lady Bertram MP II 8 254 9
His niece, meanwhile, did not thank him for what he had MP II 10 280 32
Fanny, meanwhile, speaking only when she could not help it, MP II 13 305 26
Meanwhile, he saw enough of Fanny's embarrassment to make MP III 3 335 6
Fanny, meanwhile, vexed with herself for not having been MP III 3 342 32
Sir Thomas, meanwhile, went on with his own hopes, and his MP III 6 368 7
Emma, in the meanwhile, could not be satisfied without a E II 16 290 4
Mr. Weston meanwhile, perfectly unsuspicious of the E II 17 303 24
In the meanwhile the lame horse recovered so fast, that E III 6 357 32
In the meanwhile, she resolved against seeing Harriet.-- E III 12 416 2
in the meanwhile, we need not talk much on the subject." E III 18 471 16
Charles, in the meanwhile, was very decidedly declaring P III 10 86 17
by one, and in the meanwhile were to be all together, and P III 12 107 22
In the meanwhile she was in the carriage. P III 12 116 70

MEASLES (4)
Mr. Perry said, so many years ago, when I had the measles? E II 11 252 37
You were very bad with the measles; that is, you would E II 11 253 38
great comfort; but the measles are a dreadful complaint. E II 11 253 38
little ones have the measles, she will send for Perry." E II 11 253 38

MEASURE (46)
of adopting so harsh a measure, merely propose to make it LS 7 253 2
Poor Reginald was beyond measure concerned to see his fair LS 17 270 3
dear madam Your letter has surprised me beyond measure. LS 41 309 1
to fill up the measure of curiosity to be raised in the NA I 15 120 25
And it was in a great measure his own doing, for had not NA II 7 173 3
not catch at the measure so eagerly as she had expected. NA II 11 209 2
in forcing her on such a measure, General Tilney had acted NA II 14 234 10
objections against such a measure only a few days before! SS II 4 159 1
more eagerly bent on this measure by perceiving after SS II 5 171 38
as resembling, in some measure, your sister Marianne." SS II 9 205 22
must in some measure be always at the mercy of chance. SS II 14 248 6
it, therefore, as a measure which would fix the time of SS III 3 280 6
diverted him beyond measure;--and when to that was added SS III 5 298 33
By one measure I might have saved myself. SS III 8 323 40
dissipation, had in some measure quieted it, and I had SS III 8 326 53
The girls, dressing in some measure together, grew W 323 3
declined any share in a measure which carried quite as W 347 22
but attribute in some measure to jealousy. had the late Mr. PP I 16 80 32
measure for both, and could very sincerely wish him happy. PP II 5 150 26
allow him to pursue any measure in the best and safest way, PP III 4 276 5
any success from this measure, but as his brother was PP III 6 295 5
she added, "in a great measure, to his kindness. PP III 7 306 46
Fanny thought it a bold measure, but offered no farther MP I 2 16 20
The necessity of the measure in a pecuniary light, and the MP I 3 32 62
of coming to her, a measure quite as welcome on one side, MP I 4 41 15
yet so much in love as to measure distance, or reckon time, MP I 9 94 61
Can you mention any other measure by which I have a chance MP I 16 155 18
A weariness arising probably, in great measure, from the MP II 10 278 20
very ball had in great measure sprung, were well founded. MP II 10 280 32
imparted to her aunts; a measure which he would still have MP III 2 331 19
It had been, as he before presumed, too hasty a measure on MP III 5 356 1
as a right and desirable measure; but before he absolutely MP III 6 368 9
When he had really resolved on any measure, he could MP III 6 370 14
from objecting to such a measure, would have been the MP III 12 419 9
Maria was owing, in some measure, to a favourable MP III 17 466 17
should in a just measure attend his share of the offence, MP III 17 468 22
of his own little circle, in a great measure as he liked. E I 3 20 1
It seemed to him a very ill-judged measure." E I 12 106 58
"had been the wisest measure, every friend must rejoice in E II 5 192 28
herself--to suffer her even to think of such a measure!" E III 10 397 50
which had certainly been, in some measure, the cause. E III 12 421 17
They should lose her; and, probably, in great measure, her E III 12 422 20
the intelligence to prove, in some measure, premature. E III 18 473 27
Lady Russell was extremely sorry that such a measure P III 5 34 11
Elizabeth was, in fact, revolving a great measure. P IV 10 226 64
we can do will be to measure back our steps into the S 1 367 1

MEASURED (5)
Allen says it is nine, measured nine; but I am sure it NA I 3 29 46
We measured the dining-room, and found it would hold SS II 14 252 18
enough for the time his measured manner needed; and very MP II 7 240 10
In that very room she had been measured last September, E II 5 187 4
One complete, measured mile nearer than East Bourne. S 1 369 1

MEASUREMENTS (1)
orders and taken his measurements, had suggested and MP I 14 130 1

MEASURES (26)
But these measures are each too violent to be adopted LS 25 293 4
to disconcert their measures, my heroine was most NA I 14 106 1
known beforehand, proper measures will undoubtedly be NA I 14 112 34
measures by which their intimacy was to be continued. NA II 2 141 11
frightens away all my inclination for hasty measures." SS II 2 148 15
On her measures depended those of her two friends; Mrs. SS III 10 341 4
doomed, however, to be long in ignorance of his measures. SS III 11 353 21
to the others, proper measures would have been taken to SS III 13 371 38
in some of the measures he takes for becoming so.-- W 342 19
That he had been concerned in the measures taken to PP II 10 186 38
to adopt the measures of art so far as to conceal from him PP II 12 199 5
She then proceeded to enquire into the measures which her PP III 5 293 68
riding on horseback, no measures were taken for mounting MP I 4 35 7
in their wrong measures, her countenance of their unsafe MP II 2 188 3
measures and such amusements should have been suggested. MP II 2 188 3
at times very wrong--her measures often ill-chosen and ill- MP III 9 396 6
power to superintend his happiness or quicken his measures. E I 11 91 1
presumed on such early measures, but from the very E III 14 440 8
But these measures, however good in themselves, were P III 1 10 19
measures advised, as he meant to see finally adopted. P III 2 11 1
She wanted more vigorous measures, a more complete P III 2 12 3
be recoverable by proper measures; and this property, P IV 9 210 98
it right to change our measures--and being convinced on S 5 387 1
I dare say, but their measures seem to touch on extremes.-- S 5 388 1
the expense alas! of measures in that masterly style was S 8 405 2
looks, that you are nmot used to such quick measures."-- S 9 410 1

MEASURING (3)
too busily employed in measuring lengths of worsted for SS II 7 181 7
8
determined too easily by measuring them at once; but as SS II 12 233 20
But still he went on measuring, and still he ended with, " E II 11 249 15
16

MEAT (13)
abroad or eating cold meat at home; and great as was NA II 9 190 1
at the side-table for cold meat which was not there. NA II 11 214 27
meat, and have not a neighbour nearer than your mother. SS II 8 197 22
Collins's joints of meat were too large for her family. PP II 7 169 3
set out with such cold meat as an inn larder usually PP II 16 219 2
of servants with cold meat, cake, and a variety of all the PP III 3 268 6
purpose to order in some meat on Wednesday, and she has PP III 11 331 15
I could not tell whether you would be for some meat, or MP III 7 378 14
in the garden, there shall be cold meat in the house." E III 6 355 21
Another slice of cold meat, another draught of Madeira and E III 6 365 65
then, she ate her cold meat; and then she was well enough P III 5 39 40
But I should not like to have butcher's meat raised, S 6 393 1
of the price of butcher's meat in time--tho' you may not S 6 393 1

MECHANICALLY (4)
prepared quietly and mechanically for every evening's SS II 14 249 7
though she answered mechanically to the repeated appeals PP III 1 253 55
hand, it was not mechanically twisted about without regard. E I 7 53 22
while her fingers were mechanically at work, proceeding P III 8 72 58

MECHLIN (1)
great rent in my best Mechlin so charmingly mended, before NA II 14 238 22

MEDALS (1)
Books of engravings, drawers of medals, cameos, corals, E III 6 362 43

MEDECINAL (1)
Mrs G. did never deviate from the strict Medecinal page.-- S 11 422 1

MEDECINE (3)
an unfortunate turn for Medecine, especially quack S 10 412 1
especially quack Medecine, had given them an early S 10 412 1
& Medecine, more relaxed in air, & more subdued in voice. S 10 413 1

MEDIATION (2)
of his own, some mediation of friends, or some more SS III 12 357 1
opinion of what his own mediation in his brother's affairs SS III 13 364 11

MEDICAL (9)
subject in the world for a little medical imposition. MP III 14 429 1
Mrs. Churchill had been recommended to the medical skill E III 1 317 7
where she could have medical attendance at hand, in case P III 12 102 2
of a partnership in the medical line--in your own parish-- S 1 366 1
a wish to establish some medical man at Sanditon, which S 2 371 1
He was convinced that the advantage of a medical man at S 2 372 1
place where they could not have immediate medical advice.-- S 2 372 1
We have entirely done with the whole medical Tribe. S 5 386 1
the place, to get a medical man there, I will undertake S 5 387 1

MEDICINAL (1)
It was a medicinal project upon his niece's understanding, MP III 6 369 10

MEDICINE (3)
arms, in quest of this medicine, and as the two boys chose SS I 21 122 10
any thing that care and medicine might not remove, or at E III 1 317 6
more good than all the medicine he took; and, that being P III 12 102 2
MEDICINES (2)
and forcing proper medicines on her at night, trusted, SS III 7 307 1
His medicines had failed;--the fever was unabated; and SS III 7 313 21
MEDIOCRE (1)
honour my performance is mediocre to the last degree. E II 14 276 36
MEDIOCRITY (2)
mercenary; and the mediocrity of her fortune proved no PP II 13 207 6
mediocrity of condition which seemed to be your lot.-- MP III 1 313 12
MEDITATE (3)
Come, Miss Morland, let us leave him to meditate over our NA I 14 108 17
of her chamber had to meditate upon Charlotte's degree of PP II 5 157 10
Elizabeth that she must meditate an application to her PP III 15 360 2
MEDITATED (8)
Thorpe talked to his horse, and she meditated, by turns, NA I 11 87 51
When he gave his promise to his father, he meditated SS I 1 5 8
extent of the injury I meditated, because I did not then SS III 8 320 32
equally surprised to find that he meditated a quick return. PP I 22 124 11
had ever reached her of Miss Darcy's meditated elopement. PP III 3 270 10
and she worked and meditated in the east room, undisturbed, MP I 18 168 14
knowing what was felt, what was meditated, what was done. E II 15 284 11
her, and professions of Mrs. Elton's meditated activity. E II 17 299 1
MEDITATING (8)
I have been meditating on the very great pleasure which a PP I 6 27 48
you really serious in meditating a dance at Netherfield?-- PP I 11 55 5
6
Mr. Collins, meanwhile, was meditating in solitude on what PP I 20 112 24
While each of the Miss Bertrams were meditating how best, MP I 8 80 29
each thoughtful; Fanny meditating on the different sorts MP III 5 360 13
before her; and she was meditating much upon silver forks, MP III 15 446 35
meditating, in a fixed attitude, for a few minutes. E III 11 407 32
which she had been meditating over, and say, "thank you. P IV 9 204 76
77
MEDITATION (8)
whole night to indulge meditation, Elinor found every day SS I 19 104 12
other, or sat down by the fire in melancholy meditation. SS II 5 172 39
He was sitting in an attitude of deep meditation, and SS III 8 317 9
in earnest meditation; his brow contracted, his air gloomy. PP III 4 278 19
There was great food for meditation in this letter, and MP III 9 394 2
chiefly for unpleasant meditation; and yet, with all the MP III 9 394 2
An interval of meditation, serious and grateful, was the P IV 11 245 77
to form themselves into such a meditation as this.-- S 7 402 1
MEDITATIONS (10)
shake of the head, your meditations are not satisfactory." NA I 3 29 47
of his meditations, he could still smile with them. NA II 8 182 1
walks and silent meditations, still produced occasional SS I 16 83 4
way, wrapt in her own meditations, and scarcely ever SS II 4 160 2
In her earnest meditations on the contents of the letter, SS II 7 184 16
and meditations which had at length closed her eyes. PP II 12 195 1
or pain, might occupy the meditations of almost all. MP I 10 106 58
flow of her own meditations, unbiassed by his bewildering MP III 6 370 14
of her secret meditations; and nothing was more MP III 14 431 8
Emma's pensive meditations, as she walked home, were not E III 9 385 1
MEDITERRANEAN (5)
years ago from the Mediterranean by William, with H. M. S. MP I 16 152 2
return from the Mediterranean, &c.; and the good luck MP II 6 232 13
He had been in the Mediterranean--in the West Indies--in MP II 6 236 21
West Indies--in the Mediterranean again--had been often MP II 6 236 21
when I had still the same luck in the Mediterranean." P III 8 67 23
MEDIUM (4)
be indistinct through the soft medium of a lazy atmosphere. SS I 18 97 4
her size a most becoming medium, between fat and thin, E II 2 167 12
and Miss Bates and I that he is just the happy medium. E II 3 174 38
maintaining the loveliest medium of fortitude and P IV 11 241 61
MEDLEY (2)
style, and the same medley of trusts, hopes, and fears, MP III 13 427 12
Emma wondered on what, of all the medley, she would fix. E II 9 237 50
MEEKLY (1)
that the consciousness of it should be so meekly born. NA II 2 141 12
MEET (157)
unadvisable for them to meet at present; & yet if you do LS 26 295 3
Adeiu till we meet. LS 29 299 4
We must not meet. LS 30 301 4
therefore I say that we ought not, we must not yet meet. LS 30 301 4
meet, and nothing in the world advances intimacy so much." NA I 3 29 51
were over, and ready to meet him with a smile:--but no NA I 4 31 1
I assure you, if it had not been to meet you, I would not NA I 6 40 7
You must not betray me, if you should ever meet with one NA I 6 42 30
too; but I chanced to meet him on Magdalen Bridge, as he NA I 7 46 11
"Did you meet Mr. Tilney, my dear?" said Mrs. Allen. NA I 8 58 28
You would hardly meet with a man who goes beyond his four NA I 9 64 24
You would not often meet with any thing like it in Oxford-- NA I 9 64 24
they will certainly meet with an accident if we go on. NA I 9 65 29
Catherine's resolution of endeavouring to meet Miss Tilney NA I 10 71 8
a crowd they should even meet with the Tilneys in any NA I 10 75 24
to buy a good horse when I meet with one; but it would not NA I 10 76 28
was not one of the family whom she need now fear to meet.-- NA I 12 96 24
to me this evening; we shall meet them at the rooms." NA II 1 130 10
whom he expected to meet here, and as he is now pretty NA II 2 138 2
for him, and he would meet them by another course." NA II 7 179 29
to descend and meet him under the protection of visitors. NA II 9 192 4
at least they should not meet under such circumstances as NA II 13 222 8
Who could say when they might meet again?-- NA II 13 226 25
"If so, my dear, I dare say you will meet again some time NA II 14 236 17
but he might forget her; and in that case to meet!---- NA II 14 236 18
whom he had chanced to meet again in town, and who, under NA II 15 246 12
miles of each other, and shall meet every day of our lives. SS I 3 17 17
at being unable to get any smart young men to meet them. SS I 7 33 4
And was hastening to meet him, when Elinor cried out, " SS I 16 86 17
18
I am so sorry we cannot stay longer; however we shall meet SS I 20 110 2
do but meet him of a morning, he is not fit to be seen.-- SS I 21 123 28
him so seldom--we can hardly meet above twice a-year. SS I 22 133 42
could not be supposed to meet for the sake of conversation. SS II 1 142 8
"it would have gave me such pleasure to meet you there! SS II 2 150 38
last night that did not meet your approbation; and though SS II 7 183 13
I was prepared to meet you with the pleasure which our SS II 7 187 42
When he told me that it might be many weeks before we meet SS II 7 189 46
in this way: and if ever I meet him again, I will give him SS II 8 192 3
"I could meet him in no other way. SS II 9 211 38
He would not speak another word to him, meet him where he SS II 10 214 9
was one who would meet her without feeling any curiosity SS II 10 215 12
their mutual impatience to meet, was not to be told, they SS II 11 230 4
They were to meet Mrs. Ferrars; but Elinor could not learn SS II 12 230 6
for though she could now meet Edward's mother without that SS II 12 230 6
But now, there is one good thing, we shall be able to meet, SS II 13 240 15
shall be able to meet, and meet pretty often, for Lady SS II 13 240 15
of bitterness;--to meet Lucy without betraying the SS III 1 264 32
"I am so glad to meet you;" said Miss Steele, taking her SS III 2 271 8
respective homes, to meet, by appointment, on the road. SS III 6 301 3
You had better meet every night, & break up two hours W 325 4
to be expected, or she cd meet with any chance conveyance, W 338 18
Elizabeth, "that we shall meet him at the assemblies, and PP I 2 6 4
That the Miss Lucases and the Miss Bennets should meet to PP I 5 18 3
But though Bingley and Jane meet tolerably often, it is PP I 6 22 6
as he told Elizabeth, to meet with folly and conceit in PP I 15 71 6
it always gives me pain to meet him, but I have no reason PP I 16 78 20
that I had better not meet Mr. Darcy;--that to be in the PP I 21 115 4
are scarcely less eager to meet her again. I really do not PP I 21 117 14
and instantly set out to meet him accidentally in the lane. PP I 22 121 1
should meet at all, unless he really comes to see her." PP II 2 141 12
I hope they will not meet at all. PP II 2 141 14
"We shall often meet, I hope, in Hertfordshire." PP II 3 146 15
that he had never been so fortunate as to meet Miss Bennet. PP II 7 171 12
her ramble within the park, unexpectedly meet Mr. Darcy.-- PP II 10 182 1
Bennet's carriage was to meet them, they quickly perceived, PP II 16 219 1
all the Lucases came to meet Maria and hear the news: and PP II 16 222 21
If I was to go through the world, I could not meet with a PP III 1 249 33
to speak with calmness, if he really intended to meet them. PP III 1 254 57
Her brother, whose eye she feared to meet, scarcely PP III 3 270 11
with him at the next ball we meet, with great pleasure. PP III 5 291 60
mother, went forward to meet her; but, instead of the PP III 7 301 1
The particulars, I reserve till we meet. PP III 7 302 14
How merry we shall be together when we meet!" PP III 7 306 44
with him; when it was no longer likely they should meet. PP III 8 311 13
The carriage was sent to meet them at ----, and they were PP III 9 315 1
go together; and the others were to meet us at the church. PP III 9 319 24
where he was reduced to meet, frequently meet, reason with, PP III 10 326 3
to meet, frequently meet, reason with, persuade, and PP III 10 326 3
"Oh! my dear Lydia," she cried, "when shall we meet again?" PP III 11 330 3
It will then be publicly seen, that on both sides, we meet PP III 12 339 6
I hope we may often meet again." PP III 12 343 30
good luck, I may meet with another Mr. Collins in time." PP III 13 350 54
the sadler's, and the child be appointed to meet her there. MP I 1 8 8
If I can but make both ends meet, that's all I ask for." MP I 3 29 48
to meet them with a great anxiety to avoid the suspicion. MP I 7 68 17
more spacious and more meet for walking about in, and MP I 16 150 1
get it over; and when we meet at breakfast we shall be all MP I 16 156 27
away immediately, being to meet his uncle at Bath without MP II 2 192 11
"Upon my word, Fanny, you are in high luck to meet with MP II 5 220 28
here's a carriage! who have they got to meet us?" MP II 5 222 46
but she would now meet him with his own cool feelings. MP II 5 227 69
to meet him with any feeling answerable to his own? MP III 4 353 45
'When two sympathetic hearts meet in the marriage state, MP III 5 358 9
and trusting, that when we meet again, it will be under MP III 5 364 30
Fanny, with doubting feelings, had risen to meet him, but MP III 7 379 20
me, and I acknowledge that they did not meet as friends. MP III 13 423 2
from the drawing room to meet her; came with no indolent MP III 15 447 37
consequence, and he was to meet Mrs. Rushworth there. MP III 17 467 20
it was that he should ever meet with such another woman, MP III 17 470 25
He could not meet her in conversation, rational or playful. E I 1 7 7
I dare say Mr. Knightley will be so kind as to meet him." E I 1 14 47
Six years hence, if he could meet with a good sort of E I 4 30 18
"Only think of our happening to meet him!-- E I 4 32 29
So very odd we should happen to meet! E I 4 32 29
did meet, his grave looks shewed that she was not forgiven. E I 9 69 1
every sort that she could meet with, into a thin quarto of E I 9 69 3
and he found it easier to meet her eye than her friend's. E I 9 71 12
this," thought Emma; "to meet in a charitable scheme; this E I 10 87 32
only persons invited to meet them;--the hours were to be E I 13 108 4
as to allow them all to meet again in the common routine E I 17 142 11
If she were to meet Miss Bates in her way!--and upon its E II 3 177 51
was sure just to meet with him, or just to miss him, just E II 4 184 10
But she had made up her mind how to meet this presumption E II 7 207 7
observe it whenever I meet you under those circumstances. E II 8 213 10
of asking Mr. Perry; I happened to meet him in the street. E II 9 237 46
Quite delightful to have you all meet so!-- E II 10 243 31
change; but when they did meet, her composure was odious. E II 12 263 42
meet with any thing at all like what one has left behind. E II 14 273 19
timidity--and I am sure one does not often meet with it.-- E II 15 283 7
If I meet with no insuperable difficulties therefore, E II 16 296 36
and leave his horses to meet him by another road, a mile E III 3 334 7
I do not care whether I meet him or not--except that of E III 4 337 6
Disingenuousness and double-dealing seemed to meet him at E III 5 348 21
highly entertained her: but his gaiety did not meet her's. E III 5 351 38
have spoken to some others whom I would wish to meet you." E III 6 354 11
"You certainly will meet them if I can prevail; and I E III 6 355 19
meet Mr. and Mrs. Elton, and any other of his neighbours.-- E III 6 356 30
Little expecting to meet Miss Woodhouse so soon, there was E III 6 362 43
the next day to tell me that we never were to meet again.-- E III 14 442 8
How much worse, had they been obliged to meet! E III 16 451 1
When the Campbells are returned, we shall meet them in E III 18 477 57
tenants as any set of people one should meet with. P III 3 17 4
I meet them wherever I go; and I declare, I never go twice P III 6 45 9
she supposed, they must meet; and soon she began to wish P III 7 53 1
His father very much wished him to meet Captain Wentworth, P III 7 55 7
Charles's being to meet him to breakfast at his father's. P III 7 58 22
same view of escaping introduction when they were to meet. P III 7 59 23
seriously described the woman he should wish to meet with. P III 7 62 40
they now moved forward to meet the party, "he had not, P III 11 97 13
The nights were too dark for the ladies to meet again till P III 11 99 22
She was actually forced to exert herself, to meet Lady P IV 1 124 11
assiduous endeavours to meet, and, when they did meet, by P IV 3 138 6
meet, and, when they did meet, by such great openness of P IV 3 138 6
particularly unfit to meet any extraordinary expense. P IV 5 154 9
He could meet even Lady Russell in a discussion of her P IV 5 159 21
she had the good fortune to meet with the Admiral. P IV 6 168 25
as every body was to meet every body in Bath, Lady Russell P IV 7 178 26
Sir Walter and his two ladies stepped forward to meet her. P IV 8 184 17
But "they should meet again. P IV 8 185 18
be exceedingly pleased to meet with you again in Camden- P IV 9 206 88
She was particularly asked to meet Mr. Elliot, and be P IV 10 220 29
asked on purpose to meet Lady Dalrymple and her daughter, P IV 10 223 43
to meet the heartless elegance of her father and sister. P IV 10 226 63
"To-morrow evening, to meet a few friends, no formal party. P IV 10 226 64
away and says, "God knows whether we ever meet again!" P IV 11 234 31
for their releif, provided it meet with her approbation.--" S 12 423 1
him--and they parted, to meet again within a few hours.-- S 12 425 1
MEETING (161)
not only prevent our meeting this Christmas, but be the LS 13 263 1
at the idea of the meeting, received her with perfect self- LS 17 269 2
for the hour of meeting, I yet feel myself under the LS 30 299 1
before, but this happy meeting will make us young again. LS 40 309 1
This correspondence, by a meeting between some of the LS 42 311 1
Their joy on this meeting was very great, as well it might, NA I 4 31 2
they had thought of meeting in Bath, and what a pleasure NA I 4 32 2
were still resolute in meeting in defiance of wet and dirt, NA I 5 37 4
Catherine, by whom this meeting was wholly unexpected, NA I 7 44 4
the usual ceremonial of meeting her friend with the most NA I 8 52 1
having missed such a meeting with both brother and sister. NA I 9 69 51
apprehension of really meeting with what he related. NA II 5 160 23
had depended upon meeting with features, air, complexion NA II 9 191 3
to attend the parish meeting, and shall probably be NA II 11 209 5
as would make their meeting materially painful. NA II 13 222 8
Very little passed between them on meeting; each found her NA II 13 227 27
destroy the pleasure of a meeting with those she loved NA II 14 231 5
The hope of meeting again in the course of a few years NA II 14 236 18
happen within that time to make a meeting dreadful to her. NA II 14 236 18
the first day of their meeting, it will not appear, after NA II 16 252 7
Another meeting will suffice to explain his sentiments on SS I 10 47 4
In every meeting of the kind Willoughby was included; and SS I 11 53 1
To Marianne, indeed, the meeting between Edward and her SS I 16 87 23
surprise and inquiries of meeting, Marianne asked Edward SS I 16 87 24
schemes for their meeting were effectual, he had not a SS I 21 124 33
prevented their meeting in conversation on terms of SS I 22 127 2
The insipidity of the meeting was exactly such as Elinor SS II 1 143 10
I had quite depended upon meeting you there. SS II 2 151 40
from meeting her mother or the Miss Dashwoods again. SS II 4 164 21
of him not to give you the meeting when he was invited." SS II 5 171 36
As for Marianne, on the pangs which so unhappy a meeting SS II 6 179 18
One meeting was unavoidable. SS II 9 211 35

We returned unwounded, and the meeting, therefore, never SS II 9 211 38
Their affection and pleasure in meeting, was just enough SS II 11 221 7
recent meeting--and this she had every reason to expect. SS II 13 245 47
Within a few days after this meeting, the newspapers SS II 14 246 1
being so deceived!--meeting with such ingratitude, where SS III 1 265 36
had a constant dread of meeting them, chose rather to stay SS III 2 271 4
great satisfaction in meeting them, and on receiving SS III 2 271 5
that I should soon have the pleasure of meeting you again. SS III 4 288 27
He expressed great pleasure in meeting Elinor, told her SS III 5 294 4
Delaford, was all that foretold any meeting in the country. SS III 6 301 1
his open pleasure in meeting her after an absence of only SS III 6 305 16
Elinor's delight, as she saw what each felt in the meeting, SS III 9 334 5
at first accidentally meeting, the vanity of the one had SS III 13 364 11
A very stiff meeting between these near neighbours ensued-- W 327 8
On meeting her long-absent sister, as on every occasion of W 349 23
mind, at the moment of meeting;--& she cd. not but feel W 349 24
dreaded the meeting, & at the same time longed for it.-- W 356 28
I could never dread a meeting with Miss Emma Watson,--or W 356 28
"Would he give robt the meeting, they shd be very happy." W 359 28
there were; but as to not meeting with many people in this PP I 9 43 25
tedious in the usual process of such a meeting. PP I 11 55 8
other, was all astonishment at the effect of the meeting. PP I 15 73 8
might, the very cold manner of our meeting yesterday.-- PP I 16 77 12
The certainty of meeting him had not been checked by any PP I 18 89 1
Who would have thought of my meeting with--perhaps--a PP I 18 96 57
I am particularly unlucky in meeting with a person so well PP II 8 174 15
saw on looking up that Colonel Fitzwilliam was meeting her. PP II 10 182 2
walking in the grove some time in the hope of meeting you. PP II 12 195 2
of the young man, who, on meeting him accidentally in town, PP II 13 205 4
and possibly a mutual desire of never meeting again. PP II 18 235 39
The possibility of meeting Mr. Darcy, while viewing the PP II 19 240 16
house, all her apprehensions of meeting its owner returned. PP III 1 245 4
again and again over the perverseness of the meeting. PP III 1 252 54
spoken with such gentleness as on this unexpected meeting. PP III 1 252 54
on this accidental meeting, most eager to preserve the PP III 2 265 16
of his meeting some of the gentlemen at Pemberley by noon. PP III 2 266 18
What a meeting for her, when she first sees my aunt!" PP III 7 305 36
her own inclination, any meeting with him would have been PP III 8 314 22
She knew but little of their meeting in Derbyshire, and PP III 11 334 36
"Now," said she, "that this first meeting is over, I feel PP III 12 339 6
his hopes of their all meeting frequently at St. James's, PP III 18 384 26
Their eager affection in meeting, their exquisite delight MP I 2 21 34
The two families will be meeting every day in the year. MP I 3 27 31
The meeting was very satisfactory on each side. MP I 4 41 17
The second meeting proved him not so very plain; he was MP I 5 44 2
The next meeting of the two Mansfield families produced MP I 8 79 28
when the young people, meeting with an outward door, MP I 9 89 32
three on this unexpected meeting; and as Edmund was come MP I 18 169 23
to witness the first meeting of his father and his friend. MP II 1 182 22
After a little while I dare say we shall be meeting again MP II 3 199 14
A friendly meeting, and not a fine dinner, is all we have MP II 4 215 49
A very cordial meeting passed between him and Edmund; and MP II 5 223 48
to delay the moment of meeting, she was with him as he MP II 6 233 15
The meeting was generally felt to be a pleasant one, being MP II 7 238 3
opportunities of meeting, but my daughters would be happy MP II 7 245 34
any other appointed meeting of the two families might be. MP II 8 256 13
In every meeting there was a hope of receiving farther MP II 8 256 13
his seat and his pen, and meeting her with something in MP II 9 261 2
The stiffness of the meeting soon gave way before their MP II 10 273 8
When the meeting with which she was threatened for the MP III 1 324 59
I am sure of meeting again and again, and all but you. MP III 5 364 32
At last, after various attempts at meeting, I have seen MP III 9 393 1
That Miss Crawford should endeavour to secure a meeting MP III 12 418 4
manner, however, rather than any unfrequency of meeting. MP III 13 421 2
Fanny began to dread the meeting with her aunts and Tom, MP III 15 446 35
of; and as to his ever meeting with any other woman who MP III 16 460 31
We shall be always meeting! E I 1 8 14
half a mile apart, and were sure of meeting every day." E I 1 11 35
that morning, and meeting with Harriet and pleading his E I 8 67 56
poor family, however, were the first subject on meeting. E I 10 87 31
for the happiness of meeting her again, when he hoped to E I 13 111 14
that she knew the first meeting must be rather alarming.-- E I 14 121 14
the anxiety of a first meeting at the time talked of: "for E I 14 121 14
they would give them the meeting in Dublin, and take them E II 1 159 20
never, as a first meeting, occur again, and therefore you E II 3 180 55
to be rather glad that there had been such a meeting. E II 3 180 58
to feel that the first meeting was over, and to give her E II 4 182 7
had been the cure of the agitation of meeting Mr. Martin. E II 4 184 11
the sort of meeting, and the sort of pain it was creating. E II 5 186 4
quick amendment; and so ended a most satisfactory meeting. E II 5 189 16
numbers enough for such a meeting; and even when E II 6 198 5
could hardly believe it to be only their second meeting. E II 6 203 42
Another accidental meeting with the Martins was possible, E II 9 233 23
seemed to give fresh pleasure to the present meeting. E II 9 233 25
Short had been the notice--short their meeting; he was E II 12 261 37
They had been meeting almost every day since his arrival. E II 12 262 38
the very last time of its meeting her eye, unadorned as it E II 13 266 5
the third time of their meeting, she heard all Mrs. E II 15 282 4
I had the pleasure of meeting you; and Henry and John had E II 16 293 15 16
doubt of very soon meeting with something that would do." E II 17 301 15
good fortune in meeting with so many of your friends at E II 18 312 50
No second meeting had there yet been between him and Emma. E III 2 319 2
it would be better than a common meeting in a crowd. E III 2 319 2
This is meeting quite in fairy-land!-- E III 2 323 19
I have no objection at all to meeting the Hartfield family. E III 6 355 18
she would still avoid a meeting with her, and communicate E III 14 435 4
to find Harriet as desirous as herself to avoid a meeting. E III 16 451 1
"Oh! no, it is a meeting at the crown, a regular meeting. E III 16 456 27
I am almost certain that the meeting at the crown is not E III 16 456 28
"Oh! no; the meeting is certainly to-day," was the abrupt E III 16 456 29
You mean the crown; you come from the meeting at the crown. E III 16 457 39
was ready, on the first meeting, to consider the subject E III 17 467 30
I would not have missed this meeting for the world. E III 18 479 72
by meeting her with the most unqualified congratulations.-- E III 19 481 2
This meeting of the two parties proved highly satisfactory, P III 5 32 2
The two families were so continually meeting, so much in P III 5 36 21
whom they recollected meeting, once or twice, after their P III 6 52 33
like to leave the little boy, to give him the meeting.-- P III 7 54 5
She would have liked to know how he felt as to a meeting. P III 7 58 21
of curiosity, he had no desire of meeting her again. P III 7 61 37
Lady Russell and Captain Wentworth never meeting any where. P III 11 93 3
and this second meeting, short as it was, also proved P III 12 104 7
some anxiety mixed with Lady Russell's joy in meeting her. P IV 1 123 10
So ended all danger to Anne of meeting Captain Wentworth P IV 1 128 32
Mary spoke with animation of their meeting with, or rather P IV 2 132 22
They went through the particulars of their first meeting a P IV 4 148 9
was uncomfortable in the meeting had soon passed away, and P IV 5 153 6
She longed to see the Crofts, but when the meeting took P IV 6 168 22
We are always meeting with some old friend or other; the P IV 6 170 29
Their last meeting had been most important in opening his P IV 10 221 32
I have no pleasure in the sort of meeting, and should be P IV 10 224 53
To-night we may have the pleasure of all meeting again, at P IV 11 236 36
she felt almost certain of meeting him) could not be borne. P IV 11 238 47
in the very hour of first meeting her in Bath; that had P IV 11 241 60
Their first meeting in Milsom-Street afforded much to be P IV 11 244 71
danger, because the wind meeting with nothing to oppose or S 4 381 1
Heaven defend me from meeting such a man un-armed."-- S 7 397 1
D. having been defeated by meeting with her beforehand. S 12 423 1
it was a very friendly meeting between Sidney & his sister S 12 425 1

MEETINGS (17)
One or two meetings of this kind had taken place, without SS II 1 143 9
and what he meant, before many meetings had taken place. SS II 4 159 1
had marked their several meetings in Derbyshire; and as PP III 4 279 23
in the course of their meetings she must sometimes think PP III 18 384 26
him decidedly in the meetings which were now becoming MP I 6 52 1
again for the almost daily meetings they lately had. MP II 11 286 15
in yearly meetings at Sotherton and Everingham.' MP III 16 456 23
with such frequent meetings at Hartfield, was foundation E I 4 35 45
This is quite the season indeed for friendly meetings. E I 13 115 39
awkwardness of future meetings, the difficulties of E I 16 137 12
and have regular weekly meetings at your house, or ours. E II 14 277 38
the uncertainty of our meetings, the sort of constant E II 18 309 30
it was not more productive than such meetings usually are. E III 2 326 33
was but the beginning of other dinings and other meetings. P III 8 63 1
as might in two meetings extinguish every past hope, and P III 9 77 19
had witnessed former meetings which would be brought too P III 11 93 3
It was in one of these short meetings, each apparently P IV 11 246 79 80

MEETLY (1)
Can either of us be more meetly employed? NA II 8 187 15

MEETS (5)
For now we have a quiet little whist club that meets three W 325 4
Affectation of candour is common enough;--one meets it PP I 4 14 9
fight Wickham, wherever he meets him, and then he will be PP III 5 287 35
delicacy which one seldom meets with now-a-days, Mrs. MP I 12 117 14
He meets with a young woman at a watering-place, gains her E III 13 428 23

MELANCHOLY (61)
in, would undergo so speedy, so melancholy a reverse! LS 24 285 1
of the delightful melancholy which such a grove inspired. NA II 7 179 29
its affliction by melancholy remembrances, she was SS I 3 14 1
was performed in too melancholy a disposition to be SS I 6 28 1
When is she dejected or melancholy? SS I 8 39 18
in the most melancholy order of disastrous love. SS I 11 57 17
"Something very melancholy must be the matter, I am sure," SS I 14 70 2
few days into a calmer melancholy; but these employments, SS I 16 83 4
Edward--whether it be melancholy or gay, I love to recall SS I 17 92 26
You are in a melancholy humour, and fancy that any one SS I 19 103 7
but it made him so melancholy, not being able to stay more SS I 22 134 52
near Plymouth, his melancholy state of mind, his SS II 1 139 1
upon his patience; but melancholy was the state of the SS II 1 140 3
death, which is a melancholy and shocking extremity?-- SS II 2 148 14
the card table with the melancholy persuasion that Edward SS II 2 151 41
other, or sat down by the fire in melancholy meditation. SS II 5 172 39
on the contrary, with a melancholy impression of Colonel SS II 5 174 47
in his disturbed and melancholy look, and in his anxious SS II 9 204 17
her; but the search was as fruitless as it was melancholy. SS II 9 207 26
could I believe the melancholy and sickly figure before me, SS II 9 207 26
It is a melancholy consideration. SS III 1 268 50
the admission of every melancholy idea, and he could not SS III 7 309 7
soon discovered in his melancholy eye and varying SS III 10 340 2
with her tears, my uncle's melancholy state of health.-- W 352 26
as possible, when the melancholy event takes place--which, PP I 19 106 10
"Pray do, my dear Miss Lucas," she added in a melancholy PP II 3 113 26
the melancholy scene so lately gone through at Rosings. PP II 14 210 1
Poor Charlotte!--it was melancholy to leave her to such PP II 15 216 7
consoled her for the melancholy conviction of her PP II 18 233 23
feel a most melancholy difference in the change of masters. MP I 6 52 1
There is nothing awful here, nothing melancholy, nothing MP I 9 85 6
melancholy truth--that they had not yet got any Anhalt. MP I 15 143 28
to grieve over the melancholy change; and there her uncle MP II 11 282 2
It was a heavy, melancholy day.-- MP II 11 282 4
ready to feed on melancholy remembrances, and tender MP III 3 334 1
withstand the melancholy influence of the word "last." MP III 5 359 10
man cut off in the flower of his days, is most melancholy. MP III 14 434 13
made her still more melancholy; for sun-shine appeared to MP III 15 439 9
Employment, even melancholy, may dispel melancholy, and MP III 15 443 25
It made her melancholy again; and the knowledge of what MP III 15 447 36
and well situated as it was, with a melancholy aspect. MP III 15 447 36
be given in his then melancholy state of spirits, of his MP III 17 461 2
a subject of most melancholy and momentous consultation. MP III 17 464 13
It was a melancholy change; and Emma could not but sigh E I 1 7 10
Mr. Woodhouse, with a melancholy shake of the head and a E I 11 93 5
Papa, if you speak in that melancholy way, you will be E I 11 94 14
of it, save the melancholy remembrance of him dying in E II 2 163 2
lamenting, with tender melancholy, over the departure of E III 5 347 20
could be ventured on, and it was all melancholy stagnation. E III 6 353 6
The evening of this day was very long, and melancholy, at E III 12 421 18
soon after tea, and dissipated every melancholy fancy. E III 12 422 19
and the same melancholy, seemed to reign at Hartfield--but E III 13 424 1
to which time must be giving increase of melancholy! E III 15 450 36
subject of misery to him, by a melancholy tone herself. E III 17 465 28
had, indeed, made a melancholy change: but she was not E III 17 466 29
solitariness and the melancholy of so altered a village, P III 5 36 19
by the now deserted and melancholy looking rooms, and P III 11 96 10
He had a pleasing face and a melancholy air, just as he P III 11 97 14
Indeed I think it quite melancholy to have such excellent P III 12 102 2
melancholy, just as satire or morality might prevail.-- S 7 396 1
you to mention a very melancholy case to Lady D. which has S 12 424 1

MELODIES (1)
And here are a new set of Irish melodies. E II 10 242 21

MELT (1)
it, was enough to melt Catherine's pride in a moment, and NA II 13 229 30

MELTED (1)
so little disconcerted by the melted butter's being oiled. NA II 11 215 27

MELTING (1)
Can you conceive any thing more subduing, more melting, S 7 397 1

MEMBER (7)
For any member of your family I must always feel a degree LS 24 290 13
The luck of one member of a family is luck to all.--" W 321 2
by the voice of every member of their respective houses; PP III 14 356 50
to think of every member of that home as she directed, or MP II 6 234 18
in the autumn, than any member of the old intimacy had MP II 7 238 1
unworthy member of the one she was now transplanted into.-- P III 6 43 3
Most families have such a member among them I beleive Miss S 4 382 1

MEMBERS (5)
with one of its members, and his own views on another, (NA II 15 245 12
Some members of their society sent away and the spirits of MP II 3 196 1
But though she had <u>seen</u> all the members of the family, she MP III 7 381 26
and success of the other members of the family, all MP III 17 473 31
be to <u>his</u>, and those members of the denham family, whom S 3 376 1

MEMENTO (4)
allow, that an occasional memento of past folly, however NA II 10 201 4
dear lock--all, every memento was torn from me." SS III 8 329 63
wipe away every outward memento of what had been, even to MP II 2 190 9
of Edmund, such a memento made her particularly awake to MP II 4 207 10

MEMOIRS (2)
into whose hands these memoirs of the wretched Matilda may NA II 5 160 21
the finest letters, such memoirs of characters of worth P III 11 101 24

MEMORABLE (1)
and Margaret one memorable morning direct their steps, SS I 9 40 3

MEMORANDUM (1)
a memorandum in his pocket-book; it was about spruce beer. E III 4 339 18

MEMORANDUMS (2)
There were the pencilled marks and memorandums on the E II 5 187 4
and memorandums of real importance had been destroyed. P IV 9 203 70

MEMORIAL (1)
to them both--a standing memorial of the beauty of one, E I 6 47 27

MEMORIALS (2)
some awful memorials of an injured and ill-fated nun. NA II 2 141 11
and the cross, those memorials of the two most beloved of MP II 9 271 40

MEMORIES (6)
read to supply their memories with those quotations which NA I 1 15 3
impressed on their memories than that their brother's PP I 4 15 11

They seemed each of them to have the happiest memories in PP III 9 316 6
memories, and your poor cousin has probably none at all. MP I 2 19 27
There is a vast deal of difference in memories, as well as MP I 2 19 27
to exercise their memories, practise their duets, and grow MP I 2 20 33

MEMORY (45)

blame on the memory of one, whose name is sacred with me." LS 24 288 11
endebted to my husband's memory for any happiness derived LS 30 300 3
But her memory endears it now." NA II 7 180 32
be, as certainly as her memory could guide her, exactly NA II 8 188 17
elegant monument to the memory of Mrs. Tilney, which NA II 9 190 1
as described by Eleanor, which does honour to her memory. NA II 9 196 23
times; and had Elinor's memory been equal to her means of SS I 11 54 6
and engross her memory, her reflection, and her fancy. SS I 19 105 12
it must nearly have escaped her memory by this time." SS III 5 296 21
The event has been unfortunate, but my uncle's memory is W 352 26
of their existence; in memory & in prospect, but for the W 361 31
seem disrespectful to his memory for me to be on good PP I 13 62 12
the hopes and disgracing the memory of his father." PP I 16 78 20
He may live in my memory as the most amiable man of my PP II 1 134 7
He was storing his memory with anecdotes and noble names. PP II 6 166 41
living was fresh in her memory, and as she recalled his PP II 13 205 3
Many of his expressions were still fresh in her memory. PP II 13 206 5
Elizabeth was pleased to find his memory so exact; and he PP III 2 262 9
But in such cases as these, a good memory is unpardonable. PP III 17 373 7
so as not to disgrace the memory of the dear departed-- MP I 3 29 46
her respect for her aunt's memory which misleads her here. MP I 7 63 7
in it by the domestic chaplain, within the memory of many. MP I 9 86 9
My feelings are not quite so evanescent, nor my memory of MP I 10 98 10
to make an artificial memory for him, and learning every MP I 18 166 4
more wonderful than the rest, I do think it is memory. MP II 4 208 12
of memory, than in any other of our intelligences. MP II 4 208 12
The memory is sometimes so retentive, so serviceable, so MP II 4 209 12
"You have a good memory. MP II 7 241 18
"There is hardly any desiring to refresh such a memory as E I 5 37 9
Emma assisted with her invention, memory and taste; and as E I 9 70 4
If I had but her memory! E I 9 78 54
Well, time does fly indeed!--and my memory is very bad. E I 11 96 24
Perfect happiness, even in memory, is not common; and E II 9 231 2
in the place, within her memory; no recontre, no alarm of E III 3 335 10
refresh and correct her memory with more particular E III 6 357 34
The impression of it is strong on my memory." E III 11 406 23
which her own memory brought in favour of Mr. Knightley's E III 11 409 34
Much that lived in Harriet's memory, many little E III 11 409 35
with Frederick Wentworth, as he stood in her memory. P III 4 28 7
her imagination, her memory, and all her ideas in as much P III 6 43 3
might dare to judge from memory and experience, that P III 10 82 1
hope, and spring, all gone together, blessed her memory. P III 10 85 12
some sweetness to the memory of her two months visit there, P III 11 93 4
If I had such a memory as benwick, I could bring you fifty P IV 11 234 27
I owe to poor Mr Hollis's memory, I should never keep up S 6 393 1

MEN (199)

house the affections of two men who were neither of them LS 4 248 2
scarcely possible that two men should be so grossly LS 6 252 2
I know that young men in general do not admit of any LS 12 260 1
Her neglect of her husband, her encouragement of other men, LS 12 260 2
Young men are often hasty in their resolutions--& not more LS 23 284 6
surprise at there being any men in the world who could NA I 2 20 8
way through the throng of men by the door, as swiftly as NA I 2 21 9
She was now seen by many young men who had not been near NA I 2 23 27
obliged to the two young men for this simple praise than a NA I 2 24 28
write better letters than men, than that they sing better NA I 3 28 34
"Men commonly take so little notice of those things," said NA I 3 28 39
and I am so vexed with the men for not admiring her!-- NA I 6 40 12
The men think us incapable of real friendship you know, NA I 6 40 14
the kind of girl to be a great favourite with the men." NA I 6 40 14
The men take notice of that sometimes you know." NA I 6 42 25
Do you know, there are two odious young men who have been NA I 6 43 33
to watch the proceedings of these alarming young men. NA I 6 43 34
she added, "perhaps we may overtake the two young men." NA I 6 43 40
I have no notion of treating men with such respect. NA I 6 43 43
fast as they could walk, in pursuit of the two young men. NA I 6 43 44
the present case) of young men, are not detained on one NA I 7 44 1
the two offending young men in Milsom-Street, she was so NA I 7 47 18
talked, like the married men to whom she had been used; he NA I 8 53 3
But you men are all so immoderately lazy! NA I 8 56 14
You men have such restless curiosity! NA I 8 57 18
But when you men have a point to carry, you never stick at NA I 8 57 23
her general notions of what men ought to be, she could not NA I 9 66 32
duties of both; and those men who do not chuse to dance or NA I 10 76 29
are hardly three young men in the room besides him, that I NA I 10 78 38
he had never seen two men so much alike in his life, and NA I 11 87 53
I dare say we would do very well without you; but you men NA I 11 90 63
Young men and women driving about the country in open NA I 13 104 31
in them by young men, to whom they are not even related?" NA I 13 104 33
But I really thought before, young men despised novels NA I 14 107 10
in every page; the men all so good for nothing, and hardly NA I 14 108 22
will only add in justice to men, that though to the larger NA I 14 111 29
a mob of three hundred men assembling in St. George's NA I 14 113 39
Your brother is the most charming of men. NA I 15 117 6
they would be at, young men especially, they are so NA II 3 146 20
You men have none of you any hearts." NA II 3 147 24
the taste of ladies in regard to places as well as men. NA II 7 175 15
They are a set of very worthy men. NA II 11 210 6
and young men never know their minds two days together. NA II 12 216 2
to see him connected with some of the great men of the day. SS I 3 16 6
But Edward had no turn for great men or barouches. SS I 3 16 6
at being unable to get any smart young men to meet them. SS I 7 33 4
Miss Marianne must not expect to have all the men to SS I 9 44 23
Men are very safe with us, let them be ever so rich. SS I 9 44 24
The law was allowed to be genteel enough; many young men, SS I 19 102 4
not as many genteel young men in Devonshire as Sussex?" SS I 21 123 27
prettiest behaved young men I ever saw; but as for Lucy, SS II 2 148 22
I shall speak a good word for you to all the young men, SS II 3 154 2
can ever be given up by the young men of this age." SS II 8 194 10
as any I ever saw; and as likely to attract the men. SS II 11 227 50
on her, "you think young men never stand upon engagements, SS II 13 243 38
among a group of young men, the very he, who had given SS II 14 250 11
difference of the two young men, she did not find that the SS II 14 250 12
two maids and two men; and I believe I could help them to SS III 1 260 7
Two maids and two men indeed!--as I talked of t'other day.- SS III 2 277 28
There are not many men who would act as he has done. SS III 4 285 2
men, I do not know that one is superior to the other." SS III 5 297 29
as the most worthless of men, Willoughby, in spite of all SS III 9 333 2
is enough to prove him one of the worthiest of men." SS III 9 337 16
of the dearest of our friends, and the best of men!-- SS III 11 350 7
reality of reason and truth, one of the happiest of men. SS III 13 361 3
many very disagreable men;--I think I could like any good W 318 2
Among the increasing numbers of military men, one now made W 328 8
seemed to call the young men to their duty, & people the W 328 9
Carr, & a party of young men were standing engaged in ver W 330 11
men of four thousand a year come into the neighbourhood." PP I 1 5 31
consequence to young ladies who are slighted by other men. PP I 3 11 13
men of any consideration in the world," replied Darcy. PP I 8 37 19
their own; and with many men, I dare say, it succeeds. PP I 8 40 56
The wisest and the best of men, nay, the wisest and best PP I 11 57 20
Darcy, was one of the best men that ever breathed, and the PP I 16 78 20
But the fact is, that we are very different sort of men, PP I 16 80 27
in the way of other rich men; and lastly, it was so PP I 18 99 63
to make him the happiest of men; and though such a PP I 22 121 2
Without thinking highly either of men or of matrimony, PP I 22 122 3
to name an early day for making him the happiest of men. PP I 23 128 10
"And men take care that they should." PP II 1 136 15
everybody else Mr. Darcy was condemned as the worst of men. PP II 1 138 31
would be fixed that was to make him the happiest of men. PP II 2 139 1
men must have something to live on, as well as the plain." PP II 3 150 29
very poor opinion of young men who live in Derbyshire; and PP II 4 154 19
Stupid men are the only ones worth knowing, after all." PP II 4 154 19
What are men to rocks and mountains? PP II 4 154 23
There could not exist in the world two men, over whom Mr. PP II 10 186 38
But I am particularly attached to these young men; and PP II 14 210 3
made a point of her having two men servants go with her.-- PP II 14 211 13
Have you seen any pleasant men? PP II 16 221 17
of the men came in, they did not know him in the least. PP II 16 221 17
And that made the men suspect something, and then they PP II 16 221 17
mismanagement in the education of those two young men. PP II 17 225 15
Not like the wild young men now-a-days, who think of PP III 1 249 38
only because he does not rattle away like other young men." PP III 1 249 38
"Your great men often are; and therefore I shall not take PP III 1 258 72
of the most worthless young men in Great Britain to be her PP III 8 308 1
And there are several of the young men, too, that she PP III 8 313 21
whisper, "the men shan't come and part us, I am determined. PP III 12 341 16
17
"If you were to give me forty such men, I never could be PP III 13 350 54
the room, "if any young men come for Mary or Kitty, send PP III 17 377 40
and young men, her father would never consent to her going. PP III 19 385 4
But there certainly are not so many men of large fortune MP I 1 3 1
all the grandeur of men in the eyes of their little cousin. MP I 2 12 3
they were in the company of men of fortune, and MP I 4 38 9
were very fine young men, that two such young men were not MP I 5 47 27
men, that two such young men were not often seen together MP I 5 47 27
Sneyd was surrounded by men, attached myself to one of her MP I 5 51 40
Post captains may be very good sort of men, but they do MP I 6 60 49
for men and women, her talents for the light and lively. MP I 8 81 31
time would ever come when men and women might lie another MP I 9 87 15
Men love to distinguish themselves, and in either of the MP I 9 92 44
as one finds to be the case with men of the world." MP I 10 98 10
Nobody can wonder that men are soldiers and sailors." MP I 11 109 19
the trouble of being agreeable, which make men clergymen. MP I 11 110 23
with very few of a set of men you condemn so conclusively. MP I 11 110 24
"Where any one body of educated men, of whatever MP I 11 110 26
of the most correct men in England, would not hear of it." MP I 13 122 4
Such a forward young lady may well frighten the men." MP I 15 144 32
I could name at this moment at least six young men within MP I 15 148 58
There are his own two men pushing it back into its old MP II 5 222 46
much between the two young men about hunting, so much of MP II 5 223 48
the eyes of the two young men assured him, that the MP II 10 272 4
"We miss our two young men," was Sir Thomas's observation MP II 11 284 9
It is the general way; all young men do." MP II 11 287 20
The two young men were the only talkers, but they, MP III 3 339 22
degree of ignorance men, when suddenly called to the MP III 3 339 22
and bustle upon bustle, men and boys at last all in motion MP III 7 384 36
The men appeared to her all coarse, the women all pert, MP III 9 395 3
she knows but three men in town who have so good a person, MP III 12 416 2
Tom had gone from London with a party of young men to MP III 13 426 10
house of one of these young men, to the comforts of MP III 13 426 10
If he is to die, there will be two poor young men less in MP III 14 434 13
"Well, and that is as early as most men can afford to E I 4 30 20
had very good specimens of well educated, well bred men. E I 4 32 32
It is so with some men. E I 7 51 5
and till it appears that men are much more philosophic on E I 8 63 44
Men of sense, whatever you may chuse to say, do not want E I 8 64 47
Men of family would not be very fond of connecting E I 8 64 47
obscurity--and most prudent men would be afraid of the E I 8 64 47
when there are only men present, I am convinced that he E I 8 66 53
I believe he is one of the very best tempered men that E I 11 95 19
As to men and women, our opinions are sometimes very E I 12 98 3
nature in your estimate of men and women, and as little E I 12 98 4
is, I believe, in many men, especially single men, such an E I 13 111 13
many men, especially single men, such an inclination--such E I 13 111 13
With men he can be rational and unaffected, but when he E I 13 111 16
I wish her extremely well: and, no doubt, there are men E I 15 132 35
often look upon fine young men, well-bred and agreeable. E I 18 149 29
chiefly among the single men, had already taken place. E II 7 207 6
of gentlemen-like, sensible men; and spoke so handsomely E II 8 220 48
sort of thing that so few men would think of. E II 8 223 63
The ladies here probably exchanged looks which meant, "men E II 11 253 43
men and women; and Mrs. Weston must not speak of it again. E II 11 254 45
every morning (one of our men, I forget his name) shall E II 16 295 34
And it is a kindness to employ our men." E II 16 296 38
away before the other men!--what a dear creature he is;--I E II 17 302 22
"Aye, we men are sad fellows. E II 18 305 7
shoulders of the elderly men, was such as Emma felt must E III 2 326 32
whole row of young men who could be compared with him.-- E III 2 326 32
She had given them neither men, nor names, nor places, E III 6 358 35
men and women, I cannot imagine them to be very frequent. E III 7 373 44
could be in love with more than three men in one year. E III 15 450 38
How very few of those men in a rank of life to address E III 17 467 31
a comparison of the two men, she felt, that pleased as she E III 18 480 80
and few navy officers, or men of any other description, P III 3 18 8
claim with any other set of men, for all the comforts and P III 3 19 11
12
distinction, and raising men to honours which their P III 3 19 16
I was in company with two men, striking instances of what P III 3 19 16
Have a little mercy on the poor men. P III 3 20 17
I know no other set of men but what lose something of P III 3 20 17
they as to the names of men or ships, that it had made P III 6 51 31
If there is any thing disagreeable going on, men are P III 7 56 10
for I have thought on the subject more than most men." P III 7 62 41
a few hundred men to sea, in a ship not fit to be employed. P III 8 65 11
He knows there must have been twenty better men than P III 8 65 12
and of all the young men who came near them, seemed to P III 9 74 9
Winthrop, however, or its environs--for young men are, P III 10 85 13
than any other set of men in England; that they only knew P III 11 99 19
He is one of the dullest young men that ever lived. P IV 2 132 16
Mr. Elliot was better to look at than most men, and he had P IV 3 141 12
in Bath; and as for the men! they were infinitely worse. P IV 3 142 13
There are several odd-looking men walking about here, who, P IV 6 166 16
me a pitiful trick once--got away some of my best men. P IV 6 170 29
But the men are all wild after Miss Elliot. P IV 7 178 23
There were many other men about him, many groups walking P IV 7 179 28
standing among a cluster of men at a little distance. P IV 8 188 41
her more from other men, than their final separation. P IV 9 192 2
But he was careless and immethodical, like other men, P IV 9 203 70
of his attentions being beyond those of other men." P IV 10 213 7
does all this so soon for men, (which, however, I do not P IV 11 232 20
But perhaps you will say, these were all written by men." P IV 11 234 27
Men have had every advantage of us in telling their own P IV 11 234 28
I speak, you know, only of such men as have hearts!" P IV 11 235 31
that there is true attachment and constancy "among men. P IV 11 237 42
Like other great men under reverses," he added with a P IV 11 247 84
field, men, women, women & children--not very far off.-- S 1 364 1
& while one or two of the men lent their help to the S 1 365 1

MEN'S (7)

and, on catching the young men's eyes, the horse was NA I 7 44 3
You women are always thinking of men's being in liquor. NA I 9 63 20
opinion, respecting young men's open carriages, made her NA II 5 156 5
"I do not want to pry into other men's concerns. SS I 13 65 39
I have no notion of men's going on in this way: and if SS II 8 192 3
there are so many young men's claims to be attended to in MP III 5 364 29
well-tied parcels of "men's beavers" and "York tan" were E II 6 200 16

MEND (10)

Now however, we begin to mend; our party is enlarged by LS 7 254 3
Marianne continued to mend every day, and the brilliant SS III 9 335 7
though slowly, to mend; and in the evening Elizabeth PP I 10 47 1

Let me mend it for you. PP I 10 47 11
I mend pens remarkably well." PP I 10 47 11
"Thank you--but I always mend my own." PP I 10 47 12
you would tell sally to mend a great slit in my worked PP III 5 292 60
wished Rebecca would mend it; and Fanny was first roused MP III 15 439 9
untowardly one month, they are sure to mend the next." E II 18 308 27
in her deserted nursery to mend stockings, and dress all P IV 1 121 3
MENDED (3)
Mechlin so charmingly mended, before I left Bath, that one NA II 14 238 22
I wish we could get the bell mended--but Betsey is a very MP III 7 379 15
"My appetite is very much mended I assure you lately. S 9 411 1
MENDING (2)
At fifteen, appearances were mending; she began to curl NA I 1 14 2
But I told a man mending a hedge that it was Thornton MP II 7 241 17
MENS' (1)
"Oh! dear! one never thinks of married mens' being beaux-- SS I 21 124 30
MENTAL (12)
it) the conversation of a woman of high mental powers. LS 14 263 2
Morland's personal and mental endowments, when about to be NA I 2 18 1
and her deficiency of all mental improvement, her want of SS I 22 127 2
she might inhale a breeze of mental strength herself. MP I 16 152 3
he had acknowledged Fanny's mental superiority. MP III 17 471 28
at present, the only mental provision she was making for E I 9 69 3
"My dear, dear, anxious friend,"--said she, in mental E II 5 189 20
Personal size and mental sorrow have certainly no P III 8 68 30
to converse, she was soon sensible of some mental change. P IV 1 124 11
our bodily frames and our mental; and that as our bodies P IV 11 233 22
for her cheerfulness and mental alacrity did not fail her; P IV 12 252 12
The whole of their mental vivacity was evidently not so S 10 412 1
MENTION (104)
me, & makes very gracious mention of my children, but I am LS 3 247 1
she took occasion to mention before Mr. Allen the half- NA I 13 103 29
And as for dancing, do not mention it I beg; that is quite NA II 1 130 13
made her blush at the mention of such a plan, and her NA II 5 156 5
was proceeding to mention the costly gilding of one in NA II 5 162 27
must always tremble;--the mention of a chest or a cabinet, NA II 10 201 4
to mention the circumstance which had produced it. NA II 10 207 41
of it; and as long as all mention of Bath scenes were NA II 13 222 8
the house without some mention of one whose name had not NA II 13 229 31
from Fanny's occasional mention of her conduct and SS I 4 21 15
It was only necessary to mention any favourite amusement SS I 10 47 3
Dashwood's happening to mention her design of improving SS I 14 72 6
The slightest mention of any thing relative to Willoughby SS I 15 82 47
and herself, he would not have ventured to mention it. SS I 18 100 30
sought nor avoided the mention of his name, appeared to SS I 19 104 10
I should never have heard him even mention your name." SS I 22 131 31
as I know the very mention of such a thing would do. SS I 22 133 44
even partly determined never to mention the subject again. SS II 2 150 35
I would not mention a word about it to her for the world. SS II 8 196 18
she was resolved never to mention his name again, and she SS II 10 215 10
Fanny voluntarily to mention his name before her, till SS II 12 229 4
but I shall not mention it at present to any body else." SS III 4 286 13
You will not mention the matter to Fanny, however, for SS III 5 295 16
I mention this, in hopes of Yr being drawn out to see W 347 21
I have heard you mention them with consideration these PP I 1 5 29
between him and Mr. Robinson; did not I mention it to you? PP I 5 19 7
defied her friend to mention such a subject to him, which PP I 6 24 17
18
large fortune, the mention of which gave animation to PP I 7 29 4
And, if I may mention so delicate a subject, endeavour to PP I 10 52 55
daughter, she must just mention--she felt it incumbent on PP I 15 71 3
She dared not even mention that gentleman. PP I 16 77 8
not time for her even to mention his name as they went, PP I 16 84 59
she were authorised to mention it, when Sir William Lucas PP I 23 126 1
The very mention of any thing concerning the match threw PP I 23 129 16
one I will not mention; the other is Charlotte's marriage. PP II 1 135 11
We had better not mention it. PP II 3 149 26
Indeed, Mr. Darcy, it is very ungenerous in you to mention PP II 8 174 15
the mention of his misfortunes with contempt and ridicule." PP II 11 192 21
I must now mention a circumstance which I would wish to PP II 12 201 5
I am glad it occurred to me to mention it; for it would PP II 14 212 13
If you mention my name at the bell, you will be attended PP II 14 212 15
was no escaping the frequent mention of Wickham's name. PP II 16 222 18
"It was a subject which they could not mention before me." PP II 17 228 34
reasonable as not to mention an officer above once a day, PP II 19 238 6
With the mention of Derbyshire, there were many ideas PP II 19 239 9
more that might lead to the mention of her, had he dared. PP III 2 262 8
In Darcy's presence she dared not mention Wickham's name; PP III 3 269 10
again, till he had something of importance to mention." PP III 5 286 28
habit of saying; made no mention of the business that had PP III 6 299 18
But of course she did not mention my name to you." PP III 10 327 11
"I mention it, because it is the living which I ought to PP III 10 328 26
Did you ever hear Darcy mention the circumstance, when you PP III 10 328 28
You know, sister, we agreed long ago never to mention a PP III 11 331 14
She had been unwilling to mention Bingley; and the PP III 17 374 19
mention of such a thing she was sure would distract him. MP I 1 9 10
Edmund, you have heard me mention Charles anderson. MP I 5 49 35
to oblige him, the mention of Sotherton Court, and the MP I 6 52 1
on, but she could not mention the number of years that he MP I 6 60 47
Can you mention any other measure by which I have a chance MP I 16 155 18
nature had honourable mention--her taste and her time were MP I 17 160 6
mention without some necessity of defence or palliation. MP II 2 187 1
a great favour of you never to mention the subject again. MP II 13 307 31
sake, she could scarcely dare mention to their father. MP III 1 317 38
a moment) I shall make no mention below of what has passed; MP III 1 322 48
must intreat him never to mention it again, to allow her MP III 2 327 5
once more obliged to mention the subject to his niece, to MP III 2 331 19
and not even to mention the name of Crawford again, except MP III 4 354 48
to be at peace from all mention of the Crawfords, safe MP III 6 370 11
mention of the handsome letter Mrs. Weston had received. E I 2 18 9
which you have heard me mention; I can only recollect the E I 9 78 54
of myself--but you mention them in most of your letters. E I 12 102 31
deal the case, my dear; but not to the degree you mention. E I 12 102 34
I did not mention a syllable of it in the other room. E I 14 120 11
The mention of the Coles was sure to be followed by that E II 1 156 5
sooner did I come to the mention of her being unwell, than E II 1 162 31
"Yes, Oh! yes--he replied; I was just going to mention it. E II 6 198 7
The unpersuadable point, which he did not mention, Emma E II 8 221 50
you have any better foundation than what you mention. E II 8 224 72
Miss Woodhouse will be so good as not to mention it. E II 9 238 51
I mention no names; but happy the man who changes Emma for E II 13 269 16
"Thank you, but I would rather you did not mention the E II 17 300 11
I shall only just mention the circumstance to the others E II 17 304 27
and for the reasons you mention; exactly as you say, she E III 8 380 15
warmest friendship, do I mention Miss Woodhouse; my father E III 14 438 8
"John does not even mention your friend," said Mr. E III 17 464 17
and that he did mention, without its being much to the E III 18 472 20
Could I mention any thing more fit to be done, than to go E III 18 474 30
"No, ma'am,--he did not mention no particular family; but P III 12 106 15
She would not, upon any account, mention her having met P III 12 106 19
"Oh course," said Mary, "you will mention our seeing Mr. P III 12 107 20
certainly ought to hear of it; do mention all about him." P III 12 107 20
"I declare, Charles, I never heard him mention Anne twice P IV 2 131 8
to smile about it; and at last to mention "Elizabeth." P IV 4 147 7
He would mention no names now; but such, he could assure P IV 8 187 34
I shall mention to him your being in Bath? P IV 9 198 43
whom I have heard you mention, came to Bath with Miss P IV 9 206 88
she determined to mention it; and it seemed to her that P IV 10 228 70
Pray be so good as to mention to the other gentlemen that P IV 11 239 49
Will you promise me to mention it, when you see them again? P IV 11 239 51
You must have heard me mention Miss Capper, the particular S 9 408 1
think you had better mention the poor Mullins's situation, S 12 423 1
Mary, I will thank you to mention a very melancholy case S 12 424 1
If you wd mention the circumstance to Lady Denham!-- S 12 424 1
I could no more mention these things to Lady D.-- than I S 12 424 1
MENTIONED (115)
manners; but when he has mentioned her of late, it has LS 8 255 2
I have never before mentioned the likelihood of it's LS 20 277 5
but yet he had lately mentioned Frederica spontaneously & LS 22 280 1
an end--his name merely mentioned to say that he was not LS 42 312 3
Yet he had not mentioned that his stay would be so short! NA I 5 35 2
You hardly mentioned any thing of her, when you wrote to NA I 7 50 48
never mentioned a wife, and he had acknowledged a sister. NA I 8 53 3
Catherine had never heard Mrs. Tilney mentioned in the NA II 7 179 31
No, James should never hear Isabella's name mentioned by NA II 12 218 3
eyes were turned to the ground as she mentioned his name. NA II 13 223 13
her faith before he mentioned the subject; and as he NA II 15 244 11
in short, to be mentioned; but till that one was removed, NA II 16 249 1
"I have never mentioned it to her, but of course she must." SS I 8 39 16
it is, because he looked so conscious when I mentioned her. SS I 14 70 2
It was several days before Willoughby's name was mentioned SS I 16 85 11
12
Sir John would have mentioned it to the Colonel, and we SS I 20 116 62
when alluded to, or even openly mentioned by Sir John. SS I 21 126 41
and I never should have mentioned it to you, if I had not SS I 22 129 16
was mentioned by Sir John, lest she should out with it all. SS I 22 133 42
By whom can you have heard it mentioned?" SS II 5 173 43
I hardly ever heard her mentioned; except that Mrs. Taylor SS II 8 194 12
hearing Willoughby's name mentioned, was not thrown away. SS II 10 214 8
and had already mentioned their wishes to their kind SS III 3 279 1
then it was that he mentioned with regret, that the house SS III 3 283 20
I think it ought not to be mentioned to any body else. SS III 4 286 15
to be thought of or mentioned--as to any attachment you SS III 5 297 31
gave her likewise no concern, she never mentioned her name. SS III 7 309 6
mother, and whenever she mentioned her name, it gave a SS III 7 312 18
was not even mentioned in any of the succeeding letters. SS III 11 353 21
Neither of them was ever again to be mentioned to Mrs. SS III 13 371 38
He thus continued: "Mrs. Ferrars has never yet mentioned SS III 13 371 38
39
"I wonder I never mentioned it when I wrote. W 321 2
She once mentioned Sam, & certainly with a little W 341 19
Mary had heard herself mentioned to Miss Bingley as the PP I 3 12 15
She mentioned this to her friend Miss Lucas. PP I 6 21 1
that morning should be mentioned, and the request made. PP I 12 59 1
cried his wife, "I cannot bear to hear that mentioned. PP I 13 61 7
names, facts, every thing mentioned without ceremony.-- PP I 17 85 5
to hear George Wickham mentioned, and that though my PP I 18 94 45
perhaps I ought to have mentioned earlier, that it is the PP I 19 105 10
I do not know whether I ever before mentioned to you my PP I 21 118 14
Mr. Darcy's house, and mentioned with raptures, some plans PP II 1 133 2
You mentioned two instances. PP II 1 136 14
Bingley's name was scarcely ever mentioned between them. PP II 1 137 25
comforts, and mentioned nothing which she could not praise. PP II 3 146 19
person, who was merely mentioned to me, and the family are PP II 6 165 32
manner in which he had mentioned Mr. Wickham, his cruelty PP II 11 193 31
The first mentioned was, that, regardless of the PP II 12 196 5
in which her family were mentioned, in terms of such PP II 13 208 10
passed at Hunsford, she mentioned Colonel Fitzwilliam's PP II 18 233 26
name had been last mentioned between them; and if she PP III 1 256 62
His name had never been voluntarily mentioned before them PP III 6 298 16
that the subject might never be mentioned to him again. PP III 8 312 18
I thought him very sly;--he hardly ever mentioned your PP III 10 325 2
It was many months since she had mentioned his name to PP III 11 331 16
17
Elizabeth had mentioned her name to her mother, on her PP III 14 351 3
your name will never even be mentioned by any of us." PP III 14 355 46
or allow their names to be mentioned in your hearing." PP III 15 364 22
Darcy mentioned his letter. PP III 16 368 18
of promise, for I ought not to have mentioned the subject? PP III 18 381 13
such a thing must be, he mentioned its probability to his MP I 3 24 7
I could see it in her eyes, when he was mentioned. MP I 5 45 14
proved the contrary, she never mentioned him. MP I 5 48 30
The Sotherton scheme was mentioned of course. MP I 8 75 2
I could not, when the scheme was first mentioned the other MP I 8 77 9
Mr. Rushworth mentioned his curricle. MP I 9 84 1
Crawford were mentioned in my last letters from Mansfield. MP II 1 185 29
By all the others it was mentioned with regret, and his MP II 2 194 20
him, as soon as he mentioned the name of Cardinal Wolsey, MP III 3 336 10
to Crawford should be mentioned between them or not; and MP III 4 345 1
I should not have mentioned the subject, though very MP III 4 351 36
ever be mentioned between them with any remains of liberty. MP III 6 373 26
how Mrs. Rushworth looked when your name was mentioned? MP III 9 393 1
of a friend when he mentioned it, and led the way to her MP III 10 405 17
Nobody thought of Hannah till you mentioned her--James is E I 1 9 18
and was always mentioned with approbation for his great E I 4 27 5
He had never heard of such books before I mentioned them, E I 4 29 10
in nothing; and I have not heard him mentioned lately." E I 11 95 21
Miss Smith should be mentioned at all,--he resumed the E I 15 130 28
Her name was not mentioned;--and there was so striking a E I 17 140 3
She never mentioned it before, because she would not alarm E II 1 161 29
Hawkins's name was first mentioned in Highbury, before she E II 4 181 2
to attend, were mentioned; but he was not satisfied. E II 6 198 5
But when you mentioned Mrs. Dixon, I felt how much more E II 8 219 42
points on which his influence failed, he then mentioned. E II 8 221 49
but unluckily, I had mentioned it before I was aware." E II 9 239 51
I do not see why Miss Fairfax should not be mentioned too. E II 10 245 49
William Larkins mentioned it here. E II 10 245 52
and it would have been a pity not to have mentioned . . . . E II 10 245 52
you at Kingston?" said he; so I just mentioned . . . . E II 10 245 54
of herself, she had not mentioned it; but now she was too E II 12 258 7
'My friend Knightley' had been so often mentioned, that I E II 14 278 50
You mentioned it as what was certainly to be very soon. E III 5 344 9
I really was persuaded of Mrs. Weston's having mentioned E III 5 345 13
for Mrs. Perry herself mentioned it to my mother, and the E III 5 345 16
who is not--and she had mentioned it to her in confidence; E III 5 346 16
day to this, I never mentioned it to a soul that I know of. E III 5 346 16
latest occurrences to be mentioned, the two of strongest E III 11 410 35
whisper, "I mentioned no names, you will observe.-- E III 16 454 14
15
Harriet was very seldom mentioned between them. E III 17 463 15
settled in Cheshire; how mentioned in Dugdale--serving the P III 1 3 3
4
Mr. Shepherd had once mentioned the word, "advertise;"-- P III 2 15 14
gentleman's family, and mentioned a place; and Anne, after P III 3 21 20
21
with Sir Walter, he mentioned it no more; returning, with P III 3 23 34
of cousins already mentioned, were apparently admitted to P III 8 71 57
to particularize, mentioned such works of our best P III 11 101 24
and Captain Wentworth's name must be mentioned by both. P IV 1 124 12
through Mr. Elliot, had mentioned one or two things P IV 3 139 8
Anne mentioned the glimpses she had had of him at Lyme, P IV 3 140 12
She mentioned nothing of what she had heard, or what she P IV 5 153 5
and Louisa Musgrove was mentioned, and Captain Benwick too, P IV 6 168 22
he had not mentioned it, or she could not recollect it. P IV 7 178 26
You never mentioned it before. P IV 9 194 23
She had been necessarily often mentioned at Willingden,-- S 3 375 1
day to Fanny Noyce and mentioned it to her--& Fanny all S 9 408 1
MENTIONING (21)
and the unfortunate dread of me I have been mentioning. LS 24 289 12
imprudent kindness by mentioning the offer, and to tell SS I 12 59 5
occasion for ever mentioning my name to you, and as he was SS I 22 131 32
that was reason enough for his not mentioning it." SS I 22 131 32
at the time, at his mentioning nothing farther of those SS I 22 134 49
by his manner of mentioning a country neighbourhood. PP I 9 43 19

hearing her brother mentioning a ball to Miss Bennet, she PP I 11 55 5
6
I happened to overhear the gentleman himself mentioning to PP I 18 96 57
confirm his account, by mentioning her prior knowledge of PP I 23 126 4
"You may depend upon my not mentioning it." PP II 10 185 27
marriage, but without mentioning names or any other PP II 10 185 28
"After mentioning the likelihood of this marriage to her PP III 15 363 22
through the hall, of mentioning Miss Price as one who MP I 8 79 23
"You were mentioning may. E II 18 308 30
that Jane would name--mentioning that she had Mr. Perry's E III 9 390 16
I should not think of mentioning it to any body but you, E III 11 404 6
of that service, and mentioning even what your sensations E III 11 406 23
laughing eyes, after mentioning the expected return of the E III 18 477 51
any thing amiss, you need not be afraid of mentioning it." P III 6 45 9
under his care, and mentioning him in strong, though not P III 6 52 33
need not be afraid of mentioning poor dick before me, for P III 8 66 20
MENUS PLAISIRS (2)
be all for his menus plaisirs; and a sermon at Christmas MP II 5 226 61
You would look rather blank, Henry, if your menus plaisirs MP II 5 226 62
MERCANTILE (1)
of the profits of his mercantile life appeared so very E II 4 183 9
MERCENARY (8)
I should be sorry to think our friend mercenary." PP II 4 153 8
affairs, between the mercenary and the prudent motive? PP II 4 153 9
pounds, you want to find out that he is mercenary." PP II 4 153 9
He shall be mercenary, and she shall be foolish." PP II 4 153 17
solely and hatefully mercenary; and the mediocrity of her PP II 13 207 6
supporter of every thing mercenary and ambitious, provided MP III 13 421 2
provided it be only mercenary and ambitious enough. MP III 13 421 2
Sick of ambitious and mercenary connections, prizing more MP III 17 471 29
MERCHANDIZE (1)
who can afford to buy, and she disposes of my merchandize. P IV 5 155 9
MERCHANT (1)
daughters of a Bristol--merchant, of course, he must be E II 4 183 9
MERCHANT-TAYLORS' (1)
at Oxford, Edward at Merchant-Taylors', and William at sea, NA I 4 32 2
MERCIFUL (4)
them merciful or just, to give them honour or compassion. MP I 17 162 19
William was not very merciful to the first lieutenant) was MP III 7 375 2
seems to have been the merciful appointment of Providence MP III 16 455 23
instances in which, by a merciful appointment, it seems P IV 5 154 8
MERCY (12)
have my character at the mercy of a man whose passions LS 25 292 1
& I could not bear to have her at the mercy of her mother. LS 27 296 1
Catherine was left to the mercy of Mrs. Thorpe and Mrs. NA I 8 52 2
should be abandoned to the mercy of Marianne for all the SS II 3 156 15
must in some measure be always at the mercy of chance. SS II 14 248 6
he had to dispose of, or any part of it at her mercy."-- W 352 26
event, and without mercy wishing poor Sir Thomas had been MP II 1 176 4
I leave him entirely to your mercy; and when he has got MP III 5 363 24
They have no mercy on her." E II 8 229 97
as if he had very little doubt and very little mercy. E II 10 241 11
must be always at the mercy of chance,) who will suffer an E III 7 373 44
Have a little mercy on the poor men. P III 3 20 17
MERE (62)
Sir James may seem to have drawn an harder lot than mere LS 42 313 10
be nothing to put off a mere walk for one day longer, and NA I 13 97 1
The mere habit of learning to love is the thing; and a NA II 7 174 10
rest, for the purpose of mere domestic economy; and would NA II 8 184 4
We are considering it as a mere parsonage, small and NA II 11 213 19
mere calmness of manner with which sense had nothing to do. SS I 11 55 6
no real satisfaction, as far as mere self is concerned." SS I 17 91 10
admiration of landscape scenery is become a mere jargon. SS I 18 97 7
couple, with two violins, and a mere side-board collation. SS II 5 170 29
our past attachment as a mere idle, trifling, business, SS III 8 326 53
he perhaps, thinking that mere friendship, as the world SS III 9 336 12
me, to be resorted to for anything beyond mere amusement. SS III 10 343 9
to domestic happiness, than the mere temper of a wife." SS III 11 351 13
a mere nothing, that had great effect at a card table. W 359 28
mere trifle, and begged she would not make herself uneasy. PP I 16 83 49
miraculous virtue, and the mere stateliness of money and PP II 6 161 9
his studying the law was a mere pretence, and being now PP II 12 201 5
the mere ceremonious salutation attending his entrance. PP III 12 340 14
Though Elizabeth would not, for the mere purpose of PP III 14 356 55
56
where he spoke ten, by the mere aid of a good-humoured MP I 2 12 2
and it was a mere nothing before repton took it in hand. MP I 6 55 15
In extent it is a mere nothing--you would be surprised at MP I 6 61 54
something grander than a mere, spacious, oblong room, MP I 9 85 6
For mere amusement among ourselves, we should want nothing MP I 13 124 8
is a nothing of a part, a mere nothing, not above half a MP I 15 145 47
the last week, to get up a few scenes, a mere trifle. MP II 1 181 16
of a something above a mere parsonage house, above the MP II 7 243 27
From being the mere gentleman's residence, it becomes, by MP II 7 244 27
She considered it all as nonsense, as mere trifling and MP II 13 301 7
I had, for this is to be a mere letter of business, penned MP III 12 415 2
as tranquil as their tempers, was now become a mere name. MP III 13 428 15
be some mere farmer's daughter, without education." E I 4 31 24
a mere joke; he was afraid they would find no difficulty. E I 15 126 11
in strange hands--a mere common coachman--no James; and E I 15 132 38
passed as his way, as a mere error of judgment, of E I 16 134 5
sacrifice of mere pleasure you will always find me ready E I 18 146 16
and of leading a life of mere idle pleasure, and fancying E I 18 148 24
as a mere trifle, and quite unworthy of being dwelt on. E II 3 180 54
trying her native air, I look upon that as a mere excuse.-- E II 8 217 32
It is a mere nothing after all; and not the least draught E II 11 254 48
or were left as mere trifles to be settled at any time E II 11 255 59
This is a matter of mere common politeness and good- E II 14 280 60
Her own attachment had really subsided into a mere nothing; E III 1 315 1
There could be no harm in a scheme, a mere passive scheme. E III 3 335 11
"it all meant nothing; a mere joke among ourselves." E III 5 350 29
the mere proposal of going out seemed to make her worse.-- E III 9 390 18
in mere charitable caution, be kept at a distance from. E III 15 450 37
much better than to any mere Mr. ----; a Mr. (save, P III 3 24 36
letters; all the rest had been mere applications for money. P III 6 51 30
It was mere lively chat,--such as any young persons, on an P III 10 84 7
I see that more than a mere dutiful morning-visit to your P III 10 87 26
on it--(they never got beyond) was become a mere nothing. P III 11 99 21
Marlborough-Buildings--a mere pretty, silly, expensive, P IV 5 156 13
thirty and forty--a mere Mrs. Smith, an every day Mrs. P IV 5 158 19
with the Elliots as a mere matter of form, and not in the P IV 6 168 24
It is not a mere bit of gossip. P IV 6 172 41
The rain was a mere trifle, and Anne was most sincere in P IV 7 174 3
But the rain was also a mere trifle to Mrs. Clay; she P IV 7 174 3
The mere trash of the common circulating library, I hold S 8 403 1
a mere name with you all, that it can do you no good.-- S 9 411 1
"Not, as to mere distance, but the hill is so steep!-- S 10 416 1
might be a mere trifle of reproach remaining for herself.-- S 11 420 1
MERELY (129)
is in all probability merely an affair of convenience, it LS 3 246 1
so harsh a measure, merely propose to make it her own LS 7 253 2
him not merely to forget, but to justify her conduct. LS 11 259 1
me beleive, that it was merely an impatience of restraint, LS 17 271 7
any doubt of the fact--but merely to see how she looked. LS 41 310 1
at an end--his name merely mentioned to say that he was LS 42 312 3
preferred cricket not merely to dolls, but to the more NA I 1 13 1
she had not consulted merely her own gratification; that NA I 13 101 25
he wanted merely to dance, he wanted to be with me. NA II 1 134 39
all your happiness merely to oblige my brother, because he NA II 3 146 20
her doubts and anxieties were merely sportive irritations. NA II 13 221 6
increasing; and by merely adding twice as much for the NA II 15 245 12
which proceeded not merely from interest, but from SS I 1 3 1
he now offered her was merely a cottage, he assured her SS I 4 23 20
of a sick chamber, merely because he chanced to complain SS I 8 38 11
appeared to her not merely an unnecessary effort, but a SS I 11 53 2
It came from town, and is merely a letter of business." SS I 13 63 11
To Marianne, he merely bowed and said nothing. SS I 13 66 49
in all probability not merely giving way to as a relief, SS I 15 77 20
Are no probabilities to be accepted, merely because they SS I 15 78 28
I thought our judgments were given us merely to be SS I 17 94 38
contenting herself with merely giving her husband a gentle SS I 21 118 2
She merely observed that he was perfectly good humoured SS I 21 122 16
highly in her praise, not merely from Lucy's assertion, SS II 1 142 7
to the plan, and merely referred it to her mother's SS II 3 154 6
and care; nor was it a matter of pleasure merely to her. SS II 3 157 19
know who they were, and merely nodded to Mrs. Jennings SS II 5 171 30
and probability, that on merely hearing the name of the SS II 14 248 6
superiority by nature, merely from the advantage of a SS II 14 250 12
from something more than merely malice against herself; SS II 14 254 27
young women to her house; merely because she thought they SS III 1 266 36
grounds, and an evening merely cold or damp would not have SS III 6 303 11
of her being there, not merely on the dry gravel of the SS III 6 305 17
He merely meant to persuade her to give up the engagement; SS III 14 376 11
To be so bent on marriage--to pursue a man merely for the W 318 2
that was perhaps merely oweing to the consciousness of his W 341 19
out of his road merely to call for ten minutes at Stanton. W 355 28
Sir William and Lady Lucas are determined to go, merely on PP I 1 4 24
His brother-in-law, Mr. Hurst, merely looked the gentleman; PP I 3 10 5
Had she merely dined with him, she might only have PP I 6 22 8
precipitance merely to shew off before the ladies." PP I 10 49 28
delay of his plan, has merely desired it, asked it without PP I 10 50 34
conversation; he merely answered her question, and read on. PP I 11 55 4
the universities, he had merely kept the necessary terms, PP I 15 70 1
it--or to treat it as a merely conditional recommendation. PP I 16 79 27
"Merely to the illustration of your character," said she, PP I 18 93 38
your refusal of my addresses is merely words of course. PP I 19 108 19
It appeared to her merely the suggestion of Caroline's PP I 21 120 28
an audience not merely wondering, but incredulous; for Mrs. PP I 23 126 1
2
explained that it was merely with the view of enjoying her PP I 23 128 10
to Jane had been merely the effect of a common and PP II 1 137 26
Lizzy, to fall in love merely because you are warned PP II 3 144 2
I would advise you merely to put on whatever of your PP II 6 160 6
young person, who was merely mentioned to me, and the PP II 6 165 32
Elizabeth merely curtseyed to him, without saying a word. PP II 7 171 9
and then they were merely asked on leaving church to come PP II 8 172 1
occasions it was not merely a few formal enquiries and an PP II 10 182 1
What he told me was merely this; that he congratulated PP II 10 185 28
"But it is not merely this affair," she continued, "on PP II 11 191 17
My objections to the marriage were not merely those, which PP II 12 198 5
ever take place, I shall merely be able to tell what PP II 17 227 25
have been alluding, is merely adopted on his visits to his PP II 18 234 38
"If it were merely a fine house richly furnished," said PP II 19 240 15
Gratitude, not merely for having once loved her, but for PP III 2 265 16
the hint; but she had merely intended to discompose PP III 3 269 10
He merely added, that he should not write again, till he PP III 5 286 28
I should not have merely my own gratitude to express." PP III 16 365 3
loved him, or merely from my information last spring?" PP III 16 371 42
Was it merely to ride to Longbourn and be embarrassed? or PP III 18 381 15
woods had received, not merely from the presence of such a PP III 19 388 12
contented herself with merely giving up her sister, and MP I 1 4 1
Fanny's age, seeming not merely to do away any former MP I 3 24 7
I was merely joking. MP I 11 108 12
to do in five minutes, by merely moving the book-case in MP I 13 125 14
before; and it was not merely Tom, for the requisition was MP I 15 146 53
leave to learn his sentiments merely through his conduct. MP II 2 187 3
She was then merely a quiet, modest, not plain looking MP II 6 229 5
and it was not merely for the use of it in the hunting MP II 7 246 37
my business, which is merely to beg your acceptance of MP II 9 261 2
to recommend him; not merely situation in life, fortune, MP III 1 315 27
in you, beyond what--not merely beyond what one sees, MP III 3 344 41
more is necessary than merely pacing this gravel together. MP III 4 346 8
and said, "it is not merely in temper that I consider him MP III 4 349 25
probability of its being merely to give her notice that MP III 15 437 2
steady and quiet, and not living merely for himself. MP III 17 462 4
depend upon it, a lucky guess is never merely luck. E I 1 13 43
There is health, not merely in her bloom, but in her air, E I 5 39 20
There were not merely no grammatical errors, but as a E I 7 50 4
A woman is not to marry a man merely because she is asked, E I 7 54 31
of none, except what are merely personal; that he is well E I 18 149 28
I merely called, because I would not pass the door without E II 1 162 32
merely to announce--but cheerful, exulting, of course."-- E II 3 174 31
32
of ingratitude, merely glossed over-- it must be done, or E II 4 185 14
It was not merely in fine words or hyperbolical compliment E II 6 196 2
"I merely asked, whether you had known much of Miss E II 6 200 17
he was gone off to London, merely to have his hair cut. E II 7 205 1
"I am not speaking of its prudence; merely its probability. E II 8 224 71
Mrs. Weston proposed having no regular supper; merely E II 11 254 45
And it is not merely the house--the grounds, I assure you, E II 14 273 21
He seemed not merely happy with her, but proud. E II 15 281 2
Not merely when a state of warfare with one young lady E II 15 282 4
"But I have never fixed on June or any other month--merely E II 17 299 3
in a hurry, merely to give us notice--it tells us that E II 18 305 7
were merely imaginary, or that she was as strong as ever. E III 1 317 6
She merely said, in the course of some trivial chat, "well, E III 4 340 28
He made no answer; merely looked, and bowed in submission; E III 7 373 45
46
She asked no more questions therefore, merely employed her E III 10 393 18
at present, to be allowed merely to write to Miss Fairfax E III 12 417 5
It was merely a blind to conceal his real situation with E III 13 427 19
merely because I would be as angry with her as possible. E III 14 441 8
or disapprobation; or merely of love, as the subject E III 15 445 14
15
And again, on Emma's merely turning her head to look at E III 16 454 14
15
This, on his side, might merely proceed from her not being E III 17 463 15
I have been silent from surprise merely, excessive E III 18 473 24
Elizabeth; for Mary had merely connected herself with an P III 1 6 10
But it was not a merely selfish caution, under which she P III 4 27 5
attractions than any merely personal might have been. P III 5 34 12
she considered as not merely unnecessary to be P III 12 107 21
"Merely Gowland," he supposed. P IV 4 145 3
It was not merely complaisance, it must be a liking to the P IV 4 148 10
And it is not merely in its follies, that they are well P IV 5 156 10
they were succeeded, not merely by friendship and regard, P IV 8 185 21
conversations had been merely hinted at, were dwelt on now P IV 9 210 97
agitations which she had merely laid her account of P IV 11 229 2
with him--; it was merely in consequence of a wish to S 2 371 1
"Oh! my dear Mary, merely a joke of his. S 4 382 1
to his sister--not merely for moving, but for walking on S 7 395 1
air so cold that he had merely walked from one house to S 10 414 1
It is merely to "introduce the bearer, Mrs G.-- from S 10 419 1
MEREST (4)
park; as to a stable, the merest shed would be sufficient. SS I 12 58 3
The merest awkward country girl, without style, or SS III 5 299 37
The most trivial, paltry, insignificant part; the merest MP I 14 134 13
and nothing beyond the merest common-place had been talked E II 5 186 4
MERGED (1)
"All merged in my friendship, Sophia. P III 8 69 40
MERIT (59)
deepest conviction of my merit, is satisfied that whatever LS 16 269 3
every Bath season, yet the merit of their being spoken NA I 10 72 8
could no longer claim any merit from its amendment, the NA I 11 83 16

But the merit of the curricle did not all belong to the NA II 5 157 5
or what had she omitted to do, to merit such a change? NA II 14 230 2
She could never do justice to Henry and Eleanor's merit; NA II 14 232 5
I know no one more entitled, by unpretending merit, or NA II 16 251 5
his merit before, in believing him incapable of generosity. SS I 3 14 2
and that Elinor's merit should not be acknowledged by SS I 3 15 5
short, to be such as his merit, and the suspicion--the SS I 4 21 15
for every new print of merit to be sent you--and as for SS I 17 92 25
it was impossible, with calm ones it could have no merit. SS I 19 104 11
of having done nothing to merit her present unhappiness, SS II 1 140 4
own merit, than on the merit of his nearest relations! SS II 14 250 12
Because your merit cries out upon myself, I have been SS III 1 264 31
but only Elinor and Marianne understood its true merit. SS III 2 270 1
to your own merit, and Colonel Brandon's discernment of it. SS III 4 289 35
manner which it was no merit to possess; and by that still SS III 9 333 2
that even John and Fanny are not entirely without merit." SS III 13 372 45
years enjoyment, had some merit in chearfully undertaking W 315 1
the persuasion of a friend is no merit with you." PP I 10 50 35
less sensible of your merit than when he took leave of you PP I 21 119 20
Miss Bennet eagerly disclaimed all extraordinary merit, PP II 1 135 10
can be placed on the appearance of either merit or sense. PP II 1 135 11
Wickham had allowed him merit as a brother, and that she PP II 13 207 6
There is but such a quantity of merit between them; just PP II 17 225 10
she had refused, and whose merit she had undervalued; but PP III 11 334 36
of character which could so well distinguish merit. MP I 4 39 10
Her merit in being gifted by nature with strength and MP I 7 69 23
her gratitude, and whose merit in making them was spoken MP I 17 159 6
absent, dwelling on his merit and affection, and longing MP II 11 286 15
he claims no merit in it, perhaps is entitled to none. MP III 2 330 14
You are infinitely my superior in merit; all that I know.-- MP III 3 343 41
It is not by equality of merit that you can be won. MP III 3 344 41
It is he who sees and worships your merit the strongest, MP III 3 344 41
object, she had had the merit of withdrawing herself from MP III 17 466 18
With so much true merit and true love, and no want of MP III 17 473 32
of success? where is your merit?--what are you proud of?-- E I 1 12 42
to make his merit and prospects a kind of common concern. E I 2 17 7
and probable, for her to have much merit in planning it. E I 4 34 44
There will be very little merit in making a good wife to E I 5 38 12
man may be a weston in merit, and a Churchill in fortune,-- E I 5 38 15
There was merit in every drawing--in the least finished, E I 6 44 20
all his sense and all his merit Mr. Martin is nothing more, E I 8 62 39
supposed it could make him unjust to the merit of another. E I 18 150 37
there, not to be vulgar, was distinction, and merit. E II 2 167 12
of perfect beauty and merit, was in possession of an E II 4 181 4
there was no positive merit, they shewed, altogether, a E II 6 197 3
which must be very like a merit to those he was with. E II 6 197 3
on his side, for I think the merit will be all on her's." E III 12 420 13
creature who would so designedly suppress her own merit.-- E III 14 439 8
on your side of the question; all the merit on mine. E III 17 464 24
now armed with the idea of merit in maintaining her own P III 11 94 7
her merit, and excited the warmest curiosity to know her." P IV 8 187 34
It is, perhaps, our fate rather than our merit. P IV 11 232 19
merit and activity could place him, was no longer nobody. P IV 12 248 1
Clara had returned with her--& by her good Sence & merit S 3 379 1
Such poverty & dependance joined to such beauty & merit, S 6 391 1
merit to his civility in wishing her to take his chair.-- S 10 414 1

MERITED (5)
seem to have drawn an harder lot than mere folly merited. LS 42 313 10
of his reception, and consious that he merited no kind one. SS III 12 359 11
yet merited reproach, her sense of shame was severe. PP II 13 208 10
to you at the time, had merited the severest reproof. PP III 16 367 12
this is a punishment beyond what you can have merited!-- E II 15 284 10

MERITORIOUS (1)
own, appeared no more meritorious to Marianne, than her SS I 19 104 11

MERITS (37)
good opinion merits a better return than it has received. LS 14 265 5
the price and weigh the merits of a new muff and tippet. NA I 7 51 54
Thorpe's ideas then all reverted to the merits of his own NA I 9 64 27
from her on that lady's merits, closed the subject.-- NA I 14 110 28
The domestic, unpretending merits of a person never known, NA II 9 196 23
never enough valued her merits or kindness: and never NA II 14 235 14
Any further definition of his merits must be unnecessary; NA II 16 251 5
She speedily comprehended all his merits; the persuasion SS I 3 16 13
is not in every thing equal to your sense of his merits. SS I 4 19 5
6
lively nor young, seemed resolved to undervalue his merits. SS I 10 50 13
a confirmation of his merits as might remove the SS I 20 114 43
within herself--to his wishes than to his merits. SS III 9 333 2
His own merits must soon secure it." SS III 9 337 18
merits, and a temper irritated by their very attention.-- SS III 10 346 28
Brandon's injuries and merits, warm as friendship and SS III 11 352 18
dictate;--and among the merits and the happiness of Elinor SS III 14 380 21
The morng passed quietly away in discussing the merits of W 338 17
merits, as they proceeded together up the great staircase. PP III 1 249 37
with regret, and his merits honoured with due gradation of MP II 2 194 20
But he was deceived in her; he gave her merits which she MP II 9 264 17
was scarcely beyond her merits, rejoice in her prospects. MP II 12 294 18
half Mr. Crawford's estate, or a tenth part of his merits. MP III 1 319 39
own children's merits set off by the depreciation of her. MP III 1 323 57
out his sense of her merits, describing and describing MP III 2 328 6
himself, and thoroughly investigate the merits of the case. MP III 10 404 15
to every body's merits; thought herself a most fortunate E I 3 21 4
doated on, full of their merits, blind to their faults, E I 17 140 1
ready to acknowledge his merits as any other man; but I E I 18 149 28
circulate the fame of her merits, there was very little E II 4 181 2
her for Miss Taylor's merits, without seeming quite to E II 5 192 29
insensible of half his merits, and quarrelling with him E III 12 415 1
But poor Mrs. Clay, who, with all her merits, can never P III 5 35 14
exactly alike of the merits of either, till something P III 12 107 23
in a discussion of her merits; and Anne could not be given P IV 5 159 21
of Captain Wentworth's merits could be allowed to prefer P IV 6 167 21
to her merits, because he had been a sufferer from them. P IV 11 241 61
who bid fair by her merits to vie in favour with Sir S 3 377 1

MERMAID (2)
Or a trident? or a mermaid? or a shark? E I 9 73 17
us a charade made by a friend upon a mermaid or a shark? E I 9 73 18

MERMAIDS (1)
"Mermaids and sharks! E I 9 73 18

MERRIER (1)
or not, only the more the merrier say I, and I thought it SS II 3 154 4

MERRIMENT (8)
The stage could no longer excite genuine merriment--no NA I 12 92 4
young brood, she found fresh sources of merriment. SS III 6 303 10
Tom, than that sort of merriment which a young man of MP I 2 17 22
a doubt, for the sound of merriment ascended even to her. MP I 7 67 16
full of conversation and merriment; and to see only his MP I 8 81 32
however, for the indulgence of any images of merriment. MP II 1 183 23
Even Emma grew tired at last of flattery and merriment, E III 7 374 54
smiles, the sneers, the merriment it would prompt at his E III 11 413 48

MERRY (15)
Sir James's carriage was at the door, & he, merry as usual, LS 24 291 15
was a good-humoured, merry, fat, elderly woman, who talked SS I 7 34 5
and that every body should be extremely merry all day long. SS I 13 67 61
always with animation--but she is not often really merry." SS I 17 93 35
at the other, looking as good humoured and merry as before. SS I 20 110 1
And then we were so merry all the way home! we talked and PP II 16 222 22
How merry we shall be together when we meet!" PP III 7 306 44
all have a bowl of punch, to make merry at her wedding." PP III 7 307 49
with Maria and Julia, and being as merry as possible. MP I 2 17 20
formerly were ever merry, except when my uncle was in town. MP II 3 197 3
their moonlight walks and merry evening games; and dwelt a E I 4 28 6
I would much rather have been merry than wise." E II 12 260 18
young ladies, living to be fashionable, happy, and merry. P III 5 40 45
So we must all be as merry as we can, that she may not be P III 6 50 27
It was a merry, joyous party, and no one seemed in higher P III 8 71 57

MERYTON (57)
The manner in which they spoke of the Meryton assembly was PP I 4 16 15
Sir William Lucas had been formerly in trade in Meryton, PP I 5 18 1
a house about a mile from Meryton, denominated from that PP I 5 18 1
Mr. Robinson's asking him how he liked our Meryton PP I 5 19 7
She danced four dances with him at Meryton; she saw him PP I 6 22 7
was teazing Colonel Forster to give us a ball at Meryton?" PP I 6 24 17
18
"You saw me dance at Meryton, I believe, sir." PP I 6 25 29
Her father had been an attorney in Meryton, and had left PP I 7 28 1
The village of Longbourn was only one mile from Meryton; a PP I 7 28 3
better offered, a walk to Meryton was necessary to amuse PP I 7 28 3
remain the whole winter, and Meryton was the head quarters. PP I 7 28 3
to go to Meryton; and the Hursts have no horses to theirs." PP I 7 30 23
"We will go as far as Meryton with you," said Catherine PP I 7 32 39
In Meryton they parted; the two youngest repaired to the PP I 7 32 41
heard you say, that their uncle is an attorney in Meryton." PP I 8 36 15
time most likely Captain Carter would be at Meryton again. PP I 9 45 38
I shall walk to Meryton to-morrow to hear more about it, PP I 14 68 14
Lydia's intention of walking to Meryton was not forgotten; PP I 15 71 6
his cousins, their time passed till they entered Meryton. PP I 15 72 7
at a suitable hour to Meryton; and the girls had the PP I 16 75 1
He inquired how far Netherfield was from Meryton; and, PP I 16 77 8
Mr. Wickham began to speak on more general topics, Meryton, PP I 16 78 22
and excellent acquaintance Meryton had procured them. PP I 16 79 23
of rain as prevented their walking to Meryton once. PP I 17 88 15
if she and her sisters did not very often walk to Meryton. PP I 18 93 18
"No; he never saw him till the other morning at Meryton." PP I 18 96 52
After breakfast, the girls walked to Meryton to inquire if PP I 21 115 3
no other way than as a piece of news to spread at Meryton. PP I 23 127 7
shortly prevailed in Meryton of his coming no more to PP I 23 129 12
Here are officers enough at Meryton to disappoint all the PP II 1 138 27
beyond the walks to Meryton, sometimes dirty and sometimes PP II 4 151 1
While there was an officer in Meryton, they would flirt PP II 14 213 17
flirt with him; and while Meryton was within a walk of PP II 14 213 17
have left Meryton, and they are going in a fortnight." PP II 16 219 4
regiment of militia, and the monthly balls of Meryton." PP II 16 220 7
of the girls to walk to Meryton and see how every body PP II 16 223 25
in Meryton, to attempt to place him in an amiable light. PP II 17 226 23
It was the last of the regiment's stay in Meryton, and all PP II 18 229 1
regiment's remaining in Meryton, he dined with others of PP II 18 233 26
with Mrs. Forster to Meryton, from whence they were to set PP II 18 235 40
as to be able to enter Meryton without tears; an event of PP II 19 238 6
another regiment should be quartered in Meryton. PP II 19 238 6
Eliza, are not the ----shire militia removed from Meryton? PP III 3 269 8
9
Since the ----shire were first quartered in Meryton, PP III 5 283 10
was to leave Meryton in a week or fortnight's time. PP III 5 285 16
Every girl in, or near Meryton, was out of her senses PP III 5 285 18
Meryton greatly in debt; but I hope this may be false." PP III 5 291 54
All Meryton seemed striving to blacken the man, who, but PP III 6 294 4
"I will go to Meryton," said she, "as soon as I am dressed, PP III 7 307 49
Girls, can I do any thing for you in Meryton? PP III 7 307 49
spiteful old ladies in Meryton, lost but little of their PP III 8 309 6
to his creditors in Meryton, of whom I shall subjoin a PP III 8 313 19
Mrs. Bennet and Lydia are going in the carriage to Meryton. PP III 10 327 9
"for Mrs. Nicholls was in Meryton last night; I saw her PP III 11 331 15
to do the same by all her neighbours in Meryton. PP III 13 350 55
through Meryton, thought she might as well call on you. PP III 14 359 76
So near a vicinity to her mother and Meryton relations was PP III 19 385 3

MESS (2)
regard which his social powers had gained him in the mess. PP II 13 206 4
I have been to Turner's about your mess; it is all in a to MP III 7 380 20

MESS-ROOM (1)
The mess-room will drink Isabella Thorpe for a fortnight, NA II 4 153 29

MESSAGE (42)
engagement, without sending her any message of excuse. NA I 11 86 50
had asked whether any message had been left for her; and NA I 11 89 62
Mr. Thorpe had no business to invent any such message. NA I 13 100 20
Catherine found that John Thorpe had given the message; NA I 13 102 26
the bearer of such a message, I seem guilty myself of all NA II 13 225 19
The possibility of some conciliatory message from the NA II 13 227 27
dignity was put to the trial--Eleanor brought no message. NA II 13 227 27
Lady Middleton had sent a very civil message by him, SS I 6 30 7
and as this message was answered by an invitation equally SS I 6 30 7
The chance proved a lucky one, for a message from Mrs. SS II 13 238 3
off his servant with a message to Mr. Harris, and an order SS III 7 311 15
as I went there with a message from sally at the park to SS III 11 354 27
She recognised the whole of Lucy in the message, and was SS III 11 355 39
seeing her mother's servant, on hearing Lucy's message! SS III 12 357 2
malice against him in her message by thomas, was perfectly SS III 13 366 21
was commissioned with a message of excuse to osborne W 348 22
great satisfaction, a message from her ladyship, importing PP II 14 210 1
forgotten to leave any message for the ladies of Rosings. PP II 15 217 8
but was too angry with Lydia, to send any message to her. PP III 8 309 5
purport of the message than on any thing else. MP I 13 129 39
chanced to send him of a message to father, and then MP I 15 141 22
Fanny told of their departure, and delivered their message. MP II 1 182 20
no return, no letter, no message--no symptom of a softened MP II 3 201 24
There had, in fact, been so much of message, of allusion, MP III 7 376 4
from aunt Norris, but a message to say she hoped her god- MP III 7 387 45
"Have you no message for anybody?" MP III 11 412 26
If Mr. Crawford remembered her message to her cousin, she MP III 12 418 5
no notice, no message from the uncle on whom all depended. MP III 14 430 6
about of his housekeeper--no message from my father." E I 10 83 7
me for my friend--any message to Miss Smith I shall be E I 15 130 25
"Miss Smith!--message to Miss Smith!--what could she E I 15 130 26
illnesses for her, she could make no figure in a message. E III 3 336 12
The invitation was refused, and by a verbal message. E III 9 389 16
thing that message could do was tried--but all in vain. E III 9 390 18
but by some letter or message--and it was the discovery of E III 10 398 51
him this morning, and the message he returned, that he E III 16 457 38
And no apology left, no message for me. E III 16 457 40
My dear Mr. E., he must have left a message for you, I am E III 16 458 42
kind forgiving message in one of Mrs. Weston's letters. E III 18 476 46
47
Shall I take any message?" P IV 9 198 43
Make a civil message. P IV 10 215 16
Harville any where, remember to give Miss Anne's message. P IV 11 239 52

MESSAGES (8)
But perseverance in humility of conduct and messages, in SS III 14 377 11
calling off his attention by messages to his sister. PP I 10 47 1
quick in carrying messages, and fetching what she wanted." MP I 2 20 31
and send back proper messages, with cheerful looks. MP III 7 375 1
saved her, and how many messages she might have carried. MP III 14 432 10
I have not time or patience to give half Henry's messages; MP III 14 435 14
and messages; but if he wished to do it, it might be done. E I 18 146 16
messages enough to make everything appear what it was not. S 11 420 1

MESSENGER (8)
friend, she exclaimed, "'tis a messenger from Woodston!" NA II 13 223 12
I am indeed a most unwilling messenger. NA II 13 223 13
and dispatching a messenger to Barton for her mother. SS III 7 311 14
himself as the messenger who should fetch Mrs. Dashwood. SS III 7 311 15
not find a more willing or speedy messenger than myself--. W 338 18
bell mended--but Betsey is a very handy little messenger." MP III 7 379 15
Randall's, was, that a messenger had come over from E III 8 383 31
from box hill--which messenger, however, had been no more E III 8 383 31

MET (206)
met before, I should have imagined her an attached friend. LS 6 251 1

I met her on the stairs & saw that she was crying. LS 24 285 2
was going to my own room I met him in the passage, & then LS 24 286 5
arrival in town; & she was met with such an easy & LS 42 311 2
He was no where to be met with; every search for him was NA I 5 35 2
been only two days in Bath before they met with Mrs. Allen. NA I 5 36 2
They were changed into--"how glad I am we have met with NA I 5 36 3
They met by appointment; and as Isabella had arrived NA I 6 39 2
face of every woman they met; and Catherine, after NA I 7 48 32
affectionate son, as they met Mrs. Thorpe, who had NA I 7 49 43
so I thought perhaps he would ask you, if he met with you." NA I 8 58 30
In the Pump-Room, one so newly arrived in Bath must be met NA I 9 60 1
there I met her, and we had a great deal of talk together. NA I 9 68 38
met Mrs. Hughes, and Mr. and Miss Tilney walking with her." NA I 9 68 40
The Allens, Thorpes, and Morlands, all met in the evening NA I 10 70 1
Miss Tilney met her with great civility, returned her NA I 10 72 8
At the head of them she was met by Mr. Allen, who, on NA I 11 89 62
I have met him for ever at the Bedford; and I knew his NA I 12 96 20
to be more horrible than any thing we have met with yet." NA I 14 112 31
her confidence; she was met by one with the same kindness, NA II 1 131 14
When the young ladies next met, they had a far more NA II 1 135 42
into scenes, where pleasures of every kind had met her. NA II 2 141 11
She has been in love with him ever since they first met, NA II 4 151 13
and met with every mile-stone before she expected it. NA II 5 155 4
at last by mutual consent--happy for me had we never met! NA II 10 202 7
The last time we met was in Bath-Street, and I turned NA II 12 217 2
case, she would have met with very different treatment." NA II 12 219 13
It was not four-and-twenty hours ago since they had met NA II 13 228 27
She met with nothing, however, to distress or frighten her. NA II 14 232 6
and though, when they all met the next morning, her NA II 14 235 13
"Very true: we soon met with Mrs. Thorpe, and then we NA II 14 238 24
days before, he had been met near the Abbey by his NA II 15 244 10
Mrs. Dashwood and her daughters were met at the door of SS I 7 33 4
every day since they first met on high-church down; and SS I 12 60 10
Elinor had met his eye, and looked conscious likewise. SS I 18 98 13
I met Colonel Brandon Monday morning in Bond-Street, just SS I 20 115 48
When we met him, he turned back and walked with us; and so SS I 20 115 50
In a morning's excursion to Exeter, they had met with two SS I 21 118 2
in the world were to be met with in every part of England, SS I 21 119 3
the others; and though they met at least every other SS II 1 142 8
They met for the sake of eating, drinking, and laughing SS II 1 143 8
his behaviour to me when we met, or any lowness of spirits SS II 2 147 12
she had met and invited in the morning, dined with them. SS II 4 166 31
Mrs. Jennings, when they met at breakfast the following SS II 5 167 1
Sir John met him somewhere in the street this morning." SS II 5 171 38
in love with each other from the first moment they met? SS II 7 182 10
"I met Mrs. Jennings in Bond-Street," said he, after the SS II 9 204 18
at him anxiously, saying, "what? have you met him to-----" SS II 9 211 36
37
met by appointment, he to defend, I to punish his conduct. SS II 9 211 38
It was only the last time they met that he had offered him SS II 10 215 9
of uncordial address, who met her husband's sisters SS II 12 229 3
She met him with a hand that would be taken, and a voice SS II 13 242 23
But what was that, when such friends were to be met?" SS II 13 243 37
He had met Mrs. Jennings at the door in her way to the SS III 4 287 25
to be guided in everything, met him with a look of forced SS III 12 359 11
You must have a sweet temper indeed;--I never met with any W 320 2
ten minutes ago, said he--I met her in the village of W 338 18
And when T. Musgrave was met with again, he was W 348 22
wait, said she, so I put on the first thing I met with.-- W 353 26
She might perhaps have met with some unexpected W 355 28
Upon my honour, I never met with so many pleasant girls in PP I 3 11 10
Bingley had never met with pleasanter people or prettier PP I 4 16 15
It was generally evident whenever they met, that he did PP I 6 21 1
and when they next met, he looked at her only to criticise. PP I 6 23 12
I never met with anybody who delighted me so much. PP I 8 38 42
who does not greatly surpass what is usually met with. PP I 8 39 50
Bingley met them with hopes that Mrs. Bennet had not found PP I 9 41 2
without exception, the sweetest temper I ever met with. PP I 9 42 7
a variety of people to be met with in the country as in PP I 9 43 24
At that moment they were met from another walk, by Mrs. PP I 10 53 59
met with so much attention in the whole course of his life. PP I 15 74 13
You could not have met with a person more capable of PP I 16 77 10
it an age since they had met, and repeatedly asked what PP I 17 86 9
added, "when you met us there the other day, we had just PP I 18 92 18
Jane met her with a smile of such sweet complacency, a PP I 18 95 48
She was met in the vestibule by Lydia, who, flying to her, PP I 20 112 25
I have met with two instances lately; one I will not PP II 1 135 11
Every time they met, it was more decided and remarkable. PP II 2 141 9
about me, we must have met long, long ago. she said PP II 3 148 26
She opened the door, and met Maria in the landing place, PP II 5 158 11
12
a husband and such a neighbour as were not often met with. PP II 7 168 1
her friend, met her with every appearance of composure. PP II 7 171 9
well rejoice in his having met with one of the very few PP II 9 178 15
That they might have met without ill consequence, is PP II 12 199 5
On Saturday morning Elizabeth and Mr. Collins met for PP II 15 215 1
over to the gardener, who met them at the hall door. PP III 1 251 49
Their eyes instantly met, and the cheeks of each were PP III 1 251 51
on the other side, allowed them to see him before they met. PP III 1 254 57
she began, as they met, to admire the beauty of the place; PP III 1 254 57
liked him better when they met in Kent than before, and PP III 1 258 71
We have not met since the 26th of November, when we were PP III 2 262 8
stairs from her mother's apartment, immediately met her. PP III 5 286 22
mother, when they were met by the butler, who said, "if PP III 7 301 4
5
They met several times, for there was much to be discussed. PP III 10 323 2
They met again on Sunday and then I saw him too. PP III 10 324 2
please than when they last met, were plainly expressed. PP III 11 336 43
Her mother impatiently met her at the door of the dressing- PP III 14 358 74
going down stairs, she was met by her father, who came out PP III 15 361 6
of asking what you thought of me; when we met at Pemberley. PP III 16 369 29
and at Northampton was met by Mrs. Norris, who thus MP I 2 12 1
As soon as she met with Edmund, she told him her distress. MP I 3 25 17
where such a one was to be met with, and having once made MP I 4 37 8
Mr. Bertram, I dare say you have sometimes met with such MP I 5 49 32
I met her at Mrs. Holford's--and did not recollect her. MP I 5 50 35
taken a different route to the house, they had not met him. MP I 8 75 2
In the drawing-room they were met with equal cordiality by MP I 9 84 1
leaving them, they had been met by the gardener, with whom MP I 10 103 50
He has met with great kindness from the chaplain of the MP I 11 111 27
as ours, is not to be met with, I believe, above ground! MP I 13 125 14
of hand-shaking had already met him, and with pointed MP II 1 179 8
in the house, for he was burning all that met his eye. MP II 2 190 9
I wish they met more frequently!-- MP II 3 199 13
give something that Rushworth and Maria had never met." MP II 3 200 19
Edmund met them with particular pleasure. MP II 4 211 25
disappointing and unfeeling kind friends I ever met with! MP II 4 212 30
Never met with a girl who looked so grave on me! MP II 6 230 7
She met Miss Crawford within a few yards of the parsonage, MP II 8 257 15
parcel, which Fanny had observed in her hand when they met. MP II 8 257 15
with her in the garden, met him at last most impatiently MP II 12 291 1
her uncle, nor of her aunt Norris, till they met at dinner. MP III 1 323 53
a variety of excellence beyond what she had ever met with. MP III 3 337 10
met, was Fanny's only support in looking forward to it. MP III 5 356 4
the small, diminished party met at breakfast, William and MP III 6 374 29
in her mother's arms, who met her there with looks of true MP III 7 377 9
dear, her daughter never met with greater kindness from MP III 8 389 4
the crown, had accidentally met with a navy officer or two MP III 10 400 7
high street, before they met her father, whose appearance MP III 10 401 11
day and the next; he had met with some acquaintance at the MP III 10 406 22
It was her public place; there she met her acquaintance, MP III 11 408 4
again or not, till they met, and might never hear from his MP III 14 433 12

He was alone, and met her instantly; and she found herself MP III 15 444 28
deal more indifference than she met with from the others. MP III 16 448 3
additional blow which had met him on his arrival in London, MP III 16 451 13
She had met him, he said, with a serious--certainty a MP III 16 454 18
the joyful consent which met Edmund's application, the MP III 17 471 29
ago) that Miss Taylor and I met with him in Broadway-Lane, E I 1 12 41
They met Mr. Martin the very next day, as they were E I 4 31 27
I never met with a disposition more truly amiable." E I 6 43 7
from Clayton Park, he had met Mr. Elton, and found to his E I 8 68 58
houses where it was never met with tolerable;--but, E I 12 104 50
door, when she was met by Mr. Elton himself, evidently E I 13 109 6
I remember she said she was sorry we never met now; which E II 3 178 52
I met her frequently at Weymouth. E II 6 200 20
moment! for, if we had met first in the drawing-room, I E II 8 213 9
ladies; Mrs. Weston and Miss Bates met them at the door. E II 9 235 43
same musician engaged, met with the readiest acquiescence. E II 11 247 3
I never met with her equal. E II 14 279 52
she appeared whenever they met again,-- self-important, E II 15 281 1
her proposals of intimacy met with, she drew back in her E II 15 281 3
He had met her before breakfast as he was returning from a E II 16 293 10
and to herself; he had met with it in his way, and had E II 17 303 24
I met the letters in my way this morning, and seeing my E II 18 305 5
nor of the treatment I have met with; and, between E II 18 309 33
They met with the utmost friendliness. E III 1 316 3
She was now met by Mrs. Weston.-- E III 2 322 19
He had met with them in a little perplexity, which must be E III 2 325 29
plaister, one of the very last times we ever met in it!-- E III 4 338 12
son, Miss Bates and her niece, who had accidentally met. E III 5 344 3
I met one as I came--madness in such weather!--absolute E III 6 364 55
no young woman before ever met with on first going out--do E III 8 379 8
He met her at the parlour door, and hardly asking her how E III 10 392 1
2
She met Mr. Weston on his entrance, with a smiling E III 10 400 67
68
I met him just now. E III 11 404 6
allowed to pass before they met again, except in the E III 12 416 2
I have already met with such success in two applications E III 14 437 8
When I think of the kindness and favour I have met with, E III 14 439 8
I was late; I met her walking home by herself, and wanted E III 14 440 8
Had we been met walking together between Donwell and E III 14 441 8
a moment afterwards she was met on the stairs by Jane E III 16 452 8
body; and as Mrs. Elton met her with unusual graciousness, E III 16 453 11
"I met William Larkins," continued Mr. Elton, "as I got E III 16 458 43
They met readily and smiling, but with a consciousness E III 18 476 46
Till this morning, we have not once met since the day of E III 18 477 57
like a good father, (having met with one or two private P III 1 5 8
his overtures had not been met with any warmth, he had P III 1 7 14
sailor he had ever met with, and went so far as to say, P III 5 32 4
far as possible, for they met every morning, and hardly P III 6 46 12
Her eye half met Captain Wentworth's; a bow, a curtsey P III 7 59 25
They had met. P III 7 60 27
away to the Laconia, and there he met with our poor boy.-- P III 8 66 18
Wentworth where it was he first met with your poor brother. P III 8 66 18
ailed me, and I never met with the smallest inconvenience." P III 8 71 54
Charles Hayter had met with much to disquiet and mortify P III 9 77 19
men are, sometimes, to be met with, strolling about near P III 10 85 13
and though they all met at the great house at rather an P III 11 95 8
They all met, and were introduced. P III 11 97 14
She would not, upon any account, mention her having met P III 12 106 19
They were not off the Cobb, before the Harvilles met them. P III 12 111 50
Mrs. Croft always met her with a kindness which gave her P IV 1 126 19
her the house and furniture, and met her with kindness. P IV 3 137 2
Mr. Smiths whose names are to be met with every where. P IV 5 157 15
It is a great while since we met." P IV 9 194 22
business, and they met no more while Anne belonged to them. P IV 10 227 68
Only think, Miss Elliot, to my great surprise I met with P IV 10 228 71
and my brother hayter had met again and again to talk it P IV 11 230 5
He met with a clever young German artist at the Cape, and P IV 11 232 15
of those who had never met before, and those who met too P IV 11 245 78
met before, and those who met too often--a common-place P IV 11 245 78
a great deal more than they met with, for there was little P IV 12 248 1
the prompt welcome which met her in his brothers and P IV 12 251 10
The prejudices which had met her at first in some quarters, S 3 379 1
When they met before dinner, Mr P. was looking over S 5 385 1
than are often met with, either separate or together.-- S 5 385 1
the library they were met by two ladies whose arrival made S 6 390 1
I am very sorry you met with your accident, but upon my S 6 393 1
such young ladies as may be met with, in at least one S 11 421 1

METAL (1)
of the lid, was a mysterious cypher, in the same metal. NA II 6 163 2

METALS (1)
Mythology, and all the Metals, Semi-metals, Planets, and MP I 2 18 25

METAMORPHOSIS (1)
stage, and the gradual metamorphosis of the impassioned MP II 1 182 22

METAPHOR (1)
Every line, every word, was--in the hackneyed metaphor SS III 8 325 50

METHOD (24)
Isabella then tried another method. NA I 13 98 2
aim; and that by their method and style, they are NA I 14 109 25
I observed to be your own method, instead of 'to instruct,' NA I 14 109 25
and that she had by that method been informed that they SS I 13 67 65
method of understanding the affair as satisfactory as this. SS I 15 78 26
But there was one method so direct, so simple, and in her SS I 16 84 7
she did not adopt the method so judiciously employed by SS I 19 104 9
I cannot compare my aunt's method with any other persons, W 318 2
times more good will than method in her guidance of the W 348 23
"You either chuse this method of passing the evening PP I 11 56 15
directions as to the best method of packing, and was so PP II 14 213 20
this was not the best method of recommending herself; but PP III 3 271 16
of a trial to the latter method, in her partiality for PP III 4 279 24
"You have insulted me, in every possible method. PP III 14 357 63
time to devise any other method of assisting them, an MP I 1 3 1
at length determined on a method of proceeding which would MP I 4 37 8
in finding out such a method of pleasing her, as well as MP II 6 232 13
reason, should err in the method of reform was not MP III 9 395 4
a letter will be decidedly the best method of explanation. MP III 13 422 2
own affection in some better method than by match-making. E I 17 142 10
hit upon the very best method in the world of preserving E I 18 148 24
well as the route and the method of his journey; and she E II 5 188 9
While Lady Elliot lived, there had been method, moderation, P III 1 9 19
Charles had a little of your method with those children. P III 6 44 8

METHODICAL (4)
but active and methodical, he had not only done all this MP II 2 190 9
Her aunt was no very methodical narrator; but with the MP III 16 449 7
what he saw, for he was slow, constant, and methodical.-- E III 6 362 43
Methodical, or well arranged, or very well delivered, it E III 11 409 34

METHODICALLY (1)
collectedly or methodically as I have repeated it to you. MP III 16 458 30

METHODISTS (1)
of Methodists, or as a missionary into foreign parts.' MP III 16 458 30

METHODS (1)
I have had a little knowledge of their methods of doing P III 3 17 4

METROPOLIS (1)
"The metropolis, I imagine, is a pretty fair sample of the MP I 9 93 48

MICHAELMAS (14)
not be married till Michaelmas, and by the end of a week SS II 10 216 15
Michaelmas; and I am sure I sha'nt go if Lucy an't there." SS III 4 292 57
together in Delaford parsonage before Michaelmas. SS III 5 293 2
in their parsonage by Michaelmas, and she found in Elinor SS III 14 374 7
take possession before Michaelmas, and some of his PP I 1 3 10
at Michaelmas; but, however, I hope it is not true. PP III 11 336 49
which I had been doctoring him for, ever since Michaelmas. MP II 2 189 5

And at Michaelmas, perhaps, a fourth may be added, some MP III 10 405 19
who did not know him, to speak to him, at Michaelmas! E I 9 75 26
The Crofts were to have possession at Michaelmas, and as P III 5 33 5
Michaelmas came; and now Anne's heart must be in Kellynch P III 6 47 16
in very good health, and very good looks since Michaelmas." P IV 3 142 15
her from London last Michaelmas a Miss Brereton, who bid S 3 377 1
to go there last Michaelmas with the certainty of being S 3 378 1
MICKLEHAM (1)
Let my accents swell to Mickleham on one side, and Dorking E III 7 369 16
MID-DAY (1)
Under a bright mid-day sun, at almost midsummer, Mr. E III 6 357 33
MID-SUMMER (1)
Campbell are to be in town again by mid-summer," said Jane. E II 17 300 9
MIDDLE (40)
The middle seat of the chaise was not drawn out, though NA II 5 155 4
The place in the middle alone remained now unexplored; and NA II 6 169 11
of Eleanor's being in the middle of a speech about NA II 13 220 2
Before the middle of the day, they were visited by Sir SS I 18 99 15
Elinor was obliged to turn from her, in the middle of her SS I 19 106 21
About the middle of the day, Mrs. Jennings went out by SS II 5 172 39
Lady Middleton, though in the middle of a rubber, on being SS II 6 178 16
to be in town before the middle of February, and she SS II 10 213 5
Emma watson was not more than of the middle height--well W 328 9
About the middle of the next day, as she was in her room PP II 5 158 11
serenity, and by the middle of June Kitty was so much PP II 19 238 6
I was in the middle before I knew that I had begun." PP III 18 380 2
say, just now, in the middle of a very late hay harvest, MP I 6 58 36
to the door in the middle which opened to the wilderness. MP I 9 91 37
It would probably be the middle of November at least; the MP I 11 107 3
at least; the middle of November was three months off. MP I 11 107 3
Her conscience stopt her in the middle, but Edmund was MP I 16 156 26
"To own the truth, Sir Thomas, we were in the middle of a MP II 1 185 28
You know the distance to Sotherton; it was in the middle MP II 2 189 3
the spot--and before the middle of the same month the MP II 3 202 28
Honesty, in the something between, in the middle state of MP II 4 214 41
her seat, and was in the middle of his further explanation MP II 13 301 7
books and she was in the middle of a very fine speech of MP III 3 336 9
were to pass all their middle and latter life together. MP III 7 375 2
be permitted before the middle of next week, that is, he MP III 12 417 3
Her youth had passed without distinction, and her middle E I 3 21 4
Though now the middle of December, there had yet been no E I 10 83 1
I am as confident of seeing Frank here before the middle E I 14 120 11
Standing up in the middle of the room, I suppose, and E I 18 147 17
But about the middle of the day she gets hungry, and there E II 9 237 46
Before the middle of the next day, he was at Hartfield; E II 11 250 20
down the middle, and was in a continual course of smiles. E III 2 328 41
as he was to be at home by the middle of the day. E III 3 332 2
It was now the middle of June, and the weather fine; and E III 6 353 6
He did not suppose they could be damp now, in the middle E III 6 356 30
She seemed to be in the middle of some eager speech. P III 10 87 22
considered, a day in the middle of November would not P III 11 94 8
gentlemanlike man, of middle age, the proprietor of the S 1 364 1
Lady D. was of middle height, stout, upright & alert in S 6 391 1
Walking up that hill, in the middle of the day, would S 10 416 1
MIDDLETON (87)
She instantly wrote Sir John Middleton her acknowledgment SS I 4 24 20
arrival; for as Lady Middleton was entirely unknown to Mrs. SS I 5 26 6
Sir John Middleton was a good looking man about forty. SS I 6 30 6
Lady Middleton had sent a very civil message by him, SS I 6 30 7
Lady Middleton was not more than six or seven and twenty; SS I 6 31 8
very chatty, and Lady Middleton had taken the wise SS I 6 31 9
Sir John was a sportsman, Lady Middleton a mother. SS I 7 32 1
Lady Middleton had the advantage of being able to spoil SS I 7 32 1
Lady Middleton piqued herself upon the elegance of her SS I 7 32 2
be his friend, than Lady Middleton was to be his wife, or SS I 7 34 6
cold insipidity of Lady Middleton was so particularly SS I 7 34 7
Lady Middleton seemed to be roused to enjoyment only by SS I 7 34 7
of the songs which Lady Middleton had brought into the SS I 7 35 8
Lady Middleton frequently called him to order, wondered SS I 7 35 9
Sir John Middleton, who called on them every day for the SS I 9 40 1
by such women as Lady Middleton and Mrs. Jennings, that SS I 10 50 17
amends for the regard of Lady Middleton and her mother. SS I 10 50 18
Neither Lady Middleton nor Mrs. Jennings could supply to SS I 11 54 6
Lady Middleton was more agreeable than her mother, only in SS I 11 54 6
Most grateful did Elinor feel to Lady Middleton for SS I 12 62 27
"I hope he has had no bad news," said Lady Middleton. SS I 13 63 6
"My dear madam," said Lady Middleton, "recollect what you SS I 13 64 13
said he, addressing Lady Middleton, "that I should receive SS I 13 64 19
for we must walk to the park, to call on Lady Middleton." SS I 14 74 21
Mrs. Dashwood's visit to Lady Middleton took place the SS I 15 75 1
Amongst them were Sir John and Lady Middleton and Mrs. SS I 19 105 13
rest of the party; Lady Middleton introduced the two SS I 19 106 21
Mrs. Palmer was several years younger than Lady Middleton, SS I 19 106 22
Lady Middleton could no longer endure such a conversation, SS I 19 108 32
When Lady Middleton rose to go away, Mr. Palmer rose also, SS I 19 108 37
Lady Middleton too, though she did not press their mother, SS I 19 109 40
Sir John and Lady Middleton wished it very much. SS I 20 116 62
an invitation, and Lady Middleton was thrown into no SS I 21 118 2
their coming, Lady Middleton resigned herself to the idea SS I 21 118 2
they were making themselves agreeable to Lady Middleton. SS I 21 120 6
Lady Middleton without the smallest surprise or distrust. SS I 21 120 6
ineffectual till Lady Middleton luckily remembering that SS I 21 121 10
"What a sweet woman Lady Middleton is!" said Lucy Steele. SS I 21 122 13
on, by speaking of Lady Middleton with more warmth than SS I 21 122 14
it is so natural in Lady Middleton; and for my part, I SS I 21 122 19
for the use of Sir John Middleton, his family, and all his SS I 21 124 33
would all dine with Lady Middleton that day, as he was SS II 1 143 9
direction of Lady Middleton than when her husband united SS II 1 143 9
The young ladies went, and Lady Middleton was happily SS II 1 143 10
"I am glad," said Lady Middleton to Lucy, "you are not SS II 1 144 11
very much mistaken, Lady Middleton; I am only waiting to SS II 1 144 12
Lady Middleton proposed a rubber of Casino to the others. SS II 1 144 15
Lady Middleton looked as if she thanked heaven that she SS II 1 145 16
"You are very kind," said Lady Middleton to Elinor: "and SS II 1 145 22
her own end, and pleased Lady Middleton at the same time. SS II 1 145 23
will almost always appear in public with Lady Middleton." SS II 3 156 13
Even Lady Middleton took the trouble of being delighted, SS II 3 157 19
John and Lady Middleton in town by the end of next week." SS II 5 167 4
It was from Lady Middleton, announcing their arrival in SS II 5 170 28
This was an affair, however, of which Lady Middleton did SS II 5 170 29
have it known that Lady Middleton had given a small dance SS II 5 170 29
"So my daughter Middleton told me, for it seems Sir John SS II 5 171 38
that time to attend Lady Middleton to a party, from which SS II 6 175 1
they were told that Lady Middleton waited for them at the SS II 6 175 1
and doing less, Lady Middleton sat down to Casino, and as SS II 6 175 2
would entreat Lady Middleton to take them home, as she was SS II 6 178 15
Lady Middleton, though in the middle of a rubber, on being SS II 6 178 16
The pity of such a woman as Lady Middleton! SS II 7 191 64
The calm and polite unconcern of Lady Middleton on the SS II 10 215 12
Lady Middleton expressed her sense of the affair about SS II 10 215 14
and introduce him to Sir John and Lady Middleton. SS II 11 223 15
They were lucky enough to find Lady Middleton at home, and SS II 11 228 52
fellow: while Lady Middleton saw enough of fashion in his SS II 11 228 52
"Lady Middleton is really a most elegant woman! SS II 11 228 53
notice; and as for Lady Middleton, she found her one of SS II 12 229 1
Lady Middleton was equally pleased with Mrs. Dashwood. SS II 12 229 2
the good opinion of Lady Middleton, did not suit the fancy SS II 12 229 3
So well had they recommended themselves to Lady Middleton, SS II 12 230 8
particular desire, Lady Middleton set her down in Berkeley- SS II 13 238 2
sister--besides, Lady Middleton and Mrs. Ferrars will SS II 13 240 15
Their hours were therefore made over to Lady Middleton and SS II 14 246 2
Lady Middleton was ashamed of doing nothing before them, SS II 14 247 4
"without affronting Lady Middleton, for they spend every SS II 14 253 21
Conduit-Street, and Lady Middleton could not be displeased SS II 14 253 22
Harley-Street, as soon as Lady Middleton could spare them. SS II 14 253 26
and the visit to Lady Middleton, which had not before had SS II 14 254 26
the pride of Lady Middleton, and made an entry into the SS II 14 254 27
And Lady Middleton, is she angry?" SS III 2 272 10
against us, and Lady Middleton the same; and if any thing SS III 2 275 25
I suppose Lady Middleton won't ask us any more this bout. SS III 2 276 25
to Sir John, and Lady Middleton, and the dear children, SS III 2 278 30
I ran against Sir John Middleton, and when he saw who I SS III 8 330 69
MIDDLETONS (16)
The house was large and handsome; and the Middletons lived SS I 7 32 1
was returned by the Middletons dining at the cottage, the SS I 8 36 1
Are the Middletons pleasant people?" SS I 16 88 38
"you think the little Middletons rather too much indulged; SS I 21 122 19
When you and the Middletons are gone, we shall go on so SS II 3 155 8
The Middletons were to follow in about a week. SS II 3 158 22
intimate, Mrs. Jennings, Mrs. Palmer, and the Middletons. SS II 5 173 44
The Middletons and Palmers--how am I to bear their pity? SS II 7 191 64
not be easy till the Middletons and Palmers were able to SS II 9 203 10
And the Middletons too, you must introduce me to them. SS II 11 222 9
delighted with the Middletons, that though not much in the SS II 12 230 6
together--for the Middletons arrived so directly after Mrs. SS II 12 231 13
Middletons, spent the whole of every day in Conduit-Street. SS II 14 246 2
I avoided the Middletons as much as possible, as well as SS III 8 326 55
To Mrs. Jennings, to the Middletons, he has been long and SS III 9 337 17
To the Middletons, the Palmers, the Steeles, to every SS III 10 346 28
MIDDLETONS' (2)
be gathered from the Middletons' partial acquaintance with SS I 20 114 43
after the dance at the Middletons', was in these words:-- " SS II 7 187 39 40
MIDDLING (4)
He was a stout young man of middling height, who, with a NA I 7 45 5
down to a middling one for one day could not signify." NA II 11 211 13
"Middling, my dear; I cannot compliment you. E I 12 103 40
Miss Diana P. was about 4 & 30, of middling height & S 9 407 1
MIDLAND (1)
in the midland counties of England, was to be looked for. NA II 10 200 3
MIDNIGHT (5)
She had nothing to dread from midnight assassins or NA II 6 167 9
Till midnight, she supposed it would be in vain to watch; NA II 8 189 19
We are always at home before midnight. W 325 4
late; they are but just rising from dinner at midnight."-- W 325 4
say we shall be all safe at Hartfield before midnight." E I 15 126 10
MIDNIGHT BELL (1)
Midnight Bell, Orphan of the Rhine, and Horrid Mysteries. NA I 6 40 10
MIDSHIPMAN (4)
for he was still only a midshipman; and as his parents, MP II 6 233 14
a smart place as that--poor scrubbery midshipman as I am." MP II 7 245 33
One might as well be nothing as a midshipman. MP II 7 249 52
in London, and the other midshipman on board an indiaman. MP III 7 381 26
MIDSHIPMEN (2)
removals to which all midshipmen are liable, and P III 6 51 30
and especially such midshipmen as every captain wishes to P III 6 51 30
MIDST (26)
still more interesting, in the midst of an heavy rain. SS I 9 42 10
Elinor had just been congratulating herself, in the midst SS III 4 287 26
A tap at the door roused her in the midst of this attempt MP I 16 153 3
stay, she might be in the midst of their noise, or retreat MP I 17 159 6
exhibition in the midst of theatrical nonsense, and forced MP II 1 183 23
perhaps till in the midst of some tender ejaculation of MP II 4 208 11
hand shirt button in the midst of her nephew's account of MP II 6 236 21
They had been hunting together, and were in the midst of a MP II 7 240 13
downy field, in the midst of a retired little village MP II 7 241 13
at such a time, in the midst of all the rich ornaments MP II 8 254 8
shook back, and in the midst of all this, still speaking MP II 12 296 31
that, brought up in the midst of negligence and error, she MP III 9 397 8
because she was in the midst of closeness and noise, to MP III 14 432 9
was escaping her, in the midst of all the agitating, MP III 15 443 24
a dash of evil--for in the midst of it she could exclaim ' MP III 16 455 23
Even in the midst of his late infatuation, he had MP III 17 471 28
her father was yet in the midst of his very civil welcome E II 5 190 21
in the midst of the pangs of disappointed affection. E II 8 219 44
as you are, in the midst of every dearest connection, and E II 16 293 17 18
with two people in the midst of us who may have been E III 10 399 61
no preventing a laugh, sometimes in the very midst of them. E III 18 475 40
"I do suspect that in the midst of your perplexities at E III 18 478 64 65
She would be placed in the midst of those who loved her, E III 19 482 4
indifference, even in the midst of the serious anxiety P III 7 53 2
stopped her short in the midst of the Elliot countenance. P IV 2 133 24
"To see you," cried he, "in the midst of those who could P IV 11 244 72
MIDSUMMER (5)
Mind me, now, if they an't married by midsummer. SS II 8 196 22
think that, instead of midsummer, they would not be SS II 10 216 15
to stay at least till midsummer, and fresh invitations had E II 15 285 14
and August, instead of midsummer, fixed for it, she was E III 5 343 1
Under a bright mid-day sun, at almost midsummer, Mr. E III 6 357 33
MIEN (1)
handsome features, noble mien; and the report which was in PP I 3 10 5
MIGHTILY (1)
And yet, here are two gentlemen stuck up in it mightily at P IV 6 169 25
MIGHTY (4)
"A mighty concession indeed! SS I 15 80 42
"Sir Thomas is to achieve mighty things when he comes home, MP I 17 161 15
agreeable day and find it all mighty delightful. MP II 5 220 30
them all in high and mighty claims: but in herself, I E II 18 310 33
MILCH (2)
milk--& I have two Milch Asses at this present time.-- S 6 393 1
for Sir Edward's sake, & the sake of her Milch Asses. S 11 422 1
MILCH-ASSES (1)
There is the sea & the downs & my Milch-Asses--& I have S 6 393 1
MILD (22)
that no one less amiable & mild than himself could have LS 3 247 1
is absolutely sweet, & her voice & manner winningly mild. LS 6 251 1
the oval face & mild dark eyes, & there is peculiar LS 17 270 5
mild day of February, with the consciousness of safety. NA I 9 62 10
It represented a very lovely woman, with a mild and NA II 9 191 3
Their tempers were mild, but their principles were steady, NA II 16 249 2
His manners, though serious, were mild; and his reserve SS I 10 50 12
was a something in it's mild seriousness, as well as in W 346 21
of Hertfordshire; her mild and steady candour always PP II 1 138 31
It was a beautiful evening, mild and still, and the drive MP I 10 106 58
that when he inquired with mild gravity after the fate of MP II 1 183 24
weather being unusually mild for the time of year; and MP II 4 208 11
"And really," added Edmund, "the day is so mild, that your MP II 4 212 29
because the nights are so mild, and I know the end of it MP II 4 212 31
of saying to her, with a mild gravity, intended to be MP III 2 330 14
It was really March; but it was April in its mild air, MP III 11 409 6
It is a beautiful, moonlight night; and so mild that I E I 1 10 23
more yielding, complying, mild disposition than would suit E I 18 148 23
So mild and ladylike--and with such talents!-- E II 15 282 5
Selina, who is mild almost to a fault, bore with them much E III 2 321 15
her delicate features and mild dark eyes from his own); P III 1 6 10
steady conduct & mild, gentle temper was felt by everybody. S 3 379 1
MILDER (1)
as to want only a milder air to produce a very white world E I 13 112 24
MILDEST (1)
her-- and with all his mildest urbanity, said, "I am very E II 16 294 24 25
MILDLY (3)

yet so rationally and so mildly, to receive her and her PP III 8 314 22
and given so mildly and considerately as not to irritate MP III 9 397 8
Mr. P. spoke too mildly of her.-- S 7 402 1
MILDNESS (12)
tell tales; but if the mildness of her uncle should get LS 16 268 2
by such unlooked-for mildness, it was not just at that NA II 15 242 8
He replied with his accustomary mildness to all her SS II 4 163 19
In another day or two perhaps; this extreme mildness can SS II 5 167 3
And Marianne was in spirits; happy in the mildness of the SS II 5 168 7
she is all gentleness & mildness when anybody is by.-- W 318 2
Jane with all possible mildness declined interfering;--and PP I 20 112 23
It needed all Jane's steady mildness to bear these attacks PP I 23 129 14
office of governess, the mildness of her temper had hardly E I 1 5 3
but the engaging mildness of her countenance, and P III 11 100 23
mildness, or the sound of his artificial good sentiments. P IV 10 214 11
though with more decision & less mildness in her tone. S 9 407 1
MILE (49)
the truth in the course of a thirty mile journey. LS 17 271 6
Every mile, as it brought her nearer Woodston, added to NA II 14 230 1
The two houses were only a quarter of a mile apart; and, NA II 14 236 19
After winding along it for more than a mile, they reached SS I 6 28 1
Barton Park was about half a mile from the cottage. SS I 7 32 1
About a mile and a half from the cottage, along the narrow SS I 9 40 2
and only a quarter of a mile from the turnpike-road, so SS II 8 197 22
uncle is going within a mile of Guilford the next day.--" W 341 19
home, & he had come half a mile out of his road merely to W 355 28
family to a house about a mile from Meryton, denominated PP I 5 18 1
The village of Longbourn was only one mile from Meryton; a PP I 7 28 3
has a pleasant walk of about half a mile across the park.-- PP II 6 161 8
It was not in their direct road, nor more than a mile or PP II 19 240 12
They gradually ascended for half a mile, and then found PP III 1 245 3
Mr. and Mrs. Gardiner were half a quarter of a mile behind. PP III 1 257 65
The houses, though scarcely half a mile apart, were not MP I 7 67 16
of a mile, I cannot think I was unreasonable to ask it. MP I 7 73 53
gates; but we have nearly a mile through the park still. MP I 8 82 34
at; for we must have walked at least a mile in this wood. MP I 9 94 60
"Not half a mile," was his sturdy answer; for he was not MP I 9 94 61
wood itself must be half a mile long in a straight line, MP I 9 94 62
we have walked a mile in it, I must speak within compass." MP I 9 95 64
that it cannot be half a mile long, or half half a mile." MP I 9 96 74
saw a knoll not half a mile off, which would give them MP I 10 97 4
now going only half a mile and only to three people, still MP II 5 219 27
It was true that her friend was going only half a mile E I 1 6 7
a Mrs. Weston only half a mile from them, and a Miss E I 1 6 7
He lived about a mile from Highbury, was a frequent E I 1 9 21
half a mile apart, and were sure of meeting every day." E I 1 11 35
then, about a quarter of a mile down the lane rose the E I 10 83 2
from the sea--a quarter of a mile off--very comfortable. E I 12 106 56
and the three-quarters of a mile would have seemed but one. E I 15 129 23
About half a mile beyond Highbury, making a sudden turn, E III 3 333 5
him by another road, a mile or two beyond Highbury--and E III 3 334 7
its grounds; and at half a mile distant was a bank of E III 6 360 38
of the great house, about a quarter of a mile farther on. P III 5 36 20
half a mile distant, making himself agreeable to others! P III 7 58 20
and after another half mile of gradual ascent through P III 10 85 13
her full a mile, and they were going through Uppercross. P III 10 90 38
Wentworth, within half a mile of him; they would have to P III 11 93 2
mile or two of a Willingden, I sought no farther . . . S 1 367 1
One complete, measured mile nearer than East Bourne. S 1 369 1
Only conceive sir, the advantage of saving a whole mile, S 1 369 1
never heard of half a mile from home."-- S 1 370 1
air or veiw, only one mile & 3 qrs from the noblest S 4 380 1
If we any of us want to bathe, we have not a qr of a mile S 4 381 1
to regard the walk of a mile as any thing requiring rest, S 6 390 1
it was 1/2 a qr of a mile round about, & added two steps S 11 422 1
at the end of a qr of a mile through second gates into the S 12 426 1
MILE-STONE (1)
and met with every mile-stone before she expected it. NA II 5 155 4
MILES (92)
it is so far to go;--eight miles is a long way; Mr. Allen NA I 3 29 46
Her brother told her that it was twenty-three miles." NA I 7 45 6
my horse go less than ten miles an hour in harness; that NA I 7 45 7
only three-and-twenty miles! look at that creature, and NA I 7 46 9
than ten miles an hour: tie his legs and he will get on. NA I 7 46 11
"Rest! he has only come three-and-twenty miles to-day; all NA I 7 47 27
Catherine very seriously, "that will be forty miles a day." NA I 7 48 28
inevitable pace was ten miles an hour) by no means NA I 9 62 10
I would not be bound to go two miles in it for fifty NA I 9 65 28
"The finest place in England--worth going fifty miles at NA I 11 85 23
miles; and, I suppose, we have at least eight more to go. NA I 11 88 54
for my heart, you know, will be some forty miles off. NA II 1 130 13
of fixing mine, when my thoughts are an hundred miles off. NA II 3 143 4
a journey of thirty miles: such was the distance of NA II 5 155 4
which is nearly twenty miles from my father's, and some of NA II 5 157 7
miles off--could you shrink from so simple an adventure? NA II 5 159 21
drive of almost twenty miles, they entered Woodston, a NA II 11 212 17
be at Salisbury, and then I am only nine miles from home." NA II 13 224 17
but a journey of seventy miles, to be taken post by you, NA II 13 225 23
she was conveyed some miles beyond the walls of the Abbey NA II 14 230 1
and, for fourteen miles, every bitter feeling was rendered NA II 14 230 1
spire which would announce her within twenty miles of home. NA II 14 232 6
We shall live within a few miles of each other, and shall SS I 3 17 17
It was within four miles northward of Exeter. SS I 5 25 1
fine place about twelve miles from Barton, belonging to a SS I 12 62 28
"Our dear Willoughby is now some miles from Barton, Elinor, SS I 15 77 22
Not above ten miles, I dare say." SS I 20 111 12
are forced to send three miles for their meat, and have SS II 8 197 22
From Cleveland, which was within a few miles of Bristol, SS III 3 280 6
of being only eighty miles from Barton, and not thirty SS III 6 302 8
Palmer's, who lived a few miles on the other side of Bath; SS III 7 308 3
What had Edward felt on being within four miles of Barton, SS III 12 357 2
a village about 3 miles distant, were poor & had no close W 314 1
is nothing, when one has a motive; only three miles. PP I 7 32 37
That she should have walked three miles so early in the PP I 7 32 42
"To walk three miles, or four miles, or five miles, or PP I 8 36 10
rich, and living but three miles from them, were the first PP I 18 99 63
It was a journey of only twenty-four miles, and they began PP II 4 152 5
It is nearly fifty miles." PP II 9 178 17
"And what is fifty miles of good road? PP II 9 178 18
loud, that any body might have heard us ten miles off!" PP II 16 222 22
country; and within five miles of Lambton, Elizabeth found PP II 19 240 12
smile, they were told, that it was ten miles round. PP III 1 253 57
My dear Lizzy, they must have passed within ten miles of PP III 4 274 3
I could not bear to have her ten miles from me; and as for PP III 8 310 8
After walking several miles in a leisurely manner, and too PP III 16 370 35
of happiness, were within thirty miles of each other. PP III 19 385 3
You speak as if you were going two hundred miles off, MP I 3 26 31
ten miles of indifferent road, to pay a morning visit. MP I 4 39 10
a park, a real park five miles round, a spacious modern- MP I 5 48 28
this will not do seventy miles from London--but this MP I 6 57 33
Ten miles there, and ten back, you know. MP I 8 76 3
For the first seven miles Miss Bertram had very little MP I 8 81 32
"Do you think we are walking four miles an hour?" MP I 9 95 65
all happening two hundred miles off, I think there would MP I 13 122 4
six young men within six miles of us, who are wild to be MP I 15 148 58
"His going, though only eight miles, will be an unwelcome MP II 7 247 42
thinking of as seventy miles off, and as farther, much MP III 3 334 1
My poor aunt always felt affected, if within ten miles of MP III 12 416 3
a family above an hundred miles off--not even Mrs. Price, MP III 13 428 14
in London, only sixteen miles off, was much beyond her E I 1 7 9
"He had gone three miles round one day, in order to bring E I 4 28 6
were needless; the sixteen miles being happily E I 11 91 3
A hundred miles, perhaps, instead of forty." E I 12 106 57
is not much to chuse between forty miles and an hundred.-- E I 12 106 58
altogether than travel forty miles to get into a worse air. E I 12 106 58
of an hundred and thirty miles with no greater expense or E I 12 106 60
twenty miles off would administer most satisfaction. E II 4 182 7
in his travelling sixteen miles twice over on such an E II 7 205 1
"Yes, they are about 190 miles from London. E II 18 306 9
Sixty-five miles farther than from Maple Grove to London. E II 18 306 10
What were nine miles to a young man?-- E III 1 317 10
Sixteen miles--nay, eighteen--it must be full eighteen to E III 1 318 10
Seven miles were travelled in expectation of enjoyment, E III 7 367 1
neighbourhood:--lives only four miles from Maple Grove. E III 8 380 13
Jane will be only four miles from Maple Grove." E III 8 380 13
moment before, as unquestionably sixteen miles distant.-- E III 13 424 1
from Kellynch, only fifty miles, and Lady Russell's P III 2 14 10
and Mary fixed only three miles off, must be anticipated, P III 4 31 12
a distance of only three miles, will often include a total P III 6 42 1
by being removed three miles from Kellynch: Mary's P III 6 46 12
at his father's house, only two miles from Uppercross. P III 9 73 4
instead of going six miles another way; of his having, in P III 9 78 19
quite unknowingly, within twenty miles of each other. P III 11 94 6
it was only seventeen miles from Uppercross; though P III 11 94 7
And at Lyme too,--only seventeen miles off,--he would be P III 12 103 2
Lady Russell lived three miles off, his heart failed him, P IV 2 130 6
expected him, but for his known engagement seven miles off. P IV 10 216 17
"only five-and-twenty miles from Uppercross, and in a very P IV 10 217 20
Abbots, & lies 7 miles off, on the other side of Battel-- S 1 366 1
good dish of tea within 3 miles of the place--& as for the S 1 369 1
a sheltered Dip within 2 miles of the sea, they passed S 4 379 1
MILES' (2)
you with Irish anecdotes during a ten miles' drive." MP I 10 99 14
Dinner was soon followed by tea and coffee, a ten miles' MP I 10 104 52
MILESTONES (1)
innkeepers, and milestones; but his friend disregarded NA I 7 45 7
MILITARY (5)
like every military man, had a very large acquaintance. NA I 12 95 17
Among the increasing numbers of military men, one now made W 328 8
and society. a military life is not what I was intended PP I 16 79 23
when the chances of his military life had introduced him E I 2 15 2
Wallis, (who was a fine military figure, though sandy- P IV 3 142 13
MILITATE (1)
stay would therefore militate against her own happiness, SS II 10 214 7
MILITATED (1)
of manner which militated against all her established SS I 3 16 13
MILITIA (8)
the recent arrival of a militia regiment in the PP I 7 28 3
into the ----shire militia, in which he had engaged at the PP II 13 205 4
regiment of militia, and the monthly balls of Meryton." PP II 16 220 7
Eliza, are not the ----shire militia removed from Meryton? PP III 3 269 8
9
since he had been in the militia, it did not appear that PP III 6 297 12
that Mr. Wickham had resolved on quitting the militia. PP III 8 312 18
by entering into the militia of his country, then embodied. E I 2 15 1
He quitted the militia and engaged in trade, having E I 2 16 5
MILK (4)
wiped in streaks, the milk a mixture of motes floating in MP III 15 439 9
milk--& I have two Milch Asses at this present time.-- S 6 393 1
was ordered to drink Asses milk I could supply her)--and S 7 401 1
or any complaint which Asses milk cd possibly releive. S 11 422 1
MILK-MEN (1)
newsmen, muffin-men and milk-men, and the ceaseless clink P IV 2 135 33
MILKINESS (1)
to have all the vernon milkiness; but on receiving the LS 16 268 1
MILL (3)
into a certain mill, which I design for somebody else.-- MP III 11 411 20
leave her at the Abbey mill, while she drove a little E II 4 185 13
Perhaps to Hartfield, perhaps to the Abbey mill, perhaps E III 16 458 40
MILLER (2)
It was seen by some farmer, and he told the miller, and MP I 6 57 33
told the miller, and the miller told the butcher, and the MP I 6 57 33
MILLINER (1)
in visiting an opposite milliner, watching the sentinel on PP II 16 219 1
MILLINER'S (2)
to their aunt and to a milliner's shop just over the way. PP I 7 28 3
In this row were the best milliner's shop & the library--a S 4 384 1
MILLINERY (1)
in quest of pastry, millinery, or even (as in the present NA I 7 44 1
MILLION (3)
not one in a million, I suppose, actually lost! E II 16 296 42
You must think one five hundred million times more above E III 11 407 28
a "million times better than marrying among the Hayters." P IV 6 165 8
MILLIONS (2)
here for a few weeks, we would not live here for millions. NA I 10 70 3
Had I the command of millions, were I mistress of the NA I 15 119 18
MILMANS (1)
that was--and of the two Milmans, now Mrs. Bird and Mrs. E II 14 277 40
MILSOM-STREET (16)
in a shop window in Milsom-Street just now--very like NA I 6 39 4
offending young men in Milsom-Street, she was so far from NA I 7 47 18
believed they were in Milsom-Street, she was not certain NA I 12 91 3
To Milsom-Street she was directed; and having made herself NA I 12 91 3
remaining ground till she gained the top of Milsom-Street. NA I 13 101 25
from her visit in Milsom-Street were so very high, that NA II 1 129 1
Having heard the day before in Milsom-Street, that their NA II 1 131 15
Mr. Allen attended her to Milsom-Street, where she was to NA II 5 154 1
general had fixed to be out of Milsom-Street by that hour. NA II 5 155 4
Milsom-Street; I am naturally indifferent about flowers." NA II 7 174 7
But no wonder; Milsom-Street you know."-- NA II 14 238 27
and in walking up Milsom-Street, she had the good fortune P IV 6 168 25
She had hoped, when clear of Milsom-Street, to have her P IV 6 170 30
They were in Milsom-Street. P IV 7 174 2
and whom he must have joined a little below Milsom-Street. P IV 7 175 6
Their first meeting in Milsom-Street afforded much to be P IV 11 244 71
MILTON (1)
some dozen lines of Milton, Pope, and prior, with a paper NA I 5 37 4
MIMIC (1)
Do not mimic her. E II 8 225 78
MINCE (1)
I fancy she was wanted about the mince pies. PP I 9 44 29
MINCED (1)
help and recommend the minced chicken and scalloped E I 3 24 11
MIND (599)
situation & state of mind; & I impatiently look forward to LS 1 243 1
But I was determined to be discreet, to bear in mind my LS 2 244 1
I cannot make up my mind, till I better understand her LS 3 247 1
attend an impudent mind; at least I was myself prepared LS 6 251 1
of triumphing over a mind prepared to dislike me, & LS 10 257 1
that of relieving my own mind, by this letter; but I felt LS 12 261 5
my dear sir to quiet your mind, & no longer harbour a LS 14 263 1
her on that article, with every mind of common candour. LS 14 265 4
my mind was entirely satisfied with the posture of affairs. LS 22 281 4
You know his eager manner, my dear madam, when his mind is LS 23 283 3
She is an amiable girl, & has a very superior mind to what LS 23 284 4
I should not be surprised if he were to change his mind at LS 23 284 6
genius, or vigour of mind which will force itself forward." LS 24 288 11
Flexibility of mind, a disposition easily biassed by LS 25 294 5
idea to remain long on my mind, I do not feel very eager LS 29 299 2
not less unpropitious for heroism seemed her mind. NA I 1 13 1
looks, pretty--and her mind about as ignorant and NA I 2 18 1
and uninformed as the female mind at seventeen usually is. NA I 2 18 1
and a trifling turn of mind, were all that could account NA I 2 20 8
the greatest powers of the mind are displayed, in which NA I 5 38 4

I make it a rule never to mind what they say. NA I 6 42 26
"Oh! never mind that. NA I 6 43 41
Well, I will drive you up Lansdown to-morrow; mind, I am NA I 7 48 29
of the youthful female mind, fearful of hazarding an NA I 7 48 32
begin; I know you will not mind my going away, and I dare NA I 8 52 2
delicacy of a generous mind making light of the obligation; NA I 8 55 10
hear what your sister says, and yet you will not mind her. NA I 8 58 25
Allen, whose vacancy of mind and incapacity for thinking NA I 9 60 1
just passed through her mind, when she suddenly found NA I 10 75 24
"Oh! that will not signify; I never mind dirt." NA I 11 82 6
her friend very placidly, "I know you never mind dirt." NA I 11 82 7
mind, and so very inadequate was the comfort she offered. NA I 11 90 64
I never mind going through any thing, where a friend is NA I 11 90 64
Catherine's mind was greatly eased by this information, NA I 12 94 11
"Well done, General, said I, I am quite of your mind." NA I 12 96 22
These painful ideas crossed her mind, though she said NA I 13 98 3
information to her mind, and made her think with pleasure NA I 13 102 27
To ease her mind, and ascertain by the opinion of an NA I 13 103 29
It always puts me in mind of the country that Emily and NA I 14 106 4
To come with a well-informed mind, is to come with an NA I 14 110 28
heart and a very ignorant mind, cannot fail of attracting NA I 14 111 29
"Miss Morland, do not mind what he says;--but have the NA I 14 112 37
suddenly darted into her mind; and, with the natural blush NA I 15 117 7
a source of some real agitation to the mind of Isabella. NA I 15 119 14
truth, there are not many that I know my own mind about." NA I 15 124 45
"Your brother will not mind it I know," said she, "because NA II 1 132 17
something occupied her mind so much, that she drew back NA II 1 133 29
"And did Isabella never change her mind before?" NA II 1 133 32
Amusing enough, if my mind had been disengaged; but I NA II 1 134 37
With a mind thus full of happiness, Catherine was hardly NA II 3 143 1
Ah! here he comes; never mind, he will not see us, I am NA II 3 147 20
of that boasted absence of mind which Catherine had never NA II 4 149 1
that the inquietude of his mind, on Isabella's account, NA II 5 155 3
Will not your mind misgive you, when you find yourself in NA II 5 158 15
Thus wisely fortifying her mind, as she proceeded up NA II 6 167 9
announced a happy state of mind, but whose gentle hint of NA II 7 175 11
speak a mind at ease, or a conscience void of reproach."-- NA II 8 182 1
was convinced, that, to a mind like Miss Morland's, a view NA II 8 184 4
the gloomy workings of a mind not wholly dead to every NA II 8 187 13
bend to one purpose by a mind which, before she entered NA II 10 199 2
Her mind made up on these several points, and her NA II 10 201 4
that she suffered her mind to be at ease as to the NA II 11 208 2
Catherine's mind was too full, as she entered the house, NA II 11 212 18
so well assured was her mind on the subject of his NA II 11 215 28
I believe if I could see you I should not mind the rest, NA II 12 216 2
But your mind is warped by an innate principle of general NA II 12 219 15
of such a weight on her mind, she very soon resolved to NA II 13 220 1
as the human mind can never do comfortably without. NA II 13 221 6
Catherine walked on to her chamber, making up her mind as NA II 13 222 8
A new idea now darted into Catherine's mind, and turning NA II 13 223 12
in probability; and with a mind so occupied in the NA II 13 227 26
at that instant on her mind with peculiar force, made her NA II 13 228 27
one article of which her mind was incapable of more than NA II 14 231 5
But, whatever might be the distress of Catherine's mind, NA II 14 233 8
impress on her daughter's mind the happiness of having NA II 14 239 28
situations of the human mind in which good sense has very NA II 14 239 28
Henry, in an agitation of mind which many solitary hours NA II 15 248 16
in _her_ mind there was a sense of honour so keen, a SS I 1 6 9
all, that eagerness of mind in Mrs. Dashwood which must SS I 1 6 11
her of former delight, was exactly what suited her mind. SS I 2 8 2
began to revive, and her mind became capable of some other SS I 3 14 1
He did not disturb the wretchedness of her mind by ill- SS I 3 16 7
propensities of his mind, his inclinations and tastes as SS I 4 19 6
to pronounce that his mind is well-informed, his enjoyment SS I 4 20 9
It would not be likely to produce that dejection of mind SS I 4 22 18
could want to make her mind as captivating as her person. SS I 7 33 3
than he could describe to her the shades of his mind. SS I 9 44 21
but a natural ardour of mind which was now roused and SS I 10 48 7
Her mother too, in whose mind not one speculative thought SS I 10 49 11
world; has been abroad; has read, and has a thinking mind. SS I 10 51 20
of a strong affection in a young and ardent mind. SS I 11 54 4
the prejudices of a young mind, that one is sorry to see SS I 11 56 12
refinements of a young mind are obliged to give way, how SS I 11 56 17
I once knew a lady who in temper and mind greatly SS I 11 57 17
"There is no persuading you to change your mind, brandon, SS I 13 65 32
But you had better change your mind." SS I 13 65 43
a tolerable composure of mind by driving about the country. SS I 13 66 60
its cause, filled the mind and raised the wonder of Mrs. SS I 14 70 1
sometimes entered her mind of their being really engaged, SS I 14 71 4
silence, for Marianne's _mind_ could not be controuled, and SS I 16 85 15
and it ended in an absence of mind still more settled. SS I 18 99 14
This desponding turn of mind, though it could not be SS I 19 104 9
Her mind was inevitably at liberty; her thoughts could not SS I 19 105 12
"Never mind if they do. SS I 19 105 16
and integrity of mind, which her attentions, her SS I 22 127 2
her mind, she could have none of its being Edward's face. SS I 22 132 26
You can't think how much I go through in my mind from it SS I 22 133 42
his melancholy state of mind, his dissatisfaction at his SS II 1 139 1
and well-informed mind, be satisfied with a wife like her-- SS II 1 140 1
to-morrow, and then I hope she will not much mind it." SS II 1 144 11
will change her mind by and bye, why so much the better." SS II 3 154 4
cheerless her own state of mind in the comparison, and how SS II 4 159 1
party were engaged, her mind was equally abstracted from SS II 4 164 24
From this moment her mind was never quiet; the expectation SS II 5 169 15
But still I might not have believed it, for where the mind SS II 5 173 44
the uneasiness of her mind on other points; she was left, SS II 5 174 47
Elinor was robbed of all presence of mind by such an SS II 6 176 7
be divided in future, her mind might be always supported. SS II 6 179 18
state of Marianne's mind not only prevented her from SS II 7 180 5
on the depravity of that mind which could dictate it, and, SS II 7 184 16
on the very different mind of a very different person, who SS II 7 184 16
slept; and now, when her mind was no longer supported by SS II 7 185 16
and in restless pain of mind and body she moved from one SS II 7 191 65
Mind me, now, if they an't married by midsummer. SS II 8 196 22
refinement of her own mind, and the too great importance SS II 9 201 4
conviction, lasting conviction to your sister's mind. SS II 9 204 18
strong resemblance between them, as well in mind as person. SS II 9 205 23
24

The consequence of this, upon a mind so young, so lively, SS II 9 206 24
been guarded by a firmer mind, or an happier marriage, she SS II 9 208 28
as her own, and with a mind tormented by self-reproach, SS II 9 210 32
rest; for it irritates her mind more than the most perfect SS II 9 211 34
carried home to her mind, though she saw with satisfaction SS II 10 212 1
Her mind did become settled, but it was settled in a SS II 10 212 1
most likely change your mind when it came to the point. SS II 10 217 21
low, but eager, voice, "dear, dear Elinor, don't mind them. SS II 12 236 39
40

they have no mind to keep them, little as well as great." SS II 13 243 38
his eldest sister, his mind was equally at liberty to fix SS II 14 252 20
of her own composure of mind, and a very earnest SS III 1 261 12
had all this hanging on my mind, without being at liberty SS III 1 263 29
The composure of mind with which I have brought myself at SS III 1 264 29
In such a frame of mind as she was now in, Elinor had no SS III 1 264 32
Her mind was so much weakened that she still fancied SS III 2 270 2
if she had the least mind for it, to put an end to the SS III 2 273 16
she had not the least mind in the world to be off, for she SS III 2 273 16
a couple of minutes, from what was uppermost in her mind. SS III 2 275 21
had been already foreseen and foreplanned in her own mind. SS III 2 276 26
a man has once made up his mind to such a thing, somehow SS III 4 285 5
I do not ask you to go with me, for I dare say your mind SS III 4 286 11
that suspicion in his mind which had recently entered it. SS III 4 290 36
a great deal to say, her mind was so much more occupied by SS III 4 291 46
her nerves and fill her mind;--and she was therefore glad SS III 5 297 32
see its influence on her mind, in the something like SS III 5 300 38
restoring Marianne's peace of mind, and confirming her own. SS III 6 302 5
was not in a state of mind to resist their influence. SS III 7 309 7
mind the persuasion that he should see Marianne no more. SS III 7 309 7
pre-arranged in his mind, he offered himself as the SS III 7 311 15
firmness of a collected mind, made every necessary SS III 7 312 17
her's; and whose mind--Oh! how infinitely superior!"-- SS III 8 322 36
luxury, had made in the mind, the character, the happiness, SS III 8 331 70
She felt that his influence over her mind was heightened SS III 9 333 2
Such a noble mind!--such openness, such sincerity!-- no SS III 9 337 14
scenes of misery to his mind, brought back by that SS III 10 340 2
her daughter, but with a mind very differently influenced, SS III 10 340 3
an apparent composure of mind, which, in being the result SS III 10 341 6
traced the direction of a mind awakened to reasonable SS III 10 342 7
On the contrary, with a mind and body alike strengthened SS III 10 343 8
might again unsettle the mind of Marianne, and ruin at SS III 10 343 10
My peace of mind is doubly involved in it;--for not only SS III 10 345 20
she now sought; and with a mind anxiously pre-arranging SS III 10 348 34
Elinor, "exactly as a good mind and a sound understanding SS III 11 350 9
was very well; and to my mind she was always a very SS III 11 355 44
the mind may be told to consider it, and certainty itself. SS III 12 357 1
from the impatience of her mind to have something going on. SS III 12 358 5
disposed as is the human mind to be easily familiarized SS III 13 363 8
to Barton in a temper of mind which needed all the SS III 13 369 35
Some doubts always lingered in her mind when they parted, SS III 14 376 11
her society restored his mind to animation, and his SS III 14 379 17
a modest unpretending mind, & a great wish of obliging--& W 323 3
Miss Emma Watson puts me very much in mind of her eldest W 324 3
bravery "Oh! I do not mind it"--it was very evident by the W 330 11
of this gratified state of mind, in the course of the W 336 14
any chance conveyance, or did not mind walking so far.-- W 338 18
more to my mind--continued Mr W. or one better delivered.-- W 343 20
very little;--her simpler mind, or juster reason saved her W 345 21
after hard labour of mind, he produced the remark of it's W 345 21
was uppermost in her mind, at the moment of meeting;--& W 349 24
present, the employment of mind, the dissipation of W 361 31
uncle who had formed her mind with the care of a parent, & W 361 31
Her mind was less difficult to develope. PP I 1 5 34
"I do not mind his not talking to Mrs. Long," said Miss PP I 5 20 15
My mind was more agreeably engaged. PP I 6 27 48
in the improvement of her mind by extensive reading." PP I 8 39 51
I have therefore made up my mind to tell you, that I do PP I 10 52 50
Teaze calmness of temper and presence of mind! PP I 11 57 18
But pride--where there is a real superiority of mind, PP I 11 57 24
"Louisa, you will not mind my waking Mr. Hurst." PP I 11 58 33
My mind however is now made up on the subject, for having PP I 13 62 12
want of presence of mind; Charlotte tried to console her. PP I 18 90 5
make haste he will change his mind and not have _her_." PP I 20 111 7
If it was not for the entail I should not mind _it_. PP I 23 130 20
"What should not you mind?" PP I 23 130 21
"I should not mind any thing at all." PP I 23 130 21
immediately to Elizabeth's mind; and from the observation PP II 6 162 11
likely to promote sisterly affection or delicacy of mind." PP II 6 165 35
manners, she believed he might have the best informed mind. PP II 9 180 28
in it, and sometimes it seemed nothing but absence of mind. PP II 9 181 29
Her understanding excellent, her mind improved, and her PP II 10 186 40
from the serenity of a mind at ease with itself, and PP II 11 188 1
the disturbance of his mind was visible in every feature. PP II 11 190 8
The tumult of her mind was now painfully great. PP II 11 193 31
In this perturbed state of mind, with thoughts that could PP II 13 205 3
have made a stronger impression on his mind than on hers. PP II 13 209 10
You know I always speak my mind, and I cannot bear the PP II 14 211 13
a mind so occupied, she might have forgotten where she was. PP II 14 212 16
My dear Charlotte and I have but one mind and one way of PP II 15 216 6
The tumult of Elizabeth's mind was allayed by this PP II 17 227 25
and emptiness of her mind, wholly unable to ward off any PP II 18 231 18
not mean that either his mind or manners were in a state PP II 18 234 35
36

and illiberal mind, had very early in their marriage put PP II 19 236 1
even if incapable of enlarging the mind of his wife. PP II 19 236 2
Elizabeth said no more--but her mind could not acquiesce. PP II 19 240 16
Elizabeth's mind was too full for conversation, but she PP III 1 245 3
There was certainly at this moment, in Elizabeth's mind, a PP III 1 250 48
there, recurring to her mind, the few minutes in which PP III 1 252 52
moment was passing in his mind; in what manner he thought PP III 1 253 55
on her absence of mind roused her, and she felt the PP III 1 253 56
complexion, _his_ mind was not very differently engaged. PP III 1 256 62
change his mind another day, and warn me off his grounds." PP III 1 258 72
struck so forcibly on her mind, that she could hardly PP III 2 263 10
to speak, she, in whose mind every idea was superseded by PP III 4 276 6
letter remained on her mind, she was all surprise--all PP III 4 279 24
must be of all others most afflicting to a parent's mind. PP III 6 296 11
considering the event, shews some greatness of mind." PP III 6 299 26
ease and liveliness, his mind might have been softened, PP III 8 312 15
cause where her peace of mind must be materially concerned. PP III 10 326 3
In future, I hope we shall be always of one mind." PP III 10 329 34
shortly relieved, and her mind opened again to the PP III 11 331 13
But her mind was so busily engaged, that she did not PP III 11 338 56
painful to Elizabeth's mind; and she would, at times, have PP III 12 340 13
Never mind Miss Lizzy's hair." PP III 13 344 7
of Miss Bennet's mind gave a glow of such sweet animation PP III 13 348 34
But I hope you will not mind it: it is all for Jane's PP III 17 375 26
Elizabeth's mind was now relieved from a very heavy weight; PP III 17 377 41
"For the liveliness of your mind, I did." PP III 18 380 4
Her mind received knowledge which had never before fallen PP III 19 388 11
sense and uprightness of mind, bid most fairly for utility, MP I 2 20 33
the improvement of her mind, and extending its pleasures. MP I 2 22 35
will be as good for your mind, as riding has been for your MP I 3 27 37
"Then you will not mind living by yourself quite alone?" MP I 3 29 47
unspeakably welcome to a mind which had seldom known a MP I 4 35 6
made up his mind, the whole business was soon completed. MP I 4 37 8
of their progress, her mind became so pleasantly occupied MP I 4 38 9
"The right of a lively mind, Fanny, seizing whatever may MP I 7 64 11
Having formed her mind and gained her affections, he had a MP I 7 64 12
good horsemanship has a great deal to do with the mind." MP I 7 69 25
be seen, the pain of her mind had been much beyond that in MP I 7 74 59
trying to make up her mind as to whether Miss Crawford's MP I 8 77 8
She had none of Fanny's delicacy of taste, of mind, of MP I 8 81 31
lively mind can hardly be serious even on serious subjects. MP I 9 87 16
"The mind which does not struggle against itself under _one_ MP I 9 88 18
I admit to be sometimes too hard a stretch upon the mind. MP I 9 88 18
will be at what she said just now," passed across her mind. MP I 9 89 26
Come, do change your mind. MP I 9 93 53
Miss Bertram had made up her mind to something different, MP I 10 105 52
"but it does put me in mind of the old Heathen heroes, who MP I 11 108 10
an amusement to his sated mind; and finding nothing in MP I 12 115 3
has quite made up his own mind, will distinguish the MP I 12 116 10
carry fascination to the mind of genius; and with the MP I 13 129 39
I only wish Tom had known his own mind when the carpenters MP I 15 141 22
she placed herself, "never mind, my dear Miss Price--this MP I 15 147 56
teasing--but do not let us mind them;" and with pointed MP I 15 147 56
morning, to such a willing mind as Fanny's, and while MP I 16 151 2
Her mind had been never farther from peace. MP I 17 159 6
and make him know his own mind; and if he means nothing, MP I 17 162 18
a very absent, anxious mind; and about noon she made her MP I 18 168 14
though almost every mind was ruffled; and the music which MP II 2 191 11
Her spirit supported her, but the agony of her mind was MP II 2 193 18
and trust to his seeing as much beauty of mind in time." MP II 3 197 6
You must try not to mind growing up into a pretty woman." MP II 3 198 8
She was in a state of mind to be glad that she had secured MP II 3 201 23
from separation--her mind became cool enough to seek all MP II 3 201 24

Her mind was quite determined and varied not. MP II 3 202 25
In all the important preparations of the mind she was MP II 3 202 26
a very desponding state of mind, sighing over the ruin of MP II 4 205 3
Miss Crawford, calling to mind an early-expressed wish on MP II 4 206 5
operations of time, and the changes of the human mind!" MP II 4 208 12
back her own mind to what she thought must interest. MP II 4 209 13
in Lady Bertram's mind, that half an hour afterwards, on MP II 5 217 11
mind to what may happen, and take your things accordingly." MP II 5 221 34
as her own propriety of mind directed, in spite of her MP II 5 223 48
soon in possession of his mind, and which he seemed to MP II 5 223 48
Oh! what a corrupted mind!" MP II 5 225 56
Henry Crawford had quite made up his mind by the next MP II 6 229 1
exercise only to my body, and I must take care of my mind. MP II 6 229 3
could give to the peace of mind he was attacking, his MP II 6 231 11
timidity of her mind by the flow of her love for William. MP II 6 232 13
the first ardours of her young, unsophisticated mind! MP II 6 235 20
such bodily hardships, and given such proofs of mind. MP II 6 236 22
His mind, now disengaged from the cares which had pressed MP II 7 238 1
But never mind it, William. MP II 7 249 53
You must think of that; you must try to make up your mind MP II 7 249 53
full of cares; his mind being deeply occupied in the MP II 8 254 10
He knew his own mind, but he was not always perfectly MP II 8 255 10
The sister is not to be in your mind without bringing the MP II 8 259 19
her to bring down her mind from its heavenly flight by MP II 9 262 10
over his own mind, though it might have its drawback. MP II 9 262 11
William could make up his mind to leave Mansfield half a MP II 9 265 21
They have injured the finest mind!--for sometimes, Fanny, MP II 9 269 33
than manner; it appears as if the mind itself was tainted." MP II 9 269 33
William's good fortune returned again upon her mind, and MP II 9 270 40
were playing, and her mind was in a flutter that forbad MP II 10 275 10
His mind was fagged, and her happiness sprung from being MP II 10 278 20
Sleep as long as you can and never mind me." MP II 10 279 25
could afterwards bring her mind without much effort into MP II 11 283 7
To Fanny's mind, Edmund's absence was really in its cause MP II 11 285 15
My mind is entirely made up. MP II 12 291 4
Mary was in a state of mind to rejoice in a connection MP II 12 292 5
to consult the Admiral, before you made up your mind." MP II 12 292 8
manners were the mirror of her own modest and elegant mind. MP II 12 294 16
sanguine and pre-assured mind to stand in the way of the MP II 13 302 9
was passing in his niece's mind, conceived that by such MP III 1 314 16
Her mind was in too much confusion. MP III 1 314 16
it not improbable that her mind might be in such a state, MP III 1 320 44
having passed across his mind and cheered it, "well," said MP III 1 320 44
Her mind was all disorder. MP III 1 321 46
endeavour to reason yourself into a stronger frame of mind. MP III 1 321 48
try to compose her spirits, and strengthen her mind. MP III 1 322 50
her could distress him long; his mind was not of that sort. MP III 1 324 59
While Fanny's mind was engaged in these sort of hopes, her MP III 1 324 60
suspicion rushed over her mind which drove the colour from MP III 1 325 60
by youth, a youth of mind as lovely as of person; whose MP III 2 326 3
every exertion of mind--but he did not think he could have MP III 3 336 7
She could not abstract her mind five minutes; she was MP III 3 337 10
and more than half a mind to take orders and preach myself. MP III 3 341 28
her from a grievous imprisonment of body and mind. MP III 3 344 43
mind, and try what his influence might do for his friend. MP III 4 345 1
I know you have something on your mind. MP III 4 346 8
"Yes; that is, it was the fault of my own mind if I did MP III 4 355 52
assiduities, and the natural workings of her own mind. MP III 5 356 2
the strong effect on her mind which the finding herself in MP III 5 357 6
Her mind was entirely self-engrossed. MP III 5 358 8
In their house I shall call to mind the conjugal manners MP III 5 361 16
as might warrant strong suspicion in a predisposed mind. MP III 5 362 17
Poor Fanny's mind was thrown into the most distressing of MP III 5 364 30
nothing, would awaken very wholesome regrets in her mind.-- MP III 6 366 1
Crawford, still shewn a mind led astray and bewildered, MP III 6 367 5
he absolutely made up his mind, he consulted his son. MP III 6 368 9
Park, would bring her mind into a sober state, and incline MP III 6 369 9
you will teach Betsey, and make the boys love and mind you. MP III 6 372 20
She must say that she had more than half a mind to go with MP III 6 372 21
The vicissitudes of the human mind had not yet been MP III 6 374 27
the high glee of William's mind, and he was full of frolic MP III 7 375 2
Tom, however, had no mind for such treatment: he came home, MP III 7 381 25
servants?"--soon led her mind away from Northamptonshire, MP III 7 385 38
Here was another strange revolution of mind!-- MP III 9 393 1
the natural light of the mind which could so early MP III 9 395 4
a mind so much in need of help, and so much deserving it. MP III 9 397 8
were too apt to seize her mind if her fingers only were MP III 9 398 10
silence, between which her mind was in fluctuation; each MP III 10 399 1
a relief to her worn mind to be at any certainty; and the MP III 10 401 9
he had secured agreeable recollections for his own mind. MP III 10 404 15
I have a great mind to go back into Norfolk directly, and MP III 11 412 20
way of being starved, both mind and body, into a much MP III 11 413 30
hundredth part of my great mind on paper, so I will MP III 12 415 2
and perhaps you would not mind passing through London, and MP III 12 416 3
times, dwelt more on her mind than the pages of Goldsmith; MP III 12 419 7
the support of their own bad sense to her too lively mind. MP III 13 421 2
but it will not be a less faithful picture of my mind. MP III 13 422 2
and where the mind is any thing short of perfect decision, MP III 13 423 2
He thoroughly knows his own mind, and acts up to his MP III 13 423 2
added that there must be a mind to be properly guided. MP III 14 430 2
my mind, and fear to trust the influence of friends. MP III 14 430 4
What animation both of body and mind, she had derived from MP III 14 432 9
what was, and prepare her mind for what might be; and how MP III 14 432 10
convey to the sanguine mind of her correspondent, the hope MP III 14 436 16
The horror of a mind like Fanny's, as it received the MP III 15 440 19
of a hope to soothe her mind, and was reduced to so low MP III 15 442 22
but it could not occupy her, could not dwell on her mind. MP III 15 443 24
state of his own mind made him find relief only in motion. MP III 15 445 29
Her affections were not acute, nor was her mind tenacious. MP III 16 449 6
to her in such a state of mind, so softened, so devoted, MP III 16 454 18
in a perversion of mind which made it natural to her to MP III 16 456 25
Fanny, of blunted delicacy and a corrupted, vitiated mind. MP III 16 456 25
coming in such a state of mind into that house, as I had MP III 16 457 30
that, as far as related to mind, it had been the creature MP III 16 457 30
which such a disappointment must make on his mind. MP III 16 460 31
made an impression on his mind which, at the age of six- MP III 17 462 4
he had so well talked his mind into submission, as to be MP III 17 462 5
no useful influence that way, no moral effect on the mind. MP III 17 463 8
What can exceed the misery of such a mind in such a MP III 17 464 11
was too strong for a mind unused to make any sacrifice to MP III 17 467 20
the smallest inconstancy of mind towards her cousin.-- MP III 17 468 21
purity of her mind, and the excellence of her principles. MP III 17 468 21
being ten years old, her mind in so great a degree formed MP III 17 470 27
Her mind, disposition, opinions, and habits wanted no half MP III 17 471 28
for it by a readiness of mind, and an inclination for MP III 17 472 31
life, without activity of mind or body, he was a much E I 1 7 8
from Farmer Mitchell's, I made up my mind on the subject. E I 1 12 41
A worthy employment for a young lady's mind! E I 1 12 42
an active cheerful mind and social temper by entering into E I 2 15 1
the real good-will of a mind delighted with its own ideas, E I 3 24 11
give any strength of mind, or tend at all to make a girl E I 5 39 15
"Oh! you would rather talk of her person than her mind, E I 5 39 17
Yes, I understand the sort of mind. E I 7 51 5
themselves unbidden to *your* mind, I am persuaded. E I 7 51 11
that--as you say, one's mind ought to be quite made up-- E I 7 52 20
and really almost made up my mind--to refuse Mr. Martin. E I 7 53 22
23

I hope he will not mind it so very much." E I 7 56 43
had previously made up his mind to walk out, was persuaded E I 8 57 2
It crossed my mind immediately that you would not regret E I 8 61 38
Till you chose to turn her into a friend, her mind had no E I 8 63 42
to recommend them; and his mind has more true gentility E I 8 65 49

settled her with her own mind, and convinced her, that let E I 8 67 56
an attachment as her youth and sort of mind admitted. E I 9 69 2
Her views of improving her little friend's mind, by a E I 9 69 3
is clear; the state of his mind is as clear and decided. E I 9 73 20
The most satisfactory comparisons were rising in her mind. E I 9 76 34
Harriet submitted, though her mind could hardly separate E I 9 77 43
"Never mind, Harriet, I shall not be a poor old maid; and E I 10 85 19
has a tendency to contract the mind, and sour the temper. E I 10 85 19
Poverty certainly has not contracted her mind: I really E I 10 85 19
"If I know myself, Harriet, mine is an active, busy mind, E I 10 85 21
Woman's usual occupations of eye and hand and mind will be E I 10 85 21
yet, who can say how soon it may all vanish from my mind?" E I 10 87 25
He had all the clearness and quickness of mind which she E I 11 93 5
a mind to take it up; but she struggled, and let it pass. E I 11 96 27
call to mind exactly the present line of the path . . . . E I 12 106 61
but as he has made up his mind, and does not seem to feel E I 13 110 9
Mr. Woodhouse had so completely made up his mind to the E I 13 112 24
towards Harriet, from her mind, while he not only sat at E I 14 118 4
the amusement afforded her mind by the expectation of Mr. E I 15 124 2
I should not mind walking half the way. I could change my E I 15 127 14
Elton's sanguine state of mind, he tried to take her hand E I 15 131 32
33

But her mind had never been in such perturbation, and it E I 15 133 38
her equal in connection or mind!--look down upon her E I 16 135 8
was her inferior in talent, and all the elegancies of mind. E I 16 136 9
should not have liberty of mind or limb to that amount. E I 18 146 12
the real liberality of mind which she was always used to E I 18 150 37
the greatest presence of mind, caught hold of her habit--(E II 1 160 23
could her higher powers of mind be unfelt by the parents. E II 2 165 7
of body and mind to be discharged with tolerable comfort. E II 2 165 9
whether of person or of mind, she saw so little in E II 2 167 12
of perfection in Highbury, both in person and mind." E II 3 174 38
amused, at such a state of mind in poor Harriet--such a E II 3 180 56
of person and mind; to be handsome, elegant, highly E II 4 181 2
humiliation to her own mind, she would have been thankful E II 4 182 7
many vacancies of Harriet's mind was not to be talked away. E II 4 183 10
mind, Emma would have been amused by its variations. E II 4 184 11
Her mind was quite sick of Mr. Elton and the Martins. E II 5 187 4
being the commonest process of a not ill-disposed mind. E II 5 187 6
strong possession of her mind, had ever crossed his; and E II 5 192 33
confusion of rank, bordered too much on inelegance of mind. E II 6 198 5
But Emma, in her own mind, determined that he *did* know E II 6 204 43
She had half a mind to resent; but an instant's E II 7 206 4
But she had made up her mind how to meet this presumption E II 7 207 7
evasions of a mind too weak to defend its own vanities.-- E II 8 212 3
gaining ground over the mind of her friend; for Mrs. E II 8 226 85
soon drew away half Emma's mind; and she fell into a train E II 8 227 87
changing her mind, Emma went to the door for amusement.-- E II 9 233 24
A mind lively and at ease, can do with seeing nothing, and E II 9 233 24
all the force of her own mind, to convince her that if she E II 9 235 35
William did not seem to mind it himself, he was so pleased E II 9 239 51
He told Patty this, but bid her not mind it, and be sure E II 9 239 51
accrue either to body or mind;--but when a beginning is E II 11 247 1
Miss Bates's powerful, argumentative mind might have E II 12 260 26
to do otherwise, as my own mind is quite made up. E II 13 265 4
Mr. Elton; and Harriet's mind, she had been willing to E II 13 267 8
and occupation of mind to shorten it, that Emma would not E II 14 270 3
And now, Miss Woodhouse, I do not think I shall mind E II 14 271 15
When the visit was returned, Emma made up her mind. E II 14 272 16
with a bench round it, which put me so exactly in mind! E II 14 273 21
Frank Churchill comes as regularly into my mind!"---- E II 14 279 52
Her mind returned to Mrs. Elton's offences, and long, very E II 14 280 61
by her superiority both of mind and manner; and that face E II 15 286 23
in the triumph of Miss Fairfax's mind over Mrs. Elton. E II 15 288 39
I think it is the state of mind which gives most spirit E II 18 309 30
there was a restlessness, which showed a mind not at ease. E III 2 320 7
a ground-work of anticipation as her mind had already made. E III 3 335 9
And knowing, as she did, the favourable state of mind of E III 3 335 10
It's tendency would be to raise and refine her mind--and E III 4 342 40
A variety of evils crossed his mind. E III 5 350 31
It was a sweet view--sweet to the eye and the mind. E III 6 360 39
Harriet's sweet easy temper will not mind it." E III 6 364 58
say, she had made up her mind to close with nothing till E III 8 380 15
that she would change her mind!--but that good Mrs. Elton, E III 8 380 15
aware of it, had been making up her mind the whole day." E III 8 381 20
it united with the subject which already engaged her mind. E III 8 384 32
mind when it was all but done, she could not perceive.-- E III 9 386 7
He always moved with the alertness of a mind which could E III 9 386 7
He had long made up his mind to Jane Fairfax's going out E III 9 387 9
grief of her husband--her mind glanced over them both with E III 9 388 13
Well, well, never mind." E III 10 394 22
Her mind was divided between two ideas--her own former E III 10 395 36
She understood it all; and as far as her mind could E III 11 403 2
mind, producing reserve and self-command, it would.-- E III 11 403 2
really--if *he* does not mind the disparity, I hope, dear E III 11 407 28
A mind like her's, once opening to suspicion, made rapid E III 11 407 32
Her voice was not unsteady; but her mind was in all the E III 11 409 34
allowed, and every moment of involuntary absence of mind. E III 11 412 44
Every other part of her mind was disgusting. E III 11 412 46
Her inferiority, whether of mind or situation, seemed E III 11 414 50
and thorough excellence of mind, he had loved her, and E III 12 415 1
pent up within her own mind as every thing had so long E III 12 418 5
it had been the agony of a mind that would bear no more. E III 12 421 17
distant from her mind, that it had been all her own work? E III 12 422 20
There was time only for the quickest arrangement of mind. E III 13 424 1
intolerable than any alternative to such a mind as his.-- E III 13 429 30
While he spoke, Emma's mind was most busy, and, with all E III 13 430 38
distressed state of mind, to something so like perfect E III 13 432 40
were very great--and her mind had to pass again and again E III 14 435 4
the most upright female mind in the creation to stoop in E III 14 437 8
The delicacy of her mind throughout the whole engagement, E III 14 439 8
from the confusion of my mind, and the multiplicity of E III 14 442 8
Natural enough!--his own mind full of intrigue, that he E III 15 446 15
Ever since I left you this morning, Emma, my mind has been E III 15 448 30
to the place in her mind which Harriet had occupied. E III 16 452 6
A fortnight, at least, of leisure and peace of mind, to E III 16 452 6
of the two recommendations to Mr. Woodhouse's mind.-- E III 17 467 30
enough to familiarize the idea to his quickness of mind.-- E III 17 468 33
Her mind was in a state of flutter and wonder, which made E III 18 475 37
in the same style; but his mind was the next moment in his E III 18 478 60
61

very promising step of the mind on its way to resignation. E III 19 483 9
of Mr. Woodhouse's mind, or any wonderful change of his E III 19 483 10
The strength, resolution, and presence of mind of the Mr. E III 19 484 10
Anne, with an elegance of mind and sweetness of character, P III 1 5 8
But now, another occupation and solicitude of mind was P III 1 9 19
She had a cultivated mind, and was, generally speaking, P III 2 11 2
made up my mind as to the privileges to be annexed to it. P III 3 18 8
a toil and a labour of the mind, if not of the body, which P III 3 20 17
of birth, beauty, and mind, to throw herself away at P III 4 26 3
His sanguine temper, and fearlessness of mind, operated P III 4 27 4
to the nice tone of her mind, the fastidiousness of her P III 4 28 7
found a more willing mind in her younger sister; and Lady P III 4 28 7
and possessed, in an acute mind and assiduous pleasing P III 5 34 12
Little Charles does not mind a word I say, and Walter is P III 5 38 27
elegant and cultivated mind for all their enjoyments; and P III 5 41 45
extraordinary bursts of mind which do sometimes occur. P III 6 51 31
in tolerable ease of mind; and then it was, just before P III 7 54 4
Wentworth, and I know you do not mind being left alone. P III 7 55 16
"A strong mind, with sweetness of manner," made the first P III 7 62 40
from her knowledge of his mind, that he could be unvisited P III 8 63 2
she heard the same voice, and discerned the same mind. P III 8 64 4

The only time that I ever really suffered in body or mind, P III 8 71 54
he should know his own mind, early enough not to be P III 9 77 18
influence on the mind of taste and tenderness, that season P III 10 84 7
She occupied her mind as much as possible in such like P III 10 84 7
When I have made up my mind, I have made it. P III 10 87 23
"Happy for her, to have such a mind as yours at hand!-- P III 10 87 26
fortitude and strength of mind, if she have not resolution P III 10 87 26
of life, she will cherish all her present powers of mind." P III 10 88 26
too, long enough, one would think, to make up his mind. P III 10 92 44
exactly adapted to Captain Benwick's state of mind. P III 11 97 12
much exercise; but a mind of usefulness and ingenuity P III 11 99 18
a broken heart, or a mind destroyed by wretchedness, and P III 11 100 23
the right of seniority of mind, she ventured to recommend P III 11 101 24
to rouse and fortify the mind by the highest precepts, and P III 11 101 24
of the mind, it should have its proportions and limits. P III 12 116 72
a mind to go with him, but the ladies could not consent. P IV 1 121 3
There could not be a doubt, to her mind there was none, of P IV 1 123 7
I think she would be so much pleased with his mind, that P IV 2 132 17
was all the operation of a sensible, discerning mind. P IV 3 143 19
To your fine mind, I well know the sight of beauty is a P IV 4 145 1
fine mind did not appear to excite a thought in her sister. P IV 4 145 2
Lady Russell's composed mind and polite manners were put P IV 4 146 5
no happiness to sour his mind, nor (she began pretty soon P IV 4 147 6
was that elasticity of mind, that disposition to be P IV 5 154 8
in her temper, manners, mind, a model of female excellence. P IV 5 159 21
How could it ever be ascertained that his mind was truly P IV 5 161 27
presence of mind never varied, whose tongue never slipped. P IV 5 161 28
putting us in mind of those we first had at North Yarmouth. P IV 6 170 29
Admiral had made up his mind not to begin, till they had P IV 6 170 30
over Lady Russell's mind, the difficulty it must be for P IV 7 179 28
When you had the presence of mind to suggest that benwick P IV 8 182 6
a disparity, and in a point no less essential than mind.-- P IV 8 182 9
10
involved in--the stretch of mind, the wear of spirits!-- P IV 8 183 15
passed to their seats, her mind took a hasty range over it. P IV 8 185 21
Anne's mind was in a most favourable state for the P IV 8 186 24
at the composure of her friend's usual state of mind. P IV 9 210 97
be in that quarter of the mind which could not be opened P IV 10 212 1
only a buzz of words in her ear, her mind was in confusion. P IV 11 231 11
from thorough absence of mind, became gradually sensible P IV 11 231 12
Her character was now fixed on his mind as perfection P IV 11 241 61
perfect excellence of the mind with which Louisa's could P IV 11 242 63
of heedlessness and the resolution of a collected mind. P IV 11 242 63
a smile, "I must endeavour to subdue my mind to my fortune. P IV 11 247 84
advantage of maturity of mind, consciousness of right, and P IV 12 248 1
result of the most correct opinions and well regarded mind. P IV 12 249 3
of as lively pain as her mind could well be sensible of, P IV 12 251 10
to his ancle--but never mind, my dear--(looking up at her S 1 364 1
turn of mind, with more imagination than judgement. S 2 372 1
She has a fine active mind, as well as a fine healthy S 3 376 1
& soften Lady D--who wd enlarge her mind & open her hand.-- S 3 379 1
emotions they excite in the mind of sensibility.-- S 7 396 1
of high toned genius, the grovellings of a common mind.-- S 7 398 1
through Charlotte's mind--but a civil answer was easy. S 9 410 1
some degree of strength of mind is given, it is not a S 9 410 1
The world is pretty much divided between the weak of mind S 9 410 1
for the refreshment the mind receives in doing it's duty.-- S 9 410 1
you to be pressing matters upon a mind at all unwilling."-- S 12 425 1

MINDED (3)
I am sure John and I should not have minded it. NA I 11 90 64
of his features that he minded it as much as ever.-- W 330 11
"you ought to have minded me, Walter; I told you not to P III 9 80 34

MINDFUL (3)
who was on every occasion mindful of the feelings of SS I 12 62 27
go away, Mrs. Bennet was mindful of her intended civility, PP III 11 338 57
Charles, being somewhat more mindful of the probabilities P III 8 66 21

MINDING (1)
It is not worth minding. MP II 7 249 53

MINDS (26)
I had fifty minds to buy it myself, for it is one of my NA I 10 76 28
Tilney says it is always the case with minds of a certain NA II 3 144 4
and young men never know their minds two days together. NA II 12 216 2
involved filling the minds of both, scarcely another word NA II 13 229 31
The change which a few hours had wrought in the minds and SS III 13 363 6
The most liberal & enlightened minds are always the most W 352 26
surrounded by inferior minds with little chance of W 361 31
is so well fixed in the minds of the surrounding families, PP I 1 3 2
in these attentions; their minds were more vacant than PP I 7 28 3
always seen a great similarity in the turn of our minds.-- PP I 18 91 15
doubtless be congenial with the generality of female minds. PP II 16 222 23
up; how to preserve in the minds of my daughters the MP I 1 10 17
to form her nieces' minds; and it is not very wonderful MP I 2 19 30
reading in her two nieces' minds their little approbation MP I 6 61 58
Do you think the minds which are suffered, which are MP I 9 87 16
cause, must be imputed to the fulness of their own minds. MP I 17 163 21
for him; but as nobody minds having what is too good for MP III 17 471 28
in love with well-informed minds instead of handsome faces, E I 8 63 44
regularly, their little minds would bend to his." E I 18 147 18
You are very fond of bending little minds; but where E I 18 147 19
minds; but where little minds belong to rich people in E I 18 147 19
Their children had more modern minds and manners. P III 5 40 45
You can make little Charles do any thing; he always minds P III 7 57 16
Their minds most dissimilar! P IV 6 166 19
They have only weaker constitutions & stronger minds than S 5 385 1
the amusement of eager minds in want of employment than of S 10 412 1

MINE (113)
to her own child, should be attached to any of mine. LS 3 247 1
of the letter--& is his judgement inferior to mine? LS 15 267 4
That horrid girl of mine has been trying to run away.-- LS 16 268 1
be her real sentiments, said nothing in opposition to mine. LS 22 280 1
ever, while mine will be found still fresh & implacable. LS 22 282 7
in his apartment, whither I heard him go, on leaving mine. LS 22 282 8
mine as I listened to him, I need not attempt to describe. LS 23 284 5
With feelings so poignant as mine, the conviction of LS 30 300 3
mine, it will unite us again in the same intimacy as ever. LS 39 307 1
"Yes, quite sure; for a particular friend of mine, a Miss NA I 6 40 12
It was built for a Christchurch man, a friend of mine, a NA I 7 46 11
directly, threw down the money, and the carriage was mine." NA I 7 46 13
"I am glad of it; I will drive you out in mine every day." NA I 7 47 23
No, no; I shall exercise mine at the average of four hours NA I 7 48 27
Mine is famous good stuff to be sure. NA I 9 64 24
Here is a friend of mine, Sam Fletcher, has got one to NA I 10 76 28
A pretty good thought of mine--hey?" NA I 13 100 15
"A particular friend of mine had an account of it in a NA I 14 112 33
Oh! how different to your brother and to mine! NA II 1 130 7
of fixing mine, when my thoughts are an hundred miles off. NA II 3 143 4
"This is so favourite a walk of mine," said Miss Tilney, " NA II 7 179 28
as that staircase can be from the stables to mine." NA II 9 195 8
is quite unnecessary upon your sister's account and mine. NA II 11 211 13
Anne Mitchell had tried to put on a turban like mine, as I NA II 12 217 2
make her character better known to me than mine is to her. NA II 12 218 4
have united for their ease what they must divide for mine. NA II 15 247 14
As it is, without any addition of mine, they will each SS I 2 10 14
If we find they correspond, every fear of mine will be SS I 15 80 41
Your ideas are only more noble than mine. SS I 17 91 11
and this prepared a future mine of raillery against the SS I 18 99 15
Mine is a misery which nothing can do away." SS II 7 186 28
"No, no," cried Marianne, "misery such as mine has no SS II 7 189 52
"But for my mother's sake and mine"----- SS II 7 190 53
The doctor is no beau of mine." SS II 10 218 26
Then, you must be no friend of mine; for those who will SS II 13 244 40
But I don't think mine would be, to make one son SS III 1 269 54
said about them, and I took care to keep mine out of sight. SS III 2 275 22
As a friend of mine, of my family, he may perhaps--indeed SS III 4 289 35
in the constancy of mine as ever, awakened all my remorse. SS III 8 325 53
It happened to catch Sophia's eye before it caught mine-- SS III 8 328 61
like mine, any thing was to be done to prevent a rupture. SS III 8 328 63
His heart was softened in seeing mine suffer; and so much SS III 8 330 69
What in a situation like mine, but a most shamefully SS III 10 345 20
ungraciously delivered as mine were on the occasion, he SS III 13 368 30
Your pleasure would be greater than mine. W 320 2
of your company than of mine, & I shd most readily return W 320 2
"Mine is all to come I am sure--said eliz: giving another W 321 2
are quite safe, the danger is only mine."-- W 339 18
He is no favourite of mine, as you well know, Emma;--but W 342 19
forgive his pride, if he had not mortified mine." PP I 5 20 19
your porridge,"--and I shall keep mine to swell my song. PP I 6 24 22
"This was a lucky idea of mine, indeed!" said Mrs. Bennet, PP I 7 31 29
chuse to call mine, but which I have never acknowledged. PP I 10 50 34
case, or do you imagine that you are gratifying mine?" PP I 18 91 14
"How near it may be to mine, I cannot pretend to say.-- PP I 18 91 16
"Yes, there can; for mine is totally different.-- PP I 21 118 16
a more happy idea, since you will not take comfort in mine. PP I 21 119 22
His own father did not long survive mine, and within half PP II 12 200 5
The liberty of communication cannot be mine till it has PP II 17 227 25
"I am sure I shall break mine," said Lydia. PP II 18 229 5
"But you are not entitled to know mine; nor will such PP III 14 354 39
you have certainly no right to concern yourself in mine. PP III 14 357 61
"Your surprise could not be greater than mine in being PP III 16 370 31
a case, but his reliance on mine, made every thing easy. PP III 16 371 45
But, in short, it is not a favourite profession of mine. MP I 6 60 51
aromatic vinegar; I always forget to have mine filled." MP I 7 72 45
Rushworth, "what would you do with such a part as mine? MP I 15 145 48
if any son of mine could reconcile himself to doing less. MP II 7 247 42
Do you think Henry will claim the necklace as mine, and MP II 8 259 20
No doubt it is handsomer than mine, and fitter for a ball- MP II 9 263 14
the noisy ones gone, your brother and mine and myself. MP II 11 288 30
her own feelings, to furnish a tolerable guess at mine.-- MP III 13 420 2
sisters, as the greatest misfortune of her life and mine. MP III 13 421 2
With real affection, Fanny like mine, more might be MP III 14 434 13
to every body and a mine of felicity to herself. E I 3 21 4
Don't pretend to be in raptures about mine. E I 6 43 15
I assure you mine are very different. E I 8 62 39
sure I should be a fool to change such a situation as mine. E I 10 84 15
"If I know myself, Harriet, mine is an active, busy mind, E I 10 85 21
"And mine," said Mr. Knightley warmly, "is, that if he E I 18 150 32
your thoughts on this subject are very much like mine." E II 8 216 26
I told you that your suspicions would guide mine." E II 8 217 29
"It is not fair," said Emma in a whisper, "mine was a E II 10 241 10
"You are speaking of letters of business; mine are letters E II 16 293 20
"here comes this dear old beau of mine, I protest!-- E II 17 302 21
22
These amazing engagements of mine--what have they been? E II 18 312 50
And I see very few pearls in the room except mine.-- E III 2 324 21
supply him; and so I took mine out and cut him a piece; E III 4 338 12
"I will answer for it, that mine thinks herself full as E III 6 356 25
Mine, I confess, are exhausted. E III 6 363 50
your temper under your own command rather than mine." E III 7 369 11
Do not let mine continue longer. E III 10 394 27
and let his behaviour be the rule of mine--and so I have. E III 11 411 39
scruple of mine with multiplied strength and refinement.-- E III 14 440 8
on her side, abominable on mine; and I returned the same E III 14 441 8
You must get his consent before you ask mine." E III 15 449 33
on your side of the question; all the merit on mine. E III 17 464 24
"The shame," he answered, "is all mine, or ought to be. E III 18 477 53
You can have no superior, but most true on mine.-- E III 18 479 70
"Such an extraordinary dream of mine!" he cried. E III 18 480 77
should be sorry to see any friend of mine belonging to it." P III 3 19 13
14
a friend of mine who was standing near, (Sir Basil Morley.) P III 3 20 16
A friend of mine, and I, had such a lovely cruise together P III 8 67 23
your feelings are less reconciled to the change than mine. P IV 1 125 15
16
It had been my doing--solely mine. P IV 8 183 13
Your peace will not be shipwrecked as mine has been. P IV 9 196 32
"And mine," added Sir Walter. P IV 10 215 16
"your feelings, as I think you must have penetrated mine. P IV 11 237 42
of mine, which you shot with one day, round Winthrop." P IV 11 240 58
past, as I did; and one encouragement happened to be mine. P IV 11 244 70
My sister's complaints & mine are happily not often of a S 9 410 1
the world, shall you stir a step on any business of mine.-- S 9 411 1
whom some friends of mine are exceedingly interested about, S 12 424 1

MINEHEAD (1)
When we came back from Minehead, he was gone down to P IV 6 171 33

MINGLE (1)
they were permitted to mingle in the croud, and take their SS II 6 175 2

MINGLED (4)
and the fair ladies mingled in embraces and tears of joy. NA I 15 118 8
an expression of mingled incredulity and mortification. PP II 11 193 27
the discourse while he mingled among the others with the MP II 1 184 25
her sister as an object of mingled compassion and respect. MP III 9 396 6

MINGLING (1)
her as his patroness, mingling with a very good opinion of PP I 15 70 1

MINIATURE (3)
it turned out to be only the miniature of our great uncle." SS I 12 60 10
Then taking a small miniature from her pocket, she added, " SS I 22 131 35
a small miniature painting, "do you know who that is?" P IV 11 232 13

MINIATURES (5)
amongst several other miniatures, over the mantle-piece. PP III 1 247 9
of the miniatures, "is my master--and very like him. PP III 1 247 11
and these miniatures are just as they used to be then. PP III 1 247 18
Miniatures, half-lengths, whole-lengths, pencil, crayon, E I 6 44 19
that one among many miniatures in another part of the room, S 12 427 1

MINISTER (1)
Oh! no; cautious as a minister of state. E III 16 454 15

MINOR (3)
cause;--but whatever minor feelings less pure, less SS III 3 283 20
she never heard of Asia Minor--or she does not know the MP I 2 18 23
All the minor arrangements of table and chair, lights and E II 11 255 59

MINORITY (1)
But I am quite in the minority, I believe; few people seem E II 17 302 22

MINUTE (71)
For a minute or two I remained in the same spot, LS 23 284 5
necessity of a long and minute detail from Mrs. Thorpe NA I 4 34 9
Half a minute conducted them through the Pump-Yard to the NA I 7 44 1
and having only one minute in sixty to bestow even on the NA I 7 51 54
afterwards, been half a minute earlier, he might have NA I 8 54 10
the rest for a minute; but he will soon know his master. NA I 9 62 9
of patience, had he staid with you half a minute longer. NA I 10 76 29
out of the house the next minute after my leaving it; I NA I 12 94 9
to forget that she had for a minute thought otherwise. NA II 1 137 50
way, they could have passed it with ease in half a minute. NA II 5 156 5
being late; and in half a minute they ran down stairs NA II 6 165 5
suggestion for half a minute, till the possibility of the NA II 7 173 4
was called back in half a minute to receive a strict NA II 7 181 41
lingering only half a minute behind her friend to throw a NA II 13 227 27
They saw him step into his carriage, and in a minute it SS I 15 76 17
after listening half a minute, returned into the room in SS II 4 161 7
home, as she was too miserable to stay a minute longer. SS II 6 178 15
every engagement however minute, and however it may make SS II 13 243 40
have given her a full and minute account of the whole SS II 14 247 4
to give so exact, so minute a detail of her situation, as SS II 14 247 5
Nothing escaped her minute observation and general SS II 14 249 8
Mrs. Dashwood declared they should not stay a minute SS III 1 259 7

saw, on her frequent and minute examination, that every SS III 7 315 25
He took the opposite chair, and for half a minute not a SS III 8 317 7
over the keys for a minute complained of feebleness in her SS III 10 342 7
and was carefully minute in every particular of speech and SS III 10 348 34
another minute was led by Col. Beresford to begin the set. W 330 11
in, returned in half a minute, with a look of awkward W 344 21
Emma" that she could hardly speak a word in a minute.-- W 349 24
In another minute Mr. Bingley, but without seeming to have PP I 15 73 9
them again, after the pause of half a minute began another. PP I 18 100 68
all her family were very minute, and then by a little PP I 20 114 31
of Pemberley, with the minute description which Wickham PP II 2 143 20
to hear, in reply to her minute enquiries, that though PP II 4 152 6
would not do; in half a minute the letter was unfolded PP II 13 205 3
more than half a minute, and never attended to Mary at all. PP II 16 223 24
"I will not detain you a minute, but let me, or let the PP III 4 276 7
face, returned for half a minute with an additional glow, PP III 11 334 37
judges of time, and every half a minute seems like five." MP I 10 102 46
was spoken for half a minute; each with an altered MP II 1 175 1
on his looking in for a minute in his way from his MP II 5 217 11
The coachman drove round to a minute; another minute MP II 5 222 41
could give her direct and minute information of the father MP II 6 234 18
when the animal was one minute tendered to his use again; MP II 6 237 23
she anticipated, in another minute alone with Mr. Crawford. MP III 1 325 62
clouded for a minute; and every thing looked so beautiful MP III 11 409 6
prepared herself for a minute detail of happiness and a MP III 13 420 1
but she was within half a minute of starting the idea, MP III 13 424 4
and butter growing every minute more greasy than even MP III 15 439 9
Half a minute brought it all out. E I 7 50 1
goodness to walk on, and she would follow in half a minute. E I 10 88 33
It had a most favourable aspect; and, for half a minute, E I 10 90 39
Emma was rather in dismay when only half a minute E I 13 115 36
I stood for a minute, feeling dreadfully, you know, one E II 3 179 52
had called in for half a minute, in order to hear that his E II 6 196 2
very minute directions, or wrote to Broadwood himself. E II 10 241 8
Her approbation, at once general and minute, warm and E II 11 256 60
left him not another minute to lose; and Emma engaging to E III 3 334 8
They walked off, followed in half a minute by Mr. E III 7 374 54
In half a minute they were together. E III 13 424 1
She will give you all the minute particulars, which only E III 18 472 20
In half a minute they were in the room. E III 18 476 46
she had been within half a minute of sending for Mr. Perry. E III 18 479 73
in the very first half minute, in the instant even of P III 6 48 18
Another minute brought another addition. P III 9 79 28
must be decided, and without the loss of another minute. P III 12 113 57
58

Every minute is valuable. P III 12 113 58
Hayter for all the minute knowledge of Louisa, which it P IV 1 122 4
that is, Harville, if you are ready, I am in half a minute. P IV 11 236 38
I shall be at your service in half a minute." P IV 11 236 38
In half a minute, Charles was at the bottom of Union- P IV 11 240 59

MINUTE'S (3)

He made no answer; but after a minute's silence burst out NA I 15 122 30
Mr. Crawford contrived a minute's privacy for telling MP III 10 406 21
more of it, till after a minute's silence she heard E III 4 340 28

MINUTELY (7)

my dear sister, too minutely on this point--continued she, LS 24 289 12
it personally in town, ceased writing minutely or often. LS 42 311 1
which had passed twenty years before, be minutely repeated. NA I 4 34 9
and to question him more minutely on the objects that had SS I 18 96 4
concerns familiarly and minutely, and gave her a great PP II 6 163 15
ladyship again enquired minutely into the particulars of PP II 14 213 20
very often and very minutely to her mother and Kitty; but PP II 19 238 5

MINUTENESS (4)

of the satin; and all minuteness of praise, all praise NA II 8 182 2
no sweet elation of spirits can lead me into minuteness. NA II 14 232 7
speech and look, where minuteness could be safely indulged. SS III 10 348 34
out with a minuteness which left beauty entirely behind. PP II 5 156 4

MINUTER (2)

of estimating the minuter propensities of his mind, his SS I 4 19 6
But of his minuter propensities as you call them, you have SS I 4 20 9

MINUTES (286)

In about ten minutes after my return to the parlour, Lady LS 23 284 6
Every five minutes, by removing some of the crowd, gave NA I 2 23 27
one can step out of doors and get a thing in five minutes." NA I 3 29 46
had she been seated ten minutes before a lady of about her NA I 4 31 2
attentively for several minutes, addressed her with great NA I 4 31 2
had arrived nearly five minutes before her friend, her NA I 6 39 2
"But if we only wait a few minutes, there will be no NA I 6 43 42
The Thorpes and James Morland were there only two minutes NA I 8 52 1
The dancing began within a few minutes after they were NA I 8 52 2
as they were for three minutes longer, when Isabella, who NA I 8 52 2
roused, at the end of ten minutes, to a pleasanter feeling, NA I 8 53 3
them; and after a few minutes consideration, he asked NA I 8 54 10
In a very few minutes she re-appeared, having scarcely NA I 9 62 7
A silence of several minutes succeeded their first short NA I 9 63 10
and yet she lay awake ten minutes on Wednesday night NA I 10 73 22
Catherine went every five minutes to the clock, NA I 11 83 14
five minutes, she would give up the matter as hopeless. NA I 11 83 14
There, it is twenty minutes after twelve, and now I shall NA I 11 83 15
Ten minutes more made it certain that a bright afternoon NA I 11 83 16
And in two minutes they were off. NA I 11 86 49
inquired for her a few minutes after her setting off; that, NA I 11 89 62
In a few minutes the servant returned, and with a look NA I 12 91 3
She was right; in a few minutes he appeared, and, making NA I 12 93 5
part of the house for ten minutes together, was engaged in NA I 12 95 17
daughter, rather than postpone his own walk a few minutes. NA I 12 95 17
She had left them for a few minutes to speak to Miss NA I 13 97 1
Thus passed a long ten minutes, till they were again NA I 13 100 13
made only five minutes before, and on a false pretence too, NA I 13 101 25
A clean gown is not five minutes wear in them. NA I 13 104 32
called away for only five minutes to answer a note, NA I 14 107 8
to wait only five minutes for my sister; breaking the NA I 14 107 9
Such was the information of the first five minutes; the NA I 15 116 1
affair became in a few minutes as nearly settled, as this NA II 2 140 10
her seeing Isabella for more than a few minutes together. NA II 3 143 1
were ever alone for five minutes--however, it is not worth NA II 3 145 13
of the first five minutes, she could almost have wished to NA II 5 154 1
in the course of a few minutes, she found herself with NA II 5 156 5
pronounce it with surprize within twenty minutes of five! NA II 5 162 27
having harboured for some minutes an absurd expectation, NA II 6 165 4
that of stopping five minutes to order refreshments to be NA II 8 182 1
it was some minutes before she could advance another step. NA II 9 193 6
Nothing further was said for a few minutes; and then NA II 10 204 11
employ herself for ten minutes together, walking round the NA II 15 240 1
work; but, after a few minutes, sunk again, without NA II 15 241 7
within the last few minutes, till, on entering the room, NA II 15 241 7
he remained for some minutes most civilly answering all NA II 15 242 8
After a couple of minutes unbroken silence, Henry, turning NA II 15 242 9
daughter, was, for a few minutes, considerable; it having NA II 16 249 1
minutes, she believed it to be no more than friendship. SS I 4 22 18
In the present case it took up ten minutes to determine SS I 6 31 9
delight for about twenty minutes longer, when suddenly the SS I 9 41 6
once in ten minutes, this reproach would have been spared." SS I 10 48 5
and what he said to his wife a few minutes before he died. SS I 11 54 6
after a silence of some minutes, he said with a faint SS I 11 55 8
In about five minutes he returned. SS I 13 63 7
And now after only ten minutes notice--gone too without SS I 15 77 23
In a few minutes they could distinguish him to be a SS I 16 86 16
17

As Elinor was certain of seeing her in a couple of minutes, SS I 19 105 17
at her some minutes, and then returned to his newspaper. SS I 19 108 35
a noise for the last two minutes; "and she is always so SS I 21 121 9

reply, and they walked on for a few minutes in silence. SS I 21 128 8
"To be sure," continued Lucy, after a few minutes silence SS I 22 133 46
After sitting with them a few minutes, the Miss Steeles SS I 22 135 56
They were again silent for many minutes. SS II 2 149 29
Marianne's was finished in a very few minutes; in length SS II 4 161 5
at the door, and in a few minutes she came laughing into SS II 4 164 21
She sometimes endeavoured for a few minutes to read; but SS II 4 166 31
After a pause of several minutes, their silence was broken, SS II 5 172 40
It was some minutes before she could go on with her letter, SS II 7 180 4
she had not been five minutes earlier, was satisfied with SS II 8 198 29
and rising hastily walked for a few minutes about the room. SS II 9 206 25
A few minutes more of silent exertion enabled him to SS II 9 207 25
she sat at least seven minutes and a half in silence. SS II 12 229 3
In a few minutes, however, Marianne was recovered enough SS II 12 236 42
she loitered away several minutes on the landing-place, SS II 13 241 23
five minutes of their being together, when it was finished. SS II 14 249 8
were ready to enter five minutes after it stopped at the SS II 14 249 9
as it was within ten minutes after its arrival, it gave SS II 14 254 27
your brother, only five minutes before, that she thought SS III 1 258 7
A few minutes more spent in the same kind of effusion, SS III 1 269 57
a couple of minutes, from what was uppermost in her mind. SS III 2 275 21
meaning, and conversed with her there for several minutes. SS III 3 280 9
They then talked on for a few minutes longer without her SS III 3 281 9
10

made her feel particularly uncomfortable for some minutes. SS III 4 288 26
Colonel Brandon, who was here only ten minutes ago, has SS III 4 288 28
They had scarcely been two minutes by themselves, before SS III 5 298 33
to drop in for ten minutes; and I saw quite enough of her. SS III 5 299 37
before she had been five minutes within its walls, while SS III 6 302 8
for half an hour--for ten minutes--I entreat you to stay." SS III 8 317 1
2

o'clock, and the only ten minutes I have spent out of my SS III 8 318 20
at the end of some minutes by Willoughby, who, rousing SS III 8 331 70
71

first desire; and in two minutes she was with her beloved SS III 9 334 5
health;--and they crept on for a few minutes in silence. SS III 10 345 23
Emma expressed her gratitude, & for a few minutes they W 320 2
been only five & thirty minutes coming.--which I think is W 322 2
the door; & in a very few minutes, the party were W 327 7
After some minutes of extraordinary bustle without, & W 329 9
suited her--& in a few minutes afterwards, the value of W 333 13
followed her with Mary, in less than five minutes.-- W 333 13
say two minutes before that you were not engaged."-- W 336 14
of Miss Watson only ten minutes ago, said he--I met her in W 338 18
with them only a few minutes,--"now my dear Emma, said W 341 19
On the 3d day after the ball, as Nanny at five minutes W 344 21
sat in silence for some minutes longer, while Tom Musgrave W 346 21
when she heard Margt 5 minutes afterwards say to eliz: in W 351 24
The wheels rapidly approached;--in two minutes the general W 354 28
out of his road merely to call for ten minutes at Stanton. W 355 28
supper in less than ten minutes--which to a man whose W 359 28
visit, and sat about ten minutes with him in his library. PP I 3 9 3
circulation within five minutes after his entrance, of his PP I 3 10 5
dance for a few minutes, to press his friend to join it. PP I 3 11 7
quit Netherfield, I should probably be off in five minutes. PP I 9 42 8
should be gone in five minutes, you meant it to be a sort PP I 10 49 27
After a few minutes reflection, however, she continued, "I PP I 16 80 34
After a pause of some minutes she addressed him a second PP I 18 91 8
9

and he detained her some minutes at the gate to hear and PP II 5 155 3
After sitting a few minutes, they were all sent to one of PP II 6 162 13
after listening for a few minutes, said to Darcy, "Miss PP II 8 176 27
28

minutes longer without saying much to any body, went away. PP II 9 179 26
frequently sat there ten minutes together without opening PP II 9 180 29
After a silence of several minutes he came towards her in PP II 11 189 3
4

Mr. Darcy, only for a few minutes to take leave. but that PP II 13 209 13
met for breakfast a few minutes before the others appeared; PP II 15 215 1
"Good gracious!" cried Maria, after a few minutes silence, PP II 15 217 11
agitated look; for a few minutes he was silent; till, PP II 18 234 37
38

She stood several minutes before the picture in earnest PP III 1 250 47
to her mind, the few minutes in which they continued PP III 1 252 52
Had they been only ten minutes sooner, they should have PP III 1 252 54
minutes convinced her, that she was only exceedingly shy. PP III 2 261 3
to it, and for a few minutes could not speak another word. PP III 4 277 11
after a pause of several minutes, was only recalled to a PP III 4 278 20
all repaired, after a few minutes conversation together, PP III 5 287 34
He could not speak a word for full ten minutes. PP III 5 292 62
have spent ten minutes of every day in a rational manner." PP III 6 300 30
But luckily, he came back again in ten minutes time, and PP III 9 319 25
But now several minutes elapsed, without bringing the PP III 11 335 43
five minutes seemed to be giving her more of his attention. PP III 11 337 56
He stood by her, however, for some minutes, in silence; PP III 12 342 25
She then sat still five minutes longer; but unable to PP III 13 345 12
13

In a few minutes, Mrs. Bennet half opened the door and PP III 13 345 13
14

In a few minutes she was joined by Bingley, whose PP III 13 347 30
In a few minutes he approached the table where she was PP III 17 375 28
Nor was it under many, many minutes, that she could PP III 17 378 42
But before she had been three minutes in her own room, her PP III 17 378 44
After a few minutes, they stopt entirely, Edmund was close MP I 7 67 16
For a few minutes, the brother and sister were too eager MP I 7 71 31
might lie another ten minutes in bed, when they woke with MP I 9 87 15
seemed likely to assist them, and be back in a few minutes. MP I 9 96 76
A quarter of an hour, twenty minutes, passed away, and MP I 10 97 1
After some minutes spent in this way, Miss Bertram MP I 10 97 4
her eye; and for some minutes longer she remained without MP I 10 100 23
He joined her within five minutes after Julia's exit; and MP I 10 101 33
had talked of only a few minutes, nor to banish the sort MP I 10 103 49
a weak voice, always hoarse after the first ten minutes! MP I 13 122 2
may be made to do in five minutes, by merely moving the MP I 13 125 14
not talked down in five minutes by her eldest nephew and MP I 13 129 40
In a few minutes Mr. Bertram was called out of the room to MP I 15 139 11
round the fire a few minutes, Miss Crawford returned to MP I 15 143 27
"Can I speak with you, Fanny for a few minutes?" said he. MP I 16 153 4
By the bye, I looked in upon them five minutes ago, and it MP I 18 169 21
She had been almost fluttered for a few minutes, and still MP II 1 179 9
minutes seemed to mark him the most at home of the two. MP II 1 183 23
A few minutes were enough for such unsatisfactory MP II 1 183 24
and so were they a few minutes afterwards upon hearing MP II 2 192 11
end of a few minutes, she exclaimed, "Ah! here he is." MP II 4 210 22
down for a few minutes can be hardly thought imprudent. MP II 4 212 29
Will twenty minutes after four suit you?" MP II 5 221 37
of being late, been many minutes seated in the drawing MP II 5 222 41
exclaimed, breaking forth again after a few minutes musing. MP II 5 225 55
the house, and the first minutes of exquisite feeling had MP II 6 233 15
formed by the last thirty minutes of expectation and the MP II 6 233 17
of the game in three minutes, he had yet to inspirit her MP II 7 240 8
many minutes to form it in: but you must do a good deal. MP II 7 243 27
"Mr. Bertram," said Miss Crawford, a few minutes MP II 7 244 30
observing them for a few minutes; himself in the meanwhile MP II 7 249 49
required some minutes silence to be settled into composure. MP II 8 253 4
able to talk another five minutes, there is no saying that MP II 9 270 40
In a few minutes Sir Thomas came to her, and asked if she MP II 10 275 11
himself, in every five minutes that she could walk about MP II 10 278 20
did, and be back in ten minutes--but he was gone above an MP II 12 291 1
"She must not go, she must allow him five minutes longer," MP II 13 301 7
I must speak to you for a few minutes, but I will not MP III 1 313 12
He talked therefore for several minutes without Fanny's MP III 1 314 16

And for a few minutes he did say nothing. MP III 1 316 33
alone, be it only five minutes; a request too natural, a MP III 1 321 48
butler re-appeared ten minutes afterwards, and advancing MP III 1 324 60
She could not abstract her mind five minutes; she was MP III 3 337 10
fixed on him for minutes, fixed on him in short till the MP III 3 337 11
not by dint of several minutes of supplication and waiting. MP III 3 341 27
After leaving him to his happier thoughts for some minutes, MP III 4 349 25
not been in the room five minutes, before she began, MP III 4 351 36
speak to you for a few minutes somewhere;" words that MP III 5 357 5
After this speech, the two girls sat many minutes silent, MP III 5 360 13
that though within five minutes afterwards the three boys MP III 7 383 31
and Susan, within ten minutes, walking towards the high MP III 10 401 10
against the wall, some minutes, to look and admire; and MP III 11 409 7
And it would not be ten minutes work." MP III 15 440 18
Mrs. Price talked of her poor sister for a few minutes-- MP III 15 444 26
She could say nothing; nor for some minutes could he say MP III 15 444 28
in time to spend a few minutes with the family, and be a MP III 15 445 31
listen to him for a few minutes, he should be very brief, MP III 16 453 17
"Five and twenty minutes. MP III 16 456 29
words, that for five minutes she thought they had done. MP III 16 459 31
They remained but a few minutes together, as Miss E I 4 32 28
minutes against the earnest pressing of both the others. E I 6 44 19
assurances,--and a very few minutes settled the business. E I 6 49 41
Some minutes passed in this unpleasant silence, with only E I 8 65 50
After a mutual silence of some minutes, Harriet thus began E I 10 84 8
9
But she had not been there two minutes when she found that E I 10 88 33
For ten minutes she could hear nothing but herself. E I 10 89 38
After an interval of some minutes, however, he began with, E I 12 105 51
52
After a few minutes of entire silence between them, John E I 13 111 15
16
A few minutes more, and Emma hoped to see one troublesome E I 15 128 21
continue together a few minutes longer, for the fears of E I 15 132 37
just called in for ten minutes, and had been so good as to E II 1 155 4
more than five minutes, when I first entered the house. E II 1 162 32
For it is not five minutes since I received Mrs. Cole's E II 3 173 27
I shall not stop three minutes: and, Jane, you had better E II 3 176 50
it had not been over five minutes, when in came Harriet, E II 3 177 52
in the world, full ten minutes, perhaps--when, all of a E II 3 178 52
Fourteen minutes to be given to those with whom she had E II 5 187 4
They had been arrived only a few minutes, and Mr. Weston E II 5 190 21
on, he stopt for several minutes at the two superior E II 6 197 5
Ten minutes would have been all that was necessary, E II 6 199 7
return from him for a few minutes, and listen to Mr. Cole. E II 8 222 54
but soon (within five minutes) the proposal of dancing-- E II 8 229 98
"coming at least ten minutes earlier than I had calculated. E II 10 240 3
he in a deliberating manner, "for five minutes, perhaps." E II 10 244 43
I could not stay two minutes. E II 10 244 45
He sat really lost in thought for the first few minutes; E II 12 259 12
13
"Not five minutes to spare even for your friends Miss E II 12 260 26
I went in for three minutes, and was detained by Miss E II 12 260 27
A very few minutes more, however, completed the present E II 12 261 35
again; and after a few minutes silence, he said, "another E II 15 286 22
23
After Emma had talked about it for ten minutes, Mr. E II 16 291 4
be; and within a few minutes were joined by the contents E III 2 319 3
In a few minutes the carriage returned.-- E III 2 321 14
her speech under many minutes after her being admitted E III 2 322 18
The impertinence of the Eltons, which for a few minutes E III 3 332 1
A few minutes made Emma acquainted with the whole. E III 3 333 4
and go in for a few minutes: he was therefore later than E III 3 334 7
to be heard the last two minutes, "if I must speak on this E III 5 345 16
I shall be at home in twenty minutes." E III 6 362 46
It can be round in five minutes." E III 6 362 47
In two minutes, however, he relented in his own favour; E III 6 364 57
she had left her ten minutes earlier;--it would have been E III 9 386 8
five minutes, and wanted particularly to speak with her."-- E III 10 392 1
meditating, in a fixed attitude, for a few minutes. E III 11 407 32
A few minutes were sufficient for making her acquainted E III 11 407 32
as her own heart, was before her in the same few minutes. E III 11 408 33
he could not stay five minutes--and his having told her, E III 11 410 35
Remember how few minutes I was at Randall's, and in how E III 14 439 8
Mr. Weston had his five minutes share of it; but five E III 17 468 33
share of it; but five minutes were enough to familiarize E III 17 468 33
In ten minutes, however, the child had been perfectly well E III 18 479 73
visit;--staying five minutes behind their father and P III 7 54 4
to wait on her for a few minutes, if not inconvenient; and P III 7 59 24
In two minutes after Charles's preparation, the others P III 7 59 25
of persons and voices--but a few minutes ended it. P III 7 59 25
more; and for a few minutes, therefore, could not keep P III 8 64 7
thus they continued a few minutes, when, to her very great P III 9 79 25
just run down for a few minutes, to see their aunt and P III 10 86 18
Lady Russell had not been arrived five minutes the day P IV 1 124 12
down close to her for ten minutes, talking with a very P IV 2 134 29
Ten minutes were enough to certify that. P IV 3 143 19
The first ten minutes had its awkwardness and its emotion. P IV 5 153 6
take them home, and would call for them in a few minutes. P IV 7 174 2
For a few minutes she saw nothing before her. P IV 7 175 5
If she could only have a few minutes conversation with him P IV 7 180 32
She had learnt, in the last ten minutes, more of his P IV 8 184 17
They talked for a few minutes more; the improvement held; P IV 8 190 47
A few minutes, though a few as possible, were inevitably P IV 8 190 48
for a couple of minutes; but Anne convinced herself that a P IV 10 220 30
One five minutes brought a note, the next a parcel, and P IV 10 221 32
And yet, a few minutes afterwards, she felt as if their P IV 10 221 33
After the waste of a few minutes in saying the proper P IV 10 226 64
solicitude never appeased for five minutes together. P IV 10 227 69
Two minutes after her entering the room, Captain Wentworth P IV 11 229 2
3
I shall have done in five minutes." P IV 11 234 26
her; but the ten minutes only, which now passed before she P IV 11 238 44
Within the first five minutes I said, 'I will be at Bath P IV 11 243 70
One of these good people can be with him in three minutes S 1 365 1
herself the first 5 minutes with fancying the persecutions S 6 391 1
of my right side, before I had swallowed it 5 minutes.-- S 10 418 1
I wish I could go with you myself--but in 5 minutes I must S 12 424 1
opposite to them, & they all stopped for a few minutes. S 12 425 1

MINUTES' (7)
and, after a few minutes' silence, renewed the NA I 7 47 19
Her suspense was of full five minutes' duration; and she NA II 1 132 16
had she felt a five minutes' longing of friendship, before NA II 3 143 1
to her; and after a ten minutes' interval of earnest SS I 13 69 76
Another pause therefore of many minutes' duration, SS II 2 150 35
almost every day. minutes' conversation with Charlotte, PP II 7 168 2
In the few minutes' conversation which she had yet had E III 3 335 11

MINUTEST (2)
as to defy the minutest inspection, and on opening it, a NA II 5 159 19
in her own parish, the minutest concerns of which were PP II 7 169 4

MINUTIA (1)
"Upon my word, I am not acquainted with the minutia of her SS I 11 56 16

MINUTIAE (4)
Whenever she had thought on the minutiae of the evening, MP II 10 275 11
The minutiae of the business Anne could not attempt to P III 10 89 36
past sad scenes, all the minutiae of distress upon P IV 9 210 97
communication--minutiae which, even with every advantage P IV 11 230 5

MIRACLE (3)
and it must seem to you a miracle that my life has been SS I 8 37 7
We are to be sure a miracle every way--but our powers of MP II 4 209 12
is quite a miracle if one keeps them more than half-a-year. MP III 7 385 39

MIRACULOUS (2)
talents or miraculous virtue, and the mere stateliness of PP II 6 161 9
miraculous consequence of travelling in the summer. PP III 3 271 14

MIRROR (3)
for home by great acquaintance--'the mirror' I think. NA II 15 241 6
lay aside the first volume of the mirror for a future hour. NA II 15 242 8
manners were the mirror of her own modest and elegant mind. MP II 12 294 16

MIRRORS (1)
the others to admire mirrors and china; but Anne had heard P IV 10 219 27

MIRTH (10)
mirth of Sir John and his mother-in-law was interesting. SS I 7 34 7
This increased the mirth of the company, and Margaret was SS I 12 61 20
seen a check to all mirth, she could have been entertained SS II 8 193 7
now arrived to be read with less emotion than mirth. SS III 13 370 37
assent, and indulged their mirth for some time at the PP I 8 37 20
happiness overflows in mirth; and Elizabeth, agitated and PP III 17 372 2
their hours of happy mirth, and moments of serious MP I 2 21 34
"Not quite so miserable as to be insensible to mirth. E III 18 478 67
did not seem fit for the mirth of the party in general. P III 11 100 22
theirs; had heard voices--mirth continually; thought they P IV 3 144 19

MIS-JUDGING (1)
grossly mistaken and mis-judging in all her ideas on one E I 17 141 5

MIS-JUDGMENT (1)
disgraced by mis-judgment, than she actually was, could E I 16 134 1

MISAPPLIED (1)
But while she smiled at a graciousness so misapplied, she SS II 12 233 16

MISAPPLY (1)
Better be without sense, than misapply it as you do." E I 8 64 45

MISAPPREHENSION (8)
From whence arose so astonishing a misapprehension of your LS 24 289 12
implied, the fault must have been in her misapprehension. NA II 4 149 1
Elinor, "in a total misapprehension of character in some SS I 17 93 37
is explained--some dreadful misapprehension or other.-- SS II 6 177 13
such behaviour to mistake or misapprehension of any kind. SS II 6 178 17
be broken by any mistake or misapprehension of my actions. SS II 7 183 13
Here is some great misapprehension which must be rectified. MP III 1 312 10
It had originated in misapprehension entirely. P IV 3 138 7

MISBEHAVE (1)
and hardy; and if they misbehave, can give them a sharp E I 9 81 73

MISCELLANEOUS (1)
& looking over the miscellaneous foreground of unfinished S 4 384 1

MISCHANCE (4)
journey without any mischance; and were within view of the NA I 11 88 54
If, indeed, by any strange mischance his father should NA II 14 231 3
She felt all the perverseness of the mischance that should PP II 10 182 1
some mischance, to damp the perfection of her felicity. P IV 11 239 53

MISCHEIF (1)
they may not be doing mischeif by raising the price of S 6 392 1

MISCHIEF (22)
for the pleasure of mischief--at least so it was NA I 1 13 1
and yours preparing by rest for the future mischief." NA II 8 187 15
had been created, the mischief settled long before her NA II 10 200 2
real cause of all the mischief; and the other, that she PP I 21 127 5
keep her out of any real mischief; and she is luckily too PP II 18 232 20
The mischief of neglect and mistaken indulgence towards PP III 4 280 25
seven years hence, and I dare say there would be mischief. MP I 1 7 6
about in the flower-garden, that did the mischief." MP I 7 73 55
Perhaps you are not so much aware as I am, of the mischief MP I 16 154 14
and judging more clearly of the mischief that must ensue. MP II 1 177 5
at the ball, I am sure the mischief was done that evening. MP III 2 333 28
The mischief such a man does on an estate, both as to the MP III 11 412 20
working on a weak head, produces every sort of mischief. E I 8 64 47
bodies, which (as you well know, sir) does the mischief." E II 11 251 29
How could he tell what mischief he might be doing?-- E III 10 396 44
original author of the mischief; with having suggested E III 11 402 1
she had not quite done nothing--for she had done mischief. E III 11 413 47
I had been too deeply concerned in the mischief to be soon P IV 8 183 13
In spite of the mischief of his attentions, she owed him P IV 9 192 2
officious, to be giving bad impressions, making mischief. P IV 9 198 53
night, the irremediable mischief he might have done, was P IV 10 212 1
Currents which do more mischief in a valley, when they do S 4 381 1

MISCHIEF'S (1)
"And only made believe to do so for mischief's sake?" NA II 12 219 10

MISCHIEVOUS (4)
mischievous creature, do you want to attract every body? NA I 10 70 1
and mischievous tricks to which her cousins submitted. SS I 21 120 6
mischievous which her imagination had suggested at first. E II 2 168 13
and misconstructions of the most mischievous kind. P IV 10 221 33

MISCHIEVOUSLY (1)
of Pemberley from her, might be mischievously construed. PP III 1 254 57

MISCHIEVOUSNESS (1)
of their general mischievousness, and was wholly NA I 2 18 2

MISCONCEIVED (1)
of so many, to be misconceived by folly in one, and P IV 9 205 85

MISCONCEPTION (2)
the grounds of that misconception of your sentiments, MP III 1 320 44
have been led into a misconception of your views; not E I 15 132 36

MISCONCEPTIONS (1)
a second time the dupe of her misconceptions and flattery. E III 11 402 1

MISCONDUCT (17)
of great misconduct on her side, so very generally known. LS 12 260 2
the accounts of your misconduct during the life & since LS 36 305 1
all innocence, and the misconduct of another the true NA I 8 53 2
all the shame of misconduct, or at least of its appearance, NA I 12 93 4
in their father's misconduct, Mrs. Morland had been always NA II 15 242 7
of his own misconduct, and prevented her from believing SS II 6 178 17
They proceed from no misconduct, and can be no disgrace. SS II 9 210 32
I acquit Edward of all essential misconduct. SS III 1 263 27
That his repentance of misconduct, which thus brought its SS III 14 379 18
deter him from such foul misconduct as I have suffered by. PP II 18 234 38
felicity, nor humbled by any remembrance of her misconduct. PP III 7 306 43
in Mr. Crawford's misconduct, that she could not give his MP III 1 318 38
But after all the punishment that misconduct can bring, it E III 12 419 8
that misconduct can bring, it is still not less misconduct. E III 12 419 8
which I have of misconduct, very great misconduct, it is E III 16 459 47
misconduct, very great misconduct, it is particularly E III 16 459 47
to so much misconduct and misery, both in young and old! P IV 10 218 23

MISCONSTRUCTION (2)
and this misconstruction produced within a day or two SS II 14 248 6
and stopped, fearing she hardly knew what misconstruction. P IV 10 225 60

MISCONSTRUCTIONS (1)
and misconstructions of the most mischievous kind. P IV 10 221 33

MISCONSTRUED (1)
a point could not be misconstrued, and as it must be E III 14 442 8

MISERABLE (65)
delicious gratification of making a whole family miserable. LS 4 248 1
of being able to make a worthy man completely miserable. LS 14 264 4
I am very miserable about Sir James Martin, & have no LS 21 279 1
My dear aunt, you do not know how miserable I have been." LS 24 286 5
to make my own child miserable, & that I had forbidden her LS 24 289 12
He is absolutely miserable about you, & jealous to such a LS 26 295 3
make me, even with you, the most miserable of beings. LS 30 300 3
It makes me miserable--but Mr Johnson vows that if I LS 38 306 1
was to fetch her away; & miserable as it made the poor LS 41 310 3
I am sure you would be miserable if you thought so." NA I 6 41 18
to read, I feel as if nobody could make me miserable. NA I 6 41 19
Catherine was restlessly miserable; she could almost have NA I 12 93 4
her eyes; and Morland, miserable at such a sight, could NA I 13 98 3
"I am sure I shall be miserable if we do not. NA I 15 120 22
have been miserable if I had sat down the whole evening. NA II 1 134 39
have no hope here, and it is only staying to be miserable." NA II 4 150 4
But now--in short, she made herself as miserable as NA II 10 199 1
She has made me miserable for ever! NA II 10 202 7

I cannot bear the thoughts of making him so miserable, as SS I 22 133 44
He was so miserable when he left us at Longstaple, to go SS I 22 133 46
His imprudence had made her miserable for a while; but it SS II 1 140 1
though it would make us miserable for a time, we should be SS II 2 149 30
home, as she was too miserable to stay a minute longer. SS II 6 178 15
"Oh! Elinor, I am miserable indeed," before her voice was SS II 7 185 19
But to appear happy when I am so miserable--Oh! who can SS II 7 190 54
he had made poor and miserable; but had he known it, what SS II 9 209 30
I saw her, and saw her miserable, and left her miserable-- SS III 8 323 40
her miserable--and left her hoping never to see her again." SS III 8 323 40
I was miserable. SS III 8 324 45
an unbounded affection, to be miserable for my sake." SS III 10 346 28
his sisters declared that they were miserable. PP I 8 40 59
would have been very miserable; but being satisfied on PP I 9 41 2
When I have a house of my own, I shall be miserable if I PP I 11 55 4
greatest honor; and I should be miserable to forfeit it. PP II 3 144 7
Only think what a miserable summer else we shall have!" PP II 16 220 6
If such goodness does not make her miserable now, she will PP III 7 305 36
I must live within my income, or I shall be miserable; and MP I 3 30 50
part of her education, made her miserable under it. MP I 9 91 36
had seen her influence in every speech, and was miserable. MP I 16 156 28
increased, and she was miserable in considering how much MP II 1 178 7
which I should be miserable if I thought myself without MP II 4 214 45
They were now a miserable trio, confined within doors by a MP II 11 286 15
happy, miserable, infinitely obliged, absolutely angry. MP II 13 302 10
make him happy, and that I should be miserable myself." MP III 1 320 43
that great black word miserable, which served to introduce MP III 1 320 44
She was miserable for ever. MP III 1 321 46
We should be miserable." MP III 4 348 22
for such a house, and it would not make me miserable. MP III 12 416 2
He will marry her, and be poor and miserable. MP III 13 424 4
of being exquisitely happy, while so many were miserable. MP III 15 443 24
She had not time to be miserable. MP III 15 443 25
It had been a miserable party, each of the three believing MP III 16 448 1
each of the three believing themselves most miserable. MP III 16 448 1
It makes me envious and miserable;--I who have never seen E I 12 101 23
away, and Emma sat sat down to think and be miserable.-- E I 16 134 1
Mr. Woodhouse would have been miserable had his daughter E I 16 138 17
Oh! dear; I was so miserable! E II 3 178 52
Dear, Miss Woodhouse, I was absolutely miserable! E II 3 179 52
"You are not quite so miserable, though, as when you first E III 6 365 65
short, put an end to the miserable state of concealment E III 10 398 51
Jane, Jane, you will be a miserable creature." E III 13 426 16
I was the most miserable wretch!" E III 18 478 66
"Not quite so miserable as to be insensible to mirth. E III 18 478 67
When first sounded on the subject, he was so miserable, E III 19 483 9
most miserable, when time had disclosed all, too late? P IV 9 211 102

MISERABLY (7)
There she fell miserably short of the true heroic height. NA I 1 16 10
herself, and looking so miserably ill, that it was PP III 4 276 9
My present state is miserably irksome. MP III 13 422 2
tolerate the prospect of being miserably crowded at supper. E II 11 254 44
Deceived myself, I did very miserably deceive you--and it E II 13 268 10
But you are miserably behind-hand. E II 15 287 28
Yet so miserably had he conducted himself, that though she P III 1 8 17

MISERIES (2)
that in enumerating the miseries of a marriage with one, PP III 15 360 2
slow progress, and to feel the miseries of waiting. MP I 18 164 1

MISERLY (2)
being a d---- thing to be miserly; and that if people who NA I 11 89 61
of an illiterate and miserly father; and though he PP I 15 70 1

MISERY (92)
She said something of her misery, but that was all. LS 22 280 1
have not an idea of the misery I have been in, & mama had LS 24 286 5
Am I capable of consigning her to everlasting misery, LS 24 289 12
misery enough; & come yourself to town, as soon as you can. LS 26 295 1
the latter was spared the misery of her friend's NA I 9 67 33
smiles of most exquisite misery, and the laughing eye of NA I 9 67 33
and, setting aside the misery of his quitting their box, NA I 12 95 16
foreboding of future misery to herself, or one moment's NA II 5 161 25
in room, gave her fresh misery, and strengthened her NA II 13 228 27
in comparison of the misery of continuing her daughter-in- SS I 4 24 20
misery of disappointed love had already been known by him. SS I 11 55 8
You had rather look out for misery for Marianne and guilt SS I 15 78 28
In books too, as well as in music, she courted the misery SS I 16 83 3
misery of her feelings, by exclamations of wretchedness. SS II 6 177 15
uniting to heighten the misery of Marianne in a final SS II 6 179 18
Think of your mother; think of her misery while you suffer; SS II 7 185 21
Mine is a misery which nothing can do away." SS II 7 186 28
"No, no," cried Marianne, "misery such as mine has no SS II 7 189 52
With an hasty exclamation of misery, and a sign to her SS II 8 193 7
room, leaning, in silent misery, over the small remains of SS II 8 197 23
consciousness of misery in which she had closed her eyes. SS II 9 201 1
it did; but at last the misery of her situation, for she SS II 9 205 24
She resigned herself at first to all the misery of her SS II 9 206 24
of Miss Williams, the misery of that poor girl, and the SS II 10 212 1
"What!--while attending me in all my misery, has this been SS III 1 262 20
my misery, who have seemed to be only suffering for me!-- SS III 1 264 31
In such moments of precious, of invaluable misery, she SS III 6 303 9
of the idea, and it gave fresh misery to her reflections. SS III 7 314 21
of the comfort it gives me to look back on my own misery. SS III 8 324 45
But I hardly know--the misery that you have inflicted--I SS III 8 330 66
Tell her of my misery and my penitence--tell her that my SS III 8 330 67
left her sister to misery, was likely to prove a source of SS III 8 331 70
of many past scenes of misery to his mind, brought back by SS III 10 340 2
Had I died,--in what peculiar misery should I have left SS III 10 346 28
which had long formed his misery, from a woman whom he had SS III 13 361 3
or suspense, but from misery to happiness;--and the change SS III 13 361 3
be the means of spreading misery farther in the family.-- SS III 13 371 38
her all the shame and misery which a disagreeable partner PP I 18 90 4
you find that the misery of disobliging his two sisters is PP I 21 119 24
unhappy, there may be error, and there may be misery. PP II 1 136 17
Mr. Darcy's shameful boast of what misery he had been able PP II 11 188 1
and involving them both in misery of the acutest kind." PP II 11 191 12
and Lydia, whose own misery was extreme, and who could not PP II 18 229 1
Lydia--the humiliation, the misery, she was bringing on PP III 4 278 20
entered the room, the misery of her impatience was severe. PP III 4 280 26
Elizabeth, after all the misery of the morning, found PP III 4 281 29
with such an husband, her misery was considered certain. PP III 8 309 6
such misery of shame, that she could hardly keep her seat. PP III 11 337 52
Elizabeth's misery increased, at such unnecessary, such PP III 11 337 54
Yet the misery, for which years of happiness were to offer PP III 11 337 56
and she sat in misery till Mr. Darcy appeared again, when, PP III 17 375 28
You could scarcely escape discredit and misery. PP III 17 376 35
and her consciousness of misery was therefore increased by MP I 2 13 4
to the last, and the misery of the girl when he left her. MP I 2 21 34
harp is come, he heard so much of my misery about it. MP I 6 59 41
obliged to yield--no matter--it was all misery now. MP I 16 157 28
his part, and that it was misery to have any thing to do MP I 18 164 2
and tranquillity; by the misery of disappointed affection, MP II 3 202 26
But Fanny shewed such reluctance, such misery, at the idea MP III 1 320 45
did come; and the first misery over, and Miss Crawford MP III 5 357 5
It was the greatest misery of all. MP III 8 391 11
of the misery that must ensue, can hardly be described. MP III 15 440 19
The evening passed, without a pause of misery, the night MP III 15 441 20
He so near her, and in misery. MP III 15 444 28
who was not at this time a source of misery to him. MP III 16 451 13
Let other pens dwell on guilt and misery. MP III 17 461 1
Rushworth's side for the misery she had occasioned, MP III 17 461 4
What can exceed the misery of such a mind in such a MP III 17 464 11
misery in another man's family, as he had known himself. MP III 17 465 13
it had not been for the misery of her leaving Hartfield, I E I 11 95 19
never known any thing of; but it must be a life of misery. E I 14 121 17
not recur again--but the misery of having a very E II 6 202 33
I can sit and admire him now without any great misery. E II 14 271 15
greater misery of the victims, I do not know where it lies. E II 17 300 15
From perfect misery to perfect happiness." E III 4 342 38
or two spent at Donwell, be tempted away to his misery. E III 6 356 29
which constituted the real misery of the business to her. E III 11 402 1
"On the misery of what she had suffered, during the E III 12 418 6
better yet; still insane either from happiness or misery. E III 14 439 8
of repentance and misery to each: she dissolved it.-- E III 14 442 8
of repentance and misery to each--she dissolved it.-- E III 15 447 22
She must not make it a more decided subject of misery to E III 17 465 28
consolation, under the misery of a parting--a final P III 4 28 5
misery, and could never be remembered with indifference. P IV 5 152 2
Anne saw the misery of such feelings. P IV 5 156 12
pain, pleasure, a something between delight and misery. P IV 7 175 6
It was misery to think of Mr. Elliot's attentions.-- P IV 8 191 51
shudder at the idea of the misery which must have followed. P IV 9 211 102
to so much misconduct and misery, both in young and old! P IV 10 218 23
She was deep in the happiness of such misery, or the P IV 11 229 2
of such misery, or the misery of such happiness, instantly. P IV 11 229 2
the very person who had guided you in that year of misery. P IV 11 245 74

MISFORTUNE (28)
A woman especially, if she have the misfortune of knowing NA I 14 111 28
By some means or other she must have had the misfortune to NA II 13 226 25
that any injury or any misfortune could provoke such ill- NA II 13 226 25
will always be a heavy misfortune to me, that I have had SS I 19 102 4
had since fallen into misfortune, carried me to visit him SS II 9 207 26
she would bear up with fortitude under this misfortune. SS II 10 213 2
I come now to the relation of a misfortune, which about SS II 14 248 6
deficiency, than to the misfortune of a private education; SS II 14 250 12
man that it would be quite a misfortune to be liked by him. PP I 5 19 10
since I have had the misfortune to lose him, I have PP I 13 62 12
That would be the greatest misfortune of all!-- PP I 18 90 7
But the misfortune of speaking with bitterness, is a most PP II 17 226 21
but , under such a misfortune as this, one cannot see too PP III 5 293 67
alleviate so severe a misfortune; or that may comfort you, PP III 6 296 11
does one good; it gives such an elegance to misfortune! PP III 6 299 28
had been generally proved to be marked out for misfortune. PP III 13 350 56
thinking his return a misfortune; and when, on having MP II 1 178 7
learnt to think it no misfortune to be quietly employed. MP III 9 398 9
rather put up with the misfortune of being sought by a MP III 10 402 11
sisters, as the greatest misfortune of her life and mine. MP III 13 421 2
The misfortune of your birth ought to make you E I 4 30 22
At ten years old, she had the misfortune of being able to E I 5 37 9
The misfortune of Harriet's cold had been pretty well gone E I 14 117 3
her friend, he had the misfortune to fall in love with her, E II 8 217 32
No misfortune occurred, again to prevent the ball. E III 2 319 1
She must not appear to think it a misfortune.-- E III 17 465 28
it would be quite a misfortune to have the existing P III 9 75 12
she thought it was the misfortune of poetry, to be seldom P III 11 100 23

MISFORTUNES (7)
"Who that knows what his misfortunes have been, can help PP II 11 191 19
"His misfortunes!" repeated Darcy contemptuously; "yes, PP II 11 191 20
"yes, his misfortunes have been great indeed." PP II 11 191 20
the mention of his misfortunes with contempt and ridicule." PP II 11 192 21
"These are heavy misfortunes," replied Elizabeth. PP III 14 355 46
they did not by any means rank as misfortunes with her. E I 1 5 4
personal misfortunes, though I know you must fifty times. P III 5 35 14

MISGAVE (1)
My heart misgave me instantly. LS 24 287 8

MISGIVE (2)
Will not your mind misgive you, when you find yourself in NA II 5 158 15
my heart did misgive me that you would like him too well. W 343 19

MISINFORMED (2)
hope, so far as concerns my brother, you are misinformed. NA II 10 204 20
You have perhaps been misinformed, or purposely deceived, SS II 7 188 42

MISINTERPRETED (2)
If she had so misinterpreted his feelings, she had little E I 16 136 9
He had misinterpreted the feelings which had kept her face E III 7 375 62

MISINTERPRETING (1)
self-consequence; and misinterpreting Fanny's blushes, MP II 10 277 17

MISLAID (2)
I would write to him myself, but have mislaid his NA II 12 217 2
A key was mislaid, Betsey accused of having got at his new MP III 7 381 26

MISLEAD (2)
once or twice, could not mislead her here; and what the NA II 8 186 6
If his own vanity, however, did not mislead him, he was PP II 10 186 38

MISLEADING (1)
partiality is not misleading me, I think, when I call PP I 21 118 14

MISLEADS (3)
I suspect his gratitude misleads him, and that in spite of PP I 16 83 57
her respect for her aunt's memory which misleads her here. MP I 7 63 7
His own goodnature misleads him. S 7 402 1

MISLED (14)
longer time--had been misled (perhaps by her wishes) to NA II 13 221 2
appearances of alarm, or misled by a raised imagination, NA II 13 223 9
John Thorpe had first misled him. NA II 15 244 12
and character, misled by the rhodomontade of his friend to NA II 15 246 12
It taught him that he had been scarcely more misled by by NA II 16 251 6
She found that she had been misled by the careful, the SS III 11 355 46
If it be so, if I have been misled by such error, to PP II 12 197 5
misled Sir Thomas to suppose it really intended for Fanny. MP I 3 28 38
that her judgment had not misled her; for the purity of MP III 1 324 58
If she has fancied otherwise, her own wishes have misled E I 15 130 31
wavering, dubious, or she could not have been so misled. E I 16 134 3
You misled me by the term gentleman. P III 3 23 33
He will not be led astray, he will not be misled by others P IV 9 196 32
be captiously irritable, misled by every moment's P IV 10 221 33

MISMANAGEMENT (3)
"There certainly was some great mismanagement in the PP II 17 225 15
house was the scene of mismanagement and discomfort from MP III 8 390 6
Here had been grievous mismanagement; but, bad as it was, MP III 17 463 8

MISPLACED (2)
A misplaced shame. NA I 14 110 28
in some points, a misplaced distinction; but I think too MP III 1 313 12

MISREPRESENTATION (2)
some malevolent misrepresentation of her, which he now NA II 1 132 16
Or under what misrepresentation, can you here impose upon PP II 11 191 17

MISREPRESENTED (2)
Interested people have perhaps misrepresented each to the PP I 17 85 2
that, you know, things are strangely misrepresented." PP III 10 327 14

MISS (39)
I need not tell you how much I miss him--how perpetually LS 5 250 3
from her seat she should miss her sisters, she was NA II 3 147 28
"To be sure you must miss him very much." NA II 7 180 35
We shall miss her; but she will be happy." SS I 3 17 15
My sister will be equally sorry to miss the pleasure of SS II 10 219 38
who would certainly miss her, and who, when it came to the PP II 4 151 2
she finds Miss Pope a treasure. PP II 6 165 32
that she would not miss the opportunity of enjoying PP II 18 235 40
Miss Lydia is going to be married; and you shall all have PP III 7 307 49
quite as handsome as Miss Maria, did not scruple to MP I 1 3 1
away--he had told her he should miss her very much indeed." MP I 2 16 12
in their society, and to miss him decidedly in the MP I 6 52 1
Very different from you, miss, when you first began, six MP I 7 69 22
"That is Miss Maria's concern. MP I 10 101 32
"I must entreat Miss Julia Bertram," said he, "not to MP I 14 133 11
"We miss our two young men," was Sir Thomas's observation MP II 11 284 9
You must miss him. MP II 11 287 18
You cannot wish me to marry; for you would miss me, me, MP III 2 333 25
Yes, I am sure you would miss me too much for that." MP III 2 333 25

Text	Work	Vol	Ch	Page	Line
are very right, but I am sure I shall miss her very much."	MP	III	6	371	16
She clung to her aunt, because she would miss her; she	MP	III	6	374	28
I miss you more than I can express.	MP	III	13	423	2
I am sure she will miss her more than she thinks for."	E	I	1	11	36
"It is impossible that Emma should not miss such a	E	I	1	11	38
Miss Harriet Smith may not find offers of marriage flow in	E	I	8	64	47
he had been never known to miss before; and Mr. Perry had	E	I	8	68	58
cried she with ready sympathy, "how you must miss her!	E	I	11	93	7
soon try for miss somebody else with twenty, or with ten.	E	I	16	135	7
regiment of infantry, and Miss Jane Bates, had had its day	E	II	2	163	2
with him, or just to miss him, just to hear his voice, or	E	II	4	184	10
"And now we shall just miss them; too provoking!--	E	II	5	187	6
Somebody said that Miss Gilbert was expected at her	E	II	11	248	9
She will be extremely sorry to miss seeing you, Miss	E	III	8	379	8
Miss Harville only died last June.	P	IV	2	131	10
he had ever thought of this Miss (what's her name?) for	P	IV	6	173	47
They never miss a concert."	P	IV	9	193	6
"Give me joy: I have got rid of Sir Walter and Miss.	P	IV	9	203	72
regretting that he should miss my father this morning, I	P	IV	10	213	5
I told you my sisters were excellent women, miss h----."	S		5	388	1
MISS ---- (4)					
"And what are you reading, Miss ----?"	NA	I	5	38	4
To Miss ----.	E	I	9	71	14
"For Miss ----, read Miss Smith.	E	I	9	73	18
Only think of those sweet verses--'to Miss ----.'	E	I	9	74	22
MISS A. E.-- (1)					
legible, to "Miss A. E.--." was evidently the one which he	P	IV	11	237	41
MISS ANDERSON (4)					
You are quizzing me and Miss Anderson."	MP	I	5	49	33
Miss Anderson! I do not know who or what you mean.	MP	I	5	49	34
You must have had Miss Anderson in your eye, in describing	MP	I	5	49	35
truth in it, I dare say, than does credit to Miss Anderson.	MP	I	5	50	36
MISS ANDREWS (6)					
friend of mine, a Miss Andrews, a sweet girl, one of the	NA	I	6	40	12
I wish you knew Miss Andrews, you would be delighted with	NA	I	6	40	12
he would allow Miss Andrews to be as beautiful as an angel.	NA	I	6	40	14
is exactly what Miss Andrews wants, for I must confess	NA	I	6	41	16
I remember Miss Andrews could not get through the first	NA	I	6	42	22
"I remember too, Miss Andrews drank tea with us that	NA	I	15	118	13
MISS ANNE (14)					
"They set off at eight this morning," said Miss Anne, "and	NA	I	14	115	50
What Miss Anne says, is very true," was Mr. Shepherd's	P	III	3	19	13
					14
Mrs. Musgrove--"so, Miss Anne, Sir Walter and your sister	P	III	6	42	1
Anne, to say, "Oh! Miss Anne, I cannot help wishing Mrs.	P	III	6	44	8
I assure you, Miss Anne, it prevents my wishing to see	P	III	6	45	8
I shall tell you, Miss Anne, because you may be able to	P	III	6	45	9
done, Miss Anne! very well done indeed!	P	III	6	47	15
help saying, "Ah! Miss Anne, if it had pleased heaven to	P	III	8	64	5
					6
have said, that "now Miss Anne was come, she could not	P	IV	4	145	1
much thicker than Miss Anne's; and, in short, her civility	P	IV	7	174	3
hard-hearted sister, Miss Anne, seems bent on cruelty."	P	IV	10	213	4
we should be losing Miss Anne too, if there is a party at	P	IV	10	224	51
at all for the play, if Miss Anne could not be with us."	P	IV	10	224	51
Harville any where, remember to give Miss Anne's message.	P	IV	11	239	52
MISS ANNE ELLIOT (6)					
Miss Anne Elliot to be visiting in Westgate-Buildings?--	P	IV	5	157	15
Upon my word, Miss Anne Elliot, you have the most	P	IV	5	157	15
friend of Miss Anne Elliot, and to be preferred by her, to	P	IV	5	158	19
something of Miss Anne Elliot; and I do regard her as one	P	IV	8	187	28
description of Miss Anne Elliot, as had inspired him with	P	IV	8	187	34
as Miss Anne Elliot, and from that moment, I have no doubt,	P	IV	9	206	88
MISS ATKINSON (1)					
"Yes, and Miss Atkinson, who dined with him once at the	P	IV	7	177	20
MISS AUGUSTA (2)					
Miss Augusta ought not to have been noticed for the next	MP	I	5	51	40
Miss Augusta should have been with her governess.	MP	I	5	51	41
MISS B-- (1)					
in spite of the mist; Miss B-- seated, not far before her,	S		12	426	1
MISS B. (4)					
but observe Lady D. & Miss B. walking by--& there was	S		7	395	1
one end of the bench, & Sir Edw: & Miss B. at the other.--	S		7	395	1
immediately brought Miss B. into her head--& stepping to	S		12	426	1
the tallest of the two, Miss B.'s white ribbons might not	S		12	426	1
MISS BATES (95)					
Miss Bates stood in the very worst predicament in the	E	I	3	21	4
Miss Bates, let Emma help you to a little bit of tart--a	E	I	3	24	14
"But then, to be an old maid at last, like Miss Bates!" "	E	I	10	84	16
should ever be like Miss Bates! so silly--so satisfied--so	E	I	10	84	16
This does not apply, however, to Miss Bates; she is only	E	I	10	85	19
And that excellent Miss Bates!--such thorough worthy	E	I	12	102	31
hurried off by Miss Bates, she jumped away from him at	E	II	1	156	6
All this spoken extremely fast obliged Miss Bates to stop	E	II	1	158	11
"You are extremely kind," replied Miss Bates highly	E	II	1	158	12
Miss Bates turned to her again and seized her attention.	E	II	1	158	13
Miss Bates was very chatty and good-humoured, as she	E	II	3	171	12
open, and Miss Bates and Miss Fairfax walked into the room.	E	II	3	172	22
					23
Full of thanks, and full of news, Miss Bates knew not	E	II	3	172	23
"But where could you hear it?" cried Miss Bates.	E	II	3	173	27
Woodhouse!" said Miss Bates, joyfully; "my mother is so	E	II	3	174	35
and Miss Bates and I that he is just the happy medium.	E	II	3	174	38
Miss Woodhouse," said Miss Bates, "four weeks yesterday.--	E	II	3	176	44
If she were to meet Miss Bates in her way!--and upon its	E	II	3	177	51
we passed her house--I saw Miss Bates at the window.	E	II	5	194	38
in the evening, with Miss Bates, Miss Fairfax, and Miss	E	II	8	214	13
had been calling on Miss Bates, and as soon as she entered	E	II	8	214	13
en passant to Miss Bates and her niece, made his way	E	II	8	220	47
Do you know how Miss Bates and her niece came here?"	E	II	8	222	59
my way directly to Miss Bates, to assure her that the	E	II	8	223	63
than I do; for while Miss Bates was speaking, a suspicion	E	II	8	224	65
How would he bear to have Miss Bates belonging to him?--	E	II	8	225	78
think Mr. Knightley would be much disturbed by Miss Bates.	E	II	8	225	78
And touching Miss Bates, who at the moment passed near-- "	E	II	8	229	97
passed near-- "Miss Bates, are you mad, to let your niece	E	II	8	229	97
Miss Bates, in her real anxiety for Jane, could hardly	E	II	8	229	98
It was growing late, and Miss Bates became anxious to get	E	II	8	230	101
Miss Bates last night, that I would come this morning.	E	II	9	234	26
ladies; Mrs. Weston and Miss Bates met them at the door.	E	II	9	235	43
delay from Miss Bates than, "how do you do, Mrs. Ford?	E	II	9	237	47
					48
Miss Bates had just done as Patty opened the door; and her	E	II	9	239	52
Shortly afterwards Miss Bates, passing near the window,	E	II	10	243	30
So began Miss Bates; and Mr. Knightley seemed determined	E	II	10	244	34
					35
commandingly did he say, "how is your niece, Miss Bates?--	E	II	10	244	34
					35
And Miss Bates was obliged to give a direct answer before	E	II	10	244	36
much obliged to you for the carriage," resumed Miss Bates.	E	II	10	244	37
Or Miss Bates?	E	II	11	254	50
And I do not know whether Miss Bates is not as likely to	E	II	11	254	50
Suppose I go and invite Miss Bates to join us?"	E	II	11	255	50
"You will get nothing to the purpose from Miss Bates,"	E	II	11	255	52
I see no advantage in consulting Miss Bates."	E	II	11	255	52
I am very fond of hearing Miss Bates talk.	E	II	11	255	53
Go and fetch Miss Bates, and let us end the matter at once.	E	II	11	255	55
Fetch Miss Bates.	E	II	11	255	55
Most cordially, when Miss Bates arrived, did she agree	E	II	11	256	60
spare even for your friends Miss Fairfax and Miss Bates?	E	II	12	260	26
According to Miss Bates--it all came from her--Mrs. Dixon	E	II	15	285	14
Poor Miss Bates may very likely have committed her niece	E	II	15	286	21
of getting away from Miss Bates, than I can believe in the	E	II	15	288	39
"But Miss Bates and Miss Fairfax!" said Mr. Weston,	E	III	2	320	12
"Miss Bates must not be forgotten:" and away he went.	E	III	2	321	14
"I have no doubt of its being our carriage with Miss Bates	E	III	2	321	17
Miss Bates and Miss Fairfax, escorted by the two gentlemen,	E	III	2	322	18
incessant flow of Miss Bates, who came in talking, and had	E	III	2	322	18
Emma; and as soon as Miss Bates was quiet, she found	E	III	2	323	20
The move began; and Miss Bates might be heard from that	E	III	2	328	44
the night before of Miss Bates, and to have forgotten to	E	III	3	334	7
son, Miss Bates and her niece, who had accidentally met.	E	III	5	344	3
long speech from Miss Bates, which few persons listened to,	E	III	5	344	3
"Why, to own the truth," cried Miss Bates, who had been	E	III	5	345	16
prevail; and I shall call on Miss Bates in my way home."	E	III	6	355	19
Jane, Miss Bates, and me--and my caro sposo walking by.	E	III	6	356	26
Emma and Harriet went together; Miss Bates and her niece,	E	III	7	367	1
took charge of Miss Bates and Jane; and Emma and Harriet	E	III	7	367	1
Miss Bates said a great deal; Mrs. Elton swelled at the	E	III	7	369	17
"Oh! very well," exclaimed Miss Bates, "then I need not be	E	III	7	370	24
Miss Bates, deceived by the mock ceremony of her manner,	E	III	7	371	27
How could you be so unfeeling to Miss Bates?	E	III	7	374	56
How could she have been so brutal, so cruel to Miss Bates!-	E	III	7	376	62
Miss Bates should never again--no, never!	E	III	8	377	1
them out, she heard Miss Bates saying, "well, my dear, I	E	III	8	378	4
She had a moment's fear of Miss Bates keeping away from	E	III	8	378	7
But Miss Bates soon came--"very happy and obliged"--but	E	III	8	378	7
she collected from Miss Bates to be now actually	E	III	8	380	9
"So very kind!" replied Miss Bates.	E	III	8	380	10
Miss Bates would hardly give Emma time to say how	E	III	8	383	30
Emma could not regret her having gone to Miss Bates, but	E	III	9	386	8
it would not do;--Miss Bates came to the carriage door,	E	III	9	390	18
Miss Bates was obliged to return without success; Jane was	E	III	9	390	18
could hint the wish, Miss Bates made it appear that she	E	III	9	390	18
and only questioned Miss Bates farther as to her niece's	E	III	9	390	19
On that subject poor Miss Bates was very unhappy, and very	E	III	9	391	19
despatched to Miss Bates with a most friendly note.	E	III	9	391	20
thousand thanks from Miss Bates, but "dear Jane would not	E	III	9	391	20
How shocked had he been by her behaviour to Miss Bates!	E	III	12	415	1
poor Miss Bates had before made so happily intelligible.--	E	III	16	452	8
Miss Bates was out, which accounted for the previous	E	III	16	453	11
Soon after this Miss Bates came in, and Emma could not	E	III	16	455	19
"Upon my word it is, Miss Bates.--	E	III	16	455	23
Miss Bates looked about her, so happily!--	E	III	16	456	24
must tell her; and Miss Bates being present, it passed, of	E	III	17	468	35
MISS BATES'S (10)					
"Do you know Miss Bates's niece?	E	I	10	86	22
explanations on Miss Bates's, was, that this pianoforte	E	II	8	214	13
that at first, by Miss Bates's account, Jane herself was	E	II	8	214	13
Miss Bates's powerful, argumentative mind might have	E	II	12	260	26
minutes, and was detained by Miss Bates's being absent.	E	II	12	260	27
the lead of Miss Bates's good-will or taking it for	E	II	15	281	2
Miss Bates's gratitude for Mrs. Elton's attentions to Jane	E	II	15	284	12
Mr. Knightley's eyes had preceded Miss Bates's in a glance	E	III	5	346	17
She heard Miss Bates's voice, some thing was to be done in	E	III	8	378	4
till roused by Miss Bates's saying, "ay, I see what you	E	III	8	384	32
					33
MISS BEAUFORT'S (1)					
the hope on Miss Beaufort's side, of praise & celebrity	S		11	421	1
MISS BEAUFORTS (4)					
The other girls, two Miss Beauforts were just such young	S		11	421	1
the Miss Beauforts were soon satisfied with "the circle in	S		11	421	1
favourable spot for the seclusions of the Miss Beauforts.	S		11	422	1
a place; the Miss Beauforts, who wd have been nothing at	S		11	422	1
MISS BENNET (60)					
room," said Mr. Darcy, looking at the eldest Miss Bennet.	PP	I	3	11	11
Miss Bennet, he could not conceive an angel more beautiful.	PP	I	4	16	15
Miss Bennet he acknowledged to be pretty, but she smiled	PP	I	4	16	15
Miss Bennet was therefore established as a sweet girl, and	PP	I	4	17	16
Oh! the eldest Miss Bennet beyond a doubt, there cannot be	PP	I	5	19	7
with a note for Miss Bennet; it came from Netherfield, and	PP	I	7	30	14
Miss Bennet had slept ill, and though up, was very	PP	I	7	33	43
in the morning, if Miss Bennet were not decidedly better.	PP	I	8	40	59
Bennet had not found Miss Bennet worse than she expected.	PP	I	9	41	2
civility, "that Miss Bennet shall receive every possible	PP	I	9	41	5
you must remember, Miss Bennet, that the friend who is	PP	I	10	50	34
in the argument, Miss Bennet, than you may be aware of.	PP	I	10	50	39
If you and Miss Bennet will defer yours till I am out of	PP	I	10	51	42
Bennet, to seize such an opportunity of dancing a reel?"	PP	I	10	51	47
					48
He addressed himself directly to Miss Bennet, with a	PP	I	11	54	2
and then in her brother's conversation with Miss Bennet.	PP	I	11	54	3
a ball to Miss Bennet, she turned suddenly towards him and	PP	I	11	55	5
					6
tried to persuade Miss Bennet that it would not be safe	PP	I	12	59	3
Bingley was the principal spokesman, and Miss Bennet the	PP	I	15	72	8
"You may well be surprised, Miss Bennet, at such an	PP	I	16	77	12
His father, Miss Bennet, the late Mr. Darcy, was one of	PP	I	16	78	20
Miss Bennet, that you were not to sketch my character at	PP	I	18	94	41
it came from Netherfield, and was opened immediately.	PP	I	21	116	6
Miss Bennet eagerly disclaimed all extraordinary merit,	PP	II	1	135	10
Miss Bennet was the only creature who could suppose there	PP	II	1	138	31
Miss Bennet accepted her aunt's invitation with pleasure;	PP	II	2	142	17
Do you play and sing, Miss Bennet?"	PP	II	6	164	16
Are any of your younger sisters out, Miss Bennet?"	PP	II	6	165	32
that he had never been so fortunate as to meet Miss Bennet.	PP	II	7	171	12
What are you telling Miss Bennet?	PP	II	8	173	4
I have told Miss Bennet several times, that she will never	PP	II	8	173	10
said to Darcy, "Miss Bennet would not play at all amiss,	PP	II	8	176	27
					28
his intruding on Miss Bennet, and after sitting a few	PP	II	9	179	26
Miss Bennet was beyond what I had ever witnessed in him.	PP	II	12	197	5
Lady Catherine observed, after dinner, that Miss Bennet	PP	II	14	211	5
					6
Miss Bennet paused a little and then replied, "surely	PP	II	17	226	22
to dinner at Pemberly, before they left the country.	PP	III	2	263	11
separate him from Miss Bennet, it is probable that it	PP	III	3	270	10
but certain, and Miss Bennet could not assert to be wholly	PP	III	5	290	45
They were interrupted by Miss Bennet, who came to fetch	PP	III	6	299	27
her, she said to Miss Bennet, "I beg your pardon, madam,	PP	III	7	301	1
Elizabeth was disgusted, and even Miss Bennet was shocked.	PP	III	9	315	4
Miss Bennet had not been able to hear of his coming,	PP	III	11	331	16
the table, where Miss Bennet was making tea, and Elizabeth	PP	III	12	341	16
"It has been a very agreeable day," said Miss Bennet to	PP	III	12	343	30
Here, Sarah, come to Miss Bennet this moment, and help her	PP	III	13	344	7
prevailed on Miss Bennet to avoid the confinement of such	PP	III	14	351	1
stiffly to Elizabeth, "I hope you are well, Miss Bennet.	PP	III	14	351	4
					5
said to Elizabeth, "Miss Bennet, there seemed to be a	PP	III	14	352	16
					17
Miss Bennet, to understand the reason of my journey hither.	PP	III	14	353	22
					23
"Miss Bennet," replied her ladyship, in any angry tone, "	PP	III	14	353	26
Miss Bennet, I insist on being satisfied.	PP	III	14	354	34
"Miss Bennet, do you know who I am?	PP	III	14	354	38
Yes, Miss Bennet, interest; for do not expect to be	PP	III	14	355	45
You are to understand, Miss Bennet, that I came here with	PP	III	14	355	48
"Miss Bennet I am shocked and astonished.	PP	III	14	356	60
Do not imagine, Miss Bennet, that your ambition will ever	PP	III	14	358	71
round, she added, "I take no leave of you, Miss Bennet.	PP	III	14	358	72
					73
Miss Bennet still looked all amazement.	PP	III	17	373	8
When convinced on that article, Miss Bennet had nothing	PP	III	17	373	17
MISS BENNET'S (5)					

Miss Bennet's pleasing manners grew on the good will of PP I 6 21 1
Miss Bennet's lovely face confirmed his views, and PP I 15 70 3
Miss Bennet's astonishment was soon lessened by the strong PP II 17 224 2
satisfaction of Miss Bennet's mind gave a glow of such PP III 13 348 34
Though suspicion was very far from Miss Bennet's general PP III 17 372 3

MISS BENNETS (7)
That the Miss Lucases and the Miss Bennets should meet to PP I 5 18 3
because the Miss Bennets were come away, when her civility PP I 15 73 11
of, the younger Miss Bennets would have been in a pitiable PP I 17 88 15
It should not be said, that the Miss Bennets could not be PP II 16 223 25
The elder Miss Bennets alone were still able to eat, drink, PP II 18 229 1
In the afternoon, the two elder Miss Bennets were able to PP III 5 289 45
Their arrival was dreaded by the elder Miss Bennets; and PP III 9 315 1

MISS BERTRAM (43)
to make her remember that she is not a Miss Bertram. MP I 1 10 17
with the beauty of Miss Bertram, and being inclined to MP I 4 38 10
she had ever seen, Miss Bertram seemed, by her amiable MP I 4 39 10
the expediency of Mr. Rushworth's marrying Miss Bertram. MP I 4 39 11
marry the youngest Miss Bertram, a nice, handsome, good- MP I 4 42 19
"But do you really? for Miss Bertram is in general thought MP I 5 45 7
Miss Bertram is certainly the handsomest, and I have found MP I 5 45 8
"And besides, Miss Bertram is engaged. MP I 5 45 11
"But Miss Bertram does not care three straws for him; that MP I 5 45 14
I am sure Miss Bertram is very much attached to Mr. MP I 5 45 14
I think too well of Miss Bertram to suppose she would ever MP I 5 45 14
Miss Bertram, calmly, "would be Mr. Repton, I imagine." MP I 6 53 7
know," turning to Miss Bertram particularly as he spoke. MP I 6 55 17
But Miss Bertram thought it most becoming to reply: "the MP I 6 55 17
18
brother's; and as Miss Bertram caught at the idea likewise, MP I 6 61 58
Miss Bertram was the one. MP I 7 70 30
on a hint from Miss Bertram, Mr. Rushworth discovered that MP I 8 75 1
For the first seven miles Miss Bertram had very little MP I 8 81 32
Bertram, who might be said to have two strings to her bow. MP I 8 81 33
Miss Bertram could now speak with decided information of MP I 8 83 37
had all the distinction with each that she could wish. MP I 9 84 1
acceptable, for Miss Bertram was pleased to have its size MP I 9 84 2
her, "I do not like to see Miss Bertram so near the altar." MP I 9 88 20
Miss Bertram, displeased with her sister, led the way, and MP I 9 89 30
Mr. Crawford was soon followed by Miss Bertram and Mr. MP I 9 90 36
she wanted, when Miss Bertram, Mr. Rushworth, and Mr. MP I 10 97 1
After some minutes spent in this way, Miss Bertram MP I 10 97 4
Miss Bertram began again. MP I 10 98 11
"You will hurt yourself, Miss Bertram," she cried, "you MP I 10 99 21
astonished at Miss Bertram, and angry with Mr. Crawford. MP I 10 100 23
"Miss Bertram thought you would follow her." MP I 10 102 39
Mr. Crawford and Miss Bertram were much more gay, and she MP I 10 104 51
Miss Bertram had made up her mind to something different, MP I 10 105 52
"If Miss Bertram were not engaged." said Fanny, cautiously, MP I 12 116 9
Miss Bertram did indeed look happy, her eyes were MP I 12 117 15
out, "no want of hands in our theatre, Miss Bertram. MP I 13 129 38
Miss Bertram feeling all the interest of an Agatha in the MP I 14 132 8
choose, and wanted Miss Bertram to direct him, but upon MP I 15 138 1
Miss Bertram approved the decision, for the less he had to MP I 15 138 1
"You had better tell Miss Bertram to think of Mr. MP I 17 161 13
Such a match as Miss Bertram has made is a public blessing, MP II 4 210 21
to suffer in seeing him on the stage with Miss Bertram. MP III 3 337 10
should resent any former supposed slight to Miss Bertram. MP III 13 423 2

MISS BERTRAM'S (6)
Miss Bertram's engagement made him in equity the property MP I 5 44 2
Miss Bertram's attention and opinion was evidently his MP I 6 52 1
well guessed Miss Bertram's feelings, and made it a point MP I 8 82 35
They could not get through; and as Miss Bertram's MP I 10 98 4
theatre, and Miss Bertram's resolving to go down to the MP I 14 136 22
and soon after Miss Bertram's return from the parsonage, MP I 15 138 1

MISS BERTRAMS (24)
The holiday allowed to the Miss Bertrams the next day on MP I 2 14 7
In the country, therefore, the Miss Bertrams continued to MP I 2 20 33
The Miss Bertrams were much to be pitied on the occasion; MP I 3 32 64
The Miss Bertrams were now fully established among the MP I 4 34 4
them;" and as the Miss Bertrams regularly wanted their MP I 4 35 7
If your Miss Bertrams do not like to have their hearts MP I 4 43 21
beauty did her no disservice with the Miss Bertrams. MP I 5 44 1
any danger; the Miss Bertrams were worth pleasing, and MP I 5 44 3
"I like your Miss Bertrams exceedingly, sister," said he, MP I 5 45 4
by the Miss Bertrams; her delight in riding was like their MP I 7 69 23
The Miss Bertrams laughed at the idea, assuring her that MP I 8 77 8
While each of the Miss Bertrams were meditating how best, MP I 8 80 29
"The Miss Bertrams have never seen the wilderness yet." MP I 9 90 35
It was late before the Miss Bertrams and the two gentlemen MP I 10 104 51
afforded the Miss Bertrams much more agreeable feelings MP I 11 107 1
scene, while the Miss Bertrams, Mr. Rushworth, and Henry MP I 11 108 4
invited by the Miss Bertrams to join in a glee, she MP I 11 112 33
dulness to the Miss Bertrams, as ought to have put them MP I 12 114 3
Bertrams, "and for a theatre, what signifies a theatre? MP I 13 123 6
On the tragic side were the Miss Bertrams, Henry Crawford, MP I 14 130 3
called till the Miss Bertrams would not allow it to be MP I 16 150 1
that the Miss Bertrams, with every superiority in their MP I 16 151 1
and though the Miss Bertrams had latterly added little to MP II 3 204 33
happy without the Miss Bertrams, as if he had never known MP II 5 224 49

MISS BERTRAMS' (2)
The Miss Bertrams' admiration of Mr. Crawford was more MP I 5 47 27
after the Miss Bertrams' going away, an intimacy resulting MP II 4 207 11

MISS BICKERTON (3)
Miss Smith, and Miss Bickerton, another parlour boarder at E III 3 333 5
them to beg; and Miss Bickerton, excessively frightened, E III 3 333 5
abominable folly of Miss Bickerton in the warmest terms. E III 3 335 11

MISS BINGLEY (71)
and once with Miss Bingley, declined being introduced to PP I 3 11 6
Mary had heard herself mentioned to Miss Bingley as the PP I 3 12 15
Miss Bingley is to live with her brother and keep his PP I 4 15 10
only as a tenant, Miss Bingley was by no means unwilling PP I 4 15 13
"Miss Bingley told me," said Jane, "that he never speaks PP I 5 19 13
of Mrs. Hurst and Miss Bingley; and though the mother was PP I 6 21 1
by Miss Bingley, "I can guess the subject of your reverie." PP I 6 27 44
45
Miss Bingley immediately fixed her eyes on his face, and PP I 6 27 49
50
"Miss Elizabeth Bennet!" repeated Miss Bingley. PP I 6 27 51
"It is from Miss Bingley," said Jane, and then read it PP I 7 30 16
to Mrs. Hurst and Miss Bingley; and Elizabeth was PP I 7 32 42
and when Miss Bingley left them together, could attempt PP I 7 33 43
Miss Bingley offered her the carriage, and she only wanted PP I 7 33 45
with her, that Miss Bingley was obliged to convert the PP I 7 33 45
Miss Bingley was engrossed by Mr. Darcy, her sister PP I 8 35 2
began abusing her as soon as she was out of the room. PP I 8 35 3
I am sure," said Miss Bingley; "and I am inclined to think PP I 8 36 7
"I am afraid, Mr. Darcy," observed Miss Bingley, in a half PP I 8 36 12
"Miss Eliza Bennet," said Miss Bingley, "despises cards. PP I 8 37 23
"I am astonished," said Miss Bingley, "that my father PP I 8 38 29
said Miss Bingley; "will she be as tall as I am?" PP I 8 38 40
Mrs. Hurst and Miss Bingley both cried out against the PP I 8 40 55
"Eliza Bennet," said Miss Bingley, when the door was PP I 8 40 56
Miss Bingley was not so entirely satisfied with this reply PP I 8 40 58
"You may depend upon it, madam," said Miss Bingley, with PP I 9 41 5
Mrs. Hurst and Miss Bingley had spent some hours of the PP I 10 47 1
Mr. Darcy was writing, and Miss Bingley, seated near him, PP I 10 47 1
"Oh!" cried Miss Bingley, "Charles writes in the most PP I 10 48 22
Miss Bingley warmly resented the indignity he had received, PP I 10 51 40
When that business was over, he applied to Miss Bingley PP I 10 51 45
Miss Bingley moved with alacrity to the piano-forte, and PP I 10 51 45
After playing some Italian songs, Miss Bingley varied the PP I 10 51 47
48
Miss Bingley saw, or suspected enough to be jealous; and PP I 10 52 53
Bingley, in some confusion, lest they had been overheard. PP I 10 53 60
Darcy took up a book; Miss Bingley did the same; and Mrs. PP I 11 54 3
Miss Bingley made no answer; and soon afterwards got up PP I 11 56 10
Miss Bingley succeeded no less in the real object of her PP I 11 56 12
Miss Bingley, however, was incapable of disappointing Mr. PP I 11 56 14
"Oh! shocking!" cried Miss Bingley. PP I 11 56 16
"Miss Bingley," said he, "has given me credit for more PP I 11 57 20
said Miss Bingley;--"and pray what is the result?" PP I 11 57 26
"Do let us have a little music,"--cried Miss Bingley, PP I 11 58 33
Miss Bingley was then sorry that she had proposed the PP I 12 59 2
She attracted him more than he liked--and Miss Bingley was PP I 12 59 4
made Elizabeth smile, as she thought of poor Miss Bingley. PP I 16 83 56
They had not long separated when Miss Bingley came towards PP I 18 94 44
45
"I beg your pardon," replied Miss Bingley, turning away PP I 18 95 47
Mrs. Hurst or Miss Bingley; and even Lydia was too much PP I 18 103 75
happiness to which Miss Bingley looks forward, may arrive PP I 21 117 9
"It is only evident that Miss Bingley does not mean he PP I 21 117 13
Miss Bingley sees that her brother is in love with you, PP I 21 118 18
Miss Bingley I am sure cannot. PP I 21 119 20
that because Miss Bingley tells you her brother greatly PP I 21 119 20
"If we thought alike of Miss Bingley," replied Jane, "your PP I 21 119 21
when the visit was paid, and she had seen Miss Bingley. PP II 3 147 23
Miss Bingley said something of his never returning to PP II 3 149 26
this comfort for Miss Bingley, that he might have been PP II 8 176 29
ladies of my acquaintance, Mrs. Hurst and Miss Bingley. PP II 10 184 21
Miss Bingley the principal design and arrangement of them. PP II 10 186 38
I knew it myself, as it was known to Miss Bingley, but her PP II 12 199 5
Miss Bingley, and the lady with whom she lived in London. PP III 3 267 3
By Mrs. Hurst and Miss Bingley, they were noticed only by PP III 3 267 4
closely watched by Miss Bingley, and that she could not PP III 3 268 5
Miss Bingley saw all this likewise; and, in the imprudence PP III 3 269 8
9
Had Miss Bingley known what pain she was then giving her PP III 3 269 10
emotion; and as Miss Bingley, vexed and disapppointed, PP III 3 270 11
to their carriage, Miss Bingley was venting her feelings PP III 3 270 12
When Darcy returned to the saloon, Miss Bingley could not PP III 3 270 12
Persuaded as Miss Bingley was that Darcy admired Elizabeth, PP III 3 271 16
He then went away, and Miss Bingley was left to all the PP III 3 271 19
Miss Bingley was very deeply mortified by Darcy's marriage; PP III 19 387 10

MISS BINGLEY'S (15)
After sitting a little while with Jane, on Miss Bingley's PP I 9 41 2
in spite of all Miss Bingley's witticisms on fine eyes. PP I 9 46 39
Miss Bingley's eyes were instantly turned towards Darcy, PP I 11 54 2
Miss Bingley's attention was quite as much engaged in PP I 11 54 4
Miss Bingley's civility to Elizabeth increased at last PP I 12 60 5
Miss Bingley's letter arrived, and put an end to doubt. PP II 1 133 1
she could no longer be blind to Miss Bingley's inattention. PP II 3 147 25
been entirely deceived in Miss Bingley's regard for me. PP II 3 148 26
also of Miss Bingley's visit in Gracechurch-Street, and PP II 4 152 6
how hopeless Miss Bingley's designs on him were, by his PP II 7 170 6
Convinced as Elizabeth now was that Miss Bingley's dislike PP III 3 267 1
without hearing Miss Bingley's voice, Elizabeth was roused PP III 3 268 5
marked as in Miss Bingley's, in spite of the smiles which PP III 3 269 8
see you again the dupe of Miss Bingley's pretended regard." PP III 13 350 48
Miss Bingley's congratulations to her brother, on his PP III 18 383 24

MISS BRERETON (8)
Lady D. had been a rich Miss Brereton, born to wealth but S 3 375 1
last Michaelmas a Miss Brereton, who bid fair by her S 3 377 1
The Lady Denham, Miss Brereton, Mr & Mrs P---- Sir Edw: S 6 389 1
an alteration necessary, Lady Denham & Miss Brereton.-- S 6 390 1
feel;--and as for Miss Brereton, her appearance so S 6 391 1
It was done to pique Miss Brereton. S 7 398 1
Poor Miss Brereton!-- S 7 402 1
to skirt along;--Miss Brereton seated, apparently very S 12 426 1

MISS BS-- (2)
account--and the Miss Bs--, though naturally preferring S 11 421 1
of a glimpse of the Miss Bs--, though it was 1/2 a qr of a S 11 422 1

MISS CAMPBELL (12)
be telling Miss Campbell about his own home in Ireland. E II 1 159 20
Miss Campbell always was absolutely plain--but extremely E II 1 161 27
attachment of Miss Campbell in particular, was the more E II 2 164 7
the marriage of Miss Campbell, who by that chance, that E II 2 165 7
for the sake of the future twelve thousand pounds. E II 2 169 16
the business on Miss Campbell's account--we shall not E II 3 175 42
And as it is some months since Miss Campbell married, the E II 3 175 43
"My dear, you said that Miss Campbell would not allow him E II 3 176 48
49
"Yes Mr. Dixon and Miss Campbell were the persons; and I E II 6 202 30
been Miss Campbell, would have been at all agreeable to me. E II 6 202 31
How did Miss Campbell appear to like it?" E II 6 202 31
I was not very flattering to Miss Campbell; but she really E II 6 202 34

MISS CAPPER (5)
You must have heard me mention Miss Capper, the particular S 9 408 1
Fanny Noyce;--now, Miss Capper is extremely intimate with S 9 408 1
Miss Capper happened to be staying with Mrs D. when Mrs G. S 9 408 1
had heard from Miss Capper, who by a letter from Mrs S 9 409 1
to Mrs Darling, Miss Capper, Fanny Noyce, Mrs D. dupuis & S 11 420 1

MISS CAREYS (1)
Consider, here are the two Miss Careys come over from SS I 13 65 32

MISS CAROLINE (1)
good Mr. Otway, and Miss Otway and Miss Caroline.-- E III 2 323 19

MISS CARR (8)
Miss Osborne; Miss Carr, her daughter's friend, Mr Howard W 329 9
On the other side of Emma, Miss Osborne, Miss Carr, & a W 330 11
she turned again to Miss Carr, & in another minute was led W 330 11
It gained her a broad stare from Miss Osborne & Miss Carr W 331 11
Tom Musgrave who was dancing with Miss Carr, gave her many W 331 11
The dancing now recommended; Miss Carr being impatient to W 335 13
From Miss Osborne & Miss Carr she received something like W 336 13
but Miss Osborne & Miss Carr were likewise fair, & his W 357 28

MISS CARTERET (12)
the honourable Miss Carteret; and all the comfort of no. -- P IV 4 148 10
Dalrymple and Miss Carteret;" "our cousins, the Dalrymples, P IV 4 148 11
and the hon. Miss Carteret, to be arranged wherever they P IV 4 149 13
Dalrymple and Miss Carteret," were talked of to every body. P IV 4 149 13
Miss Carteret, with still less to say, was so plain and so P IV 4 150 14
Miss Carteret was with her mother; consequently it was not P IV 7 174 3
Lady Dalrymple and Miss Carteret, escorted by Mr. Elliot P IV 8 184 17
Elizabeth, arm in arm with Miss Carteret, and looking on P IV 8 185 20
by Elizabeth and Miss Carteret, in a manner not to be P IV 8 189 46
Miss Carteret was very anxious to have a general idea of P IV 8 190 47
Dalrymple and Miss Carteret, who were fortunately already P IV 10 220 29
Lady Dalrymple and Miss Carteret; they would soon be P IV 11 246 78

MISS CHARLOTTE HEYWOOD (1)
Their invitation was to Miss Charlotte Heywood, a very S 2 374 1

MISS CHURCHILL (4)
him to Miss Churchill, of a great Yorkshire family, and E I 2 15 2
family, and Miss Churchill fell in love with him, nobody E I 2 15 2
Miss Churchill, however, being of age, and with the full E I 2 15 3
the wife of Captain Weston, and Miss Churchill of Enscombe. E I 2 15 3

MISS CLARA (5)
No, no, Miss Clara & I will get back to our own tea.-- S 6 390 1
always calling her Miss Clara--nor anything objectionable S 6 392 1
very neighbourly, I beleive Miss Clara & I must stay."---- S 6 394 1
I have Miss Clara with me now, which makes a great S 7 401 1
They have Miss Clara's room to put to rights as well as my S 7 401 1

MISS COXES (2)
two Miss Coxes five," had been repeated many times over. E II 11 248 4
three, and the two Miss Coxes five; and for five couple E II 11 248 4

MISS CRAWFORD / MISS CRAWFORD'S

MISS CRAWFORD (210)

Context	Work	Vol.	Ch.	Page	Para.
Miss Crawford was not entirely free from similar	MP	I	4	41	16
Miss Crawford found a sister without preciseness or	MP	I	4	41	17
Miss Crawford was glad to find a family of such	MP	I	4	42	18
Dr. Grant laughingly congratulated Miss Crawford on	MP	I	4	43	26
young woman like Miss Crawford, is always pleasant society	MP	I	5	47	26
Miss Crawford soon felt, that he and his situation might	MP	I	5	48	28
Miss Crawford, as she was walking with the Mr. Bertrams.	MP	I	5	48	30
time--and Miss Crawford, it is plain, has heard the story."	MP	I	5	50	35
"I do not know," replied Miss Crawford hesitatingly.	MP	I	5	50	39
Mr. Bertram set off for ----, and Miss Crawford was	MP	I	6	52	1
exactly opposite Miss Crawford, and who had been	MP	I	6	56	19
					20
"I collect," said Miss Crawford, "that Sotherton is an old	MP	I	6	56	25
Miss Crawford listened with submission, and said to	MP	I	6	56	27
Edmund was sorry to hear Miss Crawford, whom he was much	MP	I	6	57	32
you both," said Miss Crawford; "at least, as long as you	MP	I	6	59	41
Miss Crawford civilly wished him an early promotion.	MP	I	6	60	47
"Well Fanny, and how do you like Miss Crawford now?" said	MP	I	7	63	1
amiable that Miss Crawford should acquit her aunt entirely.	MP	I	7	63	7
manner of Miss Crawford, nothing sharp, or loud, or coarse.	MP	I	7	64	11
which might lead him where Fanny could not follow.	MP	I	7	64	12
integrity, which Miss Crawford might be equal to feel,	MP	I	7	65	13
many hours with Miss Crawford, and not see more of the	MP	I	7	66	14
Edmund was fond of speaking to her of Miss Crawford, but	MP	I	7	66	14
The first actual pain which Miss Crawford occasioned her,	MP	I	7	66	14
Miss Crawford made her first essay with great credit to	MP	I	7	66	15
group--Edmund and Miss Crawford both on horseback, riding	MP	I	7	67	16
At first Miss Crawford and her companion made the circuit	MP	I	7	67	16
disperse, and Miss Crawford still on horseback, but	MP	I	7	68	17
"My dear Miss Price," said Miss Crawford, as soon as she	MP	I	7	68	18
In the drawing-room Miss Crawford was also celebrated.	MP	I	7	69	23
at home, I think Miss Crawford would be glad to have her	MP	I	7	69	28
Before his return Mrs. Grant and Miss Crawford came in.	MP	I	8	75	2
to include Miss Crawford in the invitation; and though Mrs.	MP	I	8	76	7
Probably, Miss Crawford will choose the barouche box	MP	I	8	78	15
but a value for Edmund, Miss Crawford was very unlike her.	MP	I	8	80	31
was addressed to Miss Crawford, as they gained the summit	MP	I	8	81	32
so much," and Miss Crawford could hardly answer, before	MP	I	8	81	32
She could not tell Miss Crawford that "those woods	MP	I	8	81	33
"Now we shall have no more rough road, Miss Crawford, our	MP	I	8	82	34
Miss Crawford was not slow to admire; she pretty well	MP	I	8	82	35
chiefly to Miss Crawford and Fanny, but there was no	MP	I	9	85	3
attention, for Miss Crawford, who had seen scores of great	MP	I	9	85	3
improvements," said Miss Crawford; with a smile, to Edmund.	MP	I	9	86	10
Fanny, and Miss Crawford remained in a cluster together.	MP	I	9	86	11
"Very fine indeed!" said Miss Crawford, laughing.	MP	I	9	86	13
he stood with Miss Crawford and Fanny; "my dear Edmund, if	MP	I	9	89	25
"Ordained!" said Miss Crawford; "what, are you to be a	MP	I	9	89	27
Miss Crawford rallying her spirits, and recovering her	MP	I	9	89	29
by Edmund, Miss Crawford and Fanny, who seemed as	MP	I	9	90	36
"This is insufferably hot," said Miss Crawford when they	MP	I	9	91	37
At length, after a short pause, Miss Crawford began with, "	MP	I	9	91	38
public manners, Miss Crawford must not misunderstand me,	MP	I	9	93	49
"There," cried Miss Crawford, "you have quite convinced	MP	I	9	93	51
"I wish I could convince Miss Crawford too."	MP	I	9	93	52
Perhaps," turning to Miss Crawford, "my dear companion may	MP	I	9	94	58
Every sort of exercise fatigues her so soon, Miss Crawford,	MP	I	9	95	68
After sitting a little while, Miss Crawford was up again.	MP	I	9	96	73
"Now, Miss Crawford, if you will look up the walk, you	MP	I	9	96	74
Crawford, and herself, without interruption from any one.	MP	I	10	97	1
that Edmund and Miss Crawford had left it, but that it was	MP	I	10	100	23
whether she had seen any thing of Miss Crawford and Edmund.	MP	I	10	101	33
and the laugh of Miss Crawford once more caught her ear;	MP	I	10	103	49
Miss Crawford, on walking up with her brother to spend the	MP	I	11	108	4
but after tea, as Miss Crawford was standing at an open	MP	I	11	108	4
Miss Crawford in esteeming it their general character.	MP	I	11	110	24
my uncle," said Miss Crawford, "that I can hardly suppose:-	MP	I	11	111	28
Fanny turned farther into the window; and Miss Crawford	MP	I	11	112	33
served, or Miss Crawford demanded, to tell of races and	MP	I.	12	114	1
the property of Miss Crawford if she would accept it.	MP	I	14	133	10
It is fit for Miss Crawford and Miss Crawford only.	MP	I	14	135	16
"Miss Crawford must be Amelia.--	MP	I	14	136	19
offer of Amelia to Miss Crawford; and Fanny remained alone.	MP	I	14	136	22
Miss Crawford accepted the part very readily, and soon	MP	I	15	138	1
and (with a bolder eye) Miss Crawford is to be Amelia."	MP	I	15	139	8
a few minutes, Miss Crawford returned to the party round	MP	I	15	143	27
"You chose very wisely, I am sure," replied Miss Crawford,	MP	I	15	144	30
"I am not at all surprised," said Miss Crawford, after a	MP	I	15	144	32
Miss Crawford talked of something else, and soon	MP	I	15	144	36
Miss Crawford was silenced; and with some feelings of	MP	I	15	145	42
Edmund was too angry to speak; but Miss Crawford looking	MP	I	15	147	56
Fanny did not love Miss Crawford; but she felt very much	MP	I	15	147	57
was married, Miss Crawford proceeded to inquire if she had	MP	I	15	147	57
After a moment's thought, Miss Crawford calmly replied, "	MP	I	15	148	59
our play"--said Miss Crawford in an under voice, to Fanny,	MP	I	15	149	61
Miss Crawford had protected her only for the time; and if	MP	I	16	150	1
"I am sorry for Miss Crawford; but I am more sorry to see	MP	I	16	155	15
change in Edmund; Miss Crawford looked very lovely in	MP	I	17	159	6
request of Miss Crawford, Mrs. Grant had with her usual	MP	I	17	159	6
it, for it was Miss Crawford to whom she was obliged, it	MP	I	17	159	6
obliged, it was Miss Crawford whose kind exertions were to	MP	I	17	159	6
Miss Crawford came with looks of gaiety which seemed an	MP	I	17	159	6
Edmund and Miss Crawford would then be acting together for	MP	I	18	167	12
at the door was followed by the entrance of Miss Crawford.	MP	I	18	168	14
part I mean?" continued Miss Crawford, opening her book.	MP	I	18	168	19
With such an Anhalt, however, Miss Crawford had courage	MP	I	18	169	22
that had brought Miss Crawford, consciousness and pleasure	MP	I	18	169	23
without knowing Miss Crawford to be in the house; and	MP	I	18	170	23
Why was not Miss Crawford to be applied to as well?	MP	I	18	171	29
"Where did you leave Miss Crawford, Fanny?"	MP	II	1	182	19
"Miss Crawford was very right in what she said of you the	MP	II	3	198	13
and to poor Miss Crawford, who had just been contemplating	MP	II	4	205	3
thus extended to Miss Crawford, and might carry on her	MP	II	4	206	3
she should; but Miss Crawford, calling to mind an early-	MP	II	4	206	5
"Another quarter of an hour," said Miss Crawford, "and we	MP	II	4	207	7
Miss Crawford, untouched and inattentive, had nothing to	MP	II	4	209	13
"Yes," replied Miss Crawford carelessly, "it does very	MP	II	4	209	15
"To say the truth," replied Miss Crawford, "I am something	MP	II	4	209	17
Miss Crawford however, with renewed animation, soon went	MP	II	4	210	20
					21
Fanny was silent--and Miss Crawford relapsed into	MP	II	4	210	22
"Well," said Miss Crawford, "and do not you scold us for	MP	II	4	211	26
"Upon my word," cried Miss Crawford, "you are two of the	MP	II	4	212	30
in a country village!" said Miss Crawford archly.	MP	II	4	212	32
Miss Crawford may chuse her degree of wealth.	MP	II	4	213	39
No, Miss Crawford," he added, in a more serious tone, "	MP	II	4	214	45
last; and though Miss Crawford is in a manner at home, at	MP	II	5	221	32
Has not Miss Crawford a gown something the same?"	MP	II	5	222	44
Miss Crawford, who had been repeatedly eyeing Dr. Grant	MP	II	5	226	60
Miss Crawford could have said that there would be a	MP	II	5	226	64
supposed so--and Miss Crawford took her harp, she had	MP	II	5	227	68
Miss Crawford was too much vexed by what had passed to be	MP	II	5	227	68
unsuspected by Miss Crawford, might have been a little	MP	II	6	231	11
living, as Miss Crawford well knew; and her interest in a	MP	II	7	241	19
Miss Crawford, a little suspicious and resentful of a	MP	II	7	242	25
Miss Crawford listened, and Edmund agreed to this.	MP	II	7	243	27
"Mr. Bertram," said Miss Crawford, a few minutes	MP	II	7	244	30
of his most attentive listeners, Miss Crawford and Fanny.--	MP	II	7	248	47
Miss Crawford was soon to leave Mansfield, and on this	MP	II	8	255	12
She met Miss Crawford within a few yards of the parsonage,	MP	II	8	257	15
Miss Crawford appeared gratified by the application, and	MP	II	8	257	15
Miss Crawford, pleased with the appeal, gave her all her	MP	II	8	257	15
shall you have by way of necklace?" said Miss Crawford.	MP	II	8	257	15
Such had been the parcel with which Miss Crawford was	MP	II	8	258	15
But, Miss Crawford persevered, and argued the case with so	MP	II	8	258	17
to be chusing what Miss Crawford least wished to keep.	MP	II	8	258	17
Miss Crawford smiled her perfect approbation; and hastened	MP	II	8	258	17
Miss Crawford had anticipated her wants with a kindness	MP	II	8	258	18
too when you wear that necklace," replied Miss Crawford.	MP	II	8	259	19
Miss Crawford thought she had never seen a prettier	MP	II	8	259	20
"Well then," replied Miss Crawford more seriously but	MP	II	8	259	22
he had not, for Miss Crawford, complaisant as a sister,	MP	II	8	260	24
with what Miss Crawford had done, so gratified by such a	MP	II	9	262	11
He would marry Miss Crawford.	MP	II	9	264	17
Could she believe Miss Crawford to deserve him, it would	MP	II	9	264	17
To think of him as Miss Crawford might be justified in	MP	II	9	264	18
"I wished to engage Miss Crawford for the two first dances,	MP	II	9	268	28
would by no means go through the ring of the cross.	MP	II	9	270	40
Miss Crawford had a claim; and when it was no longer to	MP	II	9	271	40
first time near Miss Crawford, whose eyes and smiles were	MP	II	10	274	9
Miss Crawford listened; and all her intended compliments	MP	II	10	274	9
would begin with Miss Crawford, and the impression was so	MP	II	10	275	11
Miss Crawford saw much of Sir Thomas's thoughts as he	MP	II	10	276	14
Miss Crawford knew Mrs. Norris too well to think of	MP	II	10	277	16
Miss Crawford blundered most towards Fanny herself, in her	MP	II	10	277	17
"Well, then," replied Miss Crawford laughing, "I must	MP	II	10	277	19
discontent; while Miss Crawford wondered she did not smile,	MP	II	10	277	20
Miss Crawford had been in gay spirits when they first	MP	II	10	279	21
Mrs. Grant and Miss Crawford, in a very handsome style,	MP	II	11	283	7
immediately Miss Crawford thus began, with a voice as well	MP	II	11	287	18
"That is the first question, you know," said Miss Crawford,	MP	II	11	288	28
Miss Crawford turned her eye on her, as if wanting to hear	MP	II	11	289	32
to speak, and Miss Crawford was disappointed; for she had	MP	II	11	289	33
"Not at all!"--cried Miss Crawford with alacrity.	MP	II	11	289	36
"I am very much obliged to you, my dear Miss Crawford, for	MP	II	13	307	31
your note, I remain, dear Miss Crawford, &c. &c."	MP	II	13	307	31
you will be so good as to give that to Miss Crawford."	MP	II	13	307	34
not devise, for Miss Crawford certainly wanted no delay.--	MP	III	1	311	1
beyond a fortnight purposely to avoid Miss Crawford.	MP	III	3	334	1
"It is above a week since I saw Miss Crawford."	MP	III	4	352	39
Miss Crawford made us laugh by her plans of encouragement	MP	III	4	354	46
You and Miss Crawford have made me too nice."	MP	III	4	355	54
as Edmund called Miss Crawford, was a formidable threat to	MP	III	5	356	4
her aunt, when Miss Crawford did come; and the first	MP	III	5	357	5
misery over, and Miss Crawford looking and speaking with	MP	III	5	357	5
But here she hoped too much, Miss Crawford was not the	MP	III	5	357	5
She cried as if she had loved Miss Crawford more than she	MP	III	5	359	10
could; and Miss Crawford, yet farther softened by the	MP	III	5	359	10
Oh! Miss Crawford, that was not fair."	MP	III	5	362	19
I had not, Miss Crawford, been an inattentive observer of	MP	III	5	363	21
In their very last conversation, Miss Crawford, in spite	MP	III	6	367	5
had still been Miss Crawford, still shewn a mind led	MP	III	6	367	5
them, and could never speak of Miss Crawford without pain.	MP	III	6	367	6
discourse about Miss Crawford; and Fanny was the more	MP	III	6	373	26
she trusted that Miss Crawford would have no motive for	MP	III	7	376	4
to hear from Miss Crawford now, at the rapid rate in which	MP	III	9	393	1
Crawford alone--or, he was too happy for letter writing!	MP	III	10	399	1
How Miss Crawford really felt--how she meant to act, or	MP	III	12	417	4
was that Miss Crawford, after proving herself cooled and	MP	III	12	417	4
Yet there was no saying what Miss Crawford might not ask.	MP	III	12	417	4
That Miss Crawford should endeavour to secure a meeting	MP	III	12	418	4
So very fond of you as Miss Crawford is, it is most	MP	III	13	420	2
written to Miss Crawford before this summons came, but no	MP	III	13	427	12
she thought of Miss Crawford--but Miss Crawford gave her	MP	III	14	430	3
Crawford--but Miss Crawford gave her the idea of being the	MP	III	14	430	3
She saw the proof of it in Miss Crawford, as well as in	MP	III	14	433	12
any thing of Miss Crawford or of her other connections in	MP	III	14	433	12
She thanked Miss Crawford, but gave a decided negative.--	MP	III	14	436	15
Miss Crawford need not be alarmed for her.	MP	III	15	438	4
from what Miss Crawford said, it was not likely that any	MP	III	15	438	4
and must continue till she heard from Miss Crawford again.	MP	III	15	438	7
Miss Crawford need not have urged secrecy with so much	MP	III	15	438	7
she could believe Miss Crawford to be the woman!	MP	III	15	441	19
Miss Crawford herself--Edmund; but it was dangerous,	MP	III	15	441	21
the first, from Miss Crawford; there was no intelligence	MP	III	15	442	22
interview with Miss Crawford had taken place, from which	MP	III	16	452	15
That Edmund must be for ever divided from Miss Crawford,	MP	III	16	453	16
He had seen Miss Crawford.	MP	III	16	454	18
imagination, not Miss Crawford, that I had been too apt to	MP	III	16	457	30
to talk of Miss Crawford alone, and how she had attached	MP	III	16	459	31
of it, for Edmund was no longer the dupe of Miss Crawford.	MP	III	17	461	2
to care about Miss Crawford, and became as anxious to	MP	III	17	470	26

MISS CRAWFORD'S (50)

Context	Work	Vol.	Ch.	Page	Para.
Miss Crawford's beauty did her no disservice with the Miss	MP	I	5	44	1
thing which Miss Crawford's habits made her likely to feel.	MP	I	5	47	27
admiration to Miss Crawford's beauty; but as she still	MP	I	5	48	30
Miss Crawford's attractions did not lessen.	MP	I	7	64	12
Miss Crawford's enjoyment of riding was such, that she did	MP	I	7	66	15
his comments on Miss Crawford's great cleverness as a	MP	I	7	69	21
of Miss Crawford's, that it should never happen again.	MP	I	7	74	58
as to whether Miss Crawford's being of the party were	MP	I	8	77	8
Miss Crawford's countenance, as Julia spoke, might have	MP	I	9	89	26
Agatha, began to be scrupulous on Miss Crawford's account.	MP	I	14	133	8
brother again interposed with Miss Crawford's better claim.	MP	I	14	135	15
went on, and Miss Crawford's attention was first called	MP	I	15	148	58
It was not in Miss Crawford's power to talk Fanny into any	MP	I	16	150	1
Put yourself in Miss Crawford's place, Fanny.	MP	I	16	154	14
would have entered more into Miss Crawford's feelings."	MP	I	16	155	22
Alas! it was all Miss Crawford's doing.	MP	I	16	156	28
part, between Miss Crawford's claims and his own conduct,	MP	I	17	163	21
untouched all Miss Crawford's resources, her	MP	II	3	199	16
Miss Crawford's kind opinion of herself deserved at least	MP	II	3	199	16
from Miss Crawford's desire of something new, and which	MP	II	4	207	11
of manner on Miss Crawford's side as she made some	MP	II	4	214	46
Miss Crawford's direction, were arranged round the other.	MP	II	7	239	8
not always perfectly assured of knowing Miss Crawford's.	MP	II	8	255	10
confirmation of Miss Crawford's attachment; but the whirl	MP	II	8	256	13
Miss Crawford's eyes which she could not be satisfied with.	MP	II	8	260	23
Miss Crawford's attentions to you have been--not more than	MP	II	9	263	16
of judging of Miss Crawford's character and the privilege	MP	II	9	265	18
been Miss Crawford's, "you are all considerate thought!--	MP	II	9	269	38
talked away all Miss Crawford's faults and his own	MP	II	9	270	40
effort, to resolve on wearing Miss Crawford's necklace too.	MP	II	9	271	40
leisure for thinking long even of Miss Crawford's feelings.	MP	II	10	275	10
Miss Crawford's uneasiness was much lightened by this	MP	II	12	291	1
judgment of Miss Crawford's meaning, it was evident that	MP	II	13	304	16
She had read Miss Crawford's note only once; and how to	MP	II	13	307	30
Miss Crawford's power was all returning.	MP	III	4	349	24
and to have Miss Crawford's liveliness repeated to her at	MP	III	4	354	47
restraint of countenance was over on Miss Crawford's side.	MP	III	5	357	6
change in Miss Crawford's ideas; by the strong effect on	MP	III	5	357	6
little of it, she was the more overcome by Miss Crawford's.	MP	III	5	365	33
Crawford's marrying Edmund than it had ever been before.--	MP	III	6	366	4
the chance of Miss Crawford's future improvement as nearly	MP	III	6	367	5
have denied to Miss Crawford's nature, that participation	MP	III	6	367	6
time in which Miss Crawford's name would ever be mentioned	MP	III	6	373	26
Miss Crawford's style of writing, lively and affectionate,	MP	III	7	376	4
knowledge of Miss Crawford's temper, of being urged again;	MP	III	15	437	1
jealousy, in Miss Crawford's apprehension, if she heard it.	MP	III	15	438	4
Miss Crawford's letter, which she had read so often as to	MP	III	15	441	19
it possibility--Miss Crawford's letter stampt it a fact.	MP	III	15	441	20
Sir Thomas not in the secret of Miss Crawford's character.	MP	III	16	453	15
Long, long would it be ere Miss Crawford's name passed his	MP	III	16	453	16

MISS D (86)
of marrying Miss De Courcy, & the event has justified me. LS 5 249 1
honour of calling to-morrow to inquire after Miss Dashwood. SS I 9 42 10
I can tell you, Miss Dashwood; he has a pretty little SS I 9 44 23
Miss Dashwood had a delicate complexion, regular features, SS I 10 46 2
"Miss Dashwood," cried Willoughby, "you are now using me SS I 10 51 28
had he not convinced Miss Dashwood that what concerned her SS I 11 57 17
This was all overheard by Miss Dashwood; and in the whole SS I 12 59 7
you and your sisters in town this winter, Miss Dashwood?" SS I 13 66 46
"Do not be alarmed," said Miss Dashwood, "nothing of the SS I 14 72 8
You, Miss Dashwood, would give a general commission for SS I 17 92 25
in a low voice, to miss Dashwood, by whom he was sitting. SS I 18 100 22
"Oh! my dear Miss Dashwood," said Mrs. Palmer soon SS I 20 112 29
abruptly, "and how do you like Devonshire, Miss Dashwood? SS I 21 123 21
I suppose your brother was quite a beau, Miss Dashwood, SS I 21 124 28
will make Miss Dashwood believe you think of nothing else." SS I 21 124 31
What! your sister-in-law's brother, Miss Dashwood? a very SS I 21 126 39
not be concealed from Miss Dashwood, in spite of her SS I 22 127 2
Though you do not know him so well as me, Miss Dashwood, SS I 22 130 28
What would you advise me to do in such a case, Miss SS I 22 133 44
so near them that Miss Dashwood now judged, she might SS II 1 145 23
But you will not give me your advice, Miss Dashwood?" SS II 2 150 30
"Shall you be in town this winter, Miss Dashwood?" said SS II 2 150 36
a little pleasure, because Miss Dashwood does not wish it. SS II 3 154 3
Barton, without saying a word to Miss Dashwood about it." SS II 3 154 3
company, whether Miss Dashwood will go or not, only the SS II 3 154 4
upon the bargain, and if Miss Dashwood will change her SS II 3 154 4
satisfaction at finding Miss Dashwood alone, as if he had SS II 5 172 40
Excuse me, Miss Dashwood. SS II 5 173 44
"For shame, for shame, Miss Dashwood! how can you talk so! SS II 7 182 10
as this must be read by Miss Dashwood, may be imagined. SS II 7 183 14
"How is she, Miss Dashwood?-- SS II 8 192 3
You will find me a very awkward narrator, Miss Dashwood; I SS II 9 204 20
Ah! Miss Dashwood--a subject such as this--untouched for SS II 9 208 28
were repeated by Miss Dashwood to her sister, as they very SS II 10 212 1
inquiries were never unwelcome to Miss Dashwood. SS II 10 216 15
The good understanding between the Colonel and Miss SS II 10 216 15
your brother and sister, Miss Dashwood, when they come to SS II 10 218 30
"I am sorry we cannot see your sister, Miss Dashwood," SS II 10 219 37
"Pity me, dear Miss Dashwood!" said Lucy, as they walked SS II 12 231 13
one fell to the share of Miss Dashwood, whom she eyed with SS II 12 232 15
any thing painted by Miss Dashwood; and the curiosity of SS II 12 234 28
her at the same time, that they were done by Miss Dashwood. SS II 12 235 28
"Are you ill, Miss Dashwood?--you seem low--you don't SS II 13 239 11
my dear Miss Dashwood! have you heard the news!" SS III 1 257 2
3
"Well, but Miss Dashwood," speaking triumphantly, "people SS III 2 272 14
Miss Dashwood, do you think people make love when any body SS III 2 274 18
March. I hope my dear Miss Dashwood will excuse the SS III 2 277 29
30
for the delicacy of Miss Dashwood;--but it was inforced SS III 3 279 1
"Well, Miss Dashwood," said Mrs. Jennings, sagaciously SS III 4 285 1
to enter, by saying that Miss Dashwood was above, and SS III 4 287 25
You must not judge him, Miss Dashwood, from your slight SS III 5 299 35
and though encouraging Miss Dashwood to expect that a few SS III 7 307 3
of an evening, while Miss Dashwood was above with her SS III 7 309 5
able to assist or advise Miss Dashwood in any emergence. SS III 7 309 5
a speedy recovery, and Miss Dashwood was equally sanguine; SS III 7 309 7
the ear, but could not enter the heart, of Miss Dashwood. SS III 7 313 21
than supplication, "Miss Dashwood, for half an hour--for SS III 8 317 1
2
For once, Miss Dashwood--it will be the last time, perhaps- SS III 8 318 15
Miss Dashwood at this point, turning her eyes on him with SS III 8 320 30
31
look, even of yours, Miss Dashwood, can ever reprobate too SS III 8 320 32
Miss Dashwood, you cannot have an idea of the comfort it SS III 8 324 45
If you can pity me, Miss Dashwood, pity my situation as it SS III 8 327 55
And now do you pity me, Miss Dashwood?--or have I said all SS III 8 329 65
assured of his fate with Miss Dashwood; and by his SS III 13 366 20
him from marrying Miss Dashwood, by every argument in her SS III 14 373 3
thousand pounds, while Miss Dashwood was only the daughter SS III 14 373 3
that he & his sister Miss D-- who lived with him, wd be S 3 377 1
Miss Denham had a very small provision--& her brother was S 3 377 1
P---- Sir Edw: Denham & Miss Denham, whose names might be S 6 389 1
Miss D. was a fine young woman, but cold & reserved, S 7 394 1
The difference in Miss Denham's countenance, the change S 7 396 1
the change from Miss Denham sitting in cold grandeur in S 7 396 1
efforts of others, to Miss D. at Lady D.'s elbow, S 7 396 1
Miss Denham's character was pretty well decided with S 7 396 1
than the simple enquiry of--"Sir Edward & Miss Denham?"-- S 7 399 1
And here they were obliged to part--Miss D. being too much S 8 404 1
room, and she was soon introduced to Miss Diana Parker. S 9 406 1
Miss Diana P. was about 4 & 30, of middling height & S 9 407 1
It was not a week, since Miss Diana Parker had been told S 10 412 1
two or three veiws of Miss Diana posting over the down S 10 413 1
one sort of Herb-Tea & Miss Diana another, & turning S 10 416 1
Miss Diana herself derived an immediate advantage to S 10 419 1
Miss D. probably felt a little awkward on being first S 11 420 1
The particular introduction of Mrs G. to Miss Diana Parker, S 11 421 1
was the one in which Miss D. P. had the pleasure of S 11 422 1
"The easiest thing in the world--cried Miss Diana Parker S 12 423 1

MISS D. P-- (1)
Soon after tea, a letter was brought to Miss D. P-- from S 10 418 1

MISS D. P.'S (1)
young ladies under her care, to Miss D. P.'s notice.-- S 10 419 1

MISS DARCY (34)
"Is Miss Darcy much grown since the spring?" said Miss PP I 8 38 40
"How delighted Miss Darcy will be to receive such a letter! PP I 10 47 3
"What sort of a girl is Miss Darcy?" PP I 16 82 42
is in love with you, and wants him to marry Miss Darcy. PP I 21 118 18
more anxious to get Miss Darcy for her brother, from the PP I 21 119 20
greatly admires Miss Darcy, he is in the smallest degree PP I 21 119 20
the attractions of Miss Darcy and the amusements of London, PP I 23 129 13
brother's being partial to Miss Darcy she paid no credit. PP II 1 133 3
"Beyond a doubt, they do wish him to chuse Miss Darcy," PP II 1 137 24
I found that Miss Darcy was expected to dinner. PP II 3 147 23
persuade herself that he is really partial to Miss Darcy. PP II 3 148 26
I am joined with him in the guardianship of Miss Darcy." PP II 10 184 18
her why she supposed Miss Darcy likely to give them any PP II 10 184 20
of his designs on Miss Darcy, received some confirmation PP II 13 206 4
Miss Darcy, the daughter of Mr. Darcy, of Pemberly and PP II 14 212 13
one of miss Darcy, drawn when she was only eight years old. PP III 1 247 20
"And is Miss Darcy as handsome as her brother?" said Mr. PP III 1 248 21
here; and Miss Darcy is always down for the summer months." PP III 1 248 25
to give pleasure to Miss Darcy, who had taken a liking to PP III 1 249 43
She immediately felt that whatever desire Miss Darcy might PP III 1 256 64
Miss Darcy and her brother appeared, and this formidable PP III 2 261 3
Since her being at Lambton, she had heard that Miss Darcy PP III 2 261 3
Miss Darcy was tall, and on a larger scale than Elizabeth; PP III 2 261 4
to Miss Darcy, who had been set up as a rival of Jane. PP III 2 262 8
Miss Darcy, though with a diffidence which marked her PP III 2 263 11
In this room they were received by Miss Darcy, who was PP III 3 267 3
Miss Darcy looked as if she wished for courage enough to PP III 3 267 4
especially to Miss Darcy, without calling her attention. PP III 3 268 5
Mrs. Annesley to Miss Darcy had been given, to remind her PP III 3 268 6
Miss Darcy, on her brother's entrance, exerted herself PP III 3 269 8
Be so kind as to apologize for us to Miss Darcy. PP III 4 278 21
From what he said of Miss Darcy, I was thoroughly prepared PP III 5 284 14
ago governess to Miss Darcy, and was dismissed from her PP III 10 322 2
The joy which Miss Darcy expressed on receiving similar PP III 18 383 25

MISS DARCY'S (5)
Miss Darcy's praise occupied the chief of it. PP II 1 133 2
Mrs. Reynolds anticipated Miss Darcy's delight, when she PP III 1 250 45
some drawings of Miss Darcy's, in crayons, whose subjects PP III 1 250 46
civility as Miss Darcy's, in coming to them on the very PP III 2 266 17
Not a syllable had ever reached her of Miss Darcy's PP III 3 270 10

MISS DASHWOOD'S (5)
Here too, Miss Dashwood's commendation, being only simple SS I 21 122 16
"I can answer for it that Miss Dashwood's is not," said SS II 2 148 22
is quite as modest and pretty behaved as Miss Dashwood's." SS II 2 148 23
the effect of Miss Dashwood's communication, in such an SS II 8 200 43
their good on Miss Dashwood's part, either present or SS III 5 293 2

MISS DASHWOODS (24)
And what possible claim could the Miss Dashwoods, who were SS I 2 8 3
The Miss Dashwoods were young, pretty, and unaffected. SS I 7 33 3
the three Miss Dashwoods walked up from the cottage, and SS I 13 65 32
took his usual place between the two elder Miss Dashwoods. SS I 13 67 61
As the Miss Dashwoods entered the drawing-room of the park SS I 20 110 1
me persuade the Miss Dashwoods to go to town this winter." SS I 20 110 9
you long to have the Miss Dashwoods come to Cleveland?" SS I 20 113 29
to tell the Miss Dashwoods of the Miss Steeles' arrival, SS I 21 119 3
only afraid the Miss Dashwoods might find it dull at SS I 21 123 28
and the other Miss Dashwoods, quite as his own sisters."-- SS I 22 130 16
by them, asked the elder Miss Dashwoods to accompany her. SS II 3 153 1
from meeting her mother or the Miss Dashwoods again. SS II 4 164 21
The Miss Dashwoods had no greater reason to be SS II 5 168 11
towards the Miss Dashwoods to express his surprise on SS II 5 171 30
only to see the Miss Dashwoods from the first without the SS II 10 215 14
On ascending the stairs, the Miss Dashwoods found so many SS II 11 220 3
glance on the Miss Dashwoods, but such a one as seemed SS II 11 221 5
to be where the Miss Dashwoods were, received his eager SS II 12 230 6
evening; and at the Miss Dashwoods, at the particular request SS II 14 246 2
the name of the Miss Dashwoods, and understanding them to SS II 14 248 6
carriage for the Miss Dashwoods; but, what was still worse, SS II 14 248 6
Miss Dashwoods very ready to reassume their former share. SS III 1 257 1
The Miss Dashwoods had now been rather more than two SS III 3 279 1
do without the Miss Dashwoods;"--was Mrs. Jennings's SS III 3 280 8

MISS DE BOURGH (20)
of true beauty, Miss de Bourgh is far superior to the PP I 14 67 7
"Her daughter, Miss de Bourgh, will have a very large PP I 16 83 55
cousin Miss de Bourgh, and of her mother lady Catherine. PP I 18 96 57
was arranging Miss de Bourgh's foot-stool, that she said, ' PP I 19 105 10
it would succeed, if Miss de Bourgh were out of the way. PP I 21 119 20
The other is Miss de Bourgh. PP II 5 158 15
It is the greatest of favours when Miss de Bourgh comes in. PP II 5 158 17
constantly bowing whenever Miss de Bourgh looked that way. PP II 5 158 19
Miss de Bourgh was pale and sickly; her features, though PP II 6 162 12
Charlotte and Miss de Bourgh--the former of whom was PP II 6 163 14
how little Miss de Bourgh ate, pressing her to try some PP II 6 163 14
Down to quadrille; and as Miss de Bourgh chose to play at PP II 6 166 41
her fears of Miss de Bourgh's being too hot or too cold, PP II 6 166 41
often especially Miss de Bourgh drove by in her phaeton, PP II 7 168 2
his behavior to Miss de Bourgh she derived this comfort PP II 8 176 29
next year; and Miss de Bourgh exerted herself so far as to PP II 14 214 21
de Bourgh, which I am certain he has very much at heart." PP II 18 235 38
"Perhaps preparing for his marriage with Miss de Bourgh," PP III 10 328 17
To his tacit engagement with Miss de Bourgh? PP III 14 355 43
his mother and aunt wished him to marry Miss de Bourgh. PP III 14 355 44

MISS DIANA P-- (1)
in the cause by the vigilance & caution of Miss Diana P--. S 11 420 1

MISS DIANA PARKER'S (1)
Miss Diana Parker's two large families were not forgotten. S 6 392 1

MISS DRUMMOND (2)
Mrs. Tilney was a Miss Drummond, and she and Mrs. Hughes NA I 9 68 46
and Miss Drummond had a very large fortune; and, when she NA I 9 68 46

MISS E (54)
"Is Sam. attached to Miss Edwardes?"-- W 320 2
"Do you suppose Miss Edwardes inclined to like him?" W 321 2
There was nothing in the manners of mrs or Miss Edwardes W 322 3
The discussion led to more intimate remarks, & Miss W 324 3
solemn scene, said to Miss Edwardes, "the gentleman we W 327 8
We shall greatly Miss Edmund in our small circle, but I MP III 13 426 11
It was so with Elizabeth; still the same handsome Miss P III 1 6 11
herself so acceptable to Miss Elliot, as to have been P III 2 15 15
intimates within Miss Elliot's reach, was therefore an P III 2 16 17
You need not be afraid, Miss Elliot, of your own sweet P III 3 18 7
and I should recommend Miss Elliot to be on her guard with P III 3 18 8
But Mrs. Clay was talking so eagerly with Miss Elliot, P III 3 23 26
was to draw Sir Walter, Miss Elliot, and Mrs. Clay to Bath. P III 5 35 18
having asked his partner whether Miss Elliot never danced? P III 8 72 58
"Miss Elliot, I am sure you are tired," cried Mrs. Croft. P III 10 91 40
We sailors, Miss Elliot, cannot afford to make long P III 10 92 44
pleasantly; "for if Miss Elliot were to hear how soon we P III 10 92 45
"Miss Elliot," said he, speaking rather low, "you have P III 12 107 24
You may think, Miss Elliot, whether he is dear to us!" P III 12 108 28
expressed his hope of Miss Elliot's not being the worse P IV 1 126 20
his mistress's head!--is not it, Miss Elliot!-- P IV 1 126 22
I should think, Miss Elliot" (looking with serious P IV 1 127 28
to your good father, Miss Elliot, pray give my compliments P IV 1 128 29
then "Miss Elliot" was spoken of in the highest terms!-- P IV 2 131 9
beauty," Oh! there was no end of Miss Elliot's charms." P IV 2 131 9
general observance as "Miss Elliot," that any P IV 4 147 8
which a visit from Miss Elliot would give Mrs. Smith, and P IV 5 153 5
and no doubt is well known to convey a Miss Elliot.-- P IV 5 158 19
of Bath as it might suit Miss Elliot and himself to visit P IV 6 165 9
How do you like Bath, Miss Elliot? P IV 6 170 29
Do not you think, Miss Elliot, we had better try to get P IV 6 173 49
it very desirable for Miss Elliot to have the advantage of P IV 7 174 2
There could be no doubt as to Miss Elliot. P IV 7 174 3
to settle it for them; Miss Elliot maintaining that Mrs. P IV 7 174 3
Lady Dalrymple's carriage, for which Miss Elliot was P IV 7 176 10
that Lady Dalrymple was calling to convey Miss Elliot. P IV 7 176 10
At last Miss Elliot and her friend, unattended but by the P IV 7 176 10
But the men are all wild after Miss Elliot. P IV 7 178 23
Miss Elliot, surrounded by her cousins, and the principal P IV 8 186 23
the goodness, my dear Miss Elliot, to make it an object to P IV 9 195 24
But now, my dear Miss Elliot, as an old friend, do give me P IV 9 195 27
Well, my dear Miss Elliot, I hope and trust you will be P IV 9 196 32
At last, "I beg your pardon, my dear Miss Elliot," she P IV 9 198 52
53
He described one Miss Elliot, and I thought very P IV 9 201 59
came to Bath with Miss Elliot and Sir Walter as long ago P IV 9 206 88
that Miss Elliot should be apparently blind to the danger." P IV 9 206 88
Dear Miss Elliot, may I not say father and son?" P IV 10 213 6
"My dear Miss Elliot!" exclaimed Mrs. Clay, lifting up her P IV 10 213 8
Miss Elliot was to have the honour of calling on Mrs. P IV 10 220 29
Miss Elliot, whose entrance seemed to give a general chill. P IV 10 226 63
provided herself, the "Miss Elliot at home," were laid on P IV 10 226 64
Only think, Miss Elliot, to my great surprise I met with P IV 10 228 71
But (in a deep tone) it was not done for her. Miss Elliot, P IV 11 232 15
Well, Miss Elliot," (lowering his voice) "as I was saying, P IV 11 234 27

MISS E. (4)
Emma found in Miss E.--the shew of good sense, a modest W 323 3
How do you do Miss E.?--he cried, with an easy air;--you W 327 7
Miss E. answered hesitatingly--"yes--he is very much liked W 328 8
were to drink tea;--Miss E. gave her a caution to be at W 331 11

MISS E. MATHEWS (1)
Mathews--Miss Mathews, Miss E. Mathews, miss h. mathews.-- S 6 389 1

MISS E.'S (1)
to see a blush on Miss E.'s cheek, & in remembering what W 326 5

MISS EDWARDS (7)
ladies; & tho' Miss Edwards was rather discomposed at the W 326 7
her followers, & Miss Edwards on hazarding the anxious W 327 7
made his way to Miss Edwards, with an air of Empressement, W 328 8

dear Miss Edwards--how soon it is at an end!-- W 336 14
Won't he Miss Edwards?"-- W 340 18
Miss Edwards accompanied her home, but as it was dinner W 341 19
me, you will not encourage him to think of Miss Edwards.-- W 341 19
MISS ELIZA (9)
to her, "my dear Miss Eliza, why are not you dancing?-- PP I 6 26 37
38
"You excel so much in the dance, Miss Eliza, that it is PP I 6 26 41
inducement, my dear Miss Eliza, we cannot wonder at his PP I 6 26 43
"Miss Eliza Bennet," said Miss Bingley, "despises cards. PP I 8 37 23
"Miss Eliza Bennet, let me persuade you to follow my PP I 11 56 11
event, my dear Miss Eliza, (glancing at her sister and PP I 18 92 23
accosted her, "so, Miss Eliza, I hear you are quite PP I 18 94 44
45
I pity you, Miss Eliza, for the discovery of your PP I 18 94 45
Eliza, are not the ----shire militia removed from Meryton? PP III 3 269 8
9
MISS ELIZABETH (7)
yours, Miss Elizabeth, for the two first dances especially, PP I 17 87 13
thus, "my dear Miss Elizabeth, I have the highest opinion PP I 18 97 60
61
"Believe me, my dear Miss Elizabeth, that your modesty, so PP I 19 105 8
Mrs. Bennet rang the bell, and Miss Elizabeth was summoned PP I 20 111 14
observed, "yes, Miss Elizabeth, you will have the honour PP II 5 157 6
7
"I know not, Miss Elizabeth," said he, "whether Mrs. PP II 15 215 2
Only let me assure you, my dear Miss Elizabeth, that I can PP II 15 216 6
MISS ELIZABETH BENNET (4)
replied with great intrepidity, "Miss Elizabeth Bennet." PP I 6 27 49
50
"Miss Elizabeth Bennet!" repeated Miss Bingley. PP I 6 27 51
I thought Miss Elizabeth Bennet looked remarkably well, PP I 8 36 7
that Miss Elizabeth Bennet, would, in all likelihood, be PP III 14 353 26
MISS ELIZABETH BENNET'S (1)
She is now about Miss Elizabeth Bennet's height, or rather PP I 8 38 41
MISS EMMA (8)
"You are paying Miss Emma no great compliment I think Mary, W 324 3
"Your father, Miss Emma, is one of my oldest friends--said W 324 4
began with, "I think Miss Emma, I remember your aunt very W 325 4
into that country Miss Emma--but it must be a great W 326 5
be extremely happy Miss Emma, if you can give us the W 339 18
Fine open weather Miss Emma!-- W 357 28
you must have a little cheek-glowing now & then Miss Emma. W 358 28
'If Miss Taylor undertakes to wrap Miss Emma up, you need E II 11 252 37
MISS EMMA WATSON (4)
their friends; Miss Emma Watson who was very recently W 315 1
Miss Emma Watson puts me very much in mind of her eldest W 324 3
him to Miss Emma Watson, left that good lady without any W 334 13
I could never dread a meeting with Miss Emma Watson,--or W 356 28
MISS ESTHER (4)
of arch sagacity--"Miss Esther wants me to invite her & S 7 399 1
"And Miss Esther must marry somebody of fortune too--she S 7 401 1
But--after a short pause--if Miss Esther thinks to talk me S 7 401 1
dear, the next time Miss Esther begins talking about the S 7 402 1
MISS F-- (1)
absolutely unknown to Miss F--, who would never have E III 14 439 8
MISS F. (1)
W., in being unpleasant to Miss F., were highly blamable. E III 14 440 8
MISS FAIRFAX (109)
interest----- "have you heard from Miss Fairfax so lately? E II 1 157 8
9
"Are you expecting Miss Fairfax here soon?" E II 1 158 15
chance of my hearing any thing of Miss Fairfax to-day." E II 1 159 19
Fairfax should be allowed to come to you at such a time. E II 1 160 21
22
Fairfax prefers devoting the time to you and Mrs. Bates?" E II 1 161 24
is not, by any means, to be compared with Miss Fairfax." E II 1 161 26
You and Miss Fairfax gave us some very good music. E II 3 170 2
I am sure Miss Fairfax must have found the evening E II 3 170 2
enough;" but she said only, "Miss Fairfax is reserved." E II 3 171 6
"True, sir; and Emma, because she had Miss Fairfax." E II 3 171 13
open, and Miss Bates and Miss Fairfax walked into the room. E II 3 172 22
23
When you have been here a little longer, Miss Fairfax, you E II 3 174 38
I hope you mean to take an interest in this news. E II 3 175 41
42
True, true, you are acquainted with Miss Fairfax; I E II 5 194 38
"And how did you think Miss Fairfax looking?" E II 6 199 8
And, seriously, Miss Fairfax is naturally so pale, as E II 6 199 9
"I cannot separate Miss Fairfax and her complexion." E II 6 199 12
had known much of Miss Fairfax and her party at Weymouth." E II 6 200 17
Miss Fairfax must already have given her account.-- E II 6 200 18
than Miss Fairfax would have vouchsafed in half a year." E II 6 202 29
I think, who must have felt it: Miss Fairfax herself. E II 6 202 35
But you, who have known Miss Fairfax from a child, must be E II 6 203 38
Intimacy between Miss Fairfax and me is quite out of the E II 6 203 41
with Miss Bates, Miss Fairfax, and Miss Smith; but already, E II 8 214 13
"Perhaps Miss Fairfax has never been staying here so long E II 8 216 23
Mr. Dixon or Miss Fairfax, but I cannot help suspecting E II 8 217 32
but the fact, that Miss Fairfax was nearly dashed from the E II 8 218 37
"No, I am sure it is not form the Campbells. Miss Fairfax E II 8 218 41
Miss Fairfax; but it was most prudent to avoid speech. E II 8 220 48
the room at Miss Fairfax, who was sitting exactly opposite. E II 8 222 54
"I believe I have been very rude; but really Miss Fairfax E II 8 222 56
standing before Miss Fairfax, and talking to her; but as E II 8 222 57
of Miss Fairfax, she could absolutely distinguish nothing. E II 8 222 57
found a seat by Miss Fairfax, followed Mr. Cole, to add E II 8 227 85
her place to Miss Fairfax, whose performance, both vocal E II 8 227 86
"One more;--they would not fatigue Miss Fairfax on any E II 8 229 95
Miss Woodhouse and Miss Fairfax were the only young-lady- E II 8 229 98
"I must have asked Miss Fairfax, and her languid dancing E II 8 230 102
"Oh! if I could play as well as you and Miss Fairfax!" E II 9 231 5
"I hope Mrs. Bates and Miss Fairfax are"----- E II 9 236 45
been assisting Miss Fairfax in trying to make her E II 10 240 5
I dare say, Miss Fairfax, that he either gave his friend E II 10 241 8
be enjoying your pleasure on this occasion, Miss Fairfax. E II 10 241 11
12
of a word--Miss Fairfax said something about conjecturing. E II 10 242 15
who was still sitting at it, to play something more. E II 10 242 16
He knew Miss Fairfax could have no music here. E II 10 242 21
How is Miss Fairfax?-- E II 10 244 35
Tell me how Miss Fairfax is." E II 10 244 35
I do not see why Miss Fairfax should not be mentioned too. E II 10 245 49
I think Miss Fairfax dances very well; and Mrs. Weston is E II 10 245 49
"You and Miss Smith, and Miss Fairfax, will be three, and E II 11 248 4
You and Miss Smith, and Miss Fairfax, will be three, and E II 11 248 4
spare even for your friends Miss Fairfax and Miss Bates? E II 12 260 26
or the pride of Miss Fairfax could endure such society and E II 15 285 12
We must consider what Miss Fairfax quits, before we E II 15 286 17
Knightley warmly, "Miss Fairfax is as capable as any of us E II 15 286 18
imagined, would rather disgust than gratify Miss Fairfax. E II 15 286 19
20
"I should not wonder," said Mrs. Weston, "if Miss Fairfax E II 15 286 21
does not talk to Miss Fairfax as she speaks of her. E II 15 286 22
23
may be sure that Miss Fairfax awes Mrs. Elton by her E II 15 286 23
Miss Fairfax, I dare say, would not have me if I were to E II 15 287 30
they waited for dinner, he was talking to Miss Fairfax. E II 16 292 10
information--but Miss Fairfax was an old acquaintance and E II 16 292 10
this morning, or I am sure you must have been wet.-- E II 16 293 10
11
As an old friend, you will allow me to hope, Miss Fairfax, E II 16 294 23
Miss Fairfax, of your being out this morning in the rain. E II 16 294 24
25
"My dear Miss Fairfax, young ladies are very sure to be E II 16 294 27
Miss Fairfax, you must not run such risks.-- E II 16 295 33
have proceeded to Miss Fairfax, but she was so deep in E II 17 304 30
"But Miss Bates and Miss Fairfax!" said Mr. Weston, E III 2 320 12
Miss Bates and Miss Fairfax, escorted by the two gentlemen, E III 2 322 18
Miss Fairfax, who were standing a little way behind her.-- E III 2 323 20
"That is easy--but Miss Fairfax does not disapprove it, I E III 2 324 24
"Come Miss Woodhouse, Miss Otway, Miss Fairfax, what are E III 2 331 57
a single look, at Miss Fairfax, which, from the admirer of E III 5 343 2
Frank Churchill placed a word before Miss Fairfax. E III 5 347 21
over the word to Miss Fairfax, and with a particular E III 5 348 23
sting of the last word given to you and Miss Fairfax? E III 5 349 27
"Between Mr. Frank Churchill and Miss Fairfax? E III 5 350 33
negative, though Miss Fairfax continued to assure her that E III 6 359 37
Miss Fairfax, who had seldom spoken before, except among E III 7 372 41
A very friendly inquiry after Miss Fairfax, she hoped, E III 8 378 7
inquiry of-- "where--may I ask?--is Miss Fairfax going?" E III 8 380 11
12
has been the person to whom Miss Fairfax owes-----" E III 8 380 14
"Miss Fairfax, I suppose, though you were not aware of it, E III 8 381 20
"And when is Miss Fairfax to leave you?" E III 8 382 26
"Miss Fairfax was not well enough to write;" and when Mr. E III 9 389 16
He very much feared that Miss Fairfax derived more evil E III 9 389 16
Churchill and Miss Fairfax are engaged;--nay, that they E III 10 395 32
with him about Miss Fairfax; and poor Harriet;--and for E III 10 395 36
good opinion of Miss Fairfax, I never could, under any E III 10 399 64
then induced Miss Fairfax to join her in an airing, was E III 12 417 4
merely to write to Miss Fairfax instead, and to defer this E III 12 417 5
his approbation to Miss Fairfax and her family, and did E III 12 417 5
up of the evil and the good I have done Miss Fairfax!-- E III 12 420 13
and her sense of past injustice towards Miss Fairfax. E III 12 420 17
that attention to Miss Fairfax, which was every way her E III 12 421 17
them no more; and Miss Fairfax, it was reasonable to E III 12 422 20
Fairfax and Frank Churchill, I have heard that already." E III 13 425 6
7
did not come till Miss Fairfax was in Highbury; and as you E III 14 437 8
Mrs. Elton gratitude for her attentions to Miss Fairfax.-- E III 14 439 8
much in love with Miss Fairfax, and she was so happy E III 15 444 1
Very true; he did not come till Miss Fairfax was here." E III 15 445 11
really attached to Miss Fairfax, and will soon, it may be E III 15 448 30
of this holiday of spirits in calling on Miss Fairfax.-- E III 16 452 7
reading aloud to Miss Fairfax, and return it into the E III 16 453 12
13
She was pleased, on taking leave, to find Miss Fairfax E III 16 459 45
46
"It is Frank and Miss Fairfax," said Mrs. Weston. E III 18 476 45
He stays till to-morrow, and Miss Fairfax has been E III 18 476 45
MISS FAIRFAX'S (16)
civil about the excellence of Miss Fairfax's handwriting. E II 1 158 11
and began a warm defence of Miss Fairfax's complexion. E II 6 199 10
"You know Miss Fairfax's situation in life, I conclude; E II 6 201 21
to say when you speak of Miss Fairfax's situation in life. E II 6 201 23
Miss Fairfax's sensations from you, or from any body else. E II 6 202 37
Quite otherwise indeed, if I understood Miss Fairfax's E II 9 234 33
acquainted with Miss Fairfax's situation and understand E II 15 283 6
you or any of Miss Fairfax's acquaintance here, any of E II 15 283 8
in the triumph of Miss Fairfax's mind over Mrs. Elton. E II 15 288 39
on Miss Fairfax's disappearance being explained. E III 6 366 74
much for Miss Fairfax's advantage and comfort as possible. E III 8 380 9
The answer was only in this short note: "Miss Fairfax's E III 9 390 16
17
Miss Fairfax's recent illness had offered a fair plea for E III 12 418 5
admitted into Miss Fairfax's confidence on this important E III 12 421 17
it was being in Miss Fairfax's confidence, and fancying E III 16 453 12
Emma, and trying, as he spoke, to catch Miss Fairfax's eye. E III 18 479 75
MISS FANNY (1)
said, "I do not quite know what to make of Miss Fanny. MP II 6 230 7
MISS FISHER (1)
Miss Fisher. S 6 389 1
MISS FRANCES (3)
Miss Ward and Miss Frances quite as handsome as Miss Maria, MP I 1 3 1
any private fortune, and Miss Frances fared yet worse. MP I 1 3 1
But Miss Frances married, in the common phrase, to MP I 1 3 1
MISS FREDERICA (2)
& I mean to give Miss Frederica a hint of my intentions LS 10 258 4
Miss Frederica therefore must wait a little. yours LS 19 275 4
MISS FREDERICA SUSANNA VERNON (1)
Miss Frederica Susanna Vernon, & if we consider that it LS 19 274 2
MISS GODBY (1)
more than one; for Miss Godby told Miss Sparks, that SS III 2 272 16
MISS GRANTLEY'S (1)
and I think it infinitely superior to Miss Grantley's." PP I 10 48 15
MISS GREY (8)
particular friend of Miss Grey herself, else I am sure I SS II 8 192 3
"The lady then--Miss Grey I think you called her--is very SS II 8 194 9
"Do you know what kind of a girl Miss Grey is? SS II 8 194 11
not be sorry to have Miss Grey married, for she and Mrs. SS II 8 194 12
forced calmness, "Mr. Willoughby's marriage with Miss Grey. SS II 8 199 36
his marriage with Miss Grey--it was no longer to be a SS II 8 199 37
But have you likewise heard that Miss Grey has fifty SS II 8 199 38
But everything was then just settled between Miss Grey and SS III 8 326 53
MISS GREY'S (2)
been since informed, is the name of Miss Grey's guardian." SS II 8 199 37
and at what warehouse Miss Grey's clothes might be seen. SS II 10 215 11
MISS H. (5)
we now & then, see things differently, Miss H.-- S 3 376 1
Sidney is a saucy fellow, Miss H.-- S 5 385 1
Miss H., if you will give me leave, I will read Diana's S 5 386 1
what think you Miss H. of Burns lines to his Mary?-- S 7 397 1
But Burns--I confess my Sence of his pre-eminence Miss H.-- S 7 397 1
MISS H. MATHEWS (1)
Mathews--Miss Mathews, Miss E. Mathews, miss h. mathews.-- S 6 389 1
MISS HAMILTON (4)
Miss Hamilton, now Mrs. Smith, had shewn her kindness in P IV 5 152 2
such a time; and Miss Hamilton, three years older than P IV 5 152 2
Miss Hamilton had left school, had married not long P IV 5 152 3
well-grown Miss Hamilton, in all the glow of health and P IV 5 153 6
MISS HAWKINS (16)
A Miss Hawkins--that's all I know. E II 3 173 27
A Miss Hawkins of Bath. E II 3 173 27
A Miss Hawkins"----- E II 3 173 27
state, that he was going to be married to a Miss Hawkins. E II 3 174 32
Miss Hawkins,--I dare say, an excellent young woman. E II 3 175 39
Now, here will be Mr. Elton and Miss Hawkins; and there E II 3 175 39
to who, or what Miss Hawkins is, or how long he has been E II 3 175 39
40
your being indifferent about Mr. Elton and Miss Hawkins." E II 3 175 42
A Miss Hawkins.-- E II 3 176 44
Mr. Elton, and Miss Hawkins.-- E II 3 177 50
to this fortunate Miss Hawkins, which could conduce to E II 3 180 57
Miss Hawkins was the youngest of the two daughters of a E II 4 183 9
wind-up of the history; that was the glory of Miss Hawkins. E II 4 183 9
Miss Hawkins perhaps wanted a home, and thought this the E II 14 271 14
who were; but Miss Hawkins, it might be fairly supposed E II 14 272 17
and conceived Miss Hawkins to have held such a place in E II 15 281 1
MISS HAWKINS'S (2)
A week had not passed since Miss Hawkins's name was first E II 4 181 2
repetitions of Miss Hawkins's happiness, and continual E II 4 184 10
MISS HAYTERS (1)
The Miss Hayters, the females of the family of cousins P III 8 71 57

MISS HEYWOOD (9)
have such a member among them I beleive Miss Heywood.-- S 4 382 1
can you, loveliest Miss Heywood--(speaking with an air of S 7 398 1
Miss Heywood, or any other young woman with any S 8 405 2
Miss Heywood must have seen our carriage standing at the S 9 407 1
I knew Miss Heywood the moment I saw her before me on the S 9 407 1
a week certain.-- Miss Heywood, I astonish you.-- you S 9 410 1
But my dear Miss Heywood, we are sent into this world to S 9 410 1
besides, he only wanted it now for Miss Heywood.-- S 10 417 1
proper address to Miss Heywood on her being named to him-- S 12 425 1
MISS HEYWOOD'S (1)
"Happy, happy wind, to engage Miss Heywood's thoughts!--" S 7 398 1
MISS JANE FAIRFAX (2)
I like old friends; and Miss Jane Fairfax is a very pretty E II 3 171 12
"You are acquainted with Miss Jane Fairfax, sir, are you?" E II 5 194 45
MISS JULIA (2)
"Oh! dear--Miss Julia and Mr. Crawford. MP I 12 118 18
steady young man, so I hope Miss Julia will be very happy." MP I 12 118 20
MISS JULIA BERTRAM (1)
it was calling his attention from Miss Julia Bertram. MP I 6 60 53
MISS KING (5)
Then, the two third he danced with Miss King, and the two PP I 3 13 16
towards him; they are even impartial towards Miss King. PP II 3 150 29
Elizabeth," she added, "what sort of girl is Miss King? PP II 4 153 8
"If you will only tell me what sort of girl Miss King is, PP II 4 153 10
His attentions to Miss King were now the consequence of PP II 13 207 6
MISS L. (2)
Mrs G. would not allow Miss L. to have the smallest S 11 422 1
"Miss L. was under the constant care of an experienced S 11 422 1
MISS LAMBE (7)
account of a certain Miss Lambe a young lady (probably a S 9 409 1
Miss Lambe has an immense fortune--richer than all the S 9 409 1
Miss Lambe too!--a young Westindian of large fortune.-- S 10 419 1
under her care, a Miss Lambe, a young W. Indian of large S 10 419 1
Of these three, & indeed of all, Miss Lambe was beyond S 11 421 1
In Miss Lambe, here was the very young lady, sickly & rich, S 11 422 1
Mrs G.-- to encourage Miss Lambe in taking her first Dip. S 12 424 1
MISS LAMBE'S (1)
like Sanditon, on Miss Lambe's account--and the Miss Bs--, S 11 421 1
MISS LAROLLES (2)
herself with Miss Larolles, the inimitable Miss Larolles,-- P IV 8 189 46
the inimitable Miss Larolles,--but still she did it, and P IV 8 189 46
MISS LEE (9)
be just the same to Miss Lee, whether she has three girls MP I 1 9 12
It will be much the best place for her, so near Miss Lee, MP I 1 9 12
with her cousins; if Miss Lee taught her nothing, she MP I 1 10 15
noticing her shyness; Miss Lee wondered at her ignorance, MP I 2 14 8
Miss Lee taught her French, and heard her read the daily MP I 2 22 35
Miss Lee any longer, when Fanny goes to live with you?" MP I 3 28 38
39
of the family; and as Miss Lee had left Mansfield, she MP I 4 35 6
There Miss Lee had lived, and there they had read and MP I 15 150 1
had spoken for her, or Miss Lee had been encouraging, or MP I 16 152 2
MISS LETITIA'S (1)
instrument, & on Miss Letitia's, of curiosity & rapture in S 11 421 1
MISS LIZZY (1)
But I tell you what, Miss Lizzy, if you take it into your PP I 20 113 28
MISS LIZZY'S (1)
Never mind Miss Lizzy's hair." PP III 13 344 7
MISS LOUISA (3)
in being allowed to go and help nurse dear Miss Louisa. P IV 1 121 3
"Ay, ay, Miss Louisa Musgrove, that is the name. P IV 6 171 33
Well, this Miss Louisa, we all thought, you know, was to P IV 6 171 33
MISS LUCAS (23)
First of all, he asked Miss Lucas. PP I 3 13 16
said Mrs. Bennet with civil self-command to Miss Lucas. PP I 5 18 4
said Miss Lucas, "but I wish he had danced with Eliza." PP I 5 20 15
"His pride," said Miss Lucas, "does not offend me so much PP I 5 20 18
She mentioned this to her friend Miss Lucas. PP I 6 21 1
of speaking, Miss Lucas defied her friend to mention such PP I 6 24 17
18
will be her turn soon to be teazed," said Miss Lucas. PP I 6 24 21
withdrew to Miss Lucas; to whose inquiry after the PP I 18 96 56
She owed her greatest relief to her friend Miss Lucas, who PP I 18 102 73
subject, calling on Miss Lucas for her compassion, and PP I 20 113 26
"Pray do, my dear Miss Lucas," she added in a melancholy PP II 3 113 26
rest of the day to Miss Lucas, whose civility in listening PP I 21 115 1
day, was Miss Lucas so kind as to listen to Mr. Collins. PP I 22 121 1
Miss Lucas perceived him from an upper window as he walked PP I 22 121 1
its continuance; and Miss Lucas, who accepted him solely PP I 22 122 2
Miss Lucas called soon after breakfast, and in a private PP I 22 124 11
The steady countenance which Miss Lucas had commanded in PP I 22 124 14
15
Kitty and Lydia were far from envying Miss Lucas, for Mr. PP I 23 127 7
amiable neighbour, Miss Lucas, and then explained that it PP I 23 128 10
The sight of Miss Lucas was odious to her. PP I 23 129 16
and on Wednesday Miss Lucas paid her farewell visit; and PP II 3 145 11
had already been frequently seen by Miss Lucas and herself. PP II 7 170 6
Miss Lucas is married and settled. and one of my own PP III 11 336 49
MISS LUCAS'S (2)
On Miss Lucas's persevering, however, she added, "very PP I 6 24 22
Such was Miss Lucas's scheme; and appearances were so PP I 22 121 1
MISS LUCASES (2)
That the Miss Lucases and the Miss Bennets should meet to PP I 5 18 3
all to the younger Miss Lucases; and Lydia, in a voice PP II 16 222 21
MISS LUCY (2)
warmth than she felt, though with far less than Miss Lucy. SS I 21 122 14
"They come straight from town, as Miss Lucy--Mrs. Ferrars SS III 11 354 36
MISS LUCY STEELE (3)
of some use to Miss Lucy Steele, in rolling her papers for SS II 1 145 19
Miss Lucy Steele is, I dare say, a very deserving young SS III 1 267 45
lately married to--to the youngest--to Miss Lucy Steele." SS III 12 360 22
23
MISS LYDIA BENNET (2)
had Miss Lydia Bennet come upon the town; or, as the PP III 8 309 6
Esq. to Miss Lydia Bennet,' without there being a syllable PP III 11 336 49
MISS LYDIA'S (1)
bows, in spite of Miss Lydia's pressing entreaties that PP I 15 73 10
MISS MADDOXES (1)
about one of the Miss Maddoxes, or what it was that Lady MP II 11 283 4
MISS MANWARING (8)
a little notice in order to detach him from Miss Manwaring. LS 2 244 1
man engaged to Miss Manwaring distractedly in love with LS 11 259 1
Miss Manwaring's lover was scarcely better founded. LS 14 264 4
It is well known that Miss Manwaring is absolutely on the LS 14 264 4
how warmly Miss Manwaring resented her lover's defection, LS 14 265 4
said she had been at pains to detach from Miss Manwaring. LS 20 275 2
Miss Manwaring is just come to town to be with her aunt, & LS 38 307 3
can pity only Miss Manwaring, who coming to town & putting LS 42 313 10
MISS MARGARET (1)
"Oh! pray, Miss Margaret, let us know all about it," said SS I 12 61 21
MISS MARGT (2)
Miss Penelope & Miss Margt were, when he first came in?-- W 347 22
How long have you been in the country Miss Margt?"-- W 356 28
MISS MARIA WARD (1)
About thirty years ago, Miss Maria Ward of Huntingdon, MP I 1 3 1
MISS MARIANNE (16)
Miss Marianne must not expect to have all the men to SS I 9 44 23
I hope you like your house, Miss Marianne. SS I 13 67 64
"And that will tempt you, Miss Marianne." SS I 18 99 18
"I am afraid, Miss Marianne," said Sir John, "you have not SS I 20 111 10
"I have a notion," said Sir John, "that Miss Marianne SS II 3 154 3
Come, Miss Marianne, let us strike hands upon the bargain, SS II 3 154 4
Your friend Miss Marianne, too--which you will not be SS II 4 163 18
but as for Miss Marianne, she is quite an altered creature. SS II 7 181 8
But there is one comfort, my dear Miss Marianne; he is not SS II 8 192 3
I warrant you, Miss Marianne would have been ready to wait SS II 8 194 10
"Perhaps, Miss Marianne," cried Lucy, eager to take some SS II 13 243 38
Good bye; I am sorry Miss Marianne was not here. SS III 2 276 25
to see them, and love to Miss Marianne, I am, &c. &c. SS III 2 278 30
The servant, who saw only that Miss Marianne was taken ill, SS III 11 353 25
especially Miss Marianne, and bid me I should give her SS III 11 354 27
him to Barton, and Miss Marianne must try to comfort him." SS III 13 371 37
MISS MARIANNE'S (1)
glad of Miss Marianne's company, whether Miss Dashwood SS II 3 154 4
MISS MARTIN (2)
I shall always have a great regard for the Miss Martins, E I 4 31 25
She came solitarily down the gravel walk-- a Miss Martin E II 5 186 3
MISS MATHEWS (1)
Mathews--Miss Mathews, Miss E. Mathews, miss h. mathews.-- S 6 389 1
MISS MERRYWEATHER (1)
Mrs Davis. & Miss Merryweather.-- S 6 389 1
MISS MORLAND (55)
woman, fond of Miss Morland, and probably aware that if NA I 1 17 12
below; and hence Miss Morland had a comprehensive view of NA I 2 21 9
"Well, Miss Morland," said he, directly, "I hope you have NA I 2 23 23
Allen; "and so I told Miss Morland when she bought it." NA I 3 28 44
account or other; Miss Morland will get enough out of it NA I 3 28 45
The Miss Thorpes were introduced; and Miss Morland, who NA I 4 32 4
rest, "how excessively like her brother Miss Morland is!" NA I 4 32 4
years older than Miss Morland, and at least four years NA I 4 33 7
should accompany Miss Morland to the very door of Mr. NA I 4 34 7
think we have been running it from Tetbury, Miss Morland?" NA I 7 45 5
out of my senses, Miss Morland; do but look at my horse; NA I 7 46 9
What do you think of my gig, Miss Morland? a neat one, is NA I 7 46 11
And how much do you think he did, Miss Morland?" NA I 7 46 11
find, however, Miss Morland, it would be reckoned a cheap NA I 7 47 19
Are you fond of an open carriage, Miss Morland?" NA I 7 47 21
"I beg your pardon, Miss Morland," said she, "for this NA I 8 55 10
of such goodness, Miss Morland with the real delicacy of a NA I 8 55 10
and said, "well, Miss Morland, I suppose you and I are to NA I 8 59 35
up stairs, calling out, "well, Miss Morland, here I am. NA I 9 61 1
Come, Miss Morland, be quick, for the others are in a NA I 9 61 1
"You will not be frightened, Miss Morland," said Thorpe, NA I 9 62 9
"Hey-day, Miss Morland!" said he, "what is the meaning of NA I 10 75 25
the stairs he was calling out to Miss Morland to be quick. NA I 11 84 18
You see, Miss Morland, the injustice of your suspicions. NA I 14 107 9
Miss Morland, he is treating you exactly as he does his NA I 14 107 14
Come, Miss Morland, let us leave him to meditate over our NA I 14 108 17
"Miss Morland, do not mind what he says;--but have the NA I 14 112 37
Miss Morland has been talking of nothing more dreadful NA I 14 113 39
And you, Miss Morland--my stupid sister has mistaken all NA I 14 113 39
may as well make Miss Morland understand yourself--unless NA I 14 113 40
Miss Morland is not used to your odd ways." NA I 14 113 40
"Miss Morland, I think very highly of the understanding of NA I 14 113 45
"Miss Morland, no one can think more highly of the NA I 14 114 47
shall get nothing more serious from him now, Miss Morland. NA I 14 114 48
"Well, Miss Morland," said he, on finding her alone in the NA I 15 122 29
What do you think of it, Miss Morland? NA I 15 122 30
"But I say, Miss Morland, I shall come and pay my respects NA I 15 123 40
"And I hope--I hope, Miss Morland, you will not be sorry NA I 15 123 42
But I have a notion, Miss Morland, you and I think pretty NA I 15 124 44
My daughter, Miss Morland," he continued, without leaving NA II 2 139 7
"My dear Miss Morland," said Henry, "in this amiable NA II 4 152 28
with parcels, that Miss Morland would not have room to sit; NA II 5 155 4
to be of use to Miss Morland; and though Catherine NA II 6 164 3
It is a family living, Miss Morland; and the property in NA II 7 176 15
sure your father, Miss Morland, would agree with me in NA II 7 176 15
extension of their walk, if Miss Morland were not tired. NA II 7 179 27
Miss Morland will get wet. NA II 7 179 27
information of Miss Morland, as to what she neither NA II 8 183 3
Had not Miss Morland already seen all that could be worth NA II 8 185 6
Dear Miss Morland, consider the dreadful nature of the NA II 9 197 29
Dearest Miss Morland, what ideas have you been admitting?" NA II 9 198 29
is a rule with me, Miss Morland, never to give offence to NA II 11 210 6
attention to Miss Morland, had accidentally inquired of NA II 15 244 12
Already had he discerned a liking towards Miss Morland in NA II 15 245 12
as in affection to Miss Morland, and believing that heart NA II 15 247 15
MISS MORLAND'S (8)
"And pray, sir, what do you think of Miss Morland's gown?" NA I 3 28 41
Yes, he certainly read in Miss Morland's eyes a judicious NA II 7 177 17
to a mind like Miss Morland's, a view of the NA II 8 184 4
making Miss Morland's time at Northanger pass pleasantly. NA II 11 209 5
for an hour of Miss Morland's company, and anxiously NA II 13 220 1
to be assured of Miss Morland's having reached her home in NA II 15 241 7
Morland's departure, and ordered to think of her no more. NA II 15 244 10
childless, of Miss Morland's being under their care, and-- NA II 15 245 12
MISS MORTON (13)
The lady is the Hon. Miss Morton, only daughter of the SS II 11 224 28
his marriage with Miss Morton was resolved on, or till her SS II 12 229 4
kind!--what is Miss Morton to us?--who knows, or who cares, SS II 12 235 34
35
bitter phillippic; "Miss Morton is Lord Morton's daughter." SS II 12 235 37
of his marrying Miss Morton; told him that she would SS III 1 266 38
a-year, (for Miss Morton has thirty thousand pounds,) I SS III 1 268 50
up a woman like Miss Morton, with thirty thousand pounds SS III 2 272 16
or of wishing to marry Miss Morton, or anything like it. SS III 2 273 16
a short pause, "of Robert's marrying Miss Morton." SS III 5 296 24
same to Miss Morton whether she marry Edward or Robert." SS III 5 296 28
be unable to marry Miss Morton, and his chusing herself SS III 13 369 33
him, that in Miss Morton he would have a woman of higher SS III 14 373 3
by observing that Miss Morton was the daughter of a SS III 14 373 3
MISS MORTON'S (2)
of its being Miss Morton's mother, rather than her own, SS II 12 232 14
are something in Miss Morton's style of painting, ma'am?-- SS II 12 235 31
32
MISS MUSGROVE (6)
be listened for, when the youngest Miss Musgrove walked in. P III 6 50 26
A most improper match for Miss Musgrove, of Uppercross." P III 9 76 13
any attendance on Miss Musgrove, there need not be the P III 12 113 56
The Miss Musgrove, on whom all this has been happening to. P IV 6 170 31
lady, this same Miss Musgrove, instead of being to marry P IV 6 171 33
I find, is bespoke by her cousin, the young parson. P IV 6 173 49
MISS MUSGROVE'S (1)
think, how long Miss Musgrove's recovery might yet be P IV 1 126 21
MISS MUSGROVES (20)
It did not happen to suit the Miss Musgroves, I suppose, P III 5 38 29
both the Miss Musgroves, at Mary's particular invitation. P III 5 41 46
with only the Miss Musgroves, one of them, after talking P III 6 46 10
either of the Miss Musgroves; but having no voice, no P III 6 46 13
something to the Miss Musgroves, enough to mark an easy P III 7 59 25
was gone; the Miss Musgroves were gone too, suddenly P III 7 59 25
for after the Miss Musgroves had returned and finished P III 7 60 31
32
He had a heart for either of the Miss Musgroves, if they P III 7 61 38
by the two Miss Musgroves, who seemed hardly to have any P III 8 64 4
she found the Miss Musgroves just fetching the navy-list,-- P III 8 64 7
alone: but the Miss Musgroves could be as open as they P III 8 66 17
air which he wished to give the Miss Musgroves an idea of. P III 8 72 58
Musgroves, as made them pleased to improve their cousins.-- P III 9 74 6
"I thought the Miss Musgroves had been here--Mrs. Musgrove P III 9 78 22
of Mary and the Miss Musgroves to make over her little P III 9 80 34
It was a very fine November day, and the Miss Musgroves P III 10 83 4
chosen by the Miss Musgroves, who evidently considered the P III 10 83 6

either of the Miss Musgroves, she should not try to hear P III 10 84 7
The Miss Musgroves were not at all tired, and Mary was P III 10 90 38
The Miss Musgroves agreed to it; and having all kindly P III 12 105 10
MISS MUSGROVES' (2)
times in the Miss Musgroves' company, and Charles Hayter P III 9 75 9
to accept the Miss Musgroves' much more cordial invitation P III 10 83 4
MISS NASH (12)
the three teachers, Miss Nash, and Miss Prince, and Miss E I 4 28 8
I am sure Miss Nash would--for Miss Nash thinks her own E I 7 55 40
I dare say Miss Nash would envy you such an opportunity as E I 7 56 41
Miss Nash had been telling her something, which she E I 8 68 58
a sick child, and Miss Nash had seen him, and he had told E I 8 68 58
him, and he had told Miss Nash, that as he was coming back E I 8 68 58
Miss Nash had told her all this, and had talked a great E I 8 68 58
Miss Nash, head-teacher at Mrs. Goddard's, had written out E I 9 69 4
Miss Nash has put down all the tests he has ever preached E I 9 75 26
he was going by, and Miss Nash came and scolded us away, E I 9 75 26
There are the yellow curtains that Miss Nash admires so E I 10 83 4
Miss Nash thinks either of the Coxes would be very glad to E II 9 233 21
MISS OSBORNE (12)
great; Miss Osborne perhaps, or something in that stile.--" W 319 2
her daughter Miss Osborne; Miss Carr, her daughter's W 329 9
Miss Osborne has been so very kind as to promise to dance W 330 11
On the other side of Emma, Miss Osborne, Miss Carr, & a W 330 11
the dance, while Miss Osborne passing before her, to her W 330 11
It gained her a broad stare from Miss Osborne & Miss Carr W 331 11
Do you think Miss Osborne will keep her word with me, when W 332 12
give than that Miss Osborne had not kept it before.-- W 332 12
From Miss Osborne & Miss Carr she received something like W 336 13
Miss Osborne is a charming girl, is not she?" W 340 19
her; but Miss Osborne & Miss Carr were likewise fair, & W 357 28
You have seen Miss Osborne?--she is my model for a truly W 357 28
MISS OSBORNE'S (1)
the prospect of Miss Osborne's second promise;--but tho' W 330 11
MISS OTWAY (2)
good Mr. Otway, and Miss Otway and Miss Caroline.-- E III 2 323 19
"Come Miss Woodhouse, Miss Otway, Miss Fairfax, what are E III 2 331 57
MISS OWENS (5)
How many Miss Owens are there?" MP II 11 288 24
"I know nothing of the Miss Owens," said Fanny calmly. MP II 11 288 29
"The Miss Owens," said she soon afterwards--"suppose you MP II 11 289 34
Owens settled at Thornton Lacey; how should you like it? MP II 11 289 34
"The Miss Owens--you liked them, did not you?" MP III 4 355 53
MISS P-- (1)
Miss P-- whom, remembering the three teeth drawn in one S 10 413 1
MISS P. (1)
persons in company, Miss P. drinking one sort of Herb-Tea S 10 416 1
MISS PARKERS (1)
do think the Miss Parkers carry it too far sometimes--& so S 5 388 1
MISS PENELOPE (3)
I see a look of Miss Penelope--& once or twice there has W 324 3
But did not you hear him ask where Miss Penelope & Miss W 347 22
I fancy she'll come back 'Miss Penelope' as she went.--" W 351 24
MISS PRICE (41)
"I begin now to understand you all, except Miss Price," MP I 5 48 30
But now I must be satisfied about Miss Price. MP I 5 51 41
Miss Price is not out." MP I 5 51 43
"Miss Price has a brother at sea," said Edmund, "whose MP I 6 59 45
"My dear Miss Price," said Miss Crawford, as soon as she MP I 7 68 18
Miss Price, I give way to you with a very bad grace; but I MP I 7 68 20
the young lady too, Miss Price, who had never been at MP I 8 76 4
hall, of mentioning Miss Price as one who would probably MP I 8 79 23
Crawford, "you have quite convinced Miss Price already." MP I 9 93 51
Miss Price has found it so, though she did not know it." MP I 9 96 71
"Miss Price all alone!" and "my dear Fanny, how comes this? MP I 10 97 2
"Or if we are, Miss Price will be so good as to tell him, MP I 10 99 20
"Pray, Miss Price, are you such a great admirer of this Mr. MP I 10 102 41
"No, my dear Miss Price, and for reasons good. MP I 11 109 19
you a better fate Miss Price, than to be the wife of a man MP I 11 112 31
manner, "I fancy Miss Price has been more used to deserve MP I 11 112 33
"never mind, my dear Miss Price--this is a cross evening,-- MP I 15 147 56
My dear Miss Price, I beg your pardon, but I have made my MP I 18 168 15
"if Miss Price would be so good as to read the part." MP I 18 171 28
Price dripping with wet in the vestibule, was delightful. MP II 4 205 3
nothing frightful in such a picture, is there, Miss Price? MP II 4 210 21
But Miss Price and Mr. Edmund Bertram, I dare say, would MP II 4 215 49
Mrs. Grant's shewing civility to Miss Price, to Lady MP II 5 218 18
"Yes, they have been there--about a fortnight, Miss Price, MP II 5 224 50
in the letters to Mansfield Park; do you, Miss Price?-- MP II 5 224 52
"We are unlucky, Miss Price," he continued in a lower tone, MP II 5 225 57
I think, Miss Price, we would have indulged ourselves with MP II 5 225 57
Miss Price, will not you join me in encouraging your MP II 5 227 65
her ladyship and Miss Price, and teach them, it was MP II 7 239 8
Thomas, as you have perhaps heard me telling Miss Price. MP II 7 247 38
in company who does not like to have Miss Price spoken of." MP II 7 251 61
Miss Price, known only by name to half the people invited, MP II 9 266 22
Who could be happier than Miss Price? MP II 9 267 22
But Miss Price had not been brought up to the trade of MP II 9 267 22
attic floor, when Miss Price came out of her room MP II 9 271 41
Is not there a something wanted, Miss Price, in our MP II 11 287 22
You don't speak, Fanny--Miss Price--you don't speak.-- MP II 11 289 34
been stumbling at Miss Price for at least the last six MP II 13 303 15
Baddeley, I am sure; Sir Thomas wants me, not Miss Price." MP III 1 325 60
"No, ma'am, it is Miss Price, I am certain of its being MP III 1 325 61
it is Miss Price, I am certain of its being Miss Price." MP III 1 325 61
MISS PRICE'S (1)
began to dance, to compliment her on Miss Price's looks. MP II 10 276 14
MISS PRICES (2)
himself of, if the Miss Prices were not afraid of the MP III 10 402 13
to consider the Miss Prices as his peculiar charge; and MP III 11 409 5
MISS PRINCE (1)
and Miss Prince, and Miss Richardson, to sup with her." E I 4 28 8
MISS PS-- (1)
The Miss Ps-- & Arthur had also seen something;--they S 10 414 1
MISS RICHARDSON (1)
and Miss Prince, and Miss Richardson, to sup with her." E I 4 28 8
MISS S. (1)
Miss S. writes word that she could not get the young lady LS 16 268 1
MISS SCROGGS (1)
Miss Scroggs.-- S 6 389 1
MISS SMITH (50)
not the young lady he danced with on Monday a Miss Smith?" NA I 10 73 13
be allowed to bring Miss Smith with her; a most welcome E I 3 22 7
welcome request: for Miss Smith was a girl of seventeen E I 3 22 7
The happiness of Miss Smith was quite equal to her E I 3 25 15
"You have given Miss Smith all that she required," said he; E I 6 42 2
"The expression of the eye is most correct, but Miss Smith E I 6 47 31
the placing of Miss Smith out of doors; and the tree is E I 6 48 39
stopt a moment-- "or Miss Smith could inspire him." E I 9 71 9
This is saying very plainly--'pray, Miss Smith, give me E I 9 72 15
"For Miss ----, read Miss Smith. E I 9 73 18
Smith was not better, by no means better, rather worse. E I 13 114 31
little friend, Miss Smith, and my son--and then I should E I 14 119 7
Churchill and Miss Smith making their party quite complete. E I 14 119 8
message to Miss Smith I shall be happy to deliver; but no E I 15 130 25
"Miss Smith!--message to Miss Smith!--what could she E I 15 130 26
upon his respect for Miss Smith as her friend,--but E I 15 130 28
his wonder that Miss Smith should be mentioned at all,--he E I 15 130 28
the last month, to Miss Smith--such attentions as I have E I 15 130 30
Miss Smith!-- E I 15 130 31
I never thought of Miss Smith in the whole course of my E I 15 130 31
sorry--but, Miss Smith, indeed!--Oh! Miss Woodhouse! who E I 15 130 31
who can think of Miss Smith, when Miss Woodhouse is near! E I 15 130 31
Smith?--that you have never thought seriously of her?" E I 15 131 34
I think seriously of Miss Smith?--Miss Smith is a very E I 15 131 35
alliance, as to be addressing myself to Miss Smith!-- E I 15 132 35
Had the same behaviour continued, Miss Smith might have E I 15 132 36
Miss Smith would do them the favour to eat a piece too." E II 1 155 4
How does Miss Smith do? E II 3 176 44
caring nothing for Miss Woodhouse, and defying Miss Smith. E II 4 181 3
gate again; and Miss Smith receiving her summons, was with E II 5 186 3
that she thought Miss Smith was grown, had brought on a E II 5 186 4
Miss Fairfax, and Miss Smith; but already, at dinner, they E II 8 214 13
She introduced him to her friend, Miss Smith, and, at E II 8 220 47
us your opinion of our new instrument; you and Miss Smith. E II 9 235 44
How do you do, Miss Smith?-- E II 9 236 44
Miss Smith, pray take care. E II 9 239 53
Miss Smith, the step at the turning." E II 9 239 53
Miss Woodhouse and Miss Smith; so kind as to call to hear E II 10 244 42
"You and Miss Smith, and Miss Fairfax, will be three, and E II 11 248 4
You and Miss Smith, and Miss Fairfax, will be three, and E II 11 248 4
He did not omit being sometimes directly before Miss Smith, E III 2 327 34
whom I should be very glad to see dancing--Miss Smith." E III 2 327 37
"Miss Smith!--Oh!--I had not observed.-- E III 2 327 37
"Knightley has taken pity on poor little Miss Smith!-- E III 2 328 42
43
Miss Smith, and Miss Bickerton, another parlour boarder at E III 3 333 5
after), as well as Miss Smith, were coming in during the E III 3 336 12
persuaded--Miss Smith, you walk as if you were tired. E III 5 345 11
to be our brother and sister, Henry, John--and Miss Smith. E III 18 471 20
and he followed with Miss Smith and Henry; and that at one E III 18 472 20
were in such a crowd, as to make Miss Smith rather uneasy." E III 18 472 20
MISS SMITH'S (7)
clever in Miss Smith's conversation, but she found her E I 3 23 10
of her part, and lessen the irksomeness of Miss Smith's." E I 6 46 25
one exactly the idea of such a height as Miss Smith's. E I 6 48 35
The naivete of Miss Smith's manners--and altogether--Oh, E I 6 48 39
"I do not offer it for Miss Smith's collection," said he. E I 9 71 11
I have ventured to write it into Miss Smith's collection. E I 9 82 80
were certain that Miss Smith's disorder had no infection? E I 15 125 4
MISS SMITHS (1)
"When Miss Smiths and Mr. Eltons get acquainted--they do E I 9 74 25
MISS SNEYD (2)
months, and Miss Sneyd, I believe, has never forgiven me. MP I 5 51 40
Poor Miss Sneyd! MP I 5 51 41
MISS SNEYDS (1)
Mrs. and the two Miss Sneyds, with others of their MP I 5 51 40
MISS SPARKS (2)
for Miss Godby told Miss Sparks, that nobody in their SS III 2 272 16
had nothing at all; and I had it from Miss Sparks myself. SS III 2 272 16
MISS STEELE (27)
"Poor little creature!" said Miss Steele, as soon as they SS I 21 122 11
was first broken by Miss Steele, who seemed very much SS I 21 123 21
prodigious beautiful place, is not it?" added Miss Steele. SS I 21 123 23
in telling the name, as Miss Steele had in hearing it. SS I 21 125 37
"Ferrars!" repeated Miss Steele; "Mr. Ferrars is the happy SS I 21 126 39
The manner in which Miss Steele had spoken of Edward, SS I 21 126 41
when alluded to, or even openly mentioned by Sir John. SS I 21 126 41
"Oh! that would be terrible indeed," said Miss Steele-- " SS II 1 145 21
"A great coxcomb!" repeated Miss Steele, whose ear had SS II 2 148 20
"Oh!" cried Miss Steele, looking significantly round at SS II 2 148 23
"Not in the stage, I assure you," replied Miss Steele, SS II 10 218 24
"There now," said Miss Steele, affectedly simpering, " SS II 10 218 26
would not, and Miss Steele was made completely happy. SS II 10 218 29
cannot see your sister, Miss Dashwood," said Miss Steele. SS II 10 219 37
"Oh, if that's all," cried Miss Steele, "we can just as SS II 10 219 41
distinguished; and Miss Steele wanted only to be teazed SS II 12 233 17
between them; and Miss Steele, with yet greater address SS II 12 234 24
Miss Steele was the lest discomposed of the three, by SS II 14 247 4
as only Miss Steele had curiosity enough to desire. SS II 14 247 5
it received from Miss Steele in the first five minutes of SS II 14 249 8
accosted by Miss Steele, who, though looking rather shy, SS III 2 271 5
"I am so glad to meet you;" said Miss Steele, taking her SS III 2 271 8
Elinor tried to talk of something else; but Miss Steele SS III 2 275 21
Miss Steele was going to reply on the same subject, but SS III 2 275 24
and fortunately she had heard his address from Miss Steele. SS III 3 283 20
morning in Exeter, and his lady too, Miss Steele as was. SS III 11 354 27
it was the youngest Miss Steele; so I took off my hat, and SS III 11 354 27
MISS STEELE'S (1)
on his taking Miss Steele's pocket handkerchief, and SS I 21 121 7
MISS STEELES (26)
attractions to the Miss Steeles, as he had been already SS I 21 119 5
he had been already boasting of the Miss Steeles to them. SS I 21 119 5
endurance of the Miss Steeles towards her offspring, were SS I 21 120 6
the alarm of the Miss Steeles, and every thing was SS I 21 121 10
by one of the Miss Steeles, who was on her knees to attend SS I 21 121 10
This speciman of the Miss Steeles was enough. SS I 21 124 32
Not so, the Miss Steeles.-- SS I 21 124 33
on the side of the Miss Steeles, their party would be too SS I 21 124 33
by making the Miss Steeles acquainted with whatever he SS I 21 125 34
The Miss Steeles, as she expected, had now all the benefit SS I 21 125 37
pleased with the Miss Steeles, or to encourage their SS I 22 127 1
After sitting with them a few minutes, the Miss Steeles SS I 22 135 56
knowledge of the Miss Steeles as to Norland and their SS II 1 139 1
be quite alone, except her mother and the two Miss Steeles. SS II 1 143 9
The visit of the Miss Steeles at Barton Park was SS II 2 151 43
and as for the Miss Steeles, especially Lucy, they had SS II 3 157 19
The Miss Steeles kept their station at the park, and were SS II 3 158 22
About this time, the two Miss Steeles, lately arrived at SS II 10 217 19
by her hearing that the Miss Steeles were also to be at it. SS II 12 230 7
convenient to the Miss Steeles, as soon as the Dashwoods' SS II 12 230 8
with which the Miss Steeles courted its continuance, SS II 12 233 16
and the two Miss Steeles, by whom their company was in SS II 14 246 2
myself to ask the Miss Steeles to spend a few days with us. SS II 14 253 24
you know; but the Miss Steeles may not be in town any more. SS II 14 253 24
He saw the necessity of inviting the Miss Steeles SS II 14 253 25
The Miss Steeles removed to Harley-Street, and all that SS II 14 254 28
MISS STEELES' (1)
Dashwoods of the Miss Steeles' arrival, and to assure them SS I 21 119 3
MISS SUMMERS (8)
under the care of Miss Summers in Wigmore Street, till she LS 2 246 1
to be attended to, while she remains with Miss Summers. LS 7 252 1
He is if possible to prevail on Miss Summers to let LS 15 266 4
in my life as by a letter this morning from Miss Summers. LS 16 268 1
If Miss Summers will not keep her, you must find me out LS 16 268 1
informing her that Miss Summers had absolutely refused to LS 17 269 1
had, but while Miss Summers declares that Miss Vernon LS 17 271 7
which prevented Miss Summers from keeping the girl; & it LS 19 274 2
MISS TAYLOR (41)
Sixteen years had Miss Taylor been in Mr. Woodhouses's E I 1 5 3
Even before Miss Taylor had ceased to hold the nominal E I 1 5 3
Miss Taylor married. E I 1 6 5
The want of Miss Taylor would be felt every hour of every E I 1 6 6
from them, and a Miss Taylor in the house; and with all E I 1 6 7
be accepted in lieu of Miss Taylor for even half a day. E I 1 7 10
to part with Miss Taylor too; and from his habits of E I 1 7 10
disposed to think Miss Taylor had done as sad a thing for E I 1 7 10
exactly as he had said at dinner, "poor Miss Taylor!-- E I 1 8 10
11
would not have had Miss Taylor live with us for ever and E I 1 8 12
Taylor to have somebody about her that she is used to see. E I 1 9 19
"Ah! poor Miss Taylor! 'tis a sad business." E I 1 10 28
please; but I cannot possibly say 'poor Miss Taylor.' E I 1 10 29
Miss Taylor has been used to have two persons to please; E I 1 11 34

sorry to lose poor Miss Taylor, and I am sure she will E I 1 11 36
Every friend of Miss Taylor must be glad to have her so E I 1 11 38
Ever since the day (about four years ago) that Miss Taylor E I 1 12 41
very good thing for Miss Taylor if Mr. Weston were to E I 1 12 42
Taylor, may be safely left to manage their own concerns. E I 1 13 44
portionless even as Miss Taylor, and to live according to E I 2 16 5
It was now some time since Miss Taylor had begun to E I 2 16 6
able to pity "poor Miss Taylor," when they left her at E I 2 18 12
giving a gentle sigh, and saying: "Ah! poor Miss Taylor. E I 2 19 12 13
There was no recovering Miss Taylor--nor much likelihood E I 2 19 14
Where Miss Taylor failed to stimulate, I may safely affirm E I 5 37 7
him a wife, I should certainly have named Miss Taylor." E I 5 38 11
she will be when she comes, not to see Miss Taylor here!" E I 9 79 58
"Ah! my dear," said he, "poor Miss Taylor--it is a E I 11 93 6
Every body must be aware that Miss Taylor must be missed, E I 11 94 14
have thought of Miss Taylor but as the most fortunate E I 11 95 19
If any body can deserve him, it must be Miss Taylor." E I 11 95 19
marriage with Miss Taylor--that if she were to marry, he E I 14 119 5
supposed that Miss Taylor had formed Miss Woodhouse's E II 5 192 29
reproach--"Ah! Miss Taylor, if you had not married, you E II 7 209 10
"Well, sir," cried Mr. Weston, "as I took Miss Taylor away, E II 7 209 11
Mrs. Weston (poor Miss Taylor that was) would suffer it." E II 11 252 30
'If Miss Taylor undertakes to wrap Miss Emma up, you need E II 11 252 37
voices; and nobody speaks like you and poor Miss Taylor. E II 14 279 54
is going to be to this new lady what Miss Taylor was to us. E III 9 387 10
Nature gave you understanding:--Miss Taylor gave you E III 17 462 7
single; and told of poor Isabella, and poor Miss Taylor.-- E III 17 466 29

MISS TAYLOR'S (8)
Miss Taylor's judgment, but directed chiefly by her own. E I 1 5 3
It was Miss Taylor's loss which first brought grief. E I 1 6 5
But she knows how much the marriage is to Miss Taylor's E I 1 11 38
it must be at Miss Taylor's time of life to be settled in E I 1 11 38
thanking her for Miss Taylor's merits, without seeming E II 5 192 29
Woodhouse's character, than Miss Woodhouse Miss Taylor's. E II 5 192 29
object, as I am sure poor Miss Taylor's always was with me. E III 9 387 10
I may, or, I have Miss Taylor's leave'--something which, E III 17 462 9

MISS THORPE (25)
Miss Thorpe, and take a turn with her about the room. NA I 4 33 6
almost forgot Mr. Tilney while she talked to Miss Thorpe. NA I 4 33 6
Miss Thorpe, however, being four years older than Miss NA I 4 33 7
it together, that Miss Thorpe should accompany Miss NA I 4 34 7
nods and smiles of Miss Thorpe, though they certainly NA I 5 35 1
the independence of Miss Thorpe, and her resolution of NA I 6 43 44
the bright eyes of Miss Thorpe were incessantly NA I 7 44 4
of such a girl as Miss Thorpe even you, Catherine," taking NA I 7 50 47
part, in praise of Miss Thorpe, till they reached Pulteney- NA I 7 51 54
any how get to Miss Thorpe, and Mrs. Thorpe said she was NA I 8 55 10
her brother driving Miss Thorpe in the second, before John NA I 9 61 1
in her to write to Miss Thorpe, and explain the indecorum NA I 13 105 40
overtook the second Miss Thorpe, as she was loitering NA I 14 114 50
thought her friend, Miss Thorpe, would have any objection NA II 1 132 16
she was very sure Miss Thorpe did not mean to dance at all. NA II 1 132 16
of dancing with Miss Thorpe to good-nature alone, NA II 1 133 28
I really think Miss Thorpe has by no means chosen ill in NA II 1 134 36
partiality for Miss Thorpe, and entreating him to make NA II 4 150 1
I have myself told him that Miss Thorpe is engaged. NA II 4 150 6
"Is it my brother's attentions to Miss Thorpe, or Miss NA II 4 151 10
that every thing is at an end between Miss Thorpe and me.-- NA II 10 202 6 7
His marrying Miss Thorpe is not probable. NA II 10 204 20
He has his vanities as well as Miss Thorpe, and the chief NA II 12 218 7
be much distressed by the disappointment of Miss Thorpe. NA II 12 219 15
She trusted he would never speak of Miss Thorpe; and NA II 13 222 8

MISS THORPE'S (8)
easy gaiety of Miss Thorpe's manners, and her frequent NA I 4 33 7
and watched Miss Thorpe's progress down the street from NA I 4 34 7
stilishness of Miss Thorpe's, had more real elegance. NA I 8 55 11
or Miss Thorpe's admission of them, that gives the pain?" NA II 4 151 10
own account or Miss Thorpe's, for supposing that her NA II 4 152 28
in which Miss Thorpe's name was included, passed his lips. NA II 10 204 18
began to inquire into Miss Thorpe's connexions and fortune. NA II 10 205 25
Moreover, I have too good an opinion of Miss Thorpe's NA II 10 206 31

MISS THORPES (4)
The Miss Thorpes were introduced; and Miss Morland, who NA I 4 32 4
were said by the Miss Thorpes of their wish of being NA I 4 33 6
The younger Miss Thorpes being also dancing, Catherine was NA I 8 52 2
The two youngest Miss Thorpes were by themselves in the NA I 15 116 1

MISS TILNEY (81)
Tilney with seats, as they had agreed to join their party. NA I 8 54 10
behind her, attended by Miss Tilney and a gentleman. NA I 8 55 10
to each other, Miss Tilney expressing a proper sense of NA I 8 55 10
Miss Tilney had a good figure, a pretty face, and a very NA I 8 55 11
of his partner; Miss Tilney, though belonging to it, did NA I 8 59 38
acquaintance with Miss Tilney, and almost her first NA I 9 60 1
desire of seeing Miss Tilney again could at that moment NA I 9 61 6
Miss Tilney was in a very pretty spotted muslin, and I NA I 9 68 42
and that Miss Tilney had got now, for they were put by for NA I 9 68 48
Catherine's resolution of endeavouring to meet Miss Tilney NA I 10 71 8
of speaking to Miss Tilney, whom she most joyfully saw NA I 10 72 8
Miss Tilney met her with great civility, returned her NA I 10 72 8
Miss Tilney could only bow. NA I 10 72 11
Mrs. Hughes now joined them, and asked Miss Tilney if she NA I 10 73 19
In chatting with Miss Tilney before the evening concluded, NA I 10 80 61
Miss Tilney, to whom all the commonly-frequented environs NA I 10 80 61
rain for Miss Tilney to venture, must yet be a question. NA I 11 83 16
cannot go indeed, for you know Miss Tilney may still call." NA I 11 84 18
and her brother to call on me to take a country walk. NA I 11 85 32
Catherine looked round and saw Miss Tilney leaning on her NA I 11 87 53
she impatiently cried, it is Miss Tilney; it is indeed.-- NA I 11 87 53
I must go back to Miss Tilney." NA I 11 87 53
there be any harm in my calling on Miss Tilney to-day? NA I 12 91 1
only put on a white gown; Miss Tilney always wears white." NA I 12 91 2
looked at the door, and inquired for Miss Tilney. NA I 12 91 3
The man believed Miss Tilney to be at home, but was not NA I 12 91 3
he had been mistaken, for that Miss Tilney was walked out. NA I 12 91 3
She felt almost persuaded that Miss Tilney was at home, NA I 12 91 3
but issuing from the door, she saw Miss Tilney herself. NA I 12 91 3
"Oh! do not say Miss Tilney was not angry," cried NA I 12 94 9
had left them for a few minutes to speak to Miss Tilney. NA I 13 97 1
She had that moment settled with Miss Tilney to take their NA I 13 97 1
I am engaged to Miss Tilney. NA I 13 97 1
"It would be so easy to tell Miss Tilney that you had just NA I 13 98 1
more affection for Miss Tilney, though she had known her NA I 13 98 2
I have been to Miss Tilney, and made your excuses." NA I 13 100 13
I must run after Miss Tilney directly and set her right." NA I 13 100 18
When every thing was settled, when Miss Tilney herself NA I 13 100 19
to put it off, I could have spoken to Miss Tilney myself. NA I 13 100 20
her engagement to Miss Tilney, to have retracted a promise NA I 13 101 25
she had spoken to Miss Tilney she could not be at ease; NA I 13 101 25
that moment, and hurrying by him proceeded up stairs. NA I 13 102 25
the message; and Miss Tilney had no scruple in owning NA I 13 102 26
was introduced by Miss Tilney to her father, and received NA I 13 102 27
Miss Tilney added her own wishes. NA I 13 103 28
"No; I had just engaged myself to walk with Miss Tilney NA I 13 104 30
"Yes," added Miss Tilney, "and I remember that you NA I 14 107 8
"Henry," said Miss Tilney, "you are very impertinent. NA I 14 107 14
"Historians, you think," said Miss Tilney, "are not happy NA I 14 109 23
Miss Tilney, to whom this was chiefly addressed, was NA I 14 112 30
"And now, Henry," said Miss Tilney, "that you have made us NA I 14 113 40
into the house, and Miss Tilney, before they parted, NA I 14 114 49
I dine with Miss Tilney to-day, and must now be going home. NA I 15 123 35
acquaintance with Miss Tilney, from the intercourse of the NA II 1 129 1
as heretofore: Miss Tilney took pains to be near her, and NA II 1 131 14
visited Miss Tilney, and poured forth her joyful feelings. NA II 2 138 1
stay, than Miss Tilney told her of her father's having NA II 2 138 1
"Perhaps," said Miss Tilney in an embarrassed manner, "you NA II 2 139 4
Miss Tilney was earnest, though gentle, in her secondary NA II 2 140 10
eager to make of Miss Tilney; but so active were her NA II 2 141 13
Her happiness in going with Miss Tilney, however, NA II 5 154 1
the door; for with Miss Tilney she felt no restraint; and, NA II 5 155 4
"Miss Tilney, she was sure, would never put her into such NA II 5 160 23
hurried away by Miss Tilney in such a manner as convinced NA II 5 162 27
quadrangle, before Miss Tilney led the way into a chamber, NA II 5 162 28
of surprize, when Miss Tilney, anxious for her friend's NA II 6 165 4
is not it?" said Miss Tilney, as Catherine hastily closed NA II 6 165 4
Miss Tilney gently hinted her fear of being late; and in NA II 6 165 5
on perceiving that Miss Tilney slept only two doors from NA II 6 167 9
been pointed out to her by Miss Tilney the evening before. NA II 7 173 5
Why was Miss Tilney embarrassed? NA II 7 177 18
"This is so favourite a walk of mine," said Miss Tilney, " NA II 7 179 28
Miss Tilney continuing silent, she ventured to say, "her NA II 7 180 33
Miss Tilney, understanding in part her friend's curiosity NA II 8 182 1
doors, which Miss Tilney, advancing, had thrown open, and NA II 8 185 6
Miss Tilney drew back directly, and the heavy doors were NA II 8 185 5
"No," said Miss Tilney, sighing; "I was unfortunately from NA II 8 186 12
proposed to Miss Tilney the accomplishment of her promise. NA II 9 191 3
Miss Tilney, at Catherine's invitation, now read the NA II 10 205 25
There was yet another point which Miss Tilney was anxious NA II 13 229 31
her promise to Miss Tilney, whose trust in the effect of NA II 14 235 14

MISS TILNEY'S (10)
they parted--on Miss Tilney's side with some knowledge of NA I 10 73 21
only a proviso of Miss Tilney's, that it did not rain, NA I 10 80 61
Such insolence of behaviour as Miss Tilney's she had never NA II 1 130 1
Tilney's concluding words, "by the end of another week!" NA II 2 138 1
Miss Tilney's manners and Henry's smiles soon did away NA II 5 154 2
This ill-timed intruder was Miss Tilney's maid, sent by NA II 6 164 3
she was stopt by Miss Tilney's saying, with a little NA II 7 177 17
short sentence of Miss Tilney's, as they followed the NA II 8 186 6
his figure so repeatedly, as to catch Miss Tilney's notice. NA II 8 187 13
Miss Tilney's meaning, in her own calculation! NA II 9 193 6

MISS VERNON (7)
Miss Vernon is to be placed at a school in town before her LS 3 247 1
I am glad to find that Miss Vernon does not come with her LS 4 248 2
worthy notice, & Miss Vernon shall be consigned to LS 4 248 2
to request that Miss Vernon might be immediately removed, LS 15 266 2
declares that Miss Vernon shewed no sign of obstinacy or LS 17 271 7
Miss Vernon to Mr De Courcy. LS 21 279 1
to interfere--Miss Vernon was mistaken in applying to me. LS 24 287 9

MISS VERNON'S (1)
to allow of Miss Vernon's continuance in her academy. LS 17 269 1

MISS W. (8)
"There was a reason for that--replied Miss W. changing W 316 2
"When first we knew Tom Musgrave, continued Miss W. W 316 2
"Penelope however has had her troubles--continued Miss W.-- W 317 2
my dear Emma, said Miss W., as soon as they were alone, W 341 19
give--& tho' charged by Miss W. to let nobody in, returned W 344 21
And here I can admit, that my manners to Miss W., in being E III 14 440 8
apparent devotion to Miss W., as it would have been E III 14 441 8
Miss W. calls me the child of good fortune. E III 14 443 8

MISS WALKER (1)
that one day Miss Walker hinted to her, that she believed SS II 8 194 12

MISS WARD (2)
as thought Miss Ward and Miss Frances quite as handsome as MP I 1 3 1
Miss Ward, at the end of half a dozen years, found herself MP I 1 3 1

MISS WARD'S (1)
Miss Ward's match, indeed, when it came to the point, was MP I 1 3 1

MISS WATSON (12)
As they splashed along the dirty lane Miss Watson thus W 315 1
"I see the likeness between her & Miss Watson, replied Mr W 324 3
the family but Miss Watson; but I am very sure there is no W 324 3
my dear Miss Watson, brings all his family upon you. W 333 13
leave my father"--"Miss Watson the only one at home!-- W 334 13
"I received that note from the fair hands of Miss Watson W 338 18
& what do you thing of Ld Osborne Miss Watson?" W 340 19
meal concluded, Miss Watson could not help observing how W 343 19
& I fancy Miss Watson--when once they had the inclination, W 345 21
able to tell the Miss Watsons, whom he depended on finding W 355 28
round the fire, & Miss Watson sitting at the best Pembroke W 355 28
from the beaufit by Miss Watson, the general voice was so W 357 28

MISS WATSON'S (2)
Such were the last audible sounds of Miss Watson's voice, W 321 2
go so often to Miss Watson's as they did when they first PP I 7 30 13

MISS WEBBS (1)
The Miss Webbs all play, and their father has not so good PP II 6 164 20

MISS WESTON (1)
She had been decided in wishing for a Miss Weston. E III 17 461 1

MISS WHITBY (1)
body, as soon as Miss Whitby could be hurried down from S 6 390 1

MISS WILLIAMS (6)
"Yes; it is about Miss Williams, I am sure." SS I 13 66 55
"And who is Miss Williams?" asked Marianne. SS I 13 66 56
"What! do not you know who Miss Williams is? SS I 13 66 57
Perhaps it is about Miss Williams--and, by the bye, I dare SS I 14 70 2
I would lay any wager it is about Miss Williams. SS I 14 70 2
and desertion of Miss Williams, the misery of that poor SS II 10 212 1

MISS WOODHOUSE (161)
Miss Woodhouse was so great a personage in Highbury, that E I 3 25 15
with which Miss Woodhouse had treated her all the evening, E I 3 25 15
"Six years hence! dear Miss Woodhouse, he would be thirty E I 4 30 19
Miss Woodhouse, I am not afraid of what any body can do." E I 4 31 23
as to be independent even of Hartfield and Miss Woodhouse. E I 4 31 24
together, as Miss Woodhouse must not be kept waiting; and E I 4 32 28
spirits, which Miss Woodhouse hoped very soon to compose. E I 4 32 28
Well, Miss Woodhouse, is he like what you expected? E I 4 32 29
Let me entreat you, Miss Woodhouse, to exercise so E I 6 43 14
"Miss Woodhouse has given her friend the only beauty she E I 6 47 31
as she could to ask Miss Woodhouse what she should do."-- E I 7 50 1
Dear Miss Woodhouse, do advise me." E I 7 51 10
Pray, dear Miss Woodhouse, tell me what I ought to do?" E I 7 52 16
Harriet said-- "Miss Woodhouse, as you will not give me E I 7 53 22 23
Dear Miss Woodhouse, I would not give up the pleasure and E I 7 54 26
He was afraid not even Miss Woodhouse"--he stopt a moment-- E I 9 71 9
"What can it be, Miss Woodhouse?--what can it be? I have E I 9 72 17
Do try to find it out, Miss Woodhouse. E I 9 72 17
Oh! Miss Woodhouse, do you think we shall ever find it out? E I 9 73 17
"Dear Miss Woodhouse"--and "dear Miss Woodhouse," was all E I 9 74 21
out?-- Oh! Miss Woodhouse, what can we do about that?" E I 9 76 37
"Oh! Miss Woodhouse, what a pity that I must not write E I 9 77 39
"I do so wonder, Miss Woodhouse, that you should not be E I 10 84 8 9
his, to induce Miss Woodhouse not to go to Mrs. Goddard's, E I 15 125 4
indeed!--Oh! Miss Woodhouse! who can think of Miss Smith, E I 15 130 31
who can think of Miss Smith, when Miss Woodhouse is near! E I 15 130 31
allow me to interpret this interesting silence. E I 15 131 32 33
himself; and if Miss Woodhouse of Hartfield, the heiress E I 16 135 7
a friend as Miss Woodhouse would have thought it possible. E I 17 141 8
up her place to Miss Woodhouse, and her more active, E II 1 155 4
she hoped Miss Woodhouse and Miss Smith would do them the E II 1 155 4
Ma'am," addressing her, "do you hear what Miss Woodhouse E II 1 158 12
You may guess, dear Miss Woodhouse, what a flurry it has E II 1 161 31
My dear Miss Woodhouse--I come quite overpowered. E II 3 172 24

"A new neighbour for us all, Miss Woodhouse!" said Miss E II 3 174 35
"Very true, Miss Woodhouse, so she will. E II 3 174 39
Miss Woodhouse," said Miss Bates, "four weeks yesterday.-- E II 3 176 44
Woodhouse lets me chatter on, so good-humouredly. E II 3 176 44
my dear Miss Woodhouse; but we really must take leave. E II 3 176 50
and the "Oh! Miss Woodhouse, what do you think has E II 3 177 52
Dear Miss Woodhouse! only think. E II 3 178 52
Oh! dear, Miss Woodhouse--well, at last, I fancy, he E II 3 178 52
think he was, Miss Woodhouse?)--for presently she came E II 3 178 52
Dear, Miss Woodhouse, I was absolutely miserable! E II 3 179 52
Oh! Miss Woodhouse, I would rather done any thing than E II 3 179 52
Oh! Miss Woodhouse, do talk to me and make me comfortable E II 3 179 52
caring nothing for Miss Woodhouse, and defying Miss Smith. E II 4 181 3
Woodhouse's character, than Miss Woodhouse Miss Taylor's. E II 5 192 29
Woodhouse revived the former good old days of the room?-- E II 6 198 5
beg your pardon, Miss Woodhouse, you were speaking to me, E II 6 200 16
We are in great hopes that Miss Woodhouse may be prevailed E II 8 216 16
Miss Woodhouse made the proper acquiescence; and finding E II 8 216 17
where sat Miss Woodhouse; and till he could find a seat by E II 8 220 47
Miss Woodhouse would do them the honour of trying it. E II 8 226 85
the evening, for Miss Woodhouse and Miss Fairfax were the E II 8 229 98
Miss Woodhouse looks as if she did not want me. E II 9 234 30
She says I fidget her to death; and Miss Woodhouse looks E II 9 234 30
I think, Miss Woodhouse, I may just as well have it sent E II 9 235 40
"My dear Miss Woodhouse," said the latter, "I am just run E II 9 235 44
I am sure Miss Woodhouse will allow me just to run across E II 9 236 46
For, would you believe it, Miss Woodhouse, there he is, in E II 9 236 46
Miss Woodhouse will be so good as not to mention it. E II 9 238 51
Pray take care, Miss Woodhouse, ours is rather a dark E II 9 239 53
Miss Woodhouse, I am quite concerned, I am sure you hit E II 9 239 53
What nonsense one talks, Miss Woodhouse, when hard at work, E II 10 242 15
Miss Woodhouse and Miss Smith; so kind as to call to hear E II 10 244 42
Miss Woodhouse and Mr. Frank Churchill; I never saw any E II 10 245 48
for I suppose Miss Woodhouse and Mr. Frank Churchill are E II 10 245 49
Oh! Miss Woodhouse, must you be going?-- E II 10 245 54
Churchill and Miss Woodhouse danced--for doing that in E II 11 247 2
A crowd in a little room--Miss Woodhouse, you have the art E II 11 249 18
"Well, Miss Woodhouse," he almost immediately began, "your E II 11 250 21
Miss Woodhouse, I hope nothing may happen to prevent the E II 12 258 5
Oh! Miss Woodhouse, why are you always so right?" E II 12 259 17
"In short," said he, "perhaps, Miss Woodhouse-----I think E II 12 260 29
Miss Woodhouse appeared more than once, and never without E II 13 266 5
it was just as Miss Woodhouse described--it was not worth E II 13 267 9
for Miss Woodhouse, whom she really loved extremely, made E II 13 268 13
Oh! Miss Woodhouse, how ungrateful I have been!" E II 13 268 14
"Well, Miss Woodhouse," said Harriet, when they had E II 14 271 6
(with a gentle sigh,) what do you think of her?-- E II 14 271 6
And now, Miss Woodhouse, I do not think I shall mind E II 14 271 15
No, indeed, Miss Woodhouse, you need not be afraid; I can E II 14 271 15
I assure you, Miss Woodhouse, it is very delightful to me, E II 14 273 19
Whenever you are transplanted, like me, Miss Woodhouse, E II 14 273 19
sort, you know, Miss Woodhouse, one naturally wishes them E II 14 274 28
that kind here, I suppose, Miss Woodhouse, every summer?" E II 14 274 28
however, Miss Woodhouse--(looking towards Mr. Woodhouse)-- E II 14 275 30
I assure you, Miss Woodhouse, where the waters do agree, E II 14 275 32
The dignity of Miss Woodhouse, of Hartfield, was sunk E II 14 276 33
You, Miss Woodhouse, I well know, play delightfully. E II 14 276 36
I think, Miss Woodhouse, you and I must establish a E II 14 277 38
as not even Miss Woodhouse would equal; and the greater E II 15 281 2
do, unimpeded by Miss Woodhouse, who readily continued her E II 15 281 2
to begin abusing Miss Woodhouse; and the enmity which they E II 15 282 3
"Jane Fairfax is absolutely charming, Miss Woodhouse.-- E II 15 282 5
Miss Woodhouse, we must exert ourselves and endeavour to E II 15 282 5
"Oh! but dear Miss Woodhouse, she is now in such E II 15 283 7
"My dear Miss Woodhouse, a vast deal may be done by those E II 15 283 9
disgustingly decorated with a "dear Miss Woodhouse." E II 15 284 11
If Miss Woodhouse would not be displeased, she would E II 16 291 5
Miss Woodhouse, he will, of course, put forth his best." E II 16 298 55
Ah! here's Miss Woodhouse.-- E III 2 323 19
Dear Miss Woodhouse, how do you do?-- E III 2 323 19
Woodhouse, you do look--how do you like Jane's hair?-- E III 2 323 19
the way, Mr. Frank Churchill and Miss Woodhouse followed. E III 2 325 31
Miss Woodhouse, who would be so very much concerned!-- E III 2 329 45
"Come Miss Woodhouse, Miss Otway, Miss Fairfax, what are E III 2 331 57
himself and Miss Woodhouse (for his neighbours knew that E III 3 336 12
thus began: "Miss Woodhouse--if you are at leisure--I have E III 4 337 1
2
However, I assure you, Miss Woodhouse, I wish her no evil.- E III 4 337 6
"Oh! Miss Woodhouse, believe me I have not the presumption E III 4 341 36
admirer of Miss Woodhouse, seemed somewhat out of place. E III 5 343 2
"Miss Woodhouse," said Frank Churchill, after examining a E III 5 347 19
Little expecting to meet Miss Woodhouse so soon, there was E III 6 362 43
but Miss Woodhouse was the very person she was in quest of. E III 6 362 43
Miss Woodhouse, we all know at times what it is to be E III 6 363 50
words, "Oh! Miss Woodhouse, the comfort of being sometimes E III 6 363 51
I am serious, Miss Woodhouse, whatever your penetrating E III 6 365 62
"Mr. Frank Churchill and Miss Woodhouse flirted together E III 7 368 3
Ladies and gentlemen, I am ordered by Miss Woodhouse (who, E III 7 369 16
"Is Miss Woodhouse sure that she would like to hear what E III 7 369 18
Ladies and gentlemen--I am ordered by Miss Woodhouse to E III 7 370 23
Miss Woodhouse must excuse me. E III 7 372 37
that can entertain Miss Woodhouse, or any other young lady. E III 7 372 38
say my daughter will be here presently, Miss Woodhouse. E III 8 378 6
"Ah! Miss Woodhouse, how kind you are!-- E III 8 378 8
us ungrateful, Miss Woodhouse, for such surprising good E III 8 379 8
you, Miss Woodhouse, but your kindness will excuse her. E III 8 379 8
'Oh!' said I, 'it is Miss Woodhouse: I am sure you will E III 8 379 8
Such kind friends, you know, Miss Woodhouse, one must E III 8 381 19
"Thank you, dear Miss Woodhouse. yes, indeed, there is E III 8 382 23
cannot venture to name her salary to you, Miss Woodhouse. E III 8 382 23
promised her niece on no account to let Miss Woodhouse in. E III 9 390 18
"Well, Miss Woodhouse!" cried Harriet, coming eagerly into E III 11 404 4
Dear Miss Woodhouse, how could you so mistake me?" turning E III 11 405 14
"Oh! Miss Woodhouse, how you do forget!" E III 11 406 22
"I do not wonder, Miss Woodhouse," she resumed, "that you E III 11 407 28
But I hope, Miss Woodhouse, that supposing--that if-- E III 11 407 28
I hope, dear Miss Woodhouse, you will not set yourself E III 11 407 28
such a friend as Miss Woodhouse, and only wanted E III 11 408 34
But as soon as she (Miss Woodhouse) appeared likely to E III 11 410 35
Woodhouse, to say whether she had not good ground for hope. E III 11 411 38
do I mention Miss Woodhouse; my father perhaps will think E III 14 438 8
My behaviour to Miss Woodhouse indicated, I believe, more E III 14 438 8
I cannot deny that Miss Woodhouse was my ostensible object- E III 14 438 8
Amiable and delightful as Miss Woodhouse is, she never E III 14 438 8
Whether Miss Woodhouse began really to understand me E III 14 438 8
When he came to Miss Woodhouse, he was obliged to read the E III 15 445 14
15
'Miss Woodhouse calls me the child of good fortune.'-- E III 15 447 28
Miss Woodhouse, it is impossible for me to express----- E III 16 453 9
not you think, Miss Woodhouse, our saucy little friend E III 16 454 16
17
of seeing you, Miss Woodhouse," she shortly afterwards E III 16 454 18
"Thank you, dear Miss Woodhouse, you are all kindness.-- E III 16 455 20
Elton, but to Miss Woodhouse, as the latter plainly saw. E III 16 457 34
Miss Woodhouse, this is not like our friend Knightley.-- E III 16 458 40
Indeed, Miss Woodhouse, (speaking more collectedly,) with E III 16 459 47
to thank you, Miss Woodhouse, for a very kind forgiving E III 18 476 46
47
a distance from her--is not it hard, Miss Woodhouse?-- E III 18 477 57
She hears us, she hears us, Miss Woodhouse. E III 18 480 77
to join the hands of Mr. Knightley and Miss Woodhouse. E III 19 484 11

MISS WOODHOUSE'S (11)
A likeness pleases every body; and Miss Woodhouse's E I 6 45 20
with Miss Woodhouse's help, to get a great many more. E I 9 69 4
that could give us so much pleasure as Miss Woodhouse's. E II 1 158 12
Woodhouse's character, than Miss Woodhouse Miss Taylor's. E II 5 192 29
and Miss Woodhouse's doing it would be more thought of E II 7 210 19
opinion of the instrument will be worth having.'-- E II 9 236 46
as you know, for Miss Woodhouse's beautiful little friend. E II 13 266 5
to accept dear Miss Woodhouse's most obliging invitation. E III 5 344 3
at the idea of Miss Woodhouse's presiding; Mr. Knightley's E III 7 369 17
the time of Miss Woodhouse's encouraging her to think of E III 11 409 35
Those were Miss Woodhouse's words, were they?-- E III 15 448 28

MISS'D (1)
when she was fortunately miss'd, pursued, & overtaken. LS 19 273 1

MISSED (38)
She seemed to have missed by so little the very object she NA I 8 59 35
having missed such a meeting with both brother and sister. NA I 9 69 51
her ability reached; and missed no opportunity of SS I 8 36 1
her the conversation she missed; although the latter was SS I 11 54 6
especially of Lucy, who missed no opportunity of engaging SS I 22 127 1
on by Lucy, who seldom missed an opportunity of SS II 2 151 42
disappointment in having missed you the day before SS II 7 187 39
40
had called; and still more pleased that she had missed him. SS II 12 230 5
but were not missed till yesterday morning at eight. PP III 4 274 3
at your surprise tomorrow morning, as soon as I am missed. PP III 5 291 60
Mr. Bennet missed his second daughter exceedingly; his PP III 19 385 2
could be only nominally missed; and Lady Bertram was soon MP I 4 34 1
was missed, they would have jumped with joy and envy. MP I 9 87 15
on the other, had missed Mr. Crawford grievously; and MP I 12 115 4
solitude of the east room, without being seen or missed. MP I 17 159 6
dreadfully she must have missed him, and how impossible it MP II 1 179 9
added little to its gaiety, they could not but be missed. MP II 3 204 33
Even their mother missed them--and how much more their MP II 3 204 33
work in such a state as to prevent her being missed. MP II 5 220 29
"You cannot doubt your being missed by many," said she. MP II 11 289 31
"You will be very much missed. MP II 11 289 31
said, "Oh! yes, missed as every noisy evil is missed when MP II 11 289 32
as every noisy evil is missed when it is taken away; that MP II 11 289 32
If I am missed, it will appear. MP II 11 289 32
was, that he should be missed, and he entertained great MP III 6 366 1
there she might be missed to a degree that she did not MP III 6 370 13
and in short could not really be wanted or missed. MP III 6 371 15
the conviction of being missed, by her best friends, and MP III 14 432 9
She knew that at times she must be missed; and could not E I 2 18 11
"Oh! papa, we have missed seeing them but one entire day E I 11 94 14
Every body must be aware that Miss Taylor must be missed, E I 11 94 14
She will be missed every moment." E I 13 114 35
to bed, and got back again, and nobody missed me.-- E III 2 329 45
"Will you be so kind," said she, "when I am missed, as to E III 6 362 44
Till they come in I shall not be missed; and when they do, E III 6 362 44
I would not have missed this meeting for the world. E III 18 479 72
sorry that she had missed the opportunity of seeing them. P III 5 32 1
them to distinguish the very set who may be least missed." P III 8 65 11

MISSENT (2)
one of which was marked that it had been missent elsewhere. PP III 4 273 1
The one missent must be first attended to; it had been PP III 4 273 2

MISSES (3)
mistresses and misses of Highbury and their card-parties. E II 1 156 6
She never misses, I know; and you must have seen her. P IV 9 193 10
But perhaps the little misses may hurt the furniture.-- S 6 393 1

MISSING (10)
Emma could not help missing the party, by whom she had W 336 14
concern in missing him; she really rejoiced at it. PP II 13 209 13
unemployed, felt all the right of missing him much more. MP I 12 115 4
"No, my dear, I should not think of missing you, when such MP III 2 333 26
And as to the not missing her, which under Mrs. Norris's MP III 6 371 14
the disappointment of her missing such an opportunity; and MP III 6 373 24
anger, nor from missing the luxuries of her former home. E I 2 15 3
do really prevent our missing her by any means to the E I 11 94 14
comfortless visit, and of their all missing her very much. E I 13 109 6
with, or rather missing, Mr. Elliot so extraordinarily. P IV 2 132 22

MISSIONARY (1)
of Methodists, or as a missionary into foreign parts.' MP III 16 458 30

MISSISH (1)
You are not going to be Missish, I hope, and pretend to be PP III 15 364 22

MISSPENT (1)
morning more completely misspent, more totally bare of E III 8 377 1

MIST (3)
could do was to throw a mist over it, and hope when the MP I 11 107 3
when the mist cleared away, she should see nothing else. MP I 11 107 3
decidedly, in spite of the mist; Miss B-- seated, not far S 12 426 1

MISTAKE (58)
There has been some very great mistake--we have been all LS 24 287 9
"But what was this mistake, to which your ladyship so LS 24 289 12
My dear Alicia, of what a mistake were you guilty in LS 29 298 1
mistake, why should you be so ready to take offence?" NA I 12 94 11
led me into one act of rudeness by his mistake on Friday. NA I 13 101 20
"I am come in a great hurry--it was all a mistake--I never NA I 13 102 25
thing like it, there must be some unaccountable mistake. NA II 3 144 11
It must be all and completely a mistake--for I did not see NA II 3 145 11
forgotten that he could mistake, and his assertion of the NA II 3 148 29
Yet, though smiling within herself at the mistake, she SS I 4 19 3
but surely there must be some mistake of person or name. SS I 22 131 29
possibility of mistake, be so good as to look at this face. SS I 22 131 35
"Here is some mistake I am sure--some dreadful mistake. SS II 6 177 10
such behaviour to mistake or misapprehension of any kind. SS II 6 178 17
be broken by any mistake or misapprehension of my actions. SS II 7 183 13
no space in a cottage; but this is all a mistake. SS II 14 252 18
The consideration of Mrs. Dennison's mistake, in supposing SS II 14 252 20
that the others were likewise aware of the mistake. SS III 12 358 9
"Yes--but--there was a mistake--I had misunderstood--I did W 337 14
"You mistake me, my dear. PP I 1 5 29
ma'am?--is not there a little mistake?" said Jane.-- PP I 5 19 11
and never open their mouths, quite mistake the matter." PP I 9 44 27
or mistake, whatever could not be otherwise explained. PP I 17 85 1
"La! my dear," said Maria quite shocked at the mistake, " PP II 5 158 15
Mr. Darcy related the mistake which had occasioned his PP II 9 179 26
Wretched, wretched, mistake!" PP III 4 278 18
"He made a little mistake to be sure; but it is to the PP III 13 350 50
You paint too accurately for mistake. MP I 5 49 35
Not a hope of imposition or mistake was harboured any MP II 1 175 1
"How comes this about; here must be some mistake. MP III 1 312 10
hear there has been any mistake, but the report is so MP III 14 433 13
Depend upon it there is some mistake, and that a day or MP III 15 437 3
"It is a mistake, sir," said Fanny instantly; "it must be MP III 15 440 15
cannot be true--it must mean some other people." MP III 15 440 15
Now she could see her own mistake as to who were gone--or MP III 15 441 19
not been the most direful mistake in his plan of education. MP III 17 463 8
I beg your pardon, perhaps I have been under a mistake. E I 7 52 13
with many people, but indeed it is quite a mistake, sir.-- E I 12 105 55
says it is entirely a mistake to suppose the place E I 12 105 55
I am exceedingly sorry: but it is well that the mistake E I 15 132 36
If I mistake not that was danced at Weymouth." E II 10 242 19
You could not give me a greater reproof for the mistake I E II 13 268 10
interposed with, "Oh! Mr. Weston, do not mistake me. E II 18 306 14
15
The mistake had been slight. E III 2 320 13
Dear Miss Woodhouse, how could you so mistake me?" turning E III 11 405 14
Mistake you!-- E III 11 405 15
each other now, without the possibility of farther mistake. E III 11 406 19
has been a most unfortunate--most deplorable mistake!-- E III 11 407 25
entirely groundless, a mistake, a delusion, as complete a E III 13 430 38

"You mistake me, you quite mistake me," she replied, E III 18 471 17
you, in the confusion of so many subjects, mistake him?-- E III 18 473 26
it as a prejudice and mistake, arising first form the P III 2 14 11
A moment's reflection shewed her the mistake she had been P IV 9 194 21
I am afraid there has been some mistake; and I wish you P IV 11 239 49
Do not mistake me, however. P IV 11 246 80
myself with; and if I mistake not, a strong sense of duty P IV 11 246 80
Your mistake is in the place.-- S 1 366 1
little awkward on being first obliged to admit her mistake. S 11 420 1

MISTAKEN (118)
You were mistaken my dear Alicia, in supposing me fixed at LS 2 244 1
It grieves me to say how greatly you were mistaken, for I LS 2 244 1
am much mistaken if a syllable of his uttering, escape her. LS 18 272 1
my mother; but I was mistaken; they have had a dreadful LS 24 286 7
some very great mistake--we have been all mistaken I fancy. LS 24 287 9
to interfere--Miss Vernon was mistaken in applying to me. LS 24 287 9
but I flattered myself that you would be mistaken." LS 24 287 11
I was mistaken, it is true, but I beleived myself to be LS 24 289 12
had perhaps been equally mistaken in each other's meaning, LS 24 290 13
madam, I cannot be mistaken; it is a long time since I had NA I 4 31 2
he had been mistaken, for that Miss Tilney was walked out. NA I 12 91 3
Thorpe has-----he may be mistaken again perhaps; he led me NA I 13 101 20
And you, Miss Morland--my stupid sister has mistaken all NA I 14 113 39
partner; but he is quite mistaken, for she would not dance NA II 1 132 17
your brother's comfort, may you not be a little mistaken? NA II 4 152 28
own inclination, under a mistaken idea of pleasing her; NA II 7 177 17
She could not be mistaken as to the room; but how grossly NA II 9 193 6
room; but how grossly mistaken in every thing else!--in NA II 9 193 6
"You are mistaken, indeed," returned Eleanor, looking at NA II 13 223 13
was not entirely mistaken in his object in wishing it. NA II 15 243 9
Under a mistaken persuasion of her possessions and claims, NA II 15 244 11
to have been totally mistaken in his opinion of their NA II 15 246 12
and I am very much mistaken if Edward is not himself aware SS I 4 21 15
"I rather think you are mistaken, for when I was talking SS I 8 39 17
subjection of reason to common-place and mistaken notions. SS I 11 53 2
"You are mistaken, Elinor," said she warmly, "in supposing SS I 12 58 4
cried out, "indeed, Marianne, I think you are mistaken. SS I 16 86 17
18
Surely you must be mistaken. SS I 20 115 49
you are very much mistaken, Lady Middleton; I am only SS II 1 144 12
"No, sister," cried Lucy, "you are mistaken there, our SS II 2 148 21
which could not be mistaken for one at any other house. SS II 4 161 7
ma'am," said Elinor, very seriously, "you are mistaken. SS II 7 182 11
the very excess of her mistaken confidence in Willoughby, SS II 9 203 9
wrong, formed on mistaken grounds, and that by requiring SS II 10 214 6
"You are mistaken, Elinor; you are very much mistaken. SS II 11 223 24
She will be mistaken, however. SS II 11 227 50
of hearing Marianne's mistaken warmth, nor to the SS II 13 245 47
"You are very much mistaken. SS III 4 289 35
began to feel, her own mistaken judgment in encouraging SS III 9 335 7
There, however, he is quite mistaken. SS III 9 338 20
He had just dismounted;--she could not be mistaken;--it SS III 12 358 8
I am sure she is mistaken, & that he will no more follow W 319 2
his house; and I am much mistaken if we shall not find a PP I 4 15 10
"Indeed, mama, you are mistaken," said Elizabeth, blushing PP I 9 43 24
"You are mistaken. PP I 10 47 6
present party; I am much mistaken if there are not some PP I 11 55 6
"You are much mistaken if you expect to influence me by PP I 18 95 48
my attentions have been too marked to be mistaken. PP I 19 105 8
at least could not be mistaken for the affectation and PP I 19 109 22
he must be entirely mistaken, and Lydia, always unguarded PP I 23 126 1
2
I am not ashamed of having been mistaken--or, at least, it PP II 1 137 24
"I shall not say that you are mistaken," he replied, " PP II 8 174 14
when she said, "you are mistaken, Mr. Darcy, if you PP II 11 192 23
24
If _you_ have not been mistaken here, _I_ must have been in an PP II 12 197 5
"Indeed you are mistaken. PP II 18 231 18
She dreaded lest the chambermaid had been mistaken. PP III 1 245 4
Elizabeth felt that they had entirely mistaken his PP III 1 258 73
The mischief of neglect and mistaken indulgence towards PP III 4 280 25
He generously imputed the whole to his mistaken pride, and PP III 10 322 2
"Indeed, you are mistaken, madam. PP III 14 353 25
You have widely mistaken my character, if you think I can PP III 14 357 61
what may, in a mistaken light, have given you uneasiness. PP III 16 365 4
ill-founded, formed on mistaken premises, my behaviour to PP III 16 367 12
I told him, moreover, that I believed myself mistaken in PP III 16 371 40
children of her own; but he found himself wholly mistaken. MP I 1 9 10
him how much he had mistaken his sister-in-law's views; MP I 3 30 57
it possible to be mistaken as to a girl's being out or not. MP I 5 49 32
Fanny supposed she must have been mistaken, and meant to MP I 12 116 11
I was sorry for _him_ that he should have so mistaken his MP I 13 122 2
he was mistaken _in_ supposing she would wish to make any. MP I 13 129 40
a curtain--and I am much mistaken if you do not find it MP I 18 167 11
but he was quite mistaken in supposing she had the MP II 3 200 21
Well, I am much mistaken if his lovely Maria will ever MP II 5 224 53
No, Mary, you are quite mistaken. MP II 12 293 10
"You are mistaken, sir,"--cried Fanny, forced by the MP III 1 315 19
tell her uncle that he was wrong--"you are quite mistaken. MP III 1 315 19
He deprecated her mistaken, but well-meaning zeal. MP III 2 332 19
who are always doing mistaken and very disagreeable things. MP III 2 332 19
Your ladyship is quite mistaken. MP III 3 339 20
found herself sadly mistaken, and that it was only a MP III 3 343 40
they were quite mistaken who wished you to do otherwise. MP III 4 347 18
"You are mistaken, Fanny. MP III 4 348 23
"Before the play, I am much mistaken, if _Julia_ did not MP III 4 350 29
She was mistaken, however, in supposing that Edmund gave MP III 16 452 15
I am much mistaken if Emma's doctrines give any strength E I 5 39 15
madness, if it is so; but I hope you are mistaken." E I 8 60 34
I am very much mistaken if your sex in general would not E I 8 63 44
in your life you would obliged to own yourself mistaken. E I 9 72 15
"I thank you; but I assure you you are quite mistaken. E I 13 112 23
you have been entirely mistaken in supposing it. E I 15 132 35
36
to feel yet more mistaken--more in error--more disgraced E I 16 134 1
self-interest to blind him, should have mistaken her's. E I 16 136 9
herself grossly mistaken and mis-judging in all her ideas E I 17 141 5
"you are very much mistaken if you suppose Mr. Perry to be E II 11 251 28
that Mrs. Weston was quite mistaken in that surmise. E II 12 258 6
He gave me a quiet hint; I told him he was mistaken; he E II 15 288 38
"I do own myself to have been completely mistaken in Mr. E III 2 330 54
You are quite mistaken. E III 6 365 64
"No, indeed you are mistaken."-- E III 10 393 11
And that you should have been so mistaken, is amazing!-- E III 11 405 18
She was proved to have been universally mistaken; and she E III 11 413 47
kind--but you are mistaken--and I must set you right.-- E III 13 426 14
15
disguised, or a little mistaken; but where, as in this E III 13 431 39
though the conduct is mistaken, the feelings are not, it E III 13 431 39
So it appeared to me at least, but I might be mistaken. E III 16 454 18
"Have not you mistaken the day?" said Emma. E III 16 456 28
Henrietta found herself mistaken in the nature of her P III 9 77 18
Do not you think it is quite a mistaken point of P III 12 103 2
"You are mistaken," said he gently, "that is not good P IV 4 150 17
Indeed you are mistaken there, sir. P IV 6 171 38
In the warmth of the moment, and under a mistaken P IV 9 198 44
How sure to be mistaken! P IV 9 201 63
that is all--or I may be mistaken; I might not attend;" P IV 10 223 39
She had not mistaken him. P IV 11 241 60
She must learn to feel that she had been mistaken with P IV 12 249 3
of the fact;--stay--can I be mistaken in the place?-- S 1 365 1
A common idea--but a mistaken one. S 1 368 1

& stay at Sanditon house, she will find herself mistaken.-- S 7 401 1

MISTAKES (7)
no time in clearing up these mistakes as far as I could. LS 24 288 11
dogs had repaired the mistakes of the most experienced NA I 9 66 31
her that his mistakes could sometimes be very egregious. NA II 3 148 29
myself in such kind of mistakes," said Elinor, "in a total SS I 17 93 37
the possibility of mistakes--but by everybody else Mr. PP II 1 138 31
speaking--stating the mistakes of the three others, or PP II 6 166 41
of circumstances, of the mistakes which people of high E I 13 112 23

MISTAKING (1)
walking the same way, but there was no mistaking him. P IV 7 179 28

MISTOOK (1)
"You quite mistook Mr. Darcy. PP I 9 43 24

MISTRESS (54)
time away; to be mistress of French, Italian, German, LS 7 253 1
Mistress of deceit however she appeared perfectly LS 23 284 6
Had I the command of millions, were I mistress of the NA I 15 119 18
maid, sent by her mistress to be of use to Miss Morland; NA II 6 164 3
Till she had made herself mistress of its contents, NA II 6 170 12
Of the way to the apartment she was now perfectly mistress; NA II 9 193 5
a nominal mistress of it, that my real power is nothing." NA II 13 225 19
Mrs. John Dashwood now installed herself mistress of SS I 2 8 1
to inhabit or visit it while such a woman was its mistress. SS I 4 24 20
"No, ma'am, for my mistress." SS II 5 169 18
to tell her that his mistress waited for them at the door. SS II 11 222 12
I should be very glad to get her so good a mistress. SS III 4 287 22
anxious to be alone, than to be mistress of the subject. SS III 4 287 23
her more, by hints of what her mistress had always thought. SS III 7 312 17
the inquiries of his mistress as to the event of his SS III 11 353 22
23
I _will_ be calm; I _will_ be mistress of myself." SS III 12 358 8
much attention, as _to_ be entirely mistress of the subject. SS III 13 368 31
the mistress of a family, and the patroness of a village. SS III 14 378 16
of his hopes, that a mistress for it might be found at PP I 15 70 3
as worthy of being the mistress of Hunsford parsonage, and PP I 17 88 14
Lucas should ever be mistress of this house, that I should PP I 23 130 17
her grandfather's death made her mistress of this fortune." PP II 4 153 12
felt, that to be mistress of Pemberly might be something! PP III 1 245 3
of this place," thought she, "I might have been mistress! PP III 1 246 6
to fetch his master and mistress home, instantly. PP III 4 276 8
as for Mary, she was mistress enough of herself to whisper PP III 5 289 41
the presence of such a mistress, but the visits of her PP III 19 388 12
his niece, to bring his mistress under his own roof; and MP I 4 41 15
"If the master and mistress do _not_ attend themselves, MP I 9 87 14
she had now for some time been _almost_ equally mistress. MP I 16 150 1
to show herself mistress of the room by her civilities, MP I 18 168 16
had taken place, which gave Sotherton another mistress. MP II 3 202 28
not to feel herself mistress of the rules of the game in MP II 7 240 8
And yet, I do not think I am a very difficult mistress to MP III 7 385 39
pleased as she was to be mistress of property which she MP III 9 397 7
the fortunate creature, who was now mistress of his fate. MP III 13 420 1
improvements till I know that it will ever have a mistress. MP III 13 423 2
and, supported by her mistress, was not to be silenced. MP III 16 450 10
been mistress of his house from a very early period. E I 1 5 2
Mrs. Goddard was the mistress of a school--not of a E I 3 21 5
no longer dreaded by the fair mistress of the mansion. E I 3 22 7
And ever since she was twelve, Emma has been mistress of E I 5 37 9
quite certain, and quite mistress of the lines, and then E I 9 72 15
women are half as much mistress of their husband's house, E I 10 84 15
bear to have the poor old vicarage without a mistress. E II 3 174 35
that neither "master nor mistress was at home;" they had E II 5 187 5
Jane Fairfax, who is mistress of music, has not any thing E II 8 215 16
Jane Fairfax mistress of the Abbey!-- E II 8 225 72
Thirteen years had seen her mistress of Kellynch Hall, P III 1 6 12
of the lodge, and to gladden the eyes of its mistress. P IV 1 123 9
that woman, who had been mistress of Kellynch Hall, P IV 3 138 5
regard you as the future mistress of Kellynch, the future P IV 5 159 25
and when her own mistress again, when able to turn and P IV 8 190 48
of seniority, and the mistress of a very pretty P IV 12 250 5

MISTRESS'S (5)
the house for their mistress's arrival; for as Lady SS I 5 26 6
every thing bespoke the mistress's inclination to shew, SS II 12 233 18
ladies, and the barking of pug in his mistress's arms. MP I 8 80 30
Here is the rivet of your mistress's spectacles out. E II 9 236 46
his mistress's head!--is not it, Miss Elliot!-- P IV 1 126 22

MISTRESSES (2)
and waited on by mistresses and maids, being also obliged MP II 4 206 3
mistresses and misses of Highbury and their card-parties. E II 1 156 6

MISTY (2)
or even notice through the misty glasses the last humble P IV 1 123 8
It was a close, misty morng, & when they reached the brow S 12 425 1

MISUNDERSTAND (5)
replied with a smile, "is wilfully to misunderstand them." PP I 11 58 32
"Sir, you quite misunderstand me," said Mrs. Bennet, PP I 20 111 5
I cannot misunderstand you, but I intreat you, dear Lizzy, PP II 1 136 14
Miss Crawford must not misunderstand me, or suppose I mean MP I 9 93 49
Did not you misunderstand him?-- E III 18 473 26

MISUNDERSTANDING (2)
he went to Oxford; and am fearful of some misunderstanding. NA II 12 216 2
I certainly have been misunderstanding you, if you feel in E I 7 52 13

MISUNDERSTANDINGS (4)
"There were misunderstandings between them, Emma; he said E III 10 397 47
that there had been misunderstandings he decidedly said. E III 10 397 47
by them; and those misunderstandings might very possibly E III 10 397 47
misunderstandings which he had given us hints of before. E III 12 419 12

MISUNDERSTOOD (14)
I have entirely misunderstood Lady Susan, & was on the LS 24 287 9
We misunderstood each other. LS 24 290 13
But I do assure you that he must be entirely misunderstood, NA I 14 114 48
I could not have misunderstood a thing of that kind, you NA II 3 144 11
disposition in such matters misunderstood by his children. NA II 11 208 1
Such was the sentence which, when misunderstood, so justly SS III 3 284 24
"Yes--but--there was a mistake--I had misunderstood--I did W 337 14
the best, and that his character has been misunderstood. PP III 4 273 3
inclined to hope, he might have been misunderstood before." PP III 5 290 48
character had been so misunderstood, and consequently that PP III 10 324 2
motives had been often misunderstood, her feelings MP I 16 152 2
she began, "that you could have misunderstood me! E III 11 405 18
as she had hitherto misunderstood even those she was E III 12 416 2
and he had "been quite misunderstood,"--and he had P IV 2 130 5

MISUSE (1)
misuse, when a knock at the door suspended every thing. P IV 3 142 17

MITCHELLS (2)
I know the Mitchells will not be there. NA I 11 90 63
We happened to sit by the Mitchells, and they pretended to NA II 12 217 2

MITE (2)
in the world to withhold my mite upon such an occasion. MP I 1 6 6
very glad that she had contributed her mite towards it." MP II 13 305 19

MIX (11)
entreaties that they would mix more in the neighbourhood, SS I 9 40 2
infirm to mix with the world, and never stirred from home. SS I 9 40 2
was as well fitted to mix in the world as any other man. SS II 14 250 12
to move; and if I do mix in other society it will be only SS III 10 347 30
Mary was obliged to mix more with the world, but she could PP III 19 386 5
if Edmund were not there to mix the wine and water for her, MP I 7 65 14
which nature had denied--to mix up an understanding for MP II 5 224 53
is much more advisable to mix in the world in a proper E II 14 275 30
many rooms as you like, and mix in the family as much as E II 17 301 18
Your neighbourhood is increasing, and you mix more with it. E II 18 311 46
Mr. and Mrs. Elton, indeed, showed no unwillingness to mix, E III 7 367 1

MIXED (12)
I doubt not) she must have mixed, or have been left in LS 27 296 1

Among the Alps and Pyrenees, perhaps, there were no mixed NA II 10 200 3
I do not much attend the balls, they are rather too mixed,- W 350 24
see each other in large mixed parties, it is impossible PP I 6 22 6
She was even sensible of some pleasure, though mixed with PP III 10 327 3
equal of every body she mixed with, but here she is with a E II 5 194 40
With mixed feelings, she seated herself at a little E II 8 227 87
for the sake of being in mixed company till bed-time, of E II 17 302 23
If meant to be immediately mixed with the others, and E III 5 348 21
across, for it was not mixed; and Harriet, eager after E III 5 348 21
staid at home, under the mixed plea of a head-ache of her P III 9 77 17
There was some anxiety mixed with Lady Russell's joy in P IV 1 123 10
MIXING (7)
in coming to Churchill, mixing more frequent laughter with LS 20 276 3
He then told me, mixing in his speech a few insolent LS 22 281 4
believed kept him from mixing in proper society, he SS II 14 250 12
attachment, especially by mixing more with the world, as SS III 13 362 5
mixing with them many instructions on execution and taste. PP II 8 176 30
her of mixing in society without having horses to hire. MP I 4 35 5
distinct, or very rarely mixing--and Emma only E I 12 100 15
MIXTURE (24)
it as a very happy mixture of circumspection & tenderness. LS 7 253 2
so thoroughly that with a mixture of true girlish LS 19 273 1
speedily paid, with a mixture of joy and embarrassment NA I 7 44 4
there was a general though unequal mixture of good and bad. NA II 10 200 3
Mr. Bennet was so odd a mixture of quick parts, sarcastic PP I 1 5 34
to be very bad indeed, a mixture of pride and impertinence; PP I 8 35 3
but there was a mixture of sweetness and archness in her PP I 10 52 52
There is a mixture of servility and self-importance in his PP I 13 64 18
made him altogether a mixture of pride and obsequiousness, PP I 15 70 1
feelings by this happy mixture of reason and weakness, she MP II 9 265 20
habits, that he could do nothing without a mixture of evil. MP II 13 302 10
impatience, a judicious mixture of all on the lover's side, MP III 1 320 44
in streaks, the milk a mixture of motes floating in thin MP III 15 439 9
I imagined I saw a mixture of many feelings--a great, MP III 16 458 30
presented a very sweet mixture of youthful expression to E I 6 46 24
Accordingly, with a mixture of the serious and the playful, E I 15 129 24
25
society, and a judicious mixture of home and amusement, E II 2 164 6
had been an interesting mixture of wounded affection and E II 3 179 53
mixture of pique and pretension, now spread over his air. E II 4 182 7
style to touch; a small mixture of reproach, with a great E II 4 184 11
inconvenience of such a mixture would be any thing, or E II 6 198 5
Little Henry was in her thoughts, and a mixture of alarm E II 15 287 24
It was but a card-party, it was but a mixture of those who P IV 11 245 78
exemplification of that mixture of character, that union S 3 378 1
MIZZLE (1)
when, because it began to mizzle, he darted away with so E I 1 12 41
MIZZLING (1)
worse than a thick mizzling rain; and having given a good NA II 5 161 25
MOAN (1)
is gone to her own room I suppose to moan by herself. SS II 8 195 14
MOANS (1)
once her blood was chilled by the sound of distant moans. NA II 6 171 12
MOB (3)
the card-room, and left them to enjoy a mob by themselves. NA I 2 20 9
pictured to herself a mob of three hundred men assembling NA I 14 113 39
You must get a brown gown, and a white apron, and a mob MP I 15 146 52
MOBS (1)
He must not head mobs, or set the ton in dress. MP I 9 92 45
MOCK (3)
"Dr. Grant is ill," said she, with mock solemnity. MP I 18 171 27
honour;" was Crawford's answer, with a bow of mock gravity. MP III 3 338 15
Miss Bates, deceived by the mock ceremony of her manner, E III 7 371 27
MOCKERY (1)
to censure those who "bear about the mockery of woe." NA I 1 15 4
MODE (14)
recollect on the different mode of life which she led with LS 6 252 2
nor splendour, for our mode of living, as you see, is NA II 2 139 7
this mode of approach which she certainly had not expected. NA II 5 161 25
Has my sister a pleasant mode of instruction?" NA II 7 174 10
choice as to the time or mode of her travelling; of two NA II 13 226 25
people are determined on a mode of conduct which they know SS II 14 248 6
the relief which a fresh mode of treatment must procure, SS III 7 312 19
indignation at such a mode of passing the evening, to the PP I 6 25 25
I believe, the established mode to express a sense of PP II 11 189 6
7
if you suppose that the mode of your declaration affected PP II 11 192 23
24
her to seek the other less interesting mode of attachment. PP III 4 279 24
curiosity as to the mode of her intelligence was all alive. PP III 5 284 13
journey, for when the mode of it came to be talked of, and MP III 6 372 21
would be; and perhaps the mode of it, the mystery, the E II 8 217 29
MODEL (14)
You have seen Miss Osborne?--she is my model for a truly W 357 28
that neighbourhood, and take Pemberley for a kind of model. PP I 8 38 35
he must always be her model of the amiable and pleasing. PP II 4 151 3
and it is so useful to have any thing of a model!-- MP I 15 139 6
He wished him to be a model of constancy; and fancied the MP III 4 345 3
you will be the perfect model of a woman, which I have MP III 4 347 18
idea of taking him for a model in dress; but (as Fanny MP III 10 402 12
be very safely recommended to take Mr. Elton as a model. E I 4 34 42
busy, might have been a model of right feminine happiness. E I 17 140 1
would make them the safest model for any young woman." E II 14 278 47
Maple Grove will probably by my model more than it ought E II 15 283 9
in whatever way he might choose to model his household." P III 2 13 7
by report, to the Admiral, as a model of good breeding. P III 5 32 2
in her temper, manners, mind, a model of female excellence. P IV 5 159 21
MODERATE (18)
admiration but what was very moderate and very transient. NA I 1 16 10
"my wishes are so moderate, that the smallest income in NA I 15 119 20
my dear Isabella, are so moderate, you do not consider how NA II 1 135 44
the rent so uncommonly moderate, as to leave her no right SS I 4 24 21
Your wishes are all moderate." SS I 17 91 5
"As moderate as those of the rest of the world, I believe. SS I 17 91 7
"And yet two thousand a-year is a very moderate income," SS I 17 91 14
consequently, after a moderate period of extravagant and PP III 5 285 18
had been more reasonable, her expressions more moderate! PP III 17 376 30
to be endured than an half-hour of moderate agitation. MP III 5 357 5
Where a man does his best with only moderate powers, he E I 13 111 17
and there, in the very moderate sized apartment, which was E II 1 155 4
his fortune was moderate and must be all his daughter's; E II 2 164 5
attraction to what is moderate rather than to what is E II 2 165 7
life appeared so very moderate, it was not unfair to guess E II 4 183 9
dignity of his line of trade had been very moderate also. E II 4 183 9
His ideas seemed more moderate--his feelings warmer. E II 6 203 42
He was steady, observant, moderate, candid; never run away P IV 4 146 6
MODERATE-SIZED (3)
An elegant, moderate-sized house in the centre of family MP II 4 210 21
Uppercross was a moderate-sized village, which a few years P III 5 36 20
passed close by a moderate-sized house, well fenced & S 4 379 1
MODERATED (1)
her to think of her cousin Edmund with moderated feelings. MP III 8 391 10
MODERATELY (4)
many--perhaps with most people, unless taken moderately. E I 2 19 14
our's, and eaten very moderately of, with a boiled turnip, E II 3 172 19
were of low origin, in trade, and only moderately genteel. E II 7 207 6
repeated--or two things moderately clever--or three things E III 7 370 23
MODERATION (14)
with a degree of moderation and composure, which seemed NA I 2 19 3
thing; her sorrows, her joys, could have no moderation. SS I 1 6 12
know no moderation, and leave him no sense of fatigue." SS I 9 45 28
proved no longer the moderation of his wishes, but his PP II 13 207 6
not avoid recommending moderation to her, as well in her PP III 5 288 39
the better; but then there is moderation in all things." MP I 2 13 5
moderation myself in being satisfied with the old butler. MP I 14 134 14
"By moderation and economy, and bringing down your wants MP II 4 213 40
"Moderation itself!" said Mary. MP II 6 231 10
but there should be moderation in every thing.-- MP III 1 312 12
him spoken of with cooling moderation or repellant truth. E I 17 143 15
of plan, the moderation in expense, or even the unselfish E II 7 205 1
While Lady Elliot lived, there had been method, moderation, P III 1 9 19
The more wine I drink (in moderation) the better I am.-- S 10 415 1
MODERN (25)
"Bravo!--an excellent satire on modern language." NA II 1 133 24
To pass between lodges of a modern appearance, to find NA II 5 161 25
was in all the profusion and elegance of modern taste. NA II 5 162 26
An inventory of linen, in coarse and modern characters, NA II 7 172 2
a room such as that, so modern, so habitable!--or that she NA II 7 173 2
furniture of a more modern date than the fifteenth century. NA II 8 182 2
not loitered here: every modern invention to facilitate NA II 8 183 3
use, and with modern furniture it would be delightful. SS I 13 69 76
there are others of more modern production which I know I SS III 10 343 9
to approve of every modern extravagance however sanctioned- W 323 3
drawing, dancing, and the modern languages, to deserve the PP I 8 39 50
It was a handsome modern building, well situated on rising PP II 5 156 4
in meaning to give it a modern dress, and I have no doubt MP I 6 56 26
man of education, taste, modern manners, good connections. MP II 7 244 27
which prevails so much in modern days, even in young women, MP III 1 318 39
invested even the house, modern, airy, and well situated MP III 15 447 36
The contrivances of modern days indeed have rendered a E I 13 115 37
neat and pretty; and the house was modern and well-built. E II 14 272 18
my taste than modern ease; modern ease often disgusts me. E II 17 302 22
the rest round the large modern circular table which Emma E III 5 347 18
Their children had more modern minds and manners. P III 5 40 45
Her first return, was to resume her place in the modern P IV 1 123 9
brings us to Sanditon--modern Sanditon--a beautiful spot.-- S 4 380 1
A little higher up, the modern began; & in crossing the S 4 384 1
formed on a more general knowledge of modern literature.-- S 8 404 1
MODERN-BUILT (2)
Cleveland was a spacious, modern-built house, situated on SS III 6 302 7
round, a spacious modern-built house, so well placed and MP I 5 48 28
MODERNIZED (1)
respectable, elegant, modernized, and occasional residence MP II 7 248 47
MODES (5)
relate of the different modes of dancing which had fallen MP II 7 251 63
observe in their various modes, till other subjects were E III 2 320 5
He was giving Harriet information as to modes of E III 6 361 40
up to, as regulating the modes of life, in whatever way he P III 2 13 7
fait as to the newest modes of being trifling and silly. P IV 5 155 9
MODEST (30)
her spirits were gradually raised to a modest tranquillity. NA II 10 199 2
is quite as modest and pretty behaved as Miss Dashwood's." SS II 2 148 23
"Lord! my dear, you are very modest! SS III 4 285 3
shew of good sense, a modest unpretending mind, & a great W 323 3
opinions tho' Margaret's modest smiles imported that she W 355 28
to the happy, though modest hopes which Jane entertained PP I 18 96 56
Bingley is most unaffectedly modest. PP III 16 371 45
you should always be modest; for, much as you know already, MP I 2 19 27
Girls should be quiet and modest. MP I 5 49 32
"A pretty modest request upon my word!" he indignantly MP I 12 119 26
She began, and Fanny joined in with all the modest feeling MP I 18 169 22
is the sort of amiable modest young man who wants a great MP II 2 188 3
not without some modest reluctance on her part, to come in. MP II 4 205 3
She was then merely a quiet, modest, not plain looking MP II 6 229 5
of it was so proper and modest, so calm and uninviting, MP II 7 246 37
and having with modest reluctance given her consent, MP II 8 258 17
She was attractive, she was modest, she was Sir Thomas's MP II 10 276 13
manners were the mirror of her own modest and elegant mind. MP II 12 294 16
that, however, in so modest a girl might be very MP III 1 316 32
thing in the power of her modest gentle nature, to repulse MP III 3 342 32
This is my modest request and expectation, for you are so MP III 14 433 13
horror, no feminine--shall I say? no modest loathings!-- MP III 16 455 18
No, my dear little modest Harriet, depend upon it the E I 7 56 46
for she is as modest and humble as I used to think him. E I 16 137 11
yourself;--I know what a modest creature you are; but it E II 17 301 16
making allowance for the modest drawing back of youth; and P III 1 7 14
Modest Sir Walter! P IV 3 142 13
her as one who is too modest, for the world in general to P IV 8 187 28
necessary to kindle his modest cousin's vanity; he found, P IV 10 214 12
soft blue eyes, a sweetly modest & yet naturally graceful S 6 391 1
MODESTEST (2)
"for he is one of the modestest, prettiest behaved young SS II 2 148 22
It is certainly the modestest part of the business. MP I 5 50 39
MODESTLY (4)
before;--and he then modestly owned that, "without any NA II 7 178 21
"I hope I am not ungrateful, aunt," said Fanny, modestly. MP I 3 25 13
Fanny could not help modestly presuming that her mother MP III 7 385 38
"Yes," replied Harriet modestly, but not fearfully--"I E III 11 407 31
MODESTY (22)
thing--even your modesty cannot doubt his attachment now; NA I 10 70 1
Modesty such as your's--but not for the world would I pain NA II 2 139 7
Modesty, and all that, is very well in its way, but really NA II 3 144 10
and perceiving that her modesty declined what her SS I 9 42 8
all out of charity with the modesty and worth of the other. SS II 14 250 12
Brandon, in spite of the modesty with which he rated his SS III 13 366 20
two do you call my little recent piece of modesty?" PP I 10 48 26
"Believe me, my dear Miss Elizabeth, that your modesty, so PP I 19 105 8
your modesty, economy, and other amiable qualifications." PP I 19 107 15
bashful modesty and the genuine delicacy of her character. PP I 20 110 1
But Bingley has great natural modesty, with a stronger PP II 12 199 5
to be sure; but it is to the credit of his modesty." PP III 13 350 50
there is no more real modesty in their behaviour before MP I 5 50 38
Fanny found that it was not to be, and in the modesty of MP I 12 118 22
expressed by any woman of modesty, that she could hardly MP I 14 137 23
gales dispense to Templars modesty, to parsons sense.' MP I 17 161 15
The gentleness, modesty, and sweetness of her character MP II 12 294 16
her at a moment when her modesty alone seemed to his MP II 13 302 9
as of person; whose modesty had prevented her from MP III 2 326 3
Emma was in the humour to value simplicity and modesty to E I 17 141 8
girl, with gentleness, modesty, taste, and feeling.-- P III 4 26 1
accomplished for modesty to be natural in any other woman." P IV 8 187 28
MODIFY (1)
difference to modify of all that "this indenture sheweth." P III 5 32 3
MODULATION (1)
of the voice, of proper modulation and emphasis, of MP III 3 339 22
MOHRS (1)
to the existence of nabobs, gold mohrs, and palanquins." SS I 10 51 23
MOIETY (1)
for the remaining moiety of his first wife's fortune was SS I 1 4 2
MOLLAND'S (1)
therefore, turned into Molland's, while Mr. Elliot stepped P IV 7 174 2
MOMENT (564)
have you encumber one moment of your precious time by LS 7 252 1
I cannot for a moment imagine that she has anything more LS 8 256 4
He caught all your fears the moment he had read your LS 13 262 1
My dear sir I have this moment received your letter, LS 14 263 1
this lenity, I have for a moment given up my plan of her LS 19 275 4
At that moment we were interrupted by a knock at the door; LS 20 275 1
must depend on that moment, I forced myself to give it. LS 24 286 5
At that moment, how great was my astonishment at seeing LS 24 287 8
Will you let me speak to you a moment? LS 24 287 8
if it had not at that moment occurred <to> me, that his LS 24 287 11
This idea struck me at the moment, & I instantly LS 24 288 11
by so little, as every moment that you can be saved from LS 24 291 18

Context	Work	Vol	Ch	Page	Para
on reading the note, this moment received from you.	LS		35	304	1
I shall count every moment till your arrival. S. V.	LS		35	305	1
must, at such a moment, relieve the fulness of her heart.	NA	I	2	18	2
of people were every moment passing in and out, up the	NA	I	4	31	1
For a moment Catherine was surprized; but Mrs. Thorpe and	NA	I	4	33	5
I should fire up in a moment:--but that is not at all	NA	I	6	40	14
more, for at the very moment of coming opposite to Union-	NA	I	7	44	1
was uttered at the same moment by Catherine; and, on	NA	I	7	44	3
be back in a moment, and then you may easily find me out."	NA	I	8	52	2
Let me look at her this moment.	NA	I	8	57	16
again could at that moment bear a short delay in favour of	NA	I	9	61	6
at one moment what they would contradict the next.	NA	I	9	65	31
his own life for a moment, had been constantly leading	NA	I	9	66	31
fact; to have doubted a moment longer then, would have	NA	I	9	67	33
morning; and till usual moment of going to the Pump-Room,	NA	I	10	71	8
heroine in this critical moment, for every young lady has	NA	I	10	74	23
John is just walked off, but he will be back in a moment."	NA	I	10	75	23
to each other till the moment of its dissolution; that it	NA	I	10	77	33
put on your hat this moment--there is not time to be lost--	NA	I	11	84	18
because I am engaged; I expect some friends every moment."	NA	I	11	84	19
"Well, I saw him at that moment turn up the Lansdown road,-	NA	I	11	85	37
Stop, stop, I will get out this moment and go to them."	NA	I	11	87	53
look after her, were in a moment out of sight round the	NA	I	11	87	53
moment she was herself whisked into the market-place.	NA	I	11	87	53
again to-day the moment he came into the billiard-room.	NA	I	12	96	20
She had that moment settled with Miss Tilney to take their	NA	I	13	97	1
At one moment she was softened, at another irritated;	NA	I	13	99	9
Left her this moment.	NA	I	13	100	15
that moment, and hurrying by him proceeded up stairs.	NA	I	13	102	25
Mr. and Mrs. Allen would expect her back every moment.	NA	I	13	103	28
Frederick Tilney, in the moment of charging at the head of	NA	I	14	113	39
Well, and so you guessed it the moment you had my note?--	NA	I	15	117	6
"that I quite doated on you the first moment I saw you.	NA	I	15	118	11
But so it always is with me; the first moment settles	NA	I	15	118	11
first moment I beheld him--my heart was irrecoverably gone.	NA	I	15	118	11
three lines, and in one moment all was joyful security.	NA	I	15	121	26
sensible of them for a moment--except just his asking me	NA	II	3	144	11
never suspected him of liking me till this moment?"	NA	II	3	146	17
her sisters every moment; so that her dearest Catherine	NA	II	3	147	28
are so, at this moment; but be as little uneasy as you can.	NA	II	4	152	28
heart; but that at such a moment was allowable; and once	NA	II	4	153	31
for her to forget for a moment that she was a visitor.	NA	II	5	154	2
made Catherine grow every moment more in awe of him, and	NA	II	5	156	4
in so favourable a moment for indulging it, you will	NA	II	5	159	19
Her fearful curiosity was every moment growing greater;	NA	II	6	164	3
a few inches; but at that moment a sudden knocking at the	NA	II	6	164	3
she dared not waste a moment upon a second attempt, she	NA	II	6	164	3
One moment surely might be spared; and, so desperate	NA	II	6	164	3
means, the lid in one moment should be thrown back.	NA	II	6	164	3
She paused a moment in breathless wonder.	NA	II	6	168	10
and her feelings at that moment were indescribable.	NA	II	6	169	11
rising with sudden fury, added fresh horror to the moment.	NA	II	6	170	12
The very curtains of her bed seemed at one moment in	NA	II	6	171	12
from the bed in the very moment of the maid's going away,	NA	II	7	172	1
joyful haste, and she was ready to attend him in a moment.	NA	II	7	176	17
and would fetch his hat and attend them in a moment."	NA	II	7	177	17
She stopped for a moment, and then added, with great	NA	II	7	180	34
The name of "Eleanor" at the same moment, in his loudest	NA	II	9	191	4
to lose a moment, she passed through and closed the door.	NA	II	9	194	6
The letter was one moment in her hand, then in her lap,	NA	II	10	203	8
and were at that moment deep in consultation about her.	NA	II	10	203	8
Upon looking round it then, she perceived in a moment that	NA	II	11	213	18
her admiration at the moment with all the honest	NA	II	11	213	21
other, she would at each moment of each day have been	NA	II	13	220	1
to the door, and the next moment confirmed the idea by the	NA	II	13	222	7
At that moment Catherine thought she heard her step in the	NA	II	13	222	9
doorway--and in another moment a slight motion of the lock	NA	II	13	222	9
which just at this moment seems important; but which I can	NA	II	13	225	21
thing to startle and recall them to the present moment.	NA	II	13	228	27
Catherine's pride in a moment, and she instantly said, "Oh,	NA	II	13	229	30
on the subject till that moment; but upon examining her	NA	II	13	229	31
by either, she paused a moment, and with quivering lips	NA	II	13	229	31
into the chaise, and in a moment was driven from the door.	NA	II	13	229	31
than she did at that moment; but he might forget her; and	NA	II	14	236	18
that moment in his power to say any thing to the purpose.	NA	II	15	242	8
for the grandeur of the moment, by doubling what he chose	NA	II	15	245	12
formed almost at the moment, to promote the dismissal of	NA	II	15	248	16
her husband's from the moment of his father's decease; but	SS	I	1	6	9
mother conjectured one moment, they believed the next--	SS	I	4	21	11
those words again and I will leave the room this moment."	SS	I	4	21	14
more especially at a moment when she was suffering under	SS	I	4	23	20
diverted from music for a moment, and asked Marianne to	SS	I	7	35	9
Marianne, after pausing a moment, "can never hope to feel	SS	I	8	38	10
which the exigence of the moment gave more than usual	SS	I	9	41	6
Marianne was softened in a moment.	SS	I	10	48	6
From that moment she doubted not of their being engaged to	SS	I	12	60	7
for observing at this moment, "that it rained very hard,"	SS	I	12	62	27
we are all offending every moment of all our lives.	SS	I	13	68	74
"Almost this moment."	SS	I	15	76	8
One moment she feared that no serious design had ever been	SS	I	15	77	19
It seems but the work of a moment.	SS	I	15	77	23
giving pain every moment to her mother and sisters, and	SS	I	16	83	1
be a gentleman; and in a moment afterwards Marianne	SS	I	16	86	16
					17
world who could at that moment be forgiven for not being	SS	I	16	86	21
Mrs. Dashwood was surprised only for a moment at seeing	SS	I	17	90	1
her contradicted one moment what a more animated look had	SS	I	18	96	1
to be true, so from that moment I set it down as certain.	SS	I	20	115	52
What felt Elinor at that moment?	SS	I	22	129	15
always thinking of every moment of my life, your	SS	II	2	146	5
moment of parting, her grief on that score was excessive.	SS	II	3	158	21
the room, pausing for a moment whenever she came to the	SS	II	4	166	33
be out in a moment; and we shall have a clear afternoon."	SS	II	5	168	9
From this moment her mind was never quiet; the expectation	SS	II	5	169	15
fire after tea, till the moment of Lady Middleton's	SS	II	6	175	1
At that moment she first perceived him, and her whole	SS	II	6	176	3
to be composed at such a moment was not only beyond the	SS	II	6	176	6
painful to him, and he held her hand only for a moment.	SS	II	6	177	8
Elinor, expecting every moment to see her faint, tried to	SS	II	6	177	12
Oh go to him this moment."	SS	II	6	177	13
polite to object for a moment to her wish of going away,	SS	II	6	178	16
remaining in the room a moment after she was dressed, but	SS	II	7	180	5
to speak than at that moment, obliged herself to answer	SS	II	7	181	9
in love with each other from the first moment they met?	SS	II	7	182	10
look, his manner, had you heard his voice at that moment!	SS	II	7	189	46
For a moment or two she could say no more; but when this	SS	II	7	189	47
					48
Elinor advised her to lie down again, and for a moment she	SS	II	7	191	65
Elinor, pleased to have her governed for a moment by such	SS	II	8	193	5
What now," after pausing a moment--"your poor sister is	SS	II	8	195	14
I think"--he stopped a moment; then added in a voice which	SS	II	8	199	39
At one moment she was absolutely indifferent to the	SS	II	9	201	2
In one moment her imagination placed before her a letter	SS	II	9	202	7
The work of one moment was destroyed by the next.	SS	II	9	202	7
He stopt a moment for recollection, and then, with another	SS	II	9	205	21
the circumstances of the moment, to more than its real	SS	II	10	215	13
In a moment I shall see the person that all my happiness	SS	II	12	232	13
Perhaps Fanny thought for a moment that her mother had	SS	II	12	235	30
					31
she moved, after a moment, to her sister's chair, and	SS	II	12	236	39
					40
seeing her;--but the very moment I was introduced, there	SS	II	13	239	4
"I am sure I should have seen it in a moment, if Mrs.	SS	II	13	240	17
It was a very awkward moment; and the countenance of each	SS	II	13	240	19
"Dear Edward!" she cried, " this is a moment of great	SS	II	13	242	24
Again they all sat down, and for a moment or two all were	SS	II	13	242	25
knowing till the last moment, where it was to take her.	SS	II	14	249	7
Fanny paused a moment, and then, with fresh vigour, said, "	SS	II	14	253	23
					24
They all looked their assent; it seemed too awful a moment	SS	III	1	265	35
And away she went; but returning again in a moment, "I	SS	III	4	287	21
					22
amusement for the moment, without any material loss of	SS	III	4	292	54
moment--"but upon my soul, it is a most serious business.	SS	III	5	298	35
Elinor's satisfaction at the moment of removal, was more	SS	III	6	302	5
The comfort of such a friend at that moment as Colonel	SS	III	7	311	16
Not a moment was lost in delay of any kind.	SS	III	7	312	17
his fears in a moment, proposed to call in farther advice.	SS	III	7	313	21
degrees, and left her no moment of tranquillity till the	SS	III	7	314	22
of sleep at that moment about her, and she was not to be	SS	III	7	315	27
convinced that at that moment she heard a carriage driving	SS	III	7	316	29
Elinor found it so difficult to be calm, as at that moment.	SS	III	7	316	30
"Your sister," said he, with abruptness, a moment	SS	III	8	318	10
off, from day to day, the moment of doing it, from an	SS	III	8	321	34
But I thought of her, I believe, every moment of the day,	SS	III	8	327	55
will, that at this moment she is dearer to me than ever."	SS	III	8	330	67
usual warmth, was in a moment as much overcome by her	SS	III	9	334	4
of his sharing with herself in the bliss of the moment.	SS	III	9	334	4
with another; and for a moment wished Willoughby a widower.	SS	III	9	335	5
were then expected every moment to fetch Margaret away, as	SS	III	9	335	6
He has loved her, my Elinor, ever since the first moment	SS	III	9	336	12
Marianne might at that moment be dying.	SS	III	9	337	18
I shall divide every moment between music and reading.	SS	III	10	343	9
really suffered, and in a moment afterwards, alike	SS	III	11	353	24
In a moment she perceived that the others were likewise	SS	III	12	358	9
the gravel path; in a moment he was in the passage; and in	SS	III	12	359	10
mother's, and when the moment of action was over, she	SS	III	12	359	12
From the moment of learning that Lucy was married to	SS	III	13	363	8
Edward was free, to the moment of his justifying the hopes	SS	III	13	363	8
But when the second moment had passed, when she found	SS	III	13	363	8
Emma for a moment made no answer--at last she said--"I	W			319	2
briskness, till Mrs E.'s moment for dressing arrived, &	W			323	3
lengthened the ceremony almost to the wished for moment.	W			326	7
The candles are but this moment lit"--"I like to get a	W			327	7
"I am this moment going to dress, said he--I am waiting	W			327	7
but watch her at such a moment, saw her looking rather	W			328	8
The boy in one moment restored to all his first delight--	W			331	11
"I was determining on it this very moment my Lord, I'll be	W			333	13
I will go this moment.	W			333	13
their being joined at the moment by Tom Musgrave, who	W			334	13
heads--she was at that moment in quest of a person to	W			338	18
No visitors would have been welcome at such a moment; but	W			344	21
in her mind, at the moment of meeting;--& she cd. not but	W			349	24
A sound like a distant carriage was at this moment caught;	W			354	28
at a greater distance are probably doing at this moment.--	W			357	28
she supposed her sister in law's feelings at that moment.--	W			357	28
At this interesting moment he was called on by the others,	W			359	28
In a moment afterwards--"that is if I can possibly get	W			360	28
the moment, she ceased to be tortured by their effects.--	W			361	31
round, he looked for a moment at Elizabeth, till catching	PP	I	3	11	13
every moment should be employed in conversing together.	PP	I	6	22	6
admiration to love, from love to matrimony in a moment.	PP	I	6	27	52
Elizabeth did not quit her room for a moment, nor were the	PP	I	7	33	44
after looking at her for a moment, turned silently away.	PP	I	9	43	20
said of myself to be true, and I believe it at this moment.	PP	I	10	49	28
of no very great moment, should you think ill of that	PP	I	10	50	37
At that moment they were met from another walk, by Mrs.	PP	I	10	53	59
I must speak to him, this moment."	PP	I	13	61	3
of the moment, or are the result of previous study?"	PP	I	14	68	10
The moment of her release from him was exstacy.	PP	I	18	90	4
At that moment Sir William Lucas appeared close to them,	PP	I	18	92	22
character at the present moment, as there is reason to	PP	I	18	94	41
Elizabeth instantly read her feelings, and at that moment	PP	I	18	95	48
to himself even at the moment, he set about it in a very	PP	I	19	104	1
and she could not for a moment suppose that those wishes,	PP	I	21	120	28
In a moment they were all out of the chaise, rejoicing at	PP	II	5	155	3
and after listening a moment, she heard somebody running	PP	II	5	158	11
Make haste, and come down this moment."	PP	II	5	158	12
Maria's alarm was every moment increasing, and even Sir	PP	II	6	161	9
but neither at that moment nor at any other could she	PP	II	8	176	29
"No, I should have turned in a moment."	PP	II	10	183	5
Elizabeth felt herself growing more angry every moment;	PP	II	11	192	23
					24
"From the very beginning, from the first moment I may	PP	II	11	193	28
him the next moment open the front door and quit the house.	PP	II	11	193	30
consideration of his attachment had for a moment excited.	PP	II	11	193	31
From that moment I observed my friend's behaviour	PP	II	12	197	5
had been given, was scarcely the work of a moment.--	PP	II	12	199	5
Till this moment, I never knew myself."	PP	II	13	208	8
him; nor could she for a moment repent her refusal, or	PP	II	14	212	17
I am growing every moment more unconcerned and indifferent.	PP	II	17	225	13
admiration; and at that moment she felt, that to be	PP	III	1	245	3
his sister any pleasure, is sure to be done in a moment.	PP	III	1	250	45
There was certainly at this moment, in Elizabeth's mind, a	PP	III	1	250	48
He absolutely started, and for a moment seemed immoveable	PP	III	1	251	51
plain that he was that moment arrived, that moment	PP	III	1	252	54
that moment alighted from his horse or his carriage.	PP	III	1	252	54
She longed to know what at that moment was passing in his	PP	III	1	253	55
of Elizabeth's feelings was every moment increasing.	PP	III	2	260	1
heard on the stairs, and in a moment he entered the room.	PP	III	2	261	5
He observed to her, at a moment when the others were	PP	III	2	262	8
She expected every moment that some of the gentlemen would	PP	III	3	268	5
and then, though but a moment before she had believed her	PP	III	3	268	7
him, without losing a moment of the time so precious; but	PP	III	4	276	6
I must find Mr. Gardiner this moment, on business that	PP	III	4	276	6
think so?" cried Elizabeth, brightening up for a moment.	PP	III	5	282	2
eyes of both, lost not a moment in asking whether any	PP	III	5	286	23
"What a letter is this, to be written at such a moment.	PP	III	5	292	61
Consider how important every moment is, in such a case."	PP	III	7	303	20
I will put on my things in a moment.	PP	III	7	306	44
from the distress of the moment, been led to make Mr.	PP	III	8	311	11
I was only confused for the moment, because I felt that I	PP	III	11	331	17
not let me smile, and are provoking me to it every moment."	PP	III	12	343	33
Here, Sarah, come to Miss Bennet this moment, and help her	PP	III	13	344	7
She will be down in a moment I dare say."	PP	III	13	347	32
At that moment, she cared for no other.	PP	III	13	349	41
After sitting for a moment in silence, she said very	PP	III	14	351	4
					5
such moment as this, I shall certainly not depart from it.	PP	III	14	353	26
But your arts and allurements may, in a moment of	PP	III	14	354	36
Lady Catherine hesitated for a moment, and then replied, "	PP	III	14	354	42
					43
union: and now, at the moment, in their marriage, to be	PP	III	14	355	43
Now was the moment for her resolution to be executed, and,	PP	III	16	365	2
					3
was to him, made his affection every moment more valuable.	PP	III	16	366	8
At such a moment, the arrival of her friend was a sincere	PP	III	18	384	26
Mr. Norris took up every moment of her time, and the very	MP	I	1	9	10
a matter of very serious moment; but as it is, I hope	MP	I	1	10	14
moment, making artificial flowers or wasting gold paper.	MP	I	2	14	7
remember your goodness, to the last moment of my life."	MP	I	3	26	30
and she was from that moment perfectly safe from all	MP	I	3	30	57
Unfavourable circumstances had suddenly arisen at a moment	MP	I	4	38	9
mother in and out every moment with letters of business;	MP	I	5	50	35

know of." replied Mrs. Norris; "she was here a moment ago."	MP	I	7	71	32
The former was on the barouche-box in a moment, the latter	MP	I	8	80	30
broke at the same moment from them both, more than once.	MP	I	8	81	31
recovering herself in a moment, affected to laugh, and	MP	I	9	88	21
Julia joining them at the moment, carried on the joke.	MP	I	9	88	23
Mr. Rushworth will be here in a moment you know--we shall	MP	I	10	99	19
"But, Julia, Mr. Rushworth will be here in a moment with	MP	I	10	100	27
Why, child, I have but this moment escaped from his	MP	I	10	100	28
excuse, but I went the very moment she said she wanted it."	MP	I	10	102	45
At the same moment Mr. Crawford approaching Julia, said, "	MP	I	10	105	52
of others! joining them the moment she is asked.	MP	I	11	112	34
bad example, he would not look beyond the present moment.	MP	I	12	114	3
Dear ma'am, only look at her face at this moment;--how	MP	I	12	117	14
pleasure--but that I am this moment going to dance.	MP	I	12	119	24
This, though the thought of the moment, did not end with	MP	I	13	123	6
did not end with the moment; for the inclination to act	MP	I	13	123	6
be fool enough at this moment to undertake any character	MP	I	13	123	6
From this moment I make no difficulties.	MP	I	14	131	5
was ringing at the very moment over our heads, and as I	MP	I	15	142	22
For a moment no one spoke; and then many spoke together to	MP	I	15	143	28
Fanny was up in a moment, expecting some errand, for the	MP	I	15	145	44
to find herself at that moment the only speaker in the	MP	I	15	145	49
Crawford looking for a moment with astonished eyes at Mrs.	MP	I	15	147	56
I could name at this moment at least six young men within	MP	I	15	148	58
in the complaisance of the moment, to promise any thing.	MP	I	17	158	2
From this moment there was a return of his former jealousy,	MP	I	18	165	4
the entrance of Edmund the next moment, suspended it all.	MP	I	18	169	22
He is in the hall at this moment."	MP	I	18	172	33
To the greater number it was a moment of absolute horror.	MP	II	1	175	1
common cause; but at the moment of her appearance,	MP	II	1	175	2
Her going roused the rest; and at the same moment, the two	MP	II	1	176	3
Henry Crawford's retaining her hand at such a moment, a	MP	II	1	176	3
hand at such a moment, a moment of such peculiar proof and	MP	II	1	176	3
door, and after pausing a moment for what she knew would	MP	II	1	177	7
Sir Thomas was at that moment looking round him, and	MP	II	1	177	7
in the most interesting moment of his passage to England,	MP	II	1	180	10
He stept to the door, rejoicing at that moment in having	MP	II	1	182	22
At the very moment of Yates perceiving Sir Thomas, and	MP	II	1	182	22
forced in so untoward a moment to admit the acquaintance	MP	II	1	183	23
could then, in a soberer moment, feel his motives to	MP	II	2	187	1
It was well at that moment that Tom had to speak and not	MP	II	2	193	13
expressions of the moment, that she could define many as	MP	II	3	198	13
Do not run away the first moment of its holding up.	MP	II	4	207	7
In the moment of parting, Edmund was invited by Dr. Grant	MP	II	4	215	47
Thomas, stop a moment--I have something to say to you."	MP	II	5	217	11
fearfulness to delay the moment of meeting, she was with	MP	II	6	233	15
Fanny's eyes were turned on Crawford for a moment with an	MP	II	7	244	31
of them, appear of less moment in his eyes than in those	MP	II	8	254	10
then called out, "Oh! cousin, stop a moment, pray stop."	MP	II	9	261	3
It comes too in such an acceptable moment.	MP	II	9	262	8
Edmund, after waiting a moment, obliged her to bring down	MP	II	9	262	10
"Fanny," said a voice at that moment near her.	MP	II	9	267	24
I am only vexed for a moment.	MP	II	9	268	31
perhaps at the happiest moment; had he been able to talk	MP	II	9	270	40
laughed, and every moment had its pleasure and its hope.	MP	II	10	273	6
essential good--for the moment of beginning was now	MP	II	10	274	8
his eye glancing for a moment at her necklace--with a	MP	II	10	274	8
found herself the next moment conducted by Mr. Crawford to	MP	II	10	275	11
"Poor Fanny!" cried William, coming for a moment to visit	MP	II	10	279	23
of Branxholm Hall, "one moment and no more," to view the	MP	II	10	280	33
After seeing William to the last moment, Fanny walked back	MP	II	11	282	2
she was not to have a moment at her own command, her hair	MP	II	12	296	31
without losing another moment, turned instantly to Fanny,	MP	II	13	298	2
Here are the letters which announce it, this moment come	MP	II	13	298	2
I have not lost a moment, however.	MP	II	13	299	5
She had burst away from him, and at that moment Sir Thomas	MP	II	13	302	9
to part with her at a moment when her modesty alone seemed	MP	II	13	302	9
moment, and saying, "have you nothing to send to Mary?	MP	II	13	306	28
will be ready in a moment--I am very much obliged to you--	MP	II	13	307	34
to be sent for every moment; but as no footsteps	MP	III	1	311	3
For a moment he ceased, but she had barely become	MP	III	1	314	16
by the anxiety of the moment even to tell her uncle that	MP	III	1	315	19
And, Fanny, (turning back again for a moment) I shall make	MP	III	1	322	48
It is me, Baddeley, you mean; I am coming this moment.	MP	III	1	325	60
it kindly; and at that moment she thought that, but for	MP	III	3	335	5
Nay, nay, I entreat you; for one moment put down your work.	MP	III	3	342	33
know yourself as well as you seemed to do at that moment."	MP	III	3	343	39
the whim of the moment--easily tempted--easily put aside.	MP	III	3	343	41
tightened for the moment by the very idea of separation.	MP	III	4	347	21
right to every thing he may wish for, at the first moment.	MP	III	4	352	40
How then was I to be--to be in love with him the moment he	MP	III	4	353	45
a moment, and on such a subject, was a bitter aggravation.	MP	III	4	354	47
becoming, she turned away for a moment to recover herself.	MP	III	5	358	9
over Fanny's face at that moment, as might warrant strong	MP	III	5	362	17
When it came to the moment of parting, he would take her	MP	III	5	365	36
At the moment she could only thank and accept.	MP	III	6	369	11
her there to the last moment before he sailed, and perhaps	MP	III	6	372	18
Edmund, at a convenient moment, then added, in a whisper, "	MP	III	6	373	26
nor think, when the last moment came with him, and it was	MP	III	6	374	28
The moment they stopt, a trollopy-looking maid-servant,	MP	III	7	377	7
Another moment, and Fanny was in the narrow entrance-	MP	III	7	377	9
and she stood for a moment expecting to be invited on; but	MP	III	7	377	10
seat, looked at him for a moment in speechless admiration,	MP	III	7	384	34
in motion together, the moment came for setting off; every	MP	III	7	384	36
There had been at one moment a slight murmur in the	MP	III	7	387	45
There was no recovering the complexion from the moment	MP	III	9	394	1
herself capable of uttering a syllable at such a moment.	MP	III	10	399	4
Fanny was doubly silenced here; though when the moment was	MP	III	10	406	20
moment, lead it to do what it may afterwards regret.	MP	III	13	423	2
but you. at this very moment, he is wild to see you, and	MP	III	14	435	14
conduct, at the present moment, she saw so much to condemn;	MP	III	14	435	15
channel, that the subject was for a moment out of her head.	MP	III	15	438	8
At first, it was a sort of stupefaction; but every moment	MP	III	15	440	19
feel such an instance of his kindness at such a moment!	MP	III	15	443	23
house again at the same moment, just in time to spend a	MP	III	15	445	31
deadened at the moment, must, she knew, be sorely felt.	MP	III	16	451	13
At such a moment to give way to gaiety and to speak with	MP	III	16	456	24
on points too, of some moment, it had not entered my	MP	III	16	457	30
I resisted; it was the impulse of the moment to resist,	MP	III	16	459	30
I have since--sometimes--for a moment--regretted that I	MP	III	16	459	30
Fanny, even at the moment, but regretting her infinitely	MP	III	17	468	21
Knightley, feelingly; and for a moment or two he had done.	E	I	5	37	9
Does any body else occur to you at this moment under such	E	I	7	53	21
At this moment whom are you thinking of?"	E	I	7	53	21
way at that moment, he would have been accepted after all.	E	I	7	55	35
"At this moment, perhaps, Mr. Elton is shewing your	E	I	7	56	44
"Thank you, sir, thank you; I am going this moment myself;	E	I	8	58	8
"Almost every moment.	E	I	8	58	15
He was afraid not even Miss Woodhouse"--he stopt a moment--	E	I	9	71	9
He was gone the next moment:--after another moment's pause,	E	I	9	71	12
					13
With the view of passing off an awkward moment, Emma	E	I	9	82	81
					82
he would consider it as the proudest moment of his life."	E	I	9	82	83
she was at that moment very happy to assist in praising.	E	I	12	104	45
except now and then for a moment accidentally in town!	E	I	12	104	46
succeeded of similar moment, and passed away with similar	E	I	12	104	50
He paused--and growing cooler in a moment, added, with	E	I	12	106	60
pleasure than at this moment; never had his smile been	E	I	13	111	12
Actually snowing at this moment!--	E	I	13	113	26
She will be missed every moment."	E	I	13	114	35
my shoes, you know, the moment I got home; and it is not	E	I	15	127	14
It would not have been the awkwardness of a moment, it	E	I	15	129	23
Angry as she was, the thought of the moment made her	E	I	15	129	24
error with respect to your views, till this moment.	E	I	15	131	34
with particular advantage at that moment to her friend.	E	I	17	141	7
had never before for a moment supposed it could make him	E	I	18	150	37
At this moment, an ingenious and animating suspicion	E	II	1	160	21
					22
reasonable excuse for not hurrying on the wretched moment.	E	II	2	165	9
Mr. Knightley soon saw that he had lost his moment, and	E	II	3	172	23
heard it? for the very moment Mr. Cole told Mrs. Cole of	E	II	3	173	27
it would pour down every moment--but she thought she might	E	II	3	177	52
not seem to stay half a moment there, soon after she came	E	II	3	177	52
"It might be distressing, for the moment," said she; "but	E	II	3	180	55
very spot where, at that moment, a trunk, directed to The	E	II	5	186	1
at the moment were speaking a very different conviction.	E	II	5	189	13
At this moment they were approaching Ford's, and he	E	II	6	199	14
at the very moment of this burst of my amor patriae.	E	II	6	200	16
The circumstance was told him at Hartfield; for the moment,	E	II	7	206	4
I will step to Mrs. Goddard in a moment, if you wish it."	E	II	7	209	11
But the idea of any thing to be done in a moment, was	E	II	7	209	12
should arrive at the same moment! for, if we had met first	E	II	8	213	9
It was the work of a moment.	E	II	8	218	37
at the same moment Mr. Cole approaching to entreat Miss	E	II	8	226	85
From that moment, Emma could have taken her oath that Mr.	E	II	8	228	93
And touching Miss Bates, who at the moment passed near-- "	E	II	8	229	97
Mrs. Weston had been speaking to her at the same moment.	E	II	10	241	9
She looked up at him for a moment, coloured deeply, and	E	II	10	242	20
She is playing Robin Adair at this moment--his favourite."	E	II	10	243	29
"Oh! Mr. Knightley, one moment more; something of	E	II	10	245	50
It can be allowable only as the thought of the moment."	E	II	11	248	8
"My father and Mrs. Weston are at the crown at this moment,	E	II	11	253	39
I am almost afraid that every moment will bring him."	E	II	12	260	25
words--"I had not a spare moment on Tuesday, as you know,	E	II	13	266	5
In a moment he went on-- "that will never be, however, I	E	II	15	287	29
					30
Did not keep the horses a moment.	E	III	2	322	19
Must go and speak to Dr. and Mrs. Hughes for a moment.--	E	III	2	323	19
At this moment Frank began talking so vigorously, that	E	III	2	324	22
I was this moment telling Jane, I thought you would begin	E	III	2	324	23
expecting him every moment to escape into the card-room.	E	III	2	326	33
She looked round for a moment; he had joined Mr. Knightley	E	III	2	328	38
In another moment a happier sight caught her;-- Mr.	E	III	2	328	40
might be heard from that moment, without interruption,	E	III	2	328	44
She hesitated a moment, and then replied, "with you, if	E	III	2	331	60
A moment sufficed to convince her that something	E	III	3	333	3
as to bring him to her assistance at this critical moment.	E	III	3	334	7
of that till this moment--but the cutting the finger, and	E	III	4	338	13
it up, and never parted with it again from that moment."	E	III	4	339	18
Emma was not thinking of it at the moment, which made the	E	III	4	340	28
In one moment such a change!	E	III	4	342	38
"Upon my word I never heard of it till this moment."	E	III	5	345	10
him seize every possible moment for darting his eyes	E	III	5	348	23
twentieth part of a moment, did such an idea occur to me.	E	III	5	350	35
who was expected every moment from Richmond; and Mrs.	E	III	6	358	35
I am going this moment.--	E	III	6	362	44
He might even have Harriet in his thoughts at the moment;	E	III	7	373	51
and the pride of the moment, laugh at her, humble her--and	E	III	7	375	61
carriage, sunk back for a moment overcome--then	E	III	7	376	62
pleased to wait a moment, and then ushered her in too soon.	E	III	8	378	4
Elton at the same moment came congratulating me upon it!	E	III	8	382	29
She was warmly gratified--and in another moment still more	E	III	9	385	7
He left them immediately afterwards--gone in a moment.	E	III	9	386	7
She saw in a moment all the possible good.	E	III	9	388	13
Her health seemed for the moment completely deranged--	E	III	9	389	16
This moment, if you please.	E	III	10	392	5
Tell me, I charge you tell me this moment what it is."	E	III	10	393	10
For a moment he was silent; and then added, in a tone much	E	III	10	394	23
					24
increased; and the moment they were alone, she eagerly	E	III	10	394	26
					27
Emma pondered a moment, and then replied, "I will not	E	III	10	396	39
At this moment Mr. Weston appeared at a little distance	E	III	10	400	65
fondness, which at that moment would have been dreadful	E	III	11	411	42
another door--and the moment she was gone, this was the	E	III	11	411	42
Every moment had brought a fresh surprise; and every	E	III	11	411	43
To that point went every leisure moment which her father's	E	III	11	412	44
allowed, and every moment of involuntary absence of mind.	E	III	11	412	44
She had been thinking of him the moment before, as	E	III	13	424	1
"After waiting a moment, as if to be sure she intended to	E	III	13	425	6
					7
For a moment or two nothing was said, and she was	E	III	13	425	12
					13
will not ask, though I may wish it unsaid the next moment."	E	III	13	429	27
almost ready to sink under the agitation of this moment.	E	III	13	430	36
The rest had been the work of the moment, the immediate	E	III	13	432	40
that I was within a moment of confessing the truth, and I	E	III	14	438	8
which any picture of love must have for her at that moment.	E	III	15	444	1
how much might at that moment, and at a little distance,	E	III	16	451	4
her to walk up;"--and a moment afterwards she was met on	E	III	16	452	8
forget the poem at this moment: "for when a lady's in the	E	III	16	454	13
He paused a moment, again smiling, with his eyes fixed on	E	III	18	470	8
She must wait a moment, or he would think her mad.	E	III	18	472	21
Martin was, at this moment, so strong to Emma's feelings,	E	III	18	473	27
demure for the moment--"I hope Mr. Knightley is well?"	E	III	18	477	58
					59
but his mind was the next moment in his own concerns and	E	III	18	478	60
					61
the slightest degree disordered, were it only for a moment.	E	III	18	479	73
Jane was forced to smile completely, for a moment; and the	E	III	18	480	78
					79
to hope for at the moment, she was able to fix her wedding-	E	III	19	484	11
clergyman--" she stopt a moment to consider what might do	P	III	3	20	17
At this moment I cannot recollect his name, though I have	P	III	3	23	25
After waiting another moment-- "you mean Mr. Wentworth, I	P	III	3	23	29
					30
More than I can recollect in a moment: but I can tell you	P	III	5	38	34
to be checking every moment; 'don't do this, and don't do	P	III	6	45	8
and courage, till for a moment electrified by Mrs. Croft's	P	III	6	49	18
					19
&c. to have another moment for finishing or recollecting	P	III	6	49	25
at that moment brought home in consequence of a bad fall.	P	III	7	53	2
The next moment she was tapping at her husband's dressing-	P	III	7	57	17
					18
And the next moment she was hating herself for the folly	P	III	7	60	30
and, in the first moment of appeal, had spoken as he felt.	P	III	7	61	36
than herself; in another moment he was perfectly collected	P	III	8	67	28
moment, and released Captain Wentworth as well as herself.	P	III	9	79	23
"Walter," said she, "get down this moment.	P	III	9	80	30
In another moment, however, she found herself in the state	P	III	9	80	33
Mary sat down for a moment, but it would not do; she was	P	III	10	87	21
her arm almost every moment, to cut off the heads of some	P	III	10	90	37
the hedge in a moment to say something to his sister.--	P	III	10	91	39
as occurred to her at the moment as calculated to rouse	P	III	11	101	24
a gentleman at the same moment preparing to come down,	P	III	12	104	6
I, at this moment, see something like Anne Elliot again."	P	III	12	104	6
The horror of that moment to all who stood around!	P	III	12	109	33
and in another moment, Henrietta, sinking under the	P	III	12	109	34
Captain Benwick obeyed, and Charles at the same moment,	P	III	12	110	37
					38
of the idea, and in a moment (it was all done in rapid	P	III	12	110	42
She paused a moment to recover from the emotion of hearing	P	III	12	114	62
first seen Mr. Elliot; a moment seemed all that could now	P	III	12	115	66

that I had not given way to her at the fatal moment! P III 12 116 71
either!" continued the Admiral, after thinking a moment. P IV 1 127 28
and finances at that moment particularly unfit to meet any P IV 5 154 9
at that moment with propriety have spoken for himself!-- P IV 5 160 26
"I have this moment heard that the Crofts are going to P IV 6 163 7
of calmness, and answer the common questions of the moment. P IV 6 165 9
to be upset the next moment, which they certainly must be. P IV 6 169 25
She was sent back, however, in a moment by the entrance of P IV 7 175 6
He will be here in a moment, I am sure." P IV 7 177 15
increased; and in another moment they walked off together, P IV 7 177 16
anxiously; and when the moment approached which must point P IV 7 179 28
have lost the right moment for seeing whether he saw them. P IV 7 179 31
expecting him to go every moment; but he did not; he P IV 8 181 3
4
too painful; but in a moment half smiling again, added, " P IV 8 182 6
breathe very quick, and feel a hundred things in a moment. P IV 8 183 11
of the moment, with exquisite, though agitated sensations. P IV 8 184 17
She seemed as if she had been one moment too late; and as P IV 8 188 41
occupying; when, at that moment, a touch on her shoulder P IV 8 190 47
For a moment the gratification was exquisite. P IV 8 191 51
you do not design to be cruel, when the right moment comes. P IV 9 195 30
In the warmth of the moment, and under a mistaken P IV 9 198 44
Elliot, and from that moment, I have no doubt, had a P IV 9 206 88
Here Mrs. Smith paused a moment; but Anne had not a word P IV 9 206 89
90
latter could not be more than the surprise of the moment. P IV 10 221 32
to wait, had gone out the moment it had cleared, but would P IV 11 229 2
over her, and at the same moment that her eyes P IV 11 231 10
The peace turned him on shore at the very moment, and he P IV 11 233 20
you fifty quotations in a moment on my side the argument, P IV 11 234 27
fixed on her for a moment, and hastily collecting his P IV 11 236 40
Every moment rather brought fresh agitation. P IV 11 238 44
to the last possible moment, that I might see it; and if I P IV 11 240 58
preceded the present moment, which were so poignant and so P IV 11 241 59
The moment of her stepping forward in the Octagon-Room to P IV 11 244 71
to speak to him, the moment of Mr. Elliot's appearing and P IV 11 244 71
All done in a moment;--the advertisements did not catch my S 1 367 1
at this important moment, & learning her situation, S 3 378 1
omission is supplied in a moment by Ly D.'s Gardiner--but S 4 381 1
I remember none at this moment, of the sea, in either of S 7 397 1
Nor can I exactly recall the beginning at this moment--but- S 7 397 1
me in the face at this very moment, numbers 3, 4 & 8. S 7 402 1
astonishment--but another moment brought Mr P. into the S 9 406 1
I knew Miss Heywood the moment I saw her before me on the S 9 407 1
"I will come to you the moment I have dined, said he, & we S 9 410 1
lodgings, & probably the moment dinner is over, shall be S 9 411 1
I had forgotten them for the moment, but I had a letter 3 S 9 411 1
stream--and at the same moment, his sisters both crying S 10 417 1
on, & then seize an odd moment for adding a great dab just S 10 417 1
Parker who happened to be calling on them at the moment--. S 12 423 1
I really have not a moment to spare--besides that (between S 12 424 1

MOMENT'S (69)
Allen, for after only a moment's consideration, she said, NA I 8 59 34
It was ages since she had had a moment's conversation with NA I 9 67 33
"You cannot think," added Catherine after a moment's NA I 10 72 11
Isabella; and after a moment's thought, asked Mr. Allen NA I 13 105 40
must be bought without a moment's delay, walked out into NA I 14 114 50
to herself, or one moment's suspicion of any past scenes NA II 5 161 25
A moment's glance was enough to satisfy Catherine that her NA II 6 163 1
a moment's attention, she found no stage of it tedious. NA II 14 231 5
and, after a moment's silence, said, "Oh! Edward! SS I 18 100 28
29
she said; but after a moment's reflection, she added with SS I 22 131 29
I can safely say that he has never gave me one moment's SS II 2 147 10
their absence; but a moment's glance at her sister when SS II 5 169 16
After a moment's pause, he spoke with calmness. SS II 6 177 8
I cannot rest--I shall not have a moment's peace till this SS II 6 177 13
scenes as must prevent her ever knowning a moment's rest. SS II 10 214 6
forced herself, after a moment's recollection, to welcome SS II 13 241 20
whom it would give her a moment's regret to be divided for SS III 6 302 5
After a moment's recollection, therefore, concluding that SS III 8 317 7
she said, after a moment's recollection, "Mr. Willoughby, SS III 8 318 21
22
Eager to save her mother from every unnecessary moment's SS III 9 333 3
an injunction--and a moment's consideration making her PP I 19 104 7
She answered him in the usual way, and after a moment's PP II 7 171 10
11
alarmed; but with a moment's recollection and a returning PP II 18 233 27
with him gave her a moment's distress; but, exerting PP III 3 269 10
not but say, after a moment's deliberation, "I am not." PP III 14 356 55
56
it would not give me one moment's concern--and the world PP III 14 358 70
After a moment's embarrassment the lady replied, "you are MP I 10 98 8
After a moment's thought, Miss Crawford calmly replied, " MP I 15 148 59
of our acting," said Tom after a moment's thought. MP II 1 184 26
Maria had a moment's struggle as she listened, and only a MP II 3 200 21
listened, and only a moment's: when her father ceased, she MP II 3 200 21
There is no giving you a moment's uneasiness. MP II 4 212 30
Sir Thomas, after a moment's thought, recommended MP II 7 239 6
and Lady Bertram felt a moment's indecision again--but MP II 7 239 8
application, and after a moment's thought, urged Fanny's MP II 8 257 15
and therefore, after a moment's consideration, said, "if MP II 9 269 34
They will be angry," he added, after a moment's silence, MP II 12 297 33
morning, but there has not been since, a moment's delay. MP II 13 299 5
After a moment's pause, Sir Thomas, trying to suppress a MP III 1 313 13
Sir Thomas, after a few moment's silence, "that you mean MP III 1 315 21
had a moment's share in your thoughts on this occasion. MP III 1 318 39
After half a moment's pause--"and I should have been very MP III 1 319 39
"Oh!" said Mrs. Norris with a moment's check, "that was MP III 1 323 56
After a moment's reflection, Mr. Crawford replied, "I know MP III 11 410 16
of a moment's etourderie thinks of nobody but you. MP III 15 437 3
A moment's recollection enabled her to say, "Rushworth, MP III 15 439 10
He was gone the next moment:--after another moment's pause, E I 9 71 12
13
cannot have a moment's doubt as to Mr. Elton's intentions. E I 9 73 20
her father's being given a moment's uneasiness about it. E I 16 138 15
the rapidity of half a moment's thought, she hoped Mr. E II 5 188 8
after a moment's pause, Mrs. Elton chose another subject. E II 14 278 43
is not obtained at a moment's notice; indeed, indeed, we E II 17 300 12
will not give me another moment's pang: and to convince E III 4 337 6
how it was; and after a moment's debate, as to whether it E III 4 341 29
30
She had a moment's fear of Miss Bates keeping away from E III 8 378 7
"Harriet!" cried Emma, after a moment's pause--"what do E III 11 405 15
and no moment's uneasiness can ever occur between us again. E III 14 443 8
"Oh! well;"--and after a moment's pause, "but you have P III 5 39 35
You can send for us, you know, at a moment's notice, if P III 7 57 16
After a moment's pause, Captain Wentworth said, "do you P III 10 89 29
30
Anne had a moment's astonishment on the subject herself; P III 11 98 17
She gave a moment's recollection, as they hurried along, P III 12 115 66
After a moment's pause he said, "though I came only P IV 7 177 14
but after standing in a moment's suspense, was obliged, P IV 7 180 36
He was gone--he had disappeared: she felt a moment's P IV 8 184 18
A moment's reflection shewed her the mistake she had been P IV 9 194 21
misled by every moment's inadvertence, and wantonly P IV 10 221 33
it did not give her a moment's regret; but to have no P IV 12 251 10
on seeing her, were a moment's astonishment--but another S 9 406 1

MOMENTARY (24)
For half an hour I was in momentary expectation of his LS 24 285 2
her book with affected indifference, or momentary shame.-- NA I 5 38 4
who, having seen, in a momentary glance beyond them, a NA II 8 185 5
incapable of more than momentary repose, the hours passed NA II 14 231 5
He coloured very deeply, and giving a momentary glance at SS I 18 98 12
But this, from the momentary perverseness of impatient SS II 8 197 25
her story, gave way to a momentary confusion here on PP I 22 124 14
15
avoidance spoke rather a momentary embarrassment, than any PP III 2 264 11
her daughter sat in momentary dread, Bingley, who wanted PP III 16 365 1
pleasure were likely to be more than momentary in them. MP I 18 169 23
to her"--adding, with a momentary seriousness, "she is too MP II 5 224 53
dance, made more than a momentary impression on his uncle. MP II 8 252 1
of the united voices gave only momentary interruptions. E II 8 227 87
Emma felt that Mrs. Weston was giving her a momentary E II 15 286 19
had only, in the momentary conquest of eagerness over E III 13 432 40
and, excepting one momentary glance at her, instantly E III 15 447 21
feeling for Harriet, a momentary doubt of its being E III 19 481 1
There was a momentary expression in Captain Wentworth's P III 8 67 28
a weasel which he had a momentary glance of; and they P III 10 90 37
He gave her a momentary glance,--a glance of brightness, P III 12 104 6
Louisa, and had even a momentary look of his own arch P IV 7 176 8
mouth form itself into a momentary expression of contempt, P IV 10 227 67
Another momentary vexation occurred. P IV 11 239 54
momentary apprehensions of its being impossible to last. P IV 11 245 77

MOMENTOUS (2)
spirit of reproach, exerted on a more momentous subject. MP III 1 323 53
a subject of most melancholy and momentous consultation. MP III 17 464 13

MOMENTS (77)
to attend me for a few moments in my dressing room, as she LS 20 276 5
and after remaining a few moments silent, was on the point NA I 6 42 33
In a few moments Catherine, with unaffected pleasure, NA I 6 43 36
and even then, even in moments of languor or restraint, a NA II 6 166 8
Catherine, for a few moments, was motionless with horror. NA II 6 170 12
and certainly there are moments when we could all wish him NA II 7 176 15
staircase, and in a few moments it gave Henry to her view. NA II 9 194 6
heart sink, and for a few moments she hardly supposed NA II 13 223 13
There are moments when the extent of it seems doubtful; SS I 4 21 15
For a few moments every one was silent. SS I 15 76 13
into a reverie for a few moments;--but rousing herself SS I 16 88 33
Marianne in a low voice, "nor how many painful moments." SS I 16 88 41
There were moments in abundance, when, if not by the SS I 19 105 12
Elinor for a few moments remained silent. SS I 22 130 17
nothing else; for a few moments, she was almost overcome-- SS I 22 134 53
In a few moments Marianne did the same. SS II 4 160 4
observing her for a few moments with silent anxiety, said, SS II 7 180 1
2
within her reach in her moments of happiest eloquence, SS II 9 202 8
of her short life; I was with her in her last moments." SS II 9 207 26
In such moments of precious, of invaluable misery, she SS III 6 303 9
would of course, in some moments, occur to remind her of SS III 7 315 25
They were both silent for a few moments. SS III 8 324 43
hating me in her latest moments--for how could I tell what SS III 8 330 69
For some moments her voice was lost; but recovering SS III 11 350 6
Mrs E. & her party were for a few moments hemmed in. W 332 11
after a few moments recollection, was not sorry for it. PP I 11 58 34
Mr. Wickham, after a few moments, touched his hat--a PP I 15 73 8
Mr. Collins for a few moments, he asked Elizabeth in a low PP I 16 83 51
He sat down for a few moments, and then getting up walked PP II 11 189 3
him in unguarded moments, which Mr. Darcy could not have. PP II 12 200 5
moments, she flattered herself that her wishes did not err. PP II 13 205 3
and, after standing a few moments without saying a word, PP III 1 252 53
For a few moments, indeed, she felt that he would probably PP III 1 254 57
as such pauses must always be, succeeded for a few moments. PP III 3 267 4
or herself amends, for moments of such painful confusion. PP III 11 337 54
in a few moments after seated with the rest of the party. PP III 12 342 26
hours of happy mirth, and moments of serious conference, MP I 2 21 34
For a few moments she was unanswered. MP I 9 87 16
A few moments of feverish enjoyment was followed by hours MP II 2 192 11
He was surprized; but after a few moments silent MP II 5 226 59
Excepting the moments of peculiar delight, which any MP II 6 234 18
quite agree, there were moments in which she did not seem MP II 8 255 10
pills, it will have two moments ill-flavour, and then be MP II 12 297 33
distressed, and for some moments unable to speak. MP II 13 301 7
from the woman whom, two moments before, he had been MP III 3 334 1
Its object was unquestionable; and two moments were enough MP III 15 437 2
If two moments, however, can surround with difficulties, a MP III 15 437 2
The event was so shocking, that there were moments even MP III 15 441 20
as made it for a few moments impossible to Fanny's fears, MP III 16 454 18
to Mrs. Weston, and of moments only of regret; and her E I 2 18 12
asperity, added, a few moments afterwards, "no, he is not E I 8 61 38
of talking in unreserved moments, when there are only men E I 8 66 53
He called for a few moments, just to leave a piece of E I 9 71 10
interrupting, for a few moments, her busy labours for some E I 12 100 18
able to reply: and two moments of silence being ample E I 15 131 32
33
at the time, there were moments of self-examination in E II 2 166 11
moments afterwards, heard what each thought of the other. E II 8 220 47
A few awkward moments passed, and he sat down again; and E II 12 261 32
33
She paused a few moments. E III 11 407 27
I have not had some happy moments; but I can say, that I E III 12 418 6
will be down in a few moments, I dare say,"--had been P III 9 79 23
(it was all done in rapid moments) Captain Benwick had P III 12 110 42
In such moments Anne had no power of saying to herself, " P IV 1 126 18
to believe that she had moments only of languor and P IV 5 154 8
For a few moments her imagination and her heart were P IV 5 160 26
of him, in the preparation of the last few moments. P IV 7 175 6
moments, that no flagrant open crime could have been worse. P IV 9 210 97
the Pump-Room, could not but have her moments of imagining. P IV 10 220 31
After waiting a few moments he said--and as if it were the P IV 10 225 60
two moments preparation for the sight of Captain Wentworth. P IV 11 239 55
That evening seemed to be made up of exquisite moments. P IV 11 244 71
and one or two subsequent moments, marked by returning P IV 11 244 71
Captain Wentworth, some moments of communication P IV 11 246 78
it, was obliged in a few moments to cut short, both his S 1 364 1
offensive;--& there are moments, there are points, when S 3 376 1
I had a few moments indecision;--whether to offer to write S 9 409 1
It appeared at different moments to be everything from the S 12 425 1

MOMENTS' (5)
"Well," said Catherine, after some moments' consideration, NA II 4 152 27
"No," said Catherine, after a moments' reflection, "I do NA II 10 207 39
A few moments' reflection, however, produced a very happy SS III 4 286 16
17
After a few moments' chat, John Dashwood, recollecting SS III 5 298 32
for the sake of a few moments' free observation of the E III 6 362 43

MONARCH (4)
No signs that a 'Scottish monarch sleeps below.'" MP I 9 86 6
second brings, behold him there, the monarch of the seas! E I 9 71 14
Behold him there, the monarch of the seas! E I 9 72 17
second brings; behold him there, the monarch of the seas! E I 9 73 18

MONASTERIES (1)
compared with the old chapels of castles and monasteries. MP I 9 86 7

MONASTIC (1)
than that which yet bore the traces of monastic division? NA II 8 188 17

MONDAY (35)
enough to call on her on Monday, but she beleived he had LS 41 310 2
"Yes, sir, I was there last Monday." NA I 3 26 11
Was not the young lady he danced with on Monday a Miss NA I 10 73 13
from what had attended her thither the Monday before. NA I 10 74 23
I firmly believe you were engaged to me ever since Monday. NA I 10 75 26
Monday, Tuesday, Wednesday, Thursday, Friday and Saturday NA I 13 97 1
I must be at Woodston on Monday to attend the parish NA II 11 209 5
Let me see; Monday will be a busy day with you, we will NA II 11 210 6
not come on Monday; and Tuesday will be a busy one with me. NA II 11 210 6

an engagement that takes our whole family away on Monday. NA II 13 224 13
aloud, "Monday--so soon as Monday;--and you all go. NA II 13 224 17
Do not be distressed, Eleanor, I can go on Monday very NA II 13 224 17
I met Colonel Brandon Monday morning in Bond-Street, just SS I 20 115 48
afraid I had offended you by what I told you that Monday." SS II 2 146 3
that he came down on Monday in a chaise and four to see PP I 1 3 10
on you and your family, Monday, November 18th, by four PP I 13 63 12
Saturday, Sunday and Monday, endurable to Kitty and Lydia. PP I 17 88 15
to be able to return on Monday fortnight; for Lady PP I 23 128 10
Mr. Collins returned most punctually on the Monday PP I 23 129 15
On the following Monday, Mrs. Bennet had the pleasure of PP II 2 139 2
"Gracechurch-Street, Monday, August 2. PP III 7 302 14
Well, Monday morning came, and I was in such a fuss! PP III 9 319 24
It was not all settled before Monday: as soon as it was, PP III 10 324 2
about green goose from Monday morning till Saturday night." MP I 11 112 31
the cause, I came away on Monday, trusting that many posts MP II 13 299 5
principle, he soon afterwards observed, "they go on Monday. MP III 4 354 48
They really go on Monday! and I was within a trifle of MP III 4 354 48
that the Grants go to Bath; they leave Mansfield on Monday. MP III 13 423 2
the Monday following--as you will find from Jane's letter. E II 1 161 31
From Monday next to Saturday, I assure you we have not a E II 16 290 2
She sat an hour with me on Monday evening, and gave me the P IV 9 197 40
On Monday evening my good friend Mrs. Rooke let me thus P IV 9 205 82
I got more acquainted with him last Monday than ever I did P IV 10 219 26
time, for a week; from Monday to Monday; and very S 7 399 1
to Monday; and very delighted & thankful they were.-- S 7 399 1

MONEY (124)

has once got his name in a banking house he rolls in money. LS 5 250 2
not at present in want of money, & might perhaps till the LS 10 257 1
lady to be governed by the fear of never getting her money. LS 19 274 2
Nothing but my being in the utmost distress for money, LS 26 296 4
keep some account of the money you spend;--I will give you NA I 2 18 2
directly, threw down the money, and the carriage was mine." NA I 7 46 13
I would give any money for a real good hunter. NA I 10 76 28
"Because he has not money enough." NA I 11 89 59
if people who rolled in money could not afford things, he NA I 11 89 61
to be resigned, or funded money made over, was a matter in NA I 15 122 28
And to marry for money I think the wickedest thing in NA I 15 124 47
has a right to do what they like with their own money." NA II 1 136 47
It is not the want of more money that makes me just at NA II 1 136 48
out of spirits; I hate money; and if our union could take NA II 1 136 48
that romancers may say, there is no doing without money. NA II 3 146 16
and not so much about money; and had not looked so well NA II 3 148 28
The money is nothing, it is not an object, but employment NA II 7 176 15
up; every thing that money and taste could do, to give NA II 8 185 5
He told me the other day, that he only valued money as it NA II 10 205 30
on the subject of money, which she had more than once NA II 11 208 1
might not be provided with money enough for the expenses NA II 13 229 31
The money therefore which Eleanor had advanced was NA II 14 236 14
no more inclined than entitled to demand his money. NA II 16 249 2
Harry, by giving away all his money to his half sisters? SS I 2 8 3
Consider," she added, "that when the money is once parted SS I 2 9 7
because, otherwise, the money would have been entirely at SS I 2 11 20
ever being distressed for money, and will, I think, be SS I 2 11 23
father had no idea of your giving them any money at all. SS I 2 12 24
money himself than to have any design of giving money away. SS I 5 27 6
she had at this time ready money enough to supply all that SS I 6 29 4
Perhaps in the spring, if I have plenty of money, as I SS I 6 29 4
notice; who has more money than he can spend, more time SS I 10 51 25
I do think he must have been sent for about money matters, SS I 14 70 2
for my mother will never have money enough to attempt it." SS I 14 72 8
"Elinor, for shame!" said Marianne; "money can only give SS I 17 91 10
You are very right in supposing how my money would be SS I 17 92 26
But when there is plenty of money on one side, and next to SS II 8 194 8
it, I would not have joked her about it for all my money. SS II 8 195 16
came to town, aware that money could not be very plenty SS II 11 224 28
convenience; and it has cost me a vast deal of money." SS II 11 225 31
a man who had got all his money in a low way; and Fanny SS II 11 228 53
And I protest, if I had any money to spare, I should buy a SS II 14 251 17
of people's making such a to-do about money and greatness. SS III 1 259 7
He makes a monstrous deal of money, and they keep their SS III 2 275 25
knowing that her son has money enough to live upon,--for SS III 5 296 19
In honest words, her money was necessary to me, and in a SS III 8 328 63
it seems borrowed all her money before she went off to be SS III 13 370 37
If Mr E. does not lose his money at cards, you will stay W 315 1
A woman should never be trusted with money. W 351 26
"But that would have been trusting me with money, replied W 351 26
and generous,--to give his money freely, to display PP I 16 81 41
that he considered the money as a mere trifle, and begged PP I 16 83 49
all the importance of money, great connections, and pride." PP II 1 136 23
because I had no money, what occasion could there be for PP II 4 153 13
the mere stateliness of money and rank, she thought she PP II 6 161 9
When have you been prevented by want of money from going PP II 10 183 11
of greater weight, I may suffer from the want of money. PP II 10 183 12
who can afford to marry without some attention to money." PP II 10 183 14
money, for we have just spent ours at the shop out there." PP II 16 219 3
They will never be distressed for money. PP II 17 228 33
She has no money, no connections, nothing that can tempt PP III 4 277 11
he could marry for money; and how Lydia could ever have PP III 4 279 24
It is not likely that money should be very abundant on PP III 5 282 7
Wickham will never marry a woman without some money. PP III 5 283 8
money as she chuses, to buy them, after they are married. PP III 5 288 38
there will be some little money, even when all his debts PP III 7 302 14
to know;--one is, how much money your uncle has laid down, PP III 7 304 27
"Money! my uncle!" cried Jane, "what do you mean, sir?" PP III 7 304 28
he has pledged himself to assist Mr. Wickham with money." PP III 7 306 46
must have had all his money you know, and it is the first PP III 7 306 47
We will settle with your father about the money afterwards; PP III 7 306 47
the continual presents in money, which passed to her, PP III 8 309 4
and all money matters were then to receive the last finish. PP III 10 324 2
Imprudence or thoughtlessness in money matters, would be PP III 13 348 39
up the match, gave the money, paid the fellow's debts, and PP III 17 377 39
have quite money enough to live upon without some help. PP III 19 386 7
money and baby-linen, and Mrs. Norris wrote the letters. MP I 1 5 3
to others: but her love of money was equal to her love of MP I 1 8 9
might never have saved her money; but having no care of MP I 1 8 9
ought, and I am glad her love of money does not interfere. MP I 3 26 23
Court deserves every thing that taste and money can do. MP I 6 53 9
beauty as he could for my money; and I should never look MP I 6 57 29
thing is to be got with money, I was a little embarrassed MP I 6 58 39
will be all so much money thrown away--and I am sure that MP I 15 141 22
to make money--how to turn a good income into a better. MP II 5 226 61
an ornament which his money purchased three years ago, MP II 8 259 20
save her brother-in-law's money was vain, and that in MP III 6 372 21
or speculations upon prize money, which was to be MP III 7 375 2
her, that a small sum of money might, perhaps, restore MP III 9 396 7
had only learnt to think nothing of consequence but money. MP III 14 436 16
his own, with a little money, it might be very desirable." E I 4 30 18
Whatever money he might come into when his father died, E I 4 30 20
I would give any money for it. E I 6 43 13
He cannot want money--he cannot want leisure. E I 18 146 12
reason to wish the money unspent, to improve his spirits. E II 8 212 2
having little spare money and a great deal of health, E II 8 213 7
"Business, you know, may bring money, but friendship E II 16 293 21
immediately promised them money, and taking out her purse, E III 3 334 6
of its being some money concern--something just come to E III 10 393 18
Her father was growing distressed for money. P III 1 9 19
agreed in the want of more money, and a strong inclination P III 6 43 5
uses for his money, and a right to spend it as he liked. P III 6 43 5
letters; all the rest had been mere applications for money. P III 6 51 30
How fast I made money in her.-- P III 8 67 23
You know how much he wanted money--worse than myself. P III 8 67 23
They had each had money, but their marriages had made a P III 9 74 5
Without that attraction, not all her money would have P IV 3 139 9
She has plenty of money, and I intend she shall buy all P IV 5 156 13
Mr. Elliot married, then, completely for money? P IV 9 201 63
marrying for money is too common to strike one as it ought. P IV 9 201 64
Money, money, was all that he wanted. P IV 9 202 66
Having long had as much money as he could spend, nothing P IV 9 206 90
weakness, and from employing others by her want of money. P IV 9 210 98
Money, you know, coming down with money--two daughters at P IV 10 218 22
Where people can be found with money or time to go to them! S 1 368 1
who knew the value of money, was very much looked up to & S 3 375 1
points, when her love of money is carried greatly too far. S 3 376 1
her to be spending all her money the very first evening. S 6 390 1
That will bring money."-- S 6 392 1
But then, they who scatter their money so freely, never S 6 392 1
of money among us, as must do us more good than harm.-- S 6 392 1
will think so--for Sir Edwd must marry for money.-- S 7 400 1
compliments, but he knows he must marry for money.-- S 7 400 1
Ah! young ladies that have no money are very much to be S 7 401 1

MONEY-MATTERS (2)

be wanting; & as to money-matters, it has not with-held LS 5 250 1
disposition as to money-matters; he might naturally be E I 8 67 57

MONKEY (1)

throwing it out of window--"he is full of monkey tricks." SS I 21 121 7

MONKFORD (8)

to the gentleman who lived a few years back, at Monkford. P III 3 22 25
gentleman who lived at Monkford--Mrs. Croft's brother?" P III 3 23 25
resident at Monkford since the time of old Governor Trent." P III 3 23 27
He had the curacy of Monkford, you know, Sir Walter, some P III 3 23 32
Oh! ay,--Mr. Wentworth, the curate of Monkford. P III 3 23 33
the former curate of Monkford, however suspicious P III 4 26 1
parent living, found a home for half a year, at Monkford. P III 4 26 1
Mr. Wentworth, of Monkford, Captain Wentworth's brother. P IV 8 187 35

MONOPOLIZE (1)

and sharing the kindness which they wanted to monopolize. SS II 14 246 3

MONOSYLLABLE (1)

to obtain even a word from her beyond a monosyllable. PP III 2 261 3

MONOTONOUS (1)

he had, with very monotonous solemnity, read three pages, PP I 14 68 13 14

MONOTONY (1)

monotony of Lady Bertram's, only worn into fretfulness.)-- MP III 8 392 11

MONSTROUS (14)

A monstrous deal of good-nature, and it is not only good- NA I 15 123 38
"Now, palmer, you shall see a monstrous pretty girl." SS I 19 108 34
I am monstrous glad of it, for then I shall have her for a SS I 20 114 44
She is a monstrous lucky girl to get him, upon my honour; SS I 20 116 58
Lucy is monstrous pretty, and so good humoured and SS I 21 119 4
"I am sure I shall be monstrous glad of Miss Marianne's SS II 3 154 4
cheerfulness, "I am monstrous glad to see you--sorry I SS II 4 163 14
as it turns out, I am monstrous glad there never was any SS III 1 258 7
for they say he is monstrous fond of her, as well he may. SS III 1 259 7
"I am monstrous glad of it. SS III 2 272 12
So then he was monstrous happy, and talked on some time SS III 2 274 16
He makes a monstrous deal of money, and they keep their SS III 2 275 25
There is a monstrous curious stuff'd fox there, & a Badger- W 333 12
But Heiresses are monstrous scarce! S 7 401 1

MONTGOMERY (1)

Montgomery has all the fire of poetry, Wordsworth has the S 7 397 1

MONTH (55)

you had no doubt of it's authenticity a month ago. LS 12 261 5
Well hung; town built; I have not had it a month. NA I 7 46 11
I dare say she will not be in good humour again this month; NA I 15 117 3
with your brother over poor tilney's passion for a month." NA II 4 153 29
were beautiful even in the leafless month of March. NA II 7 177 19
"I was at Norland about a month ago." SS I 16 87 28
at Barton, that you should not stay above a month. SS II 10 217 21
I was last month at my friend Elliott's neat Dartford. SS II 14 252 18
The first month after their marriage was spent with their SS III 14 374 7
she has gone to spend a month with Robert and Jane on W 319 2
Mrs Robert Smartly--but we think a month very little. W 356 28
I assure you we bring her home at the end of a month, much W 356 28
"A month! have you really been gone a month! 'tis amazing W 356 28
probably not go--and, at another word, might stay a month." PP I 10 49 29
"About a month ago I received this letter, and about a PP I 13 61 6
"About a month," said Elizabeth; and then, unwilling to PP I 16 77 9
without scolding her, a month passed away before she could PP I 23 127 5
and I had not known you a month before I felt that you PP II 11 193 28
And if you will stay another month complete, it will be in PP II 14 211 10
in London again within a month; and as that left too short PP II 19 238 7
said, "I was surprised to see Darcy in town last month. PP III 10 328 15 16
Such was the state of affairs in the month of July, and MP I 4 40 15
November was the black month fixed for his return. MP I 11 107 2
she had been living a month at her own cost, and take up MP I 13 129 40
is a still more serious month, and I can see that Mrs. MP II 3 199 15
the middle of the same month the ceremony had taken place, MP II 3 202 28
that I should be spending month after month here, as I MP II 4 210 17
be spending month after month here, as I have done, I MP II 4 210 17
could rationally be hoped in the dirty month of February. MP III 7 376 5
"You have been here a month, I think?" said he. MP III 11 410 8
Not quite a month.-- MP III 11 410 9
I should call that a month." MP III 11 410 10
I am sure, a month ago, I had no more idea myself!-- E I 9 74 24
for her grandmother, one hears of nothing else for a month. E I 10 86 23
But poor Mrs. Bates had a bad cold about a month ago." E I 12 102 32
witnessed during the last month, to Miss Smith--such E I 15 130 30
"To chuse to remain here month after month, under E II 15 285 13
"But I have never fixed on June or any other month--merely E II 17 299 3
untowardly one month, they are sure to mend the next." E II 18 308 27
May is the very month which Mrs. Churchill is ordered, or E II 18 308 30
stay longer; her fortnight was likely to be month at least. E III 17 463 16
The intermediate month was the one fixed on, as far as E III 19 483 8
was called on, within a month from the marriage of Mr. and E III 19 484 11
the day of the month on which he had lost his wife. P III 1 3 2
course of the preceding month, there was no time to be P III 5 33 5
note down the day of the month, exclaimed, "dear me! is P III 6 48 16
He declares himself, that coming to Lyme for a month, did P III 12 102 2
Though they had now been acquainted a month, she could not P IV 5 160 27
and Anne, having been a month in Bath, was growing very P IV 6 162 1
at the great house very well, for a month "or six weeks. P IV 6 163 7
though they were here a month: and I dare say it would be P IV 10 219 29
roads, an occasional month at Tunbridge Wells, & symptoms S 2 373 1
This is new within the month. S 4 383 1
There was no blue shoe when we passed this way a month ago. S 4 383 1
have been at the point of death within the last month."-- S 5 385 1

MONTH'S (2)

he would hardly think a month's ablution enough to cleanse PP II 2 141 13
"He is a person I never think of from one month's end to E I 18 150 36

MONTHLY (2)

house, on every monthly return throughout the winter.-- W 314 1
regiment of militia, and the monthly balls of Meryton." PP II 16 220 7

MONTHS (151)

months more agreably than those which have just flown away. LS 2 244 1
mind my being only four months a widow, & to be as quiet LS 2 244 1
she had not staid three months there before she discovered LS 6 252 2
that he is in no danger of doing so three months hence. LS 15 266 1
to present, in having been scarcely ten months a widow. LS 29 299 3
I have now been but a few months a widow; & however little LS 30 300 3
By a removal for some months from each other, we shall LS 30 301 4
in town for several months, she could not be easy if her LS 41 310 3
& in the course of two months ceased to write of her LS 42 313 7

Three months might have done it in general. but Reginald's LS 42 313 8
Her mother was three months in teaching her only to repeat NA I 1 14 1
family were here three months; so I tell Mr. Allen he must NA I 8 54 9
I should be tired, if I were to stay here six months." NA I 10 78 44
good night's rest in the course of the next three months. NA I 11 90 65
It was not three months ago since, wild with joyful NA II 14 237 20
Three months ago had seen her all this; and now, how NA II 14 237 20
Mrs. Dashwood remained at Norland several months; not from SS I 3 14 1
"In a few months, my dear Marianne," said she, "Elinor SS I 3 17 15
farther than their maintenance for six months at Norland. SS I 5 27 6
and leave her perhaps for months, without telling her of SS I 15 80 36
But it may be months, perhaps, before that happens." be SS I 16 85 12
happens." be months, perhaps, before that happens." SS I 16 85 12
"Months!" cried Marianne, with strong surprise. SS I 16 85 13
How much may not a few months do?" SS I 19 103 7
"I think," replied Edward, "that I may defy many months to SS I 19 103 8
on to stay nearly two months at the park, and to assist in SS II 2 151 43
had been carried on for months and months, as it might SS II 7 186 29
carried on for months and months, as it might have been, SS II 7 186 29
as I then was, a few months must have reconciled me to it, SS II 9 206 24
father lived only a few months after their marriage, and I SS II 9 206 24
it had been made over some months before to another person. SS II 9 207 26
At last, however, and after I had been six months in SS II 9 207 26
the rest, for eight long months, was left to conjecture. SS II 9 209 28
where they had taken a very good house for three months. SS II 12 230 6
A few months ago it would have hurt her exceedingly; but SS II 12 232 16
handsome a few months ago; quite as handsome as Elinor.-- SS II 12 237 43
"I have known it these four months. SS III 1 262 16
After a pause of wonder, she exclaimed, "four months!-- SS III 1 262 17
18
Have you known of this four months?"-- SS III 1 262 18
"Four months!"--cried Marianne again.-- SS III 1 262 22
"Four months!--and yet you loved him!"-- SS III 1 262 26
For four months, Marianne, I have had all this hanging on SS III 1 263 29
own folly, within three months have been in the receipt of SS III 1 268 50
been rather more than two months in town, and Marianne's SS III 3 279 1
suppose two or three months will complete his ordination." SS III 4 291 50
"Two or three months!" cried Mrs. Jennings; "Lord! my dear, SS III 4 291 51
talk of it; and can the Colonel wait two or three months! SS III 4 291 51
it is not worth while to wait two or three months for him. SS III 4 291 51
with hope to what a few months of tranquillity at Barton SS III 6 302 5
She had been for three months her companion, was still SS III 7 313 20
was--for the first time these two months--he spoke to me.-- SS III 8 330 69
from her for a few months, I should very soon have SS III 13 362 5
it was earned by them before many months had passed away. SS III 14 375 10
They passed some months in great happiness at Dawlish; for SS III 14 376 11
you with us--if it be for months together.--& I am sorry, (W 350 24
at Netherfield, in the course of three or four months. PP I 18 103 77
A thousand things may arise in six months!" PP I 21 120 27
being rude, and many months were gone before she could at PP I 23 127 5
"my eldest sister has been in town these three months. PP II 7 171 10
11
recital which I received many months ago from Mr. Wickham. PP II 11 191 17
love with her for so many months! so much in love as to PP II 11 193 31
I expected you to stay two months. PP II 14 211 8
here; and Miss Darcy is always down for the summer months." PP III 1 248 25
she could reply, he added, "it is above eight months. PP III 2 262 8
any intercourse a few months ago would have been a PP III 2 263 10
knew her, for it is many months since I have considered PP III 3 271 18
him for the first two months; but he never distinguished PP III 5 285 18
but three months before, had been almost an angel of light. PP III 6 294 4
proudly spurned only four months ago, would now have been PP III 8 311 14
"Only think of its being three months," she cried, "since PP III 9 316 7
It was many months since she had mentioned his name to PP III 11 331 16
17
them so many previous months of suspense and vexation. PP III 13 347 28
now, and has been many months, inexpressibly painful to me. PP III 16 367 14
had been in town three months last winter, that I had PP III 16 371 45
stood the test of many months suspense, and enumerating PP III 17 376 36
It was some months before Sir Thomas's consent could be MP I 4 39 12
protegee, after some months further trial at her uncle's MP I 4 40 15
months, and Miss Sneyd, I believe, has never forgiven me. MP I 5 51 40
improved; and for three months we were all dirt and MP I 6 57 31
age three months before Everingham was all that it is now. MP I 6 61 56
at least; the middle of November was three months off. MP I 11 107 3
Three months comprised thirteen weeks. MP I 11 107 3
I have now been here nearly five months! and moreover the MP II 4 210 17
and moreover the quietest five months I ever passed." MP II 4 210 17
of her in the last few months had excited, Fanny had never MP II 6 234 18
So many months acquaintance!-- MP II 11 288 22
the guest of neither brother nor sister many months longer. MP II 12 295 24
returning for a couple of months to the scenes of her MP III 6 369 11
Edmund too--to be two months from him, (and perhaps, she MP III 6 370 12
My uncle talked of two months. MP III 11 410 13
Two months is an ample allowance, I should think six weeks MP III 11 410 16
waiting for the two months to be ended--that must not be MP III 11 411 16
Seven weeks of the two months were very nearly gone, when MP III 13 420 1
soon be almost three months instead of two that she had MP III 14 430 6
She felt that she had, indeed, been three months there; MP III 15 439 9
A woman married only six months ago, a man professing MP III 15 441 20
you to invite Susan to go with you, for a few months. MP III 15 443 23
It was three months, full three months, since her quitting MP III 15 446 35
that I had been too apt to dwell on for many months past. MP III 16 457 30
was over, and a very few months had taught him, by the MP III 17 468 21
of the latter, for some months purposely lengthened, ended MP III 17 469 23
had spent two very happy months with them, and now loved E I 4 27 4
and it was therefore many months since they had been seen E I 11 91 2
little girl about eight months old, who was now making her E I 12 98 2
coming two or three months later would be a much better E I 18 144 2
she is to be three months with us at least. E II 1 159 20
Three months, she says so, positively, as I am going to E II 1 159 20
a distance from us, for months together--not able to come E II 1 160 23
doubt that three or four months at Highbury will entirely E II 1 161 29
spend, perhaps, her last months of perfect liberty with E II 2 166 10
depended more on a few months spent in her native air, for E II 2 166 10
like through three long months!--to be always doing more E II 2 166 11
And as it is some months since Miss Campbell married, the E II 3 175 43
she had thankfully passed six weeks not six months ago?-- E II 5 187 4
do for them in the months of January, February, and March? E II 8 217 32
people passing many, many months successively, without E II 11 247 1
months ago, to lace up her boot, without recollecting. E II 14 270 3
I have spent so many happy months there!(with a little E II 14 273 19
Jane had come to Highbury professedly for three months; E II 15 285 14
gone to Ireland for three months; but now the Campbells E II 15 285 14
For two or three months longer I shall remain where I am, E II 17 301 19
If a separation of two months should not have cooled him, E III 1 315 1
blessing of having two months before him of such near E III 1 317 8
Two months must bring it to the proof. E III 1 317 9
to remain there full two months longer, provided at least E III 5 343 1
You wrote me word of it three months ago." E III 5 344 7
whom she had been so many months neglecting, was now the E III 9 389 16
for at least these three months, cared nothing about him. E III 10 396 41
so many months," continued Mrs. Weston, "she was energetic. E III 12 418 6
his mother-in-law a few months ago, Emma, it would not E III 15 444 6
There must be three months, at least, of deep mourning; E III 16 460 56
by passing all the warm months with her at Kellynch-Lodge, P III 2 14 12
few months more, and he, perhaps, may be walking here." P III 3 24 38
A few months had seen the beginning and the end of their P III 4 28 6
with a few months ended Anne's share of suffering from it. P III 4 28 6
so sad of the autumnal months in the country, did not P III 5 33 6
With the prospect of spending at least two months at P III 6 43 3
She had no dread of these two months. P III 6 43 4
to get rid of, been six months on board Captain Frederick P III 6 51 30
Dick's having been six months under his care, and P III 6 52 33
to the memory of her two months visit there, but he was P III 11 93 4
A few months hence, and the room now so deserted, occupied P IV 1 123 7
an imprisonment of many months, and anxiously saying to P IV 3 137 2
the constant use of Gowland, during the spring months. P IV 4 146 3
it must be remembered, had not been a widower seven months. P IV 4 147 8
three months, in laura-place, and would be living in style. P IV 4 149 12
to take place in a few months, quite as soon as Louisa's. P IV 10 217 20
in six months, or even in twelve, but a long engagement!" P IV 11 231 8
The invitation was to one, for six months--with the S 3 379 1
The six months had long been over--& not a syllable was S 3 379 1
& September were the months;--and besides, the promised S 6 389 1

MONTHS' (3)
months' acquaintance they had been intimate two. PP II 18 230 11
"And it is to be a two months' visit, is not it?" MP III 11 410 12
for me to be fetched exactly at the two months' end." MP III 11 410 15

MONTONI (1)
It was the air and attitude of a Montoni!-- NA II 8 187 13

MONUMENT (4)
-----"like patience on a monument "smiling at grief." NA I 1 16 9
sight of a very elegant monument to the memory of Mrs. NA II 9 190 1
That the General, having erected such a monument, should NA II 9 190 2
The erection of the monument itself could not in the NA II 9 190 2

MOOD (5)
He is not in a sober mood. NA I 14 114 48
in a most humble mood, concerned for his children, and NA II 6 165 6
I am in a fine mood for gaiety.-- SS III 8 318 15
and, in an unhappy mood, thus spoke Mary;--"I do believe P III 6 44 7
And therefore, if you find her in a giving mood, you might S 12 424 1

MOON (1)
drive back, only the moon was not up, and it rained a NA I 15 116 1

MOONLIGHT (6)
But it does not signify, the nights are moonlight, and we NA I 11 84 19
it was moonlight and every body was full of engagements. SS I 7 33 4
your mother, and have a pleasant drive home by moonlight. MP I 6 62 58
a cave in Italy, and a moonlight lake in Cumberland; a MP I 16 152 2
It is a beautiful, moonlight night; and so mild that I E I 1 10 23
he had had in their moonlight walks and merry evening E I 4 28 6

MOOR (4)
"Sir, it is a moor park, we bought it as a moor park, and MP I 6 54 11
it cost seven shillings, and was charged as a moor park." MP I 6 54 11
of a moor park apricot, as the fruit from that tree. MP I 6 54 12
a stagnant marsh, a bleak moor & the constant effluvia of S 1 369 1

MOORINGS (1)
to say she had slipped her moorings and was coming out. MP III 7 380 20

MORAL (13)
such kind of moral extractions from the evil before them. PP III 5 289 44
for what becomes of the moral, if our comfort springs from PP III 18 381 13
The moral will be perfectly fair. PP III 18 381 14
by the same rule of moral obligation, her evident duty to MP I 4 38 10
Edmund had descended from that moral elevation which he MP I 17 158 1
moral, so infamously tyrannical as Sir Thomas. MP II 2 191 10
It was a picture which Henry Crawford had moral taste MP II 6 235 20
You have moral and literary tastes in common. MP III 4 348 23
no useful influence that way, no moral effect on the mind. MP III 17 463 8
feelings, that except in a moral light, as a penance, a E II 4 182 7
the strongest examples of moral and religious endurances. P III 11 101 24
fix on any one article of moral duty evidently P IV 5 160 27
it at all, not very moral--& being moreover by no means S 7 398 1

MORALISING (1)
Among other points of moralising reflection which the S 12 426 1

MORALISTS (2)
such works of our best moralists, such collections of the P III 11 101 24
like many other great moralists and preachers, she had P III 11 101 26

MORALITY (8)
I believe, to doubt the morality of my conduct in general, SS III 8 323 40
In the height of her morality, good woman! she offered to SS III 8 323 40
some new observations of thread-bare morality to listen to. PP I 12 60 7
We do not look in great cities for our best morality. MP I 9 93 49
with elegant morality upon new principles and new systems-- E I 3 21 5
This may be bad morality to conclude with, but I believe P IV 12 248 1
melancholy, just as satire or morality might prevail.-- S 7 396 1
from lessons of morality, & incentives to vice from the S 8 404 1

MORALIZE (1)
the world, but she could moralize over every morning visit; PP III 19 386 5

MORALIZED (1)
seeing him, Emma thus moralized to herself:-- "I do not E II 8 212 2
3

MORALIZING (3)
From such a moralizing strain as this, she was suddenly NA I 8 55 10
young ladies, in a very moralizing strain, to observe that NA II 11 210 7
wife sat sighing and moralizing over her broad hems with a E III 9 388 13

MORALLY (1)
It is morally impossible. MP I 1 6 6

MORALS (3)
of religion and morals, and consequently of the manners MP I 9 92 45
were not always on subjects so high as history or morals. MP III 12 419 8
manners, and probably of morals and discretion to suit-- MP III 16 450 8

MORBID (1)
by the tranquil & morbid virtues of any opposing character. S 8 404 1

MOREOVER (47)
I meant moreover to have reminded him of our being quite LS 13 262 1
If she is with her mother moreover, she must alas! in all LS 27 297 1
of tyranny; she was moreover noisy and wild, hated NA I 1 14 1
An estate of at least equal value, moreover, was assured NA II 1 135 42
To raise your spirits, moreover, she gives you reason to NA II 5 158 17
he promised himself moreover the pleasure of accompanying NA II 7 176 17
Moreover, I have too good an opinion of Miss Thorpe's NA II 10 206 31
her feelings moreover with some alarm towards herself. NA II 11 208 1
and professing myself moreover convinced, that the NA II 16 252 7
He insisted moreover on conveying all their letters to and SS I 6 30 6
He is moreover aware that she does disapprove the SS I 15 78 26
one could wish for: and, moreover, it is close to the SS II 8 197 22
The impertinence of these kind of scrutinies, moreover, SS II 14 249 8
him as a saint, but was moreover truly anxious that he SS III 5 293 2
in general, and was moreover discontented with the very SS III 8 323 40
As a clergyman, moreover, I feel it my duty to promote and PP I 13 63 12
It was, moreover, such a promising thing for her younger PP I 18 99 63
for marrying--and moreover for coming into Hertfordshire PP I 19 105 8
The journey would moreover give her a peep at Jane; and, PP II 4 151 1
there (an invitation moreover including the whole party) PP II 6 160 2
pretty friend has moreover caught his fancy very much. PP II 8 172 3
In his present behaviour to herself, moreover, she had a PP II 18 233 25
And this consideration leads me moreover to reflect with PP III 6 297 11
and my sister; and, moreover, to enter into an engagement PP III 7 302 14
"Mr. Collins moreover adds," "I am truly rejoiced that my PP III 15 363 22
I told him, moreover, that I believed myself mistaken in PP III 16 371 40
He had said to her moreover, on the very last morning, MP I 3 33 64
of any one, and who, moreover, if the cook makes a blunder, MP I 11 111 28
There was a great deal of needle-work to be done moreover, MP I 18 166 6
I have now been here nearly five months! and moreover the MP II 4 210 17
She had, moreover, to contend with one disagreeable MP II 11 286 17
Sir Thomas, feeling, moreover, his own replies, and his MP III 1 314 16
His sister, moreover, is your intimate friend, and he has MP III 1 316 27
In this occupation she hoped, moreover, to bury some of MP III 9 398 10
"And, moreover, if you must go to the sea, it had better E I 12 105 54
She was, moreover, perpetually hearing about him; for, E II 4 184 10
she could not take--and, moreover, she insisted on her E III 9 391 20
and such happiness moreover as she believed must still be E III 14 434 1
pretty nearly promised, moreover, to think of it, with the E III 15 449 34
She had had a disappointment, moreover, which that book, P III 1 7 13

And moreover, Sir Walter, I found she was not quite P III 3 22 25
a sensible man, and, moreover, a single man at the time, P III 4 30 10
She had this communication, moreover, from Mary. P III 6 45 9
Bride of Abydos; and moreover, how the Giaour was to be P III 11 100 23
moreover, assured of her having been a very fine woman. P IV 3 139 9
and quite as much so, moreover, for the opportunity it P IV 10 224 52
53
not very moral--& being moreover by no means pleased with S 7 398 1

MORGAN (2)
pleasanter still--Morgan, with his "dinner on table."-- S 5 389 1
The ease of the lady, her "how do you do Morgan?--" & S 9 406 1

MORGAN'S (1)
do you do Morgan?--" & Morgan's looks on seeing her, were S 9 406 1

MORLAND (25)
No one who had ever seen Catherine Morland in her infancy, NA I 1 13 1
Such was Catherine Morland at ten. NA I 1 14 2
Morland remonstrated, pleaded the authority of road-books, NA I 7 45 7
"You have lost an hour," said Morland; "it was only ten NA I 7 45 8
bid me sixty at once; Morland was with me at the time." NA I 7 47 19
"Yes," said Morland, who overheard this; "but you forget NA I 7 47 20
Morland must take care of you." NA I 7 48 31
Here is Morland and I come to stay a few days with you, so NA I 7 49 43
The Thorpes and James Morland were there only two minutes NA I 8 52 1
reason or reality, till Morland produced his watch, and NA I 9 67 33
family, attended by James Morland, appeared among the NA I 10 71 8
"I doubt our being able to do so much," said Morland. NA I 11 84 20
when a halloo from Morland, who was behind them, made his NA I 11 88 54
for conversation, and Morland said, "we had better go back, NA I 11 88 54
Morland is a fool for not keeping a horse and gig of his NA I 11 89 56
private partnership with Morland, a very good equivalent NA I 11 89 63
to her eyes; and Morland, miserable at such a sight, could NA I 13 98 3
Thorpe would have darted after her, but Morland withheld NA I 13 101 22
The very first day that Morland came to us last Christmas-- NA I 15 118 11
"Morland says exactly the same," replied Isabella; "and NA I 15 119 15
Morland says that by sending it to-night to Salisbury, we NA I 15 120 22
"Indeed, Morland, I must drive you away. NA I 15 120 24
means of injuring my dear Morland, making him sit down NA II 1 135 45
The expectations of his friend Morland, therefore, from NA II 15 245 12
a reconciliation between Morland and Isabella, convinced NA II 15 246 12

MORLAND'S (5)
said of Catherine Morland's personal and mental endowments, NA I 2 18 1
more attached to my dear Morland's family than to my own." NA I 15 118 9
A clever fancy of Morland's and Belle's. NA I 15 122 30
James Morland's second letter was then received, and the NA II 1 135 42
in daily expectation of Morland's engaging Isabella, but NA II 15 244 12

MORLANDS (6)
for the number; but the Morlands had little other right to NA I 1 13 1
in Wiltshire where the Morlands lived, was ordered to Bath NA I 1 17 12
done, on the part of the Morlands, with a degree of NA I 2 19 3
was, that, when the two Morlands, after sitting an hour NA I 7 50 44
The Allens, Thorpes, and Morlands, all met in the evening NA I 10 70 1
to the advantage of the Morlands;--confessed himself to NA II 15 246 12

MORNG (18)
her finery in the old chair to d. on the important morng.-- W 315 1
Emma had seen the Edwardses only one morng at Stanton, W 322 3
upon that for I was with Ld Osborne this morng--" W 327 7
The next morng brought a great many visitors. W 337 16
to call on Mrs E. on the morng after a ball, & this W 337 16
The morng passed quietly away in discussing the merits of W 338 17
home till the following morng, unless the Edwardses wd W 338 18
"We came only this morng.-- W 356 28
My kind brother & sister brought me home this very morng.-- W 356 28
for a short time the next morng; & had proceeded so far as W 360 29
Gazette, only yesterday morng in London--I think you will S 1 366 1
of the morng had given her a great curiosity to see. S 6 391 1
their house was cleared of morng visitors was to get out S 7 395 1
enough of Sir Edw: for one morng, & very gladly accepted S 7 398 1
time taken up all the morng, in dusting out bed rooms.-- S 7 401 1
we were off yesterday morng at 6--, left Chichester at the S 9 409 1
At any rate, she was seen all the following morng walking S 11 420 1
It was a close, misty morng, & when they reached the brow S 12 425 1

MORNING (469)
His answer came this morning, which I shall enclose to you, LS 13 262 1
She had this morning a letter from the lady with whom she LS 15 266 2
in my life as by a letter this morning from Miss Summers. LS 16 268 1
Reginald came this morning into my dressing room, with a LS 22 281 4
Is it true that he leaves Churchill this morning?" LS 23 284 6
said she laughing, or even this morning at breakfast. LS 23 284 6
I got up this morning before it was light--I was two hours LS 24 286 5
in which we had been this morning engaged, & which had LS 24 287 11
sent off my letter this morning, you might have been LS 40 308 1
Every morning now brought its regular duties;--shops were NA I 3 25 1
which every morning brought, of her knowing nobody at all. NA I 3 25 1
in a slight slumber, or a morning doze at most; for if it NA I 3 29 52
Tilney there before the morning were over, and ready to NA I 4 31 1
and say their prayers in the same chapel the next morning. NA I 4 34 7
by seeing a beautiful morning, she hardly felt a doubt of NA I 5 35 1
equally unsuccessful, in morning lounges or evening NA I 5 35 2
the horseman, or the curricle-drivers of the morning. NA I 5 35 2
the set; and if a rainy morning deprived them of other NA I 5 37 4
in the Pump-Room one morning, after an acquaintance of NA I 6 39 1
afraid it would rain this morning, just as I wanted to set NA I 6 39 4
what have you been doing with yourself all this morning?-- NA I 6 39 4
morning after his having had the pleasure of seeing her. NA I 8 54 4
Her plan for the morning thus settled, she sat quietly NA I 9 60 1
Did not we agree together to take a drive this morning? NA I 9 61 3
the busy idleness of the morning, and was immediately NA I 9 67 34
be got at market this morning, it is so uncommonly scarce." NA I 9 68 38
him this morning you know: you must introduce him to me. NA I 10 70 1
and I were agreeing this morning that, though it is vastly NA I 10 70 3
in full force the next morning; and till usual moment of NA I 10 71 8
"Yes, sometimes; but he has rid out this morning with my NA I 10 73 18
The morning had answered all her hopes, and the evening of NA I 10 73 22
they they should join in a walk, some morning or other. NA I 10 80 61
The morrow brought a very sober looking morning; the sun NA I 11 82 1
A bright morning so early in the year, she allowed would NA I 11 82 1
"It was such a nice looking morning! NA I 11 83 12
few people in the Pump-Room, if it rains all the morning. NA I 11 83 13
"Mrs. Allen," said Catherine the next morning, "will there NA I 12 91 1
she would not see me this morning when I called; I saw her NA I 12 94 9
place on the following morning; and they were to set off NA I 13 97 1
The next morning was fair, and Catherine almost expected NA I 14 106 1
they can be for a whole morning together, and how tired my NA I 14 109 26
The morning had passed away so charmingly as to banish all NA I 14 114 50
Towards the end of the morning however, Catherine having NA I 14 114 50
the world, who had been her dear friends all the morning. NA I 14 114 50
"They set off at eight this morning," said Miss Anne, "and NA I 14 115 50
Good morning to you." NA I 15 123 39
In the course of the morning which saw this business NA II 2 138 1
The past suspense of the morning had been ease and quiet NA II 2 138 1
The circumstances of the morning had led Catherine's NA II 2 140 11
along the Pump-Room one morning, by Mrs. Allen's side, NA II 3 143 1
a mistake--for I did not see him once that whole morning." NA II 3 145 11
for you spent the whole morning in Edgar's Buildings--it NA II 3 145 12
been only in jest in what he had told her that morning. NA II 6 167 6
a bright morning had succeeded the tempest of the night. NA II 7 172 1
"But we have a charming morning after it," she added, NA II 7 174 5
be wisest to take the morning while it is so fine; and do NA II 7 177 17
of his morning walks, and boded nothing good. NA II 8 187 14
that she might that morning have passed near the very spot NA II 8 188 17
It was Sunday, an the whole time between morning and NA II 9 190 1
The succeeding morning promised something better. NA II 9 191 3
fatal morning, shewn something like affection for her.-- NA II 10 199 1
which each morning became more severe: but, on the tenth. NA II 10 201 6
The General, meanwhile, though offended every morning by NA II 11 209 5
in his telling Henry one morning, that when he next went NA II 11 209 5
with his report in the morning; and afterwards I cannot in NA II 11 210 6
The next morning brought the following very unexpected NA II 12 216 1
2
To-morrow morning is fixed for your leaving us, and not NA II 13 224 18
now left her with "I shall see you in the morning." NA II 13 226 24
the morning, that he might not be obliged even to see her. NA II 13 226 25
they all met the next morning, her recovery was not equal NA II 14 235 13
He had been to several families that morning in hopes of SS I 7 33 4
in the course of the last morning, and each time did he SS I 8 39 18
Margaret one memorable morning direct their steps, SS I 9 40 3
of fair weather that morning allowed him to get out of SS I 9 43 12
early the next morning to make his personal inquiries. SS I 10 46 1
"for one morning I think you have done pretty well. SS I 10 47 4
walking together the next morning the latter communicated SS I 12 58 1
The morning was rather favourable, though it had rained SS I 13 63 2
He wished her a good morning, and attended by Sir John, SS I 13 66 51
I know where you spent the morning." SS I 13 67 61
I never spent a pleasanter morning in my life." SS I 13 68 70
called him out in the morning was almost certain of ending SS I 14 71 5
"I do not ask you to come in the morning, for we must walk SS I 14 74 21
Mrs. Smith has this morning exercised the privilege of SS I 15 75 6
"To London!--and are you going this morning?" SS I 15 76 7
in his manners this morning;--he did not speak like SS I 15 81 43
in the face the next morning, had she not risen from her SS I 16 83 1
over the present reverse for the chief of the morning. SS I 16 83 2
One morning, about a week after his leaving the country, SS I 16 85 15
breakfast-room the next morning before the others were SS I 18 96 2
He was particularly grave the whole morning. SS I 18 99 14
at breakfast the last morning, "you would be a happier man SS I 19 102 3
she was roused one morning, soon after Edward's leaving SS I 19 105 13
I wanted her to stay at home and rest this morning, but SS I 19 107 29
I met Colonel Brandon Monday morning in Bond-Street, just SS I 20 115 48
with a smile, "from what I have witnessed this morning." SS I 21 122 18
do but meet him of a morning, he is not fit to be seen.-- SS I 21 123 28
their morning discourse, mush have left at least doubtful. SS II 1 141 7
called at the cottage one morning, to beg in the name of SS II 1 143 9
Marianne rose the next morning with recovered spirits and SS II 4 164 21
she had business that morning, to which Mrs. Jennings and SS II 4 164 23
It was late in the morning before they returned home; and SS II 4 165 25
she had met and invited in the morning, dined with them. SS II 4 166 31
breakfast the following morning, "Sir John will not like SS II 5 167 1
The morning was chiefly spent in leaving cards at the SS II 5 168 8
"Don't you find it colder than it was in the morning, SS II 5 168 9
of the fire, and every morning in the appearance of the SS II 5 168 10
She insisted on being left behind, the next morning, when SS II 5 169 15
Sir John met him somewhere in the street this morning." SS II 5 171 38
to write the next morning to her mother, and hoped by SS II 5 171 38
power over a cold, gloomy morning in January, Marianne, SS II 7 180 1
Her second note, which had been written on the morning SS II 7 187 39
40
The morning that we parted too! SS II 7 189 46
Mrs. Taylor did say this morning, that one day Miss Walker SS II 8 194 12
"what I heard this morning may be--there may be more truth SS II 8 198 33
elucidation, for this very morning first unfolded it to us. SS II 8 199 36
Marianne awoke the next morning to the same consciousness SS II 9 201 1
attendance, went out alone for the rest of the morning. SS II 9 203 10
I received it on the very morning of our intended party to SS II 9 209 30
papers, which she saw her eagerly examining every morning. SS II 10 217 16
with her and Mrs. Jennings one morning for half an hour. SS II 11 220 1
This morning I had fully intended to call on you, if I SS II 11 221 9
over again the next morning more openly, for at her SS II 13 238 2
she went thither every morning as soon as she was dressed, SS II 14 246 2
at least all the morning, in Mrs. Jennings's house; but it SS II 14 246 2
it, wrote the next morning to Lucy, to request her company SS II 14 253 26
About the third or fourth morning after their being thus SS III 1 257 2
3
matter;--till this very morning, poor Nancy, who, you know, SS III 1 258 7
The next morning brought a farther trial of it, in a visit SS III 1 265 33
I left her this morning with her lawyer, talking over the SS III 1 269 53
However this morning he came just as we came home from SS III 2 273 16
The next morning brought Elinor a letter by the two-penny SS III 2 277 29
she come this way any morning, 'twould be a great kindness, SS III 2 277 30
and the rest of the morning was easily whiled away, in SS III 6 303 10
The morning was fine and dry, and Marianne, in her plan of SS III 6 303 11
morning of the same continued rain had reduced very low. SS III 6 304 14
Marianne got up the next morning at her usual time; to SS III 7 307 1
On the morning of the third day however, the gloomy SS III 7 310 8
did Mrs. Jennings hear in the morning of what had passed. SS III 7 313 20
"Yes--I left London this morning at eight o'clock, and the SS III 8 318 20
was to go the next morning--was spent by me in SS III 8 323 40
all safely out of the house one morning, and left my name." SS III 8 326 53
The next morning brought another short note from Marianne-- SS III 8 327 55
sister wrote to me again, you know the very next morning. SS III 8 328 61
Cleveland-- a letter that morning received from Mrs. SS III 8 330 69
and at eight o'clock this morning I was in my carriage. SS III 8 331 69
The next morning produced no abatement in these happy SS III 10 342 8
But at last a soft, genial morning appeared; such as might SS III 10 344 11
morning--I have now heard exactly what I wished to hear."-- SS III 11 350 5
6
Their man-servant had been sent one morning to Exeter on SS III 11 353 22
23
"I see Mr. Ferrars myself, ma'am, this morning in Exeter, SS III 11 354 27
usually returned in the morning, early enough to interrupt SS III 13 369 34
were walking together one morning before the gates of SS III 14 375 9
by a young man in a morning dress & boots, who was W 327 7
the question of, "have you been walking this morning?" W 345 21
the morning in the kitchen herself directing & scolding.-- W 360 30
If I had known as much this morning, I certainly would not PP I 2 7 22
this morning, and never said a word about it till now." PP I 2 7 24
necessary; and the morning after the assembly brought the PP I 5 18 3
Meryton; she saw him one morning at his own house, and has PP I 6 22 7
necessary to amuse their morning hours and furnish PP I 7 28 3
After listening one morning to their effusions on this PP I 7 29 5
6
of the day, as he was going the next morning to London. PP I 7 29 7
Till the next morning, however, she was not aware of all PP I 7 31 29
myself very unwell this morning, which, I I suppose, is to PP I 7 31 29
30
I shall never forget her appearance this morning. PP I 8 35 4
remarkably well, when she came into the room this morning. PP I 8 36 7
in the morning, if Miss Bennet were not decidedly better. PP I 8 40 59
sister's room, and in the morning had the pleasure of PP I 9 41 1
spent some hours of the morning with the invalid, who PP I 10 47 1
When you told Mrs. Bennet this morning that if you ever PP I 10 49 27
night all the foolish things that were said in the morning. PP I 10 49 28
Elizabeth wrote the next morning to her mother, to beg PP I 12 59 1
that morning should be mentioned, and the request made. PP I 12 59 1
On Sunday, after morning service, the separation, so PP I 12 60 5
at breakfast the next morning, "that you have ordered a PP I 13 61 1
The next morning, however, made an alteration; for in a PP I 15 70 3
"No; he never saw him till the other morning at Meryton." PP I 18 96 52
private audience with her in the course of this morning?" PP I 19 104 1
2
What do you think has happened this morning?-- PP I 20 112 25
Longbourn house the next morning with admirable slyness, PP I 22 121 1
But on the following morning, every hope of this kind was PP I 22 124 11
spend a morning with her, without any danger of seeing him. PP II 2 142 17
After waiting at home every morning for a fortnight, and PP II 3 147 25

The day passed most pleasantly away; the morning in bustle	PP	II	4	152	5
the whole day or next morning, but their visit to Rosings.	PP	II	6	160	4
was walking the whole morning within view of the lodges	PP	II	7	170	7
On the following morning he hastened to Rosings to pay his	PP	II	7	170	7
Elizabeth was sitting by herself the next morning, and	PP	II	9	177	1
They called at various times of the morning, sometimes	PP	II	9	180	28
Elizabeth awoke the next morning to the same thoughts and	PP	II	12	195	1
the morning, to stop at the gates and look into the park.	PP	II	12	195	2
It was dated from Rosings, at eight o'clock in the morning,	PP	II	12	196	3
this letter in your hands in the course of the morning.	PP	II	12	203	5
and herself only the morning before; and at last she was	PP	II	13	206	4
The two gentlemen left Rosings the next morning; and Mr.	PP	II	14	210	1
all the work of the morning, and pack her trunk afresh.	PP	II	14	213	20
On Saturday morning Elizabeth and Mr. Collins met for	PP	II	15	215	1
pleasures of the morning to any body who would hear her.	PP	II	16	222	21
related to her the next morning the chief of the scene	PP	II	17	224	1
from whence they were to set out early the next morning.	PP	II	18	235	40
morning with Elizabeth in pursuit of novelty and amusement.	PP	II	19	239	11
was revived the next morning, and she was again applied to,	PP	II	19	241	17
by the exercise of the morning, found Elizabeth's arm	PP	III	1	256	61
that she had never seen him so pleasant as this morning.	PP	III	1	258	71
to be out of sight of the inn the whole of that morning.	PP	III	2	260	1
But her conclusion was false; for on the very morning	PP	III	2	260	1
to wait on her at Pemberley the following morning.	PP	III	2	266	17
of the family intended a visit to Georgiana that morning.	PP	III	3	268	8
"How very ill Eliza Bennet looks this morning, Mr. Darcy, "	PP	III	3	270	13
but were not missed till yesterday morning at eight.	PP	III	4	274	3
all the misery of the morning, found herself, in a shorter	PP	III	4	281	29
end well, and that every morning would bring some letter,	PP	III	5	287	33
at your surprise tomorrow morning, as soon as I am missed.	PP	III	5	291	60
walked here on Wednesday morning to condole with us, and	PP	III	5	292	66
from Mr. Bennet the next morning, but the post came in	PP	III	6	294	1
One morning, soon after their arrival, as she was sitting	PP	III	9	318	21
					22
Well, Monday morning came, and I was in such a fuss!	PP	III	9	319	24
shall devote this whole morning to answering it, as I	PP	III	10	321	2
was still with him, but would quit town the next morning.	PP	III	10	323	2
believe your letter this morning gave him great pleasure,	PP	III	10	324	2
But on the third morning after his arrival in	PP	III	11	333	30
His friend had left him that morning for London, but was	PP	III	13	344	1
for his coming next morning to shoot with her husband.	PP	III	13	345	19
Bennet spent the morning together, as had been agreed on.	PP	III	13	346	21
One morning, about a week after Bingley's engagement with	PP	III	14	351	1
It was too early in the morning for visitors, and besides,	PP	III	14	351	1
The next morning, as she was going down stairs, she was	PP	III	15	361	6
He then said, "I have received a letter this morning that	PP	III	15	362	9
					10
at a window the next morning, "if that disagreeable Mr.	PP	III	17	374	20
said Mrs. Bennet, "to walk to oakham mount this morning.	PP	III	17	374	23
could moralize over every morning visit; and as she was no	PP	III	19	386	5
Norris, "and what I was saying to my husband this morning.	MP	I	1	10	15
when she was found one morning by her cousin Edmund, the	MP	I	2	15	9
He had said to her moreover, on the very last morning,	MP	I	3	33	64
ten miles of indifferent road, to pay a morning visit.	MP	I	4	39	10
I sat there an hour one morning waiting for anderson, with	MP	I	5	50	35
London--but this morning we heard of it in the right way.	MP	I	6	57	33
favourite instrument; one morning secured an invitation	MP	I	7	64	12
at the parsonage every morning; she would gladly have been	MP	I	7	65	14
have her for a longer time--for a whole morning in short.	MP	I	7	69	28
But any morning will do for this.	MP	I	7	70	29
took place the next morning;--the party included all the	MP	I	7	70	30
a pleasant fresh-feeling morning, less hot than the	MP	I	8	75	1
and was formerly in constant use both morning and evening.	MP	I	9	86	9
we have been doing this morning--seeing a great house,	MP	I	9	95	71
seemed to enjoy your drive here very much this morning.	MP	I	10	98	11
I have had enough of the family for one morning.	MP	I	10	100	28
had been hoping the whole morning to reach at last; and	MP	I	10	103	49
nieces, she had found a morning of complete enjoyment--for	MP	I	10	103	50
about green goose from Monday morning till Saturday night."	MP	I	11	112	31
of speaking the next morning, were quite as impatient of	MP	I	13	128	38
who had been out all the morning, knew any thing of the	MP	I	15	138	2
my horse early to-morrow morning, and ride over to Stoke,	MP	I	15	148	58
found it quite as puzzling when she awoke the next morning.	MP	I	16	150	1
spring, and late autumn morning, to such a willing mind as	MP	I	16	151	2
And the morning wore away in satisfactions very sweet, if	MP	I	17	159	6
Edmund's first object the next morning was to see his	MP	II	2	187	1
It was a busy morning with him.	MP	II	2	190	9
guns the chief of the morning, and Tom had taken the	MP	II	2	191	10
She had been expecting to see him the whole morning--and	MP	II	2	192	11
plan of exercise for that morning, and of every chance of	MP	II	4	205	3
up his mind by the next morning to give another fortnight	MP	II	6	229	1
of ship news, the next morning, seemed the reward of his	MP	II	6	232	13
of it appeared the next morning at breakfast, when, after	MP	II	8	252	1
passing around him on the subject, from morning till night.	MP	II	8	256	13
Thursday was the day of the ball: and on Wednesday morning,	MP	II	8	256	14
Fanny's spirits lived on it half the morning, deriving	MP	II	9	266	21
in the course of a long morning, spent principally with	MP	II	9	267	22
I have been pained by her manner this morning, and cannot	MP	II	9	268	31
expressions of tender gallantry as had blessed the morning.	MP	II	10	278	20
had acknowledged in the morning, was peculiarly to be	MP	II	10	278	20
It will be the last time you know, the last morning."	MP	II	10	280	28
had hoped to have William all to herself, the last morning.	MP	II	10	280	32
cheerfully, and as the morning afforded her an opportunity	MP	II	11	283	7
"Had you seen her this morning, Mary," he continued, "	MP	II	12	296	31
Park again the next morning, and at an earlier hour than	MP	II	13	298	1
The post was late this morning, but there has not been	MP	II	13	299	5
when she awoke the next morning; but she remembered the	MP	III	1	311	1
have had a visitor this morning--I had not been long in my	MP	III	1	313	14
for after so stormy a morning; but she trusted, in the	MP	III	1	324	58
Fanny, I have had a very agreeable surprise this morning.	MP	III	2	332	23
begin very early in the morning; and when the small,	MP	III	6	374	29
The next morning saw them off again at an early hour; and	MP	III	7	376	6
The thrush went out of harbour this morning.	MP	III	7	377	7
The thrush went out of harbour this morning.	MP	III	7	380	20
here in the morning to see the thrush go out of harbour.	MP	III	7	380	20
night's rest, a pleasant morning, the hope of soon seeing	MP	III	8	388	1
to spend the chief of the morning up stairs, at first only	MP	III	9	398	9
One morning about this time, Fanny having now been nearly	MP	III	10	399	2
walk;--"it was a lovely morning, and at the season of the	MP	III	10	401	10
season of the year a fine morning so often turned off,	MP	III	10	401	10
after morning service and staying till dinner-time.	MP	III	11	408	4
symptoms and Mrs. Grant's morning calls, it was very hard	MP	III	13	425	6
he saw her this morning, she returns to Wimpole-Street to-	MP	III	14	435	14
She could still think of little else all the morning; but	MP	III	15	438	8
I shall be at Portsmouth the morning after you receive	MP	III	15	442	23
By eight in the morning, Edmund was in the house.	MP	III	15	444	28
The next morning produced a little more.	MP	III	15	446	34
For a few days every morning visit in Highbury included	E	I	2	18	9
As she sat one morning, looking forward to exactly such a	E	I	3	22	7
likeness, to every morning visitor in Brunswick-Square;--	E	I	6	46	21
She was obliged to go the next morning for an hour or two	E	I	8	57	1
"You are expecting her again, you say, this morning?"	E	I	8	58	14
"Good morning to you,"--said he, rising and walking off	E	I	8	66	55
to Mrs. Goddard's that morning, and meeting with Harriet	E	I	8	67	56
A piece of paper was found on the table this morning-- (	E	I	9	78	50
Later in the morning, and just as the girls were going to	E	I	9	81	78
Either in the morning or evening of every day, excepting	E	I	11	94	14
I shall see you at the Abbey to-morrow morning I hope, and	E	I	12	107	61
going about every morning among her old acquaintance with	E	I	13	108	1
such a cordial as I knew had been given in the morning."	E	I	13	114	31
morning will bring us both a more comfortable report.	E	I	13	114	34
I had a letter from him this morning, and he will be with	E	I	14	119	7
The youth and cheerfulness of morning are in happy analogy,	E	I	16	137	13
for exercise, every morning beginning in rain or snow, and	E	I	16	138	17
Highbury the following morning in his way to Bath, where,	E	I	17	140	2
Emma and Harriet had been walking together one morning,	E	II	1	155	1
we had a letter this very morning,' I do not know that I	E	II	1	157	7
Now, however, we must wish you and Mrs. Bates good morning.	E	II	1	162	32
was expressing the next morning, being at Hartfield again	E	II	3	170	1
"Oh! my dear sir, how are you this morning?	E	II	3	172	24
Good morning to you, my dear sir.	E	II	3	177	50
Good morning to you."	E	II	3	177	50
and on the very morning of his setting off for Bath again,	E	II	4	185	11
Frank comes to-morrow--I had a letter this morning--we see	E	II	5	188	7
The morning of the interesting day arrived, and Mrs.	E	II	5	189	19
"There is no necessity for my calling this morning," said	E	II	5	194	39
					40
The next morning brought Mr. Frank Churchill again.	E	II	6	196	1
as their visit included all the rest of the morning.	E	II	6	196	2
body's returning into their proper place the next morning.	E	II	6	198	5
this morning was in another respect particularly opportune.	E	II	7	206	5
Miss Bates last night, that I would come this morning.	E	II	9	234	26
The rivet came out, you know, this morning.--	E	II	9	236	46
other hindered me all the morning; first one thing, then	E	II	9	236	46
Mr. Knightley called one morning, and Jane was eating	E	II	9	238	51
watches, so much of the morning was perceived to be gone,	E	II	10	246	55
morning, we may talk it over, and see what can be done."	E	II	11	252	32
"And you must be off this very morning?"	E	II	12	260	24
of seeing him which every morning had brought, the	E	II	12	262	38
nor, after the first morning, to be less disposed for	E	II	13	264	1
I believe I was half an hour this morning shut up with my	E	II	14	278	40
this morning, or I am sure you must have been wet.--	E	II	16	293	10
					11
Miss Fairfax, of your being out this morning in the rain.	E	II	16	294	24
					25
The man who fetches our letters every morning (one of our	E	II	16	295	34
my word, I have scarcely ever had a bad morning before."	E	II	16	296	35
know whether the wet walk of this morning had produced any.	E	II	16	298	58
eight o'clock in the morning, and might now have been	E	II	17	303	23
I met the letters in my way this morning, and seeing my	E	II	18	305	5
one morning, I remember*, he came to me quite in despair."	E	II	18	308	28
The day approached, the day arrived; and, after a morning	E	III	2	319	1
she walked about the lawn the next morning to enjoy.--	E	III	3	332	1
She was not to see Frank Churchill this morning.	E	III	3	332	2
The pleasantness of the morning had induced him to walk	E	III	3	334	7
when Harriet came one morning to Emma with a small parcel	E	III	4	337	1
					2
"Do not you remember one morning?--no, I dare say you do	E	III	4	339	18
But one morning--I forget exactly the day--but perhaps it	E	III	4	339	18
spirits one morning because she thought she had prevailed.	E	III	5	346	16
We had great amusement with those letters on morning.	E	III	5	347	19
had agreed to choose some fine morning and drive thither.	E	III	6	352	2
It is to be a morning scheme, you know, Knightley; quite a	E	III	6	355	20
specious pretence of a morning drive, and an hour or two	E	III	6	356	29
"Some very fine morning, he, and Emma, and Harriet, could	E	III	6	356	30
Emma's, and Harriet's, going there some very fine morning.	E	III	6	357	30
for him by a fire all the morning, he was happily placed,	E	III	6	357	33
Morning decidedly the best time--never tired--every sort	E	III	6	358	35
Mrs. Elton had received notice of it that morning, and was	E	III	6	359	37
away the morning; and the kindness had perfectly answered.	E	III	6	362	43
not like a man who is so soon discomposed by a hot morning.	E	III	6	364	58
I feel a strong persuasion, this morning, that I shall	E	III	6	365	62
"But you may come again in the cool of to-morrow morning."	E	III	6	365	69
but in her view it was a morning more completely misspent,	E	III	8	377	1
upon her the very next morning, and it should be the	E	III	8	377	1
just now, writing all the morning:--such long letters, you	E	III	8	378	8
yesterday, the very morning we were at Donwell,) when Jane	E	III	8	380	15
back beyond the next morning early; but that Mr. Frank	E	III	8	383	31
at Hartfield, the same morning, it appeared that she was	E	III	9	389	16
good; and the following morning she wrote again to say, in	E	III	9	390	16
One morning, about ten days after Mrs. Churchill's decease,	E	III	10	392	1
"can you come to Randall's at any time this morning?--	E	III	10	392	1
					2
Frank came over this morning, just to ask us how we did."	E	III	10	394	23
					24
"He has been here this very morning, on a most	E	III	10	395	30
last night, and Frank was off with the light this morning.	E	III	10	398	57
her visit, the very last morning of his being at Hartfield-	E	III	11	410	35
same all the following morning; and the same loneliness,	E	III	13	424	1
Only that morning.	E	III	13	424	1
from Mr. Weston this morning, and at the end of them he	E	III	13	425	9
but it was an ungenial morning; and though you will never	E	III	14	436	7
afternoon and yesterday morning, but had the comfort of	E	III	14	436	7
Do you remember the morning spent at Donwell?--	E	III	14	440	8
with you till the next morning, merely because I would be	E	III	14	441	8
This letter reached me on the very morning of my poor	E	III	14	442	8
Ever since I left you this morning, Emma, my mind has been	E	III	15	448	30
Larkins the whole morning, to have his thoughts to himself.	E	III	15	449	32
into the house since the morning after Box-Hill, when poor	E	III	16	452	8
like morning visits, and Mr. Elton's time is so engaged."	E	III	16	455	22
He really is engaged from morning to night.--	E	III	16	455	23
the note I sent him this morning, and the message he	E	III	16	457	38
Such a dreadful broiling morning!--	E	III	16	457	40
He went to Highbury the next morning, and satisfied	E	III	17	468	35
was thinking of it one morning as what must bring a great	E	III	18	470	1
"Have you heard from her yourself this morning?" cried he.	E	III	18	470	10
and was with me this morning immediately after breakfast,	E	III	18	472	20
our agreeable surprise in seeing him arrive this morning.	E	III	18	476	45
Till this morning, we have not once met since the day of	E	III	18	477	57
Has he been here this morning?--	E	III	18	479	75
said Mr. Shepherd one morning at Kellynch Hall, as he laid	P	III	3	17	1
On the morning appointed for Admiral and Mrs. Croft's	P	III	5	32	1
I have not seen a creature the whole morning!	P	III	5	37	22
all this morning--very unfit to be left alone, I am sure.	P	III	5	37	24
you, I have not seen a soul this whole long morning."	P	III	5	37	25
"You will see them yet, perhaps, before the morning is	P	III	5	38	30
nothing at all the matter with me till this morning.	P	III	5	39	37
for they met every morning, and hardly ever spent an	P	III	6	46	12
When the Crofts called this morning, (they called here	P	III	6	50	27
is ill; and you saw, this morning, that if I told him to	P	III	7	56	12
he was coming the very next morning to shoot with Charles.	P	III	7	58	22
The morning hours of the cottage were always later than	P	III	7	59	24
come, particularly in the morning, when he had no	P	III	9	73	2
One morning, very soon after the dinner at the Musgroves,	P	III	9	78	21
One morning, about this time, Charles Musgrove and Captain	P	III	10	83	3
They meant to take a long drive this morning; perhaps we	P	III	10	84	8
The first heedless scheme had been to go in the morning	P	III	11	94	8
of the party the next morning, agreed to stroll down to	P	III	12	102	1
They praised the morning; gloried in the sea; sympathized	P	III	12	102	1
					2
lateness of the morning,--an hour already gone since they	P	III	12	113	57
to be sent home the next morning early, when there would	P	III	12	114	64
which the same spots had witnessed earlier in the morning.	P	III	12	115	66
They had an early account from Lyme the next morning.	P	IV	1	121	2
Mary had been hysterical again this morning.	P	IV	1	121	2
could not spend her last morning at Uppercross better than	P	IV	1	122	5
It had been a frosty morning, to be sure, a sharp frost,	P	IV	3	142	13
On going down to breakfast the next morning, she found	P	IV	4	145	1
In the course of the same morning, Anne and her father	P	IV	4	145	3
The Bath paper one morning announced the arrival of the	P	IV	4	148	10
Sir Walter, Elizabeth and Mrs. Clay returned one morning	P	IV	5	156	14
the next morning that they had had a delightful evening.--	P	IV	5	158	21
her carriage almost every morning, and she never failed to	P	IV	6	168	24
it so happened that one morning, about a week or ten days	P	IV	6	168	25

full of them every morning; sure to have plenty of chat; P IV 6 170 29
glance, and a "good morning to you," being all that she P IV 7 177 16
The following morning Anne was out with her friend, and P IV 7 178 28
Anne recollected with pleasure the next morning her P IV 9 192 1
her friend seemed this morning particularly obliged to her P IV 9 192 4
how to value your kindness in coming to me this morning. P IV 9 194 18
the greater part of the morning, was, that Anne had full P IV 9 211 103
and paid them a long morning visit; but hardly had she P IV 10 212 2
miss my father this morning, I gave way immediately, for I P IV 10 213 5
out of Bath the next morning, going early, and that he P IV 10 214 13
On Friday morning she meant to go very early to Lady P IV 10 215 14
she began to talk of spending the morning in Rivers-Street. P IV 10 215 14
Morning visits are never fair by women at her time of life, P IV 10 215 16
We had a famous set-to at rat-hunting all the morning, in P IV 10 219 26
in the course of the morning, and Anne walked off with P IV 10 220 29
A morning of thorough confusion was to be expected. P IV 10 221 32
He was to leave Bath at nine this morning, and does not P IV 10 222 35
whole of the following morning, therefore, she closed the P IV 10 227 69
matter of course the next morning, still to defer her P IV 11 229 1
her account of tasting a little before the morning closed. P IV 11 229 2
She had the kindest "good morning, God bless you," from P IV 11 236 39
You will see them both again this morning, I dare say P IV 11 239 51
She is rather done for this morning, and must not go so P IV 11 240 58
My spirits rallied with the morning, and I felt that I had P IV 11 245 76
other painful part of the morning dissipated by this P IV 11 245 77
I cut out myself from the morning post & the Kentish S 1 366 1
this morning on poor Arthur's trying to suppress a cough. S 5 387 1
visitors the very next morning;--amongst them, Sir Edwd S 7 394 1
on her feet the whole morning, on Mrs G.'s business or S 10 414 1
I shall be out every morning before breakfast--& take S 10 416 1

MORNING'S (14)
morning's prediction, how was it to be accounted for?-- NA II 6 170 12
In the course of this morning's reflections, she came to a NA II 9 192 5
form a great part of the morning's amusement; cold SS I 12 62 28
In a morning's excursion to Exeter, they had met with two SS I 21 118 2
on the table, when they came in from the morning's drive. SS II 5 169 13
table, when they returned from their morning's engagements. SS II 12 230 5
of news which his morning's lounge had supplied him with, W 323 3
If the morning's tolerable, pray do us the honour of W 347 21
Fatigued as she had been by the morning's walk, they had PP III 1 259 76
was the first grand object of every morning's impatience. PP III 6 296 9
was in spirits from the morning's rehearsal, and little MP I 18 171 25
the match; but it was a black morning's work for her. E I 1 6 6
every body seemed rather fagged after the morning's party. E III 8 381 19
morning's post had conveyed the history of Jane Fairfax.-- E III 13 433 41

MORNING-ROOM (1)
That room was the very shape and size of the morning-room E II 14 272 18

MORNING-VISIT (1)
I see that more than a mere dutiful morning-visit to your P III 10 87 26

MORNINGS (9)
people that had surprized her so much a few mornings back. NA I 11 84 17
For nine successive mornings, Catherine wondered over the NA II 10 201 6
it; and idled away the mornings at billiards, which ought SS III 6 304 15
"While I can have my mornings to myself," said she, "it is PP I 17 87 11
Mr. Collins devoted his mornings to driving him out in his PP II 7 168 1
renewed on each of the mornings that had now been spent PP III 4 273 1
They took their cheerful rides in the fine mornings of MP I 4 36 7
Four fine mornings successively were spent in this manner, MP I 7 70 30
with friends than their mornings: but one complete dinner E I 13 108 2

MORROW (36)
The morrow brought a very sober looking morning; the sun NA I 11 82 1
was expected on the morrow, there was no time to be lost. NA II 9 193 5
when he returned on the morrow to Northanger and heard of NA II 14 231 4
after breakfast on the morrow, that Marianne was again SS II 5 171 38
on Jane; and till the morrow, their going was deferred. PP I 12 59 2
The morrow produced no abatement of Mrs. Bennet's ill PP I 21 115 2
As he was to begin his journey too early on the morrow to PP I 22 123 4
determine what weather they were to have on the morrow. PP II 6 166 42
But the morrow passed off much better than she expected; PP III 17 378 46
going to him early on the morrow; and though Julia, who MP I 15 148 60
the morrow might produce in continuation of the subject. MP I 16 150 1
she thought of the morrow a great deal,--for if the three MP I 18 167 12
The morrow came, the plan for the evening continued, and MP I 18 167 14
It was a sad anxious day; and the morrow, though differing MP II 2 192 11
evening's comfort for the morrow, was so much uppermost in MP II 5 217 11
when she came on the morrow, in consequence of an early MP II 5 219 27
On the morrow they were walking about together with true MP II 6 234 17
and every succeeding morrow renewed a tete-a-tete, which MP II 6 234 17
to go to London on the morrow for a few days, he could not MP II 9 265 21
was threatened for the morrow was past, she could not but MP III 1 324 59
himself to wait till the morrow for a knowledge of what MP III 2 329 11
On the morrow the Crawfords were gone. MP III 5 365 37
on them again on the morrow, &c. and so they parted--Fanny MP III 10 406 22
back to London, on the morrow, for nothing more was seen MP III 12 415 1
2
duly accomplished, and the girls were ready for the morrow. MP III 15 444 27
took place on the morrow, and accompanied the whole E I 6 47 30
to return till the morrow, though it was the whist-club E I 8 68 58
exercise; and on the morrow, Emma had a charitable visit E I 10 83 1
Emma got up on the morrow more disposed for comfort than E I 16 138 14
be begun cutting on the morrow, or, at any rate, have the E III 6 361 42
She was just as determined when the morrow came, and went E III 8 377 2
dine with them on the morrow, actually on the morrow!-- P III 7 54 4
other house; and on the morrow the difference was so great, P III 7 59 24
to meet again till the morrow, but Captain Harville had P III 11 99 22
Anne was to leave them on the morrow, an event which they P IV 1 122 5
the more decided promise of a longer visit on the morrow. P IV 7 180 33

MORROW'S (2)
authorized to write an acquiescence by the morrow's post.-- E III 6 359 37
and Mrs. Clay for the morrow's party, the frequent P IV 10 227 69

MORTAL (2)
But while he was mortal, there must be a triumph. PP III 8 312 14
every thing the heart of mortal can most desire,--splendid PP III 15 362 15

MORTALS (4)
she called herself without scruple the happiest of mortals. NA I 15 121 26
plans and decisions of mortals, for their own instruction, MP III 17 471 29
regard, must, I think, be the happiest of mortals.-- E III 13 428 23
to mortals given with less of earth in them than heaven" &c S 7 397 1

MORTGAGE (1)
He had condescended to mortgage as far as he had the power, P III 1 10 20

MORTIFICATION (35)
was, produced severe mortification to the lady; and in NA I 8 54 10
her acquaintance;--one mortification succeeded another, NA I 8 55 10
Catherine, with a blush of mortification, left the house. NA I 12 91 3
Catherine, in deep mortification, proceeded on her way. NA I 12 92 3
have been spared the mortification of a walk through NA II 8 184 4
resist insult, or return mortification--but I cannot. SS II 7 189 52
His mother, stifling her own mortification, tried to sooth W 330 11
saved her from such mortification--& tho' shrinking under W 345 21
a return of distress; they were dances of mortification. PP I 18 90 4
of, and she had the mortification of seeing Mary, after PP I 18 100 68
an expression of mingled incredulity and mortification. PP II 11 193 27
the mortification of Kitty, are scarcely to be described. PP II 18 230 12
all the trouble and mortification attendant on such a PP III 10 326 3
might converse without mortification; and though the PP III 18 384 27
way to sink her in sad mortification, by adding, "if MP I 3 33 64
within, in gloom and mortification; and the carriage drove MP I 8 80 30
advanced, she had the mortification of seeing him advance MP I 11 113 42
of resentment and mortification, moved her chair MP I 15 145 42
at a distance, was felt with resentment and mortification. MP II 5 227 69
place to the infinite mortification of Mr. and Mrs. E I 2 15 3
and mutually deep mortification, they had to continue E I 15 132 37
to his "very great mortification and regret; but still he E I 18 144 1
peace and hope, to penance and mortification for ever. E II 2 165 8
to have purchased the mortification of having loved--yes, E II 8 219 44
And now to chuse the mortification of Mrs. Elton's notice E II 15 285 13
and mortification she must be returning to her seat. E III 2 327 38
obliged to endure the mortification of hearing that they E III 6 352 1
of anger against herself, mortification, and deep concern. E III 7 375 62
at his expense; the mortification and disdain of his E III 11 413 48
"Thank you," said he, in an accent of deep mortification, E III 13 429 29
pleasure for their sakes, than mortification for her own. P III 6 47 13
Anne fully submitted, in silent, deep mortification. P III 7 60 34
mortification of finding such words applied to her father. P IV 9 204 76
the various sources of mortification preparing for them! P IV 10 215 13
She had soon the mortification of seeing Mr. Elliot P IV 12 250 6

MORTIFICATIONS (6)
its hopes and fears, mortifications and pleasures have NA I 13 97 1
from the dreadful mortifications of unequal society, & W 361 31
so many mortifications, for the sake of discovering them." PP III 16 366 5
be with the rich; my mortifications, I think, would only E II 17 301 17
Anne herself would have found the mortifications of it P III 2 14 11
be feeling, for the mortifications which must be hanging P IV 10 212 1

MORTIFIED (29)
mortified to find it as I thought so ill bestowed. LS 24 290 13
were closed upon the mortified Catherine, who, having seen, NA II 8 185 5
natural consequence of mortified feelings, and of the NA II 14 235 13
His coldness and reserve mortified her severely; she was SS I 16 89 42
She was mortified, shocked, confounded. SS I 22 135 55
"Oh!--(in a soften'd voice, & rather mortified to find she W 351 25
forgive his pride, if he had not mortified mine." PP I 5 20 19
of a sister's frailty would have mortified her so much. PP III 8 311 12
Her father had most cruelly mortified her, by what he said PP III 15 364 25
and as she was no longer mortified by comparisons between PP III 19 386 5
Miss Bingley was very deeply mortified by Darcy's marriage; PP III 19 387 10
Her elder cousins mortified her by reflections on her size, MP I 2 14 8
though Fanny was often mortified by their treatment of her, MP I 2 20 32
was evidently mortified and displeased in no common degree. MP I 10 101 33
Sir Thomas would have been deeply mortified by a suspicion MP I 11 107 4
should have been deeply mortified, if any son of mine MP II 7 247 42
describe; how severely mortified, how cruelly disappointed, MP II 13 299 5
She was mortified. MP III 14 436 15
He was released from the engagement to be mortified and MP III 17 464 12
for ever; but he was mortified, he could not bear to be MP III 17 467 20
"To be sure," said Harriet, in a mortified voice, "he is E I 4 32 31
I should be mortified indeed if I did not believe I had E I 8 58 13
the young man, and was mortified to have been the means of E I 8 66 55
Ambition, as well as love, had probably been mortified. E II 3 179 53
He had gone away rejected and mortified--disappointed in a E II 4 181 3
I suppose," interrupted Mrs. Elton, rather mortified. E III 6 354 16
Never had she felt so agitated, mortified, grieved, at any E III 7 376 62
of powers; and it mortified her that she was given so E III 9 391 21
were shocked and mortified by the loss of their companion, P IV 12 251 9

MORTIFIES (2)
serious in veiw, but it mortifies me to see a young man of LS 8 256 4
It mortifies me. PP III 12 343 32

MORTIFY (6)
mortify & distress me.-- I am &c. R. De Courcy. LS 14 265 6
have been most anxious to mortify; while she herself, who SS II 12 232 16
did not seem to offend or mortify his fair companion in SS III 3 281 13
14
any thing for you, or to mortify you by the contrast of MP II 4 213 40
You would not wish to disappoint and mortify the Coles, I E II 7 210 19
Charles Hayter had met with much to disquiet and mortify P III 9 77 19

MORTIFYING (26)
as must bring the most mortifying conviction of the LS 34 304 1
with some hesitation, from the fear of mortifying him. NA I 7 49 37
It would be mortifying to the feelings of many ladies, NA I 10 74 22
It was as incomprehensible as it was mortifying and NA II 13 226 25
that sister, in spite of this mortifying conviction. SS I 19 104 11
talk of fortitude! mortifying and humiliating must be the SS II 10 213 2
& imagine him mortifying with his Barrel of oysters, in W 336 14
To this discovery succeeded some others equally mortifying. PP I 6 23 12
heart, but for the mortifying supposition of his viewing PP I 13 65 26
and not yet open to the mortifying conviction that PP II 3 150 29
she again began the mortifying perusal of all that related PP II 13 205 3
in terms of such mortifying, yet merited reproach, her PP II 13 208 10
though it was very mortifying to know that her neighbours PP III 11 333 27
therefore not to wear the cross might be mortifying him. MP II 8 254 8
upon no account. it would be mortifying her severely. MP II 9 262 11
We had better put an end to this most mortifying MP III 1 318 39
adverse passion of the man she did, was cruelly mortifying. MP III 7 376 4
but it is mortifying to be with Rushworth as a brother. MP III 13 423 2
it must have been very mortifying to her to see it fall to MP III 13 425 6
It was dreadfully mortifying; but Mr. Elton was proving E I 16 135 6
A real injury to the children--a most mortifying change, E II 8 228 87
on by others in a most mortifying degree; that she had E III 11 411 43
in a degree yet more mortifying; that she was wretched, E III 11 411 43
it is, in fact, a most mortifying retrospect for me. E III 14 440 8
listened to, made but a mortifying reception of Anne; or P III 12 115 68
How mortifying to feel that it was so! P IV 10 226 63

MOSQUITOES (1)
the climate is hot, and the mosquitoes are troublesome." SS I 10 51 21

MOSS (1)
grey moss and brush wood, but these are all lost on me. SS I 18 97 4

MOSTLY (6)
in learning what was mostly worn, and her chaperon was NA I 2 20 8
person whose society she mostly prized--and, in addition NA II 2 141 11
of the person who had mostly engaged their attention. PP III 3 272 20
habits of a young woman who had been mostly used to London. MP I 4 41 15
Norfolk was what he had mostly to talk of; there had been MP III 10 404 15
he seemed mostly fearful of not being incommoded enough. E I 6 49 42

MOTES (1)
the milk a mixture of motes floating in thin blue, and the MP III 15 439 9

MOTHER (586)
I have been called an unkind mother, but it was the sacred LS 2 245 1
My dear mother I am very sorry to tell you that it LS 3 246 1
school in town before her mother comes to us, which I am LS 3 247 1
to be separated from her mother; & a girl of sixteen who LS 3 247 1
does not come with her mother to Churchill, as she has not LS 4 248 2
My dear mother You must not expect Reginald back again LS 8 254 1
I really grow quite uneasy my dearest mother about LS 11 259 1
without acquainting your mother & myself or at least LS 12 260 1
Kiss the dear children for me. your affec: mother C. LS 13 263 1
As a mother she is unexceptionable. LS 14 265 5
My dear mother I return you Reginald's letter, & LS 15 266 1
her mother insinuates I am afraid she is a perverse girl. LS 15 266 3
She has been sadly neglected however, & her mother ought LS 15 266 3
My dear mother Mr Vernon returned on Thursday night, LS 17 269 1
She is very pretty, tho' not so handsome as her mother, LS 17 270 5
Her mother has insinuated that her temper is untractable, LS 17 270 5
where she may see her mother walking for an hour together, LS 17 271 7
detach him from her mother, we might bless the day which LS 18 272 2
example of levity in her mother; but yet I can pronounce LS 18 273 2
Her mother leaves her more to herself now than she did, & LS 18 273 3
opens her lips before her mother, she talks enough when LS 18 273 3
To disobey her mother by refusing an unexceptionable offer LS 19 274 2
a very unexpected guest with us at present, my dear mother. LS 20 275 1
& then addressed Frederica, but more frequently her mother. LS 20 276 3
tho' to me as a mother, it is highly flattering. LS 20 276 5
What can one say of such a woman, my dear mother?--such LS 20 278 8
of her injured mother. Yrs affec:ly S. Vernon. LS 22 282 8
Let me congratulate you, my dearest mother. LS 23 283 1
It is a great while since I have seen my father & mother. LS 23 283 4

Context	Work	Vol	Ch	Page	Line
He wants to marry her--her mother promotes the match--but	LS		23	284	4
He is only a fool--but what her mother can mean, heaven	LS		23	284	4
I trust however my dear mother, that we have no reason to	LS		23	284	7
Little did I imagine my dear mother, when I sent off my	LS		24	285	1
My dear mother, every hope which but two hours ago made me	LS		24	285	1
could do anything with my mother; but I was mistaken; they	LS		24	286	7
Frederica does not know her mother--Lady Susan means	LS		24	287	9
reconciliation with her mother precludes every dearer hope.	LS		24	291	16
This letter my dear mother, will be brought you by	LS		27	296	1
& I could not bear to have her at the mercy of her mother.	LS		27	296	1
be injured, even by her mother, or all her mother's	LS		27	296	1
If she is with her mother moreover, she must alas! in all	LS		27	297	1
for any other woman in the world, than her own mother.	LS		27	297	2
no great distance. Yr affec: mother C. De Courcy.	LS		40	309	1
removed from such a mother, & placed under her own care; &	LS		42	311	2
in the presence of her mother as heretofore, assured her	LS		42	311	3
for six weeks; but her mother, tho' inviting her to return	LS		42	313	7
of his attachment to her mother, for his abjuring all	LS		42	313	8
of her father and mother, her own person and disposition,	NA	I	1	13	1
Her mother was a woman of useful plain sense, with a good	NA	I	1	13	1
Her mother was three months in teaching her only to repeat	NA	I	1	14	1
Her mother wished her to learn music; and Catherine was	NA	I	1	14	1
of a letter from her mother, or seize upon any other odd	NA	I	1	14	1
her father; French by her mother; her proficiency in	NA	I	1	14	1
her father and mother remark on her personal improvement.	NA	I	1	15	2
"The very picture of him indeed!" cried the mother--and "I	NA	I	4	32	5
well-meaning woman, and a very indulgent mother.	NA	I	4	34	8
"Ah, mother! how do you do?" said he, giving her a hearty	NA	I	7	49	43
it, though I am his mother, that there is not a more	NA	I	8	58	33
with a pun, and her mother with a proverb; they were not	NA	I	9	65	31
both dead; at least the mother is; yes, I am sure Mrs.	NA	I	9	68	48
now, for they were put by for her when her mother died."	NA	I	9	68	48
My mother says he is the most delightful young man in the	NA	I	10	70	1
Young people will be young people, as your good mother	NA	I	13	104	36
what she is about; and if not, has a mother to advise her.	NA	I	13	105	40
and how tired my poor mother is at the end of it, as I am	NA	I	14	109	26
But what will your excellent father and mother say?--	NA	I	15	117	6
father and mother would never oppose their son's wishes.--	NA	I	15	119	14
My father and mother will be very glad to see you."	NA	I	15	123	41
and mother, and her kind compliments to all the Skinners.	NA	I	15	125	48
"A mother would have been always present.	NA	II	7	180	36
A mother would have been a constant friend; her influence	NA	II	7	180	36
"And how long ago may it be that your mother died?"	NA	II	8	186	9
bearing always an equal resemblance of mother and child.	NA	II	9	191	3
as to return only to see her mother in her coffin."	NA	II	9	197	25
"Her mother was a very good sort of woman," was Catherine's	NA	II	10	205	26
Good God! what will your father and mother say!	NA	II	13	225	19
Her father, mother, Sarah, George, and Harriet, all	NA	II	14	233	9
trouble," said her mother at last; "depend upon it, it is	NA	II	14	234	10
"Well," continued her philosophic mother, "I am glad I did	NA	II	14	234	12
so renewed; and her mother, perceiving her comfortable	NA	II	14	236	18
contradicted almost every position her mother advanced.	NA	II	14	239	28
defects of that sort, her mother could not but perceive	NA	II	15	240	1
brightened eye made her mother trust that this good-	NA	II	15	242	8
a silencing nod from her mother; for Mrs. Morland,	NA	II	15	243	9
for by the fortune of his mother, which had been large,	SS	I	1	3	2
Their mother had nothing, and their father only seven	SS	I	1	4	2
with his father and mother at Norland, had so far gained	SS	I	1	4	3
be the counsellor of her mother, and enabled her	SS	I	1	6	11
was a knowledge which her mother had yet to learn, and	SS	I	1	6	11
The resemblance between her and her mother was strikingly	SS	I	1	6	12
could strive to rouse her mother to similar exertion, and	SS	I	1	7	13
of Norland; and her mother and sisters-in-law were	SS	I	2	8	1
to do something for their mother while she lives rather	SS	I	2	10	16
of annuities; for my mother was clogged with the payment	SS	I	2	10	20
My mother was quite sick of it.	SS	I	2	11	20
One's fortune, as your mother justly says, is not one's	SS	I	2	11	21
they will pay their mother for their board out of it.	SS	I	2	12	24
When my mother removes into another house my services	SS	I	2	12	25
When your father and mother moved to Norland, though the	SS	I	2	12	26
plate, and linen was saved, and is now left to your mother.	SS	I	2	12	26
for their income, which her mother would have approved.	SS	I	3	14	1
whole of his fortune depended on the will of his mother.	SS	I	3	15	5
answer the wishes of his mother and sister, who longed to	SS	I	3	15	6
His mother wished to interest him in political concerns,	SS	I	3	16	6
contrast which recommended him most forcibly to her mother.	SS	I	3	16	7
"Like him!" replied her mother with a smile.	SS	I	3	16	10
Why should you be less fortunate than your mother?	SS	I	3	18	21
engrossed on the most affectionate principle by my mother.	SS	I	4	20	9
She knew that what Marianne and her mother conjectured one	SS	I	4	21	11
What his mother really is we cannot know; but, from	SS	I	4	21	15
of her mother and herself had outstripped the truth.	SS	I	4	22	16
She knew that his mother neither behaved to him so as to	SS	I	4	22	18
which her mother and sister still considered as certain.	SS	I	4	22	18
her mother from sending her letter of acquiescence.	SS	I	4	24	21
Mr. John Dashwood told his mother again and again how	SS	I	5	25	4
him questions which his mother answered for him, while he	SS	I	6	31	9
most like his father or mother, and in what particular he	SS	I	6	31	9
Sir John was a sportsman, Lady Middleton a mother.	SS	I	7	32	1
Luckily Lady Middleton's mother had arrived at Barton	SS	I	7	34	4
The young ladies, as well as their mother, were perfectly	SS	I	7	34	4
Mrs. Jennings, Lady Middleton's mother, was a good-	SS	I	7	34	5
his wife, or Mrs. Jennings to be Lady Middleton's mother.	SS	I	7	34	6
greater to you than to my mother; but you can hardly	SS	I	8	37	5
"My dearest child," said her mother laughing, "at this	SS	I	8	37	7
mother and Elinor from sharing such delightful sensations.	SS	I	9	41	4
Elinor and her mother rose up in amazement at their	SS	I	9	42	9
"My love," said her mother, "you must not be offended with	SS	I	10	48	6
Her mother too, in whose mind not one speculative thought	SS	I	10	49	11
amends for the regard of Lady Middleton and her mother.	SS	I	10	50	18
Lady Middleton was more agreeable than her mother, only in	SS	I	11	54	6
Towards her husband and mother she was the same as to them;	SS	I	11	55	6
But by an appeal to her affection for her mother, by	SS	I	12	59	5
which tnat indulgent mother must draw on herself, if (as	SS	I	12	59	5
promised not to tempt her mother to such imprudent	SS	I	12	59	5
subjects of raillery as delighted her husband and mother.	SS	I	12	62	27
Why they should not openly acknowledge to her mother and	SS	I	14	71	3
for my mother will never have money enough to attempt it."	SS	I	14	72	8
of employment; and her mother, who concluded that a	SS	I	15	75	1
In about half an hour her mother returned, and though her	SS	I	15	77	21
"You must remember, my dear mother, that I have never	SS	I	15	80	41
representations of her mother, to acknowledge the	SS	I	15	82	45
pain every moment to her mother and sisters, and	SS	I	16	83	1
Her mother was surprised, and Elinor again became uneasy.	SS	I	16	84	5
that she could not help suggesting it to her mother.	SS	I	16	84	7
From you, her mother, and so kind, so indulgent a mother,	SS	I	16	84	8
want of liberality in his mother, sat down to table	SS	I	17	90	1
I hope my mother is now convinced that I have no more	SS	I	17	90	3
for her that he had a mother whose character was so	SS	I	19	101	2
extorted from her, for Willoughby's service, by her mother.	SS	I	19	101	2
same inevitable necessity of temporising with his mother.	SS	I	19	102	2
Your mother will secure to you, in time, that independence	SS	I	19	103	7
increase, and her mother and sisters were spared much	SS	I	19	104	10
not by the absence of her mother and sisters, at least by	SS	I	19	105	12
Lady Middleton too, though she did not press their mother,	SS	I	19	109	40
I contradicted any body in calling your mother ill-bred."	SS	I	20	112	24
of Sir John's proposal to your mother before it was made?	SS	I	20	117	63
husband and mother on that subject went for nothing at all.	SS	I	21	118	2
such foibles, a fond mother, though, in pursuit of praise	SS	I	21	120	6
entreated by their mother to stay behind, the four young	SS	I	21	122	10
with your sister-in-law's mother, Mrs. Ferrars?"	SS	I	22	128	3
real opinion of Edward's mother, and not very desirous of	SS	I	22	128	6

Context	Work	Vol	Ch	Page	Line
and approbation of his mother; but I was too young and	SS	I	22	130	28
his mother; for she would never approve of it, I dare say.	SS	I	22	132	39
inquiries about Edward's mother; and I am so unfortunate,	SS	I	22	132	42
on both sides, "his mother must provide for him sometime	SS	I	22	133	46
Her mother, sisters, Fanny, all had been conscious of his	SS	II	1	139	1
his difficulties from his mother had seemed great, how	SS	II	1	140	3
every suspicion of the truth from her mother and sisters.	SS	II	1	140	4
The necessity of concealing from her mother and Marianne,	SS	II	1	141	5
be quite alone, except her mother and the two Miss Steeles.	SS	II	1	143	9
was persuaded by her mother, who could not bear to have	SS	II	1	143	9
Ferrars, I believe, is entirely dependent on his mother."	SS	II	2	147	6
that his mother might give him if he married to please her.	SS	II	2	147	7
of not leaving their mother at that time of year.	SS	II	3	153	1
Lord, I am sure your mother can spare you very well, and I	SS	II	3	153	2
I am sure your mother will not object to it; for I have	SS	II	3	153	2
But my mother, my dearest, kindest mother,--I feel the	SS	II	3	154	5
Whatever Marianne was desirous of, her mother would be	SS	II	3	155	6
"That is very true," replied her mother; "but of her	SS	II	3	156	13
not, and when she saw her mother so thoroughly pleased	SS	II	3	158	20
Her unwillingness to quit her mother was her only	SS	II	3	158	21
which Marianne and her mother equally shared, been	SS	II	4	159	1
in writing to her mother, and sat down for that purpose.	SS	II	4	160	4
"I am not going to write to my mother," replied Marianne	SS	II	4	160	5
from meeting her mother or the Miss Dashwoods again.	SS	II	4	164	21
After an hour or two spent in what her mother called	SS	II	4	164	23
Oh! my dear mother, you must be wrong in permitting an	SS	II	4	165	29
strongest manner to her mother the necessity of some	SS	II	4	165	30
company of her mother and cousins the following evening.	SS	II	5	170	28
the next morning to her mother, and hoped by awakening her	SS	II	5	171	38
Elinor was very earnest in her application to her mother,	SS	II	5	172	39
to her mother; for Willoughby neither came nor wrote.	SS	II	6	175	1
Think of your mother; think of her misery while you suffer;	SS	II	7	185	21
meat, and have not a neighbour nearer than your mother.	SS	II	8	197	22
The hand writing of her mother, never till then unwelcome,	SS	II	9	202	7
Her mother, still confident of their engagement, and	SS	II	9	202	8
again now returned; her mother was dearer to her than ever;	SS	II	9	203	9
sat down to write her mother an account of what had passed,	SS	II	9	203	10
grieving still more fondly over its effect on her mother.	SS	II	9	203	10
My regard for her, for yourself, for your mother--will you	SS	II	9	204	18
between the fate of mother and daughter! and so	SS	II	9	211	40
affliction be, when her mother could talk of fortitude!	SS	II	10	213	2
From all danger of seeing Willoughby again, her mother	SS	II	10	213	4
personal sympathy of her mother, and doomed her to such	SS	II	10	214	6
the exchange of a few old-fashioned jewels of her mother.	SS	II	11	220	1
inquiries after their mother were respectful and attentive.	SS	II	11	221	7
so much engaged with her mother, that really she had no	SS	II	11	222	14
And her mother too, Mrs. Ferrars, a very good-natured	SS	II	11	224	24
He has a most excellent mother.	SS	II	11	224	28
A thousand a-year is a great deal for a mother to give	SS	II	11	224	28
at Norland (and very valuable they were) to your mother.	SS	II	11	225	35
could now meet Edward's mother without that strong anxiety	SS	II	12	230	6
Edward who lived with his mother, must be asked as his	SS	II	12	231	10
must be asked as his mother was, to a party given by his	SS	II	12	231	10
all my happiness depends on--that is to be my mother!"--	SS	II	12	232	13
its being Miss Morton's mother, rather than her own, whom	SS	II	12	232	14
the graciousness of both mother and daughter towards the	SS	II	12	232	16
presented them to her mother, considerately informing her	SS	II	12	235	28
Perhaps Fanny thought for a moment that her mother had	SS	II	12	235	30
					31
disgusted with his mother, till they were more in private.	SS	II	13	243	34
the ill-humour of his mother and sister would have begun.	SS	II	14	250	12
so I often tell my mother, when she is grieving about it.	SS	II	14	251	13
matter, and my mother is perfectly convinced of her error."	SS	II	14	251	13
does my mother; and they are such favourites with Harry!"	SS	II	14	253	24
of a fortnight, that her mother felt it no longer	SS	III	1	257	1
undeceive yourself and my mother," added Elinor; "and once	SS	III	1	262	25
it would make you and my mother most unhappy whenever it	SS	III	1	263	29
and the insolence of his mother; and have suffered the	SS	III	1	264	29
His mother explained to him her liberal designs, in case	SS	III	1	266	38
good mother, in like circumstances, would adopt.	SS	III	1	268	45
be worse than all--his mother has determined, with a very	SS	III	1	269	53
and been talked to by his mother and all of them, and how	SS	III	2	273	16
What an ill-natured woman his mother is, an't she?	SS	III	2	275	22
returning to that dear mother, whom she so much wished to	SS	III	3	280	6
As Marianne's affection for her mother was sincere, it	SS	III	3	280	6
place, depend upon it his mother will feel as much as if	SS	III	5	296	20
My mother was the first person who told me of it, and I,	SS	III	5	299	35
as I directly said to my mother, I am not in the least	SS	III	5	299	35
My poor mother was half frantic."	SS	III	5	299	35
I offered immediately, as soon as my mother related the	SS	III	5	299	37
rude to his wife and her mother; she found him very	SS	III	6	304	15
was almost equally urgent with her mother to accompany her.	SS	III	7	308	3
to her the place of the mother she had taken her from; and	SS	III	7	308	3
taken their mother by surprise on the following forenoon.	SS	III	7	308	4
in her letters to her mother, she had pursued her own	SS	III	7	310	8
and dispatching a messenger to Barton for her mother.	SS	III	7	311	14
post-horses directly, she wrote a few lines to her mother.	SS	III	7	311	15
such a companion for her mother,--how gratefully was it	SS	III	7	311	16
fixed incoherently on her mother, and whenever she	SS	III	7	312	18
to herself her suffering mother arriving too late to see	SS	III	7	312	18
her;--and as for their mother, when Mrs. Jennings	SS	III	7	313	20
She was calm, except when she thought of her mother, but	SS	III	7	313	21
and to her doating mother, was an idea to fill her heart	SS	III	7	315	24
least not much later, her mother would be relieved from	SS	III	7	315	26
The knowledge of what her mother must be feeling as the	SS	III	7	316	30
Then came your dear mother to torture me farther, with all	SS	III	8	324	45
"Your poor mother too!--doting on Marianne."	SS	III	8	327	59
Eager to save her mother from every unnecessary moment's	SS	III	9	333	3
joyful relief;--and her mother, catching it with all her	SS	III	9	334	4
satisfied in knowing her mother was near her, and	SS	III	9	334	5
Margaret away, as her mother was unwilling to take her	SS	III	9	335	6
wondering whether her mother ever recollected Edward.	SS	III	9	335	7
could be given;--but her mother must always be carried	SS	III	9	336	11
"I know it is"--replied her mother seriously, "or after	SS	III	9	337	16
Elinor could not remember it;--but her mother, without	SS	III	9	338	21
					22
her mother, Colonel Brandon was invited to visit her.	SS	III	10	340	1
My mother too!	SS	III	10	346	28
But you,--you above all, above my mother, had been wronged	SS	III	10	346	28
You, my mother, and Margaret, must henceforth be all the	SS	III	10	347	30
"I know it--I know it," cried her mother.	SS	III	11	350	7
to the remark; and her mother was led by it to an	SS	III	11	352	18
By that time, Marianne was rather better, and her mother	SS	III	11	353	25
She observed, in a low voice, to her mother, that they	SS	III	11	355	39
She saw her mother and Marianne change colour; saw them	SS	III	12	358	9
with an air of surprise-- "no, my mother is in town."	SS	III	12	359	18
She dared not look up;--but her mother and Marianne both	SS	III	12	360	20
by Marianne and her mother, in an accent of the utmost	SS	III	12	360	22
Had my mother given me some active profession when I was	SS	III	13	362	5
myself in love; and as my mother did not make my home in	SS	III	13	362	5
And your mother has brought on herself a most appropriate	SS	III	13	366	18
I was renounced by my mother, and stood to all appearance	SS	III	13	367	22
favourable change in his mother towards him; and on that	SS	III	13	369	33
and by her shewn to her mother, might not be taken amiss;	SS	III	13	371	39
Lucy, who had owed his mother no duty, and therefore could	SS	III	14	376	11
entirely useless, for her mother and sisters spent much	SS	III	14	378	13
even for ever with her mother, and finding her only	SS	III	14	378	16
Not that her father or mother like officers, but if she	W			320	2
Her father & mother wd never consent to it.	W			320	2
to these ideas;--the mother tho' a very friendly woman,	W			322	3
of the stile of the mother who had brought her up.--	W			322	3
very early hour which her mother always fixed for going,	W			326	7

& mother think it has given him rather an unsettled turn.-- W 328 8
before his mother, wondering when they should begin.-- W 330 11
His mother, stifling her own mortification, tried to sooth W 330 11
joyfully at his mother and stepping forwards with an W 331 11
made both the boy & his mother; the latter of whom was W 331 11
with either of the Mr Tomlinsons, Mary?--said her mother. W 336 14
The father is decidedly against him, the mother shews him W 341 19
"You are very good--replied her mother--& I assure you it W 350 24
said her mother resentfully, "since we are not to visit." PP I 2 6 3
"Aye, so it is," cried her mother, "and Mrs. Long does not PP I 2 6 13
Jane was as much gratified by this, as her mother could be, PP I 3 12 15
"Another time, Lizzy," said her mother, "I would not dance PP I 5 20 16
Bingley; and though the mother was found to be intolerable PP I 6 21 1
gave animation to their mother, was worthless in their PP I 7 29 4
such girls to have the sense of their father and mother.-- PP I 7 29 12
go on horseback, and her mother attended her to the door PP I 7 31 28
Her sisters were uneasy for her, but her mother was PP I 7 31 28
"How can you be so silly," cried her mother, "as to think PP I 7 32 34
But with such a father and mother, and such low PP I 8 36 14
Longbourn, desiring her mother to visit Jane, and form her PP I 9 41 1
and invitation, the mother and three daughters all PP I 9 41 2
"Lizzy," cried her mother, "remember where you are, and do PP I 9 42 14
you are mistaken," said Elizabeth, blushing for her mother. PP I 9 43 24
tremble lest her mother should be exposing herself again. PP I 9 45 35
a favourite with her mother, whose affection had brought PP I 9 45 36
the next morning to her mother, to beg that the carriage PP I 12 59 1
They were not welcomed home very cordially by their mother. PP I 12 60 6
As for their mother, Mr. Collins's letter had done away PP I 13 64 20
was not long before her mother gave her to understand that PP I 17 88 14
cousin Miss de Bourgh, and of her mother lady Catherine. PP I 18 96 57
vexed to find that her mother was talking to that one PP I 18 98 63
Her mother only scolded her for being nonsensical. PP I 18 99 64
Her mother would talk of her views in the same PP I 18 100 67
not always looking at her mother, she was convinced that PP I 18 100 67
he addressed the mother in these words, "may I hope, madam, PP I 19 104 1
2
Your mother insists upon your accepting it. PP I 20 111 17
Your mother will never see you again if you do not marry PP I 20 112 19
and occasionally from some peevish allusion of her mother. PP I 21 115 1
as an occasion of introducing him to her father and mother. PP I 21 116 5
Elizabeth was sitting with her mother and sisters, PP I 23 126 1
the exclamations of her mother and sisters, by the PP I 23 126 4
But as no such delicacy restrained her mother, an hour PP I 23 129 14
"Oh! that my dear mother had more command over herself; PP II 1 134 4
5
affectionate mother who will always make the most of it." PP II 1 138 29
At least, you should not remind your mother of inviting PP II 3 145 7
and as, with such a mother and such uncompanionable PP II 4 151 1
When, after examining the mother, in whose countenance and PP II 6 162 12
Your mother should have taken you to town every spring for PP II 6 164 24
"My mother would have had no objection, but my father PP II 6 164 25
Your mother must have been quite a slave to your education. PP II 6 164 28
and if I had known your mother, I should have advised her PP II 6 165 32
When she thought of her mother indeed, her confidence gave PP II 10 187 40
which were kindly smiled on by the mother and daughter. PP II 14 210 4
to your mother to beg that you may stay a little longer. PP II 14 211 5
6
your father of course may spare you, if your mother can.-- PP II 14 211 10
daughters; and her mother, with manners so far from right PP II 14 213 17
and equivocal, that her mother, though often disheartened, PP II 16 223 26
"Well, Lizzy," continued her mother soon afterwards, "and PP II 17 228 31
If she is half as sharp as her mother, she is saving PP II 17 228 31
Their affectionate mother shared all their grief; she PP II 18 229 3
same feelings as in her mother and Lydia, that she PP II 18 230 14
Had Lydia and her mother known the substance of her PP II 18 232 22
They could have been understood only by her mother, who PP II 18 232 23
and at home she had a mother and sister whose constant PP II 19 237 3
discontentedness of her mother and Kitty made inevitable; PP II 19 237 3
and very minutely to her mother and Kitty; but her letters PP II 19 238 5
Those to her mother, contained little else, than that they PP II 19 238 5
a beauty!--I should as soon call her mother a wit.' PP III 3 271 16
17
Our poor mother is sadly grieved. PP III 4 274 3
I must conclude, for I cannot be long from my poor mother. PP III 4 274 3
My father and mother believe the worst, but I cannot think PP III 4 275 5
My poor mother is really ill and keeps her room. PP III 4 275 5
a father absent, a mother incapable of exertion, and PP III 4 280 26
"And my mother--how is she? PP III 5 286 29
"My mother is tolerably well, I trust; though her spirits PP III 5 286 30
My father and mother knew nothing of that, they only felt PP III 5 290 50
My mother was taken ill immediately, and the whole house PP III 5 292 62
My mother was in hysterics, and though I endeavoured to PP III 5 292 64
a father and mother, both of whom had been dead many years. PP III 6 296 8
to call them to their mother, went forward to meet her; PP III 7 301 1
him up stairs with their mother, when they were met by the PP III 7 301 4
5
It now occurred to the girls that their mother was in all PP III 7 305 39
"Well," cried her mother, "it is all very right; who PP III 7 306 47
mother was too happy, to be quite so obstinate as usual. PP III 7 307 48
mother.--your's, &c. "E. Gardiner." PP III 8 313 19
And their mother had the satisfaction of knowing, that she PP III 8 314 22
Her mother stepped forwards, embraced her, and welcomed PP III 9 315 3
The bride and her mother could neither of them talk fast PP III 9 316 6
"I should like it beyond any thing!" said her mother. PP III 9 317 14
My mother means well; but she does not know, no one can PP III 11 333 28
Elizabeth, to satisfy her mother, went to the window--she PP III 11 333 31
for themselves; and their mother talked on, of her dislike PP III 11 334 36
Elizabeth particularly, who knew that her mother owed to PP III 11 335 42
married," continued her mother, "but at the same time, Mr. PP III 11 336 51
Mr. Bingley," said her mother, " I beg you will come here, PP III 11 337 53
Her prudent mother, occupied by the same ideas, forbore to PP III 12 340 11
He was on one side of her mother. PP III 12 340 12
But when her mother was gone, Jane would not be prevailed PP III 13 344 10
you know;" said her mother as soon as she was in the hall. PP III 13 345 16
Elizabeth made no attempt to reason with her mother, but PP III 13 345 17
officiousness of the mother, and heard all her silly PP III 13 345 18
to fear that her mother had been too ingenious for her. PP III 13 346 22
"I must go instantly to my mother;" she cried. PP III 13 347 26
She then hastened away to her mother, who had purposely PP III 13 347 27
"With my mother up stairs. PP III 13 347 32
Elizabeth had mentioned her name to her mother, on her PP III 14 351 3
That lady I suppose is your mother." PP III 14 351 5
"Go, my dear," cried her mother, "and shew her ladyship PP III 14 352 18
It was the favourite wish of his mother, as well as of PP III 14 355 43
his mother and aunt wished him to marry Miss de Bourgh. PP III 14 355 44
But who was your mother? PP III 14 356 52
I send no compliments to your mother. PP III 14 358 73
Her mother impatiently met her at the door of the dressing- PP III 14 358 74
her mother should be always giving him such an epithet. PP III 17 374 21
She could not determine how her mother would take it; PP III 17 375 27
When her mother went up to her dressing-room at night, she PP III 17 377 42
three minutes in her own room, her mother followed her. PP III 17 378 44
So near a vicinity to her mother and Meryton relations was PP III 19 385 3
more attention than her poor mother could possibly give? MP I 1 5 4
of temper--her poor mother had a good deal; but we must MP I 2 13 5
her mother (of whom he was the darling) in every distress. MP I 2 15 12
Mrs. Norris is much better fitted than my mother for MP I 3 27 33
by the supineness of his mother, or the economy of his MP I 4 36 7
his aunt than with his mother, as evincing least regard MP I 4 37 8
with the gentleman's mother, who at present lived with him, MP I 4 39 10
Crawford, the children of her mother by a second marriage. MP I 4 40 15
sisters, a quiet mother, and an agreeable man himself-- MP I 5 48 28
sick or run away, and the mother in and out every moment MP I 5 50 35
father and mother and sisters were there, all new to me. MP I 5 51 40
My mother seldom goes into company herself, and dines no MP I 5 51 42
to wait upon your good mother again; nothing but having no MP I 6 62 58
your mother, and have a pleasant drive home by moonlight. MP I 6 62 58
only be sullen to her mother, aunt, and cousin, and throw MP I 7 70 30
Even your mother was out to-day for above an hour." MP I 7 72 41
significantly at his mother, "it was cutting the roses, MP I 7 73 55
Vexed as Edmund was with his mother and aunt, he was still MP I 7 74 58
arrived, escorting his mother, who came to be civil, and MP I 8 75 1
said he, addressing his mother, "for wishing Fanny not to MP I 8 78 18
equal cordiality by the mother, and Miss Bertram had all MP I 9 84 1
of Mr. Rushworth and his mother, and expose her sister to MP I 9 88 24
I have but this moment escaped from his horrible mother. MP I 10 100 28
The mother I could not avoid, as long as my tiresome aunt MP I 10 101 32
And if I have good luck, your mother shall have some." MP I 10 106 57
Your mother is quite anxious about it but cannot very well MP I 12 119 23
if possible, though his mother, who equally heard the MP I 13 124 13
very anxious period to my mother, and if we can be the MP I 13 126 18
As he said this, each looked towards their mother. MP I 13 126 19
"To be sure, my dear mother, your anxiety--I was unlucky MP I 13 126 21
Their mother had no objection to the plan, and they were MP I 13 128 38
occasion than Julia, to consult either father or mother. MP I 13 128 38
to the fire where sat his mother, aunt, and Fanny, and MP I 15 139 9
Read only the first act aloud, to either your mother or MP I 15 140 12
father, you may be sure; mother had chanced to send him of MP I 15 141 22
idea of that except his mother--she, indeed, regretted MP I 18 166 4
something, and amusing my mother, just within the last MP II 1 181 16
being introduced to his mother, and then prevailed on my MP II 2 188 3
to the unconcern of his mother speaking entirely by rote. MP II 2 194 20
great attention to my mother and sisters while he was away. MP II 3 196 2
father gave her away--her mother stood with salts in her MP II 3 203 29
Even their mother missed them--and how much more their MP II 3 204 33
to recollect, that his mother had been inquiring for her, MP II 4 214 46
not imagine that his mother would make any difficulty of MP II 4 215 47
but I am sure, my dear mother, she would like to go; and I MP II 5 217 2
"But my mother will have my father with her all the MP II 5 217 5
of the father and mother, brothers and sisters, of whom MP II 6 234 18
that an affectionate mother must feel in promoting her MP II 11 285 10
to be sure his father and mother would be able to put him MP II 13 305 19
the drawing-room, his mother and Fanny were sitting as MP III 3 336 8
have not been so silent all the time," replied his mother. MP III 3 336 9
going near a father and mother who had done without her so MP III 6 370 14
to forbear, and when her mother could be no longer MP III 6 371 17
soon be what mother and daughter ought to be to each other. MP III 6 371 17
You will tell my mother how it all ought to be, and you MP III 6 372 20
not leave his father and mother just when every body else MP III 6 373 25
Her mother, however, could not stay long enough to suspect MP III 7 378 10
Come, mother, you have hardly looked at your own dear MP III 7 378 12
"Dear me!" continued the anxious mother, "what a sad fire MP III 7 379 17
of the second story, for his mother and for Rebecca. MP III 7 381 26
followed not far behind by his mother and Betsey. MP III 7 384 34
well composed, and the mother having lamented again over MP III 7 385 37
her mother meant to part with her when her year was up. MP III 7 385 38
have pained her mother by alluding to her, for the world.-- MP III 7 386 40
back again to the door to say, "take care of Fanny, mother. MP III 8 388 2
Her disappointment in her mother was greater; there she MP III 8 389 4
respectable mother of nine children, on a small income. MP III 8 390 5
and did feel that her mother was a partial, ill-judging MP III 8 390 6
Her continual disagreements with her mother, her rash MP III 8 391 9
and that both her mother and Betsey were restrained from MP III 9 395 4
In every argument with her mother, Susan had in point of MP III 9 396 5
mother, which Fanny had almost feared to be impossible. MP III 9 396 7
able to name him to her mother, and recal her remembrance MP III 10 399 4
himself entirely to her mother, addressing her, and MP III 10 399 5
Her poor mother now did not look so very unworthy of being MP III 11 408 2
so much, and that her mother, as handsome as Lady Bertram, MP III 11 408 2
My mother desires her best love, and hopes to hear from MP III 13 423 2
safe, as to make his mother perfectly easy; for being now MP III 14 429 1
and looked fearfully towards her father and mother. MP III 14 431 8
to Bath, to fetch his mother; but how will she and the MP III 14 435 13
Her father read his newspaper, and her mother lamented MP III 15 439 9
a condition as no mother--not unkind, except Mrs. Price, MP III 15 442 22
be gone; her father and mother must be spoken to, Susan MP III 15 443 25
consent of her father and mother to Susan's going with her- MP III 15 444 25
pass a few days with his mother, and bring her back to MP III 16 450 8
which her father and mother were now disposed to attribute MP III 16 450 8
mother, that the worst consequences might be apprehended. MP III 16 450 9
The servant of Mrs. Rushworth, the mother, had exposure in MP III 16 450 10
in the room, except his mother, who, after hearing an MP III 16 453 17
Her mother had died too long ago for her to have more than E I 1 5 2
who had fallen little short of a mother in affection. E I 1 5 2
that he had written to his new mother on the occasion. E I 2 18 9
to the care of a failing mother, and the endeavour to make E I 3 21 4
in such an excellent mother and so many good neighbours E I 3 21 4
She had taken up a wrong idea, fancying it was a mother E I 4 27 5
His mother and sisters were very fond of him. E I 4 28 6
His mother is perfectly right not to be in a hurry. E I 4 30 18
In her mother she lost the only person able to cope with E I 5 37 9
of speech that Emma's mother might have had) the liberty E I 5 40 24
so much of what his mother and sisters would think and say, E I 7 55 35
your picture to his mother and sisters, telling how much E I 7 56 44
Your dear mother was so clever at all those things! E I 9 78 54
a devoted wife, a doating mother, and so tenderly attached E I 11 92 4
he was but two years old when he lost his poor mother! E I 11 96 24
reading it again to my mother, for it is such a pleasure E II 1 157 10
My mother often wonders that I can make it out so well. E II 1 157 10
My mother does not hear; she is a little deaf you know. E II 1 158 12
to come here so soon. my mother is so delighted!--for she E II 1 159 20
Mrs. Dixon has persuaded her father and mother to come E II 1 159 20
urgent letter to her mother--or her father, I declare I do E II 1 159 20
I read them aloud to my mother, you know, for fear of E II 1 162 31
is ill!--which my mother, being on the watch, heard E II 1 162 31
years old, on losing her mother, she became the property, E II 2 163 3
Neither father nor mother could promote, and the daughter E II 2 164 6
for her mother and herself; and Jane's offences rose again. E II 2 168 15
not you, Jane?--for my mother was so afraid that we had E II 3 173 27
My mother desires her very best compliments and regards, E II 3 173 29
as my mother says, our friends are only too good to us. E II 3 173 30
31
Miss Bates, joyfully; "my mother is so pleased!--she says E II 3 174 35
His extreme attention to my mother--wanting her to sit in E II 3 175 39
hear the better, for my mother is a little deaf, you know-- E II 3 175 39
My dear sir, if there is one thing my mother loves better E II 3 175 39
40
for though the father and mother had died some years ago, E II 4 183 9
absolute neglect of the mother and sisters, when invited E II 4 185 12
My mother is delightfully well; and Jane caught no cold E II 9 236 46
her to come in; my mother will be so very happy to see her- E II 9 236 46
For my mother had no use of her spectacles--could not put E II 9 236 46
I dare not let my mother know how little she eats--so I E II 9 237 46
My mother says the orchard was always famous in her E II 9 238 51
He was very warmly thanked both by mother and daughter; to E II 10 242 16
We were just in time; my mother just ready for us. E II 10 243 33
Frank's mother would never have been slighted as she was E II 18 309 33
I said to my mother, 'upon my word, ma'am-----.' E III 2 322 19
Thank you, my mother is remarkably well. E III 2 322 19
So kind of her to think of my mother! E III 2 322 19
My mother often talks of your goodnature. E III 2 323 19
mentioned it to my mother, and the Coles knew of it as E III 5 345 16
carriage, and came to my mother in great spirits one E III 5 346 16
Mrs. Perry was always particularly fond of my mother-- E III 5 346 16

off, he did not;--but my mother, and Jane, and I, were all E III 8 381 19
My poor mother does not know how to bear it. E III 8 382 27
it was by knowing her to be the mother of a little girl. E III 17 461 1
that a daughter would suit both father and mother best. E III 17 461 1
was an awful legacy for a mother to bequeath; and awful P III 1 4 6
in Anne that she could fancy the mother to revive again. P III 1 6 9
The father and mother were in the old English style, and P III 5 40 45
deal more than their mother, she had an object of interest, P III 6 43 4
the loss of her dear mother, known the happiness of being P III 6 47 13
which his father and mother had ever received from him P III 6 51 30
pursued and informed--the mother to support and keep from P III 7 53 3
behind their father and mother, to endeavour to express P III 7 54 4
boy!"--both father and mother were in much too strong and P III 7 55 5
and because I am the poor mother, I am not to be allowed P III 7 56 10
My being the mother is the very reason why my feelings P III 7 56 10
"I hope I am as fond of my child as any mother--but I do P III 7 56 12
"It was at Gibraltar, mother, I know. P III 8 66 19
by her father and mother without any disapprobation. P III 9 74 6
wishes of her father and mother for putting it off till P III 11 94 7
the bitterest agony, "Oh God! her father and mother!" P III 12 110 37 38
thought of her father and mother, she gave it up; she P III 12 114 59
had seen the father and mother quite as composed as could P III 12 117 76
No, except when she thought of her mother, and remembered P IV 1 126 18
home; and her father and mother, who must return in time P IV 2 129 1
Her mother could even think of her being able to join P IV 2 134 31
for the loss of a mother whom she had dearly loved, P IV 5 152 2
The idea of becoming what her mother had been; of having P IV 5 160 26
"Mrs. Harville must be an odd mother to part with them so " P IV 6 163 7
Miss Carteret was with her mother; consequently it was not P IV 7 174 3
But then, it had been taken up by his father and mother. P IV 10 216 19
His mother had some old friends in Bath, whom she wanted P IV 10 217 19
I hope your father and mother are quite happy with regard P IV 10 218 21
Your father and mother seem so totally free from all those P IV 10 218 23
mother, I have done something for you that you will like. P IV 10 223 40 41
Have not I done well, mother?" P IV 10 223 41
in attaching herself as a mother to the man who was P IV 12 249 4
family, many a careful mother, many a pretty daughter, S 4 382 1
hooping cough, and whose mother would not let them be S 4 383 1

MOTHER'S (131)

worthy than she has yet done, of her mother's tender care. LS 14 265 5
idea of her must be drawn from the mother's description. LS 15 267 7
must likewise be given without her mother's approbation. LS 19 274 2
In such a point as this, your mother's prohibition ought LS 24 286 7
fearful perhaps of her mother's anger, & tho' dreading my LS 24 291 16
of her whims, at the expense of her mother's inclination. LS 25 294 5
her mother, or all her mother's friends; but with those LS 27 296 1
am sorry to add that her mother's errand hither was to LS 41 310 3
were written under her mother's inspection, & therefore LS 42 311 1
fondest wishes of the mother's heart, for she received him NA I 7 49 43
"It was my mother's favourite walk." NA II 7 179 30
you into what was my mother's room--the room in which she NA II 8 186 6
said Catherine, looking down, "to see your mother's room." NA II 9 195 9
"My mother's room!-- NA II 9 195 10
My mother's room is very commodious, is it not? NA II 9 196 21
of respect for my mother's character, as described by NA II 9 196 23
"My mother's illness," he continued, "the seizure which NA II 9 196 25
My father and mother's having no notice of it is of very NA II 13 224 17
agreed to her mother's next counsel of going early to bed. NA II 14 235 13
the first time since her mother's entrance, asked her, NA II 15 242 9
to be sure," was her mother's foreboding remark; but quick NA II 16 249 1
half of his own mother's fortune, warmed his heart and SS I 1 5 8
thousand pounds on their mother's death--a very SS I 2 10 14
at my mother's disposal, without any restriction whatever. SS I 2 11 20
oppose her mother's intention of removing into Devonshire. SS I 4 24 21
music, although by her mother's account she had played SS I 7 35 8
Without considering that it was not in her mother's plan SS I 12 58 1
Elinor's uneasiness was at least equal to her mother's. SS I 15 77 19
to accept her mother's invitation, a backwardness so SS I 15 77 19
after some time, on her mother's silently pressing her SS I 15 82 46
way of acting to his mother's account; and it was happy SS I 19 101 2
The mother's consternation was excessive; but it could not SS I 21 121 10
She was seated in her mother's lap, covered with kisses, SS I 21 121 10
She was carried out of the room therefore in her mother's SS I 21 122 10
Margaret, with her mother's permission, was equally SS II 1 143 9
referred it to her mother's decision, from whom however SS II 3 154 6
attempting to weaken her mother's dependence on the SS II 3 157 17
Her mother's affliction was hardly less, and Elinor was SS II 3 158 21
at their accepting her mother's invitation after having SS II 4 164 21
"But for my mother's sake and mine"----- SS II 7 190 53
of patience till their mother's wishes could be known; and SS II 9 203 9
Marianne had promised to be guided by her mother's opinion, SS II 10 214 6
information about her mother's health, their coming to SS II 13 241 22
his mother's threats, for a woman who could not reward him. SS III 1 268 46
Edward is dismissed for ever from his mother's notice. SS III 1 268 48
had went away from his mother's house, he had got upon his SS III 2 273 16
he did not regard his mother's anger, while he could have SS III 2 277 30
day's journey; and their mother's servant might easily SS III 3 280 6
their design; and their mother's concurrence being readily SS III 3 280 7
unfair a division of his mother's love and liberality, to SS III 5 298 32
some rest before her mother's arrival, and allow her to SS III 7 315 27
the excess of her poor mother's alarm, gave some SS III 7 316 29
safety, and her mother's expected arrival, threw her SS III 9 333 3
in compliance with her mother's entreaty, went to bed. SS III 9 334 5
embellishments of her mother's active fancy, which SS III 9 336 13
strength, and her mother's presence in aid, it proceeded SS III 10 340 1
wishes and the mother's confidence; and Marianne, leaning SS III 10 344 11
"Rather say your mother's imprudence, my child," said Mrs. SS III 11 352 15
seeing her mother's servant, on hearing Lucy's message! SS III 12 357 2
Elinor's lips had moved with her mother's, and when the SS III 12 359 12
contracted without his mother's consent, as he had already SS III 13 361 1
his lady, engaged her mother's consent, and was not only SS III 13 361 3
it laid him open to his mother's anger, had been a SS III 13 367 21
of her mother's language, to make it cheerful. SS III 13 369 35
they have me beg my mother's pardon for Robert's SS III 13 372 41
the engagement which drew on you your mother's anger." SS III 13 372 42
proud of marrying privately without his mother's consent. SS III 14 376 11
relation; and their mother's fortune, though ample for her PP I 7 28 1
said Elizabeth, "my mother's purpose will be answered." PP I 7 31 27
that might turn her mother's thoughts, now asked her if PP I 9 43 26
to this sudden attack was delightful to their mother's ear. PP I 9 45 36
Her mother's thoughts she plainly saw were bent the same PP I 18 98 63
the rapidity of her mother's words, or persuade her to PP I 18 99 64
I have your respected mother's permission for this address. PP I 19 105 8
mother's decease, is all that you may ever be entitled to. PP I 19 106 10
her mother's reproach prevented his feeling any regret. PP I 20 112 24
this week. you know my mother's ideas as to the necessity PP II 3 145 9
ashamed of her mother's ungracious and reluctant good PP II 3 145 11
father kept, and what had been her mother's maiden name?-- PP II 6 163 15
The situation of your mother's family, though PP II 12 198 5
of my mother's nephew, Colonel Fitzwilliam, and myself. PP II 12 201 5
were supported by their mother's indulgence, what chance PP II 14 213 17
stairs from her mother's apartment, immediately met her. PP III 5 286 22
by Miss Bennet, who came to fetch her mother's tea. PP III 6 299 27
to her, through her mother's hands, Lydia's expences had PP III 8 309 4
parade, walk up to her mother's right hand, and hear her PP III 9 317 9
But, perhaps he could not in her mother's presence be what PP III 11 335 40
Her mother's ungraciousness, made the sense of what they PP III 12 340 13
him fall a victim to her mother's rapacity for whist PP III 12 342 26
she could not be wanted to counteract her mother's schemes. PP III 13 346 21
reserved to herself the application for her mother's. PP III 17 375 27
This was a sad omen of what her mother's behaviour to the PP III 17 378 46
She was too indolent even to accept a mother's MP I 4 35 5
But it was entirely the mother's fault. MP I 5 51 41
very time about your mother's dairymaid, by her desire, MP I 7 73 53
Why is not use to be made of my mother's chaise? MP I 8 77 9
to speak and fill up the blanks in his mother's story. MP II 5 218 16
Fanny wrote to offer herself; and her mother's answer, MP III 6 371 17
of the house, and in her mother's arms, who met her there MP III 7 377 9
boys, in spite of their mother's intreaty, determined to MP III 7 384 36
but the child ran to her mother's protection, and Susan MP III 7 386 42
was wounded by her sister's speech and her mother's reply. MP III 7 386 43
(excepting, perhaps, her mother's, which resembled the MP III 8 392 11
of her father's and mother's acquaintance to afford her MP III 9 395 3
A line occasionally added by Edmund to his mother's letter MP III 14 430 5
The mother's sufferings, the father's--there, she paused. MP III 15 442 21
He is anxious to get you there for my mother's sake. MP III 15 442 23
lingering illness of his mother's, been the means of a E I 2 16 4
She inherits her mother's talents, and must have been E I 5 37 9
feelings: standing in a mother's place, but without a E I 18 149 26
place, but without a mother's affection to blind her. E I 18 149 26
communications about her mother's, and sweet-cake from the E II 1 155 4
And, indeed, though my mother's eyes are not so good as E II 1 157 10
My mother's are really very good indeed. E II 1 158 10
"My mother's deafness is very trifling you see--just E II 1 158 14
a great deal at my mother's time of life--and it really is E II 1 158 14
And then fly off, through half a sentence, to her mother's E II 8 225 78
Bates became anxious to get home, on her mother's account. E II 8 230 101
world, fastening in the rivet of my mother's spectacles.-- E II 9 236 46
Oh! my mother's spectacles. E II 9 237 51
you all cold; but I can go into my mother's room you know. E II 10 243 31
Oh! Mr. Frank Churchill, I must tell you my mother's E III 2 323 19
was possible, of her mother's rights and consequence; and P III 1 5 8
school there, after her mother's death, and, secondly, P III 2 14 11
mother's love, and mother's rights, it would be prevented. P III 4 27 3
A sick child is always the mother's property, her own P III 7 56 11
You, who have not a mother's feelings, are a great deal P III 7 57 16
you occupying your dear mother's place, succeeding to all P IV 5 159 25
You are your mother's self in countenance and disposition; P IV 5 160 25
it ended in being his mother's party, that every thing P IV 10 217 19
& the one, who under her mother's directions had been S 2 374 1

MOTHER-IN-LAW (12)

command, the interest of his mother-in-law and sisters. SS I 1 5 5
mother-in-law, arrived with her child and their attendants. SS I 1 5 9
comfortable your mother-in-law and her daughters may live SS I 2 12 24
of affronting her mother-in-law on the occasion, talking SS I 4 23 19
mirth of Sir John and his mother-in-law was interesting. SS I 7 34 7
With the assistance of his mother-in-law, Sir John was not SS I 18 99 15
any attention to his mother-in-law, and therefore never SS II 5 171 30
the two young ladies to this formidable mother-in-law. SS II 12 231 12
You will have a charming mother-in-law, indeed, and of PP I 6 27 53
"you will give your mother-in-law a few hints, when this PP I 10 52 55
of introducing his mother-in-law, and speaking of her with E II 5 191 28
letters to his mother-in-law a few months ago, Emma, it E III 15 444 6

MOTHER-IN-LAW'S (3)

As my mother-in-law's relations, I shall be happy to shew SS II 11 222 9
father's hints, his mother-in-law's guarded silence; it E III 5 343 2
the journey in her mother-in-law's carriage with four P IV 10 219 28

MOTHERBANK (1)

Motherbank; he swore and he drank, he was dirty and gross. MP III 8 389 3

MOTHERLY (4)

You will be under the care of a motherly good sort of SS II 3 156 8
expressed so natural and motherly a joy in the prospect of MP III 6 371 17
She was a plain, motherly kind of woman, who had worked E I 3 22 5
is something so motherly and kind-hearted about her, that E II 14 278 44

MOTHERS (8)

Some mothers would have insisted on their daughter's LS 7 253 2
mothers, she is accused of wanting maternal tenderness. LS 14 265 5
Yet Reginald still thinks Lady Susan the best of mothers-- LS 17 271 7
Some mothers might have encouraged the intimacy from SS I 3 15 5
The parties stood thus: the two mothers, though each SS II 12 234 21 22
Mrs. Ferrars is one of the most affectionate mothers in SS III 5 296 22
pains which they, their mothers, (very clever women,) as MP I 4 42 21
Mothers certainly have not yet got quite the right way of MP I 5 50 36

MOTION (24)

Every body was shortly in motion for tea, and they must NA I 2 21 10
excellence of the springs, gave the motion of the carriage. NA I 9 64 27
With what sparkling eyes and ready motion she granted his NA I 10 75 24
The window curtains seemed in motion. NA II 6 167 10
seemed at one moment in motion, and at another the lock of NA II 6 171 12
motion of the lock proved that some hand must be on it. NA II 13 222 9
again, as if nothing but motion was voluntary; and it NA II 15 240 1
but judged from the motion of her lips that she did not SS III 3 281 9
She is so pretty!" as they were immediately in motion W 332 11
it all, and saw in the motion of his lips the words " PP I 18 98 61
Last night it had been hope and smiles, bustle and motion, MP II 11 283 6
and boys at last all in motion together, the moment came MP III 7 384 36
state of his own mind made him find relief only in motion. MP III 15 445 29
second carriage was in motion, a few flakes of snow were E I 13 112 24
the felicities of rapid motion have once been, though E II 11 247 1
A man who had been in motion since eight o'clock in the E II 17 303 23
He had turned away, and the horses were in motion. E III 7 376 62
herself made the first motion, she could not say--she E III 9 386 7
afterwards collected, and once more in motion together. P III 10 89 35
putting his horse into motion again, when Captain P III 10 91 39
a last look at the picture, as they began to be in motion. P IV 6 169 27
He looked at her with a smile, and a little motion of the P IV 11 231 12
disregarding his sister's motion to go, & persisting in S 7 395 1
of which rototory motion, is perhaps to be attributed the S 11 421 1

MOTIONLESS (8)

in motionless wonder, while these thoughts crossed her:-- NA II 6 163 1 2
Catherine, for a few moments, was motionless with horror. NA II 6 170 12
motionless although we can observe you no longer!-- SS I 5 27 8
returned, she continued on the bed quiet and motionless. SS II 7 191 65
The hand and the heart were alike motionless and passive MP II 2 193 18
her hand while she sat motionless over it--and at last, MP III 3 337 11
for not having been as motionless as she was speechless, MP III 3 342 32
which had kept her face averted, and her tongue motionless. E III 7 375 62

MOTIONS (1)

upright & alert in her motions, with a shrewd eye, & self- S 6 391 1

MOTIVE (61)

But if the world could know my motive there, they they LS 2 245 1
disposition to dislike a motive will never be wanting; & LS 5 250 1
And this circumstance while it explains the true motive of LS 14 264 3
I have still another motive for your coming. LS 26 295 4
you to understand the motive of other people's actions." NA II 1 132 18
tried to find in it a motive sufficient for their silence. SS I 16 84 7
The motive was too common to be wondered at; but the means SS I 20 112 28
Could you have a motive for the trust, that was not SS II 2 146 4
the motive of her own disinclination for going to London. SS II 3 155 6
for a moment by such a motive, though believing it hardly SS II 8 193 5
what she said--"what could be the Colonel's motive?" SS III 5 295 14
or what diabolical motive you may have imputed to me.-- SS III 8 319 29
And even now, I cannot comprehend on what motive she acted, SS III 13 367 22
conduct, nor more self-evident than the motive of it. SS III 13 367 24
had had the additional motive of being able to tell the W 355 28
The distance is nothing, when one has a motive; only three PP I 7 32 37
motive?--what can have induced him to behave so cruelly?" PP I 16 80 31
If from no better motive, that he should not have been too PP I 16 81 38
the influence of the Pemberley house, is a powerful motive. PP I 16 81 41
This has been my motive, my fair cousin, and I flatter PP I 19 106 10

Context	Work	Vol.	Ch.	Page	Line
to comprehend on what motive his cousin could refuse him;	PP	I	20	112	24
affairs, between the mercenary and the prudent motive?	PP	II	4	153	9
And to be kept back on such a motive!--	PP	II	6	165	35
No motive can excuse the unjust and ungenerous part you	PP	II	11	191	12
It adds even another motive.	PP	II	12	200	5
now have had no tolerable motive; he had either been	PP	II	13	207	6
and esteem, there was a motive within her of good will	PP	III	2	265	16
there was a very powerful motive for secrecy, in addition	PP	III	6	297	12
The motive professed, was his conviction of its being	PP	III	10	321	2
If he had another motive, I am sure it would never	PP	III	10	322	2
as it seemed the only probable motive for her calling.	PP	III	14	352	15
"My motive for cautioning you, is as follows.	PP	III	15	363	17
journey to Longbourn, its motive, and the substance of her	PP	III	16	367	9
I consider it rather as a motive; for the expectation of	MP	I	13	126	18
All who can distinguish, will understand your motive.--	MP	I	15	140	15
Fanny, from a different motive, was exceedingly pleased:	MP	II	9	266	21
given her another strong motive for exertion, in keeping	MP	III	1	322	50
to his son, for his prime motive in sending her away, had	MP	III	6	368	9
Crawford would have no motive for writing, strong enough	MP	III	7	376	4
I am refused, that, I think, will be the honest motive.	MP	III	13	422	2
from considering her residence there as the motive.	MP	III	17	465	13
This had been her motive in going to her cousins.	MP	III	17	466	18
as (supposing her real motive unperceived) might warrant a	E	I	16	136	9
whatever might be their motive or motives, whether single,	E	II	2	166	10
more than may be pardoned, in consideration of the motive."	E	II	14	277	37
"She must have some motive, more powerful than appears,	E	II	15	285	15
there would have been a motive; but his coming would	E	II	17	303	23
I can have no self-command without a motive.	E	III	7	369	12
I have no motive for wishing him ill--and for her sake,	E	III	13	428	21
without vouchsafing any motive, because he could not marry	E	III	13	431	38
situations increasing every other motive of good will.	E	III	16	452	7
all the motive of their attention just as he ought!--	P	III	7	54	4
Why was she to suspect herself of another motive?	P	IV	7	175	6
It was the only intelligible motive.	P	IV	8	190	51
That was his motive for drawing back, I can assure you.	P	IV	9	201	59
I have now another motive for being glad that I can	P	IV	9	203	70
I have no doubt, had a double motive in his visits there.	P	IV	9	206	88
added another motive) to watch Sir Walter and Mrs. Clay.	P	IV	9	207	90
I have always wanted some other motive for his conduct as	P	IV	9	207	91
and I felt that I had still a motive for remaining here."	P	IV	11	245	76
the decided want of some motive for action, some powerful	S		10	415	1
MOTIVES (34)					
from the most selfish motives, take all possible pains to	LS		12	260	2
worst, where the motives of her conduct have been doubtful.	LS		14	264	2
I must have unanswerable motives for all that I had done!	LS		22	282	6
"I have very little to say for Frederick's motives, such	NA	II	12	218	7
and explain the motives of his father's conduct, her	NA	II	15	244	11
the intimacy from motives of interest, for Edward Ferrars	SS	I	3	15	5
have repressed it from motives of prudence, for, except a	SS	I	3	15	5
To the possibility of motives unanswerable in themselves,	SS	I	15	79	28
and she judged of their motives by the immediate effect of	SS	II	9	202	4
Colonel Brandon, on motives of equal delicacy, declining	SS	III	3	283	20
Mrs. Dashwood was acting on motives of policy as well as	SS	III	14	378	13
he could imagine but two motives for their chusing to walk	PP	I	11	56	12
either of which motives his joining them would interfere.	PP	I	11	56	12
therefore in requiring an explanation of his two motives.	PP	I	11	56	14
account of my actions and their motives has been read.--	PP	II	12	196	5
done; and though the motives which governed me may to you	PP	II	12	199	5
Elizabeth told her the motives of her secrecy.	PP	III	17	374	19
They are always acting upon motives of vanity--and there	MP	I	5	50	38
"But the motives of a man who takes orders with the	MP	I	11	109	20
of examining his own motives, and of reflecting to what	MP	I	12	114	3
to her--though her motives had been often misunderstood,	MP	I	16	152	2
soberer moment, feel his motives to deserve, and	MP	II	2	187	1
interest, in twofold motives, in views and wishes more	MP	II	13	300	7
been governed by motives of selfishness and worldly wisdom.	MP	III	17	461	4
of a strong passion at war with all interested motives.	E	I	8	67	57
might be their motive or motives, whether single, or	E	II	2	166	10
the best, the purest of motives, might now be denying	E	II	2	168	13
to settle early in life, and to marry, from worthy motives.	E	II	6	204	43
These are the motives which I have been pressing on you.	E	II	13	268	12
the same motives which she had been used to urge before.--	E	III	6	359	37
of Lady Russell's motives in this, over those of her	P	III	4	30	10
nothing to require more motives than appeared, in Mr.	P	IV	4	147	7
Her motives for such a match could be little understood at	S		3	375	1
Lady Denham had other motives for calling on Mrs G.	S		11	422	1
MOTTO (3)					
It is a sort of prologue to the play, a motto to the	E	I	9	74	23
with the arms and motto: "principal seat, Kellynch Hall,	P	III	1	3	3
					4
for fifty pounds, arms and motto, name and livery included;	P	IV	9	202	66
MOULDING (1)					
lamps, silver moulding, all you see complete; the iron-	NA	I	7	46	13
MOUND (1)					
mound,--there I fell; and there I first saw Willoughby."	SS	III	10	344	12
					13
MOUNT (5)					
They all attended in the hall to see him mount his horse,	NA	II	7	175	13
said Mrs. Bennet, "to walk to oakham mount this morning.	PP	III	17	374	23
the view from the mount, and Elizabeth silently consented.	PP	III	17	375	25
hunt; and Crawford could mount him without the slightest	MP	II	6	237	23
and her first attempt to mount the bank brought on such a	E	III	3	333	5
MOUNTAIN-ASH (1)					
of the fir, the mountain-ash, and the acacia, and a thick	SS	III	6	302	7
MOUNTAINS (4)					
round the neighbouring mountains--and during the frightful	NA	II	5	159	19
What are men to rocks and mountains?	PP	II	4	154	23
Lakes, mountains, and rivers, shall not be jumbled	PP	II	4	154	23
them at the rocks and mountains, as if they were not to be	P	IV	6	169	25
MOUNTED (5)					
the servant had just mounted the carriage and was driving	NA	I	7	46	9
mounted, sunk a little under this consequent inconvenience.	NA	II	5	156	4
which being now just mounted and brought home, ornamented	SS	II	12	234	26
mounted his horse for Peterborough, and then all were gone.	MP	II	11	282	4
Emma's spirits were mounted quite up to happiness; every	E	II	5	189	16
MOUNTING (2)					
and if, as you were mounting your horse, a friend were to	PP	I	10	49	29
measures were taken for mounting her again, "because," as	MP	I	4	35	7
MOUNTS (1)					
Bond-Street till just before he mounts his horse to-morrow.	E	I	7	56	46
MOURN (1)					
'Ye fallen avenues, once more I mourn your fate unmerited.'	MP	I	6	56	20
MOURNED (2)					
How many a time have we mourned over the dead body of	MP	I	13	126	25
anxious for its success & mourned over its Discomfitures	S		8	404	1
MOURNER (1)					
be called a young mourner--only last summer, I understand."	P	III	12	108	25
MOURNFUL (1)					
that Emma first sat in mournful thought of any continuance.	E	I	1	6	5
MOURNFULLY (1)					
then--how mournfully superior in reality and substance!	NA	II	13	227	26
MOURNING (9)					
sisters, that Elinor was mourning in secret over obstacles	SS	II	1	141	4
and resolved, that his mourning should be as handsome as	E	III	9	388	13
There must be three months, at least, of deep mourning;	E	III	16	460	56
Captain Harville's sister, and was now mourning her loss.	P	III	11	96	12
Both master and man being in mourning, assisted the idea.	P	III	12	104	7
It was driven by a servant in mourning."	P	III	12	105	8
his own, the servant in mourning roused Anne's curiosity,	P	III	12	105	9
In mourning, you see, just as our Mr. Elliot must be.	P	III	12	105	14
been in mourning, one should have known him by the livery."	P	III	12	106	16
MOUTH (17)					
her, and her mouth stuffed with sugar plums by the other.	SS	I	21	121	10
the information by word of mouth, when her visitor entered,	SS	III	4	287	26
concessions by word of mouth than on paper, it was	SS	III	13	372	45
He has a long face, & a wide mouth.--	W			324	3
there is something pleasing about his mouth when he speaks.	PP	III	1	258	74
up her mouth, and turned from me with such an air!	MP	I	5	50	35
about the corners of the mouth, and seemed to think it as	MP	I	17	158	2
I observed of her eyes and mouth, I do not despair of	MP	II	6	229	5
and the lines about the mouth which one ought to catch."	E	I	6	44	15
lines about the mouth--I have not a doubt of your success.	E	I	6	44	16
in every body's mouth, and Frank Churchill was forgotten.	E	II	13	267	8
praise passed from one mouth to another as it ought to do,	E	II	15	281	2
as soon as ever I open my mouth, shan't I?--(looking round	E	III	7	370	24
and curl of his handsome mouth, which convinced Anne, that	P	III	8	67	28
Anne caught his eye, saw his cheeks glow, and his mouth	P	IV	10	227	67
stream, & formed at its mouth, a 3d habitable division, in	S		4	383	1
adding a great dab just before it went into his mouth.--	S		10	417	1
MOUTHFULS (2)					
but she had appetite, and could not swallow many mouthfuls.	NA	II	13	228	27
scarcely swallow two mouthfuls before tears interrupted	MP	I	2	13	4
MOUTHS (4)					
The speeches that are put into the heroes' mouths, their	NA	I	14	108	22
and never open their mouths, quite mistake the matter."	PP	I	9	44	27
Mrs. Hurst and her sister scarcely opened their mouths	PP	I	18	102	75
said she, "with their mouths open to catch the music; like	P	IV	9	193	6
MOVE (60)					
sake! let us move away from this end of the room.	NA	I	6	42	33
Mrs. Allen, that she would move a little to accommodate	NA	I	8	54	10
light horses disposed to move, that, had not the General	NA	II	5	156	5
She had no power to move.	NA	II	9	194	6
for them, helping them to move their things, and sending	SS	I	2	12	24
from any disinclination to move when the sight of every	SS	I	3	14	1
the smallest incitement to move; and if I do mix in other	SS	III	10	347	30
players being disposed to move exactly the different way.	W			333	13
conclusion the Osbornes & their train were all on the move.	W			335	13
In a country neighbourhood you move in a very confined and	PP	I	9	43	17
are not puffed about with every attempt to move them.	PP	I	11	58	28
"My fingers," said Elizabeth, "do not move over this	PP	II	8	175	25
The rooms were too large for her to move in with ease;	MP	I	2	14	9
no inclination to move in any plan, or to any distance.	MP	I	9	90	36
Mr. Crawford was the first to move forward, to examine the	MP	I	9	90	36
"I must move," said she, "resting fatigues me.--	MP	I	9	96	73
Mrs. Norris had been too well employed to move faster.	MP	I	10	103	50
Julia was the first to move and speak again.	MP	II	1	175	2
as to put away her work, move pug from her side, and give	MP	II	1	179	9
I was ready to move heaven and earth to persuade my sister,	MP	II	2	189	3
to move all the chaperons to a better part of the room.	MP	II	10	277	16
I saw your lips move.	MP	III	3	340	25
and in vain did she try to move away--in the same low	MP	III	3	342	34
Mr. Crawford was obliged to move.	MP	III	3	344	43
himself very much, for I know the parties he had to move.	MP	III	5	364	29
broke up, being unable to move, had been left by himself	MP	III	13	426	10
to shift as she can;--to move, in short, in Mrs. Goddard's	E	I	8	62	42
Better not move at all, better stay in London altogether	E	I	12	106	58
did he move to those with whom he was always comfortable.	E	I	14	122	18
The weather soon improved enough for those to move who	E	I	17	140	1
for those to move who must move; and Mr. Woodhouse having,	E	I	17	140	1
still when he ought to move, and of leading a life of mere	E	I	18	148	24
"We had better move on, Mr. Weston," said she, "we are	E	II	5	189	12
A reasonable visit paid, Mr. Weston began to move.--	E	II	5	193	36
At last he was persuaded to move on from the front of the	E	II	6	198	6
I will move a little farther off."	E	II	6	201	23
Jane Fairfax did look and move superior; but Emma	E	II	8	219	44
always the first to move when he could--that his father,	E	II	8	220	48
&c." and they did at last move out of the shop, with no	E	II	9	237	47
'I really cannot get this girl to move form the house.	E	II	14	274	30
talents, you have a right to move in the first circle.	E	II	17	301	18
they are all to move southward without loss of time."	E	II	18	305	7
He was on the move immediately; but coming back, said, "I	E	III	2	320	9
					10
The move began; and Miss Bates might be heard from that	E	III	2	328	44
passed pleasantly, and nobody seemed in a hurry to move.	E	III	5	347	18
For herself--she feared to move, lest she should be seen.	P	III	10	88	27
She had much to recover from, before she could move.	P	III	10	89	34
You may depend upon it, that they will move in the first	P	IV	4	150	17
Anne was one of the few who did not choose to move.	P	IV	8	189	44
her own embarrassment, Anne did move quietly to the window.	P	IV	10	222	39
They were obliged to move.	P	IV	10	225	62
The present was that Captain Wentworth would move about	P	IV	10	226	64
Wentworth's pen ceased to move, his head was raised,	P	IV	11	231	10
She had only time, however, to move closer to the table	P	IV	11	236	40
A twinge or two, in trying to move his foot disposed the	S		1	367	1
P.'s sprain proving too serious for him to move sooner.--	S		2	370	1
be seen, who was forced to move early & walk for health--	S		6	389	1
You shd not move again after dinner."	S		9	411	1
for every body must now "move in a circle",--to the	S		11	421	1
at Brighton, could not move here without notice;--and even	S		11	422	1
MOVED (53)					
Still they moved on--something better was yet in view; and	NA	I	2	21	9
with which his horse moved along, and the ease which his	NA	I	9	64	27
follow the General, as he moved through the crowd, and "	NA	I	10	80	60
the Pump-Room; and if she moved from her seat she should	NA	II	3	147	28
not, but I have not had it moved, because I thought it	NA	II	6	165	4
She moved on towards the gallery.	NA	II	9	194	8
of weariness, much oftener than she moved her needle.--	NA	II	15	241	7
When your father and mother moved to Norland, though the	SS	I	2	12	26
approach, and Marianne starting up moved towards the door.	SS	II	4	161	7
delight, she would have moved towards him instantly, had	SS	II	6	176	3
pain of mind and body she moved from one posture to	SS	II	7	191	65
Marianne moved to the window----- "it is Colonel Brandon!"	SS	II	9	203	13
					14
sensibility, she moved, after a moment, to her sister's	SS	II	12	236	39
					40
already come, that she moved into the adjoining dressing-	SS	III	7	316	29
She moved away and sat down.	SS	III	12	358	8
Elinor's lips had moved with her mother's, and when the	SS	III	12	359	12
both close to her when she moved into the Tearoom; & Emma	W			331	11
I entreat you not to suppose that I moved this way in	PP	I	6	26	39
"She is a great deal too ill to be moved.	PP	I	9	41	3
Miss Bingley moved with alacrity to the piano-forte, and	PP	I	10	51	45
of it he only made him a slight bow, and moved another way.	PP	I	18	98	61
performed when the ladies moved for the night; and Mrs.	PP	I	22	123	4
it to be Mr. Darcy, she moved again towards the gate.	PP	II	12	195	2
Yet time and her aunt moved slowly--and her patience and	PP	III	1	257	66
And on the gentlemen's approaching, one of the girls moved	PP	III	12	341	16
					17
and moved away from each other, would have told it all.	PP	III	13	346	22
the circles in which they moved so distinct, as almost to	MP	I	1	4	2
Starting, the lady instinctively moved a step or two, but	MP	I	9	88	21
Fanny said she was rested, and would have moved too, but	MP	I	9	96	76
to good I can have them moved to my own house and borrow a	MP	I	10	106	57
being moved from one side of the room to the other.--	MP	I	13	127	29
and mortification, moved her chair considerably nearer the	MP	I	15	145	42
is too hot for me"--and moved away her chair to the	MP	I	15	147	56
All were alert and impatient; the ladies moved soon, the	MP	I	18	171	25
The farm-yard must be moved, I grant you; but I am not	MP	II	7	241	22
a parting worry to dress, moved as languidly towards her	MP	II	9	267	22
Dearest, dearest William!" she jumped up and moved in	MP	II	13	300	7
and moved forwards to the fire, before she was aware.	E	I	3	24	11
Once, I felt the fire rather too much; but then I moved	E	II	3	171	12
When Mr. Cole had moved away, and her attention could be	E	II	8	222	54

what she did say, and soon moved away to make the rest of	E II 17 304 29
He moved a few steps nearer, and those few steps were	E III 2 326 32
He always moved with the alertness of a mind which could	E III 9 386 7
spirits; and till she had moved about, and talked to	E III 18 475 37
He got up and moved away.	P III 8 70 50
"And yet," said Anne to herself, as they now moved forward	P III 11 97 13
She coloured deeply; and he recollected himself, and moved	P III 12 114 63
suited, and there remain till dear Louisa could be moved.	P IV 1 122 5
When she could give another glance, he had moved away.	P IV 8 188 42
rubbish it collects in the turnings. is easily moved away.	P IV 9 204 82
it, now left his seat, and moved to a window; and Anne	P IV 11 231 12
When his toils were over however, he moved back his chair	S 10 416 1
"the circle in which they moved in Sanditon" to use a	S 11 421 1
MOVEMENT (3)	
her first instinctive movement on perceiving him, yet she	NA II 9 192 4
it a second time, by any word, or look, or movement.	MP III 3 335 6
movement of more than common friendliness on his part.--	E III 9 385 7
MOVEMENTS (7)	
An inquiry now took place into the intended movements of	NA I 7 47 18
So rapid had been her movements, that in spite of the	NA I 13 102 25
and took the seat to which her movements invited him.	NA II 3 147 21
of the uneasy movements of many of his friends as they sat,	MP II 1 184 27
Her gestures and movements might be understood by any one	E III 2 322 18
glowed, and the movements which had hesitated were decided.	P IV 11 240 55
numerous family, their movements had been long limitted to	S 2 373 1
MOVER (1)	
of the family; principal Mover & actor;--she had been on	S 10 414 1
MOVES (4)	
his loins; only see how he moves; that horse cannot go	NA I 7 46 11
Your cousin Edmund moves slowly; detained, perchance, by	MP III 9 394 1
The sphere in which she moves is much above his.--	E I 8 62 39
to be in her family, for she moves in the first circle.	E II 17 299 8
MOVING (42)	
females, who, arm in arm, were then moving towards her.	NA I 4 32 3
they sat; he seemed to be moving that way, but he did not	NA I 8 53 3
to the key, and after moving it in every possible way for	NA II 6 168 10
the noise of something moving close to her door made her	NA II 13 222 9
languor and listlessness, moving herself in her chair,	NA II 15 241 7
was not in spirits for moving about, she and Elinor	SS II 6 175 2
She listened to her praise of Lucy with only moving from	SS III 1 265 33
gained; for, on Elinor's moving to the window to take more	SS III 3 280 9
soon afterwards, and moving different ways, Mrs. Jennings	SS III 3 281 13 14
"Here we are--said eliz:--as the carriage ceased moving--	W 322 2
Elizabeth at that instant moving towards them, he was	PP I 6 26 37 38
Mr. Jones says we must not think of moving her.	PP I 9 41 3
of attending, and often moving wrong without being aware	PP I 18 90 4
walked away from her, and moving with his usual	PP II 8 174 12
edged the park; he was moving that way; and fearful of its	PP II 12 195 2
They were always moving from place to place in quest of a	PP III 19 387 8
"Well, Lady Bertram," said Mrs. Norris, moving to go, "I	MP I 3 30 56
answer, before they were moving again at a good pace.	MP I 8 81 32
seeing him advance too, moving forward by gentle degrees	MP I 11 113 42
very fond of change and moving about, that I thought	MP I 12 115 5
five minutes, by merely moving the book-case in my	MP I 13 125 14
just now, such as moving a book-case, or unlocking a door,	MP I 13 127 29
You have not the smallest chance of moving me.	MP II 4 212 31
When the company were moving into the ball-room she found	MP II 10 274 9
"I was up stairs, mamma, moving my things;" said Susan, in	MP III 7 379 18
uniform, looking and moving all the taller, firmer, and	MP III 7 384 34
as well she may, with moving the queen of a palace, though	MP III 9 394 1
heat, in a cloud of moving dust; and her eyes could only	MP III 15 439 9
telling you of my idea of moving the path to Langham, of	E I 12 106 61
very soon after their moving into the drawing-room:	E I 14 121 14
"My dear Emma," said he, moving from his chair into one	E II 3 171 9
in a family not moving in a certain circle, or able to	E II 17 301 16
by no means moving slowly, could hardly be out of hearing.	E III 2 321 14
but slowly, and was moving away--but her terror and her	E III 3 334 6
Jane's alertness in moving, proved her as ready as her	E III 5 349 25
but so many were also moving, that she could not get away;	E III 5 349 25
There was a bustle on her approach; a good deal of moving	E III 8 378 4
till just as they were moving, she heard the Admiral say	P III 6 49 23 24
low rambling holly protected her, and they were moving on.	P III 10 88 27
with no possibility of moving from one to the other	P IV 5 154 8
The party were very soon moving after dinner.	S 6 389 1
sister--not merely for moving, but for walking on together	S 7 395 1
MR BEARD (1)	
Mr Beard--Solicitor, Grays Inn.--	S 6 389 1
MR CHARLES VERNON (1)	
of Mr Charles Vernon; and yet in spite of his generous	LS 12 260 2
MR CURTIS (1)	
to our balls--but Mr Curtis won't often spare him, & just	W 321 2
MR DARCY (1)	
assuring him that Mr Darcy would consider his addressing	PP I 18 97 60
MR DE COURCY (20)	
Mr De Courcy to Mrs Vernon. Parklands.	LS 4 248 1
Mrs Vernon to Mr De Courcy. Churchill.	LS 6 250 1
you my dearest Susan, Mr De Courcy may be worth having.	LS 9 256 1
advice respecting Mr De Courcy, which I know was given	LS 10 257 1
Mr De Courcy to Sir Reginald. Churchill.	LS 14 263 1
Miss Vernon to Mr De Courcy.	LS 21 279 1
"I find from Wilson that we are going to lose Mr De Courcy.	LS 23 284 6
"My dear aunt, said she, he is going, Mr De Courcy is	LS 24 286 3
I thought that Mr De Courcy could do anything with my	LS 24 286 7
She wrote to Mr De Courcy."	LS 24 289 12
Her applying to Mr De Courcy hurt me particularly."	LS 24 289 12
if my acquaintance with Mr De Courcy had ended so gloomily.	LS 24 290 13
by marrying Mr De Courcy, than to irritate him & the rest	LS 26 295 1
Lady Susan to Mr De Courcy. Upper Seymour St.	LS 30 299 1
Mr De Courcy arrived, just when he should not.	LS 32 302 1
Mr De Courcy to Lady Susan. hotel.	LS 34 304 1
Lady Susan to Mr De Courcy. Upper Seymour St. I	LS 35 304 1
Mr De Courcy to Lady Susan. hotel.	LS 36 305 1
Lady Susan to Mr De Courcy. Upper Seymour St.	LS 37 306 1
De Courcy; he had just informed Mr Johnson of it by letter.	LS 38 306 1
MR DE COURCY'S (1)	
My dearest friend I congratulate you on Mr De Courcy's	LS 9 256 1
MR E. (7)	
If Mr E. does not lose his money at cards, you will stay	W 315 1
Mr E. lived in the best house in the street, & the best in	W 322 2
Mr E.s house was higher than most of its neighbours with	W 322 2
qualified admiration; & Mr E. not less satisfied with Mary,	W 323 3
in the manner in which Mr E. took up the subject.--	W 324 3
E.--, very strongly--but I am not sensible of the others.--	W 324 3
Mr E. having play'd with good luck, they were some of the	W 336 14
MR EDWARD'S (1)	
milleners, before she drew up towards Mr Edward's door.--	W 322 2
MR EDWARDES (3)	
'Mr Watson!--cried Mr Edwardes, well, you astonish me.--	W 324 3
friends--said Mr Edwardes, as he helped her to wine, when	W 324 4
how they make a second choice." observed Mr Edwardes.--	W 326 6
MR EDWARDS (5)	
Mr Edwards had a much easier, & more communicative air	W 323 3
Mr Edwards proceeded to relate every other little article	W 323 3
that point; & Mr Edwards now turned to something else.--	W 325 4
eveng so much--& Mr Edwards was as warm as herself, in	W 336 14
themselves so many dances beforehand, Mr Edwards."--	W 337 15
MR H (2)	
for us."--turned again to Mr H--& said--"before we accept	S 1 367 1
Rev: Mr Hanking.	S 6 389 1
MR H. (10)	
Give me leave to introduce my brother--Mr H."	W 333 13
gentlemanlike air in Mr H. which suited her--& in a few	W 333 13
little interruption till she heard of Mr H. as a partner.--	W 342 19
"Dance with Mr H.--good heavens!	W 342 19
Mr H. read like a scholar & a gentleman."--	W 344 20
Mr H. looked very much astonished--& replied--"what sir!	S 1 365 1
"Yes--I have heard of sanditon. replied Mr H.--	S 1 368 1
to any place in particular sir, answered Mr H.--	S 1 368 1
of such surgeon--nor (as Mr H. had been apt to suppose)	S 2 371 1
receive his Dividends, Mr H. went no farther than his feet	S 2 373 1
MR HEMMINGS (1)	
Mr Marshall & Mr Hemmings change their dress every day of	W 353 26
MR HEYWOOD (6)	
Mr Heywood, such was the name of the said proprietor,	S 1 365 1
"The surgeon sir!--replied Mr Heywood--I am afraid you	S 1 365 1
"Sir--said Mr Heywood with a good humoured smile--if you	S 1 366 1
In a most friendly manner Mr Heywood here interposed.	S 1 367 1
heard it spoken of in my life before, said Mr Heywood.	S 1 369 1
All that Mr Heywood himself could be persuaded to promise	S 2 374 1
MR HOLLIS (5)	
Her first husband had been a Mr Hollis, a man of	S 3 375 1
nursed & pleased Mr Hollis, that at his death he left her	S 3 375 1
the legal heirs of Mr Hollis, who must hope to be more	S 3 376 1
of the room, little conspicuous, represented Mr Hollis.--	S 12 427 1
Poor Mr Hollis!--	S 12 427 1
MR HOLLIS' (3)	
to say that Mr Hollis' kindred were the least in favour &	S 3 376 1
what I owe to poor Mr Hollis's memory, I should never keep	S 6 393 1
a fair rate--(poor Mr Hollis's Chamber-Horse, as good as	S 6 393 1
MR HOWARD (10)	
daughter's friend, Mr Howard formerly Tutor to Ld Osborne,	W 329 9
Mr Howard was an agreable-looking man, a little more than	W 330 10
Cassino Table; Mr Howard who belonged to it spoke to his	W 332 11
Among these was Mr Howard--his sister leaning on his arm--	W 333 13
appeased, on seeing Mr Howard come forward and claim	W 335 13
the only objection she could make to Mr Howard.--	W 335 13
when she heard Mr Howard spoken of as the preacher, & as	W 343 20
But what pleased me as much as anything was Mr Howard's	W 344 20
my gouty foot--& Mr Howard walked by me from the bottom to	W 344 20
to her to wonder why Mr Howard had not taken the same	W 347 22
MR JAMES (1)	
"I thought you were to have stood up with Mr James, the	W 336 14
MR JOHNSON (15)	
If I am as little in favour with Mr Johnson as ever, you	LS 2 245 1
be the case, for as Mr Johnson with all his faults is a	LS 2 245 1
to be assured that Mr Johnson suspected nothing of your	LS 5 249 1
in spite of Mr Johnson, to make opportunities of seeing me.	LS 26 295 3
Mr Johnson leaves London next Tuesday.	LS 26 295 4
my promise to Mr Johnson as comprehending only (at least	LS 26 296 4
so great, that tho' Mr Johnson was her guardian & I do not	LS 26 296 5
Mr Johnson has hit on the most effectual manner of	LS 28 297 1
to make me detest Mr Johnson; but now the extent of my	LS 29 298 1
Mr Johnson, while he waited in the drawing room for me.	LS 32 302 1
time known to de courcy, who is now alone with Mr Johnson.	LS 32 303 1
Mr Johnson has for some time suspected de courcy of	LS 32 303 1
De Courcy; he had just informed Mr Johnson of it by letter.	LS 38 306 1
It makes me miserable--but Mr Johnson vows that if I	LS 38 306 1
Mr Johnson & he are the greatest friends in the world.	LS 38 307 3
MR JOHNSON'S (1)	
I received my information in Mr Johnson's house, from Mrs	LS 34 304 1
MR MANWARING (2)	
By her behaviour to Mr Manwaring, she gave jealousy &	LS 4 248 1
of having made Mr Manwaring & a young man engaged to Miss	LS 11 259 1
MR MANWARING'S (1)	
Manwaring's sister, deprived an amiable girl of her lover.	LS 4 248 1
MR MARSHALL (1)	
Mr Marshall & Mr Hemmings change their dress every day of	W 353 26
MR MUSGRAVE (6)	
seat by the fire you know, Mr Musgrave." replied Mrs E.	W 327 7
we passed in the passage, was Mr Musgrave, then?--	W 327 8
Mr Musgrave was shortly afterwards announced;--& mrs	W 338 17
& the convenient Mr Musgrave in high spirits at his own	W 345 21
"You may call a fortnight a great while Mr Musgrave, said	W 356 28
Musgrave?--" said Emma, as they were taking their seats.--	W 358 28
MR NORTON (2)	
"Mr Norton, & Mr Styles."	W 337 15
"Mr Norton is a cousin of Capt. Hunter's"--	W 337 15
MR P (2)	
at Denham Park; & Mr P-- had little doubt, that he & his	S 3 377 1
"Civilization, civilization indeed!--cried Mr P--,	S 4 383 1
MR P. (23)	
"Our coast too full"--repeated Mr P.--	S 1 369 1
Upon the whole, Mr P. was evidently an aimable, family-man,	S 2 372 1
library, which Mr P. was anxiously wishing to support.--	S 2 374 1
that she had married--& Mr P. acknowledged there being	S 3 376 1
these three divisions, Mr P. did not hesitate to say that	S 3 376 1
Till within the last twelvemonth, Mr P. had considered Sir	S 3 377 1
"Ah!--said Mr P.--	S 4 379 1
day had been caught, as Mr P. observed with delight to	S 4 383 1
Such sights & sounds were highly Blissful to Mr P.--	S 4 383 1
amused curiosity, & by Mr P. with the eager eye which	S 4 384 1
When they met before dinner, Mr P. was looking over	S 5 385 1
"Well--said Mr P.--as he finished.	S 5 387 1
Mr P. could not be satisfied without an early visit to the	S 6 389 1
Mr P. could not but feel that the list was not only	S 6 389 1
so much good will for Mr P. to encourage expenditure,	S 6 390 1
so completely justified Mr P.'s praise that Charlotte	S 6 391 1
another moment brought Mr P. into the hall to welcome the	S 9 406 1
Here Mr P. drew his chair still nearer to his sister, &	S 9 408 1
be of use to you?"--and Mr P. warmly offered his	S 9 410 1
"I think you are doing too much, said Mr P.	S 9 411 1
coming to Sanditon, said Mr P. as he walked with her to	S 9 411 1
Mr P. was confident of another new family.--	S 10 414 1
opening my love, said Mr P. (who did not mean to go with	S 12 423 1
MR PARKER (14)	
Mr Parker of Sanditon; this lady, my wife Mrs Parker.--	S 1 368 1
"Not at all sir, not at all--cried Mr Parker eagerly.	S 1 368 1
Mr Parker was therefore carried into the house, and his	S 1 370 1
Mr Parker could not think of very little besides.--	S 2 371 1
to the coast, Mr Parker gave Charlotte a more detailed	S 3 375 1
"He is a warm friend to Sanditon--said Mr Parker--& his	S 3 377 1
Mr Parker spoke warmly of Clara Brereton, & the interest	S 3 378 1
delighted to see Mr Parker again, whose manners	S 6 390 1
freely, I beleive, than W. Indians." observed Mr Parker.--	S 6 392 1
of life, we shall not much thank them Mr Parker."--	S 6 392 1
Well Mr Parker--and the other is a Boarding school, a	S 6 393 1
Poor Mr Parker got no more credit from Lady D. than he had	S 6 393 1
I beseech you Mr Parker, no Doctors here."--	S 6 394 1
"Excellent!--excellent!--cried Mr Parker.--	S 9 409 1
MR PARKER'S (1)	
Mr Parker's character & history were soon unfolded.	S 2 371 1
MR RICHARD PRATT (1)	
Dr & Mrs Brown--Mr Richard Pratt.--	S 6 389 1
MR SAMUEL (1)	
Robert--but I cannot perceive any likeness to Mr Samuel."	W 324 3
MR SMITH (1)	
I learnt all this from a Mr Smith now in this	LS 4 248 1
MR SMITH'S (4)	
& according to Mr Smith's account, is equally dull & proud.	LS 4 248 2
Your friend Mr Smith's story however cannot be quite true,	LS 6 252 2
Mr Smith's account of her proceedings at Langford, where	LS 11 259 1

for disbeleiving Mr Smith's intelligence; you had no doubt LS 12 261 5
MR STYLES (2)
"Mr Norton, & Mr Styles." W 337 15
"And who is Mr Styles?" W 337 15
MR TOM MUSGRAVE (2)
Well, we shall see how irresistable Mr Tom Musgrave & I W 319 2
years old, & Mr Tom Musgrave; who probably imprisoned W 329 9
MR TOMLINSON (1)
in the place, if Mr Tomlinson the banker might be indulged W 322 2
MR TOMLINSON'S (1)
she should, that "Mr Tomlinson's family were in the room." W 327 7
MR TOMLINSONS (1)
with either of the Mr Tomlinsons, Mary?--said her mother. W 336 14
MR TURNER (1)
"Mr Turner had not been dead a great while I think? W 325 5
MR VERNON (21)
Lady Susan Vernon to Mr Vernon. Langford, Decr. LS 1 243 1
Mr Vernon I think was a great deal too kind to her, when LS 3 246 1
My dear sister I congratulate you & Mr Vernon on being LS 4 248 1
of my reception from Mr Vernon; but I confess myself not LS 5 249 1
me for marrying Mr Vernon, & that we had never met before, LS 6 251 1
of such a husband as Mr Vernon, to whom her own behaviour LS 6 252 2
wish of hunting with Mr Vernon, & of course I cannot LS 8 255 1
the happiness of Mr Vernon, to whom she was always much LS 14 264 3
her regard for Mr Vernon equal even to his deserts, & her LS 14 265 5
Mr Vernon set off for town as soon as she had determined LS 15 266 4
Mr Vernon declares that he never saw deeper distress than LS 15 267 4
My dear mother Mr Vernon returned on Thursday night, LS 17 269 1
to acquaint yourself and Mr Vernon with the whole business. LS 20 277 5
After I had sent off my letter to you, I went to Mr Vernon LS 24 285 2
You will find Mr Vernon in his own room." LS 24 287 8
You had forbidden her speaking to Mr Vernon or to me on LS 24 289 12
be still more insupportable, the displeasure of Mr Vernon. LS 30 300 3
& since the death of Mr Vernon which had reached me in LS 36 305 1
I hope nothing will make it inconvenient to Mr Vernon, & LS 40 309 1
kind & proper--& Mr Vernon beleives that Frederica will LS 41 310 3
visit to London; & Mr Vernon who, as it must have already LS 42 311 2
MR VERNON'S (3)
more strongly they operate on Mr Vernon's generous temper. LS 6 251 2
him to accept Mr Vernon's invitation to prolong his stay LS 8 254 1
his visit, I should regret Mr Vernon's giving him any. LS 8 256 3
MR W. (2)
more to my mind--continued Mr W. or one better delivered.-- W 343 20
My dear Mr W.--(to her husband) you have not put any fresh W 353 26
MR W.'S (1)
On the present occasion, as only two of Mr W.'s children W 315 1
MR WATSON (7)
'Mr Watson!--cried Mr Edwardes, well, you astonish me.-- W 324 3
Mr Watson returned in the evening, not the worse for the W 343 19
not offend Mr Watson--which I thought very kind of him.-- W 344 20
of doing himself the honour of waiting on Mr Watson.-- W 344 21
Mr Watson, as the gentlemen had already heard from Nanny, W 345 21
Mr Watson had not been well enough to join the party at W 354 28
of observing to Mr Watson that he should leave him at W 359 28
MR WATSON'S (1)
plea of Mr Watson's infirm state of health.-- W 348 22
MR WOODCOCK'S (1)
well, with only Mr Woodcock's assistance--& when I left S 9 407 1
MR. ---- (1)
than to any mere Mr. ---- ; a Mr. (save, perhaps, some P III 3 24 36
MR. ALLEN (35)
Mr. Allen, who owned the chief of the property about NA I 1 17 12
the choice of a sensible, intelligent man, like Mr. Allen. NA I 2 20 8
As for Mr. Allen, he repaired directly to the card-room, NA I 2 20 9
They saw nothing of Mr. Allen; and after looking about NA I 2 22 10
discovered and joined by Mr. Allen when the dance was over. NA I 2 23 22
never get Mr. Allen to know one of my gowns from another. NA I 3 28 39
miles is a long way; Mr. Allen says it is nine, measured NA I 3 29 46
"Yes, very much indeed, I fancy; Mr. Allen thinks her the NA I 7 51 50
any man who is a better judge of beauty than Mr. Allen. NA I 7 51 51
I tell Mr. Allen, when he talks of being sick of it, that NA I 8 54 5
"And I hope, madam, that Mr. Allen will be obliged to like NA I 8 54 6
so I tell Mr. Allen he must not be in a hurry to get away." NA I 8 54 9
"Oh! Mr. Allen, you mean. NA I 9 63 11
took place; Mr. Allen, after drinking his glass of water, NA I 10 71 8
to the wish of Mr. Allen, which took them rather early NA I 10 81 61
She applied to Mr. Allen for confirmation of her hopes, NA I 11 82 1
of her hopes, but Mr. Allen not having his own skies and NA I 11 82 1
I hope Mr. Allen will put on his great coat when he goes, NA I 11 83 13
At the head of them she was met by Mr. Allen, who, on NA I 11 89 62
Tilney's, was not sorry to be called away by Mr. Allen. NA I 12 96 23
to mention before Mr. Allen the half-settled scheme of her NA I 13 103 29
Mr. Allen caught at it directly. NA I 13 104 29
no harm done," said Mr. Allen; "and I would only advise NA I 13 105 38
thought, asked Mr. Allen whether it would not be both NA I 13 105 40
Mr. Allen however discouraged her from doing any such NA I 13 105 40
With Mr. Allen to support her, she felt no dread of the NA I 14 106 1
"You are fond of history!--and so are Mr. Allen and my NA I 14 109 24
Mr. Allen attended her to Milsom-Street, where she was to NA II 5 154 1
Neither her father nor Mr. Allen did so. NA II 7 177 18
Mr. Allen, he supposed, must feel these inconveniences as NA II 7 178 21
Mr. Allen did not care about the garden, and never went NA II 7 178 22
"Mr. Allen had only one small hot-house, which Mrs. Allen NA II 7 178 25
characters, which Mr. Allen had been used to call NA II 7 181 40
Mr. Allen expressed himself on the occasion with the NA II 14 237 22
uttered twice after Mr. Allen left the room, without any NA II 14 238 22
MR. ALLEN'S (14)
another evening I hope," was Mr. Allen's consolation. NA I 2 23 26
yet perhaps entered Mr. Allen's head, but that he was not NA I 3 30 52
to the very door of Mr. Allen's house; and that they NA I 4 34 7
to walk together to Mr. Allen's, and James, as the door NA I 7 50 44
greatly relieved by Mr. Allen's approbation of her own NA I 13 105 41
No sooner had she expressed her delight in Mr. Allen's NA II 2 138 1
The remembrance of Mr. Allen's opinion, respecting young NA II 5 156 5
been used to much better sized apartments at Mr. Allen's?" NA II 6 166 6
honest assurance; "Mr. Allen's dining-parlour was not more NA II 6 166 7
Mr. Allen's house, he was sure, must be exactly of the NA II 6 166 7
the extent of all Mr. Allen's, as well as her father's, NA II 7 178 21
"How were Mr. Allen's succession-houses worked?" NA II 7 178 24
before they reached Mr. Allen's grounds he had done it so NA II 15 243 9
give her, would be a pretty addition to Mr. Allen's estate. NA II 15 245 12
MR. AND MISS CRAWFORD (5)
Crawford, the children of her mother by a second marriage. MP I 4 40 15
of Mr. and Miss Crawford, who, late and dark and dirty as MP I 15 142 25
Crawford were mentioned in my last letters from Mansfield. MP II 1 185 29
trying to understand what Mr. and Miss Crawford were at. MP II 13 305 26
of Mr. and Miss Crawford's having applied to her uncle and MP III 15 437 2
MR. AND MISS TILNEY (1)
met Mrs. Hughes, and Mr. and Miss Tilney walking with her." NA I 9 68 40
MR. AND MISS WOODHOUSE (1)
"Poor Mr. and Miss Woodhouse, if you please; but I cannot E I 1 10 29
MR. AND MRS. ALLEN (7)
kindness by Mr. and Mrs. Allen, invited by the former to NA I 7 51 54
Mr. and Mrs. Allen would expect her back every moment. NA I 13 103 28
claims of Mr. and Mrs. Allen were not to be superseded; NA I 13 103 28
Mrs. Allen, by the communication of the wonderful event. NA I 15 124 48
Mr. and Mrs. Allen were sorry to lose their young friend, NA II 5 154 1
as Mr. and Mrs. Allen, and the very little consideration NA II 14 239 28
alacrity, if Mr. and Mrs. Allen were now at Fullerton? and NA II 15 242 9
MR. AND MRS. BENNET (1)
of leaving Mr. and Mrs. Bennet for a single evening during PP I 16 75 1
MR. AND MRS. CHARLES MUSGROVE (1)
"Mr. and Mrs. Charles Musgrove" were ushered into the room. P IV 10 216 17
MR. AND MRS. CHURCHILL (2)
Mr. and Mrs. Churchill, who threw her off with due decorum. E I 2 15 3
and Mr. and Mrs. Churchill, having no children of their E I 2 16 4
MR. AND MRS. COLE (3)
I am sorry Mr. and Mrs. Cole should have done it. E II 7 209 10
Cole, you would stay a little longer than you might wish. E II 7 210 20
promoted by Mr. and Mrs. Cole, that every thing was E II 8 229 98
MR. AND MRS. COLLINS (4)
Lady Catherine, Sir William, and Mr. and Mrs. Collins sat PP II 6 166 41
Mr. and Mrs. Collins have a comfortable income, but not PP II 9 179 22
opinion of Mr. and Mrs. Collins's happiness; and that in PP II 10 182 1
your ladyship whether you left Mr. and Mrs. Collins well." PP III 14 352 12
13
MR. AND MRS. DASHWOOD (1)
though he had arrived in town with Mr. and Mrs. Dashwood. SS II 11 230 4
MR. AND MRS. DIXON (3)
They want her (Mr. and Mrs. Dixon) excessively to come E II 1 160 23
that it must be the joint present of Mr. and Mrs. Dixon. E II 8 217 31
soon hear that it is a present from Mr. and Mrs. Dixon." E II 8 218 39
MR. AND MRS. ELLISON (1)
believed Mr. and Mrs. Ellison would not be sorry to have SS II 8 194 12
MR. AND MRS. ELTON (3)
Mr. and Mrs. Elton appeared; and all the smiles and the E III 2 320 11
meet Mr. and Mrs. Elton, and any other of his neighbours.-- E III 6 356 30
Mr. and Mrs. Elton, indeed, showed no unwillingness to mix, E III 7 367 1
MR. AND MRS. GARDINER (11)
his compliments to Mr. and Mrs. Gardiner, though unknown. PP II 15 217 8
But they did pass away, and Mr. and Mrs. Gardiner, with PP II 19 239 10
Mr. and Mrs. Gardiner smiled. PP III 1 248 29
Mr. and Mrs. Gardiner were half a quarter of a mile behind. PP III 1 257 65
To Mr. and Mrs. Gardiner he was scarcely a less PP III 2 261 6
of seeing Mr. and Mrs. Gardiner, and Miss Bennet, to PP III 2 263 11
let me, or let the servant, go after Mr. and Mrs. Gardiner. PP III 4 276 7
Mr. and Mrs. Gardiner had hurried back in alarm, supposing, PP III 4 280 26
Mr. and Mrs. Gardiner could not but be deeply affected. PP III 4 280 26
while Mr. and Mrs. Gardiner were engaged with their PP III 5 286 32
Darcy, after enquiring of her how Mr. and Mrs. Gardiner PP III 11 335 43
MR. AND MRS. GARDINER'S (2)
On Mr. and Mrs. Gardiner's coming up, they were all PP III 1 257 66
But she had no reason to fear Mr. and Mrs. Gardiner's PP III 2 264 13
MR. AND MRS. HENRY DASHWOOD (1)
The constant attention of Mr. and Mrs. Henry Dashwood to SS I 1 3 1
MR. AND MRS. JOHN DASHWOOD (1)
to Mr. and Mrs. John Dashwood to visit her at Barton; and SS I 5 25 3
MR. AND MRS. JOHN KNIGHTLEY (5)
Mr. and Mrs. John Knightley, from having been longer than E I 11 91 2
and Mr. and Mrs. John Knightley, their five children, and E I 11 91 3
Mr. and Mrs. John Knightley were not detained long at E I 17 140 1
and Mrs. John Knightley came--I think the very evening.-- E III 4 338 12
Mr. and Mrs. John Knightley were to come down in August, E III 17 464 16
MR. AND MRS. MORLAND (6)
Mr. and Mrs. Morland were all compliance, and Catherine NA I 1 17 12
Mr. and Mrs. Morland, relying on the discretion of the NA II 2 140 11
Mr. and Mrs. Morland--your brothers and sisters--I hope NA II 10 203 9
that if Mr. and Mrs. Morland were aware of the pleasure it NA II 13 221 2
journey, Mr. and Mrs. Morland could not but feel that it NA II 14 234 10
Mr. and Mrs. Morland never did--they had been too kind to NA II 16 250 3
MR. AND MRS. MORLAND'S (1)
Mr. and Mrs. Morland's surprize on being applied to by Mr. NA II 16 249 1
MR. AND MRS. MUSGROVE (16)
Mr. and Mrs. Musgrove took me, and we were so crowded! P III 5 39 39
Mr. and Mrs. Musgrove were a very good sort of people; P III 5 40 45
remark of Mr. and Mrs. Musgrove--"so, Miss Anne, Sir P III 6 42 1
sight of Mr. and Mrs. Musgrove's respectable forms in the P III 6 46 12
and Mr. and Mrs. Musgrove's fond partiality for their own P III 6 47 13
notice of Mr. and Mrs. Musgrove more than any thing else, P III 6 47 15
Mr. and Mrs. Musgrove cannot think it wrong, while I P III 7 57 15
Mr. and Mrs. Musgrove, either from seeing little, or from P III 9 74 9
him, Mr. and Mrs. Musgrove were sure all could not be P III 10 82 2
broken to Mr. and Mrs. Musgrove--the lateness of the P III 12 113 57
Though it was rather desirable that Mr. and Mrs. Musgrove P III 12 114 64
her, while I go in and break it to Mr. and Mrs. Musgrove. P III 12 117 74
which, in Mr. and Mrs. Musgrove's distressed state of P IV 1 121 1
after Mr. and Mrs. Musgrove's going, than Anne conceived P IV 2 129 1
"We have had a very dull Christmas; Mr. and Mrs. Musgrove " P IV 6 162 7
"Such excellent parents as Mr. and Mrs. Musgrove," P IV 10 218 23
MR. AND MRS. NORRIS (1)
and Mr. and Mrs. Norris began their career of conjugal MP I 1 3 1
MR. AND MRS. PALMER (2)
But they had no curiosity to see how Mr. and Mrs. Palmer SS I 19 108 40
Mr. and Mrs. Palmer were of the party; from the former, SS II 5 171 30
MR. AND MRS. PERRY (2)
was a happier or a better couple than Mr. and Mrs. Perry. E II 3 175 39
friends, then I begin dreaming of Mr. and Mrs. Perry." E III 5 345 13
MR. AND MRS. PHILIPS (1)
of Mr. and Mrs. Philips, protesting that he did not in the PP I 16 84 59
MR. AND MRS. ROBERT MARTIN (1)
to join the hands of Mr. Knightley and Miss Woodhouse. E III 19 484 11
MR. AND MRS. RUSHWORTH (3)
of Mr. and Mrs. Rushworth in a supernumerary glass or two, MP II 3 203 30
dear Mr. and Mrs. Rushworth will be at home, and I am sure MP II 7 245 32
It was not Mr. and Mrs. Rushworth, it was Mrs. Rushworth MP III 15 441 19
MR. AND MRS. SUCKLING (1)
form Mr. and Mrs. Suckling, the Highbury world were E III 6 352 1
MR. AND MRS. TILNEY (1)
"And are Mr. and Mrs. Tilney in Bath?" NA I 9 68 47
MR. AND MRS. WESTON (18)
"We must ask Mr. and Mrs. Weston to dine with us, while E I 9 79 61
that Mr. and Mrs. Weston do really prevent our missing her E I 11 94 14
and gave Mr. and Mrs. Weston a great deal of pleasure. E I 11 96 24
would be so great a disappointment to Mr. and Mrs. Weston. E I 13 110 9
she;--"we will make your apologies to Mr. and Mrs. Weston." E I 13 110 11
Charming people, Mr. and Mrs. Weston;--Mrs. Weston indeed E I 13 116 43
That Mr. and Mrs. Weston did think of it, she was very E I 14 119 5
warmly into Mr. and Mrs. Weston's disappointment, as might E I 18 144 4
My love for Mr. and Mrs. Weston gives me a decided E I 18 150 35
by Mr. and Mrs. Weston, who were standing to speak to her. E II 5 188 6
tidings, Mr. and Mrs. Weston's visit this morning was in E II 7 206 5
that nobody can object to, if Mr. and Mrs. Weston do not. E II 11 251 24
If Mr. and Mrs. Weston will be so obliging as to call here E II 11 252 32
There were Mr. and Mrs. Weston; delighted to see her and E II 11 253 40
in seeing Mr. and Mrs. Weston; she was very often thinking E II 13 264 1
After tea, Mr. and Mrs. Weston, and Mr. Elton sat down E II 18 311 36
but was quickly back again with both Mr. and Mrs. Weston. E III 2 325 29
rain; Mr. and Mrs. Weston and their son, Miss Bates and E III 5 344 3
MR. ARTHUR (1)
Such a host of friends!--and Mr. George and Mr. Arthur!-- E III 2 323 19
MR. BENNET (80)
"My dear Mr. Bennet," said his lady to him one day, "have PP I 1 3 3
Mr. Bennet replied that he had not. PP I 1 3 4
Mr. Bennet made no answer. PP I 1 3 6
"My dear Mr. Bennet," replied his wife, "how can you be so PP I 1 4 16
"Mr. Bennet, how can you abuse your own children in such a PP I 1 5 28
Mr. Bennet was so odd a mixture of quick parts, sarcastic PP I 1 5 34
Mr. Bennet was among the earliest of those who waited on PP I 2 6 1
"No more have I," said Mr. Bennet; "and I am glad to find PP I 2 6 6
"Impossible, Mr. Bennet, impossible, when I am not PP I 2 7 15
"How good it was in you, my dear Mr. Bennet! PP I 2 7 24
as you chuse," said Mr. Bennet; and, as he spoke, he left PP I 2 8 25
They found Mr. Bennet still up. PP I 3 12 15
"Oh! my dear Mr. Bennet," as she entered the room, "we PP I 3 12 16

Mr. Bennet protested against any description of finery. PP I 3 13 19
on this subject, Mr. Bennet coolly observed, "from all PP I 7 29 5
6
"My dear Mr. Bennet, you must not expect such girls to PP I 7 29 12
They are wanted in the farm, Mr. Bennet, are not they?" PP I 7 31 25
"Well, my dear," said Mr. Bennet, when Elizabeth had read PP I 7 31 31
"I hope, my dear," said Mr. Bennet to his wife, as they PP I 13 61 1
affair," said Mr. Bennet, "and nothing can clear Mr. PP I 13 62 8
gentleman," said Mr. Bennet, as he folded up the letter. PP I 13 63 13
Mr. Bennet indeed said little; but the ladies were ready PP I 13 64 21
During dinner, Mr. Bennet scarcely spoke at all; but when PP I 14 66 1
Mr. Bennet could not have chosen better. PP I 14 66 1
"You judge very properly," said Mr. Bennet, "and it is PP I 14 68 10
had been enough, and Mr. Bennet was glad to take his guest PP I 14 68 13
Then turning to Mr. Bennet, he offered himself as his PP I 14 69 17
Mr. Bennet accepted the challenge, observing that he acted PP I 14 69 17
another table with Mr. Bennet, and prepared for backgammon. PP I 14 69 17
at the request of Mr. Bennet, who was most anxious to get PP I 15 71 6
really talking to Mr. Bennet, with little cessation, of PP I 15 71 6
Such doings discomposed Mr. Bennet exceedingly. PP I 15 71 6
Many smiled; but no one looked more amused than Mr. Bennet PP I 18 101 71
Mr. Bennet, in equal silence, was enjoying the scene. PP I 18 103 75
I will go directly to Mr. Bennet, and we shall very soon PP I 20 111 5
"Oh! Mr. Bennet, you are wanted immediately; we are all in PP I 20 111 7
Mr. Bennet raised his eyes from his book as she entered, PP I 20 111 8
"What do you mean, Mr. Bennet, by talking in this way? PP I 20 112 21
paid yourself and Mr. Bennet the compliment of requesting PP I 20 114 32
many years longer Mr. Bennet was likely to live; and Sir PP I 22 122 3
They were all astonished; and Mr. Bennet, who could by no PP I 22 123 6
7
out of the house, as soon as Mr. Bennet were dead. PP I 23 130 16
"Indeed, Mr. Bennet," said she, "it is very hard to think PP I 23 130 17
"I never can be thankful, Mr. Bennet, for any thing about PP I 23 130 24
"I leave it to yourself to determine" said Mr. Bennet. PP I 23 130 25
Mr. Bennet treated the matter differently. PP II 1 137 27
"True," said Mr. Bennet, "but it is a comfort to think PP II 1 138 29
during dinner did Mr. Bennet say voluntarily to Elizabeth, PP II 16 222 19
20
"Already arisen!" repeated Mr. Bennet. PP II 18 231 17
Mr. Bennet saw that her whole heart was in the subject; PP II 18 231 19
20
But Mr. Bennet was not of a disposition to seek comfort PP II 19 236 1
And now here's Mr. Bennet gone away, and I know he will PP III 5 287 35
assist Mr. Bennet in every endeavour for recovering Lydia. PP III 5 287 36
And, above all things, keep Mr. Bennet from fighting. PP III 5 288 38
The whole party were in hopes of a letter from Mr. Bennet PP III 6 294 1
to prevail on Mr. Bennet to return to Longbourn, as soon PP III 6 294 2
That Mr. Bennet had been to Epsom and Clapham, before his PP III 6 295 5
hotels in town, as Mr. Bennet thought it possible they PP III 6 295 5
He added, that Mr. Bennet seemed wholly disinclined at PP III 6 295 5
to London, at the same time that Mr. Bennet came from it. PP III 6 298 15
When Mr. Bennet arrived, he had all the appearance of his PP III 6 299 18
Mr. Bennet made no answer, and each of them, deep in PP III 7 304 33
Mr. Bennet had very often wished, before this period of PP III 8 308 1
When first Mr. Bennet had married, economy was held to be PP III 8 308 3
to be settled, and Mr. Bennet could have no hesitation in PP III 8 308 4
A long dispute followed this declaration; but Mr. Bennet PP III 8 310 10
Mr. Bennet and his daughters saw all the advantages of PP III 8 313 20
When Mr. Bennet wrote again to his brother, therefore, he PP III 8 314 22
Their reception from Mr. Bennet, to whom they then turned, PP III 9 315 4
Though Mr. Bennet was not imagined to be very rich, he PP III 10 323 2
"He is as fine a fellow," said Mr. Bennet, as soon as they PP III 11 330 8
After tea, Mr. Bennet retired to the library, as was his PP III 13 344 11
Bennet spent the morning together, as had been agreed on. PP III 13 346 21
an hour; and when Mr. Bennet joined them at supper, his PP III 13 348 34
My dear Mr. Bennet," cried his wife, "what are you talking PP III 13 348 40
said aloud, "Mr. Bennet, have you no more lanes here- PP III 17 374 22
In the evening soon after Mr. Bennet withdrew to the PP III 17 375 28
with him; and Mr. Bennet soon assured her that he was PP III 17 379 47
what Mr. Bennet sent to Mr. Collins, in reply to his last. PP III 18 383 22
Mr. Bennet missed his second daughter exceedingly; his PP III 19 385 2

MR. BENNET'S (10)
he would return Mr. Bennet's visit, and determining when PP I 2 8 28
In a few days Mr. Bingley returned Mr. Bennet's visit, and PP I 3 9 3
Mr. Bennet's property consisted almost entirely in an PP I 7 28 1
Mr. Bennet's expectations were fully answered. PP I 14 68 12
Mr. Bennet's emotions were much more tranquil on the PP I 23 127 6
inn where Mr. Bennet's carriage was to meet them, they PP II 16 219 1
Two days after Mr. Bennet's return, as Jane and Elizabeth PP III 7 301 1
To Mr. Bennet's acknowledgments he briefly replied, with PP III 8 312 18
and shoot as many as you please, on Mr. Bennet's manor. PP III 11 337 53
During their walk, it was resolved that Mr. Bennet's PP III 17 375 27

MR. BERTRAM (26)
and having seen Mr. Bertram in town, she knew that MP I 4 42 18
She acknowledged, however, that the Mr. Bertrams were very MP I 5 47 27
Miss Crawford, as she was walking with the Mr. Bertrams. MP I 5 48 30
Mr. Bertram, I dare say you have sometimes met with such MP I 5 49 32
be," said Mr. Bertram, gallantly, "are doing a a great MP I 5 50 37
"Yes, that is very inconvenient," said Mr. Bertram. MP I 5 50 40
Mr. Bertram set off for ----, and Miss Crawford was MP I 6 52 1
"Mr. Bertram," said she, "I have tidings of my harp at MP I 6 57 33
Now, Mr. Bertram, if you write to your brother, I entreat MP I 6 59 41
began with, "so you are to be a clergyman, Mr. Bertram. MP I 9 91 38
It is indolence Mr. Bertram, indeed. MP I 11 110 23
The approach of September brought tidings of Mr. Bertram MP I 12 114 1
The season and duties which brought Mr. Bertram back to MP I 12 114 3
for a time, for Mr. Bertram was in the room again, and MP I 12 118 22
"An after-piece instead of a comedy," said Mr. Bertram. MP I 13 122 5
In a few minutes Mr. Bertram was called out of the room to MP I 15 139 11
"No, indeed, Mr. Bertram, you must excuse me. MP I 15 146 51
It was, indeed, a triumphant day to Mr. Bertram and Maria. MP I 17 158 1
my uncle dines at Sotherton, and you and Mr. Bertram too. MP II 3 199 17
"My sister and Mr. Bertram--I am so glad your eldest MP II 4 211 22
eldest cousin is gone that he may be Mr. Bertram again. MP II 4 211 22
But I have long thought Mr. Bertram one of the worst MP II 4 212 30
"Mr. Bertram," said Miss Crawford, a few minutes MP II 7 244 30
son, your cousin, Mr. Bertram, is to marry early; but at MP III 1 317 34
poor Mr. Bertram has a bad chance of ultimate recovery. MP III 14 433 13
'Mr. Bertram,' said she, with a smile--but it was a smile MP III 16 459 30

MR. BERTRAM'S (3)
seemed likely to disappoint Mr. Bertram's calculations. MP I 3 24 5
intimate friend of Mr. Bertram's just arrived on a visit. MP I 12 117 11
Mr. Bertram's acquaintance with him had begun at Weymouth, MP I 13 121 1

MR. BINGLEY (94)
of them, Mr. Bingley might like you the best of the party." PP I 1 4 19
"But, my dear, you must indeed go and see Mr. Bingley when PP I 1 4 22
I dare say Mr. Bingley will be very glad to see you; and I PP I 1 4 25
was among the earliest of those who waited on Mr. Bingley. PP I 2 6 1
her with, "I hope Mr. Bingley will like it Lizzy." PP I 2 6 1
2
"We are not in a way to know what Mr. Bingley likes," said PP I 2 6 3
of your friend, and introduce Mr. Bingley to her." PP I 2 7 14
her ideas," he continued, "let us return to Mr. Bingley." PP I 2 7 20
"I am sick of Mr. Bingley," cried his wife. PP I 2 7 21
dare say Mr. Bingley will dance with you at the next ball." PP I 2 8 26
her husband any satisfactory description of Mr. Bingley. PP I 3 9 1
In a few days Mr. Bingley returned Mr. Bennet's visit, and PP I 3 9 3
Mr. Bingley was obliged to be in town the following day, PP I 3 9 4
soon followed that Mr. Bingley was to bring twelve ladies PP I 3 10 4
five altogether; Mr. Bingley, his two sisters, the husband PP I 3 10 4
Mr. Bingley was good looking and gentlemanlike; he had a PP I 3 10 5
much handsomer than Mr. Bingley, and he was looked at with PP I 3 10 5
Mr. Bingley had soon made himself acquainted with all the PP I 3 10 6
between him and Mr. Bingley, who came from the dance for a PP I 3 11 7
Mr. Bingley followed his advice. PP I 3 12 14
Mr. Bingley had danced with her twice, and she had been PP I 3 12 15
Every body said how well she looked; and Mr. Bingley PP I 3 12 16
in her praise of Mr. Bingley before, expressed to her PP I 4 14 1
Mr. Bingley inherited property to the amount of nearly an PP I 4 15 11
Mr. Bingley intended it likewise, and sometimes made PP I 4 15 12
Mr. Bingley had not been of age two years, when he was PP I 4 16 13
was all in pursuit of Mr. Bingley, and under your orders." PP I 7 31 31
Mr. Bingley and his eldest sister, to observe the game. PP I 8 38 39
early received from Mr. Bingley by a housemaid, and some PP I 9 41 1
You have a sweet room here, Mr. Bingley, and a charming PP I 9 42 7
is a vast deal pleasanter, is not it, Mr. Bingley?" PP I 9 43 21
What an agreeable man Sir William is, Mr. Bingley--is not PP I 9 44 27
For my part, Mr. Bingley, I always keep servants that can PP I 9 44 29
her thanks to Mr. Bingley for his kindness to Jane, with PP I 9 45 35
Mr. Bingley was unaffectedly civil in his answer, and PP I 9 45 35
youngest should tax Mr. Bingley with having promised on PP I 9 45 35
She was very equal therefore to address Mr. Bingley on the PP I 9 45 36
Mr. Hurst and Mr. Bingley were at piquet, and Mrs. Hurst PP I 10 47 1
"Your humility, Mr. Bingley," said Elizabeth, "must disarm PP I 10 48 24
Mr. Bingley did not do justice to his own disposition. PP I 10 49 30
of such a case as you have supposed about Mr. Bingley. PP I 10 50 37
was added, that if Mr. Bingley and his sister pressed them PP I 12 59 1
It is Mr. Bingley I am sure. PP I 13 61 3
I am sure I shall be extremely glad to see Mr. Bingley.-- PP I 13 61 3
"It is not Mr. Bingley," said her husband; "it is a person PP I 13 61 4
In another minute Mr. Bingley, but without seeming to have PP I 15 73 9
his intimacy with Mr. Bingley! how can Mr. Bingley, who PP I 16 82 44
45
Bingley! how can Mr. Bingley, who seems good humour itself, PP I 16 82 44
45
Do you know Mr. Bingley?" PP I 16 82 45
one point,-- that Mr. Bingley, if he had been imposed on, PP I 17 86 8
had been speaking; Mr. Bingley and his sisters came to PP I 17 86 9
from Mr. Bingley himself, instead of a ceremonious card. PP I 17 86 10
to Mr. Bingley, whose blind partiality provoked her. PP I 18 89 3
Mr. Bingley does not know the whole of his history, and is PP I 18 95 50
"Mr. Bingley does not know Mr. Wickham himself?" PP I 18 96 51
being joined by Mr. Bingley himself, Elizabeth withdrew to PP I 18 96 56
on her sister and Mr. Bingley, and the train of agreeable PP I 18 98 63
that Jane would be soon married to Mr. Bingley.-- PP I 18 98 63
was complimenting Mr. Bingley and his sisters on the PP I 18 102 75
Mr. Bingley and Jane were standing together, a little PP I 18 103 75
particularly to Mr. Bingley, to assure him how happy he PP I 18 103 76
worth of each was eclipsed by Mr. Bingley and Netherfield. PP I 18 103 77
Mr. Bingley will not be detained in London by them." PP I 21 117 9
of thinking that Mr. Bingley would be soon down again and PP I 21 120 30
Mrs. Bennet's best comfort was, that Mr. Bingley must be PP II 1 137 26
"for Jane would have got Mr. Bingley, if she could. PP II 2 140 4
A young man, such as you describe Mr. Bingley, so easily PP II 2 140 6
and depend upon it, Mr. Bingley never stirs without him." PP II 2 141 13
could discover to Mr. Bingley her sister's being in town. PP II 3 147 24
It must have been a most agreeable surprise to Mr. Bingley PP II 9 177 4
understood that Mr. Bingley has not much idea of ever PP II 9 177 6
7
But perhaps Mr. Bingley did not take the house so much for PP II 9 178 9
Mr. Bingley, and takes a prodigious deal of care of him." PP II 10 184 23
taken to separate Mr. Bingley and Jane, she had never PP II 10 186 38
partly by the wish of retaining Mr. Bingley for his sister. PP II 10 187 40
I had detached Mr. Bingley from your sister,--and the PP II 12 196 5
not but allow that Mr. Bingley, when questioned by Jane, PP II 13 207 6
such an amiable man as Mr. Bingley, was incomprehensible. PP II 13 208 6
an acquaintance with you,--Mr. Bingley and his sisters." PP III 1 256 61
"Well, well, and so Mr. Bingley is coming down, sister," (PP III 11 331 14
"As soon as ever Mr. Bingley comes, my dear," said Mrs. PP III 11 332 22
see Mr. Bingley in consequence of it, before they did. PP III 11 333 27
Mr. Bingley arrived. PP III 11 333 30
"It is a long time, Mr. Bingley, since you went away," PP III 11 336 47
it is very hard to have her taken such a way from me. PP III 11 336 51
"When you have killed all your own birds, Mr. Bingley," PP III 11 337 53
"You are quite a visit in my debt, Mr. Bingley," she added, PP III 11 338 58
A few days after this visit, Mr. Bingley called again, and PP III 13 344 1
He is come--Mr. Bingley is come.-- PP III 13 344 7
half expected Mr. Bingley to do, he was able to bring PP III 16 365 1
"What could become of Mr. Bingley and Jane!" was a wonder PP III 16 370 36
Elizabeth longed to observe that Mr. Bingley had been a PP III 16 371 46
"It may do very well for the others," replied Mr. Bingley; PP III 17 374 24
Mr. Bingley and Jane remained at Netherfield only a PP III 19 385 3

MR. BINGLEY'S (20)
very lively hopes of Mr. Bingley's heart were entertained. PP I 3 9 1
"You were Mr. Bingley's first choice." PP I 5 18 4
Occupied in observing Mr. Bingley's attentions to her PP I 6 23 12
They could talk of nothing but officers; and Mr. Bingley's PP I 7 29 4
"Oh! but the gentlemen will have Mr. Bingley's chaise to PP I 7 30 23
Mr. Bingley's, she could not make a very favourable answer. PP I 8 35 1
Jane to borrow Mr. Bingley's carriage immediately, and at PP I 12 59 1
be so unworthy of Mr. Bingley's regard; and yet, it was PP I 17 85 1
"I can much more easily believe Mr. Bingley's being PP I 17 85 5
to accept Mr. Bingley's invitation, and if he did, whether PP I 17 87 12
"I have not a doubt of Mr. Bingley's sincerity," said PP I 18 96 55
Mr. Bingley's defence of his friend was a very able one I PP I 18 96 55
would prevent Mr. Bingley's being there; and as to the PP I 21 116 8
to the greater distress of Mr. Bingley's continued absence. PP I 23 128 11
"I am far from attributing any part of Mr. Bingley's PP II 1 136 17
Bingley's name was scarcely ever mentioned between them. PP II 1 137 25
Pray, how violent was Mr. Bingley's love?" PP II 2 141 8
to the time when Mr. Bingley's name had been last PP III 1 256 62
Well, any friend of Mr. Bingley's will always be welcome PP III 11 334 35
Bingley's friend, without being heard by either of them. PP III 11 334 36

MR. BRANDON (2)
"But if you write a note to the housekeeper, Mr. Brandon," SS I 13 64 23
"Mr. Brandon was very well I hope." SS I 20 115 53

MR. C. (1)
known and captivating Mr. C. the intimate friend and MP III 15 440 14

MR. CAMPBELL (3)
And Mr. Campbell was here at four o'clock, to ask for you; MP III 7 377 7
The next bustle brought in Mr. Campbell, the surgeon of MP III 7 384 36
their brother and Mr. Campbell to the sally-port; and Mr. MP III 7 384 36

MR. CHARLES MADDOX (1)
Yes, Mr. Charles Maddox dined at my sister's one day, did MP I 15 148 59

MR. CHURCHILL (21)
longer knowledge than they had yet had of Mr. Churchill. E II 2 169 17
'Open the windows!--but surely, Mr. Churchill, nobody E II 11 251 30
A letter arrived from Mr. Churchill to urge his nephew's E II 12 258 7
Mr. Churchill has pride; but his pride is nothing to his E II 18 309 33
Mr. Churchill, Oh! you are too obliging! E III 2 329 45
Well, I am sure, Mr. Churchill--only it seems too good-- E III 2 330 45
Emma, "will there be a beginning of Mr. Churchill?" E III 4 340 27
gravely, "seemed confined to you and Mr. Churchill." E III 5 350 30
Pass us, if you please, Mr. Churchill. E III 7 372 37
and that Mr. Churchill had sent his nephew a few lines, E III 8 383 31
all her faults, what would Mr. Churchill do without her? E III 9 388 13
Mr. Churchill would never get over it".-- E III 9 388 13
Mr. Churchill, independent of his wife, was feared by E III 9 388 13
Mr. Churchill was better than could be expected; and their E III 9 388 15
Churchill had been promising a visit the last ten years. E III 9 388 15
Well, and how did Mr. Churchill take it?" E III 10 398 54
It is not a connexion to gratify; but if Mr. Churchill E III 10 400 65
Mr. Churchill had made a point of it, as a token of E III 11 403 2
had passed, and Mr. Churchill could be reconciled to the E III 12 417 5

Context	Work	Vol	Ch	Page	Line
our living with Mr. Churchill at Enscombe, it is settled.	E	III	16	460	56
The Mr. Churchills were also in town; and they were only	E	III	19	483	7
MR. CHURCHILL'S (1)					
Mr. Churchill's loss would be dreadful indeed.	E	III	9	388	13
MR. COLE (24)					
He was arm in arm with Mr. Cole."	E	I	9	75	26
There was intimacy between them, and Mr. Cole had heard	E	II	1	156	5
Cole told Mrs. Cole of it, she sat down and wrote to me.	E	II	3	173	27
"I was with Mr. Cole on business an hour and half ago.	E	II	3	173	28
better go round by Mr. Cole's stables. for I should find	E	II	3	179	52
Perry tells me that Mr. Cole never touches malt liquor.	E	II	7	210	20
look at him, but he is bilious--Mr. Cole is very bilious.	E	II	7	210	20
scene being laid at Mr. Cole's; and without being able to	E	II	8	213	5
her more than his propensity to dine with Mr. Cole.	E	II	8	213	5
She followed another carriage to Mr. Cole's door; and was	E	II	8	213	7
I was telling Mr. Cole, I really was ashamed to look at	E	II	8	215	16
I was saying this to Mr. Cole but yesterday, and he quite	E	II	8	216	16
Mr. Cox, and Mr. Cole, were left very busy over parish	E	II	8	220	48
return from him for a few minutes, and listen to Mr. Cole.	E	II	8	222	54
When Mr. Cole had moved away, and her attention could be	E	II	8	222	54
at the same moment Mr. Cole approaching to entreat Miss	E	II	8	226	85
Miss Fairfax, followed Mr. Cole, to add his very pressing	E	II	8	227	85
Mr. Cole said how much taste you had; and Mr. Frank	E	II	9	232	9
in at the office door, Mr. Cole's carriage horses	E	II	9	233	24
the dance begun at Mr. Cole's should be finished there--	E	II	11	247	3
Mr. Cole gave me a hint of it six weeks ago."	E	II	15	287	28
"Well," said she, "and you soon silenced Mr. Cole, I	E	II	15	288	37
She calls you, Knightley--what can she do for Mr. Cole?	E	II	15	288	39
Account of fresh gaieties; dinners at Mr. Cole's, or balls	E	II	18	312	46
MR. COLLINS (129)					
It is from my cousin, Mr. Collins, who, when I am dead,	PP	I	13	61	6
clear Mr. Collins from the guilt of inheriting Longbourn.	PP	I	13	62	8
Mr. Collins was punctual to his time, and was received	PP	I	13	64	21
enough to talk, and Mr. Collins seemed neither in need of	PP	I	13	64	21
Mr. Collins was eloquent in her praise.	PP	I	14	66	1
Mr. Collins readily assented, and a book was produced; but	PP	I	14	68	13
her tongue; but Mr. Collins, much offended, laid aside his	PP	I	14	69	15
					16
his book; but Mr. Collins, after assuring them that he	PP	I	14	69	17
Mr. Collins was not a sensible man, and the deficiency of	PP	I	15	70	1
Mr. Collins had only to change from Jane to Elizabeth--and	PP	I	15	71	4
to go with her; and Mr. Collins was to attend them, at the	PP	I	15	71	6
for thither Mr. Collins had followed him after breakfast,	PP	I	15	71	6
prompt in inviting Mr. Collins to join his daughters in	PP	I	15	71	6
in their walk; and Mr. Collins, being in fact much better	PP	I	15	71	6
claimed towards Mr. Collins by Jane's introduction of him.	PP	I	15	73	11
Mr. Collins repeated his apologies in quitting the room,	PP	I	15	74	11
Mr. Collins on his return highly gratified Mrs. Bennet by	PP	I	15	74	13
taken their seats, Mr. Collins was at leisure to look	PP	I	16	75	2
and the officers, Mr. Collins seemed likely to sink into	PP	I	16	76	5
other table, and Mr. Collins took his station between his	PP	I	16	82	49
and after observing Mr. Collins for a few moments, he	PP	I	16	83	51
I hardly know how Mr. Collins was first introduced to her	PP	I	16	83	52
"Mr. Collins," said she, "speaks highly both of Lady	PP	I	16	83	57
went, for neither Lydia nor Mr. Collins were once silent.	PP	I	16	84	59
she had won, and Mr. Collins, in describing the civility	PP	I	16	84	59
unnecessarily to Mr. Collins, she could not help asking	PP	I	17	87	12
instead! her liveliness had been never worse timed.	PP	I	17	87	14
Mr. Collins might never make the offer, and till he did,	PP	I	17	88	14
Mr. Collins, awkward and solemn, apologising instead of	PP	I	18	90	4
replied, before Mr. Collins came up to them and told her	PP	I	18	96	56
Mr. Collins listened to her with the determined air of	PP	I	18	97	60
					61
and when at last Mr. Collins allowed him time to speak,	PP	I	18	98	61
Mr. Collins, however, was not discouraged from speaking	PP	I	18	98	61
Mr. Collins then returned to Elizabeth.	PP	I	18	98	61
"If I," said Mr. Collins, "were so fortunate as to be able	PP	I	18	101	71
seriously commended Mr. Collins for having spoken so	PP	I	18	101	71
She was teazed by Mr. Collins, who continued most	PP	I	18	102	73
long speeches of Mr. Collins, who was complimenting Mr.	PP	I	18	102	75
Of having another daughter married to Mr. Collins, she	PP	I	18	103	77
Mr. Collins made his declaration in form.	PP	I	19	104	1
Mr. Collins must excuse me.--	PP	I	19	104	5
I insist upon your staying and hearing Mr. Collins."	PP	I	19	104	6
off, and as soon as they were gone Mr. Collins began.	PP	I	19	105	7
The idea of Mr. Collins, with all his solemn composure,	PP	I	19	105	9
					10
foot-stool, that she said, 'Mr. Collins, you must marry.	PP	I	19	105	10
"I am not now to learn," replied Mr. Collins, with a a	PP	I	19	107	13
think so," said Mr. Collins very gravely--"but I cannot	PP	I	19	107	15
"Indeed. Mr. Collins, all praise of me will be unnecessary.	PP	I	19	107	16
the room, had not Mr. Collins thus addressed her, "when I	PP	I	19	108	16
					17
"Really. Mr. Collins," cried Elizabeth with some warmth, "	PP	I	19	108	18
Mr. Collins was not left long to the silent contemplation	PP	I	20	110	1
Mr. Collins received and returned these felicitations with	PP	I	20	110	1
"But depend upon it, Mr. Collins," she added, "that Lizzy	PP	I	20	110	3
"Pardon me for interrupting you, madam," cried Mr. Collins;	PP	I	20	110	4
You must come and make Lizzy marry Mr. Collins, for she	PP	I	20	111	7
"Of Mr. Collins and Lizzy. Lizzy declares she will not	PP	I	20	111	10
she will not have Mr. Collins, and Mr. Collins begins to	PP	I	20	111	10
and Mr. Collins begins to say that he will not have Lizzy."	PP	I	20	111	10
I understand that Mr. Collins has made you an offer of	PP	I	20	111	15
Mr. Collins, and I will never see you again if you do."	PP	I	20	112	19
Mr. Collins, meanwhile, was meditating in solitude on what	PP	I	20	112	24
Mr. Collins has made an offer to Lizzy, and she will not	PP	I	20	112	25
they were joined by Mr. Collins, who entered with an air	PP	I	20	113	29
					30
Mr. Collins and me have a little conversation together."	PP	I	20	113	30
by the civility of Mr. Collins, whose inquiries after	PP	I	20	114	31
"Oh! Mr. Collins!"--	PP	I	20	114	31
Mr. Collins was also in the same state of angry pride.	PP	I	21	115	2
day, was Miss Lucas so kind as to listen to Mr. Collins.	PP	I	22	121	1
that whenever Mr. Collins should be in possession of the	PP	I	22	122	3
Mr. Collins to be sure was neither sensible nor agreeable;	PP	I	22	122	3
therefore charged Mr. Collins when he returned to	PP	I	22	123	3
"My dear sir," replied Mr. Collins, "I am particularly	PP	I	22	123	8
to Mr. Collins! my dear Charlotte,--impossible!"	PP	I	22	124	12
					13
Do you think it incredible that Mr. Collins should be able	PP	I	22	125	15
lately as Mr. Collins was wishing to marry you.	PP	I	22	125	17
Charlotte the wife of Mr. Collins, was a most humiliating	PP	I	22	125	18
Do not you know that Mr. Collins wants to marry Lizzy?"	PP	I	23	126	2
and the convenient distance of Hunsford from London.	PP	I	23	126	4
was very sure that Mr. Collins had been taken in; thirdly,	PP	I	23	127	5
Miss Lucas, for Mr. Collins was only a clergyman; and it	PP	I	23	127	7
The promised letter of thanks from Mr. Collins arrived on	PP	I	23	128	10
Mr. Collins returned most punctually on the Monday	PP	I	23	129	15
in a low voice to Mr. Collins, was convinced that they	PP	I	23	130	16
understand; and all for the sake of Mr. Collins too!--	PP	I	23	130	24
My dear Jane, Mr. Collins is a conceited, pompous, narrow-	PP	II	1	135	13
of felicity, Mr. Collins was called from his amiable	PP	II	2	139	1
Mr. Collins returned into Hertfordshire soon after it had	PP	II	3	145	11
Charlotte again, and weakened her disgust of Mr. Collins.	PP	II	4	151	1
Mr. Collins and Charlotte appeared at the door, and the	PP	II	5	155	3
When Mr. Collins said any thing of which his wife might	PP	II	5	156	4
happened in London, Mr. Collins invited them to take a	PP	II	5	156	4
From his garden, Mr. Collins would have led them round his	PP	II	5	156	5
When Mr. Collins could be forgotten, there was really a	PP	II	5	157	5
at dinner, when Mr. Collins joining in, observed, "yes,	PP	II	5	157	6
					7
and the gaieties of their intercourse with Rosings.	PP	II	5	157	10
Mr. Collins and Charlotte were both standing at the gate	PP	II	5	158	19
Mr. Collins no sooner saw the two girls than he began to	PP	II	5	159	20
Mr. Collins was carefully instructing them in what they	PP	II	6	160	4
in such raptures as Mr. Collins expected the scene to	PP	II	6	161	8
From the entrance hall, of which Mr. Collins pointed out,	PP	II	6	161	10
to admire the view, Mr. Collins attending them to point	PP	II	6	162	13
of plate which Mr. Collins had promised; and, as he had	PP	II	6	162	14
"your father's estate is entailed on Mr. Collins, I think.	PP	II	6	164	15
					16
Mr. Collins was employed in agreeing to every thing her	PP	II	6	166	41
by no means satisfy Mr. Collins, and he was very soon	PP	II	6	167	42
While Sir William was with them, Mr. Collins devoted his	PP	II	7	168	1
what she did, for Mr. Collins would undoubtedly have been	PP	II	7	168	1
were indebted to Mr. Collins for the knowledge of what	PP	II	7	168	2
Very few days passed in which Mr. Collins did not walk to	PP	II	7	168	3
carried to her by Mr. Collins; and whenever any of the	PP	II	7	169	4
the parsonage, for Mr. Collins was walking the whole	PP	II	7	170	7
when Mr. Collins returned the gentlemen accompanied him.	PP	II	7	170	7
great deal to it when mr. collins first came to Hunsford."	PP	II	9	178	12
"Mr. Collins appears very fortunate in his choice of a	PP	II	9	178	14
her marrying Mr. Collins as the wisest thing she ever did.	PP	II	9	178	15
pressing her, but Mr. Collins could not conceal his	PP	II	10	187	41
next morning; and Mr. Collins having been in waiting near	PP	II	14	210	1
Mr. Collins had a compliment, and an allusion to throw in	PP	II	14	210	4
On Saturday morning Elizabeth and Mr. Collins met for	PP	II	15	215	1
Mr. Collins was gratified; and with a more smiling	PP	II	15	215	3
					4
to the carriage by Mr. Collins, and as they walked down	PP	II	15	217	8
She says Lizzy had better have taken Mr. Collins; but I do	PP	II	16	221	17
quarter, from Mr. Collins; which, as Jane had received	PP	III	6	296	10
good luck, I may meet with another Mr. Collins in time."	PP	III	13	350	54
This letter is from Mr. Collins."	PP	III	15	362	12
"From Mr. Collins! and what can he have to say?"	PP	III	15	362	13
"Mr. Collins moreover adds," "I am truly rejoiced that my	PP	III	15	363	22
what Mr. Bennet sent to Mr. Collins, in reply to his last.	PP	III	18	383	22
Before any answer could arrive from Mr. Collins, or any	PP	III	18	383	26
MR. COLLINS'S (20)					
As for their mother, Mr. Collins's letter had done away	PP	I	13	64	20
They were not the only objects of Mr. Collins's admiration.	PP	I	13	65	26
aunt, and all Mr. Collins's scruples of leaving Mr. and	PP	I	16	75	1
proposal accepted with as good a grace as she could.	PP	I	17	87	14
engaged Mr. Collins's conversation to herself.	PP	I	18	102	73
The discussion of Mr. Collins's offer was now nearly at an	PP	I	21	115	1
Mr. Collins's addresses, by engaging them towards herself.	PP	I	22	121	1
In as short a time as Mr. Collins's long speeches would	PP	I	22	121	2
Mr. Collins's present circumstances made it a most	PP	I	22	122	3
The possibility of Mr. Collins's fancying himself in love	PP	I	22	124	12
					13
and considering Mr. Collins's character, connections, and	PP	I	22	125	17
The strangeness of Mr. Collins's making two offers of	PP	I	22	125	18
Mr. Collins's return into Hertfordshire was no longer a	PP	I	23	128	11
Consider Mr. Collins's respectability, and Charlotte's	PP	II	1	135	12
might have been Mr. Collins's wife by this time, had not	PP	II	2	140	4
It was Mr. Collins's picture of Hunsford and Rosings	PP	II	3	147	19
Mr. Collins's triumph in consequence of this invitation	PP	II	6	160	1
side, and as many bows on Sir William's, they departed.	PP	II	6	166	42
give up Mr. Collins's correspondence for any consideration.	PP	III	15	364	24
on his reading Mr. Collins's letter; and after laughing at	PP	III	17	377	40
MR. COX (1)					
father, Mr. Knightley, Mr. Cox, and Mr. Cole, were left	E	II	8	220	48
MR. COX'S (1)					
the male part of Mr. Cox's family, the lawyer of Highbury.	E	II	8	214	13
MR. CRAWFORD (161)					
her situation--Mr. Crawford must take care of himself."	MP	I	5	44	3
Mr. Crawford did not mean to be in any danger; the Miss	MP	I	5	44	3
The Miss Bertrams' admiration of Mr. Crawford was more	MP	I	5	47	27
continued to think Mr. Crawford very plain, in spite of	MP	I	5	48	30
assistance; and Mr. Crawford after properly depreciating	MP	I	6	61	58
to take Mr. Crawford away, interposed with an amendment.	MP	I	6	61	58
I dare say Mr. Crawford would take my two nieces and me in	MP	I	6	62	58
their home, while Mr. Crawford was devoted to the ladies	MP	I	7	65	14
Mrs. Grant, and Mr. Crawford, with two or three grooms,	MP	I	7	67	16
She could not but think indeed that Mr. Crawford might as	MP	I	7	67	16
it himself; but Mr. Crawford, with all his boasted good-	MP	I	7	67	16
to, provided Mr. Crawford should be disengaged; the young	MP	I	8	75	1
and inquire whether Wednesday would suit him or not.	MP	I	8	75	1
were given that he would find Mr. Crawford at home.	MP	I	8	75	2
"Besides," said Maria, "I know that Mr. Crawford depends	MP	I	8	77	11
barouche arrived, Mr. Crawford driving his sisters; and as	MP	I	8	80	29
always ended in Mr. Crawford and her sister sitting side	MP	I	8	81	32
How would Mr. Crawford like, in what manner would he	MP	I	9	84	1
Mr. Crawford suggested the greater desirableness of some	MP	I	9	84	1
her lesson to Mr. Crawford; and Edmund, Fanny, and Miss	MP	I	9	86	11
Mr. Crawford smiled his acquiescence, and stepping forward	MP	I	9	88	20
"Query," said Mr. Crawford, looking round him, "whether we	MP	I	9	90	34
Mr. Crawford was the first to move forward, to examine the	MP	I	9	90	36
Mr. Crawford was soon followed by Miss Bertram and Mr.	MP	I	9	90	36
Mr. Rushworth, and Mr. Crawford, issued from the same path	MP	I	10	97	1
the house already," said Mr. Crawford, when he was gone.	MP	I	10	98	5
astonished at Miss Bertram, and angry with Mr. Crawford.	MP	I	10	100	23
I thought Maria and Mr. Crawford were with you."	MP	I	10	100	24
a great admirer of this Mr. Crawford as some people are?	MP	I	10	102	41
Mr. Crawford and Miss Bertram were much more gay, and she	MP	I	10	104	51
At the same moment Mr. Crawford approaching Julia, said, "	MP	I	10	105	52
Bertram back to Mansfield, took Mr. Crawford into Norfolk.	MP	I	12	114	3
other, had missed Mr. Crawford grievously; and Julia,	MP	I	12	115	4
she wished, and Maria by the hints of Mr. Crawford himself.	MP	I	12	115	4
could never see Mr. Crawford with either sister without	MP	I	12	115	5
"I am rather surprised," said she, "that Mr. Crawford	MP	I	12	115	5
and her partner, Mr. Crawford, were close to her; they	MP	I	12	117	15
"Oh! dear--Miss Julia and Mr. Crawford.	MP	I	12	118	18
and me, but here is nothing for your sister, Mr. Crawford."	MP	I	14	133	9
Mr. Crawford desired that might not be thought of; he was	MP	I	14	133	10
by Maria and Mr. Crawford, and Mr. Yates, with an urgency	MP	I	15	146	53
between her and Mr. Crawford, that she had soon all the	MP	I	18	164	2
As far as she could judge, Mr. Crawford was considerably	MP	I	18	165	3
"Mr. Crawford was a most pleasant gentleman-like man;--his	MP	II	1	186	30
In the drawing-room Mr. Crawford certainly was; having	MP	II	5	223	48
politics between Mr. Crawford and Dr. Grant, and of every	MP	II	5	223	48
together between Mr. Crawford and Mrs. Grant, as to leave	MP	II	5	223	48
except when Mr. Crawford now and then addressed to her a	MP	II	5	227	68
that obligation to Mr. Crawford for lending the horse	MP	II	6	237	23
careless way that Mr. Crawford was somewhat distinguishing	MP	II	7	238	1
nothing to do with Mr. Crawford, but as being one in an	MP	II	7	238	2
thought that Mr. Crawford was the admirer of Fanny Price.	MP	II	7	238	2
I am never to see my cards; and Mr. Crawford does all the	MP	II	7	240	12
should not have thought much on the subject, Mr. Crawford.	MP	II	7	247	42
Mr. Crawford bowed his acquiescence.	MP	II	7	248	43
not be happy to wait on Mr. Crawford as occupier."	MP	II	7	248	44
Mr. Crawford bowed his thanks.	MP	II	7	248	45
really produce on Mr. Crawford, it raised some awkward	MP	II	7	248	47
reason to think Mr. Crawford likewise out, she walked down	MP	II	8	256	14
was brought from Mr. Crawford to William stating, that as	MP	II	9	265	21
Mr. Crawford meant to be in town by his uncle's	MP	II	9	266	21
a great deal with Mr. Crawford, to see William enjoy	MP	II	9	267	22
end on perceiving Mr. Crawford before her, and her	MP	II	10	274	8
to think, that if Mr. Crawford had not asked her, she must	MP	II	10	274	8
to Mr. Crawford," was exactly what he had intended to hear.	MP	II	10	275	11
Mr. Crawford was not far off; Sir Thomas brought him to	MP	II	10	275	11
conducted by Mr. Crawford to the top of the dancers,	MP	II	10	275	11
to be opening the ball--and with Mr. Crawford too!	MP	II	10	276	12
niece, and she was soon said to be admired by Mr. Crawford.	MP	II	10	276	13

From that time, Mr. Crawford sat down likewise. MP II 10 279 22
Mr. Crawford, I think you call for him at half past nine?" MP II 10 280 29
Mr. Crawford was in love with Fanny. MP II 10 280 32
It might occur to him, that Mr. Crawford had been sitting MP II 10 281 34
Mr. Crawford had, as he foretold, been very punctual, and MP II 11 282 1
been talking of Mr. Crawford or of William, when he said MP II 11 283 4
Oh! Mr. Crawford, we are infinitely obliged to you. MP II 13 300 7
with much agitation, "don't, Mr. Crawford, pray don't. MP II 13 301 7
Mr. Crawford would certainly never address her so again: MP II 13 302 11
was engaged to return and dine there that very day. MP II 13 303 12
Mr. Crawford was not only in the room; he was soon close MP II 13 303 14
whenever Mr. Crawford spoke to her, and he spoke to her MP II 13 304 16
of this before Sir Thomas and Mr. Crawford joined them. MP II 13 306 26
absolutely after Mr. Crawford was in the room; for once or MP II 13 306 26
I have seen too much of Mr. Crawford not to understand his MP II 13 307 31
for she found that Mr. Crawford, under pretence of MP II 13 307 32
Fanny had by no means forgotten Mr. Crawford, when she MP III 1 311 1
If Mr. Crawford would but go away!-- MP III 1 311 1
astonished to see Mr. Crawford, as she accidentally did, MP III 1 311 2
able to hope that Mr. Crawford had come, and would go MP III 1 311 3
room, after breakfast, when Mr. Crawford was shewn in.-- MP III 1 313 14
Mr. Crawford, as you have perhaps foreseen, is yet in the MP III 1 314 16
Mr. Crawford ought to know--he must know that--I told him MP III 1 314 17
How could Mr. Crawford say such a thing? MP III 1 315 19
silence, "that you mean to refuse Mr. Crawford?" MP III 1 315 21
"Refuse Mr. Crawford! MP III 1 315 25
as her uncle had drawn, for not liking Mr. Crawford. MP III 1 316 28
Mr. Crawford must not be kept longer waiting. MP III 1 318 39
do not feel for Mr. Crawford exactly what a young, heated MP III 1 318 39
Maria is nobly married--but had Mr. Crawford sought MP III 1 319 39
Mr. Crawford has been kept waiting too long already. MP III 1 320 44
resentment against Mr. Crawford; yet, if he really loved MP III 1 321 46
he began with, "Mr. Crawford is gone; he has just left me. MP III 1 321 47
Even to see Mr. Crawford would be less overpowering. MP III 1 322 49
concluded, and Mr. Crawford once gone from Mansfield, that MP III 1 324 59
she anticipated, in another minute alone with Mr. Crawford. MP III 1 325 62
Mr. Crawford was no longer the Mr. Crawford who, as the MP III 2 327 6
He was now the Mr. Crawford who was addressing herself MP III 2 328 6
the Mr. Crawford who had procured William's promotion! MP III 2 328 6
Here was again a something of the same Mr. Crawford whom MP III 2 328 6
able to love Mr. Crawford, and the felicity of having a MP III 2 329 9
He then saw Mr. Crawford, and received his account.-- MP III 2 329 10
At Mansfield Park Mr. Crawford would always be welcome; he MP III 2 329 11
Fanny, I have seen Mr. Crawford again, and learn from him MP III 2 329 12
"I am very sorry that Mr. Crawford should continue to----- MP III 2 330 14
feelings of Mr. Crawford, as to any secrecy of proceeding. MP III 2 330 15
were married to a man of such good estate as Mr. Crawford. MP III 2 331 19
"You have a great turn for acting, I am sure, Mr. Crawford, MP III 2 333 26
nature, to repulse Mr. Crawford, and avoid both his looks MP III 3 338 19
In vain was her "pray, sir, don't--pray, Mr. Crawford," MP III 3 342 32
Mr. Crawford was obliged to move. MP III 3 342 34
returned to Mr. Crawford, and said, "it is not merely in MP III 3 344 43
But even supposing it is so, allowing Mr. Crawford to have MP III 4 349 25
of vanity to be forming expectations on Mr. Crawford. MP III 4 353 45
I could not but see that Mr. Crawford allowed himself in MP III 4 353 45
decision against Mr. Crawford; and she sat thinking deeply MP III 5 363 21
Mr. Crawford gone, Sir Thomas's next object was, that he MP III 5 364 30
involved Mr. Crawford, made no part of their conversation. MP III 6 366 1
to suppose herself not yet forgotten by Mr. Crawford.-- MP III 7 375 3
sure of her, and been delighted with his own sagacity. MP III 7 375 4
turning pale about, when Mr. Crawford walked into the room. MP III 8 388 1
never tire; and Mr. Crawford was as warm in his MP III 10 399 3
walking towards the high street, with Mr. Crawford. MP III 10 400 7
looked, Fanny was obliged to introduce him to Mr. Crawford. MP III 10 401 10
a doubt of the manner in which Mr. Crawford must be struck. MP III 10 401 11
Mr. Crawford probably could not regard his future father- MP III 10 402 11
good manners of Mr. Crawford; and be the consequence what MP III 10 402 12
Price's to take Mr. Crawford into the dock-yard, which Mr. MP III 10 402 12
dock-yard, which Mr. Crawford, desirous of accepting as a MP III 10 402 13
go; and, but for Mr. Crawford, Mr. Price would have turned MP III 10 402 13
their walk back, Mr. Crawford contrived a minute's privacy MP III 10 402 13
for church the next day when Mr. Crawford appeared again. MP III 10 406 21
In chapel they were obliged to divide, but Mr. Crawford MP III 11 408 1
Thither they now went; Mr. Crawford most happy to consider MP III 11 408 3
and but for Mr. Crawford and the beauty of the weather, MP III 11 409 5
After a moment's reflection, Mr. Crawford replied, "I know MP III 11 409 6
Though tolerably secure of not seeing Mr. Crawford again, MP III 11 410 16
still fancied in Mr. Crawford, was the nearest to MP III 11 413 31
It was presumed that Mr. Crawford was travelling back to MP III 11 413 32
MP III 12 415 1
2

Crawford and herself, touched her in comparison, slightly. MP III 12 418 4
Whether Mr. Crawford went into Norfolk before or after the MP III 12 418 4
If Mr. Crawford remembered her message to her cousin, she MP III 12 418 5
never know whether Mr. Crawford had gone into Norfolk MP III 14 433 12
Wimpole Street and Mr. Crawford, and only conjecture that MP III 15 438 4
As to Mr. Crawford, she hoped it might give him a MP III 15 438 5
and Mrs. Rushworth, it was Mrs. Rushworth and Mr. Crawford. MP III 15 441 19
Had Fanny accepted Mr. Crawford, this could not have MP III 16 448 2
house Mr. Crawford had constant access at all times. MP III 16 450 8
somewhere with Mr. Crawford, who had quitted his uncle's MP III 16 450 11
Mr. Crawford would have fully acquitted her conduct in MP III 16 452 14
she was safe from Mr. Crawford, and when Sir Thomas came MP III 17 461 2
She was not to be prevailed on to leave Mr. Crawford. MP III 17 464 10

MR. CRAWFORD'S (36)

man; and Mr. Crawford's being his guest was an excuse for MP I 5 47 26
the favour of Mr. Crawford's assistance; and Mr. Crawford MP I 6 61 58
Mr. Rushworth then began to propose Mr. Crawford's doing MP I 6 61 58
"There can be no doubt of Mr. Crawford's willingness; but MP I 6 62 58
like to hear Mr. Crawford's opinion on the spot, and that MP I 6 62 58
reason for using Mr. Crawford's," said Maria; "but the MP I 8 77 13
Julia called Mr. Crawford's attention to her sister, by MP I 9 88 19
Mr. Crawford's choice, she knew not always what to think. MP I 12 116 11
We must rather adopt Mr. Crawford's views, and make the MP I 13 124 9
Sir Thomas had been quite indifferent to Mr. Crawford's MP II 2 194 21
to remark in Mr. Crawford's behaviour; but when the whist MP II 7 246 36
was seized by Mr. Crawford's quicker hand, and she was MP II 7 251 66
her to be insensible of Mr. Crawford's change of manners. MP II 8 260 24
this offer of Mr. Crawford's would rob her of many hours MP II 9 266 21
Since the first joy from Mr. Crawford's note to William MP II 9 270 40
rise and, with Mr. Crawford's very cordial adieus, pass MP II 10 280 33
her feelings with the broken egg-shells in Mr. Crawford's. MP II 11 282 2
the dread of Mr. Crawford's interpretation; for though MP II 13 304 16
imposed on, nor gratified by Mr. Crawford's attentions. MP II 13 308 36
pause, proceeded in his account of Mr. Crawford's visit. MP III 1 313 15
Mr. Crawford's business had been to declare himself the MP III 1 314 16
aware of a particularity in Mr. Crawford's manners to you. MP III 1 316 29
"Independently of the interest which Mr. Crawford's choice MP II 13 317 34
any reason, child, to think ill of Mr. Crawford's temper?" MP III 1 317 36
implicated in Mr. Crawford's misconduct, that she could MP III 1 318 38
half Mr. Crawford's estate, or a tenth part of his merits. MP III 1 319 39
She would not, could not believe, that Mr. Crawford's MP III 1 324 59
Mr. Crawford's steadiness was honoured, and Fanny was MP III 2 329 12
but to bear with Mr. Crawford's endeavours to convince you, MP III 2 331 16
suppose Mr. Crawford's attachment would hold out for ever; MP III 2 331 18
to have been Mr. Crawford's choice; and, independently of MP III 2 332 20
well; but in Mr. Crawford's reading there was a variety of MP III 3 337 10
the perfection of Mr. Crawford's character in that point. MP III 4 345 3
(according to Mr. Crawford's opinion) in a singular manner, MP III 10 403 14
juster value for Mr. Crawford's good company and good MP III 11 413 30
And had it been possible for her to return Mr. Crawford's MP III 12 419 9

MR. DARCY (241)

but his friend Mr. Darcy soon drew the attention of the PP I 3 10 5
Mr. Darcy danced only once with Mrs. Hurst and once with PP I 3 11 6
part of that time, Mr. Darcy had been standing near enough PP I 3 11 7
room," said Mr. Darcy, looking at the eldest Miss Bennet. PP I 3 11 11
Mr. Darcy walked off; and Elizabeth remained with no very PP I 3 12 14
and some exaggeration, the shocking rudeness of Mr. Darcy. PP I 3 13 19
"Mr. Darcy is not so well worth listening to as his friend, PP I 5 19 9
"I certainly saw Mr. Darcy speaking to her." PP I 5 19 11
"If I were as rich as Mr. Darcy," cried a young Lucas who PP I 5 20 21
Mr. Darcy had at first scarcely allowed her to be pretty; PP I 6 23 12
"What does Mr. Darcy mean," said she to Charlotte, "by PP I 6 24 14
"That is a question which Mr. Darcy only can answer." PP I 6 24 15
"did not you think, Mr. Darcy, that I expressed myself PP I 6 24 17
18

And gravely glancing at Mr. Darcy, "there is a fine old PP I 6 24 22
Mr. Darcy stood near them in silent indignation at such a PP I 6 25 25
charming amusement for young people this is, Mr. Darcy!-- PP I 6 25 26
that you are an adept in the science yourself, Mr. Darcy." PP I 6 25 28
Mr. Darcy bowed. PP I 6 26 35
Mr. Darcy, you must allow me to present this young lady to PP I 6 26 38
39

And taking her hand, he would have given it to Mr. Darcy, PP I 6 26 38
Mr. Darcy with grave propriety requested to be allowed the PP I 6 26 40
"Mr. Darcy is all politeness," said Elizabeth, smiling. PP I 6 26 42
Mr. Darcy replied with great intrepidity, "Miss Elizabeth PP I 6 27 49
50

Darcy said very little, and Mr. Hurst nothing at all. PP I 7 33 42
Miss Bingley was engrossed by Mr. Darcy, her sister PP I 8 35 2
"you observed it, Mr. Darcy, I am sure," said Miss Bingley; PP I 8 36 7
"I am afraid, Mr. Darcy," observed Miss Bingley, in a half PP I 8 36 12
What a delightful library you have at Pemberley, Mr. Darcy! PP I 8 38 29
"You quite mistook Mr. Darcy. PP I 9 43 24
her eye towards Mr. Darcy with a very expressive smile. PP I 9 43 26
of the two ladies and Mr. Darcy; the latter of whom, PP I 9 46 39
Mr. Darcy was writing, and Miss Bingley, seated near him, PP I 10 47 1
write such charming long letters to her, Mr. Darcy?" PP I 10 48 17
"Would Mr. Darcy then consider the rashness of your PP I 10 49 32
"You appear to me, Mr. Darcy, to allow nothing for the PP I 10 50 37
Mr. Darcy smiled; but Elizabeth thought she could perceive PP I 10 51 40
my side; and Mr. Darcy had much better finish his letter." PP I 10 51 43
"Mr. Darcy took her advice, and did finish his letter. PP I 10 51 44
and soon afterwards Mr. Darcy, drawing near Elizabeth, PP I 10 51 47
48

Then taking the disengaged arm of Mr. Darcy, she left PP I 10 53 62
Mr. Darcy felt their rudeness and immediately said,-- " PP I 10 53 62
63

She had obtained private intelligence that Mr. Darcy did PP I 11 54 3
in the real object of her civility; Mr. Darcy looked up. PP I 11 56 12
of disappointing Mr. Darcy in any thing, and persevered PP I 11 56 14
Mr. Darcy may hug himself." PP I 11 57 18
"Mr. Darcy is not to be laughed at!" cried Elizabeth. PP I 11 57 19
"Your examination of Mr. Darcy is over, I presume," said PP I 11 57 26
"I am perfectly convinced by it that Mr. Darcy has no PP I 11 57 27
To Mr. Darcy it was welcome intelligence--Elizabeth had PP I 12 59 4
Mr. Darcy corroborated it with a bow, and was beginning to PP I 15 73 8
hat--a salutation which Mr. Darcy just deigned to return. PP I 15 73 8
to be told, the history of his acquaintance with Mr. Darcy. PP I 16 77 8
manner how long Mr. Darcy had been staying there. PP I 16 77 8
Are you much acquainted with Mr. Darcy?" PP I 16 77 12
no--it is not for me to be driven away by Mr. Darcy. PP I 16 78 20
His father, Miss Bennet, the late Mr. Darcy, was one of PP I 16 78 20
in company with this Mr. Darcy without being grieved to PP I 16 78 20
"Yes--the late Mr. Darcy bequeathed me the next PP I 16 79 25
the intention, but Mr. Darcy chose to doubt it--or to PP I 16 79 27
had the late Mr. Darcy liked me less, his son might have PP I 16 80 32
"I had not thought Mr. Darcy so bad as this--though I have PP I 16 80 33
be of use to the late Mr. Darcy, and devoted all his time PP I 16 81 37
He was most highly esteemed by Mr. Darcy, a most intimate, PP I 16 81 37
Mr. Darcy often acknowledged himself to be under the PP I 16 81 37
my father's death, Mr. Darcy gave him a voluntary promise PP I 16 81 37
I wonder that the very pride of this Mr. Darcy has not PP I 16 81 38
He cannot know what Mr. Darcy is." PP I 16 82 47
"Probably not;--but Mr. Darcy can please where he chuses. PP I 16 82 48
consequently that she is aunt to the present Mr. Darcy." PP I 16 83 53
how to believe that Mr. Darcy could be so unworthy of Mr. PP I 17 85 1
light it places Mr. Darcy, to be treating his father's PP I 17 85 4
If it be not so, let Mr. Darcy contradict it. PP I 17 86 5
suddenly addressed by Mr. Darcy, who took her so much by PP I 18 90 5
to stand opposite to Mr. Darcy, and reading in her PP I 18 90 8
"it is your turn to say something now, Mr. Darcy.-- PP I 18 91 8
9

but on perceiving Mr. Darcy he stopt with a bow of PP I 18 92 22
I appeal to Mr. Darcy:--but let me not interrupt you, sir.- PP I 18 92 23
hearing you once say, Mr. Darcy, that you hardly ever PP I 18 93 32
Wickham has treated Mr. Darcy in a most infamous manner. PP I 18 94 45
I know very well that Mr. Darcy is not in the least to PP I 18 94 45
but your own wilful ignorance and the malice of Mr. Darcy." PP I 18 95 48
principally offended Mr. Darcy; but he will vouch for the PP I 18 95 50
less attention from Mr. Darcy than he has received; and I PP I 18 95 50
"This account then is what he has received from Mr. Darcy. PP I 18 96 53
has heard them from Mr. Darcy more than once, but he PP I 18 96 54
"You are not going to introduce yourself to Mr. Darcy?" PP I 18 97 58
it must belong to Mr. Darcy, the superior in consequence, PP I 18 97 60
And with a low bow he left her to attack Mr. Darcy, whose PP I 18 97 61
Mr. Darcy was eyeing him with unrestrained wonder, and PP I 18 98 61
Mr. Darcy seemed much pleased with the attention. he PP I 18 98 62
of it was overheard by Mr. Darcy, who sat opposite to them. PP I 18 99 64
"What is Mr. Darcy to me, pray, that I should be afraid of PP I 18 99 65
What advantage can it be to you to offend Mr. Darcy?-- PP I 18 99 66
glancing her eye at Mr. Darcy, though every glance PP I 18 100 67
And with a bow to Mr. Darcy, he concluded his speech, PP I 18 101 71
That his two sisters and Mr. Darcy, however, should have PP I 18 102 72
I had better not meet Mr. Darcy;--that to be in the same PP I 21 115 4
"Mr. Darcy is impatient to see his sister, and to confess PP I 21 117 14
Could she have seen half as much love in Mr. Darcy for PP I 21 119 20
heard, his claims on Mr. Darcy, and all that he had PP II 1 138 30
Mr. Darcy before they had known any thing of the matter. PP II 1 138 30
everybody else Mr. Darcy was condemned as the worst of men. PP II 1 138 31
of his friend, and Mr. Darcy would no more suffer him to PP II 2 141 13
Mr. Darcy may perhaps have heard of such a place as PP II 2 141 13
and known the late Mr. Darcy by character perfectly well. PP II 2 143 20
Oh! that abominable Mr. Darcy!--my father's opinion of me PP II 3 144 7
He was well, but so much engaged with Mr. Darcy, that they PP II 3 147 23
some resemblance of Mr. Darcy, she turned her eyes on the PP II 6 162 12
Elizabeth had heard soon after her arrival, that Mr. Darcy PP II 7 170 6
to require them, for Mr. Darcy had brought with him a PP II 7 170 7
Mr. Darcy would never have come so soon to wait upon me." PP II 7 170 8
Mr. Darcy looked just as he had been used to look in PP II 7 171 9
the time, but Mr. Darcy they had only seen at church. PP II 8 172 1
of Lady Catherine herself, as well as of Mr. Darcy. PP II 8 172 3
Mr. Darcy spoke with affectionate praise of his sister's PP II 8 173 7
Mr. Darcy looked a little ashamed of his aunt's ill PP II 8 173 11
me, Mr. Darcy, by coming in all this state to hear me? PP II 8 174 12
13

Indeed, Mr. Darcy, it is very ungenerous in you to mention PP II 8 174 15
Mr. Darcy, you cannot deny the fact." PP II 8 175 18
surprise, Mr. Darcy, and Mr. Darcy only, entered the room. PP II 9 177 1
you all quitted Netherfield last November, Mr. Darcy! PP II 9 177 3
4

Mr. Darcy drew his chair a little towards her, and said, " PP II 9 179 23
Mr. Darcy related the mistake which had occasioned his PP II 9 179 26
But why Mr. Darcy came so often to the parsonage, it was PP II 9 180 29
these advantages, Mr. Darcy had considerable patronage in PP II 9 181 31

her ramble within the park, unexpectedly meet Mr. Darcy.-- PP II 10 182 1
again surprised by Mr. Darcy, she saw on looking up that PP II 10 182 2
to enjoy the power of doing what he likes than Mr. Darcy." PP II 10 183 9
"Oh! yes," said Elizabeth drily--"Mr. Darcy is uncommonly PP II 10 184 23
"Did Mr. Darcy give you his reasons for this interference?" PP II 10 185 29
"I do not see what right Mr. Darcy had to decide on the PP II 10 185 36
so just a picture of Mr. Darcy, that she would not trust PP II 10 186 38
over whom Mr. Darcy could have such boundless influence. PP II 10 186 38
has abilities which Mr. Darcy himself need not disdain, PP II 10 187 40
material weight with Mr. Darcy, whose pride, she was PP II 10 187 40
unwillingness to see Mr. Darcy, it determined her not to PP II 10 187 41
as possible against Mr. Darcy, chose for her employment PP II 11 188 1
her utter amazement, she saw Mr. Darcy walk into the room. PP II 11 188 3
Mr. Darcy, who was leaning against the mantle-piece with PP II 11 190 8
As she pronounced these words, Mr. Darcy changed colour; PP II 11 191 11
"you are mistaken, Mr. Darcy, if you suppose that the mode PP II 11 192 23
24

of marriage from Mr. Darcy! that he should have been in PP II 11 193 31
of its being Mr. Darcy, she was directly retreating. PP II 12 195 2
it to be Mr. Darcy, she moved again towards the gate. PP II 12 195 2
him in unguarded moments, which Mr. Darcy could not have. PP II 12 200 5
If Elizabeth, when Mr. Darcy gave her the letter, did not PP II 13 204 1
kindness of the late Mr. Darcy, though she had not before PP II 13 205 3
from the attacks of Mr. Darcy; or at least, by the PP II 13 206 4
to class, what Mr. Darcy had described as the idleness and PP II 13 206 4
the conviction that Mr. Darcy would never have hazarded PP II 13 206 4
no fear of seeing Mr. Darcy--that Mr. Darcy might leave PP II 13 207 5
Mr. Darcy--that Mr. Darcy might leave the country, but PP II 13 207 5
justification of Mr. Darcy, she could not but allow that PP II 13 207 6
during her absence; Mr. Darcy, only for a few minutes to PP II 13 209 13
Miss Darcy, the daughter of Mr. Darcy, of Pemberly and PP II 14 212 13
the chief of the scene between Mr. Darcy and herself. PP II 17 224 1
She was sorry that Mr. Darcy should have delivered his PP II 17 224 2
And poor Mr. Darcy! dear Lizzy, only consider what he must PP II 17 225 12
"I never thought Mr. Darcy so deficient in the appearance PP II 17 225 16
Mr. Darcy, for now they do appear wholly undeserved." PP II 17 226 20
Mr. Darcy has not authorised me to make his communication PP II 17 226 23
The general prejudice against Mr. Darcy is so violent, PP II 17 226 23
But I think Mr. Darcy improves on acquaintance." PP II 18 234 32
my feelings towards Mr. Darcy, will readily comprehend how PP II 18 234 37
38

The possibility of meeting Mr. Darcy, while viewing the PP II 19 240 16
"Does that young lady know Mr. Darcy?" PP III 1 247 14
"Can this be Mr. Darcy!" thought she. PP III 1 249 34
resemblance of Mr. Darcy, with such a smile over the face, PP III 1 250 47
two that they now saw Mr. Darcy, the gardener's expression PP III 1 251 52
house, whichever it might be, where Mr. Darcy then was. PP III 1 253 55
of Mr. Darcy approaching them, and at no great distance. PP III 1 254 57
and she heard Mr. Darcy invite him, with the greatest PP III 1 255 60
Mr. Darcy took her place by her niece, and they walked on PP III 1 256 61
Mr. Darcy handed the ladies into the carriage, and when it PP III 1 257 66
Elizabeth had settled it that Mr. Darcy would bring his PP III 2 260 1
an observer as ever Mr. Darcy had been, was much relieved PP III 2 261 4
The suspicions which had just arisen of Mr. Darcy and PP III 2 261 6
It was often that she could turn her eyes on Mr. Darcy PP III 2 263 10
they arose to depart, Mr. Darcy called on his sister to PP III 2 263 11
acquainted with Mr. dArcy than they had before any idea of; PP III 2 264 13
Of Mr. Darcy it was now a matter of anxiety to think well; PP III 2 264 14
he was known, would not have recognised it for Mr. Darcy. PP III 2 264 14
debts behind him, which Mr. Darcy afterwards discharged. PP III 2 265 15
for the appearance of Mr. Darcy, by the feelings which PP III 3 268 7
and her attentions to Mr. Darcy were by no means over. PP III 3 269 8
and while Mr. Darcy was attending them to their carriage, PP III 3 270 12
"How very ill Eliza Bennet looks this morning, Mr. Darcy, " PP III 3 270 13
However little Mr. Darcy might have liked such an address, PP III 3 271 14
door, it was opened by a servant, and Mr. Darcy appeared. PP III 4 276 6
"John told us Mr. Darcy was here when you sent for us;-- PP III 4 280 26
infamous behaviour to Mr. Darcy; and you, yourself, when PP III 5 284 14
Till I was in Kent, and saw so much both of Mr. Darcy and PP III 5 284 16
been led to make Mr. Darcy acquainted with their fears for PP III 8 311 11
to be supposed that Mr. Darcy would connect himself with a PP III 8 311 12
not be put off, for Mr. Darcy might have done as well." PP III 9 319 25
"Mr. Darcy!" repeated Elizabeth, in utter amazement. PP III 9 319 26
Mr. Darcy had been at her sister's wedding. PP III 9 320 32
Mr. Darcy called, and was shut up with him several hours. PP III 10 321 2
Mr. Darcy asked him why he had not married your sister at PP III 10 323 2
But Mr. Gardiner could not be seen, and Mr. Darcy found, PP III 10 323 2
Mr. Darcy was punctual in his return, and as Lydia PP III 10 325 2
had produced of what Mr. Darcy might have been doing to PP III 10 326 3
and confidence subsisted between Mr. Darcy and herself. PP III 10 327 3
saw Mr. Darcy with him, and sat down again by her sister. PP III 11 333 31
"Good gracious! Mr. Darcy!--and so it does I vow. PP III 11 334 35
on, of her dislike of Mr. Darcy, and her resolution to be PP III 11 334 36
How Mr. Darcy looked, therefore, she could not tell. PP III 11 336 50
Elizabeth, who knew this to be levelled at Mr. Darcy, was PP III 11 337 52
Mr. Darcy, with an expression of half-laughing alarm. PP III 12 340 12
Mr. Darcy was almost as far from her, as the table could PP III 12 340 13
last week; and even Mr. Darcy acknowledged, that the PP III 12 342 28
unless Mr. Darcy returned within the stated time. PP III 13 345 20
afterwards united to my nephew, my own nephew, Mr. Darcy. PP III 14 353 26
Mr. Darcy is engaged to my daughter. PP III 14 354 40
If Mr. Darcy is neither by honour nor inclination confined PP III 14 355 44
"But the wife of Mr. Darcy must have such extraordinary PP III 14 355 46
Your ladyship wants Mr. Darcy to marry your daughter; but PP III 14 357 61
of either, would be violated by my marriage with Mr. Darcy. PP III 14 358 70
of breaking off her supposed engagement with Mr. Darcy. PP III 15 360 1
"Mr. Darcy, you see, is the man! PP III 15 363 18
Mr. Darcy, who never looks at any woman but to see a PP III 15 363 18
immediately said, "Mr. Darcy, I am a very selfish creature; PP III 16 365 2
3

This cannot be?--engaged to Mr. Darcy! PP III 17 372 4
Mr. Darcy is not coming here again with our dear Bingley! PP III 17 374 20
"I advise Mr. Darcy, and Lizzy, and Kitty," said Mrs. PP III 17 374 23
It is a nice long walk, and Mr. Darcy has never seen the PP III 17 374 23
no more bear that Mr. Darcy should hear the first raptures PP III 17 375 27
the library, she saw Mr. Darcy rise also and follow him, PP III 17 375 28
sat in misery till Mr. Darcy appeared again, when, looking PP III 17 375 28
him with some confusion, of her attachment to Mr. Darcy. PP III 17 376 30
assurances that Mr. Darcy was really the object of her PP III 17 376 36
told him what Mr. Darcy had voluntarily done for Lydia. PP III 17 377 38
Lord bless me! only think! dear me! Mr. Darcy! PP III 17 378 43
But my dearest love, tell me what dish Mr. Darcy is PP III 17 378 45
to account for his having ever fallen in love with her. PP III 18 380 1
her intimacy with Mr. Darcy had been over-rated, Elizabeth PP III 18 382 20
Mr. Darcy sends you all the love in the world, that he can PP III 18 383 21
Elizabeth will soon be the wife of Mr. Darcy. PP III 18 383 23
bought, when she saw Mr. Darcy exposed to all the parading PP III 18 384 26
If you love Mr. Darcy half as well as I do my dear Wickham, PP III 19 386 7
But, however, do not speak to Mr. Darcy about it, if you PP III 19 386 7

MR. DARCY'S (30)
how frequently Mr. Darcy's eyes were fixed on her. PP I 10 51 46
engaged in watching Mr. Darcy's progress through his book, PP I 11 54 4
of every thing in Mr. Darcy's looks and behaviour. PP I 17 86 10
omitted for Mr. Darcy's pleasure in the Bingleys' PP I 18 89 1
2

was the son of old Wickham, the late Mr. Darcy's steward. PP I 18 94 45
for as to Mr. Darcy's using him ill, it is perfectly false; PP I 18 94 45
of being the son of Mr. Darcy's steward, and of that, I PP I 18 95 46
imprudent, and has deserved to lose Mr. Darcy's regard." PP I 18 95 50
speaking again, and Mr. Darcy's contempt seemed abundantly PP I 18 98 61
She was at least free from the offence of Mr. Darcy's PP I 18 102 74
being an inmate of Mr. Darcy's house, and mentioned with PP II 1 133 2
On being made acquainted with the present Mr. Darcy's PP II 2 143 20
really soon marry Mr. Darcy's sister, as, by Wickham's PP II 3 149 27
Mr. Darcy's shameful boast of what misery he had been able PP II 11 188 1
the recollection of Mr. Darcy's sometimes coming there PP II 12 195 1
as to render Mr. Darcy's conduct in it less than infamous, PP II 13 205 3
scruples in sinking Mr. Darcy's character, though he had PP II 13 207 5
recollection that Mr. Darcy's explanation there, had PP II 13 208 9
Mr. Darcy's letter, she was in a fair way of soon knowing PP II 14 212 17
concern, and Mr. Darcy's explanation, by restoring Bingley PP II 14 213 18
before she told her sister of Mr. Darcy's proposals. PP II 15 217 17
For my part, I am inclined to believe it all Mr. Darcy's, PP II 17 225 10
She dared not relate the other half of Mr. Darcy's letter, PP II 17 227 25
She felt anew the justice of Mr. Darcy's objections; and PP II 18 229 10
Fitzwilliam's and Mr. Darcy's having both spent three PP II 18 233 26
with wonder, of Mr. Darcy's civility, and above all, of PP III 1 259 77
Every thing being settled between them, Mr. Darcy's next PP III 10 323 2
Mr. Darcy's behaviour astonished and vexed her. PP III 12 339 1
by what he said of Mr. Darcy's indifference, and she could PP III 15 364 25
Mr. Darcy's letter to Lady Catherine, was in a different PP III 18 383 22

MR. DASHWOOD (12)
Mr. Dashwood had wished for it more for the sake of his SS I 1 4 3
known, and to him Mr. Dashwood recommended, with all the SS I 1 5 5
"to have those kind of yearly drains on one's income. SS I 2 11 21
Do but consider, my dear Mr. Dashwood, how excessively SS I 2 12 24
"Upon my word," said Mr. Dashwood, "I believe you are SS I 2 12 25
Mr. Dashwood attended them down stairs, was introduced to SS II 11 222 13
and though Mr. Dashwood did not seem to know much about SS II 11 228 52
having; and Mr. Dashwood went away delighted with both. SS II 11 228 52
Mr. Dashwood introduced him to her as Mr. Robert Ferrars. SS II 14 250 11
Mr. Dashwood was convinced. SS II 14 253 25
I beg your pardon, Mr. Dashwood, but if he had done SS III 1 267 43
"We think now"--said Mr. Dashwood, after a short pause, " SS III 5 296 24

MR. DASHWOOD'S (3)
Mr. Dashwood's disappointment was, at first, severe; but SS I 1 4 4
them to be Mr. Dashwood's sisters, she immediately SS II 14 248 6
Mr. Dashwood's strains were more solemn. SS III 13 371 38

MR. DE COURCY (1)
"It is Mr. De Courcy, said she, colouring violently, Mama LS 20 275 1

MR. DENNY (6)
about it, and to ask when Mr. Denny comes back from town." PP I 14 68 14
The officer was the very Mr. Denny, concerning whose PP I 15 72 8
Mr. Denny addressed them directly, and entreated PP I 15 72 8
Mr. Denny and Mr. Wickham walked with the young ladies to PP I 15 73 10
already knew, that Mr. Denny had brought him from London, PP I 15 73 11
by his friend Mr. Denny, to whom Lydia eagerly applied, PP I 18 89 1
2

MR. DIXON (20)
Jane has heard a great deal of its beauty; from Mr. Dixon E II 1 159 20
out often with only Mr. Dixon, for which I do not at all E II 1 159 20
this charming Mr. Dixon, and the not going to Ireland, she E II 1 160 21
22

Dixon does not seem in the least backward in any attention. E II 1 160 23
history of that day, I have been so fond of Mr. Dixon!" E II 1 161 23
the affections of Mr. Dixon, a young man, rich and E II 2 165 7
Mr. Dixon, which she had so naturally started to herself. E II 2 167 13
her own preference; Mr. Dixon, perhaps, had been very near E II 2 169 16
And Mr. Dixon seems a very charming young man, quite E II 3 175 39
Jane, do you know I always fancy Mr. Dixon like Mr. John E II 3 176 44
One takes up a notion, and runs away with it. Mr. Dixon, E II 3 176 46
"Mr. Dixon is very musical, is he? E II 6 201 29
"Yes Mr. Dixon and Miss Campbell were the persons; and I E II 6 202 30
she was asked by Mr. Dixon, one may guess what one chuses." E II 6 202 37
"Mr. Dixon.-- E II 8 217 31
intentions of either Mr. Dixon or Miss Fairfax, but I E II 8 217 32
dashed from the vessel and that Mr. Dixon caught her.-- E II 8 218 37
myself that Mr. Dixon is a principal in the business." E II 8 218 41
You may have done wrong with regard to Mr. Dixon, but this E II 15 284 10
attachment to Mr. Dixon, which she had not only so E III 12 421 17

MR. DIXON'S (5)
letter--wrote in Mr. Dixon's name as well as her own, to E II 1 159 20
of having seduced Mr. Dixon's affections from his wife, or E II 2 168 13
She seemed bent on giving no real insight into Mr. Dixon's E II 2 169 16
Mr. Dixon's preference of her music to her friend's, I can E II 8 217 33
Bought at Weymouth, you know--Mr. Dixon's choice. E III 2 322 19

MR. DONAVAN (3)
But Charlotte, she would not be satisfied, so Mr. Donavan SS III 1 257 5
and Mr. Donavan found the house in all this uproar. SS III 1 259 7
of a passion!--and Mr. Donavan thinks just the same. SS III 1 259 7

MR. DRUMMOND (1)
set of pearls that Mr. Drummond gave his daughter on her NA I 9 68 48

MR. E. (10)
I honestly said as much to Mr. E. when he was speaking of E II 14 276 36
A little upstart, vulgar being, with her Mr. E., and her E II 14 279 52
I shall speak to Mr. E. E II 16 295 34
As I tell Mr. E., you are a thorough humourist.-- E III 6 356 28
Pass Mr. E., Knightley, Jane, and myself. E III 7 372 37
'Upon my word, Mr. E., I often say, rather you than I.-- E III 16 455 23
Mr. E. is knightley's right hand." E III 16 456 25
I fancy Mr. E. and Knightley have every thing their own E III 16 456 27
"Donwell!" cried his wife?"my dear Mr. E., you have not E III 16 457 39
My dear Mr. E., he must have left a message for you, I am E III 16 458 42

MR. E.'S (1)
particular a friend of Mr. E.'s, I had a great curiosity. E II 14 278 50

MR. EDMUND (1)
Mr.--and Mr. Edmund is no more than Mr. John or Mr. Thomas. MP II 4 211 24

MR. EDMUND BERTRAM (2)
Mr. Edmund Bertram, as you do not act yourself, you will MP I 15 144 36
But Miss Price and Mr. Edmund Bertram, I dare say, would MP II 4 215 49

MR. EDWARD (4)
Lord! what a taking poor Mr. Edward will be in when he SS III 1 259 7
There is no reason on earth why Mr. Edward and Lucy should SS III 1 259 7
towards poor Mr. Edward, who, she was sure, had quite SS III 13 370 37
Poor Mr. Edward! SS III 13 371 37

MR. EDWARD FERRARS (5)
companion's falsehood--"engaged to Mr. Edward Ferrars?-- SS I 22 131 29
"Mr. Edward Ferrars, the eldest son of Mrs. Ferrars of SS I 22 131 30
"Is Mr. Edward Ferrars," said Elinor, with resolution, " SS II 11 224 27
Mr. Edward Ferrars, the very young man I used to joke with SS III 1 258 7
in it), Mr. Edward Ferrars, it seems, has been engaged SS III 1 258 7

MR. ELLIOT (146)
bloom, Mr. Elliot had been forced into the introduction. P III 1 7 14
Mr. Elliot had attempted no apology, and shewn himself as P III 1 8 16
This very awkward history of Mr. Elliot, was still, after P III 1 8 17
"Yes, sir, a Mr. Elliot; a gentleman of large fortune,-- P III 12 105 12
cousin;--it must be our Mr. Elliot, it must, indeed!-- P III 12 105 14
In mourning, you see, just as our Mr. Elliot must be. P III 12 105 14
Anne, must not it be our Mr. Elliot; my father's next heir? P III 12 105 14
their father and Mr. Elliot had not, for many years, been P III 12 106 18
our seeing Mr. Elliot, the next time you write to Bath. P III 12 107 20
she had first seen Mr. Elliot; a moment seemed all that P III 12 115 66
with, or rather missing, Mr. Elliot so extraordinarily. P IV 2 132 22
Mr. Elliot was in Bath. P IV 2 135 35
and perplexity about Mr. Elliot, already recanting the P IV 2 135 35
she would rather see Mr. Elliot again than not, which was P IV 2 136 36
They had Mr. Elliot, too. P IV 3 138 6
Anne had a great deal to hear of Mr. Elliot. P IV 3 138 6
acquaintance through Mr. Elliot, had mentioned one or two P IV 3 139 8
Colonel Wallis had known Mr. Elliot long, had been well P IV 3 139 9
Mr. Elliot had called repeatedly, had dined with them once, P IV 3 139 10
been penetrated by Mr. Elliot, knowing her but in public, P IV 3 140 11
"Oh! yes, perhaps, it had been Mr. Elliot. P IV 3 141 12
Mr. Elliot appeared to think that he (Sir Walter) was P IV 3 141 12

Mr. Elliot was better to look at than most men, and he had P IV 3 141 12
Mr. Elliot, and his friends in Marlborough buildings, were P IV 3 141 13
to them! and Mr. Elliot so anxious that he should!" P IV 3 141 13
her confinement; but Mr. Elliot spoke of her as "a most P IV 3 141 13
Could it be Mr. Elliot? P IV 3 142 17
foot-boy could give, Mr. Elliot was ushered into the room. P IV 3 142 17
Sir Walter talked of his youngest daughter; "Mr. Elliot P IV 3 143 18
becomingly shewed to Mr. Elliot the pretty features which P IV 3 143 18
She could only compare Mr. Elliot to Lady Russell, in the P IV 3 144 22
same tale, before Mr. Elliot or any of them seemed to feel P IV 3 144 23
As Mr. Elliot became known to her, she grew more P IV 4 146 6
"can this be Mr. Elliot?" and could not seriously picture P IV 4 146 6
Her satisfaction in Mr. Elliot outweighed all the plague P IV 4 147 6
natural that Mr. Elliot, at a mature time of life, should P IV 4 147 7
Mr. Elliot, too, it must be remembered, had not been a P IV 4 147 8
neither Lady Russell nor Mr. Elliot thought unimportant. P IV 4 149 12
Neither Lady Russell nor Mr. Elliot could admire the P IV 4 149 13
opinion of them to Mr. Elliot, he agreed to their being P IV 4 150 15
Anne smiled and said, "my idea of good company, Mr. Elliot, P IV 4 150 15
16

Lady Russell and Mr. Elliot; and Mr. Elliot had made a P IV 5 158 21
and Mr. Elliot; and Mr. Elliot had made a point of leaving P IV 5 158 21
her friend and Mr. Elliot, in having been wished for, P IV 5 158 21
and reduced, seemed to have quite delighted Mr. Elliot. P IV 5 158 21
was now perfectly decided in her opinion of Mr. Elliot. P IV 5 159 22
I only mean that if Mr. Elliot should some time hence pay P IV 5 159 23
"Mr. Elliot is an exceedingly agreeable man, and in many P IV 5 159 24
that, could Mr. Elliot at that moment with propriety have P IV 5 160 26
The same image of Mr. Elliot speaking for himself, brought P IV 5 160 26
the possibilities of such a case, was against Mr. Elliot. P IV 5 160 26
Mr. Elliot was rational, discreet, polished,--but he was P IV 5 161 28
Mr. Elliot was too generally agreeable. P IV 5 161 29
he ought to be than Mr. Elliot; nor did she ever enjoy a P IV 5 161 30
"I am glad you find Mr. Elliot so agreeable, and wish I " P IV 6 163 7
Mr. Elliot was attending his two cousins and Mrs. Clay. P IV 7 174 2
stepped to Lady Dalrymple, to request her assistance. P IV 7 174 2
Anne was most sincere in preferring a walk with Mr. Elliot. P IV 7 174 3
be left to walk with Mr. Elliot, as Anne could be, and it P IV 7 174 3
cold already, and Mr. Elliot deciding on appeal, that his P IV 7 174 3
the carriage, and Mr. Elliot (always obliging) just P IV 7 175 5
at present, and adding, "I am only waiting for Mr. Elliot. P IV 7 177 15
She had hardly spoken the words, when Mr. Elliot walked in. P IV 7 177 16
"Mr. Elliot does not dislike his cousin, I fancy?" P IV 7 177 18
Lady Dalrymple and Miss Carteret, escorted by Mr. Elliot P IV 8 184 17
on the foremost, and Mr. Elliot had manoeuvred so well, P IV 8 186 23
song, she explained the words of the song to Mr. Elliot.-- P IV 8 186 24
"Perhaps," said Mr. Elliot, speaking low, "I have had a P IV 8 187 30
Mr. Elliot was not disappointed in the interest he hoped P IV 8 187 33
of getting rid of Mr. Elliot; and she did not mean, what P IV 8 189 44
Colonel Wallis declined sitting down again, and Mr. Elliot P IV 8 189 46
It came from Mr. Elliot. P IV 8 190 47
Jealousy of Mr. Elliot! P IV 8 190 51
at the time when Mr. Elliot would be most likely to call; P IV 9 192 1
to call; for to avoid Mr. Elliot was almost a first object. P IV 9 192 1
I did not see them myself, but I heard Mr. Elliot say they P IV 9 193 7
Smith, "is Mr. Elliot aware of your acquaintance with me? P IV 9 194 19
20

"Mr. Elliot!" repeated Anne, looking up surprised. P IV 9 194 21
more composedly, "are you acquainted with Mr. Elliot?" P IV 9 194 21
I want you to talk about me to Mr. Elliot. P IV 9 195 24
a higher claim on Mr. Elliot--a greater right to influence P IV 9 195 25
I am not going to marry Mr. Elliot. P IV 9 195 28
Let me recommend Mr. Elliot. P IV 9 196 30
Mrs. Smith, archly, "Mr. Elliot is safe, and I shall give P IV 9 196 32
Mr. Elliot has sense to understand the value of such a P IV 9 196 32
I assure you Mr. Elliot had not the share which you have P IV 9 197 33
afford:--not Mr. Elliot; it is not Mr. Elliot that-----" P IV 9 197 33
she was to marry Mr. Elliot, where she could have received P IV 9 197 34
and she it was who told me you were to marry Mr. Elliot. P IV 9 197 40
having this claim on Mr. Elliot, I should be extremely P IV 9 198 43
"I think you spoke of having known Mr. Elliot many years?" P IV 9 198 45
I have a great curiosity to know what Mr. Elliot was as a P IV 9 198 51
"I have not seen Mr. Elliot these three years," was Mrs. P IV 9 198 52
Mr. Elliot is a man without heart or conscience; a P IV 9 199 53
Mr. Elliot, and entertained the highest opinion of him. P IV 9 199 55
very seriously, but Mr. Elliot appeared to me quite as P IV 9 199 55
Why did Mr. Elliot draw back?" P IV 9 200 58
"Mr. Elliot," replied Mrs. Smith, "at that period of his P IV 9 200 59
a sudden idea, "you sometimes spoke of me to Mr. Elliot?" P IV 9 201 60
"This accounts for something which Mr. Elliot said last P IV 9 201 63
Mr. Elliot married, then, completely for money? P IV 9 201 63
I saw nothing reprehensible in what Mr. Elliot was doing. P IV 9 201 64
Depend upon it, whatever esteem Mr. Elliot may have for P IV 9 202 66
to what Mr. Elliot appeared to be some years ago. P IV 9 202 67
The letter I am looking for, was one written by Mr. Elliot P IV 9 203 70
satisfied with Mr. Elliot, I was determined to preserve P IV 9 203 70
I have shewn you Mr. Elliot, as he was a dozen years ago, P IV 9 204 80
Mr. Elliot talks unreservedly to Colonel Wallis of his P IV 9 205 82
but his regard for Mr. Elliot gave him an interest in P IV 9 206 90
on there, and when Mr. Elliot came to Bath for a day or P IV 9 206 90
Mr. Elliot came back accordingly; and on application was P IV 9 207 90
a representation of Mr. Elliot, who would have difficulty P IV 9 207 91
Elliot marry, that your father is not to marry Mrs. Clay. P IV 9 208 92
Mr. Elliot if evidently a disingenuous, artificial, P IV 9 208 93
But Mr. Elliot was not yet done with. P IV 9 208 94
always together, and Mr. Elliot had led his friend into P IV 9 208 95
Mr. Elliot, raised by his marriage to great affluence, and P IV 9 209 95
of his will; but Mr. Elliot would not act, and the P IV 9 209 96
Mr. Elliot would do nothing, and she could do nothing P IV 9 210 98
she hoped to engage Anne's good offices with Mr. Elliot. P IV 9 210 99
After listening to this full description of Mr. Elliot, P IV 9 211 100
her feelings were relieved by this knowledge of Mr. Elliot. P IV 10 212 1
escaped seeing Mr. Elliot; that he had called and paid P IV 10 212 2
Mr. Elliot looking up with so much respect!" P IV 10 231 5
hate the sight of Mr. Elliot; and yet she could assume a P IV 10 213 10
To Anne herself it was most distressing to see Mr. Elliot P IV 10 214 11
at all hours, of Mr. Elliot, would have expected him, but P IV 10 216 17
She was particularly asked to meet Mr. Elliot, and be P IV 10 220 29
It is Mr. Elliot himself." P IV 10 222 34
"No," cried Anne quickly, "it cannot be Mr. Elliot, I P IV 10 222 35
that it was Mr. Elliot, calling again upon Anne to come P IV 10 222 37
Not know Mr. Elliot, indeed!-- P IV 10 222 38
that it really was Mr. Elliot (which she had never P IV 10 222 39
she calmly said, "yes, it is Mr. Elliot certainly. P IV 10 222 39
her daughter, and Mr. Elliot--all the principal family P IV 10 223 43
We are quite near relations, you know: and Mr. Elliot too, P IV 10 224 47
Every attention is due to Mr. Elliot. P IV 10 224 47
What is Mr. Elliot to me?" P IV 10 224 48
had been seen with Mr. Elliot three hours after his being P IV 10 228 70
my great surprise I met with Mr. Elliot in Bath-Street! P IV 10 228 71
Jealousy of Mr. Elliot had been the retarding weight, the P IV 11 241 60
The passing admiration of Mr. Elliot had at least roused P IV 11 242 62
Mr. Elliot was there; she avoided, but she could pity him. P IV 11 245 78
and relinquishing Mr. Elliot, and be making some struggles P IV 12 249 3
She had soon the mortification of seeing Mr. Elliot P IV 12 250 6
Anne's engagement burst on Mr. Elliot most unexpectedly. P IV 12 250 7

MR. ELLIOT'S (27)

and that Mr. Elliot's idea always produced irritation in P III 12 107 21
appeared, in Mr. Elliot's wishing, after an interval of so P IV 3 140 11
them, while Mr. Elliot's frequent visits were talked of. P IV 3 140 11
Mrs. Clay decidedly thought it Mr. Elliot's knock." P IV 3 142 17
even than Mr. Elliot's being in love with Elizabeth, which P IV 4 145 1
appeared, in Mr. Elliot's great desire of a reconciliation. P IV 4 147 7
He might have been in Mr. Elliot's company, but she had P IV 8 187 35
Mr. Elliot's speech too distressed her. P IV 8 188 43
It was misery to think of Mr. Elliot's attentions.-- P IV 8 191 51
You must consider me only as Mr. Elliot's relation. P IV 9 195 25
build my own selfish schemes on Mr. Elliot's good fortune." P IV 9 195 27
"My dear Mrs. Smith, Mr. Elliot's wife has not been dead P IV 9 196 31
so soon in Mr. Elliot's failure, but from the perception P IV 9 197 34
to be made acquainted with Mr. Elliot's real character. P IV 9 199 53
very period of Mr. Elliot's life," said Anne, "which has P IV 9 200 56
by chance into Mr. Elliot's company, and fell in love with P IV 9 202 66
Mr. Elliot's having any views on me will not in the least P IV 9 205 83
in Mr. Elliot's opinions as to the value of a baronetcy. P IV 9 206 90
unimpaired by Mr. Elliot's marriage) they had been as P IV 9 208 95
and to prove that Mr. Elliot's had better not be tried; P IV 9 209 96
With a confidence in Mr. Elliot's regard, more creditable P IV 9 209 96
observances due to Mr. Elliot's character would allow, P IV 9 210 99
of Mr. Elliot's subtleties, in endeavouring to prevent it. P IV 10 215 13
little touched by Mr. Elliot's conduct, except by its P IV 11 229 1
Her faith was plighted, and Mr. Elliot's character, like P IV 11 229 1
him, the moment of Mr. Elliot's appearing and tearing her P IV 11 244 71
and that because Mr. Elliot's manners had precisely P IV 12 249 3

MR. ELTON (190)

"Only one more, papa; only for Mr. Elton. E I 1 13 46
Poor Mr. Elton! E I 1 13 46
You like Mr. Elton, papa,--I must look about for a wife E I 1 13 46
I think very well of Mr. Elton, and this is the only way I E I 1 13 46
"Mr. Elton is a very pretty young man to be sure, and a E I 1 14 47
Mr. Knightley; and by Mr. Elton, a young man living alone E I 3 20 2
What say you to Mr. Weston and Mr. Elton? E I 4 33 34
be very safely recommended to take Mr. Elton as a model. E I 4 34 42
Mr. Elton is good humoured, cheerful, obliging, and gentle. E I 4 34 42
she had drawn from Mr. Elton, and now did full justice to; E I 4 34 43
and said she had always thought Mr. Elton very agreeable. E I 4 34 43
Mr. Elton was the very person fixed on by Emma for driving E I 4 34 44
to contradict a lady," said the gallant Mr. Elton-- E I 6 42 4
"Let me entreat you," cried Mr. Elton; "it would indeed be E I 6 43 14
"Well, if you give me such kind encouragement, Mr. Elton, E I 6 43 15
"But I am afraid, Mr. Elton, Harriet will not like to sit. E I 6 44 17
Mr. Elton seemed very properly struck and delighted by the E I 6 46 22
But there was no doing anything, with Mr. Elton fidgetting E I 6 46 24
Mr. Elton was only too happy. E I 6 47 26
Harriet was to sit again the next day; and Mr. Elton, just E I 6 47 28
Every body who saw it was pleased, but Mr. Elton was in E I 6 47 30
would not own it, and Mr. Elton warmly added, "Oh, no! E I 6 48 34
35

"You, sir, may say any thing," cried Mr. Elton; "but I E I 6 48 39
But no sooner was the distress known to Mr. Elton, than it E I 6 49 40
Mr. Elton was to take the drawing to London, chuse the E I 6 49 42
sometimes by bringing forward the idea of Mr. Elton. E I 7 55 36
The idea of Mr. Elton was certainly cheering; but still, E I 7 56 42
"At this moment, perhaps, Mr. Elton is shewing your E I 7 56 44
Then I know nothing of Mr. Elton. E I 7 56 46
and advisor, and she knew Mr. Elton looked up to him. E I 8 59 24
He had frightened her a little about Mr. Elton; but when E I 8 67 57
He certainly might have heard Mr. Elton speak with more E I 8 67 57
had ever done, and Mr. Elton might not be of an imprudent, E I 8 67 57
of prudence, she was very sure did not belong to Mr. Elton. E I 8 67 57
back, not to think of Mr. Martin, but to talk of Mr. Elton. E I 8 68 58
Park, he had met Mr. Elton, and found to his great E I 8 68 58
great surprize that Mr. Elton was actually on his road to E I 8 68 58
but it would not do; Mr. Elton had been determined to go E I 8 68 58
he told him so; and Mr. Elton only looked very conscious E I 8 68 58
great deal more about Mr. Elton; and said, looking so very E I 8 68 58
that any woman whom Mr. Elton could prefer, she should E I 8 68 58
Mr. Elton had not his equal for beauty or agreeableness." E I 8 68 58
with Mr. Elton, of the utmost advantage to the latter. E I 9 69 2
Mr. Elton was the only one whose assistance she asked. E I 9 70 7
"Why will not you write one yourself for us, Mr. Elton?" E I 9 71 8
hope and dulness, "very well, Mr. Elton, very well, indeed. E I 9 72 15
you and Mr. Elton were most desirable or most natural. E I 9 74 20
Mr. Elton, who might marry any body! E I 9 74 22
You and Mr. Elton are by situation called together; you E I 9 75 25
"That Mr. Elton should really be in love with me,--me, of E I 9 75 26
You and Mr. Elton are one as clever as the other. E I 9 76 28
Mr. Elton certainly did not very well know what to say. E I 9 82 81
"I have no hesitation in saying," replied Mr. Elton, E I 9 82 83
may be inferred, containing the blessed abode of Mr. Elton. E I 10 83 2
yet. to be tempted; Mr. Elton, you know, (recollecting E I 10 84 13
that bend was passed, Mr. Elton was immediately in sight; E I 10 87 29
30

Mr. Elton then turned back to accompany them. E I 10 87 31
Mr. Elton was speaking with animation, Harriet listening E I 10 88 33
Mr. Elton was still talking, still engaged in some E I 10 88 34
Mr. Elton, I must beg leave to stop at your house, and ask E I 10 89 37
Mr. Elton looked all happiness at this proposition; and E I 10 89 38
it; but she fully intended that Mr. Elton should close it. E I 10 89 38
Mr. Elton must now be left to himself. E I 11 91 1
Harriet, Mr. Elton, and Mr. Knightley, their own especial E I 13 108 4
when she was met by Mr. Elton himself, evidently coming E I 13 109 6
Mr. Elton looked all alarm on the occasion, as he E I 13 109 6
7

But, upon my word, Mr. Elton, in your case, I should E I 13 110 9
Mr. Elton looked as if he did not very well know what E I 13 110 10
only objection, and Mr. Elton actually accepting the offer E I 13 110 12
It was a done thing; Mr. Elton was to go, and never had E I 13 111 12
must be the case with Mr. Elton; a most valuable, amiable, E I 13 111 13
Soon afterwards Mr. Elton quitted them, and she could not E I 13 111 14
saw a man more intent on being agreeable than Mr. Elton. E I 13 111 15
16

temper and good will in Mr. Elton as one cannot but value." E I 13 112 17
"Mr. Elton in love with me!-- E I 13 112 21
Mr. Elton and I are very good friends, and nothing more;" E I 13 112 23
Elton, spruce, black, and smiling, was with them instantly. E I 13 114 28
Mr. Elton was all obligation and cheerfulness; he was so E I 13 114 28
"Christmas weather," observed Mr. Elton. E I 13 115 39
drawing-room;-- Mr. Elton must compose his joyous looks, E I 14 117 1
Mr. Elton must smile less, and Mr. John Knightley more, to E I 14 117 1
Emma's project of forgetting Mr. Elton for a while, made E I 14 118 4
she could quiet Mr. Elton, the subject was so completely E I 14 118 4
So it proved;--for when happily released from Mr. Elton, E I 14 119 6
7

Mr. Elton, in very good spirits, was one of the first to E I 15 124 1
She had not time to know how Mr. Elton took the reproof, E I 15 125 7
second carriage by Mr. Elton, that the door was to be E I 15 128 23
demanded, and Mr. Elton actually making violent love to E I 15 129 24
apparent diffidence, Mr. Elton, the lover of Harriet, was E I 15 129 24
state, she replied, "I am very much astonished, Mr. Elton. E I 15 129 24
25

with quickness, "Mr. Elton, this is the most extraordinary E I 15 130 26
27

But Mr. Elton had only drunk wine enough to elevate his E I 15 130 28
Mr. Elton, my astonishment is much beyond any thing I can E I 15 130 30
"Good heaven!" cried Mr. Elton, "what can be the meaning E I 15 130 31
said to her about Mr. Elton, the caution he had given, the E I 16 135 6
he had professed that Mr. Elton would never marry E I 16 135 6
It was dreadfully mortifying; but Mr. Elton was proving E I 16 135 6
neighbourhood which Mr. Elton had first entered not two E I 16 136 9
Mr. Elton, in fancying himself a very decided favourite. E I 16 136 9
It was a great consolation that Mr. Elton should not be E I 16 138 15
why do not you stay at home like poor Mr. Elton?" E I 16 138 18
19

brought a note from Mr. Elton to Mr. Woodhouse, a long, E I 17 140 2
and his fears that Mr. Elton might never get safely to the E I 17 141 4
The affection of such a man as Mr. Elton would have been E I 17 141 8
and conversation, to drive Mr. Elton from her thoughts. E I 17 142 10
in an attachment to Mr. Elton in particular; but it seemed E I 17 142 11
If Mr. Elton, on his return, made his own indifference as E I 17 143 13
at Mrs. Goddard's; Mr. Elton being the adoration of all E I 17 143 15
opinion, been talking enough of Mr. Elton for that day. E II 1 155 1
a very plaintive--"Mr. Elton is so good to the poor!" she E II 1 155 1
of the Coles was sure to be followed by that of Mr. Elton. E II 1 156 5
and Mr. Cole had heard from Mr. Elton since his going away. E II 1 156 5
Jane Fairfax succeed Mr. Elton; but he was actually E II 1 156 6
"Oh! yes--Mr. Elton, I understood--certainly as to dancing- E II 1 156 7
Mr. Elton is going to be married." E II 3 173 24
Emma had not had time even to think of Mr. Elton, and she E II 3 173 25
"Mr. Elton going to be married!" said Emma, as soon as she E II 3 174 33
Jane, you have never seen Mr. Elton!--no wonder that you E II 3 174 35
"No--I have never seen Mr. Elton," she replied, starting E II 3 174 37
will understand that Mr. Elton is the standard of E II 3 174 38
Now, here will be Mr. Elton and Miss Hawkins; and there E II 3 175 39
your being indifferent about Mr. Elton and Miss Hawkins." E II 3 175 42
"When I have seen Mr. Elton," replied Jane, "I dare say I E II 3 175 43
said, 'no, Mr. Elton is a most worthy young man--but'---- E II 3 176 44
At the same time, nobody could wonder if Mr. Elton should E II 3 176 44
Mr. Elton, and Miss Hawkins.-- E II 3 177 50
news, as proving that Mr. Elton could not have suffered E II 3 177 51
amiable: and when Mr. Elton himself arrived to triumph in E II 4 181 2
Mr. Elton returned, a very happy man. E II 4 181 3
She was good enough for Mr. Elton, no doubt; accomplished E II 4 183 9
considerably worse from this re-appearance of Mr. Elton. E II 4 184 10
who saw no fault in Mr. Elton, and found nothing so E II 4 184 10
Sometimes Mr. Elton predominated, sometimes the Martins; E II 4 184 11
of kindness; and till Mr. Elton himself appeared, she had E II 4 184 11
But Mr. Elton, in person, had driven away all such cares. E II 4 185 11
Her mind was quite sick of Mr. Elton and the Martins. E II 5 187 4
she hoped Mr. Elton would now be talked of no more. E II 5 188 8
among the failings of Mr. Elton, even in the days of his E II 8 213 5
while politics and Mr. Elton were talked over, Emma could E II 8 214 13
of having loved even Mr. Elton in vain--by the surrender E II 8 219 44
did think there were some looks a little like Mr. Elton." E II 8 220 47
had told her, though fearful of its producing Mr. Elton. E II 9 232 14
He would soon be among them again; Mr. Elton and his bride. E II 13 267 8
from Enscombe before "Mr. Elton and his bride" was in E II 13 267 8
She had had three weeks of happy exemption from Mr. Elton; E II 13 267 8
less, talk less of Mr. Elton for my sake; because for your E II 13 268 11
12

As for Mr. Elton, his manners did not appear--but no, she E II 14 270 5
unlucky poor Mr. Elton was in being in the same room at E II 14 271 5
present to engage Mr. Elton, she had a quarter of an hour E II 14 272 16
and that her society would certainly do Mr. Elton no good. E II 14 272 16
Mr. Elton was appealed to.-- E II 14 272 18
"We cannot suppose," said Emma, smiling, "that Mr. Elton E II 14 277 37
Mr. Elton knows you." E II 14 280 55
There was no reason to suppose Mr. Elton thought at all E II 15 281 2
Elton, was disposed to pay him attention on his marriage. E II 16 290 1
I am sure Mr. Elton will lose no time in calling on him; E II 18 305 4
After tea, Mr. and Mrs. Weston, and Mr. Elton sat down E II 18 311 36
Mr. Elton had just joined them, and his wife was E III 2 324 22
23

soon afterwards, on seeing Mr. Elton sauntering about. E III 2 326 33
eyes to watch; but Mr. Elton was so near, that she heard E III 2 327 34
"do not you dance, Mr. Elton?" to which his prompt reply E III 2 327 34
This was Mr. Elton! the amiable, obliging, gentle Mr. E III 2 328 38
was Mr. Elton! the amiable, obliging, gentle Mr. Elton.-- E III 2 328 38
Mr. Elton had retreated into the cardroom, looking (Emma E III 2 328 42
her first partner was Mr. Elton, I do not know who will E III 2 329 45
own myself to have been completely mistaken in Mr. Elton. E III 2 330 54
Elton was not the superior creature she had believed him. E III 3 332 1
herself, she just recovering from her mania for Mr. Elton. E III 3 335 10
Mr. Elton was sitting here, I remember, much about where I E III 4 340 20
goes, and there is an end, thank heaven! of Mr. Elton." E III 4 340 26
I hope it is not in compliment to Mr. Elton?" E III 4 341 32
"Mr. Elton indeed!" cried Harriet indignantly.-- E III 4 341 33
could just catch the words, "so superior to Mr. Elton!" E III 4 341 33
Mr. Elton was called out of the room before tea, old John E III 8 383 29
And poor John's son came to talk to Mr. Elton about relief E III 8 383 29
help; and so, when Mr. Elton came back, he told us what E III 8 383 29
What Mr. Elton had learnt from the ostler on the subject, E III 8 383 31
me to dance, when Mr. Elton would not stand up with me; E III 11 406 24
be doing nothing to assist the cure;--not like Mr. Elton. E III 15 450 38
are we to have the pleasure of a call from Mr. Elton?-- E III 16 455 22
and only said, "is Mr. Elton gone on foot to Donwell?-- E III 16 456 26
Mr. Elton made his appearance. E III 16 457 35
Mr. Elton was so hot and tired, that all this wit seemed E III 16 457 37
"I met William Larkins," continued Mr. Elton, "as I got E III 16 458 43
towards Mr. Elton, if not towards William Larkins. E III 16 458 44
Mr. Elton cared little about it, compared with his wife; E III 17 469 36
for the Churchills--or even for Mr. Elton!-- E III 19 482 3
with Mr. Elton as he stood before them, could impair.-- E III 19 482 6
Perhaps, indeed, at that time she scarcely saw Mr. Elton, E III 19 482 6
her wedding-day--and Mr. Elton was called on, within a E III 19 484 11

MR. ELTON'S (39)

respect, perhaps, Mr. Elton's manners are superior to Mr. E I 4 34 41
42

Mr. Elton's situation was most suitable, quite the E I 4 35 44
might very well be conquered by Mr. Elton's admiration. E I 4 35 45
than before of Mr. Elton's being a remarkably handsome man, E I 6 42 1
She was quite convinced of Mr. Elton's being in the E I 6 42 1
as Mr. Elton's very promising attachment was likely to add. E I 6 47 27
The very day of Mr. Elton's going to London produced a E I 7 50 1
Emma was more than half in hopes of Mr. Elton's having E I 8 59 24
"If I had set my heart on Mr. Elton's marrying Harriet, it E I 8 66 54
to hand soon after Mr. Elton's return, and being hung over E I 9 69 2
cannot have a moment's doubt as to Mr. Elton's intentions. E I 9 73 20
Mr. Elton's superiority had very ample acknowledgment. E I 9 74 21
a proof of love, with Mr. Elton's seeing ready wit in her. E I 10 83 6
how much Mr. Elton's would be depressed when he knew her E I 13 109 6
if the weather were Mr. Elton's only objection, and Mr. E I 13 110 12
"Mr. Elton's manners are not perfect," replied Emma; "but E I 13 111 17
"are you imagining me to be Mr. Elton's object?" E I 13 112 19
astonished now at Mr. Elton's spirits for other feelings. E I 13 115 42
as possible of Mr. Elton's oddities, or of any thing else E I 14 117 2
nonsense, which she particularly wished to listen to. E I 14 118 4
With such sensations, Mr. Elton's civilities were E I 14 119 6
encouragement for Mr. Elton's sanguine state of mind, he E I 15 131 32
33

Contrary to the usual course of things, Mr. Elton's E I 16 135 7
no need to find excuses for Mr. Elton's absenting himself. E I 16 138 17
note, to say, with Mr. Elton's best compliments, "that he E I 17 140 2
Mr. Elton's absence just at this time was the very thing E I 17 140 3
by the time of Mr. Elton's return, as to allow them all to E I 17 142 11
a conclusion of Mr. Elton's importance with her! E II 3 180 56
Mr. Elton's rights, however, gradually revived. E II 3 180 57
Mr. Elton's engagement had been the cure of the agitation E II 4 184 11
of considering Mr. Elton's house, which, as well as the E II 6 203 42
As Frank Churchill's arrival had succeeded Mr. Elton's E II 13 267 8
concerns were assuming the most irresistible form.-- E II 13 267 8
so unhappy about Mr. Elton's marrying, Harriet, is the E II 13 268 10
Her manners too--and Mr. Elton's, were unpleasant towards E II 15 281 3
He was warm in his reprobation of Mr. Elton's conduct; it E III 2 330 46
and Mr. Elton's seeming resolved to learn to like it too. E III 4 339 19
She had seemed more sensible of Mr. Elton's being to stoop E III 11 414 50
like morning visits, and Mr. Elton's time is so engaged." E III 16 455 22

MR. ELTONS (1)

"When Miss Smiths and Mr. Eltons get acquainted--they do E I 9 74 25

MR. FERRARS (27)

They are a very respectable family, Mr. Ferrars; and SS I 16 88 40
"Ferrars!" repeated Miss Steele; "Mr. Ferrars is the happy SS I 21 126 39
And I do not think Mr. Ferrars can be displeased, when he SS I 22 130 16
We cannot mean the same Mr. Ferrars." SS I 22 131 29
Mr. Ferrars, I believe, is entirely dependent on his SS II 2 147 6
and friendship for Mr. Ferrars; but do not you perceive SS II 2 149 26
had for some time ceased to think at all of Mr. Ferrars. SS II 10 216 15
Mr. Ferrars, and Edward's immediately walking in. SS II 13 240 18
senses could expect Mr. Ferrars to give up a woman like SS III 2 272 16
he was afraid Mr. Ferrars would be off; and when Edward SS III 2 272 16
your friend Mr. Ferrars has suffered from his family; for SS III 3 282 17
I have seen Mr. Ferrars two or three times in Harley- SS III 3 282 19
no more than make Mr. Ferrars comfortable as a bachelor; SS III 3 284 23
I think it ought not to be mentioned to any body else. SS III 4 286 15
Why Mr. Ferrars was to be written to about it in such a SS III 4 286 16
Mr. Ferrars is to be the man. SS III 4 286 17
one to announce his intention to Mr. Ferrars than himself." SS III 4 287 19
a kindness by poor Mr. Ferrars, I do think it is not worth SS III 4 291 51
Brandon's only object is to be of use to Mr. Ferrars." SS III 4 291 52
you for the sake of giving ten guineas to Mr. Ferrars!" SS III 4 291 53
"A very simple one--to be of use to Mr. Ferrars." SS III 5 295 15
friend of Mr. Ferrars, and the kind confidante of himself, SS III 6 305 16
"I suppose you know, ma'am, that Mr. Ferrars is married." SS III 11 353 22
23

"Who told you that Mr. Ferrars was married, thomas?" SS III 11 354 26
"I see Mr. Ferrars myself, ma'am, this morning in Exeter, SS III 11 354 27
"Was Mr. Ferrars in the carriage with her?" SS III 11 354 30
since eventually it promoted the interest of Elinor. SS III 13 370 35

MR. FERRARS'S (4)

was taken of Mr. Ferrars's name by Miss Steele when SS I 21 126 41
they chuse about Mr. Ferrars's declaring he would not have SS III 2 272 14
was considering Mr. Ferrars's marriage as the certain SS III 3 284 22
compliments and Mr. Ferrars's, their best compliments and SS III 11 354 27

MR. FITZWILLIAM DARCY (1)

Darcy formerly spoken of as a very proud, ill-natured boy. PP II 2 143 20

MR. FRANK CHURCHILL (45)

Mr. Frank Churchill was one of the boasts of Highbury, and E I 2 17 8
Now was the time for Mr. Frank Churchill to come among E I 2 18 9
letter Mr. Frank Churchill had written to Mrs. Weston? E I 2 18 9
idea of Mr. Frank Churchill, which always interested her. E I 14 118 5
Churchill and Miss Smith making their party quite complete. E I 14 119 8
Mr. Frank Churchill, in my opinion, as his father thinks. E I 14 121 16
of Mr. Frank Churchill, was willing to forget his late E I 15 124 2
Mr. Frank Churchill did not come. E I 18 144 1
What has Mr. Frank Churchill done, to make you suppose him E I 18 145 9
Mr. Frank Churchill to be making such a speech as that to E I 18 147 17
Frank Churchill; we shall think and speak of nobody else." E I 18 149 29
it--Mr. Frank Churchill--must put up for the present with E II 2 166 10
She and Mr. Frank Churchill had been at Weymouth at the E II 2 169 17
"Will Mr. Frank Churchill pass through Bath as well as E II 5 189 17
Mr. Frank Churchill still declined it, looking as serious E II 5 195 48
The next morning brought Mr. Frank Churchill again. E II 6 196 1
Mr. Frank Churchill hardly knows what to say when you E II 6 201 23
had; and Mr. Frank Churchill talked a great deal about E II 9 232 9
'Aye, pray do,' said Mr. Frank Churchill, 'Miss E II 9 236 46
So very obliging of Mr. Frank Churchill! E II 9 237 51
"And here is Mrs. Weston and Mr. Frank Churchill too!-- E II 10 244 44
Miss Woodhouse and Mr. Frank Churchill; I never saw any E II 10 245 48
Mr. Frank Churchill are hearing every thing that passes. E II 10 245 49
Mr. Frank Churchill and Miss Woodhouse danced--for doing E II 11 247 2
writes one of the best gentlemen's hands I ever saw." E II 16 297 49
"Oh! when a gallant young man, like Mr. Frank Churchill," E II 16 298 55
I have heard so much in praise of Mr. Frank Churchill.-- E II 18 309 31
Mr. Frank Churchill was so extremely--and there was a mat E III 2 323 19
Oh! Mr. Frank Churchill, I must tell you my mother's E III 2 323 19
Do not we often talk of Mr. Frank Churchill?-- E III 2 323 19
Mr. Weston and Mrs. Elton led the way, Mr. Frank Churchill E III 2 325 31
that Mr. Frank Churchill might have--I do not mean to say E III 5 345 16
"Between Mr. Frank Churchill and Miss Fairfax? E III 5 350 33
"Mr. Frank Churchill and Miss Woodhouse flirted together E III 7 368 3
sent to Randall's to take Mr. Frank Churchill to Richmond. E III 8 383 29
but that Mr. Frank Churchill having resolved to go home E III 8 383 31
"So far as that it relates to Mr. Frank Churchill, I do E III 10 394 29
Fairfax and Mr. Frank Churchill are to be married, and E III 11 404 8
You do not think I care about Mr. Frank Churchill." E III 11 405 12
Mr. Frank Churchill, indeed! E III 11 405 18
of Mr. Frank Churchill, who is like nobody by his side. E III 11 405 18
almost assert that you had named Mr. Frank Churchill. E III 11 406 21
I am sure the service Mr. Frank Churchill had rendered you, E III 11 406 21
It was not the gipsies--it was not Mr. Frank Churchill E III 11 406 24
between Mr. Frank Churchill and me; and, therefore, it E III 11 407 28

MR. FRANK CHURCHILL'S (5)

not coming, except as a disappointment at Randalls. E I 18 144 4
once in Mr. Frank Churchill's situation, you would be able E I 18 147 19
after Mr. Frank Churchill's accommodation on his journey, E II 5 193 35
of Mr. Frank Churchill's going, she proceeded to give them E III 8 383 30
Frank Churchill's of having the least regard for Jane Fairfax. E III 11 405 11

MR. FRASER (2)

is a daughter of Mr. Fraser by a first wife, whom she is MP III 5 360 16
and she was decidedly in favour of Mr. Fraser. MP III 5 361 16

MR. GARDINER (30)

Mr. Gardiner was a sensible, gentlemanlike man, greatly PP II 2 139 2
Mr. Gardiner would be prevented by business from setting PP II 19 238 7
Mr. Gardiner declared his willingness, and Elizabeth was PP II 19 240 12
Miss Darcy as handsome as her brother?" said Mr. Gardiner. PP III 1 248 21
Mr. Gardiner, whose manners were easy and pleasant, PP III 1 248 23
Mr. Gardiner, highly amused by the kind of family PP III 1 249 37
Mr. Gardiner expressed a wish of going round the whole PP III 1 253 57
was slow, for Mr. Gardiner, though seldom able to indulge PP III 1 254 57
with them, and entered into conversation with Mr. Gardiner. PP III 1 255 59
Mr. Gardiner left them soon after breakfast. PP III 2 266 18
He had been some time with Mr. Gardiner, who, with two or PP III 3 268 8
I must find Mr. Gardiner this moment, on business that PP III 4 276 6
Gardiner readily promised every assistance in his power.-- PP III 4 280 26
completed; and Mr. Gardiner meanwhile having settled his PP III 4 281 29
"In the first place," replied Mr. Gardiner, "there is no PP III 5 282 5
ideas; and Mr. Gardiner, after general assurances of his PP III 5 287 36
But Mr. Gardiner, though he assured her again of his PP III 5 288 39
Mr. Gardiner had waited only for the letters before he set PP III 6 294 1
Mr. Gardiner left Longbourn on Sunday; on Tuesday, his PP III 6 295 5
Mr. Gardiner himself did not expect any success from this PP III 6 295 5
But before they heard again from Mr. Gardiner, a letter PP III 6 296 10
Mr. Gardiner did not write again, till he had received an PP III 6 297 12
Mr. Gardiner did not attempt to conceal these particulars PP III 6 298 12
Mr. Gardiner added in his letter, that they might expect PP III 6 298 13
there is an express come for master from Mr. Gardiner! PP III 7 301 3
exactly know what Mr. Gardiner has done for them, because PP III 7 305 36
Mr. Gardiner soon wrote again to his brother. PP III 8 312 18
from the ----shire, as clearly as Mr. Gardiner could do. PP III 8 313 20
He came to tell Mr. Gardiner that he had found out where PP III 10 321 2
But Mr. Gardiner could not be seen, and Mr. Darcy found, PP III 10 323 2

MR. GARDINER'S (4)

As they drove to Mr. Gardiner's door, Jane was at a PP II 4 152 5
Mr. Gardiner's house, where they were to remain a few days. PP II 15 217 15
As soon as Jane had read Mr. Gardiner's hope of Lydia's PP III 7 305 43
which Mr. Gardiner's behaviour laid them all under. PP III 7 306 45

MR. GEORGE (1)

Such a host of friends!--and Mr. George and Mr. Arthur!-- E III 2 323 19

MR. GEORGE OTWAY (1)
dancing with Mr. George Otway; she will love to tell you E III 2 329 45
MR. GRAHAM'S (1)
"about your friend Mr. Graham's intending to have a E I 12 104 44
MR. GRAY'S (2)
around her, in Mr. Gray's shop, as in her own bed-room. SS II 11 221 4
to make a very creditable appearance in Mr. Gray's shop. SS II 11 221 7
MR. GREEN (1)
and I was talking to Mr. Green at that very time about MP I 7 73 53
MR. GREEN'S (1)
to the dinner at Mr. Green's, and the party at Mrs. E II 4 181 4
MR. HARDING (2)
to him (Mr. Harding), for his advice; Mr. Harding feared MP III 16 450 9
for his advice; Mr. Harding feared there had been at least, MP III 16 450 9
MR. HARRIS (8)
Mr. Harris, who attended her every day, still talked SS III 7 309 7
Harris arrived, he declared his patient materially better. SS III 7 310 8
and dispatching a messenger to Barton for her mother. SS III 7 311 14
with a message to Mr. Harris, and an order for post-horses SS III 7 311 15
most cruel anxiety on Elinor's, before Mr. Harris appeared. SS III 7 312 17
She was on the point of sending again for Mr. Harris, or SS III 7 312 19
Mr. Harris was punctual in his second visit;--but he came SS III 7 313 21
till the arrival of Mr. Harris at four o'clock;--when his SS III 7 314 22
MR. HARRIS'S (2)
very grave on Mr. Harris's report, and confirming SS III 7 307 3
an hour after Mr. Harris's arrival, she set off, with her SS III 7 308 3
MR. HENRY DASHWOOD (2)
his nephew Mr. Henry Dashwood, the legal inheritor of the SS I 1 3 1
By a former marriage, Mr. Henry Dashwood had one son: by SS I 1 3 2
MR. HENRY TILNEY (2)
sudden view of Mr. Henry Tilney and his father, joining a NA I 12 92 4
daughter as "Mr. Henry Tilney," with the embarrassment of NA II 15 241 7
MR. HOLLIS'S (1)
at the time of Mr. Hollis's death;--the latter, to the S 3 377 1
MR. HUME (1)
if the production of Mr. Hume or Mr. Robertson, than if NA I 14 109 23
MR. HURST (12)
His brother-in-law, Mr. Hurst, merely looked the gentleman; PP I 3 10 5
Darcy said very little, and Mr. Hurst nothing at all. PP I 7 33 42
less so; and as for Mr. Hurst, by whom Elizabeth sat, he PP I 8 35 2
Mr. Hurst looked at her with astonishment. PP I 8 37 21
description, when Mr. Hurst called them to order, with PP I 8 40 55
Mr. Hurst and Mr. Bingley were at piquet, and Mrs. Hurst PP I 10 47 1
congratulation; Mr. Hurst also made her a slight bow, and PP I 11 54 2
When tea was over, Mr. Hurst reminded his sister-in-law of PP I 11 54 3
and Mr. Hurst soon found even his open petition rejected. PP I 11 54 3
Mr. Hurst had therefore nothing to do, but to stretch PP I 11 54 3
"Louisa, you will not mind my waking Mr. Hurst." PP I 11 58 33
that day in Grosvenor street, where Mr. Hurst had a house. PP I 21 116 8
MR. IMPUDENCE (1)
"Yes, yes, Mr. Impudence, I know that very well, and I was SS I 13 67 64
MR. JAMES MORLAND (1)
with Mr. James Morland, before she remembered that her NA I 4 33 5
MR. JENNINGS'S (1)
particulars of Mr. Jennings's last illness, and what he SS I 11 54 6
MR. JOHN (1)
Mr.--and Mr. Edmund is no more than Mr. John or Mr. Thomas. MP II 4 211 24
MR. JOHN DASHWOOD (3)
Mr. John Dashwood had not the strong feelings of the rest SS I 1 5 6
and Mr. John Dashwood had then leisure to consider how SS I 1 5 6
Mr. John Dashwood told his mother again and again how SS I 5 25 4
MR. JOHN KNIGHTLEY (28)
last and my best--my brother, Mr. John Knightley.-- E I 6 45 21
Mr. John Knightley must be in town again on the 28th, and E I 9 79 63
Mr. John Knightley is an affectionate father. E I 9 81 73
Mr. John Knightley was a tall, gentleman-like, and very E I 11 92 5
It did not often happen; for Mr. John Knightley had really E I 11 93 5
Mr. John Knightley here asked Emma quietly whether there E. I 11 94 9
"Just as it should be," said Mr. John Knightley, "and just E I 11 94 15
Churchills, I fancy," observed Mr. John Knightley coolly. E I 11 96 26
I think Mr. John Knightley very far from looking well." E I 12 103 40
Did you speak to me?" cried Mr. John Knightley, hearing E I 12 103 41
overtaken by Mr. John Knightley returning from the daily E I 13 109 6
"Yes," said Mr. John Knightley presently, with some E I 13 112 18
least, which Mr. John Knightley did not by any means like; E I 13 113 25
Mr. John Knightley looked as if he did not comprehend the E I 13 115 40
41
looks, and Mr. John Knightley disperse his ill-humour. E I 14 117 1
Mr. Elton must smile less, and Mr. John Knightley more, to E I 14 117 1
succeed; for Mr. John Knightley now came into the room E I 15 125 7
go well: for Mr. John Knightley, ashamed of his ill-humour, E I 15 132 38
To Mr. John Knightley was she indebted for her first idea E I 16 135 6
you know I always fancy Mr. Dixon like Mr. John Knightley? E II 3 176 44
It would be a great disappointment to Mr. John Knightley; E II 8 227 87
and Mr. John Knightley seemed early to devote himself to E II 16 292 10
Mr. John Knightley smiled, and replied, "that is to say, E II 16 293 15
16
I know Mr. John Knightley too well--I am very sure he E II 16 293 22
answering, she began speaking again to Mr. John Knightley. E II 16 296 39
Mr. John Knightley proved more talkative than his brother. E II 18 311 37
I can understand you--(nodding at Mr. John Knightley)-- E II 18 312 50
But Mr. John Knightley must be in London again by the end E III 19 484 10
MR. JOHN KNIGHTLEY'S (2)
like Mr. John Knightley's, and was destined, if she could E I 6 46 23
Mr. John Knightley's being a lawyer is very inconvenient.-- E I 9 79 58
MR. JONES (3)
They insist also on my seeing Mr. Jones--therefore do not PP I 7 31 30
it was settled that Mr. Jones should be sent for early in PP I 8 40 59
Mr. Jones says we must not think of moving her. PP I 9 41 3
MR. JONES'S (2)
Bingley urged Mr. Jones's being sent for immediately; PP I 8 40 59
not happened to see Mr. Jones's shop boy in the street, PP I 15 73 11
MR. K. (1)
elegant terseness of Mrs. Elton, by calling you Mr. K.-- E III 17 463 14
MR. KING (1)
man, introduced by Mr. King; had a great deal of NA I 3 27 26
MR. KNIGHTLEY (266)
Mr. Knightley, a sensible man about seven or eight-and- E I 1 9 21
Mr. Knightley had a cheerful manner which always did him E I 1 9 21
Knightley, to come out at this late hour to call upon us. E I 1 10 21
22
mean you, or suppose Mr. Knightley to mean you. E I 1 10 32
Mr. Knightley loves to find fault with me you know--in a E I 1 10 32
Mr. Knightley, in fact, was one of the few people who E I 1 11 33
"Emma knows I never flatter her," said Mr. Knightley; "but E I 1 11 34
"But, Mr. Knightley, she is really very sorry to lose poor E I 1 11 36
Emma should not miss such a companion," said Mr. Knightley. E I 1 11 38
Mr. Knightley shook his head at her. E I 1 12 40
what you mean by 'success;'" said Mr. Knightley. E I 1 12 42
I dare say Mr. Knightley will be so kind as to meet him." E I 1 14 47
any time," said Mr. Knightley laughing; "and I agree with E I 1 14 48
the seat of Mr. Knightley, comprehended many such. E I 3 20 1
the Westons and Mr. Knightley; and by Mr. Elton, a young E I 3 20 2
a large farm of Mr. Knightley, and residing in the parish E I 3 23 10
knew Mr. Knightley thought highly of them--but they must E I 3 23 10
"Certainly, he is not like Mr. Knightley. E I 4 33 33
not such a fine air and way of walking as Mr. Knightley. E I 4 33 33
But Mr. Knightley is so very fine a man!" E I 4 33 33
with gentlemen so plainly written as in Mr. Knightley. E I 4 33 34
Weston," said Mr. Knightley, "of this great intimacy E I 5 36 1
of one of our quarrels about Emma, Mr. Knightley." E I 5 36 4
Mr. Knightley, I shall not allow you to be a fair judge in E I 5 36 6
Knightley, feelingly; and for a moment or two he had done. E I 5 37 9
"I should have been sorry, Mr. Knightley, to be dependent E I 5 37 10
Mr. Knightley, is not she?" E I 5 39 20
"And I, Mr. Knightley, am equally stout in my confidence E I 5 39 22
but excuse me, Mr. Knightley, if I take the liberty (I E I 5 40 24
Mr. Knightley, at this little remains of office." E I 5 40 24
transition which Mr. Knightley soon afterwards made to " E I 5 41 31
"You have made her too tall, Emma," said Mr. Knightley. E I 6 48 33
While she was gone, Mr. Knightley called, and sat some E I 8 57 2
his own civility, to leave Mr. Knightley for that purpose. E I 8 57 2
Mr. Knightley, who had nothing of ceremony about him, was E I 8 57 2
"Well, I believe, if you will excuse me, Mr. Knightley, if E I 8 57 3
I treat you without ceremony Mr. Knightley. E I 8 57 3
of your company, Mr. Knightley, but I am a very slow E I 8 58 7
Mr. Woodhouse at last was off; but Mr. Knightley, instead E I 8 58 9
Mr. Knightley was a sort of general friend and advisor, E I 8 59 24
"Pray, Mr. Knightley," said Emma, who had been smiling to E I 8 60 28
be believed; and Mr. Knightley actually looked red with E I 8 60 31
32
"Not Harriet's equal!" exclaimed Mr. Knightley loudly and E I 8 61 38
"Whoever might be her parents," said Mr. Knightley, " E I 8 62 42
intimacy," said Mr. Knightley presently, "though I have E I 8 64 47
"We think so very differently on this point, Mr. Knightley, E I 8 65 48
nonsense, as ever was talked!" cried Mr. Knightley.-- E I 8 65 49
were right and her adversary's wrong, as Mr. Knightley. E I 8 67 56
her, that let Mr. Knightley think or say what he would, E I 8 67 56
considered that Mr. Knightley could not have observed him E I 8 67 57
them; but then, Mr. Knightley did not make the allowance E I 8 67 57
Mr. Knightley saw no such passion, and of course thought E I 8 67 57
Mr. Knightley might quarrel with her, but Emma could not E I 9 69 1
Ah! Mr. Knightley, I wish you had the benefit of this; I E I 9 72 15
Mr. Knightley promises to give up his claim this Christmas- E I 9 79 63
Mr. Knightley was to dine with them--rather against the E I 12 98 1
and herself, in procuring him the proper invitation. E I 12 98 1
Now, Mr. Knightley, a word or two more, and I have done. E I 12 99 11
I trust, at least, that you do not think Mr. Knightley E I 12 103 39
"True, true," cried Mr. Knightley, with most ready E I 12 106 61
Harriet, Mr. Elton, and Mr. Knightley, their own especial E I 13 108 4
though Mr. Knightley perhaps, from being used to the large E I 13 116 43
the point, when Mr. Knightley, who had left the room E I 15 127 16
and recommending, Mr. Knightley and Emma settled it in a E I 15 128 17
18
to his own by Mr. Knightley and Mr. Weston; but not all E I 15 128 22
She remembered what Mr. Knightley had once said to her E I 16 135 6
hear him say to Mr. Knightley, whom no weather could keep E I 16 138 18
19
why do not you stay at home like poor Mr. Elton?" E I 16 138 18
19
She was the first to announce it to Mr. Knightley; and E I 18 145 5
disagreement with Mr. Knightley; and, to her great E I 18 145 5
coolly; "but I dare say he might come if he would." E I 18 145 6
You are the worst judge in the world, Mr. Knightley, of E I 18 146 11
Nobody but you, Mr. Knightley, would imagine it possible E I 18 147 17
I can imagine, that if you, as you are, Mr. Knightley, E I 18 147 19
"Me!--not at all," replied Mr. Knightley, rather E I 18 149 28
Cannot you imagine, Mr. Knightley, what a sensation his E I 18 149 29
"And mine," said Mr. Knightley warmly, "is, that if he E I 18 150 32
to another," said Mr. Knightley, with a degree of vexation, E I 18 150 36
She had had many a hint from Mr. Knightley and some from E II 1 155 3
to answer; Mr. Knightley had once told her it was because E II 2 166 11
than saying to Mr. Knightley, "she certainly is handsome; E II 2 168 15
were discerned by Mr. Knightley, who had been of the party, E II 3 170 1
"No," said Mr. Knightley, nearly at the same time; "you E II 3 170 5
She must have found the evening agreeable, Mr. Knightley, E II 3 171 12
Mr. Knightley looked as if he were more gratified than he E II 3 171 16
17
"Emma," said Mr. Knightley presently, "I have a piece of E II 3 172 20
Mr. Knightley soon saw that he had lost his moment, and E II 3 172 23
you," said Mr. Knightley, with a smile which implied a E II 3 173 26
"Where could you possibly hear it, Mr. Knightley? E II 3 173 27
But, Mr. Knightley, how could you possibly have heard it? E II 3 173 27
Well, Mr. Knightley, and so you actually saw the letter; E II 3 174 31
32
"My father would say 'yes,' Mr. Knightley, 'no;' and Miss E II 3 174 38
Oh! Mr. Knightley is coming too. E II 3 177 50
and that Mr. Knightley certainly had not done him justice. E II 6 197 4
its power of censure, by bows or smiles--Mr. Knightley. E II 7 206 4
she had little hope of Mr. Knightley, none of Mr. Weston. E II 7 207 6
be there, and Mr. Knightley too, to take care of her, I E II 7 209 10
Mr. Knightley, he is not a trifling, silly young man. E II 8 212 3
Knightley's; for Mr. Knightley keeping no horses, having E II 8 213 7
satisfied with the rest of the party as with Mr. Knightley. E II 8 214 12
his father, Mr. Knightley, Mr. Cox, and Mr. Cole, were E II 8 220 48
I know no man more likely than Mr. Knightley to do the E II 8 223 64
is nobody whom I would fix on more than on Mr. Knightley. E II 8 223 64
In short, I have made a match between Mr. Knightley and E II 8 224 65
"Mr. Knightley and Jane Fairfax!" exclaimed Emma. E II 8 224 66
Mr. Knightley!-- E II 8 224 66
Mr. Knightley must not marry!-- E II 8 224 66
and if Mr. Knightley really wished to marry, you would not E II 8 224 67
Mr. Knightley marry!-- E II 8 224 68
"But Mr. Knightley does not want to marry. E II 8 225 74
And, upon my word, I do not think Mr. Knightley would be E II 8 225 78
from the Campbells, may it not be from Mr. Knightley? E II 8 226 79
Mr. Knightley does nothing mysteriously." E II 8 226 80
Mr. Knightley has any thought of marrying Jane Fairfax." E II 8 226 84
But the sight of Mr. Knightley among the most attentive, E II 8 227 87
No--Mr. Knightley must never marry. E II 8 228 87
Presently Mr. Knightley looked back, and came and sat down E II 8 228 88
Mr. Knightley had had no concern in giving the instrument. E II 8 228 93
Mr. Knightley grew angry. E II 8 229 96
taste, to look about, and see what became of Mr. Knightley. E II 8 229 99
other day--for Mr. Knightley called one morning, and Jane E II 9 238 51
I would not have Mr. Knightley know any thing about it for E II 9 239 51
window, descried Mr. Knightley on horseback not far off. E II 10 243 30
"Mr. Knightley I declare!-- E II 10 243 31
So began Miss Bates; and Mr. Knightley seemed determined E II 10 244 34
35
Oh! Mr. Knightley, what a delightful party last night; how E II 10 245 48
"Oh! Mr. Knightley, one moment more; something of E II 10 245 50
Mr. Knightley cannot stop. E II 10 245 52
and the window was open, and Mr. Knightley spoke loud. E II 10 245 54
young Cox, my father, and myself, besides Mr. Knightley. E II 11 248 4
was soon no leisure for quarrelling with Mr. Knightley. E II 12 258 7
not for Frank Churchill; but Mr. Knightley will be happy. E II 12 262 39
Mr. Knightley, however, shewed no triumphant happiness. E II 12 262 40
Actually to discover that Mr. Knightley is a gentleman! E II 14 279 52
"You are right, Mrs. Weston," said Mr. Knightley warmly, " E II 15 286 18
Mr. Knightley was hard at work upon the lower buttons of E II 15 287 27
28
enough to exclaim, "you are not vain, Mr. Knightley. E II 15 287 31
Mr. Knightley was thoughtful again. E II 15 288 36
"Jane Fairfax has feeling," said Mr. Knightley--"I do not E II 15 289 40
the Westons and Mr. Knightley; so far it was all of course- E II 16 291 5
Mrs. Weston and Mr. Knightley, she was more conscience- E II 16 291 5
"I do not admire it," said Mr. Knightley. E II 16 297 50
and can shew it after dinner to convince Mr. Knightley." E II 16 298 54
Churchill," said Mr. Knightley drily, "writes to a fair E II 16 298 55
Mr. Woodhouse or Mr. Knightley particularly delighted. E II 17 304 30
on very well; for Mr. Knightley seemed little disposed for E II 18 311 36
"No," cried Mr. Knightley, "that need not be the E II 18 312 49
But you, (turning to Mr. Knightley,) who know how very, E II 18 312 50

Mr. Knightley seemed to be trying not to smile; and E II 18 312 51
She looked round for a moment; he had joined Mr. Knightley E III 2 328 38
caught her;-- Mr. Knightley leading Harriet to the set!-- E III 2 328 40
Emma had no opportunity of speaking to Mr. Knightley till E III 2 330 46
"Whom are you going to dance with?" asked Mr. Knightley. E III 2 331 59
This little explanation with Mr. Knightley gave Emma E III 3 332 1
much in love, and Mr. Knightley not wanting to quarrel E III 3 332 1
neighbourhood to Mr. Knightley, he set off, with all the E III 3 334 8
Mr. Knightley had been telling him something about brewing E III 4 339 18
Oh! yes--Mr. Knightley and I both saying we liked it, and E III 4 339 19
Stop; Mr. Knightley was standing just here, was not he?-- E III 4 340 19
Mr. Knightley, who, for some reason best known to himself, E III 5 343 2
over to Harriet, Mr. Knightley began to suspect him of E III 5 343 2
Mr. Knightley suspected in Frank Churchill the E III 5 346 17
The dream must be borne with, and Mr. Knightley must take E III 5 347 18
to them--and Mr. Knightley so placed as to see them all; E III 5 341 21
Mr. Knightley connected it with the dream; but how it E III 5 348 21
not get away; and Mr. Knightley thought he saw another E III 5 349 25
and how they parted, Mr. Knightley could not tell. E III 5 349 25
with a satisfaction which silenced, Mr. Knightley. E III 5 351 38
"You had better explore to Donwell," replied Mr. Knightley. E III 6 354 8
If Mr. Knightley did not begin seriously, he was obliged E III 6 354 9
Mr. Knightley had another reason for avoiding a table in E III 6 356 29
He thought it very well done of Mr. Knightley to invite E III 6 357 30
Mr. Knightley was fortunate in every body's most ready E III 6 357 31
Mr. Knightley was then obliged to say the he should be E III 6 357 31
Would not Mr. Knightley show them the gardens--all the E III 6 359 37
perceived Mr. Knightley and Harriet distinct from the rest, E III 6 360 40
Mr. Knightley and Harriet!-- E III 6 360 40
Mr. Knightley had done all in his power for Mr. E III 6 361 43
The Eltons walked together; Mr. Knightley took charge of E III 7 367 1
Yes, I see what she means, (turning to Mr. Knightley,) and E III 7 371 28
about it, and Mr. Knightley gravely said, "this explains E III 7 371 35
36

walked off, followed in half a minute by Mr. Knightley. E III 7 374 54
While waiting for the carriage, she found Mr. Knightley by E III 7 374 55
she might see Mr. Knightley in her way; or, perhaps, he E III 8 377 2
the hill, while we were walking about with Mr. Knightley. E III 8 381 17
"Mr. Knightley was there too, was he?" E III 8 381 18
"No, not Mr. Knightley; he declined it from the first; and E III 8 381 19
Mr. Knightley and Harriet had arrived during her absence, E III 9 385 1
Mr. Knightley immediately got up, and in a manner E III 9 385 1
2

Mrs. and Miss Bates, Mr. Knightley, as I told you before. E III 9 385 6
the head, which spoke much, she looked at Mr. Knightley.-- E III 9 385 7
to talk over Jane Fairfax's situation with Mr. Knightley.-- E III 9 386 8
that could Mr. Knightley have been privy to all her E III 9 391 21
Mr. Knightley had spoken prophetically, when he once said, E III 11 402 1
Are you speaking of--Mr. Knightley?" E III 11 406 19
as to--if Mr. Knightley should really--if he does not mind E III 11 407 28
be in love with Mr. Knightley, than with Frank Churchill? E III 11 408 32
arrow, that Mr. Knightley must marry no one but herself! E III 11 408 32
herself loved by Mr. Knightley--but justice required that E III 11 408 33
Neither of them thought but of Mr. Knightley and E III 11 408 33
to declare, that Mr. Knightley is the last man in the E III 11 411 40
41

How long had Mr. Knightley been so dear to her, as every E III 11 412 45
did not consider Mr. Knightley as infinitely the superior, E III 11 412 45
the one revealed to her--her affection for Mr. Knightley.-- E III 11 412 46
on herself, and she too much feared, on Mr. Knightley.-- E III 11 413 47
Mr. Knightley and Harriet Smith!-- E III 11 413 48
Mr. Knightley and Harriet Smith!-- E III 11 413 48
the presumption to raise her thoughts to Mr. Knightley!-- E III 11 414 50
with Mr. Knightley, first in interest and affection.-- E III 12 415 1
exclusively, passionately loved by Mr. Knightley. E III 12 415 1
Let him but continue the same Mr. Knightley to her and her E III 12 416 1
father, the same Mr. Knightley to all the world; let E III 12 416 1
would not marry, even if she were asked by Mr. Knightley. E III 12 416 1
wedding-day; but Mr. Knightley had walked in then, soon E III 12 422 19
Mr. Knightley to be no longer coming there for his evening E III 12 422 20
when she saw Mr. Knightley passing through the garden door, E III 13 424 1
"Mr. Knightley," said Emma, trying to be lively, but E III 13 426 17
"He is a most fortunate man!" returned Mr. Knightley, with E III 13 428 23
to begin, when Mr. Knightley startled her, by saying, "you E III 13 429 26
27

just now, Mr. Knightley, and, I am afraid, gave you pain.-- E III 13 429 32
"As a friend!"--repeated Mr. Knightley.-- E III 13 429 33
She felt its inconsistency; but Mr. Knightley was so E III 13 431 38
Mr. Knightley could not impute to Emma a more relenting E III 13 431 39
As long as Mr. Knightley remained with them, Emma's fever E III 14 434 4
She hardly knew yet what Mr. Knightley would ask; but a E III 14 435 4
nearly sad, that Mr. Knightley, in walking up to Hartfield E III 14 435 5
She thought so well of the letter, that when Mr. Knightley E III 15 444 2
Mr. Knightley, had seen so much to blame in his conduct. E III 15 444 2
Mr. Knightley returned to his reading with greater E III 15 445 10
"I hope he does," replied Mr. Knightley coolly, and E III 15 447 24
English, such as Mr. Knightley used even to the woman he E III 15 448 31
her father, Mr. Knightley felt as strongly as herself; but E III 15 448 31
In time, of course, Mr. Knightley would be forgotten, that E III 15 450 38
Mr. Knightley himself would be doing nothing to assist the E III 15 450 38
Mr. Knightley, always so kind, so feeling, so truly E III 15 450 38
Mr. Knightley was at Hartfield yesterday, and spoke of it E III 16 456 28
for there; and Mr. Knightley might be preserved from E III 16 458 44
"That is," replied Mr. Knightley, "she will indulge her E III 17 461 3
saucy looks--'Mr. Knightley, I am going to do so and so; E III 17 462 9
"'Mr. Knightley.'-- E III 17 462 11
You always called me, 'Mr. Knightley;' and, from habit, it E III 17 462 11
I never can call you any thing but 'Mr. Knightley.' E III 17 463 14
does not even mention your friend," said Mr. Knightley. E III 17 464 17
continued Mr. Knightley, "but he is no complimenter; and E III 17 464 19
put it off; but Mr. Knightley was to come at such a time, E III 17 465 28
of all--she and Mr. Knightley meant to marry; by which E III 17 465 28
for having Mr. Knightley always at hand, when he were once E III 17 466 29
Did not he love Mr. Knightley very much?-- E III 17 466 29
he ever want to consult on business but Mr. Knightley?-- E III 17 466 29
Mr. Knightley could not be there too often; he should be E III 17 466 29
She had such a regard for Mr. Knightley, as to think he E III 17 467 31
And who but Mr. Knightley could know and bear with Mr. E III 17 467 31
Knightley came in, and distressing thoughts were put by. E III 18 470 1
"It is so, indeed," continued Mr. Knightley; "I have it E III 18 471 14
"I mean that he has done it," answered Mr. Knightley, with E III 18 471 18
best," replied Mr. Knightley; "but I should say she was a E III 18 473 25
But, Mr. Knightley, are you perfectly sure that she has E III 18 473 26
and air of Mr. Knightley and Robert Martin was, at this E III 18 473 27
"Do you dare say this?" cried Mr. Knightley. E III 18 474 28
of concealment from Mr. Knightley would soon be over. E III 18 475 42
demure for the moment--"I hope Mr. Knightley is well?" E III 18 477 58
59

her attachment to Mr. Knightley, and really able to accept E III 19 481 1
Knightley, and was now forming all her views of happiness. E III 19 481 1
for the Churchills--or even for Mr. Elton!-- E III 19 482 3
on, as far as they dared, by Emma and Mr. Knightley.-- E III 19 483 8
to join the hands of Mr. Knightley and Miss Woodhouse. E III 19 484 11

MR. KNIGHTLEY'S (30)

"Mr. Knightley's air is so remarkably good, that it is not E I 4 33 34
manners are superior to Mr. Knightley's or Mr. Weston's. E I 4 34 41
42

Neither would Mr. Knightley's downright, decided, E I 4 34 42
in spite of Mr. Knightley's pretensions) with the skill of E I 8 67 57
Mr. Woodhouse could never allow for Mr. Knightley's claims E I 9 80 65
see that it was Mr. Knightley's; for Mr. Knightley keeping E II 8 213 7
trouble us, for Mr. Knightley's carriage had brought, and E II 8 223 63
I cannot at all consent to Mr. Knightley's marrying; and I E II 8 224 66
Her objections to Mr. Knightley's marrying did not in the E II 8 227 87
from Donwell--some of Mr. Knightley's most liberal supply. E II 9 238 51
called Mr. Knightley's attention, and every syllable of E II 10 243 32
vexation Mr. Knightley's provoking indifference about it. E II 12 257 2
do you say now to Mr. Knightley's marrying Jane Fairfax?" E II 15 289 41
Mr. Knightley's words dwelt with her. E II 16 291 5
She was more disturbed by Mr. Knightley's not dancing, E III 2 325 32
Mr. Knightley's eyes had preceded Miss Bates's in a glance E III 5 346 17
Mr. Knightley's excessive curiosity to know what this word E III 5 348 23
presiding; Mr. Knightley's answer was the most distinct. E III 7 369 17
of Mr. Knightley's going to London; and going so suddenly; E III 9 386 9
Knightley's going to London had been an unexpected blow. E III 9 387 9
Mr. Knightley's coming and asking me to dance, when Mr. E III 11 406 24
you any idea of Mr. Knightley's returning your affection?" E III 11 407 29
30

favour of Mr. Knightley's most improved opinion of Harriet. E III 11 409 34
in marrying her, than she now seemed of Mr. Knightley's.-- E III 11 414 50
Had she followed Mr. Knightley's known wishes, in paying E III 12 421 17
dislike of Mr. Knightley's marrying Jane Fairfax, or any E III 15 449 35
Now Emma could, indeed, enjoy Mr. Knightley's visits; now E III 16 451 4
such an hour of Mr. Knightley's absence, or when it came E III 17 465 28
succeeded Mr. Knightley's, whose fond praise of her gave E III 17 466 30
sensible of Mr. Knightley's high superiority of character. E III 18 480 80

MR. KNIGHTLEYS (4)

other the two Mr. Knightleys; their subjects totally E I 12 100 15
that both the Mr. Knightleys were as unpersuadable on that E I 12 101 19
of both the Mr. Knightleys, that when once the event were E III 19 483 9
of the Mr. Knightleys, commanded his fullest dependance. E III 19 484 10

MR. MADDOX (1)

"and I can tell Mr. Maddox, that I shall shorten some of MP I 15 149 61

MR. MARTIN (35)

it appeared that the Mr. Martin, who bore a part in the E I 4 27 5
of Mr. Martin,--and there was evidently no dislike to it. E I 4 28 6
"Mr. Martin, I suppose, is not a man of information beyond E I 4 29 9
question was: "what sort of looking man is Mr. Martin?" E I 4 29 10
11

Mr. Martin, I imagine, has his fortune entirely to make-- E I 4 30 20
in this country when Mr. Martin marries, I wish you may E I 4 31 24
Not that I think Mr. Martin would ever marry any body but E I 4 31 25
They met Mr. Martin the very next day, as they were E I 4 31 27
Mr. Martin looked as if he did not know what manner was. E I 4 32 27
must yourself be struck with the difference in Mr. Martin. E I 4 32 32
be in company with Mr. Martin again without perceiving him E I 4 32 32
that it is not fair to compare Mr. Martin with <u>him</u>. E I 4 33 34
Compare Mr. Martin with either of <u>them</u>. E I 4 33 34
Mr. Martin is now awkward and abrupt; what will he be at E I 4 33 36
Mrs. Goddard's, that Mr. Martin had been there an hour E I 7 50 1
Mr. Martin, and contained a direct proposal of marriage. E I 7 50 1
If you prefer Mr. Martin to every other person; if you E I 7 53 21
and really almost made up my mind--to refuse Mr. Martin. E I 7 53 22
23

must have been the consequence of your marrying Mr. Martin. E I 7 53 24
However, I do really think Mr. Martin a very amiable young E I 7 54 30
was tender-hearted again towards the rejected Mr. Martin. E I 7 56 42
"how do you know that Mr. Martin did not speak yesterday?" E I 8 60 28
Mr. Martin is a very respectable young man, but I cannot E I 8 61 37
and all his merit Mr. Martin is nothing more,) a good E I 8 62 39
as well as myself; Mr. Martin may be the richest of the E I 8 62 39
"You are a very warm friend to Mr. Martin; but, as I said E I 8 63 44
back, not to think of Mr. Martin, but to talk of Mr. Elton. E I 8 68 58
I only want to know that Mr. Martin is not very, very E I 12 99 11
had been the cure of the agitation of meeting Mr. Martin. E II 4 184 11
"They told me--that Mr. Martin dined with them last E II 9 232 15
Martin--he might have Mr. Martin's interest in view?"-- E III 11 410 36
"Mr. Martin! E III 11 410 37
There was not a hint of Mr. Martin. E III 11 410 37
I hope I know better now, than to care for Mr. Martin, or E III 11 411 37
the terms on which Mr. Martin and Harriet now are?" E III 18 474 29

MR. MARTIN'S (3)

Emma was soon perfectly satisfied of Mr. Martin's being no E I 9 69 2
desired a more spirited rejection of Mr. Martin's prose. E I 9 76 36
Martin--he might have Mr. Martin's interest in view?"-- E III 11 410 36

MR. MORLAND (17)

Mr. Morland and my brother!" NA I 7 44 2
Do go and see for her, Mr. Morland, said I--but all in NA I 8 56 14
Was not it so, Mr. Morland? NA I 8 56 14
Mr. Morland, you are not to listen. NA I 8 57 16
"I tell you, Mr. Morland," she cried, "I would not do such NA I 8 57 21
"Now, Mr. Morland," for he was close to her on the other NA I 10 70 1
But I dare say, Mr. Morland, you long to be at it, do not NA I 11 90 63
He not only bestowed on Mr. Morland the high commendation NA I 15 121 27
A living, of which Mr. Morland was himself patron and NA II 1 135 42
"Mr. Morland has behaved vastly handsome indeed," said the NA II 1 135 44
and I dare say when Mr. Morland sees you, my dear child-- NA II 1 136 46
Mr. Morland has behaved so very handsome you know. NA II 1 136 46
"Nobody can think better of Mr. Morland than I do, I am NA II 1 136 47
"I think Mr. Morland would acknowledge a difference. NA II 4 151 12
I am very sorry for Mr. Morland--sorry that any one you NA II 10 204 20
to summon him; but Mr. Morland was from home--and being NA II 15 242 9
worded in a page full of empty professions to Mr. Morland. NA II 16 252 7

MR. MORLAND'S (7)

Morland's horse was so tired he could hardly get it along. NA I 15 116 1
only to want Mr. Morland's consent, to consider Isabella's NA I 15 120 25
The needful was comprised in Mr. Morland's promise; his NA I 15 122 28
material share in bringing on Mr. Morland's disappointment. NA II 10 204 20
Desirous of Mr. Morland's assistance, as well in giving NA II 15 242 9
the amount of Mr. Morland's preferment, trebling his NA II 15 245 12
understanding of Mr. Morland's circumstances which, as NA II 16 251 6

MR. MORRIS (1)

that he agreed with Mr. Morris immediately; that he is to PP I 1 3 10

MR. MUSGROVE (22)

I have not seen one of them to-day, except Mr. Musgrove, P III 5 38 29
And Mr. Musgrove always sits forward. P III 5 39 39
The Mr. Musgroves had their own game to guard, and to P III 6 42 3
Mr. Musgrove was, in a lesser degree, affected likewise; P III 6 51 32
at Kellynch, and Mr. Musgrove had called on him, and come P III 7 53 1
It had been a great disappointment to Mr. Musgrove, to P III 7 53 1
Captain Wentworth made a very early return to Mr. P III 7 53 2
enquiries; and Mr. Musgrove, no longer under the first P III 7 54 5
They were soon dining in company together at Mr. P III 8 63 1
<u>I</u> know what it is, for Mr. Musgrove always attends the P III 8 71 55
compared with Mr. Musgrove's; and while the Musgroves were P III 9 74 5
A dinner at Mr. Musgrove's had been the occasion, when all P III 9 77 17
on the occasion by Mr. Musgrove with some large books P III 10 82 2
night, but to this Mr. Musgrove, for the sake of his P III 11 94 8
the two carriages, Mr. Musgrove's coach containing the P III 11 95 8
the inn, and leave Mr. Musgrove's carriage and horses to P III 12 114 64
their visit; and Mr. Musgrove made a point of paying his P IV 2 134 29
an "answer from Mr. Musgrove; for it was all settled P IV 6 164 8
Hayter; and Mr. Musgrove has written "his consent, and P IV 6 165 8
remained with Mr. Musgrove and Louisa at Uppercross. P IV 10 217 19
such as "how Mr. Musgrove and my brother hayter had met P IV 11 230 5
one day, and what Mr. Musgrove had proposed the next, and P IV 11 230 5

MR. NORRIS (6)

attached to the Rev. Mr. Norris, a friend of her brother- MP I 1 3 1
I am sure Mr. Norris is too just--but you know I am a MP I 1 6 6
but just now, poor Mr. Norris took up every moment of her MP I 1 9 10
was the death of Mr. Norris, which happened when Fanny was MP I 3 23 1
my sister always meant to take you when Mr. Norris died. MP I 3 25 9
A great many things were due from poor Mr. Norris as MP I 3 30 50

MR. NORRIS'S (5)

Poor Mr. Norris's indifferent state of health made it an MP I 1 9 10
On Mr. Norris's death, the presentation became the right MP I 3 24 5
been done, but for poor Mr. Norris's sad state of health. MP I 6 54 9
It was only the spring twelvemonth before Mr. Norris's MP I 6 54 9
twice a year since Mr. Norris's death, she became a MP II 4 205 2

MR. OR MRS. ELTON (1)
I have never seen either Mr. or Mrs. Elton. E III 2 320 10

MR. OTWAY (1)
Mrs. Otway, I protest!--and good Mr. Otway, and Miss Otway E III 2 323 19

MR. OWEN (2)
His friend Mr. Owen had sisters--he might find them MP II 11 286 17
"He did not, the only time he went to see Mr. Owen before." MP II 11 287 21

MR. P.'S (1)
P.'s sprain proving too serious for him to move sooner.-- S 2 370 1

MR. PALMER (32)
Should not you, Mr. Palmer?" SS I 19 107 24
Mr. Palmer made her no answer, and did not even raise his SS I 19 107 25
"Mr. Palmer does not hear me," said she, laughing, "he SS I 19 107 26
to ask Mr. Palmer if there was any news in the paper. SS I 19 108 32
Mr. Palmer looked up on her entering the room, stared at SS I 19 108 35
When Lady Middleton rose to go away, Mr. Palmer rose also, SS I 19 108 37
then Mr. Palmer asked me if I would go with him to Barton. SS I 20 110 2
"As vile a spot as I ever saw in my life," said Mr. Palmer. SS I 20 111 15
"Then you would be very ill-bred," cried Mr. Palmer. SS I 20 111 22
"Mr. Palmer is so droll!" said she, in a whisper, to SS I 20 112 27
"There now"--said his lady, "you see Mr. Palmer expects SS I 20 113 31
are so gay now, for Mr. Palmer is always going about the SS I 20 113 33
Don't you, Mr. Palmer?" SS I 20 113 35
Mr. Palmer took no notice of her. SS I 20 113 36
asking her whether she did not like Mr. Palmer excessively. SS I 20 113 40
I thought you would, he is so pleasant; and Mr. Palmer is SS I 20 114 42
I do not think Mr. Palmer would visit him, for he is in SS I 20 114 44
pretty, and so does Mr. Palmer too I am sure, though we SS I 20 116 58
Mr. Palmer is just the kind of man I like." SS I 20 117 64
"Mr. Palmer will be so happy to see you," said she; "what SS II 4 164 22
After they had been assembled about an hour, Mr. Palmer SS II 5 171 30
Mr. Palmer maintained the common, but unfatherly opinion SS II 14 248 5
Mr. Palmer, or any friend that may be able to assist us.-- SS III 2 277 30
real politeness by Mr. Palmer himself, as, joined to the SS III 3 279 1
their journey, and Mr. Palmer, travelling more SS III 6 301 3
and wondered whether Mr. Palmer and Colonel Brandon would SS III 6 303 12
Elinor had seen so little of Mr. Palmer, and in that SS III 6 304 15
with her infant; and Mr. Palmer, though treating their SS III 7 307 3
Their party was now farther reduced; for Mr. Palmer, SS III 7 308 5
warmly seconded by Mr. Palmer, who seemed to feel a relief SS III 7 309 5
forgot to tell you that Mr. Palmer was not in the house." SS III 8 317 3
vehemence, "that Mr. Palmer and all his relations were at SS III 8 317 4

MR. PALMER'S (5)
a cause, at Mr. Palmer's acting so simply, with good SS I 21 118 1
"I had the pleasure of hearing it at Mr. Palmer's, where I SS II 4 163 15
When I got to Mr. Palmer's, I found Charlotte quite in a SS III 1 257 5
a near relation of Mr. Palmer's, who lived a few miles on SS III 7 308 3
Two days passed away from the time of Mr. Palmer's SS III 7 309 7

MR. PERRY (36)
He had been at the pains of consulting Mr. Perry, the E I 2 19 14
Mr. Perry was an intelligent, gentlemanlike man, whose E I 2 19 14
Mr. Perry had been to Mrs. Goddard's to attend a sick E I 8 68 58
to miss before; and Mr. Perry had remonstrated with him E I 8 68 58
Mr. Perry could not quite understand him, but he was very E I 8 68 58
Mr. Wingfield in town as her father could be of Mr. Perry. E I 11 92 4
one inquiry after Mr. Perry yet; and he never forgets you." E I 12 101 23
"Oh! good Mr. Perry--how is he, sir?" E I 12 101 24
I have a great regard for Mr. Perry. E I 12 101 26
"Mr. Perry," said he, in a voice of very strong E I 12 106 60
I hope, the use of my judgment as well as Mr. Perry.-- E I 12 106 60
dryness, "if Mr. Perry can tell me how to convey a wife E I 12 106 60
care and affection, Mr. Perry was talked of, and Harriet E I 13 109 5
Mr. Perry has been with her, as you probably heard." E I 13 114 32
till he had seen Mr. Perry and learnt his opinion; and E I 15 125 4
If Jane does not get well soon, we will call in Mr. Perry. E II 1 162 31
you yesterday he was precisely the height of Mr. Perry. E II 3 174 39
part of Highbury;--Mr. Perry walking hastily by, Mr. E II 9 233 24
of asking Mr. Perry; I happened to meet him in the street. E II 9 237 46
Mr. Perry might have reason to regret the alteration, but E II 11 251 27
if you suppose Mr. Perry to be that sort of character. E II 11 251 28
Mr. Perry is extremely concerned when any of us are ill. E II 11 251 28
Do not you remember what Mr. Perry said, so many years ago, E II 11 252 37
Mr. Perry did say so. E II 11 253 38
any benefit; and Mr. Perry, whose name, I dare say, is not E II 14 275 31
As they were turning into the grounds, Mr. Perry passed by E III 5 344 4
to write;" and when Mr. Perry called at Hartfield, the E III 9 389 16
apprehension of the family, Mr. Perry was uneasy about her. E III 9 389 16
eat any thing:--Mr. Perry recommended nourishing food; but E III 9 391 19
Mr. Perry is not gone." E III 13 429 32
he had received from Mr. Perry, and talked on with much E III 14 434 3
last night, by Mr. Perry, that it had not made him ill. E III 14 436 7
I mean good Mr. Perry!--such attention to Jane!"-- E III 16 455 20
she had been within half a minute of sending for Mr. Perry. E III 18 479 73
"My friend Mr. Perry! E III 18 479 75
What are they saying about Mr. Perry?-- E III 18 479 75

MR. PERRY'S (3)
became of Mr. Perry's plan of setting up his carriage?" E III 5 344 5
that she had Mr. Perry's decided opinion, in favour of E III 9 390 16
introduce; and on Mr. Perry's coming in soon after dinner, E III 13 424 1

MR. PHILIPS (2)
Mr. Philips visited them all, and this opened to his PP I 7 28 4
which your uncle, Mr. Philips, appears to do so much PP I 16 81 37

MR. PHILIPS'S (2)
to the door of Mr. Philips's house, and then made their PP I 15 73 10
and herself, in their first evening at Mr. Philips's. PP II 13 206 5

MR. PHILLIPS (1)
She had a sister married to a Mr. Phillips, who had been a PP I 7 28 2

MR. PRATT (5)
"Yes; Mr. Pratt. SS I 22 130 26
Did you never hear him talk of Mr. Pratt?" SS I 22 130 26
in the house of Mr. Pratt was a foundation for the rest, SS II 1 139 1
what little matter Mr. Steele and Mr. Pratt can give her.-- SS III 2 276 28
from the care of Mr. Pratt, I think-- nay, I am sure, it SS III 13 362 5

MR. PRATT'S (4)
him to Mr. Pratt's, all this would have been prevented.' SS II 14 251 13
abode in Mr. Pratt's family, with any satisfaction. SS II 14 251 14
were probably going down to Mr. Pratt's, near Plymouth. SS III 11 355 39
"He comes from Mr. Pratt's purposely to see us. SS III 12 358 8

MR. PRICE (12)
your sister dance, Mr. Price," said Henry Crawford, MP II 7 250 61
the door of a small house now inhabited by Mr. Price. MP III 7 376 6
and lastly in walked Mr. Price himself, his own loud voice MP III 7 379 19
had quite forgot her, Mr. Price now received his daughter; MP III 7 380 22
the sally-port; and Mr. Price walked off at the same time MP III 7 384 36
Mr. Price was out, which she regretted very much. MP III 10 400 6
man, a very different Mr. Price in his behaviour to this MP III 10 402 12
but for Mr. Crawford, Mr. Price would have turned thither MP III 10 402 13
singular manner, had Mr. Price been allowed the entire MP III 10 403 14
or any crowd, when Mr. Price was only calling out, "come MP III 10 403 14
When Mr. Price and his friend had seen all that they MP III 10 406 21
Mr. Price cared too little about the report, to make her MP III 15 440 17

MR. PRICE'S (3)
was an offer of Mr. Price's to take Mr. Crawford into the MP III 10 402 13
brother lounger of Mr. Price's, who was come to take his MP III 10 403 15
was seen of him at Mr. Price's; and two days afterwards, MP III 12 415 1

MR. R. (2)
in the family of Mr. R. of Wimpole Street; the beautiful MP III 15 440 14
friend and associate of Mr. R. and it was not known, even MP III 15 440 14

MR. REPTON (2)
Miss Bertram, calmly, "would be Mr. Repton, I imagine." MP I 6 53 7
most thankful to any Mr. Repton who would undertake it, MP I 6 57 29

MR. RICHARD (2)
Where's dear Mr. Richard?-- E III 2 323 19
How do you do, Mr. Richard?-- E III 2 323 19

MR. ROBERT FERRARS (4)
Are you acquainted with Mr. Robert Ferrars? SS I 22 129 13
"Do you know Mr. Robert Ferrars?" asked Elinor. SS II 2 148 18
Mr. Dashwood introduced him to her as Mr. Robert Ferrars. SS II 14 250 11
from her brother, by the entrance of Mr. Robert Ferrars. SS III 5 297 32

MR. ROBERT MARTIN (2)
quick eye sufficiently acquainted with Mr. Robert Martin. E I 4 31 27
She is superior to Mr. Robert Martin." E I 8 62 41

MR. ROBERTSON (1)
of Mr. Hume or Mr. Robertson, than if the genuine words of NA I 14 109 23

MR. ROBINSON (4)
it-- but I hardly know what--something about Mr. Robinson. PP I 5 18 6
between him and Mr. Robinson; did not I mention it to you? PP I 5 19 7
and though Mr. Robinson felt and felt, and rubbed, and P III 7 54 4
to the spine, but Mr. Robinson found nothing to increase P III 7 55 7

MR. ROBINSON'S (2)
Mr. Robinson's asking him how he liked our Meryton PP I 5 19 7
I perfectly understand Mr. Robinson's directions, and have P III 7 56 11

MR. ROSE (1)
Now there's Mr. Rose at Exeter, a prodigious smart young SS I 21 123 28

MR. RUSHWORTH (110)
Mr. Rushworth was from the first struck with the beauty of MP I 4 38 10
a marriage with Mr. Rushworth would give her the enjoyment MP I 4 38 10
her evident duty to marry Mr. Rushworth if she could. MP I 4 38 10
an acquaintance, Mr. Rushworth appeared precisely the MP I 4 39 10
induce him to find Mr. Rushworth a desirable companion. MP I 4 39 13
"Why as to that--Mr. Rushworth is a very good sort of MP I 5 45 13
sure Miss Bertram is very much attached to Mr. Rushworth. MP I 5 45 14
and in observing Mr. Rushworth, who was now making his MP I 6 52 1
by an improver, Mr. Rushworth was returned with his head MP I 6 52 1
"No wonder that Mr. Rushworth should think so at present," MP I 6 53 5
"I must try to do something with it," said Mr. Rushworth, " MP I 6 53 6
After a short interruption, Mr. Rushworth began again. MP I 6 55 15
"Mr. Rushworth," said Lady Bertram, "if I were you, I MP I 6 55 16
Mr. Rushworth was eager to assure her ladyship of his MP I 6 55 17
Mr. Rushworth, however, though not usually a great talker, MP I 6 55 17
Mr. Rushworth is quite right, I think, in meaning to give MP I 6 56 26
"I do not wish to influence Mr. Rushworth," he continued, " MP I 6 56 28
I am inclined to envy Mr. Rushworth for having so much MP I 6 61 56
Instead of envying Mr. Rushworth, you should assist him MP I 6 61 57
professional man, Mr. Rushworth was very ready to request MP I 6 61 58
Mr. Rushworth then began to propose Mr. Crawford's doing MP I 6 61 58
my dear Mr. Rushworth, and that would like to hear Mr. MP I 6 62 58
As Mr. Rushworth did not come, the injury was increased, MP I 7 70 30
While she was gone, Mr. Rushworth arrived, escorting his MP I 8 75 1
Miss Bertram, Mr. Rushworth discovered that the properest MP I 8 75 1
Mr. Rushworth came back from the parsonage successful; and MP I 8 77 7
Mr. Rushworth has made it since he succeeded to the estate. MP I 8 82 34
Mr. Rushworth talked of the west front." MP I 8 82 35
about, when Mr. Rushworth had asked her opinion, and her MP I 8 83 37
Mr. Rushworth was at the door to receive his fair lady, MP I 9 84 1
Mr. Rushworth mentioned his curricle. MP I 9 84 1
But the late Mr. Rushworth left it off." MP I 9 86 9
"do look at Mr. Rushworth and Maria, standing side by side, MP I 9 88 19
comprehension of Mr. Rushworth and his mother, and expose MP I 9 88 24
How unlucky that you are not ordained, Mr. Rushworth and MP I 9 89 25
Mr. Rushworth, shall we summon a council on this lawn?" MP I 9 90 34
Miss Bertram and Mr. Rushworth, and when after a little MP I 9 90 36
Miss Bertram, Mr. Rushworth, and Mr. Crawford, issued from MP I 10 97 1
her, and then by Mr. Rushworth, whose principal business MP I 10 97 3
Mr. Rushworth wished he had brought the key; he had been MP I 10 98 4
"Mr. Rushworth is so long fetching this key!" MP I 10 99 17
Mr. Rushworth will be here in a moment you know--we shall MP I 10 99 19
She expected Mr. Rushworth, but it was Julia, who hot and MP I 10 100 24
"But, Julia, Mr. Rushworth will be here in a moment with MP I 10 100 27
Do wait for Mr. Rushworth." MP I 10 100 27
notice, only asked her if she had not seen Mr. Rushworth. MP I 10 101 29
now sat of seeing Mr. Rushworth prevented her thinking so MP I 10 101 33
Mr. Rushworth was worked on. MP I 10 103 48
She felt, as she looked at Julia and Mr. Rushworth, that MP I 10 104 51
Miss Bertrams, Mr. Rushworth, and Henry Crawford, were all MP I 11 108 4
the group and saying, "how happy Mr. Rushworth looks! MP I 11 108 4
Edmund looked round at Mr. Rushworth too, but had nothing MP I 11 108 5
Maria, with only Mr. Rushworth to attend to her, and MP I 12 115 4
directed towards Mr. Rushworth and Maria, who were MP I 12 117 12
Mr. Rushworth is never remiss. MP I 12 117 14
Mr. Rushworth has set a good example, and such things are MP I 12 118 16
now cast, besides Mr. Rushworth, who was always answered MP I 14 133 8
arrived, and another character was consequently cast. MP I 15 138 1
Mr. Rushworth liked the idea of his finery very well, MP I 15 138 1
Mr. Yates; and Mr. Rushworth stepped forward with great MP I 15 138 2
his only reply to Mr. Rushworth; and he turned towards his MP I 15 139 5
Mr. Rushworth followed him to say, "I come in three times, MP I 15 139 10
afterwards by Mr. Rushworth, Edmund almost immediately MP I 15 139 11
As Mr. Rushworth is to act too, there can be no harm.-- MP I 15 141 22
company, and Mr. Rushworth having only his own part, and MP I 15 142 24
"Mr. Rushworth was to be Count Cassel, but no one had yet MP I 15 143 28
"I had my choice of the parts," said Mr. Rushworth; "but I MP I 15 143 29
speeches," returned Mr. Rushworth, "which is no trifle." MP I 15 144 31
Rushworth, "what would you do with such a part as mine?" MP I 15 145 48
and Mr. Rushworth undertook to count his speeches. MP I 17 158 2
Think of Mr. Rushworth." MP I 17 161 12
had better tell Miss Bertram to think of Mr. Rushworth. MP I 17 161 13
shameful towards herself, as well as towards Mr. Rushworth. MP I 17 162 19
Rushworth, who was wanting a prompter through every speech. MP I 18 164 2
She knew, also, that poor Mr. Rushworth could seldom get MP I 18 164 2
at last, when Mr. Rushworth turned to her with a black MP I 18 165 3
to herself, and of avoiding the sight of Mr. Rushworth. MP I 18 168 14
trying not to embrace, and Mr. Rushworth was with me. MP I 18 169 21
the evening, and Mr. Rushworth might imagine it a blessing, MP II 1 175 1
Mr. Rushworth was not forgotten; a most friendly reception MP II 1 179 8
Mr. Rushworth could be silent no longer. MP II 1 186 31
"If I must say what I think," continued Mr. Rushworth, "in MP II 1 186 33
a genius in Mr. Rushworth; but as a well-judging steady MP II 1 186 35
Mr. Rushworth hardly knew what to do with so much meaning; MP II 1 186 35
come of it--for Mr. Rushworth is the sort of amiable MP II 2 188 3
other day, 'if Mr. Rushworth were a son of your own he MP II 2 190 7
Mr. Rushworth had set off early with the great news for MP II 2 192 11
I hope my uncle may continue to like Mr. Rushworth." MP II 3 199 17
his good-will for Mr. Rushworth, not all Mr. Rushworth's MP II 3 200 19
the truth--that Mr. Rushworth was an inferior young man, MP II 3 200 19
Her behaviour to Mr. Rushworth was careless and cold. MP II 3 200 20
Mr. Rushworth had perhaps been accepted on too short an MP II 3 200 20
Mr. Rushworth was young enough to improve;--Mr. Rushworth MP II 3 201 22
cautiously to Mr. Rushworth in future, that her father MP II 3 201 23
been an evil, and Mr. Rushworth could hardly be more MP II 3 202 26
which Mr. Rushworth had used for a twelvemonth before. MP II 3 203 29
Some other companion than Mr. Rushworth was of the first MP II 3 204 32
It was not Mr. Rushworth, however, but Edmund, who then MP II 4 211 22
their relations, and Mr. Rushworth is a most amiable man. MP II 7 245 32
and you will find Mr. Rushworth most sincerely disposed to MP II 7 245 34
satisfaction than I gave Maria's to Mr. Rushworth." MP III 1 319 39
He who had married a daughter to Mr. Rushworth. MP III 2 331 17
by poor Mr. Rushworth, not seeming to care how he exposed MP III 4 349 25

I do think that Mr. Rushworth was sometimes very jealous." MP III 4 350 27
sense, Fanny, as Mr. Rushworth, but much worse looking, MP III 5 361 16
I was sorry that Mr. Rushworth should resent any former MP III 13 423 2
Mr. Rushworth had been gone, at this time, to Bath, to MP III 16 450 8
remarks, and evidently making Mr. Rushworth uneasy. MP III 16 450 8
Mrs. Rushworth had left her husband's house; Mr. Rushworth MP III 16 450 9
Mr. Rushworth had no difficulty in procuring a divorce; MP III 17 464 12
MR. RUSHWORTH'S (25)
the expediency of Mr. Rushworth's marrying Miss Bertram. MP I 4 39 11
to himself, in Mr. Rushworth's company, "if this man had MP I 4 40 13
good humour, on Mr. Rushworth's account, who was partly MP I 7 70 30
Mr. Rushworth's consequence was hers. MP I 8 81 33
it was now all Mr. Rushworth's property on each side of MP I 8 81 33
declaring outright that he would go and fetch the key. MP I 10 98 4
key and without Mr. Rushworth's authority and protection, MP I 10 99 18
to receive Mr. Rushworth's parting attentions as she ought. MP I 10 105 52
I often think of Mr. Rushworth's property and independence, MP I 17 161 13
"I would not give much for Mr. Rushworth's chance, if MP I 17 162 17
the chances of Mr. Rushworth's ever attaining to the MP I 18 165 4
to contrive Mr. Rushworth's cloak without sending for any MP I 18 166 6
They walked off, utterly heedless of Mr. Rushworth's MP II 1 176 3
There was nothing disagreeable in Mr. Rushworth's MP II 1 179 8
whisked away Mr. Rushworth's pink satin cloak as her MP II 1 179 10
Sir Thomas meant to be giving Mr. Rushworth's opinion in MP II 1 186 35
bringing Mr. Rushworth's admiration of Maria to any effect. MP II 2 188 3
There is nothing very striking in Mr. Rushworth's manners, MP II 2 190 6
not all Mr. Rushworth's deference for him, could prevent MP II 3 200 19
She had the highest esteem for Mr. Rushworth's character MP II 3 200 21
pleasures of Mr. Rushworth's wife must be to fill her MP II 4 210 21
Fanny, he said, "you were Mr. Rushworth's best friend. MP II 5 224 53
as Mr. Rushworth's fine fortune gives them a right to be. MP II 7 245 32
influence of Mr. Rushworth's mother, that the worst MP III 16 450 9
in town, and Mr. Rushworth's house became Crawford's MP III 17 466 18
MR. SCOTT (1)
talking as before of Mr. Scott and Lord Byron, and still P III 12 107 23
MR. SHEPHERD (22)
hints of Mr. Shepherd, his agent, from his thoughts. P III 1 9 19
Their two confidential friends, Mr. Shepherd, who lived in P III 1 10 21
Mr. Shepherd, a civil, cautious lawyer, who, whatever P III 2 11 1
The hint was immediately taken up by Mr. Shepherd, whose P III 2 13 7
of London, but Mr. Shepherd felt that he could not be P III 2 14 10
Mr. Shepherd had once mentioned the word, "advertise;"-- P III 2 15 14
It was with a daughter of Mr. Shepherd, who had returned, P III 2 15 15
Sir Walter," said Mr. Shepherd one morning at Kellynch P III 3 17 1
Mr. Shepherd laughed, as he knew he must, at this wit, and P III 3 17 2
3
After a short pause, Mr. Shepherd presumed to say, "in all P III 3 18 9
10
It seemed as if Mr. Shepherd, in this anxiety to bespeak P III 3 21 18
he had foretold, Mr. Shepherd observed, Sir Walter's P III 3 21 18
feel; and given Mr. Shepherd, in his explicit account of P III 3 21 18
Mr. Shepherd answered for his being of a gentleman's P III 3 21 20
21
Mr. Shepherd hastened to assure him, that Admiral Croft P III 3 22 23
Mr. Shepherd was eloquent on the subject; pointing out all P III 3 22 24
A house was never taken good care of, Mr. Shepherd P III 3 22 24
Mr. Shepherd was all gratitude. P III 3 23 31
As Mr. Shepherd perceived that this connexion of the P III 3 23 34
into allowing Mr. Shepherd to proceed in the treaty, and P III 3 24 35
Mr. Shepherd was completely empowered to act; and no P III 3 24 38
thinks it the greatest improvement the house ever had. P IV 1 127 28
MR. SHEPHERD'S (4)
What Miss Anne says, is very true," was Mr. Shepherd's P III 3 19 13
14
his (Mr. Shepherd's) connection with the owner, he had P III 3 21 18
behaviour by Mr. Shepherd's assurances of his being known, P III 5 32 2
was right; and Mr. Shepherd's clerks were set to work, P III 5 32 3
MR. SIMPSON (1)
a beau, clerk to Mr. Simpson you know, and yet if you do SS I 21 123 28
MR. SMALLRIDGE'S (1)
to Mr. Smallridge's, near Bristol, stared me in the face. E III 14 442 8
MR. SMITHS (1)
One of the five thousand Mr. Smiths whose names are to be P IV 5 157 15
MR. STEELE (1)
what little matter Mr. Steele and Mr. Pratt can give her.-- SS III 2 276 28
MR. SUCKLING (9)
possible; and Mr. Suckling is extremely fond of exploring. E II 14 274 28
all affect to equal my brother, Mr. Suckling, in income.-- E II 15 283 9
A cousin of Mr. Suckling, Mrs. Bragge, had such an E II 17 299 8
Mr. Suckling was always rather a friend to the abolition." E II 17 300 14
You would be amazed to hear how my brother, Mr. Suckling, E II 18 306 10
who happens to be one of their nearest neighbours. E II 18 310 34
Mr. Suckling, who has been eleven years a resident at E II 18 310 34
Mr. Suckling had completed the purchase before his death." E II 18 310 34
Neither Mr. Suckling nor me had ever any patience with E III 2 321 15
MR. SUCKLING'S (1)
Suckling's seat"--a comparison of Hartfield to Maple Grove. E II 14 272 18
MR. THOMAS (1)
Mr.--and Mr. Edmund is no more than Mr. John or Mr. Thomas. MP II 4 211 24
MR. THORPE (26)
it was, "have you ever read Udolpho, Mr. Thorpe?" NA I 7 48 32
non-appearance of Mr. Thorpe, for she not only longed to NA I 8 53 2
by seeing, not Mr. Thorpe, but Mr. Tilney, within three NA I 8 53 3
in her going with Mr. Thorpe, as Isabella was going at the NA I 9 61 6
"You do not really think, Mr. Thorpe," said Catherine, NA I 9 65 27
Do let us turn back, Mr. Thorpe; stop and speak to my NA I 9 65 29
of requesting from Mr. Thorpe a clearer insight into his NA I 9 66 31
But I really had been engaged the whole day to Mr. Thorpe." NA I 10 72 11
"Mr. Thorpe is such a very particular friend of my NA I 10 78 38
"Isabella, my brother, and Mr. Thorpe, I declare! NA I 11 84 18
"Stop, stop, Mr. Thorpe, she impatiently cried, it is Miss NA I 11 87 53
"Pray, pray stop, Mr. Thorpe.-- NA I 11 87 53
But Mr. Thorpe only laughed, smacked his whip, encouraged NA I 11 87 53
"How could you deceive me so, Mr. Thorpe?-- NA I 11 87 53
was gone out with Mr. Thorpe, the lady had asked whether NA I 11 89 62
thing; but I begged Mr. Thorpe so earnestly to stop; I NA I 12 94 8
I did; and, if Mr. Thorpe would only have stopped, I would NA I 12 94 8
"How came Mr. Thorpe to know your father?" was her anxious NA I 12 95 17
"But why cannot Mr. Thorpe drive one of his other sisters? NA I 13 99 6
Mr. Thorpe had no business to invent any such message. NA I 13 100 20
how do I know that Mr. Thorpe has-----he may be mistaken NA I 13 101 20
Let me go, Mr. Thorpe; Isabella, do not hold me." Tilneys; NA I 13 101 20
not have gone with Mr. Thorpe at all; but I always hoped NA I 13 104 35
you, my dear, not to go out with Mr. Thorpe any more." NA I 13 105 38
of every thought of Mr. Thorpe's being in love with her, NA II 3 144 11
and thankful for Mr. Thorpe's communication, he almost NA II 15 245 12
MR. TILNEY (35)
guessed it, madam," said Mr. Tilney, looking at the muslin. NA I 3 28 36
Mr. Tilney was polite enough to seem interested in what NA I 3 29 47
How proper Mr. Tilney might be as a dreamer or a lover, NA I 3 30 52
herself of seeing Mr. Tilney there before the morning were NA I 4 31 1
no smile was demanded--Mr. Tilney did not appear. NA I 4 31 1
almost forgot Mr. Tilney while she talked to Miss Thorpe. NA I 4 33 6
an inquiring eye for Mr. Tilney in every box which her eye NA I 5 35 1
Mr. Tilney was no fonder of the play than the Pump-Room. NA I 5 35 1
about Mr. Tilney, for perhaps I may never see him again." NA I 6 41 17
I have not forgot your description of Mr. Tilney;--"a NA I 6 42 30
not Mr. Thorpe, but Mr. Tilney, within three yards of the NA I 8 53 3
her head that Mr. Tilney could be married; he had not NA I 8 53 3
Mr. Tilney and his companion, who continued, though slowly, NA I 8 54 4
This was accordingly done, Mr. Tilney still continuing NA I 8 54 10
that part of the room where she had left Mr. Tilney. NA I 8 55 10
her relationship to Mr. Tilney, was desirous of being NA I 8 56 11
of all Isabella's impatient desire to see Mr. Tilney. NA I 8 57 21
ever willing to give Mr. Tilney an opportunity of NA I 8 58 25
"Did you meet Mr. Tilney, my dear?" said Mrs. Allen. NA I 8 58 28
The rest of the evening she found very dull; Mr. Tilney NA I 8 59 38
"And is Mr. Tilney, my partner, the only son?" NA I 9 69 49
already; and as for Mr. Tilney--but that is a settled NA I 10 70 1
not expect that Mr. Tilney should ask her a third time to NA I 10 74 23
and again solicited to dance, by Mr. Tilney himself. NA I 10 75 24
her, asked by Mr. Tilney, as if he had sought her on NA I 10 75 24
Mr. Tilney was very much amused. NA I 10 79 55
saw him presently address Mr. Tilney in a familiar whisper. NA I 10 80 59
the latter: "Oh! Mr. Tilney, I have been quite wild to NA I 12 93 5
Did not they tell me that Mr. Tilney and his sister were NA I 12 93 5
Tilney, why were you less generous than your sister? NA I 12 94 11
"Oh! Mr. Tilney, how frightful!-- NA II 5 159 18
"Mr. Tilney!" she exclaimed in a voice of more than common NA II 9 194 6
"Oh! why do not you fit up this room, Mr. Tilney? NA II 11 214 21
Mr. Tilney drank tea with us, and I always thought him a NA II 14 238 26
being applied to by Mr. Tilney, for their consent to his NA II 16 249 1
MR. TILNEY'S (3)
been assured of Mr. Tilney's being a clergyman, and of a NA I 3 30 52
catching Mr. Tilney's eye, instantly received from him the NA I 8 54 4
her friend from James--"it is Mr. Tilney's sister." NA I 8 56 15
MR. VERNON (1)
he appears both to Mr. Vernon & me a very weak young man. LS 20 276 2
MR. WENTWORTH (7)
After waiting another moment-- "you mean Mr. Wentworth, I P III 3 23 29
30
Mr. Wentworth was the very man. P III 3 23 32
Oh! ay,--Mr. Wentworth, the curate of Monkford. P III 3 23 33
Mr. Wentworth was nobody, I remember; quite unconnected; P III 3 23 33
He was not Mr. Wentworth, the former curate of Monkford, P III 4 26 1
it to be Mr. Wentworth of whom she spoke, that she had P III 6 49 22
Mr. Wentworth, of Monkford, Captain Wentworth's brother. P IV 8 187 35
MR. WESTON (144)
Mr. Weston was a man of unexceptionable character, easy E I 1 6 6
What a pity it is that Mr. Weston ever thought of her!" E I 1 8 11
Mr. Weston is such a good-humoured, pleasant, excellent E I 1 8 12
We talked it all over with Mr. Weston last night. E I 1 8 18
would never marry again, may comfort me for any thing." E I 1 11 39
Every body said that Mr. Weston would never marry again. E I 1 12 41
Mr. Weston, who had been a widower so long, and who seemed E I 1 12 41
always cheerful--Mr. Weston need not spend a single E I 1 12 41
Mr. Weston certainly would never marry again. E I 1 12 41
for Miss Taylor if Mr. Weston were to marry her,' and E I 1 12 42
Mr. Weston was a native of Highbury, and born of a E I 2 15 1
What say you to Mr. Weston and Mr. Elton? E I 4 33 34
But Mr. Weston is almost an old man. E I 4 33 35
Mr. Weston must be between forty and fifty." E I 4 33 35
a bluntness in Mr. Weston, which every body likes in him E I 4 34 42
"Mr. Weston would undoubtedly support me, if he were here, E I 5 36 6
merit in making a good wife to such a man as Mr. Weston." E I 5 38 12
have we seen either Mr. Weston or Mrs. Weston, and E I 11 94 14
Mr. Weston is really as kind as herself. E I 11 94 14
"It would be very hard upon Mr. Weston if she did not, E I 11 95 17
You quite forget poor Mr. Weston." E I 11 95 17
pleasantly, "that Mr. Weston has some little claim. E I 11 95 18
of putting all the Mr. Westons aside as much as she can." E I 11 95 18
and as to slighting Mr. Weston, that excellent Mr. Weston, E I 11 95 19
Mr. Weston, I think there is nothing he does not deserve. E I 11 95 19
I never can comprehend how Mr. Weston could part with him. E I 11 96 25
"But you need not imagine Mr. Weston to have felt what you E I 11 96 26
Mr. Weston is rather an easy, cheerful tempered man, than E I 11 96 26
on a reflection on Mr. Weston, and had half a mind to take E I 11 96 27
Mr. Weston would take no denial; they must all dine at E I 13 108 2
Mr. Weston was a great favourite, and there was not a E I 14 117 1
She heard enough to know that Mr. Weston was giving some E I 14 118 4
or the substance of it, from the open-hearted Mr. Weston.-- E I 14 119 6
Elton, and seated by Mr. Weston, at dinner, he made use of E I 14 119 6
7
"He has been wanting to come to us," continued Mr. Weston, E I 14 119 9
Emma; "but am disposed to side with you, Mr. Weston. E I 14 120 12
I cannot be so sanguine as Mr. Weston. E I 14 121 14
Mr. Weston, I dare say, has been telling you exactly how E I 14 121 14
on his coming, and I wish Mr. Weston were less sanguine." E I 14 122 21
Mr. Weston was chatty and convivial, and no friend to E I 15 124 1
Mr. Weston, with triumph of a different sort, was E I 15 126 11
by Mr. Knightley and Mr. Weston; but not all that either E I 15 128 22
For half an hour Mr. Weston was surprized and sorry; but E I 18 144 2
Mr. Weston would not be blind to folly, though in his own E I 18 148 23
in sound--for Mr. Weston immediately accosted her with, " E II 5 188 6
7
Mr. Weston gave her the history of the engagements at E II 5 188 9
"We had better move on, Mr. Weston," said she, "we are E II 5 189 12
gentlemen sitting with her father--Mr. Weston and his son. E II 5 190 21
They had been arrived only a few minutes, and Mr. Weston E II 5 190 21
"I told you yesterday," cried Mr. Weston with exultation, " E II 5 190 24
She had no doubt of what Mr. Weston was often thinking E II 5 192 34
A reasonable visit paid, Mr. Weston began to move.-- E II 5 193 36
Emma had hardly expected them: for Mr. Weston, who had E II 6 196 2
Mr. Weston, on his side, added a virtue to the account E II 7 206 3
she had little hope of Mr. Knightley, none of Mr. Weston. E II 7 207 6
"Well, sir," cried Mr. Weston, "as I took Miss Taylor away, E II 7 209 11
Mr. Weston must be quiet, and every thing deliberately E II 7 209 12
"But my dear sir," cried Mr. Weston, "if Emma comes away E II 7 210 17
Mr. Weston, I am much obliged to you for reminding me. E II 7 210 20
I could not bear the idea of it; so, as soon as Mr. Weston E II 8 223 63
in spite of all that Mr. Weston could say of their exactly E II 11 247 2
Mr. Weston entered into the idea with thorough enjoyment, E II 11 247 3
Cox; and at last, Mr. Weston naming one family of cousins E II 11 248 9
And Mr. Weston at the same time, walking briskly with long E II 11 254 47
48
Here Mr. Weston joined them, and on hearing what was E II 11 255 54
Mr. Weston whisper to his wife, "he has asked her, my dear. E II 11 256 60
Mr. Weston, always alert when business was to be done, and E II 12 261 35
Mr. Weston seems an excellent creature--quite a first-rate E II 14 278 44
John Knightley came; but Mr. Weston was unexpectedly E II 16 292 9
when Mr. Weston made his appearance among them. E II 17 302 23
Mr. Weston meanwhile, perfectly unsuspicious of the E II 17 303 24
Mr. Weston, however, too eager to be very observant, too E II 17 304 29
pleasure of introducing my son to you," said Mr. Weston. E II 18 305 1
affectedly) I must protest against that.-- E II 18 305 6
Oh! Mr. Weston, I could not have believed it of you!" E II 18 305 6
But what is distance, Mr. Weston, to people of large E II 18 306 10
"The evil of the distance from Enscombe," said Mr. Weston, E II 18 306 11
Mrs. Elton eagerly interposed with, "Oh! Mr. Weston, do E II 18 306 14
15
in what way she had best retract, when Mr. Weston went on. E II 18 307 17
"If she is really ill, why not go to Bath, Mr. Weston?-- E II 18 307 19
to be passed by, and Mr. Weston, with a very good grace, E II 18 307 24
25
"Very true, Mr. Weston, perfectly true. E II 18 308 28
Mr. Weston instantly seized the opportunity of going on. E II 18 308 29
"And I assure you, Mr. Weston, I have very little doubt E II 18 309 31
Mr. Weston was musing. E II 18 309 32
which is not a place to promise much, you know, Mr. Weston. E II 18 310 34
Tea was carrying round, and Mr. Weston, having said all E II 18 310 35
It was not very long, though rather longer than Mr. Weston E III 1 315 3
Emma saw how Mr. Weston understood these joyous prospects. E III 1 317 9
Mr. Weston had been so very earnest in his entreaties for E III 2 319 2
only taste on which Mr. Weston depended, and felt, that to E III 2 319 4

"But Miss Bates and Miss Fairfax!" said Mr. Weston, E III 2 320 12
Mr. Weston was following; but Mrs. Elton detained him, to E III 2 321 14
"A very fine young man indeed, Mr. Weston. E III 2 321 15
Oh! Mr. Weston, you must really have had Aladdin's Lamp. E III 2 322 19
we to do for a proper partner for her?" said Mr. Weston. E III 2 325 30
Mr. Weston and Mrs. Elton led the way, Mr. Frank Churchill E III 2 325 31
Mr. Weston might be his son's superior.-- E III 2 325 32
They were interrupted by the bustle of Mr. Weston calling E III 2 331 56
What is this?" cried Mr. Weston, "about Perry and a E III 5 345 12
Mr. Weston had walked in. E III 5 346 17
animated sort, which Mr. Weston had occasionally E III 5 347 20
seeing, and she and Mr. Weston had agreed to choose some E III 6 352 2
on hearing from Mr. Weston that he had been proposing to E III 6 353 3
Mrs. Elton, of which Mr. Weston must already be perfectly E III 6 353 3
day, and settle with Mr. Weston as to pigeon-pies and cold E III 6 353 6
from it; and Mr. Weston, unasked, promised to get Frank E III 6 357 31
glad to see him; and Mr. Weston engaged to lose no time in E III 6 357 31
In this walk Emma and Mr. Weston found all the others E III 6 360 40
Mr. Weston directed the whole, officiating safely between E III 7 367 1
And Mr. Weston tried, in vain, to make them harmonize E III 7 367 1
any cold collation, or any cheerful Mr. Weston, to remove. E III 7 367 1
There are one or two, perhaps, (glancing at Mr. Weston and E III 7 370 19
"I like your plan," cried Mr. Weston. E III 7 371 29
"I doubt it's being very clever myself," said Mr. Weston. E III 7 371 32
that is wanted, and Mr. Weston has done very well for E III 7 371 35
36
Mr. Weston, his son, Emma, and Harriet, only remained; and E III 7 374 54
Even Mr. Weston shook his head, and looked solemn, and E III 9 388 13
down stairs to Mr. Weston, who "could not stay five E III 10 392 1
walk now, she and Mr. Weston were soon out of the house E III 10 392 7
gates,--"now Mr. Weston, do let me know what has happened." E III 10 392 8
"Good God!--Mr. Weston, tell me at once.-- E III 10 393 10
"Mr. Weston do not trifle with me.-- E III 10 393 12
Mr. Weston in keeping his secret, than with any other view. E III 10 394 19
"Mr. Weston will be almost as much relieved as myself," E III 10 396 43
At this moment Mr. Weston appeared at a little distance E III 10 400 65
She met Mr. Weston on his entrance, with a smiling E III 10 400 67
68
I congratulate you, Mr. Weston, with all my heart, on the E III 10 400 68
of owning it to me, for Mr. Weston has told me himself. E III 11 404 6
"What did Mr. Weston tell you?"--said Emma, still E III 11 404 7
Mr. Weston had accompanied her to Mrs. Bates's, and gone E III 12 417 4
to reports:--but Mr. Weston had thought differently; he E III 12 417 5
Emma smiled, and felt that Mr. Weston had very good reason E III 12 417 5
towards herself and Mr. Weston, must necessarily open the E III 12 418 5
"I have a few lines on parish business from Mr. Weston E III 13 425 9
He was the son of Mr. Weston--he was continually here--I E III 13 427 19
Mr. Weston was to call in the evening, and she must return E III 15 444 4
exertions; but Mr. Weston earned every present comfort E III 15 445 11
It would be a great comfort to Mr. Weston as he grew older- E III 17 461 1
grew older--and even Mr. Weston might be growing older ten E III 17 461 1
acknowledged by Mr. Weston than by herself--but even he E III 17 467 31
it spread; and Mr. Weston had his five minutes share of it; E III 17 468 33
When Mr. Weston joined the party, however, and when the E III 18 476 46
47
Perhaps she ought to be ashamed, but Mr. Weston had been E III 18 479 73

MR. WESTON'S (24)

"They are to be put into Mr. Weston's stable, papa. E I 1 8 18
If I had not promoted Mr. Weston's visits here and given E I 1 13 43
but it was not in Mr. Weston's nature to imagine that any E I 2 17 7
walking, and in Mr. Weston's disposition and circumstances, E I 2 18 11
and abrupt; what will he be at Mr. Weston's time of life?" E I 4 33 36
manners are superior to Mr. Knightley's or Mr. Weston's. E I 4 34 41
42
own and Mr. Weston's on the subject, as much as possible. E I 5 41 31
Mr. Weston's dining-room does not accommodate more than E I 13 116 43
She believed he had been drinking too much of Mr. Weston's E I 15 129 23
a happy face as Mr. Weston's, confirmed as it all was by E II 5 188 8
by three," was Mr. Weston's quick amendment; and so ended E II 5 189 16
because you were Mr. Weston's son--but lay out half-a- E II 6 200 15
for, in spite of Mr. Weston's confidence, she could not E II 12 257 1
With Mr. Weston's ball in view at least, there had been a E II 13 267 8
Mr. Weston's own happiness was indisputable. E III 1 317 10
Mr. Weston's ball was to be a real thing. E III 1 318 12
desire, to help Mr. Weston's judgement; and they were so E III 2 319 3
Emma found that it was not Mr. Weston's fault that the E III 2 320 6
While she talked of his son, Mr. Weston's attention was E III 2 321 16
appearance, and was beyond the reach of Mr. Weston's hint. E III 5 345 15
on the unmanageable good-will of Mr. Weston's temper. E III 6 353 3
A conundrum of Mr. Weston's shall clear him and his next E III 7 371 31
An injunction of secresy had been among Mr. Weston's E III 11 403 2
Mr. Weston's sanguine temper was a blessing on all his E III 15 445 11

MR. WICKHAM (58)

his friend, Mr. Wickham, who had returned with him the day PP I 15 72 8
Mr. Wickham, after a few moments, touched his hat--a PP I 15 73 8
Mr. Denny and Mr. Wickham walked with the young ladies to PP I 15 73 10
the street, and had Mr. Wickham appeared Kitty and Lydia PP I 15 74 11
her husband call on Mr. Wickham, and give him an PP I 15 74 11
drawing-room, that Mr. Wickham had accepted their uncle's PP I 16 75 1
The gentlemen did approach; and when Mr. Wickham walked PP I 16 76 3
present party; but Mr. Wickham was as far beyond them all PP I 16 76 3
Mr. Wickham was the happy man towards whom almost every PP I 16 76 4
of the fair, as Mr. Wickham and the officers, Mr. Collins PP I 16 76 5
Mr. Wickham did not play at whist, and with ready delight PP I 16 76 8
Allowing for the common demands of the game, Mr. Wickham PP I 16 77 8
Mr. Wickham began the subject himself. PP I 16 77 8
Mr. Wickham began to speak on more general topics, Meryton, PP I 16 78 22
She could think of nothing but of Mr. Wickham, and of what PP I 16 84 59
next day, what had passed between Mr. Wickham and herself. PP I 17 85 1
on, than that Mr. Wickham should invent such a history of PP I 17 85 5
a great deal with Mr. Wickham, and of seeing a PP I 17 86 10
the evening with Mr. Wickham, he was by no means the only PP I 17 86 10
acquaintance with Mr. Wickham; and nothing less than a PP I 17 88 15
looked in vain for Mr. Wickham among the cluster of red PP I 18 89 1
"Mr. Wickham is blessed with such happy manners as may PP I 18 92 20
than her sister's, "what you have learnt about Mr. Wickham. PP I 18 95 49
convinced that Mr. Wickham has deserved much less PP I 18 95 50
Mr. Wickham is by no means a respectable young man. PP I 18 95 50
"Mr. Bingley does not know Mr. Wickham himself?" PP I 18 96 51
of her allusions to Mr. Wickham, and rejoiced in it. PP I 18 102 74
to inquire if Mr. Wickham were returned, and to lament PP I 21 115 3
of which officers Mr. Wickham was sure to be one; and on PP II 2 142 18
I will take care of myself, and of Mr. Wickham too. PP II 3 144 5
At present I am not in love with Mr. Wickham; no, I PP II 3 144 7
My father, however, is partial to Mr. Wickham. PP II 3 144 7
The farewell between herself and Mr. Wickham was perfectly PP II 4 151 3
and brought Mr. Wickham immediately to Elizabeth's mind; PP II 6 162 11
recital which I received many months ago from Mr. Wickham. PP II 11 191 17
he had mentioned Mr. Wickham, his cruelty towards whom he PP II 11 193 31
prosperity, and blasted the prospects of Mr. Wickham.-- PP II 12 196 5
of having injured Mr. Wickham, I can only refute it by PP II 12 199 5
Mr. Wickham is the son of a very respectable man, who had PP II 12 199 5
But whatever may be the sentiments which Mr. Wickham has PP II 12 200 5
his attachment to Mr. Wickham was to the last so steady, PP II 12 200 5
from these events, Mr. Wickham wrote to inform me that, PP II 12 200 5
I knew that Mr. Wickham ought not to be a clergyman. PP II 12 201 5
thither also went Mr. Wickham, undoubtedly by design; for PP II 12 201 5
but I wrote to Mr. Wickham, who left the place immediately, PP II 12 202 5
hope, acquit me henceforth of cruelty towards Mr. Wickham. PP II 12 202 5
by his account of Mr. Wickham, when she read with somewhat PP II 13 204 2
Elizabeth was now to see Mr. Wickham for the last time. PP II 18 233 25
She approached, and saw the likeness of Mr. Wickham PP III 1 247 9
Imprudent as a marriage between Mr. Wickham and our poor PP III 4 274 3
has thrown herself into the power of--of Mr. Wickham. PP III 4 277 11
he has pledged himself to assist Mr. Wickham with money." PP III 7 306 46
that Mr. Wickham had resolved on quitting the militia. PP III 8 312 18
creditors of Mr. Wickham in and near Brighton, with PP III 8 313 19
Mr. Wickham had received his commission before he left PP III 9 318 17
your sister and Mr. Wickham were, and that he had seen and PP III 10 321 2
"come, Mr. Wickham, we are brother and sister, you know. PP III 10 329 33
34
Mr. Wickham was so perfectly satisfied with this PP III 11 330 1

MR. WICKHAM'S (10)

Mr. Wickham's attention was caught; and after observing Mr. PP I 16 83 51
rest of the ladies their share of Mr. Wickham's attentions. PP I 16 84 59
Mr. Wickham's happiness and her own was per force delayed PP I 17 87 14
Mr. Wickham's society was of material service in PP II 1 138 30
Mr. Wickham's chief object was unquestionably my sister's PP II 12 202 5
not to lay to Mr. Wickham's charge, exceedingly shocked PP II 13 205 4
This accounted to Elizabeth for Mr. Wickham's being among PP III 1 247 19
particulars, that Mr. Wickham's circumstances are not so PP III 7 302 14
It is Mr. Wickham's intention to go into the regulars; and, PP III 8 312 19
Mr. Wickham's adieus were much more affectionate than his PP III 11 330 7

MR. WILLIAM COX (2)

hastily by, Mr. William Cox letting himself in at the E II 9 233 24
not know who will ask her next, perhaps Mr. William Cox.' E III 2 329 45

MR. WILLIAM PRICE'S (1)

of Mr. William Price's commission as second lieutenant of MP II 13 298 3

MR. WILLOUGHBY (33)

told them that Mr. Willoughby had no property of his own SS I 9 44 23
smile, "that Mr. Willoughby will be incommoded by the SS I 9 44 24
the affection of Mr. Willoughby, an equally striking SS I 10 49 12
I am sure she will be married to Mr. Willoughby very soon." SS I 12 60 9
the cottage, and Mr. Willoughby got up two hours before SS I 13 65 32
there, and with no other companion than Mr. Willoughby." SS I 13 68 69
"Mr. Willoughby however is the only person who can have a SS I 13 68 70
to Allenham; but Mr. Willoughby wanted particularly to SS I 13 69 76
"Well then, I guess that Mr. Willoughby hunts." SS I 18 100 27
and herself, he would not have ventured to mention it. SS I 18 100 30
She began by inquiring if they saw much of Mr. Willoughby SS I 20 114 43
is going to be married to Mr. Willoughby of Combe Magna. SS I 20 115 50
"Is Mr. Willoughby much known in your part of SS I 20 116 57
Nobody is more liked than Mr. Willoughby wherever he goes, SS I 20 116 58
I do not know what you and Mr. Willoughby will do between SS II 4 163 18
engagement to Mr. Willoughby is very generally known." SS II 5 173 40
hand, directed to Mr. Willoughby in your sister's writing. SS II 5 173 44
persuasion of my sister's being engaged to Mr. Willoughby? SS II 7 181 9
ever naming Mr. Willoughby, or making the slightest SS II 8 195 17
I must do this justice to Mr. Willoughby--he has broken no SS II 8 196 19
Mr. Willoughby is unfathomable! SS II 8 199 36
"You have something to tell me of Mr. Willoughby, that SS II 9 204 19
your sister to Mr. Willoughby, and it was, though from a SS II 9 205 24
Little did Mr. Willoughby imagine, I suppose, when his SS II 9 209 30
"ever seen Mr. Willoughby since you left him at Barton?" SS II 9 211 34
Marianne and Mr. Willoughby, she would have thought SS II 14 247 4
Willoughby, I advise you at present to return to Combe.-- SS III 8 318 16
17
recollection, "Mr. Willoughby, you ought to feel, and I SS III 8 318 21
22
for you to relate, or for me to listen any longer. SS III 8 320 30
31
"Why did you call, Mr. Willoughby?" said Elinor, SS III 8 324 41
"This is not right, Mr. Willoughby.-- SS III 8 325 52
"But the letter, Mr. Willoughby, your own letter; have you SS III 8 328 60
"You are very wrong, Mr. Willoughby, very blameable," said SS III 8 329 64

MR. WILLOUGHBY'S (6)

the colour of Mr. Willoughby's pointer, than he could SS I 9 44 21
You have already ascertained Mr. Willoughby's opinion in SS I 10 47 4
enquire of Mr. Willoughby's groom, and that she had by SS I 13 67 65
They will one day be Mr. Willoughby's, and" . . . SS I 13 68 74
75
forced calmness, "Mr. Willoughby's marriage with Miss Grey. SS II 8 199 36
what painter Mr. Willoughby's portrait was drawn, and at SS II 10 215 11

MR. WINGFIELD (9)

Mr. Wingfield in town as her father could be of Mr. Perry. E I 11 92 4
"Mr. Wingfield most strenuously recommended it, sir--or we E I 12 101 21
Mr. Wingfield told me that he had never known them more E I 12 102 33
"No, I do not know that Mr. Wingfield considers it very E I 12 102 35
Mr. Wingfield thinks the vicinity of Brunswick Square E I 12 103 37
for I assure you Mr. Wingfield told me, that he did not E I 12 103 39
that you had seen Mr. Wingfield before you left home." E I 12 103 42
from the mud; and Mr. Wingfield says it is entirely a E I 12 105 55
she was quite eager to have Harriet under her care.-- E III 16 451 3

MR. WINGFIELD'S (1)

embrocation of Mr. Wingfield's, which we have been E I 12 102 28

MR. WOODHOUSE (110)

Sixteen years had Miss Taylor been in Mr. Woodhouses's E I 1 5 3
their ages (and Mr. Woodhouse had not married early) was E I 1 7 8
It was a happy circumstance and animated Mr. Woodhouse for E I 1 9 21
When this was over, Mr. Woodhouse gratefully observed, "it E I 1 10 21
22
true, my dear, indeed," said Mr. Woodhouse with a sigh. E I 1 10 31
others;" rejoined Mr. Woodhouse, understanding but in part. E I 1 13 45
Mr. Woodhouse told me of it. E I 2 18 9
Mr. Woodhouse saw the letter, and he says he never saw E I 2 18 9
but a few weeks brought some alleviation to Mr. Woodhouse. E I 2 19 14
of his own, Mr. Woodhouse hoped to influence every visitor E I 2 19 14
in their hands: but Mr. Woodhouse would never believe it. E I 2 19 15
Mr. Woodhouse was fond of society in his own way. E I 3 20 1
thought it no hardship for either James or the horses. E I 3 20 3
full of trivial communications and harmless gossip. E I 3 21 4
"It is very pretty," said Mr. Woodhouse. E I 6 48 36
was December, and Mr. Woodhouse could not bear the idea of E I 6 48 40
some time with Mr. Woodhouse and Emma, till Mr. Woodhouse, E I 8 57 2
and Emma, till Mr. Woodhouse, who had previously made up E I 8 57 2
Mr. Woodhouse at last was off; but Mr. Knightley, instead E I 8 58 9
Mr. Woodhouse was almost as much interested in the E I 9 70 5
Mr. Woodhouse came in, and very soon led to the subject E I 9 78 49
Mr. Woodhouse could never allow for Mr. Knightley's claims E I 9 80 65
Unwelcome as it was, Mr. Woodhouse could only give a E I 9 80 68
or seen at all by Mr. Woodhouse, who could not be induced E I 11 91 2
and composed when Mr. Woodhouse, with a melancholy shake E I 11 93 5
Mr. Woodhouse hesitated.-- E I 11 94 13
"Why to be sure," said Mr. Woodhouse--"yes, certainly--I E I 11 94 16
inclination of Mr. Woodhouse, who did not like that any E I 12 98 1
The evening was quiet and conversible, as Mr. Woodhouse E I 12 100 15
While they were thus comfortably occupied Mr. Woodhouse E I 12 100 17
Mr. Woodhouse agreed to it all, but added, "our little E I 12 104 47
48
"Ah!" said Mr. Woodhouse, shaking his head and fixing his E I 12 105 51
Mr. Woodhouse was rather agitated by such harsh E I 12 107 62
one day;--even Mr. Woodhouse was persuaded to think it a E I 13 108 2
great event that Mr. Woodhouse should dine out, on the E I 13 108 5
Mr. Woodhouse had so completely made up his mind to the E I 13 112 24
have done, for Mr. Woodhouse would hardly have ventured E I 13 115 39
Mr. Woodhouse had been safely seated long enough to give E I 14 117 3
Mr. Woodhouse very soon followed them into the drawing- E I 14 122 18
Mr. Woodhouse was soon ready for his tea; and when he had E I 15 124 1
wind; concluding with these words to Mr. Woodhouse: E I 15 125 7
Poor Mr. Woodhouse was silent from consternation; but E I 15 126 9
it should make Mr. Woodhouse uncomfortable, and be an E I 15 126 11
The carriages came: and Mr. Woodhouse, always the first E I 15 128 22
fears of Mr. Woodhouse had confined them to a foot pace. E I 15 132 37
Mr. Woodhouse would have been miserable had his daughter E I 16 138 17

MRS HILLIER (1)
I remember seeing Mrs Hillier after one of those dreadful S 4 381 1
MRS JANE FISHER (1)
Mrs Jane Fisher. S 6 389 1
MRS JOHNSON (19)
Lady Susan to Mrs Johnson. Langford. LS 2 244 1
Lady Susan to Mrs Johnson. Churchill. LS 5 249 1
Lady Susan to Mrs Johnson. Churchill. LS 7 252 1
Mrs Johnson to Lady Susan. Edward St. LS 9 256 1
Lady Susan to Mrs Johnson. Churchill. LS 10 257 1
Lady Susan to Mrs Johnson. Churchill. LS 16 268 1
Lady Susan to Mrs Johnson. Churchill. LS 19 273 1
times that he had seen Mrs Johnson a few evenings before. LS 20 276 3
Lady Susan to Mrs Johnson. Churchill. LS 22 280 1
Lady Susan to Mrs Johnson. Churchill. LS 25 291 1
Mrs Johnson to Lady Susan. Edward St. LS 26 295 1
going to town, to see her particular friend, Mrs Johnson. LS 27 296 1
Mrs Johnson to Lady Susan. Edward St. LS 28 297 1
Lady Susan to Mrs Johnson. Upper Seymour St. LS 29 298 1
Lady Susan to Mrs Johnson. Upper Seymour St. LS 31 301 1
Mrs Johnson to Lady Susan. Edward St. LS 32 302 1
Lady Susan to Mrs Johnson. Upper Seymour St. LS 33 303 1
Mrs Johnson to Lady Susan. Edward St. LS 38 306 1
Lady Susan to Mrs Johnson. Upper Seymour St. LS 39 307 1
MRS M. (1)
are to part; I am afraid Mrs M. will come home to us again. LS 38 307 2
MRS MANWARING (11)
incensed, and Mrs Manwaring insupportably jealous; so LS 2 245 1
attachment to Mrs Manwaring, that I was very far from LS 3 246 1
regularly with Mrs Manwaring; at any rate it must be LS 6 252 2
As to Mrs Manwaring's jealousy, it was totally his own LS 14 264 4
Manwaring's most earnest entreaties, to leave the family. LS 14 265 4
Mrs Manwaring had that instant entered the house, & forced LS 32 302 1
That detestable Mrs Manwaring, who for your comfort, has LS 32 303 2
in Mr Johnson's house, from Mrs Manwaring herself. LS 34 304 1
of what Mrs Manwaring can have told you, to occasion so LS 35 304 1
I cannot suppose that the old story of Mrs Manwaring's LS 35 304 1
But the unfortunate Mrs Manwaring, whose agonies while she LS 36 306 1
MRS MATHEWS (1)
Mathews--Miss Mathews, Miss E. Mathews, miss h. mathews.-- S 6 389 1
MRS P-- (2)
strangers easy--and as Mrs P--was exceedingly anxious for S 1 370 1
The Lady Denham, Miss Brereton, Mr & Mrs P---- Sir Edw: S 6 389 1
MRS P. (12)
And Mrs P. was as evidently a gentle, amiable, sweet S 2 372 1
were born--where Mrs P. & I lived till within the last 2 S 4 379 1
"Why to own the truth, said Mrs P.--I do think the Miss S 5 388 1
to hear a word of Mrs P.'s orders to the servant as they S 6 391 1
Mrs P.-- in the drawing room in time to see them all.-- S 7 394 1
Delighted to have such good news for Mr & Mrs P., who had S 9 406 1
Mr & Mrs P. spent a great part of the eveng at the hotel; S 10 413 1
Mr & Mrs P.-- & Charlotte had seen two post chaises S 10 414 1
"My dear Diana! exclaimed Mrs P.-- S 12 424 1
Mrs P. was delighted at this release, & set off very happy S 12 425 1
Mrs P. entered into all her husband's joy on the occasion, S 12 426 1
about, & to be told by Mrs P. that the whole-length S 12 427 1
MRS PARKER (6)
Mr Parker of Sanditon; this lady, my wife Mrs Parker.-- S 1 368 1
When Mr & Mrs Parker therefore ceased from soliciting a S 2 374 1
"It was always a very comfortable house--said Mrs Parker-- S 4 380 1
"Oh! my dear Mrs Parker--you should not indeed--why should S 6 394 1
in cold grandeur in Mrs Parker's Drawg-Room to be kept S 7 396 1
been discerned by Mrs Parker; if Charlotte had not been S 12 426 1
MRS R. (5)
Mrs R. W. eyed her with much familiar curiosity & W 349 24
you in such a hurry to run away from her? cried Mrs R.-- W 350 24
Mrs R. W. was indeed wondering what sort of a home Emma cd W 350 24
Dinner came, & except when Mrs R. looked at her husband's W 353 27
tonight," said Eliz. to Mrs R. after seeing her father W 354 28
MRS ROBERT (6)
"Mrs Robert ferrars!"--was repeated by Marianne and her SS III 12 360 22
three days from Mr & Mrs Robert Watson, who undertook to W 348 23
"How charming Emma is!--" whispered Margt to Mrs Robert in W 350 24
Mrs Robert exactly as smart as she had been at her own W 353 26
Croydon now, said Mrs Robert--we never think of any other. W 358 28
Mrs Robert offered not another word in support of the game. W 358 28
MRS ROBERT SMARTLY (1)
Mrs Robert Smartly--but we think a month very little. W 356 28
MRS ROBT (1)
Mrs Robt was not less pleased with herself for having had W 349 23
MRS SHAW (1)
I considered her engagement to Mrs Shaw just at that time W 317 2
MRS SHELDON (1)
Two years ago I happened to be calling on Mrs Sheldon when S 5 386 1
MRS TOMLINSON (1)
last two dances; Mrs Tomlinson told me he was gone to ask W 336 14
MRS VERNON (29)
convenient to you & Mrs Vernon to receive me at present, I LS 1 243 1
Mrs Vernon to Lady De Courcy. Churchill. LS 3 246 1
Mr De Courcy to Mrs Vernon. Parklands. LS 4 248 1
Mrs Vernon to Mr De Courcy. Churchill. LS 6 250 1
party is enlarged by Mrs Vernon's brother, a handsome LS 7 254 3
lower, to convince Mrs Vernon that her sisterly cautions LS 7 254 3
Mrs Vernon to Lady De Courcy. Churchill. LS 8 254 1
Mrs Vernon's consciousness of deserving every sort of LS 10 258 2
Mrs Vernon to Lady De Courcy. LS 11 259 1
Lady De Courcy to Mrs Vernon. Parklands. LS 13 262 1
If Mrs Vernon would allow something to my affection for LS 14 264 2
Mrs Vernon to Lady De Courcy. Churchill. LS 15 266 1
Mrs Vernon to Lady De Courcy. Churchill. LS 17 269 1
Mr & Mrs Vernon; & I cannot just now afford to go to town. LS 19 275 4
Mrs Vernon to Lady De Courcy. Churchill. LS 20 275 1
professions, my dear Mrs Vernon, & I never had the LS 20 277 6
7
Mrs Vernon to Lady De Courcy. Churchill. LS 23 283 1
"Heaven knows my dearest Mrs Vernon, how fully I am aware LS 24 288 11
pleasure to Mr & Mrs Vernon which your society must; & my LS 25 293 3
Mrs Vernon to Lady De Courcy. Churchill. LS 27 296 1
sisterly fears of Mrs Vernon, who, accustomed herself to LS 30 301 4
Lady De Courcy to Mrs Vernon. Parklands. LS 40 308 1
Mrs Vernon to Lady De Courcy. Churchill. LS 41 309 1
intercourse of Mrs Vernon & her neice, for the former soon LS 42 311 1
With a heart full of the matter, Mrs Vernon waited on Lady LS 42 311 2
Mrs Vernon surprised & incredulous, knew not what to LS 42 312 4
Mrs Vernon encouraging the doubt, directly proposed her LS 42 312 5
Mrs Vernon however persevered in the offer of it, & tho' LS 42 312 5
Mrs Vernon was then convinced of what she had only LS 42 313 7
MRS WHITBY (5)
house & without, and Mrs Whitby at the library was sitting S 6 389 1
Mrs Whitby came forward without delay from her literary S 6 390 1
vol:s they had left behind them on Mrs Whitby's shelves.-- S 6 391 1
I have told Mrs Whitby that if any body enquires for a S 6 393 1
Whitby to secure them a house?--but neither pleased me.-- S 9 409 1
MRS. ADMIRAL MAXWELL (1)
Maxwell, only six weeks before she was taken for death. MP III 7 387 44
MRS. ALLEN (70)
It is now expedient to give some description of Mrs. Allen, NA I 2 19 7
Mrs. Allen was one of that numerous class of females, NA I 2 20 8
with care, and both Mrs. Allen and her maid declared she NA I 2 20 8
Mrs. Allen was so long in dressing, that they did not NA I 2 20 9
of her protegee, Mrs. Allen made her way through the NA I 2 21 9
Mrs. Allen did all that she could do in such a case by NA I 2 21 9
Mrs. Allen congratulated herself, as soon as they were NA I 2 22 11
"Yes, my dear," replied Mrs. Allen, with perfect serenity, NA I 2 22 13
But, dear Mrs. Allen, are you sure there is nobody you NA I 2 23 20
still uppermost with Mrs. Allen, and she repeated it after NA I 3 25 1
They were interrupted by Mrs. Allen:--"my dear Catherine," NA I 3 28 35
Mrs. Allen was quite struck by his genius. NA I 3 28 39
"I am quite of your opinion, sir," replied Mrs. Allen; " NA I 3 28 44
"What a delightful place Bath is," said Mrs. Allen, as NA I 4 31 1
often in vain, that Mrs. Allen had no particular reason to NA I 4 31 2
to be Thorpe; and Mrs. Allen immediately recognized the NA I 4 31 2
as a talker, over Mrs. Allen, in a family of children; and NA I 4 32 2
beings ever were, Mrs. Allen had no similar information to NA I 4 32 2
"My dear Mrs. Allen, I long to introduce them; they will NA I 4 32 3
been only two days in Bath before they met with Mrs. Allen. NA I 5 36 2
Mrs. Allen was now quite happy--quite satisfied with Bath. NA I 5 36 3
chiefly of her children, and Mrs. Allen of her gowns. NA I 5 36 3
Mrs. Thorpe and Mrs. Allen, between whom she now remained. NA I 8 52 2
and Mrs. Allen, by whom he was very civilly acknowledged. NA I 8 54 4
from Mrs. Thorpe to Mrs. Allen, that she would move a NA I 8 54 10
made her way to Mrs. Allen and Mrs. Thorpe as fast as she NA I 8 58 25
"Did you meet Mr. Tilney, my dear?" said Mrs. Allen. NA I 8 58 28
asked you," said Mrs. Allen; and after a short silence, NA I 8 58 32
"Indeed he is, Mrs. Allen," said Mrs. Thorpe, smiling NA I 8 58 33
it did not puzzle Mrs. Allen, for after only a moment's NA I 8 59 34
and ejaculations of Mrs. Allen, whose vacancy of mind and NA I 9 60 1
How do you do, Mrs. Allen? a famous ball last night, was NA I 9 61 1
Allen for her opinion; "but really I did not expect you." NA I 9 61 4
thrown away, for Mrs. Allen, not being at all in the habit NA I 9 61 6
"Do just as you please, my dear," replied Mrs. Allen, with NA I 9 61 7
Catherine found Mrs. Allen just returned from all the busy NA I 9 67 34
enough to feel that Mrs. Allen had no real intelligence to NA I 9 69 51
street, and there I can only go and call on Mrs. Allen." NA I 10 79 54
"Only go and call on Mrs. Allen!" he repeated. NA I 10 79 55
something to talk of again to Mrs. Allen, or any body else. NA I 10 79 56
She applied to Mrs. Allen, and Mrs. Allen's opinion was NA I 11 82 1
"I thought how it would be," said Mrs. Allen. NA I 11 82 3
of Mrs. Allen, who had "always thought it would clear up." NA I 11 83 16
It was too dirty for Mrs. Allen to accompany her husband NA I 11 84 17
Mrs. Allen agreed to it. NA I 11 84 18
How d'ye do, Mrs. Allen?" NA I 11 84 18
as no reason at all; Mrs. Allen was called on to second NA I 11 84 19
Shall I go, Mrs. Allen?" NA I 11 86 47
"Mrs. Allen, you must persuade her to go," was the general NA I 11 86 49
Mrs. Allen was not inattentive to it:--"well, my dear," NA I 11 86 49
"Mrs. Allen," said Catherine the next morning, "will there NA I 12 91 1
with like calm politeness to Mrs. Allen and her friend.-- NA I 12 93 5
but indeed it was not my own fault,--was it, Mrs. Allen? NA I 12 93 5
rather have been with you; now had not I, Mrs. Allen?" NA I 12 93 5
as soon as ever I saw you; now, Mrs. Allen, did not----- NA I 12 94 8
Mrs. Allen, are not you of my way of thinking? NA I 13 104 31
form, as much to Mrs. Allen as to Catherine, petitioned NA I 14 114 49
to little effect; Mrs. Allen had no intelligence to give NA I 14 114 50
the day before, did raise some emotion in Mrs. Allen. NA I 15 125 48
saying she should join Mrs. Allen, proposed their walking. NA II 3 147 28
But Catherine could be stubborn too; and Mrs. Allen just NA II 3 147 28
Mrs. Allen used to take pains, year after year, to make me NA II 7 174 7
"Mr. Allen had only one small hot-house, which Mrs. Allen NA II 7 178 25
had often amazed Mrs. Allen; and, when Catherine saw what NA II 8 184 4
to Oxford; and Mrs. Allen had given her no hopes of a NA II 10 201 5
I am sorry it happens so, for Mrs. Allen thought them very NA II 14 236 15
restoring her spirits, that they should call on Mrs. Allen. NA II 14 236 18
sensible friend; and Mrs. Allen thought his expressions NA II 14 237 22
of other subjects, Mrs. Allen again returned to--"I really NA II 14 238 27
A very short visit to Mrs. Allen, in which Henry talked at NA II 15 243 10
MRS. ALLEN'S (10)
Nothing more alarming occurred than a fear on Mrs. Allen's NA I 2 19 4
of soothing Mrs. Allen's fears on the delay of an expected NA I 7 51 54
in a fit on Mrs. Allen's bosom, Catherine sat erect, in NA I 8 53 3
had procured Mrs. Allen's admiration of his gig; and then NA I 9 62 7
When they arrived at Mrs. Allen's door, the astonishment NA I 9 67 33
She applied to Mrs. Allen, and Mrs. Allen's opinion was NA I 11 82 1
Allen's wavering convictions only made it more doubtful. NA I 12 91 3
"My dear, you tumble my gown," was Mrs. Allen's reply. NA I 12 93 6
No difficulty was made on Mrs. Allen's side--and the only NA I 14 114 49
one morning, by Mrs. Allen's side, without any thing to NA II 3 143 1
MRS. AND MISS BATES (7)
Miss Bates, or when Mrs. and Miss Bates returned the visit. E I 2 17 9
whom were Mrs. and Miss Bates and Mrs. Goddard, three E I 3 20 3
"You seem to me to have forgotten Mrs. and Miss Bates," E I 12 102 30
just approaching the house where lived Mrs. and Miss Bates. E II 1 155 2
attention; Mrs. and Miss Bates loved to be called on, and E II 1 155 2
Mrs. and Miss Bates occupied the drawing-room floor; and E II 1 155 4
Dear Emma has been to call on Mrs. and Miss Bates, Mr. E III 9 385 6
MRS. AND THE MISS MUSGROVES (1)
with people I know so well as Mrs. and the Miss Musgroves." P III 5 40 42
MRS. ANNESLEY (3)
It was first broken by Mrs. Annesley, a genteel, agreeable- PP III 3 267 4
and smile from Mrs. Annesley to Miss Darcy had been given, PP III 3 268 6
"Mrs. Annesley is with her. PP III 12 342 24
MRS. BATES (21)
Mrs. Bates, the widow of a former vicar of Highbury, was a E I 3 21 4
Bates, let me propose your venturing on one of these eggs. E I 3 24 13
14
Good old Mrs. Bates--I will call upon her to-morrow, and E I 12 102 31
But poor Mrs. Bates had a bad cold about a month ago." E I 12 102 32
Fairfax prefers devoting the time to you and Mrs. Bates?" E II 1 161 24
after Mrs. Bates; but I have been so pleasantly detained! E II 1 162 32
Now, however, we must wish you and Mrs. Bates good morning. E II 1 162 32
However, she is very agreeable, and Mrs. Bates too, in a E II 3 171 12
"To be sure we do," cried his father; "Mrs. Bates-- we E II 5 194 38
Mrs. Goddard, if not Mrs. Bates, might be depended on for E II 7 208 9
Her father's comfort was amply secured, Mrs. Bates as well E II 8 213 6
"I hope Mrs. Bates and Miss Fairfax are"----- E II 9 236 45
Emma would be "very happy to wait on Mrs. Bates, &c." and E II 9 237 47
48
tranquillity itself; Mrs. Bates, deprived of her usual E II 10 240 1
I have the pleasure, madam, (to Mrs. Bates,) of restoring E II 10 242 15
Mrs. Bates, Mrs. Perry, Mrs. Goddard and others, were a E II 16 290 3
Mrs. Bates was engaged to spend the evening at Hartfield, E III 1 318 13
Poor old Mrs. Bates, civil and humble as usual, looked as E III 8 378 5
Mrs. Bates and Mrs. Elton were together. E III 16 453 11
own compliments to Mrs. Bates, and appearing to attend to E III 16 453 12
13
And when Mrs. Bates was saying something to Emma, E III 16 454 17
MRS. BATES'S (10)
Jane Fairfax was an orphan, the only child of Mrs. Bates's E II 2 163 1
sees it, and as to Mrs. Bates's, he may get there from the E II 5 195 48
and he might think it too large for Mrs. Bates's house." E II 8 216 25
the first place at Mrs. Bates's; whose house was a little E II 9 233 25
reward him, returned with Mrs. Weston to Mrs. Bates's door. E II 9 235 35
They had stopped at Mrs. Bates's door to offer the use of E III 2 320 6
and drove to Mrs. Bates's, in the hope that Jane would be E III 9 390 18
Mr. Weston had accompanied her to Mrs. Bates's, and gone E III 12 417 4
an hour spent in Mrs. Bates's parlour, with all the E III 12 417 4
head to look at Mrs. Bates's knitting, she added, in a E III 16 454 14
15
MRS. BENNET (138)
Mrs. Bennet deigned not to make any reply; but unable to PP I 2 6 7
Mrs. Bennet said only, "nonsense, nonsense!" PP I 2 7 17
he wished; that of Mrs. Bennet perhaps surpassing the rest; PP I 2 7 23
Not all that Mrs. Bennet, however, with the assistance of PP I 3 9 1
Netherfield," said Mrs. Bennet to her husband, "and all PP I 3 9 2

and already had Mrs. Bennet planned the courses that were PP I 3 9 4
Mrs. Bennet was quite disconcerted. PP I 3 9 4
Amongst the most violent against him was Mrs. Bennet, PP I 3 11 6
Mrs. Bennet had seen her eldest daughter much admired by PP I 3 12 15
"Oh! my dear," continued Mrs. Bennet, "I am quite PP I 3 13 18
not too clever to be a valuable neighbour to Mrs. Bennet.-- PP I 5 18 2
"You began the evening well, Charlotte," said Mrs. Bennet PP I 5 18 4
you ought," said Mrs. Bennet; "and if I were to see you at PP I 5 20 22
"I am astonished, my dear," said Mrs. Bennet, "that you PP I 7 29 8
Mrs. Bennet was prevented replying by the entrance of the PP I 7 30 14
"Dining out," said Mrs. Bennet, "that is very unlucky." PP I 7 30 19
indeed!" said Mrs. Bennet, more than once, as if the PP I 7 31 29
Mrs. Bennet, accompanied by her two youngest girls, PP I 9 41 1
Had she found Jane in any apparent danger, Mrs. Bennet PP I 9 41 2
Bingley met them with hopes that Mrs. Bennet had not found PP I 9 41 2
Mrs. Bennet was profuse in her acknowledgments. PP I 9 42 6
"Yes, indeed," cried Mrs. Bennet, offended by his manner PP I 9 43 19
Mrs. Bennet, who fancied she had gained a complete victory PP I 9 43 20
a short silence Mrs. Bennet began repeating her thanks to PP I 9 45 35
graciousness, but Mrs. Bennet was satisfied, and soon PP I 9 45 35
Mrs. Bennet and her daughters then departed, and Elizabeth PP I 9 46 39
When you told Mrs. Bennet this morning that if you ever PP I 10 49 27
But Mrs. Bennet, who had calculated on her daughters PP I 12 59 1
Mrs. Bennet sent them word that they could not possibly PP I 12 59 1
Mrs. Bennet wondered at their coming, and thought them PP I 12 60 6
a subject on which Mrs. Bennet was beyond the reach of PP I 13 62 8
"There, Mrs. Bennet."-- PP I 13 62 12
he complimented Mrs. Bennet on having so fine a family of PP I 13 64 21
of his hearers, but Mrs. Bennet, who quarrelled with no PP I 13 65 21
22
But here he was set right by Mrs. Bennet, who assured him PP I 13 65 26
Mrs. Bennet, "and I dare say she is a very agreeable woman. PP I 14 66 2
"Ah!" cried Mrs. Bennet, shaking her head, "then she is PP I 14 67 6
Mrs. Bennet and her daughters apologised most civilly for PP I 14 69 17
tete-a-tete with Mrs. Bennet before breakfast, a PP I 15 70 3
soon done--done while Mrs. Bennet was stirring the fire. PP I 15 71 4
Mrs. Bennet treasured up the hint, and trusted that she PP I 15 71 5
Mr. Collins on his return highly gratified Mrs. Bennet by PP I 15 74 13
attention; avoiding Mrs. Bennet as much as possible, PP I 17 86 9
Mrs. Bennet chose to consider it as given in compliment to PP I 17 86 10
It was an animating subject, and Mrs. Bennet seemed PP I 18 99 63
less likely than Mrs. Bennet to find comfort in staying at PP I 18 99 63
At length however Mrs. Bennet had no more to say; and Lady PP I 18 100 68
by a manoeuvre of Mrs. Bennet had to wait for their PP I 18 102 75
They repulsed every attempt of Mrs. Bennet at conversation, PP I 18 102 75
When at length they arose to take leave, Mrs. Bennet was PP I 18 103 76
Mrs. Bennet was perfectly satisfied; and quitted the house PP I 18 103 77
On finding Mrs. Bennet, Elizabeth, and one of the younger PP I 19 104 1
2
of surprise, Mrs. Bennet instantly answered, "Oh dear!-- PP I 19 104 3
4
Mrs. Bennet and Kitty walked off, and as soon as they were PP I 19 105 7
love; for Mrs. Bennet, having dawdled about in the PP I 20 110 1
This information, however, startled Mrs. Bennet;--she PP I 20 110 2
"Sir, you quite misunderstand me," said Mrs. Bennet, PP I 20 111 5
Mrs. Bennet rang the bell, and Miss Elizabeth was summoned PP I 20 111 14
Is not it so, Mrs. Bennet?" PP I 20 111 17
a beginning; but Mrs. Bennet, who had persuaded herself PP I 20 112 20
in her husband, did Mrs. Bennet give up the point. PP I 20 112 23
where Mrs. Bennet was alone, than she likewise began on PP I 20 113 26
"Aye, there she comes," continued Mrs. Bennet, "looking as PP I 20 113 28
In a doleful voice Mrs. Bennet thus began the projected PP I 20 114 31
They agreed that Mrs. Bennet should only hear of the PP I 21 120 30
for the night; and Mrs. Bennet with great politeness and PP I 22 123 4
Mrs. Bennet wished to understand by it that he thought of PP I 22 124 11
incredulous; for Mrs. Bennet, with more perseverance than PP I 23 126 1
2
Mrs. Bennet was in fact too much overpowered to say a PP I 23 126 5
able to retort on Mrs. Bennet the comfort of having a PP I 23 127 8
was no longer a matter of pleasure to Mrs. Bennet. PP I 23 128 11
Such were the gentle murmurs of Mrs. Bennet, and they gave PP I 23 128 11
highly incensed Mrs. Bennet, and which she never failed to PP I 23 129 12
Mrs. Bennet was really in a most pitiable state. PP I 23 129 16
This was not very consoling to Mrs. Bennet, and, therefore, PP I 23 130 19
Mrs. Bennet still continued to wonder and repine at his PP II 1 137 26
On the following Monday, Mrs. Bennet had the pleasure of PP II 2 139 2
years younger than Mrs. Bennet and Mrs. Philips, was an PP II 2 139 2
Mrs. Bennet had many grievances to relate, and much to PP II 2 139 3
Mrs. Bennet had so carefully provided for the PP II 2 142 18
his arrival was no great inconvenience to Mrs. Bennet. PP II 3 145 11
Mrs. Bennet could certainly spare you for another PP II 14 211 8
Mrs. Bennet rejoiced to see Jane in undiminished beauty; PP II 16 222 19
20
eldest daughter; Mrs. Bennet was doubly engaged, on one PP II 16 222 21
"Well, Lizzy," said Mrs. Bennet one day, "what is your PP II 17 227 27
"If one could but go to Brighton!" observed Mrs. Bennet. PP II 18 229 6
the delight of Mrs. Bennet, and the mortification of Kitty, PP II 18 230 12
Mrs. Bennet was diffuse in her good wishes for the PP II 18 235 40
Mrs. Bennet was restored to her usual querulous serenity, PP II 19 238 6
Mrs. Bennet, to whose apartment they all repaired, after a PP III 5 287 34
"Oh! my dear brother," replied Mrs. Bennet, "that is PP III 5 288 38
She shared in their attendance on Mrs. Bennet, and was a PP III 6 294 3
of yourself and Mrs. Bennet, I am inclined to think that PP III 6 297 11
When Mrs. Bennet was told of this, she did not express so PP III 6 298 13
Mary and Kitty were both with Mrs. Bennet: one PP III 7 305 43
Mrs. Bennet could hardly contain herself. PP III 7 305 43
was to come; and Mrs. Bennet, for many years after Lydia's PP III 8 308 3
Mrs. Bennet had no turn for economy, and her husband's PP III 8 308 3
by marriage articles on Mrs. Bennet and the children. PP III 8 308 4
It was a fortnight since Mrs. Bennet had been down stairs, PP III 8 310 7
But when they had withdrawn, he said to her, "Mrs. Bennet, PP III 8 310 9
led to another; and Mrs. Bennet found, with amazement and PP III 8 310 10
Mrs. Bennet could hardly comprehend it. PP III 8 310 10
But Mrs. Bennet, was not so well pleased with it. PP III 8 313 20
Smiles decked the face of Mrs. Bennet, as the carriage PP III 9 315 2
No one but Mrs. Bennet, regretted that their stay would be PP III 9 318 18
Mrs. Bennet and Lydia are going in the carriage to Meryton. PP III 10 327 9
soon came, and Mrs. Bennet was forced to submit to a PP III 11 330 2
The loss of her daughter made Mrs. Bennet very dull for PP III 11 330 9
Mrs. Bennet was quite in the fidgets. PP III 11 331 13
dear," said Mrs. Bennet, "you will wait on him of course." PP III 11 332 22
Mrs. Bennet, through the assistance of servants, contrived PP III 11 333 30
He was received by Mrs. Bennet with a degree of civility, PP III 11 335 41
time, Mr. Bingley, since you went away," said Mrs. Bennet. PP III 11 336 47
When the gentlemen rose to go away, Mrs. Bennet was PP III 11 338 57
till Tuesday; and Mrs. Bennet, in the meanwhile, was PP III 12 339 10
Mrs. Bennet had designed to keep the two Netherfield PP III 12 342 27
'Ah! Mrs. Bennet, we shall have her at Netherfield at last. PP III 12 342 28
Mrs. Bennet, in short, was in very great spirits; she had PP III 12 343 29
Mrs. Bennet invited him to dine with them; but, with many PP III 13 344 1
In ran Mrs. Bennet to her daughter's room, in her dressing PP III 13 344 6
7
Two obstacles of the five being thus removed, Mrs. Bennet PP III 13 345 11
In a few minutes, Mrs. Bennet half opened the door and PP III 13 345 13
14
Mrs. Bennet could not give her consent, or speak her PP III 13 348 34
Mrs. Bennet was privileged to whisper it to Mrs. Philips, PP III 13 350 55
and on the part of Mrs. Bennet and Kitty, though she was PP III 14 351 2
Mrs. Bennet all amazement, though flattered by having a PP III 14 351 4
"Yes, madam," said Mrs. Bennet, delighted to speak to a PP III 14 352 8
Mrs. Bennet assured her that they never sat there after PP III 14 352 12
13
Mrs. Bennet, with great civility, begged her ladyship to PP III 14 352 16
17
The gentlemen arrived early; and, before Mrs. Bennet had PP III 16 365 1
It was agreed to. Mrs. Bennet was not in the habit of PP III 16 365 1
"Good gracious!" cried Mrs. Bennet, as she stood at a PP III 17 374 20
said Mrs. Bennet, "to walk to oakham mount this morning. PP III 17 374 23
As she went up stairs to get ready, Mrs. Bennet followed PP III 17 375 25
26
Bennet sat quite still, and unable to utter a syllable. PP III 17 378 42
she expected; for Mrs. Bennet luckily stood in such awe of PP III 17 378 46
Mrs. Bennet got rid of her two most deserving daughters. PP III 19 385 1

MRS. BENNET'S (13)
Mrs. Bennet's eyes sparkled with pleasure, and she was PP I 7 30 14
15
Mrs. Bennet's eyes sparkled.-- PP I 13 61 3
have touched Mrs. Bennet's heart, but for the mortifying PP I 13 65 26
off as if eager to escape from Mrs. Bennet's civilities. PP I 17 86 9
The morrow produced no abatement of Mrs. Bennet's ill PP I 21 115 2
she was, though Mrs. Bennet's sour looks and ill-natured PP I 23 127 8
but at last on Mrs. Bennet's leaving them together, after PP II 1 134 4
5
Mrs. Bennet's best comfort was, that Mr. Bingley must be PP II 1 137 26
Mrs. Bennet's schemes for this day were ineffectual. PP III 13 345 18
his own and Mrs. Bennet's means, for his coming next PP III 13 345 19
in the evening Mrs. Bennet's invention was again at work PP III 13 346 21
had appeased Mrs. Bennet's curiosity; and Elizabeth was PP III 15 361 5
by Mrs. Bennet's being quite unable to sit alone. PP III 19 386 5

MRS. BINGLEY (1)
Mrs. Bingley and talked of Mrs. Darcy may be guessed. PP III 19 385 1

MRS. BIRD (1)
the two Milmans, now Mrs. Bird and Mrs. James Cooper; and E II 14 277 40

MRS. BRAGGE (4)
A cousin of Mr. Suckling, Mrs. Bragge, had such an E II 17 299 8
It was not with Mrs. Suckling, it was not with Mrs. Bragge, E III 6 359 37
with a cousin of Mrs. Bragge, an acquaintance of Mrs. E III 6 359 37
of your sister and Mrs. Bragge; the only school, and not E III 16 456 32

MRS. BRAGGE'S (2)
Of all houses in the kingdom Mrs. Bragge's is the one I E II 17 300 8
own family, and Mrs. Bragge's; but Mrs. Smallridge is E III 8 380 13

MRS. BRANDON (1)
in after-days as bearing no comparison with Mrs. Brandon. SS III 14 379 19

MRS. BRANDON'S (1)
so inexperienced as Mrs. Brandon's, was but too natural. SS II 9 206 24

MRS. BRIDGETS (1)
The young Mrs. Eleanors and Mrs. Bridgets--starched up MP I 9 87 15

MRS. BROWN (1)
believe it, and when Mrs. Brown, and the other women, at MP II 6 235 19

MRS. BROWN'S (1)
and the party at Mrs. Brown's--smiles and blushes rising E II 4 181 4

MRS. BURGESS (1)
or four weeks with Mrs. Burgess, in hopes, as I tell her, SS III 13 370 37

MRS. CAMPBELL (11)
and Mrs. Campbell will not be able to part with her at all. E I 12 104 46
Colonel and Mrs. Campbell were very particular about their E II 1 159 20
to be excused from accompanying Colonel and Mrs. Campbell." E II 1 160 22
with Colonel and Mrs. Campbell; quite depend upon it; E II 1 160 23
and Colonel and Mrs. Campbell think she does quite right, E II 1 161 25
The good sense of Colonel and Mrs. Campbell could not E II 2 165 9
Col. Campbell is a very agreeable man, and Mrs. Campbell a E II 6 201 20
with Col. and Mrs. Campbell, I have no idea that you will E II 15 283 6
"Col. and Mrs. Campbell are to be in town again by mid- E II 17 300 9
not Colonel and Mrs. Campbell be sorry to find that she E III 8 382 28
I am here till claimed by Colonel and Mrs. Campbell." E III 16 460 53

MRS. CHAPMAN (2)
Mrs. Chapman had just reached the attic floor, when Miss MP II 9 271 41
as much as Lady Bertram or Mrs. Chapman do themselves. MP II 9 271 41

MRS. CHARLES (8)
by becoming Mrs. Charles Musgrove; but Anne, with an P III 1 5 8
Charles had a little of your method with those children. P III 6 44 8
Mrs. Charles knows no more how they should be treated!-- P III 6 45 8
I believe Mrs. Charles is not quite pleased with my not P III 6 45 8
Mrs. Charles quite swears by her, I know; but I just give P III 6 45 9
afraid of being in Mrs. Charles musgrove's way, on account P III 7 58 22
Mrs. Charles Musgrove will, of course, wish to get back to P III 12 114 61
an enquiry after Mrs. Charles Musgrove, and her fine P IV 6 166 17

MRS. CHARLES'S (1)
good opinion of Mrs. Charles's nursery-maid: I hear P III 6 45 9

MRS. CHURCHILL (29)
ill-humour of Mrs. Churchill, which I imagine to be the E I 14 121 15
Mrs. Churchill rules at Enscombe, and is a very odd- E I 14 121 16
"Oh, Mrs. Churchill; every body knows Mrs. Churchill," E I 14 121 17
Now, according to my idea of Mrs. Churchill, it would be E I 14 123 24
resolutely, to Mrs. Churchill--'every sacrifice of mere E I 18 146 16
even chance that Mrs. Churchill were not in health or E II 8 221 48
Mrs. Churchill was unwell--far too unwell to do without E II 12 258 7
anticipated: Mrs. Churchill was recovering, and he dared E II 13 266 5
"is, that Mrs. Churchill, as we understand, has not been E II 18 306 11
Does Mrs. Churchill do the same?" E II 18 306 12
"Depend on it, Mrs. Churchill does every thing that any E II 18 306 13
Mrs. Churchill will not be second to any lady in the land E II 18 306 13
Then she is no rule for Mrs. Churchill, who is as thorough E II 18 306 16
"Mrs. Churchill is not much in my good graces, as you may E II 18 307 18
And Mrs. Churchill probably has not health or spirits like E II 18 307 21
May is the very month which Mrs. Churchill is ordered, or E II 18 308 30
"I have not been severe upon poor Mrs. Churchill. E II 18 309 33
Your description of Mrs. Churchill made me think of them E II 18 310 34
Mrs. Churchill had been recommended to the medical skill E III 1 317 7
last accounts of Mrs. Churchill, whose health seemed every E III 6 352 1
attack of Mrs. Churchill that he was prevented coming.-- E III 6 361 41
were right who had named Mrs. Churchill as the cause. E III 6 363 53
account of Mrs. Churchill, and only wishing him not to E III 8 383 31
at Randall's to announce the death of Mrs. Churchill! E III 9 387 11
The great Mrs. Churchill was no more. E III 9 387 11
Mrs. Churchill, after being disliked at least twenty-five E III 9 387 12
"Poor Mrs. Churchill! no doubt she had been suffering a E III 9 387 13
The character of Mrs. Churchill, the grief of her husband-- E III 9 388 13
While poor Mrs. Churchill lived, I suppose there could not E III 10 398 55

MRS. CHURCHILL'S (10)
and with Mrs. Churchill's temper, before we pretend to E I 18 146 15
He thought principally of Mrs. Churchill's illness, and E II 12 259 11
directly, on Mrs. Churchill's account--she has not been E II 18 305 7
Mrs. Churchill's making incredible exertions to avoid it. E II 18 306 12
but I have not much faith in Mrs. Churchill's illness." E II 18 307 18
inferred that Mrs. Churchill's removal to London had been E III 1 316 6
Mrs. Churchill's state, however, as many were ready to E III 6 361 41
The contrast between Mrs. Churchill's importance in the E III 8 384 32
33
They spoke, therefore, of Mrs. Churchill's death with E III 9 388 14
One morning, about ten days after Mrs. Churchill's decease, E III 10 392 1

MRS. CLARKE (1)
You see I cannot leave Mrs. Clarke." SS III 2 271 6

MRS. CLAY (57)
in this selection of Mrs. Clay; turning from the society P III 2 16 16
From situation, Mrs. Clay was, in Lady Russell's estimate, P III 2 16 17
that would leave Mrs. Clay behind, and bring a choice of P III 2 16 17
good fortune," said Mrs. Clay, for Mrs. Clay was present; P III 3 18 7
said Mrs. Clay, for Mrs. Clay was present; her father had P III 3 18 7
"Nay, Sir Walter," cried Mrs. Clay, "this is being severe P III 3 20 17
But Mrs. Clay was talking so eagerly with Miss Elliot, P III 3 23 26
Mrs. Clay had freckles, and a projecting tooth, and a P III 5 34 12
"Mrs. Clay," said she warmly, "never forgets who she is; P III 5 35 14
If Mrs. Clay were a very beautiful woman, I grant you, it P III 5 35 14

But poor Mrs. Clay, who, with all her merits, can never P III 5 35 14
I really think poor Mrs. Clay may be staying here in P III 5 35 14
was to draw Sir Walter, Miss Elliot, and Mrs. Clay to Bath. P III 5 35 18
and her regret that Mrs. Clay should still be with them, P IV 1 124 11
Camden-Place, or her own sister's intimacy with Mrs. Clay. P IV 1 124 11
Mrs. Clay was very pleasant, and very smiling; but her P IV 3 137 3
and that her friend Mrs. Clay was encouraging the idea, P IV 3 140 11
His daughter and Mrs. Clay united in hinting that Colonel P IV 3 142 13
Mrs. Clay decidedly thought it Mr. Elliot's knock." P IV 3 142 17
Mrs. Clay was right. P IV 3 142 17
being in love with Mrs. Clay; and she was very far from P IV 4 145 1
She could imagine Mrs. Clay to have said, that "now Miss P IV 4 145 1
see Mrs. Clay stealing, a glance at Elizabeth and herself. P IV 4 145 2
Mrs. Clay has been using it at my recommendation, and you P IV 4 146 3
The sight of Mrs. Clay in such favour, and of Anne so P IV 4 146 5
in Mr. Elliot outweighed all the plague of Mrs. Clay. P IV 4 147 6
He looked, as he spoke, to the seat which Mrs. Clay had P IV 4 151 22
him for not liking Mrs. Clay; and her conscience admitted P IV 4 151 22
Sir Walter, Elizabeth and Mrs. Clay returned one morning P IV 5 156 14
Mrs. Clay, who had been present while all this passed, now P IV 5 158 20
degree of openness of Mrs. Clay; had appeared completely P IV 5 161 29
to see what Mrs. Clay was about, and to hold her in P IV 5 161 29
and yet Mrs. Clay found him as agreeable as anybody. P IV 5 161 29
"What an immense time Mrs. Clay has been staying with " P IV 6 163 7
in the letter; when Mrs. Clay had paid her tribute of more P IV 6 166 17
Mr. Elliot was attending his two cousins and Mrs. Clay. P IV 7 174 2
she, Anne, and Mrs. Clay, therefore, turned into Molland's, P IV 7 174 2
But the rain was also a mere trifle to Mrs. Clay; she P IV 7 174 3
maintaining that Mrs. Clay had a little cold already, and P IV 7 174 3
It was fixed accordingly that Mrs. Clay should be of the P IV 7 175 4
and insinuations highly rational against Mrs. Clay. P IV 7 178 24
Sir Walter, his two daughters, and Mrs. Clay, were the P IV 8 181 1
added another motive) to watch Sir Walter and Mrs. Clay. P IV 9 207 90
"He thinks Mrs. Clay afraid of him, aware that he sees P IV 9 208 92
Elliot marry, that your father is not to marry Mrs. Clay. P IV 9 208 92
"but he gave so many hints; so Mrs. Clay says, at least." P IV 10 213 3
"Quite delightful!" cried Mrs. Clay, not daring, however, P IV 10 213 6
"My dear Miss Elliot!" exclaimed Mrs. Clay, lifting up her P IV 10 213 8
It was impossible but that Mrs. Clay must hate the sight P IV 10 213 10
It was bad enough that a Mrs. Clay should be always before P IV 10 215 13
breakfast but that Mrs. Clay was also going out on some P IV 10 215 14
She saw Mrs. Clay fairly off, therefore, before she began P IV 10 215 14
her window, "there is Mrs. Clay, I am sure, standing under P IV 10 222 34
on one side, as Mrs. Clay walked quickly off on the other; P IV 10 222 39
of Elizabeth and Mrs. Clay for the morrow's party, the P IV 10 227 69
agitation, to let Mrs. Clay know that she had been seen P IV 10 228 70
She cared not for Mrs. Clay, and had nothing to blush for P IV 11 246 78

MRS. CLAY'S (9)
of so much use to Mrs. Clay's health as a drive to P III 3 18 7
on her, which was Mrs. Clay's being engaged to go to Bath P III 5 34 11
to Anne, in Mrs. Clay's being of so much use, while Anne P III 5 34 11
You must have heard him notice Mrs. Clay's freckles." P III 5 35 14
off for Union-Street on a commission of Mrs. Clay's. P IV 7 175 5
Mrs. Clay's selfishness was not so complicate nor so P IV 10 215 13
that there was guilt in Mrs. Clay's face as she listened. P IV 10 228 70
He soon quitted Bath; and on Mrs. Clay's quitting it P IV 12 250 7
Mrs. Clay's affections had overpowered her interest, and P IV 12 250 8

MRS. COLE (24)
from the beaufet--"Mrs. Cole had just been there, just E II 1 155 4
as to dancing--Mrs. Cole was telling me that dancing at E II 1 156 7
rooms at Bath was-----Mrs. Cole was so kind as to sit some E II 1 156 7
Whenever she is with us, Mrs. Cole does not know how to E II 1 157 7
I was reading it to Mrs. Cole, and since she went away, I E II 1 157 10
Cole, we shall hardly know how to make enough of her now." E II 1 158 14
Cole told Mrs. Cole of it, she sat down and wrote to me. E II 3 173 27
not that I ever-----Mrs. Cole once whispered to me--but I E II 3 176 44
which he had to give Mrs. Cole of the rise and progress of E II 4 181 4
of all, there must be an answer written to Mrs. Cole." E II 7 209 13
Mrs. Cole seemed to be relating something of her that was E II 8 214 13
Mrs. Cole was telling that she had been calling on Miss E II 8 214 13
"One can suppose nothing else," added Mrs. Cole, "and I E II 8 215 14
Mrs. Cole had many to agree with her; every body who spoke E II 8 215 15
Emma to think her own way, and still listen to Mrs. Cole. E II 8 215 15
I am sure he was particularly silent when Mrs. Cole told E II 8 226 83
No; he was talking to Mrs. Cole--he was looking on E II 8 230 99
by somebody else, and he was still talking to Mrs. Cole. E II 8 230 99
Mrs. Cole was saying the other day she wanted something E II 10 244 40
"Mrs. Cole has servants to send. E II 10 244 41
'It is only Mrs. Cole,' said I, 'depend upon it. E III 8 379 8
resolve on seeing Mrs. Cole or any other steady friend, E III 8 379 9
not be denied--and Mrs. Cole had made such a point--and E III 9 390 18
Cole, Mrs. Perry, and Mrs. Elton, immediately afterwards. E III 17 468 35

MRS. COLE'S (5)
For it is not five minutes since I received Mrs. Cole's E II 3 173 27
I shall just go round by Mrs. Cole's; but I shall not stop E II 3 176 50
a certain glance of Mrs. Cole's did not seem to contradict, E II 4 182 6
communication of Mrs. Cole's, turned to Frank Churchill. E II 8 216 17
You can borrow Mrs. Cole's. E III 6 356 27

MRS. COLES (1)
Mrs. Perrys, and the Mrs. Coles, who would force E III 9 390 19

MRS. COLLINS (23)
Mrs. Collins welcomed her friend with the liveliest PP II 5 155 3
them; and as Mrs. Collins had settled it with her husband PP II 6 161 10
In the intervals of her discourse with Mrs. Collins, she PP II 6 163 15
to Mrs. Collins, was a very genteel, pretty kind of girl. PP II 6 163 15
Mrs. Collins, did I tell you of Lady Metcalfe's calling PP II 6 165 32
Mrs. Collins, gratefully accepted, and immediately ordered. PP II 6 166 42
usual reserve, to Mrs. Collins; and whatever might be his PP II 7 171 9
Collins, sat for some time without speaking to any body. PP II 7 171 10
more; and though Mrs. Collins has no instrument, she is PP II 8 173 10
to Jane, while Mrs. Collins and Maria were gone on PP II 9 177 1
"I should never have said Mrs. Collins was settled _near_ PP II 9 179 19
Mrs. Collins knew not what to make of him. PP II 9 180 29
at the idea; and Mrs. Collins did not think it right to PP II 9 181 30
Mrs. Collins, seeing that she was really unwell, did not PP II 10 187 41
Mrs. Collins will be very glad of your company, I am sure." PP II 14 211 6
I told Mrs. Collins so before you came. PP II 14 211 8
"Mrs. Collins, you must send a servant with them. PP II 14 211 13
You must send John with the young ladies, Mrs. Collins. PP II 14 212 13
said he, "whether Mrs. Collins has yet expressed her sense PP II 15 215 2
Lady Catherine's great attentions to Mrs. Collins you have PP II 15 216 6
Be assured, my dear sir, that Mrs. Collins and myself PP III 6 296 11
not only joined by Mrs. Collins, but likewise by Lady PP III 6 297 11
congratulations of Mrs. Collins and myself on this happy PP III 15 362 14

MRS. COLLINS'S (2)
Collins's joints of meat were too large for her family. PP II 7 169 3
pretty friend has moreover caught his fancy very much. PP II 8 172 3

MRS. CRAWFORD (5)
Admiral and Mrs. Crawford, though agreeing in nothing else, MP I 4 40 15
The Admiral delighted in the boy, Mrs. Crawford doated on MP I 4 40 15
for Mrs. Crawford, without throwing a shade on the Admiral. MP I 7 63 7
as her niece has been entirely brought up by her? MP I 7 63 8
suppose the next Mrs. Crawford would have half the reason MP II 12 296 29

MRS. CROFT (33)
He had seen Mrs. Croft, too; she was at Taunton with the P III 3 22 24
The sister, Mrs. Croft, had then been out of England, P III 4 31 11
way when Admiral and Mrs. Croft first arrived, she had P III 5 36 19
as it chanced that Mrs. Croft fell to the share of Anne, P III 6 48 17
Mrs. Croft, though neither tall nor fat, had a squareness, P III 6 48 18
may not have heard that he is married," added Mrs. Croft. P III 6 49 21
it was, that Mrs. Croft should be thinking and speaking of P III 6 49 22
With the exception, perhaps, of Admiral and Mrs. Croft, P III 8 63 3
must have been, ma'am!" said Mrs. Musgrove to Mrs. Croft. P III 8 70 51
"And I do assure you, ma'am," pursued Mrs. Croft, "that P III 8 70 54
opinion, Mrs. Croft," was Mrs. Musgrove's hearty answer. P III 8 71 55
for the Admiral and Mrs. Croft were generally out of doors P III 9 73 2
Elliot, I am sure _you_ are tired," cried Mrs. Croft. P III 10 91 40
my dear," replied _Mrs._ Croft, pleasantly; "for if Miss P III 10 92 45
girls, indeed," said Mrs. Croft, in a tone of calmer P III 10 92 47
must call on Mrs. Croft; I really must call upon her soon. P IV 1 125 14
Mrs. Croft always met her with a kindness which gave her P IV 1 126 19
Lady Russell and Mrs. Croft were very well pleased with P IV 1 128 31
"In the first place, I had a note from Mrs. Croft " P IV 6 164 8
off the gout, and Mrs. Croft seemed to go shares with him P IV 6 168 24
knot of the navy, Mrs. Croft looking as intelligent and P IV 6 168 24
not really Mrs. Croft, she must let him have his own way. P IV 6 170 30
letter to make you and Mrs. Croft particularly uneasy. P IV 6 172 42
Before Mrs. Croft had written, he was arrived; and the P IV 7 174 1
Musgrove, talking to Mrs. Croft, and Captain Harville to P IV 11 229 2
Mrs. Musgrove was giving Mrs. Croft the history of her P IV 11 230 5
Mrs. Croft was attending with great good humour, and P IV 11 230 5
precisely what I was going to observe," cried Mrs. Croft. P IV 11 230 7
"Oh! dear Mrs. Croft," cried Mrs. Musgrove, unable to let P IV 11 230 8
"Yes, dear ma'am," said Mrs. Croft, "or an uncertain P IV 11 231 9
Mrs. Croft was taking leave. P IV 11 236 35
Mrs. Croft left them, and Captain Wentworth having sealed P IV 11 236 39
with Admiral and Mrs. Croft, every thing of peculiar P IV 11 246 78

MRS. CROFT'S (8)
gentleman who lived at Monkford--Mrs. Croft's brother?" P III 3 23 25
On the morning appointed for Admiral and Mrs. Croft's P III 5 32 1
suspicion of Mrs. Croft's side, to give a bias of any sort. P III 6 48 18
electrified by Mrs. Croft's suddenly saying,-- "it was you, P III 6 49 18
19

to feel, when Mrs. Croft's next words explained it to be P III 6 49 22
Mrs. Croft's here soon; I dare say you know him by name." P III 6 49 23
24

my compliments and Mrs. Croft's, and say that we are P IV 1 128 29
and surprise, with Admiral and Mrs. Croft's compliments. P IV 6 162 1

MRS. DARCY (1)
Mrs. Bingley and talked of Mrs. Darcy may be guessed. PP III 19 385 1

MRS. DASHWOOD (119)
and to a woman in Mrs. Dashwood's situation, with only SS I 1 6 9
So acutely did Mrs. Dashwood feel this ungracious SS I 1 6 10
Mrs. Dashwood which must generally have led to imprudence. SS I 1 6 11
but by Mrs. Dashwood it was valued and cherished. SS I 1 7 13
so eligible to Mrs. Dashwood as remaining there till she SS I 2 8 1
But then if Mrs. Dashwood should live fifteen years, we SS I 2 10 18
Mrs. Dashwood remained at Norland several months; not from SS I 3 14 1
Mrs. Dashwood had been informed by her husband of the SS I 3 14 2
of Mrs. Dashwood, to her daughters' continuance at Norland. SS I 3 14 3
But Mrs. Dashwood was alike uninfluenced by either SS I 3 15 5
engaged much of Mrs. Dashwood's attention; for she was, at SS I 3 16 7
Mrs. Dashwood now took pains to get acquainted with him. SS I 3 16 13
him in; that Mrs. Dashwood could neither pretend to be SS I 4 23 19
No sooner was her answer dispatched, than Mrs. Dashwood SS I 5 25 1
it hard that as Mrs. Dashwood's income would be so SS I 5 26 4
Mrs. Dashwood took the house for a twelvemonth; it was SS I 5 26 5
unknown to Mrs. Dashwood, she preferred going directly to SS I 5 26 6
But Mrs. Dashwood began shortly to give over every hope of SS I 5 27 6
Mrs. Dashwood and her daughters to begin their journey. SS I 5 27 7
With the size and furniture of the house Mrs. Dashwood was SS I 6 29 4
of waiting on Mrs. Dashwood as soon as she could be SS I 6 30 7
Mrs. Dashwood and her daughters were met at the door of SS I 7 33 4
Mrs. Dashwood, who could not think a man five years SS I 8 37 3
you any idea of his coming so soon?" said Mrs. Dashwood. SS I 8 39 15
independence of Mrs. Dashwood's spirit overcame the wish SS I 9 40 2
and kindness of Mrs. Dashwood would have been secured by SS I 9 42 9
Mrs. Dashwood then begged to know to whom she was obliged. SS I 9 42 10
"You know him then," said Mrs. Dashwood. SS I 9 43 14
"I do not believe," said Mrs. Dashwood, with a good SS I 9 44 24
He was received by Mrs. Dashwood with more than politeness; SS I 10 46 1
In Mrs. Dashwood's estimation, he was as faultless as in SS I 10 48 9
Little had Mrs. Dashwood or her daughters imagined, when SS I 11 53 1
Mrs. Dashwood entered into all their feelings with a SS I 11 54 4
fortnight;--and Mrs. Dashwood, who had already a cold, was SS I 12 62 29
him: and on Mrs. Dashwood's happening to mention her SS I 14 72 6
Mrs. Dashwood looked with pleasure at Marianne, whose fine SS I 14 73 16
said, "and yet this house you would spoil, Mrs. Dashwood? SS I 14 73 17
Mrs. Dashwood again assured him that no alteration of the SS I 14 74 18
to dinner?" said Mrs. Dashwood when he was leaving them. SS I 14 74 21
Mrs. Dashwood's visit to Lady Middleton took place the SS I 15 75 1
Dashwood was convinced that her conjecture had been just. SS I 15 75 2
"Is any thing the matter with her?" cried Mrs. Dashwood as SS I 15 75 3
Mrs. Dashwood looked at Elinor with surprise. SS I 15 76 13
Mrs. Dashwood first spoke. SS I 15 76 13
Mrs. Dashwood was too much astonished to speak, and SS I 15 76 16
Mrs. Dashwood felt too much for speech, and instantly SS I 15 77 18
But Mrs. Dashwood could find explanations whenever she SS I 16 84 5
were all sunk in Mrs. Dashwood's romantic delicacy. SS I 16 85 10
one evening, Mrs. Dashwood, accidentally taking up a SS I 16 85 11
12

Mrs. Dashwood was surprised only for a moment at seeing SS I 17 90 1
quite overcome by the captivating manners of Mrs. Dashwood. SS I 17 90 1
The whole family perceived it, and Mrs. Dashwood, SS I 17 90 1
"if my children were all to be rich without my help." SS I 17 92 23
his tea from Mrs. Dashwood, his hand passed so directly SS I 18 98 10
pressed by Mrs. Dashwood to stay longer; but as if he were SS I 19 101 1
"I think, Edward," said Mrs. Dashwood, as they were at SS I 19 102 3
will be," said Mrs. Dashwood, "since leisure has not SS I 19 103 5
communicated to Mrs. Dashwood, gave additional pain to SS I 19 104 9
How does Mrs. Dashwood do? SS I 19 106 20
two strangers; Mrs. Dashwood and Margaret came down stairs SS I 19 106 21
to Mrs. Dashwood,) but you have made it so charming! SS I 19 107 24
This was quite a new idea to Mrs. Dashwood, she had never SS I 19 107 27
Mrs. Dashwood, who did not chuse to dine with them oftener SS I 19 108 40
if Mrs. Dashwood should not like to go into public." SS I 20 110 4
Mrs. Jennings repeated her assurance that Mrs. Dashwood SS II 3 154 6
On being informed of the invitation, Mrs. Dashwood, SS II 3 155 7
"And what," said Mrs. Dashwood, "is my dear prudent Elinor SS II 3 156 11
"I will have you _both_ go," said Mrs. Dashwood; "these SS II 3 157 16
Mrs. Dashwood _smiled_ and said nothing. SS II 3 157 18
Mrs. Dashwood, and asked how long they had been in town. SS II 6 176 7
To give the feelings or the language of Mrs. Dashwood on SS II 10 212 2
comfort, Mrs. Dashwood had determined that it would be SS II 10 213 3
marriage, which Mrs. Dashwood, from foreseeing at first as SS II 10 213 4
"What a charming thing it is that Mrs. Dashwood can spare SS II 10 218 34
Lady Middleton was equally pleased with Mrs. Dashwood. SS II 12 229 2
never hear you say how agreeable Mrs. Dashwood was!" SS II 13 239 9
delighted with Mrs. Dashwood, so we shall be a good deal SS II 13 240 15
Mrs. Dashwood seemed actually working for her, herself; SS II 14 254 26
Mrs. Dashwood had never been so much pleased with any SS II 14 254 28
reason for alarm; I hope Mrs. Dashwood will do very well." SS III 1 258 5
my dear, 'Lord!' says I, 'is Mrs. Dashwood ill?' SS III 1 258 7
Mrs. Dashwood declared they should not stay a minute SS III 1 259 7
Mrs. Dashwood was denied; but before the carriage could SS III 5 294 4
himself as the messenger who should fetch Mrs. Dashwood. SS III 7 311 15
Mrs. Dashwood, whose terror as they drew near the house SS III 9 334 4
As soon as Mrs. Dashwood had recovered herself, to see SS III 9 334 5
sleep;--but Mrs. Dashwood could be calm, could be even SS III 9 334 5
Mrs. Dashwood _would_ sit up with her all night, and Elinor, SS III 9 334 5
much softened to Mrs. Dashwood by her own previous alarm; SS III 9 334 6
cheerfulness of Mrs. Dashwood's looks and spirits proved SS III 9 335 7
But Mrs. Dashwood, trusting to the temperate account of SS III 9 335 7
of me," added Mrs. Dashwood, "even if I remain at Barton; SS III 9 338 24

Mrs. Dashwood, not less watchful of what passed than her SS III 10 340 3
twelve hours, Mrs. Dashwood, urged equally by her own and SS III 10 340 4
in return, Mrs. Dashwood was prevailed on to accept the SS III 10 341 4
invitation of Mrs. Dashwood and Mrs. Jennings, whose SS III 10 341 4
Mrs. Dashwood and Elinor then followed, and the others SS III 10 341 5
Mrs. Dashwood did not hear unmoved the vindication of her SS III 11 349 1
Had Mrs. Dashwood, like her daughter, heard Willoughby's SS III 11 349 2
Mrs. Dashwood would have interrupted her instantly with SS III 11 349 5
child," said Mrs. Dashwood; "she must be answerable." SS III 11 352 15
Mrs. Dashwood, whose eyes, as she answered the servant's SS III 11 353 24
Dashwood's assistance, supported her into the other room. SS III 11 353 25
Mrs. Dashwood immediately took all that trouble on herself; SS III 11 353 25
and Mrs. Dashwood probably found the same explanation. SS III 11 354 32
Mrs. Dashwood now looked at her daughter; but Elinor knew SS III 11 355 39
Mrs. Dashwood could think of no other question, and Thomas SS III 11 355 45
Mrs. Dashwood's and Elinor's appetites were equally lost, SS III 11 355 45
arranged, and Mrs. Dashwood and Elinor were left by SS III 11 355 46
Mrs. Dashwood feared to hazard any remark, and ventured SS III 11 355 46
Mrs. Dashwood, however, conforming, as she trusted, to the SS III 12 359 11
It was put an end to by Mrs. Dashwood, who felt obliged to SS III 12 359 14
address of Mrs. Dashwood could penetrate, and at last, SS III 12 360 26
Mrs. Dashwood, too happy to be comfortable, knew not how SS III 13 363 6
impossible that Mrs. Dashwood should advance anything, and SS III 13 369 32
to complete Mrs. Dashwood's satisfaction, and to give her SS III 13 369 34
Every thing was explained to him by Mrs. Dashwood, and he SS III 13 370 35
Mrs. Dashwood was acting on motives of policy as well as SS III 14 378 13
Mrs. Dashwood was prudent enough to remain at the cottage, SS III 14 380 20

MRS. DENNISON'S (1)
The consideration of Mrs. Dennison's mistake, in supposing SS II 14 252 20

MRS. DIXON (12)
Mrs. Dixon has persuaded her father and mother to come E II 1 159 20
between her and Mrs. Dixon, you could hardly have expected E II 1 160 22
But Mrs. Dixon must be very much disappointed. E II 1 161 26
Mrs. Dixon, I understand, has no remarkable degree of E II 1 161 26
Poor Mrs. Dixon! E II 6 202 33
"What do you say to Mrs. Dixon?" E II 8 216 28
"Mrs. Dixon! very true indeed. E II 8 217 29
I had not thought of Mrs. Dixon. E II 8 217 29
It is Mrs. Dixon I dare say. E II 8 217 29
But when you mentioned Mrs. Dixon, I felt how much more E II 8 219 42
According to Miss Bates--it all came from her--Mrs. Dixon E II 15 285 14
know, to be written to Colonel Campbell, and Mrs. Dixon. E III 8 378 8

MRS. DIXON'S (1)
warm--her large new shawl--Mrs. Dixon's wedding present.-- E III 2 322 19

MRS. ELEANORS (1)
The young Mrs. Eleanors and Mrs. Bridgets--starched up MP I 9 87 15

MRS. ELLISON (2)
married, for she and Mrs. Ellison could never agree."-- SS II 8 194 12
were gone, was a Mrs. Ellison, and that, as I have been SS II 8 199 37

MRS. ELTON (121)
A Mrs. Elton would be an excuse for any change of E II 4 182 8
Mrs. Elton was first seen at church: but though devotion E II 14 270 1
convinced her that Mrs. Elton was a vain woman, extremely E II 14 272 16
Mrs. Elton seemed most favourably impressed by the size of E II 14 272 18
for Mrs. Elton, who only wanted to be talking herself. E II 14 273 20
"No, I fancy not," replied Mrs. Elton, with a most E II 14 274 26
Mrs. Elton; "and that will be our time for exploring. E II 14 274 28
The idea of her being indebted to Mrs. Elton for what was E II 14 275 33
and only thanked Mrs. Elton coolly; "but their going to E II 14 276 34
"I do not ask whether you are musical, Mrs. Elton. E II 14 276 34
35
"Well," said Mrs. Elton, laughing, "we shall see." E II 14 278 42
after a moment's pause, Mrs. Elton chose another subject. E II 14 278 43
Elton hardly waited for the affirmative before she went on. E II 14 278 45
"Knightley!" continued Mrs. Elton;--"Knightley himself!-- E II 14 278 50
to wait on him and Mrs. Elton on this happy occasion; I E II 14 280 54
discovery, to retract her ill opinion of Mrs. Elton. E II 15 281 1
Such as Mrs. Elton appeared to her on this second E II 15 281 1
In one respect Mrs. Elton grew even worse than she had E II 15 281 3
Mrs. Elton took a great fancy to Jane Fairfax; and from E II 15 282 4
The kindness and protection of Mrs. Elton!-- E II 15 284 10
particular friend of Mrs. Elton, nor, under Mrs. Elton's E II 15 284 11
and condescending as Mrs. Elton meant to be considered. E II 15 284 12
attentions and tolerate Mrs. Elton as she seemed to do. E II 15 285 12
of Mrs. Elton, Mrs. Weston ventured this apology for Jane. E II 15 285 16
as any of us of forming a just opinion of Mrs. Elton. E II 15 286 18
attentions from Mrs. Elton, which nobody else pays her." E II 15 286 18
consideration too-- Mrs. Elton does not talk to Miss E II 15 286 22
23
Miss Fairfax awes Mrs. Elton by her superiority both of E II 15 286 23
that face to face Mrs. Elton treats her with all the E II 15 286 23
"In that respect how unlike dear Mrs. Elton, who wants to E II 15 288 39
in the triumph of Miss Fairfax's mind over Mrs. Elton. E II 15 288 39
attentions from Mrs. Elton which nobody else paid her. E II 16 291 5
Mrs. Elton, as elegant as lace and pearls could make her, E II 16 292 10
By this time, the walk in the rain had reached Mrs. Elton, E II 16 295 29
not do such a thing again," eagerly rejoined Mrs. Elton. E II 16 295 34
Mrs. Elton, before she could be spoken to, was ready; and E II 16 298 56
57
ill did Mrs. Elton engross Jane Fairfax and slight herself. E II 17 299 1
Mrs. Elton left them no choice. E II 17 299 1
Mrs. Elton, who can have thought of it as I have done?" E II 17 299 7
"Something that would do!" repeated Mrs. Elton. E II 17 301 16
I am exceedingly obliged to you, Mrs. Elton, I am obliged E II 17 301 19
assure you," replied Mrs. Elton gaily, "in resolving to be E II 17 302 20
himself close to Mrs. Elton, and her attention disengaged, E II 17 304 30
Mrs. Elton, very willing to suppose a particular E II 18 305 2
You must take care of yourself, Mrs. Elton.-- E II 18 305 7
ladies have very extraordinary constitutions, Mrs. Elton. E II 18 306 11
Mrs. Elton eagerly interposed with, "Oh! Mr. Weston, do E II 18 306 14
15
Mrs. Elton began to think she had been wrong in E II 18 307 17
I would not say so to every body, Mrs. Elton, but I have E II 18 307 18
lately have been full of very little else than Mrs. Elton." E II 18 308 25
I have observed, Mrs. Elton, in the course of my life, E II 18 308 27
and I do not know, Mrs. Elton, whether the uncertainty of E II 18 309 30
You cannot be ignorant, Mrs. Elton, of my connection with E II 18 309 33
for conversation; Mrs. Elton was wanting notice, which E II 18 311 36
Mrs. Elton was spoken of. E III 2 320 8
"I have a great curiosity to see Mrs. Elton, I have heard E III 2 320 8
first opinion of Mrs. Elton might be; how he was affected E III 2 320 13
Mr. Weston was following; but Mrs. Elton detained him, to E III 2 321 14
Mrs. Elton turned to Mrs. Weston. E III 2 321 17
into the room; and Mrs. Elton seemed to think it as much E III 2 322 18
Ah! dear Mrs. Elton, so obliged to you for the carriage!-- E III 2 322 19
Mrs. Elton had most kindly sent Jane a note, or we should E III 2 322 19
the discourse of Mrs. Elton and Miss Fairfax, who were E III 2 323 20
and properly taken, Mrs. Elton was evidently wanting to be E III 2 324 20
Mrs. Elton then said, "nobody can think less of dress in E III 2 324 20
21
"How do you like Mrs. Elton?" said Emma in a whisper. E III 2 324 25
It had just occurred to Mrs. Weston that Mrs. Elton must E III 2 325 29
to dance with Mrs. Elton himself, and that their business E III 2 325 31
Mr. Weston and Mrs. Elton led the way, Mr. Frank Churchill E III 2 325 31
Emma must submit to stand second to Mrs. Elton, though she E III 2 325 31
Mrs. Elton had undoubtedly the advantage, at this time, in E III 2 325 32
Stop, stop, let us stand a little back, Mrs. Elton is E III 2 329 45
Elton is going; dear Mrs. Elton, how elegant she looks!-- E III 2 329 45
first-rate qualities, which Mrs. Elton is totally without. E III 2 331 55
any man of sense and taste to such a woman as Mrs. Elton. E III 2 331 55
Mrs. Elton was very much disappointed. E III 6 352 2
been proposing to Mrs. Elton, as her brother and sister E III 6 353 3
and that as Mrs. Elton had very readily acceded to it, so E III 6 353 3
great dislike of Mrs. Elton, of which Mr. Weston must E III 6 353 3
weather fine; and Mrs. Elton was growing impatient to name E III 6 353 6
"--Mrs. Weston, I suppose," interrupted Mrs. Elton, rather E III 6 354 16
seemed as if, like Mrs. Elton, they were all taking the E III 6 357 31
from Richmond; and Mrs. Elton, in all her apparatus of E III 6 358 35
what Mrs. Elton and Jane Fairfax were talking of.-- E III 6 359 37
Mrs. Elton had received notice of it that morning, and was E III 6 359 37
Elton was wild to have the offer closed with immediately.-- E III 6 359 37
Still Mrs. Elton insisted on being authorized to write an E III 6 359 37
Miss Bates said a great deal; Mrs. Elton swelled at the E III 7 369 17
"It is a sort of thing," cried Mrs. Elton emphatically, " E III 7 370 20
be excused," said Mrs. Elton; "I really cannot attempt--I E III 7 371 37
ma'am," said Jane to her aunt, "shall we join Mrs. Elton?" E III 7 374 52
the solicitude of Mrs. Elton to have her carriage first, E III 7 374 54
"Mrs. Elton, I suppose, has been the person to whom Miss E III 8 380 14
"Yes, our good Mrs. Elton. E III 8 380 15
so she told Mrs. Elton over and over again--and I am sure E III 8 380 15
that good Mrs. Elton, whose judgement never fails her, saw E III 8 380 15
Jane took Mrs. Elton aside, and told her at once, that E III 8 381 15
"You spent the evening with Mrs. Elton?" E III 8 381 16
"Yes, all of us; Mrs. Elton would have us come. E III 8 381 17
would come, because Mrs. Elton declared she would not let E III 8 381 19
had been saying to Mrs. Elton, and when Mrs. Elton at the E III 8 382 29
Elton at the same moment came congratulating me upon it! E III 8 382 29
It was after tea that Jane spoke to Mrs. Elton." E III 8 383 29
Mrs. Elton is very good-natured and agreeable, and I dare E III 9 387 10
at all--Mrs. Elton, indeed, could not be denied--and Mrs. E III 9 390 18
Emma did not want to be classed with the Mrs. Eltons, the E III 9 390 19
Mrs. Elton gratitude for her attentions to Miss Fairfax.-- E III 14 439 8
of that officious Mrs. Elton; the whole system of whose E III 14 441 8
the bye, I wonder how Mrs. Elton bears the disappointment." E III 15 447 25
Emma, while you oblige me to read--not even of Mrs. Elton. E III 15 447 26
Mrs. Bates and Mrs. Elton were together. E III 16 453 11
Emma could have wished Mrs. Elton elsewhere; but she was E III 16 453 11
every body; and as Mrs. Elton met her with unusual E III 16 453 11
delight towards Mrs. Elton for being there, Emma guessed E III 16 455 20
it beyond a guess, Mrs. Elton, speaking louder, said, "yes, E III 16 455 20
21
Elton, but to Miss Woodhouse, as the latter plainly saw. E III 16 457 34
"I cannot imagine," cried Mrs. Elton, (feeling the E III 16 458 42
elegant terseness of Mrs. Elton, by calling you Mr. K.-- E III 17 463 14
Cole, Mrs. Perry, and Mrs. Elton, immediately afterwards. E III 17 468 35
But Mrs. Elton was very much discomposed indeed.-- E III 17 469 36
or parade; and Mrs. Elton, from the particulars detailed E III 19 484 12

MRS. ELTON'S (27)
of a friend of Mrs. Elton's, probably some vulgar, dashing E II 14 275 33
Her mind returned to Mrs. Elton's offences, and long, very E II 14 280 61
in society as Mrs. Elton's consequence only could surpass. E II 15 281 1
satisfied; so that Mrs. Elton's praise passed from one E II 15 281 2
heard all Mrs. Elton's knight-errantry on the subject.-- E II 15 282 4
The change on Mrs. Elton's side soon afterwards appeared, E II 15 284 11
Elton, nor, under Mrs. Elton's guidance, the very active E II 15 284 11
Miss Bates's gratitude for Mrs. Elton's attentions to Jane E II 15 284 12
And now to chuse the mortification of Mrs. Elton's notice E II 15 285 13
attentions as Mrs. Elton's, I should have imagined, would E II 15 286 19
20
Mrs. Elton's invitations I should have imagined any thing E II 15 286 20
eagerness in accepting Mrs. Elton's civilities for her. E II 15 286 21
never fell in Mrs. Elton's way before--and no degree of E II 15 287 23
I have no faith in Mrs. Elton's acknowledging herself the E II 15 288 39
especially on Mrs. Elton's side, there was no avoiding a E II 17 299 1
her, and professions of Mrs. Elton's meditated activity. E II 17 299 1
difficulty, upon Mrs. Elton's beginning to talk to him. E II 18 312 51
brought Mrs. Elton's tones again distinctly forward.-- E III 2 324 22
Mrs. Elton's looks also received the due share of censure. E III 2 330 46
able to defeat Mrs. Elton's activity in her service, and E III 5 343 1
degradation of being said to be of Mrs. Elton's party! E III 6 353 3
Mrs. Elton's resources were inadequate to such an attack. E III 6 353 6
so liberal and elegant, in all Mrs. Elton's acquaintance. E III 8 382 23
dear friend of Mrs. Elton's--a neighbour of Maple Grove; E III 15 447 25
if the sound of Mrs. Elton's voice from the sitting-room E III 16 453 10
She soon believed herself to penetrate Mrs. Elton's E III 16 453 12
the impossibility of any blunder on Mrs. Elton's side.-- E III 16 456 29

MRS. F. (2)
Though Lydia's short letter to Mrs. F. gave them to PP III 4 274 5
I am sincerely grieved for him and Mrs. F. but no one can PP III 4 275 5

MRS. FERRAR'S (1)
better knowledge of Mrs. Ferrar's disposition and designs. SS I 19 102 2

MRS. FERRARS (61)
to yield,--when Mrs. Ferrars would be reformed, and her SS I 19 102 2
with your sister-in-law's mother, Mrs. Ferrars?" SS I 22 128 3
it, as she answered that she had never seen Mrs. Ferrars. SS I 22 128 4
I am sorry you do not happen to know Mrs. Ferrars." SS I 22 128 9
Mrs. Ferrars is certainly nothing to me at present,--but SS I 22 129 11
Ferrars, must seem so odd, that it ought to be explained. SS I 22 129 16
"Mr. Edward Ferrars, the eldest son of Mrs. Ferrars of SS I 22 131 30
But Mrs. Ferrars is a very headstrong proud woman, and in SS II 2 148 15
and we spent the rest of the day with Mrs. Ferrars. SS II 11 221 9
And her mother too, Mrs. Ferrars, a very good-natured SS II 11 224 24
Mrs. Ferrars, with the utmost liberality, will come SS II 11 224 28
to make over for ever; but Mrs. Ferrars has a noble spirit. SS II 11 224 28
way; and Fanny and Mrs. Ferrars were both strongly SS II 11 228 53
They were to meet Mrs. Ferrars; but Elinor could not learn SS II 12 230 6
in company with Mrs. Ferrars, her curiosity to know what SS II 12 230 6
envy to Elinor. Mrs. Ferrars was a little, thin woman, SS II 12 232 14
which she offended Mrs. Ferrars and Fanny still more, did SS II 12 234 25
Mrs. Ferrars, not aware of their being Elinor's work, SS II 12 235 28
"Hum"--said Mrs. Ferrars--"very pretty,"--and without SS II 12 235 29
She was already greatly displeased with Mrs. Ferrars; and SS II 12 235 34
35
Mrs. Ferrars looked exceedingly angry, and drawing herself SS II 12 235 37
Elinor's curiosity to see Mrs. Ferrars was satisfied.-- SS II 13 238 1
by the civility of Mrs. Ferrars;--that her interest and SS II 13 238 2
in the world why Mrs. Ferrars should seem to like me, if SS II 13 239 9
Mrs. Ferrars is a charming woman, and so is your sister. SS II 13 239 9
Lady Middleton and Mrs. Ferrars will visit now;--and Mrs. SS II 13 240 15
visit now;--and Mrs. Ferrars and your sister were both so SS II 13 240 15
it in a moment, if Mrs. Ferrars had took a dislike to me. SS II 13 240 17
for fear of Mrs. Ferrars, and neither she nor your brother SS III 1 258 7
within call when Mrs. Ferrars is told of it, for she was SS III 1 259 7
for I am sure Mrs. Ferrars may afford to do very well by SS III 1 259 7
and I dare say, if Mrs. Ferrars would only allow him five SS III 1 259 7
What Mrs. Ferrars would say and do, though there could not SS III 1 260 9
Mrs. Ferrars too--in short it has been a scene of such SS III 1 265 36
"What poor Mrs. Ferrars suffered, when first Fanny broke SS III 1 266 38
All that Mrs. Ferrars could say to make him put an end to SS III 1 266 38
Mrs. Ferrars, is perhaps altogether a little extraordinary. SS III 1 267 45
is terrible-- Mrs. Ferrars does not know what she may be SS III 3 282 19
"Mrs. Ferrars," added he, lowering his voice to the tone SS III 5 295 18
Though it is not to be supposed that Mrs. Ferrars can have SS III 5 296 19
Mrs. Ferrars can never forget that Edward is her son." SS III 5 296 20
Mrs. Ferrars is one of the most affectionate mothers in SS III 5 296 22
precisely heard Mrs. Ferrars say it herself--but her SS III 5 297 31
I was exceedingly pleased to hear that Mrs. Ferrars SS III 5 297 31
"They come straight from town, as Miss Lucy--Mrs. Ferrars SS III 11 354 36
"Did Mrs. Ferrars look well?" SS III 11 355 43
obliged to hope that he had left Mrs. Ferrars very well. SS III 12 359 14
her own voice, now said, "is Mrs. Ferrars at Longstaple?" SS III 12 359 16
17
fright for fear of Mrs. Ferrars, as well as not knowing SS III 13 370 37
Mrs. Ferrars was the most unfortunate of women--poor Fanny SS III 13 371 38

Context	Work	Vol.	Ch.	Page	Line
to be mentioned to Mrs. Ferrars; and even, if she might	SS	III	13	371	38
He thus continued: "Mrs. Ferrars has never yet mentioned	SS	III	13	371	38
					39
After a proper resistance on the part of Mrs. Ferrars,	SS	III	14	373	1
Mrs. Ferrars at first reasonably endeavoured to dissuade	SS	III	14	373	3
and Elinor; and Mrs. Ferrars herself, by her shuffling	SS	III	14	374	5
Mrs. Ferrars came to inspect the happiness which she was	SS	III	14	375	8
But though Mrs. Ferrars did come to see them, and always	SS	III	14	375	10
reconciled Mrs. Ferrars to his choice, and re-established	SS	III	14	375	10
the forgiveness of Mrs. Ferrars, by the simple expedient	SS	III	14	376	11
Lucy became as necessary to Mrs. Ferrars, as either Robert	SS	III	14	377	11
assistance from Mrs. Ferrars, were on the best terms	SS	III	14	377	11

MRS. FERRARS' (1)

Context	Work	Vol.	Ch.	Page	Line
Or have you none but that of waiting for Mrs. Ferrars'	SS	II	2	148	14

MRS. FERRARS'S (11)

Context	Work	Vol.	Ch.	Page	Line
expectations, of Mrs. Ferrars's resolution that both her	SS	I	4	23	19
"What are Mrs. Ferrars's views for you at present, Edward?"	SS	I	17	90	2
being rich, and how acceptable Mrs. Ferrars's kindness is."	SS	II	11	226	35
it was not in Mrs. Ferrars's power to distress her by it	SS	II	12	232	16
The cold insolence of Mrs. Ferrars's general behaviour to	SS	II	12	236	39
					40
any other of Mrs. Ferrars's creation, preserved her from	SS	II	13	238	1
Could any thing be so flattering as Mrs. Ferrars's way of	SS	II	13	239	4
We all wish her extremely happy, and Mrs. Ferrars's	SS	III	1	268	45
Mrs. Ferrars's conduct, the Dashwoods' and Edward's.	SS	III	1	269	57
spoken of in Mrs. Ferrars's flattering language as only a	SS	III	13	369	33
tenderness of Mrs. Ferrars's heart, and that she wishes	SS	III	13	371	39

MRS. FORD (6)

Context	Work	Vol.	Ch.	Page	Line
I send it to Mrs. Goddard's, ma'am?" asked Mrs. Ford.	E	II	9	235	36
You could make it into two parcels, Mrs. Ford, could not	E	II	9	235	36
"It is not worth while, Harriet, to give Mrs. Ford the	E	II	9	235	37
trouble in the world, ma'am," said the obliging Mrs. Ford.	E	II	9	235	39
To Hartfield, if you please, Mrs. Ford."	E	II	9	235	41
delay from Miss Bates than, "how do you do, Mrs. Ford?	E	II	9	237	47
					48

MRS. FORSTER (12)

Context	Work	Vol.	Ch.	Page	Line
Kitty and me were to spend the day there, and Mrs. Forster	PP	II	16	221	17
(by the bye, Mrs. Forster and me are such friends!) and so	PP	II	16	221	17
Not a soul knew of it, but Col. and Mrs. Forster, and	PP	II	16	221	17
Lord! how I laughed! and so did Mrs. Forster.	PP	II	16	221	17
an invitation from Mrs. Forster, the wife of the Colonel	PP	II	18	230	11
her adoration of Mrs. Forster, the delight of Mrs. Bennet,	PP	II	18	230	12
"I cannot see why Mrs. Forster should not ask me as well	PP	II	18	230	13
of such a woman as Mrs. Forster, and the probability of	PP	II	18	230	14
When the party broke up, Lydia returned with Mrs. Forster	PP	II	18	235	40
violent hurry, as Mrs. Forster called her, and they were	PP	II	19	238	5
should go with Mrs. Forster, the necessity of opening her	PP	III	5	285	16
"She is so fond of Mrs. Forster," said she, "it will be	PP	III	8	313	21

MRS. FRANKLAND (1)

Context	Work	Vol.	Ch.	Page	Line
Alicia and Mrs. Frankland were telling me of last night.	P	IV	7	179	30

MRS. FRASER (8)

Context	Work	Vol.	Ch.	Page	Line
Mrs. Fraser has been my intimate friend for years.	MP	III	5	359	12
I wish I had settled with Mrs. Fraser not to go to her	MP	III	5	359	12
to Mrs. Fraser in consequence of his situation with you.	MP	III	5	360	16
My friend Mrs. Fraser is mad for such a house, and it	MP	III	12	416	2
Mrs. Fraser (no bad judge), declares she knows but three	MP	III	12	416	2
deriving support from the commendations of Mrs. Fraser!	MP	III	12	417	4
I do not like Mrs. Fraser.	MP	III	13	421	2
My greatest danger would lie in her consulting Mrs. Fraser,	MP	III	13	422	2

MRS. FRASER'S (2)

Context	Work	Vol.	Ch.	Page	Line
The last time I saw Crawford was at Mrs. Fraser's party.	MP	III	13	423	2
But he was pressed to stay for Mrs. Fraser's party; his	MP	III	17	467	20

MRS. GARDINER (39)

Context	Work	Vol.	Ch.	Page	Line
Mrs. Gardiner, who was several years younger than Mrs.	PP	II	2	139	2
Mrs. Gardiner, to whom the chief of this news had been	PP	II	2	140	5
"I hope," added Mrs. Gardiner, "that no consideration with	PP	II	2	141	12
these occasions, Mrs. Gardiner, rendered suspicious by	PP	II	2	142	18
To Mrs. Gardiner, Wickham had one means of affording	PP	II	2	142	19
Mrs. Gardiner had seen Pemberley, and known the late Mr.	PP	II	2	143	20
Mrs. Gardiner about this time reminded Elizabeth of her	PP	II	3	149	28
All this was acknowledged to Mrs. Gardiner; and after	PP	II	3	150	29
Mrs. Gardiner gave her the particulars also of Miss	PP	II	4	152	6
Mrs. Gardiner then rallied her niece on Wickham's	PP	II	4	153	7
carry us," said Mrs. Gardiner, "but perhaps to the lakes."	PP	II	4	154	22
arrived from Mrs. Gardiner, which at once delayed its	PP	II	19	238	7
and to Mrs. Gardiner it had a peculiarly strong attraction.	PP	II	19	239	7
Gardiner expressed an inclination to see the place again.	PP	II	19	240	12
Mrs. Gardiner abused her stupidity.	PP	II	19	240	15
Mrs. Gardiner looked at her niece with a smile, but	PP	III	1	247	10
Gardiner, looking at the picture; "it is a handsome face.	PP	III	1	247	12
"His father was an excellent man," said Mrs. Gardiner.	PP	III	1	249	35
from the house, Mrs. Gardiner, who was not a great walker,	PP	III	1	254	57
Mrs. Gardiner was standing a little behind; and on her	PP	III	1	254	58
Mrs. Gardiner, who was walking arm in arm with Elizabeth,	PP	III	1	255	60
It originated in Mrs. Gardiner, who, fatigued by the	PP	III	1	256	61
"From what we have seen of him," continued Mrs. Gardiner, "	PP	III	1	258	74
Mrs. Gardiner was surprised and concerned; but as they	PP	III	1	258	76
Mrs. Gardiner looked at her niece, desirous of knowing how	PP	III	2	263	11
Mrs. Gardiner and her niece, however, did her justice, and	PP	III	3	267	3
between her and Mrs. Gardiner, with occasional help from	PP	III	3	267	4
Mrs. Gardiner and Elizabeth talked of all that had	PP	III	3	271	20
to know what Mrs. Gardiner thought of him, and Mrs.	PP	III	3	272	20
of him, and Mrs. Gardiner would have been highly gratified	PP	III	3	272	20
what is to be done about Pemberley?" cried Mrs. Gardiner.	PP	III	4	280	26
"Upon my word," said Mrs. Gardiner, "I begin to be of your	PP	III	5	282	3
"And do you really know all this?" cried Mrs. Gardiner,	PP	III	5	284	13
Mrs. Gardiner and the children were to remain in	PP	III	6	294	3
As Mrs. Gardiner began to wish to be at home, it was	PP	III	6	298	15
Mrs. Gardiner went away in all the perplexity about	PP	III	6	298	16
which Mrs. Gardiner had formed, of their being followed by	PP	III	6	298	16
I understand from Mrs. Gardiner, that my niece is very	PP	III	8	313	19
I did not think Mrs. Gardiner was so little to be trusted.	PP	III	16	366	4

MRS. GARDINER'S (5)

Context	Work	Vol.	Ch.	Page	Line
The first part of Mrs. Gardiner's business on her arrival,	PP	II	2	139	3
Mrs. Gardiner's caution to Elizabeth was punctually and	PP	II	3	144	1
					2
the scene of Mrs. Gardiner's former residence, and where	PP	II	19	240	12
courage to shew Mrs. Gardiner's letter, or to relate her	PP	III	11	334	36
yet answered Mrs. Gardiner's long letter, but now, having	PP	III	18	382	20

MRS. GILBERT (3)

Context	Work	Vol.	Ch.	Page	Line
"If Mrs. Gilbert wishes to dance," said he, "I shall have	E	III	2	327	36
any time to stand up with an old friend like Mrs. Gilbert."	E	III	2	327	36
"Mrs. Gilbert does not mean to dance, but there is a young	E	III	2	327	37

MRS. GODDARD (25)

Context	Work	Vol.	Ch.	Page	Line
and Miss Bates and Mrs. Goddard, three ladies almost	E	I	3	20	3
Mrs. Goddard was the mistress of a school--not of a	E	I	3	21	5
was brought from Mrs. Goddard, requesting, in most	E	I	3	22	7
Mrs. Goddard, what say you to half a glass of wine?	E	I	3	25	14
what Mrs. Goddard chose to tell her; and looked no farther.	E	I	4	27	3
Mrs. Goddard, and the teachers, and the girls, and the	E	I	4	27	4
kind as to send Mrs. Goddard a beautiful goose: the finest	E	I	4	28	8
goose: the finest goose Mrs. Goddard had ever seen.	E	I	4	28	8
Mrs. Goddard had dressed it on a Sunday, and asked all the	E	I	4	28	8
Some time afterwards it was, "I think Mrs. Goddard would	E	I	7	55	40
Emma could not have allowed her to leave the house.	E	I	13	108	5
a bad sore-throat: Mrs. Goddard was full of care and	E	I	13	109	5
sorry to find from Mrs. Goddard that Harriet was liable to	E	I	13	109	6
I shall not attempt calling on Mrs. Goddard, for I really	E	II	3	177	50
how certainly Mrs. Goddard, if not Mrs. Bates, might be	E	II	7	208	9
I will step to Mrs. Goddard in a moment, if you wish it."	E	II	7	209	11
"He should be happy to see Mrs. Goddard.	E	II	7	209	13
He had a great regard for Mrs. Goddard; and Emma should	E	II	7	209	13
your not being exceedingly comfortable with Mrs. Goddard.	E	II	7	211	21
Bates as well as Mrs. Goddard being able to come; and her	E	II	8	213	6
But then, Mrs. Goddard will want to see it.--	E	II	9	235	36
Mrs. Bates, Mrs. Perry, Mrs. Goddard and others, were a	E	II	16	290	3
of her safety to Mrs. Goddard, and notice of there being	E	III	3	334	8
He knew of no one but Mrs. Goddard to whom he could apply	E	III	18	474	30
any thing more fit to be done, than to go to Mrs. Goddard?	E	III	18	474	30

MRS. GODDARD'S (33)

Context	Work	Vol.	Ch.	Page	Line
Mrs. Goddard's school was in high repute--and very	E	I	3	22	5
years back, at Mrs. Goddard's school, and somebody had	E	I	3	22	8
as large as Mrs. Goddard's drawing-room; and of her having	E	I	4	27	4
She had heard, as soon as she got back to Mrs. Goddard's,	E	I	7	50	1
hour or two to Mrs. Goddard's, but it was then to be	E	I	8	57	1
he should be at Mrs. Goddard's to day; and she may be	E	I	8	60	27
she is left in Mrs. Goddard's hands to shift as she can;--	E	I	8	62	42
Mrs. Goddard's line, to have Mrs. Goddard's acquaintance.	E	I	8	62	42
at Mrs. Goddard's all the rest of her life--or, at least, (	E	I	8	64	47
man's coming to Mrs. Goddard's that morning, and meeting	E	I	8	67	56
Mr. Perry had been to Mrs. Goddard's to attend a sick	E	I	8	68	58
Miss Nash, head-teacher at Mrs. Goddard's, had written out	E	I	9	69	4
to attend her in Mrs. Goddard's unavoidable absences, and	E	I	13	109	6
She had not advanced many yards from Mrs. Goddard's door,	E	I	13	109	6
by assurances of Mrs. Goddard's experience and care; but	E	I	13	110	8
should call at Mrs. Goddard's for news of her fair friend,	E	I	13	111	14
"My report from Mrs. Goddard's," said she presently, "was	E	I	13	114	29
when I called at Mrs. Goddard's door, which I did the very	E	I	13	114	31
not to go to Mrs. Goddard's, till it were certain that	E	I	15	125	4
She went to Mrs. Goddard's accordingly the very next day,	E	I	17	141	5
companions at Mrs. Goddard's; Mr. Elton being the	E	I	17	143	15
detaining her at Mrs. Goddard's, and that the intelligence	E	II	3	177	51
"She had set out from Mrs. Goddard's half an hour ago--	E	II	3	177	52
never been at Mrs. Goddard's; and a twelvemonth might pass	E	II	3	180	58
Martin's calling at Mrs. Goddard's a few days afterwards.	E	II	4	184	11
for her at Mrs. Goddard's, her evil stars had led her to	E	II	5	186	1
"Should I send it to Mrs. Goddard's, ma'am?" asked Mrs.	E	II	9	235	36
"Yes--no--yes, to Mrs. Goddard's.	E	II	9	235	36
send it all to Mrs. Goddard's --I do not know--no, I think,	E	II	9	235	40
should not at all like to have it sent to Mrs. Goddard's."	E	II	9	235	42
boarder at Mrs. Goddard's, who had been also at the ball,	E	III	3	333	5
her that he might have called at Mrs. Goddard's in his way.	E	III	13	425	8
The difference of Harriet at Mrs. Goddard's, or in London,	E	III	16	452	5

MRS. GRANT (87)

Context	Work	Vol.	Ch.	Page	Line
every day; and Mrs. Grant, instead of contriving to	MP	I	3	31	59
might have been good enough for Mrs. Grant to go into.	MP	I	3	31	59
Mrs. Grant had ever had more than five thousand pounds."	MP	I	3	31	59
and sister of Mrs. Grant, a Mr. and Miss Crawford, the	MP	I	4	40	15
Mrs. Grant knew nothing, she had scarcely seen them since.	MP	I	4	40	15
roof; and to this Mrs. Grant was indebted for her sister's	MP	I	4	41	15
on the other; for Mrs. Grant having by this time run	MP	I	4	41	15
well fitted up; and Mrs. Grant received in those whom she	MP	I	4	41	17
Grant immediately gave them credit for every thing else.	MP	I	4	41	17
which Mrs. Grant foresaw in her; and being a warm-hearted,	MP	I	4	42	17
"And now," added Mrs. Grant, "I have thought of something	MP	I	4	42	19
"There, Mrs. Grant, you see how he dwells on one word, and	MP	I	4	43	24
"I pay very little regard," said Mrs. Grant, "to what any	MP	I	4	43	25
be married, my dear Mrs. Grant, there is not one in a	MP	I	5	46	20
It delighted Mrs. Grant to keep them both with her, and Dr.	MP	I	5	47	26
but with Mrs. Grant, and Fanny stays at home with her."	MP	I	5	51	42
so at present," said Mrs. Grant to Mrs. Norris, with a	MP	I	6	53	5
"The truth is, ma'am," said Mrs. Grant, pretending to	MP	I	6	54	13
the others; and Mrs. Grant could not help addressing her	MP	I	6	60	53
Mrs. Grant hearing the latter part of this speech,	MP	I	6	61	58
Mrs. Grant and her tambour frame were not without their	MP	I	7	65	13
it right to attend Mrs. Grant and her sister to their home,	MP	I	7	65	14
by side, Dr. and Mrs. Grant, and Mr. Crawford, with two or	MP	I	7	67	16
as Mansfield common, Mrs. Grant has been telling her of	MP	I	7	69	28
It was meant and done by Mrs. Grant, with perfect good	MP	I	7	70	30
Before his return Mrs. Grant and Miss Crawford came in.	MP	I	8	75	2
and though Mrs. Grant, who had not been at the trouble of	MP	I	8	76	7
Mrs. Grant offered herself as companion for the day to	MP	I	8	79	28
and was on the point of proposing it when Mrs. Grant spoke.	MP	I	8	80	28
Mrs. Grant to alight and the others to take their places.	MP	I	8	80	29
by the hints of Mrs. Grant, inclined to credit what she	MP	I	12	115	4
Mrs. Grant, I believe, suspects him of a preference for	MP	I	12	116	8
with the help of Mrs. Grant and a new intimate friend of	MP	I	12	117	11
but Yates and Mrs. Grant--and, between ourselves, she,	MP	I	12	119	22
of Miss Crawford, Mrs. Grant had with her usual good	MP	I	17	159	6
Mrs. Grant was of consequence; her good nature had	MP	I	17	160	6
and shewed her that Mrs. Grant was entitled to respect,	MP	I	17	160	6
long have raised expectations in more than Mrs. Grant.--	MP	I	17	160	9
Will not that do, Mrs. Grant?	MP	I	17	162	15
Julia did suffer, however, though Mrs. Grant discerned it	MP	I	17	162	19
unintelligible, that Mrs. Grant spoilt every thing by	MP	I	18	164	2
in the evening; Mrs. Grant and the Crawfords were engaged	MP	I	18	171	25
only the arrival of Mrs. Grant and the Crawfords to begin.	MP	I	18	171	25
wait long for the Crawfords, but there was no Mrs. Grant.	MP	I	18	171	26
could put Mrs. Grant right the other day in twenty places.	MP	I	18	172	31
'Upon my word, Mrs. Norris,' said Mrs. Grant, the other	MP	II	2	190	7
congratulation and inquiry from Mrs. Grant to Lady Bertram.	MP	II	2	192	11
Dr. and Mrs. Grant would enliven us, and make our evenings	MP	II	3	196	2
and I can see that Mrs. Grant is very anxious for her not	MP	II	3	199	15
Mrs. Grant, really eager to get any change for her sister,	MP	II	4	205	2
I must admire the taste Mrs. Grant has shewn in all this.	MP	II	4	209	14
who then appeared walking towards them with Mrs. Grant.	MP	II	4	211	22
"They cannot have been sitting long," cried Mrs. Grant, "	MP	II	4	211	28
the first; but you, Mrs. Grant, my sister, my own sister,	MP	II	4	212	30
as she ought to Mrs. Grant, by whose side she was now	MP	II	4	214	46
the occasion, when Mrs. Grant, with sudden recollection,	MP	II	4	215	47
were heard to the contrary, Mrs. Grant might expect her.	MP	II	4	215	47
"And you know what your dinner will be," said Mrs. Grant,	MP	II	4	215	48
"But why should Mrs. Grant ask Fanny?" said Lady Bertram.	MP	II	5	217	1
"I cannot imagine why Mrs. Grant should think of asking	MP	II	5	217	3
it a right thing by Mrs. Grant, as well as by Fanny, that	MP	II	5	217	9
But he will be very much surprized that Mrs. Grant should	MP	II	5	217	10
Mrs. Grant has asked Fanny to dinner!"	MP	II	5	218	12
add, "so strange! for Mrs. Grant never used to ask her."	MP	II	5	218	16
Edmund, "that Mrs. Grant should wish to procure so	MP	II	5	218	17
You ought to be very much obliged to Mrs. Grant for	MP	II	5	220	28
Mrs. Grant thinks it a civility due to us to take a little	MP	II	5	220	28
lady as Mrs. Grant should not contrive better!	MP	II	5	220	30
Mr. Crawford and Mrs. Grant, as to leave her to fairest	MP	II	5	223	48
to engross them, and Mrs. Grant occupied at the tea-table,	MP	II	5	224	49
predetermination of Mrs. Grant and her sister, that after	MP	II	7	239	4
answer--"then speculation if you please, Mrs. Grant.	MP	II	7	239	7
Norris, and Dr. and Mrs. Grant, being seated at the table	MP	II	7	239	8
could be known till Mrs. Grant was able, at the end of the	MP	II	7	240	10
had heard her tell Mrs. Grant that she should leave her	MP	II	8	256	12
and apply to Mrs. Grant and her sister, whose acknowledged	MP	II	8	256	14
Dr. and Mrs. Grant, who were together in the drawing-room.	MP	II	8	257	15
out of the room; and Mrs. Grant coming up to the two girls	MP	II	10	275	9
Thursday night with Mrs. Grant and Miss Crawford, in a	MP	II	11	283	7
I do not like the idea of leaving Mrs. Grant now the time	MP	II	11	289	30
he; "I cannot admit Mrs. Grant to have an equal claim with	MP	II	12	295	23
Mrs. Grant laughed at her for her rapidity."	MP	III	4	352	36
"Was Mrs. Grant in the room, then?"	MP	III	4	352	37
"And Mrs. Grant, did she say--did she speak--was she there	MP	III	4	352	43
to your friend and Mrs. Grant, and they were both better	MP	III	4	353	46
And the other, that you will often call on Mrs. Grant and	MP	III	5	364	32
Mrs. Grant, with a temper to love and be loved, must have	MP	III	17	469	24

MRS. GRANT'S (10)

Context	Work	Vol.	Ch.	Page	Line
of beauty in Mrs. Grant's being so well settled in life	MP	I	3	31	60
of her sister, and Mrs. Grant's wasteful doings to	MP	I	4	34	3

Mrs. Grant's manners are just what they ought to be. MP I 7 64 9
was settled by Mrs. Grant's saying, as she stepped from MP I 8 80 29
Mrs. Grant's non-attendance was sad indeed. MP I 18 171 28
an half hour in Mrs. Grant's shrubbery, the weather being MP II 4 208 11
Mrs. Grant's shewing civility to Miss Price, to Lady MP II 5 218 18
done away all Mrs. Grant's part of the favour, that Fanny, MP II 5 220 29
against Dr. and Mrs. Grant's great hands, she called out MP II 7 245 32
gouty symptoms and Mrs. Grant's morning calls, it was very MP III 13 425 6

MRS. HARVILLE (18)
"But you, yourself, brought Mrs. Harville, her sister, her P III 8 69 39
my taking Mrs. Harville, and all her family, to Plymouth." P III 8 69 44
Harville, and a Captain Benwick, who was staying with them. P III 11 96 11
Mrs. Harville, a degree less polished than her husband, P III 11 97 15
by Captain and Mrs. Harville, and Captain Benwick, with P III 12 107 22
from Captain and Mrs. Harville at their door, and still P III 12 108 30
Mrs. Harville was a very experienced nurse; and her P III 12 113 56
to Captain and Mrs. Harville; but as to leaving his sister P III 12 113 58
to assist Mrs. Harville, I think it need be only one.-- P III 12 114 61
sufficient for her, if Mrs. Harville would but think so." P III 12 114 63
was, that Mrs. Harville left nothing for any body to do." P IV 1 121 2
at least relieve Mrs. Harville from the care of her own P IV 1 122 5
and at first, Mrs. Harville had always given Mrs. Musgrove P IV 2 129 3
"Mrs. Harville must be an odd mother to part with them so " P IV 6 163 7
"Mrs. Harville says her husband feels a good deal on his " P IV 6 165 8
"Indeed Mrs. Harville and I quite agree that we love her P IV 6 165 8
with him, and Mrs. Harville had seemed to like the idea of P IV 10 216 19
Mrs. Harville, her children, and Captain Benwick, remained P IV 10 217 19

MRS. HARVILLE'S (6)
Mrs. Harville's giving it as her opinion that her husband P III 12 108 30
Louisa, under Mrs. Harville's direction, was conveyed up P III 12 111 50
uneasiness in leaving her to Mrs. Harville's care entirely. P III 12 113 56
especially of Mrs. Harville's exertions as a nurse. P IV 1 121 2
Mrs. Musgrove had got Mrs. Harville's children away as P IV 2 129 2
with them Mrs. Harville's little children, to improve the P IV 2 133 27

MRS. HAYTER (1)
Mrs. Musgrove and Mrs. Hayter were sisters. P III 9 74 5

MRS. HILL (3)
"Dear madam," cried Mrs. Hill, in great astonishment, " PP III 7 301 3
Mrs. Hill began instantly to express her joy. PP III 7 307 50
of being married, to Mrs. Hill and the two housemaids. PP III 9 317 10

MRS. HODGES (5)
than any thing; but Mrs. Hodges, he said, was quite E II 9 239 51
to us about it, for Mrs. Hodges would be cross sometimes, E II 9 239 51
Mrs. Hodges may well be angry. E II 10 245 52
If you wish me to talk to Mrs. Hodges, or to inspect E III 6 355 22
And as for Mrs. Hodges, Wright holds her very cheap indeed. E III 16 458 42

MRS. HOLFORD'S (1)
I met her at Mrs. Holford's--and did not recollect her. MP I 5 50 35

MRS. HUGHES (16)
to accommodate Mrs. Hughes and Miss Tilney with seats, as NA I 8 54 10
round, perceived Mrs. Hughes directly behind her, attended NA I 8 55 10
Mrs. Hughes could not have applied to any creature in the NA I 8 55 10
the obligation; and Mrs. Hughes, satisfied with having so NA I 8 55 10
met Mrs. Hughes, and Mr. and Miss Tilney walking with her." NA I 9 68 40
Mrs. Hughes talked to me a great deal about the family." NA I 9 68 42
Mrs. Tilney was a Miss Drummond, and she and Mrs. Hughes NA I 9 68 46
Mrs. Hughes saw all the clothes after they came from the NA I 9 68 46
is dead, because Mrs. Hughes told me there was a very NA I 9 68 48
young man Mrs. Hughes says, and likely to do very well." NA I 9 69 50
the room with Mrs. Hughes, and whom she instantly joined, NA I 10 72 8
"Yes, an acquaintance of Mrs. Hughes." NA I 10 73 14
Mrs. Hughes now joined them, and asked Miss Tilney if she NA I 10 73 19
Besides, I thought Mrs. Hughes, who introduced him, might NA II 1 134 39
Ah! Dr. Hughes I declare--and Mrs. Hughes. E III 2 323 19
Must go and speak to Dr. and Mrs. Hughes for a moment.-- E III 2 323 19

MRS. HURST (20)
Mr. Darcy danced only once with Mrs. Hurst and once with PP I 3 11 6
his table, nor was Mrs. Hurst, who had married a man of PP I 4 15 13
Mrs. Hurst and her sister allowed it to be so--but still PP I 4 17 16
on the good will of Mrs. Hurst and Miss Bingley; and PP I 6 21 1
almost incredible to Mrs. Hurst and Miss Bingley; and PP I 7 32 42
Mrs. Hurst thought the same, and added, "she has nothing, PP I 8 35 3
4

A short pause followed this speech, and Mrs. Hurst began PP I 8 36 13
Mrs. Hurst and Miss Bingley both cried out against the PP I 8 40 55
Mrs. Hurst and Miss Bingley had spent some hours of the PP I 10 47 1
Mr. Hurst and Mr. Bingley were at piquet, and Mrs. Hurst PP I 10 47 1
Mrs. Hurst sang with her sister, and while they were thus PP I 10 51 46
met from another walk, by Mrs. Hurst and Elizabeth herself. PP I 10 53 59
"You used us abominably ill," answered Mrs. Hurst, "in PP I 10 53 61
did the same; and Mrs. Hurst, principally occupied in PP I 11 54 3
Mrs. Hurst and her sister scarcely opened their mouths PP I 18 102 75
a silence as either Mrs. Hurst or Miss Bingley; and even PP I 18 103 75
My visit was not long, as Caroline and Mrs. Hurst were PP II 3 147 23
ladies of my acquaintance, Mrs. Hurst and Miss Bingley. PP II 10 184 21
sitting there with Mrs. Hurst and Miss Bingley, and the PP III 3 267 3
By Mrs. Hurst and Miss Bingley, they were noticed only by PP III 3 267 4

MRS. HURST'S (1)
I dare say the lace upon Mrs. Hurst's gown-----" PP I 3 13 18

MRS. JAMES COOPER (1)
and Mrs. James Cooper; and of more than I can enumerate. E II 14 277 40

MRS. JEFFEREYS (1)
And the same may be said of Mrs. Jeffereys-- Clara E II 14 277 40

MRS. JEFFERIES (1)
to write to Mrs. Jefferies about his son, and the poor MP I 7 73 53

MRS. JENKINSON (8)
quadrille, while Mrs. Jenkinson was arranging Miss de PP I 19 105 10
The old lady is Mrs. Jenkinson, who lives with them. PP II 5 158 15
Catherine, her daughter, and Mrs. Jenkinson were sitting.-- PP II 6 161 10
a low voice, to Mrs. Jenkinson, in whose appearance there PP II 6 162 12
Mrs. Jenkinson was chiefly employed in watching how little PP II 6 163 14
Four nieces of Mrs. Jenkinson are most delightfully PP II 6 165 32
honour of assisting Mrs. Jenkinson to make up her party. PP II 6 166 41
except when Mrs. Jenkinson expressed her fears of Miss de PP II 6 166 41

MRS. JENKINSON'S (1)
day, and play on the piano forte in Mrs. Jenkinson's room. PP II 8 173 10

MRS. JENNINGS (200)
Mrs. Jennings, Lady Middleton's mother, was a good- SS I 7 34 5
his wife, or Mrs. Jennings to be Lady Middleton's mother. SS I 7 34 6
Mrs. Jennings was a widow, with an ample jointure. SS I 8 36 1
Mrs. Jennings had been anxious to see Colonel Brandon well SS I 8 36 1
ventured to clear Mrs. Jennings from the probability of SS I 8 37 3
Colonel Brandon is certainly younger than Mrs. Jennings, SS I 8 37 4
sentiments which Mrs. Jennings had assigned him for her SS I 10 49 12
Middleton and Mrs. Jennings, that could command the SS I 10 50 17
Neither Lady Middleton nor Mrs. Jennings could supply to SS I 11 54 6
When Mrs. Jennings attacked her one evening at the park, SS I 12 61 15
composure to become a standing joke with Mrs. Jennings. SS I 12 61 16
Margaret, let us know all about it," said Mrs. Jennings. SS I 12 61 21
"No bad news, Colonel, I hope;" said Mrs. Jennings, as SS I 13 63 8
Mrs. Jennings, without attending to her daughter's reproof. SS I 13 64 14
"In town!" cried Mrs. Jennings. SS I 13 64 20
"we might see whether it could be put off or not." SS I 13 64 27
"Aye, so do, Sir John," cried Mrs. Jennings, "and then SS I 13 65 38
"Come, Colonel," said Mrs. Jennings, "before you go, do SS I 13 66 50
his business is, however," said Mrs. Jennings exultingly. SS I 13 66 53
Mrs. Jennings sat on Elinor's right hand; and they had not SS I 13 67 61
Mrs. Jennings laughed heartily; and Elinor found that in SS I 13 67 65
circumstance related by Mrs. Jennings was perfectly true. SS I 13 68 67
"If the impertinent remarks of Mrs. Jennings are to be the SS I 13 68 74
the wonder of Mrs. Jennings for two or three days; she was SS I 14 70 1
So wondered, so talked Mrs. Jennings, her opinion varying SS I 14 70 3
away, which Mrs. Jennings was desirous of her feeling; for SS I 14 71 3
Sir John and Mrs. Jennings, indeed, were not so nice; SS I 16 85 11
12

by Sir John and Mrs. Jennings, who, having heard of the SS I 18 99 15
Mrs. Jennings enforced the necessity. SS I 18 99 18
Middleton and Mrs. Jennings, but there were two others, a SS I 19 105 13
They were now joined by Mrs. Jennings, who had not SS I 19 106 20
another, while Mrs. Jennings continued her story as she SS I 19 106 21
Mrs. Jennings, in the mean time, talked on as loud as she SS I 19 107 28
see them," added Mrs. Jennings, leaning forwards towards SS I 19 107 29
to be confined in February," continued Mrs. Jennings. SS I 19 108 31
Mrs. Jennings asked her, as soon as she appeared, if she SS I 19 108 35
Mrs. Jennings and Mrs. Palmer joined their entreaties, all SS I 19 109 40
"You and I, Sir John," said Mrs. Jennings, "should not SS I 20 111 21
ladies, whom Mrs. Jennings had the satisfaction of SS I 21 118 2
life, she thought Mrs. Jennings deficient either in SS I 21 126 41
is not," said Mrs. Jennings, laughing heartily; "for he is SS II 2 148 22
Though Mrs. Jennings was in the habit of spending a large SS II 3 153 1
Mrs. Jennings received the refusal with some surprize, and SS II 3 153 1
"Nay," cried Mrs. Jennings. "I am sure I shall be SS II 3 154 4
Mrs. Jennings repeated her assurance that Mrs. Dashwood SS II 3 154 6
acquainted with Mrs. Jennings' manners, and invariably SS II 3 155 6
very well of Mrs. Jennings' heart, she is not a woman SS II 3 156 12
by her dislike of Mrs. Jennings," said Marianne, "at least SS II 3 156 14
judgment, or that Mrs. Jennings should be abandoned to the SS II 3 156 15
Mrs. Jennings received the information with a great deal SS II 3 157 19
the carriage with Mrs. Jennings, and beginning a journey SS II 4 159 1
companionableness to Mrs. Jennings might be expected to be. SS II 4 160 2
attention to Mrs. Jennings, talked with her, laughed with SS II 4 160 2
she could; and Mrs. Jennings on her side treated them both SS II 4 160 2
It was a great satisfaction to Elinor that Mrs. Jennings, SS II 4 161 7
had caused to Mrs. Jennings, and she was fearful that her SS II 4 162 13
Mrs. Jennings soon came in. SS II 4 163 14
and Mrs. Jennings could not prevail on him to stay long. SS II 4 163 20
morning, to which Mrs. Jennings and Elinor readily SS II 4 164 23
longer," said Mrs. Jennings, when they met at breakfast SS II 5 167 1
to prevent Mrs. Jennings from seeing her sister's thoughts SS II 5 167 4
"It is indeed for Mrs. Jennings; how provoking!" SS II 5 169 20
Mrs. Jennings soon appeared, and the note being given her, SS II 5 170 28
civility to Mrs. Jennings, that they should both attend SS II 5 170 28
nodded to Mrs. Jennings from the other side of the room. SS II 5 171 30
"Aye,aye," said Mrs. Jennings, "we know the reason of all SS II 5 171 36
About the middle of the day, Mrs. Jennings went out by SS II 5 172 39
intimate, Mrs. Jennings, Mrs. Palmer, and the Middletons. SS II 5 173 44
party, from which Mrs. Jennings was kept away by the SS II 6 175 1
enough to find yourselves and Mrs. Jennings at home. SS II 6 177 9
for tears; but as Mrs. Jennings was luckily not come home, SS II 6 178 16
Jennings, had leisure enough for thinking over the past. SS II 6 178 16
As this was a favourite meal with Mrs. Jennings, it lasted SS II 7 181 7
Mrs. Jennings laughed again, but Elinor had not spirits to SS II 7 182 12
Mrs. Jennings, on account of her sister being indisposed. SS II 7 184 16
Mrs. Jennings, with a thoroughly good-humoured concern for SS II 7 185 16
An opportunity of coming hither, though with Mrs. Jennings, SS II 7 187 38
We owe Mrs. Jennings much more than civility; and civility SS II 7 191 63
that time till Mrs. Jennings returned, she continued on SS II 7 191 65
Mrs. Jennings came immediately to their room on her return, SS II 8 192 1
"Poor soul!" cried Mrs. Jennings, as soon as she was gone, SS II 8 194 8
After a short silence on both sides, Mrs. Jennings, with SS II 8 196 21
with a wine-glass, full of something, in her hand. SS II 8 197 26
Mrs. Jennings, though regretting that she had not been SS II 8 198 29
Mrs. Jennings was not struck by the same thought; for, SS II 8 198 30
Mrs. Jennings, who had watched them with pleasure while SS II 8 200 43
the presence of Mrs. Jennings, and in a determined silence SS II 9 201 2
sunk the heart of Mrs. Jennings still lower in her SS II 9 202 4
herself, though Mrs. Jennings was governed in it by an SS II 9 202 4
The cruelty of Mrs. Jennings no language, within her reach SS II 9 202 8
Mrs. Jennings left them earlier than usual; for she could SS II 9 203 10
"He will not come in, as Mrs. Jennings is from home." SS II 9 204 15
"I met Mrs. Jennings in Bond-Street," said he, after the SS II 9 204 18
their visit to Mrs. Jennings; the length of which, though SS II 10 213 3
for neither Mrs. Jennings, nor Sir John, nor even Mrs. SS II 10 214 8
hereafter; but Mrs. Jennings, who knew nothing of all this, SS II 10 216 15
to her; and Mrs. Jennings had for some time ceased to SS II 10 216 15
"Well, my dear," said Mrs. Jennings, "and how did you SS II 10 218 23
"Oh, Oh!" cried Mrs. Jennings; "very pretty, indeed! and SS II 10 218 25
Mrs. Jennings directly gave her the gratifying assurance SS II 10 218 29
"Long a time, indeed!" interposed Mrs. Jennings. SS II 10 219 35
with her and Mrs. Jennings one morning for half an hour. SS II 11 220 1
When they stopped at the door, Mrs. Jennings recollected SS II 11 220 2
and be introduced to your friend Mrs. Jennings. SS II 11 222 9
was introduced to Mrs. Jennings at the door of the SS II 11 222 13
Mrs. Jennings, however, assured him directly, that she SS II 11 223 14
kind; to Mrs. Jennings most attentively civil; and on SS II 11 223 14
Elinor on having such a friend as Mrs. Jennings. SS II 11 226 41
was the easiest means of atoning for his own neglect. SS II 11 228 51
And Mrs. Jennings too, an exceeding well-behaved woman, SS II 11 228 53
we only knew that Mrs. Jennings was the widow of a man who SS II 11 228 53
next day both on Mrs. Jennings and her daughter; and her SS II 12 229 1
suit the fancy of Mrs. Jennings, and to her she appeared SS II 12 229 3
There sisters and Mrs. Jennings were invited likewise, and SS II 12 230 6
so directly after Mrs. Jennings, that they all followed SS II 12 231 13
Mrs. Jennings, with a very intelligent "Ah! poor dear," SS II 12 236 41
Palmer soon after she arrived, carried Mrs. Jennings away. SS II 13 238 3
unsuspected by Mrs. Jennings, that she thought it a SS II 14 247 5
two sisters with Mrs. Jennings were first calling on her SS II 14 248 6
Berkeley-Street, Mrs. Jennings, on returning from her SS III 1 257 2
3

Here Mrs. Jennings ceased, and as Elinor had had time SS III 1 260 8
in it; that Mrs. Jennings (as she had of late often hoped SS III 1 260 8
As Mrs. Jennings could talk on no other subject, Elinor SS III 1 260 10
She attended to all that Mrs. Jennings had to say upon the SS III 1 265 33
another, and when Mrs. Jennings talked of Edward's SS III 1 265 33
"Then," cried Mrs. Jennings with blunt sincerity, no SS III 1 267 43
of any person whom you have a regard for, Mrs. Jennings. SS III 1 268 45
"Well, sir," said Mrs. Jennings, "and how did it end?" SS III 1 268 47
"Poor young man!" cried Mrs. Jennings, "I am sure he SS III 1 268 51
"Well!" said Mrs. Jennings, "that is her revenge. SS III 1 269 54
unnecessary in Mrs. Jennings, they all joined in a very SS III 1 269 58
Mrs. Jennings was very warm in her praise of Edward's SS III 2 270 1
already, that Mrs. Jennings might have had enough to do in SS III 2 270 3
Mrs. Jennings and Elinor were of the number; but Marianne, SS III 2 271 4
An intimate acquaintance of Mrs. Jennings joined them soon SS III 2 271 5
left her own party for a short time, to join their's. SS III 2 271 5
Mrs. Jennings immediately whispered to Elinor, "get it all SS III 2 271 5
6

And then lowering her voice, "I suppose Mrs. Jennings has SS III 2 271 8
I have not time to speak to Mrs. Jennings about it myself, SS III 2 275 25
sister away, and Mrs. Jennings should want company, I am SS III 2 275 25
compliments to Mrs. Jennings, before her company was SS III 2 276 26
As soon as they returned to the carriage, Mrs. Jennings SS III 2 276 27
produced from Mrs. Jennings the following natural remark. SS III 2 276 27
as likewise dear Mrs. Jennings, I spent two happy hours SS III 2 277 30
us, and dear Mrs. Jennings too, trust she will speak a SS III 2 277 30
say nothing; hope Mrs. Jennings won't think it too much SS III 2 277 30
in the hands of Mrs. Jennings, who read it aloud with many SS III 2 278 31
She calls me dear Mrs. Jennings, you see. SS III 2 278 32
holidays; and Mrs. Jennings, with both her friends, SS III 3 279 1
Mrs. Jennings was so far from being weary of her guests, SS III 3 280 7
Perhaps Mrs. Jennings was in hopes, by this vigorous SS III 3 280 9
Jennings commended her in her heart for being so honest. SS III 3 281 9
different ways, Mrs. Jennings very plainly heard Elinor SS III 3 281 13
14

Mrs. Jennings was delighted with her gratitude, and only SS III 3 282 15
Her emotion was such as Mrs. Jennings had attributed to a SS III 3 283 20
which Elinor, as Mrs. Jennings had supposed her to do, SS III 3 283 20
feelings of Mrs. Jennings; but after this narration of SS III 3 284 24
"Well, Miss Dashwood," said Mrs. Jennings, sagaciously SS III 4 285 1
"Opportunity!" repeated Mrs. Jennings--"Oh! as to that, SS III 4 285 5
at the door; and Mrs. Jennings immediately preparing to go, SS III 4 286 10
11
"Oh! very well," said Mrs. Jennings rather disappointed. SS III 4 286 14
This speech at first puzzled Mrs. Jennings exceedingly. SS III 4 286 16
He had met Mrs. Jennings at the door in her way to the SS III 4 287 25
"Mrs. Jennings told me," said he, "that you wished to SS III 4 288 27
Mrs. Jennings was quite right in what she said. SS III 4 288 28
When Mrs. Jennings came home, though she returned from SS III 4 291 46
"Two or three months!" cried Mrs. Jennings; "Lord! my dear, SS III 4 291 51
to either, for Mrs. Jennings only exchanged one form of SS III 4 292 54
able to assure Mrs. Jennings, who called on her again the SS III 5 293 1
and she joined Mrs. Jennings most heartily in her SS III 5 293 2
going at all; and Mrs. Jennings, though her carriage was SS III 5 294 3
her brother and Mrs. Jennings, but even Lucy, when they SS III 6 301 2
Mrs. Palmer had her child, and Mrs. Jennings her carpet- SS III 6 303 12
he must feel himself to be to Mrs. Jennings and Charlotte. SS III 6 304 15
his eyes, while Mrs. Jennings thought only of his SS III 6 305 16
Mrs. Jennings, who had been inclined from the first to SS III 7 307 3
Mrs. Jennings, however, with a kindness of heart which SS III 7 308 3
by a servant of Mrs. Jennings, were to have taken their SS III 7 308 4
Here, however, the kindness of Mrs. Jennings interposed SS III 7 309 5
Mrs. Jennings had determined very early in the seisure SS III 7 309 7
Mrs. Jennings, knowing nothing of any change in the SS III 7 310 9
would not allow Mrs. Jennings to be called, only tortured SS III 7 312 17
did Mrs. Jennings hear in the morning of what had passed. SS III 7 313 20
mother, when Mrs. Jennings considered that Marianne might SS III 7 313 20
conversation of Mrs. Jennings, who scrupled not to SS III 7 313 21
Mrs. Jennings, though forced, on examination, to SS III 7 314 22
Mrs. Jennings, perhaps satisfied with the partial SS III 7 314 23
she joined Mrs. Jennings in the drawing-room to tea. SS III 7 315 27
Mrs. Jennings would have persuaded her at its conclusion SS III 7 315 27
Mrs. Jennings therefore attending her up stairs into the SS III 7 316 27
received from Mrs. Jennings declared her danger most SS III 8 330 69
To Mrs. Jennings, to the Middletons, he has been long and SS III 9 337 17
her two friends; Mrs. Jennings could not quit Cleveland SS III 10 341 4
Mrs. Dashwood and Mrs. Jennings, whose active good-nature SS III 10 341 4
a leave of Mrs. Jennings, one so earnestly grateful, so SS III 10 341 5
own dulness, till Mrs. Jennings was summoned to her chaise SS III 10 341 5
The kindness, the unceasing kindness of Mrs. Jennings, I SS III 10 346 28
Brandon, of Mrs. Jennings, and of every wealthy friend. SS III 12 357 3
Mrs. Jennings wrote to tell the wonderful tale, to vent SS III 13 370 37
for Sir John and Mrs. Jennings, when Marianne was taken SS III 14 380 20

MRS. JENNINGS'S (33)

arise from such common-place raillery as Mrs. Jennings's. SS I 7 34 5
Sir John's and Mrs. Jennings's active zeal in the cause of SS I 21 118 1
the worse; and Mrs. Jennings's attempts at consolation SS I 21 118 2
acquaintance on Mrs. Jennings's side, and in laughter SS II 4 164 23
Mrs. Palmer and two elderly ladies of Mrs. Jennings's SS II 4 166 31
the houses of Mrs. Jennings's acquaintance to inform them SS II 5 168 8
with Mrs. Jennings's style of living, and set of SS II 5 168 11
Mrs. Jennings's entrance, escaped with the precious card. SS II 5 169 14
to engage Mrs. Jennings's notice entirely to herself. SS II 7 181 6
her fear it impossible to escape Mrs. Jennings's notice. SS II 7 181 7
chariot, which she knew had not been ordered till one. SS II 7 184 16
of half Mrs. Jennings's well-meant but ill-judged SS II 8 193 6
Elinor, who did justice to Mrs. Jennings's kindness, SS II 8 193 7
entertained by Mrs. Jennings's endeavours to cure a SS II 8 193 7
drawing-room on Mrs. Jennings's going away, remained fixed SS II 9 203 10
the arrival of Mrs. Jennings's servant, who came to tell SS II 11 222 12
This event, highly important to Mrs. Jennings's happiness, SS II 14 246 2
the morning, in Mrs. Jennings's house; but it was not a SS II 14 246 2
such, while Mrs. Jennings's engagements kept her from home. SS II 14 252 20
engaging all Mrs. Jennings's conversation, she was herself SS III 2 271 5
It was lucky, however, for Mrs. Jennings's curiosity and SS III 2 271 7
Mrs. Jennings's address to him when he first called on her, SS III 3 280 8
beginning of Mrs. Jennings's speech; neither did she think SS III 4 286 18
well justify Mrs. Jennings's persuasion of his attachment, SS III 6 305 16
head, except by Mrs. Jennings's suggestion; and she could SS III 6 305 16
Jennings's advice, of sending for the Palmers' apothecary. SS III 7 307 2
especially as Mrs. Jennings's entreaty was warmly seconded SS III 7 309 5
in listening to Mrs. Jennings's forebodings, was not in a SS III 7 309 7
On Mrs. Jennings's compassion she had other claims. SS III 7 313 20
Jennings's maid with her sister, she hurried down stairs. SS III 7 316 30
coming, and the day after I had called at Mrs. Jennings's. SS III 8 326 55
At his and Mrs. Jennings's united request in return, Mrs. SS III 10 341 4
Mrs. Jennings's prophecies, though rather jumbled together, SS III 14 374 7

MRS. JOHN DASHWOOD (24)

But Mrs. John Dashwood was a strong caricature of himself;- SS I 1 5 7
over, than Mrs. John Dashwood, without sending any notice SS I 1 5 9
Mrs. John Dashwood had never been a favourite with any of SS I 1 6 9
Mrs. John Dashwood now installed herself mistress of SS I 2 8 1
Mrs. John Dashwood did not at all approve of what her SS I 2 8 3
"Certainly," returned Mrs. John Dashwood. SS I 2 12 26
brother of Mrs. John Dashwood, a gentlemanlike and SS I 3 15 4
Mrs. John Dashwood wished it likewise; but in the mean SS I 3 16 6
Mrs. John Dashwood said nothing; but her husband civilly SS I 5 25 1
to shew Mrs. John Dashwood by this pointed invitation to SS I 5 25 3
Mrs. John Dashwood saw the packages depart with a sigh: SS I 5 26 4
Mrs. John Dashwood, is the person I mean; you must allow SS I 22 131 30
He is brother to Mrs. John Dashwood--that must be SS II 2 149 26
"But Mrs. John Dashwood would not much approve of Edward's SS II 2 149 27
John Dashwood very soon, and bring her sisters to see her. SS II 11 223 14
Mrs. John Dashwood had so much confidence in her husband's SS II 12 229 1
recommended Mrs. John Dashwood to the good opinion of Lady SS II 12 229 3
Their claims to the notice of Mrs. John Dashwood, as the SS II 12 231 9
life than she was on receiving Mrs. John Dashwood's card. SS II 12 231 9
which about this time befell Mrs. John Dashwood. SS II 14 248 6
The consequence of which was, that Mrs. John Dashwood was SS II 14 248 6
heart of Mrs. John Dashwood; and these were effects that SS II 14 254 27
disliked Mrs. John Dashwood, that not even her curiosity SS III 5 294 3
entrance of Mrs. John Dashwood put an end to the subject. SS III 5 300 38

MRS. JOHN KNIGHTLEY (9)

"Mrs. John Knightley is easily alarmed, and might be made E I 5 40 26
by Mrs. John Knightley, that in spite of maternal E I 11 92 3
Mrs. John Knightley was a pretty, elegant little woman, of E I 11 92 4
of him!" cried the good-hearted Mrs. John Knightley. E I 11 96 25
said Mrs. John Knightley--"it is so long since I have seen E I 12 104 46
world, than Mrs. John Knightley, in this short visit to E I 13 108 1
Have you heard from Mrs. John Knightley lately? E II 3 176 44
Mrs. John Knightley was delighted to be of use; any thing E III 16 451 3
charge of Mrs. John Knightley and little John, and the E III 18 472 20

MRS. KNIGHTLEY (4)

know, my dear Mrs. Knightley, that we are by no means so E I 14 121 16
A Mrs. Knightley for them all to give way to!-- E II 8 228 87
"No--Mrs. Knightley;--and, till she is in being, I will E III 6 355 17
Oh! no; there would be a Mrs. Knightley to throw cold E III 17 469 36

MRS. LONG (14)

"But it is," returned she; "for Mrs. Long has just been PP I 1 3 5
"Why, my dear, you must know, Mrs. Long says that PP I 1 3 10
and that Mrs. Long has promised to introduce him." PP I 2 6 4
"I do not believe Mrs. Long will do any such thing. PP I 2 6 5
"Aye, so it is," cried her mother, "and Mrs. Long does not PP I 2 6 13
will; and after all, Mrs. Long and her neices must stand PP I 2 7 16
Mrs. Long told me last night that he sat close to her for PP I 5 19 10
been so very agreeable he would have talked to Mrs. Long. PP I 5 19 14
heard somehow that Mrs. Long does not keep a carriage, and PP I 5 19 14
"I do not mind his not talking to Mrs. Long," said Miss PP I 5 20 15
And as I come back, I can call on Lady Lucas and Mrs. Long. PP III 7 307 49
We must have Mrs. Long and the Gouldings soon. PP III 11 333 26
Mrs. Long said so too, for I asked her whether you did not. PP III 12 342 28
I do think Mrs. Long is as good a creature as ever lived-- PP III 12 342 28

MRS. MARTIN (6)

there was no young Mrs. Martin, no wife in the case; she E I 4 27 5
Mrs. Martin had told her one day, (and there was a blush E I 4 28 6
"Well done, Mrs. Martin!" thought Emma. E I 4 28 7
"And when she had come away, Mrs. Martin was so very kind E I 4 28 8
thing; and Mrs. Martin talks of taking a boy another year." E I 4 30 21
She had seen only Mrs. Martin and the two girls. E II 5 186 4

MRS. MARTIN'S (3)

exultation of Mrs. Martin's having "two parlours, two very E I 4 27 4
indeed; and of Mrs. Martin's saying, as she was so fond of E I 4 27 4
at last, when Mrs. Martin's saying, all of a sudden, that E II 5 186 4

MRS. MORLAND (23)

not bear it;--and Mrs. Morland, who did not insist on her NA I 1 14 1
Mrs. Morland was a very good woman, and wished to see her NA I 1 15 3
Mrs. Morland will be naturally supposed to be most severe. NA I 2 18 2
But Mrs. Morland knew so little of lords and baronets, NA I 2 18 2
before; but I suppose Mrs. Morland objects to novels." NA I 6 41 20
of going; I am sure Mrs. Morland would not be pleased. NA I 13 104 31
it; for as I told Mrs. Morland at parting, I would always NA I 13 104 36
tea-table, which Mrs. Morland had hurried for the comfort NA II 14 233 9
"I am sorry for the young people," returned Mrs. Morland; " NA II 14 234 12
observed Mrs. Morland, as the letter was finished; "soon NA II 14 236 15
Mrs. Morland was not happy in her attempt at consolation. NA II 14 236 18
as they walked, Mrs. Morland quickly dispatched all that NA II 14 236 19
treated,--though Mrs. Morland's account of it was no NA II 14 237 21
I do not suppose, Mrs. Morland, you ever saw a better-bred NA II 14 238 26
As they walked home again, Mrs. Morland endeavoured to NA II 14 239 28
and while Mrs. Morland was successfully confirming her own NA II 14 239 28
For two days Mrs. Morland allowed it to pass even without NA II 15 240 2
Mrs. Morland watched the progress of this relapse; and NA II 15 241 7
misconduct, Mrs. Morland had been always kindly disposed NA II 15 242 7
Mrs. Morland's common remarks about the weather and roads. NA II 15 242 8
earnestly pitied, Mrs. Morland had very early dispatched NA II 15 242 9
her mother; for Mrs. Morland, thinking it probable, as a NA II 15 243 9
They began their walk, and Mrs. Morland was not entirely NA II 15 243 9

MRS. MUSGROVE (45)

And Mrs. Musgrove took the first opportunity of being P III 6 44 8
"Mrs. Musgrove thinks all her servants so steady, that it P III 6 45 9
Again; it was Mary's complaint, that Mrs. Musgrove was P III 6 45 10
time; and that Mrs. Musgrove should have been suddenly P III 6 51 31
kindly, while Mrs. Musgrove relieved her heart a little P III 8 64 7
"And so then, I suppose," said Mrs. Musgrove, in a low P III 8 66 18
"And I am sure, sir," said Mrs. Musgrove, "it was a lucky P III 8 67 24
"Poor dear fellow!" continued Mrs. Musgrove; "he was grown P III 8 67 27
on which she and Mrs. Musgrove were sitting, took a place P III 8 67 28
They were actually on the same sofa, for Mrs. Musgrove had P III 8 68 29
room for him;--they were divided only by Mrs. Musgrove. P III 8 68 29
Mrs. Musgrove was of a comfortable substantial size, P III 8 68 29
must have been, ma'am!" said Mrs. Musgrove to Mrs. Croft. P III 8 70 51
Mrs. Musgrove had not a word to say in dissent; she could P III 8 70 53
Mrs. Musgrove and Mrs. Hayter were sisters. P III 9 74 5
had been here--Mrs. Musgrove told me I should find them P III 9 78 22
before to Mrs. Musgrove and Henrietta; but without Anne, P IV 1 122 3
Mrs. Musgrove had got Mrs. Harville's children away as P IV 2 129 2
had always given Mrs. Musgrove precedence; but then, she P IV 2 129 3
Immediately surrounding Mrs. Musgrove were the little P IV 2 134 29
shaken; but Mrs. Musgrove, who got Anne near her on P IV 2 134 30
and, like Mrs. Musgrove, she was feeling, though not P IV 2 135 33
my opinion; but "Mrs. Musgrove seems to like them quite as P IV 6 163 7
the day "after, Mrs. Musgrove is so afraid of her being P IV 6 163 7
"Mrs. Musgrove protests solemnly that she knew nothing of " P IV 6 165 8
They were come to Bath for a few days with Mrs. Musgrove, P IV 10 216 18
She then found that it consisted of Mrs. Musgrove, P IV 10 216 19
She felt that Mrs. Musgrove and all her party ought to be P IV 10 219 29
to Mrs. Musgrove--put her quite out of her way. P IV 10 219 29
of calling on Mrs. Musgrove in the course of the morning. P IV 10 220 29
They found Mrs. Musgrove and her daughter within, and by P IV 10 220 31
were seated round Mrs. Musgrove, and Charles came back P IV 10 221 32
Mrs. Musgrove was good humouredly beginning to express her P IV 10 223 42
43
Mrs. Musgrove interposed. P IV 10 224 50
The party before her were Mrs. Musgrove, talking to Mrs. P IV 11 229 2
with Mrs. Musgrove, to keep her there till they returned. P IV 11 229 2
Mrs. Musgrove was giving Mrs. Croft the history of her P IV 11 230 5
which good Mrs. Musgrove could not give, could be properly P IV 11 230 5
considered," said Mrs. Musgrove in her powerful whisper, " P IV 11 230 6
"Oh! dear Mrs. Croft," cried Mrs. Musgrove, unable to let P IV 11 230 8
his back towards Mrs. Musgrove, he drew out a letter from P IV 11 236 40
almost before Mrs. Musgrove was aware of his being in it-- P IV 11 236 40
Mrs. Musgrove had little arrangements of her own at her P IV 11 237 41
42
"By all means, my dear," cried Mrs. Musgrove, "go home P IV 11 238 46
against; and Mrs. Musgrove, who thought only of one sort P IV 11 238 47

MRS. MUSGROVE'S (6)

And on Mrs. Musgrove's side, it was,--"I make a rule of P III 6 45 9
by a whisper of Mrs. Musgrove's, who, overcome by fond P III 8 64 5
6
of sharing in Mrs. Musgrove's kind wishes, as to her son, P III 8 67 28
opinion, Mrs. Croft," was Mrs. Musgrove's hearty answer. P III 8 71 55
at all; and Mrs. Musgrove's real affection had been won by P IV 10 220 31
listening to Mrs. Musgrove's history of Louisa, and to P IV 10 220 31

MRS. NICHOLLS (1)

the other, "for Mrs. Nicholls was in Meryton last night; I PP III 11 331 15

MRS. NORRIS (157)

of the matter: but Mrs. Norris had a spirit of activity, MP I 1 4 1
of Sir Thomas, as Mrs. Norris could not possibly keep to MP I 1 4 1
to Sir Thomas, that Mrs. Norris should ever have it in her MP I 1 4 2
money and baby-linen, and Mrs. Norris wrote the letters. MP I 1 5 3
Mrs. Norris was often observing to the others, that she MP I 1 5 4
objections, than Mrs. Norris interrupted him with a reply MP I 1 6 5
"I thoroughly understand you," cried Mrs. Norris; "you are MP I 1 7 8
selected child, and Mrs. Norris had not the least MP I 1 8 9
Had there been a family to provide for, Mrs. Norris might MP I 1 8 9
Mrs. Norris was sorry to say, that the little girl's MP I 1 9 10
"Very true," cried Mrs. Norris, "which are both very MP I 1 9 12
girl," continued Mrs. Norris, "and be sensible of her MP I 1 10 13
"That is exactly what I think," cried Mrs. Norris, "and MP I 1 10 15
"There will be some difficulty in our way, Mrs. Norris," MP I 1 10 17
Mrs. Norris was quite at his service; and though she MP I 1 11 18
It will be readily believed that Mrs. Norris did not write MP I 1 11 19
was met by Mrs. Norris, who thus regaled in the credit of MP I 2 12 1
Mrs. Norris had been talking to her the whole way from MP I 2 13 4
prognostications of Mrs. Norris that she would be a good MP I 2 13 4
"This is not a very promising beginning," said Mrs. Norris MP I 2 13 5
It required a longer time, however, than Mrs. Norris was MP I 2 14 6
Sir Thomas and Mrs. Norris thought with greater MP I 2 18 23
Such were the counsels by which Mrs. Norris assisted to MP I 2 19 30
Mrs. Norris, on quitting the parsonage, removed first to MP I 3 23 1
Mrs. Norris is much better fitted than my mother for MP I 3 27 33
"And I am quite convinced that your being with Mrs. Norris, MP I 3 27 37
Mrs. Norris had not the smallest intention of taking her. MP I 3 28 38
observing to Mrs. Norris,-- "I think, sister, we need not MP I 3 28 38
39
Mrs. Norris almost started. MP I 3 28 40
"Well, Lady Bertram," said Mrs. Norris, moving to go, "I MP I 3 30 56
Mrs. Norris took possession of the white house, the Grants MP I 3 31 58
They had their faults, and Mrs. Norris soon found them out. MP I 3 31 59

Mrs. Norris could not speak with any temper of such	MP	I	3	31	59
not so diffusely, as Mrs. Norris discussed the other.	MP	I	3	31	60
though not before Mrs. Norris had been indulging in very	MP	I	4	34	2
good;--and Mrs. Norris in promoting gaieties for her	MP	I	4	34	3
to herself; and Mrs. Norris, who was walking all day,	MP	I	4	36	7
Mrs. Norris could not help thinking that some steady old	MP	I	4	36	7
Mrs. Norris could not see it in the same light.	MP	I	4	36	7
property of Edmund, Mrs. Norris could tolerate its being	MP	I	4	37	9
very little purpose, as far as Mrs. Norris was concerned.	MP	I	4	38	9
Mrs. Norris was most zealous in promoting the match, by	MP	I	4	39	10
Mrs. Norris accepted the compliment, and admired the nice	MP	I	4	39	10
but yet as far as Mrs. Norris could allow herself to	MP	I	4	39	10
"Oh! for shame!" cried Mrs. Norris.	MP	I	6	53	3
said Mrs. Grant to Mrs. Norris, with a smile; "but depend	MP	I	6	53	5
"Well, and if they were ten," cried Mrs. Norris, "I am	MP	I	6	53	9
across the table to Mrs. Norris, "that Dr. Grant hardly	MP	I	6	54	13
Mrs. Norris, who had begun to redden, was appeased, and,	MP	I	6	55	14
Dr. Grant and Mrs. Norris were seldom good friends; their	MP	I	6	55	14
a bed there; when Mrs. Norris, as if reading in her two	MP	I	6	61	58
Fanny was ready and waiting, and Mrs. Norris was beginning	MP	I	7	67	15
asleep; and even Mrs. Norris, discomposed by her niece's	MP	I	7	71	31
"No, not that I know of," replied Mrs. Norris; "she was	MP	I	7	71	32
Mrs. Norris began scolding.	MP	I	7	71	33
"Go out! to be sure she did," said Mrs. Norris; "would you	MP	I	7	72	41
"There was no help for it certainly," rejoined Mrs. Norris,	MP	I	7	72	45
Mrs. Norris was talking to Julia, and did not hear.	MP	I	7	72	48
done better," cried Mrs. Norris, unable to be longer deaf;	MP	I	7	73	53
Mrs. Norris and her nieces were all well pleased with its	MP	I	8	75	1
and though Mrs. Norris would willingly have answered for	MP	I	8	75	1
be talked of, for Mrs. Norris was in high spirits about it,	MP	I	8	75	2
dear madam," cried Mrs. Norris; "but as to Fanny, she will	MP	I	8	76	5
On his return to the breakfast-room, he found Mrs. Norris	MP	I	8	77	8
"And my dear Edmund," added Mrs. Norris, "taking out two	MP	I	8	77	12
"Fanny!" repeated Mrs. Norris; "my dear Edmund, there is	MP	I	8	78	17
Mrs. Norris was very ready with the only objection which	MP	I	8	78	23
Mrs. Norris had no affection for Fanny, and no wish of	MP	I	8	79	23
for his cousin, Mrs. Norris was too much vexed to submit	MP	I	8	79	23
of the party; and Mrs. Norris thought it an excellent plan,	MP	I	8	80	28
Mrs. Norris was all delight and volubility; and even Fanny	MP	I	8	82	35
fully agitated, and Mrs. Norris was beginning to arrange	MP	I	9	89	32
The remaining three, Mrs. Rushworth, Mrs. Norris, and	MP	I	9	90	36
Mrs. Rushworth and Mrs. Norris presented themselves at the	MP	I	10	103	50
Mrs. Norris had been too well employed to move faster.	MP	I	10	103	50
to the door, and Mrs. Norris, having fidgetted about, and	MP	I	10	104	52
word!" said Mrs. Norris, as they drove through the park.	MP	I	10	105	53
make it; but when Mrs. Norris ceased speaking it was	MP	I	10	106	58
Mrs. Norris gave the particulars of the letters, and the	MP	I	11	108	4
"I think, ma'am," said Mrs. Norris--her eyes directed	MP	I	12	117	12
Mrs. Norris continued, "it is quite delightful, ma'am, to	MP	I	12	118	16
Opposition was vain; and as to Mrs. Norris, he was	MP	I	13	129	40
and been cut out by Mrs. Norris (with a saving, by her	MP	I	14	130	1
just going to say the very same thing," said Mrs. Norris.	MP	I	15	141	22
Mrs. Norris related again her triumph over Dick Jackson,	MP	I	15	142	24
madam, as well as Mrs. Norris, and every body else who is	MP	I	15	143	26
all her attention to Mrs. Norris, who was presiding there.	MP	I	15	145	42
breathe after it, Mrs. Norris completed the whole, by thus	MP	I	15	146	53
"I am not going to urge her,"--replied Mrs. Norris sharply,	MP	I	15	147	55
astonished eyes at Mrs. Norris, and then at Fanny, whose	MP	I	15	147	56
approving it;--and Mrs. Norris having stipulated for there	MP	I	16	151	1
Mrs. Norris offered to contrive his dress, Mr. Yates	MP	I	17	158	2
is at home; and nobody else can keep Mrs. Norris in order.	MP	I	17	162	16
unobservant; and Mrs. Norris was too busy in contriving	MP	I	17	163	21
wanted; and that Mrs. Norris thought her quite as well off	MP	I	18	166	6
hung," interposed Mrs. Norris--"the curtain will be hung	MP	I	18	167	11
of Lady Bertram, Mrs. Norris, and Julia, every body was in	MP	I	18	171	25
Mrs. Norris was by no means to be compared in happiness to	MP	II	1	179	10
Mrs. Norris felt herself defrauded of an office on which	MP	II	1	180	10
Still Mrs. Norris was at intervals urging something	MP	II	1	180	10
every body's comfort, my dear Mrs. Norris," was his answer.	MP	II	1	180	11
He could not help giving Mrs. Norris a hint of his having	MP	II	2	188	3
Mrs. Norris was a little confounded, and as nearly being	MP	II	2	188	3
'Upon my word, Mrs. Norris,' said Mrs. Grant, the other	MP	II	2	190	7
Mrs. Norris began to look about her and wonder that his	MP	II	2	194	20
Mrs. Norris contrived to remove one article from his sight	MP	II	2	195	22
Mrs. Norris, most happy to assist in the duties of the day,	MP	II	3	203	30
to any body, and Mrs. Norris, when she came on the morrow,	MP	II	5	219	27
Mrs. Norris had now so ingeniously done away all Mrs.	MP	II	5	220	29
Mrs. Norris fetched breath and went on again.	MP	II	5	221	31
as low even as Mrs. Norris could; and when Sir Thomas,	MP	II	5	221	35
"My dear Sir Thomas!" cried Mrs. Norris, red with anger, "	MP	II	5	221	36
a criminal towards Mrs. Norris; and not bearing to remain	MP	II	5	221	38
					39
to; and though Mrs. Norris could fidget about the room,	MP	II	6	236	21
any emotion in Mrs. Norris, who could never behold either	MP	II	7	238	3
and Sir Thomas, Mrs. Norris, and Dr. and Mrs. Grant, being	MP	II	7	239	8
Sotherton was a word to catch Mrs. Norris, and being just	MP	II	7	245	32
Mrs. Norris was beginning an eager assurance of the	MP	II	7	245	34
Dr. Grant and Mrs. Norris to dispute over their last play,	MP	II	7	246	36
called to the knowledge of it by the bustle of Mrs. Norris.	MP	II	7	251	63
Norris, who must fancy that she settled it all herself.	MP	II	7	251	65
"Ah! my dear Sir Thomas," interrupted Mrs. Norris, "I knew	MP	II	8	252	2
Mrs. Norris had not another word to say.	MP	II	8	253	4
Mrs. Norris was ready with her suggestions as to the rooms	MP	II	8	253	7
Mrs. Norris was obliged to be satisfied with thinking just	MP	II	8	254	7
gave orders and Mrs. Norris ran about, but all this gave	MP	II	8	254	9
the worrying of Mrs. Norris, who was cross because the	MP	II	9	267	22
Oh yes," cried Mrs. Norris, "she has good reason to look	MP	II	10	272	3
with Edmund; and what was the restlessness of Mrs. Norris?	MP	II	10	273	5
personal beauty, as Mrs. Norris seemed to do, to her	MP	II	10	276	13
Miss Crawford knew Mrs. Norris too well to think of	MP	II	10	277	16
to-night!" and Mrs. Norris paid her with as many smiles	MP	II	10	277	16
inquiries of Mrs. Norris, about the supper-hour, were all	MP	II	10	278	20
Mrs. Norris often talks of her luck; what will she say now?	MP	II	12	292	7
Mrs. Norris seemed as much delighted with the saving it	MP	II	13	304	19
"Indeed!" cried Mrs. Norris, reddening.	MP	II	13	305	21
Mrs. Norris being not at all inclined to question its	MP	II	13	305	23
Norris, and she carefully refused him every opportunity.	MP	II	13	306	27
sent for; and as Mrs. Norris was still in the house, there	MP	III	1	311	2
"Oh!" said Mrs. Norris with a moment's check, "that was	MP	III	1	323	56
could succeed; for Mrs. Norris had not discernment enough	MP	III	1	323	57
to obey, when Mrs. Norris called out, "stay, stay, Fanny!	MP	III	1	325	60
Mrs. Norris, much discontented, was obliged to compose	MP	III	1	325	62
the communication to Mrs. Norris was as much as Fanny herself.	MP	III	2	332	19
far from classing Mrs. Norris as one of those well-meaning	MP	III	2	332	19
Mrs. Norris, however, relieved him.	MP	III	2	332	20
But Mrs. Norris wanted to persuade her that Fanny could be	MP	III	6	371	15
be talked of, and Mrs. Norris found that all her anxiety	MP	III	6	372	21
Mrs. Norris was left to settle the matter by herself; and	MP	III	6	373	23
Mrs. Norris, however, had gone home and taken down two old	MP	III	7	387	45
very much more resembled Lady Bertram than Mrs. Norris.	MP	III	8	390	5
Lady Bertram, but Mrs. Norris would have been a more	MP	III	8	390	5
Mrs. Norris, however, as most attached to Maria, was	MP	III	16	448	1
to her aunt; but Mrs. Norris, instead of having comfort	MP	III	16	448	2
differently from Mrs. Norris, would now be done away.	MP	III	16	452	14
what was wrong in Mrs. Norris, by its reverse in himself,	MP	III	17	463	7
Mrs. Norris, whose attachment seemed to augment with the	MP	III	17	464	13
MRS. NORRIS'S (16)					
power to take any share in the personal charge of her.	MP	I	1	9	10
looks, and quite overcome by Mrs. Norris's admonitions.	MP	I	2	14	8
the change in Mrs. Norris's situation, and the improvement	MP	I	3	24	7
her own; but in Mrs. Norris's watchful attention, and in	MP	I	3	32	62
at secrecy, than Mrs. Norris's talking of it every where	MP	I	4	39	12
sharp reprimand to Fanny; "I was out above an hour.	MP	I	7	72	42
to come, till Mrs. Norris's more numerous words and louder	MP	I	8	76	2
scolded away by Mrs. Norris's threats of catching cold.	MP	I	11	113	43
they both advised Mrs. Norris's continuing where she was,	MP	II	6	233	15
It was only better than Mrs. Norris's sharp answers would	MP	II	11	283	4
And as to the not missing her, which under Mrs. Norris's	MP	III	6	371	14
Mrs. Norris's inclination for it, or any of her activity.	MP	III	8	390	5
have caught from Mrs. Norris's lips the cant of its being	MP	III	13	428	15
Sir Thomas would not hear of it, and Mrs. Norris's anger	MP	III	17	465	13
It ended in Mrs. Norris's resolving to quit Mansfield, and	MP	III	17	465	14
Mrs. Norris's removal from Mansfield was the great	MP	III	17	465	15
MRS. OTWAY (1)					
Mrs. Otway, I protest!--and good Mr. Otway, and Miss Otway	E	III	2	323	19
MRS. PALMER (36)					
Mrs. Palmer was several years younger than Lady Middleton,	SS	I	19	106	22
Mrs. Palmer, on the contrary, who was strongly endowed by	SS	I	19	106	23
Mrs. Palmer laughed heartily at the recollection of their	SS	I	19	107	28
Mrs. Palmer laughed, and said it would not do her any harm.	SS	I	19	107	30
to Allenham; and Mrs. Palmer laughed so heartily at the	SS	I	19	108	35
Mrs. Palmer's eye was now caught by the drawings which	SS	I	19	108	35
Mrs. Jennings and Mrs. Palmer joined their entreaties, all	SS	I	19	109	40
day, at one door, Mrs. Palmer came running in at the other,	SS	I	20	110	1
"Not go to town!" cried Mrs. Palmer, with a laugh, "I	SS	I	20	110	4
"Oh! my love," cried Mrs. Palmer to her husband, who just	SS	I	20	110	9
"Oh! don't be so sly before us," said Mrs. Palmer; "for we	SS	I	20	111	12
"Is it very ugly?" continued Mrs. Palmer--"then it must be	SS	I	20	111	17
or more determined to be happy than Mrs. Palmer.	SS	I	20	112	26
"Oh! my dear Miss Dashwood," said Mrs. Palmer soon	SS	I	20	112	29
in the same county, Mrs. Palmer might be able to give some	SS	I	20	114	43
well," replied Mrs. Palmer--"not that I ever spoke to him	SS	I	20	114	44
"My dear Mrs. Palmer!"	SS	I	20	115	47
Mrs. Palmer's information respecting Willoughby was not	SS	I	20	116	59
"Mrs. Palmer appeared quite well, and I am commissioned to	SS	II	4	163	17
breakfast before Mrs. Palmer's barouche stopt at the door,	SS	II	4	164	21
without cause on Mrs. Palmer's, it was proposed by the	SS	II	4	164	23
the tediousness of Mrs. Palmer, whose eye was caught by	SS	II	4	165	24
Mrs. Palmer and two elderly ladies of Mrs. Jennings's	SS	II	4	166	31
intimate, Mrs. Jennings, Mrs. Palmer, and the Middletons.	SS	II	5	173	44
for you to caution Mrs. Palmer and Sir John against ever	SS	II	8	195	17
nor even Mrs. Palmer herself, ever spoke of him before her.	SS	II	10	214	8
Mrs. Palmer, in her way, was equally angry.	SS	II	10	215	10
The rest of Mrs. Palmer's sympathy was shewn in procuring	SS	II	10	215	11
Palmer soon after she arrived, carried Mrs. Jennings away.	SS	II	13	238	3
Mrs. Palmer was so well at the end of a fortnight, that	SS	III	1	257	1
ordinary visit to Mrs. Palmer, entered the drawing-room,	SS	III	1	257	2
					3
Mrs. Palmer had her child, and Mrs. Jennings her carpet-	SS	III	6	303	12
Nothing was wanting on Mrs. Palmer's side that constant	SS	III	6	304	13
gave instant alarm to Mrs. Palmer on her baby's account.	SS	III	7	307	3
she saw nothing of Mrs. Palmer; and as it gave her	SS	III	7	309	6
arrival of the latter, into Mrs. Palmer's dressing-room.	SS	III	10	340	1
MRS. PARTRIDGE (2)					
friend, Mrs. Partridge, the lady I have always resided	E	II	14	275	32
I shall write Mrs. Partridge in a day or two, and shall	E	II	17	300	10
MRS. PERRY (11)					
subject, either when Mrs. Perry drank tea with Mrs. and	E	I	2	17	9
"And Mrs. Perry and the children, how are they? do the	E	I	12	101	26
Mrs. Bates, Mrs. Perry, Mrs. Goddard and others, were a	E	II	16	290	3
Mrs. Perry had told somebody, and was extremely happy	E	III	5	344	9
last spring; for Mrs. Perry herself mentioned it to my	E	III	5	345	16
Mrs. Perry was very anxious that he should have a carriage,	E	III	5	346	16
Mrs. Perry was always particularly fond of my mother--	E	III	5	346	16
Perfectly remember Mrs. Perry's coming.--	E	III	5	346	16
such a point--and Mrs. Perry had said so much--but, except	E	III	9	390	18
the Mrs. Eltons, the Mrs. Perrys, and the Mrs. Coles, who	E	III	9	390	19
Cole, Mrs. Perry, and Mrs. Elton, immediately afterwards.	E	III	17	468	35
MRS. PHILIPS (14)					
Their visits to Mrs. Philips were now productive of the	PP	I	7	28	4
even in spite of Mrs. Philips' throwing up the parlour	PP	I	15	73	10
Mrs. Philips was always glad to see her nieces, and the	PP	I	15	73	11
Mrs. Philips was quite awed by such an excess of good	PP	I	15	73	11
This was agreed to, and Mrs. Philips protested that they	PP	I	15	74	11
but when Mrs. Philips understood from him what Rosings was,	PP	I	16	75	2
and he found in Mrs. Philips a very attentive listener,	PP	I	16	75	3
a kind listener in Mrs. Philips, and was, by her	PP	I	16	76	5
Mrs. Philips was very thankful for his compliance, but	PP	I	16	76	7
station between his cousin Elizabeth and Mrs. Philips.--	PP	I	16	82	49
point; but when Mrs. Philips began to express her concern	PP	I	16	83	49
Mrs. Bennet and Mrs. Philips, was an amiable, intelligent,	PP	II	2	139	2
Mrs. Bennet was privileged to whisper it to Mrs. Philips,	PP	III	13	350	55
and though Mrs. Philips, as well as her sister, stood in	PP	III	18	384	27
MRS. PHILIPS'S (3)					
Bennet by admiring Mrs. Philips's manners and politeness.	PP	I	15	74	13
in the noise of Mrs. Philips's supper party, but his	PP	I	16	84	59
Mrs. Philips's vulgarity was another, and perhaps a	PP	III	18	384	27
MRS. PHILLIPS (2)					
She longed to see Mrs. Phillips, the Lucasses, and all	PP	III	9	317	10
sister," (for Mrs. Phillips first brought her the news.)	PP	III	11	331	14
MRS. PRICE (28)					
To save herself from useless remonstrance, Mrs. Price	MP	I	1	4	1
Mrs. Price in her turn was injured and angry; and an	MP	I	1	4	1
By the end of eleven years, however, Mrs. Price could no	MP	I	1	4	2
a more important advantage to Mrs. Price resulted from it.	MP	I	1	5	4
her wish, that poor Mrs. Price should be relieved from the	MP	I	1	5	4
serviceable to Mrs. Price, and creditable to ourselves, we	MP	I	1	7	7
Mrs. Price seemed rather surprised that a girl should be	MP	I	1	11	19
for the children of Mrs. Price; he assisted her liberally	MP	I	2	21	34
In they both came, and Mrs. Price having kindly kissed her	MP	III	7	378	13
Mrs. Price, Rebecca, and Betsey, all went up to defend	MP	III	7	382	27
the tea-things, and Mrs. Price had walked about the room	MP	III	7	385	37
"Her year!" cried Mrs. Price; "I am sure I hope I shall be	MP	III	7	385	39
"Now, Susan," cried Mrs. Price in a complaining voice, "	MP	III	7	386	44
Mrs. Price was not unkind--but, instead of gaining on her	MP	III	8	389	4
Of her two sisters, Mrs. Price very much more resembled	MP	III	8	390	5
They talked of William, a subject on which Mrs. Price	MP	III	10	400	7
recommendation to Mrs. Price and her daughters, to take	MP	III	10	401	10
Mrs. Price, it appeared, scarcely ever stirred out of	MP	III	10	401	10
Mrs. Price was greatly obliged, and very complying.--	MP	III	10	401	10
cheerful looking Mrs. Price, coming abroad with a fine	MP	III	11	408	2
Mrs. Price took her weekly walk on the ramparts every fine	MP	III	11	408	4
miles off--not even Mrs. Price, beyond a brief question or	MP	III	13	428	14
Mrs. Price did quite as much for Lady Bertram, as Lady	MP	III	13	428	15
Bertram, as Lady Bertram would have done for Mrs. Price.	MP	III	13	428	15
"Indeed, I hope it is not true," said Mrs. Price	MP	III	15	440	18
unkind, except Mrs. Price, could have overlooked, when the	MP	III	15	442	22
Mrs. Price talked of her poor sister for a few minutes--	MP	III	15	444	26
As nothing was really left for the decision of Mrs. Price,	MP	III	15	444	27
MRS. PRICE'S (3)					
By the time Mrs. Price's answer arrived, there remained	MP	III	6	372	21
satisfied, and Mrs. Price's attachment had no other source.	MP	III	8	389	4
Mrs. Price's manners were also at their best.	MP	III	10	400	6
MRS. R. (3)					
Mrs. R. has been spending Easter with the Aylmers at	MP	III	14	434	13
Mrs. R. knows a decline is apprehended; he saw her this	MP	III	14	435	14
Street; the beautiful Mrs. R. whose name had not long been	MP	III	15	440	14
MRS. R.'S (1)					
I suppose, Mrs. R.'s Easter holidays will not last much	MP	III	14	434	13
MRS. RADCLIFF (1)					
"Udolpho was written by Mrs. Radcliff," said Catherine,	NA	I	7	49	37
MRS. RADCLIFF'S (1)					
No, if I read any, it shall be Mrs. Radcliff's; her novels	NA	I	7	49	36
MRS. RADCLIFFE (1)					

Then the baked apples came home, Mrs. Wallis sent them by E II 9 236 46
people say that Mrs. Wallis can be uncivil and give a very E II 9 236 46
Indeed they are very delightful apples, and Mrs. Wallis E II 9 238 51
And there was a Mrs. Wallis, at present only known to them P IV 3 141 13
Sir Walter thought much of Mrs. Wallis; she was said to be P IV 3 141 13
You must stay to be acquainted with Mrs. Wallis, the P IV 4 145 1
be acquainted with Mrs. Wallis, the beautiful Mrs. Wallis. P IV 4 145 1
She is only nursing Mrs. Wallis of Marlborough-Buildings-- P IV 5 156 13
I mean to make my profit of Mrs. Wallis, however. P IV 5 156 13
She had had it from Mrs. Wallis herself, which did not P IV 9 197 40
He was to be introduced, and Mrs. Wallis was to be P IV 9 207 90
Mrs. Wallis has an amusing idea, as nurse tells me, that P IV 9 208 92
MRS. WALLIS'S (2)
A scheme, worthy of Mrs. Wallis's understanding, by all P IV 9 208 92
next Lady Elliot, through Mrs. Wallis's recommendation?" P IV 9 208 92
MRS. WESTON (213)
between a Mrs. Weston only half a mile from them, and a E I 1 6 7
Mrs. Weston ought to have found more in it, for she had a E I 2 15 3
mention of the handsome letter Mrs. Weston had received. E I 2 18 9
letter Mr. Frank Churchill had written to Mrs. Weston? E I 2 18 9
Mrs. Weston had, of course, formed a very favourable idea E I 2 18 10
of gratitude to Mrs. Weston, and of moments only of regret; E I 2 18 12
it was not remedy for the absence of Mrs. Weston. E I 3 22 6
Such a friend as Mrs. Weston was out of the question. E I 4 26 2
Mrs. Weston was the object of a regard, which had its E I 4 26 2
For Mrs. Weston there was nothing to be done; for Harriet E I 4 27 2
"I do not know what your opinion may be, Mrs. Weston," E I 5 36 1
"I dare say," replied Mrs. Weston, smiling, "that I E I 5 37 8
Mrs. Weston, I am not to be talked out of my dislike of E I 5 39 21
"So do I," said Mrs. Weston gently; "very much." E I 5 41 28
at present," said Mrs. Weston, "as can well be; and while E I 5 41 30
and has not Mrs. Weston some inimitable figure-pieces in E I 6 43 14
Mrs. Weston again, and again, and again, you see. E I 6 45 21
Dear Mrs. Weston! always my kindest friend on every E I 6 45 21
likeness of it-- (Mrs. Weston and I were quite agreed in E I 6 45 21
wanted,"--observed Mrs. Weston to him--not in the least E I 6 47 31
I never saw Mrs. Weston better in my life--never looking E I 11 94 10
Mr. Weston or Mrs. Weston, and generally both, either at E I 11 94 14
cannot deny that Mrs. Weston, poor Mrs. Weston, does come E I 11 94 16
Mrs. Weston, poor Mrs. Weston, don't come and see us pretty E I 11 94 16
"He wrote a letter to poor Mrs. Weston, to congratulate E I 11 96 22
Charming people, Mr. and Mrs. Weston;--Mrs. Weston indeed E I 13 116 43
She could tell nothing of Hartfield, in which Mrs. Weston E I 14 117 1
the very sight of Mrs. Weston, her smile, her touch, her E I 14 117 2
appeared, and Mrs. Weston, who had been almost wholly E I 14 117 3
so delighted with Mrs. Weston; and at last would begin E I 14 118 4
be to you! and Mrs. Weston is so anxious to be acquainted E I 14 120 10
began upon it, to Mrs. Weston, very soon after their E I 14 121 14
Mrs. Weston agreed to it; but added, that she should be E I 14 121 14
"My Emma!" replied Mrs. Weston, smiling, "what is the E I 14 121 16
Emma wished she had been alone with Mrs. Weston. E I 14 122 18
She should then have heard more: Mrs. Weston would speak E I 14 122 18
one decides upon what he can do," replied Mrs. Weston. E I 14 123 23
points," continued Mrs. Weston, "and on others, very E I 14 123 27
Mrs. Weston and Emma were sitting together on a sopha. E I 15 124 1
He turned to Mrs. Weston to implore her assistance, "would E I 15 125 4
Is this fair, Mrs. Weston?-- E I 15 125 5
Mrs. Weston and Emma tried earnestly to cheer him and turn E I 15 126 9
Isabella turned to Mrs. Weston for her approbation of the E I 15 127 16
Mrs. Weston could only approve. E I 15 127 16
Mrs. Weston was exceedingly disappointed--much more E I 18 144 2
his comfort, while Mrs. Weston, of a more apprehensive E I 18 144 3
"I suspect they do not satisfy Mrs. Weston. E I 18 149 26
deserved by Mrs. Weston; but undoubtedly he could know E II 5 191 28
that I was to find a pretty young woman in Mrs. Weston." E II 5 192 30
"You cannot see too much perfection in Mrs. Weston for my E II 5 192 31
that in addressing Mrs. Weston I should understand whom I E II 5 192 32
Weston at Ford's; but he need not hurry any body else." E II 5 193 6
He came with Mrs. Weston, to whom and to Highbury he E II 6 196 1
Highbury, with Mrs. Weston, stood for Hartfield; and she E II 6 196 1
him in company with Mrs. Weston, upon his behaviour to E II 6 196 2
But the expression is hardly admissible, Mrs. Weston, is E II 6 199 9
"You get upon delicate subjects, Emma," said Mrs. Weston E II 6 201 23
Mrs. Weston laughed, and said he did not know what he was E II 6 204 43
of his father and Mrs. Weston, indifference as to how his E II 7 205 1
story; but that Mrs. Weston did not like it, was clear E II 7 205 1
Mrs. Weston was very ready to say how attentive and E II 7 205 2
As Mrs. Weston observed, "all young people would have E II 7 206 3
The turning to Mrs. Weston, with a look of gentle reproach- E II 7 209 10
of staying as late as Mrs. Weston, but on your account. E II 7 211 21
at Hartfield; for Mrs. Weston was too anxious for his E II 8 212 1
Mrs. Weston, kind-hearted and musical, was particularly E II 8 220 46
But just got acquainted with Mrs. Weston, and others?-- E II 8 222 51
he could return to his chair, it was taken by Mrs. Weston. E II 8 222 58
"Well," said Mrs. Weston, smiling, "you give him credit E II 8 224 65
"Dear Mrs. Weston, how could you think of such a thing?-- E II 8 224 66
My dear Mrs. Weston, do not take to match-making. E II 8 225 72
"Well," said Mrs. Weston, laughing, "perhaps the greatest E II 8 225 77
"You take up an idea, Mrs. Weston, and run away with it; E II 8 226 84
of her friend; for Mrs. Weston was the most used of the E II 8 226 85
conversation with Mrs. Weston, she had been seeing nothing, E II 8 227 85
thought, but for Mrs. Weston, it would not have struck her. E II 8 228 88
Mrs. Weston, capital in her country-dances, was seated, E II 8 229 98
to thank Mrs. Weston, look sorrowful, and have done. E II 8 230 101
The scene enlarged; two persons appeared; Mrs. Weston and E II 9 233 25
Mrs. Weston informed her that she was going to call on the E II 9 233 25
"And while Mrs. Weston pays her visit, I may be allowed, I E II 9 234 27
Mrs. Weston was disappointed. E II 9 234 28
But you had better go with Mrs. Weston and hear the E II 9 234 31
I shall be no support to Mrs. Weston. E II 9 234 32
"Do come with me," said Mrs. Weston, "if it be not very E II 9 234 34
reward him, returned with Mrs. Weston to Mrs. Bates's door. E II 9 235 35
ladies; Mrs. Weston and Miss Bates met them at the door. E II 9 235 43
And I begged Mrs. Weston to come with me, that I might be E II 9 236 44
Mrs. Weston told me you were here.-- E II 9 236 46
Well, Mrs. Weston, you have prevailed, I hope, and these E II 9 237 46
I do congratulate you, Mrs. Weston, most warmly. E II 9 238 51
Pray take care, Mrs. Weston, there is a step at the E II 9 239 53
"What!" said Mrs. Weston, "have not you finished it yet? E II 10 240 4
Mrs. Weston had been delighted before, and was delighted E II 10 241 7
Mrs. Weston had been speaking to her at the same moment. E II 10 241 9
The listeners were amused; and Mrs. Weston gave Emma a E II 10 244 36
"And here is Mrs. Weston and Mr. Frank Churchill too!-- E II 10 244 44
I think Miss Fairfax dances very well; and Mrs. Weston is E II 10 245 49
to be gone, that Mrs. Weston and her companion taking E II 10 246 55
enjoyment, and Mrs. Weston most willingly undertook to E II 11 247 3
Emma said it would be awkward; Mrs. Weston was in distress E II 11 248 10
Mrs. Weston, you would be quite laid up; do not let them E II 11 249 11
Mrs. Weston was sorry for such a charge. E II 11 249 12
Mrs. Weston sees no objection to it, provided you are E II 11 250 23
I am sure, neither your father nor Mrs. Weston (poor Miss E II 11 252 30
Mrs. Weston undertakes to direct the whole." E II 11 252 36
Now you must be satisfied--our own dear Mrs. Weston, who E II 11 252 37
"My father and Mrs. Weston are at the crown at this moment, E II 11 253 39
Mrs. Weston was afraid of draughts for the young people in E II 11 254 44
Mrs. Weston proposed having no regular supper; merely E II 11 254 45
men and women; and Mrs. Weston must not speak of it again. E II 11 254 45
"I wish," said Mrs. Weston, "one could know which E II 11 254 49
"Well--if you please," said Mrs. Weston rather hesitating, E II 11 255 51
her elegant niece,--Mrs. Weston, like a sweet-tempered E II 11 255 59
settled at any time between Mrs. Weston and Mrs. Stokes.-- E II 11 255 59
No!--she was more and more convinced that Mrs. Weston was E II 12 258 6
forwarded to Emma, in a note from Mrs. Weston, instantly. E II 12 258 8
Mrs. Weston added, "that he could only allow himself time E II 12 258 9
I have engaged Mrs. Weston to correspond with me. E II 12 261 36
When his letter to Mrs. Weston arrived, Emma had the E II 13 265 5
feelings towards Mrs. Weston; and the transition from E II 13 265 5
up and returned to Mrs. Weston, that it had not added any E II 13 266 6
And Mrs. Weston!-- E II 14 279 52
of Mrs. Elton, Mrs. Weston ventured this apology for Jane. E II 15 285 16
"You are right, Mrs. Weston," said Mr. Knightley warmly, " E II 15 286 18
Emma felt that Mrs. Weston was giving her a momentary E II 15 286 19
"I should not wonder," said Mrs. Weston, "if Miss Fairfax E II 15 286 21
Emma felt her foot pressed by Mrs. Weston, and did not E II 15 287 29
Mrs. Weston, your argument weighs most with me. E II 15 288 39
"Well, Mrs. Weston," said Emma triumphantly when he left E II 15 289 41
Since her last conversation with Mrs. Weston and Mr. E II 16 291 5
Mrs. Weston, did you ever hear the like? E II 16 295 32
"My advice," said Mrs. Weston kindly and persuasively, "I E II 16 295 33
You know, Mrs. Weston, you and I must be cautious how we E II 16 296 36
And so does poor Mrs. Weston"--with half a sigh and half a E II 16 297 47
looking also at Mrs. Weston; but stopped, on perceiving E II 16 297 48
on perceiving that Mrs. Weston was attending to some one E II 16 297 48
Mrs. Weston was disengaged and Emma began again-- "Mr. E II 16 297 49
Had not Mrs. Weston any letter about her to produce?" E II 16 298 51
Do not you remember, Mrs. Weston, employing him to write E II 16 298 52
She and Mrs. Weston were obliged to be almost always E II 17 299 1
addressed to Mrs. Weston, he had not the smallest doubt of E II 17 303 24
Mrs. Weston was most comfortably pleased on the occasion. E II 17 304 28
They were the first entitled, after Mrs. Weston and Emma, E II 17 304 30
it was not directed to me--it was to Mrs. Weston. E II 18 305 5
He and Mrs. Weston were both dreadfully desponding. E II 18 308 27
Mrs. Elton turned to Mrs. Weston. E III 2 321 17
She was now met by Mrs. Weston.-- E III 2 322 19
Oh! and I am sure our thanks are due to you, Mrs. Weston, E III 2 322 19
It had just occurred to Mrs. Weston that Mrs. Elton must E III 2 325 29
then appeared that Mrs. Weston was wanting him to dance E III 2 325 31
The anxious cares, the incessant attentions of Mrs. Weston, E III 2 326 33
between him and Mrs. Weston; and she perceived that his E III 2 327 34
The kind-hearted, gentle Mrs. Weston had left her seat to E III 2 327 34
was, "most readily Mrs. Weston, if you will dance with me." E III 2 327 34
But my dancing days are over, Mrs. Weston. E III 2 327 37
Mrs. Weston said no more; and Emma could imagine with what E III 2 327 38
Mrs. Weston begs you to put on your tippet. E III 2 328 45
"By the bye," said Frank Churchill to Mrs. Weston E III 5 344 5
Mrs. Weston looked surprised, and said, "I did not know E III 5 344 6
the situation of Mrs. Weston, whose happiness it was to be E III 6 352 1
"--Mrs. Weston, I suppose," interrupted Mrs. Elton, rather E III 6 354 16
Mrs. Weston, while the dear girls walked about the gardens. E III 6 356 30
Mrs. Weston, who seemed to have walked there on purpose to E III 6 357 33
only once by Mrs. Weston, who came out, in her solicitude E III 6 359 36
Mrs. Weston looked, and looked in vain. E III 6 361 41
dependence--and Mrs. Weston was at last persuaded to E III 6 361 41
with him, that Mrs. Weston might be persuaded away by her E III 6 361 42
Mrs. Weston had been showing them all to him, and now he E III 6 362 43
Mrs. Weston would be at ease. E III 6 363 53
Mrs. Weston remained with Mr. Woodhouse. E III 7 367 1
Mrs. Weston wants to see you. E III 10 392 2
Mrs. Weston was looking so ill, and had an air of so much E III 10 394 26
27
"Have you indeed no idea?" said Mrs. Weston in a trembling E III 10 394 28
"More than an attachment, indeed," resumed Mrs. Weston; " E III 10 395 32
"You may well be amazed," returned Mrs. Weston, still E III 10 395 35
Mrs. Weston looked up, afraid to believe; but Emma's E III 10 396 40
You may believe me, Mrs. Weston. E III 10 396 41
Mrs. Weston kissed her with tears of joy; and when she E III 10 396 42
But this does not acquit him, Mrs. Weston; and I must say, E III 10 396 44
Oh! Mrs. Weston--it is too calm a censure. E III 10 397 48
"I am to hear from him soon," continued Mrs. Weston. E III 10 398 53
"I am quite easy on that head," replied Mrs. Weston. E III 10 399 62
which Mrs. Weston had just gone through by herself. E III 11 403 3
Mrs. Weston felt when she was approaching Randall's. E III 11 404 3
twenty-four hours--Mrs. Weston, who had been calling on E III 12 417 3
Mrs. Weston had set off to pay the visit in a good deal of E III 12 417 5
a fair plea for Mrs. Weston to invite her to an airing; E III 12 418 5
of their drive, Mrs. Weston had, by gentle encouragement, E III 12 418 5
Mrs. Weston was convinced that such conversation must be E III 12 418 5
so many months," continued Mrs. Weston, "she was energetic. E III 12 418 6
thanks;--for, Oh! Mrs. Weston, if there were an account E III 12 420 13
Such a conclusion could not pass unanswered by Mrs. Weston. E III 12 420 14
to listen; and when Mrs. Weston ended with, "we have not E III 12 420 14
so;--a note from Mrs. Weston to herself, ushered in the E III 14 436 6
herself, ushered in the letter from Frank to Mrs. Weston. E III 14 436 6
To Mrs. Weston. Windsor-July. My dear Madam, "if I E III 14 436 8
to do it all the justice that Mrs. Weston foretold. E III 15 444 1
was so grateful to Mrs. Weston, and so much in love with E III 15 444 1
She had resolved to defer the disclosure till Mrs. Weston E III 16 452 6
of the weather and Mrs. Weston, she found herself abruptly E III 16 454 16
17
from home; and Mrs. Weston--no one could doubt that a E III 17 461 1
As soon as Mrs. Weston was sufficiently recovered to admit E III 17 465 28
next to his daughters and Mrs. Weston, best in the world. E III 17 465 28
with Isabella and Mrs. Weston, whose marriages taking them E III 17 466 29
approbation; and Mrs. Weston was ready, on the first E III 17 467 30
Mrs. Weston was acting no part, feigning no feelings in E III 17 467 31
Mrs. Weston, with her baby on her knee, indulging in such E III 17 468 32
every day, or poor Mrs. Weston would be disappointed. E III 18 476 43
Mrs. Weston was alone in the drawing-room:--but hardly had E III 18 476 44
"It is Frank and Miss Fairfax," said Mrs. Weston. E III 18 476 45
You see how my father and Mrs. Weston doat upon her." E III 18 477 50
The others had been talking of the child, Mrs. Weston E III 18 479 73
MRS. WESTON'S (25)
with a slice of Mrs. Weston's wedding-cake in their hands: E I 2 19 15
In that respect Mrs. Weston's loss had been important. E I 4 26 1
Weston's marriage her exercise had been too much confined. E I 4 26 1
they walked into Mrs. Weston's drawing-room;-- Mr. Elton E I 14 117 1
Emma saw Mrs. Weston's surprize, and felt that it must be E I 15 125 6
When the time proposed drew near, Mrs. Weston's fears were E I 18 144 1
and making use of Mrs. Weston's arguments against herself. E I 18 145 5
o'clock," was Mrs. Weston's parting injunction; spoken E II 5 189 15
day arrived, and Mrs. Weston's faithful pupil did not E II 5 189 19
and herself; and Mrs. Weston's accounting for it with "I E II 7 207 7
on the subject of Mrs. Weston's suspicions, to which the E II 8 227 87
nature, sir, because it will be under Mrs. Weston's care. E II 11 252 36
"Mrs. Weston's manners," said Emma, "were always E II 14 278 47
I believe Mrs. Weston's letters lately have been full of E II 18 308 25
Mrs. Weston's partiality for him is very great, and, as E II 18 309 30
think it as much her duty as Mrs. Weston's to receive them. E III 2 322 18
I really was persuaded of Mrs. Weston's having mentioned E III 5 345 13
"Are you well, my Emma?" was Mrs. Weston's parting E III 12 420 15
Mrs. Weston's communications furnished Emma with more food E III 12 420 17
on the evening of Mrs. Weston's wedding-day; but Mr. E III 12 422 19
and Mrs. Weston's heart and time would be occupied by it. E III 12 422 20
She was sure of Mrs. Weston's wishing it to be E III 15 444 2
Mrs. Weston's friends were all made happy by her safety; E III 17 461 1
kind forgiving message in one of Mrs. Weston's letters. E III 18 476 46
47
Mrs. Weston's poultry-house was robbed one night of all E III 19 483 10
MRS. WHITAKER (3)
Nothing would satisfy that good old Mrs. Whitaker, but my MP I 10 105 55
That Mrs. Whitaker is a treasure! MP I 10 105 55
eggs, which Mrs. Whitaker would quite force upon me; she MP I 10 106 57
MRS. WICKHAM (3)
Mrs. Wickham! PP III 7 306 47

herself called "Mrs. Wickham," by each of them; and in the PP III 9 317 10
kept, and though Mrs. Wickham frequently invited her to PP III 19 385 4
MRS. WILLOUGHBY (2)
John) that as Mrs. Willoughby would at once be a woman of SS II 10 215 14
speak in this way, either of Mrs. Willoughby or my sister. SS III 8 329 64
MRS. WILLOUGHBY'S (1)
and wished any thing rather than Mrs. Willoughby's death. SS III 9 335 5
MRS. YOUNGE (4)
between him and Mrs. Younge, in whose character we were PP II 12 201 5
and Mrs. Younge was of course removed from her charge. PP II 12 202 5
There is a lady, it seems, a Mrs. Younge, who was some PP III 10 322 2
This Mrs. Younge was, he knew intimately acquainted with PP III 10 322 2
MUCH (2088)
dispositions lead them too much into society for my LS 1 243 1
dictated, & I have but too much reason to fear that the LS 1 244 1
The price is immense, & much beyond what I can ever LS 2 246 1
powers which can do so much--engaging at the same time & LS 4 248 2
I need not tell you how much I miss him--how perpetually LS 5 250 3
if I had not known how much she has always disliked me for LS 6 251 1
She speaks of her with so much tenderness & anxiety, LS 6 251 1
heart, you may guess how much more strongly they operate LS 6 251 2
I was so much indulged in my infant years that I was never LS 7 253 1
return, is occasioned as much by a degree of fascination LS 8 255 1
know that Reginald is too much at home at Churchill to LS 8 256 3
I am much obliged to you my dear friend, for your advice LS 10 257 1
if I were not already as much attached to another person LS 10 258 2
of character is one so much more serious, that the LS 12 260 2
which affected my eyes so much as to prevent my reading it LS 13 262 1
quite alone now, & very much in need of him to keep up our LS 13 262 1
but be the occasion of so much vexation & trouble. LS 13 263 1
to whom she was always much attached, would be absolutely LS 14 264 3
present as she is in real distress, & with too much cause. LS 15 266 2
Frederica must be as much as sixteen, & ought to know LS 15 266 3
Frederica is too shy I think, & too much in awe of me, to LS 16 268 2
eyes looked very red, & she was as much agitated as before. LS 17 270 2
& watched her with so much tender solicitude that I, who LS 17 270 3
some pains are taken to prevent her being much with me. LS 17 270 6
am much mistaken if a syllable of his uttering, escape her. LS 18 272 1
& I have her with me as much as possible, & have taken LS 18 273 3
Susan she would always appear to much greater advantage. LS 18 273 3
she is about; nor is it of much consequence; she is not an LS 19 274 3
Her beauty is much admired by the Vernons, but it has no LS 19 274 3
to prevent her seeing much of her aunt, but I have since LS 19 274 3
character; a little too much of the rattle perhaps, but a LS 20 276 5
me when I declare that much as I had heard in your praise LS 20 277 6
7
feelings are much as both her uncle & I beleive them to be. LS 20 278 11
Much good, may such love do him! LS 22 282 6
The affair which has given us so much anxiety is drawing LS 23 283 1
I am so much agitated by delight that I can scarcely hold LS 23 283 2
We have much to do, but it shall be done. LS 23 285 8
myself) I know my father wants very much to see him. LS 24 286 4
& which had ended very much to his dissatisfaction from LS 24 287 11
I might probably be as much to blame as himself, should LS 24 288 11
known her to possess so much as she does, I should not LS 24 288 11
value her own happiness as much as I do, if she judge LS 24 290 13
I could have said "not much indeed;"--but I left her LS 24 291 14
relations to whom you are so much attached & are so dear. LS 25 292 3
It would surely be much more to the purpose to get LS 26 295 1
I am pleased to find that my letter had so much effect on LS 28 298 2
or look forward with much impatience to the time when LS 29 299 2
it, while there is so much reason to fear the connection LS 30 300 1
Much as I wish him away however, I cannot help being LS 31 302 1
& I allow you to flirt with him as much as you like. LS 31 302 1
But she is still so fond of her husband & frets so much LS 38 307 2
I have given up too much--have been too easily worked on; LS 39 308 1
Frederica runs much in my thoughts, & when Reginald has LS 40 309 1
Lady Susan's maternal fears were then too much awakened LS. 42 312 6
and strong features;--so much for her person;--and not NA I 1 13 1
trees, hens and chickens, all very much like one another.-- NA I 1 14 1
to be; but her time was so much occupied in lying-in and NA I 1 15 3
black shoes--appeared to much advantage; but was strangely NA I 3 26 22
ladies do write so much better letters than gentlemen! NA I 3 27 29
himself a little too much with the foibles of others.-- NA I 3 29 47
meet, and nothing in the world advances intimacy so much." NA I 3 29 51
Whether she thought of him so much, while she drank her NA I 3 29 52
The others are very much admired too, but I believe NA I 4 32 3
discussion has generally much to do in perfecting a sudden NA I 4 33 7
Catherine was not so much engaged at the theatre that NA I 5 35 1
they certainly claimed much of her leisure, as to forget NA I 5 35 1
conversation;--they talked much, and with much enjoyment; NA I 5 35 2
talked much, and with much enjoyment; but again was NA I 5 35 2
world, no species of composition has been so much decried. NA I 5 37 4
"Dear creature! how much I am obliged to you; and when you NA I 6 40 8
"I know you very well; you have so much animation, which NA I 6 41 16
"But you should not persuade me that I think so very much NA I 6 41 17
I do not pretend to say that I was not very much pleased NA I 6 41 19
the world, and think themselves of so much importance!-- NA I 6 42 28
I never much thought about it. NA I 6 42 29
I believe I have said too much. NA I 6 42 32
dress of a groom, and too much like a gentleman unless he NA I 7 45 5
And how much do you think he did, Miss Morland?" NA I 7 46 11
horses so much as rest; nothing knocks them up so soon. NA I 7 47 27
replied, "I like him very much; he seems very agreeable." NA I 7 50 44
"Very, very much indeed: Isabella particularly." NA I 7 50 46
attached to; she has so much good sense, and is so NA I 7 50 47
general favourite; and how much she must be admired in NA I 7 51 49
"Yes, very much indeed, I fancy; Mr. Allen thinks her the NA I 7 51 50
Catherine, though a little disappointed, had too much good- NA I 8 52 2
a place, that it is much better to be here than at home at NA I 8 54 5
on the occasion so very much as if she really felt it, NA I 8 54 10
them, interest her so much as to prevent her looking very NA I 8 55 10
the other liked Bath, how much she admired its buildings NA I 8 56 11
"No, not at all; but if you think it wrong, you had much NA I 8 58 24
This inapplicable answer might have been too much for the NA I 8 59 34
"Oh, no; I am much obliged to you, our two dances are over; NA I 8 59 36
James and Isabella were so much engaged in conversing NA I 8 59 38
"But you are always very much with them." NA I 9 63 16
"Yes, very much." NA I 9 63 17
However, I am sure James does not drink so much." NA I 9 64 25
She reflected on the affair for some time in much NA I 9 66 31
vivacity attended with so much laughter, that though NA I 10 72 8
her, hid herself as much as possible from his view, and NA I 10 74 23
But certainly there is much more sameness in a country NA I 10 79 48
"But then you spend your time so much more rationally in NA I 10 79 49
"I do not believe there is much difference." NA I 10 79 52
"And so I am at home--only I do not find so much of it. NA I 10 79 54
Mr. Tilney was very much amused. NA I 10 79 55
when I am at home again--I do like it so very much. NA I 10 79 56
I would much rather take a chair at any time." NA I 11 83 11
there had not been too much rain for Miss Tilney to NA I 11 83 16
people that had surprized her so much a few mornings back. NA I 11 84 17
and quiet!--so much better than going to the Lower Rooms. NA I 11 84 19
"I doubt our being able to do so much," said Morland. NA I 11 84 20
"And well they might, for I never saw so much dirt in my NA I 11 85 41
had never seen two men so much alike in his life, and NA I 11 87 53
We had much better put it off till another day, and turn NA I 11 88 54
brother had so much sense; I am glad you are come back. NA I 11 89 62
was at home, and too much offended to admit her; and as NA I 12 91 3
the second, that it was a play she wanted very much to see. NA I 12 92 4
reserve:--"we were much obliged to you at any rate for NA I 12 93 7
She was very much vexed, and meant to make her apology as NA I 12 94 10
There are few people much about town that I do not know. NA I 12 96 20
Here, Catherine, who was much less gratified by his NA I 12 96 23
The evening had done more, much more, for her, than could NA I 12 96 24
The sacrifice is not much; and to oblige such a friend--I NA I 13 99 3
addressed herself as much to one as to the other in her NA I 13 102 26
"Yes, very much so indeed. NA I 13 104 32
"To say the truth, I do not much like any other." NA I 14 108 18
records, which may be as much depended on, I conclude, as NA I 14 109 23
be made--and probably with much greater, if the production NA I 14 109 23
very well, but to be at so much trouble in filling great NA I 14 109 24
but if you had been as much used as myself to hear poor NA I 14 109 26
of wearying her with too much wisdom at once, Henry NA I 14 111 29
There must be murder; and government cares not how much." NA I 14 112 35
In my opinion, nature has given them so much, that they NA I 14 114 47
with respectful form, as much to Mrs. Allen as to NA I 14 114 49
from the first not to go, if they pressed me ever so much." NA I 14 115 52
she bade her adieu without much uneasiness, and returned NA I 14 115 55
the second unfolded thus much in detail,--that they had NA I 15 116 1
I feel that I shall be so much more attached to my dear NA I 15 118 9
This charming sentiment, recommended as much by sense as NA I 15 119 19
but you have so much, so much of every thing; and then you NA I 15 123 38
but you have so much, so much of every thing; and then you NA I 15 123 38
you and I think pretty much alike upon most matters." NA I 15 124 44
own; and if she had not a penny, why so much the better." NA I 15 124 46
towards them again, and, much to Catherine's NA II 1 132 16
occupied her mind so much, that she drew back for some NA II 1 133 29
"It is as much as should be said of any one. NA II 1 134 36
"I only wish I could do as much. NA II 1 135 44
my father has promised to do as much as he can afford." NA II 1 136 47
to be sure that a much smaller income would satisfy me. NA II 1 136 48
I know how much your heart is in it. NA II 2 139 7
I cannot suppose your brother cares so very much about me. NA II 3 145 13
check is still in view--at once too much and too little." NA II 3 147 27
With much uneasiness did she thus leave them. NA II 3 148 28
her usual self, and not so much about money; and had not NA II 3 148 28
to torment, for she is very much attached to my brother. NA II 4 151 13
not believe Isabella so very much attached to my brother?" NA II 4 151 17
to the offence; and much was her concern increased, when NA II 5 154 2
and even afterwards, so much were his spirits affected, NA II 5 155 3
have room to sit; and, so much was he influenced by this NA II 5 155 4
At last, however, the order of release was given; and much NA II 5 156 4
anxious for her seeing as much of the country as possible." NA II 5 156 4
"No, indeed; I should be too much frightened to do any NA II 5 159 20
But Henry was too much amused by the interest he had NA II 5 160 23
in its dimensions to a much larger drawing-room than the NA II 6 165 6
been used to much better sized apartments at Mr. Allen's?" NA II 6 166 6
absence of General Tilney, with much positive cheerfulness. NA II 6 166 8
"How much better is this," said she, as she walked to the NA II 6 167 9
walked to the fender--"how much better to find a fire NA II 6 167 9
her candle, the yellow had very much the effect of gold. NA II 6 168 10
size, and much less than she supposed it to be at first. NA II 7 172 1
So much the better. NA II 7 174 8
The manufacture was much improved since that time; he had NA II 7 175 12
it was a proposal of too much happiness in itself; for she NA II 7 176 17
He turned away; and Catherine was shocked to find how much NA II 7 179 29
"To be sure you must miss him very much." NA II 7 180 35
so much wished for, struck Catherine as very remarkable. NA II 7 181 41
all praise that had much meaning, was supplied by the NA II 8 182 2
might be glad of some refreshment after so much exercise? NA II 8 185 5
"So much the worse!" thought Catherine; such ill-timed NA II 8 187 14
Catherine had read too much not to be perfectly aware of NA II 9 191 2
of this drawback, with much emotion; and, but for a yet NA II 9 191 3
the great gallery was too much for any endeavour at NA II 9 191 4
It could be much better in every respect that Eleanor NA II 9 192 5
had certainly too much wit to let them Sue for detection. NA II 9 194 6
seemed always at hand when least wanted,) much worse!-- NA II 9 194 6
"No, and I am very much surprized. NA II 9 195 20
That is--no, not much, but what she did say, was very NA II 9 196 24
might not often have had much to bear, but though his NA II 9 197 27
lenient hand of time did much for her by insensible NA II 10 201 4
the sight of him; his honest heart would feel so much. NA II 10 202 7
as much attached to me as ever, and laughed at my fears. NA II 10 202 7
"Your brother is certainly very much to be pitied at NA II 10 206 38
so very, very much afflicted as one would have thought." NA II 10 207 39
found her spirits so very much relieved by this NA II 10 207 41
"Aye, and sadly too--for I had much rather stay." NA II 11 211 11
if he had not said half so much as he did, he has always NA II 11 211 13
He went; and, it being at any time a much simpler NA II 11 211 15
of the General's conduct dwelt much on her thoughts. NA II 11 211 15
three terriers, was ready to receive and make much of them. NA II 11 212 17
When she had finished it,--"so much for Isabella," she NA II 12 218 3
But, suppose he had made her very much in love with him?" NA II 12 219 12
be much distressed by the disappointment of Miss Thorpe. NA II 12 219 15
it might seem an intrusion if she staid much longer. NA II 13 220 1
Aware that if she gave herself much time, she might feel NA II 13 220 2
Eleanor looked and declared herself much concerned. NA II 13 221 2
She had "hoped for the pleasure of her company for a much NA II 13 221 2
wishes) to suppose that a much longer visit had been NA II 13 221 2
as left her only just so much solicitude as the human mind NA II 13 221 6
to see him, and have so much to say, for half an hour was NA II 13 222 8
and her journey advanced much faster than she looked for. NA II 14 231 5
Reluctantly, and with much hesitation, did she then begin NA II 14 233 10
have been productive of much unpleasantness to her; that NA II 14 234 10
wits about you, with so much changing of chaises and so NA II 14 234 12
after long thought and much perplexity, to be very brief NA II 14 235 14
Your head runs too much upon Bath; but there is a time for NA II 15 240 2
voice, that "her head did not run upon Bath-----much." NA II 15 240 3
you talk so much about the French-bread at Northanger." NA II 15 241 4
the books up stairs upon much such a subject, about young NA II 15 241 6
of weariness, much oftener than she moved her needle.-- NA II 15 241 7
down stairs with the volume from which so much was hoped. NA II 15 241 7
With a look of much respect, he immediately rose, and NA II 15 241 7
by merely adding twice as much for the grandeur of the NA II 15 245 12
I leave it to my reader's sagacity to determine how much NA II 15 247 14
time to Catherine, how much of it he could have learnt NA II 15 247 14
He felt himself bound as much in honour as in affection to NA II 15 247 15
every other will, gave as much disappointment as pleasure. SS I 1 4 3
much there might prudently be in his power to do for them. SS I 1 5 6
of her conduct was so much the greater, and to a woman in SS I 1 6 9
romance, without having much of her sense, she did not, at SS I 1 7 14
and by her husband with as much kindness as he could feel SS I 2 8 1
What brother on earth would do half so much for his SS I 2 9 11
"One had rather, on such occasions, do too much than too SS I 2 9 12
It will certainly be much the best way. SS I 2 11 23
They will be much more able to give you something." SS I 2 12 24
she was persuaded that a much smaller provision than 7000l. SS I 3 14 2
daughter-in-law, was very much increased by the farther SS I 3 14 3
house before he engaged much of Mrs. Dashwood's attention; SS I 3 16 7
Elinor's drawings very much, it is not the admiration of a SS I 3 17 18
Yet she bore it with so much composure, she seemed SS I 3 18 18
I require so much! SS I 3 18 20
He distrusts his own judgment in such matters so much, SS I 4 19 2
His abilities in every respect improve as much upon SS I 4 20 9
her amiable; and I am very much mistaken if Edward is not SS I 4 21 15
Marianne was astonished to find how much the imagination SS I 4 22 16
by them in their last adieus to a place so much beloved. SS I 5 27 8
I shall see how much I am before-hand with the world in SS I 6 29 4
He said much of his earnest desire of their living in the SS I 6 30 6
to see a person on whom so much of their comfort at Barton SS I 6 31 8
But Sir John's satisfaction in society was much more real; SS I 7 32 2
Brandon was very much in love with Marianne Dashwood. SS I 8 36 1
I can easily suppose that his age may appear much greater SS I 8 37 5

Context	Work	Vol.	Ch.	Page	Line
fever, you would not have despised him half so much.	SS	I	8	38	13
not in the habit of seeing much occupation at home, could	SS	I	9	40	1
"Upon my soul," said he, "I do not know much about him as	SS	I	9	44	20
Sir John did not much understand this reproof; but he	SS	I	9	45	31
					32
I have been too much at my ease, too happy, too frank.	SS	I	10	48	5
her sister, of saying too much what he thought on every	SS	I	10	48	9
I have found him capable of giving me much information on	SS	I	10	51	20
have stretched much farther than your candour.	SS	I	10	51	24
"You decide on his imperfections so much in the mass,"	SS	I	10	51	27
replied Elinor, "and so much on the strength of your own	SS	I	10	51	27
deny me the privilege of disliking him as much as ever."	SS	I	10	52	28
Her heart was not so much at ease, nor her satisfaction in	SS	I	11	54	6
think that he had said too much, and by his countenance	SS	I	11	57	17
This was too much.	SS	I	12	58	3
I have not known him long indeed, but I am much better	SS	I	12	59	4
and much was said on the subject of rain by both of them.	SS	I	12	62	27
"But how came the hand to discompose you so much, if it	SS	I	13	63	12
it wanted it very much, when I was there six years ago."	SS	I	13	67	64
Mrs. Dashwood was too much astonished to speak, and	SS	I	15	76	16
Mrs. Dashwood felt too much for speech, and instantly	SS	I	15	77	18
Is nothing due to the man whom we have all so much reason	SS	I	15	79	28
of any one; of a child much less; because a sense of duty	SS	I	16	84	9
"Dear, dear Norland," said Elinor, "probably looks much as	SS	I	16	87	30
off, and driven as much as possible from the sight."	SS	I	16	88	31
little," said Elinor, "but wealth has much to do with it."	SS	I	17	91	9
Your competence and my wealth are very much alike, I dare	SS	I	17	91	11
other: fancying people so much more gay or grave, or	SS	I	17	93	37
but I am afraid my practice is much more on your sister's.	SS	I	17	94	42
the village itself, in a much higher situation than the	SS	I	18	96	4
I admire them much more if they are tall, straight and	SS	I	18	98	8
felt--but when she saw how much she had pained Edward, her	SS	I	18	98	12
would not be able to give them so much of your time.	SS	I	19	102	3
How much may not a few months do?"	SS	I	19	103	7
interest herself almost as much as ever in the general	SS	I	19	104	10
and sisters were spared much solicitude on her account.	SS	I	19	104	10
as her sister's, but they were much more prepossessing.	SS	I	19	106	22
would come with us; she longed so much to see you all!"	SS	I	19	107	29
Dulness is as much produced within doors as without, by	SS	I	20	111	8
your taste very much, for I think he is extremely handsome.	SS	I	20	111	12
"Much nearer thirty," said her husband.	SS	I	20	111	13
"Ah! well! there is not much difference.	SS	I	20	111	14
She surprised Elinor very much as they returned into the	SS	I	20	113	40
She began by inquiring if they saw much of Mr. Willoughby	SS	I	20	114	43
but if he were ever so much there, I do not think Mr.	SS	I	20	114	44
"Upon my word," replied Elinor, "you know much more of the	SS	I	20	114	45
"You surprise me very much.	SS	I	20	115	49
"Oh!--he did not say much; but he looked as if he knew it	SS	I	20	115	52
"Is Mr. Willoughby much known in your part of	SS	I	20	116	57
honour; not but that he is much more lucky in getting her,	SS	I	20	116	58
You can't think how much I longed to see you!	SS	I	20	116	60
Sir John and Lady Middleton wished it very much.	SS	I	20	116	62
However I am much happier as I am.	SS	I	20	117	64
Their being her relations too made it so much the worse;	SS	I	21	118	2
however, there was not much to be learned; Elinor well	SS	I	21	119	3
Middletons rather too much indulged; perhaps they may be	SS	I	21	122	19
Steele, who seemed very much disposed for conversation,	SS	I	21	123	21
best affections with so much significancy and so many nods	SS	I	21	125	36
for he had at least as much pleasure in telling the name,	SS	I	21	125	37
it is rather too much to pretend to know him very well."	SS	I	21	126	40
She wished very much to have the subject continued, though	SS	I	21	126	41
Marianne, who had never much toleration for any thing like	SS	I	22	127	1
But if I dared tell you all, you would not be so much	SS	I	22	129	11
And she did not feel much delighted with the idea of such	SS	I	22	129	13
"Yes; and heaven knows how much longer we may have to wait.	SS	I	22	131	35
in return, which I am very much vexed at, for he has been	SS	I	22	132	37
You can't think how much I go through in my mind from it	SS	I	22	133	42
than a fortnight with us, and seeing me so much affected.--	SS	I	22	134	52
How much could it not tempt her to forgive!	SS	II	1	140	1
if he had injured her, how much more had he injured	SS	II	1	140	1
had seemed great, how much greater were they now likely to	SS	II	1	140	3
Much as she had suffered from her first conversation with	SS	II	1	141	7
a friend, which she very much feared her involuntary	SS	II	1	141	7
She had little difficulty in understanding thus much of	SS	II	1	142	7
to-morrow, and then I hope she will not much mind it."	SS	II	1	144	11
"indeed you are very much mistaken, Lady Middleton; I am	SS	II	1	144	12
the offence; "and I do not much wonder at it; for it is	SS	II	1	145	17
for her; and there is so much still to be done to the	SS	II	1	145	19
"Indeed I shall be very much obliged to you for your help,"	SS	II	1	145	20
in life, from his being so much more in the world than me,	SS	II	2	147	12
"But Mrs. John Dashwood would not much approve of Edward's	SS	II	2	149	27
It raises my influence much too high; the power of	SS	II	2	150	33
tenderly attached is too much for an indifferent person."	SS	II	2	150	33
will change her mind by and bye, why so much the better."	SS	II	3	154	4
would be productive of much amusement to both her	SS	II	3	155	7
attention to herself, how much the heart of Marianne was	SS	II	3	155	7
Margaret and I shall be as much benefited by it as	SS	II	3	155	8
You will have much pleasure in being in London, and	SS	II	3	157	16
like Edward Ferrars very much, and shall always be glad to	SS	II	3	157	17
prevented their giving much pleasure to her sister, and	SS	II	4	161	6
Mrs. Jennings, by being much engaged in her own room,	SS	II	4	161	7
Elinor wished very much to ask whether Willoughby were	SS	II	4	162	12
much more curiosity on the subject than she had ever felt.	SS	II	4	162	13
"Aye, to be sure, I thought as much.	SS	II	4	163	18
In Bond-Street especially, where much of their business	SS	II	4	164	24
"If this open weather holds much longer," said Mrs.	SS	II	5	167	1
them when they do; they seem to take it so much to heart."	SS	II	5	167	1
"How much they must enjoy it!	SS	II	5	167	3
compound for the want of much real enjoyment from any of	SS	II	5	168	11
time with much concern his continued regard for her sister.	SS	II	5	168	12
"Yes, a little--not much."	SS	II	5	169	22
it was risking too much for the gratification of a few	SS	II	5	170	29
that evening, and never so much fatigued by the exercise.	SS	II	5	171	35
I believe I have been wrong in saying so much, but I	SS	II	5	173	44
avowal of his love for her sister, affected her very much.	SS	II	5	173	45
it, she might be as liable to say too much as too little.	SS	II	5	173	45
last Tuesday, and very much regretted that I was not	SS	II	6	177	9
Marianne was in a silent agony, too much oppressed even	SS	II	6	178	16
could esteem Edward as much as ever, however they might be	SS	II	6	179	18
he wo'nt keep her waiting much longer, for it is quite	SS	II	7	181	8
I am much concerned to find there was any thing in my	SS	II	7	183	13
This, as every thing else would have been, was too much	SS	II	7	185	19
Much as you suffer now, think of what you would have	SS	II	7	186	29
letters which now raised a much stronger curiosity than	SS	II	7	186	37
You must be very much altered indeed since we parted, if	SS	II	7	187	40
over every sentence, exclaimed-----"it is too much!	SS	II	7	190	55
					56
We owe Mrs. Jennings much more than civility; and civility	SS	II	7	191	63
though Marianne might lose much, he could gain very little	SS	II	8	196	21
nothing will be of so much service to her as rest, if you	SS	II	8	198	28
Elinor encouraged her as much as possible to talk of what	SS	II	9	201	2
were able to grieve as much as herself; and positively	SS	II	9	203	10
Her fortune was large, and our family estate much	SS	II	9	205	24
to describe it--I have pained you too much already.	SS	II	9	207	26
been suspected of a much nearer connection with her.	SS	II	9	208	28
Now, though at first she will suffer much, I am sure she	SS	II	9	211	34
preyed altogether so much on her spirits, that she could	SS	II	10	212	1
much as the idea of both might now be spurned by her.	SS	II	10	213	3
to visit; she hated him so much that she was resolved	SS	II	10	215	10
you; but she has been very much plagued lately with	SS	II	10	219	38
Elinor began to find this impertinence too much for her	SS	II	10	219	42
though it did not give much sweetness to the manners of	SS	II	10	219	42
"I wished very much to call upon you yesterday," said he, "	SS	II	11	221	9
but one has always so much to do on first coming to town.	SS	II	11	221	9
too; "but she was so much engaged with her mother, that	SS	II	11	222	14
all my heart, it were twice as much, for your sake."	SS	II	11	223	22
"You are mistaken, Elinor; you are very much mistaken.	SS	II	11	223	24
have too much sense not to see all that.	SS	II	11	224	24
for she has your interest very much at heart, I assure you.	SS	II	11	224	24
give her great pleasure; she said as much the other day."	SS	II	11	224	24
"Another year or two may do much towards it," he gravely	SS	II	11	226	37
Whereas, in my opinion, by her taking so much notice of	SS	II	11	227	46
and I am very much deceived if you do not do better.	SS	II	11	227	50
was an expectation of too much pleasure to himself to be	SS	II	11	228	51
did not seem to know much about horses, he soon set him	SS	II	11	228	52
Mrs. John Dashwood had so much confidence in her husband's	SS	II	12	229	1
Elinor wanted very much to know, though she did not chuse	SS	II	12	229	4
them still so very much attached to each other, that they	SS	II	12	229	4
that though not much in the habit of giving any thing,	SS	II	12	230	6
civilities with some surprise, but much more pleasure.	SS	II	12	230	6
might not have done much, however, towards procuring them	SS	II	12	231	9
others, had they known as much as she did, they would have	SS	II	12	232	16
John Dashwood had not much to say for himself that was	SS	II	12	233	18
in this, for it was very much the case with the chief of	SS	II	12	233	18
Elinor was much more hurt by Marianne's warmth, than she	SS	II	12	236	38
She wondered that Lucy's spirits could be so very much	SS	II	13	238	2
her vanity should so very much blind her, as to make the	SS	II	13	238	2
him, and that she had very much regretted being from home,	SS	II	13	241	20
I expected much pleasure in it, but I have found none.	SS	II	13	242	29
But I have much to say to you on that head, which cannot	SS	II	13	243	33
her persuasion that Lucy could not stay much longer.	SS	II	13	244	43
for as she wished to be as much as possible with Charlotte,	SS	II	14	246	2
For their own comfort, they would much rather have	SS	II	14	246	2
They had too much sense to be desirable companions to the	SS	II	14	246	3
Marianne had now been brought by degrees, so much into the	SS	II	14	249	7
before they parted, how much her washing cost per week,	SS	II	14	249	8
and how much she had every year to spend upon herself.	SS	II	14	249	8
generously attributed it much less to any natural	SS	II	14	250	12
is always so much comfort, so much elegance about them.	SS	II	14	251	17
like them, you know, very much already, and so does my	SS	II	14	253	24
Mrs. Dashwood had never been so much pleased with any	SS	II	14	254	28
For him she felt much compassion;--for Lucy very little--	SS	III	1	260	9
herself as suffering much, any otherwise than as the self-	SS	III	1	261	12
"It was not fit that you should then know how much I was	SS	III	1	262	21
Marianne seemed much struck.--	SS	III	1	262	24
me, I was glad to spare them from knowing how much I felt.	SS	III	1	263	27
borne it as much as possible without spreading it farther.	SS	III	1	263	27
You do not suppose that I have ever felt much.--	SS	III	1	263	29
injured, no reparation could be too much for her to make.	SS	III	1	265	32
But I would not alarm you too much.	SS	III	1	265	36
such ingratitude, where so much kindness had been shewn,	SS	III	1	265	36
had been shewn, so much confidence had been placed!	SS	III	1	265	36
we both wished very much to have invited you and Marianne	SS	III	1	266	36
Her mind was so much weakened that she still fancied	SS	III	2	270	2
But though so much of the matter was known to them already,	SS	III	2	270	3
Poor Anne was much to blame for what she did, but she did	SS	III	2	277	30
won't think it too much trouble to give us a call, should	SS	III	2	277	30
their removal, and only so much less bent on its being	SS	III	3	279	1
to Elinor altogether much more eligible than any other.	SS	III	3	279	1
it was inforced with so much real politeness by Mr. Palmer	SS	III	3	279	1
dear mother, whom she so much wished to see, in a more	SS	III	3	280	6
"I shall always think myself very much obliged to you."	SS	III	3	281	13
					14
three times in Harley-Street, and am much pleased with him.	SS	III	3	282	19
will of course have much to do relative to his ordination."	SS	III	4	286	15
Well, so much the better for him.	SS	III	4	286	17
"Certainly, ma'am," replied Elinor, not hearing much of	SS	III	4	287	23
equally feared to say too much or too little, and sat	SS	III	4	287	24
He too was much distressed, and they sat down together in	SS	III	4	288	26
to get over what she so much dreaded as soon as possible, "	SS	III	4	288	28
two hundred a-year--were much more considerable, and such	SS	III	4	289	28
"You are very much mistaken.	SS	III	4	289	35
between the parsonage and the mansion-house much greater.	SS	III	4	290	39
to say, her mind was so much more occupied by the	SS	III	4	291	46
Elinor's service, so very much disliked Mrs. John Dashwood,	SS	III	5	294	3
whom neither of the others had so much reason to dislike.	SS	III	5	294	3
vastly well,--she will not like to hear it much talked of."	SS	III	5	295	16
it his mother will feel as much as if she had never	SS	III	5	296	20
event, must be concealed from her as much as possible.	SS	III	5	296	20
you of this, because I knew how much it must please you.	SS	III	5	297	31
the necessity of saying much in reply herself, and from	SS	III	5	297	32
in that little had seen so much variety in his address to	SS	III	6	304	15
to fancy himself as much superior to people in general, as	SS	III	6	304	15
She liked him, however, upon the whole much better than	SS	III	6	305	15
on a sofa, did not speak much in favour of her amendment;	SS	III	7	307	1
a much greater exertion, began to talk of going likewise.--	SS	III	7	308	5
while his love was in so much uneasiness on her sister's	SS	III	7	309	5
Her pulse was much stronger, and every symptom more	SS	III	7	310	8
to be found at a much later hour than the present.	SS	III	7	311	14
At ten o'clock, she trusted, or at least not much later,	SS	III	7	315	26
reverse, from eating much;--and the present refreshment,	SS	III	7	315	27
"Had I known as much half an hour ago--but since I am here"	SS	III	8	318	15
I had always been too much in the habit of indulging, I	SS	III	8	320	29
can ever reprobate too much--I was acting in this manner,	SS	III	8	320	32
all likelihood much more than was justified by the future.	SS	III	8	324	45
I avoided the Middletons as much as possible, as well as	SS	III	8	326	55
You have proved your heart less wicked, much less wicked.	SS	III	8	329	66
I was too much shocked to be able to pass myself off as	SS	III	8	330	69
His heart was softened in seeing mine suffer; and so much	SS	III	8	330	69
died away, remained too much oppressed by a croud of ideas,	SS	III	9	333	1
warmth, was in a moment as much overcome by her happiness,	SS	III	9	334	4
errand at Barton had been much softened to Mrs. Dashwood	SS	III	9	335	6
ever felt or feigned, as much more warm, as more sincere	SS	III	9	336	14
His age is only so much beyond her's, as to be an	SS	III	9	338	20
there is something much more pleasing in his countenance.--	SS	III	9	338	20
unstudied simplicity is much more accordant with her real	SS	III	9	338	22
as she did so, that she should in future practise much.	SS	III	10	342	7
"I am not wishing him too much good," said Marianne at	SS	III	10	345	24
supported by an affection, on his side, much less certain.	SS	III	11	350	9
Her daughter did not look, however, as if much of it were	SS	III	11	352	18
studies with quite so much vigour as when they first came	SS	III	11	352	20
Elinor's countenance how much she really suffered, and in	SS	III	11	353	24
Elinor, who, though still much disordered, had so far	SS	III	11	353	25
not look up;--he never was a gentleman much for talking."	SS	III	11	354	31
well off, that with so much uneasiness as both her sisters	SS	III	11	355	45
had lately experienced, so much reason as they had often	SS	III	11	355	45
had so well understood, much slighter in reality, than she	SS	III	11	355	46
before her, had too much engrossed her tenderness, and led	SS	III	11	356	46
suffering almost as much, certainly with less self-	SS	III	11	356	46
which so much heightened the pain of the intelligence.	SS	III	12	357	1
Delaford,--that place in which so much conspired to give	SS	III	12	357	3
Marianne had retreated as much as possible out of sight,	SS	III	12	359	13
really did, so much in need of encouragement and fresh air.	SS	III	13	361	2
and on the same principle will forgive him much sooner."	SS	III	13	366	19
for having spent so much time with them at Norland, when	SS	III	13	368	25
wrong in remaining so much in Sussex, and the arguments	SS	III	13	368	28
herself, who had heard so much of it from Colonel Brandon,	SS	III	13	368	31
much attention, as to be entirely mistress of the subject.	SS	III	13	368	31
nothing so much as to be on good terms with her children."	SS	III	13	371	39
to him, as he declared a much greater willingness to make	SS	III	13	372	45
It was as much, however, as was desired, and more than was	SS	III	14	374	5
would be saying too much, for certainly you have been one	SS	III	14	375	9
when people are much thrown together, and see little of	SS	III	14	375	9
or bringing himself too much;--and if Edward might be	SS	III	14	377	12

and sisters spent much more than half their time with her. SS III 14 378 13
she desired nothing so much as to give up its constant SS III 14 378 13
heart became, in time, as much devoted to her husband, as SS III 14 379 17
to hear her, I was very much attached to a young man of W 316 2
"Not much indeed--but you know we must marry.-- W 317 2
Penelope will laugh at you very much." W 318 2
But I doubt whether ridicule,--has Penelope much wit?"-- W 318 2
He has been very much in love with her these two years, & W 321 2
The Edwardes look much higher. W 321 2
I have been unlucky enough, & I cannot say much for you, W 321 2
Mr Edwards had a much easier, & more communicative air W 323 3
they entered it with much easier feelings & more natural W 323 3
has been rather too much exposed to all weathers, to make W 324 3
Miss Emma Watson puts me very much in mind of her eldest W 324 3
I do not much think she is like any of the family but Miss W 324 3
& if he cd but have his health, how much he wd enjoy it." W 325 4
Miss E. answered hesitatingly--"yes--he is very much liked W 328 8
Of the females, Ly. Osborne had by much the finest person;- W 329 9
of his features that he minded it as much as ever.-- W 330 11
"Aye do--& if you find she does not want much talking to, W 333 13
here Mrs E.; she is by much too nice a judge of decorum to W 334 13
"We are off at last, said his Lordship to Tom--how much W 335 13
I shall retreat in as much secrecy as possible to the most W 335 13
enjoyed the eveng so much--& Mr Edwards was as warm as W 336 14
herself very unwilling to give him so much trouble. W 339 18
"It is making it too much of a fatigue I think, to stay so W 340 19
of as much;--for I am rather fond of dancing than not.-- W 340 19
You had said so much against him that I could not wish W 341 19
shews him in general as much encouragement as is W 341 19
"His manners are of a kind to give me much more ease & W 342 19
not come on to pay you much attention; it is a hard thing W 343 19
Nobody can tell how much I hate quarrelling. W 343 19
I own, I do not like much action in the pulpit--I do not W 343 20
A simple delivery is much better calculated to inspire W 344 20
to inspire devotion, & shews a much better taste.-- W 344 20
But what pleased me as much as anything was Mr Howard's W 344 20
to be down stairs;--with much concern they took their W 345 21
Emma was not inclined to give herself much trouble for his W 345 21
"If they knew how much it became them, they would all have W 345 21
quite as much impertinence in it's form as Goodbreeding.-- W 347 22
with much sentiment, as they were sitting together.-- W 349 24
Mrs R. W. eyed her with much familiar curiosity & W 349 24
she cd. not but feel how much better it was to be the W 349 24
who regretted very much her not being of the party.-- W 350 24
I do not much attend the balls, they are rather too mixed,- W 350 24
"Very much"--replied Emma, who thought a comprehensive W 350 24
as it makes me nervous to be much alone." W 351 25
He was persuaded without much difficulty to throw off his W 355 28
I assure you we bring her home at the end of a month, much W 356 28
I think it is a much better game than speculation. W 358 28
"Do you see much of the parsonage family at the castle, Mr W 358 28
made for his entertainment much exceeding what had been W 360 30
She was very much pressed by Robert & Jane to return with W 362 32
see the place, and was so much delighted with it that he PP I 1 3 10
"In such cases, a woman has not often much beauty to think PP I 1 4 21
"They have none of them much to recommend them," replied PP I 1 5 27
If I had known as much this morning, I certainly would not PP I 2 7 22
"Now, Kitty, you may cough as much as you chuse," said Mr. PP I 2 8 25
whose beauty he had heard much; but he saw only the father. PP I 3 9 3
the ladies declared he was much handsomer than Mr. Bingley, PP I 3 10 5
You had much better dance." PP I 3 11 8
Mrs. Bennet had seen her eldest daughter much admired by PP I 3 12 15
Jane was as much gratified by this, as her mother could be, PP I 3 12 15
impatiently, "he would not have danced half so much! PP I 3 13 17
subject, and related, with much bitterness of spirit and PP I 3 13 19
"that Lizzy does not lose much by not suiting his fancy; PP I 3 13 20
expressed to her sister how very much she admired him. PP I 4 14 1
much ease, with such perfect good breeding!" PP I 4 14 2
"I was very much flattered by his asking me to dance a PP I 4 14 4
keep his house; and I am much mistaken if we shall not PP I 4 15 10
he acknowledged to be pretty, but she smiled too much. PP I 4 16 15
never speaks much unless among his intimate acquaintance. PP I 5 19 13
"His pride," said Miss Lucas, "does not offend me so much PP I 5 20 18
was in a way to be very much in love; but she considered PP I 6 21 1
There is so much of gratitude or vanity in almost every PP I 6 21 2
"But she does help him on, as much as her nature will PP I 6 22 3
will be leisure for falling in love as much as she chuses." PP I 6 22 6
I do not imagine that much has been unfolded." PP I 6 22 9
had been listened to with much more pleasure, though not PP I 6 25 24
conversation, and was too much engrossed by his own PP I 6 25 25
You cannot refuse to dance, I am sure, when so much beauty PP I 6 26 38
"You excel so much in the dance, Miss Eliza, that it is PP I 6 26 41
"I had much rather go in the coach." PP I 7 30 24
"They are wanted in the farm much oftener than I can get PP I 7 31 26
and head-ache there is not much the matter with me. PP I 7 31 30
expressing in her note how much she longed for such a PP I 7 33 43
She was not equal, however, to much conversation, and when PP I 7 33 43
saw how much affection and solicitude they shewed for Jane. PP I 7 33 44
of distinguishing the much superior solicitude of Mr. PP I 8 35 1
three or four times how much they were grieved, how PP I 8 35 1
her feeling herself so much an intruder as she believed PP I 8 35 2
"And then you have added so much to it yourself, you are PP I 8 38 31
Elizabeth was so much caught by what passed, as to leave PP I 8 38 39
"Is Miss Darcy much grown since the spring?" said Miss PP I 8 38 40
I never met with anybody who delighted me so much. PP I 8 38 42
of accomplishments," said Darcy, "has too much truth. PP I 8 39 46
"But people themselves alter so much, that there is PP I 9 43 18
"I assure you there is quite as much of that going on in PP I 9 43 19
leave it; and when I am in town it is pretty much the same. PP I 9 43 22
so much the man of fashion! so genteel and so easy!-- PP I 9 44 27
Gardiner's in town, so much in love with her, that my PP I 9 44 31
She performed her part indeed without much graciousness, PP I 9 45 35
"Oh! yes--it would be much better to wait till Jane was PP I 9 45 38
The day passed much as the day before had done. PP I 10 47 1
He studies too much for words of four syllables.-- PP I 10 48 20
The power of doing any thing with quickness is always much PP I 10 49 27
"Nay," cried Bingley, "this is too much, to remember at PP I 10 49 28
You have shewn him off now much more than he did himself." PP I 10 49 30
with myself, I should not pay him half so much deference. PP I 10 50 39
Arguments are too much like disputes. PP I 10 51 42
my side; and Mr. Darcy had much better finish his letter." PP I 10 51 43
Jane was already so much recovered as to intend leaving PP I 10 53 66
Miss Bingley's attention was quite as much engaged in PP I 11 54 4
How much sooner one tires of any thing than of a book!-- PP I 11 55 4
of the present party; I am much mistaken if there are not PP I 11 55 6
It would surely be much more rational if conversation PP I 11 55 8
"Much more rational, my dear Caroline, I dare say but it PP I 11 56 9
I dare say but it would not be near so much like a ball." PP I 11 56 9
He was as much awake to the novelty of attention in that PP I 11 56 12
second, I can admire you much better as I sit by the fire." PP I 11 56 15
He began to feel the danger of paying Elizabeth too much PP I 11 58 34
resolved--nor did she much expect it would be asked; and PP I 12 59 1
of one sister much exceeded her affection for the other. PP I 12 59 2
them very wrong to have so much trouble, and was sure Jane PP I 12 60 6
all assembled, had lost much of its animation, and almost PP I 12 60 6
Much had been done, and much had been said in the regiment PP I 12 60 7
father, always gave me much uneasiness, and since I have PP I 13 62 12
letter had done away much of her ill-will, and she was PP I 13 64 20
said he had heard much of their beauty, but that, in this PP I 13 64 21
This gallantry was not much to the taste of some of his PP I 13 65 21
22
cousins,--and could say much on the subject, but that I am PP I 13 65 25
tongue; but Mr. Collins, much offended, laid aside his PP I 14 69 15
16
Mr. Collins, being in fact much better fitted for a walker PP I 15 71 6
which he returned with as much more, apologising for his PP I 15 73 11
met with so much attention in the whole course of his life. PP I 15 74 13
and admire, and he was so much struck with the size and PP I 16 75 2
did not at first convey much gratification; but when Mrs. PP I 16 75 2
tickets, she soon grew too much interested in the game, PP I 16 76 8
Are you much acquainted with Mr. Darcy?" PP I 16 77 12
"As much as I ever wish to be," cried Elizabeth warmly,-- " PP I 16 77 13
"whether he is likely to be in this country much longer." PP I 16 78 18
Philips, appears to do so much credit to--but he gave up PP I 16 81 37
that he felt it to be as much a debt of gratitude to him, PP I 16 81 37
But she is too much like her brother,--very, very proud.-- PP I 16 82 43
he assured her with much earnest gravity that it was not PP I 16 83 49
"Laugh as much as you chuse, but you will not laugh me out PP I 17 85 4
"I can much more easily believe Mr. Bingley's being PP I 17 85 5
would have much to suffer when the affair became public. PP I 17 86 8
avoiding Mrs. Bennet as much as possible, saying not much PP I 17 86 9
not much to Elizabeth, and nothing at all to the others. PP I 17 86 9
Mr. Darcy, who took her so much by surprise in his PP I 18 90 5
that private balls are much pleasanter than public ones.-- PP I 18 91 11
considering his descent, one could not expect much better." PP I 18 94 45
"You are much mistaken if you expect to influence me by PP I 18 95 48
Mr. Wickham has deserved much less attention from Mr. PP I 18 95 50
Mr. Darcy seemed much pleased with the attention. he PP I 18 98 62
Upon the whole, I am much pleased with him." PP I 18 98 62
not to venture near her, lest she might hear too much. PP I 18 98 63
they must desire the connection as much as she could do. PP I 18 99 63
justified in devoting too much of our time to music, for PP I 18 101 71
The rector of a parish has much to do.-- PP I 18 101 71
remains will not be too much for his parish duties, and PP I 18 101 71
to expose themselves as much as they could during the PP I 18 101 72
much distressed by the folly which he must have witnessed. PP I 18 101 72
and even Lydia was too much fatigued to utter more than PP I 18 103 75
Thus much for my general intention in favour of matrimony; PP I 19 106 10
you have even now said as much to encourage my suit as PP I 19 108 16
17
of temper, she could not contribute much to my felicity." PP I 20 110 4
Not that I have much pleasure indeed in talking to any PP I 20 113 28
all wish the connection as much as his own, and a sister's PP I 21 118 14
Could she have seen half as much love in Mr. Darcy for PP I 21 119 20
in love with you, he is very much in love with her friend." PP I 21 119 20
I cannot consider your situation with much compassion." PP I 21 120 26
But little had she dared to hope that so much love and PP I 22 121 1
"You cannot be too much on your guard. PP I 22 123 9
She rated his abilities much higher than any of the others; PP I 22 124 11
must be surprised, very much surprised,--so lately as Mr. PP I 22 125 17
Charlotte did not stay much longer, and Elizabeth was then PP I 22 125 18
With many compliments to them, and much self-gratulation PP I 23 126 1
2
Mrs. Bennet was in fact too much overpowered to say a PP I 23 126 5
Mr. Bennet's emotions were much more tranquil on the PP I 23 127 6
On the contrary she was as much disposed to complain of it PP I 23 128 11
too much, she feared, for the strength of his attachment. PP I 23 129 13
He was too happy, however, to need much attention; and PP I 23 129 15
she had ever done; and much as she had always been PP II 1 133 3
being so much design in the world as some persons imagine." PP II 1 136 16
They have known her much longer than they have known me; PP II 1 137 24
was pleased to think how much they had always disliked Mr. PP II 1 138 30
He took leave of his relations at Longbourn with as much PP II 2 139 1
Mrs. Bennet had many grievances to relate, and much to PP II 2 139 3
and that Longbourn estate is just as much entailed as ever. PP II 2 140 4
"So much the better. PP II 2 141 14
body had as much to say or to hear on the subject as usual. PP II 3 146 19
He was well, but so much engaged with Mr. Darcy, that they PP II 3 147 23
that I have never been much in love; for had I really PP II 3 150 29
Kitty and Lydia take his defection much more to heart than PP II 3 150 29
to with about as much delight as the rattle of the chaise. PP II 4 152 4
friends who live in Hertfordshire are not much better. PP II 4 154 19
exercise, and owned she encouraged it as much as possible. PP II 5 156 4
of woman whom one cannot regard with too much deference." PP II 5 157 9
very much objected to be kept waiting for her dinner.-- PP II 6 161 7
at Rosings, with as much apprehension, as her father had PP II 6 161 7
and Elizabeth saw much to be pleased with, though she PP II 6 161 8
that it was much better worth looking at in the summer. PP II 6 162 13
The party did not supply much conversation. PP II 6 163 14
Perhaps she is full young to be much in company. PP II 6 165 35
ever dared to trifle with so much dignified impertinence. PP II 6 166 38
hot or too cold, or having too much or too little light. PP II 6 166 41
Sir William did not say much. PP II 6 166 41
undoubtedly have been much less in his own apartment, had PP II 7 168 1
Colonel Fitzwilliam's manners were very much admired at PP II 8 172 1
to Darcy, much more than to any other person in the room. PP II 8 172 2
pretty friend has moreover caught his fancy very much. PP II 8 172 3
and they conversed with so much spirit and flow, as to PP II 8 172 3
"So much the better. PP II 8 173 10
It cannot be done too much; and when I next write to her, PP II 8 173 10
You have employed your time much better. PP II 8 176 26
has not much idea of ever returning to Netherfield again?" PP II 9 177 6
7
But perhaps Mr. Bingley did not take the house so much for PP II 9 178 9
minutes longer without saying much to any body, went away. PP II 9 179 26
and whenever he came to Hunsford; but without much success. PP II 9 181 29
doubted whether there were much admiration in it, and PP II 9 181 29
of talking or of listening much; but it struck her in the PP II 10 182 1
Are you going much farther?" PP II 10 183 4
Does your charge give you much trouble? PP II 10 184 19
I have reason to think Bingley very much indebted to him. PP II 10 185 24
"And remember that I have not much reason for supposing it PP II 10 185 28
It is not to be supposed that there was much affection in PP II 10 186 36
a headach; and it grew so much worse towards the evening PP II 10 187 41
press her to go, and as much as possible prevented her PP II 10 187 41
to exasperate herself as much as possible against Mr. PP II 11 188 1
Forgive me for having taken up so much of your time, and PP II 11 193 29
for so many months! so much in love as to wish to marry PP II 11 193 31
I cannot blame myself for having done thus much. PP II 12 199 5
Having said thus much, I feel no doubt of your secrecy. PP II 12 201 5
had latterly brought them much together, and given her a PP II 13 207 6
believe nobody feels the loss of friends so much as I do. PP II 14 210 3
young men; and know them to be so much attached to me!-- PP II 14 210 3
"I am much obliged to your ladyship for your kind PP II 14 211 7
Daughters are never of so much consequence to a father. PP II 14 211 10
before, were now so much affected as to make it almost PP II 14 213 19
The favour of your company has been much felt, I assure PP II 15 215 2
How much I shall have to tell!" PP II 15 217 13
Elizabeth privately added, "and how much I shall have to PP II 15 217 14
Their journey was performed without much conversation, or PP II 15 217 15
there were two or three much much uglier in the shop; and PP II 16 219 4
were two or three much much uglier in the shop; and when I PP II 16 219 4
Besides, it will not much signify what one wears this PP II 16 219 4
but consider how much it must increase his disappointment." PP II 17 224 3
without believing that so much wickedness existed in the PP II 17 224 9
of man; and of late it has been shifting about pretty much. PP II 17 225 10
him much longer, my heart will be as light as a feather." PP II 17 225 13
was meant to be kept as much as possible to myself; and if PP II 17 226 23
Bingley may tell in a much more agreeable manner himself. PP II 17 227 25
Well, much good may it do them! PP II 17 228 33
estate that is not lawfully their own, so much the better. PP II 17 228 35
had she before been so much disposed to pardon his PP II 18 229 10
I have just as much right to be asked as she has, and more PP II 18 230 13
essentials, I believe, he is very much what he ever was." PP II 18 234 34

Context	Work	Vol	Ch	Page	Line
of whose good opinion and judgment he stands much in awe.	PP	II	18	234	38
de Bourgh, which I am certain he has very much at heart."	PP	II	18	235	38
of enjoying herself as much as possible; advice, which	PP	II	18	235	40
much too full of lines under the words to be made public.	PP	II	19	238	5
of June Kitty was so much recovered as to be able to enter	PP	II	19	238	6
to go so far, and see so much as they had proposed, or at	PP	II	19	238	7
a place of which you have heard so much?" said her aunt.	PP	II	19	240	13
elderly woman, much less fine, and more civil, than she	PP	III	1	246	5
"I have heard much of your master's fine person," said Mrs.	PP	III	1	247	12
"Is your master much at Pemberley in the course of the	PP	III	1	248	24
"Not so much as I could wish, sir; but I dare say he may	PP	III	1	248	25
Elizabeth could not help saying, "it is very much to his	PP	III	1	248	29
"there are very few people of whom so much can be said.	PP	III	1	248	31
					32
How much of pleasure or pain it was in his power to bestow!	PP	III	1	251	48
How much of good or evil must be done by him!	PP	III	1	251	48
Nor did he seem much more at ease; when he spoke, his	PP	III	1	252	52
of fishing, and was so much engaged in watching the	PP	III	1	254	57
allow me, or do I ask too much, to introduce my sister to	PP	III	1	256	63
At such a time, much might have been said, and silence was	PP	III	1	257	66
and she was too much engaged in pointing out to her	PP	III	1	258	76
to leave Elizabeth much attention for any of these new	PP	III	1	259	77
should have said too much in her favour; and more than	PP	III	2	260	1
acquaintance was at least as much embarrassed as herself.	PP	III	2	261	3
was much relieved by discerning such different feelings.	PP	III	2	261	4
Elizabeth, on her side, had much to do.	PP	III	2	262	7
There was not much in the question, nor in the preceding	PP	III	2	263	9
It was evident that she was much better acquainted with Mr.	PP	III	2	264	13
of; it was evident that he was very much in love with her.	PP	III	2	264	13
They saw much to interest, but nothing to justify enquiry.	PP	III	2	264	13
he was a liberal man, and did much good among the poor.	PP	III	2	265	14
he was not held there in much estimation; for though the	PP	III	2	265	15
Such a change in a man of so much pride, excited not only	PP	III	2	265	16
curious to know with how much civility on that lady's side,	PP	III	3	267	1
was not sorry to be spared the necessity of saying much.	PP	III	3	268	5
entrance, exerted herself much more to talk; and Elizabeth	PP	III	3	269	8
and forwarded, as much as possible, every attempt at	PP	III	3	269	8
saw any one so much altered as she is since the winter.	PP	III	3	270	13
but too much reason to fear they are not gone to Scotland.	PP	III	4	274	3
But I knew not--I was afraid of doing too much.	PP	III	4	278	18
consideration, I am much more inclined than I was to judge	PP	III	5	282	1
Till I was in Kent, and saw so much both of Mr. Darcy and	PP	III	5	284	16
How much you must have gone through!"	PP	III	5	286	31
Lydia she shall have as much money as she chuses, to buy	PP	III	5	288	38
unfortunate affair; and will probably be much talked of.	PP	III	5	289	42
that she cannot be too much guarded in her behaviour	PP	III	5	289	43
in amazement, but was too much oppressed to make reply.	PP	III	5	289	44
I am afraid I did not do so much as I might have done!	PP	III	5	292	64
"Your attendance upon her, has been too much for you.	PP	III	5	292	65
Kitty is slight and delicate, and Mary studies so much,	PP	III	5	292	66
that I had difficulty in finding out even so much as this."	PP	III	5	293	69
to console yourself as much as possible, to throw off your	PP	III	6	297	11
she did not express so much satisfaction as her children	PP	III	6	298	13
No, Lizzy, let me once in my life feel how much I have	PP	III	6	299	21
gown, and give as much trouble as I can,--or, perhaps, I	PP	III	6	300	28
Jane, who was not so light, nor so much in the habit of	PP	III	7	301	7
					8
"I dislike it very much," he replied; "but it must be done.	PP	III	7	303	22
But there are two things that I want very much to know;--	PP	III	7	304	27
much to know;--one is, how much money your uncle has laid	PP	III	7	304	27
said Elizabeth, "and how much is settled on his side on	PP	III	7	305	36
down to your father, and ask him how much he will give her.	PP	III	7	306	44
But there was much to be talked of, in marrying her; and	PP	III	8	309	6
of a sister's frailty would have mortified her so much.	PP	III	8	311	12
several of the young men, too, that she likes very much.	PP	III	8	313	21
Your uncle is as much surprised as I am--and nothing but	PP	III	10	321	2
some time or other, and it did not much signify when.	PP	III	10	323	2
They met several times, for there was much to be discussed.	PP	III	10	323	2
I was never bold enough to say before) how much I like him.	PP	III	10	325	2
revolt from the connection. he had to be sure done much.	PP	III	10	326	3
She was ashamed to think how much.	PP	III	10	326	3
I believe it would be too much for me, or else I could	PP	III	10	327	11
"Very much."	PP	III	10	328	21
But you know married women have never much time for	PP	III	11	330	6
Mr. Wickham's adieus were much more affectionate than his	PP	III	11	330	7
"Well, so much the better.	PP	III	11	331	14
know, no one can know how much I suffer from what she says.	PP	III	11	333	28
a sufferer is denied me, because you have always so much."	PP	III	11	333	29
relief, from observing how much the beauty of her sister	PP	III	11	337	56
and was really persuaded that she talked as much as ever.	PP	III	11	337	56
Much disappointed that you did not come back and keep your	PP	III	11	338	58
danger of making him as much in love with you as ever."	PP	III	12	339	9
The latter was much more agreeable than his companion	PP	III	13	346	21
" tis too much!" she added, "by far too much.	PP	III	13	346	24
my dear family! how shall I bear so much happiness!"	PP	III	13	347	26
"I suspected as much," replied Elizabeth.	PP	III	13	349	46
have chosen so much more advantageously in many respects.	PP	III	13	349	47
I assure you it is much larger than Sir William Lucas's."	PP	III	14	352	10
I would not injure him so much as to suppose the truth of	PP	III	14	353	26
You both did as much as you could, in planning the	PP	III	14	355	44
in general would have too much sense to join in the scorn."	PP	III	14	358	70
to suppose the he thought much higher of her ladyship than	PP	III	15	360	2
ridiculous, contained much good sense and solid reasoning.	PP	III	15	361	2
and Elizabeth was spared from much teazing on the subject.	PP	III	15	361	5
"Something very much to the purpose of course.	PP	III	15	362	14
Much as I abominate writing, I would not give up Mr.	PP	III	15	364	24
even over Wickham, much as I value the impudence and	PP	III	15	364	24
seeing too little, she might have fancied too much.	PP	III	15	364	25
Very little was said by either; Kitty was too much afraid	PP	III	16	365	1
own feelings, care not how much I may be wounding your's.	PP	III	16	365	2
					3
induced you to take so much trouble, and bear so many	PP	III	16	366	5
Much as I respect them, I believe, I thought only of you."	PP	III	16	366	6
Elizabeth was too much embarrassed to say a word.	PP	III	16	366	7
There was too much to be thought, and felt, and said, for	PP	III	16	366	9
not of philosophy, but what is much better, of ignorance.	PP	III	16	369	24
I guessed as much."	PP	III	16	370	39
the term, she found that it had been pretty much the case.	PP	III	16	370	39
I know how much you dislike him."	PP	III	17	372	6
"Very, very much.	PP	III	17	373	11
Mr. Bingley; "but I am sure it will be too much for Kitty.	PP	III	17	374	24
So much the better.	PP	III	17	377	39
pray apologise for my having disliked him so much before.	PP	III	17	378	43
But the morrow passed off much better than she expected;	PP	III	17	378	46
are to exaggerate them as much as possible; and, in return,	PP	III	18	381	7
Too much, I am afraid; for what becomes of the moral, if	PP	III	18	381	13
From an unwillingness to confess how much her intimacy	PP	III	18	382	20
But now suppose as much as you chuse; give a loose to your	PP	III	18	382	21
her a much kinder answer than she knew was deserved.	PP	III	18	383	24
her sister, stood in too much awe of him to speak with the	PP	III	18	384	27
the season of courtship much of its pleasure, it added to	PP	III	18	384	27
that she submitted to the change without much reluctance.	PP	III	19	386	5
I am sure Wickham would like a place at court very much,	PP	III	19	386	7
As it happened that Elizabeth had much rather not, she	PP	III	19	386	8
in a letter which spoke so much contrition and despondence,	MP	I	1	4	2
out of her head, and that much as they had all done for	MP	I	1	5	4
her, in any respect, so much my own, I should hate myself	MP	I	1	7	8
It will be much the best place for her, so near Miss Lee,	MP	I	1	9	12
We shall probably see much to wish altered in her, and	MP	I	1	10	14
though there might not be much in her first appearance to	MP	I	2	12	2
and Sir Thomas seeing how much she needed encouragement,	MP	I	2	12	2
without taking half so much trouble, or speaking one word	MP	I	2	12	2
very well, with much good humour, and no embarrassment, at	MP	I	2	12	3
But they were too much used to company and praise, to have	MP	I	2	12	3
better; I told her how much might depend upon her	MP	I	2	13	5
as yet understand how much she has changed for the better;	MP	I	2	13	5
away--he had told her he should miss her very much indeed."	MP	I	2	16	12
which she felt very much, a kindness to her brother, which	MP	I	2	16	20
nor did her aunt Norris's voice make her start very much.	MP	I	2	17	21
always be modest; for, much as you know already, there is	MP	I	2	19	27
is much more desirable that there should be a difference."	MP	I	2	19	29
to transfer in its favour much of her attachment to her	MP	I	2	20	32
and had already given him much uneasiness; but his other	MP	I	2	20	33
or any fear of doing too much, he was always true to her	MP	I	2	21	34
he had not been half so much in debt as some of his	MP	I	3	24	4
Fanny was too much surprised to do more than repeat her	MP	I	3	25	8
I hope it does not distress you very much, Fanny."	MP	I	3	26	23
But you will belong to us almost as much as ever.	MP	I	3	26	31
Mrs. Norris is much better fitted than my mother for	MP	I	3	27	33
than myself, and I am very much obliged to you for trying	MP	I	3	27	34
Ah! cousin, when I remember how much I used to dread	MP	I	3	27	36
your health--and as much for your ultimate happiness, too."	MP	I	3	27	37
Sir Thomas is too much my friend.	MP	I	3	28	42
My situation is as much altered as my income.	MP	I	3	30	50
It is unknown how much was consumed in our kitchen by odd	MP	I	3	30	50
to convince him how much he had mistaken his sister-in-	MP	I	3	30	57
Lady Bertram listened without much interest to this sort	MP	I	3	31	60
The Miss Bertrams were much to be pitied on the occasion;	MP	I	3	32	64
"Sir Thomas, who had done so much for her and her brothers,	MP	I	3	33	64
sixteen in some respects too much like his sister at ten."	MP	I	3	33	64
future husbands, had so much to do as, in addition to all	MP	I	4	34	3
the never failing hope of his arrival was worth much.	MP	I	4	35	6
walking all day, thinking every body ought to walk as much.	MP	I	4	36	7
Though Edmund was much more displeased with his aunt than	MP	I	4	37	8
thinking he had done too much, and at the same time	MP	I	4	37	8
Thomas, was entered into, much to the satisfaction of	MP	I	4	39	11
and poultry, was very much in want of some variety at home.	MP	I	4	41	15
On each side there was much to attract, and their	MP	I	5	44	1
so too, and were almost as much charmed as their brothers,	MP	I	5	44	1
sure, but then he had so much countenance, and his teeth	MP	I	5	44	2
I am sure Miss Bertram is very much attached to Mr.	MP	I	5	45	14
are all apt to expect too much; but then, if one scheme of	MP	I	5	46	23
dearest Mary, who make much of a little, are more taken in	MP	I	5	46	23
He had been much in London, and had more liveliness and	MP	I	5	47	27
of being tied up from much gaming at present, by a promise	MP	I	5	48	28
Much was said on his side to induce her to attend the	MP	I	5	48	29
It is much worse to have girls not out, give themselves	MP	I	5	50	39
not saying much to the purpose, could talk of nothing else.	MP	I	6	52	1
I never saw a place that wanted so much improvement in my	MP	I	6	53	4
You young ones do not remember much about it, perhaps.	MP	I	6	54	9
"these potatoes have as much the flavour of a moor park	MP	I	6	54	12
"Smith has not much above a hundred acres altogether in	MP	I	6	55	17
if so much could be done at Compton, we need not despair.	MP	I	6	55	17
it, and give me as much beauty as he could for my money;	MP	I	6	57	29
Edmund was sorry to hear Miss Crawford, whom he was much	MP	I	6	57	32
never heard the harp at all, and wished for it very much.	MP	I	6	59	40
like to listen; probably much longer, for I dearly love	MP	I	6	59	41
harp is come, he heard so much of my misery about it.	MP	I	6	59	41
too little--I should like to have been busy much longer."	MP	I	6	61	54
I am inclined to envy Mr. Rushworth for having so much	MP	I	6	61	56
"Very well--very much.	MP	I	7	63	2
She did not think very much about it, however; he pleased	MP	I	7	65	13
in the conviction of very much surpassing her sex in	MP	I	7	66	15
I wish you may not be fatigued by so much exercise.	MP	I	7	68	19
did her attendant do her much good by his comments on Miss	MP	I	7	69	21
but herself, and was much enjoyed at the time, and doubly	MP	I	7	70	30
"I was afraid it would be too much for her," said Lady	MP	I	7	72	49
my house for me, it is not much above a quarter of a mile,	MP	I	7	73	53
overheard her, "I am very much afraid she caught the	MP	I	7	74	56
It was as much as I could bear myself.	MP	I	7	74	56
keep him from the flower-beds, was almost too much for me."	MP	I	7	74	56
pain of her mind had been much beyond that in her head;	MP	I	7	74	59
"The fatigue would be too much for my sister, a great deal	MP	I	8	76	3
a great deal too much I assure you, my dear Mrs. Rushworth.	MP	I	8	76	3
I know she wishes it very much.	MP	I	8	78	21
Mrs. Norris was too much vexed to submit with a very good	MP	I	8	79	23
"I am sure she ought to be very much obliged to you,"	MP	I	8	79	25
heard the plan, was in fact much greater than her pleasure.	MP	I	8	79	27
let me press you ever so much," and Miss Crawford could	MP	I	8	81	32
Much was said, and much was ate, and all went well.	MP	I	9	84	1
the possibility of much prospect from any of the rooms,	MP	I	9	85	4
There is something in a chapel and chaplain so much in	MP	I	9	86	12
in a tone not much louder, "if he would give her away?"	MP	I	9	88	21
though laid out with too much regularity, was darkness and	MP	I	9	91	38
One does not see much of this influence and importance in	MP	I	9	92	46
arch smile; "I am just as much surprised now as I was at	MP	I	9	93	53
"Go into the law! with as much ease as I was told to go	MP	I	9	94	54
for he was not yet so much in love as to measure distance,	MP	I	9	94	61
"Oh! you do not consider how much we have wound about.	MP	I	9	94	62
the possibility of improvements with much animation.	MP	I	10	97	3
ever see Sotherton again with so much pleasure as I do now.	MP	I	10	98	7
lady replied, "you are too much a man of the world not to	MP	I	10	98	8
"I am afraid I am not quite so much the man of the world	MP	I	10	98	10
"You seemed to enjoy your drive here very much this	MP	I	10	98	11
I think I am equal to as much as Maria, even without help."	MP	I	10	100	26
"It is a pity that he should have so much trouble for	MP	I	10	101	31
prevented her thinking so much of their continued absence,	MP	I	10	101	33
had wished for her very much, and that he should certainly	MP	I	10	103	49
to have been as much too late for re-establishing harmony,	MP	I	10	104	51
Mr. Crawford and Miss Bertram were much more gay, and she	MP	I	10	104	51
I am sure you ought to be very much obliged to your aunt	MP	I	10	105	53
afforded the Miss Bertrams much more agreeable feelings	MP	I	11	107	1
It was much pleasanter to think of Henry Crawford than of	MP	I	11	107	1
Sir Thomas wrote of it with as much decision as experience	MP	I	11	107	2
Much might happen in thirteen weeks.	MP	I	11	107	3
can have given you much knowledge of the clergy.	MP	I	11	110	24
Though I have not seen much of the domestic lives of	MP	I	11	110	25
of Fanny's, very much to the purpose of her own feelings,	MP	I	11	111	27
It is a lovely night, and they are much to be pitied who	MP	I	11	113	36
his indifference was so much more than equalled by her own,	MP	I	12	114	2
unemployed, felt all the right of missing him much more.	MP	I	12	115	4
He is used to much gayer places than Mansfield."	MP	I	12	116	5
never seen much symptom of it, but I wish it may be so.	MP	I	12	116	8
Crawford has too much sense to stay here if he found	MP	I	12	116	10
sense of propriety, so much of that true delicacy which	MP	I	12	117	14
so properly happy, so well suited, and so much the thing!	MP	I	12	118	16
"I am glad of it," said he in a much brisker tone, and	MP	I	12	118	22
poor woman! must want a lover as much as any one of them.	MP	I	12	119	22
impossible for her to feel much gratitude towards her	MP	I	12	119	25
The honourable John Yates, this new friend, had not much	MP	I	13	121	1
"I do think you were very much to be pitied;" were the	MP	I	13	122	3
house; and who having so much leisure as to make almost	MP	I	13	123	6
than you do, or can have gone much farther to see one."	MP	I	13	124	11
as only raising her so much more above restraint, and	MP	I	13	128	38
herself with the play of which she had heard so much.	MP	I	14	137	23
of his being very much dressed, and choosing his colours.	MP	I	15	138	1
to despise it, and was too much engaged with what his own	MP	I	15	138	1
Thus much was settled before Edmund, who had been out all	MP	I	15	138	2
But I do not much like the idea of being so fine.--	MP	I	15	139	10
humour she answered, "I am much obliged to you, Edmund;--	MP	I	15	140	14
will be all so much money thrown away--and I am sure that	MP	I	15	141	22
preparation were otherwise much talked of, for Edmund's	MP	I	15	142	24
best--though I do not much relish the finery I am to have."	MP	I	15	143	29
and it will not much signify if nobody hears a word you	MP	I	15	145	47

Context	Reference
Fanny did not love Miss Crawford; but she felt very much	MP I 15 147 57
when she was alone much less so,--especially with the	MP I 16 150 1
there had been sometimes much of suffering to her--though	MP I 16 152 2
Perhaps you are not so much aware as I am, of the mischief	MP I 16 154 14
"They will not have much cause of triumph, when they see	MP I 16 155 16
much smaller circle than they are now in the high road for.	MP I 16 155 16
both as much the better as the happier for the descent.	MP I 17 158 1
his tranquillity by too much admiration there, and then	MP I 17 161 9
"I would not give much for Mr. Rushworth's chance, if	MP I 17 162 17
Fanny saw and pitied much of this in Julia; but there was	MP I 17 163 20
and delight, as had been almost too much for her at first.	MP I 18 164 1
town, and was at work, much to the increase of the	MP I 18 164 1
Fanny believed herself to derive as much innocent	MP I 18 165 3
knowledge of his two and forty speeches became much less.	MP I 18 165 4
his part herself, but without his being much the forwarder.	MP I 18 166 4
useful to all; she was perhaps as much at peace as any.	MP I 18 166 5
a curtain--and I am much mistaken if you do not find it	MP I 18 167 11
I did not think much of it at first--but, upon my word--.	MP I 18 168 19
for a theatre, I dare say; much more fitted for little	MP I 18 169 21
She believed herself to feel too much of it in the	MP I 18 170 24
They did begin--and being too much engaged in their own	MP I 18 172 33
Sir Thomas's affection was much too humble to give her any	MP II 1 176 4
with those who thought much of parental claims, or family	MP II 1 177 5
observing with decided pleasure how much she was grown!	MP II 1 177 7
in considering how much unsuspected vexation was probably	MP II 1 178 7
"Sure, my dear Sir Thomas, a basin of soup would be a much	MP II 1 180 10
pheasants, sir, I assure you, as much as you could desire.	MP II 1 181 16
Sir Thomas listened most politely, but found much to	MP II 1 184 25
It is having too much of a good thing.	MP II 1 186 33
to find our sentiments on this subject so much the same.	MP II 1 186 34
which shuts out noisy pleasures, should much exceed theirs.	MP II 1 186 34
Mr. Rushworth hardly knew what to do with so much meaning;	MP II 1 186 35
he must; he felt it too much indeed for many words; and	MP II 2 187 2
impression, and forget how much he had been forgotten	MP II 2 187 2
and comfort of his family, much exertion and many	MP II 2 188 3
said, 'coachman, you had much better not go, your lady and	MP II 2 189 5
It might not be saving them much, but it was something,	MP II 2 189 5
To her he soon turned, repeating much of what he had	MP II 2 193 18
As well as I can recollect, it was always much the same.	MP II 3 197 3
There was never much laughing in his presence; or, if	MP II 3 197 3
and trust to his seeing as much beauty of mind in time."	MP II 3 197 6
have gained so much countenance!--and your figure-----	MP II 3 198 8
Could they be much together I feel sure of their liking	MP II 3 199 13
day, if there were not a much greater evil to follow--the	MP II 3 199 18
He cannot much longer deceive himself.	MP II 3 200 19
unfixed, and without seeming much aware of it himself.	MP II 3 200 19
To such feelings, delay, even the delay of much	MP II 3 202 26
was indeed experiencing much of the agitation which his	MP II 3 203 30
been gradually recovering much of their former good	MP II 3 203 32
have struggled through so much to obtain them, and could	MP II 3 204 32
Even their mother missed them--and how much more their	MP II 3 204 33
regret which they had never done much to deserve!	MP II 3 204 33
to be done but to be very much ashamed and to get into the	MP II 4 205 3
of her wishing very much to hear it, and a confession,	MP II 4 206 5
a listener who seemed so much obliged, so full of wonder	MP II 4 207 6
in the plan of the walk!--not too much attempted!"	MP II 4 209 14
I expect we shall be all very much at Sotherton another	MP II 4 210 21
You do not know how much we have been suffering, nor what	MP II 4 212 30
Sunday, because I know how much more Dr. Grant would enjoy	MP II 4 212 31
You have not much time before you; and your relations are	MP II 4 213 40
not envy you; I do not much think I shall even respect you.	MP II 4 213 40
I have a much greater respect for those that are honest	MP II 4 213 40
"That is not much to the purpose now; and as to my being	MP II 4 214 45
that she had really been much longer absent than usual,	MP II 4 214 46
which he saw with so much pleasure established, it was a	MP II 4 216 50
But he will be very much surprized that Mrs. Grant should	MP II 5 217 10
for the morrow, was so much uppermost in Lady Bertram's	MP II 5 217 11
pleasure, both present and future, as much as possible.	MP II 5 219 27
You ought to be very much obliged to Mrs. Grant for	MP II 5 220 28
only say that she was very much obliged to her aunt	MP II 5 220 29
would have been! and how much more he would have been	MP II 5 220 30
any part--there was so much to be said between the brother	MP II 5 223 48
and sister about Bath, so much between the two young men	MP II 5 223 48
men about hunting, so much of politics between Mr.	MP II 5 223 48
She could not wish him to stay, and would much rather not	MP II 5 224 48
Her two absent cousins, especially Maria, were much in her	MP II 5 224 48
I do not imagine he figures much in the letters to	MP II 5 224 52
Well, I am much mistaken if his lovely Maria will ever	MP II 5 224 53
seriousness, "she is too good for him--much too good."	MP II 5 224 53
She had never spoken so much at once to him in her life	MP II 5 225 59
ducks and drakes with, and earned without much trouble.	MP II 5 226 61
Miss Crawford was too much vexed by what had passed to be	MP II 5 227 68
so much taller, and produces all these charms and graces!	MP II 6 230 8
or to think that with so much tenderness of disposition,	MP II 6 231 11
of disposition, and so much taste as belonged to her, she	MP II 6 231 11
and much less incumbered by refinement or self-distrust.	MP II 6 234 17
Fanny had never known so much felicity in her life, as in	MP II 6 234 18
Henry Crawford was as much struck with it as any.	MP II 6 235 19
have been at sea, and seen and done and suffered as much.	MP II 6 236 22
and consequence with so much self-respect and happy ardour,	MP II 6 236 22
of William price, had much to do with it, but much was	MP II 7 238 1
much to do with it, but much was still owing to Sir	MP II 7 238 1
of the Grants, and too much according to the usual habits	MP II 7 238 3
that it would not much amuse him to have her for a partner.	MP II 7 239 6
I had forgotten having ever told you half so much of the	MP II 7 241 18
"Very much indeed.	MP II 7 241 21
not satisfied with much less than it is capable of.--(	MP II 7 243 27
which had in itself so much the air of a gentleman's	MP II 7 243 27
gentleman's residence, so much the look of a something	MP II 7 243 27
But it is capable of much more.	MP II 7 243 27
and imposing on her as much as he could; but Crawford	MP II 7 244 28
"And Fanny had much rather it were William's," said Edmund.	MP II 7 244 29
"I cannot say there was much done at Sotherton; but it was	MP II 7 245 31
Edmund, am I saying too much?"	MP II 7 247 39
should not have thought much on the subject, Mr. Crawford.	MP II 7 247 42
"She was checked by the sight of her uncle much nearer to	MP II 7 250 56
The fatigue would be too much for your aunt.	MP II 8 252 1
quickly restored so much of her good humour as enabled her	MP II 8 253 4
ways, look and speak as much grateful pleasure in the	MP II 8 253 5
own account, think very much of the evening, which the	MP II 8 256 13
to the parsonage without much fear of wanting an	MP II 8 256 14
returning with her in a much more cordial manner than	MP II 8 257 15
argued the case with so much affectionate earnestness	MP II 8 258 17
imagining he would be too much flattered by seeing round	MP II 8 259 20
possession what she had so much wished for, did not bring	MP II 8 260 25
wished for, did not bring much satisfaction, she now	MP II 8 260 25
I feel much more than I can possibly express.	MP II 9 262 5
dear Fanny, you feel these things a great deal too much.	MP II 9 262 9
characters there is so much general resemblance in true	MP II 9 263 16
and nature, let her not be much wondered at if, after	MP II 9 265 19
her, it would very much have lessened her comfort by	MP II 9 267 22
To dance without much observation or any extraordinary	MP II 9 267 22
was often under the influence of much less sanguine views.	MP II 9 267 22
Edmund, she had too much reason to suppose, was at the	MP II 9 267 22
his lips, with almost as much warmth as if it had been	MP II 9 269 38
it with much of the happy flutter which belongs to a ball.	MP II 9 270 40
as much as Lady Bertram or Mrs. Chapman do themselves.	MP II 9 271 41
own gaiety of heart was much subdued; the sight of so many	MP II 10 273 7
Her happiness on this occasion was very much a-la-mortal,	MP II 10 274 8
she was a great deal too much frightened to have any	MP II 10 276 13
down the dance with much complacency; he was proud of his	MP II 10 276 13
Miss Crawford saw much of Sir Thomas's thoughts as he	MP II 10 276 14
admired; but she was so much more struck with her own	MP II 10 277 15
ma'am, how much we want dear Mrs. Rushworth and Julia to-	MP II 10 277 16
she had time for, amid so much occupation as she found for	MP II 10 277 16
She would much rather not have been asked by him again so	MP II 10 278 20
had been last together; much less could her feelings	MP II 11 282 3
their little party, though it could not boast much beside.	MP II 11 283 4
bring her mind without much effort into its everyday state,	MP II 11 283 7
every hour; and was too much in want of it to derive any	MP II 11 285 15
Does he give you much account of what he is doing?--	MP II 11 288 22
"You will be very much missed.	MP II 11 289 31
Miss Crawford's uneasiness was much lightened by this	MP II 12 291 1
That Mansfield should have done so much for--that you	MP II 12 293 11
Henry Crawford had too much sense not to feel the worth of	MP II 12 294 16
Few fathers would have let me have my own way half so much.	MP II 12 296 28
gentleness, so much as if it were a matter of course that	MP II 12 296 31
in his face, "how glad I am to see you so much in love!	MP II 12 297 32
by any means to take so much trouble in vain, she still	MP II 13 298 1
that Sir Charles was much delighted in having such an	MP II 13 298 3
with much agitation, "don't, Mr. Crawford, pray don't.	MP II 13 301 7
for though she read in too much haste and confusion to	MP II 13 304 16
her, and he spoke to her much too often; and she was	MP II 13 304 16
Mrs. Norris seemed as much delighted with the saving it	MP II 13 304 19
for it was unknown how much he had cost his uncle; and	MP II 13 304 19
"It is amazing," said she, "how much young people cost	MP II 13 305 24
They little think how much it comes to, or what their	MP II 13 305 24
"I am very much obliged to you, my dear Miss Crawford, for	MP II 13 307 31
I have seen too much of Mr. Crawford not to understand his	MP II 13 307 31
in a moment--I am very much obliged to you--if you will be	MP II 13 307 34
said, with much surprise, "why have you no fire to-day?"	MP III 1 312 5
remarks to have been very much to the purpose--was	MP III 1 314 16
Her mind was in too much confusion.	MP III 1 314 16
I understand), received as much encouragement to proceed	MP III 1 315 18
I was very much pleased with what I collected to have been	MP III 1 315 18
I am sure I said as much as that and more; and I should	MP III 1 315 19
This is so much my opinion, that I am sorry to think how	MP III 1 317 34
"Edmund I consider from his disposition and habits as much	MP III 1 317 34
spirit, which prevails so much in modern days, even in	MP III 1 318 39
I should have been very much surprised had either of my	MP III 1 319 39
I should have been much surprised, and much hurt, by such	MP III 1 319 39
might be as much lost as gained by an immediate interview.	MP III 1 320 45
A fire! it seemed too much; just at that time to be giving	MP III 1 322 51
and when she found how much and how unpleasantly her	MP III 1 323 53
Mrs. Norris, much discontented, was obliged to compose	MP III 1 325 62
He was in love, very much in love; and it was a love which,	MP III 2 326 2
distance; and he had so much delight in the idea of	MP III 2 327 4
To Fanny, however, who had known too much opposition all	MP III 2 327 5
aware how much it concealed the sternness of her purpose.	MP III 2 327 6
to be giving nearly as much pain to herself as to him.	MP III 2 327 6
in the same manner, and as much as you can, dismissing the	MP III 2 331 16
was all that Fanny could think of with much satisfaction.	MP III 2 331 17
when she considered how much of the truth was unknown to	MP III 2 331 17
How much time she might, in her own fancy, allot for its	MP III 2 331 18
the communication to Mrs. Norris was as much as Fanny herself.	MP III 2 332 19
fortune, raised her, therefore, very much in her opinion.	MP III 2 332 22
Yes, I am sure you would miss me too much for that."	MP III 2 333 25
miles off, and as farther, much farther from him in	MP III 3 334 1
They sat so much longer than usual in the dining parlour,	MP III 3 334 5
inclined to hope that so much could not have been said and	MP III 3 344 44
might have as much hope to sustain them as possible.	MP III 4 345 2
they would be found as much alike as they have been used	MP III 4 346 12
He is lively, you are serious; but so much the better; his	MP III 4 348 23
in the inclination for much or little company, in the	MP III 4 349 23
"Before the play, I am much mistaken, if Julia did not	MP III 4 350 29
to acknowledge, have hitherto been too much his guides.	MP III 4 351 32
to anything!--fancying every thing too much for you!	MP III 4 351 34
Edmund first began again:-- "I was very much pleased by	MP III 4 351 35
	36
worldly maxims, which she was been too much used to hear.	MP III 4 351 36
and ingenuousness, which are so much a part of herself.	MP III 4 351 36
She feared she had been doing wrong, saying too much,	MP III 4 354 47
looking and speaking with much less particularity of	MP III 5 357 5
But here she hoped too much, Miss Crawford was not the	MP III 5 357 5
You have all so much more heart among you, than one finds	MP III 5 359 12
her till after Easter, a much better time for the visit--	MP III 5 359 12
but I have not cared much for her these three years."	MP III 5 359 12
I have not so much to say for my friend Flora, who jilted	MP III 5 361 16
who has about as much sense, Fanny, as Mr. Rushworth, but	MP III 5 361 16
but much worse looking, and with a blackguard character.	MP III 5 361 16
you at Everingham, I do not care how much you lecture him.	MP III 5 363 24
a woman for ever, I think Henry will do as much for you."	MP III 5 363 24
"I know he must have exerted himself very much, for I know	MP III 5 364 29
There was no resisting so much apparent affection.	MP III 5 365 33
a tete so much less painful than her fears had predicted.	MP III 5 365 33
been so much to her, should not be more visibly regretted.	MP III 6 366 3
be as distant as she was much inclined to think his, she	MP III 6 366 4
amiable sensations, and much personal kindness, had still	MP III 6 367 5
she suffered very much from them, and could never speak of	MP III 6 367 6
are very right, but I am sure I shall miss her very much."	MP III 6 371 16
And besides, he wanted her so very much to see the thrush	MP III 6 372 18
She knew so much already, that she must know every thing.	MP III 6 373 26
She had tears for every room in the house, much more for	MP III 6 374 28
There had, in fact, been so much of message, of allusion,	MP III 7 376 4
of recollection, so much of Mansfield in every letter,	MP III 7 376 4
"To be sure, I had much rather she had stayed in harbour,	MP III 7 378 12
soon, seemed very much inclined to forget her again.	MP III 7 380 22
reports from the kitchen, much hope of any under a	MP III 7 381 24
the friends who had done so much--the dear, dear friends!	MP III 7 382 29
Fanny's spirit was as much refreshed as her body; her head	MP III 7 384 33
Was she as much plagued as herself to get tolerable	MP III 7 385 38
whom Susan had also much to depose, and little Betsey a	MP III 7 385 38
she had left there not much younger when she went into	MP III 7 385 40
there she had hoped much, and found almost nothing.	MP III 8 389 4
Her daughters never had been much to her.	MP III 8 389 4
was the first of her girls whom she had ever much regarded.	MP III 8 389 4
Of her two sisters, Mrs. Price very much more resembled	MP III 8 390 5
would have been much more suited to her capacity, than the	MP III 8 390 5
Much of all this, Fanny could not but be sensible of.	MP III 8 390 6
and great dispatch, did so much, that the boy was shipped	MP III 8 390 7
whom she had never felt so much curiosity as now, and she	MP III 9 394 2
Susan saw that much was wrong at home, and wanted to set	MP III 9 395 4
full possession of her so much prettier herself, she	MP III 9 396 7
a mind so much in need of help, and so much deserving it.	MP III 9 397 8
knowledge--but that so much better knowledge, so many good	MP III 9 397 8
Mr. Price was out, which she regretted very much.	MP III 10 400 6
"Her daughters were very much confined--Portsmouth was a	MP III 10 401 10
though she had been so much wanting his affection to be	MP III 10 402 11
again; and hoping to be so much the longer with Fanny, was	MP III 10 402 13
with the hope of spending much, very much of his time	MP III 10 405 18
of spending much, very much of his time there--always	MP III 10 405 18
she had seen him; he was much more gentle, obliging, and	MP III 10 406 21
should have made so much, and that her mother, as handsome	MP III 11 408 2
have an appearance so much more worn and faded, so	MP III 11 408 2
happiness, and his in seeing her, must be so much greater.	MP III 11 410 7
say much, or even to be certain of what she ought to say.--	MP III 11 411 19
"Nothing, I am much obliged to you."	MP III 11 412 25
her looks were not much more affected than he found them.	MP III 11 412 30
both mind and body, into a much juster value for Mr.	MP III 11 413 30
just seeing him, nor how much might be owing to contrast,	MP III 11 413 32
not much longer persevere in a suit so distressing to her?	MP III 11 414 32
I have not time for writing much, but it would be out of	MP III 12 415 2
are very much struck with his gentleman-like appearance.	MP III 12 416 2
to supply matter for much reflection, and to leave every	MP III 12 417 4

in the end too much attached to him, to give him up. MP III 12 417 4
readings and conversation with Susan were much suspended. MP III 12 418 5
Fanny, with a disposition much less inclined to sedentary MP III 12 418 7
My hopes are much weaker.-- MP III 13 420 2
I shall be able to write much that I could not say, and MP III 13 422 2
You are very much wanted. MP III 13 423 2
but if they are so much fonder of her than she is of them, MP III 13 424 4
writing, without having much to say, which will include a MP III 13 425 6
which I make no doubt will give you much concern." MP III 13 425 7
8
Poor Tom, I am quite grieved for him, and very much MP III 13 427 12
Mrs. Price did quite as much for Lady Bertram, as Lady MP III 13 428 15
as she now learnt, nerves much affected, spirits much MP III 14 430 2
much affected, spirits much depressed to calm and raise; MP III 14 430 2
"I cannot but say, I much regret your being from home at MP III 14 431 8
She had not known before, how much the beginnings and MP III 14 431 9
London very much at war with all respectable attachments. MP III 14 433 12
I suppose, Mrs. R.'s Easter holidays will not last much MP III 14 434 13
present moment, she saw so much to condemn; the sister's MP III 14 435 15
for her to understand much of this strange letter. MP III 15 438 4
Miss Crawford need not have urged secrecy with so much MP III 15 438 7
There, (holding out the paper to her)--much good may such MP III 15 439 13
matters; he may be too much of the courtier and fine MP III 15 439 13
cared too little about the report, to make her much answer. MP III 15 440 17
She had so much to do, that not even the horrible story of MP III 15 443 25
boxes and spoilt them, was much more in her thoughts, and MP III 15 444 26
much as ought to be expected from human virtue at fourteen. MP III 15 444 26
The advantage of much sleep to prepare them for their MP III 15 444 27
table, which by dint of much unusual activity, was quite MP III 15 445 31
to Oxford; but the second was over at a much earlier hour. MP III 15 446 35
much upon silver forks, napkins, and finger glasses. MP III 15 446 35
at hand, and when, while much is actually given to the MP III 15 446 35
Lady Bertram could not give her much time, or many words, MP III 16 448 3
never do enough for one who seemed so much to want her. MP III 16 449 4
to understand quite as much as she wished of the MP III 16 449 7
return, but was so much counteracted in Wimpole Street by MP III 16 450 9
perhaps, arise almost as much from the personal disrespect MP III 16 450 10
and his recovery so much thrown back by it, that even Lady MP III 16 451 13
His letters expressed how much he deplored it. MP III 16 451 13
It was of a much less poignant nature than what the others MP III 16 452 15
had sometimes been too much for her before, it would be MP III 16 453 16
protection, there will be much less chance of his marrying MP III 16 457 29
After repeating this, Edmund was so much affected, that MP III 16 457 30
so tending to ease, and so much in harmony with every MP III 17 461 3
rather more, and his debts much less, than he had feared, MP III 17 462 4
or time would have worn away much of its ill effect. MP III 17 463 8
another--and he had been very much aware that it was so. MP III 17 464 12
anger against Fanny was so much the greater, from MP III 17 465 13
either time had done her much disservice, or that he had MP III 17 465 15
He had felt her as an hourly evil, which was so much the MP III 17 465 15
to secure herself from being again too much attracted. MP III 17 466 18
must vary much as to time in different people.-- MP III 17 470 26
With so much true merit and true love, and no want of MP III 17 473 32
power of having rather too much her own way, and a E I 1 5 4
had not married early) was much increased by his E I 1 7 8
of mind or body, he was a much older man in ways than in E I 1 7 8
sixteen miles off, was much beyond her daily reach; and E I 1 7 8
from himself, he was very much disposed to think Miss E I 1 7 9
she knew it would be so much less so to her father, that E I 1 7 10
But she knows how much the marriage is to Miss Taylor's E I 1 11 33
cannot allow herself to feel so much pain as pleasure. E I 1 11 38
he darted away with so much gallantry, and borrowed two E I 1 12 41
to-day, he looked so very much as if he would like to have E I 1 13 46
That will be a much better thing. E I 1 14 47
with you entirely that it will be a much better thing. E I 1 14 48
It was an unsuitable connection, and did not produce much E I 2 15 3
match, was proved to have much the worst of the bargain: E I 2 16 4
There was no recovering Miss Taylor--nor much likelihood E I 2 19 14
He liked very much to have his friends come and see him; E I 3 20 1
He had not much intercourse with any families beyond that E I 3 20 1
in the world for having much of the public favour; and she E I 3 21 4
and having formerly owed much to Mr. Woodhouse's kindness, E I 3 22 5
look comfortable, and very much pleased with herself for E I 3 22 6
the evening, Emma was as much pleased with her manners as E I 3 23 9
supplied her visitors in a much more satisfactory style; E I 3 25 15
introduction had given as much panic as pleasure--but the E I 3 25 15
Weston's marriage her exercise had been too much confined. E I 4 26 1
which could speak with so much exultation of Mrs. Martin's E I 4 27 4
as much above my notice as in every other he is below it." E I 4 29 14
I had no right to expect much, and I did not expect much; E I 4 32 30
"How much his business engrosses him already, is very E I 4 33 40
because there is so much good humour with it--but that E I 4 34 42
and probable, for her to have much merit in planning it. E I 4 34 44
He was reckoned very handsome; his person much admired in E I 4 35 45
You are so much used to live alone, that you do not know E I 5 36 6
it did her judgment so much credit, that I preserved it E I 5 37 7
You never could persuade her to read half so much as you E I 5 37 7
She is a flatterer in all her ways; and so much the worse, E I 5 38 15
I am much mistaken if Emma's doctrines give any strength E I 5 39 15
intimacy being made a matter of much discussion among you. E I 5 40 24
"Not at all," cried he; "I am much obliged to you for it. E I 5 40 25
"So do I," said Mrs. Weston gently; "very much." E I 5 41 28
It would not be a bad thing for her to be very much in E I 5 41 29
own and Mr. Weston's on the subject, as much as possible. E I 5 41 31
confident of creating as much liking on Harriet's side, as E I 6 42 1
So much superadded decision of character! E I 6 42 6
She was not much deceived as to her own skill either as an E I 6 44 19
but had there been much less, or had there been ten times E I 6 44 20
This did not want much of being finished, when I put it E I 6 45 21
Any other situation would have been much less in character. E I 6 48 39
It was impossible to say how much he should be gratified E I 6 49 40
ensure its safety without much incommoding him, while he E I 6 49 42
And he wrote as if he really loved her very much--but she E I 7 50 1
The style of the letter was much above her expectation. E I 7 50 4
it conveyed very much to the credit of the writer. E I 7 50 4
"Oh, no, no! the letter had much better be all your own. E I 7 51 11
"I had no notion that he liked me so very much," said E I 7 52 18
a friend, and older than yourself, to say thus much to you. E I 7 52 19
and I shall always feel much obliged to him, and have a E I 7 54 30
of him; and his being so much attached to me--and his E I 7 54 30
and she was so very much concerned at the idea of making E I 7 55 35
unhappy, and thought so much of his mother and E I 7 55 35
would be very much surprized if she knew what had happened. E I 7 55 40
about wondering that people should like her so much. E I 7 56 42
I hope he will not mind it so very much." E I 7 56 43
and sisters, telling how much more beautiful is the E I 7 56 44
to keep her with them as much as possible just at present. E I 8 57 1
making so much of her) as in a line of society above him. E I 8 59 27
I was very much pleased with all that he said. E I 8 59 27
Now, as we may fairly suppose, he would not allow much E I 8 60 27
for he is as much her superior in sense as in situation. E I 8 61 38
probability he might do much better; and that as to a E I 8 61 38
I much think your statement by no means fair. E I 8 62 39
The sphere in which she moves is much above his.-- E I 8 62 39
He has too much real feeling to address any woman on the E I 8 63 42
it appears that men are much more philosophic on the E I 8 63 44
I am very much mistaken if your sex in general would not E I 8 63 44
His appearance is so much against him, and his manner so E I 8 65 48
feeling uncomfortable and wanting him very much to be gone. E I 8 65 50
"I am very much obliged to you," said Emma, laughing again. E I 8 66 54
He was very much vexed. E I 8 66 55
effects; but she saw too much of it, to feel a doubt of E I 8 67 57
himself, and tried very much to persuade him to put off E I 8 68 58
He was so much displeased, that it was longer than usual E I 9 69 1
It was much easier to chat than to study; much pleasanter E I 9 69 3
Mr. Woodhouse was almost as much interested in the E I 9 70 5
much, something, he thought, might come from that quarter. E I 9 70 6
A man must be very much in love indeed, to describe her so. E I 9 72 15
An excellent charade indeed! and very much to the purpose. E I 9 72 15
Harriet, you cannot find much difficulty in comprehending. E I 9 73 18
It is so much beyond any thing I deserve. E I 9 74 22
to have his charade slighted, much better than his passion. E I 9 77 42
It will be giving him so much pleasure! E I 9 77 45
"My dear Harriet, you must not refine too much upon this E I 9 77 47
proceeded--and he was very much pleased, and, as she had E I 9 78 51
I am sure I was very much surprized when I first heard she E I 9 79 60
"Harriet must give us as much of her company as she can E I 9 80 69
they like it, papa; there is nothing they like so much. E I 9 81 75
Cole had been saying so much about his dining with him-- E I 9 81 78
We admired it so much, that I have ventured to write it E I 9 82 80
It had no advantage of situation; but had been very much E I 10 83 2
are the yellow curtains that Miss Nash admires so much." E I 10 83 4
married women are half as much mistress of their husband's E I 10 84 15
And the distinction is not quite so much against the E I 10 85 19
in general, she is very much to the taste of everybody, E I 10 85 19
all the children of a sister I love so much, to care about. E I 10 85 21
ever bore people half so much about all the Knightleys E I 10 86 23
gave her assistance with as much intelligence as good-will. E I 10 86 24
again find something very much amiss about her boot, and E I 10 89 36
had been the occasion of much present enjoyment to both, E I 10 90 41
He thought much of the evils of the journey for her, and E I 11 91 3
cause, nor have endured much longer even for this; but the E I 11 92 3
father, she inherited also much of his constitution; was E I 11 92 4
"Very much to the honour of both," was the handsome reply. E I 11 94 11
of putting all the Mr. Westons aside as much as she can." E I 11 95 18
depending, I suspect, much more upon what is called E I 11 96 26
"If you were as much guided by nature in your estimate of E I 12 98 4
no doubt you were much my superior in judgment at that E I 12 99 7
elder, whose temper was by much the most communicative, E I 12 100 16
was entered into with as much equality of interest by John, E I 12 100 16
I never had much opinion of the sea air." E I 12 101 20
"Oh! my dear sir, her throat is so much better that I have E I 12 102 28
The gruel came and supplied a great deal to be said--much E I 12 104 50
is not much to chuse between forty miles and an hundred.-- E I 12 106 58
It was a delightful visit;--perfect, in being much too E I 13 108 1
and she had gone home so much indisposed with a cold, that, E I 13 108 5
by representing how much Mr. Elton's would be depressed E I 13 109 6
comfortless visit, and of their all missing her very much. E I 13 109 6
complaint;--"a throat very much inflamed, with a great E I 13 109 6
looks and feels so very much like snow, that if it were to E I 13 110 9
the case; for though very much gratified by the kind care E I 13 110 10
actually accepting the offer with much prompt satisfaction. E I 13 110 12
man undoubtedly, and very much in love with Harriet; but E I 13 111 13
that left the balance of approbation much in his favour. E I 13 111 14
and the answer had been, "much the same--not better." E I 13 114 28
Very much grieved and concerned--I had flattered myself E I 13 114 31
much snow on the ground; but now it is of no consequence. E I 13 115 39
amused, but she was too much astonished now at Mr. Elton's E I 13 115 42
Weston indeed is much beyond praise, and he is exactly E I 13 116 43
her drawings with so much zeal and so little knowledge as E I 14 118 4
other half-syllables very much suspected that he was E I 14 118 4
She does not depend upon his coming so much as I do: but E I 14 120 11
I am very much afraid that it will all end in nothing. E I 14 121 14
man's not having it in his power to do as much as that. E I 14 122 22
to go home; and it was as much as his three companions E I 15 124 1
at Randalls?--he felt much anxiety--he must confess that E I 15 124 3
time very properly, not much attending to any answer, but E I 15 124 3
for herself, she was too much provoked and offended to E I 15 125 6
"I admired your resolution very much, sir," said he, "in E I 15 126 10
who was immediately set as much at ease on the subject as E I 15 128 17
of a much darker night than he had been prepared for. E I 15 128 22
They must keep as much together as they could;" and James E I 15 128 22
She believed he had been drinking too much of Mr. Weston's E I 15 129 23
To restrain him as much as might be, by her own manners, E I 15 129 24
effect, and in short, very much resolved on being E I 15 129 24
Without scruple--without apology--without much apparent E I 15 129 24
state, she replied, "I am very much astonished, Mr. Elton. E I 15 129 24
25
Mr. Elton, my astonishment is much beyond any thing I can E I 15 130 30
If there had not been so much anger, there would have been E I 15 132 37
and blushed to think how much truer a knowledge of his E I 16 135 6
him to feel how very much he was her inferior in talent, E I 16 136 9
It was adventuring too far, assuming too much, making E I 16 137 10
poor Harriet into being very much attached to this man. E I 16 137 11
disappointment so very much, I am sure I have not an idea E I 16 137 11
a few weeks, and very much regretted the impossibility he E I 17 140 2
him much credit for the manner in which it was announced. E I 17 140 3
that she should have as much time as possible for getting E I 17 141 5
Mrs. Weston was exceedingly disappointed--much more E I 18 144 2
the young man had been so much more sober: but a sanguine E I 18 144 2
months later would be a much better plan; better time of E I 18 144 2
took care to express as much interest in the circumstance, E I 18 144 4
and exclaimed quite as much as was necessary, (or, being E I 18 145 5
cannot be without the means of doing as much as that. E I 18 145 10
We know, on the contrary, that he has so much of both that E I 18 146 12
"You will excuse my being so much overpowered. E I 18 150 30
coxcomb, he will not occupy much of my time or thoughts." E I 18 150 30
"But I am very much, and without being at all ashamed of E I 18 150 35
to say she liked it very much; and therefore she hoped E II 1 155 4
he had been gone, and how much he was engaged in company, E II 1 156 5
I must say that Jane deserves it as much as anybody can. E II 1 157 7
as you do--and so much fine work as you have done too!-- E II 1 158 10
that could give us so much pleasure as Miss Woodhouse's. E II 1 158 12
never away from them so much as a week, which must make it E II 1 159 20
But Mrs. Dixon must be very much disappointed. E II 1 161 26
of it now to her, that she does not think much about it. E II 1 162 31
She regained the street--happy in this, that though much E II 1 162 33
herself; but she was too much beloved to be parted with. E II 2 164 6
and every thing was relapsing much into its usual state. E II 2 168 15
safely judged of, under a much longer knowledge than they E II 2 169 17
I was glad you made her play so much, for having no E II 3 170 2
Once, I felt the fire rather too much; but then I moved E II 3 171 12
know--it is not much, but she does not hear quite quick. E II 3 175 39
You, who have been hearing and seeing so much of late on E II 3 175 42
he thought I had much better go round by Mr. Cole's E II 3 179 52
So I said, I was very much obliged to him: you know I E II 3 179 52
had meant to give with so much tender caution; hardly E II 3 180 56
She was, in fact, beginning very much to wonder that she E II 4 182 7
observation of, how much he seemed attached?--his air as E II 4 184 10
his hat, being all in proof of how much he was in love! E II 4 184 10
appeared, she had been much occupied by it, continually E II 4 184 11
After much thinking, she could determine on nothing better, E II 4 185 13
which had given her so much pleasure the autumn before. E II 5 186 2
She was feeling too much; but at last Emma collected from E II 5 186 4
of pain in the process--so much to herself at this time, E II 5 187 4
a question, however, which did not augur much. E II 5 189 17
and she did not think too much had been said in his praise; E II 5 190 22
He was very much pleased with Randalls, thought it a most E II 5 191 26
speaking of her with so much handsome praise, so much warm E II 5 191 28
much handsome praise, so much warm admiration, so much E II 5 191 28
much warm admiration, so much gratitude for the happiness E II 5 191 28
"You cannot see too much perfection in Mrs. Weston for my E II 5 192 31
houses; you might be very much at a loss, and it is a very E II 5 195 47
and interest much oftener than Emma could have supposed. E II 6 196 2

He argued like a young man very much bent on dancing; and E II 6 198 5
confusion of rank, bordered too much on inelegance of mind. E II 6 198 5
felt very much obliged to you for your preparatory hint. E II 6 198 7
"I merely asked, whether you had known much of Miss E II 6 200 17
But her account of every thing leaves so much to be E II 6 200 19
in town; and at Weymouth we were very much in the same set. E II 6 200 20
You forget how much she belongs to Highbury. E II 6 201 27
"So much the better--or so much the worse:--I do not know E II 6 202 35
so long, and thinking so much alike, Emma felt herself so E II 6 203 42
at, and would not join them in finding much fault with. E II 6 203 42
up much of wealth to be allowed an early establishment. E II 6 204 43
much she saw to like in his disposition altogether. E II 7 205 2
very charming; and with so much to be said for him E II 7 206 3
This lesson, she very much feared, they would receive only E II 7 207 6
so properly--there was so much real attention in the E II 7 208 9
in the manner of it--so much consideration for her father. E II 7 208 9
I think it would be much better if they would come in one E II 7 209 10
Mr. Weston, I am much obliged to you for reminding me. E II 7 210 20
Emma had as much reason to be satisfied with the rest of E II 8 214 12
your thoughts on this subject are very much like mine." E II 8 216 26
Good fires and carriages would be much more to the purpose E II 8 217 32
alarm was very great and much more durable-- indeed I E II 8 218 37
But when you mentioned Mrs. Dixon, I felt how much more E II 8 219 42
downright silly, but by much the larger proportion neither E II 8 219 43
pianoforte, she felt too much in the secret herself, to E II 8 220 45
the subject; and having so much to ask and to say as to E II 8 220 46
she had been used to despise the place rather too much. E II 8 220 48
He had wanted very much to go abroad--had been very eager E II 8 221 49
And, in short, from knowing his usual ways, I am very much E II 8 223 63
think Mr. Knightley would be much disturbed by Miss Bates. E II 8 225 78
I am sure I had much rather hear you. E II 9 231 7
to be praised, but Jane Fairfax's is much beyond it." E II 9 232 8
Mr. Cole said how much taste you had; and Mr. Frank E II 9 232 9
taste, and that he valued taste much more than execution." E II 9 232 9
Much could not be hoped from the traffic of even the E II 9 233 24
They would be very much pleased." E II 9 234 29
"Oh! but indeed I would much rather have it only in one. E II 9 235 40
"Aye, that will be much best," said Harriet, quite E II 9 235 42
"Very well, I am much obliged to you. E II 9 236 46
Indeed I must say that, much as I had heard of him before E II 9 237 51
heard of him before and much as I had expected, he very E II 9 237 51
about them and said how much she enjoyed them, and he E II 9 238 51
Oh! said I, my dear, I did say as much as I could. E II 9 239 51
at least, and I was very much obliged, and went down and E II 9 239 51
Soon afterwards he began again, "how much your friends in E II 10 241 11
12

amusement, and much less compunction with respect to her.-- E II 10 243 22
"I do not see much sign of it. E II 10 243 29
"So obliged to you!--so very much obliged to you for the E II 10 244 37
on examining watches, so much of the morning was perceived E II 10 246 55
an improvement--a very bad plan--much worse than the other. E II 11 251 26
cold--so much less danger at the crown than at Randalls! E II 11 251 27
warmly, "you are very much mistaken if you suppose Mr. E II 11 251 28
Another room of much better size might be secured for the E II 11 254 44
and found the evils of it much less than she had supposed E II 11 255 59
approver, (a much safer character,) she was truly welcome. E II 11 256 60
refuse; and I will keep as much awake as I can; but I E II 12 257 3
William Larkins's week's account; much rather, I confess.-- E II 12 257 3
He felt the going away almost too much to speak of it. E II 12 259 12
I would much rather have been merry than wise." E II 12 260 18
I am sure you did not much expect to like us. E II 12 260 22
to be afraid of being too sorry, and feeling it too much. E II 12 261 37
are really out of luck; you are very much out of luck!" E II 12 262 40
41

Her ideas only varied as to the how much. E II 13 264 1
though thinking of him so much, and, as she sat drawing or E II 13 264 1
that she could not be very much in love; for in spite of E II 13 264 1
So much the better. E II 13 264 2
"He is undoubtedly very much in love--every thing denotes E II 13 265 3
thing denotes it--very much in love indeed!--and when he E II 13 265 3
it was felt, and how much more might have been said but E II 13 265 5
but he had been very much struck with the loveliness of E II 13 266 6
Emma felt that she could not do too much for her, that E II 13 267 9
Harriet felt this too much to utter more than a few words E II 13 268 11
The visit was of course short; and there was so much E II 14 270 3
young woman, a stranger, a bride, there was too much ease. E II 14 270 4
as much affectedly, and as little really easy as could be. E II 14 271 5
again, "I dare say she was very much attached to him." E II 14 271 13
with herself, and thinking much of her own importance; E II 14 272 16
as here, and stand very much in the same way--just across E II 14 273 21
the barouche-landau; it will be so very much preferable. E II 14 274 28
wishes them to see as much as possible; and Mr. Suckling E II 14 274 28
bad thing; and that it is much more advisable to mix in E II 14 275 30
degree, without living in it either too much or too little. E II 14 275 30
spirits, which, I understand, are sometimes much depressed. E II 14 275 32
I fancy I need not take much pains to dwell on them. E II 14 275 32
It was as much as Emma could bear, without being impolite. E II 14 275 33
I honestly said as much to Mr. E. when he was speaking of E II 14 276 36
Emma was almost too much astonished to answer; but Mrs. E II 14 278 45
"Having understood as much, I was rather astonished to E II 14 278 46
I like him very much. E II 14 279 50
Much beyond my hopes. E II 14 279 52
lady; and I dare say she was very much pleased with you. E II 14 279 54
It is encouraging people to marry if you make so much of E II 14 280 57
turn and gradually became much more cold and distant; and E II 15 281 3
could prompt such behaviour sunk them both very much.-- E II 15 281 3
way, in doing too much, and being too careless of expense. E II 15 283 9
You have scolded me too much for match-making, for me to E II 15 288 35
I can much more readily enter into the temptation of E II 15 288 39
"Why really, dear Emma, I say that he is so very much E II 15 289 42
it would be a ninth very much out of humour at not being E II 16 292 7
said she, "and reached home before the rain was much. E II 16 293 12
are very little to you, much less than to me, but it is E II 16 294 22
"Yes, sir, I did indeed; and I am very much obliged by E II 16 294 26
Yes, I am sure you are much too reasonable. E II 16 295 33
I am advised to be out of doors as much as I can, I must E II 16 296 35
"Oh! my dear; but so much as Patty has to do!-- E II 16 296 38
Isabella and Emma, I think, do write very much alike. E II 16 297 45
distinct parties;--with so much perseverance in judging E II 17 299 1
began again; and though much that passed between them was E II 17 299 1
"But you have not seen so much of the world as I have. E II 17 299 8
and mix in the family as much as you chose;--that is--I do E II 17 301 18
politeness; it is much more to my taste than modern ease; E II 17 302 22
He had been too much expected by the best judges, for E II 17 302 23
"Mrs. Churchill is not much in my good graces, as you may E II 18 307 18
but I have not much faith in Mrs. Churchill's illness." E II 18 307 18
I have heard so much in praise of Mr. Frank Churchill.-- E II 18 309 31
which is not a place to promise much, you know, Mr. Weston. E II 18 310 34
My charge would be much more concise than her's, and E II 18 311 38
her's, and probably not much in the same spirit; all that E II 18 311 38
continue to increase as much as they have done lately." E II 18 311 42
"There can be no doubt of your being much more engaged E II 18 311 46
at once here, delights you too much to pass unnoticed. E II 18 312 50
not think they would fare much better with Uncle Knightley, E II 18 312 50
undoubtedly been always so much the most in love of the E III 1 315 1
if he did not call, and much as he wished to stay longer E III 1 316 4
Though much might be fancy, he could not doubt, when he E III 1 317 6
was engaged, and much benefit expected from the change. E III 1 317 7
that his aunt felt already much better for the change, and E III 1 318 11
and though he did not say much, his eyes declared that he E III 2 319 3
much of her. it cannot be long, I think, before she comes." E III 2 320 8
Selina, who is mild almost to a fault, bore with them much E III 2 321 15
think it as much her duty as Mrs. Weston's to receive them. E III 2 322 18
by so often, and knowing how much trouble you must have. E III 2 322 19
Much better employed talking to the young ladies. E III 2 323 19
Quite well, I am much obliged to you. E III 2 323 19
everybody's eyes are so much upon me, and in compliment to E III 2 324 20
21

said much, as soon as she could catch his eye again. E III 2 328 40
Miss Woodhouse, who would be so very much concerned!-- E III 2 329 45
"And, in return for your acknowledging so much, I will do E III 2 331 55
so much brother and sister as to make it at all improper." E III 2 331 62
husband and wife were so much alike; and his praise of E III 3 332 1
Harriet rational, Frank Churchill not too much in love, E III 3 332 1
She had suffered very much from cramp after dancing, and E III 3 333 5
How much more must an imaginist, like herself, be on fire E III 3 335 9
Harriet not much otherwise, Emma would not interfere with. E III 3 336 12
as much as her words, for something more than ordinary. E III 4 337 3
I do not want to say more than is necessary--I am too much E III 4 337 4
gifts: but they are things that I have valued very much." E III 4 338 8
Mr. Elton was sitting here, I remember, much about where I E III 4 340 20
asking her to hear too much; and against any thing like E III 4 341 34
one seemed so much disposed to employ as their two selves. E III 5 347 20
as much as he could, with as little apparent observation. E III 5 341 21
and his feelings were too much irritated for talking. E III 5 351 38
might eventually be as much increased by the arrival of a E III 6 352 1
Mrs. Elton was very much disappointed. E III 6 352 2
She promised him again and again to come--much oftener E III 6 354 9
I would wish every thing to be as much to your taste as E III 6 356 27
kind and sensible--much cleverer than dining out.-- E III 6 357 30
too rich to be eaten much of--inferior to cherries-- E III 6 358 35
"His aunt was so much better, that he had not a doubt of E III 6 361 41
be something for a young man so much in want of a change. E III 6 365 67
himself increased so much, that his last words to Emma E III 6 366 74
75

They separated too much into parties. E III 7 367 1
"How much I am obliged to you," said he, "for telling me E III 7 368 4
or you would not have been so much out of humour before." E III 7 369 13
and it is rather too much to be talking nonsense for the E III 7 369 15
"It is too much a matter of fact, but here it is.-- E III 7 371 32
prosperous, I could allow much for the occasional E III 7 375 61
This does not seem much like joy, indeed, in me--(E III 8 378 8
much for Miss Fairfax's advantage and comfort as possible. E III 8 380 9
say that any of them seemed very much to have enjoyed it. E III 8 381 19
that so much could be given to a young person like Jane." E III 8 382 23
they must have been very much obliged to you for coming. E III 9 385 6
the head, which spoke much, she looked at Mr. Knightley.-- E III 9 385 7
Square, for she knew how much his visit would be enjoyed-- E III 9 386 8
appeared that she was so much indisposed as to have been E III 9 389 16
He very much feared that Miss Fairfax derived more evil E III 9 389 16
so much--but, except them, Jane would really see nobody." E III 9 390 18
a disagreeable business--but things might be much worse.-- E III 10 393 17
For a moment he was silent; and then added, in a tone much E III 10 394 23
24

Mrs. Weston was looking so ill, and had an air of so much E III 10 394 26
27

It has hurt me, Emma, very much. E III 10 395 38
like him, when I was very much disposed to be attached to E III 10 396 41
"Mr. Weston will be almost as much relieved as myself," E III 10 396 43
He had not time to enter into much explanation. E III 10 397 47
Much, much beyond impropriety!-- E III 10 397 48
Emma drily, "do not appear to have done him much harm. E III 10 398 54
"Ah!" thought Emma, "he would have done as much for E III 10 398 56
He was very much agitated--very much, indeed--to a degree E III 10 399 57
And how much may be said in her situation for even that E III 10 400 65
"Much, indeed!" cried Emma, feelingly. E III 10 400 66
ways,--but it was not so much his behaviour as her own, E III 11 402 1
No! (with some elevation) I was thinking of a much more E III 11 406 24
Why was it so much worse that Harriet should be in love E III 11 408 32
She listened with much inward suffering, but with great E III 11 409 34
Emma knew that he had, on that occasion, found her much E III 11 409 35
of his talking to her much more than he had been used to E III 11 409 35
Emma knew it to have been very much the case. E III 11 409 35
Much that lived in Harriet's memory, many little E III 11 409 35
go to London, it was very much against his inclination E III 11 410 35
home at all, which was much more (as Emma felt) than he E III 11 410 35
Harriet was too much agitated to encounter him. E III 11 411 42
on herself, and she too much feared, on Mr. Knightley.-- E III 11 413 47
Emma had never known how much of her happiness depended on E III 12 415 1
a slight one, at times much stronger,) that Harriet might E III 12 416 1
in her way home, almost as much in duty to Emma as in E III 12 417 3
was now returned with much more to say, and much more to E III 12 417 4
with much more to say, and much more to say with E III 12 417 4
sensation; thought so much of Jane; so much of everybody, E III 12 418 5
so much of Jane; so much of everybody, and so little of E III 12 418 5
encouragement, overcome so much of her embarrassment, as E III 12 418 5
much pleased with all that she had said on the subject. E III 12 418 5
much--for every wish and every endeavour to do her good. E III 12 419 12
him very much, and her defence was, therefore, earnest. E III 12 420 14
affection--but she had too much to urge for Emma's E III 12 420 14
by exertions which had never cost her half so much before. E III 12 422 19
The weather continued much the same all the following E III 13 424 1
me--I am pleased that you can say even so much.-- E III 13 426 16
an impression, I have as much reason to be ashamed of E III 13 426 17
The superior hopes which gradually opened were so much the E III 13 432 40
wrong place. there was too much domestic happiness in his E III 13 432 41
in it; Isabella was too much like Emma--differing only in E III 13 432 41
much to have been done, even had his time been longer.-- E III 13 432 41
Emma, was there so much fond solicitude, so much keen E III 13 433 41
so much keen anxiety for her, that he could stay no longer. E III 13 433 41
Perry, and talked on with much self-contentment, totally E III 14 434 3
I felt for your dear father very much in the storm of E III 14 436 7
attached to me, was as much my conviction as my wish.-- E III 14 438 8
whom I regard with so much brotherly affection, as to long E III 14 439 8
Of the pianoforte so much talked of, I feel it only E III 14 439 8
my dear madam, is much beyond my power of doing justice to. E III 14 439 8
mad a state: and I am not much better yet; still insane E III 14 439 8
as much happiness in the marriage state as he had done.-- E III 14 443 8
But it is done; we are reconciled, dearer, much dearer, E III 14 443 8
to Mrs. Weston, and so much in love with Miss Fairfax, and E III 15 444 1
Mr. Knightley, had seen so much to blame in his conduct. E III 15 444 2
Too much indebted to the event for his acquittal.-- E III 15 445 15
of it might not very much exceed the pleasure. E III 15 446 18
She must have had much more to contend with, in carrying E III 15 446 20
"There is no saying much for the delicacy of our good E III 15 447 22
You will find how very much he suffers." E III 15 447 23
'Dearer, much dearer than ever.' E III 15 447 28
and I am very much of his opinion in thinking him likely E III 15 448 30
I have another person's interest at present so much at E III 15 448 30
his own, there would be much, very much, to be borne with. E III 15 449 32
now; and it really was too much to hope even of Harriet, E III 15 450 38
How much worse, had they been obliged to meet! E III 16 451 1
Harriet expressed herself very much as might be supposed, E III 16 451 2
a heart was near her, how much might at that moment, and E III 16 451 4
tone of great ill usage,) which made it so much the worse. E III 16 457 40
Oh! if you knew how much I love every thing that is E III 16 460 57
I could not think about you so much without doating on you, E III 17 462 7
humanity in you to do as much for her as you have done for E III 17 462 8
a sort of serious smile--"much less, perhaps, than he is E III 17 464 22
Depend upon it, he will be much farther from doing you E III 17 464 24
I believe I did not play with the children quite so much E III 17 465 27
Did not he love Mr. Knightley very much?-- E III 17 466 29
But Mrs. Elton was very much discomposed indeed.-- E III 17 469 36
his features, "I am very much afraid, my dear Emma, that E III 18 470 6

in the meanwhile, we need not talk much on the subject."	E III	18	471	16
Your friend Harriet will make a much longer history when	E III	18	472	20
mention, without its being much to the purpose, that on	E III	18	472	20
determined against him, much more, than she was before."	E III	18	473	24
much in love with her as ever,) to get acquainted with her.	E III	18	474	34
Much of this, I have no doubt, she may thank you for."	E III	18	474	34
It would have been a much better transgression had I	E III	18	477	55
us with two characters so much superior to our own."	E III	18	478	69
who commended her very much for thinking of sending for	E III	18	479	73
Nay, he appeared so much otherwise, that his daughter's	E III	19	483	9
The result of this distress was, that, with a much more	E III	19	484	11
The wedding was very much like other weddings, where the	E III	19	484	12
any thing, which he had not been very much tempted to do.	P III	1	5	8
He had never indulged much hope, he had now none, of ever	P III	1	6	10
the book of books with as much enjoyment as in her early	P III	1	7	12
on the subject, and gave it much serious consideration.	P III	2	11	2
release from debt, a much higher tone of indifference for	P III	2	12	3
Lady Russell, looking over her paper, "much may be done.	P III	2	12	4
It was a much safer place for a gentleman in his	P III	2	14	10
It would be too much to expect Sir Walter to descend into	P III	2	14	11
Sir Walter, was certainly much strengthened by one part,	P III	2	15	13
stronger heads than Sir Walter's have found too much.--	P III	2	15	13
"that the present juncture is much in our favour.	P III	3	17	1
elude--and therefore, thus much I venture upon, that I	P III	3	17	4
over, nothing being of so much use to Mrs. Clay's health	P III	3	18	7
Here Anne spoke,-- "the navy, I think, who have done much	P III	3	19	11
				12
to be sure, but not much; and quite the gentleman in all	P III	3	22	23
in danger of suffering as much where there was no lady, as	P III	3	22	24
sound extremely well; very much better than to any mere Mr.	P III	3	24	36
and time had softened down much, perhaps nearly all of	P III	4	28	7
in Mrs. Clay's being of so much use, while Anne could be	P III	5	34	11
such a reverse would be so much more to be pitied than	P III	5	34	12
be wrong to have her so much with me; not that any thing	P III	5	35	14
Freckles do not disgust me so very much as they do him: I	P III	5	35	14
The two families were so continually meeting, so much in	P III	5	36	21
They talk and laugh a great deal too much for me.	P III	5	38	31
been so busy, have had so much to do, that I could not	P III	5	38	32
They are both so very large, and take up so much room!	P III	5	39	39
and hospitable, not much educated, and not at all elegant.	P III	5	40	45
in?" and this, without much waiting for an answer;--or in	P III	6	42	1
and all her ideas in as much of Uppercross as possible.	P III	6	43	3
As it was, he did nothing with much zeal, but sport; and	P III	6	43	5
He had very good spirits, which never seemed much affected	P III	6	43	5
much better than his wife's, and his practice not so bad.--	P III	6	44	6
her being treated with too much confidence by all parties,	P III	6	44	7
too much in the secret of the complaints of each house.	P III	6	44	7
degree, and gives them so much trash and sweet things,	P III	6	44	8
was to be considered so much at home as to lose her place.	P III	6	45	10
other person's, gave her much more pleasure for their	P III	6	47	13
any where; and Anne, very much preferring the office of	P III	6	47	15
She could not think of much else on the 29th of September;	P III	6	48	16
"Nobody knew how much she should suffer.	P III	6	48	17
her having been almost as much at sea as her husband, made	P III	6	48	18
not go; and being too much engrossed by proposals of	P III	6	49	25
mamma; she is thinking so much of poor Richard!	P III	6	50	27
family, though quite as much as he deserved; seldom heard	P III	6	50	28
To hear them talking so much of Captain Wentworth,	P III	6	52	33
they were with him, how much handsomer, how infinitely	P III	7	54	4
father and mother were in much too strong and recent alarm	P III	7	55	5
so well--and he wished so much to be introduced to Captain	P III	7	55	6
His father very much wished him to meet Captain Wentworth,	P III	7	55	7
I ought if I can, quite as much as Charles, for they want	P III	7	57	16
Mary, very much gratified by this attention, was delighted	P III	7	59	25
I shall of course put up with, but it must not be much.	P III	7	62	41
Once so much to each other!	P III	8	63	3
the party; and he was very much questioned, and especially	P III	8	64	4
the great nation not having much improved our condition.	P III	8	66	16
You know how much he wanted money--worse than myself.	P III	8	67	23
He felt it all, so much for her sake.--	P III	8	67	23
her son, doing it with so much sympathy and natural grace,	P III	8	67	28
I believe I have lived as much on board as most women, and	P III	8	69	37
There was so much of friendliness, and of flattery, and of	P III	9	73	1
by it, and to think Captain Wentworth very much in the way.	P III	9	73	3
from that time cousin Charles had been very much forgotten.	P III	9	74	7
however, and I never think much of your new creations."	P III	9	75	11
and therefore it is very much to be wished that Captain	P III	9	76	16
Charles Hayter had met with much to disquiet and mortify	P III	9	77	19
but it proved to be one much less calculated for making	P III	9	79	25
had bent down her head so much, that his little sturdy	P III	9	80	33
too wise to acknowledge as much at home, where she knew it	P III	10	82	1
like to join you very much, I am very fond of a long walk,"	P III	10	83	4
accept the Miss Musgroves' much more cordial invitation to	P III	10	83	4
She occupied her mind as much as possible in such like	P III	10	84	7
sure Louisa had got a much better somewhere,--and nothing	P III	10	86	21
If you value her conduct or happiness, infuse as much of	P III	10	88	26
She has a great deal too much of the Elliot pride.--	P III	10	88	28
She had much to recover from, before she could move.	P III	10	89	34
they walked side by side, nearly as much as the other two.	P III	10	90	37
She was very much affected by the view of his disposition	P III	10	91	42
other hand, he spent so much of his time at Uppercross,	P III	11	93	2
that he had too much self-possession, and she too little.	P III	11	93	3
November would not leave much time for seeing a new place,	P III	11	94	8
very punctually, it was so much past noon before the two	P III	11	95	8
want of health, looking much older than Captain Wentworth.	P III	11	97	14
There was so much attachment to Captain Wentworth in all	P III	11	98	16
His lameness prevented him from taking much exercise; but	P III	11	99	18
Anne found herself by this time growing so much more	P III	11	99	21
time; luckily Mary did not much attend to their having	P III	12	106	19
done a good deed in making that poor fellow talk so much.	P III	12	107	24
decision, and said as much in reply as her own feelings	P III	12	108	29
to bear, for he was too much affected to renew the subject-	P III	12	108	29
There was too much wind to make the high part of the new	P III	12	109	32
The Harvilles silenced all scruples; and, as much as they	P III	12	112	56
agreed, that it would be much better for him to take a	P III	12	114	64
She was so wretched, and so vehement, complained so much	P III	12	115	65
much in favour of happiness, as a very resolute character.	P III	12	116	72
Louisa was much the same.	P IV	1	121	2
and a much better scheme followed and was acted upon.	P IV	1	121	3
And so much was said in this way, that Anne thought she	P IV	1	122	5
to have it known, how much more she was thinking of Lyme,	P IV	1	124	11
acquaintance there; how much more interesting to her was	P IV	1	124	11
been the consequence of much thoughtlessness and much	P IV	1	126	21
much thoughtlessness and much imprudence; that its effects	P IV	1	126	21
we have made have been all very much for the better.	P IV	1	127	28
A very good man, and very much the gentleman I am sure--	P IV	1	127	28
Though Charles and Mary had remained at Lyme much longer	P IV	2	129	1
children away as much as she could, every possible supply	P IV	2	129	2
was, and there had been so much going on every day, there	P IV	2	129	3
that the balance had certainly been much in favour of Lyme.	P IV	2	129	3
I think she would be so much pleased with his mind, that	P IV	2	132	17
Benwick seemed much more disposed to ride over to Kellynch.	P IV	2	133	25
had been taking as much pains to seek the acquaintance,	P IV	2	135	35
Elizabeth were settled there, much to their satisfaction.	P IV	3	137	1
should find so much to be vain of in the littlenesses of a	P IV	3	138	5
his marriage too were found to admit of much extenuation.	P IV	3	139	8
had had of him at Lyme, but without being much attended to.	P IV	3	140	12
lament his being very much under-hung, a defect which time	P IV	3	141	12
Sir Walter thought much of Mrs. Wallis; she was said to be	P IV	3	141	13
down with them, and improved their conversation very much.	P IV	3	143	19
He spoke and looked so much in earnest, that Anne was not	P IV	4	145	2
The evil of the marriage would be much diminished, if	P IV	4	146	4

there; and vexed her as much when she was away, as a	P IV	4	146	5
there was but too much reason to apprehend that the	P IV	4	149	12
"She was very much honoured, and should be happy in their	P IV	4	149	13
by far too much trouble taken to procure the acquaintance.	P IV	4	150	18
she had lived very much in the world, nor the restrictions	P IV	5	153	7
She had seen too much of the world, to expect sudden or	P IV	5	154	9
To me, who live so much alone, her conversation I assure	P IV	5	155	9
will furnish much either to interest or edify me.--	P IV	5	156	12
				13
They were not much interested in any thing relative to	P IV	5	157	14
and Anne could have said much and did long to say a little,	P IV	5	158	20
be, in having been very much talked of between her friend	P IV	5	158	21
be given to understand so much by her friend, could not	P IV	5	159	21
She was as much convinced of his meaning to gain Anne in	P IV	5	159	22
said Lady Russell, "being much too well aware of the	P IV	5	159	23
She felt that she could so much more depend upon the	P IV	5	161	28
She wanted to hear much more than Mary communicated.	P IV	6	162	1
who has been "calling much oftener than was welcome.	P IV	6	163	7
be much "more convenient to me to dine there to-morrow.	P IV	6	163	7
butcher says there is a "bad sore-throat very much about.	P IV	6	164	8
put into an envelop, containing nearly as much more.	P IV	6	164	8
She did not mean, however, to derive much more from it to	P IV	6	167	19
They were too much like joy, senseless joy!	P IV	6	168	21
Anne was too much engaged with Lady Russell to be often	P IV	6	168	25
man to whine and complain; he has too much spirit for that.	P IV	6	172	45
at benwick; does not so much as say, "I wonder at it, I	P IV	6	173	47
It began to rain, not much, but enough to make shelter	P IV	7	174	2
her boots were so thick! much thicker than Miss Anne's;	P IV	7	174	3
should not be always so much wiser than the other half, or	P IV	7	175	6
neither of them, probably, much the wiser for what they	P IV	7	176	8
They had, by dint of being so very much together, got to	P IV	7	176	8
"I am much obliged to you," was her answer, "but I am not	P IV	7	176	11
She was very much obliged to him, but declined it all,	P IV	7	177	15
he were really suffering much from disappointment or not;	P IV	7	178	24
All this is much, very much in favour of their happiness;	P IV	8	182	8
"I should very much like to see Lyme again," said Anne.	P IV	8	183	14
So much novelty and beauty!	P IV	8	184	16
and flurried her too much to leave her any power of	P IV	8	186	22
"For shame! for shame!--this is too much of flattery.	P IV	8	187	29
enabled to place herself much nearer the end of the bench	P IV	8	189	46
she had been before, much more within reach of a passer-by.	P IV	8	189	46
she did it, and not with much happier effect; though by	P IV	8	189	46
She could not help thinking much of the extraordinary	P IV	9	192	2
There was much to regret.	P IV	9	192	2
Mr. Elliot's wife has not been dead much above half a year.	P IV	9	196	31
so much; but less would hardly have been sufficient.	P IV	9	197	34
Smith, "upon finding how much you were together, and	P IV	9	197	36
"And--were you much acquainted?"	P IV	9	198	49
as good as others, and much more agreeable than most	P IV	9	199	55
the temple, and it was as much as he could do to support	P IV	9	199	55
let me thus much into the secrets of Marlborough-Buildings.	P IV	9	205	82
you see, I was not romancing so much as you supposed."	P IV	9	205	82
and ignorance in another, can hardly have much truth left."	P IV	9	205	85
Having long had as much money as he could spend, nothing	P IV	9	206	90
own family concerns, how much had been originally implied	P IV	9	208	94
had led his friend into expenses much beyond his fortune.	P IV	9	208	95
not strong understanding, much more amiable than his	P IV	9	209	95
wait the event with as much composure as possible; and	P IV	10	212	1
"Oh!" cried Elizabeth, "I have been rather too much used	P IV	10	213	5
They appear to so much advantage in company with each	P IV	10	213	5
Mr. Elliot looking up with so much respect!"	P IV	10	231	5
as much to Sir Walter as she would have done otherwise.	P IV	10	213	10
praised; wanted very much to be gratified by more	P IV	10	214	12
So much was pretty soon understood; but till Sir Walter	P IV	10	216	18
like the idea of it very much, as an advantage to her	P IV	10	216	19
to so much misconduct and misery, both in young and old!	P IV	10	218	23
"yes, I believe I do--very much recovered; but she is	P IV	10	218	24
"That cannot be much to your taste, I know," said she; "	P IV	10	218	25
I will ask them all for an evening; that will be much	P IV	10	220	29
She was intreated to give them as much of her time as	P IV	10	220	31
course; and tried to dwell much on this argument of	P IV	10	221	33
her regret that she had said so much, simple as it was.	P IV	10	222	36
Charles, you had much better go back, and change the box	P IV	10	224	51
kindness; and quite as much so, moreover, for the	P IV	10	224	52
				53
"I am not yet so much changed," cried Anne, and stopped,	P IV	10	225	60
in a hurry, and could not much attend, and I can only	P IV	10	228	71
much on her own, before she was able to attempt the walk.	P IV	11	229	2
Anne hoped the gentlemen might each be too much self-	P IV	11	230	5
Captain Harville smiled, as much as to say, "do you claim	P IV	11	232	19
Education has been theirs in so much higher a degree; the	P IV	11	234	28
her heart was too full, her breath too much oppressed.	P IV	11	235	33
Thus much indeed he was obliged to acknowledge--that he	P IV	11	241	61
Their first meeting in Milsom-Street afforded much to be	P IV	11	244	71
to yourself might have spared you much or all of this."	P IV	11	245	75
believe that I was right, much as I suffered from it, that	P IV	11	246	79
				80
eyed him well, he was very much struck by his personal	P IV	12	248	2
He had grumbled & shaken his shoulders so much indeed, and	S	1	364	1
a very civil salutation--much concern for the accident--	S	1	365	1
Mr H. looked very much astonished--& replied--"what sir!	S	1	365	1
to say that he has not much business--to be sure, if	S	1	366	1
So much for the celebrity of Brinshore!--	S	1	370	1
husband by this time, not much less disposed for it--a	S	1	370	1
their getting out into the world, as much as possible.	S	2	374	1
value of money, was very much looked up to & had a poor	S	3	375	1
very much with the introduction of such a character.	S	3	378	1
He lives too much in the world to be settled; that is his	S	4	382	1
useful women & have so much energy of character that,	S	5	385	1
with them, & who is not much above 20, I am sorry to say,	S	5	385	1
"My dear Tom, we were all much greived at your accident, &	S	5	386	1
She has been suffering much from the headache and six	S	5	387	1
on examination that much of the evil lay in her Gum, I	S	5	387	1
With all their sufferings, you perceive how much they are	S	5	388	1
see as much, & as quickly as possible, where all was new.	S	6	389	1
temptations, & with so much good will for Mr P. to	S	6	390	1
Her situation with Lady Denham so very much in favour of	S	6	391	1
I have heard that's very much the case with your West-	S	6	392	1
of life, we shall not much thank them Mr Parker."--	S	6	392	1
Sir Edwd was much her superior in air & manner;--certainly	S	7	394	1
He came into the room remarkably well, talked much--& very	S	7	394	1
well, talked much--& very much to Charlotte, by whom he	S	7	394	1
to mean to detach her as much as possible from the rest of	S	7	396	1
why he shd talk so much nonsense, unless he could do no	S	7	398	1
feelings or other, & very much addicted to all the newest-	S	7	398	1
call them sometimes, for I take them very much by the hand.	S	7	399	1
or trust me, they wd not be so much in my company.--	S	7	399	1
Ah! young ladies that have no money are very much to be	S	7	401	1
And here they were obliged to part--Miss D. being too much	S	8	404	1
had confined very much to one spot had read more	S	8	404	1
Trafalgar house with as much alacrity as could remain,	S	9	406	1
himself, but there is so much wind that I did not think he	S	9	407	1
the West-Indians were very much disposed to go thither.--	S	9	408	1
The world is pretty much divided between the weak of mind	S	9	410	1
of your foot, that you have used it too much already.--	S	9	411	1
I have not much confidence in poor Arthur's skill for	S	9	411	1
"I think you are doing too much, said Mr P.	S	9	411	1
"My appetite is very much mended I assure you lately.	S	9	411	1
as for Arthur, he is only too much disposed for food.	S	9	411	1
Disorders & Recoveries so very much out of the common way,	S	10	412	1
as he could,--& boasted much of sitting by the fire till	S	10	414	1
She had been too successful however for much fatigue; for	S	10	414	1

declining it, and he sat down again with much satisfaction. S 10 415 1
I am not afraid of any thing so much as damp.--" S 10 415 1
"But you do not call a walk to traf: h. much exercise?--" S 10 416 1
"I am much obliged to you, replied Charlotte--but I prefer S 10 417 1
over it, very much--said Charlotte--but not otherwise.--" S 10 417 1
of eating a great deal too much, & declaring he was not to S 10 417 1
scraped off almost as much butter as he put on, & then S 10 417 1
into her cheeks, & with much perturbation she added--"the S 10 419 1
immediate reflections--& much worse than all the rest, S 11 420 1
could dress in a stile much beyond what they ought to have S 11 421 1
captivate some man of much better fortune than their own.-- S 11 421 1
his wife--but you would do it so much better yourself. S 12 423 1
I & a few more, have very much at heart--the establishment S 12 424 1
These entrance gates were so much in a corner of the S 12 426 1

MUD (3)
six inches deep in mud, I am absolutely certain; and the PP I 8 36 6
inconvenience from the mud; and Mr. Wingfield says it is E I 12 105 55
yards from the shore--no mud--no weeds--no slimey rocks-- S 1 369 1

MUFF (2)
the price and weigh the merits of a new muff and tippet. NA I 7 51 54
I can hardly keep my hands warm even in my muff. SS II 5 168 9

MUFFIN (3)
& ate an additional muffin when they were going to sit up W 326 7
most abundantly supplied with coffee and muffin. PP I 16 76 5
The muffin last night--if it had been handed round once, I E II 3 170 4

MUFFIN-MEN (1)
the bawling of newsmen, muffin-men and milk-men, and the P IV 2 135 33

MULATTO (1)
She was about 17, half Mulatto, chilly & tender, had a S 11 421 1

MULBERRY (1)
in the country: and such a mulberry tree in one corner! SS II 8 196 22

MULBERRY-TREE (1)
the honours of the mulberry-tree, the canal, and the yew SS II 10 216 15

MULE (1)
letter-boy on an obstinate mule, were the liveliest E II 9 233 24

MULES (1)
the rough horses and mules he had ridden, or his many MP II 6 237 23

MULL (1)
the spotted, the sprigged, the mull or the jackonet. NA I 10 74 22

MULLINS'S (2)
better mention the poor Mullins's situation, & sound her S 12 423 1
I will not trouble you to speak about the Mullins's.-- S 12 425 1

MULTIPLICITY (2)
expectation, by their multiplicity and their convenience. NA II 8 184 4
of my mind, and the multiplicity of business falling on me E III 14 442 8

MULTIPLIED (3)
so heavy, so multiplied, so rising in dreadful gradation! MP III 1 319 40
relation, and contained multiplied proofs to her who had E III 11 410 35
scruple of mine with multiplied strength and refinement.-- E III 14 440 8

MULTIPLY (1)
It would be going only to multiply trouble to the others, P IV 1 121 3

MULTITUDE (3)
there is nobody you know in all this multitude of people? NA I 2 23 20
the admiring multitude what connubial felicity really was. PP III 8 312 16
But still, there certainly were a dreadful multitude of P IV 3 142 13

MURDER (3)
I shall expect murder and every thing of the kind." NA I 14 112 33
There must be murder; and government cares not how much." NA I 14 112 35
Murder was not tolerated, servants were not slaves, and NA II 10 200 3

MURDERED (1)
to waft the sighs of the murdered to her; it had wafted NA II 5 161 25

MURDERER (1)
If aware of her having viewed him as a murderer, she could NA II 14 231 3

MURDERING (2)
on from crime to crime, murdering whomsoever they chose, NA II 9 190 2
General Tilney of either murdering or shutting up his wife, NA II 15 247 14

MURMUR (3)
Catherine had fortitude too; she suffered, but no murmur NA I 8 53 2
There had been at one moment a slight murmur in the MP III 7 387 45
"Not at all, not at all; there is not an oath or a murmur P IV 6 172 43

MURMURED (1)
and he murmured, in reply, "very true, my love, very true. E III 7 370 21

MURMURING (2)
overthrown there was no spirit of murmuring within her. MP II 10 280 32
of his voice but the murmuring of a few broken sentences S 10 416 1

MURMURINGS (1)
days; who had known all the murmurings of my heart!-- SS III 10 346 28

MURMURS (4)
Hollow murmurs seemed to creep along the gallery, and more NA II 6 171 12
Such were the gentle murmurs of Mrs. Bennet, and they gave PP I 23 128 11
business from himself in murmurs of his own, over the MP III 3 341 31
And she leaned back in the corner, to indulge her murmurs, E II 5 187 6

MUSGROVE (33)
son and heir of Charles Musgrove, Esq. of Uppercross, in P III 1 3 2
by becoming Mrs. Charles Musgrove; but Anne, with an P III 1 5 8
her refusal; for Charles Musgrove was the eldest son of a P III 4 28 7
Charles Musgrove was civil and agreeable; in sense and P III 6 43 5
unprofitable Dick Musgrove, who had never done any thing P III 6 51 29
Charles Musgrove, indeed, afterwards shewed more of P III 7 55 6
alarm, and Charles Musgrove began consequently to feel no P III 7 55 7
probably not having Dick Musgrove at all near his thoughts, P III 8 67 25
One morning, about this time, Charles Musgrove and Captain P III 10 83 3
but "no," said Charles Musgrove, and "no, no," cried P III 10 85 16
If Louisa Musgrove would be beautiful and happy in her P III 10 88 26
favour with any of the Musgrove family; she had only time, P III 12 103 5
The word curricle made Charles Musgrove jump up, that he P III 12 105 9
Musgrove, take care of the others." P III 12 111 48
Musgrove, either you or I must go." P III 12 113 58
"Then it is settled, Musgrove," cried Captain Wentworth, " P III 12 114 61
Mrs. Charles Musgrove will, of course, wish to get back to P III 12 114 61
proposed, and Charles Musgrove agreed, that it would be P III 12 114 64
of Lyme, and Louisa Musgrove, and all her acquaintance P IV 1 124 11
eight years afterwards, be charmed by a Louisa Musgrove. P IV 1 125 13
The name of Musgrove would have told him enough. P IV 3 144 19
"Certainly not a great match for Louisa Musgrove; but a " P IV 6 165 8
Captain Benwick and Louisa Musgrove! P IV 6 165 9
Musgrove, and her fine little boys, Anne was at liberty. P IV 6 166 17
Captain Benwick and Louisa Musgrove! P IV 6 166 19
The high-spirited, joyous, talking Louisa Musgrove, and P IV 6 166 19
The idea of Louisa Musgrove turned into a person of P IV 6 167 20
and returned, and Louisa Musgrove was mentioned, and P IV 6 168 22
"Ay, ay, Miss Louisa Musgrove, that is the name. P IV 6 171 33
between him and Louisa Musgrove; but I hope it may be P IV 6 172 42
Russell that Louisa Musgrove was to marry Captain Benwick. P IV 7 178 27
I regard Louisa Musgrove as a very amiable, sweet-tempered P IV 8 182 10
attach himself to Louisa Musgrove (the attempts of angry P IV 11 242 63

MUSGROVES (17)
The Musgroves, like their houses, were in a state of P III 5 40 45
The neighbourhood was not large, but the Musgroves were P III 6 47 14
who depended on the Musgroves for all their pleasures: P III 6 47 15
history were, that the Musgroves had had the ill fortune P III 6 50 28
and speedily, but the Musgroves, in their warm gratitude P III 6 52 33
The Musgroves could hardly be more ready to invite than he P III 9 73 2
Wentworth, among the Musgroves and their dependencies. P III 9 73 3
and while the Musgroves were in the first class of society P III 9 74 5
the alliances which the Musgroves have made, she has no P III 9 75 13
One morning, very soon after the dinner at the Musgroves, P III 9 78 21
the Musgroves, were now become but of secondary interest. P IV 1 124 11
The Musgroves came back to receive their happy boys and P IV 2 133 27
of Uppercross, of the Musgroves, nay, even of Louisa, and P IV 7 176 8
The Musgroves are behaving like themselves, most P IV 8 182 8
was to comprise all the remaining dues of the Musgroves. P IV 10 226 64
She had promised to be with the Musgroves from breakfast P IV 11 229 1
With the Musgroves, there was the happy chat of perfect P IV 11 246 78

MUSH (1)
their morning discourse, mush have left at least doubtful. SS II 1 141 7

MUSIC (69)
French, Italian, German, music, singing, drawing &c. will LS 7 253 1
Her mother wished her to learn music; and Catherine was NA I 1 14 1
Music seems scarcely to attract him, and though he admires SS I 3 17 18
the same books, the same music must charm us both. SS I 3 17 18
that event by giving up music, although by her mother's SS I 7 35 8
could be diverted from music for a moment, and asked SS I 7 35 9
His pleasure in music, though it amounted not to that SS I 7 35 9
heard him declare that of music and dancing he was SS I 10 46 2
enjoyment of dancing and music was mutual, and that it SS I 10 47 3
gazing on every line of music that he had written out for SS I 16 83 3
In books too, as well as in music, she courted the misery SS I 16 83 3
there would not be music enough in London to content her. SS I 17 92 25
be employed in improving my collection of music and books." SS I 17 92 26
wrapt up in her own music and her own thoughts, had by SS II 1 145 23
caught those words by a sudden pause in Marianne's music.-- SS II 2 148 20
and happily together with our books and our music! SS II 3 155 8
As John Dashwood had no more pleasure in music than his SS II 14 252 20
She went to it; but the music on which her eye first SS III 10 342 7
She shook her head, put the music aside, and after running SS III 10 342 7
I shall divide every moment between music and reading. SS III 10 343 9
to the sound of the music, for the last half hour. W 329 9
A woman must have a thorough knowledge of music, singing, PP I 8 39 50
Bingley and Elizabeth for the indulgence of some music. PP I 10 51 45
as she turned over some music books that lay on the PP I 10 51 46
"Do let us have a little music,"--cried Miss Bingley, PP I 11 58 33
an air; for I consider music as a very innocent diversion, PP I 18 101 71
too much of our time to music, for there are certainly PP I 18 101 71
at home, of new books and music, that Elizabeth had never PP II 8 172 3
"We are speaking of music, madam," said he, when no longer PP II 8 173 5
"Of music! PP II 8 173 6
my share in the conversation, if you are speaking of music. PP II 8 173 6
enjoyment of music than myself, or a better natural taste. PP II 8 173 6
I often tell young ladies, that no excellence in music is PP II 8 173 10
says she does not want to learn either music or drawing." MP I 2 19 28
longer, for I dearly love music myself, and where the MP I 6 59 41
Here's what may leave all painting and all music behind, MP I 11 113 35
mind was ruffled; and the music which Sir Thomas called MP II 2 191 11
what had passed to be in a humour for any thing but music. MP II 5 227 68
both in drawing and music than many might have done with E I 6 44 19
If I draw less, I shall read more; if I give up music, I E I 10 85 21
to me, of drawing or music; and so on to every body, E I 18 150 31
They had music; Emma was obliged to play; and the thanks E II 2 168 15
You and Miss Fairfax gave us some very good music. E II 3 170 2
sometimes with music and sometimes with conversation. E II 3 170 2
christian name, and say whose music she principally played. E II 4 181 2
I am excessively fond of music, but without the smallest E II 6 201 28
I could not excuse a man's having more music than love -- E II 6 202 31
who is mistress of music, has not any thing of the nature E II 8 215 16
is so particularly fond of music that he could not help E II 8 216 16
Mr. Dixon's preference of her music to her friend's, I can E II 8 217 33
and a perfect knowledge of music; which was properly E II 8 227 86
He took some music from a chair near the pianoforte, and E II 10 242 20 21
He knew Miss Fairfax could have no music here. E II 10 242 21
He brought all the music to her, and they looked it over E II 10 243 23
and chair, lights and music, tea and supper, made E II 11 255 59
I am doatingly fond of music--passionately fond;--and my E II 14 276 36
I absolutely cannot do without music. E II 14 276 36
I condition for nothing else; but without music, life E II 14 277 36
They are but too apt to give up music." E II 14 277 38
Selina has entirely given up music--never touches the E II 14 277 40
Emma, finding her so determined upon neglecting her music, E II 14 278 43
I know enough of music to speak decidedly on that point. E II 15 282 5
to arrange--books and music to divide, and all my trunks P III 5 38 34
of house-keeping, neighbours, dress, dancing, and music. P III 6 42 3
In music she had been always used to feel alone in the P III 6 47 13
There had been music, singing, talking, laughing, all that P III 7 58 22
a good one, and Captain Wentworth was very fond of music. P IV 7 180 32
set out, another hour of music was to give delight or the P IV 8 189 45
catch the music; like unfledged sparrows ready to be fed. P IV 9 193 6

MUSIC-MASTER (1)
The day which dismissed the music-master was one of the NA I 1 14 1

MUSIC-SELLERS (1)
What a happy day for booksellers, music-sellers, and print- SS I 17 92 25

MUSICAL (22)
In the evening, as Marianne was discovered to be musical, SS I 7 35 8
They read, they talked, they sang together; his musical SS I 10 48 8
brother and sister, to a small musical party at her house. SS II 14 248 6
The party, like other musical parties, comprehended a SS II 14 250 10
As Elinor was neither musical, nor affecting to be so, she SS II 14 250 11
If my vanity had taken a musical turn, you would have been PP I 6 24 22
"Are they musical?" MP II 11 288 26
Was it a musical society?" E II 5 191 27
play well:--a man, a very musical man, and in love with E II 6 201 28
That I thought, in a man of known musical talent, was some E II 6 201 28
"Mr. Dixon is very musical, is he? E II 6 201 29
Mrs. Weston, kind-hearted and musical, was particularly E II 8 220 46
"I do not ask whether you are musical, Mrs. Elton. E II 14 276 34 35
to me, to hear what a musical society I am got into. E II 14 276 36
been used to a very musical society, both at Maple Grove E II 14 276 36
think I can live without something of a musical society. E II 14 277 36
of there being a very musical society in Highbury; and I E II 14 277 37
and I must establish a musical club, and have regular E II 14 277 38
that she and I should unite to form a musical club! E II 14 279 52
I can, shall have musical parties to draw out her talents, E II 15 284 9
Your musical knowledge alone would entitle you to name E II 17 301 18
always recommended her musical powers to the notice of Mr. P III 6 47 15

MUSICIAN (3)
either as an artist or a musician, but she was not E I 6 44 19
same musician engaged, met with the readiest acquiescence. E II 11 247 3
preferring the office of musician to a more active post, P III 6 47 15

MUSING (8)
if nothing but musing would do, she could scarcely see an MP I 16 151 2
exclaimed, breaking forth again after a few minutes musing. MP II 5 225 55
sober sadness, as she sat musing over that too great MP III 2 329 10
complacently, and then musing on something else, suddenly MP III 5 364 30
She was deep in other musing. MP III 15 439 9
He sat musing a little while, and then said, "but I do not E I 9 80 65 66
Mr. Weston was musing. E II 18 309 32
nothing--and she sat musing on the difference of woman's E III 8 384 32 33

MUSINGS (6)
She was again roused from disagreeable musings by sudden MP I 10 100 24
Her own musings were brought to an end on perceiving Mr. MP II 10 274 8
in one of his dignified musings, as a right and desirable MP III 6 368 9
as possible in such like musings and quotations; but it P III 10 84 7
Prettier musings of high-wrought love and eternal P IV 9 192 3
Already had he had many musings on the subject. S 8 405 2

MUSLIN (15)
It is such a delicate muslin.-- NA I 2 22 11
Rooms; wore my sprigged muslin robe with blue trimmings-- NA I 3 26 22
guessed it, madam," said Mr. Tilney, looking at the muslin. NA I 3 28 36
five shillings a yard for it, and a true Indian muslin." NA I 3 28 38
"But then you know, madam, muslin always turns to some NA I 3 28 45
Muslin can never be said to be wasted. NA I 3 28 45

Text	Work	Vol	Ch	Page	Line
Miss Tilney was in a very pretty spotted muslin, and I	NA	I	9	68	42
spotted and her tamboured muslin, and nothing but the	NA	I	10	73	22
by the texture of their muslin, and how unsusceptible of	NA	I	10	74	22
first came, not to buy that sprigged muslin, but you would.	NA	I	13	105	36
La! if you have not got your spotted muslin on!--	SS	III	2	276	25
or a really new muslin in a shop window, could recal them.	PP	I	15	72	7
slit in my worked muslin gown, before they are packed up.	PP	III	5	292	60
particulars of calico, muslin, and cambric, and would	PP	III	7	307	48
that if she wanted plain muslin it was of no use to look	E	II	9	235	35
MUSLINS (4)					
"Do you understand muslins, sir?"	NA	I	3	28	37
him on the subject of muslins till the dancing recommenced.	NA	I	3	29	47
nuptials, fine muslins, new carriages, and servants.	PP	III	8	310	7
was still hanging over muslins and changing her mind, Emma	E	II	9	233	24
MUSTARD (1)					
cold pork bones and mustard in William's place, might but	MP	II	11	282	2
MUSTERED (1)					
Not more than five couple could be mustered; but the	E	II	8	230	100
MUTE (1)					
John Knightley only was in mute astonishment.--	E	II	17	302	23
MUTTERED (2)					
Poor Edward muttered something, but what it was, nobody	SS	II	13	243	32
easy, voluble friend, he muttered something of doing	W			344	21
MUTTERING (2)					
well satisfied with his muttering acknowledgment of its	E	I	13	110	10
and muttering something about spruce beer, walked off.	E	III	6	364	57
MUTTERINGS (1)					
Her mutterings were chiefly to her husband; and he	E	III	7	370	21
MUTTON (8)					
there some day or other, and eat their mutton with him.	NA	II	11	209	5
One shoulder of mutton, you know, drives another down.	SS	II	8	197	22
by Dr. Grant to eat his mutton with him the next day; and	MP	II	4	215	47
A turkey or a goose, or a leg of mutton, or whatever you	MP	II	4	215	49
the honour of taking his mutton with them, and Fanny had	MP	III	10	406	22
roast mutton and rice pudding they were hastening home for.	E	I	13	109	6
from the saddle of mutton, to say to her, "we want only	E	I	14	119	6 7
and how small a slice of mutton for dinner, as well as to	E	II	2	168	15
MUTUAL (45)					
after learning, to their mutual relief, that they should	NA	I	4	34	7
We have entered into a contract of mutual agreeableness	NA	I	10	76	29
You have no doubt of the mutual attachment of your brother	NA	II	4	152	28
We parted at last by mutual consent--happy for me had we	NA	II	10	202	7
She believed the regard to be mutual; but she required	SS	I	4	21	11
of the sense, elegance, mutual affection, and domestic	SS	I	10	46	1
of dancing and music was mutual, and that it arose from a	SS	I	10	47	3
together by mutual consent, while the others were dancing.	SS	I	11	55	8
they should part without a mutual exchange of confidence?"	SS	I	15	80	36
had often observed at Norland in their mutual behaviour.	SS	I	16	87	23
of all your mutual affection to support you under them.	SS	II	2	146	6
A mutual silence took place for some time.	SS	II	2	149	24
with each other, of their mutual affection she had no	SS	II	5	174	45
and though their mutual impatience to meet, was not to be	SS	II	11	230	4
of her finding their mutual relatives more disagreeable	SS	II	13	243	34
A short pause of mutual thoughtfulness succeeded.	SS	III	8	327	56
be restored, of their mutual pursuits and cheerful society	SS	III	10	343	8
They were brought together by mutual affection, with the	SS	III	13	369	32
of each other, made that mutual regard inevitable and	SS	III	13	370	36
of the two sisters, whose mutual regard was increasing	W			348	23
was very cheering, and they parted in mutual good spirits.	PP	I	15	74	11
talking together with mutual satisfaction till supper put	PP	I	16	84	59
they parted at last with mutual civility, and possibly a	PP	II	18	235	39
and possibly a mutual desire of never meeting again.	PP	II	18	235	39
Their mutual affection will steady them; and I flatter	PP	III	7	305	37
more engaging, and they talked with mutual satisfaction.	MP	I	9	96	76
they had parted at last with mutual vexation.	MP	II	10	279	21
dissimilar, as to make mutual affection incompatible; and	MP	III	2	327	5
last, and that, united by mutual affection, it would	MP	III	3	335	6
but after a day or two of mutual reserve, he was induced	MP	III	4	345	1
some fifty yards in mutual silence and abstraction.	MP	III	4	351	35
supposed that their tempers became their mutual punishment.	MP	III	17	465	14
friends finding their mutual consolation in each other for	MP	III	17	471	29
each other, their mutual attachment became very strong.	MP	III	17	472	30
as coming directly from their mutual connections in London.	E	I	1	9	21
After a mutual silence of some minutes, Harriet thus began	E	I	10	84	8 9
of Mrs. Churchill's death with mutual forbearance.	E	III	9	388	14
She asked after their mutual friends; they were all well.--	E	III	13	424	1
to increase, their mutual good to outweigh every drawback.	E	III	15	450	36
that good-humoured mutual affection, of which she had	P	III	5	41	45
Their mutual friend answered for the satisfaction which a	P	IV	5	153	5
Mutual enquiries on common subjects passed; neither of	P	IV	7	176	8
by some complication of mutual trick, or some overbearing	P	IV	10	228	70
I always think that no mutual-----"	P	IV	11	230	7
nor his wife entertained a doubt of our mutual attachment.	P	IV	11	242	65
MUTUALLY (5)					
on both sides, which mutually attracted them; and they	SS	II	12	229	2
which kept them mutually silent on the subject; and	PP	I	23	127	9
friend and friend very mutually attached, and Emma doing	E	I	1	5	3
swelling resentment, and mutually deep mortification, they	E	I	15	132	37
them to be very mutually and very sincerely attached."	E	III	13	428	22
MYRTLE (1)					
It certainly may secure all the myrtle and turkey part of	MP	II	4	213	36
MYSTERIES OF UDOLPHO (1)					
The Mysteries of Udolpho, when I had once begun it, I	NA	I	14	106	7
MYSTERIOUS (6)					
significant looks and mysterious expressions to fill up	NA	I	15	120	25
of the lid, was a mysterious cypher, in the same metal.	NA	II	6	163	2
how strangely mysterious!--the door was still immoveable.	NA	II	6	168	10
In this there was surely something mysterious, and she	NA	II	7	173	4
for the proposed examination of the mysterious apartments.	NA	II	9	190	1
to be carried on in so doubtful, so mysterious a manner!	SS	II	4	165	29
MYSTERIOUS WARNINGS (1)					
Castle of Wolfenbach, Clermont, Mysterious Warnings,	NA	I	6	40	10
MYSTERIOUSLY (3)					
a cabinet so mysteriously closed in her immediate vicinity.	NA	II	6	168	10
was, that however mysteriously they might wish to conduct	SS	II	4	160	5
Mr. Knightley does nothing mysteriously."	E	II	8	226	80
MYSTERIOUSNESS (1)					
This sort of mysteriousness, which is always so becoming	NA	I	5	35	2
MYSTERY (12)					
you mean to infer said I, by this appearance of mystery?	LS		24	290	12
on one side in the mystery of an affected secret, on the	NA	I	15	121	25
dressing-gown around you, proceed to examine this mystery.	NA	II	5	159	19
mystery, to proceed in her dressing without further delay.	NA	II	6	164	3
of instantly removing all mystery, that she could not help	SS	I	16	84	7
her in throwing off this last incumbrance of mystery.	PP	II	17	227	25
in, when the mystery of her parentage came to be revealed.	E	I	8	64	47
the mode of it, the mystery, the surprize, is more like a	E	II	8	217	29
Mystery; finesse--how they pervert the understanding!	E	III	15	446	15
sort of anxious parade of mystery fold up a letter which	E	III	16	453	12 13
The disguise, equivocation, mystery, so hateful to her to	E	III	18	475	42
No one can withstand the charm of such a mystery.	P	IV	8	187	33
MYTHOLOGY (1)					
deal of the Heathen Mythology, and all the Metals, Semi-	MP	I	2	18	25

N. (2)
the building in which N. takes M. for better, for worse." E III 17 463 14
Lieut: Smith r.N. capt: little,--Limehouse.-- S 6 389 1
NABOBS (1)
to the existence of nabobs, gold mohrs, and palanquins." SS I 10 51 23
NAIL (2)
to drive it to York and back again, without losing a nail." NA I 9 65 30
"To want to nail me to a card table for the next two hours MP I 12 119 26
NAILED (1)
has been done--one door nailed up--quantities of matting-- E III 2 328 45
NAIVE (1)
You can imagine nothing more naive or piquante; & what do W 340 19
NAIVETE (4)
with a very interesting naivete, "Oh! dear, no, never." E I 6 43 10
11
The naivete of Miss Smith's manners--and altogether--Oh, E I 6 48 39
so lovely a face, and was delighted with with her naivete." E II 8 220 47
spoken of her terror, her naivete, her fervor as she E III 3 335 11
NAME (250)
has once got his name in a banking house he rolls in money. LS 5 250 2
that of your parents, and the credit of your name. LS 12 260 1
introduced to me by the name of Sir James Martin, the very LS 20 275 2
blame on the memory of one, whose name is sacred with me." LS 24 288 11
entirely at an end--his name merely mentioned to say that LS 42 312 3
his name was Richard--and he had never been handsome. NA I 1 13 1
without altering her name as far as she can?) must from NA I 2 19 3
gentlemanlike young man as a partner;--his name was Tilney. NA I 3 25 2
the pleasure of seeing you, but is not your name Allen?" NA I 4 31 2
The name seemed to strike them all; and, after speaking to NA I 4 32 4
of his own college, of the name of Thorpe; and that he had NA I 4 33 5
His name was not in the Pump-Room book, and curiosity NA I 5 35 2
They called each other by their christian name, were NA I 5 37 4
the book, and told its name; though the chances must be NA I 5 38 4
That gentleman knows your name, and you have a right to NA I 10 80 59
Would she be pleased to send up her name? NA I 12 91 3
"dears" at once before the name of Isabella were not more NA I 15 121 27
at her command, a new name on her tickets, and a brilliant NA I 15 122 28
she was at no loss for the name of a very fashionable- NA II 1 131 15
Though his looks did not please her, his name was a NA II 4 149 1
The name of "Eleanor" at the same moment, in his loudest NA II 9 191 4
in which Miss Thorpe's name was included, passed his lips. NA II 10 204 18
No, James should never hear Isabella's name mentioned by NA II 12 218 3
eyes were turned to the ground as she mentioned his name. NA II 13 223 13
Sleep, or repose that deserved the name of sleep, was out NA II 13 227 26
some mention of one whose name had not yet been spoken by NA II 13 229 31
But with this approach to his name ended all possibility NA II 13 229 31
inquired of Thorpe, if he knew more of her than her name. NA II 15 244 12
The terrified General pronounced the name of Allen with an NA II 15 246 13
direction; under another name, and in another course, it SS I 6 29 3
they had to inquire his name and age, admire his beauty, SS I 6 31 9
His name, he replied, was Willoughby, and his present home SS I 9 42 10
His name was good, his residence was in their favourite SS I 9 43 11
knew any gentleman of the name of Willoughby at Allenham. SS I 9 43 12
sister by her christian name alone, she instantly saw an SS I 12 59 7
at the park, to give the name of the young man who was SS I 12 61 15
fixed on a person, whose name she could not bear with SS I 12 61 16
"What is the gentleman's name?" SS I 12 61 21
there was such a man once, and his name begins with an F." SS I 12 62 26
It was several days before Willoughby's name was mentioned SS I 16 85 11
12
in discovering that the name of ferrars began with an F. SS I 18 99 15
patience--or give it a more fascinating name, call it hope. SS I 19 103 7
avoided the mention of his name, appeared to interest SS I 19 104 10
a curiosity to know the name of the gentleman alluded to, SS I 21 125 37
in telling the name, as Miss Steele had in hearing it. SS I 21 125 37
"His name is ferrars," said he, in a very audible whisper; SS I 21 125 38
was taken of Mr. Ferrars's name by Miss Steele when SS I 21 126 41
but surely there must be some mistake of person or name. SS I 22 131 29
as to the name of the man on who all my happiness depends." SS I 22 131 30
I should never have heard him even mention your name." SS I 22 131 31
for ever mentioning my name to you, and as he was always SS I 22 131 32
t'other day, when Edward's name was mentioned by Sir John, SS I 22 133 42
one morning, to beg in the name of charity, that they SS II 1 143 9
his name in a tone of affection, held out her hand to him. SS II 6 176 7
Let her name her own supper, and go to bed. SS II 8 195 16
The name of Willoughby, John Willoughby, frequently SS II 8 199 37
been since informed, is the name of Miss Grey's guardian." SS II 8 199 37
most reluctantly, the name of her lover; and when he SS II 9 211 38
hearing Willoughby's name mentioned, was not thrown away. SS II 10 214 8
never to mention his name again, and she should tell SS II 10 215 10
voluntarily to mention his name before her, till able to SS II 12 229 4
that on merely hearing the name of the Miss Dashwoods, and SS II 14 248 6
determined to find out his name from the latter, when they SS II 14 250 11
Lucy by her christian name; and did not know whether she SS II 14 254 28
gave her likewise no concern, she never mentioned her name. SS III 7 309 6
whenever she mentioned her name, it gave a pang to the SS III 7 312 18
all safely out of the house one morning, and left my name." SS III 8 326 53
copying such sentences as I was ashamed to put my name to. SS III 8 328 63
on its outward leaf her own name in his hand writing.-- SS III 10 342 7
correspondence, for his name was not even mentioned in any SS III 11 353 21
She smiled, and said how she had changed her name since SS III 11 354 29
yet mentioned Edward's name, which does not surprise us; SS III 13 371 38
39
to a young man of the name of Purvis a particular friend W 316 2
"I forget what her name is now?"-- W 325 5
could not be slighted--her name was whispered from one W 328 9
"His name is howard." W 343 19
allow'd to send Emma the name of her shoemaker--& W 347 21
to me?"--said Emma, who had caught her own name.-- W 356 28
"What is his name?" PP I 1 3 11
you shall if you please name the very day of the ball. PP I 9 45 37
I do not remember her name among the ladies at court." PP I 14 67 8
her even to mention his name as they went, for neither PP I 16 84 59
earnestly entreated her to name the day that was to make PP I 22 121 2
to name an early day for making him the happiest of men. PP I 23 128 10
Bingley's name was scarcely ever mentioned between them. PP II 1 137 25
detest his very name, and wish him all manner of evil. PP II 3 150 29
father kept, and what had been her mother's maiden name?-- PP II 6 163 15
and stepping forward with eagerness, pronounced her name. PP II 12 195 2
If you mention my name at the bell, you will be attended PP II 14 212 15
was no escaping the frequent mention of Wickham's name. PP II 16 222 18
It was consequently necessary to name some other period PP II 19 237 3
fine place, what was the name of its proprietor, and with PP II 19 241 17
his tenants or servants but what will give him a good name. PP III 1 249 38
time when Mr. Bingley's name had been last mentioned PP III 1 256 62
In Darcy's presence she dared not mention Wickham's name; PP III 3 269 10
when I write to them, and sign my name Lydia Wickham. PP III 5 291 60
His name had never been voluntarily mentioned before them PP III 6 298 16
full powers to act in your name, throughout the whole of PP III 7 303 14
He did not leave his name, and till the next day, it was PP III 10 323 2
thought him very sly;--he hardly ever mentioned your name. PP III 10 325 2
and whose very name it was punishment to him to pronounce. PP III 10 326 3
But of course she did not mention my name to you." PP III 10 327 11
It was many months since she had mentioned his name to PP III 11 331 16
17
Mr. what's his name. PP III 11 334 34
Elizabeth had mentioned her name to her mother, on her PP III 14 351 3
Your alliance will be a disgrace; your name will never PP III 14 355 46
your sagacity, to discover the name of your admirer. PP III 15 362 12
will not long bear the name of Bennet, after her elder PP III 15 362 14
of our acquaintance, whose name would have given the lie PP III 15 363 18
Let me thank your again and again, in the name of all my PP III 16 366 5
feelings had made her equally avoid the name of his friend. PP III 17 374 19
His daughters he felt, while they retained the name of MP I 2 20 33
As the horse continued in name as well as fact, the MP I 4 37 9
And I am sure, my name was Norval, every evening of my MP I 13 126 25
I could name at this moment at least six young men within MP I 15 148 58
As she entered, her own name caught her ear. MP II 1 177 7
But there is nobleness in the name of Edmund. MP II 4 211 23
It is a name of heroism and renown--of kings, princes, and MP II 4 211 23
"I grant you the name is good in itself, and Lord Edmund MP II 4 211 24
Thornton Lacey was the name of his impending living, as MP II 7 241 19
Miss Price, known only by name to half the people invited, MP II 9 266 22
in addition, for the sake of at least hearing his name. MP II 11 287 17
know them by their proper name; but when he talked of her MP II 12 294 16
I could name three people now, who would give me my own MP II 12 295 20
aunt had to abhor the very name, I would prevent the MP II 12 296 29
his name, Fanny?--when we heard your footsteps." MP III 3 336 9
name of Cardinal Wolsey, that he had got the very speech.-- MP III 3 336 10
Perhaps I have as yet no right--but by what other name can MP III 3 344 41
You have given the name such reality of sweetness, that MP III 3 344 41
not even to mention the name of Crawford again, except as MP III 4 354 48
in which Miss Crawford's name would ever be mentioned MP III 6 373 26
Shall I tell you how Mrs. Rushworth looked when your name MP III 9 393 1
her, I shall never force your name upon her again. MP III 9 394 1
that she had been able to name him to her mother, and MP III 10 399 4
her remembrance of the name, as that of "William's friend," MP III 10 399 4
If I avoided his name entirely, it would look suspicious. MP III 12 416 2
as tranquil as their tempers, was now become a mere name. MP III 13 428 15
It will be but the loss of the Esquire after his name. MP III 14 434 13
near Bedford Square; but I forgot their name and street. MP III 14 434 13
the name of your great cousins in town, fan?" MP III 15 439 9
beautiful Mrs. R. whose name had not long been enrolled in MP III 15 440 14
Long, long would it be ere Miss Crawford's name passed his MP III 16 453 16
To hear the woman whom--no harsher name than folly given!-- MP III 16 454 18
and name, did really belong, afforded her no equals. E I 1 7 10
to have him assume the name of Churchill on coming of age. E I 2 17 7
They were a family of the name of Martin, whom Emma well E I 3 23 10
him fifty times, but without having any idea of his name. E I 4 29 14
I only name possibilities. E I 5 38 15
allowing them to hear your name, your own dear name." E I 7 56 44
The name makes me think of poor Isabella; for she was very E I 9 79 56
One is sick of the very name of Jane Fairfax. E I 10 86 23
to me?" cried Mr. John Knightley, hearing his own name. E I 12 103 41
there was something in the name, in the idea of Mr. Frank E I 14 118 5
Her name was not mentioned;--and there was so striking a E I 17 140 3
in Mr. Dixon's name as well as her own, to press their E II 1 159 20
A week had not passed since Miss Hawkins's name was first E II 4 181 2
christian name, and say whose music she principally played. E II 4 181 2
She brought no name, no blood, no alliance. E II 4 183 9
in or near Highbury; a family of the name of fairfax. E II 5 193 37
not the proper name--I should rather say Barnes, or Bates. E II 5 193 37
Do you know any family of that name?" E II 5 194 37
come for you again; and you had better name an early hour. E II 7 210 14
herself obliged to attend, was the name of Jane Fairfax. E II 8 214 13
the name of "my excellent friend Col. Campbell." E II 8 220 45
And left a name behind her that would not soon die away. E II 9 231 1
The charm of her own name was not wanting. E II 13 266 5
and Mr. Perry, whose name, I dare say, is not unknown to E II 14 275 31
name) shall inquire for your's too and bring them to you. E II 16 295 34
Am I unequal to speaking his name at once before all these E II 16 297 48
No, I can pronounce his name without the smallest distress. E II 16 297 48
Your musical knowledge alone would entitle you to name E II 17 301 18
know him to be my son, though he does not bear my name." E II 18 305 3
People of the name of Tupman, very lately settled there, E II 18 310 34
time, induced them to name as early a day as possible. E III 1 318 11
Let no name ever pass our lips. E III 4 342 39
was growing impatient to name the day, and settle with Mr. E III 6 353 6
Name your day, and I will come. E III 6 354 10
"I cannot name a day," said he, "till I have spoken to E III 6 354 11
I had an acrostic once sent to me upon my own name, which E III 7 372 37
I really cannot venture to name her salary to you, Miss E III 8 382 23
any hour that Jane would name--mentioning that she had Mr. E III 9 390 16
connected with any human being of the name of Knightley." E III 10 393 15
Emma could not speak the name of Dixon without a little E III 10 399 59
I know we agreed never to name him--but considering how E III 11 405 18
and she was ready to give it every bad name in the world. E III 11 408 33
She had no hope, nothing to deserve the name of hope, that E III 12 416 1
He is a disgrace to the name of man.-- E III 13 426 16
like perfect happiness, that it could bear no other name. E III 13 432 40
indulged myself in calling her by that name, even to you. E III 14 441 8
I knew the name, the place, I knew all about it, and E III 14 442 8
As soon as she came to her own name, it was irresistible; E III 15 444 1
That was your name for him, was it?" E III 15 448 28
at home, to wait in the passage, and send up her name.-- E III 16 452 8
will promise to call you once by your christian name. E III 17 463 14
No sacrifice on any side worth the name. E III 17 468 31
Her cheeks flushed at the name, and she felt afraid of E III 18 470 9
return of the Campbells, he named the name of Dixon.-- E III 18 477 51
Frank Churchill caught the name. E III 18 479 74
reading her name in any other page of his favourite work. P III 1 6 10
No; he would never disgrace his name so far. P III 1 10 20
'In the name of heaven, who is that old fellow?' said I, P III 3 20 16
Bless me! what was his name? P III 3 23 25
At this moment I cannot recollect his name, though I have P III 3 23 25
Penelope, my dear, can you help me to the name of the P III 3 23 25
I shall forget my own name soon, I suppose. P III 3 23 28
A name that I am so very well acquainted with; knew the P III 3 23 28
"Wentworth was the very name! P III 3 23 32
to change her name, by the young man, who not long P III 4 28 7
Mrs. Croft's here soon; I dare say you know him by name." P III 6 49 23
24
very like it, was the name of poor Richard's captain, at P III 6 50 27
to more than the abbreviation of his name, living or dead. P III 6 51 29
with a recollection of the name of Wentworth, as connected P III 6 51 31
Wentworth, repeating his name so often, puzzling over past P III 6 52 33
little statement of her name and rate, and present non- P III 8 66 22
tell us the name of the gentleman who is just gone away?" P III 12 105 11
and many had repeated the name, before all this had been P III 12 105 13
What, in heaven's name, is to be done next?" P III 12 111 45
and Captain Wentworth's name must be mentioned by both. P IV 1 124 12
She could not speak the name, and look straight forward to P IV 1 124 12
When this was told, his name distressed her no longer. P IV 1 125 12
The name of Musgrove would have told him enough. P IV 3 144 19
Lady Dalrymple had acquired the name of "a charming woman," P IV 4 150 14
Mrs. Smith, such a name!" P IV 5 158 19
she was, in situation, and name, and home, presiding and P IV 5 160 25
of having the precious name of "Lady Elliot" first revived P IV 5 160 26
But first of all, you must tell me the name of the young P IV 6 170 31
Her christian name--I always forget her christian name." P IV 6 170 31
did; but now she could safely suggest the name of "Louisa." P IV 6 170 32
"Ay, ay, Miss Louisa Musgrove, that is the name. P IV 6 171 33
he had ever thought of this Miss (what's her name?) for P IV 6 173 47
"The name of Anne Elliot," said he, "has long had an P IV 8 188 36
would breathe my wishes that the name might never change." P IV 8 188 36
"No, I just know his name. P IV 8 188 40
or notoriety in Bath was well known by name to Mrs. Smith. P IV 9 193 5
pounds, arms and motto, name and livery included; but I P IV 9 202 66
"I wish I had any name but Elliot. P IV 9 203 73
"The name of walter I can drop, thank God! and I desire " P IV 9 203 73
by his well-sounding name, enabled Sir Walter at last to P IV 12 248 2
Mr Heywood, such was the name of the said proprietor, S 1 365 1
My name is Parker.-- S 1 368 1
We are on our road home from London;--my name perhaps-- S 1 368 1

What in the name of common sense is to recommend Brinshore? S 1 369 1
Waterloo Crescent--& the name joined to the form of the S 4 380 1
Charlotte having added her name to the list as the first S 6 390 1
The very name of Sir Edward he thought, carried some S 8 405 2
a mere name with you all, that it can do you no good.-- S 9 411 1
That good woman (I do not know her name) not being so S 9 411 1
That both should have the same name.-- S 10 418 1
Camberwell--& her name happens to be griffiths too.--" S 10 419 1
better,--& Lady Denham's name at the head of the list will S 12 423 1

NAMED (22)
The breakfast-room was gay with company; and she was named NA II 9 192 4
and the gentleman having named the last day on which his SS II 11 221 5
I do not think Tom Musgrave should be named with him in W 316 2
made; and as she named their relationship to herself, she PP III 1 255 59
and an early day was named, and agreed to, provided Mr. MP I 8 75 1
visit, to hear the day named; but he had only spoken of MP III 1 311 1
was too impossible to be named but with indignation. MP III 16 460 31
woman, and a woman whom no one named without good-will. E I 3 21 4
him a wife, I should certainly have named Miss Taylor." E I 5 38 11
Henry is the eldest, he was named after me, not after his E I 9 80 72
John, the second, is named after his father. E I 9 80 72
told you all that he would be here before the time named. E II 5 190 24
His wedding-day was named. E II 13 267 8
were right who had named Mrs. Churchill as the cause. E III 6 363 53
heard named as a salary on such occasions, dearly earned." E III 8 382 24
I could almost assert that you had named Mr. Frank E III 11 406 21
return of the Campbells, he named the name of Dixon.-- E III 18 477 51
could not but be named by him, in the little narratives or P III 8 63 2
arch significance as he named her; but yet it was Captain P IV 7 176 8
Anne named them all. P IV 7 180 35
not named Trafalgar--for Waterloo is more the thing now. S 4 380 1
Miss Heywood on her being named to him--and they parted, S 12 425 1

NAMELESS (4)
except that of one gentleman, who shall be nameless. NA I 6 41 16
because a certain person that shall be nameless is gone!" SS I 18 100 20
person who shall be nameless, had been there, you would SS II 5 171 36
recent acquaintance, by nameless people, is irresistible; P IV 8 187 33

NAMES (29)
children; I know all their names already, & am going to LS 5 250 2
"I will read you their names directly; here they are, in NA I 6 40 10
Isabella examined the names, it was Catherine's employment NA I 6 43 34
manner; addressing her by the most endearing names. NA I 13 98 2
the post-masters for the names of the places which were NA II 14 232 6
at his total silence with respect even to their names. SS I 22 134 49
the stairs, heard their names announced from one landing- SS II 6 175 2
to their knowledge of the officers' names and connections. PP I 7 28 4
names, facts, every thing mentioned without ceremony.-- PP I 17 85 5
honours of this house the names of his cousin Miss de PP I 18 96 57
He was storing his memory with anecdotes and noble names. PP II 6 166 41
but without mentioning names or any other particulars, and PP II 10 185 28
or allow their names to be mentioned in your hearing." PP III 15 364 22
with the names of people and parties, that fill up my time. MP III 12 415 2
I mention no names; but happy the man who changes Emma for E II 13 269 16
did not know that proper names were allowed," pushed away E III 5 349 23
She had given them neither men, nor names, nor places, E III 6 358 35
whisper, "I mentioned no names, you will observe.-- E III 16 454 14
15
One wonders how the names of many of our nobility become P III 3 23 33
were they as to the names of men or ships, that it had P III 6 51 31
like his, noted down the names of those she recommended, P III 11 101 25
One of the five thousand Mr. Smiths whose names are to be P IV 5 157 15
of all people and all names in the world, to be the chosen P IV 5 158 19
The names which occasionally dropt of former associates, P IV 5 161 27
young ladies had not such a number of fine christian names. P IV 6 171 33
He would mention no names now; but such, he could assure P IV 8 187 34
& Miss Denham, whose names might be said to lead off the S 6 389 1
as to names--which have but lately transpired.-- S 9 408 1
An accidental resemblance of names & circumstances, S 10 419 1

NAMING (7)
General, after slightly naming a few of the distinguished NA II 8 185 5
and Sir John against ever naming Mr. Willoughby, or making SS II 8 195 17
without actually naming her authority, but stating it to PP III 1 258 75
without fear; there can be no difficulties worth naming. MP II 13 303 15
in his manner of naming Harriet at parting; in the tone of E I 13 111 14
had the advantage of naming among their acquaintance, and E II 8 214 13
and at last, Mr. Weston naming one family of cousins who E II 11 248 9

NANCY (7)
'Lord! here comes your beau, Nancy,' my cousin said SS II 10 218 26
creature knowing a syllable of the matter except Nancy!-- SS III 1 258 7
this very morning, poor Nancy, who, you know, is a well- SS III 1 258 7
Nancy, she fell upon her knees, and cried bitterly; and SS III 1 259 7
she could hardly walk; and Nancy, she was almost as bad. SS III 1 259 7
of the matter, not even Nancy, who, poor soul! came crying SS III 13 370 37
make a shew with, and poor Nancy had not seven shillings SS III 13 370 37

NANKIN (2)
a half-boot; nankin galoshed with black looks very well.-- W 345 21
Blue shoes, & nankin boots!-- S 4 383 1

NANNY (10)
But first of all Nanny shall bring in the dinner. W 341 19
Nanny brought in the dinner;--"we will wait upon ourselves, W 341 19
On the 3d day after the ball, as Nanny at five minutes W 344 21
Mr Watson, as the gentlemen had already heard from Nanny, W 345 21
briskly after Nanny "to tell Betty to take up the fowls."-- W 346 21
I am glad Nanny had not laid the cloth however, it wd have W 347 22
agreably occupied; & when Nanny came in with her master's W 359 28
I will send Nanny to London on purpose, and she may have a MP I 1 8 8
their own trouble; and Nanny shall fetch her, however it MP I 1 9 12
house with some orders for Nanny," said she, "which I have MP III 1 323 54

NANNY'S (2)
they were interrupted by Nanny's approach, who half W 346 21
Except to the attack on Nanny's cousin, Sir Thomas no MP I 1 8 9

NAPKINS (1)
much upon silver forks, napkins, and finger classes. MP III 15 446 35

NARRATION (7)
Her narration was clear and simple; and though it could SS III 1 261 12
Jennings; but after this narration of what really passed SS III 3 284 24
speedily hazarding her narration, without feeling at all SS III 10 347 32
Emma concluded her narration.-- W 342 19
having any regular narration to attend to, pursued only by E II 9 239 52
and tautology of the narration, a substance to sink her E III 11 409 34
account of the whole; a narration in which she saw a great P IV 10 216 19

NARRATIVE (4)
This, madam, is a faithful narrative of every event in PP II 12 202 5
of devotion to Agatha's narrative, and pressing her hand MP II 1 175 2
She carried this point, and Sir Thomas's narrative MP II 1 180 12
who bore a part in the narrative, and was always mentioned E I 4 27 5

NARRATIVES (2)
filled by his narratives, that she began particularly to MP II 1 179 9
narratives or descriptions which conversation called forth. P III 8 63 2

NARRATOR (2)
You will find me a very awkward narrator, Miss Dashwood; I SS II 9 204 20
Her aunt was no very methodical narrator; but with the MP II 16 449 7

NARROW (21)
his brother's widow & in narrow circumstances it was LS 3 247 1
in their way along narrow, winding vaults, by a low, NA I 11 88 54
Its long, damp passages, its narrow cells and ruined NA II 2 141 11
It was a narrow winding path through a thick grove of old NA II 7 179 29
A narrow passage led directly through the house into the SS I 6 28 2
such as society produced, within a very narrow compass. SS I 7 32 1
About a mile and a half from the cottage, along the narrow SS I 9 40 2
"With dark narrow stairs, and a kitchen that smokes, I SS I 14 72 12
for the stream, and a narrow walk amidst the rough coppice- PP III 1 253 57
complains bitterly of the narrow lanes scratching his MP I 8 77 12
find no inconvenience from narrow roads on Wednesday." MP I 8 77 13
had ridden, or his many narrow escapes from dreadful falls, MP II 6 237 23
they were rattled into a narrow street, leading from the MP III 7 376 6
Another moment, and Fanny was in the narrow entrance- MP III 7 377 9
A single woman, with a very narrow income, must be a E I 10 85 19
at first; for a very narrow income has a tendency to E I 10 85 19
footstep which ended the narrow, slippery path through the E I 10 87 27
took possession of a narrow footpath, a little raised on E I 10 88 33
any body, and where the narrow paths across the fields P III 10 84 7
knowledge of their narrow income & pecuniary difficulties, S 3 378 1
of the paling & which a narrow path seemed to skirt along;- S 12 426 1

NARROW-MINDED (3)
He blushed for the narrow-minded counsel which he was NA II 15 247 15
caricature of himself;-- more narrow-minded and selfish. SS I 1 5 7
a conceited, pompous, narrow-minded, silly man; you know PP II 1 135 13

NARROWER (3)
glance beyond them, a narrower passage, more numerous NA II 8 185 5
Having married on a narrower income than she had been used MP I 1 8 9
staircase--rather darker and narrower than one could wish. E II 9 239 53

NARROWEST (1)
to the edge of the water, in one of its narrowest parts. PP III 1 253 57

NARROWLY (6)
To escape, and, as she believed, so narrowly escape John NA I 10 75 24
and gold, which, though narrowly examining the furniture NA II 5 160 21
I observed him narrowly, and am convinced of it. SS II 11 223 20
though she soon perceived them to be narrowly watching her. SS II 13 241 20
warm commendation of him, narrowly observed them both. PP II 2 142 18
I had narrowly observed her during the two visits which I PP III 16 371 43

NARROWNESS (2)
below indeed, and the narrowness of the passage and MP III 7 387 47
their slow pace & the narrowness of the lane, & the S 1 364 1

NASTY (3)
Open carriages are nasty things. NA I 13 104 32
But I can't bear to see them dirty and nasty. SS I 21 123 28
Who could about such a nasty little freckled thing?" PP II 16 220 14

NATION (8)
on the state of the nation, was put an end to by Catherine, NA I 14 111 29
(the hope of the nation,) called up from Northampton to NA I 14 113 39
the affairs of the nation for hours after you are asleep. NA II 8 187 15
of London, I am speaking of the nation at large." MP I 9 93 47
not what they ought to be, so are the rest of the nation." MP I 9 93 49
dozen in the nation,) always needs a note of explanation. P III 3 24 36
the great nation not having much improved our condition. P III 8 66 16
with all new poems and states of the nation that come out. P IV 10 215 15

NATIONAL (2)
to the less national, & important demands of the women.-- W 356 28
in its domestic virtues than in its national importance. P IV 12 252 12

NATIVE (7)
of her career, to her native village, in the triumph of NA II 14 232 7
Mr. Weston was a native of Highbury, and born of a E I 2 15 1
wish her to try her native air, as she has not been quite E II 1 161 25
a few months spent in her native air, for the recovery of E II 2 166 10
As to the pretence of trying her native air, I look upon E II 8 217 32
but what can any body's native air do for them in the E II 8 217 32
make, Admiral Croft was a native of Somersetshire, who P III 3 21 18

NATURAL (189)
but no more than was natural; & I did not wonder at his LS 8 255 2
to be excellent, & her natural abilities very good. LS 18 273 2
Do you think me destitute of every honest, every natural LS 24 289 12
"Why, indeed!" said he, in his natural tone--"but some NA I 3 26 8
Feelings rather natural than heroic possessed her; instead NA I 12 93 4
a more cordial, more natural smile into his countenance, NA I 12 93 7
The advantages of natural folly in a beautiful girl have NA I 14 111 29
satisfied of her having a great deal of natural taste. NA I 14 111 29
all her friendship and natural affection; for no thought NA I 14 114 50
her mind; and, with the natural blush of so new an emotion, NA I 15 117 7
natural course of things, she must ere long be released. NA II 8 188 16
his silence would be the natural result of the suspected NA II 11 209 5
of actual and natural evil, the solitude of her situation, NA II 13 227 26
What so natural, as that anger should pass away and NA II 13 227 27
and agitation, but the natural consequence of mortified NA II 14 235 13
after all, could be more natural than Catherine's being NA II 16 249 1
to himself; but when his natural shyness was overcome, his SS I 3 15 6
by no means deficient in natural taste, though he has not SS I 4 19 2
of improving that natural taste for your favourite pursuit SS I 4 22 17
captivating person, but a natural ardour of mind which was SS I 10 48 7
of spirits, than of any natural gloominess of temper. SS I 10 50 12
To her it was but the natural consequence of a strong SS I 11 54 4
little, she said to Elinor, "she is his natural daughter." SS I 13 66 57
It would be the natural result of your affection for her. SS I 16 84 8
Barton was, in her opinion, of all things the most natural. SS I 17 90 1
when I am only kept back by my natural awkwardness. SS I 17 94 42
of enough; but it is so natural in Lady Middleton; and for SS I 21 122 19
probabilities to make it natural that Lucy should be SS II 1 142 7
Jennings, with all her natural hilarity, burst forth again. SS II 8 196 21
so inexperienced as Mrs. Brandon's, was but too natural. SS II 9 206 24
be the same; and had the natural sweet disposition of the SS II 9 208 28
and face, of strong natural, sterling insignificance, SS II 11 220 3
of sense, either natural or improved--want of elegance-- SS II 12 233 18
It is but natural that he should like to see her as well SS II 13 244 45
it much less to any natural deficiency, than to the SS II 14 250 12
She would not even admit it to have been natural; and SS III 1 261 13
Your exclamation is very natural." SS III 1 267 40
determined, with a very natural kind of spirit, to settle SS III 1 269 53
produced from Mrs. Jennings the following natural remark. SS III 2 276 27
in a point of such common, such natural, concern!-- SS III 5 295 12
Do not think yourself excused by any weakness, any natural SS III 8 322 37
more natural, more gentle, less dignified, forgiveness. SS III 8 330 67
Colonel Brandon, but the natural embellishments of her SS III 9 336 13
slow; and with youth, natural strength, and her mother's SS III 10 340 1
saw only an emotion too natural in itself to raise SS III 10 342 7
could have been more natural than Lucy's conduct, nor more SS III 13 367 24
feelings & more natural smiles than they had taken away.-- W 323 3
time as must do away all natural affection among us & W 352 26
What could be more natural than his asking you again? PP I 4 14 5
slight preference is natural enough; but there are very PP I 6 21 2
She had high animal spirits, and a sort of natural self- PP I 9 45 36
some particular evil, a natural defect, which not even the PP I 11 58 30
discourse, however your natural delicacy may lead you to PP I 19 105 8
combated by the more natural influence Jane's attractions. PP II 2 142 16
was, my confidence was as natural as your suspicion. PP II 3 148 26
anxiety she may feel on his behalf, is natural and amiable. PP II 3 148 26
Nothing, on the contrary, could be more natural; and while PP II 5 150 26
enjoyment of music than myself, or a better natural taste. PP II 8 173 6
It is natural that obligation should be felt, and if I PP II 11 190 7
They were natural and just. PP II 11 192 22
But Bingley has great natural modesty, with a stronger PP II 12 199 5
appear perfectly natural; and all surprise was shortly PP II 17 224 2
bitterness, is a most natural consequence of the PP II 17 226 21
might in time regain her natural degree of sense, since PP II 19 237 3
front, a stream of some natural importance was swelled PP III 1 245 3
had done more, or where natural beauty had been so little PP III 1 245 3
But now it was all too natural. PP III 4 279 24
Kitty then owned, with a very natural triumph on knowing PP III 5 290 50
so natural as abhorrence against relationship with Wickham. PP III 10 326 3
her judgment, but it was natural to suppose the he thought PP III 15 360 2
It was the natural result of the conduct of each party, MP I 1 4 1
to have any thing like natural shyness, and their MP I 2 12 3
have been beyond his natural claims on us, and that MP I 3 23 3
"Yes, I dare say you will; that's natural enough. MP I 3 25 12
she will force you to do justice to your natural powers." MP I 3 27 33

Context	Work	Vol	Ch	Page	Line
hardly knows what the natural taste of our apricot is; he	MP	I	6	54	13
myself, and where the natural taste is equal, the player	MP	I	6	59	41
Its natural beauties, I am sure, are great.	MP	I	6	61	53
"Excessively: but what with the natural advantages of the	MP	I	6	61	56
of his wife: but it is natural and amiable that Miss	MP	I	7	63	7
this; what could be more natural than that Edmund should	MP	I	7	67	16
darkness and shade, and natural beauty, compared with the	MP	I	9	91	38
There was no natural disinclination to be overcome, and I	MP	I	11	109	17
feel, is perfectly natural; and equally so that my value	MP	II	1	186	34
is so very natural, that she can argue nothing from that.	MP	II	3	199	14
To Fanny herself it appeared a very simple and natural	MP	II	4	206	5
One cannot fix one's eyes on the commonest natural	MP	II	4	209	16
"But is not it very natural," observed Edmund, "that Mrs.	MP	II	5	218	17
"Nothing can be more natural," said Sir Thomas, after a	MP	II	5	218	18
in the case, could any thing in my opinion be more natural.	MP	II	5	218	18
temper, made it as natural for him to express as to feel.	MP	II	6	234	17
It is perfectly natural that you should not have thought	MP	II	7	247	42
in true generosity and natural delicacy as to make the few	MP	II	9	263	16
Every thing natural, probable, reasonable was against it;	MP	II	13	305	26
a request too natural, a claim too just to be denied.	MP	III	1	321	48
boys, the consequently natural--yet in some instances	MP	III	3	339	22
I consider it as most natural that all your family should	MP	III	4	346	12
the wish to love him--the natural wish of gratitude.	MP	III	4	348	21
assiduities, and the natural workings of her own mind.	MP	III	5	356	2
simple lines expressed so natural and motherly a joy in	MP	III	6	371	17
soon produced their natural effect on Fanny's spirits,	MP	III	7	375	1
growth, began with very natural solicitude to feel for	MP	III	7	378	13
disposed to admire the natural light of the mind which	MP	III	9	395	4
She was nice only from natural delicacy, but he had been	MP	III	10	407	23
Crawford is, it is most natural that she should tell you	MP	III	13	420	2
Believe me, they are not only natural, they are	MP	III	14	434	13
made it natural to her to treat the subject as she did.	MP	III	16	456	25
time when it was quite natural that it should be so, and	MP	III	17	470	26
growing worth, what could be more natural than the change?	MP	III	17	470	27
had to deal with, and no natural timidity to restrain any	MP	III	17	472	31
with all her advantages, natural and domestic, she was now	E	I	1	6	7
Harriet Smith was the natural daughter of somebody.	E	I	3	22	8
Those soft blue eyes and all those natural graces should	E	I	3	23	10
too palpably desirable, natural, and probable, for her to	E	I	4	34	44
She had all the natural grace of sweetness of temper and	E	I	6	42	3
and I suppose may have a natural talent for--thinks	E	I	7	51	5
She is the natural daughter of nobody knows whom, with	E	I	8	61	38
you and Mr. Elton were most desirable or most natural.	E	I	9	74	20
"Very well," replied Emma, "a most natural feeling; and	E	I	9	77	45
her, was the most natural thing in the world, or would	E	I	10	88	33
would have been the most natural, had she been acting just	E	I	10	88	33
that any natural defects in it should not be increased.	E	I	11	92	5
being taken away from his parents and natural home!	E	I	11	96	25
the little party made two natural divisions; on one side	E	I	12	100	15
it would be most natural, that while she makes no	E	I	14	123	24
To youth and natural cheerfulness like Emma's, though	E	I	16	137	13
yet it appeared to her so natural, so inevitable to strive	E	I	17	142	12
It is a great deal more natural than one could wish, that	E	I	18	145	10
else; but it was very natural, you know, that he should	E	II	1	159	20
give way to all his natural kind-hearted civility in	E	II	5	193	35
women together; and it is natural to suppose that we	E	II	6	203	39
and thought it the most natural thing in the world.	E	II	8	219	42
right; it was most natural to pay your visit, then"-----	E	II	12	261	30
					31
It was natural for him to feel that he had cause to sigh.	E	II	12	261	32
and respect which was natural and honourable, and	E	II	13	265	5
with expressing a natural and reasonable admiration--but	E	II	15	282	4
in spite of the very natural wish of a little change."	E	II	15	286	21
Her Bath habits made evening-parties perfectly natural to	E	II	16	290	3
It was natural to have some civil hopes on the subject,	E	II	16	293	10
					11
and where the same master teaches, it is natural enough.	E	II	16	297	45
like a bride, but my natural taste is all for simplicity;	E	II	17	302	22
had produced this very natural and very desirable effect.	E	III	1	316	3
a manner, with what natural grace, he must have danced,	E	III	2	326	32
Every thing was to take its natural course, however,	E	III	3	335	11
"It is very natural.	E	III	4	342	39
It is natural, and it is honourable.--	E	III	4	342	39
Every thing as natural and simple as possible.	E	III	6	355	20
My idea of the simple and the natural will be to have the	E	III	6	355	21
her how she did, in the natural key of his voice, sunk it	E	III	10	392	1
					2
Half a dozen natural children, perhaps--and poor Frank cut	E	III	10	393	18
you, it was extremely natural:--and you agreed to it,	E	III	11	406	23
One natural consequence of the evil she had involved	E	III	12	419	12
of, as it might be natural for a woman to feel in	E	III	13	426	17
Now, however, I see nothing in it but a very natural and	E	III	14	441	8
maintain itself, by the natural return of her former	E	III	15	444	1
"It will be natural for me," he added shortly afterwards, "	E	III	15	445	8
Natural enough!--his own mind full of intrigue, that he	E	III	15	446	15
"His feelings are natural.--	E	III	15	447	22
It was very natural for you to say, what right has he to	E	III	17	462	7
I am afraid very natural for you to feel that it was done	E	III	17	462	7
which appeared perfectly natural, as there was a dentist	E	III	17	463	16
already beginning, and in the most gradual, natural manner.	E	III	19	482	5
seldom leaves a man's looks to the natural effect of time.	P	III	3	20	17
No second attachment, the only thoroughly natural, happy,	P	III	4	28	7
grew older--the natural sequel of an unnatural beginning.	P	III	4	30	9
Anne found it most natural to take her almost daily walk	P	III	5	32	1
when she found it most natural to be sorry that she had	P	III	5	32	1
and oblivion of the past--how natural, how certain too!	P	III	7	60	28
but, except from some natural sensation of curiosity, he	P	III	7	61	37
When she could let her attention take its natural course	P	III	8	64	7
with so much sympathy and natural grace, as shewed the	P	III	8	67	28
the confusion that was natural; and if the child had not	P	III	9	79	23
It was all quite natural, however.	P	III	12	116	70
In Lady Russell's view, it was perfectly natural that Mr.	P	IV	4	147	7
"I love your indignation," said he; "it is very natural.	P	IV	4	151	21
accomplished for modesty to be natural in any other woman."	P	IV	8	187	28
which it is very natural for him now, with so many affairs	P	IV	9	196	32
to avoid and get rid of as he can--very natural, perhaps.	P	IV	9	196	32
she cried, in her natural tone of cordiality, "I beg your	P	IV	9	198	52
					53
hinted at, were dwelt on now with a natural indulgence.	P	IV	9	210	97
She had no natural connexions to assist her even with	P	IV	9	210	98
thoughtful expression which seemed its natural character.	P	IV	11	232	12
of character, a natural penetration, in short, which no	P	IV	12	249	4
no pretensions; but some natural advantages in its	S		2	371	1
now, as to give her conduct that natural explanation.	S		3	376	1
She has good natural sense, but quite uncultivated.--	S		3	376	1
veiw, as with all her natural endowments & powers, to have	S		3	379	1
conscious importance or a natural love of talking, she	S		7	399	1
Some natural delicacy of constitution in fact, with an	S		10	412	1

NATURALLY (73)

Context	Work	Vol	Ch	Page	Line
She is poor, & may naturally seek an alliance which may be	LS		12	261	4
Mrs. Morland will be naturally supposed to be most severe.	NA	I	2	18	2
After chatting some time on such matters as naturally	NA	I	3	25	2
the respect which they naturally inspired might have been	NA	I	4	33	7
her first address naturally was--"my dearest creature,	NA	I	6	39	2
Milsom-Street; I am naturally indifferent about flowers."	NA	II	7	174	7
horrid suggestions which naturally sprang from these words.	NA	II	8	186	13
steady affection, would naturally call forth; and great	NA	II	14	237	21
Catherine's disposition was not naturally sedentary, nor	NA	II	15	240	1
future heiress of Fullerton naturally followed.	NA	II	15	245	12
and familiarity which naturally attended these parties	SS	I	11	53	1
Lucy was naturally clever; her remarks were often just and	SS	I	22	127	2
The youthful infatuation of nineteen would naturally blind	SS	II	1	140	2
many circumstances it naturally would during a four years'	SS	II	2	147	8
having heard him would naturally produce; in the extasy of	SS	II	4	161	7
which our separation naturally produced, with the	SS	II	7	187	42
visiting her, very naturally; for we only knew that Mrs.	SS	II	11	228	53
without beauty, and naturally without expression; but a	SS	II	12	232	15
as the subject might naturally be supposed to produce.	SS	III	1	260	8
of riches, which I was naturally inclined to feel, and	SS	III	8	323	40
united a disposition naturally open and honest, and a	SS	III	8	331	70
affection of both, he naturally expected that one or two	SS	III	14	376	11
family affection would naturally dictate;--and among the	SS	III	14	380	21
pause went on--"you will naturally ask why it did not take	W			316	2
the papers, seemed very naturally to have caught something	W			322	3
It was well for her that she was naturally cheerful;--for	W			362	31
and leading naturally to the avowal of his hopes, that a	PP	I	15	70	3
given him would naturally flow from her bashful modesty	PP	I	20	110	1
who naturally looks for happiness in the marriage state.	PP	I	20	110	4
me may to you very naturally appear insufficient, I have	PP	II	12	199	5
discharge of his trust, naturally inclined my father to be	PP	II	12	199	5
anxious to please, she naturally suspected that every	PP	III	2	260	1
In seeing Bingley, her thoughts naturally flew to her	PP	III	2	262	8
to her feelings; which are naturally lively enough.	PP	III	5	284	10
own disposition must be naturally bad, or she could not be	PP	III	6	297	11
over, he naturally returned to all his former indolence.	PP	III	8	309	5
This naturally introduced a panegyric from Jane on his	PP	III	13	350	51
interruption; which naturally leading to the cause of that	PP	III	16	370	33
acquirements, a manner naturally easy, and carefully	MP	I	4	34	4
had left Mansfield, she naturally became every thing to	MP	I	4	35	6
and improving, for naturally I am excessively fond of it.	MP	I	6	53	9
and Fanny, who seemed as naturally to unite, and who after	MP	I	9	90	36
"Naturally, I believe, I am as lively as Julia, but I have	MP	I	10	99	15
"It falls as naturally, as necessarily to her," said he, "	MP	I	14	133	10
to oppose her, had so naturally and so artlessly worked	MP	I	16	151	1
to Mansfield must naturally hold out the greatest	MP	II	3	201	22
Fanny naturally turned up stairs, and took her guest to	MP	III	5	357	6
Her disposition was naturally easy and indolent, like Lady	MP	III	8	390	5
Her temper was naturally the easiest of the two, her	MP	III	17	466	17
removal, succeeded so naturally to her influence over the	MP	III	17	472	31
in general, formed naturally a great part of her	E	I	4	27	4
Consider, she is sitting down--which naturally presents a	E	I	6	48	35
a pen in hand, his thoughts naturally find proper words.	E	I	7	51	5
money-matters; he might naturally be rather attentive than	E	I	8	67	57
in after his wife very naturally; so that Emma found, on	E	I	15	128	23
as might naturally belong to their friendship.	E	I	18	144	4
Mr. Dixon, which she had so naturally started to herself.	E	II	2	167	13
they might resent, how naturally Harriet must suffer.	E	II	5	187	4
And, seriously, Miss Fairfax is naturally so pale, as	E	II	6	199	9
He did not boast, but it naturally betrayed itself, that	E	II	8	221	49
Miss Woodhouse, one naturally wishes them to see as much	E	II	14	274	28
I am sure I never suspected it, you did it so naturally."	E	III	4	339	14
that Jane might very naturally resolve on seeing Mrs. Cole	E	III	8	379	9
Randall's, and falling naturally into a comparison of the	E	III	18	480	80
affairs, changed naturally into pity and contempt, as he	P	III	1	3	1
which had naturally grown out of their conversation.	P	III	11	100	23
naturally clear, and only erring in the heyday of youth.	P	IV	4	147	7
They were people whom her heart turned to very naturally.	P	IV	6	162	2
acquaintance with you, very naturally brings it all to me.	P	IV	9	205	82
and in return, she naturally fell into all her wonted ways	P	IV	10	220	31
a sweetly modest & yet naturally graceful address,	S		6	391	1
If he were constrained so to act, he must naturally wish	S		8	405	2
the Miss Bs--, though naturally preferring any thing to	S		11	421	1

NATURE (201)

Context	Work	Vol	Ch	Page	Line
engagement of that nature without acquainting your mother	LS		12	260	1
a simpleton who has it either by nature or affectation.	LS		19	274	3
his feelings must be; the nature of mine as I listened to	LS		23	284	5
not in his nature to refuse, when urged in such a manner?"	LS		24	290	12
whose sensibilities are not of a nature to comprehend ours.	LS		30	301	4
Catherine, who had by nature nothing heroic about her,	NA	I	1	15	3
important and applicable nature must of course flow from	NA	I	2	18	2
Nature may have done something, but I am sure it must be	NA	I	3	27	28
knowledge of human nature, the happiest delineation of its	NA	I	5	38	4
no notion of loving people by halves, it is not my nature.	NA	I	6	40	14
of so impertinent a nature, so unfortunately connected	NA	I	7	44	1
they are worth reading; some fun and nature in them."	NA	I	7	49	36
all acquainted with human nature in a civilized state can	NA	I	14	109	25
and hastily replied, "indeed!--and of what nature?"	NA	I	14	112	30
In my opinion, nature has given them so much, that they	NA	I	14	114	47
express; the nature of them, however, contented her friend.	NA	I	15	118	8
that the smallest income in nature would be enough for me.	NA	I	15	119	20
by any thing in his nature to urge; and she hurried away,	NA	I	15	124	47
that no syllable of such a nature ever passed between us.	NA	II	3	144	11
Human nature could support no more.	NA	II	6	170	12
describing the nature of his own as they entered them.	NA	II	7	178	24
to hide from herself the nature of the feelings which, in	NA	II	7	181	40
Dear Miss Morland, consider the dreadful nature of the	NA	II	9	197	29
them perhaps that human nature, at least in the midland	NA	II	10	200	3
always do, what is most to the credit of human nature.--	NA	II	10	207	40
enjoyment of no every-day nature for those to whom she	NA	II	14	233	8
recommendation of such a nature at such a time, and he	SS	I	1	5	6
more doubtful seemed the nature of his regard; and	SS	I	4	22	18
all the deficiencies of nature and education; supported	SS	I	7	32	1
yet apprehensive of losing him in the course of nature.	SS	I	8	37	8
with the readiness of good-breeding and good nature."	SS	I	10	51	20
"are of such a nature--that--I dare not flatter myself"--	SS	I	15	76	15
doubt the nature of the terms on which they are together.	SS	I	15	80	38
have been intended by nature to be fond of low company, I	SS	I	17	94	42
of the beauties of nature than they really feel, and is	SS	I	18	97	6
sisters, at least by the nature of their employments,	SS	I	19	105	12
was strongly endowed by nature with a turn for being	SS	I	19	106	23
but her beauty and good nature; but the four succeeding	SS	II	1	140	2
"I am rather of a jealous temper too by nature, and from	SS	II	2	147	12
would be of a different nature--she must then learn to	SS	II	4	159	1
opinion, than believe his nature capable of such cruelty.	SS	II	7	189	50
Her kindness is not sympathy; her good nature in not	SS	II	9	201	3
education myself, had the nature of our situations allowed	SS	II	9	208	28
Bad indeed must the nature of Marianne's affliction be,	SS	II	10	213	2
The nature of her commendation, in the present case,	SS	II	13	244	41
material superiority by nature, merely from the advantage	SS	II	14	250	12
not be a doubt of its nature, she was anxious to hear; and	SS	III	1	260	9
John Dashwood was greatly astonished; but his nature was	SS	III	1	267	44
very good, but it is founded on ignorance of human nature.	SS	III	5	296	20
His manners are certainly not the happiest in nature.--	SS	III	5	299	35
Poor Marianne, languid and low from the nature of her	SS	III	7	308	4
of unhappiness to himself of a far more incurable nature.	SS	III	8	331	70
in Shropshire, what is passing of that nature in Surry?--	W			320	2
of nature that she should suffer from it many years."	W			326	6
By nature inoffensive, friendly and obliging, his	PP	I	5	18	1
common indeed, that human nature is particularly prone to	PP	I	5	20	20
"But she does help him on, as much as her nature will	PP	I	6	22	3
thorough bass and human nature; and have some new extracts	PP	I	12	60	7
Jane and Elizabeth attempted to explain to her the nature	PP	I	13	62	8
and the deficiency of nature had been but little assisted	PP	I	15	70	1
yet, it was not in her nature to question the veracity of	PP	I	17	85	1
make no demand of that nature on your father, since I am	PP	I	19	106	10
that if she suspects the nature of my feelings for him,	PP	I	21	118	15
The stupidity with which he was favoured by nature, must	PP	I	22	122	2
superior to his sister as well by nature as education.	PP	II	2	139	2
say that I have experienced many hardships of that nature.	PP	II	10	183	12
"Two offences of a very different nature, and by no means	PP	II	12	196	5
a suspicion of their nature shall not prevent me from	PP	II	12	200	5
It was not in her nature, however, to increase her	PP	II	18	232	21
She had never seen a place for which nature had done more,	PP	III	1	245	3
bestowed on him by Mrs. Reynolds was of no trifling nature.	PP	III	1	250	48

somewhat of a friendlier nature, by the testimony so PP III 2 265 16
unexpected and serious nature; but I am afraid of alarming PP III 4 273 3
of so satisfactory a nature, as the compliment deserved. PP III 6 295 7
and then he had nothing of a pleasant nature to send. PP III 6 297 12
Human nature is so prone to fall into it! PP III 6 299 21
A report of a most alarming nature, reached me two days PP III 14 353 26
of an excellent nature, "what can be the matter?" MP I 2 15 10
were sometimes of a nature to make a third very useful, MP I 2 17 21
but a more tender nature suggested that her feelings were MP I 3 32 64
of happiness fails, human nature turns to another; if the MP I 5 46 23
highly the love or good nature of a brother, who will not MP I 7 64 10
same nature whenever she was in her company; but so it was. MP I 7 66 14
nature it was most astonishing to see how well she sat. MP I 7 67 16
Her merit in being gifted by nature with strength and MP I 7 69 23
mind, of feeling; she saw nature, inanimate nature, with MP I 8 81 31
she saw nature, inanimate nature, with little observation; MP I 8 81 31
You have given us an amusing sketch, and human nature MP I 9 87 16
a bon-mot, for there is not the least wit in my nature. MP I 9 94 56
as the serenity of nature could make it; but when Mrs. MP I 10 106 58
both if the sublimity of nature were more attended to, and MP I 11 113 35
not at least been given a taste for nature in early life. MP I 11 113 36
and in the modesty of her nature immediately felt that she MP I 12 118 22
"For every thing of that nature, I will be answerable,"-- MP I 13 127 29
and we must not suffer her good nature to be imposed on. MP I 14 134 15
Mrs. Grant was of consequence; her good nature had MP I 17 160 6
would, indeed, have such nature and feeling in it, as must MP I 18 170 24
of even fond dependence on her good nature, she must yield. MP I 18 172 32
any one faculty of our nature may be called more wonderful MP II 4 208 12
When one thinks of it, how astonishing a variety of nature! MP II 4 209 16
to give him a brain which nature had denied--to mix up an MP II 5 224 53
an agitation of a higher nature--watching in the hall, in MP II 6 233 14
He knows that human nature needs more lessons than a MP II 7 248 42
have the meaning, is not in your nature I am sure. MP II 9 263 16
the feelings of youth and nature, let her not be much MP II 9 265 19
though in her own good nature she would not have prevented MP II 11 284 10
her children's enjoyment, was attributed to her nature. MP II 11 285 10
any thing of a serious nature in such a quarter? MP II 13 306 26
unfitted for each other by nature, education, and habit. MP III 2 327 5
varying, unsteady nature of love, as it generally exists, MP III 2 330 14
and wit, and good nature together, could do; or at least, MP III 3 340 24
of her modest gentle nature, to repulse Mr. Crawford, and MP III 3 342 32
And, and--we think very differently of the nature of women, MP III 4 353 45
Oh, I am sure it is not in woman's nature to refuse such a MP III 5 363 22
denied to Miss Crawford's nature, that participation of MP III 6 367 6
of the general nature of women, which would lead her to MP III 6 367 6
his knowledge of human nature, to expect to see the effect MP III 6 368 7
The instinct of nature was soon satisfied, and Mrs. MP III 8 389 4
Nature had given them no inconsiderable share of beauty, MP III 11 408 2
them--to think that where nature had made no little MP III 11 408 2
of nature, and very well able to express his admiration. MP III 11 409 7
It was parting with somebody of the nature of a friend; MP III 11 413 31
wanting, but nothing of that nature was ever in my power.-- MP III 13 420 2
intelligence was of a nature to promise occupation for the MP III 13 426 9
of evil, for human nature, not in a state of utter MP III 15 441 20
It was of a much less poignant nature than what the others MP III 16 452 15
For where, Fanny, shall we find a woman whom nature had so MP III 16 455 18
No, her's is not a cruel nature. MP III 16 456 25
him, and how delightful nature had made her, and how MP III 16 459 31
Nature resisted it for a while. MP III 16 459 31
was not in Mr. Weston's nature to imagine that any caprice E I 2 17 7
Hartfield, and his good nature, from his fortune, his E I 3 20 1
The simplicity and cheerfulness of her nature, her E I 3 21 4
are infinitely superior to what she received from nature." E I 6 42 2
of our nature, eager curiosity and warm prepossession. E I 7 56 46
What are Harriet Smith's claims, either of birth, nature E I 8 61 38
not my way, or my nature; and I do not think I ever shall. E I 10 84 15
"If you were as much guided by nature in your estimate of E I 12 98 4
understands the nature of the air, and his own brother and E I 12 105 55
Emma was just describing the nature of her friend's E I 13 109 6
defiance of the voice of nature, which tells man, in every E I 13 113 26
Emma only might be as nature prompted, and shew herself E I 14 117 1
that the nature of her complaint alarmed him considerably." E I 15 124 3
him--that Harriet's nature should not be of that superior E I 16 138 15
to be engrafted on what nature had given her in a pleasing E II 2 163 3
That nature had given it in feature could not be unseen by E II 2 165 7
Jane's curiosity did not appear of that absorbing nature E II 3 174 36
Human nature is so well disposed towards those who are in E II 4 181 1
has not any thing of the nature of an instrument, not even E II 8 215 16
Emma perceived that the nature of his gallantry was a E II 11 250 19
"I can answer for every thing of that nature, sir, because E II 11 252 36
Something of that nature would be particularly desirable E II 14 277 38
to satisfy Emma as to the nature of her agitation on E III 1 315 1
of a very serious nature; but yet, Harriet, more wonderful E III 4 342 39
of a totally different nature:--it is impossible exactly E III 5 350 37
The nature and the simplicity of gentlemen and ladies, E III 6 355 21
It was with him, of so simple, yet so dignified a nature.-- E III 9 386 7
A sudden seizure of a different nature from any thing E III 9 387 11
light, of a disagreeable nature in the circumstances of E III 10 393 18
Something of a very unpleasant nature, I find, has E III 10 394 27
Never had the exquisite sight, smell, sensation of nature, E III 13 424 1
said he quietly, and looking at her; "of what nature?" E III 13 425 4
"Oh! the best nature in the world--a wedding." E III 13 425 5
She did not think it in Harriet's nature to escape being E III 14 435 4
You must all endeavour to comprehend the exact nature of E III 14 437 8
Nature gave you understanding:--Miss Taylor gave you E III 17 462 7
every fear of that nature, by meeting her with the most E III 19 481 2
Mary, of a more trying nature; going to almost every house P III 5 39 34
infinitely more fitted by nature to express good cheer and P III 8 68 29
herself mistaken in the nature of her feelings, the P III 9 77 18
nature of the country required, for going and returning. P III 11 94 8
her nature obliged her to begin an acquaintance with him. P III 11 100 23
was going on as well as the nature of the case admitted. P IV 1 121 2
on topics which had by nature the first claim on her. P IV 1 124 11
carried her out of herself, which was from nature alone. P IV 5 154 8
Hers is a line for seeing human nature; and she has a fund P IV 5 155 9
Such varieties of human nature as they are in the habit of P IV 5 156 10
Here and there, human nature may be great in times of P IV 5 156 11
But there is nothing at all of that nature in the letter. P IV 6 173 47
would be an insult to the nature of Anne's felicity, to P IV 8 185 20
I wish nature had made such hearts as yours more common, " P IV 9 203 72
made no attempt of that nature, since he did not even know P IV 9 210 99
however, with a very tolerable imitation of nature. P IV 10 228 70
71
"It was not in her nature. P IV 11 232 17
"It would not be the nature of any woman who truly loved." P IV 11 232 18
from within; it must be nature, man's nature, which has P IV 11 233 21
nature, which has done the business for Captain Benwick." P IV 11 233 21
"No, no, it is not man's nature. P IV 11 233 22
I will not allow it to be more man's nature than woman's P IV 11 233 22
explains my view of the nature of their attachments. P IV 11 233 23
is allowable in human nature, nothing to reproach myself P IV 11 246 80
by nature, & promising to be the most chosen by man."-- S 1 368 1
Nature had marked it out--had spoken in most intelligible S 1 369 1
more palpably designed by nature for the resort of the S 1 369 1
at Sanditon, which the nature of the advertisement induced S 2 371 1
alone was evidently designed by nature for the cure.-- S 2 373 1
For objections of this nature, Charlotte was not prepared, S 7 401 1
This poor Sir Edward & his sister.--how far nature meant S 7 402 1
are such as display human nature with grandeur--such as S 8 403 1
to his not having by nature a very strong head, the graces, S 8 404 1
happily not often of a nature, to threaten existence S 9 410 1

NATURED (4)
In every thing else she is as good natured a girl as ever PP I 20 111 5
natured, and as unaffected, though not quite so chatty. PP III 11 337 56
"at least he is very good natured, and I shall always feel E I 7 54 30
she is only too good natured and too silly to suit me; but, E I 10 85 19

NAVAL (7)
the paper esteemed to have the earliest naval intelligence. MP II 6 232 13
than begin upon the last naval regulations, or settle the MP III 10 403 13
think any from our wealthy naval commanders particularly P III 3 17 4
goodwill towards a naval officer as tenant, had been P III 3 21 18
The Crofts took possession with true naval alertness, and P III 6 48 17
There was a very general ignorance of all naval matters P III 8 64 4
Louisa had fine naval fervour to begin with, and they P IV 6 167 20

NAVY (19)
As for the navy, it had fashion on its side, but I was too SS I 19 103 4
You have a large acquaintance in the navy, I conclude?" MP I 6 60 48
an Admiral to go into the navy, or the son of a general to MP I 11 109 18
The profession, either navy or army, is its own MP I 11 109 19
as he must either in the navy or army have had a great MP I 11 111 30
accidentally met with a navy officer or two of his MP III 10 400 7
This peace will be turning all our rich navy officers P III 3 17 1
of business, gentlemen of the navy are well to deal with. P III 3 17 2
3
among the gentlemen of the navy, I imagine, who would not P III 3 18 5
6
The park would be open to him of course, and few navy P III 3 18 8
Here Anne spoke,-- "the navy, I think, who have done much P III 3 19 11
12
A man is in greater danger in the navy of being insulted P III 3 19 16
She had only navy lists and newspapers for her authority, P III 4 30 8
and a few compliments to the navy, and I am a lost man. P III 7 62 39
the navy-list,--(their own navy list, the first that had P III 8 64 7
a man to distinguish himself as any officer in the navy. P III 9 75 10
on the character of the navy--their friendliness, their P III 11 99 19
into a little knot of the navy, Mrs. Croft looking as P IV 6 168 24
Wentworth--Captain Wentworth of the navy. P IV 8 188 40

NAVY-LIST (2)
the newspaper and the navy-list; he talked only of the MP III 8 389 3
just fetching the navy-list,--(their own navy list, the P III 8 64 7

NAY (68)
Nay, I know not whether I ought to be quite tranquil now, LS 25 292 1
Nay, more, I am assured that a connection, of which I I LS 36 305 1
Nay, I cannot blame you--(speaking more seriously)--your NA I 6 41 16
"Nay, do not distress me. NA I 6 42 32
"Nay, I am sure you cannot have a better; for if I do not NA I 10 78 40
"Nay, I am sure by your look, when you came into the box, NA I 12 95 13
at such a sight, could not help saying, "nay, Catherine. NA I 13 98 3
"Nay, my beloved, sweetest friend," continued the other, " NA I 15 117 6
"Nay, but there is no such confounded hurry.-- NA I 15 123 36
"Nay, since you make such a point of it, I can refuse you NA II 1 130 13
"Nay, my sweetest Catherine, this is being quite absurd! NA II 3 144 10
Nay, if it is to be guess-work, let us all guess for NA II 4 151 26
Nay, perverse as it seemed, she doubted whether she might NA II 5 154 2
look so fearlessly around, nay, that he should even enter NA II 9 190 2
in the General; nay, that he was even looking at the side- NA II 11 214 27
"Nay, if you can use such a word, I can urge you no NA II 13 221 5
for the abruptness, the rudeness, nay, the insolence of it. NA II 13 226 25
"Nay, mama, if he is not to be animated by Cowper!--but we SS I 3 18 20
Nay, the longer they were together the more doubtful SS I 4 22 18
Nay, more, I consider it as the only form of building in SS I 14 72 11
"Nay, Edward," said Marianne, "you need not reproach me. SS I 17 93 33
"Nay, my dear, I'm sure I don't pretend to say that there SS I 21 123 28
"Nay," cried Mrs. Jennings. "I am sure I shall be SS II 3 154 4
hardly last longer--nay, perhaps it may freeze to-night!" SS II 5 167 3
"Nay, Elinor, this reproach from you--you who have SS II 5 170 24
been unjust, inattentive, nay, almost unkind, to her SS III 11 356 46
of Mr. Pratt, I think-- nay, I am sure, it would never SS III 13 362 5
"Nay, if you are so serious about it, I shall consider the PP I 6 27 53
my girls, I shall not say nay to him; and I thought PP I 7 29 12
"Nay," cried Bingley, "this is too much, to remember at PP I 10 49 28
The wisest and the best of men, nay, the wisest and best PP I 11 57 20
Nay, were your friend Lady Catherine to know me, I am PP I 19 107 14
"Nay," said Elizabeth, "this is not fair. PP II 1 135 11
and imprudent manner; nay, which has already arisen from PP II 18 231 16
and for the last half year, nay, for a twelvemonth, she PP III 5 283 10
"Because honour, decorum, prudence, nay, interest, forbid PP III 14 355 45
Nay, when I read a letter of his, I cannot help giving him PP III 15 364 24
"Nay," said Edmund, who began to listen with alarm. MP I 13 124 10
Nay, Fanny, do not turn away about it--it is but an uncle. MP II 3 198 8
"Nay, Henry, not by all, not forgotten by all, not MP II 12 297 34
acting before her again; nay, perhaps with greater MP III 3 337 10
Nay, nay, I entreat you; for one moment put down your work. MP III 3 342 33
Fanny--nay--(seeing her draw back displeased) forgive me. MP III 3 344 41
Nay, in sober sadness, I believe I now love you all." MP III 5 358 9
circumstance; nay, it seemed a relief to her worn mind to MP III 10 401 9
Nay, had she been without his arm, she would soon have MP III 11 409 6
"Why do you smile?" said she. "nay, why do you?" E II 8 216 18
"Nay, she has always been a first favourite with him, as E II 8 224 69
Sixteen miles--nay, eighteen--it must be full eighteen to E III 1 318 10
"Nay, I had it from you. E III 5 344 7
"Nay, how could I help saying what I did?-- E III 7 374 58
are engaged;--nay, that they have been long engaged!" E III 10 395 32
to be attached to him--nay, was attached--and how it came E III 10 396 41
"Nay, dear Emma, now I must take his part; for though he E III 10 397 49
Then, with the gladness which must be felt, nay, which he E III 13 433 41
"Nay, nay, read on.-- E III 15 447 23
Nay, he appeared so much otherwise, that his daughter's E III 19 483 9
"Nay, Sir Walter," cried Mrs. Clay, "this is being severe P III 3 20 17
Now they were as strangers; nay, worse than strangers, for P III 8 64 3
sight of a dead young lady, nay, two dead young ladies, P III 12 111 49
for Scott and Lord Byron; nay, that was probably learnt P IV 6 167 20
Nay, most likely they are married already, for I do not P IV 6 171 35
of the Musgroves, nay, even of Louisa, and had even a P IV 7 176 8
"Nay," said Anne, "I have no particular enquiry to make P IV 9 200 58
Nay, it would be too hard upon you, if it were otherwise. P IV 11 233 23
constant unconsciously, nay unintentionally; that he had P IV 11 241 61
nay, perhaps herself, I was no longer at my own disposal. P IV 11 242 65
"Nay sir, if he is not in the way, his partner will just S 1 365 1

NEAR (233)
whole of your family, far & near, must highly reprobate. LS 12 260 1
near me incog.--but I forbid anything of the kind. LS 16 269 3
When the hour of departure drew near, the maternal anxiety NA I 2 18 2
She was now seen by many young men who had not been near NA I 2 23 27
lively eye, and, if not quite handsome, was very near it. NA I 3 25 2
Allen, as they sat down near the great clock, after NA I 4 31 1
of the Christmas vacation with his family, near London. NA I 4 33 5
must look out for a couple of good beds some where near." NA I 7 49 43
the attention of every man near her, and without NA I 8 56 11
to it, did not sit near her, and James and Isabella were NA I 8 59 38
Her partner now drew near, and said, "that gentleman would NA I 10 76 29
oak which he had placed near its summit, to oaks in NA I 14 111 29
"You must settle near Fullerton. NA I 15 120 21
You must be near us." NA I 15 120 21
If I can but be near you, I shall be satisfied. NA I 15 120 22
expectation drew near, Isabella became more and more NA I 15 121 26
took pains to be near her, and Henry asked her to dance. NA II 1 131 14
As they drew near the end of their journey, her impatience NA II 5 161 24
that morning have passed near the very spot of this NA II 8 188 17
We are going to Lord Longtown's, near Hereford, for a NA II 13 224 13
and thought of Henry, so near, yet so unconscious, her NA II 14 230 1
before, he had been met near the Abbey by his impatient NA II 15 244 10
The Allens, he believed, had lived near them too long, and NA II 15 247 13
The ladies had passed near it in their way along the SS I 7 32 1

of thirty-five any thing near enough to love, to make him SS I 8 38 11
"It shall not be put off when we are so near it. SS I 13 64 25
She is a relation of the Colonel's, my dear; a very near SS I 13 66 57
We will not say how near, for fear of shocking the young SS I 13 66 57
that he had been staying with some friends near Plymouth. SS I 16 87 26
She was sitting near the window, and as soon as Sir John SS I 19 105 13
with my uncle, who lives at Longstaple, near Plymouth. SS I 22 130 28
been staying a fortnight with some friends near Plymouth." SS I 22 134 49
and Edward's visit near Plymouth, his melancholy state of SS II 1 139 1
to see in every carriage which drove near their house. SS II 1 141 4
Lucy directly drew her work table near her and reseated SS II 1 144 14
herself, was luckily so near them that Miss Dashwood now SS II 1 145 23
in a house in one of the streets near Portman-Square. SS II 3 153 1
hour of appointment drew near, necessary as it was in SS II 5 170 28
and therefore never came near her, they received no mark SS II 5 171 30
Elinor drew near, but without saying a word; and seating SS II 7 182 12
lying-in, for I found her near her delivery, I removed her SS II 9 211 42
She wished with all her heart Combe Magna was not so near SS II 10 215 10
his next observation, "in a cottage near Dawlish." SS II 14 251 15
could live in Devonshire, without living near Dawlish. SS II 14 251 16
giving the same number of days to such near relations." SS II 14 253 22
when Edward did not come near us for three days, I could SS III 2 272 16
as you will be such very near neighbours, (for I SS III 4 290 38
nurse, for the house of a near relation of Mr. Palmer's, SS III 7 308 3
have felt it too certain a thing, to trust myself near him. SS III 8 327 55
Mrs. Dashwood, whose terror as they drew near the house SS III 9 334 4
in knowing her mother was near her, and conscious of being SS III 9 334 5
was very confident that Edward would never come near them. SS III 11 355 39
were probably going down to Mr. Pratt's, near Plymouth. SS III 11 355 39
good friends, as our near relationship now makes proper. SS III 13 365 14
A very stiff meeting between these near neighbours ensued-- W 327 8
in love to station himself near any fair creature seemed W 328 8
near her, when you know what a partner he is to have. W 330 11
lounging on a vacant table near her, call Tom Musgrave W 333 13
they would make me sit near the fire, & as the partridges W 344 20
their seats--Ld. Osborne near Emma, & the convenient Mr W 345 21
I would endite it if I lived near you. W 349 24
been a party of such very near relations as could have W 359 28
Darcy had been standing near enough for her to overhear a PP I 3 11 7
Mr. Darcy stood near them in silent indignation at such a PP I 6 25 25
"Yes; and they have another, who lives somewhere near PP I 8 36 16
it wholly aside, she drew near the card-table, and PP I 8 38 39
Mr. Darcy was writing, and Miss Bingley, seated near him, PP I 10 47 1
Mr. Darcy, drawing near Elizabeth, said to her-- "do not PP I 10 51 47
48
I dare say but it would not be near so much like a ball." PP I 11 56 9
Hunsford, near Westerham, Kent, 15th October. PP I 13 62 12
Does she live near you, sir?" PP I 14 67 2
"How near it may be to <u>mine</u>, I cannot pretend to say.-- PP I 18 91 16
there is now in the room a near relation of my patroness. PP I 18 96 57
not to venture near her, lest she might hear too much. PP I 18 98 63
her, quite disengaged, he never came near enough to speak. PP I 18 102 74
made Elizabeth so near laughing that she could not use the PP I 19 105 9
10
"I found," said he, "as the time drew near, that I had PP I 21 115 4
drew near, she would have been very sorry for any delay. PP II 4 151 1
He drew a chair near her. PP II 8 174 12
"I should never have said Mrs. Collins was settled <u>near</u> PP II 9 179 19
to say that a woman may not be settled too near her <u>family</u>. PP II 9 179 22
The far and the near must be relative, and depend on many PP II 9 179 22
would not call herself <u>near</u> her family under less than PP II 9 179 22
that she had somehow or other got pretty near the truth. PP II 10 184 20
But the person who advanced, was now near enough to see PP II 12 195 2
Fitzwilliam, who from our near relationship and constant PP II 12 202 5
the information of his near concern in all his cousin's PP II 13 206 4
having been in waiting near the lodges, to make them his PP II 14 210 1
and, as they drew near the appointed inn where Mr. PP II 16 219 1
"They are going to be encamped near Brighton; and I do so PP II 16 219 6
Every girl in, or near Meryton, was out of her senses PP III 5 285 18
and it was certain that he had no near one living. PP III 6 297 12
I would not trust you so near it as East Bourne, for fifty PP III 6 300 30
of Mr. Wickham in and near Brighton, with assurances of PP III 8 313 19
who happened to sit near Elizabeth, began enquiring after PP III 9 316 6
As the day of his arrival drew near, "I begin to be sorry PP III 11 333 27
28
She was not near enough to hear any of their discourse, PP III 12 340 13
a single vacancy near her, which would admit of a chair. PP III 12 341 16
advice and intreaty of so near a relation might settle PP III 15 361 3
So near a vicinity to her mother and Meryton relations was PP III 19 385 3
child in the little white attic, near the old nurseries. MP I 1 9 12
It will be much the best place for her, so near Miss Lee, MP I 1 9 12
Fanny, whether near or from her cousins, whether in the MP I 2 14 8
and without any near prospect of finishing his business. MP I 4 37 9
such consequence so very near them, and not at all MP I 4 42 18
retook her chosen place near the bottom of the table, MP I 6 52 1
cut down that grew too near the house, and it opens the MP I 6 55 17
herself; and both placed near a window, cut down to the MP I 7 65 13
the present; she liked to have him near her; it was enough. MP I 7 65 13
her, "I do not like to see Miss Bertram so near the altar." MP I 9 88 20
the key; he had been very near thinking whether he should MP I 10 98 4
find us near that knoll, the grove of oak on the knoll." MP I 10 99 20
her to dance, drew a chair near her, and gave her an MP I 12 118 22
To be so near happiness, so near fame, so near the long MP I 13 121 1
and being so near, to lose it all, was an injury to be MP I 13 121 1
On the 23d he was going to a friend near Peterborough in MP II 8 255 10
her usual employments near her aunt Bertram, and pay her MP II 9 265 20
As for the ball so near at hand, she had too many MP II 9 266 22
"Fanny," said a voice at that moment near her. MP II 9 267 24
was now growing seriously near, and she so little MP II 10 274 8
herself for the first time near Miss Crawford, whose eyes MP II 10 274 9
He was not near, he was attending a party of ladies out of MP II 10 275 9
her on a sofa very near, turned round before she began to MP II 10 276 14
a week, when her own departure from Mansfield was so near. MP II 11 286 15
the idea of leaving Mrs. Grant now the time draws near. MP II 11 289 30
a page or two, quite near enough to satisfy Lady Bertram, MP III 3 336 10
"You were near staying there?" MP III 4 354 49
But I have not the least inclination to go near her. MP III 5 359 12
for Fanny's ever going near a father and mother who had MP III 6 370 14
Near the Canopus? MP III 7 378 12
him so agreeable--so <u>near</u> being agreeable; his behaviour MP III 10 406 21
without feelings so near akin to envy, as made her hate MP III 11 413 31
Such sensations, however, were too near a kin to MP III 13 424 5
near Bedford Square; but I forgot their name and street. MP III 14 434 13
to another--that other her near relation--the whole family, MP III 15 441 20
He so near her, and in misery. MP III 15 444 28
been expected, and for his sake been more near doing right. MP III 16 459 31
of his near approach afraid, so fatal to my suit before. E I 9 78 54
very near being christened Catherine after her grandmama. E I 9 79 56
in sight; and so near as to give Emma time only to say E I 10 87 29
30
thing will serve as introduction to what is near the heart. E I 10 89 35
The coming of her sister's family was so very near at hand, E I 11 91 1
"Not near so often, my dear, as I could wish." E I 11 94 13
"But still, not near enough to give me a chance of being E I 12 99 9
who can think of Miss Smith, when Miss Woodhouse is near! E I 15 130 31
When the time proposed drew near, Mrs. Weston's fears were E I 18 144 1
on them for ever, and therefore she seldom went near them. E II 1 155 3
However, when I read on, I found it was not near so bad as E II 1 162 31
perhaps, had been very near changing one friend for the E II 2 169 16
Randalls; I have not been near Randalls," when the door E II 3 172 22
23
I was sitting near the door--Elizabeth saw me directly; E II 3 178 52
end of the shop; and I kept sitting near the door!--
for I should find the near way quite floated by this rain. E II 3 178 52
in a <u>great way</u>, near Bristol, who kept two carriages! E II 3 179 52
He got as near as he could to thanking her for Miss E II 4 183 9
in or near Highbury; a family of the name of Fairfax. E II 5 192 29
of being at least very near it, and saved only be her own E II 5 193 37
near at hand, and spending the whole evening away from him. E II 7 206 2
great families, none very near; and that even when days E II 7 208 9
she:--"one can get near every body, and say every thing. E II 8 221 48
And touching Miss Bates, who at the moment passed near-- " E II 8 222 59
Churchill, at a table near her, most deedily occupied E II 8 229 97
He took some music from a chair near the pianoforte, and E II 10 240 1
E II 10 242 20
21
Shortly afterwards Miss Bates, passing near the window, E II 10 243 30
They will be so near their own stable." E II 11 252 34
The rich brother-in-law near Bristol was the pride of the E II 14 272 17
"But, my dear child, the time <u>is</u> drawing near; here is E II 17 300 12
is very near, with such business to accomplish before us. E II 17 300 12
thing to have Frank among us again, so near as town. E II 17 304 27
months before him of such near neighbourhood to many dear E III 1 317 8
to begin, or afraid of being always near her. E III 2 320 7
but Mr. Elton was so near, that she heard every syllable E III 2 327 34
stray letter near him, how beautifully Emma had written it. E III 5 347 20
He looked around, as if to see that no one were near, and E III 7 374 55
56
They would be married, and settled either at or near E III 12 422 20
to Mr. Smallridge's, near Bristol, stared me in the face. E III 14 442 8
By doing it, I shall feel that I am near you. E III 15 445 8
disappointed a heart was near her, how much might at that E III 16 451 4
Mr. Elton, "as I got near the house, and he told me I E III 16 458 43
She knew a family near Maple Grove who had tried it, and E III 17 469 36
through the blind, of two figures passing near the window. E III 18 476 44
Frank Churchill to draw near her and say, "I have to thank E III 18 476 46
47
I was once very near--and I wish I had--it would have been E III 18 477 55
death, and they were still near neighbours and intimate P III 1 5 7
left it open on the table near her, had she closed it, P III 1 7 12
society, still be near Mary, and still have the pleasure P III 2 14 9
a friend of mine who was standing near, (Sir Basil Morley.) P III 3 20 16
father's house, and settled so permanently near herself. P III 4 28 7
told him how ill I was, not one of them have been near me. P III 5 38 29
that she is enough to ruin any servants she comes near. P III 6 45 9
necessary between such near neighbours, and make those P III 6 46 11
child--and not a creature coming near us all the evening! P III 7 56 10
Dick Musgrove at all near his thoughts, looked rather in P III 8 67 25
near them, seemed to leave every thing to take its chance. P III 9 74 9
acres, besides the farm near Taunton, which is some of the P III 9 76 15
by seating himself near the table, and taking up the P III 9 79 27
met with, strolling about near home, was their destination; P III 10 85 13
aunt, now that he was so near; and very evidently, though P III 10 86 17
They were speaking as they drew near. P III 10 87 22
as near giving it up, out of nonsensical complaisance!" P III 10 87 23
for in a small house, near the foot of an old pier of P III 11 96 10
miles off,--he would be near enough to hear, if people P III 12 103 2
near the two inns as they came back, should be his servant. P III 12 104 7
while she had never been near him at all; no, that P III 12 106 19
Anne found Captain Benwick getting near her, as soon as P III 12 107 23
for this; but as they drew near the Cobb, there was such a P III 12 108 30
Anne found Captain Benwick again drawing near her. P III 12 109 31
and many were collected near them, to be useful if wanted, P III 12 111 49
him afterwards, as he sat near a table, leaning over it P III 12 112 54
and bruises she could get near her, and who, consequently, P IV 1 121 3
one corner, and another great thing that I never go near." P IV 1 128 28
Musgrove, who got Anne near her on purpose to thank her P IV 2 134 30
but "he could not be so near without wishing to know that P IV 3 143 18
but still from the want of near relations and a settled P IV 5 152 2
and was now in lodgings near the hot-baths, living in a P IV 5 152 4
happy to convey her as near to Mrs. Smith's lodgings in P IV 5 153 5
She is not so near her end, I presume, but that she may P IV 5 157 15
drawn up near its pavement!" observed Sir Walter.-- P IV 5 157 19
when Anne, as she sat near the window, descried, most P IV 7 175 4
the straight line to stand near her, and make enquiries in P IV 8 181 1
She wished him not so near her. P IV 8 188 43
very slow degrees came at last near enough to speak to her. P IV 8 189 47
the marriage from being near at hand; but she learned from P IV 10 217 20
He did not seem to want to be near enough for conversation. P IV 10 221 32
We are quite near relations, you know: and Mr. Elliot too, P IV 10 224 47
and Henrietta was pretty near as bad; and so we thought P IV 11 230 6
though nearer to Captain Wentworth's table, not very near. P IV 11 231 12
Are you going near Camden-Place? P IV 11 240 58
the only gentleman's house near the lane--a house, which S 1 364 1
never put them too near the fire at first--& yet, you see, S 10 417 1
& rapture in all who came near her while she sketched--and S 11 421 1
the grounds or paddock, so near one of its Boundaries, S 12 426 1
They were sitting so near each other & appeared so closely S 12 426 1

NEARER (41)

and then advancing still nearer, he spoke both to her and NA I 8 54 4
and her partner coming nearer, said, "I see that you guess NA I 10 80 59
Every mile, as it brought her nearer Woodston, added to NA II 14 230 1
There was a thought yet nearer, a more prevailing, more NA II 14 231 4
the cold and unfeeling behaviour of her nearer connections. SS I 4 23 20
turn back, for no shelter was nearer than their own house. SS I 9 41 6
"Much nearer thirty," said her husband. SS I 20 111 13
meat, and have not a neighbour nearer than your mother. SS II 8 197 22
been suspected of a much nearer connection with her. SS II 9 208 28
to the family, to have a nearer view of their characters SS II 12 231 9
without feeling at all nearer decision than at first, SS III 10 347 32
it became more decided; it certainly drew nearer.-- W 354 28
It has connected him nearer with virtue than any other PP I 16 81 39
terms on the happy prospect of their nearer connection. PP I 20 110 1
and, while examining the nearer aspect of the house, all PP III 1 245 4
dared not approach nearer to Wickham, Georgiana also PP III 3 270 11
If that had been nearer, she would not have gone so soon." PP III 11 331 12
therefore without an idea of any nearer concern in them. MP I 4 35 6
Fanny seemed nearer being right than Edmund had supposed. MP I 14 130 1
her chair considerably nearer the tea-table, and gave all MP I 15 145 42
He led her nearer the light and looked at her again-- MP II 1 178 7
arrival, as to place her nearer agitation than she had MP II 1 179 9
"She was checked by the sight of her uncle much nearer to MP II 7 250 56
be nearer her uncle, "I must get up and breakfast with him. MP II 10 279 28
Draw your chair nearer, my dear. MP III 7 379 17
I had imagined him, I confess, a degree or two nearer E I 4 32 30
Can you imagine any thing nearer perfect beauty than Emma E I 5 39 18
years bring our understandings a good deal nearer?" E I 12 99 7
"Yes--a good deal <u>nearer</u>." E I 12 99 8
whose house was a <u>little</u> nearer Randalls than Ford's; and E II 9 233 25
She is still nearer.-- E II 11 254 50
draws nearer, I do not wish to be giving any body trouble." E II 17 300 11
Better than nearer! E III 1 318 10
He moved a few steps nearer, and those few steps were E III 2 326 32
He could not have come nearer to her if he would; she was P IV 8 188 42
to place herself much nearer the end of the bench than she P IV 8 189 46
though nearer to Captain Wentworth's table, not very near. P IV 11 231 12
startled at finding him nearer than she had supposed, and P IV 11 233 24
One complete, measured mile nearer than East Bourne. S 1 369 1
them be nearer the shore for fear of their tumbling in.-- S 4 383 1
Here Mr P. drew his chair still nearer to his sister, & S 9 408 1

NEAREST (21)

enquiry even from their nearest relations, into affairs of LS 12 260 1
Tilney, "that I always think it the best and nearest way. NA II 7 179 28
"Because it is my nearest way from the stable-yard to my NA II 9 194 7
he felt for us the attachment of the nearest relation? SS I 15 80 36

Context	Work	Vol	Ch	Page	Line
This lady was one of my nearest relations, an orphan from	SS	II	9	205	24
own merit, than on the merit of his nearest relations!	SS	II	14	250	12
object before him, the nearest road to Barton, had had no	SS	III	13	366	20
But amidst your concern for the defects of your nearest	PP	II	12	198	5
fact been the work of her nearest relations, and reflected	PP	II	13	209	11
side of the river, in the nearest direction; but their	PP	III	1	254	57
of the nearest kind with the man whom he so justly scorned.	PP	III	8	311	12
I am almost the nearest relation he has in the world, and	PP	III	14	354	38
death of one of the nearest connections of the family had	MP	I	13	121	1
and his gardens, and nearest plantations; but active and	MP	II	2	190	9
him driven away by the vulgarity of her nearest relations.	MP	III	10	402	11
in Mr. Crawford, was the nearest to administering comfort	MP	III	11	413	32
who happens to be one of their nearest neighbours.	E	II	18	310	34
It had then seemed the object nearest her heart, that Dr.	P	III	9	78	19
Anne was the nearest to him, and making yet a little	P	IV	8	181	1
clear that these, their nearest relations, were not	P	IV	10	216	18
very lofty cliff--and the nearest to it, of every building,	S		4	384	1

NEARLY (83)

Context	Work	Vol	Ch	Page	Line
She staid nearly two hours, was as affectionate & agreable	LS		41	309	1
as Isabella had arrived nearly five minutes before her	NA	I	6	39	2
if they do--for they read nearly as many as women.	NA	I	14	107	11
in a few minutes as nearly settled, as this necessary	NA	II	2	140	10
of an hour, had seemed too nearly impossible for desire.	NA	II	2	141	11
in Woodston, which is nearly twenty miles from my father's,	NA	II	5	157	7
way, and your lamp being nearly exhausted, you will return	NA	II	5	160	21
her toilette seemed so nearly finished, that the	NA	II	6	164	3
and folding them up as nearly as possible in the same	NA	II	7	173	3
pleasure of sitting down nearly twenty to table, which Sir	SS	I	13	67	61
of the eldest, who was nearly thirty, with a very plain	SS	I	21	120	6
were prevailed on to stay nearly two months at the park,	SS	II	2	151	43
nearly twenty young people, and to amuse them with a ball.	SS	II	5	170	29
Our ages were nearly the same, and from out earliest years	SS	II	9	205	24
"It was nearly three years after this unhappy period	SS	II	9	207	26
second son William, who were nearly of the same age.	SS	II	12	233	19
"You surprise me; I should think it must nearly have	SS	III	5	296	21
the finest person;--tho' nearly 50, she was very handsome,	W			329	9
was now rapidly forming, with nearly equal complacency.--	W			331	11
Mr. Bingley inherited property to the amount of nearly an	PP	I	4	15	11
The discussion of Mr. Collins's offer was now nearly at an	PP	I	21	115	1
bordered the park nearly opposite the front of his house.	PP	II	5	156	4
It is nearly fifty miles."	PP	II	9	178	17
of a young man of nearly the same age with himself, and	PP	II	12	200	5
only by her mother, who might have felt nearly the same.	PP	II	18	232	23
"Nearly three weeks."	PP	II	18	234	28
ideas were nearly worn out before the tete-a-tete was over.	PP	III	1	257	66
supposed the girls so nearly of an age as they really were.	MP	I	2	13	4
as a child; but it was the same with us all, or nearly so.	MP	I	3	26	25
They left England with the probability of being nearly a	MP	I	3	32	61
Now we are coming to the lodge gates; but we have nearly a	MP	I	8	82	34
His business was so nearly concluded as to justify him in	MP	I	11	107	2
felt herself becoming too nearly nothing to both, to have	MP	I	18	170	24
She was nearly fainting: all her former habitual dread of	MP	II	1	176	4
have been nearly confined to the house for days together.	MP	II	1	181	16
Mrs. Norris was a little confounded, and as nearly being	MP	II	2	188	3
I have now been here nearly five months! and moreover the	MP	II	4	210	17
the others, she had nearly resolved on going home	MP	II	4	214	46
was at this period more nearly restored to what it had	MP	II	7	238	1
She had hardly ever been in a state so nearly approaching	MP	II	10	272	4
Nearly half an hour had passed, and she was growing very	MP	III	1	312	4
Her uncle's behaviour to her was then as nearly as	MP	III	1	323	53
to be giving nearly as much pain to herself as to him.	MP	III	2	327	6
would not be won by them nearly so soon, without the	MP	III	3	340	24
I was most kindly pressed, and had nearly consented.	MP	III	4	354	50
heart, and will love you as nearly for ever as possible.	MP	III	5	363	24
future improvement as nearly desperate, for thinking that	MP	III	6	367	5
like these received for nearly half an hour, was from a	MP	III	7	383	30
One morning about this time, Fanny having now been nearly	MP	III	10	399	2
Seven weeks of the two months were very nearly gone, when	MP	III	13	420	1
I have nearly determined on explaining myself by letter.	MP	III	13	422	2
existence; and had lived nearly twenty-one years in the	E	I	1	5	1
She had reason to believe her nearly recovered from her	E	I	17	141	5
"No," said Mr. Knightley, nearly at the same time; "you	E	II	3	170	5
sitting with them very nearly three quarters of an hour.	E	II	6	199	7
that Miss Fairfax was nearly dashed from the vessel and	E	II	8	218	37
owned the apples were so nearly gone; she wished I had	E	II	9	238	51
The considerable slope, at nearly the foot of which the	E	III	6	360	38
water, will make you nearly on a par with the rest of us."	E	III	6	365	65
did speak, it was in a voice nearly as agitated as Emma's.	E	III	11	405	17
sat talking with her nearly half an hour before Emma came	E	III	11	410	35
in one scheme more--nearly resolve, that it might be	E	III	14	435	4
her so very serious, so nearly sad, that Mr. Knightley, in	E	III	14	435	5
She promised, however, to think of it; and pretty nearly	E	III	15	449	34
one--well aware of the nearly equal importance of the two	E	III	17	467	30
down much, perhaps nearly all of peculiar attachment to	P	III	4	28	7
of Anne's side, produced nearly a cure on Mary's.	P	III	5	39	40
children, who loved her nearly as well, and respected her	P	III	6	43	4
It was certainly carried nearly as far as possible, for	P	III	6	46	12
It included nearly a third part of her own life.	P	III	7	60	28
they walked side by side, nearly as much as the other two.	P	III	10	90	37
to their dining-room, had nearly run against the very same	P	III	12	104	7
They had nearly done breakfast, when the sound of a	P	III	12	105	8
Mrs. Smith told her, when her spirits had nearly failed.	P	IV	5	154	9
put into an envelop, containing nearly as much more.	P	IV	6	164	8
Russell would perceive him till they were nearly opposite.	P	IV	7	179	28
arrive nearly at the same instant, advanced into the room.	P	IV	8	184	17
"This," said she, "is nearly the sense, or rather the	P	IV	8	186	25
talked of,--but it is as nearly the meaning as I can give;	P	IV	8	186	25
table; he went to it, and nearly turning his back on them	P	IV	11	229	4
The sea air & sea bathing together were nearly infallible,	S		2	373	1
If the village could attract, the hill might be nearly	S		4	383	1
was not very violent--nearly over by the time we reached	S		9	407	1

NEARNESS (3)

Context	Work	Vol	Ch	Page	Line
however positive, of the nearness of that meal, now jumped	W			346	21
within doors; and in the nearness of the parsonage, or the	PP	II	9	180	28
her own family, and the nearness of Sotherton to Mansfield	MP	II	3	201	22

NEAT (25)

Context	Work	Vol	Ch	Page	Line
What do you think of my gig, Miss Morland? a neat one, is	NA	I	7	46	11
taste, confessed it to be neat and simple, thought it	NA	II	7	175	12
great admiration at every neat house above the rank of a	NA	II	11	212	17
in front; and a neat wicket gate admitted them into it.	SS	I	6	28	1
and several neat farm houses scattered here and there.	SS	I	18	97	4
I was last month at my friend Elliott's neat Dartford.	SS	II	14	252	18
were prepared, & the neat upper maid was lighting the	W			336	14
very un-smart family equipage perceived a neat curricle.--	W			338	17
After another pause, "nothing sets off a neat ankle more	W			345	21
But though every thing seemed neat and comfortable, she	PP	II	5	156	4
Her figure is as neat as her brother's."	MP	I	7	69	24
It appears a neat job, however, as far as I could judge by	MP	II	1	184	25
simple and neat, she could not help bursting forth again.	MP	II	9	262	8
claim on her to leave her neat parlour hung round with	E	I	3	22	5
His appearance was very neat, and he looked like a	E	I	4	31	27
welcomed; the quiet neat old lady, who with her knitting	E	II	1	155	4
at the end of the broad, neat gravel-walk, which led	E	II	5	186	2
Long before he re-appeared, attending the short, neat,	E	II	11	255	59
The grounds of Hartfield were small, but neat and pretty;	E	II	14	272	18
they are so neat and careful in all their ways!	P	III	3	18	7
enclosed in its own neat garden, with a vine and a pear-	P	III	5	36	20
Such a young man as Sidney, with his neat equipage &	S		4	382	1
They were now approaching the church & neat village of	S		4	382	1
for the eveng in a small neat drawing room, with a	S		10	413	1
Mr Sidney Parker driving his servant in a very neat	S		12	425	1

NEAT-LOOKING (1)

Context	Work	Vol	Ch	Page	Line
cure"--pointing to the neat-looking end of a cottage,	S		1	364	1

NEATEST (2)

Context	Work	Vol	Ch	Page	Line
England, his carriage the neatest, his horse the best goer,	NA	I	9	64	27
"The nicest;--by which I suppose you mean the neatest.	NA	I	14	107	13

NEATLY (2)

Context	Work	Vol	Ch	Page	Line
her hair arranged as neatly as it always is, and one	MP	II	12	296	31
well chosen, and very neatly arranged--sometimes	E	I	5	37	7

NEATLY-PAINTED (1)

Context	Work	Vol	Ch	Page	Line
wardrobes and neatly-painted chairs, on which the warm	NA	II	9	193	6

NEATNESS (6)

Context	Work	Vol	Ch	Page	Line
Neatness and fashion are enough for the former, and a	NA	I	10	74	22
Originally perhaps it was applied only to express neatness,	NA	I	14	108	16
his pointing out the neatness of the entrance, taken into	PP	II	5	155	3
up and arranged with a neatness and consistency of which	PP	II	5	157	5
The neatness and propriety of her dress was all that he	MP	II	10	272	1
conscious of such an overthrow of all order and neatness!	P	III	5	40	44

NECESSARIES (4)

Context	Work	Vol	Ch	Page	Line
enough to find one in the common necessaries of life.	NA	II	1	135	45
as one of the necessaries of life; he supposed, however, "	NA	II	6	166	6
the necessaries of life, than do an ungenerous thing.	MP	I	1	7	8
raise the price of our necessaries of life, we shall not	S		6	392	1

NECESSARILY (25)

Context	Work	Vol	Ch	Page	Line
impudent address will necessarily attend an impudent mind;	LS		6	251	1
to a ball, does not necessarily increase either the	NA	I	8	55	10
father's, and some of my time is necessarily spent there."	NA	II	5	157	7
coarse food, was the conclusion which necessarily followed.	NA	II	8	187	16
inconvenience, to which their arrival must necessarily add.	SS	II	6	175	2
of the card parties, the subject was necessarily dropped.	SS	II	8	200	43
necessarily produced between Elinor's conduct and her own.	SS	III	2	270	1
It does not necessarily follow that a deep, intricate	PP	I	9	42	13
uncomfortable feelings necessarily attending it, and	PP	I	21	115	1
sources of happiness necessarily attached to her situation,	PP	III	14	355	46
at home; and she was necessarily drawn from the pursuit of	PP	III	19	386	5
not least of herself, necessarily wore away, and she was	MP	I	2	17	21
and necessarily introduced alterations and novelties.	MP	I	3	23	1
will necessarily be brought forward, as you ought to be.	MP	I	3	27	31
"It falls as naturally, as necessarily to her," said he, "	MP	I	14	133	10
thanks and praise which necessarily followed appeared to	E	II	2	168	15
produced it was necessarily increasing Emma's dislike.	E	II	15	281	3
disengaged, he necessarily began on the subject with her.	E	II	17	304	30
she found herself necessarily overhearing the discourse of	E	III	2	323	20
and Mr. Weston, must necessarily open the cause; but when	E	III	12	418	5
Harriet, necessarily drawn away by her engagements with	E	III	19	482	5
and least complaisance, Anne necessarily belonged.	P	III	10	90	37
in which Anne found herself also necessarily included.	P	IV	8	184	17
had conceived to be necessarily their object, & had with	S		1	364	1
She had been necessarily often mentioned at Willingden,--	S		3	375	1

NECESSARY (174)

Context	Work	Vol	Ch	Page	Line
which are now necessary to finish a pretty woman.	LS		7	253	1
"It will be absolutely necessary, said she, as you my dear	LS		15	267	6
seem to have the sort of temper to make severity necessary.	LS		17	270	4
Lady Susan finds it necessary for her own justification	LS		17	272	8
"My love, replied I, do not think it necessary to	LS		24	286	4
which it has since been necessary for me to shew, has	LS		24	288	11
my disfavour; in this light, condescension was necessary.	LS		25	292	1
it will be indispensably necessary for you to get	LS		26	295	3
such a resolution, I feel that absence will be necessary.	LS		30	301	4
considers fortune as necessary every where, & whose	LS		30	301	4
door, as swiftly as the necessary caution would allow;	NA	I	2	21	9
he should think it necessary to alarm her with a relation	NA	I	9	62	10
it is all very right and necessary, I have often wondered	NA	I	14	109	24
that they never find it necessary to use more than half."	NA	I	14	114	47
as this necessary reference to Fullerton would allow.	NA	II	2	140	10
think any profession necessary for him; and certainly	NA	II	7	176	15
no uniformity of architecture had been thought necessary.	NA	II	8	184	4
what was necessary here, she began to be amazed herself.	NA	II	8	184	4
to think an apology necessary for the flatness of the	NA	II	11	212	17
must be so indispensably necessary to your future felicity.	SS	I	4	22	17
she might think necessary, if the situation pleased her.	SS	I	4	23	20
It was necessary to the happiness of both; for however	SS	I	7	32	1
her situation rendered necessary, took her up in his arms	SS	I	9	42	8
It was only necessary to mention any favourite amusement	SS	I	10	47	3
presence is necessary to gain your admittance at Whitwell."	SS	I	13	64	21
from his character, where the deviation is necessary.	SS	I	15	79	30
We have already agreed that secrecy may be necessary, and	SS	I	16	84	6
me, that I have had no necessary business to engage me, no	SS	I	19	102	4
think some apology necessary for the freedom of her sister.	SS	I	21	123	24
was indispensably necessary, and she struggled so	SS	I	22	134	53
appointment drew near, necessary as it was in common	SS	II	5	170	28
A short account of myself, I believe, will be necessary,	SS	II	9	205	20
not happened to have the necessary sum in my banker's	SS	II	11	225	33
mother felt it no longer necessary to give up the whole of	SS	III	1	257	1
But unwelcome as such a task must be, it was necessary to	SS	III	1	261	11
the approach of her own party made another more necessary.	SS	III	2	275	24
She wondered indeed at his thinking it necessary to do so;-	SS	III	3	281	9
time, or the preparation necessary; but I suppose two or	SS	III	4	291	50
Elinor began to feel it necessary to pay her a visit.--	SS	III	5	293	3
stay at Cleveland was necessary to herself, that she	SS	III	7	309	5
mind, made every necessary arrangement with the utmost	SS	III	7	312	17
was therefore necessary for my breaking the engagement.	SS	III	8	323	40
Why was it necessary to call?"	SS	III	8	324	41
"It was necessary to my own pride.	SS	III	8	324	42
Relate only what in your conscience you think necessary	SS	III	8	325	52
In honest words, her money was necessary to me, and in a	SS	III	8	328	63
"I will tell her all that is necessary to what may	SS	III	8	330	68
Lucy became as necessary to Mrs. Ferrars, as either Robert	SS	III	14	377	11
home, & one was always necessary as companion to himself,	W			315	1
It is quite as necessary to young ladies in their first."--	W			326	6
what had been deemed necessary the day before; and taking	W			360	30
a ball was absolutely necessary; and the morning after the	PP	I	5	18	3
a walk to Meryton was necessary to amuse their morning	PP	I	7	28	3
which must leave very necessary business undone, and can	PP	I	10	49	27
he had merely kept the necessary terms, without forming at	PP	I	15	70	1
Society, I own, is necessary to me.	PP	I	16	79	23
it was not in the least necessary there should be any	PP	I	18	97	60
It was necessary to make this circumstance a matter of	PP	I	18	99	63
that, allowing for the necessary preparations of	PP	I	18	103	77
It was absolutely necessary to interrupt him now.	PP	I	19	106	11
long enough to render it necessary, I shall now take the	PP	I	22	124	10
apologies and thanks which he would have thought necessary.	PP	II	6	161	10
It was not thought necessary in Sir Lewis de Bourgh's	PP	II	6	164	16
to read, and had all the masters that were necessary.	PP	II	6	165	31
wife did not think it necessary to go likewise; and till	PP	II	7	168	3
house, they could not be necessary; and it was not till	PP	II	8	172	1
It was absolutely necessary, therefore, to think of	PP	II	9	177	3
					4
thought it necessary to turn back and walk with her.	PP	II	10	182	1
herself, attention was necessary, which Elizabeth believed	PP	II	14	212	16
parting civilities which he deemed indispensably necessary.	PP	II	15	215	1
It was consequently necessary to name some other period	PP	II	19	237	3
resolution the more necessary to be made, but perhaps not	PP	III	3	268	8
whole, nor I, thought it necessary to make our knowledge	PP	III	5	285	16
would be necessary to clear his expences at Brighton.	PP	III	6	298	12
his flight was rendered necessary by distress of	PP	III	9	318	19
Lydia seems to think necessary; and then I must endeavour	PP	III	9	320	33
imagined such enquiries to be necessary on your side.	PP	III	10	321	2
supplication had been necessary to a woman whom he must	PP	III	10	326	3
His wife represented to him how absolutely necessary such	PP	III	11	332	24
It was necessary to laugh, when she would rather have	PP	III	15	364	25
what I wrote must give you pain, but it was necessary.	PP	III	16	368	20
give; but they were now necessary, and she assured him	PP	III	17	376	30
strict line of economy necessary; and what was begun as a	MP	I	1	8	9

you, it is not at all necessary that she should be as MP I 2 19 29
of the next presentation necessary, and the younger MP I 3 23 2
alive and well, made it necessary to lay by her agitation MP I 4 34 2
to its being considered necessary by his father;--she only MP I 4 36 7
it was soon found necessary to be improved; and for three MP I 6 57 31
"But why is it necessary," said Edmund, "that Crawford's MP I 8 77 9
was over, it was first necessary to eat, and the doors MP I 9 84 1
expression and subject necessary, as Fanny, in spite of MP I 12 119 22
nothing more would be necessary on such a plan as this. MP I 13 123 8
what scenery would be necessary--while Maria and Henry MP I 14 136 21
It will not be necessary to send you to your father's MP I 15 140 11
need not be so scrupulous as I might feel necessary. MP I 15 141 21
amongst them--but now she was absolutely necessary. MP I 18 171 28
thing of the kind was necessary, and therefore, thanking MP II 1 177 5
It was necessary for him to step forward too and assist MP II 1 183 23
Little observation there was necessary to tell him that MP II 3 200 20
his absence had given was now become absolutely necessary. MP II 3 202 25
it necessary to be done, if no objection arose at home. MP II 4 207 10
her into the house, through which it was necessary to pass. MP II 4 215 47
she was glad to find it necessary to come to a conclusion MP II 7 248 48
of, and each found it necessary to talk of something else. MP II 7 250 56
he calculated, with all necessary allowance for the MP II 8 253 7
only civilities were necessary--but Fanny felt her aunt's MP II 9 271 41
his watch with all necessary caution--"it is three o'clock, MP II 10 279 24
kind to her, she is now quite as necessary to us." MP II 11 285 11
It became absolutely necessary for her to get to Fanny and MP II 11 287 17
fancy imagines to be necessary for happiness, you resolve MP III 1 318 39
but which became necessary from the totally opposite MP III 2 331 19
him to stay dinner; it was really a necessary compliment. MP III 3 335 7
more is necessary than merely pacing this gravel together. MP III 4 346 8
she had been fancying necessary, in guarding against one MP III 4 354 47
of time and habit were necessary for her, she might not MP III 5 356 3
she was a great deal too necessary to Sir Thomas and Lady MP III 6 373 23
his dress, and make the necessary preparations for his MP III 7 381 24
brought in every thing necessary for the meal; Susan MP III 7 383 32
the purchase necessary for the tranquillity of the house. MP III 9 397 7
the purpose of conveying necessary information, which MP III 12 415 2
her being thought at all necessary, she must suppose her MP III 14 436 15
her father awoke, and made it necessary to be cheerful. E I 1 7 10
that it was particularly necessary to brace her up with a E I 7 55 35
You are a great deal too necessary at Hartfield, to be E I 7 55 38
he should be in the smallest degree necessary at Hartfield. E I 9 81 78
Some change of countenance was necessary for each E I 14 117 1
and though it is thought necessary to invite them once in E I 14 120 11
next day, to undergo the necessary penance of E I 17 141 5
quite as much as was necessary, (or, being acting a part, E I 18 145 5
As long as they lived, no exertions would be necessary, E II 2 165 9
talked into what was necessary, told that he understood, E II 3 170 2
and nothing but the necessary preparations to wait for; E II 4 182 6
would be necessary--and what might be safest, had been a E II 4 185 12
The refreshment of Randalls was absolutely necessary. E II 5 187 4
Ten minutes would have been all that was necessary, E II 6 199 7
how soon it might be necessary for her to throw coldness E II 8 212 4
In so large a party it was not necessary that Emma should E II 8 220 45
neighbours, when it is necessary; but there is no reason E II 9 234 33
representations were necessary to make it acceptable. E II 11 251 25
I do suspect that he is not really necessary to my E II 13 264 2
It is a necessary of life to me; and having always been E II 14 276 36
within myself, the world was not necessary to me. E II 14 276 36
necessary to my happiness, nor were spacious apartments. E II 14 277 36
Is it necessary for me to use any roundabout phrase?-- E II 16 297 48
her:--caution for him and for herself would be necessary. E III 1 315 1
I do not want to say more than is necessary--I am too much E III 4 337 4
"But, Harriet, is it necessary to burn the court plaister?- E III 4 340 25
but no plea was necessary; cabbage-beds would have been E III 6 354 9
In a country life I conceive it to be a sort of necessary; E III 6 356 26
them till it was necessary to do as the others did, and E III 6 358 35
own way, and only say that I am gone when it is necessary." E III 6 363 50
Happily it was not necessary to speak. E III 7 376 63
whom he is just now more necessary than ever, that, as I E III 10 398 57
made the utmost exertion necessary on Emma's side, to E III 11 411 40
41

figuratively, was quite necessary to reinstate her in a E III 14 435 5
of, I feel it only necessary to say, that its being E III 14 439 8
else I should think it necessary to apologize: but the E III 16 455 20
21

every profession is necessary and honourable in its turn, P III 3 20 17
a sigh were necessary to dispel the agitation of the idea. P III 4 30 10
own circle, was become necessary for her;--for certainly, P III 6 42 1
hints of the forbearance necessary between such near P III 6 46 11
and mental sorrow have certainly no necessary proportions. P III 8 68 30
separations necessary, to keep with her brother and sister. P III 10 84 7
many divisions were necessary, or even where they were not, P III 10 90 37
It now became necessary for the party to consider what was P III 12 112 56
It had not been necessary, and the few occasions of its P IV 1 123 9
said he, "as to what is necessary in manners to make him P IV 3 144 20
At last, it became necessary to speak of her.-- P IV 5 156 14
of a public room was necessary to kindle his modest P IV 10 214 12
and accomplish the necessary communication; and she would P IV 10 215 14
likely to be necessary to each other's ultimate comfort. P IV 12 248 1
I could soon put the necessary Irons in the fire.-- S 5 387 1
an alteration necessary, Lady Denham & Miss Brereton.-- S 6 390 1
the head of the list will be a very necessary beginning.-- S 12 423 1

NECESSITOUS (3)

They were, in fact, a necessitous family; numerous too NA II 15 246 12
of the word were they necessitous or poor, and that NA II 16 251 6
would have been always necessitous-- always poor; and SS III 11 351 13

NECESSITY (84)

as to prevent the necessity of our leaving the castle, LS 5 249 1
painful necessity, but I will endeavour to submit to it. LS 15 267 6
urge the necessity of reproof, if you see me too lenient." LS 15 267 6
feel myself under the necessity of delaying that hour LS 30 299 1
Cruel as this sentence may appear, the necessity of LS 30 301 4
necessity of an immediate & eternal separation from you. LS 34 304 1
potent intelligence, as to supersede the necessity of more. LS 35 305 1
my dear Alicia I yeild to the necessity which parts us. LS 39 307 1
to supersede the necessity of a long and minute detail NA I 4 34 9
friend, by the avowed necessity of speaking to Miss Tilney, NA I 10 72 8
repeatedly regretted the necessity of its concealment, NA I 15 125 48
gratitude; and the necessity of waiting between two and NA II 1 135 43
ease as to the necessity of any sudden removal of her own. NA II 11 208 2
regretting that any necessity should rob him even for an NA II 13 220 1
had saved her from the necessity of a conscientious NA II 15 244 11
Mrs. Jennings enforced the necessity. SS I 18 99 18
same inevitable necessity of temporising with his mother. SS I 19 102 2
length, as there was no necessity for my having any SS I 19 103 4
The necessity of concealing from her mother and Marianne, SS II 1 141 5
in spite of the absolute necessity of their returning to SS II 2 151 43
the necessity of some serious inquiry into the affair. SS II 4 165 30
talking, he felt the necessity of instant exertion, he SS II 6 177 11
Elinor sighed over the fancied necessity of this; but to a SS II 9 211 39
sorry to be spared the necessity of answering him, by the SS II 11 222 12
and to do away the necessity of buying a pair of ear-rings SS II 11 226 41
perceive the necessity of her remembering them farther. SS II 11 227 46
more, did not see the necessity of enforcing it by any SS II 12 234 25
He saw the necessity of inviting the Miss Steeles SS II 14 253 25
saw the necessity of preparing Marianne for its discussion. SS III 1 260 10
to be spared from the necessity of saying much in reply SS III 5 297 32
and caution, urged the necessity of her immediate removal SS III 7 307 3
those false ideas of the necessity of riches, which I was SS III 8 323 40
its offspring, necessity, had required to be sacrificed. SS III 8 331 70
far beyond the necessity of regarding little matters." PP I 16 83 50
the necessity of his absence had been self imposed. PP I 21 115 3
as to the necessity of constant company for her friends. PP II 3 145 9
it seemed the effect of necessity rather than of choice--a PP II 9 180 29
myself, I am under the necessity of relating feelings PP II 12 197 5
The necessity must be obeyed--and farther apology would be PP II 12 197 5
and was so urgent on the necessity of placing gowns in the PP II 14 213 20
and she felt the necessity of appearing more like herself. PP III 1 253 56
attentive; and there was not necessity for such attention. PP III 1 257 69
was not sorry to be spared the necessity of saying much. PP III 3 268 5
with Mrs. Forster, the necessity of opening her eyes to PP III 5 285 16
of income by the evident necessity of stricter economy. MP I 3 23 1
wanted, but the absolute necessity of a spare-room for a MP I 3 28 38
The necessity of the measure in a pecuniary light, and the MP I 3 32 62
with her son as to the necessity of it, and as to its MP I 4 36 7
but upon the most urgent necessity in the world; and when MP I 6 59 43
"Yes," he continued, "there is no necessity for my going, MP I 8 78 21
her sister, the absolute necessity of distrusting his MP I 12 114 3
and having made the necessity of an enlargement of plan MP I 14 130 1
pointing out the necessity of his being very much dressed, MP I 15 138 1
stepped forward, feeling the necessity of doing something. MP II 1 176 3
from pleased with the necessity of the acquaintance as MP II 1 183 23
mention without some necessity of defence or palliation. MP II 2 187 1
He might talk of necessity, but she knew his independence.- MP II 2 193 18
way of the happiness he sought, was a cruel necessity.-- MP II 13 302 9
When Sir Thomas understood this, he felt the necessity of MP III 2 332 19
suddenly called to the necessity of reading aloud, which MP III 3 339 22
not acknowledge any necessity for Fanny's ever going near MP III 6 370 14
She was a manager by necessity, without any of Mrs. MP III 8 390 5
disposition; and of the necessity of self-denial and MP III 17 463 8
very fortunately in the necessity, or at least the MP III 17 469 23
they cannot stay longer--but it seems a case of necessity. E I 9 79 63
and this being of necessity so short might be hoped to E I 11 93 5
that there could be no necessity for any body's knowing E I 16 138 15
again, with any necessity, or even any power of speech. E II 3 180 58
that she soon felt the necessity of a little consolation, E II 5 187 4
"There is no necessity for my calling this morning," said E II 5 194 39
40

Mr. Woodhouse soon followed; and the necessity of exertion E II 12 261 34
must contain, and deprecated the necessity of reading it.-- E III 14 436 6
a peculiarly cruel necessity that was to be placing her in E III 15 450 37
the reflection that all necessity of concealment from Mr. E III 18 475 42
Mary deplored the necessity for herself. P III 6 48 17
consequently to feel no necessity for longer confinement. P III 7 55 7
again the sort of necessity which the family-habits seemed P III 10 83 4
"Uppercross,--the necessity of some one's going to P III 12 113 57
and ashamed for the necessity of the removal, she could P IV 1 125 17
the absolute necessity of having a regular nurse, and P IV 5 154 9
a pause, feeling the necessity of speaking, and having not P IV 8 183 11
12

Here they were interrupted by the absolute necessity of P IV 10 219 27
The absolute necessity of seeming like herself produced P IV 11 238 45
He had very early seen the necessity of the case, & had S 8 405 2

NECK (8)

wore his picture round her neck; but it turned out to be SS I 12 60 10
scratching the child's neck, produced from this pattern of SS I 21 121 10
arms round her sister's neck; "I know you feel for me; I SS II 7 185 24
putting one arm round her neck, and one cheek close to SS II 12 236 39
40

put them round her neck, and seen and felt how full of MP II 9 271 40
neck to sob out her various emotions of pain and pleasure. MP III 7 384 34
her neck, said, "dear Fanny! now I shall be comfortable." MP III 15 447 37
unfastened from around her neck, and he was resolutely P III 9 80 33

NECKLACE (25)

shall you have by way of necklace?" said Miss Crawford. MP II 8 257 15
I offer nothing but an old necklace. MP II 8 258 16
fancying there was one necklace more frequently placed MP II 8 258 17
necklace round her and making her see how well it looked. MP II 8 258 17
"When I wear this necklace I shall always think of you," MP II 8 258 18
too when you wear that necklace," replied Miss Crawford. MP II 8 259 19
He gave it to me, and with the necklace I make over to you MP II 8 259 19
she laid down the necklace again on its cotton, and seemed MP II 8 259 20
Do you think Henry will claim the necklace as mine, and MP II 8 259 20
found you, take the necklace, and say no more about it. MP II 8 259 22
And as for this necklace, I do not suppose I have worn it MP II 8 260 22
thanks accepted the necklace again, for there was an MP II 8 260 23
he might not have some concern in this necklace!-- MP II 8 260 24
this doubtful good of a necklace, in some favourite box in MP II 9 261 1
It was about the necklace, which she was now most MP II 9 262 11
she wished. "return the necklace! no, my dear Fanny, upon MP II 9 262 11
cross beyond all comparison better than the necklace." MP II 9 263 15
Wear the necklace, as you are engaged to do to-morrow MP II 9 263 16
effort, to resolve on wearing Miss Crawford's necklace too. MP II 9 271 40
The necklace really looked very well; and Fanny left her MP II 9 271 40
for a moment at her necklace--with a smile--she thought MP II 10 274 8
the explanation of the second necklace--the real chain. MP II 10 274 9
And then before the ball, the necklace! MP III 5 362 18
"Do you mean then that your brother knew of the necklace MP III 5 362 19
it, nothing should have induced me to accept the necklace. MP III 5 362 21

NECKLACES (2)

to chuse from among several gold chains and necklaces. MP II 8 257 15
and when she came to the necklaces again, her good fortune MP II 9 270 40

NECKS (1)

which he calmly concluded had broken the necks of many. NA I 9 66 31

NECROMANCER OF THE BLACK FORES (1)

Necromancer of the Black Forest, Midnight Bell, Orphan of NA I 6 40 10

NECTARINES (1)

pyramids of grapes, nectarines, and peaches, soon PP III 3 268 6

NEED (152)

I need not tell you how much I miss him--how perpetually LS 5 250 3
at home at Churchill to need an invitation for lengthening LS 8 256 3
alone now, & very much in need of him to keep up our LS 13 262 1
mine as I listened to him, I need not attempt to describe. LS 23 284 5
My spirits are not so high as to need being repressed. LS 30 301 5
"You need not give yourself that trouble, sir." NA I 3 25 3
I need not have been afraid of disclaiming the compliment. NA I 3 27 33
assured her that she need not be longer uneasy, as the NA I 6 43 36
I need not ask you whether you are happy here, my dear NA I 7 51 51
age? but I need not ask you, for you look delightfully. NA I 10 70 1
With a yet sweeter smile, he said every thing that need be NA I 12 94 9
was not one of the family whom she need now fear to meet.-- NA I 12 96 24
upon this conviction she need not fear to acknowledge some NA II 10 200 3
need of my being played off to make her secure of Tilney. NA II 10 202 7
"No," said he, "my father's hands need not be strengthened, NA II 11 209 2
Frederick's confession of folly need not be forestalled. NA II 11 209 2
There is no need to fix. NA II 11 210 6
I need not go till just before you do, you know. NA II 13 224 17
but that something need not be three thousand pounds. SS I 2 9 7
A doubt of her regard, supposing him to feel it, need not SS I 4 22 18
He understood that she was in need of a dwelling, and SS I 4 23 20
seemed rather to stand in need of more money himself than SS I 5 27 6
bed in more need of repose than when she lay down in it. SS I 16 83 1
"Nay, Edward," said Marianne, "you need not reproach me. SS I 17 93 33
and you will have need of all your mutual affection to SS II 2 146 6
least it need not prevent my accepting her invitation. SS II 3 156 14
Your sister need not have any scruple even of visiting her, SS II 11 228 53
and that they need not therefore be very uneasy about it, SS III 1 269 57
"This is very strange!--sure he need not wait to be older." SS III 3 281 12
a connection--but I need not explain myself farther," he SS III 8 321 34
Well, at last, as I need not tell you, you were forced on SS III 8 327 55
really did, so much in need of encouragement and fresh air. SS III 13 361 2
and how he was received, need not be particularly told. SS III 13 361 3
This only need be said;--that when they all sat down to SS III 13 361 3

punishment, was sincere, need not be doubted;--nor that he SS III 14 379 18
need of encouragement, nor inclined to be silent himself. PP I 13 64 21
He can have nothing to say to me that any body need not PP I 19 104 5
He was too happy, however, to need much attention; and PP I 23 129 15
You need not. PP II 1 135 11
"Well, then, you need not be under any alarm. PP II 3 144 5
I need not explain myself farther; and though we know this PP II 3 148 26
church, and I need not say you will be delighted with her. PP II 5 157 6
7
I am sure,--therefore you need not conceal your age." PP II 6 166 39
"I assure you, madam," he replied, "that she does not need PP II 8 173 9
She directly replied, "you need not be frightened. PP II 10 184 20
21
which Mr. Darcy himself need not disdain, and PP II 10 187 40
waiter was told that he need not stay. Lydia laughed, and PP II 16 220 9
she had some relations for whom there was no need to blush. PP III 1 255 59
You need not send them word at Longbourn of my going, if PP III 5 291 60
but that it was no worse, she had need to be thankful. PP III 7 307 51
Had he done his duty in that respect, Lydia need not have PP III 8 308 1
going, the wedding need not be put off, for Mr. Darcy PP III 9 319 25
This was enough to prove that her approbation need not be PP III 17 378 44
"You need not distress yourself. PP III 18 381 14
Even your constant little heart need not take fright at MP I 3 27 35
"I think, sister, we need not keep Miss Lee any longer, MP I 3 28 38
39
very age of all others to need most attention and care, MP I 3 28 42
cried Mrs. Norris, "I am sure you need not regard it. MP I 6 53 9
The expense need not be any impediment. MP I 6 53 9
if so much could be done at Compton, we need not despair. MP I 6 55 17
him the hearing, that she need not distress herself on Mrs. MP I 8 79 23
"You need not hurry when the object is only to prevent my MP I 9 94 56
"No," replied Fanny, "but we need not give up his MP I 11 111 30
They had need be all in love, to find any amusement in MP I 12 118 22
and above all, such a need that the play should be at once MP I 14 130 2
need not be so scrupulous as I might feel necessary. MP I 15 141 21
It need not frighten you; it is a nothing of a part, a MP I 15 145 47
saying "I need not be afraid of appearing before him." MP II 1 175 2
himself, observed, that he need not inquire, for her MP II 1 178 7
One need not envy the new Mrs. Rushworth with such a home MP II 4 210 21
Its being a gift of my brother's need not make the MP II 8 259 22
protest against such an office, but you need not be afraid. MP II 9 269 35
either you or me, that we need be afraid of, for I can MP II 9 269 38
You need not fear me. MP II 9 270 38
unsaid; but there was no need of confusion, for her MP II 12 295 22
I need not repeat what has passed. MP III 1 321 47
If she did not need counsel, she must need the comfort of MP III 4 345 4
a mind so much in need of help, and so much deserving it. MP III 9 397 8
Our confidences in you need not clash.-- MP III 13 420 2
I need not particularize. MP III 13 421 2
She need not have been uneasy. MP III 14 431 8
I need not say how rejoiced I shall be to hear there has MP III 14 433 13
Miss Crawford need not be alarmed for her. MP III 15 438 4
Miss Crawford need not have urged secrecy with so much MP III 15 438 7
in the same way again--she need not fear a repetition--it MP III 16 453 17
last half year, to be in need of the true kindness of her MP III 17 469 24
opposition of taste, no need of drawing new hopes of MP III 17 471 28
cheerful--Mr. Weston need not spend a single evening in E I 1 12 41
by any body else--but you need not be afraid--they are E I 3 24 14
You need not be afraid of unwholesome preserves here. E I 3 25 14
But a farmer can need none of my help, and is therefore in E I 4 29 14
his being illiterate and coarse need not disturb us." E I 4 34 40
You need not be prompted to write with the appearance of E I 7 52 11
man that everybody says he need not eat a single meal by E I 9 75 26
every sort of sensation that declining life can need. E I 10 86 21
"But you need not imagine Mr. Weston to have felt what you E I 11 96 26
I need not so totally despair of an equal alliance, as to E I 15 132 35
not suffering any disappointment that need be cared for. E I 16 135 7
She need not trouble herself to pity him. he only wanted E I 16 135 7
no need to find excuses for Mr. Elton's absenting himself. E I 16 138 17
occur again, and therefore you need not think about it." E II 3 180 55
Weston at Ford's; but he need not hurry any body else." E II 5 193 6
he need not attempt to describe what the effect was. E II 6 199 10
I need not tell you what is to be done. E II 7 210 14
It need not detain us long. E II 9 234 34
doing that in which she need not blush to compare herself E II 11 247 2
to wrap Miss Emma up, you need not have any fears, sir.' E II 11 252 37
And I need not bring the whole family, you know." E II 11 255 53
had need be all grace to acquit himself well through it. E II 14 271 5
No, indeed, Miss Woodhouse, you need not be afraid; I can E II 14 271 15
And as to its recommendations to you, I fancy I need not E II 14 275 32
justice to say that he need not be ashamed of his friend. E II 14 278 50
You and I need not be afraid. E II 15 283 9
A woman with fewer resources than I have, need not have E II 16 290 2
"No," cried Mr. Knightley, "that need not be the E II 18 312 49
convinced her that every thing need not be put off. E III 6 352 2
But consider;--you need not be afraid of delegating power E III 6 354 14
the exercise and variety which her spirits seemed to need. E III 6 361 42
"Oh! very well," exclaimed Miss Bates, "then I need not be E III 7 370 24
Harriet would be anxiety enough; she need no longer be E III 11 403 2
Oh!--you need not be afraid of owning it to me, for Mr. E III 11 404 6
would be no need of compassion to the girl who believed E III 11 408 33
her, and to resolve that it need not and should not.-- E III 13 431 38
She said enough to show there need not be despair--and to E III 13 431 38
and communicate all that need be told by letter; that it E III 14 435 4
You are all goodness, and I believe there will be need of E III 14 436 8
If you need farther explanation, I have the honour, my E III 14 437 8
in the meanwhile, we need not talk much on the subject." E III 18 471 16
"You need not be at any pains to reconcile me to the match. E III 18 473 24
You need not be afraid, Miss Elliot, of your own sweet P III 3 18 7
anticipated, need not involve any particular awkwardness. P III 4 31 12
single so long for our sakes, need be suspected now. P III 5 35 14
any thing amiss, you need not be afraid of mentioning it." P III 6 45 9
Had he wished ever to see her again, he need not have P III 7 58 21
"Oh!--but, Charles, tell Captain Wentworth, he need not be P III 8 66 20
was in company with him, I need not affect to have no P III 10 87 26
on Miss Musgrove, there need not be the least uneasiness P III 12 113 56
to assist Mrs. Harville, I think it need be only one.-- P III 12 114 61
Mary need not have feared her sister's being in any degree P IV 6 165 9
She was in need of a little interval for recollection." P IV 8 185 18
You need not say anything more of your ignorance.-- P IV 8 186 26
I need not ask after her. P IV 9 193 10
You need not tell me that you had a pleasant evening. P IV 9 194 14
"At present, believe me, I have no need of your services, " P IV 9 203 72
at all hours--but I need not be particular on this subject. P IV 9 207 90
"Well, my dear Penelope, you need not be so alarmed about P IV 10 213 9
You need not tell her so, but I thought her dress hideous P IV 10 215 15
a very enviable one, you need not covet it) is that of P IV 11 235 32
But indeed, my dear, you need not be uneasy. P IV 11 239 52
I need not ask whether I see the house; (looking towards S 1 365 1
invalid--the very spot which thousands seemed in need of.-- S 1 369 1
it need not have been binding, if I had not chose it.--" S 7 400 1

NEEDED (22)

My dear Alicia There needed not this last fit of the LS 29 298 1
Catherine's swelling heart needed relief. NA II 13 226 25
The General needed no more. NA II 15 247 13
place of experience, his character needed no attestation. NA II 16 249 1
dear to him, and who most needed a provision, by any SS I 1 4 3
She needed no time for deliberation or inquiry. SS I 4 23 20
Elinor needed little observation to perceive that her SS I 11 55 6
Elinor had not needed this to be assured of the injustice SS II 9 201 4
in a temper of mind which needed all the improvement in SS III 13 369 35
on what improvements were needed to it; and from thence, SS III 13 372 46
It needed all Jane's steady mildness to bear these attacks PP I 23 129 14
She had scarcely needed her present observation to be PP III 9 318 19
He scarcely needed an invitation to stay supper; and PP III 13 345 19
seeing how much she needed encouragement, tried to be all MP I 2 12 2
for speech; and he needed a little recollection before he MP I 9 87 16
unwelcome; and it needed all the felicity of being again MP II 1 183 23
time his measured manner needed; and very little of her MP II 7 240 10
soon have known that she needed it, for she wanted MP III 11 409 6
such perturbation, and it needed a very strong effort to E I 15 133 38
clearness and delicacy which really needed no fuller bloom. E II 2 167 12
were supplied by her husband to all who needed them. P III 12 111 50
her own husband sometimes needed, & so entirely waiting to S 2 372 1

NEEDFUL (6)

expressing every thing needful; attention to his words, NA I 10 80 60
of the letters; a needful exertion, for as the time of NA I 15 121 26
The needful was comprised in Mr. Morland's promise; his NA I 15 122 28
needful solicitude, which there were no children to supply. MP I 1 8 9
Independence was more needful than ever; the want of it at MP II 3 202 25
of the party, to the needful civilities of the moment, P IV 8 184 17

NEEDLE (4)

her work, if she lost her needle or broke her thread, if NA I 9 60 1
of weariness, much oftener than she moved her needle.-- NA II 15 241 7
had given each of them a needle book, made by some SS II 14 254 28
an excellent housemaid, and works very well at her needle. SS III 4 287 22

NEEDLE-WORK (3)

greater inclination for needle-work, she could no longer NA II 15 240 2
There was a great deal of needle-work to be done moreover, MP I 18 166 6
slackened in the needle-work, which, at the beginning, MP III 3 337 11

NEEDLEFULLS (1)

body in quest of two needlefulls of thread or a second MP II 6 236 21

NEEDLESS (11)

"My dear, you give yourself a great deal of needless NA II 14 234 10
make the invitation needless, by bringing Elinor to town SS II 14 253 25
in them the quick feelings, and needless alarm of a lover. SS III 6 305 16
now alike needless, were soon afterwards dismissed. SS III 11 355 45
It would be needless to say, that the gentlemen advanced SS III 13 370 36
assume the character of needless precipitance merely to PP I 10 49 28
with unwearying civility that they were perfectly needless. PP I 15 74 11
this anxiety to be quite needless, yet if she feels it, it PP II 3 148 26
way; but his alarms were needless; the sixteen miles being E I 11 91 3
will have their little nonsenses and needless cares." E II 11 253 43
all the vulgarity of needless repetition, and all the E III 14 442 8

NEEDLESSLY (3)

as intruding themselves needlessly long, she urged Jane to PP I 12 59 1
of him, and so needlessly often the rehearsal of the first MP I 18 164 2
an arrangement, so needlessly troublesome to your servant. E II 16 296 37

NEEDLEWORK (3)

Elizabeth took up some needlework, and was sufficiently PP I 10 47 2
some long piece of needlework, of little use and no beauty, MP I 2 19 31
have had her here to do needlework, I observe she always E I 1 9 19

NEEDS (6)

He knows that human nature needs more lessons than a MP II 7 248 42
worth a great deal more than any little exertion it needs." E II 5 190 24
the affair burst out, needs explanation; for though the E III 14 440 8
of a second marriage, needs no apology to the public, P III 1 5 8
dozen in the nation,) always needs a note of explanation. P III 3 24 36
And poor young man, he needs it bad enough;--for though I S 7 400 1

NEGATIVE (10)

She was answered in the negative. SS II 4 165 26
to her father, whose negative might be uttered in such a PP I 19 109 22
A most welcome negative followed the last question--and PP II 19 241 17
off for the north, received at first an absolute negative. PP III 8 313 22
Fanny gave a quick negative, and tried to hide her MP II 7 244 28
of any consultation, put a decided negative on it. MP III 1 319 39
She thanked Miss Crawford, but gave a decided negative.-- MP III 14 436 15
to take her friend's negative, though Miss Fairfax E III 6 359 37
be, gave it all the negative of great astonishment, great P III 4 26 2
negative, he was not to be induced to sit down again. P III 8 72 58
59

NEGATIVED (2)

politely and more earnestly negatived, she seated herself. PP I 10 51 45
being absolutely negatived, it was "and when shall we see S 9 410 1

NEGATIVES (1)

negatives, is there any allusion to making a sacrifice. E II 13 264 2

NEGLECT (41)

lamenting so bitterly the neglect of her education, I am LS 6 251 1
Her neglect of her husband, her encouragement of other men, LS 12 260 2
with the servant whose neglect had reduced her to open the NA I 13 102 27
consideration which the neglect or unkindness of slight NA II 14 239 28
He could hardly suppose I should neglect them. SS I 2 9 6
Elinor saw, and pitied her for, the neglect of abilities SS I 22 127 2
was the easiest means of atoning for his own neglect. SS II 11 228 51
indifference is no apology for your cruel neglect of her. SS III 8 322 37
by them, that we do not know how to take this neglect."-- W 334 13
"Yes, yes, we must not neglect our old neighbours. W 337 15
I was sure you loved your girls too well to neglect such PP I 2 7 24
"I cannot comprehend the neglect of a family library in in PP I 8 38 32
"Neglect! I am sure you neglect nothing that can add to PP I 8 38 33
You had better neglect your relations, than run the risk PP I 22 123 7
her, I shall charge her not to neglect it on any account. PP II 8 173 10
one, and offended by the neglect of the other, on the very PP II 13 208 8
The mischief of neglect and mistaken indulgence towards PP III 4 280 25
But of every other neglect I can believe him capable. PP III 5 282 4
I am sure there was some great neglect or other on their PP III 5 287 35
I must not, however, neglect the duties of my station, or PP III 15 363 22
us all in poverty and neglect, would be enough to make MP I 1 7 6
grown into a habit from neglect, what could be expected MP I 9 87 16
If the man who holds it is so, it is by the neglect of his MP I 9 92 45
and consideration make me more sensible of my own neglect. MP I 9 95 70
tyranny, of ridicule, and neglect, yet almost every MP I 16 152 2
of notice and praise as other women were of neglect. MP II 3 198 13
was concerned at her own neglect;--and "shall I play to MP II 4 206 5
ashamed of their own abominable neglect and unkindness. MP II 12 297 33
over the too common neglect of the qualification, the MP III 3 339 22
Her aunt did not neglect her; she wrote again and again; MP III 13 427 12
consideration. absolute neglect of the mother and sisters, E II 4 185 12
of pointed neglect that could be further requisite.-- E III 3 332 1
rather than the remembrance of neglect in such a cause. E III 5 350 31
Abbey, with all the old neglect of prospect, had scarcely E III 6 358 35
such shameful, insolent neglect of her, and such apparent E III 14 441 8
Bad enough as it is, for I absolutely neglect them both to E III 16 456 23
connection, as he had formerly taken pains to shew neglect. P IV 2 135 35
He had explained away all the appearance of neglect on his P IV 3 138 7
The neglect had been visited on the head of the sinner, P IV 4 149 12
he can neglect and desert without the smallest compunction. P IV 9 199 53
"I am not one of those who neglect the reigning power to P IV 10 224 48

NEGLECTED (21)

to be imputed to her neglected education & early marriage, LS 8 255 2
She has been sadly neglected however, & her mother ought LS 15 266 3
Her father was a clergyman, without being neglected, or NA I 1 13 1
Since he had neglected to do it on first coming to the SS I 5 27 6
past, I saw some duty neglected, or some failing indulged. SS III 10 346 28
Without a governess you must have been neglected." PP II 6 165 30
But I have an aunt, too, who must not be longer neglected." PP III 18 382 19
To be neglected before one's time, must be very vexatious. MP I 5 51 41
for she had been feeling neglected, and been struggling MP I 7 74 59
I am afraid they may feel themselves neglected. MP II 3 196 2
Now she is dependent, helpless, friendless, neglected, MP II 12 297 33
Fanny, because she had neglected her; and she would have MP III 2 332 20
had been promised to have done for him, entirely neglected. MP III 7 381 26
I am unwilling to fancy myself neglected for a young one. MP III 9 394 1
to Newmarket, where a neglected fall, and a good deal of MP III 13 426 10

a lady--and a bride, especially, is never to be neglected. E II 14 280 58
I have neglected her too long. E II 16 291 6
him fancying himself neglected; and though her E III 19 483 9
Elliot, of your own sweet flower-garden's being neglected." P III 3 18 7
distress that of fancying herself neglected and ill-used. P III 5 37 21
that nothing might be neglected of attention to Lady D. or S 12 423 1

NEGLECTING (5)
Pardon me for neglecting to profit by your advice, which PP I 18 97 61
"Not perhaps of neglecting his own interest. PP III 5 282 4
I should hate myself if I were capable of neglecting her. MP I 1 7 8
Emma, finding her so determined upon neglecting her music, E II 14 278 43
had been so many months neglecting, was now the very one E III 9 389 16

NEGLIGENCE (8)
then suppose, by the negligence of a servant in the place NA II 7 172 2
probability of some negligence--some--(involuntarily she NA II 9 196 25
in each other's way: negligence could never leave them SS II 10 213 4
on by myself, by such negligence of my own health, as I SS III 10 345 28
I hear dreadful complaints of my negligence wherever I go, W 335 13
the housemaid in negligence; and if she accepted any PP II 7 169 3
up in the midst of negligence and error, she should have MP III 9 397 8
"So seldom that any negligence or blunder appears! E II 16 296 42

NEGLIGENT (12)
& perhaps may think me negligent for not writing before. LS 19 273 1
I have been very negligent--but are you now at leisure to NA I 3 25 2
the very gentleman whose negligent servant left behind him NA II 16 251 5
shy, that I often seem negligent, when I am only kept back SS I 17 94 42
common occasions, a most negligent and dilatory PP III 6 294 1
but he was more negligent of his family, his habits were MP III 8 389 3
"Certainly; and if he is lazy or negligent, I will write MP III 11 412 28
he will have the advantage over negligent superiority. E I 13 111 17
in her, as rather negligent in that respect, and as not E II 1 155 2
They were sneering and negligent. E II 15 281 3
She had not deserved it; she had often been negligent or E III 12 415 1
cannot even weary her by negligent treatment--and had he E III 13 428 23

NEGOCIATION (3)
was carrying on a negociation for the exchange of a few SS II 11 220 1
in a negociation for William price's knave increased. MP II 7 241 19
all the former doubt and solicitude of the negociation. P III 9 78 19

NEGUS (2)
in her bar to make fresh negus for the happy dancers above. W 336 14
hopes and fears, soup and negus, sore-footed and fatigued, MP II 10 280 33

NEICE (9)
returned on Thursday night, bringing his neice with him. LS 17 269 1
any conversation with my neice; she is shy, & I think I LS 17 270 6
& your dear neice is included of course; I long to see her. LS 40 309 1
of Mrs Vernon & her neice, for the former soon perceived LS 42 311 1
in Croydon, than the neice of an old woman who threw W 349 24
There was a little neice at Croydon, to be fondly enquired W 350 24
I was her own neice, & he left to herself the power & the W 352 26
she had chosen clara, a neice--, more helpless & more S 3 379 1
a young lady (probably a neice) under her care, than on S 9 409 1

NEICE'S (1)
proposed her Neice's returning with them into the country. LS 42 312 5

NEICES (2)
She has two neices of her own. PP I 2 6 5
all, Mrs. Long and her neices must stand their chance; and PP I 2 7 16

NEIGHBOUR (32)
A neighbour of ours, Dr. Skinner, was here for his health NA I 8 54 7
of it, for then I shall have her for a neighbour you know." SS I 20 114 44
meat, and have not a neighbour nearer than your mother. SS II 8 197 22
and agreeable a neighbour, and then it was that he SS III 3 283 20
she turned to her neighbour with repeated & fervent W 331 11
But I am afraid I have been a very sad neighbour of late. W 334 13
his eye by occasional glances at his fair neighbour.-- W 345 21
the second-hand intelligence of their neighbour Lady Lucas. PP I 3 9 1
if we shall not find a very charming neighbour in her." PP I 4 15 10
not too clever to be a valuable neighbour to Mrs. Bennet.-- PP I 5 18 2
Lucas was his neighbour, till Sir William thus began. PP I 6 25 25
of their amiable neighbour, Miss Lucas, and then explained PP I 23 128 10
indeed," added Charlotte, "and a most attentive neighbour." PP II 5 157 8
a husband and such a neighbour as were not often met with. PP II 7 168 1
when some barbarous neighbour, who could not be enough PP III 13 349 43
his fair neighbour with a look of considerable earnestness. MP II 7 246 37
"I want to be your neighbour, Sir Thomas, as you have MP II 7 247 38
as a permanent neighbour; but I hope, and believe, that MP II 7 247 39
to refresh her spirits by a change of place and neighbour. MP II 7 248 48
accustomary loan of a neighbour, applied himself to MP III 7 382 28
"A new neighbour for us all, Miss Woodhouse!" said Miss E II 3 174 35
I have the honour of being acquainted with a neighbour of E II 5 193 37
all her attention to the pleasantness of her neighbour. E II 8 214 13
But he always had been such a very kind neighbour!' E II 8 225 78
but resolve never to expose them to her neighbour again. E II 10 240 6
I wish my health allowed me to be a better neighbour. E II 16 294 27
of Mr. Weston's shall clear him and his next neighbour. E III 7 371 31
of Mrs. Elton's--a neighbour of Maple Grove; and, by the E III 15 447 25
an attentive neighbour, an obliging landlord, the husband P III 2 11 2
amazingly, and wish we had such a neighbour at Uppercross." P III 12 103 4
very obliging, friendly neighbour; a chearful, independant, S 3 376 1
D. dupuis & Mrs C. D's neighbour, there might be a mere S 11 420 1

NEIGHBOUR'S (2)
at the same time to carry back his neighbour's newspaper. MP III 7 384 36
former neighbour's present state, with proper interest. P III 6 49 22

NEIGHBOURHOOD (98)
Mr Smith now in this neighbourhood--(I have dined with him LS 4 248 1
There was not one Lord in the neighbourhood; no--not even NA I 1 16 10
man is surrounded by a neighbourhood of voluntary spies, NA II 9 197 29
the number of young dancing people in the neighbourhood. NA II 11 209 5
when once beyond the neighbourhood of Woodston, saved her NA II 14 231 5
respected in their own neighbourhood, as he had lately had NA II 15 246 12
a house in the neighbourhood, his invitation was accepted. SS I 2 8 1
dwelling in the neighbourhood of Norland; for to remove SS I 3 14 1
To quit the neighbourhood of Norland was no longer an evil; SS I 4 24 20
of every kind than any other family in the neighbourhood. SS I 7 32 1
juvenile part of the neighbourhood, for in summer he was SS I 7 32 2
would mix more in the neighbourhood, and repeated SS I 9 40 2
Is Allenham the only house in the neighbourhood to which SS I 15 76 11
"Have you an agreeable neighbourhood here? SS I 16 88 38
not . . . . that it is not in the neighbourhood of . . . ." SS III 3 279 4
or the rest of the neighbourhood, to suspect any part of SS III 8 324 42
appearance in the neighbourhood; & her eldest sister, W 315 1
his first entering a neighbourhood, this truth is so well PP I 1 3 2
and see Mr. Bingley when he comes into the neighbourhood." PP I 1 4 22
men of four thousand a year come into the neighbourhood." PP I 1 5 31
Accomplished girl in the neighbourhood; and Catherine and PP I 3 12 15
regiment in the neighbourhood; it was to remain the whole PP I 7 28 3
that neighbourhood, and take Pemberley for a kind of model. PP I 8 38 35
In a country neighbourhood you move in a very confined and PP I 9 43 17
by his manner of mentioning a country neighbourhood. PP I 9 43 19
many people in this neighbourhood, I believe there are few PP I 9 43 25
in the society of the neighbourhood, nor to his leaving PP I 14 66 1
House in the neighbourhood, except Netherfield. PP I 16 77 15
will not be affected by his being in the neighbourhood." PP I 16 78 19
topics, Meryton, the neighbourhood, the society, appearing PP I 16 78 22
instead of my own neighbourhood, where I assure you there PP I 19 106 10
The house, furniture, neighbourhood, and roads, were all PP II 3 146 19
neighbourhood in general, was beyond the Collinses' reach. PP II 7 169 5
be better for the neighbourhood that he should give up the PP II 9 178 9
the convenience of the neighbourhood as for his own, and PP II 9 178 9
Any thing beyond the very neighbourhood of Longbourn, I PP II 9 179 20
approbation of the neighbourhood, and the regard which his PP II 13 206 4
the young ladies in the neighbourhood were drooping apace. PP II 18 229 1
he continued in the neighbourhood, offering at the same PP III 1 255 60
the neighbourhood had of him, should then be overthrown? PP III 5 285 16
and with proportionate speed through the neighbourhood. PP III 8 309 6
She was busily searching through the neighbourhood for a PP III 8 310 7
Into one house in this neighbourhood, they shall never PP III 8 310 9
in the neighbourhood, before she was banished to the north. PP III 8 314 22
acquaintance in that neighbourhood, with a good humoured PP III 9 316 6
A great many changes have happened in the neighbourhood, PP III 11 336 49
not grow up in this neighbourhood without many advantages. MP I 1 6 6
and they entered the neighbourhood with the usual fair MP I 3 24 6
the belles of the neighbourhood; and as they joined to MP I 4 34 4
lookers-on of the neighbourhood, who had, for many weeks MP I 4 39 11
on her coming into the neighbourhood, civilly declined it MP I 8 76 7
in his parish and his neighbourhood, where the parish and MP I 9 93 49
where the parish and neighbourhood are of a size capable MP I 9 93 49
enliven the whole neighbourhood exceedingly"--Edmund still MP I 15 148 60
the discussion of the neighbourhood, except that the MP II 3 203 29
first society in the neighbourhood--looked-up to perhaps MP II 4 210 21
of his own in that neighbourhood; and it was not merely MP II 7 246 37
his attachment to that neighbourhood did not depend upon MP II 7 246 37
the only house in the neighbourhood in which I should not MP II 7 248 44
rent a place in this neighbourhood--perhaps Stanwix Lodge. MP II 12 295 20
and the same close neighbourhood, he went on, re-urging MP III 3 342 34
The postman's knock within the neighbourhood was beginning MP III 9 398 10
of his time there--always there, or in the neighbourhood. MP III 10 405 18
His having been in the same neighbourhood, Fanny already MP III 16 450 8
insult to the neighbourhood, as to expect it to notice her. MP III 17 465 13
Grants in such close neighbourhood would have been most MP III 17 469 23
The neighbourhood of Brunswick Square is very different E I 12 103 37
consideration of the neighbourhood which Mr. Elton had E I 16 136 9
Had they a large neighbourhood?-- E II 5 191 27
the convenience of the neighbourhood than from any run on E II 6 197 5
and while the neighbourhood had been in a particularly E II 6 197 5
the extent of the neighbourhood about Enscombe, and the E II 8 221 48
and improve a country neighbourhood; and conceived Miss E II 15 281 1
I saw a vast deal of that in the neighbourhood round Maple E II 17 299 8
is a family in that neighbourhood who are such an E II 18 310 34
Your neighbourhood is increasing, and you mix more with it. E II 18 311 46
him of such near neighbourhood to many dear friends--for E III 1 317 8
it would be really having Frank in their neighbourhood. E III 1 317 10
a set of people in the neighbourhood to Mr. Knightley, he E III 3 334 8
neighbourhood:--lives only four miles from Maple Grove. E III 8 380 13
Other poultry-yards in the neighbourhood also suffered.-- E III 19 483 10
Anne haggard, Mary coarse, every face in the neighbourhood P III 1 6 11
credit which a scanty neighbourhood afforded; and thirteen P III 1 7 12
A small house in their own neighbourhood, where they might P III 2 14 9
to descend into a small house in his own neighbourhood. P III 2 14 11
house in the same neighbourhood for Sir Walter, was P III 2 15 13
in that immediate neighbourhood, which, however, had not P III 3 21 18
The neighbourhood was not large, but the Musgroves were P III 6 47 14
He was in orders, and having a curacy in the neighbourhood P III 9 73 4
The scenes in its neighbourhood, Charmouth, with its high P III 11 95 9
they were in the neighbourhood of Uppercross, and there P III 12 117 73
By remaining in the neighbourhood, I am become inured to P IV 1 125 16
regretted in their old neighbourhood, which Anne could not P IV 3 137 3
to one or two very poor families in this neighbourhood. P IV 5 155 9
"Our neighbourhood cannot spare such a pleasant family. P IV 6 164 8
Every neighbourhood should have a great lady.-- S 3 375 1
of Denham Park in the neighbourhood of Sanditon had S 3 375 1
ascertain whether the neighbourhood of Tombuctoo might not S 8 405 2

NEIGHBOURHOODS (1)
I believe there are few neighbourhoods larger. PP I 9 43 25

NEIGHBOURING (6)
will roll round the neighbouring mountains--and during the NA II 5 159 19
once by a rap at a neighbouring door, when a loud one was SS II 4 161 7
neighbouring gentlemen, on his returning to Netherfield. PP III 11 332 24
bought an estate in a neighbouring country to Derbyshire, PP III 19 385 3
He had been visiting a friend in a neighbouring county, MP I 6 52 1
who lived in the neighbouring market town, and Lady P III 1 10 21

NEIGHBOURLY (4)
such kind of neighbourly acts as his own wife pointed out. SS I 2 13 29
after a ball, & this neighbourly inclination was increased W 337 16
toleration of the neighbourly attempts at the parsonage. MP II 7 238 1
But since you are so very neighbourly, I beleive Miss S 6 394 1

NEIGHBOURS (48)
tea from one of their neighbours; it was thankfully NA I 2 23 22
business with the partners or wives of their neighbours." NA I 10 76 29
perfections of their neighbours, or fancying that they NA I 10 77 33
offence to any of my neighbours, if a small sacrifice of NA II 11 210 6
waiting on their worthy neighbours, that he might have NA II 15 243 9
us merely to be subservient to those of our neighbours. SS I 17 94 38
They are excellent neighbours to you in the country, I SS II 11 222 9
will be such very near neighbours, (for I understand the SS III 4 290 38
Mr E.s house was higher than most of its neighbours with W 322 2
A very stiff meeting between these near neighbours ensued-- W 327 8
her dancing with some of our old neighbours I confess.--" W 337 15
"Yes, yes, we must not neglect our old neighbours. W 337 15
"Well, I only beg you will not set your neighbours against W 350 24
retail it all among her neighbours as soon as she could. PP I 16 75 3
neighbours who think of themselves before anybody else. PP II 2 140 4
as this, one cannot see too little of one's neighbours. PP III 5 293 67
and all their other neighbours, and to hear herself called PP III 9 317 10
neighbours every time they go away, and come back again." PP III 11 332 25
to know that her neighbours might all see Mr. Bingley in PP III 11 333 27
to do the same by all her neighbours in Meryton. PP III 13 350 55
equipage did not answer to that of any of their neighbours. PP III 14 351 1
And her neighbours at Lucas Lodge, therefore, (for through PP III 15 360 1
For what do we live, but to make sport for our neighbours, PP III 15 364 22
his jealousy of his neighbours, his doubts of their MP I 12 115 4
The compliments of his neighbours were over; he was no E I 2 19 14
neighbours and friends, and a home that wanted for nothing. E I 3 21 4
playing whist with his neighbours five times a-week, than E I 11 96 26
I always say, we are quite blessed in our neighbours.-- E II 3 175 39
and who have been your neighbours these ten years." E II 7 210 19
that some of our good neighbours might be so obliging E II 8 216 16
be as insincere as your neighbours, when it is necessary; E II 9 234 33
does not want to be wiser or wittier than his neighbours." E II 15 288 38
I beg you will not let your neighbours follow your example. E II 18 305 6
who happens to be one of their nearest neighbours. E II 18 310 34
Never were such neighbours. E III 2 322 19
Miss Woodhouse (for his neighbours knew that he loved to E III 3 336 12
as that of all her neighbours was by the approach of it. E III 6 352 1
meet Mr. and Mrs. Elton, and any other of his neighbours.-- E III 6 356 30
never had anybody such good neighbours) was distasteful. E III 9 391 19
they were still near neighbours and intimate friends; and P III 1 5 7
trespass of one of his neighbours; farmer's man breaking P III 3 23 28
How are your neighbours at the great house?" P III 5 38 28
of house-keeping, neighbours, dress, dancing, and music. P III 6 42 3
between such near neighbours, and make those hints P III 6 46 11
"I do not think they improve at all as neighbours. P IV 6 164 7
abdication in her next neighbours, she found herself at P IV 8 189 46
now & then to visit her neighbours, in the old coach which S 2 373 1
My early hours are not to put my neighbours to S 6 390 1

NEIGHBOURS' (3)
neighbours' looks their equal amazement in beholding it. PP I 18 90 8
their own instruction, and their neighbours' entertainment. MP III 17 471 29
You want your neighbours' opinions. E II 11 254 50

NEPHEW (46)
house the family of his nephew Mr. Henry Dashwood, the SS I 1 3 1
In the society of his nephew and niece, and their children, SS I 1 3 1
leave his estate from his nephew;--but he left it to him SS I 1 4 3
to it spoke to his nephew; & Emma on perceiving herself W 332 11
from the pride of her nephew, who chuses that every one PP I 16 84 58

nephew of Lady Catherine de Bourgh in this assembly!-- PP I 18 96 57
I believe him to be Lady Catherine's nephew. PP I 18 97 59
as before, to her other nephew; till the latter walked PP II 8 174 12
of my mother's nephew, Colonel Fitzwilliam, and myself. PP II 12 201 5
"How could I ever think her like her nephew?" said she, as PP III 14 353 21
afterwards united to my nephew, my own nephew, Mr. Darcy. PP III 14 353 26
Has he, has my nephew, made you an offer of marriage?" PP III 14 354 34
If there is no other objection to my marrying your nephew, PP III 14 355 44
My daughter and my nephew are formed for each other. PP III 14 356 50
"In marrying your nephew, I should not consider myself as PP III 14 356 51
said Elizabeth, "if your nephew does not object to them, PP III 14 356 53
How far your nephew might approve of your interference in PP III 14 357 61
no regard, then for the honour and credit of my nephew! PP III 14 357 65
an application to her nephew; and how he might take a PP III 15 360 2
being a letter from the nephew, instead of the aunt; and PP III 15 362 11
12
promise from her nephew, which she had refused to give. PP III 16 367 9
But, if I were you, I would stand by the nephew. PP III 18 383 23
on the marriage of her nephew; and as she gave way to all PP III 19 388 12
minutes by her eldest nephew and niece, who were all- MP I 13 129 40
who knew better than his nephew the value of such a loan, MP II 6 237 23
and listening to what his nephew could relate of the MP II 7 251 63
and commending what his nephew had said, he added, "I do MP II 8 252 1
The first was from the Admiral to inform his nephew, in a MP II 13 298 3
the infinite joy of her nephew and niece, in the MP III 6 373 23
The being left with her sister and nephew, and all the MP III 16 448 2
"But she is so fond of the nephew: he is so very great a E I 14 123 24
governed by the nephew, to whom she owes nothing at all." E I 14 123 24
before we pretend to decide upon what her nephew can do. E I 18 146 15
They would feel that they could trust him; that the nephew, E I 18 147 18
allow their nephew to remain a day beyond his fortnight. E II 12 257 1
when writing to her nephew two days before, though from E II 12 258 7
as might disappoint her nephew in the most reasonable E III 6 361 41
Churchill had sent his nephew a few lines, containing, E III 8 383 31
Though her nephew had had no particular reason to hasten E III 9 387 11
guidable man, to be persuaded into any thing by his nephew. E III 9 388 13
All that remained to be wished was, that the nephew should E III 9 388 13
"Most favourably for his nephew--gave his consent with E III 10 398 55
sense of injury to her nephew Henry, whose rights as heir E III 15 449 35
Sir Edward, the present baronet, nephew to Sir Harry, S 3 377 1
not bequeath it to his nephew, my dear--it was no bequest. S 7 400 1
that he shd wish his nephew to have his watch; but it need S 7 400 1
NEPHEW'S (7)
And is such a girl to be my nephew's sister? PP III 14 357 62
by the contents of her nephew's letter, that Charlotte, PP III 18 383 26
in the midst of her nephew's account of a shipwreck or an MP II 6 236 21
His nephew's introduction to Admiral Crawford might be of MP II 9 266 21
A letter arrived from Mr. Churchill to urge his nephew's E II 12 258 7
nephew's letter to Randall's communicated a change of plan. E III 1 317 7
to digress from their nephew's state, as to give the P III 7 54 4
NEPHEWS (6)
There were two nephews of Lady Catherine to require them, PP II 7 170 7
almost engrossed by her nephews, speaking to them, PP II 8 172 2
My nephews and nieces!--I shall often have a niece with me. E I 10 86 21
it is, that we think alike about our nephews and nieces. E I 12 98 2
3
but to Emma and her nephews:--in her imagination it E III 3 336 13
nephews taken away their alphabets--their box of letters? E III 5 347 19
NEPTUNE (1)
Can it be Neptune? E I 9 72 17
NERVE (1)
would have made every nerve in Elinor's body thrill with SS III 13 370 37
NERVES (35)
her irritation of nerves and shortness of breath--no NA I 13 102 25
Nerves fit for sliding pannels and tapestry?" NA II 5 158 13
when Marianne, whose nerves could not then bear any sudden SS II 9 203 11
to agitate her nerves and fill her mind;--and she was SS III 5 297 32
You have no compassion on my poor nerves." PP I 1 5 28
I have a high respect for your nerves. PP I 1 5 29
Have a little compassion on my nerves. PP I 2 6 8
me, I am cruelly used, nobody feels for my poor nerves." PP II 3 113 26
of her eldest niece, as tolerably to quiet her nerves. MP I 4 38 9
to bed full of it, her nerves still agitated by the shock MP I 16 150 1
dependence perhaps on the nerves of his wife and children, MP II 1 180 10
with her uncle, was more than her nerves could bear. MP II 5 218 12
felt all over her, in all her pulses, and all her nerves. MP III 5 357 5
also, as she now learnt, nerves much affected, spirits MP III 14 430 2
Her more fearless disposition and happier nerves made MP III 17 472 31
was no rest for his benevolent nerves till it was all gone. E I 2 19 14
and confusion which his nerves could not have born under E I 11 92 3
had many fears and many nerves, and was as fond of her own E I 11 92 4
from the state of her nerves; she had not yet possessed E II 10 240 6
as the utmost that his nerves could bear--and here would E II 16 292 7
Her nerves were under continual irritation and suffering; E III 1 317 7
she could harden her nerves sufficiently to feel the P III 4 30 10
eight years ago,--was a new sort of trial to Anne's nerves. P III 6 52 33
I have not nerves for the sort of thing." P III 7 56 12
he brought senses and nerves that could be instantly P III 12 111 50
exceedingly weak, and her nerves susceptible to the P IV 2 129 1
"Though he had not nerves for coming away with us and P IV 2 131 12
a bad restorative of the nerves, which Louisa's illness P IV 2 134 30
influence her health, her nerves, her courage, her P IV 6 167 20
overlooked him; her nerves were strengthened by these P IV 7 180 32
But in truth, I doubt whether Susan's nerves wd be equal S 5 387 1
decidedly better, but her nerves are a good deal deranged. S 5 387 1
That man who can read them unmoved must have the nerves of S 7 396 1
To say the truth nerves are the worst part of my S 10 415 1
What nerves you must have!-- S 10 418 1
NERVOUS (31)
nervous irritability, not to speak to her for the world. SS II 7 180 5
head, a weakened stomach, and a general nervous faintness. SS II 7 185 16
much plagued lately with nervous head-aches, which make SS II 10 219 38
"She is not well, she has had a nervous complaint on her SS II 11 227 49
the author of this nervous distress, that he instantly SS II 12 236 41
her sister,--she is very nervous,--she has not Elinor's SS II 12 236 43
as it makes me nervous to be much alone." W 351 25
When she was discontented she fancied herself nervous. PP I 1 5 34
People who suffer as I do from nervous complaints can have PP I 20 113 28
It makes me very nervous and poorly, to be thwarted so in PP II 2 140 4
she still was occasionally nervous and invariably silly. PP III 19 385 1
He knew her to be very timid, and exceedingly nervous; and MP III 1 320 44
was yet to come, and in a nervous agitation which made MP III 2 329 10
and temper, delicate and nervous like Fanny's, an evil MP III 8 391 11
He was a nervous man, easily depressed; fond of every body E I 1 7 10
his picture made him so nervous, that I could only take E I 6 45 21
excepting those little nervous head-aches and palpitations E I 12 103 39
visit was of use to the nervous part of her complaint, I E I 13 114 32
on the subject as his nervous constitution allowed; but E I 15 128 17
Her father was growing nervous, and could not understand E II 14 280 61
no service to the wilful or nervous part of her disorder. E III 1 316 6
of illness in her; a nervous seizure, which had lasted E III 6 363 53
severe headachs, and a nervous fever to a degree, which E III 9 389 16
was unfavourable to a nervous disorder:--confined always E III 9 389 16
wonderful change of his nervous system, but by the E III 19 483 10
repeated to herself again, and again, in nervous gratitude. P III 7 60 26
quite ashamed of being so nervous, so overcome by such a P III 9 81 34
She felt its application to herself, felt it in a nervous P IV 11 231 10
But perhaps you are nervous." S 10 415 1
"I am very nervous.-- S 10 415 1
as I can understand what nervous complaints are, I have a S 10 416 1
NERVOUSLY (1)
was now most nervously and apprehensively happy in E I 11 91 2
NERVOUSNESS (3)
At last--it seemed an at last to Fanny's nervousness, MP II 13 306 28
of all the little nervousness I have been feeling lately.-- E III 14 436 7
and there cannot be a surer sign of nervousness.--" S 10 416 1
NEST (1)
To this nest of comforts Fanny now walked down to try its MP I 16 152 3
NESTLED (1)
He had nestled down his head most conveniently. E I 6 45 21
NESTS (1)
by hens forsaking their nests, or being stolen by a fox, SS III 6 303 10
NET (1)
They all paint tables, cover skreens and net purses. PP I 8 39 45
NETHERFIELD (72)
Mrs. Long says that Netherfield is taken by a young man of PP I 1 3 10
happily settled at Netherfield," said Mrs. Bennet to her PP I 3 9 2
and never settled at Netherfield as he ought to be. PP I 3 10 4
so early, and talked of giving one himself at Netherfield. PP I 3 10 6
her eldest daughter much admired by the Netherfield party. PP I 3 12 15
at Netherfield, and leave the next generation to purchase. PP I 4 15 12
an accidental recommendation to look at Netherfield house. PP I 4 16 13
at last how he liked Netherfield, and he could not help PP I 5 19 12
ladies of Longbourn soon waited on those of Netherfield. PP I 6 21 1
from Netherfield, and the servant waited for an answer. PP I 7 30 14
when a servant from Netherfield brought the following note PP I 7 31 29
30
an invitation to remain at Netherfield for the present. PP I 7 33 45
girls, reached Netherfield soon after the family breakfast. PP I 9 41 1
to health would probably remove her from Netherfield. PP I 9 41 2
know a place in the country that is equal to Netherfield. PP I 9 42 7
quit Netherfield, I should probably be off in five minutes. PP I 9 42 8
coming into the country to give a ball at Netherfield. PP I 9 45 35
resolved on quitting Netherfield you should be gone in PP I 10 49 27
you really serious in meditating a dance at Netherfield?-- PP I 11 55 5
6
daughters remaining at Netherfield till the following PP I 12 59 1
design of leaving Netherfield that morning should be PP I 12 59 1
had been at Netherfield long enough. PP I 12 59 4
either at Longbourn or Netherfield, and embracing her most PP I 12 60 5
any more draughts to Netherfield because the Miss Bennets PP I 15 73 11
He inquired how far Netherfield was from Meryton; and, PP I 16 77 8
House in the neighbourhood, except Netherfield. PP I 16 77 15
nothing of his going away when I was at Netherfield. PP I 16 78 19
boasting one day, at Netherfield, of the implacability of PP I 16 80 34
at Netherfield, which was fixed for the following Tuesday. PP I 17 86 9
The prospect of the Netherfield ball was extremely PP I 17 86 10
If there had not been a Netherfield ball to prepare for PP I 17 88 15
very shoe-roses for Netherfield were got by proxy. PP I 17 88 15
Till Elizabeth entered the drawing-room at Netherfield and PP I 18 89 1
at Netherfield, in the course of three or four months. PP I 18 103 77
worth of each was eclipsed by Mr. Bingley and Netherfield. PP I 18 103 77
and to lament over his absence from the Netherfield ball. PP I 21 115 3
it came from Netherfield, and was opened immediately. PP I 21 116 6
The whole party have left Netherfield by this time, and PP I 21 116 7
that their absence from Netherfield would prevent Mr. PP I 21 116 8
return to Netherfield and answer every wish of her heart. PP I 21 120 29
his coming no more to Netherfield the whole winter; a PP I 23 129 12
than usual about Netherfield and its master, she could not PP II 1 134 4
5
The Netherfield ladies would have had difficulty in PP II 2 139 2
his never returning to Netherfield again, of giving up the PP II 3 149 26
you all quitted Netherfield last November, Mr. Darcy! PP II 9 177 3
4
has not much idea of ever returning to Netherfield again?" PP II 9 177 6
7
"If he means to be but little at Netherfield, it would be PP II 9 178 9
of Jane and Netherfield, and she blushed as she answered. PP II 9 179 21
evening of the dance at Netherfield that I had any PP II 12 197 5
He left Netherfield for London, on the day following, as PP II 12 198 5
she began his account of what had happened at Netherfield. PP II 13 204 1
yet he had avoided the Netherfield ball the very next week. PP II 13 207 5
She remembered also, that till the Netherfield family had PP II 13 207 5
as having passed at the Netherfield ball, and as PP II 13 209 10
There is no talk of his coming to Netherfield again in the PP II 17 228 27
"I do not believe that he will ever live at Netherfield PP II 17 228 28
when we were all dancing together at Netherfield." PP III 2 262 8
of his dear friends at Netherfield, or his dignified PP III 2 263 10
and censure of the ladies both of Netherfield and Rosings. PP III 2 263 10
they had been dining at Netherfield, 'she a beauty!--I PP III 3 271 16
17
The housekeeper at Netherfield had received orders to PP III 11 331 13
But, however, he is very welcome to come to Netherfield, PP III 11 331 14
neighbouring gentlemen, on his returning to Netherfield. PP III 11 332 24
Happy shall I be, when his stay at Netherfield is over!" PP III 11 333 28
his coming to Netherfield, to Longbourn, and voluntarily PP III 11 334 36
Mrs. Bennet had designed to keep the two Netherfield PP III 12 342 27
'Ah! Mrs. Bennet, we shall have her at Netherfield at last. PP III 12 342 28
Mary petitioned for the use of the library at Netherfield; PP III 13 349 42
to Bingley of coming again to Netherfield must give way. PP III 15 361 3
behaviour to Jane, while she was ill at Netherfield?" PP III 18 380 6
But tell me, what did you come down to Netherfield for? PP III 18 381 15
Mr. Bingley and Jane remained at Netherfield only a PP III 19 385 3
NETHERFIELD PARK (1)
"have you heard that Netherfield Park is let at last?" PP I 1 3 3
NETTING (2)
She is netting herself the sweetest cloak you can conceive. NA I 6 40 12
no otherwise than by netting a purse, or covering a skreen. PP I 8 39 46
NETTING-BOX (1)
The netting-box, just leisurely drawn forth, was closed NA II 7 176 17
NETTING-BOXES (1)
with work-boxes and netting-boxes, which had been given MP I 16 153 3
NETTING-COTTON (1)
matched some fine netting-cotton, on which she had left NA II 10 201 5
NETTLED (1)
somewhat nettled, she had all the success she expected. PP III 3 271 16
NETTLES (2)
I am not fond of nettles, or thistles, or heath blossoms. SS I 18 98 8
cut off the heads of some nettles in the hedge with his P III 10 90 37
NEVER-CEASING (1)
and engage in the never-ceasing inquiry of 'have you read NA I 14 107 11
NEVER-ENDING (1)
in secret with the never-ending question, of whether P IV 10 227 69
NEVER-FAILING (3)
and jokes, was his never-failing subject, and to boast of MP I 13 121 1
matters of equal and never-failing interest, while the MP III 10 403 15
Fanny watched him with never-failing solicitude, and MP III 15 445 34
NEVERTHELESS (1)
hammer. "the baronet, nevertheless, is not unlikely to P IV 9 203 72
NEW (224)
the character of every new acquaintance, nor a detail of NA I 2 19 3
With more care for the safety of her new gown than for the NA I 2 21 9
were to be visited; some new part of the town to be looked NA I 3 25 1
rectify the opinions of her new friend in many articles of NA I 4 33 7
to whom they were entirely new; and the respect which they NA I 4 33 7
leisure, and over every new novel to talk in threadbare NA I 5 37 4
Grandison herself; but new books do not fall in our way." NA I 6 41 21
to Edgar's Buildings with me, and looking at my new hat? NA I 6 43 39
you see complete; the iron-work as good as new, or better. NA I 7 46 13
they withdrew to see the new hat, that John thought her NA I 7 50 44
the price and weigh the merits of a new muff and tippet. NA I 7 51 54
could strike out nothing new in commendation, but she NA I 9 64 27
every new face, and almost every new bonnet in the room. NA I 10 71 8
with some knowledge of her new acquaintance's feelings, NA I 10 73 21

of the time prevented her buying a new one for the evening. NA I 10 73 22
be aware of the insensibility of man towards a new gown. NA I 10 73 22
by what is costly or new in their attire; how little it is NA I 10 74 22
evening concluded, a new source of felicity arose to her. NA I 10 80 61
o'clock," was her parting speech to her new friend. NA I 10 80 61
more dreadful than a new publication which is shortly to NA I 14 113 39
the natural blush of so new an emotion, she cried out, " NA I 15 117 7
New to such circumstances, the importance of it appeared NA I 15 117 8
and admiration of every new acquaintance at Fullerton, the NA I 15 122 28
carriage at her command, a new name on her tickets, and a NA I 15 122 28
have spread a new grace and inspired a warmer interest. NA II 4 149 1
kindest welcome among her new friends; but so great was NA II 5 154 1
new writing-desk from being thrown out into the street.-- NA II 5 155 4
interest of a road entirely new to her, of an Abbey before, NA II 5 155 4
on the welfare of her new straw bonnet:--and she was NA II 5 161 25
a third, a fourth, and a fifth presented nothing new. NA II 7 172 2
You have gained a new source of enjoyment, and it is well NA II 7 174 8
of that kind, might have been tempted to order a new set. NA II 7 175 12
The new building was not only new, but declared itself to NA II 8 184 4
the expectations of its new observer; but they were not in NA II 9 191 3
A new idea now darted into Catherine's mind, and turning NA II 13 223 12
Well, we must live and learn; and the next new friends you NA II 14 236 15
I put them on new the first time of our going to the Lower NA II 14 238 24
It is a new circumstance in romance, I acknowledge, and NA II 15 243 9
dignity; but if it be as new in common life, the credit of NA II 15 243 9
them whenever they leave Norland and settle in a new home." SS I 2 9 6
an entrance; this, with a new drawing-room which may be SS I 6 29 4
The arrival of a new family in the country was always a SS I 7 33 3
her yesterday of getting a new grate for the spare SS I 8 39 17
the delight of your conversation with our new friend."-- SS I 10 48 6
than he knows how to employ, and two new coats every year." SS I 10 51 25
In Colonel Brandon alone, of all her new acquaintance, did SS I 11 55 7
commission for every new print of merit to be sent you-- SS I 17 92 25
silent, till a new object suddenly engaged her attention. SS I 18 98 10
This, and Marianne's blushing, gave new suspicions to SS I 18 100 22
This was quite a new idea to Mrs. Dashwood, she had never SS I 19 107 27
'so, Colonel, there is a new family come to Barton cottage, SS I 20 115 50
her some other new acquaintance to see and observe. SS I 21 118 1
patterns of some elegant new dress, in which her SS I 21 120 6
not only upon gaining very new light as to his character SS II 4 159 1
thing pretty, expensive, or new; who was wild to buy all, SS II 4 165 24
She could soon tell at what coachmaker's the new carriage SS II 10 215 11
Nothing new was heard by them, for a day or two afterwards, SS III 2 270 3
She vowed at first she would never trim me up a new bonnet, SS III 2 272 12
to the doctor, to get Edward the curacy of his new living. SS III 2 275 22
remained, busy in new engagements, and new schemes, in SS III 6 302 4
in new engagements, and new schemes, in which <u>she</u> could SS III 6 302 4
Poor Elinor!--here was a new scheme for getting her to SS III 9 339 25
we will walk to Sir John's new plantations at Barton-Cross, SS III 10 343 9
her leaving London, nothing new of his plans, nothing SS III 11 352 21
They was stopping in a chaise at the door of the new SS III 11 354 27
in my brother, and disliked new acquaintance, it was not SS III 13 362 5
said Marianne, in her new character of candour, "in SS III 13 372 45
at nineteen, submitting to new attachments, entering on SS III 14 378 16
attachments, entering on new duties, placed in a new home, SS III 14 378 16
on new duties, placed in a new home, a wife, the mistress SS III 14 378 16
He generally pays attention to every new girl, but he is a W 315 1
went thro' the winter, & a new cap from the milliners, W 323 3
A new face & a very pretty one, could not be slighted--her W 328 9
Maam was instantly ready to attend his new acquaintance.-- W 331 11
How nice Mary Edwards looks in her new pelisse!-- W 341 19
It was a new thing with him to wish to please a woman; it W 346 21
this visit, before any new bustle arose to interrupt even W 348 23
And what was the use of my putting up your last new coat, W 353 26
disagreeable ways are new to <u>you</u>, & they would vex you more W 362 32
account, for in general you know they visit no new comers. PP I 1 4 24
can tell you, to be making new acquaintance every day; but PP I 2 8 26
there is something new to be observed in them for ever." PP I 9 43 18
human nature; and had some new extracts to admire, and PP I 12 60 7
some new observations of thread-bare morality to listen to. PP I 12 60 7
The idea of the olive branch perhaps is not wholly new, PP I 13 64 19
or a really new muslin in a shop window, could recal them. PP I 15 72 7
other day, we had just been forming a new acquaintance." PP I 18 92 18
of settlements, new carriages and wedding clothes, she PP I 18 103 77
The next day opened a new scene at Longbourn. PP I 19 104 1
some plans of the latter with regard to new furniture. PP II 1 133 2
how she would speak of her new home, how she would like PP II 3 146 19
He could tell her nothing new of the wonders of his PP II 4 152 4
Every object in the next day's journey was new and PP II 5 155 1
furnish one comparatively new to look at in their Rosings PP II 7 170 6
and staying at home, of new books and music, that PP II 8 172 3
quite wild; that she had a new gown, or a new parasol, PP II 19 238 5
she had a new gown, or a new parasol, which she would have PP II 19 238 5
In the next room is a new instrument just come down for PP III 1 248 22
attention for any of these new friends; and she could do PP III 1 259 77
place with some of their new friends, and were just PP III 2 260 1
preceding day, opened to them a new idea on the business. PP III 2 260 1
With astonishment did Elizabeth see, that her new PP III 2 261 3
nuptials, fine muslins, new carriages, and servants. PP III 8 310 7
She was more alive to the disgrace, which the want of new PP III 8 310 10
Bertram, must be giving it new grace, and in quitting it MP I 2 20 33
satisfaction in the main among their new acquaintance. MP I 3 31 59
The new mare proved a treasure; with a very little trouble, MP I 4 37 8
only to be completely new furnished--pleasant sisters, a MP I 5 48 28
father and mother and sisters were there, all new to me. MP I 5 51 40
"but had I a place to new fashion, I should not put myself MP I 6 56 28
There is all the new calico that was bought last week, not MP I 7 71 34
all that was new, and admiring all that was pretty. MP I 8 80 31
as interesting as it was new, attended with unaffected MP I 9 85 3
She looked almost aghast under the new idea she was MP I 9 89 26
"I believe the wilderness will be new to all the party. MP I 9 90 35
help of Mrs. Grant and a new intimate friend of Mr. MP I 12 117 11
The honourable John Yates, this new friend, had not much MP I 13 121 1
vary the scene, and exercise our powers in something new. MP I 13 125 18
be delighted; it is all new to her, you know,--you and I MP I 18 167 7
8

returned to what they were, than assuming a new character. MP II 3 197 4
Such language was so new to Fanny that it quite MP II 3 197 7
The preparations of new carriages and furniture might wait MP II 3 202 26
Every public place was new to Maria, and Brighton is MP II 3 203 31
She played accordingly; happy to have a new listener, and MP II 4 207 6
new, and which had little reality in Fanny's feeling. MP II 4 207 11
One need not envy the new Mrs. Rushworth with such a home MP II 4 210 21
This was so new an attention, so perfectly new a MP II 4 215 47
of having that absurd new one of his own, which is wider, MP II 5 220 30
"The new dress that my uncle was so good as to give me on MP II 5 222 43
a new gown, and you never saw her so well dressed before. MP II 6 230 6
You must make you a new garden at what is not the back of MP II 7 242 23
hurried in making up a new dress for her; Sir Thomas gave MP II 8 254 9
I do not offer them as new. MP II 8 258 16
one disagreeable emotion entirely new to her--jealousy. MP II 11 286 17
His situation was new and animating. MP III 2 327 4
who can say any thing new or striking, any thing that MP III 3 341 28
Their being so new and so recent was all in their MP III 4 354 46
to look around her, and wonder at the new buildings.-- MP III 7 376 6
proud to shew her abilities before her fine new sister. MP III 7 379 16
A key was mislaid, Betsey accused of having got at his new MP III 7 381 26
from introductions either to old or new acquaintance. MP III 9 395 3
for her good opinion; and new as any thing like an office MP III 9 396 6
of authority was to Fanny, new as it was to imagine MP III 9 396 6
use, and Susan was entertained in a way quite new to her. MP III 10 404 15
was received to revive old, and create some new sensations. MP III 14 433 12

But <u>your's</u>--your regard was new compared with----- MP III 15 446 34
of old vulgarisms and new gentilities were before her; and MP III 15 446 35
new hopes of happiness from dissimilarity of temper. MP III 17 471 28
wife; and was beginning a new period of existence with E I 2 17 6
that he had written to his new mother on the occasion. E I 2 18 9
with elegant morality upon new principles and new systems-- E I 3 21 5
upon new principles and new systems--and where young E I 3 21 5
Emma must do Harriet good: and by supplying her with a new E I 5 36 4
have a bailiff from Scotland, to look after his new estate. E I 12 104 44
Something new for your coachman and horses to be making E I 15 126 8
of looking at some body new; the gala-day to Highbury E I 18 145 5
as to see exhibitions of new caps and new work-bags for E II 2 168 15
exhibitions of new caps and new work-bags for her mother E II 2 168 15
"A new neighbour for us all, Miss Woodhouse!" said Miss E II 3 174 35
There was one person among his new acquaintance in Surry, E II 7 206 4
Their love of society, and their new dining-room, prepared E II 7 207 6
We have never been there above once since the new approach E II 7 210 14
was ashamed to look at our new grand pianoforte in the E II 8 215 16
nothing of course, for it seems to be a new idea to you.-- E II 8 218 36
call on the Bateses, in order to hear the new instrument. E II 9 233 25
us your opinion of our new instrument; you and Miss Smith. E II 9 235 44
I hear you have a charming collection of new ribbons from E II 9 237 48
turning to Emma, said, "here is something quite new to me. E II 10 242 20
21

And here are a new set of Irish melodies. E II 10 242 21
Miss Smith; so kind as to call to hear the new pianoforte. E II 10 244 42
I bring a new proposal on the subject:--a thought of my E II 11 250 21
and then, being quite new, further representations were E II 11 251 25
the actual approach--new carriage, bell ringing and all. E II 13 267 8
and the greater part of her new acquaintance, disposed to E II 15 281 2
warm--her large new shawl--Mrs. Dixon's wedding present.-- E III 2 322 19
Do not you remember his cutting his finger with your new E III 4 338 12
This is a new resolution." E III 4 341 30
time to say how perfectly new this circumstance was to her; E III 8 383 30
You know, my dear, she is going to be to this new lady E III 9 387 10
Was it a new circumstance for a man of first-rate E III 11 413 48
Was it new for one, perhaps too busy to seek, to be the E III 11 413 48
Was it new for any thing in this world to be unequal, E III 11 413 48
shows of cattle, or new drills--and might not you, in the E III 18 473 26
They are to be new set. E III 18 479 70
now could the valet of any new made Lord be more delighted P III 1 4 5
worse to anticipate the new hands they were to fall into; P III 5 36 19
in the old English style, and the young people in the new. P III 5 40 45
to herself; but this was no new sensation: excepting one P III 6 47 13
eight years ago,--was a new sort of trial to Anne's nerves. P III 6 52 33
Her brother and sister came back delighted with their new P III 7 58 22
themselves in their new possessions, their grass, and P III 9 73 2
It would be but a new creation, however, and I never think P III 9 75 11
however, and I never think much of your new creations." P III 9 75 11
much time for seeing a new place, after deducting seven P III 11 94 8
itself, its old wonders and new improvements, with the P III 11 95 9
On quitting the Cobb, they all went indoors with their new P III 11 98 17
the children, he fashioned new netting-needles and pins P III 11 99 18
course of events and the new interests of Henrietta's P III 12 103 5
There was too much wind to make the high part of the new P III 12 109 32
A new sort of way this, for a young fellow to be making P IV 1 126 22
and grow coarse, I would send her a new hat and pelisse." P IV 3 142 16
the water, gets all the new publications, and has a very P IV 4 146 5
you see," (pointing to a new umbrella) "I wish you would P IV 7 177 14
"The Ibbotsons--were they there? and the two new beauties, P IV 9 193 8
I really cannot be plaguing myself for ever with all new P IV 10 215 15
Lady Russell quite bores one with her new publications. P IV 10 215 15
It is a sort of pain, too, which is new to me. P IV 11 247 84
wrong, and to take up a new set of opinions and of hopes. P IV 12 249 3
Every five years, one hears of some new place or other S 1 368 1
old coach which had been new when they married & fresh S 2 373 1
them to have indulged in a new carriage & better roads, an S 2 373 1
she went with--& to buy new parasols, new gloves, & new S 2 374 1
to buy new parasols, new gloves, & new Broches, for her S 2 374 1
new parasols, new gloves, & new Broches, for her sisters & S 2 374 1
within the last 2 years--till our new house was finished.-- S 4 379 1
open down where the new Buildgs might soon be looked for. S 4 382 1
This is new within the month. S 4 383 1
see as much, & as quickly as possible, where all was new. S 6 389 1
as good as new)--and what can people want for more?-- S 6 393 1
to strike out something new, to exceed those who had gone S 8 405 2
Mr P. was confident of another new family.-- S 10 414 1
inevitable expence of six new dresses each for a three S 11 421 1
pleasure of settling her new friends, & considering that S 11 422 1
& extremely well kept, than new or shewey--and as Lady D. S 12 427 1
NEW-BUILT (1)
stood the parsonage, a new-built substantial stone house, NA II 11 212 17
NEW-COMERS (1)
while? and what was <u>her</u> opinion of the new-comers? MP I 5 48 30
NEW-FORMED (1)
it took from her the new-formed hope of succeeding in the P IV 9 210 99
NEW-FURNISHED (1)
I hope you will have new-furnished it, for it wanted it SS I 13 67 64
NEW-FURNISHING (1)
and to refrain from new-furnishing the drawing-room; to P III 1 9 19
NEW-MARRIED (1)
every visitor of the new-married pair; but still the cake E I 2 19 14
NEWBURY (1)
where, till they reached Newbury, where a comfortable meal, MP III 7 376 5
NEWCASTLE (4)
We shall be at Newcastle all the winter, and I dare say PP III 9 317 13
for me, or else I could take it in my way to Newcastle. PP III 10 327 11
Newcastle, was likely to continue at least a twelvemonth. PP III 11 330 2
They are gone down to Newcastle, a place quite northward, PP III 11 336 51
NEWER (1)
the two, as being somewhat newer and more conjectural; and SS I 21 125 36
NEWEST (3)
chaperon was provided with a dress of the newest fashion. NA I 2 20 8
distribute her presents and describe the newest fashions. PP II 2 139 3
fait as to the newest modes of being trifling and silly. P IV 5 155 9
NEWEST-FASHIONED (1)
addicted to all the newest-fashioned hard words--had not a S 7 398 1
NEWFOUNDLAND (1)
his solitude, a large Newfoundland puppy and two or three NA II 11 212 17
NEWLY (3)
In the Pump-Room, one so newly arrived in Bath must be met NA I 9 60 1
furniture,--but if it were newly fitted up-----a couple of SS I 13 69 76
be indulged in calling his newly erected house at the end W 322 2
NEWLY-ARRIVED (1)
She could not compliment the newly-arrived gentleman MP II 5 223 48
NEWLY-BORN (1)
While these newly-born notions were passing in their heads, PP III 2 260 1
NEWMARKET (1)
a party of young men to Newmarket, where a neglected fall, MP III 13 426 10
NEWNESS (2)
which nothing but the newness of their acquaintance with SS I 18 99 15
with great delight, its newness giving it every advantage MP III 9 396 7
NEWS (117)
Manwaring is just gone; he brought me the news of his LS 33 303 1
My dear Catherine I have charming news for you, & if I LS 40 308 1
With such news to communicate, and such a visit to prepare NA I 15 124 47
to be receiving unpleasant news; and Henry, earnestly NA II 10 202 8
Eleanor said, "no bad news from Fullerton, I hope? NA II 10 203 9
send me some news of the latter--I am quite unhappy about NA II 12 217 2
That is good news however; I will ride over to-morrow, and SS I 9 43 13
communicated a piece of news to her sister, which in spite SS I 12 58 1
"I hope he has had no bad news," said Lady Middleton. SS I 13 63 6

"No bad news, Colonel, I hope;" said Mrs. Jennings, as SS I 13 63 8
there must be some bad news, and thought over every kind SS I 14 70 1
How little did I then think that the very first news I SS I 14 73 17
to ask Mr. Palmer if there was any news in the paper. SS I 19 108 32
to be amused by the relation of all the news of the day. SS II 8 193 7
Lord! how he'll chuckle over this news! SS II 8 196 22
"The first news that reached me of her," he continued, " SS II 9 209 30
She received the news with resolute composure; made no SS II 10 217 17
my dear Miss Dashwood! have you heard the news!" SS III 1 257 2
3

but it came into my head to ask him if there was any news. SS III 1 257 5
over the dreadful affair, and bring them news of his wife. SS III 1 265 33
to his daughter with "well Mary, I bring you good news.-- W 323 3
other little article of news which his morning's lounge W 323 3
friend carried him the news--& he was continually at W 335 13
report as to public news, & the general opinion of the day W 356 28
her daughters married; its solace was visiting and news. PP I 1 5 34
and however bare of news the country in general might be, PP I 7 28 3
At present, indeed, they were well supplied both with news PP I 7 28 3
No aunt, no officers, no news could be sought after;--the PP I 17 88 15
who came to tell the same news, and no sooner had they PP I 20 113 26
no other way than as a piece of news to spread at Meryton. PP I 23 127 7
Mrs. Gardiner, to whom the chief of this news had been PP II 2 140 5
talking over Hertfordshire news, and telling again what PP II 5 157 10
"Now I have got some news for you," said Lydia, as they PP II 16 220 8
It is excellent news, capital news, and about a certain PP II 16 220 8
Well, but now for my news: it is about dear Wickham; too PP II 16 220 10
meet Maria and hear the news: and various were the PP II 16 222 21
and engagements, with such news as the country afforded; PP III 4 273 2
but I have bad news for you, and it cannot be delayed. PP III 4 274 5
I am only distressed by some dreadful news which I have PP III 4 277 10
have just had a letter from Jane, with such dreadful news. PP III 4 277 11
In a few days more, we may gain some news of them, and PP III 5 288 37
they must in all probability have gained some news of them. PP III 6 295 4
day was expected to bring some news of importance. PP III 6 296 9
could be pointed out, as likely to give any news of him. PP III 6 297 12
news from town, so I took the liberty of coming to ask." PP III 7 301 1
what news? what news? have you heard from my uncle?" PP III 7 301 7
8

"Well, and what news does it bring? good or bad?" PP III 7 302 10
After a slight preparation for good news, the letter was PP III 7 305 43
and tell the good, good news to my sister Phillips. PP III 7 307 49
My dear hill, have you heard the good news? PP III 7 307 49
The good news quickly spread through the house; and with PP III 8 309 6
an article of news, which then began to be in circulation. PP III 11 331 13
sister," (for Mrs. Phillips first brought her the news.) PP III 11 331 14
I do assure you, that the news does not affect me either PP III 11 332 17
The news was as disagreeable to Fanny as it had been MP I 3 25 10
Park, heard the good news; and though seeming to have no MP I 11 108 4
to help wishing, that the news could have been suppressed MP I 13 122 4
forward with great alacrity to tell him the agreeable news. MP I 15 138 2
most unwelcome news; and she could think of nothing else. MP I 16 156 28
having to spread the happy news through the house, Sir MP II 1 180 10
Mr. Rushworth had set off early with the great news for MP II 2 192 11
The good news soon followed her. MP II 5 219 24
early examination of ship news, the next morning, seemed MP II 6 232 13
with you in the first knowledge of the news I now bring. MP II 13 298 2
more intent on telling the news, than giving them any help, MP III 7 377 7
Have you heard the news? MP III 7 380 20
her to Susan; and when the news of her death had at last MP III 7 386 40
heard a little news, talked over the badness of the MP III 11 408 4
I have no news for you. MP III 12 415 2
of Mansfield news should fall to my pen instead of her's. MP III 13 424 2
capital piece of Mansfield news, as the certainty of the MP III 13 425 6
call at Mrs. Goddard's for news of her fair friend, the E I 13 111 14
Mr. Knightley presently, "I have a piece of news for you. E II 3 172 20
You like news--and I heard an article in my way hither E II 3 172 20
"News! E II 3 172 21
Oh! yes, I always like news. E II 3 172 21
Full of thanks, and full of news, Miss Bates knew not E II 3 172 23
Have you heard the news? E II 3 173 24
"There is my news:--I thought it would interest you," said E II 3 173 26
there never was a piece of news more generally interesting. E II 3 173 29
This is great news, indeed. E II 3 174 35
I hope you mean to take an interest in this news. E II 3 175 41
42

This has been a most agreeable piece of news indeed. E II 3 176 50
a very welcome piece of news, as proving that Mr. Elton E II 3 177 51
obliged to hurry on the news, which she had meant to give E II 3 180 56
There was no resisting such news, no possibility of E II 5 188 8
day remarks, dull repetitions, old news, and heavy jokes. E II 8 219 43
Oh! said I, Patty do not come with your bad news to me. E II 9 236 46
spread abroad what public news he had heard, was E II 17 303 24
"Well, he is coming, you see; good news, I think. E II 17 303 27
Well, pretty good news, is not it? E II 17 304 27
see him again, which makes this day's news doubly welcome. E II 18 308 27
of her agitation on hearing this news of Frank Churchill. E III 1 315 1
in the place were soon in the happiness of frightful news. E III 3 336 12
In the daily interchange of news, they must be again E III 6 352 1
bad; Emma communicated her news of Jane Fairfax, and her E III 9 386 9
The following day brought news from Richmond to throw E III 9 387 11
the room--"is not this the oddest news that ever was?" E III 11 404 4
"What news do you mean?" replied Emma, unable to guess, by E III 11 404 5
began-- "you have some news to hear, now you are come back, E III 13 425 2
3

all the articles of news he had received from Mr. Perry, E III 14 434 3
"And the next news, I suppose, will be, that we are to E III 16 460 52
The time was coming when the news must be spread farther, E III 17 465 28
The news was universally a surprise wherever it spread; E III 17 468 33
He told her the news. E III 17 468 35
with, "I have something to tell you, Emma; some news." E III 18 470 1
2

I assure you that I have heard the news with the warmest E III 18 477 59
There the news must follow him, but who was to tell it? P III 12 108 28
going to Uppercross,--the news to be conveyed--how it P III 12 113 57
Elizabeth's last letter had communicated a piece of news P IV 2 135 35
was growing very eager for news from Uppercross and Lyme. P IV 6 162 1
her sister's being in any degree prepared for the news. P IV 6 165 9
evident that no rumour of the news had yet reached them. P IV 6 168 22
I think, of one such little article of unfounded news." P IV 9 197 41
You may guess therefore that the news he heard from his P IV 9 207 90
The news of his cousin Anne's engagement burst on Mr. P IV 12 250 7
Delighted to have such good news for Mr & Mrs P., who had S 9 406 1

NEWSMEN (1)

and drays, the bawling of newsmen, muffin-men and milk-men, P IV 2 135 33

NEWSPAPER (23)

The General, between his cocoa and his newspaper, had NA II 10 203 8
the satisfaction of sending them his newspaper every day. SS I 6 30 6
apartments, took up a newspaper from the table and SS I 19 106 22
answer, and did not even raise his eyes from the newspaper. SS I 19 107 25
at her some minutes, and then returned to his newspaper. SS I 19 108 35
newspaper, stretched himself, and looked at them all round. SS I 19 108 37
back his chair, took a newspaper from the table, and, PP II 9 179 24
25

newspaper, watch the weather, and quarrel with his wife. MP I 11 110 23
When he had told of his horse, he took a newspaper from MP I 12 118 22
down the newspaper again--"for I am tired to death. MP I 12 118 22
walked up with the newspaper in his hand, which he had MP II 4 232 12
his back, and took up a newspaper, very sincerely wishing MP III 3 341 31
and he taking out a newspaper--the accustomary loan of a MP III 7 382 28
at the same time to carry back his neighbour's newspaper. MP III 7 384 36
he read only the newspaper and the navy-list; he talked MP III 8 389 3
afternoon with the daily newspaper as usual, she was so MP III 15 438 8
that room, of her father and his newspaper came across her. MP III 15 439 9
Her father read his newspaper, and her mother lamented MP III 15 439 9
infinite concern the newspaper had to announce to the MP III 15 440 14
to the editor of the newspaper, whither they were gone." MP III 15 440 14
say to himself, over a newspaper he held in his hand, "hum! E II 7 206 4
as he laid down the newspaper, "that the present juncture P III 3 17 1
newspaper; and Captain Wentworth returned to his window. P III 9 79 27

NEWSPAPERS (7)

the accounts of their newspapers; and the ladies walked NA I 10 71 8
and where roads and newspapers lay every thing open? NA II 9 197 29
Within a few days after this meeting, the newspapers SS II 14 246 1
She had only navy lists and newspapers for her authority, P III 4 30 8
own horses, dogs, and newspapers to engage them; and the P III 6 42 3
at one corner of the newspapers; and being lost in only a P III 8 66 16
were to shew me all the newspapers that are printed in one S 1 366 1

NEWTON (1)

Careys come over from Newton, the three Miss Dashwoods SS I 13 65 32

NEXT (344)

When I next write, I shall be able I hope to tell you that LS 23 285 8
Mr Johnson leaves London next Tuesday. LS 26 295 4
May the next gouty attack be more favourable. LS 39 308 2
& on Thursday next, we & our little ones will be with you. LS 41 310 2
her next sister, sally, could say it better than she did. NA I 1 14 1
to the Pump-Room the next day, secure within herself of NA I 4 31 1
and say their prayers in the same chapel the next morning. NA I 4 34 7
She hoped to be more fortunate the next day; and when her NA I 5 35 1
for ten guineas more the next day; Jackson, of Oriel, bid NA I 7 47 19
"A famous thing for his next heirs. NA I 9 63 14
at one moment what they would contradict the next. NA I 9 65 31
in full force the next morning; and till usual moment of NA I 10 71 8
to get a house in Leicestershire, against the next season. NA I 10 76 28
good night's rest in the course of the next three months. NA I 11 90 65
"Mrs. Allen," said Catherine the next morning, "will there NA I 12 91 1
walk out of the house the next minute after my leaving it; NA I 12 94 9
going to Clifton the next day, in spite of what had passed. NA I 13 105 40
The next morning was fair, and Catherine almost expected NA I 14 106 1
of her company to dinner on the day after the next. NA I 14 114 49
Early the next day, a note from Isabella, speaking peace NA I 15 116 1
Catherine was with her friend again the next day, NA I 15 121 26
When the young ladies next met, they had a far more NA II 1 135 42
when she saw her at their next interview as cheerful and NA II 1 137 50
Her passion for ancient edifices was next in degree to her NA II 2 141 11
one means one day, you know, one may not mean the next. NA II 3 146 18
without any thing to see, next followed--and her NA II 5 156 4
To be driven by him, next to being dancing with him, was NA II 5 157 5
at eight o'clock the next day, was the sound which first NA II 7 172 1
The kitchen-garden was to be next admired, and he led the NA II 7 178 20
She ventured, when next alone with Eleanor, to express her NA II 8 186 7
The next day afforded no opportunity for the proposed NA II 9 190 1
of making her next attempt on the forbidden door alone. NA II 9 192 5
others were called in the next day, and remained in almost NA II 9 197 25
one morning, that when he next went to Woodston, they NA II 11 209 5
The next morning brought the following very unexpected NA II 12 216 1
2

call at Putney when next in town, might set all to rights. NA II 12 217 2
up to the door, and the next moment confirmed the idea by NA II 13 222 7
agreed to her mother's next counsel of going early to bed. NA II 14 235 13
when they all met the next morning, her recovery was not NA II 14 235 13
Well, we must live and learn; and the next new friends you NA II 14 236 15
himself, he set out the next day for the Abbey, where his NA II 15 247 13
moment, they believed the next--that with them, to wish SS I 4 21 11
soon after breakfast the next day by the entrance of their SS I 6 30 6
polite, her ladyship was introduced to them the next day. SS I 6 30 7
securing their promise of dining at the park the next day. SS I 6 31 10
Sir John called on them as soon as the next interval of SS I 9 43 12
early the next morning to make his personal inquiries. SS I 10 46 1
As Elinor and Marianne were walking together the next SS I 12 58 1
Willoughby when she saw him next, that it must be declined. SS I 12 59 5
Margaret related something to her the next day, which SS I 12 60 8
to her eldest sister, when they were next by themselves. SS I 12 60 8
from Mrs. Smith, when I next came into the country, would SS I 14 73 17
Middleton took place the next day, and two of her SS I 15 75 1
on his side; and the next that some unfortunate quarrel SS I 15 77 19
her family in the face the next morning, had she not risen SS I 16 83 1
He joined her and Marianne in the breakfast-room the next SS I 18 96 2
park the next day, or to drink tea with them that evening. SS I 18 99 16
urgent with them all to spend the next day at the park. SS I 19 108 40
of the park the next day, at one door, Mrs. Palmer came SS I 20 110 1
We must go, for the Westons come to us next week you know. SS I 20 110 2
I could get the nicest house in the world for you, next SS I 20 110 4
The Palmers returned to Cleveland the next day, and the SS I 21 118 1
Marianne rose the next morning with recovered spirits and SS II 4 164 21
not like leaving Barton next week; 'tis a said thing for SS II 5 167 1
John and Lady Middleton in town by the end of next week." SS II 5 167 4
She insisted on being left behind, the next morning, when SS II 5 169 15
resolved to write the next morning to her mother, and SS II 5 171 38
Nothing occurred during the next three or four days, to SS II 6 175 1
Before the house-maid had lit their fire the next day, or SS II 7 180 1
But when there is plenty of money on one side, and next to SS II 8 194 8
Marianne awoke the next morning to the same consciousness SS II 9 201 1
The work of one moment was destroyed by the next. SS II 9 202 7
of being able to call on them the next day, took leave. SS II 11 222 13
I might have sold it again the next day, for more than I SS II 11 225 33
of his sisters, in his next visit at Gray's, his thoughts SS II 11 226 41
that she waited the very next day both on Mrs. Jennings SS II 12 229 1
declared over again the next morning more openly, for at SS II 13 238 2
next to Edward's love, it is the greatest comfort I have.-- SS II 13 240 14
15

"You reside in Devonshire, I think"--was his next SS II 14 251 15
had procured it, wrote the next morning to Lucy, to SS II 14 253 26
son, and though Lucy has next to nothing herself, she SS III 1 259 7
The next morning brought a farther trial of it, in a visit SS III 1 265 33
The next morning brought Elinor a letter by the two-penny SS III 2 277 29
called on her again the next day with her congratulations, SS III 5 293 1
"Very well--and for the next presentation to a living of SS III 5 295 12
The two gentlemen arrived the next day to a very late SS III 6 304 14
Marianne got up the next morning at her usual time; to SS III 7 307 1
The next day produced little or no alteration in the state SS III 7 308 5
The night following this affair--I was to go the next SS III 8 323 40
The next morning brought another short note from Marianne-- SS III 8 327 55
Your sister wrote to me again, you know the very next SS III 8 328 61
The next morning produced no abatement in these happy SS III 10 342 8
their income, was next to be considered; and here it SS III 14 374 4
The next turning will bring us to the turnpike. W 321 2
honour of her hand in the next two dances, to which as W 333 13
The next morng brought a great many visitors. W 337 16
uncle is going within a mile of Guilford the next day.--" W 341 19
be hunting this country next week--I beleive they will W 347 21
calling his next meal a dinner, was quite insupportable.-- W 359 28
alone for a short time the next morng; & had proceeded so W 360 29
day, & the whole of the next, which comprised the length W 360 30
servants are to be in the house by the end of next week." PP I 1 3 10
"When is your next ball to be, Lizzy?" PP I 2 6 11
dare say Mr. Bingley will dance with you at the next ball." PP I 2 8 26
he meant to be at the next assembly with a large party. PP I 3 9 1
was, and got introduced, and asked her for the two next. PP I 3 13 16
at Netherfield, and leave the next generation to purchase. PP I 4 15 12
and when they next met, he looked at her only to criticise. PP I 6 23 12
of the day, as he was going the next morning to London. PP I 7 29 7
Till the next morning, however, she was not aware of all PP I 7 31 29
you had better stay till next week,' you would probably do PP I 10 49 29

Context	Reference
in the shrubbery the next day, "you will give your mother-	PP I 10 52 55
Put them next to your great uncle the judge.	PP I 10 53 57
Elizabeth wrote the next morning to her mother, to beg	PP I 12 59 1
they were at breakfast the next morning, "that you have	PP I 13 61 1
circumstance of my being next in the entail of Longbourn	PP I 13 63 12
And what can he mean by apologizing for being next in the	PP I 13 64 17
It was next to impossible that their cousin should come in	PP I 13 64 20
The next morning, however, made an alteration; for in a	PP I 15 70 3
Elizabeth, equally next to Jane in birth and beauty,	PP I 15 71 4
Some of them were to dine with the Philipses the next day,	PP I 15 74 11
the next evening, although utterly unknown to her before.	PP I 15 74 13
"I wonder," said he, at the next opportunity of speaking, "	PP I 16 78 18
"Yes--the late Mr. Darcy bequeathed me the next	PP I 16 79 25
Elizabeth related to Jane the next day, what had passed	PP I 17 85 1
She danced next with an officer, and had the refreshment	PP I 18 90 5
success, and what we are to talk of next I cannot imagine."	PP I 18 93 26
whither he was obliged to go the next day for a short time.	PP I 18 103 76
The next day opened a new scene at Longbourn.	PP I 19 104 1
honour of speaking to you next on this subject I shall	PP I 19 108 16
	17
The next was in these words.	PP I 21 116 8
out of Longbourn house the next morning with admirable	PP I 22 121 1
Next to being married, a girl likes to be crossed in love	PP II 1 137 27
that shortly after his next return into Hertfordshire, the	PP II 2 139 1
Her fellow-travellers the next day, were not of a kind to	PP II 4 152 4
Every object in the next day's journey was new and	PP II 5 155 1
About the middle of the next day, as she was in her room	PP II 5 158 11
the whole party was asked to dine at Rosings the next day.	PP II 5 159 20
Scarcely any thing was talked of the whole day or next	PP II 6 160 4
It cannot be done too much; and when I next write to her,	PP II 8 173 10
Well, Colonel Fitzwilliam, what do I play next?	PP II 8 175 20
Elizabeth was sitting by herself the next morning, and	PP II 9 177 1
end on the day after the next, and a still greater, that	PP II 11 188 1
him the next moment open the front door and quit the house.	PP II 11 193 30
Elizabeth awoke the next morning to the same thoughts and	PP II 12 195 1
of knowing what the next sentence might bring, was	PP II 13 204 1
yet he had avoided the Netherfield ball the very next week.	PP II 13 207 5
The two gentlemen left Rosings the next morning; and Mr.	PP II 14 210 1
I must be in town next Saturday."	PP II 14 211 7
to come to Hunsford again next year; and Miss de Bourgh	PP II 14 214 21
she related to her the next morning the chief of the scene	PP II 17 224 1
it, when I have told you what happened the very next day."	PP II 17 224 8
from whence they were to set out early the next morning.	PP II 18 235 40
Longbourn, and set off the next morning with Elizabeth in	PP II 19 239 11
subject was revived the next morning, and she was again	PP II 19 241 17
In the next room is a new instrument just come down for	PP III 1 248 22
her attendance, and the day after the next was fixed on.	PP III 2 264 11
The next variation which their visit afforded was produced	PP III 3 268 6
on the road, reached Longbourn by dinner-time the next day.	PP III 5 285 20
to be in London the very next day, and would assist Mr.	PP III 5 287 36
with him at the next ball we meet, with great pleasure.	PP III 5 291 60
letter from Mr. Bennet the next morning, but the post came	PP III 6 294 1
If you are a good girl for the next ten years, I will take	PP III 6 300 32
I let down the side glass next to him, and took off my	PP III 9 316 8
them, Mr. Darcy's next step was to make your uncle	PP III 10 323 2
was still with him, but would quit town the next morning.	PP III 10 323 2
He did not leave his name, and till the next day, it was	PP III 10 323 2
He dined with us the next day, and was to leave town again	PP III 10 325 2
seeing him there again the next day, to make his proposals.	PP III 12 343 29
"Next time you call," said she, "I hope we shall be more	PP III 13 344 2
for his coming next morning to shoot with her husband.	PP III 13 345 19
The next morning, as she was going down stairs, she was	PP III 15 361 6
she stood at a window the next morning, "if that	PP III 17 374 20
The holiday allowed to the Miss Bertrams the next day on	MP I 2 14 7
different disposal of the next presentation necessary, and	MP I 3 23 2
Miss Augusta ought not to have been noticed for the next	MP I 5 51 40
had still more to say on the subject next his heart.	MP I 6 55 17
next day, after thinking some time on the subject himself.	MP I 7 63 1
an invitation for the next, for the lady could not be	MP I 7 64 12
miss, when you first began, six years ago come next Easter.	MP I 7 69 22
Edmund asked Fanny whether she meant to ride the next day.	MP I 7 69 26
he; "but whenever you are next inclined to stay at home, I	MP I 7 69 28
common took place the next morning;--the party included	MP I 7 70 30
Fanny's rides recommenced the very next day, and as it was	MP I 8 75 1
Mrs. Rushworth proceeded next, under the conviction that	MP I 8 76 7
The next meeting of the two Mansfield families produced	MP I 8 79 28
Her next proposition, of shewing the house to such of them	MP I 9 84 2
this sweet wood; but the next time we come to a seat, if	MP I 9 94 57
"To want to nail me to a card table for the next two hours	MP I 12 119 26
walk from this room to the next to look at the raw efforts	MP I 13 124 12
up her spirits for the next few weeks, I shall think our	MP I 13 126 18
of speaking the next morning, were quite as impatient of	MP I 13 128 38
found it quite as puzzling when she awoke the next morning.	MP I 16 150 1
the entrance of Edmund the next moment, suspended it all.	MP I 18 169 22
He inquired next after her family, especially William; and	MP II 1 178 7
Edmund's first object the next morning was to see his	MP II 2 187 1
"Whose stables do you use at Bath?" was the next question;	MP II 2 193 17
beyond themselves for the next twenty-four hours; the	MP II 4 205 3
his mutton with him the next day; and Fanny had barely	MP II 4 215 47
Henry Crawford had quite made up his mind by the next	MP II 6 229 1
of ship news, the next morning, seemed the reward of his	MP II 6 232 13
as to his plans for the next day's hunting; and he found	MP II 6 236 23
to his use again; and the next, with the greatest	MP II 6 237 23
William, you are quite out of luck; but the next time you	MP II 7 245 32
result of it appeared the next morning at breakfast, when,	MP II 8 252 1
and she found herself the next moment conducted by Mr.	MP II 10 275 11
heard in the room for the next two hours beyond the	MP II 11 283 6
She could think of William the next day more cheerfully,	MP II 11 283 7
And the next day did bring a surprize to her.	MP II 12 291 1
if I could suppose the next Mrs. Crawford would have half	MP II 12 296 29
Henry Crawford was at Mansfield Park again the next	MP II 13 298 1
by his turning to her the next moment, and saying, "have	MP II 13 306 28
when she awoke the next morning; but she remembered the	MP III 1 311 1
next time pug has a litter you shall have a puppy."	MP III 2 333 28
Crawford called the next day, and on the score of Edmund's	MP III 3 335 7
Next to your happiness, Fanny, his has the first claim on	MP III 4 351 34
Mr. Crawford gone, Sir Thomas's next object was, that he	MP III 6 366 1
The next step was to communicate with Portsmouth.	MP III 6 371 17
was to give himself the next step as soon as possible, or	MP III 7 375 2
The next morning saw them off again at an early hour; and	MP III 7 376 6
The next opening of the door brought something more	MP III 7 383 32
The next bustle brought in Mr. Campbell, the surgeon of	MP III 7 384 36
had begun; Mary's next letter was after a decidedly longer	MP III 9 393 1
She wished the next day over, she wished he had come only	MP III 10 406 21
both for that day and the next; he had met with some	MP III 10 406 22
The prices were just setting off for church the next day	MP III 11 408 1
which he may have laid down for the next quarter of a year.	MP III 11 410 16
He went to while away the next three hours as he could,	MP III 11 412 29
more to be dwelt on the next day, on the ramparts; when	MP III 12 415 1
	2
before the middle of next week, that is, he cannot any how	MP III 12 417 3
The next day came and brought no second letter.	MP III 15 438 8
Nothing happened the next day, or the next, to weaken her	MP III 15 442 22
The next morning produced a little more.	MP III 15 446 34
what followed the receipt of the next letters from London.	MP III 16 450 10
and when I hear of you next, it may be as a celebrated	MP III 16 458 30
Christmas brought the next visit from Isabella and her	E I 1 7 9
pleasures of society, the next eighteen or twenty years of	E I 2 16 5
garden, where some day next year they were all to drink	E I 4 27 4
The next question was: "what sort of looking man is Mr.	E I 4 29 10
	11
may be rich in time, it is next to impossible that he	E I 4 30 20
They met Mr. Martin the very next day, as they were	E I 4 31 27
Her next beginning was, "in one respect, perhaps, Mr.	E I 4 34 41
	42
Harriet was to sit again the next day; and Mr. Elton, just	E I 6 47 28
The next thing wanted was to get the picture framed; and	E I 6 48 40
She was obliged to go the next morning for an hour or two	E I 8 57 1
to her by the general appearances of the next few days.	E I 9 69 1
The very next day however produced some proof of	E I 9 71 10
He was gone the next moment:--after another moment's pause,	E I 9 71 12
	13
I hope we shall have her here next week.	E I 9 79 56
every field was to bear next year, and to give all such	E I 12 100 16
Emma called on her the next day, and found her doom	E I 13 109 5
nor his eyes more exulting than when he next looked at her.	E I 13 111 12
She went to Mrs. Goddard's accordingly the very next day,	E I 17 141 5
"Oh, yes; next week."	E II 1 159 16
Yes, next week.	E II 1 159 18
Oh, yes, Friday or Saturday next.	E II 1 159 18
not have heard from her before next Tuesday or Wednesday."	E II 1 159 18
"And so she is to come to us next Friday or Saturday, and	E II 1 161 31
he was expressing the next morning, being at Hartfield	E II 3 170 1
when he next entered Highbury he would bring his bride.	E II 4 182 6
The next morning brought Mr. Frank Churchill again.	E II 6 196 1
body's returning into their proper place the next morning.	E II 6 198 5
come in one afternoon next summer, and take their tea with	E II 7 209 10
pleasant recollections the next day; and all that she	E II 9 231 1
if I thought I should go and stay there again next summer."	E II 9 232 19
Before the middle of the next day, he was at Hartfield;	E II 11 250 20
began to adopt as the next vexation Mr. Knightley's	E II 12 257 2
could avail, and the next half hour saw her as anxious and	E II 13 267 9
From Monday next to Saturday, I assure you we have not a	E II 16 290 2
In town next week, you see--at the latest, I dare say; for	E II 17 304 27
He is to be in town next week, if not sooner.	E II 18 305 5
untowardly one month, they are sure to mend the next."	E II 18 308 27
He was to leave them early the next day; and he soon began	E II 18 311 37
	38
not know who will ask her next, perhaps Mr. William Cox.	E III 2 329 45
she walked about the lawn the next morning to enjoy.--	E III 3 332 1
Frank was next to Emma, Jane opposite to them--and Mr.	E III 5 341 21
He heard Frank Churchill next say, with a glance towards	PP II 11 348 22
hill for the next,--the weather appearing exactly right.	E III 6 357 32
The next remove was to the house; they must all go in and	E III 6 361 41
final arrangement for the next day's scheme, they parted.	E III 6 366 74
A conundrum of Mr. Weston's shall clear him and his next	E III 7 371 31
call upon her the very next morning, and it should be the	E III 8 377 1
coming back beyond the next morning early; but that Mr.	E III 8 383 31
will not ask, though I may wish it unsaid the next moment."	E III 13 429 27
she to be consenting the next to a proposal which might	E III 14 441 8
I doubted it more the next day on Box-Hill; when, provoked	E III 14 441 8
staid with you till the next morning, merely because I	E III 14 441 8
the next day to tell me that we never were to meet again.--	E III 14 442 8
She was deeply ashamed, and a little afraid of his next	E III 15 447 21
our good friends, the Eltons," was his next observation.--	E III 15 447 22
"And the next news, I suppose, will be, that we are to	E III 16 460 52
next to his daughters and Mrs. Weston, best in the world.	E III 17 465 28
He went to Highbury the next morning, and satisfied	E III 17 468 35
him to dine with them the next day--which he did--and in	E III 18 472 20
but his mind was the next moment in his own concerns and	E III 18 478 60
	61
with his own Jane, and his next words were, "did you ever	E III 18 478 60
	61
and the dinner the next day; she could dwell on it all	E III 19 481 2
whose blessing at the altar might next fall on herself.--	E III 19 482 6
by baronet-blood within the next twelvemonth or two.	P III 1 7 12
not come; and the next tidings were that he was married.	P III 1 8 15
to feel, when Mrs. Croft's next words explained it to be	P III 6 49 22
The child had a good night, and was going on well the next	P III 7 55 7
The next moment she was tapping at her husband's dressing-	P III 7 57 17
	18
he was coming the very next morning to shoot with Charles.	P III 7 58 22
And the next moment she was hating herself for the folly	P III 7 60 30
in my passage home the next autumn, to fall in with the	P III 8 65 16
I wished for him again the next summer, when I had still	P III 8 67 23
I should hear from him next; but as long as we could be	P III 8 71 54
been out of the room the next moment, and released Captain	P III 9 79 23
and not to be expected back till the next day's dinner.	P III 11 94 8
at one of the inns, the next thing to be done was	P III 11 95 9
earliest of the party the next morning, agreed to stroll	P III 12 102 1
Anne, must not it be our Mr. Elliot; my father's next heir?	P III 12 105 14
our seeing Mr. Elliot, the next time you write to Bath.	P III 12 107 20
"Anne, Anne," cried Charles, "what is to be done next?	P III 12 111 45
What, in heaven's name, is to be done next?"	P III 12 111 45
horses to be sent home the next morning early, when there	P III 12 114 64
They had an early account from Lyme the next morning.	P IV 1 121 2
They were indebted, the next day, to Charles Hayter for	P IV 1 122 4
again, to say, "the next time you write to your good	P IV 1 128 29
On going down to breakfast the next morning, she found	P IV 4 145 1
the next morning that they had had a delightful evening.--	P IV 5 158 21
to be upset the next moment, which they certainly must be.	P IV 6 169 25
and the very next time Anne walked out, she saw him.	P IV 7 174 1
I forget what we are to have next," turning to the bill.	P IV 8 187 29
an early abdication in her next neighbours, she found	P IV 8 189 46
anxious to have a general idea of what was next to be sung.	P IV 8 190 47
Anne recollected with pleasure the next morning her	P IV 9 192 1
Next week?	P IV 9 195 27
To be sure by next week I may be allowed to think it all	P IV 9 195 27
"No," replied Anne, "nor next week, nor next, nor next.	P IV 9 195 28
next Lady Elliot, through Mrs. Wallis's recommendation?"	P IV 9 208 92
going out of Bath the next morning, going early, and that	P IV 10 214 13
One five minutes brought a note, the next a parcel, and	P IV 10 221 32
a matter of course the next morning, still to defer her	P IV 11 229 1
Musgrove had proposed the next, and what had occurred to	P IV 11 230 5
and he turned round the next instant to give a look--one	P IV 11 231 10
soon afterwards, and being next heard of as established	P IV 12 250 7
Send me more particulars in your next.--	S 5 386 1
some visitors the very next morning;--amongst them, Sir	S 7 394 1
so, my dear, the next time Miss Esther begins talking	S 7 402 1
Mrs Charles Dupuis lives almost next door to a lady, who	S 9 412 1
by Arthur, who was sitting next to the fire with a degree	S 10 414 1
to have a fine young woman next to him, requiring in	S 10 415 1
NICE (62)	
I can get you however a very nice Drawingroom-apartment in	LS 26 296 4
"No, indeed, it looks very nice.--	NA I 2 23 20
"It was such a nice looking morning!	NA I 11 83 12
it is a nice book, and why should not I call it so?"	NA I 14 108 15
"Very true," said Henry, "and this is a very nice day, and	NA I 14 108 16
a very nice walk, and you are two very nice young ladies.	NA I 14 108 16
Oh! it is a very nice word indeed!--it does for every	NA I 14 108 16
nice in their dress, in their sentiments, or their choice.	NA I 14 108 16
You are more nice than wise.	NA I 14 108 17
Bath is a nice place, Catherine, after all.	NA II 14 238 22
room up stairs; of a nice comfortable size for constant	SS I 13 69 76
indeed, were not so nice; their witticisms added pain to	SS I 16 85 11
	12
Elinor could not suppose that Sir John would be more nice	SS I 21 125 36
Delaford is a nice place, I can tell you; exactly what I	SS II 8 196 22
you; exactly what I call a nice old fashioned place, full	SS II 8 196 22
Oh! 'tis a nice place!	SS II 8 197 22
He was nice in his eating, uncertain in his hours; fond of	SS III 6 304 15
Is not it a nice town?--	W 322 2
Mrs E.; she is by much too nice a judge of decorum to give	W 334 13
How nice Mary Edwards looks in her new pelisse!--	W 341 19

of getting you home; besides it won't do to be too nice.-- W 341 19
Mrs Blake is a nice little good-humoured woman, she & I W 358 28
that they would have a nice comfortable noisy game of PP I 15 74 11
park, where there was a nice sheltered path, which no one PP II 7 169 5
"is not this nice? is not this an agreeable surprise?" PP II 16 219 2
A low phaeton, with a nice little pair of ponies, would be PP III 10 325 2
It is a nice long walk, and Mr. Darcy has never seen the PP III 17 374 23
Mrs. Norris accepted the compliment, and admired the nice MP I 4 39 10
youngest Miss Bertram, a nice, handsome, good-humoured, MP I 4 42 19
thing done in the best style, and made as nice as possible. MP I 6 53 9
Here is a nice little wood, if one can but get into it. MP I 9 91 37
little heath, which that nice old gardener would make me MP I 10 105 55
We must not be so nice. MP I 14 131 5
Tom would be quite angry; and if we are so very nice, we MP I 15 141 21
You and Miss Crawford have made me too nice." MP III 4 355 54
Flora, who jilted a very nice young man in the blues, for MP III 5 361 16
want some of your nice ways and orderliness at my father's. MP III 6 372 20
She was nice only from natural delicacy, but *he* had been MP III 10 407 23
choosing from among many, consequently a claim to be nice. E I 8 63 44
with her--the youngest, a nice little girl about eight E I 12 98 2
You and I will have a nice basin of gruel together. E I 12 100 18
by a basin of nice smooth gruel, thin, but not too thin. E I 12 104 50
We must not be nice and ask for all the virtues into the E I 18 149 29
you know, which is so very nice, and the loin to be E II 3 172 18
her-- and now we are such a nice party, she cannot refuse. E II 9 236 46
We are growing a little too nice. E II 11 255 55
But I believe I am nice; I do not like strange voices; and E II 14 279 54
I shall be a little more nice, and I am sure the good E II 17 301 18
had been possible to the nice tone of her mind, the P III 4 28 7
they are particularly nice; and that she reprobates all P III 5 35 14
who has had no society among women to make him nice?" P III 7 62 39
conviction that he was nice; and Anne Elliot was not out P III 7 62 40
Anne found a nice seat for her, on a dry sunny bank, under P III 10 87 21
And very nice young ladies they both are; I hardly know P III 10 92 46
ingenious contrivances and nice arrangements of Captain P III 11 98 17
Most earnestly did she wish that he might not be too nice, P IV 3 140 11
and manners, and with regard to education is not very nice. P IV 4 150 17
"They are not at all nice children, in my opinion; but " P IV 6 163 7
"It may not be felt in Bath, with your nice pavements; " P IV 6 163 7
And such a nice garden--such an excellent garden." S 4 380 1
But it was a nice place for the children to run about in. S 4 380 1
of the two others are nice little snug houses, very fit S 7 402 1

NICELY (8)
"How nicely we are crammed in!" cried Lydia. PP II 16 221 17
She was a woman who spent her days in sitting nicely MP I 2 19 31
as I can judge by this light, you look very nicely indeed. MP II 5 222 42
How nicely you talk; I love to hear you. E I 9 76 28
making it into steaks, nicely fried, as our's are fried, E II 3 171 16
17
To be in company, nicely dressed herself and seeing others E II 8 219 44
herself and seeing others nicely dressed, to sit and smile E II 8 219 44
"Very nicely dressed, indeed; a remarkably elegant gown." E II 14 271 10

NICENESS (1)
before her, in all the niceness of jeweller's packing, a MP II 9 262 8

NICER (2)
"Yes, ma'am, I thank you; we could not have had a nicer NA I 9 68 35
comfortably clearing the nicer things, to say: "Mrs. E I 3 24 13
14

NICEST (7)
But now really, do not you think Udolpho the nicest book NA I 14 107 12
"The nicest;--by which I suppose you mean the neatest. NA I 14 107 13
The word 'nicest,' as you used it, did not suit him; and NA I 14 108 14
got the nicest little black bitch of a pointer I ever saw. SS I 9 44 20
I could get the nicest house in the world for you, next SS I 20 110 4
believing herself the nicest observer of the two;-- she SS III 6 305 16
the other three with the nicest cold luncheon in the world, PP II 16 222 22

NICETY (5)
extraordinary a peice of nicety, considering what are my LS 19 274 2
But unfortunately my own nicety, and the nicety of my SS I 19 102 4
It requires great powers, great nicety, to give her MP I 14 135 15
to her--and I believe I have caught a little of her nicety. E II 18 306 12
There is a quickness of perception in some, a nicety in P IV 12 249 4

NICHOLLS (2)
thing; and as soon as Nicholls has made white soup enough PP I 11 55 7
the other, "for Mrs. Nicholls was in Meryton last night; I PP III 11 331 15

NIECE (84)
In the society of his nephew and niece, and their children, SS I 1 3 1
years, he had received from his niece and her daughters. SS I 1 4 3
preference for his niece, yet had I then had any pursuit, SS III 13 362 5
Mrs. Gardiner then rallied her niece on Wickham's PP II 4 153 7
to her, as her future niece; nor could she think, without PP II 14 210 2
When my niece Georgiana went to ramsgate last summer, I PP II 14 211 13
Mrs. Gardiner looked at her niece with a smile, but PP III 1 247 10
he was talking to their niece, who, astonished and PP III 1 251 52
Her niece was, therefore, obliged to submit, and they took PP III 1 254 57
Mr. Darcy took her place by her niece, and they walked on PP III 1 256 61
a quarter, than by supposing a partiality for their niece. PP III 2 260 1
of Mr. Darcy and their niece, directed their observation PP III 2 261 6
Mrs. Gardiner looked at her niece, desirous of knowing how PP III 2 263 11
between the aunt and niece, that such a striking civility PP III 2 266 17
Mrs. Gardiner and her niece, however, did her justice, and PP III 3 267 3
account, that their niece was taken suddenly ill;--but PP III 4 280 26
before them by her niece; and the kind of half-expectation PP III 6 298 16
you some tidings of my niece, and such as, upon the whole, PP III 7 302 14
to settle on my niece, in addition to her own fortune. PP III 7 302 14
We have judged it best, that my niece should be married PP III 7 303 14
Mrs. Gardiner, that my niece is very desirous of seeing PP III 8 313 19
"My dear niece, PP III 10 321 2
to be of use to his niece, was forced to put up with only PP III 10 324 2
A niece of our's, Sir Thomas, I may say, or, at least of MP I 1 6 6
claim her share in their niece, the change in Mrs. MP I 3 24 7
to do any thing for a niece, whom she had been so forward MP I 3 30 57
least regard for her niece, he could not help paying more MP I 4 37 8
of her eldest niece, as tolerably to quiet her nerves. MP I 4 38 9
instead of retaining his niece, to bring his mistress MP I 4 41 15
as her niece has been entirely brought up by her? MP I 7 63 8
Yes, we must suppose the faults of the niece to have been MP I 7 64 9
by her eldest nephew and niece, who were all-powerful with MP I 13 129 40
of the niece who had been brought up under her eye. MP II 3 203 30
to Lady Bertram's niece, could never want explanation. MP II 5 218 18
Her niece thought it perfectly reasonable. MP II 5 221 35
"My niece walk to a dinner engagement at this time of the MP II 5 221 37
distinguishing his niece--nor perhaps refrain (though MP II 7 238 1
at the other, he found his niece the object of attentions, MP II 7 246 36
niece, and she was soon said to be admired by Mr. Crawford. MP II 10 276 13
he was proud of his niece, and without attributing all her MP II 10 276 13
His niece, meanwhile, did not thank him for what he had MP II 10 280 32
Sir Thomas paused, half smiled, glanced at his niece, and MP II 11 285 13
She is niece to Sir Thomas Bertram; that will be enough MP II 12 293 11
His niece was deep in thought likewise, trying to harden MP III 1 316 33
But the removal of his alarm did his niece no service; as MP III 1 317 36
but when he looked at his niece, and saw the state of MP III 1 320 45
himself, leaving his poor niece to sit and cry over what MP III 1 320 45
he thought well of his niece, or how very far he was from MP III 1 323 57
with his niece, and to shew no open interference. MP III 2 330 14
mention the subject to his niece, to prepare her briefly MP III 2 331 19
their niece; she not only promised, but did observe it. MP III 2 332 20
it made her feel a sort of credit in calling her niece. MP III 2 332 22
I give you joy, my dear niece."-- MP III 2 333 23
the inference of what her niece, alive and enlightened as MP III 3 338 18
great hope that his niece would find a blank in the loss MP III 6 366 1
joy of her nephew and niece, in the recollection that she MP III 6 373 23
Lady Bertram had been telling her niece in the evening to MP III 6 373 26
might have thought his niece in the most promising way of MP III 11 413 30
write about, even to her niece, and being so soon to lose MP III 13 425 6
Lady Bertram wrote her daily terrors to her niece, who MP III 13 427 13
and an indigent niece, and every thing most odious. MP III 16 448 3
with the demerits of her niece, would have had her MP III 17 464 13
No happiness of son or niece could make her wish the MP III 17 472 31
Susan became the stationary niece--delighted to be so!-- MP III 17 472 31
My nephews and nieces!--I shall often have a niece with me. E I 10 86 21
"Do you know Miss Bates's niece? E I 10 86 22
is almost enough to put one out of conceit with a niece. E I 10 86 23
abruptly to the Coles, to usher in a letter from her niece. E II 1 156 6
of both aunt and niece--entirely unexpected; that at first, E II 8 214 13
to Miss Bates and her niece, made his way directly to the E II 8 220 47
Do you know how Miss Bates and her niece came here?" E II 8 222 59
in conveying the aunt and niece; and though his answer was E II 8 228 88
mad, to let your niece sing herself hoarse in this manner? E II 8 229 97
commandingly did he say, "how is your niece, Miss Bates?-- E II 10 244 34
35
want to inquire after you all, but particularly your niece. E II 10 244 35
blockhead, Frank, if you bring the aunt without the niece." E II 11 255 57
aunt, and her elegant niece,--Mrs. Weston, like a sweet- E II 11 255 59
Poor Miss Bates may very likely have committed her niece E II 15 286 21
but the aunt and niece were to be brought by the Eltons. E III 2 320 6
son, Miss Bates and her niece, who had accidentally met. E III 5 344 3
Emma and Harriet went together; Miss Bates and her niece, E III 7 367 1
humble her--and before her niece, too --and before others, E III 7 375 61
The aunt and niece seemed both escaping into the adjoining E III 8 378 4
promised her niece on no account to let Miss Woodhouse in. E III 9 390 18

NIECE'S (10)
been highly gratified by her niece's beginning the subject. PP III 3 272 20
as highly advisable, both on his account and my niece's. PP III 8 312 19
discomposed by her niece's ill-humour, and having asked MP I 7 71 31
only on lessening her niece's pleasure, both present and MP II 5 219 27
what was passing in his niece's mind, conceived that by MP III 1 314 16
In all his niece's family and friends there could be but MP III 2 329 12
and consequence, on his niece's spirits, and the past MP III 6 368 7
It was a medicinal project upon his niece's understanding, MP III 6 369 10
Could Sir Thomas have seen all his niece's feelings, when MP III 8 388 1
Bates farther as to her niece's appetite and diet, which E III 9 390 19

NIECES (15)
John Dashwood, as the nieces of the gentleman who for many SS II 12 231 9
opened to his nieces a source of felicity unknown before. PP I 7 28 4
Mrs. Philips was always glad to see her nieces, and the PP I 15 73 11
she could only tell her nieces what they already knew, PP I 15 73 11
woman, and a great favourite with all her Longbourn nieces. PP II 2 139 2
and in compassion to her nieces turned the conversation. PP II 2 140 5
Four nieces of Mrs. Jenkinson are most delightfully PP II 6 165 32
thought her presence might be serviceable to her nieces. PP III 6 294 3
as ever lived-- and her nieces are very pretty behaved PP III 12 342 28
gaieties for her nieces, assisting their toilettes, MP I 4 34 3
I dare say Mr. Crawford would take my two nieces and me in MP I 6 62 58
Mrs. Norris and her nieces were all well pleased with its MP I 8 75 1
the pleasures of her nieces, she had found a morning of MP I 10 103 50
My nephews and nieces!--I shall often have a niece with me. E I 10 86 21
it is, that we think alike about our nephews and nieces. E I 12 98 2
3

NIECES' (2)
assisted to form her nieces' minds; and it is not very MP I 2 19 30
as if reading in her two nieces' minds their little MP I 6 61 58

NIGGARDLY (2)
income, no niggardly assignment to one of ten children. NA II 1 135 42
his relations, and no niggardly proportion was now dealt SS I 21 124 33

NIGHT (199)
My dear mother Mr Vernon returned on Thursday night, LS 17 269 1
"He told us nothing of all this last night, said she LS 23 284 6
I arrived last night about five, & had scarcely swallowed LS 29 299 2
you come from the rooms at night; and I wish you would try NA I 2 18 2
across the theatre at night, and say their prayers in the NA I 4 34 7
if he was to tease me all night, I would not dance with NA I 6 40 14
How do you do, Mrs. Allen? a famous ball last night, was NA I 9 61 1
What a delightful ball we had last night. NA I 9 62 7
man, and you could not fancy him in liquor last night?" NA I 9 63 19
ten minutes on Wednesday night debating between her NA I 10 73 22
south of France!--the night that poor St. Aubin died!-- NA I 11 83 15
You are talking of the man you danced with last night, are NA I 11 85 35
others to the theatre that night; but it must be confessed NA I 12 92 4
her; I could not sleep a wink all night for thinking of it. NA I 15 118 13
further to alarm perhaps may occur the first night. NA II 5 159 19
But on the second, or at farthest the *third* night after NA II 5 159 19
The night was stormy; the wind had been rising at NA II 6 166 9
not know that, in such a night as this, I could have NA II 6 167 9
To close her eyes in sleep that night, she felt must be NA II 6 170 12
a bright morning had succeeded the tempest of the night. NA II 7 172 1
play, except going in last night with the Hodges's, for a NA II 12 217 2
Heavily past the night. NA II 13 227 26
of coming till Saturday night; for General Tilney, from NA II 14 237 21
The General, perceiving his son one night at the theatre NA II 15 244 12
how tame was Edward's manner in reading to us last night! SS I 3 17 18
If dancing formed the amusement of the night, they were SS I 11 54 3
Last night after tea, when you and mama went out of the SS I 12 60 13
though it had rained all night, as the clouds were then SS I 13 63 2
made by Willoughby the night before of calling on her SS I 15 75 1
And last night he was with us so happy, so cheerful, so SS I 15 77 23
sleep at all the first night after parting from Willoughby. SS I 16 83 1
She was awake the whole night, and she wept the greatest SS I 16 83 1
"You *must* drink tea with us to night," said he, "for we SS I 18 99 17
or lying awake the whole night to indulge meditation, SS I 19 104 12
I thought I heard a carriage last night, while we were SS I 19 106 20
am sure, though we could not get him to own it last night." SS I 20 116 58
persevered, and saw every night in the brightness of the SS II 5 168 10
in Conduit-Street the night before, and requesting the SS II 5 170 28
thing in my behaviour last night that did not meet your SS II 7 183 13
We were last night at Lady Middleton's, where there was a SS II 7 187 40
am I to imagine, Willoughby, by your behaviour last night? SS II 7 187 41
42
I have passed a wretched night in endeavouring to excuse a SS II 7 187 42
From a night of more sleep than she had expected, Marianne SS II 9 201 1
her young friends every night, on having escaped the SS II 14 247 5
me this bow to my hat, and put in the feather last night. SS III 2 272 12
Colonel Brandon would get farther than reading that night. SS III 6 303 12
proper medicines on her at night, trusted, like Marianne, SS III 7 307 1
A very restless and feverish night, however, disappointed SS III 7 307 2
the apothecary, and to watch by her the rest of the night. SS III 7 312 17
It was a night of almost equal suffering to both. SS III 7 312 17
The night was cold and stormy. SS III 7 316 28
The night following this affair--I was to go the next SS III 8 323 40
"Last night, in Drury-Lane lobby, I ran against Sir John SS III 8 330 69
Mrs. Dashwood *would* sit up with her all night, and Elinor, SS III 9 334 5
But the rest, *which* one night entirely sleepless, and many SS III 9 334 5
promised them all, the satisfaction of a sleepless night. SS III 13 363 6
therefore walked every night to his old quarters at the SS III 13 369 34
"What! would you come late at night in this chair?"-- W 319 2
You had better meet every night, & break up two hours W 325 4
girl who had been admired the night before by Ld Osborne.-- W 337 16
"What a famous ball we had last night!--he cried, after a W 340 19
man who was here last night my dear Emma & returns today, W 360 29
Mrs. Long told me last night that he sat close to her for PP I 5 19 10
the other night at Sir William's in his regimentals." PP I 7 29 12
it seems likely to rain; and then you must stay all night." PP I 7 30 21
Elizabeth passed the chief of the night in her sister's PP I 9 41 1
night all the foolish things that were said in the morning. PP I 10 49 28

only on its being a wet night, and on the probability of a PP I 16 76 4
himself as he gave me last night; names, facts, every PP I 17 85 5
his interference, lest Mary should be singing all night. PP I 18 100 68
was but the very Saturday night before I left Hunsford-- PP I 19 105 10
that when they parted at night, she would have felt almost PP I 22 121 1
the ladies moved for the night; and Mrs. Bennet with great PP I 22 123 4
The improvement of spending a night in London was added in PP II 4 151 1
those offers, which were last night so disgusting to you. PP II 12 196 4
means of equal magnitude you last night laid to my charge. PP II 12 196 5
But from the severity of that blame which was last night PP II 12 196 5
merely those, which I last night acknowledged to have PP II 12 198 5
possibly wonder why all this was not told you last night. PP II 12 202 5
The Gardiners staid only one night at Longbourn, and set PP II 19 239 11
Accordingly, when she retired at night, she asked the PP II 19 241 17
recollect your saying one night, after they had been PP III 3 271 16
17
An express came at twelve last night, just as we were all PP III 4 273 3
They were off Saturday night about twelve, as is PP III 4 274 3
They left Brighton together on Sunday night, and were PP III 4 277 14
possible; and sleeping one night on the road, reached PP III 5 285 20
at heart, that I can get no rest by night nor by day. PP III 5 288 38
not keeping my engagement, and dancing with him to night. PP III 5 291 60
It would have spared her, she thought, one sleepless night PP III 6 299 17
sit in my library, in my night cap and powdering gown, and PP III 6 300 28
was in Meryton last night; I saw her passing by, and went PP III 11 331 15
took his leave for the night; but as soon as he was gone, PP III 13 348 35
36
I am sure I sha'nt get a wink of sleep all night. PP III 13 348 40
I saw them the night before last." PP III 14 352 14
to her ladyship last night, she immediately, with her PP III 15 363 22
At night she opened her heart to Jane. PP III 17 372 2
All was acknowledged, and half the night spent in PP III 17 374 19
When her mother went up to her dressing-room at night, she PP III 17 377 42
when she left it at night, as seeming as desirably MP I 2 14 9
Do you know, we asked her last night, which way she would MP I 2 18 25
to Lady Bertram during the night of a ball or a party. MP I 4 35 6
When they parted at night, Edmund asked Fanny whether she MP I 7 69 26
in their praise of the night and their remarks on the MP I 7 71 31
No banners, cousin, to be 'blown by the night wind of MP I 9 86 6
about green goose from Monday morning till Saturday night." MP I 11 112 31
night, and the contrast of the deep shade of the woods. MP I 11 112 35
When I look out on such a night as this, I feel as if MP I 11 113 35
It is a lovely night, and they are much to be pitied who MP I 11 113 36
I heard enough of what she said to you last night, to MP I 16 154 14
more amiable than in her behaviour to you last night. MP I 16 156 24
or waking, my head has been full of this matter all night. MP I 16 156 27
flirted as she did last night with Mr. Yates; and though MP I 17 162 16
but I was pleased last night with what appeared to be his MP II 2 190 6
not you hear me ask him about the slave trade last night?" MP II 3 198 10
And as to coming away at night, you are to stay just as MP II 5 221 32
I certainly do not go home to night, and, therefore, the MP II 5 221 34
I observed he was hoarse on Thursday night." MP II 5 222 39
When we talked of her last night, you none of you seemed MP II 6 229 5
"This is the assembly night," said William. MP II 7 249 50
night with her head full of happy cares as well as Fanny.-- MP II 8 254 8
passing around him on the subject, from morning till night. MP II 8 256 13
"For one night, Fanny, for only one night, if it be a MP II 9 263 16
Northampton the following night, which would not have MP II 9 266 21
"I have been talking incessantly all night, and with MP II 10 278 20
Nothing remained of last night but remembrances, which she MP II 11 282 4
It must be sitting up so late last night. MP II 11 283 5
Last night it had been hope and smiles, bustle and motion, MP II 11 283 6
of talking over Thursday night with Mrs. Grant and Miss MP II 11 283 7
as to its effect, than she had been the night before. MP III 1 311 1
that I think of all day, and dream of all night.-- MP III 3 344 41
the other night, will think you unfitted as companions? MP III 4 348 23
All this passed over night, for the journey was to begin MP III 6 374 29
He had reached it late the night before, was come for a MP III 10 400 7
The evening passed, without a pause of misery, the night MP III 15 441 20
We talked it all over with Mr. Weston last night. E I 1 8 18
It is a beautiful, moonlight night; and so mild that I E I 1 10 23
He had his shepherd's son into the parlour one night on E I 4 28 6
How well she looked last night!" E I 5 39 16
Harriet slept at Hartfield that night. E I 8 57 1
This happened the night before last. E I 8 60 27
it was the whist-club night, which he had been never known E I 8 68 58
note, at twelve o'clock at night, on purpose to assure me E I 11 95 19
I went for only one night, and could not get away till E I 13 115 39
of a much darker night than he had been prepared for. E I 15 128 22
of the weather and the night; but scarcely had she begun, E I 15 129 24
Emma then felt it indispensable to wish him a good night. E I 15 132 37
under temporary gloom at night, the return of day will E I 16 137 13
The muffin last night--if it had been handed round once, I E II 3 170 4
to feel quite assured of himself till after another night. E II 5 193 35
could get away, or introduce an acquaintance for a night. E II 8 221 48
home again, late at night, and cold as the nights are now. E II 8 223 63
Every body last night said how well you played." E II 9 231 7
The Coxes were wondering last night whether she would get E II 9 232 11
Miss Bates last night, that I would come this morning. E II 9 234 26
indeed, if I understood Miss Fairfax's opinion last night." E II 9 234 33
it sent to Hartfield, and take it home with me at night. E II 9 235 40
is delightfully well; and Jane caught no cold last night. E II 9 236 46
waltzes we danced last night;--let me live them over again. E II 10 242 17
So obliged to you for the carriage last night. E II 10 243 33
I hope she caught no cold last night. E II 10 244 35
Oh! Mr. Knightley, what a delightful party last night; how E II 10 245 48
a pair of scissars the night before of Miss Bates, and to E III 3 334 7
shall never forget her look the other night!-- E III 4 337 6
We really must wish you good night." E III 5 349 24
"This was settled last night, and Frank was off with the E III 10 398 57
The rest of the day, the following night, were hardly E III 11 411 43
course of the sleepless night, which was the tax for such E III 14 434 4
comfort of hearing last night, by Mr. Perry, that it had E III 14 436 7
I will take it home with me at night." E III 15 444 3
He really is engaged from morning to night.-- E III 16 455 23
It was a pity, perhaps, that he had not come last night; E III 18 479 73
Mrs. Weston's poultry-house was robbed one night of all E III 19 483 10
have been under wretched alarm every night of his life. E III 19 483 10
The child had a good night, and was going on well the next P III 7 55 7
might be at rest for the night, and kindly urged her to P III 7 58 20
the morning and return at night, but to this Mr. Musgrove, P III 11 94 8
They were consequently to stay the night there, and not to P III 11 94 8
fortune,--came in last night from Sidmouth,--dare say you P III 12 105 12
the return, travelled night and day till he got to P III 12 108 28
two, she could want no possible attendance by day or night. P III 12 113 56
farther advantage of sending an account of Louisa's night. P III 12 114 64
had been persuaded to go early to their inn last night. P IV 1 121 2
when behold! on Tuesday night, he made a very awkward sort P IV 2 130 5
Alicia and Mrs. Frankland were telling me of last night. P IV 7 179 30
"He must wish her good night. P IV 8 190 48
you were in company last night with the person, whom you P IV 9 194 16
the concert of last night might afford:--not Mr. Elliot; P IV 9 197 33
something which Mr. Elliot said last night," cried Anne. P IV 9 201 63
of his attentions last night, the irremediable mischief he P IV 10 212 1
guarded, and more cool, than she had been the night before. P IV 10 214 11
her so, but I thought her dress hideous the other night. P IV 10 215 15
They had arrived late the night before. P IV 10 217 19
been to the theatre, and secured a box for to-morrow night. P IV 10 223 41
Take a box for to-morrow night! P IV 10 223 43
to Camden-Place to-morrow night? and that we were most P IV 10 223 43
her cheerfully, and depend on finding her better at night. P IV 11 238 47
She had not a wink of sleep either the night before we set S 9 407 1
before we set out, or last night at Chichester, and as S 9 407 1
"Keep you awake perhaps all night"--replied Charlotte, S 10 418 1

NIGHT'S (7)
good night's rest in the course of the next three months. NA I 11 90 65
and alarm, and robbed her of half her night's rest! NA II 7 172 2
a hint; but when a third night's rest had neither restored NA II 15 240 2
and a sore throat, a good night's rest was to cure her SS III 6 306 17
A good night's rest improved her spirits. MP II 11 283 7
for though a good night's rest, a pleasant morning, the MP III 8 388 1
The last night's ball seemed lost in the gipsies. E III 3 336 12

NIGHTLY (1)
hands of her husband a nightly supply of coarse food, was NA II 8 187 16

NIGHTS (14)
But it does not signify, the nights are moonlight, and we NA I 11 84 19
Oh! Catherine, the many sleepless nights I have had on NA I 15 118 13
him to leave them on Saturday for a couple of nights. NA II 13 221 7
any appetite, and many nights since she had really slept; SS II 7 185 16
couple of nights, he was to proceed on his journey to town. SS III 13 372 46
for two or three nights, without making a peice of work. W 351 25
Margaret & I have played at cribbage, most nights that we W 354 28
leave out because the nights are so mild, and I know the MP II 4 212 31
sad evils of sleeping two nights on the road, and express E II 5 193 35
home again, late at night, and cold as the nights are now. E II 8 223 63
that she means to sleep only two nights on the road.-- E II 18 306 11
lasted four days and nights, and which would have done for P III 8 66 16
The nights were too dark for the ladies to meet again till P III 11 99 22
one of those dreadful nights, when we had been literally S 4 381 1

NIMBLY (3)
for the curricle, and so nimbly were the light horses NA II 5 156 5
she saw a lady walking nimbly behind her at no great S 9 406 1
one house to the other as nimbly as he could,--& boasted S 10 414 1

NINE (31)
favourite gown, though it cost but nine shillings a yard." NA I 3 28 35
way; Mr. Allen says it is nine, measured nine; but I am NA I 3 29 46
says it is nine, measured nine; but I am sure it cannot be NA I 3 29 46
acquaintance of eight or nine days, is given as a specimen NA I 6 39 1
a sound sleep which lasted nine hours, and from which she NA I 9 60 1
"She has been dead these nine years." NA II 8 186 10
And nine years, Catherine knew was a trifle of time, NA II 8 186 10
For nine successive mornings, Catherine wondered over the NA II 10 201 6
be at Salisbury, and then I am only nine miles from home." NA II 13 224 17
a small dance of eight or nine couple, with two violins, SS II 5 170 29
No, tho' I am nine years older than you are, I would not W 320 2
The clock struck nine, while he was thus agreably occupied; W 359 28
In nine cases out of ten, a woman had better show more PP I 6 22 2
"We have dined nine times at Rosings, besides drinking tea PP II 15 217 13
daughter, a girl now nine years old, of an age to require MP I 1 5 4
Poor Julia, the only one out of the nine not tolerably MP I 9 91 36
He is not five foot nine. MP I 10 102 43
He is to have breakfasted and be gone by half past nine.-- MP II 10 280 29
Mr. Crawford, I think you call for him at half past nine?" MP II 10 280 29
"Yes, half past nine," said Crawford to William, as the MP II 10 280 31
A residence of eight or nine years in the abode of wealth MP III 6 369 10
and dirty, about eight and nine years old, rushed into it MP III 7 381 25
respectable mother of nine children, on a small income. MP III 8 390 5
past nine, there was little intermission of noise or grog. MP III 11 413 32
all; and, before she was nine years old, his daughter's E II 2 163 4
certainly would make them nine, yet he always said so E II 16 292 8
What were nine miles to a young man?-- E III 1 317 10
all lines and wrinkles, nine grey hairs of a side, and P III 3 19 16
be feeling that eight or nine years should have passed P IV 7 179 28
He was to leave Bath at nine this morning, and does not P IV 10 222 35
It holds nine. P IV 10 223 41

NINE-AND-TWENTY (1)
of being nine-and-twenty, to give her some regrets and P III 1 7 12

NINE-HUNDREDTH (1)
And while the abilities of the nine-hundredth abridger of NA I 5 37 4

NINETEEN (14)
her, though only nineteen, to be the counsellor of her SS I 1 6 11
The youthful infatuation of nineteen would naturally blind SS II 1 140 2
me, for I was not entered at Oxford till I was nineteen. SS III 13 362 5
there from eighteen to nineteen: Lucy appeared everything SS III 13 362 5
found herself at nineteen, submitting to new attachments, SS III 14 378 16
One does not like to see a girl of eighteen or nineteen so MP I 5 49 32
a glance at Fanny) that nineteen times out of twenty I am MP III 3 340 25
do; and at eighteen or nineteen she was, as far as such an E II 2 164 6
to throw herself away at nineteen; involve herself at P III 4 26 3
involve herself at nineteen in an engagement with a young P III 4 26 3
more, while Anne was nineteen, she would have rejoiced to P III 4 28 7
from what she had been made to think at nineteen.-- P III 4 29 8
Louisa, young ladies of nineteen and twenty, who had P III 5 40 45
At nineteen, you know, one does not think very seriously, P IV 9 199 55

NINETY-NINE (2)
must be thought so by ninety-nine people out of an hundred; E I 8 63 44
Ninety-nine out of a hundred would do the same. P IV 9 196 32

NINNY (1)
"The Colonel is a ninny, my dear; because he has two SS III 4 292 57

NINTH (3)
She was preparing for her ninth lying-in, and after MP I 1 5 2
bear--and here would be a ninth--and Emma apprehended that E II 16 292 7
that it would be a ninth very much out of humour at not E II 16 292 7

NIPPED (1)
unwarily exposed, and nipped by the lingering frost, SS III 6 303 10

NO 10 (1)
you must come to me at No 10 Wigmore St--but I hope this LS 2 245 1

NO 2. DENHAM PLACE (1)
other, for No 2. Denham Place--or the end house of the S 5 388 1

NOBILITY (4)
The stain of illegitimacy, unbleached by nobility or E III 19 482 3
One wonders how the names of many of our nobility become P III 3 23 33
nobility, and she must acknowledge herself disappointed. P IV 4 148 11
connections among the nobility of England and Ireland! P IV 5 158 19

NOBLE (36)
A sacrifice was always noble; and if she had given way to NA I 13 103 29
They determined on walking round Beechen Cliff, that noble NA I 14 106 1
No--I will be noble. NA I 14 112 36
love you the better for such a noble honest affection." NA II 1 136 49
The dining-parlour was a noble room, suitable in its NA II 6 165 6
It was very noble--very grand--very charming!--was all NA II 8 182 2
with a long train of noble relations in their several NA II 14 232 7
They contained a noble piece of water; a sail on which was SS I 12 62 28
Your ideas are only more noble than mine. SS I 17 91 11
to make over for ever; but Mrs. Ferrars has a noble spirit. SS II 11 224 28
Such a noble mind!--such openness, such sincerity!-- no SS III 9 337 14
The Edwards' have a noble house you see, & they live quite W 322 2
person, handsome features, noble mien; and the report PP I 3 10 5
nothing that can add to the beauties of that noble place. PP I 8 38 33
"Yes," replied Wickham;--"his estate there is a noble one. PP I 16 77 10
recommendation of the very noble lady whom I have the PP I 19 105 10
He was storing his memory with anecdotes and noble names. PP II 6 166 41
He bore it with noble indifference, and she would have PP III 12 340 12
room for her parasol, attended her noble guest down stairs. PP III 14 352 19
side, from the same noble line; and, on the father's, from PP III 14 356 50
property, noble kindred, and extensive patronage. PP III 15 362 15
cousin, that she and her noble admirer may be aware of PP III 15 363 22
your feelings were always noble and just; and in your PP III 18 380 5
which is now grown such a noble tree, and getting to such MP I 6 54 9
Edmund again felt grave, and only replied, "it is a noble MP I 6 60 50
and be dragged up at the expense of those noble animals. MP II 2 189 5
and injuring the noble fire which the butler had prepared. MP II 10 272 4
capable of every thing noble, and I am ready to blame MP III 13 421 2
though you make so noble a profession of doing it, but I E II 8 217 32

And such a noble fire!-- E III 2 323 19
saw him coming--his noble look--and my wretchedness before. E III 4 342 38
"You are so noble in your ideas!" E III 8 382 25
That was the kind action; that was the noble benevolence E III 11 406 24
Many a noble fortune has been made during the war. P III 3 17 1
That would be a noble thing, indeed, for Henrietta! P III 9 75 11
He would be a noble Coadjutor!-- S 3 377 1
NOBLEMAN (2)
was the daughter of a nobleman with thirty thousand pounds, SS III 14 373 3
least, a nobleman & a stranger, was really distressing.-- W 344 21
NOBLEMEN (1)
Cautions against the violence of such noblemen and NA I 2 18 2
NOBLENESS (2)
Henry's astonishing generosity and nobleness of conduct, NA II 10 201 4
But there is nobleness in the name of Edmund. MP II 4 211 23
NOBLER (1)
was bringing forward a nobler fall of ground, or a finer PP III 1 253 55
NOBLEST (3)
his conduct in the noblest light, seemed most improbable. PP III 9 320 32
Sotherton Court is the noblest old place in the world." MP I 6 53 3
one mile & 3 qrs from the noblest expanse of ocean between S 4 380 1
NOBLY (4)
dear sister, by seeing how nobly the consciousness of your SS II 7 189 51
Elinor honoured her for a plan which originated so nobly SS III 10 343 10
nobly settled, as will, probably, never occur to you again. MP III 1 318 39
Maria is nobly married--but had Mr. Crawford sought MP III 1 319 39
NOBODY (198)
Reginald, & seeing nobody from Churchill; I never found LS 40 309 1
But, dear Mrs. Allen, are you sure there is nobody you NA I 2 23 20
which every morning brought, of her knowing nobody at all. NA I 3 25 1
and down; people whom nobody cared about, and nobody NA I 4 31 1
about, and nobody wanted to see; and he only was absent. NA I 4 31 1
to read, I feel as if nobody could make me miserable. NA I 6 41 19
Nobody drinks there. NA I 9 64 24
Nobody can fasten themselves on the notice of one, without NA I 10 76 29
that she might find nobody to go with her, it was proposed NA I 10 80 61
"Well, nobody would have thought you had no right who saw NA I 12 95 15
as I used to think, nobody would willingly ever look into, NA I 14 109 24
scheme in the world; that nobody could imagine how NA I 15 116 1
to my hand, there was nobody else in the room he could NA II 1 134 39
"Nobody can think better of Mr. Morland than I do, I am NA II 1 136 47
body speaks well of, and nobody cares about; whom all are SS I 10 50 14
all are delighted to see, and nobody remembers to talk to." SS I 10 50 14
Nobody could tell. SS I 13 63 5
What! you thought nobody could dance because a certain SS I 18 100 20
Nobody is more liked than Mr. Willoughby wherever he goes, SS I 20 116 58
great solemnity; "I know nobody of whose judgment I think SS II 2 150 32
Because you are so sly about it yourself, you think nobody SS II 7 182 10
is nobody here but you, that can feel for me.-- SS II 12 231 13
Some kindness as fell to the share of nobody but me!-- SS II 13 239 6
Poor Edward muttered something, but what it was, nobody SS II 13 243 32
brought so forward between them, and nobody suspect it! SS III 1 258 7
told Miss Sparks, that nobody in their senses could expect SS III 2 272 16
loved nobody but Lucy, and nobody but Lucy would he have. SS III 2 273 16
himself, he thinks that nobody else can marry on less. SS III 4 292 57
Nobody was there. SS III 5 294 4
a great deal at home, nobody can tell what may happen--for, SS III 14 375 9
I am a stranger here, & know nobody but the Edwardses; my W 320 2
I know nobody who likes a game of cards in a social way, W 325 4
Nobody could have thought of the Edwards' letting you have W 341 19
You are like nobody else in the world.-- W 342 19
Nobody can tell how much I hate quarrelling. W 343 19
charged by Miss W. to let nobody in, returned in half a W 344 21
& spirit! he lets nobody dream over their cards--I wish W 358 28
her at all: indeed, nobody can, you know; and he seemed PP I 3 13 16
"Certainly, my dear, nobody said there were; but as to not PP I 9 43 25
I know of nobody that is coming I am sure, unless PP I 13 61 2
in favour of a man whom nobody cared anything about. "it PP I 13 62 8
a melancholy tone, "for nobody is on my side, nobody takes PP II 3 113 26
nobody is on my side, nobody takes part with me, I am PP II 3 113 26
me, I am cruelly used, nobody feels for my poor nerves." PP II 3 113 26
Nobody can tell what I suffer!-- PP I 20 113 28
instruction, and nobody but a governess can give it. PP II 6 165 32
as when she could get nobody else; and she was, in fact, PP II 8 172 2
"True; and nobody can ever be introduced in a ball room. PP II 8 175 20
believe nobody feels the loss of friends so much as I do. PP II 14 210 3
and pretended there was nobody in the coach; and I should PP II 16 222 22
Nobody wants him to come. PP II 17 228 29
but poor dear Lydia had nobody to take care of her. PP III 5 287 35
My sole dependence was on you; and I am sure nobody else PP III 17 372 5
To be sure, you know no actual good of me--but nobody PP III 18 380 5
benevolent, and nobody knew better how to dictate MP I 1 8 9
Nobody meant to be unkind, but nobody put themselves out MP I 2 14 6
Of the rest she saw nothing; nobody seemed to think of her MP I 2 21 34
again, even for a visit, nobody at home seemed to want her; MP I 2 21 34
Nobody that wishes me well, I am sure, would propose it. MP I 3 28 42
I have nobody else to care for, but I should be very glad MP I 3 30 52
"Nobody loved plenty and hospitality more than herself-- MP I 3 31 59
more than herself--nobody more hated pitiful doings--the MP I 3 31 59
Nobody can think more highly of the matrimonial state than MP I 4 43 23
could nobody be employed on such an errand but Fanny?-- MP I 7 73 52
I think nobody can justly accuse me of sparing myself upon MP I 7 73 53
thing, and what nobody likes: and if the good people who MP I 9 87 15
Nobody can call such an under-sized man handsome. MP I 10 102 43
to be in the army, and nobody sees any thing wrong in that. MP I 11 109 18
Nobody wonders that they should prefer the line where MP I 11 109 18
Nobody can wonder that men are soldiers and sailors." MP I 11 109 19
"Nobody loves a play better than you do, or can have gone MP I 13 124 11
"Oh! dear, ma'am--nobody suspected you----- MP I 13 126 23
Nobody is fonder of the exercise of talent in young people, MP I 13 126 25
Don't imagine that nobody in this house can see or judge MP I 13 128 31
rhyming butler for me--if nobody else wants it--a trifling MP I 14 132 7
Nobody was at the trouble of an answer; the others soon MP I 15 142 23
will not much signify if nobody hears a word you say, so MP I 15 145 47
having the use of what nobody else wanted, though the MP I 16 151 1
been nobody to put him in the way of doing any thing yet." MP I 17 161 14
is at home; and nobody else can keep Mrs. Norris in order. MP I 17 162 16
expedient, for which nobody thanked her, and saying, with MP I 17 163 21
too long or too short;--nobody would attend as they ought, MP I 18 165 2
attend as they ought, nobody would remember on which side MP I 18 165 2
in--nobody but the complainer would observe any directions. MP I 18 165 2
tolerable of them, nobody had the smallest idea of that MP I 18 166 4
You are best off, I can tell you; but if nobody did more MP I 18 166 6
You will find nobody there." MP II 2 193 13
I know nobody who distinguishes characters better.-- MP II 3 198 13
sought after now when nobody else was to be had; and MP II 4 208 11
"Nobody can ever forget them. MP II 5 224 53
of dress and your having nobody else to look at; and MP II 6 230 6
you if you would, for nobody would know who I was here, MP II 7 250 59
night but remembrances, which she had nobody to share in. MP II 11 282 4
all together, I dare say nobody would believe what a sum MP II 13 305 24
seemed all done away--nobody could tell how; and the MP III 6 367 4
Nobody was in their right place, nothing was done as it MP III 8 388 3
done without a clatter, nobody sat still, and nobody could MP III 8 392 11
still, and nobody could command attention when they spoke. MP III 8 392 11
satisfaction; she saw nobody in whose favour she could MP III 9 395 3
She loves nobody but herself and her brother. MP III 13 424 4
Nobody else could be interested in so remote an evil as MP III 13 428 14
be assured, he cares for nobody but you. at this very MP III 14 435 14
of a moment's etourderie thinks of nobody but you. MP III 15 437 3
his sister still said that he cared for nobody else. MP III 15 438 6
She was of course only too good for him; but as nobody MP III 17 471 28
"No, papa, nobody thought of your walking. E I 1 8 16
Nobody thought of Hannah till you mentioned her--James is E I 1 9 18
There is nobody in Highbury who deserves him--and he has E I 1 13 46
fell in love with him, nobody was surprized except her E I 2 15 2
that Emma, accountable to nobody but her father, who E I 5 40 24
But there is nobody hereabouts to attach her; and she goes E I 5 41 29
Nobody cares for a letter; the thing is, to be always E I 7 55 34
She is the natural daughter of nobody knows whom, with E I 8 61 38
she may be called nobody, it will not hold in common sense. E I 8 62 41
while, nobody within her reach will be good enough for her. E I 8 64 47
altogether, having seen nobody better (that must have been E I 8 65 48
"It is a sort of thing which nobody could have expected. E I 9 74 24
Nobody could have written so prettily, but you, Emma." E I 9 78 52
of it; and nobody is afraid of her: that is a great charm." E I 10 85 19
I am sure nobody ought to be, or can be, a greater E I 11 95 19
"Nobody ever did think well of the Churchills, I fancy," E I 11 96 26
Nobody is healthy in London, nobody can be. E I 12 102 36
of a very ancient family--and that the Eltons were nobody. E I 16 136 9
Harriet bore the intelligence very well--blaming nobody-- E I 17 141 7
She never could have deserved him--and nobody but so E I 17 141 8
Nobody, who has not been in the interior of a family, can E I 18 146 15
Nobody but you, Mr. Knightley, would imagine it possible E I 18 147 17
Frank Churchill; we shall think and speak of nobody else." E I 18 149 29
out herself, if she had nobody to do it for her --every E II 1 157 10
Nobody could nurse her, as we should do." E II 1 161 29
would think tall, and nobody could think very tall; her E II 2 167 12
nobody that she could wish to scheme about for her. E II 2 168 14
There is nobody half so attentive and civil as you are. E II 3 170 4
Nobody had any information to give; and, after a few more E II 3 175 41
42

At the same time, nobody could wonder if Mr. Elton should E II 3 176 44
I see nobody else looking like her!-- E II 8 222 56
'Nobody was ever so fortunate as herself!'--but many, many E II 8 223 63
is nobody whom I would fix on more than on Mr. Knightley. E II 8 223 64
of dancing--originating nobody exactly knew where-- was so E II 8 229 98
if there is any difference nobody would ever find it out. E II 9 232 9
Nobody talked about it. E II 9 232 11
"It appears to me a plan that nobody can object to, if Mr. E II 11 251 24
reason to regret the alteration, but nobody else could." E II 11 251 27
'Open the windows!--but surely, Mr. Churchill, nobody E II 11 251 30
Nobody would be so imprudent! E II 11 252 30
Nobody is equal to you!-- E II 13 268 14
I care for nobody as I do for you!-- E II 13 268 14
"Yes," said Harriet earnestly, "and well she might, nobody E II 14 271 15
Nobody can be more devoted to home than I am. E II 14 274 30
voices; and nobody speaks like you and poor Miss Taylor. E II 14 279 54
attentions from Mrs. Elton, which nobody else pays her." E II 15 286 18
attentions from Mrs. Elton which nobody else paid her. E II 16 291 5
Nobody but yourself could imagine such a thing possible. E II 18 308 25
something favourable would turn up--but nobody believed me. E II 18 308 27
She thinks nobody equal to him." E II 18 309 30
of pride that would harm nobody, and only make himself a E II 18 309 33
She was nobody when he married her, barely the daughter of E II 18 310 33
at west hall; and how they got their fortune nobody knows. E II 18 310 34
was wanting notice, which nobody had inclination to pay, E II 18 311 36
Mrs. Elton then said, "nobody can think less of dress in E III 2 324 20
21

to bed, and got back again, and nobody missed me.-- E III 2 329 45
Is there nobody you would not rather?-- E III 2 329 45
his son, laughing, "I seem to have had it from nobody.-- E III 5 345 13
known to nobody else, and only thought of about three days. E III 5 345 16
Tea passed pleasantly, and nobody seemed in a hurry to E III 5 347 18
But (lowering her voice)--nobody speaks except ourselves, E III 7 369 15
Nobody could have helped it. E III 7 374 58
To look at her, nobody would think how delighted and happy E III 8 379 8
Nobody else would come so early.' E III 8 379 8
'I can see nobody,' said she; and up she got, and would go E III 8 379 8
or say, besides the 'love,' which nobody carries?" E III 9 385 2
his wife, was feared by nobody; an easy, guidable man, to E III 9 388 13
so much--but, except them, Jane would really see nobody." E III 9 390 18
who can see into everybody's heart; but nobody else-----" E III 11 404 10
of Mr. Frank Churchill, who is like nobody by his side. E III 11 405 18
And nobody knew at all which way he was gone. E III 16 458 40
real understanding, was nobody with either father or P III 1 5 8
and she did, what nobody else thought of doing, she P III 2 12 3
that I chose, for nobody would think it worth their while P III 3 17 4
Mr. Wentworth was nobody, I remember; quite unconnected; P III 3 23 33
Anne had better stay, for nobody will want her in Bath." P III 5 33 7
Nobody doubts her right to have precedence of mamma, but P III 6 46 10
"Nobody knew how much she should suffer. P III 6 48 17
lost in only a sloop, nobody would have thought about me." P III 8 66 16
over the destiny of a son, whom alive nobody had cared for. P III 8 68 29
But nobody heard, or, at least, nobody answered her. P III 10 85 12
Nobody could do it, but that good fellow, (pointing to P III 12 108 28
what he did, and nobody else could have saved poor James. P III 12 108 28
in Bath; she saw nobody equal to him; and it was a great P IV 4 148 9
Nobody supposed that you were his first inducement. P IV 9 205 86
But there was nobody to stir in it. P IV 9 210 98
Nobody doubts it; and I hope you do not think I am so P IV 10 218 26
he would go to the play to-morrow, if nobody else would." P IV 10 225 55
merit and activity could place him, was no longer nobody. P IV 12 248 1
Nobody could catch cold by the sea, nobody wanted appetite S 2 373 1
the sea, nobody wanted spirits, nobody wanted strength.-- S 2 373 1
Nobody could live happier together than us--& he was a S 7 400 1
I know nobody like you.-- S 9 409 1
NOBODY'S (4)
"Nobody's, that I know of." NA I 11 89 61
body's good word and nobody's notice; who has more money SS I 10 51 25
She would be in nobody's way, you know, in that part of PP II 8 173 10
I am sure there is nobody's praise that could give us so E II 1 158 12
NOD (4)
gentleman, and a silencing nod from her mother; for Mrs. NA II 15 243 9
On finding him determined to go, Margt began to wink & nod W 359 28
as Lady Bertram began to nod again--"but this I will MP I 13 126 23
They were permitted to go alone; and with a cordial nod E II 5 195 49
NODDED (4)
nodded to Mrs. Jennings from the other side of the room. SS II 5 171 30
Emma only nodded, and smiled.-- E I 9 78 53
Sir Walter only nodded. P III 3 18 5
of the case, only nodded in reply, and walked away. P III 8 66 21
NODDING (7)
business, for you know (nodding significantly and pointing SS I 19 107 29
Between ourselves, Edmund," nodding significantly at his MP I 7 73 55
your good friend there (nodding towards the upper end of E I 14 120 11
such a thing again:"--and nodding significantly--"there E II 16 295 34
I can understand you--(nodding at Mr. John Knightley)-- E II 18 312 50
You know who I mean--(nodding to her husband). E III 7 372 37
and that you know--(nodding towards her father)----- E III 10 392 4
NODS (4)
evening, in returning the nods and smiles of Miss Thorpe, NA I 5 35 1
and so many nods and winks, as to excite general attention. SS I 21 125 36
the house, amidst the nods and smiles of the whole party. PP II 5 155 3
gold ridicule by her side, saying, with significant nods, E III 16 453 12
13

NOISE (45)
called, but I seldom hear any noise when I pass that way. LS 17 271 7
with the least possible noise through the folding doors, NA II 9 193 6
the idea by the loud noise of the house-bell. after the NA II 13 222 7
fancy of error, when the noise of something moving close NA II 13 222 9
Her avocations above having shut out all noise but what NA II 15 241 7
and a great deal of noise, as to outweigh all the value of SS I 1 4 3
shy before company as he could make noise enough at home. SS I 6 31 9

old, who had not made a noise for the last two minutes; " SS I 21 121 9
under the shelter of its noise, introduce the interesting SS II 1 145 23
her young friend's affliction could be increased by noise. SS II 8 192 4
bear any sudden noise, was startled by a rap at the door. SS II 9 203 11
by some accidental noise in the house, started hastily up, SS III 7 310 10
11

the town--the jumbling & noise of which made farther W 321 2
parlour, to the bustle, noise & draughts of air of the W 327 7
You would be astonished to hear the noise we make there.-- W 358 28
The insipidity and yet the noise; the nothingness and yet PP I 6 27 47
There could be no conversation in the noise of Mrs. PP I 16 84 59
ready for a walk, a sudden noise below seemed to speak the PP II 5 158 11
he could no more bear the noise of a child than he could MP I 1 9 10
as heroism, and noise, and fashion are all against him, he MP I 11 110 22
am sure you must be sick of all our noise and difficulties. MP I 15 143 26
be in the midst of their noise, or retreat from it to the MP I 17 159 6
much engaged in their own noise, to be struck by unusual MP I 18 172 33
to be struck by unusual noise in the other part of the MP I 18 172 33
smiles, bustle and motion, noise and brilliancy in the MP II 11 283 6
to run about and make a noise; and both boys had soon MP III 7 381 25
she had not yet heard all the noise they could make. MP III 7 381 26
intervals by the superior noise of Sam, Tom, and Charles MP III 7 382 27
between the gentlemen, noise rising upon noise, and bustle MP III 7 384 36
noise rising upon noise, and bustle upon bustle, men and MP III 7 384 36
all below in confusion and noise again, the boys begging MP III 7 387 46
It was the abode of noise, disorder, and impropriety. MP III 8 388 3
The living in incessant noise was to a frame and temper, MP III 8 391 11
past nine, there was little intermission of noise or grog. MP III 11 413 32
the midst of closeness and noise, to have confinement, bad MP III 14 432 9
disposed of, produced a noise and confusion which his E I 11 92 3
You will not like the noise." E II 7 210 16
that the increase of noise would be very immaterial. E II 16 292 8
noise of numbers, was a circumstance to strike him deeply. E II 17 302 23
She could not endure its noise. E III 1 317 7
"Yes, as long as I could bear their noise; but they are so P III 5 38 27
soon forced on her by the noise he was studiously making P III 9 80 34
improve the noise of Uppercross, and lessen that of Lyme. P IV 2 133 27
to be heard, in spite of all the noise of the others. P IV 2 134 29
to say, when a slight noise called their attention to P IV 11 233 24
NOISES (8)
his horse, made odd noises, and drove on; and Catherine, NA I 11 87 53
The storm still raged, and various were the noises, more NA II 6 170 12
The various ascending noises convinced her that the NA II 8 189 19
strange and sudden noises throughout the house, she heard NA II 13 227 26
the hall as soon as the noises of the arrival reached them. MP II 6 233 15
Every body has their taste in noises as well as in other P IV 2 135 33
No, these were noises which belonged to the winter P IV 2 135 33
spite of all the various noises of the room, the almost P IV 8 183 11
NOISIER (1)
hold, and the noisier they were the better was he pleased. SS I 7 32 2
NOISY (18)
tyranny; she was moreover noisy and wild, hated NA I 1 14 1
the entrance of her four noisy children after dinner, who SS I 7 34 7
could hardly be outdone by any creature professedly noisy. SS I 21 121 10
or any other game that was sufficiently noisy. SS II 1 143 8
them together in one noisy purpose, immediately accepted SS II 1 143 9
"Oh! Colonel," said she, with her usual noisy cheerfulness, SS II 4 163 14
have a nice comfortable noisy game of lottery tickets, and PP I 15 74 11
The separation between her and her family was rather noisy PP II 18 235 40
Lydia was Lydia still; untamed, unabashed, wild, noisy, PP III 9 315 4
which shuts out noisy pleasures, should much exceed theirs. MP II 1 186 34
We were getting too noisy." MP II 5 226 59
opinion, and more noisy abuse of their aunt Norris--and MP II 6 234 18
the noisy ones gone, your brother and mine and myself. MP II 11 288 30
yes, missed as every noisy evil is missed when it is taken MP II 11 289 32
Here, every body was noisy, every voice was loud, (MP III 8 392 11
trouble for a few hours of noisy entertainment, I have E II 12 257 3
"I hope I am aware that they may be too noisy for your E II 18 311 42
Her accommodations were limited to a noisy parlour, and a P IV 5 154 8
NOMINAL (5)
a nominal mistress of it, that my real power is nothing." NA II 13 225 19
I had not even the nominal employment, which belonging to SS III 13 362 5
little heart need not take fright at such a nominal change. MP I 3 27 35
Even before Miss Taylor had ceased to hold the nominal E I 1 5 3
days;--just to have a nominal supply you know, that poor S 4 382 1
NOMINALLY (5)
Frederica's visit was nominally for six weeks; but her LS 42 313 7
there he would continue, nominally engaged with one of the PP I 15 71 6
that he could be only nominally missed; and Lady Bertram MP I 4 34 1
every Sunday, to a house nominally inhabited, and go MP II 7 247 42
for though we shall nominally part in the breakfast MP III 5 364 30
NON-APPEARANCE (1)
She could not help being vexed at the non-appearance of Mr. NA I 8 53 2
NON-ATTENDANCE (1)
Mrs. Grant's non-attendance was sad indeed. MP I 18 171 28
NON-CONVICTION (1)
of discussion, explanation, and probably non-conviction. MP III 1 317 38
NON-EXISTENCE (1)
and maintain the non-existence of any body equal to him in E I 17 142 12
NONSENSE (58)
it is surely my duty to discourage such romantic nonsense. LS 25 294 5
make me dance with him, and distressed me by his nonsense." NA I 3 26 22
miles to-day; all nonsense; nothing ruins horses so much NA I 7 47 27
are all so full of nonsense and stuff; there had not been NA I 7 48 34
you; it is the horridest nonsense you can imagine; there NA I 7 49 42
"Nonsense, how can you say so? NA I 8 57 23
for each other, or some nonsense of that kind, which would NA I 10 71 5
"Oh! nonsense! how can you say so?" NA I 12 96 21
Oh! such nonsense!-- NA II 1 134 39
My spirits are quite jaded with listening to his nonsense: NA II 1 134 39
"Psha, nonsense!" was Isabella's answer in the same half NA II 3 147 22
as he is now, it may be nonsense to appear to doubt; I SS III 3 282 19
"Nonsense."-- W 353 26
to make such nonsense easy) began to admire her gown.-- W 353 26
"Design! nonsense, how can you talk so! PP I 1 4 18
Mrs. Bennet said only, "nonsense, nonsense!" PP I 2 7 17
and the stress that is laid on them, as nonsense? PP I 2 7 18
so honestly blind to the follies and nonsense of others! PP I 4 14 9
expostulation with her brother for talking such nonsense. PP I 10 51 40
Follies and nonsense, whims and inconsistencies do divert PP I 11 57 21
"No, no, nonsense, Lizzy.-- PP I 19 104 6
rule, he talked no nonsense, he paid no compliments, his MP I 7 65 13
"Prohibited! nonsense! I certainly can get out that way, MP I 10 99 19
Absolute nonsense!" MP I 13 127 29
nonsense of acting, and sit comfortably down to your table. MP I 16 156 27
the midst of theatrical nonsense, and forced in so MP II 1 183 23
"The nonsense and folly of people's stepping out of their MP II 5 221 32
Nonsense! MP II 6 229 4
how little you will care for any nonsense of this kind." MP II 7 249 53
She considered it all as nonsense, as mere trifling and MP II 13 301 7
"This is all nonsense. MP II 13 301 8
and independence, and nonsense, about her, which I would MP III 1 323 56
years--but I am writing nonsense--were I refused, I must MP III 13 422 2
"'So very fond of me!' 'tis nonsense all. MP III 13 424 4
All manner of solemn nonsense was talked on the subject, E I 1 12 41
sentences of refined nonsense, to combine liberal E I 3 21 5
"Nonsense! a man does not imagine any such thing. E I 8 60 34
"Nonsense, errant nonsense, as ever was talked!" cried Mr. E I 8 65 49
Nonsense! E I 9 73 18
it him back, and some nonsense or other will pass between E I 9 76 38
nonsense, which she particularly wished to listen to. E I 14 118 4
and felt sure that he would want to be talking nonsense. E I 15 129 23
Who could have seen through such thick-headed nonsense? E I 16 134 4
of foppery and nonsense in it which she could not approve. E II 7 205 1
"Nonsense! E II 8 225 76
What nonsense one talks, Miss Woodhouse, when hard at work, E II 10 242 15
And so then, in my nonsense, I could not help making a E III 4 338 12
appear to censure; for she said, "nonsense! for shame!" E III 5 348 22
is a good deal of nonsense in it--but the part which is E III 5 350 37
and, at last, made himself talk nonsense very agreeably. E III 6 364 59
nonsense for the entertainment of seven silent people." E III 7 369 15
Any nonsense will serve. E III 7 369 16
by the sports and the nonsense, the freaks and the fancies E III 17 461 1
"Now you are talking nonsense, Mary," was therefore his P III 9 76 15
well as Henrietta, it is nonsense to say so; for he P III 9 77 16
she should be frightened from the visit by such nonsense. P III 10 87 23
by her nonsense and her pride; the Elliot pride. P III 10 88 28
why he shd talk so much nonsense, unless he could do no S 7 398 1
NONSENSES (1)
will have their little nonsenses and needless cares." E II 11 253 43
NONSENSICAL (8)
this was too idle & nonsensical an idea to remain long on LS 29 299 2
go," said Mrs. Dashwood; "these objections are nonsensical. SS II 3 157 16
Very nonsensical to come at all! PP I 8 36 5
Her mother only scolded her for being nonsensical. PP I 18 99 64
so very weak and vain and nonsensical as I knew I had! PP II 17 226 19
"Nonsensical girl!" was his reply, but not at all in anger. E II 8 214 11
to you, how nonsensical some persons are about their place, P III 6 46 10
as near giving it up, out of nonsensical complaisance!" P III 10 87 23
NOOK (1)
Here were we, pent down in this little contracted Nook, S 4 380 1
NOON (7)
to seek her for that purpose, in the Pump-Room at noon. NA I 9 60 1
state she continued till noon, scarcely stirring from her SS III 7 313 21
About noon, however, she began--but with a caution--a SS III 7 314 22
began it so early as to be in Gracechurch-Street by noon. PP II 4 152 5
of his meeting some of the gentlemen at Pemberley by noon. PP III 2 266 18
anxious mind; and about noon she made her escape with her MP I 18 168 14
it was so much past noon before the two carriages, Mr. P III 11 95 8
NORFOLK (18)
would settle on him the Norfolk estate, which, clear of SS III 1 266 38
The son had a good estate in Norfolk, the daughter twenty MP I 4 40 15
Bertram back to Mansfield, took Mr. Crawford into Norfolk. MP I 12 114 3
and finding nothing in Norfolk to equal the social MP I 12 115 3
"From Bath, Norfolk, London, York--wherever I may be," MP II 2 193 12
for his hunters from Norfolk, which, suggested by Dr. MP II 5 223 48
a theatre, some time or other, at your house in Norfolk. MP III 3 338 19
I think you will fit up a theatre at your house in Norfolk. MP III 3 339 19
world, for Henry is in Norfolk; business called him to MP III 9 393 1
after his return from Norfolk, before he set off again; MP III 10 400 8
Norfolk was what he had mostly to talk of; there had been MP III 10 404 15
Norfolk at all, at this unusual time of year, was given. MP III 10 404 15
I have half an idea of going into Norfolk again soon. MP III 11 411 20
I have a great mind to go back into Norfolk directly, and MP III 11 412 20
Henry I find has some idea of going into Norfolk again MP III 12 417 3
Whether Mr. Crawford went into Norfolk before or after the MP III 12 418 4
Crawford had gone into Norfolk again or not, till they met, MP III 14 433 12
he resolved to defer his Norfolk journey, resolved that MP III 17 467 20
NORLAND (51)
legal inheritor of the Norland estate, and the person to SS I 1 3 1
To him therefore the succession to the Norland estate was SS I 1 3 2
his father and mother at Norland, had so far gained on the SS I 1 4 3
herself mistress of Norland; and her mother and sisters-in- SS I 2 8 1
earnestness, to consider Norland as their home; and, as no SS I 2 8 1
them whenever they leave Norland and settle in a new home." SS I 2 9 6
When your father and mother moved to Norland, though the SS I 2 12 26
Mrs. Dashwood remained at Norland several months; not from SS I 3 14 1
in the neighbourhood of Norland; for to remove far from SS I 3 14 1
of Mrs. Dashwood, to her daughters' continuance at Norland. SS I 3 14 3
sister's establishment at Norland, and who had since spent SS I 3 15 4
To quit the neighbourhood of Norland was no longer an evil; SS I 4 24 20
at some distance from Norland than immediately amongst SS I 4 24 21
from the vicinity of Norland beyond her wishes, she made SS I 4 24 21
hoped that she would not be settled far from Norland. SS I 5 25 1
resolve on remaining at Norland no longer than was SS I 5 25 3
at such a distance from Norland as to prevent his being of SS I 5 25 4
of her effects at Norland, and to determine her future SS I 5 26 5
those who had formed their establishment at Norland. SS I 5 26 5
Her eagerness to be gone from Norland was preserved from SS I 5 27 6
farther than their maintenance for six months at Norland. SS I 5 27 6
first letter to Norland, every thing was so far settled in SS I 5 27 7
"Dear, dear Norland!" said Marianne, as she wandered alone SS I 5 27 8
In comparison of Norland, it was poor and small indeed!-- SS I 6 28 2
What else can detain him at Norland?" SS I 8 39 14
And Elinor, in quitting Norland and Edward, cried not as I SS I 8 39 18
which had given to Norland half its charm, were engaged in SS I 9 40 1
greater enjoyment than Norland had been able to afford, SS I 9 40 1
them a little of Norland, interested their imagination and SS I 9 40 2
the fond attachment to Norland, which she brought with her SS I 11 54 5
teach her to think of Norland with less regret than ever. SS I 11 54 6
guess where he is; at his own house at Norland to be sure. SS I 12 61 23
had often observed at Norland in their mutual behaviour. SS I 16 87 23
"I was at Norland about a month ago." SS I 16 87 28
"And how does dear, dear Norland look?" cried Marianne. SS I 16 87 29
"Dear, dear Norland," said Elinor, "probably looks much as SS I 16 87 30
He had no pleasure at Norland; he detested being in town; SS I 19 101 1
being in town; but either to Norland or London, he must go. SS I 19 101 1
"Norland is a prodigious beautiful place, is not it?" SS I 21 123 23
there might be about Norland; and I was only afraid the SS I 21 123 28
for I thought you must have seen her at Norland sometimes. SS I 22 128 5
of the Miss Steeles as to Norland and their family SS II 1 139 1
her at Norland; it was not an illusion of her own vanity. SS II 1 139 1
in remaining at Norland after he first felt her influence SS II 1 140 1
be persuaded to give him Norland living; which I SS II 2 149 25
expenses too we have had on first coming to Norland. SS II 11 225 35
at Norland (and very valuable they were) to your mother. SS II 11 225 35
which were making to the Norland estate, and in spite of SS II 12 233 18
Before her removing from Norland, Elinor had painted a SS II 12 234 26
invitation from Fanny, to Norland whenever it should SS III 6 301 1
at Norland, when he must have felt his own inconstancy. SS III 13 368 25
NORLAND COMMON (1)
The inclosure of Norland Common, now carrying on, is a SS II 11 225 31
NORLAND PARK (1)
residence was at Norland park, in the centre of their SS I 1 3 1
NORTH (14)
sheltered from the north and east by rising woods of oak. NA II 2 141 13
of large fortune from the north of England; that he came PP I 1 3 10
They were of a respectable family in the north of England; PP I 4 15 11
in general ----'s regiment, now quartered in the north. PP III 8 312 19
Lydia's being settled in the north, just when she had PP III 8 313 20
off for the north, received at first an absolute negative. PP III 8 313 22
in the neighbourhood, before she was banished to the north. PP III 8 314 22
"South or north, I know a black cloud when I see it; and MP II 4 207 9
the east instead of the north--the entrance and principal MP II 7 242 23
on the north, that I will be master of my own property. MP III 11 411 20
the Stilton cheese, the north Wiltshire, the butter, the E I 10 88 34
the Admiral (captain Croft then) was in the north seas. P III 8 71 54
only when the wind is due north and blows hard, which may P IV 1 128 30
the connexions in the north of the country, and probably P IV 1 128 31
NORTH YARMOUTH (3)
sitting down together in our lodgings at North Yarmouth?" P III 10 92 44
ay, or as we used to be even at North Yarmouth and deal. P IV 6 170 29
putting us in mind of those we first had at North Yarmouth. P IV 6 170 29
NORTH-EAST (2)

lane I stood in to the north-east, that is, to the MP II 7 242 23
by weather, I think every body feels a north-east wind.-- E III 14 436 7
NORTHAMPTON (13)
nation,) called up from Northampton to quell the NA I 14 113 39
Park, in the country of Northampton, and to be thereby MP I 1 3 1
in safety, and at Northampton was met by Mrs. Norris, who MP I 2 12 1
her the whole way from Northampton of her wonderful good MP I 2 13 4
I am assured that it is safe at Northampton; and there it MP I 6 57 33
baize had arrived from Northampton, and been cut out by MP I 14 130 1
of his being then at least as far off as Northampton. MP II 2 190 9
Have you never any balls at Northampton?-- MP II 7 250 59
You spoke of the balls at Northampton. MP II 8 252 1
I believe, we must not think of a Northampton ball. MP II 8 252 1
William were gone to Northampton, and she had reason to MP II 8 256 14
and I have only just now received it at Northampton. MP II 9 261 2
go up by the mail from Northampton the following night, MP II 9 266 21
NORTHAMPTONSHIRE (16)
with his sister in Northamptonshire, before he went to sea. MP I 2 21 34
kindness, into Northamptonshire, and as readily engaged to MP I 4 41 16
use entirely so long as he remained in Northamptonshire. MP II 6 237 23
of strengthening his views in favour of Northamptonshire. MP II 7 247 37
you should leave Northamptonshire without this indulgence. MP II 8 252 1
I will not take her from Northamptonshire. MP II 12 295 20
"Ha!" cried Mary, "settle in Northamptonshire! MP II 12 295 21
divide your year between London and Northamptonshire?" MP II 12 295 25
He leaves Northamptonshire so soon, that even this slight MP III 2 331 16
likely wish me in Northamptonshire again; for there is a MP III 5 360 16
to be given to the Northamptonshire, and was coming, the MP III 6 368 7
her mind away from Northamptonshire, and fixed it on her MP III 7 385 38
into Northamptonshire, who had died a few years afterwards. MP III 7 385 40
I mean about our taking you back into Northamptonshire. MP III 12 416 3
longing to go into Northamptonshire, seemed almost to MP III 12 419 8
"when I go back into Northamptonshire, or when I return to MP III 14 431 8
NORTHANGER (30)
court, and cottage, Northanger turned up an Abbey, and she NA II 2 141 11
And so you are going to Northanger!-- NA II 3 143 2
be of the party to Northanger, he was to continue at Bath. NA II 4 150 1
was the distance of Northanger from Bath, to be now NA II 5 155 4
"Northanger is not more than half my home; I have an NA II 5 157 7
the very grounds of Northanger, without having discerned NA II 5 161 24
to the family hours would be expected at Northanger. NA II 5 162 27
How glad I am that Northanger is what it is! NA II 6 167 9
estimation of Northanger had waited unfixed till that hour. NA II 7 178 19
certainly larger than Northanger, all the dirty work of NA II 8 184 4
Half an hour at Northanger must be enough." NA II 9 195 18
feelings she had prepared for a knowledge of Northanger. NA II 10 200 2
I wish your visit at Northanger may be over before Captain NA II 10 202 7
less likely to come to Northanger than at the present time, NA II 11 208 2
making Miss Morland's time at Northanger pass pleasantly. NA II 11 209 5
They have half a buck from Northanger twice a year; and I NA II 11 210 6
are not comparing it with Fullerton and Northanger----- NA II 11 213 19
for a week; and he left Northanger earnestly regretting NA II 13 220 1
of remaining wholly at Northanger in attendance on the NA II 13 221 7
on the morrow to Northanger and heard of her being gone, NA II 14 231 4
be her point on leaving Northanger; but after the first NA II 14 232 6
must have arrived at Northanger; now he must have heard of NA II 14 239 28
hope, my Catherine, you are not so grand as Northanger. NA II 15 240 4
you talk so much about the French-bread at Northanger." NA II 15 241 4
at Northanger, and designed her for his daughter in law. NA II 15 244 11
the late explanation at Northanger that they had the NA II 15 245 12
The conversation between them at Northanger had been of NA II 15 247 15
evils of such a home as Northanger had been made by NA II 16 250 5
from a long visit at Northanger, by which my heroine was NA II 16 251 5
his son to return to Northanger, and thence made him the NA II 16 252 7
NORTHANGER ABBEY (4)
our side to make Northanger Abbey not wholly disagreeable." NA II 2 139 7
Northanger Abbey!-- NA II 2 140 8
at her heart, and Northanger Abbey on her lips, she NA II 2 140 11
than before, of Northanger Abbey having been a richly- NA II 2 141 13
NORTHERN (4)
would have yielded the northern and western extremities. NA II 10 200 3
of her northern tour was a constant source of delight. PP II 5 155 1
The time fixed for the beginning of their northern tour PP II 19 238 7
whose northern aspect rendered it delightful for summer. PP III 3 267 2
NORTHWARD (4)
It was within four miles northward of Exeter. SS I 5 25 1
plan, were to go no farther northward than Derbyshire. PP II 19 238 7
They are gone down to Newcastle, a place quite northward, PP III 11 336 51
continue there, I trust, till we may carry her northward.-- E III 18 477 57
NORVAL (1)
And I am sure, my name was Norval, every evening of my MP I 13 126 25
NOSE (2)
Her nose wants character; there is nothing marked in its PP III 3 271 15
"The last time I saw her, she had a red nose, but I hope P IV 3 142 14
NOSEGAY (1)
the room, beautifying a nosegay; then, she ate her cold P III 5 39 40
NOSES (1)
The Portsmouth girls turn up their noses at any body who MP II 7 249 52
NOTCH (1)
being but a sort of notch in the Donwell Abbey estate, to E I 16 136 9
NOTE (83)
I received your note my dear Alicia, just before I left LS 5 249 1
He will carry this note himself, which is to serve as an LS 31 302 1
on reading the note, this moment received from you. LS 35 304 1
five minutes to answer a note, instead of waiting for me, NA I 14 107 8
Early the next day, a note from Isabella, speaking peace NA I 15 116 1
Well, and so you guessed it the moment you had my note?-- NA I 15 117 6
only wanted me to answer a note," she began to hope that NA II 9 192 4
"But if you write a note to the housekeeper, Mr. Brandon," SS I 13 64 23
it could be no more than a note; it was then folded up, SS II 4 161 5
that no servant, no porter has left any letter or note?" SS II 4 165 26
A note was just then brought in, and laid on the table. SS II 5 169 16
Mrs. Jennings soon appeared, and the note being given her, SS II 5 170 28
Her second note, which had been written on the morning SS II 7 187 39
40
any answer to a note which I sent you above a week ago. SS II 7 187 39
40
The contents of her last note to him were these:-- "what SS II 7 187 41
42
When the note was shewn to Elinor, as it was within ten SS II 14 254 27
herself in her note to Edward, was now all her concern. SS III 4 287 24
reproachfully; "a note would have answered every purpose.-- SS III 8 324 41
"Yes, I saw every note that passed." SS III 8 325 49
"Marianne's note, by assuring me that I was still as dear SS III 8 325 53
But this note made me know myself better. SS III 8 326 53
The next morning brought another short note from Marianne-- SS III 8 327 55
Emma, presented her a note, which he had the honour of W 338 17
The note, which Emma was beginning to read rather before W 338 18
"I received that note from the fair hands of Miss Watson W 338 18
of the footman with a note for Miss Bennet; it came from PP I 7 30 14
brought the following note for elizabeth: "my dearest PP I 7 31 29
30
Elizabeth had read the note aloud, "if your daughter PP I 7 31 31
from expressing in her note how much she longed for such a PP I 7 33 43
she requested to have a note sent to Longbourn, desiring PP I 9 41 1
The note was immediately dispatched, and its contents as PP I 9 41 1
and not a note, not a line, did I receive in the mean time. PP II 3 148 26
repeat the particulars of Lydia's note to his wife?" PP III 5 291 57
tidings beyond a friendly note of congratulation and MP II 2 192 11
just to note down any sentence pre-eminently beautiful? MP II 5 227 65
You will find the beginning of a note to yourself; but I MP II 9 261 2
breakfast a very friendly note was brought from Mr. MP II 9 265 21
Upon the whole, it was a very joyous note. MP II 9 266 21
Since the first joy from Mr. Crawford's note to William MP II 9 270 40
to her seat to finish a note which she was previously MP II 12 296 31
He had a note to deliver from his sister. MP II 13 303 14
She opened her note immediately, glad to have any thing to MP II 13 303 14
No answer to her note? MP II 13 306 28
She had read Miss Crawford's note only once; and how to MP II 13 307 30
The rest of your note I know means nothing; but I am so MP II 13 307 31
With thanks for the honour of your note, I remain, MP II 13 307 31
pretence of receiving the note, was coming towards her. MP II 13 307 32
made up the note; "you cannot think I have any such object. MP II 13 307 33
The note was held out and must be taken; and as she MP II 13 307 35
She had no doubt that her note must appear excessively ill- MP II 13 308 36
the purport of her note, and was not less sanguine, as to MP III 1 311 1
Having so satisfactorily settled the conviction her note MP III 1 311 2
He had received a note from Lady Stornaway to beg him to MP III 16 454 18
of the present day, a note was brought from Mrs. Goddard, E I 3 22 7
A Hartfield edition of Shakespeare would have a long note E I 9 75 25
in writing that note, at twelve o'clock at night, on E I 11 95 19
No intercourse with Harriet possible but by note; no E I 16 138 17
which they went, brought a note from Mr. Elton to Mr. E I 17 140 2
a long, civil, ceremonious note, to say, with Mr. Elton's E I 17 140 2
It was a very useful note, for it supplied them with fresh E I 17 141 4
I received Mrs. Cole's note--no, it cannot be more than E II 3 173 27
""Oh! my dear, said I--well, and just then came the note. E II 3 173 27
Harriet had not been at home; but a note had been prepared E II 4 184 11
James could take the note. E II 7 209 13
while I do not know one note from another, and our little E II 8 215 16
forwarded to Emma, in a note from Mrs. Weston, instantly. E II 12 258 8
This wretched note was the finale of Emma's breakfast. E II 12 259 10
I have a note of his.-- E II 16 298 52
"Well, well, I have that note; and can shew it after E II 16 298 54
Mrs. Elton had most kindly sent Jane a note, or we should E III 2 322 19
A note was written to urge it. E III 9 389 16
The answer was only in this short note: "Miss Fairfax's E III 9 390 16
17
Emma felt that her own note had deserved something better; E III 9 390 18
despatched to Miss Bates with a most friendly note. E III 9 391 20
She opened the packet; it was too surely so;--a note from E III 14 436 6
Very odd! very unaccountable! after the note I sent him E III 16 457 38
dozen in the nation,) always needs a note of explanation. P III 3 24 36
who, on having occasion to note down the day of the month, P III 6 48 16
excepting the receipt of a note or two from Lyme, which P IV 1 125 14
had brought Anne the last note, which she had not been P IV 1 126 20
"In the first place, I had a note from Mrs. Croft " P IV 6 164 8
a very "kind, friendly note indeed, addressed to me, just P IV 6 164 8
One five minutes brought a note, the next a parcel, and P IV 10 221 32
NOTE-WRITING (1)
Quite unpractised in such sort of note-writing, had there MP II 13 307 30
31
NOTED (2)
ought to be, unless noted down every evening in a journal? NA I 3 27 28
books on grief like his, noted down the names of those she P III 11 101 25
NOTES (6)
"But have you not received my notes?" cried Marianne in SS II 6 177 10
were, you will return my notes, and the lock of my hair SS II 7 188 42
Her three notes--unluckily they were all in my pocket-book, SS III 8 329 63
the rest there were notes to be written to all their PP III 4 281 29
actually give William notes for the purpose, she was MP III 6 372 21
the softness of the upper notes I am sure is exactly what E II 10 241 8
NOTHING (1237)
At present nothing goes smoothly. LS 2 244 1
that Mr Johnson suspected nothing of your engagement the LS 5 249 1
She is a stupid girl, & has nothing to recommend her. LS 7 252 1
impropriety in it,--nothing of vanity, of pretension, of LS 8 255 2
with her, had he known nothing of her previous to this LS 8 255 2
brother, & conclude that nothing will be wanting on her LS 10 257 1
superior to such as allow nothing for a father's anxiety, LS 12 260 1
but can expect nothing better while he is so very eager in LS 15 266 2
entirely convinced me that she did in fact feel nothing. LS 17 270 3
Nothing satisfactory transpires as to her reason for LS 17 270 6
my hands, and having now nothing else to employ her, is LS 19 274 2
but I see nothing in it more like encouragement. LS 20 278 11
be her real sentiments, said nothing in opposition to mine. LS 22 280 1
"He told us nothing of all this last night, said she LS 23 284 6
mother--Lady Susan means nothing but her good--but LS 24 287 9
Nothing but my being in the utmost distress for money, LS 26 296 4
for Bath, nothing could induce him to have a gouty symptom. LS 28 298 1
You may be, you must be well assured that nothing but the LS 30 301 4
Nothing is wanting but to have you here, & it is our LS 40 309 1
I hope nothing will make it inconvenient to Mr Vernon, & LS 40 309 1
was resolved to leave nothing unattempted that might offer LS 42 311 2
She had nothing against her, but her husband, & her LS 42 313 9
cleanliness, and loved nothing so well in the world as NA I 1 14 1
who had by nature nothing heroic about her, should prefer NA I 1 15 3
provided that nothing like useful knowledge could be NA I 1 15 3
Nothing more alarming occurred than a fear on Mrs. Allen's NA I 2 19 4
just the same; they saw nothing of the dancers but the NA I 2 21 9
of whose faces possessed nothing to interest, and with all NA I 2 21 10
They saw nothing of Mr. Allen; and after looking about NA I 2 22 10
meet, and nothing in the world advances intimacy so much." NA I 3 29 51
are told to "despair of nothing we would attain," as " NA I 4 31 2
to know nothing of each other for the last fifteen years. NA I 4 31 2
feeling of awe, and left nothing but tender affection. NA I 4 33 7
From the Thorpes she could learn nothing, for they had NA I 5 36 2
There is nothing I would not do for those who are really NA I 6 40 14
Catherine had nothing to oppose against such reasoning; NA I 6 43 44
to-day; all nonsense; nothing ruins horses so much as rest; NA I 7 47 27
horses so much as rest; nothing knocks them up so soon. NA I 7 47 27
animated pitch, to nothing more than a short decisive NA I 7 48 32
you can imagine; there is nothing in the world in it but NA I 7 49 42
to speak to a friend, and nothing, she declared, should NA I 8 52 2
longed to point out that gentleman, she could see nothing. NA I 8 55 10
Talk of the curiosity of women, indeed!--'tis nothing. NA I 8 57 18
well in his time, I dare say; he is not gouty for nothing. NA I 9 63 18
she could strike out nothing new in commendation, but she NA I 9 64 27
Could she have foreseen such a circumstance, nothing NA I 9 69 51
But nothing of that kind occurred, no visitors appeared to NA I 10 71 8
her tamboured muslin, and nothing but the shortness of the NA I 10 73 22
her wishes, hopes and plans all centered in nothing less. NA I 10 74 23
beginning, and she saw nothing of the Tilneys. NA I 10 74 23
you, there would be nothing to restrain you from NA I 10 78 37
and those who go to London may think nothing of Bath. NA I 10 78 46
and done all day long, which I can know nothing of there." NA I 10 78 46
it may come to nothing, or it may hold up before twelve." NA I 11 82 4
It was nothing more than that my father-----they were just NA I 12 94 10
He knew nothing about it; but his father, like every NA I 12 95 17
without her, it would be nothing to put off a mere walk NA I 13 97 1
This availed nothing. NA I 13 98 1
painful ideas crossed her mind, though she said nothing. NA I 13 98 3
I read it a little as a duty, but it tells me nothing that NA I 14 108 22
the men all so good for nothing, and hardly any women at NA I 14 108 22
soon engaged in another on which she had nothing to say. NA I 14 110 28
She knew nothing of drawing--nothing of taste:--and she NA I 14 110 28
Miss Morland has been talking of nothing more dreadful NA I 14 113 39
"We shall get nothing more serious from him now, Miss NA I 14 114 48
relieve her anxiety, she had heard nothing of any of them. NA I 14 114 50
rest, there was nothing to regret for half an instant.-- NA I 15 116 2
Catherine felt that nothing could have been safer; but NA I 15 119 14
The difference of fortune can be nothing to signify." NA I 15 119 17
I know it would signify nothing; but we must not expect NA I 15 119 18
Fortune is nothing. NA I 15 124 46

you make such a point of it, I can refuse you nothing. NA II 1 130 13
For myself, it is nothing; I never think of myself." NA II 1 136 45
so soon, was an evil which nothing could counterbalance. NA II 2 138 1
old friends, there is nothing to detain me longer in Bath. NA II 2 139 7
'tis true, we can offer you nothing like the gaieties of NA II 2 139 7
Tilney says, there is nothing people are so often deceived NA II 3 147 20
come across her; but had nothing worse appeared, that NA II 4 149 1
to be secured by her seeing nothing of Captain Tilney? NA II 4 152 28
in Pulteney-Street, and nothing passed between the lovers NA II 4 153 31
fears of her seeing nothing to her taste--though never in NA II 5 154 2
she could distinguish nothing but these words, in a NA II 5 155 3
in which there was nothing to be done but to eat without NA II 5 156 4
the delay would have been nothing; but General Tilney, NA II 5 156 4
"Nothing further to alarm perhaps may occur the first NA II 5 159 19
torture; but there being nothing in all this out of the NA II 5 160 21
nothing but a considerable hoard of diamonds. NA II 5 160 21
to her; it had wafted nothing worse than a thick mizzling NA II 5 161 25
She had nothing to dread from midnight assassins or NA II 6 167 9
guarded, she could have nothing to explore or to suffer; NA II 6 167 9
now, to be sure, there is nothing to alarm one." NA II 6 167 9
It could be nothing but the violence of the wind NA II 6 167 10
behind each curtain, saw nothing on either low window seat NA II 6 167 10
and though there could be nothing really in it, there was NA II 6 168 10
a third, a fourth, and a fifth presented nothing new. NA II 7 172 2
Nothing could now be clearer than the absurdity of her NA II 7 173 2
storms and sleeplessness are nothing when they are over. NA II 7 174 5
The money is nothing, it is not an object, but employment NA II 7 176 15
Catherine had seen nothing to compare with it; and her NA II 7 177 19
fitting-up could be nothing to her; she cared for no NA II 8 182 2
walks about the room in this way; it is nothing unusual." NA II 8 187 13
of his morning walks, and boded nothing good. NA II 8 187 14
the company left them, and nothing occurred to disturb it. NA II 9 192 4
respect that Eleanor should know nothing of the matter. NA II 9 192 5
remain to tell what nothing else was allowed to whisper? NA II 9 194 6
"No, nothing at all.-- NA II 9 195 11
ago I had the pleasure of finding nothing to detain me.-- NA II 9 195 12
Catherine said nothing--after a short silence, during NA II 9 196 23
he added, "as there is nothing in the room in itself to NA II 9 196 23
terror felt and done, nothing could shortly be clearer, NA II 10 199 2
good sense, she had nothing to do but to forgive herself NA II 10 201 4
Nothing further was said for a few minutes; and then NA II 10 204 11
feel a void in your heart which nothing else can occupy. NA II 10 207 38
a point of your providing nothing extraordinary:--besides, NA II 11 211 13
Now, there was nothing so charming to her imagination as NA II 11 212 16
the paper and hangings, nothing like an opinion on the NA II 11 214 25
but in this horrid place one can find time for nothing. NA II 12 216 2
I wear nothing but purple now: I know I look hideous in it, NA II 12 218 2
She said nothing; and Eleanor endeavouring to collect NA II 13 223 13
a nominal mistress of it, that my real power is nothing." NA II 13 225 19
"Oh, the journey is nothing. NA II 13 226 24
She met with nothing, however, to distress or frighten her. NA II 14 232 6
Her parents seeing nothing in her ill-looks and agitation, NA II 14 235 13
post by herself, and knew nothing of coming till Saturday NA II 14 237 21
soon met with Mrs. Thorpe, and then we wanted for nothing. NA II 14 238 24
again and again, as if nothing but motion was voluntary; NA II 15 240 1
at the end of a quarter of an hour she had nothing to say. NA II 15 242 9
affection originated in nothing better than gratitude, or, NA II 15 243 9
The General had had nothing to accuse her of, nothing to NA II 15 244 11
Henry and Eleanor, perceiving nothing in her situation NA II 15 245 12
on either side; but as nothing, after all, could be more NA II 16 249 1
of there being nothing like practice. there was but one NA II 16 249 1
Their mother had nothing, and their father only seven SS I 1 4 2
I'll lay my life that he meant nothing farther; indeed, it SS I 2 12 24
Their housekeeping will be nothing at all. SS I 2 12 24
My father certainly could mean nothing more by his request SS I 2 12 25
she draws, that in fact he knows nothing of the matter. SS I 3 17 18
Mrs. John Dashwood said nothing; but her husband civilly SS I 5 25 1
reserved, cold, and had nothing to say for herself beyond SS I 6 31 8
There was nothing in any of the party which could SS I 7 34 7
nothing to do but to marry all the rest of the world. SS I 8 36 1
But thirty-five has nothing to do with matrimony." SS I 8 37 8
such a woman therefore there would be nothing unsuitable. SS I 8 38 10
it would be no marriage at all, but that would be nothing. SS I 8 38 10
Nothing but real indisposition could occasion this SS I 8 39 14
marriages, and then you can have nothing farther to ask."-- SS I 10 47 4
and Elinor saw nothing to censure in him but a propensity, SS I 10 48 9
mere calmness of manner with which sense had nothing to do. SS I 11 55 6
She had nothing to say one day that she had not said the SS I 11 55 6
To Marianne, he merely bowed and said nothing. SS I 13 66 49
soon out of sight; and nothing more of them was seen till SS I 13 67 60
"On the contrary, nothing can be a stronger proof of it, SS I 13 68 72
I did not see it to advantage, for nothing could be more SS I 13 69 76
May be she is ill in town; nothing in the world more SS I 14 70 2
which in fact concealed nothing at all, she could not SS I 14 71 4
Nothing could be more expressive of attachment to them all, SS I 14 71 5
"Do not be alarmed," said Miss Dashwood, "nothing of the SS I 14 72 8
in the event, which nothing but a kind of prescience of SS I 14 73 17
"Nothing, for you have anticipated my answer." SS I 15 78 27
Is nothing due to the man whom we have all so much reason SS I 15 79 28
Nothing in my opinion has ever passed to justify doubt; no SS I 15 80 42
They saw nothing of Marianne till dinner time, when she SS I 15 82 46
She read nothing but what they had been used to read SS I 16 83 3
only give happiness where there is nothing else to give it. SS I 17 91 10
I know nothing of the picturesque." SS I 18 97 4
the devoted Elinor, which nothing but the newness of their SS I 18 99 15
only on a something or a nothing between Mr. Willoughby SS I 18 100 30
to resist the solicitations of his friends to do nothing. SS I 19 103 4
You want nothing but patience--or give it a more SS I 19 103 7
I thought of nothing but whether it might not be Colonel SS I 19 106 20
21

coming at all, and I knew nothing of it till the carriage SS I 20 110 2
Marianne looked very grave and said nothing. SS I 20 111 11
your praises, he did nothing but say fine things of you." SS I 20 115 54
and agreeable, that nothing can be good enough for her. SS I 20 116 58
Nothing can be like it to be sure! SS I 20 116 60
husband and mother on that subject went for nothing at all. SS I 21 118 2
and not a sensible face, nothing to admire; but in the SS I 21 120 6
alarm, where there is nothing to be alarmed at in reality." SS I 21 122 12
"Lord! Anne," cried her sister, "you can talk of nothing SS I 21 124 31
will make Miss Dashwood believe you think of nothing else." SS I 21 124 31
join in it herself; but nothing more of it was said, and SS I 21 126 41
what seemed impertinent curiosity--"I know nothing of her." SS I 22 128 6
Mrs. Ferrars is certainly nothing to me at present,--but SS I 22 129 11
You knew nothing of me, or my family, and therefore there SS I 22 131 32
time, at his mentioning nothing farther of those friends, SS I 22 134 49
could be authorised by nothing else; for a few moments, SS I 22 134 53
and proofs, and contradicted by nothing but her own wishes. SS II 1 139 1
Supported by the conviction of having done nothing to SS II 1 140 4
that Edward had done nothing to forfeit her esteem, she SS II 1 140 4
And as she could now have nothing more painful to hear on SS II 1 142 7
or expression, and nothing could be less interesting than SS II 1 143 10
the truest sincerity, "nothing could be farther from my SS II 2 146 4
affection and constancy nothing can deprive me of I know." SS II 2 147 7
any reluctance, for nothing had been said on either side, SS II 2 151 41
absence--Oh! no, nothing should tempt me to leave her. SS II 3 154 5
Mrs. Dashwood smiled and said nothing. SS II 3 157 18
nothing but grief and disappointment in seeing him. SS II 4 162 8
come confusion; "indeed, Marianne, I have nothing to tell." SS II 5 170 25
because you communicate, and I, because I conceal nothing." SS II 5 170 26
for still she had seen nothing of Willoughby; and SS II 5 170 28
"By many--by some of whom you know nothing, by others with SS II 5 173 44
Nothing occurred during the next three or four days, to SS II 6 175 1
Nothing but a thorough change of sentiment could account SS II 6 178 17
"No, Elinor," she replied, "ask nothing; you will soon SS II 7 180 3
My girls were nothing to her, and yet they used to be SS II 7 181 8
I do assure you that nothing would surprise me more than SS II 7 182 9
Mine is a misery which nothing can do away." SS II 7 186 28
her that they contained nothing but what any one would SS II 7 188 43
Whatever may have changed him now, (and nothing but the SS II 7 188 46
Cruel, cruel--nothing can acquit you. SS II 7 190 56
Elinor, nothing can. SS II 7 190 56
Lord! nothing seems to do her any good. SS II 8 194 8
But that won't do, now-a-days; nothing in the way of SS II 8 194 10
Is there nothing one can get to comfort her? SS II 8 195 14
I made sure of its being nothing but a common love letter, SS II 8 195 16
asleep; and as I think nothing will be of so much service SS II 8 198 28
He knows nothing of it; do tell him, my dear." SS II 8 198 30
"A man who has nothing to do with his own time has no SS II 9 204 16
some circumstances, which nothing but a very sincere SS II 9 204 18
very sincere regard--nothing but an earnest desire of SS II 9 204 18
promised me that nothing-----but how blindly I relate! SS II 9 205 24
of trifling weight--was nothing--to what I felt when I SS II 9 206 24
Life could do nothing for her, beyond giving time for a SS II 9 207 26
I seem to have been distressing you for nothing. SS II 9 208 28
nothing, would give no clue, though she certainly knew all. SS II 9 209 28
In short, I could learn nothing but that she was gone; all SS II 9 209 28
She will feel her own sufferings to be nothing. SS II 9 210 32
Mrs. Jennings, who knew nothing of all this, who knew only SS II 10 216 15
settled in your little cottage and want for nothing! SS II 11 222 11
and nothing but the plan of the flower-garden marked out." SS II 11 226 37
"Nothing at all, I should rather suppose; for she has only SS II 11 226 43
Nothing can be kinder than her behaviour; and she can SS II 11 227 46
He had just compunction enough for having done nothing for SS II 11 228 51
to her she appeared nothing more than a little proud- SS II 12 229 3
was then in town; but nothing would have induced Fanny SS II 12 229 4
not to be told, they could do nothing at present but write. SS II 11 230 4
to sell out at a loss, nothing gave any symptom of that SS II 12 233 18
Did you see nothing but only civility?-- SS II 13 239 6
engagement," said she, "nothing could be more flattering SS II 13 239 8
Though nothing could be more polite than Lady Middleton's SS II 14 246 3
Lady Middleton was ashamed of doing nothing before them, SS II 14 247 4
Nothing escaped her minute observation and general SS II 14 249 8
"Upon my soul," he added, "I believe it is nothing more; SS II 14 251 13
The expense would be nothing, the inconvenience not more; SS II 14 252 20
dear,' says I, 'it is nothing in the world but the red-gum; SS III 1 257 5
as we did, that it was nothing in the world but the red- SS III 1 257 5
though Lucy has next to nothing herself, she knows better SS III 1 259 7
Nothing has proved him unworthy; nor has any thing SS III 1 264 29
bound to silence, perhaps nothing could have kept me SS III 1 264 29
nothing, and was heard three times to say, "yes, ma'am."-- SS III 1 265 33
Donavan says there is nothing materially to be apprehended; SS III 1 265 36
Nothing should prevail on him to give up his engagement. SS III 1 267 42
in his proper situation, and would have wanted for nothing. SS III 1 269 53
Nothing new was heard by them, for a day or two afterwards, SS III 2 270 3
as soon as she could; and nothing but the hindrance of SS III 2 270 3
She saw nothing of the Willoughbys, nothing of Edward, and SS III 2 271 5
Edward, and for some time nothing of anybody who could by SS III 2 271 5
being asked, for nothing would otherwise have been learnt. SS III 2 271 7
on which Elinor had nothing to say, and therefore soon SS III 2 272 13
had nothing at all; and I had it from Miss Sparks myself. SS III 2 272 16
on Wednesday, and we saw nothing of him not all Thursday, SS III 2 272 16
he had no fortune, and no nothing at all, it would be SS III 2 273 16
for her loss, for he had nothing but two thousand pounds, SS III 2 273 16
thoughts, he could get nothing but a curacy, and how was SS III 2 273 16
"Oh, la! there is nothing in that. SS III 2 274 20
two before; but however, nothing was said about them, and SS III 2 275 22
it for the best, so I say nothing; hope Mrs. Jennings SS III 2 277 30
What I am now doing indeed, seems nothing at all, since it SS III 3 284 23
thought of late, there was nothing more likely to happen." SS III 4 285 3
it; but, upon my word, you owe nothing to my solicitation." SS III 4 289 35
a subject, "knows nothing about it at present, and I SS III 5 295 18
she would be glad to compound now for nothing worse.' SS III 5 297 31
and Mary brown, he could conceive nothing more ridiculous. SS III 5 298 33
way at first, and knew nothing of it till after the breach SS III 5 299 37
Nothing was wanting on Mrs. Palmer's side that constant SS III 6 304 13
It gave her no surprise that she saw nothing of Mrs. SS III 7 309 6
attribute the change to nothing more than the fatigue of SS III 7 310 9
Mrs. Jennings, knowing nothing of any change in the SS III 7 310 9
to suppose that I have nothing to urge-- that because she SS III 8 322 36
that nothing else in common prudence remained for me to do. SS III 8 323 40
one or other of you; and nothing but the most prevailing SS III 8 326 55
I, you may well believe, could talk of nothing but my SS III 9 336 12
different effect, saw nothing in the Colonel's behaviour SS III 10 340 3
with him last autumn, nothing but a series of imprudence SS III 10 345 28
that as reflection did nothing, resolution must do all, SS III 10 347 32
to speak it, talked of nothing but Willoughby, and their SS III 10 348 34
Nothing could restore him with a faith unbroken--a SS III 11 349 1
Nothing could do away the knowledge of what the latter had SS III 11 349 1
Nothing could replace him, therefore, in her former esteem, SS III 11 349 1
Nothing could have done it away to my feelings." SS III 11 350 6
which, because they are removed, he now reckons as nothing. SS III 11 351 13
"and I have nothing to regret--nothing but my own folly." SS III 11 352 14
She had heard nothing of him since her leaving London, SS III 11 352 21
since her leaving London, nothing new of his plans, SS III 11 352 21
of his plans, nothing certain even of his present abode. SS III 11 352 21
this sentence:--"we know nothing of our unfortunate Edward, SS III 11 353 21
had already sent to say that she should eat nothing more. SS III 11 355 45
see;--happy or unhappy,--nothing pleased her; she turned SS III 12 357 4
for more than four years, nothing less could be expected SS III 13 361 1
I had therefore nothing in the world to do, but to fancy SS III 13 362 5
He could do nothing till he were assured of his fate with SS III 13 366 20
Nothing but such a persuasion could have prevented his SS III 13 367 21
In such a situation as that, where there seemed nothing to SS III 13 367 22
And at any rate, she lost nothing by continuing the SS III 13 367 23
her friends; and, if nothing more advantageous occurred, SS III 13 367 23
Edward was of course immediately convinced that nothing SS III 13 367 24
she, "because--to say nothing of my own conviction, our SS III 13 368 26
yet reached him;--he knew nothing of what had passed; and SS III 13 370 35
"I do think," she continued, "nothing was ever carried on SS III 13 370 37
nothing so much as to be on good terms with her children." SS III 13 371 39
He had nothing to urge against it, but still resisted the SS III 13 372 45
secured to them, they had nothing to wait for after Edward SS III 14 374 6
They had in fact nothing to wish for, but the marriage of SS III 14 374 7
and as there could be nothing to overcome but the SS III 14 376 11
and Lucy themselves, nothing could exceed the harmony in SS III 14 377 11
if not in its cause; for nothing ever appeared in Robert's SS III 14 377 12
to her, she desired nothing so much as to give up its SS III 14 378 13
There is nothing she wd not do to get married--she would W 316 2
At least I believe so--but she tells me nothing. W 318 2
think of nothing worse) than marry a man I did not like."-- W 318 2
doing pretty well, tho' it would be nothing for Penelope.-- W 322 2
There was nothing in the manners of mrs or Miss Edwardes W 322 3
It is more than they deserve, for in fact they add nothing W 323 3
"I know nothing of my brother's beauty, said Emma, for I W 324 3
"That is nothing to the purpose.-- retorted the lady W 325 4
"Aye--there is nothing like your officers for captivating W 326 5
With nothing to do but to expect the hour of setting off, W 326 7
that she had heard nothing of her father's chair. W 338 17
Remember, I say nothing of my disinterestedness.-- W 339 18
You can imagine nothing more naive or piquante; & what do W 340 19
did yesterday, for we have nothing but some fried beef.-- W 341 19
But I see nothing else to admire in him.-- W 342 19
Now, tho' we have had nothing but fried beef, how good it W 343 19
rather have quarrelling going on, than nothing at all."-- W 343 19

Text	Work	Vol	Ch	Page	Line
cold at the ball, he had nothing more to say for some time,	W			345	21
After another pause, "nothing sets off a neat ankle more	W			345	21
Tom had nothing to say for himself, he knew it very well,	W			346	21
He is very handsome--but Tom Musgrave looks all to nothing,	W			347	22
that he had either known nothing about it, or had declined	W			347	22
In her person there was nothing remarkable; her manners	W			349	23
observed him, perceived nothing that did not justify eliz.	W			355	28
osborne castle; I have played nothing but vingt-un of late.	W			358	28
a mere nothing, that had great effect at a card table.	W			359	28
pretending to understand nothing extraordinary in the	W			360	29
Nothing could be more delightful!	PP	I	3	9	1
equally well married, I shall have nothing to wish for."	PP	I	3	9	2
Jane was so admired, nothing could be like it.	PP	I	3	12	16
better, and say nothing of the bad--belongs to you alone.	PP	I	4	14	9
as if-- but however, it may all come to nothing you know."	PP	I	5	19	8
replied Elizabeth, "where nothing is in question but the	PP	I	6	22	7
There is nothing like dancing after all.--	PP	I	6	25	26
their sisters', and when nothing better offered, a walk to	PP	I	7	28	3
They could talk of nothing but officers; and Mr. Bingley's	PP	I	7	29	4
The distance is nothing, when one has a motive; only three	PP	I	7	32	37
Darcy said very little, and Mr. Hurst nothing at all.	PP	I	7	33	42
being out, they had in fact nothing to do elsewhere.	PP	I	7	33	44
prefer a plain dish to a ragout, had nothing to say to her.	PP	I	8	35	2
Mrs. Hurst thought the same, and added, "she has nothing,	PP	I	8	35	3
					4
"Neglect! I am sure you neglect nothing that can add to	PP	I	8	38	33
I often tell my other girls they are nothing to her.	PP	I	9	42	7
at Darcy, "seemed to think the country was nothing at all."	PP	I	9	43	23
Nothing but concern for Elizabeth could enable Bingley to	PP	I	9	43	26
She longed to speak, but could think of nothing to say;	PP	I	9	45	35
"Nothing is more deceitful," said Darcy, "than the	PP	I	10	48	25
"You appear to me, Mr. Darcy, to allow nothing for the	PP	I	10	50	37
and of a Sunday evening when he has nothing to do."	PP	I	10	50	39
Mr. Hurst had therefore nothing to do, but to stretch	PP	I	11	54	3
way of disappointing him, will be to ask nothing about it."	PP	I	11	56	13
"Nothing so easy, if you have but the inclination," said	PP	I	11	57	17
now escape him, nothing that could elevate her with the	PP	I	12	60	4
said Mr. Bennet, "and nothing can clear Mr. Collins from	PP	I	13	62	8
and that her daughters had nothing to do in the kitchen.	PP	I	13	65	26
can be nothing so advantageous to them as instruction.	PP	I	14	69	16
of the officers, and nothing less than a very smart bonnet	PP	I	15	72	7
she should have known nothing about, if she had not	PP	I	15	73	11
their cousin, and who had nothing to do but to wish for an	PP	I	16	75	3
ladies he certainly was nothing; but he had still at	PP	I	16	76	5
"I do not at all know; but I heard nothing of his going	PP	I	16	78	19
by extravagance, imprudence, in short any thing or nothing.	PP	I	16	79	27
I can recal nothing worse.	PP	I	16	80	27
But she is nothing to me now.	PP	I	16	82	43
I knew nothing at all of Lady Catherine's connections. I	PP	I	16	83	54
She could think of nothing but of Mr. Wickham, and of what	PP	I	16	84	59
her tender feelings; and nothing therefore remained to be	PP	I	17	85	1
not much to Elizabeth, and nothing at all to the others.	PP	I	17	86	9
with Mr. Wickham; and nothing less than a dance on Tuesday,	PP	I	17	88	15
heard you accuse him of nothing worse than of being the	PP	I	18	95	46
I see nothing in it but your own wilful ignorance and the	PP	I	18	95	48
forgotten him; but I have nothing satisfactory to tell you.	PP	I	18	95	50
freely, openly, and of nothing else but of her expectation	PP	I	18	98	63
to be obliged to say nothing he may not like to hear."	PP	I	18	99	65
Nothing that she could say, however, had any influence.	PP	I	18	99	67
Darcy said nothing at all.	PP	I	18	103	75
He can have nothing to say to me that any body need not	PP	I	19	104	5
And now nothing remains for me but to assure you in the	PP	I	19	106	10
surprised her, she saw nothing in it really to lament; it	PP	I	21	116	8
favour an attachment and nothing to prevent it, am I wrong,	PP	I	21	118	14
of;--its object was nothing less, than to secure her from	PP	I	22	121	1
days, was nothing in comparison of his being now accepted.	PP	I	22	125	18
Nothing less than the complaisance of a courtier could	PP	I	23	126	3
Nothing could console and nothing appease her.--	PP	I	23	127	5
now been gone a week, and nothing was heard of his return.	PP	I	23	128	9
She could think of nothing else, and yet whether Bingley's	PP	II	1	134	3
her sister with incredulous solicitude, but said nothing.	PP	II	1	134	6
I have nothing either to hope or fear, and nothing to	PP	II	1	134	7
It is very often nothing but our own vanity that deceives	PP	II	1	136	14
it is slight, it is nothing in comparison of what I should	PP	II	1	137	24
point of marriage, and after all there was nothing in it.	PP	II	2	139	3
I have nothing to say against him; he is a most	PP	II	3	144	2
comforts, and mentioned nothing which she could not praise.	PP	II	3	146	19
Four weeks passed away, and Jane saw nothing of him.	PP	II	3	147	25
Nothing, on the contrary, could be more natural; and while	PP	II	5	150	26
as himself, had nothing to say that could be worth hearing,	PP	II	4	152	4
He could tell her nothing new of the wonders of his	PP	II	4	152	4
Maria would tell her nothing more, and down they ran into	PP	II	5	158	13
and here is nothing but Lady Catherine and her daughter!"	PP	II	5	158	14
At length there was nothing more to be said; the ladies	PP	II	5	159	20
She had heard nothing of Lady Catherine that spoke her	PP	II	6	161	9
appearance there was nothing remarkable, and who was	PP	II	6	162	12
as if he felt that life could furnish nothing greater.--	PP	II	6	162	14
question, and the gentlemen did nothing but eat and admire.	PP	II	6	163	14
Elizabeth found that nothing was beneath this great lady's	PP	II	6	163	15
I always say that nothing is to be done in education	PP	II	6	165	32
From the drawing room they could distinguish nothing in	PP	II	7	168	2
from her ladyship, and nothing escaped her observation	PP	II	7	169	3
his friend; and, having nothing else to say, was now	PP	II	9	178	11
in it, and sometimes it seemed nothing but absence of mind.	PP	II	9	181	29
She saw him start at this, but he said nothing, and she	PP	II	11	192	25
					26
though objectionable, was nothing in comparison of that	PP	II	12	198	5
On this subject I have nothing more to say, no other	PP	II	12	199	5
that could rest on nothing, she walked on; but it would	PP	II	13	205	3
Of his former way of life, nothing had been known in	PP	II	13	206	4
temptation to openness as nothing could have conquered,	PP	II	15	217	17
there could be nothing more to plague her on his account.	PP	II	16	223	25
At present I will say nothing about it."	PP	II	17	226	23
and she was sensible that nothing less than a perfect	PP	II	17	227	25
There is nothing extravagant in their housekeeping, I dare	PP	II	17	228	31
"No, nothing at all."	PP	II	17	228	32
young men now-a-days, who think of nothing but themselves.	PP	III	1	249	38
There is nothing he would not do for her."	PP	III	1	250	45
but Elizabeth knew nothing of the art; and from such as	PP	III	1	250	46
Elizabeth said nothing, but it gratified her exceedingly;	PP	III	1	255	60
people may call him proud, I have seen nothing of it."	PP	III	1	257	68
they had entirely mistaken his character, but said nothing.	PP	III	1	258	73
friends; and she could do nothing but think, and think	PP	III	1	259	77
Nothing had ever suggested it before, but they now felt	PP	III	2	260	1
Nothing occurred between them that could justify the hopes	PP	III	2	262	8
They saw much to interest, but nothing to justify enquiry.	PP	III	2	264	13
They had nothing to accuse him of but pride; pride he	PP	III	2	265	14
Her nose wants character; there is nothing marked in its	PP	III	3	271	15
(and let us rejoice over it) marks nothing bad at heart.	PP	III	4	273	3
at least, for he must know my father can give her nothing.	PP	III	4	273	3
Is there nothing you could take, to give you present	PP	III	4	276	9
"There is nothing the matter with me.	PP	III	4	276	10
She has no money, no connections, nothing that can tempt	PP	III	4	277	11
But nothing can be done; I know very well that nothing can	PP	III	4	277	16
his self-conquest brought nothing consolatory to her bosom,	PP	III	4	278	19
have been exchanged, nothing can be said in her defence,	PP	III	4	279	24
almost persuaded that nothing could be done for Lydia, her	PP	III	4	280	26
his account at the inn, nothing remained to be done but to	PP	III	4	281	29
know nothing of the effects that such a step might produce.	PP	III	5	283	8
she has been given up to nothing but amusement and vanity.	PP	III	5	283	10
quartered in Meryton, nothing but love, flirtation, and	PP	III	5	283	10
"But does Lydia know nothing of this?	PP	III	5	284	15

Text	Work	Vol	Ch	Page	Line
on Lydia's side, but nothing to give him any alarm.	PP	III	5	290	46
My father and mother knew nothing of that, they only felt	PP	III	5	290	50
At present we have nothing to guide us.	PP	III	6	295	6
and then he had nothing of a pleasant nature to send.	PP	III	6	297	12
being followed by a letter from him, had ended in nothing.	PP	III	6	298	16
her spirits unnecessary; nothing, therefore, could be	PP	III	6	298	17
that, had she known nothing of Darcy, she could have borne	PP	III	6	298	17
he must have endured, he replied, "say nothing of that.	PP	III	6	299	19
We have heard nothing from town."	PP	III	7	301	2
There is nothing else to be done.	PP	III	7	304	27
Nothing of the past was recollected with pain; and Lydia	PP	III	9	316	6
"Oh, Lord! yes;--there is nothing in that.	PP	III	9	317	13
Your uncle is as much surprised as I am--and nothing but	PP	III	10	321	2
know where, and he knew he should have nothing to live on.	PP	III	10	323	2
Nothing was to be done that he did not do himself; though	PP	III	10	324	2
be thanked, therefore say nothing about it,) your uncle	PP	III	10	324	2
all please me; he wants nothing but a little more	PP	III	10	325	2
of my duty, and the exertion would soon have been nothing.	PP	III	10	328	28
They will have nothing else to do."	PP	III	11	330	6
"I often think," said she, "that there is nothing so bad	PP	III	11	330	10
He is nothing to us, you know, and I am sure I never want	PP	III	11	331	14
But that is nothing to us.	PP	III	11	331	14
But it ended in nothing, and I will not be sent on a	PP	III	11	332	23
"It would be nothing; I could see him with perfect	PP	III	11	333	28
of speaking, which nothing else had so effectually done	PP	III	11	337	52
She could think of nothing more to say; but if he wished	PP	III	12	342	25
tables, and she had nothing to hope, but that his eyes	PP	III	12	342	26
"Nothing child, nothing.	PP	III	13	345	12
There was nothing of presumption or folly in Bingley, that	PP	III	13	346	21
she talked to Bingley of nothing else, for half an hour;	PP	III	13	348	34
You are each of you so complying, that nothing will ever	PP	III	13	348	38
I was sure you could not be so beautiful for nothing!	PP	III	13	348	40
he really loved me, and nothing but a persuasion of my	PP	III	13	350	49
"It is nothing in comparison of Rosings, my lady, I dare	PP	III	14	352	10
to you last spring! is nothing due to me on that score?	PP	III	14	355	47
does not object to them, they can be nothing to you."	PP	III	14	356	53
"You can now have nothing farther to say," she resentfully	PP	III	14	357	63
"Lady Catherine, I have nothing farther to say.	PP	III	14	358	66
I suppose she had nothing particular to say to you, Lizzy?"	PP	III	14	359	76
Had they fixed on any other man it would have been nothing;	PP	III	15	364	24
and she could do nothing but wonder at such a want of	PP	III	15	364	25
But your family owe me nothing.	PP	III	16	366	6
"No indeed; I felt nothing but surprise."	PP	III	16	370	30
I speak nothing but the truth.	PP	III	17	372	5
"You know nothing of the matter.	PP	III	17	373	7
Nothing could give either Bingley or myself more delight.	PP	III	17	373	11
When convinced on that article, Miss Bennet had nothing	PP	III	17	373	17
Were it for nothing but his love of you, I must always	PP	III	17	374	18
of man; but this would be nothing if you really liked him."	PP	III	17	376	33
Jane's is nothing to it--nothing at all.	PP	III	17	378	43
"My dearest child," she cried, "I can think of nothing	PP	III	17	378	45
you have nothing else to do, I hope you will think of us.	PP	III	19	386	7
The trouble and expense of it to them, would be nothing	MP	I	1	5	4
of that kind, there was nothing to impede her frugality,	MP	I	1	8	9
take her turn, and think nothing of the inconvenience; but	MP	I	1	9	10
is, I hope there can be nothing to fear for them, and	MP	I	1	10	14
if Miss Lee taught her nothing, she would learn to be good	MP	I	1	10	15
there was, at least, nothing to disgust her relations.	MP	I	2	12	2
as your uncle will frank it, it will cost William nothing."	MP	I	2	16	17
Edmund was uniformly kind himself, and she had nothing	MP	I	2	17	22
but she had been taught nothing more; and as her cousins	MP	I	2	18	23
She thinks of nothing but the Isle of Wight, and she calls	MP	I	2	18	25
with proper masters, and could want nothing more.	MP	I	2	20	31
but his other children promised him nothing but good.	MP	I	2	20	33
Of the rest she saw nothing; nobody seemed to think of her	MP	I	2	21	34
claims on us, and that nothing can, in fact, be an	MP	I	3	23	3
I shall love nothing there.	MP	I	3	26	24
"I can say nothing for her manner to you as a child; but	MP	I	3	26	25
those persons who think nothing can be dangerous or	MP	I	3	32	63
her sister, who desired nothing better than a post of such	MP	I	4	35	5
sense; but as there was nothing disagreeable in his figure	MP	I	4	38	10
he heard nothing but the perfectly good and agreeable.	MP	I	4	40	14
Mrs. Grant knew nothing, she had scarcely seen them since.	MP	I	4	40	15
Admiral and Mrs. Crawford, though agreeing in nothing else,	MP	I	4	40	15
promised well, and there was nothing to call him elsewhere.	MP	I	5	47	26
"And yet in general, nothing can be more easily	MP	I	5	49	32
look from the young lady--nothing like a civil answer--she	MP	I	5	50	35
describe so well, (and nothing was ever juster,) tell one	MP	I	5	51	40
In comparison with his brother, Edmund would have nothing	MP	I	6	52	1
not saying much to the purpose, could talk of nothing else.	MP	I	6	52	1
and it was a mere nothing before repton took it in hand.	MP	I	6	55	15
Not by a waggon or cart;--Oh! no, nothing of that kind	MP	I	6	58	35
it is nothing more than, 'dear Mary, I am just arrived.	MP	I	6	59	43
"My dear Henry, have you nothing to say?	MP	I	6	60	53
"Nothing could be so gratifying to me as to hear your	MP	I	6	61	54
In extent it is a mere nothing--you would be surprised at	MP	I	6	61	54
your good mother again; nothing but having no horses of my	MP	I	6	62	58
excepting Edmund, who heard it all and said nothing.	MP	I	6	62	59
But was there nothing in her conversation that struck you	MP	I	7	63	3
manner of Miss Crawford, nothing sharp, or loud, or coarse.	MP	I	7	64	11
probably knew nothing of the matter, and had no active	MP	I	7	67	16
you waiting--but I have nothing in the world to say for	MP	I	7	68	18
Nothing ever fatigues me, but doing what I do not like.	MP	I	7	68	20
ride, and that I may have nothing but good to hear of this	MP	I	7	68	20
It is nothing but the heat."	MP	I	7	72	39
There is nothing so likely to give it as standing and	MP	I	7	72	45
ay and in all weathers too, and say nothing about it."	MP	I	7	73	53
the roses; for there is nothing so refreshing as a walk	MP	I	7	73	55
Nothing of this would have happened had she been properly	MP	I	7	74	58
woman, who thought nothing of consequence, but as it	MP	I	8	75	2
do, would be trouble for nothing; and between ourselves,	MP	I	8	77	12
"There is no hardship, I suppose, nothing unpleasant,"	MP	I	8	78	14
in seeing Sotherton would be nothing without him.	MP	I	8	79	27
body was ready, there was nothing to be done but for Mrs.	MP	I	8	80	29
of what she had known nothing about, when Mr. Rushworth	MP	I	8	83	37
purpose of devotion--with nothing more striking or more	MP	I	9	85	6
There is nothing awful here, nothing melancholy, nothing	MP	I	9	85	6
and nothing in the world could be more snug and pleasant."	MP	I	9	88	24
A clergyman is nothing."	MP	I	9	92	44
"The nothing of conversation has its gradations, I hope,	MP	I	9	92	45
But I cannot call that situation nothing, which has the	MP	I	9	92	45
No one here can call the office nothing.	MP	I	9	92	45
"Oh! I know nothing of your furlongs, but I am sure it is	MP	I	9	95	64
no surprise; for there is nothing in the course of one's	MP	I	9	95	71
Nothing was fixed on--but Henry Crawford was full of ideas	MP	I	10	97	3
"Yes, there is nothing else to be done.	MP	I	10	98	6
is a pity that he should have so much trouble for nothing."	MP	I	10	101	31
go any further," said he sullenly; "I see nothing of them.	MP	I	10	101	35
For my part, I can see nothing in him."	MP	I	10	102	41
"Nothing could be more obliging than your manner, I am	MP	I	10	102	46
it may be improved; and nothing of that sort, you know,	MP	I	10	102	47
go; it would be foolish to bring the key for nothing."	MP	I	10	103	48
"Nothing but pleasure from beginning to end!	MP	I	10	105	53
Nothing would satisfy that good old Mrs. Whitaker, but my	MP	I	10	105	55
It is nothing but four of those beautiful pheasant's eggs,	MP	I	10	106	57
when the mist cleared away, she should see nothing else.	MP	I	11	107	3
Edmund looked round at Mr. Rushworth too, but had nothing	MP	I	11	108	5
best intentions of doing nothing all the rest of his days	MP	I	11	110	23
A clergyman has nothing to do but to be slovenly and	MP	I	11	110	23
sated mind; and finding nothing in Norfolk to equal the	MP	I	12	115	3
Mrs. Rushworth, who saw nothing but her son, was quite at	MP	I	12	118	17
But when my aunt has got a fancy in her head, nothing can	MP	I	12	120	26

be keenly felt, and Mr. Yates could talk of nothing else. MP I 13 121 1
nothing more would be necessary on such a plan as this. MP I 13 123 8
For mere amusement among ourselves, we should want nothing MP I 13 124 8
"Let us do nothing by halves. MP I 13 124 10
If we do not out do Ecclesford, we do nothing." MP I 13 124 10
of the rest; and though nothing was settled but that Tom MP I 13 124 13
a tragedy, and that nothing in the world could be easier MP I 13 124 13
I may say, that nothing shall ever tempt me to it again. MP I 13 125 14
We mean nothing but a little amusement among ourselves, MP I 13 125 18
take care that his daughters do nothing to distress him. MP I 13 127 27
Nothing but buffoonery from beginning to end. MP I 14 131 3
Let it but be comic, I condition for nothing more." MP I 14 131 5
with every body was, that nothing had been proposed before MP I 14 132 8
and me, but here is nothing for your sister, Mr. Crawford." MP I 14 133 9
There is nothing of tragedy about her. MP I 14 134 12
and I am sure I will do nothing else; and as to Amelia, it MP I 14 136 20
we find there is nothing that will suit us altogether so MP I 15 139 6
so well, nothing so unexceptionable, as Lovers' Vows. MP I 15 139 6
of course, I can see nothing objectionable in it; and I am MP I 15 140 12
"If every play is to be objected to, you will act nothing-- MP I 15 141 22
and "Oh! we can do nothing without you," followed the MP I 15 143 26
civilly answered by Lady Bertram, but Edmund said nothing. MP I 15 143 27
It need not frighten you; it is a nothing of a part, a MP I 15 145 47
nothing of a part, a mere nothing, not above half a dozen MP I 15 145 47
of work here is about nothing,--I am quite ashamed of you, MP I 15 146 53
all their first protestations; but Edmund said nothing.-- MP I 15 148 59
time there; and having nothing to oppose her, had so MP I 16 151 1
for employment, if nothing but musing would do, she could MP I 16 151 2
I am well aware that nothing else will quiet Tom." MP I 16 154 10
As I am now, I have no influence, I can do nothing; I have MP I 16 155 16
most unwelcome news; and she could think of nothing else. MP I 16 156 28
wrapt in such gravity as nothing could subdue, no MP I 17 160 8
own mind; and if he means nothing, we will send him off, MP I 17 162 18
and saw nothing that did not immediately relate to it. MP I 17 163 21
but the others aspired at nothing beyond his remembering MP I 18 166 4
It would be lucky for me if I had nothing but the MP I 18 166 6
becoming too nearly nothing to both, to have any comfort MP I 18 170 24
There was nothing disagreeable in Mr. Rushworth's MP II 1 179 8
It had left her nothing to do. MP II 1 180 10
where nothing was wanted but tranquillity and silence. MP II 1 180 10
all dinner; he would take nothing, nothing till tea came-- MP II 1 180 10
nothing till tea came--he would rather wait for tea. MP II 1 180 10
"But indeed I would rather have nothing but tea." MP II 1 180 11
being gone home, that nothing more can be done to-night; MP II 1 185 28
comfortably here among ourselves, and doing nothing." MP II 1 186 33
He was anxious, while vindicating himself, to say nothing MP II 2 187 1
as I sit here, that nothing would have come of it--for Mr. MP II 2 188 3
There is nothing very striking in Mr. Rushworth's manners, MP II 2 190 6
with Julia had come to nothing; and could almost fear that MP II 2 194 20
is so very natural, that she can argue nothing from that. MP II 3 199 14
but it was safer to say nothing, and leave untouched all MP II 3 199 16
Nothing could be objected to when it came under the MP II 3 203 29
an umbrella, there was nothing to be done but to be very MP II 4 205 3
occasion at home, she had nothing to suffer on that score; MP II 4 206 4
Three years ago, this was nothing but a rough hedgerow MP II 4 208 12
Miss Crawford, untouched and inattentive, had nothing to MP II 4 209 13
of such amusements to nothing worse than a tete-a-tete MP II 4 210 21
There is nothing frightful in such a picture, is there, MP II 4 210 21
"Oh! you can do nothing but what you do already; be MP II 4 213 34
was soon settled that if nothing were heard to the MP II 4 215 47
There was nothing more to be said, or that could be said MP II 5 217 11
"Nothing can be more natural," said Sir Thomas, after a MP II 5 218 18
No, I see no finery about you; nothing but what is MP II 5 222 44
Oh! we hear nothing of Mr. Yates. MP II 5 224 52
Fanny coloured, and said nothing. MP II 5 225 54
her feelings by saying, "nothing amuses me more than the MP II 5 226 62
will have seven hundred a year, and nothing to do for it." MP II 5 226 63
"No, he can feel nothing as he ought." MP II 5 227 67
took her harp, she had nothing to do but to listen, and MP II 5 227 68
her, she must have a constitution which nothing could save. MP II 6 231 9
I want nothing more." MP II 6 231 9
almost every thing, is at others worse than nothing. MP II 6 235 18
good-will alone, and had nothing to do with Mr. Crawford, MP II 7 238 2
I know nothing about it, but Fanny must teach me." MP II 7 239 7
body's assuring her that nothing could be so easy, that it MP II 7 239 8
Nothing can be easier. MP II 7 242 23
I am not born to sit still and do nothing. MP II 7 243 25
She will have nothing to say to it. MP II 7 243 27
As yet Sir Thomas had seen nothing to remark in Mr. MP II 7 246 36
calm and uninviting, that he had nothing to censure in her. MP II 7 246 37
One might as well be nothing as a midshipman. MP II 7 249 52
One is nothing indeed. MP II 7 249 52
a time when you will have nothing of that sort to endure. MP II 7 249 53
My uncle says nothing, but I am sure he will do every MP II 7 250 55
of all, for she had nothing but a bit of ribbon to fasten MP II 8 254 8
nothing but the friends she was to visit, was before her. MP II 8 256 12
I offer nothing but an old necklace. MP II 8 258 16
To her, he could be nothing under any circumstances-- MP II 9 264 18
under any circumstances--nothing dearer than a friend. MP II 9 264 18
And even if it should--there will be nothing to be MP II 9 269 38
She had felt nothing like it for hours. MP II 9 270 40
She had nothing more to wish for. MP II 10 272 4
talking incessantly all night, and with nothing to say. MP II 10 278 20
Nothing remained of last night but remembrances, which she MP II 11 282 4
of Fanny's swimming eyes, nothing more was said on the MP II 11 284 9
and snow, with nothing to do and no variety to hope for. MP II 11 286 15
unless she had Fanny to herself she could hope for nothing. MP II 11 287 18
he comes there will be nothing to detain me at Mansfield. MP II 11 287 22
"I know nothing of the Miss Owens," said Fanny calmly. MP II 11 288 29
"You know nothing and you care less, as people say. MP II 11 288 30
usual cheerfulness, she had nothing further to try her own. MP II 12 291 1
Nothing could be more impossible than to answer such a MP II 12 292 8
though nothing be more agreeable than to have it asked. MP II 12 292 8
all interference, he shall know nothing of the matter. MP II 12 293 10
though he had in fact nothing to relate but his own MP II 12 293 16
own sensations, nothing to dwell on but Fanny's charms.-- MP II 12 293 16
in the hope of it, for nothing less dear to me than such MP II 13 299 5
I know it is all nothing." MP II 13 302 8
But such were his habits, that he could do nothing without MP II 13 302 10
as to make her feel as if nothing had occurred to vex her, MP II 13 303 12
though he might think nothing of what had passed, it would MP II 13 303 12
for though nothing could have tempted her to turn her eyes MP II 13 304 16
every year, to say nothing of what I do for them." MP II 13 305 24
Nothing could be more unnatural in either. MP II 13 306 26
moment, and saying, "have you nothing to send to Mary? MP II 13 306 28
She will be disappointed if she received nothing from you. MP II 13 306 28
The rest of your note I know means nothing; but I am so MP II 13 307 31
the others, he had nothing to do but to go in good earnest. MP II 13 307 35
His coming might have nothing to do with her, but she must MP III 1 311 2
I thought it might all pass for nothing with him." MP III 1 315 19
Well, there is nothing more to be said." MP III 1 316 32
And for a few minutes he did say nothing. MP III 1 316 33
in such an establishment for you--is nothing to you. MP III 1 318 39
the disappointment; say nothing about it yourself." MP III 1 322 48
She saw nothing more of her uncle, nor of her aunt Norris, MP III 1 323 53
Fanny, Sir Thomas thought nothing could be more unjust, MP III 1 323 57
her, and she thought nothing of it till the butler re- MP III 1 324 60
agitation which made nothing clear to her but the MP III 2 329 10
Nothing was omitted, on his side, of civility, compliment, MP III 2 329 12
There is nothing more to be said or done. MP III 2 330 16
You will have nothing to fear, or to be agitated about. MP III 2 330 16
that I have in view, and nothing is required of you but to MP III 2 331 16
as you might have done, had nothing of this sort occurred. MP III 2 331 16
If her aunt's feelings were against her, nothing could be MP III 2 333 27
there was hope in nothing else) that he was almost ready MP III 3 336 7
silently at work as if there was nothing else to care for. MP III 3 336 8
She seemed determined to be interested by nothing else. MP III 3 337 10
she could not help half a smile, but she said nothing. MP III 3 343 37
I see nothing alarming in the word. MP III 3 343 38
that nothing else can now be descriptive of you." MP III 3 344 41
every body, cousin, there can be nothing for me to tell." MP III 4 346 9
You did not love him--nothing could have justified your MP III 4 347 16
Nothing could be more improper than the whole business. MP III 4 350 28
There could be nothing very striking, because it is clear MP III 4 350 30
by a different conduct; nothing else will satisfy them. MP III 4 352 44
must have thought it so, supposing he had meant nothing. MP III 4 353 45
that you could tolerate nothing that you were not used to; MP III 4 354 46
have stayed; but I knew nothing that had happened here for MP III 4 354 50
recommended there being nothing more said to her, no MP III 5 356 2
There was nothing to be done, however, but to submit MP III 5 356 3
to hope there would be nothing worse to be endured than an MP III 5 357 5
She said nothing, however, but, "sad, sad girl! MP III 5 357 6
in you; which, in common intercourse, one knows nothing of. MP III 5 359 12
he was rich, and she had nothing; but he turns out ill- MP III 5 361 16
There is a spirit of irritation, which, to say nothing MP III 5 361 16
but of that, I shall see nothing with the Frasers. MP III 5 361 16
in; and yet there was nothing improper on her side; she MP III 5 361 16
This seems as if nothing were a security for matrimonial MP III 5 361 16
And had I had an idea of it, nothing should have induced MP III 5 362 21
considered it as meaning nothing, I put it down as simply MP III 5 362 21
allowed himself in gallantries which did mean nothing." MP III 5 363 21
Fanny could not avoid a faint smile, but had nothing to MP III 5 363 25
not be denied it; he said nothing, however, or nothing MP III 5 365 36
said nothing, however, or nothing that she heard, and when MP III 5 365 36
nothing, would awaken very wholesome regrets in her mind.-- MP III 6 366 1
Edmund considered it every way, and saw nothing but what MP III 6 368 9
and nothing at all with any idea of making her happy. MP III 6 368 9
taken to Portsmouth for nothing, it would be hardly MP III 6 373 24
Portsmouth their correspondence would dwindle into nothing. MP III 7 376 4
convenience; but she had nothing to do, and was glad to MP III 7 382 28
Fanny had indeed nothing to convey from aunt Norris, but a MP III 7 387 45
There was nothing to raise her spirits in the confined and MP III 7 387 47
of all that they had planned and depended on. MP III 8 388 2
Nobody was in their right place, nothing was done as it MP III 8 388 3
there she had hoped much, and found almost nothing. MP III 8 389 4
On the contrary, she could think of nothing but Mansfield, MP III 8 391 10
were never at rest, nothing was done without a clatter, MP III 8 392 11
for, take away his rants, and the poor Baron has nothing. MP III 9 394 1
and prospect, there was nothing alike in the two MP III 9 398 9
Susan had read nothing, and Fanny longed to give her a MP III 9 398 9
be supposed in town, and Fanny had heard nothing of him. MP III 10 399 1
Nothing of all that she had been used to think of as the MP III 10 400 7
and such hints producing nothing, he soon proceeded to a MP III 10 401 10
Nothing could be more grateful to her, and she was on the MP III 10 404 15
I have heard nothing about it yet from my aunt. MP III 11 410 15
"Is there nothing I can do for you in town?" MP III 11 412 24
"Nothing, I am much obliged to you." MP III 11 412 25
on the morrow, for nothing more was seen of him at Mr. MP III 12 415 1
2
The only certainty to be drawn from it was, that nothing MP III 12 417 4
wanting, but nothing of that nature was ever in my power.-- MP III 12 420 2
resolved on doing nothing till she returns to Mansfield. MP III 13 422 2
As for the main subject of the letter--there was nothing MP III 13 424 4
He is blinded, and nothing will open his eyes, nothing can, MP III 13 424 4
situated, the ties of blood were little more than nothing. MP III 13 428 15
Lady Bertram could think nothing less, and Fanny shared MP III 14 429 1
She could do nothing but glide in quietly and look at him; MP III 14 429 2
It came, and she had yet heard nothing of her return-- MP III 14 430 6
nothing of her return--nothing even of the going to London, MP III 14 430 6
secret meditations; and nothing was more consolatory to MP III 14 431 8
and her husband away, she can have nothing but enjoyment. MP III 14 434 13
Henry is not at hand, so I have nothing to say from him. MP III 14 435 13
She had only learnt to think nothing of consequence but MP III 14 436 16
Say not a word of it--hear nothing, surmise nothing, MP III 15 437 3
surmise nothing, whisper nothing, till I write again. MP III 15 437 3
I am sure it will be all hushed up, and nothing proved by MP III 15 437 3
Nothing happened the next day, or the next, to weaken her MP III 15 442 22
We have been here two days, but there is nothing to be MP III 15 442 23
Now it seems nothing, yet it is an heavy aggravation. MP III 15 442 23
There is nothing like employment, active, indispensable MP III 15 443 25
of her heart, and knowing nothing personally of those who MP III 15 444 26
As nothing was really left for the decision of Mrs. Price, MP III 15 444 27
She could say nothing; nor for some minutes could he say MP III 15 444 28
witness--but that he saw nothing--of the tranquil manner MP III 15 445 31
perfectly aware, that nothing but ill humour was to be MP III 16 448 3
"Nothing, nothing to be understood. MP III 16 455 21
very like it, and nothing less than Lady Bertram's rousing MP III 16 459 31
Mr. Yates's convenience had had nothing to do with it. MP III 17 466 18
to happiness, there was nothing on the side of prudence to MP III 17 471 28
They lived beyond their income, but still it was nothing E I 2 15 3
His own stomach could bear nothing rich, and he could E I 2 19 14
neighbours and friends, and a home that wanted for nothing. E I 3 21 4
For Mrs. Weston there was nothing to be done; for Harriet E I 4 27 2
order of people with whom I feel I can have nothing to do. E I 4 29 14
is nothing, compared with his entire want of gentility. E I 4 32 30
appearances, and thinking of nothing but profit and loss." E I 4 33 38
I may safely affirm that Harriet Smith will do nothing.-- E I 5 37 7
disposition to bear, there will be nothing to be borne. E I 5 38 13
She knows nothing herself, and looks upon Emma as knowing E I 5 38 15
never marry, which, of course, means just nothing at all. E I 5 41 29
that he had nothing more to say or surmise about Hartfield. E I 5 41 31
You know nothing of drawing. E I 6 43 15
been wanting; and in nothing had she approached the degree E I 6 44 19
I will have nothing to do with it. E I 7 52 17
degree wavering, I said nothing about it, because I would E I 7 53 24
Then I know nothing of Mr. Elton. E I 7 56 46
Mr. Knightley, who had nothing of ceremony about him, was E I 8 57 2
was too true for contradiction, and therefore said nothing. E I 8 58 19
"I saw her answer, nothing could be clearer." E I 8 60 35
She has been taught nothing useful, and is too young and E I 8 61 38
is nothing more,) a good match for my intimate friend! E I 8 62 39
Her allowance is very liberal; nothing has ever been E I 8 62 41
She desired nothing better herself. E I 8 63 42
Nothing so easy as for a young lady to raise her E I 8 64 47
her to be satisfied with nothing less than a man of E I 8 64 47
She knows now what gentlemen are; and nothing but a E I 8 65 48
he would, she had done nothing which woman's friendship E I 8 67 56
and of course thought nothing of its effects; but she saw E I 8 67 57
earnestly careful that nothing ungallant, nothing that did E I 9 70 7
that nothing ungallant, nothing that did not breathe a E I 9 70 7
for its freshness; and nothing could be easier to you." E I 9 71 8
This is a connection which offers nothing but good. E I 9 74 20
You do nothing. E I 9 76 38
But I can remember nothing;--not even that particular E I 9 78 54
"But they like it, papa; there is nothing they like so E I 9 81 75
She pondered, but could think of nothing. E I 10 84 8
for her grandmother, one hears of nothing else for a month. E I 10 86 23
as if I could think of nothing but these poor creatures E I 10 87 25
"Poor creatures! one can think of nothing else." E I 10 87 26
at this proposition; and nothing could exceed his E I 10 89 38
For ten minutes she could hear nothing but herself. E I 10 89 38
and allusions had been dropt, but nothing serious. E I 10 90 39
and will hazard nothing till he believes himself secure." E I 10 90 40
Nothing wrong in him escaped her. E I 11 93 5

Mr. Weston, I think there is nothing he does not deserve.	E	I	11	95	19
in nothing; and I have not heard him mentioned lately."	E	I	11	95	21
and sister, she had nothing worse to hear than Isabella's	E	I	12	104	45
health is at stake, nothing else should be considered; and	E	I	12	106	58
She had nothing to wish otherwise, but that the days did	E	I	13	108	1
Mr. Elton and I are very good friends, and nothing more;"	E	I	13	112	23
like; he anticipated nothing in the visit that could be at	E	I	13	113	25
another man's house, with nothing to say or to hear that	E	I	13	113	26
servants taken out for nothing but to convey five idle,	E	I	13	113	26
in this carriage we know nothing of the matter.--	E	I	13	115	37
Nothing could be pleasanter.	E	I	13	115	39
"I know nothing of the large parties of London, sir--I	E	I	13	116	44
She could tell nothing of Hartfield, in which Mrs. Weston	E	I	14	117	1
I am very much afraid that it will all end in nothing.	E	I	14	121	14
"Yes--it seems to depend upon nothing but the ill-humour	E	I	14	121	15
But at present there was nothing more to be said.	E	I	14	122	18
governed by the nephew, to whom she owes nothing at all."	E	I	14	123	24
both agreed with him in there being nothing to apprehend.	E	I	15	128	16
way to any feelings-----nothing could be farther from my	E	I	15	131	34
She thought nothing of his attachment, and was insulted by	E	I	16	135	7
went to bed at last with nothing settled but the	E	I	16	137	12
end of it, and saw nothing extraordinary in his language.	E	I	17	141	4
disposition, foresaw nothing but a repetition of excuses	E	I	18	144	3
about him," cried Emma; "but that is nothing extraordinary.	E	I	18	148	23
of other people: nothing really amiable about him."	E	I	18	149	26
"Well, if he have nothing else to recommend him, he will	E	I	18	149	29
deafness is very trifling you see--just nothing at all.	E	II	1	158	14
quite depend upon it; nothing can be more kind or pressing	E	II	1	160	23
hope and interest; but nothing now remained of it, save	E	II	2	163	2
She had fallen into good hands, known nothing but kindness	E	II	2	164	6
to her aunt contained nothing but truth, though there	E	II	2	166	10
In that case, nothing could be more pitiable or more	E	II	2	168	13
of politeness, she seemed determined to hazard nothing.	E	II	2	169	15
It was all general approbation and smoothness; nothing	E	II	2	169	16
You left nothing undone.	E	II	3	170	2
with her," said Emma, "nothing I suppose can be known.	E	II	3	175	39
					40
"Oh! as for me, my judgment is worth nothing.	E	II	3	176	48
					49
and I was determined that nothing should stop me from	E	II	3	179	52
she could talk of nothing else; and Emma, at last, in	E	II	3	180	56
caring nothing for Miss Woodhouse, and defying Miss Smith.	E	II	4	181	3
themselves to please, and nothing but the necessary	E	II	4	182	6
vaunted claims and disdain of Harriet, he had done nothing.	E	II	4	183	9
the law line--nothing more distinctly honourable was	E	II	4	183	9
certainly would indeed; nothing could be clearer; even a	E	II	4	183	10
sufficient; but nothing else, she feared, would cure her.	E	II	4	183	10
in Mr. Elton, and found nothing so interesting as the	E	II	4	184	10
After much thinking, she could determine on nothing better,	E	II	4	185	13
She could think of nothing better: and though there was	E	II	4	185	14
if not coolly; and nothing beyond the merest common-place	E	II	5	186	4
I dare say he is really nothing extraordinary:"-- though	E	II	5	189	13
innocent, and answer in a manner that appropriated nothing.	E	II	5	189	14
was very handsome, knew nothing of their plans; and it was	E	II	6	196	2
If he were deficient there, nothing should make amends for	E	II	6	196	2
that he paid his duty; nothing could be more proper or	E	II	6	196	2
his whole manner to her--nothing could more agreeably	E	II	6	196	2
father, and nothing of the pride or reserve of Enscombe.	E	II	6	198	5
must confess, that to him nothing could make amends for	E	II	6	199	10
Then I will speak the truth, and nothing suits me so well.	E	II	6	200	20
taste, but I know nothing of the matter myself.--	E	II	6	201	28
one; she could observe nothing wrong in his notions, a	E	II	7	205	2
his hair cut, there was nothing to denote him unworthy of	E	II	7	206	2
Nothing should tempt her to go, if they did; and she	E	II	7	207	6
Now you have nothing to try for.	E	II	8	214	10
"One can suppose nothing else," added Mrs. Cole, "and I	E	II	8	215	14
and finding that nothing more was to be entrapped from any	E	II	8	216	17
But you observed nothing of course, for it seems to be a	E	II	8	218	36
"I dare say you would; but I, simple I, saw nothing but	E	II	8	218	37
the one nor the other--nothing worse than every day	E	II	8	219	43
nothing, was enough for the happiness of the present hour.	E	II	8	219	44
where his uncle could do nothing, and on her laughing and	E	II	8	221	49
of Miss Fairfax, she could absolutely distinguish nothing.	E	II	8	222	57
"Very likely," said Emma--"nothing more likely.	E	II	8	223	64
a boy of six years old, who knows nothing of the matter?"	E	II	8	224	67
a little disparity of age, I can see nothing unsuitable."	E	II	8	225	73
Mr. Knightley does nothing mysteriously."	E	II	8	226	80
I see no sign of attachment--I believe nothing of the	E	II	8	226	84
she had been seeing nothing, except that he had found a	E	II	8	227	85
denied; and that he knew nothing of the matter, and had no	E	II	8	227	86
She could see nothing but evil in it.	E	II	8	227	87
"That fellow," said he, indignantly, thinks of nothing but	E	II	8	229	97
hesitatingly, "but it is nothing of any consequence."	E	II	9	232	13
A mind lively and at ease, can do with seeing nothing, and	E	II	9	233	24
seeing nothing, and can see nothing that does not answer.	E	II	9	233	24
she really eats nothing--makes such a shocking breakfast,	E	II	9	237	46
gets hungry, and there is nothing she likes so well as	E	II	9	237	46
he directly, 'there is nothing in the way of fruit half so	E	II	9	238	51
send you some more, before they get good for nothing.'	E	II	9	238	51
calmness, "I can imagine nothing with any confidence.	E	II	10	241	14
Nothing hastily done; nothing incomplete.	E	II	10	242	21
"Oh! very delightful indeed; I can say nothing less, for I	E	II	10	245	49
Five couple are nothing, when one thinks seriously about	E	II	11	248	8
Nothing can be farther from pleasure than to be dancing in	E	II	11	249	17
They can do nothing satisfactorily without you."	E	II	11	253	39
You will see nothing of it by candle-light.	E	II	11	253	42
It is a mere nothing after all; and not the least draught	E	II	11	254	48
"You will get nothing to the purpose from Miss Bates,"	E	II	11	255	52
all delight and gratitude, but she will tell you nothing.	E	II	11	255	52
The preparations must take their time, nothing could be	E	II	12	257	1
entertainment, I have nothing to say against it, but that	E	II	12	257	3
Miss Woodhouse, I hope nothing may happen to prevent the	E	II	12	258	5
"There is nothing to be compared to it.	E	II	13	269	16
"Oh! no--there is nothing to surprize one at all.--	E	II	14	271	12
"Ah! there is nothing like staying at home, for real	E	II	14	274	30
I condition for nothing else; but without music, life	E	II	14	277	36
neglecting her music, had nothing more to say; and, after	E	II	14	278	43
nothing to do with any encouragement to people to marry."	E	II	14	280	60
When they had nothing else to say, it must be always easy	E	II	15	282	3
upon my word, I talk of nothing but Jane Fairfax.--	E	II	15	282	5
off, for there really is nothing in the manners of either	E	II	15	284	9
What I said just now, meant nothing.	E	II	15	288	35
If this is living in the country, it is nothing very	E	II	16	290	2
"But have you really heard of nothing?"	E	II	17	299	4
serious in wishing nothing to be done till the summer.	E	II	17	301	19
also, that nothing really unexceptionable may pass us."	E	II	17	302	20
As to her illness, all nothing of course.	E	II	17	304	27
Her looks and words had nothing to restrain them.	E	II	17	304	28
"No, indeed, I shall grant you nothing.	E	II	18	306	12
Nothing can stand more retired from the road than Maple	E	II	18	307	21
Mr. Churchill has pride; but his pride is nothing to his	E	II	18	309	33
direful in the sound: but nothing more is positively known	E	II	18	310	34
Her own attachment had really subsided into a mere nothing;	E	III	1	315	1
again; and then, having nothing else to do, formed a sort	E	III	2	320	5
Nothing to signify.	E	III	2	322	19
Nothing wanting.	E	III	2	322	19
There was nothing like flirtation between her and her	E	III	2	326	32
Now there is nothing grandmamma loves better than	E	III	2	329	45
I have seen nothing like it since--well, where shall we	E	III	2	330	45
To that surmise, you say nothing, of course; but confess,	E	III	2	330	48
Nothing of the sort had ever occurred before to any young	E	III	3	335	10
I can see nothing at all extraordinary in him now.--	E	III	4	337	6
this relick--I knew nothing of that till this moment--but	E	III	4	338	13
and this was left upon the table as good for nothing.	E	III	4	339	18
I have nothing more to show you, or to say--except that I	E	III	4	340	22
she let it pass, and seem to suspect nothing?--	E	III	4	341	34
Henceforward I know nothing of the matter.	E	III	4	342	39
"it all meant nothing; a mere joke among ourselves."	E	III	5	350	29
Now, as her objection was nothing but her very great	E	III	6	353	3
Such schemes as these are nothing without numbers.	E	III	6	353	4
The year will wear away at this rate, and nothing done.	E	III	6	354	7
Nothing can be more simple, you see.	E	III	6	355	20
It led to nothing; nothing but a view at the end over a	E	III	6	360	38
I have said nothing about it to any body.	E	III	6	362	44
he had staid at home--nothing killed him like heat--he	E	III	6	363	53
I am tired of doing nothing.	E	III	6	365	62
She smiled her acceptance; and nothing less than a summons	E	III	6	366	76
Nothing was wanting but to be happy when they got there.	E	III	7	367	1
He said nothing worth hearing--looked without seeing--	E	III	7	367	2
her own estimation, meant nothing, though in the judgment	E	III	7	368	3
"I say nothing of which I am ashamed," replied he, with	E	III	7	369	16
We have nothing clever to say--not one of us."	E	III	7	372	37
"I have nothing to say that can entertain Miss Woodhouse,	E	III	7	372	38
An old married man--quite good for nothing.	E	III	7	372	38
can give--it is all nothing; there can be no knowledge.	E	III	7	372	40
I care for nothing else.	E	III	7	373	50
came, and went early, that nothing might prevent her.	E	III	8	377	2
suspicion, and left her nothing but pity; and the	E	III	8	379	9
up her mind to close with nothing till Colonel Campbell's	E	III	8	380	15
Campbell's return, and nothing should induce her to enter	E	III	8	380	15
It will be nothing but pleasure, a life of pleasure.--	E	III	8	382	23
There was nothing in all this either to astonish or	E	III	8	384	32
every thing, the other nothing--and she sat musing on the	E	III	8	384	32
					33
"Nothing at all.	E	III	9	385	3
it happened, but she thought nothing became him more.--	E	III	9	386	7
stoops to folly, she has nothing to do but to die; and	E	III	9	387	12
Now, an attachment to Harriet Smith would have nothing to	E	III	9	388	13
she might feel of brighter hope, she betrayed nothing.	E	III	9	388	14
At present, there was nothing to be done for Harriet; good	E	III	9	388	15
alarming symptoms, nothing touching the pulmonary	E	III	9	389	16
your honour, that it has nothing to do with any of them?	E	III	10	393	14
for at least these three months, cared nothing about him.	E	III	10	396	41
"He knew nothing about it, Emma.	E	III	10	397	51
She was afraid she had done her nothing but disservice.--	E	III	11	402	1
and Harriet had done nothing to forfeit the regard and	E	III	11	408	33
she had not quite done nothing--for she had done mischief.	E	III	11	413	47
no disparity, affording nothing to be said or thought.--	E	III	11	413	48
She had no hope, nothing to deserve the name of hope, that	E	III	12	416	1
Wish it she must, for his sake--be the consequence nothing	E	III	12	416	1
Nothing should separate her from her father.	E	III	12	416	1
A cold stormy rain set in, and nothing of July appeared	E	III	12	421	18
For a moment or two nothing was said, and she was	E	III	13	425	12
					13
I thought them a habit, a trick, nothing that called for	E	III	13	427	19
She could really say nothing.--	E	III	13	430	35
You hear nothing but truth from me.--	E	III	13	430	37
her own--that Harriet was nothing; that she was every	E	III	13	430	38
Emma Woodhouse, I could deserve nothing from either.	E	III	14	439	8
Now, however, I see nothing in it but a very natural and	E	III	14	441	8
He knows he is wrong, and has nothing rational to urge.--	E	III	15	445	11
"Say nothing, my dear Emma, while you oblige me to read--	E	III	15	447	26
Mr. Knightley himself would be doing nothing to assist the	E	III	15	450	38
but she would have nothing to do with it at present.--	E	III	16	452	6
No; she heard nothing but the instant reply of, "beg her	E	III	16	452	8
heat he was suffering, and the walk he had had for nothing.	E	III	16	457	37
The housekeeper declared she knew nothing of my being	E	III	16	458	40
I have nothing to do with William's wants, but it really	E	III	16	458	43
"Oh! as to all that, of course nothing can be thought of	E	III	16	460	53
"Nothing can be actually settled yet, perhaps," replied	E	III	16	460	54
over, I imagine there will be nothing more to wait for."	E	III	16	460	56
"Nothing very bad.--	E	III	17	461	5
But here there was nothing to be shifted off in a wild	E	III	17	468	31
of it was very soon nothing; and by the end of an hour he	E	III	17	468	33
"Does nothing occur to you?--	E	III	18	470	8
"No, I have not; I know nothing; pray tell me."	E	III	18	470	11
there was no obscurity, nothing doubtful, in the words he	E	III	18	474	30
and reflected, she could be fit for nothing rational.	E	III	18	475	37
Nothing, but to grow more worthy of him, whose intentions	E	III	18	475	39
Nothing, but that the lessons of her past folly might	E	III	18	475	39
nothing else, though pretending to listen to the others?"	E	III	18	480	77
his own); there could be nothing in them now that she was	P	III	1	6	10
spend less; he had done nothing but what Sir Walter Elliot	P	III	1	9	19
Elizabeth had nothing to propose of deeper efficacy.	P	III	1	10	19
There will be nothing singular in his case; and it is	P	III	2	12	4
that nothing would be done without a change of abode.--	P	III	2	13	7
than outward attention, nothing beyond the observances of	P	III	2	16	16
been nothing to her but the object of distant civility.	P	III	2	16	16
had driven her over, nothing being of so much use to Mrs.	P	III	3	18	7
hairs of a side, and nothing but a dab of powder at top.--	P	III	3	19	16
quite unconnected; nothing to do with the Strafford family.	P	III	3	23	33
appear as if they ranked nothing beyond the happiness of	P	III	3	23	34
Nothing could be done without a reference to Elizabeth;	P	III	3	24	37
been enough, for he had nothing to do, and she had hardly	P	III	4	26	1
a professed resolution of doing nothing for his daughter.	P	III	4	26	2
with a young man, who had nothing but himself to recommend	P	III	4	26	3
freely, what had come freely, had realized nothing.	P	III	4	27	4
But in this case, Anne had left nothing for advice to do;	P	III	4	29	7
for an agreement, and saw nothing, therefore, but good	P	III	5	32	2
I was very well yesterday; nothing at all the matter with	P	III	5	39	37
"Nothing remarkable.	P	III	5	39	39
and envied them nothing but that seemingly perfect good	P	III	5	41	45
Nothing seemed amiss on the side of the great house family,	P	III	5	41	46
As it was, he did nothing with much zeal, but sport; and	P	III	6	43	5
she had said nothing which might not do for either brother.	P	III	6	49	22
him "poor Richard," been nothing better than a thick-	P	III	6	51	29
but Mr. Robinson found nothing to increase alarm, and	P	III	7	55	7
"Nothing can be going on better than the child," said he, "	P	III	7	55	8
She said nothing, therefore, till he was out of the room,	P	III	7	56	9
					10
I dare say we shall have nothing to distress us.	P	III	7	56	11
matter; but I dare say there will be nothing to alarm you.	P	III	7	57	16
feelings eight years may be little more than nothing.	P	III	7	60	29
Now nothing!	P	III	8	63	3
nothing superior to the accommodations of a man of war.	P	III	8	69	37
"Nothing to the purpose," replied her brother.	P	III	8	69	38
pursued Mrs. Croft, "that nothing can exceed the	P	III	8	70	54
While we were together, you know, there was nothing to be	P	III	8	70	54
as we could be together, nothing ever ailed me, and I	P	III	8	71	54
"There is nothing so bad as a separation.	P	III	8	71	55
and desired nothing in return but to be unobserved.	P	III	8	71	56
occupied by him, that nothing but the continued appearance	P	III	8	71	57
Nothing but a country curate.	P	III	9	76	13
past hope, and leave him nothing to do but to keep away	P	III	9	77	19
There being nothing to be eat, he could only have some	P	III	9	79	29
nothing of it--she would as lieve be tossed out as not."	P	III	10	84	8
would be always with him, nothing should ever separate us,	P	III	10	85	9
better somewhere,--and nothing could prevent her from	P	III	10	86	21
for Captain Wentworth; nothing could be plainer; and where	P	III	10	90	37
strength apace, and she had nothing else to stay for.	P	III	11	93	4
left--and, as there is nothing to admire in the buildings	P	III	11	95	9
same good feelings; and nothing could be more pleasant	P	III	11	97	15
on it--(they never got beyond) was become a mere nothing.	P	III	11	99	21
At first, they were capable of nothing more to the purpose	P	III	12	113	57

58
of Anne;--Anne, who was nothing to Louisa, while she was P III 12 115 65
"She really left nothing for Mary to do. P IV 1 121 2
was, that Mrs. Harville left nothing for any body to do." P IV 1 121 2
all she had gone through, nothing was so likely to do her P IV 2 134 30
long in the country, nothing could be so good for her as a P IV 2 135 33
having cards left by people of whom they knew nothing. P IV 3 138 4
in his change; should see nothing to regret in the duties P IV 3 138 5
In a worldly view, he had nothing to gain by being on P IV 3 140 11
with Sir Walter, nothing to risk by a state of variance. P IV 3 140 11
She is nothing to me, compared with you;" and she was in P IV 4 145 1
As yet, you have seen nothing of Bath. P IV 4 145 1
"No, nothing." P IV 4 145 3
"No, nothing at all." P IV 4 146 3
Lady Russell should see nothing suspicious or inconsistent, P IV 4 147 7
or inconsistent, nothing to require more motives than P IV 4 147 7
She could determine nothing at present. P IV 4 147 8
of the agitation they created, but they were nothing. P IV 4 149 14
he agreed to their being nothing in themselves, but still P IV 4 150 15
She mentioned nothing of what she had heard, or what she P IV 5 153 5
education in the world," know nothing worth attending to. P IV 5 155 9
will have nothing to report but of lace and finery.-- P IV 5 156 13
"She sees nothing to blame in it," replied Anne; "on the P IV 5 157 18
her young friend, for she saw nothing to excite distrust. P IV 5 161 30
"We see nothing of them, and this is really an instance of P IV 6 164 7
"Mrs. Musgrove protests solemnly that she knew nothing of " P IV 6 165 8
another man, there was nothing in the engagement to excite P IV 6 167 21
lost no friend by it, certainly nothing to be regretted. P IV 6 167 21
We have seen nothing of him since November. P IV 6 171 33
Admiral, I hope there is nothing in the style of Captain P IV 6 172 42
But what I mean is, that I hope there is nothing in P IV 6 172 46
But there is nothing at all of that nature in the letter. P IV 6 173 47
and there is nothing very unforgiving in that, I think." P IV 6 173 47
For a few minutes she saw nothing before her. P IV 7 175 5
Nothing that I regard." P IV 7 177 13
the rain would come to nothing at present, and adding, "I P IV 7 177 15
to listen to him, though nothing could exceed his P IV 7 178 24
sick of knowing nothing, and fancying herself stronger P IV 7 180 32
support to Anne; she knew nothing of their looks, and felt P IV 8 181 1
was yet better than nothing, and her spirits improved. P IV 8 181 2
has been all suffering, nothing but suffering--which was P IV 8 184 16
Dalrymple before her, had nothing to wish for which did P IV 8 185 20
Anne saw nothing, thought nothing of the brilliancy of the P IV 8 185 21
and her cheeks glowed,--but she knew nothing about it. P IV 8 185 21
I see you know nothing of the matter. P IV 8 186 26
"No!" he replied impressively, "there is nothing worth my P IV 8 190 50
large party in yourselves, and you wanted nothing beyond." P IV 9 193 12
She could say nothing. P IV 9 194 17
Anne heard nothing of this. P IV 9 194 19
I assure you that nothing of the sort you are thinking of P IV 9 195 28
I am sure you hear nothing but good of him from Colonel P IV 9 196 30
of him, Mrs. Smith, convince you that he is nothing to me? P IV 9 196 33
And, upon my word, he is nothing to me. P IV 9 196 33
the semblance of seeing nothing beyond; and Anne, eager to P IV 9 197 34
Mrs. Smith said nothing. P IV 9 198 42
But not now: no, I thank you, I have nothing to trouble P IV 9 198 44
that she had gained nothing but an increase of curiosity. P IV 9 198 52
preserving, though there may be nothing durable beneath. P IV 9 198 53
I saw nothing reprehensible in what Mr. Elliot was doing. P IV 9 201 64
grandfather had been a butcher, but that was all nothing. P IV 9 202 66
"You have asserted nothing contradictory to what Mr. P IV 9 202 67
that; it takes a bend or two, but nothing of consequence. P IV 9 204 82
Having long had as much money as he could spend, nothing P IV 9 206 90
"Yes," said Anne, "you tell me nothing which does not P IV 9 207 91
but I have heard nothing which really surprises me. P IV 9 207 91
Mr. Elliot would do nothing, and she could do nothing P IV 9 210 98
"My dear," was Mrs. Smith's reply, "there was nothing else P .IV 9 211 101
"Very well," said Elizabeth, "I have nothing to send but P IV 10 215 15
Nothing ever happened on either side that was not P IV 10 224 47
The usual character of them has nothing for me. P IV 10 225 58
The past was nothing. P IV 10 226 64
her speech, "there is nothing I so abominate for young P IV 11 230 8
but Anne heard nothing distinctly; it was only a buzz of P IV 11 231 11
It was nothing more than that his pen had fallen down, but P IV 11 233 24
(smiling at Anne) "well supplied, and want for nothing.-- P IV 11 234 27
of her situation, could do nothing towards tranquillity. P IV 11 238 44
whether to join or to pass on, said nothing--only looked. P IV 11 239 55
Of what he had then written, nothing was to be retracted P IV 11 241 61
She cared not for Mrs. Clay, and had nothing to blush for P IV 11 246 78
in human nature, nothing to reproach myself with; and if I P IV 11 246 80
Sir Walter made no objection, and Elizabeth did nothing P IV 12 248 1
There was nothing less for Lady Russell to do, than to P IV 12 249 3
The disproportion in their fortune was nothing; it did not P IV 12 251 10
estimate him properly; nothing of respectability, of P IV 12 251 10
their master--to say nothing of all the rest of the field, S 1 364 1
the poor good for nothing--as I dare say you find, sir." S 1 368 1
sea weed, can end in nothing but their own disappointment. S 1 369 1
to bring a prodigious influx;--nothing else was wanting. S 2 372 1
asked his advice, & that nothing should ever induce him (S 2 374 1
though she had got nothing but her title from the family, S 3 375 1
from the family, still she had given nothing for it."-- S 3 375 1
the wind meeting with nothing to oppose or confine it S 4 381 1
down in this Gutter--nothing is known of the state of the S 4 381 1
the beach, he had done nothing there--but it was a most S 4 383 1
If indeed a simple sprain, as you denominate it, nothing S 5 386 1
that they can do nothing for us & that we must trust to S 5 .386 1
I have heard nothing of Sidney since your being together S 5 387 1
I by myself, can see nothing in it but what is either very S 5 387 1
season, were followed by nothing better than--Mrs Mathews-- S 6 389 1
She cd see nothing worse in Lady Denham, than the sort of S 6 392 1
Had he written nothing more, he wd have been Immortal. S 7 397 1
gravely answered "I really know nothing of the matter.-- S 7 398 1
Charlotte cd think of nothing more harmless to be said, S 7 399 1
even to affect simpathy, that she cd say nothing.-- S 7 401 1
Emanations which detail nothing but discordant principles S 8 403 1
Alembic;--we distil nothing which can add to science.-- S 8 403 1
to say that he read nothing else, or that his language S 8 404 1
Nothing cd be kinder than her reception from both husband S 9 406 1
Nothing else to be done.-- S 9 407 1
present I shall want nothing; I never eat for about a week S 9 411 1
There was nothing dubious in her manner of declining it, S 10 415 1
was all done, she heard nothing of his voice but the S 10 416 1
nothing really incredible--and so it was settled.-- S 10 419 1
A long journey from Hampshire taken for nothing--a brother S 11 420 1
the Balcony, or look at nothing through a Telescope, S 11 422 1
who wd have been nothing at Brighton, could not move here S 11 422 1
a more early hour, that nothing might be neglected of S 12 423 1
Nothing can be more simple. S 12 423 1
nothing to do but to step back again, & say not a word.-- S 12 426 1
She was glad to perceive that nothing had been discerned S 12 426 1

NOTHING-MEANING (2)
is so cold and nothing-meaning--so entirely without warmth MP II 4 211 23
give one, beyond the nothing-meaning terms of being " E II 14 270 3

NOTHING-SAYING (1)
after a period of nothing-saying amongst the party, some P IV 8 188 44

NOTHINGNESS (3)
The insipidity and yet the noise; the nothingness and yet PP I 6 27 47
the prosperity and the nothingness, of her scene of life-- P III 1 9 18
art of knowing our own nothingness beyond our own circle, P III 6 42 1

NOTHINGS (3)
In pompous nothings on his side, and civil assents on that PP I 15 72 7
quick succession of busy nothings till the carriage came MP I 10 104 52
in saying the proper nothings, she began to give the P IV 10 226 64

NOTICE (169)
a little notice in order to detach him from Miss Manwaring. LS 2 244 1
no dissimulation worthy notice, & Miss Vernon shall be LS 4 248 2
My dear Alicia You are very good taking notice of LS 7 252 1
"Men commonly take so little notice of those things," said NA I 3 28 39
The men take notice of that sometimes you know." NA I 6 42 25
challenging his notice; and to her his devoirs were NA I 7 44 4
notice, that she looked back at them only three times. NA· I 7 47 18
gave her very little share in the notice of either. NA I 10 71 8
Nobody can fasten themselves on the notice of one, without NA I 10 76 29
Confused by his notice, and blushing from the fear of its NA I 10 80 59
down the street, when her notice was claimed by the NA I 11 84 17
for a play; his notice was never withdrawn from the stage NA I 12 92 4
thus to expose her feelings to the notice of others? NA I 13 98 3
he trusted, when longer notice could be given, they would NA I 13 103 28
such happy importance, as engaged all her friend's notice. NA I 15 117 4
fixing her eye on him as she spoke, soon caught his notice. NA II 3 147 21
share with James in her notice and smiles, the alteration NA II 4 149 1
unawares, without giving any notice, as generally happens." NA II 5 158 14
Abbey not unworthy her notice--and was proceeding to NA II 5 162 27
conspicuous enough, had never caught her notice before. NA II 6 168 10
itself on Catherine's notice when they were seated at NA II 7 175 12
Morland already seen all that could be worth her notice?-- NA II 8 185 6
of something worth her notice; and felt, as she NA II 8 185 5
his figure so repeatedly, as to catch Miss Tilney's notice. NA II 8 187 13
here, you will give me notice of it, that I may go away." NA II 10 204 15
Davis: I pitied his taste, but took no notice of him. NA II 12 217 2
My father and mother's having no notice of it is of very NA II 13 224 17
looks soon caught her notice, before any inquiry so direct NA II 14 233 9
without sending any notice of her intention to her mother- SS I 1 5 9
with so much composure, she seemed scarcely to notice it. SS I 3 18 18
good word and nobody's notice; who has more money than he SS I 10 51 25
And now after only ten minutes notice--gone too without SS I 15 77 23
Elinor took no notice of this, and directing her attention SS I 16 89 42
and affecting to take no notice of what passed, by SS I 18 98 13
Mr. Palmer took no notice of her. SS I 20 113 36
beauty, courting their notice, and humouring all their SS I 21 120 6
But her curiosity was unavailing, for no farther notice SS I 21 126 41
Perhaps you might notice the ring when you saw him?" SS I 22 135 54
to engage Mrs. Jennings's notice entirely to herself. SS II 7 181 6
her fear it impossible to escape Mrs. Jennings's notice. SS II 7 181 7
"You had better leave me," was all the notice that her SS II 8 197 24
not receive the first notice of it from the public papers, SS II 10 217 16
broad stares; a kind of notice which served to imprint on SS II 11 220 3
Whereas, in my opinion, by her taking so much notice of SS II 11 227 46
by no means unworthy her notice; and as for Lady Middleton, SS II 12 229 1
Their claims to the notice of Mrs. John Dashwood, as the SS II 12 231 9
never after had took any notice of me, and never looked at SS II 13 240 17
Edward was the first to speak, and it was to notice SS II 13 242 25
Edward is dismissed for ever from his mother's notice. SS III 1 268 48
and as since that time no notice had been taken by them of SS III 5 293 3
on the concern of every body, and the notice of herself. SS III 6 305 17
upon my notice, requires a very particular excuse.-- SS III 8 318 21
22
myself from her farther notice; and for some time I was SS III 8 326 53
from their notice, sat earnestly gazing through the window. SS III 10 342 7
her in time the haughty notice which overcame her by its SS III 14 377 11
Perhaps Tom Musgrave may take notice of you--but I would W 315 1
I defy you not to be delighted with him if he takes notice W 319 2
"You will take notice who Mary Edwards dances with."-- W 320 2
called general notice, & "the Osbornes are coming, the W 329 9
than Mrs B. calling her notice by a friendly touch, said " W 333 13
No notice was taken. W 340 18
his coming was a sort of notice which might please her W 347 22
His doing so drew her notice. PP I 6 24 13
She had very little notice from any but him. PP I 8 35 2
Her dirty petticoat quite escaped my notice." "you PP I 8 36 7
last, that she drew his notice because there was a PP I 10 51 46
of horses drew their notice, and Darcy and Bingley were PP I 15 72 8
to the young ladies who introduced him to her notice. PP I 15 73 11
With such rivals for the notice of the fair, as Mr. PP I 16 76 5
to her notice, but he certainly has not known her long." PP I 16 83 52
her cousin, and to point him out to her particular notice. PP I 18 90 4
there should be any notice on either side, and that if it PP I 18 97 60
had escaped his notice, and that his feelings were not of PP I 18 101 72
of Mr. Darcy's farther notice; though often standing PP I 18 102 74
that I do not reckon the notice and kindness of Lady PP I 19 106 10
He was anxious to avoid the notice of his cousins, from a PP I 22 121 1
me for giving her no notice of my coming to London. PP II 3 147 23
with some portion of her notice when service is over. PP II 5 157 7
summer he was again most painfully obtruded on my notice. PP II 12 201 5
arise from the public notice of Lydia's unguarded and PP II 18 231 16
The officers will find women better worth their notice. PP II 18 232 20
round the room, took notice of some little alteration in PP III 9 315 4
him from the frequent notice of either, and was ever PP III 18 384 27
shy, and shrinking from notice; but her air, though MP I 2 12 2
half an hour's notice, whenever she was weary of the place. MP I 4 41 16
The notice which she excited herself, was to this effect. MP I 5 48 30
notice, only asked her if she had not seen Mr. Rushworth. MP I 10 101 29
and the warmth which might excite general notice. MP I 12 115 4
and when from taking notice of her work and wishing she MP I 15 147 57
To be called into notice in such a manner, to hear that it MP I 16 150 1
it escaped the notice of many of her own family likewise. MP I 17 162 19
and as soon as she could notice this, and see that, in MP II 1 175 2
from notice herself, saw all that was passing before her. MP II 1 185 27
attend you from any place in England, at an hour's notice." MP II 2 193 12
soon called his notice from her, and the farewell visit, MP II 2 193 18
of notice and praise as other women were of neglect. MP II 3 198 13
us to take a little notice of you, or else it would never MP II 5 220 28
You do not seem properly aware of her claims to notice. MP II 6 229 5
You see her every day, and therefore do not notice it, but MP II 6 229 5
in company for you to notice, and you must have a somebody. MP II 6 230 6
for the shortness of the notice, to collect young people MP II 8 253 7
The very gown you have been taking notice of, is your own MP II 10 272 3
could be safe from the notice of her aunt Norris, who was MP II 10 272 4
you will excuse my begging you to take no further notice. MP II 13 307 31
had fallen within their notice, giving instances of MP III 3 339 22
love him (you having due notice of his intentions), must MP III 4 347 21
because he was taking, what seemed, very idle notice of me. MP III 4 353 45
was all the voluntary notice which this brother bestowed;-- MP III 7 377 8
her tears, was able to notice and admire all the striking MP III 7 384 35
kind and proper in the notice he took of Susan. MP III 10 406 21
I am at your service and Henry's, at an hour's notice. MP III 12 416 3
they had received notice by express, a few hours before. MP III 13 426 9
no notice, no message from the uncle on whom all depended. MP III 14 430 6
being merely to give her notice that they should be in MP III 15 437 2
that quarter to draw the notice of the world, and to MP III 15 438 4
She had not spirits to notice her in more than a few MP III 16 448 3
insult to the neighbourhood, as to expect it to notice her. MP III 17 465 13
She would notice her; she would improve her; she would E I 3 23 10
as much above my notice as in every other he is below it." E I 4 29 14
that he might marry any body at all fit for you to notice. E I 4 30 22
happy countenance on her notice, and solicitously E I 14 118 4
do, to entertain away his notice of the lateness of the E I 15 124 1
him to notice but his situation and his civility.-- E I 16 136 9
did return, he sought out the child and took notice of her. E II 2 163 4
directly, and took no notice; and they both went to quite E II 3 178 52
by distinguishing notice; the history which he had to give E II 4 181 4
"But they would have done better had they given her notice E II 8 228 92
Short had been the notice--short their meeting; he was E II 12 261 37
And now to chuse the mortification of Mrs. Elton's notice E II 15 285 13

notice; indeed, indeed, we must begin inquiring directly." E II 17 300 12
I fancy I am rather a favourite; he took notice of my gown. E II 17 302 22
We have notice of it in a letter to-day. E II 18 305 5
hurry, merely to give us notice--it tells us that they are E II 18 305 7
I give you notice----- E II 18 306 12
I give you notice that as I find your son, so I shall E II 18 309 31
Mrs. Elton was wanting notice, which nobody had E II 18 311 36
Hartfield, James had due notice, and he sanguinely hoped E III 1 318 13
to Mrs. Goddard, and notice of there being such a set of E III 3 334 8
Mrs. Elton had received notice of it that morning, and was E III 6 359 37
out for them to give notice of the carriages was a joyful E III 7 374 54
up from a period when her notice was an honour, to have E III 7 375 61
have had longer notice of it, would have been pleasanter.-- E III 9 386 8
little particulars of the notice she had received from him, E III 11 409 35
I am amused by one part of John's letter--did you notice E III 17 465 25
of the world from the notice and curiosity of the other,-- P III 3 17 4
You must have heard him notice Mrs. Clay's freckles." P III 5 35 14
world, but I know it is taken notice of by many persons." P III 6 46 10
her musical powers to the notice of Mr. and Mrs. Musgrove P III 6 47 15
by his good-humoured notice of her little boys, she was P III 6 48 17
I am come on to give you notice, that papa and mamma are P III 6 50 27
recollected it, proper notice to the other house, which P III 7 53 3
"Well--if you do not think it too late to give notice for P III 7 57 15
You can send for us, you know, at a moment's notice, if P III 7 57 16
not be satisfied without his running on to give notice. P III 7 59 24
She took hardly any notice of Charles Hayter yesterday. P III 9 77 16
Louisa certainly put more forward for his notice than her P III 10 84 7
veranda, or even notice through the misty glasses the last P IV 1 123 8
So, I give you notice, Lady Russell." P IV 2 131 12
every proof of cousinly notice, and placing his whole P IV 3 139 10
to give me any notice, or offer to take "any thing. P IV 6 164 7
as well as address him before she could catch his notice. P IV 6 169 25
eager to escape farther notice, was impatient to know why P IV 9 197 34
disposed to take very kind and proper notice of him. P IV 9 200 58
the better half, of the pair)--not unworthy notice.-- S 7 394 1
of one who felt that any notice from her was an honour, & S 7 399 1
I wd not have you think that I only notice them, for poor S 7 399 1
young ladies under her care, to Miss D. P.'s notice.-- S 10 419 1
not move here without notice;--and even Mr Arthur Parker, S 11 422 1
The rest was common enquiries & remarks, with kind notice S 12 425 1

NOTICED (23)
in the events of the evening, to be noticed and admired. NA I 2 23 27
His attentions were such as a child must have noticed. NA II 3 144 10
to Elinor, when it ceased to be noticed by them. SS I 10 49 12
declared that he noticed only what was amiable in it, the SS II 12 236 38
It was a partnership which cd not be noticed without W 331 11
I have lived here 14 years without being noticed by any of W 348 22
without seeming to have noticed what passed, took leave PP I 15 73 9
Elizabeth noticed every sentence conveying the idea of PP II 11 188 1
By Mrs. Hurst and Miss Bingley, they were noticed only by PP III 3 267 4
Could he expect to be noticed again by the regiment, after PP III 5 282 1
that she should be noticed on her marriage by her parents, PP III 8 314 22
that he had been received and noticed as he was. PP III 10 324 2
for do not expect to be noticed by his family or friends, PP III 14 355 45
could not be greater than mine in being noticed by you. PP III 16 370 31
Miss Augusta ought not to have been noticed for the next MP I 5 51 40
which she occasionally noticed in some of the others, and MP I 12 116 11
that Lady Prescott had noticed in Fanny; she was not sure MP II 11 283 4
noticed her, but to make her the object of a coarse joke. MP III 8 389 3
she had voluntarily noticed her father's gentleness with E I 4 32 27
of being longer noticed by the family, as Sir Walter P III 1 8 16
when they sat down to dinner, was noticed as an advantage. P IV 3 137 2
is going on; always the last of my family to be "noticed. P IV 6 163 7
having noticed & caressed them all,--she prepared to go.-- S 9 410 1

NOTICING (11)
walked about together, noticing every new face, and almost NA I 10 71 8
luckily no leisure for noticing her; but to the other two NA II 10 203 8
which prevented her from noticing any thing before her, NA II 14 231 5
at her eyes; and without noticing them ran up stairs. SS I 15 75 2
Elizabeth disdained the appearance of noticing this civil PP II 11 191 16
size, and abashed her by noticing her shyness; Miss Lee MP I 2 14 8
Edmund could not help noticing their apparently deep MP III 3 336 8
her father was fondly noticing the beauty of her dress, to E II 8 213 6
and on her laughing and noticing it, he owned that he E II 8 221 49
However, my resolution is taken as to noticing Jane E II 15 284 9
at her instantly in a way which shewed his noticing of it. P III 12 104 6

NOTIFICATION (1)
The promised notification was hanging over her head. MP III 9 398 10

NOTION (41)
I had not a notion of her being such a little devil before; LS 16 268 1
I have communicated a notion that has recently struck me, LS 18 272 1
in the pencil--she had no notion of drawing--not enough NA I 1 16 10
that she entertained no notion of their general NA I 2 18 2
I have no notion of loving people by halves, it is not my NA I 6 40 14
I have no notion of treating men with such respect. NA I 6 43 43
But this will just give you a notion of the general rate NA I 9 64 24
"Yes, it does give a notion," said Catherine, warmly, "and NA I 9 64 25
Upon recollection, however, I have a notion they are both NA I 9 68 48
I say it is no bad notion." NA I 15 122 30
But I have a notion, Miss Morland, you and I think pretty NA I 15 124 44
My notion of things is simple enough. NA I 15 124 46
Eleanor had wished to spare her form so painful a notion, NA II 13 226 25
I have a notion you danced with him, but am not quite sure. NA II 14 238 26
I have erred against every common-place notion of decorum; SS I 10 48 5
likely, for I have a notion she is always rather sickly. SS I 14 70 2
"I have a notion," said Lucy, "you think the little SS I 21 122 19
"I have a notion," said Sir John, "that Miss Marianne SS II 3 154 3
I have no notion of men's going on in this way: and if SS II 8 192 3
I am sure if I had had a notion of it, I would not have SS II 8 195 16
though she had not any notion of what was principally SS II 12 235 34, 35
I have no notion of people's making such a to-do about SS III 1 259 7
tried to drive away the notion of its being possible to SS III 1 260 9
But as it was, such a notion had scarcely ever entered her SS III 6 305 16
Poor creature! she is possessed with the notion of Tom W 319 2
he was struck with the notion of doing a very gallant PP I 6 26 37, 38
for her brother, from the notion that when there has been PP I 21 119 20
notion of me, and teach you not to believe a word I say. PP II 8 174 15
She has a very good notion of fingering, though her taste PP II 8 176 28
and more civil, than she had any notion of finding her. PP III 1 246 5
pleased herself with the notion that as he looked at her, PP III 2 262 8
"That is his notion of christian forgiveness! PP III 15 364 22
I had no notion but he would go a shooting, or something PP III 17 374 20
know a great deal that she has not the least notion of yet. MP I 2 18 25
of conduct, such a high notion of honour, and such an MP II 12 294 16
With this inspiriting notion, her questions increased in E I 4 28 6
"I had no notion that he liked me so very much," said E I 7 52 18
One takes up a notion, and runs away with it. Mr. Dixon, E II 3 176 46
I have a very strong notion that it comes from him. E II 8 226 83
I have some notion of putting such a trimming as this to E II 17 302 22
am sure you have, somehow or other, imbibed such a notion. P IV 9 195 25

NOTIONS (36)
as were her general notions of what men ought to be, she NA I 9 66 32
thence infer, that your notions of the duties of the NA I 10 77 37
very few notions she had entertained on the matter before. NA I 14 110 28
You know I carry my notions of friendship pretty high. NA II 3 146 20
that at once answered her notions of comfort and ease, and SS I 3 14 1
subjection of reason to common-place and mistaken notions. SS I 11 53 2
The purity of her life, the formality of her notions, her SS III 8 323 40
all his strictest notions of what was due to seniority; PP I 15 70 3
While these newly-born notions were passing in their heads, PP III 2 260 1
With his notions of dignity he would probably feel that PP III 15 361 2
and delicacy of your notions, which indeed are quite of a MP I 1 6 6
Maria's notions on the subject were more confused and MP I 5 44 2
They are given wrong notions from the beginning. MP I 5 50 38
She cannot have given her right notions of what was due to MP I 7 64 8
young man, with better notions than his elocution would do MP II 1 186 35
for adhering to his own notions and acting on them in MP II 11 286 15
all her high and worldly notions of matrimony, would be MP II 13 306 26
and regulating her notions, his worth would be finally MP III 6 367 5
her advantage the juster notions of what was due to every MP III 9 396 6
knowledge, so many good notions, should have been hers at MP III 9 397 8
inclinations and doubtful notions of right; there was no MP III 14 436 15
than would suit your notions of man's perfection. E I 18 148 23
the world in some of his notions, less of the spoiled E II 6 203 42
nothing wrong in his notions, a great deal decidedly right; E II 7 205 2
familiar; that all her notions were drawn from one set of E II 14 272 16
Who had been at pains to give Harriet notions of self- E III 11 414 50
girl, with very good notions, very seriously good E III 18 474 34
conduct, strict in her notions of decorum, and with P III 2 11 2
they have very liberal notions, and are as likely to make P III 3 17 4
the gentleman in all this notions and behaviour;--not P III 3 22 23
He is so very strict and scrupulous in his notions; over- P III 12 103 2
who can give occasion to such directly opposite notions. P IV 2 132 20
"The notions of a young man of one or two and twenty," P IV 3 144 20
have given me other notions; but, at that period, I must P IV 9 201 64
"Old fashioned notions--country hospitality--we do not P IV 10 219 29
very steady man in the main, & has got very good notions." S 7 400 1

NOTORIETY (1)
Every body of any consequence or notoriety in Bath was P IV 9 193 5

NOTORIOUS (1)
were so gross & notorious, that no one could be ignorant LS 12 260 2

NOUGHT (2)
of setting propriety at nought; and a better acquaintance SS I 11 56 13
set all their claims on his gratitude and regard at nought. E I 18 148 19

NOURISH (1)
folly it had helped to nourish and perfect, was the only NA II 11 212 16

NOURISHES (1)
Every thing nourishes what is strong already. PP I 9 44 34

NOURISHING (1)
Perry recommended nourishing food; but every thing they E III 9 391 19

NOURISHMENT (4)
unwilling to take any nourishment; giving pain every SS I 16 83 1
and this nourishment of grief was every day applied. SS I 16 83 3
a still-born son, nov. 5, 1789; mary, born nov. 20, 1791." P III 1 3 1
but such as called for warm rooms & good nourishment.-- S 10 418 1

NOV. 20, 1791 (1)
a still-born son, nov. 5, 1789; mary, born nov. 20, 1791." P III 1 3 1

NOVEL (10)
custom so common with novel writers, of degrading by their NA I 5 37 4
novel, is sure to turn over its insipid pages with disgust. NA I 5 37 4
Alas! if the heroine of one novel be not patronized by the NA I 5 37 4
and over every new novel to talk in threadbare strains of NA I 5 37 4
"I am no novel reader--I seldom look into novels--do not NA I 5 37 4
I often read novels--it is really well for a novel."-- NA I 5 37 4
Oh! it is only a novel!" replies the young lady; while she NA I 5 38 4
not pleasure in a good novel, must be intolerably stupid. NA I 14 106 7
"I wish," said Margaret, striking out a novel thought, " SS I 17 92 18
& gave him probably the novel sensation of doubting his W 335 13

NOVEL-READER (1)
I am no indiscriminate Novel-Reader. S 8 403 1

NOVELIST (1)
the labour of the novelist, and of slighting the NA I 5 37 4

NOVELS (18)
and dirt, and shut themselves up, to read novels together. NA I 5 37 4
Yes, novels;--for I will not adopt that ungenerous and NA I 5 37 4
"I am no novel reader--I seldom look into novels--do not NA I 5 37 4
I often read novels--it is really well for a novel."-- NA I 5 37 4
before; but I suppose Mrs. Morland objects to novels." NA I 6 41 20
Oh, Lord! not I; I never read novels; I have something NA I 7 48 33
prevented her by saying, "novels are all so full of NA I 7 48 34
No, if I read any, it shall be Mrs. Radcliff's; her novels NA I 7 49 36
But you never read novels, I dare say?" NA I 14 106 4
But I really thought before, young men despised novels NA I 14 107 10
and begging pardon, protested that he never read novels.-- PP I 14 68 13
reading one of her own novels, for want of employment.-- S 6 389 1
sufficiently well-read in novels to supply her imagination S 6 391 1
But if you will describe the sort of novels which you do S 8 403 1
The novels which I approve are such as display human S 8 403 1
These are the novels which enlarge the Primitive S 8 404 1
Charlotte--our taste in novels is not at all the same." S 8 404 1
spot had read more sentimental novels than agreed with him. S 8 404 1

NOVELTIES (2)
and necessarily introduced alterations and novelties. MP I 3 23 1
No such importation of novelties could enrich their E III 6 352 1

NOVELTY (27)
as much by sense as novelty, gave Catherine a most NA I 15 119 19
it produced not one novelty of thought or expression, and SS II 1 143 10
girls in the room, there is a great deal in novelty. W 315 1
common voice, when the novelty of her own appearance were W 351 25
He was as much awake to the novelty of attention in that PP I 11 56 12
There was novelty in the scheme, and as, with such a PP II 4 151 1
when any dish on the table proved a novelty to them. PP II 6 163 14
morning with Elizabeth in pursuit of novelty and amusement. PP II 19 239 11
It may be easily believed, that however little of novelty PP III 5 285 19
to reconcile Fanny to the novelty of Mansfield Park, and MP I 2 14 6
as to make almost any novelty a certain good, had likewise MP I 13 123 6
taste, as were exactly adapted to the novelty of acting. MP I 13 123 6
The novelty was in their being lively.-- MP II 3 197 4
When the novelty of amusement there were over, it would be MP II 3 203 31
was quite as eager for novelty and pleasure as Maria, MP II 3 204 32
in other eyes, it had novelty and importance in her's, for MP II 5 219 27
circumstances of less novelty, less interest, less MP II 9 266 22
unexpected, and the novelty of a situation which her fancy MP III 2 326 3
habit had most power, and novelty least; and that the very MP III 4 354 46
of the novelty of Crawford's addresses was against him. MP III 4 354 46
The novelty of travelling, and the happiness of being with MP III 7 375 1
of welcoming that perfect novelty which had been so long E II 2 166 10
escape being benefited by novelty and variety, by the E III 14 435 4
rupture.) or in any novelty or enlargement of society.-- P III 4 28 7
So much novelty and beauty! P IV 8 184 16
will be much better--that will be a novelty and a treat. P IV 10 220 29
A little novelty has a great effect in so small a place; S 11 422 1

NOVEMBER (29)
When Lucy first came to Barton-Park last November, she SS III 1 262 16
you all quitted Netherfield last November, Mr. Darcy! PP II 9 177 3, 4
We have not met since the 26th of November, when we were PP III 2 262 8
a certain event of last November, for had it been PP III 6 297 11
he went to town last November, he really loved me, and PP III 13 350 49
November was the black month fixed for his return. MP I 11 107 2
of being with his beloved family again early in November. MP I 11 107 2
It would hardly be early in November, there were generally MP I 11 107 3
It would probably be the middle of November at least; the MP I 11 107 3
at least; the middle of November was three months off. MP I 11 107 3
He is thinking of November." MP I 11 108 4
Sir Thomas was to return in November, and his eldest son MP I 12 114 1
the country; and November is a still more serious month, MP II 3 199 15
very early in November removed herself, her maid, her MP II 3 202 28
dirt of a November day, most acceptable to Mary Crawford. MP II 4 205 2
We may sometimes take greater liberties in November than MP II 4 212 29
has staid a year, for that will not be up till November. MP III 7 385 39
many a long October and November evening must be struggled E I 1 7 9

not so heavy as he has very often known them in November. E I 12 102 34
long ago as the 7th of November, (as I am going to read to E II 1 161 29
were also in town; and they were only waiting for November. E III 19 483 7
in London again by the end of the first week in November. E III 19 484 10
It was a very fine November day, and the Miss Musgroves P III 10 83 4
and happy in her November of life, she will cherish all P III 10 88 26
from Uppercross; though November, the weather was by no P III 11 94 7
a day in the middle of November would not leave much time P III 11 94 8
as these, on a dark November day, a small thick rain P IV 1 123 8
passed through Bath in November, in his way to London, P IV 3 138 6
We have seen nothing of him since November. P IV 6 171 33

NOVEMBER 18 (1)
your family, Monday, November 18th, by four o'clock, and PP I 13 63 12

NOVICIATE (1)
With the fortitude of a devoted noviciate, she had E II 2 165 8

NOW-A-DAYS (6)
will support a family now-a-days; and after all that NA II 3 146 16
But that won't do, now-a-days; nothing in the way of SS II 8 194 10
Not like the wild young men now-a-days, who think of PP III 1 249 38
one seldom meets with now-a-days, Mrs. Rushworth, that MP I 12 117 14
Luckily there is no distinction of dress now-a-days to MP III 12 416 2
were going to the devil now-a-days that way, that there MP III 15 440 17

NUISANCE (3)
They are seen only as a nuisance, swept hastily off, and SS I 16 88 31
of that terrible nuisance, I never saw a house of the kind MP II 7 243 27
or the yearly nuisance of its decaying vegetation.-- S 4 380 1

NUISANCES (1)
improvements in hand as the greatest of nuisances. MP I 6 57 31

NUMBER (55)
and legs enough for the number; but the Morlands had NA I 1 13 1
very performances, to the number of which they are NA I 5 37 4
herself perfect in the number; hastened away with eager NA I 12 91 3
than its spaciousness and the number of their attendants. NA II 6 165 6
The number of acres contained in this garden was such as NA II 7 178 21
The walls seemed countless in number, endless in length; a NA II 7 178 21
The number of servants continually appearing, did not NA II 8 184 4
did not strike her less than the number of their offices. NA II 8 184 4
the number of young dancing people in the neighbourhood. NA II 11 209 5
Her wisdom too limited the number of their servants to SS I 5 26 5
some addition to their number, but it was moonlight and SS I 7 33 4
two, to the number of inhabitants in London, was something. SS II 3 157 19
proportioned them to the number of her ideas; and of the SS II 12 232 15
could have guessed the number of her gowns altogether with SS II 14 249 8
giving the same number of days to such near relations." SS II 14 253 22
Mrs. Jennings and Elinor were of the number; but Marianne, SS III 2 271 4
from his chair Elinor told him the number of the house. SS III 4 290 40
41
I am really frightened out of my wits with the number of W 354 27
The girls grieved over such a number of ladies; but were PP I 3 10 4
remark on the size of the room, or the number of couples." PP I 18 91 9
He could number the fields in every direction, and could PP II 5 156 4
His principal object must be, to discover the number of PP III 5 293 69
impossible to find out the stand and number of the coach. PP III 5 293 69
and expense of one child entirely out of her great number. MP I 1 5 4
After dancing with each other at a proper number of balls, MP I 4 39 11
she could not mention the number of years that he had been MP I 6 60 47
were shewn through a number of rooms, all lofty, and many MP I 9 84 3
"Here are the greatest number of our plants, and here are MP I 9 90 33
To the greater number it was a moment of absolute horror. MP II 1 175 1
She has only to fix on her number of thousands a year, and MP II 4 213 39
the wide table or the number of dishes on it with patience, MP II 7 238 3
years ago, the larger number, to judge by their MP III 3 339 23
Edmund was not sorry to be admitted again among the number MP III 3 344 44
or settle the number of three deckers now in commission, MP III 10 403 13
questions increased in number and meaning; and she E I 4 28 6
number of nursery-maids, all reaching Hartfield in safety. E I 11 91 3
to her, "we want only two more to be just the right number. E I 14 119 6
7
It would hold the very number for comfort. E II 6 198 5
They added to their house, to their number of servants, to E II 7 207 6
that the number of privy counsellors was not yet larger. E III 2 320 6
had been hitherto the number of dancers, that how there E III 2 326 33
Pardon me--but you will be limited as to number--only E III 7 370 26
number of embarrassing recollections on each side. E III 18 476 46
favour; their age, and number, and fortune; the high idea P III 3 23 34
Such a number of women and children have no right to be P III 8 69 42
Such a number of looking-glasses! Oh Lord! there was no P IV 1 128 28
The worst of Bath was, the number of its plain women. P IV 3 141 13
but the number of the plain was out of all proportion. P IV 3 141 13
to calculate the number of weeks which would free him from P IV 5 159 22
I wish young ladies had not such a number of fine P IV 6 171 33
not recollect the exact number, and I have been trying to P IV 7 179 30
are trying to add to the number, are in my opinion S 1 369 1
present number of Visitants & the chances of a good season. S 6 392 1
And out of such a number, who knows but some may be S 6 393 1
to stagger her by the number of his quotations, & the S 7 396 1

NUMBERS (13)
besides of all the numbers resorting hither, except Sir LS 2 244 1
Among the increasing numbers of military men, one now made W 328 8
might be found among the numbers belonging to the park, MP I 4 36 7
of all possible numbers to sit down to table; and I cannot MP II 5 220 30
be early, as well as the numbers few; Mr. Woodhouse's E I 13 108 4
determined to call upon them and seek safety in numbers. E II 1 155 2
him, could not furnish numbers enough for such a meeting; E II 6 198 5
distance from the numbers round the instrument, to listen. E II 8 227 87
noise of numbers, was a circumstance to strike him deeply. E II 17 302 23
Such schemes as these are nothing without numbers. E III 6 353 4
no change in their numbers or their comforts but for the E III 17 466 29
the solitude and silence which only numbers could give. P III 10 89 35
me in the face at this very moment, numbers 3, 4 & 8. S 7 402 1

NUMEROUS (20)
Mrs. Allen was one of that numerous class of females, NA I 2 20 8
The wish of a numerous acquaintance in Bath was still NA I 3 25 1
in their stirrups, and numerous out-riders properly NA II 5 156 4
a narrower passage, more numerous openings, and symptoms NA II 8 185 5
They were, in fact, a necessitous family; numerous too NA II 15 246 12
If he should have a numerous family, for instance, it SS I 2 9 8
his private balls were numerous enough for any young lady SS I 7 32 2
and in spite of their numerous and long arranged SS II 2 151 43
The dinner was a grand one, the servants were numerous, SS II 12 233 18
your beaux will be so numerous as to prevent your feeling PP I 21 117 11
His former acquaintance had been numerous; but since he PP III 6 297 12
numerous words and louder tone convinced her of the truth. MP I 8 76 2
the hours would be too late, and the party too numerous. E II 7 208 9
at dinner, they were too numerous for any subject of E II 8 214 13
I should like to know how many of all my numerous E II 18 312 50
There was a numerous family; but the only two grown up, P III 5 40 45
business, too numerous for intimacy, too small for variety; P IV 11 245 78
Marrying early & having a very numerous family, their S 2 373 1
without distinction, but less numerous than he had hoped. S 6 389 1
& bewitching, in all the numerous vol:s they had left S 6 391 1

NUN (1)
some awful memorials of an injured and ill-fated nun. NA II 2 141 11

NUNCHEON (1)
since that time, procured me a nuncheon at Marlborough." SS III 8 318 20

NUPTIALS (3)
nuptials, fine muslins, new carriages, and servants. PP III 8 310 7
on her daughter's nuptials, than to any sense of shame at PP III 8 310 10
He begins with congratulations on the approaching nuptials PP III 15 362 14

NURSE (28)
To have you confined, a nurse in his apartment! LS 29 298 1
submit to the offices of a nurse, for the sake of the SS I 8 38 10
the world but the red-gum;' and nurse said just the same. SS III 1 257 5
her little boy and his nurse, for the house of a near SS III 7 308 3
the silence and quiet prescribed by every nurse around her. SS III 9 334 5
should I have left you, my nurse, my friend, my sister!-- SS III 10 346 28
instructress, and nurse, the despondence that sunk her MP I 2 14 8
supernumerary jellies to nurse a sick maid, there was MP II 11 283 4
nurse, and now felt a particular pleasure in seeing again. MP III 7 381 25
for those who had to nurse him; but now it is confidently MP III 14 433 13
She wanted me to nurse my cold by staying at home to-day, E I 15 125 5
Nobody could nurse her, as we should do." E II 1 161 29
be left at home by herself, to nurse our sick child." P III 7 58 19
Mrs. Harville was a very experienced nurse; and her P III 12 113 56
"You will stay, I am sure; you will stay and nurse her;" P III 12 114 63
especially of Mrs. Harville's exertions as a nurse. P IV 1 121 2
in being allowed to go and help nurse dear Miss Louisa. P IV 1 121 3
of having a regular nurse, and finances at that moment P IV 5 154 9
fortunate in her nurse, as a sister of her landlady, a P IV 5 154 9
sister of her landlady, a nurse by profession, and who had P IV 5 154 9
and nurse Rooke thoroughly understands when to speak. P IV 5 155 9
Call it gossip if you will; but when nurse Rooke has half P IV 5 155 9
"It was my friend, Mrs. Rooke--nurse Rooke, who, by the by, P IV 9 197 40
repeats it all to her nurse; and the nurse, knowing my P IV 9 205 82
all to her nurse; and the nurse, knowing my acquaintance P IV 9 205 82
Mrs. Wallis has an amusing idea, as nurse tells me, that P IV 9 208 92
but my sensible nurse Rooke sees the absurdity of it.-- P IV 9 208 92
And indeed, to own the truth, I do not think nurse in her P IV 9 208 92

NURSED (8)
At Bath, his old aunts would have nursed him, but here it LS 28 298 2
After being nursed up at Mansfield, it was too late in the MP III 11 413 30
how nursed her through the various illnesses of childhood. E I 1 6 6
own earnest wish of being nursed by Mrs. Goddard, Emma E I 13 108 5
that an old woman who had nursed him was still living, E II 6 197 3
agree that we love her the "better for having nursed her. P IV 6 165 8
He was waited on & nursed, & she cheered & comforted with S 2 371 1
but she had so well nursed & pleased Mr Hollis, that at S 3 375 1

NURSERIES (1)
child in the little white attic, near the old nurseries. MP I 1 9 12

NURSERY (8)
should be wanted left the nursery soon afterwards & was LS 20 275 1
her all his choicest nursery of plants, and actually MP I 10 103 50
the nursery for the children,--just as usual, you know.-- E I 9 79 57
there is not such another nursery establishment, so E III 8 382 23
go twice into my nursery without seeing something of them. P III 6 45 9
living in her deserted nursery to mend stockings, and P IV 1 121 3
place, the buildings, the nursery grounds, the demand for S 1 368 1
for a situation little better than a nursery maid.-- S 3 379 1

NURSERY-MAID (3)
of Mrs. Charles's nursery-maid: I hear strange stories of P III 6 45 9
nurse; and her nursery-maid, who had lived with her long P III 12 113 56
person in the old nursery-maid of the family, one who P IV 1 121 3

NURSERY-MAIDS (2)
number of nursery-maids, all reaching Hartfield in safety. E I 11 91 3
flirting girls, nor nursery-maids and children, they could P IV 11 241 59

NURSERYMAN (3)
"Commend me to the nurseryman and the poulterer." MP II 4 212 32
as glad of your nurseryman and poulterer as you could be. MP II 4 212 33
yours, in spite of the nurseryman and the poulterer--or MP II 4 213 35

NURSES (1)
was one of the principal nurses, was recreating herself in SS III 7 310 9

NURSING (8)
enjoyments of infancy, nursing a dormouse, feeding a NA I 1 13 1
who, though attending and nursing her the whole day, SS III 7 307 1
often by her better experience in nursing, of material use. SS III 7 308 3
"In nursing your sister I am sure you have pleasure," said PP I 8 37 25
gone in attending and nursing him, my spirits still worse, MP I 3 29 46
Nursing does not belong to a man, it is not his province. P III 7 56 11
"And she," said Mrs. Smith, "besides nursing me most P IV 5 155 9
She is only nursing Mrs. Wallis of Marlborough-Buildings-- P IV 5 156 13

NURTURE (1)
and the same sun should nurture plants differing in the MP II 4 209 16

NUT (3)
Here is a nut," said he, catching one down from an upper P III 10 88 26
"To exemplify,--a beautiful glossy nut, which, blessed P III 10 88 26
This nut," he continued, with playful solemnity,--"while P III 10 88 26

NUTMEG (1)
It irritates & acts like a nutmeg grater.--" S 10 417 1

NUTS (1)
to try for a gleaning of nuts in an adjoining hedge-row, P III 10 86 21

O'BRIEN (2)
"O'brien." W 326 5
It did not suit them, it did not suit Capt. O'brien that I W 326 5
O'CLOCK (53)
"it was only ten o'clock when we came from Tetbury." NA I 7 45 8
"Ten o'clock! it was eleven, upon my soul! NA I 7 46 9
the house:--"past three o'clock!" it was inconceivable, NA I 9 67 33
At twelve o'clock, they were to call for her in Pulteney- NA I 10 80 61
o'clock," was her parting speech to her new friend. NA I 10 80 61
At about eleven o'clock however, a few specks of small NA I 11 82 2
window-shutters at eight o'clock the next day, was the NA II 7 172 1
always to be seen at five o'clock, the General could not NA II 8 183 3
sky between six and seven o'clock, or by the yet more NA II 9 190 1
The day was bright, her courage high; at four o'clock, the NA II 9 193 5
By ten o'clock, the chaise-and-four conveyed the trio from NA II 11 212 17
o'clock, when Catherine scarcely thought it could be three. NA II 11 214 26
at six o'clock, the General having taken his coffee, the NA II 11 215 28
that it was eleven o'clock, rather a late hour at the NA II 13 222 7
here at seven o'clock, and no servant will be offered you." NA II 13 224 18
o'clock in the evening found herself entering Fullerton. NA II 14 232 6
from eight o'clock till four, without once sitting down." SS I 9 44 25
By ten o'clock the whole party were assembled at the park, SS I 13 63 2
He engaged to be with them by four o'clock. SS I 14 74 22
They reached town by three o'clock the third day, glad to SS II 4 160 2
It was then about twelve o'clock, and she returned to her SS III 7 312 17
when the former--but not till after five o'clock--arrived. SS III 7 312 19
of Mr. Harris at four o'clock;--when his assurances, his SS III 7 314 22
and saw Marianne at six o'clock sink into a quiet, steady, SS III 7 315 25
At ten o'clock, she trusted, or at least not much later, SS III 7 315 26
At seven o'clock, leaving Marianne still sweetly asleep, SS III 7 315 27
"Yes--I left London this morning at eight o'clock, and the SS III 8 318 20
My resolution was soon made, and at eight o'clock this SS III 8 331 69
sat down to table at four o'clock, about three hours after SS III 13 361 3
The entrance of the tea things at 7 o'clock was some W 326 7
"What o'clock was it?"-- W 332 12
by finding it two o'clock, & considering that she had W 338 17
will throw off at Stanton wood on Wednesday at 9 o'clock.-- W 347 21
after tea, that he was going home to an 8 o'clock dinner.-- W 355 28
warm last Saturday about 9 or 10 o'clock in the eveng--? W 358 28
At five o'clock the two ladies retired to dress, and at PP I 8 35 1
November 18th, by four o'clock, and shall probably PP I 13 63 12
"At four o'clock, therefore, we may expect this PP I 13 63 13
It was dated from Rosings, at eight o'clock in the morning, PP II 12 196 3
was settled that we should all be there by eleven o'clock. PP III 9 318 24
caution--"it is three o'clock, and your sister is not used MP II 10 279 24
And Mr. Campbell was here at four o'clock, to ask for you; MP III 7 377 7
there; and from six o'clock to half past nine, there was MP III 11 413 32
for the regular four o'clock dinner, the hero of this E I 9 81 78
that note, at twelve o'clock at night, on purpose to E I 11 95 19
"Think of me to-morrow, my dear Emma, about four o'clock," E II 5 189 15
"Four o'clock!--depend upon it he will be here by three," E II 5 189 16
or twelve o'clock, that she was to think of her at four. E II 5 189 19
A man who had been in motion since eight o'clock in the E II 17 303 23
"Dating from three o'clock yesterday. E III 7 369 13
"Three o'clock yesterday! E III 7 369 14
I have not seen him since seven o'clock. P III 5 37 25
It was ten o'clock. P IV 3 142 17
OAK (6)
fragment and the withered oak which he had placed near its NA I 14 111 29
sheltered from the north and east by rising woods of oak. NA II 2 141 13
broad staircase of shining oak, which, after many flights NA II 5 162 28
It is oak entirely." MP I 8 83 36
find us near that knoll, the grove of oak on the knoll." MP I 10 99 20
and lingering leaves of an oak just beyond their premises, MP II 4 205 3
OAKS (3)
placed near its summit, to oaks in general, to forests, NA I 14 111 29
amidst a grove of ancient oaks, with the last beams of the NA II 5 161 24
and of the beautiful oaks and Spanish chesnuts which were PP III 3 267 2
OATH (5)
I will take my oath he never dropt a syllable of being SS III 2 273 16
as with something of the oath kind he kicked away his MP III 7 379 19
the open air, and there was not a single oath to be heard. MP III 10 402 12
From that moment, Emma could have taken her oath that Mr. E II 8 228 93
"Not at all, not at all; there is not an oath or a murmur P IV 6 172 43
OATHS (1)
amounting almost to oaths, which adorned it, and Catherine NA I 9 64 26
OBEDIENCE (3)
this act of filial obedience, & I flatter myself with the LS 37 306 1
of early obedience and long observance to break through. E I 18 147 19
sample of true conjugal obedience--for who can say, you E III 16 457 36
OBEDIENT (2)
I am, dear madam, your most obedient humble servant, John SS II 7 183 13
so serviceable, so obedient--at others, so bewildered and MP II 4 209 12
OBEISANCE (1)
to make them his parting obeisance, was able to bring home PP II 14 210 1
OBEY (5)
Henry was not able to obey his father's injunction of NA II 13 221 7
He was not ill inclined to obey this request, for, though NA II 15 242 8
It is with great regret that I obey your commands of SS II 7 183 13
You refuse to obey the claims of duty, honour, and PP III 14 358 69
she was preparing to obey, when Mrs. Norris called out, " MP III 1 325 60
OBEYED (9)
at the sight of him, obeyed the first impulse of her heart SS III 8 317 1
2
Emma obeyed her--& eliz: listened with very little W 342 19
The necessity must be obeyed--and farther apology would be PP II 12 197 5
little in the habit of giving invitations, readily obeyed. PP III 2 263 11
Elizabeth obeyed, and running into her own room for her PP III 14 352 19
Fanny obeyed, with eyes cast down and colour rising.-- MP III 1 313 13
This was an order to be most joyfully obeyed; this was an MP III 1 322 49
Captain Benwick obeyed, and Charles at the same moment, P III 12 110 37
38
They would not listen to scruples: he was obeyed; they P III 12 111 50
OBJECT (253)
she is not an object of indifference to him, she would be LS 19 274 3
that it was my object to make my own child miserable, & LS 24 289 12
that does not relate to the beloved object! NA I 6 41 16
She seemed to have missed by so little the very object she NA I 8 59 35
day was now the object of expectation, the future good. NA I 10 73 22
herself the object of their attention and discourse. NA I 12 95 17
Catherine was the immediate object of his gallantry; and, NA I 12 95 18
it so striking an object from almost every opening in Bath. NA I 14 106 1
if they do not object, as I dare say they will not"----- NA II 2 140 8
of friendship, before the object of it appeared, and NA II 3 143 1
given him her heart, to her it was always an object. NA II 4 149 1
were still bent on the object so well calculated to NA II 6 164 3
The money is nothing, it is not an object, but employment NA II 7 176 15
be more agreeable to her to make those her first object. NA II 7 176 17
object must occasion so serious a delay of proper repose. NA II 8 187 16
object was a letter, held out by Henry's willing hand. NA II 10 201 6
"You like it--you approve it as an object;--it is enough. NA II 11 214 24
to his children as their chief object in his absence. NA II 13 220 1
well-known cherished object, and went down to the NA II 13 227 27
progress; and though no object on the road could engage a NA II 14 231 5
the room, the first object she beheld was a young man whom NA II 15 241 7
was not entirely mistaken in his object in wishing it. NA II 15 243 9
involuntary, unconscious object of a deception which his NA II 15 244 11
For Catherine, however, the peculiar object of the NA II 15 245 12
longer an evil; it was an object of desire; it was a SS I 4 24 20
was as far from being her object as ever; and she wished SS I 5 25 3
their comfort to be an object of real solicitude to him. SS I 6 30 6
In the promotion of this object she was zealously active, SS I 8 36 1
and when its object was understood, she hardly knew SS I 8 36 2
But I must object to your dooming Colonel Brandon and his SS I 8 38 11
and reserve, she beheld in him an object of interest. SS I 10 50 12
the inconstancy of its object, or the perverseness of SS I 11 56 15
she was sure would never object to it; and any horse would SS I 12 58 3
silent, till a new object suddenly engaged her attention. SS I 18 98 10
I can't imagine why you should object to it." SS I 20 114 42
to divine the reason or object of such a declaration, and SS I 22 129 15
likely to be, when the object of his engagement was SS II 1 140 3
her for ever from the object of her love, and that SS II 1 141 4
I am sure your mother will not object to it; for I have SS II 3 153 2
Miss Marianne would not object to such a scheme, if her SS II 3 154 3
in her pursuit of one object, was such a proof, so strong, SS II 3 155 6
of the importance of that object to her, as Elinor, in SS II 3 155 6
animating object in view, the same possibility of hope. SS II 4 159 1
speaking, except when any object of picturesque beauty SS II 4 160 2
unwell, was too polite to object for a moment to her wish SS II 6 178 16
so entirely lost on its object, that after many SS II 9 202 8
My object--my wish--my sole wish in desiring it--I hope, I SS II 9 204 18
It will be a very fine object from many parts of the park, SS II 11 226 39
hoped at least to be an object of irrepressible envy to SS II 12 232 14
would fix them at pleasure on any other object in the room. SS II 14 250 11
good reason to think her object gained; for, on Elinor's SS III 3 280 9
what must be his principal, his only object of happiness. SS III 3 284 23
Why, Colonel Brandon's only object is to be of use to Mr. SS III 4 291 52
She had no such object for her lingering thoughts to fix SS III 6 302 5
The Colonel too!--perhaps scarcely less an object of pity!- SS III 7 315 26
Brandon's marrying one of you as the object most desirable. SS III 9 336 10
to the sight of every object with which the remembrance of SS III 10 342 7
Myhappiness never was his object." SS III 11 351 12
then had any pursuit, any object to engage my time and SS III 13 362 5
and with only one object before him, the nearest road to SS III 13 366 20
It was now her darling object. SS III 14 378 13
guess at the object that could take her away, from Stanton W 317 2
on perceiving herself the object of attention both to Ly. W 332 11
Eliz. was the usual object of both. W 360 30
From being the first object of hope & solicitude of an W 361 31
girl, and one whom they should not object to know more of. PP I 4 17 16
the same skill from the object of it, she may lose the PP I 6 21 2
an object of some interest in the eyes of his friend. PP I 6 23 12
his complaisance; for who would object to such a partner?" PP I 6 26 43
I declare I do not know a more aweful object than Darcy, PP I 10 50 39
She hardly knew how to suppose that she could be an object PP I 10 51 46
the gentlemen entered, Jane was no longer the first object. PP I 11 54 2
Miss Bingley succeeded no less in the real object of her PP I 11 56 12
by a person whose first object in life is a joke." PP I 11 57 20
principal spokesman, and Miss Bennet the principal object. PP I 15 72 8
in such circumstances as to make five shillings any object. PP I 16 83 50
to it; that his chief object was by delicate attentions to PP I 18 102 73
My object has been to secure an amiable companion for PP I 20 114 32
any conception of;--its object was nothing less, than to PP I 22 121 1
had always been her object; it was the only honourable PP I 22 122 3
will not be in a hurry to believe myself his first object. PP II 3 145 7
be a more interesting object to all my acquaintance, were PP II 3 150 29
If she does not object to it, why should we?" PP II 4 153 15
Every object in the next day's journey was new and PP II 5 155 1
not have bestowed her kindness on a more grateful object." PP II 9 178 13
effect of love, and the object of that love, her friend PP II 9 180 29
Mr. Wickham's chief object was unquestionably my sister's PP II 12 202 5
Colonel Fitzwilliam was no longer an object. PP II 13 209 13
and as Dawson does not object to the barouche box, there PP II 14 211 10
to be cool, I should not object to taking you both, as you PP II 14 211 10
his disappointed feelings became the object of compassion. PP II 14 212 17
any one abiding in it an object of compassion, while they PP II 15 216 4
is luckily too poor to be an object of prey to any body. PP II 18 232 20
She saw herself the object of attention, to tens and to PP II 18 232 22
thus selected as the object of such idle and frivolous PP II 18 233 25
Her tour to the lakes was now the object of her happiest PP II 19 237 3
was probably as great an object of her curiosity, as all PP II 19 239 7
It is not the object of this work to give a description of PP II 19 240 12
abruptness form the distance, was a beautiful object. PP III 1 246 5
to all; and in the latter object, where she feared most to PP III 2 262 7
first interview with its object, and even before two words PP III 4 279 24
been continually fluctuating, but never without an object. PP III 4 280 25
that she was serious in the object of her journey. PP III 5 292 61
His principal object must be, to discover the number of PP III 5 293 69
The arrival of letters was the first grand object of every PP III 6 296 9
which had been the first object of her wishes, since Jane PP III 8 310 7
with him would have been the last object of her wishes. PP III 8 314 22
His first object with her, he acknowledged, had been to PP III 10 322 2
as at herself, and frequently on no object but the ground. PP III 11 335 43
does not object to them, they can be nothing to you." PP III 14 356 53
"My object then," replied Darcy, "was to shew you, by PP III 16 370 32
Mr. Darcy was really the object of her choice, by PP III 17 376 36
her affection, she now saw the object of open pleasantry. PP III 19 388 61
a matter of choice, as an object of that needful MP I 1 8 9
and her cousin began to find her an interesting object. MP I 2 16 20
"My object, Lady Bertram, is to be of use to those that MP I 3 30 52
Their father was no object of love to them, he had never MP I 3 32 64
which was now a prime object, it became, by the same rule MP I 4 38 10
but Mary was her dearest object; and having never been MP I 4 42 17
Matrimony was her object, provided she could marry well, MP I 4 42 18
and he began with no object but of making them like him. MP I 5 44 3
interested in one object--cheerful beyond a doubt, for the MP I 7 67 16
The particular object of the day was then considered. MP I 9 84 1
"Shall any of us object to being comfortable? MP I 9 91 37
"You need not hurry when the object is only to prevent my MP I 9 94 56
of any thing useful with regard to the object of the day. MP I 10 104 51
make the performance, not the theatre, our object. MP I 13 124 9
as well suppose he would object to our sitting more in MP I 13 127 29
she could scarcely see an object in that room which had MP I 16 151 2
My object is to confine it to Mrs. Rushworth and the MP I 16 155 16
important, each had their object of interest, their part, MP I 17 159 6
Edmund's first object the next morning was to see his MP II 2 187 1
had been cleared of every object enforcing the remembrance, MP II 2 187 2
My object was accomplished in the visit." MP II 2 190 5
to be rid of the worst object connected with the scheme, MP II 2 194 21
She was the first object of his love, but it was a love MP II 6 234 17
Sir Thomas, but the chief object in seeking them, was to MP II 6 236 21
he found his niece the object of attentions, or rather of MP II 7 246 36
provided, and such the object of her intended visit; and MP II 8 258 15
To the former she was an interesting object, and he saw MP II 10 272 1
disturb her, though his object seemed then to be only MP II 10 274 8
her feel that she was the object of all; though she could MP II 10 278 20
irritation from considering the object for which he went. MP II 11 285 15
than other women's, though I was the object of them. MP II 12 297 33
having succeeded in the object he had undertaken, the MP II 13 298 3
object would have detained me half the time from Mansfield. MP II 13 299 5
made up the note; "you cannot think I have any such object. MP II 13 307 33
look or manner was now an object worth attaining; and she MP III 1 322 50
and trick of composition are oftener an object of study. MP III 3 341 28
one object of curiosity and one set of words to another. MP III 3 343 40
there is something in him which I object to still more. MP III 4 349 25
secure, she was in every way an object of painful alarm. MP III 5 356 4
Mr. Crawford gone, Sir Thomas's next object was, that he MP III 6 366 1
noticed her, but to make her the object of a coarse joke. MP III 8 389 3
her sister as an object of mingled compassion and respect. MP III 9 396 6
his arrival, but had no object of that kind in coming. MP III 10 400 7
all about it, a dearer object than it had ever been yet. MP III 10 404 15
To be at an early certainty is a material object. MP III 13 422 2
Its object was unquestionable; and two moments were enough MP III 15 437 2
His great object was to be off as soon as possible. MP III 15 445 29

eyes were fixed on any object but himself, may be imagined. MP III 16 454 18
have been too happy and too busy to want any other object. MP III 16 455 23
authorised object of their youth--could have had no useful MP III 17 463 8
house became Crawford's object, she had had the merit of MP III 17 466 18
a knowledge of what was passing became his first object. MP III 17 468 21
affections for an object worthy to succeed her in them. MP III 17 470 25
on his kindness, an object to him of such close and MP III 17 470 27
to her comfort, the object of almost every day was to see MP III 17 472 30
Mrs. Weston was the object of a regard, which had its E I 4 26 2
that could fairly object to the doubtful birth of Harriet. E I 4 35 44
object of interest, Harriet may be said to do Emma good. E I 5 36 4
thing for her to be very much in love with a proper object. E I 5 41 29
to a young lady, the object of his admiration, but which, E I 9 71 10
You are his object--and you will soon receive the E I 9 73 20
and if their only object is that you should, in the common E I 9 75 27
But here is my father coming: you will not object to my E I 9 77 45
henceforth her prime object of interest; and during the E I 11 91 1
"are you imagining me to be Mr. Elton's object?" E I 13 112 19
always the first object on such occasions, was carefully E I 15 128 22
from gratified in being the object of such professions." E I 15 130 30
are men who might not object to-----every body has their E I 15 132 35
but one interest--one object of curiosity; it will be all E I 18 149 29
The charm of an object to occupy the many vacancies of E II 4 183 10
travelling round to its object, he wound it all up with E II 5 192 29
Some of the object of his curiosity spoke very amiable E II 6 197 3
her as his peculiar object, and at dinner she found him E II 8 214 12
She was his object, and every body must perceive it. E II 8 220 47
"It appears to me a plan that nobody can object to, if Mr. E II 11 251 24
be our object--if one could but tell what that would be." E II 11 254 49
It will be the object of all my thoughts and cares!-- and E II 12 259 15
She was, of course, the object of their joint dislike.-- E II 15 282 3
and the post-office is an object; and upon my word, I have E II 16 296 35
it would be no object to me to be with the rich; my E II 17 301 17
had then a change of object, and Emma heard her saying in E II 17 302 21
22
It was by no means her object to have it believed that her E II 18 307 17
That Emma was his object appeared indisputable. E III 5 343 2
them all; and it was his object to see as much as he could, E III 5 341 21
grew talkative and gay, making her his first object. E III 7 367 3
It ought to be a first object, as I am sure poor Miss E III 9 387 10
Considering the very superior claims of the object, it E III 11 403 2
He is no object of regret, indeed! and it will not be very E III 13 426 16
It was his object to blind all about him; and no one, I am E III 13 427 19
In one respect he is the object of my envy." E III 13 428 25
was my ostensible object--but I am sure you will believe E III 14 438 8
I was not disappointed either in the object of my journey. E III 14 443 8
first object to prevent her from suffering unnecessarily.-- E III 15 446 20
paid; but his subsequent object was to lament over himself E III 16 457 37
The good was all to myself, by making you an object of the E III 17 462 7
the constant object of his warmest respect and devotion. P III 1 4 5
and groves of Kellynch, was the object of her ambition. P III 2 14 9
been nothing to her but the object of distant civility. P III 2 16 16
reach, was therefore an object of first-rate importance. P III 2 16 17
an object of disgust himself, than in any other line. P III 3 19 16
an object of interest, amusement, and wholesome exertion. P III 6 43 4
It was now his object to marry. P III 7 61 38
It was a great object with me, at that time, to be at sea,- P III 8 65 13
with me, at that time, to be at sea,--a very great object. P III 8 65 13
being as thoroughly the object of the Admiral's fraternal P III 9 73 1
It had then seemed the object nearest her heart, that Dr. P III 9 78 19
Anne's object was, not to be in the way of any body, and P III 10 84 7
the Cobb, equally their object in itself and on Captain P III 11 96 10
in Bath, and his first object, on arriving, had been to P IV 3 138 6
very sensible man, why should it be an object to him? P IV 3 140 11
If Elizabeth were his object; and that Elizabeth was P IV 3 140 11
feel it a most desirable object, and what would very P IV 4 147 7
But here you are in Bath, and the object is to be P IV 4 151 21
would have the same object, I have no doubt, though the P IV 4 151 21
Then, she had indeed been a pitiable object--for she had P IV 5 154 9
object of Colonel Wallis's gallantry, was quite contented. P IV 8 186 23
to call; for to avoid Mr. Elliot was almost a first object. P IV 9 192 1
of looking about; that the object only had been deficient. P IV 9 193 13
to make it an object to yourself, of course it is done." P IV 9 195 24
of his life, had one object in view--to make his fortune, P IV 9 200 59
there it was his constant object, and his only object (P IV 9 207 90
object, and his only object (till your arrival added P IV 9 207 90
hope of succeeding in the object of her first anxiety, P IV 9 210 99
presence must really be interfering with her prime object. P IV 10 213 10
It was a great object with her to escape all enquiry or P IV 10 214 11
be allowed the expression, so long as you have an object. P IV 11 235 32
But she was a very good woman, and if her second object P IV 12 249 4
to be necessarily their object, & had with most unwilling S 1 364 1
bathing place was the object, for which he seemed to live. S 2 371 1
His object in quitting the high road, to hunt for an S 2 371 1
sisters, for the object which had taken him to Willingden. S 6 393 1
The first object of the parkers, when their house was S 7 395 1
because their object in that line is the same, he fancies S 7 402 1
Sir Edw:'s great object in life was to be seductive.-- S 8 405 2
for the object of his affections, to the more renowned.-- S 8 405 2
While I have been travelling, with this object in veiw, I S 9 410 1
for action, some powerful object of animation for him, S 10 415 1
change of fashion--& the object of all, was to captivate S 11 421 1
of hers, which was his object, as he felt all their S 12 425 1
Privacy was certainly their object.-- S 12 426 1

OBJECTED (7)
"Oh! no; but if mama had not objected to it, I dare say he SS I 20 117 64
very much objected to be kept waiting for her dinner.-- PP II 6 161 7
"If every play is to be objected to, you will act nothing-- MP I 15 141 22
Nothing could be objected to when it came under the MP II 3 203 29
are not to be altogether objected to, it does not follow E I 4 30 22
company of others--she objected only to a tete-a-tete-- E III 12 416 2
"Yes; which I objected to, but he would not regard. P IV 9 202 66

OBJECTING (7)
to Reginald, her objecting to Sir James could not less LS 24 290 12
of her objecting had been a consciousness of his folly. LS 24 290 12
Catherine is far from objecting to my occasional absence PP I 13 63 12
and I am so far from objecting to dancing myself that I PP I 17 87 13
"Her not objecting, does not justify him. PP II 4 153 16
his being very far from objecting to such a measure, would MP III 12 419 9
Though always objecting to every marriage that was E II 5 193 35

OBJECTION (75)
Lady Susan's age is itself a material objection, but her LS 12 260 2
When your choice is so fixed as that no objection can be LS 12 261 3
Our difference of age must be an insuperable objection, & LS 14 263 1
no reflection, she had never any objection to books at all. NA I 1 15 3
the least objection to letting in this young lady by you." NA I 8 55 10
ridiculous, quite absurd to make any further objection. NA I 13 100 19
objection, and she should have great pleasure in coming." NA I 13 103 28
Thorpe, would have any objection to dancing, as his NA II 1 132 16
independent of the objection that might be raised against NA II 11 208 1
alone were concerned, had not a single objection to start. NA II 16 249 1
have been a sufficient objection to outweigh every SS I 4 23 20
to leave her no right of objection on either point; and, SS I 4 24 21
being thirty-five any objection to his marrying her." SS I 8 38 9
difference appeared, any objection arose, it lasted no SS I 10 47 3
No one made any objection but Marianne, who, with her SS II 1 144 15
you, there is still one objection which, in my opinion, SS II 3 156 9
"My objection is this; though I think very well of Mrs. SS II 3 156 12
attention, made neither objection nor remark, attempted no SS II 10 212 1
great humility, did not see the force of her objection. SS II 14 253 22
that any material objection;--and Mrs. Jennings commended SS III 3 281 9
have the least objection in the world to seeing you.-- SS III 5 294 6
a-year, not the smallest objection was made against SS III 14 374 4
the only objection she could make to Mr Howard.-- W 335 13
"You want to tell me, and I have no objection to hearing PP I 1 3 8
no objection, I am sure, to oblige us for one half hour." PP I 6 26 41
"I have not the smallest objection to explaining them," PP I 11 56 15
Her sister made not the smallest objection, and the piano PP I 11 58 34
If you should have no objection to receive me into your PP I 13 63 12
made not the smallest objection to his joining in the PP I 14 66 1
As no objection was made to the young people's engagement PP I 16 75 1
will be very happy--I am sure she can have no objection.-- PP I 19 104 4
"My mother would have had no objection, but my father PP II 6 164 25
she exclaimed, "there could be no possibility of objection. PP II 10 186 40
Elizabeth made no objection;--the door was then allowed to PP II 15 217 10
But as to your other objection, I am afraid it will hardly PP III 5 283 8
where to every other objection would now be added, an PP III 8 311 12
If there is no other objection to my marrying your nephew, PP III 14 355 44
"Have you any other objection," said Elizabeth, "than your PP III 17 376 32
no longer made any objection, and a more respectable, MP I 1 8 9
to do away any former objection to their living together, MP I 3 24 7
thought about her own objection again, he might have been MP I 4 37 9
in town, she knew that objection could no more be made to MP I 4 42 18
Lady Bertram made no objection, and every one concerned in MP I 6 62 59
"There can be no objection then to Fanny's going with you; MP I 8 78 16
"Oh! yes, very glad, if your aunt sees no objection." MP I 8 78 22
Mrs. Norris was very ready with the only objection which MP I 8 78 23
No objection was made, but for some time there seemed no MP I 9 90 36
say you will have no objection to join us in a rubber; MP I 12 119 23
it is so far from an objection, that I consider it rather MP I 13 126 18
Their mother had no objection to the plan, and they were MP I 13 128 38
"I should have no objection," she replied; "for though I MP I 15 144 38
have no objection to any thing that you all think eligible. MP I 15 148 59
it necessary to be done, if no objection arose at home. MP II 4 207 10
that she had no objection but on her aunt's account, could MP II 4 215 47
Always some little objection, some little doubt, some MP II 5 225 55
he made no objection to her kissing him, though still MP III 7 377 8
I can imagine your objection to Harriet Smith. E I 5 36 6
were Mr. Elton's only objection, and Mr. Elton actually E I 13 110 12
"Yes; if you and Mr. Woodhouse see no objection, and I E II 11 250 23
Mrs. Weston sees no objection to it, provided you are E II 11 250 23
confidence; she had no objection to her telling us, of E III 5 346 16
acceded to it, so it was to be, if she had no objection. E III 6 353 3
Now, as her objection was nothing but her very great E III 6 353 3
I have no objection at all to meeting the Hartfield family. E III 6 355 18
He could not see any objection at all to his, and Emma's, E III 6 357 30
more refreshing-- only objection to gathering strawberries E III 6 358 35
She had no objection. E III 8 377 2
you; but, as you made no objection, I never did it again." E III 17 462 12
objection raised, except in one habitation, the vicarage.-- E III 17 468 36
No objection was raised on the father's side; the young E III 19 482 4
to me; I have two strong grounds of objection to it. P III 3 19 16
"I have not the smallest objection on that account," P III 5 39 42
and he had no objection to being seen with him any where." P IV 3 141 12
There could not be an objection. P IV 11 240 59
Sir Walter made no objection, and Elizabeth did nothing P IV 12 248 1

OBJECTIONABLE (11)
but that he was not objectionable as a common acquaintance NA I 3 30 52
Do not you think these kind of projects objectionable?" NA I 13 104 31
My conduct may I fear be objectionable in having accepted PP I 20 114 32
to do it, unless there were something very objectionable? PP II 1 137 24
family, though objectionable, was nothing in comparison of PP II 12 198 5
The most objectionable part is, that the alteration of MP I 5 49 32
I can see nothing objectionable in it; and I am not the MP I 15 140 12
objectionable, the more than intimacy--the familiarity. MP I 16 153 8
behaving one hour with objectionable particularity to E III 14 441 8
find in any respect objectionable; it was, that he should E III 15 449 31
Clara--nor anything objectionable in the degree of S 6 392 1

OBJECTIONS (34)
But I was persuaded that her objections to him did not LS 24 289 12
and prepare his objections on a fairer ground than NA II 11 208 2
no distinction in her objections against a second SS I 11 56 14
15
I will not raise objections against any one's conduct on SS I 15 81 43
go," said Mrs. Dashwood; "these objections are nonsensical. SS II 3 157 16
objections against such a measure only a few days before! SS II 4 159 1
But these objections had all, with that happy ardour of SS II 4 159 1
of the question, the objections are insurmountable--you SS II 11 224 24
in short, whatever objections there might be against a SS III 5 297 31
"I understood that there were some very strong objections PP II 10 185 30
"There were some very strong objections against the lady," PP II 10 186 39
words, and these strong objections probably were, her PP II 10 186 39
not allow that any objections there had material weight PP II 10 187 40
her in spite of all the objections which had made him PP II 11 193 31
My objections to the marriage were not merely those, which PP II 12 198 5
of the real, the worst objections to the match, made her PP II 13 204 1
She felt anew the justice of Mr. Darcy's objections; and PP II 18 229 10
But against this, there were objections; and she finally PP II 19 241 16
To all the objections I have already urged, I have still PP III 14 357 62
score of some family objections on the part of my cousin, PP III 15 363 22
begun to state his objections, than Mrs. Norris MP I 1 6 5
are open to some objections, but as we are circumstanced, MP I 13 125 17
were successively dismissed with yet warmer objections. MP I 14 130 3
I do not wish to make objections, I shall be happy to be MP I 14 131 3
After all his objections--objections so just and so public! MP I 16 156 28
quiescent and contented, and had no objections to make. MP II 8 253 6
His objections, the scruples of his integrity, seemed all MP III 6 367 4
I hope I foresee two objections, two fair, excellent, MP III 10 405 19
two fair, excellent, irresistible objections to that plan." MP III 10 405 19
Her objections to Mr. Knightley's marrying did not in the E II 8 227 87
and there do seem objections and obstacles of a very E III 4 342 39
imprudence, or smooth objections; and by the time they had E III 10 401 69
"Oh! if these are your only objections," cried Mrs. Smith, P IV 9 196 32
For objections of this nature, Charlotte was not prepared, S 7 401 1

OBJECTS (38)
naturally arose from the objects around them, he suddenly NA I 3 25 2
before; but I suppose Mrs. Morland objects to novels." NA I 6 41 20
ever have been closed, on objects of cheerfulness; her NA II 7 172 1
from the surrounding objects, she soon began to walk with NA II 7 181 41
from the sight of such objects as that room must contain; NA II 8 186 6
to all the gloomy objects to which they were advancing. NA II 9 191 4
The influence of fresh objects and fresh air, however, was NA II 11 214 25
severe by the review of objects on which she had first NA II 14 230 1
affliction as rendered her careless of surrounding objects. SS I 3 16 7
The house and the garden, with all the objects surrounding SS I 9 40 1
of attachment to the objects around him; and on Mrs. SS I 14 72 6
Amongst the objects in the scene, they soon discovered an SS I 16 86 16
"How can you think of dirt, with such objects before you?" SS I 16 88 35
rest of the objects before me, I see a very dirty lane." SS I 16 88 36
him more minutely on the objects that had particularly SS I 18 96 4
and rugged; and distant objects out of sight, which ought SS I 18 97 4
Their means were as different as their objects, and SS I 19 104 9
from one, or discerning objects through the other; and SS II 7 190 55
56
A variety of occupations, of objects, and of company, SS II 10 213 3
They were not the only objects of Mr. Collins's admiration. PP I 13 65 26
the same amusements, objects of the same parental care. PP I 16 81 37
As they passed into other rooms, these objects were taking PP III 1 246 5
direct her eyes to such objects as they pointed out, she PP III 1 253 55
she spoke to one of its objects; for jealousy had not yet PP III 3 269 8
interest with her for objects of happiness which she might PP III 13 349 41
and felt, and said, for attention to any other objects. PP III 16 366 9
with the super-added objects of professing attention to MP I 6 55 17
circumstance, would find objects to distract it in the MP I 9 88 18

in the objects most intimately connected with Mansfield. MP II 1 179 8
little, "between the two dearest objects I have on earth." MP II 9 264 16
with these objects in view, till they were accomplished. E I 2 16 6
And as for objects of interest, objects for the affections, E I 10 85 21
mule, were the liveliest objects she could presume to E II 9 233 24
hence you may have as many concentrated objects as I have." E II 16 294 23
of her in London without objects of curiosity and E III 16 452 5
to recognise the same hills and the same objects so soon. P III 12 117 73
blotting out the very few objects ever to be discerned P IV 1 123 8
every man to have the same objects and pleasures as myself. P IV 10 218 26

OBLIGATION (31)

I shall feel myself under an obligation to anyone who is LS 24 286 4
making light of the obligation; and Mrs. Hughes, satisfied NA I 8 55 10
to start forth her obligation of going away very soon. NA II 13 220 2
as she assented to the hardship of such an obligation. SS I 20 113 34
pain of receiving an obligation from her, she would have SS III 3 283 20
ready to own all their obligation to her, and openly SS III 5 293 2
This was an obligation, however, which not only opposed SS III 5 293 3
and the warm acknowledgment of peculiar obligation. SS III 10 340 2
not wish either for the obligation, or the intimacy which W 341 19
to express a sense of obligation for the sentiments avowed, PP II 11 189 6
7
It is natural that obligation should be felt, and if I PP II 11 190 7
myself, and which no obligation less than the present PP II 12 201 5
breach of conjugal obligation and decorum which, in PP II 19 236 2
and to discharge the obligation as soon as he could. PP III 8 308 2
just, from the pain of obligation, were proved beyond PP III 10 326 3
of her support, and the obligation of her future provision. MP I 3 24 7
the same rule of moral obligation, her evident duty to MP I 4 38 10
The obligation of attendance, the formality, the restraint, MP I 9 87 15
have had less time and obligation--where he might have MP I 11 111 30
without any sense of obligation for being sought after now MP II 4 208 11
out her great obligation, and her--"but she did not MP II 4 215 47
or feel any of that obligation to Mr. Crawford for lending MP II 6 237 23
had been conferring an obligation, which no want of MP II 13 301 7
so expressive of obligation and concern, that to a temper MP III 2 328 7
while seeing all the obligation and expediency of MP III 9 397 8
to keep ahead, without any obligation of waiting for her. E I 10 88 33
Mr. Elton was all obligation and cheerfulness; he was so E I 13 114 28
as having conferred the highest obligation on him." E II 5 192 28
"Service! Oh! it was such an inexpressible obligation!-- E III 4 342 38
but in conferring obligation, or of deriving it, except in E III 8 378 3
with such a powerful discharge of unexpected obligation. S 10 414 1

OBLIGATIONS (7)

You totally disallow any similarity in the obligations; NA I 10 77 37
They each felt his sorrows, and their own obligations, and SS III 14 378 13
be under the greatest obligations to my father's active PP I 16 81 37
her thoughts to the obligations which Mr. Gardiner's PP III 7 306 45
obligations to a person who could never receive a return. PP III 10 326 3
imagine any interfering obligations, Julia was certainly MP III 14 432 11
line of Primitive obligations)--to hazard all, dare, all, S 8 403 1

OBLIGE (29)

was very ready to oblige the whole party by consenting to LS 42 313 7
in the room more happy to oblige her than Catherine. NA I 8 55 10
The sacrifice is not much; and to oblige such a friend--I NA I 13 99 3
of public triumph and oblige your friend Eleanor with your NA II 2 139 7
your happiness merely to oblige my brother, because he is NA II 3 146 20
Eleanor was ready to oblige her; and Catherine reminding NA II 9 191 3
she was obliged, or could oblige herself to speak to him. SS II 10 216 15
the others, inclined to oblige her, that if Sir John dined SS II 14 247 4
Emma was not more disposed to oblige him for all this.-- W 340 18
Only do not oblige me to chuse the game, that's all. W 354 28
no objection, I am sure, to oblige us for one half hour." PP I 6 26 41
to her partner to oblige him to talk, she made some slight PP I 18 91 8
very little entreaty, preparing to oblige the company. PP I 18 100 68
"To oblige you, I would try to believe almost any thing. PP II 1 135 13
I am sure he will be vastly happy to oblige you, and will PP III 11 337 53
You refuse, then to oblige me. PP III 14 358 69
than any solicitude to oblige him, the mention of MP I 6 52 1
"But were there roses enough to oblige her to go twice?" MP I 7 73 50
as to oblige one to do the very thing--whatever it be! MP I 12 120 26
"You must oblige us," said he, "indeed you must. MP I 14 135 17
I only puzzle them, and oblige them to make civil speeches. MP I 15 144 36
said Tom, "Fanny may be more disposed to oblige us now. MP I 17 158 3
means of conferring a kindness where he wished to oblige. MP II 6 237 23
You must forgive the liberty and oblige me." MP II 8 258 16
She had, to oblige Edmund, resolved to wear it--but it was MP II 9 271 40
have prevailed, I hope, and these ladies will oblige us." E II 9 237 46
It was not to oblige Jane Fairfax therefore that he would E II 12 258 6
"Say nothing, my dear Emma, while you oblige me to read-- E III 15 447 26
She had given him up to oblige others. P III 7 61 36

OBLIGED (305)

me. Yr most obliged & affec: sister S. Vernon. LS 1 244 1
we should at some future period be obliged to receive her. LS 3 246 1
castle when we were obliged to sell it, but it was a LS 5 249 1
years that I was never obliged to attend to anything, & LS 7 253 1
I am much obliged to you my dear friend, for your advice LS 10 257 1
more obliged to you than it is possible for me to express. LS 21 279 1
which I have found myself imperiously obliged to place it. LS 30 301 4
But since it must be so, I am obliged to declare that all LS 36 305 1
For some time her young friend felt obliged to her for NA I 2 21 9
eligible situation, were obliged to sit down at the end of NA I 2 22 10
contented--she felt more obliged to the two young men for NA I 2 24 28
"Dear creature! how much I am obliged to you; and when you NA I 6 40 8
of one friend, and obliged him to hurry away as soon as he NA I 7 51 54
"And I hope, madam, that Mr. Allen will be obliged to like NA I 8 54 6
"Oh, no; I am much obliged to you, our two dances are over; NA I 8 59 36
time with James, was therefore obliged to speak plainer. NA I 9 61 6
acute on finding herself obliged to go directly home.-- NA I 9 67 33
getting away, was obliged to give up the point and submit. NA I 11 87 53
that she might not be obliged to see her beloved Isabella NA I 12 91 3
reserve:--"we were much obliged to you at any rate for NA I 12 93 7
Catherine was greatly obliged; but it was quite out of her NA I 13 103 28
and I was obliged to stay till you had finished it." NA I 14 107 8
of a wood fire--nor be obliged to spread our beds on the NA II 5 158 15
subject or voice, and was obliged to entreat her to use NA II 5 160 23
many poor girls have been obliged to do, and then to have NA II 6 167 9
she found herself again obliged to walk with him, listen NA II 7 181 41
But here she was obliged to look and consider and study NA II 9 191 3
were busy in it, and she was obliged to come down again. NA II 10 203 8
and shall probably be obliged to stay two or three days." NA II 11 209 5
she was very soon obliged to give him credit for being NA II 11 211 15
Soon after this, the General found himself obliged to go NA II 13 220 1
by silent attention; obliged her to be seated, rubbed her NA II 13 223 9
think the worse of me for the part I am obliged to perform. NA II 13 223 13
the morning, that he might not be obliged even to see her. NA II 13 226 25
the narrow-minded counsel which he was obliged to expose. NA II 15 247 15
Chagrined and surprised, they were obliged, though SS I 9 41 6
Mrs. Dashwood then begged to know to whom she was obliged. SS I 9 42 10
Elinor was obliged, though unwillingly, to believe that SS I 10 49 12
half the time; and when obliged to separate for a couple SS I 11 54 3
of a young mind are obliged to give way, how frequently SS I 11 56 17
on being obliged to forego the acceptance of his present. SS I 12 59 6
"My own loss is great," he continued, "in being obliged to SS I 13 64 21
But Mrs. Smith must be obliged;--and her business will not SS I 15 76 9
and he feels himself obliged, from his dependent situation, SS I 15 78 26
and if he felt obliged, from a fear of offending Mrs. SS I 15 81 43
stepping across the turf, obliged her to open the casement SS I 19 105 13
Elinor was obliged to turn from her, in the middle of her SS I 19 106 21
a family party; and the young ladies were obliged to yield. SS I 19 109 40
They were obliged to put an end to such an expectation. SS I 20 110 3
They thanked her; but were obliged to resist all her SS I 20 110 5
Elinor was again obliged to decline her invitation; and by SS I 20 114 43
to herself, though it obliged her to unceasing exertion, SS II 1 141 5
that day, as he was obliged to attend the club at Exeter, SS II 1 143 9
"Indeed I shall be very much obliged to you for your help," SS II 1 145 20
Elinor now began to make the tea, and Marianne was obliged SS II 4 163 19
obliged to assist in making a whist-table for the others. SS II 4 166 31
no answer ready, was obliged to adopt the simple and SS II 5 172 40
of grief which still obliged her, at intervals, to SS II 7 180 4
than at that moment, obliged herself to answer such an SS II 7 181 9
It would grieve me indeed to be obliged to think ill of SS II 7 188 42
and in a determined silence when obliged to endure it. SS II 9 201 2
had obliged her to dispose of it for some immediate relief. SS II 9 207 26
impossible, and she was obliged to listen day after day to SS II 10 214 8
she was obliged, or could oblige herself to speak to him. SS II 10 216 15
to attend to their orders; and they were obliged to wait. SS II 11 220 3
impossible, for we were obliged to take Harry to see the SS II 11 221 9
But, in consequence of it, we have been obliged to make SS II 11 225 35
thousand pounds of being obliged to sell out at a loss, SS II 12 233 18
for her happiness; and Elinor was obliged to go on.-- SS II 13 239 7
from Elinor, who was obliged to volunteer all the SS II 13 241 22
in an error might be, she was obliged to submit to it. SS II 13 244 47
Mrs. John Dashwood was obliged to submit not only to the SS II 14 248 6
My promise to Lucy, obliged me to be secret. SS III 1 262 23
"I shall always think myself very much obliged to you." SS III 3 281 13
14
returning herself, had obliged him to enter, by saying SS III 4 287 25
Truth obliged her to acknowledge some small share in the SS III 4 290 36
which it was given, obliged him to submit to her authority. SS III 5 295 13
pleasantly while I was obliged to remain in Devonshire, SS III 8 319 29
I told her that I was obliged to leave Devonshire so SS III 8 324 42
she had never been obliged to go without her dinner before. SS III 11 355 45
and was obliged to leave all to their own discretion. SS III 12 358 9
It was put an end to by Mrs. Dashwood, who felt obliged to SS III 12 359 14
be, by eliz.'s being obliged to hurry away--& some very, W 322 3
obliged to listen to Tom Musgrave's farther account. W 338 18
firm, & the gentleman found himself obliged to submit. W 340 18
Emma gave him no encouragement, & he was obliged to keep W 340 19
He was also obliged to put an end to his visit--for Mrs W 340 19
stile in which they were obliged to live; & having in her W 345 21
Emma was greatly obliged. W 350 24
they were obliged to sit down without their guest.-- W 360 30
and they were at last obliged to accept the second-hand PP I 3 9 1
Mr. Bingley was obliged to be in town the following day, PP I 3 9 4
Elizabeth Bennet had been obliged, by the scarcity of PP I 3 11 7
She was therefore obliged to seek another branch of the PP I 3 13 19
Jane was therefore obliged to go on horseback, and her PP I 7 31 28
that Miss Bingley was obliged to convert the offer of the PP I 7 33 45
Do clear them too, or we shall be obliged to think ill of PP I 17 85 3
that Wickham had been obliged to go to town on business PP I 18 89 1
2
not be obliged to go into company more than she liked. PP I 18 99 63
to be obliged to say nothing he may not like to hear." PP I 18 99 65
whither he was obliged to go the next day for a short time. PP I 18 103 76
obliged to spend his vacant hours in a comfortless hotel. PP I 21 117 10
11
she, "and I am more obliged to you than I can express." PP I 22 121 1
"I am particularly obliged to you for this friendly PP I 22 123 8
obliged to take her ladyship's praise into his own hands. PP II 6 167 42
which she had been obliged to give in the other?-- PP II 13 208 9
"I am much obliged to your ladyship for your kind PP II 14 211 7
Maria thought herself obliged, on her return, to undo all PP II 14 213 20
she had received, must make her feel the obliged. PP II 15 215 3
his feelings; and he was obliged to walk about the room, PP II 15 216 5
more fully, but was obliged to leave off in a violent PP II 19 238 5
had built on, they were obliged to give up the lakes, and PP II 19 238 7
and was obliged to assume a disinclination for seeing it. PP II 19 240 14
Her niece was, therefore, obliged to submit, and they took PP III 1 254 57
is obliged to be at Brighton again to-morrow evening. PP III 4 276 5
He confessed himself obliged to leave the regiment, on PP III 10 323 2
to dinner, which he thought himself obliged to accept. PP III 13 349 43
I was obliged to confess one thing, which for a time, and PP III 16 371 45
Mary was obliged to mix more with the world, but she could PP III 19 386 5
years, found herself obliged to be attached to the Rev. Mr. MP I 1 3 1
now obliged to forego through the urgency of your debts." MP I 3 23 3
obliged to you for trying to reconcile me to what must be. MP I 3 27 34
be obliged to take daily refuge in the dining of the park. MP I 4 38 9
lady's death which now obliged her protegee, after some MP I 4 40 15
and been obliged to put up with exactly the reverse! MP I 5 46 22
in the world; and when obliged to take up the pen to say MP I 6 59 43
his determined silence obliged her to relate her brother's MP I 6 60 47
and bring away the key, so she was obliged to go again." MP I 7 73 51
to Fanny, and obliged her to drink the greater part. MP I 7 74 57
Mrs. Rushworth being obliged to yield to Lady Bertram's MP I 8 76 4
"I am sure she ought to be very much obliged to you," MP I 8 79 25
no longer prevailed, was obliged to keep by the side of MP I 9 90 36
I am not obliged to punish myself for her sins. MP I 10 101 32
I am sure you ought to be very much obliged to your aunt MP I 10 105 53
letters obliged them to do, was a most unwelcome exercise. MP I 11 107 1
she have been not to be obliged to listen, for it was MP I 12 116 11
it was rather a pity they should have been obliged to part. MP I 12 117 13
And Edmund silenced, was obliged to acknowledge that the MP I 13 129 39
of fancying herself obliged to leave her own house, where MP I 13 129 40
Frederick and his knapsack would be obliged to run away." MP I 14 133 11
she answered, "I am much obliged to you, Edmund;--you mean MP I 15 140 14
but she felt very much obliged to her for her present MP I 15 147 57
of her cousins to being obliged, were strengthened by the MP I 16 153 3
She was beyond their reach; and if at last obliged to MP I 16 157 28
Crawford to whom she was obliged, it was Miss Crawford MP I 17 159 6
but rehearse it with me, I should be so obliged! MP I 18 168 17
by her flattery; and was obliged to rest satisfied with MP II 2 190 8
and Fanny, after being obliged to submit to all this MP II 4 206 3
and maids, being also obliged on returning down stairs, to MP II 4 206 3
who seemed so much obliged, so full of wonder at the MP II 4 207 6
Edmund found himself obliged to speak and fill up the MP II 5 218 16
You ought to be very much obliged to Mrs. Grant for MP II 5 220 28
that she was very much obliged to her aunt Bertram for MP II 5 220 29
her very soon to dislike him less than formerly. MP II 6 231 11
been obliged to give up, and make the best of his way back. MP II 7 240 13
was obliged to be indebted to his more prominent attention. MP II 7 251 66
Mrs. Norris was obliged to be satisfied with thinking just MP II 8 254 7
that her friend, though obliged to insist on turning back, MP II 8 257 15
Fanny found herself obliged to yield that she might not be MP II 8 258 17
She would rather perhaps have been obliged to some other MP II 8 258 18
after waiting a moment, obliged her to bring down her mind MP II 9 262 10
expectation; and she was obliged to repeat again and again MP II 9 264 17
that as he found himself obliged to go to London on the MP II 9 265 21
wished she had not been obliged to suspect that his MP II 10 278 20
Fanny felt obliged to speak. MP II 11 289 31
she felt, that he was obliged to repeat what he had said, MP II 12 291 5
myself infinitely obliged to any creature who gives me MP II 13 298 2
Oh! Mr. Crawford, we are infinitely obliged to you. MP II 13 300 7
Your kindness to William makes me more obliged to you than MP II 13 302 8
happy, miserable, infinitely obliged, absolutely angry. MP II 13 302 10
"I am very much obliged to you, my dear Miss Crawford, for MP II 13 307 31
a moment--I am very much obliged to you--if you will be so MP II 13 307 34
without her being obliged to know any thing of the matter. MP III 1 311 3
Fanny would rather have been silent, but being obliged to MP III 1 312 11
great inconvenience, been obliged to go and carry myself. MP III 1 323 54
Mrs. Norris, much discontented, was obliged to compose MP III 1 325 62
she felt herself obliged to use, was not to be understood. MP III 2 327 5
Sir Thomas was obliged or obliged himself to wait till the MP III 2 329 11
found himself once more obliged to mention the subject to MP III 2 331 19

Mr. Crawford was obliged to move. MP III 3 344 43
I wish he had not been obliged to tell you what he was MP III 4 348 21
own inconvenience, in being obliged to hurry away so soon. MP III 7 378 11
Mrs. Price was greatly obliged, and very complying.-- MP III 10 401 10
looked, Fanny was obliged to introduce him to Mr. Crawford. MP III 10 401 11
In chapel they were obliged to divide, but Mr. Crawford MP III 11 408 3
"Nothing, I am much obliged to you." MP III 11 412 25
She was obliged to call herself to think of it, and MP III 15 443 24
things to extremity, and obliged her brother to give up MP III 16 455 19
He was obliged to pause more than once as he continued. MP III 16 456 29
together till she was obliged to be convinced that such MP III 17 464 10
when he was now obliged to part with Miss Taylor too; and E I 1 7 10
till you mentioned her--James is so obliged to you!" E I 1 9 18
Emma was obliged to fancy what she liked--but she could E I 4 27 3
"Not at all," cried he; "I am much obliged to you for it. E I 5 40 25
offence; but was really obliged to put an end to it, and E I 6 46 24
I shall always feel much obliged to him, and have a great E I 7 54 30
She was obliged to go the next morning for an hour or two E I 8 57 1
This was obliged to be repeated before it could be E I 8 60 31
32
"I am very much obliged to you," said Emma, laughing again. E I 8 66 54
never loth to be first, was obliged to examine it herself. E I 9 71 14
For once in your life you would obliged to own yourself E I 9 72 15
She was obliged to break off from these very pleasant E I 9 72 16
should be obliged to go back so soon, though he does. E I 9 80 65
66
they both looked around, and she was obliged to join them. E I 10 88 33
a ditch, was presently obliged to entreat them to stop, E I 10 89 36
She was obliged to leave the door ajar as she found it; E I 10 89 38
She was then obliged to be finished and make her E I 10 89 38
often--but then--she is always obliged to go away again." E I 11 94 16
If we were obliged to go out such an evening as this, by E I 13 113 26
conceited head, Emma was obliged in common honesty to stop E I 16 136 9
all her children, was obliged to see the whole party set E I 17 140 1
forward to prevent Harriet's being obliged to say a word. E II 1 156 5
All this spoken extremely fast obliged Miss Bates to stop E II 1 158 11
They had music; Emma was obliged to play; and the thanks E II 2 168 15
to rain, Emma was obliged to expect that the weather would E II 3 177 51
So I said, I was very much obliged to him: you know I E II 3 179 52
She was obliged to stop and think. E II 3 179 53
out of her head, was obliged to hurry on the news, which E II 3 180 56
felt very much obliged to you for your preparatory hint. E II 6 198 7
Mr. Weston, I am much obliged to you for reminding me. E II 7 210 20
might have obliged them to practise during the meal.-- E II 8 213 6
The first remote sound to which she felt herself obliged E II 8 214 13
between the courses, and obliged to as formal and as E II 8 218 38
39
room, Emma found herself obliged to return from him for a E II 8 222 54
to begin again, they were obliged to thank Mrs. Weston, E II 8 230 101
than she is obliged to do, because she will have to teach. E II 9 232 11
Emma was obliged to ask what they had told her, though E II 9 232 14
"Very well, I am much obliged to you. E II 9 236 46
and I was very much obliged, and went down and spoke to E II 9 239 51
She was not obliged to hear. E II 10 241 9
So obliged to you for the carriage last night. E II 10 243 33
And Miss Bates was obliged to give a direct answer before E II 10 244 36
"So obliged to you!--so very much obliged to you for the E II 10 244 37
She was obliged to repeat and explain it, before it was E II 11 251 25
"Yes, sir, I did indeed; and I am very much obliged by E II 16 294 26
She and Mrs. Weston were obliged to be almost always E II 17 299 1
I am exceedingly obliged to you, Mrs. Elton, I am obliged E II 17 301 19
Ah! dear Mrs. Elton, so obliged to you for the carriage!-- E III 2 322 19
Quite well, I am much obliged to you. E III 2 323 19
and exceedingly terrified, she had been obliged to remain. E III 3 333 5
restore them, he had been obliged to stop at her door, and E III 3 334 7
the Highbury world were obliged to endure the E III 6 352 1
found herself therefore obliged to consent to an E III 6 353 3
If Mr. Knightley did not begin seriously, he was obliged E III 6 354 9
Mr. Knightley was then obliged to say the he should be E III 6 357 31
found; and now Emma was obliged to overhear what Mrs. E III 6 359 37
"How much I am obliged to you," said he, "for telling me E III 7 368 4
But Miss Bates soon came--"very happy and obliged"--but E III 8 378 7
sensations of the past, obliged her to admit that Jane E III 8 379 9
obliged to the kind friends who included me in it." E III 8 381 19
Now Emma was obliged to think of the piano forte; and the E III 8 384 34
they must have been very much obliged to you for coming. E III 9 385 6
Miss Bates was obliged to return without success; Jane was E III 9 390 18
will soon come," she was obliged to pause before she E III 12 420 14
she answered, and at last obliged to answer at random, E III 12 420 14
case to be obliged still to lower herself in his opinion. E III 13 427 18
Here, my dear madam, I was obliged to leave off abruptly, E III 14 440 8
obliged and affectionate son, F. C. Weston Churchill. E III 14 443 8
She was obliged, in spite of her previous determination to E III 15 444 1
When he came to Miss Woodhouse, he was obliged to read the E III 15 445 14
15
How much worse, had they been obliged to meet! E III 16 451 1
The pain of being obliged to practise concealment towards E III 17 463 15
obliged to separate before the end of the first quarter. E III 17 469 36
persuasion of his being obliged to go to Randall's every E III 18 476 43
found himself obliged to confess to her soon afterwards. P III 1 10 19
Lady Russell felt obliged to oppose her dear Anne's known P III 2 14 11
clergyman, you know, is obliged to go into infected rooms, P III 3 20 17
lot of those who are not obliged to follow any, who can P III 3 20 17
concluded you must have been obliged to give up the party." P III 5 39 36
with one, that one is obliged to be checking every moment; P III 6 45 8
She was obliged to kneel down by the sofa, and remain P III 9 79 25
and quietly obliged her to be assisted into the carriage. P III 10 91 41
her nature obliged her to begin an acquaintance with him. P III 11 100 23
Anne was obliged to turn away, to rise, to walk to a P IV 5 160 26
him unseen, but was obliged to touch as well as address P IV 6 169 25
but she was still obliged to wait, for the Admiral had P IV 6 170 30
that the others were obliged to settle it for them; Miss P IV 7 174 3
"I am much obliged to you," was her answer, "but I am not P IV 7 176 11
She was very much obliged to him, but declined it all, P IV 7 177 15
Anne would have been particularly obliged to her cousin, P IV 7 178 24
She had already been obliged to tell Lady Russell that P IV 7 178 27
was obliged, and not sorry to be obliged, to hurry away. P IV 7 180 36
a touch on her shoulder obliged Anne to turn round.-- P IV 8 190 47
this morning particularly obliged to her for coming, P IV 9 192 4
She was obliged to recollect that her seeing the letter P IV 9 204 76
77
Anne felt truly obliged to her for such kindness; and P IV 10 224 52
53
They were obliged to move. P IV 10 225 62
authority of his, been obliged to attend (perhaps for half P IV 10 228 70
absence perhaps, and obliged to put into another port, he P 1 6 235 31
and was obliged to plead indisposition and excuse herself. P IV 11 238 45
Thus much indeed he was obliged to acknowledge--that he P IV 11 241 61
gentleness; but he was obliged to acknowledge that only at P IV 11 241 61
house so happy as to be obliged to find an alloy in some P IV 11 245 77
While he was not obliged to say that he believed her to P IV 12 251 10
sensible of it, was obliged in a few moments to cut short, S 1 364 1
obliged them to be stationary and healthy at Willingden. S 2 373 1
a distance, she had been obliged to go there last S 3 378 1
into their house, & obliged to take her tea with him them, S 6 390 1
are <u>obliged</u> to be mean in their servility to her.-- S 7 402 1
And here they were obliged to part--Miss D. being too much S 8 404 1
to his purse, & prudence obliged him to prefer the S 8 405 2
We are often obliged to check him."-- S 9 411 1
"I am much obliged to you, replied Charlotte--but I <u>prefer</u> S 10 417 1
little awkward on being first obliged to admit her mistake. S 11 420 1
him hardly used; to be obliged to stand back in his own S 12 427 1

OBLIGING (66)
or more obliging manners, when acting without restraint. LS 18 273 3
The whole being explained, many obliging things were said NA I 4 33 6
his curate at Woodston obliging him to leave them on NA II 13 221 7
"You are very obliging. SS I 13 65 36
Lucy appeared everything that was amiable and obliging. SS III 13 362 5
mind, & a great wish of obliging--& when they returned to W 323 3
By nature inoffensive, friendly and obliging, his PP I 5 18 1
of obliging her in return, by sitting down to whist. PP I 16 76 6
pleasure, I am sure, in obliging the company with an air; PP I 18 101 71
Lady Catherine's behaviour was most friendly and obliging. PP II 3 146 19
for the mere purpose of obliging Lady Catherine, have PP III 14 356 55
56
that third was of an obliging, yielding temper; and they MP I 2 17 21
idea of carrying their obliging manners to the sacrifice MP I 4 35 7
with most appearance of obliging the others, to secure it, MP I 8 80 29
"Nothing could be more obliging than your manner, I am MP I 10 102 46
And though Dr. Grant is most kind and obliging to me, and MP I 11 111 28
her obliging manners down to her light and graceful tread. MP I 11 112 33
to dwell more on the obliging, accommodating purport of MP I 13 129 39
such a difficulty of obliging your cousins in a trifle of MP I 15 146 53
of some use, and obliging her aunt: it is all her fault. MP III 1 323 56
delight in the idea of obliging her to love him in a very MP III 2 327 4
she did not love, and obliging her administer to the MP III 7 376 4
he was much more gentle, obliging, and attentive to other MP III 10 406 21
deal upon his being so very good-humoured and obliging. E I 4 28 6
of them--and in every thing else he was so very obliging! E I 4 28 6
Mr. Elton is good humoured, cheerful, obliging, and gentle. E I 4 34 42
"He is very obliging," said Emma; "but is he sure that E I 8 59 26
the charade you were so obliging as to leave with us; E I 9 81 79
80
been so complaisant and obliging, so full of courtesy and E I 16 136 9
He was always agreeable and obliging, and speaking E I 16 139 20
Woodhouse is so obliging to say about Jane's handwriting?" E II 1 158 12
every body says the same obliging things. I am sure she E II 1 159 18
"So obliging of you! E II 1 159 20
You are very obliging to say such things-- but certainly E II 1 161 27
be uneasy. you are too obliging, my dear Miss Woodhouse; E II 3 176 50
must decline their obliging invitation; beginning with my E II 7 209 14
neighbours might be so obliging occasionally to put it to E II 8 216 16
'So very kind and obliging!-- E II 8 225 78
"No trouble in the world, ma'am," said the obliging Mrs. E II 9 235 39
there he is, in the most obliging manner in the world, E II 9 236 46
So very obliging!-- E II 9 236 46
are extremely civil and obliging to us, the Wallises, E II 9 236 46
So very obliging of Mr. Frank Churchill! E II 9 237 51
friends would be so very obliging as to take some, 'Oh!' E II 9 238 51
You seem but just come--so very obliging of you." E II 10 245 54
If Mr. and Mrs. Weston will be so obliging as to call here E II 11 252 32
However, she seems a very obliging, pretty-behaved young E II 14 279 54
"You are very obliging; but as to all that, I am very E II 17 301 17
"You are very obliging.-- E II 18 305 5
As the door opened she was heard, "so very obliging of you! E III 2 322 18
19
You are extremely obliging--and if I were not an old E III 2 327 37
This was Mr. Elton! the amiable, obliging, gentle Mr. E III 2 328 38
Mr. Churchill, Oh! you are too obliging! E III 2 329 45
My dear sir, you are too obliging.-- E III 2 329 45
to accept dear Miss Woodhouse's most obliging invitation. E III 5 344 3
My dear sir, you are too obliging. E III 5 349 24
but Mr. Knightley was so obliging as to put up with it, E III 13 431 38
attentive neighbour, an obliging landlord, the husband of P III 2 11 2
was a perfect gentleman, unaffected, warm, and obliging. P III 11 97 15
and Mr. Elliot (always obliging) just setting off for P IV 7 175 5
she could assume a most obliging, placid look, and appear P IV 10 213 10
also going out on some obliging purpose of saving her P IV 10 215 14
proper alacrity, a most obliging compliance for public P IV 11 240 59
are extremely obliging sir, & I take you at your word.-- S 1 365 1
particularly useful & obliging to them; who had attended S 2 374 1
woman,--a very obliging, friendly neighbour; a cheerful, S 3 376 1

OBLIGINGLY (3)
the lock of hair, which you so obligingly bestowed on me. SS II 7 183 13
you so obligingly bestowed on me'--that is unpardonable. SS II 7 190 56
very great; but they obligingly satisfied it, with the PP III 15 361 5

OBLIGINGNESS (2)
general civility and obligingness, they possessed its MP I 4 34 4
with the greatest obligingness, with an expression and MP I 7 64 12

OBLIQUELY (1)
A branch only, of the valley, winding more obliquely S 4 383 1

OBLIVION (2)
the general air of oblivion among them was highly P III 4 30 10
and oblivion of the past--how natural, how certain too! P III 7 60 28

OBLONG (2)
than a mere, spacious, oblong room, fitted up for the MP I 9 85 6
length sir"--offering him the two little oblong extracts.-- S 1 366 1

OBSCURE (1)
First, as being the means of bringing persons of obscure P III 3 19 16

OBSCURITY (4)
with obscurity when it might rise to distinction." MP II 4 214 42
with a girl of such obscurity--and most prudent men would E I 8 64 47
now in such retirement, such obscurity, so thrown away.-- E II 15 283 7
and that there was no obscurity, nothing doubtful, in the E III 18 474 30

OBSEQUIOUS (1)
to all the parading and obsequious civility of her husband. PP III 18 384 26

OBSEQUIOUSNESS (1)
of pride and obsequiousness, self-importance and humility. PP I 15 70 1

OBSERVABLE (2)
long after it was observable to everybody else--burst on SS III 14 378 14
for any thing of peculiar anxiety to be observable. E II 8 218 37

OBSERVANCE (7)
no smile, no continued observance attended it; his eyes NA I 12 93 4
of honour, and such an observance of decorum as might MP II 12 294 16
you wish to shew me any observance, you will not give way MP III 1 321 48
of early obedience and long observance to break through. E I 18 147 19
with the closest observance; and wretchedly as she had E III 12 416 2
habit of such general observance as "Miss Elliot," that P IV 4 147 8
in the degree of observance & attention which clara paid.-- S 6 392 1

OBSERVANCES (4)
manner, with all the observances which he supposed a PP I 19 104 1
the usual observances without any apparent want of spirits. MP II 9 265 20
nothing beyond the observances of complaisance; had never P III 2 16 16
feelings, as far as the observances due to Mr. Elliot's P IV 9 210 99

OBSERVANT (8)
I do not mean to say that I am particularly observant or SS II 2 148 12
were his due, by the observant eyes of Lucy, though she SS II 13 241 20
Mr. Weston, however, too eager to be very observant, too E II 17 304 29
Be observant of him. E III 4 342 39
resenting the suspicion, might yet be made observant by it. P III 5 35 17
not be too nice, or too observant, if Elizabeth were his P IV 3 140 11
He was steady, observant, moderate, candid; never run away P IV 4 146 6
fallen within the ken of <u>her</u> more observant eyes.-- S 12 426 1

OBSERVATION (86)
all probability not an observation was made, nor an NA I 10 72 8
could not from her own observation help thinking, that NA I 11 86 50
pass under one's own observation; and as for the little NA I 14 109 23
Perhaps they may want observation, discernment, judgment, NA I 14 112 36
but by himself; the observation of which, with his NA II 5 156 4
her observation, would have given her the consciousness. NA II 5 161 26
which was to escape her observation at first, immediately NA II 6 168 10
for her observation which sent his daughter to the bell. NA II 8 187 15
and from our own observation can bear witness to her NA II 9 197 25
the probable, your own observation of what is passing NA II 9 197 29

by her own unassisted observation, already discovered; but NA II 11 211 15
imagination lively, his observation just and correct, and SS I 4 20 9
Elinor needed little observation to perceive that her SS I 11 55 6
of common sense and observation; and then they may be more SS I 11 56 11
Elinor was not inclined, after a little observation, to SS I 20 112 28
character which her own observation or the intelligence of SS II 4 159 1
beginning with the observation of "your sister looks SS II 5 172 40
to screen her from the observation of others, while SS II 6 177 12
indifferent to the observation of all the world, at SS II 9 201 2
composure; made no observation on it, and at first shed no SS II 10 217 17
Nothing escaped her minute observation and general SS II 14 249 8
his next observation, "in a cottage near Dawlish." SS II 14 251 15
could not escape her observation, for though she was too SS III 3 281 9
to be driven by the observation of his epicurism, his SS III 6 305 15
the latter lady's observation;--she could discover in them SS III 6 305 16
had passed within her observation the preceding evening SS III 8 328 61
To Elinor, the observation of the latter was particularly SS III 10 341 6
continued, "one observation may, I think, be fairly drawn SS III 11 352 16
17
was exactly like Robert,"--was his immediate observation.-- SS III 13 364 12
observation of others, that it was an excellent ball.-- W 329 9
Tho' rather distressed by such observation, Emma could not W 331 11
with more quickness of observation and less pliancy of PP I 4 15 11
him to talk, she made some slight observation on the dance. PP I 18 91 8
it had escaped his observation; whichever were the case, PP II 1 134 3
mind; and from the observation of the day altogether, she PP II 6 162 11
and nothing escaped her observation that was passing in PP II 7 169 3
addressed a slight observation on the house and garden to PP II 7 171 10
Charlotte's observation, and hurried her away to her room. PP II 11 194 32
could not escape the observation of a young man of nearly PP II 12 200 5
at Longbourn there would be leisure enough for observation. PP II 14 217 16
proud; but the observation of a very few minutes convinced PP III 2 261 3
niece, directed their observation towards each with an PP III 2 261 6
This observation would not have prevented her from trying PP III 3 268 5
She had scarcely needed her present observation to be PP III 9 318 19
"Did you speak from your own observation," said she, "when PP III 16 371 42
from my own observation, it is a manoeuvring business. MP I 5 46 22
nature, with little observation; her attention was all for MP I 8 81 31
last seemed, to Fanny's observation, to have been as much MP I 10 104 51
It is impossible that your own observation can have given MP I 11 110 24
either sister without observation, and seldom without MP I 12 115 5
is not in love with Henry," was her observation to Mary. MP I 17 161 10
Little observation there was necessary to tell him that MP II 3 200 20
food for Fanny's observation; and finding herself quite MP II 4 214 46
or observation, which she could not avoid answering. MP II 5 227 68
had fallen within his observation, that he had not heard MP II 7 251 63
To dance without much observation or any extraordinary MP II 9 267 22
"We miss our two young men," was Sir Thomas's observation MP II 11 284 9
there is more general observation and taste, a more MP III 3 340 23
, on farther observation, admit no right of superiority. MP III 9 395 3
now and then the quiet observation of "my poor sister MP III 13 428 14
from personal observation, better than herself; not one MP III 14 429 2
at a window, in eager observation of the departure of a MP III 15 446 34
a man of ordinary observation and delicacy, like Mr. Elton, E I 16 136 9
is very young to settle," was Mr. Woodhouse's observation. E II 3 174 34
and continual observation of, how much he seemed attached?- E II 4 184 10
points of pursuit or observation there was no positive E II 6 197 3
but an instant's observation convinced her that it was E II 7 206 4
Her observation had been pretty correct. E II 15 281 1
exercise all her quick observation, and speedily determine E III 1 315 3
as much as he could, with as little apparent observation. E III 5 341 21
with more particular observation, more exact understanding E III 6 357 34
of a few moments' free observation of the entrance and E III 6 362 43
in tranquil observation of the beautiful views beneath her. E III 7 374 54
The power of observation would be soon given--frightfully E III 12 416 2
our good friends, the Eltons," was his next observation.-- E III 15 447 22
With a great deal of quiet observation, and a knowledge, P III 5 34 12
and without any observation of what he might be P III 8 68 31
32
yet quite doubtful, as far as Anne's observation reached. P III 9 74 8
Anne, after a little observation, felt she must submit to. P IV 4 147 8
fund of good sense and observation which, as a companion, P IV 5 155 9
leave her any power of observation; and she passed along P IV 8 186 22
that has fallen within my observation, to do otherwise. P IV 9 196 33
that had fallen within their observation, but Anne heard P IV 11 231 11
admit from subsequent observation, that they appeared to S 6 391 1
Sir Edward's required longer observation. S 7 396 1
perfectly secure from observation!--the whole field open S 12 427 1

OBSERVATIONS (23)

The result of her observations was not agreeable. NA II 4 149 1
His son and daughter's observations were of a different NA II 11 214 27
"Perhaps," said Willoughby, "his observations may have SS I 10 51 23
"I may venture to say that his observations have stretched SS I 10 51 24
had opportunity for observations, which, with a most SS I 12 60 8
Should the result of her observations be unfavourable, she SS II 4 159 1
answer, and make such observations, as the subject might SS III 1 260 8
some new observations of thread-bare morality to listen to. PP I 12 60 7
reflections which her observations gave birth to, made her PP I 18 98 63
The observations of her uncle and aunt now began; and each PP III 1 257 67
betray her into any observations seemingly unhandsome. MP II 3 199 16
the habit of such idle observations would have thought MP II 7 238 2
Her ill opinion of him was founded chiefly on observations, MP III 1 317 38
own hopes, and his own observations, still feeling a right, MP III 6 368 7
these very pleasant observations, which were otherwise of E I 9 72 16
one subject, all her observations, all her convictions, E I 17 141 5
of fancying what the observations of all those might be, E II 8 212 4
were farther talked of, and the usual observations made. E II 16 297 44
nor could he avoid observations which, unless it were like E III 5 344 2
came to assist his observations, he must--yes, he E III 5 349 26
case: but, from all my observations, I am convinced of her E III 18 474 34
Other opportunities of making her observations could not P III 10 82 1
did but confirm my own observations, the last time I was P III 10 87 26

OBSERVE (78)

intimacy, especially to observe his altered manner in LS 10 257 2
upon her gown, she must observe it aloud, whether there NA I 9 60 1
That she might not appear, however, to observe or expect NA I 10 75 24
One thing, however, I must observe. NA I 10 77 37
you are to observe, was her own, particularly her own. NA I 14 107 9
historians, I must observe, that they might well be NA I 14 109 25
it impossible for her to observe any thing farther, and NA II 5 161 25
moralizing strain, to observe that our pleasures in this NA II 11 210 7
house, for her either to observe or to say a great deal; NA II 11 212 18
She could not but observe that the abundance of the dinner NA II 11 214 27
"Certainly not; but if you observe, people always live for SS I 2 10 20
She was first called to observe and approve him farther, SS I 3 16 7
motionless although we can observe you no longer!-- SS I 5 27 8
her some other new acquaintance to see and observe. SS I 21 118 1
side glance at her companion to observe its effect on her. SS I 22 129 12
and determined not to observe her attitude, inquired in a SS II 6 176 7
from which it sprung, nor observe the studied attentions SS II 12 233 16
It amused her to observe that all her friends seemed SS III 6 301 2
time; and anxious to observe the result of it herself, she SS III 7 310 9
"Only observe whether she dances with Capt. Hunter, more W 320 2
& she heard Ly. Osborne observe that they had made a point W 329 9
but to which he must observe that a verbal postscript from W 338 17
Mr. Bingley and his eldest sister, to observe the game. PP I 8 38 39
Perhaps by and bye I may observe that private balls are PP I 18 91 11
for give me leave to observe that I consider the clerical PP I 18 97 60
61
Allow me, by the way, to observe, my fair cousin, that I PP I 19 106 10
all those elegant decorums which other people may observe. PP II 4 153 15
and could observe the three ladies before her composedly.-- PP II 6 162 11

leisure to observe the real state of her sister's spirits. PP II 17 227 26
of his concern, and observe her in compassionate silence. PP III 4 277 11
Elizabeth would not observe her; and when at last Kitty PP III 13 345 11
Elizabeth longed to observe that Mr. Bingley had been a PP III 16 371 46
I only meant to observe, that it ought not to be lightly MP I 1 7 7
she could not carelessly observe that "she believed it was MP I 8 81 33
push me so hard, I must observe, that I am not entirely MP I 11 111 28
Fanny looked on and listened, not unamused to observe the MP I 14 131 4
in--nobody but the complainer would observe any directions. MP I 18 165 2
Fanny was wanted only to prompt and observe them. MP I 18 170 24
But I must observe, that five is the very awkwardest of MP II 5 220 30
of having such another to observe her, was a great MP II 5 223 47
Sir Thomas could not but observe with complacency, even MP II 6 234 17
their niece; she not only promised, but did observe it. MP III 2 332 20
here to do needlework, I observe she always turns the lock E I 1 9 19
Did not you observe her manner of answering me? E I 6 44 17
wives in the case at present indeed, as you observe. E I 6 46 22
regard to these children, I observe we never disagree." E I 12 98 3
"Yes, he has been gone just four weeks, as you observe, E II 3 176 44
and lively one; she could observe nothing wrong in his E II 7 205 2
observe it whenever I meet you under those circumstances. E II 8 213 10
"I was going to observe, sir," said Frank Churchill, "that E II 11 251 27
assure you, as far as I could observe, are strikingly like. E II 14 273 21
silence--wanting only to observe enough for Isabella's E II 16 292 10
At the same time it is fair to observe, that I am one of E II 18 309 31
circle round the fire, to observe in their various modes, E III 2 320 5
With great indignation did he continue to observe him; E III 5 348 22
and distrust, to observe also his two blinded companions. E III 5 348 22
"I was only going to observe, that though such unfortunate E III 7 373 44
Emma was gratified, to observe such a proof in her of E III 9 388 14
Her present home, he could not but observe, was E III 9 389 16
You told me to observe him carefully, and let his E III 11 411 39
You will observe that I have not yet indulged myself in E III 14 441 8
whisper, "I mentioned no names, you will observe.-- E III 16 454 14
15
He might observe that it was so. E III 17 463 15
Observe the turn of her throat. E III 18 479 70
Observe her eyes, as she is looking up at my father.-- E III 18 479 70
"I must take leave to observe, Sir Walter," said Mr. P III 3 17 1
then added, "I presume to observe, Sir Walter, that, in P III 3 17 2
3
it worth their while to observe me, but Sir Walter Elliot P III 3 17 4
which, as I was going to observe, since applications will P III 3 17 4
an old friend, and observe their eagerness of conversation P IV 6 168 24
It did not surprise, but it grieved Anne to observe that P IV 7 176 9
and as long as she dared observe, he did not look again: P IV 8 188 41
"Did you observe the woman who opened the door to you, P IV 9 197 38
to, and daring not even to try to observe their effect. P IV 10 225 54
"That is precisely what I was going to observe," cried Mrs. P IV 11 230 7
But let me observe that all histories are against you, all P IV 11 234 27
information, to such of the Heywoods as could observe.-- S 2 371 1
they sat, could not but observe Lady D. & Miss B. walking S 7 395 1

OBSERVED (132)

of her disposition, he observed that whatever might have LS 8 255 2
Reginald observed all that passed, in perfect silence. LS 20 276 3
that I have always observed his attachment with the LS 20 276 5
my visitor; and at first observed Sir James with an LS 22 280 2
the eldest young lady observed aloud to the rest, "how NA I 4 32 4
Well, I never observed that. NA I 6 42 27
them how they did, and observed they both looked very ugly. NA I 7 49 43
While talking to each other, she had observed with some NA I 12 95 17
I use the verb 'to torment,' as I observed to be your own NA I 14 109 25
your brother's fortitude," observed the General to Eleanor. NA II 7 175 13
which he had closely observed her, he added, "as there is NA II 9 196 23
"But perhaps," observed Catherine, "though she has behaved NA II 10 206 33
"This has been a strange acquaintance," observed Mrs. NA II 14 236 15
spare bedchamber, she observed that there was no immediate SS I 8 39 17
to table, which Sir John observed with great contentment. SS I 13 67 61
as far as it can be observed, may now be very advisable." SS I 15 81 44
had often observed at Norland in their mutual behaviour. SS I 16 87 23
"You must begin your improvements on this house," observed SS I 17 92 24
He made her no answer; and only observed, after again SS I 19 108 39
observed with regret that they were only eight altogether. SS I 20 111 18
fingers, she fondly observed, "how playful William is!" SS I 21 121 8
She merely observed that he was perfectly good humoured SS I 21 122 16
by him, that he even observed Marianne as she quitted the SS II 4 162 8
Perhaps he has not observed you yet." SS II 6 176 5
finished the letters, observed to her that they contained SS II 7 188 43
which Marianne sometimes observed him, and the gentleness SS II 10 216 15
I observed him narrowly, and am convinced of it. SS II 11 223 20
She observed, in a low voice, to her mother, that they SS III 11 355 39
I have observed it ever since you came home, & I am afraid W 318 2
"I am glad of it--observed Mrs E., because their coming W 323 3
how they make a second choice." observed Mr Edwardes.-- W 326 6
"I am sure we shall be great friends"--she observed, with W 349 24
Emma who closely observed him, perceived nothing that did W 355 28
"For whether he dined at 8 or 9, as he observed, was a W 356 28
"Pride," observed Mary, who piqued herself upon the PP I 5 20 20
Mr. Bennet coolly observed, "from all that I can collect PP I 7 29 5
6
"I admire the activity of your benevolence," observed Mary, PP I 7 32 38
my notice." "you observed it, Mr. Darcy, I am sure," said PP I 8 36 7
"I am afraid, Mr. Darcy," observed Miss Bingley, in a half PP I 8 36 12
"Then," observed Elizabeth, "you must comprehend a great PP I 8 39 48
there is something new to be observed in them for ever." PP I 9 43 18
I have more than once observed to Lady Catherine, that her PP I 14 67 9
and said, "I have often observed how little young ladies PP I 14 69 15
16
The idea soon reached to conviction, as she observed his PP I 17 88 14
spoken so sensibly, and observed in a half-whisper to Lady PP I 18 101 71
hand; for I have often observed that resignation is never PP I 20 114 32
warm commendation of him, narrowly observed them both. PP II 2 142 18
Mr. Collins joining in, observed, "yes, Miss Elizabeth, PP II 5 157 6
7
the least, and who she observed to Mrs. Collins, was a PP II 6 163 15
Lady Catherine then observed, "your father's estate is PP II 6 164 15
16
hasty departure, she observed, "how very suddenly you all PP II 9 177 3
4
As she spoke, she observed him looking at her earnestly, PP II 10 184 20
From that moment I observed my friend's behaviour PP II 12 197 5
Lady Catherine observed, after dinner, that Miss Bennet PP II 14 211 5
6
"If one could but go to Brighton!" observed Mrs. Bennet. PP II 18 229 6
But I have always observed, that they who are good-natured PP III 1 249 33
He observed to her, at a moment when the others were PP III 2 262 8
Elizabeth soon observed, and instantly understood it. PP III 4 278 19
One day's delay she observed, would be of small importance; PP III 7 307 48
alteration in it, and observed, with a laugh, that it was PP III 9 315 4
I had narrowly observed her during the two visits which I PP III 16 371 43
our way, Mrs. Norris," observed Sir Thomas, "as to the MP I 1 10 17
was present, she calmly observed to her, "so, Fanny, you MP I 3 24 7
"because," as it was observed by her aunts, "she might MP I 4 35 7
which he had already observed, and of which she was almost MP I 7 66 14
it would be Anhalt," observed the lady, archly, after a MP I 15 144 40
opened her lips before, observed in a sarcastic manner, MP I 15 148 60
her kinder aunt Bertram observed on her behalf, "one MP I 18 167 7
8
then correcting himself, observed, that he need not MP II 1 178 7
"But they," he observed to Fanny, "have a claim. MP II 3 196 2
"But is not it very natural," observed Edmund, "that Mrs. MP II 5 218 17
I observed he was hoarse on Thursday night." MP II 5 222 39

Grant and Edmund, now observed, "those gentlemen must have MP II 5 226 60
beauty; and from what I observed of her eyes and mouth, I MP II 6 229 5
Finding by whom he was observed, Henry Crawford addressed MP II 7 247 37
himself in the meanwhile observed by Sir Thomas, who was MP II 7 249 49
her business at once and observed that if she would be so MP II 8 257 15
parcel, which Fanny had observed in her hand when they met. MP II 8 257 15
spontaneously observed, "Sir Thomas, I have been thinking-- MP II 11 285 10
Thomas good humouredly observed, that joy had taken away MP II 13 304 16
You must have observed his attentions; and though you MP III 1 316 29
Fanny, I have often observed it before,--she likes to go MP III 1 323 56
that he observed to pass before, and at, and after dinner. MP III 3 336 7
"Our liturgy," observed Crawford, "has beauties, which not MP III 3 340 25
And I observed that she always spoke of you as 'Fanny,' MP III 4 352 42
On this principle, he soon afterwards observed, "they go MP III 4 354 48
more she recollected and observed, the more deeply was she MP III 6 366 4
her a cordial hug, and observed that she was grown into a MP III 7 380 22
as you may suppose," observed her ladyship, after giving MP III 13 426 11
When this was over, Mr. Woodhouse gratefully observed, "it E I 1 10 21
22
Oh! yes, it is not likely you should ever have observed E I 4 29 15
"Oh! yes, I observed it, I assure you. E I 6 44 18
beauty she wanted,"--observed Mrs. Weston to him--not in E I 6 47 31
Knightley could not have observed him as she had done, E I 8 67 57
Churchills, I fancy," observed Mr. John Knightley coolly. E I 11 96 26
"Christmas weather," observed Mr. Elton. E I 13 115 39
when they parted, Emma observed her to be looking around E II 5 186 2
As Mrs. Weston observed, "all young people would have E II 7 206 3
But you observed nothing of course, for it seems to be a E II 8 218 36
room, observed, "I do not think it is so very small. E II 11 254 45
46
"And the staircase--you know, as I came in, I observed how E II 14 273 19
I have observed, Mrs. Elton, in the course of my life, E II 18 308 27
"Miss Smith!--Oh!--I had not observed.-- E III 2 327 37
side, which, having once observed, he could not persuade E III 5 343 2
"It is odd though," observed his father, "that you should E III 5 345 14
furniture, I think is best observed by meals within doors. E III 6 355 21
She had often observed the change, to almost the same E III 11 409 35
for "such things," he observed, "always got about." E III 12 417 5
observed the same beautiful effect of the western sun!-- E III 14 434 2
and then, with a smile, observed, "humph!--a fine E III 15 445 7
all, I have often observed, extremely awkward and remiss.-- E III 16 458 42
been seen together," he observed, "once at Tattersal's, P III 1 8 16
and pacing the room, he observed sarcastically, "there are P III 3 18 5
6
sooner than any other man; I have observed it all my life. P III 3 19 16
I have often observed it; they soon lose the look of youth. P III 3 20 17
foretold, Mr. Shepherd observed, Sir Walter's concerns P III 3 21 18
"Then I take it for granted," observed Sir Walter, "that P III 3 22 22
care of, Mr. Shepherd observed, without a lady: he did not P III 3 22 24
sympathetic cordiality, observed to his wife as they drove P III 5 32 4
Charles's attentions to Henrietta had been observed by her P III 9 74 6
I am sure, I should have observed them, and the livery too; P III 12 106 16
He had frequently observed, as he walked, that one P IV 3 141 13
She watched--observed--reflected--and finally determined P IV 5 154 8
drawn up near its pavement!" observed Sir Walter.-- P IV 5 157 19
than she had ever observed before; he looked quite red. P IV 7 175 6
I observed no one in particular." P IV 9 197 39
I called, I observed the blinds were let down immediately." P IV 10 215 16
Not that he will value it as he ought," he observed, " P IV 10 217 20
been caught, as Mr P. observed with delight to Charlotte, S 4 383 1
She observed them well.-- S 6 391 1
freely, I beleive, than W. Indians." observed Mr Parker.-- S 6 392 1
animation for him, observed with considerable pleasure.-- S 10 415 1

OBSERVER (8)
expectations of its new observer; but they were not in NA II 9 191 3
herself the nicest observer of the two;-- she watched his SS III 6 305 16
given the most acute observer, a conviction that, however PP II 12 197 5
and unembarrassed an observer as ever Mr. Darcy had been, PP III 2 261 4
as Julia spoke, might have amused a disinterested observer. MP I 9 89 26
I had not, Miss Crawford, been an inattentive observer of MP III 5 363 21
the skill of such an observer on such a question as E I 8 67 57
Isabella, to be sure, was no very quick observer; yet if E III 17 463 16

OBSERVERS (1)
those evil-minded observers, dearest Mary, who make much MP I 5 46 23

OBSERVES (1)
I see how closely she observes him & Lady Susan. LS 24 291 16

OBSERVING (63)
occasionally caught her observing his countenance with LS 17 270 3
observing the rules I have laid down for their discourse. LS 19 274 3
Compliments on good looks now passed; and, after observing NA I 4 32 2
her care, that no one, observing her during the first four NA I 12 92 4
Catherine, observing that Isabella's eyes were continually NA II 3 143 2
cells pointed out, and observing several doors, that were NA II 8 183 2
to Lady Middleton for observing at this moment, "that it SS I 12 62 27
concluding however by observing, that as they were all got SS I 13 66 60
Elinor, without observing the varying complexion of her SS II 3 153 1
was all the time busy in observing the direction of the SS II 5 168 8
perceived her; and after observing her for a few moments SS II 7 180 1
2
Elinor had some difficulty here to refrain from observing, SS III 5 295 17
the assertion, by observing that Miss Morton was the SS III 14 373 3
the persuasion and delight of each observing friend. SS III 14 379 17
could not help observing how comfortably it had passed. W 343 19
he had the pleasure of observing to Mr Watson that he W 359 28
Observing his second daughter employed in trimming a hat, PP I 2 6 1
2
Occupied in observing Mr. Bingley's attentions to her PP I 6 23 12
were at piquet, and Mrs. Hurst was observing their game. PP I 10 47 1
Elizabeth could not help observing as she turned over some PP I 10 51 46
but he declined it, observing, that he could imagine but PP I 11 56 12
observing that he seemed very fortunate in his patroness. PP I 14 66 1
Mr. Bennet accepted the challenge, observing that he acted PP I 14 69 17
Mr. Wickham's attention was caught; and after observing Mr. PP I 16 83 51
him often; and after observing that he was a very PP II 18 233 27
and accordingly began by observing, that his arrival had PP III 1 256 61
material relief, from observing how much the beauty of her PP III 11 337 56
she yet received pleasure from observing his behaviour. PP III 12 340 13
Mrs. Norris was often observing to the others, that she MP I 1 5 4
certainty, by carelessly observing to Mrs. Norris,-- "I MP I 3 28 38
39
end of the table, and in observing Mr. Rushworth, who was MP I 6 52 1
and was very happy in observing all that was new, and MP I 8 80 31
best companions; and in observing the appearance of the MP I 8 80 31
a view of the house, and observing that "it was a sort of MP I 8 82 35
private character, and observing his general conduct, MP I 9 93 49
Edmund, observing her; "why would not you speak sooner? MP I 9 95 68
this way, Miss Bertram observing the iron gate, expressed MP I 10 97 4
on her to decide it, by observing to Mr. Yates, that this MP I 14 132 8
Edmund, who was kindly observing her, but unwilling to MP I 15 146 53
observing with decided pleasure how much she was grown! MP II 1 177 7
It was beginning to look brighter, when Fanny, observing a MP II 4 206 5
and he sat silently observing them for a few minutes; MP II 7 249 49
intimacy I have been observing with the greatest pleasure, MP II 9 263 16
Fanny, not able to refrain entirely from observing them, MP II 10 279 21
ample opportunity for observing how he sped with Fanny, MP III 3 336 7
he had the happiness of observing its good effects not MP III 9 397 8
Mary Crawford, and observing to Fanny how impossible it MP III 17 470 25
passing it without a slackened pace and observing eyes.-- E I 10 83 2
wishing her joy--yet observing, that she knew the first E I 14 121 14
in the daily habit of observing--to be addressing me in E I 15 130 30
door without going in--observing, as she proposed it to E II 1 155 3
he thanked her, observing, "how lucky that we should E II 8 213 9
He seemed often observing her. E III 2 326 32
some of her feelings, by observing audibly to her partner, E III 2 328 42
43
Her silence disturbed him; and after observing her a E III 18 472 21
22
"I have no scruple of observing to you, how nonsensical P III 6 46 10
non-commissioned class, observing over it, that she too P III 8 66 22
was looking at herself--observing her altered features, P III 8 72 58
felt as she said, in observing, "I think you are very P IV 1 125 15
16
had suffered herself, by observing, with a happy glance P IV 2 134 30
sandy-haired) without observing that every woman's eye was P IV 3 142 13
for him, of her being in short intently observing him. P IV 7 179 28
a glow; and Mrs. Smith, observing the high colour in her P IV 9 204 74
75

OBSTACLE (5)
of fine gravel, without obstacle, alarm or solemnity of NA II 5 161 25
there was but one obstacle, in short, to be mentioned; but NA II 16 249 1
What formidable obstacle is she now to bring forward? SS II 3 156 11
sake, that one greater obstacle preserved her from SS II 13 238 1
full eighteen to Manchester-Street--was a serious obstacle. E III 1 318 10

OBSTACLES (4)
mourning in secret over obstacles which must divide her SS II 1 141 4
of the family obstacles which judgment had always opposed PP II 11 189 5
Two obstacles of the five being thus removed, Mrs. Bennet PP III 13 345 11
do seem objections and obstacles of a very serious nature; E III 4 342 39

OBSTINACY (6)
Vernon shewed no sign of obstinacy or perverseness during LS 17 271 7
the obstinacy which could resist such arguments as these. SS III 1 267 40
as atoned for by your obstinacy in adhering to it?" PP I 10 49 32
I fancy, Lizzy, that obstinacy is the real defect of his PP III 10 324 2
to have the charge of obstinacy and ingratitude of her MP I 16 150 1
of principle and the obstinacy of self-will, between the P IV 11 242 63

OBSTINATE (13)
"I did not think you had been so obstinate, Catherine," NA I 13 99 10
"She is as obstinate as-----" NA I 13 101 23
To be always firm must be to be often obstinate. NA II 1 134 36
for, with a most obstinate and ill-judged secrecy, she SS II 9 209 28
right, do not think me obstinate if I still assert, that, PP II 3 148 26
mother was too happy, to be quite so obstinate as usual. PP III 7 307 48
But our visitor was very obstinate. PP III 10 324 2
"Obstinate, headstrong girl! PP III 14 355 47
I shall think her a very obstinate, ungrateful girl, if MP I 15 147 55
Self-willed, obstinate, selfish, and ungrateful. MP III 1 319 40
But had she been less obstinate, or of less weight with MP III 16 450 11
a stray letter-boy on an obstinate mule, were the E II 9 233 24
She would not have been obstinate if I had not been weak. P IV 8 183 13

OBSTRUCTED (1)
may be apparently obstructed, will do in securing every SS III 14 376 11

OBTAIN (11)
though whenever she could obtain the outside of a letter NA I 1 14 1
He could only obtain a promise of their calling at the SS I 21 119 5
her sister could never obtain her opinion of any article SS II 4 165 24
been always a rascal, to obtain something like forgiveness SS III 8 319 23
She found it difficult to obtain even a word from her PP III 2 261 3
assist her endeavours to obtain that promise from her PP III 16 367 9
the past; and I hoped to obtain your forgiveness, to PP III 16 370 32
obtain them, and could better bear a subordinate situation. MP II 3 204 32
return, and hoped to obtain his approbation of her doing. MP II 9 262 11
it was so essential to obtain every twenty-four hours. P IV 1 122 4
hazard all, dare, all, atcheive all, to obtain her.-- S 8 403 1

OBTAINED (22)
Pulteney-Street, and obtained their sanction of his wishes. NA II 2 140 9
Soon after her death I obtained it for my own, and hung it NA II 7 181 39
yielded, and that once obtained--and their own hearts made NA II 16 249 2
till after Eleanor had obtained his forgiveness of Henry, NA II 16 250 4
have been accidentally obtained; it might not have been SS I 22 134 53
obtained her sister's consent to wait for that knowledge. SS II 9 203 9
place been so unfairly obtained, she confined herself to SS III 2 276 27
She had obtained private intelligence that Mr. Darcy did PP I 11 54 3
This preservative she had now obtained; and at the age of PP I 22 123 3
his happiness in having obtained the affection of their PP I 23 128 10
me, when he might have obtained my affections and hand, I PP III 15 361 4
For a long while no answer could be obtained beyond a "no, MP I 2 15 10
fidgetted about, and obtained a few pheasant's eggs and a MP I 10 104 52
William had obtained a ten days' leave of absence to be MP III 6 368 7
After sitting some time longer, a candle was obtained; but, MP III 7 381 24
her uncle and obtained his permission, was giving her ease. MP III 15 437 2
more would have been obtained; especially when that MP III 17 467 19
He had made his fortune, bought his house, and obtained E I 2 17 6
were not quite so easily obtained as he had fancied, he E I 16 135 7
and amused to think how little information I obtained." E II 3 171 10
day occurrence, is not obtained at a moment's notice; E II 17 300 12
approbation could be obtained--which, she trusted, would E III 17 465 28

OBTAINING (10)
deserts, & her wish of obtaining my sister's good opinion LS 14 265 5
am not very desirous of obtaining; nor has Frederica any LS 25 294 5
a chance of obtaining her sister in law's consent to it. LS 42 311 2
had no difficulty in obtaining from her whatever promise SS III 1 264 32
of obtaining--but they are of a different character." MP II 4 214 45
There could be no doubt of his obtaining leave of absence MP II 6 233 14
his wife to let her go; obtaining it rather from MP III 6 370 14
eyes could not be very long in obtaining the pre-eminence. MP III 17 470 27
in obtaining her promises of faith and correspondence. E III 14 437 8
present curacy, and obtaining that of Uppercross instead. P III 9 78 19

OBTRUDE (1)
They will sometimes obtrude--but how you can court them!" E III 18 480 79

OBTRUDED (2)
But last summer he was again most painfully obtruded on my PP II 12 201 5
unlucky recollections obtruded, and she fancied that PP III 1 254 57

OBTRUDING (1)
but was continually obtruding his happy countenance on her E I 14 118 4

OBTRUSIVE (1)
but not obtrusive, and adapting themselves more and more MP II 6 231 11

OBTRUSIVENESS (2)
others with the least obtrusiveness himself, would keep MP II 1 184 25
all his own unwelcome obtrusiveness; and the evil of his P IV 10 212 1

OBVIATE (4)
of proceeding which would obviate the risk of his father's MP I 4 37 8
only some scruples to obviate in Sir Thomas, who knew MP II 6 237 23
she could think of to obviate the scruples which were MP II 8 258 15
That will obviate all difficulties you know; and from us I E II 16 295 34

OBVIATED (1)
were instantly obviated, for with a readiness that seemed SS III 7 311 15

OBVIATING (1)
Elinor, "you have been obviating every impediment to the SS II 3 156 9

OBVIOUS (2)
Again his astonishment was obvious; and he looked at her PP II 11 193 27
How clara received it, was less obvious--but she was S 7 395 1

OBVIOUSLY (1)
He was more obviously struck and confused by the sight of P IV 7 175 6

OCCASION (179)
I shall soon have occasion for all my fortitude, as I am LS 1 244 1
She will have occasion for all those attractive powers for LS 3 247 1
on the occasion--but all in vain--she does not like me. LS 5 249 1
but be the occasion of so much vexation & trouble. LS 13 263 1
his tender feelings I suppose on this distressing occasion. LS 15 267 4
But what is it that you have done to occasion all this?" LS 24 286 4
to occasion so extraordinary a change in your sentiments. LS 35 304 1
world appears on such an occasion to walk about and tell NA I 5 35 1
her sorrow on the occasion so very much as if she really NA I 8 54 10
she should wear on the occasion became her chief concern. NA I 10 73 22

really been, she took occasion to mention before Mr. Allen NA I 13 103 29
Catherine having occasion for some indispensable yard of NA I 14 114 50
on one side, there can be no occasion for any on the other. NA I 15 124 47
that they felt on the occasion was comprehended in a wish NA I 15 124 48
James expressed himself on the occasion with becoming NA II 1 135 43
on the present occasion, I assure you I can only guess at." NA II 4 151 24
there was not the least occasion for hurry in the world: NA II 6 165 6
its ancient date might occasion, she hastily snuffed it. NA II 6 169 12
object must occasion so serious a delay of proper repose. NA II 8 187 16
taking an early occasion of saying to her, "my father only NA II 9 192 4
unusually tidy on the occasion; an afterwards into what NA II 11 213 21
Mr. Allen expressed himself on the occasion with the NA II 14 237 22
The General, accustomed on every ordinary occasion to give NA II 15 247 15
My own joy on the occasion is very sincere. NA II 16 251 5
of other people she could act when occasion required it. SS I 1 6 9
her mother-in-law on the occasion, talking to her so SS I 4 23 19
He really felt conscientiously vexed on the occasion; for SS I 5 26 4
or the regret you occasion, and insensible of any change SS I 5 27 8
a respect for him on the occasion, which the others had SS I 7 35 9
Nothing but real indisposition could occasion this SS I 8 39 14
occasion, without attention to persons or circumstances. SS I 10 48 9
who was on every occasion mindful of the feelings of SS I 12 62 27
all that a lover ought to look and say on such an occasion. SS I 16 87 23
On the present occasion, for the better entertainment of SS I 18 99 16
Marianne, on a similar occasion, to augment and fix her SS I 19 104 9
however trivial the occasion; and upon Elinor therefore SS I 21 122 14
I am; but however there is no occasion to trouble you. SS I 22 128 9
there could be no occasion for ever mentioning my name to SS I 22 131 32
on such an occasion would be perfectly unnecessary? SS II 2 149 26
was solicitous on every occasion for their ease and SS II 4 160 2
of Lady Middleton on the occasion was an happy relief to SS II 10 215 12
too sedulously divided in word and deed on every occasion. SS II 12 229 4
dismissed on the present occasion of her brother's SS II 14 249 9
on the present occasion, as far at least as it regarded SS III 1 269 57
and as there could be no occasion for their staying above SS III 3 280 6
approbation of your behaviour on the present occasion." SS III 4 289 31
may intend to do on the occasion, but as for myself, I SS III 5 299 35
found her on every occasion a most willing and active SS III 7 308 3
that seemed to speak the occasion, and the service pre- SS III 7 311 15
as mine were on the occasion, he must think I have never SS III 13 368 30
not a line has been received from him on the occasion. SS III 13 371 38
39

On the present occasion, as only two of Mr W.'s children W 315 1
"I think there is no occasion for their engaging W 337 15
What occasion could there be for Ld O.'s coming. W 348 22
On meeting her long-absent sister, as on every occasion of W 349 23
"I see no occasion for that. PP I 1 4 19
time; and on the present occasion he had a good deal of PP I 3 12 15
to be civil also, and say what the occasion required. PP I 9 45 35
"How many letters you must have occasion to write in the PP I 10 47 7
that I am happy on every occasion to offer those little PP I 14 67 9
Elizabeth's spirits were so high on the occasion, that PP I 17 87 12
of my conscience on this occasion, which leads me to PP I 18 97 61
man who should omit an occasion of testifying his respect PP I 18 101 71
"And what am I to do on the occasion?-- PP I 20 111 11
on the present occasion; and secondly, of my room. PP I 20 112 22
as an occasion of introducing him to her father and mother. PP I 21 116 5
family in short were properly overjoyed on the occasion. PP I 22 122 3
was the surprise it must occasion to Elizabeth Bennet, PP I 22 123 3
more tranquil on the occasion, and such as he did PP I 23 127 6
The letter which she wrote on this occasion to her sister, PP II 3 147 25
I had no money, what occasion could there be for making PP II 4 153 13
to the rest, there is no occasion for any thing more. PP II 6 160 6
could furnish her with an occasion of dictating to others. PP II 6 163 15
no occasion for entailing estates from the female line.-- PP II 6 164 16
of this letter must occasion, should have been spared, had PP II 12 196 4
There can be no occasion for your going so soon. PP II 14 211 8
there can be no occasion for exposing him so dreadfully. PP II 17 226 22
endured on a similar occasion, five and twenty years ago. PP II 18 229 3
The rapture of Lydia on this occasion, her adoration of PP II 18 230 12
and he afterwards took occasion to ask her, when PP III 2 262 9
the worst, there is no occasion to look on it as certain. PP III 5 288 37
that there was no real occasion for such a seclusion from PP III 5 288 40
to him to do, whatever occasion might suggest to be PP III 6 298 13
There will not be the smallest occasion for your coming to PP III 7 303 14
from him no mark of affection whatever, on the occasion. PP III 8 310 10
He was her dear Wickham on every occasion; no one was to PP III 9 318 20
to waste such a precious occasion, she suddenly got up, PP III 13 345 12
13

what she felt on the occasion; when it became apparent, PP III 15 363 22
and as Elizabeth saw no occasion for making it a general PP III 16 365 2
expressed himself on the occasion as sensibly and as PP III 16 366 8
no occasion for talking to him, except just now and then. PP III 17 375 26
She wrote even to Jane on the occasion, to express her PP III 18 383 24
in the world to withhold my mite upon such an occasion. MP I 1 6 6
on the occasion with rather an injudicious particularity. MP I 2 12 3
Fanny's feelings on the occasion were such as she believed MP I 2 16 20
I may pity your feelings as a brother on the occasion. MP I 3 23 3
It had never occurred to her, on the present occasion, but MP I 3 28 38
The Miss Bertrams were much to be pitied on the occasion; MP I 3 32 64
occasion to be occupied even in fears for the absent. MP I 4 34 3
"Your best friend upon such an occasion," said Miss MP I 6 53 7
but I do not at present foresee any occasion for writing." MP I 6 59 42
The occasion would never be foreseen. MP I 6 59 43
any occasion, but really I cannot do every thing at once. MP I 7 73 53
You must excuse my sister on this occasion, and accept of MP I 8 76 3
"Fanny will feel quite as grateful as the occasion MP I 8 79 26
On the present occasion, she addressed herself chiefly to MP I 9 85 3
and gallant again as occasion served, or Miss Crawford MP I 12 114 1
occasion than Julia, to consult either father or mother. MP I 13 128 38
There is no occasion to put them so very close together. MP I 15 141 22
to him on the occasion, betraying no exultation beyond the MP I 17 158 2
had not, and giving occasion of discontent to the others.-- MP I 18 165 2
of cheerfulness on the occasion; Tom was enjoying such an MP I 18 171 25
in such weather might occasion at home, she had nothing to MP II 4 206 4
feeling on the occasion, when Mrs. Grant, with sudden MP II 4 215 47
that there is no real occasion for your going into company MP II 5 220 28
There was no occasion, there was no time for Fanny to say MP II 5 223 47
to afford a reason, an occasion for such a thing, you MP II 8 252 2
for to-morrow: but your thanks are far beyond the occasion. MP II 9 262 9
so perfectly gratifying in the occasion and the style. MP II 9 265 19
Her aunt Bertram had recollected her on this occasion, MP II 9 271 41
Her happiness on this occasion was very much a-la-mortal, MP II 10 274 8
to her it was, as the occasion offered,--"Ah! ma'am, how MP II 10 277 16
occasion; it shewed a discretion highly to be commended. MP III 1 315 18
had a moment's share in your thoughts on this occasion. MP III 1 318 39
There is no occasion for spreading the disappointment; say MP III 1 322 48
"My dear," interrupted Sir Thomas, "there is no occasion MP III 2 330 16
for discretion on the occasion than she deserved; and MP III 2 332 21
affected on the present occasion, and whether she were MP III 6 366 1
of circumstances occasion in this world of changes. MP III 6 374 27
You know all that would be felt on the occasion." MP III 11 411 16
The value of a man like Henry on such an occasion, is what MP III 12 417 3
distressing occasion, as it would be too trying for me. MP III 13 426 11
Fanny's feelings on the occasion were indeed considerably MP III 13 427 12
of right; there was no occasion to determine, whether she MP III 14 436 15
which, as affording an occasion for leaving Mansfield, an MP III 17 469 23
I purposely abstain from dates on this occasion, that MP III 17 470 26
that he had written to his new mother on the occasion. E I 2 18 9
on Harriet's side, as there could be any occasion for. E I 6 42 1
Mrs. Weston! always my kindest friend on every occasion. E I 6 45 21
a fresh occasion for Emma's services towards her friend. E I 7 50 1

that it had been the occasion of much present enjoyment to E I 10 90 41
"Has he been here on this occasion--or has he not?" E I 11 95 20
Mr. Elton looked all alarm on the occasion, as he E I 13 109 6
7

and solicitously addressing her upon every occasion. E I 14 118 4
in such a mark of respect to him on the present occasion. E I 18 146 16
if this be the first occasion of his carrying through a E I 18 148 22
hour, the party, the occasion--to feel the same E II 5 187 4
There was no occasion to press the matter farther. E II 8 219 43
thanks,--'there was no occasion to trouble us, for Mr. E II 8 223 63
He has no occasion to marry, either to fill up his time or E II 8 225 74
be enjoying your pleasure on this occasion, Miss Fairfax. E II 10 241 11
12

We shall have no occasion to open the windows at all--not E II 11 251 29
Mrs. Elton on this happy occasion; I said that I hoped I E II 14 280 54
Mrs. Weston was most comfortably pleased on the occasion. E II 17 304 28
I do--but upon such an occasion as this, when everybody's E III 2 324 20
21

evening, had been the occasion of some of its highest E III 3 332 1
and alarm it would occasion;: but she soon felt that E III 3 335 12
Harriet behaved extremely well on the occasion, with great E III 9 388 14
not, on this occasion, have found any thing to reprove. E III 9 391 21
In short, my dear Emma, there is no occasion to be so E III 10 393 17
remember the substance of what I said on the occasion. E III 11 406 23
Emma knew that he had, on that occasion, found her much E III 11 409 35
a palpable display, repeated on every possible occasion. E III 16 454 16
used to be talked to by each, on every fair occasion.-- E III 17 466 30
Mary, who, on having occasion to note down the day of the P III 6 48 16
there would be no occasion for putting Captain P III 7 54 5
A dinner at Mr. Musgrove's had been the occasion, when all P III 9 77 17
having been found on the occasion by Mr. Musgrove with P III 10 82 2
willing upon the present occasion; he did it, however; she P III 12 109 32
perhaps, be the occasion of continuing their acquaintance. P III 12 115 67
her compliments on the occasion, had the amusement of P IV 1 124 10
and on the present occasion, receiving her in that house, P IV 1 126 19
who can give occasion to such directly opposite notions. P IV 2 132 20
daughter"--(there was no occasion for remembering Mary) P IV 3 143 18
Anne was shewn some letters of his on the occasion, P IV 9 209 97
him really happy on the occasion, was very far from P IV 12 248 2
to be guided on every occasion, that whether he were S 2 372 1
told me that this was an occasion which called for me. S 9 409 1
Mrs P. entered into all her husband's joy on the occasion, S 12 426 1

OCCASION'S (1)
as to the occasion's justifying her coming so far alone. PP I 7 33 42

OCCASIONAL (25)
and, in the occasional absence of General Tilney, with NA II 6 166 8
the court, which, with occasional passages, not wholly NA II 8 183 2
could allow, that an occasional memento of past folly, NA II 10 201 4
of this child, who, in occasional visits with his father SS I 1 4 3
know; but, from Fanny's occasional mention of her conduct SS I 4 21 15
produced occasional effusions of sorrow as lively as ever. SS I 16 83 4
&c. extorting from him occasional questions and remarks. SS I 16 89 42
in spite of every occasional doubt of Willoughby's SS II 4 159 1
his eye by occasional glances at his fair neighbour.-- W 345 21
from objecting to my occasional absence on a Sunday, PP I 13 63 12
and except in an occasional glance at Elizabeth, requiring PP I 14 68 12
and her mansion, with occasional digressions in praise of PP I 16 75 3
to utter more than the occasional exclamation of "Lord, PP I 18 103 75
engaged in watching the occasional appearance of some PP III 1 254 57
and Mrs. Gardiner, with occasional help from Elizabeth, PP III 3 267 4
I can perceive, from occasional lively hints, the MP II 3 198 13
her conversation than occasional amusement, and that often MP II 4 208 11
modernized, and occasional residence of a man of MP II 7 248 47
The terror of his former occasional visits to that room MP III 1 312 4
she did resolve to give occasional hints to Susan, and MP III 9 396 6
herself entitled to the occasional holiday of a tea-visit; E I 3 22 5
any thing beyond occasional, fortuitous assistance could E I 11 91 1
the occasional prevalence of the ridiculous over the good. E III 7 375 61
affected by his wife's occasional lowness; bore with her P III 6 43 5
& better roads, an occasional month at Tunbridge Wells, & S 2 373 1

OCCASIONALLY (37)
ask him to your house occasionally, & talk to him about LS 7 253 1
solicitude that I, who occasionally caught her observing LS 17 270 3
for she was often inattentive, and occasionally stupid. NA I 1 14 1
heard of before, would occasionally come across her; but NA II 4 149 1
I may give them occasionally will be of far greater SS I 2 11 23
his visitors, and only occasionally rude to his wife and SS III 6 304 15
the room, speaking occasionally to one of his own party. PP I 3 11 6
occasionally for a week or two, to visit his relations. PP I 14 66 1
I think it no sacrifice to join occasionally in evening PP I 17 87 11
and occasionally from some peevish allusion of her mother. PP I 21 115 1
her brother, she might occasionally spend a morning with PP II 2 142 17
great enjoyment in occasionally professing opinions which PP II 8 174 14
Colonel Fitzwilliam's occasionally laughing at his PP II 9 180 29
younger sisters, and occasionally even by your father.-- PP II 12 198 5
overspreading many, and occasionally part of the stream. PP III 1 253 57
of his voice; and when occasionally, unable to resist the PP III 11 335 43
she still was occasionally nervous and invariably silly. PP III 19 385 1
Lydia was occasionally a visitor there, when her husband PP III 19 387 9
To her cousins she became occasionally an acceptable MP I 2 17 21
and hints which she occasionally noticed in some of the MP I 12 116 11
She was occasionally useful to all; she was perhaps as MP I 18 166 5
Your cousins have occasionally attended them; but they MP II 8 252 1
herself occasionally called on to endure something worse. MP II 10 273 7
He was able to introduce some improvement occasionally, MP III 10 403 14
wind, and bright sun, occasionally clouded for a minute; MP III 11 409 6
A line occasionally added by Edmund to his mother's letter MP III 14 430 5
Emma only occasionally joining in one or the other. E I 12 100 15
and each was occasionally useful as a check to the other. E II 4 184 11
state, had been occasionally used as such;--but such E II 6 197 5
might be so obliging occasionally to put it to a better E II 8 216 16
which Mr. Weston had occasionally introduced, and who now E III 5 347 20
ended, occasionally, in an unpremeditated little ball. P III 6 47 15
occasionally thinking of Captain Benwick, from this time. P IV 2 133 26
read; for they see it occasionally under every P IV 5 156 10
The names which occasionally dropt of former associates, P IV 5 161 27
of conversation when occasionally forming into a little P IV 6 168 24
or words, or actions occasionally encouraged; it had been P IV 11 241 60

OCCASIONED (25)
the path of propriety, occasioned her removal from a LS 6 252 2
for his return, is occasioned as much by a degree of LS 8 255 1
to me at least what has occasioned so great an alteration LS 12 261 6
of going might be occasioned by a conversation in which we LS 24 287 11
all the dreadful delays occasioned by the General's NA II 16 252 2
the settled rain of the two preceding days had occasioned. SS I 9 40 3
concern and alarm which this sudden departure occasioned. SS I 15 77 18
that he was already aware of what occasioned her absence. SS II 8 198 30
those regrets which the remembrance of me occasioned. SS II 9 206 24
by the fire after dinner, which their arrival occasioned. SS II 14 247 4
Mr. Darcy related the mistake which had occasioned his PP II 9 179 26
The agitation and tears which the subject occasioned, PP II 10 187 41
I am sorry to have occasioned pain to any one. PP II 11 190 7
with his steward had occasioned his coming forward a few PP III 1 256 61
The first actual pain which Miss Crawford occasioned her, MP I 7 66 14
occasioned, made her hardly know how to support herself. MP I 7 74 5
the inconveniences they occasioned, but never in the whole MP II 2 191 10
question to answer, and occasioned an "Oh!" of some length MP II 4 214 4
for the misery she had occasioned, comfort was to be found MP III 17 461 1
some of the distress it occasioned, judged it best for her E II 4 185 1
on domestic peace to be occasioned by no housekeeper's E II 6 204 4
The bitter feelings occasioned by this speech, the many E III 11 411 4
4

all the uneasiness I occasioned her, and how little I E III 14 439 8
of the sufferings it occasioned; but if Henrietta found P III 9 77 18
either, till something occasioned an almost general change P III 12 107 23
OCCASIONING (2)
that you will be occasioning, of the curiosity there will MP III 5 360 16
not in the least aware of the pain he was occasioning. P III 10 82 1
OCCASIONS (24)
"One had rather, on such occasions, do too much than too SS I 2 9 12
Marianne was of no use on these occasions, as she would SS II 4 166 31
which now, as on many occasions, though it did not give SS II 10 219 42
Darcy, on particular occasions, and in particular places; PP I 10 50 39
be adapted to ordinary occasions, I always wish to give PP I 14 68 11
because on such occasions it is the etiquette; but no one PP I 18 99 63
to be one; and on these occasions, Mrs. Gardiner, rendered PP II 2 142 18
penance, for on these occasions it was not merely a few PP II 10 182 1
less than on former occasions, and once or twice pleased PP III 2 262 8
His family knew him to be on all common occasions, a most PP III 6 294 1
it belongs to me to find occasions for teazing and PP III 18 381 7
a choice as on such occasions they always are, speculation MP II 7 239 4
any reference to the ball, be kept for commoner occasions. MP II 9 263 16
and listener on this, as on more common occasions. MP III 13 428 14
Upon such occasions poor Mr. Woodhouse's feelings were in E I 3 24 12
the first object on such occasions, was carefully attended E I 15 128 22
not make our carriage more useful on such occasions. E II 8 228 89
Upon these occasions, a lady's character generally E II 14 276 35
to his custom on such occasions, making the circle of his E II 16 294 24
25
heard named as a salary on such occasions, dearly earned." E III 8 382 24
her, on a thousand occasions, unnecessarily scrupulous and E III 14 440 8
out, and on many lesser occasions had endeavoured to give P III 2 16 16
It had not been necessary, and the few occasions of its P IV 1 123 9
go elsewhere upon such occasions--& that old Stringer & S 4 381 1
OCCUPATION (20)
two girls agreeing in occupation, and improving in NA II 13 222 7
habit of seeing much occupation at home, could not conceal SS I 9 40 1
the happy occupation, the first bliss of a ball began.-- W 323 3
have continued the occupation, but unluckily no one passed PP I 15 74 11
time for, amid so much occupation as she found for herself, MP II 10 277 16
that, but for the occupation and the scene which the tea MP III 3 335 5
In this occupation she hoped, moreover, to bury some of MP III 9 398 10
of a nature to promise occupation for the pen for many MP III 13 426 9
and between useful occupation and the pleasures of society, E I 2 16 5
down in complete occupation of the footpath, begged them E I 10 88 33
exactly right, and occupation and ease were generally E II 8 218 38
39
much embarrassment and occupation of mind to shorten it, E II 14 270 3
there he found occupation for an idle hour, and P III 1 3 1
But now, another occupation and solicitude of mind was P III 1 9 19
and depression, to hours of occupation and enjoyment. P IV 5 154 8
evening: it was just occupation enough: she had feelings P IV 8 186 24
continual occupation and change soon weaken impressions." P IV 11 232 19
his Hobby Horse; his occupation his hope & his futurity.-- S 2 372 1
any occupation that may be of use to himself or others.-- S 5 388 1
said "you may perceive what has been our occupation. S 8 403 1
OCCUPATIONS (4)
A variety of occupations, of objects, and of company, SS II 10 213 3
may dispel melancholy, and her occupations were hopeful. MP III 15 443 25
interest in the usual occupations; but whenever Lady MP III 16 449 6
Woman's usual occupations of eye and hand and mind will be E I 10 85 21
OCCUPIED (55)
but her time was so much occupied in lying-in and teaching NA I 1 15 3
be against her being occupied by any part of that NA I 5 38 4
and that something occupied her mind so much, that she NA II 1 133 29
and with a mind so occupied in the contemplation of actual NA II 13 227 26
them, from all that interested and occupied the others. SS II 4 164 24
mind was so much more occupied by the important secret in SS III 4 291 46
The clock struck nine, while he was thus agreably occupied; W 359 28
Occupied in observing Mr. Bingley's attentions to her PP I 6 23 12
Mrs. Hurst, principally occupied in playing with her PP I 11 54 3
Miss Darcy's praise occupied the chief of it. PP II 1 133 2
a mind so occupied, she might have forgotten where she was. PP II 14 212 16
were the subjects which occupied them; Lady Lucas was PP II 16 222 21
Her prudent mother, occupied by the same ideas, forbore to PP III 12 340 11
occasion to be occupied even in fears for the absent. MP I 4 34 3
became so pleasantly occupied in superintending the MP I 4 38 9
Conversation with any of them occupied but a small part of MP II 2 190 9
them, and Mrs. Grant occupied at the tea-table, he began MP II 5 224 49
his mind being deeply occupied in the consideration of two MP II 8 254 10
could be no longer occupied by the incessant demands of a MP III 6 371 17
Sam, Tom, and Charles, occupied all the rest of her MP III 8 389 4
is wild to see you, and occupied only in contriving the MP III 14 435 14
The first division of their journey occupied a long day, MP III 15 446 35
were shut up, or wholly occupied each with the person MP III 16 449 4
a wife, so constantly occupied either in his business in E I 1 12 41
But the Martins occupied her thoughts a good deal; she had E I 4 27 4
to be little occupied with it; her vanity lies another way. E I 5 39 21
was the one he chiefly occupied, and looking forwards; E I 10 89 38
While they were thus comfortably occupied Mr. Woodhouse E I 12 100 17
Mrs. and Miss Bates occupied the drawing-room floor; and E II 1 155 4
she had been much occupied by it, continually pondering E II 4 184 11
near her, most deedily occupied about her spectacles, and E II 10 240 1
"Your allowing yourself to be so occupied and so unhappy E II 13 268 10
that he is so very much occupied by the idea of not being E II 15 289 42
She was a little occupied in weighing her own feelings, E II 17 304 28
and who now sat happily occupied in lamenting, with tender E III 5 347 20
Frank Churchill had once, for a short period, occupied?-- E III 11 412 45
and Mrs. Weston's heart and time would be occupied by it. E III 12 422 20
to the place in her mind which Harriet had occupied. E III 16 452 6
enough for safety, and occupied enough for cheerfulness. E III 19 482 4
the females were fully occupied in all the other common P III 6 42 3
both seemed so entirely occupied by him, that nothing but P III 8 71 57
These were some of the thoughts which occupied Anne, while P III 8 72 58
She occupied her mind as much as possible in such like P III 10 84 7
A few months hence, and the room now so deserted, occupied P IV 1 123 7
How unworthily occupied! P IV 1 126 18
On one side was a table, occupied by some chattering girls, P IV 2 134 29
must suffer none, but it occupied a little time to settle P IV 7 174 3
attendant visions, which occupied and flurried her too P IV 8 186 22
because he had been occupied by them, striving to catch P IV 11 233 24
the chair which he had occupied, succeeding to the very P IV 11 237 41
42
each apparently occupied in admiring a fine display of P IV 11 246 79
80
uch they are occupied in promoting the good of others!-- S 5 388 1
ody, & they were fully occupied in their various S 6 390 1
s concerned, had since occupied the greater part of his S 8 404 1
he best place by the fire constantly occupied by Sir H. D. S 12 427 1
UPIER (2)
rawing-room, the only occupier of that interesting MP II 4 205 1
ot be happy to wait on Mr. Crawford as occupier." MP II 7 248 44
UPIES (2)
The present always occupies you in such scenes--does it?" PP I 18 93 31
have given it up you know to the man who occupies the S 4 380 1
UPY (20)
therwise be expected to occupy the three or four NA I 4 34 9
eel a void in your heart which nothing else can occupy. NA II 10 207 38
o brighten every eye and occupy every fancy--a pleasure NA II 14 233 8
ould arise to occupy their time as shortly presented SS I 11 53 1
ccupy himself solely in being civil to all the world. PP I 5 18 1
n that county, there was enough to be seen, to occupy the PP II 19 239 7
he had been used to occupy every spring, and remained MP I 2 20 33
r pain, might occupy the meditations of almost all. MP I 10 106 58
that Edmund will occupy his own house at Thornton Lacey. MP II 7 247 39
the beginning, seemed to occupy her totally; how it fell MP III 3 337 11
but it could not occupy her, could not dwell on her mind. MP III 15 443 24
to a doubt; nor did it occupy Emma long to convince him E I 13 108 3
eclat, were enough to occupy her in most unmirthful E I 16 137 12
kindness, striving to occupy and amuse her, and by books E I 17 142 10
coxcomb, he will not occupy much of my time or thoughts." E I 18 150 30
appear of that absorbing nature as wholly to occupy her. E II 3 174 36
The charm of an object to occupy the many vacancies of E II 4 183 10
Elton's offences, and long, very long, did they occupy her. E II 14 280 61
abroad, no talents, or accomplishments for home, to occupy. P III 1 9 18
anecdotes in abundance to occupy and entertain the others, P III 11 100 23
OCCUPYING (4)
had been completely occupying both houses in Kellynch for P III 6 42 1
Clay had been lately occupying, a sufficient explanation P IV 4 151 22
look forward and see you occupying your dear mother's P IV 5 159 25
a place on it well worth occupying; when, at that moment, P IV 8 190 47
OCCUR (38)
A little harmless flirtation or so will occur, and one is NA II 3 146 18
"Nothing further to alarm perhaps may occur the first NA II 5 159 19
ere long occur of selecting one--though not for himself. NA II 7 175 12
How could such a thought occur to you? SS I 15 80 36
not occur to relieve my spirits at first--no, Marianne.-- SS III 1 264 29
not foresee that the opportunity would so very soon occur." SS III 4 285 4
was the most unlikely to occur, with a more warm, though SS III 6 301 1
course, in some moments, occur to remind her of what SS III 7 315 25
that something would occur to prevent his marrying Lucy; SS III 12 357 1
Comparisons would occur--regrets would arise;--and her joy, SS III 13 363 7
"No, but she might suppose that something would occur in SS III 13 367 23
that it should not occur again, if he would resume his PP I 14 69 17
How wonderfully these sort of things occur! PP I 18 96 57
How it could occur a second time therefore was very odd!-- PP II 10 182 1
in those hours of separation that must sometimes occur. PP III 13 349 44
occur when he was once gone, to take him elsewhere. MP I 12 115 5
of your improved plan that may occur to you this spring." MP II 7 247 41
Why did such an idea occur to her even enough to be MP II 9 264 18
It might occur to him, that Mr. Crawford had been sitting MP II 10 281 34
nobly settled, as will, probably, never occur to you again. MP III 1 318 39
none such might occur again before his leaving Mansfield. MP III 3 343 40
the Grants going to Bath, occur at a time when she could MP III 13 425 6
done, that any thing could occur to make me suffer more, MP III 16 457 30
Does any body else occur to you at this moment under such E I 7 53 21
occur again, and therefore you need not think about it." E II 3 180 55
just to have something occur to preserve him in her fancy, E II 4 184 10
occurred, all that might occur in the arrangement of his E II 4 184 10
would, in the common course of things, occur to him." E II 8 226 81
twentieth part of a moment, did such an idea occur to me. E III 5 350 35
"Such things do occur, undoubtedly."-- E III 7 373 42
circumstances do sometimes occur both to men and women, I E III 7 373 44
and no moment's uneasiness can ever occur between us again. E III 14 443 8
"Does nothing occur to you?-- E III 18 470 8
"can we retrench? does it occur to you that there is any P III 1 9 19
an absurd suspicion should occur to her; and indignantly P III 5 34 13
extraordinary bursts of mind which do sometimes occur. P III 6 51 31
of making her observations could not fail to occur. P III 10 82 1
A sudden recollection seemed to occur, and to give him P IV 8 182 9
OCCURRED (94)
had not at that moment occurred <to> me, that his LS 24 287 11
Nothing more alarming occurred than a fear on Mrs. Allen's NA I 2 19 4
other whenever a thought occurred, and supplying the place NA I 8 52 1
But nothing of that kind occurred, no visitors appeared to NA I 10 71 8
"That never occurred to me; and of course, not seeing him NA I 10 73 13
This was the only comfort that occurred. NA II 7 173 3
conjecture, it further occurred to her, that the forbidden NA II 8 188 17
the company left them, and nothing occurred to disturb it. NA II 9 192 4
Isabella's conduct, it occurred to her as highly expedient NA II 11 208 2
This was a painful consideration whenever it occurred; and NA II 13 220 1
His temper is not happy, and something has now occurred to NA II 13 225 21
from the General occurred to her as his daughter appeared. NA II 13 227 27
It had occurred to her, that after so long an absence from NA II 13 229 31
for never had it occurred to him to doubt its authority. NA II 15 245 12
particular circumstance occurred to give still greater SS I 3 14 3
As these considerations occurred to her in painful SS II 1 140 4
advantage of any that occurred; for the weather was not SS II 1 142 8
the present scheme which occurred to you, there is still SS II 3 156 9
Nothing occurred during the next three or four days, to SS II 6 175 1
Thus a circumstance occurred, while the sisters were SS II 9 202 4
or twice, if the subject occurred very often, by saying, " SS II 10 215 14
vacant; nor had it ever occurred to me that he might have SS III 4 289 35
private--a circumstance occurred--an unlucky circumstance, SS III 8 321 34
opportunity of private conference between them occurred. SS III 9 335 7
of exercising it occurred, in what manner he expressed SS III 13 361 3
Not the smallest suspicion, therefore, had ever occurred SS III 13 364 13
more advantageous occurred, it would be better for her to SS III 13 367 23
had any suspicion of it occurred to the others, proper SS III 13 371 38
Among other unsatisfactory feelings it once occurred to W 347 22
a doubt of his being present had never occurred to her. PP I 18 89 1
with her friend had once occurred to Elizabeth within the PP I 22 124 12
13
I am glad it occurred to me to mention it; for it would PP II 14 212 13
Nothing occurred between them that could justify the hopes PP III 2 262 8
little circumstances occurred ere they parted, which, in PP III 2 262 8
Neither had any thing occurred in the intelligence of PP III 2 264 14
talked of all that had occurred, during their visit, as PP III 3 271 20
Lizzy, something has occurred of a most unexpected and PP III 4 273 3
of opening her eyes to his character never occurred to me. PP III 5 285 16
said Elizabeth; "though it had not occurred to me before. PP III 7 304 30
It now occurred to the girls that their mother was in all PP III 7 305 39
their marriage, it occurred to Elizabeth that she must PP III 15 360 2
I told him of all that had occurred to make my former PP III 16 371 40
It had never occurred to her, on the present occasion, but MP I 3 28 38
"Very true; but, in short, it had not occurred to me. MP I 9 92 40
Whatever cross accidents had occurred to intercept the MP I 10 103 50
this was all that occurred to gladden her heart during the MP I 17 159 6
But this had occurred on the first day of its being MP II 8 256 12
Such a sight having never occurred before, was almost as MP II 9 261 1
am very sorry that any thing has occurred to distress you. MP II 9 268 30
It had really occurred to her, unprompted, that Fanny, MP II 9 271 41
the ball; an idea that had never occurred to her before. MP II 10 275 11
feel as if nothing had occurred to vex her, till she found MP II 13 303 12
Then it occurred to her what might be going on; a MP III 1 325 60
as you might have done, had nothing of this sort occurred. MP III 2 331 16
The first that occurred was not least in interest,--the MP III 3 334 1
In the evening a few circumstances occurred which he MP III 3 336 8
None such had occurred since his seeing her in her uncle's MP III 3 343 40
It had occurred to Sir Thomas, in one of his dignified MP III 6 368 9
It had, in fact, occurred to her, that, though taken to MP III 6 373 24
It had very early occurred to her, that a small sum of MP III 9 396 7
the terrors that occurred of what this visit might lead to, MP III 10 399 4
very imprudent had just occurred in that quarter to draw MP III 15 438 4
other for all that had occurred of disappointment to MP III 17 471 29
the death of Dr. Grant, occurred just after they had been MP III 17 473 32
It then occurred to her to employ him in reading. E I 6 46 24
Emma; and if it never occurred to you before, you may as E I 13 112 20
that had already occurred, all that might occur in the E II 4 184 10
Something occurred while they were at Hartfield, to make E II 7 206 5
was dearest to her, occurred again and again, she did not E II 7 208 7
Well, a little while ago it occurred to me how very sad it E II 8 223 63
Oh! and I had almost forgotten one idea that occurred to E II 8 226 79
He knew her illnesses; they never occurred but for her own E II 12 258 8
A circumstance rather unlucky occurred. E II 16 292 7
No misfortune occurred, again to prevent the ball. E III 2 319 1

It had just occurred to Mrs. Weston that Mrs. Elton must E III 2 325 29
Nothing of the sort had ever occurred before to any young E III 3 335 10
I find, has occurred;--do let my know directly what it is. E III 10 394 27
even as this, may have occurred before--and if I should be E III 11 407 28
felicity, occurred to her, to institute the comparison.-- E III 11 412 45
for while she spoke, it occurred to her that he might have E III 13 425 8
There every little dissatisfaction that had occurred E III 14 440 8
but such an alternative as this had not occurred to her. E III 15 449 32
at school while it all occurred--and never admitted by the P III 4 31 11
Something occurred, however, to give her a different duty. P III 5 33 7
to sea in the year six," occurred in the course of the P III 8 63 2
worth and suffering, as occurred to her at the moment as P III 11 101 24
Anne wondered whether it ever occurred to him now, to P III 12 116 72
Vague wishes of getting Sarah thither, had occurred before P IV 1 122 3
him she felt all over courage if the opportunity occurred. P IV 7 180 32
in Bath, it immediately occurred, that something might be P IV 9 210 99
the next, and what had occurred to my sister hayter, and P IV 11 230 5
favour of it which has occurred within our own circle; P IV 11 234 30
Another momentary vexation occurred. P IV 11 239 54
I sounded Susan--the same thought had occurred to her.-- S 9 409 1
OCCURRENCE (7)
inconceivable vexation on every little trifling occurrence. NA I 8 56 11
from any other daily occurrence, but who saw at the same SS II 5 168 12
thought it a lucky occurrence, as quietly putting an end MP I 17 160 9
out of the room; an occurrence too common to strike her, MP III 1 324 60
This was the occurrence:--the Coles had been settled some E II 7 207 6
you, is no every day occurrence, is not obtained at a E II 17 300 12
It was not possible that the occurrence should not be E III 3 335 10
OCCURRENCES (8)
She shall not soon forget the occurrences of this day. LS 22 282 8
to herself in the occurrences of a visitation--but when W 343 20
she was satisfied with the occurrences of the evening.-- PP I 18 95 48
occurrences had thrown on many of the Longbourn family. PP II 1 138 30
occurrences, or any communication of present suffering. PP II 11 188 1
The occurrences of the day were too full of interest to PP III 1 259 77
but the two latest occurrences to be mentioned, the two of E III 11 410 35
occurrences from which no useful Deductions can be drawn.-- S 8 403 1
OCCURRING (6)
the same difficulty occurring in the management of this NA II 6 169 11
and other family matters occurring to detain her, a NA II 15 241 7
repeated conversations occurring at different times PP II 4 152 6
time of the subject's occurring to her again, happening to MP I 3 24 7
this week's absence, occurring as it did at the very time MP II 11 286 15
continually occurring, and always the hope of more, and P IV 11 246 78
OCCURS (3)
We may as well wait, perhaps, till the circumstance occurs, PP I 10 50 37
expecting more good than occurs, does not always pay for E I 18 144 2
Ly D.'s Gardiner--but it occurs to me that we ought to go S 4 381 1
OCEAN (3)
as a drop of water to the ocean, compared with the MP III 8 392 11
the noblest expanse of ocean between the south foreland & S 4 380 1
The terrific grandeur of the ocean in a storm, its glassy S 7 396 1
OCLOCK (1)
to have Leaches at one oclock--which will be a three hours S 12 424 1
OCTAGON ROOM (3)
The time of the two parties uniting in the Octagon Room NA I 7 51 54
took their station by one of the fires in the Octagon Room. P IV 8 181 1
it had been in the Octagon Room was strikingly great.-- P IV 8 190 47
OCTAGON-ROOM (1)
The moment of her stepping forward in the Octagon-Room to P IV 11 244 71
OCTOBER (13)
and accomplished as often as a showery October would allow. SS I 11 53 1
I quitted Barton last October,--but this will give you no SS II 9 204 20
he continued, "came in a letter from herself, last October. SS II 9 209 30
Hunsford, near Westerham, Kent, 15th October. PP I 13 62 12
We have had such incessant rains almost since October MP II 1 181 16
"This is the first October that she has passed in the MP II 3 199 15
She must be grown two inches, at least, since October." MP II 6 230 5
She is just what she was in October, believe me. MP II 6 230 6
reach; and many a long October and November evening must E I 1 7 9
till she married, last October, she was never away from E II 1 159 20
between them ever since October--formed at Weymouth, and E III 10 395 35
"Engaged since October,--secretly engaged.-- E III 10 395 38
Who can endure a Cabbage bed in October?" S 4 380 1
OCTR YE 13TH (1)
be held on Tuesday Octr Ye 13th, & it was generally W 314 1
ODD (82)
hoped we would not think it odd, was aware of it's being LS 20 278 10
"It is odd that you alone should be ignorant of your LS 24 288 11
or seize upon any other odd piece of paper, she did what NA I 1 14 1
What an odd gown she has got on!-- NA I 2 23 21
"It is so odd to me, that you should never have read NA I 6 41 20
"He must have thought it very odd to hear me say I was NA I 10 72 11
"It is very odd! but I suppose they thought it would be NA I 11 85 40
encouraged his horse, made odd noises, and drove on; and NA I 11 87 53
Do not you think it has an odd appearance, if young ladies NA I 13 104 33
"Yes, my dear, a very odd appearance indeed. NA I 13 104 34
and yet I often think it odd that it should be so dull, NA I 14 108 22
Miss Morland is not used to your odd ways." NA I 14 113 40
To Catherine's simple feelings, this odd sort of reserve NA I 15 121 25
the whole of their conversation her manner had been odd. NA II 3 148 28
solemnity of any kind, struck her as odd and inconsistent. NA II 5 161 25
thing, but it was so very odd, after what Henry had said. NA II 6 168 10
Perhaps it may seem odd, that with only two younger NA II 7 176 15
And was not it odd that he should always take his walk so NA II 7 177 18
happened to become my odd face I believe, at least Tilney NA II 12 217 2
from her first excursion from home, was odd enough! NA II 14 235 13
General Tilney, from some odd fancy or other, all of a NA II 14 237 21
Very unfriendly, certainly; and he must be a very odd man;- NA II 14 237 21
it might have been odd that he should leave us without SS I 15 81 44
"You will think my question an odd one, I dare say," said SS I 22 128 3
Elinor did think the question a very odd one, and her SS I 22 128 4
Ferrars, must seem so odd, that it ought to be explained. SS I 22 129 16
to one another, and laugh at my odd ways behind my back. SS II 3 154 4
always a world of little odd things to do after one has SS II 4 163 14
"How very odd!" said she in a low and disappointed voice, SS II 4 165 28
"How odd indeed!" repeated Elinor within herself, SS II 4 165 29
in town, how odd that he should neither come nor write! SS II 4 165 29
Well, that is an odd kind of delicacy! SS III 4 287 20
thing, & describe a very odd young lady; but the W 347 22
It must seem odd enough to you to be here.-- W 351 26
"That's odd sort of talking!-- W 352 26
"It is very odd you should not like to do what other W 353 26
Mr. Bennet was so odd a mixture of quick parts, sarcastic PP I 1 5 34
It would look odd to be entirely silent for half an hour PP I 18 91 13
Very odd!-- PP II 6 165 34
How it could occur a second time therefore was very odd!-- PP II 10 182 1
that he was asking some odd unconnected questions--about PP II 10 182 1
But I must tell you another thing of Fanny, so odd and so MP I 2 19 28
It is unknown how much was consumed in our kitchen by odd MP I 3 30 50
"It seems very odd," said Maria, "that you should be MP I 8 79 24
A very odd game. MP II 7 240 12
which followed securing the odd trick by Sir Thomas's MP II 7 245 32
or thought her odd, or thought her any thing rather than MP II 10 277 20
my odd humours, when she might have a house of her own?" E I 1 8 12
And you have never any odd humours, my dear." E I 1 8 13
a fortnight and a day's difference! which is very odd!" E I 4 30 17
be advisable to have as few odd acquaintance as may be; E I 4 31 24
How very odd! E I 4 32 29
So very odd we should happen to meet! E I 4 32 29
"Dear me!--it is so odd to hear a woman talk so!"-- E I 10 84 14
She is an odd woman!-- E I 14 120 13
"How odd you are! E I 18 145 9
"Very odd! but one never does form a just idea of any body E II 3 176 46
be sure it was so very odd!--but they always dealt at E II 3 178 52
has done her hair in so odd a way--so very odd a way-- E II 8 222 56
very odd a way-- that I cannot keep my eyes from her. E II 8 222 56
I have now a key to all her odd looks and ways. E II 10 243 27
Emma could hardly understand him; he seemed in an odd E III 2 325 29
How very odd! E III 2 329 45
It is very odd, but I cannot recollect.-- E III 4 340 20
Very odd!-- E III 5 345 13
"It is odd though," observed his father, "that you should E III 5 345 14
"Ah! you are an odd creature!" she cried, satisfied to E III 6 355 18
It was an odd tete-a-tete; but she was glad to see it.-- E III 6 360 40
How very odd!" E III 11 404 8
It was, indeed, so odd; Harriet's behaviour was so E III 11 404 9
extremely odd, that Emma did not know how to understand it. E III 11 404 9
Very odd! very unaccountable! after the note I sent him E III 16 457 38
"Bless me! how very odd! P III 3 23 28
Very odd indeed!" P III 3 23 28
is very well, I believe, but he is a very odd young man. P IV 2 130 5
"Mrs. Harville must be an odd mother to part with them so " P IV 6 163 7
But even then, there was something odd in their way of P IV 6 171 33
dare say she thinks me an odd sort of a creature,--but she S 6 393 1
to dissipate theirs in the invention of odd complaints.-- S 10 412 1
made a great many odd faces & contortions, Charlotte could S 10 413 1
he put on, & then seize an odd moment for adding a great S 10 417 1
"It sounds rather odd to be sure--answered Charlotte S 10 418 1
ODD-LOOKING (1)
There are several odd-looking men walking about here, who, P IV 6 166 16
ODD-TEMPERED (1)
and is a very odd-tempered woman; and his coming now, E I 14 121 16
ODDEST (5)
Well, it is the oddest thing to me, that a man should use SS II 8 194 8
I must be in love; I should be the oddest creature in the E II 12 262 39
sure I have sometimes the oddest dreams in the world--but E III 5 345 16
the room--"is not this the oddest news that ever was?" E III 11 404 4
she added--"the oddest thing that ever was!--a Miss Lambe S 10 419 1
ODDITIES (2)
transition to the oddities of her cousin, and to point him PP I 18 90 4
possible of Mr. Elton's oddities, or of any thing else E I 14 117 2
ODDITY (1)
"He must be an oddity, I think," said she. PP I 13 64 17
ODDLY (3)
Things are settled so oddly." PP I 13 65 22
They were gone, she hoped, to be happy, however oddly P III 7 58 20
The acquaintance, thus oddly begun, was neither short nor S 2 370 1
ODDS (2)
of him at first: the odds were five to four against me; NA I 12 96 20
Now, if he were here, I know he wd be offering odds that S 5 385 1
ODIOUS (17)
Do you know, there are two odious young men who have been NA I 6 43 33
"Oh, these odious gigs!" said Isabella, looking up, "how I NA I 7 44 2
She was so amazingly tired, and it was so odious to parade NA II 3 147 28
His cruelty to such a charming woman made him odious to NA II 7 181 40
or 'making a conquest,' are the most odious of all. SS I 9 45 30
ran away from a subject which was odious to her feelings.-- W 360 29
How odious I should think them!" PP I 10 47 7
Pray do not talk of that odious man. PP I 13 61 7
The sight of Miss Lucas was odious to her. PP I 23 129 16
An odious, little, pert, unnatural, impudent girl. MP I 14 136 20
His presence was beginning to be odious to her; and if MP II 2 194 19
and an indigent niece, and every thing most odious. MP III 16 448 3
I quit such odious subjects as soon as I can, impatient to MP III 17 461 1
change; but when they did meet, her composure was odious. E II 12 263 42
she should be exposed to odious suspicions, and imagined E II 16 290 4
These delays and disappointments are quite odious. E III 6 353 7
his former language, was odious; and when she thought of P IV 10 214 11
OFFENCE (40)
She knew not how such an offence as her's might be classed NA I 12 92 3
mistake, why should you be so ready to take offence?" NA I 12 94 11
"Me!--I take offence!" NA I 12 94 12
disproportionate to the offence; and much was her concern NA II 5 154 2
Morland, never to give offence to any of my neighbours, if NA II 11 210 6
is, that you can have given him no just cause of offence. NA II 13 225 21
The only offence against him of which she could accuse NA II 14 230 3
so romantic, that any offence of the kind, by whomsoever SS I 1 6 9
assured that I meant no offence to you, by speaking, in so SS I 4 21 15
perseverance beyond civility, they could not give offence. SS I 6 30 6
so indulgent a mother, the question could not give offence. SS I 16 84 8
had she known how little offence it had given her sister. SS I 18 99 14
to smooth away the offence; "and I do not much wonder at SS II 1 145 17
to every body, and which I believe gave offence to some. SS II 9 209 30
"She taxed me with the offence at once, and my confusion SS III 8 323 40
her dissent was not heard, and therefore gave no offence. SS III 9 338 23
offence against virtue, in his behaviour to Eliza Williams. SS III 11 352 16
17
offence would serve no other purpose than to enrich Fanny. SS III 13 369 33
Robert's offence was unpardonable, but Lucy's was SS III 13 371 38
for Robert's offence, and gratitude for the unkindness she SS III 14 377 11
wherever he appeared, Darcy was continually giving offence. PP I 4 16 14
She was at least free from the offence of Mr. Darcy's PP I 18 102 74
home, and be satisfied that we shall take no offence." PP I 22 124 9
leave her to reap the fruits of her own heinous offence. PP III 6 297 11
on to overlook the offence, and seek a reconciliation; and, PP III 19 388 12
might be some ground of offence--that there might be some MP II 1 183 24
is offensive and disgusting beyond all common offence. MP III 1 318 39
deeply involved in the offence of his sister and friend, MP III 16 452 15
it was the detection, not the offence which she reprobated. MP III 16 455 19
his share of the offence, is, we know, not one of the MP III 17 468 22
and gaze again without offence; but was really obliged to E I 6 46 24
She is not to pay for the offence of others, by being held E I 8 62 41
frequently to be endured, though the offence came not. E I 11 93 5
going away directly after tea might be giving offence. E II 7 210 19
It was kindly said, and very far from giving offence. E II 16 294 24
account, that gave the deepest hue to his offence.-- E III 11 402 1
Not too strongly for the offence--but far, far too E III 12 415 1
among your friends who have had any ground of offence.-- E III 14 437 8
of offence, neither family could now do without it. P III 5 40 44
The offence which had been given her father, many years P III 12 107 21
OFFENCES (6)
forgave all his offences in compassion for his punishment. SS III 2 270 1
so soon as I ought, nor their offences against myself. PP I 11 58 28
towards her, "these offences might have been overlooked, PP II 11 192 22
"Two offences of a very different nature, and by no means PP II 12 196 5
for her mother and herself; and Jane's offences rose again. E II 2 168 15
Her mind returned to Mrs. Elton's offences, and long, very E II 14 280 6
OFFEND (18)
or other she must have had the misfortune to offend him. NA II 13 226 25
you will never offend me by talking of former times. SS I 17 92 2
I never wish to offend, but I am so foolishly shy, that I SS I 17 94 4
picturesque, and I shall offend you by my ignorance and SS I 18 96
be so unfortunate as to offend you, I entreat your SS II 7 183 1
to offend anybody, especially anybody of good fortune. SS III 1 267 4
however, did not seem to offend or mortify his fair SS III 3 281 1
1
You do not offend me, tho' I hardly know how to beleive W 342 1
not offend Mr Watson--which I thought very kind of him.-- W 344 2
"His pride," said Miss Lucas, "does not offend me so much PP I 5 20 1
What advantage can it be to you to offend Mr. Darcy?-- PP I 18 99 6
It pains me to offend you. PP II 12 198
but found much to offend his ideas of decorum and confirm MP II 1 184 2
to her father could not offend, and there was something MP III 10 406 2

of pride and importance, which the connection would offend. E I 2 15 2
She knows I would not offend for the world. E II 3 176 44
I did it because I thought it would offend you; but, as E III 17 462 12
She spoke, and seemed only to offend. P III 5 34 13
FENDED (36)
at home, and too much offended to admit her; and as she NA I 12 91 3
any thing more of the offended party; and now that she had NA I 13 103 29
that they might well be offended at being supposed to have NA I 14 109 25
No man is offended by another man's admiration of the NA II 4 151 12
The General, meanwhile, though offended every morning by NA II 11 209 5
so suddenly too; but I am not offended, indeed I am not. NA II 13 224 14
"Have I offended the General?" said Catherine in a NA II 13 225 20
"I am sure," said she, "I am very sorry if I have offended NA II 13 225 22
At length she replied: "do not be offended, Elinor, if my SS I 4 19 5
6
"My love," said her mother, "you must not be offended with SS I 10 48 6
afraid I had offended you by what I told you that Monday." SS II 2 146 3
'Offended me! SS II 2 146 4
'Your sister, I hope, cannot be offended," said he, by the SS II 9 208 28
side, by which she offended Mrs. Ferrars and Fanny still SS II 12 234 25
called on for her's, offended them all, by declaring that SS II 12 234 25
misunderstood, so justly offended the delicate feelings of SS III 3 284 24
'because you have offended;--and I should think you might SS III 13 372 42
'Yes, indeed." cried Mrs. Bennet, offended by his manner PP I 9 43 19
he was rather offended; and therefore checked her laugh. PP I 10 51 40
herself not at all offended; but he continued to apologise PP I 13 65 26
but Mr. Collins, much offended, laid aside his book, and PP I 14 69 15
16
which have principally offended Mr. Darcy; but he will PP I 18 95 50
at his own ball he offended two or three young ladies, by PP II 2 141 9
'leased with the preference of one, and offended by the PP II 13 208 8
himself at all, or offended that his letter was not rather PP III 15 362 11
12
thing, which for a time, and not unjustly, offended him. PP III 16 371 45
not out, and had most excessively offended the eldest. MP I 5 51 40
thing in the world, had offended all the farmers, all the MP I 6 58 37
Sir Thomas heard and was not offended. MP II 7 246 37
family, were soon offended by what they termed "airs"--for MP III 9 395 3
much provoked and and offended to have the power of E I 15 125 6
e had gone away deeply offended--he came back engaged to E II 4 181 3
offended, probably, by the little encouragement which her E II 15 281 3
very feeling was offended; and the forbearance of her E III 6 353 3
ou that Mrs. S. admits our apology, and is not offended. E III 16 453 13
nd Mary was either offended, by not being asked before P III 10 90 38
ENDING (10)
nd passed the two offending young men in Milsom-Street, NA I 7 47 18
arianne was afraid of offending, and said no more on the SS I 4 19 3
e are all offending every moment of all our lives. SS I 13 68 74
bliged, from a fear of offending Mrs. Smith, to resist SS I 15 81 43
ilent by his fear of offending, and I shall, therefore, SS III 13 371 39
elations, than run the risk of offending your patroness." PP I 22 123 7
o evident a design of offending and insulting me, you PP II 11 190 10
he idea of grieving and offending a brother whom she PP II 12 202 5
he attention, without offending the taste, or wearing out MP III 3 341 28
anner which might be offending her every hour of the day, E I 7 54 33
ENSIVE (9)
e beneficial to himself and not offensive to his patron. PP I 18 101 71
e offensive to your's, I can only say that I am sorry.-- PP II 12 197 5
riend of Tom and the admirer of Julia he became offensive. MP II 2 194 21
s offensive and disgusting beyond all common offence. MP III 1 318 39
dmund knew to be most offensive to Fanny, he had true MP III 3 340 24
ome excesses of very offensive indulgence and vulgarity. MP III 9 395 4
Yes; it is in two points offensive to me; I have two P III 3 19 16
here is always something offensive in the details of P IV 9 207 91
t is not offensive;--& there are moments, there are S 3 376 1
ER (113)
ccepting so great an offer on the first overture, but I LS 7 253 2
o disobey her mother by refusing an unexceptionable offer LS 19 274 2
nattempted that might offer a chance of obtaining her LS 42 311 2
rs Vernon however persevered in the offer of it, & tho' LS 42 312 5
fter some time they received an offer of tea from one of NA I 2 23 22
rom a doubt of the propriety of accepting such an offer. NA I 7 47 24
ntirely decided, and to offer some little variation on NA I 9 65 27
tis true, we can offer you nothing like the gaieties of NA II 2 139 7
e as good as made you an offer, and that you received his NA II 3 144 10
nd as to making me an offer, or any thing like it, there NA II 3 144 11
nd his assertion of the offer and of her encouragement NA II 3 148 29
t was the offer of a small house, on very easy terms, SS I 4 23 20
hem to Barton, and to offer them every accommodation from SS I 6 30 6
hich an evident wish of improving it could offer. SS I 10 48 7
indness by mentioning the offer, and to tell Willoughby SS I 12 59 5
f their declining the offer upon her account; insisted on SS II 3 155 7
revail on him to make the offer himself, nor commission SS II 10 216 15
o a great deal; and an offer from Colonel Brandon, or a SS II 11 228 51
rovoke him to make that offer, which might give himself SS III 3 280 9
he Colonel been really making her an offer of his hand. SS III 3 283 20
orded than if it had arisen from an offer of marriage. SS III 3 284 24
linor did not offer to detain him; and they parted, with SS III 4 290 43
mployed in conveying the offer from Colonel Brandon to SS III 5 295 13
anger would not allow her to offer the comfort of hope. SS III 7 313 20
mean to offer some kind of explanation, some kind of SS III 8 319 23
azard any remark, and ventured not to offer consolation. SS III 11 355 46
or; & she accepted the offer most thankfully; W 339 18
situation, to suppose to offer could appear in a less W 362 32
o disposition could offer a greater contrast to his own, PP I 4 16 14
ou were sure that they would not offer to send her home." PP I 7 30 22
as obliged to convert the offer of the chaise into an PP I 7 33 45
as sure he would make her an offer before we came away. PP I 9 44 31
appy on every occasion to offer those little delicate PP I 14 67 9
r. Collins might never make the offer, and till he did, PP I 17 88 14
d offer to introduce him to any young lady in the room. PP I 18 102 73
s among the least of the advantages in my power to offer. PP I 19 106 10
n making me the offer, you must have satisfied the PP I 19 107 16
he establishment I can offer would be any other than PP I 19 108 19
hat another offer of marriage may ever be made you. PP I 19 108 19
understand that Mr. Collins has made you an offer of PP I 20 111 15
'ery well--and this offer of marriage you have refused?" PP I 20 111 15
r. Collins has made an offer to Lizzy, and she will not PP I 20 112 25
o go on refusing every offer of marriage in this way, you PP I 20 113 28
he discussion of Mr. Collins's offer was now nearly at an PP I 21 115 1
e made her an offer in this very room, and she refused PP II 2 140 4
ould not have made me the offer of your hand in any PP II 11 192 25
26
at she should receive an offer of marriage from Mr. PP II 11 193 31
have nothing more to say, no other apology to offer. PP II 12 199 5
at a contrast did it offer to his last address in PP III 1 252 54
om his pride had revolted, in his offer to herself. PP III 1 254 58
part, that might offer consolation to such distress.-- PP III 4 278 20
t the misery, for which years of happiness were to offer PP III 11 337 56
s he, has my nephew, made you an offer of marriage?" PP III 14 354 34
n have no reason to suppose he will make an offer to me." PP III 14 354 41
shall offer to pay him to-morrow; he will rant and storm PP III 17 377 39
was in her power to offer him any attention, or mark PP III 17 378 46
ould offer as you are so sanguine in expecting." MP I 1 7 7
ys, but accepted the offer most thankfully, assuring MP I 1 11 19
e wish, and the offer of his own quiet mare for the MP I 7 66 14
is offer: she was not to lose a day's exercise by it. MP I 7 66 14
at she ought to offer to stay at home herself. MP I 8 79 25
e it, &c." but her only offer of exchange was addressed MP I 8 81 32
th more than a equal civility the offer was declined;-- MP I 12 118 22
th the greatest alacrity offer his services for the part. MP I 14 132 8
fer of Amelia to Miss Crawford; and Fanny remained alone. MP I 14 136 22
He had the offer of Count Cassel and Anhalt, and at first MP I 15 138 1
variety of danger, which sea and war together could offer. MP II 6 236 21
too dearly, and your brother does not offer half her value. MP II 7 244 28
and he knew what he had to offer her--he had many anxious MP II 8 255 10
I do not offer them as new. MP II 8 258 16
I offer nothing but an old necklace. MP II 8 258 16
coach; and though this offer of Mr. Crawford's would rob MP II 9 266 21
for having received such an offer, than for refusing it. MP III 2 332 20
missing you, when such an offer as this comes in your way. MP III 2 333 26
duty to accept such a very unexceptionable offer as this." MP III 2 333 26
Not a look, or an offer of help had Fanny given; not a MP III 3 337 10
Her acceptance must be as certain as his offer; and yet, MP III 6 367 4
permanence, and equal comfort, of which she had the offer. MP III 6 369 9
uncle first made her the offer of visiting the parents and MP III 6 369 11
Fanny wrote to offer herself; and her mother's answer, MP III 6 371 17
civilities was an offer of Mr. Price's to take Mr. MP III 10 402 13
whether the concluding offer might be accepted or not. MP III 14 435 15
If he wanted, he would send for her; and even to offer an MP III 14 436 15
she had again a home to offer Mary; and Mary had had MP III 17 469 24
Smith will soon have an offer of marriage, and from a most E I 8 59 25
"Well, well, means to make her an offer then. E I 8 59 27
a man that a woman should ever refuse an offer of marriage. E I 8 60 33
because she does not accept the first offer she receives? E I 8 64 46
"I do not offer it for Miss Smith's collection," said he. E I 9 71 11
actually accepting the offer with much prompt satisfaction. E I 13 110 12
and had some question to ask, or some comfort to offer. E I 15 126 9
united to produce an offer from Colonel Campbell of E II 2 163 4
and thought this the best offer she was likely to have." E II 14 271 14
such society and friendship as the vicarage had to offer. E II 15 285 12
up with any thing that may offer, any inferior, E II 17 301 16
They had stopped at Mrs. Bates's door to offer the use of E III 2 320 6
I understand you were so kind as to offer, but another E III 2 321 17
Elton was wild to have the offer closed with immediately.-- E III 6 359 37
against accepting the offer, and for the reasons you E III 8 380 15
thing she could offer of assistance or regard be repulsed. E III 11 403 2
Emma, I accept your offer--extraordinary as it may seem, I E III 13 429 33
she closed with the offer of that officious Mrs. Elton; E III 14 441 8
She closed with this offer, resolving to break with me E III 14 442 8
than Admiral Croft bid fair to be, could hardly offer. P III 3 24 36
as a public place, might offer; the rooms were shut up, P III 11 95 9
She could only offer one solution; it was, perhaps, for P IV 3 140 11
to give me any notice, or offer to take "any thing. P IV 6 164 7
not yet have made the offer, and I could no more speak the P IV 9 211 101
"I offer myself to you again with a heart even more your " P IV 11 237 42
harmony, of good-will to offer in return for all the worth P IV 12 251 10
house in a very inferior part of London, cd offer.-- S 3 378 1
I had a few moments indecision;--whether to offer to write S 9 409 1
the hotel, to investigate the truth & offer her services.-- S 10 419 1
OFFERED (55)
your father when he offered to read it to me, by which LS 13 262 1
doubt if I could resist even matrimony offered by him. LS 39 308 1
with the gentleman who offered it, which was the only time NA I 2 23 22
mind, and so very inadequate was the comfort she offered. NA I 11 90 64
as readily as they were offered, and allowing him almost NA II 4 149 1
the house, and he now offered himself as her conductor; NA II 7 176 17
The shock however being less real than the relief, offered NA II 7 179 29
here at seven o'clock, and no servant will be offered you." NA II 13 224 18
Such was the permission upon which he had now offered her NA II 15 244 11
though the house he now offered her was merely a cottage, SS I 4 23 20
The gentleman offered his services, and perceiving that SS I 9 42 8
in London or at Barton, offered no counsel of her own SS II 9 203 9
refusing Elinor's offered attendance, went out alone for SS II 9 203 10
It was only the last time they met that he had offered him SS II 10 215 9
from every charge but of imprudence, was readily offered. SS III 1 261 12
a good thousand a-year; offered even, when matters grew SS III 1 266 38
I offered immediately, as soon as my mother related the SS III 5 299 37
in his mind, he offered himself as the messenger who SS III 7 311 15
In the height of her morality, good woman! she offered to SS III 8 323 40
to decline what he offered--Mrs E. continued silent, W 339 18
Mrs Robert offered not another word in support of the game. W 358 28
and when nothing better offered, a walk to Meryton was PP I 7 28 3
Miss Bingley offered her the carriage, and she only wanted PP I 7 33 45
He immediately offered to fetch her others; all that his PP I 8 37 26
side, and not lead you to reject the offered olive branch. PP I 13 63 12
Then turning to Mr. Bennet, he offered himself as his PP I 14 69 17
all the compliment it offered to herself, and it was most PP I 21 116 5
up, the carriage was offered to Mrs. Collins, gratefully PP II 6 166 42
to condole with us, and offered her services, or any of PP III 5 292 66
"Having thus offered you the sincere congratulations of PP III 15 362 14
Fanny thought it a bold measure, but offered no farther MP I 2 16 20
Henry, who is good-nature itself, has offered to fetch it MP I 6 58 39
Mrs. Grant offered herself as companion for the day to MP I 8 79 28
land, offered sacrifices to the gods on their safe return." MP I 11 108 10
and though Lord Ravenshaw offered to resign his to me, it MP I 13 122 2
We all agreed that it could not be offered to any body MP I 14 134 13
Mrs. Norris offered to contrive his dress, Mr. Yates MP I 17 158 2
having such an happiness offered, and ascertaining with MP II 4 215 47
it was, as the occasion offered,--"Ah! ma'am, how much we MP II 10 277 16
Julia had offered to return if wanted--but this was all.-- MP III 14 432 11
he would never have offered so great an insult to the MP III 17 465 13
kindred to care for, offered to take the whole charge of E I 2 16 4
her as the source of all the happiness they offered. E III 1 317 9
to be engaged by no other word that could be offered, E III 5 349 23
perhaps, have rather offered it--but he took her hand, E III 9 386 7
Miss Fairfax's recent illness had offered a fair plea for E III 12 418 5
to say, "had I been offered the sight of one of this E III 15 444 6
She came forward with an offered hand; and said, in a low, E III 16 453 8
9
him, and in the home he offered, there would be the hope E III 19 482 4
the idea of its being offered in any manner; forbad the P III 2 15 14
On its being proposed, Anne offered her services, as usual, P III 8 71 56
engaged in, they kindly offered a seat to any lady who P III 10 90 38
for what could be offered but general acquiescence?-- P III 12 103 3
of gratitude to heaven had been offered, may be conceived. P III 12 112 53
offered his assistance in taking the house for Mrs G.-- S 9 410 1
OFFERING (27)
steadily declared his intention of offering her his hand. NA II 15 248 16
and an opportunity now offering of disposing of her SS I 5 26 5
her two brothers for offering to touch her, and all their SS I 21 121 10
times, she feared they would despise her for offering. SS II 14 247 4
he has great pleasure in offering you the living of SS III 4 288 28
he must think I have never forgiven him for offering." SS III 13 368 30
without offering one argument in favour of its propriety." PP I 10 50 34
in the neighbourhood, offering at the same time to supply PP III 1 255 60
her, offering his assistance, as far as it would go. PP III 10 322 2
The boy looked very silly and turned away without offering MP I 15 142 22
was not prevented from offering, nor you from taking it on MP II 9 263 14
meaning even to her, offering himself, hand, fortune, MP II 13 301 7
there will be no little offering of love at the end, no MP III 9 393 1
ceremony about him, was offering by his short, decided E I 8 57 2
It seemed too precious an offering for any degree of E I 9 77 43
her brother was civilly offering a seat in his carriage, E I 13 110 12
And now I can see it in no other light than as an offering E II 8 219 42
attachment had been an offering to conjugal unreserve, and E II 15 282 3
"Will you?" said he, offering his hand. E III 2 331 61
repeated attentions were offering to another woman, before E III 10 397 46
excused himself from offering the slightest hint, and only P III 2 11 1
Mrs. Croft "yesterday, offering to convey any thing to you; P IV 6 164 8
rather than words, was offering his services to her. P IV 7 176 10
offering, as atonement for all the insolence of the past. P IV 10 226 65
length sir"--offering him the two little oblong extracts.-- S 1 366 1
Now, if he were here, I know he wd be offering odds that S 5 385 1

to the list as the first offering to the success of the S 6 390 1
OFFERS (15)
offers of accommodation, it proved to be exactly the case. NA II 13 229 31
The strangeness of Mr. Collins's making two offers of PP I 22 125 18
punctually repeated all his wife's offers of refreshment. PP II 5 155 3
to give it up, as soon as any eligible purchase offers." PP II 9 178 10
those offers, which were last night so disgusting to you. PP II 12 196 4
contain a renewal of his offers, she had formed no PP II 13 204 1
use of such words and offers, if they meant but to trifle? MP II 13 302 10
Miss Harriet Smith may not find offers of marriage flow in E I 8 64 47
This is a connection which offers nothing but good. E I 9 74 20
"Yes," said Jane, "we heard his kind offers, we heard E II 10 245 53
encouragement, and offers of service; that she will not be E II 15 288 39
But two such offers in one day!-- E III 2 322 19
course among us, that every man is refused--till he offers. P IV 9 195 30
that road in a carriage--& ready offers of assistance. S 1 365 1
recommend their father's offers; & in an unaffected manner S 1 370 1
OFFICE (38)
detriment of the post office revenue, be continued longer. LS 42 311 1
must wring her heart, could not be the office of a friend. NA II 9 192 5
painful office of informing her sister that he was married. SS II 10 216 16
Elinor's office was a painful one.-- SS III 1 261 11
his wish to put off so agreeable an office to another. SS III 3 283 20
It was an office in short, from which, unwilling to give SS III 3 283 20
I am charged with a most agreeable office, (breathing SS III 4 288 28
her comfortable, was the office of each watchful companion, SS III 10 341 6
before; and taking the office of superintendance intirely W 360 30
if you decline the office, I will take it on myself." PP I 2 7 16
which had been let down to hide it, not doing its office." PP I 8 36 6
I consider the clerical office as equal in point of PP I 18 97 60
61
with her husband that the office of introduction should be PP II 6 161 10
I readily engaged in the office of pointing out to my PP II 12 198 5
No one here can call the office nothing. MP I 9 92 45
You do not deserve the office, if you cannot appreciate MP I 14 134 13
She was invested, indeed, with the office of judge and MP I 18 170 24
Mrs. Norris felt herself defrauded of an office on which MP II 1 180 10
"You are right, Fanny, to protest against such an office, MP II 9 269 35
accent--"in such an office of high responsibility!" MP III 4 351 33
was clerk in a public office in London, and the other MP III 7 381 26
dread of being thought to demean herself by such an office. MP III 7 383 32
new as any thing like an office of authority was to Fanny, MP III 9 396 6
returning to every former office, with more than former MP III 16 449 4
to hold the nominal office of governess, the mildness of E I 1 5 3
he would like to have the same kind office done for him! E I 1 13 46
I am sure you always thought me unfit for the office I E I 5 38 10
Mr. Knightley, at this little remains of office." E I 5 40 24
him such a troublesome office for the world"--brought on E I 6 49 41
fully competent to the office of instruction herself; but E II 2 164 6
letting himself in at the office door, Mr. Cole's carriage E II 9 233 24
distressing and delicate office to perform by Harriet, E III 11 403 3
in Dugdale--serving the office of High Sheriff, P III 1 3 3
4
The last office of the four carriage-horses was to draw P III 5 35 18
very much preferring the office of musician to a more P III 6 47 15
all the duties of his office, but was now growing too P III 9 78 19
she would shrink unnecessarily from the office of a friend. P III 12 116 69
kindness--and as every office of hospitality & S 2 371 1
OFFICER (17)
dance with a brother officer, introduced by Capt. Hunter.-- W 328 9
she saw the smartest officer of the sett, walking off to W 330 11
walking with an officer on the other side of the way. PP I 15 72 8
The officer was the very Mr. Denny, concerning whose PP I 15 72 8
She danced next with an officer, and had the refreshment PP I 18 90 5
as Wickham and another officer walked back with them to PP I 21 115 5
While there was an officer in Meryton, they would flirt PP II 14 213 17
as not to mention an officer above once a day, unless by PP II 19 238 6
Sometimes one officer, sometimes another had been her PP III 4 280 25
No officer is ever to enter my house again, nor even to PP III 6 300 30
met with a navy officer or two of his acquaintance, since MP III 10 400 7
Fairfax, as an excellent officer and most deserving young E II 2 163 4
goodwill towards a naval officer as tenant, had been P III 3 21 18
a man to distinguish himself as any officer in the navy. P III 9 75 10
young man and an officer, whom he had always valued highly, P III 11 96 12
a very active, zealous officer too, which is more than you P IV 6 171 37
the tall Irish officer, who is talked of for one of them." P IV 9 193 8
OFFICER'S (1)
I would assist any brother officer's wife that I could, P III 8 69 40
OFFICERS (38)
& among so many officers, you will hardly want partners. W 315 1
Not that her father or mother like officers, but if she W 320 2
"Aye--there is nothing like your officers for captivating W 326 5
while three or four officers were lounging together, W 327 8
officers joined eagerly in dancing at one end of the room. PP I 6 25 24
and at length they began to know the officers themselves. PP I 7 28 4
They could talk of nothing but officers; and Mr. Bingley's PP I 7 29 4
say they will not think about officers any more than we do. PP I 7 29 12
"With the officers!" cried Lydia. PP I 7 30 18
the attentions of the officers, to whom her uncle's good PP I 9 45 36
do cure the younger girls of running after the officers.-- PP I 10 52 55
several of the officers had dined lately with their uncle, PP I 12 60 7
street in quest of the officers, and nothing less than a PP I 15 72 7
now except a few of the officers, who in comparison with PP I 15 74 11
The officers of the ----shire were in general a very PP I 16 76 3
as Mr. Wickham and the officers, Mr. Collins seemed likely PP I 16 76 5
No aunt, no officers, no news could be sought after;--the PP I 17 88 15
invitation to the officers; and though this was not PP I 18 89 1
2
in his invitation to the officers, he was excessively glad PP I 18 94 45
Here are officers enough at Meryton to disappoint all the PP II 1 138 27
the officers, there was not a day without its engagement. PP II 2 142 18
When the engagement was for home, some of the officers PP II 2 142 18
part of it, of which officers Mr. Wickham was sure to be PP II 2 142 18
half a day before they were in pursuit of the officers. PP II 16 223 25
The officers will find women better worth their notice. PP II 18 232 20
streets of that gay bathing place covered with officers. PP II 18 232 22
tent, tenderly flirting with at least six officers at once. PP II 18 232 22
dined with others of the officers at Longbourn; and so PP II 18 233 26
where such and such officers had attended them, and where PP II 19 238 5
Scotland with one of his officers; to own the truth, with PP III 4 273 3
but love, flirtation, and officers, have been in her head. PP III 5 283 10
The officers may not be so pleasant in general ----'s PP III 8 313 21
please sir, and one of the officers has been here to"----- MP III 7 377 7
and after a time the two officers seemed very well MP III 10 403 15
This peace will be turning all our rich navy officers P III 3 17 1
of course, and few navy officers, or men of any other P III 3 18 8
as intelligent and keen as any of the officers around her. P IV 6 168 24
town, or half pay officers, or Widows with only a jointure. S 7 401 1
OFFICERS' (2)
to their knowledge of the officers' names and connections. PP I 7 28 4
lodgings of one of the officers' wives, and Elizabeth PP I 7 32 41
OFFICES (21)
kind offices have implanted, he may be an agreable flirt. LS 7 254 3
be so; intended only for offices, and enclosed behind by NA II 8 184 4
in the arrangement of his offices; and as he was convinced, NA II 8 184 4
did not strike her less than the number of their offices. NA II 8 184 4
aware of their leading from the offices in common use?" NA II 9 195 12
Your kind offices will set all right:--he is the only man NA II 12 216 2
square; and beyond them were the offices and the stairs. SS I 6 28 2
herself to submit to the offices of a nurse, for the sake SS I 8 38 10
with tall Lombardy poplars, shut out the offices. SS III 6 302 7
taking any part in those offices of general complaisance SS III 10 346 28
think only of procuring his good offices in my favour. SS III 13 364 12
am sure you will be too generous to do us any ill offices. SS III 13 365 14
and personally intreat her good offices in his favour.-- SS III 13 372 45
Mansfield Park, and was scarcely ever seen in her offices. MP I 3 31 59
sympathizing in praise of Fanny's kind offices. MP I 18 170 23
Mrs. Price, or the good offices of Rebecca, every thing MP III 15 444 27
There are places in town, offices, where inquiry would E II 17 300 13
soon produce something--offices for the sale--not quite of E II 17 300 13
But I only mean to say that there are advertising offices, E II 17 301 15
she hoped to engage Anne's good offices with Mr. Elliot. P IV 9 210 99
Her recent good offices by Anne had been enough in P IV 12 251 11
OFFICIAL (1)
I ought to have waited for official information. P IV 9 195 27
OFFICIATING (1)
Mr. Weston directed the whole, officiating safely between E III 7 367 1
OFFICIOUS (11)
worried down by officious condolence to rate good-breeding SS II 10 215 13
are rather disposed to call his interference officious?" PP II 10 185 35
increased, at such unnecessary, such officious attention! PP III 11 337 54
sick of civility, of deference, of officious attention. PP III 18 380 5
Sir Thomas, and all the officious prognostications of Mrs. MP I 2 13 4
hate to be worrying and officious, I said no more; but my MP II 2 189 5
evil of a restless, officious companion, too apt to be MP III 14 432 10
If by any officious exertions of his, she is induced to MP III 16 457 29
with the offer of that officious Mrs. Elton; the whole E III 14 441 8
One hates to be officious, to be giving bad impressions, P IV 9 198 53
Her intimate friends must be officious like herself, & the S 11 420 1
OFFICIOUSLY (1)
into the room, were officiously handed by him to Colonel SS II 12 234 26
OFFICIOUSNESS (2)
with the ill-judged officiousness of the mother, and heard PP III 13 345 18
The words "unaccountable officiousness!-- S 9 410 1
OFFSPRING (4)
Miss Steeles towards her offspring, were viewed therefore SS I 21 120 6
a little girl, the offspring of her first guilty SS II 9 208 28
its offspring, necessity, had required to be sacrificed. SS III 8 331 70
it perpetuated by offspring, have been got over, had he P III 1 8 17
OFTEN (389)
is too often used I believe to make black appear white. LS 6 251 1
I am afraid I have been often too indulgent, but my poor LS 15 267 6
to my brother, I so very often see her eyes fixed on his LS 18 272 1
Young men are often hasty in their resolutions--& not more LS 23 284 6
was this mistake, to which your ladyship so often alludes? LS 24 289 12
But the influence of reason is often acknowledged too late LS 30 300 2
I charged her to write to me very often, & to remember LS 41 310 4
it personally in town, ceased writing minutely or often. LS 42 311 1
for she was often inattentive, and occasionally stupid. NA I 1 14 1
but they were repeated so often, and proved so totally NA I 2 21 9
and my sister has often trusted me in the choice of a gown. NA I 3 28 38
This sentiment had been uttered so often in vain, that Mrs. NA I 4 31 2
It was a subject, however, in which she often indulged NA I 5 36 2
of opinion, and not often any resemblance of subject, for NA I 5 36 3
I often read novels--it is really well for a novel."-- NA I 5 37 4
substance of its papers so often consisting in the NA I 5 38 4
She very often reads Sir Charles Grandison herself; but NA I 6 41 21
They are very often amazingly impertinent if you do not NA I 6 42 26
prevent her looking very often towards that part of the NA I 8 55 10
"in these public assemblies, it is as often done as not." NA I 8 57 22
You would not often meet with any thing like it in Oxford-- NA I 9 64 24
excessive solicitude about it often destroys its own aim. NA I 10 73 22
way to which he had often recourse, about its being a d---- NA I 11 89 61
very tiresome: and yet I often think it odd that it should NA I 14 108 22
and necessary, I have often wondered at the person's NA I 14 109 24
To be always firm must be to be often obstinate. NA II 1 134 36
and remembering how often she had been falsely accused of NA II 3 143 2
so will occur, and one is often drawn on to give more NA II 3 146 18
Tilney says, there is nothing people are so often deceived NA II 3 147 20
"I used to walk here so often with her!" added Eleanor; " NA II 7 179 32
for, it is impossible for me not to be often solitary." NA II 7 180 34
She had often read of such characters; characters, which NA II 7 181 40
failed, his own had often produced the perfection wanted. NA II 8 183 3
How they could get through it all, had often amazed Mrs. NA II 8 184 4
"My father," she whispered, "often walks about the room in NA II 8 187 13
But it is not often that virtue can boast an interest such NA II 9 196 23
person never known, do not often create that kind of NA II 9 196 23
The malady itself, one from which she had often suffered, NA II 9 196 25
she lived, she might not often have had much to bear, but NA II 9 197 27
He often expressed his uneasiness on this head, feared the NA II 11 209 5
be paid for, and that we often purchase them at a great NA II 11 210 7
brother, whose arrival was often as sudden, if not quite NA II 13 222 7
the wind was high, and often produced strange and sudden NA II 13 227 26
did not think it could ever be repeated too often. NA II 15 243 9
happened pretty often, they always looked another way. NA II 16 250 3
him often enough to engage him in unreserved conversation. SS I 4 20 9
only by that shyness which too often keeps him silent. SS I 4 20 9
friends as I hope to see often collected here; and I have SS I 6 29 4
sportsmen likewise, is not often desirous of encouraging SS I 7 33 3
and accomplished as often as a showery October would allow. SS I 11 53 1
Is not it what you have often wished to do yourself?" SS I 13 68 68
of those fine bold hills that we have so often admired. SS I 13 69 76
equal, and he had himself often complained of his poverty. SS I 14 71 4
"How often did I wish," added he, "when I was at Allenham SS I 14 73 17
and crying; her voice often totally suspended by her tears. SS I 16 83 3
"Remember, Elinor," said she, "how very often Sir John SS I 16 84 6
had often observed at Norland in their mutual behaviour. SS I 16 87 23
"No; my feelings are not often shared, not often SS I 16 88 33
always with animation--but she is not often really merry." SS I 17 93 35
I am guilty, I confess, of having often wished you to SS I 17 94 39
so foolishly shy, that I often seem negligent, when I am SS I 17 94 42
unsuitableness which often existed between husband and SS I 21 118 1
alluded to, which, though often impertinently expressed, SS I 21 125 37
Lucy was naturally clever; her remarks were often just and SS I 22 127 2
for my sister and me was often staying with my uncle, and SS I 22 130 28
connections, which had often surprised her, the picture, SS II 1 139 1
for the weather was not often fine enough to allow of SS II 1 142 8
a person, to whom she had often had difficulty in SS II 3 156 15
Elinor had often wished for an opportunity of attempting SS II 3 157 17
and talk to Elinor, who often derived more satisfaction SS II 5 168 12
It grieved her to see the earnestness with which he often SS II 5 169 12
though its effusions were often distressing, and sometimes SS II 8 193 7
to which her sister was often led in her opinion of others, SS II 9 201 4
as they often were by the clamorous kindness of the others. SS II 10 215 12
the subject occurred very often, by saying, "it is very SS II 10 215 14
(though it did not often happen) she was obliged, or could SS II 10 216 15
to repeat it over and over again as often as they liked. SS II 12 233 20
to meet, and meet pretty often, for Lady Middleton's SS II 13 240 15
"What can bring her here so often! "said Marianne, on her SS II 13 244 44
All that she could hope, was that Edward would not often SS II 13 245 4
granted; for though she often threw out expressions of SS II 14 247
from any, and very often without knowing till the last SS II 14 249
so I often tell my mother, when she is grieving about it. SS II 14 251 1
(as she had of late often hoped might be the case) had SS III 1 260
"I have very often wished to undeceive yourself and my SS III 1 262 2
in the world, for I have often thought of late, there was SS III 4 285
elegance, which made her often deficient in the forms of SS III 6 304 1
often by her better experience in nursing, of material use. SS III 7 308
better treatment, and I often, with great self-reproach, SS III 8 322 3
You would be surprised to hear how often I watched you, SS III 8 326 5
you, how often I was on the point of falling in with you. SS III 8 326 5
artificial, and often ill-timed of the other. SS III 9 338 2
the Abbeyland; and we will often go to the old ruins of SS III 10 343
so much reason as they had often had to be careless of SS III 11 355 4

for me to be very often at Longstaple, where I always felt SS III 13 362 5
balls--but Mr Curtis won't often spare him, & just now it W 321 2
were not often reckoned very like her youngest brother.-- W 324 3
So far, the subject was very often carried;--but Mr & Mrs W 325 4
"In such cases, a woman has not often much beauty to think PP I 1 4 21
as pride often does, because there is an excuse for it. PP I 5 20 18
things, though the words are often used synonimously. PP I 5 20 20
But though Bingley and Jane meet tolerably often, it is PP I 6 22 6
Do you often dance at St. James's?" PP I 6 25 30
Carter do not go so often to Miss Watson's as they did PP I 7 30 13
she sees them now very often standing in Clarke's library." PP I 7 30 13
nor were the ladies often absent; the gentlemen being out, PP I 7 33 44
I often tell my other girls they are nothing to her. PP I 9 42 7
Lady Lucas herself has often said so, and envied me Jane's PP I 9 44 31
sure, Jane--one does not often see any body better looking. PP I 9 44 31
It is often only carelessness of opinion, and sometimes an PP I 10 48 25
by the possessor, and often without any attention to the PP I 10 49 27
A regard for the requester would often make one readily PP I 10 50 37
She often tried to provoke Darcy into disliking her guest, PP I 10 52 54
which often expose a strong understanding to ridicule." PP I 11 57 22
I do not believe she often sees such at home." PP I 13 61 2
They had often attempted it before, but it was a subject PP I 13 62 8
But she is perfectly amiable, and often condescends to PP I 14 67 7
book, and said, "I have often observed how little young PP I 14 69 15
16
but with him I believe it does not often happen. PP I 16 78 16
we stood--the sort of preference which was often given me." PP I 16 80 32
Mr. Darcy often acknowledged himself to be under the PP I 16 81 37
traced to pride;--and pride has often been his best friend. PP I 16 81 39
It has often led him to be liberal and generous,--to give PP I 16 81 41
that though she did not often speak unnecessarily to Mr. PP I 17 87 12
instead of attending, and often moving wrong without being PP I 18 90 4
if she and her sisters did not very often walk to Meryton. PP I 18 93 18
Such very superior dancing is not often seen. PP I 18 92 23
hope to have this pleasure often repeated, especially when PP I 18 92 23
her friend Miss Lucas, who often joined them, and PP I 18 102 73
farther notice; though often standing within a very short PP I 18 102 74
with her hand; for I have often observed that resignation PP I 20 114 32
in his reflections which often struck her, and though by PP I 22 124 11
and often uncivil, boisterously exclaimed, "good Lord! PP I 23 126 1
2
It is very often nothing but our own vanity that deceives PP II 1 136 14
They saw him often, and to his other recommendations was PP II 1 138 30
But these things happen so often! PP II 2 140 6
It does not often happen that the interference of friends PP II 2 140 7
It is as often applied to feelings which arise from an PP II 2 140 8
as well, if you discourage his coming here so very often. PP II 3 145 7
But do not imagine that he is always here so often. PP II 3 145 9
"I shall depend on hearing from you very often, Eliza." PP II 3 146 11
12
"We shall often meet, I hope, in Hertfordshire." PP II 3 146 15
of it, Elizabeth supposed he must be often forgotten. PP II 5 157 5
a husband and such a neighbour as were not often met with. PP II 7 168 1
went along, and how often especially Miss de Bourgh drove PP II 7 168 2
of year, that she had often great enjoyment out of doors. PP II 7 169 5
I often tell young ladies, that no excellence in music is PP II 8 173 10
is very welcome, as I have often told her, to come to PP II 8 173 10
appear interested in their concerns, as I often see done." PP II 8 175 24
But why Mr. Darcy came so often to the parsonage, it was PP II 9 180 29
It was an earnest, steadfast gaze, but she often doubted PP II 9 181 29
like women of fortune, which I think they very often do." PP II 10 183 13
I had often seen him in love before.-- PP II 12 197 5
brother, and that she had often heard him speak so PP II 13 207 6
my abilities! who have often disdained the generous PP II 13 208 8
air and manner, not often united with great sensibility. PP II 13 208 9
I dare say he often hears worse things said than I am PP II 16 220 10
that her mother, though often disheartened, had never yet PP II 16 223 26
than first attachments often boast; and so fervently did PP II 17 227 26
And so, I suppose, they often talk of having Longbourn PP II 17 228 33
But I make no doubt, they often talk of it between PP II 17 228 35
What are we to do!" would they often exclaim in the PP II 18 229 2
their sisters will not be often involved in the disgrace?" PP II 18 231 18
he had formerly seen him often; and after observing that PP II 18 233 27
those pleasures which too often console the unfortunate PP II 19 236 1
When Lydia went away, she promised to write very often and PP II 19 238 5
her stay in Derbyshire, so often, and in so hurried a way, PP III 1 252 52
civility, to fish there as often as he chose, while he PP III 1 255 60
"Your great men often are; and therefore I shall not take PP III 1 258 72
It was often that she could turn her eyes on Mr. Darcy PP III 2 263 10
comparison of what is so often described as arising on a PP III 4 279 24
"And have you heard from him often?" PP III 5 286 27
"Colonel Forster did own that he had often suspected some PP III 5 290 46
Mr. Bennet had very often wished, before this period of PP III 8 308 1
What a triumph for him, as she often thought, could he PP III 8 311 14
"Write to me very often, my dear." PP III 11 330 5
"As often as I can. PP III 11 330 6
"I often think," said she, "that there is nothing so bad PP III 11 330 10
They were more disturbed, more unequal, than she had often PP III 11 332 20
her work, with an eagerness which it did not often command. PP III 11 335 40
eyes to his face, she as often found him looking at Jane, PP III 11 335 43
but that his eyes were so often turned towards her side of PP III 12 342 26
I hope we may often meet again." PP III 12 343 30
he should do, which had often seemed likely, the advice PP III 15 361 3
I never meant to deceive you, but my spirits might often PP III 16 369 27
quarrelling with you as often as may be; and I shall begin PP III 18 381 7
though at first she often listened with an astonishment PP III 19 387 11
Mrs. Norris was often observing to the others, that she MP I 1 5 4
of something or other; often retreating towards her own MP I 2 14 9
and though Fanny was often mortified by their treatment of MP I 2 20 32
all; and though you have often persuaded me to be MP I 3 25 18
on that point almost as often, though not so diffusely, as MP I 3 31 60
well married," she very often thought; always when they MP I 4 38 9
nor could he refrain from often saying to himself, in Mr. MP I 4 40 13
such young men were not often seen together even in London, MP I 5 47 27
set people right, but I do see that they are often wrong." MP I 5 50 36
assurances we have so often received to the contrary." MP I 6 57 33
page in a letter; and very often it is nothing more than, ' MP I 6 59 43
been out very often lately, and would rather stay at home. MP I 7 70 29
How often do I pace it three times a-day, early and late, MP I 7 73 53
She has not often a gratification of the kind, and I am MP I 8 78 21
She was not often invited to join in the conversation of MP I 8 80 31
so close to the great house as often happens in old places. MP I 8 82 34
may often rouse better feelings than are begun with. MP I 9 88 18
conversation which means not very often, I do think it. MP I 9 92 44
scholar and clever, and often preaches good sermons, and MP I 11 111 28
"I think the man who could often quarrel with Fanny," said MP I 11 112 32
be aware; for I believe it often happens, that a man, MP I 12 116 10
her motives had been often misunderstood, her feelings MP I 16 152 2
I often think of Mr. Rushworth's property and independence, MP I 17 161 13
Fanny, being always a very courteous listener, and often MP I 18 164 2
of him, and so needlessly often the rehearsal of the first MP I 18 164 2
prompter, sometimes as spectator--was often very useful.-- MP I 18 165 3
so often encouraged the sort of thing in us formerly, MP II 1 184 26
leaders so often now, that I am sure there is no fear.' MP II 2 189 5
He had known many disagreeable fathers before, and often MP II 2 191 10
amusement, and that often at the expense of her judgment, MP II 4 208 11
already; be plagued very often and never lose your temper." MP II 4 213 34
Too often, alas! it is so.-- MP II 6 235 18
William was often called on by his uncle to be the talker. MP II 6 236 21
again--had been often taken on shore by the favour of his MP II 6 236 21
unmanageable days often volunteer, for soon after MP II 9 265 21
was often under the influence of much less sanguine views. MP II 9 267 22

So often as she had heard them wish for a ball at home as MP II 10 276 12
Mrs. Norris often talks of her luck; what will she say now? MP II 12 292 7
He had often seen it tried. MP II 12 294 16
he spoke to her much too often; and she was afraid there MP II 13 304 16
no more than what he might often have expressed towards MP II 13 306 26
she had trembled at it as often, and began to tremble MP III 1 312 4
about Fanny, I have often observed it before,--she likes MP III 1 323 56
that even this slight sacrifice cannot be often demanded. MP III 2 331 16
"She often reads to me out of those books and she was in MP III 3 336 9
be fond of preaching often; now and then, perhaps, once or MP III 3 341 30
too great; his spirits often oppress me--but there is MP III 4 349 25
I have often scolded him for it, but it is his only fault; MP III 5 363 22
feelings; and there may often be a great deal more MP III 5 363 23
And the other, that you will often call on Mrs. Grant and MP III 5 364 32
to write to her soon and often, and promising to be a good MP III 6 373 26
away, but Tom she had often helped to nurse, and now felt MP III 7 381 25
a girl under her, and I often do half the work myself." MP III 7 385 39
very wrong--her measures often ill-chosen and ill-timed, MP III 9 396 6
looks and language very often indefensible, Fanny could MP III 9 396 6
two apartments; and she often heaved a sigh at the MP III 9 398 9
the year a fine morning so often turned off, that it was MP III 10 401 10
a sad place--they did not often get out--and she knew they MP III 10 401 10
enough inured to, for her often to make a tolerable meal. MP III 10 407 23
It often grieved her to the heart--to think of the MP III 11 408 2
They often stopt with the same sentiment and taste, MP III 11 409 7
forks, that she was very often constrained to defer her MP III 11 413 30
matters, none returned so often, or remained so long MP III 12 419 8
three weeks in London, and saw her (for London) very often. MP III 13 420 2
Her aunt often expressed a wish for her, but there was no MP III 14 430 6
Miss Crawford's letter, which she had read so often as to MP III 15 441 19
Edmund's deep sighs often reached Fanny. MP III 15 445 33
of our acquaintance, been often sensible of some MP III 16 457 30
first inclination, and brought them very often together. MP III 17 467 19
"How often we shall be going to see them and they coming E I 1 8 14
His coming to visit his father had been often talked of E I 2 17 8
and carried home so often that Mr. Woodhouse thought it no E I 3 20 3
telling her to come very often; and as their acquaintance E I 4 26 1
He has passed you very often." E I 4 29 13
your fate has often found; for it shall be attended to." E I 5 40 25
for accomplishment often higher than it deserved. E I 6 44 19
You do not often overpower me with it." E I 8 58 13
very often to recollect something worth their putting in. E I 9 70 5
I think their father is too rough with them very often." E I 9 81 72
"I do not often walk this way now," said Emma, as they E I 10 83 5
My nephews and nieces!--I shall often have a niece with me. E I 10 86 21
to you both, but I hope I am not often so ill-equipped. E I 10 89 37
He was not an ill-tempered man, not so often unreasonably E I 11 92 5
It did not often happen; for Mr. John Knightley had really E I 11 93 5
due to him; but it was too often for Emma's charity, E I 11 93 5
"And do you see her, sir, tolerably often?" asked Isabella E I 11 94 12
"Not near so often, my dear, as I could wish." E I 11 94 13
often--but then--she is always obliged to go away again." E I 11 94 16
not so heavy as he has very often known them in November. E I 12 102 34
Often as she had wished for and ordered it, she had never E I 12 105 50
bad sore-throats, and had often alarmed her with them."-- E I 13 109 6
of the blunders which often arise from a partial knowledge E I 13 112 23
Certainly she had often, especially of late, thought his E I 16 134 5
Do you suppose she does not often say all this to herself? E I 18 149 26
often look upon fine young men, well-bred and agreeable. E I 18 149 29
of himself, which she had often laid to his charge, she E I 18 150 37
she can never hear it often enough; so I knew it could not E II 1 157 10
My mother often wonders that I can make it out so well. E II 1 157 10
She often says, when the letter is first opened, 'well, E II 1 157 10
Jane often says, when she is here, 'I am sure, grandmama, E II 1 158 10
as Jane used to be very often walking out with them--for E II 1 159 20
daughter's not walking out often with only Mr. Dixon, for E II 1 159 20
chance, that luck which so often defies anticipation in E II 2 165 7
not often deficient in what is due to guests at Hartfield." E II 3 170 3
same time; "you are not often deficient; not often E II 3 170 5
not often deficient either in manner or comprehension. E II 3 170 5
pity indeed! and I have often wished--but it is so little E II 3 171 16
17
She had no doubt of what Mr. Weston was often thinking E II 5 192 34
not to look, she was confident that he was often listening. E II 5 193 34
"Did you see her often at Weymouth?" E II 6 199 13
Were you often in the same society?" E II 6 199 13
man--one who smiled so often and bowed so well; but there E II 7 206 4
his carriage so often as became the owner of Donwell Abbey. E II 8 213 7
"I often feel concerned," said she, "that I dare not make E II 8 228 89
he replied;--"but you must often wish it, I am sure." E II 8 228 90
not enhanced, and the inconvenience is often considerable. E II 8 228 92
Not that I had any doubt before--I have so often heard Mr. E II 9 237 46
We have apple dumplings, however, very often. E II 9 237 46
I dare say they often think of you, and wonder which will E II 10 241 12
He has been opening doors very often this evening, and E II 11 249 11
I have often known it done myself." E II 11 252 31
out of the world, and am often astonished at what I hear. E II 11 252 32
How often have I heard you speak of it as such a E II 11 252 37
How often is happiness destroyed by preparation, foolish E II 12 259 17
Mrs. Weston; she was very often thinking of him, and quite E II 13 264 1
'My friend Knightley' had been so often mentioned, that I E II 14 278 50
timidity--and I am sure one does not often meet with it.-- E II 15 283 7
I shall certainly have her very often at my house, shall E II 15 284 9
I shall have her very often indeed while they are with me, E II 15 284 9
about Jane Fairfax than she had often been.-- E II 16 291 5
"I have often thought them the worst of the two," replied E II 16 293 21
same sort of hand-writing often prevails in a family; and E II 16 297 45
my taste than modern ease; modern ease often disgusts me. E II 17 302 22
He was often hoping, intending to come--but was always E III 1 316 6
often with them, almost as often as he could even wish. E III 1 317 8
by so often, and knowing how much trouble you must have. E III 2 322 19
My mother often talks of your goodnature. E III 2 323 19
Do not we often talk of Mr. Frank Churchill?-- E III 2 323 19
He seemed often observing her. E III 2 326 32
He had walked up one day after dinner, as he very often E III 5 344 3
for Mr. Woodhouse, who had often been distressed by the E III 5 347 20
eating and drinking were often the cure of such incidental E III 6 364 56
She had been often remiss, her conscience told her so; E III 8 377 1
When they had been all walking together, he had so often E III 11 409 35
She had often observed the change, to almost the same E III 11 409 35
She had not deserved it; she had often been negligent or E III 12 415 1
"I am afraid," returned Emma, sighing, "that I must often E III 12 419 11
She thought he was often looking at her, and trying for a E III 13 425 2
round the same table--how often it had been collected!-- E III 14 434 2
been collected!--and how often had her eyes fallen on the E III 14 434 2
thither as often as might be, and with the least suspicion. E III 14 439 8
'Upon my word, Mr. E., I often say, rather you than I.-- E III 16 455 23
evident, though it could not often proceed beyond a look. E III 16 457 34
all, I have often observed, extremely awkward and remiss.-- E III 16 458 42
"I was very often influenced rightly by you--oftener than E III 17 462 8
"How often, when you were a girl, have you said to me, E III 17 462 9
Mr. Knightley could not be there too often; he should be E III 17 466 29
I have often talked to her a good deal. E III 18 474 34
not be too soon alarmed, nor send for Perry too often. E III 18 479 73
but was hearing of it so often, that it became vain to P III 1 9 19
it is singularity which often makes the worst part of our P III 2 12 4
I have often observed it; they soon lose the look of youth. P III 3 20 17
in the wit which often expressed it, must have been enough P III 4 27 3
She often told herself it was folly, before she could P III 4 30 10
Mary, often a little unwell, and always thinking a great P III 5 33 7
and a knowledge, which she often wished less, of her P III 5 34 12
Here Anne had often been staying. P III 5 36 21

of only three miles, will often include a total change of P III 6 42 1
though there was very often a little disagreement, (in P III 6 43 5
what Anne often heard him say, and had a good deal of P III 6 44 6
to see them at our house so often as I otherwise should. P III 6 45 8
than any thing else, and often drew this compliment;--" P III 6 47 15
repeating his name so often, puzzling over past years, and P III 6 52 33
poor sailors' wives, who often want to be conveyed to one P III 8 69 43
with all the four together often enough to have an opinion, P III 10 82 1
Oh! it does happen very often, I assure you--but my sister P III 10 84 8
and changed them so often, that the balance had certainly P IV 2 129 3
The folly of the means they often employ is only to be P IV 3 144 20
A sick chamber may often furnish the worth of volumes." P IV 5 156 10
lessons are not often in the elevated style you describe. P IV 5 156 11
me more delight than is often felt at my time of life!" P IV 5 160 25
Anne was too much engaged with Lady Russell to be often P IV 6 168 25
is over, the remembrance of it often becomes a pleasure. P IV 8 183 16
"More air than one often sees in Bath.-- P IV 8 188 39
purse was open to him; I know that he often assisted him." P IV 9 199 55
"To be sure I did, very often. P IV 9 201 61
I have often heard him declare, that if baronetcies were P IV 9 202 66
and I could not help often saying, was this for me?" P IV 11 244 70
and those who met too often--a common-place business, too P IV 11 245 78
of such friends to be often with, for her cheerfulness and P IV 12 252 12
if gentlemen were to be often attempting this lane in post- S 1 366 1
She had been necessarily often mentioned at Willingden,-- S 3 375 1
such addition, and long & often enjoyed the repeated S 3 377 1
not be amiss to have them often wanted, to have something S 4 382 1
than are often met with, either separate or together.-- S 5 385 1
often makes me laugh at them all in spite of myself.-- S 5 385 1
You often think they wd better, if they wd leave S 5 388 1
He & I often talk that matter over.-- S 7 400 1
My sister's complaints & mine are happily not often of a S 9 410 1
We are often obliged to check him."-- S 9 411 1
the terrace, & you will often see me at Trafalgar house."-- S 10 416 1
it has happened to me so often that I cannot doubt it.-- S 10 418 1
OFTEN-EXPRESSED (1)
would eat, and his often-expressed fears of her seeing NA II 5 154 2
OFTENER (17)
of weariness, much oftener than she moved her needle.-- NA II 15 241 7
Mrs. Dashwood, who did not chuse to dine with them oftener SS I 19 108 40
"They are wanted in the farm much oftener than I can get PP I 7 31 26
at Longbourn rather oftener than usual to say how happy PP I 23 127 8
drew him oftener from home than any thing else could do. PP III 19 385 2
was of the kind to be oftener found agreeable than some MP I 5 47 28
I have no doubt that he oftener endeavours to restrain MP I 11 112 30
and trick of composition are oftener an object of study. MP III 3 341 28
and might have been there oftener, but it is mortifying to MP III 13 423 2
and interest much oftener than Emma could have supposed. E II 6 196 2
no instrument repeatedly; oftener than I should suppose E II 8 226 81
She promised him again and again to come--much oftener E III 6 354 9
"I was very often influenced rightly by you--oftener than E III 17 462 8
with my not inviting them oftener; but you know it is very P III 6 45 8
I wish he could have such company oftener. P III 12 107 24
Charles Hayter had been at Lyme oftener than suited her, P IV 2 129 3
who has been "calling much oftener than was welcome. P IV 6 163 7
OFTENEST (3)
their voices had been oftenest joined, and sat at the SS I 16 83 3
oftenest answered with a "yes," had sometimes its "no." MP II 8 255 11
The idea that returned the oftenest, was that Miss MP III 12 417 4
OFTENTIMES (1)
"Oftentimes very convenient, no doubt, but never pleasing. E II 6 203 40
OILED (1)
so little disconcerted by the melted butter's being oiled. NA II 11 215 27
OLD (323)
& might perhaps till the old gentleman's death, be very LS 10 257 1
that Frederica is too old ever to submit to school LS 20 277 5
At Bath, his old aunts would have nursed him, but here it LS 28 298 2
a man of his age!--just old enough to be formal, LS 29 298 1
have the gout--too old to be agreeable, & too young to die. LS 29 298 1
If the old man would die, I might not hesitate; but a LS 29 299 3
I cannot suppose that the old story of Mrs Manwaring's LS 35 304 1
the old forlorn spinnet; so, at eight years old she began. NA I 1 14 1
of profligacy at ten years old, she had neither a bad NA I 1 14 1
How old fashioned it is! NA I 2 23 21
a pleasure it was to see an old friend, they proceeded to NA I 4 32 2
the family of a most worthy old friend; and, as the NA I 5 36 3
And old man playing at see-saw! NA I 7 49 40
in the world in it but an old man's playing at see-saw and NA I 7 49 42
that quiz of a hat, it makes you look like an old witch? NA I 7 49 43
my fault, if we set all the old ladies in Bath in a bustle. NA I 8 58 25
We could not come before; the old devil of a coachmaker NA I 9 61 1
very abruptly, "old Allen is as rich as a Jew--is not he?" NA I 9 63 10
adding in explanation, "old Allen, the man you are with." NA I 9 63 10
He seems a good kind of old fellow enough, and has lived NA I 9 63 18
"What, is it really a castle, an old castle?" NA I 11 85 24
Tilney:--"he is a fine old fellow, upon my soul!--stout, NA I 12 95 18
"You had better leave her alone, my dear, she is old NA I 13 105 40
the envy of every valued old friend in Putney, with a NA I 15 122 28
Did you ever hear the old song, 'going to one wedding NA I 15 122 32
then you know, we may try the truth of this same old song." NA I 15 123 34
son as soon as he should be old enough to take it; no NA II 1 135 42
old friends, there is nothing to detain me longer in Bath. NA II 2 139 7
It is one of the finest old places in England, I NA II 3 143 2
It not it a fine old place, just like what one reads about? NA II 5 157 12
beneath the shelter of the old porch, and had even passed NA II 5 161 25
"That is a curious old chest, is not it?" said Miss Tilney, NA II 6 165 4
his children, and detesting old chests; and the General NA II 6 165 6
old servant frightening one by coming in with a faggot! NA II 6 167 9
A glance at the old chest, as she turned away from this NA II 6 167 10
But this was quite an old set, purchased two years ago. NA II 7 175 12
The remainder was shut off by knolls of old trees, or NA II 7 177 19
It was a narrow winding path through a thick grove of old NA II 7 179 29
Because no time is to be lost in frightening my old NA II 11 211 9
old, who expected a brother or sister in every carriage. NA II 14 233 8
children, the old gentleman's days were comfortably spent. SS I 1 3 1
The old gentleman died; his will was read, and like almost SS I 1 4 3
son, a child of four years old, it was secured, in such a SS I 1 4 3
of two or three years old; an imperfect articulation, an SS I 1 4 3
the payment of three to old superannuated servants by my SS I 2 10 20
little boy about six years old, by which means there was SS I 6 31 9
and Margaret an absolute old bachelor, for he was on the SS I 7 34 6
years, and on his forlorn condition as an old bachelor. SS I 8 36 2
Mrs. Jennings, but he is old enough to be my father; and SS I 8 37 4
I know very well that Colonel Brandon is not old enough to SS I 8 37 8
of ailment that can afflict the old and the feeble." SS I 8 38 12
Had he been even old, ugly, and vulgar, the gratitude and SS I 9 42 9
while he was visiting the old lady at Allenham Court, to SS I 9 44 23
mind, brandon, I know of old," said Sir John, "when once SS I 13 65 32
book that tells her how to admire an old twisted tree. SS I 17 92 25
to shew you that I had not forgot our old disputes." SS I 17 92 25
The old, well established grievance of duty against will, SS I 19 102 2
on its side, but I was too old when the subject was first SS I 19 103 4
said the good-natured old lady, "you have taken Charlotte SS I 20 112 25
about her already, as if she was an old acquaintance. SS I 21 119 4
little girl of three years old, who had not made a noise SS I 21 121 9
I saw you, I felt almost as if you was an old acquaintance. SS I 22 132 42
plan, and excepting a few old city friends, whom, to Lady SS II 5 168 11
exactly what I call a nice old fashioned place, full of SS II 8 196 22
only go and sit up in an old yew arbour behind the house, SS II 8 197 22
I have some of the finest old Constantia wine in the house, SS II 8 197 27
Whenever he had a touch of his old cholicky gout, he said SS II 8 198 27
guilty connection, who was then about three years old. SS II 9 208 28
"Oh, dear, that is a great pity! but such old friends as SS II 10 219 39
you must remember the place, where old Gibson used to live. SS II 11 225 31
The old walnut trees are all come down to make room for it. SS II 11 226 39
We have cleared away all the old thorns that grew in SS II 11 226 39
having escaped the company of a stupid old woman so long. SS II 14 247 5
She had not thought her old friend could have made so SS III 3 282 15
late incumbent to have been old and sickly, and likely to SS III 5 295 12
really sold the presentation, is old enough to take it.-- SS III 5 295 12
and though the death of my old cousin, Mrs. Smith, was to SS III 8 320 32
he reminded me of an old promise about a pointer puppy. SS III 8 330 69
and we will often go to the old ruins of the Priory, and SS III 10 343 9
walked every night to his old quarters at the park; from SS III 13 369 34
she had many relations and old acquaintance to cut--and he SS III 14 376 11
she had considered too old to be married,--and who still SS III 14 378 15
her finery in the old chair to d. on the important morng.-- W 315 1
us, & it is very bad to grow old & be poor & laughed at.-- W 317 2
but I beleive it is a rich old Dr Harding, uncle to the W 317 2
be at all afraid to drive this quiet old creature, home. W 320 2
The old mare trotted heavily on, wanting no direction of W 322 2
since he was 7 years old--but my father reckons us alike." W 324 3
This was an old greivance.-- W 325 4
her in the old rooms at Bath, the year before I married--. W 325 4
your officers for captivating the ladies, young or old.-- W 326 5
When an old lady plays the fool, it is not in the course W 326 6
son a fine boy of 10 years old, & Mr Tom Musgrave; who W 329 9
That stiff old Mrs E. has never done tea."-- W 333 13
Emma & Mrs Blake parted as old acquaintance, & Charles W 335 13
her dancing with some of our old neighbours I confess.--" W 337 15
"Yes, yes, we must not neglect our old neighbours. W 337 15
old coachman will look as black as his horses--". W 340 18
a very comfortable day; my old friends were quite W 344 20
an old woman who threw herself away on an Irish captain.-- W 349 24
I hope the old woman will smart for it." W 352 26
you, but you know every body must think her an old fool.-- W 352 26
of his carriage--but the old card table being set out, & W 357 28
The fine old, lofty drawing-room rings again. W 358 28
They are my old friends. PP I 1 5 29
And gravely glancing at Mr. Darcy, "there is a fine old PP I 6 24 22
was the son of old Wickham, the late Mr. Darcy's steward. PP I 18 94 45
from their apprehension of Charlotte's dying an old maid. PP I 22 122 3
The old lady is Mrs. Jenkinson, who lives with them. PP II 5 158 15
Jane will be quite an old maid soon, I declare. PP II 16 221 17
She saw that he wanted to engage her on the old subject of PP II 18 235 39
The children, two girls of six and eight years old, and PP II 19 239 10
one of miss Darcy, drawn when she was only eight years old. PP III 1 247 20
and I have known him ever since he was four years old." PP III 1 248 30
him since he was four years old, and whose own manners PP III 2 264 14
from all the spiteful old ladies in Meryton, lost but PP III 8 309 6
And you saw the old housekeeper, I suppose? PP III 10 327 11
Her eldest was a boy of ten years old, a fine spirited MP I 1 5 2
a girl now nine years old, of an age to require more MP I 1 5 4
child in the little white attic, near the old nurseries. MP I 1 9 12
Fanny Price was at this time just ten years old, and MP I 2 12 2
I had not known better long before I was so old as she is. MP I 2 18 25
of her sons as they became old enough for a determinate MP I 2 21 34
to some friend to hold till he were old enough for orders. MP I 3 23 2
Yes, dear old grey pony. MP I 3 27 36
of her valued friend the old grey poney, and for some time MP I 4 35 7
Mrs. Norris could not help thinking that some steady old MP I 4 36 7
ever suit her like the old grey poney; but her delight in MP I 4 37 8
it looked like a prison--quite a dismal old prison." MP I 6 53 2
Sotherton Court is the noblest old place in the world." MP I 6 53 3
There have been two or three fine old trees cut down that MP I 6 55 17
it is now, in its old state; but I do not suppose I shall." MP I 6 56 22
"I collect," said Miss Crawford, "that Sotherton is an old MP I 6 56 25
either Fanny or the steady old coachman, who always MP I 7 66 15
The old coachman, who had been waiting about with his own MP I 7 69 21
is a stupid old fellow, and does not know how to drive. MP I 8 77 13
so close to the great house as often happens in old places. MP I 8 82 34
compared with the old chapels of castles and monasteries. MP I 9 86 7
ridiculous stories of an old Irish groom of my uncle's. MP I 10 99 12
heath, which that nice old gardener would make me take; MP I 10 105 55
Nothing would satisfy that good old Mrs. Whitaker, but my MP I 10 105 55
does put me in mind of the old Heathen heroes, who after MP I 11 108 10
old woman, who knows no more of whist than of algebra. MP I 12 119 26
but to be sure the poor old dowager could not have died at MP I 13 122 4
to take the part of any old Duenna or tame confidante, MP I 13 129 38
She had better do the old countrywoman; the Cottager's MP I 14 134 12
The old lady relieves the high-flown benevolence of her MP I 14 134 12
moderation myself in being satisfied with the old butler. MP I 14 134 14
fellow of ten years old you know, who ought to be ashamed MP I 15 142 22
eyes, and you will be a very proper, little old woman." MP I 15 146 52
pay his respects to the old gentleman handsomely since he MP II 1 177 5
It was like treading old ground again." MP II 1 184 26
horses of course; and poor old coachman would attend us, MP II 2 189 5
There are his own two men pushing it back into its old MP II 5 222 46
I am grown too old to go out more than three times a week; MP II 6 229 1
of the old intimacy had thought ever likely to be again. MP II 7 238 1
"I told you I lost my way after passing that old farm MP II 7 241 13
might suppose a respectable old country family had lived MP II 7 243 27
I cannot bear to keep good old Wilcox waiting. MP II 7 251 64
I offer nothing but an old necklace. MP II 8 258 16
For as to secrecy, Henry is quite the hero of an old MP III 5 360 16
able to take leave of the old coachman, and send back MP III 7 375 1
She was interrupted by a fine tall boy of eleven years old, MP III 7 377 7
But old Scholey was saying just now, that he thought you MP III 7 380 20
Old Scholey ran in at breakfast time, to say she had MP III 7 380 20
about eight and nine years old, rushed into it just MP III 7 381 25
It was the gift of her good godmother, old Mrs. Admiral MP III 7 387 44
Mrs. Norris, however, had gone home and taken down two old MP III 7 387 45
There may be some old woman at Thornton Lacey to be MP III 9 394 1
from introductions either to old or new acquaintance. MP III 9 395 3
was received to revive old, and create some new sensations. MP III 14 433 12
she returns to Wimpole-Street to-day, the old lady is come. MP III 14 435 14
Visions of good and ill breeding, of old vulgarisms and MP III 15 446 35
received a letter from an old and most particular friend MP III 16 450 8
since her being ten years old, her mind in so great a MP III 17 470 27
with her from five years old--how she had devoted all her E I 1 6 6
was not only a very old and intimate friend of the family, E I 1 9 21
old lady, almost past every thing but tea and quadrille. E I 3 21 4
old lady, under such untoward circumstances, can excite. E I 3 21 4
dear Miss Woodhouse, he would be thirty years old!" E I 4 30 19
But Mr. Weston is almost an old man. E I 4 33 35
meaning to read more ever since she was twelve years old. E I 5 37 7
At ten years old, she had the misfortune of being able to E I 5 37 9
But I am a partial old friend." E I 5 39 19
of three or four years old stand still you know; nor can E I 6 45 21
and is glad to catch at the old writing master's son." E I 8 64 47
lane rose the vicarage; an old and not very good house, E I 10 83 2
"But then, to be an old maid at last, like Miss Bates!" " E I 10 84 16
"But still, you will be an old maid! and that's so E I 10 85 18
"Never mind, Harriet, I shall not be a poor old maid; and E I 10 85 19
a ridiculous, disagreeable, old maid! the proper sport of E I 10 85 19
you do? how shall you employ yourself when you grow old?" E I 10 85 20
and a strong habit of regard for every old acquaintance. E I 11 92 4
he was but two years old when he lost his poor mother! E I 11 96 24
girl about eight months old, who was now making her first E I 12 98 2
I was sixteen years old when you were born." E I 12 99 6
example than to be renewing old grievances, and that if E I 12 99 10
Good old Mrs. Bates--I will call upon her to-morrow, and E I 12 102 31
Will not the old prejudice be too strong?" E I 12 104 44
What happiness it must be to her good old grandmother and E I 12 104 46

every morning among her old acquaintance with her five E I 13 108 1
welcomed; the quiet neat old lady, who with her knitting E II 1 155 4
twice over before the good old lady could comprehend it. E II 1 158 13
and when at three years old, on losing her mother, she E II 2 163 3
before she was nine years old, his daughter's great E II 2 163 4
I like old friends; and Miss Jane Fairfax is a very pretty E II 3 171 12
bear to have the poor old vicarage without a mistress. E II 3 174 35
to an old servant who was married, and settled in Donwell. E II 5 186 2
a poor old grandmother, who has barely enough to live on. E II 5 194 40
and on recollecting that an old woman who had nursed him E II 6 197 3
Woodhouse revived the former good old days of the room?-- E II 6 198 5
old spinnet in the world, to amuse herself with.-- E II 8 215 16
day remarks, dull repetitions, old news, and heavy jokes. E II 8 219 43
a boy of six years old, who knows nothing of the matter?" E II 8 224 67
through half a sentence, to her mother's old petticoat. E II 8 225 78
'Not that it was such a very old petticoat either--for E II 8 225 78
with his tray, a tidy old woman travelling homewards from E II 9 233 24
William Larkins is such an old acquaintance! E II 9 239 51
and another of very old acquaintance who could not be left E II 11 248 9
Can the old lady?" . . . E II 11 255 56
"The old lady! E II 11 255 57
The tone implied some old acquaintance--and how could she E II 14 278 49
Miss Fairfax was an old acquaintance and a quiet girl, and E II 16 292 10
As an old friend, you will allow me to hope, Miss Fairfax, E II 16 294 23
They are some of my very old friends. E II 16 294 27
The kind-hearted, polite old man might then sit down and E II 16 295 28
"here comes this dear old beau of mine, I protest!-- E II 17 302 21
22
But this good old Mr. Woodhouse, I wish you had heard his E II 17 302 22
to be on a footing with the old established families. E II 18 310 34
am almost sure that old Mr. Suckling had completed the E II 18 310 34
and recur to old stories: and he was not without agitation. E III 1 316 4
"He had seen a group of old acquaintance in the street as E III 1 316 4
that it was a family of old friends, who were coming, like E III 2 319 3
to feel myself rather an old married man, and that my E III 2 327 36
any time to stand up with an old friend like Mrs. Gilbert." E III 2 327 36
You are extremely obliging--and if I were not an old E III 2 327 37
It was the end of an old pencil,--the part without any E III 4 339 17
I have not a word to say for the bit of old pencil, but E III 4 340 25
He should like to see the old house again exceedingly, and E III 6 356 30
the Abbey, with all the old neglect of prospect, had E III 6 358 35
It was too old a story.-- E III 6 361 40
had not yet been seen, the old Abbey fish-ponds; perhaps E III 6 361 42
had been prepared for his old friend, to while away the E III 6 362 43
or she would not have said such a thing to an old friend." E III 7 371 28
An old married man--quite good for nothing. E III 7 372 38
to; and, if she live to old age, must probably sink more. E III 7 375 61
Poor old Mrs. Bates, civil and humble as usual, looked as E III 8 378 5
she hoped, might lead the way to a return of old feelings. E III 8 378 7
Mr. Elton was called out of the room before tea, old John E III 8 383 29
Poor old John, I have a great regard for him; he was clerk E III 8 383 29
years; and now, poor old man, he is bed-ridden, and very E III 8 383 29
And how did you find my worthy old friend and her daughter? E III 9 385 6
be to the house of a very old friend in Windsor, to whom E III 9 388 15
good aunt, though his very old friend, he must acknowledge E III 9 389 16
The quiet, heartfelt satisfaction of the old lady, and the E III 12 418 5
And old story, probably--a common case--and no more than E III 13 427 19
On his side, there had been a long-standing jealousy, old E III 13 432 41
to attend to the good old lady's replies, she saw her with E III 16 453 12
13
connected herself with an old country family of P III 1 6 10
he could plainly see how old all the rest of his family P III 1 6 11
of his claims as an old acquaintance, an attentive P III 2 11 2
horribly; a sailor grows old sooner than any other man; I P III 3 19 16
'In the name of heaven, who is that old fellow?' said I, P III 3 20 16
'Old fellow'! cried Sir Basil, 'it is Admiral Baldwin. P III 3 20 16
The sea is no beautifier, certainly; sailors do grow old P III 3 20 17
resident at Monkford since the time of old Governor Trent." P III 3 23 27
had been completely in the old English style; containing P III 5 36 20
walls, great gates, and old trees, substantial and P III 5 36 20
The father and mother were in the old English style, and P III 5 40 45
clinging to him like an old friend, and declaring he P III 6 49 25
For an old built sloop, you would not see her equal. P III 8 65 12
to the Asp, to see what an old thing they had given you." P III 8 65 16
fashion and strength of any old pelisse, which you had P III 8 65 16
Ah! she was a dear old Asp to me. P III 8 65 16
would have done for poor old Asp, in half the time; our P III 8 66 16
in his reception there; the old were so hospitable, the P III 9 73 1
She had too old a regard for him to be so wholly estranged, P III 9 77 19
forward child, of two years old, having got the door P III 9 79 28
the Cobb itself, its old wonders and new improvements, P III 11 95 9
of an old pier of unknown date, were the Harvilles settled. P III 11 96 10
more useful person in the old nursery-maid of the family, P IV 1 121 3
course of streets from the old bridge to Camden-Place, P IV 2 135 33
deeply regretted in their old neighbourhood, which Anne P IV 3 137 3
from her of there being an old school-fellow in Bath, who P IV 5 152 2
remembering former partialities and talking over old times. P IV 5 153 6
was engaged to spend the evening with an old schoolfellow." P IV 5 157 14
it understood what this old schoolfellow was; and P IV 5 157 14
That she is old and sickly.-- P IV 5 157 15
But surely, you may put off this old lady till to-morrow. P IV 5 157 15
Her kind, compassionate visits to this old schoolfellow, P IV 5 158 21
man, grown old enough to appreciate a fair character? P IV 5 161 27
"Poor old gentleman." P IV 6 166 12
hand when he encountered an old friend, and observe their P IV 6 168 24
their lives in such a shapeless old cockleshell as that. P IV 6 169 25
There comes old Sir Archibald drew and his grandson. P IV 6 170 29
Poor old Sir Archibald! P IV 6 170 29
We are always meeting with some old friend or other; the P IV 6 170 29
"Old Lady Mary Maclean? P IV 9 193 10
But now, my dear Miss Elliot, as an old friend, do give me P IV 9 195 27
reward for not slighting an old friend like Mrs. Smith, P IV 10 212 1
His mother had some old friends in Bath, whom she wanted P IV 10 217 19
to so much misconduct and misery, both in young and old! P IV 10 218 23
"Old fashioned notions--country hospitality--we do not P IV 10 219 29
filled: a party of steady old friends were seated round P IV 10 221 32
Shepherd lives at one end, & three old women at the other." S 1 366 1
his feet or his well-tried old horse could carry him, and S 2 373 1
her neighbours, in the old coach which had been new when S 2 373 1
& that she was a very rich old lady, who had buried two S 3 375 1
This is my old house--the house of my Forefathers--the S 4 379 1
It is an honest old place--and Hillier keeps it in very S 4 380 1
at an old friend, at a place where one has been happy.-- S 4 381 1
that old Stringer & his son have a higher claim. S 4 381 1
supply you know, that poor old Andrew may not lose his S 4 382 1
is always complaining of old Andrew now, & says he never S 4 381 2
There--now the old house is quite left behind.-- S 4 381 1
little green court of an old farm house, two females in S 4 383 1
Who wd have expected such a sight at a Shoemaker's in old S 4 383 1
attack than usual of my old greivance, Spasmodic Bile & S 5 386 1
of welcome towards her old friends, which was inspiring S 6 391 1
themselves equal, may be, to your old country families. S 6 392 1
came within sight of poor old Sanditon--and the attack was S 9 407 1
of the Luggage, & helping old Sam uncord the trunks.-- S 9 407 1
rows of old thorns following its line almost every where.-- S 12 426 1
-FASHIONED (7)
towards a large, old-fashioned cabinet of ebony and gold, NA II 5 160 21
appearance of a high, old-fashioned black cabinet, which, NA II 6 168 10
the exchange of a few old-fashioned jewels of her mother. SS II 11 220 1
herself too old-fashioned to approve of every modern W 323 3
real, honest, old-fashioned Boarding-School, where a E I 3 21 5
admire all that quaint, old-fashioned politeness; it is E II 17 302 22
full half hour in the old-fashioned square parlour, with a P III 5 40 44

OLDER (27)
five & twenty, tho' she must in fact be ten years older. LS 6 251 1
of her due by a woman ten years older than herself. LS 42 313 10
Miss Thorpe, however, being four years older than Miss NA I 4 33 7
Had she been older or vainer, such attacks might have done NA I 7 50 44
Of her other, her older, her more established friend, NA I 10 81 61
is very strange!--sure he need not wait to be older."-- SS III 3 281 12
No, tho' I am nine years older than you are, I would not W 320 2
I suppose she is grown somewhat older since that time.-- W 325 4
she had, whether they were older or younger than herself, PP II 6 163 15
asked as she has, and more too, for I am two years older." PP II 18 230 13
Julia Bertram was only twelve, and Maria but a year older. MP I 2 13 4
William, the eldest, a year older than herself, her MP I 2 15 12
and she may be forgiven by older sages, for looking on the MP III 6 367 5
their journey to have her older head to manage for them; MP III 6 372 21
or body, he was a much older man in ways than in years; E I 1 7 8
The older a person grows, Harriet, the more important it E I 4 33 36
I thought it my duty as a friend, and older than yourself, E I 7 52 19
growing older should make me indifferent about letters." E II 16 293 17
18
not your being ten years older than myself which makes the E II 16 294 22
to Mr. Weston as he grew older--and even Mr. Weston might E III 17 461 1
Weston might be growing older ten years hence--to have his E III 17 461 1
in infancy, and correct herself as she grows older. E III 17 461 5
grew older--the natural sequel of an unnatural beginning. P III 4 30 9
want of health, looking much older than Captain Wentworth. P III 11 97 14
Miss Hamilton, three years older than herself, but still P IV 5 152 2
denoted the feelings of an older acquaintance than he P IV 11 231 12
small circle; & they were older in habits than in age.-- S 2 373 1

OLDEST (5)
"The oldest in the kingdom." NA I 11 85 25
than for her best and oldest friends; with being grown NA I 13 98 2
where the trees were the oldest, and the grass was the SS III 6 305 17
"Your father, Miss Emma, is one of my oldest friends--said W 324 4
is, a token of the love of one of your oldest friends." MP II 9 261 2

OLDFASHIONED (1)
than the sort of oldfashioned formality of always calling S 6 392 1

OLIVE (3)
side, and not lead you to reject the offered olive branch. PP I 13 63 12
The idea of the olive branch perhaps is not wholly new, PP I 13 64 19
Colonel Campbell rather preferred an olive. E III 2 323 19

OLIVE-BRANCH (1)
situation, and his expectation of a young olive-branch. PP III 15 364 22

OLIVERS (1)
I should not be afraid to trust either of the Olivers or MP I 15 148 58

OLIVES (1)
by a variety of sweetmeats and olives, and a good fire. SS II 8 193 7

OMEN (2)
This was a sad omen of what her mother's behaviour to the PP III 17 378 46
This was an evil omen. MP III 15 442 22

OMISSION (4)
is doubly due, and she must doubly feel the omission. E I 18 149 26
even supposing the omission to be intended as a compliment, E II 7 208 7
same time, there had been an unlucky omission at Kellynch. P IV 4 148 12
that any accidental omission is supplied in a moment by Ly S 4 381 1

OMISSIONS (1)
you--and with a very few omissions, and so forth, which MP I 15 140 12

OMIT (4)
well of the man who should omit an occasion of testifying PP I 18 101 71
He did not omit being sometimes directly before Miss Smith, E III 2 327 34
for I would never really omit an opportunity of bringing P IV 10 213 5
Anxious to omit no possible precaution, Anne struggled, P IV 11 239 48
49

OMITTED (6)
And now--what had she done, or what had she omitted to do, NA II 14 230 2
not recollect that I had omitted to give her my direction; SS III 8 322 38
of his being purposely omitted for Mr. Darcy's pleasure in PP I 18 89 1
2
Nothing was omitted, on his side, of civility, compliment, MP III 2 329 12
He omitted no opportunity of being with them, threw P IV 9 207 90
omitted to say and do, in the last four-and-twenty hours. P IV 11 241 60

OMITTING (2)
never remember Emma's omitting to do any thing I wished." E I 5 37 8
opposing it, and not omitting to make it known, that P IV 10 224 50

ONE (2002)
I have therefore resolved on placing her at one of the LS 1 244 1
him myself, & were he but one degree less contemptibly LS 2 245 1
first in agitation, that no one less amiable & mild than LS 3 247 1
to think the best of every one, her display of Greif, & LS 3 247 1
The house is a good one, the furniture fashionable, & LS 5 250 2
the great sensibility to one in particular, a young LS 5 250 2
& from her appearance one would not suppose her more than LS 6 251 1
One is apt I beleive to connect assurance of manner with LS 6 251 1
Unfortunately one knows her too well. LS 6 251 1
I would not therefore on any account have you encumber one LS 7 252 1
some applause, but will not add one lover to her list. LS 7 253 1
that he considered her as one entitled neither to delicacy LS 8 255 1
I hear the young man well spoken of, & tho' no one can LS 9 256 1
representations of any one to the disadvantage of another LS 10 257 1
person as I can be to any one, I should make a point of LS 10 258 2
which put one in good humour with oneself & all the world. LS 10 258 3
her want of character is one so much more serious, that LS 12 260 2
gross & notorious, that no one could be ignorant of them LS 12 260 2
an event, which no one but herself I can affirm, would LS 14 263 1
the general report of any one ought to be credited, since LS 14 264 3
catch for a husband, & no one therefore can pity her, for LS 14 264 4
This is one sort of love--but I confess it does not LS 16 269 3
know with the shrubbery on one side, where she may see her LS 17 271 7
by no means so ignorant as one might expect to find her, LS 18 273 3
be one of contempt were he to understand her emotions. LS 19 274 3
of it's taking place to any one, because I thought that LS 20 277 5
What can one say of such a woman, my dear mother?--such LS 20 278 8
by wishing with a laugh, that he might be really one soon. LS 20 278 10
How unpleasant, one would think, must his reflections be! LS 22 282 8
& with still greater energy, I must warn you of one thing. LS 23 283 4
One point only is gained; Sir James Martin is dismissed. LS 24 285 1
blame on the memory of one, whose name is sacred with me." LS 24 288 11
when one wishes to influence the passions of another. LS 25 293 3
One title I know she might have had, besides baronets. LS 26 296 5
countenance that one cannot help loving him at first sight. LS 38 307 3
it, but after all that I have seen, how can one be secure? LS 41 309 1
no consciousness of guilt, gave one look of embarrassment. LS 42 311 2
inviting her to return in one or two affectionate letters, LS 42 313 7
No one who had ever seen Catherine Morland in her infancy, NA I 1 13 1
The day which dismissed the music-master was one of the NA I 1 14 1
trees, hens and chickens, all very much like one another.-- NA I 1 14 1
without having seen one amiable youth who could call forth NA I 1 16 10
without having inspired one real passion, and without NA I 1 16 10
There was not one Lord in the neighbourhood; no--not even NA I 1 16 10
There was not one family among their acquaintance who had NA I 1 16 10
at their door--not one young man whose origin was unknown. NA I 1 16 10
Neither robbers nor tempests befriended them, nor one NA I 2 19 4
Mrs. Allen was one of that numerous class of females, NA I 2 20 8
In one respect she was admirably fitted to introduce a NA I 2 20 8
But I think we had better sit still, for one gets so NA I 2 22 19
After some time they received an offer of tea from one of NA I 2 23 22
Not one, however, started with rapturous wonder on NA I 2 23 27
for an hour, looking at every body and speaking to no one. NA I 3 25 1
"Now I must give one smirk, and then we may be rational NA I 3 26 18
to understand the tenour of your life in Bath without one? NA I 3 27 28
I bought one for her the other day, and it was pronounced NA I 3 28 38

never get Mr. Allen to know one of my gowns from another. NA I 3 28 39
Now here one can step out of doors and get a thing in five NA I 3 29 46
Mrs. Thorpe, however, had one great advantage as a talker, NA I 4 32 2
Mrs. Thorpe was a widow, and not a very rich one; she was NA I 4 34 8
Alas! if the heroine of one novel be not patronized by the NA I 5 37 4
Let us not desert one another; we are an injured body. NA I 5 37 4
which no longer concern any one living; and their language, NA I 5 38 4
friends in the Pump-Room one morning, after an NA I 6 39 1
It is but just one. NA I 6 39 3
Miss Andrews, a sweet girl, one of the sweetest creatures NA I 6 40 12
creatures in the world, has read every one of them. NA I 6 40 12
I told Capt. Hunt at one of our assemblies this winter, NA I 6 40 14
except that of one gentleman, who shall be nameless. NA I 6 41 16
one can be pleased with the attention of any body else. NA I 6 41 16
You must not betray me, if you should ever meet with one NA I 6 42 30
"One was a very good-looking young man." NA I 6 43 37
on one side or other by carriages, horsemen, or carts. NA I 7 44 1
It is now half after one; we drove out of the inn-yard at NA I 7 45 7
What do you think of my gig, Miss Morland? a neat one, is NA I 7 46 11
a capital one of the kind, but I am cursed tired of it.' NA I 7 46 11
"Neither one nor t'other; I might have got it for less I NA I 7 46 15
"Oh! d---- it, when one has the means of doing a kind NA I 7 47 17
of being in one; but I am particularly fond of it." NA I 7 47 22
not been a tolerably decent one come out since Tom Jones, NA I 7 48 34
and continued, with only one small digression on James's NA I 7 51 54
accepting the invitation of one friend, and obliged him to NA I 7 51 54
and having only one minute in sixty to bestow even on the NA I 7 51 54
of her debasement, is one of those circumstances which NA I 8 53 2
from all her acquaintance;--one mortification succeeded NA I 8 55 10
by the frequent want of one or more of these requisites, NA I 8 56 11
than one smile, one squeeze, and one "dearest Catherine." NA I 8 59 38
In the Pump-Room, one so newly arrived in Bath must be met NA I 9 60 1
till the clock struck one; and from habitude very little NA I 9 60 1
whether there were any one at leisure to answer her or not. NA I 9 60 1
one, but they break down before we are out of the street. NA I 9 61 1
"Not expect me! that's a good one! NA I 9 61 5
Catherine did not think the portrait a very inviting one, NA I 9 62 10
without a plunge or a caper, or any thing like one. NA I 9 62 10
at one moment what they would contradict the next. NA I 9 65 31
(though without having one good shot) than all his NA I 9 66 31
frequently called for by one or the other, she was never NA I 10 72 8
of the time prevented her buying a new one for the evening. NA I 10 73 22
not uncommon, from which one of the other sex rather than NA I 10 73 22
But not one of these grave reflections troubled the NA I 10 74 22
from the pursuit of some one whom they wished to avoid; NA I 10 74 23
for the attentions of some one whom they wished to please. NA I 10 74 23
"That is a good one, by Jove!-- NA I 10 75 26
Here is a friend of mine, Sam Fletcher, has got one to NA I 10 76 28
I had fifty minds to buy it myself, for it is one of my NA I 10 76 28
good horse when I meet with one; but it would not answer NA I 10 76 28
Nobody can fasten themselves on the notice of one, without NA I 10 76 29
that they should have been better off with any one else. NA I 10 77 33
"In one respect, there certainly is a difference. NA I 10 77 35
One thing, however, I must observe. NA I 10 77 37
One day in the country is exactly like another." NA I 10 79 48
but a cloudy one foretold improvement as the day advanced. NA I 11 82 1
"But is it like what one reads of?" NA I 11 85 26
regret for the loss of one great pleasure, and the hope of NA I 11 86 50
"It is all one to me," replied Thorpe rather angrily; and NA I 11 88 55
street, could not withhold one glance at the drawing-room NA I 12 91 3
of seeing her there, but no one appeared at them. NA I 12 91 3
suspended her care, that no one, observing her during the NA I 12 92 4
the whole, left one of the happiest creatures in the world. NA I 12 95 16
One of the best players we have, by the bye; and we had a NA I 12 96 20
me; and, if I had not made one of the cleanest strokes NA I 12 96 20
was not one of the family whom she need now fear to meet.-- NA I 12 96 24
for one day longer, and they would not hear of a refusal. NA I 13 97 1
"But why cannot Mr. Thorpe drive one of his other sisters? NA I 13 99 6
At one moment she was softened, at another irritated; NA I 13 99 9
Isabella, however, caught hold of one hand; Thorpe of the NA I 13 100 19
led me into one act of rudeness by his mistake on Friday. NA I 13 101 20
the simile, for it could hardly have been a proper one. NA I 13 101 24
herself as much to one as to the other in her vindication, NA I 13 102 26
her dancing, and making her one of the most graceful bows NA I 13 103 28
But one must not be over particular. NA I 13 104 36
Her escape from being one of the party to Clifton was now NA I 13 105 41
if she had been guilty of one breach of propriety, only to NA I 13 105 41
on every subject is comprised in that one word." NA I 14 108 16
said Henry, "is what no one at all acquainted with human NA I 14 109 25
"Miss Morland, no one can think more highly of the NA I 14 114 47
unjust thing of any woman at all, or an unkind one of me." NA I 14 114 48
and she contemplated it as one of those grand events, of NA I 15 117 8
by the urgent entreaties of his fair one that he would go. NA I 15 120 24
of family ingenuity; on one side in the mystery of an NA I 15 121 25
three lines, and in one moment all was joyful security. NA I 15 121 26
high commendation of being one of the finest fellows in NA I 15 121 27
"I am sure I think it a very good one." NA I 15 122 31
Did you ever hear the old song, 'going to one wedding NA I 15 122 32
If there is a good fortune on one side, there can be no NA I 15 124 47
I hate the idea of one great fortune looking out for NA I 15 124 47
Henry was at home, and no one else of the party, she found, NA II 1 129 1
Ten to one but he guesses the reason, and that is exactly NA II 1 131 13
confidence; she was met by one with the same kindness, and NA II 1 131 14
"With you, it is not, how is such a one likely to be NA II 1 132 20
"It is as much as should be said of any one. NA II 1 134 36
income, no niggardly assignment to one of ten children. NA II 1 135 42
One could not expect more from him you know. NA II 1 135 44
enough to find one in the common necessaries of life. NA II 1 135 45
To see and explore either the ramparts and keep of the one, NA II 2 141 11
walked along the Pump-Room one morning, by Mrs. Allen's NA II 3 143 1
continually bent towards one door or the other, as in NA II 3 143 2
It is one of the finest old places in England, I NA II 3 143 2
of one man more than another--he is not the person." NA II 3 145 13
"Yes, yes," (with a blush) "there are more ways than one NA II 3 145 14
A little harmless flirtation or so will occur, and one is NA II 3 146 18
on to give more encouragement than one wishes to stand by. NA II 3 146 18
What one means one day, you know, one may not mean the NA II 3 146 18
A woman in love with one man cannot flirt with another." NA II 4 151 15
constant to him only when unsolicited by any one else?-- NA II 4 152 28
you may be certain, that one will never tease the other NA II 4 152 28
as they were to remain only one more week in Bath NA II 5 154 1
in finding herself as one of the family, and so fearful NA II 5 154 1
It not it a fine old place, just like what one reads about? NA II 5 157 12
building such as 'what one reads about' may produce?-- NA II 5 157 13
Not tables, toilettes, wardrobes, or drawers, but on one NA II 5 158 17
lamp is not extinguished) one part of the hanging more NA II 5 159 19
In one perhaps there may be a dagger, in another a few NA II 5 160 21
her, without feeling one aweful foreboding of future NA II 5 161 25
misery to herself, or one moment's suspicion of any past NA II 5 161 25
the costly gilding of one in particular, when taking out NA II 5 162 27
On one side it had a range of doors, and it was lighted on NA II 5 162 28
was very unlike the one which Henry had endeavoured to NA II 6 163 1
back in a deep recess on one side of the fire-place. NA II 6 163 1
At length, however, having slipped one arm into her gown, NA II 6 164 3
One moment surely might be spared; and, so desperate NA II 6 164 3
means, the lid in one moment should be thrown back. NA II 6 164 3
at one end of the chest in undisputed possession! NA II 6 164 3
drawing-room than the one in common use, and fitted up in NA II 6 165 6
large eating-room as one of the necessaries of life; he NA II 6 166 6
of her friends in Bath without one wish of being with them. NA II 6 166 8
old servant frightening one by coming in with a faggot! NA II 6 167 9
now, to be sure, there is nothing to alarm one." NA II 6 167 9
Not one was left unsearched, and in not one was any thing NA II 6 169 11
Alas! it was snuffed and extinguished in one. NA II 6 170 12
The very curtains of her bed seemed at one moment in NA II 6 171 12
ere long occur of selecting one--though not for himself. NA II 7 175 12
Catherine was probably the only one of the party who did NA II 7 175 12
you may believe I take care that it shall not be a bad one. NA II 7 176 15
The pinery had yielded only one hundred in the last year. NA II 7 178 21
"Mr. Allen had only one small hot-house, which Mrs. Allen NA II 7 178 25
"A great and increasing one," replied the other, in a low NA II 7 180 34
loss perhaps as strongly as one so young could feel it, I NA II 7 180 34
the common drawing-room and one useless anti-chamber, into NA II 8 182 2
one on the same plan, but superior in length and breadth. NA II 8 184 5
to look or breathe, rushed forward to the one in question. NA II 9 193 6
to be one end of what the General's father had built. NA II 9 193 6
was hastily opened; some one seemed with swift steps to NA II 9 194 6
The malady itself, one from which she had often suffered, NA II 9 196 25
and one in whom she had always placed great confidence. NA II 9 196 25
thing forced to bend to one purpose by a mind which, NA II 10 199 2
The letter was one moment in her hand, then in her lap, NA II 10 203 8
"I have one favour to beg," said Catherine, shortly NA II 10 204 15
I am very sorry for Mr. Morland--sorry that any one you NA II 10 204 20
Stay-----there is one part-----" recollecting with a blush NA II 10 205 21
She must be an unprincipled one, or she could not have NA II 10 205 30
would part with one gentleman before the other was secured. NA II 10 206 31
so very, very much afflicted as one would have thought." NA II 10 207 39
And it all ended, at last, in his telling Henry one NA II 11 209 5
"Well, well, we will take our chance some one of those NA II 11 210 6
not come on Monday; and Tuesday will be a busy one with me. NA II 11 210 6
a quarter before one on Wednesday, you may look for us." NA II 11 210 6
down to a middling one for one day could not signify." NA II 11 211 13
but why he should say one thing so positively, and mean NA II 11 211 15
ourselves, if there is one thing more than another my NA II 11 213 19
but in this horrid place one can find time for nothing. NA II 12 216 2
is beyond any thing; and every body one cares for is gone. NA II 12 216 2
I knew their spite:--at one time they could not be civil NA II 12 217 2
"There is but one thing that I cannot understand. NA II 12 218 6
expedient to leave the one, and an apprehension of not NA II 13 220 1
start; it seemed as if some one was touching the very NA II 13 222 9
at her most compassionately--"it is no one from Woodston. NA II 13 223 13
For one letter, at all risks, all hazards, I must entreat. NA II 13 228 28
without some mention of one whose name had not yet been NA II 13 229 31
Leaning back in one corner of the carriage, in a violent NA II 14 230 1
The day which she had spent at that place had been one of NA II 14 230 2
it was not, however, the one on which she dwelt most. NA II 14 231 4
and inquiries, on any one article of which her mind was NA II 14 231 5
It is ten to one but you are thrown together again in the NA II 14 236 17
before I left Bath, that one can hardly see where it was. NA II 14 238 22
of you; for ten to one whether you ever see him again. NA II 15 240 4
"There is a very clever essay in one of the books up NA II 15 241 6
had very early dispatched one of the children to summon NA II 15 242 9
reply, the meaning, which one short syllable would have NA II 15 242 9
The General, perceiving his son one night at the theatre NA II 15 244 12
approaching connection with one of its members, and his NA II 15 245 12
practice. there was but one obstacle, in short, to be NA II 16 249 1
be mentioned; but till that one was removed, it must be NA II 16 249 1
I know no one more entitled, by unpretending merit, or NA II 16 251 5
Concerning the one in question therefore I have only to NA II 16 251 5
was involved in one of her most alarming adventures. NA II 16 251 5
By a former marriage, Mr. Henry Dashwood had one son: by SS I 1 3 2
had been so tardy in coming, was his only one twelvemonth. SS I 1 4 4
No one could dispute her right to come; the house was her SS I 1 6 9
which one of her sisters had resolved never to be taught. SS I 1 6 11
say; ten to one but he was light-headed at the time. SS I 2 9 5
for all parties if the sum were diminished one half.-- SS I 2 9 10
"One had rather, on such occasions, do too much than too SS I 2 9 12
No one, at least, can think I have not done enough for SS I 2 10 12
it to them; and then one of them was said to have died, SS I 2 11 20
pin myself down to the payment of one for all the world." SS I 2 11 20
"But, however, one thing must be considered. SS I 2 12 26
one who knew her, was to her comprehension impossible. SS I 3 15 5
but in the mean while, till one of these superior SS I 3 16 6
which Elinor chanced one day to make on the difference SS I 3 16 7
In one circumstance only, my Marianne, may your destiny be SS I 3 18 21
"Of his sense and his goodness," continued Elinor, "no one SS I 4 20 9
She knew that what Marianne and her mother conjectured one SS I 4 21 11
and to Edward she gave one with still greater affection. SS I 5 25 3
The man and one of the maids were sent off immediately SS I 5 26 6
The village of Barton was chiefly on one of these hills, SS I 6 29 3
throwing the passage into one of them with perhaps a part SS I 6 29 4
But one must not expect every thing; though I suppose it SS I 6 29 4
by which means there was one subject always to be recurred SS I 6 31 9
They would see, he said, only one gentleman there besides SS I 7 33 4
day) of a slight rheumatic feel in one of his shoulders." SS I 8 38 11
the girls had, in one of their earliest walks, discovered SS I 9 40 2
beauties; and towards one of these hills did Marianne and SS I 9 40 3
did Marianne and Margaret one memorable morning direct SS I 9 40 3
One consolation however remained for them, to which the SS I 9 41 6
man, and one whose acquaintance will not be ineligible." SS I 9 44 24
will make conquests enough, I day say, one way or other. SS I 9 45 31
32

"for one morning I think you have done pretty well. SS I 10 47 4
Her mother too, in whose mind not one speculative thought SS I 10 49 11
opposed by a very lively one of five and twenty? and as SS I 10 50 12
"Brandon is just the kind of man," said Willoughby one day, SS I 10 50 14
When he was present she had no eyes for any one else. SS I 11 53 3
She had nothing to say one day that she had not said the SS I 11 55 6
accidentally dropt from him one evening at the park, when SS I 11 55 8
of a young mind, that one is sorry to see them give way to SS I 11 56 12
had given her a horse, one that he had bred himself on his SS I 12 58 1
he might always get one at the park; as to a stable, the SS I 12 58 3
When Mrs. Jennings attacked her one evening at the park, SS I 12 61 15
Among the rest there was one for Colonel Brandon;--he took SS I 13 63 3
But it is not in my power to delay my journey for one day!" SS I 13 64 26
"I cannot afford to lose one hour."-- SS I 13 64 29
Brandon is one of them. SS I 13 65 30
It is a very large one I know, and when I come to see you, SS I 13 67 64
They will one day be Mr. Willoughby's, and" . . . SS I 13 68 74
75

"If they were one day to be your own, Marianne, you would SS I 13 69 75
There is one remarkably pretty sitting room up stairs; of SS I 13 69 76
On one side you look across the bowling-green, behind the SS I 13 69 76
make it one of the pleasantest summer-rooms in England." SS I 13 69 76
a great wonderer, as every one must be who takes a very SS I 14 70 1
One evening in particular, about a week after Colonel SS I 14 72 6
But you may be assured that I would not sacrifice one SS I 14 72 10
one whom I loved, for all the improvements in the world. SS I 14 72 10
belonging to it;--in no one convenience or inconvenience SS I 14 73 13
this place will always have one claim on my affection, SS I 14 73 15
its situation, and grieving that no one should live in it. SS I 14 73 17
For a few moments every one was silent. SS I 15 76 13
One moment she feared that no serious design had ever been SS I 15 77 19
every circumstance except one is in favour of their SS I 15 80 37
engagement; but that one is the total silence of both on SS I 15 80 37
But there was one method so direct, so simple, and in her SS I 16 84 7
what is meant at present to be unacknowledged to any one. SS I 16 84 9
I would not attempt to force the confidence of any one; of SS I 16 84 9
many a painful hour;--but one evening, Mrs. Dashwood, SS I 16 85 11
12

One morning, about a week after his leaving the country, SS I 16 85 15
with gaining one point, would not then attempt more. SS I 16 85 15
one; it was a man on horseback riding towards them. SS I 16 86 16
being Willoughby; the only one who could have gained a SS I 16 86 21

Context	Work	Vol	Ch	Page	Line
Now there is no one to regard them.	SS	I	16	88	31
"It is not every one," said Elinor, "who has your passion	SS	I	16	88	32
You may see one end of the house.	SS	I	16	88	33
One is my wealth!	SS	I	17	91	13
favorite maxim, that no one can ever be in love more than	SS	I	17	93	29
Sometimes one is guided by what they say of themselves,	SS	I	17	93	37
Do not you know that she calls every one reserved who does	SS	I	17	95	49
towards her contradicted one moment what a more animated	SS	I	18	96	1
what a more animated look had intimated the preceding one.	SS	I	18	96	1
say it is a picturesque one too, because you admire it; I	SS	I	18	97	4
"I suspect," said Elinor, "that to avoid one kind of	SS	I	18	97	6
hair in the centre, very conspicuous on one of his fingers.	SS	I	18	98	10
be materially benefited in one particular at least--you	SS	I	19	102	3
red coat on my back as with one, idleness was pronounced	SS	I	19	103	4
You are in a melancholy humour, and fancy that any one	SS	I	19	103	7
she was roused one morning, soon after Edward's leaving	SS	I	19	105	13
possible to speak at one without being heard at the other.	SS	I	19	105	13
all sat down to look at one another, while Mrs. Jennings	SS	I	19	106	21
one, and could not help looking with surprise at them both.	SS	I	19	107	27
she meant to be heard by no one else, though they were	SS	I	19	107	29
whenever any one is staying either with them, or with us."	SS	I	19	109	41
the park the next day, at one door, Mrs. Palmer came	SS	I	20	110	1
It makes one detest all one's acquaintance.	SS	I	20	111	8
It was impossible for any one to be more thoroughly good-	SS	I	20	112	26
were not likely to attach any one to him except his wife.	SS	I	20	112	28
was eager to gain from any one, such a confirmation of his	SS	I	20	114	43
my brother and sister, and one thing and another, and I	SS	I	20	115	50
are very pretty, and that one of them is going to be	SS	I	20	115	50
they were all cousins and must put up with one another.	SS	I	21	118	2
boy's violently pinching one of the same lady's fingers,	SS	I	21	121	8
with lavender-water, by one of the Miss Steeles, who was	SS	I	21	121	10
"I think every one must admire it," replied Elinor, "who	SS	I	21	123	25
supposed that any one can estimate its beauties as we do."	SS	I	21	123	25
before he he married, he is one still, for there is not	SS	I	21	124	29
"Oh! dear! one never thinks of married mens' being beaux--	SS	I	21	124	30
"You will think my question an odd one, I dare say," said	SS	I	22	128	3
dare say," said Lucy to her one day as they were walking	SS	I	22	128	3
Elinor did think the question a very odd one, and her	SS	I	22	128	4
amiably bashful, with only one side glance at her	SS	I	22	129	12
"You know his hand, I dare say, a charming one it is; but	SS	I	22	134	52
Yes, I have one other comfort in his picture; but poor	SS	I	22	135	54
all her dearest hopes, no one would have supposed from the	SS	II	1	141	4
wish of renewing it; and this for more reasons than one.	SS	II	1	141	7
One or two meetings of this kind had taken place, without	SS	II	1	143	9
John called at the cottage one morning, to beg in the name	SS	II	1	143	9
united them together in one noisy purpose, immediately	SS	II	1	143	9
expected; it produced not one novelty of thought or	SS	II	1	143	10
No one made any objection but Marianne, who, with her	SS	II	1	144	15
Your case is a very unfortunate one; you seem to me to be	SS	II	2	146	6
I can safely say that he has never gave me one moment's	SS	II	2	147	10
or if he had talked more of one lady than another, or	SS	II	2	147	12
heartily; "for he is one of the modestest, prettiest	SS	II	2	148	22
"I will honestly tell you of one scheme which has lately	SS	II	2	149	25
I understand is a very good one, and the present incumbent	SS	II	2	149	25
me from giving any opinion on the subject had I formed one.	SS	II	2	150	33
in a house in one of the streets near Portman-Square.	SS	II	3	153	1
thoughts, and thither she one day abruptly, and very	SS	II	3	153	1
well and good, you may always go with one of my daughters.	SS	II	3	153	2
of you; and if I don't get one of you at least well	SS	II	3	153	2
to one another, and laugh at my odd ways behind my back.	SS	II	3	154	4
But one or the other, if not both of them, I must have.	SS	II	3	154	4
feelings, in her pursuit of one object, was such a proof,	SS	II	3	155	6
may now be performed without inconvenience to any one.	SS	II	3	155	8
to you, there is still one objection which, in my opinion,	SS	II	3	156	9
and Elinor was the only one of the three, who seemed to	SS	II	3	158	21
door, when a loud one was suddenly heard which could not	SS	II	4	161	7
which could not be mistaken for one at any other house.	SS	II	4	161	7
been at home, and you know one has always a world of	SS	II	4	163	14
odd things to do after one has been away for any time; and	SS	II	4	163	14
see but one of them now, but there is another somewhere.	SS	II	4	163	18
dropped, she visited no one, to whom an introduction could	SS	II	5	168	11
from you--you who have confidence in no one!"	SS	II	5	170	24
Marianne gave one glance round the apartment as she	SS	II	5	171	30
conversation, walked from one window to the other, or sat	SS	II	5	172	39
without one look of hope, or one expression of pleasure.	SS	II	6	175	1
started as if she had forgotten that any one was expected.	SS	II	6	175	1
their names announced from one landing-place to another in	SS	II	6	175	2
was kneeling against one of the window-seats for the sake	SS	II	7	180	1
almost choked by grief, one letter in her hand, and two or	SS	II	7	182	12
chariot, which she knew had not been ordered till one.	SS	II	7	184	16
earlier another time, because we are generally out by one.	SS	II	7	187	40
but what any one would have written in the same situation.	SS	II	7	188	43
This woman of whom he writes--whoever she be--or any one,	SS	II	7	189	50
she received warmth from one, or discerning objects	SS	II	7	190	55
					56
her head leaning against one of its post, again took up	SS	II	7	190	55
					56
Oh! no one, no one--he talked to me only of myself."	SS	II	7	190	58
and body she moved from one posture to another, till	SS	II	7	191	65
But there is one comfort, my dear Miss Marianne; he is not	SS	II	8	192	3
But when there is plenty of money on one side, and next to	SS	II	8	194	8
did say this morning, that one day Miss Walker hinted to	SS	II	8	194	12
Is there nothing one can get to comfort her?	SS	II	8	195	14
for the sake of every one concerned in it, make it unfit	SS	II	8	196	19
It will be all to one a better match for your sister.	SS	II	8	196	22
in the country: and such a mulberry tree in one corner!	SS	II	8	196	22
every thing, in short, that one could wish for: and,	SS	II	8	197	22
One shoulder of mutton, you know, drives another down.	SS	II	8	197	22
Two ladies were waiting for their carriage, and one of	SS	II	8	199	37
One thing, especially, I remember, because it served to	SS	II	8	199	37
At one moment she was absolutely indifferent to the	SS	II	9	201	2
In one thing, however, she was uniform, when it came to	SS	II	9	201	2
In one moment her imagination placed before her a letter	SS	II	9	202	7
The work of one moment was destroyed by the next.	SS	II	9	202	7
will be necessary, and it shall be a short one.	SS	II	9	205	20
conversation between us one evening at Barton Park-- it	SS	II	9	205	22
This lady was one of my nearest relations, an orphan from	SS	II	9	205	24
the conduct of one, who was at once her uncle and guardian.	SS	II	9	205	24
and the blow was a severe one--but had her marriage been	SS	II	9	206	24
sweet disposition of the one been guarded by a firmer mind,	SS	II	9	208	28
desire, to go to Bath with one of her young friends, who	SS	II	9	208	28
away to the relief of one, whom he had made poor and	SS	II	9	209	30
One meeting was unavoidable.	SS	II	9	211	35
event, had brought herself to expect as a certain one.	SS	II	10	213	4
one of Folly's puppies! and this was the end of it!"	SS	II	10	215	9
exciting no interest in one person at least among their	SS	II	10	215	12
to know that there was one who would meet her without	SS	II	10	215	12
I never think about him from one hour's end to another.	SS	II	10	218	26
sweetness to the manners of one sister, was of advantage	SS	II	10	219	42
with her and Mrs. Jennings one morning for half an hour.	SS	II	11	220	1
the quickest succession; one gentleman only was standing	SS	II	11	220	3
Miss Dashwoods, but such a one as seemed rather to demand	SS	II	11	221	5
but one has always so much to do on first coming to town.	SS	II	11	221	9
certainly be considerable, but your income is a large one."	SS	II	11	225	29
					30
a comfortable one, and I hope will in time be better.	SS	II	11	225	31
Her's has been a very short one!	SS	II	11	227	50
found her one of the most charming women in the world!	SS	II	12	229	1
that did escape her, not one fell to the share of Miss	SS	II	12	232	15
The dinner was a grand one, the servants were numerous,	SS	II	12	233	18
almost all laboured under one or other of these	SS	II	12	233	18
then it was all over; and one subject only engaged the	SS	II	12	233	19
Lucy, who was hardly less anxious to please one parent	SS	II	12	234	24
sister's chair, and putting one arm round her neck, and	SS	II	12	236	39
					40
one arm round her neck, and one cheek close to her's said	SS	II	12	236	39
					40
changed his seat to one close by Lucy Steele, and gave her,	SS	II	12	236	41
Elinor's constitution;--and one must allow that there is	SS	II	12	236	43
for her own sake, that one greater obstacle preserved her	SS	II	13	238	1
The chance proved a lucky one, for a message from Mrs.	SS	II	13	238	3
But now, there is one good thing, we shall be able to meet,	SS	II	13	240	15
She paused--no one spoke.	SS	II	13	243	30
It checked the idleness of one, and the business of the	SS	II	14	247	4
One thing did disturb her; and of that she made her daily	SS	II	14	247	5
between this baby and every one of his relations on both	SS	II	14	248	5
In one of these excursive glances she perceived among a	SS	II	14	250	11
and conceit of the one, put her at all out of charity with	SS	II	14	250	12
buy a little land and build one myself, within a short	SS	II	14	251	17
There is no great wonder in their liking one another; but	SS	III	1	258	7
impartiality on the conduct of every one concerned in it.	SS	III	1	260	8
Elinor's office was a painful one.--	SS	III	1	261	11
for ever, without hearing one circumstance that could make	SS	III	1	264	29
speak of the affair to any one with the least appearance	SS	III	1	264	32
Lucy with only moving from one chair to another, and when	SS	III	1	265	33
is a good one, and her resolution equal to any thing.	SS	III	1	265	36
well of anybody again; and one cannot wonder at it, after	SS	III	1	265	36
in the world, nor one who more deserves a good husband."	SS	III	1	267	43
has drawn his own lot, and I fear it will be a bad one."	SS	III	1	268	45
And there is one thing more preparing against him, which	SS	III	1	269	53
But I don't think mine would be, to make one son	SS	III	1	269	54
very well, and by more than one; for Miss Godby told Miss	SS	III	2	272	16
and all that--Oh, la! one can't repeat such kind of things	SS	III	2	273	16
her coach, and would take one of us to Kensington Gardens;	SS	III	2	274	16
and as happy as we must always be in one another's love.	SS	III	2	277	29
					30
to Barton was not beyond one day, though a long day's	SS	III	3	280	6
Lord! we shall sit and gape at one another as dull as two	SS	III	3	280	8
she might not hear, to one close by the piano forte on	SS	III	3	281	9
of Marianne's turning from one lesson to another, some	SS	III	3	281	9
He is not a young man with whom one can be intimately	SS	III	3	282	19
It is a rectory, but a small one; the late incumbent, I	SS	III	3	282	19
thinking that no one could so well perform it as himself.	SS	III	3	283	20
And as to the house being a bad one, I do not know what	SS	III	4	285	7
would be at, for it is as good a one as ever I saw."	SS	III	4	285	7
One day's delay will not be very material; and till I have	SS	III	4	286	15
one to announce his intention to Mr. Ferrars than himself."	SS	III	4	287	19
it cannot be expected that any one else should say for him.	SS	III	4	289	29
And though one would be very glad to do a kindness by poor	SS	III	4	291	51
Jennings only exchanged one form of delight for another,	SS	III	4	292	54
"Aye, aye, the parsonage is but a small one," said she,	SS	III	4	292	55
he should be treated as one in all worldly concerns;	SS	III	5	293	2
indisposition, beyond one verbal inquiry, Elinor began to	SS	III	5	293	3
pay a visit, for which no one could really have less	SS	III	5	294	3
"A very simple one--to be of use to Mr. Ferrars."	SS	III	5	295	15
Mrs. Ferrars is one of the most affectionate mothers in	SS	III	5	296	22
men, I do not know that one is superior to the other."	SS	III	5	297	29
"Of one thing, my dear sister," kindly taking her hand,	SS	III	5	297	31
such a one as your family are unanimous in disapproving.'	SS	III	5	300	37
One other short call in Harley-Street, in which Elinor	SS	III	6	301	1
to bed, to try one or two of the simplest of the remedies.	SS	III	6	306	17
really believed herself, that it would be a very short one.	SS	III	7	308	4
to bed; her maid, who was one of the principal nurses, was	SS	III	7	310	9
her thoughts wandering from one image of grief, one	SS	III	7	313	21
from one image of grief, one suffering friend to another,	SS	III	7	313	21
to make you hate me one degree less than you do now.	SS	III	8	319	23
But one thing may be said for me, even in that horrid	SS	III	8	320	32
softened, "believe yourself at one time attached to her."	SS	III	8	321	33
Could it be an impartial one?	SS	III	8	322	36
herself; and I have injured one, whose affection for me--(	SS	III	8	322	36
By one measure I might have saved myself.	SS	III	8	323	40
in a more simple one--perhaps too simple to raise any	SS	III	8	325	50
all safely out of the house one morning, and left my name."	SS	III	8	326	53
did not catch a glimpse of one or other of you; and	SS	III	8	326	55
Marianne, beautiful as an angel on one side, calling me	SS	III	8	327	55
is delightful in a woman one loves, she opened the letter	SS	III	8	328	61
It must have been only to one end.	SS	III	8	328	63
letter will only make them think me a blackguard one.'	SS	III	8	328	63
Am I--by it only one degree--am I less guilty in your	SS	III	8	329	65
One person I was sure would represent me as capable of	SS	III	8	331	69
I shall now go away and live in dread of one event."	SS	III	8	332	79
"But she will be gained by some one else.	SS	III	8	332	83
And if that some one should be the very he whom, of all	SS	III	8	332	83
But the rest, which one night entirely sleepless, and many	SS	III	9	334	5
declared herself, one of the happiest women in the world.	SS	III	9	335	7
Brandon's marrying one of you as the object most desirable.	SS	III	9	336	10
such sincerity!-- no one can be deceived in him."	SS	III	9	337	14
is enough to prove him one of the worthiest of men."	SS	III	9	337	16
Elinor, "does not rest on one act of kindness, to which	SS	III	9	337	17
is exactly the very one to make your sister happy.	SS	III	9	338	20
know, what it really is, I am sure it must be a good one."	SS	III	9	339	26
a leave of Mrs. Jennings, one so earnestly grateful, so	SS	III	10	341	5
there"--pointing with one hand, "on that projecting mound,-	SS	III	10	344	12
					13
At present, if I could be satisfied on one point, if I	SS	III	10	344	17
sprung up from her heart, but she dared not urge one.	SS	III	10	347	33
With one who had so injured the peace of the dearest of	SS	III	11	350	7
immediately continued, "one observation may, I think, be	SS	III	11	352	16
					17
That crime has been the origin of every lesser one, and of	SS	III	11	352	17
Their man-servant had been sent one morning to Exeter on	SS	III	11	353	22
					23
had sense enough to call one of the maids, who, with Mrs.	SS	III	11	353	25
at the park to her brother, who is one of the post-boys.	SS	III	11	354	27
"Was there no one else in the carriage?"	SS	III	11	354	33
think the attachment, which one she had so well understood,	SS	III	11	355	46
Elinor flattered herself that some one of their	SS	III	12	358	4
Though uncertain that any one were to blame, she found	SS	III	12	358	4
of his reception, and consious that he merited no kind one.	SS	III	12	359	11
the blessings of one imprudent engagement, contracted	SS	III	13	361	1
His errand at Barton, in fact, was a simple one.	SS	III	13	361	2
reality of reason and truth, one of the happiest of men.	SS	III	13	361	3
them all, formed of course one of the earliest discussions	SS	III	13	364	10
to her in every view, as one of the most extraordinary and	SS	III	13	364	10
it was even a ridiculous one, but to her reason, her	SS	III	13	364	10
meeting, the vanity of the one had been so worked on by	SS	III	13	364	11
we could not live without one another, we are just	SS	III	13	365	14
has actually been bribing one son with a thousand a-year,	SS	III	13	366	18
arrived, and with only one object before him, the nearest	SS	III	13	366	20
The connection was certainly a respectable one, and	SS	III	13	367	23
One question after this only remained undecided, between	SS	III	13	369	32
between them, one difficulty only was to be overcome.	SS	III	13	369	32
Edward had two thousand pounds, and Elinor one, which,	SS	III	13	369	32
ago, had robbed her of one; the similar annihilation of	SS	III	14	373	2
and now, by the resuscitation of Edward, she had one again.	SS	III	14	373	2
really believed, one of the happiest couple in the world.	SS	III	14	374	7
they were walking together one morning before the gates of	SS	III	14	375	9
for certainly you have been one of the most fortunate	SS	III	14	375	9
that one or two interviews would settle the matter.	SS	III	14	376	11
expected to be a very good one; a long list of country	W			314	1
children were at home, & one was always necessary as	W			315	1
sickly & had lost his wife, one only could profit by the	W			315	1
I should not be surprised if you were to be thought one of	W			315	1
I believe I am the only one among them that have escaped	W			316	1

Context	Work	Vol	Ch	Page	Line
always behaving in a particular way to one or another."--	W			316	1
"And how came your heart to be the only cold one?"--said	W			316	2
would be enough for me, if one could be young for ever,	W			317	2
The luck of one member of a family is luck to all.--"	W			321	2
turning, & making only one blunder, in proposing to stop	W			322	2
Emma had seen the Edwardses only one morng at Stanton,	W			322	3
respectably attired in one of the two Sattin gowns which	W			323	3
"Your father, Miss Emma, is one of my oldest friends--said	W			324	4
it, changed the subject to one of less anxiety to all.--	W			326	6
but the first scrape of one violin, blessed the ears of	W			327	7
at the upper end, where one party only were formally	W			327	8
small cluster of females at one end of it began soon to	W			328	8
Among the increasing numbers of military men, one now made	W			328	8
A new face & a very pretty one, could not be slighted--her	W			328	9
name was whispered from one party to another, & no sooner	W			328	9
The boy in one moment restored to all his first delight--	W			331	11
quite alone at the end of one, as if retreating as far as	W			332	11
happened to be increased by one or two of the card parties	W			333	13
"My eldest sister is the only one at home--& she could not	W			334	13
leave my father"--"Miss Watson the only one at home!--	W			334	13
in the same room, with only one change of chairs, it might	W			336	14
"One of his particular friends,"--"all in the same Regt	W			337	15
I suppose your set was not a very full one."--	W			340	19
Why--he is quite one of the great & grand ones;--did not	W			342	19
more to my mind--continued Mr W. or one better delivered.--	W			343	20
By the bye, he enquired after one of my daughters, but I	W			344	20
visitors as these--such a one as Ld Osborne at least, a	W			344	21
but it cannot turn a small income into a large one."--	W			346	21
& to busy the hours of one of them at least--for as Jane	W			348	23
I am one of those who always take things as they find them.	W			351	25
I shall wear one tomorrow that I think you will prefer to	W			353	26
Have you seen the one I gave Margaret?"--	W			353	26
a formal circle, but one never wants them among friends."	W			354	28
When there is only one or two of you at home, you must be	W			354	28
the smart sayings of one lady, detailed the oversights of	W			359	28
consequence of the death of one friend and the imprudence	W			361	31
become of importance to no one, a burden on those, whose	W			361	31
rightful property of some one or other of their daughters.	PP	I	1	3	2
"My dear Mr. Bennet," said his lady to him one day, "have	PP	I	1	3	3
You must know that I am thinking of his marrying one of	PP	I	1	4	16
may fall in love with one of them, and therefore you must	PP	I	1	4	18
Only think what an establishment it would be for one of	PP	I	1	4	24
to contain herself, began scolding one of her daughters.	PP	I	2	6	7
One cannot know what a man really is by the end of a	PP	I	2	7	16
"If I can but see one of my daughters happily settled at	PP	I	3	9	2
be always flying about from one place to another, and	PP	I	3	10	4
so early, and talked of giving one himself at Netherfield.	PP	I	3	10	6
the room, speaking occasionally to one of his own party.	PP	I	3	11	6
resentment, by his having slighted one of her daughters.	PP	I	3	11	6
But there is one of her sisters sitting down just behind	PP	I	3	11	12
I wish you had been there, my dear, to have given him one	PP	I	3	13	20
But that is one great difference between us.	PP	I	4	14	5
"I would wish not to be hasty in censuring any one; but I	PP	I	4	14	8
Affectation of candour is common enough;--one meets it	PP	I	4	14	9
They were rather handsome, had been educated in one of the	PP	I	4	15	11
girl, and one whom they should not object to know more of.	PP	I	4	17	16
One cannot wonder that so very fine a young man, with	PP	I	5	20	18
"Your plan is a good one," replied Elizabeth, "where	PP	I	6	22	7
him at Meryton; she saw him one morning at his own house,	PP	I	6	22	7
Though he had detected with a critical eye more than one	PP	I	6	23	12
of being the only plain one in the family, worked hard for	PP	I	6	25	23
officers joined eagerly in dancing at one end of the room.	PP	I	6	25	24
I consider it as one of the first refinements of polished	PP	I	6	25	26
no objection, I am sure, to oblige us for one half hour."	PP	I	6	26	41
The village of Longbourn was only one mile from Meryton; a	PP	I	7	28	3
After listening one morning to their effusions on this	PP	I	7	29	5
					6
a year, should want one of my girls, I shall not say nay	PP	I	7	29	12
The distance is nothing, when one has a motive; only three	PP	I	7	32	37
repaired to the lodgings of one of the officers' wives,	PP	I	7	32	41
Their brother, indeed, was the only one of the party whom	PP	I	8	35	2
Bingley, "it would not make them one jot less agreeable."	PP	I	8	37	18
I scarcely know any one who cannot do all this, and I am	PP	I	8	39	45
"Oh! certainly," cried his faithful assistant, "no one can	PP	I	8	39	50
door was closed on her, "is one of those young ladies who	PP	I	8	40	56
an express to town for one of the most eminent physicians.	PP	I	8	40	59
is more or less estimable than such a one as yours."	PP	I	9	42	13
sure, Jane--one does not often see any body better looking.	PP	I	9	44	31
"There has been many a one, I fancy, overcome in the same	PP	I	9	44	32
that one good sonnet will starve it entirely away."	PP	I	9	44	34
ball," she added, "I shall insist on their giving one also.	PP	I	9	46	38
can be of no real advantage to yourself or any one else?"	PP	I	10	49	27
without offering one argument in favour of its propriety."	PP	I	10	50	34
A regard for the requester would often make one readily	PP	I	10	50	37
without waiting for arguments to reason one into it.	PP	I	10	50	37
friend and friend, where one of them is desired by the	PP	I	10	50	37
He then sat down by her, and talked scarcely to any one	PP	I	11	54	2
She assured him that no one intended to play, and the	PP	I	11	54	3
to stretch himself on one of the sophas and go to sleep.	PP	I	11	54	3
How much sooner one tires of any thing than of a book!--	PP	I	11	55	4
No one made any reply.	PP	I	11	55	5
In the desperation of her feelings she resolved on one	PP	I	11	56	10
					11
is very refreshing after sitting so long in one attitude."	PP	I	11	56	11
"We can all plague and punish one another.	PP	I	11	57	17
are such people, but I hope I am not one of them.	PP	I	11	57	21
"Perhaps that is not possible for any one.	PP	I	11	57	22
of one sister much exceeded her affection for the other.	PP	I	12	59	2
and though they were at one time left by themselves for	PP	I	12	60	4
be on good terms with any one, with whom it had always	PP	I	13	62	12
"She has one only daughter, the heiress of Rosings, and of	PP	I	14	67	5
told Lady Catherine myself one day, has deprived the	PP	I	14	67	9
and though he belonged to one of the universities, he had	PP	I	15	70	1
view, as he meant to chuse one of the daughters, if he	PP	I	15	70	2
he thought it an excellent one, full of eligibility and	PP	I	15	70	2
nominally engaged with one of the largest folios in the	PP	I	15	71	6
Both changed colour, one looked white, the other red.	PP	I	15	73	8
but her contemplation of one stranger was soon put an end	PP	I	15	73	11
but unluckily no one passed the windows now except a few	PP	I	15	74	11
to the description of only one of Lady Catherine's drawing	PP	I	16	75	2
after prizes, to have attention for any one in particular.	PP	I	16	76	8
"Yes," replied Wickham;--"his estate there is a noble one.	PP	I	16	77	10
I am not qualified to form one.	PP	I	16	77	14
You will not find him more favourably spoken of by any one.	PP	I	16	78	15
His father, Miss Bennet, the late Mr. Darcy, was one of	PP	I	16	78	20
remember his boasting one day, at Netherfield, of the	PP	I	16	80	34
contented herself with "and one, too, who had probably	PP	I	16	80	36
who chuses that every one connected with him should have	PP	I	16	84	58
whom his father had promised to provide for.--	PP	I	17	85	4
One does not know what to think."	PP	I	17	86	6
"I beg your pardon;--one knows exactly what to think."	PP	I	17	86	7
But Jane could think with certainty on only one point,--	PP	I	17	86	8
Society has claims on us all; and I profess myself one of	PP	I	17	87	11
To find a man agreeable whom one is determined to hate!--	PP	I	18	90	7
One must speak a little, you know.	PP	I	18	91	13
considering his descent, one could not expect much better."	PP	I	18	94	45
Mr. Bingley's defence of his friend was a very able one I	PP	I	18	96	55
She then changed the discourse to one more gratifying to	PP	I	18	96	56
which placed them within one of each other; and deeply was	PP	I	18	98	63
mother was talking to that one person (Lady Lucas) freely,	PP	I	18	98	63
it is the etiquette; but no one was less likely than Mrs.	PP	I	18	99	63
Many smiled; but no one looked more amused than Mr. Bennet	PP	I	18	101	71
On finding Mrs. Bennet, Elizabeth, and one of the younger	PP	I	19	104	1
					2
be complied with; and that one thousand pounds in the 4	PP	I	19	106	10
hope is rather an extraordinary one after my declaration.	PP	I	19	107	14
I do assure you that I am not one of those young ladies (	PP	I	19	107	14
in such a way as may convince you of its being one."	PP	I	19	108	18
From this day you must be a stranger to one of your	PP	I	20	112	19
of making one in the croud, but of that I despair.	PP	I	21	117	11
No one who has ever seen you together, can doubt his	PP	I	21	119	20
that when there has been one intermarriage, she may have	PP	I	21	119	20
Caroline is incapable of wilfully deceiving any one; and	PP	I	21	119	21
influence a young man so totally independent of every one.	PP	I	21	120	28
of paying his addresses to one of her younger girls, and	PP	I	22	124	11
deduced from the whole; one, that Elizabeth was the real	PP	I	21	127	5
How any one could have the conscience to entail away an	PP	I	23	130	24
side, and that it has done no harm to any one but myself."	PP	II	1	134	8
I have met with two instances lately; one I will not	PP	II	1	135	11
Remember that she is one of a large family; that as to	PP	II	1	135	12
almost any thing, but no one else could be benefited by	PP	II	1	135	13
You shall not, for the sake of one individual, change the	PP	II	1	135	13
"So, Lizzy," said he one day, "your sister is crossed in	PP	II	1	137	27
the still more interesting one of Bingley's being withheld	PP	II	2	142	16
Mr. Wickham was sure to be one; and on these occasions,	PP	II	2	142	18
To Mrs. Gardiner, Wickham had one means of affording	PP	II	2	142	19
attentions were over, he was the admirer of some one else.	PP	II	3	149	28
and shopping, and the evening at one of the theatres.	PP	II	4	152	5
find a man who has not one agreeable quality, who has	PP	II	4	154	19
without being able to give one accurate idea of anything.	PP	II	4	154	23
The paling of Rosings Park was their boundary on one side.	PP	II	5	155	2
To work in his garden was one of his most respectable	PP	II	5	156	4
I should say, one of her ladyship's carriages, for she has	PP	II	5	157	7
of woman whom one cannot regard with too much deference."	PP	II	5	157	9
After sitting a few minutes, they were all sent to one of	PP	II	6	162	13
Our instrument is a capital one, probably superior to----	PP	II	6	164	18
"One of them does."	PP	II	6	164	19
"Not one."	PP	II	6	164	23
I should have advised her most strenuously to engage one.	PP	II	6	165	32
"I am not one and twenty."	PP	II	6	166	40
apartment, had they sat in one equally lively; and she	PP	II	7	168	1
and there being only one card table in the evening, every	PP	II	7	169	5
sheltered path, which no one seemed to value but herself,	PP	II	7	169	5
his coming would furnish one comparatively new to look at	PP	II	7	170	6
than one young lady was sitting down in want of a partner.	PP	II	8	175	18
No one admitted to the privilege of hearing you, can think	PP	II	8	176	26
in his having met with one of the very few sensible women	PP	II	9	178	15
"I should never have considered the distance as one of the	PP	II	9	179	19
income, but not such a one as will allow of frequent	PP	II	9	179	22
should bring him where no one else was brought; and to	PP	II	10	182	1
She was engaged one day as she walked, in re-perusing	PP	II	10	182	2
I never heard any harm of her; and I dare say she is one	PP	II	10	184	21
one could say how lasting an evil he might have inflicted.	PP	II	10	186	38
probably were her having one uncle who was a country	PP	II	10	186	39
disposed towards every one, had been scarcely ever clouded.	PP	II	11	188	1
I am sorry to have occasioned pain to any one.	PP	II	11	190	7
each other, of exposing one to the censure of the world	PP	II	11	191	12
The park paling was still the boundary on one side, and	PP	II	12	195	1
side, and she soon passed one of the gates into the ground.	PP	II	12	195	1
There is but one part of my conduct in the whole affair,	PP	II	12	199	5
I can summon more than one witness of undoubted veracity.	PP	II	12	199	5
There was also a legacy of one thousand pounds.	PP	II	12	200	5
aware that the interest of one thousand pounds would be a	PP	II	12	200	5
intimacy, and still more as one of the executors of my	PP	II	12	202	5
incapable of attending to the sense of one before her eyes.	PP	II	13	204	1
was gross duplicity on one side or the other; and, for a	PP	II	13	205	3
At one time she had almost resolved on applying to him,	PP	II	13	206	4
he had told his story to no one but herself; but that	PP	II	13	207	5
Pleased with the preference of one, and offended by the	PP	II	13	208	8
How could she deny that credit to his assertions, in one	PP	II	13	208	9
will be in my power to take one of you as far as London,	PP	II	14	211	10
will be very good room for one of you--and indeed, if the	PP	II	14	211	10
We know how little there is to tempt any one to our humble	PP	II	15	215	2
I should not think any one abiding in it an object of	PP	II	15	216	4
My dear Charlotte and I have but one mind and one way of	PP	II	15	216	6
Besides, it will not much signify what one wears this	PP	II	16	219	4
been overset already by one poor regiment of militia, and	PP	II	16	220	7
I was in great hopes that one of you would have got a	PP	II	16	221	17
we were forced to borrow one of her gowns; and you cannot	PP	II	16	221	17
was doubly engaged, on one hand collecting an account of	PP	II	16	222	21
race of mankind, as was here collected in one individual.	PP	II	17	224	9
error, and seek to clear one, without involving the other.	PP	II	17	225	9
Take your choice, but you must be satisfied with only one.	PP	II	17	225	10
them; just enough to make one good sort of man; and of	PP	II	17	225	10
One has got all the goodness, and the other all the	PP	II	17	225	15
One may be continually abusive without saying any thing	PP	II	17	226	17
saying any thing just; but one cannot be always laughing	PP	II	17	226	17
And with no one to speak to, of what I felt, no Jane to	PP	II	17	226	19
There is one point, on which I want your advice.	PP	II	17	226	21
Here was knowledge in which no one could partake; and she	PP	II	17	227	25
"Well, Lizzy," said Mrs. Bennet one day, "what is your	PP	II	17	227	27
I should be ashamed of having one that was only entailed	PP	II	17	228	35
"If one could but go to Brighton!" observed Mrs. Bennet.	PP	II	18	229	6
"Oh, yes!--if one could but go to Brighton!	PP	II	18	229	7
Kitty was the only one who shed tears; but she did weep	PP	II	18	235	40
But here, by carrying with me one ceaseless source of	PP	II	19	237	4
The Gardiners staid only one night at Longbourn, and set	PP	II	19	239	11
One enjoyment was certain--that of suitableness as	PP	II	19	239	11
They entered it in one of its lowest points, and drove for	PP	III	1	245	2
Mrs. Reynolds then directed their attention to one of miss	PP	III	1	247	20
There is not one of his tenants or servants but what will	PP	III	1	249	38
said Elizabeth, as she walked towards one of the windows.	PP	III	1	250	44
Her thoughts were all fixed on that one spot of Pemberley	PP	III	1	253	55
to the edge of the water, in one of its narrowest parts.	PP	III	1	253	57
"There is also one other person in the party," he	PP	III	1	256	63
that would not give one an unfavourable idea of his heart.	PP	III	1	258	74
that one of them at least knew what it was to love.	PP	III	2	261	6
its existence might prove, had at least outlived one day.	PP	III	2	263	10
her feelings towards one in that mansion; and she lay	PP	III	2	265	16
face whenever she spoke to one of its objects; for	PP	III	3	269	8
saw any one so much altered as she is since the winter.	PP	III	3	270	13
recollect your saying one night, after they had been	PP	III	3	271	16
					17
and I believe you thought her rather pretty at one time."	PP	III	3	271	17
her as one of the handsomest women of my acquaintance."	PP	III	3	271	18
forced him to say what gave no one any pain but herself.	PP	III	3	271	19
one of which was marked that it had been missent elsewhere.	PP	III	4	273	1
The one missent must be first attended to; it had been	PP	III	4	273	2
gone off to Scotland with one of his officers; to own the	PP	III	4	273	3
I am sincerely grieved for him and Mrs. F. but no one can	PP	III	4	275	5
but as it was a matter of confidence one cannot wonder.	PP	III	4	275	5
glass of wine;--shall I get you one?--you are very ill."	PP	III	4	276	9
It cannot be concealed from any one.	PP	III	4	277	11
relations, with only one serious, parting, look, went away.	PP	III	4	278	22
meaning to marry her. no one but Jane, she thought, could	PP	III	4	279	24
Sometimes one officer, sometimes another had been her	PP	III	4	280	25
all three being actuated by one spirit, every thing	PP	III	4	280	26
was impossible to one so wretched as herself; but she had	PP	III	4	281	29
it apparently be to any one, that the good opinion which	PP	III	5	285	16
as possible; and sleeping one night on the road, reached	PP	III	5	285	20
and judged it better that one only of the household, and	PP	III	5	288	40
of the household, and the one whom they could most trust,	PP	III	5	288	40
One came from her books, and the other from her toilette.	PP	III	5	289	41
is irretrievable--that one false step involves her in	PP	III	5	289	43

"And till Colonel Forster came himself, not one of you PP III 5 290 49
is but one man in the world I love, and he is an angel. PP III 5 291 60
"I never saw any one so shocked. PP III 5 292 62
as this, one cannot see too little of one's neighbours. PP III 5 293 67
and lady's removing from one carriage into another, might PP III 5 293 69
they might have gone to one of them, on their first coming PP III 6 295 5
If there were any one, that one could apply to, with a PP III 6 295 6
that this false step in one daughter, will be injurious to PP III 6 297 11
and it was certain that he had no near one living. PP III 6 297 12
There was no one therefore who could be pointed out, as PP III 6 297 12
It would have spared her, she thought, one sleepless night PP III 6 299 17
"This is a parade," cried he, "which does one good; it PP III 6 299 28
prohibited, unless you stand up with one of your sisters. PP III 6 300 30
his way towards a small wood on one side of the paddock. PP III 7 301 6
her, during your life, one hundred pounds per annum. PP III 7 302 14
I want very much to know;--one is, how much money your PP III 7 304 27
so slight a temptation as one hundred a-year during my PP III 7 304 29
Mary and Kitty were both with Mrs. Bennet: one PP III 7 305 43
One day's delay she observed, would be of small importance; PP III 7 307 48
The satisfaction of prevailing on one of the most PP III 8 308 1
so little advantage to any one, should be forwarded at the PP III 8 308 2
This was one point, with regard to Lydia at least, which PP III 8 308 4
Into one house in this neighbourhood, they shall never PP III 8 310 9
the same time, there was no one, whose knowledge of a PP III 8 311 12
"And then when you go away, you may leave one or two of my PP III 9 317 15
No one but Mrs. Bennet, regretted that their stay would be PP III 9 318 18
He was her dear Wickham on every occasion; no one was to PP III 9 318 20
One morning, soon after their arrival, as she was sitting PP III 9 318 21
22
However, I did not hear above one word in ten, for I was PP III 9 319 24
Not one party, or scheme, or any thing. PP III 9 319 25
she sat down on one of the benches, and prepared to be PP III 10 321 1
From what I can collect, he left Derbyshire only one day PP III 10 321 2
faults at different times; but this is the true one. PP III 10 324 2
One ought not repine;--but, to be sure, it would have been PP III 10 328 28
In future, I hope we shall be always of one mind." PP III 10 329 34
One seems so forlorn without them." PP III 11 330 10
I am glad of one thing, that he comes alone; because we PP III 11 332 17
if I went to see him, he should marry one of my daughters. PP III 11 332 23
My mother means well; but she does not know, no one can PP III 11 333 28
She had ventured only one glance at Darcy. PP III 11 335 40
She was in no humour for conversation with any one but PP III 11 336 45
Miss Lucas is married and settled. and one of my own PP III 11 336 49
Let me never see either one or the other again!" PP III 11 337 56
the appetite and pride of one who had ten thousand a-year. PP III 11 338 60
He was on one side of her mother. PP III 12 340 12
And on the gentlemen's approaching, one of the girls moved PP III 12 341 16
17
She followed him with her eyes, envied every one to whom PP III 12 341 18
Is there one among the sex, who would not protest against PP III 12 341 19
"The party seemed so well selected, so suitable one with PP III 12 343 30
not be prevailed on to go down without one of her sisters. PP III 13 344 10
or allow her to hear it from any one but myself. PP III 13 347 26
attention to bestow on any one else; but she found herself PP III 13 349 44
"He has made me so happy," said she, one evening, "by PP III 13 349 45
One morning, about a week after Bingley's engagement with PP III 14 351 1
"And that I suppose is one of your sisters." PP III 14 352 7
"She is my youngest girl but one. PP III 14 352 8
kind of a little wilderness on one side of your lawn. PP III 14 352 16
17
You will be censured, slighted, and despised, by every one PP III 14 355 45
me, it would not give me one moment's concern--and the PP III 14 358 70
when the expectation of one wedding, made every body eager PP III 15 360 1
of a marriage with one, whose immediate connections were PP III 15 360 2
as one of the most illustrious personages in this land." PP III 15 362 14
pleasantry, but could only force one most reluctant smile. PP III 15 363 19
My affections and wishes are unchanged, but one word from PP III 16 366 7
There was one part especially, the opening of it, which I PP III 16 368 20
I was obliged to confess one thing, which for a time, and PP III 16 371 45
she was aware that no one liked him but Jane; and even PP III 17 372 2
I could not have parted with you, my Lizzy, to any one PP III 17 377 37
My avowed one, or what I avowed to myself, was to see PP III 18 382 16
Perhaps other people have said so before, but not one with PP III 18 383 21
or to lose one connection that might possibly assist her. MP I 1 4 2
and expense of one child entirely out of her great number. MP I 1 5 4
of doing every thing one could by way of providing for a MP I 1 6 6
of providing for a child one had in a manner taken into MP I 1 6 6
into the world, and ten to one but she has the means of MP I 1 6 6
I am not one of those that spare their own trouble; and MP I 1 9 12
much trouble, or speaking one word where he spoke ten, by MP I 2 12 2
to their address; and no one would have supposed the girls MP I 2 13 4
manner, when she was found one morning by her cousin MP I 2 15 9
one among them who ran more in her thoughts than the rest. MP I 2 15 12
to you, whether you are in one house or the other." MP I 3 25 16
not unpleasant to you, I should call it an excellent one." MP I 3 25 21
"I can never be important to any one." MP I 3 26 26
for his comfort, being one of those persons who think MP I 3 32 63
and without aiming at one gratification that would MP I 3 32 64
her aunts, "she might ride one of her cousins' horses at MP I 4 35 7
at home the whole day with one aunt, or walked beyond her MP I 4 36 7
there seemed with him but one thing to be done, and that " MP I 4 36 7
do vastly well, or that one might be borrowed of the MP I 4 36 7
He had three horses of his own, but not one that would MP I 4 37 8
he resolved to exchange for one that his cousin might ride; MP I 4 37 8
ride; he knew where such a one was to be met with, and MP I 4 37 8
possessing worth, which no one but herself could ever MP I 4 37 8
had recently succeeded to one of the largest estates and MP I 4 38 9
in the mean while, as no one felt a doubt of his most MP I 4 39 12
Edmund was the only one of the family who could see a MP I 4 39 13
measure quite as welcome on one side, as it could be MP I 4 41 15
"There, Mrs. Grant, you see how he dwells on one word, and MP I 4 43 24
he was so well made, that one soon forgot he was plain; MP I 5 44 2
Mrs. Grant, there is not one in a hundred of either sex, MP I 5 46 20
of all transactions, the one in which people expect most MP I 5 46 20
and confidence of some one particular advantage in the MP I 5 46 22
too much; but then, if one scheme of happiness fails, MP I 5 46 23
One does not like to see a girl of eighteen or nineteen so MP I 5 49 32
when one has seen her hardly able to speak the year before. MP I 5 49 32
I sat there an hour one morning waiting for anderson, with MP I 5 50 35
"It leads one astray; one does not know what to do. MP I 5 51 40
was ever juster,) tell one what is expected; but I got MP I 5 51 40
by men, attached myself to one of her daughters, walked by MP I 5 51 40
cut up without supplying one pleasant anecdote of any MP I 6 52 1
a single entertaining story about "my friend such a one." MP I 6 52 1
The approach now is one of the finest things in the MP I 6 53 2
scarcely ever indulged with one, for it is so valuable a MP I 6 54 13
One likes to get out into a shrubbery in fine weather." MP I 6 55 16
insinuating, that there was one only whom he was anxious MP I 6 55 17
It stands in one of the lowest spots of the park; in that MP I 6 56 26
I told my maid to speak for one directly; and as I cannot MP I 6 58 37
without seeing one farm yard, nor walk in the shrubbery MP I 6 58 37
be best off, for she is gratified in more ways than one. MP I 6 59 41
You have but one style among you. MP I 6 59 43
perhaps at Cambridge, and at one and twenty executed. MP I 6 61 56
Lady Bertram made no objection, and every one concerned in MP I 6 62 59
conduct might incline one to the side of his wife: but it MP I 7 63 7
one more sensible of the disadvantages she has been under. MP I 7 64 9
his favourite instrument; one morning secured an MP I 7 64 12
A happy party it appeared to her--all interested in one MP I 7 67 16
himself useful, and proving his good-nature by any one? MP I 7 67 16
Her feelings for one and the other were soon a little MP I 7 67 17
"I never see one sit a horse better. MP I 7 69 22
the happiness of one of the party was exceedingly clouded. MP I 7 70 30
Miss Bertram was the one. MP I 7 70 30
and having asked one or two questions about the dinner, MP I 7 71 31
was a very long one, told them that she was on the sofa. MP I 7 71 33
but they were so full blown, that one could not wait." MP I 7 72 44
independent of the box, on which one might go with him. MP I 8 77 8
two carriages when one will do, would be trouble for MP I 8 77 12
his carriage, and you know one should not like to have MP I 8 77 12
of mentioning Miss Price as one who would probably be of MP I 8 79 23
plan, and one that was admitted with general approbation. MP I 8 79 28
you, it will be better that one should sit with Henry, and MP I 8 80 29
open to admit them through one or two intermediate rooms MP I 9 84 1
against itself under one circumstance, would find objects MP I 9 88 18
One wishes it were not so--but I have not yet left Oxford MP I 9 88 18
one impulse, one wish for air and liberty, all walked out. MP I 9 89 32
Poor Julia, the only one out of the nine not tolerably MP I 9 91 36
when they had taken one turn on the terrace, and were MP I 9 91 37
Here is a nice little wood, if one can but get into it. MP I 9 91 37
I am one of the exceptions, and being one, must do MP I 9 92 41
No one here can call the office nothing. MP I 9 92 45
to the clergyman than one has been used to hear given, or MP I 9 92 46
One does not see much of this influence and importance in MP I 9 92 46
One scarcely sees a clergyman out of his pulpit." MP I 9 93 46
great house, dawdling from one room to another--straining MP I 9 95 71
attention--hearing what one does not understand--admiring MP I 9 95 71
does not understand--admiring what one does not care for.-- MP I 9 95 71
They would go to one end of it, in the line they were then MP I 9 96 76
Crawford, and herself, without interruption from any one. MP I 10 97 1
as one finds to be the case with men of the world." MP I 10 98 10
I have had enough of the family for one morning. MP I 10 100 28
at last; and had been sitting down under one of the trees. MP I 10 103 49
of being really the one preferred, comforted her under it, MP I 10 105 52
cream cheese, just like the excellent one we had at dinner. MP I 10 105 55
good old Mrs. Whitaker, but my taking one of the cheeses. MP I 10 105 55
the trouble of working for one; and has the best MP I 11 110 23
"Where any one body of educated men, of whatever MP I 11 110 26
for the convenience of any one, and who, moreover, if the MP I 11 111 28
without some talent on one side, or some attachment on the MP I 12 115 4
Fanny was the only one of the party who found any thing to MP I 12 115 5
She was privy, one evening, to the hopes of her aunt MP I 12 116 11
It had, however, been a very happy one to Fanny through MP I 12 117 11
of that true delicacy which one seldom meets with now-a- MP I 12 117 14
poor woman! must want a lover as much as any one of them. MP I 12 119 22
as to oblige one to do the very thing--whatever it be! MP I 12 120 26
when the sudden death of one of the nearest connections of MP I 13 121 1
all to my taste, and such a one as I certainly would not MP I 13 122 2
Ravenshaw, who I suppose is one of the most correct men in MP I 13 122 4
act was awakened, and in no one more strongly than in him MP I 13 123 6
than you do, or can have gone much farther to see one." MP I 13 124 11
But one good thing I have just ascertained. MP I 13 125 14
delicate one, considering every thing, extremely delicate." MP I 13 125 17
Lady Bertram, sunk back in one corner of the sofa, the MP I 13 126 19
in the heavy tone of one half roused,--"I was not asleep." MP I 13 126 22
every evening of my life through one Christmas holidays." MP I 13 126 25
being moved from one side of the room to the other.-- MP I 13 127 29
with a difficulty, and on one side or the other it was a MP I 14 131 3
One could not expect any body to take such a part----- MP I 14 131 3
same speaker, who taking up one of the many volumes of MP I 14 132 7
said he, "as Agatha does to one or other of my sisters. MP I 14 133 10
We cannot have two Agathas, and we must have one MP I 14 134 14
of provisions--though one might have supposed--but it is MP I 14 136 18
feelings to more than one, but exciting small compassion MP I 14 136 20
situation of one, and language of the other, so unfit to MP I 14 137 23
had some effect, for no one loved better to lead than MP I 15 140 14
There should always be one steady head to superintend so MP I 15 141 22
about the house for one while,--I hate such greediness--so MP I 15 142 22
For a moment no one spoke; and then many spoke together to MP I 15 143 28
"Mr. Rushworth was to be Count Cassel, but no one had yet MP I 15 143 28
itself, is, perhaps, one of the last who would wish to MP I 15 145 41
and there are one or two that would not disgrace us.-- MP I 15 148 58
and ride over to Stoke, and settle with one of them." MP I 15 148 58
Yes, Mr. Charles Maddox dined at my sister's one day, did MP I 15 148 59
her plants, or wanted one of the books, which she was MP I 16 151 1
smallness of the one making the use of the other so MP I 16 151 1
the three lower panes of one window, where Tintern Abbey MP I 16 152 2
of one, before whom all her doubts were wont to be laid. MP I 16 153 3
"There is but one thing to be done, Fanny. MP I 16 154 10
into the whole affair, as could have but one effect on him. MP I 17 159 6
One advantage resulted from it to Fanny; at the earnest MP I 17 159 6
Fanny's heart was not absolutely the only saddened one MP I 17 160 7
to have time for more than one flirtation, he grew MP I 17 160 9
he took every trifling one that could be united with the MP I 18 164 1
not be always walking from one room to the other and doing MP I 18 166 6
observed on her behalf, "one cannot wonder, sister, that MP I 18 167 7
8
not one of those who can talk and work at the same time.-- MP I 18 167 9
happened to be exactly at one of the times when they were MP I 18 169 21
and every one concerned was looking forward with eagerness. MP I 18 171 25
him and for almost every one of the party on the MP II 1 176 4
By not one of the circle was he listened to with such MP II 1 179 9
joyfully around him, now at one, now at another of the MP II 1 180 13
Some one was talking there in a very loud accent--he did MP II 1 182 22
Tom was the only one at all ready with an answer, but he MP II 1 185 30
others; but there was only one amongst them whose conduct MP II 2 187 1
less to blame," said he, "every one of us, excepting Fanny. MP II 2 187 1
Fanny is the only one who has judged rightly throughout, MP II 2 187 1
There was one person, however, in the house whom he could MP II 2 187 3
always arisen, and more than one bad servant been detected. MP II 2 188 3
to be his opinion on one subject--his decided preference MP II 2 190 6
He seemed to feel exactly as one could wish." MP II 2 190 6
spoilt only the floor of one room, ruined all the MP II 2 190 9
of his life, had he seen one of that class, so MP II 2 191 10
But they had seen no one from the parsonage--not a MP II 2 192 11
it then became openly acknowledged, was a very short one.-- MP II 2 193 18
Mrs. Norris contrived to remove one article from his sight MP II 2 195 22
at this time, for any engagements but in one quarter. MP II 3 196 1
You are one of those who are too silent in the evening MP II 3 198 9
done every thing--and no one would have supposed, from her MP II 3 203 30
and being descried from one of the windows endeavouring to MP II 4 205 3
even to sit down on one of the benches now comparatively MP II 4 208 11
were thus sitting together one day: "every time I come MP II 4 208 12
afterwards added: "if any one faculty of our nature may be MP II 4 208 12
One does not think of extent here--and between ourselves, MP II 4 209 15
When one thinks of it, how astonishing a variety of nature! MP II 4 209 16
One cannot fix one's eyes on the commonest natural MP II 4 209 16
with the person one feels most agreeable in the world. MP II 4 210 21
One need not envy the new Mrs. Rushworth with such a home MP II 4 210 21
But I have long thought Mr. Bertram one of the worst MP II 4 212 30
and I shall lose every one; and what is worse, cook has MP II 4 212 31
I assure you a very fine one; for, my dear"--turning to MP II 4 215 48
He had but one opinion. MP II 5 219 25
of having that absurd new one of his own, which is wider, MP II 5 220 30
your opinion as if you were one of your cousins--as if you MP II 5 221 32
And then changing his tone again to one of gentle MP II 5 224 53
Another week, only one other week, would have been enough MP II 5 225 57
and never so angrily to any one; and when her speech was MP II 5 225 59
as people say; a sort of beauty that grows on one. MP II 6 230 6
ladies of eighteen (or one should not read about them) as MP II 6 231 11
to believe Fanny one of them, or to think that with so MP II 6 231 11
different person from the one he had equipped seven years MP II 6 233 16
In one respect it was better, as it gave him the means of MP II 6 237 23
a smile when the animal was one minute tendered to his use MP II 6 237 23

possibilities of any one most dear to him, and disdaining MP II 7 238 1
Mr. Crawford, but as being one in an agreeable group; for MP II 7 238 2
began to think, that any one in the habit of such idle MP II 7 238 2
The meeting was generally felt to be a pleasant one, being MP II 7 238 3
house to be seen excepting one--to be presumed the MP II 7 241 13
also," said Edmund, "and one of them is that very little MP II 7 242 24
looking house, such as one might suppose a respectable old MP II 7 243 27
by our all going with him one hot day in August to drive MP II 7 244 30
They are at Brighton now, you know--in one of the best MP II 7 245 32
did not depend upon one amusement or one season of the MP II 7 246 37
upon one amusement or one season of the year: he had set MP II 7 246 37
One of whom, having never before understood that thornton MP II 7 248 47
One might as well be nothing as a midshipman. MP II 7 249 52
One is nothing indeed. MP II 7 249 52
make up your mind to it as one of the hardships which fall MP II 7 249 53
There is one person in company who does not like to have MP II 7 251 61
be very quickly followed by one of them, appear of less MP II 8 254 10
The issue of all depended on one question. MP II 8 255 11
now urged Fanny's taking one for the cross and to keep for MP II 8 258 15
last, by fancying there was one necklace more frequently MP II 8 258 17
happened to fix on the very one which, if I have a choice, MP II 8 260 22
is, a token of the love of one of your oldest friends." MP II 9 261 2
to speak; but quickened by one sovereign wish she then MP II 9 261 3
the superior power of one pleasure over his own mind, MP II 9 262 11
"For one night, Fanny, for only one night, if it be a MP II 9 263 16
give pain to one who has been so studious of your comfort. MP II 9 263 16
She was one of his two dearest--that must support her. MP II 9 264 17
and again that she was one of his two dearest, before the MP II 9 264 17
The proposal was a very pleasant one to William himself, MP II 9 266 21
but of one errand, which turned her too sick for speech.-- MP II 9 268 28
"One thing more. MP II 9 269 36
for upon trial the one given her by Miss Crawford would by MP II 9 270 40
and had no composure till he turned away to some one else. MP II 10 274 8
forgotten; she felt only one thing; and her eyes, bright MP II 10 274 9
lady of Branxholm Hall, "one moment and no more," to view MP II 10 280 33
that she had heard about one of the Miss Maddoxes, or what MP II 11 283 4
not see that--I should not know one from the other." MP II 11 283 4
of disposition and habit--one so easily satisfied, the MP II 11 285 15
She had, moreover, to contend with one disagreeable MP II 11 286 17
Was his letter a long one?-- MP II 11 288 22
sisters just grown up; for one knows, without being told, MP II 11 288 28
very accomplished and pleasing, and one very pretty. MP II 11 288 28
Two play on the piano-forte, and one on the harp--and all MP II 11 288 28
Indeed how can one care for those one has never seen?-- MP II 11 288 30
of her power, from one who she thought must know; and her MP II 11 289 33
you were to have one of the Miss Owens settled at Thornton MP II 11 289 34
Was there one of the family, excepting Edmund, who had not MP II 12 294 16
I am now persuaded she is the very one to make you happy. MP II 12 294 19
I must have them love one another." MP II 12 296 28
neatly as it always is, and one little curl falling MP II 12 296 31
hardly have borne that any one in the house should share MP II 13 298 2
and inclosing two more, one from the secretary of the MP II 13 298 3
her eye running from one to the other, and her heart MP II 13 299 4
from the absence of one friend, and the engagements of MP II 13 299 5
so plain as to bear but one meaning even to her, offering MP II 13 301 7
She rushed out at an opposite door from the one her uncle MP II 13 302 9
every body, and seemed to find no one essential to him?-- MP II 13 305 26
written, and with only one decided feeling, that of MP II 13 307 30
31

her eyes fixed intently on one of the windows, was MP III 1 314 16
Fanny, having performed one part of my commission, and MP III 1 314 16
to your finding one still better worth listening to.-- MP III 1 314 16
Young as you are, and having seen scarcely any one, it is MP III 1 316 31
She had no one to take her part, to counsel, or speak for MP III 1 321 46
He considered her rather as one who had never thought on MP III 2 326 3
friends there could be but one opinion, one wish on the MP III 2 329 12
could be but one opinion, one wish on the subject; the MP III 2 329 12
the influence of all who loved her must incline one way. MP III 2 329 12
Intreaty should be from one quarter only. MP III 2 330 14
classing Mrs. Norris as one of those well-meaning people, MP III 2 332 19
to one whom she had been always trying to depress. MP III 2 332 20
But Shakespeare one gets acquainted with without knowing MP III 3 338 13
His thoughts and beauties are so sread abroad that one MP III 3 338 13
them every where, one is intimate with him by instinct.-- MP III 3 338 13
No man of any brain can open at a good part of one of his MP III 3 338 13
"No doubt, one is familiar with Shakespeare in a degree," MP III 3 338 14
I can never hear such a one without the greatest MP III 3 341 28
whom one could not (in his public capacity) honour enough. MP III 3 341 28
Nay, nay, I entreat you; for one moment put down your work. MP III 3 342 33
one object of curiosity and one set of words to another. MP III 3 343 40
merely beyond what one sees, because one never sees any MP III 3 344 41
what one sees, because one never sees any thing like it-- MP III 3 344 41
any thing like it--but beyond what one fancies might be. MP III 3 344 41
it might be as well to make one more effort for the young MP III 4 345 2
No one but you can tell me them. MP III 4 346 10
We have not one taste in common. MP III 4 348 22
"Julia!--I have heard before from some one of his being in MP III 4 350 30
possible that they might, one or both, be more desirous of MP III 4 350 30
not being loved by some one of her sex, at least, let him MP III 4 353 45
I told them, that you were of all human creatures the one, MP III 4 354 46
in guarding against one evil, laying herself open to MP III 4 354 47
If I had the power of recalling any one week of my MP III 5 358 9
I shall see no one half so amiable where I am going. MP III 5 359 10
"but you are only going from one set of friends to another. MP III 5 359 11
You have all so much more heart among you, than one finds MP III 5 359 12
in you; which, in common intercourse, one knows nothing of. MP III 5 359 12
Thinking, I hope, of one who is always thinking of you. MP III 5 360 16
her judgment, which makes one feel there is attachment; MP III 5 361 16
And then, Fanny, the glory of fixing one who has been shot MP III 5 363 22
I have two favours to ask, Fanny; one is your MP III 5 364 32
It had occurred to Sir Thomas, in one of his dignified MP III 6 368 9
She was of use to no one else; but there she might be MP III 6 370 13
a larger share than any one among so many could deserve. MP III 6 371 17
Mansfield; and for part of one of those days the young MP III 6 372 21
No one interfered to encourage or dissuade. MP III 6 373 23
It made the substance of one other confidential discourse MP III 6 373 26
and Fanny were talked of as already advanced one stage. MP III 6 374 29
please sir, and one of the officers has been here to"----- MP III 7 377 7
to ask for you; he has got one of the Thrush's boats, and MP III 7 377 7
The doctor has been here enquiring for you; he has got one MP III 7 380 20
If ever there was a perfect beauty afloat, she is one; and MP III 7 380 20
between herself and Susan, one of whom was clerk in a MP III 7 381 26
But here, one subject swallowed up all the rest. MP III 7 382 29
A few enquiries began; but one of the earliest--"how did MP III 7 385 38
is quite a miracle if one keeps them more than half-a-year. MP III 7 385 39
There had been at one moment a slight murmur in the MP III 7 387 45
One was found to have too small a print for a child's eyes, MP III 7 387 45
allowed to sit up only one hour extraordinary in honour of MP III 7 387 46
of the one, which her imprudent marriage had placed her in. MP III 8 390 5
interest her, a letter from one belonging to the set where MP III 9 393 1
Then she will be in beauty, for she will open one of the MP III 9 394 1
am unwilling to fancy myself neglected for a young one. MP III 9 394 1
London; write me a pretty one in reply to gladden Henry's MP III 9 394 1
of guiding or informing any one, she did resolve to give MP III 9 396 6
more was not expected by one, who, while seeing all the MP III 9 397 8
One morning about this time, Fanny having now been nearly MP III 10 399 2
the severe one of shame for the home in which he found her. MP III 10 400 6
comprehension of one half of his meaning, and encouraged MP III 10 406 20
wished he had come only for one day--but it was not so MP III 10 406 21
thank him for another pleasure, and one of no trivial kind. MP III 10 406 22
and Fanny had time for only one thrill of horror, before MP III 10 406 22
them, and made one in the family party on the ramparts. MP III 11 408 3
and she turned in to her more simple one immediately. MP III 11 412 29
of a friend; and though in one light glad to have him gone, MP III 11 413 31
last Saturday, and one still more to be dwelt on the next MP III 12 415 1
2

so very ill-looking as I did, at least one sees many worse. MP III 12 416 2
more than does me good), one very material thing I had to MP III 12 416 3
What a long letter!--one word more. MP III 12 417 3
very nearly gone, when the one letter, the letter from MP III 13 420 1
They have all, perhaps, been corrupting one another; but MP III 13 424 4
of one of the last epistolary uses she could put them to. MP III 13 425 6
Edmund's letter, Fanny had one from her aunt, beginning MP III 13 425 7
8

by himself at the house of one of these young men, to the MP III 13 426 10
There was hardly any one in the house who might have not MP III 14 429 2
not one who was not more useful at times to her son. MP III 14 429 2
It appeared from one of her aunt's letters, that Julia had MP III 14 432 11
One should be a brute not to feel for the distress they MP III 14 433 13
voice would I say to any one, that wealth and consequence MP III 14 434 13
but you are now the only one I can apply to for the truth, MP III 14 434 1
3000

but how will she and the dowager agree in one house? MP III 14 435 13
the spirit of each and every one is unalterable affection." MP III 14 435 14
steadily attached to any one woman in the world, and shame MP III 15 438 5
her correspondent was not of a sort to regard a slight one. MP III 15 438 6
greatest blessing to every one of kindred with Mrs. MP III 15 442 21
Never had she felt such a one as this letter contained. MP III 15 443 24
their agitated spirits, one all happiness, the other all MP III 15 444 27
The journey was likely to be a silent one. MP III 15 445 33
By one of the suffering party within, they were expected MP III 15 447 37
never do enough for one who seemed so much to want her. MP III 16 449 4
she could see it only in one light, as comprehending the MP III 16 449 6
There was but one of his children who was not at this time MP III 16 451 13
in reason to think that one interview with Miss Crawford MP III 16 452 15
and every thing told--no one else in the room, except his MP III 16 453 17
one of whose affectionate sympathy he was quite convinced. MP III 16 453 17
he had been able to speak one intelligible sentence, she MP III 16 454 18
She would not voluntarily give unnecessary pain to any one, MP III 16 456 25
now hope to succeed with one of her stamp, and therefore I MP III 16 457 29
As a daughter--he hoped a penitent one--she should be MP III 17 465 13
with little society, on one side no affection, on the MP III 17 465 14
She was regretted by no one at Mansfield. MP III 17 466 16
Could he have been satisfied with the conquest of one MP III 17 467 19
not one of the barriers, which society gives to virtue. MP III 17 468 22
institutionary dinners in one week, they still lived MP III 17 469 24
and her 20,000l. any one who could satisfy the better MP III 17 469 24
this occasion, that every one may be at liberty to fix MP III 17 470 26
with her than any one else at Mansfield, what was there MP III 17 470 27
Let no one presume to give the feelings of a young woman MP III 17 471 28
every scheme of her's;--one to whom she could speak every E I 1 6 6
universally civil, but not one among them who could be E I 1 7 10
At any rate, it must be better to have only one to please, E I 1 10 29
"Especially when one of those two is such a fanciful, E I 1 10 30
We always say what we like to one another." E I 1 10 32
Mr. Knightley, in fact, was one of the few people who E I 1 11 33
Woodhouse, and the only one who ever told her of them: and E I 1 11 33
to have two persons to please; she will now have but one. E I 1 11 34
"And you have forgotten one matter of joy to me," said E I 1 11 39
"and a very considerable one--that I made the match myself. E I 1 11 39
it, your saying to yourself one idle day, 'I think it E I 1 12 42
"Only one more, papa; only for Mr. Elton. E I 1 13 46
though she had one sort of spirit, she had not the best. E I 2 15 3
one so dear, and, as he believed, so deservedly dear. E I 2 17 7
Mr. Frank Churchill was one of the boasts of Highbury, and E I 2 17 8
whose frequent visits were one of the comforts of Mr. E I 2 19 14
And yet she was a happy woman, and a woman whom no one E I 3 21 4
one of the long evenings she had fearfully anticipated. E I 3 22 6
As she sat one morning, looking forward to exactly such a E I 3 22 7
Bates, let me propose your venturing on one of these eggs. E I 3 24 13
14

small, you see--one of our small eggs will not hurt you. E I 3 24 14
a Harriet Smith, therefore, one whom she could summon at E I 4 26 1
and only desiring to be guided by any one she looked up to. E I 4 26 2
Harriet would be loved as one to whom she could be useful. E I 4 26 2
very good parlours indeed; one of them quite as large as E I 4 27 4
two of them Alderneys, and one a little Welch cow, a very E I 4 27 4
"He had gone three miles round one day, in order to bring E I 4 28 6
He had his shepherd's son into the parlour one night on E I 4 28 6
Mrs. Martin had told her one day, (and there was a blush E I 4 28 6
other books, that lay in one of the window seats--but he E I 4 29 10
One does not, you know, after a time. E I 4 29 13
help, and is therefore in one sense as much above my E I 4 29 14
You might not see one in a hundred, with gentlemen so E I 4 33 34
Her next beginning was, "in one respect, perhaps, Mr. E I 4 34 41
42

This will certainly be the beginning of one of our E I 5 36 4
of one of her own sex, after being used to it all her life. E I 5 36 6
One hears sometimes of a child being 'the picture of E I 5 39 20
she will never lead any one really wrong; she will make so E I 5 40 22
There is an anxiety, a curiosity in what one feels for E I 5 40 27
at Hartfield, was not one of the least agreeable proofs of E I 6 42 1
But from one cause or another, I gave it up in disgust. E I 6 43 13
and the lines about the mouth which one ought to catch." E I 6 44 15
at portraits, for not one of them had ever been finished, E I 6 44 19
and John and Bella, from one end of the sheet to the other, E I 6 45 21
and any one of them might do for any one of the rest. E I 6 45 21
memorial of the beauty of one, the skill of the other, and E I 6 47 27
We shall be most happy to consider you as one of the party. E I 6 47 29
Oh, no! it gives one exactly the idea of such a height as E I 6 48 35
her shoulders--and it makes one think she must catch cold." E I 6 48 36
little parcel for her from one of his sisters, and gone E I 7 50 1
I think one of his sisters must have helped him. E I 7 51 5
should not be hesitating--it is a very serious thing.-- E I 7 52 20
I have seen people--and if one comes to compare them, E I 7 54 30
at all, one is so very handsome and agreeable. E I 7 54 30
"One should be sorry to see greater pride or refinement in E I 7 56 41
I can think of but one thing--who is in love with her? E I 8 59 23
and, I believe, considers me as one of his best friends. E I 8 59 27
I never heard better sense from any one than Robert Martin. E I 8 59 27
gentlemen's daughters, no one, I apprehend, will deny.-- E I 8 62 41
that it will be a very unfortunate one for Harriet. E I 8 64 47
silence, with only one attempt on Emma's side to talk of E I 8 65 50
to put off his journey only one day; but it would not do; E I 8 68 58
Mr. Elton was the only one whose assistance she asked. E I 9 70 7
"Why will not you write one yourself for us, Mr. Elton?" E I 9 71 8
Do you think it is a good one? E I 9 72 17
Oh, no! shark is only one syllable. E I 9 73 17
one another by every circumstance of your respective homes. E I 9 75 25
You and Mr. Elton are one as clever as the other. E I 9 76 28
"I never read one more to the purpose, certainly." E I 9 76 31
"It is one thing," said she, presently--her cheeks in a E I 9 76 35
I am sure I have not got one half so good." E I 9 77 39
a very depressed tone)--she is coming for only one week. E I 9 79 62
One half of the world cannot understand the pleasures of E I 9 81 77
but so good a charade must not be confined to one or two. E I 9 82 81
82

There go you and your riddle-book one of these days."-- E I 10 83 3
must find other people charming--one other person at least. E I 10 84 10
11

"I must see somebody very superior to any one I have seen E I 10 84 13
By the bye, that is almost enough to put one out of E I 10 86 23
One is sick of the very name of Jane Fairfax. E I 10 86 23
for her grandmother, one hears of nothing else for a month. E I 10 86 23

away, "these are the sights, Harriet, to do one good. E I 10 86 24
25
"Poor creatures! one can think of nothing else." E I 10 87 26
a little raised on one side of the lane, leaving them E I 10 88 33
The room they were taken into was the one he chiefly E I 10 89 38
The lovers were standing together at one of the windows. E I 10 90 39
"Oh! papa, we have missed seeing them but one entire day E I 11 94 14
of every day, excepting one, have we seen either Mr. E I 11 94 14
I believe he is one of the very best tempered men that E I 11 95 19
Whether it was his own idea you know, one cannot tell. E I 11 96 22
that any one should share with him in Isabella's first day. E I 12 98 1
came into the room she had one of the children with her-- E I 12 98 2
two natural divisions; on one side he and his daughter; on E I 12 100 15
Emma only occasionally joining in one or the other. E I 12 100 15
her busy labours for some one of her five children--"how E I 12 100 18
My dear Isabella, I have not heard you make one inquiry E I 12 101 23
said Emma, "I have not heard one inquiry after them." E I 12 102 30
"I am most happy to hear it--but only Jane Fairfax one E I 12 104 49
be considered; and if one is to travel, there is not much E I 12 106 58
my taking my family to one part of the coast or another?-- E I 12 106 60
the immediate alertness of one brother, and better E I 12 107 62
than their mornings: but one complete dinner engagement, E I 13 108 2
must all dine at Randalls one day;--even Mr. Woodhouse was E I 13 108 2
might in one of the carriages find room for Harriet also. E I 13 108 3
one ought to overlook, and one does overlook a great deal. E I 13 111 17
temper and good will in Mr. Elton as one cannot but value." E I 13 112 17
One is so fenced and guarded from the weather, that not a E I 13 115 37
I went for only one night, and could not get away till E I 13 115 39
and he is exactly what one values, so hospitable, and so E I 13 116 43
as to his wife; not any one, to whom she related with such E I 14 117 1
life depends, was one of the first gratifications of each. E I 14 117 1
"Yes; and every delay makes one more apprehensive of other E I 14 122 21
days, he ought to come; and one can hardly conceive a E I 14 122 22
she wants to be with; but one cannot comprehend a young E I 14 122 22
"One ought to be at Enscombe, and know the ways of the E I 14 123 23
one decides upon what he can do," replied Mrs. Weston. E I 14 123 23
"One ought to use the same caution, perhaps, in judging of E I 14 123 23
of the conduct of any one individual of any one family; E I 14 123 23
any one individual of any one family; but Enscombe, I E I 14 123 23
temper, to understand a bad one, or to lay down rules for E I 14 123 25
Mr. Elton, in very good spirits, was one of the first to E I 15 124 1
we are two carriages; if one is blown over in the bleak E I 15 126 10
A few minutes more, and Emma hoped to see one troublesome E I 15 128 21
and the three-quarters of a mile would have seemed but one. E I 15 129 23
can account for it only in one way; you are not yourself, E I 15 130 26
27
against having paid the smallest attention to any one else. E I 15 131 31
of knowledge of taste, as one proof among others that he E I 16 134 5
some one worth having; I ought not to have attempted more. E I 16 137 11
penance of communication; and a severe one it was.-- E I 17 141 5
ungracious character of the one preferred--and acknowledge E I 17 141 5
in all her ideas on one subject, all her observations, all E I 17 141 5
Not one of them had the power of removal, or of effecting E I 17 143 14
It is a great deal more natural than one could wish, that E I 18 145 10
"There is one thing, Emma, which a man can always do, if E I 18 146 16
There will be but one subject throughout the parishes of E I 18 149 29
Donwell and Highbury; but one interest--one object of E I 18 149 29
Highbury; but one interest--one object of curiosity; it E I 18 149 29
"He is a person I never think of from one month's end to E I 18 150 36
Emma and Harriet had been walking together one morning, E II 1 155 1
will be wanting the carriage himself one of those days. E II 1 159 18
He was a married man, with only one living child, a girl, E II 2 163 4
had been very near changing one friend for the other, or E II 2 169 16
"My dear Emma," said he, moving from his chair into one E II 3 171 9
with a sincerity which no one could question----- "she is E II 3 171 14
of elegant creature that one cannot keep one's eyes from. E II 3 171 14
15
wished--but it is so little one can venture to do--small, E II 3 171 16
17
my dear Emma, unless one could be sure of their making it E II 3 171 16
17
the precise words--one has no business to remember them. E II 3 174 32
My dear sir, if there is one thing my mother loves better E II 3 175 39
40
One feels that it cannot be a very long acquaintance. he E II 3 175 40
"Very odd! but one never does form a just idea of any body E II 3 176 46
One takes up a notion, and runs away with it. Mr. Dixon, E II 3 176 46
with their buyings, they began whispering to one another. E II 3 178 52
dreadfully, you know, one can't tell how; and then I took E II 3 179 52
finding himself debased to the level of a very wrong one. E II 4 181 3
Harriet was one of those, who, having once begun, would be E II 4 184 10
One cannot creep upon a journey; one cannot help getting E II 5 190 24
help getting on faster than one has planned; and the E II 5 190 24
"It is a great pleasure where one can indulge in it," said E II 5 190 25
a falsehood, it was a pleasant one, and pleasantly handled. E II 5 191 26
They will be extremely glad to see you, I am sure, and one E II 5 195 45
and with a cordial nod from one, and a graceful bow from E II 5 195 49
quest of her cottage from one end of the street to the E II 6 197 3
house, though the principal one of the sort, where a E II 6 197 5
your question, I must pronounce it to be a very unfair one. E II 6 200 18
I wanted the opinion of some one who could really judge. E II 6 201 28
I have been used to hear her's admired; and I remember one E II 6 201 28
seemed to like to hear one if he could hear the other. E II 6 201 28
"One would rather have a stranger preferred than one's E II 6 202 33
hand, to do every thing better than one does oneself!-- E II 6 202 33
of feeling--there was one person, I think, who must have E II 6 202 35
she was asked by Mr. Dixon, one may guess what one chuses." E II 6 202 37
could attach myself to any one so completely reserved." E II 6 203 39
One cannot love a reserved person." E II 6 203 40
trouble of conquering any body's reserve to procure one. E II 6 203 41
of the privations inevitably belonging to a small one. E II 6 204 43
a very cheerful and lively one; she could observe nothing E II 7 205 2
There was one person among his new acquaintance in Surry, E II 7 206 4
such a handsome young man--one who smiled so often and E II 7 206 4
so well; but there was one spirit among them not to be E II 7 206 4
Although in one instance the bearers of not good tidings, E II 7 206 5
I think it would be much better if they would come in one E II 7 209 10
The party was rather large, as it included one other E II 8 214 13
one quarter; --of course it must be from Col. Campbell. E II 8 214 13
"One can suppose nothing else," added Mrs. Cole, "and I E II 8 215 14
while I do not know one note from another, and our little E II 8 215 16
One might guess twenty things without guessing exactly the E II 8 217 32
I was there--one of the party." E II 8 218 35
proportion neither the one nor the other--nothing worse E II 8 219 43
that he believed (excepting one of two points) he could E II 8 221 49
One of those points on which his influence failed, he then E II 8 221 49
"Perhaps you may now begin to regret that you spent one E II 8 222 52
"This is the luxury of a large party," said she:--"one can E II 8 222 59
He is not a gallant man, but he is a very humane one; and E II 8 223 64
Oh! and I had almost forgotten one idea that occurred to E II 8 226 79
"Very well; and if he had intended to give her one, he E II 8 226 82
One accompaniment to her song took her agreeably by E II 8 227 86
"You have sung quite enough for one evening--now, be quiet. E II 8 229 94
"One more;--they would not fatigue Miss Fairfax on any E II 8 229 95
Fairfax on any account, and would only ask for one more." E II 8 229 95
"Oh! but indeed I would much rather have it only in one. E II 9 235 40
Voices approached the shop--or rather one voice and two E II 9 235 43
But, said I, I shall be more sure of succeeding if one of E II 9 236 46
one thing, then another, there is no saying what, you know. E II 9 236 46
At one time Patty came to say she thought the kitchen E II 9 236 46
I say one thing and then I say another, and it passes off. E II 9 237 46
where as one of his trees--I believe there is two of them. E II 9 238 51
Mr. Knightley called one morning, and Jane was eating E II 9 238 51
all--and now his master had not one left to bake or boil. E II 9 239 51
staircase--rather darker and narrower than one could wish. E II 9 239 53
employment, slumbering on one side of the fire, Frank E II 10 240 1
You see we have been wedging one leg with paper. E II 10 240 5
"Conjecture--aye, sometimes one conjectures right, and E II 10 242 15
one conjectures right, and sometimes one conjectures wrong. E II 10 242 15
What nonsense one talks, Miss Woodhouse, when hard at work, E II 10 242 15
when hard at work, if one talks at all;--your real workmen, E II 10 242 15
"If you are very kind," said he, "it will be one of the E II 10 242 17
the worlds one ever has to give--for another half hour." E II 10 242 17
is to hear a tune again which has made one happy!-- E II 10 242 19
That, from such a quarter, one might expect. E II 10 242 21
"Oh! Mr. Knightley, one moment more; something of E II 10 245 50
You said you had a great many, and now you have not one E II 10 245 52
But soon it came to be on one side, "but will there be E II 11 248 5
6
Five couple are nothing, when one thinks seriously about E II 11 248 8
at last, Mr. Weston naming one family of cousins who must E II 11 248 9
Still, however, having proceeded so far, one is unwilling E II 11 250 18
said Frank Churchill, "that one of the great E II 11 251 27
One cannot resolve upon them in a hurry. E II 11 252 32
so obliging as to call here one morning, we may talk it E II 11 252 32
One perplexity, however, arose, which the gentlemen did E II 11 253 44
"I wish," said Mrs. Weston, "one could know which E II 11 254 49
be our object--if one could but tell what that would be." E II 11 254 49
If one could ascertain what the chief of them--the Coles, E II 11 254 50
One thing was wanting to make the prospect of the ball E II 12 257 1
All was safe and prosperous; and as the removal of one E II 12 257 2
She is a woman that one may, that one must laugh at; but E II 12 260 27
must laugh at; but that one would not wish to slight. E II 12 260 27
Oh! the blessing of a female correspondent, when one is E II 12 261 36
"In not one of all my clever replies, my delicate E II 13 264 2
and on no account to give one, beyond the nothing-meaning E II 14 270 3
"Oh! no--there is nothing to surprize one at all.-- E II 14 271 12
her notions were drawn from one set of people, and one E II 14 272 16
from one set of people, and one style of living; that if E II 14 272 16
meet with any thing at all like what one has left behind. E II 14 273 19
I always say this is quite one of the evils of matrimony." E II 14 273 19
you know, Miss Woodhouse, one naturally wishes them to see E II 14 274 28
Upon my word it is enough to put one in a fright. E II 14 277 40
and kind-hearted about her, that it wins upon one directly. E II 14 278 44
One would fancy we were bosom friends! E II 14 279 52
Elton's praise passed from one mouth to another as it E II 15 281 2
In one respect Mrs. Elton grew even worse than she had E II 15 281 3
Not merely when a state of warfare with one young lady E II 15 282 4
And her situation is so calculated to affect one!-- E II 15 282 5
I am a great advocate for timidity--and I am sure one does E II 15 283 7
She was quite one of her worthies--the most amiable, E II 15 284 12
One says those sort of things, of course, without any idea E II 15 288 35
return their civilities by one very superior party--in E II 16 290 3
bringing them, and staying one whole day at Hartfield-- E II 16 292 7
one day would be the very day of this party.-- E II 16 292 7
The post-office has a great charm at one period of our E II 16 293 16
I consider one as including the other. E II 16 294 23
The man who fetches our letters every morning (one of our E II 16 295 34
If one thinks of all that it has to do, and all that it E II 16 296 40
not one in a million, I suppose, actually lost! E II 16 296 42
And when one considers the variety of hands, and of bad E II 16 296 42
was attending to some one else--and the pause gave her E II 16 297 48
writes one of the best gentlemen's hands I ever saw." E II 16 297 49
Mrs. Weston, employing him to write for you one day?" E II 16 298 52
from some one very dear, and that it had not been in vain. E II 16 298 58
and to them succeeded one, which must be at least equally E II 17 299 1
Of all houses in the kingdom Mrs. Bragge's is the one I E II 17 300 8
been in more than one crowd, and might have been alone!-- E II 17 303 23
You will hardly believe me--but twice in one week he and E II 18 306 10
untowardly one month, they are sure to mend the next." E II 18 308 27
one morning, I remember*, he came to me quite in despair." E II 18 308 28
season of the year which one should have chosen for it: E II 18 308 30
always inviting one out, and never too hot for exercise. E II 18 308 30
At the same time it is easy to observe, that I am one of E II 18 309 31
And what inclines one less to bear, she has no fair E II 18 310 33
One has not great hopes from Birmingham. E II 18 310 34
who happens to be one of their nearest neighbours. E II 18 310 34
Here am I come down for only one day, and you are engaged E II 18 311 46
hours where she is absent one--and who, when he is at home, E II 18 312 50
One good thing was immediately brought to a certainty by E III 1 318 11
Her gestures and movements might be understood by any one E III 2 322 18
But two such offers in one day!-- E III 2 322 19
own partner, there was not one among the whole row of E III 2 326 32
There was one, however, which Emma thought something of.-- E III 2 326 33
how there could be any one disengaged was the wonder!-- E III 2 326 33
every thing has been done--one door nailed up--quantities E III 2 328 45
Upon my word, Jane on one arm, and me on the other!-- E III 2 329 45
Oh! no, there is but one. E III 2 329 45
I was convinced there were two, and there is but one. E III 2 329 45
If one leads you wrong, I am sure the other tells you of E III 2 330 53
It was one of the agreeable recollections of the ball, E III 3 332 1
when Harriet came one morning to Emma with a small parcel E III 4 337 1
2
As I am happily quite an altered creature in one respect, E III 4 337 4
plaister, one of the very last times we ever met in it!-- E III 4 338 12
One of my senseless tricks!-- E III 4 339 13
"Do not you remember one morning?--no, I dare say you do E III 4 339 18
But one morning--I forget exactly the day--but perhaps it E III 4 339 18
"It is one that I shall never change, however." E III 4 341 31
In one moment such a change! E III 4 342 38
He had walked up one day after dinner, as he very often E III 5 344 3
having mentioned it in one of her letters to Enscombe, E III 5 345 13
spirits one morning because she thought she had prevailed. E III 5 346 16
one seemed so much disposed to employ as their two selves. E III 5 347 20
to the one, and so very distressing to the other." E III 5 349 27
for one another, as any two beings in the world can be. E III 5 350 37
One cannot have too large a party. E III 6 353 4
One could not leave her out." E III 6 353 4
"No,"--he calmly replied,--"there is but one married woman E III 6 354 15
what guests she pleases to Donwell, and that one is-----" E III 6 354 15
she cried, satisfied to have no one preferred to herself.-- E III 6 355 18
I shall wear a large bonnet, and bring one of my little E III 6 355 20
Donwell was settled for one day, and box hill for the next, E III 6 357 32
in his carriage, with one window down, to partake of this E III 6 357 33
al-fresco party; and in one of the most comfortable rooms E III 6 357 33
with many comfortable and one or two handsome rooms.-- E III 6 358 35
they insensibly followed one another to the delicious E III 6 360 38
I met one as I came--madness in such weather!--absolute E III 6 364 55
a letter to Maple Grove by one lady, to Ireland by another. E III 7 368 3
Let my accents swell to Mickleham on one side, and Dorking E III 7 369 16
There are one or two, perhaps, (glancing at Mr. Weston and E III 7 370 19
from each of you either one thing very clever, be it prose E III 7 370 23
be indulgent--especially to any one who leads the way." E III 7 371 30
These kind of things are very well at Christmas, when one E III 7 372 37
opinion, when one is exploring about the country in summer. E III 7 372 37
I am not one of those who have witty things at every E III 7 372 37
We have nothing clever to say--not one of us." E III 7 372 37
I am really tired of exploring so long on one spot. E III 7 372 39
were out of hearing:--"how well they suit one another!-- E III 7 372 40
That's one of the ladies in the Irish car party, not at E III 7 374 53
He looked around, as if to see that no one were near, and E III 7 374 55
56
herself to such ill opinion in any one she valued! E III 7 376 62

Context	Ref
And how suffer him to leave her without saying one word of	E III 7 376 62
She hoped no one could have said to her, "how could you be	E III 8 377 1
One cannot wonder, one cannot wonder.	E III 8 379 8
When one is in great pain, you know one cannot feel any	E III 8 379 8
Such kind friends, you know, Miss Woodhouse, one must	E III 8 381 19
Jane Fairfax's, struck her; one was every thing, the other	E III 8 384 32
	33
And I hope she will be better off in one respect, and not	E III 9 387 10
In one point she was fully justified.	E III 9 387 12
allowed of no delay in any one at Highbury, who wished to	E III 9 389 16
was now the very one on whom she would have lavished every	E III 9 389 16
always to one room;--he could have wished it otherwise--	E III 9 389 16
One morning, about ten days after Mrs. Churchill's decease,	E III 10 392 1
to me, that does not relate to one of that family?"	E III 10 393 14
One of the Otways.--	E III 10 394 20
did--to distinguish any one young woman with persevering	E III 10 396 44
I must love him; and now that I am satisfied on one point,	E III 10 398 53
satisfied on one point, the one material point, I am	E III 10 398 53
"None; not one.	E III 10 399 60
of this one great deviation from the strict rule of right.	E III 10 400 65
Of such, one may almost say, that 'the world is not	E III 10 400 66
of condolence, it turns out to be one of congratulation.--	E III 10 400 68
on the prospect of having one of the most lovely and	E III 10 400 68
hundred chances to one against his ever caring for her.--	E III 11 402 1
have been privately engaged to one another this long while.	E III 11 404 8
You must think one five hundred million times more above	E III 11 407 28
Harriet was standing at one of the windows.	E III 11 407 29
arrow, that Mr. Knightley must marry no one but herself!	E III 11 408 32
a speech, a removal from one chair to another, a	E III 11 409 35
which this one article marked, gave her severe pain.	E III 11 410 35
the one revealed to her--her affection for Mr. Knightley.--	E III 11 412 46
Was it new for one, perhaps too busy to seek, to be the	E III 11 413 48
a hope (at times a slight one, at times much stronger,)	E III 12 416 1
soon it appeared when her thoughts were in one course.	E III 12 416 2
discussion of <u>one</u> topic had better be avoided; and hoping,	E III 12 416 2
thoughts a little from the one subject which had engrossed	E III 12 417 3
This was one of her expressions.	E III 12 418 6
never known the blessing of one tranquil hour:'--and the	E III 12 418 6
No one, I believe, can blame her more than she is disposed	E III 12 419 8
One natural consequence of the evil she had involved	E III 12 419 12
had been equally marking one as an associate for her, to	E III 12 421 17
excusable in one who sets up as I do for understanding.	E III 13 427 19
It was his object to blind all about him; and no one, I am	E III 13 427 19
in every point but one--and that one, since the purity of	E III 13 428 23
point but one--and that one, since the purity of her heart	E III 13 428 23
a better home than the one he takes her from; and he who	E III 13 428 23
In one respect he is the object of my envy."	E III 13 428 25
He <u>had</u> despaired at one period; he had received such an	E III 13 431 38
This one half hour had given to each the same precious	E III 13 432 41
from about the same period, one sentiment having probably	E III 13 432 41
from about the same period, one sentiment having probably	E III 13 432 41
such an evening, she found one or two such very serious	E III 14 434 4
Highbury, and--indulging in one scheme more--nearly	E III 14 435 4
But I have been forgiven by one who had still more to	E III 14 436 8
hope, lay me open to reprehension, excepting on one point.	E III 14 438 8
but the suddenness, and, in one light, the	E III 14 440 8
engagement, was behaving one hour with objectionable	E III 14 441 8
One thing only.--	E III 14 443 8
In one respect, my good fortune is undoubted, that of	E III 14 443 8
communicated; especially to one, who, like Mr. Knightley,	E III 15 444 2
I been offered the sight of one of this gentleman's	E III 15 444 6
One man's style must not be the rule of another's.	E III 15 445 7
Ah! that was the act of a very, very young man, one too	E III 15 446 18
We must look to her one fault, and remember that she had	E III 15 446 20
remark; and, excepting one momentary glance at her,	E III 15 447 21
Only one page more.	E III 15 447 26
Emma, my mind has been hard at work on one subject."	E III 15 448 30
"Ah! there is one difficulty unprovided for," cried Emma.	E III 15 449 33
could be in love with more than <u>three</u> men in one year.	E III 15 450 38
However, I think it answered so <u>far</u> as to tempt one to go	E III 16 454 18
you know, quite the same party, not <u>one</u> exception."	E III 16 455 18
Weston and Cole will be there too; but one is apt to speak	E III 16 456 27
he returned, that he should certainly be at home till one."	E III 16 457 38
The very last person whom one should expect to be	E III 16 458 42
home; and Mrs. Weston--no one could doubt that a daughter	E III 17 461 1
be quite a pity that any one who so well knew how to teach,	E III 17 461 1
have you said to me, with one of your saucy looks--'Mr.	E III 17 462 9
was giving you two bad feelings instead of one."	E III 17 462 9
"I remember once calling you 'George,' in one of my	E III 17 462 12
Emma grieved that she could not be more openly just to one	E III 17 463 15
I am amused by one part of John's letter--did you notice	E III 17 465 25
I remember one evening the poor boys saying, 'uncle seems	E III 17 465 27
and secondly, as a good one--well aware of the nearly	E III 17 467 30
a connexion, and in one respect, one point of the highest	E III 17 467 31
and in one respect, one point of the highest importance,	E III 17 467 31
one real, rational difficulty to oppose or delay it.	E III 17 468 31
as these, was one of the happiest women in the world.	E III 17 468 32
One set might recommend their all removing to Donwell, and	E III 17 468 36
objection raised, except in one habitation, the vicarage.--	E III 17 468 36
It was an alarming change; and Emma was thinking of it one	E III 18 470 1
"There is one subject," he replied, "I have but one, on	E III 18 470 8
Time, you may be very sure, will make one or the other of	E III 18 471 16
and Henry; and that at one time they were in such a crowd,	E III 18 472 20
He knew of no one but Mrs. Goddard to whom he could apply	E III 18 474 30
kind forgiving message in one of Mrs. Weston's letters.	E III 18 476 46
	47
One cannot call her fair.	E III 18 478 61
an opportunity of being one hour alone with Harriet, than	E III 19 481 1
The intermediate month was the one fixed on, as far as	E III 19 483 8
Mrs. Weston's poultry-house was robbed one night of all	E III 19 483 10
consolation in a distressed one; there his faculties were	P III 1 3 1
His good looks and his rank had one fair claim on his	P III 1 4 6
She had, however, one very intimate friend, a sensible,	P III 1 5 6
friends; and one remained a widower, the other a widow.	P III 1 5 7
father, (having met with one or two private	P III 1 5 8
For one daughter, his eldest, he would really have given	P III 1 5 8
none: Elizabeth would, one day or other, marry suitably.	P III 1 6 10
back of youth; and in one of their spring excursions to	P III 1 7 14
uneventful residence in one country circle, to fill the	P III 1 9 18
to you that there is any one article in which we can	P III 1 9 19
should be struck out by one or the other to remove their	P III 1 10 21
think that the sacrifice of one pair of horses would be	P III 2 13 5
much strengthened by one part, and a very material part of	P III 2 15 13
Lady Russell had another excellent one at hand, for being	P III 2 15 15
affection and confidence on one who ought to have been	P III 2 16 16
Walter," said Mr. Shepherd one morning at Kellynch Hall,	P III 3 17 1
tenants as any set of people one should meet with.	P III 3 17 4
the actions and designs of one part of the world from the	P III 3 17 4
insulted by the rise of one whose father, his father might	P III 3 19 16
One day last spring, in town, I was in company with two	P III 3 19 16
about a trespass of one of his neighbours; farmer's man	P III 3 23 28
One wonders how the names of many of our nobility become	P III 3 23 33
with an evil eye on any one intending to inhabit that	P III 3 24 35
of exquisite felicity followed, and but a short one.--	P III 4 26 2
pardonable pride, received it as a most unfortunate one.	P III 4 26 2
any representations from one who had almost a mother's	P III 4 27 3
though unsoftened by one kind word or look on the part of	P III 4 27 5
change of place, (except in one visit to Bath soon after	P III 4 28 7
No one had ever come within the Kellynch circle, who could	P III 4 28 7
or its change, on the one leading point of Anne's conduct,	P III 4 29 8
startled by the wrong of one part of the Kellynch-Hall	P III 5 34 11
One would imagine you had never heard my father speak of	P III 5 35 14
an agreeable manner might not gradually reconcile one to."	P III 5 35 15
long; but he has never come back, and now it is almost one.	P III 5 37 25
I have not seen one of them to-day, except Mr. Musgrove,	P III 5 38 29
told him how ill I was, not one of them have been near me.	P III 5 38 29
And one thing I have had to do, Mary, of a more trying	P III 5 39 34
me one word about our dinner at the Pooles yesterday."	P III 5 39 35
One always knows beforehand what the dinner will be, and	P III 5 39 39
learn that a removal from one set of people to another,	P III 6 42 1
having one such truly sympathising friend as Lady Russell.	P III 6 42 2
unworthy member of the one she was now transplanted into.--	P III 6 43 3
One of the least agreeable circumstances of her residence	P III 6 44 7
bad to have children with one, that one is obliged to be	P III 6 45 8
children with one, that one is obliged to be checking	P III 6 45 8
don't do that;'--or that one can only keep in tolerable	P III 6 45 8
And one day, when Anne was walking with only the Miss	P III 6 46 10
only the Miss Musgroves, one of them, after talking of	P III 6 46 10
no new sensation: excepting one short period of her life,	P III 6 47 13
Her manners were open, easy, and decided, like one who had	P III 6 48 18
poor Richard's captain, at one time, I do not know when or	P III 6 50 27
with her son, seemed one of those extraordinary bursts of	P III 6 51 31
She found, however, that it was one to which she must	P III 6 52 33
and the poor suffering one to attend and soothe;--besides	P III 7 53 3
On one other question, which perhaps her utmost wisdom	P III 7 60 31
	32
found it most difficult to cease to speak to one another.	P III 8 63 3
in a small paragraph at one corner of the newspapers; and	P III 8 66 16
that she too had been one of the best friends man ever had.	P III 8 66 22
"My brother," whispered one of the girls; "mamma is	P III 8 67 26
want to be conveyed to one port or another, after our	P III 8 69 43
may be perfectly happy in one of them; and I can safely	P III 8 70 54
It was a merry, joyous party, and no one seemed in higher	P III 8 71 57
Hitherto there had been but one opinion of Captain	P III 9 73 3
A short absence from home had left his fair one unguarded	P III 9 74 4
there being no pride on one side, and no envy on the other,	P III 9 74 6
brother and sister, as to <u>which</u> was the one liked best.	P III 9 75 9
It suited Mary best to think Henrietta the one preferred,	P III 9 75 12
not be; he is the only one that could be possible; but he	P III 9 76 15
One morning, very soon after the dinner at the Musgroves,	P III 9 78 21
house; but it proved to be one much less calculated for	P III 9 79 25
door opened for him by some one without, made his	P III 9 79 28
released from him; some one was taking him from her,	P III 9 80 33
He had even refused one regular invitation to dinner; and	P III 10 82 2
One morning, about this time, Charles Musgrove and Captain	P III 10 83 3
in this manner on purpose to ask us, how can one say no?"	P III 10 83 5
This distinction appeared to increase, and there was one	P III 10 84 7
After one of the many praises of the day, which were	P III 10 84 7
	8
another path, "is not this one of the ways to Winthrop?"	P III 10 85 12
But this was one of the points on which the lady shewed	P III 10 86 17
Here is a nut," said he, catching one down from an upper	P III 10 88 26
could not endure to make a third in a one horse chaise.	P III 10 90 38
"He certainly means to have one or other of those two	P III 10 92 44
He has been running after them, too, long enough, one	P III 10 92 44
and bring us home one of these young ladies to Kellynch.	P III 10 92 46
ladies they both are; I hardly know one from the other."	P III 10 92 46
One could not be connected with better people.--	P III 10 92 47
and ordering a dinner at one of the inns, the next thing	P III 11 95 9
down to his large fishing-net at one corner of the room.	P III 11 99 18
While Captain Wentworth and Harville led the talk on one	P III 11 100 23
the tenderest songs of the one poet, and all the	P III 11 100 23
been in mourning, one should have known him by the livery."	P III 12 106 16
They ought to be setting off for Uppercross by one, and in	P III 12 107 22
"Is there no one to help me?" were the first words which	P III 12 110 35
Every one capable of thinking felt the advantage of the	P III 12 110 42
only turn his eyes from one sister, to see the other in a	P III 12 110 43
But as to the rest;--as to the others;--if one stays to	P III 12 114 61
to assist Mrs. Harville, I think it need be only one.--	P III 12 114 61
if Anne will stay, no one so proper, so capable as Anne!"	P III 12 114 61
One thing more, and all seemed arranged.	P III 12 114 64
one but Louisa, or those who were wrapt up in her welfare.	P III 12 115 66
at the substitution of one sister for the other--the	P III 12 115 68
nursery-maid of the family, one who having brought up all	P IV 1 121 3
They were wretched comforters for one another!"	P IV 1 122 5
last, the only remaining one of all that had filled and	P IV 1 123 6
could be canvassed only in one style by a couple of steady,	P IV 1 126 21
One man's ways may be as good as another's, but we all	P IV 1 127 26
one corner, and another great thing that I never go near."	P IV 1 128 28
can judge, there is not one that we like better than this.	P IV 1 128 30
out something or other in one of them which he thinks--Oh!	P IV 2 131 9
over to Kellynch one day by himself, you may depend on it.	P IV 2 131 12
He is one of the dullest young men that ever lived.	P IV 2 132 16
He has walked with me, sometimes, from one end of the	P IV 2 132 16
when one drops one's scissors, or any thing that happens.	P IV 2 132 19
that my opinion of any one could have admitted of such	P IV 2 132 20
On one side was a table, occupied by some chattering girls,	P IV 2 134 29
walked with exultation from one drawing-room to the other,	P IV 3 138 5
Mr. Elliot, had mentioned one or two things relative to	P IV 3 139 8
She could only offer one solution; it was, perhaps, for	P IV 3 140 11
time of life was another concern, and rather a fearful one.	P IV 3 140 11
He had frequently observed, as he walked, that one	P IV 3 141 13
eighty-seven women go by, one after another, without there	P IV 3 141 13
hardly one woman in a thousand could stand the test of.	P IV 3 142 13
They could think of no one else.	P IV 3 142 17
compare them in excellence to only one person's manners.	P IV 3 143 18
"The notions of a young man of one or two and twenty,"	P IV 3 144 20
There was one point which Anne, on returning to her family,	P IV 4 145 1
she was the inexcusable one, in attributing to him such	P IV 4 147 8
The Bath paper one morning announced the arrival of the	P IV 4 148 10
In one point, I am sure, my dear cousin, (he continued,	P IV 4 151 21
lower, though there was no one else in the room) in one	P IV 4 151 21
in the room) in one point, I am sure, we must feel alike.	P IV 4 151 21
had shewn her kindness in one of those periods of her life	P IV 5 152 2
possibility of moving from one to the other without	P IV 5 154 8
which there was only one servant in the house to afford,	P IV 5 154 8
Anne viewed her friend as one of those instances in which,	P IV 5 154 8
to one or two very poor families in this neighbourhood.	P IV 5 155 9
to have something that makes one know one's species better.	P IV 5 155 9
One likes to hear what is going on, to be <u>au fait</u> as to	P IV 5 155 9
rather than generosity and fortitude, that one hears of.	P IV 5 156 11
Sir Walter, Elizabeth and Mrs. Clay returned one morning	P IV 5 156 14
One of the five thousand Mr. Smiths whose names are to be	P IV 5 157 15
"No, sir, she is not one and thirty; but I do not think I	P IV 5 157 16
She had been the only one of the set absent; for Sir	P IV 5 158 21
consider it--but I think it might be a very happy one."	P IV 5 159 23
adverse to any man save one; her judgment, on a serious	P IV 5 160 26
nor could she fix on any one article of moral duty	P IV 5 160 27
(and probably not a short one) when he had been, at least,	P IV 5 161 27
of them all very intently one evening, when a thicker	P IV 6 162 1
Musgrove "have not had one dinner-party all the holidays.	P IV 6 162 7
but it so happened that one morning, about a week or ten	P IV 6 168 25
She has a blister on one of her heels, as large as a three	P IV 6 170 29
The wind blows through one of the cupboards just in the	P IV 6 170 29
She left her seat, she would go, one half of her should	P IV 7 175 6
One can guess what will happen there.	P IV 7 177 19
Anne Elliot; very pretty, when one comes to look at her.	P IV 7 177 21
service too, without robbing him of one personal grace!	P IV 7 179 28
They described the drawing-room window-curtains of one of	P IV 7 179 30
It was really expected to be a good one, and Captain	P IV 7 180 32
took their station by one of the fires in the Octagon Room.	P IV 8 181 1
eventually one of those most concerned in her recovery."	P IV 8 182 6
One does not love a place the less for having suffered in	P IV 8 184 16
and to pity every one, as being less happy than herself.	P IV 8 184 17

er sister's; the origin of one all selfish vanity, of the   P IV 8 185 20
nd look, had been such as she could see in only one light.   P IV 8 185 21
nd I do regard her as one who is too modest, for the   P IV 8 187 28
o one can withstand the charm of such a mystery.   P IV 8 187 33
nne could think of no one so likely to have spoken with   P IV 8 187 35
More air than one often sees in Bath.--   P IV 8 188 39
he seemed as if she had been one moment too late; and as   P IV 8 188 41
nne was one of the few who did not choose to move.   P IV 8 189 44
nce more, without the interchange of one friendly look.   P IV 8 189 45
ut the all was little for one who had been there, and   P IV 9 192 5
he tall Irish officer, who is talked of for one of them."   P IV 9 193 8
ot to be supposed to be paying his addresses to any one."   P IV 9 196 31
observed no one in particular."   P IV 9 197 39
She could not make a very long history, I think, of one   P IV 9 197 41
he hates to be officious, to be giving bad impressions,   P IV 9 198 53
nineteen, you know, one does not think very seriously,   P IV 9 199 55
e was then the poor one; he had chambers in the temple,   P IV 9 199 55
eriod of his life, had one object in view--to make his   P IV 9 200 59
e described one Miss Elliot, and I thought very   P IV 9 201 59
hat wild imaginations one forms, where dear self is   P IV 9 201 63
hen one lives in the world, a man or woman's marrying for   P IV 9 201 64
arrying for money is too common to strike one as it ought.   P IV 9 201 64
he letter I am looking for, was one written by Mr. Elliot   P IV 9 203 70
nd happened to be saved; why, one can hardly imagine.   P IV 9 203 70
e laws of honour, that no one ought to be judged or to   P IV 9 204 76
77
e misconceived by folly in one, and ignorance in another,   P IV 9 205 85
here was one circumstance in the history of her   P IV 9 210 98
e no longer deceived; and one of the concluding   P IV 9 211 103
n one point, her feelings were relieved by this knowledge   P IV 10 212 1
any evils, without knowing how to avert any one of them.--   P IV 10 212 1
rs. Smith had been able to tell her what no one else   P IV 10 212 1
ady Russell quite bores one with her new publications.   P IV 10 215 15
e pleasant prospects of one should not be dimming those   P IV 10 217 21
one happens only to shut the door a little hard, she   P IV 10 218 24
have a great value for benwick; and when one can but get   P IV 10 218 26
e five minutes brought a note, the next a parcel, and   P IV 10 221 32
efore he disappeared on one side, as Mrs. Clay walked   P IV 10 222 39
am not one of those who neglect the reigning power to   P IV 10 224 48
r jealous eye was satisfied in one particular.   P IV 10 226 64
mile to all; and one smile and one card more decidedly   P IV 10 226 64
mile and one card more decidedly for Captain Wentworth.   P IV 10 226 64
e day only had passed since Anne's conversation with Mrs.   P IV 11 229 1
cept by its effects in one quarter, that it became a   P IV 11 229 1
brother hayter had said one day, and what Mr. Musgrove   P IV 11 230 5
stant to give a look--one quick, conscious look at her.   P IV 11 231 10
t is not a very enviable one, you need not covet it) is   P IV 11 235 32
e revolution which one instant had made in Anne, was   P IV 11 237 41
s evidently the one which he had been folding so hastily.   P IV 11 237 41
o thought only of one sort of illness, having assured   P IV 11 238 47
mine, which you shut with one day, round Winthrop."   P IV 11 240 58
Lyme, he had received lessons of more than one sort.   P IV 11 242 62
ar, that she has not lost one charm of earlier youth: P IV 11 243 68
st, as I did; and one encouragement happened to be mine.   P IV 11 244 70
at you had refused one man at least, of better   P IV 11 244 70
d tearing her away, and one or two subsequent moments,   P IV 11 244 71
could think of you only as one who had yielded, who had   P IV 11 245 74
, who had been influenced by any one rather than by me.   P IV 11 245 74
last Anne was at home again, and happier than any one   P IV 11 245 77
was in one of these short meetings, each apparently   P IV 11 246 79
80
was, perhaps, one of those cases in which advice is   P IV 11 246 80
ve been one person more my enemy even than that lady?   P IV 11 247 82
ght to make me forgive every one sooner than myself.   P IV 11 247 84
nsciousness of right, and one independent fortune   P IV 12 248 1
e only one among them, whose opposition of feeling could   P IV 12 249 3
all the family, Mary was probably the one most   P IV 12 249 5
. Elliot withdraw; and no one of proper condition has   P IV 12 250 6
mself from being cut out by one artful woman, at least.   P IV 12 250 7
stead of depriving her of one friend, secured her two.   P IV 12 251 11
gratitude & while one or two of the men lent their help   S 1 365 1
u to send off one of these good people for the surgeon."   S 1 365 1
e of these good people can be with him in three minutes   S 1 365 1
at are printed in one week throughout the kingdom, you   S 1 366 1
epherd lives at one end, & three old women at the other."   S 1 366 1
tend a short stay there--one is never able to complete   S 1 367 1
ery five years, one hears of some new place or other   S 1 368 1
common idea--but a mistaken one.   S 1 368 1
e complete, measured mile nearer than East Bourne.   S 1 369 1
s not more good will on one side than gratitude on the   S 2 371 1
had strong reason to beleive that one family had been   S 2 372 1
at every one of them wd be benefited by the sea.--   S 2 373 1
re nearly infallible, one or the other of them being a   S 2 373 1
st as was wanted--sometimes one, sometimes the other.--   S 2 373 1
d been long limitted to one small circle; & they were   S 2 373 1
ck one daughter with them, no difficulties were started.   S 2 374 1
ughters at home, & the one, who under her mother's   S 2 374 1
e of the girls of the family to pass the winter with her.   S 3 378 1
e invitation was to one, for six months--with the   S 3 379 1
selecting the one, Lady D. had shewn the good art of   S 3 379 1
an encumbered circle--& one, who had been so low in   S 3 379 1
ther better situation!--one other hill brings us to   S 4 380 1
thout air or veiw, only one mile & 3 qrs from the   S 4 380 1
t you know, (still looking back) one loves to look at an   S 4 381 1
an old friend, at a place where one has been happy.--   S 4 381 1
remember seeing Mrs Hillier after one of those dreadful   S 4 381 1
ken totally unawares, by one of those dreadful Currents   S 4 381 1
e whole summer, excepting one family of children who   S 4 383 1
ery building, excepting one short row of smart-looking   S 4 384 1
t here is a letter from one of my sisters.   S 5 385 1
u two large families, one a rich West Indian from Surry,   S 5 387 1
o large families--one, for prospect house probably, the   S 5 388 1
ading one of her own novels, for want of employment.--   S 6 389 1
one side it seemed protecting kindness, on the other   S 6 392 1
d never seen one neither, he wd have been alive now.--   S 6 394 1
n fees, one after another, did the man take who sent him   S 6 394 1
ving the idea of one who felt her consequence with pride   S 7 394 1
rrace, & there, seated on one of the two green benches   S 7 395 1
e end of the bench, & Sir Edw: & Miss B. at the other.--   S 7 395 1
! there is pathos to madden one!--   S 7 397 1
ough of Sir Edw: for one morng, & very gladly accepted   S 7 398 1
king hold of Charlotte's arm with the ease of one who   S 7 399 1
I can learn, it is not one in an hundred of them that   S 7 401 1
come & take one of these lodgings for a fortnight.--   S 7 402 1
d confined very much to one spot had read more   S 8 404 1
e day soon after Charlotte's arrival at Sanditon, she   S 9 406 1
ere was but one thing for me to do.--   S 9 408 1
e sees clearly enough by all this, the sort of woman Mrs   S 9 409 1
shall take only one however, & that, but for a week   S 9 410 1
got that man a hare from one of Sidney's friends--and he   S 9 412 1
ey were in one of the terrace houses--& she found them   S 10 413 1
ss P-- whom, remembering the three teeth drawn in one   S 10 413 1
o or three times from one, out of the several Phials   S 10 413 1
the drops & the salts by means of one or the other.   S 10 413 1
had merely walked from one house to the other as nimbly   S 10 414 1
the fire till he had cooked up a very good one.--   S 10 414 1
e shd not have one at home, said he, but the sea air is   S 10 415 1
mpany, Miss P. drinking one sort of Herb-Tea & Miss   S 10 416 1
one particular however, she soon found that he had   S 10 418 1
on two dishes of strong green tea in one eveng?--   S 10 418 1
w, if I were to swallow only one such dish--what do you   S 10 418 1
comodation & comfort of one of the young ladies under   S 10 419 1
Surry & the family from Camberwell were one & the same.--   S 11 420 1
be met with, in at least one family out of three,   S 11 421 1
There, with the hire of a harp for one, & the purchase of   S 11 421 1
The corner house of the terrace was the one in which Miss   S 11 422 1
visitors at Sanditon, & on one side, whatever might be   S 11 422 1
Susan is to have Leaches at one oclock--which will be a   S 12 424 1
gig to the Pheaton,--from one horse to 4; & just as they   S 12 425 1
grounds or paddock, so near one of its Boundaries, that an   S 12 426 1
vacant spaces--& through one of these, Charlotte as soon   S 12 426 1
of Sir H. Denham--and that one among many miniatures in   S 12 427 1

ONE'S (52)

I have admitted no one's attentions but Manwaring's, I   LS 2 244 1
pre-determined to dislike, acknowledge one's superiority.   LS 7 254 3
not actually pass under one's own observation; and as for   NA I 14 109 23
for two or three years of one's life, for the sake of   NA I 14 110 27
One's eyes must be somewhere, and you know what a foolish   NA II 3 143 4
I never was so deceived in any one's character in my life   NA II 10 206 32
She trembled a little at the idea of any one's approaching   NA II 13 223 9
"to have those kind of yearly drains on one's income.   SS I 2 11 21
One's fortune, as your mother justly says, is not one's   SS I 2 11 21
fortune, as your mother justly says, is not one's own.   SS I 2 11 21
by no means desirable: it takes away one's independence."   SS I 2 11 21
to order, wondered how any one's attention could be   SS I 7 35 9
intended; and 'setting one's cap at a man,' or 'making a   SS I 9 45 30
objections against any one's conduct on so illiberal a   SS I 15 81 43
It makes one detest all one's acquaintance.   SS I 20 111 8
it by slight appearances, one's happiness must in some   SS II 14 248 6
all that can be said of one's happiness depending entirely   SS III 1 263 27
entail away an estate from one's own daughters I cannot   PP I 23 130 24
It is such a spur to one's genius, such an opening for wit   PP II 17 225 17
ecstacy, calling for every one's congratulations, and   PP II 18 230 12
as this, one cannot see too little of one's neighbours.   PP III 5 293 67
her reflections, by some one's approach; and before she   PP III 10 327 4
there is nothing so bad as parting with one's friends.   PP III 11 330 10
had in a manner taken into one's own hands; and I am sure   MP I 1 6 6
To be neglected before one's time, must be very vexatious.   MP I 5 51 41
There can be no comparison as to one's view of the country.   MP I 8 78 15
with one's ideas of what such a household should be!   MP I 9 86 12
nothing in the course of one's duties so fatiguing as what   MP I 9 95 71
room to another--straining one's eyes and one's attention--   MP I 9 95 71
one's eyes and one's attention--hearing what one does not   MP I 9 95 71
unabated eagerness, every one's inclination increasing by   MP I 13 124 13
even without her being wanted for any one's convenience.   MP II 4 205 1
One cannot fix one's eyes on the commonest natural   MP II 4 209 16
in a degree," said Edmund, "from one's earliest years.   MP III 3 338 14
it in one's power to pay off the debts of one's sex!   MP III 5 363 22
And to be having any one's improvement in view in her   MP III 9 398 9
silly things, and break up one's family circle grievously."   E I 1 13 45
not mean that--as you say, one's mind ought to be quite   E I 7 52 20
To give up one's child!   E I 11 96 25
sir, than sitting at one's ease to be entertained a whole   E II 3 170 2
of elegant creature that one cannot keep one's eyes from.   E II 3 171 14
15
pleasure of coming in upon one's friends before the look-   E II 5 190 24
the country which none but one's own country gives, and   E II 5 191 26
"One would rather have a stranger preferred than one's   E II 6 202 33
What a pleasure it is to send one's carriage for a friend!-   E III 2 321 17
Delightful to gather for one's self--the only way of   E III 6 358 35
so very uncomfortable, not having a carriage of one's own.   P III 5 39 39
impossible it is, with all one's efforts, and all one's   P III 8 68 35
all one's efforts, and all one's sacrifices, to make the   P III 8 68 35
"Uppercross,--the necessity of some one's going to   P III 12 113 57
when one drops one's scissors, or any thing that happens.   P IV 2 132 19
to have something that makes one know one's species better.   P IV 5 155 9

ONE-AND-TWENTY (4)

want of employment at forty or fifty than one-and-twenty.   E I 10 85 21
does not the lapse of one-and-twenty years bring our   E I 12 99 7
She had long resolved that one-and-twenty should be the   E II 2 165 8
she had resolved at one-and-twenty to complete the   E II 2 165 8

ONES (25)

& on Thursday next, we & our little ones will be with you.   LS 41 310 2
very kind to the little ones, with few interruptions of   NA I 1 14 1
and teaching the little ones, that her elder daughters   NA I 1 15 3
beauty, and the younger ones, by pretending to be as   NA I 4 34 8
The embraces, tears, and promises of the parting fair ones   NA II 4 153 31
it was impossible, with calm ones it could have no merit.   SS I 19 104 11
Why--he is quite one of the great & grand ones;--did not   W 342 19
The attention of the younger ones was then no longer to be   PP I 15 72 7
that private balls are much pleasanter than public ones.--   PP I 18 91 11
Stupid men are the only ones worth knowing, after all."   PP II 4 154 19
The younger ones out before the elder are married!--   PP II 6 165 34
As soon as all had ate, and the elder ones paid, the   PP II 16 220 16
You young ones do not remember much about it, perhaps.   MP I 6 54 9
be one steady head to superintend so many young ones.   MP I 15 141 22
the noisy ones gone, your brother and mine and myself.   MP II 11 288 30
best of the three younger ones was gone in him; Tom and   MP III 8 390 8
learn to prefer soft light eyes to sparkling dark ones.--   MP III 17 470 27
enjoyment of her little ones, and for their having   E I 11 92 3
He will be so pleased to see my little ones."   E I 12 101 26
out, till they are quite as unmanageable as great ones.   E I 18 147 19
I hope whenever poor Isabella's little ones have the   E II 11 253 38
set off handsome features, but can never alter plain ones.   P III 5 35 16
at last: I believe no "children ever had such long ones.   P IV 6 163 7
"And I am sure they must be very extraordinary ones.--said   S 5 388 1
The Denhams were the only ones to excite particular   S 7 394 1

ONESELF (6)

which put one in good humour with oneself & all the world.   LS 10 258 3
so delightful to have an evening now and then to oneself.   NA I 11 90 63
them, without giving oneself time to deliberate and judge."   SS I 17 93 37
hand, to do every thing better than one does oneself!--   E II 6 202 33
"Not till the reserve ceases towards oneself; and then the   E II 6 203 41
Oh Lord! there was no getting away from oneself.   P IV 1 128 28

OPEN (187)

Were there another place in England open to me, I would   LS 2 246 1
He desires me to tell you that the present open weather   LS 8 254 1
Manwaring, & with such an open, goodhumoured countenance   LS 38 307 3
disposition cheerful and open, without conceit or   NA I 2 18 1
Are you fond of an open carriage, Miss Morland?"   NA I 7 47 21
shy, nor affectedly open; and she seemed capable of being   NA I 8 56 11
of there being two open carriages at the door, in the   NA I 9 61 1
approach of the same two open carriages, containing the   NA I 11 84 17
"Make haste! make haste!" as he threw open the door--" put   NA I 11 84 18
still remaining at the open door, she used only the   NA I 13 102 25
had reduced her to open the door of the apartment herself.   NA I 13 102 27
Young men and women driving about the country in open   NA I 13 104 31
Open carriages are nasty things.   NA I 13 104 32
I hate an open carriage myself."   NA I 13 104 32
I know I shall never have courage to open the letter.   NA I 15 120 22
The fairness of your friend was an open attraction; her   NA II 1 133 34
not for the world would I pain it by open praise.   NA II 2 139 7
Their hearts are open to each other, as neither heart can   NA II 4 152 28
respecting young men's open carriages, made her blush at   NA II 5 156 5
chest which no efforts can open, and over the fire-place   NA II 5 158 17
an inner compartment will open--a roll of paper appears:--   NA II 5 160 21
worst of it is that its weight makes it difficult to open.   NA II 6 165 4
victory, and having thrown open each folding door, the   NA II 6 168 10
but at length it did open; and not vain, as hitherto, was   NA II 6 169 11
of unlocking a cabinet, the key of which was open to all!   NA II 7 173 2
Why the locks should have been so difficult to open   NA II 7 173 4
advancing, had thrown open, and passed through, and seemed   NA II 8 185 6
but she had no inclination to open either.   NA II 9 194 6
and where roads and newspapers lay every thing open?   NA II 9 197 29

Open, candid, artless, guileless, with affections strong NA II 10 206 31
being ordered to acquiesce in them, had been open and bold. NA II 15 247 15
was consequently open to every greedy speculation. NA II 16 251 6
gave every indication of an open affectionate heart. SS I 3 15 6
of which were open downs, the others cultivated and woody. SS I 6 28 3
of which had been left open by Margaret, he bore her SS I 9 42 8
of decorum; I have been open and sincere where I ought to SS I 10 48 5
lively spirits, and open, affectionate manners. SS I 10 48 7
were to be taken, open carriages only to be employed, and SS I 12 62 28
and as we went in an open carriage, it was impossible to SS I 13 68 70
seemed more than usually open to every feeling of SS I 14 72 6
been attempted; all has been uniformly open and unreserved. SS I 15 80 42
In such a case, a plain and open avowal of his SS I 15 81 43
was less wild and more open, a long stretch of the road SS I 16 85 15
she heard the parlour door open, and , turning round, was SS I 18 96 2
the turf, obliged her to open the casement to speak to him, SS I 19 105 13
I see her instrument is open." SS I 19 105 18
at all events to open the eyes of her sister; should it be SS II 4 159 1
"If this open weather holds much longer," said Mrs. SS II 5 167 1
The triumph of seeing me so may be open to all the world. SS II 7 189 52
me of Mr. Willoughby, that will open his character farther. SS II 9 204 19
by the most open and most frequent confession of them. SS II 10 212 1
by the door's being thrown open, the servant's announcing SS II 13 240 18
almost easy, and almost open; and another struggle, SS II 13 241 20
my love and esteem, must submit to my open commendation." SS II 13 244 40
the library may be open for tea and other refreshments; SS II 14 252 18
were effects that laid open the probability of greater. SS II 14 254 27
his nature was calm, not open to provocation, and he never SS III 1 267 44
of importance, it had its open shrubbery, and closer wood SS III 6 302 7
other particular, his open pleasure in meeting her after SS III 6 305 16
apology, for the past; to open my whole heart to you, and SS III 8 319 23
still affectionate, open, artless, confiding--everything SS III 8 327 55
open and honest, and a feeling, affectionate temper. SS III 8 331 70
uncommon attraction, that open, affectionate, and lively SS III 9 333 2
Elinor tenderly invited her to be open. SS III 10 344 16
the simple truth, and lay open such facts as were really SS III 11 349 2
to be open, she sat down again and talked of the weather. SS III 12 359 12
His heart was now open to Elinor, all its weaknesses, all SS III 13 362 4
discovery of it laid him open to his mother's anger, had SS III 13 367 21
family, had made her more open to disagreeable impressions W 322 3
eye, a sweet smile, & an open countenance, gave beauty to W 328 9
to open a door which was never shut, made their appearance. W 329 9
hold the parlour door open for Ld Osborne & Tom Musgrave.-- W 344 21
of all that must be open to the ridicule of richer people W 345 21
than the other was thrown open, & he beheld a circle of W 355 28
Fine open weather Miss Emma!-- W 357 28
"I am going to open the instrument, Eliza, and you know PP I 6 24 21
and never open their mouths, quite mistake the matter." PP I 9 44 27
and Mr. Hurst soon found even his open petition rejected. PP I 11 54 3
no sooner saw Elizabeth open the door and with quick step PP I 20 110 1
They are young in the ways of the world, and not yet open PP II 3 150 29
Catherine, was along the open grove which edged that side PP II 7 169 5
composure, and would not open his lips, till he believed PP II 11 190 8
him the next moment open the front door and quit the house. PP II 11 193 30
Her look and manners were open, cheerful and engaging as PP II 12 197 5
chosen it with her eyes open; and though evidently PP II 15 216 7
When all of the house that was open to general inspection PP III 1 251 49
had received directions to open all that came for him in PP III 6 296 10
the door was thrown open, and she ran into the room. PP III 9 315 3
was rather thin, but however the little theatre was open. PP III 9 319 25
beneath him, to lay his private actions open to the world. PP III 10 322 2
till the door was thrown open, and their visitor entered. PP III 14 351 1
her affection, she now saw the object of open pleasantry. PP III 19 388 61
and the doors were thrown open to admit them through one MP I 9 84 1
outward door, temptingly open on a flight of steps which MP I 9 89 32
was standing at an open window with Edmund and Fanny MP I 11 108 4
In a general light, private theatricals are open to some MP I 13 125 17
table, with the play open before them, and were just MP I 15 142 25
of the room was thrown open, and Julia appearing at it, MP I 18 172 33
entreated her to be open and sincere, and assured her that MP II 3 200 21
therefore gave his decided open advice that the invitation MP II 4 215 47
continuance of the open weather, but her answers were as MP II 5 223 48
ago, but a young man of an open, pleasant countenance, and MP II 6 233 16
Edmund, who was holding open the door, said as she passed MP II 10 272 4
was to lead the way and open the ball; an idea that had MP II 10 275 11
seemed so little open to serious impressions, even where MP II 13 305 26
with his niece, and to shew no open interference. MP III 2 330 14
No man of any brain can open at a good part of one of his MP III 3 338 13
are in half the books we open, and we all talk Shakespeare, MP III 3 338 14
of service to her, whom else had she to open her heart to? MP III 4 345 4
I was playing the fool with my eyes open." MP III 4 350 26
one evil, laying herself open to another, and to have Miss MP III 4 354 47
circumstances which may open our hearts to each other MP III 5 364 30
door in the house was open, could be plainly distinguished MP III 7 382 27
Susan had an open, sensible countenance; she was like MP III 7 384 33
Then she will be in beauty, for she will open one of the MP III 9 394 1
Her temper was open. MP III 9 397 8
the open air, and there was not a single oath to be heard. MP III 10 402 12
that he was sufficiently open to the charms of nature, and MP III 11 409 7
He is blinded, and nothing will open his eyes, nothing can, MP III 13 424 4
I had gone a few steps, Fanny, when I heard the door open MP III 16 459 30
regular features, open countenance, with a complexion! Oh! E I 5 39 20
I will fetch your great coat and open the garden door for E I 8 58 8
He always speaks to the purpose; open, straight forward, E I 8 59 27
have been very kind to open my eyes; but at present I only E I 8 66 54
and then seeing the book open on the table, took it up, E I 9 82 81
hand and mind will be as open to me then, as they are now; E I 10 85 21
the door between them was open, and Emma passed into it E I 10 89 38
A fine open sea, he says, and very pure air. E I 12 106 56
to open to sensations of softened pain and brighter hope. E I 16 137 13
open, and Miss Bates and Miss Fairfax walked into the room. E II 3 172 22
23
sashed windows which were open to look in and contemplate E II 6 197 5
He appeared to have a very open temper--certainly a very E II 7 205 2
I will not open the window here; it would give you all E II 10 243 31
you know the door was open, and the window was open, and E II 10 245 54
and the window was open, and Mr. Knightley spoke loud. E II 10 245 54
this evening, and keeping them open very inconsiderately. E II 11 249 11
We shall have no occasion to open the windows at all--not E II 11 251 29
'Open the windows!--but surely, Mr. Churchill, nobody E II 11 251 30
Dancing with open windows!-- E II 11 252 30
It made her animated--open hearted--she voluntarily said;-- E II 12 258 4
5
Warmth and tenderness of heart, with an affectionate, open E II 13 269 16
they dared not shew in open disrespect to her, found a E II 15 282 3
She has not the open temper which a man would wish for in E II 15 288 36
I think, than she used to be--and I love an open temper. E II 15 289 40
Her congratulations were warm and open; but Emma could not E II 17 304 28
my son's hand, presumed to open it--though it was not E II 18 305 5
She liked his open manners, but a little less of open- E III 2 320 4
as had been, such an open and frequent discussion of hopes E III 4 341 34
"Never, never!"--she cried with a most open eagerness--" E III 5 350 35
They were laying themselves open to that very phrase--and E III 7 368 3
things as soon as ever I open my mouth, shan't I?--(E III 7 370 24
in her general conduct, be open to any severe reproach. E III 8 377 1
This discovery laid many smaller matters open. E III 11 403 2
Weston, must necessarily open the cause; but when these E III 12 418 5
which may well lay me open to unpleasant conjectures, but E III 13 426 15
hope, lay me open to reprehension, excepting on one point. E III 14 438 8
how much I love every thing that is decided and open!-- E III 16 460 57
It was all right, all open, all equal. E III 17 468 31
her father had left it open on the table near her, had she P III 1 7 12
visit to London, sensibly open to all the injustice and P III 2 16 1
The park would be open to him of course, and few navy P III 3 18
good humour, such an open, trusting liberality on the P III 5 32
Her manners were open, easy, and decided, like one who had P III 6 48 1
open look, in no respect lessening his personal advantages. P III 7 61 3
have been no two hearts so open, no tastes so similar, no P III 8 63
Miss Musgroves could be as open as they were sincere, in P III 8 66 1
not but hear what followed, for the parlour door was open. P III 12 114 6
too, as Elizabeth threw open the folding-doors, and walked P IV 3 138
Every body's heart is open, you know, when they have P IV 5 155
him at liberty to exert his most open powers of pleasing. P IV 5 159 2
was rational, discreet, polished,--but he was not open. P IV 5 161 2
"I kept my letter open, that I might send you word how " P IV 6 164
she, "with their mouths open to catch the music; like P IV 9 193
He seems to have a calm, decided temper, not at all open P IV 9 196 3
purse was open to him; I know that he often assisted him." P IV 9 199 5
moments, that no flagrant open crime could have been worse. P IV 9 210 9
and the door was thrown open for Sir Walter and Miss P IV 10 226 6
that he might have been open to the suspicion of S 1 364
& soften Lady D--who wd enlarge her mind & open her hand.-- S 3 379
an open country ever experiences in the heaviest gale.-- S 4 381
open down where the new Buildgs might soon be looked for. S 4 382
Now Mary, (smiling at his wife)--before I open it, what S 5 385
saw that it was laying her open to suspicion by Lady D's S 7 400
only was there no open window, but the sopha & the table, S 10 413
fond of standing at an open window when there is no wind-- S 10 415
to close the blinds, or open the blinds, to arrange a S 11 422
whole field open before them--a steep bank & pales never S 12 427

OPEN-HEARTED (4)

"A straight-forward, open-hearted man, like weston, and a E I 1 13 4
or the substance of it, from the open-hearted Mr. Weston.-- E I 14 119
She prized the frank, the open-hearted, the eager P IV 5 161 2
in the same style of open-hearted communication--minutiae P IV 11 230

OPEN-HEARTEDNESS (1)

open-heartedness would have made him a higher character.-- E III 2 320

OPENED (80)

roused Catherine; and she opened her eyes, wondering that NA II 7 172
doors, that were neither opened nor explained to her;--by NA II 8 183
At that instant a door underneath was hastily opened; some NA II 9 194
been, had more thoroughly opened her eyes to the NA II 10 199
She opened it; it was from Oxford; and to this purpose:-- " NA II 10 202
the book he had just opened; "if I had suspected the NA II 10 204 1
she stepped quietly forward, and opened the door. NA II 13 223
happiness, scarcely opened her lips, dismissed them to the NA II 15 243 1
Willoughby opened the piano-forte, and asked Marianne to SS I 12 62 2
till the door was opened before she told her story. SS I 19 106 2
He immediately went into the passage, opened the front SS I 19 108 3
understanding, must have opened his eyes to her defects of SS II 1 140
borne many seconds, she opened the door, advanced a few SS II 4 161
opened the door and walked in with a look of real concern. SS II 8 192
and opened a window-shutter, to be satisfied of the truth. SS III 7 316 2
she opened the letter directly, and read its contents. SS III 8 328 6
"He opened his whole heart to me yesterday as we travelled. SS III 9 336 1
Though his eyes had been long opened, even before his SS III 13 366 2
The door will be opened by a man in livery with a powder'd W 322
Elizth as she opened the door of the spare bedchamber.-- W 351 2
The door opened, & displayed Tom Musgrave in the wrap of a W 355 2
Mr. Philips visited them all, and this opened to his PP I 7 28
and the piano forte was opened, and Darcy, after a few PP I 11 58 3
Lydia gaped as he opened the volume, and before he had, PP I 14 68 1
1
Mrs. Hurst and her sister scarcely opened their mouths PP I 18 102 7
The next day opened a new scene at Longbourn. PP I 19 104
it came from Netherfield, and was opened immediately. PP I 21 116
She opened the door, and met Maria in the landing place, PP II 5 158 1
1
questions, when the door opened, and to her very great PP II 9 177
curiosity, Elizabeth opened the letter, and to her still PP II 12 196
preceding day, opened to them a new idea on the business. PP III 2 260
door, it was opened by a servant, and Mr. Darcy appeared. PP III 4 276
"When my eyes were opened to his real character.--Oh! had PP III 4 277 1
gained in austerity; and he scarcely opened his lips. PP III 9 315
relieved, and her mind opened again to the agitation of PP III 11 331 1
In a few minutes, Mrs. Bennet half opened the door and PP III 13 345 1
1
"Where is your sister?" said he hastily, as he opened the PP III 13 347 3
As they passed through the hall, Lady Catherine opened the PP III 14 352 1
At night she opened her heart to Jane. PP III 17 372
to the door in the middle which opened to the wilderness. MP I 9 91 3
Julia, who had scarcely opened her lips before, observed MP I 15 148 6
and enjoyment, came; and opened with more kindness to MP II 9 265 2
She opened her note immediately, glad to have any thing to MP II 13 303 1
It was indeed Sir Thomas, who opened the door, and asked MP III 1 312
astonishment when he opened the door at seeing me here! MP III 5 360 1
of enjoyment so suddenly opened, she could speak more MP III 6 369 1
letter from his sister, opened and read by her, on another MP III 12 415
As she opened and saw its length she prepared herself for MP III 13 420
them; and before she had opened the letter, the MP III 15 437
Had he been alone with her, his heart must have opened in MP III 15 445 3
at hand the heart must be opened, and every thing told--no MP III 16 453 1
My eyes are opened." MP III 16 456 2
the weather, and opened on them all with the information E I 15 125
She often says, when the letter is first opened, 'well, E II 1 157 1
She opened the parlour door, and saw two gentlemen sitting E II 5 190 2
Miss Bates had just done as Patty opened the door; and her E II 9 239 5
Mrs. Elton, and her remonstrances now opened upon Jane. E II 16 295 2
"And so you absolutely opened what was directed to her! Oh! E II 18 305
As the door opened she was heard, "so very obliging of you! E III 2 322 1
1
It seemed as if her eyes were suddenly opened, and she E III 3 332
the great iron sweepgate opened, and two persons entered E III 3 332
box, which Harriet opened: it was well lined with the E III 4 338
and hopes, and connivance, June opened upon Hartfield. E III 5 343
closing, while Harriet's opened, and whose engagements now E III 9 389 1
The superior hopes which gradually opened were so much the E III 13 432 4
She opened the packet; it was too surely so;--a note from E III 14 436
conclude, immediately opened to me the happiest prospects, E III 14 440
so, than when Emma first opened the affair to her; but she E III 17 467 3
favourite volume always opened: "Elliot of Kellynch- P III 1 3
old, having got the door opened for him by some one P III 9 79 2
Louisa had once opened her eyes, but soon closed them P III 12 112 5
But hardly were they so settled, when the door opened P IV 8 181
As she ceased, the entrance door opened again, and the P IV 8 184 1
"Did you observe the woman who opened the door to you, P IV 9 197 3
The circumstance, probably, which first opened your eyes P IV 9 201 6
mind which could not be opened to Lady Russell, in that P IV 10 212
and I do not think I ever opened a book in my life which P IV 11 234 2
were heard returning; the door opened; it was himself. P IV 11 236 4
but the door was not opened, when the other crossed the S 9 406
Mrs G.--; she had also opened so many Treaties with cooks, S 10 414

OPENHEARTED (2)

Having learnt enough in the meanwhile from her openhearted LS 42 311
told, for he was very openhearted;--& where he might be S 2 371

OPENING (65)

The poor girl sat all this time without opening her lips; LS 20 276
Then, opening the first door before her, which happened to NA I 13 102 2
it so striking an object from almost every opening in Bath. NA I 14 106
inspection, and on opening it, a door will appear--which NA II 5 159 1
a few efforts, succeed in opening,--and, with your lamp in NA II 5 159 1
Elinor, who foresaw a fairer opening for the point she had SS II 1 143

er sister was concerned, impatiently expected its opening. SS II 5 172 40
o their room, where, on opening the door, she saw SS II 7 182 12
s your loss such as leaves no opening for consolation? SS II 7 186 29
s soon as the smallest opening was given for their SS III 14 375 10
pproach, who half opening the door & putting in her head, W 346 21
o her for half an hour without once opening his lips." PP I 5 19 10
osings, afforded by an opening in the trees that bordered PP II 5 156 4
lizabeth was ready to speak whenever there was an opening, PP II 6 163 14
ithin view of the lodges opening into Hunsford lane, in PP II 7 170 7
inutes together without opening his lips; and when he did PP II 9 180 29
: is such a spur to one's genius, such an opening for wit PP II 17 225 17
n spots where the opening of the trees gave the eye power PP III 1 253 57
:s windows opening to the ground, admitted a most PP III 3 267 2
eized the other, and opening it with the utmost PP III 4 274 4
f opening her eyes to his character never occurred to me. PP III 5 285 16
n opening the door, she perceived her sister and Bingley PP III 13 346 22
here was one part especially, the opening of it, which I PP III 16 368 20
was not in a humour to wait for any opening of your's. PP III 18 381 14
rembled at my uncle's opening his lips if horses were MP I 3 27 36
own to the ground, and opening on a little lawn, MP I 7 65 13
ow does Lord Macartney go on?--(opening a volume on the MP I 16 156 27
art I mean?" continued Miss Crawford, opening her book. MP I 18 168 19
ounds of opening doors and passing footsteps. MP II 1 175 1
ommunication, and opening it, found himself on the stage MP II 1 182 22
oon afterwards, just opening the door, said, "Fanny, at MP II 5 221 35
ntent upon opening the proper doors could be called such. MP II 6 233 15
nd friend, who was opening all his heart to her, telling MP II 6 234 18
maller treasures; but on opening the door, what was her MP II 9 261 1
o be opening the ball--and with Mr. Crawford too! MP II 10 276 12
t for comfortable use; opening the door, however, with a MP III 5 357 6
nd while William was opening the chaise door himself, MP III 7 377 7
he next opening of the door brought something more MP III 7 383 32
nd it was the means of opening Susan's heart to her, and MP III 9 397 7
er aunt's garden, to the opening of leaves of her uncle's MP III 14 432 9
ep she had taken, as opening the worst probabilities of MP III 16 452 13
he opening was alarming. MP III 16 454 18
nce it had, by an opening undesigned and unmerited, led MP III 17 467 19
ay in London, which afforded him a favourable opening. E I 2 16 5
nd gone away; and on opening this parcel, she had E I 7 50 1
ere was a dangerous opening. E I 12 105 50
asses, and wrapped herself up, without opening her lips. E I 13 114 27
he had not even a share in his opening compliments.-- E I 17 140 3
n general were such as belong to an opening acquaintance. E II 5 191 27
he still spoke, and opening the casement there, E II 10 243 32
e has been opening doors very often this evening, and E II 11 249 11
s that dreadful habit of opening the windows, letting in E II 11 251 29
body would think of opening the windows at Randalls. E II 11 251 30
: in his way, and had taken the liberty of opening it. E II 17 303 24
mind like her's, once opening to suspicion, made rapid E III 11 407 32
he allowed him an opening, to soothe or to counsel her.-- E III 13 432 40
must have suffered in opening the cause to him, for my E III 14 443 8
ne complimentary opening:--but it is his way. E III 15 445 7
irteen winters' revolving frosts had seen her opening P III 1 7 12
he inconvenience of its opening as it did, so long!-- P IV 1 127 28
he concert being just opening, she must consent for a P IV 8 186 22
heir last meeting had been most important in opening his P IV 10 221 32
putting out the fire, opening the window, & disposing S 10 413 1
the delight of opening the first Trenches of an S 10 414 1
and if you should find a favourable opening my love, said S 12 423 1
INGS (2)
me of the crowd, gave greater openings for her charms. NA I 2 23 27
ssage, more numerous openings, and symptoms of a winding NA II 8 185 5
LY (33)
ow them too; and on her openly fearing that she might NA I 10 80 61
his was the first time of her brother's openly siding NA I 13 99 4
at even laughed openly at Henry for finding it possible. NA II 1 131 15
he only wished that it were less openly shewn; and once SS I 11 53 2
ay they should not openly acknowledge to her mother and SS I 14 71 3
after all that has openly passed between them, you can SS I 15 80 38
hen alluded to, or even openly mentioned by Sir John. SS I 21 126 41
ecrecy intended, as they openly correspond, and their SS II 5 173 42
he next morning more openly, for at her particular desire, SS II 13 238 2
enly shewing that I was very unhappy."-- SS III 1 264 29
ligation to her, and openly declared that no exertion SS III 5 293 2
variably paid her, and openly assure her of an affection SS III 8 321 34
he change was openly spoken in such a genuine, flowing, SS III 13 361 3
nd always openly acknowledged, to be a favourite child. SS III 14 377 11
ady Lucas) freely, openly, and of nothing else but of PP I 18 98 63
ose wishes, however openly or artfully spoken, could PP I 21 120 28
om him, was now openly acknowledged and publicly PP II 1 138 30
; and, therefore, I am not afraid of speaking openly. PP II 3 144 2
he feeling, was more openly acknowledged, for she did not PP II 8 172 3
4
speak openly to her aunt, than to run such a risk. PP II 19 240 16
lations whom he had openly disdained, and recollected PP III 2 263 10
knowledged it to Lady Catherine, frankly and openly." PP III 16 367 10
being so surprised, and persuade her to speak openly. MP I 2 15 10
then became openly acknowledged, was a very short one.-- MP II 2 193 18
he had never heard him speak so openly before, and though MP II 9 264 17
ne it all so well, so openly, so liberally, so properly, MP III 1 314 16
anny, now at liberty to speak openly, felt more than MP III 16 459 31
the whole; not so openly as he might have done had her E II 3 170 1
u to give way to your own feelings?-- E III 11 404 11
t if you have any wish to speak openly to me as a friend, E III 13 429 32
dared not address her openly; my difficulties in the E III 14 437 8
eak more openly than might have been strictly correct.-- E III 16 459 46
mma grieved that she could not be more openly just to one E III 17 463 15
NESS (18)
t more--there is an openness in his manner that must be LS 18 272 1
th almost equal openness,) seemed sufficient vouchers NA II 15 245 12
s want of spirits, of openness, and of consistency, were SS I 19 102 2
rcumstances, to press for greater openness in Marianne. SS II 5 170 27
om Marianne greater openness towards them both; and this, SS II 9 202 8
he openness and heartiness of her manner, more than SS III 6 304 13
ch a noble mind!--such openness, such sincerity!-- no SS III 9 337 14
ngley was endeared to Darcy by the easiness, openness, PP I 4 16 14
s such a temptation to openness as nothing could have PP II 15 217 17
ch an openness and gentleness in his manner." PP II 17 225 14
with all that openness of heart, and sweet peculiarity MP III 4 351 36
here is an openness, a quickness, almost a bluntness in E I 4 34 42
tience, self-controul; but it wants openness. E II 15 289 40
come among us with professions of openness and E III 10 399 61
otherliness, their openness, their uprightness; P III 11 99 19
d meet, by such great openness of solicitude to be P IV 3 138 6
th great openness, and Anne's astonishment increased. P IV 5 153 8
had spoken to her with some degree of openness of Mrs. P IV 5 161 29
S (3)
are very good friends, & tho' she never opens her lips LS 18 273 3
o near the house, and it opens the prospect amazingly MP I 6 55 17
opens his designs to his family, it introduces you E I 7 56 46
A (1)
e first rested was an opera, procured for her by SS III 10 342 7
ATE (4)
re strongly they operate on Mr Vernon's generous temper. LS 6 251 2
ange! and here were claims which could not but operate. MP III 2 328 7
at had begun to operate in the very hour of first P IV 11 241 60
not want the imagination of a man to operate upon. S 3 378 1
ATED (2)
s fear of her, has always operated, I know, when they PP II 18 235 38
s sanguine temper, and fearlessness of mind, operated P III 4 27 4
ATING (1)
d it was a love which, operating on an active, sanguine MP III 2 326 2

OPERATION (10)
any time a much simpler operation to Catherine to doubt NA II 11 211 15
analogy, and of powerful operation; and if the distress be E I 16 137 13
was to be seen under the operation of being lifted into E II 5 186 1
And besides the operation of this, as a general principle, E II 15 286 23
but by the operation of the same system in another way.-- E III 19 483 10
was all the operation of a sensible, discerning mind. P IV 3 143 19
the matter to its own operation; and believing that, could P IV 5 160 26
operation, and it streightens him as to many things. P IV 10 218 22
"Oh!--they are so used to the operation--to every S 5 388 1
operation--to every operation--& have such fortitude!--" S 5 388 1
OPERATIONS (2)
How wonderful, how very wonderful the operations of time, MP II 4 208 12
The gipsies did not wait for the operations of justice; E III 3 336 13
OPINION (356)
His opinion of her I am sure, was as low as of any woman LS 8 255 1
my progress in the good opinion of her brother, & conclude LS 10 257 1
the justice of her opinion of me, I think I may defy her. LS 10 257 1
in your opinion of her. I am &c. Regd De Courcy. LS 12 261 6
as to injure me in your opinion, & give you all this alarm. LS 14 263 1
good opinion merits a better return than it has received. LS 14 265 5
to themselves & the opinion of the world. S. Vernon. LS 16 269 3
"I should not have hazarded such an opinion, returned she, LS 24 287 11
"Good God!--she exclaimed, what an opinion must you have LS 24 289 12
I trust I am in no danger of sinking in your opinion." LS 24 290 13
Let me know your opinion on this point. LS 25 294 5
Send me your opinion on all these matters, my dear Alicia, LS 25 294 7
the claims of our friends, or the opinion of the world. LS 30 300 1
tho' but an hour, in your opinion, is an humiliation to LS 35 305 1
I had almost forgot to give you my opinion of de courcy, I LS 38 307 3
lower than ever in her opinion, she was proportionably LS 42 311 2
"I am quite of your opinion, sir," replied Mrs. Allen; " NA I 3 28 44
ever any exchange of opinion, and not often any NA I 5 36 3
fearful of hazarding an opinion of its own in opposition NA I 7 48 32
Allen for her opinion; "but really I did not expect you." NA I 9 61 4
insight into his real opinion on the subject; but she NA I 9 66 31
Catherine's supporting opinion was not frequently called NA I 10 72 8
She applied to Mrs. Allen, and Mrs. Allen's opinion was NA I 11 82 1
and justified the opinion of Mrs. Allen, who had "always NA I 11 83 16
due to others, and to her own character in their opinion. NA I 13 101 25
To ease her mind, and ascertain by the opinion of an NA I 13 103 29
it, and I think it must establish me in your good opinion." NA I 14 107 9
and a great brute in your opinion of women in general. NA I 14 113 40
In my opinion, nature has given them so much, that they NA I 14 114 47
Isabella's opinion of the Tilneys did not influence her NA II 1 131 14
might be our heroine's opinion of him, his admiration of NA II 1 131 15
"But my opinion of your brother never did alter; it was NA II 3 146 19
"I can have no opinion on that subject." NA II 4 151 18
to preserve their good opinion, that, in the embarrassment NA II 5 154 1
be now able to form her opinion of him; but she scarcely NA II 5 155 3
The remembrance of Mr. Allen's opinion, respecting young NA II 5 156 5
"What say you, Eleanor?--speak your opinion, for ladies NA II 7 175 15
to reproach her for her opinion of him, was most urgent NA II 7 181 41
Upon his opinion of her danger, two others were called in NA II 9 197 25
Moreover, I have too good an opinion of Miss Thorpe's NA II 10 206 31
form a cool and impartial opinion, and prepare his NA II 11 208 2
on by the General for her opinion of it, she had very NA II 11 212 18
like an opinion on the subject could be drawn from her. NA II 11 214 25
the good opinion and affection of her earliest friends. NA II 14 239 28
totally mistaken in his opinion of their circumstances and NA II 15 246 12
the general good opinion of their surrounding acquaintance. SS I 1 3 1
A great deal too handsome, in my opinion, for any place SS I 2 13 28
Edward Ferrars was not recommended to their good opinion SS I 3 15 6
I have the highest opinion in the world of Edward's heart. SS I 3 17 17
unwilling to give his opinion on any picture; but he has SS I 4 19 2
which, in her opinion, could alone be called taste. SS I 4 19 3
your opinion, I am sure you could never be civil to him." SS I 4 19 4
the highest opinion in the world of his goodness and sense. SS I 4 19 6
sentiments and heard his opinion on subjects of literature SS I 4 20 9
She felt that Edward stood very high in her opinion. SS I 4 21 11
Elinor had given her real opinion to her sister. SS I 4 22 18
and every body was astonished at the opinion of the others. SS I 6 31 9
It was enough to secure his good opinion; for to be SS I 7 33 3
spite of his being in the opinion of Marianne and Margaret SS I 7 34 6
You have already ascertained Mr. Willoughby's opinion in SS I 10 47 4
In hastily forming and giving his opinion of other people, SS I 10 49 9
subject would only attach her the more to her own opinion. SS I 12 59 5
So wondered, so talked Mrs. Jennings, her opinion varying SS I 14 70 3
did not in her opinion justify such lasting amazement or SS I 14 71 3
Nothing in my opinion has ever passed to justify doubt; no SS I 15 80 42
so simple, and in her opinion so eligible of knowing the SS I 16 84 7
Barton was, in her opinion, of all things the most natural. SS I 17 90 1
your opinion on that point is unchanged, I presume?" SS I 17 93 29
"to be guided wholly by the opinion of other people. SS I 17 93 38
Lady Middleton's good opinion was engaged in their favour SS I 21 119 3
be together was, in his opinion, to be intimate, and while SS I 21 124 33
"No;" returned Elinor, cautious of giving her real opinion SS I 22 128 6
person whose good opinion is so well worth having as yours. SS I 22 128 9
could be of any use to you to know my opinion of her. SS I 22 128 10
I know he has the highest opinion in the world of all your SS I 22 130 16
You know every well that my opinion would have no weight SS II 2 150 31
me from giving any opinion on the subject had I formed one. SS II 2 150 33
your own feelings, your opinion would not be worth having." SS II 2 150 34
which, in my opinion, cannot be so easily removed." SS II 3 156 9
could never obtain her opinion of any article of purchase, SS II 4 165 24
concerning me, which may have lowered me in your opinion. SS II 7 188 42
opinion, than believe his nature capable of such cruelty. SS II 7 189 50
was often led in her opinion of others, by the irritable SS II 9 201 4
Marianne had promised to be guided by her mother's opinion, SS II 10 214 6
rather against the opinion of Sir John) that as Mrs. SS II 10 215 14
Whereas, in my opinion, by her taking so much notice of SS II 11 227 46
John Dashwood to the good opinion of Lady Middleton, did SS II 12 229 3
indifference as to her opinion of herself, her desire of SS II 12 230 6
equally positive in their opinion, and to repeat it over SS II 12 233 20
Elinor, having once delivered her opinion on William's SS II 12 234 25
had no opinion to give, as she had never thought about it. SS II 12 234 25
upon her caprice, or any solicitude for her good opinion. SS II 13 238 1
Mr. Palmer maintained the common, but unfatherly opinion SS II 14 248 5
Elinor would not oppose his opinion, because, whatever SS II 14 251 14
him for ever in her good opinion,--and to make Marianne, SS III 1 261 11
Elinor was quite of her opinion, as to the probability of SS III 4 292 58
her most unfavourable opinion of his head and heart. SS III 5 298 32
and his deference for her opinion, might very well justify SS III 6 305 16
His opinion, however, made some little amends for his SS III 7 312 19
to my character in the opinion of Marianne and her friends, SS III 8 328 63
'I am ruined for ever in their opinion--said I to myself-- SS III 8 328 63
I less guilty in your opinion than I was before?-- SS III 8 329 65
Let me be a little lightened too in her opinion as well as SS III 8 330 67
and sobered her own opinion of Willoughby's deserts;--she SS III 11 349 2
unbiassed opinion, by an eager sign, engaged her silence. SS III 11 349 5
in Harley-Street, of his opinion of what his own mediation SS III 13 364 11
"I will not ask your opinion of it as a composition," said SS III 13 365 17
advanced in the good opinion of each other, as they SS III 13 370 36
you to ask Mary Edwards's opinion if you are all at a W 315 1
able to win a more favourable opinion of poor osborne.--" W 340 19
"My uncle's sense is not at all impeached in my opinion, W 352 26
news, & the general opinion of the day must be understood, W 356 28
Margt had just respect enough for her Br & Sr's opinion, W 360 30
selfish, hypocritical woman, and I have no opinion of her." PP I 2 6 5
own he reliance, and of his judgment the highest opinion. PP I 4 16 14
Pride relates more to our opinion of ourselves, vanity to PP I 5 20 20
such society; and indeed I am quite of your opinion. PP I 6 27 47

by reason; and, in my opinion, exertion should always be PP I 7 32 38
But, in my opinion, it is a paltry device, a very mean art. PP I 8 40 56
and was exactly in unison with her opinion of each. PP I 10 47 2
It is often only carelessness of opinion, and sometimes an PP I 10 48 25
My good opinion once lost is lost for ever." PP I 11 58 28
mingling with a very good opinion of himself, of his PP I 15 70 1
attentive listener, whose opinion of his consequence PP I 16 75 3
"I have no right to give my opinion." said Wickham, "as to PP I 16 77 14
But I believe your opinion of him would in general PP I 16 77 14
spoken my opinion of him, and to him, too freely. PP I 16 80 27
as you chuse, but you will not laugh me out of my opinion. PP I 17 85 4
"I am by no means of opinion, I assure you," said he, " PP I 17 87 13
their opinion, to be secure of judging properly at first." PP I 18 93 36
I have the highest opinion in the world of your excellent PP I 18 97 60
61
to give me her opinion (unasked too!) on this subject; and PP I 19 105 10
She shall hear my opinion." PP I 20 111 13
Can there be any other opinion on the subject?" PP I 21 118 15
gave it as his decided opinion, that whenever Mr. Collins PP I 22 122 3
to procure any woman's opinion, because he was not so PP I 22 125 15
She had always felt that Charlotte's opinion of matrimony PP I 22 125 18
delicacy she was sure her opinion could never be shaken, PP I 23 128 9
were the case, though her opinion of him must be PP II 1 134 3
person to blame, and saying your opinion of him is sunk. PP II 1 136 14
Mr. Darcy!--my father's opinion of me does me the greatest PP II 3 144 7
and trusting their opinion of her--their opinion of every PP II 4 151 3
opinion of her--their opinion of every body--would always PP II 4 151 3
"Oh! if that is all, I have a very poor opinion of young PP II 4 154 19
came in, delivering her opinion on every subject in so PP II 6 163 15
"Upon my word," said her ladyship, "you give your opinion PP II 6 165 36
her cousin, to give her opinion of all that she had seen PP II 6 166 42
for in her opinion it admitted not of a doubt, that all PP II 9 181 30
solitary walks, and her opinion of Mr. and Mrs. Collins's PP II 10 182 1
"In my opinion, the younger son of an earl can know very PP II 10 183 11
But I cannot--I have never desired your good opinion, and PP II 11 190 7
Long before it had taken place, my opinion of you was PP II 11 191 17
with quick steps across the room, "is your opinion of me! PP II 11 192 22
passed that evening, my opinion of all parties was PP II 12 198 5
he had also the highest opinion of him, and hoping the PP II 12 200 5
overthrow every cherished opinion of his worth, and which PP II 13 204 2
remembering what Charlotte's opinion had always been.-- PP II 13 208 9
good opinion, heightened the sense of what Jane had lost. PP II 14 213 18
the knowledge of your ill opinion too! and having to PP II 17 225 12
What is your own opinion?" PP II 17 226 22
is your opinion now of this sad business of Jane's? PP II 17 227 27
be content; but her own opinion continued the same, and PP II 18 232 21
of whose good opinion and judgment he stands much in awe. PP II 18 234 38
Had Elizabeth's opinion been all drawn from her own family, PP II 19 236 1
was not a good-tempered man, had been her firmest opinion. PP III 1 248 31
and courting the good opinion of people, with whom any PP III 2 263 10
opinion of Bingley, and then hurried away to dress. PP III 2 264 12
was soliciting the good opinion of her friends, and bent PP III 2 265 16
injure her in Darcy's opinion, and perhaps to remind the PP III 3 269 10
favourite, as their attentions raised them in her opinion. PP III 4 280 25
said Mrs. Gardiner, "I begin to be of your uncle's opinion. PP III 5 282 3
to any one, that the good opinion which all the PP III 5 285 16
their plan, and would not give his real opinion about it. PP III 5 290 48
to be pitied, in which opinion I am not only joined by Mrs. PP III 6 297 11
"And this is your real opinion! PP III 14 358 71
to lessen your ill opinion, by letting you see that your PP III 16 370 32
him any attention, or mark her deference for his opinion. PP III 17 378 46
Georgiana had the highest opinion in the world of PP III 19 387 11
A mean opinion of her abilities was not confined to them. MP I 2 18 23
for him; that is your opinion of your intimate friend. MP I 5 45 14
while? and what was her opinion of the new-comers? MP I 5 48 30
could be less called on to speak their opinion than Fanny. MP I 5 48 30
Miss Bertram's attention and opinion was evidently his MP I 6 52 1
to me as to hear your opinion of it," was his answer. MP I 6 61 54
Mr. Rushworth, you should assist him with your opinion." MP I 6 61 57
declaring that in her opinion it was infinitely better to MP I 6 61 58
to hear Mr. Crawford's opinion on the spot, and that might MP I 6 62 58
Rushworth had asked her opinion, and her spirits were in MP I 8 83 37
in Henry Crawford's opinion; and he directly saw a knoll MP I 10 97 4
In my opinion, these Crawfords are no addition at all. MP I 10 102 43
"I speak what appears to me the general opinion; and where MP I 11 110 25
and where an opinion is general, it is usually correct. MP I 11 110 25
and the opinion of the groom, from whom he had just parted. MP I 12 118 22
What is your opinion?-- MP I 12 119 22
If I must give my opinion, I have always thought it the MP I 14 131 3
I want your opinion." MP I 16 153 6
"My opinion!" she cried, shrinking from such a compliment, MP I 16 153 7
"Yes, your advice and opinion. MP I 16 153 8
With no material fault of temper, or difference of opinion, MP I 17 162 19
set up for a fine actor, is very ridiculous in my opinion." MP I 18 165 3
The case admitted no difference of opinion; they must go MP II 1 176 3
cousins; and as her own opinion of her claims on Sir MP II 1 176 4
and confirm his ill opinion of Mr. Yates's habits of MP II 1 184 25
my opinion it is very disagreeable to be always rehearsing. MP II 1 186 33
Sir Thomas meant to be giving Mr. Rushworth's opinion in MP II 1 186 35
with Sir Thomas's good opinion, and saying scarcely any MP II 1 186 35
best towards preserving that good opinion a little longer. MP II 1 186 35
what appeared to be his opinion on one subject--his MP II 2 190 6
"In my opinion, my uncle would not like any addition. MP II 3 196 3
Miss Crawford's kind opinion of herself deserved at least MP II 3 199 16
any change of opinion or inclination since her forming it. MP II 3 200 21
power," was looking at Edmund for his opinion and help.-- MP II 4 215 47
"Suppose you take my father's opinion, ma'am." MP II 5 217 7
but I meant my father's opinion as to the propriety of the MP II 5 217 9
in the case, could any thing in my opinion be more natural. MP II 5 218 18
He had but one opinion. MP II 5 219 25
talking and giving your opinion as if you were one of your MP II 5 221 32
of her aunt Norris's opinion, to being the principal lady MP II 5 223 48
Her opinion was sought as to the probable continuance of MP II 5 223 48
that in my opinion, every thing had gone quite far enough." MP II 5 225 58
only by a less scrupulous opinion, and more noisy abuse of MP II 6 234 18
An affection so amiable was advancing each in the opinion MP II 6 235 19
be so kind as to give her opinion, it might be all talked MP II 8 257 15
to her demand of his opinion; he was in a reverie of fond MP II 9 262 11
you have always known my opinion of her; you can bear me MP II 9 270 38
To be urging her opinion against Sir Thomas's, was a proof MP II 10 275 11
she really did that his opinion of Fanny Price was MP II 12 294 18
will influence her in her opinion of the wants of others. MP III 1 313 12
I am sure you will not disappoint my opinion of you, by MP III 1 313 12
me, and quite out of my power to return his good opinion." MP III 1 314 17
"Out of your power to return his good opinion! what is all MP III 1 315 18
This is so much my opinion, that I am sorry to think how MP III 1 317 34
Her ill opinion of him was founded chiefly on observations, MP III 1 317 38
it my duty to mark my opinion of your conduct--that you MP III 1 318 39
opinion of you from the period of my return to England. MP III 1 318 39
and without paying my opinion or my regard the compliment MP III 1 319 39
deceived his expectations; she had lost his good opinion. MP III 1 319 40
favourable opinion of his understanding, heart, and temper. MP III 1 321 47
And when farther pressed, had added, that in her opinion MP III 2 327 5
there could be but one opinion, one wish on the subject; MP III 2 329 12
fortune, raised her, therefore, very much in her opinion. MP III 2 332 22
proceeded to ask his opinion and give his own as to the MP III 3 340 24
because I now understand more clearly your opinion of me. MP III 3 343 41
With such an opinion, no wonder that----- MP III 3 343 41
being for you, has raised him inconceivably in my opinion. MP III 4 350 30
He gave this opinion as the result of the conversation, to MP III 5 356 2
connected with her, whose opinion was worth having; and MP III 5 361 16
all the changes of opinion and sentiment, which the MP III 6 374 27
and wished for her good opinion; and new as any thing like MP III 9 396
inclined to seek her good opinion and refer to her MP III 9 397
to Mr. Crawford's opinion) in a singular manner, had Mr. MP III 10 403
When you give me your opinion, I always know what is right. MP III 11 412
unhappy differences of opinion may exist between us, we MP III 13 420
You will wish to hear my opinion of Maria's degree of MP III 13 423
I want you at home, that I may have your opinion about MP III 13 423
Such was his opinion of the set into which she had thrown MP III 16 452
quite agreed in their opinion of the lasting effect, the MP III 16 460
His opinion of her had been sinking from the day of his MP III 17 465
a contrast with his early opinion on the subject when the MP III 17 471
a civil, pretty-spoken girl; I have a great opinion of her. E I 1 9
With such an opinion, in confirmation of his own, Mr. E I 2 19
However, I do not mean to set up my opinion against your's- E I 4 31
"I do not know what your opinion may be, Mrs. Weston," E I 5 36
came to you, but, in my opinion, the attractions you have E I 6 42
watching for her opinion, with a "well, well," and was at E I 7 51
you will not give me your opinion, I must do as well as I E I 7 53
He must have a pretty good opinion of himself." E I 7 54
man, and have a great opinion of him; and his being so E I 7 54
If he had never esteemed my opinion before, he would have E I 8 59
and manner, a very humble opinion of herself, and a great E I 8 63
I never had much opinion of the sea air." E I 12 101
"would do as well to keep his opinion till it is asked for. E I 12 106
will look them over, and you shall give me your opinion." E I 12 107
"A man," said he, "must have a very good opinion of E I 13 113
And it is no small credit, in my opinion, to him, that he E I 14 121
Mr. Frank Churchill, in my opinion, as his father thinks. E I 14 121
Mr. Perry and learnt his opinion; and though she tried to E I 15 125
to pay his addresses to her had sunk him in her opinion. E I 16 135
of disposition and lowly opinion of herself, as must E I 17 141
question from her real opinion, and making use of Mrs. E I 18 145
for with all the high opinion of himself, which she had E I 18 150
opinion, been talking enough of Mr. Elton for that day. E II 1 155
There was no getting at her real opinion. E II 2 169
his company, or opinion of the suitableness of the match. E II 2 169
But I gave what I believed the general opinion, when I E II 3 176
And at last, as if resolved to qualify his opinion E II 5 192
his behaviour to whom her opinion of him was to depend. E II 6 196
I wanted the opinion of some one who could really judge. E II 6 201
Emma's very good opinion of Frank Churchill was a little E II 7 205
was too apt, in Emma's opinion, to get about as he could, E II 8 213
indeed, if I understood Miss Fairfax's opinion last night." E II 9 234
us your opinion of our new instrument; you and Miss Smith. E II 9 235
opinion of the instrument will be worth having.'-- E II 9 236
impatient for your opinion, and hoping you might be E II 11 253
her opinion, the great risk, of its being all in vain. E II 12 257
entirely to form an opinion of the lady, and on no account E II 14 270
discovery, to retract her ill opinion of Mrs. Elton. E II 15 281
the few who knew her opinion of Mrs. Elton, Mrs. Weston E II 15 285
as any of us of forming a just opinion of Mrs. Elton. E II 15 286
doubt that my opinion will be decidedly in his favour. E II 18 309
of forming some opinion of Frank Churchill's feelings. E III 1 315
the purpose of taking her opinion as to the propriety and E III 2 319
Emma longed to know what Frank's first opinion of Mrs. E III 2 320
He was immediately qualifying himself to form an opinion, E III 2 321
to gratify him by her opinion of his son; and so briskly E III 2 321
You know I candidly told you I should form my own opinion; E III 2 321
or my housekeeper be of any use to you with our opinion?-- E III 6 355
opinion, when one is exploring about the country in summer. E III 7 372
How could she have exposed herself to such ill opinion in E III 7 376
assure her that she had fully recovered his good opinion.-- E III 9 386
opinion, in favour of such exercise for his patient. E III 9 390
sunk him, I cannot say how it has sunk him in my opinion. E III 10 397
But as I have always had a thoroughly good opinion of Miss E III 10 399
favour of Mr. Knightley's most improved opinion of Harriet. E III 11 409
with what she had known of his opinion of Harriet. E III 11 409
sink him in the general opinion, to foresee the smiles, E III 11 413
case to be obliged still to lower herself in his opinion. E III 13 427
"I have never had a high opinion of Frank Churchill.-- E III 13 427
as a friend, or to ask my opinion of any thing that you E III 13 429
opinion, and some censure I acknowledge myself liable to.-- E III 14 438
I want to have your opinion of her looks. E III 14 439
to be happier than I deserve, I quite of your opinion.-- E III 14 443
shortly afterwards, "to speak my opinion aloud as I read. E III 15 445
and I am very much of his opinion in thinking him likely E III 15 448
could alter his wishes or his opinion on the subject. E III 15 449
and churchwardens, are always wanting his opinion. E III 16 455
of my friends, whose good opinion is most worth preserving, E III 16 459
till my dear father is in the secret, and hear his opinion. E III 17 464
He asked my opinion as to what he was now to do. E III 18 474
with such steadiness of opinion, and such tenderness of P III 4 27
They knew not each other's opinion, either its constancy P III 4 29
include a total change of conversation, opinion, and idea. P III 6 42
that I have no very good opinion of Mrs. Charles's nursery- P III 6 45
Yes, indeed, Oh yes, I am quite of your opinion, Mrs. P III 8 71
I am quite of your opinion. P III 8 71
Hitherto there had been but one opinion of Captain P III 9 73
often enough to have an opinion, though too wise to P III 10 82
a brief comparison of opinion as to the first-rate poets, P III 11 100
Mrs. Harville's giving it as her opinion that her husband P III 12 108
of his own previous opinion as to the universal felicity P III 12 116
had in fact so high an opinion of the Crofts, and P IV 1 125
not have supposed that my opinion of any one could have P IV 2 132
opinion; but I am determined not to judge him before-hand." P IV 2 132
defying public opinion in any point of worldly decorum. P IV 4 146
the Dalrymples (in Anne's opinion, most unfortunately) P IV 4 148
ventured to speak her opinion of them to Mr. Elliot, he P IV 4 150
Lady Russell was now perfectly decided in her opinion of P IV 5 159
"They are not at all nice children, in my opinion; but " P IV 6 163
His opinion of Louisa Musgrove's inferiority, an opinion P IV 8 185
Mr. Elliot, and entertained the highest opinion of him. P IV 9 199
It is a difference of opinion which does not admit of P IV 11 234
cases to have a surgeon's opinion without loss of time; S 1 365
to the number, are in my opinion excessively absurd, & S 1 369
that she is quite of my opinion & thinks it a pity to lose S 1 370
& wrote to ask the opinion of her friend Mrs Darling.-- S 9 408
are the worst part of my complaints in my opinion. S 10 415

OPINIONS (67)

could rectify the opinions of her new friend in many NA I 4 33
other place; really, our opinions were so exactly the same, NA I 10 71
Circumstances change, opinions alter." NA II 3 146
confirming her own opinions by the justness of her own NA II 14 239
according to the opinions of Mrs. Dashwood, to her SS I 3 14
of her conduct and opinions, we have never been disposed SS I 4 21
examination of his opinions, she proceeded to question him SS I 10 47
at all times, was an illustration of their opinions. SS I 11 53
"No," replied Elinor, "her opinions are all romantic." SS I 11 56
A few years however will settle her opinions on the SS I 11 56
them give way to the reception of more general opinions." SS I 11 56
such opinions as are but too common, and too dangerous! SS I 11 56
to their general opinions and practice, that a doubt SS I 14 71
At my time of life opinions are tolerably fixed. SS I 17 93
feelings and varying opinions on Marianne's, as before. SS II 9 201
She expected from other people the same opinions and SS II 9 202
me!--her taste, her opinions--I believe they are better SS III 8 325
can be overcome by no change of circumstances or opinions. SS III 10 347
in some of her opinions--they had been equally imputed, by SS III 13 366
She was born to discover the falsehood of her own opinions, SS III 14 378
said Emma,--but I do not like her plans or her opinions. W 318

f my opinions are wrong, I must correct them--if they are W 318 2
id not justify eliz.'s opinions tho' Margaret's modest W 355 28
doubt, there cannot be two opinions on that point." PP I 5 19 7
You expect me to account for opinions which you chuse to PP I 10 50 34
e may compare our different opinions." PP I 18 93 29
rofessing opinions which in fact are not your own." PP II 8 174 14
anner, and to adopt any opinions that came in her way. PP III 5 283 10
is understanding and opinions all please me; he wants PP III 10 325 2
oth reason to think my opinions not entirely unalterable, PP III 16 368 21
ow earnestly did she then wish that her former opinions PP III 17 376 30
ome meanness of opinions, and very distressing vulgarity MP I 1 10 14
hese opinions had been hardly canvassed a year, before MP I 3 32 61
eople justified these opinions, and an engagement, with a MP I 4 39 11
you with <u>their</u> opinions; and for my own part I have MP I 6 62 58
do not censure her <u>opinions</u>; but there certainly <u>is</u> MP I 7 63 7
aid no compliments, <u>his</u> opinions were unbending, <u>his</u> MP I 7 65 13
hose opinions you have been in the habit of hearing. MP I 11 110 24
I have been so little addicted to take my opinions from MP I 11 111 28
in books, with opinions in general unfixed, and without MP II 3 200 19
her professed opinions, sometimes a tinge of wrong. MP II 9 269 31
ny of his foolish opinions, or learnt to sit over your MP II 12 295 27
dare say, that on a comparison of our opinions, they MP III 4 346 12
pinions of the man she loved and respected, as her own.-- MP III 6 367 6
ave formed such proper opinions of what ought to be--she, MP III 9 397 8
ome difference in our opinions, on points too, of some MP III 16 457 30
er mind, disposition, opinions, and habits wanted no half MP III 17 471 28
ood society; she would form her opinions and her manners. E I 3 23 10
am sure of having their opinions with me." E I 5 40 23
nvinced that her opinions were right and her adversary's E I 8 67 56
here cannot be two opinions about <u>him</u>. E I 9 74 22
to men and women, our opinions <u>are</u> sometimes very E I 12 98 3
u want your neighbours' opinions. E II 11 254 50
, without being able to make their opinions the same. E II 13 267 9
tons, and that their opinions of both husband and wife E III 3 332 1
wish our opinions were the same. E III 18 471 16
e additional pain of opinions, on his side, totally P III 4 28 5
d to listen to the opinions of her brother and sister, P III 9 75 9
s a strong proof of his opinions on the subject. P IV 3 139 7
me, wanting to compare opinions respecting the place, P IV 3 143 19
rrect opinions, knowledge of the world, and a warm heart. P IV 4 146 6
ll, professed good opinions, seemed to judge properly P IV 5 160 27
cts or opinions which are to pass through the hands of P IV 9 205 85
Mr. Elliot's opinions as to the value of a baronetcy. P IV 9 206 90
herself, giving opinions of business, and P IV 10 220 31
sult of the most correct opinions and well regarded mind. P IV 12 249 3
ong, and to take up a new set of opinions and of hopes. P IV 12 249 3

RTUNE (1)

is morning was in another respect particularly opportune. E II 7 206 5

RTUNITIES (15)

spite of Mr Johnson, to make opportunities of seeing me. LS 26 295 3
tely had particular opportunities of discovering; aiming NA II 15 246 12
ste, though he has not had opportunities of improving it. SS I 4 19 2
have not had so many opportunities of estimating the SS I 4 19 6
s continually making opportunities of addressing her W 331 11
mself, and who had opportunities of seeing him in PP II 12 200 5
ly afforded more frequent opportunities of proving them. MP I 2 21 34
e will have opportunities in plenty of seeing Sotherton. MP I 8 76 5
r the most important opportunities of improvement in MP II 4 205 2
ll, you will have opportunities enough of endeavouring MP II 6 231 10
ve more convenient opportunities of meeting, but my MP II 7 245 34
ma, who have so few opportunities of dancing, you are E II 12 262 40
41
u and I shall not want opportunities. E III 16 453 13
her opportunities of making her observations could not P III 10 82 1
men of that class have great opportunities, and if they P IV 5 155 10

RTUNITY (138)

opportunity of leaving her myself, in my way to you. LS 1 244 1
th as little opportunity as inclination to do evil, LS 14 264 3
d here I have opportunity enough for the exercise of my LS 16 268 2
ster I beleive wanted only opportunity for doing so. LS 22 281 3
have not a doubt but that the girl took this opportunity LS 22 282 6
s far as I have had opportunity of judging, it appears NA I 3 27 30
es, very; I have hardly ever an opportunity of being in NA I 7 47 22
rowing away a fair opportunity of considering him lost NA I 8 53 3
give Mr. Tilney an opportunity of repeating the NA I 8 58 25
ere was then an opportunity for the latter to utter some NA I 10 70 1
s only eager for an opportunity of explaining its cause. NA I 12 93 4
therine took the opportunity of asking the other for NA I 15 116 1
e present a fine opportunity for being really so; and NA II 3 143 2
ther opportunity or comprehension was always against her. NA II 4 150 1
trusted, however, that an opportunity might ere long NA II 7 175 12
e next day afforded no opportunity for the proposed NA II 9 190 1
e took the first opportunity of being suddenly alone NA II 13 220 2
t she had had no opportunity, till the present, of SS I 1 6 9
ll have greater opportunity of improving that natural SS I 4 22 17
e took the first opportunity of affronting her mother-in- SS I 4 23 19
ter his death, and an opportunity now offering of SS I 5 26 5
opportunity was soon to be given to the Dashwoods of SS I 6 31 10
ached; and missed no opportunity of projecting weddings SS I 8 36 1
afford him opportunity of witnessing the excellencies SS I 11 53 1
is not time or opportunity that is to determine SS I 12 59 4
d Marianne, had had opportunity for observations, which, SS I 12 60 8
catch every opportunity of eyeing the hair and of SS I 18 98 13
Lucy, who missed no opportunity of engaging her in SS I 22 127 1
am determined to set for it the very first opportunity." SS I 22 132 37
eir opportunity of acquaintance in the house of Mr. SS II 1 139 1
t it was not immediately that an opportunity of doing so SS II 1 142 8
o seldom missed an opportunity of introducing it, and SS II 2 151 42
inor had often wished for an opportunity of attempting SS II 3 157 17
opportunity of coming hither, though with Mrs. Jennings, SS II 7 187 38
d to have an opportunity of endeavouring to please them, SS II 12 231 9
ch an opportunity of being with Edward and his family SS II 14 254 26
t foresee that the opportunity would so very soon occur." SS III 4 285 4
pportunity!" repeated Mrs. Jennings--"Oh! as to that, SS III 4 285 5
thing, somehow or other he will soon find an opportunity. SS III 4 285 5
r a possible opportunity of making myself contemptible SS III 8 321 34
fore I could have an opportunity of speaking with her in SS III 8 321 34
was thus imparted to her, as soon as any opportunity of SS III 9 335 7
some more eligible opportunity of establishment for the SS III 12 357 1
wever, how soon an opportunity of exercising it occurred, SS III 13 361 3
d will return your picture the first opportunity. SS III 13 365 15
m, but to have an opportunity of convincing him that he SS III 13 368 30
pleased with the opportunity of seeing your sister."-- W 339 18
ve met with some unexpected opportunity of returning."-- W 355 28
it, she may lose the opportunity of fixing him; and it PP I 6 21 2
nnet, to seize such an opportunity of dancing a reel?" PP I 10 51 47
48
en the card tables were placed, he had an opportunity of PP I 16 76 6
wonder," said he, at the next opportunity of speaking, " PP I 16 78 18
d I take this opportunity of soliciting yours, Miss PP I 17 87 13
ur likeness now, I may never have another opportunity." PP I 18 94 42
em; such an opportunity of exhibiting was delightful to PP I 18 100 68
ould have such an opportunity of ridiculing her PP I 18 102 72
r taking the earliest opportunity of waiting on her, PP I 18 103 76
will have frequent opportunity now of seeing her on the PP I 21 118 14
izabeth took an opportunity of thanking her. PP I 22 121 1
the first favourable opportunity of speaking to her PP II 3 144 1
2
all take the opportunity of calling in Grosvenor-Street." PP II 3 147 22
e opportunity of shewing it without her husband's help. PP II 5 156 5
shed for; and that an opportunity of doing it should be PP II 6 160 1
t I suppose you had no opportunity. PP II 6 164 24
endeavour to find some opportunity of putting this letter PP II 12 203 5
and he took the opportunity of paying the parting PP II 15 215 1
Jane looked well, and Elizabeth had little opportunity of PP II 15 217 16
she would not miss the opportunity of enjoying herself as PP II 18 235 40
While thus engaged, Elizabeth had a fair opportunity of PP III 3 268 7
anger, took the first opportunity of saying, with sneering PP III 3 269 8
9
availed herself of the opportunity of making many PP III 5 289 45
young man to resist an opportunity of having a companion. PP III 9 318 19
Lizzy, if I take this opportunity of saying (what I was PP III 10 325 2
would afford some opportunity of bringing them together; PP III 12 340 14
and she seized the opportunity of saying, "is your sister PP III 12 341 20
21
the others, and she had no opportunity of detaining them. PP III 12 342 27
leave, would take an early opportunity of waiting on them. PP III 13 344 3
he had taken the opportunity as he walked with her through MP I 8 79 23
this will be a good opportunity for you to take a lesson." MP I 8 80 29
The same evening afforded him an opportunity of trying his MP I 13 124 14
His sisters, to whom he had an opportunity of speaking the MP I 13 128 38
immediately took the opportunity of saying, "I cannot MP I 15 139 11
give you an opportunity of seeing all the actors at once." MP I 18 167 10
having had an opportunity of making his passage thither in MP II 1 178 8
and Tom had taken the opportunity of explaining, with MP II 2 191 10
I might not have such another opportunity all the winter. MP II 5 222 43
afterwards, taking the opportunity of a little languor in MP II 7 240 13
perhaps we may have an opportunity of doing ere long." MP II 7 250 60
The hope of an opportunity, which Sir Thomas had then MP II 8 252 1
much fear of wanting an opportunity for private discussion; MP II 8 256 14
herself to him, took an opportunity of stepping aside to MP II 10 276 14
morning afforded her an opportunity of talking over MP II 11 283 7
"For--for very little more than opportunity. MP II 12 293 14
who gives me such an opportunity of seeing you alone: I MP II 13 298 2
in having such an opportunity of proving his regard for MP II 13 298 3
The opportunity was too fair, and his feelings too MP II 13 300 7
Norris, and she carefully refused him every opportunity. MP II 13 306 27
away from you such an opportunity of being settled in life, MP III 1 318 39
Thomas took the first opportunity of saying to her, with a MP III 2 330 14
He staid of course, and Edmund had then ample opportunity MP III 3 336 7
The opportunity was too fair. MP III 3 343 40
I will take the first opportunity of speaking to her alone, MP III 4 345 5
too much, Miss Crawford was not the slave of opportunity. MP III 5 357 5
it very unkind of her not to come by such an opportunity. MP III 6 372 21
of her missing such an opportunity; and another twenty MP III 6 373 24
he had yet procured no opportunity of seeing Miss Crawford MP III 10 399 1
Emma was not sorry to have such an opportunity of survey; E I 4 31 27
I dare say Miss Nash would envy you such an opportunity as E I 7 56 41
to Isabella, however, Emma found an opportunity of saying, E I 14 122 19
himself of the precious opportunity, declaring sentiments E I 15 129 24
and giving her the opportunity of pleasing some one worth E I 16 137 11
he contrived to find an opportunity, while their two E II 5 191 28
sir, I will take the opportunity of paying a visit, which E II 5 193 36
37
She had an opportunity now of speaking her approbation E II 8 213 7
for I took the opportunity the other day of asking Mr. E II 9 237 46
Emma took the opportunity of whispering, "you speak too E II 10 243 23
24
Mr. Weston instantly seized the opportunity of going on. E II 18 308 29
that he wanted, soon took the opportunity of walking away. E II 18 310 35
Emma had no opportunity of speaking to Mr. Knightley till E III 2 330 46
me, whenever I had an opportunity, to thank you--I could E III 12 419 12
stairs; it gave her an opportunity which she immediately E III 16 459 45
46
understand) he found an opportunity of speaking to Harriet; E III 18 472 20
of courage and opportunity for Frank Churchill to draw E III 18 476 46
47
she had no sooner an opportunity of being one hour alone E III 19 481 1
sorry that she had missed the opportunity of seeing them. P III 5 32 1
And Mrs. Musgrove took the first opportunity of being P III 6 44 8
It might have been an opportunity of watching the loves P III 9 80 34
on this, the first opportunity of reconciliation, to be P IV 3 139 7
lost such an opportunity of paying his respects to her. P IV 3 143 19
This was an opportunity which Anne could not resist; she P IV 6 172 42
him she felt all over courage if the opportunity occurred. P IV 7 180 32
with Captain Wentworth, if he gave her the opportunity. P IV 8 189 44
He omitted no opportunity of being with them, threw P IV 9 207 90
an opportunity of bringing him and Sir Walter together. P IV 10 213 5
it was thought a good opportunity for Henrietta to come P IV 10 217 19
so, moreover, for the opportunity it gave her of decidedly P IV 10 224 52
53
to let no opportunity of being useful escape them.-- S 9 410 1
I will take an opportunity of seeing Lady D. myself.-- S 12 425 1

OPPOSE (24)

but it is my duty to oppose a match, which deep art only LS 12 261 3
Catherine had nothing to oppose against such reasoning; NA I 6 43 44
father and mother would never oppose their son's wishes.-- NA I 15 119 14
against her character, oppose the connexion, turned her NA II 11 208 1
On <u>that</u> head, therefore, it was not for her to oppose her SS I 4 24 21
and though she did not oppose the parties arranged by her SS I 11 55 6
Elinor would not oppose his opinion, because, whatever SS II 14 251 14
This person's suspicions, therefore, I have had to oppose, SS III 1 263 29
Elizabeth would not oppose such an injunction--and a PP I 19 104 7
Elizabeth could not oppose such a wish; and from this time PP II 1 137 25
they did not attempt to oppose it, for they knew that she PP III 5 288 40
expectation that he must oppose such an enlargement of the MP I 15 148 59
and having nothing to oppose her, had so naturally and so MP I 16 151 1
After being known to oppose the scheme from the beginning, MP I 16 154 12
side to oppose any friendly arrangement of her own. E I 4 31 26
not oppose such a resolution, though their feelings did. E II 2 165 9
and that he would rather oppose than lose the pleasure of E II 11 250 19
Emma had not another word to oppose. E III 6 363 51
one real, rational difficulty to oppose or delay it. E III 17 468 31
Lady Russell felt obliged to oppose her dear Anne's known P III 2 14 11
none of the others could oppose when he gave way, there P III 12 115 65
She had only meant to oppose the too-common idea of spirit P IV 6 172 40
41
"I will not oppose such kind politeness; but I should be P IV 8 187 27
meeting with nothing to oppose or confine it around our S 4 381 1

OPPOSED (22)

opposed to the immediate influence of intellect and manner. LS 10 257 1
would be opposed by those friends on whom you depend. LS 30 300 1
and thirty hope, when opposed by a very lively one of five SS I 10 50 12
in the spring, he warmly opposed every alteration of a SS I 14 72 6
This was an obligation, however, which not only opposed SS III 5 293 3
The plan was warmly opposed by their visitor. W 339 18
in their eyes when opposed to the regimentals of an ensign. PP I 7 29 4
is very unlikely they should have opposed their brother's. PP II 1 137 24
which judgment had always opposed to inclination, were PP II 11 189 5
body went on; but Elizabeth steadily opposed the scheme. PP II 16 223 25
of Longbourn, I should very strenuously have opposed it. PP III 15 364 22
declaration with which he opposed whatever could be urged MP I 4 36 7
But this was immediately opposed by Tom Bertram, who MP I 14 133 10
stage of a theatre, and opposed to a ranting young man, MP II 1 182 22
In some points of interest they were exactly opposed to MP II 11 285 15
He ought to have opposed the first attempt on their side E I 18 148 22
Mr. Woodhouse opposed it earnestly, on the score of health. E II 11 248 10
longer evidently did not please; but it was not opposed. E II 12 257 2
conversation opposed to her instead of his brother. E II 16 292 8
But in this he was eagerly opposed by his wife, with "Oh, P III 7 55 6
He stood, as opposed to Captain Wentworth, in all his own P IV 10 212 1
religious Cottager, as opposed to Voltaire--"<u>she</u>, never S 1 370 1

OPPOSER (1)

strenuous opposer of Sir Walter's making a second match. P IV 9 208 92

OPPOSING (11)
but of feeling, no opposing desire that should dare to NA II 15 247 15
he was very decided in opposing what she wished. "return MP II 9 262 11
many counteractions of opposing habits, she had certainly MP III 16 459 31
Harriet, her conscience opposing such censure; "at least E I 7 54 30
to feel in directly opposing those, whom as child and boy E I 18 148 21
clearly heard Emma opposing it with eager laughing warmth. PP II 11 348 22
advice, or even wilfully opposing him, insensible of half E III 12 415 1
and yet had no authority for opposing Harriet's confidence. E III 12 416 2
of generosity run mad, opposing all that could be probable E III 13 431 38
serious, most warmly opposing it, and not omitting to make P IV 10 224 50
by the tranquil & morbid virtues of any opposing character. S 8 404 1
OPPOSITE (44)
opposite Union-Passage; but here they were stopped. NA I 7 44 1
very moment of coming opposite to Union-Passage, and NA I 7 44 1
People that dance, only stand opposite each other in a NA I 10 77 32
in the opposite box, recalled her to anxiety and distress. NA I 12 92 4
was directed towards the opposite box; and, for the space NA I 12 92 4
top, they turned in an opposite direction from the gallery NA II 8 184 5
to her belief, just opposite her own, it struck her that, NA II 8 188 19
the influence of exactly opposite feelings, irritated by NA II 15 246 12
He took the opposite chair, and for half a minute not a SS III 8 317 7
& they were immediately impelled in opposite directions.-- W 333 13
of his own head in an opposite glass,--said with equal W 357 28
Elizabeth, at work in the opposite corner, saw it all with PP I 11 54 2
wanting something in an opposite shop, and fortunately had PP I 15 72 8
being allowed to stand opposite to Mr. Darcy, and reading PP I 18 90 8
of it was overheard by Mr. Darcy, who sat opposite to them. PP I 18 99 64
bordered the park nearly opposite the front of his house. PP II 5 156 4
herself at the gate in the pales opposite the parsonage. PP II 10 182 1
employed in visiting an opposite milliner, watching the PP II 16 219 1
house, situated on the opposite side of the valley, into PP III 1 245 3
all others most extraordinary, most opposite to her ideas. PP III 1 248 31
views of the valley, the opposite hills, with the long PP III 1 253 57
towards the house on the opposite side of the river, in PP III 1 254 57
time from reserve to quite the opposite--to confidence! MP I 5 49 32
side of Edmund, exactly opposite Miss Crawford, and who MP I 6 56 19
20
away her chair to the opposite side of the table close to MP I 15 147 56
She rushed out at an opposite door from the one her uncle MP II 13 302 9
from the totally opposite feelings of Mr. Crawford, as to MP III 2 331 19
by the prevalence of every thing opposite to them here. MP III 8 391 10
weigh and decide between opposite inclinations and MP III 14 436 15
must be the totally opposite treatment which Maria and MP III 17 463 7
just opposite to her in angry state, was very disagreeable. E I 8 65 50
is requisite in situations directly opposite to your own. E I 18 147 17
his way directly to the opposite side of the circle, where E II 8 220 47
the room at Miss Fairfax, who was sitting exactly opposite. E II 8 222 54
The doors of the two rooms were just opposite each other. E II 11 248 10
Frank was next to Emma, Jane opposite to them--and Mr. E III 5 341 21
to act exactly opposite to what she would have required. E III 10 398 55
something very opposite from her inclination fixed on. P III 2 14 9
and were surmounting an opposite stile; and the Admiral P III 10 91 39
who can give occasion to such directly opposite notions. P IV 2 132 20
Russell would perceive him till they were nearly opposite. P IV 7 179 28
two persons of totally opposite interests, she calmly said, P IV 10 222 39
to defy the suggestions of very opposite feelings. P IV 10 227 69
opposite to them, & they all stopped for a few minutes. S 12 425 1
OPPOSITION (43)
poor Frederica's temper could never bear opposition well. LS 15 267 6
be her real sentiments, said nothing in opposition to mine. LS 22 280 1
opinion of its own in opposition to that of a self-assured NA I 7 48 32
good-nature to make any opposition, and the others rising NA I 8 52 2
she drew away her arm, and Isabella made no opposition. NA I 13 100 13
health in vain, was too polite to make further opposition. NA II 7 179 29
could ill brook the opposition of his son, steady as the NA II 15 247 15
an equally striking opposition of character was no SS I 10 49 12
Opposition on so tender a subject would only attach her SS I 12 59 5
were to cease, this opposition was to yield,--when Mrs. SS I 19 102 2
the opposition you know, and besides it is such a way off. SS I 20 114 44
would be too strong for opposition, and that kind of SS I 21 124 33
opposition and unkindness, could be felt as a relief! SS II 1 140 3
made no further direct opposition to the plan, and merely SS II 3 154 6
to it therefore without opposition, though it proved SS II 10 214 6
Elinor would not humour her by farther opposition. SS II 10 218 33
After some opposition, Marianne yielded to her sister's SS II 11 220 1
think he deserved the compliment of rational opposition. SS II 14 252 19
twelve hundred; and in opposition to this, if he still SS III 1 266 38
that she would not on any account make farther opposition. SS III 3 283 20
friendship, in spite of a great opposition of character,-- PP I 4 16 14
There was another reason too for her opposition. PP II 16 223 25
She did not fear her father's opposition, but he was going PP III 17 375 28
Lady Bertram made no opposition. MP I 1 10 13
at any time, but her opposition to Edmund now arose more MP I 8 79 23
Opposition was vain; and as to Mrs. Norris, he was MP I 13 129 40
his own way, and feel the folly of it without opposition. MP II 2 191 10
wounded by no opposition of interest, cooled by no MP II 6 235 18
Fanny dared not make any further opposition; and with MP II 8 260 23
To Fanny, however, who had known too much opposition all MP III 2 327 5
of all the too public opposition she foresaw to it, had it MP III 3 344 42
Some opposition here is, I am thoroughly convinced, MP III 4 349 23
no fears from opposition of taste, no need of drawing new MP III 17 471 28
a man, there would be no opposition made to his going." E I 18 146 16
to act in direct opposition to Jane Fairfax's sense of E III 15 446 20
were great, from the opposition of two leading principles. P III 2 11 2
it in more decided opposition to Lady Russell, than in P III 2 16 16
Such opposition, as these feelings produced, was more than P III 4 27 5
Husbands and wives generally understand when opposition P III 7 55 9
with at home, no opposition, no caprice, no delays.-- P IV 8 182 8
between them, fail of bearing down every opposition? P IV 12 248 1
The only one among them, whose opposition of feeling could P IV 12 249 3
in defiance of every opposition of feeling & convenience S 8 404 1
OPPRESS (4)
terrific separation must oppress her heart with sadness, NA I 2 18 2
herself; but it did not oppress them by any means so long; NA II 14 234 10
great; his spirits often oppress me--but there is MP III 4 349 25
a thousand thanks, and says you really quite oppress her." E II 3 173 29
OPPRESSED (17)
Marianne was in a silent agony, too much oppressed even SS II 6 178 16
to Elinor's spirits, oppressed as they often were by the SS II 10 215 12
another, and her spirits oppressed to the utmost by the SS III 7 313 21
Anxiety and hope now oppressed her in equal degrees, and SS III 7 314 22
away, remained too much oppressed by a croud of ideas, SS III 9 333 1
so constantly suffering, oppressed by anguish of heart SS III 10 341 6
it to be,--she was oppressed, she was overcome by her own SS III 13 363 8
Astonishment, apprehension, and even horror, oppressed her. PP II 13 204 2
in amazement, but was too much oppressed to make reply. PP III 5 289 44
She was quite oppressed. MP II 1 178 7
Still, however, Fanny, was oppressed and wearied; he saw MP III 4 355 55
He was evidently oppressed, and Fanny must grieve for him, MP III 5 365 35
To be the friend of the poor and oppressed! MP III 10 404 15
the view of cheerfulness oppressed him, and the lovely MP III 15 447 35
His tender compassion towards oppressed worth can go no E III 17 465 24
of being oppressed by the presence of so many strangers. P III 11 99 22
her heart was too full, her breath too much oppressed. P IV 11 235 33
OPPRESSION (5)
the result of some oppression of spirits, than of any SS I 10 50 12
This violent oppression of spirits continued the whole SS I 15 82 47
resolutely against the oppression of her feelings, that SS I 22 134 53
to be an inconvenience, an oppression for ever." E III 7 373 44
Anne felt an instant oppression, and, wherever she looked, P IV 10 226 63
OPPRESSIVE (2)
She sat in a blaze of oppressive heat, in a cloud of MP III 15 439
comfort, seen under a sun bright, without being oppressive. E III 6 360 3
OPPRESSIVELY (1)
at the head of her table, and in spirits oppressively high. PP III 8 310
OPTION (1)
feelings, to give her the option of continuing the SS III 13 367 2
ORACLE (1)
Fanny was her oracle. MP III 12 418
ORAL (1)
I can give as authentic oral testimony as you can desire, P IV 9 204 8
ORANGE (1)
is about as orange as the cuffs and capes of my livery." P III 3 22 2
ORATOR (2)
"are you still to be a great orator in spite of yourself?" SS I 17 90
it if I could--but as you well know, I am no orator." SS III 4 289 3
ORCHARD (6)
as well as her father's, including church-yard and orchard. NA II 7 178 2
round the garden and orchard again and again, as if NA II 15 240
My mother says the orchard was always famous in her E II 9 238 5
orchard in blossom, and light column of smoke ascending.-- E III 6 360 4
man breaking into his orchard--wall torn down--apples P III 3 23 2
& rich in the garden, orchard & meadows which are the best S 4 379
ORCHARDS (1)
forest trees and orchards of luxuriant growth declare that P III 11 95
ORCHESTRA (4)
When the orchestra struck up a fresh dance, James would NA I 8 57 2
sett, walking off to the orchestra to order the dance, W 330 1
her attention to the orchestra, and look straight forward. P IV 8 188 4
in the seats of grandeaur; round the orchestra, of course." P IV 9 193 1
ORCHESTRA'S (1)
been given, by the Orchestra's striking up a favourite air, W 328
ORDAINED (7)
as soon as he can light upon a Bishop, he will be ordained. SS III 2 275 2
for the best; he will be ordained shortly, and should it SS III 2 277 3
Aye, to be sure, he must be ordained in readiness; and I SS III 4 286 1
resolved on being ordained, if I would present him to the PP II 12 201
How unlucky that you are not ordained, Mr. Rushworth and MP I 9 89 2
"Ordained!" said Miss Crawford; "what, are you to be a MP I 9 89 2
but among those who were ordained twenty, thirty, forty MP III 3 339 2
ORDER (63)
a little notice in order to detach him from Miss Manwaring. LS 2 244
on the subject of it, in order to understand the LS 22 281
Her father, instead of giving her an unlimited order on NA I 2 19
to set off very early, in order to be at home in good time. NA I 13 97
her promise to them in order to do what was wrong in NA I 13 105 4
At last, however, the order of release was given; and much NA II 5 156
of that kind, might have been tempted to order a new set. NA II 7 175 1
stopping five minutes to order refreshments to be in the NA II 8 182
Lady Middleton frequently called him to order, wondered SS I 7 35
in the most melancholy order of disastrous love. SS I 11 57 1
to Mr. Harris, and an order for post-horses directly, she SS III 7 311 1
signal for Mrs Edwards to order hers to the door; & in a W 327
off to the orchestra to order the dance, while Miss W 330 1
I shall order a Barrel of oysters, & be famously snug." W 335 1
that I moved this way in order to beg for a partner." PP I 6 26 3
Mr. Hurst called them to order, with bitter complaints of PP I 8 40 5
conversation instead of dancing made the order of the day." PP I 11 55
into Hunsford lane, in order to have the earliest PP II 7 170
He was coming to us, in order to assure us of his concern, PP III 5 290 4
Kitty, run down and order the carriage. PP III 7 307 4
she told me, on purpose to order in some meat on Wednesday, PP III 11 331 1
repeat the chronological order of the kings of England, MP I 2 18 2
Their vanity was in such good order, that they seemed to MP I 4 35
but I shall always like Julia best, because you order me." MP I 5 45
is at home; and nobody else can keep Mrs. Norris in order. MP I 17 162 1
in order to look about me; and saw how it might all be. MP II 7 242 2
This was an order to be most joyfully obeyed; this was an MP III 1 322 4
"But, Fanny," he presently added, "in order to have a MP III 4 346
better order than she could, acquitted herself very well. MP III 7 383 3
be heightening danger in order to enhance her own MP III 14 432 1
It was settled that he should order the carriage to the MP III 15 445 2
to give up every dearer plan, in order to fly with her." MP III 16 455 1
in order to subdue me; at least, it appeared so to me. MP III 16 459 3
to her other friends, in order to secure herself from MP III 17 466 1
"He had gone three miles round one day, in order to bring E I 4 28
The yeomanry are precisely the order of people with whom I E I 4 29 1
be done in London; the order must go through the hands of E I 6 48 4
of the first order, in form as well as quantity. E I 9 70
"You had better order the carriage directly, my love," E I 15 127 1
and Emma, at last, in order to put the Martins out of her E II 3 180 5
in for half a minute, in order to hear that his son was E II 6 196
call on the Bateses, in order to hear the new instrument. E II 9 233 2
a general direction, an order indefinite as to time, to E II 10 241 1
at exactly the proper hour, and in the proper order. E II 16 290
Let me order the carriage. E III 6 362 4
I must order the carriage. E III 6 363 4
You order me, whether you speak or not. E III 7 369 1
In order to assist a concealment so essential to me, I was E III 14 438
would be kept in almost as high order as they are now. P III 3 18
come down to Taunton in order to look at some advertised P III 3 21 1
himself to him in order to make particular inquiries, and P III 3 21 1
conscious of such an overthrow of all order and neatness! P III 5 40 4
I cannot get them into any order,"--she never had the P III 6 44
in tolerable order by more cake than is good for them." P III 6 45
him, being called to order by his wife, now came up to P III 8 68 3
3
She roused herself to say, as they struck by order into P III 10 85 1
all her evening engagements in order to wait on her. P IV 5 158 2
Charles, ring and order a chair. P IV 11 238 4
hospitality sir,--& in order to do away with any S 1 367
honest old place--and Hillier keeps it in very good order. S 4 380
low windows upstairs, in order to close the blinds, or S 11 422
& every thing had a suitable air of property & order.-- S 12 427
in the order and the importance of her style of living.-- S 12 427
ORDERED (36)
Reginald was all but gone; his horse was ordered, & almost LS 24 285
have been in, & mama had ordered me never to speak to you LS 24 286
the Morlands lived, was ordered to Bath for the benefit of NA I 1 17 1
violence, ordered "dinner to be on table directly!" NA II 6 165
the very carriage is ordered, and will be here at seven NA II 13 224 1
Morland's departure, and ordered to think of her no more. NA II 15 244 1
being ordered to acquiesce in them, had been open and bold. NA II 15 247 1
The carriages were then ordered; Willoughby's was first, SS I 13 66 6
chariot, which she knew had not been ordered till one. SS II 7 184 1
Horses for two carriages are ordered from the White Hart, W 323
Mrs Edwards having ordered her carriage, there was no time W 340 1
The carriage was ordered to the door--& no entreaties for W 359 2
was satisfied, and soon afterwards ordered her carriage. PP I 9 45 3
morning, "that you have ordered a good dinner to-day, PP I 13 61
for herself, she would have ordered her wedding clothes. PP I 21 119 2
Her ladyship's carriage is regularly ordered for us. PP II 5 157
Mrs. Collins, gratefully accepted, and immediately ordered. PP II 6 166 4
paid, the carriage was ordered; and after some contrivance, PP II 16 220 1
afterwards; but the things should be ordered immediately." PP III 7 306 4
carriage was unluckily ordered before any of the others, PP III 12 342 2
the chain, which was not ordered with any reference to the MP II 9 263 1
that article as herself;--and two basins only were ordered. E I 12 101 1
Often as she had wished for and ordered it, she had never E I 12 105 5
who could possibly have ordered it--but now, they were E II 8 214 1
May is the very month which Mrs. Churchill is ordered, or E II 18 308 3
is ordered, or has ordered herself, to spend in some E II 18 308 3
Ladies and gentlemen, I am ordered by Miss Woodhouse (who, E III 7 369 1

Ladies and gentlemen--I am ordered by Miss Woodhouse to E III 7 370 23
In spite of the answer, therefore, she ordered the E III 9 390 18
She would have ordered the carriage, and come to you, but E III 10 392 4
to say, that its being ordered was absolutely unknown to E III 14 439 8
She spoke to him--ordered, intreated, and insisted in vain. P III 9 80 29
The dinner, already ordered at the inn, was at last, P III 11 98 15
He was ordered to walk, to keep off the gout, and Mrs. P IV 6 168 24
health--(and if she was ordered to drink Asses milk I S 7 401 1
Our dinner is not ordered till six--& by that time I hope S 9 411 1
ORDERING (1)
After securing accommodations, and ordering a dinner at P III 11 95 9
ORDERLINESS (2)
want some of your nice ways and orderliness at my father's. MP III 6 372 20
course of cheerful orderliness; every body had their due MP III 8 391 11
ORDERLY (3)
he set about it in a very orderly manner, with all the PP I 19 104 1
to the steady sobriety and orderly silence of the other. MP II 7 240 9
to as formal and as orderly as the others; but when the E II 8 218 38
39
ORDERS (50)
John Thorpe, who in the mean time had been giving orders NA I 7 45 5
Catherine followed her orders and turned away, but not too NA I 9 62 8
who was then abroad, had left strict orders on that head. SS I 12 62 28
"What magnificent orders would travel from this family to SS I 17 92 25
is that he should take orders as soon as he can, and then SS II 2 149 25
would not much approve of Edward's going into orders." SS II 2 149 27
to attend to their orders; and they were obliged to wait. SS II 11 220 3
He was giving orders for a toothpick-case for himself, and SS II 11 220 3
and if he was to go into orders, as he had some thoughts, SS III 2 273 16
agreed he should take orders directly, and they must wait SS III 2 274 16
I understand that he intends to take orders. SS III 3 282 19
you mean to take orders, he has great pleasure in offering SS III 4 288 28
that would do as well; somebody that is in orders already." SS III 4 291 51
imagined) he could be in orders, and consequently before SS III 12 357 2
against Edward's taking orders for the sake of two hundred SS III 14 374 4
written down, I bring your sister's orders for the same.--" W 339 18
was all in pursuit of Mr. Bingley, and under your orders." PP I 7 31 31
My fingers wait your orders." PP II 8 175 20
allow, and if he took orders, desired that a valuable PP II 12 200 5
resolved against taking orders, he hoped I should not PP II 12 200 5
some very plentiful orders, had not Jane, though with some PP III 7 307 48
of never taking orders, and that the business had been PP III 10 329 31
The housekeeper at Netherfield had received orders to PP III 11 331 13
to some friend to hold till he were old enough for orders. MP I 3 23 2
"If Edmund were but in orders!" cried Julia, and running MP I 9 89 25
but in orders now, you might perform the ceremony directly. MP I 9 89 25
"Yes, I shall take orders soon after my father's return-- MP I 9 89 28
as I was at first that you should intend to take orders. MP I 9 93 53
events; your sister's marriage, and your taking orders." MP I 11 108 8
"My taking orders I assure you is quite as voluntary as MP I 11 108 13
"But the motives of a man who takes orders with the MP I 11 109 20
"What! take orders without a living! MP I 11 109 21
man is neither to take orders with a living, nor without? MP I 11 109 22
had received his orders and taken his measurements, had MP I 14 130 1
I find he takes orders in a few weeks. MP II 5 226 61
The assurance of Edmund's being so soon to take orders, MP II 5 227 69
for her; Sir Thomas gave orders and Mrs. Norris ran about, MP II 8 254 9
at her side, gave his orders for her sitting down entirely. MP II 10 279 22
Sir Thomas had given orders for it. MP III 1 322 51
far as my house with some orders for Nanny," said she, " MP III 1 323 54
and more than half a mind to take orders and preach myself. MP III 3 341 28
They are two distinct orders of being. MP III 4 355 54
And they think she will have her orders in a day or two. MP III 7 377 7
in time; for she may have her orders to-morrow, perhaps. MP III 7 378 10
I should not wonder if you had your orders to-morrow; but MP III 7 380 20
The thrush had had her orders, the wind had changed, and MP III 8 388 2
to orders, with her pitcher, to fetch broth from Hartfield. E I 10 88 33
He was in orders, and having a curacy in the neighbourhood P III 9 73 4
letters, but the Grappler was under orders for Portsmouth. P III 12 108 28
hear a word of Mrs P.'s orders to the servant as they S 6 391 1
ORDINARILY (1)
Fairfax could be thought only ordinarily gifted with it. E II 5 194 43
ORDINARY (18)
the Pump-Room, where the ordinary course of events and NA I 10 71 8
the ordinary course of life can hardly afford a return. NA I 15 117 8
After being used to such a home as the Abbey, an ordinary NA II 5 157 10
The General, accustomed on every ordinary occasion to give NA II 15 247 15
with propriety in the discharge of his ordinary duties. SS I 1 5 7
become familiar, and the ordinary pursuits which had given SS I 9 40 1
requires a more than ordinary share of private balls and SS II 2 151 43
on returning from her ordinary visit to Mrs. Palmer, SS III 1 257 2
3
He had more than the ordinary triumph of accepted love to SS III 13 361 3
were now added to his ordinary means of entertainment; he W 359 28
But in general and ordinary cases between friend and PP I 10 50 37
as may be adapted to ordinary occasions, I always wish to PP I 14 68 11
Has he deigned to add ought of civility to his ordinary PP II 18 234 33
to it, in the ordinary school-system for boys, the MP III 3 339 22
At a more than ordinary pitch of thumping and hallooing in MP III 7 383 30
might warrant a man of ordinary observation and delicacy, E I 16 136 9
as much as her words, for something more than ordinary. E III 4 337 3
those vapid tissues of ordinary occurrences from which no S 8 403 1
ORDINATION (6)
will of course have much to do relative to his ordination." SS III 4 286 15
suppose two or three months will complete his ordination." SS III 4 291 50
for having received ordination at Easter, I have been so PP I 13 62 12
fix his fate in life--ordination and matrimony--events of MP II 8 254 10
to receive ordination in the course of the Christmas week. MP II 8 255 10
service once since his ordination; and upon this being MP III 3 340 24
ORIEL (1)
the next day; Jackson, of Oriel, bid me sixty at once; NA I 7 47 19
ORIGIN (13)
at their door--not one young man whose origin was unknown. NA I 1 16 10
Its origin--jealousy perhaps, or wanton cruelty--was yet NA II 8 188 16
Her partiality for this gentleman was not of recent origin; NA II 16 251 5
humiliation must be the origin of those regrets, which she SS II 10 213 2
That crime has been the origin of every lesser one, and of SS III 11 352 17
"This was in fact the origin of our acting," said Tom MP II 1 184 26
Such was the origin of the sort of intimacy which took MP II 4 207 11
Matrimony, as the origin of change, was always E I 1 7 10
were of low origin, in trade, and only moderately genteel. E II 7 207 6
feelings, whatever their origin, and could not but resolve E II 10 240 6
of course, the same origin, must be equally under cure.-- E III 11 403 2
might have no origin but in the language of the relators. P IV 3 140 11
it and her sister's; the origin of one all selfish vanity, P IV 8 185 20
ORIGINAL (17)
lasted some time, the original subject seemed entirely NA I 8 57 21
The original was all her own--her own happy thoughts and SS III 8 328 63
Elizabeth to the enjoyment of all her original dislike. PP I 8 35 1
the rashness of your original intention as atoned for by PP I 10 49 32
was settled that their original design of leaving PP I 12 59 1
madam; but I believe we must abide by our original plan." PP II 14 211 11
sensation towards the original, than she had ever felt in PP III 1 250 48
who scarcely risked an original thought of his own beyond MP I 10 97 3
over to you all the duty of remembering the original giver. MP II 8 259 19
pleased: for the original plan was that William should go MP II 9 266 21
more beautiful is the original, and after being asked for E I 7 56 44
and lament that its original purpose should have ceased. E II 6 197 5
in the slightest particular from the original recital. E III 3 336 13
be it prose or verse, original or repeated--or two things E III 7 370 23
with being the sole and original author of the mischief; E III 11 402 1
original strength, has outlived all the storms of autumn. P III 10 88 26
reasonably wish for her original thirty thousand pounds S 3 376 1
ORIGINALITY (1)
delicacy, discretion, originality of thought, and literary NA I 6 39 1
ORIGINALLY (14)
here beyond the time originally fixed for his return, is LS 8 255 1
of delaying that hour beyond the time originally fixed. LS 30 299 1
Originally perhaps it was applied only to express neatness, NA I 14 108 16
If not originally their's, by what strange events could it NA II 6 164 2
him up, had given him originally great humility of manner, PP I 15 70 1
glazing altogether had originally cost Sir Lewis de Bourgh. PP II 6 161 8
though what had been originally plain, had suffered all MP I 16 152 2
and its having been originally her brother's gift makes no MP II 9 263 14
An attachment, originally as tranquil as their tempers, MP III 13 428 15
prudence might originally suggest; and more than a E I 8 67 57
Precisely such had the paragraph originally stood from the P III 1 3 2
how much had been originally implied against him; but her P IV 9 208 94
to have been right in originally dividing them, he was P IV 12 251 10
it was furniture rather originally good & extremely well S 12 427 1
ORIGINALS (1)
Oh! could the originals of the portraits against the P III 5 40 44
ORIGINATE (1)
their engagement could originate, Elizabeth was at a loss PP III 15 360 1
ORIGINATED (9)
"It originated in an action of my daughter's, which LS 24 289 12
that his affection originated in nothing better than NA II 15 243 9
I can hardly tell why, or in what the deception originated. SS I 17 93 37
in leaving them, originated in the same fettered SS I 19 102 2
Elinor honoured her for a plan which originated so nobly SS III 10 343 10
It originated in Mrs. Gardiner, who, fatigued by the PP III 1 256 61
dislike of her had originated in jealousy, she could not PP III 3 267 1
and use of it, originated in an act of kindness by Susan, MP III 9 396 7
It had originated in misapprehension entirely. P IV 3 138 7
ORIGINATING (2)
very far was it, from originating in anxiety for Reginald. LS 11 259 2
proposal of dancing--originating nobody exactly knew where- E II 8 229 98
ORNAMENT (9)
of every well-known ornament, they proceeded into the NA II 8 182 2
must ornament his goodness with every possible charm." SS I 3 18 20
has deprived the British court of its brightest ornament. PP I 14 67 9
as a convenience or an ornament; and perhaps in another MP II 4 208 12
I must be satisfied with rather less ornament and beauty. MP II 7 242 24
and the almost solitary ornament in her possession, a very MP II 8 254 8
your lovely throat an ornament which his money purchased MP II 8 259 20
is the only ornament I have ever had a desire to possess. MP II 9 262 8
I am resolved to have some in an ornament for the head. E III 18 479 70
ORNAMENTAL (1)
and, having reached the ornamental part of the premises, NA II 11 214 25
ORNAMENTED (2)
and brought home, ornamented her present drawing room; and SS II 12 234 26
up by her friend, and ornamented with cyphers and trophies. E I 9 69 3
ORNAMENTS (9)
and ornaments over it of the prettiest English china. NA II 5 162 26
rich in Gothic ornaments, stood forward for admiration. NA II 7 177 19
beauty of its wood, and ornaments of rich carving might be NA II 8 184 5
its size, shape, and ornaments were determined, all of SS II 11 220 3
proportion and finished ornaments, they followed the PP II 6 161 10
had seen such beautiful ornaments as made her quite wild; PP II 19 238 5
greatest elegancies and ornaments were a faded footstool MP I 16 152 2
midst of all the rich ornaments which she supposed all the MP II 8 254 8
I must put on a few ornaments now, because it is expected E II 17 302 22
ORNEE (1)
a tasteful little cottage Ornee, on a strip of waste S 3 377 1
ORPHAN (2)
This lady was one of my nearest relations, an orphan from SS II 9 205 24
Jane Fairfax was an orphan, the only child of Mrs. Bates's E II 2 163 1
ORPHAN OF THE RHINE (1)
Midnight Bell, Orphan of the Rhine, and Horrid Mysteries. NA I 6 40 10
ORTHOGRAPHY (1)
his penknife or his orthography, as either were wanted; MP I 2 16 20
OSBORNE-CASTLE (1)
She was quite vanquished, & the fashions of Osborne-Castle W 358 28
OSBORNES (12)
entertained that the Osbornes themselves would be there.-- W 314 1
till late; & if the Osbornes are coming, he will wait in W 319 2
The Osbornes will certainly be at the ball tonight.-- W 323 3
The Osbornes being known to have been at the first ball, W 323 3
The Osbornes are to be no rule for us. W 325 4
We shall have a famous ball, the Osbornes are certainly W 327 7
general notice, & "the Osbornes are coming, the Osbornes W 329 9
the Osbornes are coming"--was repeated round the room.-- W 329 9
At their conclusion the Osbornes & their train were all on W 335 13
spirits, her head full of Osbornes, Blakes & Howards.-- W 337 15
How long did you keep it up, after the Osbornes & I went W 340 19
"Yes, quite as full as ever, except the Osbornes. W 340 19
OSTENSIBLE (3)
His ostensible reason, however, was to ask whether Mr. E I 9 81 78
cheek which gave it a meaning not otherwise ostensible. E III 5 348 21
I cannot deny that Miss Woodhouse was my ostensible object- E III 14 438 8
OSTENTATION (3)
But to be candid without ostentation or design--to take PP I 4 14 9
there was indelicacy or ostentation in his manner--and MP II 10 278 20
There would have been either the ostentation of a coxcomb, E II 8 212 3
OSTENTATIOUS (2)
whole evening, & so ostentatious & artful a display had LS 17 270 3
a second time with ostentatious formality to his humble PP II 5 155 3
OSTENTATIOUSLY (1)
which had been ostentatiously dropped by Mary, as well as P IV 10 216 18
OSTLER (4)
head man at the crown, ostler, and every thing of that E III 8 383 29
he told us what John ostler had been telling him, and then E III 8 383 29
What Mr. Elton had learnt from the ostler on the subject, E III 8 383 31
the crown chaise, and the ostler had stood out and seen it E III 8 383 31
OSTLER'S (1)
the accumulation of the ostler's own knowledge, and the E III 8 383 31
OTHELLO (1)
Neither Hamlet, nor Macbeth, nor Othello, nor Douglas, nor MP I 14 130 3
OTHER'S (13)
from our not rightly understanding each other's meaning. LS 24 287 11
equally mistaken in each other's meaning, I resolved to LS 24 290 13
walked, pinned up each other's train for the dance, and NA I 5 37 4
Design could never bring them in each other's way: SS II 10 213 4
each other's acquaintance, for it could not be otherwise. SS III 13 370 36
because you are in each other's confidence and have secret PP I 11 56 15
of ever hearing of each other's existence during the MP I 1 4 2
were still kicking each other's shins, and hallooing out MP III 7 383 31
other's punishment, and then induce a voluntary separation. MP III 17 464 10
They knew not each other's opinion, either its constancy P III 4 29 8
in and out of each other's house at all hours, that it was P III 5 36 21
in a knowledge of each other's character, truth, and P IV 11 240 59
likely to be necessary to each other's ultimate comfort. P IV 12 248 1
OTHERS (356)
But in this case, as well as in many others, the world has LS 14 264 2
& at others that her temper only is in fault. LS 17 271 8
easily biassed by others, is an attribute which you know I LS 25 294 5
will to the caprices of others--of resigning my own LS 39 308 1
& separation between the others, could not, to the great LS 42 311 1
himself a little too much with the foibles of others.-- NA I 3 29 47
The others are very much admired too, but I believe NA I 4 32 3
all the others, they are the stupidest things in creation." NA I 7 48 34
any opposition, and the others rising up, Isabella had NA I 8 52 2
Come, Miss Morland, be quick, for the others are in a NA I 9 61 1
scarcely allowed the two others time enough to get through NA I 9 62 7

been constantly leading others into difficulties, which he NA I 9 66 31
her to go out with the others; and, as it was, she could NA I 9 69 51
The others walked away, John Thorpe was still in view, and NA I 10 75 24
and the two others walked in, to give their assistance. NA I 11 84 19
The others then came close enough for conversation, and NA I 11 88 54
of not going with the others to the theatre that night; NA I 12 92 4
thus to expose her feelings to the notice of others? NA I 13 98 3
The three others still continued together, walking in a NA I 13 99 9
due to others, and to her own character in their opinion. NA I 13 101 25
others, which a sensible person would always wish to avoid. NA I 14 110 28
through this into several others, without perceiving any NA II 5 160 21
Two others, penned by the same hand, marked an expenditure NA II 7 172 2
affirmative, the two others were passed by; and NA II 7 180 37
and, when the genius of others had failed, his own had NA II 8 183 3
My eyes will be blinding for the good of others; and yours NA II 8 187 15
Upon his opinion of her danger, two others were called in NA II 9 197 25
forced to return; and the others withdrew, after Eleanor NA II 10 203 8
and at others that it was wholly incompatible with it. NA II 11 209 5
I rejoice to say, that the young man whom, of all others, NA II 12 216 2
calm acquiescence, and at others was answered by the NA II 14 231 4
each for the sake of the others resolved to appear happy. SS I 6 28 2
of which were open downs, the others cultivated and woody. SS I 6 28 3
and every body was astonished at the opinion of the others. SS I 6 31 9
his conversation with the others while every song lasted. SS I 7 35 9
the occasion, which the others had reasonably forfeited by SS I 7 35 9
insensibility of the others; and she was reasonable enough SS I 7 35 9
The weather was not tempting enough to draw the two others SS I 9 41 3
others, and with an energy which always adorned her praise. SS I 9 43 11
for the esteem of the others, it is a reproach in itself. SS I 10 50 17
to the pleasure of the others, by any share in their SS I 11 55 6
together by mutual consent, while the others were dancing. SS I 11 55 8
each other, and seven days are more than enough for others. SS I 12 59 4
of the feelings of others; and much was said on the SS I 12 62 27
had kept in the lanes, while the others went on the downs. SS I 13 67 60
interruption from the others, she would have described SS I 13 69 77
hills, and could never be found when the others set off. SS I 16 85 15
next morning before the others were down; and Marianne, SS I 18 96 2
not only the meaning of others, but such of Marianne's SS I 18 100 23
but there were two others, a gentleman and lady, who were SS I 19 105 13
by finding, like many others of his sex, that through some SS I 20 112 28
and whose conduct towards others, made every shew of SS I 22 127 2
themselves from the others; and though they met at least SS II 1 142 8
Lady Middleton proposed a rubber of Casino to the others. SS II 1 144 15
or the intelligence of others could give her, but likewise SS II 4 159 1
them, from all that interested and occupied the others. SS II 4 164 24
obliged to assist in making a whist-table for the others. SS II 4 166 31
left behind, the next morning, when the others went out. SS II 5 169 15
"By many--by some of whom you know nothing, by others with SS II 5 173 44
of others, while reviving her with lavender water. SS II 6 177 12
letter in her hand, and two or three others lying by her. SS II 7 182 12
as herself, and at others, lost every consolation in the SS II 9 201 2
led in her opinion of others, by the irritable refinement SS II 9 201 4
time has no conscience in his intrusion on that of others." SS II 9 204 16
been intended to raise myself at the expense of others." SS II 9 210 32
as they often were by the clamorous kindness of the others. SS II 10 215 12
of all others, had they known as much as she did, they SS II 12 232 16
and the curiosity of the others being of course excited, SS II 12 234 28
to the comfort of the others, and would not say a word; SS II 13 241 22
Marianne, to leave the others by themselves: and she SS II 13 241 23
But so little were they, any more than the others, SS II 14 247 4
to hear it talked of by others, without betraying that she SS III 1 260 10
Elinor was to be the comforter of others in her own SS III 1 261 12
while the comfort of others was dear to me, I was glad to SS III 1 263 27
them by working on others;--and represented it, therefore, SS III 3 280 6
whom neither of the others had so much reason to dislike. SS III 5 294 3
place, in which, of all others, she would now least chuse SS III 6 301 2
its walls, while the others were busily helping Charlotte SS III 6 302 8
She returned just in time to join the others as they SS III 6 303 10
the expectation of the others was by no means so cheerful. SS III 7 309 7
Others even arose to confirm it. SS III 7 314 22
with some others, was brought to me there from my lodgings. SS III 8 328 61
be the very he whom, of all others, I could least bear----- SS III 8 332 83
of its being known to others; and she soon discovered in SS III 10 340 2
Mrs. Dashwood and Elinor then followed, and the others SS III 10 341 5
the park; and there are others of more modern production SS III 10 343 9
imprudence towards myself, and want of kindness to others. SS III 10 345 28
They shall no longer worry others, nor torture myself. SS III 10 347 30
In a moment she perceived that the others were likewise SS III 12 358 9
the village--leaving the others in the greatest SS III 12 360 26
of it occurred to the others, proper measures would have SS III 13 371 38
E.--, very strongly--but I am not sensible of the others.-- W 324 3
observation of others, that it was an excellent ball.-- W 329 9
came back after the others were out of the room, to "beg W 336 13
ball, were rather flat, in comparison with the others.-- W 336 14
of every grace, & others could never be persuaded that she W 337 17
Emma was glad when they were joined by the others; it was W 353 26
be the worst of all parties; & the others were delighted.-- W 357 28
At this interesting moment he was called on by the others, W 359 28
Lizzy is not a bit better than the others; and I am sure PP I 1 4 26
her husband, "and all the others equally well married, I PP I 3 9 2
so honestly blind to the follies and nonsense of others! PP I 4 14 9
entitled to think well of themselves, and meanly of others. PP I 4 15 11
vanity to what we would have others think of us." PP I 5 20 20
To this discovery succeeded some others equally mortifying. PP I 6 23 12
with her himself, attended to her conversation with others. PP I 6 24 13
intruder as she believed she was considered by the others. PP I 8 35 2
He immediately offered to fetch her others; all that his PP I 8 37 26
I cannot forget the follies and vices of others so soon as PP I 11 58 28
not much to Elizabeth, and nothing at all to the others. PP I 17 86 9
Others of the party were now applied to. PP I 18 101 70
him again, put it out of her power to dance with others. PP I 18 102 73
She rated his abilities much higher than any of the others; PP I 22 124 11
and luckily for the others, the business of love-making PP I 23 129 15
for her sister, and resentment against all the others. PP II 1 133 3
to do wrong, or to make others unhappy, there may be error, PP II 1 136 17
ladies drove on, and the others returned into the house. PP II 5 159 20
could furnish her with an occasion of dictating to others. PP II 6 163 15
of the three others, or relating some anecdote of herself. PP II 6 166 41
frequently went while the others were calling on Lady PP II 7 169 5
that never can bear to be frightened at the will of others. PP II 8 174 13
many others, because he is rich, and many others are poor. PP II 10 183 10
what misrepresentation, can you here impose upon others?" PP II 11 191 17
of the feelings of others, were such as to form that PP II 11 193 28
I saw, in common with others, that Bingley preferred your PP II 12 197 5
his abuse of me to others, as in his reproaches to myself. PP II 12 201 5
a few minutes before the others appeared; and he took the PP II 15 215 1
in Meryton, he dined with others of the officers at PP II 18 233 26
not to himself, to many others, for it must deter him from PP II 18 234 38
This was praise, of all others most extraordinary, most PP III 1 248 31
The others then joined her, and expressed their admiration PP III 1 252 54
They soon outstripped the others, and when they had PP III 1 257 65
He observed to her, at a moment when the others were PP III 2 262 8
account, as well as some others, found herself, when their PP III 2 264 12
bred than either of the others; and between her and Mrs. PP III 3 267 4
for him gave way, and others of the regiment, who treated PP III 5 285 18
of course repeated by the others, and they soon found that PP III 5 287 33
must be of all others most afflicting to a parent's mind. PP III 6 296 11
the fortunes of all the others, for who, as Lady Catherine PP III 6 297 11
You were not by, when I told mamma, and the others, all PP III 9 318 22
go together; and the others were to meet us at the church. PP III 9 319 24
Are the others coming out?" PP III 10 327 8
The others have been gone on to Scarborough, these three PP III 12 342 24
the others, and she had no opportunity of detaining them. PP III 12 342 27
"And how impossible in others!" PP III 12 343 35
after tea; for as the others were all going to sit down to PP III 13 346 21
Its completion depended on others. PP III 14 355 44
Bingley and Jane, however, soon allowed the others to PP III 16 365 1
room, and from all the others when they sat down to table. PP III 17 372 1
even feared that with the others it was a dislike which PP III 17 372 2
"It may do very well for the others," replied Mr. Bingley; PP III 17 374 24
she was able to join the others with tolerable composure. PP III 17 377 41
Mrs. Norris was often observing to the others, that she MP I 1 5 4
to dictate liberality to others: but her love of money was MP I 1 8 9
fair to expect Ellis to wait on her as well as the others. MP I 1 9 12
in to the others, and recommending her to their kindness. MP I 2 12 1
the very age of all others to need most attention and care, MP I 3 28 42
of others at their present most interesting time of life. MP I 3 32 62
of breaking it to all the others, when Sir Thomas's MP I 4 34 2
expect most from others, and are least honest themselves." MP I 5 46 20
Mrs. and the two Miss Sneyds, with others of their MP I 5 51 40
consideration among the others; and Mrs. Grant could not MP I 6 60 53
own amusement or that of others; perfectly allowable, when MP I 7 64 11
she looked back, that the others were walking down the MP I 7 69 21
Mrs. Grant to alight and the others to take their places. MP I 8 80 29
of obliging the others, to secure it, the matter was MP I 8 80 29
in the conversation of the others, nor did she desire it. MP I 8 80 31
Fanny and some of the others were attending Mrs. Rushworth, MP I 9 85 4
after a little time the others began to form into parties, MP I 9 90 36
just consideration of others, that knowledge of her own MP I 9 91 36
seemed to be to hear the others, and who scarcely risked MP I 10 97 3
It was the very thing of all others to be wished, it was MP I 10 97 4
Where are the others? MP I 10 100 24
till the return of the others, and the arrival of dinner. MP I 10 104 51
in the habit of teaching others their duty every week, MP I 11 112 30
of others! joining them the moment she is asked. MP I 11 112 34
noticed in some of the others, and which seemed to say MP I 12 116 11
trying to persuade the others that there were some fine MP I 14 131 6
would be, to think of the others, or draw any of those MP I 15 138 1
If others have blundered, it is your place to put them MP I 15 140 13
Nobody was at the trouble of an answer; the others soon MP I 15 142 23
Is it practicable for any of the others to double it? MP I 15 144 36
It will be such a triumph to the others!" MP I 16 155 15
a volume on the table and then taking up some others.) MP I 16 156 27
to him alone, and ridiculing the acting of the others. MP I 17 160 8
had not, and giving occasion of discontent to the others.-- MP I 18 165 2
all his scenes, but the others aspired at nothing beyond MP I 18 166 4
most palpitating heart, while the others prepared to begin. MP I 18 172 32
delay, sent him after the others with delighted haste. MP II 1 176 3
would be fair by the others to have every body run away." MP II 1 177 5
he mingled among the others with the least obtrusiveness MP II 1 184 25
Look so to all the others, but not to him!" MP II 1 185 27
It was impossible for many of the others not to smile. MP II 1 186 35
say nothing unkind of the others; but there was only one MP II 2 187 1
By all the others it was mentioned with regret, and his MP II 2 194 20
and the spirits of many others saddened, it was all MP II 3 196 1
was in hopes the question would be followed up by others. MP II 3 198 11
and with regard to some others, I can perceive, from MP II 3 198 13
quite so far as his judgment might have dictated to others. MP II 3 201 22
so obedient--at others, so bewildered and so weak--and at MP II 4 209 12
at others again, so tyrannic, so beyond controul!-- MP II 4 209 12
she was now following the others, she had nearly resolved MP II 4 214 46
looks of the three others standing round him, shewed how MP II 5 223 48
Fraternal love, sometimes almost every thing, is at others MP II 6 235 18
sensations in two of the others, two of his most attentive MP II 7 248 47
absence of some is not to debar the others of amusement." MP II 8 252 3
her to join in with the others, before their happiness and MP II 8 253 4
did, for now the others are away, we feel the good of it." MP II 11 285 10
different from what they were when he talked to the others. MP II 13 304 16
the others, he had nothing to do but to go in good earnest. MP II 13 307 35
will influence her in her opinion of the wants of others. MP III 1 313 12
Here was again a want of delicacy and regard for others MP III 2 328 9
the dependence of having others present when they met, was MP III 5 356 4
a year or two, and sees others made commanders before him? MP III 6 368 8
With such thoughts as these among ten hundred others, MP III 7 376 5
disappeared with the others, there were soon only her MP III 7 382 28
to make her better bear with its excesses to the others. MP III 9 396 5
or had time for, the others were ready to return; and in MP III 10 406 21
Fanny after all the others were in the house; "I wish I MP III 11 411 20
more gentle, and regardful of others, than formerly. MP III 11 413 32
Others had their hour; and of lesser matters, none MP III 12 419 8
others only established her superiority in wretchedness. MP III 16 448 2
deal more indifference than she met with from the others. MP III 16 448 3
go with him; and the others had been left in a state of MP III 16 450 10
It was of a much less poignant nature than what the others MP III 16 452 15
on that account as on others, to get him out of town, and MP III 16 452 15
very time of all others when if a friend is at hand the MP III 16 453 17
She was speaking only, as she had been used to hear others MP III 16 456 25
and others of the son and the uncle not letting him. E I 1 12 41
others;" rejoined Mr. Woodhouse, understanding but in part. E I 1 13 45
minutes against the earnest pressing of both the others. E I 6 44 19
was not unwilling to have others deceived, or sorry to E I 6 44 19
They would be estimated very differently by others as well E I 8 62 39
She is not to pay for the offence of others, by being held E I 8 62 41
and by this means the others were still able to keep ahead, E I 10 88 33
Our part of London is so very superior to most others!-- E I 12 103 37
This topic was discussed very happily, and others E I 12 104 50
than either of the others; too full of the wonder of his E I 13 112 24
his daughter, when the others appeared, and Mrs. Weston, E I 14 117 3
was going on amongst the others, in the most overpowering E I 14 118 4
I believe you did not hear me telling the others in the E I 14 119 7
Mrs. Weston, "and on others, very little: and among those, E I 14 123 27
"So scrupulous for others," he continued, "and yet so E I 15 125 5
to stay; and while the others were variously urging and E I 15 128 17
18

"I am ready, if the others are." E I 15 128 19
taste, as one proof among others that he had not always E I 16 134 5
claims, and little concerned about the feelings of others. E I 16 135 6
and thaw, which is of all others the most unfriendly for E I 16 138 17
be able to do a great deal more than he can at others." E I 18 146 15
a resolution to do right against the will of others. E I 18 148 22
off from some advantages, it will secure him many others." E I 18 148 23
brought up for educating others; the very few hundred E II 2 164 5
herself, to save her from hearing it abruptly from others. E II 3 177 51
and as orderly as the others; but when the table was again E II 8 218 38
39

To be in company, nicely dressed herself and seeing others E II 8 219 44
at a distance; but by the others, the subject was almost E II 8 220 45
But just got acquainted with Mrs. Weston, and others?-- E II 8 222 51
the others, as if it had passed within the same apartment." E II 10 243 32
Well! evil to some is always good to others. E II 12 262 39
the disappointment of the others, and with considerable E II 12 262 40
41

avoid the suspicions of others, to save your health and E II 13 268 11
12

the first in company, let the others be who they may." E II 14 280 58
and only sharing with others in a general way, in knowing E II 15 284 11
Mrs. Bates, Mrs. Perry, Mrs. Goddard and others, were a E II 16 290 3
They must not do less than others, or she should be E II 16 290 4
I shall only just mention the circumstance to the others E II 17 304 27
too communicative to want others to talk, was very well E II 17 304 29
and are by no means implicitly guided by others. E II 18 309 31
There were three others, Jane says, which they hesitated E III 2 323 19
to do me honour--I would not wish to be inferior to others. E III 2 324 20
21

And at others, what a heap of absurdities it is! E III 5 345 14
If meant to be immediately mixed with the others, and E III 5 348 21
have spoken to some others whom I would wish to meet you." E III 6 354 11
remained, when all the others were invited or persuaded E III 6 357 33
as the others did, and collect round the strawberry beds.-- E III 6 358 35
comparison--the others hardly eatable--hautboys very E III 6 358 35
In this walk Emma and Mr. Weston found all the others E III 6 360 40
alone!--I, who may so soon have to guard others!" E III 6 362 48
sight of Frank Churchill; others took it very composedly; E III 6 366 74
about with any of the others, or sitting almost alone, and E III 7 374 54
niece, too --and before others, many of whom (certainly E III 7 375 61
The first, was his walking with her apart from the others, E III 11 410 35
had been imposed on by others in a most mortifying degree; E III 11 411 43
except in the company of others--she objected only to a E III 12 416 2
full of intrigue, that he should suspect it in others.-- E III 15 446 15
Some might think him, and others might think her, the most E III 17 468 36
The others had been talking of the child, Mrs. Weston E III 18 479 73
nothing else, though pretending to listen to the others?" E III 18 480 77
by the others as having any interest in the question. P III 2 12 3
to see it in the hands of others; a trial of fortitude, P III 2 15 13
of others, to the smallest knowledge of it afterwards. P III 4 31 11
must involve least suffering, to go with the others. P III 5 33 6
civility, or to refresh the others, as she was well aware. P III 6 46 13
A beloved home made over to others; all the precious rooms P III 6 47 16
half a mile distant, making himself agreeable to others! P III 7 58 20
In two minutes after Charles's preparation, the others P III 7 59 25
She had given him up to oblige others. P III 7 61 36
could not keep pace with the conversation of the others.-- P III 8 64 7
him do as you and I, and a great many others, have done. P III 8 70 46
The others will be here presently." P III 9 79 26
satisfied so long as the others all stood about her; but P III 10 86 21
asked before any of the others, or what Louisa called the P III 10 90 38
the others walked on, and he was to join them on the Cobb. P III 11 96 10
occupy and entertain the others, it fell to Anne's lot to P III 11 100 23
to suggest comfort to the others, tried to quiet Mary, to P III 12 111 44
Musgrove, take care of the others." P III 12 111 48
arranged every thing, before the others began to reflect. P III 12 113 56
But as to the rest;--as to the others;--if one stays to P III 12 114 61
and as none of the others could oppose when he gave way, P III 12 115 65
It would be going only to multiply trouble to the others, P IV 1 121 3
to be heard, in spite of all the noise of the others. P IV 2 134 29
but the complaisance of the others was unlooked for. P IV 3 137 3
advantages over all the others which they had either seen P IV 3 137 4
Anne drew a little back, while the others received his P IV 3 143 18
diffused again among the others, and it was only at P IV 3 144 21
more charitable, or more indifferent, towards the others. P IV 4 146 6
Anne kept her appointment; the others kept theirs, and of P IV 5 158 21
by her in collecting others, and had been at the trouble P IV 5 158 21
of indignation or delight, at the evil or good of others. P IV 5 161 28
the open-hearted, the eager character beyond all others. P IV 5 161 28
so determined, that the others were obliged to settle it P IV 7 174 3
her senses, she found the others still waiting for the P IV 7 175 5
The others joined them, and it was a group in which Anne P IV 8 184 17
The others returned, the room filled again, benches were P IV 8 189 45
He will not be led astray, he will not be misled by others P IV 9 196 32
He has no feeling for others. P IV 9 199 53
to me quite as good as others, and much more agreeable P IV 9 199 55
than most others, and we were almost always together. P IV 9 199 55
papers, I found it with others still more trivial from P IV 9 203 70
could bear the eye of others, before she could recover P IV 9 204 76
77
weakness, and from employing others by her want of money. P IV 9 210 98
could hazard among the too-commanding claims of the others. P IV 10 214 12
glad to see them; and the others were not so sorry but P IV 10 216 18
Charles's following the others to admire mirrors and china; P IV 10 219 27
if Henrietta and all the others liked it, when Mary P IV 10 223 42
43
make the best of it, as many others have done before them. P IV 11 230 6
Their attention was called towards the others.-- P IV 11 236 35
tones of "that voice, when they would be lost on others.-- P IV 11 237 42
I began to reflect that others might have felt the same-- P IV 11 242 65
be loved and sought by others, but I knew to a certainty P IV 11 244 70
which no experience in others can equal, and Lady Russell P IV 12 249 4
to flatter and follow others, without being flattered and P IV 12 251 9
much they are occupied in promoting the good of others!-- S 5 388 1
any occupation that may be of use to himself or others.-- S 5 388 1
silence by the efforts of others, to Miss D. at Lady D.'s S 7 396 1
The others all left them, Sir Edw: with looks of very S 7 399 1
but either of the two others are nice little snug houses, S 7 402 1
is the same, he fancies she feels like him in others.-- S 7 402 1
till rejoined by the others, who as they issued from the S 8 403 1
I know them only through others.-- S 9 408 1
I hate to employ others, when I am equal to act myself-- S 9 409 1
ourselves to be of use of others, I am convinced that the S 9 410 1
cannot answer for it; the others will be at the hotel all S 9 411 1
for the good of others, or else extremely ill themselves. S 10 412 1
She was not made acquainted with the others till the S 10 413 1
to Sanditon, but the others all happened to be absent.-- S 11 421 1

THERWISE (104)

visit which my brother's company would otherwise give me. LS 8 255 1
which would be otherwise spent in endeavouring to overcome LS 10 258 3
at least, I cannot otherwise account for her doing it. LS 16 268 1
Under such circumstances you could not act otherwise. LS 39 307 1
following pages should otherwise fail of giving any idea NA I 2 18 1
sufferings, which might otherwise be expected to occupy NA I 4 34 9
otherwise; and the Allens I am sure are very kind to you?" NA I 7 51 51
that Isabella might otherwise perhaps be going to Clifton NA I 13 105 40
to forget that she had for a minute thought otherwise. NA II 1 137 50
might otherwise create both for him and her brother. NA II 3 148 28
their wishing it otherwise; and, as they were to remain NA II 5 154 1
to more frequent exercise than you would otherwise take. NA II 7 174 8
Far be it from me to say otherwise; and any thing in NA II 11 213 19
"We are sorry for him," said she; "but otherwise there is NA II 14 236 19
in my father, because, otherwise, the money would have SS I 2 11 20
Ashamed of being otherwise. SS I 4 21 14
a disposition to be otherwise than tedious and unpleasant. SS I 6 28 1
which might not otherwise have entered Elinor's head. SS I 11 57 17
inconveniences and hardships rather than be otherwise. SS I 13 63 2
of speculation, her wonder was otherwise disposed of. SS I 14 71 3
good enough for me, otherwise Sir John would have SS I 20 116 62
deprived himself of all chance of ever being otherwise. SS II 1 140 1
on it, that she was no otherwise interested in it than as SS II 1 141 7
at Exeter, and she would otherwise be quite alone, except SS II 1 143 9
He will be there in February, otherwise London would have SS II 2 151 40
her sister; should it be otherwise, her exertions would be SS II 4 159 1
"And you will never see me otherwise. SS II 7 186 28
assurance of its being otherwise." M. D. SS II 7 187 40
and herself, had he been otherwise free;--and she had seen SS II 13 238 1
with her; otherwise I should be exceedingly glad to do it. SS II 14 253 21
otherwise at last, than in the marriage of Edward and Lucy. SS III 1 260 9
as suffering much, any otherwise than as the self-command SS III 1 261 12
pleasant companions; for otherwise we both wished very SS III 1 266 36
he had done otherwise, I should have thought him a rascal. SS III 1 267 43
being asked, for nothing would otherwise have been learnt. SS III 2 271 7
not repeat it, for otherwise it would be very wrong to say SS III 5 297 31
such manners, seemed no otherwise intelligible; and with SS III 8 318 16
17
each other's acquaintance, for it could not be otherwise. SS III 13 370 36
otherwise have waited the effect of time and judgment. SS III 13 370 36
no otherwise than by netting a purse, or covering a skreen. PP I 8 39 46
I cannot be otherwise than concerned at being the means of PP I 13 63 12
which she could not otherwise have failed of; as I am PP I 11 67 7
said Wickham, "as to his being agreeable or otherwise. PP I 16 77 14
or mistake, whatever could not be otherwise explained. PP I 17 85 1
it is impossible for me to do otherwise than decline them." PP I 19 107 12
hand, do all in my power to prevent your being otherwise. PP I 19 107 16
sooner than they might otherwise have done; and the boys PP I 22 122 3
and the Bingleys were no otherwise in her thoughts at the PP II 2 142 17
Longbourn family, and otherwise diversified by little PP II 4 151 1
"I am glad of it; but otherwise I see no occasion for PP II 6 164 16
To his wife he was very little otherwise indebted, than as PP II 19 236 1
the power of finding her otherwise than lovely and amiable. PP III 3 270 12
But if otherwise, if the regard springing from such PP III 4 279 24
for had it been otherwise, I must have been involved in PP III 6 297 11
"Could I expect it to be otherwise!" said she. PP III 11 336 44
but his attentions were otherwise of the highest MP I 2 22 35
"No, indeed, far otherwise. MP I 10 98 7
there may be to wish otherwise in Dr. Grant, would have MP I 11 111 30
nor preparation were otherwise much talked of, for MP I 15 142 24
attempt it; had she been otherwise qualified for criticism, MP I 18 170 24
They remained together at the otherwise deserted card- MP II 7 249 49
it might be settled otherwise; in vain however;--Sir MP II 10 275 11
which would otherwise have taken place about this time. MP II 11 284 10
honestly now, do not you rather expect it than otherwise?" MP II 11 289 34
"If it were possible for me to do otherwise," said she MP III 1 320 43
they were quite mistaken who wished you to do otherwise. MP III 4 347 18
How could it be otherwise, with such an education and MP III 4 350 32
She could not do otherwise than accept him, for he was MP III 5 361 16
not like to be supposed otherwise; but take it all in all, MP III 11 410 7
forward stains and dirt that might otherwise have slept. MP III 15 439 9
while those who might otherwise have attended to her, were MP III 16 449 4
To be otherwise comforted was out of the question. MP III 16 449 5
be rather attentive than otherwise to them; but then, Mr. E I 8 67 57
of Mr. Martin's being no otherwise remembered, than as he E I 9 69 2
observations, which were otherwise of a sort to run into E I 9 72 16
it must be so; but otherwise I could not have imagined it. E I 9 74 22
If he were, every thing else must give way; but otherwise E I 9 81 78
She had nothing to wish otherwise, but that the days did E I 13 108 1
If she has fancied otherwise, her own wishes have misled E I 15 130 31
To provide for her otherwise was out of Colonel Campbell's E II 2 164 5
but as it was, how could she have done otherwise?-- E II 5 187 4
Quite otherwise indeed, if I understood Miss Fairfax's E II 9 234 33
It would be most inexcusable to do otherwise, as my own E II 13 265 4
person there, and had otherwise a fancy for the place. E III 1 317 7
Harriet not much otherwise, Emma would not interfere with. E III 3 336 12
cheek which gave it a meaning not otherwise ostensible. E III 5 348 21
could have wished it otherwise--and her good aunt, though E III 9 389 16
such feelings as might otherwise never have entered E III 11 402 1
towards myself; but, otherwise, I should loudly protest E III 14 441 8
a dead weight than otherwise; but for the poor girl E III 15 450 37
It could not be otherwise. E III 18 473 27
Nay, he appeared so much otherwise, that his daughter's E III 19 483 9
sport; and his time was otherwise trifled away, without P III 6 43 5
to see them at our house so often as I otherwise should. P III 6 45 8
hid the arms; so it did, otherwise, I am sure, I should P III 12 106 16
wish to believe myself otherwise, for our pride, if P IV 4 151 21
that has fallen within my observation, to do otherwise. P IV 9 196 33
as much to Sir Walter as she would have done otherwise. P IV 10 213 10
Nay, it would be too hard upon you, if it were otherwise. P IV 11 233 23
and that if I had done otherwise, I should have suffered P IV 11 246 80
of, under circumstances of otherwise strong felicity. P IV 12 251 10
no excuse for her doing otherwise--& that it wd not do for S 6 390 1
over it, very much--said Charlotte--but not otherwise.--" S 10 417 1
Impossible to be otherwise. S 10 419 1

OTWAYS (1)

One of the Otways.-- E III 10 394 20

OUGHT (363)

I might have been rewarded for my exertions as I ought.-- LS 2 245 1
his marriage--& everybody ought to respect the delicacy of LS 5 249 1
general report of any one ought to be credited, since no LS 14 264 3
Frederica must be as much as sixteen, & ought to know LS 15 266 3
She has been sadly neglected however, & her mother ought LS 15 266 3
Ought he not to have felt assured that I must have LS 22 282 6
"Frederica, said I, you ought to have told me all your LS 24 286 6
In such a point as this, your mother's prohibition ought LS 24 286 7
wisely & command herself as she ought, she may now be easy. LS 24 290 13
Nay, I know not whether I ought to be quite tranquil now, LS 25 292 1
& am doubtful whether I ought not to punish him, by LS 25 293 4
Again therefore I say that we ought not, we must not yet LS 30 301 4
children every thing they ought to be; but her time was so NA I 1 15 3
of a heroine from her family ought always to excite. NA I 2 19 3
"Shall I tell you what you ought to say?" NA I 3 26 24
ought to be, unless noted down every evening in a journal? NA I 3 27 28
he were easy where he ought to be civil, and impudent NA I 7 45 5
the wine consumed in this kingdom, that there ought to be. NA I 9 64 22
notions of what men ought to be, she could not entirely NA I 9 66 32
I tell him he ought to be ashamed of himself, but you and NA I 10 75 23
You ought to be tired at the end of six weeks." NA I 10 78 43
The engagement which ought to have kept her from joining NA I 13 97 1
"While, in fact," cried his sister, "it ought only to be NA I 14 108 17
"You know what you ought to do. NA I 14 113 44
is--I do not know what I ought to say--but make him NA II 3 145 13
to the sense of what she ought to be doing, and forced her, NA II 6 164 3
"And ought it not," reflected Catherine, "to endear it to NA II 7 180 33
after a moments' reflection, "I do not--ought I? NA II 10 207 39
Such feelings ought to be investigated, that they may know NA II 10 207 40
attentions you would have received but half what you ought. NA II 13 224 18
correspondence as I ought to do, I will not expect more. NA II 13 228 28
like the Tilneys ought to have with her, while she could NA II 14 239 28
what a young man's address ought to be, was no longer SS I 3 16 13
On every formal visit a child ought to be of the party, by SS I 6 31 9
"That is what I like; that is what a young man ought to be. SS I 9 45 28
their beauties as he ought, and you have received every SS I 10 47 4
open and sincere where I ought to have been reserved, SS I 10 48 5
that what concerned her ought not to escape his lips. SS I 11 57 17
of the allowances which ought to be made for him, and it SS I 15 79 29
all that a lover ought to look and say on such an occasion. SS I 16 87 23
thought he ought to be treated from the family connection. SS I 16 89 42
I shall call hills steep, which ought to be bold; surfaces SS I 18 97 4
strange and uncouth, which ought to be irregular and SS I 18 97 4
out of sight, which ought only to be indistinct through SS I 18 97 4
Ferrars, must seem so odd, that it ought to be explained. SS I 22 129 16
him too well to be so prudent as I ought to have been.-- SS I 22 130 28
felt her influence over him to be more than it ought to be. SS II 1 140 1
Whatever he might have heard against me--ought he not to SS II 7 190 56
suspended his belief? ought he not to have told me of it, SS II 7 190 56
were not what they ought to have been, and from the first SS II 9 206 24
of the street, on whom she ought to call; and as she had SS II 11 220 2
But so it ought to be; they are people of large fortune, SS II 11 222 11
hands, to admire them herself as they ought to be admired. SS II 12 235 36
had Lucy been more amiable, she ought to have rejoiced. SS II 13 238 1
which Edward ought to have inquired about, but never did. SS II 13 241 22
to be the case, you ought to recollect that I am the last SS II 13 244 46
a conversation which you ought not to have known yourself. SS III 2 274 19
I think it ought not to be mentioned to any body else. SS III 4 286 15
at billiards, which ought to have been devoted to business. SS III 6 304 15
"Mr. Willoughby, you ought to feel, and I certainly do-- SS III 8 318 21
22
"Then she has forgiven me before she ought to have done it. SS III 8 319 27
I acknowledge that her situation and her character ought SS III 8 322 36
emotion; "you ought not to speak in this way, either of SS III 8 329 64
of telling me what he knew ought to--though probably he SS III 8 330 69
by circumstances which ought not in reason to have weight; SS III 9 333 2
I can talk of it now, I hope, as I ought to do."-- SS III 10 344 15

Context	Reference
I compare it with what it ought to have been; I compare it	SS III 10 345 26
all that the conscience of her husband ought to have felt."	SS III 11 350 7
& feeling it ought not, it cannot be the greatest.--	W 318 2
I always said she ought to have settled something on you,	W 351 26
"Indeed you ought to make some alteration in your dress	W 353 26
When a woman has five grown up daughters, she ought to	PP I 1 4 20
and never settled at Netherfield as he ought to be.	PP I 3 10 4
"He is just what a young man ought to be," said she, "	PP I 4 14 2
a young man ought likewise to be, if he possibly can.	PP I 4 14 3
of spending more than they ought, and of associating with	PP I 4 15 11
"Then you would drink a great deal more than you ought,"	PP I 5 20 22
"It ought to be good," he replied. "it has been the work	PP I 8 38 30
so soon as I ought, nor their offences against myself.	PP I 11 58 28
The church ought to have been my profession--I was brought	PP I 16 79 23
I talked about the dance, and you ought to make some kind	PP I 18 91 9
of some, conversation ought to be so arranged as that they	PP I 18 91 13
thirdly--which perhaps I ought to have mentioned earlier,	PP I 19 105 10
"Indeed, Jane, you ought to believe me.--	PP I 21 119 20
he ought to have, I should think you could not do better.	PP II 3 144 2
told her how every thing ought to be regulated in so small	PP II 6 163 15
You ought all to have learned	PP II 6 164 20
But I ought to beg his pardon, for I have no right to	PP II 10 185 24
I knew that Mr. Wickham ought not to be a clergyman.	PP II 12 201 5
of myself to know what could or ought to be revealed.	PP II 12 202 5
said she; "and certainly ought not to have appeared; but	PP II 17 224 3
I want to be told whether I ought, or ought not to make	PP II 17 226 21
"That it ought not to be attempted.	PP II 17 226 23
Has he deigned to add ought of civility to his ordinary	PP II 18 234 33
only to a late breakfast, ought to be imitated, though it	PP III 2 266 17
had I known what I ought, what I dared, to do?	PP III 4 277 18
It has been my own doing, and I ought to feel it."	PP III 6 299 19
been exactly what they ought his smiles and his easy	PP III 9 316 5
I ought not to have said a word about it.	PP III 9 319 27
"I mention it, because it is the living which I ought to	PP III 10 328 26
One ought not repine;--but, to be sure, it would have been	PP III 10 328 28
I know; though it was not put in as it ought to be.	PP III 10 336 49
tone, "you ought to know, that I am not to be trifled with.	PP III 14 353 26
"It ought to be so; it must be so, while he retains the	PP III 14 354 36
As it principally concerns yourself, you ought to know its	PP III 15 362 10
You ought certainly to forgive them as a christian, but	PP III 15 364 22
circumstance attending it, ought to be forgotten.	PP III 16 368 23
will intrude, which cannot, which ought not to be repelled.	PP III 16 369 24
to him, which I believe I ought to have made long ago.	PP III 16 370 40
Are you quite sure that you feel what you ought to do?"	PP III 17 373 11
You will only think I feel more than I ought to do, when I	PP III 17 373 12
of promise, for I ought not to have mentioned the subject?	PP III 18 381 13
"Lady Catherine has been of infinite use, which ought to	PP III 18 381 15
But it ought to be done, and if you will give me a sheet	PP III 18 382 18
"I would have thanked you before, my dear aunt, as I ought	PP III 18 382 21
cheap situation, and always spending more than they ought.	PP III 19 387 8
I only meant to observe, that it ought not to be lightly	MP I 1 7 7
The division of gratifying sensations ought not, in strict	MP I 1 8 9
good behaviour which it ought to produce, and her	MP I 2 13 4
life, of more than half the income which ought to be his.	MP I 3 23 3
ought, and I am glad her love of money does not interfere.	MP I 3 26 23
You will be what you ought to be to her.	MP I 3 26 23
I ever thank you as I ought, for thinking so well of me?	MP I 3 26 30
will necessarily be brought forward, as you ought to be.	MP I 3 27 31
things as you do; but I ought to believe you to be right	MP I 3 27 34
walking all day, thinking every body ought to walk as much.	MP I 4 36 7
sense and temper which ought to have made him judge and	MP I 5 45 3
Miss Augusta ought not to have been noticed for the next	MP I 5 51 40
"Oh! yes, she ought not to have spoken of her uncle as she	MP I 7 63 4
Mrs. Grant's manners are just what they ought to be.	MP I 7 64 9
persuaded, that when she does not ride, she ought to walk.	MP I 7 73 55
"I am sure she ought to be very much obliged to you,"	MP I 8 79 25
that she ought to offer to stay at home herself.	MP I 8 79 25
The rest of the way is such as it ought to be.	MP I 8 82 34
chapel, which properly we ought to enter from above, and	MP I 9 85 5
out of his place to appear what he ought not to appear."	MP I 9 92 45
not what they ought to be, so are the rest of the nation."	MP I 9 93 49
to receive Mr. Rushworth's parting attentions as she ought.	MP I 10 105 52
I am sure you ought to be very much obliged to your aunt	MP I 10 105 53
are all against him, he ought to be less liable to the	MP I 11 110 22
to the Miss Bertrams, as ought to have put them both on	MP I 12 114 3
the gentleman that he ought to keep longer away, had he	MP I 12 114 3
way; and I think a theatre ought not to be attempted.--	MP I 13 127 28
in which height and figure ought to be considered, and	MP I 14 132 8
will be given up, and your delicacy honoured as it ought."	MP I 15 140 15
years old you know, who ought to be ashamed of himself,)	MP I 15 142 22
undecided as to what she ought to do; and as she walked	MP I 16 152 3
Her feelings ought to be respected.	MP I 16 155 14
"If you are against me, I ought to distrust myself--and	MP I 16 155 22
sister so reasonable as ought to have been their cure; and	MP I 17 160 8
would attend as they ought, nobody would remember on which	MP I 18 165 2
in forming the plan; they ought to have been capable of a	MP II 2 188 3
prejudice, the blindness of love, she ought to be believed.	MP II 3 201 22
before she could add "you ought to be in Parliament, or	MP II 4 214 44
unable to attend as she ought to Mrs. Grant, by whose side	MP II 4 214 46
anxious perhaps than she ought to be--for what was it	MP II 5 218 12
She appears to feel as she ought.	MP II 5 219 18
assistance from those who ought to have entered into her	MP II 5 219 27
You ought to be very much obliged to Mrs. Grant for	MP II 5 220 28
letting you go, and you ought to look upon it as something	MP II 5 220 28
I hope it is not too fine; but I thought I ought to wear	MP II 5 222 43
"No, he can feel nothing as he ought."	MP II 5 227 67
You ought to be satisfied with her two cousins."	MP II 6 229 4
is not very far off, you ought to go over and pay your	MP II 7 245 32
herself, as to what she ought to wear, determined to seek	MP II 8 256 14
You ought to have had it a week ago, but there has been a	MP II 9 261 2
it on that account, it ought not to affect your keeping it.	MP II 9 263 14
It ought not to have touched on the confines of her	MP II 9 264 18
in anticipation which she ought to have had, or must have	MP II 9 266 22
This ought to be a day of pleasure.	MP II 9 268 30
Every thing that a considerate parent ought to feel was	MP II 11 285 10
And they will now see their cousin treated as she ought to	MP II 12 297 33
of what you ought to have known before all the world.	MP II 13 299 5
My uncle ought to know it as soon as possible."	MP II 13 300 7
Mr. Crawford ought to know--he must know that--I told him	MP III 1 314 17
Had her own affections been as free--as perhaps they ought	MP III 2 329 9
It was an injury and affront to Julia, who ought to have	MP III 2 332 20
always so attentive as I ought to be--(here was a glance	MP III 3 340 25
thinking how such a prayer ought to be read, and longing	MP III 3 340 25
I fancied you might be going to tell me I ought to be more	MP III 3 340 25
Did you think I ought?"	MP III 3 343 38
cannot, you have done exactly as you ought in refusing him.	MP III 4 346 12
"I am persuaded that he does not think as he ought, on	MP III 4 350 31
She spoke of you, Fanny, just as she ought.	MP III 4 351 36
in the world, I think it ought not to be set down as	MP III 4 353 45
composed as Anhalt ought, through the two long speeches.	MP III 5 358 9
thought Fanny ought to go, and therefore that she must.	MP III 6 370 14
soon be what mother and daughter ought to be to each other.	MP III 6 371 17
You will tell my mother how it all ought to be, and you	MP III 6 372 20
and she ought to have had it to keep herself long ago.	MP III 7 386 42
his rum and water, and Rebecca never where she ought to be.	MP III 7 387 46
in their right place, nothing was done as it ought to be.	MP III 8 388 3
She ought to do better.	MP III 9 394 1
proper opinions of what ought to be--she, who had no	MP III 9 397 8
so properly; here, he had been acting as he ought to do.	MP III 10 404 15
completely unsuited to her, and ought not to think of her.	MP III 10 405 16
as ever, her face was less blooming than it ought to be.--	MP III 11 409 7
she does, and that she ought never to be long banished	MP III 11 410 16
say much, or even to be certain of what she ought to say.--	MP III 11 411 19
I ought to have sent you an account of your cousin's first	MP III 12 416 2
every thing was just as it ought to be, in a style that	MP III 12 416 2
He acknowledged no such inducement, and his sister ought	MP III 12 418 4
whether she ought to keep Edmund and Mary asunder or not.	MP III 14 436 15
agitation of doubting what she ought to do in such a case.	MP III 15 437 2
much as ought to be expected from human virtue at fourteen.	MP III 15 444 26
which Crawford's sister ought to have known, he had gone	MP III 16 454 18
Had she accepted him as she ought, they might now have	MP III 16 455 23
He felt that he ought not to have allowed the marriage,	MP III 17 461 4
He became what he ought to be, useful to his father,	MP III 17 462 4
Had he done as he intended, and as he knew he ought, by	MP III 17 467 20
her with a coldness which ought to have been repulsive,	MP III 17 467 20
Mrs. Weston ought to have found more in it, for she had a	E I 2 15 3
The misfortune of your birth ought to make you	E I 4 30 22
the superior young woman which Emma's friend ought to be.	E I 5 36 6
and the lines about the mouth which one ought to catch."	E I 6 44 15
have been glad to command, and ought not to have failed of.	E I 6 44 19
and Mr. Elton, just as he ought, entreated for the	E I 6 47 28
"You think I ought to refuse him then," said Harriet,	E I 7 52 12
"Ought to refuse him!	E I 7 52 13
Pray, dear Miss Woodhouse, tell me what I ought to do?"	E I 7 52 16
accept a man or not, she certainly ought to refuse him.	E I 7 52 18
	19
If she can hesitate as to 'yes,' she ought to say 'no'	E I 7 52 19
you say, one's mind ought to be quite made up--one should	E I 7 52 20
my dearest Harriet; you are doing just what you ought.	E I 7 53 24
of admiration just as he ought; and as for Harriet's	E I 9 69 2
saw, felt, anticipated, and remembered just as she ought.	E I 9 74 21
and sends it into the very channel where it ought to flow.	E I 9 75 25
again on the 28th, and we ought to be thankful, papa, that	E I 9 79 63
be missed, but every body ought also to be assured that Mr.	E I 11 94 14
I am sure nobody ought to be, or can be, a greater	E I 11 95 19
Tell your aunt, little Emma, that she ought to set you a	E I 12 99 10
one ought to overlook, and one does overlook a great deal.	E I 13 111 17
"He ought to come," said Emma.	E I 14 122 22
If he could stay only a couple of days, he ought to come;	E I 14 122 22
"One ought to be at Enscombe, and know the ways of the	E I 14 123 23
"One ought to use the same caution, perhaps, in judging of	E I 14 123 23
ought to be serious, a trick of what ought to be simple.	E I 16 137 10
some one worth having; I ought not to have attempted more.	E I 16 137 11
that was amiable, all that ought to be attaching, seemed	E I 17 141 8
We ought to be acquainted with Enscombe, and with Mrs.	E I 18 146 15
world must know, that he ought to pay this visit to his	E I 18 147 18
It ought to have been an habit with him by this time, of	E I 18 148 22
As he became rational, he ought to have roused himself and	E I 18 148 22
He ought to have opposed the first attempt on their side	E I 18 148 22
Had he begun as he ought, there would have been no	E I 18 148 22
"Yes; all the advantages of sitting still when he ought to	E I 18 148 24
what she ought to the stock of their scanty comforts.	E II 1 155 2
doing more than she wished, and less than she ought!	E II 2 166 11
part of her reserve which ought to be overcome, all that	E II 3 171 7
was just the happy man he ought to be; talking only of	E II 4 182 5
They ought to have balls there at least every fortnight	E II 6 198 5
in their way, but they ought to be taught that it was not	E II 7 207 6
be what it ought, neither damp, nor cold, nor windy."	E II 7 209 10
"I do not know whether it ought to be so, but certainly	E II 8 212 2
	3
bought--or else I am sure we ought to be ashamed of it.--	E II 8 216 16
to be quite certain that she ought to have held her tongue.	E II 9 231 2
And, by the bye, every body ought to have two pair of	E II 9 236 46
If she does wrong, she ought to feel it."	E II 10 243 27
But I ought to have gone before.	E II 14 280 54
"Yes: but a young lady--a bride--I ought to have paid my	E II 14 280 56
It ought to be no recommendation to you.	E II 14 280 57
one mouth to another as it ought to do, unimpeded by Miss	E II 15 281 2
Maple Grove will probably by my model more than it ought	E II 15 283 9
would soon shew them how every thing ought to be arranged.	E II 16 290 3
Of the same age--and always knowing her--I ought to have	E II 16 291 6
Liable as you have been to severe colds, indeed you ought	E II 16 295 33
She was happy, she knew she was happy, and knew she ought	E II 17 304 28
not general friendship, made a man what he ought to be.--	E III 2 320 4
"She will think Frank ought to ask her."	E III 2 325 30
There he was, among the standers-by, where he ought not to	E III 2 325 32
he ought not to be; he ought to be dancing,--not classing	E III 2 325 32
no answer, added, "she ought not to be angry with you, I	E III 2 330 48
going to destroy--what I ought to have destroyed long ago--	E III 4 337 6
destroyed long ago--what I ought never to have kept--I	E III 4 337 6
This is a sort of dull-looking evening, that ought to be	E III 5 347 19
It was just what it ought to be, and it looked what it was-	E III 6 358 35
I ought to travel.	E III 6 365 62
Time, however, she thought, would tell him that they ought	E III 9 385 5
I dare say her acquaintance are just what they ought to be.	E III 9 387 10
It ought to be a first object, as I am sure poor Miss	E III 9 387 10
And now she was very conscious that she ought to have	E III 11 402 1
claims of the object, it ought; and judging by its	E III 11 403 2
Had she left her where she ought, and where he had told	E III 11 413 49
where she ought, and where he had told her she ought!--	E III 11 413 49
line of life to which she ought to belong--all would have	E III 11 413 49
been a state of perpetual suffering to me; and so it ought.	E III 12 419 8
receiving, is what my conscience tells me ought not to be.	E III 12 419 8
said she, 'which I ought to have done, for his temper and	E III 12 419 12
in knowing her as she ought, and as she might, she must	E III 12 421 17
Just what she ought, of course.	E III 13 431 38
will think I ought to add, with the deepest humiliation.--	E III 14 438 8
Miss Woodhouse indicated, I believe, more than it ought.--	E III 14 438 8
You have not heard all that you ought to hear.	E III 14 440 8
enough to make the rest of my letter what it ought to be.--	E III 14 440 8
She disapproved them, which ought to have been enough.--	E III 14 440 8
He ought not to have formed the engagement.--	E III 15 445 11
No, he felt that it ought not to be attempted.	E III 15 449 31
She ought to go--and she was longing to see her; the	E III 16 452 7
the indignity as a wife ought to do,) "I cannot imagine	E III 16 458 42
"I do not know which it ought to be called."	E III 18 470 4
"You ought to know your friend best," replied Mr.	E III 18 473 25
"The shame," he answered, "is all mine, or ought to be.	E III 18 477 53
Perhaps she ought to be ashamed, but Mr. Weston had been	E III 18 479 73
and, fortunately, what ought to be, and must be, seemed	E III 19 482 5
They had determined that their marriage ought to be	E III 19 483 8
As the head of the house, he felt that he ought to have	P III 1 8 16
many of our first families have done,--or ought to do?--	P III 2 12 4
in the very quarter which ought to dictate, he had no	P III 2 13 7
and confidence on one who ought to have been nothing to	P III 2 16 16
"Oh! but they ought to call upon you as soon as possible.	P III 5 40 43
They ought to feel what is due to you as my sister.	P III 5 40 43
She could now answer as she ought; and was happy to feel,	P III 6 49 22
all the motive of their attention just as he ought!--	P III 7 54 4
reason against it, he ought to go; and it ended in his	P III 7 55 7
Oh! I will certainly go; I am sure I ought if I can, quite	P III 7 57 16
the accommodations on board, such as women ought to have.	P III 8 68 35
to recollect himself, and feel how he ought to behave.	P III 9 78 22
interference, "you ought to have minded me, Walter; I told	P III 9 80 34
Wentworth should do what he ought to have done himself.	P III 9 80 34
just as he ought to have, and drew back from conversation.	P III 11 97 14
the very feelings which ought to taste it but sparingly.	P III 11 100 23
I really think they ought.	P III 12 102 2
Shirley to repose, as she ought; saw how very desirable it	P III 12 103 3
I think my father certainly ought to hear of it; do	P III 12 107 20
to be communicated, but as what ought to be suppressed.	P III 12 107 21
They ought to be setting off for Uppercross by one, and in	P III 12 107 22
already gone since they ought to have been off,--the	P III 12 113 57
his sister in such a state, he neither ought, nor would.	P III 12 113 58

Had I done as I ought! P III 12 116 71
saying to herself, "these rooms ought to belong only to us. P IV 1 126 18
were so exactly what they ought to be, so polished, so P IV 3 143 18
and dignity which ought to belong to Sir Walter Elliot. P IV 4 151 21
The husband had not been what he ought, and the wife had P IV 5 156 12
She could not imagine a man more exactly what he ought to P IV 5 161 30
to me, just as it "ought; I shall therefore be able to P IV 6 164 8
Situated as we are with Lady Dalrymple, cousins, we ought P IV 6 166 16
He ought not--he does not." P IV 8 183 10
"But I ought to have looked about me more," said Anne, P IV 9 193 13
I ought to have waited for official information. P IV 9 195 27
He ought not to be supposed to be paying his addresses to P IV 9 196 31
giving you, but I have been uncertain what I ought to do. P IV 9 198 52 53
I have been doubting and considering as to what I ought to P IV 9 198 53
I am right; I think you ought to be made acquainted with P IV 9 199 53
marrying for money is too common to strike one as it ought. P IV 9 201 64
And yet you ought to have proof; for what is all this but P IV 9 202 66
of honour, that no one ought to be judged or to be known P IV 9 204 76 77
rich, just as his friend ought to have found himself to be P IV 9 209 95
To feel that she ought to be in better circumstances, that P IV 9 210 98
Not that he will value it as he ought," he observed, " P IV 10 217 20
admire every thing as she ought, and enter most readily P IV 10 219 28
She felt that Mrs. Musgrove and all her party ought to be P IV 10 219 29
whom you ought so particularly to be acquainted with! P IV 10 224 47
she generally thought he ought; but it was a case which P IV 10 227 69
And I ought to be at that fellow's in the market-place. P IV 11 240 58
"Perhaps I ought to have reasoned thus," he replied, "but P IV 11 244 74
This is a recollection which ought to make me forgive P IV 11 247 84
Captain Wentworth as she ought, had no other alloy to the P IV 12 251 10
was received as it ought--as there was not more good will S 2 371 1
it occurs to me that we ought to go elsewhere upon such S 4 381 1
the persecutions which ought to be the lot of the S 6 391 1
much beyond what they ought to have afforded; they were S 11 421 1
that (between ourselves) I ought to be in bed myself at S 12 424 1
eat & drink more than he ought; --but you see Mary, how S 12 424 1

OUR'S (5)
the world for you, next door to our's, in Hanover-Square. SS I 20 110 4
A niece of our's, Sir Thomas, I may say, or, at least of MP I 1 6 6
steaks, nicely fried, as our's are fried, without the E II 3 171 16 17
just as Serle boils our's, and eaten very moderately of, E II 3 172 19
imagined a certain friend of our's in love with the lady." E III 10 399 63

OURS (14)
whose sensibilities are not of a nature to comprehend ours. LS 30 301 4
A neighbour of ours, Dr. Skinner, was here for his health NA I 8 54 7
money, for we have just spent ours at the shop out there." PP II 16 219 3
ours is not a family, on which it could be thrown away. PP III 5 285 18
a little assistance, and ours is such a remarkably large, MP I 6 54 13
"Such a horribly vile billiard-table as ours, is not to be MP I 13 125 14
Ours are all apple tarts. E I 3 25 14
So I begged he would not--for really as to ours being gone, E II 9 238 51
Pray take care, Miss Woodhouse, ours is rather a dark E II 9 239 53
and have regular weekly meetings at your house, or ours. E II 14 277 38
she would feel scrupulous as to any proposal of ours. P IV 6 166 16
this kind soon makes a stir in a lonely place like ours.-- S 1 370 1
In ours, it is Sidney; who is a very clever young man,-- S 4 382 1
be ours eventually in the increased value of our houses." S 6 393 1

OUT-CHURCHILL'D (1)
a Churchill she has Out-Churchill'd them all in high and E II 18 310 33

OUT-RIDERS (1)
stirrups, and numerous out-riders properly mounted, sunk a NA II 5 156 4

OUT-STRETCHED (1)
With a letter in her out-stretched hand, and countenance SS II 9 202 5 6

OUT-TALK (1)
that he could hardly out-talk the interest of his hearers. MP I 13 121 2

OUTCRY (1)
"Be satisfied," said he, "I will not raise any outcry. E I 5 40 27

OUTDONE (2)
could hardly be outdone by any creature professedly noisy. SS I 21 121 10
You will hardly bear to be long outdone by Jane. PP III 1 138 27

OUTER (3)
this inner lock as of the outer; but at length it did open; NA II 6 169 11
seize the advantage of an outer door, and then expressing NA II 7 179 27
She now felt a great inclination to go to the outer door; P IV 7 175 6

OUTGROWN (2)
I should very soon have outgrown the fancied attachment, SS III 13 362 5
the baby would soon have outgrown its first set of caps. E III 17 468 32

OUTLINE (2)
shaping a very complete outline of the business; and as MP II 8 253 7
and the first outline of this important change made out. P III 2 13 8

OUTLIVED (8)
thirty might well have outlived all acuteness of feeling SS I 7 35 9
love, must have long outlived every sensation of the kind. SS I 8 37 4
Her joy and expressions of regard long outlived her wonder. SS I 17 90 1
its existence might prove, had at least outlived one day. PP III 2 263 10
of the earliest attachments are ever entirely outlived. MP II 6 235 18
therefore till I have outlived all my affections, a post- E II 16 294 22
Anne hoped she had outlived the age of blushing; but the P III 6 49 20
original strength, has outlived all the storms of autumn. P III 10 88 26

OUTRAGE (1)
And then, to prevent further outrage and indignation, E II 14 276 34 35

OUTRAGED (1)
truth was less violently outraged than usually happens. SS I 10 46 2

OUTREE (1)
I never saw any thing so outree!-- E II 8 222 56

OUTRIGHT (1)
declaring outright that he would go and fetch the key. MP I 10 98 4

OUTRUN (2)
her fancy so far to outrun truth and probability, that on SS II 14 248 6
They will take care not to outrun their income. PP II 17 228 33

OUTS (2)
She has the age and sense of a woman, but the outs and not MP I 5 49 31
sense of a woman, but the outs and not outs are beyond me." MP I 5 49 31

OUTSET (1)
Tilneys' advantage in the outset, they were but just NA I 13 102 25

OUTSIDE (5)
she could obtain the outside of a letter from her mother, NA I 1 14 1
perhaps they may be the outside of enough; but it is so SS I 21 122 19
for a courage which the outside of no door had ever MP II 1 177 7
its Boundaries, that an outside fence was at first almost S 12 426 1
sloped down from the outside of the paling & which a S 12 426 1

OUTSTAID (1)
and Lucy, who would have outstaid him had his visit lasted SS II 13 244 43

OUTSTEPPED (1)
will not find he has outstepped the truth more than may be E II 14 277 37

OUTSTRIP (1)
Jane, however, soon allowed the others to outstrip them. PP III 16 365 1

OUTSTRIPPED (3)
favourably thought of, outstripped even her wishes in the NA II 2 141 11
of her mother and herself had outstripped the truth. SS I 4 22 16
They soon outstripped the others, and when they had PP III 1 257 65

OUTWARD (14)
dissimilar in temper and outward behaviour, they strongly SS I 7 32 1
to no outward demonstrations of joy, no words, no smiles. SS III 7 315 24
the hall, and reached the outward door just in time to SS III 9 333 3
on its outward leaf her own name in his hand writing.-- SS III 10 342 7
people, meeting with an outward door, temptingly open on a MP I 9 89 32
in Julia; but there was no outward fellowship between them. MP I 17 163 20
to wipe away every outward memento of what had been, even MP II 2 190 9
or frighten those who might hate her, into outward respect. E I 3 21 4
look once more at all the outward wretchedness of the E I 10 87 27
the forbearance of her outward submission left a heavy E III 6 353 3
hill; and all the other outward circumstances of E III 7 367 1
but with great outward patience, to Harriet's detail.-- E III 11 409 34
She had never received from her more than outward P III 2 16 16
If the change be not from outward circumstances, it must P IV 11 233 21

OUTWARDLY (4)
better interest he had outwardly torn himself, now, when SS III 8 331 70
father, he was not outwardly affectionate, and the reserve MP I 2 19 30
I can only say that there was smoothness outwardly. E II 6 202 38
She had only to submit, sit down, be outwardly composed, P IV 11 229 2

OUTWEIGH (4)
deal of noise, as to outweigh all the value of all the SS I 1 4 3
sufficient objection to outweigh every possible advantage SS I 4 23 20
was all insufficient to outweigh that dread of poverty, or SS III 8 323 40
to increase, their mutual good to outweigh every drawback. E III 15 450 36

OUTWEIGHED (2)
Her satisfaction in Mr. Elliot outweighed all the plague P IV 4 147 6
villain of the story outweighed all his absurdities & all S 8 404 1

OUTWEIGHS (1)
the subject, and with me it almost outweighs every other." SS I 15 80 37

OVAL (1)
cast of countenance, the oval face & mild dark eyes, & LS 17 270 5

OVER-ANXIOUS (2)
smile, and thought her over-anxious, or thought her odd, MP II 10 277 20
futurity, against that over-anxious caution which seems to P III 4 30 9

OVER-CAREFUL (2)
in her own health, over-careful of that of her children, E I 11 92 4
her own room, "always over-careful for every body's E II 5 189 20

OVER-CHARGED (1)
to burst from an over-charged heart, and to describe E III 6 363 51

OVER-PERSUASION (1)
It had been the effect of over-persuasion. P III 7 61 36

OVER-RATED (4)
from the first over-rated, had ever since his introduction NA II 15 245 12
with Mr. Darcy had been over-rated, Elizabeth had never PP III 18 382 20
he had considerably over-rated her sense, and wonderfully MP III 17 465 15
I am afraid you will think you have over-rated Hartfield. E II 14 273 22 23

OVER-RATING (1)
herself, and be over-rating his regard for her.-- E III 12 416 1

OVER-REACHED (1)
I do not think I was ever over-reached in my life; & that S 7 399 1

OVER-RULED (2)
for the benefit of masters, but we over-ruled her there. LS 27 296 1
the charge of her; but I was over-ruled, as I always am. PP III 5 287 35

OVER-SALT (1)
They must not over-salt the leg; and then, if it is not E II 3 172 19

OVER-SALTED (1)
and then, if it is not over-salted, and if it is very E II 3 172 19

OVER-SCRUPULOUS (2)
and scrupulous in his notions; over-scrupulous, I must say. P III 12 103 2
Do not you think, Anne, it is being over-scrupulous? P III 12 103 2

OVER-SET (1)
my cold beef at Marlborough was enough to over-set me." SS III 8 318 18

OVER-TRIMMED (2)
know whether it is not over-trimmed; I have the greatest E II 17 302 22
the idea of being over-trimmed--quite a horror of finery. E II 17 302 22

OVERACTING (1)
wrong, saying too much, overacting the caution which she MP III 4 354 47

OVERBEARING (3)
me to be selfish and overbearing, to care for none beyond PP III 16 369 24
Sam, loud and overbearing as he was, she rather regretted MP III 8 390 8
mutual trick, or some overbearing authority of his, been P IV 10 228 70

OVERBOARD (1)
and by some accident she was falling overboard. E II 8 218 34

OVERBORNE (1)
were to be braved or overborne by a defiance of decency MP III 16 457 30

OVERCAME (9)
they were to inhabit overcame their dejection, and a view SS I 6 28 1
Mrs. Dashwood's spirit overcame the wish of society for SS I 9 40 2
a body of evidence, as overcame every fear of condemning SS II 1 139 1
great unkindness, overcame all her resolution, and though SS II 9 205 24
the haughty notice which overcame her by its graciousness, SS III 14 377 11
of affection sometimes overcame the hope, that Bingley PP I 21 120 29
attempted to deny, soon overcame the pity which the PP II 11 193 31
a respect which almost overcame her affection, she now saw PP III 19 388 61
The heat overcame me." E III 7 368 6

OVERCHARGED (1)
appearance of being so overcharged as to want only a E I 13 112 24

OVERCOME (57)
spent in endeavouring to overcome my sister in law's LS 10 258 3
& have taken great pains to overcome her timidity. LS 18 273 3
be overcome; & I hope I was afterwards sufficiently keen. LS 22 282 7
will, I trust, gradually overcome this youthful attachment. LS 27 297 2
scarcely believe it, or overcome the suspicion of there NA II 8 183 2
not to be again overcome by trivial appearances of alarm, NA II 13 223 9
his natural shyness was overcome, his behaviour gave every SS I 3 15 6
was quite overcome, she burst into tears and left the room. SS I 15 82 46
quite overcome by the captivating manners of Mrs. Dashwood. SS I 17 90 1
moments, she was almost overcome--her heart sunk within SS I 22 134 53
equally shared, been overcome or overlooked; and Elinor, SS II 4 159 1
have determined him to overcome it, but that such a regard SS II 6 179 17
if she had not lived to overcome those regrets which the SS II 9 206 24
She could say no more; her spirits were quite overcome, SS II 12 236 41
be weathered without our being any of us quite overcome. SS III 1 265 36
overcome her unwillingness to be in her company again. SS III 5 294 3
Elinor made no resistance that was not easily overcome. SS III 7 311 15
was in a moment as much overcome by her happiness, as she SS III 9 334 4
at first I was quite overcome--that if she lived, as I SS III 9 337 18
His remembrance can be overcome by no change of SS III 10 347 30
was oppressed, she was overcome by her own felicity;--and SS III 13 363 8
between them, one difficulty only was to be overcome. SS III 13 369 32
could be nothing to overcome but the affection of both, he SS III 14 376 11
She was born to overcome an affection formed so late in SS III 14 378 15
"There has been many a one, I fancy, overcome in the same PP I 9 44 32
defect, which not even the best education can overcome." PP I 11 58 30
so great as to overcome at first the bounds of decorum, PP I 22 124 12 13
could no longer be overcome; and at length resolving to PP II 17 224 1
with an embarrassment impossible to be overcome. PP III 1 251 52
overcome with confusion, and unable to lift up her eyes. PP III 3 269 10
refused him, as able to overcome a sentiment so natural as PP III 10 326 3
could not be easily overcome; nor could she for many hours, PP III 15 360 1
would be enough to overcome her abhorrence of the man. PP III 17 375 27
good humour was overcome, and he proceeded so far as to PP III 19 387 9
looks, and quite overcome by Mrs. Norris's admonitions. MP I 2 14 8
And sitting down by her, was at great pains to overcome MP I 2 15 10
There was no natural disinclination to be overcome, and I MP I 11 109 17
was not yet overcome, in spite of all that Edmund could do. MP I 15 145 44
be overcome, had not her affection been engaged elsewhere. MP II 6 231 11
be her duty, to try to overcome all that was excessive, MP II 9 264 18
A little difficulty to be overcome, was no evil to Henry MP III 2 327 4
little of it, she was the more overcome by Miss Crawford's. MP III 5 365 33
strong enough to overcome the trouble, and that at MP III 7 376 4
she could wish to overcome her own shyness and reserve. MP III 9 395 3
felt; but as they were overcome by other considerations, E I 2 16 4
but you will soon overcome all that part of her reserve E II 3 171 7
to be overcome, all that has its foundation in diffidence. E II 3 171 7
to reach Hartfield, before her spirits were quite overcome. E III 3 334 7

sunk back for a moment overcome--then reproaching herself E III 7 376 62
Her spirits seemed overcome. E III 9 389 16
by gentle encouragement, overcome so much of her E III 12 418 5
the vicarage quarter, which was now graciously overcome.-- E III 16 455 20
but the worst was overcome, the idea was given; time and E III 17 466 30
of Mrs. Musgrove's, who, overcome by fond regrets, could P III 8 64 5
6
of being so nervous, so overcome by such a trifle; but so P III 9 81 34
overcome-- "don't talk of it, don't talk of it," he cried. P III 12 116 70
71
to the game to be soon overcome by a gentleman's hints. P IV 10 213 5
OVERCOMING (6)
Elinor would not argue upon the propriety of overcoming SS III 3 280 6
every reproach, overcoming every scruple, by secretly SS III 8 326 53
little difficulty in overcoming it after this explanation." PP II 11 190 7
gravity, intended to be overcoming, "well, Fanny, I have MP III 2 330 14
exultation in overcoming the reluctance, in working MP III 17 467 19
to feel a doubt of its overcoming any hesitations that a E I 8 67 57
OVERDRAW (1)
wish you could see him overdraw himself on both his own W 358 28
OVERDRAWING (1)
Ld Osborne's stile of overdrawing himself on both cards.-- W 359 28
OVERDRAWN (1)
and overdrawn; but here was proof positive of the contrary. NA II 7 181 40
OVERFLOWING (5)
Her heart was overflowing with tenderness. NA I 15 121 27
was overflowing with admiration was evident enough. PP III 2 262 6
before him, she was overflowing with gratitude, artless, MP III 10 400 6
and to me, very overflowing; and that he did mention, E III 18 472 20
She, in the overflowing spirits of her recovery, repeats P IV 9 205 82
OVERFLOWS (1)
in which happiness overflows in mirth; and Elizabeth, PP III 17 372 2
OVERGROWN (1)
It may apply to your large, overgrown places, like S 1 368 1
OVERHEAR (4)
had believed herself to overhear in the Pump-Room, his NA II 4 149 1
near enough for her to overhear a conversation between him PP I 3 11 7
I happened to overhear the gentleman himself mentioning to PP I 18 96 57
now Emma was obliged to overhear what Mrs. Elton and Jane E III 6 359 37
OVERHEARD (10)
"Yes," said Morland, who overheard this; "but you forget NA I 7 47 20
This was all overheard by Miss Dashwood; and in the whole SS I 12 59 7
"Perhaps you mean what I overheard between him and Mr. PP I 5 19 7
Bingley, in some confusion, lest they had been overheard. PP I 10 53 60
of it was overheard by Mr. Darcy, who sat opposite to them. PP I 18 99 64
Lady Bertram, who had overheard her, "I am very much MP I 7 74 56
I wish you could have overheard her tribute of praise; I MP III 4 352 42
of what the whole room must have overheard already. E II 17 304 29
not but imagine he had overheard his own praises, and did E III 2 324 22
something very fine--I overheard him telling Henrietta all P IV 2 131 9
OVERHEARING (3)
nor without her overhearing Mr. Weston whisper to his wife, E II 11 256 60
herself necessarily overhearing the discourse of Mrs. E III 2 323 20
Whether he were overhearing too, she could not determine. E III 2 324 20
OVERHEARINGS (1)
"My overhearings were more to the purpose than yours, PP I 5 19 9
OVERJOYED (3)
I should be overjoyed if I dared depend on it, but after LS 41 309 1
The whole family in short were properly overjoyed on the PP I 22 122 3
Henry, overjoyed to have her go, bowed and watched her off, MP II 13 298 2
OVERLOOK (12)
Elinor has not my feelings, and therefore she may overlook SS I 3 18 20
would make you overlook every thing else I am sure." SS II 2 146 5
by them, should overlook every inconvenience of that kind, SS II 3 155 6
him, should overlook every thing but the risk of delay. SS III 12 357 2
what she could not overlook, and to banish from her PP II 19 236 2
I hope he will overlook it. PP III 17 378 43
he was prevailed on to overlook the offence, and seek a PP III 19 388 12
wasteful doings to overlook, left her very little occasion MP I 4 34 3
pacify her, and make her overlook the previous affront? MP I 14 135 18
while you do wrong together I can overlook a great deal." MP II 4 211 28
one ought to overlook, and one does overlook a great deal. E I 13 111 17
These were claims which he did not learn to overlook, E II 2 163 4
OVERLOOKED (12)
than himself could have overlooked it at all; & tho' as LS 3 247 1
was an insult not to be overlooked, nor, for the first NA II 14 233 10
been overcome or overlooked; and Elinor, in spite of every SS II 4 159 1
estate, will be kindly overlooked on your side, and not PP I 13 63 12
might have been overlooked, had not your pride been hurt PP II 11 192 22
within her of good will which could not be overlooked. PP III 2 265 16
She had been quite overlooked by her cousins; and as her MP II 1 176 4
agitation, had quite overlooked the deficiences of her MP III 1 312 5
real affection, Fanny like mine, more might be overlooked. MP III 14 434 13
Mrs. Price, could have overlooked, when the third day did MP III 15 442 22
favour, and of Anne so overlooked, was a perpetual P IV 4 146 5
Elizabeth had turned from him, Lady Russell overlooked him; P IV 7 180 32
OVERLOOKING (1)
her station at a window overlooking the entrance to the P IV 10 220 31
OVERLOOKS (1)
for that room overlooks the lawn you know with the LS 17 271 7
OVERPOWER (5)
"My dearest Jane--do not overpower me with your raillery.-- W 350 24
and so splendid a dinner might not wholly overpower them. PP II 6 160 4
stake, her kindness did sometimes overpower her judgment. MP II 2 190 8
You do not often overpower me with it." E I 8 58 13
almost ready to overpower them with care and kindness, E II 1 155 4
OVERPOWERED (22)
in the same spot, overpowered by wonder--of a most LS 23 284 5
you can, or we shall be overpowered with Johnson and Blair NA I 14 108 14
The agony of grief which overpowered them at first, was SS I 1 7 13
strongly partook of the emotion which overpowered Marianne. SS I 15 75 2
relative to Willoughby overpowered her in an instant; and SS I 15 82 47
led him to beleive her not overpowered with applications.-- W 334 13
Mrs. Bennet was in fact too much overpowered to say a PP I 23 126 5
She was overpowered by shame and vexation. PP III 1 252 54
I am not afraid of being overpowered by the impression. PP III 6 299 21
slighted, was almost overpowered with gratitude that he MP I 7 66 14
away, before Fanny, overpowered by a thousand feelings of MP II 9 261 3
and who was still overpowered by the suddenness of MP III 2 326 3
My father is not overpowered. MP III 15 442 23
and say, and this conclusion of it almost overpowered her. MP III 16 448 1
Do not be overpowered by such a little tribute of E I 9 77 47
She was too completely overpowered to be immediately able E I 15 131 32
33
"You will excuse my being so much overpowered. E I 18 150 30
My dear Miss Woodhouse--I come quite overpowered. E II 3 172 24
Her affection must have overpowered her judgment." E III 12 419 9
question, and the expression of his eyes overpowered her. E III 13 430 34
face concealed, as if overpowered by the various feelings P III 12 112 54
Mrs. Clay's affections had overpowered her interest, and P IV 12 250 8
OVERPOWERING (11)
This declaration brought on a loud and overpowering reply, NA I 9 64 26
gracious return to the overpowering delight of Lucy in SS II 10 217 20
sisters and of his overpowering friend, assisted by the PP I 23 129 13
it is only as Agatha that I was to be so overpowering!"-- MP I 14 136 18
altogether was quite overpowering to Fanny; and before she MP I 15 146 53
Even to see Mr. Crawford would be less overpowering. MP III 1 322 49
might lead to, were overpowering, and she fancied herself MP III 10 399 4
others, in the most overpowering period of Mr. Elton's E I 14 118 4
All the overpowering, blinding, bewildering, first effects P IV 7 175 6
and the more from its not overpowering you at the time." P IV 8 181 4
It was an overpowering happiness. P IV 11 238 44
OVERPOWERS (2)
"Your kindness almost overpowers me. P IV 9 203 72
"I am every instant hearing something which overpowers me. P IV 11 237 42
OVERSEERS (1)
The magistrates, and overseers, and churchwardens, are E III 16 455 23
OVERSET (2)
Why you do not suppose a man is overset by a bottle? NA I 9 63 20
to us, who have been overset already by one poor regiment PP II 16 220 7
OVERSIGHTS (1)
one lady, detailed the oversights of another, & indulged W 359 28
OVERSPREAD (4)
A deeper shade of hauteur overspread his features, but he PP I 18 92 19
the cheeks of each were overspread with the deepest blush. PP III 1 251 51
of the smiles which overspread her face whenever she spoke PP III 3 269 8
A blush overspread Anne's cheeks. P IV 9 194 17
OVERSPREADING (2)
Tell me honestly"--a deeper glow overspreading his cheeks-- SS III 8 318 15
overspreading many, and occasionally part of the stream. PP III 1 253 57
OVERSTOCKED (1)
in an house, already overstocked, surrounded by inferior W 361 31
OVERSTRAINED (2)
I have no idea of being so overstrained! NA II 3 144 10
Elinor thought this generosity overstrained, considering SS I 16 85 10
OVERTAKE (2)
"Only," she added, "perhaps we may overtake the two young NA I 6 43 40
We shall soon overtake her. E III 7 374 53
OVERTAKEN (6)
when she was fortunately miss'd, pursued, & overtaken. LS 19 273 1
when he had overtaken them, and were at home by this time. NA I 13 101 20
strike into another path, she was overtaken by Wickham. PP III 10 327 4
by her aunt Norris, was overtaken by a heavy shower close MP II 4 205 3
in her power, being overtaken by a child from the cottage, E I 10 88 33
to Hartfield--they were overtaken by Mr. John Knightley E I 13 109 6
OVERTHREW (1)
grew stronger, it overthrew caution, and she found herself MP III 14 431 8
OVERTHROW (7)
his subsequent malicious overthrow of it; that in no sense NA II 16 251 6
which, if true, must overthrow every cherished opinion of PP II 13 204 2
Such an overthrow of every thing she had been wishing for!- E I 16 134 1
were immediately followed by the overthrow of every thing. E II 12 258 7
conscious of such an overthrow of all order and neatness! P III 5 40 44
from the history of it's overthrow, he gathered only hard S 8 404 1
Charlotte, meaning to overthrow his attempts at surprise, S 10 418 1
OVERTHROWING (1)
I always delight in overthrowing those kind of schemes, PP I 10 52 50
OVERTHROWN (4)
and all his views of domestic happiness were overthrown. PP II 19 236 1
the neighbourhood had of him, should then be overthrown? PP III 5 285 16
when all her views were overthrown, by seeing him fall a PP III 12 342 26
But though her wishes were overthrown there was no spirit MP II 10 280 32
OVERTOOK (4)
that, though they overtook and passed the two offending NA I 7 47 18
town, and in Bond-Street overtook the second Miss Thorpe, NA I 14 114 50
I was afraid they might not; and we overtook William PP III 9 316 8
somewhere else, and she would go on, till she overtook her. P III 10 87 21
OVERTURE (2)
an offer on the first overture, but I could not answer it LS 7 253 2
forward on the first overture of a marriage between the NA II 15 246 12
OVERTURES (3)
myself that my present overtures of good-will are highly PP I 13 63 12
But now, when he has made his overtures so properly, and MP III 1 315 18
and though his overtures had not been met with any warmth, P III 1 7 14
OVERTURN (1)
them, nor one lucky overturn to introduce them to the hero. NA I 2 19 4
OVERTURNED (2)
be overturned by him, than driven safely by anybody else." P III 10 85 9
a very rough lane, were overturned in toiling up it's long S 1 363 1
OVERTURNING (1)
to the suspicion of overturning them on purpose (S 1 364 1
OVERWHELMED (2)
I could not bring it into play: it was overwhelmed, buried, P IV 11 245 74
it in sunshine & overwhelmed by the sudden tempest, all S 7 396 1
OWE (20)
I beleive I owe it to my own character, to complete the LS 25 294 5
My own folly has endangered me, my preservation I owe to LS 36 305 1
those, to whom I owe no duty, & for whom I feel no respect. LS 39 308 1
And I must say this: that you owe no particular gratitude SS I 2 13 28
We owe Mrs. Jennings much more than civility; and civility SS II 7 191 63
be ignorant that you to your goodness I owe it all.-- SS III 4 289 34
I do assure you that you owe it entirely, at least almost SS III 4 289 35
it; but, upon my word, you owe nothing to my solicitation." SS III 4 289 35
I owe such a grudge to myself for the stupid, rascally SS III 8 324 45
I can safely say I owe you no ill-will, and am sure you SS III 13 365 14
I am sure we owe him no such particular civility as to be PP I 18 99 65
would in general wish to owe to his wife; but where other PP II 19 236 1
But your family owe me nothing. PP III 16 366 6
What do I not owe you! PP III 16 369 24
I owe all that I know of it, to another, not to you." PP III 17 374 18
You do not owe me the duty of a child. MP III 1 319 39
think more justly, and not owe the most valuable knowledge MP III 16 458 30
"You owe me no apologies; and every body to whom you might E III 16 459 48
you might be supposed to owe them, is so perfectly E III 16 459 48
& if it was not for what I owe to poor Mr Hollis's memory, S 6 393 1
OWED (27)
on your time, but I owed it to my own character; & after LS 24 290 13
You have owed us a visit many long weeks. LS 40 309 1
Marianne, how many pleasant days we have owed to them?" SS I 16 88 40
I owed it to her, therefore, to avoid giving any hint of SS III 1 262 23
hint of the truth; and I owed it to my family and friends, SS III 1 262 23
entirely--not even what I owed to my dearest friends--from SS III 1 264 29
in the matter, that he owed all his knowledge of the house, SS III 13 368 31
an ungracious delay as she owed to her own dignity, and as SS III 14 373 3
Robert; and Lucy, who had owed his mother no duty, and SS III 14 376 11
She owed her greatest relief to her friend Miss Lucas, who PP I 18 102 73
happy to add, that I owed the knowledge of it to herself. PP II 12 202 5
He owed a good deal in the town, but his debts of honour PP III 6 298 12
They owed the restoration of Lydia, her character, every PP III 10 326 3
Elizabeth particularly, who knew that her mother owed to PP III 11 335 42
the sense of what they owed him more painful to PP III 12 340 13
she owed the greatest complaisance, had set their hearts? MP I 16 153 3
every thing else;--education and manners she owed to him. MP II 10 276 13
and having formerly owed much to Mr. Woodhouse's kindness, E I 3 22 5
They owed to him their two or three politest puzzles; and E I 9 70 7
He owed it to her, to risk any thing that might be E III 5 350 31
It would be incompatible with what she owed to her father, E III 12 416 1
I remember her telling me at the ball, that I owed Mrs. E III 14 439 8
since to them he must have owed a wife of very superior P III 1 4 6
had done it, that she owed it to his perception of her P III 10 91 42
these circumstances; she felt that she owed him attention. P IV 7 180 32
In spite of the mischief of his attentions, she owed him P IV 9 192 2
Though he owed many of his ideas to this sort of reading, S 8 404 1
OWEING (2)
that was perhaps merely oweing to the consciousness of his W 341 19
Perhaps it might be partly oweing to her having just S 6 391
OWES (5)
especially towards those to whom he owes his preferment. PP I 18 101 7
him forget what he owes to himself and to all his family. PP III 14 354 3
the husband, to whom she owes every thing, while she E I 14 123 2
governed by the nephew, to whom she owes nothing at all." E I 14 123 2
has been the person to whom Miss Fairfax owes-----" E III 8 380 1
OWING (15)
her that it was entirely owing to the peculiarly judicious NA I 9 62 1

his fair cousins, the excellence of its cookery was owing. PP I 13 65 26
the errors of her daughter must be principally owing. PP III 5 287 34
conviction of its being owing to himself that Wickham's PP III 10 321 2
It was owing to him, to his reserve, and want of proper PP III 10 324 2
so, for, though you know (owing to me) your papa and mamma MP I 2 19 29
to our owing her a great many gay, brilliant, happy hours. MP II 4 210 21
it, but much was still owing to Sir Thomas's more than MP II 7 238 1
him, nor how much might be owing to contrast, she was MP III 11 413 32
a material drawback, to be owing such felicity to persons MP III 14 435 15
That Julia escaped better than Maria was owing, in some MP III 17 466 17
A large debt of gratitude was owing here; but the E I 1 6 6
It was owing to her persuasion, as she thought his being E III 5 344 9
I, who am owing all my happiness to you, would not it be E III 17 461 5
it very likely that my illness to-day may be owing to it." P III 5 39 39
OWN (1511)
as I am on the point of separation from my own daughter. LS 1 244 1
should, but I must own myself rather romantic in that LS 2 245 1
to her own child, should be attached to any of mine. LS 3 247 1
comes to us, which I am glad of, for her sake and my own. LS 3 247 1
I hope you will soon be able to form your own judgement. LS 6 250 1
longer young, I must for my own part declare that I have LS 6 251 1
as Mr Vernon, to whom her own behaviour was far from LS 6 252 2
Upon the whole I commend my own conduct in this affair LS 7 253 2
propose to make it her own choice by rendering her LS 7 253 2
coquetry to subdue his judgement to her own purposes. LS 11 259 1
as common decency will allow me to do in my own house. LS 11 259 1
everything at stake; your own happiness, that of your LS 12 260 1
To the fortune of your wife, the goodness of my own, will LS 12 261 3
You know your own rights, & that it is out of my power to LS 12 261 4
I may perhaps do no good, but that of relieving my own LS 12 261 5
injurious to your own peace than to our understandings. LS 14 263 1
As to Mrs Manwaring's jealousy, it was totally his own LS 14 264 4
between ourselves, I must own it has only convinced me of LS 15 266 1
which confirms me in my own private explanation of it. LS 16 268 1
Lady Susan finds it necessary for her own justification LS 17 272 8
been perfectly right in attributing it to my own letter. LS 19 273 1
as ashes came running up, & rushed by me into her own room. LS 20 275 1
After breakfast however, as I was going to my own room I LS 24 286 5
You will find Mr Vernon in his own room." LS 24 287 8
it was my object to make my own child miserable, & that I LS 24 289 12
Neither for your sake, for hers, nor for my own, could LS 24 289 12
Where my own resolution was taken, I could not wish for LS 24 289 12
I honestly own that there is something to conceal. LS 24 289 12
a degree of affection, & I own it would have sensibly hurt LS 24 290 13
to make; if she value her own happiness as much as I do, LS 24 290 13
time, but I owed it to my own character; & after this LS 24 290 13
This Reginald has a proud spirit of his own!--a spirit too, LS 25 292 1
I beleive I owe it to my own character, to complete the LS 25 294 5
When my own will is effected, contrary to his, I shall LS 25 294 6
During his absence we shall be able to chuse our own LS 26 296 4
for any other woman in the world, than her own mother. LS 27 297 2
much effect on you, & that de courcy is certainly your own. LS 28 298 2
could induce me to wound my own feelings by urging a LS 30 301 4
Depend upon it, I can make my own story with Reginald. LS 33 303 1
My own folly has endangered me, my preservation I owe to LS 36 305 1
of others--of resigning my own judgement in deference to LS 39 308 1
mother, & placed under her own care; & tho' with little LS 42 311 2
& without any change in her own veiws, only feared greater LS 42 312 4
daughter; & as, tho' her own plans were not yet wholly LS 42 312 5
own person and disposition, were all equally against her. NA I 1 13 1
on the pianoforte, of her own composition, she could NA I 1 16 10
At present she did not know her own poverty, for she had NA I 1 16 10
befal a young lady in her own village, she must seek them NA I 1 17 12
admiration; for, in her own hearing, two gentlemen NA I 2 24 28
"Particularly well; I always buy my own cravats, and am NA I 3 28 38
before a lady of about her own age, who was sitting by her, NA I 4 31 2
pelisse was not half so handsome as that on her own. NA I 4 32 2
with a young man of his own college, of the name of Thorpe; NA I 4 33 5
them to be read by their own heroine, who, if she NA I 5 37 4
simply engrossed by her own, that her brother thought her NA I 7 44 4
hazarding an opinion of its own in opposition to that of a NA I 7 48 32
where the beauty of her own sex is concerned, ventured at NA I 7 48 32
her own felicity, in being already engaged for the evening. NA I 7 51 54
and she was too young to own herself frightened; so, NA I 9 62 10
Thorpe's ideas then all reverted to the merits of his own NA I 9 64 27
Her own family were plain matter-of-fact people, who NA I 9 65 31
talk, began and ended with himself and his own concerns. NA I 9 66 31
it had never endangered his own life for a moment, had NA I 9 66 31
would neither believe her own watch, nor her brother's, NA I 9 67 33
Her own feelings entirely engrossed her; her wretchedness NA I 9 67 33
not look amiss; the sleeves were entirely my own thought. NA I 10 70 3
excessive solicitude about it often destroys its own aim. NA I 10 73 22
other sex rather than her own, a brother rather than a NA I 10 73 22
Woman is fine for her own satisfaction alone. NA I 10 74 22
best interest to keep their own imaginations from NA I 10 77 33
a place as this, than in my own home; for here are a NA I 10 78 46
Mr. Allen not having his own skies and barometer about him, NA I 11 82 1
she could not from her own observation help thinking, that NA I 11 86 50
is a fool for not keeping a horse and gig of his own." NA I 11 89 56
the resentful sensation; she remembered her own ignorance. NA I 12 92 3
She was not deceived in her own expectation of pleasure; NA I 12 92 4
instead of considering her own dignity injured by this NA I 12 93 4
but indeed it was not my own fault,--was it, Mrs. Allen? NA I 12 93 5
daughter, rather than postpone his own walk a few minutes. NA I 12 95 17
they are too strong for my own peace; and to see myself NA I 13 98 2
friendship by strangers, does cut me to the quick, I own. NA I 13 98 2
regardless of every thing but her own gratification. NA I 13 98 3
Setting her own inclination apart, to have failed a second NA I 13 101 25
not consulted merely her own gratification; that might NA I 13 101 25
due to others, and to her own character in their opinion. NA I 13 101 25
Miss Tilney added her own wishes. NA I 13 103 28
person what her own conduct had really been, she took NA I 13 103 29
Allen's approbation of her own conduct, and truly rejoiced NA I 13 105 41
you are to observe, was her own, particularly her own. NA I 14 107 9
actually pass under one's own observation; and as for the NA I 14 109 23
as I observed to be your own method, instead of 'to NA I 14 109 25
But Catherine did not know her own advantages--did not NA I 14 111 29
"My dear Eleanor, the riot is only in your own brain. NA I 14 113 39
more attached to my dear Morland's family than to my own." NA I 15 118 9
"For my own part," said Isabella, "my wishes are so NA I 15 119 20
truth, there are not many that I know my own mind about." NA I 15 124 45
I am sure of a good income of my own; and if she had not a NA I 15 124 46
of his own happy address, and her explicit encouragement. NA I 15 124 47
the latter she could only attribute to her own stupidity. NA II 1 129 1
in the business, I must own, has been no more than I NA II 1 133 34
"It is not on my own account I wish for more; but I cannot NA II 1 135 45
has a right to do what they like with their own money." NA II 1 136 47
of their own affections, and I believe he is very right. NA II 3 147 20
would at least restore peace to every heart but his own. NA II 4 150 1
Pray advise him for his own sake, and for every body's NA II 4 150 4
He knows what he is about, and must be his own master." NA II 4 150 6
Would he thank you, either on his own account or Miss NA II 4 152 28
of whose enjoyment their own had been gently increased. NA II 5 154 1
difficulty in saving her own new writing-desk from being NA II 5 155 4
General chosen to have his own carriage lead the way, they NA II 5 156 5
that of listening to her own praise; of being thanked at NA II 5 157 5
have an establishment at my own house in Woodston, which NA II 5 157 7
While they snugly repair to their own end of the house, NA II 5 158 15
exhausted, you will return towards your own apartment. NA II 5 160 21
precious treasure into your own chamber, but scarcely have NA II 5 160 21
her to use her own fancy in the perusal of Matilda's woes. NA II 5 160 23
and a good appetite of her own, restored her to peace. NA II 6 165 6
as securely as if it had been her own chamber at Fullerton. NA II 6 167 9
And it was in a great measure his own doing, for had not NA II 7 173 3
the place being chiefly my own, you may believe I take NA II 7 176 15
out of doors against his own inclination, under a mistaken NA II 7 177 17
The proposal was his own. NA II 7 177 18
and it seemed as if his own estimation of Northanger had NA II 7 178 19
describing the nature of his own as they entered them. NA II 7 178 24
art of her own question, "hangs in your father's room?" NA II 7 180 38
Soon after her death I obtained it for my own, and hung it NA II 7 181 39
When the General had satisfied his own curiosity, in a NA II 8 182 2
failed, his own had often produced the perfection wanted. NA II 8 183 3
Catherine sometimes started at the boldness of her own NA II 8 188 18
belief, just opposite her own, it struck her that, if NA II 8 188 19
she ran for safety to her own room, and, locking herself NA II 9 192 4
from the angry General to attend him in his own apartment. NA II 9 192 4
Miss Tilney's meaning, in her own calculation! NA II 9 193 6
but to be safe in her own room, with her own heart only NA II 9 194 6
in her own room, with her own heart only privy to its NA II 9 194 6
to my own chamber; and why should I not come up it?" NA II 9 194 7
rather wonder that Eleanor should not take it for her own. NA II 9 196 21
repeatedly; and from our own observation can bear witness NA II 9 197 25
Consult your own understanding, your own sense of the NA II 9 197 29
sense of the probable, your own observation of what is NA II 9 197 29
and with tears of shame she ran off to her own room. NA II 9 198 30
Catherine dared not doubt beyond her own country, and even NA II 10 200 3
she hurried away to her own room; but the house-maids were NA II 10 203 8
then their own brother so closely concerned in it!-- NA II 10 203 9
"My own disappointment and loss in her is very great; but, NA II 10 206 37
ease as to the necessity of any sudden removal of her own. NA II 11 208 2
He must tell his own story." NA II 11 209 2
"I wish I could reason like you, for his sake and my own. NA II 11 211 14
to Catherine to doubt her own judgment than Henry's, she NA II 11 211 15
his eating, she had, by her own unassisted observation, NA II 11 211 15
at any table but his own; and never before known him so NA II 11 215 27
Pray write to me soon, and direct to my own home. NA II 12 216 2
You know I have a pretty good spirit of my own. NA II 12 217 2
and fatigues at their own command, made her thoroughly NA II 13 220 1
For my own pleasure, I could stay with you as long again."- NA II 13 221 6
any reference to her own convenience, or allowing her even NA II 13 226 25
I will trust to your own kindness of heart when I am at a NA II 13 229 30
Henry and her own heart only were privy to the shocking NA II 14 230 3
that would not increase her own grief by the confession of NA II 14 231 5
to feel an interest in her own amendment, but her spirits NA II 14 235 13
up in the reflection of her own change of feelings and NA II 14 237 20
successfully confirming her own opinions by the justness NA II 14 239 28
by the justness of her own representations, Catherine was NA II 14 239 28
was already entirely his own; for, though Henry was now NA II 15 243 9
credit of a wild imagination will at least be all my own. NA II 15 243 9
in the contemplation of her own unutterable happiness, NA II 15 243 10
and which a better pride would have been ashamed to own. NA II 15 244 11
likely to be connected, his own consequence always NA II 15 245 12
curiosity, and his own speculations, he had yet something NA II 15 245 12
one of its members, and his own views on another, (NA II 15 245 12
ignorant at the time of all this, than his own children. NA II 15 245 12
no means respected in their own neighbourhood, as he had NA II 15 246 12
father, in what points his own conjectures might assist NA II 15 247 14
that heart to be his own which he had been directed to NA II 15 247 15
once obtained--and their own hearts made them trust that NA II 16 249 2
My own joy on the occasion is very sincere. NA II 16 251 5
But her death, which happened ten years before his own, SS I 1 3 1
By his own marriage, likewise, which happened soon SS I 1 3 2
thousand pounds in his own disposal; for the remaining SS I 1 4 2
desire of having his own way, many cunning tricks, and a SS I 1 4 3
the remaining half of his own mother's fortune, warmed his SS I 1 5 8
propriety of going, and her own tender love for all her SS I 1 6 10
you to give away half your fortune from your own child." SS I 2 9 5
Her income was not her own, she said, with such perpetual SS I 2 11 20
fortune, as your mother justly says, is not one's own. SS I 2 11 21
If I were you, whatever I did should be done at my own SS I 2 11 22
a hundred, or even fifty pounds from our own expences." SS I 2 11 22
have been a very pleasant addition to our own stock here." SS I 2 13 27
such kind of neighbourly acts as his own wife pointed out. SS I 2 13 29
For their brother's sake too, for the sake of his own SS I 3 14 2
whose taste did not in every point coincide with my own. SS I 3 17 18
He distrusts his own judgment in such matters so much, SS I 4 19 2
to you, by speaking, in so quiet a way, of my own feelings. SS I 4 21 15
own partiality, by believing or calling it more than it is. SS I 4 21 15
own, a gentleman of consequence and property in Devonshire. SS I 4 23 20
park, the place of his own residence, from whence she SS I 4 23 20
own, she should have any handsome article of furniture. SS I 5 26 4
had she consulted only her own wishes, she would have kept SS I 5 26 5
to examine it herself till she entered it as her own. SS I 5 26 6
it for more than a mile, they reached their own house. SS I 6 28 1
accommodation from his own house and garden in which SS I 6 30 6
by admitting them to a residence within his own manor. SS I 7 33 3
played extremely well, and by her own was very fond of it. SS I 7 35 8
could sympathize with her own, was estimable when SS I 7 35 9
They gaily ascended the downs, rejoicing in their own SS I 9 41 4
turn back, for no shelter was nearer than their own house. SS I 9 41 6
had no property of his own in the country; that he resided SS I 9 44 23
pretty little estate of his own in Somersetshire besides; SS I 9 44 23
account of him and her own gratitude prompted; and every SS I 10 46 1
by the example of her own, and which recommended him to SS I 10 48 7
had assigned him for her own satisfaction, were now SS I 10 49 12
on the strength of your own imagination, that the SS I 10 51 27
She had already repeated her own history to Elinor three SS I 11 54 6
regard, was all his own; but he was a lover; his SS I 11 55 7
of her own father, who had himself two wives, I know not. SS I 11 56 11
subject would only attach her the more to her own opinion. SS I 12 59 5
When you leave Barton to form your own establishment in a SS I 12 59 6
"Yes, yes, we can guess where he is; at his own house at SS I 12 61 23
your own, and that there is no such person in existence." SS I 12 61 25
"My own loss is great," he continued, "in being obliged to SS I 13 64 21
I would lay fifty guineas the letter was of his own SS I 13 65 30
she had actually made her own woman enquire of Mr. SS I 13 67 65
now begin to doubt the discretion of your own conduct?" SS I 13 68 73
"If they were one day to be your own, Marianne, you would SS I 13 69 75
find your own house as faultless as you now do this." SS I 14 73 14
happiness forgot for a time her own disappointment. SS I 16 86 21
happy; but like every body else it must be in my own way. SS I 17 91 7
"She knows her own worth too well for false shame," SS I 17 94 44
while his own enjoyment in it appeared so imperfect. SS I 18 96 1
beginning to describe her own admiration of these scenes, SS I 18 96 4
He is fastidious and will have an affectation of his own." SS I 18 97 6
she had pained Edward, her own vexation at her want of SS I 18 98 12
That the hair was her own, she instantaneously felt as SS I 18 98 13
beyond all doubt, that it was exactly the shade of her own. SS I 18 98 13
what she had said; but her own forgiveness might have been SS I 18 99 14
wishes and his own, and without any restraint on his time. SS I 19 101 1
But unfortunately my own nicety, and the nicety of my SS I 19 102 4
has not promoted your own happiness, that your sons will SS I 19 103 5
Know your own happiness. SS I 19 103 7
she did not lessen her own grief, it was at least SS I 19 104 10
Such behaviour as this, so exactly the reverse of her own, SS I 19 104 11
to Marianne, than her own had seemed faulty to her. SS I 19 104 11
and of the strength of her own, she gave a very striking SS I 19 104 11
on her own account; her daughters might do as they pleased. SS I 19 108 40
am sure, though we could not get him to own it last night." SS I 20 116 58
Sir John's confidence in his own judgment rose with this SS I 21 119 3
and the other Miss Dashwoods, quite as his own sisters."-- SS I 22 130 16
And on my own account too--so dear as he is to me--I don't SS I 22 133 44
Your own judgment must direct you." SS I 22 133 45

She remembered too, her own surprise at the time, at his SS I 22 134 49
and proofs, and contradicted by nothing but her own wishes. SS II 1 139 1
his dissatisfaction at his own prospects, his uncertain SS II 1 139 1
His affection was all her own. SS II 1 139 1
her at Norland; it was not an illusion of her own vanity. SS II 1 139 1
And so well was she able to answer her own expectations, SS II 1 141 4
She was stronger alone, and her own good sense so well SS II 1 141 6
directed, to combat her own affection for Edward and to SS II 1 142 7
she did not mistrust her own ability of going through a SS II 1 142 7
her own end, and pleased Lady Middleton at the same time. SS II 1 145 23
The piano-forte, at which Marianne, wrapt up in her own SS II 1 145 23
up in her own music and her own thoughts, had by this time SS II 1 145 23
But I am very glad to find it was only my own fancy, and SS II 2 146 5
"He has only two thousand pounds of his own; it would be SS II 2 147 7
upon that, though for my own part, I could give up every SS II 2 147 7
"And for your own sake too, or you are carrying your SS II 2 148 16
your own feelings, your opinion would not be worth having." SS II 2 150 34
she was not without a settled habitation of her own. SS II 3 153 1
good luck in getting my own children off my hands, that SS II 3 153 2
on her own account she had particular reasons to avoid. SS II 3 154 6
the motive of her own disinclination for going to London. SS II 3 155 6
to the sole guidance of her own judgment, or that Mrs. SS II 3 156 15
without wondering at her own situation, so short had their SS II 4 159 1
feeling how blank was her own prospect, how cheerless her SS II 4 159 1
prospect, how cheerless her own state of mind in the SS II 4 159 1
to his character which her own observation or the SS II 4 159 1
She sat in silence almost all the way, wrapt in her own SS II 4 160 2
not make them choose their own dinners at the inn, nor SS II 4 160 2
in her own room, could see little of what was passing. SS II 4 161 7
after having declined her own, though at the same time she SS II 4 164 21
time was therefore at her own disposal, the evening was by SS II 4 166 31
Mary always has her own way." SS II 5 167 5
Business on Sir John's part, and a violent cold on her own, SS II 5 170 28
returned Elinor, "for her own family do not know it." SS II 5 173 41
her attitude, lost in her own thoughts and insensible of SS II 6 175 1
own room, where hartshorn restored her a little to herself. SS II 6 178 16
might still feed her own wishes, she could not attribute SS II 6 178 17
a consciousness of his own misconduct, and prevented her SS II 6 178 17
Her own situation gained in the comparison; for while she SS II 6 179 18
Oh! how easy for those who have no sorrow of their own to SS II 7 185 22
it,) I was once as dear to him as my own soul could wish. SS II 7 188 46
"By all the world, rather than by his own heart. SS II 7 189 50
any one, in short, but your own dear self, mama, and SS II 7 189 50
own innocence and good intentions supports your spirits. SS II 7 189 51
"I would do more than for my own. SS II 7 190 54
is gone to her own room I suppose to moan by herself. SS II 8 195 14
Let her name her own supper, and go to bed. SS II 8 195 16
Their own good-nature must point out to them the real SS II 8 195 17
as she expected, in her own room, leaning, in silent SS II 8 197 23
irritable refinement of her own mind, and the too great SS II 9 201 4
and feelings as her own, and she judged of their motives SS II 9 202 4
were together in their own room after breakfast, which SS II 9 202 4
because, through her own weakness, it chanced to prove a SS II 9 202 4
offered no counsel of her own except of patience till SS II 9 203 9
"I will not trust to that," retreating to her own room. SS II 9 204 16
"A man who has nothing to do with his own time has no SS II 9 204 16
Regard for a former servant of my own, who had since SS II 9 207 26
with gratitude towards her own condition, when she SS II 9 210 32
still as strong as her own, and with a mind tormented by SS II 9 210 32
She will feel her own sufferings to be nothing. SS II 9 210 32
Use your own discretion, however, in communicating to her SS II 9 210 32
Against the interest of her own individual comfort, Mrs. SS II 10 213 3
militate against her own happiness, it would be better for SS II 10 214 7
the dignity of her own sex, and spoken her decided censure SS II 10 215 14
to the interest of her own assemblies, and therefore SS II 10 215 14
finally arranged by his own inventive fancy, he had no SS II 11 220 3
around her, in Mr. Gray's shop, as in her own bed-room. SS II 11 221 4
my own property, that I felt it my duty to buy it. SS II 11 225 31
undoubted right to dispose of his own property as he chose. SS II 11 225 35
was the easiest means of atoning for his own neglect. SS II 11 228 51
of their characters and her own difficulties, and to have SS II 12 231 9
They were relieved however, not by her own recollection, SS II 12 231 11
mother, rather than her own, whom they were about to SS II 12 232 14
really convinced that her own son was the tallest, SS II 12 234 21
22
were equally earnest in support of their own descendant. SS II 12 234 23
to Elinor, as her own wounded heart taught her to think of SS II 12 236 39
40
to be thankful for her own sake, that one greater obstacle SS II 13 238 1
Lucy still pressed her to own that she had reason for her SS II 13 239 7
to make a civil answer, though doubting her own success. SS II 13 240 14
she, for his sake and her own, to do it well, that she SS II 13 241 20
For their own comfort, they would much rather have SS II 14 246 2
and sometimes at her own house; but wherever it was, she SS II 14 247 5
well doing to her own care, and ready to give so exact, so SS II 14 247 5
were, as usual, in their own estimation, and that of their SS II 14 250 10
own merit, than on the merit of his nearest relations! SS II 14 250 12
now irremediable, and it has been entirely your own doing. SS II 14 251 13
sir Robert, against your own judgment, to place Edward SS II 14 251 13
"For my own part," said he, "I am excessively fond of a SS II 14 251 17
from that period to her own home, and her own habits, in SS III 1 257 1
to her own home, and her own habits, in which she found SS III 1 257 1
as he was sitting in his own dressing-room down stairs, SS III 1 259 7
She could hardly determine what her own expectation of its SS III 1 260 9
seem strong, feel all her own disappointment over again. SS III 1 261 11
She was very far from dwelling on her own feelings, or to SS III 1 261 12
Elinor was to be the comforter of others in her own SS III 1 261 12
given by assurances of her own composure of mind, and a SS III 1 261 12
by any imprudence of my own, and I have borne it as much SS III 1 263 27
His own two thousand pounds she protested should be his SS III 1 267 38
Edward has drawn his own lot, and I fear it will be a bad SS III 1 268 45
that he might, but for his own folly, within three months SS III 1 268 50
It is not fit that he should be living about at his own SS III 1 268 51
Everybody has a way of their own. SS III 1 269 54
in possession of an estate which might have been his own? SS III 1 269 56
necessarily produced between Elinor's conduct and her own. SS III 2 270 1
left her own party for a short time, to join their's. SS III 2 271 5
that he said a word about being off, and not upon his own. SS III 2 273 16
in their own chariot, which was more than I looked for. SS III 2 275 22
the approach of her own party made another more necessary. SS III 2 275 24
a monstrous deal of money, and they keep their own coach. SS III 2 275 25
had been already foreseen and foreplanned in her own mind. SS III 2 276 26
the sake of her own consequence, would chuse to have known. SS III 2 276 27
own sake, and as a friend of yours, I wish it still more. SS III 3 282 19
began to talk of his own advantage in securing so SS III 3 283 20
You know your own concerns best. SS III 4 287 20
"The unkindness of your own relations has made you SS III 4 289 33
to your own merit, and Colonel Brandon's discernment of it. SS III 4 289 35
and, of course, to reflect on her own with discontent. SS III 4 291 45
Her own happiness, and her own spirits, were at least very SS III 5 293 2
warmth, was ready to own all their obligation to her, and SS III 5 293 2
which not only opposed her own inclination, but which had SS III 5 293 3
"Fanny is in her own room, I suppose," said he;--"I will SS III 5 294 6
brother, earned only by his own dissipated course of life, SS III 5 298 32
relieved her own feelings, and gave no intelligence to him. SS III 5 298 34
not by any reproof of her's, but by his own sensibility. SS III 5 298 34
But though she never spoke of it out of her own family, SS III 5 300 38
restoring Marianne's peace of mind, and confirming her own. SS III 6 302 5
she knew not what to expect to find him in his own family. SS III 6 304 15
and of endeavouring, by her own attentive care, to supply SS III 7 308 3
the first wish of his own heart by a compliance, could not SS III 7 309 5
mother, she had pursued her own judgment rather than her SS III 7 310 8
and retired to her own room to write letters and sleep. SS III 7 316 27
and thoughtfulness on his own,--"how you may have SS III 8 319 29
Careless of her happiness, thinking only of my own SS III 8 320 29
In that point, however, I undervalued my own magnanimity, SS III 8 323 40
"It was necessary to my own pride. SS III 8 324 42
of the comfort it gives me to look back on my own misery. SS III 8 324 45
rascally folly of my own heart, that all my past SS III 8 324 45
My journey to town--travelling with my own horses, and SS III 8 325 45
creature to speak to--my own reflections so cheerful--when SS III 8 325 45
known to me than my own,--and I am sure they are dearer." SS III 8 325 50
she was as constant in her own feelings, and as full of SS III 8 325 53
"But the letter, Mr. Willoughby, your own letter; have you SS III 8 328 60
The letter was in your own hand-writing." SS III 8 328 62
The original was all her own--her own happy thoughts and SS III 8 328 63
You have made your own choice. SS III 8 329 64
can I suppose it a relief to your own conscience." SS III 8 329 64
Vanity, while seeking its own guilty triumph at the SS III 8 331 70
shared it, however, in a silence even greater than her own. SS III 9 334 4
to Mrs. Dashwood by her own previous alarm; for so great SS III 9 335 6
temperate account of her own disappointment which Elinor SS III 9 335 7
she now began to feel, her own mistaken judgment in SS III 9 335 7
I saw that it equalled my own, and he perhaps, thinking SS III 9 336 12
respect him; and even my own knowledge of him, though SS III 9 337 17
His own merits must soon secure it." SS III 9 337 18
When there, at her own particular request, for she was SS III 10 340 1
urged equally by her own and her daughter's wishes began SS III 10 340 4
request, to consider his own abode there as equally SS III 10 341 4
wishes as seemed due to her own heart from a secret SS III 10 341 5
travellers, and feel their own dulness, till Mrs. Jennings SS III 10 341 5
on its outward leaf her own name in his hand writing.-- SS III 10 342 7
Our own library is too well known to me, to be resorted to SS III 10 343 9
secret reflections may be no more unpleasant than my own. SS III 10 345 24
I considered the past; I saw in my own behaviour since the SS III 10 345 28
I saw that my own feelings had prepared my sufferings, and SS III 10 345 28
my own health, as I had felt even at the time to be wrong. SS III 10 345 28
I cannot express my own abhorrence of myself. SS III 10 346 28
judgment, and sobered her own opinion of Willoughby's SS III 11 349 2
retrenched only on your own comfort, you might have been SS III 11 350 9
would have lessened your own influence on his heart, and SS III 11 351 9
which afterwards, when his own were engaged, made him SS III 11 351 11
His own enjoyment, or his own ease, was, in every SS III 11 351 11
"and I have nothing to regret--nothing but my own folly." SS III 11 352 14
that each felt their own error, wished to avoid any survey SS III 11 352 16
17
that some resolution of his own, some mediation of friends, SS III 12 357 1
practices;-- pursuing her own interest in every thought, SS III 12 357 3
and was obliged to leave all to their own discretion. SS III 12 358 9
her own voice, now said, "is Mrs. Ferrars at Longstaple?" SS III 12 359 16
17
had no means of lessening but by their own conjectures. SS III 12 360 26
she was overcome by her own felicity;--and happily SS III 13 363 8
To her own heart it was a delightful affair, to her SS III 13 364 10
of his opinion of what his own mediation in his brother's SS III 13 364 11
at liberty to bestow my own on another, and have no doubt SS III 13 365 14
it in his power to make his own choice; and she has SS III 13 366 18
with which he rated his own deserts, and the politeness SS III 13 366 20
in your favour; that your own family might in time relent. SS III 13 367 23
at Norland, when he must have felt his own inconstancy. SS III 13 368 25
say nothing of my own conviction, our relations were all SS III 13 368 26
is my own; I am doing no injury to anybody but myself." SS III 13 368 28
that they could call their own; for it was impossible that SS III 13 369 32
delay as she owed to her own dignity, and as served to SS III 14 373 3
interest even equal to his own; and in short, it became SS III 14 376 11
They each felt his sorrows, and their own obligations, and SS III 14 378 13
She was born to discover the falsehood of her own opinions, SS III 14 378 15
and that Marianne found her own happiness in forming his, SS III 14 379 17
which thus brought its own punishment, was sincere, need SS III 14 379 18
Do not trust her with any secrets of your own, take W 317 2
no scruples, if she can promote her own advantage.-- W 317 2
I could do very well single for my own part--a little W 317 2
She professes to keep her own counsel; she says, & truly W 318 2
with respect to her own family, had made her more open to W 322 3
After bringing you up like a child of her own."-- W 326 5
had just recovered from her own perturbation in time to W 326 5
Mrs Edwards carefully guarding her own dress, while she W 327 7
imprisoned within his own room, had been listening in W 329 9
His mother, stifling her own mortification, tried to sooth W 330 11
& had a horse of his own given him by Ld Osborne; & that W 331 11
to enjoy his own thoughts, & gape without restraint.-- W 332 11
sensation of doubting his own influence, & of wishing for W 335 13
make his pupil's manners as unexceptionable as his own.-- W 335 13
I must own however that it is a releif to me, to find you W 343 19
he had done, & glad to talk of it, over his own fireside.-- W 343 19
I own, I do not like much action in the pulpit--I do not W 343 20
in high spirits at his own importance, on the other side W 345 21
"Your Lordship thinks we always have our own way.-- W 346 21
when the novelty of her own appearance were over; the tone W 351 25
I was her own neice, & he left to herself the power & the W 352 26
Mrs Robert exactly as smart as she had been at her own W 353 26
to me?"--said Emma, who had caught her own name.-- W 356 28
giving a glance over his own person, I am highly endebted W 357 28
stealing a veiw of his own head in an opposite glass,-- W 357 28
both his own cards--it is worth anything in the world!"-- W 358 28
to resist hints, which her own hospitable, social temper W 359 28
thought too highly of their own kindness & situation, to W 362 32
tho' evidently against her own, in privately urging Emma W 362 32
she ought to give over thinking of her own beauty." PP I 1 4 20
"Mr. Bennet, how can you abuse your own children in such a PP I 1 5 28
She has two neices of her own. PP I 2 6 5
"I do not cough for my own amusement," replied Kitty PP I 2 6 10
the room, speaking occasionally to one of his own party. PP I 3 11 6
her eye, he withdrew his own and coldly said, "she is PP I 3 11 13
brother's fortune and their own had been acquired by trade. PP I 4 15 11
his having an estate of his own; but though he was now PP I 4 15 13
a greater contrast to his own, and though with his own he PP I 4 16 14
own he reliance, and of his judgment the highest opinion. PP I 4 16 14
think with pleasure of his own importance, and unshackled PP I 5 18 1
of the degree of her own regard, nor of its reasonableness. PP I 6 22 7
saw him one morning at his own house, and has since dined PP I 6 22 7
too much engrossed by his own thoughts to perceive that PP I 6 25 25
you should be so ready to think your own children silly. PP I 7 29 8
any body's children, it should not be of my own however." PP I 7 29 8
once, as if the credit of making it rain were all her own. PP I 7 31 29
for your benefit and my own credit; but I am an idle PP I 8 38 27
"Are you so severe upon your own sex, as to doubt the PP I 8 40 53
their own; and with many men, I dare say, it succeeds. PP I 8 40 56
to visit Jane, and form her own judgment of her situation. PP I 9 41 1
own work; my daughters are brought up differently. PP I 9 44 29
"Oh! dear, yes;--but you must own she is very plain. PP I 9 44 31
I do not like to boast of my own child, but to be sure, PP I 9 44 31
I do not trust my own partiality. PP I 9 44 31
good dinners and her own easy manners recommended her, had PP I 9 45 36
to Jane, leaving her own and her relations' behaviour to PP I 9 46 39
"Thank you--but I always mend my own." PP I 10 47 12
Mr. Bingley did not do justice to his own disposition. PP I 10 49 30
particular places; at his own house especially, and of a PP I 10 50 39
book, as in reading her own; and she was perpetually PP I 11 54 4
to be amused with her own book, which she had only chosen PP I 11 55 4
When I have a house of my own, I shall be miserable if I PP I 11 55 4
divert me, I own, and I laugh at them whenever I can.-- PP I 11 57 21
be entailed away from your own children; and I am sure if PP I 13 61 7
time I was kept back by my own doubts, fearing lest it PP I 13 62 12

of his viewing it all as his own future property.	PP	I	13	65	26
in leaving the girls to their own trifling amusements.	PP	I	14	69	17
and excessively generous and disinterested on his own part.	PP	I	15	70	2
home, which, as their own carriage had not fetched them,	PP	I	15	73	11
in praise of his own humble abode, and the improvements it	PP	I	16	75	3
and examine their own indifferent imitations of china on	PP	I	16	75	3
Here you are in your own family."	PP	I	16	77	14
Society, I own, is necessary to me.	PP	I	16	79	23
who had probably been his own companion from childhood,	PP	I	16	80	36
Mr. Wickham's happiness and her own was per force delayed	PP	I	17	87	14
every prospect of her own was destroyed for the evening,	PP	I	18	90	4
was left to fret over her own want of presence of mind;	PP	I	18	90	5
"Are you consulting your own feelings in the present case,	PP	I	18	91	14
"This is no very striking resemblance of your own	PP	I	18	91	16
"I must not decide on my own performance."	PP	I	18	91	17
blaming herself for her own weakness, could not go on.	PP	I	18	92	19
I see nothing in it but your own wilful ignorance and the	PP	I	18	95	48
air of following his own inclination, and when she ceased	PP	I	18	97	60
					61
As Elizabeth had no longer any interest of her own to	PP	I	18	98	63
he must write his own sermons; and the time that remains	PP	I	18	101	71
my sake; and for your own, let her be an active, useful	PP	I	19	105	10
to Longbourn instead of my own neighbourhood, where I	PP	I	19	106	10
and my relationship to your own, are circumstances highly	PP	I	19	108	19
know her own interest; but I will make her know it."	PP	I	20	110	3
if we were at York, provided she can have her own way.--	PP	I	20	113	28
dismission from your daughter's lips instead of your own.	PP	I	20	114	32
When they had gained their own room, Jane taking out the	PP	I	21	116	6
					7
It must be his own doing.--	PP	I	21	117	14
He is his own master.	PP	I	21	117	14
connection as much as his own, and a sister's partiality	PP	I	21	118	14
was not exactly like her own, but she could not have	PP	I	22	125	18
away an estate from one's own daughters I cannot	PP	I	23	130	24
his own happiness to the caprice of their inclinations.	PP	II	1	133	3
Had his own happiness, however, been the only sacrifice,	PP	II	1	133	3
It is very often nothing but our own vanity that deceives	PP	II	1	136	14
But, whatever may be their own wishes, it is very unlikely	PP	II	1	137	24
own warehouses, could have been so well bred and agreeable.	PP	II	2	139	2
by this time, had not it been for her own perverseness.	PP	II	2	140	4
to be thwarted so in my own family, and to have neighbours	PP	II	2	140	4
At his own ball he offended two or three young ladies, by	PP	II	2	141	9
she must wait for her own visit there, to know the rest.	PP	II	3	147	19
a little change was not unwelcome for its own sake.	PP	II	4	151	1
smiling, "your ladyship can hardly expect me to own it."	PP	II	6	166	37
obliged to take her ladyship's praise into his own hands.	PP	II	6	167	42
out of window in his own book room, which fronted the road.	PP	II	7	168	1
have been much less in his own apartment, had they sat in	PP	II	7	168	1
active magistrate in her own parish, the minutest concerns	PP	II	7	169	4
professing opinions which in fact are not your own."	PP	II	8	174	14
of knowing any lady in the assembly beyond my own party."	PP	II	8	175	19
But then I have always supposed it to be my own fault--	PP	II	8	175	25
neighbourhood as for his own, and we must expect him to	PP	II	9	178	9
within so easy a distance of her own family and friends."	PP	II	9	178	16
"It is a proof of your own attachment to Hertfordshire.	PP	II	9	179	20
was reminded by her own satisfaction in being with him, as	PP	II	9	180	28
different, which her own knowledge of him could not have	PP	II	9	180	29
"He likes to have his own way very well," replied Colonel	PP	II	10	183	10
the true Darcy spirit, she may like to have her own way."	PP	II	10	184	19
"He did not talk to me of his own arts," said Fitzwilliam	PP	II	10	185	32
or why, upon his own judgment alone, he was to determine	PP	II	10	185	36
There, shut into her own room, as soon as their visitor	PP	II	10	186	38
If his own vanity, however, did not mislead him, he was	PP	II	10	186	38
Had not my own feelings decided against you, had they been	PP	II	11	190	10
whose condition in life is so decidedly beneath my own?"	PP	II	11	192	22
and have now only to be ashamed of what my own have been.	PP	II	11	193	29
with equal force in his own case, was almost incredible!	PP	II	11	193	31
passion to put aside, in my own case; the want of	PP	II	12	198	5
equally excited with my own; our coincidence of feeling	PP	II	12	198	5
a stronger dependence on my judgment than on his own.--	PP	II	12	199	5
assistance, as his own father, always poor from the	PP	II	12	200	5
His own father did not long survive mine, and within half	PP	II	12	200	5
alarming an affinity to his own history of himself, her	PP	II	13	204	2
known its extent, agreed equally well with his own words.	PP	II	13	205	3
That among his own connections he was esteemed and valued--	PP	II	13	207	6
In her own past behaviour, there was a constant source of	PP	II	14	212	17
deprived, by the folly and indecorum of her own family!	PP	II	14	213	18
gratify whatever of her own vanity she had not yet been	PP	II	15	217	17
own breast had formerly harboured and fancied liberal!	PP	II	16	220	15
What is your own opinion?"	PP	II	17	226	22
been injurious to her own health and their tranquillity.	PP	II	17	227	26
They look upon it quite as their own, I dare say, whenever	PP	II	17	228	33
estate that is not lawfully their own, so much the better.	PP	II	17	228	35
by Kitty and Lydia, whose own misery was extreme, and who	PP	II	18	229	1
that her being there may teach her her own insignificance.	PP	II	18	232	20
to be content; but her own opinion continued the same, and	PP	II	18	232	21
Had Elizabeth's opinion been all drawn from her own family,	PP	II	19	236	1
disappointment which his own imprudence had brought on, in	PP	II	19	236	1
contempt of her own children, was so highly reprehensible.	PP	II	19	236	2
She must own that she was tired of great houses; after	PP	II	19	240	14
own, and welcomed to them as visitors my uncle and aunt.--	PP	III	1	246	6
How rejoiced was Elizabeth that their own journey had not	PP	III	1	247	8
who had been brought up by him at his own expence.--	PP	III	1	247	9
engrossed by her own feelings, followed them in silence.	PP	III	1	252	54
after their own arrival at Lambton, these visitors came.	PP	III	2	260	1
She was quite amazed at her own discomposure; but amongst	PP	III	2	260	1
she wanted to compose her own, and to make herself	PP	III	2	262	7
his character from their own feelings, and his servant's	PP	III	2	264	14
four years old, and whose own manners indicated	PP	III	2	264	14
Her own thoughts were employing her.	PP	III	3	268	5
ago attributed to him, of their becoming hereafter her own.	PP	III	3	270	10
"For my own part," she rejoined, "I must confess that I	PP	III	3	271	15
to own the truth, with Wickham!--imagine our surprise.	PP	III	4	273	3
shock is over, shall I own that I long for your return?	PP	III	4	275	5
of it only--some part of what I learnt, to my own family!	PP	II	4	7	12
to make her understand her own wishes; and never had she	PP	III	4	278	19
"Not perhaps of neglecting his own interest.	PP	III	5	282	4
and complaints of her own sufferings and ill usage;	PP	III	5	287	34
"Colonel Forster did own that he had often suspected some	PP	III	5	290	46
inclined to think that her own disposition must be	PP	III	6	297	11
leave her to reap the fruits of her own heinous offence.	PP	III	6	297	11
And in the wretched state of his own finances, there was a	PP	III	6	297	12
well acquainted with her own feelings, was perfectly aware,	PP	III	6	298	17
It has been my own doing, and I ought to feel it."	PP	III	6	299	19
to settle on my niece, in addition to her own fortune.	PP	III	7	302	14
He has children of his own, and may have more.	PP	III	7	304	35
done for them, because Wickham has not sixpence of his own.	PP	III	7	305	36
"it is all very right; who should do it but her own uncle?	PP	III	7	306	47
If he had not had a family of his own, I and my children	PP	III	7	306	47
refuge in her own room, that she might think with freedom.	PP	III	7	307	50
His understanding and temper, though unlike her own, would	PP	III	8	312	15
had she consulted only her own inclination, any meeting	PP	III	8	314	22
ill-consequences of Lydia's flight, on her own folly alone.	PP	III	10	323	2
her own settled upon her, and his commission purchased.	PP	III	10	324	2
or to relate her own change of sentiment towards him.	PP	III	11	334	36
had undervalued; but to her own more extensive information,	PP	III	11	334	36
Miss Lucas is married and settled. and one of my own	PP	III	11	336	49
"When you have killed all your own birds, Mr. Bingley,"	PP	III	11	337	53
I know my own strength, and I shall never be embarrassed	PP	III	12	339	6
Jane's happiness, and his own, would be speedily secured.	PP	III	12	340	13
formed, chiefly through his own and Mrs. Bennet's means,	PP	III	13	345	19
all he had to say, of his own happiness, and of Jane's	PP	III	13	347	33
and the little value he put on his own good qualities.	PP	III	13	350	51
Elizabeth obeyed, and running into her own room for her	PP	III	14	352	19
Your own heart, your own conscience, must tell you why I	PP	III	14	353	23
afterwards united to my nephew, my own nephew, Mr. Darcy.	PP	III	14	353	26
If you were sensible of your own good, you would not wish	PP	III	14	356	50
manner, which will, in my own opnion, constitute my	PP	III	14	358	68
to his own, his aunt would address him on his weakest side.	PP	III	15	360	2
own feelings, care not how much I may be wounding your's.	PP	III	16	365	2
					3
I should not have merely my own gratitude to express."	PP	III	16	365	3
to care for none beyond my own family circle, to think	PP	III	16	369	24
think meanly of their sense and worth compared with my own.	PP	III	16	369	24
"Did you speak from your own observation," said she, "when	PP	III	16	371	42
His diffidence had prevented his depending on his own	PP	III	16	371	45
to be inferior only to his own, he continued the	PP	III	16	371	46
had wandered about, till she was beyond her own knowledge.	PP	III	17	372	1
the unsettled state of her own feelings had made her	PP	III	17	374	19
these violent young lovers carry every thing their own way.	PP	III	17	377	39
quiet reflection in her own room, she was able to join the	PP	III	17	377	41
But before she had been three minutes in her own room, her	PP	III	17	378	44
her sisters' beauty and her own, it was suspected by her	PP	III	19	386	5
in her own private expences, she frequently sent them.	PP	III	19	387	8
at length she could not but own it to be her wish, that	MP	I	1	5	4
He thought of his own four children--of his two sons--of	MP	I	1	6	5
a manner taken into one's own hands; and I am sure I	MP	I	1	6	6
Having no children of my own, who should I look to in any	MP	I	1	6	6
of the regard I bear your own dear children, nor consider	MP	I	1	7	8
in any respect, so much my own, I should hate myself if I	MP	I	1	7	8
My own trouble, you know, I never regard.	MP	I	1	7	8
well how to save her own as to spend that of her friends.	MP	I	1	8	9
children of her own; but he found himself wholly mistaken.	MP	I	1	9	10
companions of her own age, and of a regular instructress."	MP	I	1	9	11
I am not one of those that spare their own trouble; and	MP	I	1	9	12
"we must not, for our own children's sake, continue her in	MP	I	1	10	14
retreating towards her own chamber to cry; and the little	MP	I	2	14	9
he begun to revert to her own home, than her increased	MP	I	2	15	10
He wrote with his own hand his love to his cousin William,	MP	I	2	16	20
and they could not but own, when their aunt inquired into	MP	I	2	17	21
thought too lowly of her own claims to feel injured by it.	MP	I	2	20	32
Amid the cares and the complacency which his own children	MP	I	2	21	34
eligibility; and as his own circumstances were rendered	MP	I	3	24	7
If I could wish it for my own sake, I would not do so	MP	I	3	29	46
I shall be miserable; and I own it would give me great	MP	I	3	30	50
what should have been her own; but in Mrs. Norris's	MP	I	3	32	62
immediately at their own disposal, and to have every	MP	I	3	32	64
as, in addition to all her own household cares, some	MP	I	4	34	3
thought too lowly of her own situation to imagine she	MP	I	4	35	6
lady's horse of her own in the style of her cousins.	MP	I	4	36	7
He had three horses of his own, but not one that would	MP	I	4	37	8
ever thought about her own objection again, he might have	MP	I	4	37	9
He could allow his sister to be the best judge of her own	MP	I	4	40	13
fond of them; but, as her own marriage had been soon	MP	I	4	40	15
his mistress under his own roof; and to this Mrs. Grant	MP	I	4	41	15
to settle with her at his own country-house, that she	MP	I	4	41	16
to glory in beauty of her own, she thoroughly enjoyed the	MP	I	4	42	17
from my own observation, it is a manoeuvring business.	MP	I	5	46	22
eager to be improving his own place in the same way; and	MP	I	6	52	1
For my own part, if I had any thing within the fiftieth	MP	I	6	53	9
of beauty, or my own choice, and acquired progressively.	MP	I	6	56	28
I would rather abide by my own blunders than by his."	MP	I	6	56	28
me; and had I a place of my own in the country, I should	MP	I	6	57	29
remained to be done, and my own consequent resolutions, I	MP	I	6	61	56
I have been a devourer of my own."	MP	I	6	61	56
properly depreciating his own abilities, was quite at his	MP	I	6	61	58
opinions; and for my own part I have been long wishing to	MP	I	6	62	58
but having no horses of my own, could have made me so	MP	I	6	62	58
may contribute to its own amusement or that of others;	MP	I	7	64	11
own remarks to him, lest it should appear like ill-nature.	MP	I	7	66	14
wish, and the offer of his own quiet mare for the purpose	MP	I	7	66	14
"I am come to make my own apologies for keeping you	MP	I	7	68	18
The old coachman, who had been waiting about with his own	MP	I	7	69	21
had been watching with an interest almost equal to her own.	MP	I	7	69	21
in riding was like their own; her early excellence in it	MP	I	7	69	23
like their own, and they had great pleasure in praising it.	MP	I	7	69	23
Her own gentle voice speaking from the other end of the	MP	I	7	71	33
If you have no work of your own, I can supply you from the	MP	I	7	71	34
His own forgetfulness of her was worse than any thing	MP	I	7	74	58
but as it related to her own and her son's concerns, had	MP	I	8	75	2
civilly declined it on her own account, she was glad to	MP	I	8	76	7
party, but as it relates to yourself, to your own comfort.	MP	I	8	78	18
for Mrs. Rushworth, whose own manners were such a pattern	MP	I	8	78	23
from partiality for her own scheme because it was her own,	MP	I	8	79	23
because it was her own, than from any thing else.	MP	I	8	79	23
settle it your own way, I am sure I do not care about it."	MP	I	8	79	23
gave her pain, and her own satisfaction in seeing	MP	I	8	79	27
Her own thoughts and reflections were habitually her best	MP	I	8	80	31
her own sense of propriety could but just smooth over.	MP	I	8	81	32
"At any rate, it is safer to leave people to their own	MP	I	9	87	15
Every body likes to go their own way--to choose their own	MP	I	9	87	15
that knowledge of her own heart, that principle of right	MP	I	9	91	36
to prefer Blair's to his own, do all that you speak of?	MP	I	9	92	46
and consideration make me more sensible of my own neglect.	MP	I	9	95	70
an original thought of his own beyond a wish that they had	MP	I	10	97	3
By their own accounts they had been all walking after each	MP	I	10	104	51
I can have them moved to my own house and borrow a coop;	MP	I	10	106	57
at the piano-forte again, "it is entirely her own doing."	MP	I	11	108	11
The profession, either navy or army, is its own	MP	I	11	109	19
beg some advantage to the clergyman from your own argument.	MP	I	11	109	22
His curate does all the work, and the business of his own	MP	I	11	110	23
It is impossible that your own observation can have given	MP	I	11	110	24
purpose of her own feelings, if not of the conversation.	MP	I	11	111	27
this present time the guest of my own brother, Dr. Grant.	MP	I	11	111	28
To own the truth, Henry and I were partly driven out this	MP	I	11	111	28
depends upon his own sermons; for though he may preach	MP	I	11	112	31
pleasure in view, and his own will to consult, made it	MP	I	12	114	2
more than equalled by her own, that were he now to step	MP	I	12	114	2
the habit of examining his own motives, and of reflecting	MP	I	12	114	3
had her confidence in her own judgment been equal to her	MP	I	12	115	5
he has quite made up his own mind, will distinguish the.	MP	I	12	116	10
on whom all her own hopes of a partner then depended.	MP	I	12	116	11
did, between the selfishness of another person and his own.	MP	I	12	119	25
respectable author than in chattering in words of our own.	MP	I	13	125	18
Manage your own concerns, Edmund, and I'll take care of	MP	I	13	127	27
obliged to leave her own house, where she had been living	MP	I	13	129	40
been living a month at her own cost, and take up her abode	MP	I	13	129	40
For her own gratification she could have wished that	MP	I	14	131	4
and been forced to re-rant it all in his own room.	MP	I	14	132	8
She must not be left to her own complaisance.	MP	I	14	135	15
much engaged with what his own appearance would be, to	MP	I	15	138	1
I only wish Tom had known his own mind when the carpenters	MP	I	15	141	22
Rushworth having only his own part, and his own dress in	MP	I	15	142	24
only his own part, and his own dress in his head, had soon	MP	I	15	142	24
a great many of my own, before we rehearse together.--	MP	I	15	149	61
every superiority in their own apartments, which their own	MP	I	16	151	1
own apartments, which their own sense of superiority could	MP	I	16	151	1
But she had more than fears of her own perseverance to	MP	I	16	152	3
the truth and purity of her own scruples, and as she	MP	I	16	153	3
The doubts and alarms as to her own conduct, which had	MP	I	16	156	28
"To have it quite in their own family circle was what they	MP	I	17	158	2
be the best judge of his own, and as he did assure her,	MP	I	17	161	9
and make him know his own mind; and if he means nothing,	MP	I	17	162	18
it escaped the notice of many of her own family likewise.	MP	I	17	162	19

cause, must be imputed to the fulness of their own minds. MP I 17 163 21
Crawford's claims and his own conduct, between love and MP I 17 163 21
Or why had not she rather gone to her own room, as she had MP I 18 172 29
too much engaged in their own noise, to be struck by MP I 18 172 33
by her cousins; and as her own opinion of her claims on MP II 1 176 4
As she entered, her own name caught her ear. MP II 1 177 7
in being again in his own house, in the centre of his MP II 1 178 8
cloud her pleasure; her own time had been irreproachably MP II 1 179 9
and useful pursuits of all the young people as for her own. MP II 1 179 9
into his own dear room, every agitation was returning. MP II 1 181 17
which was due to his own character, but was really as far MP II 1 183 23
thus bewildered in his own house, making part of a MP II 1 183 23
Its vicinity to my own room--but in every respect indeed MP II 1 184 25
of the face on which his own eyes were fixed--from seeing MP II 1 184 27
"To own the truth, Sir Thomas, we were in the middle of a MP II 1 185 28
scheme, defending his own share in it as far only as he MP II 2 187 1
She had a great deal to insinuate in her own praise as to MP II 2 188 3
sudden removals from her own fire-side, and many excellent MP II 2 188 3
own he could not hold Sir Thomas in greater respect.'" MP II 2 190 7
his own way, and feel the folly of it without opposition. MP II 2 191 10
The Rushworths were the only addition to his own domestic MP II 3 196 1
that the repose of his own family-circle is all he wants. MP II 3 196 3
information which he must wish his own daughters to feel." MP II 3 198 12
the more attached to her own family, and the nearness of MP II 3 201 22
and spring, when her own taste could have fairer play. MP II 3 202 26
was concerned at her own neglect;--and "shall I play to MP II 4 206 5
back her own mind to what she thought must interest. MP II 4 209 13
here is better than his own, and so it appears from the MP II 4 209 16
own sister, I think I had a right to alarm you a little." MP II 4 212 30
you by the contrast of their own wealth and consequence. MP II 4 213 40
involving, as it did, her own evening's comfort for the MP II 5 217 11
Edmund knocked at her door in his way to his own. MP II 5 219 24
that absurd new one of his own, which is wider, literally MP II 5 220 30
She rated her own claims to comfort as low even as Mrs. MP II 5 221 35
as good time as his own correctly punctual habits required. MP II 5 222 41
There are his own two men pushing it back into its old MP II 5 222 46
she must submit, as her own propriety of mind directed, in MP II 5 223 48
understanding for him out of the superfluity of your own! MP II 5 224 53
was over, she trembled and blushed at her own daring. MP II 5 225 59
but she would now meet him with his own cool feelings. MP II 5 227 69
proceeds from any thing but your own idleness and folly." MP II 6 230 6
on his side as warm as her own, and much less incumbered MP II 6 234 17
of endurance, made his own habits of selfish indulgence MP II 6 236 22
that he could relate of his own horsemanship in various MP II 6 237 23
of being applied to for her own choice between the games, MP II 7 239 4
protestations of her own equal ignorance; she had never MP II 7 239 8
to manage as well as his own--for though it was impossible MP II 7 240 8
capital play and her own, against Dr. and Mrs. Grant's MP II 7 245 32
to regard all the connections of our family as his own." MP II 7 245 34
he might have a home of his own in that neighbourhood; and MP II 7 246 37
that Edmund will occupy his own house at Thornton Lacey. MP II 7 247 39
Consider the house as half your own every winter, and we MP II 7 247 41
add to the stables on your own improved plan, and with all MP II 7 247 41
he does very little either for their good or his own." MP II 7 248 42
her own cheeks in a glow of indignation as she spoke.) MP II 7 249 53
Sir Thomas could not dissent, as it had been his own MP II 7 251 65
and no confidence in her own taste--the "how she should be MP II 8 254 8
He knew his own mind, but he was not always perfectly MP II 8 255 10
Edmund could not, on his own account, think very much of MP II 8 256 13
Fanny, being more than half ashamed of her own solicitude. MP II 8 256 14
over his own mind, though it might have its drawback. MP II 9 262 11
was a stab;--for it told of his own convictions and views. MP II 9 264 17
had not words strong enough to satisfy her own humility. MP II 9 264 18
house-keeper would have her own way with the supper, and MP II 9 267 22
as languidly towards her own room, and felt as incapable MP II 9 267 22
For my own sake, I could wish there had been no ball just MP II 9 268 29
sweet and faultless as your own, but the influence of her MP II 9 269 31
sometimes, Fanny, I own to you, it does appear more than MP II 9 269 33
can never be ashamed of my own scruples; and if they are MP II 9 269 38
Crawford's faults and his own despondence. but as it was, MP II 9 270 40
All went well--she did not dislike her own looks; and when MP II 9 270 40
she actually sent her own maid to assist her; too late of MP II 9 271 41
The very gown you have been taking notice of, is your own MP II 10 272 3
really to assemble, her own gaiety of heart was much MP II 10 273 7
Her own musings were brought to an end on perceiving Mr. MP II 10 274 8
so little understood her own claims as to think, that if MP II 10 274 8
not at home to take their own place in the room, and have MP II 10 275 12
much more struck with her own kindness in sending Chapman MP II 10 277 15
Your brother will find my ideas of time and his own very MP II 10 280 31
and cheerlessness of her own small house, without MP II 11 282 3
body's dress, or any body's place at supper, but her own. MP II 11 282 4
Lady Bertram, though in her own good nature she would not MP II 11 284 10
Angry as she was with Edmund for adhering to his own MP II 11 286 15
a week, when her own departure from Mansfield was so near. MP II 11 286 15
son is somebody; and now, he is in their own line. MP II 11 289 34
usual cheerfulness, she had nothing further to try her own. MP II 12 291 1
progress in her affections; but my own are entirely fixed." MP II 12 292 6
now delicacy of language enough to embody his own ideas. MP II 12 293 10
Does she know her own happiness?" MP II 12 293 11
her disposition would secure her all your own immediately. MP II 12 293 15
own sensations, nothing to dwell on but Fanny's charms.-- MP II 12 293 16
manners were the mirror of her own modest and elegant mind. MP II 12 294 16
I could name three people now, who would give me my own MP II 12 295 20
to his own house, and to claim the best right in her. MP II 12 295 22
of course, a house of your own; no longer with the Admiral. MP II 12 295 27
Few fathers would have let me have my own way half so much. MP II 12 296 28
not to have a moment at her own command, her hair arranged MP II 12 296 31
ashamed of their own abominable neglect and unkindness. MP II 12 297 33
"I will not talk of my own happiness," said he, "great as MP II 13 299 5
I have almost grudged myself my own prior knowledge of MP II 13 299 5
of his joy as well as her own, and all the benefit of his MP II 13 302 12
the subject of William's appointment in their own style. MP II 13 304 18
habits and ways of thinking, and all her own demerits.-- MP II 13 305 26
had not been long in my own room, after breakfast, when Mr. MP III 1 313 14
impossible, turned away his own eyes, and without any MP III 1 313 15
feeling, moreover, his own replies, and his own remarks to MP III 1 314 16
his own replies, and his own remarks to have been very MP III 1 314 16
Fanny, that you do not quite know your own feelings." MP III 1 316 29
She would rather die than own the truth, and she hoped by MP III 1 317 33
think how little likely my own eldest son, your cousin, Mr. MP III 1 317 34
for really examining your own inclinations--and are, in a MP III 1 318 39
Gladly would I have bestowed either of my own daughters on MP III 1 319 39
You must give him your own answer; we cannot expect him to MP III 1 320 44
and that it was only her own conscience that could fancy MP III 1 323 53
likes to go her own way to work; she does not like to be MP III 1 323 56
dictated to; she takes her own independent walk whenever MP III 1 323 56
own children's merits set off by the depreciation of her. MP III 1 323 57
Thomas wishes to speak with you, ma'am, in his own room." MP III 1 324 60
admit that she did know her own present feelings, MP III 2 326 1
Fanny knew her own meaning, but was no judge of her own MP III 2 327 6
and humanity where his own pleasure was concerned--and, MP III 2 329 9
Had her own affections been as free--as perhaps they ought MP III 2 329 9
he had only to consult his own judgment and feelings as to MP III 2 329 12
He proceeds at his own risk. MP III 2 331 16
How much time she might, in her own fancy, allot for its MP III 2 331 18
into a young lady's exact estimate of her own perfections. MP III 2 331 18
the necessity of making his own wife and sister-in-law MP III 2 332 19
associations, when her own fair self was before him, MP III 3 334 1
of comfort within his own breast to help the joy, he found MP III 3 334 3
his opinion and give his own as to the properest manner in MP III 3 340 24
himself in murmurs of his own, over the various MP III 3 341 31
can get your heart for his own use, he has to unfasten it MP III 4 347 21
You must be sorry for your own indifference." MP III 4 348 21
who firm as a rock in her own principles, has a gentleness MP III 4 351 32
to meet him with any feeling answerable to his own? MP III 4 353 45
"Yes; that is, it was the fault of my own mind if I did MP III 4 355 52
assiduities, and the natural workings of her own mind. MP III 5 356 2
My own sister as a wife, Sir Thomas Bertram as a husband, MP III 5 361 16
"Knew of it! it was his own doing entirely, his own MP III 5 362 20
accede to it more readily than her own judgment authorised. MP III 5 364 33
Her secret was still her own; and while that was the case, MP III 5 365 34
opinions of the man she loved and respected, as her own.-- MP III 6 367 6
Sir Thomas, meanwhile, went on with his own hopes, and his MP III 6 368 7
with his own hopes, and his own observations, still MP III 6 368 7
of seeing it, all its own freshness, and all the freshness MP III 6 368 8
to Portsmouth, and spend a little time with her own family. MP III 6 368 9
In the calmness of her own dressing room, in the impartial MP III 6 370 14
the impartial flow of her own meditations, unbiassed by MP III 6 370 14
ready to give up all her own time to her as requested) and MP III 6 371 15
suppose to have been her own fault, or her own fancy. MP III 6 371 17
for her to avoid paying her own expenses back again. MP III 6 373 24
own inconvenience, in being obliged to hurry away so soon. MP III 7 378 11
Come, mother, you have hardly looked at your own dear MP III 7 378 12
he would manage all his own way; and lastly in walked Mr. MP III 7 379 19
Mr. Price himself, his own loud voice preceding him, as MP III 7 379 19
She could not but own that she should be very glad of a MP III 7 383 33
and fixed it on her own domestic grievances; and the MP III 7 385 38
her own two were the very worst, engrossed her completely. MP III 7 385 38
Up jumped Susan, claiming it as her own, and trying to get MP III 7 386 42
"It was very hard that she was not to have her own knife; MP III 7 386 42
own knife; it was her own knife; little sister Mary had MP III 7 386 42
it, and get it for her own, though mamma had promised her MP III 7 386 42
her that Betsey should not have it in her own hands." MP III 7 386 42
My own Betsey, (fondling her), you have not the luck of MP III 7 387 44
She soon learnt to think with respect of her own little MP III 7 387 47
Sam on some project of his own, and her father on his MP III 8 388 1
her own perfect consciousness, many drawbacks suppressed. MP III 8 388 1
sure of her, and been delighted with his own sagacity. MP III 8 388 1
she could wish to overcome her own shyness and reserve. MP III 9 395 3
understand a disposition so totally different from her own. MP III 9 395 4
That a girl of fourteen, acting only on her own unassisted MP III 9 395 4
the same system, which her own judgment acknowledged, but MP III 9 395 4
which her own more favoured education had fixed in her. MP III 9 396 6
persona, amazed at her own doings in every way; to be a MP III 9 398 9
to give her a share in her own first pleasures, and MP III 9 398 9
stranger, from what he was in his own family at home. MP III 10 402 12
while they walked on together at their own hasty pace. MP III 10 403 14
he had secured agreeable recollections for his own mind. MP III 10 404 15
though on his own estate, had been hitherto unknown to him. MP III 10 404 15
allowed her to gratify her own heart in the warmest MP III 10 405 17
at Mansfield, where her own happiness, and his in seeing MP III 11 410 7
only at the door of their own house, when he knew them to MP III 11 411 19
and get a cousin of his own into a certain mill, which I MP III 11 411 20
on the north, that I will be master of my own property. MP III 11 411 20
that her own dress and manners did her the greatest credit. MP III 12 416 2
and pleasant in his own family, and I do not think him so MP III 12 416 2
He will see the Rushworths, which I own I am not sorry for- MP III 12 417 3
to have given him credit for better feelings than her own. MP III 12 418 4
Time did something, her own exertions something more, and MP III 12 418 6
began to feel that when her own release from Portsmouth MP III 12 419 9
have been the greatest increase of all her own comforts. MP III 12 419 9
her own feelings, to furnish a tolerable guess at mine.-- MP III 13 420 2
I will not be prevented, however, from making my own MP III 13 420 2
the support of their own bad sense to her too lively mind. MP III 13 421 2
Her ideas are not higher than her own fortune may warrant, MP III 13 421 2
Fraser, and I at a distance, unable to help my own cause. MP III 13 422 2
This long letter, full of my own concerns alone, will be MP III 13 423 2
He thoroughly knows his own mind, and acts up to his MP III 13 423 2
it to spread over the largest part of a page of her own.-- MP III 13 425 6
and her own eyes had beheld his altered appearance. MP III 13 427 12
to calm and raise; and her own imagination added that MP III 14 430 2
in order to enhance her own importance, her being there MP III 14 432 10
yourself to be ashamed of either my feelings or your own. MP III 14 434 13
own amusements cut up, as to shut their eyes to the truth. MP III 14 434 13
exactly according to her own belief of it, and such as she MP III 14 436 16
give him a knowledge of his own disposition, convince him MP III 15 438 5
every line her own, was in frightful conformity with it. MP III 15 441 19
Now she could see her own mistake as to who were gone--or MP III 15 441 19
must be suffering, brought back all her own first feelings. MP III 15 444 28
state of his own mind made him find relief only in motion. MP III 15 445 29
all; the match had been her own contriving, as she had MP III 16 448 1
Edmund trying to bury his own feelings in exertions for MP III 16 449 4
He was aware of what Edmund must be suffering on his own MP III 16 452 15
that he felt the same, her own conviction was insufficient. MP III 16 453 16
That his judgment submitted to all his own peculiar and MP III 16 453 16
and how carefully her own eyes were fixed on any object MP III 16 454 18
properly supported by her own family, people of MP III 16 457 29
Do not let him injure his own cause by interference. MP III 16 457 29
had been the creature of my own imagination, not Miss MP III 16 457 30
in his own conduct as a parent, was the longest to suffer. MP III 17 461 4
from the conviction of his own errors in the education of MP III 17 462 6
aunt had been continually contrasted with his own severity. MP III 17 463 7
Maria had destroyed her own character, and he would not by MP III 17 465 13
he might have been deciding his own happy destiny. MP III 17 467 20
He was entangled by his own vanity, with as little excuse MP III 17 468 21
for Mrs. Rushworth's credit than he felt it for his own.-- MP III 17 468 21
Mary had had enough of her own friends, enough of vanity, MP III 17 469 24
be at liberty to fix their own, aware that the cure of MP III 17 470 26
interest, dearer by all his own importance with her than MP III 17 470 27
Their own inclinations ascertained, there were no MP III 17 471 29
their own instruction, and their neighbours' entertainment. MP III 17 471 29
Miss Taylor's judgment, but directed chiefly by her own. E I 1 5 3
having rather too much her own way, and a disposition to E I 1 5 4
means yet reconciled to his own daughter's marrying, nor E I 1 7 10
my odd humours, when she might have a house of her own?" E I 1 8 12
"A house of her own!--but where is the advantage of a E I 1 8 13
own!--but where is the advantage of a house of her own? E I 1 8 13
the evening, and be attacked by no regrets but her own. E I 1 9 20
be settled in a home of her own, and how important to her E I 1 11 38
Taylor, may be safely left to manage their own concerns. E I 1 13 44
fish and the chicken, but leave him to chuse his own wife. E I 1 14 48
She had resolution enough to pursue her own will in spite E I 2 15 3
having no children of their own, nor any other young E I 2 16 4
and he had only his own comfort to seek and his own E I 2 16 4
to seek and his own situation to improve as he could. E I 2 16 4
to the wishes of his own friendly and social disposition. E I 2 16 5
He had never been an unhappy man; his own temper had E I 2 17 6
choice: his fortune was his own; for as to Frank, it was E I 2 17 7
attended by her pleasant husband to a carriage of her own. E I 2 18 12
His own stomach could bear nothing rich, and he could E I 2 19 14
With such an opinion, in confirmation of his own, Mr. E I 2 19 14
Mr. Woodhouse was fond of society in his own way. E I 3 20 1
of his own little circle, in a great measure as he liked. E I 3 20 1
acquaintance, but such as would visit him on his own terms. E I 3 20 1
any vacant evening of his own blank solitude for the E I 3 20 2
It was her own universal good-will and contented temper E I 3 21 4
and in winter dressed their chilblains with her own hands. E I 3 22 5
her own situation in life, her leisure, and powers. E I 3 24 10
a mind delighted with its own ideas, did she then do all E I 3 24 11
Such another small basin of this gruel as his own, was all E I 3 24 13
14
a man of information beyond the line of his own business. E I 4 29 9
his own, with a little money, it might be very desirable." E I 4 30 18
by every thing within your own power, or there will be E I 4 30 22

side to oppose any friendly arrangement of her own. E I 4 31 26
to be out, and that you must still fight your own battle." E I 5 36 5
of one of her own sex, after being used to it all her life. E I 5 36 6
point of submitting your own will, and doing as you were E I 5 38 11
"Why, to own the truth, I am afraid you are rather thrown E I 5 38 13
own and Mr. Weston's on the subject, as much as possible. E I 5 41 31
As you will do it, it will indeed, to use your own words, E I 6 44 16
She thinks so little of her own beauty. E I 6 44 17
She was not much deceived as to her own skill either as an E I 6 44 19
"I had only my own family to study from. E I 6 45 21
There is my sister; and really quite her own little E I 6 45 21
But for Harriet's sake, or rather for my own, and as there E I 6 46 21
Emma knew that she had, but would not own it, and Mr. E I 6 48 34
35

well, if left quite to his own powers, and yet it is not E I 7 51 5
"Oh, no, no! the letter had much better be all your own. E I 7 51 11
That is a point which you must settle with your own E I 7 52 17
You must be the best judge of your own happiness. E I 7 53 21
Harriet had not surmised her own danger, but the idea of E I 7 53 25
"Thank you, thank you, my own sweet little friend. E I 7 54 31
them by speaking of her own affection, sometimes by E I 7 55 36
I am sure Miss Nash would--for Miss Nash thinks her own E I 7 55 40
allowing them to hear your name, your own dear name." E I 7 56 44
his own civility, to leave Mr. Knightley for that purpose. E I 8 57 2
whom I could never admit as an acquaintance of my own! E I 8 62 39
no distaste for her own set, nor any ambition beyond it. E I 8 63 42
chose rather to take up her own line of the subject again. E I 8 63 43
You will puff her up with such ideas of her own beauty, E I 8 64 47
He is as well acquainted with his own claims, as you can E I 8 66 53
I could never hope to equal my own doings at Randalls. E I 8 66 54
Harriet and pleading his own cause, gave alarming ideas. E I 8 67 56
which settled her with her own mind, and convinced her, E I 8 67 56
his manner, Emma was immediately convinced must be his own. E I 9 71 10
Take your own." E I 9 71 13
For once in your life you would obliged to own yourself E I 9 72 15
Your soft eyes shall chuse their own time for beaming. E I 9 76 38
"I shall never let that book go out of my own hands," said E I 9 77 44
"Oh! yes--she will have her own room, of course; the room E I 9 79 57
brother, or any body's claims on Isabella, except his own. E I 9 80 65
for him to chuse his own subject in the adjoining room. E I 10 89 38
of the fatigues of his own horses and coachman who were to E I 11 91 3
was delicate in her own health, over-careful of that of E I 11 92 4
and was as fond of her own Mr. Wingfield in town as her E I 11 92 4
Papa is only speaking his own regret." E I 11 94 10
Whether it was his own idea you know, one cannot tell. E I 11 96 22
been in the wrong, and he would never own that he had. E I 12 98 2
The brothers talked of their own concerns and pursuits, E I 12 100 16
I should be unwilling, I own, to live in any other part of E I 12 103 37
to me?" cried Mr. John Knightley, hearing his own name. E I 12 103 41
most prominent, was in her own cook at south end, a young E I 12 104 50
to restore him to the relish of his own smooth gruel. E I 12 105 51
and his own brother and family have been there repeatedly." E I 12 105 55
attributing many of his own feelings and expressions;--but E I 12 107 62
Harriet, Mr. Elton, and Mr. Knightley, their own especial E I 13 108 4
a cold, that, but for her own earnest wish of being nursed E I 13 108 5
too eager and busy in her own previous conceptions and E I 13 110 10
"Such an imagination has crossed me, I own, Emma; and if E I 13 112 20
his eldest daughter in his own carriage, with less E I 13 112 24
full of the wonder of his own going, and the pleasure it E I 13 112 24
asks people to leave their own fireside, and encounter E I 13 113 26
all the history of his own and Isabella's coming, and of E I 14 117 3
For her own sake she could not be rude; and for Harriet's, E I 14 118 4
has been full of it; but he cannot command his own time. E I 14 119 9
the young man, of which her own imagination had already E I 14 122 18
to lay down rules for it: you must let it go its own way. E I 14 123 25
companion deposited in his own house, to get sober and E I 15 128 21
carefully attended to his own by Mr. Knightley and Mr. E I 15 128 22
To restrain him as much as might be, by her own manners, E I 15 129 24
He perfectly knew his own meaning; and having warmly E I 15 130 28
own passion, and was very urgent for a favourable answer. E I 15 130 28
If she has fancied otherwise, her own wishes have misled E I 15 130 31
conceited; very full of his own claims, and little E I 16 135 6
to stop and admit that her own behaviour to him had been E I 16 136 9
She stopt to blush and laugh at her own relapse, and then E I 16 137 12
his being all alone in his own house, too wise to stir out; E I 16 138 18
19

to be attaching, seemed on Harriet's side, not her own. E I 17 141 8
her would be more for her own welfare and happiness than E I 17 142 9
own affection in some better method than by match-making. E I 17 142 10
If Mr. Elton, on his return, made his own indifference as E I 17 143 13
for any thing but his own pleasure, from living with those E I 18 145 10
easily felt by you, who have always been your own master. E I 18 145 11
is requisite in situations directly opposite to your own. E I 18 147 17
Mr. Weston would not be blind to folly, though in his own E I 18 148 23
to the display of his own superiority; to be dispensing E I 18 150 32
My dear Emma, your own good sense could not endure such a E I 18 150 32
She could not think that Harriet's solace or her own sins E II 1 155 1
Knightley and some from her own heart, as to her E II 1 155 3
And Emma had the advantage of hearing her own silly E II 1 158 13
Dixon's name as well as her own, to press their coming E II 1 159 20
should like to speak of his own place while he was paying E II 1 159 20
be telling Miss Campbell about his own home in Ireland. E II 1 159 20
"But, in spite of all her friend's urgency, and her own E II 1 161 24
Yes--entirely her own doing, entirely her own choice; and E II 1 161 25
own story a great deal better than I can tell it for her." E II 1 162 31
his own return to England put any thing in his power. E II 2 163 4
fondness for her, and his own wish of being a real friend, E II 2 163 4
sobering suggestions of her own good understanding to E II 2 164 6
the age which her own judgment had fixed on for beginning. E II 2 165 8
for ever; and for their own comfort they would have E II 2 165 9
It was her own choice to give the time of their absence to E II 2 166 10
shew off in higher style her own very superior performance. E II 2 168 15
Dixon's character, or her own value for his company, or E II 2 169 16
more to conceal than her own preference; Mr. Dixon, E II 2 169 16
"Oh! no; I was pleased with my own perseverance in asking E II 3 171 10
other half she could give to her own view of the subject. E II 3 177 51
only of himself and his own concerns --expecting to be E II 4 182 5
humiliation to her own mind, she would have been thankful E II 4 182 7
that after all his own vaunted claims and disdain of E II 4 183 9
something in it which her own heart could not approve -- E II 4 185 14
though his own sparkling eyes at the moment were speaking E II 5 189 13
down stairs from her own room, "always over-careful for E II 5 189 20
body's comfort but your own; I see you now in all your E II 5 189 20
which none but one's own country gives, and the greatest E II 5 191 26
Her own father's perfect exemption from any thought of the E II 5 193 35
and your popularity will stand upon your own virtues." E II 6 200 15
"Certainly--very strong it was; to own the truth, a great E II 6 202 31
But Emma, in her own mind, determined that he did know E II 6 204 43
it, and saved only be her own indifference--(for still her E II 7 206 2
said only to relieve his own feelings, and not meant to E II 7 206 4
and think little of their own claims; but still they must E II 7 210 19
something to eat; that her own maid should sit up for her; E II 7 211 22
evasions of a mind too weak to defend its own vanities.-- E II 8 212 3
Emma to think her own way, and still listen to Mrs. Cole. E II 8 215 15
"Or that he did not give her the use of their own E II 8 216 24
Emma watched the entree of her own particular little E II 8 219 44
This must be a fancy of her own. E II 8 222 56
For his own sake, I would not have him do so mad a thing." E II 8 225 72
She knew the limitations of her own powers too well to E II 8 227 86
acceptable, and could accompany her own voice well. E II 8 227 86
conceal from herself, was infinitely superior to her own. E II 8 227 86
his disinclination to dwell on any kindness of his own. E II 8 228 88

thinks of nothing but shewing off his own voice. E II 8 229 97
regret the inferiority of her own playing and singing. E II 9 231 3
"I am here on no business of my own," said Emma, "I am E II 9 234 31
with all the force of her own mind, to convince her that E II 9 235 35
It is his own idea. E II 11 250 23
They will be so near their own stable." E II 11 252 34
Now you must be satisfied--our own dear Mrs. Weston, who E II 11 252 37
Fine dancing, I believe, like virtue, must be its own E II 12 258 3
I do look forward to it, I own, with very great pleasure." E II 12 258 5
He knew her illnesses; they never occurred but for her own E II 12 258 8
He could not say that he was sorry on his own account; his E II 12 262 40
41

of a struggle than she could foresee in her own feelings. E II 13 264 1
It would be most inexcusable to do otherwise, as my own E II 13 265 4
shake her head over her own sensations, and think she had E II 13 265 5
The charm of her own name was not wanting. E II 13 266 5
own imagination, fix a time for coming to Randalls again. E II 13 266 5
my sake; because for your own sake rather, I would wish it E II 13 268 11
12

but the man had only his own good sense to depend on; and E II 14 271 5
and thinking much of her own importance; that she meant to E II 14 272 16
from her easy conceit, had been the best of her own set. E II 14 272 17
own good will, would never stir beyond the park paling.' E II 14 274 30
conjugal unreserve, and her own share in the story, under E II 15 282 3
been drawn on beyond her own inclination, by her aunt's E II 15 286 21
of intimacy than her own good sense would have dictated, E II 15 286 21
her acknowledging her own comparative littleness in action, E II 15 287 23
any restraint beyond her own scanty rule of good-breeding. E II 15 288 39
for the evening than their own establishment could furnish, E II 16 290 3
not six yards from your own door when I had the pleasure E II 16 293 15
16

Jane's solicitude about fetching her own letters had not E II 16 298 58
entitle you to name your own terms, have as many rooms as E II 17 301 18
and independence of his own fire-side, and on the evening E II 17 303 23
She was a little occupied in weighing her own feelings, E II 17 304 28
I always take the part of my own sex. E II 18 306 12
She always travels with her own sheets; and excellent E II 18 306 12
that indeed, by her own account, she has always been. E II 18 307 18
The remaining five were left to their own powers, and Emma E II 18 311 36
Her own attachment had really subsided into a mere nothing; E III 1 315 1
She did not mean to have her own affections entangled E III 1 315 1
Such was his own account at Randall's. E III 1 316 6
Mr. Weston's own happiness was indisputable. E III 1 317 10
in all the certainty of his own self, reached Randall's E III 2 319 1
You know I candidly told you I should form my own opinion; E III 2 321 15
Good Mrs. Stokes would not know her own room again. E III 2 322 19
he had overheard his own praises, and did not want to hear E III 2 324 22
eyes; and, excepting her own partner, there was not one E III 2 326 32
I leave you to your own reflections." E III 2 330 51
"I do own myself to have been completely mistaken in Mr. E III 2 330 54
had been creating in Harriet was then their own portion. E III 3 334 7
at last, after Harriet's own account had been given, he E III 3 335 11
the judicious law of her own brain laid down with speed.-- E III 4 341 34
Every thing declared it; his own attentions, his father's E III 5 343 2
"Why, to own the truth," cried Miss Bates, who had been E III 5 345 16
A large party secures its own amusement. E III 6 353 4
a smile which seemed to say, "these are my own concerns. E III 6 361 40
His father would not own himself uneasy, and laughed at E III 6 361 41
own way, and only say that I am gone when it is necessary." E III 6 363 50
In two minutes, however, he relented in his own favour; E III 6 364 57
Choose your own degree of crossness. E III 6 366 73
but which now, in her own estimation, meant nothing, E III 7 368 3
and run away from your own management; but to-day you are E III 7 369 11
your temper under your own command rather than mine." E III 7 369 11
I had an acrostic once sent to me upon my own name, which E III 7 372 37
I have a great deal of vivacity in my own way, but I E III 7 372 37
It is only by seeing women in their own homes, among their E III 7 372 40
own homes, among their own set, just as they always are, E III 7 372 40
before, except among her own confederates, spoke now. E III 7 372 41
so little confidence in my own judgment, that whenever I E III 7 373 45
46

into her own room--I want her to lie down upon the bed. E III 8 379 8
perhaps, Mrs. Suckling's own family, and Mrs. Bragge's; E III 8 380 13
of the ostler's own knowledge, and the knowledge of the E III 8 383 31
visited, though against her own consent, by himself, and E III 9 389 16
that she felt it so herself, though she would not own it. E III 9 389 16
Emma felt that her own note had deserved something better; E III 9 390 18
Emma wished she could have seen her, and tried her own E III 9 390 18
merely employed her own fancy, and that soon pointed out E III 10 393 18
Her mind was divided between two ideas--her own former E III 10 395 36
to come forward at once, own it all to his uncle, throw E III 10 398 51
behaviour as her own, which made her so angry with him. E III 11 402 1
Emma could now imagine why her own attentions had been E III 11 403 2
you to give way to your own feelings?-- E III 11 404 11
But you know they were your own words, that more wonderful E III 11 407 28
sufficient for making her acquainted with her own heart. E III 11 407 32
Her own conduct, as well as her own heart, was before her E III 11 408 33
concern for her own appearance, and a strong sense of E III 11 408 33
For her own advantage indeed, it was fit that the utmost E III 11 408 33
circumstances, which her own memory brought in favour of E III 11 409 34
The blunders, the blindness of her own head and heart!-- E III 11 411 43
walked about, she tried her own room, she tried the E III 11 411 43
To understand, thoroughly understand her own heart, was E III 11 412 44
totally ignorant of her own heart--and, in short, that she E III 11 412 45
Alas! was not that her own doing too? E III 11 414 50
no female connexions of his own, there had been only E III 12 415 1
insolent estimate of her own--but still, from family E III 12 415 1
pent up within her own mind as every thing had so long E III 12 418 5
The error has been all my own; and I do assure you that, E III 12 419 8
as if ever willing to change his own home for their's!-- E III 12 422 20
distant from her mind, that it had been all her own work? E III 12 422 20
in the resolution of her own better conduct, and the hope E III 12 423 21
Your own excellent sense--your exertions for your father's E III 13 426 13
"I have very little to say for my own conduct.-- E III 13 427 19
by representing to him his own independence, relieve him E III 13 429 30
a delusion as any of her own--that Harriet was nothing; E III 13 430 38
as the language of her own feelings; and that her E III 13 430 38
He had, in fact, been wholly unsuspicious of his own E III 13 432 40
She was his own Emma, by hand and word, when they returned E III 13 433 42
very short parley with her own heart produced the most E III 14 435 4
and though you will never own being affected by weather, I E III 14 436 7
my own anxiety, or requires very solicitous explanation. E III 14 438 8
creature who would so designedly suppress her own merit.-- E III 14 439 8
She gives a good account of her own health; but as she E III 14 439 8
a parcel from her, my own letters all returned!--and a few E III 14 442 8
my own blunder, I raved at the blunders of the post.-- E III 14 443 8
As soon as she came to her own name, it was irresistible; E III 15 444 1
No judge of his own manners by you.-- E III 15 445 15
Always deceived in fact by his own wishes, and regardless E III 15 445 15
and regardless of little besides his own convenience.-- E III 15 445 15
Natural enough!--his own mind full of intrigue, that he E III 15 446 15
Her own behaviour had been so very improper! E III 15 447 21
to Donwell, Emma had already had her own passing thoughts. E III 15 449 32
his own, there would be much, very much, to be borne with. E III 15 449 32
His evils seemed to lessen, her own advantages to increase, E III 15 450 36
but every blessing of her own seemed to involve and E III 15 450 37
her future absence as any deduction from her own enjoyment. E III 15 450 37
It might be only her own consciousness; but it seemed as E III 16 451 2
face; and while paying her own compliments to Mrs. Bates, E III 16 453 12
13

I fancy Mr. E. and Knightley have every thing their own E III 16 456 27
And I will own to you, (I am sure it will be safe), that E III 16 460 56

her own little adelaide educated on a more perfect plan." E III 17 461 2
I doubt whether my own sense would have corrected me E III 17 462 6
rightly by you--oftener than I would own at the time. E III 17 462 8
Emma would have renounced their own home for Hartfield! E III 17 467 31
plans and her own, for a marriage between Frank and Emma. E III 17 467 31
his proceedings, first on my affairs, and then on his own. E III 18 472 20
and judgment had been ever so superior to her own. E III 18 475 39
was the next moment in his own concerns and with his own E III 18 478 60 61
own concerns and with his own Jane, and his next words E III 18 478 60 61
us with two characters so much superior to our own." E III 18 478 69
the very passage of her own letter, which sent me the E III 18 480 77
it all extremely shabby, and very inferior to her own.-- E III 19 484 12
was a man who, for his own amusement, never took up any P III 1 3 1
he could read his own history with an interest which never P III 1 3 1
very superior character to any thing deserved by his own. P III 1 4 6
and mild dark eyes from his own); there could be nothing P III 1 6 10
Always to be presented with the date of her own birth, and P III 1 7 12
of her own family, must ever present the remembrance of. P III 1 7 13
to, and the honours which were hereafter to be his own. P III 1 8 17
of self-denial, which her own conscience prompted, she P III 2 13 5
A small house in their own neighbourhood, where they might P III 2 14 9
to descend into a small house in his own neighbourhood. P III 2 14 11
profound secret; no to be breathed beyond their own circle. P III 2 15 13
applicant, on his own terms, and as a great favor, that he P III 2 15 14
the advantage of her own better judgment and experience-- P III 2 16 16
Elizabeth would go her own way--and never had she pursued P III 2 16 16
You need not be afraid, Miss Elliot, of your own sweet P III 3 18 7
so jealous for his own, as John Shepherd will be for him." P III 3 19 10
the country, choosing their own hours, following their own P III 3 20 17
own hours, following their own pursuits, and living on P III 3 20 17
and living on their own property, without the torment of P III 3 20 17
wishing to settle in his own country, and had come down to P III 3 21 18
I shall forget my own name soon, I suppose. P III 3 23 28
An Admiral speaks his own consequence, and, at the same P III 3 24 36
Such confidence, powerful in its own warmth, and P III 4 27 3
more than her own, she could hardly have given him up.-- P III 4 28 5
satisfied as ever with her own discretion, never wished P III 4 29 7
among the only three of her own friends in the secret of P III 4 30 10
a foreign station, and her own sister, Mary, had been at P III 4 31 11
far as to say, that, if his own man might have had the P III 5 32 4
having engagements of her own, which must take her from P III 5 33 6
a great deal of her own complaints, and always in the P III 5 33 7
country, and her own dear country, readily agreed to stay. P III 5 33 9
Their respectability was as dear to her as her own; and a P III 5 36 19
her own absence from home begin when she must give up Anne. P III 5 36 19
parsonage, enclosed in its own neat garden, with a vine P III 5 36 20
I have had all my own little concerns to arrange--books P III 5 38 34
so very uncomfortable, not having a carriage of one's own. P III 5 39 39
would not have given up her own more elegant and P III 5 41 45
in the art of knowing our own nothingness beyond our own P III 6 42 1
own nothingness beyond our own circle, was become P III 6 42 1
The Mr. Musgroves had their own game to guard, and to P III 6 42 3
and to destroy; their own horses, dogs, and newspapers to P III 6 42 3
should dictate its own matters of discourse; and hoped, P III 6 43 3
I really am very ill--a great deal worse than I ever own." P III 6 44 7
upon the gad: and from my own knowledge, I can declare, P III 6 45 9
Her own spirits improved by change of place and subject, P III 6 46 12
fond partiality for their own daughters' performance, and P III 6 47 13
pleasure for their sakes, than mortification for her own. P III 6 47 13
prospects, beginning to own other eyes and other limbs! P III 6 47 16
and with shame at her own forgetfulness, applied herself P III 6 49 22
Captain Wentworth under his own roof, and welcoming him to P III 7 53 1
A sick child is always the mother's property, her own P III 7 56 11
It is Anne's own proposal, and so I shall go with you, P III 7 57 18
Anne was now at hand to take up her own cause, and the P III 7 58 20
It included nearly a third part of her own life. P III 7 60 28
which his own decided, confident temper could not endure. P III 7 61 36
the navy-list,--(their own navy list, the first that had P III 8 64 7
precious volume into his own hands to save them the P III 8 66 22
Mr. Hayter had some property of his own, but it was P III 9 74 5
way of living, and their own defective education, have P III 9 74 5
own, and some return of indisposition in little Charles. P III 9 77 17
that he should know his own mind, early enough not to be P III 9 77 18
sister, or impeaching his own honour, than that he should P III 9 77 18
her, till she had a little better arranged her own. P III 9 81 34
and lessening the interference in any plan of their own. P III 10 83 4
she quarrelled with her own seat,--was sure Louisa had got P III 10 86 21
which did but confirm my own observations, the last time I P III 10 87 26
infuse as much of your own spirit into her, as you can. P III 10 88 26
Her own emotions still kept her fixed. P III 10 89 34
She saw how her own character was considered by Captain P III 10 89 34
it was a proof of his own warm and amiable heart, which P III 10 91 42
think how her own comfort was likely to be affected by it. P III 11 93 1
of merit in maintaining her own way, bore down all the P III 11 94 7
party as friends of their own, because the friends of P III 11 97 15
point in which her own conduct would ill bear examination. P III 11 101 26
afterwards quickly from her own chamber to their dining- P III 12 104 7
might compare it with his own, the servant in mourning P III 12 105 9
as much in reply as her own feelings could accomplish, or P III 12 108 29
with a face as pallid as her own, in an agony of silence. P III 12 109 34
and contributing with his own horror to make him P III 12 109 34
tone of despair, and as if all his own strength were gone. P III 12 110 35
and given possession of her own bed, assistance, cordials, P III 12 111 50
of her own insensibility. Mary, too, was growing calmer. P III 12 112 51
the justness of his own previous opinion as to the P III 12 116 72
unable to satisfy his own sense of their kindness, P IV 1 121 2
others, and increase his own distress; and a much better P IV 1 121 3
from the care of her own children; and in short they were P IV 1 122 5
Captain Benwick, than her own father's house in Camden- P IV 1 124 11
Camden-Place, or her own sister's intimacy with Mrs. Clay. P IV 1 124 11
These convictions must unquestionably have their own pain, P IV 1 125 17
may be as good as another's, but we all like our own best. P IV 1 127 26
Anne, judging from her own temperament, would have deemed P IV 2 134 30
Russell then drove to her own lodgings, in Rivers-Street. P IV 2 136 37
enquiries to make, before the talk must be all their own. P IV 3 137 3
away all the appearance of neglect on his own side. P IV 3 138 7
buildings, and had, at his own particular request, been P IV 3 139 8
the same time, to give his own route, understand something P IV 3 143 19
their high ideas of their own situation in life, and was P IV 4 148 11
Sir Walter, however, would choose his own means, and at P IV 4 149 13
"Pardon me, my dear cousin, you are unjust to your own P IV 4 151 19
she declined on her own account with great alacrity--"she P IV 5 157 14
be preferred by her, to her own family connections among P IV 5 158 19
only said in rejoinder, "I own that to be able to regard P IV 5 159 25
to leave the matter to its own operation; and believing P IV 5 160 26
We had better leave the Crofts to find their own level. P IV 6 166 16
In her own room she tried to comprehend it. P IV 6 166 18
not really Mrs. Croft, she must let him have his own way. P IV 6 170 30
at it, I have a reason of my own for wondering at it." P IV 6 173 47
or quiet attention, and the Admiral had it all his own way. P IV 6 173 48
a momentary look of his own arch significance as he named P IV 7 176 8
to look again (for her own countenance she knew was unfit P IV 7 179 28
you might hear me previously spoken of in my own family." P IV 8 187 31
a little scheming of her own, Anne was enabled to place P IV 8 189 46
consumed; and when her own mistress again, when able to P IV 8 190 48
by his own sentiments, by his early prepossession. P IV 9 192 2
She must have been in your own circle, for as you went P IV 9 193 10
"Oh! you saw enough for your own amusement.-- P IV 9 193 12
build my own selfish schemes on Mr. Elliot's good fortune." P IV 9 195 27
and engagements of his own, to avoid and get rid of as he P IV 9 196 32
of himself; who, for his own interest or ease, would be P IV 9 199 53
I used to boast of my own Anne Elliot, and vouch for your P IV 9 201 61
but, at that period, I must own I saw nothing P IV 9 201 64
Mr. Elliot may have for his own situation in life now, as P IV 9 202 66
to use her own words, without knowing it to be you?" P IV 9 205 86
And indeed, to own the truth, I do not think nurse in her P IV 9 208 92
in the interest of her own family concerns, how much had P IV 9 208 94
for the payment of its own incumbrances, might be P IV 9 210 98
least the comfort of telling the whole story her own way. P IV 9 210 99
He stood, as opposed to Captain Wentworth, in all his own P IV 10 212 1
She was most thankful for her own knowledge of him. P IV 10 212 1
four horses, and with her own complete independence of P IV 10 219 28
does; did not even ask her own sister's family, though P IV 10 219 29
inadvertence, and wantonly playing with our own happiness." P IV 10 221 33
be supposed not to know her own cousin, began talking very P IV 10 222 37
To pacify Mary, and perhaps screen her own embarrassment, P IV 10 222 39
have found, in all her own sensations for her cousin, in P IV 10 225 62
The gentlemen had their own pursuits, the ladies proceeded P IV 10 227 68
ladies proceeded on their own business, and they met no P IV 10 227 68
much on her own, before she was able to attempt the walk. P IV 11 229 2
Neither time, nor health, nor life, to be called your own. P IV 11 233 23
Men have had every advantage of us in telling their own P IV 11 234 28
We each begin probably with a little bias towards our own P IV 11 234 30
has occurred within our own circle; many of which P IV 11 234 30
such men as have hearts!" pressing his own with emotion. P IV 11 235 31
All the privilege I claim for my own sex (it is not a very P IV 11 235 32
Mrs. Musgrove had little arrangements of her own at her P IV 11 237 41 42
of her own at her own table; to their protection she must P IV 11 237 41 42
recollections of their own future lives could bestow. P IV 11 240 59
or the perfect, unrivalled hold it possessed over his own. P IV 11 242 63
have felt the same--her own family, nay, perhaps herself, P IV 11 242 65
nay, perhaps herself, I was no longer at my own disposal. P IV 11 242 65
the blindness of his own pride, and the blunders of his P IV 11 243 69
and the blunders of his own calculations, till at once P IV 11 243 69
Even, if your own feelings were reluctant or indifferent, P IV 11 244 72
My own self. P IV 11 247 82
manners had not suited her own ideas, she had been too P IV 12 249 3
She loved Anne better than she loved her own abilities; P IV 12 249 4
in the autumn; and as her own sister must be better than P IV 12 249 5
do something for his own interest and his own enjoyment. P IV 12 250 7
There she felt her own inferiority keenly. P IV 12 251 10
was not his masters own) if the road had not indisputably S 1 364 1
cottage) for excepting your own, we have passed none in S 1 365 1
the medical line--in your own parish--extensive business-- S 1 366 1
A little of our own bracing sea air will soon set me on my S 1 367 1
the dupes of their own fallacious calculations.-- S 1 369 1
sea weed, can end in nothing but their own disappointment. S 1 369 1
very many more--and his own sisters who were sad invalids, S 2 372 1
cooler reflection which her own husband sometimes needed, S 2 372 1
many of the family as his own house wd contain, to follow S 2 373 1
He had been an elderly man when she married him;--her own S 3 375 1
man when she married him;--her own own age about 30.-- S 3 375 1
& her large income to his own Domains, but he cd not S 3 375 1
She had been too wary to put anything out of her own power- S 3 375 1
she returned again to her own house at Sanditon, she was S 3 375 1
Those who tell their own story you know must be listened S 3 376 1
to be courted by; her own relations, who might very S 3 376 1
She had gone to an hotel--living by her own account as S 3 378 1
born & bred--& where my own 3 eldest children were born-- S 4 379 1
He longed to be on the sands, the cliffs, at his own house, S 4 384 1
I rubbed his ancle with my own hand for six hours without S 5 386 1
& that we must trust to our own knowledge of our own S 5 386 1
of our own wretched constitutions for any releif.-- S 5 386 1
"Why to own the truth, said Mrs P.--I do think the Miss S 5 388 1
20, on the interest of his own little fortune, without any S 5 388 1
reading one of her own novels, for want of employment.-- S 6 389 1
No, no, Miss Clara & I will get back to our own tea.-- S 6 390 1
being really come--, but we get back to our own tea."-- S 6 391 1
Sanditon house as I do;--it is not for my own pleasure.-- S 6 393 1
face of a doctor in all my life, on my own account.-- S 6 394 1
talked & talked only of her own concerns, & Charlotte S 7 399 1
room to put to rights as well as my own every day.-- S 7 401 1
His own goodnature misleads him. S 7 402 1
entitled (according to his own veiws of society) to S 8 405 2
be no acquaintance of her own, she resolved to hurry on & S 9 406 1
under her care, than on her own account or her daughters.-- S 9 409 1
little panegyric on her own disposition--& after having S 9 410 1
Arthur has done about our own lodgings, & probably the S 9 411 1
I have been taking some Bitters of my own decocting, which S 9 411 1
she, in the boldness of her own good health, wd not have S 10 413 1
or their own, & was still the most alert of the three.-- S 10 414 1
but who, by her own account, had not once sat down during S 10 414 1
He took his own cocoa from the tray,--which seemed S 10 416 1
and cooking it to his own satisfaction & toasting some S 10 416 1
was done, & he took his own in hand, Charlotte cd hardly S 10 417 1
at surprise, by the grandeur of her own conceptions.-- S 10 418 1
& tender, had a maid of her own, was to have the best room S 11 421 1
captivate some man of much better fortune than their own.-- S 11 421 1
which a cousin of her own had a property in, Mrs G. did S 11 422 1
certainty of their ill effect upon his own better claim.-- S 12 425 1
to stand back in his own house & see the best place by the S 12 427 1

OWNED (15)

Mr. Allen, who owned the chief of the property about NA I 1 17 12
he then modestly owned that, "without any amibition of NA II 7 178 21
Something more than what he owned to us must have happened. SS I 15 77 23
Had he never owned his affection to yourself?" SS I 20 117 63
exercise, and owned she encouraged it as much as possible. PP II 5 156 4
Kitty then owned, with a very natural triumph on knowing PP III 5 290 50
Kitty owned that she had rather stay at home. PP III 17 375 25
even by his brother, though he would not have owned it. MP I 15 142 24
except of a Sunday; she owned she could seldom, with her MP III 10 401 10
the subject in a manner which he owned had shocked him. MP III 16 454 18
She owned that, considering every thing, she was not E II 7 208 9
and noticing it, he owned that he believed (excepting one E II 8 221 49
distressed that I had owned the apples were so nearly gone; E II 9 238 51
at first; but having once owned that she had been E III 19 481 2
Wentworth of Uppercross; owned himself disappointed, had P IV 8 190 47

OWNER (14)

boasted knowledge of its owner, she sat peaceably down, NA I 9 62 10
The late owner of this estate was a single man, who lived SS I 1 3 1
and in spite of its owner having once been within some SS II 12 233 18
what the owner said in its praise, and took it immediately. PP I 4 16 13
see the word without thinking of Pemberley and its owner. PP II 19 239 9
house, all her apprehensions of meeting its owner returned. PP III 1 245 4
date of the building, the owner of it himself suddenly PP III 1 251 50
he now to step forth the owner of Mansfield Park, the Sir MP I 12 114 2
and even reward the owner with a smile when the animal was MP II 6 237 23
such an air as to make its owner be set down as the great MP II 7 244 27
his carriage so often as became the owner of Donwell Abbey. E II 8 213 7
connection with the owner, he had introduced himself to P III 3 21 18
to look, by the time the owner of the curricle was to be P III 12 105 9
to know that the future owner of Kellynch was undoubtedly P III 12 106 19

OWNERS (2)

the means of sending the owners of Cleveland away, in SS III 7 309 6
each of its two former owners, Fanny had never been able MP III 17 473 33

OWNERS' (1)

had passed into better hands than its owners'. P IV 1 125 17

OWNING (4)

had no scruple in owning herself greatly surprized by it. NA I 13 102 26
a dark little room, owning Henry's authority, and strewed NA II 8 183 2

Context	Work	Vol.	Ch.	Page	Line
risk of her displeasure for a while by owning the truth?"	SS	II	2	148	14
Oh!--you need not be afraid of owning it to me, for Mr.	E	III	11	404	6
OWNS (3)					
very snappish, & Penelope owns she had rather have	W			343	19
He owns it himself without disguise."	PP	I	11	57	27
"Yes, she laments it; yet owns it may have been best.	MP	III	4	352	40
OX (1)					
was certain of--it was the dimensions of some famous ox."	E	III	18	473	26
OXFORD (32)					
views,--that John was at Oxford, Edward at Merchant-	NA	I	4	32	2
with the great London and Oxford roads, and the principal	NA	I	7	44	1
as he was driving into Oxford, last term: 'Ah! Thorpe,'	NA	I	7	46	11
heard that there is a great deal of wine drank in Oxford."	NA	I	9	64	23
"Oxford!	NA	I	9	64	24
There is no drinking at Oxford now, I assure you.	NA	I	9	64	24
You would not often meet with any thing like it in Oxford--	NA	I	9	64	24
deal of wine drank in Oxford, and the same happy	NA	I	9	64	26
I had entered on my studies at Oxford, while you were a	NA	I	14	107	11
to her till his return to Oxford; and Mrs. Allen had given	NA	II	10	201	5
She opened it; it was from Oxford; and to this purpose:-- "	NA	II	10	202	6
					7
My letter was from my brother at Oxford."	NA	II	10	203	10
he went to Oxford; and am fearful of some misunderstanding.	NA	II	12	216	2
I was therefore entered at Oxford and have been properly	SS	I	19	103	4
"Edward talks of going to Oxford soon," said she, "but now	SS	III	2	275	22
Edward have got some business at Oxford, he says; so he	SS	III	2	275	22
I go to Oxford to-morrow."	SS	III	4	288	27
him to be still at Oxford;" which was all the intelligence	SS	III	11	353	21
me, for I was not entered at Oxford till I was nineteen.	SS	III	13	362	5
to make out; for at Oxford, where he had remained by	SS	III	13	364	13
He had quitted Oxford within four and twenty hours after	SS	III	13	366	20
now, by all accounts, almost broken-hearted, at Oxford.--	SS	III	13	370	37
him a hint, by a line to Oxford, that his sister and I	SS	III	13	371	39
their route thither lay; Oxford, Blenheim, Warwick,	PP	II	19	240	12
her: his leaving Eton for Oxford made no change in his	MP	I	2	21	34
One wishes it were not so--but I have not yet left Oxford	MP	I	9	88	18
At Oxford I have been a good deal used to have a man lean	MP	I	9	94	59
They entered Oxford, but she could take only a hasty	MP	III	7	376	5
Just before their setting out from Oxford, while Susan was	MP	III	15	446	34
to Oxford; but the second was over at a much earlier hour.	MP	III	15	446	35
to a certainty--he is at Oxford to-day, and he comes for a	E	II	5	188	7
through Bath as well as Oxford?"--was a question, however,	E	II	5	189	17
OYSTERS (3)					
I shall order a Barrel of oysters, & be famously snug."	W			335	13
with his Barrel of oysters, in dreary solitude--or gladly	W			336	14
chicken and scalloped oysters with an urgency which she	E	I	3	24	11

P. (27)
Upon the whole, Mr P. was evidently an aimable, family-man, S 2 372 1
And Mrs P. was as evidently a gentle, amiable, sweet S 2 372 1
library, which Mr P. was anxiously wishing to support.-- S 2 374 1
that she had married--& Mr P. acknowledged there being S 3 376 1
these three divisions, Mr P. did not hesitate to say that S 3 376 1
Till within the last twelvemonth, Mr P. had considered Sir S 3 377 1
were born--where Mrs P. & I lived till within the last 2 S 4 379 1
day had been caught, as Mr P. observed with delight to S 4 383 1
amused curiosity, & by Mr P. with the eager eye which S 4 384 1
When they met before dinner, Mr P. was looking over S 5 385 1
Mr P. could not be satisfied without an early visit to the S 6 389 1
Mr P. could not but feel that the list was not only S 6 389 1
so much good will for Mr P. to encourage expenditure, S 6 390 1
Mr. P. spoke too mildly of her.-- S 7 402 1
another moment brought Mr P. into the hall to welcome the S 9 406 1
Miss Diana P. was about 4 & 30, of middling height & S 9 407 1
Here Mr P. drew his chair still nearer to his sister, & S 9 408 1
be of use to you?"--and Mr P. warmly offered his S 9 410 1
coming to Sanditon, said Mr P. as he walked with her to S 9 411 1
Mr & Mrs P. spent a great part of the eveng at the hotel; S 10 413 1
Mr P. was confident of another new family.-- S 10 414 1
persons in company, Miss P. drinking one sort of Herb-Tea S 10 416 1
the one in which Miss D. P. had the pleasure of settling S 11 422 1
opening my love, said Mr P. (who did not mean to go with S 12 423 1
Mrs P. was delighted at this release, & set off very happy S 12 425 1
Mrs P. entered into all her husband's joy on the occasion, S 12 426 1
about, & to be told by Mrs P. that the whole-length S 12 427 1

PACE (25)
is tolerable, we pace the shrubbery for hours together. LS 16 268 2
its inevitable pace was ten miles an hour) by no means NA I 9 62 10
pulling him in to that cursed broken-winded jade's pace. NA I 11 88 56
ease; and quickening her pace when she got clear of the NA I 13 101 25
they set off at the sober pace in which the handsome, NA II 5 155 4
being Willoughby, quickened her pace and kept up with her. SS I 16 86 20
The sisters set out at a pace, slow as the feebleness of SS III 10 344 12
13
after field at a quick pace, jumping over stiles and PP I 7 32 41
was not small, at a foot's pace; then, at her apparent MP I 7 67 16
How often do I pace it three times a-day, early and late, MP I 7 73 53
answer, before they were moving again at a good pace. MP I 8 81 32
feet to that lady's slow pace, while her aunt, having MP I 9 90 36
was coming at a quick pace down the principal walk. MP I 10 100 24
for even her activity to keep pace with her wishes? MP II 2 194 20
alone; but the general pace was quickened, and they all MP II 4 215 47
while they walked on together at their own hasty pace. MP III 10 403 14
a very slow walker, and my pace would be tedious to you; E I 8 58 7
passing it without a slackened pace and observing eyes.-- E I 10 83 2
involuntarily; the child's pace was quick, and theirs E I 10 88 33
fears of Mr. Woodhouse had confined them to a foot pace. E I 15 132 37
by, the boy going a good pace, and driving very steady. E III 8 383 31
together and on their way at a quick pace for Randall's. E III 10 392 7
could not keep pace with the conversation of the others.-- P III 8 64 7
The severity of the fall was broken by their slow pace & S 1 364 1
But the stranger's pace did not allow this to be S 9 406 1

PACED (2)
felt, as she unwillingly paced back the gallery, that she NA II 8 185 5
And there, as they slowly paced the gradual ascent, P IV 11 241 59

PACES (4)
and the ease which his paces, as well as the excellence of NA I 9 64 27
attempt, she could not remain many paces from the chest. NA II 6 164 3
have been within a few paces of the cell in which she NA II 8 188 17
They then proceeded a few paces in silence. SS I 22 132 38

PACIFIED (1)
and his conscience was pacified by the resolution of SS II 14 253 25

PACIFY (3)
Manwaring will storm of course, but you may easily pacify LS 9 256 1
Julia wavered: but was he only trying to soothe and pacify MP I 14 135 18
To pacify Mary, and perhaps screen her own embarrassment, P IV 10 222 39

PACING (6)
for General Tilney was pacing the drawing-room, his watch NA II 6 165 5
forego the pleasure of pacing out the length, for the more NA II 8 183 3
with her friend, slowly pacing the drawing-room for an NA II 8 187 13
more is necessary than merely pacing this gravel together. MP III 4 346 8
assist him first in pacing out the room they were in to E II 11 247 2
But soon afterwards, rising and pacing the room, he P III 3 18 5
6

PACK (4)
with a tolerably clean pack brought forward from the W 357 28
I would keep a pack of foxhounds, and drink a bottle of PP I 5 20 21
all the work of the morning, and pack her trunk afresh. PP II 14 213 20
Emma thought she could so pack it as to ensure its safety E I 6 49 42

PACKAGE (1)
to unpin the linen package, which she chaise-seat had NA II 6 163 1

PACKAGES (1)
Mrs. John Dashwood saw the packages depart with a sigh: SS I 5 26 4

PACKED (2)
her to let them stay till they had packed up their clothes. SS III 1 259 7
slit in my worked muslin gown, before they are packed up. PP III 5 292 60

PACKET (3)
passage in the September packet, and he consequently MP I 11 107 2
of waiting for the packet; and all the little particulars MP II 1 178 8
She opened the packet; it was too surely so;--a note from E III 14 436 6

PACKING (3)
she was almost dressed, and her packing almost finished. NA II 13 227 27
as to the best method of packing, and was so urgent on the PP II 14 213 20
niceness of jeweller's packing, a plain gold chain MP II 9 262 8

PACKS (1)
candles and unbroken packs in the true style--and more E II 16 290 3

PADDOCK (4)
as they entered the paddock; and when the carriage drove PP III 5 286 21
his way towards a small wood on one side of the paddock. PP III 7 301 6
window, enter the paddock, and ride towards the house. PP III 11 333 30
corner of the grounds or paddock, so near one of its S 12 426 1

PADLOCK (1)
by massy bars and a padlock, you will, after a few efforts, NA II 5 159 19

PAGE (15)
or pestilences, in every page; the men all so good for NA I 14 108 22
Her greedy eye glanced rapidly over a page. NA II 7 172 2
worded in a page full of empty professions to Mr. Morland. NA II 16 252 7
Willoughby filled every page. SS II 9 202 8
either making some inquiry, or looking at his page. PP I 11 54 4
any thing of the last page or two, put it hastily away, PP II 13 204 2
has never yet turned the page in a letter; and very often MP I 6 59 43
closed the page and turned away exactly as he wanted help. MP I 18 170 24
did find it, or within a page or two, quite near enough to MP III 3 336 10
it to spread over the largest part of a page of her own.-- MP III 13 425 6
"Yes, papa, it is written out in our second page. E I 9 79 55
Only one page more. E III 15 447 26
never failed--this was the page at which the favourite P III 1 3 1
reading her name in any other page of his favourite work. P III 1 6 10
Mrs G. did never deviate from the strict Medecinal page.-- S 11 422 1

PAGES (12)
lest the following pages should otherwise fail of giving NA I 2 18 1
novel, is sure to turn over its insipid pages with disgust. NA I 5 37 4
imagination over the pages of Udolpho, lost from all NA I 7 51 54
hundred and seventy-six pages in each, with a frontispiece NA I 14 113 39
were, they conveyed pages of intelligence to Catherine. NA II 8 186 6
compression of the pages before them, that we are all NA II 16 250 4
I have blushed over the pages of her writing!--and I SS III 13 365 17
solemnity, read three pages, she interrupted him with, "do PP I 14 68 13
14
more on her mind than the pages of Goldsmith; and she paid MP III 12 419 7
that they had transcribed it some pages ago already. E I 9 70 7
short a letter--only two pages you see--hardly two--and in E II 1 157 10
two handsome duodecimo pages, and concluding with the arms P III 1 3 3
4

PAID (74)
his devoirs were speedily paid, with a mixture of joy and NA I 7 44 4
her, was that he paid her rather more attention than usual. NA II 10 199 1
world are always to be paid for, and that we often NA II 11 210 7
there is any annuity to be paid them; and she is very SS I 2 10 20
Twice every year these annuities were to be paid; and then SS I 2 11 20
He paid her only the compliment of attention; and she felt SS I 7 35 9
inform her, that Willoughby had paid no second visit there. SS II 5 169 16
When they had paid their tribute of politeness by SS II 6 175 2
Elinor paid her every quiet and unobtrusive attention in SS II 7 180 5
and paid ten or twelve shillings more than we did." SS II 10 218 24
His visit was duly paid. SS II 11 222 14
which seemed only paid her because she was not Elinor, SS II 13 238 2
Her apprehensions once raised, paid by the excess for all SS III 7 312 17
I had so invariably paid her, and openly assure her of an SS III 8 321 34
She was well paid for her impudence. SS III 8 328 61
and yet I was the first he paid attention to, when he came W 316 1
less satisfied with Mary, paid some compliments of good W 323 3
Not at all dismayed however by her chilling air, he paid W 338 17
I must say that everybody paid me great attention, & W 344 20
after the visit was paid, she had no knowledge of it. PP I 2 6 1
It is very unlucky; but as I have actually paid the visit, PP I 2 7 22
attention might be paid to the sick lady and her sister. PP I 8 40 59
discretion; and had once paid him a visit in his humble PP I 14 66 1
To the rest of the family they paid little attention; PP I 17 86 9
utmost civility, and even paid me the compliment of saying, PP I 18 98 62
I would rather be paid the compliment of being believed PP I 19 108 20
favour, without having paid yourself and Mr. Bennet the PP I 20 114 32
brother's being partial to Miss Darcy she paid no credit. PP II 1 133 3
on Wednesday Miss Lucas paid her farewell visit; and when PP II 3 145 11
She wrote again when the visit was paid, and she had seen PP II 3 147 23
"But he paid her not the smallest attention, till her PP II 4 153 12
to look in Hertfordshire, paid his compliments, with his PP II 7 171 9
As soon as all had ate, and the elder ones paid, the PP II 16 220 16
the hundred that was to be paid them; for, what with her PP III 8 309 4
His debts are to be paid, amounting, I believe, to PP III 10 324 2
paid the fellow's debts, and got him his commission! PP III 17 377 39
I must and would have paid him; but these violent young PP III 17 377 39
and paid off every arrear of civility to Elizabeth. PP III 19 387 10
To the education of her daughters, Lady Bertram paid not MP I 2 19 31
In a quiet way, very little attended to, she paid her MP I 5 48 30
he talked no nonsense, he paid no compliments, his MP I 7 65 13
that this should be the first time of its being paid. MP II 5 218 18
and Mrs. Norris paid her with as many smiles and courteous MP II 10 277 16
the driver came to be paid--then there was a squabble MP III 7 379 19
of Goldsmith; and she paid her sister the compliment of MP III 12 419 7
Well, sir, the time must come when you will be paid for E I 13 116 45
of my existence--never paid her any attentions, but as E I 15 130 31
I protest against having paid the smallest attention to E I 15 131 31
when the due visit was paid, on her arrival, after a two E II 2 167 12
A reasonable visit paid, Mr. Weston began to move.-- E II 5 193 36
a visit, which must be paid some day or other, and E II 5 193 36
37
some day or other, and therefore may as well be paid now. E II 5 193 36
37
compliment that he paid his duty; nothing could be more E II 6 196 2
visit the day before, and asked him if he had paid it. E II 6 198 6
form which were then to be paid, to settle whether she E II 14 270 1
"Yes: but a young lady--a bride--I ought to have paid my E II 14 280 56
attentions from Mrs. Elton which nobody else paid her. E II 16 291 5
explanation," continued he, smiling, "they are paid for it. E II 16 296 43
Every distinguishing attention that could be paid, was E III 7 368 3
attention that could be paid, was paid to her. E III 7 368 3
such a visit could not be paid without leading to reports:- E III 12 417 5
of wrong, for that visit might have been sooner paid. E III 14 437 8
Perhaps it is paid already. E III 14 439 8
His civilities to the other ladies must be paid; but his E III 16 457 37
returned to England, or paid off, or something, and is P III 6 50 27
Lady Russell and Anne paid their compliments to them once, P IV 2 134 28
The visit was paid, their acquaintance re-established, P IV 5 153 6
letter; when Mrs. Clay had paid her tribute of more decent P IV 6 166 17
The visit of ceremony was paid and returned, and Louisa P IV 6 168 22
that he had called and paid them a long morning visit; but P IV 10 212 2
possible attention was paid in the kindest & most S 2 370 1
farther solicitation & paid for what she bought.-- S 6 390 1
in the degree of observance & attention which clara paid.-- S 6 392 1
& precious, as she paid in proportion to her fortune.-- S 11 421 1

PAIN (156)
falls upon me--& he bears pain with such patience that I LS 28 298 2
I am grown wretchedly thin I know; but I will not pain you NA I 15 118 13
which repaid her for the pain of confusion; and that NA II 1 133 29
Modesty such as your's--but not for the world would I pain NA II 2 139 7
guard, and prevent all the pain which her too lively NA II 3 148 28
Isabella could not be aware of the pain she was inflicting; NA II 4 149 1
"he does not know the pain he is giving my brother. NA II 4 150 7
or Miss Thorpe's admission of them, that gives the pain?" NA II 4 151 10
worth knowing however, since it can deceive and pain you. NA II 9 196 21
I shall not enter into particulars, they would only pain NA II 10 202 7
It was with pain that Catherine could speak at all; and it NA II 13 225 22
She tried to eat, as well to save herself from the pain of NA II 13 228 27
What had she to say that would not humble herself and pain NA II 14 231 5
which gave Elinor far more pain than could arise from such SS I 7 34 5
pleasant, and the pain of a sprained ancle was disregarded. SS I 9 43 11
which must give me some pain, you cannot deny me the SS I 10 52 28
any nourishment; giving pain every moment to her mother SS I 16 83 1
their witticisms added pain to many a painful hour;--but SS I 16 85 11
12
But remember that the pain of parting from friends will be SS I 19 103 7
Dashwood, gave additional pain to them all in the parting, SS I 19 104 9
her husband gave her no pain: and when he scolded or SS I 20 112 26
was afraid of giving him pain by any inquiry after his SS II 4 162 12
the anxiety of expectation and the pain of disappointment. SS II 4 166 31
her ease; and in restless pain of mind and body she moved SS II 7 191 65
to prove a source of fresh pain to herself, though Mrs. SS II 9 202 4
Elinor, with a very heavy heart, aware of the pain she was SS II 9 203 10
in silence, gave more pain to her sister than could have SS II 10 212 1
Their presence always gave her pain, and she hardly knew SS II 10 217 20
hoped to be carrying the pain still farther by persuading SS II 12 231 11
He is the most fearful of giving pain, of wounding SS II 13 244 40
of any other part of the pain that had attended their SS II 13 245 47
she felt it with all the pain of continual self-reproach, SS III 2 270 2
to give Edward the pain of receiving an obligation from SS III 3 283 20
which were now extinguished for ever, without great pain. SS III 6 301 4
Though heavy and feverish, with a pain in her limbs, a SS III 6 306 17
Hour after hour passed away in sleepless pain and delirium SS III 7 312 17
I can look with so little pain on the spot!--shall we ever SS III 10 344 14
15
which so much heightened the pain of the intelligence. SS III 12 357 1
beg your pardon, if I have unthinkingly given you pain."-- W 316 2
Of the pain of such feelings, eliz: knew very little;--her W 345 21
peevish under immediate pain, & ill disposed to be pleased, W 348 22
The supposition did not pain her. PP I 10 51 46
We are not on friendly terms, and it always gives me pain PP I 16 78 20
It gives me pain to speak ill of a Darcy. PP I 16 82 43
mean while may lessen the pain of separation by a very PP I 21 116 8
the pain she gives me by her continual reflections on him. PP II 1 134 4
5

They must be separated; but there was a great deal of pain E II 5 187 4
I should be extremely sorry to be giving them any pain. E II 7 210 20
No, I would not be the means of giving them any pain. E II 7 210 20
unwillingness to give pain, and constant habit of never E II 12 258 7
My being saved from pain is a very secondary consideration. E II 13 268 12
I want you to save yourself from greater pain. E II 13 268 12
him, which would be giving pain to his wife; and she found E III 6 353 3
anger, though a slight blush showed that it could pain her. E III 7 371 27
When one is in great pain, you know one cannot feel any E III 8 379 8
had ever supposed--and continual pain would try the temper. E III 9 387 13
which this one article marked, gave her severe pain. E III 11 410 35
Pain is no expiation. E III 12 419 8
been spared from every pain which pressed on her now.-- E III 12 421 17
Emma could not bear to give him pain. E III 13 429 30
just now, Mr. Knightley, and, I am afraid, gave you pain.-- E III 13 429 32
She felt for Harriet, with pain and with contrition; but E III 13 431 38
her from any unnecessary pain; how to make her any E III 14 435 4
of giving pain--no remembrance of Box-Hill seemed to exist. E III 15 447 21
The pain of being obliged to practise concealment towards E III 17 463 15
little inferior to the pain of having made Harriet unhappy. E III 17 463 15
but I am afraid it gives you more pain than you expected. E III 18 472 21
22
self-deceived, before, her pain and confusion seemed to E III 19 481 2
A second allusion, indeed, gave less pain.-- E III 19 483 9
it done with the least possible pain to him and Elizabeth. P III 2 12 3
all the additional pain of opinions, on his side, totally P III 4 28 5
a revival of former pain; and many a stroll and many a P III 4 30 10
she was very far from conceiving it to be of equal pain. P III 8 63 2
he came back he had the pain of finding very altered P III 9 74 4
not in the least aware of the pain he was occasioning. P III 10 82 1
of pleasure and pain, that she knew not which prevailed. P III 10 91 42
It stood the record of many sensations of pain, once P IV 1 123 8
These convictions must unquestionably have their own pain, P IV 1 125 17
but they precluded that pain which Lady Russell would P IV 1 125 17
under severe and constant pain; and all this among P IV 5 154 9
escaped from severe pain, or are recovering the blessing P IV 5 155 9
It was agitation, pain, pleasure, a something between P IV 7 175 6
it, and she had the pain of seeing her sister turn away P IV 7 176 9
replied Anne: "but when pain is over, the remembrance of P IV 8 183 16
She was concerned for the disappointment and pain Lady P IV 10 212 1
I was really in pain for him; for your hard-hearted sister, P IV 10 213 4
It is a sort of pain, too, which is new to me. P IV 11 247 84
Anne knew that Lady Russell must be suffering some pain in P IV 12 249 3
was a source of as lively pain as her mind could well be P IV 12 251 10
It gives me no pain while I am quiet,--and as soon as S 1 367 1

PAINED (17)

in the right, and though pained by such tender, such NA I 13 98 2
She was quite pained by the severity of his father's NA II 5 154 2
to understand or be pained by it; and other subjects being NA II 11 213 20
Eleanor might not be pained by the perusal of--and, above NA II 14 235 14
she saw how much she had pained Edward, her own vexation SS I 18 98 12
Elinor was alternately diverted and pained; but Marianne SS II 5 168 10
to describe it--I have pained you too much already. SS II 9 207 26
"I have been more pained," said she, "by her endeavours to SS II 9 211 34
Do not let me be pained by hearing any thing more on the SS III 8 320 31
Her daughter, feeling by turns both pleased and pained, SS III 9 336 9
I have been pained by her manner this morning, and cannot MP II 9 268 31
again, she had absolutely pained him by her manner of MP II 10 279 21
Fanny shrunk back to her seat, with feelings sadly pained MP III 7 380 23
have pained her mother by alluding to her, for the world.-- MP III 7 386 40
was pained by the manner in which they had been received. E III 13 424 1
delicacy which must be pained by any lightness of conduct P III 9 77 18
His looks shewing him not pained, but pleased with this P III 11 101 24

PAINFUL (74)

It would indeed give me most painful sensations to know LS 1 244 1
painful necessity, but I will endeavour to submit to it. LS 15 267 6
I have not <u>that</u> pain. PP II 1 134 7
you, dear <u>Lizzy</u>, not to pain me by thinking <u>that person</u> to PP II 1 136 14
The pain of separation, however, might be alleviated on PP II 2 139 1
This letter gave Elizabeth some pain; but her spirits PP II 3 149 27
but she could see it and write of it without material pain. PP II 3 149 28
The only pain was in leaving her father, who would PP II 4 151 2
I am sorry to pain you--but so it was. PP II 8 175 18
was at first sorry for the pain he was to receive; till, PP II 11 189 6
I am sorry to have occasioned pain to any one. PP II 11 190 7
pain on her, your resentment has not been unreasonable. PP II 12 197 5
Here again I shall give you pain--to what degree you only PP II 12 200 5
She had always seen it with pain; but respecting his PP II 19 236 2
How much of pleasure or pain it was in his power to bestow! PP III 1 251 48
Whether he had felt more of pain or of pleasure in seeing PP III 1 253 55
Had Miss Bingley known what pain she was then giving her PP III 3 269 10
forced him to say what gave no one any pain but herself. PP III 3 271 19
Nothing of the past was recollected with pain; and Lydia PP III 9 316 6
therefore what I now tell you, can give you no fresh pain. PP III 10 325 2
determine whether pleasure or pain bore the greatest share. PP III 10 326 3
to be just, from the pain of obligation, were proved PP III 10 326 3
the news does not affect me either with pleasure or pain. PP III 11 332 17
"I knew," said he, "that what I wrote must give you pain, PP III 16 368 20
You do not know what he really is; then pray do not pain PP III 17 376 34
to you without rather wishing to give you pain than not. PP III 18 380 3
He had never knowingly given her pain, but he now felt MP I 2 17 20
The first actual pain which Miss Crawford occasioned her, MP I 7 66 14
No pain, no injury, however, was designed by him to his MP I 7 66 14
she might not be seen, the pain of her mind had been much MP I 7 74 59
on her account gave her pain, and her own satisfaction in MP I 8 79 27
sufficient to do away the pain of having been left a whole MP I 10 103 49
or pain, might occupy the meditations of almost all. MP I 10 106 58
"There goes a temper which would never give pain! MP I 11 112 34
not have relinquished without pain; and thus he reasoned. MP II 3 201 22
certain of seeing or hearing something there to pain me?" MP II 5 219 26
pain and pleasure retraced with the fondest recollection. MP II 6 234 18
by a thousand feelings of pain and pleasure, could attempt MP II 9 261 3
give pain to one who has been so studious of your comfort. MP II 9 263 16
the right hand too, and there was pain in the connection. MP II 13 304 17
greater agitation, both of pain and pleasure; but happily MP II 13 308 36
whereas the pain she hoped would return no more. MP II 13 308 36
But her uncle's anger gave her the severest pain of all. MP III 1 321 46
to be giving nearly as much pain to herself as to him. MP III 2 327 6
them, and could never speak of Miss Crawford without pain. MP III 6 367 6
heal every pain that had since grown out of the separation. MP III 6 370 11
It did pain her to have Mansfield forgotten; the friends MP III 7 382 29
neck to sob out her various emotions of pain and pleasure. MP III 7 384 34
It was soon pain upon pain, confusion upon confusion; for MP III 10 401 11
seemed to distance every pain, and make her incapable of MP III 15 443 24
in supposing that Edmund gave his father no present pain. MP III 16 452 15
and concern, what pain and what delight, how the agitation MP III 16 454 18
I hope more pleasure than pain by this retrospect of what MP III 16 455 21
She would not voluntarily give unnecessary pain to any one, MP III 16 456 25
Gladly would I submit to all the increased pain of losing MP III 16 456 25
prefer any increase of the pain of parting, for the sake MP III 16 458 30
had given him pain before--improvement in his spirits. MP III 17 462 5
cannot allow herself to feel so much pain as pleasure. E I 1 11 38
could not think, without pain, of Emma's losing a single E I 2 18 11
and concern for the pain you are inflicting as propriety E I 7 51 11
as there was all the pain of apprehension frequently to be E I 11 93 5
Every part of it brought pain and humiliation, of some E I 16 134 1
to open to sensations of softened pain and brighter hope. E I 16 137 13
wonder and regret, pain and pleasure, as to this fortunate E II 3 180 57
She wished him very well; but he gave her pain, and his E II 4 182 7
The pain of his continued residence in Highbury, however, E II 4 182 8
had there been no pain to his friend, or reproach to E II 4 184 11
the sort of meeting, and the sort of pain it was creating. E II 5 186 4

To feel herself slighted by them was very painful. NA I 11 86 50
These painful ideas crossed her mind, though she said NA I 13 98 3
It was painful to her to disappoint and displease them, NA I 13 101 25
where victory itself was painful; and was heartily NA I 14 106 1
of past folly, however painful, might not be without use. NA II 10 201 4
The very painful reflections to which this thought led, NA II 11 208 1
The painful remembrance of the folly it had helped to NA II 11 212 16
This was a painful consideration whenever it occurred; and NA II 13 220 1
as would make their meeting materially painful. NA II 13 222 8
Eleanor had wished to spare her form so painful a notion, NA II 13 226 25
and sometimes, for a few painful minutes, she believed it SS I 4 22 18
place would be less painful than to inhabit or visit it SS I 4 24 20
But the effort was painful. SS I 12 61 16
by than dispose of it in a manner so painful to you. SS I 14 72 10
integrity cannot be more painful to yourself than to me. SS I 15 81 43
added pain to many a painful hour;--but one evening, Mrs. SS I 16 85 11
12
"No," said Marianne in a low voice, "nor how many painful SS I 16 88 41
It was painful to him to keep a third cousin to himself. SS I 21 119 3
Astonishment, that would have been as painful as it was SS I 22 129 15
"It is strange," replied Elinor in a most painful SS I 22 131 31
As these considerations occurred to her in painful SS II 1 140 4
And as she could now have nothing more painful to hear on SS II 1 142 7
He could not then avoid it, but her touch seemed painful SS II 6 177 8
hardly less painful than Marianne's, and an indignation SS II 10 212 2
His chief reward for the painful exertion of disclosing SS II 10 216 15
painful office of informing her sister that he was married. SS II 10 216 16
convince Marianne; and painful as the consequences of her SS II 13 244 47
Elinor's office was a painful one.-- SS III 1 261 11
effect of constant and painful exertion;--they did not SS III 1 264 29
to rouse her from so painful a slumber, when Marianne, SS III 7 310 10
11
raise any emotion--my feelings were very, very painful.-- SS III 8 325 50
reverie at least equally painful, started up in SS III 8 331 70
71
of relating it to her sister was invariably painful. SS III 9 335 5
some peculiar, some painful recollection, she grew silent SS III 10 342 7
usage, and most painful regrets at his being what he is. PP I 16 78 20
Elizabeth's eyes were fixed on her with most painful PP I 18 100 68
was, of course, more painful than Elizabeth's; but PP I 23 129 14
endeavour to banish every painful thought, and think only PP II 3 148 26
yet more acutely painful and more difficult of definition. PP II 13 204 2
It was painful, exceedingly painful, to know that they PP III 10 326 3
It was a painful, but not an improbable, conjecture. PP III 11 335 40
to a most painful degree by a distinction so ill applied. PP III 11 335 42
or herself amends, for moments of such painful confusion. PP III 11 337 54
what they owed him more painful to Elizabeth's mind; and PP III 12 340 13
now, and has been many months, inexpressibly painful to me. PP III 16 367 14
Painful recollections will intrude, which cannot, which PP III 16 369 24
She expressed her gratitude again, but it was too painful PP III 16 370 34
it, must be exceedingly painful to such feelings as your's. MP I 11 111 29
She had read, and read the scene again with many painful, MP I 18 167 13
dressed" was a point of painful solicitude; and the almost MP II 8 254 8
To Mary it was every way painful. MP II 11 285 15
to give her so many painful sensations on the first day of MP II 13 303 13
such an indulgence, was exciting even painful gratitude. MP III 1 322 51
that the subject was most painful to her, that she must MP III 2 327 5
secure, she was in every way an object of painful alarm. MP III 5 356 4
a tete so much less painful than her fears had predicted. MP III 5 365 33
to approach but with some painful sensation of restraint MP III 17 473 33
you--and it will be a painful reflection to me for ever. E II 13 268 10
That would be so very painful a conclusion of their E III 1 315 2
She must communicate the painful truth, however, and as E III 11 403 2
Their intercourse was painful enough by letter. E III 16 451 1
guilt, of something most painful, which had haunted her E III 16 451 4
would be hardly less painful than of both, and so on, P III 2 13 5
It was painful to look upon their deserted grounds, and P III 5 36 19
of varying, but very painful agitation, as she could not P III 9 80 34
she had heard a great deal of very painful import. P III 10 89 34
were still too painful; but in a moment half smiling again, P IV 8 182 6
"The last few hours were certainly very painful," replied P IV 8 183 16
Flattering, but painful. P IV 9 192 2
"It will be more painful to me in some respects to be in P IV 9 208 93
and quite painful to have him approach and speak to her. P IV 10 214 11
All the surprise and suspense, and every other painful P IV 11 245 77

PAINFULLY (4)

had been rather more painfully extorted from her, for SS I 19 101 2
The tumult of her mind was now painfully great. PP II 11 193 31
But last summer he was again most painfully obtruded on my PP II 12 201 5
would be brought too painfully before her; but she was yet P III 11 93 3

PAINING (1)

I write without any intention of paining you, or humbling PP II 12 196 4

PAINS (47)

that I <u>did</u> take some pains to prevent my brother-in-law's LS 5 249 1
take all possible pains to prevent his marrying Catherine. LS 12 260 2
some pains are taken to prevent her being much with me. LS 17 270 6
& have taken great pains to overcome her timidity. LS 18 273 3
When she first came, I was at some pains to prevent her LS 19 274 3
said she had been at pains to detach from Miss Manwaring. LS 20 275 2
early in the evening taken pains to know who her partner NA I 3 30 52
took pains to be near her, and Henry asked her to dance. NA II 1 131 14
Mrs. Allen used to take pains, year after year, to make me NA II 7 174 7
determined to spare no pains in weakening his boasted NA II 15 245 12
which he was at some pains to procure, that the Fullerton NA II 16 251 6
Mrs. Dashwood now took pains to get acquainted with him. SS I 3 16 13
see him myself without taking pains to converse with him." SS I 10 50 16
it cost her some pains to procure that little;-- for the SS III 1 260 9
affection which I had already taken such pains to display. SS III 8 321 34
T. Musgrave never came, & Margt was at no pains to conceal W 360 30
It pains me to offend you. PP II 12 198 5
spasms in my side, and pains in my head, and such beatings PP III 5 288 38
seeing her father taking pains to get acquainted with him; PP III 17 379 47
it; but in spite of the pains you took to disguise PP III 18 380 5
And sitting down by her, was at great pains to overcome MP I 2 15 10
and Fanny must take more pains; she did not know what else MP I 2 20 31
and then think of the kind pains you took to reason and MP I 3 27 36
him in their turn; and the pains which they, their mothers, MP I 4 42 21
and after being at some pains to get a view of the house, MP I 8 82 35
who had been at great pains to learn all that the MP I 9 84 3
he was taking particular pains, during dinner, to do away MP I 10 104 51
though she had known the pains of tyranny, of ridicule, MP I 16 152 2
of Crawford, was at little pains to remove; and the MP I 18 165 4
was at great pains to teach him how to learn, giving him MP I 18 166 4
impressions, even where pains had been taken to please him- MP II 13 305 26
might have some pains, Portsmouth could have no pleasures. MP III 8 392 12
He would have taken no pains to be on terms with Mrs. MP III 16 456 23
He had been at the pains of consulting Mr. Perry, the E I 2 19 14
take any pains to marry him, she would probably repent it. E I 4 30 18
I could not help being provoked; for after all my pains, E I 6 45 21
He was the brother of her friends, and he took pains to E I 8 65 48
I fancy I need not take much pains to dwell on them. E II 14 275 32
Oh! the pains I have been at to dispel those gloomy ideas E II 18 308 28
came, and he had taken pains (as she was convinced) to E III 11 410 35
Who had been at pains to give Harriet notions of self- E III 11 414 50
"You need not be at any pains to reconcile me to the match. E III 18 473 24
I have taken some pains for your sake, and for Robert E III 18 474 34
had probably been at some pains to get rid of him; but it P III 8 67 28
had been taking as much pains to seek the acquaintance, P IV 2 135 35
connection, as he had formerly taken pains to shew neglect. P IV 2 135 35
him; and, certainly, the pains he had been taking on this, P IV 3 139 7

PAINT (3)

<u>She does</u> paint most delightfully!-- SS II 12 235 32

They all paint tables, cover skreens and net purses. PP I 8 39 45
You paint too accurately for mistake. MP I 5 49 35
PAINTED (4)
heaviest stone-work, for painted glass, dirt and cobwebs, NA II 5 162 26
window shutters were not painted green, nor were the walls SS I 6 28 2
Before her removing from Norland, Elinor had painted a SS II 12 234 26
would have done any thing painted by Miss Dashwood; and SS II 12 234 28
PAINTER (6)
was building, by what painter Mr. Willoughby's portrait SS II 10 215 11
what painter could do justice to those beautiful eyes?" PP I 10 53 57
Entirely against his judgment, a scene painter arrived MP I 18 164 1
room, and given the scene painter his dismissal, long MP II 2 190 9
The scene painter was gone, having spoilt only the floor MP II 2 190 9
The painter was sent off yesterday, and very little will MP II 2 193 13
PAINTER'S (1)
Tom himself began to fret over the scene painter's slow MP I 18 164 1
PAINTERS (1)
What queer fellows your fine painters must be, to think P IV 6 169 25
PAINTING (5)
with the painting, and for some time it had no place. NA II 7 180 39
and when Elinor saw the painting, whatever other doubts SS I 22 132 26
are something in Miss Morton's style of painting, ma'am?-- SS II 12 235 31
32
Here's what may leave all painting and all music behind, MP I 11 113 35
a small miniature painting, "do you know who that is?" P IV 11 232 13
PAINTINGS (1)
In the former were many good paintings; but Elizabeth knew PP III 1 250 46
PAIR (16)
was to be done by two pair of female hands at the utmost. NA II 8 184 4
the necessity of buying a pair of ear-rings for each of SS II 11 226 41
had painted a very pretty pair of screens for her sister- SS II 12 234 26
pair of silk stockings, and came off with the Richardsons." SS III 2 274 16
what to do; took up a pair of scissars that lay there, and SS III 12 360 22
23
great pleasure which a pair of fine eyes in the face of a PP I 6 27 48
A low phaeton, with a nice little pair of ponies, would be PP III 10 325 2
visitor of the new-married pair; but still the cake was E I 2 19 14
of a stomacher, or knit a pair of garters for her E I 10 86 23
sort, where a couple of pair of post-horses were kept, E II 6 197 5
I do suspect he would not have had a pair of horses for E II 8 223 63
While waiting till the other young people could pair E II 8 229 99
And, by the bye, every body ought to have two pair of E II 9 236 46
to have borrowed a pair of scissars the night before of E III 3 334 7
that the sacrifice of one pair of horses would be hardly P III 2 13 5
the better half, of the pair)--not unworthy notice.-- S 7 394 1
PALACE (1)
moving the queen of a palace, though the king may appear MP III 9 394 1
PALANQUINS (1)
to the existence of nabobs, gold mohrs, and palanquins." SS I 10 51 23
PALATABLE (1)
sermon-making was not so palatable to you as it seems to PP III 10 329 31
PALATE (2)
part, to his uncritical palate, the tea was as well NA II 7 175 12
vivant, who must have his palate consulted in every thing, MP I 11 111 28
PALATEABLE (1)
A disagreeable truth would be palateable through her lips, E II 9 234 32
PALE (19)
stairs, when Frederica as pale as ashes came running up, & LS 20 275 1
which he spoke, and sat pale and breathless, in a most NA II 6 165 6
fluttered, her knees trembled, and her cheeks grew pale. NA II 6 169 11
You look pale.-- NA II 9 195 12
cheeks were pale, and her manner greatly agitated. NA II 13 223 9
mind, and turning as pale as her friend, she exclaimed, " NA II 13 223 12
the poor traveller, whose pale and jaded looks soon caught NA II 14 233 9
and in receiving the pale hand which she immediately held SS III 10 340 2
her turning pale, and fell back in her chair in hysterics. SS III 11 353 24
Miss de Bourgh was pale and sickly; her features, though PP II 6 162 12
His complexion became pale with anger, and the disturbance PP II 11 190 8
Her pale face and impetuous manner made him start, and PP III 4 276 6
"You look pale. PP III 5 286 31
turning pale about, when Mr. Crawford walked into the room. MP III 10 399 3
the children were rather pale before they went to bed, it E I 12 103 39
And, seriously, Miss Fairfax is naturally so pale, as E II 6 199 9
she behaved very well, and was only rather pale and silent. E II 14 270 3
time when you found fault with her for being so pale?-- E III 18 478 62
The cheeks which had been pale now glowed, and the P IV 11 240 55
PALENESS (4)
turning of a deathlike paleness, and falling in a fit on NA I 8 53 3
of a death-like paleness, instantly ran out of the room. SS II 7 181 7
not stand your countenance dressed up in woe and paleness. MP I 14 133 11
A fine blush having succeeded the previous paleness of her MP II 1 178 7
PALER (1)
Jane looked a little paler than usual, but more sedate PP III 11 335 39
PALES (6)
standing in it, the green pales and the laurel hedge, PP II 5 155 3
herself at the gate in the pales opposite the parsonage. PP II 10 182 1
view of the vicarage pales, when a sudden resolution, of E I 10 89 36
caught a glimpse over the pales of something white & S 12 426 1
head--& stepping to the pales, she saw indeed--& very S 12 426 1
them--a steep bank & pales never crossed by the foot of S 12 427 1
PALING (5)
The paling of Rosings Park was their boundary on one side. PP II 5 155 2
The park paling was still the boundary on one side, and PP II 12 195 1
own good will, would never stir beyond the park paling.' E II 14 274 30
The fence was a proper park paling in excellent condition; S 12 426 1
from the outside of the paling & which a narrow path S 12 426 1
PALISADES (1)
avenue immediately beyond tall iron palisades and gates. MP I 9 85 4
PALISSADES (1)
walk, backed by iron palissades, and commanding a view MP I 9 90 36
PALL MALL (2)
"In a stationer's shop in Pall Mall, where I had business. SS II 8 199 37
said she, "but now he is lodging at no.--, Pall Mall. SS III 2 275 22
PALLIATE (1)
His companions suggested only what could palliate E III 10 401 69
PALLIATION (2)
to her bosom, afforded no palliation of her distress. PP III 4 278 19
mention without some necessity of defence or palliation. MP II 2 187 1
PALLID (1)
with a face as pallid as her own, in an agony of silence. P III 12 109 34
PALM (1)
Don't palm all your abuses of language upon me." SS I 20 113 38
PALMERS (9)
It is only the Palmers. SS I 19 105 16
The Palmers returned to Cleveland the next day, and the SS I 21 118 1
The Middletons and Palmers--how am I to bear their pity? SS II 7 191 64
till the Middletons and Palmers were able to grieve as SS II 9 203 10
The Palmers were to remove to Cleveland about the end of SS III 3 279 1
upon going home from the Palmers;--and how forlorn we SS III 3 280 8
the Palmers, in the indulgence of such solitary rambles. SS III 6 303 9
most imminent--the Palmers all gone off in a fright, &c.-- SS III 8 330 69
To the Middletons, the Palmers, the Steeles, to every SS III 10 346 28
PALMERS' (1)
Jennings's advice, of sending for the Palmers' apothecary. SS III 7 307 2
PALPABLE (1)
It was a palpable display, repeated on every possible E III 16 454 16
PALPABLY (5)
This threat was so palpably disregarded, that though MP III 7 383 31
match; and only too palpably desirable, natural, and E I 4 34 44
what is so evidently, so palpably desirable-- what courts E I 9 74 25
enjoyed with the Campbells are so palpably at an end! E II 15 283 7
was there a place more palpably designed by nature for the S 1 369 1
PALPITATING (1)
most palpitating heart, while the others prepared to begin. MP I 18 172 32
PALPITATIONS (1)
nervous head-aches and palpitations which I am never E I 12 103 39
PALTRY (5)
But, in my opinion, it is a paltry device, a very mean art. PP I 8 40 56
you expect to influence me by such a paltry attack as this. PP I 18 95 48
The most trivial, paltry, insignificant part; the merest MP I 14 134 13
Every thing that revolts other people, low company, paltry P IV 5 157 15
last year, to raise that paltry Hamlet, lying, as it does S 1 369 1
PAMPHLETS (2)
"I have many pamphlets to finish," said he to Catherine, " NA II 8 187 15
were in bed, by stupid pamphlets, was not very likely. NA II 8 187 16
PANE (1)
every pane was so large, so clear, so light! NA II 5 162 26
PANEGYRIC (4)
Catherine assented--and a very warm panegyric from her on NA I 14 110 28
meant it to be a sort of panegyric, of compliment to PP I 10 49 27
This naturally introduced a panegyric from Jane on his PP III 13 350 51
The entrance of the children ended this little panegyric S 9 410 1
PANES (1)
for the three lower panes of one window, where Tintern MP I 16 152 2
PANG (9)
feels a pang as great "as when a giant dies." NA I 1 16 8
her name, it gave a pang to the heart of poor Elinor, who, SS III 7 312 18
and yet in wishing it, to feel a pang for Willoughby. SS III 9 339 27
Willoughby could not hear of her marriage without a pang; SS III 14 379 18
And to the pang of a friend disgracing herself and sunk in PP I 22 125 18
wondered that Edmund should forget her, and felt a pang. MP I 7 67 16
by Edmund brought a pang with it, for it was Miss Crawford MP I 17 159 6
"Indeed, Harriet, it would have been a severe pang to lose E I 7 54 27
give me another moment's pang: and to convince you that I E III 4 337 6
PANGS (4)
Friendship is certainly the finest balm for the pangs of NA I 4 33 6
separately stated, and the pangs of Sunday only now remain NA I 13 97 1
As for Marianne, on the pangs which so unhappy a meeting SS II 6 179 18
in the midst of the pangs of disappointed affection. E II 8 219 44
PANIC (2)
had given as much panic as pleasure--but the humble, E I 3 25 15
in safety before their panic began, and the whole history E III 3 336 13
PANNEL (1)
Oh!--the great-coat was hanging over the pannel, and hid P III 12 106 16
PANNELS (1)
Nerves fit for sliding pannels and tapestry?" NA II 5 158 13
PANTING (3)
She caught every syllable with panting eagerness; her hand, SS III 10 348 33
behind, while her sister, panting for breath, came up with PP III 7 301 7
8
which their hot faces and panting breaths seemed to prove-- MP III 7 383 31
PANTRIES (1)
The purposes for which a few shapeless pantries and a NA II 8 184 4
PANTRY (1)
room, or a bad butler's pantry, but no doubt he did E II 6 204 43
PAPA (49)
If I could but have papa and mamma, and the rest of them NA I 10 79 56
of papa and mamma's approbation, was eagerly given.-- NA II 2 140 8
"Oh! as to that, papa and mamma were in no hurry at all. NA II 13 221 2
I do so want papa to take us all there for the summer! PP II 16 219 6
But papa is so disagreeable." PP II 18 229 7
"I am not going to run away, papa," said Kitty, fretfully; PP III 6 300 29
eagerly cried out, "Oh, papa, what news? what news? have PP III 7 301 7
8
You and papa, and my sisters, must come down and see us. PP III 9 317 13
know (owing to me) your papa and mamma are so good as to MP I 2 19 29
"I cannot agree with you, papa; you know I cannot. E I 1 8 12
"No, papa, nobody thought of your walking. E I 1 8 16
"They are to be put into Mr. Weston's stable, papa. E I 1 8 18
That, was your doing, papa. E I 1 9 18
"My dearest papa! E I 1 10 32
"I promise you to make none for myself, papa; but I must, E I 1 12 41
me in this instance, dear papa, you cannot think that I E I 1 12 41
"Only one more, papa; only for Mr. Elton. E I 1 13 46
You like Mr. Elton, papa,--I must look about for a wife E I 1 13 46
"But, my dear papa, it is supposed to be summer; a warm E I 6 48 37
"Yes, papa, we have something to read you, something quite E I 9 78 50
"Yes, papa, it is written out in our second page. E I 9 79 55
"She will not be surprized, papa, at least." E I 9 79 59
we ought to be thankful, papa, that we are to have the E I 9 79 63
"Ah! papa--that is what you never have been able to E I 9 80 67
We are very proud of the children, are not we, papa? E I 9 80 69
"But they like it, papa; there is nothing they like so E I 9 81 75
"That is the case with us all, papa. E I 9 81 77
Papa is only speaking his own regret." E I 11 94 10
"Oh! papa, we have missed seeing them but one entire day E I 11 94 14
Papa, if you speak in that melancholy way, you will be E I 11 94 14
would be very hard upon Mr. Weston if she did not, papa.-- E I 11 95 17
"My dear papa, he is three-and-twenty.-- E I 11 96 23
"My dear papa, I sent the whole hind-quarter. E II 3 172 18
would not wish me to come away before I am tired, papa?" E II 7 210 15
"Oh, yes, papa. E II 7 211 21
Papa, do you not think it an excellent improvement?" E II 11 251 24
If it can be contrived to be at the crown, papa, it will E II 11 252 34
"There, papa!-- E II 11 252 37
"But, my dear papa, you are no friend to matrimony; and E II 14 280 57
"Well, papa, if this is not encouragement to marry, I do E II 14 280 59
in the spring, and their papa now proposed bringing them, E II 16 292 7
am going to do so and so; papa says I may, or, I have Miss E III 17 462 9
the winter; but remember, papa, if we do go, we must be in P III 6 42 1
I am come on to give you notice, that papa and mamma are P III 6 50 27
glad they had been to hear papa invite him to stay dinner-- P III 7 54 4
had promised in reply to papa and mamma's farther pressing P III 7 54 4
"Yes; you see his papa can, and why should not I?-- P III 7 56 14
We should all have liked her a great deal better; and papa P III 10 89 33
happiness & joy between papa & mama & their children; S 4 384 1
PAPAS (2)
But papas and mammas, and brothers and intimate friends NA I 10 79 57
him with other papas, you would not think him rough. E I 9 81 73
PAPER (50)
any other odd piece of paper, she did what she could in NA I 1 14 1
Pope, and prior, with a paper from the spectator, and a NA I 5 37 4
will open--a roll of paper appears:--you seize it--it NA II 5 160 21
directly fell on a roll of paper pushed back into the NA II 6 169 11
I will get the Bath paper, and look over the arrivals." NA II 10 206 34
prevailing colour of the paper and hangings, nothing like NA II 11 214 25
a piece of white paper, and put it into his pocket-book." SS I 12 60 13
to ask Mr. Palmer if there was any news in the paper. SS I 19 108 32
My paper reminds me to conclude, and begging to be most SS III 2 278 30
sat deliberating over her paper, with the pen in her hand, SS III 4 287 24
you of, which I was on the point of communicating by paper. SS III 4 288 28
size, the elegance of the paper, the hand-writing SS III 8 328 61
by word of mouth than on paper, it was resolved that, SS III 13 372 45
little, hot pressed paper, well covered with a lady's fair, PP I 21 116 6
paper, written quite through, in a very close hand.-- PP II 12 196 3
he then delivered on paper his perfect approbation of all PP III 8 309 4
hastily seizing a sheet of paper, wrote a short letter to PP III 9 320 32
will give me a sheet of paper, it shall be done directly." PP III 18 382 18
Four sides of paper were insufficient to contain all her PP III 18 383 25
moment, making artificial flowers or wasting gold paper. MP I 2 14 7
hesitatingly, "she did not know; she had not any paper." MP I 2 16 12
I will furnish you with paper and every other material, MP I 2 16 13
where Edmund prepared her paper, and ruled her lines with MP I 2 16 20
the paper esteemed to have the earliest naval intelligence. MP II 6 232 13

she seized the scrap of paper on which Edmund had begun MP II 9 265 19
The solitary candle was held between himself and the paper, MP III 7 382 28
part of my great mind on paper, so I will abstain MP III 12 415 2
light than all Lady Bertram's sheets of paper could do. MP III 14 429 2
There, (holding out the paper to her)--much good may such MP III 15 439 13
thin quarto of hot-pressed paper, made up by her friend, E I 9 69 3
just to leave a piece of paper on the table containing, as E I 9 71 10
and pushing the paper towards Harriet--"it is for you. E I 9 71 12
13
was puzzling over the paper in all the confusion of hope E I 9 72 15
Give me the paper and listen. E I 9 73 18
But how shall I ever be able to return the paper, or say I E I 9 76 37
he would not have left the paper while I was by; but he E I 9 77 47
A piece of paper was found on the table this morning-- (E I 9 78 50
his bow, when taking the paper from the table, she E I 9 81 79
80
in general she fills the whole paper and crosses half. E II 1 157 10
You see we have been wedging one leg with paper. E II 10 240 5
"Emma," said she, "this paper is worse than I expected. E II 11 253 41
Within abundance of silver paper was a pretty little E III 4 338 9
Lady Russell, looking over her paper, "much may be done. P III 2 12 4
cutting up silk and gold paper; and on the other were P IV 2 134 29
The Bath paper one morning announced the arrival of the P IV 4 148 10
from under the scattered paper, placed it before Anne with P IV 11 236 40
had seized a sheet of paper, and poured out his feelings. P IV 11 241 60
He took the peices of paper as he spoke--& having looked S 1 366 1
purchase of some drawing paper for the other & all the S 11 421 1
or with drawing paper, they had, by frequency of their S 11 422 1
PAPERED (1)
The walls were papered, the floor was carpeted; the NA II 6 163 1
PAPERS (14)
the substance of its papers so often consisting in the NA I 5 38 4
Such was the collection of papers, (left perhaps, as she NA II 7 172 2
folly, those detestable papers then scattered over the bed, NA II 7 173 3
Steele, in rolling her papers for her; and there is so SS II 1 145 19
papers, which she saw her eagerly examining every morning. SS II 10 217 16
chuse papers, project shrubberies, and invent a sweep. SS III 14 374 7
of formal civility--& the papers, seemed very naturally to W 322 3
have heard of it; indeed, you must have seen in the papers. PP III 11 336 49
and the papers swept away;-- "particularly pleasant. E II 3 170 2
of some papers which I was wanting to send to John.-- E III 18 471 20
He delivered these papers to John, at his chambers, and E III 18 471 20
said, "this is full of papers belonging to him, to my P IV 9 202 69
70
I came to examine his papers, I found it with others still P IV 9 203 70
fewer than three lodging papers staring me in the face at S 7 402 1
PAR (2)
Sir James is certainly under par--(his boyish manners make LS 24 288 11
water, will make you nearly on a par with the rest of us." E III 6 365 65
PARADE (13)
I am excessively provoked however at the parade of LS 19 274 2
She was so amazingly tired, and it was so odious to parade NA II 3 147 28
"This is a parade," cried he, "which does one good; it PP II 6 299 28
see Lydia, with anxious parade, walk up to her mother's PP III 9 317 9
to Bath--there to parade over the wonders of Sotherton in MP II 3 202 28
there was a sort of parade in his speeches which was very E I 9 82 84
a part, or making a parade of insincere professions; and E II 6 197 4
It was the delay of a great deal of pleasure and parade. E III 6 352 2
and pic-nic parade of the Eltons and the Sucklings. E III 6 352 2
There is to be no form or parade--a sort of gipsy party.-- E III 6 355 20
with a sort of anxious parade of mystery fold up a letter E III 16 453 12
13
no taste for finery or parade; and Mrs. Elton, from the E III 19 484 12
I am not a woman of parade, as all the world knows, & if S 6 393 1
PARADED (1)
be attended, where they paraded up and down for an hour, NA I 3 25 1
PARADING (4)
the great clock, after parading the room till they were NA I 4 31 1
any disturbance, without parading to her, or swearing at NA II 5 157 5
enough to make any parading stipulation; but the decent NA II 16 249 2
to all the parading and obsequious civility of her husband. PP III 18 384 26
PARADINGS (1)
Emma had not to listen to such paradings again--to any so E III 15 284 11
PARAGRAPH (7)
and satisfactory paragraph, at least to all those intimate SS II 14 246 1
This paragraph was of some importance to the prospects and SS III 13 371 40
fame, so near the long paragraph in praise of the private MP I 13 121 1
over a particular paragraph--"what's the name of your MP III 15 439 9
she dared not indulge a hope of the paragraph being false. MP III 15 440 19
Precisely such had the paragraph originally stood from the P III 1 3 2
Wentworth, in a small paragraph at one corner of the P III 8 66 16
PARALIZED (1)
of generous emotions for him;--our hearts are paralized--. S 8 403 1
PARASOL (4)
had a new gown, or a new parasol, which she would have PP II 19 238 5
room for her parasol, attended her noble guest down stairs. PP III 14 352 19
doors--& you can get a parasol at Whitby's for little Mary S 4 381 1
a little parasol, which will make her as proud as can be. S 4 381 1
PARASOLS (2)
dressed, with veils and parasols like other girls; but I MP I 5 51 40
went with--& to buy new parasols, new gloves, & new S 2 374 1
PARCEL (16)
There Fanny, you shall carry that parcel for me--take MP I 10 105 55
Now I can manage the other parcel and the basket very well. MP I 10 106 55
parcel by you that I want to get conveyed to your cousins." MP II 7 245 32
And as she spoke she was undoing a small parcel, which MP II 8 257 15
Such had been the parcel with which Miss Crawford was MP II 8 258 15
Almost unconsciously she had now undone the parcel he had MP II 9 262 8
had left a little parcel for her from one of his sisters, E I 7 50 1
away; and on opening this parcel, she had actually found, E I 7 50 1
it was all settled, even to the destination of the parcel. E II 9 235 35
to Emma with a small parcel in her hand, and after sitting E III 4 337 1
2
Cannot you guess what this parcel holds?" said she, with a E III 4 338 6
She held the parcel towards her, and Emma read the words E III 4 338 9
Harriet unfolded the parcel, and she looked on with E III 4 338 9
afterwards I received a parcel from her, my own letters E III 14 442 8
One five minutes brought a note, the next a parcel, and P IV 10 221 32
"Look here," said he, unfolding a parcel in his hand, and P IV 11 232 13
PARCELS (7)
had so crowded it with parcels, that Miss Morland would NA II 5 155 4
said she to the footman who then entered with the parcels. SS II 4 165 26
parcels placed within, and it was pronounced to be ready. PP II 15 216 8
boxes, workbags, and parcels, and the unwelcome PP II 16 220 16
They went in; and while the sleek, well-tied parcels of " E II 6 200 16
You could make it into two parcels, Mrs. Ford, could not E II 9 235 36
Harriet, to give Mrs. Ford the trouble of two parcels." E II 9 235 37
PARDON (55)
"I beg your pardon sir, for the liberty I have taken in LS 25 292 3
"I beg your pardon, Miss Morland," said she, "for this NA I 8 55 10
and tell him I beg his pardon--that is--I do not know what NA II 3 145 13
"Persuasion is not at command; but pardon me if I cannot NA II 4 150 6
She drew back, trying to beg their pardon, but was, with NA II 10 203 8
which his pride could not pardon, and which a better pride NA II 15 244 11
that really--I beg your pardon; but surely there must be SS I 22 131 29
Your secret is safe with me; but pardon me if I express SS I 22 132 40
"Pardon me," replied Elinor, startled by the question; " SS I 22 133 45
not come before--beg your pardon, but I have been forced SS II 4 163 14
He looked surprised and said, "I beg your pardon, I am SS II 5 173 42
to pardon, any former affection of Edward for her. SS III 1 261 13
I beg your pardon, Mr. Dashwood, but if he had done SS III 1 267 43
Whether he had asked her pardon for his intrusion on first SS III 4 288 26
have me beg my mother's pardon for Robert's ingratitude to SS III 13 372 41
"Dear sister, I beg your pardon, if I have unthinkingly W 316 2
I beg your pardon for not keeping my engagement, but I am W 330 11
of the room, to "beg her pardon", & look in the window W 336 13
He begged pardon for having displeased her. PP I 13 65 26
and begging pardon, protested that he never read novels.-- PP I 14 68 13
"I beg your pardon;--one knows exactly what to think." PP I 17 86 7
her pardon, and directed all his anger against another. PP I 18 94 43
"I beg your pardon," replied Miss Bingley, turning away PP I 18 95 47
third person; in which case you may be sure of my pardon." PP I 18 95 49
I shall intreat his pardon for not having done it earlier. PP I 18 97 59
Pardon me for neglecting to profit by your advice, which PP I 18 97 61
"Pardon me for interrupting you, madam," cried Mr. Collins; PP I 20 110 4
"I beg your pardon. PP II 3 144 7
But I ought to beg his pardon, for I have no right to PP II 10 185 24
You must, therefore, pardon the freedom with which I PP II 12 196 4
Pardon me.-- PP II 12 198 5
to pardon his interference in the views of his friend. PP II 18 229 10
exclaimed, "I beg your pardon, but I must leave you. PP III 4 276 6
Miss Bennet, "I beg your pardon, madam, for interrupting PP III 7 301 1
I beg your pardon, but I cannot quite believe you. MP I 5 46 23
My dear Miss Price, I beg your pardon, but I have made my MP I 18 168 15
something in his hand, "I beg your pardon for being here. MP II 9 261 2
by your desire--I beg your pardon, but I am bewildered. MP II 13 300 6
I thought--but I beg your pardon, perhaps I have been E I 7 52 13
he said--"but I beg your pardon, Miss Woodhouse, you were E II 6 200 16
Her pardon was duly begged at the close of the song, and E II 8 227 86
I beg your pardon. E II 9 237 48
"Oh! I beg your pardon, sir. E II 11 255 58
him he was mistaken; he asked my pardon and said no more. E II 15 288 38
Pardon me--but you will be limited as to number--only E III 7 370 26
in two applications for pardon, that I may be in danger of E III 14 437 8
I hope time has not made you less willing to pardon. E III 18 476 47
politeness, "I beg your pardon, madam, this is your seat;" P III 8 72 58
59
"Pardon me, my dear cousin, you are unjust to your own P IV 4 151 19
He begged her pardon, but she must be applied to, to P IV 8 190 47
I beg your pardon. P IV 9 195 27
At last, "I beg your pardon, my dear Miss Elliot," she P IV 9 198 52
53
cordiality, "I beg your pardon for the short answers I P IV 9 198 52
53
But I beg your pardon; I have interrupted you. P IV 9 201 63
He begged their pardon, but he had forgotten his gloves, P IV 11 236 40
PARDONABLE (5)
head)--or it may be of something still less pardonable." NA II 9 196 25
any instance of a second attachment's being pardonable." SS I 11 56 16
it never pardonable in a young man of independent fortune. MP II 12 292 9
Julia was yet as more pardonable than Maria as folly than MP III 16 452 13
pardonable pride, received it as a most unfortunate one. P III 4 26 2
PARDONED (4)
nor, for the first half hour, to be easily pardoned. NA II 14 233 10
more than may be pardoned, in consideration of the motive." E II 14 277 37
if they might be pardoned the youthful infatuation which P III 1 4 6
This could not be pardoned. P III 1 9 17
PARENT (19)
growing every day more & more what a parent could desire. LS 42 312 3
nor feelingly--neither as a gentleman nor as a parent. NA II 14 234 10
steady, and while his parent so expressly forbad the NA II 16 249 2
against will, parent against child, was the cause of all. SS I 19 102 2
indulgent fondness of a parent towards a favourite child SS II 8 193 7
Lucy, who was hardly less anxious to please one parent SS II 12 234 24
not be so weak as to throw away the comfort of a parent!" SS III 5 296 19
to a soothing friend--not an application to a parent. SS III 9 337 18
mind with the care of a parent, & of tenderness to an aunt W 361 31
the death of their common parent, which left them to the MP I 4 40 15
Every thing that a considerate parent ought to feel was MP II 11 285 10
a partial, ill-judging parent, a dawdle, a slattern, who MP III 8 390 6
Sir Thomas, poor Sir Thomas, a parent, and conscious of MP III 17 461 4
in his own conduct as a parent, was the longest to suffer. MP III 17 461 4
no difficulties behind, no drawback of poverty or parent. MP III 17 471 29
none can equal that of a parent, it suits my ideas of E I 10 86 21
He seems every thing the fondest parent could. . . . E II 9 238 51
parent living, found a home for half a year, at Monkford. P III 4 26 1
To me, she was in the place of a parent. P IV 11 246 80
PARENT'S (3)
must be of all others most afflicting to a parent's mind. PP III 6 296 11
seemed to her so like a parent's care, under the influence MP I 4 38 9
all that was real and unabsurd in the parent's feelings. P III 8 67 28
PARENTAGE (2)
in, when the mystery of her parentage came to be revealed. E I 8 64 47
Harriet's parentage became known. E III 19 481 3
PARENTAL (8)
by parental authority in his present application. NA II 15 243 10
him to judge--of their treating her with parental kindness. NA II 15 245 12
recommend parental tyranny, or reward filial disobedience. NA II 16 252 7
the same amusements, objects of the same parental care. PP I 16 81 37
who thought much of parental claims, or family confidence, MP II 1 177 5
Sir Thomas's parental solicitude, and high sense of honour MP III 15 442 21
true parental hearts to promote their daughter's comfort. P IV 8 182 8
unrivalled address to parental affection-- "some feelings S 7 397 1
PARENTS (31)
that of your parents, and the credit of your name. LS 12 260 1
divided the son from his parents, would make me, even with LS 30 300 3
prudent advice of your parents has not been given in vain. LS 37 306 1
"It is impossible," said she, "for parents to be more kind, NA I 15 119 14
the consent of my kind parents, and am promised that every NA I 15 121 26
Her parents seeing nothing in her ill-looks and agitation, NA II 14 235 13
her heart, which, for the parents of a young lady of NA II 14 235 13
sat down to table indignant against all selfish parents. SS I 17 90 1
parents, my proposals will not fail of being acceptable." PP I 19 109 21
this day you must be a stranger to one of your parents.-- PP I 20 112 19
the inn, was under frequent discussion between her parents. PP II 16 223 26
amongst the latter, depended on the will of the parents. PP III 8 308 4
on her marriage by her parents, urged him so earnestly, PP III 8 314 22
canvassed between their parents, about a twelvemonth ago, PP III 11 332 21
I was spoilt by my parents, who though good themselves, (PP III 16 369 24
a midshipman; and as his parents, from living on the spot, MP II 6 233 14
comes to, or what their parents, or their uncles and aunts MP II 13 305 24
stand in the place of her parents; and he had done it all MP III 1 314 16
of your family--of your parents--your brothers and sisters- MP III 1 318 39
parents and guardians"--and a "capital season'd hunter." MP III 3 341 31
of her seeing her parents again, and nothing at all with MP III 6 368 9
the offer of visiting the parents and brothers, and MP III 6 369 11
She could not respect her parents, as she had hoped. MP III 8 389 3
Delicacy to her parents made her careful not to betray MP III 14 431 8
find out who were the parents; but Harriet could not tell. E I 4 27 3
"Whoever might be her parents," said Mr. Knightley, " E I 8 62 42
being taken away from his parents and natural home! E I 11 96 25
could her higher powers of mind be unfelt by the parents. E II 2 165 7
of the harp, and no fond parents to sit by and fancy P III 6 46 13
"Such excellent parents as Mr. and Mrs. Musgrove," P IV 10 218 23
I think, all parents should prevent as far as they can." P IV 11 231 9
PARENTS' (1)
would, from their parents' inferior, retired, and P III 9 74 5
PARISH (47)
Her father had no ward, and the squire of the parish no NA I 1 16 10
and a whole parish to be at work within the inclosure. NA II 7 178 21
I must be at Woodston on Monday to attend the parish NA II 11 209 5
houses were in the same parish, could, by any alteration, SS I 4 23 20
He is the curate of the parish I dare say." SS I 12 61 23
and glebe, extent of the parish, condition of the land, SS III 13 368 31

now clergyman of the parish in which the castle stood, Mrs W 329 9
valuable rectory of this parish, where it shall be my PP I 13 62 12
nor to his leaving his parish occasionally for a week or PP I 14 66 1
"We were born in the same parish, within the same park, PP I 16 81 37
The rector of a parish has much to do.-- PP I 18 101 71
not be too much for his parish duties, and the care and PP I 18 101 71
myself) to set the example of matrimony in his parish. PP I 19 105 9
10
magistrate in her own parish, the minutest concerns of PP II 7 169 4
Her home and her housekeeping, her parish and her poultry, PP II 15 216 7
Clement's, because Wickham's lodgings were in that parish. PP III 9 318 24
buildings of Mansfield parish; the white house being only MP I 3 28 38
clergyman of the parish, that cannot be expected from me. MP I 3 30 50
the farmers, all the labourers, all the hay in the parish. MP I 6 58 37
They have been buried, I suppose, in the parish church. MP I 9 86 7
will be useful in his parish and his neighbourhood, where MP I 9 93 49
neighbourhood, where the parish and neighbourhood are of a MP I 9 93 49
hours afterwards from the parish; and so ended all the MP II 2 193 18
great land-holder of the parish, by every creature MP II 7 244 27
But a parish has want$ and claims which can be known only MP II 7 247 42
"undoubtedly understands the duty of a parish priest.-- MP II 7 248 46
Edmund moves slowly; detained, perchance, by parish duties. MP III 9 394 1
Randalls in the same parish, and Donwell Abbey in the E I 3 20 1
and Donwell Abbey in the parish adjoining, the seat of Mr. E I 3 20 1
and residing in the parish of Donwell--very creditably she E I 3 23 10
were left very busy over parish business--that as long as E II 8 220 48
his library, and all the parish to manage; and he is E II 8 225 74
about relief from the parish: he is very well to do E III 8 383 29
"I have a few lines on parish business from Mr. Weston E III 13 425 9
"this is the most troublesome parish that ever was. E III 16 456 29
"Your parish there was small," said Jane. E III 16 456 30
almost every house in the parish, as a sort of take-leave. P III 5 39 34
whether any thing could persuade him to leave his parish. P III 12 102 2
in his tenants, felt the parish to be so sure of a good P IV 1 125 17
We have neither surgeon nor partner in the parish I assure S 1 365 1
from the extent of the parish or some other cause you may S 1 365 1
a surgeon in the parish--whether you may know it or not. S 1 366 1
line--in your own parish--extensive business--undeniable S 1 366 1
tenement as any in the parish, and that my Shepherd lives S 1 366 1
landed property in the parish of Sanditon, may be unknown S 1 368 1
parish of Sanditon, with manor & mansion house made a part. S 3 375 1
last building of former days in that line of the parish. S 4 384 1

PARISHES (2)
There will be but one subject throughout the parishes of E I 18 149 29
In general he was judged, throughout the parishes of E II 7 206 4

PARISHIONERS (3)
and burying his parishioners whenever it were required. PP I 13 64 16
clergy are lost there in the crowds of their parishioners. MP I 9 93 49
not live among his parishioners and prove himself by MP II 7 248 42

PARK (151)
her of house, hall, place, park, court, and cottage, NA II 2 141 11
he led the way to it across a small portion of the park. NA II 7 178 20
Our best way is across the park." NA II 7 179 27
point of ground within the park was almost closed from her NA II 14 230 1
her daughters to Barton park, the place of his own SS I 4 23 20
being a visitor at Barton Park; and she relied so SS I 5 26 6
to dine at Barton Park every day till they were better SS I 6 30 6
and fruit arrived from the park, which was followed before SS I 6 30 6
securing their promise of dining at the park the next day. SS I 6 31 10
Barton Park was about half a mile from the cottage. SS I 7 32 1
welcomed them to Barton Park with unaffected sincerity; SS I 7 33 4
at the park, but who was neither very young nor very gay. SS I 7 33 4
At the park she laughed at the Colonel, and in the cottage SS I 8 36 2
Their visitors, except those from Barton Park, were not SS I 9 40 2
"I remember last Christmas, at a little hop at the park, SS I 9 44 25
He is highly esteemed by all the family at the park, and I SS I 10 50 16
The private balls at the park then began; and parties on SS I 11 53 1
If their evenings at the park were concluded with cards, SS I 11 54 3
him one evening at the park, when they were sitting down SS I 11 55 8
park; as to a stable, the merest shed would be sufficient. SS I 12 58 3
When Mrs. Jennings attacked her one evening at the park, SS I 12 61 15
By ten o'clock the whole party were assembled at the park, SS I 13 63 2
He drove through the park very fast, and they were soon SS I 13 67 60
Brandon's visit at the park, with his steadiness in SS I 14 70 1
collected them at the park, the exercise which called him SS I 14 71 5
for we must walk to the park, to call on Lady Middleton." SS I 14 74 21
On their return from the park they found Willoughby's SS I 15 75 2
To the left is Barton Park, amongst those woods and SS I 16 88 33
park the next day, or to drink tea with them that evening. SS I 18 99 16
urgent with them all to spend the next day at the park. SS I 19 108 40
if we are to dine at the park whenever any one is staying SS I 19 109 41
As the Miss Dashwoods entered the drawing-room of the park SS I 20 110 1
them directly to the park, as soon as their present SS I 21 118 2
in their favour before they had been an hour at the park. SS I 21 119 3
Sir John wanted the whole family to walk to the park SS I 21 119 3
of their calling at the park within a day or two, and then SS I 21 119 5
When their promised visit to the park and consequent SS I 21 120 6
"that while I am at Barton park, I never think of tame and SS I 21 123 20
her flatteries at the park betrayed; and she could have no SS I 22 127 2
walking together from the park to the cottage--"but, pray, SS I 22 128 3
Steeles returned to the park, and Elinor was then as SS I 22 135 56
evening either at the park or cottage, and chiefly at the SS II 1 142 8
a hope of finding time for conversation at the park. SS II 1 144 10
The visit of the Miss Steeles at Barton Park was SS II 2 151 43
nearly two months at the park, and to assist in the due SS II 2 151 43
The Miss Steeles kept their station at the park, and were SS II 3 158 22
To my fancy, a thousand times prettier than Barton Park, SS II 8 197 22
us one evening at Barton Park-- it was the evening of a SS II 9 205 22
It will be a very fine object from many parts of the park, SS II 11 226 39
It had no park, but the pleasure-grounds were tolerably SS III 6 302 7
But there are many works well worth reading, at the park; SS III 10 343 9
at the park to her brother, who is one of the post-boys. SS III 11 354 27
to his old quarters at the park; from whence he usually SS III 13 369 34
by a lane from Rosings Park, her ladyship's residence." PP I 14 67 3
"We were born in the same parish, within the same park, PP I 16 81 37
The paling of Rosings Park was their boundary on one side. PP II 5 155 2
bordered the park nearly opposite the front of his house. PP II 5 156 4
has a pleasant walk of about half a mile across the park.-- PP II 6 161 8
Every park has its beauty and its prospects; and Elizabeth PP II 6 161 8
edged that side of the park, where there was a nice PP II 7 169 5
into the park, hurried home with the great intelligence. PP II 7 170 7
More than once did Elizabeth in her ramble within the park, PP II 10 182 1
"I have been making the tour of the park," he replied, "as PP II 10 183 4
instead of entering the park, she turned up the lane, PP II 12 195 1
The park paling was still the boundary on one side, and PP II 12 195 1
the morning, to stop at the gates and look into the park. PP II 12 195 2
of grove which edged the park; he was moving that way; and PP II 12 195 2
The park was very large, and contained great variety of PP III 1 245 2
in rosing's park, when he put his letter into her hand! PP III 1 252 54
round the whole park, but feared it might be beyond a walk. PP III 1 253 57
never be quite happy till I have been all round the park. PP III 10 325 2
"You have a very small park here," returned Lady Catherine PP III 14 352 9
We will go round the park every day. PP III 18 382 21
Bertram, of Mansfield Park, in the country of Northampton, MP I 1 3 1
the novelty of Mansfield Park, and the separation from MP I 2 14 6
Let us walk out in the park, and you shall tell me all MP I 2 15 11
was fixed at Mansfield Park, and learning to transfer in MP I 2 20 32
removed first to the park, and afterwards to a small house MP I 3 23 1
I am to leave Mansfield Park, and go to the white house, I MP I 3 25 20
two hundred miles off, instead of only across the park. MP I 3 26 31
You will have as free a command of the park and gardens as MP I 3 27 35
Mansfield Park, and was scarcely ever seen in her offices. MP I 3 31 59
numbers belonging to the park, that would do vastly well, MP I 4 36 7
be obliged to take daily refuge in the dining of the park. MP I 4 38 9
Mansfield Park, and a baronetey, did no harm to all this. MP I 5 47 28
thing in his favour, a park, a real park five miles round, MP I 5 48 28
his favour, a park, a real park five miles round, a MP I 5 48 28
all dining together at the park soon after his going, she MP I 6 52 1
"Sir, it is a moor park, we bought it as a moor park, and MP I 6 54 11
it cost seven shillings, and was charged as a moor park." MP I 6 54 11
of a moor park apricot, as the fruit from that tree. MP I 6 54 12
It stands in one of the lowest spots of the park; in that MP I 6 56 26
to the ladies of the park; but she thought it a very bad MP I 7 65 14
of the young ladies at the park, and which, when Edmund's MP I 7 66 14
she could look down the park, and command a view of the MP I 7 67 16
into the park, and make towards the spot where she stood. MP I 7 68 17
across another part of the park; her feelings of MP I 7 69 21
was partly expected at the park that day; but it was felt MP I 7 70 30
the hot park to your house, and doing it twice, ma'am?-- MP I 7 72 47
as full as on the first evening of her arrival at the park. MP I 7 74 59
and walk half way down the park with the two other ladies. MP I 8 77 7
gates; but we have nearly a mile through the park still. MP I 8 82 34
over a ha-ha into the park, was a comfortable-sized bench, MP I 9 95 67
through it into the park, that their views and their plans MP I 10 97 4
Yes, certainly, the sun shines and the park looks very MP I 10 99 17
cannot see them any where," looking eagerly into the park. MP I 10 100 26
from that part of the park, and will be thinking how it MP I 10 102 47
They were just returned into the wilderness from the park, MP I 10 103 49
across a portion of the park into the very avenue which MP I 10 103 49
word!" said Mrs. Norris, as they drove through the park. MP I 10 105 53
the evening at Mansfield Park, heard the good news; and MP I 11 108 4
the owner of Mansfield Park, the Sir Thomas complete, MP I 12 114 2
the parsonage than at the park on this change in Edmund; MP I 17 159 6
day, by spending it at the park to support her sister's MP II 3 203 30
great clock at Mansfield Park, striking three, made her MP II 4 214 46
in the letters to Mansfield Park; do you, Miss Price?-- MP II 5 224 52
of events--if Mansfield Park had had the government of the MP II 5 225 57
Park family which was increasing in value to him every day. MP II 7 246 37
giving up Mansfield Park; he might ride over, every Sunday, MP II 7 247 42
she made her way to the park, through difficulties of MP II 11 287 17
Henry Crawford was at Mansfield Park again the next MP II 13 298 1
the theatre at Mansfield Park; but he approached her now MP III 2 328 7
At Mansfield Park Mr. Crawford would always be welcome; he MP III 2 329 12
and luxuries of Mansfield Park, would bring her mind into MP III 6 369 9
But he was master at Mansfield Park. MP III 6 370 14
be spared from Mansfield Park at present; that she was a MP III 6 373 23
He too had a sacrifice to make to Mansfield Park, as well MP III 6 373 25
last evening at Mansfield Park must still be wretchedness. MP III 6 374 28
spirits, when Mansfield Park was fairly left behind, and MP III 7 375 1
drawing-room at Mansfield Park, about sending her a prayer- MP III 7 387 45
little attic at Mansfield Park, in <u>that</u> house reckoned too MP III 7 387 47
say, that though Mansfield Park might have some pains, MP III 8 392 12
between them, as Mansfield Park, a description of the MP III 12 419 8
the manners, the amusements, the ways of Mansfield Park. MP III 12 419 8
"<u>Mansfield Park</u>. "my dear Fanny, "excuse me MP III 13 420 2
I want to know the state of things at Mansfield Park, and MP III 14 433 13
know, and be no trouble to our friends at Mansfield Park. MP III 14 435 14
they are only gone to Mansfield Park, and Julia with them. MP III 15 437 3
but, when they entered the park, her perceptions and her MP III 15 446 35
She was returned to Mansfield Park, she was useful, she MP III 17 461 2
the view and patronage of Mansfield Park, had long been. MP III 17 473 33
yesterday from Clayton Park, he had met Mr. Elton, and E I 8 68 58
own good will, would never stir beyond the park paling.' E II 14 274 30
Stevenson, Esq. of south park, Elizabeth, daughter of P III 1 3 1
stvenson, esq. of south park, in the county of Gloucester; P III 1 3 1
The park would be open to him of course, and few navy P III 3 18 8
drove back through the park, "I thought we should soon P III 5 32 4
The late Sir Harry denham, of Denham Park in the S 3 375 1
constantly at Denham Park; & Mr P-- had little doubt, that S 3 377 1
the dampness of Denham Park, & the good bathing always S 7 402 1
The fence was a proper park paling in excellent condition; S 12 426 1

PARK-STREET (1)
son of Mrs. Ferrars of Park-Street, and brother of your SS I 22 131 30

PARKER (28)
My name is Parker.-- S 1 368 1
Mr Parker of Sanditon; this lady, my wife Mrs Parker.-- S 1 368 1
"Not at all sir, not at all--cried Mr Parker eagerly. S 1 368 1
Mr Parker was therefore carried into the house, and his S 1 370 1
Mr Parker could not think of very little besides.-- S 2 371 1
When Mr & Mrs Parker therefore ceased from soliciting a S 2 374 1
to the coast, Mr Parker gave Charlotte a more detailed S 3 375 1
"He is a warm friend to Sanditon--said Mr Parker--& his S 3 377 1
Mr Parker spoke warmly of Clara Brereton, & the interest S 3 378 1
"It was always a very comfortable house--said Mrs Parker-- S 4 380 1
delighted to see Mr Parker again, whose manners S 6 390 1
freely, I beleive, than W. Indians." observed Mr Parker.-- S 6 392 1
of life, we shall not much thank them Mr Parker."-- S 6 392 1
Well Mr Parker--and the other is a Boarding school, a S 6 393 1
Poor Mr Parker got no more credit from Lady D. than he had S 6 393 1
I beseech you Mr Parker, no Doctors here."-- S 6 394 1
"Oh! my dear Mrs Parker--you should not indeed--why should S 6 394 1
room, and she was soon introduced to Miss Diana Parker. S 9 406 1
"Excellent!--excellent!--cried Mr Parker.-- S 9 409 1
It was not a week, since Miss Diana Parker had been told S 10 412 1
She had had considerable curiosity to see Mr Arthur Parker; S 10 413 1
Not all that the whole Parker race could say among S 11 420 1
The particular introduction of Mrs G. to Miss Diana Parker, S 11 421 1
even Mr Arthur Parker, though little disposed for S 11 422 1
"The easiest thing in the world--cried Miss Diana Parker S 12 423 1
Mr Sidney Parker driving his servant in a very neat S 12 425 1
Sidney Parker was about 7 or 8 & 20, very good-looking, S 12 425 1
had been discerned by Mrs Parker; if Charlotte had not S 12 426 1

PARKLANDS (6)
De Courcy to Mrs Vernon. Parklands. LS 4 248 1
Reginald de courcy to his son. Parklands. LS 12 260 1
De Courcy to Mrs Vernon. Parklands. LS 13 262 1
you, as that Reginald should be returning to Parklands. LS 23 283 2
De Courcy to Mrs Vernon. Parklands. LS 40 308 1
day of his coming to Parklands, we had a most unexpected & LS 41 309 1

PARLEY (3)
satisfy him, and a short parley of compliment ensued. MP I 14 132 8
parley about what could be done and should be done. E I 10 87 31
ask; but a very short parley with her own heart produced E III 14 435 4

PARLIAMENT (7)
to get him into Parliament, or to see him connected with SS I 3 16 6
said Charlotte, "when he is in Parliament!--won't it? SS I 20 113 35
to attend his duty in Parliament, with whatever increase MP I 2 20 33
I dare say he <u>will</u> be in Parliament soon. MP I 17 161 14
add "you ought <u>to be</u> in Parliament, or you should have MP II 4 214 44
and as to my being in Parliament, I believe I must wait MP II 4 214 45
Sir Thomas's being in Parliament, got into the way of MP III 13 425 6

PARLIAMENTS (1)
in three successive parliaments, exertions of loyalty, and P III 1 3 3
4

PARLOUR (51)
parlour, when my brother called me out of the room. LS 23 283 3
In about ten minutes after my return to the parlour, Lady LS 23 284 6
as I was tolerably composed, I returned to the parlour. LS 24 291 15
were by themselves in the parlour; and, on Anne's quitting NA I 15 116 1
her alone in the parlour, "I am come to bid you good bye." NA I 15 122 29
alone in the parlour, some time before you left the house." NA II 3 145 12
fitted up as a dining parlour; and on their quitting it to NA II 11 213 21
house rather than remain fixed for any time in the parlour. NA II 15 240 1
his hold till he had seated her in a chair in the parlour. SS I 9 42 8

eft some time in the parlour with only him and Marianne, SS I 12 60 8
nd this dear parlour, in which our acquaintance first SS I 14 73 17
ame hastily out of the parlour apparently in violent SS I 15 75 2
nd instantly quitted the parlour to give way in solitude SS I 15 77 18
o stairs she heard the parlour door open, and , turning SS I 18 96 2
hrough the passage into the parlour, attended by Sir John. SS I 19 106 21
f the parlour and every thing in it burst forth. SS I 19 106 23
oth in the dining parlour and drawing room: to the latter, SS II 1 143 10
ne dining parlour will admit eighteen couple with ease; SS II 14 252 18
urned into the parlour to fulfil her parting injunction. SS III 10 348 34
hen they returned to the parlour where Mrs E. was sitting W 323 3
uiet warmth of a snug parlour, to the bustle, noise & W 327 7
o bustle into the parlour with the tray & the knife-case, W 344 21
old the parlour door open for Ld Osborne & Tom Musgrave.-- W 344 21
mma was the first of the females in the parlour again; on W 351 26
ne door of the best parlour a foot larger each way than W 355 28
aughters all attended her into the breakfast parlour. PP I 9 41 2
o the parlour window, and loudly seconding the invitation. PP I 15 73 10
mall summer breakfast parlour at Rosings; a comparison PP I 16 75 2
oon as they were in the parlour, he welcomed them a PP II 5 155 3
ot prefer the dining parlour for common use; it was a PP II 7 168 1
itty continued in the parlour repining at her fate in PP II 18 230 12
eard them passing through the hall to the dining parlour. PP III 9 317 9
ney sat so much longer than usual in the dining parlour, MP III 3 334 5
n the breakfast parlour, I must take leave of you here. MP III 5 364 30
ne was then taken into a parlour, so small that her first MP III 7 377 10
ut no matter--here's Fanny in the parlour, and why should MP III 7 378 12
er, and slammed the parlour door till her temples ached. MP III 7 381 25
istinguished in the parlour, except when drowned at MP III 7 382 27
alling strongly into the parlour, instead of cheering, MP III 15 439 9
ne was ready to sink, as she entered the parlour. MP III 15 444 28
n her to leave her neat parlour hung round with fancy- E I 3 22 5
e had his shepherd's son into the parlour one night on E I 4 28 6
ne opened the parlour door, and saw two gentlemen sitting E II 5 190 21
mensions of the other parlour, in the hope of E II 11 247 2
ss Smith, and Miss Bickerton, another parlour boarder at E III 3 333 5
ntering the parlour, she found those who must rouse her. E III 9 385 1
e met her at the parlour door, and hardly asking her how E III 10 392 1
2
ent in Mrs. Bates's parlour, with all the incumbrance of E III 12 417 4
e old-fashioned square parlour, with a small carpet and P III 5 40 44
t but hear what followed, for the parlour door was open. P III 12 114 60
r accommodations were limited to a noisy parlour, and a P IV 5 154 8
OUR-BOARDER (3)
om the condition of scholar to that of parlour-boarder. E I 3 22 8
e is known only as parlour-boarder at a common school. E I 8 61 38
rtune, she may be a parlour-boarder at Mrs. Goddard's E I 8 64 47
OURS (3)
ese parlours are both too small for such parties of our SS I 6 29 4
rtin's having "two parlours, two very good parlours E I 4 27 4
rlours, two very good parlours indeed; one of them quite E I 4 27 4
DY (1)
will parody them: blest Knight! whose dictatorial looks MP I 17 161 15
YS (2)
last; or if the Parrys had come, as they talked of once, NA I 2 23 25
e Parrys and Sandersons luckily are coming to-night you SS II 8 192 3
NIP (1)
rrot or parsnip, I do not consider it unwholesome." E II 3 172 19
ON (2)
t imagined a country parson ever aspired to a shrubbery MP II 4 209 15
find, is bespoke by her cousin, the young parson. P IV 6 173 49
ONAGE (80)
a well-connected parsonage, something like Fullerton, NA II 11 212 16
st of it, stood the parsonage, a new-built substantial NA II 11 212 17
are considering it as a mere parsonage, small and NA II 11 213 19
vanced towards the parsonage, and whatever the NA II 14 233 8
or I understand the parsonage is almost close to the SS III 4 290 38
tween the parsonage and the mansion-house much greater. SS III 4 290 39
ye, aye, the parsonage is but a small one," said she, SS III 4 292 55
do something to the parsonage, and make it comfortable SS III 4 292 55
visit at Delaford parsonage before Michaelmas; and I am SS III 4 292 57
gether in Delaford parsonage before Michaelmas. SS III 5 293 2
r a great deal of the parsonage at Delaford, described SS III 6 305 16
e progress of the parsonage, and direct every thing as SS III 14 374 7
d his wife in their parsonage by Michaelmas, and she SS III 14 374 7
opped beyond a doubt at the garden gate of the parsonage. W 354 28
o you see much of the parsonage family at the castle, Mr W 358 28
visit in his humble parsonage; where she had perfectly PP I 14 66 1
e mistress of Hunsford parsonage, and of assisting to PP I 17 88 14
rsonage, and every turning expected to bring it in view. PP II 5 155 2
length the parsonage was discernible. PP II 5 155 3
s arrival was soon known at the parsonage, for Mr. PP II 7 170 7
ry much admired at the parsonage, and the ladies all PP II 8 172 1
lonel Fitzwilliam had called at the parsonage more than PP II 8 172 1
the nearness of the parsonage, or the pleasantness of PP II 9 180 28
t why Mr. Darcy came so often to the parsonage, it was PP II 9 180 29
rself at the gate in the pales opposite the parsonage. PP II 10 182 1
ar, and intend to close it with a call at the parsonage. PP II 10 183 4
d turn, and they walked towards the parsonage together. PP II 10 183 6
indifferent matters till they reached the parsonage. PP II 10 186 38
this humble parsonage, I should not think any one PP II 15 216 4
vely scene in Hunsford parsonage, the difference, the PP III 2 263 10
most delightful place!--excellent parsonage house! PP III 10 328 26
to walk home to the parsonage after this conversation, MP I 1 8 9
lcome addition at the parsonage, as a desirable MP I 1 9 10
s. Norris, on quitting the parsonage, removed first to MP I 3 23 1
are-rooms at the parsonage had never been wanted, but MP I 3 28 38
ants arrived at the parsonage, and these events over, MP I 3 31 58
tiful doings--the parsonage she believed had never been MP I 3 31 59
fine lady in a country parsonage was quite out of place. MP I 3 31 59
mpany with him at the parsonage, he was no longer MP I 5 44 2
ry was satisfied with the parsonage as a present home, MP I 5 47 26
e dined at the parsonage, with the rest of you, which MP I 5 48 30
did a vast deal in that way at the parsonage; we made MP I 6 54 9
mund was at the parsonage every day to be indulged with MP I 7 64 12
nny could not wonder that Edmund was at the parsonage MP I 7 65 14
e mare was only to be taken down to the parsonage half MP I 7 66 14
mmand a view of the parsonage and all its demesnes, MP I 7 67 16
mund and Julia were invited to dine at the parsonage, MP I 7 70 30
m to walk down to the parsonage directly, and call on Mr. MP I 8 75 1
. Rushworth came back from the parsonage successful; and MP I 8 77 7
ere is the parsonage; a tidy looking house, and I MP I 8 82 34
e room, fresh from the parsonage, calling out, "no want MP I 13 129 38
go down to the parsonage herself with the offer of MP I 14 136 22
turn from the parsonage, Mr. Rushworth arrived, and MP I 15 138 1
ere were not fewer smiles at the parsonage than at the MP I 17 159 6
lking up from the parsonage, made no change in her wish MP I 18 168 14
em and spending the evening at the parsonage. MP II 1 177 5
t they had seen no one from the parsonage--not a MP II 2 192 11
were talking of you at the parsonage, and those were MP II 3 198 13
home did her value increase, but at the parsonage too. MP II 4 205 2
ower close to the parsonage, and being descried from one MP II 4 205 3
e had scarcely ever been at the parsonage since the MP II 4 206 5
lked down to the parsonage on purpose to bring her back. MP II 4 214 46
the parsonage, you are not to be taking place of her. MP II 5 221 32
approaching the parsonage they passed close by the MP II 5 222 45
leration of the neighbourly attempts at the parsonage. MP II 7 238 1
reeing to dine at the parsonage, when the general MP II 7 238 2
e--to be presumed the parsonage, within a stone's throw MP II 7 241 13
something above a mere parsonage house, above the MP II 7 243 27
e walked down to the parsonage without much fear of MP II 8 256 14
e met Miss Crawford within a few yards of the parsonage, MP II 8 257 15
to suppose, was at the parsonage; and left alone to bear MP II 9 267 22
from the parsonage, and found Edmund in the east room.-- MP II 9 267 23
Mansfield, had a very different character at the parsonage. MP II 11 285 15
inmate of Mansfield parsonage, and replied but to invite MP II 12 295 22
It was all known at the parsonage, where he loved to talk MP III 2 331 19
He had dined at the parsonage only the preceding day. MP III 4 349 24
the conjugal manners of Mansfield parsonage with respect. MP III 5 361 16
He and I can go to the parsonage, you know, and be no MP III 14 435 14
On that event they removed to Mansfield, and the parsonage MP III 17 473 33
the compact, tight parsonage, enclosed in its own neat P III 5 36 20
PARSONAGE-HOUSE (5)
an ordinary parsonage-house must be very disagreeable." NA II 5 157 10
A butcher hard by in the village, and the parsonage-house SS II 8 197 22
and living in a small parsonage-house, diverted him beyond SS III 5 298 33
She saw them in an instant in their parsonage-house; saw SS III 12 357 3
beginning with his parsonage-house, and leading naturally PP I 15 70 3
PARSONAGES (1)
there are few country parsonages in England half so good. NA II 11 213 19
PARSONS (2)
parsons were very inferior even to what they are now." MP I 9 87 15
gales dispense to Templars modesty, to parsons sense.' MP I 17 161 15
PART (433)
young, I must for my own part declare that I have seldom LS 6 251 1
will be wanting on her part to counteract me; but having LS 10 257 1
& Frederica spends great part of the day there; practising LS 17 271 7
if you do not take my part, & persuade her to break it off, LS 21 279 1
kindness of taking my part with her, & persuading her to LS 21 279 1
come, no want of cordiality on my part will keep her away. LS 27 297 3
If we are to part, it will at least be handsome to take LS 35 305 1
You have heard of course that the Manwarings are to part; LS 38 307 2
No unkindness however on the part of Lady Susan appeared. LS 42 312 3
variety of reasons how to part with her daughter; & as, LS 42 312 5
journey was done, on the part of the Morlands, with a NA I 2 19 3
For my part I have not seen any thing I like so well in NA I 2 22 11
a very distinguished part in the events of the evening, to NA I 2 23 27
to be visited; some new part of the town to be looked at; NA I 3 25 1
and that they should there part with a most affectionate NA I 4 34 7
her being occupied by any part of that voluminous NA I 5 38 4
digression on James's part, in praise of Miss Thorpe, till NA I 7 51 54
that part of the room where she had left Mr. Tilney. NA I 8 55 10
There is not the hundredth part of the wine consumed in NA I 9 64 22
reply, of which no part was very distinct, except the NA I 9 64 26
"Did she tell you what part of Gloucestershire they come NA I 9 68 45
The female part of the Thorpe family, attended by James NA I 10 71 8
People that marry can never part, but must go and keep NA I 10 77 32
who was never in the same part of the house for ten NA I 12 95 17
Was it the part of a friend thus to expose her feelings to NA I 13 98 3
at a most interesting part, by running away with the NA I 14 107 9
larger and more trifling part of the sex, imbecility in NA I 14 111 29
city of Bath, as unworthy to make part of a landscape. NA I 14 111 29
she really felt on hearing this part of the arrangement. NA I 14 115 51
I cannot say I admire her taste; and for my part I was NA I 14 115 52
"For my own part," said Isabella, "my wishes are so NA I 15 119 20
Tilney, made but a small part of Catherine's speculation. NA II 2 138 1
"Since they can consent to part with you," said he, "we NA II 2 140 9
building still making a part of the present dwelling NA II 2 141 13
reason to suppose that the part of the Abbey you inhabit NA II 5 158 17
part of the hanging more violently agitated than the rest. NA II 5 159 19
having spent the best part of an hour in her arrangements, NA II 6 168 10
finding any thing in any part of the cabinet, and was not NA II 6 169 11
back into the further part of the cavity, apparently for NA II 6 169 11
his country; and for his part, to his uncritical palate, NA II 7 175 12
came in, spent, on the part of his young guest, in no very NA II 8 182 1
Miss Tilney, understanding in part her friend's curiosity NA II 8 182 1
visited the greatest part; though, on being told that, NA II 8 183 2
out her days; for what part of the Abbey could be more NA II 8 188 17
"Oh! no; she shewed me over the greatest part on Saturday-- NA II 9 195 15
But in the central part of England there was surely some NA II 10 200 3
marrying her, than at any other part of the story." NA II 10 204 20
Stay-----there is one part-----" recollecting with a blush NA II 10 205 21
would part with one gentleman before the other was secured. NA II 10 206 31
reached the ornamental part of the premises, consisting of NA II 11 214 25
A saunter into other meadows, and through part of the NA II 11 214 26
time be ashamed of the part he had acted, there could be NA II 13 222 8
think the worse of me for the part I am obliged to perform. NA II 13 223 13
My dear Catherine, we are to part. NA II 13 224 13
I am very, very sorry we are to part-- so soon, and so NA II 13 224 14
And if we are to part, a few hours sooner or later, you NA II 13 226 24
the solemn promise on the part of his son in their favour, SS I 3 14 2
who had since spent the greatest part of his time there. SS I 3 15 4
And to what part of it?" SS I 5 25 1
The first part of their journey was performed in too SS I 6 28 1
one of them with perhaps a part of the other, and so leave SS I 6 29 4
He was a blessing to all the juvenile part of the SS I 7 32 2
which was to form a great part of the morning's amusement; SS I 12 62 28
they should part without a mutual exchange of confidence?" SS I 15 80 36
Has he been acting a part in his behaviour to your sister SS I 15 80 38
ungenerous, a suspicious part by our family, he might well SS I 15 81 43
he is no stranger in this part of the world; and who has SS I 15 81 44
the whole night, and she wept the greatest part of it. SS I 16 83 1
"But gaiety never was a part of my character." SS I 17 93 34
"Nor do I think it a part of Marianne's," said Elinor; "I SS I 17 93 35
excuse for every thing strange on the part of her son. SS I 19 101 2
"Is Mr. Willoughby much known in your part of SS I 20 116 57
to be met with in every part of England, under every SS I 21 119 3
Lady Middleton; and for my part, I love to see children SS I 21 122 19
I suppose you have not so many in this part of the world; SS I 21 123 26
for my part, I think they are a vast addition always." SS I 21 123 26
For my part, I think they are vastly agreeable, provided SS I 21 123 28
falsehood of the greatest part of what she had been saying; SS I 22 132 41
that, though for my own part, I could give up every SS II 2 147 7
success in a less elegant part of the town, she had SS II 3 153 1
Business on Sir John's part, and a violent cold on her own, SS II 5 170 28
For my part, I think the less that is said about such SS II 8 196 18
distrust the truth of any part of it, for she listened to SS II 10 212 1
a conquest; but for my part I declare I never think about SS II 10 218 26
on my part, to make him pleased with you and your family. SS II 11 224 24
repetition of any other part of the pain that had attended SS II 13 245 47
knew the price of every part of Marianne's dress; could SS II 14 249 8
for some delay on their part that might inconvenience SS II 14 249 9
"For my own part," said he, "I am excessively fond of a SS II 14 251 17
not know whether she should ever be able to part with them. SS II 14 254 28
I am sure, for my part, I should never have known he did SS III 2 272 12
And for my part, I was all in a fright for fear your SS III 2 275 22
good on Miss Dashwood's part, either present or future, SS III 5 293 2
her by taking Edward's part, could overcome her SS III 5 294 3
And how you will explain away any part of your guilt in SS III 8 322 35
to suspect any part of what had really passed between Mrs. SS III 8 324 42
Have I explained away any part of my guilt?" SS III 8 329 65
not always acting a part, not always deceiving me;--but SS III 10 344 17
restraints, by taking any part in those offices of general SS III 10 346 28
She rejoiced in his being cleared from some part of his SS III 11 349 1
understanding some part, but not the whole, of the case, SS III 12 359 13
I spent the greatest part of my time there from eighteen SS III 13 362 5
After a proper resistance on the part of Mrs. Ferrars, SS III 14 373 1
husbands of course took a part, as well as the frequent SS III 14 377 11
I could do very well single for my own part--a little W 317 2
delicacy should make any part of the scanty communication W 321 2
was the only unpleasant part of her engagement, the only W 335 13
he had to dispose of, or any part of it at her mercy."-- W 352 26
to beleive it no sacrifice on her sister's part.-- W 361 30
for two dances; and during part of that time, Mr. Darcy PP I 3 11 7

country for my part, except the shops and public places. PP I 9 43 21
For my part, Mr. Bingley, I always keep servants that can PP I 9 44 29
She performed her part indeed without much graciousness, PP I 9 45 35
or society; the greatest part of his life having been PP I 15 70 1
and excessively generous and disinterested on his own part. PP I 15 70 2
he had all the best part of beauty, a fine countenance, a PP I 15 72 8
same park, the greatest part of our youth was passed PP I 16 81 37
rather believe she derives part of her abilities from her PP I 16 84 58
from her rank and fortune, part from her authoritative PP I 16 84 58
This part of his intelligence, though unheard by Lydia, PP I 18 89 3
The latter part of this address was scarcely heard by PP I 18 92 24
which he supposed a regular part of the business. PP I 19 104 1
on my side, nobody takes part with me, I am cruelly used, PP II 3 113 26
"I am far from attributing any part of Mr. Bingley's PP II 1 136 17
not try to part us; if he were so, they could not succeed. PP II 1 137 24
The first part of Mrs. Gardiner's business on her arrival, PP II 2 139 3
When this was done, she had a less active part to play. PP II 2 139 3
We live in so different a part of town, all our PP II 2 141 12
more suffer him to call on Jane in such a part of London! PP II 2 141 13
the officers always made part of it, of which officers Mr. PP II 2 142 18
time in that very part of Derbyshire, to which he belonged. PP II 2 142 19
going to-morrow into that part of the town, and I shall PP II 3 147 22
She would be in nobody's way, you know, in that part of PP II 8 173 10
my real character, in a part of the world, where I had PP II 8 174 15
No motive can excuse the unjust and ungenerous part you PP II 11 191 12
After walking two or three times along that part of the PP II 12 195 2
The part which I acted, is now to be explained.-- PP II 12 198 5
There is but one part of my conduct in the whole affair, PP II 12 199 5
When she came to that part of the letter in which her PP II 13 208 10
For my part, I am inclined to believe it all Mr. Darcy's, PP II 17 225 10
For my part, I am determined never to speak of it again to PP II 17 227 27
or augment them by anxiety, was no part of her disposition. PP II 18 232 21
which had marked the early part of their acquaintance, PP II 18 233 25
was Elizabeth disposed to part from him in good humour, PP II 18 233 26
in the scheme, every part of it would have been perfect. PP II 19 237 3
A scheme of which every part promises delight, can never PP II 19 237 4
A small part of Derbyshire is all the present concern. PP II 19 240 12
they pointed out, she distinguished no part of the scene. PP III 1 253 55
overspreading many, and occasionally part of the stream. PP III 1 253 57
some part of her family were connected with that corps. PP III 3 269 10
to him some part of what she had been saying to his sister. PP III 3 270 12
"For my own part," she rejoined, "I must confess that I PP III 3 271 15
Had I but explained some part of it only--some part of PP II 4 7 12
my part, that might offer consolation to such distress.-- PP III 4 278 20
know in what part of the town he has now concealed himself. PP III 6 295 6
most anxious part of each was when the post was expected. PP III 6 296 9
shall be wanting on my part, that can alleviate so severe PP III 6 296 11
friend, that had attended her from that part of the world. PP III 6 298 16
enough to find out in what part of London they were. PP III 7 302 14
It is an advantage to have it so far from this part of the PP III 8 313 19
I should have considered it as part of my duty, and the PP III 10 328 28
whisper, "the men shan't come and part us, I am determined. PP III 12 341 16
17
Darcy had walked away to another part of the room. PP III 12 341 18
expectation; and on the part of Mrs. Bennet and Kitty, PP III 14 351 2
man, who I believe will soon become a part of the family." PP III 14 352 8
family objections on the part of my cousin, she would PP III 15 363 22
There was one part especially, the opening of it, which I PP III 16 368 20
farther resistance on the part of his aunt, her resentment PP III 19 388 12
little girl the hundredth part of the regard I bear your MP I 1 7 8
at least on the part of the sons, who at seventeen and MP I 2 12 3
worse to endure on the part of Tom, than that sort of MP I 2 17 22
part of my future days will be spent in utter seclusion. MP I 3 29 48
at a time when a large part of his income was unsettled, MP I 4 36 7
The most objectionable part is, that the alteration of MP I 5 49 32
That is the faulty part of the present system. MP I 5 49 32
It is certainly the modestest part of the business. MP I 5 50 39
For my own part, if I had any thing within the fiftieth MP I 6 53 9
thing within the fiftieth part of the size of Sotherton, I MP I 6 53 9
It was no part of my education; and the only dose I ever MP I 6 57 31
Mrs. Grant hearing the latter part of this speech, MP I 6 61 58
opinions; and for my own part I have been long wishing to MP I 6 62 58
"No part of it fatigues me but getting off this horse, I MP I 7 68 20
set off across another part of the park; her feelings of MP I 7 69 21
to Fanny, and obliged her to drink the greater part. MP I 7 74 57
few good, but the larger part were family portraits, no MP I 9 84 3
It was a valuable part of former times. MP I 9 86 12
The lower part of the house had been now entirely shown, MP I 9 89 31
part of her education, made her miserable under it. MP I 9 91 36
They are known to the largest part only as preachers. MP I 9 93 49
For my part, I can see nothing in him." MP I 10 102 41
of the house from that part of the park, and will be MP I 10 102 47
it was rather a pity they should have been obliged to part. MP I 12 117 13
in which he had borne a part, was within two days of MP I 13 121 1
"A trifling part," said he, "and not at all to my taste, MP I 13 122 2
Sir Henry wanted the part himself; whereas it was MP I 13 122 2
will be happy to take the part of any old Duenna or tame MP I 13 129 38
Not a tolerable woman's part in the play----- MP I 14 131 3
One could not expect any body to take such a part----- MP I 14 131 3
If a part is insignificant, the greater our credit in MP I 14 131 5
I take any part you choose to give me, so as it be comic. MP I 14 131 5
else wants it--a trifling part, but the sort of thing I MP I 14 132 7
with the greatest alacrity offer his services for the part. MP I 14 132 8
Bertram, who asserted the part of Amelia to be in every MP I 14 133 10
part of Agatha, or it will be the ruin of all my solemnity. MP I 14 133 11
Cottager's wife is a very pretty part I assure you. MP I 14 134 12
The most trivial, paltry, insignificant part; the merest MP I 14 134 13
If the part is trifling she will have more credit in MP I 14 134 14
We must not allow her to accept the part. MP I 14 135 15
I have seen good actresses fail in the part. MP I 14 135 15
It is not at all the part for her. MP I 14 135 16
She looks the part, and I am persuaded will do it MP I 14 135 16
sure I would give up the part to Julia most willingly, but MP I 14 136 21
Miss Crawford accepted the part very readily, and soon MP I 15 138 1
she very kindly took his part in hand, and curtailed every MP I 15 138 1
We have cast almost every part." MP I 15 139 6
she answered, "I take the part which Lady Ravenshaw was to MP I 15 139 8
Say that, on examining the part, you feel yourself unequal MP I 15 140 15
"If I were to decline the part," said Maria with renewed MP I 15 141 19
having only his own part, and his own dress in his head, MP I 15 142 24
"Anhalt is a heavy part." MP I 15 144 30
"I should be but too happy in taking the part if it were MP I 15 144 33
"Your brother should take the part," said Mr. Yates, in a MP I 15 144 34
particularly dislike the part of Amelia if well supported-- MP I 15 144 38
"If any part could tempt you to act, I suppose it would be MP I 15 144 40
It need not frighten you; it is a nothing of a part, a MP I 15 145 47
Rushworth, "what would you do with such a part as mine? MP I 15 145 48
Learn part, and we will teach you all the rest. MP I 15 146 50
Take the part with a good grace, and let us hear no more MP I 15 146 53
for him to undertake the part of Anhalt in addition to the MP I 15 148 58
probably engaged in the part with different expectations-- MP I 16 154 14
agreed to undertake the part for which Fanny had been MP I 17 159 6
object of interest, their part, their dress, their MP I 17 159 6
Edmund, between his theatrical and his real part, between MP I 17 163 21
He had learned his part--all his parts--for he took every MP I 18 164 1
was behind-hand with his part, and that it was misery to MP I 18 164 2
Every body had a part either too long or too short;-- MP I 18 165 2
indeed, regretted that his part was not more considerable, MP I 18 166 4
his part herself, but without his being much the forwarder. MP I 18 166 4
for me if I had nothing but the executive part to do.-- MP I 18 166 6
"Have you ever happened to look at the part I mean?" MP I 18 168 19
read the part, for I can say very little of it." MP I 18 169 20

"if Miss Price would be so good as to read the part." MP I 18 171 28
"You have only to read the part," said Henry Crawford with MP I 18 172 30
Fanny, I am sure you know the part." MP I 18 172 31
unusual noise in the other part of the house, had MP I 18 172 33
in his own house, making part of a ridiculous exhibition MP II 1 183 23
Conversation with any of them occupied but a small part of MP II 2 190 9
They seem to belong to us--they seem to be part of MP II 3 196 2
understood by the greater part of those who have known you MP II 3 198 13
from soon discerning some part of the truth--that Mr. MP II 3 200 19
not without some modest reluctance on her part, to come in. MP II 4 205 3
It certainly may secure all the myrtle and turkey part of MP II 4 213 36
It began, on Lady Bertram's part, with, "I have something MP II 5 218 12
done away all Mrs. Grant's part of the favour, that Fanny, MP II 5 220 29
not required to take any part--there was so much to be MP II 5 223 48
for him to learn his part--in trying to give him a brain MP II 5 224 53
pursued with "no, no, you must not part with the queen. MP II 7 244 28
Your sister does not part with the queen. MP II 7 244 28
of appropriating any part of the compliment to herself or MP II 7 247 37
was a most important part of it to Fanny, being more than MP II 8 256 14
assure you it makes none in my willingness to part with it. MP II 8 259 22
rather part with and see in your possession than any other. MP II 8 260 22
she would rather not part with it, when it is not wanted?" MP II 9 263 13
it up with the chain, as the dearest part of the gift. MP II 9 265 19
to move all the chaperons to a better part of the room. MP II 10 277 16
for the sake of securing her at that part of the evening. MP II 10 278 20
But still his attentions made no part of her satisfaction. MP II 10 278 20
to, during the greatest part of the evening, her hand MP II 10 278 20
had made in that room, and all that part of the house. MP II 11 283 6
"I only heard a part of the letter; it was to my uncle-- MP II 11 288 23
which makes so essential a part of every woman's worth in MP II 12 294 16
no want of delicacy on his part could make a trifle to her. MP II 13 301 7
or entreaty, though to part with her at a moment when her MP II 13 302 9
saving it would be to Sir Thomas, as with any part of it. MP II 13 304 19
an unusual step in that part of the house; it was her MP III 1 312 4
things only in part, and judging partially by the event.-- MP III 1 313 12
having performed one part of my commission, and shewn you MP III 1 314 16
can judge, matrimony makes no part of his plans or thought. MP III 1 317 34
half Mr. Crawford's estate, or a tenth part of his merits. MP III 1 319 39
She had no one to take her part, to counsel, or speak for MP III 1 321 46
It is a part of an Englishman's constitution. MP III 3 338 13
No man of any brain can open at a good part of one of his MP III 3 338 13
undertake the part, we must not be surprised at the rest." MP III 4 350 28
and ingenuousness, which are so much a part of herself. MP III 4 351 36
Here we were, just in this part of the room, here was your MP III 5 358 7
Fanny roused herself, and replying only in part, said, " MP III 5 359 11
him and some part of this family in the summer and autumn. MP III 5 363 21
though we shall nominally part in the breakfast parlour, I MP III 5 364 30
like to think of; and that part of the arrangement was, MP III 6 370 13
at Mansfield; and for part of one of those days the young MP III 6 372 21
involved Mr. Crawford, made no part of their conversation. MP III 7 375 3
of being on shore some part of every day before they MP III 7 384 35
her mother meant to part with her when her year was up. MP III 7 385 38
I have no hope of ever being settled; and if I was to part MP III 7 385 39
to put an hundredth part of my great mind on paper, so I MP III 12 415 2
it to spread over the largest part of a page of her own.-- MP III 13 425 6
the most respectable part of her character, her friendship MP III 14 433 12
and that part of the family, at least, are aware of it. MP III 14 433 13
If it be so, I am sure you must be included in that part, MP III 14 433 13
that part, that discerning part, and therefore intreat you MP III 14 433 13
but the evil of a few days may be blotted out in part. MP III 14 434 13
Fanny's disgust at the greater part of this letter, with MP III 14 435 15
and began to take in some part of the misery that must MP III 15 440 19
Was it part of your last sermon? MP III 16 458 30
of what was lost, and in part reconciling him to himself; MP III 17 462 6
she seemed a part of himself, that must be borne for ever. MP III 17 465 15
But it was possible to part with her, because Susan MP III 17 472 31
and hating to part with them; hating change of every kind. E I 1 7 10
when he was now obliged to part with Miss Taylor too; and E I 1 7 10
others;" rejoined Mr. Woodhouse, understanding but in part. E I 1 13 45
never cooled, and who could ill bear to part with her! E I 2 18 10
formed naturally a great part of her conversation--and but E I 4 27 4
the Mr. Martin, who bore a part in the narrative, and was E I 4 27 5
Part of her meaning was to conceal some favourite thoughts E I 5 41 31
It would amuse away the difficulties of her part, and E I 6 46 25
"Nor if you were, could I ever bear to part with you, my E I 7 55 38
to herself through a great part of this speech, "how do E I 8 60 28
appear to have been any part of their plan to introduce E I 8 62 42
he had given; and the part which he was persuaded Emma had E I 8 66 55
with explanations of every part as she proceeded--and he E I 9 78 51
gates, pools, and pollards of this part of Highbury." E I 10 83 5
"Part of my lace is gone," said she, "and I do not know E I 10 89 37
You and I, Emma, will venture to take the part of the poor E I 11 95 18
cried his wife, hearing and understanding only in part.-- E I 11 95 19
I never can comprehend how Mr. Weston could part with him. E I 11 96 25
part of his life, and whose attachments were strong. E I 12 100 16
Our part of London is so very superior to most others!-- E I 12 103 37
I should be unwilling, I own, to live in any other part of E I 12 103 37
and Mrs. Campbell will not be able to part with her at all. E I 12 104 46
my taking my family to one part of the coast or another?-- E I 12 106 60
was of use to the nervous part of her complaint, I hope; E I 13 114 32
comfortably; and for my part, I would rather, under such E I 13 116 43
part of the common field there will be the other at hand. E I 15 126 10
Every part of it brought pain and humiliation, of some E I 16 134 1
It was foolish, it was wrong, to take so active part in E I 16 136 10
(or, being acting a part, perhaps rather more,) at the E I 18 145 5
soon overcome all that part of her reserve which ought to E II 3 171 7
a conviction of some part of what had passed between them. E II 3 173 26
Part of every winter she had been used to spend in Bath; E II 4 183 9
he had not been acting a part, or making a parade of E II 6 197 4
the male part of Mr. Cox's family, the lawyer of Highbury. E II 8 214 13
That very dear part of Emma, her fancy, received an E II 8 214 13
this without effort; the first part is so very trifling. E II 8 229 95
Here ceased the concert part of the evening, for Miss E II 8 229 98
of even the busiest part of Highbury;--Mr. Perry walking E II 9 233 24
I honour that part of the attention particularly; it shews E II 10 242 21
on Frank Churchill's part, that the space which a quarter E II 11 249 12
and Emma felt so sorry to part, and foresaw so great a E II 12 261 37
was to mark their parting; but still they were to part. E II 13 264 1
the letter in the material part, its sentiments, she yet E II 13 266 6
was; placed exactly in the same part of the house. E II 14 273 19
equal; and the greater part of her new acquaintance, E II 15 281 2
Upon her speaking her wonder aloud on that part of the E II 15 285 16
I always take the part of my own sex. E II 18 306 12
no service to the wilful or nervous part of her disorder. E III 1 316 6
He came to the part of the room where the sitters-by were E III 2 327 34
It was the end of an old pencil,--the part without any E III 4 339 17
I knew it was--but had not resolution enough to part with E III 4 340 24
chosen to conceal a deeper game on Frank Churchill's part. E III 5 348 21
twentieth part of a moment, did such an idea occur to me. E III 5 350 35
of nonsense in it--but the part which is capable of being E III 5 350 37
and Emma found it the pleasantest part of the day. E III 6 361 40
be cured of wishing that he would part with his black mare. E III 6 361 41
round in the highest part of the gardens, where no damps E III 6 361 42
be very trying for us to part with her, after having had E III 8 378 8
'You and I must part. E III 8 384 33
movement of more than common friendliness on his part.-- E III 9 385 7
Some part of his conduct we cannot excuse." E III 10 396 38
was a period in the early part of our acquaintance, when I E III 10 396 41
"Nay, dear Emma, now I must take his part; for though he E III 10 397 49
Every other part of her mind was disgusting. E III 11 412 46
better; had she done her part towards intimacy; had she E III 12 421 17
And now I come to the principal, the only important part E III 14 438 8

the whole, but her quickness must have penetrated a part. E III 14 438 8
Part only of this answer, however, was admitted. E III 15 448 31
I had always a part to act.-- E III 16 459 49
I am amused by one part of John's letter--did you notice E III 17 465 25
Mrs. Weston was acting no part, feigning no feelings in E III 17 467 31
There was only a small part of his estate that Sir Walter P III 1 10 20
part of our suffering, as it always does of our conduct. P III 2 12 4
Russell's spending some part of every winter there; and to P III 2 14 10
much strengthened by one part, and a very material part of P III 2 15 13
part, and a very material part of the scheme, which had P III 2 15 13
actions and designs of one part of the world from the P III 3 17 4
kind word or look on the part of her sister;--but Lady P III 4 27 5
by the wrong of one part of the Kellynch-Hall plan, when P III 5 34 11
sister are gone; and what part of Bath do you think they P III 6 42 1
best, and to be able to part and eat their dinner in P III 7 54 4
It included nearly a third part of her own life. P III 7 60 28
Wentworth, hearing only in part, and probably not having P III 8 67 25
happiest part of my life has been spent on board a ship. P III 8 70 54
Unintentionally she returned to that part of the room; he P III 8 72 58
59

to the principal part of her family, and be giving bad P III 9 76 13
be shut up as he is; but what can we do? we cannot part." P III 12 107 24
There was too much wind to make the high part of the new P III 12 109 32
every thing ready on his part, and to be soon followed by P III 12 115 65
convenience in the lowest part of the street; but his P III 12 115 68
delighted, and for my part, I thought it was all settled; P IV 2 130 5
politely taken as possible, but her part must follow then. P IV 3 143 18
had been led among that part of mankind which made her P IV 5 156 12
"Mrs. Harville must be an odd mother to part with them so " P IV 6 163 7
So ended the first part, which had been afterwards put P IV 6 164 8
to be situated in such a part of Bath as it might suit P IV 6 165 9
carriage, in the lower part of the town, and return alone P IV 6 168 25
as to have him in view the greater part of the street. P IV 7 178 28
side of the way, and this part of street, as being the P IV 7 179 30
The part which provoked her most, was that in all this P IV 7 179 31
voice in which the latter part had been uttered, and in P IV 8 183 11
happen to be in the same part of the room, but he was not, P IV 8 186 22
them through the greater part of the morning, was, that P IV 9 211 103
and that he would be gone the greater part of two days. P IV 10 214 13
and in a very fine country--fine part of Dorsetshire. P IV 10 217 20
part so well, that I have liked him the better ever since." P IV 10 219 26
or rather claimed as a part of the family; and in return, P IV 10 220 31
"Here, Frederick, you and I part company, I believe," said P IV 11 236 36
having had no fall, could part with her cheerfully, and P IV 11 238 47
and every other painful part of the morning dissipated by P IV 11 245 77
strong sense of duty is no bad part of a woman's portion." P IV 11 246 80
at present but a small part of the share of ten thousand P IV 12 248 1
gifted in this part of understanding than her young friend. P IV 12 249 4
Tunbridge towards that part of the Sussex coast which lies S 1 363 1
parish of Sanditon, with manor & mansion house made a part. S 3 375 1
succeeding to the greater part of all that she had to give- S 3 377 1
house in a very inferior part of London, cd offer.-- S 3 378 1
They were out in the very quietest part of a watering- S 6 389 1
And here they were obliged to part--Miss D. being too much S 8 404 1
part of his literary hours, & formed his character.-- S 8 404 1
but the inferior part of the character he had to play.-- S 8 405 2
employed; part was laid out in a zeal for being useful.-- S 10 412 1
Mr & Mrs P. spent a great part of the eveng at the hotel; S 10 413 1
To say the truth nerves are the worst part of my S 10 415 1
No part of it however seemed to trouble her long. S 11 420 1
many miniatures in another part of the room, little S 12 427 1

PARTAKE (5)
Be assured that I partake in all your feelings, & do not LS 38 306 1
Here was knowledge in which no one could partake; and she PP II 17 227 25
Her daughters were eagerly called to partake of her joy. PP III 11 333 31
having asked more than Jane Fairfax to partake of it. E II 15 283 9
with one window down, to partake of this al-fresco party; E III 6 357 33

PARTED (76)
invitation when we last parted, of spending some weeks LS 1 243 1
every feature when we last parted, were partially subdued. LS 25 292 2
Since we parted yesterday, I have received from LS 34 304 1
Lady Susan, but to tell us that they are parted forever! LS 40 308 1
she got back to town, than as if parted from him for ever. LS 41 309 1
They danced again; and, when the assembly closed, parted, NA I 3 29 52
Oh! I must tell you, that just after we parted yesterday, NA I 6 41 16
her before they parted to dance with him that evening. NA I 7 50 44
This civility was duly returned; and they parted--on Miss NA I 10 73 21
Before they parted, however, it was agreed that the NA I 12 95 16
most graceful bows she had ever beheld, when they parted. NA I 13 103 28
Miss Tilney, before they parted, addressing herself with NA I 14 114 49
Again they parted--but Eleanor was called back in half a NA II 7 181 41
We parted at last by mutual consent--happy for me had we NA II 10 202 7
of such a journey, parted from her without any doubt of NA II 14 235 13
herself with having parted from Eleanor coldly; with NA II 14 235 14
The General was furious in his anger, and they parted in NA II 15 248 16
not resent it; and they parted, endeavouring to hope that NA II 16 250 3
Consider," she added, "that when the money is once parted SS I 2 9 7
when Harry will regret that so large a sum was parted with. SS I 2 9 8
He had just parted from my sister, had seen her leave him SS I 15 81 43
But Colonel, where have you been to since we parted? SS II 4 163 18
You must be very much altered indeed since we parted, if SS II 7 187 40
The morning that we parted too! SS II 7 189 46
finding out before they parted, how much her washing cost SS II 14 249 8
sake, and would have parted for ever on the spot, would he SS III 2 277 30
Elinor did not offer to detain him; and they parted, with SS III 4 290 43
parted, gave her a pressing invitation to visit her there. SS III 6 301 2
wife's words, and parted with the last relics of Marianne. SS III 8 329 63
done away, that when we parted, he almost shook me by the SS III 8 330 69
Some doubts always lingered in her mind when they parted, SS III 14 376 11
Emma & Mrs Blake parted as old acquaintance, & Charles W 335 13
In Meryton they parted; the two youngest repaired to the PP I 7 32 41
for Jane; and when they parted, after assuring the latter PP I 12 60 5
was very cheering, and they parted in mutual good spirits. PP I 15 74 11
down the other dance and parted in silence; on each side PP I 18 94 43
favourable that when they parted at night, she would have PP I 22 121 1
of her hints, they parted; a wonderful instance of advice PP II 3 145 10
sincere regard; and she parted from him convinced, that PP II 4 151 3
When they parted, Lady Catherine, with great condescension, PP II 14 214 21
Elizabeth; and they parted at last with mutual civility, PP II 18 235 39
manner since they last parted, every sentence thet he PP III 1 252 52
and they parted on each side with the utmost politeness. PP III 1 257 66
occurred ere they parted, which, in her anxious PP III 2 262 8
In the hall they parted. PP III 16 371 46
I could not have parted with you, my Lizzy, to any one PP III 17 377 37
have passed since you parted, have not been spent on your MP I 3 33 64
and the two families parted again, he should think it MP I 7 65 14
When they parted at night, Edmund asked Fanny whether she MP I 7 69 26
and the opinion of the groom, from whom he had just parted. MP I 12 118 22
but as it was, they parted with looks on his side of MP II 9 270 40
they had parted at last with mutual vexation. MP II 10 279 21
that they had hardly parted friends at the ball,) she MP II 11 286 15
grateful joy, and the gentlemen parted the best of friends. MP III 2 329 13
Before they parted, she had to thank him for another MP III 10 406 22
morrow, &c. and so they parted--Fanny in a state of actual MP III 10 406 22
which the daughters were parted with, and just in time to MP III 15 445 31
Bertram, she could not be parted with willingly by her. MP III 17 472 31
The friends from whom she had just parted, though very E I 3 23 10
since we have parted, I can never remember Emma's omitting E I 5 37 8
We will not be parted. E I 7 54 31
herself; but she was too much beloved to be parted with. E II 2 164 6
agitation; and when they parted, Emma observed her to be E II 5 186 2
it up, and never parted with it again from that moment." E III 4 339 18
and how they parted, Mr. Knightley could not tell. E III 5 349 25
final arrangement for the next day's scheme, they parted. E III 6 366 74
They parted thorough friends, however; she could not be E III 9 386 8
to prevail, before we parted at Weymouth, and to induce E III 14 437 8
it was, just before they parted, that the two young aunts P III 7 54 4
He had been absent only two Sundays; and when they parted, P III 9 78 19
considerable hill, which parted Uppercross and Winthrop, P III 10 85 13
to feel that they had parted with Captain Wentworth long, P III 11 96 11
may be imagined, they parted from Captain and Mrs. P III 12 108 30
had done when they last parted;" but Sir Walter had "not P IV 3 141 12
Twelve years were gone since they had parted, and each P IV 5 153 6
him--and they parted, to meet again within a few hours.-- S 12 425 1

PARTIAL (36)
I cannot help fancying that she is growing partial to my LS 18 272 1
must confess herself very partial to the profession;" and NA I 5 36 2
fond of her brother, and partial to all his endowments, NA I 15 118 12
And why had she been so partial to that grove? NA II 7 180 37
partial though stronger illumination of a treacherous lamp. NA II 9 190 1
suddenly turned all his partial regard for their daughter NA II 14 234 10
steps, attracted by the partial sunshine of a showery sky, SS I 9 40 3
His visit afforded her but a very partial satisfaction, SS I 18 96 1
grew more and more partial to the house and environs-- SS I 19 101 1
from the Middletons' partial acquaintance with him; and SS I 20 114 43
from the excess of their partial affection for herself, SS II 1 141 5
hurt that a man so partial to her sister should perceive SS II 4 162 8
Mrs. Jennings, perhaps satisfied with the partial SS III 7 314 23
"But if a woman is partial to a man, and does not PP I 6 22 5
conduct; but even this partial communication gave her a PP I 21 120 30
To Caroline's assertion of her brother's being partial to PP II 1 133 3
My father, however, is partial to Mr. Wickham. PP II 3 144 7
persuade herself that he is really partial to Miss Darcy. PP II 3 148 26
possibility of his being partial to her, but Elizabeth PP II 9 181 30
that she had been blind, partial, prejudiced, absurd. PP II 13 208 7
to whom she believed her partial, to make her betray a PP III 3 269 10
but she still thought him partial to Jane, and she wavered PP III 11 332 18
your sister were still partial to Bingley, and if she were, PP III 18 382 16
disposed to give them but partial expression, began to see MP II 1 183 24
partial good as to make his judgment in it very doubtful. MP II 2 187 1
sincerity of Edmund's too partial regard, to the unconcern MP II 2 194 20
As a sister, so partial and so angry, and so little MP III 5 356 4
that her mother was a partial, ill-judging parent, a MP III 8 390 6
the only regret was for a partial separation from friends, E I 2 18 10
But I am a partial old friend." E I 5 39 19
which often arise from a partial knowledge of E I 13 112 23
him--and nobody but so partial and kind a friend as Miss E I 17 141 8
of a place I am so extremely partial to as Maple Grove. E II 14 273 19
Consider from how partial a quarter your information came. E II 14 276 36
of his friends happy by a partial communication of what E II 17 304 29
away since the first partial falling of the cliff prepared P III 11 95 9

PARTIALITIES (2)
removed from the partialities and injustice of her P III 4 28 7
remembering former partialities and talking over old times. P IV 5 153 6

PARTIALITY (39)
to tell you that your partiality for Lady Susan is no LS 12 261 5
not the blind & weak partiality of most mothers, she is LS 14 265 5
unguarded in speaking of my partiality for the church!-- NA I 15 118 13
his brother's evident partiality for Miss Thorpe, and NA II 4 150 1
of that particular partiality, which, as she was given to NA II 11 208 1
reasonings of family partiality, or a desire of revenge." NA II 12 219 15
a persuasion of her partiality for him had been the only NA II 15 243 9
Her partiality for this gentleman was not of recent origin; NA II 16 251 5
her daughter, and that Elinor returned the partiality. SS I 3 15 5
for that blind partiality to Edward which produced it. SS I 4 19 3
own partiality, by believing or calling it more than it is. SS I 4 21 15
She could not consider her partiality for Edward in so SS I 4 22 18
Colonel Brandon's partiality for Marianne, which had so SS I 10 49 12
had incurred before any partiality arose, was removed when SS I 10 49 12
partiality could set aside, his ill-treatment of herself.-- SS II 1 139 1
by the uncertainty, the partiality of tender recollection, SS II 9 205 23
24

The two grandmothers, with not less partiality, but more SS II 12 234 23
My partiality does not blind me; he certainly is not so SS III 9 338 20
I do not trust my own partiality. PP I 9 44 31
to Mr. Bingley, whose blind partiality provoked her. PP I 18 89 3
his own, and a sister's partiality is not misleading me, I PP I 21 118 14
His apparent partiality had subsided, his attentions were PP II 3 149 28
then perceive that his partiality for Miss Bennet was PP II 12 197 5
by the strong sisterly partiality which made any PP II 17 224 2
well over; the agitations of former partiality entirely so. PP II 18 233 25
a quarter, than by supposing a partiality for their niece. PP III 2 260 1
she dreaded lest the partiality of the brother, should PP III 2 260 1
latter method, in her partiality for Wickham, and that its PP III 4 279 24
that Lydia had any partiality for him, but she was PP III 4 280 25
often suspected some partiality, expecially on Lydia's PP III 5 290 46
believe, that remaining partiality for her, might assist PP III 10 326 3
now arose more from partiality for her own scheme because MP I 8 79 23
"With all your partiality for Cottager's wife," said Henry MP I 14 134 15
her partiality for Harriet, will think this a good match." E I 8 62 38
Mrs. Weston's partiality for him is very great, and, as E II 18 309 30
little dears, without partiality; but Mrs. Charles knows P III 6 45 8
Mrs. Musgrove's fond partiality for their own daughters' P III 6 47 13
likely it is all our partiality, Sophy and I cannot help P IV 6 172 39
to have spoken with partiality of her many years ago, as P IV 8 187 35

PARTIALLY (7)
every feature when we last parted, were partially subdued. LS 25 292 2
to have been more than partially agreeable, or at all MP I 10 104 51
things only in part, and judging partially by the event.-- MP III 1 313 12
while Harriet had been partially insensible, he had spoken E III 3 335 11
dispelled--that might not be even partially brightened. E III 12 422 19
concealing it longer, even partially, from his daughter. P III 1 9 19
consigned, for, though partially revived, she was quite P III 12 111 49

PARTICIPATE (1)
trying to make Edmund participate them whenever she could MP I 4 34 2

PARTICIPATION (5)
did not invite them by any participation of sentiment.-- PP II 12 197 5
and who after a short participation of their regrets and MP I 9 90 36
not have borne any participation of his feelings, but his MP II 13 300 7
He was designed only to express his participation in all MP III 3 335 6
nature, that participation of the general nature of women, MP III 6 367 6

PARTICULAR (193)
there, as from her particular attachment to Mrs Manwaring, LS 3 246 1
sensibility to one in particular, a young Frederic, whom I LS 5 250 2
They are now on terms of the most particular friendship, LS 11 259 1
perceive that she had no particular pleasure in seeing him. LS 20 276 3
& I make it my particular request that I may not in any LS 25 293 3
She is going to town, to see her particular friend, Mrs LS 27 296 1
& in particular tell me what you mean to do with Manwaring. LS 28 298 2
you here, & it is our particular wish & entreaty that you LS 40 309 1
therefore deferring all particular enquiry till she could LS 42 311 1
be remembered, and the particular state of your complexion, NA I 3 27 28
that Mrs. Allen had no particular reason to hope it would NA I 4 31 2
"Yes, quite sure; for a particular friend of mine, a Miss NA I 6 40 12
"Mr. Thorpe is such a very particular friend of my NA I 10 78 38
But one must not be over particular. NA I 13 104 36
"A particular friend of mine had an account of it in a NA I 14 112 33
every particular was deferred till James could write again. NA I 15 122 28
"Oh! my dear! it would have looked so particular; and you NA II 1 134 39
I shall depend upon a most particular description of it." NA II 3 143 2
"But I thought, Isabella, you had something in particular NA II 3 144 5
gilding of one in particular, when taking out his watch, NA II 5 162 27
to lose no time in particular examination of any thing, as NA II 6 163 1
on the effect of that particular partiality, which, as she NA II 11 208 1

PARTICULAR/PARTICULARLY

That he was very particular in his eating, she had, by her NA II 11 211 15
engage their father's particular respect, had seen with NA II 15 245 12
as he had lately had particular opportunities of NA II 15 246 12
"He did not stipulate for any particular sum, my dear SS I 2 9 6
And I must say this: that you owe no particular gratitude SS I 2 13 28
so long, had not a particular circumstance occurred to SS I 3 14 3
to his father might with particular propriety be fulfilled. SS I 5 27 6
busy in arranging their particular concerns, and SS I 6 29 5
or mother, and in what particular he resembled either, for SS I 6 31 9
besides himself; a particular friend who was staying at SS I 7 33 4
to sing a particular song which Marianne had just finished. SS I 7 35 9
received particular spirit from his exterior attractions.-- SS I 9 43 11
man who was Elinor's particular favourite, which had been SS I 12 61 15
One evening in particular, about a week after Colonel SS I 14 72 6
benefited in one particular at least--you would know where SS I 19 102 3
able to give some more particular account of Willoughby's SS I 20 114 43
He was a particular friend of Sir John's. SS I 20 116 62
after my making such particular inquiries about Edward's SS I 22 132 42
for general chat, and none at all for particular discourse. SS II 1 143 8
pique, and having a particular stress on those words, " SS II 2 150 34
on her own account she had particular reasons to avoid. SS II 3 154 6
situated in that particular than she had expected, Elinor SS II 5 168 11
if he had somewhat in particular to tell her, sat for some SS II 5 172 40
or of inquiring, something particular about her. SS II 5 172 40
she was told it by a particular friend of Miss Grey SS II 8 192 3
in every particular, is more than I can express." SS II 11 222 10
is admiration of a very particular kind!--what is Miss SS II 12 235 34
35

more openly, for at her particular desire, Lady Middleton SS II 13 238 2
Miss Dashwoods, at the particular request of the SS II 14 246 2
probably without any particular, any material superiority SS II 14 250 12
entirely on any particular person, it is not meant--it is SS III 1 263 27
encouragement from the particular kindness of Mrs. SS III 2 271 5
to it with a look of particular meaning, and conversed SS III 3 280 9
her gratitude for the particular friendship, which SS III 3 283 20
The particular circumstances between them made a SS III 4 287 24
and wanted to speak with him on very particular business. SS III 4 287 25
character, and his particular approbation of your SS III 4 289 31
well as in every other particular, his open pleasure in SS III 6 305 16
upon my notice, requires a very particular excuse.-- SS III 8 318 21
22

inquiring eye,--"your particular intimacy--you have SS III 8 321 34
"Yes, yes that in particular. SS III 8 328 61
But you have not explained to me the particular reason of SS III 8 330 68
When there, at her own particular request, for she was SS III 10 340 1
after taking so particular and lengthened a leave of Mrs. SS III 10 341 5
general complaisance or particular gratitude which you had SS III 10 346 28
minute in every particular of speech and look, where SS III 10 348 34
own ease, was, in every particular, his ruling principle." SS III 11 351 11
lovers;--and Elinor's particular knowledge of each party SS III 13 364 10
of his duties in every particular, from an increasing SS III 14 377 12
always behaving in a particular way to one or another."-- W 316 1
of the name of Purvis a particular friend of Robert's, who W 316 2
I suppose you did not know what her particular business W 317 2
"One of his particular friends,"--"all in the same Regt W 337 15
sense of inferiority, she felt no particular shame.-- W 345 21
as particular as ever in having her properly attended to." W 350 24
was sharpened into particular resentment, by his having PP I 3 11 6
coincided in every particular, but I must so far differ PP I 7 29 11
so very plain--but then she is our particular friend." PP I 9 44 29
object than Darcy, on particular occasions, and in PP I 10 50 39
occasions, and in particular places; at his own house PP I 10 50 39
a tendency to some particular evil, a natural defect, PP I 11 58 30
after prizes, to have attention for any one in particular. PP I 16 76 8
with his family in a particular manner from my infancy." PP I 16 77 10
single event, or any particular person, for though they PP I 17 86 10
her cousin, and to point him out to her particular notice. PP I 18 90 4
I am sure we owe him no such particular civility as to be PP I 18 99 65
earlier, that it is the particular advice and PP I 19 105 10
and saw her dwelling intently on some particular passages. PP I 21 116 6
especially, there subsisted a very particular regard. PP II 2 139 2
attempt to describe any particular scene, will we begin PP II 4 154 23
acquainted with every particular of these transactions. PP II 12 202 5
for the truth of every particular to Colonel Fitzwilliam PP II 13 206 4
to suppress every particular in which her sister was PP II 17 224 1
On the contrary every particular relative to his sister, PP II 17 226 23
said she, "though I am not her particular friend. PP II 18 230 13
to be left under the particular care of their cousin Jane, PP II 19 239 10
No look appeared on either side that spoke particular PP III 2 262 8
His most particular friend, you see by Jane's account, was PP III 5 283 8
her by any particular attention, and, consequently, after PP III 5 285 18
he was on terms of particular friendship with any of them. PP III 6 297 12
"It must be something particular, to take him there at PP III 10 328 17
I suppose she had nothing particular to say to you, Lizzy?" PP III 14 359 76
which she made a very particular point;--the spare-rooms MP I 3 28 38
in every particular, but that of directing her letters. MP I 4 34 1
I have three very particular friends who have been all MP I 4 42 21
confidence of some one particular advantage in the MP I 5 46 22
In any particular style of building?" MP I 6 56 25
The particular object of the day was then considered. MP I 9 84 1
that he was taking particular pains, during dinner, to do MP I 10 104 51
He is growing extremely particular in his attentions." MP I 12 118 21
situation might require particular caution and delicacy-- MP I 13 128 38
disapprove the play in particular; their point was gained; MP I 17 158 1
introduction as the "particular friend," another of the MP II 1 183 23
another of the hundred particular friends of his son, MP II 1 183 23
being entirely without particular regard for either, MP II 1 185 30
Edmund met them with particular pleasure. MP II 4 211 25
is meant as any particular compliment to you; the MP II 5 220 28
With a few words, therefore, of no particular meaning, he MP III 1 320 45
manner in which particular passages in the service should MP III 3 340 24
You are going to a very particular friend." MP III 5 359 11
was rather my most particular friend of the two; but I MP III 5 359 12
nurse, and now felt a particular pleasure in seeing again. MP III 7 381 25
look out," he would give them his particular attendance. MP III 10 403 14
For her approbation, the particular reason of his going MP III 10 404 15
Without any particular affection for her eldest cousin, MP III 13 428 13
and considering over a particular paragraph--"what's the MP III 15 439 9
from an old and most particular friend in London, who MP III 16 450 8
kindness, felt his particular claim on her to leave her E I 3 22 5
evening had particular pleasure in sending them away happy. E I 3 25 15
had said in a very particular way indeed, that he was E I 8 68 58
"There is so pointed, and so particular a meaning in this E I 9 73 20
But I can remember nothing;--not even that particular E I 9 78 54
ever since his particular kindness last September E I 11 95 19
each brother, she had particular pleasure, from the E I 12 98 1
at Enscombe, has a particular dislike to: and though it is E I 14 120 11
with particular advantage at that moment to her friend. E I 17 141 7
to Mr. Elton in particular; but it seemed to her E I 17 142 11
so equal under particular circumstances to act up to it." E I 18 148 19
had not been for this particular circumstance, of her E II 1 159 20
Mrs. Campbell were very particular about their daughter's E II 1 159 20
Considering the very particular friendship between her and E II 1 160 22
of Miss Campbell in particular, was the more honourable to E II 2 164 7
if to every well-known particular entitling her to E II 2 167 13
"It was her very particular friend, you know." E II 6 202 32
than one's very particular friend--with a stranger it E II 6 202 33
misery of having a very particular friend always at hand, E II 6 202 33
am sure there must be a particular cause for her chusing E II 8 217 32
Emma watched the entree of her own particular little E II 8 219 44
and Mrs. Weston gave Emma a look of particular meaning. E II 10 244 36
"My dear, you are too particular," said her husband. E II 11 253 42

of acquaintance; and my particular friend, Mrs. Partridge, E II 14 275 32
particular a friend of Mr. E.'s, I had a great curiosity. E II 14 278 50
forced to be the very particular friend of Mrs. Elton, nor, E II 15 284 11
guests, and paying his particular compliments to the E II 16 294 24
25

Mrs. Elton, very willing to suppose a particular E II 18 305 2
like herself, by particular desire, to help Mr. Weston's E III 2 319 3
in the slightest particular from the original recital. E III 3 336 13
it all--and it is my particular wish to do it in your E III 4 338 6
I have gone through my particular friends, then I begin E III 5 345 13
Fairfax, and with a particular degree of sedate civility E III 5 348 23
the scheme as a particular compliment to themselves.-- E III 6 357 31
her memory with more particular observation, more exact E III 6 357 34
Though her nephew had had no particular reason to hasten E III 9 387 11
talked to her in a more particular way than he had ever E III 11 410 35
done before, in a very particular way indeed!--(Harriet E III 11 410 35
of having excited any particular interest, till she found E III 13 425 12
13

but from the very particular circumstances, which left me E III 14 440 8
Harriet was most happy to give every particular of the E III 19 481 2
to him in order to make particular inquiries, and had, in P III 3 21 18
anticipated, need not involve any particular awkwardness. P III 4 31 12
both the Miss Musgroves, at Mary's particular invitation. P III 5 41 46
"No, ma'am,--he did not mention no particular family; but P III 12 106 15
she knew; Elizabeth's particular share in it she suspected; P III 12 107 21
afterwards, to bring a later and more particular account. P IV 1 121 2
her in that house, there was particular attention. P IV 1 126 19
and had, at his own particular request, been admitted to P IV 3 139 8
Had she been using any thing in particular?" P IV 4 145 3
I observed no one in particular." P IV 9 197 39
Anne, "which has always excited my particular curiosity. P IV 9 200 56
"Nay," said Anne, "I have no particular enquiry to make P IV 9 200 58
at all hours--but I need not be particular on this subject. P IV 9 207 90
in the history of her grievances of particular irritation.. P IV 9 210 98
some smiling hints of particular business, which had been P IV 10 216 18
Her jealous eye was satisfied in one particular. P IV 10 226 64
to any place in particular sir, answered Mr H.-- S 1 368 1
For her particular gratification, they were then to take a S 6 390 1
The Denhams were the only ones to excite particular S 7 394 1
You must have heard me mention Miss Capper, the particular S 9 408 1
friend of my very particular friend Fanny Noyce;--now, S 9 408 1
In one particular however, she soon found that he had S 10 418 1
The particular introduction of Mrs G. to Miss Diana Parker, S 11 421 1

PARTICULARITY (12)
screen Marianne from particularity, as she felt almost SS I 16 86 20
to give her license to such a dangerous particularity."-- W 334 13
but as to any particularity of address or emotion towards W 355 28
on the occasion with rather an injudicious particularity. MP I 2 12 3
Mrs. Rushworth, that wish of avoiding particularity!-- MP I 12 117 14
for his father's particularity, what was to be expected. MP II 2 191 10
of them with more particularity to his other sister. MP II 5 224 49
aware of a particularity in Mr. Crawford's manners to you. MP III 1 316 29
with much less particularity of expression than she had MP III 5 357 5
I was sensible of a particularity, I had been sensible of MP III 5 362 21
with objectionable particularity to another woman, was she E III 14 441 8
any particularity of attention seemed almost impossible. P IV 4 147 8

PARTICULARIZE (2)
I need not particularize. MP III 13 421 2
on being requested to particularize, mentioned such works P III 11 101 24

PARTICULARLY (191)
where she must in reality have been particularly happy. LS 6 252 2
she must imagine to be particularly prejudiced against her; LS 12 261 4
full of it all, & particularly asking for an explanation LS 13 262 1
I confess it does not particularly recommend itself to me. LS 16 269 3
towards me is more particularly gratifying, because I have LS 20 277 6
7

I have for some time been more particularly resolved on LS 22 280 1
Her applying to Mr De Courcy hurt me particularly." LS 24 289 12
"Particularly well; I always buy my own cravats, and am NA I 3 28 38
of being in one; but I am particularly fond of it." NA I 7 47 22
"Very, very much indeed: Isabella particularly." NA I 7 50 46
under it what particularly dignifies her character. NA I 8 53 2
Of her dear Isabella, to whom she particularly longed to NA I 8 55 10
and that she was most particularly unfortunate herself in NA I 9 69 51
the former of whom had particularly set her heart upon NA I 13 97 1
and displease them, particularly to displease her brother; NA I 13 101 25
you are to observe, was her own, particularly her own. NA I 14 107 9
do not altogether seem particularly friendly to very NA I 14 110 27
young man, unless circumstances are particularly untoward. NA I 14 111 29
"I am particularly fond of this spot," said her companion, NA II 7 179 30
in performing it! this made it so particularly strange! NA II 10 201 5
Perhaps, if particularly questioned, she might just give NA II 10 203 9
said? when he so particularly desired you not to give NA II 11 211 12
whom, of all others, I particularly abhor, has left Bath. NA II 12 216 2
so well-bred, and heretofore so particularly fond of her! NA II 13 226 25
post, which contained a proposal particularly well timed. SS I 4 23 20
sensible, and his address was particularly gentlemanlike. SS I 7 34 6
Lady Middleton was so particularly repulsive, that in SS I 7 34 7
thought which particularly recommended the action to her. SS I 9 43 11
said Marianne, warmly, "which I particularly dislike. SS I 9 45 30
and Sir John, who was particularly warm in their praise, SS I 12 62 28
"I am particularly sorry, ma'am," said he, addressing Lady SS I 13 64 19
Mr. Willoughby wanted particularly to shew me the place; SS I 13 69 76
On Edward's side, more particularly, there was a SS I 16 87 23
the objects that had particularly struck him, when Edward SS I 18 96 4
He was particularly grave the whole morning. SS I 18 99 14
Their manners were particularly civil, and Elinor soon SS I 21 120 6
they were particularly anxious to be better acquainted.-- SS I 21 124 33
was at this time particularly ill-disposed, from the state SS I 22 127 1
and as he was always particularly afraid of his sister's SS I 22 131 32
"We did indeed, particularly so when he first arrived." SS I 22 134 51
for him, and she particularly wanted to convince Lucy, by SS II 1 141 7
I do not mean to say that I am particularly observant or SS II 2 148 12
it, and was particularly careful to inform her confidante, SS II 2 151 42
with her, and she felt particularly hurt that a man so SS II 4 162 8
well settled; Fanny particularly, for she has your SS II 11 224 24
in her style of beauty, to please them particularly. SS II 11 227 50
and it happened to be particularly convenient to the Miss SS II 12 230 8
person--for Lucy was particularly distinguished--whom of SS II 12 232 16
this poverty was particularly evident, for the gentlemen SS II 12 233 19
being Elinor's work, particularly requested to look at SS II 12 235 38
ever, and of her being particularly disgusted with his SS II 13 243 34
happened to be particularly ill-suited to the feelings of SS II 13 244 41
made her feel particularly uncomfortable for some minutes. SS III 4 288 26
is particularly important that he should be all this." SS III 4 290 38
The distress of her sister too, particularly a favourite, SS III 7 313 20
of content as she brought to it, was particularly welcome. SS III 7 315 27
To Elinor, the observation of the latter was particularly SS III 10 341 6
and how he was received, need not be particularly told. SS III 13 361 3
herself, & he did not particularly want to compliment her; W 357 28
You know how I detest it, unless I am particularly PP I 3 11 9
a family with whom the Bennets were particularly intimate. PP I 5 18 1
that human nature is particularly prone to it, and that PP I 5 20 20
and Lydia, were particularly frequent in these attentions; PP I 7 28 3
I am not particularly speaking of such a case as you have PP I 10 50 37
He wisely resolved to be particularly careful that no sign PP I 12 60 4
recent absence, were particularly welcome, and she was PP I 15 73 11
daughter, and was particularly flattered by receiving the PP I 17 86 10
"It is particularly incumbent on those who never change PP I 18 93 36
and addressed herself particularly to Mr. Bingley, to PP I 18 103 76
and during the walk, he particularly attended to her. PP I 21 115 5
I will read you the passage which particularly hurts me. PP I 21 117 14

"this invitation is particularly gratifying, because it is PP I 22 123 5
"My dear sir," replied Mr. Collins, "I am particularly PP I 22 123 8
he addressed himself particularly to her, as if wishing to PP II 5 155 4
I am particularly unlucky in meeting with a person so well PP II 8 174 15
and might now come to enquire particularly after her. PP II 11 188 3
Of what he has particularly accused me I am ignorant; but PP II 12 199 5
that in his will he particularly recommended it to me, to PP II 12 200 5
I can appeal more particularly to the testimony of Colonel PP II 12 202 5
to which he particularly alluded, as having passed at the PP II 13 209 10
But I am particularly attached to these young men; and PP II 14 210 3
a pause, "who more particularly wishes to be known to you,- PP III 1 256 63
her brother was particularly anxious to conceal it, from PP III 3 270 10
reputed beauty; and I particularly recollect your saying PP III 3 271 16
17
except what had particularly interested them both. PP III 3 271 20
me his directions, which I particularly begged him to do. PP III 5 286 28
I do not particularly like your way of getting husbands." PP III 9 317 16
Elizabeth particularly, who knew that her mother owed to PP III 11 335 42
He should be particularly happy at any time, &c. &c.; and PP III 13 344 3
of countenance, particularly grateful to the daughter. PP III 13 345 18
themselves, (my father particularly, all that was PP III 16 369 24
is particularly fond of, that I may have it to-morrow." PP III 17 378 45
He had been considering her as a particularly welcome MP I 1 9 10
of men of fortune, and particularly on the introduction of MP I 4 38 9
manners, particularly those of the eldest, were very good. MP I 5 47 27
know," turning to Miss Bertram particularly as he spoke. MP I 6 55 17
it would have been particularly proper and becoming in a MP I 7 67 16
That is what I dislike most particularly. MP I 12 120 26
Mr. Yates was particularly pleased; he had been sighing MP I 14 132 8
though I should not particularly dislike the part of MP I 15 144 38
own family circle was what they had particularly wished. MP I 17 158 2
and that did so particularly promote the pleasure of the MP I 17 161 9
interested her most particularly, and which she was MP I 18 167 12
at her again--inquired particularly after her health, and MP II 1 178 7
that she began particularly to feel how dreadfully she MP II 1 179 9
and Edmund, dwelling particularly on the latter, and MP II 1 184 27
she happened to be particularly in want of green baize. MP II 2 195 22
in general, was particularly disinclined, at this time, MP II 3 196 1
a memento made her particularly awake to his idea, and she MP II 4 207 10
the turkey, which I particularly wished not to be dressed MP II 4 212 31
satisfaction, as so particularly desirable for her in the MP II 4 216 50
Edmund was at this time particularly full of cares; his MP II 8 254 10
perhaps was not particularly favourable to the excitement MP II 8 256 13
"Yes--I had not particularly expected it." MP II 11 287 19
stage, and explaining very particularly what he had done. MP II 13 300 7
of it yesterday, particularly pleased, because I had not MP III 4 351 35
36
could not but think particularly of another sister, a very MP III 7 385 40
He particularly built upon a very happy summer and autumn MP III 10 405 18
there was something particularly kind and proper in the MP III 10 406 21
Easter came--particularly late this year, as Fanny had MP III 14 430 6
the fire; and Edmund, particularly struck by the MP III 15 446 34
very fond of both daughters, but particularly of Emma. E I 1 5 3
of the family, but particularly connected with it as the E I 1 9 21
though this was not particularly agreeable to Emma herself, E I 1 11 33
was reckoned a particularly healthy spot: she had an ample E I 3 22 5
happened to be of a sort which Emma particularly admired. E I 3 23 9
and meaning; and she particularly led Harriet to talk more E I 4 28 6
to make you particularly careful as to your associates. E I 4 30 22
He seems to me, to be grown particularly gentle of late. E I 4 34 42
was not at home, nor particularly expected, had left a E I 7 50 1
tendency, that it was particularly necessary to brace her E I 7 55 35
"I do not consider its length as particularly in its E I 9 76 33
He recommended it for all the children, but particularly E I 12 101 21
nonsense, which she particularly wished to listen to. E I 14 118 4
to recommend yourself particularly to Miss Smith?--that E I 15 131 34
and attention; and so particularly solicitous for the E I 15 132 38
love with her, or so particularly amiable as to make it E I 16 138 15
and indeed they particularly wish her to try her native E II 1 161 25
interval, she was particularly struck with the very E II 2 167 12
very tall; her figure particularly graceful; her size a E II 2 167 12
and the papers swept away;-- "particularly pleasant. E II 3 170 2
think I am particularly quick at those sort of discoveries. E II 3 176 44
"If you were never particularly struck by her manners E II 5 194 44
had been in a particularly populous, dancing state, had E II 6 197 5
She was particularly struck by his manner of considering E II 6 203 42
this morning was in another respect particularly opportune. E II 7 206 5
with me; only he is so particularly fond of music that he E II 8 216 16
Mrs. Weston, kind-hearted and musical, was particularly E II 8 220 46
and would therefore be particularly liable to take cold. E II 8 223 63
I am sure he was particularly silent when Mrs. Cole told E II 8 226 83
what he and all that party would particularly prize. E II 10 241 8
I honour that part of the attention particularly; it shews E II 10 242 21
I want to inquire after you all, but particularly your E II 10 244 35
She had been particularly unwell, however, suffering from E II 12 263 42
Something of that nature would be particularly desirable E II 14 277 38
manners," said Emma, "were always particularly good. E II 14 278 47
I shall introduce her, of course, very particularly to my E II 15 284 9
many accounts Emma was particularly pleased by Harriet's E II 16 291 5
be particularly careful, especially at this time of year. E II 16 295 33
Mr. Woodhouse or Mr. Knightley particularly delighted. E II 17 304 30
Mrs. Perry was always particularly fond of my mother-- E III 5 346 16
The quietness of the game made it particularly eligible E III 5 347 20
five minutes, and wanted particularly to speak with her."-- E III 10 392 1
"No, no, that's to-morrow; and I particularly wanted to E III 16 457 40
misconduct, it is particularly consoling to me to know E III 16 459 47
I am particularly glad to see and shake hands with you-- E III 18 476 48
This was her history; and particularly interesting it was E III 18 479 73
naval commanders particularly worth attending to--and beg P III 3 17 4
I am not particularly disposed to favour a tenant. P III 3 18 8
of marriage they are particularly nice; and that she P III 5 35 14
Mrs. Croft, who seemed particularly attached and happy, (P III 8 63 3
than he to come, particularly in the morning, when he had P III 9 73 2
any lady who might be particularly tired; it would save P III 10 90 38
He had enquired after her, she found, particularly;--had P IV 1 126 20
polished, so easy, so particularly agreeable, that she P IV 3 143 18
explanation of what he particularly meant; and though Anne P IV 4 151 22
particularly unfit to meet any extraordinary expense. P IV 5 154 9
ill; and she had been particularly fortunate in her nurse, P IV 5 154 9
I thought them particularly pleasing, and I will answer P IV 6 172 38
letter to make you and Mrs. Croft particularly uneasy. P IV 6 172 42
Anne would have been particularly obliged to her cousin, P IV 7 178 24
seemed this morning particularly obliged to her for coming, P IV 9 192 4
"I am extremely glad, indeed," cried Anne, "particularly P IV 10 217 21
She was particularly asked to meet Mr. Elliot, and be P IV 10 220 29
and that we were most particularly asked on purpose to P IV 10 223 43
whom you ought so particularly to be acquainted with! P IV 10 224 47
and I wish you particularly to assure Captain Harville, P IV 11 239 49
he enquired after you very particularly; asked even if you P IV 11 243 67
directions had been particularly useful & obliging to them; S 2 374 1
he is a very fine young man;--particularly elegant in his S 7 400 1
there;--and she was particularly careful & scrupulous on S 9 409 1
.TICULARS (89)
.n my way to hear some particulars of her conduct at LS 4 248 1
.n his last letter he actually gave me some particulars of LS 8 255 1
he particulars & assure himself of her real wishes! LS 22 281 5
Why do you require particulars? LS 36 305 1
ot been able to learn particulars, for he is so very low, LS 40 308 1
re you now at leisure to satisfy me in these particulars? NA I 3 25 2
mong women is faultless, except in three particulars." NA I 3 27 30
ut Catherine heard neither the particulars nor the result. NA I 7 48 32
o her lot: nor did the particulars which he entered into NA I 8 55 10

If we proceed to particulars, and engage in the never- NA I 14 107 11
the other for some particulars of their yesterday's party. NA I 15 116 1
But for particulars Isabella could well afford to wait. NA I 15 122 28
Isabella, on hearing the particulars of the visit, gave a NA II 1 129 1
I shall not enter into particulars, they would only pain NA II 10 202 7
the cause, or collect the particulars of her sudden return. NA II 14 233 10
proceeded to give the particulars, and explain the motives NA II 15 244 11
He earnestly pressed her, after giving the particulars of SS I 4 23 20
acquaintance, all the particulars of Mr. Jennings's last SS I 11 54 6
From such particulars, stated on such authority, Elinor SS I 12 61 14
But whatever might be the particulars of their separation, SS I 15 77 20
my ignorance and want of taste if we come to particulars. SS I 18 96 4
in the most delicate particulars,--and Elinor had not seen SS I 21 125 34
in the most common particulars, could not be concealed SS I 22 127 2
She wanted to hear many particulars of their engagement SS II 1 141 7
going through a repetition of particulars with composure. SS II 1 142 7
with many particulars of preparations and other matters. SS II 8 199 37
When the particulars of this conversation were repeated by SS II 10 212 1
in procuring all the particulars in her power of the SS II 10 215 11
after particulars, or any anxiety for her sister's health. SS II 10 215 12
give such particulars of Edward, as she feared would ruin SS III 1 261 11
which led to farther particulars, was, "how long has this SS III 1 262 14
15
their knowledge of the particulars, was so fine, so SS III 2 271 4
suffered you to give me particulars of a conversation SS III 2 274 19
of such simple particulars, as she felt assured that Lucy, SS III 2 276 27
Elinor repeated the particulars of it, as she had given SS III 5 298 33
event, and give farther particulars,--but day after day SS III 12 358 4
She enquired into the particulars--& then said "we shall W 339 18
"let us hear all the particulars, not forgetting their PP I 10 50 39
daughter; but from some particulars that he has related of PP I 16 83 57
I do not know the particulars, but I know very well that PP I 18 94 45
proceeded to relate the particulars of their interview, PP I 20 110 1
Mrs. Gardiner gave her the particulars also of Miss PP II 4 152 6
names or any other particulars, and I only suspected it to PP II 10 185 28
none of the particulars, it is not fair to condemn him. PP II 10 186 36
closest attention, the particulars immediately following PP II 13 205 3
minutely into the particulars of their journey, gave them PP II 14 213 20
In confirmation of this, she related the particulars of PP III 1 258 75
Give me farther particulars. PP III 5 290 45
"Could Colonel Forster repeat the particulars of Lydia's PP III 5 291 57
Mr. Gardiner did not attempt to conceal these particulars PP III 6 298 12
The particulars, I reserve till we meet. PP III 7 302 14
You will easily comprehend, from these particulars, that PP III 7 302 14
She was then proceeding to all the particulars of calico, PP III 7 307 48
He begged to know farther particulars of what he was PP III 8 309 5
I am no stranger to the particulars of your youngest PP III 14 357 62
of course, I could not rest till I knew the particulars. PP III 16 366 5
satisfactory, detail of particulars; but to say the truth, PP III 18 382 21
Mrs. Norris gave the particulars of the letters, and the MP I 11 108 4
it in the aggregate for honesty or safety in particulars. MP I 18 170 24
and all the little particulars of his proceedings and MP II 1 178 8
had written to you, there would have been more particulars. MP II 11 288 24
happy to give the particulars of their conversation--and, MP III 1 314 16
William's promotion, with all its particulars, he was soon MP III 3 334 3
in detailing farther particulars of the Thrush's going out MP III 7 377 8
her with all the particulars of the Grants' intended MP III 13 426 9
Fanny learnt from her, all the particulars which had yet MP III 16 449 7
meeting; and even when particulars were given and families E II 6 198 5
It was a long, well-written letter, giving the particulars E II 13 265 5
ago, with all these particulars--but as she declares she E III 5 345 13
wanting to hear the particulars of his suspicions, every E III 5 351 38
ignorant of any of the particulars of Mr. Frank E III 8 383 30
to promise me many particulars that could not be given now. E III 10 398 53
memory, many little particulars of the notice she had E III 11 409 35
relate all the particulars of so interesting an interview. E III 12 417 3
are very kind to bring me these interesting particulars. E III 12 420 13
without delay; I am impatient for a thousand particulars. E III 14 439 8
She will give you all the minute particulars, which only E III 18 472 20
But what did such particulars explain?-- E III 19 481 2
Mrs. Elton, from the particulars detailed by her husband, E III 19 484 12
had passed--the little particulars of the circumstances-- P III 9 80 34
They went through the particulars of their first meeting a P IV 4 148 9
now asked in vain for several particulars of the company. P IV 9 192 5
by listening to some particulars which you can yourself P IV 9 205 86
She had a great deal to listen to; all the particulars of P IV 9 210 97
many undesirable particulars, such as "how Mr. Musgrove P IV 11 230 5
known, but some further particulars of her history & her S 3 375 1
He gave the particulars which had led to Clara's admission S 3 378 1
Send me more particulars in your next.-- S 5 386 1
idea;--never heard any particulars;--but I am very sure S 9 409 1
PARTIES (79)
to Reginald can be productive only of good to all parties. LS 24 287 7
between some of the parties & separation between the LS 42 311 1
day never passes in which parties of ladies, however NA I 7 44 1
The time of the two parties uniting in the Octagon Room NA I 7 51 54
the winner; of shooting parties, in which he had killed NA I 9 66 31
together as long as both parties remained in the room; and NA I 10 72 8
"Perhaps, then, it would be better for all parties if the SS I 2 9 10
These parlours are both too small for such parties of our SS I 6 29 4
vanity was her greatest enjoyment in any of their parties. SS I 7 32 2
he was for ever forming parties to eat cold ham and SS I 7 32 2
disposition between the parties might forward the SS I 10 49 12
The private balls at the park then began; and parties on SS I 11 53 1
naturally attended these parties were exactly calculated SS I 11 53 1
she did not oppose the parties arranged by her husband, SS I 11 55 6
judge, for he had formed parties to visit them, at least, SS I 12 62 28
The alteration is not in them, if their parties are grown SS I 19 109 42
to join any of their parties, was persuaded by her mother, SS II 1 143 9
from any of their evening parties, which, whether at home SS II 5 168 11
of the card parties, the subject was necessarily dropped. SS II 8 200 43
whisper--"will be exceedingly welcome to all parties." SS II 11 224 24
The parties stood thus: the two mothers, though each SS II 12 234 21
22
The party, like other musical parties, comprehended a SS II 14 250 10
early in the day, the two parties from Hanover-Square and SS III 6 301 3
by one or two of the card parties having just broken up 3 W 333 13
where she gave genteel parties, & wore fine Cloathes.-- W 349 23
too mixed,--but our parties are very select & good.-- W 350 24
be the worst of all parties; & the others were delighted.-- W 357 28
each other in large mixed parties, it is impossible that PP I 6 22 6
If the dispositions of the parties are ever so well known PP I 6 23 10
as the degree of intimacy subsisting between the parties?" PP I 10 50 38
look at in their Rosings parties, and she might be amused PP II 7 170 6
my opinion of all parties was confirmed and every PP II 12 198 5
With such kind of histories of their parties and good PP II 16 222 18
understanding between the parties could justify her in PP II 17 227 25
Their parties abroad were less varied than before; and at PP II 19 237 3
of all their little parties and engagements, with such PP III 4 273 2
her daughter, and having very frequent parties at home. PP III 9 318 18
These parties were acceptable to all; to avoid a family PP III 9 318 18
their former parties, had belonged to him, by her sister. PP III 12 340 11
more taken in and deceived than the parties themselves." MP I 5 46 23
others began to form into parties, these three were found MP I 9 90 36
races and Weymouth, and parties and friends, to which she MP I 12 114 1
of the scrambling parties in which he had been engaged, MP II 6 237 23
You would have heard of balls and parties.-- MP II 11 288 24
himself very much, for I know the parties he had to move. MP III 5 364 29
the accidental agreeableness of the parties he had been in. MP III 10 404 15
with the names of people and parties, that fill up my time. MP III 12 415 2
She was only sorry for the parties concerned and for MP III 15 438 4
good dinners, and large parties, there will always be MP III 16 457 29

which always closed such parties, and for which she had E I 3 24 11
party, but where small parties are select, they are E I 13 116 43
parties of London, may not quite enter into our feelings." E I 13 116 43
"I know nothing of the large parties of London, sir--I E I 13 116 44
as I do: but she does not know the parties so well as I do. E I 14 120 11
The wedding was no distant event, as the parties had only E II 4 182 6
dinner-company; and a few parties, chiefly among the E II 7 207 6
You have many parties of that kind here, I suppose, Miss E II 14 274 28
which attract the sort of parties you speak of; and we are E II 14 274 29
up--parties, balls, plays--for I had no fear of retirement. E II 14 276 36
I can, shall have musical parties to draw out her talents, E II 15 284 9
in the barouche-landau in some of our exploring parties." E II 15 284 9
parties which are to take place in the barouche-landau." E II 15 288 39
and there being no ice in the Highbury card parties. E II 16 290 3
their making two distinct parties;--with so much E II 17 299 1
failed her, that the two parties should unite, and go E III 6 353 3
They separated too much into parties. E III 7 367 1
between the other parties, too strong for any fine E III 7 367 1
parties--young ladies-- married women-----" E III 7 370 20
No more exploring parties to Donwell made for her. E III 17 469 36
other weddings, where the parties have no taste for finery E III 19 484 12
This meeting of the two parties proved highly satisfactory, P III 5 32 2
to by both parties) they might pass for a happy couple. P III 6 43 5
much confidence by all parties, and being too much in the P III 6 44 7
body, and had more dinner parties, and more callers, more P III 6 47 14
three distinct parties; and to that party of the three P III 10 90 37
stupidity of private parties, in which they were getting P IV 7 180 32
said he, "to enjoy the evening parties of the place." P IV 10 225 57
to be truth; and if such parties succeed, how should a P IV 12 248 1
us in the way they commonly do between those two parties.-- S 7 400 1

PARTING (58)

her wise lips in their parting conference in her closet. NA I 2 18 2
Under these unpromising auspices, the parting took place, NA I 2 19 4
parting good wishes, they both hurried down stairs. NA I 9 62 7
o'clock," was her parting speech to her new friend. NA I 10 80 61
round; the clouds were parting, and she instantly returned NA I 11 83 16
at parting, I would always do the best for you in my power. NA I 13 104 36
breathe his parting sigh before he set off for Wiltshire. NA I 15 120 24
by Isabella's behaviour in their parting interview. NA II 4 153 31
The embraces, tears, and promises of the parting fair ones NA II 4 153 31
With this parting cordial she curtseys off--you listen to NA II 5 159 17
bed, when, on giving a parting glance round the room, she NA II 6 168 10
her friend to throw a parting glance on every well-known NA II 13 227 27
"To be sure," said she, "it is better than parting with SS I 2 10 18
sleep at all the first night after parting from Willoughby. SS I 16 83 1
But remember that the pain of parting from friends will be SS I 19 103 7
pain to them all in the parting, which shortly took place, SS I 19 104 9
moment of parting, her grief on that score was excessive. SS II 3 158 21
The clouds seem parting too, the sun will be out in a SS II 5 168 9
Such was her parting concern; for after this, she had time SS III 2 276 26
he would not hear of our parting, though earnestly did I, SS III 2 277 30
by the latter on their parting, may perhaps appear in SS III 3 284 24
turned into the parlour to fulfil her parting injunction. SS III 10 348 34
Ld Osborne's parting Compts took some time, his W 347 21
testified such concern in parting with her, that Miss PP I 7 33 45
lodges, to make them his parting obeisance, was able to PP II 14 210 1
parting civilities which he deemed indispensably necessary. PP II 15 215 1
After an affectionate parting between the friends, PP II 15 217 8
relations, with only one serious, parting, look, went away. PP III 4 278 22
their uncle promised, at parting, to prevail on Mr. Bennet PP III 6 294 2
there is nothing so bad as parting with one's friends. PP III 11 330 10
to receive Mr. Rushworth's parting attentions as she ought. MP I 10 105 52
time, he had made his parting bow, and she might seek MP II 2 193 18
In the moment of parting, Edmund was invited by Dr. Grant MP II 4 215 47
and when sent off with a parting worry to dress, moved as MP II 9 267 22
William what she did at parting, very glad indeed that it MP II 13 304 19
was no look of despair in parting to bely his words, or MP III 2 328 8
In the evening there was another parting. MP III 5 365 35
When it came to the moment of parting, he would take her MP III 5 365 36
Her heart was completely sad at parting. MP III 6 374 28
given her 10l. at parting, made her as able as she was MP III 9 396 7
It was parting with somebody of the nature of a friend; MP III 11 413 31
increase of the pain of parting, for the sake of carrying MP III 16 458 30
of naming Harriet at parting; in the tone of his voice E I 13 111 14
but the clouds were parting, and there was every E I 15 127 16
and parting with her seemingly with ceremonious civility. E II 5 186 3
was Mrs. Weston's parting injunction; spoken with some E II 5 189 15
Every thing tender and charming was to mark their parting; E II 13 264 1
looks and language at parting would have been different.-- E II 13 265 4
Her parting look was grateful--and her parting words, "Oh! E III 6 363 51
no acknowledgement, parting in apparent sullenness, she E III 7 376 62
"He told me at parting, that he should soon write; and he E III 10 398 53
of secresy had been among Mr. Weston's parting words. E III 11 403 2
"Are you well, my Emma?" was Mrs. Weston's parting E III 12 420 15
She was aware herself, that, parting under any other E III 17 463 15
under the misery of a parting--a final parting; and every P III 4 28 5
of a parting--a final parting; and every consolation was P III 4 28 5
became a sort of parting proof, its value did not lessen. P III 12 117 75
They are parting, they are shaking hands. P IV 10 222 38

PARTLY (9)

The spring fashions are partly down; and the hats the most NA II 12 216 2
even partly determined never to mention the subject again. SS II 2 150 35
at last, that he had been partly governed by this worst PP II 10 187 40
partly by the wish of retaining Mr. Bingley for his sister. PP II 10 187 40
account, who was partly expected at the park that day; but MP I 7 70 30
To own the truth, Henry and I were partly driven out this MP I 11 111 28
a moment; and the smile partly remained as she turned E III 18 480 78
79
She had once partly promised Mrs. Smith to spend the P IV 7 180 33
Perhaps it might be partly owing to her having just S 6 391 1

PARTNER (78)

you could dance, my dear,--I wish you could get a partner." NA I 2 21 9
with all my heart, and then I should get you a partner.-- NA I 2 23 21
his wife, "I wish we could have got a partner for her.-- NA I 2 23 25
I am so sorry she has not had a partner!" NA I 2 23 25
gentlemanlike young man as a partner;--his name was Tilney. NA I 3 25 2
proper attentions of a partner here; I have not yet asked NA I 3 25 2
ball-room;--"not of your partner, I hope, for, by that NA I 3 29 47
pains to know who her partner was, and had been assured of NA I 3 30 52
disappointed in her hope of re-seeing her partner. NA I 5 35 2
very early engaged as a partner; and the consequence was, NA I 7 50 44
still sitting down all the discredit of wanting a partner. NA I 8 53 2
would have led his fair partner away, but she resisted. NA I 8 57 21
of her son, "I hope you have had an agreeable partner." NA I 8 58 25
"Ah! he has got a partner, I wish he had asked you," said NA I 8 58 32
to attend that of his partner; Miss Tilney, though NA I 8 59 38
"And is Mr. Tilney, my partner, the only son?" NA I 9 69 49
Her partner now drew near, and said, "that gentleman would NA I 10 76 29
He has no business to withdraw the attention of my partner NA I 10 76 29
state are not so strict as your partner might wish? NA I 10 77 37
stood among the lookers-on, immediately behind her partner. NA I 10 80 59
retreated, and her partner coming nearer, said, "I see NA I 10 80 59
she could not have her partner conveyed from her sight NA II 1 132 16
she might wish for a partner; but he is quite mistaken, NA II 1 132 17
spoke her astonishment in very plain terms to her partner. NA II 1 133 30
I begged him to excuse me, and get some other partner--but NA II 1 134 39
Having no reason to be dissatisfied with her partner, W 329 9
near her, when you know what a partner he is to have. W 330 11
to her little expecting partner hastily said--"Charles, I W 330 11
you have got a better partner than me"--to which the happy W 331 11
of talking to Charles, stood to look at his partner.-- W 331 11
Her little partner she found, tho' bent chiefly on dancing, W 331 11
whisper aloud "Oh! uncle, do look at my partner. W 332 11
The stile of her last partner had probably led him to W 334 13
little interruption till she heard of Mr H. as a partner.-- W 342 19
it, unless I am particularly acquainted with my partner. PP I 3 11 9
Do let me ask my partner to introduce you." PP I 3 11 12
You had better return to your partner and enjoy her smiles, PP I 3 12 13
this young lady to you as a very desirable partner.-- PP I 6 26 38
39
that I moved this way in order to beg for a partner." PP I 6 26 39
his complaisance; for who would object to such a partner?" PP I 6 26 43
glance at Elizabeth, requiring no partner in his pleasure. PP I 14 68 12
was by no means the only partner who could satisfy them, PP I 17 86 10
a disagreeable partner for a couple of dances can give. PP I 18 90 4
greater punishment to her partner to oblige him to talk, PP I 18 91 8
courtesy to compliment him on his dancing and his partner. PP I 18 92 22
Allow me to say, however, that your fair partner does not PP I 18 92 23
shortly, he turned to his partner, and said, "Sir PP I 18 93 24
25
pleasantness of her last partner she had scarcely replied, PP I 18 96 56
than one young lady was sitting down in want of a partner. PP II 8 175 18
it, and the chosen partner of her fate, may be reasonably PP III 15 362 14
of seeing you unable to respect your partner in life. PP III 17 376 35
on whom all her own hopes of a partner then depended. MP I 12 116 11
for Julia and her partner, Mr. Crawford, were close to her; MP I 12 117 15
that it would not much amuse him to have her for a partner. MP II 7 239 6
in going to the assembly, for I might not get a partner. MP II 7 249 52
I was here, and I should like to be your partner once more. MP II 7 250 59
To be secure of a partner at first, was a most essential MP II 10 274 8
should have received a partner only through a series of MP II 10 274 8
satisfaction of having a partner, a voluntary partner MP II 10 274 8
a voluntary partner secured against the dancing began. MP II 10 274 8
first dance at least; her partner was in excellent spirits MP II 10 276 13
He has chosen his partner, indeed, with rare felicity. MP III 4 351 32
and she found herself well matched in a partner. E II 8 230 100
Every body so happy! and she and her partner the happiest!-- E II 12 259 10
"And what are we to do for a proper partner for her?" said E III 2 325 30
and, excepting her own partner, there was not one among E III 2 326 32
was nothing like flirtation between her and her partner. E III 2 326 32
begun, and Harriet had no partner;--the only young lady E III 2 326 33
"Me!--Oh! no--I would get you a better partner than myself. E III 2 327 35
observing audibly to her partner, "Knightley has taken E III 2 328 42
43
to-morrow: her first partner was Mr. Elton, I do not know E III 2 329 45
with me; and when there was no other partner in the room. E III 11 406 24
Such a partner in all those duties and cares to which time E III 15 450 36
having asked his partner whether Miss Elliot never danced? P III 8 72 58
"Nay sir, if he is not in the way, his partner will just S 1 365 1
I wd rather see his partner indeed--I would prefer the S 1 365 1
indeed--I would prefer the attendance of his partner.-- S 1 365 1
We have neither surgeon nor partner in the parish I assure S 1 365 1

PARTNER'S (2)

The two dances seemed very short, & she had her partner's W 335 13
her and working away his partner's fan as if for life:--" MP II 10 279 23

PARTNERS (13)

the talk of the place, if we were not to change partners." NA I 8 57 21
in the room; my two younger sisters and their partners. NA I 8 59 37
business with the partners or wives of their neighbours." NA I 10 76 29
of the night, they were partners for half the time; and SS I 11 54 3
& among so many officers, you will hardly want partners. W 315 1
"I will remember her partners if I can--but you know they W 320 2
to be never without partners, which was all that they had PP I 3 12 15
For God's sake, say no more of his partners. PP I 3 13 17
and I will take care to get good partners for them all." PP III 9 317 13
and Maria, who were partners for the second time--"we MP I 12 117 12
to have strength and partners for about half the evening, MP II 9 267 22
hear his account of his partners; she was happy in knowing MP II 10 278 20
about you, how you were amused, and who were your partners. E III 2 329 45

PARTNERSHIP (5)

she shared, by private partnership with Morland, a very NA I 11 89 63
It was a partnership which cd not be noticed without W 331 11
so dear--for as to any partnership in Thornton Lacey, as MP III 10 405 19
of the dissolution of a partnership in the medical line-- S 1 366 1
design of entering into partnership with him--; it was S 2 371 1

PARTOOK (1)

strongly partook of the emotion which overpowered Marianne. SS I 15 75 2

PARTRIDGES (2)

near the fire, & as the partridges were pretty high, Dr W 344 20
acknowledged, that the partridges were remarkably well PP III 12 342 28

PARTS (32)

my dear Alicia I yeild to the necessity which parts us. LS 39 307 1
From them however the eight parts of speech shone out most NA I 15 120 24
village, he had seen many parts of the valley to advantage; SS I 18 96 4
vulgarity, inferiority of parts, or even difference of SS I 22 127 1
It will be a very fine object from many parts of the park, SS II 11 226 39
in the most distant parts of them, where there was SS III 6 305 17
how she had changed her name since she was in these parts. SS III 11 354 29
Mr. Bennet was so odd a mixture of quick parts, sarcastic PP I 1 5 34
unacquainted with several parts of the story, and has PP I 18 96 55
for them to play their parts with more spirit, or finer PP I 18 101 72
to the edge of the water, in one of its narrowest parts. PP III 1 253 57
parts of the stream where there was usually most sport. PP III 1 255 60
From the first casting of the parts, to the epilogue, it MP I 13 122 2
Many parts of our best plays are independent of scenery." MP I 13 124 9
That might do, perhaps, but for the low parts----- MP I 14 131 3
fine tragic parts in the rest of the Dramatis Personae. MP I 14 131 6
Here are two capital tragic parts for Yates and Crawford, MP I 14 132 7
She was acknowledged to be quite right, and the two parts MP I 14 132 8
wife's, and so change the parts all through; he is solemn MP I 14 134 14
it is of all parts in the world the most disgusting to me. MP I 14 136 20
"I had my choice of the parts," said Mr. Rushworth; "but I MP I 15 143 29
He had learned his part--all his parts--for he took every MP I 18 164 1
insignificance of all his parts together, and make him MP I 18 164 1
The dress being settled in all its grander parts,--"but MP II 8 257 15
admire all the striking parts of his dress--listening with MP III 7 384 35
Those parts of the letter which related only to Mr. MP III 12 418 4
of Methodists, or as a missionary into foreign parts.' MP III 16 458 30
could hardly separate the parts, so as to feel quite sure E I 9 77 43
your goodness to allow for some parts of my past conduct.-- E III 14 436 8
other component parts of the cottage inimical to comfort.-- P III 6 43 4
all those parts of his conduct which were least excusable. P IV 10 214 12
& most exceptionable parts of Richardsons; & such authors S 8 404 1

PARTY (376)

Susan, & we shall depend on his joining our party soon. LS 3 247 1
Now however, we begin to mend; our party is enlarged by LS 7 254 3
party understand that his heart was devoted to my daughter. LS 22 280 2
ready to oblige the whole party by consenting to a LS 42 313 7
of her throwing a whole party into raptures by a prelude NA I 1 16 10
awkwardness of having no party to join, no acquaintance to NA I 2 21 10
a table, at which a large party were already placed, NA I 2 22 10
we came here--we seem forcing ourselves into their party." NA I 2 22 14
dress-maker, however, the party from Pulteney-Street NA I 8 52 1
Tilney with seats, as they had agreed to join their party. NA I 8 54 10
She was separated from all her party, and away from all NA I 8 55 10
settled her young charge, returned to her party. NA I 8 55 10
was drawn away from their party at tea, to attend that of NA I 8 59 38
thing at the last party in my rooms, that upon an average NA I 9 64 24
from the rest of their party, they walked in that manner NA I 10 71 8
and his father, joining a party in the opposite box, NA I 12 92 4
the weather were fair, the party should take place on the NA I 13 97 1
said, "very well, then there is an end of the party. NA I 13 99 4
acquitted, and we shall have a most delightful party." NA I 13 100 17
thing more of the offended party; and now that she had NA I 13 103 29

Context	Work	Vol	Ch	Page	Line
Her escape from being one of the party to Clifton was now	NA	I	13	105	41
almost expected another attack from the assembled party.	NA	I	14	106	1
From her, she soon learned that the party to Clifton had	NA	I	14	115	50
home, pleased that the party had not been prevented by her	NA	I	14	115	55
the other for some particulars of their yesterday's party.	NA	I	15	116	1
as insupportably cross, from being excluded the party.	NA	I	15	116	2
party, received the delightful confession of an equal love.	NA	I	15	117	8
and no one else of the party, she found, on her return,	NA	II	1	129	1
in the ease of a family party, he had never said so little,	NA	II	1	129	1
seen before, and who now evidently belonged to their party.	NA	II	1	131	15
be of the party to Northanger, he was to continue at Bath.	NA	II	4	150	1
Had their party been perfectly agreeable, the delay would	NA	II	5	156	4
the time the party broke up, it blew and rained violently.	NA	II	6	166	9
Catherine was probably the only one of the party who did	NA	II	7	175	12
and then of having a large party to dinner, and once or	NA	II	11	209	5
On every formal visit a child ought to be of the party, by	SS	I	6	31	9
He hoped they would all excuse the smallness of the party,	SS	I	7	33	4
two entire strangers of the party, and wished for no more.	SS	I	7	34	4
There was nothing in any of the party which could	SS	I	7	34	7
Colonel Brandon alone, of all the party, heard her without	SS	I	7	35	9
and all the rest of the party to get her a good hand.	SS	I	11	54	3
A party was formed this evening for going on the following	SS	I	12	62	28
in the usual style of a complete party of pleasure.	SS	I	12	62	28
By ten o'clock the whole party were assembled at the park,	SS	I	13	63	2
to leave so agreeable a party; but I am the more concerned,	SS	I	13	64	21
"there are some people who cannot bear a party of pleasure.	SS	I	13	64	30
party; but at the same time declared it to be unavoidable.	SS	I	13	65	33
and we must put off the party to Whitwell till you return."	SS	I	13	65	35
He then took leave of the whole party.	SS	I	13	66	45
herself from being of the party under some trifling	SS	I	15	75	1
absolutely dine with us, for we shall be a large party."	SS	I	18	99	17
window, and she saw a large party walking up to the door.	SS	I	19	105	13
he left the rest of the party to the ceremony of knocking	SS	I	19	105	13
to receive the rest of the party; Lady Middleton	SS	I	19	106	21
a family party; and the young ladies were obliged to yield.	SS	I	19	109	40
of the Miss Steeles, their party would be too strong for	SS	I	21	124	33
she had in view, in such a party as this was likely to be,	SS	II	1	143	9
whether you can make your party without me, or I should	SS	II	1	144	12
to let you into the secret, for you are a party concerned.	SS	II	2	149	25
and in whatever shop the party were engaged, her mind was	SS	II	4	164	24
Mr. and Mrs. Palmer were of the party; from the former,	SS	II	5	171	30
attend Lady Middleton to a party, from which Mrs. Jennings	SS	II	6	175	1
daughter; and for this party, Marianne, wholly dispirited,	SS	II	6	175	1
I have been told that you were asked to be of the party.	SS	II	7	187	40
Colonel Brandon came in while the party were at tea, and	SS	II	8	198	30
morning of our intended party to Whitwell; and this was	SS	II	9	209	30
in breaking up the party, that I was called away to the	SS	II	9	209	30
could not learn whether her sons were to be of the party.	SS	II	12	230	6
The interest with which she thus anticipated the party,	SS	II	12	230	7
visit should begin a few days before the party took place.	SS	II	12	230	8
as his mother was, to a party given by his sister; and to	SS	II	12	231	10
brother and sister, to a small musical party at her house.	SS	II	14	248	6
The party, like other musical parties, comprehended a	SS	II	14	250	10
that little;-- for the rest of the party none at all.	SS	III	1	260	9
they all joined in a very spirited critique upon the party.	SS	III	1	269	58
left her own party for a short time, to join their's.	SS	III	2	271	5
the approach of her own party made another more necessary.	SS	III	2	275	24
Their party was small, and the hours passed quietly away.	SS	III	6	303	12
enlargement of the party, and a very welcome variety to	SS	III	6	304	14
Their party was now farther reduced; for Mr. Palmer,	SS	III	7	308	5
He asked me to a party, a dance at his house in the	SS	III	8	327	55
talking of the dear family party which would then be	SS	III	10	343	8
knowledge of each party made it appear to her in every	SS	III	13	364	10
I hope he will come with a large party, & then he will not	W			319	2
did not suit Capt. O'brien that I shd be of the party."--	W			326	5
in a very few minutes, the party were transported from the	W			327	7
The party passed on--Mrs E's Sattin gown swept along the	W			327	8
the upper end, where one party only were formally seated,	W			327	8
was whispered from one party to another, & no sooner had	W			328	9
within, the important party, preceded by the attentive	W			329	9
Osborne, Miss Carr, & a party of young men were standing	W			330	11
Mrs E. & her party were for a few moments hemmed in.	W			332	11
Emma could not help missing the party, by whom she had	W			336	14
the day which brought the party to Stanton seemed to her	W			348	23
who regretted very much her not being of the party.--	W			350	24
as she had been at her own party, came in with apologies	W			353	26
Mr Watson had not been well enough to join the party at	W			354	28
with him to join the party, that he agreed to allow	W			357	28
to feel that a family party might be the worst of all	W			357	28
You are not forgotten I assure you by any of the party.	W			358	28
him, it wd have been a party of such very near relations	W			359	28
The peace of the party for the remainder of that day, &	W			360	30
of them, Mr. Bingley might like you the best of the party."	PP	I	1	4	19
he meant to be at the next assembly with a large party.	PP	I	3	9	1
London only to get a large party for the ball; and a	PP	I	3	10	4
And when the party entered the assembly room, it	PP	I	3	10	4
the room, speaking occasionally to one of his own party.	PP	I	3	11	6
her eldest daughter much admired by the Netherfield party.	PP	I	3	12	15
It was at Sir William Lucas's, where a large party were	PP	I	6	24	13
Their brother, indeed, was the only one of the party whom	PP	I	8	35	2
On entering the drawing-room she found the whole party at	PP	I	8	37	21
evening Elizabeth joined their party in the drawing-room.	PP	I	10	47	1
said,-- "this walk is not wide enough for our party.	PP	I	10	53	62
					63
of the whole party on the subject, seemed to justify her.	PP	I	11	54	3
the wishes of the present party; I am much mistaken if	PP	I	11	55	6
He was directly invited to join their party, but he	PP	I	11	56	12
took leave of the whole party in the liveliest spirits.	PP	I	12	60	5
I have reason to expect an addition to our family party."	PP	I	13	61	1
unassuming; and the whole party were still standing and	PP	I	15	72	8
them were of the present party; but Mr. Wickham was as far	PP	I	16	76	3
The whist party soon afterwards breaking up, the players	PP	I	16	82	49
party, but his manners recommended him to every body.	PP	I	16	84	59
Others of the party were now applied to.	PP	I	18	101	70
The Longbourn party were the last of all the company to	PP	I	18	102	75
a languor over the whole party, which was very little	PP	I	18	102	75
in the same room, the same party with him for so many	PP	I	21	115	4
The whole party have left Netherfield by this time, and	PP	I	21	116	7
"Caroline decidedly says that none of the party will	PP	I	21	117	10
Charlotte, "and I hope you will consent to be of the party.	PP	II	3	146	18
the house, amidst the nods and smiles of the whole party.	PP	II	5	155	3
the whole party was asked to dine at Rosings the next day.	PP	II	5	159	20
the whole party) so immediately after your arrival!"	PP	II	6	160	2
The party did not supply much conversation.	PP	II	6	163	14
honour of assisting Mrs. Jenkinson to make up her party.	PP	II	6	166	41
The party then gathered round the fire to hear lady	PP	II	6	166	42
great surprise of all the party, when Mr. Collins returned	PP	II	7	170	7
they joined the party in Lady Catherine's drawing room.	PP	II	8	172	2
of knowing any lady in the assembly beyond my own party."	PP	II	8	175	19
first subject was the diminution of the Rosings party.--	PP	II	14	210	3
contrivance, the whole party, with all their boxes,	PP	II	16	220	16
Their party in the dining-room was large, for almost all	PP	II	16	222	21
When the party broke up, Lydia returned with Mrs. Forster	PP	II	18	235	40
we expect him tomorrow, with a large party of friends."	PP	III	1	246	8
advanced towards the party, and spoke to Elizabeth, if not	PP	III	1	251	51
the rest of the party with whom he had been travelling.	PP	III	1	256	61
"There is also one other person in the party," he	PP	III	1	256	63
The whole party before them, indeed, excited a lively	PP	III	2	261	6
employment for the whole party; for though they could not	PP	III	3	268	6
suspicions of the whole party were awakened against them,	PP	III	3	268	8
was now put an end to, by the approach of the whole party.	PP	III	5	286	32
The whole party were in hopes of a letter from Mr. Bennet	PP	III	6	294	1
Not one party, or scheme, or any thing.	PP	III	9	319	25
the belief of your being a party concerned, would have	PP	III	10	321	2
On Tuesday there was a large party assembled at Longbourn;	PP	III	12	340	11
in a few moments after seated with the rest of the party.	PP	III	12	342	26
"The party seemed so well selected, so suitable one with	PP	III	12	343	30
addition to their evening party; and he bore with the ill-	PP	III	13	345	18
up the card party, and was sitting up stairs with Kitty.	PP	III	13	347	27
comfort and elegance of their family party at Pemberley.	PP	III	18	384	27
It was the natural result of the conduct of each party,	MP	I	1	4	1
to Lady Bertram during the night of a ball or a party.	MP	I	4	35	6
desirableness to either party; and, among other means, by	MP	I	4	39	10
were made for a large party to them, with all the	MP	I	5	48	29
not we make a little party? here are many that would be	MP	I	6	62	58
A happy party it appeared to her--all interested in one	MP	I	7	67	16
by seeing the party in the meadow disperse, and Miss	MP	I	7	68	17
the next morning;--the party included all the young people	MP	I	7	70	30
A young party is always provided with a shady lane.	MP	I	7	70	30
the happiness of one of the party was exceedingly clouded.	MP	I	7	70	30
yet given over pressing Lady Bertram to be of the party.	MP	I	8	75	2
I will answer for his being most happy to join the party.	MP	I	8	76	3
Crawford's being of the party were desirable or not, or	MP	I	8	77	8
party, but as it relates to yourself, to your own comfort.	MP	I	8	78	18
would probably be of the party, and had directly received	MP	I	8	79	23
him to his share of the party; and Mrs. Norris thought it	MP	I	8	80	28
the whole party were welcomed by him with due attention.	MP	I	9	84	1
The whole party rose accordingly, and under Mrs.	MP	I	9	84	3
While this was passing, the rest of the party being	MP	I	9	88	19
"I believe the wilderness will be new to all the party.	MP	I	9	90	35
Fanny was the only one of the party who found any thing to	MP	I	12	115	5
breaking-up of a large party assembled for gaiety at the	MP	I	13	121	1
it had been a theatrical party; and the play, in which he	MP	I	13	121	1
immortalized the whole party for at least a twelvemonth!	MP	I	13	121	1
not wish to have been a party concerned, or would have	MP	I	13	122	2
When this had lasted some time, the division of the party	MP	I	14	136	22
<u>your</u> conduct must be law to the rest of the party."	MP	I	15	140	13
After continuing in chat with the party round the fire a	MP	I	15	143	27
Crawford returned to the party round the table; and	MP	I	15	143	27
else, and soon afterwards rejoined the party at the fire.	MP	I	15	144	36
enjoyment to the party themselves, and that she had not to	MP	I	18	164	1
How is the consternation of the party to be described?	MP	II	1	175	1
almost every one of the party on the development before	MP	II	1	176	4
Sir Thomas was indeed the life of the party, who at his	MP	II	1	178	8
such a scheme among such a party, and at such a time, as	MP	II	2	187	2
any time required by the party; he was going away	MP	II	2	192	11
We shall be quite a small party at home.	MP	II	3	199	17
every addition to the party must rather forward her	MP	II	5	223	48
to say that it had honour from all the rest of the party."	MP	II	5	225	53
The party being now all united, and the chief talkers	MP	II	5	227	68
The chief of the party were now collected irregularly	MP	II	7	249	49
He was not near, he was attending a party of ladies out of	MP	II	10	275	9
join the early breakfast party in that house instead of	MP	II	10	280	32
their little party, though it could not boast much beside.	MP	II	11	283	4
They were indeed a smaller party than she had ever known	MP	II	11	284	8
of general break-up of a party which had been so animated.	MP	II	11	286	15
week of the same small party in the same bad weather, had	MP	II	12	291	1
when the small, diminished party met at breakfast, William	MP	III	6	374	29
in the kitchen, the small party of females were pretty	MP	III	7	385	37
will come; we cards for her first party on the 28th.--	MP	III	9	394	1
them, and made one in the family party on the ramparts.	MP	III	11	408	3
of fifteen, who was of the party on the ramparts, taking	MP	III	12	415	2
of your cousin's first party, but I was lazy, and now it	MP	III	12	416	2
none to compare with him, and we were a party of sixteen.	MP	III	12	416	2
till after the 14th, for <u>we</u> have a party that evening.	MP	III	12	417	3
The last time I saw Crawford was at Mrs. Fraser's party.	MP	III	13	423	2
We are not a lively party.	MP	III	13	423	2
Tom had gone from London with a party of young men to	MP	III	13	426	10
on a fever; and when the party broke up, being unable to	MP	III	13	426	10
him, and the sadly small party remaining at Mansfield,	MP	III	13	427	12
By one of the suffering party within, they were expected	MP	III	15	447	37
It had been a miserable party, each of the three believing	MP	III	16	448	1
But he was pressed to stay for Mrs. Fraser's party; his	MP	III	17	467	20
We shall be most happy to consider you as one of the party.	E	I	6	47	29
it diffuses through the party those pleasantest feelings	E	I	7	56	46
whether Mr. Woodhouse's party could be made up in the	E	I	9	81	78
account of the yesterday's party at his friend Cole's, and	E	I	10	88	34
were to bring some of the party the last half of the way;	E	I	11	91	3
Isabella, and the little party made two natural divisions;	E	I	12	100	15
a possible thing in preference to a division of the party.	E	I	13	108	2
place or with any other party, I should try not to go out	E	I	13	110	9
Such a sad loss to our party to-day!"	E	I	13	114	34
and prevent this day's party, which it might very possibly	E	I	13	115	39
quite forgotten in the expectation of a pleasant party.	E	I	13	115	42
will be a small party, but where small parties are select,	E	I	13	116	43
Churchill and Miss Smith making their party quite complete.	E	I	14	119	8
know)--the case is, that a party of friends are invited to	E	I	14	120	11
at last the drawing-room party did receive an augmentation.	E	I	15	124	1
he did not belong to their party, stept in after his wife	E	I	15	128	23
and comfort to all their little party, except herself.--	E	I	15	132	38
obliged to see the whole party set off, and return to his	E	I	17	140	1
when they were out in that party on the water, and she, by	E	II	1	160	23
more honourable to each party from the circumstance of	E	II	2	164	7
who had been of the party, and had seen only proper	E	II	3	170	1
at Mr. Green's, and the party at Mrs. Brown's--smiles and	E	II	4	181	4
They all seemed to remember the day, the hour, the party,	E	II	5	187	4
had known much of Miss Fairfax and her party at Weymouth."	E	II	6	200	17
as the idea of the party to be assembled there, consisting	E	II	7	208	7
she was not absolutely without inclination for the party.	E	II	7	208	9
the hours would be too late, and the party too numerous.	E	II	7	208	9
Emma comes away early, it will be breaking up the party."	E	II	7	210	17
"The sooner every party breaks up, the better."	E	II	7	210	18
satisfied with the rest of the party as with Mr. Knightley.	E	II	8	214	12
The party was rather large, as it included one other	E	II	8	214	13
I was there--one of the party."	E	II	8	218	35
In so large a party it was not necessary that Emma should	E	II	8	220	45
"This is the luxury of a large party," said she:--"one can	E	II	8	222	59
Churchill, "to join your party and wait for her at	E	II	9	234	27
her-- and now we are such a nice party, she cannot refuse.	E	II	9	236	46
what he and <u>all that party</u> would particularly prize.	E	II	10	241	8
Oh! Mr. Knightley, what a delightful party last night; how	E	II	10	245	48
there--that the same party should be collected, and the	E	II	11	247	3
The party did not break up without Emma's being positively	E	II	11	256	60
by one very superior party--in which her card tables	E	II	16	290	3
one day would be the very day of this party.--	E	II	16	292	7
The day came, the party were punctually assembled, and Mr.	E	II	16	292	10
The whole party were but just reassembled in the drawing-	E	II	17	302	23
would probably prolong rather than break up the party.	E	II	17	303	23
without your being of the party; and why I am to be	E	II	18	312	50
time, the Randalls' party just sufficiently before them.	E	III	2	319	2
The whole party walked about, and looked, and praised	E	III	2	320	5
patch of greensward by the side, a party of gipsies.	E	III	3	333	5
was unseen by the whole party till almost close to them.	E	III	3	334	7
they fell in with a larger party, who, like themselves,	E	III	5	344	3
The Randalls' party agreed to it immediately; and after a	E	III	5	344	3
wait, and every projected party be still only talked of.	E	III	6	352	2
That there was to be such a party had been long generally	E	III	6	352	2
degradation of being said to be of Mrs. Elton's party!	E	III	6	353	3
One cannot have too large a party.	E	III	6	353	4
A large party secures its own amusement.	E	III	6	353	4
exploring party from Maple Grove to kings weston."	E	III	6	354	7
It is my party.	E	III	6	354	12
It is my party.	E	III	6	354	14
There is to be no form or parade--a sort of gipsy party.--	E	III	6	355	20

well as Emma, to join the party; and he knew that to have E III 6 356 29
so fast, that the party to box hill was again under happy E III 6 357 32
partake of this al-fresco party; and in one of the most E III 6 357 33
The whole party were assembled, excepting Frank Churchill, E III 6 358 35
The cold repast was over, and the party were to go out E III 6 361 42
You will all be going soon I suppose; the whole party E III 6 364 55
The rest of the party were now returning, and all were E III 6 366 74
you wish me to stay, and join the party, I will." E III 6 366 74
75
and punctuality, were in favour of a pleasant party. E III 7 367 1
should certainly have lost all the happiness of this party. E III 7 368 4
Though, perhaps, as the chaperon of the party--I never was E III 7 370 20
It did not seem to touch the rest of the party equally; E III 7 371 35
36
That's one of the ladies in the Irish car party, not at E III 7 374 53
How it might be considered by the rest of the party, she E III 8 377 1
every body seemed rather fagged after the morning's party. E III 8 381 19
However, I shall always think it a very pleasant party, E III 8 381 19
after the return of the party from box hill--which E III 8 383 31
The Box-Hill party had decided him on going away. E III 13 432 41
They sat down to tea--the same party round the same table-- E III 14 434 2
myself that you were not of the Box-Hill party. E III 14 441 8
Emma knew that he was now getting to the Box-Hill party, E III 15 447 21
In such a party, Harriet would be rather a dead weight E III 15 450 37
she shortly afterwards began, "since the party to Box-Hill. E III 16 454 18
Very pleasant party. E III 16 454 18
What say you both to our collecting the same party, and E III 16 455 18
It must be the same party, you know, quite the same party, E III 16 455 18
A few more to-morrows, and the party from London would be E III 18 470 1
by him to join their party the same evening to Astley's. E III 18 471 20
The party was to be our brother and sister, Henry, John-- E III 18 471 20
When Mr. Weston joined the party, however, and when the E III 18 476 46
47
A very few days brought the party from London, and she had E III 19 481 1
The party drove off in very good spirits; Sir Walter P III 5 35 18
concluded you must have been obliged to give up the party." P III 5 39 36
you were well enough, and I hope you had a pleasant party." P III 5 39 38
it, to have their walking party joined by both the Miss P III 5 41 46
The party at the great house was sometimes increased by P III 6 47 14
to think that the cottage party, probably, would not like P III 7 54 5
There had been a time, when of all the large party now P III 8 63 3
matters throughout the party; and he was very much P III 8 64 4
It was a merry, joyous party, and no one seemed in higher P III 8 71 57
rest of the party waited for them at the top of the hill. P III 10 86 18
comfort in their whole party being immediately afterwards P III 10 89 35
parties; and to that party of the three which boasted P III 10 90 37
was to cross; and when the party had all reached the gate P III 10 90 38
attended to by the party, that an earnest desire to see P III 11 94 6
The party from Uppercross passing down by the now deserted P III 11 96 10
moved forward to meet the party, "he had not, perhaps, a P III 11 97 13
of considering the whole party as friends of their own, P III 11 97 15
have brought any such party to Lyme, without considering P III 11 98 15
did not seem fit for the mirth of the party in general. P III 11 100 22
the earliest of the party the next morning, agreed to P III 12 102 1
since entering Lyme) drew half the party to the window. P III 12 105 8
change amongst their party, and instead of Captain Benwick, P III 12 107 23
the direction of all the party in what was to be their P III 12 108 30
As to the wretched party left behind, it could scarcely be P III 12 110 43
It now became necessary for the party to consider what was P III 12 112 56
being able to join their party at home, before her P IV 2 134 31
She gave him a short account of her party, and business at P IV 3 143 19
If he had but asked who the party were! P IV 3 144 19
Captain Benwick of the party, "for he had been invited as P IV 6 164 8
in the same small family party; since Henrietta's coming P IV 6 167 19
Mrs. Clay should be of the party in the carriage; and they P IV 7 175 4
Wentworth himself, among a party of gentlemen and ladies, P IV 7 175 6
ladies of Captain Wentworth's party began talking of them. P IV 7 177 17
Who is your party?" P IV 7 180 34
the earliest of all their party, at the rooms in the P IV 8 181 1
and the very party appeared for whom they were waiting. P IV 8 184 17
up to the demands of the party, to the needful civilities P IV 8 184 17
soon afterwards, the whole party was collected, and all P IV 8 185 19
The party was divided, and disposed of on two contiguous P IV 8 186 23
party, some of them did decide on going in quest of tea. P IV 8 188 44
You were a large party in yourselves, and you wanted P IV 9 193 12
should be added to their party, seemed the destruction of P IV 10 215 13
apparent confusion as to whom their party consisted of. P IV 10 216 18
in being his mother's party, that every thing might be P IV 10 217 19
She felt that Mrs. Musgrove and all her party ought to be P IV 10 219 29
It shall be a regular party--small, but most elegant." P IV 10 220 29
A large party in an hotel ensured a quick-changing, P IV 10 221 32
more than half filled: a party of steady old friends were P IV 10 221 32
"Phoo? phoo!" replied Charles, "what's an evening party? P IV 10 223 44
Anne too, if there is a party at her father's; and I am P IV 10 224 51
my inclination, ma'am, the party at home (excepting on P IV 10 224 52
53
"To-morrow evening, to meet a few friends, no formal party. P IV 10 226 64
The party separated. P IV 10 227 68
Mrs. Clay for the morrow's party, the frequent enumeration P IV 10 227 69
The party before her were Mrs. Musgrove, talking to Mrs. P IV 11 229 2
of all meeting again, at your party," (turning to Anne.) P IV 11 236 36
return "hither, or follow your party, as soon as possible. P IV 11 237 43
that we hope to see your whole party this evening. P IV 11 239 49
The party were very soon moving after dinner. S 6 389 1
found the united denham party;--but though united in the S 7 395 1
of the party & to give her the whole of his conversation. S 7 396 1
into lodgings & all the party continuing quite well, their S 10 413 1

PARTY'S (1)
for each party's perfectly knowing their situation. P III 5 34 13

PASED (1)
Miss Osborne & Miss Carr as they pased her in the dance. W 331 11

PASS (104)
You may well wonder how I contrive to pass my time here--& LS 7 254 3
make many of those hours pass very pleasantly which would LS 10 258 3
called, but I seldom hear any noise when I pass that way. LS 17 271 7
With such encouragement, Catherine hoped at least to pass NA I 2 20 8
If we make haste, we shall pass by them presently, and I NA I 6 43 41
that does not actually pass under one's own observation; NA I 14 109 23
that are to pass before your brother can hold the living." NA II 1 136 48
about, for whatever might pass on his side, you must be NA II 3 145 13
your hand, will pass through it into a small vaulted room." NA II 5 159 19
To pass between lodges of a modern appearance, to find NA II 5 161 25
she had yet to pass before she could gain the gallery. NA II 9 194 6
making Miss Morland's time at Northanger pass pleasantly. NA II 11 209 5
What so natural, as that anger should pass away and NA II 13 227 27
For two days Mrs. Morland allowed it to pass even without NA II 15 240 2
body would be eager to pass through the room which has SS I 14 73 17
correspondence were to pass through Sir John's hands." SS I 16 84 6
the house, you may see all the carriages that pass along. SS II 8 197 22
the word "infection" to pass his lips, gave instant alarm SS III 7 307 3
the acquaintance than to pass my time pleasantly while I SS III 8 319 29
few hours that were to pass, before I could have an SS III 8 321 34
I was too much shocked to be able to pass myself off as SS III 8 330 69
I know the summer will pass happily away. SS III 10 343 9
were so wise as never to pass that point; & Mr Edwards now W 325 4
defects of the person with whom you are to pass your life." PP I 6 23 10
"You are considering how insupportable it would be to pass PP I 6 27 47
to Jane what she had seen pass between the two gentlemen; PP I 15 74 12
close to them, meaning to pass through the set to the PP I 18 92 22
reproach shall ever pass my lips when we are married." PP I 19 106 10
door and with quick step pass her towards the staircase, PP I 20 110 1
and sometimes cold, did January and February pass away. PP II 4 151 1
She had also to anticipate how her visit would pass, the PP II 5 157 10
I had hoped to pass myself off with some degree of credit. PP II 8 174 15
on purpose to pass for a lady,--only think what fun! PP II 16 221 17
Four weeks were to pass away before her uncle and aunt's PP II 19 239 10
But they did pass away, and Mr. and Mrs. Gardiner, with PP II 19 239 10
any success, no such people had been seen to pass through. PP III 4 275 5
It will pass away soon enough." PP III 6 299 21
enter my house again, nor even to pass through the village. PP III 6 300 30
of the visit would not pass away without enabling them to PP III 12 340 14
They sometimes pass in such very little time from reserve MP I 5 49 32
"The soil is good; and I never pass it without regretting, MP I 6 54 10
by Edmund on foot, pass through a gate into the lane, and MP I 7 68 17
with little difficulty pass round the edge of the gate, MP I 10 99 18
allow for it, and let it pass; Julia was vexed, and her MP I 10 101 29
evenings pass away with more enjoyment even to my father." MP II 3 196 2
her into the house, through which it was necessary to pass. MP II 4 215 47
checked herself and let it pass; and tried to look calm MP II 5 226 64
very cordial adieus, pass quietly away; stopping at the MP II 10 280 33
that many posts would not pass before I should be followed MP II 13 299 5
I thought it might all pass for nothing with him." MP III 1 315 19
that he observed to pass before, and at, and after dinner. MP III 3 336 7
Oh! why will such things ever pass away?" MP III 5 358 7
were to pass all their middle and latter life together. MP III 7 375 2
Servants are come to such a pass, my dear, in Portsmouth, MP III 7 385 39
into danger, or Rebecca pass by with a flower in her hat. MP III 11 408 2
to live upon letters, and pass all her time between MP III 13 427 13
at this time, to Bath, to pass a few days with his mother, MP III 16 450 8
"Well," said Emma, willing to let it pass--"you want to E I 1 11 35
foretel things, for whatever you say always comes to pass. E I 1 12 40
Emma felt the bad taste of her friend, but let it pass E I 7 54 33
not allow much time to pass before he spoke to the lady, E I 8 60 27
not breathe a compliment to the sex should pass his lips. E I 9 70 7
will pass between us, and you shall not be committed.-- E I 9 76 38
short might be hoped to pass away in unsullied cordiality. E I 11 93 5
a mind to take it up; but she struggled, and let it pass. E I 11 96 27
wish otherwise, but that the days did not pass so swiftly. E I 13 108 1
visit could not possibly pass without bringing forward the E I 14 119 6
I merely called, because I would not pass the door without E II 1 162 32
and a twelvemonth might pass without their being thrown E II 3 180 58
"Will Mr. Frank Churchill pass through Bath as well as E II 5 189 17
and not meant to provoke; and therefore she let it pass. E II 7 206 4
also, that nothing really unexceptionable may pass us." E II 17 302 20
at once here, delights you too much to pass unnoticed. E II 18 312 50
She felt as if the spring would not pass without bringing E III 1 315 2
So afraid you might have a headach!--seeing you pass by so E III 2 322 19
very person was chancing to pass by to rescue her!-- E III 3 335 10
it should pass unnoticed or not, replied, "never marry!-- E III 4 341 29
30
Should she proceed no farther?--should she let it pass, E III 4 341 34
Let no name ever pass our lips. E III 4 342 39
The two other gentlemen waited at the door to let her pass. E III 5 346 17
Better pass it off as a joke. E III 7 370 22
Pass us, if you please, Mr. Churchill. E III 7 372 37
Pass Mr. E., Knightley, Jane, and myself. E III 7 372 37
"Yes, yes, pray pass me," added her husband, with a sort E III 7 372 38
had stood out and seen it pass by, the boy going a good E III 8 383 31
a few days were allowed to pass before they met again, E III 12 416 2
Such a conclusion could not pass unanswered by Mrs. Weston. E III 12 420 14
great--and her mind had to pass again and again through E III 14 435 4
You pass it over very handsomely--but you were perfectly E III 15 445 12
to by both parties) they might pass for a happy couple. P III 6 43 5
But a week must pass; only a week, in Anne's reckoning, P III 7 53 1
and all were contented to pass quietly and carefully down P III 12 109 32
How the long stage would pass; how it was to affect their P III 12 116 70
What instances must pass before them of ardent, P IV 5 156 10
Lady Russell let this pass, and only said in rejoinder, "I P IV 5 159 25
I shall only say, "how d'ye do," as we pass, however. P IV 6 169 29
He was preparing only to bow and pass on, but her gentle " P IV 8 181 1
Facts or opinions which are to pass through the hands of P IV 9 205 85
and intelligent glances pass between two or three of the P IV 10 222 37
whether to join or to pass on, said nothing--only looked. P IV 11 239 55
Anne smiled, and let it pass. P IV 11 243 68
with most unwilling looks been constrained to pass by--. S 1 364 1
we were actually to pass within a mile or two of a S 1 367 1
one of the girls of the family to pass the winter with her. S 3 378 1

PASSABLE (3)
polished, were more than passable; they were grateful, MP III 10 402 12
What is passable in youth, is detestable in later age. E I 4 33 36
the road to be now just passable for adventurous people, E I 15 127 13

PASSAGE (47)
own room I met him in the passage, & then as I knew that LS 24 286 5
themselves at last in the passage behind the highest bench. NA I 2 21 9
and of all the dangers of her late passage through them. NA I 2 21 9
Thorpe, who had descried them from above, in the passage. NA I 7 49 43
beyond them, a narrower passage, more numerous openings, NA II 8 185 5
In the high-arched passage, paved with stone, which NA II 8 188 17
This passage is at least as extraordinary a road from the NA II 9 195 8
"Have you looked into all the rooms in that passage?" NA II 9 195 16
A narrow passage led directly through the house into the SS I 6 28 2
thoughts of throwing the passage into one of them with SS I 6 29 4
They were no sooner in the passage than Marianne came SS I 15 75 2
through the passage into the parlour, attended by Sir John. SS I 19 106 21
He immediately went into the passage, opened the front SS I 19 108 35
he was in the passage; and in another, he was before them. SS III 12 359 10
coming, he will wait in the passage, & come in with them.-- W 319 2
we passed in the passage, was Mr Musgrave, then?-- W 327 8
the latter, where the passage was straightened by tables, W 332 11
of the house to the front door, & then within the passage. W 355 28
I will read you the passage which particularly hurts me. PP I 21 117 14
when they entered the passage she was there to welcome PP II 4 152 5
in proposing to take his passage in the September packet, MP I 11 107 2
generally delays, a bad passage or something; that MP I 11 107 3
twice as long on his passage, or were still in Antigua. MP II 1 176 4
opportunity of making his passage thither in a private MP II 1 178 8
interesting moment of his passage to England, when the MP II 1 180 10
in the parlour, and why should we stay in the passage?-- MP III 7 378 12
band-box in the passage, and called out for a candle; no MP III 7 379 19
the passage, he exclaimed, "devil take those young dogs! MP III 7 383 30
passage and staircase, struck her beyond her imagination. MP III 7 387 47
of Shakespeare would have a long note on that passage." E I 9 75 25
was standing in the passage-- were not you, Jane?--for my E II 3 173 27
not they use both rooms, and dance across the passage?" E II 11 248 10
Every door was now closed, the passage plan given up, and E II 11 249 12
a long awkward passage must be gone through to get at it. E II 11 254 44
the young people in that passage; and neither Emma nor the E II 11 254 44
long steps through the passage, was calling out, "you talk E II 11 254 47
48
talk a great deal of the length of this passage, my dear. E II 11 254 47
48
wife, had examined the passage again, and found the evils E II 11 255 59
will be draughts in the passage, though every thing has E III 2 328 45
Well, here we are at the passage. E III 2 329 45
ever before entered the passage, nor walked up the stairs, E III 8 378 3
at home, to wait in the passage, and send up her name.-- E III 16 452 8
Do not you see that, at this instant, the very passage of E III 18 480 77
had the good luck, in my passage home the next autumn, to P III 8 65 16
to give a passage to Lady Mary Grierson and her daughters." P III 8 68 31
32
run against him in the passage, and received his very P III 12 106 19
towards the sea, gave a passage to an inconsiderable S 4 383 1

PASSAGE-ROOM (1)
of its being only a passage-room to something better, and MP III 7 377 10

ASSAGES (10)
Its long, damp passages, its narrow cells and ruined NA II 2 141 11
and along many gloomy passages, into an apartment never NA II 5 158 15
which, with occasional passages, not wholly unintricate, NA II 8 183 2
"Will you take the trouble of reading to us the passages NA II 10 205 22
material passages of her letter with strong indignation. NA II 12 218 4
The same books, the same passages were idolized by each-- SS I 10 47 3
and saw her dwelling intently on some particular passages. PP I 21 116 6
and dwelling on some passages which proved that Jane had PP II 10 182 2
His celebrated passages are quoted by every body; they are MP III 3 338 14
in which particular passages in the service should be MP III 3 340 24
SSED (329)
I passed off the letter as his wife's, to the Vernons, & LS 5 250 3
Reginald observed all that passed, in perfect silence. LS 20 276 3
I am perfectly aware that after what has passed between us, LS 25 292 3
brother, of what had passed between him & Lady Susan to LS 42 311 2
Compliments on good looks now passed; and, after observing NA I 4 32 2
which had passed twenty years before, be minutely repeated. NA I 4 34 9
had been warm, and they passed so rapidly through every NA I 5 36 4
though they overtook and passed the two offending young NA I 7 47 18
other family matters, now passed between them, and NA I 7 51 54
too; she suffered, but no murmur passed her lips." NA I 8 53 2
passed away without sullying her heroic importance. NA I 8 53 3
reasonable time, had just passed through her mind, when NA I 10 75 24
They passed briskly down Pulteney-Street, and through NA I 11 86 51
and Saturday have now passed in review before the reader; NA I 13 97 1
Thus passed a long ten minutes, till they were again NA I 13 100 13
As she walked, she reflected on what had passed. NA I 13 101 25
Catherine, delighted by all that had passed, proceeded NA I 13 103 29
going to Clifton the next day, in spite of what had passed. NA I 13 105 40
The morning had passed away so charmingly as to banish all NA I 14 114 50
The cruel reply was passed on to the other, and he NA II 1 132 16
two or three days had passed away, without her seeing NA II 3 143 1
that no syllable of such a nature ever passed between us. NA II 3 144 11
A few days passed away, and Catherine, though not allowing NA II 4 149 1
had it gone no farther, it might have passed unnoticed. NA II 4 149 1
and nothing passed between the lovers to excite her NA II 4 153 31
way, they could have passed it with ease in half a minute. NA II 5 156 5
examining the furniture before, you had passed unnoticed. NA II 5 160 21
old porch, and had even passed on to the hall, where her NA II 5 161 25
The evening passed without any further disturbance, and, NA II 6 166 8
Hour after hour passed away, and the wearied Catherine had NA II 6 171 12
the two others were passed by; and Catherine's interest in NA II 7 180 37
An hour passed away before the General came in, spent, on NA II 8 182 1
had thrown open, and passed through, and seemed on the NA II 8 185 6
the dreadful scene had passed, which released his NA II 8 186 6
might that morning have passed near the very spot of this NA II 8 188 17
the lower windows, as he passed to the prison of his wife; NA II 8 188 19
Again she passed through the folding-doors, again her hand NA II 9 191 4
to lose a moment, she passed through and closed the door. NA II 9 194 6
slightest way to what had passed, was of the greatest NA II 10 201 4
in which Miss Thorpe's name was included, passed his lips. NA II 10 204 18
A day or two passed away and brought no tidings of Captain NA II 11 209 5
and at all the little chandler's shops which they passed. NA II 11 212 17
Never had any day passed so quickly! NA II 11 214 26
The happiness with which their time now passed, every NA II 13 220 1
of surprize had passed away, in a "good heaven! what can NA II 13 222 7
In such considerations time passed away, and it was NA II 13 222 8
After what has so lately passed, so lately been settled NA II 13 223 13
had passed, an apology might properly be received by her. NA II 13 227 27
Very little passed between them on meeting; each found her NA II 13 227 27
ago she had so happily passed along in going to and from NA II 14 230 1
the distance of five, she passed the turning which led to NA II 14 230 1
repose, the hours passed away, and her journey advanced NA II 14 231 5
that after what had passed he had little right to expect a NA II 15 241 7
The ladies had passed near it in their way along the SS I 7 32 1
and every thing that passed during the visit, tended to SS I 10 46 1
But when this passed away, when her spirits became SS I 10 46 2
The lady would probably have passed without suspicion, had SS I 11 57 17
I never passed within view of it without admiring its SS I 14 73 17
She thought of what had just passed with anxiety and SS I 15 77 19
after all that has openly passed between them, you can SS I 15 80 38
Nothing in my opinion has ever passed to justify doubt; no SS I 15 80 42
The evening passed off in the equal indulgence of feeling. SS I 16 83 3
Mrs. Dashwood, his hand passed so directly before her, as SS I 18 98 10
to take no notice of what passed, by instantly talking of SS I 18 98 13
Never had any week passed so quickly--he could hardly SS I 19 101 1
spite of all that had passed, was not prepared to witness. SS II 3 155 6
relating all that had passed, her suspicions of SS II 5 172 39
him with every thing that passed, Elinor forgot the SS II 7 184 16
"Yes--could that be wrong after all that had passed?-- SS II 7 186 36
I have passed a wretched night in endeavouring to excuse a SS II 7 187 42
but when this emotion had passed away, she added, in a SS II 7 189 47
48
slightest allusion to what has passed, before my sister. SS II 8 195 17
of all that had passed, satisfactory, convincing; and SS II 9 202 7
an account of what had passed, and intreat her directions SS II 9 203 10
to Marianne, from the communication of what had passed. SS II 9 211 33
Abundance of civilities passed on all sides. SS II 11 228 52
first time after all that passed, in the company of Lucy!-- SS II 12 231 10
the impression of what had passed, the whole evening. SS II 12 236 42
And now he had been so worried by what passed, that as SS III 2 273 16
what had really passed between them was to this effect. SS III 3 282 16
narration of what really passed between Colonel Brandon SS III 3 284 24
for what has lately passed--for the cruel situation in SS III 4 289 31
Their party was small, and the hours passed quietly away. SS III 6 303 12
Two days passed away from the time of Mr. Palmer's SS III 7 309 7
sounds of complaint which passed her lips, was almost SS III 7 310 10
11
Hour after hour passed away in sleepless pain and delirium SS III 7 312 17
did Mrs. Jennings hear in the morning of what had passed. SS III 7 313 20
Half an hour passed away, and the favourable symptom yet SS III 7 314 22
The bustle in the vestibule, as she passed along an inner SS III 7 316 31
after what has passed--your coming here in this manner, SS III 8 318 21
22
part of what had really passed between Mrs. Smith and SS III 8 324 42
'All!--no,--have you forgot what passed in town?-- that SS III 8 325 48
"Yes, I saw every note that passed." SS III 8 325 49
Devonshire, and what had passed within her observation the SS III 8 328 61
instead of an inquiry, she passed it off with a smile. SS III 9 336 11
Mrs. Dashwood, not less watchful of what passed than her SS III 10 340 3
her, it never passed away without the atonement of a smile. SS III 10 342 7
Some letters had passed between her and her brother, in SS III 11 353 21
after day passed off, and brought no letter, no tidings. SS III 12 358 4
Not a syllable passed aloud. SS III 12 359 10
But when the second moment had passed, when she found SS III 13 363 8
knew nothing of what had passed; and the first hours of SS III 13 370 35
am grown neither humble nor penitent by what has passed.-- SS III 13 372 41
it was earned by them before many months had passed away. SS III 14 375 10
They passed some months in great happiness at Dawlish; for SS III 14 376 11
which passed between you & me for the last 14 years." W 321 2
voice, before they passed thro' the turnpike gate & W 321 2
The party passed on--Mrs E's Sattin gown swept along the W 327 8
we passed in the passage, was Mr Musgrave, then?-- W 327 8
Emma looked at them all as they passed--but chiefly & with W 329 9
a jerking curtsey as they passed her; even Ly. Osborne W 336 13
The morng passed quietly away in discussing the merits of W 338 17
could not help observing how comfortably it had passed. W 343 19
when he heard what had passed;--a little peevish under W 348 22
The evening altogether passed off pleasantly to the whole PP I 3 12 15
Elizabeth was so much caught by what passed, as to leave PP I 8 38 39
Elizabeth passed the chief of the night in her sister's PP I 9 41 1

The day passed much as the day before had done. PP I 10 47 1
attending to what passed between Darcy and his companion. PP I 10 47 2
during the hour which passed before the gentlemen appeared. PP I 11 54 1
his cousins, their time passed till they entered Meryton. PP I 15 72 7
London Lydia came to inquire, and he bowed as they passed. PP I 15 72 8
what passed, took leave and rode on with his friend. PP I 15 73 9
but unluckily no one passed the windows now except a few PP I 15 74 11
part of our youth was passed together; inmates of the same PP I 16 81 37
Elizabeth related to Jane the next day, what had passed PP I 17 85 1
where this conversation passed, by the arrival of some of PP I 17 86 9
meanwhile, was meditating in solitude on what had passed. PP I 20 112 24
Elizabeth passed quietly out of the room, Jane and Kitty PP I 20 114 31
drop no hint of what had passed before any of the family. PP I 22 123 3
scolding her, a month passed away before she could speak PP I 23 127 5
Day after day passed away without bringing any other PP I 23 129 12
mother, an hour seldom passed in which she did not talk of PP I 23 129 14
A day or two passed before Jane had courage to speak of PP II 1 134 4
5
and though a day seldom passed in which Elizabeth did not PP II 1 137 26
Four weeks passed away, and Jane saw nothing of him. PP II 3 147 25
The day passed most pleasantly away; the morning in bustle PP II 4 152 5
A great deal more passed at the other table. PP II 6 166 41
and dinner was now passed by him either at work in the PP II 7 168 1
Very few days passed in which Mr. Collins did not walk to PP II 7 168 3
way, the first fortnight of her visit soon passed away. PP II 7 169 6
consciousness of what had passed between the Bingleys and PP II 7 171 12
affected with what had passed, she soon afterwards said, " PP II 10 184 16
17
Her astonishment, as she reflected on what had passed, was PP II 11 193 31
side, and she soon passed one of the gates into the ground. PP II 12 195 1
The five weeks which she had now passed in Kent, had made PP II 12 195 2
I will only say farther, that from what passed that PP II 12 198 5
from what had passed between Colonel Fitzwilliam and PP II 13 206 4
She perfectly remembered every thing that had passed in PP II 13 206 5
alluded, as having passed at the Netherfield ball, and as PP II 13 209 10
to hear that you have passed your time not disagreeably. PP II 15 215 3
4
But they were entirely ignorant of what had passed; and PP II 18 233 24
only serve, after what had since passed, to provoke her. PP II 18 233 25
in which her time had passed at Hunsford, she mentioned PP II 18 233 26
The rest of the evening passed with the appearance, on his PP II 18 235 39
The town where she had formerly passed some years of her PP II 19 239 7
Wickham passed all his youth there, you know." PP II 19 240 13
As they passed into other rooms, these objects were taking PP III 1 246 5
She listened most attentively to all that passed between PP III 1 255 59
the evening though as it passed it seemed long, was not PP III 2 265 16
My dear Lizzy, they must have passed within ten miles of PP III 4 274 3
Upon this information, they instantly passed through the PP III 7 301 6
"We must endeavour to forget all that has passed on either PP III 7 305 37
presents in money, which passed to her, through her PP III 8 309 4
We passed each other several times. PP III 10 328 16
Anxious and uneasy, the period which passed in the drawing- PP III 12 341 14
I think every thing has passed off uncommonly well, I PP III 12 342 28
Not a word passed between the sisters concerning Bingley; PP III 13 345 20
Not a word, however, passed his lips in allusion to it, PP III 13 348 35
36
As they passed through the hall, Lady Catherine opened the PP III 14 352 19
before many days had passed after Lady Catherine's visit. PP III 16 365 1
The evening passed quietly, unmarked by any thing PP III 17 372 2
How little did you tell me of what passed at Pemberley and PP III 17 374 18
gaiety, but the evening passed tranquilly away; there was PP III 17 377 41
But the morrow passed off much better than she expected; PP III 17 378 46
A week had passed in this way, and no suspicion of it MP I 2 15 9
the many years which have passed since you parted, have MP I 3 33 64
The winter came and passed without their being called for; MP I 4 34 3
But in general, I can assure you that they are all passed MP I 6 60 49
the meadow, she could not help watching all that passed. MP I 7 67 16
After what passed at first, he would claim it as a promise. MP I 8 77 11
will be at what she said just now," passed across her mind. MP I 9 89 26
A quarter of an hour, twenty minutes, passed away, and MP I 10 97 1
was quite unhappy in having to communicate what had passed. MP I 10 101 33
passed at table, did not evince the least disapprobation. MP I 13 124 13
and as two or three days passed away in this manner, MP I 14 130 1
Dinner passed heavily. MP I 15 142 24
Fanny into any real forgetfulness of what had passed.-- MP I 16 150 1
A glimpse, as she passed through the hall, of the two MP I 18 168 14
The evening passed with external smoothness, though almost MP II 2 191 11
Four-and-twenty hours had never passed before, since MP II 2 192 11
"This is the first October that she has passed in the MP II 3 199 15
"But they are passed over," said Fanny.-- MP II 4 207 8
and moreover the quietest five months I ever passed." MP II 4 210 17
In approaching the parsonage they passed close by the MP II 5 222 45
A very cordial meeting passed between him and Edmund; and MP II 5 223 48
Here he was again on the same ground where all had passed MP II 5 224 49
Miss Crawford was too much vexed by what had passed to be MP II 5 227 68
and scarcely ten days had passed since Fanny had been in MP II 6 233 14
He passed, however, for an admirer of her dancing; and Sir MP II 7 251 63
the door, said as she passed him, "you must dance with me, MP II 10 272 4
seen so little of what passed, and had so little curiosity, MP II 11 282 4
The week which passed so quietly and peaceably at the MP II 11 285 15
by my uncle, after the evening they passed together." MP II 13 300 5
think nothing of what had passed, it would be quite MP II 13 303 12
Nearly half an hour had passed, and she was growing very MP III 1 312 4
these reflections having passed across his mind and MP III 1 320 44
and cry over what had passed, with very wretched feelings. MP III 1 320 45
I need not repeat what has passed. MP III 1 321 47
what has passed; I shall not even tell your aunt Bertram. MP III 1 322 48
a knowledge of what had passed between the young people. MP III 2 329 11
all that had then passed, she added, "once only before. MP III 5 358 7
better pleased that such a token of friendship had passed. MP III 5 365 36
All this passed over night, for the journey was to begin MP III 6 374 29
William knew what had passed, and from his heart lamented MP III 7 375 3
the three weeks which had passed since their leaving MP III 7 375 4
Edmund's college as they passed along, and made no stop MP III 7 376 5
They passed the Drawbridge, and entered the town; and the MP III 7 376 6
time it is all settled," passed internally, without more MP III 10 401 9
when the moment was passed, could regret that she had not MP III 10 406 20
The evening passed, without a pause of misery, the night MP III 15 441 20
She passed only from feelings of sickness to shudderings MP III 15 441 20
joy and gratitude, as she passed the barriers of MP III 15 445 32
the first day's journey passed without her hearing a word MP III 15 445 34
Fanny had scarcely passed the solemn-looking servants, MP III 15 447 37
quieted, stupified, indifferent to every thing that passed. MP III 16 448 2
Long, long would it be ere Miss Crawford's name passed his MP III 16 453 16
the conversation that had passed, a saucy playful smile, MP III 16 459 30
After what had passed to wound and alienate the two MP III 17 469 23
authority being now long passed away, they had been living E I 1 5 3
or twenty years of his life passed cheerfully away. E I 2 16 5
of greater happiness than in any yet passed through. E I 2 17 6
Her youth had passed without distinction, and her middle E I 3 21 4
He has passed you very often." E I 4 29 13
Some minutes passed in this unpleasant silence, with only E I 8 65 50
A few inferior dwellings were first to be passed, and then, E I 10 83 2
The lane made a slight bend; and when that bend was passed, E I 10 87 29
30
them was open, and Emma passed into it with the E I 10 89 38
Perhaps she might have passed over more had his manners E I 11 93 5
of similar moment, and passed away with similar harmony; E I 12 104 50
John Knightley, as they passed through the sweep-gate, " E I 13 116 46
begun, scarcely had they passed the sweep-gate and joined E I 15 129 24
his house; and he was out before another syllable passed.-- E I 15 132 37
gallant; but it had passed as his way, as a mere error of E I 16 134 5

body's knowing what had passed except the three principals, E I 16 138 15
though some years passed away from the death of poor E II 2 163 4
a conviction of some part of what had passed between them. E II 3 173 26
considering all that had passed as a mere trifle, and E II 3 180 54
A week had not passed since Miss Hawkins's name was first E II 4 181 2
she had thankfully passed six weeks not six months ago?-- E II 5 187 4
The clock struck twelve as she passed through the hall. E II 5 189 20
amiable a feeling before, passed suspiciously through E II 5 191 26
we passed her house--I saw Miss Bates at the window. E II 5 194 38
brilliant days had long passed away, and now the highest E II 6 197 5
In the summer it might have passed; but what can any E II 8 217 32
the rest of the dinner passed away; the dessert succeeded, E II 8 219 43
Smiles of intelligence passed between her and the E II 8 220 48
And touching Miss Bates, who at the moment passed near-- " E II 8 229 97
the others, as if it had passed within the same apartment." E II 10 243 32
passed by the two young people in schemes on the subject. E II 11 247 2
A few awkward moments passed, and he sat down again; and E II 12 261 32
33
that Mrs. Elton's praise passed from one mouth to another E II 15 281 2
and though much that passed between them was in a half- E II 17 299 1
This was too loud a call for a compliment to be passed by, E II 18 307 24
25
in the street as he passed--he had not stopped, he would E III 1 316 4
appeared; and all the smiles and the proprieties passed. E III 2 320 11
very proper attention, after the introduction had passed. E III 2 321 13
while smiles of high glee passed between him and his wife. E III 2 328 38
the knowledge of what had passed,--aware of the anxiety E III 3 335 12
A very few days had passed after this adventure, when E III 4 337 1
2
you could forget what passed in this very room about court E III 4 338 12
As they were turning into the grounds, Mr. Perry passed by E III 5 344 4
passed between them into the hall, and looked at neither. E III 5 346 17
Tea passed pleasantly, and nobody seemed in a hurry to E III 5 347 18
be abhorred in recollection, than any she had ever passed. E III 8 377 1
her's, and all that had passed of good in her feelings E III 9 385 7
who had seen them, had passed undiscerned by her who now E III 11 410 35
friend, therefore, she passed off through another door-- E III 11 411 42
till a little time had passed, and Mr. Churchill could be E III 12 417 5
Within half an hour, he had passed from a thoroughly E III 13 432 40
still be greater when the flutter should have passed away. E III 14 434 1
Bates being present, it passed, of course, to Mrs. Cole, E III 17 468 35
Time passed on. E III 18 470 1
all that had so recently passed on Harriet's side, so E III 18 473 27
Thirteen years had passed away since Lady Elliot's death, P III 1 5 7
So passed the first three weeks. P III 6 47 16
a bow, a curtsey passed; she heard his voice--he talked to P III 7 59 25
almost eight years had passed, since all had been given up. P III 7 60 28
was the winter that I passed by myself at deal, when the P III 8 71 54
silence in which it had passed--the little particulars of P III 9 80 34
Three days had passed without his coming once to P III 10 82 2
herself, they happily passed the danger; and by once P III 10 92 48
a generation must have passed away since the first partial P III 11 95 9
They ascended and passed him; and as they passed, Anne's P III 12 104 6
half a glance at Anne; "it is they very man we passed." P III 12 105 10
attend to their having passed close by him in their early P III 12 106 19
very lately, and so light of heart, they had passed along. P III 12 111 49
informed and directed, as they passed, towards the spot. P III 12 111 50
Scenes had passed in Uppercross, which made it precious. P IV 1 123 8
The first three or four days passed most quietly, with no P IV 1 125 14
had passed into better hands than its owners'. P IV 1 125 17
He had been in Bath about a fortnight; (he had passed P IV 3 138 6
comprehending what had passed, and in the degree of P IV 3 144 22
first evening in Camden-Place could have passed so well! P IV 3 144 24
in the meeting had soon passed away, and left only the P IV 5 153 6
Mrs. Clay, who had been present while all this passed, now P IV 5 158 20
she not only might have passed him unseen, but was obliged P IV 6 169 25
Mutual enquiries on common subjects passed; neither of P IV 7 176 8
admiring Anne as she passed, except in the air and look P IV 7 177 16
you," being all that she had time for, as she passed away. P IV 7 177 16
or nine years should have passed over him, and in foreign P IV 7 179 28
A day or two passed without producing any thing.-- P IV 7 179 32
frightful day!" and he passed his hand across his eyes, as P IV 8 182 6
passed to their seats, her mind took a hasty range over it. P IV 8 185 21
of observation; and she passed along the room without P IV 8 186 22
could never have passed along the streets of Bath, than P IV 9 192 3
I perfectly see how the hours passed--that you had always P IV 9 194 14
'To do the best for himself,' passed as a duty." P IV 9 202 64
The visit passed off altogether in high good humour. P IV 10 219 28
One day only had passed since Anne's conversation with Mrs. P IV 11 229 1
He had passed out of the room without a look! P IV 11 236 39
minutes only, which now passed before she was interrupted, P IV 11 238 44
and soon words enough had passed between them to decide P IV 11 240 59
the house they had passed--& the persons who approached, S 1 364 1
your own, we have passed none in this place, which can be S 1 365 1
2 miles of the sea, they passed close by a moderate-sized S 4 379 1
There was no blue shoe when we passed this way a month ago. S 4 383 1
In ascending, they passed the Lodge-Gates of Sanditon S 4 383 1
Activity run mad!"--had just passed through Charlotte's S 9 410 1

PASSER-BY (1)
she had been before, much more within reach of a passer-by. P IV 8 189 46

PASSES (5)
city, that a day never passes in which parties of ladies, NA I 7 44 1
You forget how time passes." E I 11 96 23
I say one thing and then I say another, and it passes off. E II 9 237 46
Mr. Frank Churchill are hearing every thing that passes. E II 10 245 49
our house, simply rages & passes on--while down in this S 4 381 1

PASSING (76)
people were every moment passing in and out, up the steps NA I 4 31 1
the resistless pressure of a long string of passing ladies. NA I 10 76 29
to a man who was just passing by on horseback, that they NA I 11 86 46
a pleasant walk after our passing you in Argyle-Street: NA I 12 93 7
that she found herself passing through the great gates of NA II 5 161 24
rooms in common use, by passing through a few of less NA II 8 183 2
left them; and lastly, by passing through a dark little NA II 8 183 2
observation of what is passing around you--does our NA II 9 197 29
playing round him, was passing up the hill and within a SS I 9 42 8
Then passing through the garden, the gate of which had SS I 9 42 8
by, without claiming a share in what was passing. SS I 21 121 6
in her own room, could see little of what was passing. SS II 4 161 7
Elinor's thoughts were full of what might be passing in SS II 5 169 16
in ignorance of every thing that was passing before her. SS II 8 193 6
as ignorant of what was passing around her, in Mr. Gray's SS II 11 221 4
How should I know in Shropshire, what is passing of that W 320 2
In passing along a short gallery to the Assembly-Room, W 327 7
together, passing in & out from the adjoining card-room.-- W 327 8
dance, while Miss Osborne passing before her, to her W 330 11
within the cardroom, & in passing thro' the latter, where W 332 11
at such a mode of passing the evening, to the exclusion of PP I 6 25 25
"You either chuse this method of passing the evening PP I 11 56 15
"They arise chiefly from what is passing at the time, and PP I 14 68 11
that was passing in the room during these visits. PP II 7 169 3
She longed to know what at that moment was passing in his PP III 1 253 55
While these newly-born notions were passing in their heads, PP III 2 260 1
while it was passing, the enjoyment of it had been little. PP III 2 264 12
which had been passing while Mr. and Mrs. Gardiner were PP III 5 286 32
heard them passing through the hall to the dining parlour. PP III 9 317 9
last night; I saw her passing by, and went out myself on PP III 11 331 15
She is on her road somewhere, I dare say, and so passing PP III 14 359 76
She must try to find amusement in what was passing at the MP I 6 52 1
in the shrubbery without passing another, I thought it MP I 6 58 37
While this was passing, the rest of the party being MP I 9 88 19
gate, expressed a wish of passing through it into the park, MP I 10 97 4
sounds of opening doors and passing footsteps. MP II 1 175
from notice herself, saw all that was passing before her. MP II 1 185
to listen in quiet, and of passing a very agreeable day. MP II 5 223
some evil from the passing of the servants behind her MP II 7 238
"I told you I lost my way after passing that old farm MP II 7 241
"but which way did you turn after passing Sewell's farm?" MP II 7 241
passing around him on the subject, from morning till night. MP II 8 256
little aware of what was passing in his niece's mind, MP III 1 314
observer of what was passing between him and some part of MP III 5 363
Her dejection had no abatement from anything passing MP III 11 413
you would not mind passing through London, and seeing the MP III 12 416
that her days had been passing in a state of penance, MP III 14 430
she had to lose in passing March and April in a town. MP III 14 431
a knowledge of what was passing became his first object. MP III 17 468
of the lines, and then passing it to Harriet, sat happily E I 9 72
With the view of passing off an awkward moment, Emma E I 9 82
passing it without a slackened pace and observing eyes.-- E I 10 83
could hope that it might belong only to the passing hour. E I 15 129
poor Isabella, passing her life with those she doated on, E I 17 140
But now she made the sudden resolution of not passing E II 1 155
but then, as she was passing by the house where a young E II 3 177
excited there; but in passing it they gave the history of E II 6 197
him; and instead of passing on, he stopt for several E II 6 197
was clear enough, by her passing it over as quickly as E II 7 205
Shortly afterwards Miss Bates, passing near the window, E II 10 243
Instances have been known of young people passing many, E II 11 247
"Yes--I have called there; passing the door, I thought it E II 12 260
that are constantly passing about the kingdom, is even E II 16 296
passing through the garden door, and coming towards her.-- E III 13 424
the first thing to call for more than a word in passing. E III 15 446
to Donwell, Emma had already had her own passing thoughts. E III 15 449
through the blind, of two figures passing near the window. E III 18 476
sent me the report, is passing under her eye--that the E III 18 480
young friend's health, by passing all the warm months with P III 2 14
The party from Uppercross passing down by the now deserted P III 11 96
to the inn; and Anne in passing afterwards quickly from P III 12 104
very plain faces he was continually passing in the streets. P IV 3 141
It was but a passing emotion however with Mrs. Smith, she P IV 5 156
He might be only passing through. P IV 7 178
The passing admiration of Mr. Elliot had at least roused P IV 11 242
art of her character--for passing by the actual daughters S 3 379

PASSION (26)
can be gratified by the passion, which he never wished to LS 22 282
having inspired one real passion, and without having NA I 1 16
Dress was her passion. NA I 2 20
Her passion for ancient edifices was next in degree to her NA II 2 141
was next in degree to her passion for Henry Tilney--and NA II 2 141
with your brother over poor tilney's passion for a month." NA II 4 153
"It is not every one," said Elinor, "who has your passion SS I 16 88
without extending the passion to her; and Elinor had the SS I 17 90
of a passion!--and Mr. Donavan thinks just the same. SS III 1 259
Her wretchedness I could have borne, but her passion--her SS III 8 328
Instead of falling a sacrifice to an irresistible passion, SS III 14 378
that pure and elevating passion, I should at present PP II 3 150
the utmost force of passion to put aside, in my own case; PP II 12 198
many weeks, it would bring his passion to an early proof. MP I 5 48
adverse passion of the man she did, was cruelly mortifying. MP III 7 376
disappointments of selfish passion, can excite little pity. MP III 17 464
years ago I had a great passion for taking likenesses, and E I 6 43
to address any woman on the hap-hazard of selfish passion. E I 8 63
of a strong passion at war with all interested motives. E I 8 67
Mr. Knightley saw no such passion, and of course thought E I 8 67
to have his charade slighted, much better than his passion. E I 9 77
an inclination--such a passion for dining out--a dinner E I 13 111
love and unexampled passion could not fail of having some E I 15 129
own passion, and was very urgent for a favourable answer. E I 15 130
If Scott has a fault, it is the want of passion.-- S 7 397
the progress of strong passion from the first Germ of S 8 403

PASSIONATE (1)
from her eyes with passionate violence--a reproach, SS II 9 202

PASSIONATELY (4)
and dancing he was passionately fond, she gave him such a SS I 10 46
whom he had rationally, as well as passionately loved. MP III 17 468
I am doatingly fond of music--passionately fond;--and my E II 14 276
exclusively, passionately loved by Mr. Knightley. E III 12 415

PASSIONEES (1)
no three or four lines passionees from the most devoted H. MP III 9 393

PASSIONS (7)
of a man whose passions were so violent and resentful. LS 25 292
when one wishes to influence the passions of another. LS 25 293
representation, no studied appeal to their passions. NA II 14 237
If the violence of her passions, the weakness of her SS III 8 322
together because their passions were stronger than their PP III 8 312
The high spirit and strong passions of Mrs. Rushworth MP III 17 464
cure of unconquerable passions, and the transfer of MP III 17 470

PASSIVE (3)
it conveyed by her quiet passive manner, when she was MP I 2 15
The hand and the heart were alike motionless and passive MP II 2 193
There could be no harm in a scheme, a mere passive scheme. E III 3 335

PASSPORT (1)
her, his name was a passport to her good will, and she NA II 4 149

PASSPORTS (1)
"Oh! those letters are convenient passports. P IV 6 162

PAST (129)
to dislike me, & prejudiced against all my past actions. LS 10 257
while she related the past, seem'd to threaten her reason-- LS 36 306
Thorpe herself, of her past adventures and sufferings, NA I 4 34
At about half past twelve, a remarkably loud rap drew her NA I 9 61
friend into the house:--"past three o'clock!" it was NA I 9 67
balls and plays, and every-day sights, is past with them." NA I 10 79
He was a very handsome man, of a commanding aspect, past NA I 10 80
past the bloom, but not past the vigour of life; and with NA I 10 80
At half past twelve, when Catherine's anxious attention to NA I 11 83
to enlighten him on the past only by avoiding his sight, NA I 12 93
The past suspense of the morning had been ease and quiet NA II 2 138
what your thoughts and designs in time past may have been. NA II 3 146
smiles, the alteration became too positive to be past over. NA II 4 149
moment's suspicion of any past scenes of horror being NA II 5 161
humanity, in its fearful review of past scenes of guilt? NA II 8 187
"It is only a quarter past four, (shewing his watch) and NA II 9 195
She did not learn either to forget or defend the past; but NA II 10 199
of past folly, however painful, might not be without use. NA II 10 201
When I think of his past declarations, I give him up.-- NA II 10 206
The past, present, future, were all equally in gloom. NA II 11 212
Heavily past the night. NA II 13 227
and intreating him to say not another word of the past. NA II 15 242
be considered, in comparison with the past, as unfortunate. SS I 7 33
Sir John had dropt hints of past injuries and SS I 10 50
his emotion with the tender recollection of past regard. SS I 11 57
the recollection of past enjoyment and crying over the SS I 16 83
between the past and present was certain of giving. SS I 16 83
behaviour to him by the past rather than the present, she SS I 16 89
"I love to be reminded of the past, Edward--whether it be SS I 17 92
chained elsewhere; and the past and the future, on a SS I 19 105
Jennings, had leisure enough for thinking over the past. SS II 6 178
would be bringing back the past in the strongest and most SS II 10 213
exertion of disclosing past sorrows and present SS II 10 216
down to re-consider the past, recal the words and SS III 4 291
kind of apology, for the past; to open my whole heart to SS III 8 319
she offered to forgive the past, if I would marry Eliza. SS III 8 323

ess than was due to the past, beyond a doubt, and in all SS III 8 324 45
own heart, that all my past sufferings under it are SS III 8 324 45
lking to myself of our past attachment as a mere idle, SS III 8 326 53
e past, the present, the future, Willoughby's visit, SS III 9 333 3
currence of many past scenes of misery to his mind, SS III 10 340 2
secret acknowledgment of past inattention, and bidding SS III 10 341 5
considered the past; I saw in my own behaviour since the SS III 10 345 28
enever I looked towards the past, I saw some duty SS III 10 346 28
t the feelings of the past could not be recalled.-- SS III 11 349 1
avoid any survey of the past that might weaken her SS III 11 352 16
17
at was to be said of the past, the present, and the SS III 13 363 9
om the experience of the past, to submit--and therefore, SS III 14 373 3
was consoled for every past affliction;--her regard and SS III 14 379 17
w endeavour to make myself amends for the past."-- W 335 13
"contrasting the past & the present, the employment of W 361 31
d at half past six Elizabeth was summoned to dinner. PP I 8 35 1
s there any revival of past occurrences, or any PP II 11 188 1
her own past behaviour, there was a constant source of PP II 14 212 17
is almost past belief. PP II 17 225 12
ew; the turning past, he was immediately before them. PP III 1 254 57
may in time make their past imprudence forgotten." PP III 7 305 37
thing of the past was recollected with pain; and Lydia PP III 9 316 6
not let us quarrel about the past. PP III 10 329 34
ink only of the past as its remembrance gives you PP III 11 369 23
mean as to resent the past; and I hoped to obtain your PP III 16 370 32
o had, for many weeks past, felt the expediency of Mr. MP I 4 39 11
ruggling against discontent and envy for some days past. MP I 7 74 59
own, or warm her imagination with scenes of the past. MP I 9 85 3
is past two, and we are to dine at five." MP I 9 89 31
r my memory of they past under such easy dominion as one MP I 10 98 10
bject, and to boast of the past his only consolation. MP I 13 121 1
fore many days were past, that it was not all MP I 18 164 1
th the past; a sombre family-party rarely enlivened. MP II 3 196 1
d of forgetting, do seem peculiarly past finding out." MP II 4 209 12
e had by no means forgotten the past, and she thought as MP II 6 232 11
art had been yearning to do, through many a past year. MP II 6 233 17
is to have breakfasted and be gone by half past nine.-- MP II 10 280 29
. Crawford, I think you call for him at half past nine?" MP II 10 280 29
es, half past nine," said Crawford to William, as the MP II 10 280 31
t there was no consciousness of past folly in his voice. MP II 13 303 14
u will take in the whole of the past, you will consider MP III 1 313 12
e past, present, future, every thing was terrible. MP III 1 321 46
r the morrow was past, she could not but flatter herself MP III 1 324 59
stairs--wondering at the past and present, wondering at MP III 2 329 10
speak rather of the past, however, than the present.-- MP III 3 339 23
ece's spirits, and the past attentions of the lover MP III 6 368 7
ere was no gratitude for affection past or present, to MP III 9 396 5
st nine, there was little intermission of noise or grog. MP III 11 413 32
at I had been too apt to dwell on for many months past. MP III 16 457 30
e recalled her past kindness--the kindness, the E I 1 6 6
d lady, almost past every thing but tea and quadrille. E I 3 21 4
r some weeks past she had been spending more than half E I 8 57 1
bject was so completely past that any reviving question E I 14 118 4
ery thing that I have said or done, for many weeks past, E I 15 131 31
wards a recantation of past prejudices and errors, than E II 2 168 15
currences to the past, and give the most decided proof E II 4 185 13
to where the coaches past; and every thing in this E II 5 186 1
e worn-out past was sunk in the freshness of what was E II 5 188 8
attention, in future, could do away the past, she might E III 8 377 1
ntle sensations of the past, obliged her to admit that E III 8 379 9
e had scarcely a stronger regret than for her past E III 9 389 16
have really for some time past, for at least these three E III 10 396 41
e had herself been first with him for many years past. E III 12 415 1
d her sense of past injustice towards Miss Fairfax. E III 12 420 17
nter of her life to the past, it would yet find her more E III 12 423 21
ur goodness to allow for some parts of my past conduct.-- E III 14 436 8
st be averting the past, and carrying her out of herself. E III 16 452 5
thing, but that the lessons of her past folly might E III 18 475 39
r without a care for the past, and with the fullest E III 19 481 2
ver wished the past undone, she began now to have the P III 4 29 7
st, which seemed almost to deny any recollection of it. P III 4 30 10
ateful to her, of the past being known to those three P III 4 30 10
grace, to make the past, as they were connected P III 6 43 5
often, puzzling over past years, and at last P III 6 52 33
d oblivion of the past--how natural, how certain too! P III 7 60 28
etings extinguish every past hope, and leave him nothing P III 9 77 19
ough condemning her for the past, and considering it P III 10 91 42
nctually, it was so much past noon before the two P III 11 95 8
t a gentleness, which seemed almost restoring the past.-- P III 12 114 63
lf-threatenings of the past, became in a decided tone, " P IV 1 125 14
luded to the past, and entreated to be received as an P IV 3 143 18
her attention, of past kindness and present suffering. P IV 5 152 2
ither the dissipations of the past--and she had lived P IV 5 153 7
e distrusted the past, if not the present. P IV 5 160 27
the past; yes, some share of the tenderness of the past. P IV 8 185 21
; all the particulars of past sad scenes, all the P IV 9 210 97
e past was nothing. P IV 10 226 64
fering, as atonement for all the insolence of the past. P IV 10 226 65
ere they returned again into the past, more exquisitely P IV 11 240 59
st, as I did; and one encouragement happened to be mine. P IV 11 244 70
en thinking over the past, and trying inpartially to P IV 11 246 79
80
t I too have been thinking over the past, and a question P IV 11 247 82
is now only 1/2 past 4.-- S 9 411 1
RY (1)
ether in quest of pastry, millinery, or even (as in the NA I 7 44 1
RY-COOK'S (1)
eat ice at a pastry-cook's, and hurrying back to the NA I 15 116 1
URAGE (1)
d Marianne, and rather better pasturage for their cows. SS III 14 374 7
URE (1)
pleasant fertile spot, well wooded., and rich in pasture. SS I 6 28 1
URES (1)
d beauty, its rich pastures, spreading flocks, orchard E III 6 360 40
H (1)
tch of greensward by the side, a party of gipsies. E III 3 333 5
HED (1)
n's marrying her, was a patched up business, at the PP III 14 357 62
HED-ON (1)
re than another my aversion, it is a patched-on bow." NA II 11 213 19
NT (1)
mnant of the earliest patent; there any unwelcome P III 1 3 1
RNAL (4)
e thanked him for his great attention, his paternal MP II 3 200 21
eir distance from the paternal abode an inconvenience. MP III 17 473 32
ver, I saw it only as paternal kindness, and thought it E II 8 219 42
r having dismembered himself from the paternal tree. P IV 2 136 35
(23)
llowing, tho' late, the path of propriety, occasioned LS 6 252 2
y do you chuse that cold, damp path to it? NA II 7 179 27
was a narrow winding path through a thick grove of old NA II 7 179 29
e had just settled this point, when the end of the path NA II 7 181 41
s footsteps were heard along the gravel path; in a SS III 12 359 10
e path just admitted three. PP I 10 53 62
ere was a nice sheltered path, which no one seemed to PP II 7 169 5
lt that he would probably strike into some other path. PP III 1 254 57
rike into another path, she was overtaken by Wickham. PP III 10 327 4
e end of it yet, since we left the first great path." MP I 9 94 62
ut if you remember, before we left that first great path, MP I 9 95 63
me path which she had trod herself, and were before her. MP I 10 97 1
diminution of cares since her treading that path before. MP II 8 260 25

but you do not know how dry the path is to my house. MP III 1 323 56
ended the narrow, slippery path through the cottage garden, E I 10 87 27
of my idea of moving the path to Langham, of turning it E I 12 106 61
call to mind exactly the present line of the path . . . . E I 12 106 61
towards entering on her path of duty; though she had now E II 2 165 8
had seemed to foresee and to command his prosperous path. P III 4 29 8
another path, "is not this one of the ways to Winthrop?" P III 10 85 12
work, and the fresh-made path spoke the farmer, P III 10 85 13
Charles walking along any path, or leaning against any P III 10 85 16
paling & which a narrow path seemed to skirt along;--Miss S 12 426 1
PATHETIC (4)
This pathetic representation lasted the whole evening, & LS 17 270 3
between her and her family was rather noisy than pathetic. PP II 18 235 40
through; he is solemn and pathetic enough I am sure. MP I 14 134 14
The real circumstances of this pathetic piece of family P III 6 50 28
PATHOS (2)
as no attempt at grandeur or pathos can withstand. NA II 14 232 7
Oh! there is pathos to madden one!-- S 7 397 1
PATHS (2)
body, and where the narrow paths across the fields made P III 10 84 7
the road & all the paths across the down, Charlotte & Sir S 7 395 1
PATIENCE (52)
his countenance with exultation, was quite out of patience. LS 17 270 3
I was out of patience with her. LS 24 288 12
he bears pain with such patience that I have not the LS 28 298 2
-----"like patience on a monument "smiling at grief." NA I 1 16 9
of patience, had he staid with you half a minute longer. NA I 10 76 29
I have no patience with such of my sex as disdain to let NA I 14 112 36
really have not patience with the General"--to fill up NA II 14 237 22
And, "I really have not patience with the general," was NA II 14 238 22
to--"I really have not patience with the General! NA II 14 238 27
You want nothing but patience--or give it a more SS I 19 103 7
Jennings, who had not patience enough to wait till the SS I 19 106 20
press very hard upon his patience; but melancholy was the SS II 1 140 3
I have no patience with him. SS II 8 192 3
of her own except of patience till their mother's wishes SS II 9 203 9
I declare, I have no patience with your sister; and I hope, SS III 1 259 7
I am sure it would put me quite out of patience!-- SS III 4 291 51
It put me out of patience.-- W 347 22
have patience to be so very accomplished, as they all are." PP I 8 39 43
though with the greatest patience in the world, which is PP I 9 42 7
Even Elizabeth might have found some trial of her patience PP I 17 88 15
Attention, forbearance, patience with Darcy, was injury to PP I 18 89 3
to answer him with patience, when he should have done. PP II 11 189 6
Yet time and her aunt moved slowly--and her patience and PP III 1 257 66
and Jane, and for their sakes had patience with her. PP III 10 325 2
of preaching patience to a sufferer is denied me, because PP III 11 333 29
he spoke, had scarcely a patience enough to help anybody to PP III 12 341 18
borne it with exemplary patience, I am sure you must be MP I 15 143 26
I cannot think of it with any patience--and it does appear MP I 16 154 8
Your kindness and patience can never be forgotten, your MP II 5 224 53
your indefatigable patience in trying to make it possible MP II 5 224 53
of dishes on it with patience, and who did always contrive MP II 7 238 3
other continually exercised her patience and forbearance? MP II 12 294 16
ineffable sweetness and patience, to all the demands of MP II 12 296 31
pressing, a little patience, and a little impatience, a MP III 1 320 44
be worth every effort of patience, every exertion of mind-- MP III 3 336 7
I have not time or patience to give half Henry's messages; MP III 14 435 14
I thank you for your patience, Fanny. MP III 16 459 30
requiring industry and patience, and a subjection of the E I 5 37 7
kindness, her counsel and her patience, as from her purse. E I 10 86 24
There he had not always the patience that could have been E I 11 93 5
ingenuity and all her patience; but it was heavy work to E II 13 267 9
patience, self-controul; but it wants openness. E II 15 289 40
Neither Mr. Suckling nor me had ever any patience with E III 2 321 15
Let us have patience. E III 10 398 53
but with great outward patience, to Harriet's detail.-- E III 11 409 34
of her excellence and patience, and my uncle's generosity, E III 14 439 8
Have patience with me, I shall soon have done.-- E III 14 442 8
was in a humour to have patience with every body; and as E III 16 453 11
A little farther perseverance in patience, and forced P III 5 39 40
to Lyme, to preach patience and resignation to a young man P III 11 101 26
of heroism, fortitude, patience, resignation--of all the P IV 5 156 10
for the scientific, and patience for the wearisome; and P IV 8 186 24
PATIENT (16)
to herself, and put on her bonnet in patient discontent. NA II 7 177 18
utility, and patient endurance, as when he first hailed NA II 16 251 5
He came, examined his patient, and though encouraging Miss SS III 7 307 3
in the state of the patient; she certainly was not better, SS III 7 308 5
Harris arrived, he declared his patient materially better. SS III 7 310 8
of any change in the patient, went unusually early to bed; SS III 7 310 9
alteration in his patient, he would not allow the danger SS III 7 312 19
hours, and left both the patient and her anxious attendant SS III 7 313 19
The apothecary came, and having examined his patient, said, PP I 7 33 44
A very few lines from Edmund shewed her the patient and MP III 14 429 2
relative questions, all answered with patient politeness. E III 2 324 20
or persuaded out, his patient listener and sympathizer. E III 6 357 33
opinion, in favour of such exercise for his patient. E III 9 390 16
there to satisfy her patient; and thus they continued a P III 9 79 25
over her little patient to their cares, and leave the room. P III 9 80 34
A submissive spirit might be patient, a strong P IV 5 154 8
PATIENTLY (4)
together, nor wait very patiently while he was slowly MP I 15 138 1
Jane very patiently assured her that she had not caught E II 16 295 31
She could do little more than listen patiently, soften P III 6 46 11
she bore with him patiently enough to confirm the sort of S 8 405 2
PATRIOTISM (1)
I do admire your patriotism. E II 6 200 15
PATRON (6)
A living, of which Mr. Morland was himself patron and NA II 1 135 42
home, and assist his patron and friend in deciding on what SS III 13 372 46
be beneficial to himself and not offensive to his patron. PP I 18 101 71
with the son of his patron, were imperfectly understood, PP III 2 265 15
conditionally only, and at the will of the present patron." PP III 10 328 29
the real and consistent patron of the selected child, and MP I 1 8 9
PATRONAGE (7)
I am sorry to say that my patronage ends with this; and my SS III 3 284 23
be distinguished by the patronage of the right honourable PP I 13 62 12
Darcy had considerable patronage in the church, and his PP II 9 181 31
dependence than on our patronage, and who had been brought PP II 12 196 5
property, noble kindred, and extensive patronage. PP III 15 362 15
the view and patronage of Mansfield Park, had long been. MP III 17 473 33
speak of, as under the patronage of your sister and Mrs. E III 16 456 32
PATRONESS (10)
the mistress of a family, and the patroness of a village. SS III 14 378 16
observing that he seemed very fortunate in his patroness. PP I 14 66 1
for her as his patroness, mingling with a very good PP I 15 70 1
being his patroness, she is an arrogant, conceited woman." PP I 16 83 57
there is now in the room a near relation of my patroness. PP I 18 96 57
relations, than run the risk of offending your patroness." PP I 22 123 7
The power of displaying the grandeur of his patroness to PP II 6 160 1
the very active patroness of Jane Fairfax, and only E II 15 284 11
I am lady patroness, you know. E III 6 354 12
by her innate worth, on the affections of her patroness.-- S 3 378 1
PATRONISED (2)
sure it will never be patronised by our good friend here W 334 13
It was a concert for the benefit of a person patronised by P IV 7 180 32
PATRONIZE (1)
which reason will patronize in vain,--which taste cannot P III 8 68 30
PATRONIZED (2)
Alas! if the heroine of one novel be not patronized by the NA I 5 37 4
"That he is patronized by you," replied Willoughby, "is SS I 10 50 17

PATTENED (1)
Wherever they went, some pattened girl stopped to curtsey, NA II 8 184 4
PATTENS (1)
and the ceaseless clink of pattens, she made no complaint. P IV 2 135 33
PATTERN (9)
neck, produced from this pattern of gentleness, such SS I 21 121 10
admired;--but sometimes I think the pattern too large.-- W 353 26
own manners were such a pattern of good-breeding and MP I 8 78 23
well, and begging for the pattern, and supposing Fanny was MP I 15 147 57
They might be more safely held up as a pattern. E I 4 34 42
but send her aunt the pattern of a stomacher, or knit a E I 10 86 23
so beautiful, would still never match her yellow pattern. E II 9 235 35
Only my pattern gown is at Hartfield. E II 9 235 36
And I could take the pattern gown home any day. E II 9 235 36
PATTERNS (2)
any thing, or in taking patterns of some elegant new dress, SS I 21 120 6
But you must come up and tack on my patterns all the same." MP I 3 25 9
PATTY (12)
only gone down to speak to Patty again about the port-- E II 3 173 27
a little cold, and Patty has been washing the kitchen.' E II 3 173 27
At one time Patty came to say she thought the kitchen E II 9 236 46
Oh! said I, Patty do not come with your bad news to me. E II 9 236 46
Patty makes an excellent apple-dumpling. E II 9 237 46
But, however, I found afterwards from Patty, that William E II 9 239 51
He told Patty this, but bid her not mind it, and be sure E II 9 239 51
And so Patty told me, and I was excessively shocked indeed! E II 9 239 51
Miss Bates had just done as Patty opened the door; and her E II 9 239 52
"Oh! my dear; but so much as Patty has to do!-- E II 16 296 38
But then Patty came in, and said it was you. E III 8 379 8
She heard Patty announcing it; but no such bustle E III 16 452 8
PAUSE (94)
After a short pause, "it comes on faster and faster!" said NA I 11 82 8
The general pause which succeeded his short disquisition NA I 14 111 29
After a short pause, Catherine resumed with "then you do NA II 4 151 17
In the pause which succeeded, a sound like receding NA II 6 170 12
attentive pause with which she waited for something more. NA II 7 179 31
she could hardly tell where, made her pause and tremble. NA II 9 194 6
"But," said Eleanor, after a short pause, "would it be to NA II 10 205 30
with the General"--to fill up every accidental pause. NA II 14 237 22
After a short pause he resumed the conversation by saying-- SS I 11 56 14
15
too much astonished to speak, and another pause succeeded. SS I 15 76 16
A short pause succeeded this speech, which was first SS I 21 123 21
caught those words by a sudden pause in Marianne's music.-- SS II 2 148 20
Another pause therefore of many minutes' duration, SS II 2 150 35
After a short pause, "you have no confidence in me, SS II 5 169 23
After a pause of several minutes, their silence was broken, SS II 5 172 40
After a moment's pause, he spoke with calmness. SS II 6 177 8
Another pause ensued; Marianne was greatly agitated, and SS II 7 190 59
"Such," said Colonel Brandon, after a pause, "has been the SS II 9 211 40
After a pause of wonder, she exclaimed, "four months!-- SS III 1 262 17
18
"We think now"--said Mr. Dashwood, after a short pause, " SS III 5 296 24
"I do not know," said he, after a pause of expectation on SS III 8 319 29
A short pause of mutual thoughtfulness succeeded. SS III 8 327 56
the dryness of the season, a very awful pause took place. SS III 12 359 14
Another pause. SS III 12 359 15
said Elinor, after a pause--"they are certainly married. SS III 13 366 18
her sister after a short pause went on--"you will W 316 2
ball we had last night!--he cried, after a short pause. W 340 19
After another pause, "nothing sets off a neat ankle more W 345 21
A pause of suspense ensued.-- W 355 28
he continued after a pause, on seeing Bingley join the PP I 6 25 28
A short pause followed this speech, and Mrs. Hurst began PP I 8 36 13
Darcy only smiled; and the general pause which ensued made PP I 9 45 35
"But what," said she, after a pause, "can have been his PP I 16 80 31
After a pause of some minutes she addressed him a second PP I 18 91 8
9
them again, after the pause of half a minute began another. PP I 18 100 68
could not use the short pause he allowed in any attempt to PP I 19 105 9
10
"It is unlucky," said she, after a short pause, "that you PP I 21 117 9
an awkward pause, they returned to the rest of the family. PP I 22 125 18
way, and after a moment's pause, added, "my eldest sister PP II 7 171 10
11
at the first convenient pause, turned to him with an arch PP II 8 174 12
13
answer--and, after a short pause, added, "I think I have PP II 9 177 6
7
enquiries and an awkward pause and then away, but he PP II 10 182 1
The pause was to Elizabeth's feelings dreadful. PP II 11 190 8
he continued after a pause, "who more particularly wishes PP III 1 256 63
on their being seated, a pause, awkward as such pauses PP III 3 267 4
thing else; and, after a pause of several minutes, was PP III 4 278 20
After a short pause, her companion added, "you are too PP III 16 366 7
After a short pause, Sir Thomas added with dignity, "yes, MP I 1 9 11
had seldom known a pause in its alarms or embarrassments. MP I 4 35 6
but when the first pause came, Edmund, looking around, MP I 7 71 31
At length, after a short pause, Miss Crawford began with, " MP I 9 91 38
After another pause, he went on. MP I 10 102 41
said Fanny, after a short pause, "as for the son of an MP I 11 109 18
After a short pause, however, the subject still continued, MP I 13 124 13
The pause which followed this fruitless effort was ended MP I 14 132 7
Crawford, after a short pause, "at this want of an Anhalt. MP I 15 144 32
after a short pause--"for he is a clergyman you know." MP I 15 144 40
things when he comes home," said Mary, after a pause. MP I 17 161 15
tap at the door brought a pause, and the entrance of MP I 18 169 22
After a pause of perplexity, some eyes began to be turned MP I 18 171 28
It was a terrible pause; and terrible to every ear were MP II 1 175 1
At length there was a pause. MP II 1 180 13
beloved circle; but the pause was not long: in the elation MP II 1 180 13
there; and a pause of alarm followed his disappearance. MP II 1 181 17
his lady, but in vain; no pause was long enough for the MP II 7 240 10
After a moment's pause, Sir Thomas, trying to suppress a MP III 1 313 13
pause, proceeded in his account of Mr. Crawford's visit. MP III 1 313 15
After half a moment's pause--"and I should have been very MP III 1 319 39
"I should have thought," said Fanny, after a pause of MP III 4 353 45
The evening passed, without a pause of misery, the night MP III 15 441 20
Julia's, Tom's, Edmund's--there, a yet longer pause. MP III 15 442 21
He was obliged to pause more than once as he continued. MP III 16 456 29
He was gone the next moment:--after another moment's pause, E I 9 71 12
13
Their first pause was at the crown inn, an inconsiderable E II 6 197 5
was no getting away, no pause; and, to my utter E II 6 199 7
a most wretched discovery," said he, after a short pause.-- E II 8 221 51
have been worth while to pause and consider, and try to E II 11 250 19
after a moment's pause, Mrs. Elton chose another subject. E II 14 278 43
to some one else--and the pause gave her time to reflect, " E II 16 297 48
"Harriet!" cried Emma, after a moment's pause--"what do E III 11 405 15
come," she was obliged to pause before she answered, and E III 12 420 14
After this, he made some progress without any pause. E III 15 446 19
right, he made a fuller pause to say, "this is very bad.-- E III 15 446 20
After a short pause, Mr. Shepherd presumed to say, "in all P III 3 18 9
10
and Anne, after the little pause which followed, added-- " P III 3 21 20
21
"Oh! well;"--and after a moment's pause, "but you have P III 5 39 35
After a moment's pause, Captain Wentworth said, "do you P III 10 89 29
30
After a moment's pause he said, "though I came only P IV 7 177 14
subject; and yet, after a pause, feeling the necessity of P IV 8 183 11
12

Mrs. Smith, after a pause, "I hope you believe that I do P IV 9 194 1
wonder, made her pause, and in a calmer manner she added, P IV 9 199 5
5
had spread; and a short pause succeeded, which seemed to P IV 10 222 3
general, it was a thorough pause of company, it was S 6 389
But--after a short pause--if Miss Esther thinks to talk me S 7 401
PAUSED (25)
She paused a moment in breathless wonder. NA II 6 168 1
spoken by either, she paused a moment, and with quivering NA II 13 229 3
She paused. SS I 22 130 1
She paused over it for some time with indignant SS II 7 184 1
He paused for her assent and compassion; and she forced SS II 11 225 2
3
She paused--no one spoke. SS II 13 243 3
Fanny paused a moment, and then, with fresh vigour, said, " SS II 14 253 2
2
She paused.-- SS III 9 338 2
She paused--and added in a lower voice, "if I could but SS III 10 347 3
In their progress up the room, they paused almost W 329
He paused in hopes of an answer; but his companion was not PP I 6 26 3
3
She paused, and saw with no slight indignation that he was PP II 11 191 1
Miss Bennet paused a little and then replied, "surely PP II 17 226 2
Sir Thomas paused, half smiled, glanced at his niece, and MP II 11 285 1
saying only when he paused, "how kind! how very kind! MP II 13 300
He paused and eyed her fixedly. MP III 1 316 3
The mother's sufferings, the father's--there, she paused. MP III 15 442 2
She paused over it, while Harriet stood anxiously watching E I 7 51
He paused--and growing cooler in a moment, added, with E I 12 106 6
He paused. E II 10 241 1
She paused a few moments. E III 11 407 2
He paused a moment, again smiling, with his eyes fixed on E III 18 470
He paused.-- E III 18 477 5
She paused a moment to recover from the emotion of hearing P III 12 114 6
Here Mrs. Smith paused a moment; but Anne had not a word P IV 9 206 8
9
PAUSES (2)
After many pauses and many trials of other subjects, PP I 16 82 4
4
as such pauses must always be, succeeded for a few moments. PP III 3 267
PAUSING (8)
said Marianne, after pausing a moment, "can never hope to SS I 8 38 1
forwards across the room, pausing for a moment whenever SS II 4 166 3
What now," after pausing a moment--"your poor sister is SS II 8 195 1
hill behind, when pausing with her eyes turned towards it, SS III 10 344 1
1
After pausing on this point a considerable while, she once PP II 13 206
little behind; and on her pausing, he asked her, if she PP III 1 254 5
door, and after pausing a moment for what she knew would MP II 1 177
his head was raised, pausing, listening, and he turned P IV 11 231 1
PAVED (2)
In the high-arched passage, paved with stone, which NA II 8 188 1
Steps were distinguished, first along the paved Footway W 355 2
PAVEMENT (7)
gig, driven along on bad pavement by a most knowing- NA I 7 44
"On the right-hand pavement--she must be almost out of NA I 11 87 5
had just gained the pavement when the two gentlemen PP I 15 72
The hardness of the pavement for her feet, made him less P III 12 109 3
pavement on the lower Cobb, and was taken up lifeless! P III 12 109 3
drawn up near its pavement!" observed Sir Walter.-- P IV 5 157 1
him on the right hand pavement at such a distance as to P IV 7 178 2
PAVEMENTS (1)
"It may not be felt in Bath, with your nice pavements; " P IV 6 163
PAY (84)
is immense, & much beyond what I can ever attempt to pay. LS 2 246
in by that young lady to pay her some attention. & as he LS 14 264
"I shall not pay them any such compliment, I assure you. NA I 6 43 4
Edgar's Buildings, and pay their respects to Mrs. Thorpe. NA I 7 47 1
and a beating heart to pay her visit, explain her conduct, NA I 12 91
"But I say, Miss Morland, I shall come and pay my respects NA I 15 123 4
Why should he pay her such attentions as to make her NA II 12 218
Her youth, civil manners and liberal pay, procured her all NA II 14 232
they will pay their mother for their board out of it. SS I 2 12 2
Fortunately for those who pay their court through such SS I 21 120
their's, she should pay her visit and return for them. SS II 11 220
A man must pay for his convenience; and it has cost me a SS II 11 225 3
You know I am always ready to pay them any attention in my SS II 14 253 2
resolved from the first to pay a visit of comfort and SS III 2 270
this, she had time only to pay her farewell compliments to SS III 2 276 2
Elinor began to feel it necessary to pay her a visit.-- SS III 5 293
The consequence was, that Elinor set out by herself to pay SS III 5 294
years ago; and very great attention indeed did he pay me. W 316
that he will not come on to pay you much attention; it is W 343 1
"It is a compliment which I never pay to any place if I PP I 6 26 2
or four times a week, to pay their duty to their aunt and PP I 7 28
with myself, I should not pay him half so much deference. PP I 10 50 3
attention which I conceive myself peculiarly bound to pay." PP I 14 67
is made in time for me to pay my respects to him, which I PP I 18 97 5
You must give me leave to judge for myself, and pay me the PP I 19 107 1
at not having had time to pay his respects to his friends PP II 1 133
On the following morning he hastened to Rosings to pay his PP II 7 170
bring it about; and the other, how I am ever to pay him." PP III 7 304 2
Do you pay no regard to the wishes of his friends? PP III 14 355 4
I shall offer to pay him to-morrow; he will rant and storm PP III 17 377 3
brother must help to pay for the pleasures of the elder. MP I 3 23
from her, as no feelings could be strong enough to pay. MP I 4 37
ten miles of indifferent road, to pay a morning visit. MP I 4 39 1
"I pay very little regard," said Mrs. Grant, "to what any MP I 4 43 2
of their pay, and their bickerings and jealousies. MP I 6 60 4
enough; for she could not always pay attention to the book. MP I 18 170 2
him by all means to pay his respects to Sir Thomas without MP II 1 176
where he was that he might pay his respects to the old MP II 1 177
prevailed on my sister to pay the first visit, I am as MP II 2 188
Grant, who was anxious to pay his respects to Sir Thomas, MP II 2 192 1
of the first rubber, to go to her and pay her compliments. MP II 7 240 1
The game was her's, and only did not pay her for what she MP II 7 243 2
you ought to go over and pay your respects to them; and I MP II 7 245 3
near her aunt Bertram, and pay her the usual observances MP II 9 265 2
uncles and aunts pay for them in the course of the year. MP II 13 305 2
Here is a young man wishing to pay his addresses to you, MP III 1 315 2
it in one's power to pay off the debts of one's sex! MP III 5 363 2
"Then, there's the devil to pay among them, that's all. MP III 15 439 1
and of chusing that time to pay a visit to her other MP III 17 466 1
We must begin, we must go and pay our wedding-visit very E I 1 8 1
young ladies for enormous pay might be screwed out of E I 3 21
She is not to pay for the offence of others, by being held E I 8 62 4
Miss Smith, give me leave to pay my addresses to you. E I 9 72 1
had a charitable visit to pay to a poor sick family, who E I 10 83
of friends are invited to pay a visit at Enscombe in E I 14 120 1
to pay his addresses to her had sunk him in her opinion. E I 16 135
always pay for its hopes by any proportionate depression. E I 18 144
It is Frank Churchill's duty to pay this attention to his E I 18 146 1
must know, that he ought to pay this visit to his father; E I 18 147 1
for though his income, by pay and appointments, was E II 2 164
Emma was sorry;--to have to pay civilities to a person she E II 2 166 1
she left the house, was to pay her respects to them as E II 8 213
It was better to pay my visit, then"----- E II 12 260 2
right; it was most natural to pay your visit, then"----- E II 12 261 3
3
on not being the last to pay her respects; and she made a E II 14 270
you be so anxious to pay your respects to a bride? E II 14 280 5
but I would always wish to pay every proper attention to a E II 14 280 5

ton, was disposed to pay him attention on his marriage. E II 16 290 1
e two eldest little Knightleys were engaged to pay their E II 16 292 7
body had inclination to pay, and she was herself in a E II 18 311 36
being able to pay her such attentions, as she was for E III 7 375 59
s. Weston had set off to pay the visit in a good deal of E III 12 417 5
promised to join me here, and pay his respects to you." E III 16 455 21
a visit at Randall's; he wants to be introduced to her. E III 18 477 57
s contracted debts must pay them; and though a great P III 2 12 4
possible;--knew he must pay for his convenience;--knew P III 3 22 23
ne, have you courage to go with me, and pay a visit in P IV 1 125 14
again afterwards to pay a formal visit here, he will P IV 2 131 12
ch Anne could not pay, they had only a few faint P IV 3 137 3
ease himself, he might mean to pay his addresses to her. P IV 3 140 11
only mean that if Mr. Elliot should some time hence pay P IV 5 159 23
e gloried in being a sailor's wife, but she must pay the P IV 12 252 12
Sanditon h-- drove on to pay their compliments; & the S 7 394 1
ergymen may be, or Lawyers from town, or half pay S 7 401 1
NG (36)
e long illness of her dear father prevented my paying LS 1 244 1
s intention of paying his respects to them, and, with a NA II 15 242 9
the theatre to be paying considerable attention to Miss NA II 15 244 12
n before her while paying that visit at Allenham on his SS II 10 213 4
e expressly conditioned, however, for paying no visits, SS II 11 220 1
e would not be frightened from paying him those SS II 13 241 20
I am alive, I shall be paying a visit at Delaford SS III 4 292 57
en then, however, when fully determined on paying my SS III 8 321 34
ou are paying Miss Emma no great compliment I think Mary, W 324 3
began to feel the danger of paying Elizabeth too much PP I 11 58 34
cept my thanks for the compliment you are paying me. PP I 19 106 12
it that he thought of paying his addresses to one of PP I 22 124 11
ok the opportunity of paying the parting civilities PP II 15 215 1
ce, he could not help paying more attention to what she MP I 4 37 8
emptorily, and without paying my opinion or my regard MP III 1 319 39
now that it is paying me a very great compliment, and I MP III 2 330 15
osed or hurt him, and paying attentions to my cousin MP III 4 349 25
Julia did not think he was paying her attentions." MP III 4 350 29
e young man's inclination for paying them were over. MP III 5 356 3
her to avoid paying her own expenses back again. MP III 6 373 24
e the poor horses to be while we are paying our visit?" E I 1 8 17
place while he was paying his addresses--and as Jane E II 1 159 20
e became their guest, paying them long visits and E II 2 163 4
e the opportunity of paying a visit, which must be paid E II 5 193 36
37
it was, I was only betrayed into paying a most E II 6 199 7
handsomest; and after paying his compliments en E II 8 220 47
she,--"only to be sure it was paying him too great a E II 8 220 47
cle of his guests, and paying his particular E II 16 294 24
25
haps, he might come in while she were paying her visit. E III 8 377 2
she followed Mr. Knightley's known wishes, in paying E III 12 421 17
her face; and while paying her own compliments to Mrs. E III 16 453 12
13
grove made a point of paying his respects to Lady P IV 2 134 29
t such an opportunity of paying his respects to her. P IV 3 143 19
ought not to be supposed to be paying his addresses to P IV 9 196 31
ress & wish of paying attention & giving pleasure.-- S 7 394 1
miling about & paying girls compliments, but he knows S 7 400 1
NT (5)
clogged with the payment of three to old superannuated SS I 2 10 20
myself down to the payment of one for all the world." SS I 2 11 20
be tied down to the regular payment of such a sum, on SS I 2 11 21
speedy payment, for which I have pledged myself. PP III 8 313 19
sequestration for the payment of its own incumbrances, P IV 9 210 98
NTS (1)
Edw: has no Payments to make me. S 7 400 1
(5)
generally pays attention to every new girl, but he is a W 315 1
especially any thing that pays woman a compliment. E I 9 77 45
nd while Mrs. Weston pays her visit, I may be allowed, I E II 9 234 27
entions from Mrs. Elton, which nobody else pays her." E II 15 286 18
e public pays and must be served well." E II 16 297 43
(64)
urious to your own peace than to our understandings. LS 14 263 1
nes is gone, Lady Susan vanquished, & Frederica at peace. LS 23 285 8
restoring peace than I ever intended to submit too. LS 25 292 1
e we shall in time be at peace. LS 27 297 2
mily you robbed of it's peace, in return for the LS 36 305 1
r restoration to peace will, I doubt not, speedily LS 37 306 1
e too strong for my own peace; and to see myself NA I 13 98 2
ly the next day, a note from Isabella, speaking peace NA I 15 116 1
en I found there would be no peace if I did not stand up. NA II 1 134 39
ld at least restore peace to every heart but his own. NA II 4 150 1
a good appetite of her own, restored her to peace. NA II 6 165 6
cannot rest--I shall not have a moment's peace till this SS II 6 177 13
storing Marianne's peace of mind, and confirming her own. SS III 6 302 5
peace of mind is doubly involved in it;--for not only SS III 10 345 20
h one who had so injured the peace of the dearest of SS III 11 350 7
d she, to have things going on in peace & goodhumour. W 343 19
e peace of the party for the remainder of that day, & W 360 30
his chamber, Emma was at peace from the dreadful W 361 31
ablish the blessing of peace in all families within the PP I 13 63 12
uation remained the same, her peace equally wounded. PP II 1 134 3
the commission of the peace for the county, she was a PP II 7 169 4
shall have no peace at Longbourn if Lydia does not go PP II 18 232 20
se where her peace of mind must be materially concerned. PP III 10 326 3
ir manner of living, even when the restoration of peace PP III 19 387 8
re-established peace and kindness. MP I 1 5 3
ll worse, all my peace in this world destroyed, with MP I 3 29 46
ll held his peace, and shewed his feelings only by a MP I 15 148 60
was safe; but peace and safety were unconnected here. MP I 17 159 6
mind had been never farther from peace. MP I 17 159 6
ful to all; she was perhaps as much at peace as any. MP I 18 166 5
sipped his coffee in peace over domestic matters of a MP II 1 184 25
him could give to the peace of mind he was attacking, MP II 6 231 11
with you, Fanny, there may be peace. MP II 10 278 20
dly left her to cry in peace, conceiving perhaps that MP II 11 282 2
ick maid, there was peace and good humour in their MP II 11 283 4
r wicked project upon her peace turns out a clever MP II 12 295 19
rounded her, to be at peace from all mention of the MP III 6 370 11
haps, above all, the peace and tranquillity of MP III 8 391 10
ht, perhaps, restore peace for ever on the sore subject MP III 9 396 7
the house; Fanny had peace, and Susan learnt to think MP III 9 398 9
se peace would it not cut up for ever? MP III 15 441 21
injured family peace, so forfeited his best, most MP III 17 468 22
riet listened, and Emma drew in peace. E I 6 47 26
would keep the peace if possible; and there was E I 11 97 27
day was concluding in peace and comfort to all their E I 15 132 38
now, poor girl, her peace is cut up for some time. E I 16 137 11
way of cure, there could be no true peace for herself. E I 17 143 15
the world of preserving peace at home and preventing E I 18 148 24
ce and hope, to penance and mortification for ever. E II 2 165 8
might not be aware of the inroads on domestic peace to E II 6 204 43
she was left in peace--neither forced to be the very E II 15 284 11
confidence, and her peace would be fully secured.-- E III 12 416 1
bbed Jane Fairfax's peace in a thousand instances; and E III 12 421 17
ortnight, at least, of leisure and peace of mind, to E III 16 452 6
s peace will be turning all our rich navy officers P III 3 17 1
this comes of the peace. P III 10 92 44
Mary, however, there was an end of all peace in it. P III 12 115 65
the peace has come too soon for that younker. P IV 6 170 29
deeply concerned in the mischief to be soon at peace. P IV 8 183 13
could not quit the room in peace without seeing P IV 8 189 45

Your peace will not be shipwrecked as mine has been. P IV 9 196 32
"If he does, however, they will leave me in peace, which " P IV 9 203 72
the destruction of every thing like peace and comfort. P IV 10 215 13
The peace turned him on shore at the very moment, and he P IV 11 233 20
PEACEABLY (2)
she sat peaceably down, and saw Thorpe sit down by her. NA I 9 62 10
The week which passed so quietly and peaceably at the MP II 11 285 15
PEACEMAKING (1)
we may expect this peacemaking gentleman," said Mr. Bennet, PP I 13 63 13
PEACHES (1)
and peaches, soon collected them round the table. PP III 3 268 6
PEAK (1)
beauties of Matlock, Chatsworth, Dovedale, or the peak. PP II 19 239 7
PEALS (1)
Peals of thunder so loud as to seem to shake the edifice NA II 5 159 19
PEAR-TREE (1)
with a vine and a pear-tree trained round its casements; P III 5 36 20
PEARLS (4)
a very beautiful set of pearls that Mr. Drummond gave his NA I 9 68 48
The ivory, the gold and the pearls, all received their SS II 11 221 5
Mrs. Elton, as elegant as lace and pearls could make her, E II 16 292 10
And I see very few pearls in the room except mine.-- E III 2 324 21
PECULIAR (39)
dark eyes, & there is peculiar sweetness in her look when LS 17 270 5
and how unsusceptible of peculiar tenderness towards the NA I 10 74 22
The windows, to which she looked with peculiar dependence, NA II 5 162 26
she had trodden with peculiar awe, she well remembered the NA II 8 188 17
instant on her mind with peculiar force, made her for a NA II 13 228 27
For Catherine, however, the peculiar object of the NA II 15 245 12
good opinion by any peculiar graces of person or address. SS I 3 15 6
peculiar circumstances been kept more ignorant than myself. SS I 4 20 9
of faith, denied all peculiar affection whatever--a letter SS II 7 183 14
But there was no peculiar disgrace in this, for it was SS II 12 233 18
and the warm acknowledgment of peculiar obligation. SS III 10 340 2
every tree brought some peculiar, some painful SS III 10 342 7
Had I died,--in what peculiar misery should I have left SS III 10 346 28
duty of us all; the the peculiar duty of a young man who PP I 20 114 32
without any symptom of peculiar regard, and I remained PP II 12 197 5
It is not of peculiar, but of general evils, which I am PP II 18 231 18
off by the defence of some little peculiar vexation." PP II 19 237 4
"the engagement between them is of a peculiar kind. PP III 14 354 42
43
"This young gentleman is blessed in a peculiar way, with PP III 15 362 15
sensible of her peculiar good fortune, ended every day's MP I 2 14 9
moment, a moment of such peculiar proof and importance, MP II 1 176 3
Excepting the moments of peculiar delight, which any MP II 6 234 18
peculiar gratification than would be attributed to her. MP II 9 266 22
the Miss Prices as his peculiar charge; and before they MP III 11 409 5
That his judgment submitted to all his own peculiar and MP III 16 453 16
to him of such close and peculiar interest, dearer by all MP III 17 470 27
which gave peculiar elegance to the character of her face." E II 6 199 10
which marked her as his peculiar object, and at dinner she E II 8 214 12
for any thing of peculiar anxiety to be observable. E II 8 218 37
But whether he were entirely free from peculiar attachment- E II 8 228 93
have arisen from some peculiar circumstances--feelings E III 5 350 37
Under that peculiar sort of dry, blunt manner, I know you E III 6 356 28
or disappointment, or peculiar concern in the discovery. E III 11 404 9
perhaps nearly all of peculiar attachment to him,--but she P III 4 28 7
unsuspicious of being inflicting any peculiar wound. P III 7 60 32
autumn, that season of peculiar and inexhaustible P III 10 84 7
How, in all the peculiar disadvantages of their respective P IV 8 191 51
Croft, every thing of peculiar cordiality and fervent P IV 11 246 78
approached with a peculiar degree of respectful compassion, S 10 413 1
PECULIARITIES (2)
who, though with some peculiarities, has abilities which PP II 10 187 40
Mr. Woodhouse's peculiarities, and fidgettiness were E I 11 93 5
PECULIARITY (3)
of regard, or any peculiarity of manner, where their two PP III 2 265 16
of heart, and sweet peculiarity of manner, that spirit and MP III 4 351 36
and yet there is a peculiarity in the shape of the eye and E I 6 44 15
PECULIARLY (32)
sense of superior integrity which is peculiarly insolent. LS 25 292 1
talent of writing agreeable letters is peculiarly female. NA I 3 27 28
circumstances which peculiarly belong to the heroine's NA I 8 53 2
entirely owing to the peculiarly judicious manner in which NA I 9 62 10
of which made her peculiarly sensible of Henry's NA II 8 187 15
apartment, belonging peculiarly to the master of the house, NA II 11 213 21
strongly resembled and peculiarly delighted her sister, of SS I 10 48 9
they must know to be peculiarly interesting to them all. SS I 14 71 3
chose to consider as peculiarly propitious, would W 360 29
attention which I conceive myself peculiarly bound to pay." PP I 14 67 9
and to Mrs. Gardiner it had a peculiarly strong attraction. PP II 19 239 7
apprehension, peculiarly denoted her perverseness and PP III 16 367 9
to return, it would be peculiarly consoling to see their MP I 4 38 9
and taste which were peculiarly becoming, and there was MP I 7 64 12
the tallest, seemed to fit him peculiarly for the Baron. MP I 14 132 8
and of forgetting, do seem peculiarly past finding out." MP II 4 209 12
in the morning, was peculiarly to be respected, and they MP II 10 278 20
I had thought you peculiarly free from wilfulness of MP III 1 318 39
Her disposition was peculiarly calculated to value a fond MP III 5 365 33
all its concerns, and peculiarly interested in herself, in E I 1 6 6
when she considered how peculiarly unlucky poor Mr. Elton E II 14 271 5
she had always considered the ball as peculiarly for her. E III 2 325 31
his concession in her favour, was peculiarly gratifying. E III 3 332 1
work to make them peculiarly interesting to each other?-- E III 3 335 9
Peculiarly lucky!--for as to any real knowledge of a E III 7 372 40
not unworthy of being peculiarly, exclusively, E III 12 415 1
herself, it seemed a peculiarly cruel necessity that was E III 15 450 37
highest importance, so peculiarly eligible, so singularly E III 17 467 31
has come on me! how peculiarly unprepared I was!--for I E III 18 473 24
So peculiarly the lady in it.-- E III 18 478 61
family, which made him peculiarly desirable as a tenant. P III 3 22 24
she held her to be peculiarly fitted by her warm P III 4 29 7
PECUNIARY (7)
was proper to render her pecuniary assistance, I cannot LS 3 247 1
comfort, and under every pecuniary view, it was a match NA II 16 249 2
He would then have suffered under the pecuniary distresses SS III 11 351 13
some more immediate pecuniary advantage, in lieu of the PP II 12 200 5
particulars of all the pecuniary transactions in which PP III 1 258 75
The necessity of the measure in a pecuniary light, and the MP I 3 32 62
of their narrow income & pecuniary difficulties, to invite S 3 378 1
PEDAL (1)
say as to tone, touch, and pedal, totally unsuspicious of E II 8 220 46
PEDANTIC (1)
had given her likewise a pedantic air and conceited manner, PP I 6 25 24
PEEP (1)
The journey would moreover give her a peep at Jane; and, PP II 4 151 1
PEEPED (2)
herself of its being so, peeped courageously behind each NA II 6 167 10
The two Abbotts and I ran into the front room and peeped E I 9 75 26
PEERAGE (1)
her; independent of his peerage, his wealth, and his NA II 16 251 5
PEEVISH (3)
had passed;--a little peevish under immediate pain, & ill W 348 22
and occasionally from some peevish allusion of her mother. PP I 21 115 1
fate in terms as unreasonable as her accent was peevish. PP II 18 230 12
PEEVISHNESS (1)
disappointment, or repress the peevishness of her temper--. W 360 30
PEICE (3)
seems so extraordinary a peice of nicety, considering what LS 19 274 2
for two or three nights, without making a peice of work. W 351 25
A pretty peice of work your Aunt Turner has made of it!-- W 351 26

PEICES (1)
He took the peices of paper as he spoke--& having looked S 1 366 1
PELISSE (4)
pelisse was not half so handsome as that on her own. NA I 4 32 2
How nice Mary Edwards looks in her new pelisse!-- W 341 19
and strength of any old pelisse, which you had seen lent P III 8 65 16
and grow coarse, I would send her a new hat and pelisse." P IV 3 142 16
PELISSES (2)
we left the two gentlemen together to put on our pelisses. LS 20 276 4
pianoforte nor wore fine pelisses, they could , on farther MP III 9 395 3
PEMBERLEY (50)
and of course she will be always at Pemberley with you." PP I 6 27 53
What a delightful library you have at Pemberley, Mr. Darcy! PP I 8 38 29
house, I wish it may be half as delightful as Pemberley." PP I 8 38 33
that neighbourhood, and take Pemberley for a kind of model. PP I 8 38 35
"With all my heart; I will buy Pemberley itself if Darcy PP I 8 38 36
possible to get Pemberley by purchase than by imitation." PP I 8 38 38
and aunt Philips be placed in the gallery at Pemberley. PP I 10 52 57
devoted all his time to the care of the Pemberley property. PP I 16 81 37
the influence of the Pemberley house, is a powerful motive. PP I 16 81 41
Mrs. Gardiner had seen Pemberley, and known the late Mr. PP II 2 143 20
In comparing her recollection of Pemberley, with the PP II 2 143 20
management of all the Pemberley estates; and whose good PP II 12 199 5
I thought too ill of him, to invite him to Pemberley, or PP II 12 201 5
The account of his connection with the Pemberley family, PP II 13 205 3
see the word without thinking of Pemberley and its owner. PP II 19 239 9
Elizabeth found from her aunt, that Pemberley was situated. PP II 19 240 12
She felt that she had no business at Pemberley, and was PP II 19 240 14
the chambermaid whether Pemberley were not a very fine PP II 19 241 17
To Pemberley, therefore, they were to go. PP II 19 241 18
the first appearance of Pemberley woods with some PP III 1 245 1
was instantly caught by Pemberley house, situated on the PP III 1 245 3
"Is your master much at Pemberley in the course of the PP III 1 248 24
who had taken a liking to the room, when last at Pemberley. PP III 1 249 43
Her thoughts were all fixed on that one spot of Pemberley PP III 1 253 55
of Pemberley from her, might be mischievously construed. PP III 1 254 57
day after her reaching Pemberley; and was consequently PP III 2 260 1
As for Elizabeth, her thoughts were at Pemberley this PP III 2 265 16
day of her arrival at Pemberley, for she had reached it PP III 2 266 17
to wait on her at Pemberley the following morning. PP III 2 266 17
of his meeting some of the gentlemen at Pemberley by noon. PP III 2 266 18
her appearance at Pemberley must be to her, and was PP III 3 267 1
having the pleasure of seeing you at Pemberley to day." PP III 4 278 20
"But what is to be done about Pemberley?" cried Mrs. PP III 4 280 26
but his lies about the whole Pemberley family are endless. PP III 5 284 14
none since her return, that could come from Pemberley. PP III 6 298 16
were still staying at Pemberley; but it was agreed that he PP III 10 324 2
our uncle and aunt, that you have actually seen Pemberley." PP III 10 327 9
in Hertfordshire, than as she had seen him at Pemberley. PP III 11 335 40
of saying, "is your sister at Pemberley still?" PP III 12 341 20
21
Are the shades of Pemberley to be thus polluted?" PP III 14 357 62
of asking what you thought of me; when we met at Pemberley. PP III 16 369 29
from my first seeing his beautiful grounds at Pemberley." PP III 17 373 16
How little did you tell me of what passed at Pemberley and PP III 17 374 18
You are all to come to Pemberley at Christmas. PP III 18 383 21
comfort and elegance of their family party at Pemberley. PP III 18 384 27
He delighted in going to Pemberley, especially when he was PP III 19 385 2
Though Darcy could never receive him at Pemberley, yet, PP III 19 387 9
the right of visiting at Pemberley, she dropt all her PP III 19 387 10
Pemberley was now Georgiana's home; and the attachment of PP III 19 387 11
to wait on them at Pemberley, in spite of that pollution PP III 19 388 12
PEMBERLY (3)
Miss Darcy, the daughter of Mr. Darcy, of Pemberly and PP II 14 212 13
felt, that to be mistress of Pemberly might be something! PP III 1 245 3
to dinner at Pemberly, before they left the country. PP III 2 263 11
PEMBROKE (2)
best Pembroke table, with the best tea things before her. W 355 28
of the small-sized Pembroke, on which two of his daily E III 5 347 18
PEN (26)
that I can scarcely hold a pen, but am determined to send LS 23 283 2
set forth by the capital pen of a sister author;--and to NA I 14 111 29
I have had my pen in my hand to begin a letter to you NA II 12 216 2
is an event on which the pen of the contriver may well NA II 14 232 7
was far from assisting her pen; and never had it been NA II 14 235 14
intervals, to withhold her pen, were proofs enough of her SS II 7 180 4
the advancement of her pen, grieving over her for the SS II 9 203 10
over her paper, with the pen in her hand, till broken in SS III 4 287 24
"I am afraid you do not like your pen. PP I 10 47 11
but Harriet was ill, and so pen was forced to come by PP II 16 221 17
Adieu. I take up my pen again to do, what I have just told PP III 4 275 5
when obliged to take up the pen to say that such a horse MP I 6 59 43
"Fanny," said he directly, leaving his seat and his pen, MP II 9 261 2
Two lines more prized had never fallen from the pen of the MP II 9 265 19
reading from the brother's pen, for Edmund would never MP III 7 376 4
of Mansfield news should fall to my pen instead of her's. MP III 13 424 2
"I take up my pen to communicate some very MP III 13 425 7
8
than to have to take up the pen to acquaint her with all MP III 13 426 9
promise occupation for the pen for many days to come, MP III 13 426 9
a pen in hand, his thoughts naturally find proper words. E I 7 51 5
table, Captain Wentworth's pen ceased to move, his head P IV 11 231 10
It was nothing more than that his pen had fallen down, but P IV 11 233 24
to suspect that the pen had only fallen, because he had P IV 11 233 24
so much higher a degree; the pen has been in their hands. P IV 11 234 28
at last to prepare his pen with a very good grace for the P IV 12 248 2
instantly took up her pen & forwarded the circumstance to S 9 408 1
PEN. (1)
you heard from Pen. since she went to Chichester?-- W 351 24
PENALTY (1)
In this world, the penalty is less equal than could be MP III 17 468 22
PENANCE (16)
a little dissipation for a ten weeks' penance at Churchill. LS 25 294 4
It seemed like wilful ill-nature, or a voluntary penance, PP II 10 182 1
in a state of complete penance, and as different from the MP I 9 91 36
Such a penance as I have been enduring, while you were MP I 10 100 28
passing in a state of penance, which she loved them too MP III 14 430 6
penance of communication; and a severe one it was.-- E I 17 141 5
peace and hope, to penance and mortification for ever. E II 2 165 8
in a moral light, as a penance, a lesson, a source of E II 4 182 7
Here, she must be leading a life of privation and penance; E II 8 217 32
"She must be under some sort of penance, inflicted either E II 15 285 15
dreadful penance, by the sound of her father's footsteps. E III 11 411 42
penance compared with the happiness which brought it on! P IV 8 184 17
hour of pleasure or of penance was to be set out, another P IV 8 189 45
From that period his penance had become severe. P IV 11 242 64
other end of the bench was doing penance, was indubitable. S 7 396 1
he evidently felt it no penance to have a fine young woman S 10 415 1
PENCIL (8)
Her greatest deficiency was in the pencil--she had no NA I 1 16 10
the two others from their pencil and their book, in spite SS I 9 41 3
We will provide ourselves with tablets and a pencil. MP II 5 227 65
Miniatures, half-lengths, whole-lengths, pencil, crayon, E I 6 44 19
pencil, to jump up and see the progress, and be charmed.-- E I 6 47 26
It was the end of an old pencil,--the part without any E III 4 339 17
but when he took out his pencil, there was so little lead E III 4 339 18
I have not a word to say for the bit of old pencil, but E III 4 340 25
PENCILLED (1)
There were the pencilled marks and memorandums on the E II 5 187 4
PENDANT (1)
The shops were deserted--the straw hats & pendant lace S 6 389 1
PENELOPE (19)
But you must ask him--not me--you must ask Penelope.-- W 316
Yes Emma, Penelope was at the bottom of it all.-- W 316
Penelope makes light of her conduct, but I think such W 316
"You quite shock me by what you say of Penelope--said Emma. W 316
Appearances were against her"--"you do not know Penelope.-- W 316
Not that I can ever quite forgive Penelope."-- W 317
"Penelope however has had her troubles--continued Miss W.-- W 317
her for Margaret, & poor Penelope was very wretched--. W 317
Penelope will laugh at you very much." W 318
But I doubt whether ridicule,--has Penelope much wit?"-- W 318
doing pretty well, tho' it would be nothing for Penelope.-- W 322
I see a look of Miss Penelope--& once or twice there has W 324
is very snappish, & Penelope owns she had rather have W 343
But did not you hear him ask where Miss Penelope & Miss W 347
I fancy she'll come back 'Miss Penelope' as she went.--" W 351
Penelope was the only creature to be thought of. W 355
It could not be Penelope. W 355
Penelope, my dear, can you help me to the name of the P III 3 23
"Well, my dear Penelope, you need not be so alarmed about P IV 10 213
PENETRATE (3)
of her anxious desire to penetrate this mystery, to NA II 6 164
of Mrs. Dashwood could penetrate, and at last, without SS III 12 360
She soon believed herself to penetrate Mrs. Elton's E III 16 453
PENETRATED (4)
which astonished and penetrated her, calling her his dear MP II 1 177
the whole, but her quickness must have penetrated a part. E III 14 438
might never have been penetrated by Mr. Elliot, knowing P IV 3 140
"your feelings, as I think you must have penetrated mine. P IV 11 237
PENETRATING (4)
violence of the wind penetrating through the divisions of NA II 6 167
I am serious, Miss Woodhouse, whatever your penetrating E III 6 365
Mrs. Smith gave her a penetrating glance, and then, P IV 9 195
looking around her, or penetrating forward, she saw more P IV 10 212
PENETRATION (17)
Frederica possessed the penetration, the abilities, which LS 24 288
it is so indeed; your penetration has not deceived you.-- NA I 15 117
been as full of arch penetration and affectionate sympathy NA I 15 119
perhaps assisted her penetration; but she really felt SS I 3 16
rejoicing in their own penetration at every glimpse of SS I 9 41
penetration, founded on Margaret's instructions, extended. SS I 18 99
Young ladies have great penetration in such matters as PP III 15 362
at such a want of penetration, or fear that perhaps PP III 15 364
Her displeasure, her penetration, and her happiness were MP III 5 356
Harriet had no penetration. E I 4 27
There was no denying that those brothers had penetration. E I 16 135
him of all such sort of penetration or suspicion, was a E II 5 193
was a compliment to her penetration which made it E II 9 231
He looked with smiling penetration; and, on receiving no E III 2 330
excited by her friend's penetration, unable to imagine how P IV 9 194
of character, a natural penetration, in short, which no P IV 12 249
it the evidence of real penetration & prepared for some S 7 401
PENITENCE (3)
the torture of penitence, without the hope of amendment. SS III 2 270
Tell her of my misery and my penitence--tell her that my SS III 8 330
the appearance of the penitence, so justly and truly hers. E III 8 377
PENITENT (4)
She looks perfectly timid, dejected & penitent. LS 17 270
am grown neither humble nor penitent by what has passed.-- SS III 13 372
satisfied her; his style was not penitent, but haughty. PP II 13 204
As a daughter--he hoped a penitent one--she should be MP III 17 465
PENKNIFE (2)
to assist her with his penknife or his orthography, as MP I 2 16
your new penknife, and your recommending court plaister?-- E III 4 338
PENNED (2)
Two others, penned by the same hand, marked an expenditure NA II 7 172
mere letter of business, penned for the purpose of MP III 12 415
PENNY (2)
own; and if she had not a penny, why so much the better." NA I 15 124
phrase--that she has got her pennyworth for her penny. MP III 9 394
PENNYWORTH (1)
phrase--that she has got her pennyworth for her penny. MP III 9 394
PENS (3)
eulogized by a thousand pens,--there seems almost a NA I 5 37
I mend pens remarkably well." PP I 10 47
Let other pens dwell on guilt and misery. MP III 17 461
PENSIVE (6)
face with a remarkable expression of pensive admiration! LS 18 272
Thoughtful & pensive in general her countenance always LS 18 272
woman, with a mild and pensive countenance, justifying, so NA II 9 191
Emma's pensive meditations, as she walked home, were not E III 9 385
Anne's slender form, and pensive face, may be considered P III 8 68
but by her silent, pensive self, might be filled again P IV 1 123
PENSIVENESS (1)
yet with a degree of pensiveness which might convince him LS 25 292
PENT (2)
relief to her companion, pent up within her own mind as E III 12 418
Here were we, pent down in this little contracted Nook, S 4 380
PENURY (2)
to him the certain penury that must attend the match. SS III 1 266
Elton's notice and the penury of her conversation, rather E II 15 285
PEOPLE (384)
which satisfies most people, but aspires to the more LS 4 248
pressed against by people, the generality of whose faces NA I 2 21
there is nobody you know in all this multitude of people? NA I 2 23
hours; crowds of people were every moment passing in and NA I 4 31
up the steps and down; people whom nobody cared about, and NA I 4 31
I have no notion of loving people by halves, it is not my NA I 6 40
a cheap thing by some people, for I might have sold it for NA I 7 47
place for young people--and indeed for every body else too. NA I 8 54
You know I never stand upon ceremony with such people." NA I 8 56
"Do not you?--then let us walk about and quiz people. NA I 8 59
Her own family were plain matter-of-fact people, who NA I 9 65
They seem very agreeable people. NA I 9 68
But they are very good king of people, and very rich. NA I 9 68
People that marry can never part, but must go and keep NA I 10 77
People that dance, only stand opposite each other in a NA I 10 77
You would be told so by people of all descriptions, who NA I 10 78
"Well, other people must judge for themselves, and those NA I 10 78
here I see a variety of people in every street, and there NA I 10 79
There will be very few people in the Pump-Room, if it NA I 11 83
people that had surprized her so much a few mornings back. NA I 11 84
be miserly; and that if people who rolled in money could NA I 11 89
There are few people much about town that I do not know. NA I 12 96
Young people will be young people, as your good mother NA I 13 104
Young people do not like to be always thwarted." NA I 13 105
delicacy, or refinement;--people were nice in their dress, NA I 14 108
If people like to read their books, it is all very well, NA I 14 109
Where people wish to attach, they should always be NA I 14 110
Where people are really attached, poverty itself is wealth: NA I 15 119
"Oh! dear, there are a great many people like me, I dare NA I 15 123
There are very few people I am sorry to see. NA I 15 123
have the company of the people I love, let me only be NA I 15 123
it possible, that some people might think him handsomer NA II 1 131
I dare say people would admire him in general; but he is NA II 1 135
as happy without you, for people seldom know what they NA II 3 146
Tilney says, there is nothing people are so often deceived NA II 3 147
though there were three people to go in it, and his NA II 5 155
there would be so many people in the house--and besides, NA II 5 158
on such subjects as most people, he did look upon a NA II 6 166
by the three young people; and Catherine found, with some NA II 11 208
the number of young dancing people in the neighbourhood. NA II 11 209

How were people, at that rate, to be understood? NA II 11 211 15
love the place and the people more and more every day; and NA II 13 220 1
"I am sorry for the young people," returned Mrs. Morland; " NA II 14 234 12
It is always good for young people to be put upon exerting NA II 14 234 12
very pretty kind of your people; and you were sadly out of NA II 14 236 15
incapable of giving the young people even a decent support. NA II 15 246 12
The young people could not be surprized at a decision like NA II 16 250 3
of other people she could act when occasion required it. SS I 1 6 9
"Certainly not; but if you observe, people always live for SS I 2 10 20
the performances of other people, and I assure you he is SS I 4 19 2
by the drawings of other people, was very far from that SS I 4 19 3
about him more young people than his house would hold, and SS I 7 32 2
weddings among all the young people of her acquaintance. SS I 8 36 1
In hastily forming and giving his opinion of other people, SS I 10 49 9
"But perhaps the abuse of such people as yourself and SS I 10 50 18
Seven years would be insufficient to make some people SS I 12 59 4
different people to quit the topic, it fell to the ground. SS I 12 62 27
"there are some people who cannot bear a party of pleasure. SS I 13 64 30
Are the Middletons pleasant people?" SS I 16 88 38
Marianne coloured as she replied, "but most people do." SS I 17 92 17
point or other: fancying people so much more gay or grave, SS I 17 93 37
frequently by what other people say of them, without SS I 17 93 37
"to be guided wholly by the opinion of other people. SS I 17 93 38
Because he believes many people pretend to more admiration SS I 18 97 6
How few people know what comfort is! SS I 20 111 8
It was the desire of appearing superior to other people. SS I 20 112 28
the election; and so many people come to dine with us that SS I 20 113 33
is, I do not believe many people are acquainted with him, SS I 20 116 58
failed, as between many people and under many SS II 2 147 8
the power of dividing two people so tenderly attached is SS II 2 150 33
from that of other people, you will scarcely have any SS II 3 156 13
nearly twenty young people, and to amuse them with a ball. SS II 5 170 29
to endure the questions and remarks of all these people. SS II 7 191 64
and you know young people like to be laughed at about them. SS II 8 195 16
She expected from other people the same opinions and SS II 9 202 4
Dashwoods found so many people before them in the room, SS II 11 220 3
But so it ought to be; they are people of large fortune, SS II 11 222 11
"Not so large, I dare say, as many people suppose. SS II 11 225 31
Few people of common prudence will do that; and whatever SS II 11 227 44
"people have little, have very little in their power. SS II 11 227 48
many words: for, unlike people in general, she SS II 12 232 15
But while the imaginations of other people will carry them SS II 14 248 6
But that was not enough; for when people are determined on SS II 14 248 6
comprehended a great many people who had real taste for SS II 14 250 10
"Some people imagine that there can be no accommodations, SS II 14 252 18
So that, in fact, you see, if people do but know how to SS II 14 252 18
"Well, but Miss Dashwood," speaking triumphantly, "people SS III 2 272 14
no business of other people to set it down for certain." SS III 2 272 14
Miss Dashwood, do you think people make love when any body SS III 2 274 18
I assure you they are very genteel people. SS III 2 275 25
to divide, two young people long attached to each other, SS III 3 282 19
of all people in the world, was fixed on to bestow it!-- SS III 3 283 20
Few people who have so compassionate an heart! SS III 4 285 2
she returned from seeing people whom she had never seen SS III 4 291 46
as much superior to people in general, as he must feel SS III 6 304 15
of associating with people of better income than myself. SS III 8 320 32
Their gentleness, their genuine attention to other people, SS III 9 338 22
and hospitable for other people as well as herself, SS III 10 341 4
may happen--for, when people are much thrown together, and SS III 14 375 9
might have puzzled many people to find out; and what SS III 14 377 12
The Edward's were people of fortune who lived in the town W 314 1
Some people say that he has never seemed to like any girl W 316 1
I have lost Purvis, it is true but very few people marry W 317 2
will dispose a great many people to attend the second.-- W 323 3
go so early;--but great people have always their charm."-- W 323 3
he does; & very few people that play a fairer rubber.-- W 325 4
She was a very fine woman then--but like other people I W 325 4
whether there were many people come yet was told by the W 327 7
hesitatingly--"yes--he is very much liked by many people.-- W 328 8
men to their duty, & people the centre of the room, than W 328 9
But if these soldiers are quicker than other people in a W 337 15
He is out of luck as well as other people.-- W 342 19
to the ridicule of richer people in her present home.-- W 345 21
He loved to take people by surprise, with sudden visits at W 355 28
beheld a circle of smart people whom he cd not immediately W 355 28
with all the principal people in the room; he was lively PP I 3 10 6
a great deal too apt you know, to like people in general. PP I 4 14 7
and of associating with people of rank; and were therefore PP I 4 15 11
Bingley had never met with pleasanter people or prettier PP I 4 16 15
Darcy, on the contrary, had seen a collection of people in PP I 4 16 15
"What a charming amusement for young people this is, Mr. PP I 6 25 26
and yet the self-importance of all these people!-- PP I 6 27 47
People do not die of little trifling colds. PP I 7 31 32
"But people themselves alter so much, that there is PP I 9 43 18
He only meant that there were not such a variety of people PP I 9 43 24
to not meeting with many people in this neighbourhood, I PP I 9 43 25
"Certainly," replied Elizabeth--"there are such people, PP I 11 57 21
Lady Catherine was reckoned proud by many people he knew, PP I 14 66 1
Interested people have perhaps misrepresented each to the PP I 17 85 2
people who have probably been concerned in the business?-- PP I 17 85 3
character, to respectable people, can have any evil PP I 17 87 13
Sir William could not have interrupted any two people in PP I 18 93 26
People who suffer as I do from nervous complaints can have PP I 20 113 28
as most people can boast on entering the marriage state." PP I 22 125 17
and lovers were of all people the most disagreeable. PP I 23 128 11
There are few people whom I really love, and still fewer PP II 1 135 11
The lucases are very artful people indeed, sister. PP II 2 140 4
He was growing quite inattentive to other people, and PP II 2 141 9
there is affection, young people are seldom withheld by PP II 3 145 7
all those elegant decorums which other people may observe. PP II 4 153 15
There are few people in England, I suppose, who have more PP II 8 173 6
"I certainly have not the talent which some people possess, PP II 8 175 24
the walk to it, or of the people who lived in it, the two PP II 9 180 28
It was not to be supposed that any other people could be PP II 10 186 38
people as to the rest of his conduct, who will believe me? PP II 17 226 23
death of half the good people in Meryton, to attempt to PP II 17 226 23
"there are very few people of whom so much can be said. PP III 1 248 31
32

Some people call him proud; but I am sure I never saw any PP III 1 249 38
of some of those very people, against whom his pride had PP III 1 254 58
He takes them now for people of fashion." PP III 1 255 58
people may call him proud, I have seen nothing of it." PP III 1 257 68
the good opinion of people, with whom any intercourse a PP III 2 263 10
herself; but angry people are not always wise; and in PP III 3 271 16
any success, no such people had been seen to pass through. PP III 4 275 5
There were few people on whose secrecy she would have more PP III 8 311 12
He promises fairly, and I hope among different people, PP III 8 313 19
mamma, do the people here abouts know I am married to-day? PP III 9 316 8
It was exactly a scene, and exactly among people, where he PP III 9 320 32
well, I suppose, what has been done for the young people. PP III 10 324 2
People did say, you meant to quit the place entirely at PP III 11 336 49
Perhaps other people have said so before, but not one with PP III 18 383 21
The young people were all at home, and sustained their MP I 2 12 3
The place became less strange, and the people less MP I 2 17 21
very unlucky, but some people were stupid, and Fanny must MP I 2 20 31
fair report of being very respectable, agreeable people. MP I 3 24 6
from, the same people to look at, the same horse to ride." MP I 3 27 35
of balls, the young people justified these opinions, and MP I 4 39 11
They were young people of fortune. MP I 4 40 15
I do not like to have people throw themselves away; but MP I 4 43 27
The young people were pleased with each other from the MP I 5 44 1
the one in which people expect most from others, and are MP I 5 46 20
I do not pretend to set people right, but I do see that MP I 5 50 36
included all the young people but herself, and was much MP I 7 70 30
You should learn to think of other people; and take my MP I 7 71 34
the clergyman and his wife are very decent people. MP I 8 82 34
"At any rate, it is safer to leave people to their own MP I 9 87 15
likes: and if the good people who used to kneel and gape MP I 9 87 15
be done, when the young people, meeting with an outward MP I 9 89 32
gardeners are the only people who can go where they like." MP I 9 91 37
It is not there, that respectable people of any MP I 9 93 49
If other people think Sotherton improved, I have no doubt MP I 10 98 8
a great admirer of this Mr. Crawford as some people are? MP I 10 102 41
into the house; and when people are waiting, they are bad MP I 10 102 46
had a great many more people under his command than he has MP I 11 111 30
more attended to, and people were carried more out of MP I 11 113 35
while all the other young people were dancing, and she MP I 12 116 11
ma'am, to see young people so properly happy, so well MP I 12 118 16
I only wonder how the good people can keep it up so long.-- MP I 12 118 22
so strong among young people, that he could hardly out- MP I 13 121 2
Nobody is fonder of the exercise of talent in young people, MP I 13 126 25
be attended to, so many people to be pleased, so many best MP I 14 130 2
I hate such encroaching people, (the Jacksons are very MP I 15 142 22
so,--just the sort of people to get all they can), I said MP I 15 142 22
cheerfulness to the young people in general, and that did MP I 17 161 9
and useful pursuits of all the young people as for her own. MP II 1 179 9
people have been amusing themselves lately, Sir Thomas? MP II 1 180 13
The young people have been very inconsiderate in forming MP II 2 188 3
they are in fact exactly the sort of people he would like. MP II 3 196 2
"I suppose I am graver than other people," said Fanny. MP II 3 197 5
have done--but then I am unlike other people I dare say." MP II 3 197 5
only unlike other people in being more wise and discreet? MP II 3 197 6
on people or subjects which she wished to be respected. MP II 4 208 11
But we have no such people in Mansfield. MP II 4 213 33
to go, since all young people like to be together, I can MP II 5 219 18
a mile and only to three people, still it was dining out, MP II 5 219 27
been respected! for people are never respected when they MP II 5 220 30
as people say; a sort of beauty that grows on one. MP II 6 230 6
pleasure to the young people in general; and having MP II 8 252 1
be tempted to give the young people a dance at Mansfield. MP II 8 252 2
notice, to collect young people enough to form twelve or MP II 8 253 7
Miss Price, known only by name to half the people invited, MP II 9 266 22
"You know nothing and you care less, as people say. MP II 11 288 30
The Bertrams are undoubtedly some of the first people in MP II 12 293 11
I could name three people now, who would give me my own MP II 12 295 20
general joy through a wide circle of great people. MP II 13 298 3
"It is amazing," said she, "how much young people cost MP II 13 305 24
a knowledge of what had passed between the young people. MP III 2 329 11
one of those well-meaning people, who are always doing MP III 2 332 19
There never were two people more dissimilar. MP III 4 348 22
to be about as unhappy as most other married people. MP III 5 361 16
up to by all the young people of her acquaintance; and she MP III 5 361 16
Experience might have hoped more for any young people, so MP III 6 367 6
mind to go with the young people; it would be such an MP III 6 372 21
be a help to the young people in their journey to have her MP III 6 372 21
lives too far off, to think of such little people as you." MP III 7 387 44
absent, it told her of people and things about whom she MP III 9 394 2
interest, while the young people sat down upon some MP III 10 403 15
with the names of people and parties, that fill up my time. MP III 12 415 2
a description of the people, the manners, the amusements, MP III 12 419 8
The Aylmers are pleasant people; and her husband away, she MP III 14 434 13
cannot be true--it must mean some other people." MP III 15 440 15
in which affairs then stood with the young people. MP III 16 450 9
by her own family, people of respectability as they are, MP III 16 457 29
character of any young people, must be the totally MP III 17 463 7
from the scenes and people she had been used to; but the MP III 17 469 24
must vary much as to time in different people.-- MP III 17 470 26
to suppose that other people could feel differently from E I 1 7 10
Mr. Knightley, in fact, was one of the few people who E I 1 11 33
the right, when so many people said Mr. Weston would never E I 1 11 39
for myself, papa; but I must, indeed, for other people. E I 1 12 41
Some people even talked of a promise to his wife on her E I 1 12 41
never believe other people to be different from himself. E I 2 19 14
many--perhaps with most people, unless taken moderately. E I 2 19 14
though very good sort of people, must be doing her harm. E I 3 23 10
summer-house, large enough to hold a dozen people." E I 4 27 4
The yeomanry are precisely the order of people with whom I E I 4 29 14
plenty of people who would take pleasure in degrading you." E I 4 30 22
here I have seen people--and if one comes to compare them, E I 7 54 30
Hitherto I fancy you and I are the only people to whom his E I 7 56 41
about wondering that people should like her so much. E I 7 56 42
We invalids think we are privileged people." E I 8 57 3
thought so by ninety-nine people out of an hundred; and E I 8 63 44
and a great readiness to be pleased with other people. E I 8 63 44
pre-arrangement of other people, should so immediately E I 9 74 25
love with me,--me, of all people, who did not know him, to E I 9 75 26
Some people are surprized, I believe, that the eldest was E I 9 80 72
must find other people charming--one other person at least. E I 10 84 10
11

Heaven forbid! at least, that I should ever bore people E I 10 86 23
There are people, who the more you do for them, the less E I 11 91 1
excellent Miss Bates!--such thorough worthy people!-- E I 12 102 31
"I know there is such an idea with many people, but indeed E I 12 105 55
to the Highbury people, but if you call to mind exactly E I 12 106 61
of the mistakes which people of high pretensions to E I 13 112 23
of himself when he asks people to leave their own fireside, E I 13 113 26
The folly of not allowing people to be comfortable at home- E I 13 113 26
them, and people think little of even the worst weather. E I 13 115 39
Charming people, Mr. and Mrs. Weston;--Mrs. Weston indeed E I 13 116 43
a stone to people in general; and the devil of a temper." E I 14 121 13
passable for adventurous people, but in a state that E I 15 127 13
to take so active part in bringing any two people together. E I 16 136 10
stronger with the people he depended on, than all that a E I 18 147 18
minds belong to rich people in authority, I think they E I 18 147 19
of other people: nothing really amiable about him." E I 18 149 26
The house belonged to people in business. E II 1 155 4
and well-informed people, her heart and understanding had E II 2 164 6
If ever there were people who, without having great wealth E II 3 174 31
It is such a happiness when good people get together--and E II 3 175 39
the Coles, such very good people; and the Perrys--I E II 3 175 39
he lamented that young people would be in such a hurry to E II 3 177 51
be well meaning, worthy people before; and what difference E II 3 179 53
aunt, very worthy people; I have known them all my life. E II 5 194 45
that he had heard many people say the same--but yet he E II 6 199 10
than that "all young people would have their little whims." E II 7 205 1
As Mrs. Weston observed, "all young people would have E II 7 206 3
were very good sort of people--friendly, liberal, and E II 7 207 6
There will be a great many people talking at once. E II 7 210 16
They are good-natured people, and think little of their E II 7 210 19
friendly, good sort of people as ever lived, and who have E II 7 210 19
I know what worthy people they are. E II 7 210 20
if they are done by sensible people in an impudent way. E II 8 212 2
3

people come in a way which they know to be beneath them. E II 8 213 10
While waiting till the other young people could pair E II 8 229 99
She must have delighted the Coles--worthy people, who E II 9 231 1
always--I have heard some people say that Mrs. Wallis can E II 9 236 46
Instances have been known of young people passing many, E II 11 247 1
passed by the two young people in schemes on the subject. E II 11 247 2
But still she had inclination enough for shewing people E II 11 247 2
his life--did not know the people who kept it by sight.-- E II 11 251 26
young people set off together without delay for the crown. E II 11 253 40
Mrs. Weston was afraid of draughts for the young people in E II 11 254 44
the inclinations of the rest of the people as any body. E II 11 254 50

drawn from one set of people, and one style of living; E II 14 272 16
People who have extensive grounds themselves are always E II 14 273 21
She had a great idea that people who had extensive grounds E II 14 273 22
23
When people come into a beautiful country of this sort, E II 14 274 28
are a very quiet set of people, I believe; more disposed E II 14 274 29
on the contrary, when people shut themselves up entirely E II 14 275 30
both at home; and very pleasant people they seem to be. E II 14 278 44
It is encouraging people to marry if you make so much of E II 14 280 57
nothing to do with any encouragement to people to marry." E II 14 280 60
to speaking his name at once before all these people? E II 16 297 48
But I am quite in the minority, I believe; few people seem E II 17 302 22
But what is distance, Mr. Weston, to people of large E II 18 306 10
Maple Grove has given me a thorough disgust of people of E II 18 310 34
People of the name of Tupman, very lately settled there, E II 18 310 34
A very few to-morrows stood between the young people of E III 1 318 12
there being such a set of people in the neighbourhood to E III 3 334 8
connected dream about people whom it was not very likely E III 5 345 14
Some people were always cross when they were hot. E III 6 364 56
in the judgment of most people looking on it must have had E III 7 368 3
nonsense for the entertainment of seven silent people." E III 7 369 15
people, she hoped never to be betrayed into again. E III 7 374 54
and honour, with two people in the midst of us who may E III 10 399 61
acquainted with what was still a secret to other people. E III 16 453 12
some people may not think you perfection already.-- E III 16 457 33
could do such a thing by you, of all people in the world! E III 16 458 42
endeavours to counteract the indulgence of other people. E III 17 462 6
care of themselves; the young people will find a way."-- E III 17 467 31
placed her high with any people of real understanding, was P III 1 5 8
of sensible people, by his acting like a man of principle. P III 2 12 4
tenants as any set of people one should meet with. P III 3 17 4
of condition and rank more strongly than most people. P III 5 35 14
with people I know so well as Mrs. and the Miss Musgroves." P III 5 40 42
in the old English style, and the young people in the new. P III 5 40 45
Mr. and Mrs. Musgrove were a very good sort of people; P III 5 40 45
a removal from one set of people to another, though at a P III 6 42 1
after talking of rank, people of rank, and jealousy of P III 6 46 10
once married people begin to attack me with, 'Oh! you will P III 8 70 48
When people come in this manner on purpose to ask us, how P III 10 83 5
Upon hearing how long a walk the young people had engaged P III 10 90 38
One could not be connected with better people.-- P III 10 92 47
The young people were all wild to see Lyme. P III 11 94 7
to have such excellent people and Dr. and Mrs. Shirley, P III 12 102 2
if people thought there was any thing to complain of." P III 12 103 2
To some of the best-looking of these good people Henrietta P III 12 111 49
They must be taking off some trouble from the good people P IV 1 122 5
were a great many more people to look at in the church at P IV 2 130 3
having cards left by people of whom they knew nothing. P IV 3 138 4
a most delightful set of people--longed to be with them; P IV 3 144 19
him, among all sensible people, to be on good terms with P IV 4 147 7
of clever, well-informed people, who have a great deal of P IV 4 150 15
16
Every thing that revolts other people, low company, paltry P IV 5 157 15
day Mrs. Smith, of all people and all names in the world, P IV 5 158 19
They were people whom her heart turned to very naturally. P IV 6 162 2
"little people think of letters in such a place as Bath. P IV 6 162 7
The Crofts knew quite as many people in Bath as they P IV 6 168 24
as many whispers, and disturb as many people as they could. P IV 8 185 19
people, is irresistible; and Anne was all curiosity. P IV 8 187 33
trivial from different people scattered here and there, P IV 9 203 70
What a blessing to young people to be in such hands! P IV 10 218 23
to give dinners--few people in Bath do--Lady Alicia never P IV 10 219 29
and what the young people had wished, and what I said at P IV 11 230 5
"I would rather have young people settle on a small income P IV 11 230 7
I so abominate for young people as a long engagement. P IV 11 230 8
It is all very well, I used to say, for young people to be P IV 11 231 8
When any two young people take it into their heads to P IV 12 248 1
you to send off one of these good people for the surgeon." S 1 365 1
One of these good people can be with him in three minutes S 1 365 1
as soon as these good people have succeeded in setting the S 1 367 1
Where people can be found with money or time to go to them! S 1 368 1
be suited--and those good people who are trying to add to S 1 369 1
two or three speculating people about Brinshore, this last S 1 369 1
& three distinct sets of people to be courted by; her own S 3 376 1
her expectation worthy people--& finally was impelled by a S 3 378 1
I will not tell you how many people I have employed in the S 5 387 1
"No people spend more freely, I beleive, than W. Indians." S 6 392 1
as good as new)--and what can people want for more?-- S 6 393 1
For they are very good young people my dear. S 7 399 1
And what good can such people do anybody?--except just as S 7 401 1
If people want to be by the sea, why dont they take S 7 402 1
Thus it is, when rich people are Sordid."-- S 7 402 1
I trust there are not three people in England who have so S 9 410 1
the stomach--but there is no convincing some people.-- S 10 417 1
a totally distinct set of people as were concerned in the S 10 419 1

PEOPLE'S (19)

But some people's feelings are incomprehensible. LS 22 282 8
to other people's performance with very little fatigue. NA I 1 16 10
the development of other people's feelings, and less NA I 7 44 4
in a wish for the young people's happiness, with a remark, NA I 15 124 48
Good heavens! well, some people's feelings are NA II 1 130 3
you to understand the motive of other people's actions." NA II 1 132 18
I have no notion of people's making such a to-do about SS III 1 259 7
As no objection was made to the young people's engagement PP I 16 75 1
Thoughtlessness, want of attention to other people's PP II 1 136 17
how many people's happiness were in his guardianship!-- PP III 1 250 48
afraid of myself, but I dread other people's remarks." PP III 11 332 17
No young people's are, I suppose, when those they look up MP II 3 197 3
"The nonsense and folly of people's stepping out of their MP II 5 221 32
judiciously, for young people's being brought up without MP III 1 312 12
and attentive to other people's feelings than he had ever MP III 10 406 21
people's not staying comfortably at home when they can! E I 13 113 26
There is no end of people's coming to him, on some E III 16 455 23
consented to the young people's wishes, and that their P IV 10 217 20
Mrs G. meant to go to the sea, for her young people's S 9 408 1

PER ANNUM (3)

make more than 2001. per annum, and though it is certainly SS III 3 282 19
A clear ten thousand per annum. PP I 16 77 10
her, during your life, one hundred pounds per annum. PP III 7 302 14

PER FORCE (2)

Mr. Wickham's happiness and her own was per force delayed PP I 17 87 14
It was soon drawn per force another way. P III 12 109 31

PER WEEK (1)

and how much she had every year to spend upon herself. SS II 14 249 8

PERCEIVABLE (1)

undressed balls, was he perceivable; nor among the walkers, NA I 5 35 2

PERCEIVE (58)

alone enable her to perceive that I am actuated by any LS 10 258 2
perceive that she had no particular pleasure in seeing him. LS 20 276 3
she thought she could perceive herself the object of their NA I 12 95 17
I am amazingly agitated, as you perceive. NA I 15 117 6
How strange that she should not perceive his admiration! NA II 3 148 28
could not but perceive them now to be greatly increased. NA II 15 240 1
No sooner did she perceive any symptom of love in his SS I 3 17 14
I do not perceive how you could express yourself more SS I 4 20 7
Marianne began now to perceive that the desperation which SS I 10 49 10
Elinor needed little observation to perceive that her SS I 11 55 6
her tongue, as you must perceive, and I am sure I was in SS I 22 133 42
Ferrars; but do not you perceive that my interest on such SS II 2 149 26
to her sister should perceive that she experienced nothing SS II 4 162 8
was all astonishment to perceive Mrs. Jennings's chariot, SS II 7 184 16
perceive the necessity of her remembering them farther. SS II 11 227 46
though she could plainly perceive at different times, the SS II 14 248 5
as far as Elinor could perceive, with no traits at all SS III 6 304 15
fancy, to hope she could perceive a slight amendment in SS III 7 314 22
it; and I dare say, you perceive, as well as myself, not SS III 11 350 9
was shocked to perceive by Elinor's countenance how much SS III 11 353 24
Emma thought she could perceive a faint blush accompany W 324 3
My dear, do you perceive the least resemblance?"-- W 324 3
Robert--but I cannot perceive any likeness to Mr Samuel." W 324 3
If I can perceive her regard for him, he must be a PP I 6 22 3
by his own thoughts to perceive that Sir William Lucas was PP I 6 25 25
Mr. Darcy smiled; but Elizabeth thought she could perceive PP I 10 51 40
vexation, she could perceive that the chief of it was PP I 18 99 64
and I could then perceive that his partiality for Miss PP II 12 197 5
I never could perceive any thing extraordinary in them. PP III 3 271 15
could easily perceive that her spirits were affected by it. PP III 11 332 20
and as I could easily perceive that his attachment to her PP III 16 371 40
right; and he could perceive her to be farther entitled to MP I 2 16 20
Fanny was situated, and perceive its ill effects, there MP I 4 36 7
The house fronts the east, I perceive. MP I 8 82 35
profession, and might perceive that I am neither a lawyer, MP I 9 91 39
confidence, could not perceive that any thing of the kind MP II 1 177 5
to some others, I can perceive, from occasional lively MP II 3 198 13
said, "it is of no use, I perceive, to talk to you. MP III 1 318 39
discernment enough to perceive, either now, or at any MP III 1 323 57
this room, as you may perceive," said she presently, with MP III 5 359 9
was useful she could perceive; that things, bad as they MP III 9 395 4
She could only perceive that it must relate to Wimpole MP III 15 438 4
to myself; but I now perceive that it will be a very E I 8 64 47
same time, as she could perceive, most earnestly careful E I 9 70 7
resources; and I do not perceive why I should be more in E I 10 85 21
but then he began to perceive that Frank's coming two or E I 18 144 2
perceive them walking up to the house together, arm in arm. E II 6 196 2
Yes, I immediately perceive that it must be the joint E II 8 217 31
She was his object, and every body must perceive it. E II 8 220 47
mind when it was all but done, she could not perceive.-- E III 9 386 7
When he did perceive and acknowledge her, however, it was P IV 6 169 25
Russell would perceive him till they were nearly opposite. P IV 7 179 28
smiling, said, "I have been a little premature, I perceive. P IV 9 195 26
27
time or other, I do not perceive how he can ever be secure, P IV 9 208 92
With all their sufferings, you perceive how much they are S 5 388 1
said "you may perceive what has been our occupation. S 8 403 1
Charlotte could perceive no symptoms of illness which she, S 10 413 1
She was glad to perceive that nothing had been discerned S 12 426 1

PERCEIVED (55)

for the former soon perceived by the stile of Frederica's LS 42 311 1
and turning round, perceived Mrs. Hughes directly behind NA I 8 55 10
of the set, Catherine perceived herself to be earnestly NA I 10 80 59
Catherine, looking up, perceived Captain Tilney; and NA II 3 147 21
He perceived her inclination, and having again urged the NA II 7 179 29
lassitude; the General perceived it, and with a concern NA II 7 181 41
Upon looking round it then, she perceived in a moment that NA II 11 213 18
good, and the g sweetness of his countenance, is perceived. SS I 4 20 9
it was enough, when perceived by his sister, to make her SS I 4 23 19
The whole family perceived it, and Mrs. Dashwood, SS I 17 90 1
and as soon as Sir John perceived her, he left the rest of SS I 19 105 13
long, before Elinor perceived Willoughby, standing within SS II 6 176 3
At that moment she first perceived him, and her whole SS II 6 176 3
and sobs, first perceived her; and after observing her for SS II 7 180 1
2
though she soon perceived them to be narrowly watching her. SS II 13 241 20
In one of these excursive glances she perceived among a SS II 14 250 11
She perceived him soon afterwards looking at herself, and SS II 14 250 11
Elinor perceived with alarm that she was not quite herself, SS III 7 311 14
Here, however, Elinor perceived,--not the language, not SS III 9 336 13
In a moment she perceived that the others were likewise SS III 12 358 9
with some amusement perceived--he began to make civil W 334 13
chairs, it might have seemed a matter scarcely perceived.-- W 336 14
very un-smart family equipage perceived a neat curricle.-- W 338 17
closely observed him, perceived nothing that did not W 355 28
Miss Lucas perceived him from an upper window as he walked PP I 22 121 1
softened; and Elizabeth perceived that she must wait for PP II 3 147 19
Elizabeth soon perceived that though this great lady was PP II 7 169 4
still increasing wonder, perceived an envelope containing PP II 12 196 3
meet them, they quickly perceived, in token of the PP II 16 219 1
crossed the bridge, and perceived their distance from the PP III 1 254 57
coolly replying, that he perceived no other alteration PP III 3 271 14
She had never perceived while the regiment was in PP III 4 280 25
with us, if I had not perceived, by Jane's letter last PP III 10 325 2
Jane was anxious that no difference should be perceived in PP III 11 337 56
On opening the door, she perceived her sister and Bingley PP III 13 346 22
and they perceived a chaise and four driving up the lawn. PP III 14 351 1
French; and when they perceived her to be little struck MP I 2 14 7
than what she had long perceived, it was a stab;--for it MP II 9 264 17
that head,) I never perceived them to be unpleasant to you. MP III 1 316 29
meaning; and as Edmund perceived, by his drawing in a MP III 3 341 31
He perceived that enough had been said of Everingham, and MP III 10 405 17
to her great amusement, perceived that she was taking the E I 18 145 5
much of the morning was perceived to be gone, that Mrs. E II 10 246 55
Emma perceived that the nature of his gallantry was a E II 11 250 19
Emma perceived that her taste was not the only taste on E III 2 319 4
and Mrs. Weston; and she perceived that his wife, who was E III 2 327 34
it, they had suddenly perceived at a small distance before E III 3 333 5
deeply than he had ever perceived her, and saying only, "I E III 5 349 23
view she immediately perceived Mr. Knightley and Harriet E III 6 360 40
Emma listened, and looked, and soon perceived that Frank E III 6 364 56
every posture, she perceived that she had acted most E III 11 411 43
As Mr. Shepherd perceived that this connexion of the P III 3 23 34
His value for rank and connexion she perceived to be P IV 4 148 10
By such he was perceived to be an enthusiast;--on the S 2 371 1
to be placed--& she soon perceived that he had a fine S 7 394 1

PERCEIVING (36)

They could none of them help perceiving that Sir James was LS 22 281 3
a coachman; and perceiving that the animal continued to go NA I 9 62 10
Perceiving her still to look doubtful and grave, he added, NA II 4 152 29
without perceiving any thing very remarkable in either. NA II 5 160 21
The General, perceiving how her eye was employed, began to NA II 5 162 27
enabled, especially on perceiving that Miss Tilney slept NA II 6 167 9
instinctive movement on perceiving him, yet she could NA II 9 192 4
and her mother, perceiving her comfortable suggestions to NA II 14 236 18
The General, perceiving his son one night at the theatre NA II 15 244 12
Henry and Eleanor, perceiving nothing in her situation NA II 15 245 12
The gentleman offered his services, and perceiving that SS I 9 42 8
both her daughters, and perceiving through all her SS II 3 155 7
bent on this measure by perceiving after breakfast on the SS II 5 171 38
event, when Marianne, perceiving that she had finished the SS II 7 188 43
to communicate, and perceiving by Marianne's letter how SS II 9 203 10
first, heard this; and perceiving that as reflection did SS III 10 347 32
eyes--& Mrs Edwards on perceiving it, changed the subject W 326 6
his nephew; & Emma on perceiving herself the object of W 332 11
of the room; but on perceiving Mr. Darcy he stopt with a PP I 18 92 22
than usual, and on perceiving whom, she said to the girls, PP I 20 113 29
30
rob it of a few petrified spars without his perceiving me." PP II 19 239 9
Then, perceiving in Elizabeth no inclination of replying, PP III 5 289 43
Why do not I see my little Fanny?", and on perceiving her, MP II 1 177 7
At the very moment of Yates perceiving Sir Thomas, and MP II 1 182 22
to say; and Fanny, perceiving it, brought back her own MP II 4 209 13
he could not avoid perceiving in a grand and careless way MP II 7 238 1
Her own musings were brought to an end on perceiving Mr. MP II 10 274 8
was by the idea of his perceiving it, and had no composure MP II 10 274 8
afterwards, when Mary, perceiving her on a sofa very near, MP II 10 276 14

e, in an under voice, perceiving the amazing trepidation MP II 13 307 33
eeper; and her uncle perceiving that she was embarrassed MP III 1 313 15
f her disposition, and perceiving how fully she was MP III 9 397 8
artin again without perceiving him to be a very inferior E I 4 32 32
eston; but stopped, on perceiving that Mrs. Weston was E II 16 297 48
f any thing could increase her delight, it was perceiving E III 17 468 32
er distress returned, however, on perceiving smiles and P IV 10 222 37
CEPTIBLE (7)
ow first became perceptible to Elinor, when it ceased to SS I 10 49 12
bout it, should the least variation be perceptible. SS I 14 73 13
nd his interest in their welfare again became perceptible. SS I 17 90 1
hing of the kind been perceptible, you must be aware that PP III 5 285 18
erself from trying to make it perceptible to her sister. P III 5 34 12
er start was perceptible only to herself; but she P IV 7 175 5
inews a very little affected:--barely perceptible.-- S 9 408 1
CEPTION (9)
o him did not arise from any perception of his deficiency. LS 24 289 12
oment was quickening her perception of the horrible evil. MP III 15 440 19
is perception of the striking improvement of Harriet's E I 6 42 1
ight prevent his perception of it; but he must know that E I 16 136 9
ane Fairfax's perception seemed to accompany his; her E III 5 348 23
ithout the slightest perception of anything extraordinary E III 14 434 3
hat she owed it to his perception of her fatigue, and his P III 10 91 42
ut from the perception of there being a somebody else. P IV 9 197 34
here is a quickness of perception in some, a nicety in P IV 12 249 4
CEPTIONS (1)
er perceptions and her pleasures were of the keenest sort. MP III 15 446 35
CHANCE (1)
our cousin Edmund moves slowly; detained, perchance, by MP III 9 394 1
EMPTORILY (2)
mmediately and peremptorily, and without paying my MP III 1 319 39
o any exercise, so peremptorily refused to go out with E III 9 391 21
FECT (113)
ashion of acquiring a perfect knowledge in all the LS 7 253 1
eceived her with perfect self-command, & without LS 17 269 2
eginald observed all that passed, in perfect silence. LS 20 276 3
o which I listened with perfect indifference, that my LS 22 281 4
ake place soon, may with perfect convenience be hastened; LS 25 293 3
nd be able to watch the dances with perfect convenience. NA I 2 21 9
Yes, my dear," replied Mrs. Allen, with perfect serenity, NA I 2 22 13
erfect sincerity, "indeed, Catherine, I love you dearly." NA I 7 51 53
at erect, in the perfect use of her senses, and with NA I 8 53 3
ondering that with such perfect command of his horse, he NA I 9 62 10
o his words, and perfect reliance on their truth. NA I 10 80 60
nd having made herself perfect in the number; hastened NA I 12 91 3
he could not listen to that with perfect concealment, but NA I 15 125 48
ere now safely lodged in perfect bliss; and with spirits NA II 2 140 11
indows were neither less perfect, nor more dim than those NA II 6 163 1
or she could now manage them with perfect ease. NA II 7 173 4
ive years, they were perfect in all that would be NA II 8 185 5
ad helped to nourish and perfect, was the only emotion NA II 11 212 16
hat we are all hastening together to perfect felicity. NA II 16 250 4
o begin perfect happiness at the respective ages of NA II 16 252 7
hen she saw that to the perfect good-breeding of the SS I 10 46 2
ad ceased to be possible, by Marianne's perfect recovery. SS I 10 48 7
o direct, as marked a perfect agreement between them. SS I 12 59 7
perfect unison with what she had heard and seen herself. SS I 12 61 14
lace which affection had established as perfect with him. SS I 14 72 6
amily, it is a matter of perfect indifference to me, SS II 3 157 17
he most perfect conviction of his unworthiness can do. SS II 9 211 34
ould now see her with perfect indifference as to her SS II 12 230 6
mma with perfect truth could assure her that she could W 331 11
uch ease, with such perfect good breeding!" PP I 4 14 2
ore than one failure of perfect symmetry in her form, he PP I 6 23 12
e listened to her with perfect indifference, while she PP I 6 27 54
nswer; but Lydia, with perfect indifference, continued to PP I 7 29 7
f his letter, with the perfect unconcern with which her PP I 10 47 2
esignation is never so perfect as when the blessing PP I 20 114 32
only want to think you perfect, and you set yourself PP II 1 135 11
n time, and the plan became perfect as plan could be. PP II 4 151 1
s ugly, she added, with perfect unconcern, "Oh! but PP II 16 219 4
hat nothing less than a perfect understanding between the PP II 17 227 25
n the scheme, every part of it would have been perfect. PP II 19 237 3
erms of perfect composure, at least of perfect civility. PP III 1 251 51
as fond of society, a perfect willingness to accept it, PP III 2 264 11
elivered on paper his perfect approbation of all that was PP III 8 309 4
It would be nothing; I could see him with perfect PP III 11 333 28
een nothing; but his perfect indifference, and your PP III 15 364 24
f such evenings, her perfect security in such a tete-a- MP I 4 35 6
veringham as it used to be was perfect in my estimation; MP I 6 61 53
t was meant and done by Mrs. Grant, with perfect good MP I 7 70 30
nd look upon verdure, is the most perfect refreshment." MP I 9 96 72
e less unpleasant to me than to have a perfect stranger." MP I 15 148 59
f they are not perfect, I shall be surprised. MP I 18 169 21
nd acknowledging with perfect ingenuousness that his MP II 2 187 1
erfect in disinterested attachment as in every thing else. MP II 8 255 10
iss Crawford smiled her perfect approbation; and hastened MP II 8 258 17
ituation, no reasonable hindrance to a perfect friendship. MP II 9 263 16
nd then you will be the perfect model of a woman, which I MP III 4 347 18
f ever there was a perfect beauty afloat, she is one; and MP III 7 380 20
er own perfect consciousness, many drawbacks suppressed. MP III 8 388 1
nterest at least--which was making his manner perfect. MP III 10 399 5
s any thing short of perfect decision, an adviser may, in MP III 13 423 2
tate of spirits, of his perfect approbation and increased MP III 17 461 2
eart, and as thoroughly perfect in her eyes, as every MP III 17 473 33
he equal footing and perfect unreserve which had soon E I 1 6 6
s her not being thought perfect by every body. E I 1 11 33
little more knowledge and elegance to be quite perfect. E I 3 23 10
an you imagine any thing nearer perfect beauty than Emma E I 5 39 18
t appears to me a most perfect resemblance in every E I 6 48 32
er arms with all the unceremoniousness of perfect amity. E I 12 98 2
t was a delightful visit;--perfect, in being much too E I 13 108 1
Mr. Elton's manners are not perfect," replied Emma; "but E I 13 111 17
here is such perfect good temper and good will in Mr. E I 13 112 17
urst forth at once into perfect independence, and set all E I 18 148 19
er last months of perfect liberty with those kind E II 2 166 10
nstead of welcoming that perfect novelty which had been E II 2 166 10
he usual advantages of perfect beauty and merit, was in E II 4 181 4
er own father's perfect exemption from any thought of the E II 5 193 35
e was accused of having a delightful voice, and a perfect E II 8 227 86
erfect happiness, even in memory, is not common; and E II 9 231 2
his amiable, upright, perfect Jane Fairfax was apparently E II 10 243 22
ome little distress; and he, finding every thing perfect. E II 11 253 40
harming young woman--but not even Jane Fairfax is perfect. E II 15 288 36
way, seemed like a perfect cure; and she was rather E III 1 316 5
ather looked his most perfect approbation of--and it then E III 2 325 31
rom perfect misery to perfect happiness." E III 4 342 38
t spoke such perfect amity.-- E III 9 386 7
his boast, of my present perfect indifference," she E III 10 396 41
o have been carrying on with such perfect secresy?-- E III 10 399 58
e listened in perfect silence. E III 13 427 18
ound the world for a perfect wife for him, they could not E III 13 428 23
ike perfect happiness, that it could bear no other name. E III 13 432 40
he was now in perfect charity with Frank Churchill; she E III 14 436 6
say, Jane, what a perfect character you and I should E III 16 456 33
er own little adelaide educated on a more perfect plan." E III 17 461 2
iving him that full and perfect confidence which her E III 18 475 42
ere fully answered in the perfect happiness of the union. E III 19 484 12
he was assisted, however, by that perfect indifference P III 4 30 10
hink poor Mrs. Clay may be staying here in perfect safety. P III 5 35 14
ut that seemingly perfect good understanding and P III 5 41 45
ppearance of the most perfect good-will between P III 8 71 57

did not seem admitted to perfect confidence here; but that P III 10 89 36
was a perfect gentleman, unaffected, warm, and obliging. P III 11 97 15
cousinly little interview must remain a perfect secret. P III 12 106 19
Anne did think on the question with perfect decision, and P III 12 108 29
and with the most perfect alacrity he welcomed the P IV 3 143 18
be very sure is a matter of perfect indifference to them." P IV 4 151 18
Anne did not receive the perfect conviction which the P IV 6 173 48
Though I have forgot the exact terms, I have a perfect P IV 9 204 75
beginning to express her perfect readiness for the play, P IV 10 223 42
43
he had not understood the perfect excellence of the mind P IV 11 242 63
or the perfect, unrivalled hold it possessed over his own. P IV 11 242 63
With the Musgroves, there was the happy chat of perfect P IV 11 246 78
see in her only the most perfect representation of S 6 391 1
lead him into some Aberrations--but who is perfect?-- S 7 398 1
PERFECTED (1)
had been proved and perfected by Mr. Yates's being invited MP I 13 121 1
PERFECTING (2)
generally much to do in perfecting a sudden intimacy NA I 4 33 7
improving, and perfecting that friendhsip and intimacy MP II 7 246 37
PERFECTION (21)
failed, his own had often produced the perfection wanted. NA II 8 183 3
her ideas of perfection, had been rash and unjustifiable. SS I 10 49 10
his secret standard of perfection in woman;--and many a SS III 14 379 19
perfection, sir," addressing herself then to Dr. Grant. MP I 6 54 9
We do not expect perfection. MP I 15 146 52
Sir Thomas was most cordially anxious for the perfection MP III 4 345 3
Bertram as a husband, are my standards of perfection. MP III 5 361 16
was not his great perfection; and, indeed, with such a E I 11 92 5
Harriet did think him all perfection, and maintain the non- E I 17 142 12
than would suit your notions of man's perfection. E I 18 148 23
more than human perfection of body and mind to be E II 2 165 9
of perfection in Highbury, both in person and mind." E II 3 174 38
"You cannot see too much perfection in Mrs. Weston for my E II 5 192 31
of the alphabet are there, that express perfection?" E III 7 371 32
"What too letters!--express perfection! E III 7 371 33
Perfection should not have come quite so soon." E III 7 371 36
My liveliness and your solidity would produce perfection.-- E III 16 457 33
some people may not think you perfection already.-- E III 16 457 33
which had seen highest perfection in the other, or which P III 4 26 1
some mischance, to damp the perfection of her felicity. P IV 11 239 53
Her character was now fixed on his mind as perfection P IV 11 241 61
PERFECTIONS (8)
wandering towards the perfections of their neighbours, or NA I 10 77 33
that, amongst the many perfections of the family, a NA I 12 92 4
dwelling on the perfections of a man, of whose whole heart SS II 1 141 4
you any disservice, rather adds to your other perfections. PP I 19 105 8
and of Jane's perfections; and in spite of his being a PP III 13 347 33
into a young lady's exact estimate of her own perfections. MP III 2 331 18
Let him have all the perfections in the world, I think it MP III 4 353 45
perfections of Edward's wife upon credit a little longer. P III 9 73 1
PERFECTLY (284)
to her to visit us at Churchill perfectly unnecessary. LS 3 247 1
She is perfectly well bred indeed, & has the air of a LS 5 249 1
a gentleman who knew her perfectly well, which is true LS 8 255 1
She looks perfectly timid, dejected & penitent. LS 17 270 4
been perfectly right in attributing it to my own letter. LS 19 273 1
& from not feeling perfectly secure that a knowledge of LS 22 280 1
were alone, that I was perfectly justified, all things LS 22 281 3
Mistress of deceit however she appeared perfectly LS 23 284 6
I am perfectly aware that after what has passed between us, LS 25 292 3
an anxious doubt of London's perfectly agreeing with her. LS 42 312 4
and perfectly satisfied with her share of public attention. NA I 2 24 28
I can perfectly comprehend your feelings." NA I 6 41 16
and from which she awoke perfectly revived, in excellent NA I 9 60 1
made the matter perfectly simple by assuring her that it NA I 9 62 10
carriage to be in fact perfectly safe, and therefore would NA I 9 66 31
The business however, though not perfectly elucidated by NA I 13 102 26
subsided) to doubt whether she had been perfectly right. NA I 13 103 29
and style, they are perfectly well qualified to torment NA I 14 109 25
earnest, that he became perfectly satisfied of her having NA I 14 111 29
That he was perfectly agreeable and good-natured, and NA II 1 129 1
very unequal terms, for I understand you perfectly well." NA II 1 132 22
has been no more than I believed him perfectly equal to. NA II 1 133 34
said Mrs. Thorpe, "we perfectly see into your heart. NA II 1 136 49
We perfectly understand the present vexation; and every NA II 1 136 49
Had their party been perfectly agreeable, the delay would NA II 5 156 4
and had he not been perfectly without vanity of that kind, NA II 7 175 12
Catherine had read too much not to be perfectly aware of NA II 9 191 2
Of the way to the apartment she was now perfectly mistress; NA II 9 193 5
upon serious consideration, to be not perfectly amiable. NA II 10 200 3
two young friends were perfectly agreed in considering NA II 11 208 1
of each day have been perfectly happy; but she was now in NA II 13 220 1
perfectly unsuspicious of there being any deeper evil. NA II 14 235 13
Oh! perfectly." NA II 14 238 25
A hundred a year would make them all perfectly comfortable. SS I 2 10 16
said Mr. Dashwood, "I believe you are perfectly right. SS I 2 12 25
of taste, which in general direct him perfectly right." SS I 4 19 2
your behaviour to him is perfectly cordial, and if that SS I 4 19 4
by shewing that though perfectly well-bred, she was SS I 6 31 8
The young ladies, as well as their mother, were perfectly SS I 7 34 4
She was perfectly disposed to make every allowance for the SS I 7 35 9
She was perfectly convinced of it. SS I 8 36 1
regarded only himself, perfectly indifferent; but to the SS I 8 36 2
circumstance related by Mrs. Jennings was perfectly true. SS I 13 68 67
absent, was perfectly satisfied with her remaining at home. SS I 15 75 1
I assure you, and I can perfectly account for every thing SS I 15 78 24
"I am perfectly satisfied of both." SS I 15 79 34
Have we not perfectly understood each other? SS I 15 80 36
I wish as well as every body else to be perfectly happy; SS I 17 91 7
If I could persuade myself that my manners were perfectly SS I 17 94 44
Marianne remained perfectly silent, though her countenance SS I 20 111 16
She merely observed that he was perfectly good humoured SS I 21 122 16
for I do not perfectly comprehend the meaning of the word. SS I 21 124 29
expressed, was perfectly of a piece with her general SS I 21 125 37
and deference towards herself perfectly valueless. SS I 22 127 2
on such an occasion would be perfectly unnecessary? SS II 2 149 26
could spare them perfectly well; and Elinor, who now SS II 3 154 6
what I can assure you to have been perfectly unintentional. SS II 7 183 13
I am perfectly ready to hear your justification of it. SS II 7 187 42
and, with a look which perfectly assured her of his good SS II 8 198 31
though it proved perfectly different from what she wished SS II 10 214 6
Elinor perfectly understood her, and was forced to use all SS II 10 217 22
His manners to them, though calm, were perfectly kind; to SS II 11 223 14
only to be teazed about Dr. Davies to be perfectly happy. SS II 12 233 17
replied, "indeed I am perfectly convinced of your regard SS II 13 240 14
15
pleased herself, was perfectly satisfied, and soon talked SS II 13 243 32
To her dress and appearance she was grown so perfectly SS II 14 249 8
matter, and my mother is perfectly convinced of her error." SS II 14 251 13
sensible man, and in his manners perfectly the gentleman." SS III 4 290 37
"It is perfectly true.-- SS III 5 294 9
I remember her perfectly. SS III 5 299 37
She found him, however, perfectly the gentleman in his SS III 6 304 15
smile, and a voice perfectly calm, "yes, I am very drunk.-- SS III 8 318 18
enough recovered to talk, I was perfectly able to reflect. SS III 10 345 28
am now perfectly satisfied, I wish for no change. SS III 11 350 6
message by thomas, was perfectly clear to Elinor; and SS III 13 366 21
she found that, though perfectly admitting the truth of SS III 14 373 3
to her; & her feelings perfectly coincided with the W 329 9
Did you ever see anything more perfectly beautiful?-- W 357 28
Of this she was perfectly unaware;--to her he was only the PP I 6 23 12

she could suit herself perfectly with those in the room. PP I 8 38 28
"Oh? yes--I understand you perfectly." PP I 9 42 11
"I am perfectly ready, I assure you, to keep my engagement; PP I 9 45 37
"I am perfectly convinced by it that Mr. Darcy has no PP I 11 57 27
parsonage; where she had perfectly approved all the PP I 14 66 1
But she is perfectly amiable, and often condescends to PP I 14 67 7
at the same time perfectly correct and unassuming; and the PP I 15 72 8
with unwearying civility that they were perfectly needless. PP I 15 74 11
using him ill, it is perfectly false; for, on the contrary, PP I 18 94 45
of his friend, and is perfectly convinced that Mr. Wickham PP I 18 95 50
I am perfectly satisfied. PP I 18 96 53
perfectly compatible with the profession of a clergyman.-- PP I 18 101 71
He assured her that as to dancing, he was perfectly PP I 18 102 73
Mrs. Bennet was perfectly satisfied; and quitted the house PP I 18 103 77
To fortune I am perfectly indifferent, and shall make no PP I 19 106 10
I am perfectly serious in my refusal.-- PP I 19 107 14
her sister; that she is perfectly convinced of her PP I 21 118 15
and known the late Mr. Darcy by character perfectly well. PP II 2 143 20
perfectly resolved to continue the acquaintance no longer. PP II 3 148 26
The farewell between herself and Mr. Wickham was perfectly PP II 4 151 3
and even Sir William did not look perfectly calm.-- PP II 6 161 9
She was perfectly sensible that he never had; but she PP II 7 171 12
Darcy smiled and said, "you are perfectly right. PP II 8 176 26
"Perfectly so--I thank you." PP II 9 177 5
She seems perfectly happy, however, and in a prudential PP II 9 178 15
of Rosings and her not perfectly understanding the house, PP II 10 182 1
I perfectly comprehend your feelings, and have now only to PP II 11 193 29
at any rate, was perfectly ready to accede to his proposal. PP II 12 200 5
She perfectly remembered every thing that had passed in PP II 13 206 5
of Elizabeth appear perfectly natural; and all surprise PP II 17 224 2
"He is perfectly well behaved, polite, and unassuming," PP III 1 257 67
Wickham's countenance, for his features are perfectly good. PP III 1 257 70
face, and her manners were perfectly unassuming and gentle. PP III 2 261 4
wisely resolved to be perfectly easy and unembarrassed;--a PP III 3 268 8
Her sister, however, assured her, of her being perfectly PP III 5 286 32
her own feelings, was perfectly aware, that, had she known PP III 6 298 17
in all likelihood perfectly ignorant of what had happened. PP III 7 305 39
perfectly useless; for, of course, they were to have a son. PP III 8 308 3
dear Lizzy, you may rest perfectly assured, that your PP III 10 324 2
Mr. Wickham was so perfectly satisfied with this PP III 11 330 1
"that this first meeting is over, I feel perfectly easy. PP III 12 339 6
I am perfectly satisfied from what his manners now are, PP III 12 343 32
Kitty, though she was perfectly unknown to them, even PP III 14 351 2
"I believed myself perfectly calm and cool, but I am since PP III 16 368 22
He is perfectly amiable. PP III 17 376 34
considered, I begin to think it perfectly reasonable. PP III 18 380 5
The moral will be perfectly fair. PP III 18 381 14
"My dear Sir Thomas, I perfectly comprehend you, and do MP I 1 6 6
service; and though she perfectly agreed with him as to MP I 1 11 18
she was from that moment perfectly safe from all MP I 3 30 57
the accounts continued perfectly good;--and Mrs. Norris in MP I 4 34 3
and delight of them all--perfectly faultless--an angel; MP I 4 39 10
he heard nothing but the perfectly good and agreeable. MP I 4 40 14
I could; the young lady perfectly easy in her manners, and MP I 5 51 40
I know it perfectly. MP I 6 59 43
or that of others; perfectly allowable, when untinctured MP I 7 64 11
She is perfectly feminine, except in the instances we have MP I 7 64 11
and I have no doubt of her being perfectly equal to it. MP I 7 69 28
barouche would hold four perfectly well, independent of MP I 8 77 8
will to consult, made it perfectly clear that he did not MP I 12 114 2
choosing some play most perfectly unexceptionable, and I MP I 13 125 18
Whichever Mr. Yates did not choose, would perfectly MP I 14 132 8
cried Maria--"I am perfectly acquainted with the play, I MP I 15 140 12
do not feel, is perfectly natural; and equally so that my MP II 1 186 34
her two aunts, she was perfectly aware that none would be MP II 4 206 4
This was so new an attention, so perfectly new a MP II 4 215 47
Fanny was perfectly right in giving only a conditional MP II 5 219 18
Her niece thought it perfectly reasonable. MP II 5 221 35
no finery about you; nothing but what is perfectly proper. MP II 5 222 44
and every body being as perfectly complying, and without a MP II 7 239 4
It is perfectly natural that you should not have thought MP II 7 247 42
Lady Bertram was perfectly quiescent and contented, and MP II 8 253 6
He knew his own mind, but he was not always perfectly MP II 8 255 10
a plain gold chain perfectly simple and neat, she could MP II 9 262 8
so perfectly gratifying in the occasion and the style. MP II 9 265 19
at William, and saw how perfectly he was enjoying himself, MP II 10 278 20
of this room by way of making you perfectly comfortable.-- MP III 1 312 10
And on another account too, I can perfectly comprehend.-- MP III 1 313 12
effort, "but I am so perfectly convinced that I could MP III 1 320 43
honoured, but I am so perfectly convinced, and I have told MP III 2 330 15
imagine her to be taken perfectly unprepared, but Sir MP III 3 335 6
"As far as you have gone, Fanny, I think you perfectly MP III 4 347 16
time to attach yourself; but I think you perfectly right. MP III 4 347 16
I am perfectly persuaded that the tempers had better be MP III 4 349 23
desire rather more unguardedly than was perfectly prudent. MP III 4 350 30
Edmund now believed himself perfectly acquainted with all MP III 5 356 1
"How perfectly I remember my resolving to look for you up MP III 5 360 14
I remember it perfectly." MP III 5 362 18
"I am perfectly serious,"--he replied,--"as you perfectly MP III 11 411 18
as to make his mother perfectly easy; for being now used MP III 14 429 1
Park, and you, no doubt, are perfectly able to give it. MP III 14 433 13
satisfied, for she came perfectly aware, that nothing but MP III 16 448 3
for Mary, though perfectly resolved against ever attaching MP III 17 469 24
long, and who seemed so perfectly comfortable without a E I 1 12 41
His mother is perfectly right not to be in a hurry. E I 4 30 18
but her father, who perfectly approves the acquaintance, E I 5 40 24
"Perfectly, perfectly right, my dearest Harriet; you are E I 7 53 24
Emma was soon perfectly satisfied of Mr. Martin's being no E I 9 69 2
I remember that perfectly." E I 11 96 24
myself, I have been long perfectly convinced, though E I 12 101 22
We all had our health perfectly well there, never found E I 12 105 55
have rendered a gentleman's carriage perfectly complete. E I 13 115 37
Yet he would be so anxious for her being perfectly warm, E I 14 118 4
influence; but it may be perfectly impossible for him to E I 14 123 25
He perfectly knew his own meaning; and having warmly E I 15 130 28
him in a basin of gruel--perfectly sensible of its being E I 15 132 38
be in love; but she was perfectly easy as to his not E I 16 135 7
made it impossible for Emma to be ever perfectly at ease. E I 16 139 20
highly accomplished, and perfectly amiable: and when Mr. E II 4 181 2
As to connection, there Emma was perfectly easy; persuaded, E II 4 183 9
Emma could look perfectly unconscious and innocent, and E II 5 189 14
But on seeing them together, she became perfectly E II 6 196 2
"There appeared such a perfectly good understanding among E II 6 202 38
He perfectly agreed with her: and after walking together E II 6 203 42
but no doubt he did perfectly feel that Enscombe could not E II 6 204 43
You will be perfectly safe, you know, among your friends." E II 7 211 20
No, I am perfectly sure that he is not trifling or silly." E II 8 212 3
now, they were both perfectly satisfied that it could be E II 8 214 13
I may not have convinced you perhaps, but I am perfectly E II 8 218 41
Oh! you were perfectly right! E II 11 250 23
All the rest, in speculation at least, was perfectly E II 11 255 59
course, which holds four perfectly; and therefore, without E II 14 274 28
I perfectly understand your situation, however, Miss E II 14 275 30
and she was not perfectly convinced that the place might E II 14 276 34
I hoped I was perfectly equal to any sacrifice of that E II 14 277 36
Her Bath habits made evening-parties perfectly natural to E II 16 290 3
Mr. Weston meanwhile, perfectly unsuspicious of the E II 17 303 24
"Very true, Mr. Weston, perfectly true. E II 18 308 28
true, for she was perfectly well, and Harriet not much E III 3 336 12
"I do remember it," cried Emma; "I perfectly remember it.-- E III 4 339 19
I perfectly remember it.-- E III 4 340 19
of hopes and chances, she was perfectly resolved.-- E III 4 341 34

I remember it perfectly. E III 5 344
Perfectly remember Mrs. Perry's coming.-- E III 5 346
"do you think you perfectly understand the degree of E III 5 350
Oh! yes, perfectly.-- E III 5 350
Weston must already be perfectly aware, it was not worth E III 6 353
Donwell-Lane is never dusty, and now it is perfectly dry. E III 6 356
away the morning; and the kindness had perfectly answered. E III 6 362
I am perfectly comfortable to-day." E III 7 368
Emma time to say how perfectly new this circumstance was E III 8 383
It is so wonderful, that though perfectly convinced of the E III 10 395
each other spoken of in a way not perfectly agreeable!" E III 10 399
Hartfield, he was become perfectly reconciled, and not far E III 10 401
"My dear Harriet, I perfectly remember the substance of E III 11 406
at all, she believed she should be perfectly satisfied.-- E III 12 416
"Oh! perfectly. E III 12 420
and that she was perfectly free from any tendency to being E III 14 438
in a form of words perfectly intelligible to me.-- E III 14 441
It was perfectly accordant with that resolution of E III 14 442
You pass it over very handsomely--but you were perfectly E III 15 445
"I perfectly agree with you, sir,"--was then his remark. E III 15 446
them, is so perfectly satisfied, so delighted even-----" E III 16 459
spirits, which appeared perfectly natural, as there was a E III 17 463
He seems perfectly unprepared for that." E III 17 465
But, Mr. Knightley, are you perfectly sure that she has E III 18 473
"I am perfectly satisfied," replied Emma, with the E III 18 474
In ten minutes, however, the child had been perfectly well E III 18 479
Harriet, than she became perfectly satisfied-- E III 19 481
retrenching, and who was perfectly persuaded that nothing P III 2 13
happening to be not in perfectly good spirits the only P III 2 14
if you chose to leave them, would be perfectly safe. P III 3 18
So far all was perfectly right; but Lady Russell was P III 5 34
for each party's perfectly knowing their situation. P III 5 34
and said you were perfectly well, and in no hurry for me; P III 5 38
They were always perfectly agreed in the want of more P III 6 43
found it was so; and is perfectly sure that this must be P III 6 50
in strong, though not perfectly well spelt praise, as "a P III 6 52
endeavour to express how perfectly delighted they were P III 7 54
I perfectly understand Mr. Robinson's directions, and have P III 7 56
all to know each other perfectly, and he was coming the P III 7 58
common way; but she was perfectly unsuspicious of being P III 7 60
in another moment he was perfectly collected and serious; P III 8 67
"Depend upon it they were all perfectly comfortable." P III 8 69
reasonable woman may be perfectly happy in one of them; P III 8 70
Her sensations on the discovery made her perfectly P III 9 80
resentment, though perfectly careless of her, and though P III 10 91
him perfectly interesting in the eyes of all the ladies. P III 11 96
and Henrietta, though perfectly incapable of being in the P III 12 112
events; and it was perfectly decided that it had been the P IV 1 126
highly respectable man, perfectly the gentleman, (and not P IV 3 139
with his wife, had perfectly understood the whole story. P IV 3 139
In Lady Russell's view, it was perfectly natural that Mr. P IV 4 147
Lady Russell was now perfectly decided in her opinion of P IV 5 159
in Gay-Street, perfectly to Sir Walter's satisfaction. P IV 6 168
Captain Wentworth recollected him perfectly. P IV 7 177
to be seen), she was yet perfectly conscious of Lady P IV 7 179
It seems, on the contrary, to have been a perfectly P IV 8 183
I perfectly see how the hours passed--that you had always P IV 9 194
Your countenance perfectly informs me that you were in P IV 9 194
"I know you did; I know it all perfectly, but"----- P IV 9 205
which, if it did not perfectly justify the unqualified P IV 9 208
Anne could perfectly comprehend the exquisite relief, and P IV 9 210
I hope you think Louisa perfectly recovered now?" P IV 10 218
Anne talked of being perfectly ready, and tried to look it; P IV 10 225
was perfectly audible while it pretended to be a whisper. P IV 11 230
Wentworth's hitherto perfectly quiet division of the room. P IV 11 233
her head; that she was perfectly convinced of having had P IV 11 238
"I am afraid, ma'am, that it is not perfectly understood. P IV 11 239
from it, that I was perfectly right in being guided by the P IV 11 246
She might have been absolutely rich and perfectly healthy, P IV 12 252
"Oh! perfectly, perfectly. S 9 409
with this object in veiw, I have been perfectly well."-- S 9 410
another representation) perfectly decided, & who was S 11 420
Here perhaps they had thought themselves so perfectly S 12 427

PERFORCE (1)
Those who can barely live, and who live perforce in a very E I 10 85

PERFORM (15)
of a gentleman usually perform a journey of thirty miles: NA II 5 155
think the worse of me for the part I am obliged to perform. NA II 13 223
to be done, and Elinor therefore hastened to perform it. SS III 1 261
thinking that no one could so well perform it as himself. SS III 3 283
by Colonel Brandon to perform his promise of following her; SS III 7 308
and be ever ready to perform those rites and ceremonies PP I 13 62
leads me to perform what I look on as a point of duty. PP I 18 97
We neither of us perform to strangers." PP II 8 176
but if you are willing to perform the engagements which I PP III 7 302
with them, or rather to perform what should have been her MP I 3 32
but in orders now, you might perform the ceremony directly. MP I 9 89
she was longing and dreading to see how they would perform. MP I 18 167
to perform the dreadful duty of appearing before her uncle. MP II 1 177
more than she could perform with credit; she wanted E II 8 227
and delicate office to perform by Harriet, which Mrs. E III 11 403

PERFORMANCE (33)
to other people's performance with very little fatigue. NA I 1 16
I have heard of a faithful performance. NA II 9 196
away all her powers of performance; and, after long NA II 14 235
he had limited the performance of his promise to his SS I 5 26
rapid in the performance of every thing that interested SS I 5 26
Marianne's performance was highly applauded. SS I 7 35
coloured silks of her performance, in proof of her having SS II 4 160
had real taste for the performance, and a great many more SS II 14 250
stop in Marianne's performance brought her these words in SS III 3 281
the resolution of its performance; and as soon as she had SS III 7 311
She dreaded the performance of it, dreaded what its effect SS III 9 335
Her performance was pleasing, though by no means capital. PP I 6 25
Her performance on the piano-forte is exquisite." PP I 8 39
any attention to the imperfection of the performance. PP I 10 49
"I must not decide on my own performance." PP I 18 91
that the performance would reflect no credit on either." PP I 18 94
remarks on Elizabeth's performance, mixing with them many PP II 8 176
make the performance, not the theatre, our object. MP I 13 124
to believe their performance would, indeed, have such MP I 18 170
performance, and who shewed herself not wanting in taste. MP II 4 207
to judge by their performance, must have thought reading MP III 3 339
shew off in higher style her own very superior performance. E II 2 168
skill or right of judging of any body's performance.-- E II 6 201
know, of his being so warm an admirer of her performance." E II 8 217
Such an admirer of her performance on the pianoforte, and E II 8 226
to Miss Fairfax, whose performance, both vocal and E II 8 227
They talked at first only of the performance. E II 8 228
into the power of performance; and Emma could not but pity E II 10 240
honour my performance is mediocre to the last degree. E II 14 276
delighted, her performance was little thought of, only out P III 6 46
their own daughters' performance, and total indifference P III 6 47
not look again: but the performance was re-commencing, and P IV 8 188
Anne replied, and spoke in defence of the performance so P IV 8 190

PERFORMANCES (7)
censure the very performances, to the number of which they NA I 5 37
and of slighting the performances which have only genius, NA I 5 37
to the finer performances of the London stage, which she NA I 12 92

day for the Abbey, where his performances have been seen. NA II 15 247 13
pleasure in seeing the performances of other people, and I SS I 4 19 2
to see any of her performances before, but she is in SS II 12 234 27
body; and Miss Woodhouse's performances must be capital. E I 6 45 20
ERFORMED (18)
It was performed with suitable quietness and uneventful NA I 2 19 4
The promise, therefore, was given, and must be performed. SS I 2 9 6
The first part of their journey was performed in too SS I 6 28 1
may now be performed without inconvenience to any one. SS II 3 155 8
She performed her promise of being discreet, to admiration. SS III 1 265 33
As soon as Elinor had finished it, she performed what she SS III 2 278 31
Their journey was safely performed. SS III 6 302 6
She performed her part indeed without much graciousness, PP I 9 45 35
of leave-taking was performed when the ladies moved for PP I 22 123 4
should be her's, it was performed in a proper manner, PP II 6 161 10
I am confident that she would have performed delightfully. PP II 8 173 6
Their journey was performed without much conversation, or PP II 15 217 15
She was confident of having performed her duty, and to PP II 18 232 21
The little girl performed her long journey in safety, and MP I 2 12 1
exactly as if the ceremony were going to be performed. MP I 9 88 19
with which she performed the very aweful ceremony of MP II 5 223 47
"and now, Fanny, having performed one part of my MP III 1 314 16
which may be just as well performed by another person?-- P III 12 103 2
ERFORMER (3)
Anne would have been a delightful performer, had her PP II 8 176 28
Highbury had long known that you are a superior performer." E II 14 276 35
A superior performer!--very far from it, I assure you. E II 14 276 36
ERFORMER'S (1)
to command a full view of the fair performer's countenance. PP II 8 174 12
ERFORMERS (5)
none at all; and the performers themselves were, as usual, SS II 14 250 10
immediate friends, the first private performers in England. SS II 14 250 10
must be in the habit of hearing the very best performers." PP I 6 24 22
had destroyed the scheme and dispersed the performers. MP I 13 121 1
as young performers; we bespeak your indulgence." MP II 1 185 28
ERFORMING (4)
in performing it! this made it so particularly strange! NA II 10 201 5
the most scrupulous in performing every engagement however SS II 13 243 40
heroes, who after performing great exploits in a foreign MP I 11 108 10
and to feel, that in performing a duty, he had secured MP III 10 404 15
ERFORMS (1)
"Your friend performs delightfully;" he continued after a PP I 6 25 28
ERFUME (1)
It was almost enough to spread purification and perfume P IV 9 192 3
ERHAPS (536)
My having prevented it, may perhaps have given his wife an LS 5 250 1
in want of money, & might perhaps till the old gentleman's LS 10 257 1
tho' perhaps my desire of dominion was never more decided. LS 10 258 2
I may perhaps do no good, but that of relieving my own LS 12 261 5
& perhaps may think me negligent for not writing before. LS 19 273 1
much of the rattle perhaps, but a year or two will rectify LS 20 276 5
I may therefore expect it will sooner subside; & perhaps LS 22 282 7
the danger is over, is perhaps dearly purchased by all LS 23 283 1
But perhaps he did not know it himself. LS 23 284 6
to think that we had perhaps been equally mistaken in each LS 24 290 13
unhappy, still fearful perhaps of her mother's anger, & LS 24 291 16
society must; & my visit has already perhaps been too long. LS 25 293 3
I might perhaps harden myself in time against the LS 30 300 3
husband; but perhaps you know this already from himself. LS 32 302 1
frets so much about him that perhaps she may not live long. LS 38 307 2
"But, perhaps, I keep no journal." NA I 3 27 27
"Perhaps you are not sitting in this room, and I am not NA I 3 27 28
or a lover, had not yet perhaps entered Mr. Allen's head, NA I 3 30 52
Perhaps Catherine was wrong in not demanding the cause of NA I 5 36 2
about Mr. Tilney, for perhaps I may never see him again." NA I 6 41 17
"Only," she added, "perhaps we may overtake the two young NA I 6 43 40
Perhaps we are talking about you, therefore I would advise NA I 8 57 20
so I thought perhaps he would ask you, if he met with you." NA I 8 58 30
He will, most likely, give a plunge or two, and perhaps NA I 9 62 9
"Perhaps we----- yes, I think we certainly shall." NA I 10 73 20
"No walk for me to-day," sighed Catherine;--"but perhaps NA I 11 82 4
"Perhaps it may, but then, my dear, it will be so dirty." NA I 11 82 5
They are coming for me perhaps--but I shall not go--I NA I 11 84 18
was not to be ranked; but perhaps it was because they were NA I 12 92 4
and perhaps he might be now coming round to their box. NA I 12 93 5
Perhaps you did not know I had been there." NA I 12 94 9
reason of such incivility; but perhaps I can do it as well. NA I 12 94 10
the cleanest strokes that perhaps ever was made in this NA I 12 96 20
may be mistaken again perhaps; he led me into one act of NA I 13 101 20
happiness to both destroyed, perhaps through her means. NA I 13 103 29
Isabella might otherwise perhaps be going to Clifton the NA I 13 105 40
Originally perhaps it was applied only to express neatness, NA I 14 108 16
intense application, may perhaps be brought to acknowledge NA I 14 110 27
written in vain--or perhaps might not have written at all." NA I 14 110 27
Perhaps the abilities of women are neither sound nor acute- NA I 14 112 36
Perhaps they may want observation, discernment, judgment, NA I 14 112 36
"Perhaps we may; but it is more than I ever thought of. NA I 15 124 45
to indulge in a secret "perhaps," but in general the NA II 2 138 1
"Perhaps," said Miss Tilney in an embarrassed manner, "you NA II 2 139 4
We leave Bath, as she has perhaps told you, on Saturday NA II 2 139 7
he is my brother, and who perhaps after all, you know, NA II 3 146 20
My brother is a lively, and perhaps sometimes a NA II 4 152 26
but a very short time, perhaps only a few days behind us. NA II 4 152 29
drawers, but on one side perhaps the remains of a broken NA II 5 158 17
"Nothing further to alarm perhaps may occur the first NA II 5 159 19
In one perhaps there may be a dagger, in another a few NA II 5 160 21
nothing but a considerable hoard of diamonds. NA II 5 160 21
also of silver, broken perhaps prematurely by some strange NA II 6 163 2
Such was the collection of papers, (left perhaps, as she NA II 7 172 2
Perhaps it may seem odd, that with only two younger NA II 7 176 15
Even Frederick, my eldest son, you see, who will perhaps NA II 7 176 15
"But perhaps it might be more agreeable to her to make NA II 7 176 17
But perhaps it may be damp." NA II 7 179 28
and though I felt my loss perhaps as strongly as one so NA II 7 180 34
I can close my eyes; and perhaps may be poring over the NA II 8 187 15
Its origin--jealousy perhaps, or wanton cruelty--was yet NA II 8 188 16
Down that stair-case she had perhaps been conveyed in a NA II 8 188 17
able to face it, was not perhaps very strange, and yet NA II 9 190 2
Perhaps you did not know--you were not aware of their NA II 9 195 12
father, I thought--perhaps had not been very fond of her." NA II 9 196 24
on her's,) "you infer perhaps the probability of some NA II 9 196 25
it was not in them perhaps that human nature, at least in NA II 10 200 3
Among the Alps and Pyrenees, perhaps, there were no mixed NA II 10 200 3
Perhaps, if particularly questioned, she might just give NA II 10 203 9
"But perhaps," observed Catherine, "though she has behaved NA II 10 206 33
never to hear from her, perhaps never to see her again, I NA II 10 207 39
She was as insignificant, and perhaps as portionless as NA II 11 208 1
we allow, but decent perhaps, and habitable; and NA II 11 213 19
bow thrown out, perhaps--though, between ourselves, if NA II 11 213 19
not have written so; but perhaps this has served to make NA II 12 218 4
week would be turned, and perhaps it might seem an NA II 13 220 1
time--had been misled (perhaps by her wishes) to suppose NA II 13 221 2
useless resentment, and perhaps involve the innocent with NA II 14 231 5
she then begin what might perhaps, at the end of half an NA II 14 233 10
but now it is all over perhaps there is no great harm done. NA II 14 234 12
now, perhaps, they were all setting off for Hereford. NA II 14 239 28
was solicited, which, perhaps, they pretty equally knew NA II 15 243 9
to their felicity, was perhaps rather conducive to it, by NA II 16 252 7
Perhaps it would have been as well if he had left it SS I 2 9 6
"Perhaps, then, it would be better for all parties if the SS I 2 9 10
her family afforded; and perhaps in spite of every SS I 3 14 3
of his regard for Elinor perhaps assisted her penetration; SS I 3 16 13
"Perhaps," said Marianne, "I may consider it with some SS I 3 17 18
this spot, from whence perhaps I may view you no more!-- SS I 5 27 8
Perhaps in the spring, if I have plenty of money, as I SS I 6 29 4
into one of them with perhaps a part of the other, and so SS I 6 29 4
her marriage, and which perhaps had lain ever since in the SS I 7 35 8
"Perhaps," said Elinor, "thirty-five and seventeen had SS I 8 37 9
Perhaps she pitied and esteemed him the more because he SS I 10 50 13
"But perhaps the abuse of such people as yourself and SS I 10 50 18
"Perhaps," said Willoughby, "his observations may have SS I 10 51 23
"Perhaps it is to tell you that your cousin Fanny is SS I 13 64 14
"and then perhaps you may find out what his business is." SS I 13 65 38
with great good humour, "perhaps, Elinor, it was rather SS I 13 69 76
Perhaps it is about Miss Williams--and, by the bye, I dare SS I 14 70 2
Then, and then only, under such a roof, I might perhaps be SS I 14 73 13
disapproves of it, (perhaps because she has other views SS I 15 78 26
leave her, and leave her perhaps for months, without SS I 15 80 36
But it may be months, perhaps, before that happens." be SS I 16 85 12
happens." be months, perhaps, before that happens." SS I 16 85 12
"Perhaps," said Elinor, smiling, "we may come to the same SS I 17 91 11
A proper establishment of servants, a carriage, perhaps SS I 17 91 14
"Perhaps then you would bestow it as a reward on that SS I 17 93 29
perhaps it is Colonel Brandon come back again"----- SS I 19 106 20
21
His temper might perhaps be a little soured by finding, SS I 20 112 28
rather too much indulged; perhaps they may be the outside SS I 21 122 19
But perhaps you young ladies may not care about the beaux, SS I 21 123 28
perhaps you may have a friend in the corner already." SS I 21 125 35
Then perhaps you cannot tell me what sort of a woman she SS I 22 128 5
as she spoke; "but perhaps there may be reasons--I wish I SS I 22 128 7
in her countenance; perhaps the falsehood of the greatest SS I 22 132 41
Perhaps you might notice the ring when you saw him?" SS I 22 135 54
frivolous pursuits, had perhaps robbed her of that SS II 1 140 2
"Perhaps," continued Elinor, "if I should happen to cut SS II 1 145 19
you really like the work, perhaps you will be as well SS II 1 145 22
means of robbing him, perhaps, of all that his mother SS II 2 147 7
for a time, we should be happier perhaps in the end. SS II 2 149 30
of sources; she would perhaps expect some from improving SS II 3 157 16
In another day or two perhaps; this extreme mildness can SS II 5 167 3
hardly last longer--nay, perhaps it may freeze to-night!" SS II 5 167 3
it, for where the mind is perhaps rather unwilling to be SS II 5 173 44
Perhaps he has not observed you yet." SS II 6 176 5
You have perhaps been misinformed, or purposely deceived, SS II 7 188 42
"Well, then, another day or two, perhaps; but I cannot SS II 7 191 64
"In this affair it can only do harm; more so perhaps than SS II 8 196 19
"Perhaps, then," he hesitatingly replied, "what I heard SS II 8 198 33
regard; and even now, perhaps--but I am almost convinced SS II 8 199 40
we grew up, was such, as perhaps, judging from my present SS II 9 205 24
Had I remained in England, perhaps--but I meant to promote SS II 9 206 24
Her sister was perhaps laid down upon the bed, or in her SS II 10 219 40
Perhaps just at present he may be undecided; the smallness SS II 11 223 24
These apprehensions perhaps were not founded entirely on SS II 12 231 11
Perhaps Fanny thought for a moment that her mother had SS II 12 235 30
31
You would not think it perhaps, but Marianne was SS II 12 237 43
"Perhaps, Miss Marianne," cried Lucy, eager to take some SS II 13 243 38
fancied them satirical: perhaps without exactly knowing SS II 14 246 3
are, perhaps, a little less to be wondered at.-- SS III 1 263 28
Then, if I had not been bound to silence, perhaps nothing SS III 1 264 29
Mrs. Ferrars, is perhaps altogether a little extraordinary. SS III 1 267 45
other plan could do, and perhaps without any greater delay. SS III 3 280 6
Perhaps Mrs. Jennings was in hopes, by this vigorous SS III 3 280 9
acceptance--but that, perhaps, so unfortunately SS III 3 282 19
on their parting, may perhaps appear in general, not less SS III 3 284 24
As a friend of mine, of my family, he may perhaps--indeed SS III 4 289 35
as well, or better, perhaps, all things considered. SS III 5 297 31
as well-meaning a fellow perhaps, as any in the world. SS III 5 298 35
the Grecian temple, and perhaps all over the grounds, and SS III 6 303 11
would have been enough, perhaps, had not Elinor still, as SS III 6 305 16
Mrs. Jennings, perhaps satisfied with the partial SS III 7 314 23
The Colonel too!--perhaps scarcely less an object of pity!- SS III 7 315 26
her doubt--her dread-- perhaps her despair!--and of what SS III 7 316 30
be the last time, perhaps-- let us be cheerful together.-- SS III 8 318 15
Perhaps you will hardly think the better of me,--it is SS III 8 319 29
in a more simple one--perhaps too simple to raise any SS III 8 325 50
equalled my own, and he perhaps, thinking that mere SS III 9 336 12
to you possible; and perhaps, as long as your frugality SS III 11 350 9
some hesitation, said, "perhaps you mean--my brother--you SS III 12 360 20
21
in an hurried voice, "perhaps you do not know--you may not SS III 12 360 22
23
saw her hurry away, and perhaps saw--or even heard, her SS III 12 360 26
by supposing, that perhaps at first accidentally meeting, SS III 13 364 11
"And that," he presently added, "might perhaps be in his SS III 13 364 12
And Lucy perhaps at first might think only of procuring SS III 13 364 12
Perhaps, however, he is kept silent by his fear of SS III 13 371 39
from him, addressed perhaps to Fanny, and by her shewn to SS III 13 371 39
"And when she has forgiven you, perhaps a little humility SS III 13 372 44
And though, perhaps, Marianne may not seem exactly the SS III 14 375 9
home perhaps--but you are sure of some comfortable soup.-- W 315 1
Perhaps Tom Musgrave may take notice of you--but I would W 315 1
great; Miss Osborne perhaps, or something in that stile.--" W 319 2
"No--perhaps not--but I remember my dear when you & I did W 337 15
"Indeed! perhaps I might have looked in upon you again, if W 340 19
"Perhaps she is not critically handsome, but her manners W 340 19
were not a Lord--& perhaps--better bred; more desirous of W 340 19
with an important look, perhaps I might be able to win a W 340 19
confusion--but that was perhaps merely oweing to the W 341 19
Perhaps Emma may be tempted to go back with us, & stay W 350 24
He says his head won't bear whist--but perhaps if we make W 354 28
She might perhaps have met with some unexpected W 355 28
felt little interest, & perhaps maintained little W 359 28
interesting to me, than perhaps you may be aware--" but W 360 29
them by themselves, which perhaps will be still better, PP I 1 4 19
that of Mrs. Bennet perhaps surpassing the rest; though PP I 2 7 23
The distinction had perhaps been felt too strongly. PP I 5 18 1
"Perhaps you mean what I overheard between him and Mr. PP I 5 19 7
"It may perhaps be pleasant," replied Charlotte, "to be PP I 6 21 2
"Perhaps he must, if he sees enough of her. PP I 6 22 6
as they walked along, "perhaps we may see something of PP I 7 32 40
Perhaps he thought her too young. PP I 9 44 31
We may as well wait, perhaps, till the circumstance occurs, PP I 10 50 37
"Perhaps I do. PP I 10 51 42
"Perhaps that is not possible for any one. PP I 11 57 22
My temper would perhaps be called resentful.-- PP I 11 58 28
But if you will listen to his letter, you may perhaps be a PP I 13 62 9
The idea of the olive branch perhaps is not wholly new, PP I 13 64 19
"You allude perhaps to the entail of this estate." PP I 13 65 23
At present I will not say more, but perhaps when we are PP I 13 65 25
astonish--and perhaps you would not express it quite so PP I 16 77 14
I have a warm, unguarded temper, and I may perhaps have PP I 16 80 27
rational, honourable, and perhaps agreeable,--allowing PP I 16 82 48
Interested people have perhaps misrepresented each to the PP I 17 85 2
Perhaps by and bye I may observe that private balls are PP I 18 91 11
But perhaps you have been too pleasantly engaged to think PP I 18 95 49
Who would have thought of my meeting with--perhaps--a PP I 18 96 57
gave birth to, made her perhaps almost as happy as Jane. PP I 18 98 63
feelings on this subject, perhaps it will be advisable for PP I 19 105 8
and thirdly--which perhaps I ought to have mentioned PP I 19 105 10
first application, and perhaps you have even now said as PP I 19 108 16
17
in rejecting my suit, perhaps it were better not to force PP I 20 110 4
Perhaps not the less so from feeling a doubt of my PP I 20 114 32

Change of scene might be of service--and perhaps a little PP II 2 141 10
Mr. Darcy may perhaps have heard of such a place as PP II 2 141 13
"Perhaps it will be as well, if you discourage his coming PP II 3 145 7
less clear-sighted perhaps in his case than in Charlotte's, PP II 3 149 28
carry us," said Mrs. Gardiner, "but perhaps to the lakes." PP II 4 154 22
Perhaps she is full young to be much in company. PP II 6 165 35
"Perhaps," said Darcy, "I should have judged better, had I PP II 8 175 21
But perhaps Mr. Bingley did not take the house so much for PP II 9 178 9
"These are home questions--and perhaps I cannot say that I PP II 10 183 12
But, perhaps his sister does as well for the present, and, PP II 10 184 17
I might, perhaps, wish to be informed why, with so little PP II 11 190 9
perhaps for ever, the happiness of a most beloved sister?" PP II 11 190 10
But perhaps," added he, stopping in his walk, and turning PP II 11 192 22
ill consequence, is perhaps probable;--but his regard did PP II 12 199 5
Perhaps this concealment, this disguise, was beneath me.-- PP II 12 199 5
on you; but his success is not perhaps to be wondered at. PP II 12 202 5
He is now perhaps sorry for what he has done, and anxious PP II 17 227 24
"Perhaps we might be deceived." PP III 1 249 41
Perhaps he had been civil, only because he felt himself at PP III 1 253 55
"But perhaps he may be a little whimsical in his PP III 1 258 72
necessary to be made, but perhaps not the more easily kept, PP III 3 268 8
in Darcy's opinion, and perhaps to remind the latter of PP III 3 269 10
its ill-success might perhaps authorise her to seek the PP III 4 279 24
"Not perhaps of neglecting his own interest. PP III 5 282 4
Perhaps I am not doing her justice. PP III 5 283 10
their proceedings, and perhaps announce the marriage. PP III 5 287 33
"Perhaps it would have been better;" replied her sister. PP III 5 291 56
home," cried Elizabeth; "perhaps she meant well, but , PP III 5 293 67
But, on second thoughts, perhaps Lizzy could tell us, what PP III 6 295 6
I can,--or, perhaps, I may defer it, till Kitty runs away." PP III 6 300 28
from his pocket; "but perhaps you would like to read it." PP III 7 302 11
Perhaps there was some truth in this; though I doubt PP III 10 324 2
inducement, she could, perhaps, believe, that remaining PP III 10 326 3
"Perhaps preparing for his marriage with Miss de Bourgh," PP III 10 328 17
Not these two or three years perhaps." PP III 11 330 4
But, perhaps he could not in her mother's presence be what PP III 11 335 40
He was not seated by her; perhaps that was the reason of PP III 11 335 43
Thank heaven! he has some friends, though perhaps not so PP III 11 337 51
No, no, let me shift for myself; and, perhaps, if I have PP III 13 350 54
penetration, or fear that perhaps instead of his seeing PP III 15 364 25
resolution; and perhaps he might be doing the same. PP III 16 365 1
"The letter, perhaps, began in bitterness, but it did not PP III 11 368 23
I was angry perhaps at first, but my anger soon began to PP III 16 369 28
Perhaps I did not always love him so well as I do now. PP III 17 373 7
"Wickham, perhaps, is my favourite; but I think I shall PP III 17 379 48
Perhaps other people have said so before, but not one with PP III 18 383 21
Mrs. Philips's vulgarity was another, and perhaps a PP III 18 384 27
rest of her life; though perhaps it was lucky for her PP III 19 385 1
a charity; though perhaps she might so little know herself, MP I 1 8 9
thirty years, years, perhaps for life, of more than half MP I 3 23 3
of something better; or, perhaps, her very display of the MP I 3 28 38
and who was gone perhaps never to return! that she should MP I 3 33 64
of the steward, or that perhaps Dr. Grant might now and MP I 4 36 7
up to every thing--and perhaps when one has seen her MP I 5 49 32
You young ones do not remember much about it, perhaps. MP I 6 54 9
My plan was laid at Westminster--a little altered perhaps MP I 6 61 56
There was a charm, perhaps, in his sincerity, his MP I 7 65 13
be called conduct, perhaps, the result of good principles; MP I 9 93 49
Perhaps," turning to Miss Crawford, "my dear companion may MP I 9 94 58
side of the ha-ha,) and perhaps turn a little way in some MP I 9 96 76
It might have been as well, perhaps, if you had been in my MP I 10 100 28
Your uncle, and his brother admirals, perhaps, knew little MP I 11 110 26
"Which is, perhaps, more in favour of his liking Julia MP I 12 116 10
Well, the jointure may comfort him; and perhaps, between MP I 13 123 5
green baize for a curtain, and perhaps that may be enough." MP I 13 123 7
Perhaps it might cost a whole twenty pounds.-- MP I 13 127 31
they may not be able to find any play to suit them. MP I 13 128 34
That might do, perhaps, but for the low parts----- MP I.14 131 3
He was, perhaps, but at treacherous play with her. MP I 14 135 18
profession itself, is, perhaps, one of the last who would MP I 15 145 41
capable of; and Edmund perhaps away--what should she do? MP I 16 150 1
Perhaps you are not so much aware as I am, of the mischief MP I 16 154 14
different expectations--perhaps, without considering the MP I 16 154 14
"Perhaps," said Tom, "Fanny may be more disposed to oblige MP I 17 158 3
Perhaps you may persuade her." MP I 17 158 3
She was occasionally useful to all; she was perhaps as MP I 18 166 5
reasonable dependence perhaps on the nerves of his wife MP II 1 180 10
Sir Thomas, and giving perhaps the very best start he had MP II 1 182 22
"I may perhaps get as far as Banbury to-day." MP II 2 193 16
consistent manners; but perhaps having seen him so seldom, MP II 3 199 13
Mr. Rushworth had perhaps been accepted on too short an MP II 3 200 20
Sir Thomas was satisfied; too glad to be satisfied perhaps MP II 3 201 22
them as thoroughly perhaps in the animation of a card- MP II 3 202 28
room again and again, perhaps in the very spot where she MP II 4 207 10
unsheltered, remaining perhaps till in the midst of some MP II 4 208 11
or an ornament; and perhaps in another three years we may MP II 4 208 12
to perhaps as leading it even more than those of larger MP II 4 210 21
"Perhaps I might have scolded," said Edmund, "if either of MP II 4 211 28
and the poulterer--or perhaps on their very account. MP II 4 213 35
She was anxious, she knew--more anxious perhaps than she MP II 5 218 12
"Your sister perhaps may be prevailed on to spend the day MP II 5 219 22
"Perhaps I might; but all that you know is entirely MP II 5 226 63
a little love perhaps may animate and do her good, but I MP II 6 230 8
him and be seeing him perhaps daily, his direct holidays MP II 6 233 14
Norris--and with whom (perhaps the dearest indulgence of MP II 6 234 18
his niece--nor perhaps refrain (though unconsciously) from MP II 7 238 1
He was a whist player himself, and perhaps might feel that MP II 7 239 6
Thomas, as you have perhaps heard me telling Miss Price. MP II 7 247 38
"If I were at Portsmouth, I should be at it perhaps." MP II 7 249 50
perhaps we may have an opportunity of doing ere long." MP II 7 250 60
the whirl of a ball-room perhaps was not particularly MP II 8 256 13
She would rather perhaps have been obliged to some other MP II 8 258 18
in the world?--or perhaps--looking archly--you suspect a MP II 8 259 20
You see how it is; and could tell me, perhaps better than MP II 9 268 31
incapable of any thing else, though perhaps some might not. MP II 9 270 39
For Fanny's present comfort it was concluded perhaps at MP II 9 270 40
with a significant look, "perhaps you can tell me why my MP II 10 277 17
In thus sending her away, Sir Thomas perhaps might not be MP II 10 281 34
cry in peace, conceiving perhaps that the deserted chair MP II 11 282 2
"Perhaps he will always stay longer than he talks of. MP II 11 287 20
always imagine you are--perhaps you do not think him MP II 11 289 36
rent a place in this neighbourhood--perhaps Stanwix Lodge. MP II 12 295 20
You will, perhaps, like to see them." MP II 13 298 2
"You are not aware, perhaps, that I have had a visitor MP III 1 313 14
Mr. Crawford, as you have perhaps foreseen, is yet in the MP III 1 314 16
He might have softened his father; but all, perhaps all, MP III 1 321 46
But there is no time fixed, perhaps to-morrow, or whenever MP III 1 321 48
Had her own affections been as free--as perhaps they ought MP III 2 329 9
he claims no merit in it, perhaps is entitled to none. MP III 2 330 14
before her again; nay, perhaps with greater enjoyment, for MP III 3 337 10
pretty thoroughly, is, perhaps, not uncommon; but to read MP III 3 338 14
often; now and then, perhaps, once or twice in the spring, MP III 3 341 30
"Perhaps, sir," said Fanny, wearied at last into speaking-- MP III 3 343 39
at last into speaking--"perhaps, sir, I thought it was a MP III 3 343 39
Perhaps I have as yet no right--but by what other name can MP III 3 344 41
"Not of facts, perhaps; but of feelings, Fanny. MP III 4 346 10
"As a by-stander," said Fanny, "perhaps I saw more than MP III 4 350 27
of it some little time, perhaps two or three weeks; but MP III 5 362 21
Lacey were completed--perhaps, within a fortnight, he MP III 6 367 4
Edmund too--to be two months from him, (and perhaps, she MP III 6 370 12
before he sailed, and perhaps find her there still when he MP III 6 372 18
and another twenty years' absence, perhaps, begun. MP III 6 373 24
in time; for she may have her orders to-morrow, perhaps. MP III 7 378 10
Perhaps you would like some tea, as soon as it can be got." MP III 7 379 14
Perhaps it must be so. MP III 7 382 29
The elegance, propriety, regularity,harmony--and perhaps, MP III 8 391 10
was loud, (excepting, perhaps, her mother's, which MP III 8 392 11
ten days ago, or perhaps he only pretended the call, for MP III 9 393 1
small sum of money might, perhaps, restore peace for ever MP III 9 396 7
And at Michaelmas, perhaps, a fourth may be added, some MP III 10 405 19
Perhaps I may be to stay longer. MP III 11 410 15
in our way, and perhaps you would not mind passing through MP III 12 416 3
arise, my dear Fanny; perhaps they are some times MP III 13 422 2
They have all, perhaps, been corrupting one another; but MP III 13 424 4
little about it; or perhaps might have caught from Mrs. MP III 13 428 15
To be finding herself, perhaps, within three days, MP III 14 435 15
To have him still the acquaintance, the flirt, perhaps, of MP III 14 436 15
but it was dangerous, perhaps, to tread such ground. MP III 15 441 21
daughter-in-law might, perhaps, arise almost as much from MP III 16 450 10
Perhaps it is best for me--since it leaves me so little to MP III 16 456 25
That, perhaps, it was best for me; I had less to regret in MP III 16 458 30
to become, perhaps, the most beloved of the two.-- MP III 17 472 31
many--perhaps with most people, unless taken moderately. E I 2 19 14
Her next beginning was, "in one respect, perhaps, Mr. E I 4 34 41
42
"Perhaps you think I am come on purpose to quarrel with E I 5 36 5
value of a companion; and perhaps no man can be a good E I 5 36 6
never excited a greater interest; perhaps hardly so great. E I 5 40 27
"I have perhaps given her a little more decision of E I 6 42 5
the least finished, perhaps the most; her style was E I 6 44 20
I thought--but I beg your pardon, perhaps I have been E I 7 52 13
It will be safer to say 'no', perhaps.-- E I 7 53 20
"At this moment, perhaps, Mr. Elton is shewing your E I 7 56 44
has happened to delay her; some visitors perhaps." E I 8 58 16
having some apprehension perhaps of her being considered (E I 8 59 27
public eye, but perhaps you may not dislike looking at it." E I 9 71 11
Perhaps she might have passed over more had his manners E I 11 93 5
He is but young, and his uncle perhaps-----" E I 11 96 22
convinced, though perhaps I never told you so before, that E I 12 101 22
A hundred miles, perhaps, instead of forty." E I 12 106 57
are select, they are perhaps the most agreeable of any. E I 13 116 43
though Mr. Knightley perhaps, from being used to the large E I 13 116 43
This was a pleasure which perhaps the whole day's visit E I 14 117 2
"One ought to use the same caution, perhaps, in judging of E I 14 123 23
Perhaps it was not fair to expect him to feel how very E I 16 136 9
(or, being acting a part, perhaps rather more,) at the E I 18 145 5
"No," said Emma, laughing; "but perhaps there might be E I 18 147 17
Perhaps they began to feel it might have been kinder and E II 2 165 9
to Highbury; to spend, perhaps, her last months of perfect E II 2 166 10
preference; Mr. Dixon, perhaps, had been very near E II 2 169 16
world, full ten minutes, perhaps--when, all of a sudden, E II 3 178 52
by this time to-morrow, perhaps, or a little later, I may E II 5 190 20
Highbury, perhaps, afforded society enough?-- E II 5 191 27
Of pride, indeed, there was, perhaps, scarcely enough; his E II 6 198 5
all that was necessary, perhaps all that was proper; and I E II 6 199 7
I hardly know how it has happened; a little, perhaps, from E II 6 203 39
are but just beginning, perhaps may never make any thing E II 8 215 16
"Perhaps Miss Fairfax has never been staying here so long E II 8 216 23
instrument would be; and perhaps the mode of it, the E II 8 217 29
I may not have convinced you perhaps, but I am perfectly E II 8 218 41
"Perhaps you may now begin to regret that you spent one E II 8 222 52
Excepting inequality of fortune, and perhaps a little E II 8 225 73
"Well," said Mrs. Weston, laughing, "perhaps the greatest E II 8 225 77
"Perhaps it is as well," said Frank Churchill, as he E II 8 230 102
But, perhaps--I may be equally in the way here. E II 9 234 30
he in a deliberating manner, "for five minutes, perhaps." E II 10 244 43
However, this does make a difference; and, perhaps, when E II 11 252 32
not;" and the gentlemen perhaps thought each to himself, " E II 11 253 43
"In short," said he, "perhaps, Miss Woodhouse-----I think E II 12 260 29
the greatest compliment perhaps of all conveyed. E II 13 266 5
Perhaps I may sometimes have felt that Harriet would not E II 13 268 12
"Perhaps she might; but it is not every man's fate to E II 14 271 14
Miss Hawkins perhaps wanted a home, and thought this the E II 14 271 14
My greatest danger, perhaps, in housekeeping, may be quite E II 15 283 9
perhaps, you may hardly be aware yourself how highly it is. E II 15 287 26
was not a fine lady; perhaps there was want of spirit in E II 18 307 17
Or, perhaps she may not have resources enough in herself E II 18 307 21
But perhaps he may never have heard of there being such a E II 18 307 23
He could not have appeared to greater advantage perhaps E III 2 326 32
not know who will ask her next, perhaps Mr. William Cox.' E III 2 329 45
But one morning--I forget exactly the day--but perhaps it E III 4 339 18
Perhaps Harriet might think her cold or angry if she did; E III 4 341 34
or angry if she did; or perhaps if she were totally silent, E III 4 341 34
Perhaps it will be wisest in you to check your feelings E III 4 342 39
the old Abbey fish-ponds; perhaps get as far as the clover, E III 6 361 42
"Perhaps I intended you to say so, but I meant self- E III 7 369 11
There are one or two, perhaps, (glancing at Mr. Weston and E III 7 370 19
Though, perhaps, as the chaperon of the party--I never was E III 7 370 20
endured than allowed, perhaps, but I must still use it. E III 7 374 55
56
perhaps, more in thought than fact; scornful, ungracious. E III 8 377 1
perhaps, he might come in while she were paying her visit. E III 8 377 2
comfort; if we except, perhaps, Mrs. Suckling's own family, E III 8 380 13
could not say--she might, perhaps, have rather offered it-- E III 9 386 7
Half a dozen natural children, perhaps--and poor Frank cut E III 10 393 18
attached--and how it came to cease, is perhaps the wonder. E III 10 396 41
You, perhaps, might.-- E III 11 404 10
Was it new for one, perhaps too busy to seek, to be the E III 11 413 48
and on box hill, perhaps, it had been the agony of a mind E III 12 421 17
fears, was, that he had perhaps been communicating his E III 13 424 1
Perhaps he wanted to speak to her, of his attachment to E III 13 425 2
I cannot let you continue in your error; and yet, perhaps, E III 13 426 17
He was wishing to confide in her--perhaps to consult her;-- E III 13 429 30
the happiest dream, was perhaps the most prominent feeling. E III 13 430 36
The manner, perhaps, may have as little to recommend them. E III 13 430 37
The change had perhaps been somewhat sudden;--her proposal E III 13 431 38
Miss Woodhouse; my father perhaps will think I ought to E III 14 438 8
Perhaps it is paid already. E III 14 439 8
perhaps even of his life, which must not be hazarded. E III 15 448 31
or in London, made perhaps an unreasonable difference in E III 16 452 5
Perhaps to Hartfield, perhaps to the Abbey mill, perhaps E III 16 458 40
"it is well, perhaps, that I have not had the possibility. E III 16 459 45
46
"Nothing can be actually settled yet, perhaps," replied E III 16 460 54
I do not say when, but perhaps you may guess where;--in E III 17 463 14
smile--"much less, perhaps, than he is aware of, if we E III 17 464 22
another year or two, perhaps--it might not be so very bad E III 17 467 30
Perhaps I am the readier to suspect, because, to tell you E III 18 478 67
Perhaps she ought to be ashamed, but Mr. Weston had been E III 18 479 73
It was a pity, perhaps, that he had not come last night; E III 18 479 73
It was likely to be as untainted, perhaps, as the blood of E III 19 482 3
Perhaps, indeed, at that time she scarcely saw Mr. Elton, E III 19 482 6
The disgrace of his first marriage might, perhaps, as P III 1 8 17
'Sixty', said I, 'or perhaps sixty-two'. P III 3 20 16
the same with many other professions, perhaps most other? P III 3 20 17
---- ; a Mr. (save, perhaps, some half dozen in the nation, P III 3 24 36
few months more, and he, perhaps, may be walking here." P III 3 24 38
had softened down much, perhaps nearly all of peculiar P III 4 28 7
"You will see them yet, perhaps, before the morning is P III 5 38 30
were in a state of alteration, perhaps of improvement. P III 5 40 45
"Perhaps you may not have heard that he is married," added P III 6 49 21
Captain Wentworth, that, perhaps, he might join them in P III 7 55 6
of comfort, as were, perhaps, ever likely to be hers. P III 7 58 20
Perhaps indifferent, if indifference could exist under P III 7 58 21

acknowledged, actuated, perhaps, by the same view of — P III 7 59 23
On one other question, which perhaps her utmost wisdom — P III 7 60 31
32
With the exception, perhaps, of Admiral and Mrs. Croft, — P III 8 63 3
"I might not like them the better for that, perhaps. — P III 8 69 42
her altered features, perhaps, trying to trace in them the — P III 8 72 58
Henrietta was perhaps the prettiest, Louisa had the higher — P III 9 74 8
They meant to take a long drive this morning; perhaps we — P III 10 84 8
"he had not, perhaps, a more sorrowing heart than I have. — P III 11 97 13
impossible; but in time, perhaps--we know what time does — P III 12 108 25
"And not known to him, perhaps, so soon." — P III 12 108 27
no more; and yet perhaps by "putting the children away in — P III 12 113 56
perhaps, be the occasion of continuing their acquaintance. — P III 12 115 67
be proud of between two walls, perhaps thirty feet asunder. — P IV 3 138 5
She could only offer one solution; it was, perhaps, for — P IV 3 140 11
"Oh! yes, perhaps, it had been Mr. Elliot. — P IV 3 141 12
It might be him, perhaps." — P IV 3 141 12
They were not the same, but they were, perhaps, equally — P IV 3 143 18
Her countenance, perhaps, might express some watchfulness; — P IV 4 145 2
In London, perhaps, in your present quiet style of living, — P IV 4 151 19
"But perhaps if she were to leave the room vacant we " — P IV 6 163 7
Perhaps he had quitted the field, had given Louisa up, had — P IV 6 166 18
than you would think for, perhaps, for that soft sort of — P IV 6 171 37
much in favour of their happiness; more than perhaps-----" — P IV 8 182 8
at present, perhaps, it was as well to be asunder. — P IV 8 185 18
"Perhaps," said Mr. Elliot, speaking low, "I have had a — P IV 8 187 30
"No, no--some time or other perhaps, but not now. — P IV 8 187 34
she owed him gratitude and regard, perhaps compassion. — P IV 9 192 2
to avoid and get rid of as he can--very natural, perhaps. — P IV 9 196 32
impression, I might, perhaps, have endeavoured to interest — P IV 9 198 44
I can satisfy you, perhaps, on points which you would — P IV 9 200 57
"Perhaps," cried Anne, struck by a sudden idea, "you — P IV 9 201 60
guide, perhaps, may recollect what you have seen him do." — P IV 9 207 90
To pacify Mary, and perhaps screen her own embarrassment, — P IV 10 222 39
But, it had better not be attempted, perhaps." — P IV 10 225 53
been obliged to attend (perhaps for half an hour) to his — P IV 10 228 70
It is, perhaps, our fate rather than our merit. — P IV 11 232 19
But perhaps you will say, these were all written by men." — P IV 11 234 27
"Perhaps I shall.-- — P IV 11 234 28
of which circumstances (perhaps those very cases which — P IV 11 234 30
a twelvemonth's absence perhaps, and obliged to put into — P 1 6 235 31
more exquisitely happy, perhaps, in their re-union, than — P IV 11 240 59
nay, perhaps herself, I was no longer at my own disposal. — P IV 11 242 65
"Perhaps I ought to have reasoned thus," he replied, "but — P IV 11 244 74
It was, perhaps, one of those cases in which advice is — P IV 11 246 80
She had something to suffer perhaps when they came into — P IV 12 250 5
The very thing perhaps to be wished for. — S 1 364 1
We are on our road home from London;--my name perhaps-- — S 1 368 1
On that point perhaps we may not totally disagree;--at — S 1 369 1
But perhaps it implies that he is coming himself.-- — S 5 385 1
Perhaps it might be partly owing to her having just — S 6 391 1
But perhaps the little misses may hurt the furniture.-- — S 6 393 1
"Perhaps there was a good deal in his air & address; and — S 7 395 1
commonplace perhaps--but doing very well from the lips of — S 7 396 1
in the breast of man, are perhaps incompatible with some — S 7 398 1
An income perhaps, but no property. — S 7 401 1
the sisters were perhaps driven to dissipate theirs in the — S 10 412 1
Had there been a 3d carriage, perhaps it might; but it was — S 10 414 1
But perhaps you are nervous." — S 10 415 1
"Keep you awake perhaps all night"--replied Charlotte, — S 10 418 1
which rototory motion, is perhaps to be attributed the — S 11 421 1
Here perhaps they had thought themselves so perfectly — S 12 427 1

PERIL (1)
pray never run into Peril again, in looking for an — S 5 386 1

PERIOD (80)
we should at some future period be obliged to receive her. — LS 3 246 1
clever woman for a short period, & of yeilding admiration — LS 12 261 6
being certain for that period, the rest of her life was at — NA II 2 138 1
to equal her sisters at a more advanced period of life. — SS I 1 7 14
on as the most suitable period for its accomplishment. — SS I 5 27 6
and in every brighter period, as capable of attaching her; — SS I 10 49 10
education, while the same period of time, spent on her — SS II 1 140 2
been delayed to a later period--if your engagement had — SS II 7 186 29
"It was nearly three years after this unhappy period — SS II 9 207 26
a day, returned from that period to her own home, and her — SS III 1 257 1
denominated from that period Lucas Lodge, where he could — PP I 5 18 1
find comfort in staying at home at any period of her life. — PP I 18 99 63
will hope at some future period, to enjoy many returns of — PP I 21 116 8
But may we not hope that the period of future happiness to — PP I 21 117 9
from this period of walking thither almost every day. — PP II 9 180 28
After this period, every appearance of acquaintance was — PP II 12 201 5
It was consequently necessary to name some other period — PP II 19 237 3
as that left too short a period for them to go so far, and — PP II 19 238 7
The period of expectation was now doubled. — PP II 19 239 10
after a moderate period of extravagant and wild admiration, — PP III 5 285 18
Mr. Bennet had very often wished, before this period of — PP III 8 308 1
tidings of it, that the period of anxiety and fretfulness — PP III 11 333 30
short period saw him looking both pleased and embarrassed. — PP III 11 335 41
Anxious and uneasy, the period which passed in the drawing- — PP III 12 341 14
a change, since the period to which he alluded, as to make — PP III 16 366 8
to all intercourse between them for a considerable period. — MP I 1 4 1
Every body is taken in at some period or other." — MP I 5 46 18
like him; though at this period, and on this subject, — MP I 7 64 12
Before that period, as I understand, the pews were only — MP I 9 86 9
again within a certain period, which these letters obliged — MP I 11-107 1
must be a very anxious period to my mother, and if we can — MP I 13 126 18
It is a very anxious period for her." — MP I 13 126 18
so any longer, and inhabited as such to a later period. — MP I 16 150 1
carry on her spirits to the period of dressing and dinner. — MP II 4 206 3
as to the probable period of the Antwerp's return from the — MP II 6 232 13
correspondent through a period of seven years, and the — MP II 6 233 14
terrific scenes, which such a period, at sea, must supply. — MP II 6 235 19
The intercourse of the two families was at this period — MP II 7 238 1
opinion of you from the period of my return to England. — MP III 1 318 39
judged by what we appeared at that period of general folly. — MP III 4 349 26
any under a considerable period, William determined to go — MP III 7 381 24
formed, and such a period chosen for its completion, — MP III 16 452 13
together from that period, in their daily intercourse, in — MP III 17 465 15
a reasonable period from Edmund's marrying Mary. — MP III 17 467 19
it remained for a later period to tell him the whole — MP III 17 471 28
been mistress of his house from a very early period. — E I 1 5 2
and was beginning a new period of existence with every — E I 2 17 6
in judgment at that period of our lives; but does not the — E I 12 99 7
in the most overpowering period of Mr. Elton's nonsense, — E I 14 118 4
with the hope of coming to Randalls at no distant period." — E I 18 144 1
It was accepted; and from that period Jane had belonged to — E II 2 164 4
had long resolved that one-and-twenty should be the period. — E II 2 165 8
The post-office has a great charm at one period of our — E II 16 293 16
of mind of each at this period, it struck her the more. — E III 3 335 10
first and most animating period of their acquaintance. — E III 7 368 3
had seen grow up from a period when her notice was an — E III 7 375 61
you, that there was a period in the early part of our — E III 10 396 41
Frank Churchill had once, for a short period, occupied?-- — E III 11 412 45
"So early in life--at three and twenty--a period when, if — E III 13 428 23
He had despaired at one period; he had received such an — E III 13 431 38
from about the same period, one sentiment having probably — E III 13 432 41
from about the same period, one sentiment having probably — E III 13 432 41
forward them after that period to her at ---- : in short, — E III 14 442 8
No additional agitation should be thrown at this period — E III 16 452 6
and from that period he had been constantly exceeding it. — P III 1 9 19
A short period of exquisite felicity followed, and but a — P III 4 26 2
excepting one short period of her life, she had never, — P III 6 47 13
at this critical period, and when he came back he had the — P III 9 74 4
At the end of that period, Lady Russell's politeness could — P IV 1 125 14
that there had been a period of his life (and probably not — P IV 5 161 27
change; and, after a period of nothing-saying amongst the — P IV 8 188 44
"This must have been about that very period of Mr. — P IV 9 200 56
"Mr. Elliot," replied Mrs. Smith, "at that period of his — P IV 9 200 59
notions; but, at that period, I must own I saw nothing — P IV 9 201 64
After the usual period of suspense, the usual sounds of — P IV 10 216 17
the result of immediate feeling--"it is a period, indeed! — P IV 10 225 60
Eight years and a half is a period!" — P IV 10 225 60
From that period his penance had become severe. — P IV 11 242 64
Anne, satisfied at a very early period of Lady Russell's — P IV 12 251 10
plans were at the same period (under another — S 11 420 1

PERIODS (4)
in the room at different periods of the fashionable hours; — NA I 4 31 1
to support her spirits, there were periods of dejection. — PP II 4 152 6
Such a companion for herself in the periods of anxiety and — E III 15 450 36
those periods of her life when it had been most valuable. — P IV 5 152 2

PERMANENCE (2)
To any thing like a permanence of abode, or limitation of — MP I 4 41 16
permanence, and equal comfort, of which she had the offer. — MP III 6 369 9

PERMANENCY (1)
at Mansfield, with every appearance of equal permanency. — MP III 17 472 31

PERMANENT (6)
But how little of permanent happiness could belong to a — PP III 8 312 17
you established as a permanent neighbour; but I hope, and — MP II 7 247 39
or at least the practicability of a permanent removal. — MP III 17 469 23
from the procuring her a permanent situation to the — E II 15 288 39
of something more permanent long before the term in — P IV 10 217 20
in a state of secure & permanent health without spending — S 2 373 1

PERMANENTLY (6)
His value of her was sincere; and, if not permanently, he — NA II 9 197 27
I want to see you permanently well connected--and to that — E I 4 31 24
of her being permanently fixed there; of her being taught — E II 2 163 3
father's house, and settled so permanently near herself. — P III 4 28 7
of various kinds to recommend her quickly and permanently. — P IV 12 251 10
succeed in the veiws of permanently enriching his family, — S 3 375 1

PERMISSION (15)
As we went upstairs Lady Susan begged permission to attend — LS 20 276 5
Such was the permission upon which he had now offered her — NA II 15 244 11
and his permission for him "to be a fool if he liked it!" — NA II 16 250 4
with her mother's permission, was equally compliant, and — SS II 1 143 9
directly, and entreated permission to introduce his friend, — PP I 15 72 8
your respected mother's permission for this address. you — PP I 19 105 8
therefore, he sent his permission for them to come; and it — PP III 8 314 22
permission, or being bold enough to come without it. — PP III 11 332 18
ventured, without any permission, to do the same by all — PP III 13 350 55
"That is to say, you had given your permission. — PP III 16 370 39
it ended in a gracious, "well, well," which was permission. — MP II 10 280 30
had just applied for permission to go to town with Maria; — MP II 11 284 10
each daughter that the permission should be granted, Lady — MP II 11 284 10
her uncle and obtained his permission, was giving her ease. — MP III 15 437 2
for the permission of attending and reading to them again. — E I 6 47 28

PERMIT (5)
fast as the crowd would permit her, fearful of being — NA I 13 101 25
as fast as a continual flow of tears would permit her. — SS II 7 180 1
your understanding, but permit me to say that there must — PP I 18 97 60
61
as a well-judging your woman could permit herself to give. — MP III 1 315 18
no, she would not permit a hasty or a witty word from — E II 14 270 5

PERMITTED (11)
her wish of being permitted to see it, as well as all the — NA II 8 186 7
Eleanor's marriage, permitted his son to return to — NA II 16 252 7
of the house, they were permitted to mingle in the croud, — SS II 6 175 2
her daughter, nor be permitted to appear in her presence. — SS III 13 371 38
would have been his only choice, had fortune permitted it. — PP II 3 149 28
this cannot possibly be permitted before the middle of — MP III 12 417 3
They were permitted to go alone; and with a cordial nod — E II 5 195 49
After some attempts, therefore, to be permitted to begin — E II 8 230 101
He would save himself from witnessing again such permitted, — E III 13 432 41
her, as far as civility permitted, was very evident, — E III 16 457 34
too well off in being permitted to rent it on the highest — P III 3 24 35

PERMITTING (2)
and scarcely ever permitting them to be read by their own — NA I 5 37 4
Oh! my dear mother, you must be wrong in permitting an — SS II 4 165 29

PERPETRATED (2)
Could they be perpetrated without being known, in a — NA II 9 197 29
could be perpetrated without risk of his general character. — P IV 9 199 53

PERPETUAL (12)
Her income was not her own, she said, with such perpetual — SS I 2 11 20
housekeeping, and of the perpetual demands upon his purse, — SS I 5 27 6
The perpetual commendations of the lady either on his hand- — PP I 10 47 2
of the other, was a perpetual source of irritation, which — MP I 8 81 32
and safe from the perpetual irritation of knowing his — MP III 6 370 12
that such extreme and perpetual cautiousness of word and — E II 6 203 41
My perpetual influence could not begin earlier, or you — E III 7 369 13
been a state of perpetual suffering to me; and so it ought. — E III 12 419 8
She must have been a perpetual enemy. — E III 12 421 17
It was a perpetual estrangement. — P III 8 64 3
I lived in perpetual fright at that time, and had all — P III 8 71 54
so overlooked, was a perpetual provocation to her there; — P IV 4 146 5

PERPETUALLY (8)
I need not tell you how much I miss him--how perpetually — LS 5 250 3
I feel that I have betrayed myself perpetually;--so — NA I 15 118 13
her own; and she was perpetually either making some — PP I 11 54 4
Such were the kind of lamentations resounding perpetually — PP II 18 229 10
I can hardly bear to hear it thus perpetually talked of. — PP III 11 333 28
She was, moreover, perpetually hearing about him; for, — E II 4 184 10
blind yourself'--for tears were in her eyes perpetually. — E III 8 379 8
and still were perpetually having cards left by people of — P IV 3 138 4

PERPETUATED (1)
no reason to suppose it perpetuated by offspring, have — P III 1 8 17

PERPLEXED (4)
that must have perplexed the engagement, and retarded the — SS ·II 13 238 1
He coloured, seemed perplexed, looked doubtingly, and — SS III 12 360 20
21
did Mr. Weston tell you?"--said Emma, still perplexed. — E III 11 404 7
in the arrangement of perplexed affairs, no health to make — P IV 5 154 8

PERPLEXING (1)
confusion of sudden and perplexing emotions, must create.-- — E III 11 409 34

PERPLEXITIES (3)
perplexities and pleasures of her father and herself. — E I 14 117 1
but for her private perplexities, remarkably comfortable, — E I 16 139 20
in the midst of your perplexities at that time, you had — E III 18 478 64
65

PERPLEXITY (20)
first came, he appeared all astonishment & perplexity. — LS 20 278 9
for some time in much perplexity, and was more than once — NA I 9 66 31
end, were considerations of equal perplexity and alarm. — NA II 13 226 25
long thought and much perplexity, to be very brief was all — NA II 14 235 14
from amidst all her perplexity of words in reply, the — NA II 15 242 9
in a most painful perplexity, "that I should never have — SS I 22 131 31
in the midst of her perplexity, that however difficult it — SS III 4 287 26
astonishment and perplexity on a change in his situation, — SS III 12 360 26
and so sudden;--a perplexity which they had no means of — SS III 12 360 26
chance of her ever considering it with less perplexity. — PP II 1 137 26
Mrs. Gardiner went away in all the perplexity about — PP III 6 298 16
After a pause of perplexity, some eyes began to be turned — MP I 18 171 28
serious; there was perplexity and agitation every way. she — MP II 13 304 16
One perplexity, however, arose, which the gentlemen did — E II 11 253 44
He had met with them in a little perplexity, which must be — E III 2 325 29
On these subjects, her perplexity and distress were very — E III 14 435 4

being diverted by the perplexity of her first answer to E III 16 455 19
while it was only an interchange of perplexity and terror. P III 12 113 57
agreeable curiosity and perplexity about Mr. Elliot, P IV 2 135 35
an immediate advantage to counterbalance her perplexity. S 10 419 1
PERRY (74)
subject, either when Mrs. Perry drank tea with Mrs. and E I 2 17 9
He had been at the pains of consulting Mr. Perry, the E I 2 19 14
Mr. Perry was an intelligent, gentlemanlike man, whose E I 2 19 14
Mr. Perry had been to Mrs. Goddard's to attend a sick E I 8 68 58
to miss before; and Mr. Perry had remonstrated with him E I 8 68 58
Mr. Perry could not quite understand him, but he was very E I 8 68 58
His good friend Perry too, whom he had spoken to on the E I 9 70 6
kind; but he had desired Perry to be upon the watch, and E I 9 70 6
Mr. Wingfield in town as her father could be of Mr. Perry. E I 11 92 4
"Ah! my dear, but Perry had many doubts about the sea E I 12 101 22
one inquiry after Mr. Perry yet; and he never forgets you." E I 12 101 23
"Oh! good Mr. Perry--how is he, sir?" E I 12 101 24
Poor Perry is bilious, and he has not time to take care of E I 12 101 25
"And Mrs. Perry and the children, how are they? do the E I 12 101 26
I have a great regard for Mr. Perry. E I 12 101 26
Perry says that colds have been very general, but not so E I 12 102 34
Perry does not call it altogether a sickly season." E I 12 102 34
Perry was surprized to hear you had fixed upon south end." E I 12 105 54
Perry was a week at Cromer once, and he holds it to be the E I 12 105 56
You should have consulted Perry." E I 12 106 56
"Ah! my dear," as Perry says, "where health is at stake, E I 12 106 58
This is just what Perry said. E I 12 106 58
"Mr. Perry," said he, in a voice of very strong E I 12 106 60
I hope, the use of my judgment as well as Mr. Perry.-- E I 12 106 60
sarcastic dryness, "if Mr. Perry can tell me how to convey E I 12 106 60
reflections on his friend Perry, to whom he had, in fact, E I 12 107 62
of care and affection, Mr. Perry was talked of, and E I 13 109 5
Has Perry seen her? E I 13 109 7
Why does not Perry see her?" E I 13 109 7
Mr. Perry has been with her, as you probably heard." E I 13 114 32
till he had seen Mr. Perry and learnt his opinion; and E I 15 125 4
If Jane does not get well soon, we will call in Mr. Perry. E II 1 162 31
you yesterday he was precisely the the height of Mr. Perry. E II 3 174 39
was a happier or a better couple than Mr. and Mrs. Perry. E II 3 175 39
Perry tells me that Mr. Cole never touches malt liquor. E II 7 210 20
part of Highbury;--Mr. Perry walking hastily by, Mr. E II 9 233 24
of asking Mr. Perry; I happened to meet him in the street. E II 9 237 46
Mr. Perry might have reason to regret the alteration, but E II 11 251 27
if you suppose Mr. Perry to be that sort of character. E II 11 251 28
Mr. Perry is extremely concerned when any of us are ill. E II 11 251 28
Do not you remember what Mr. Perry said, so many years ago, E II 11 252 37
Mr. Perry did say so. E II 11 253 38
little ones have the measles, she will send for Perry." E II 11 253 38
any benefit; and Mr. Perry, whose name, I dare say, is not E II 14 275 31
Mrs. Bates, Mrs. Perry, Mrs. Goddard and others, were a E II 16 290 3
As they were turning into the grounds, Mr. Perry passed by E III 5 344 4
Mrs. Perry had told somebody, and was extremely happy E III 5 344 9
What is this?" cried Mr. Weston, "about Perry and a E III 5 345 12
Is Perry going to set up his carriage, Frank? E III 5 345 12
friends, then I begin dreaming of Mr. and Mrs. Perry." E III 5 345 13
idea last spring; for Mrs. Perry herself mentioned it to E III 5 345 16
Mrs. Perry was very anxious that he should have a carriage, E III 5 346 16
Mrs. Perry was always particularly fond of my mother-- E III 5 346 16
to write;" and when Mr. Perry called at Hartfield, the E III 9 389 16
apprehension of the family, Mr. Perry was uneasy about her. E III 9 389 16
such a point--and Mrs. Perry had said so much--but, except E III 9 390 18
hardly eat any thing:--Mr. Perry recommended nourishing E III 9 391 19
Mr. Perry is not gone." E III 13 429 32
he had received from Mr. Perry, and talked on with much E III 14 434 3
hearing last night, by Mr. Perry, that it had not made him E III 14 436 7
Do not you think her cure does Perry the highest credit?--(E III 16 454 17
Upon my word, Perry has restored her in a wonderful short E III 16 454 17
of any assistance that Perry might have; not a word of a E III 16 454 17
Oh! no; Perry shall have all the credit." E III 16 454 17
I mean good Mr. Perry!--such attention to Jane!"-- E III 16 455 20
Cole, Mrs. Perry, and Mrs. Elton, immediately afterwards. E III 17 468 35
she had been within half a minute of sending for Mr. Perry. E III 18 479 73
for Perry, and only regretted that she had not done it. E III 18 479 73
"She should always send for Perry, if the child appeared E III 18 479 73
She could not be too soon alarmed, nor send for Perry too E III 18 479 73
it would probably have been better if Perry had seen it." E III 18 479 73
"Perry!" said he to Emma, and trying, as he spoke, to E III 18 479 75
"My friend Mr. Perry! E III 18 479 75
What are they saying about Mr. Perry?-- E III 18 479 75
PERRY'S (6)
would have been very bad, but for Perry's great attention. E II 11 253 38
became of Mr. Perry's plan of setting up his carriage?" E III 5 344 5
Perry's setting up his carriage! and his wife's persuading E III 5 345 14
Perfectly remember Mrs. Perry's coming.-- E III 5 346 16
that she had Mr. Perry's decided opinion, in favour of E III 9 390 16
introduce; and on Mr. Perry's coming in soon after dinner, E III 13 424 1
PERRYS (3)
of all the little Perrys being seen with a slice of Mrs. E I 2 19 15
good people; and the Perrys--I suppose there never was a E II 3 175 39
the Mrs. Eltons, the Mrs. Perrys, and the Mrs. Coles, who E III 9 390 19
PERSECUTION (2)
Persecution on the subject of Sir James was entirely at an LS 42 312 3
free herself from the persecution of Lucy's friendship, SS III 6 302 5
PERSECUTIONS (3)
between the brothers, nor persecutions to the lady. NA II 1 131 15
We have had great trials, and great persecutions, but SS III 2 277 30
with fancying the persecutions which ought to be the lot S 6 391 1
PERSERVER (1)
Marianne's perserver, as Margaret, with more elegance than SS I 10 46 1
PERSEVERANCE (20)
perseverance beyond civility, they could not give offence. SS I 6 30 6
But perseverance in humility of conduct and messages, in SS III 14 377 11
To such perseverance in wilful self-deception Elizabeth PP I 19 109 22
Mrs. Bennet, with more perseverance than politeness, PP I 23 126 1
2
talked of Matlock and Dove Dale with great perseverance. PP III 1 257 66
But she had more than fears of her own perseverance to MP I 16 152 3
himself, must with perseverance secure a return, and at no MP III 2 327 4
Some resentment did arise at a perseverance so selfish and MP III 2 328 9
views and sanguine perseverance of the lover; and when MP III 2 329 11
in a perseverance of this sort, against discouragement. MP III 2 330 14
was almost ready to wonder at his friend's perseverance.-- MP III 3 336 7
early and late, with perseverance and great dispatch, did MP III 8 390 7
and by animated perseverance had soon re-established the MP III 17 468 21
"Oh! no; I was pleased with my own perseverance in asking E II 3 171 10
being amused at her perseverance in dwelling on the E II 8 220 46
parties;--with so much perseverance in judging and E II 17 299 1
bursts, perseverance and weariness, health and sickness. E III 14 437 8
A little farther perseverance in patience, and forced P III 5 39 40
are pretty sure by perseverance to carry their point, be P IV 12 248 1
the sagacity, & the perseverance, of the villain of the S 8 404 1
PERSEVERE (8)
her, fearful of being pursued, yet determined to persevere. NA I 13 101 25
cared enough about it to persevere against a few repulses; MP I 17 160 9
If the gentleman would but persevere, if he had but love MP III 1 320 44
had but love enough to persevere--Sir Thomas began to have MP III 1 320 44
He had all the disposition to persevere that Sir Thomas MP III 2 326 1
She found that he did mean to persevere; but how he could, MP III 2 327 5
She meant to urge him to persevere in the hope of being MP III 4 354 46
not much longer persevere in a suit so distressing to her? MP III 11 414 32
PERSEVERED (13)
Mrs Vernon however persevered in the offer of it, & tho' LS 42 312 5
She could remember dozens who had persevered in every NA II 9 190 2
pained; but Marianne persevered, and saw every night in SS II 5 168 10
Darcy in any thing, and persevered therefore in requiring PP I 11 56 14
you;" but he still persevered, and no sooner had he begun MP I 2 15 10
Tom, so public and so persevered in, and her spirits MP I 16 150 1
as they all persevered--as Edmund repeated his wish, and MP I 18 172 32
But, Miss Crawford persevered, and argued the case with so MP II 8 258 17
Would he have persevered, and uprightly, Fanny must have MP III 17 467 19
For a little while Emma persevered in her silence; but E I 7 52 18
19
very unhappy, indeed, that it could not be persevered in. E II 11 248 10
with any warmth, he had persevered in seeking it, making P III 1 7 14
Friction alone steadily persevered in, (& I rubbed his S 5 386 1
PERSEVERES (1)
Crawford's is no common attachment; he perseveres, with MP III 4 347 18
PERSEVERING (7)
cast off by them for persevering in his engagement with a SS III 3 282 17
On Miss Lucas's persevering, however, she added, "very PP I 6 24 22
"If you are resolved on acting," replied the persevering MP I 13 127 28
in the professions of persevering, assiduous, and not MP III 2 328 7
unexceptionable, I should have condemned his persevering." MP III 2 330 14
one young woman with persevering attention, as he E III 10 396 44
created so steady and persevering an affection in such a E III 19 482 4
PERSEVERINGLY (1)
who continued most perseveringly by her side, and though PP I 18 102 73
PERSIST (4)
Mr Johnson vows that if I persist in the connection, he LS 38 306 1
"You persist, then, in supposing his sisters influence him. PP II 1 136 20
Forgive me; and if you persist in indifference, do not PP III 12 343 37
If they persist in the scheme they will find something--I MP I 13 128 35
PERSISTED (7)
that if her sister persisted in going, she would go SS II 3 156 15
to this, if he still persisted in this low connection, SS III 1 266 38
determined, if he persisted in considering her repeated PP I 19 109 22
In the first place, she persisted in disbelieving the PP I 23 127 5
She persisted in placing his scruples to her account, MP III 17 465 13
She persisted in a very determined, though very silent, P IV 2 135 34
He persisted in having loved none but her. P IV 11 241 61
PERSISTING (8)
when Marianne, after persisting in rising, confessed SS III 7 307 2
consequence of her persisting in this interference. PP III 15 360 2
and enquiries; and he unrepulsable was persisting in both. MP III 3 342 32
shame him from persisting any longer in addressing herself. MP III 15 438 5
not imagine Harriet's persisting to place her happiness in E I 17 143 13
disagreement, and his persisting to act in direct E III 15 446 20
teasing his wife, by persisting that he would go to the P IV 10 225 55
to go, & persisting in his station & his discourse.-- S 7 395 1
PERSISTS (1)
If therefore she actually persists in rejecting my suit, PP I 20 110 4
PERSON (286)
spirit, in making a person pre-determined to dislike, LS 7 254 3
much attached to another person as I can be to any one, I LS 10 258 2
Every person of sense however will know how to value & LS 14 265 5
In short when a person is always to deceive, it is LS 17 272 8
James Martin, the very person, as you may remember, whom LS 20 275 2
him; and tho' his person & address are very well, he LS 20 276 2
& once had said something in praise of her person. LS 22 280 1
have dictated against the person defaming me, that person, LS 22 282 6
person defaming me, that person, too, a Chit, a child, LS 22 282 6
for the interference, however friendly, of another person. LS 24 289 12
the contract between his person & manners, & those of LS 29 299 2
own person and disposition, were all equally against her. NA I 1 13 1
much for her person;--and not less unpropitious for NA I 1 13 1
shyness of a girl; her person pleasing, and, when in good NA I 2 18 1
imagination around his person and manners, and increased NA I 5 35 2
would not disgust a young person of taste; the substance NA I 5 38 4
of an unprejudiced person what her own conduct had really NA I 13 103 29
"The person, be it gentleman or lady, who has not pleasure NA I 14 106 7
others, which a sensible person would always wish to avoid. NA I 14 110 28
the same roof with the person whose society she mostly NA II 2 141 11
abode was no more to them than their superiority of person. NA II 2 141 12
of one man more than another--he is not the person." NA II 3 145 13
But you may be assured that I am the last person in the NA II 3 146 18
"what! always to be watched, in person or by proxy!" NA II 3 147 21
did not care if she were the last person up in the house. NA II 6 167 10
The domestic, unpretending merits of a person never known, NA II 9 196 23
the courage to apply in person for his father's consent, NA II 11 208 2
such ill-will against a person not connected, or, at least, NA II 13 226 25
had learnt from the very person who had suggested them, NA II 15 246 12
estate, and the person to whom he intended to bequeath it. SS I 1 3 1
good opinion by any peculiar graces of person or address. SS I 3 15 6
the admiration of a person who can understand their worth. SS I 3 17 18
He must have all Edward's virtues, and his person and SS I 3 18 20
as much upon acquaintance as his manners and person. SS I 4 20 9
not striking; and his person can hardly be called handsome, SS I 4 20 9
They were of course very anxious to see a person on whom SS I 6 31 8
could want to make her mind as captivating as her person. SS I 7 33 3
and so grateful, that his person, which was uncommonly SS I 9 42 9
Marianne herself had seen less of his person than the rest, SS I 9 43 11
His person and air were equal to what her fancy had ever SS I 9 43 11
not only a captivating person, but a natural ardour of SS I 10 48 7
did Elinor find a person who could in any degree claim the SS I 11 55 7
She was convinced that Margaret had fixed on a person, SS I 12 61 16
your own, and that there is no such person in existence." SS I 12 61 25
"Mr. Willoughby however is the only person who can have a SS I 13 68 70
The person is not tall enough for him, and has not his air. SS I 16 86 18
He was the only person in the world who could at that SS I 16 86 21
it as a reward on that person who wrote the ablest defence SS I 17 93 29
because a certain person that shall be nameless is gone!" SS I 18 100 20
To give such intelligence to a person who could not be SS I 20 115 49
actual elegance or grace, gave distinction to her person.-- SS I 21 120 6
in the company of a person who joined insincerity with SS I 22 127 2
person whose good opinion is so well worth having as yours. SS I 22 128 9
but surely there must be some mistake of person or name. SS I 22 131 29
John Dashwood, is the person I mean; you must allow that I SS I 22 131 30
you cannot be deceived as to the person it was drew for.-- SS I 22 131 35
Anne is the only person that knows of it, and she has no SS I 22 133 42
was the state of the person, by whom the expectation of SS II 1 140 3
tenderly attached is too much for an indifferent person." SS II 2 150 33
" 'tis because you are an indifferent person," said Lucy, SS II 2 150 34
without affection for the person who was to be his wife; SS II 2 151 41
will think me a very fit person to have the charge of you; SS II 3 153 2
towards the manners of a person, to whom she had often had SS II 3 156 15
very well; if a certain person who shall be nameless, had SS II 5 171 36
for she could not suppose it to be to any other person. SS II 5 171 38
mind of a very different person, who had no other SS II 7 184 16
strong resemblance between them, as well in mind as person. SS II 9 205 23
24
it had been made over some months before to another person. SS II 9 207 26
no interest in one person at least among their circle of SS II 10 215 12
that there was not a person at liberty to attend to their SS II 11 220 3
the remembrance of a person and face, of strong natural, SS II 11 220 3
In a moment I shall see the person that all my happiness SS II 12 232 13
towards the very person--for Lucy was particularly SS II 12 232 16
but were together without the relief of any other person. SS II 13 241 19
recollect that I am the last person in the world to do it. SS II 13 244 46
on any particular person, it is not meant--it is not fit-- SS III 1 263 27
marry a woman superior in person and understanding to half SS III 1 263 27
forced on my by the very person herself, whose prior SS III 1 263 29
engaged to another person!--such a suspicion could never SS III 1 266 38
of any person whom you have a regard for, Mrs. Jennings. SS III 1 268 45
Colonel write himself?--sure, he is the proper person." SS III 4 286 17

that which to any other person would have been the easiest SS III 4 287 24
even if we had not been able to give them in person. SS III 4 288 28
Edward is only to hold the living till the person to whom SS III 5 295 12
My mother was the first person who told me of it, and I, SS III 5 299 35
in leaving behind him a person so well able to assist or SS III 7 309 5
must have struck a less interested person with concern. SS III 7 313 20
Your sister's lovely person and interesting manners could SS III 8 319 29
or deliver it in person, was a point of long debate. SS III 8 323 40
One person I was sure would represent me as capable of SS III 8 331 69
to every advantage of person and talents, united a SS III 8 331 70
to have weight; by that person of uncommon attraction, SS III 9 333 2
And his person, his manners too, are all in his favour. SS III 9 338 20
the entrance of a third person, and Elinor withdrew to SS III 9 339 27
it horrible to suspect a person, who has been what he had SS III 10 345 20
seemed the only person surprised at her not giving more. SS III 14 374 5
may not seem exactly the person to attract him--yet I SS III 14 375 9
I am sure I shd never have forgiven the person who kept me W 320 2
Of the females, Ly. Osborne had by much the finest person;- W 329 9
that moment in quest of a person to employ on the errand, W 338 18
I allow his person & air to be good--& that his manners to W 342 19
do us the honour of giving us your good wishes in person.-- W 347 21
In her person there was nothing remarkable; her manners W 349 23
a glance over his own person, I am highly endebted to your W 357 28
room by his fine, tall person, handsome features, noble PP I 3 10 5
You have liked many a stupider person." PP I 4 14 5
A person may be proud without being vain. PP I 5 20 20
defects of the person with whom you are to pass your life." PP I 6 23 10
"It is a rule with me, that a person who can write a long PP I 10 48 19
you think ill of that person for complying with the desire, PP I 10 50 37
to his ideas of right, than in any other person present. PP I 10 51 46
and cheating a person of their premeditated contempt. PP I 10 52 50
by a person whose first object in life is a joke." PP I 11 57 20
"The person of whom I speak, is a gentleman and a stranger. PP I 13 61 3
a person whom I never saw in the whole course of my life." PP I 13 61 4
any amends, I shall not be the person to discourage him." PP I 13 63 14
such behaviour in a person of rank--such affability and PP I 14 66 1
as far beyond them all in person, countenance, air, and PP I 16 76 3
You could not have met with a person more capable of PP I 16 77 10
event, or any particular person, for though they each, PP I 17 86 10
third person; in which case you may be sure of my pardon." PP I 18 95 49
was talking to that one person (Lady Lucas) freely, openly, PP I 18 98 63
an active, useful sort of person, not brought up high, but PP I 19 105 10
person. ship she valued beyond that of any other person. PP I 22 123 3
person to blame, and saying your opinion of him is sunk. PP II 1 136 14
I am always glad to get a young person well placed out. PP II 6 165 32
recommended another young person, who was merely mentioned PP II 6 165 32
give your opinion very decidedly for so young a person.-- PP II 6 165 36
but in person and address most truly the gentleman. PP II 7 170 9
to Darcy, much more than to any other person in the room. PP II 8 172 2
I am particularly unlucky in meeting with a person so well PP II 8 174 15
have no right to suppose that Bingley was the person meant. PP II 10 185 24
But the person who advanced, was now near enough to see PP II 12 195 2
that I had no other person to provide for, and I could not PP II 12 201 5
that friendship between a person capable of it, and such PP II 13 208 6
capital news, and about a certain person that we all like." PP II 16 220 8
youth and a tolerable person; and from the ignorance and PP II 18 231 18
"I have heard much of your master's fine person," said Mrs. PP III 1 247 12
"There is also one other person in the party," he PP III 1 256 63
in criticisms on Elizabeth's person, behaviour, and dress. PP III 3 270 12
of the person who had mostly engaged their attention. PP III 3 272 20
And we all know that Wickham has every charm of person and PP III 5 284 10
every body but the person to whose ill judging indulgence PP III 5 287 34
"But to expose the former faults of any person, without PP III 5 291 56
relations he had now living, better than any other person." PP III 6 295 6
must be to know how a person unconnected with any of us, PP III 9 320 33
He did not judge your father to be a person whom he could PP III 10 323 2
obligations to a person who could never receive a return. PP III 10 326 3
information, he was the person, to whom the whole family PP III 11 334 36
"If I have, I shall be the last person to confess it." PP III 14 354 37
you, or to any person so wholly unconnected with me." PP III 14 358 68
The feelings of the person who wrote, and the person who PP III 16 368 23
sure I should be the last person in the world to withhold MP I 1 6 6
care of any creditable person that may chance to be going. MP I 1 8 8
between the cousins in person, as education had given to MP I 2 13 4
finding something to fear in every person and place. MP I 2 14 8
saw them becoming in person, manner, and accomplishments, MP I 2 20 33
on being the first person made acquainted with any fatal MP I 4 34 2
more be made to his person than to his situation in life. MP I 4 42 18
"to what any young person says on the subject of marriage. MP I 4 43 25
set it down that they have not yet seen the right person." MP I 4 43 25
or good quality in the person, who have found themselves MP I 5 46 22
trick for a young person to be always lolling upon a sofa; MP I 7 71 34
did, between the selfishness of another person and his own. MP I 12 119 25
There was one person, however, in the house whom he could MP II 2 187 3
may be chiefly on your person, you must put up with it, MP II 3 197 6
with the person one feels most agreeable in the world. MP II 4 210 21
proper plan it is for a person at your time of life, with MP II 4 213 40
a very different person from the one he had equipped seven MP II 6 233 16
from the alteration of person had vanished, and she could MP II 6 233 17
There is one person in company who does not like to have MP II 7 251 61
in his eyes than in those of any other person in the house. MP II 8 254 10
rather perhaps have been obliged to some other person. MP II 8 258 18
To take what had been the gift of another person--of a MP II 8 259 20
to--I am the last person to think that could be--but they MP II 9 263 16
Being the only young person at home, I consider you as the MP II 11 287 18
I am the person to give the consequence so justly her due. MP II 12 297 33
of mind as lovely as of person; whose modesty had MP III 2 326 3
if we would attend to it, than any other person can be. MP III 11 412 23
town who have so good a person, height, and air; and I MP III 12 416 2
I looked upon him as the sort of person to be made a fuss MP III 14 433 13
by the sight of the person whom, in the blindness of her MP III 16 448 2
occupied each with the person quite dependant on them, at MP III 16 449 4
the last speaker, by the person who could get hold of and MP III 16 450 11
their indulgences to a person who had been able to attach MP III 17 463 7
had there been no young person of either sex belonging to MP III 17 465 13
person, and quite determined to continue the acquaintance. E I 3 23 9
is the very last sort of person to raise my curiosity. E I 4 29 14
young man, but his person had no other advantage; and when E I 4 31 27
The older a person grows, Harriet, the more important it E I 4 33 36
Mr. Elton was the very person fixed on by Emma for driving E I 4 34 44
He was reckoned very handsome; his person much admired in E I 4 35 45
In her mother she lost the only person able to cope with E I 5 37 9
"Oh! you would rather talk of her person than her mind, E I 5 39 17
"I have not a fault to find with her person," he replied. E I 5 39 21
hands of some intelligent person whose taste could be E I 6 48 40
If you prefer Mr. Martin to every other person; if you E I 7 53 21
comes to compare them, person and manners, there is no E I 7 54 30
The attentions of a certain person can hardly be among the E I 7 56 41
must find other people charming--one other person at least. E I 10 84 10 11
the question: and I do not wish to see any such person. E I 10 84 13
however, is just such another pretty kind of young person. E I 12 104 47 48
very person to suit her in age, character and condition. E I 14 119 5
To be constantly living with an ill-tempered person, must E I 14 121 17
any body equal to him in person or goodness --and did, in E I 17 142 12
Had she been a person of consequence herself, he would E I 18 149 26
"He is a person I never think of from one month's end to E I 18 150 36
given her in a pleasing person, good understanding, and E II 2 163 3
Emma was sorry;--to have to pay civilities to a person she E II 2 166 11
which, whether of person or of mind, she saw so little in E II 2 167 12
of perfection in Highbury, both in person and mind." E II 3 174 38

I mean in person--tall, and with that sort of look--and E II 3 176 44
Where I have a regard, I always think a person well- E II 3 176 49
situations, that a young person, who either marries or E II 4 181 1
every recommendation of person and mind; to be handsome, E II 4 181 2
But Mr. Elton, in person, had driven away all such cares. E II 4 185 11
up with astonishment at the youth and beauty of her person. E II 5 192 29
of feeling--there was one person, I think, who must have E II 6 202 35
One cannot love a reserved person." E II 6 203 40
There was one person among his new acquaintance in Surry, E II 7 206 4
If Col. Campbell is not the person, who can be?" E II 8 216 27
of visiting no fresh person; and that, though he had his E II 8 221 48
I think he is just the person to do it, even without being E II 8 226 79
with a smile at Emma, "the person has not chosen ill. E II 10 241 8
"Ah! sir--but a thoughtless young person will sometimes E II 11 252 31
properer person for shewing us how to do away difficulties. E II 11 255 55
Her person was rather good; her face not unpretty; but E II 14 270 4
would be the very person for you to go into public with." E II 14 275 32
Astonished that the person who had brought me up should be E II 14 279 52
Always the first person to be thought of! E II 14 279 52
could now invite the very person whom she really wanted to E II 16 291 5
person there, and had otherwise a fancy for the place. E III 1 317 7
had happened to the very person, and at the very hour, E III 3 335 10
very person was chancing to pass by to rescue her!-- E III 3 335 10
from an idea that the person whom you might prefer, would E III 4 341 35
but Miss Woodhouse was the very person she was in quest of. E III 6 362 43
I do not consider myself at all a fortunate person." E III 6 365 64
"Mrs. Elton, I suppose, has been the person to whom Miss E III 8 380 14
that so much could be given to a young person like Jane." E III 8 382 23
past coldness; and the person, whom she had been so many E III 9 389 16
possible that I could be supposed to mean any other person. E III 11 405 18
then said, appeared to me to relate to a different person. E III 11 406 21
had been the person; and now--it is possible -----." E III 11 407 26
by the person, whose counsels had never led her right.-- E III 11 408 33
at all attached to the person we are speaking of, as it E III 13 426 17
and as you were the person slighted, you will forgive me E III 14 437 8
but I was the injured person, injured by her coldness, and E III 14 441 8
The very last person whom one should expect to be E III 16 458 42
and shake hands with you--and to give you joy in person." E III 18 476 48
Elliot's character; vanity of person and of situation. P III 1 4 5
We must be serious and decided--for, after all, the person P III 2 12 4
felt that were any young person, in similar circumstances, P III 4 29 8
In person, she was inferior to both sisters, and had, even P III 5 37 21
and vigour of form, which gave importance to her person. P III 6 48 18
a mother's feelings, are a great deal the properest person. P III 7 57 16
not endurable to a third person, or driving out in a gig, P III 9 73 2
she heard some other person crossing the little vestibule. P III 9 79 25
of such a person?--or, of any person I may say. P III 10 87 23
which may be just as well performed by another person?-- P III 12 103 2
I always look upon her as able to persuade a person to any P III 12 103 4
thirty, and, though not handsome, had an agreeable person. P III 12 105 7
back a far more useful person in the old nursery-maid of P IV 1 121 3
book, and not know when a person speaks to him, or when P IV 2 132 19
I have really a curiosity to see the person who can give P IV 2 132 20
her "less thin in her person, in her checks; her skin, her P IV 4 145 3
when she was away, as a person in Bath who drinks the P IV 4 146 5
somewhat different person from what the other had imagined. P IV 5 153 6
the existence of such a person was known in Camden-Place. P IV 5 156 14
The idea of Louisa Musgrove turned into a person of P IV 6 167 20
It was a concert for the benefit of a person patronised by P IV 7 180 32
would be the properest person to fetch a surgeon, you P IV 8 182 6
Your person, your disposition, accomplishments, manner-- P IV 8 187 32
last night with the person, whom you think the most P IV 9 194 16
in the world, the person who interests you at this present P IV 9 194 16
arrival of the very person whose presence must really be P IV 10 213 10
I saw you with the very person who had guided you in that P IV 11 245 74
have been one person more my enemy even than that lady? P IV 11 247 82
have known of such a person, at least I may venture to say S 1 366 1
He held it indeed as certain, that no person cd be really S 2 373 1
cd be really well, no person, (however upheld for the S 2 373 1
suitable knowledge of the person with whom she might now S 3 375 1
to your Beau Monde in person, we are doing our utmost to S 5 387 1
& abrupt, as of a person who valued herself on being free- S 6 391 1
very unlike her sister in person or manner--tho' more thin S 10 413 1
all the advantage of his person as a screen, & was very S 10 415 1
her to be the sort of person who, when once she is S 12 424 1

PERSON'S (14)

person's courage that could sit down on purpose to do it." NA I 14 109 24
to act upon such a person's feelings, age, situation, and NA II 1 132 20
This person's suspicions, therefore, I have had to oppose, SS III 1 263 29
to have settled that matter before this person's death?-- SS III 5 295 12
louder than any other person's, was enumerating the PP II 16 222 21
I have not been used to submit to any person's whims. PP III 14 356 48
be more thought of than any other person's in the room. E II 7 210 19
any real knowledge of a person's disposition that Bath, or E III 7 372 40
I have another person's interest at present so much at E III 15 448 30
addition of that person's company whom she knew he loved, E III 17 465 28
to any other person's, gave her much more pleasure for P III 6 47 13
compare them in excellence to only one person's manners. P IV 3 143 18
She knew it well; and she remembered another person's look P IV 4 148 9
there was now another person's claims to be taken into S 3 377 1

PERSONABLENESS (1)

of their personableness when they cease to be quite young." P III 3 20 17

PERSONAGE (3)

was scarcely a less interesting personage than to herself. PP III 2 261 6
Miss Woodhouse was so great a personage in Highbury, that E I 3 25 15
most deplorable looking personage you can imagine, his P III 3 19 16

PERSONAGES (1)

as one of the most illustrious personages in this land." PP III 15 362 14

PERSONAL (48)

of her previous to this personal acquaintance; but against LS 8 255 2
it will at least be handsome to take your personal leave. LS 35 305 1
her father and mother remark on her personal improvement. NA I 1 15 2
of Catherine Morland's personal and mental endowments, NA I 2 18 1
Her eldest daughter had great personal beauty, and the NA I 4 34 8
without personal conceit, might be something uncommon.-- NA I 10 72 8
enhancement of their personal charms, there is a portion NA I 14 111 29
early the next morning to make his personal inquiries. SS I 10 46 1
Of their personal charms he had not required a second SS I 10 46 1
trust her on so short a personal acquaintance, with a SS II 1 142 7
soon to receive your personal assurance of its being SS II 7 187 40
of her wretchedness, the personal sympathy of her mother, SS II 10 214 6
been a beauty, in the loss of her personal attractions. SS II 12 236 43
Edward might have some personal knowledge of his future SS III 13 372 46
came to give their personal invitation for the long PP I 17 86 9
Their taking her home, and affording her their personal PP III 7 305 36
power to take any share in the personal charge of her. MP I 1 9 10
at the expense of any personal trouble, and the charge was MP I 4 35 5
attributing all her personal beauty, as Mrs. Norris seemed MP II 10 276 13
from the personal intreaty of the young man himself. MP III 1 320 44
sensations, and much personal kindness, had still been MP III 6 367 5
have not described, from personal observation, better than MP III 14 429 2
almost as much from the personal disrespect with which she MP III 16 450 10
She then repeated some warm personal praise which she had E I 4 34 43
sure of relief from her personal attention and kindness, E I 10 86 24
but hardly any degree of personal compliment could have E I 11 93 5
business, of taking a personal leave of Mr. Woodhouse, of E I 17 140 2
except what are merely personal; that he is well grown and E I 18 149 28
no remarkable degree of personal beauty; is not, by any E II 1 161 26
common civility in our personal intercourse with each E II 15 286 23
Few women could think more of their personal appearance P III 1 4 5
Elizabeth did not quite equal her father in personal P III 1 6 12
attractions than any merely personal might have been. P III 5 34 12

personal misfortunes, though I know you must fifty times. P III 5 35 14
"There is hardly any personal defect," replied Anne, " P III 5 35 15
open look, in no respect lessening his personal advantages. P III 7 61 34
Personal size and mental sorrow have certainly no P III 8 68 30
to every personal comfort high--and this is what I do. P III 8 69 35
Such personal praise might have struck her, especially as P IV 4 146 4
her sense of personal respect to her father prevented her. P IV 5 158 20
service too, without robbing him of one personal grace! P IV 7 179 28
equally disabled from personal exertion by her state of P IV 9 210 98
very much struck by his personal claims, and felt that his P IV 12 248 2
was impelled by a personal knowledge of their narrow S 3 378 1
Not that he had any personal concern in the success of the S 4 383 1
"Sir Edw: Denham, said Charlotte, with such personal S 7 400 1
With such personal advantages as he knew himself to S 8 405 2
sort of attachment which her personal charms had raised.-- S 8 405 2

PERSONALLY (9)

it personally in town, ceased writing minutely or often. LS 42 311 1
pray, are you personally acquainted with your sister-in- SS I 22 128 3
I have not known you long to be sure, personally at least, SS I 22 132 42
had long wanted to be personally known to the family, to SS II 12 231 9
and personally intreat her good offices in his favour.-- SS III 13 372 45
You can have been personally acquainted with very few of a MP I 11 110 24
and knowing nothing personally of those who had sinned, or MP III 15 444 26
add this praise, that I do not think her personally vain. E I 5 39 21
asked even if you were personally altered, little P IV 11 243 67

PERSONS (40)

They were viewing the country with the eyes of persons NA I 14 110 28
occasion, without attention to persons or circumstances. SS I 10 48 9
I cannot compare my aunt's method with any other persons, W 318 2
That is my idea of good breeding; and those persons who PP I 9 44 27
"I know very well, madam," said he, "that when persons sit PP I 16 83 50
of some of the very persons of whom they had been speaking; PP I 17 86 9
being so much design in the world as some persons imagine." PP II 1 136 16
displease you by saying what I think of persons you esteem. PP II 1 136 19
separation of two young persons, whose affection could be PP II 12 196 5
despised the persons who so assiduously courted you. PP III 18 380 5
the direction of two persons so extravagant in their wants, PP III 19 387 8
gratitude towards the persons who, by bringing her into PP III 19 388 13
being one of those persons who think nothing can be MP I 3 32 63
expected from the private devotions of such persons? MP I 9 87 16
but from prejudiced persons, whose opinions you have been MP I 11 110 24
few persons present that were not disposed to praise her. MP II 10 276 13
there could not be two persons in existence, whose MP II 12 296 29
you will consider times, persons, and probabilities, and MP III 1 313 12
be owing such felicity to persons in whose feelings and MP III 14 435 15
Miss Taylor has been used to have two persons to please; E I 1 11 34
set, were the only persons invited to meet them;--the E I 13 108 4
"Yes Mr. Dixon and Miss Campbell were the persons; and I E II 6 202 30
The scene enlarged; two persons appeared; Mrs. Weston and E II 9 233 25
The persons to be invited, required little thought. E II 16 291 5
Mr. Woodhouse considered eight persons at dinner together E II 16 292 7
rooms before any other persons came, that she could not E III 2 319 2
sweepgate opened, and two persons entered whom she had E III 3 332 3
Miss Bates, which few persons listened to, she also found E III 5 344 3
First, as being the means of bringing persons of obscure P III 3 19 16
how nonsensical some persons are about their place, P III 6 46 10
world, but I know it is taken notice of by many persons." P III 6 46 10
of persons and voices--but a few minutes ended it. P III 7 59 25
It was mere lively chat,--such as any young persons, on an P III 10 84 7
was more than she could say for many other persons in Bath. P IV 2 136 36
and ceaseless buzz of persons walking through, had P IV 8 183 11
conference between two persons of totally opposite P IV 10 222 39
enumeration of the persons invited, and the continually P IV 10 227 69
sight of several persons now coming to their assistance. S 1 364 1
they had passed--& the persons who approached, were a well- S 1 364 1
Teapots &c as there were persons in company, Miss P. S 10 416 1

PERSONS' (3)

of business, having two persons' cards to manage as well MP II 7 240 8
think so ill of any two persons' understanding as to E II 5 193 35
spread farther, and other persons' reception of it tried. E III 17 465 28

PERSPECTIVE (1)

engagement with him was in continual perspective. MP II 10 278 20

PERSPECTIVES (1)

and perspectives--lights and shades;--and Catherine was so NA I 14 111 29

PERSPIRATION (2)

of the day, would throw me into such a Perspiration!-- S 10 416 1
I am very subject to Perspiration, and there cannot be a S 10 416 1

PERSUADABLE (3)

Upon the whole, she was very persuadable; and it being E II 7 208 9
it to her friend, and found her very persuadable.-- E III 16 451 3
him to feel, that a persuadable temper might sometimes be P III 12 116 72

PERSUADABLENESS (1)

to recommend her as a wife by shewing her persuadableness. MP II 10 281 34

PERSUADE (84)

as can persuade me of her being prepossessed in my favour. LS 5 249 1
& to persuade Reginald that she has scandalously belied me. LS 7 254 3
of my sister, as to persuade her that the happiness of Mr LS 14 264 3
do not take my part, & persuade her to break it off, I LS 21 279 1
"But you should not persuade me that I think so very much NA I 6 41 17
This brother of yours would persuade me out of my senses, NA I 7 46 9
My sweet Catherine, do support me, persuade your brother NA I 8 57 23
"Mrs. Allen, you must persuade her to go," was the general NA I 11 86 49
used to be so hard to persuade; you once were the kindest, NA I 13 99 10
I do not think you would have found me hard to persuade." NA I 13 105 37
Catherine endeavoured to persuade her, as she was herself NA I 15 119 14
continued, "why do not you persuade him to go away? NA II 4 150 4
"Then you will persuade him to go away?" NA II 4 150 5
but pardon me if I cannot even endeavour to persuade him. NA II 4 150 6
curricle, and I cannot persuade him to buy my brown mare. SS I 10 52 28
If I could persuade myself that my manners were perfectly SS I 17 94 44
me persuade the Miss Dashwoods to go to town this winter." SS I 20 110 9
him herself; and to persuade her to check her agitation, SS II 6 177 15
I shall persuade her if I can to go early to bed, for I am SS II 8 195 15
his knees too, to perswade her to let them stay till they SS III 1 259 7
Sure you do not mean to persuade me that the Colonel only SS III 4 291 53
He merely meant to persuade her to give up the engagement; SS III 14 376 11
But I knew I should persuade you at last. PP I 2 7 24
"Miss Eliza Bennet, let me persuade you to follow my PP I 11 56 11
and repeatedly tried to persuade Miss Bennet that it would PP I 12 59 3
her mother's words, or persuade her to describe her PP I 18 99 64
and entreating her to persuade her friend Lizzy to comply PP I 20 113 26
and tries to persuade you that he does not care about you." PP I 21 118 18
will be in her power to persuade him that instead of being PP I 21 119 20
could Elizabeth persuade her to consider it as improbable. PP I 23 127 7
nor endeavour to persuade yourself or me, that selfishness PP II 1 135 13
of friends will persuade a young man of independent PP II 2 140 7
She endeavoured to persuade herself that she did not PP II 3 147 25
persuade herself that he is really partial to Miss Darcy. PP II 3 148 26
To persuade him against returning into Hertfordshire, when PP II 12 199 5
Whatever he might afterwards persuade her to, it was not PP III 5 292 61
had been to persuade her to quit her present disgraceful PP III 10 322 2
meet, reason with, persuade, and finally bribe, the man PP III 10 326 3
"But why should you wish to persuade me that I feel more PP III 12 343 36
without attempting to persuade her ladyship to return into PP III 14 358 74
in being so surprised, and persuade her to speak openly. MP I 2 15 10
you took to reason and persuade me out of my fears, and MP I 3 27 36
she had tried in vain to persuade her brother to settle MP I 4 41 16
"My dear sister," said Mary, "if you can persuade him into MP I 4 42 21
If you can persuade Henry to marry, you must have the MP I 4 42 21
trying to persuade the others that there were some fine MP I 14 131 6
Perhaps you may persuade her." MP I 17 158 3
I was ready to move heaven and earth to persuade my sister, MP II 2 189 3
to persuade my sister, and at last I did persuade her. MP II 2 189 3
and the roads almost impassable, but I did persuade her." MP II 2 189 3
the easiest self-deceit persuade herself that she was MP II 4 205 2
with her, you never will persuade me that it is in MP II 6 230 6
You cannot suppose me capable of trying to persuade you to MP III 2 330 16
Well, though I may not be able to persuade you into MP III 4 351 34
attempts to influence or persuade; but that every thing MP III 5 356 2
But Mrs. Norris wanted to persuade her that Fanny could be MP III 6 371 15
"Would she not then persuade her daughters to take MP III 10 401 10
"We must persuade Henry to marry her," said she, "and what MP III 16 456 29
Persuade him to let things take their course. MP III 16 457 29
hopeful undertaking to persuade her that her warm and MP III 17 470 25
You never could persuade her to read half so much as you E I 5 37 7
and tried very much to persuade him to put off his journey E I 8 68 58
I think, Emma, I shall try and persuade her to stay longer E I 9 80 66
as usual, tried to persuade his daughter to stay behind E I 17 140 1
to persuade them away with all her usual promptitude. E I 17 141 4
and falsehoods, and persuade himself that he has hit upon E I 18 148 24
points) he could with time persuade her to any thing. E II 8 221 49
Undoubtedly, if you wish it, I will endeavour to persuade E II 11 255 58
I certainly will not persuade myself to feel more than I E II 13 264 2
help to persuade him into it, which was done pretty soon.-- E III 2 325 31
observed, he could not persuade himself to think entirely E III 5 343 2
power to place there and persuade her father to use, E III 5 347 18
He wished to persuade Mr. Woodhouse, as well as Emma, to E III 6 356 29
reasonable, very just displeasure I had to persuade away. E III 14 443 8
"If we can persuade your father to all this," said Lady P III 2 12 4
"I wish you could persuade Mary not to be always fancying P III 6 44 7
I am sure, Anne, if you would, you might persuade him that P III 6 44 7
begun, Anne was left to persuade herself, as well as she P III 6 49 25
be able to persuade him to do any thing he did not like. P III 7 57 18
My doubt is, whether any thing could persuade him to leave P III 12 102 2
I always look upon her as able to persuade a person to any P III 12 103 4
she was privy, and persuade them all to go to Lyme at once. P IV 1 122 5
a week, and wanted to persuade Captain Benwick to go with P IV 2 133 25
the kingdom, you wd not persuade me of there being a S 1 366 1

PERSUADED (127)

She has already almost persuaded me of her being warmly LS 6 251 1
In short, I am persuaded that his continuing here beyond LS 8 255 1
former ill-opinion, & persuaded him not merely to forget, LS 11 259 1
is now he is persuaded only a scandalous invention. LS 11 259 1
greatest pleasure, & am persuaded that you & my brother LS 20 276 5
her heart I am persuaded, she sincerely wishes him gone. LS 20 278 10
But I was persuaded that her objections to him did not LS 24 289 12
I am persuaded the gout is brought on, or kept off at LS 28 298 1
nothing should have persuaded her to go out with the NA I 9 69 51
She felt almost persuaded that Miss Tilney was at home, NA I 12 91 3
a temper, to be so easily persuaded by those she loved. NA I 13 98 2
If I could not be persuaded into doing what I thought NA I 13 101 22
her, as she was herself persuaded, that her father and NA I 15 119 14
Of her unhappiness in marriage, she felt persuaded. NA II 7 180 37
He loved her, I am persuaded, as well as it was possible NA II 9 197 27
"I am persuaded that he never did." NA II 12 219 9
as for herself she was persuaded that a much smaller SS I 3 14 2
already a cold, was persuaded by Elinor to stay at home. SS I 12 62 29
I am persuaded that Mrs. Smith suspects his regard for SS I 15 78 26
How is it to be supposed that Willoughby, persuaded as he SS I 15 80 36
of their parties, was persuaded by her mother, who could SS II 1 143 9
your brother might be persuaded to give him Norland living; SS II 2 149 25
Mrs. Dashwood, persuaded that such an excursion would be SS II 3 155 7
Elinor, persuaded that he had some communication to make SS II 5 172 40
which she was at length persuaded to take, were of use; SS II 7 191 65
"She has been indisposed all day, and we have persuaded SS II 8 198 32
Why would you be persuaded by my uncle, sir Robert, SS II 14 251 13
that she could not be persuaded at first to believe, and SS III 1 261 13
away by his wife, was persuaded at last by Colonel Brandon SS III 7 308 5
Mrs. Jennings would have persuaded her at its conclusion SS III 7 315 27
to address her, and I persuaded myself to think that SS III 8 323 40
words of Marianne she persuaded herself to think that SS III 10 340 3
& others could never be persuaded that she were half so W 337 17
He was persuaded without much difficulty to throw off his W 355 28
as soon as she could be persuaded to beleive it no W 361 30
to know me, I am persuaded she would find me in every PP I 19 107 14
gallantry; "and I am persuaded that when sanctioned by the PP I 19 109 21
but Mrs. Bennet, who had persuaded herself that her PP I 20 112 20
their society, she was persuaded that Jane must soon cease PP I 21 116 8
and Elizabeth felt persuaded that no real confidence could PP I 23 127 9
as this; for were I persuaded that Charlotte had any PP II 1 135 13
and felt persuaded of her sister's ready acquiescence. PP II 2 141 11
journeys--and I am persuaded my friend would not call PP II 9 179 22
as a child, that she was persuaded to believe herself in PP II 12 201 5
and stedfastly was she persuaded that he could have no PP II 13 204 1
He who, she had been persuaded, would avoid her as his PP III 2 265 16
Persuaded as Miss Bingley was that Darcy admired Elizabeth, PP III 3 271 16
and though almost persuaded that nothing could be done for PP III 4 280 26
account, was persuaded of his never intending to marry her. PP III 5 283 8
Though her brother and sister were persuaded that there PP III 5 288 40
brother, and persuaded him to come to Gracechurch street. PP III 6 295 5
We are persuaded that he has pledged himself to assist Mr. PP III 7 306 46
with some difficulty, persuaded her to wait, till her PP III 7 307 48
and her uncle had been persuaded that affection and PP III 10 327 3
every thing, she was persuaded, would be hastening to the PP III 11 337 54
and was really persuaded that she talked as much as ever. PP III 11 337 56
guarded than formerly, persuaded Elizabeth, that if left PP III 12 340 13
Seriously, however, she felt tolerably persuaded that all PP III 13 346 20
"Had you then persuaded yourself that I should?" PP III 16 369 25
But his anger, I am persuaded, lasted no longer than he PP III 16 371 45
though you have often persuaded me to be reconciled to MP I 3 25 18
enforced it warmly, persuaded that no judgment could be MP I 6 61 58
persuaded, that when she does not ride, she ought to walk. MP I 7 73 55
properly pressed and persuaded, was not long in accepting MP I 8 76 7
She looks the part, and I am persuaded will do it MP I 14 135 16
do it very ill, I feel persuaded she would do it worse," MP I 14 136 21
of any body who can be persuaded to act--no matter whom; MP I 16 155 22
them) as are never to be persuaded into love against their MP II 6 231 11
I am now persuaded she is the very one to make you happy. MP II 12 294 19
little Fanny might be persuaded into explaining away that MP III 3 341 31
Edmund was not unwilling to be persuaded to engage in the MP III 4 345 4
I am perfectly persuaded that the tempers had better be MP III 4 349 23
"I am persuaded that he does not think as he ought, on MP III 4 350 31
feelings, you will be persuaded into them I trust. MP III 4 351 34
being persuaded to stay at Lessingby till that very day! MP III 4 354 48
her, she might not have persuaded herself into receiving MP III 5 356 3
contrast, she was quite persuaded of his being MP III 11 413 32
persuaded myself that you would understand my silence.-- MP III 13 420 2
little writing, and was persuaded of its having the air of MP III 15 437 2
But still I cannot imagine she would not be persuaded." E I 6 44 18
themselves unbidden to your mind, I am persuaded. E I 7 51 11
mind to walk out, was persuaded by his daughter not to E I 8 57 2
You persuaded her to refuse him." E I 8 60 36
had not felt persuaded of her not being disinclined to him. E I 8 63 42
the part which he was persuaded Emma had taken in the E I 8 66 55
Mr. Woodhouse was persuaded to think it a possible thing E I 13 108 2
she was very strongly persuaded; and though not meaning to E I 14 119 5
"If I had not persuaded Harriet into liking the man, I E I 16 134 2
Mrs. Dixon has persuaded her father and mother to come E II 1 159 20
As to connection, there Emma was perfectly easy; persuaded, E II 4 183 9
He could not be persuaded that so many good-looking houses E II 6 198 5
At last he was persuaded to move on from the front of the E II 6 198 6
itself, that he had persuaded his aunt where his uncle E II 8 221 49
"I am persuaded that you can be as insincere as your E II 9 234 33
This was very kind of you to be persuaded to come. E II 10 240 5

which Mr. Woodhouse was persuaded to spend with his E II 11 247 2
be persuaded to join them and give your advice on the spot. E II 11 253 39
Well, I was persuaded there were two. E III 2 329 45
carry you far, unless you are persuaded of his liking you. E III 4 342 39
persuaded--Miss Smith, you walk as if you were tired. E III 5 345 11
I really was persuaded of Mrs. Weston's having mentioned E III 5 345 13
or persuaded out, his patient listener and sympathizer. E III 6 357 33
Mrs. Weston was at last persuaded to believe, or to say, E III 6 361 41
Mrs. Weston might be persuaded away by her husband to the E III 6 361 42
guidable man, to be persuaded into any thing by his nephew. E III 9 388 13
to each other--and we were persuaded that it was so.-- E III 10 396 43
than her husband is persuaded to act exactly opposite to E III 10 398 55
was persuaded that she must herself have been the worst. E III 12 421 17
Miss Fairfax has been persuaded to spend the day with us.-- E III 18 476 45
he, "of my uncle's being persuaded to pay a visit at E III 18 477 57
and who was perfectly persuaded that nothing would be done P III 2 13 7
She was persuaded to believe the engagement a wrong thing-- P III 4 27 5
She was persuaded that under every disadvantage of P III 4 29 8
a long walk," Anne felt persuaded, by the looks of the two P III 10 83 4
No,--I have no idea of being so easily persuaded. P III 10 87 23
and that therefore, she persuaded Anne to refuse him." P III 10 89 33
would never be persuaded that we could be happy together. P III 10 92 45
She, however, was soon persuaded to think differently. P III 12 114 59
He and Mary had been persuaded to go early to their inn P IV 1 121 2
She was persuaded that any tolerably pleasing young woman P IV 6 167 19
She was persuaded by Lady Russell's countenance that she P IV 8 189 44
It was just possible that she might have been persuaded by P IV 9 211 102
to, but was afterwards persuaded to think might do very P IV 11 230 5
All that Mr Heywood himself could be persuaded to promise S 2 374 1
learning her situation, persuaded her to accept such a S 3 378 1
in her Gum, I persuaded her to attack the disorder there. S 5 387 1
He has persuaded her to engage in the same speculation--& S 7 402 1

PERSUADING (14)

have been very far from persuading my husband to dispose LS 5 249 1
my part with her, & persuading her to send Sir James away, LS 21 279 1
"There is no persuading you to change your mind, brandon, SS I 13 65 32
often had difficulty in persuading Marianne to behave with SS II 3 156 15
had some difficulty in persuading her sister to go, for SS II 5 170 28
pain still farther by persuading her, that he was kept SS II 12 231 11
his father of it; no persuading him to believe that it was SS II 14 248 5
am not without hopes of persuading them to confine the MP I 16 155 16
We had had a great deal of trouble in persuading him to E I 6 46 21
Oh! that I had been satisfied with persuading her not to E I 16 137 11
thinking that he was persuading her to speak to me --(do E II 3 178 52
and his wife's persuading him to it, out of care for his E III 5 345 14
She saw, that in persuading herself, in fancying, in E III 11 412 45
persuading them to a complete, than to half a Reformation. P III 2 13 5

PERSUASION (45)

had in view; and this persuasion did not incline her to a NA I 8 59 35
"Persuasion is not at command; but pardon me if I cannot NA II 4 150 6
Their persuasion that the General would, upon this ground NA II 11 208 1
had given her, and the persuasion of his being by far too NA II 13 222 8
in other words, that a persuasion of her partiality for NA II 15 243 9
Under a mistaken persuasion of her possessions and claims, NA II 15 244 11
She speedily comprehended all his merits; the persuasion SS I 3 16 13
What a softener of the heart was this persuasion! SS II 1 140 1
with the melancholy persuasion that Edward was not only SS II 2 151 41
persuasion of my sister's being engaged to Mr. Willoughby? SS II 7 181 9
Her sister's earnest, though gentle persuasion, however, SS II 8 197 25
gaily smiling, from the persuasion of bringing comfort, SS II 9 202 5
6
her persuasion that Lucy could not stay much longer. SS II 13 244 43
justify Mrs. Jennings's persuasion of his attachment, and SS III 6 305 16
mind the persuasion that he should see Marianne no more. SS III 7 309 7
and so strong was the persuasion that she did, in spite of SS III 7 316 29
She feared that under this persuasion she had been unjust, SS III 11 356 46
Nothing but such a persuasion could have prevented his SS III 13 367 21
the persuasion and delight of each observing friend. SS III 14 379 17
at all shake her purpose by his attempt at persuasion. PP I 6 26 40
"To yield readily--easily--to the persuasion of a friend PP I 10 50 35
under the delightful persuasion that, allowing for the PP I 18 103 77
in their society, a persuasion which of course recommended PP II 9 180 28
he had engaged at the persuasion of the young man, who, on PP II 13 205 4
He did not repeat his persuasion of their not marrying-- PP III 5 290 48
me, and nothing but a persuasion of my being indifferent, PP III 13 350 49
But at length, by Elizabeth's persuasion, he was prevailed PP III 19 388 12
And would Edmund's judgment, would his persuasion of Sir MP I 16 153 3
clear to her but the persuasion of her being never under MP III 2 329 10
Not unfrequently, through Emma's persuasion, he had some E I 3 20 1
Harriet could not long resist so delightful a persuasion. E I 9 73 19
equal to counteract the persuasion of its being very E II 1 155 3
of herself; and this persuasion, joined to all the rest, E II 12 262 38
That is, I always had a strong persuasion he would be here E II 18 308 27
It was owing to her persuasion, as she thought his being E III 5 344 9
I feel a strong persuasion, this morning, that I shall E III 6 365 62
He gave his consent with very little persuasion." E III 10 398 55
and persuasion to think the engagement no very bad thing. E III 10 400 69
now he confessed his persuasion, that such a E III 15 448 31
at the comfortable persuasion of his being obliged to go E III 18 476 43
poetry; and besides the persuasion of having given him at P III 11 100 23
the same unfortunate persuasion, which had hastened him P IV 10 221 32
what persuasion had once done--was it not all against me?" P IV 11 244 72
If I was wrong in yielding to persuasion once, remember P IV 11 244 73
to persuasion exerted on the side of safety, not of risk. P IV 11 244 73

ERSUASIONS (5)

you think I can be worked on by such persuasions as these. PP III 14 357 61
But as such were Fanny's persuasions, she suffered very MP III 6 367 6
services, and gentle persuasions; and she found that the MP III 8 390 8
not she add her persuasions to his, to induce Miss E I 15 125 4
These were her internal persuasions.-- P IV 10 219 29

ERSUASIVE (1)

assure her, with a most persuasive smile, that neither he MP I 17 161 9

ERSUASIVELY (1)

"My advice," said Mrs. Weston kindly and persuasively, "I E II 16 295 33

ERT (6)

nothing remarkable; her manners were pert and conceited.-- W 349 23
An odious, little, pert, unnatural, impudent girl. MP I 14 136 20
The men appeared to her all coarse, the women all pert, MP III 9 395 3
no, I could not endure William Coxe--a pert young lawyer." E I 16 137 11
formed in a bad school, pert and familiar; that all her E II 14 272 16
and all her airs of pert pretension and under-bred finery. E II 14 279 52

RTINACITY (1)

The pertinacity of her friend seemed more than she could E III 6 359 37

RTURBATION (14)

that the delightful perturbation of spirits I was then in, LS 24 285 1
after the first perturbation of surprize had passed away, NA II 13 222 7
perturbation of her spirits and her impatience to be gone. SS II 3 158 21
recovered from her own perturbation in time to see a blush W 326 5
woods with some perturbation; and when at length they PP III 1 245 1
in their heads, the perturbation of Elizabeth's feelings PP III 2 260 1
to her uncle, in the utmost perturbation and dismay.-- MP III 1 314 16
the other all varying and indescribable perturbation. MP III 15 444 27
But her mind had never been in such perturbation, and it E I 15 133 38
forth, had all the evidence of corresponding perturbation. E II 3 177 52
had an air of so much perturbation, that Emma's uneasiness E III 10 394 26
27
mind was in all the perturbation that such a developement E III 11 409 34
in all the anger & perturbation which a beleif of very S 3 378 1
cheeks, & with much perturbation she added--"the oddest S 10 419 1

RTURBED (1)

In this perturbed state of mind, with thoughts that could PP II 13 205 3

RUSAL (10)

her to use her own fancy in the perusal of Matilda's woes. NA II 5 160 23
back to enjoy the luxury of their perusal on her pillow. NA II 7 172 1
long retained; and the perusal of the highly-strained NA II 9 190 1
not be pained by the perusal of--and, above all, which she NA II 14 235 14
and again; but every perusal only served to increase her SS II 7 184 15
which it had hardly received on the first perusal. PP II 11 188 1
the formation, and the perusal of this letter must PP II 12 196 4
began the mortifying perusal of all that related to PP II 13 205 3
Widely different was the effect of a second perusal.-- PP II 13 208 9
arrived, Emma had the perusal of it; and she read it with E II 13 265 5

PERUSE (3)

to peruse every line before she attempted to rest. NA II 6 169 11
with the sun's first rays she was determined to peruse it. NA II 6 170 12
Such are the works which I peruse with delight, & I hope I S 8 403 1

PERVADING (2)

general publicity and pervading interest; yet, with all P III 6 42 1
character, the potent, pervading hero of the story, it S 8 403 1

PERVERSE (7)

her mother insinuates I am afraid she is a perverse girl. LS 15 266 3
Nay, perverse as it seemed, she doubted whether she might NA II 5 154 2
But she is a little fretful & perverse among ourselves.-- W 319 2
gloom, which the late perverse occurrences had thrown on PP II 1 138 30
you can be wilful and perverse, that you can and will MP III 1 318 39
But at last there seemed a perverse turn; it seemed all at E I 15 124 4
often been negligent or perverse, slighting his advice, or E III 12 415 1

PERVERSELY (1)

I wish matters did not go so perversely. LS 38 307 3

PERVERSENESS (12)

sign of obstinacy or perverseness during her whole stay in LS 17 271 7
of true girlish perverseness & folly, without considering LS 19 273 1
But when a young lady is to be a heroine, the perverseness NA I 1 16 11
of its object, or the perverseness of circumstances, to be SS I 11 56 15
But this, from the momentary perverseness of impatient SS II 8 197 25
of Margt's perverseness, than sit with only her father, W 361 30
it a most unlucky perverseness which placed them within PP I 18 98 63
by this time, had not it been for her own perverseness. PP II 2 140 4
She felt all the perverseness of the mischance that should PP II 10 182 1
She blushed again and again over the perverseness of the PP III 1 252 54
sighed at the perverseness of those feelings which would PP III 4 279 23
peculiarly denoted her perverseness and assurance, in the PP III 16 367 9

PERVERSION (2)

can be given, than this perversion of Reginald's judgement, LS 8 255 1
such feelings, in a perversion of mind which made it MP III 16 456 25

PERVERSITY (1)

With a perversity of judgement, which must be attributed S 8 404 1

PERVERT (1)

Mystery; finesse--how they pervert the understanding! E III 15 446 15

PERVERTED (1)

by the exertion of your perverted abilities had made me LS 36 305 1

PESTILENCES (1)

The quarrels of popes and kings, with wars or pestilences, NA I 14 108 22

PET (1)

in a pet, and vowed I would never take another likeness. E I 6 45 21

PETERBOROUGH (2)

On the 23d he was going to a friend near Peterborough in MP II 8 255 10
mounted his horse for Peterborough, and then all were gone. MP II 11 282 4

PETITION (2)

to repeat the "beggar's petition;" and after all, her next NA I 1 14 1
and Mr. Hurst soon found even his open petition rejected. PP I 11 54 3

PETITIONED (2)

Allen as to Catherine, petitioned for the pleasure of her NA I 14 114 49
Mary petitioned for the use of the library at Netherfield; PP III 13 349 42

PETRIFIED (1)

rob it of a few petrified spars without his perceiving me." PP II 19 239 9

PETTICOAT (4)

"Yes, and her petticoat; I hope you saw her petticoat, six PP I 8 36 6
Her dirty petticoat quite escaped my notice." "you PP I 8 36 7
through half a sentence, to her mother's old petticoat. E II 8 225 78
'Not that it was such a very old petticoat either--for E II 8 225 78

PETTICOATS (1)

say that their petticoats were all very strong.'" E II 8 225 78

PETTY (2)

petty information, or in a disposition to communicate it. SS I 21 126 41
seeing her through all the petty difficulties of the case, P IV 12 251 11

PETTY-FRANCE (2)

The tediousness of a two hours' bait at Petty-France, in NA II 5 156 4
easily forget its having stopped two hours at Petty-France. NA II 5 156 5

PETULANCE (2)

to forgive all the petulance and acrimony of her manner in PP III 2 265 16
Tom and Charles, and petulance with Betsey, were at least, MP III 8 391 9

PEW (2)

of Mrs. Tilney, which immediately fronted the family pew. NA II 9 190 1
satisfied by a bride in a pew, and it must be left for the E II 14 270 1

PEWS (1)

Before that period, as I understand, the pews were only MP I 9 86 9

PHAETON (7)

them--does he not drive a phaeton with bright chesnuts?" NA I 11 85 33
How could you say, you saw them driving out in a phaeton?" NA I 11 87 53
gone out in a phaeton together? and then what could I do? NA I 12 93 5
drive by my humble abode in her little phaeton and ponies." PP I 14 67 7
two ladies stopping in a low phaeton at the garden gate. PP II 5 158 13
de Bourgh drove by in her phaeton, which he never failed PP II 7 168 2
A low phaeton, with a nice little pair of ponies, would be PP III 10 325 2

PHAETONS (2)

phaetons and false hangings, Tilneys and trap-doors. NA I 11 87 51
in their several phaetons, and three waiting-maids in a NA II 14 232 7

PHEASANT (1)

ill ever since; he did not eat any of the pheasant to day. MP I 18 171 27

PHEASANT'S (2)

and obtained a few pheasant's eggs and a cream cheese from MP I 10 104 52
It is nothing but four of those beautiful pheasant's eggs, MP I 10 106 57

PHEASANTS (6)

number of our plants, and here are the curious pheasants." MP I 9 90 33
All were attracted at first by the plants or the pheasants, MP I 9 90 36
the pheasants, was lingering behind in gossip with her. MP I 9 90 36
on the subject of pheasants, had taken her to the dairy, MP I 10 103 50
pheasants, sir, I assure you, as much as you could desire. MP II 1 181 16
I never saw Mansfield wood so full of pheasants in my life MP II 1 181 16

PHEATON (1)

from the gig to the Pheaton,--from one horse to 4; & just S 12 425 1

PHIALS (1)

one, out of the several Phials already at home on the S 10 413 1

PHILANTHROPIC (2)

Benevolent, philanthropic man! SS I 21 119 3
are not only natural, they are philanthropic and virtuous. MP III 14 434 13

PHILIPPICS (1)

and pretty severe Philippics upon the many houses where it E I 12 104 50

PHILIPS (22)

Their visits to Mrs. Philips were now productive of the PP I 7 28 4
Mr. Philips visited them all, and this opened to his PP I 7 28 4
Do let the portraits of your uncle and aunt Philips be PP I 10 52 57
know, mama, that my uncle Philips talks of turning away PP I 14 68 13
14
Mrs. Philips was always glad to see her nieces, and the PP I 15 73 11
Mrs. Philips was quite awed by such an excess of good PP I 15 73 11
This was agreed to, and Mrs. Philips protested that they PP I 15 74 11
but when Mrs. Philips understood from him what Rosings was, PP I 16 75 2
and he found in Mrs. Philips a very attentive listener, PP I 16 75 3
broad-faced stuffy uncle Philips, breathing port wine, who PP I 16 76 3
a kind listener in Mrs. Philips, and was, by her PP I 16 76 5
Mrs. Philips was very thankful for his compliance, but PP I 16 76 7
which your uncle, Mr. Philips, appears to do so much PP I 16 81 37

station between his cousin Elizabeth and Mrs. Philips.-- PP I 16 82 49
point; but when Mrs. Philips began to express her concern PP I 16 83 49
civility of Mr. and Mrs. Philips, protesting that he did PP I 16 84 59
than Mrs. Bennet and Mrs. Philips, was an amiable, PP II 2 139 2
My aunt Philips wants you so to get husbands, you can't PP II 16 221 17
I told my sister Philips so the other day. PP II 17 227 27
"And my aunt Philips is sure it would do me a great deal PP II 18 229 9
Mrs. Bennet was privileged to whisper it to Mrs. Philips, PP III 13 350 55
and though Mrs. Philips, as well as her sister, stood in PP III 18 384 27
PHILIPSES (2)
Some of them were to dine with the Philipses the next day, PP I 15 74 11
and what with the Philipses, the lucases, and the officers, PP II 2 142 18
PHILLIPPIC (1)
bitter phillippic; "Miss Morton is Lord Morton's daughter." SS II 12 235 37
PHILLIPS (5)
She had a sister married to a Mr. Phillips, who had been a PP I 7 28 2
My aunt Phillips came to Longbourn on Tuesday, after my PP III 5 292 66
and tell the good, good news to my sister Phillips. PP III 7 307 49
She longed to see Mrs. Phillips, the Lucasses, and all PP III 9 317 10
sister," (for Mrs. Phillips first brought her the news.) PP III 11 331 14
PHILOSOPHER (1)
philosopher will derive benefit from such as are given. PP II 19 236 1
PHILOSOPHERS (1)
Semi-metals, Planets, and distinguished philosophers." MP I 2 18 25
PHILOSOPHIC (6)
"Well," continued her philosophic mother, "I am glad I did NA II 14 234 12
treated with all the philosophic dignity of twenty-four. SS III 13 362 4
had all the appearance of his usual philosophic composure. PP III 6 299 18
the world, Mary on something of less philosophic tendency. MP III 5 360 13
that men are much more philosophic on the subject of E I 8 63 44
the little boys and the philosophic composure of her E II 16 292 9
PHILOSOPHY (7)
said he, "we may expect philosophy from all the world." NA II 2 140 9
of it, with all the philosophy of a well bred woman, SS I 21 118 2
It was borne in the latter with decent philosophy. PP III 8 309 6
You must learn some of my philosophy. PP III 16 368 23
"I cannot give you credit for any philosophy of the kind. PP III 16 369 24
not of philosophy, but what is much better, of ignorance. PP III 16 369 24
He bore with philosophy the conviction that Elizabeth must PP III 19 386 6
PHOO (5)
disposed to be pleased, he only replied--"phoo! phoo!-- W 348 22
"Oh! phoo! MP I 15 146 52
"Phoo! phoo! MP II 6 230 6
"Phoo! phoo!" cried the Admiral, "what stuff these young P III 8 65 12
"Phoo? phoo!" replied Charles, "what's an evening party? P IV 10 223 44
PHRASE (12)
I abhor every common-place phrase by which wit is intended; SS I 9 45 30
I felt is--in the common phrase, not to be expressed; in a SS III 8 325 50
But Miss Frances married, in the common phrase, to MP I 1 3 1
Edmund might, in the common phrase, do the duty of MP II 7 247 42
phrase--that she has got her pennyworth for her penny. MP III 9 394 1
you should, in the common phrase, be well married, here is E I 9 75 27
use a most intelligible phrase, been so very ready to have E II 4 181 4
Is it necessary for me to use any roundabout phrase?-- E II 16 297 48
defined by the expressive phrase of being out of humour. E III 6 364 56
They were laying themselves open to that very phrase--and E III 7 368 3
phrase of difficult interpretation in Lady D's discourse. S 7 399 1
Sanditon" to use a proper phrase, for every body must now " S 11 421 1
PHRASES (2)
talked in phrases which conveyed scarcely any idea to her. NA I 14 110 28
through all the usual phrases employed in praise of their S 7 396 1
PHYN (1)
We have consulted physician after Phyn in vain, till we S 5 386 1
PHYSIC (3)
comprised in, do not spoil them, and do not physic them." E II 18 311 38
and happiness must preclude false indulgence and physic." E II 18 311 39
in the world & never took physic above twice--and never S 6 394 1
PHYSICIAN (8)
could be prevailed on, a physician attended her, a very NA II 9 196 25
as his physician to have a little dispatched to Mansfield. MP III 13 426 10
had imbibed from the physician, with respect to some MP III 14 429 1
but upon my honour, I never bribed a physician in my life. MP III 14 434 13
not a word of a certain young physician from Windsor.-- E III 16 454 17
The lawyer plods, quite care-worn; the physician is up at P III 3 20 17
We have consulted physician after Phyn in vain, till we S 5 386 1
care of an experienced physician;--and his prescriptions S 11 422 1
PHYSICIANS (1)
an express to town for one of the most eminent physicians. PP I 8 40 59
PHYSICS (1)
They were now advancing so deep in Physics, that Charlotte S 10 416 1
PIANO (8)
hear, to one close by the piano forte on which Marianne SS III 3 281 9
Her sister made not the smallest objection, and the piano PP I 11 58 34
day, and play on the piano forte in Mrs. Jenkinson's room. PP II 8 173 10
deliberation towards the piano forte, stationed himself so PP II 8 174 12
"ay, I see what you are thinking of, the piano forte. E III 8 384 32
33
Now Emma was obliged to think of the piano forte; and the E III 8 384 34
of confusion by a grand piano forte and a harp, flower- P III 5 40 44
benwick is rather too piano for me, and though very likely P IV 6 172 39
PIANO-FORTE (11)
Willoughby opened the piano-forte, and asked Marianne to SS I 12 62 27
I shall go to the piano-forte; I have not touched it since SS II 1 144 15
for it is the very best toned piano-forte I ever heard." SS II 1 145 17
The piano-forte, at which Marianne, wrapt up in her own SS II 1 145 23
After dinner she would try her piano-forte. SS III 10 342 7
Her performance on the piano-forte is exquisite." PP I 8 39 42
Miss Bingley moved with alacrity to the piano-forte, and PP I 10 51 45
at the piano-forte again, "it is entirely her own doing." MP I 11 108 11
Two play on the piano-forte, and one on the harp--and all MP II 11 288 28
so, but very soon stopt again to say, "the piano-forte! E III 15 446 18
harp, for it seems to amuse her more than the piano-forte. P III 6 50 27
PIANOFORTE (29)
The small pianoforte has been removed within these few LS 17 271 7
by a prelude on the pianoforte, of her own composition, NA I 1 16 10
and books, with an handsome pianoforte of Marianne's. SS I 5 26 4
Marianne's pianoforte was unpacked and properly disposed SS I 6 30 5
same position on the pianoforte, for her ladyship had SS I 7 35 8
She spent whole hours at the pianoforte alternately SS I 16 83 3
her eyes from the grand pianoforte, whenever it suited her, SS II 14 250 11
with candles at the pianoforte, she suddenly revived it by MP I 11 108 4
away, or to my sisters' pianoforte being moved from one MP I 13 127 29
neither played on the pianoforte nor wore fine pelisses, MP III 9 395 3
by the sight of a pianoforte--a very elegant looking E II 8 214 13
a large-sized square pianoforte; and the substance of the E II 8 214 13
Bates's, was, that this pianoforte had arrived from E II 8 214 13
look at our new grand pianoforte in the drawing-room, E II 8 215 16
"That is a grand pianoforte, and he might think it too E II 8 216 25
"the arrival of this pianoforte is decisive with me. I E II 8 218 38
39
She did not wish to speak of the pianoforte, she felt too E II 8 220 45
Such an admirer of her performance on the pianoforte, and E II 8 226 79
occurred to me--this pianoforte that has been sent by E II 8 226 79
believe nothing of the pianoforte--and proof only shall E II 8 226 84
"This pianoforte is very kindly given." E II 8 228 91
standing with her back to them, intent on her pianoforte. E II 10 240 1
was quite ready to sit down to the pianoforte again. E II 10 240 6
all her praise; and the pianoforte, with every proper E II 10 241 7
latter, he went to the pianoforte, and begged Miss Fairfax, E II 10 242 16
He took some music from a chair near the pianoforte, and E II 10 242 20
21
Miss Smith; so kind as to call to hear the new pianoforte. E II 10 244 42
I will call another day, and hear the pianoforte." E II 10 244 47
Of the pianoforte so much talked of, I feel it only E III 14 439 8
PIC-NIC (1)
and pic-nic parade of the Eltons and the Sucklings. E III 6 352 2
PICK (2)
"We have but to speak the word; we may pick and choose.-- MP I 15 148 58
Oh! Harriet may pick and choose. E I 8 64 46
PICTURE (73)
"The very picture of him indeed!" cried the mother--and "I NA I 4 32 5
"What a picture of intellectual poverty! NA I 10 79 55
Was there any picture of her in the Abbey? NA II 7 180 37
"Her picture, I suppose," blushing at the consummate art NA II 7 180 38
give his opinion on any picture; but he has an innate SS I 4 19 2
that Marianne wore his picture round her neck; but it SS I 12 60 10
Lucy, "to give him my picture in return, which I am very SS I 22 132 37
The picture, she had allowed herself to believe, might SS I 22 134 53
Yes, I have one other comfort in his picture; but poor SS I 22 135 54
If he had but my picture, he says he should be easy. SS I 22 135 54
some comfort to him, he said, but not equal to a picture. SS I 22 135 54
often surprised her, the picture, the letter, the ring, SS II 1 139 1
I cannot picture to myself a more wretched condition. SS III 1 268 50
picture so soothing!--Oh! it was a blessed journey!" SS III 8 325 45
and will return your picture the first opportunity. SS III 13 365 15
reverse;--he stood the picture of disappointment, with W 330 11
"Your picture may be very exact, Louisa," said Bingley; " PP I 8 36 7
As for your Elizabeth's picture, you must not attempt to PP I 10 53 57
wife of Mr. Collins, was a most humiliating picture!-- PP I 22 125 18
It was Mr. Collins's picture of Hunsford and Rosings PP II 3 147 19
Elizabeth laughed heartily at this picture of herself, and PP II 8 174 15
appeared to her so just a picture of Mr. Darcy, that she PP II 10 186 38
pleasing picture of conjugal felicity or domestic comfort. PP II 19 236 1
Her aunt now called her to look at a picture. PP III 1 247 9
and told them it was the picture of a young gentleman, the PP III 1 247 9
Gardiner, looking at the picture; "it is a handsome face. PP III 1 247 12
you will see a finer, larger picture of him than this. PP III 1 247 18
The picture gallery, and two or three of the principal bed- PP III 1 250 46
She stood several minutes before the picture in earnest PP III 1 250 47
or his resemblance to the picture they had just been PP III 1 251 52
corner of the sofa, the picture of health, wealth, ease, MP I 13 126 19
This picture of her consequence had some effect, for no MP I 15 140 14
advised Fanny to get his picture drawn before he went to MP I 15 147 57
so truly feminine, as to be no very good picture of a man. MP I 18 169 22
There is nothing frightful in such a picture, is there, MP II 4 210 21
It was a picture which Henry Crawford had moral taste MP II 6 235 20
no longer able, in the picture she had been forming of a MP II 7 248 47
After such a picture as her uncle had drawn, for not MP III 1 316 28
frown, which Fanny could picture to herself, though she MP III 1 317 36
Her heart was almost broke by such a picture of what she MP III 1 319 40
but it will not be a less faithful picture of my mind. MP III 13 422 2
and to complete the picture of good, the acquisition of MP III 17 473 32
by such a picture of another set of beings, and enjoying E I 4 27 4
One hears sometimes of a child being 'the picture of E I 5 39 20
the idea of being the complete picture of grown-up health. E I 5 39 20
seconded a sudden wish of her's, to have Harriet's picture. E I 6 43 8
Harriet?" said she: "did you ever sit for your picture?" E I 6 43 9
an exquisite possession a good picture of her would be! E I 6 43 12
13
It would be such a delight to have her picture!" E I 6 43 13
How completely it meant, 'why should my picture be drawn?'" E I 6 44 17
idea of sitting for his picture made him so nervous, that E I 6 45 21
whole progress of the picture, which was rapid and happy. E I 6 47 30
The next thing wanted was to get the picture framed; and E I 6 48 40
Mr. Elton is shewing your picture to his mother and E I 7 56 44
"My picture!-- E I 7 56 45
But he has left my picture in Bond-Street." E I 7 56 45
depend upon it the picture will not be in Bond-Street till E I 7 56 46
The picture, elegantly framed, came safely to hand soon E I 9 69 2
The picture!-- E I 16 134 4
How eager he had been about the picture!--and the charade!- E I 16 134 4
Emma could not but picture it all, and feel how justly E II 5 187 4
towards Jane; and this picture of her present sufferings E III 8 379 9
The picture which she had then drawn of the privations of E III 12 422 19
which any picture of love must have for her at that moment. E III 15 444 1
Picture to yourselves my amazement; I shall not easily P III 3 20 16
on his habits, the picture of repose and domestic P III 11 98 17
picture to herself a more agreeable or estimable man. P IV 4 146 6
try to subdue the feelings this picture excited. P IV 5 160 26
did, it was a most attractive picture of happiness to her. P IV 6 168 24
Here I am, you see, staring at a picture. P IV 6 169 25
a last look at the picture, as they began to be in motion. P IV 6 169 27
It was a dreadful picture of ingratitude and inhumanity; P IV 9 210 97
eye immediately, was the picture of Sir H. Denham--and S 12 427 1
PICTURED (4)
library, she immediately pictured to herself a mob of NA I 14 113 39
Her eyes filled with tears as she pictured her NA II 14 236 18
delayed too long, and pictured to herself her suffering SS III 7 312 18
Jane pictured to herself a happy evening in the society of PP I 17 86 10
PICTURES (8)
formed into pictures, with all the eagerness of real taste. NA I 14 110 28
of this poor girl, and pictures her to herself, with an SS II 9 210 32
She related the subject of the pictures, the dimensions of PP III 1 249 37
Of pictures there were abundance, and some few good, but MP I 9 84 3
You have drawn two pretty pictures--but I think there may E I 1 13 43
you have the art of giving pictures in a few words. E II 11 249 18
These valuable pictures of yours, Sir Walter, if you chose P III 3 18 7
of the catalogue of my father's books and pictures. P III 5 38 34
PICTURESQUE (10)
and a lecture on the picturesque immediately followed, in NA I 14 111 29
she should not know what was picturesque when she saw it. NA II 7 177 18
his sentiments on picturesque beauty, and second marriages, SS I 10 47 4
no knowledge in the picturesque, and I shall offend you by SS I 18 96 4
I dare say it is a picturesque one too, because you admire SS I 18 97 4
I know nothing of the picturesque." SS I 18 97 4
of him who first defined what picturesque beauty was. SS I 18 97 7
I like a fine prospect, but not on picturesque principles. SS I 18 98 8
when any object of picturesque beauty within their view SS II 4 160 2
The picturesque would be spoilt by admitting a fourth. PP I 10 53 65
PIECE (48)
seize upon any other odd piece of paper, she did what she NA I 1 14 1
There is not a sound piece of iron about it. NA I 9 65 28
an easy transition from a piece of rocky fragment and the NA I 14 111 29
exercise was of a piece with the strange unseasonableness NA II 8 187 14
the latter communicated a piece of news to her sister, SS I 12 58 1
a piece of white paper, and put it into his pocket-book." SS I 12 60 13
They contained a noble piece of water; a sail on which was SS I 12 62 28
was perfectly of a piece with her general inquisitiveness SS I 21 125 37
the time an unnatural, or an inexcusable piece of folly." SS III 13 362 5
two do you call my little recent piece of modesty?" PP I 10 48 26
no other way than as a piece of news to spread at Meryton. PP I 23 127 7
"I may thank you, Eliza, for this piece of civility. PP II 7 170 7
8
Dear me! we had such a good piece of fun the other day at PP II 16 221 17
home was exactly of a piece with it, and therefore what I PP III 10 325 2
indeed are quite of a piece with your general conduct; and MP I 1 6 6
on a sofa, doing some long piece of needlework, of little MP I 2 19 31
had made a most tiresome piece of work of it; and 3dly, MP I 3 24 4
"I was astonished to find what a piece of work was made of MP I 6 58 37
It must have injured the piece materially; but I was MP I 13 122 2
Luckily the strength of the piece did not depend upon him. MP I 13 122 2
be easier than to find a piece which would please them all, MP I 13 124 13
difference, they wanted a piece containing very few MP I 14 130 3
No piece could be proposed that did not supply somebody MP I 14 131 3

Amelia as the most difficult character in the whole piece. MP I 14 135 15
angry and audible: "what a piece of work here is about MP I 15 146 53
such an exhibition, such a piece of true acting as he MP II 1 182 22
pretty piece--and your cousin Edmund's prime favourite. MP II 4 207 9
himself, and entirely of a piece with what she had seen MP II 13 301 7
This was almost the only rule of conduct, the only piece MP III 2 333 27
in having such a capital piece of Mansfield news, as the MP III 13 425 6
agitation, were all of a piece with something very bad; MP III 15 441 19
anger, she could have charged as the daemon of the piece. MP III 16 448 2
He called for a few moments, just to leave a piece of E I 9 71 10
A piece of paper was found on the table this morning-- (E I 9 78 50
and she had taken a piece of cake and been so kind as to E II 1 155 4
Miss Smith would do them the favour to eat a piece too." E II 1 155 4
"Emma," said Mr. Knightley presently, "I have a piece of E II 3 172 20
there never was a piece of news more generally interesting. E II 3 173 29
This has been a most agreeable piece of news indeed. E II 3 176 50
It was to herself an amusing and a very welcome piece of E II 3 177 51
the cotton, Emma saw only a small piece of court plaister. E III 4 338 9
mine out and cut him a piece; but it was a great deal too E III 4 338 12
"And so you actually put this piece of court plaister by E III 4 339 15
of putting by in cotton a piece of court plaister that E III 4 339 15
It might be a very indifferent piece of wit; but Emma E III 7 371 35
The real circumstances of this pathetic piece of family P III 6 50 28
Elizabeth's last letter had communicated a piece of news P IV 2 135 35
on one of her heels, as large as a three shilling piece. P IV 6 170 29
PIECES (6)
more than she wanted, or careless in cutting it to pieces." NA I 3 28 45
Upon my soul, you might shake it to pieces yourself with a NA I 9 65 28
come before it's wanted; for they say he is all to pieces. SS II 8 194 10
by cutting the latter to pieces as he spoke, said, in an SS III 12 360 22
23
You tear them to pieces." PP I 2 6 8
I shall pull it to pieces as soon as I get home, and see PP II 16 219 3
PIER (2)
were out; we went after them, and found them on the pier. MP I 5 51 40
of an old pier of unknown date, were the Harvilles settled. P III 11 96 10
PIERCE (1)
"You pierce my soul. P IV 11 237 42
PIERCED (1)
With a heart pierced, wounded, almost broken! P IV 8 183 10
PIES (2)
I fancy she was wanted about the mince pies. PP I 9 44 29
weight of brawn and cold pies, where riotous boys were P IV 2 134 29
PIETY (1)
up into seeming piety, but with heads full of something MP I 9 87 15
PIGEON-PIES (1)
with Mr. Weston as to pigeon-pies and cold lamb, when a E III 6 353 6
PIGS (1)
"I expected at least that the pigs were got into the PP II 5 158 14
PILFERING (1)
Pilfering was housebreaking to Mr. Woodhouse's fears.-- E III 19 483 10
PILING (1)
The first half hour was spent in piling up the fire, lest PP I 11 54 2
PILL (1)
It will be a bitter pill to her; that is, like other MP II 12 297 33
PILLARS (1)
low stone wall with high pillars, which seemed intended, E III 6 360 38
PILLOW (3)
to a pillow strewed with thorns and wet with tears. NA I 11 90 65
back to enjoy the luxury of their perusal on her pillow. NA II 7 172 1
her aching head on the pillow, and saw her, as she hoped, SS II 8 197 25
PILLS (2)
that is, like other bitter pills, it will have two moments MP II 12 297 33
in favour of some Tonic pills, which a cousin of her own S 11 422 1
PIMPLES (1)
very ill--it cried, and fretted, and was all over pimples. SS III 1 257 5
PIN (4)
said she, "do take this pin out of my sleeve; I am afraid NA I 3 28 35
pin myself down to the payment of one for all the world." SS I 2 11 20
But unfortunately in bestowing these embraces, a pin in SS I 21 121 10
to pin his happiness upon the consequence he is heir to. P IV 9 206 90
PIN-CUSHIONS (1)
little thread-cases, pin-cushions and card-racks, which P IV 5 155 9
PIN-MONEY (1)
What pin-money, what jewels, what carriages you will have! PP III 17 378 43
PINCHING (1)
second boy's violently pinching one of the same lady's SS I 21 121 8
PINE (1)
Of the Alps and Pyrenees, with their pine forests and NA II 10 200 3
PINERY (1)
The pinery had yielded only one hundred in the last year. NA II 7 178 21
PINING (1)
He should not have to think of her as pining in the MP II 3 202 25
PINK (5)
But why should not I wear pink ribbons? SS III 2 272 12
with a blue dress, and a pink satin cloak, and afterwards MP I 15 138 3
I shall hardly know myself in a blue dress, and a pink MP I 15 139 10
away Mr. Rushworth's pink satin cloak as her brother-in- MP II 1 179 10
Here,--probably this basket with pink ribbon. E III 6 355 20
PINNED (2)
in arm when they walked, pinned up each other's train for NA I 5 37 4
and by their side and pinned against the wall, a small MP I 16 152 2
PINNY (1)
up Lyme, and, above all, Pinny, with its green chasms P III 11 95 9
PINS (1)
new netting-needles and pins with improvements; and if P III 11 99 18
PINT (1)
A pint of porter with my cold beef at Marlborough was SS III 8 318 18
PINTS (2)
with a man who goes beyond his four pints at the utmost. NA I 9 64 24
that upon an average we cleared about five pints a head. NA I 9 64 24
PIPE (1)
Holla--you there--Sam--stop your confounded pipe, or I MP III 7 383 30
PIQUANTE (1)
You can imagine nothing more naive or piquante; & what do W 340 19
PIQUE (3)
said Lucy, with some pique, and having a particular stress SS II 2 150 34
mixture of pique and pretension, now spread over his air. E II 4 182 7
It was done to pique Miss Brereton. S 7 398 1
PIQUED (2)
Lady Middleton piqued herself upon the elegance of her SS I 7 32 2
"Pride," observed Mary, who piqued herself upon the PP I 5 20 20
PIQUET (3)
want him to play at piquet of an evening, while Miss SS III 7 309 5
Mr. Hurst and Mr. Bingley were at piquet, and Mrs. Hurst PP I 10 47 1
She loves piquet, you know; but when she is gone home, I E II 7 211 21
PIT (1)
completely fitted up with pit, box, and gallery, and let MP I 13 124 10
PITCH (8)
from its hitherto animated pitch, to nothing more than a NA I 7 48 32
This was a pitch of friendship beyond Catherine. NA I 15 118 10
working himself up to a pitch of enthusiastic generosity, SS II 11 223 22
At a more than ordinary pitch of thumping and hallooing in MP III 7 383 30
young man's spirits now rose to a pitch almost unpleasant. E III 7 374 54
When it came to such a pitch as this, she was not able to E III 12 423 21
Anne was not animated to an equal pitch by the P IV 2 136 36
He was armed against the highest pitch of disdain and S 8 405 2
PITCHED (2)
is was very low pitched, and that the ceiling was crooked. SS I 19 108 39
Could he, or the lucases, have pitched on any man, within PP III 15 363 18
PITCHER (1)
to orders, with her pitcher, to fetch broth from Hartfield. E I 10 88 33

PITCHING (1)
gate & entered on the pitching of the town--the jumbling & W 321 2
PITIABLE (13)
was almost as pitiable as in their first avowal to himself. NA II 15 247 15
himself; if her case were pitiable, his was hopeless. SS II 1 140 1
your situation would have been pitiable indeed." SS II 2 147 8
pitiable than when she first learnt to expect the event. SS II 10 217 17
be sure it was pitiable enough!--but, upon my soul, I SS III 5 299 35
would have been in a pitiable state at this time, for from PP I 17 88 15
Mrs. Bennet was really in a most pitiable state. PP I 23 129 16
more pitiable; but it will have no effect on me." PP III 14 356 49
In that case, nothing could be more pitiable or more E II 2 168 13
seemed but the more pitiable from this sort of irritation E III 9 391 21
Then, she had indeed been a pitiable object--for she had P IV 5 154 9
more helpless & more pitiable of course than any--a S 3 379 1
it but what is either very pitiable or very creditable.-- S 5 387 1
PITIED (22)
"Your brother is certainly very much to be pitied at NA II 10 206 38
Davis: I pitied his taste, but took no notice of him. NA II 12 217 2
account she earnestly pitied, Mrs. Morland had very early NA II 15 242 9
south-westerly wind, they pitied the fears which had SS I 9 41 4
Perhaps she pitied and esteemed him the more because he SS I 10 50 13
Elinor saw, and pitied her for, the neglect of abilities SS I 22 127 2
Elinor assured him that she did;--that she forgave, pitied, SS III 8 332 76
Those who do not complain are never pitied." PP I 20 113 28
and her niece, however, did her justice, and pitied her. PP III 3 267 3
Howsoever that may be, you are grievously to be pitied, in PP III 6 297 11
The Miss Bertrams were much to be pitied on the occasion; MP I 3 32 64
Fanny pitied her. MP I 9 89 26
Maria was more to be pitied than Julia, for to her the MP I 11 107 3
It is a lovely night, and they are much to be pitied who MP I 11 113 36
be pitied;" were the kind responses of listening sympathy. MP I 13 122 3
Fanny saw and pitied much of this in Julia; but there was MP I 17 163 20
and she was thanked and pitied; but she deserved their MP I 18 170 24
not such a house as a man was to be pitied for having. E II 6 204 42
could not think any man to be pitied for having that house. E II 6 204 42
be so much more to be pitied than herself, should never, P III 5 34 12
so much indeed, and pitied & cut his horses so sharply, S 1 364 1
ladies that have no money are very much to be pitied!-- S 7 401 1
PITIES (1)
It is a thousand pities that he should be so deprived of W 325 4
PITIFUL (10)
of doing a kind thing by a friend, I hate to be pitiful." NA I 7 47 17
To be guided by second-hand conjecture is pitiful. NA II 4 152 26
but to be so easily seen through I am afraid is pitiful." PP I 9 42 12
Come, let me see the list of the pitiful fellows who have PP II 18 231 17
more hated pitiful doings--the parsonage she believed had MP I 3 31 59
so pitiful, so younger-brother-like, that I detest it." MP II 4 211 22
suspicions, and imagined capable of pitiful resentment. E II 16 290 4
satin, very few lace veils; a most pitiful business!-- E III 19 484 12
There was no triumph, no pitiful triumph in his manner. P III 10 82 1
They played me a pitiful trick once--got away some of my P IV 6 170 29
PITIFULLEST (1)
not even the pitifullest old spinnet in the world, to E II 8 215 16
PITILESS (1)
and receiving from the pitiless hands of her husband a NA II 8 187 16
PITY (98)
& no one therefore can pity her, for losing by the LS 14 264 4
What a pity that you should not have known his intentions! LS 22 280 1
I leave him therefore to all the pity that anybody can LS 42 313 10
For myself, I confess that I can pity only Miss Manwaring, LS 42 313 10
"How I pity the poor creatures that are going there! NA I 11 89 63
I am sure I pity every body that is. NA I 11 90 63
At this rate, I shall not pity the writers of history any NA I 14 109 24
It is a pity you could not all go." NA I 14 115 53
with a tender effusion of pity for her sister Anne, whom NA I 15 116 2
What a pity not to have it fitted up! NA II 11 214 21
"What a pity it is, Elinor," said Marianne, "that Edward SS I 4 19 1
tenderness, pity, approbation, censure, and doubt. SS I 19 104 12
He is such a charming man, that it is quite a pity he SS I 20 115 56
I always pity them when they do; they seem to take it so SS II 5 167 1
The Middletons and Palmers--how am I to bear their pity? SS II 7 191 64
The pity of such a woman as Lady Middleton! SS II 7 191 64
after many expressions of pity, she withdrew, still SS II 9 202 8
It would have been such a great pity to have went away SS II 10 217 21
"Oh, dear, that is a great pity! but such old friends as SS II 10 219 39
"Pity me, dear Miss Dashwood!" said Lucy, as they walked SS II 12 231 13
sincerity, that she did pity her,--to the utter amazement SS II 12 232 14
threw out expressions of pity for her sister to Elinor, SS II 14 247 4
I pity her. SS III 1 259 7
I have no pity for either of them. SS III 1 259 7
scarcely less an object of pity!--Oh!--how slow was the SS III 7 315 26
If you can pity me, Miss Dashwood, pity my situation as it SS III 8 327 55
And now do you pity me, Miss Dashwood?--or have I said all SS III 8 329 65
than pity, and in its unobtrusiveness entitled to praise. SS III 10 342 7
lady herself, it seems a pity to me that he should be W 321 2
It is a pity you should not see them."-- W 333 12
Pity, you can none of you get married!-- W 353 26
It is a pity they are not handsome! PP I 9 44 29
It is a pity that great ladies in general are not more PP I 14 67 2
I pity you, Miss Eliza, for the discovery of your PP I 18 94 45
I pity, though I cannot help blaming her. PP II 3 148 26
But I pity her, because she must feel that she has been PP II 3 148 26
the first to listen and to pity, the first to be admired; PP II 4 151 3
to deny, soon overcame the pity which the consideration of PP II 11 193 31
and besides, it was such a pity that Lydia should be taken PP III 8 313 20
What a pity it is, mamma, we did not all go." PP III 9 317 11
make allowance for your cousin, and pity her deficiency. MP I 2 19 27
I may pity your feelings as a brother on the occasion. MP I 3 23 3
What a pity! MP I 6 56 20
yet, and it was a pity she should not see the place." MP I 8 76 4
We go down hill to it for half-a-mile, and it is a pity, MP I 8 82 34
"It is a pity," cried Fanny, "that the custom should have MP I 9 86 12
"Upon my word, it is really a pity that it should not take MP I 9 88 24
"It is a pity that he should have so much trouble for MP I 10 101 31
said, therefore, "it is a pity you should not join them. MP I 10 102 47
What a pity," he added, after an instant's reflection, " MP I 11 112 34
it was rather a pity they should have been obliged to part. MP I 12 117 13
under the agitations of jealousy, without great pity. MP I 14 136 20
Fanny, in her pity and kind-heartedness, was at great MP I 18 166 4
their pity, more than she hoped they would ever surmise. MP I 18 170 24
Henry Crawford gone, she could even pity her sister. MP II 2 194 19
sir, I thought it was a pity you did not always know MP III 3 343 39
disappointments of selfish passion, can excite little pity. MP III 17 464 12
What a pity it is that Mr. Weston ever thought of her!" E I 1 8 11
I pity you.-- E I 1 13 43
at his being still able to pity "poor Miss Taylor," when E I 2 18 12
likelihood of ceasing to pity her: but a few weeks brought E I 2 19 14
It is a pity that they were ever got over." E I 8 61 37
"Oh! Miss Woodhouse, what a pity that I must not write E I 9 77 39
"Indeed! (in a tone of wonder and pity,) I had no idea E I 13 116 45
She need not trouble herself to pity him. he only wanted E I 16 135 7
I am always watching her to admire; and I do pity her from E II 3 171 15
said----- "it is a great pity that their circumstances E II 3 171 16
17
be so confined! a great pity indeed! and I have often E II 3 171 16
17
result of real feeling, and she could not but pity them. E II 3 179 53
and Emma could not but pity such feelings, whatever their E II 10 240 6
and it would have been a pity not to have mentioned . . . . E II 10 245 52
"Ah! that's a great pity; for I assure you, Miss Woodhouse, E II 14 275 32
"Knightley has taken pity on poor little Miss Smith!-- E III 2 328 42

					43
"I do pity you.	E	III	6	363	52
and left her nothing but pity; and the remembrance of the	E	III	8	379	9
It was a pity that she had not come back earlier!	E	III	9	386	8
Are you disposed to pity me for what I must have suffered	E	III	14	443	8
No; do not pity me till I reached Highbury, and saw how	E	III	14	443	8
Do not pity me till I saw her wan, sick looks.--	E	III	14	443	8
and it would be quite a pity that any one who so well knew	E	III	17	461	1
Do not you pity me?"	E	III	18	477	57
Emma spoke her pity so very kindly, that, with a sudden	E	III	18	477	58
					59
It was a pity, perhaps, that he had not come last night;	E	III	18	479	73
changed naturally into pity and contempt, as he turned	P	III	1	3	1
It is a pity they are not knocked on the head at once,	P	III	3	20	16
It is a pity you cannot put your sister in the way of	P	III	6	44	8
were sincere, in their exclamations of pity and horror.	P	III	8	66	17
Now, I cannot help thinking it a pity that he does not	P	III	12	102	2
What a pity that we should not have been introduced to	P	III	12	106	16
"Between ourselves, I think it a great pity Henrietta did "	P	IV	6	163	7
Anne sighed and blushed and smiled, in pity and disdain,	P	IV	7	179	31
and to pity every one, as being less happy than herself.	P	IV	8	184	17
Pity for him was all over.	P	IV	10	212	1
It would be a pity to be divided, and we should be losing	P	IV	10	224	51
the very security of his affection, wherewith to pity her.	P	IV	10	225	62
Mr. Elliot was there; she avoided, but she could pity him.	P	IV	11	245	78
my opinion & thinks it a pity to lose any more time--and	S		1	370	1
I know you think it a great pity they shd give him such a	S		5	388	1

PITYING (5)

dislike, I can not help pitying her at present as she is	LS		15	266	2
not in urging her, not in pitying her, nor in appearing to	SS	II	7	181	6
was given in the pitying eye with which Marianne sometimes	SS	II	10	216	15
"Well, sir," said Elinor, who, though pitying him, grew	SS	III	8	325	47
The effect of the whole was a manner so pitying and	MP	III	2	328	7

PLACE (510)

me fixed at this place for the rest of the winter.	LS		2	244	1
Were there another place in England open to me, I would	LS		2	246	1
Langford appeared so exactly the place for her in every	LS		3	246	1
as the sale took place exactly at the time of his marriage-	LS		5	249	1
likelihood of it's taking place to any one, because I	LS		20	277	5
In short, I found that she had in the first place actually	LS		22	281	5
When that wretched event takes place, Frederica must	LS		24	291	17
intention of leaving this place to-day, I feel it my duty	LS		25	292	3
My removal therefore, which must at any rate take place	LS		25	293	3
precisely in her proper place, at Churchill with the	LS		26	295	1
fear the separation takes place too late to do us any good.	LS		27	296	1
distress; the most unfortunate event has just taken place.	LS		28	297	1
which I have found myself imperiously obliged to place it.	LS		30	301	4
Under these unpromising auspices, the parting took place,	NA	I	2	19	4
into life could not take place till after three or four	NA	I	2	20	8
and the concert; and how you like the place altogether.	NA	I	3	25	2
"Bath is a charming place, sir; there are so many good	NA	I	3	29	46
"What a delightful place Bath is," said Mrs. Allen, as	NA	I	4	31	1
The following conversation, which took place between the	NA	I	6	39	1
In the first place, I was so afraid it would rain this	NA	I	6	39	4
An inquiry now took place into the intended movements of	NA	I	7	47	18
she must be admired in such a place as this--is not she?"	NA	I	7	51	49
and supplying the place of many ideas by a squeeze of the	NA	I	8	52	1
within three yards of the place where they sat; he seemed	NA	I	8	53	3
place for young people--and indeed for every body else too.	NA	I	8	54	5
it is so very agreeable a place, that it is much better to	NA	I	8	54	5
to like the place, from finding it of service to him."	NA	I	8	54	6
It would make us the talk of the place, if we were not to	NA	I	8	57	21
And off they went, to regain their former place.	NA	I	8	58	25
to remain in the same place and the same employment till	NA	I	9	60	1
the country to every other place; really, our opinions	NA	I	10	71	3
and conversation took place; Mr. Allen, after drinking his	NA	I	10	71	8
immediately took her usual place by the side of her friend.	NA	I	10	71	8
the quiet possession of a place, however, when her	NA	I	10	75	25
striking; but I think I could place them in such a view.--	NA	I	10	77	33
that, it is the most tiresome place in the world.'	NA	I	10	78	45
greater sameness in such a place as this, than in my own	NA	I	10	78	46
"The finest place in England--worth going fifty miles at	NA	I	11	85	23
recollected, in the first place, that she was without any	NA	I	12	92	4
the party should take place on the following morning; and	NA	I	13	97	1
of his master for ever, if not his place, by her rapidity.	NA	I	13	103	27
she soon learned that the party to Clifton had taken place.	NA	I	14	115	50
if our union could take place now upon only fifty pounds a	NA	II	1	136	48
gaieties of this lively place; we can tempt you neither by	NA	II	2	139	7
With all the chances against her of house, hall, place,	NA	II	2	141	11
"This is my favourite place," said she, as they sat down	NA	II	3	143	1
to be always together; we should be the jest of the place.	NA	II	3	143	2
was to take place within a few days, and Captain Tilney's	NA	II	4	150	1
proposal of her taking his place in his son's curricle for	NA	II	5	156	4
It not it a fine old place, just like what one reads about?	NA	II	5	157	12
The place in the middle alone remained now unexplored; and	NA	II	6	169	11
of a servant in the place whence she had taken them,"	NA	II	7	172	2
"Is it a pretty place?" asked Catherine.	NA	II	7	175	14
and the property in the place being chiefly my own, you	NA	II	7	176	15
with the painting, and for some time it had no place.	NA	II	7	180	39
the General's father, and the present erected in its place.	NA	II	8	184	4
Catherine took her place at the table, and, after a short	NA	II	10	203	9
on whose regard you can place dependence; or whose counsel,	NA	II	10	207	38
would disgust her with the place, wished the Lady Frasers	NA	II	11	209	5
she preferred it to any place she had ever been at, and	NA	II	11	212	17
but in this horrid place one can find time for nothing.	NA	II	12	216	2
Thank God! we leave this vile place to-morrow.	NA	II	12	216	2
Such ease and such delights made her love the place and	NA	II	13	220	1
embrace supplied the place of language in bidding each	NA	II	13	229	31
The day which she had spent at that place had been one of	NA	II	14	230	2
Bath is a nice place, Catherine, after all.	NA	II	14	238	22
Good-will supplying the place of experience, his character	NA	II	16	249	1
might speedily take place, to unite them again in the	NA	II	16	250	3
consequence, which took place in the course of the summer--	NA	II	16	250	4
smiled; and, as this took place within a twelve-month from	NA	II	16	252	7
A continuance in a place where every thing reminded her of	SS	I	2	8	2
A great deal too handsome, in my opinion, for any place	SS	I	2	13	28
to Barton park, the place of his own residence, from	SS	I	4	23	20
belonging to the place, was now its first recommendation.	SS	I	4	23	20
for ever from that beloved place would be less painful	SS	I	4	24	20
by them in their last adieus to a place so much beloved.	SS	I	5	27	8
and from first seeing the place under the advantage of	SS	I	6	28	2
But Marianne, in her place, would not have done so little.	SS	I	11	57	17
day to see a very fine place about twelve miles from	SS	I	12	62	28
Willoughby took his usual place between the two elder Miss	SS	I	13	67	61
me the place; and it is a charming house I assure you.--	SS	I	13	69	76
declared to have taken place, Elinor could not imagine.	SS	I	14	71	3
place which affection had established as perfect with him.	SS	I	14	72	6
But are you really so attached to this place as to see no	SS	I	14	72	10
endear it to me; but this place will always have one claim	SS	I	14	73	15
Mrs. Dashwood's visit to Lady Middleton took place the	SS	I	15	75	1
quarrel had taken place between him and her sister;--the	SS	I	15	77	19
room and took her place at the table without saying a word.	SS	I	15	82	46
doubted to what place he should go when he left them--but	SS	I	19	101	1
which shortly took place, and left an uncomfortable	SS	I	19	104	9
I always thought it such a sweet place, ma'am! (turning to	SS	I	19	107	24
was at his house; but they say it is a sweet pretty place."	SS	I	20	111	14
it must be some other place that is so pretty I suppose."	SS	I	20	111	17
You cannot think what a sweet place Cleveland is; and we	SS	I	20	113	33
When is it to take place?"	SS	I	20	115	52
It is a sweet place by all accounts."	SS	I	20	116	60
to these young ladies took place, they found in the	SS	I	21	120	6
"Norland is a prodigious beautiful place, is not it?"	SS	I	21	123	23
Elinor, "who ever saw the place; though it is not to be	SS	I	21	123	25
One or two meetings of this kind had taken place, without	SS	II	1	143	9
A mutual silence took place for some time.	SS	II	2	149	24
Their departure took place in the first week in January.	SS	II	3	158	22
and what he meant, before many meetings had taken place.	SS	II	4	159	1
of his quitting that place, with the uneasiness and	SS	II	4	162	13
They arrived in due time at the place of destination, and	SS	II	6	175	2
This is not a place for explanations.	SS	II	6	177	14
and continual change of place, made her wander about the	SS	II	7	180	5
Marianne was to have the best place by the fire, was to be	SS	II	8	193	7
Delaford is a nice place, I can tell you; exactly what I	SS	II	8	196	22
call a nice old fashioned place, full of comforts and	SS	II	8	196	22
Oh! 'tis a nice place!	SS	II	8	197	22
be a secret--it would take place even within a few weeks,	SS	II	8	199	37
her from school, to place her under the care of a very	SS	II	9	208	28
Edward brought us a most charming account of the place;	SS	II	11	222	11
settle on him a thousand a-year, if the match takes place.	SS	II	11	224	28
sides, and I have not a doubt of its taking place in time.	SS	II	11	224	28
you must remember the place, where old Gibson used to live.	SS	II	11	225	31
china, &c. to supply the place of what was taken away.	SS	II	11	225	35
visit should begin a few days before the party took place.	SS	II	12	230	8
the sacrifice of the best place by the fire after dinner,	SS	II	14	247	4
your own judgment, to place Edward under private tuition,	SS	II	14	251	13
So up he flew directly, and a terrible scene took place,	SS	III	1	259	7
has a sister out of place, that would fit them exactly."	SS	III	1	260	7
discovery that took place under our roof yesterday."	SS	III	1	265	34
to stay at home, than venture into so public a place.	SS	III	2	271	4
and the time of its taking place remained as absolutely	SS	III	2	276	26
that had in the first place been so unfairly obtained, she	SS	III	2	276	27
that if any place could give her ease, Barton must do it.	SS	III	3	279	1
calm voice, "I am afraid it cannot take place very soon."	SS	III	3	281	9
					10
least, I am afraid it cannot take place very soon.--"	SS	III	3	284	23
immediately took place, by which both gained considerable	SS	III	4	292	54
When the marriage takes place, I fear she must hear of it	SS	III	5	296	18
When Edward's unhappy match takes place, depend upon it	SS	III	5	296	20
place, when it was not for me, you know, to interfere.	SS	III	5	299	37
to send her to Delaford;-a place, in which, of all others,	SS	III	6	301	2
Nor could she leave the place in which Willoughby remained,	SS	III	6	302	4
and like every other place of the same degree of	SS	III	6	302	7
liberty, of wandering from place to place in free and	SS	III	6	303	9
of wandering from place to place in free and luxurious	SS	III	6	303	9
care, to supply to her the place of the mother she had	SS	III	7	308	3
up the maid to take her place by her sister, she hastened	SS	III	7	311	14
allow her to take her place by Marianne; but Elinor had no	SS	III	7	315	27
A discovery took place,"--here he hesitated and looked	SS	III	8	321	34
had contributed to place her;--and in her recovery she had	SS	III	9	335	7
Delaford,--that place in which so much conspired to give	SS	III	12	357	3
the dryness of the season, a very awful pause took place.	SS	III	12	359	14
for a few weeks, which place your dear brother has great	SS	III	13	365	14
astonished himself that he had never yet been to the place.	SS	III	13	368	31
ceremony took place in Barton church early in the autumn.	SS	III	14	374	6
His property here, his place, his house, every thing in	SS	III	14	375	9
had been balls in the place, the former were accustomed to	W			314	1
ask why it did not take place, & why he is married to	W			316	2
Mrs Edwards may get a good place by the fire, & he never	W			319	2
street, & the best in the place, if Mr Tomlinson the	W			322	2
do you stay in this heavenly place?--till sunrise?"--	W			335	13
It was the way of the place always to call on Mrs E. on	W			337	16
of pleasing, & shewing himself pleased in a right place.--"	W			340	19
beg you will not set your neighbours against the place.--	W			350	24
chaise and four to see the place, and was so much	PP	I	1	3	10
flying about from one place to another, and never settled	PP	I	3	10	4
not think it would be a proper compliment to the place?"	PP	I	6	26	32
"It is a compliment which I never pay to any place if I	PP	I	6	26	23
nothing that can add to the beauties of that noble place.	PP	I	8	38	33
I do not know a place in the country that is equal to	PP	I	9	42	7
this desirable event takes place, as to the advantage of	PP	I	10	52	55
the separation, so agreeable to almost all, took place.	PP	I	12	60	5
Elizabeth made no answer, and took her place in the set,	PP	I	18	90	8
(glancing at her sister and Bingley,) shall take place.	PP	I	18	92	23
In the first place, he must make such an agreement for	PP	I	18	101	71
melancholy event takes place--which, however, as I have	PP	I	19	106	10
In the first place, she persisted in disbelieving the	PP	I	23	127	5
that she wished it to take place as soon as possible,	PP	I	23	128	10
for her, and live to see her take my place in it!"	PP	I	23	130	17
Mr. Darcy may perhaps have heard of such a place as	PP	II	2	141	13
Elizabeth affected to place this point, as well as the	PP	II	2	142	16
The wedding took place; the bride and bridegroom set off	PP	II	3	146	19
She opened the door, and met Maria in the landing place,	PP	II	5	158	11
					12
that he should give up the place entirely, for then we	PP	II	9	178	9
Long before it had taken place, my opinion of you was	PP	II	11	191	17
Mr. Wickham, who left the place immediately, and Mrs.	PP	II	12	202	5
These two girls had been above an hour in the place,	PP	II	16	219	1
And in the first place, let us hear what has happened to	PP	II	16	221	17
in Meryton, to attempt to place him in an amiable light.	PP	II	17	226	23
event should ever take place, I shall merely be able to	PP	II	17	227	25
herself in some public place or other, and we can never	PP	II	18	230	14
					15
streets of that gay bathing place covered with officers.	PP	II	18	232	22
of such double danger as a watering place and a camp.	PP	II	19	237	3
place, bring all the satisfaction she had promised herself.	PP	II	19	237	3
Gardiner expressed an inclination to see the place again.	PP	II	19	240	12
"My love, should not you like to see a place of which you	PP	II	19	240	13
"A place too, with which so many of your acquaintance are	PP	II	19	240	13
the place, instantly occurred. it would be dreadful!	PP	II	19	240	16
were not a very fine place, what was the name of its	PP	II	19	241	17
She had never seen a place for which nature had done more,	PP	III	1	245	3
On applying to see the place, they were admitted into the	PP	III	1	245	4
"And of this place," thought she, "I might have been	PP	III	1	246	6
"In what an amiable light does this place him!" thought	PP	III	1	249	39
admire the beauty of the place; but she had not got beyond	PP	III	1	254	57
Mr. Darcy took her place by her niece, and they walked on	PP	III	1	256	61
before she came to the place, and accordingly began by	PP	III	1	256	61
They had been walking about the place with some of their	PP	III	2	260	1
appeared, and this formidable introduction took place.	PP	III	2	261	3
but this did not take place till after many a significant	PP	III	3	268	6
to be assured it has taken place, for there is but too	PP	III	4	274	3
for on entering that place they removed into a hackney-	PP	III	4	274	5
"In the first place," replied Mr. Gardiner, "there is no	PP	III	5	282	5
apprehension of any thing before the elopement took place?	PP	III	5	290	45
And since this sad affair has taken place, it is said,	PP	III	5	291	54
Jane, "to go to Epsom, the place where they last changed	PP	III	5	293	69
to every tradesman in the place, and his intrigues, all	PP	III	6	294	4
be her husband, might then have rested in its proper place.	PP	III	8	308	1
living with Wickham, a fortnight before they took place.	PP	III	8	310	10
"Ah! Jane, I take your place now, and you must go lower,	PP	III	9	317	9
That is the place to get husbands.	PP	III	9	317	11
more when the wedding took place, and all money matters	PP	III	10	324	2
and though she would not place herself as his principal	PP	III	10	326	3
A most delightful place!--excellent parsonage house!	PP	III	10	328	26
Jane resolutely kept her place at the table; but Elizabeth,	PP	III	11	333	31
People did say, you meant to quit the place entirely at	PP	III	11	336	49
of her father, or the place where she lived, or any thing.	PP	III	11	336	49
They are gone down to Newcastle, a place quite northward,	PP	III	11	336	51
Bingley would take the place, which, in all their former	PP	III	12	340	11
must have taken place with that gentleman's concurrence.	PP	III	13	346	20
this place, that I might make my sentiments known to you."	PP	III	14	353	26
you have the presumption to aspire, can never take place.	PP	III	14	354	40
She followed her father to the fire place, and they both	PP	III	15	362	9
the marriage took place, should be so generally known.	PP	III	15	363	22

Your lively talents would place you in the greatest danger PP III 17 376 35
beginning; but what could set you off in the first place?" PP III 18 380 1
I am sure Wickham would like a place at court very much, PP III 19 386 7
Any place would do, of about three or four hundred a hear; PP III 19 386 7
They were always moving from place to place in quest of a PP III 19 387 8
an absolute breach between the sisters had taken place. MP I 1 3 1
It will be much the best place for her, so near Miss Lee, MP I 1 9 12
Indeed, I do not see that you could possibly place her any MP I 1 10 13
finding something to fear in every person and place. MP I 2 14 8
endeavoured, in the first place, to lessen her fears of MP I 2 17 20
The place became less strange, and the people less MP I 2 17 21
Here, I know I am of none, and yet I love the place so MP I 3 27 34
"The place, Fanny, is what you will not quit, though you MP I 3 27 35
A fine lady in a country parsonage was quite out of place. MP I 3 31 59
some place in the thoughts and conversation of the ladies. MP I 3 32 61
quite equal to supply his place with them, or rather to MP I 3 32 62
Edmund could supply his place in carving, talking to the MP I 4 34 1
It was not long before a good understanding took place MP I 4 39 10
marriage should not take place before his return, which he MP I 4 40 14
half an hour's notice, whenever she was weary of the place. MP I 4 41 16
When we reached Albion Place they were out; we went after MP I 5 51 40
she retook her chosen place near the bottom of the table, MP I 6 52 1
to be improving his own place in the same way; and though MP I 6 52 1
I never saw a place so altered in my life. MP I 6 53 2
Sotherton Court is the noblest old place in the world." MP I 6 53 3
I never saw a place that wanted so much improvement in my MP I 6 53 4
Such a place as Sotherton Court deserves every thing that MP I 6 53 9
a different place from what it was when we first had it. MP I 6 54 9
other subjects took place of the improvements of Sotherton. MP I 6 55 14
"Smith's place is the admiration of all the country; and MP I 6 55 15
more surprising that the place can have been so improved. MP I 6 55 17
it is cut down, to see the place as it is now, in its old MP I 6 56 22
Sotherton is an old place, and a place of some grandeur. MP I 6 56 25
he continued, "but had I a place to new fashion, I should MP I 6 56 28
are before me; and had I a place of my own in the country, MP I 6 57 29
I hear of Everingham, it may vie with any place in England. MP I 6 60 53
to Mansfield common took place the next morning;--the MP I 7 70 30
Sotherton is the only place that could giver her a wish to MP I 8 76 3
yet, and it was a pity she should not see the place." MP I 8 76 4
The place of all places, the envied seat, the post of MP I 8 80 29
not be an ill-looking place if it had a better approach." MP I 8 82 34
and the influence of the place and of example may often MP I 9 88 18
that it should not take place directly, if we had but a MP I 9 88 24
its being a most happy event to her whenever it took place. MP I 9 88 24
out of his place to appear what he ought not to appear." MP I 9 92 45
beyond a wish that they had seen his friend Smith's place. MP I 10 97 3
But now, sincerely, do not you find the place altogether MP I 10 98 6
if you had been in my place, but you always contrive to MP I 10 100 28
junction which had taken place at last seemed, to Fanny's MP I 10 104 51
If others have blundered, it is your place to put them MP I 15 140 13
like my situation; this place is too hot for me"--and MP I 15 147 56
Put yourself in Miss Crawford's place, Fanny. MP I 16 154 14
head of such a house, and keeps every body in their place. MP I 17 162 16
acts was certainly to take place in the evening; Mrs. MP I 18 171 25
his sudden arrival, as to place her nearer agitation than MP II 1 179 9
attend you from any place in England, at an hour's notice." MP II 2 193 12
Under his government, Mansfield was an altered place. MP II 3 196 1
had taken place, which gave Sotherton another mistress. MP II 3 202 28
Every public place was new to Maria, and Brighton is MP II 3 203 31
of intimacy which took place between them within the first MP II 4 207 11
carelessly, "it does very well for a place of this sort. MP II 4 209 15
If any body told me a year ago that this place would be my MP II 4 210 17
at the parsonage, you are not to be taking place of her. MP II 5 221 32
has taken place in her looks within the last six weeks. MP II 6 229 5
due time in the very place which I had a curiosity to see. MP II 7 241 13
large and handsome for the place, and not a gentleman or MP II 7 241 13
forgotten having ever told you half so much of the place." MP II 7 241 18
for five summers at least before the place is live-able." MP II 7 241 21
The place deserves it, and you will find yourself not MP II 7 243 27
The place deserves it, Bertram. MP II 7 243 27
You may raise it into a place. MP II 7 243 27
Have you ever seen the place?" MP II 7 244 27
Yes, that is a place indeed, and we had a charming day MP II 7 245 32
a smart place as that--poor scrubbery midshipman as I am." MP II 7 245 33
to refresh her spirits by a change of place and neighbour. MP II 7 248 48
think of Henry, for it was his choice in the first place. MP II 8 259 19
had been proposed, he would accept a place in his carriage. MP II 9 265 21
at home to take their own place in the room, and have MP II 10 275 12
She was happy even when they did take place; but not from MP II 10 278 20
or to have any thing take place at all in the way she MP II 10 280 32
and mustard in William's place, might but divide her MP II 11 282 2
body's dress, or any body's place at supper, but her own. MP II 11 282 4
which would otherwise have taken place about this time. MP II 11 284 10
I shall let Everingham, and rent a place in this MP II 12 295 20
spoken of their journey as what would take place ere long. MP III 1 311 1
who seemed to stand in the place of her parents; and he MP III 1 314 16
"I recommended the shrubbery to Fanny as the dryest place," MP III 1 323 55
she trusted, in the first place, that she had done right, MP III 1 324 58
inclined him, in the first place, to think she did love MP III 2 326 1
please--and I am sure the place is easy enough, for there MP III 7 385 39
In the first place, William was gone. MP III 8 388 2
Nobody was in their right place, nothing was done as it MP III 8 388 3
good breeding supplied its place; and as to the little MP III 8 392 11
was a sad place--they did not often get out--and she knew MP III 10 401 10
Such a man could come from no place, no society, without MP III 10 404 15
Now so long divided from every body who knew the place, MP III 10 405 17
It was her public place; there she met her acquaintance, MP III 11 408 4
but it would be out of place if I had, for this is to be a MP III 12 415 2
from it was, that nothing decisive had yet taken place. MP III 12 417 4
beloved place, the hearts of both sisters sank a little. MP III 15 446 35
Miss Crawford had taken place, from which Edmund derived MP III 16 452 15
soon as Sir Thomas could place dependence on such sources MP III 17 462 5
Her beauty and acquirements had held but a second place. MP III 17 466 17
that marriage had taken place, which would have given him MP III 17 467 19
the force of contrast, to place a yet higher value on the MP III 17 468 21
of disposition must in any place and any society, secure MP III 17 469 24
with her, because Susan remained to supply her place.-- MP III 17 472 31
of her caresses, and her place had been supplied by an E I 1 5 2
She had many acquaintance in the place, for her father was E I 1 7 10
You got Hannah that good place. E I 1 9 18
ago; and to have it take place, and be proved in the right, E I 1 11 39
the marriage, and it took place to the infinite E I 2 15 3
He was looked on as sufficiently belonging to the place to E I 2 17 7
a most proper attention, that the visit should take place. E I 2 17 9
Had it taken place only once a year, it would have been a E I 3 20 3
and describe the many comforts and wonders of the place. E I 4 27 4
an end to it, and request him to place himself elsewhere. E I 6 46 24
its filling its destined place with credit to them both--a E I 6 47 27
and satisfaction, took place on the morrow, and E I 6 47 30
The strangest things do take place!" E I 9 74 24
which they have chosen to place you in, here it will be E I 9 75 27
main street of the place; and, as may be inferred, E I 10 83 2
of the place, and recal the still greater within. E I 10 87 27
I do not know but that the place agrees with her tolerably. E I 11 94 8
This had just taken place and with great cordiality, when E I 12 99 14
South end is an unhealthy place. E I 12 105 54
a mistake to suppose the place unhealthy; and I am sure he E I 12 105 55
if it were to any other place or with any other party, I E I 13 110 9
and Mr. John Knightley more, to fit them for the place.-- E I 14 117 1
though I have never been at the place in my life.-- E I 14 120 13
takes place; and the sooner it could be over, the better." E I 14 122 20
had long held a high place in the consideration of the E I 16 136 9

Harriet's persisting to place her happiness in the sight E I 17 143 13
Their being fixed, so absolutely fixed, in the same place, E I 17 143 14
place, but without a mother's affection to blind her. E I 18 149 26
even to give up her place to Miss Woodhouse, and her more E II 1 155 4
their country-seat, Balycraig, a beautiful place, I fancy. E II 1 159 20
like to speak of his own place while he was paying his E II 1 159 20
drawings of the place, views that he had taken himself. E II 1 160 20
This event had very lately taken place; too lately for any E II 2 165 8
united; the shop first in size and fashion in the place.-- E II 3 178 52
place the Martins under proper subordination in her fancy. E II 3 180 57
the young ladies of the place, to whom, a few weeks ago, E II 4 182 5
among the gentlemen and half-gentlemen of the place. E II 6 197 5
The want of proper families in the place, and the E II 6 198 5
that none beyond the place and its immediate environs E II 6 198 5
body's returning into their proper place the next morning. E II 6 198 5
to belong to the place, to be a true citizen of Highbury. E II 6 200 14
chiefly among the single men, had already taken place. E II 7 207 6
on me to supply her place, if I can; and I will step to E II 7 209 11
she had been used to despise the place rather too much. E II 8 220 48
Emma would then resign her place to Miss Fairfax, whose E II 8 227 86
They were stopping, however, in the first place at Mrs. E II 9 233 25
--every day making me less fit to bear any other place. E II 12 260 21
that had the ball taken place, she did not think Jane E II 12 263 42
and his place and his carriages were the pride of him. E II 14 272 17
of a place I am so extremely partial to as Maple Grove. E II 14 273 19
A charming place, undoubtedly. E II 14 273 19
My brother and sister will be enchanted with this place. E II 14 273 21
And it is so cheerful a place, that it could not fail of E II 14 275 32
secure you some of the best society in the place. E II 14 275 32
that the place might suit her better than her father." E II 14 276 34
to have held such a place in society as Mrs. Elton's E II 15 281 1
parties which are to take place in the barouche-landau." E II 15 288 39
It is a retired place. E II 18 307 20
I fine place, but very retired." E II 18 307 20
to spend in some warmer place than Enscombe--in short, to E II 18 308 30
They came from Birmingham, which is not a place to promise E II 18 310 34
numerous engagements take place without your being of the E II 18 312 50
Coles--and having a ball talked of, which never took place. E II 18 312 50
It soon appeared that London was not the place for her. E III 1 317 7
person there, and had otherwise a fancy for the place. E III 1 317 7
which just then took place between him and Mrs. Weston; E III 2 327 34
bring her to Hartfield: he had thought of no other place. E III 3 334 7
to any young ladies in the place, within her memory; no E III 3 335 10
in the place were soon in the happiness of frightful news. E III 3 336 12
taken place, there have been matches of greater disparity. E III 4 342 39
admirer of Miss Woodhouse, seemed somewhat out of place. E III 5 343 2
could have had power to place there and persuade her E III 5 347 18
Place, Venice, when Frank Churchill entered the room. E III 6 363 53
the fire; but quite out of place, in my opinion, when one E III 7 372 37
upon an acquaintance formed only in a public place!-- E III 7 372 40
that Bath, or any public place, can give--it is all E III 7 372 40
disparity had taken place than between Mr. Frank Churchill E III 11 407 28
the shrubbery--in every place, every posture, she E III 11 411 43
When had he succeeded to that place in her affection, E III 11 412 45
Were this most unequal of all connexions to take place, on E III 11 413 47
herself; and in the first place had wished not to go at E III 12 417 5
If all took place that might take place among the circle E III 12 422 19
My right to place myself in a situation requiring such E III 14 437 8
I knew the name, the place, I knew all about it, and E III 14 442 8
He had induced her to place herself, for his sake, in a E III 15 446 20
to the place in her mind which Harriet had occupied. E III 16 452 6
lady's in the case, "you know all other things give place." E III 16 454 13
might not be so very bad if the marriage did take place. E III 17 467 30
Lord be more delighted with the place he held in society. P III 1 4 5
In any other place, Sir Walter might judge for himself; P III 2 13 7
It was a much safer place for a gentleman in his P III 2 14 10
quite out of place, could hint of caution and reserve. P III 2 15 15
to eat; I was to give place to Lord St. Ives, and a P III 3 19 16
an inclination for the place as a man who knew it only by P III 3 21 18
family, and mentioned a place; and Anne, after the little P III 3 21 20
21

been given in change of place, (except in one visit to P III 4 28 7
and all that he had told her would follow, had taken place. P III 4 29 8
was to be considered so much at home as to lose her place. P III 6 45 10
persons are about their place, because, all the world P III 6 46 10
be always putting herself forward to take place of mamma. P III 6 46 10
Her own spirits improved by change of place and subject, P III 6 46 12
but believe that in his place she should have done long P III 7 58 21
were sitting, took a place by the latter, and entered into P III 8 67 28
She would take place of me then, and Henrietta would not P III 9 75 11
make a different sort of place of it, and live in a very P III 9 76 15
it were really so, I should do just the same in her place. P III 10 85 9
It would place her in the same village with Captain P III 11 93 2
much time for seeing a new place, after deducting seven P III 11 94 8
which Lyme, as a public place, might offer; the rooms were P III 11 95 9
would be glad to get to a place where she could have P III 12 102 2
out their last days in a place like Uppercross, where, P III 12 102 2
Her first return, was to resume her place in the modern P IV 1 123 9
Strangers filling their place!" P IV 1 126 18
A good place, is not it? P IV 1 127 26
place, for yours were always kept in the butler's room. P IV 1 127 26
liking, and have no fault at all to find with the place. P IV 1 128 29
twenty-four hours in the place, but he had not been able P IV 3 138 6
opinions respecting the place, but especially wanting to P IV 3 143 19
been engaged in there, soon after his leaving the place. P IV 3 144 22
to enjoy a welcome which depends so entirely upon place." P IV 4 151 20
your dear mother's place, succeeding to all her rights, P IV 5 159 25
"little people think of letters in such a place as Bath. P IV 6 162 7
"In the first place, I had a note from Mrs. Croft P IV 6 164 8
should not have many acquaintance in such a place as this." P IV 6 166 14
but when the meeting took place, it was evident that no P IV 6 168 22
One does not love a place the less for having suffered in P IV 8 184 16
I have travelled so little, that every fresh place would P IV 8 184 16
my impressions of the place are very agreeable." P IV 8 184 16
own, Anne was enabled to place herself much nearer the end P IV 8 189 46
the bench, as if he saw a place on it well worth occupying; P IV 8 190 47
trouble in the right place might do it, and to fear that P IV 9 210 98
to take place in a few months, quite as soon as Louisa's. P IV 10 217 20
said he, "to enjoy the evening parties of the place." P IV 10 225 57
take my place, and give Anne your arm to her father's door. P IV 11 240 58
To me, she was in the place of a parent. P IV 11 246 80
merit and activity could place him, was no longer nobody. P IV 12 248 1
cd not have happened, you know, in a better place.-- S 1 364 1
not that promise to be the very place?"-- S 1 364 1
age, the proprietor of the place, who happened to be among S 1 364 1
in this place, which can be the abode of a genlteman."-- S 1 365 1
of the fact;--stay--can I be mistaken in the place?-- S 1 365 1
Your mistake is in the place.-- S 1 366 1
Every five years, one hears of some new place or other S 1 368 1
while the growth of the place, the buildings, the nursery S 1 368 1
No sir, I assure you, Sanditon is not a place-----" S 1 368 1
"I do not mean to take exceptions to any place in S 1 368 1
Such a place as Sanditon sir, I may say was wanted, was S 1 369 1
rocks--never was there a place more palpably designed by S 1 369 1
tea within 3 miles of the place--& as for the soil--it is S 1 369 1
I did not know there was such a place in the world." S 1 369 1
This gentleman did not know there was such a place in the S 1 370 1
A thing of this kind soon makes a stir in a lonely place S 1 370 1
bathing place was the object, for which he seemed to live. S 2 371 1
rise & prosperity of the place--wd in fact tend to bring a S 2 372 1
place where they could have immediate medical advice.-- S 2 372 1
being then to take her place;--but in selecting the one, S 3 379 1

"And whose very snug-looking place is this?"--said S 4 379 1
It is an honest old place--and Hillier keeps it in very S 4 380 1
But it was a nice place for the children to run about in. S 4 380 1
at an old friend, at a place where one has been happy.-- S 4 381 1
And it would be a fine thing for the place!-- S 4 382 1
proof of the increasing fashion of the place altogether. S 4 383 1
Cottage, & a denham place were to be looked at by S 4 384 1
broad walk in front, aspiring to be the Mall of the place. S 4 384 1
for the interest of the place, to get a medical man there, S 5 387 1
not taken place, or we should have seen him in his way.-- S 5 387 1
She wanted to have the place fill faster, & seemed to have S 6 392 1
here, or even a Co--since Sanditon had been a public place. S 7 401 1
no connections in the place, & no means of ascertaining S 9 409 1
& the hotel, Charlotte's place was by Arthur, who was S 10 414 1
Mrs G. had preferred a small, retired place, like Sanditon, S 11 421 1
of meaning to be the most stylish girls in the place.-- S 11 421 1
A little novelty has a great effect in so small a place; S 11 422 1
I am not fond of charitable subscriptions in a place of S 12 423 1
in the credit which Sidney's arrival wd give to the place. S 12 426 1
the best place by the fire constantly occupied by Sir H. D. S 12 427 1

PLACED (81)
Miss Vernon is to be placed at a school in town before her LS 3 247 1
lady with whom she has placed her daughter, to request LS 15 266 2
from such a mother, & placed under her own care; & tho' LS 42 311 2
large party were already placed, without having any thing NA I 2 22 10
latter no less anxiously placed his upon pleasing her, it NA I 13 97 1
When once my affections are placed, it is not in the power NA I 13 98 2
withered oak which he had placed near its summit, to oaks NA I 14 111 29
instructions, and placed it all to judicious affection. NA II 4 153 31
Why should it be placed here?-- NA II 6 163 2
have placed him high among the benefactors of the convent. NA II 8 183 3
and one in whom she had always placed great confidence. NA II 9 196 25
day, which placed this matter in a still clearer light. SS I 12 60 8
Elinor placed all that was astonishing in this way of SS I 19 101 2
The card-table was then placed, and Elinor began to wonder SS II 1 144 10
placed themselves at no great distance from the table. SS II 6 175 2
the too great importance placed by her on the delicacies SS II 9 201 4
In one moment her imagination placed before her a letter SS II 9 202 7
I saw her placed in comfortable lodgings, and under proper SS II 9 207 26
home; and my little Eliza was therefore placed at school. SS II 9 208 28
ease; card-tables may be placed in the drawing-room; the SS II 14 252 18
had been shewn, so much confidence had been placed! SS III 1 265 36
of your family has placed you--a concern which I am sure SS III 4 289 31
entering on new duties, placed in a new home, a wife, the SS III 14 378 16
as they were all duely placed again, Emma in the low W 327 8
her disposition, & the circumstances she is placed in.-- W 341 19
and aunt Philips be placed in the gallery at Pemberley. PP I 10 52 57
When the card tables were placed, he had an opportunity of PP I 16 76 6
perverseness which placed them within one of each other; PP I 18 98 63
can be placed on the appearance of either merit or sense. PP II 1 135 11
I am always glad to get a young person well placed out. PP II 6 165 32
joined them, and tea was over, the card tables were placed. PP II 6 166 41
parcels placed within, and it was pronounced to be ready. PP II 15 216 8
He placed himself by her. PP III 12 340 11
and the card tables placed, the ladies all rose, and PP III 12 342 26
house, so well placed and well screened as to deserve to MP I 5 48 28
It is ill placed. MP I 6 56 26
as herself; and both placed near a window, cut down to the MP I 7 65 13
a kind low whisper as she placed herself, "never mind, my MP I 15 147 56
to come at all hours--and placed suddenly on a footing MP I 16 154 14
She was answered by having a small trinket-box placed MP II 8 257 15
more frequently placed before her eyes than the rest. MP II 8 258 17
To be placed above so many elegant young women! MP II 10 275 12
for William, was to be placed to the account of his MP II 13 301 7
and shewn you every thing placed on a basis the most MP III 1 314 16
of a scheme which placed Fanny's chance of seeing the 2d MP III 6 368 8
I really cannot be plaguing myself for ever with all new P IV 10 215 15

PLAIN (71)
Her mother was a woman of useful plain sense, with a good NA I 1 13 1
they were in general very plain, and Catherine, for many NA I 1 13 1
and Catherine, for many years of her life, as plain as any. NA I 1 13 1
girl who has been looking plain the first fifteen years of NA I 1 15 2
robe with blue trimmings--plain black shoes--appeared to NA I 3 26 22
height, who, with a plain face and ungraceful form, seemed NA I 7 45 5
Her own family were plain matter-of-fact people, who NA I 9 65 31
in making those things plain which he had before made NA I 9 66 31
attachment now; his coming back to Bath makes it too plain. NA I 10 70 1
spoke her astonishment in very plain terms to her partner. NA II 1 133 30
of living, as you see, is plain and unpretending; yet no NA II 2 139 7
a Rumford, with slabs of plain though handsome marble, and NA II 5 162 26
In such a case, a plain and open avowal of his SS I 15 81 43
nearly thirty, with a very plain and not a sensible face, SS I 21 120 6
very probable; it was plain that Edward had always spoken SS II 1 142 7
I heard him say all this as plain as could possibly be. SS III 2 273 16
of being the only plain one in the family, worked hard for PP I 6 25 23
prefer a plain dish to a ragout, had nothing to say to her. PP I 8 35 2
Not that I think Charlotte so very plain--but then she is PP I 9 44 29
"Oh! dear, yes;--but you must own she is very plain. PP I 9 44 31
of each other was plain enough to make her a little uneasy; PP II 2 142 18
men must have something to live on, as well as the plain." PP II 3 150 29
her features, though not plain, were insignificant; and PP II 6 162 12
Her ladyship received them civilly, but it was plain that PP II 8 172 2
It was plain to them all that Colonel Fitzwilliam came PP II 9 180 28
Our plain manner of living, our small rooms, and few PP II 15 215 2
discrimination, for it was plain that he was that moment PP III 1 252 54
saw him, he was absolutely plain, black and plain; but MP I 5 44 2
plain, black and plain; but still he was the gentleman, MP I 5 44 2
The second meeting proved him not so very plain; he was MP I 5 44 2
not so very plain; he was plain, to be sure, but then he MP I 5 44 2
one soon forgot he was plain; and after a third interview, MP I 5 44 2
to think Mr. Crawford very plain, in spite of her two MP I 5 48 30
time--and Miss Crawford, it is plain, has heard the story." MP I 5 50 35
"The error is plain enough," said the less courteous MP I 5 50 38
I am a very matter of fact, plain spoken being, and may MP I 9 94 56
what had been originally plain, had suffered all the ill- MP I 16 152 2
It was plain that he could have so serious views, no true MP II 5 228 69
She was then merely a quiet, modest, not plain looking MP II 6 229 5
of jeweller's packing, a plain gold chain perfectly simple MP II 9 262 8
and, finally, in words so plain as to bear but one meaning MP II 13 301 7
him, made it instantly plain to her, what she had to do. MP III 14 436 15
She was a plain, motherly kind of woman, who had worked E I 3 22 5
I thought him very plain at first, but I do not think him E I 4 29 13
very plain at first, but I do not think him so plain now. E I 4 29 13
Do you think him so very plain?" E I 4 32 29
"He is very plain, undoubtedly--remarkably plain:--but E I 4 32 30
I see the difference plain enough. E I 4 33 33
him already, is very plain from the circumstances of his E I 4 33 40
the language, though plain, was strong and unaffected, and E I 7 50 4
That is ship;--plain as can be.-- E I 9 73 18
Miss Campbell always was absolutely plain--but extremely E II 1 161 27
but speaking plain enough to be very intelligible to Emma. E II 3 170 1
Oh! no--far from it--certainly plain. E II 3 176 47
I told you he was plain." E II 3 176 47
would not allow him to be plain, and that you yourself----- E II 3 176 48
49
I believed the general opinion, when I called him plain." E II 3 176 49
enough--to look plain, probably, by Harriet's side. E II 4 183 9
her that if she wanted plain muslin it was of no use to E II 9 235 35
took the opportunity of whispering, "you speak too plain. E II 10 243 23
24
Plain dealing was always best. E III 4 341 34
The subject followed; it was in plain, unaffected, E III 15 448 31

Look! in places you see it is dreadfully dirty; and the E II 11 253 41
the contrast between the places in some of the first E II 13 265 5
There are places in town, offices, where inquiry would E II 17 300 13
She had given them neither men, nor names, nor places, E III 6 358 35
shall never be easy till I have seen some of these places. E III 6 364 60
look at some advertised places in that immediate P III 3 21 18
forms in the usual places, or without the talking, P III 6 46 12
places about home--Cork, and Lisbon, and Gibraltar. P III 8 70 52
Isle of Wight: these places must be visited, and visited P III 11 95 9
When their places were determined on, and they were all P IV 8 186 22
It may apply to your large, overgrown places, like S 1 368 1
If they had hard places, they would want higher wages.--" S 7 401 1

PLACID (6)
replied Mrs. Allen, with the most placid indifference. NA I 9 61 7
in excellent spirits, and Isabella most engagingly placid. NA II 4 153 31
Lady Bertram constantly declined it; but her placid manner MP I 8 76 2
"Yes, she does look very well," was Lady Bertram's placid MP II 10 277 15
In this more placid state of things William re-entered, MP III 7 384 34
assume a most obliging, placid look, and appear quite P IV 10 213 10

PLACIDITY (1)
That is a degree of placidity, which I can neither E III 10 397 46

PLACIDLY (2)
a case by saying very placidly, every now and then, "I NA I 2 21 9
"No," replied her friend very placidly, "I know you never NA I 11 82 7

PLACING (17)
I have therefore resolved on placing her at one of the LS 1 244 1
Her solid affection for her child is shewn by placing her LS 14 265 5
This was placing her in a very uncomfortable situation, NA II 5 155 2
seat to scare her, and on placing a hand against the NA II 6 167 10
So, placing the candle with great caution on a chair, she NA II 6 168 10
and endeavouring, by placing around them their books and SS I 6 29 5
manner, by constantly placing Willoughby before her, such SS II 10 213 3
writer's real design, by placing it in the hands of Mrs. SS III 2 278 31
placing a screen in the proper direction before her eyes. PP II 6 162 12
on the necessity of placing gowns in the only right way, PP II 14 213 20
Those that best pleased her, as placing his conduct in the PP III 9 320 32
She was all attention, however, in placing a chair for him, MP III 1 312 5
She persisted in placing his scruples to her account, MP III 17 465 13
a most happy thought, the placing of Miss Smith out of E I 6 48 39
to be placing her in such a state of unmerited punishment. E III 15 450 37
good principles, and placing her happiness in the E III 18 474 34
of cousinly notice, and placing his whole happiness in P IV 3 139 10

PLAGUE (13)
Leave Frederica therefore to punish herself for the plague LS 26 295 1
At any rate I hope he will plague his wife more than ever. LS 32 303 2
no Tilneys appeared to plague or please her; she feared NA I 12 92 4
Charles Hodges will plague me to death I dare say; but I NA II 1 130 13
I wish with all my soul his wife may plague his heart out. SS II 8 192 3
"We can all plague and punish one another. PP I 11 57 17
female intending to plague you, but as a rational creature PP I 19 109 20
there could be nothing more to plague her on his account. PP II 16 223 25
"How the pleasing plague had stolen on him" he could not MP II 12 292 8
it would be too bad to plague you with the names of people MP III 12 415 2
from the wantonness of comfort, or his son may plague him." E I 5 38 13
"Very well; I will not plague you any more. E I 5 40 23
Her satisfaction in Mr. Elliot outweighed all the plague P IV 4 147 6

PLAGUED (6)
ago, and I trust I shall never be plagued with him again. NA II 12 217 2
she has been very much plagued lately with nervous head- SS II 10 219 38
make one son independent, because another had plagued me." SS III 1 269 54
against common sense, that a woman could be plagued with. MP II 4 212 30
already; be plagued very often and never lose your temper." MP II 4 213 34
Was she as much plagued as herself to get tolerable MP III 7 385 38

PLAGUING (3)
has hit on the most effectual manner of plaguing us all. LS 28 297 1
My cousins have been so plaguing me!-- SS III 2 272 12
of the one, which her imprudent marriage had placed her in. MP III 8 390 5
All this became gradually evident, and gradually placed MP III 9 396 6
for its completion, placed Julia's feelings in a most MP III 16 452 13
Where she could be placed, became a subject of most MP III 17 464 13
The backgammon-table was placed; but a visitor immediately E I 1 9 20
Somebody had placed her, several years back, at Mrs. E I 3 22 8
"You are better placed here; very fit for a wife, but not E I 5 38 11
among whom birth and circumstances have placed her home. E I 5 38 15
to be transported and placed all at once in Mr. Frank E I 18 147 19
every corner dish was placed exactly right, and occupation E II 8 218 38
39
as he had improvidently placed himself exactly between E II 8 222 57
was; placed exactly in the same part of the house. E II 14 273 19
perhaps any where, than where he had placed himself. E III 2 326 32
Frank Churchill placed a word before Miss Fairfax. E III 5 347 21
Mr. Knightley so placed as to see them all; and it was his E III 5 341 21
morning, he was happily placed, quite at his ease, ready E III 6 357 33
of this bank, favourably placed and sheltered, rose the E III 6 360 38
After a few whispers, indeed, which placed it beyond a E III 16 455 20
21
She would be placed in the midst of those who loved her, E III 19 482 4
which must have placed her high with any people of real P III 1 5 8
flower-stands and little tables placed in every direction. P III 5 40 44
when they are placed in circumstances, requiring fortitude P III 10 87 26
She was in the carriage, and felt that he had placed her P III 10 91 42
fell to Anne's lot to be placed rather apart with Captain P III 11 100 23
views should have placed her friend at all in favour with P III 12 103 5
He had handed them both in, and placed himself between P III 12 116 70
The Crofts had placed themselves in lodgings in Gay-Street, P IV 6 168 23
we were exceedingly well placed--that is for hearing; I P IV 9 193 11
The box was brought and placed before her, and Mrs. Smith, P IV 9 202 69
70
the scattered paper, placed it before Anne with eyes of P IV 11 236 40
in which Providence had placed him, and who could give his P IV 12 248 1
She seemed placed with her on purpose to be ill-used. S 6 391 1
by whom he chanced to be placed--& she soon perceived that S 7 394 1
her halfhour's fever, & placed her in a more capable state S 7 395 1
two, might very fairly be placed to the account of the S 11 420 1
stately gentleman, which placed over the mantlepeice, S 12 427 1

PLACES (37)
very well; but going to inns and public places together! NA I 13 104 31
It is one of the finest old places in England, I NA II 3 143 2
If it had been like some other places, I do not know that, NA II 6 167 9
the taste of ladies in regard to places as well as men. NA II 7 175 15
for the names of the places which were then to conduct her NA II 14 232 6
country for my part, except the shops and public places. PP I 9 43 21
and in particular places; at his own house especially, and PP I 10 50 39
a disgraceful light it places Mr. Darcy, to be treating PP I 17 85 4
of any of the remarkable places through which their route PP II 19 240 12
behind, on resuming their places, after descending to the PP III 1 255 61
of the largest estates and finest places in the country. MP I 4 38 9
but I cannot be in two places at once; and I was talking MP I 7 73 53
Mrs. Grant to alight and the others to take their places. MP I 8 80 29
The place of all places, the envied seat, the post of MP I 8 80 29
so close to the great house as often happens in old places. MP I 8 82 34
it is, for in these great places, the gardeners are the MP I 9 91 37
He is used to much gayer places than Mansfield." MP I 12 116 5
could put Mrs. Grant right the other day in twenty places. MP I 18 172 31
unhappy in her marriage, places her disappointment, not to MP III 13 421 2
out of conceit with all the other places she belongs to. E I 5 38 15
to fix on times or places, but I must tell you that I have E I 8 58 19
20
he holds it to be the best of all the sea-bathing places. E I 12 105 56
they had all taken their places, that he was close to her. E I 14 118 4
half an inch deep in many places hardly enough to whiten E I 15 127 16
think there are few places with such society as Highbury. E II 3 175 39

It is very plain that he considers the good fortune of the E III 17 464 20
and, therefore, you must give me a plain, direct answer. E III 18 474 29
every thing plain and easy between landlord and tenant. P III 3 18 9
10
set off handsome features, but can never alter plain ones. P III 5 35 16
very plain faces he was continually passing in the streets. P IV 3 141 13
The worst of Bath was, the number of its plain women. P IV 3 141 13
but the number of the plain was out of all proportion. P IV 3 141 13
Miss Carteret, with still less to say, was so plain and so P IV 4 150 14
He gave her a very plain, intelligible account of the P IV 10 216 19
PLAINER (6)
time with James, was therefore obliged to speak plainer. NA I 9 61 6
Can I speak plainer? PP I 19 109 20
preferred a longer and a plainer chain as more adapted for MP II 8 258 17
Never did tone express indifference plainer. MP II 11 288 30
it of all things," was not plainer in words than manner. E III 6 354 9
nothing could be plainer; and where many divisions were P III 10 90 37
PLAINEST-SPOKEN (1)
or she and thou, the plainest-spoken amongst us; we all E II 15 286 23
PLAINLY (30)
I see plainly that she is uneasy at my progress in the LS 10 257 1
She now plainly saw that she must not expect a manuscript NA II 7 172 1
which told him almost as plainly, as he soon forced her to NA II 7 178 21
What could more plainly speak the gloomy workings of a NA II 8 187 13
letter, saw plainly that it ended no better than it began. NA II 10 202 8
Willoughby, as plainly denoted how well she understood him. SS I 14 73 16
that he wanted, Elinor; I could plainly see that. SS I 15 78 24
not wanted syllables where actions have spoken so plainly. SS I 15 79 36
Elinor, who saw as plainly by this, as if she had seen the SS II 7 181 7
and though she could plainly perceive at different times, SS II 14 248 5
bow which assured her as plainly as words could have done, SS II 14 250 12
ways, Mrs. Jennings very plainly heard Elinor say, and SS III 3 281 13
14
as she spoke--and her unsteady voice, plainly shewed. SS III 11 349 3
considered; and here it plainly appeared, that though SS III 14 374 4
Her mother's thoughts she plainly saw were bent the same PP I 18 98 63
Two inferences, however, were plainly deduced from the PP I 21 127 5
Excuse me--for I must speak plainly. PP II 18 231 18
a way, as plainly spoke the distraction of his thoughts. PP III 1 252 52
when they last met, were plainly expressed. she was PP III 11 336 43
voice and manner plainly shewed how really happy he was. PP III 13 348 34
house was open, could be plainly distinguished in the MP III 7 382 27
with gentlemen so plainly.written as in Mr. Knightley. E I 4 33 34
This is saying very plainly--'pray, Miss Smith, give me E I 9 72 15
Resentment could not have been more plainly spoken than in E I 17 140 3
which she plainly read in the fair heroine's countenance. E II 8 220 46
showed indisposition so plainly, and she thought only of E III 9 390 18
Elton, but to Miss Woodhouse, as the latter plainly saw. E III 16 457 34
body else; for he could plainly see how old all the rest P III 1 6 11
surgeon, was also plainly stated;--it had not proceeded S 2 371 1
my feelings tell me too plainly that in my present state, S 5 387 1
PLAINTIVE (3)
I shall prepare my most plaintive airs against his return, MP I 6 59 41
in the plaintive tone which just suited her father. E I 11 94 12
answer than a very plaintive--"Mr. Elton is so good to the E II 1 155 1
PLAINTIVELY (1)
Mrs. Price plaintively, "it would be so very shocking!-- MP III 15 440 18
PLAISTER (10)
the cotton, Emma saw only a small piece of court plaister. E III 4 338 9
plaister, one of the very last times we ever met in it!-- E III 4 338 12
your new penknife, and your recommending court plaister?-- E III 4 338 12
court plaister, and saying I had none about me!-- E III 4 338 13
"And so you actually put this piece of court plaister by E III 4 339 15
plaister that Frank Churchill had been pulling about!-- E III 4 339 15
once belong to him, which the court plaister never did." E III 4 339 16
"But, Harriet, is it necessary to burn the court plaister?- E III 4 340 25
bit of old pencil, but the court plaister might be useful." E III 4 340 25
This is breaking a head and giving a plaister truly!" P IV 1 127 22
PLAIT (1)
as to make a ring, with a plait of hair in the centre, SS I 18 98 10
PLAN (128)
of masters which brought on the plan of an elopement. LS 17 271 7
is busy in pursueing the plan of romance begun at Langford. LS 19 274 2
for a moment given up my plan of her marriage; no, I am LS 19 275 4
alteration of his present plan; things have gone too far. LS 23 284 7
uncomfortable, & confirmed her in the plan of altering it. LS 42 311 3
Her plan for the morning thus settled, she sat quietly NA I 9 60 1
In that interval the plan was completed, and as soon as NA I 13 97 1
at the mention of such a plan, and her first thought was NA II 5 156 5
in some way or other, by its falling short of his plan. NA II 7 178 23
one on the same plan, but superior in length and breadth. NA II 8 184 5
as their home; and, as no plan appeared so eligible to Mrs. SS I 2 8 1
a little, however, in giving her consent to this plan. SS I 2 10 17
though it was not a plan which brought any charm to her SS I 4 24 21
the spring, and we will plan our improvements accordingly." SS I 6 29 4
Without considering that it was not in her mother's plan SS I 12 58 1
and build it up again in the exact plan of this cottage." SS I 14 72 11
to your plan of general civility," said Edward to Elinor. SS I 17 94 40
other profession; now my plan is that he should take SS II 2 149 25
no indifference to the plan, immediately gave a grateful SS II 3 153 1
direct opposition to the plan, and merely referred it to SS II 3 154 6
"I am delighted with the plan," she cried, "it is exactly SS II 3 155 8
And I have a little plan of alteration for your bedrooms SS II 3 155 8
pleased with the plan, and her sister exhilarated by it in SS II 3 158 20
on the most liberal plan, and excepting a few old city SS II 5 168 11
and nothing but the plan of the flower-garden marked out." SS II 11 226 37
and the affair was arranged precisely after my plan. SS II 14 252 18
of her good-will, when a plan was suggested, which, though SS III 3 279 1
other plan could do, and perhaps without any greater delay. SS III 3 280 6
The morning was fine and dry, and Marianne, in her plan of SS III 6 303 11
I have formed my plan, and am determined to enter on a SS III 10 343 9
Elinor honoured her for a plan which originated so nobly SS III 10 343 10
I have laid down my plan, and if I am capable of adhering SS III 10 347 30
As Tom Musgrave was seen no more, we may suppose his plan W 336 14
The plan was warmly opposed by their visitor. W 339 18
"Your plan is a good one," replied Elizabeth, "where PP I 6 22 7
and the delay of his plan, has merely desired it, asked it PP I 10 50 34
This was his plan of amends--of atonement--for inheriting PP I 15 70 2
His plan did not vary on seeing them.-- PP I 15 70 3
but his plan did not appear in the least affected by it. PP I 21 115 2
plan, and she gradually learned to consider it herself with PP II 4 151 1
in time, and the plan became perfect as plan could be. PP II 4 151 1
madam; but I believe we must abide by our original plan." PP II 14 211 11
plan, were to go no farther northward than Derbyshire. PP II 19 238 7
He had certainly formed such a plan, and without meaning PP III 3 270 10
than to pursue their first plan; and even if he could form PP III 4 275 5
their plan, and would not give his real opinion about it. PP III 5 290 48
by no means given up her plan of their residing in PP III 8 313 20
impediment in the way of a plan which would be so MP I 1 7 7
of their benevolent plan; and it was pretty soon decided MP I 2 18 23
"Well, Fanny, and if the plan were not unpleasant to you, MP I 3 25 21
My plan was laid at Westminster--a little altered perhaps MP I 6 61 56
little approbation of a plan which was to take Mr. MP I 6 61 58
the execution of the plan for visiting Sotherton, which MP I 8 75 1
Fanny's gratitude when she heard the plan, was in fact MP I 8 79 27
plan, and one that was admitted with general approbation. MP I 8 79 28
thought it an excellent plan, and had it at her tongue's MP I 8 80 28
no inclination to move in any plan, or to any distance. MP I 9 90 36
nothing more would be necessary on such a plan as this. MP I 13 123 8
it will be on the simplest plan;--a green curtain and a MP I 13 127 31
Their mother had no objection to the plan, and they were MP I 13 128 38
any thing to censure in a plan like their's, comprehending MP I 13 128 38
of an enlargement of plan and expense fully evident, was MP I 14 130 1
such an enlargement of the plan as this--so contrary to MP I 15 148 59
are exceeding their first plan in every respect; but I can MP I 16 154 12
The morrow came, the plan for the evening continued, and MP I 18 167 14
in forming the plan; they ought to have been capable of a MP II 2 188 3
whether there were any plan for resuming the play after MP II 2 192 11
The plan of the young couple was to proceed after a few MP II 3 203 31
over the ruin of all her plan of exercise for that morning, MP II 4 205 3
There is such a quiet simplicity in the plan of the walk!-- MP II 4 209 14
I understand you--and a very proper plan it is for a MP II 4 213 40
times a week; but I have a plan for the intermediate days, MP II 6 229 1
No, my plan it to make Fanny Price in love with me." MP II 6 229 3
your plan for Thornton Lacey will ever be put in practice. MP II 7 242 24
"My plan may not be the best possible; I had not many MP II 7 243 27
you to proceed upon my plan, though by the bye I doubt any MP II 7 243 27
on your own improved plan, and with all the improvements MP II 7 247 41
of your improved plan that may occur to you this spring." MP II 7 247 41
It was just the plan to suit Fanny; and with a great deal MP II 8 257 15
get his attention to her plan, or any answer to her demand MP II 9 262 11
pleased: for the original plan was that William should go MP II 9 266 21
compliment, or kindness, that might assist the plan. MP III 2 329 12
William was almost as happy in the plan as his sister. MP III 6 371 18
to more than his first plan had comprehended, and was now MP III 10 404 15
a friend, a guide in every plan of utility or charity for MP III 10 404 15
two fair, excellent, irresistible objections to that plan." MP III 10 405 19
his entering into a plan of that sort, most pleasantly. MP III 12 419 9
to give up every dearer plan, in order to fly with her." MP III 16 455 19
not been the most direful mistake in his plan of education. MP III 17 463 8
her in the date of the plan, as it had entered her brain E I 4 35 44
been any part of their plan to introduce her into what you E I 8 62 42
The plan of a drain, the change of a fence, the felling of E I 12 100 16
turned to Mrs. Weston for her approbation of the plan. E I 15 127 16
would be a much better plan; better time of year; better E I 18 144 2
The plan was that she should be brought up for educating E II 2 164 5
had made him alter his plan, and travel earlier, later, E II 5 190 23
It did not accord with the rationality of plan, the E II 7 205 1
Every door was now closed, the passage plan given up, and E II 11 249 12
"It appears to me a plan that nobody can object to, if Mr. E II 11 251 24
an improvement--a very bad plan--much worse than the other. E II 11 251 26
Oh! no--a very bad plan. E II 11 251 26
himself, or because the plan had been formed without his E II 12 257 2
Will not it be a good plan? E II 14 277 38
nephew's letter to Randall's communicated a change of plan. E III 1 317 7
Escape, however, was not his plan. E III 2 327 34
became of Mr. Perry's plan of setting up his carriage?" E III 5 344 5
and said, "I did not know that he ever had any such plan." E III 5 344 6
"I like your plan," cried Mr. Weston. E III 7 371 29
She made her plan; she would speak of something totally E III 13 429 26
27
But the plan which had arisen on the sacrifice of this, he E III 15 449 31
This proposal of his, this plan of marrying and continuing E III 15 450 36
her own little adelaide educated on a more perfect plan." E III 17 461 2
difficulty, since it was a plan to promote the happiness E III 17 465 28
Shocking plan, living together. E III 17 469 36
absence in a tour to the sea-side, which was the plan.-- E III 19 483 8
agreeable, and every plan in his favour was confirmed. P III 1 8 15
part of the Kellynch-Hall plan, when it burst on her, P III 5 34 11
and lessening the interference in any plan of their own. P III 10 83 4
The plan had reached this point, when Anne, coming quietly P III 12 114 60
the two ladies. when the plan was made known to Mary, P III 12 115 65
Do you think this a good plan?" P III 12 117 74
contrary, seemed to have a plan of going away for a week P IV 2 133 25
Her plan of sitting with Lady Russell must give way for P IV 10 220 30
the extension of your plan, and all that had happened, or P IV 10 228 71
"For you alone I think and plan.-- P IV 11 237 42
It deranged his best plan of domestic happiness, his best P IV 12 250 7
Arthur made no difficulties--our plan was arranged S 9 409 1
always of the first consequence in every plan of Mrs G.-- S 11 421 1
PLANETS (1)
Semi-metals, Planets, and distinguished philosophers." MP I 2 18 25
PLANNED (10)
already had Mrs. Bennet planned the courses that were to PP I 3 9 4
In her kind schemes for Elizabeth, she sometimes planned PP II 9 181 31
While in their cradles, we planned the union: and now, at PP III 14 355 43
in the house before she told her what she had planned. MP I 4 42 17
He should not have planned such an absence--he should not MP II 11 286 15
something planned as a pleasant surprize to herself. MP II 12 291 1
of all that they had planned and depended on. MP III 8 388 2
I planned the match from that hour; and when such success E I 1 12 41
on faster than one has planned; and the pleasure of coming E II 5 190 24
they had engaged in it, & planned & built, & praised & S 2 371 1
PLANNING (8)
While she with the truest affection had been planning a SS III 1 266 38
at least planning a vigorous prosecution of them in future. SS III 11 352 20
marriage, and planning his happiness in such an alliance. PP I 10 52 54
You both did as much as you could, in planning the PP III 14 355 44
powers of planning judged of by the day at Sotherton. MP II 7 245 31
call it, means only your planning it, your saying to E I 1 12 42
and probable, for her to have much merit in planning it. E I 4 34 44
a few days they must be planning, proceeding and hoping in E II 12 257 1
PLANS (33)
To effect all this I have various plans. LS 25 294 4
& as, tho' her own plans were not yet wholly fixed, she LS 42 312 5
her wishes, hopes and plans all centered in nothing less. NA I 10 74 23
your time and give an interest to your plans and actions. SS I 19 102 3
and laid before me three different plans of Bonomi's. SS II 14 251 17
of his plans, nothing certain even of his present abode. SS III 11 352 21
cut--and he drew several plans for magnificent cottages;-- SS III 14 376 11
said Emma,--but I do not like her plans or her opinions. W 318 2
I hope your plans in favour of the ----shire will not be PP I 16 78 19
some plans of the latter with regard to new furniture. PP II 1 133 2
their views and their plans might be more comprehensive. MP I 10 97 4
all his hopes and fears, plans, and solicitudes respecting MP II 6 234 18
from Edmund as to his plans for the next day's hunting; MP II 6 236 23
according to all preceding plans, she was to remove to MP II 11 287 17
What are your plans? MP II 12 293 11
can judge, matrimony makes no part of his plans or thought. MP III 1 317 34
He should have worked upon my plans. MP III 4 348 21
Miss Crawford made us laugh by her plans of encouragement MP III 4 354 46
Edmund's plans were affected by this Portsmouth journey, MP III 6 373 25
are my present plans, if plans I can be said to have.-- MP III 13 420 2
ever producing between the plans and decisions of mortals, MP III 17 471 29
He told me every thing; his circumstances and plans, and E I 8 59 27
to suppose that views, and plans, and projects you have;-- E I 8 66 51
On the contrary, her plans and proceedings were more and E I 9 69 1
knew nothing of their plans; and it was an agreeable E II 6 196 2
I have been making discoveries and forming plans, just E II 8 222 59
that was immediately important of their state and plans. E III 9 388 15
I know he said he was in the dark as to her plans. E III 10 397 51
been communicating his plans to his brother, and was E III 13 424 1
plans and her own, for a marriage between Frank and Emma. E III 17 467 31
She drew up plans of economy, she made exact calculations, P III 2 12 3
he confided his hopes and plans, and though I did not know P IV 9 200 57
the very same Mrs G. whose plans were at the same period (S 11 420 1
PLANTATION (6)
gravel winding round a plantation, led to the front, the SS III 6 302 7
again into the plantation, and was soon out of sight. PP II 12 195 2
wall, and made the plantation to shut out the churchyard, MP I 6 54 9
in his way from his plantation to his dressing-room, she MP II 5 217 11
Such an immense plantation all round it! E II 18 307 21
lawn with a very young plantation round it, about an S 4 384 1
PLANTATIONS (8)

old trees, or luxuriant plantations, and the steep woody NA II 7 177 19
to watch over his young plantations, and extend his NA II 16 250 3
left is Barton Park, amongst those woods and plantations. SS I 16 88 33
walk to Sir John's new plantations at Barton-Cross, and SS III 10 343 9
gardens, and nearest plantations; but active and MP II 2 190 9
of her uncle's plantations, and the glory of his woods.-- MP III 14 432 9
Her eye fell every where on lawns and plantations of the MP III 15 446 35
growth of my plantations is a general astonishment. S 4 381 1
PLANTED (5)
beyond the first planted aerea, a bowling-green, and MP I 9 90 36
wilderness, which was a planted wood of about two acres, MP I 9 91 38
"The farm-yard must be cleared away entirely, and planted MP II 7 242 23
house, well fenced & planted, & rich in the garden, S 4 379 1
The road to Sanditon h. was a broad, handsome, planted S 12 426 1
PLANTING (2)
I should be always planting and improving, for naturally I MP I 6 53 9
should take a prodigious delight in improving and planting. MP I 6 54 9
PLANTS (13)
plants in winter, and there was a fire in it now and then." NA II 7 178 25
the loss of her favourite plants, unwarily exposed, and SS III 6 303 10
a choice collection of plants and poultry, was very much MP I 4 41 15
"Here are the greatest number of our plants, and here are MP I 9 90 33
All were attracted at first by the plants or the pheasants, MP I 9 90 36
his choicest nursery of plants, and actually presented her MP I 10 103 50
when she visited her plants, or wanted one of the books, MP I 16 151 1
of thought at hand.-- her plants, her books--of which she MP I 16 151 2
same sun should nurture plants differing in the first rule MP II 4 209 16
here are some of my plants which Robert will leave out MP II 4 212 31
Young ladies are delicate plants. E II 16 294 25
which of Elizabeth's plants are for Lady Russell. P III 5 38 34
display of green-house plants, that she said, "I have been P IV 11 246 79
80

PLATE (5)
plate, and linen was saved, and is now left to your mother. SS I 2 12 26
And yet some of the plate would have been a very pleasant SS I 2 13 27
It chiefly consisted of household linen, plate, china, and SS I 5 26 4
and all the articles of plate which Mr. Collins had PP II 6 162 14
He fancied it tough--sent away his plate--and has been MP I 18 171 27
PLATES (1)
of half-cleaned plates, and not half-cleaned knives and MP III 11 413 30
PLATFORM (2)
I jumped up, and made but two steps to the platform. MP III 7 380 20
I was upon the platform two hours this afternoon, looking MP III 7 380 20
PLATONIC (1)
are likely to be engaged in a kind of platonic friendship. LS 10 258 2
PLAUSIBILITY (1)
In support of the plausibility of this conjecture, it NA II 8 188 17
PLAUSIBLE (4)
get Reginald home again, under any plausible pretence. LS 11 259 1
He gives a very plausible account of her behaviour at LS 15 266 1
grown and good-looking, with smooth, plausible manners." E I 18 149 28
handsome woman, poor and plausible, and altogether such in P IV 9 206 88
PLAUSIBLY (1)
But as for myself, I am still unconvinced; & plausibly as LS 3 247 1
PLAY (140)
I want her to play & sing with some portion of taste, & a LS 7 253 1
"Yes, sir, I was at the play on Tuesday." NA I 3 26 13
Mr. Tilney was no fonder of the play than the Pump-Room. NA I 5 35 1
the second, that it was a play she wanted very much to see. NA I 12 92 4
No longer could he be suspected of indifference for a play; NA I 12 92 4
The play concluded--the curtain fell--Henry Tilney was no NA I 12 93 5
asking her to make room for him, and talking of the play. NA I 12 95 15
Could it be possible, or did not her senses play her false? NA II 7 172 2
and a charming game of play with a litter of puppies just NA II 11 214 26
I have not been to the rooms this age, nor to the play, NA II 12 217 2
was discovered to be musical, she was invited to play. SS I 7 35 8
that she had been used to play to Willoughby, every air in SS I 16 83 3
What shall we play at! SS II 8 195 14
she should want him to play at piquet of an evening, while SS III 7 309 5
I was forced to play the happy lover to another woman!-- SS III 8 327 55
he does; & very few people that play a fairer rubber.-- W 325 4
only round game at Croydon now, but I can play anything.-- W 354 28
amuse him--why do not you get him to play at cribbage?-- W 354 28
"Dear me!--cried Margt why should not we play at vingt-un?- W 358 28
me to play and sing before any body and every body!-- PP I 6 24 22
only to eat, drink, and play at cards, who when he found PP I 8 35 2
She assured him that no one intended to play, and the PP I 11 54 3
Mr. Wickham did not play at whist, and with ready delight PP I 16 76 8
impossible for them to play their parts with more spirit, PP I 18 101 72
When this was done, she had a less active part to play. PP II 2 139 3
Before they were separated by the conclusion of the play, PP II 4 154 21
Do you play and sing, Miss Bennet?" PP II 6 164 16
Do your sisters play and sing?" PP II 6 164 18
The Miss Webbs all play, and their father has not so good PP II 6 164 20
Down to quadrille; and as Miss de Bourgh chose to play at PP II 6 166 41
times, that she will never play really well, unless she PP II 8 173 10
day, and play on the piano forte in Mrs. Jenkinson's room. PP II 8 173 10
play to him; and she sat down directly to the instrument. PP II 8 173 12
But I will not be alarmed though your sister does play so PP II 8 174 13
Well, Colonel Fitzwilliam, what do I play next? PP II 8 175 20
"Miss Bennet would not play at all amiss, if she practised PP II 8 176 27
28

the room, as to make him play as unsuccessfully as herself. PP III 12 342 26
they were so good as to play, they could do no more than MP I 2 14 7
"I shall be most happy to play to you both," said Miss MP I 6 59 41
was again very happy in the prospect of hearing her play. MP I 6 60 52
She has a wonderful play of feature! MP I 7 63 3
just do; and though we play but half-crowns, you know you MP I 12 119 23
theatrical party; and the play, in which he had borne a MP I 13 121 1
The play had been Lovers' Vows, and Mr. Yates was to have MP I 13 122 2
Be it only half a play--an act--a scene; what should MP I 13 123 6
gallery, and let us have a play entire from beginning to MP I 13 124 10
end; so as it be a German play, no matter what, with a MP I 13 124 10
"Nobody loves a play better than you do, or can have gone MP I 13 124 11
We may be trusted, I think, in choosing some play most MP I 13 125 18
they may not be able to find any play to suit them. MP I 13 128 34
The business of finding a play that would suit every body, MP I 14 130 1
was already at work, while a play was still to seek. MP I 14 130 1
housemaids, and still the play was wanting; and as two or MP I 14 130 1
all, such a need that the play should be at once both MP I 14 130 2
Not a tolerable woman's part in the play----- MP I 14 131 3
it the most insipid play in the English language----- MP I 14 131 3
play, but every thing of higher consequence was against it. MP I 14 131 4
Henry Crawford, who meanwhile had taken up the play, and MP I 14 133 11
It could make no difference in the play; and as for MP I 14 134 14
He was, perhaps, but at treacherous play with her. MP I 14 135 18
eagerly looking over the play, with Mr. Yates's help, to MP I 14 136 21
herself with the play of which she had heard so much. MP I 14 137 23
that he had once seen the play in London, and had thought MP I 15 138 1
"We have got a play," said he.-- MP I 15 138 3
"I should not have thought it the sort of play to be so MP I 15 139 9
what I feel as to this play, without reflecting on his MP I 15 139 11
acquainted with the play, I assure you--and with a very MP I 15 140 12
The play will be given up, and your delicacy honoured as MP I 15 140 15
"If every play is to be objected to, you will act nothing-- MP I 15 141 22
I do not know the play; but, as Maria says, if there is MP I 15 141 22
Dick Jackson, but neither play nor preparation were MP I 15 142 24
a separate table, with the play open before them, and were MP I 15 142 25
said she, "on the play being chosen; for though you have MP I 15 143 26
"My advice," said he, calmly, "is that you change the play. MP I 15 144 37
We shall only want you in our play. MP I 15 145 45
The consultation upon the play still went on, and Miss MP I 15 148 58
"I am not very sanguine as to our play"--said Miss MP I 15 149 61
They have chosen almost as bad a play as they could; and MP I 16 153 8
and must disapprove the play in particular; their point MP I 17 158 1
soon too busy with his play to have time for more than one MP I 17 160 9
She was not pleased to see Julia excluded from the play, MP I 17 161 9
done, and as soon as the play is all over, we will talk to MP I 17 162 18
ready to regret that some other play had not been chosen. MP I 18 164 1
enjoyment from the play as any of them;--Henry Crawford MP I 18 165 3
used to be very fond of a play ourselves--and so am I MP I 18 167 7
8

What is the play about, Fanny, you have never told me?" MP I 18 167 8
is very little in a play without a curtain--and I am much MP I 18 167 11
The ruin of the play was to them a certainty, they felt MP II 1 177 5
any plan for resuming the play after the present happy MP II 2 192 11
The play should not be lost by his absence. MP II 2 192 11
are going--but as to our play, that is all over--entirely MP II 2 193 13
thing appertaining to the play; he left the house in all MP II 2 194 21
and spring, when her own taste could have fairer play. MP II 3 202 26
own neglect;--and "shall I play to you now?"--and "what MP II 4 206 5
And besides, I want to play something more to you--a very MP II 4 207 9
he had yet to inspirit her play, sharpen her avarice, and MP II 7 240 8
by Sir Thomas's capital play and her own, against Dr. and MP II 7 245 32
to dispute over their last play, he became a looker-on at MP II 7 246 36
Two play on the piano-forte, and one on the harp--and all MP II 11 288 28
His acting had first taught Fanny what pleasure a play MP III 3 337 10
"That play must be a favourite with you," said he; "you MP III 3 338 12
"It was really like being at a play," said she.-- MP III 3 338 17
I have not thought well of him from the time of the play. MP III 4 349 25
short, at the time of the play, I received an impression MP III 4 349 25
The time of the play, is a time which I hate to recollect. MP III 4 349 26
"Before the play, I am much mistaken, if Julia did not MP III 4 350 29
very curious, that we should have such a scene to play! MP III 5 358 9
It is a sort of prologue to the play, a motto to the E I 9 74 23
They had music; Emma was obliged to play; and the thanks E II 2 168 15
I was glad you made her play so much, for having no E II 3 170 2
lady we were speaking of, play?" said Frank Churchill. E II 6 201 26
She appeared to me to play well, that is, with E II 6 201 28
of her being thought to play well:--a man, a very musical E II 6 201 28
But if she continued to play whenever she was asked by Mr. E II 6 202 37
"Oh! if I could play as well as you and Miss Fairfax!" E II 9 231 5
"Oh! dear--I think you play the best of the two. E II 9 231 7
I think you play quite as well as she does. E II 9 231 7
"Well, I always shall think that you play quite as well as E II 9 232 9
Besides, if she does play so very well, you know, it is no E II 9 232 11
who was still sitting at it, to play something more. E II 10 242 16
willingly undertook to play as long as they could wish to E II 11 247 3
You, Miss Woodhouse, I well know, play delightfully. E II 14 276 36
but you sing as well as play;--yes, I really believe you E II 17 301 18
It was a child's play, chosen to conceal a deeper game on E III 5 348 21
I believe I did not play with the children quite so much E III 17 465 27
come at any time, and help play at any thing, or dance any P III 6 47 15
She had rather play. P III 8 72 58
he could only have some play; and as his aunt would not P III 9 79 29
I know you love a play; and there is room for us all. P IV 10 223 41
We all like a play. P IV 10 223 41
perfect readiness for the play, if Henrietta and all the P IV 10 223 42
43

You may do as you like, but I shall go to the play." P IV 10 223 44
the scheme for the play; and she, invariably serious, most P IV 10 224 50
very well used, if they went to the play without her. P IV 10 224 50
at all for the play, if Miss Anne could not be with us." P IV 10 224 51
should be too happy to change it for a play, and with you. P IV 10 224 53
he would go to the play to-morrow, if nobody else would." P IV 10 225 55
I could not bring it into play: it was overwhelmed, buried, P IV 11 245 74
but the inferior part of the character he had to play.-- S 8 405 2
The play of your Sinews a very little affected:--barely S 9 408 1
PLAY'D (1)
Mr E. having play'd with good luck, they were some of the W 336 14
PLAY-FELLOW (1)
been important as play-fellow, instructress, and nurse, MP I 2 14 8
PLAYED (31)
heroine, who had not yet played a very distinguished part NA I 2 23 27
whether she drew, or played or sang, and whether she was NA I 8 56 11
need of my being played off to make her secure of Tilney. NA II 10 202 7
played extremely well, and by her own was very fond of it. SS I 7 35 8
She played over every favourite song that she had been SS I 16 83 3
Margaret & I have played at cribbage, most nights that we W 354 28
"It is the only round game played at Croydon now, said Mrs W 358 28
Vingt-un is the game at osborne castle; I have played W 358 28
He played with spirit, & had a great deal to say & tho' W 359 28
When Lady Catherine and her daughter had played as long as PP II 6 166 42
and good humour, for she played with the greatest MP I 7 64 12
She played accordingly; happy to have a new listener, and MP II 4 207 6
She played till Fanny's eyes, straying to the window on MP II 4 207 6
to the favourite air, played, as it appeared to her, with MP II 4 207 10
ignorance; she had never played the game nor seen it. MP II 7 239 8
the game nor seen it played in her life; and Lady Bertram MP II 7 239 8
The cards were brought, and Fanny played at cribbage with MP II 11 283 6
as she neither played on the pianoforte nor wore fine MP III 9 395 3
taught and how she had played with her from five years old- E I 1 6 6
She played and sang;--and drew in almost every style; but E I 6 44 19
christian name, and say whose music she principally played. E II 4 181 2
Every body last night said how well you played." E II 9 231 7
She played. E II 10 242 18
for a moment, coloured deeply, and played something else. E II 10 242 20
touches the instrument--though she played sweetly. E II 14 277 40
I believe I have not played a bar this fortnight.-- E III 16 456 23
She played a great deal better than either of the Miss P III 6 46 13
She knew that when she played she was giving pleasure only P III 6 47 13
to a more active post, played country dances to them by P III 6 47 15
They played me a pitiful trick once--got away some of my P IV 6 170 29
great barns; and he played his part so well, that I have P IV 10 219 26
PLAYER (6)
You know I am no card player. W 354 28
taste is equal, the player must always be best off, for MP I 6 59 41
acquisition of a violin player in the servants' hall, and MP I 12 117 11
He was a whist player himself, and perhaps might feel that MP II 7 239 6
it was in him, their best player, to absent himself, and E I 8 68 58
best country-dance player, without exception, in England. E II 10 245 49
PLAYERS (4)
One of the best players we have, by the bye; and we had a NA I 12 96 20
players being disposed to move exactly the different way. W 333 13
The whist party soon afterwards breaking up, the players PP I 16 82 49
rapacity for whist players, and in a few moments after PP III 12 342 26
PLAYFELLOWS (1)
from out earliest years we were playfellows and friends. SS II 9 205 24
PLAYFUL (12)
He is full of spirits, playful as can be, but there is no NA I 9 62 9
fingers, she fondly observed, "how playful William is!" SS I 21 121 8
for she had a lively, playful disposition, which delighted PP I 3 12 14
and sometimes with playful gaiety replied to her attacks. PP I 20 112 23
or diversion in the playful conceits they suggested. MP I 17 159 6
quick resources, and playful impudence that could do MP II 7 240 9
she presently, with a playful smile, "but it is over now; MP III 5 359 9
myself for a too harsh construction of a playful manner. MP III 13 421 2
that had passed, a saucy playful smile, seeming to invite, MP III 16 459 30
He could not meet her in conversation, rational or playful. E I 1 7 7
Accordingly, with a mixture of the serious and the playful, E I 15 129 24
25

This nut," he continued, with playful solemnity,--"while P III 10 88 26
PLAYFULLY (2)
a fanciful, troublesome creature!" said Emma playfully. E I 1 10 30

"To be sure!" cried she playfully. E I 8 64 46

PLAYFULNESS (10)

Affecting that air of playfulness, therefore, which is SS III 8 328 61
fashionable world, he was caught by their easy playfulness. PP I 6 23 12
Elizabeth's spirits soon rising to playfulness again, she PP III 18 380 1
give her playfulness and simplicity without extravagance. MP I 14 135 15
it--speaks it in playfulness--and though I know it to be MP II 9 269 31
I know it to be playfulness, it grieves me to the soul." MP II 9 269 31
and all the laughs of playfulness which are so essential MP II 11 283 7
admiration, or playfulness, extremely judicious, they were E III 7 368 3
and that gaiety, that playfulness of disposition, which, E III 12 419 12
goodhumoured playfulness, which exactly suited me. E III 14 438 8

PLAYING (32)

And old man playing at see-saw! NA I 7 49 40
in it but an old man's playing at see-saw and learning NA I 7 49 42
playing in beautiful splendour on its high Gothic windows. NA II 5 161 24
A gentleman carrying a gun, with two pointers playing SS I 9 42 8
and laughing together, playing at cards, or consequences, SS II 1 143 8
on which Marianne was playing, she could not keep herself SS III 3 281 9
I cannot think of him, but as playing cards with ly W 343 19
more pleasure, though not playing half so well; and Mary, PP I 6 25 24
but suspecting them to be playing high she declined it, PP I 8 37 21
After playing some Italian songs, Miss Bingley varied the PP I 10 51 47
48
principally occupied in playing with her bracelets and PP I 11 54 3
Elizabeth immediately began playing again. PP II 8 176 27
way--teaching them, playing with them, and loving them. PP II 19 239 10
deal of good advice as to playing with Maria and Julia, MP I 2 17 20
only two characters worth playing before I reached MP I 13 122 2
space of a week without playing at billiards in it, you MP I 13 127 29
They were in the ball-room, the violins were playing, and MP II 10 275 10
I was playing the fool with my eyes open." MP III 4 350 26
It was a sort of playing at being frightened. MP III 13 427 12
and sleeping and playing, which they could possibly wish E I 11 92 3
eating and drinking, and playing whist with his neighbours E I 11 96 26
regret the inferiority of her own playing and singing. E II 9 231 3
My playing is no more like her's, than a lamp is like E II 9 231 6
The truth is, Harriet, that my playing is just good enough E II 9 232 8
She is playing Robin Adair at this moment--his favourite." E II 10 243 29
cut it smaller, and kept playing some time with what was E III 4 338 12
very pretty trick you have been playing me, upon my word! E III 10 400 67
68
Playing a most dangerous game. E III 15 445 15
playing with the children, it would not have escaped her. E III 17 463 16
She is never tired of playing." P III 8 72 58
inadvertence, and wantonly playing with our own happiness." P IV 10 221 33
double a game he had been playing, and how determined he P IV 12 250 7

PLAYS (17)

She was fond of all boys' plays, and greatly preferred NA I 1 13 1
balls and plays, and every-day sights, is past with them." NA I 10 79 57
the family, a fondness for plays was not to be ranked; but NA I 12 92 4
"That is, I can read poetry and plays, and things of that NA I 14 108 20
thing--a time for balls and plays, and a time for work. NA II 15 240 2
When an old lady plays the fool, it is not in the course W 326 6
She plays and sings all day long. PP III 1 248 22
Many parts of our best plays are independent of scenery." MP I 13 124 9
would never wish his grown up daughters to be acting plays. MP I 13 127 26
All the best plays were run over in vain. MP I 14 130 3
one of the many volumes of plays that lay on the table, MP I 14 132 7
every woman who plays herself is sure to ask about another. MP II 11 288 28
a good part of one of his plays, without falling into the MP III 3 338 13
She plays charmingly." E II 6 201 27
It always has quite hurt me that Jane Fairfax, who plays E II 8 215 16
up--parties, balls, plays--for I had no fear of retirement. E II 14 276 36
I do not scruple to say that she plays extremely well. E II 15 282 5

PLAYTHINGS (1)

They have brought the whole coach full of playthings for SS I 21 119 4

PLEA (13)

and having again urged the plea of health in vain, was too NA II 7 179 29
urging her by every plea of duty and affection to demand SS II 5 172 39
plea of Mr Watson's infirm state of health.-- W 348 22
Upon what plea? MP III 1 315 25
The usual plea of increasing engagements was made in MP III 9 393 1
without solicitation, or plea, or privilege, she must be E II 15 282 4
which seemed a plea for the invitation: but no plea was E III 6 354 9
for the invitation: but no plea was necessary; cabbage- E III 6 354 9
which she had, under the plea of being unequal to any E III 9 391 21
Miss Fairfax's recent illness had offered a fair plea for E III 12 418 5
My plea of concealing the truth she did not think E III 14 440 8
at home, under the mixed plea of a head-ache of her own, P III 9 77 17
Such a plea must prevail, he got the butter & spread away S 10 417 1

PLEAD (4)

My total ignorance of the connection must plead my apology. PP I 18 97 57
nor have I any thing to plead in excuse of my stay, but PP III 4 278 20
Let me plead for my--present friend I cannot call him--but P IV 9 196 30
and was obliged to plead indisposition and excuse herself. P IV 11 238 45

PLEADED (3)

Morland remonstrated, pleaded the authority of road-books, NA I 7 45 7
and steady candour always pleaded for allowances, and PP II 1 138 31
by his father;--she only pleaded against there being any MP I 4 36 7

PLEADING (2)

Harriet and pleading his own cause, gave alarming ideas. E I 8 67 56
half suspecting me of pleading poor Martin's cause, which E III 18 474 34

PLEASANT (146)

how pleasant it would be if we had any acquaintance here." NA I 4 31 1
endeavouring to ensure a pleasant walk to him who brought NA I 7 47 18
to dispute; "and I hope you have had a pleasant airing?" NA I 9 67 34
by no means been very pleasant and that John Thorpe NA I 9 69 51
'For six weeks, I allow Bath is pleasant enough; but NA I 10 78 45
rate for wishing us a pleasant walk after our passing you NA I 12 93 7
"But indeed I did not wish you a pleasant walk; I never NA I 12 94 8
that it might be too pleasant to allow either James or NA I 14 115 55
never tease the other beyond what is known to be pleasant." NA II 4 152 28
The bustle of going was not pleasant.-- NA II 5 155 4
Has my sister a pleasant mode of instruction?" NA II 7 174 10
and the view from them pleasant, though only over green NA II 11 213 21
which it must be more pleasant for him to communicate only NA II 15 243 9
And yet some of the plate would have been a very pleasant SS I 2 13 27
It was a pleasant fertile spot, well wooded., and rich in SS I 6 28 1
hills, and formed a pleasant view from the cottage windows. SS I 6 29 3
Her imagination was busy, her reflections were pleasant, SS I 9 43 11
But he is a pleasant, good humoured fellow, and had got SS I 9 44 20
Are the Middletons pleasant people?" SS I 16 88 38
Have you forgot, Marianne, how many pleasant days we have SS I 16 88 40
I thought you would, he is so pleasant; and Mr. Palmer is SS I 20 114 42
make your situation pleasant, might be reasonably expected. SS II 11 222 11
never looked at me in a pleasant way-- you know what I SS II 13 240 17
girls, and would be pleasant companions; for otherwise we SS III 1 266 36
could not fancy dry or pleasant weather for walking. SS III 6 303 11
late dinner, affording a pleasant enlargement of the party, SS III 6 304 14
very capable of being a pleasant companion, and only SS III 6 304 15
Elinor, confirmed in every pleasant hope, was all SS III 7 310 8
little company, & a pleasant ball now & then, would be W 317 2
I have had some pleasant hours at speculation in my time-- W 358 28
At our time of life, it is not so pleasant I can tell you, PP I 2 8 26
had a pleasant countenance, and easy, unaffected manners. PP I 3 10 5
Upon my honour, I never met with so many pleasant girls in PP I 3 11 10
"It may perhaps be pleasant," replied Charlotte, "to be PP I 6 21 2
right than pleasant that she should go down stairs herself. PP I 8 37 21
'She seems a very pleasant young woman," said Bingley. PP I 9 44 30
'how pleasant it is to spend an evening in this way! PP I 11 55 4
and lastly, it was so pleasant at her time of life to be PP I 18 99 63
He is a pleasant fellow, and would jilt you creditably." PP II 1 138 27
I am extremely glad that you have such pleasant accounts PP II 3 149 26
As the weather was fine, they has a pleasant walk of about PP II 6 161 8
there were half hours of pleasant conversation with PP II 7 169 5
Their brother is a pleasant gentleman-like man--he is a PP II 10 184 22
Have you seen any pleasant men? PP II 16 221 17
Mr. Gardiner, whose manners were easy and pleasant, PP III 1 248 23
that she had never seen him so pleasant as this morning. PP III 1 258 71
and then he had nothing of a pleasant nature to send. PP III 6 297 12
The officers may not be so pleasant in general ----'s PP III 8 313 21
She never knew how to be pleasant to children. MP I 3 26 25
of both were lively and pleasant, and Mrs. Grant MP I 4 41 17
Miss Crawford, is always pleasant society to an indolent, MP I 5 47 26
Tom Bertram must have been thought pleasant, indeed, at MP I 5 47 28
new furnished--pleasant sisters, a quiet mother, and an MP I 5 48 28
up without supplying one pleasant anecdote of any former MP I 6 52 1
your mother, and have a pleasant drive home by moonlight. MP I 6 62 58
it; for he was not pleasant by any common rule, he talked MP I 7 65 13
hope you will have a pleasant ride, and that I may have MP I 7 68 20
roses, and very pleasant it was I assure you, but very hot. MP I 7 72 42
day, and as it was a pleasant fresh-feeling morning, less MP I 8 75 1
Their road was through a pleasant country; and Fanny, MP I 8 80 31
and nothing in the world could be more snug and pleasant." MP I 9 88 24
and with no increase of pleasant feelings, for she was MP I 10 100 23
and the drive was as pleasant as the serenity of nature MP I 10 106 58
only time to say in a pleasant manner, "I fancy Miss Price MP I 11 112 33
and with pleasant attention was complimenting her. MP I 15 143 26
Her pleasant manners and cheerful conformity made her MP I 18 171 28
"Mr. Crawford was a most pleasant gentleman-like man;--his MP II 1 186 30
for Mr. Yates's having a pleasant journey, as he walked MP II 2 194 21
The two sisters were so kind to her and so pleasant, that MP II 4 206 4
I can even suppose it pleasant to spend half the year in MP II 4 210 21
in the country, under certain circumstances--very pleasant. MP II 4 210 21
"It is as a dream, a pleasant dream!" he exclaimed, MP II 5 225 55
It was more pleasant than prudent. MP II 5 226 59
a young man of an open, pleasant countenance, and frank, MP II 6 233 16
The meeting was generally felt to be a pleasant one, being MP II 7 238 3
The proposal was a very pleasant one to William himself, MP II 9 266 21
very punctual, and short and pleasant had been the meal. MP II 11 282 1
had hoped to hear some pleasant assurance of her power, MP II 11 289 33
but now it was a pleasant joke--suspected only of MP II 12 291 1
something planned as a pleasant surprize to herself. MP II 12 291 1
That is pleasant! MP II 12 295 21
of satisfaction, and words of simple, pleasant meaning. MP III 3 334 2
They were all very pleasant. MP III 4 355 52
Pleasant, good-humoured, unaffected girls. MP III 4 355 54
Of pleasant talk between the brother and sister, there was MP III 7 375 2
a good night's rest, a pleasant morning, the hope of soon MP III 8 388 1
Good bye; I wish you a pleasant journey to-morrow. MP III 11 412 23
I fancy Lord S. is very good-humoured and pleasant in his MP III 12 416 2
The Aylmers are pleasant people; and her husband away, she MP III 14 434 13
suitable age and pleasant manners; and there was some E I 1 6 6
to fill the house and give her pleasant society again. E I 1 7 9
Mr. Weston is such a good-humoured, pleasant, excellent E I 1 8 12
attended by her pleasant husband to a carriage of her own. E I 2 18 12
Randalls, but it was not pleasant; and a Harriet Smith, E I 4 26 1
the thing is, to be always happy with pleasant companions. E I 7 55 34
She was obliged to break off from these very pleasant E I 9 72 16
and may be as sensible and pleasant as anybody else. E I 10 85 19
presently, "was not so pleasant as I had hoped--'not E I 13 114 29
quite forgotten in the expectation of a pleasant party. E I 13 115 42
intention of finding him pleasant, of being liked by him E I 14 119 5
or other, it was very pleasant to have her father so well E I 16 138 18
19
"A very pleasant evening," he began, as soon as Mr. E II 3 170 2
and the papers swept away;-- "particularly pleasant. E II 3 170 2
Miss Fairfax must have found the evening pleasant, Emma. E II 3 170 2
to tell me, I hope, that you had not a pleasant evening." E II 3 171 9
"I hope every body had a pleasant evening," said Mr. E II 3 171 12
a falsehood, it was a pleasant one, and pleasantly handled. E II 5 191 26
Pleasant rides?-- E II 5 191 27
Pleasant walks?-- E II 5 191 27
"He did not doubt there being very pleasant walks in every E II 6 196 1
to say how attentive and pleasant a companion he made E II 7 205 2
however, it had been pleasant enough, as he found them in E II 8 220 48
The visit afforded her many pleasant recollections the E II 9 231 1
a delightful party last night; how extremely pleasant.-- E II 10 245 48
in coming, if you had had a pleasant idea of Highbury." E II 12 260 22
both at home; and very pleasant people they seem to be. E II 14 278 44
of her being "very pleasant and very elegantly dressed." E II 15 281 2
A pleasant "thank you" seemed meant to laugh it off, but a E II 16 294 24
weather genial and pleasant, always inviting one out, and E II 18 308 30
may, a fire in the evening was still very pleasant. E III 2 320 5
These were pleasant feelings, and she walked about and E III 6 358 35
Now they seemed in pleasant conversation. E III 6 360 40
and punctuality, were in favour of a pleasant party. E III 7 367 1
This is not pleasant to you, Emma--and it is very far from E III 7 375 61
it is very far from pleasant to me; but I must, I will,--I E III 7 375 61
However, I shall always think it a very pleasant party, E III 8 381 19
always found him very pleasant--and, in short, for (with a E III 13 427 19
Very pleasant party. E III 16 454 18
I hope you have pleasant accounts from Windsor?" E III 16 459 50
There would be an end of all pleasant intercourse with him. E III 17 469 36
you were well enough, and I hope you had a pleasant party." P III 5 39 38
unembarrassed and pleasant; they were of consequence at P III 5 40 45
And he had promised it in so pleasant a manner, as if he P III 7 54 4
drew from him some pleasant ridicule, which reminded Anne P III 8 64 4
"Ah! those were pleasant days when I had the Laconia! P III 8 67 23
Cobb, skirting round the pleasant little bay, which in the P III 11 95 9
nothing could be more pleasant than their desire of P III 11 97 15
part of the new Cobb pleasant for the ladies, and they P III 12 109 32
Mrs. Clay was very pleasant, and very smiling; but her P IV 3 137 3
"Our neighbourhood cannot spare such a pleasant family. P IV 6 164 8
She was sure of a pleasant reception; and her friend P IV 9 192 4
You need not tell me that you had a pleasant evening. P IV 9 194 14
such good friends, the pleasant prospects of one should P IV 10 217 21
deficiency of generally pleasant manners on either, they S 2 371 1
had at first enjoined, was now rendered pleasant by habit. S 2 374 1
The manners of the parkers were always pleasant among S 12 425 1

PLEASANT-LOOKING (1)

Mrs Blake, a lively pleasant-looking little woman of 5 or W 330 11

PLEASANTER (17)

thought the evening pleasanter than she had found it NA I 2 24 28
of ten minutes, to a pleasanter feeling, by seeing, not Mr. NA I 8 53 3
I never spent a pleasanter morning in my life." SS I 13 68 70
Bingley had never met with pleasanter people or prettier PP I 4 16 15
The country is a vast deal pleasanter, is not it, Mr. PP I 9 43 21
that private balls are much pleasanter than public ones.-- PP I 18 91 11
sized room, and had a pleasanter aspect; but she soon saw PP II 7 168 1
It was much pleasanter to think of Henry Crawford than of MP I 11 107 1
It would have been a vast deal pleasanter to have had her MP III 16 459 31
It was much easier to chat than to study; much pleasanter E I 9 69 3
Nothing could be pleasanter. E I 13 115 39
have had longer notice of it, would have been pleasanter.-- E III 9 386 8
Charles "had never seen a pleasanter man in his life; and P III 9 75 10
it was soon lost in the pleasanter feelings which spring P III 11 98 17
you must have so many pleasanter demands upon your time." P IV 9 194 18
But let us talk of pleasanter things.-- S 5 389 1
pleasanter still--Morgan, with his "dinner on table."-- S 5 389 1

PLEASANTEST (7)

make it one of the pleasantest summer-rooms in England." SS I 13 69 76
must be their pleasantest preservative from want. PP I 22 122 3

He was beyond comparison the pleasantest man; he certainly	PP II 9 181 31
and must give him the pleasantest proof of its being a	E I 2 17 6
through the party those pleasantest feelings of our nature,	E I 7 56 46
and Emma found it the pleasantest part of the day.	E III 6 361 40
any question their pleasantest acquaintance in Bath; she	P IV 4 148 9
PLEASANTLY (32)	
those hours pass very pleasantly which would be otherwise	LS 10 258 3
Isabella on having every thing so pleasantly settled.	NA II 1 135 43
making Miss Morland's time at Northanger pass pleasantly.	NA II 11 209 5
I hope you spend your time pleasantly, but am afraid you	NA II 12 216 2
In having this cause of uneasiness so pleasantly removed,	NA II 13 221 6
more powerfully than pleasantly, by her hearing that the	SS II 12 230 7
than to pass my time pleasantly while I was obliged to	SS III 8 319 29
in Devonshire, more pleasantly than I had ever done before.	SS III 8 319 29
eveng began very pleasantly to her; & her feelings	W 329 9
The evening altogether passed off pleasantly to the whole	PP I 3 12 15
But perhaps you have been too pleasantly engaged to think	PP I 18 95 49
The day passed most pleasantly away; the morning in bustle	PP II 4 152 5
man, and talked very pleasantly; but his cousin, after	PP II 7 171 10
her mind became so pleasantly occupied in superintending	MP I 4 38 9
spending their time pleasantly, and were not aware of the	MP I 10 103 49
Pleasantly, courteously it was spoken; but the manner was	MP I 14 133 12
"You spent your time pleasantly there."	MP III 4 355 51
Susan had always behaved pleasantly to herself, but the	MP III 9 395 4
his entering into a plan of that sort, most pleasantly.	MP III 12 419 9
a deference, seeming so pleasantly grateful for being	E I 3 23 10
"I think, indeed," said John Knightley pleasantly, "that	E I 11 95 18
and obliging, and speaking pleasantly of every body.	E I 16 139 20
after Mrs. Bates; but I have been so pleasantly detained!	E II 1 162 32
in seeing him behave so pleasantly and so kindly.	E II 3 179 52
a falsehood, it was a pleasant one, and pleasantly handled.	E II 5 191 26
The ball proceeded pleasantly.	E III 2 326 33
Tea passed pleasantly, and nobody seemed in a hurry to	E III 5 347 18
The half hour was chatted away pleasantly enough; and she	P III 5 41 46
replied Mrs. Croft, pleasantly; "for if Miss Elliot were	P III 10 92 45
for his feelings, so pleasantly, that his countenance	P IV 8 190 47
Each behaving so pleasantly!	P IV 10 231 5
the Weald I am sure sir, replied the traveller, pleasantly.	S 1 366 1
PLEASANTNESS (7)	
"I am afraid," replied Elinor, "that the pleasantness of	SS I 13 68 71
inquiry after the pleasantness of her last partner she had	PP I 18 96 56
the parsonage, or the pleasantness of the walk to it, or	PP II 9 180 28
was tempted, by the pleasantness of the morning, to stop	PP II 12 195 2
He sees difficulties no where; and his pleasantness and	MP III 4 348 23
all her attention to the pleasantness of her neighbour.	E II 8 214 13
The pleasantness of the morning had induced him to walk	E III 3 334 7
PLEASANTRY (6)	
was an archness and pleasantry in his manner which	NA I 3 25 2
you talking of; cried the husband with sturdy pleasantry--.	W 325 4
A great deal of goodhumoured pleasantry followed--& Emma	W 337 15
Elizabeth tried to join in her father's pleasantry, but	PP III 15 363 19
her affection, she now saw the object of open pleasantry.	PP III 19 388 61
when it was raised by pleasantry on people or subjects	MP II 4 208 11
PLEASE (95)	
"If you please."	NA I 3 26 25
These manners did not please Catherine; but he was James's	NA I 7 50 44
"Do just as you please, my dear," replied Mrs. Allen, with	NA I 9 61 7
tell a falsehood even to please Isabella; but the latter	NA I 9 67 33
for the attentions of some one whom they wished to please.	NA I 10 74 23
"Just as you please, my dear."	NA I 11 86 48
appeared to plague or please her; she feared that, amongst	NA I 12 92 4
Though his looks did not please her, his name was a	NA II 4 149 1
please me better than the finest banditti in the world."	SS I 18 98 8
his wife, but of less willingness to please or be pleased.	SS I 19 106 22
"Aye, you may abuse me as you please," said the good-	SS I 20 112 25
that his mother might give him if he married to please her.	SS II 2 147 7
There was something in her style of beauty, to please them	SS II 11 227 50
of endeavouring to please them, had seldom been happier in	SS II 12 231 9
Lucy, who was hardly less anxious to please one parent	SS II 12 234 24
"No, ma'am, not even Lucy if you please.	SS III 4 286 15
I have not heard of any thing to please me so well since	SS III 4 287 20
you of this, because I knew how much it must please you.	SS III 5 297 31
manners could not but please me; and her behaviour to me	SS III 8 319 29
Please to destroy my scrawls--but the ring with my hair	SS III 13 365 15
expedient for him to please the borough--he was not fond	W 329 10
It was a new thing with him to wish to please a woman; it	W 346 21
in her head, said "please ma'am, master wants to know why	W 346 21
of notice which might please her vanity, but did not suit	W 347 22
not been calculated to please in general; and with more	PP I 4 15 11
you shall if you please name the very day of the ball.	PP I 9 45 37
if you please, by attempting to laugh without a subject.	PP I 11 57 18
These are the kind of little things which please her	PP I 14 67 9
"Probably not;--but Mr. Darcy can please where he chuses.	PP I 16 82 48
"And if not able to please himself in the arrangement, he	PP II 10 183 9
than commonly anxious to please, she naturally suspected	PP III 2 260 1
seen him so desirous to please, so free from self-	PP III 2 263 10
raising his head, coolly replied, "just as you please."	PP III 7 305 39 40
His understanding and opinions all please me; he wants	PP III 10 325 2
More thoughfulness, and less anxiety to please than when	PP III 11 336 43
and shoot as many as you please, on Mr. Bennet's manor.	PP III 11 337 53
"Not so hasty, if you please.	PP III 14 357 62
my pretensions to please a woman worthy of being pleased."	PP III 16 369 24
whom he was anxious to please, he grew puzzled; and Edmund	MP I 6 55 17
And you may say, if you please, that I shall prepare my	MP I 6 59 41
ill; and, therefore, if you please, you must forgive me.	MP I 7 68 18
"Yes, his manners to women are such as must please.	MP I 12 116 8
find a piece which would please them all, the resolution	MP I 13 124 13
a little more justice, Mr. Manager, if you please.	MP I 14 134 13
Let <u>him</u> be applied to, if you please, for it will be less	MP I 15 148 59
"As <u>you</u> please, ma'am, on that head; but I meant my	MP II 5 217 9
answer--"then speculation if you please, Mrs. Grant.	MP II 7 239 7
He evidently tried to please her--he was gallant--he was	MP II 8 260 24
most towards Fanny herself, in her intentions to please.	MP II 10 277 17
pains had been taken to please him--who thought so	MP II 13 305 26
You must have seen that he was trying to please you, by	MP III 5 362 18
please sir, and one of the officers has been here to"-----	MP III 7 377 7
difficult mistress to please--and I am sure the place is	MP III 7 385 39
"My love to your sister, if you please; and when you see	MP III 11 412 27
"Poor Mr. and Miss Woodhouse, if you please; but I cannot	E I 1 10 29
At any rate, it must be better to have only one to please,	E I 1 10 29
Miss Taylor has been used to have two persons to please;	E I 1 11 34
He had only himself to please in his choice: his fortune	E I 2 17 7
If he means anything, it must be to please you.	E I 4 34 42
destined, if she could please herself, to hold a very	E I 6 46 23
and he took pains to please her; and altogether, having	E I 8 65 48
Do as you please."	E I 9 78 48
South end is prohibited, if you please.	E I 12 101 23
but when he has ladies to please every feature works."	E I 13 111 16
where there is a wish to please, one ought to overlook,	E I 13 111 17
He has those to please who must be pleased, and who (	E I 14 120 9
to deliver; but no more of this to <u>me</u>, if you please."	E I 15 130 25
had only themselves to please, and nothing but the	E II 4 182 6
of his knowing how to please--and of his certainly	E II 5 191 28
his certainly thinking it worth while to try to please her.	E II 5 191 28
please, and given all the consequence she could wish for.	E II 8 214 12
best, might reasonably please a young man who had more	E II 8 221 49
"Imprudent, if you please--but not mad.	E II 8 225 73
No, you shall send it to Hartfield, if you please.	E II 9 235 36
Then, if you please, you shall send it all to Mrs.	E II 9 235 40
To Hartfield, if you please, Mrs. Ford."	E II 9 235 41
"Well--if you please," said Mrs. Weston rather hesitating,	E II 11 255 51
incessant, could not but please; and for another half-hour	E II 11 256 60
His wish of staying longer evidently did not please; but	E II 12 257 2
A little tea if you please, sir, by and bye,--no hurry--Oh!	E III 2 323 19
Churchill--only it seems too good--but just as you please.	E III 2 330 45
"Well--as you please; only don't have a great set out.	E III 6 355 22
You have hit upon the very thing to please me."	E III 6 356 28
Pass us, if you please, Mr. Churchill.	E III 7 372 37
"If you please, my dear.	E III 7 374 53
This moment, if you please.	E III 10 392 5
What right had he to endeavour to please, as he certainly	E III 10 396 44
But hush!--not a word, if you please."	E III 16 457 33
pleases or amuses you, should not please and amuse me too."	E III 18 470 7
year or two; and you will please to remember, that he is	P III 9 76 15
and bookish enough to please Lady Russell, and that	P III 10 89 33
please himself, he might mean to pay his addresses to her.	P IV 3 140 11
and I will answer for it they would generally please."	P IV 6 172 38
Yes, yes, if you please, no reference to examples in books.	P IV 11 234 28
gentlemanlike, easy to please;--of a sanguine turn of mind,	S 2 372 1
PLEASED (207)	
conviction, to be so well pleased with her as I am sure he	LS 8 255 2
an attention which I was pleased to see not unmixed with	LS 22 280 2
I am pleased to find that my letter had so much effect on	LS 28 298 2
cannot help being pleased with such a proof of attachment.	LS 31 302 1
"And are you altogether pleased with Bath?"	NA I 3 26 16
one can be pleased with the attention of any body else.	NA I 6 41 16
I do not pretend to say that I was not very much pleased	NA I 6 41 19
very good-natured of you," said Catherine, quite pleased.	NA I 7 47 16
Catherine was very well pleased to have it dropped for a	NA I 8 57 21
"So Mrs. Thorpe said; she was vastly pleased at your all	NA I 9 68 36
Would she be pleased to send up her name?	NA I 12 91 3
of going; I am sure Mrs. Morland would not be pleased.	NA I 13 104 31
and returned home, pleased that the party had not been	NA I 14 115 55
not looked so well pleased at the sight of Captain Tilney.	NA II 3 148 28
"At any rate, however, I am pleased that you have learnt	NA II 7 174 10
each, and instantly, pleased by his appearance, received	NA II 15 242 7
Marianne was rejoiced to find her sister so easily pleased.	SS I 4 20 8
she might think necessary, if the situation pleased her.	SS I 4 23 20
hold, and the noisier they were the better was he pleased.	SS I 7 32 2
view of the whole, which had exceedingly pleased him.	SS I 18 96 4
his wife, but of less willingness to please or be pleased.	SS I 19 106 22
on her own account; her daughters might do as they pleased.	SS I 19 108 40
Mr. Palmer is excessively pleased with you and your	SS I 20 114 42
of her spirits, to be pleased with the Miss Steeles, or to	SS I 22 127 1
you will be as well pleased not to cut in till another	SS II 1 145 22
her own end, and pleased Lady Middleton at the same time.	SS II 1 145 23
her mother so thoroughly pleased with the plan, and her	SS II 3 158 20
Pleased to find herself more comfortably situated in that	SS II 5 168 11
Elinor, pleased to have her governed for a moment by such	SS II 8 193 5
He looked pleased by this remembrance, and added, "if I am	SS II 9 205 23 24
years I had every reason to be pleased with her situation.	SS II 9 208 28
Harry was vastly pleased.	SS II 11 221 9
on my part, to make him pleased with you and your family.	SS II 11 224 24
among the earliest and best pleased of your visitors."	SS II 11 227 50
Lady Middleton was equally pleased with Mrs. Dashwood.	SS II 12 229 2
Elinor was pleased that he had called; and still more	SS II 12 230 5
had called; and still more pleased that she had missed him.	SS II 12 230 5
as a man of taste, will, I dare say, be pleased with them.	SS II 12 234 27
it to whatever cause best pleased herself, was perfectly	SS II 13 243 32
Mrs. Dashwood had never been so much pleased with any	SS II 14 254 28
for me will make you pleased to hear such a good account	SS III 2 277 29 30
three times in Harley-Street, and am much pleased with him.	SS III 3 282 19
And I assure you I never was better pleased in my life,	SS III 4 285 1
I was exceedingly pleased to hear that Mrs. Ferrars	SS III 5 297 31
divided for ever, she was pleased to be free herself from	SS III 6 302 5
Her daughter, feeling by turns both pleased and pained,	SS III 9 336 9
to encourage such affection, or even to be pleased by it.	SS III 9 337 16
or unhappy,--nothing pleased her; she turned away her head	SS III 12 357 4
Emma was very well pleased with the circumstance;--there	W 333 13
I should have been better pleased to see her dancing with	W 337 15
be pleased with the opportunity of seeing your sister."--	W 339 18
of pleasing, & shewing himself pleased in a right place.--"	W 340 19
the day, & consequently pleased with what he had done, &	W 343 19
But what pleased me as much as anything was Mr Howard's	W 344 20
I hope you are pleased with it."--	W 346 21
disposed to be pleased, he only replied--"phoo! phoo!--	W 348 22
Mrs Robt was not less pleased with herself for having had	W 349 23
Even Emma was pleased that he would stay, for she was	W 357 28
Well, how pleased I am! and it is such a good joke, too,	PP I 2 7 24
company, and above being pleased; and not all his large	PP I 3 10 5
humour when they were pleased, nor in the power of being	PP I 4 15 11
it for half an hour, was pleased with the situation and	PP I 4 16 13
with whom it had always pleased him to be at variance.--	PP I 13 62 12
She had been graciously pleased to approve of both the	PP I 14 66 1
Her ladyship seemed pleased with the idea, and you may	PP I 14 67 9
was extremely well pleased to close his large book, and go.	PP I 15 71 6
society, appearing highly pleased with all that he had yet	PP I 16 78 22
had it pleased the gentleman we were speaking of just now."	PP I 16 79 23
She was not the better pleased with his gallantry, from	PP I 17 87 14
Mr. Darcy seemed much pleased with the attention. he	PP I 18 98 62
Upon the whole, I am much pleased with him."	PP I 18 98 62
and every body was pleased to think how much they had	PP II 1 138 30
Elizabeth was exceedingly pleased with this proposal, and	PP II 2 141 11
face, was pleased to see it healthful and lovely as ever.	PP II 4 152 5
the house, extremely well pleased, probably, to have the	PP II 5 156 5
Elizabeth saw much to be pleased with, though she could	PP II 6 161 8
it, said, in a colder voice, "are you pleased with Kent?"	PP II 9 179 24 25
Pleased with the preference of one, and offended by the	PP II 13 208 8
Elizabeth could not but be pleased, could not but triumph.	PP III 1 255 59
that was impossible, but she was flattered and pleased.	PP III 1 257 65
Georgiana was eager, and Darcy determined, to be pleased.	PP III 2 262 7
and once or twice pleased herself with the notion that as	PP III 2 262 8
Elizabeth was pleased to find his memory so exact; and he	PP III 2 262 9
speak of her sister, was pleased; and on this account, as	PP III 2 264 12
Elizabeth was pleased, though, when she asked herself the	PP III 2 266 17
But Mrs. Bennet, was not so well pleased with it.	PP III 8 313 20
Those that best pleased her, as placing his conduct in the	PP III 9 320 32
It was hardly enough; but it pleased her.	PP III 10 327 3
pleased to find that she had said enough to keep him quiet.	PP III 11 330 1
short period saw him looking both pleased and embarrassed.	PP III 11 335 41
Elizabeth was pleased to find, that he had not betrayed	PP III 13 350 52
I think she will be pleased with the hermitage."	PP III 14 352 18
Lady Catherine seemed pleased.	PP III 14 356 57
whether most to be pleased that he explained himself at	PP III 15 362 11 12
my pretensions to please a woman worthy of being pleased."	PP III 16 369 24
But are you pleased, Jane?	PP III 17 373 10
I am so pleased--so happy.	PP III 17 378 43
address, the young lady was well pleased with her conquest.	MP I 4 38 10
happiness, but he was not pleased that her happiness	MP I 4 40 13
The young people were pleased with each other from the	MP I 5 44 [illegible]
and were ready to be pleased, and were ready to be pleased;	MP I 5 44 [illegible]
and were ready to be pleased; and he began with no object	MP I 5 44 [illegible]
She did not think very much about it, however; he pleased	MP I 7 65 1[illegible]
Edmund looked pleased, which must be Fanny's comfort, and	MP I 7 70 3[illegible]
Mrs. Norris and her nieces were all well pleased with its	MP I 8 75 [illegible]
Lady Bertram was very well pleased to have it so, and the	MP I 8 80 2[illegible]
for Miss Bertram was pleased to have its size displayed,	MP I 9 84 [illegible]
He was certainly better pleased to hand her into the	MP I 10 105 5
half pleased that Sotherton should be so complimented.	MP I 10 106 5

Context	Work	Vol	Ch	Page	Line
to, so many people to be pleased, so many best characters	MP	I	14	130	2
Mr. Yates was particularly pleased; he had been sighing	MP	I	14	132	8
She was not pleased to see Julia excluded from the play,	MP	I	17	161	9
was really as far from pleased with the necessity of the	MP	II	1	183	23
felt, most exceedingly pleased with Sir Thomas's good	MP	II	1	186	35
manners, but I was pleased last night with what appeared	MP	II	2	190	6
uncle is disposed to be pleased with you in every respect;	MP	II	3	198	9
It would have pleased your uncle to be inquired of farther.	MP	II	3	198	11
expression; and though pleased with it herself, and glad	MP	II	4	207	10
and the smiles and pleased looks of the three others	MP	II	5	223	48
which must dispose her to be pleased with every body.	MP	II	6	232	12
"I hope your ladyship is pleased with the game."	MP	II	7	240	11
Miss Crawford, pleased with the appeal, gave her all her	MP	II	8	257	15
exceedingly pleased with an acquisition so very apropos.	MP	II	8	258	18
motive, was exceedingly pleased: for the original plan was	MP	II	9	266	21
to Mansfield, he was pleased with himself for having	MP	II	10	276	13
Not but that she was really pleased to have Fanny admired;	MP	II	10	277	15
I was very much pleased with what I collected to have been	MP	III	1	315	18
Crawford was excessively pleased.--	MP	III	3	338	18
with judgment, Edmund was still more and more pleased.	MP	III	3	340	24
Edmund first began again:-- "I was very much pleased by	MP	III	4	351	35
					36
yesterday, particularly pleased, because I had not	MP	III	4	351	35
					36
better pleased that such a token of friendship had passed.	MP	III	5	365	36
about making it, as if pleased to have the employment all	MP	III	7	383	33
Susan shewed that she had delicacy; pleased as she was to	MP	III	9	397	7
and very much pleased with herself for contriving things	E	I	3	22	6
evening, Emma was as much pleased with her manners as her	E	I	3	23	9
She was not less pleased another day with the manner in	E	I	6	43	8
pleased with the first day's sketch to wish to go on.	E	I	6	47	27
Every body who saw it was pleased, but Mr. Elton was in	E	I	6	47	30
Emma was half ashamed of her friend for seeming so pleased	E	I	7	50	1
I was very much pleased with all that he said.	E	I	8	59	27
and a great readiness to be pleased with other people.	E	I	8	63	44
and the longer it lasts, the better I shall be pleased.	E	I	9	77	45
he was very much pleased, and, as she had foreseen,	E	I	9	78	51
I am sure she will be pleased with the children.	E	I	9	80	69
listening with a very pleased attention; and Emma having	E	I	10	88	33
He will be so pleased to see my little ones."	E	I	12	101	26
They are always so pleased to see my children.--	E	I	12	102	31
into; and not very well pleased with her brother for	E	I	13	112	23
Emma did not find herself equal to give the pleased assent,	E	I	13	113	27
He has those to please who must be pleased, and who (	E	I	14	120	9
are sometimes to be pleased only by a good many sacrifices.	E	I	14	120	9
indifference whether she pleased or not--and then, her	E	II	2	166	11
"Oh! no; I was pleased with my own perseverance in asking	E	II	3	171	10
"my mother is so pleased!--she says she cannot bear to	E	II	3	174	35
little discerning; --what signified her praise?	E	II	3	179	53
She was pleased with the eagerness to arrive which had	E	II	5	190	23
He was very much pleased with Randalls, thought it a most	E	II	5	191	26
Emma remained very well pleased with this beginning of the	E	II	5	195	49
Mr. Cole's door; and was pleased to see that it was Mr.	E	II	8	213	7
They would be very much pleased."	E	II	9	234	29
William did not seem to mind it himself, he was so pleased	E	II	9	239	51
are always pleased with any thing in the same style."	E	II	14	273	21
lady; and I dare say she was very much pleased with you.	E	II	14	279	54
with interest; and was pleased enough to exclaim, "you are	E	II	15	287	31
which shewed him not pleased, soon afterwards said, "so	E	II	15	287	33
					34
pleased by Harriet's begging to be allowed to decline it.	E	II	16	291	5
Mrs. Weston was most comfortably pleased on the occasion.	E	II	17	304	28
I hope you will be pleased with my son; but you must not	E	II	18	309	30
I am happy to say that I am extremely pleased with him.--	E	III	2	321	15
Emma was pleased with the thought; and producing the box,	E	III	5	347	20
myself, (who, she is pleased to say, am very entertaining	E	III	7	370	23
me upon my own name, which I was not at all pleased with.	E	III	7	372	37
pleased to wait a moment, and then ushered her in too soon.	E	III	8	378	4
much pleased with all that she had said on the subject.	E	III	12	418	5
me--I am pleased that you can say even so much.--	E	III	13	426	16
by his attentions, and allowed myself to appear pleased.--	E	III	13	427	19
Isabella had been pleased with Harriet; and a few weeks	E	III	14	435	4
I assure you I am not at all pleased.	E	III	16	457	40
She was pleased, on taking leave, to find Miss Fairfax	E	III	16	459	45
					46
two men, she felt, that pleased as she had been to see	E	III	18	480	80
I believe Mrs. Charles is not quite pleased with my not	P	III	6	45	8
to Kellynch; and it pleased her: especially, as she had	P	III	6	48	18
Miss Anne, if it had pleased heaven to spare my poor son,	P	III	8	64	5
					6
Musgroves, as made them pleased to improve their cousins.--	P	III	9	74	6
not at all better pleased by the sight of Captain	P	III	9	79	25
And yet they would not have been pleased, if we had	P	III	10	83	5
Henrietta looked a little ashamed, but very well pleased;--	P	III	10	89	36
His looks shewing him not pained, but pleased with this	P	III	11	101	24
"I wish," said Henrietta, very well pleased with her	P	III	12	103	4
in angry pleasure, in pleased contempt, that the man who	P	IV	1	125	13
Lady Russell and Mrs. Croft were very well pleased with	P	IV	1	128	31
I think she would be so much pleased with his mind, that	P	IV	2	132	17
not more astonished than pleased; his eyes brightened, and	P	IV	3	143	18
sort of pride, she was pleased with him for not liking Mrs.	P	IV	4	151	22
the tempers in her father's house, he pleased them all.	P	IV	5	161	29
"We are all very well pleased, however; for though it is	P	IV	6	165	8
too, became excessively pleased with Mr. Elliot, and	P	IV	9	199	55
well as to be exceedingly pleased to meet with you again	P	IV	9	206	88
My father would be as well pleased if the gentlemen were	P	IV	10	218	22
manners had precisely pleased her in their propriety and	P	IV	12	249	3
she had so well nursed & pleased Mr Hollis, that at his	S		3	375	1
I am glad you are pleased with it.--	S		4	380	1
by them; & while she pleased herself the first 5 minutes	S		6	391	1
moreover by no means pleased with his extraordinary stile	S		7	398	1
Whitby to secure them a house?--but neither pleased me.--	S		9	409	1
"No more do I--said he exceedingly pleased--we think quite	S		10	417	1

PLEASES (7)

Context	Work	Vol	Ch	Page	Line
I hope this pleases you, (turning her back on him,) I hope	NA	II	3	147	26
may turn you all out of this house as soon as he pleases."	PP	I	13	61	6
He arranges the business just as he pleases."	PP	II	10	183	8
A likeness pleases every body; and Miss Woodhouse's	E	I	6	45	20
what guests she pleases to Donwell, and that one is-----"	E	III	6	354	15
I can hardly imagine that any thing which pleases or	E	III	18	470	7
"Charles may say what he pleases," cried Mary to Anne, as	P	III	9	76	16

PLEASING (98)

Context	Work	Vol	Ch	Page	Line
pleasing that I was not without apprehensions myself.	LS		2	244	1
deceit which must be pleasing to witness & detect.	LS		4	248	2
of a girl; her person pleasing, and, when in good looks,	NA	I	2	18	1
was rather tall, had a pleasing countenance, a very	NA	I	3	25	2
request, and with how pleasing a flutter of heart she went	NA	I	10	75	24
placed his upon pleasing her, it was agreed that, provided	NA	I	13	97	1
gave Catherine a most pleasing remembrance of all the	NA	I	15	119	19
under a mistaken idea of pleasing her; but she was stopt	NA	II	7	177	17
that would be generally pleasing, and wanting in all that	NA	II	8	185	5
His pleasing manners and good sense were self-evident	NA	II	16	249	1
a gentlemanlike and pleasing young man, who was introduced	SS	I	3	15	4
and his manners required intimacy to make them pleasing.	SS	I	3	15	6
and a far less agreeable man might have been pleasing.	SS	I	11	55	7
far that might be pleasing to Mrs. Smith; and on this head	SS	I	15	76	14
an excellent man; and I think him uncommonly pleasing."	SS	I	20	115	55
in his favour, however small, was pleasing to her.	SS	I	20	116	59
feelings less pure, less pleasing, might have a share in	SS	III	3	283	20
And with this pleasing anticipation, she sat down to re-	SS	III	4	291	45
my power, to make myself pleasing to her, without any	SS	III	8	320	29
there is something much more pleasing in his countenance.--	SS	III	9	338	20
are not only more pleasing to me than Willoughby's ever	SS	III	9	338	21
					22
of pleasing, & shewing himself pleased in a right place.--"	W			340	19
to a certain point--his address rather--is pleasing.--	W			342	19
ways of a man, when he is bent upon pleasing her.--"	W			343	19
being her constant resource when determined on pleasing.--	W			349	23
a most disagreeable, horrid man, not at all worth pleasing.	PP	I	3	13	20
But they are very pleasing women when you converse with	PP	I	4	15	10
Miss Bennet's pleasing manners grew on the good will of	PP	I	6	21	1
figure to be light and pleasing; and in spite of his	PP	I	6	23	12
Her performance was pleasing, though by no means capital.	PP	I	6	25	23
to herself most pleasing, and they prevented her feeling	PP	I	8	35	2
for her sister that is very pleasing," said Bingley.	PP	I	8	36	11
May I ask whether these pleasing attentions proceed from	PP	I	14	68	10
fine countenance, a good figure, and very pleasing address.	PP	I	15	72	8
As a child, she was affectionate and pleasing, and	PP	I	16	82	43
he must always be her model of the amiable and pleasing.	PP	II	4	151	3
able to bring home the pleasing intelligence, of their	PP	II	14	210	1
pleasing picture of conjugal felicity or domestic comfort.	PP	II	19	236	1
On the contrary, there is something pleasing about his	PP	III	1	258	74
suspected that every power of pleasing would fail her.	PP	III	2	260	1
frisks, was the first pleasing earnest of their welcome.	PP	III	5	286	21
They were forced to conclude, that he had no pleasing	PP	III	6	294	1
manners were always so pleasing, that had his character	PP	III	9	316	5
respect, been as pleasing as when we were in Derbyshire.	PP	III	10	325	2
"He could be still amiable, still pleasing, to my uncle	PP	III	12	339	4
stronger desire of generally pleasing than any other man."	PP	III	12	343	32
from society so little pleasing to either, to all the	PP	III	18	384	27
but still he was the gentleman, with a pleasing address.	MP	I	5	44	2
Miss Bertrams were worth pleasing, and were ready to be	MP	I	5	44	3
she may exert all her powers of pleasing without suspicion.	MP	I	5	45	12
She speaks of her brother with a very pleasing affection."	MP	I	7	64	9
enough to justify the pleasing belief of his being then at	MP	II	2	190	9
to forward his views of pleasing her, inasmuch as they	MP	II	6	232	12
out such a method of pleasing her, as well as of his	MP	II	6	232	13
He had a pleasing anticipation of what would be.	MP	II	10	280	32
He is a very--a very pleasing young man himself, and I	MP	II	11	287	22
very accomplished and pleasing, and one very pretty.	MP	II	11	288	28
"How the pleasing plague had stolen on him" he could not	MP	II	12	292	8
Were you even less pleasing--supposing her not to love you	MP	II	12	293	15
with address and conversation pleasing to every body.	MP	III	1	315	27
It was pleasing to hear him speak so properly; here, he	MP	III	10	404	15
young man; and such a pleasing attention was an	E	I	2	18	10
And he was really a very pleasing young man, a young man	E	I	4	35	45
seen a face or figure more pleasing to me than her's.	E	I	5	39	19
pleasing; and capable of being sometimes out of humour.	E	I	11	92	5
"How very pleasing and proper of him!" cried the good-	E	I	11	96	25
most valuable, amiable, pleasing young man undoubtedly,	E	I	13	111	13
her the opportunity of pleasing some one worth having; I	E	I	16	137	11
had given her in a pleasing person, good understanding,	E	II	2	163	3
it was not regular, but it was very pleasing beauty.	E	II	2	167	12
She believed every body found his manners pleasing."	E	II	2	169	17
proper attention and pleasing behaviour on each side, he	E	II	3	170	1
she had ever thought him pleasing at all; and his sight	E	II	4	182	7
could be more proper or pleasing than his whole manner to	E	II	6	196	2
"Oftentimes very convenient, no doubt, but never pleasing.	E	II	6	203	40
to come; and her last pleasing duty, before she left the	E	II	8	213	6
To do what would be most generally pleasing must be our	E	II	11	254	49
busy and cheerful; and, pleasing as he was, she could yet	E	II	13	264	1
without a something of pleasing connection, either a	E	II	13	266	5
terms of being "elegantly dressed, and very pleasing."	E	II	14	270	3
"Oh! yes--very--a very pleasing young woman."	E	II	14	271	8
was so little pleasing, that she soon allowed herself to	E	III	8	384	34
more she contemplated it, the more pleasing it became.	E	III	15	450	36
understood the art of pleasing; the art of pleasing, at	P	III	2	15	15
of pleasing; the art of pleasing, at least, at Kellynch-	P	III	2	15	15
acute mind and assiduous pleasing manners, infinitely more	P	III	5	34	12
heart, in short, for any pleasing young woman who came in	P	III	7	61	38
and a very amiable, pleasing young man, between whom and	P	III	9	73	4
He had a pleasing face and a melancholy air, just as he	P	III	11	97	14
him at liberty to exert his most open powers of pleasing.	P	IV	5	159	22
She was persuaded that any tolerably pleasing young woman	P	IV	6	167	19
"I thought Captain Benwick a very pleasing young man,"	P	IV	6	171	36
I thought them particularly pleasing, and I will answer	P	IV	6	172	38
It was too pleasing a blunder for a reproach.	P	IV	11	243	68
Heywood, a very pleasing young woman of two and twenty,	S		2	374	1
clever young man,--and with great powers of pleasing.--	S		4	382	1
fine countenance, a most pleasing gentleness of voice, & a	S		7	394	1
of pleasing, I know them not, & never wish to know them.--	S		7	395	1

PLEASING-LOOKING (1)

Context	Work	Vol	Ch	Page	Line
to a fashionable and pleasing-looking young woman, who	NA	I	8	53	3

PLEASURE (501)

Context	Work	Vol	Ch	Page	Line
longer refuse myself the pleasure of profitting by your	LS		1	243	1
There is exquisite pleasure in subduing an insolent spirit,	LS		7	254	3
I cannot receive that pleasure from the length of his	LS		8	255	1
that I am sure he would marry either of you with pleasure.	LS		9	257	1
& can now enjoy the pleasure of triumphing over a mind	LS		10	257	1
perceive that she had no particular pleasure in seeing him.	LS		20	276	3
with the greatest pleasure, & am persuaded that you & my	LS		20	276	5
to you; for the pleasure of learning that the danger is	LS		23	283	1
My remaining here cannot give that pleasure to Mr & Mrs	LS		25	293	3
& every domestic pleasure in my power to procure her, will,	LS		27	297	2
on, or kept off at pleasure; it was the same, when I	LS		28	298	1
I will not dissemble what real pleasure his sight afforded	LS		29	299	2
Your kind invitation is accepted by us with pleasure, & on	LS		41	310	2
sense of their kindness, & her pleasure in their society.	LS		42	311	2
it was chiefly for the pleasure of mischief--at least so	NA	I	1	13	1
smart; she had now the pleasure of sometimes hearing her	NA	I	1	15	2
the pleasure of seeing you, but is not your name Allen?"	NA	I	4	31	2
in Bath, and what a pleasure it was to see an old friend,	NA	I	4	32	2
Catherine heard with pleasure, and answered with all the	NA	I	4	33	6
extensive and unaffected pleasure than those of any other	NA	I	5	37	4
In a few moments Catherine, with unaffected pleasure,	NA	I	6	43	36
with the liveliest pleasure; and he, being of a very	NA	I	7	44	4
She returned it with pleasure, and then advancing still	NA	I	8	54	4
morning after his having had the pleasure of seeing her.	NA	I	8	54	4
an escape, spoke her pleasure aloud with grateful surprize;	NA	I	9	62	10
and to distrust his powers of giving universal pleasure.	NA	I	9	66	32
"When Henry had the pleasure of seeing you before, he was	NA	I	10	73	12
"I hope I shall have the pleasure of seeing you again soon,	NA	I	10	73	19
the loss of one great pleasure, and the hope of soon	NA	I	11	86	50
I shall have no pleasure at Clifton, nor in any thing else.	NA	I	11	87	53
looked at intervals with pleasure; though rather than be	NA	I	11	88	54
She was not deceived in her own expectation of pleasure;	NA	I	12	92	4
"That is a compliment which gives me no pleasure."	NA	I	13	99	8
not have the pleasure of walking with her till Tuesday.	NA	I	13	100	15
think with pleasure that he might be sometimes depended on.	NA	I	13	102	27
objection, and she should have great pleasure in coming."	NA	I	13	103	28
"The person, be it gentleman or lady, who has not pleasure	NA	I	14	106	7
Radcliffe's works, and most of them with great pleasure.	NA	I	14	106	7
If a speech be well drawn up, I read it with pleasure, by	NA	I	14	109	23
petitioned for the pleasure of her company to dinner on	NA	I	14	114	49
Catherine's was in concealing the excess of her pleasure.	NA	I	14	114	49
Catherine spoke the pleasure she really felt on hearing	NA	I	14	115	51
Maria desired no greater pleasure than to speak of it; and	NA	I	15	116	1
Catherine's expectations of pleasure from her visit in	NA	II	1	129	1
to her beyond the pleasure of sometimes seeing Henry	NA	II	2	138	1
The pleasure of walking and breathing fresh air is enough	NA	II	7	174	9
himself moreover the pleasure of accompanying her into the	NA	II	7	176	17
Being no longer able however to receive pleasure from the	NA	II	7	181	41
could not forego the pleasure of pacing out the length,	NA	II	8	183	3
and wanting in all that could give pleasure to Catherine.	NA	II	8	185	5

Context	Work	Vol.	Ch.	Page	Line
ago I had the pleasure of finding nothing to detain me.--	NA	II	9	195	12
do you think, sir, I may look forward to this pleasure?--	NA	II	11	209	5
Since you went away, I have had no pleasure in it--the	NA	II	12	216	2
She had "hoped for the pleasure of her company for a much	NA	II	13	221	2
were aware of the pleasure it was to her to have her there,	NA	II	13	221	2
For my own pleasure, I could stay with you as long again."-	NA	II	13	221	6
almost to destroy the pleasure of a meeting with those she	NA	II	14	231	5
at the sweep-gate was a pleasure to brighten every eye and	NA	II	14	233	8
occupy every fancy--a pleasure quite unlooked for by all	NA	II	14	233	8
was subdued, and the pleasure of seeing her, leaving them	NA	II	14	233	9
of a few years; and then what a pleasure it will be!"	NA	II	14	236	17
every other will, gave as much disappointment as pleasure.	SS	I	1	4	3
far beyond consolation as in pleasure she was beyond alloy.	SS	I	2	8	2
indeed, but he has great pleasure in seeing the	SS	I	4	19	2
could not fail of giving pleasure to his cousin; more	SS	I	4	23	20
indulged herself in the pleasure of announcing to her son-	SS	I	5	25	1
same; unconscious of the pleasure or the regret you	SS	I	5	27	8
His pleasure in music, though it amounted not to that	SS	I	7	35	9
shewed a want of pleasure and readiness in accepting my	SS	I	8	39	15
Willoughby, on his side, gave every proof of his pleasure	SS	I	10	48	7
her presence add to the pleasure of the others, by any	SS	I	11	55	6
interest of friendship, or give pleasure as a companion.	SS	I	11	55	7
in the usual style of a complete party of pleasure.	SS	I	12	62	28
"there are some people who cannot bear a party of pleasure.	SS	I	13	64	30
dinner, and they had the pleasure of sitting down nearly	SS	I	13	67	61
and with such a conviction I could have had no pleasure."	SS	I	13	68	72
Mrs. Dashwood looked with pleasure at Marianne, whose fine	SS	I	14	73	16
said; but it gave Elinor pleasure, as it produced a reply	SS	I	16	85	14
He was confused, seemed scarcely sensible of pleasure in	SS	I	16	87	23
I have more pleasure in a snug farm-house than a watch-	SS	I	18	98	8
He had no pleasure at Norland; he detested being in town;	SS	I	19	101	1
and no expectation of pleasure from them in any other way.	SS	I	19	108	40
he had at least as much pleasure in telling the name, as	SS	I	21	125	37
"it would have gave me such pleasure to meet you there!	SS	II	2	150	38
a little pleasure, because Miss Dashwood does not wish it.	SS	II	3	154	3
us pleasure, or whose protection will give us consequence."	SS	II	3	156	12
You will have much pleasure in being in London, and	SS	II	3	157	16
and care; nor was it a matter of pleasure merely to her.	SS	II	3	157	19
satisfactory, gave her pleasure, and she continued her	SS	II	4	161	5
their giving much pleasure to her sister, and this	SS	II	4	161	6
directly to speak of his pleasure at seeing them in London,	SS	II	4	162	11
"I had the pleasure of hearing it at Mr. Palmer's, where I	SS	II	4	163	15
she received most pleasure from meeting her mother or the	SS	II	4	164	21
both; she received no pleasure from any thing; was only	SS	II	4	165	24
means more productive of pleasure to her than to Elinor,	SS	II	4	166	31
'tis a said thing for sportsmen to lose a day's pleasure.	SS	II	5	167	1
equally ill-disposed to receive or communicate pleasure.	SS	II	5	171	30
without one look of hope, or one expression of pleasure.	SS	II	6	175	1
saying, "yes, I had the pleasure of receiving the	SS	II	6	177	11
the most grateful pleasure, and flatter myself it will not	SS	II	7	183	13
"I can have no pleasure while I see you in this state."	SS	II	7	186	27
I was prepared to meet you with the pleasure which our	SS	II	7	187	42
nothing in the way of pleasure can ever be given up by the	SS	II	8	194	10
Mrs. Jennings, who had watched them with pleasure while	SS	II	8	200	43
My sister will be equally sorry to miss the pleasure of	SS	II	10	219	38
Their affection and pleasure in meeting, was just enough	SS	II	11	221	7
give her great pleasure; she said as much the other day."	SS	II	11	224	24
expectation of too much pleasure to himself to be	SS	II	11	228	51
civilities with some surprise, but much more pleasure.	SS	II	12	230	6
Her pleasure in seeing him was like every other of her	SS	II	13	242	23
I expected much pleasure in it, but I have found none.	SS	II	13	242	29
and however it may make against his interest or pleasure.	SS	II	13	243	40
would fix them at pleasure on any other object in the room.	SS	II	14	250	11
As John Dashwood had no more pleasure in music than his	SS	II	14	252	20
to be unhappy, induced her to accept it with pleasure.	SS	III	3	279	1
Such as it is, however, my pleasure in presenting him to	SS	III	3	283	19
the commission with pleasure, if it were really his wish	SS	III	3	283	20
that I should soon have the pleasure of meeting you again.	SS	III	4	288	27
orders, he has great pleasure in offering you the living	SS	III	4	288	28
has, still greater pleasure in bestowing it; but, upon my	SS	III	4	289	35
He expressed great pleasure in meeting Elinor, told her	SS	III	5	294	4
particular, his open pleasure in meeting her after an	SS	III	6	305	16
as herself, engaged with pleasure to redeem it by a visit	SS	III	10	341	4
spirit, anticipating the pleasure of Margaret's return,	SS	III	10	343	8
Edward heard with pleasure of Colonel Brandon's being	SS	III	13	368	30
But, I confess, it would give me great pleasure to call	SS	III	14	375	9
of policy as well as pleasure in the frequency of her	SS	III	14	378	13
Your pleasure would be greater than mine.	W			320	2
they add nothing to the pleasure of the evening, they come	W			323	3
pities that he should be so deprived of the pleasure.	W			325	4
expressive of unexpected pleasure, & lively gratitude, she	W			331	11
not be giving greater pleasure than she felt herself--&	W			331	11
It was always the pleasure of the company to have a little	W			332	11
again a scramble for the pleasure of being first out of	W			333	13
"How comes it, that we have not the pleasure of seeing	W			334	13
A great deal of kind pleasure was expressed in her having	W			336	14
"The trouble was of course, honour, pleasure, delight.	W			339	18
if you can give us the pleasure of your company till	W			339	18
I am not to have the pleasure of your company--especially	W			351	25
to herself the power & the pleasure of providing for me."--	W			352	26
"But unluckily she has left the pleasure of providing for	W			352	26
of gruel, he had the pleasure of observing to Mr Watson	W			359	28
"With the greatest pleasure"--was his first reply.	W			360	28
Elizabeth felt Jane's pleasure.	PP	I	3	12	15
and from none received either attention or pleasure.	PP	I	4	16	15
he could think with pleasure of his own importance, and	PP	I	5	18	1
with the greatest pleasure; but Elizabeth still saw	PP	I	6	21	1
but she considered with pleasure that it was not likely to	PP	I	6	21	1
to with much more pleasure, though not playing half so	PP	I	6	25	24
"Yes, indeed, and received no inconsiderable pleasure from	PP	I	6	25	30
I have been meditating on the very great pleasure which a	PP	I	6	27	48
Mrs. Bennet's eyes sparkled with pleasure, and she was	PP	I	7	30	14
					15
which she had the pleasure of distinguishing the much	PP	I	8	35	1
She is a great reader and has no pleasure in any thing	PP	I	8	37	23
a great reader, and I have pleasure in many things."	PP	I	8	37	24
"In nursing your sister I am sure you have pleasure," said	PP	I	8	37	25
in the morning had the pleasure of being able to send a	PP	I	9	41	1
that you might have the pleasure of despising my taste;	PP	I	10	52	50
with many professions of pleasure; and Elizabeth had never	PP	I	11	54	1
whom a ball would be rather a punishment than a pleasure."	PP	I	11	55	6
not bring herself to receive them with pleasure before.	PP	I	12	59	1
the latter of the pleasure it would always give her to see	PP	I	12	60	5
in his expressions of pleasure, was really glad to see	PP	I	12	60	6
and he had the pleasure of being eagerly questioned by his	PP	I	13	61	5
pleasure from the society of a man in any other colour.	PP	I	13	64	20
glance at Elizabeth, requiring no partner in his pleasure.	PP	I	14	68	12
and the girls had the pleasure of hearing, as they entered	PP	I	16	75	1
Elizabeth thought with pleasure of dancing a great deal	PP	I	17	86	10
omitted for Mr. Darcy's pleasure in the Bingleys'	PP	I	18	89	1
					2
I must hope to have this pleasure often repeated,	PP	I	18	92	23
"I would by no means suspend any pleasure of yours," he	PP	I	18	94	43
circumstance a matter of pleasure, because on such	PP	I	18	99	63
I should have great pleasure, I am sure, in obliging the	PP	I	18	101	71
Bingley was all grateful pleasure, and he readily engaged	PP	I	18	103	76
and with considerable, though not equal, pleasure.	PP	I	18	103	77
felicitations with equal pleasure, and then proceeded to	PP	I	20	110	1
"I have not the pleasure of understanding you," said he,	PP	I	20	111	9
I have no pleasure in talking to undutiful children.--	PP	I	20	113	28
Not that I have much pleasure indeed in talking to any	PP	I	20	113	28
and had soon the pleasure of seeing its happy effect.	PP	I	21	120	29
was no longer a matter of pleasure to Mrs. Bennet.	PP	I	23	128	11
She wrote also with great pleasure of her brother's being	PP	II	1	133	2
On the following Monday, Mrs. Bennet had the pleasure of	PP	II	2	139	2
Miss Bennet accepted her aunt's invitation with pleasure;	PP	II	2	142	17
of affording pleasure, unconnected with his general powers.	PP	II	2	142	19
refuse, though she foresaw little pleasure in the visit.	PP	II	3	146	17
evident that she had no pleasure in it; she made a slight,	PP	II	3	148	26
something greater pleasure as well as greater certainty.	PP	II	3	148	26
tour of pleasure which they proposed taking in the summer.	PP	II	4	154	21
with the liveliest pleasure, and Elizabeth was more and	PP	II	5	155	3
add considerably to the pleasure of their engagements at	PP	II	8	172	1
you; and I have had the pleasure of your acquaintance long	PP	II	8	174	14
came because he had pleasure in their society, a	PP	II	9	180	28
sacrifice to propriety, not a pleasure to himself.	PP	II	9	180	29
questions--about her pleasure in being at Hunsford, her	PP	II	10	182	1
he has at least great pleasure in the power of choice.	PP	II	10	183	9
With no expectation of pleasure, but with the strongest	PP	II	12	196	3
his attentions with pleasure, she did not invite them by	PP	II	12	197	5
great enjoyment; and the pleasure of being with Charlotte,	PP	II	15	215	3
gives me the greatest pleasure to hear that you have	PP	II	15	215	3
					4
by them; but all sense of pleasure was lost in shame.	PP	II	18	229	10
by again enjoying the pleasure of anticipation, console	PP	II	19	237	3
hope to have all my expectations of pleasure realized.	PP	II	19	237	4
to enhance every pleasure--and affection and intelligence,	PP	II	19	239	11
really had no pleasure in fine carpets or satin curtains.	PP	II	19	240	14
great pleasure in talking of her master and his sister.	PP	III	1	248	23
but just done, to give pleasure to Miss Darcy, who had	PP	III	1	249	43
"Whatever can give his sister any pleasure, is sure to be	PP	III	1	250	45
How much of pleasure or pain it was in his power to bestow!	PP	III	1	251	48
Whether he had felt more of pain or of pleasure in seeing	PP	III	1	253	55
to give pleasure were prepossessed in her favour.	PP	III	2	262	7
since he had had the pleasure of seeing her;" and, before	PP	III	2	262	8
Bingley expressed great pleasure in the certainty of	PP	III	2	264	12
having the pleasure of seeing you at Pemberley to day."	PP	III	4	278	20
with him at the next ball we meet, with great pleasure.	PP	III	5	291	60
she had expected most pleasure and pride in her company,	PP	III	8	313	20
morning gave him great pleasure, because it required an	PP	III	10	324	2
determine whether pleasure or pain bore the greatest share.	PP	III	10	326	3
She was even sensible of some pleasure, though mixed with	PP	III	10	327	3
"I almost envy you the pleasure, and yet I believe it	PP	III	10	327	11
the news does not affect me either with pleasure or pain.	PP	III	11	332	17
Their society can afford no pleasure, that will atone for	PP	III	11	337	55
She could settle it in no way that gave her pleasure.	PP	III	12	339	3
she yet received pleasure from observing his behaviour.	PP	III	12	340	13
She knew how little such a situation would give pleasure	PP	III	12	340	12
all her chance of pleasure for the evening must depend.	PP	III	12	341	14
She now lost every expectation of pleasure.	PP	III	12	342	26
confidence would give pleasure; and instantly embracing	PP	III	13	346	23
to relate will give such pleasure to all my dear family!	PP	III	13	347	26
great pleasure in thinking you will be so happily settled.	PP	III	13	348	38
to Elizabeth, for the pleasure of talking of her; and when	PP	III	13	349	44
with gratitude and pleasure, his present assurances.	PP	III	16	366	8
only of the past as its remembrance gives you pleasure."	PP	III	11	369	23
her friend was a sincere pleasure to Elizabeth, though in	PP	III	18	384	26
must sometimes think the pleasure dearly bought, when she	PP	III	18	384	26
of courtship much of its pleasure, it added to the hope of	PP	III	18	384	27
"I must say it, and say it with pleasure.	MP	I	3	27	33
of any real pleasure, that time of course never came.	MP	I	4	35	7
far beyond any former pleasure of the sort; and the	MP	I	4	37	8
her pleasure sprung, was beyond all her words to express.	MP	I	4	37	8
of his most cordial pleasure in the connection, the	MP	I	4	39	12
But I will quiz you with a great deal of pleasure, if you	MP	I	5	49	34
Edmund expressed his pleasure and surprise.	MP	I	6	57	33
pretty, that I have great pleasure in looking at her."	MP	I	7	63	2
and to the pure genuine pleasure of the exercise,	MP	I	7	66	15
"It is a pleasure to see a lady with such a good heart for	MP	I	7	69	22
like their own, and they had great pleasure in praising it.	MP	I	7	69	23
She rides only for pleasure, you for health."	MP	I	7	70	29
to be talked of with pleasure--till the fourth day, when	MP	I	7	70	30
he must be to check a pleasure of Miss Crawford's, that it	MP	I	7	74	58
losses both of health and pleasure would be soon made good.	MP	I	8	75	1
was glad to secure any pleasure for her sister; and Mary,	MP	I	8	76	7
ma'am you would be glad to give her the pleasure now?"	MP	I	8	78	21
no wish of procuring her pleasure at any time, but her	MP	I	8	79	23
heard the plan, was in fact much greater than her pleasure.	MP	I	8	79	27
of heart; and it was a pleasure to increase with their	MP	I	8	81	33
might be an evil even beyond the loss of present pleasure."	MP	I	9	84	1
to leave business and pleasure, and say their prayers here	MP	I	9	86	13
I see walls of great pleasure.	MP	I	9	90	34
the bench to think with pleasure of her cousin's care, but	MP	I	9	96	76
ever see Sotherton again with so much pleasure as I do now.	MP	I	10	98	7
"Nothing but pleasure from beginning to end!	MP	I	10	105	53
day had afforded most pleasure or pain, might occupy the	MP	I	10	106	58
Fanny agreed to it, and had the pleasure of seeing him	MP	I	11	112	35
without any thing but pleasure in view, and his own will	MP	I	12	114	2
answer, "and I dare say it gives his sister pleasure.	MP	I	12	116	6
eyes were sparkling with pleasure, and she was speaking	MP	I	12	117	15
pleasure--but that I am this moment going to dance.	MP	I	12	119	24
was yet an untasted pleasure, was quite alive at the idea.	MP	I	13	123	6
quite as determined in the cause of pleasure, as Tom.--	MP	I	13	128	38
What gentleman among you am I to have the pleasure of	MP	I	15	143	27
breakfast," said he, "and am sure of giving pleasure there.	MP	I	16	156	27
promote the pleasure of the two so dear to her.	MP	I	17	161	9
acted well, and it was a pleasure to her to creep into the	MP	I	18	165	3
Surprise, consciousness, and pleasure, appeared in each of	MP	I	18	169	23
pleasure were likely to be more than momentary in them.	MP	I	18	169	23
observing with decided pleasure how much she was grown!	MP	II	1	177	7
body to cloud her pleasure; her own time had been	MP	II	1	179	9
that where the present pleasure of those she loved was at	MP	II	2	190	8
shewing a curiosity and pleasure in his information which	MP	II	3	198	12
as eager for novelty and pleasure as Maria, though she	MP	II	3	204	32
and deriving no higher pleasure from her conversation than	MP	II	4	208	11
Edmund met them with particular pleasure.	MP	II	4	211	25
to her and asked for the pleasure of her company too.	MP	II	4	215	47
he saw with so much pleasure established, it was a silent	MP	II	4	216	50
pleasure, both present and future, as much as possible.	MP	II	5	219	27
exception of Fanny, the pleasure was general; and even to	MP	II	5	223	48
look back on our theatricals with exquisite pleasure.	MP	II	5	225	55
and Sir Thomas had the pleasure of receiving in his	MP	II	6	233	16
pain and pleasure retraced with the fondest recollection.	MP	II	6	234	18
"I have had the pleasure of seeing your sister dance, Mr.	MP	II	7	250	61
Fanny dance, and to give pleasure to the young people in	MP	II	8	252	1
It would give me pleasure to see you both dance.	MP	II	8	252	1
pleasure in the promised ball, as Sir Thomas could desire.	MP	II	8	253	5
heard her speak of the pleasure of such a journey with an	MP	II	8	256	12
feelings of pain and pleasure, could attempt to speak; but	MP	II	9	261	3
Believe me, I have no pleasure in the world superior to	MP	II	9	262	9
No, I can safely say, I have no pleasure so complete, so	MP	II	9	262	9
power of one pleasure over his own mind, though it might	MP	II	9	262	11
Why should she lose a pleasure which she has shewn herself	MP	II	9	263	12
with the greatest pleasure, and in whose characters there	MP	II	9	263	16
of pleasure from its writer being himself to go away.	MP	II	9	266	21
This ought to be a day of pleasure.	MP	II	9	268	30
"Oh! yes, yes, and it will be a day of pleasure.	MP	II	9	268	31
The ball too--such an evening of pleasure before her!	MP	II	9	270	40
she could do her justice even with pleasure to herself.	MP	II	9	271	40
object, and he saw with pleasure the general elegance of	MP	II	10	272	1
laughed, and every moment had its pleasure and its hope.	MP	II	10	273	6
be brighter, she exclaimed with eager pleasure, "did he?	MP	II	10	274	9
pleasure which would have been so very delightful to them.	MP	II	10	275	12
it to be purely for the pleasure of conveying your brother	MP	II	10	277	19

rather than insensible of pleasure in Henry's attentions. MP II 10 277 20
The evening had afforded Edmund little pleasure. MP II 10 279 21
unused to have her pleasure consulted, or to have any MP II 10 280 32
There was even pleasure with the surprize. MP II 12 292 5
both of pain and pleasure; but happily the pleasure was MP II 13 308 36
but happily the pleasure was not of a sort to die with the MP II 13 308 36
humanity where his own pleasure was concerned--and, alas! MP III 2 329 9
"Let me have the pleasure of finishing that speech to your MP III 3 336 10
was capital, and her pleasure in good reading extreme. MP III 3 337 10
His acting had first taught Fanny what pleasure a play MP III 3 337 10
to Fanny, he had true pleasure in satisfying; and when MP III 3 340 24
It would be the greatest pleasure to him to have her there MP III 6 372 18
every other pleasure to that of being useful to them. MP III 6 373 23
nurse, and now felt a particular pleasure in seeing again. MP III 7 381 25
neck to sob out her various emotions of pain and pleasure. MP III 7 384 34
She had great pleasure in feeling her usefulness, but MP III 8 390 7
with the servants at her pleasure, and then encouraged to MP III 8 391 9
weather, and allow him the pleasure of attending them?"-- MP III 10 401 10
the pleasure of talking of Mansfield was so very great! MP III 10 406 21
thank him for another pleasure, and one of no trivial kind. MP III 10 406 22
You know the ease, and the pleasure with which this would MP III 11 411 16
Having once begun, it is a pleasure to me to tell you all MP III 13 422 2
Even now, she speaks with pleasure of being in Mansfield MP III 13 422 2
for doing so, and for making his pleasure conduce to yours. MP III 14 435 14
My dearest Fanny, I am giving you I hope more pleasure MP III 16 455 21
temptation of immediate pleasure was too strong for a mind MP III 17 467 20
in herself, in every pleasure, every scheme of her's;--one E I 1 6 6
cannot allow herself to feel so much pain as pleasure. E I 1 11 38
"And have you never known the pleasure and triumph of a E I 1 13 43
"With a great deal of pleasure, sir, at any time," said Mr. E I 1 14 48
Emma's losing a single pleasure, or suffering an hour's E I 2 18 11
evening had particular pleasure in sending them away happy. E I 3 25 15
given as much panic as pleasure--but the humble, grateful, E I 3 25 15
plenty of people who would take pleasure in degrading you." E I 4 30 22
have been seeing their intimacy with the greatest pleasure. E I 5 36 4
to it, so long as it is a source of pleasure to herself. E I 5 40 24
"Great has been the pleasure, I am sure. E I 6 43 7
what infinite pleasure should he have in executing it! he E I 6 49 40
Dear Miss Woodhouse, I would not give up the pleasure and E I 7 54 26
"I would ask for the pleasure of your company, Mr. E I 8 58 7
and she had the pleasure of seeing him most intently at E I 9 70 7
It will be giving him so much pleasure! E I 9 77 45
the tender and the sublime of pleasure to Harriet's share. E I 9 82 84
and gave Mr. and Mrs. Weston a great deal of pleasure. E I 11 96 24
she had particular pleasure, from the circumstance of the E I 12 98 1
face expressed more pleasure than at this moment; never E I 13 111 12
his own going, and the pleasure it was to afford at E I 13 112 24
Emma thought with pleasure of some change of subject. E I 13 114 28
did not comprehend the pleasure, but said only, coolly, "I E I 13 115 40
41
This was a pleasure which perhaps the whole day's visit E I 14 117 2
degree, and a sort of pleasure in the idea of their being E I 14 119 5
Emma spoke with a very proper degree of pleasure; and E I 14 119 8
"What a very great pleasure it will be to you! and Mrs. E I 14 120 10
It depends entirely upon his aunt's spirits and pleasure; E I 14 121 16
would have been rather a pleasure, previous to the E I 15 129 23
appeared,) gave me great pleasure, and I have been very E I 15 131 34
society in Surry; the pleasure of looking at some body new; E I 18 145 5
any thing but his own pleasure, from living with those who E I 18 145 10
his while; whenever there is any temptation of pleasure." E I 18 146 14
sacrifice of mere pleasure you will always find me ready E I 18 146 16
a life of mere idle pleasure, and fancying himself E I 18 148 24
mother, for it is such a pleasure to her--a letter from E II 1 157 10
that could give us so much pleasure as Miss Woodhouse's. E II 1 158 12
That must be a very great pleasure." E II 1 159 17
as I am going to have the pleasure of reading to you. E II 1 159 20
had its day of fame and pleasure, hope and interest; but E II 2 163 2
the sense of pleasure and the sense of rendering justice, E II 2 167 13
Jane, and had now great pleasure in marking an improvement. E II 3 170 1
I cannot have a greater pleasure than"----- "Oh! my dear E II 3 173 30
31
and regret, pain and pleasure, as to this fortunate Miss E II 3 180 57
had given her so much pleasure the autumn before, was E II 5 186 2
There was instant pleasure in the sight of them, and still E II 5 188 6
7
them, and still greater pleasure was conveyed in sound-- E II 5 188 6
7
to have her share of surprize, introduction, and pleasure. E II 5 190 21
one has planned; and the pleasure of coming in upon one's E II 5 190 24
"It is a great pleasure where one can indulge in it," said E II 5 190 25
I should listen with pleasure; but she would be ready to E II 5 192 31
heedlessness as to the pleasure of his father and Mrs. E II 7 205 1
"Me!--I suppose I smile for pleasure at Col. Campbell's E II 8 216 20
so many alleviations of pleasure, in the midst of the E II 8 219 44
of all the dangerous pleasure of knowing herself beloved E II 8 219 44
I have no pleasure in seeing my friends, unless I can E II 8 222 53
And he smiled with such seeming pleasure at the conviction, E II 8 228 90
The pleasure is not enhanced, and the inconvenience is E II 8 228 92
seemed to give fresh pleasure to the present meeting. E II 9 233 25
"This is a pleasure," said he, in rather a low voice, " E II 10 240 3
be enjoying your pleasure on this occasion, Miss Fairfax. E II 10 241 11
12
I have the pleasure, madam, (to Mrs. Bates,) of restoring E II 10 242 15
Yes, that will be quite enough for pleasure. E II 11 248 4
Nothing can be farther from pleasure than to be dancing in E II 11 249 17
oppose than lose the pleasure of dancing with her; but she E II 11 250 19
It would be the greatest pleasure to them, if you could E II 11 253 39
Pleasure in seeing dancing!--not I, indeed--I never look E II 12 257 3
look forward to it, I own, with very great pleasure." E II 12 258 5
for any thing?--why not seize the pleasure at once?-- E II 12 259 17
She had great pleasure in hearing Frank Churchill talked E II 13 264 1
for his sake, greater pleasure than ever in seeing Mr. and E II 13 264 1
read it with a degree of pleasure and admiration which E II 13 265 5
which I can already look forward to with pleasure." E II 13 267 7
to stay at home than engage in schemes of pleasure." E II 14 274 29
and pleasure always--but with no thought beyond." E II 15 289 40
that she had soon the pleasure of apprehending they were E II 16 290 1
own door when I had the pleasure of meeting you; and Henry E II 16 293 15
16
If the errand were not a pleasure to me, it could be done, E II 16 296 37
"Read it, read it," said he, "it will give you pleasure; E II 17 303 25
"I hope I shall soon have the pleasure of introducing my E II 18 305 1
both have great pleasure in seeing him at the vicarage." E II 18 305 4
There could be no doubt of his great pleasure in seeing E III 1 316 3
What a pleasure it is to send one's carriage for a friend!- E III 2 321 17
he, "I shall have great pleasure, I am sure--for, though E III 2 327 36
would give me very great pleasure at any time to stand up E III 2 327 36
She was all pleasure and gratitude, both for Harriet and E III 2 328 40
with Mr. Knightley gave Emma considerable pleasure. E III 3 332 1
not allow himself the pleasure of stopping at Hartfield, E III 3 332 2
the day; and he had the pleasure of returning for answer, E III 3 336 12
But it is a pleasure to me to admire him at a distance-- E III 4 341 36
It was the delay of a great deal of pleasure and parade. E III 6 352 2
high expectations of pleasure from it; and Mr. Weston, E III 6 357 31
ease, ready to talk with pleasure of what had been E III 6 357 33
the river, seemed the finish of the pleasure grounds.-- E III 6 360 38
have the pleasure of being hot, and growing cool again.-- E III 6 361 42
the very questionable enjoyments of this day of pleasure. E III 7 374 54
looking back on it with pleasure; but in her view it was a E III 8 377 1
there, indeed, lay real pleasure, for there she was giving E III 8 377 1
with any wish of giving pleasure, but in conferring E III 8 378 3
Even pleasure, you know, is fatiguing--and I cannot say E III 8 381 19

It will be nothing but pleasure, a life of pleasure.-- E III 8 382 23
would have been a great pleasure to talk over Jane E III 9 386 8
in duty to Emma as in pleasure to herself, to relate all E III 12 417 3
from the flutter of pleasure, excited by such tender E III 13 426 14
15
"I have the greatest pleasure, my dear Emma, in forwarding E III 14 436 7
of it might not very much exceed the pleasure. E III 15 446 18
She soon resolved, equally as a duty and a pleasure, to E III 16 452 7
"I have scarce had the pleasure of seeing you, Miss E III 16 454 18
"What! are we to have the pleasure of a call from Mr. E III 16 455 22
After the first chat of pleasure he was silent; and then, E III 18 470 1
2
Now there would be pleasure in her returning.-- E III 18 475 41
Every thing would be a pleasure. E III 18 475 41
It would be a great pleasure to know Robert Martin. E III 18 475 41
him with Jane, would yield its proportion of pleasure. E III 18 476 46
Mary, and still have the pleasure of sometimes seeing the P III 2 14 9
She knew that when she played she was giving pleasure only P III 6 47 13
pleasure for their sakes, than mortification for her own. P III 6 47 13
that my brother had the pleasure of being acquainted with, P III 6 49 18
19
pleasure of seeing them set off together in high spirits. P III 7 58 20
a pleasure to hear him talked of, by such a good friend." P III 8 66 20
not deny himself the pleasure of taking the precious P III 8 66 22
greater pleasure in getting upon her back again directly. P III 9 80 29
for this walk, and they entered into it with pleasure. P III 10 83 6
Her pleasure in the walk must arise from the exercise and P III 10 84 7
"Do let us have the pleasure of taking you home. P III 10 91 40
of pleasure and pain, that she knew not which prevailed. P III 10 91 42
to go, and besides the pleasure of doing as she liked, P III 11 94 7
towards him, and a pleasure even in thinking that it might, P III 12 115 67
But the remembrance of the appeal remained a pleasure to P III 12 117 75
her judgment, a great pleasure; and when it became a sort P III 12 117 75
heart revelled in angry pleasure, in pleased contempt, P IV 1 125 13
which gave her the pleasure of fancying herself a P IV 1 126 19
This was handsome,--and gave her more pleasure than almost P IV 1 126 20
They had the pleasure of assuring her that Bath more than P IV 3 137 4
Anne, far from wishing to cavil at the pleasure, replied, " P IV 5 155 10
her, and to quicken the pleasure and surprise, with P IV 6 162 1
and not in the least likely to afford them any pleasure. P IV 6 168 24
"None, I thank you, unless you will give me the pleasure P IV 6 169 26
It was agitation, pain, pleasure, a something between P IV 7 175 6
is over, the remembrance of it often becomes a pleasure. P IV 8 183 16
"I have not had the pleasure of visiting in Camden-Place P IV 8 187 28
Russell; but she had the pleasure of getting rid of Mr. P IV 8 189 44
and another hour of pleasure or of penance was to be set P IV 8 189 45
Anne recollected with pleasure the next morning her P IV 9 192 1
Had I known it, I would have had the pleasure of talking P IV 9 194 23
"that is exactly the pleasure I want you to have. P IV 9 195 24
supposing, in whatever pleasure the concert of last night P IV 9 197 33
every gratification of pleasure and vanity which could be P IV 9 209 95
being able to shew such pleasure as she did, in the P IV 10 213 10
I have no pleasure in the sort of meeting, and should be P IV 10 224 53
To-night we may have the pleasure of all meeting again, at P IV 11 236 36
I could have no other pleasure. P IV 11 243 67
I will answer for the pleasure it will give my wife & S 1 367 1
It was general pleasure & consent.-- S 2 374 1
receive every possible pleasure which Sanditon could be S 2 374 1
commission with pleasure, & have no doubt of succeeding.-- S 5 387 1
Sanditon house as I do;--it is not for my own pleasure.-- S 6 393 1
address & wish of paying attention & giving pleasure.-- S 7 394 1
at Sanditon, she had the pleasure of seeing just as she S 9 406 1
There was a great deal of surprise but still more pleasure S 9 406 1
I had the pleasure of hearing soon afterwards by the same S 9 408 1
animation for him, observed with considerable pleasure.-- S 10 415 1
I will have the pleasure of spreading some for you S 10 417 1
which Miss D. P. had the pleasure of settling her new S 11 422 1

PLEASURE-GROUND (1)
it prettier than any pleasure-ground she had ever been in NA II 11 214 25

PLEASURE-GROUNDS (3)
It had no park, but the pleasure-grounds were tolerably SS III 6 302 7
all the sweets of pleasure-grounds, as by one impulse, one MP I 9 89 32
I might impose on the pleasure-grounds, is another thing. P III 3 18 8

PLEASURES (47)
mortifications and pleasures have been separately stated, NA I 13 97 1
into scenes, where pleasures of every kind had met her. NA II 2 141 11
to observe that our pleasures in this world are always to NA II 11 210 7
they liked, their hours, pleasures and fatigues at their NA II 13 220 1
looking forward to pleasures untasted and unalloyed, and NA II 14 237 20
My brother had no regard for her; his pleasures were not SS II 9 206 24
and finding her only pleasures in retirement and study, as SS III 14 378 16
of his most respectable pleasures; and Elizabeth admired PP II 5 156 4
The last born has as good a right to the pleasures of PP II 6 165 35
pleasures of the morning to any body who would hear her. PP II 16 222 21
it from me, my dear sister, to depreciate such pleasures. PP II 16 222 23
on, in any of those pleasures which too often console the PP II 19 236 1
the scene of her former pleasures, every idea gave way to PP III 1 258 76
pleasures of so benevolent a scheme were already enjoyed. MP I 1 8 9
associate, their pleasures and schemes were sometimes of a MP I 2 17 21
the improvement of her mind, and extending its pleasures. MP I 2 22 35
brother must help to pay for the pleasures of the elder. MP I 3 23 2
pleasures, and his absence was unhappily most welcome. MP I 3 32 64
good-humour, from the pleasures of the day, did her the MP I 7 71 35
to intercept the pleasures of her nieces, she had found a MP I 10 103 50
to equal the social pleasures of Mansfield, he gladly MP I 12 115 3
which shuts out noisy pleasures, should much exceed theirs. MP II 1 186 34
blessing, for the first pleasures of Mr. Rushworth's wife MP II 4 210 21
all my possessions and pleasures, try to keep me longer at MP II 6 231 9
interposing, "have their pleasures at Brighton, and I hope MP II 8 252 3
the friends nor the pleasures she was going to were worth MP II 8 256 12
The remembrance of all her earliest pleasures, and of what MP III 6 370 11
might have some pains, Portsmouth could have no pleasures. MP III 8 392 12
a share in her own first pleasures, and inspire a taste MP III 9 398 9
It was sad to Fanny to lose all the pleasures of spring. MP III 14 431 9
She had not known before what pleasures she had to lose in MP III 14 431 9
To be losing such pleasures was no trifle; to be losing MP III 14 432 9
her perceptions and her pleasures were of the keenest sort. MP III 15 446 35
and attached to country pleasures, their home was the home MP III 17 473 32
occupation and the pleasures of society, the next eighteen E I 2 16 5
now loved to talk of the pleasures of her visit, and E I 4 27 4
One half of the world cannot understand the pleasures of E I 9 81 77
in the class of their pleasures, their enjoyments, their E I 13 111 13
perplexities and pleasures of her father and herself. E I 14 117 1
in all the rational pleasures of an elegant society, and a E II 2 164 6
and retire from all the pleasures of life, of rational E II 2 165 8
it, but that they shall not choose pleasures for me.-- E II 12 257 3
no friends had deserted them, no pleasures had been lost.-- E III 12 422 19
Musgroves for all their pleasures: they would come at any P III 6 47 15
belonged to the winter pleasures; her spirits rose under P IV 2 135 33
every man to have the same objects and pleasures as myself. P IV 10 218 26
of it--Campbell in his pleasures of hope has touched the S 7 397 1

PLEDGED (4)
promise; his honour was pledged to make every thing easy; NA I 15 122 28
We are persuaded that he has pledged himself to assist Mr. PP III 7 306 46
of speedy payment, for which I have pledged myself. PP III 8 313 19
recall--that she had pledged herself anew to Sotherton-- MP II 3 201 23

PLENTIFUL (3)
have dictated some very plentiful orders, had not Jane, PP III 7 307 48
itself was elegant and plentiful, according to the usual MP II 7 238 3
She had provided a plentiful dinner for them; she wished E II 8 213 6

PLENTY (18)
fashionable, & everything announces plenty & elegance. LS 5 250 2

I do not know, there are plenty of books in the room, but LS 17 271 7
and there is plenty of dirt, it will be excellent falling. NA I 9 65 30
Perhaps in the spring, if I have plenty of money, as I SS I 6 29 4
But when there is plenty of money on one side, and next to SS II 8 194 8
money could not be very plenty with us just now, she put SS II 11 224 28
their complaints, and scold them into harmony and plenty. PP II 7 169 4
"Nobody loved plenty and hospitality more than herself-- MP I 3 31 59
she will have opportunities in plenty of seeing Sotherton. MP I 8 76 5
the abode of wealth and plenty had a little disordered her MP III 6 369 10
garden, gave the children plenty of wholesome food, let E I 3 22 5
plenty of people who would take pleasure in degrading you." E I 4 30 22
five; and for five couple there will be plenty of room." E II 11 248 4
"Oh!" interrupted Emma, "there will be plenty of time for E II 11 252 34
And I had plenty all the while in my pocket!-- E III 4 339 13
She has plenty of money, and I intend she shall buy all P IV 5 156 13
morning; sure to have plenty of chat; and then we get away P IV 6 170 29
and when one can but get him to talk, he has plenty to say. P IV 10 218 26

PLIANCY (1)
of observation and less pliancy of temper than her sister, PP I 4 15 11

PLIED (1)
and, plied well with good things, would soon pop off." MP I 3 24 5

PLIGHT (1)
the common indifferent plight, were contrasted with some P III 11 98 17

PLIGHTED (2)
because my faith was plighted to another, there could be SS III 13 368 28
Her faith was plighted, and Mr. Elliot's character, like P IV 11 229 1

PLODS (1)
The lawyer plods, quite care-worn; the physician is up at P III 3 20 17

PLOTTING (1)
Poor Mr. Woodhouse little suspected what was plotting E III 14 434 3

PLOUGHS (1)
enclosures, where the ploughs at work, and the fresh-made P III 10 85 13

PLUMP (3)
She was short and plump, had a very pretty face, and the SS I 19 106 22
height--well made & plump, with an air of healthy vigour.-- W 328 9
She was short, plump and fair, with a fine bloom, blue E I 3 23 9

PLUMPNESS (2)
were softened by plumpness and colour, her eyes gained NA I 1 14 2
But happily, either Anne was improved in plumpness and P IV 1 124 10

PLUMS (1)
her, and her mouth stuffed with sugar plums by the other. SS I 21 121 10

PLUNGE (3)
He will, most likely, give a plunge or two, and perhaps NA I 9 62 9
without a plunge or a caper, or any thing like one. NA I 9 62 10
but I will not have you plunge her deep, for she is as MP II 6 230 8

PLUNGED (2)
such as might have plunged weak spirits in despondence.-- W 362 31
and feel herself plunged at once in all the agitations P IV 11 229 2

PLUNGING (1)
such a situation, plunging into such difficulties, under MP III 16 454 18

PLYMOUTH (13)
that he had been staying with some friends near Plymouth. SS I 16 87 26
with my uncle, who lives at Longstaple, near Plymouth. SS I 22 130 28
been staying a fortnight with some friends near Plymouth." SS I 22 134 49
and Edward's visit near Plymouth, his melancholy state of SS II 1 139 1
were probably going down to Mr. Pratt's, near Plymouth. SS III 11 355 39
knowing how to get to Plymouth; for Lucy it seems borrowed SS III 13 370 37
I brought her into Plymouth; and here was another instance P III 8 66 16
and the three children, round from Portsmouth to Plymouth. P III 8 69 39
my taking Mrs. Harville, and all her family, to Plymouth." P III 8 69 44
I was at Plymouth, dreading to hear of him; he sent in P III 12 108 28
The Laconia had come into Plymouth the week before; no P III 12 108 28
He had talked of going down to Plymouth for a week, and P IV 2 133 25
Instead of staying at Lyme, he went off to Plymouth, and P IV 6 171 33

POACHERS (1)
and his zeal after poachers,--subjects which will not find MP I 12 115 4

POCKET (10)
her pocket; and she looked as if she knew not what she did. NA II 10 203 8
his taking Miss Steele's pocket handkerchief, and throwing SS I 21 121 7
Then taking a small miniature from her pocket, she added, " SS I 22 131 35
her pocket and carelessly shewing the direction to Elinor. SS I 22 134 52
the letter into her pocket, "is the only comfort we have SS I 22 135 54
from his pocket; "but perhaps you would like to read it." PP III 7 302 11
what with her board and pocket allowance, and the PP III 8 309 4
And I had plenty all the while in my pocket!-- E III 4 339 13
them away in his coat pocket, &c. to have another moment P III 6 49 25
Here sir--(taking out his pocket book--) if you will do me S 1 366 1

POCKET-BOOK (6)
you their names directly; here they are, in my pocket-book. NA I 6 40 10
a piece of white paper, and put it into his pocket-book." SS I 12 60 13
Her three notes--unluckily they were all in my pocket-book, SS III 8 329 63
about me in the same pocket-book, which was now searched SS III 8 329 63
Jane then took it from her pocket-book, and gave it to PP III 5 291 59
a memorandum in his pocket-book; it was about spruce beer. E III 4 339 18

POCKETS (2)
have not left any thing behind you in any of the pockets." NA II 14 234 12
"Upon my word, he must have gone off with his pockets well MP II 13 305 21

POEM (2)
time or other, to look at--or my tour to read--or my poem. E III 6 364 60
You remember those lines--I forget the poem at this moment: E III 16 454 13

POEMS (3)
with all new poems and states of the nation that come out. P IV 10 215 15
at this moment, of the sea, in either of Scott's poems."-- S 7 397 1
"I have read several of Burn's poems with great delight, S 7 397 1

POET (6)
discreet lines of the poet, "heaven's last best gift." MP I 4 43 23
A poet in love must be encouraged in both capacities, or E I 9 77 42
I dare say you have heard those charming lines of the poet, E II 15 282 5
which has drawn form every poet, worthy of being read, P III 10 84 7
tenderest songs of the one poet, and all the impassioned P III 11 100 23
that line of the poet Cowper in his description of the S 1 370 1

POETIC (1)
to speak, but I am not poetic enough to separate a man's S 7 397 1

POETICAL (2)
some few of the thousand poetical descriptions extant of P III 10 84 7
the sweets of poetical despondence, and meaning to have P III 10 85 13

POETRY (13)
"That is, I can read poetry and plays, and things of that NA I 14 108 20
I wonder who first discovered the efficacy of poetry in PP I 9 44 32
"I have been used to consider poetry as the food of love," PP I 9 44 33
music behind, and what poetry only can attempt to describe. MP I 11 113 35
the biography and poetry which she delighted in herself. MP III 9 398 9
though principally in poetry; and besides the persuasion P III 11 100 23
and having talked of poetry, the richness of the present P III 11 100 23
did not always read only poetry; and to say, that she P III 11 100 23
it was the misfortune of poetry, to be seldom safely P III 11 100 23
already; of course they had fallen in love over poetry. P IV 6 167 20
But while we are on the subject of poetry, what think you S 7 397 1
Montgomery has all the fire of poetry, Wordsworth has the S 7 397 1
to separate a man's poetry entirely from his character;--& S 7 397 1

POETS (1)
as to the first-rate poets, trying to ascertain whether P III 11 100 23

POIGNANT (6)
With feelings so poignant as mine, the conviction of LS 30 300 3
so poignant and so fresh, it was possible for them to be. SS II 1 141 6
It was of a much less poignant nature than what the others MP III 16 452 15
if the distress be not poignant enough to keep the eyes E I 16 137 13
the great amusement, the poignant sting of the last word E III 5 349 27
which were so poignant and so ceaseless in interest. P IV 11 241 59

POINT (267)
as I am on the point of separation from my own daughter. LS 1 244 1
Charles was then on the point of marrying Miss De Courcy, LS 5 249 1
Besides, the most scrupulous point of honour could not LS 9 256 1
any one, I should make a point of not bestowing my LS 10 258 2
my eyes would let me, to point out as well as I could the LS 13 262 1
unalterably fixed on that point, tho' I have not yet quite LS 19 275 4
I made a point also of Frederica's behaving civilly to Sir LS 22 280 1
One point only is gained; Sir James Martin is dismissed. LS 24 285 1
In such a point as this, your mother's prohibition ought LS 24 286 7
Lady Susan, & was on the point of leaving the house under LS 24 287 9
point--continued she, taking me affectionately by the hand. LS 24 289 12
He was actually on the point of leaving Churchill! LS 25 292 1
Let me know your opinion on this point. LS 25 294 5
"unwearied diligence out point would gain;" and the NA I 4 31 2
and point out a quiz through the thickness of a crowd. NA I 4 33 7
moments silent, was on the point of reverting to what NA I 6 42 33
Cheap-Street at this point; it is indeed a street of so NA I 7 44 1
longed to point out that gentleman, she could see nothing. NA I 8 55 10
Point him out to me this instant, if he is. NA I 8 57 16
But when you men have a point to carry, you never stick at NA I 8 57 23
bed; such was the extreme point of her distress; for when NA I 9 60 1
was more than once on the point of requesting from Mr. NA I 9 66 31
There was not a single point in which we differed; I would NA I 10 71 3
getting away, was obliged to give up the point and submit. NA I 11 87 53
hardly give up the point of its having been Tilney himself. NA I 11 87 53
to have it put off, made a point of her being denied. NA I 12 94 10
He should make a point of inquiring into the matter." NA I 13 103 27
had carried her point and was secure of her walk, she NA I 13 103 29
no longer contest the point, nor refuse to hear been as NA I 15 119 14
"Nay, since you make such a point of it, I can refuse you NA II 1 130 13
And could we carry our selfish point with you, we should NA II 2 139 7
up Catherine's feelings to the highest point of extasy. NA II 2 140 8
Her heart instantaneously at ease on this point, she NA II 6 163 1
To retire to bed, however, unsatisfied on such a point, NA II 6 168 10
She had just settled this point, when the end of the path NA II 7 181 41
through, and seemed on the point of doing the same by the NA II 8 185 6
down stairs, seemed to point out:--"I was going to take NA II 8 186 6
folly; and she was on the point of retreating as softly as NA II 9 194 6
enough in himself, at what point of interest were the NA II 11 208 1
the General made such a point of your providing nothing NA II 11 211 13
There was yet another point which Miss Tilney was anxious NA II 13 229 31
her head; and the highest point of ground within the park NA II 14 230 1
Anxious as were all her conjectures on this point, it was NA II 14 231 4
Salisbury she had known to be her point on leaving NA II 14 232 6
on being brought to the point by the shrewdness of the NA II 15 246 12
whose taste did not in every point coincide with my own. SS I 3 17 18
of objection on either point; and, therefore, though it SS I 4 24 21
effect on her in that point to which it principally tended. SS I 5 25 3
were carried to a point of perseverance beyond civility, SS I 6 30 6
joy to him, and in every point of view he was charmed with SS I 7 33 3
On this point Sir John could give more certain SS I 9 44 23
Elinor thought it wisest to touch that point no more. SS I 12 59 5
no cavil, unless you can point out any other method of SS I 15 78 26
with gaining one point, would not then attempt more. SS I 16 85 15
them; and on reaching that point, they stopped to look SS I 16 85 15
said Elinor, smiling, "we may come to the same point. SS I 17 91 11
Marianne looked as if she had no doubt on that point. SS I 17 92 22
your opinion on that point is unchanged, I presume?" SS I 17 93 29
of character in some point or other: fancying people so SS I 17 93 37
"that I have long thought on this point, as you think now. SS I 19 102 4
Elinor, who foresaw a fairer opening for the point she had SS II 1 143 9
he had appeared on the point, either of disclosing, or of SS II 5 172 40
a loss to discover in what point I could be so unfortunate SS II 7 183 13
Their own good-nature must point out to them the real SS II 8 195 17
when it came to the point, in avoiding, where it was SS II 9 201 2
society, no amusement, till my father's point was gained. SS II 9 206 24
most likely change your mind when it came to the point. SS II 10 217 21
forward, and was on the point of concluding it, when SS II 11 221 6
not bear to see a sister slighted in the smallest point. SS II 12 236 38
that when it came to the point, he was afraid Mr. Ferrars SS III 2 272 16
you of, which I was on the point of communicating by paper. SS III 4 288 28
I wonder he should be so improvident in a point of such SS III 5 295 12
He had just settled this point with great composure, when SS III 5 300 38
not, when it came to the point, bid adieu to the house in SS III 6 301 4
She was on the point of sending again for Mr. Harris, or SS III 7 312 19
Miss Dashwood at this point, turning her eyes on him with SS III 8 320 30
31
or deliver it in person, was a point of long debate. SS III 8 323 40
In that point, however, I undervalued my own magnanimity, SS III 8 323 40
you, how often I was on the point of falling in with you. SS III 8 326 55
At present, if I could be satisfied on one point, if I SS III 10 344 17
In that point, however, and that only, he erred;--for SS III 14 376 11
body else, & is always expecting him to come to the point. W 319 2
you had not made a point of my going to this ball, I wish W 319 2
that point; & Mr Edwards now turned to something else.-- W 325 4
that they had made a point of coming early for the W 329 9
the street, & was on the point of asking leave to ring the W 338 17
to a certain point--his address rather--is pleasing.-- W 342 19
That is a point on which ladies & gentlen have long W 346 21
determine some disputable point; & his attention was so W 359 28
a doubt, there cannot be two opinions on that point." PP I 5 19 7
"This is the only point, I flatter myself, on which we do PP I 7 29 11
"In point of composition," said Mary, "his letter does not PP I 13 64 19
Lady Catherine herself says that in point of true beauty, PP I 14 67 7
It had not been very great; he had lost every point; but PP I 16 83 49
But Jane could think with certainty on only one point,-- PP I 17 86 8
her cousin, and to point him out to her particular notice. PP I 18 90 4
office as equal in point of dignity with the highest rank PP I 18 97 60
61
leads me to perform what I look on as a point of duty. PP I 18 97 61
make a point of remaining close to her the whole evening. PP I 18 102 73
We now come to the point. PP I 20 111 17
in her husband, did Mrs. Bennet give up the point. PP I 20 112 23
replied he, "let us be for ever silent on this point. PP I 20 114 32
She had gained her point, and had time to consider of it. PP I 22 122 3
Two of her girls had been on the point of marriage, and PP II 2 139 3
affected to place this point, as well as the still more PP II 2 142 16
advice being given on such a point, without being resented. PP II 3 145 10
herself on every point exactly as she might have foreseen. PP II 3 146 19
who, when it came to the point, so little liked her going, PP II 4 151 2
Collins attending them to point out its beauties, and Lady PP II 6 162 13
While settling this point, she was suddenly roused by the PP II 11 188 3
trees. she was on the point of continuing her walk, when PP II 12 195 2
that he had deceived himself, was no very difficult point. PP II 12 199 5
After pausing on this point a considerable while, she once PP II 13 206 4
made a point of her having two men servants go with her.-- PP II 14 211 13
on this point it will be as well to be silent. PP II 15 216 6
and the door was on the point of being closed, when he PP II 15 217 8
There is one point, on which I want your advice. PP II 17 226 21
to have some other point on which her wishes and hopes PP II 19 237 3
saw and admired every remarkable spot and point of view. PP III 1 245 3
Mrs. Reynolds could interest her on no other point. PP III 1 249 37
On this point she was soon satisfied; and two or three PP III 2 262 8
decency and virtue in such a point should admit of doubt. PP III 5 283 10
"If I had been able," said she, "to carry my point of PP III 5 287 35
and they were on the point of seeking him up stairs with PP III 7 301 4
5
This was one point, with regard to Lydia at least, which PP III 8 308 4
sixteen, was now on the point of accomplishment, and her PP III 8 310 7
That his anger could be carried to such a point of PP III 8 310 10
But to live in ignorance on such a point was impossible; PP III 9 320 32
You may remember what I told you on that point, when first PP III 10 329 32
She looked forward to their entrance, as the point on PP III 12 341 14
and Elizabeth was on the point of going away again, when PP III 13 346 22

I was told, that not only your sister was on the point of PP III 14 353 26
you reasonable; but depend upon it I will carry my point." PP III 14 358 71
your impatience, by reading what he says on that point. PP III 15 362 14
what made you so unwilling to come to the point at last. PP III 18 381 7
Miss Ward's match, indeed, when it came to the point, was MP I 1 3 1
angry letter to Fanny, to point out the folly of her MP I 1 4 1
and I am sure we shall never disagree on this point. MP I 1 7 8
It is a point of great delicacy, and you must assist us in MP I 1 11 17
she made a very particular point;--the spare-rooms at the MP I 3 28 38
her astonishment on that point almost as often, though not MP I 3 31 60
"Oh! then the point is clear. MP I 5 51 43
and she scrupled to point out her own remarks to him, lest MP I 7 66 14
and was on the point of proposing it when Mrs. Grant spoke. MP I 8 80 28
That was the only point of resemblance between her and the MP I 8 80 31
a point of honour to promote her enjoyment to the utmost. MP I 8 82 35
of Mrs. Rushworth, on a point of some similarity, and MP I 12 116 11
Mr. Yates, that this was a point in which height and MP I 14 132 8
"Yes, it will be a great point." MP I 16 155 17
play in particular; their point was gained; he was to act, MP I 17 158 1
on this point there were not many who differed from her. MP I 18 165 3
disrespectful, when this point was settled, and being MP II 1 177 6
for her appearance spoke sufficiently on that point. MP II 1 178 7
She carried this point, and Sir Thomas's narrative MP II 1 180 12
"If I had not been active," said she, "and made a point of MP II 2 188 3
Sir Thomas gave up the point, foiled by her evasions, MP II 2 190 8
should be gone by without seeming to advance that point. MP II 2 191 11
case, he should make a point of returning to Mansfield, at MP II 2 192 11
must have some very interesting point to discuss." MP II 5 226 60
"Bertram," said Henry Crawford, "I shall make a point of MP II 5 227 65
house to dispute the point; a circumstance between MP II 7 244 27
point of privilege and independence beyond all calculation. MP II 7 244 27
with having been on the point of proposing the 22d herself, MP II 8 254 7
should be dressed" was a point of painful solicitude; and MP II 8 254 8
Fanny acknowledged her wishes and doubts on this point; MP II 8 257 15
profession to which he was now on the point of belonging. MP II 10 279 21
in having carried her point so far, than to repine at the MP II 10 280 32
Bertram was on the very point of quitting it as he entered. MP II 13 298 1
its sufficiency, began to take the matter in another point. MP II 13 305 23
The forbearance of her family on a point, respecting which MP III 2 330 14
the perfection of Mr. Crawford's character in that point. MP III 4 345 3
been used to be: to the point--I consider Crawford's MP III 4 346 12
I have not the heart for it when it comes to the point." MP III 5 359 9
discussion was the point attempted to be proved, she set MP III 6 371 14
In every argument with her mother, Susan had in point of MP III 9 396 5
It was the only point of resemblance. MP III 9 398 9
weeks from Mansfield--a point which she never failed to MP III 10 399 2
and she fancied herself on the point of fainting away. MP III 10 399 4
and there was no introducing the main point before her. MP III 10 403 15
to her, and she was on the point of giving him an MP III 10 404 15
(now fixed to the last point of certainty), could affect MP III 15 443 25
here, was on the point of being called into action. MP III 15 446 35
might now have been on the point of marriage, and Henry MP III 16 455 23
by improvement in the only point in which he had given him MP III 17 462 5
very material matrimonial point of submitting your own E I 5 38 11
Harriet was on the point of leaving the room, and only E I 6 43 10
11
Vigorous, decided, with sentiments to a certain point, not E I 7 51 5
That is a point which you must settle with your own E I 7 52 17
Waving that point, however, and supposing her to be, as E I 8 63 44
"We think so very differently on this point, Mr. Knightley, E I 8 65 48
a better judge of such a point of female right and E I 8 65 50
with him--had made such a point of it, that he had E I 9 81 78
is in truth the great point of inferiority, the want of E I 10 85 21
But it would not do; he had not come to the point. E I 10 90 39
As a magistrate, he had generally some point of law to E I 12 100 16
when he had reached such a point as this, she could not E I 12 106 59
"Oh! no--I am grieved to find--I was on the point of E I 13 114 31
years, they always are put off when it comes to the point. E I 14 120 11
were still discussing the point, when Mr. Knightley, who E I 15 127 16
clearly they had seemed to point at Harriet. E I 16 134 4
he has not the power of coming, if he made a point of it. E I 18 145 8
could not endure such a puppy when it came to the point." E I 18 150 32
I always make a point of reading Jane's letters through to E II 1 162 31
seemed to point out the likeliest evil of the two. E II 2 167 12
always be called ten; a point of some dignity, as well as E II 4 181 4
be safest, had been a point of some doubtful consideration. E II 4 185 12
to her--on the point of marriage --would yet never ask E II 6 201 28
going; that they made a point of visiting no fresh person; E II 8 221 48
The unpersuadable point, which he did not mention, Emma E II 8 221 50
They combated the point some time longer in the same way; E II 8 226 85
be subject to, was another point; but at present she could E II 12 262 38
respects; and she made a point of Harriet's going with her, E II 14 270 2
I know enough of music to speak decidedly on that point. E II 15 282 5
difficulties therefore, consider that point as settled." E II 16 296 36
You will find me a formidable antagonist on that point. E II 18 306 12
Emma looked at Harriet while the point was under E III 6 361 41
I could very ill be spared--but such a point had been made E III 6 364 55
and certainly was on the point of carrying it to his lips-- E III 9 386 7
In one point she was fully justified. E III 9 387 12
Mrs. Cole had made such a point--and Mrs. Perry had said E III 9 390 18
"On this point we have been wretched. E III 10 396 43
Jane actually on the point of going as governess! E III 10 397 50
I must love him; and now that I am satisfied on one point, E III 10 398 53
point, the one material point, I am sincerely anxious for E III 10 398 53
Mr. Churchill had made a point of it, as a token of E III 11 403 2
To that point went every leisure moment which her father's E III 11 412 44
This point was just arranged, when a visitor arrived to E III 12 417 3
equality in every point but one--and that one, since the E III 13 428 23
saying, "you will not ask me what is the point of envy.-- E III 13 429 26
27
hope, lay me open to reprehension, excepting on one point. E III 14 438 8
that as silence on such a point could not be misconstrued, E III 14 442 8
or when it came to the point her heart would have failed E III 17 465 28
and in one respect, one point of the highest importance, E III 17 467 31
the next morning, and satisfied himself on that point. E III 17 468 35
if she could;" and, on the point of living at Hartfield, E III 17 469 36
had never succeeded in any point which she wanted to carry, P III 2 16 16
but made no great point of it;--said he sometimes took out P III 3 22 23
change, on the one leading point of Anne's conduct, for P III 4 29 8
deal more at stake on this point than any body else can P III 5 35 16
point in which her own conduct would ill bear examination. P III 11 101 26
Do not you think it is quite a mistaken point of P III 12 103 2
The plan had reached this point, when Anne, coming quietly P III 12 114 60
and Mr. Musgrove made a point of paying his respects to P IV 2 134 29
There was one point which Anne, on returning to her family, P IV 4 145 1
trial on this point, in her intercourse in Camden-Place. P IV 4 146 5
defying public opinion in any point of worldly decorum. P IV 4 146 6
In one point, I am sure, my dear cousin, (he continued, P IV 4 151 21
in the room) in one point, I am sure, we must feel alike. P IV 4 151 21
and Mr. Elliot had made a point of leaving Colonel Wallis P IV 5 158 21
That was a point which Anne had not been able to avoid P IV 6 167 19
time to settle the point of civility between the other two. P IV 7 174 3
they had just reached this point when Anne, as she sat P IV 7 175 4
that point were settled, she could not be quite herself. P IV 7 178 24
approached which must point him out, though not daring to P IV 7 179 28
a disparity, and in a point no less essential than mind.-- P IV 8 182 9
10
Before Sir Walter had reached this point, Anne's eyes had P IV 8 188 41
due to the establishment of the first point asserted. P IV 9 206 88
It was on this point that she hoped to engage Anne's good P IV 9 210 99
In one point, her feelings were relieved by this knowledge P IV 10 212 1
But this was the only point of relief. P IV 10 212 1

was saying, we shall never agree I suppose upon this point. P IV 11 234 27
We never can expect to prove any thing upon such a point. P IV 11 234 30
to carry their point, be they ever so poor, or ever so P IV 12 248 1
and it is now a doubtful point whether his cunning, or P IV 12 250 8
On that point perhaps we may not totally disagree;--at S 1 369 1
have been at the point of death within the last month."-- S 5 385 1
I was just upon the point of wishing you good evening. S 6 394 1

POINTED (29)
anxious inquiry, as she pointed them out to her companion. NA I 12 95 17
To be sure, the pointed arch was preserved--the form of NA II 5 162 26
been pointed out to her by Miss Tilney the evening before. NA II 7 173 5
having traces of cells pointed out, and observing several NA II 8 183 2
of rich carving might be pointed out: having gained the NA II 8 184 5
Yes, only ten days ago had he elated her by his pointed NA II 14 230 2
such kind of neighbourly acts as his own wife pointed out. SS I 2 13 29
John Dashwood by this pointed invitation to her brother, SS I 5 25 3
to himself, the most pointed assurance of her affection. SS I 11 53 1
of his conscience pointed out to be requisite to its SS II 14 252 20
in the manner pointed out by their brother and sister. SS III 13 371 40
Charles instantly pointed him out to Emma--"there's Lord W 332 11
asked for, every view was pointed out with a minuteness PP II 5 156 4
From the entrance hall, of which Mr. Collins pointed out, PP II 6 161 10
they pointed out, she distinguished no part of the scene. PP III 1 253 55
There was no one therefore who could be pointed out, as PP III 6 297 12
your pointed dislike, make it so delightfully absurd! PP III 15 364 24
of the ground, which pointed out even to a very young eye MP I 6 61 56
us mind them;" and with pointed attention continued to MP I 15 147 56
already met him, and with pointed attention he was now MP II 1 179 8
complacency, even before Edmund had pointed it out to him. MP II 6 234 17
or rather of professions of a somewhat pointed character. MP II 7 246 36
said that it meant something very earnest, very pointed. MP II 13 306 26
adding a something too pointed of his hoping soon to have MP III 10 404 15
"There is so pointed, and so particular a meaning in this E I 9 73 20
Emma wished he would be less pointed, yet could not help E II 10 243 22
of pointed neglect that could be further requisite.-- E III 3 332 1
in the dining-room--and she humanely pointed out the door. E III 6 364 56
own fancy, and that soon pointed out to her the E III 10 393 18

POINTEDLY (7)
directly; and, though pointedly applied to by the General NA II 11 214 25
no power to wound them, sat pointedly slighted by both. SS II 12 232 16
civility, but had even pointedly included him in her PP I 15 74 13
to her father, from which she was so pointedly excluded. E I 17 140 3
She did look vexed, she did speak pointedly--and at last, E III 6 359 37
time, a third; had been pointedly attentive: if Elizabeth P IV 2 135 35
The card was pointedly given, and Sir Walter and Elizabeth. P IV 10 226 64

POINTEDNESS (1)
same time there was a pointedness in his manner of asking MP II 10 274 8

POINTER (4)
got the nicest little black bitch of a pointer I ever saw. SS I 9 44 20
of Mr. Willoughby's pointer, than he could describe to her SS I 9 44 21
side of Marianne, and by his favourite pointer at her feet. SS I 14 71 5
he reminded me of an old promise about a pointer puppy. SS III 8 330 69

POINTERS (1)
A gentleman carrying a gun, with two pointers playing SS I 9 42 8

POINTING (16)
"Here come my dear girls," cried Mrs. Thorpe, pointing at NA I 4 32 3
hardly have forborn pointing out, had its inconsistency NA I 15 121 25
pointing to her daughter) it was wrong in her situation. SS I 19 107 29
"there, exactly there"--pointing with one hand, "on that SS III 10 344 12
13
They were then, with no other delay than his pointing out PP II 5 155 3
engaged in the office of pointing out to my friend, the PP II 12 198 5
"And that," said Mrs. Reynolds, pointing to another of the PP III 1 247 11
with fishing tackle, and pointing out those parts of the PP III 1 255 60
was too much engaged in pointing out to her husband all PP III 1 258 76
shortened;--besides pointing out the necessity of his MP I 15 138 1
boys," or in fondly pointing out, as he took up any stray E III 5 347 20
Mr. Shepherd was eloquent on the subject; pointing out all P III 3 22 24
they were about, and of pointing out some of the evils P III 10 82 1
Nobody could do it, but that good fellow, (pointing to P III 12 108 28
Bath already, you see," (pointing to a new umbrella) "I P IV 7 177 14
There, I fancy lies my cure"--pointing to the neat-looking S 1 364 1

POINTS (48)
in many other points she came on exceedingly well; for NA I 1 16 10
Her cautions were confined to the following points. NA I 2 18 2
These are points in which a doubt is equally possible. NA I 3 27 28
in discussing such points; she could compare the balls of NA I 4 33 7
Her mind made up on these several points, and her NA II 10 201 4
from his father, in what points his own conjectures might NA II 15 247 14
But there are other points to be considered besides his SS I 4 21 15
She could not be silent when such points were introduced, SS I 10 47 3
to be points on which I had been previously informed." SS I 10 51 22
of her mind on other points; she was left, on the contrary, SS II 5 174 47
He has been very deceitful! and, in some points, there SS II 8 200 40
and honestly the chief points on which Willoughby grounded SS III 10 347 33
from them, were the first points of self-gratulation; and PP I 18 99 63
points she principally dwelt during the rest of the day. PP I 21 127 5
take care of him in those points where he most wants care. PP II 10 184 24
They entered it in one of its lowest points, and drove for PP III 1 245 2
better, he allowed himself great latitude on such points. MP I 5 45 3
man of the world as might be good for me in some points. MP I 10 98 10
delicacy is.-- in all points of decorum, your conduct must MP I 15 140 13
quick-sighted on such points, he could not avoid MP II 7 238 1
There were points on which they did not quite agree, there MP II 8 255 10
had used to be essential points--did she love him well MP II 8 255 11
In some points of interest they were exactly opposed to MP II 11 285 15
unfeelingly on all such points--who was every thing to MP II 13 305 26
I am aware that there has been sometimes, in some points, MP III 1 313 12
points would be the likeliest way to produce an extreme. MP III 4 349 23
justly on all important points; and she saw, therefore, in MP III 16 449 5
more liberality and candour on those points than formerly. MP III 16 457 29
in our opinions, on points too, of some moment, it had not MP III 16 457 30
to think on points which had not fallen in her way before." E I 6 42 5
"He may have a great deal of influence on some points," E I 14 123 27
acquaintance, it was difficult to decide on such points. E II 2 169 17
But when satisfied on all these points, and their E II 5 191 28
other; and though in some points of pursuit or observation E II 6 197 3
points) he could with time persuade her to any thing. E II 8 221 49
One of those points on which his influence failed, he then E II 8 221 49
I have heard him express himself so warmly on those points! E II 8 226 79
and there were two points on which she was not quite easy. E II 9 231 2
or two such very serious points to consider, as made her E III 14 434 4
in the many, very many, points of view in which she was E III 15 449 35
"Yes; it is in two points offensive to me; I have two P III 3 19 16
she must teach herself to be insensible on such points. P III 6 52 33
But this was one of the points on which the lady shewed P III 10 86 17
These points formed her chief solicitude in anticipating P III 11 93 4
I can satisfy you, perhaps, on points which you would P IV 9 200 57
Upon all points of blood and connexion, he is a completely P IV 9 206 90
points, when her love of money is carried greatly too far. S 3 376 1
Among other points of moralising reflection which the S 12 426 1

POISON (4)
not slaves, and neither poison nor sleeping potions to be NA II 10 200 3
sucking in the sad poison, while a sharer of his E II 2 168 13
from the Hartfield store-room must have been poison. E III 11 403 2
No--it acts on me like poison and wd entirely take away S 10 418 1

POISONED (1)
I could have poisoned him; I made the best of it however, LS 22 280 1

POISONOUS (1)
and looks to all the injury of a poisonous atmosphere. P III 3 20 17

POKING (2)
Lord bless me! how do you think I can live poking by SS II 3 154 4

quarrelling, and that poking old woman, who knows no more MP I 12 119 26
POLICY (4)
She must not be sacrificed to policy or ambition, she must LS 20 278 11
of policy she should be allowed to suppose herself so. NA II 9 192 4
Mrs. Dashwood was acting on motives of policy as well as SS III 14 378 13
I with greater policy concealed my struggles, and flattered PP II 11 192 22
POLISH (1)
They only give a little polish." E I 5 39 15
POLISHED (9)
He is less polished, less insinuating than Manwaring, and LS 10 258 3
a strong sensibility, and the graces of a polished manner. SS II 9 201 4
I consider it as one of the first refinements of polished PP I 6 25 26
vogue amongst the less polished societies of the world.-- PP I 6 25 27
His manners now, though not polished, were more than MP III 10 402 12
his very best and most polished behaviour by Mr. P III 5 32 2
Mrs. Harville, a degree less polished than her husband, P III 11 97 15
they ought to be, so polished, so easy, so particularly P IV 3 143 18
Mr. Elliot was rational, discreet, polished,--but he was P IV 5 161 28
POLITE (21)
Mr. Tilney was polite enough to seem interested in what NA I 3 29 47
health in vain, was too polite to make further opposition. NA II 7 179 29
And all this by such a man as General Tilney, so polite, NA II 13 226 25
polite, her ladyship was introduced to them the next day. SS I 6 30 7
was unwell, was too polite to object for a moment to her SS II 6 178 16
The calm and polite unconcern of Lady Middleton on the SS II 10 215 12
Though nothing could be more polite than Lady Middleton's SS II 14 246 3
piano-forte, and after a polite request that Elizabeth PP I 10 51 45
to Miss Bennet, with a polite congratulation; Mr. Hurst PP I 11 54 2
"He seems to be a most conscientious and polite young man, PP I 13 63 13
tolerable civility to the polite inquiries which he PP I 18 89 3
"He is perfectly well behaved, polite, and unassuming," PP III 1 257 67
were so improved, so polite, so seriously and blamelessly MP II 6 232 11
seriously and blamelessly polite, that it was impossible MP II 6 232 11
comfort of appearing very polite, while feeling very cross- E I 14 119 6
The kind-hearted, polite old man might then sit down and E II 16 295 28
and received his very polite excuses, while she had never P III 12 106 19
Lady Russell's composed mind and polite manners were put P IV 4 146 5
them with a generosity so polite and so determined, that P IV 7 174 3
of polite acknowledgment rather than acceptance. P IV 10 226 65
Her concluding effort in the cause, had been a few polite S 10 414 1
POLITELY (12)
though she was most politely received by General Tilney, NA II 1 129 1
was the tallest, politely decided in favour of the other. SS II 12 234 21
22
She was received, however, very politely by them; and in PP I 7 33 42
politely and more earnestly negatived, she seated herself. PP I 10 51 45
resolutely, and not very politely, declined eating any PP III 14 352 16
17
wishes, though politely kept back, inclined the same way; MP I 14 130 3
Sir Thomas listened most politely, but found much to MP II 1 184 25
Sir Thomas, politely bowing, replied--"it is the only way, MP II 7 247 39
He continued at the window; and after calmly and politely P III 9 79 24
down, politely drew back, and stopped to give them way. P III 12 104 6
&c." which was all as politely done, and as politely taken P IV 3 143 18
politely taken as possible, but her part must follow then. P IV 3 143 18
POLITENESS (56)
by the laws of worldly politeness, to what a degree of NA I 12 92 3
with like calm politeness to Mrs. Allen and her friend.-- NA I 12 93 5
ready, such solicitous politeness as recalled Thorpe's NA I 13 102 27
After addressing her with his usual politeness, he turned NA II 2 139 5
General recovering his politeness as he looked at her, NA II 6 165 6
of this soothing politeness; and her spirits were NA II 10 199 2
every consideration of politeness or maternal affection on SS I 3 14 3
He was received by Mrs. Dashwood with more than politeness; SS I 10 46 1
in sacrificing general politeness to the enjoyment of SS I 10 49 9
The complaints and lamentations which politeness had SS I 13 66 52
demands which this politeness made on it, was spent in SS I 21 120 6
of telling lies when politeness required it, always fell. SS I 21 122 14
behave with tolerable politeness; and resolved within SS II 3 156 15
When they had paid their tribute of politeness by SS II 6 175 2
hopes of exciting his politeness to a quicker dispatch. SS II 11 220 3
delicacy of his taste, proved to be beyond his politeness. SS II 11 220 3
with so much real politeness by Mr. Palmer himself, as, SS III 3 279 1
in the forms of politeness; her kindness, recommended by SS III 6 304 13
Your wife has a claim to your politeness, to your respect, SS III 8 329 64
own deserts, and the politeness with which he talked of SS III 13 366 20
"Mr. Darcy is all politeness," said Elizabeth, smiling. PP I 6 26 42
something better than politeness; there was good humour PP I 7 33 42
and was received with great politeness by the whole family. PP I 13 64 21
She received him with her very best politeness, which he PP I 15 73 11
Bennet by admiring Mrs. Philips's manners and politeness. PP I 15 74 13
and the hospitality and politeness which had marked their PP I 18 102 75
Mrs. Bennet with great politeness and cordiality said how PP I 22 123 4
more perseverance than politeness, protested he must be PP I 23 126 1
2
and, to imitate his politeness, she began, as they met, to PP III 1 254 57
and they parted on each side with the utmost politeness. PP III 1 257 66
They could not be untouched by his politeness, and had PP III 2 264 14
by some exertion of politeness on their side; and, PP III 2 266 17
with more feeling than politeness; then recollecting PP III 4 276 7
politeness of her curtsey and address to his friend. PP III 11 335 41
good humour, and common politeness of Bingley, in half an PP III 12 339 10
high importance, received her with the utmost politeness. PP III 14 351 4
no extraordinary politeness, and I confess that I did not PP III 16 370 31
The politeness which she had been brought up to practise MP I 9 91 36
in the affair beyond politeness, and to have vented all MP I 11 108 4
far as discretion, and politeness, and slowness of speech MP II 10 276 14
before Sir Thomas's politeness and apologies were over, or MP II 13 302 9
to her with the utmost politeness and propriety, at the MP III 10 399 5
fewer struggles for politeness, replied, "it is impossible E I 15 130 29
30
Emma's politeness was at hand directly, to say, with E II 1 157 8
9
Wrapt up in a cloak of politeness, she seemed determined E II 2 169 15
This is a matter of mere common politeness and good- E II 14 280 60
I admire all that quaint, old-fashioned politeness; it is E II 17 302 22
step upon--I shall never forget his extreme politeness.-- E III 2 323 19
relative questions, all answered with patient politeness. E III 2 324 20
said, with studied politeness, "I beg your pardon, madam, P III 8 72 58
59
His cold politeness, his ceremonious grace, were worse P III 8 72 60
At the end of that period, Lady Russell's politeness could P IV 1 125 14
"I will not oppose such kind politeness; but I should be P IV 8 187 27
she sacrificed to politeness with a more suffering spirit. P IV 8 190 47
their general politeness and suavity, she had been too P IV 12 249 3
requiring in common politeness some attention--as his Br, S 10 415 1
POLITEST (1)
They owed to him their two or three politest puzzles; and E I 9 70 7
POLITIC (1)
when the cousins, the politic & lucky cousins, who seemed S 3 378 1
POLITICAL (1)
His mother wished to interest him in political concerns, SS I 3 16 6
POLITICIAN (1)
man--the practised politician, who is to read every body's E I 18 150 32
POLITICIANS (1)
neither sauntering politicians, bustling house-keepers, P IV 11 241 59
POLITICS (7)
to talk over the politics of the day and compare the NA I 10 71 8
found himself arrived at politics; and from politics, it NA I 14 111 29
and from politics, it was an easy step to silence. NA I 14 111 29
variety--the variety of politics, inclosing land, and SS II 12 233 19
hunting, so much of politics between Mr. Crawford and Dr. MP II 5 223 48
You have politics of course; and it would be too bad to MP III 12 415 2
to be general; and while politics and Mr. Elton were E II 8 214 13
POLLARDS (1)
gates, pools, and pollards of this part of Highbury." E I 10 83 5
POLLUTED (1)
Are the shades of Pemberley to be thus polluted?" PP III 14 357 62
POLLUTION (1)
in spite of that pollution which its woods had received, PP III 19 388 12
POMP (2)
My first displays the wealth and pomp of kings, lords of E I 9 71 14
My first displays the wealth and pomp of kings, lords of E I 9 73 18
POMPOUS (4)
There is something very pompous in his stile.-- PP I 13 64 17
In pompous nothings on his side, and civil assents on that PP I 15 72 7
My dear Jane, Mr. Collins is a conceited, pompous, narrow- PP II 1 135 13
civil, prosing, pompous woman, who thought nothing of MP I 8 75 2
PONDER (2)
With such matters to ponder over, and arrange, and re- MP II 8 256 13
to Anne's imagination to ponder over in a calmer hour; for P IV 10 225 61
PONDERED (4)
felicity, he had pondered with genuine satisfaction on the MP III 17 471 29
She cast her eye over it, pondered, caught the meaning, E I 9 72 15
She pondered, but could think of nothing. E I 10 84 8
Emma pondered a moment, and then replied, "I will not E III 10 396 39
PONDERING (5)
Pondering over these heart-rendering tidings, Catherine NA I 11 89 62
advance in posting, & pondering over a doubtful halfcrown, W 349 24
to be his home, was pondering with downcast eyes on what MP II 7 248 47
She was pondering, in the mean while, upon the possibility, E II 1 158 13
by it, continually pondering over what could be done in E II 4 184 11
PONDEROUS (2)
lute, on the other a ponderous chest which no efforts can NA II 5 158 17
the ample width and ponderous carving of former times, was NA II 5 162 26
PONDS (1)
Some are gone to the ponds, and some to the lime walk. E III 6 362 44
PONEY (3)
valued friend the old grey poney, and for some time she MP I 4 35 7
might now and then lend them the poney he sent to the post. MP I 4 36 7
suit her like the old grey poney; but her delight in MP I 4 37 8
PONIES (3)
drive by my humble abode in her little phaeton and ponies." PP I 14 67 7
A low phaeton, with a nice little pair of ponies, would be PP III 10 325 2
Your idea of the ponies is delightful. PP III 18 382 21
PONY (1)
Yes, dear old grey pony. MP I 3 27 36
POOL (2)
Isabella seemed to find a pool of commerce, in the fate of NA I 11 89 63
before, to make up her pool of quadrille in the evening. PP I 14 66 1
POOLES (1)
me one word about our dinner at the Pooles yesterday." P III 5 39 35
POOLS (2)
left Hunsford--between our pools at quadrille, while Mrs. PP I 19 105 10
gates, pools, and pollards of this part of Highbury." E I 10 83 5
POOR (480)
Poor Manwaring!-- LS 5 250 3
She is poor, & may naturally seek an alliance which may be LS 12 261 4
Poor woman! tho' I have reasons enough for my dislike, I LS 15 266 2
I am afraid I have been often too indulgent, but my poor LS 15 267 6
Reginald is so incensed against the poor silly girl! LS 15 267 7
Poor fellow! he is quite distracted by jealousy, which I LS 16 269 3
Poor Reginald was beyond measure concerned to see his fair LS 17 270 3
The poor girl looks so unhappy that my heart aches for her. LS 17 270 4
Poor creature! the prospect from her window is not very LS 17 271 7
The poor girl however I am sure dislikes him; and tho' his LS 20 276 2
The poor girl sat all this time without opening her lips; LS 20 276 3
But something must be done for this poor girl, if her LS 20 278 11
During her poor father's life she was a spoilt child; the LS 24 288 11
Poor girl, I have now no hope for her. LS 24 291 16
Poor Manwaring gives me such histories of his wife's LS 26 296 5
as it made the poor girl, it was impossible to detain her. LS 41 310 3
The poor girl's heart was almost broke at taking leave of LS 41 310 4
being neglected, or poor, and a very respectable man, NA I 1 13 1
That "the poor beetle, which we tread upon, "in NA I 1 16 8
contribute to reduce poor Catherine to all the desperate NA I 2 19 7
shall make but a poor figure in your journal to-morrow." NA I 3 26 20
say; but I hate haggling, and poor freeman wanted cash." NA I 7 46 15
was unfortunately lost on poor Catherine, brought them to NA I 7 49 43
that poor St. Aubin died!--such beautiful weather!" NA I 11 83 15
"How I pity the poor creatures that are going there! NA I 11 89 63
uncomfortable manner to poor Catherine; some times not a NA I 13 99 9
poor Valancourt when she went with her aunt into Italy. NA I 14 107 11
used as myself to hear poor little children first learning NA I 14 109 26
together, and how tired my poor mother is at the end of it, NA I 14 109 26
My poor head! NA II 3 144 6
that you are determined against poor John--is not it so?" NA II 3 145 14
For poor Captain Tilney too she was greatly concerned. NA II 4 149 1
with your brother over poor tilney's passion for a month." NA II 4 153 29
are in bed, as so many poor girls have been obliged to do, NA II 6 167 9
the state of her poor friend, and expecting a summons NA II 9 192 4
Eleanor was absent, and at such a distance as to NA II 9 197 25
Poor Thorpe is in town: I dread the sight of him; his NA II 10 202 7
Poor James is so unhappy!-- NA II 10 204 13
for poor James, I suppose he will hardly ever recover it." NA II 10 206 37
for the comfort of the poor traveller, whose pale and NA II 14 233 9
Ah! poor James! NA II 14 236 15
Just at present it comes hard to poor James; but that will NA II 14 237 19
And it is a great comfort to find that she is not a poor NA II 14 237 21
I do not know when poor Richard's cravats would be done, NA II 15 240 2
poor, and that Catherine would have three thousand pounds. NA II 16 251 6
to ruin himself, and their poor little Harry, by giving SS I 2 8 3
If, indeed, it could ever be restored to our poor little SS I 2 9 7
In comparison of Norland, it was poor and small indeed!-- SS I 6 28 2
your cap at him now, and never think of poor brandon." SS I 9 45 29
Poor brandon! he is quite smitten already, and he is very SS I 9 45 32
Poor man! SS I 14 70 2
"May she always be poor; if she can employ her riches no SS I 14 72 9
poor dependent cousin, by sending me on business to London. SS I 15 75 6
guilt for poor Willoughby, than an apology for the latter. SS I 15 78 28
But, poor fellow! it is very fatiguing to him! for he is SS I 20 113 33
"Poor little creature!" said Miss Steele, as soon as they SS I 21 122 11
Poor Edward! SS I 22 131 35
or other; but poor Edward is so cast down about it! SS I 22 133 46
Poor fellow!-- SS I 22 134 52
Yes, I have one other comfort in his picture; but poor SS I 22 135 54
are not going to finish poor little Annamaria's basket SS II 1 144 11
My poor little girl would be sadly disappointed, I know, SS II 1 144 13
Ah! poor man! he has been dead these eight years and SS II 4 163 18
Poor souls! SS II 5 167 1
by saying, "poor Elinor! how unhappy I make you!" SS II 7 185 16
17
Poor thing! she looks very bad.-- SS II 8 192 3
Well, poor thing! SS II 8 192 3
"Poor soul!" cried Mrs. Jennings, as soon as she was gone, SS II 8 194 8
he grows poor, and a richer girl is ready to have him. SS II 8 194 10
What now," after pausing a moment--"your poor sister is SS II 8 195 14
Poor dear, it seems quite cruel to let her be alone. SS II 8 195 14
Poor soul! SS II 8 195 16
My poor husband! how fond he was of it! SS II 8 198 27
I have fancied between her and my poor disgraced relation. SS II 9 208 28
of one, whom he had made poor and miserable; but had he SS II 9 209 30
it with that of my poor Eliza, when she considers the SS II 9 210 32
hopeless situation of this poor girl, and pictures her to SS II 9 210 32

the misery of that poor girl, and the doubt of what his
Mrs. Jennings, with a very intelligent "Ah! poor dear," SS II 10 212 1
"Poor Marianne!" said her brother to Colonel Brandon in a SS II 12 236 41
Poor Edward!-- SS II 12 236 43
Poor Edward muttered something, but what it was, nobody SS II 13 240 15
this very morning, poor Nancy, who, you know, is a well- SS II 13 243 32
Poor soul! SS III 1 258 7
The carriage was at the door ready to take my poor cousins SS III 1 259 7
in as he came off; poor Lucy in such a condition, he says, SS III 1 259 7
Lord! what a taking poor Mr. Edward will be in when he SS III 1 259 7
Poor Fanny! she was in hysterics all yesterday. SS III 1 259 7
'I wish with all my heart,' says poor Fanny in her SS III 1 265 36
"What poor Mrs. Ferrars suffered, when first Fanny broke SS III 1 266 36
"Poor young man!--and what is to become of him?" SS III 1 266 38
"Poor young man!" cried Mrs. Jennings, "I am sure he SS III 1 268 49
Poor Edward! SS III 1 268 51
year! and Lord help 'em! how poor they will be!-- SS III 1 269 56
Poor Anne was much to blame for what she did, but she did SS III 2 276 28
Poor soul! SS III 2 277 30
And though one would be very glad to do a kindness by poor SS III 2 278 32
Poor Edward! he is ruined for ever. SS III 4 291 51
Poor Edward!---- SS III 5 298 35
Poor fellow!--to see him in a circle of strangers!--to be SS III 5 299 35
Poor Edward!--he has done for himself completely--shut SS III 5 299 35
My poor mother was half frantic." SS III 5 299 35
of girl I should suppose likely to captivate poor Edward. SS III 5 299 37
Poor Marianne, languid and low from the nature of her SS III 7 308 4
a pang to the heart of poor Elinor, who, reproaching SS III 7 312 18
it told the excess of her poor mother's alarm, gave some SS III 7 316 29
"Your poor mother too!--doting on Marianne." SS III 8 327 59
Willoughby, "poor Willoughby," as she now allowed herself SS III 9 334 6
Poor Elinor!--here was a new scheme for getting her to SS III 9 339 25
Had you married, you must have been always poor. SS III 11 350 9
necessitous-- always poor; and probably would soon have SS III 11 351 13
her compassion towards poor Mr. Edward, who, she was sure, SS III 13 370 37
not even Nancy, who, poor soul! came crying to me the day SS III 13 370 37
to make a shew with, and poor Nancy had not seven SS III 13 370 37
Poor Mr. Edward! SS III 13 371 37
Mrs. Ferrars was the most unfortunate of women--poor Fanny SS III 13 371 38
3 miles distant, were poor & had no close carriage; & ever W 314 1
us, & it is very bad to grow old & be poor & laughed at.-- W 317 2
her for Margaret, & poor Penelope was very wretched--. W 317 2
Poor creature! she is possessed with the notion of Tom W 319 2
but if she does you know, it is all over with poor Sam.-- W 320 2
have been so busy with my poor father and our great wash W 321 2
it must be a great deprivation to her, poor lady!-- W 326 5
If the poor little boy's face had in it's happiness been W 330 11
able to win a more favourable opinion of poor osborne.--" W 340 19
Poor thing!-- W 341 19
Poor Sam!-- W 342 19
I wish everybody were as easily satisfied as you--but poor W 343 19
have been used to be; but poor Margt's disagreeable ways W 362 32
You have no compassion on my poor nerves." PP I 1 5 28
Poor Eliza!--to be only just tolerable." PP I 5 19 9
poor consolation to believe the world equally in the dark. PP I 6 21 2
It is a grievous affair to my poor girls, you must confess. PP I 13 65 24
hospitality, to assist his tenants, and relieve the poor. PP I 16 81 41
made Elizabeth smile, as she thought of poor Miss Bingley. PP I 16 83 56
me, I am cruelly used, nobody feels for my poor nerves." PP II 3 113 26
Poor Jane! I am sorry for her, because, with her PP II 2 141 10
whom he did not care about, and who was equally poor?" PP II 4 153 13
"Oh! if that is all, I have a very poor opinion of young PP II 4 154 19
discontented or too poor, she sallied forth into the PP II 7 169 4
many others, because he is rich, and many others are poor. PP II 10 183 10
as his own father, always poor from the extravagance of PP II 12 200 5
Poor Charlotte!--it was melancholy to leave her to such PP II 15 216 7
overset already by one poor regiment of militia, and the PP II 16 220 7
What a stroke was this for poor Jane! who would willingly PP II 17 224 9
And poor Mr. Darcy! dear Lizzy, only consider what he must PP II 17 225 12
"Poor Wickham; there is such an expression of goodness in PP II 17 225 14
Poor little Lizzy! PP II 18 231 17
is luckily too poor to be an object of prey to any body. PP II 18 232 20
son will be just like him--just as affable to the poor." PP III 1 249 36
quite consistent with his behaviour to our poor friend." PP III 1 249 40
so cruel a way by any body, as he has done by poor Wickham. PP III 1 258 74
he was a liberal man, and did much good among the poor. PP III 2 265 14
What I have to say relates to poor Lydia. PP III 4 273 3
Our poor mother is sadly grieved. PP III 4 274 3
I must conclude, for I cannot be long from my poor mother. PP III 4 274 3
Imprudent as a marriage between Mr. Wickham and our poor PP III 4 274 3
My poor mother is really ill and keeps her room. PP III 4 275 5
Poor Kitty has anger for having concealed their attachment; PP III 4 275 5
but poor dear Lydia had nobody to take care of her. PP III 5 287 35
Poor dear child! PP III 5 287 35
My poor father! how he must have felt it!" PP III 5 292 61
"What, is he coming home, and without poor Lydia!" she PP III 6 298 14
Poor Lydia's situation must, at best, be bad enough; but PP III 7 307 51
Poor Reynolds, she was always very fond of me. PP III 10 327 11
"Yet it is hard," she sometimes thought, "that this poor PP III 11 332 19
you for your unexampled kindness to my poor sister. PP III 16 365 3
that she could not get her poor sister and her family out MP I 1 5 4
it to be her wish, that poor Mrs. Price should be relieved MP I 1 5 4
more attention than her poor mother could possibly give? MP I 1 5 4
I have a warm heart: and, poor as I am, would rather deny MP I 1 7 8
So, if you are not against it, I will write to my poor MP I 1 7 8
Poor Mr. Norris's indifferent state of health made it an MP I 1 9 10
but just now, poor Mr. Norris took up every moment of her MP I 1 9 10
"I hope she will not tease my poor pug," said Lady Bertram; MP I 1 10 16
Poor woman! she probably thought change of air might agree MP I 1 11 19
sulkiness of temper--her poor mother had a good deal; but MP I 2 13 5
memories, and your poor cousin has probably none at all. MP I 2 19 27
she saw no harm in the poor little thing--and always found MP I 2 20 31
Me! a poor helpless, forlorn widow, unfit for any thing, MP I 3 28 42
Here am I a poor desolate widow, deprived of the best of MP I 3 29 46
sake, I would not do so unjust a think by the poor girl. MP I 3 29 46
A great many things were due from poor Mr. Norris as MP I 3 30 50
if the Antigua estate is to make such poor returns." MP I 3 30 54
"If poor Sir Thomas were fated never to return, it would MP I 4 38 9
"My poor aunt had certainly little cause to love the state; MP I 5 46 22
Poor Miss Sneyd! MP I 5 51 41
been done, but for poor Mr. Norris's sad state of health. MP I 6 54 9
He could hardly ever get out, poor man, to enjoy any thing, MP I 6 54 9
if she were forgotten the poor mare should be remembered. MP I 7 68 16
Poor thing! MP I 7 72 44
son, and the poor fellow was waiting for me half an hour. MP I 7 73 53
of good to force all the poor housemaids and footmen to MP I 9 86 13
if the poor chaplain were not worth looking at--and, in MP I 9 87 15
Poor Julia, the only one out of the nine not tolerably MP I 9 91 36
"Poor dear Fanny," cried her cousin, "how ill you have MP I 10 97 2
"Poor William! MP I 11 111 27
My poor sister was forced to stay and bear it." MP I 11 111 28
poor woman! must want a lover as much as any one of them. MP I 12 119 22
about, but to be sure the poor old dowager could not have MP I 13 122 4
She knew, also, that poor Mr. Rushworth could seldom get MP I 18 164 2
and without mercy wishing poor Sir Thomas had been twice MP II 1 176 4
"Then poor Yates is all alone," cried Tom. MP II 1 182 21
four horses of course; and poor old coachman would attend MP II 2 189 5
And then the poor horses too!-- MP II 2 189 5
fast as possible; and to poor Miss Crawford, who had just MP II 4 205 3
My intentions are only not to be poor." MP II 4 213 39
Be honest and poor, by all means--but I shall not envy you; MP II 4 213 40
"Your degree of respect for honesty, rich or poor, is MP II 4 213 41

I do not mean to be poor. MP II 4 214 41
"Poor Rushworth and his two-and-forty speeches!" continued MP II 5 224 53
Poor fellow!-- MP II 5 224 53
"Poor Fanny! not allowed to cheat herself as she wishes!" MP II 7 244 29
a smart place as that--poor scrubbery midshipman as I am." MP II 7 245 33
"Poor Fanny!" cried William, coming for a moment to visit MP II 10 279 23
half the reason which my poor ill aunt had to abhor the MP II 12 296 29
But, poor things! they cannot help it; and you know it MP II 13 305 25
by himself, leaving his poor niece to sit and cry over MP III 1 320 45
to keep it up; and poor Fanny, who had hoped to silence MP III 3 343 40
all over--so improperly by poor Mr. Rushworth, not seeming MP III 4 349 25
Poor Sir Thomas, who was glad to see you? MP III 5 358 9
Poor Margaret fraser will be at me for ever about your MP III 5 360 16
I wish Margaret were married, for my poor friend's sake, MP III 5 361 16
Poor Janet has been sadly taken in; and yet there was MP III 5 361 16
Poor Fanny's mind was thrown into the most distressing of MP III 5 364 30
to go with them--to go and see her poor dear Sister Price. MP III 6 372 21
her; she had not seen her poor dear Sister Price for more MP III 6 372 21
not help thinking her poor dear Sister Price would feel it MP III 6 372 21
So, her poor dear Sister Price was left to all the MP III 6 373 24
Poor Fanny! though going, as she did, willingly and MP III 6 374 28
"Poor dears! how tired you must both be!--and now what MP III 7 378 14
Poor little Betsey; how cross Susan is to you! MP III 7 386 44
Poor Mary little thought it would be such a bone of MP III 7 386 44
Poor little soul! she could but just speak to be heard, MP III 7 386 44
Poor little dear! she was so fond of it, Fanny, that she MP III 7 387 44
Poor little sweet creature! MP III 7 387 44
A poor honourable is no catch, and I cannot imagine any MP III 9 394 1
for, take away his rants, and the poor Baron has nothing. MP III 9 394 1
except on the very poor, so unpractised in removing evils, MP III 9 396 7
To be the friend of the poor and oppressed! MP III 10 404 15
Her poor mother now did not look so very unworthy of being MP III 11 408 2
employer, and the welfare of the poor, is inconceivable. MP III 11 412 20
My poor aunt always felt affected, if within ten miles of MP III 12 416 3
Poor Susan was very little better fitted for home than her MP III 12 419 9
And my poor aunt talking of me every hour!" MP III 13 424 3
He will marry her, and be poor and miserable. MP III 13 424 4
and apprehensive for the poor invalid, whose state Sir MP III 13 426 11
and hope he will find the poor invalid in a less alarming MP III 13 426 11
and I flatter myself, the poor sufferer will soon be able MP III 13 426 11
agitation and anxiety, and poor invalids, till Tom was MP III 13 427 12
Poor Tom, I am quite grieved for him, and very much MP III 13 427 12
poor sister Bertram must be in a great deal of trouble." MP III 13 428 14
poor dear Sister Price to have them so well provided for. MP III 13 428 15
poor Mr. Bertram has a bad chance of ultimate recovery. MP III 14 433 13
Poor Sir Thomas will feel it dreadfully. MP III 14 434 13
Poor young man!-- MP III 14 434 13
If he is to die, there will be two poor young men less in MP III 14 434 13
Mrs. Price talked of her poor sister for a few minutes-- MP III 15 444 26
to herself, would be poor consolation to Sir Thomas. MP III 16 452 14
still more the folly of--poor Maria, in sacrificing such a MP III 16 454 18
Sir Thomas, poor Sir Thomas, a parent, and conscious of MP III 17 461 4
on the subject when the poor little girl's coming had been MP III 17 471 29
exactly as he had said at dinner, "poor Miss Taylor!-- E I 1 8 10
11

are the poor horses to be while we are paying our visit?" E I 1 8 17
It was very lucky, for I would not have had poor James E I 1 9 19
will be a great comfort to poor Miss Taylor to have E I 1 9 19
his many inquiries after "poor Isabella" and her children E I 1 9 21
"Ah! poor Miss Taylor! 'tis a sad business." E I 1 10 28
"Poor Mr. and Miss Woodhouse, if you please; but I cannot E I 1 10 29
please; but I cannot possibly say 'poor Miss Taylor.' E I 1 10 29
"But, Mr. Knightley, she is really very sorry to lose poor E I 1 11 36
And as to my poor word 'success,' which you quarrel with, E I 1 13 43
Poor Mr. Elton! E I 1 13 46
being still able to pity "poor Miss Taylor," when they E I 2 18 12
giving a gentle sigh, and saying: "Ah! poor Miss Taylor. E I 2 19 12
13

Upon such occasions poor Mr. Woodhouse's feelings were in E I 3 24 12
did suspect danger to her poor little friend from all this E I 4 27 5
such difficulties, on poor Mr. Woodhouse's account. E I 5 41 30
side--after all this, came poor dear Isabella's cold E I 6 45 21
The name makes me think of poor Isabella; for she was very E I 9 79 56
Poor Isabella!--she is sadly taken away from us all!-- and E I 9 79 58
"It would be very hard indeed, my dear, if poor Isabella E I 9 80 64
"but I do not see why poor Isabella should be obliged to E I 9 80 65
66

Poor little dears, how glad they will be to come. E I 9 80 70
a poor sick family, who lived a little way out of Highbury. E I 10 83 1
"Never mind, Harriet, I shall not be a poor old maid; and E I 10 85 19
to the taste of everybody, though single and though poor. E I 10 85 19
and the distresses of the poor were as sure of relief from E I 10 86 24
think of nothing but these poor creatures all the rest of E I 10 87 25
"Poor creatures! one can think of nothing else." E I 10 87 26
The wants and sufferings of the poor family, however, were E I 10 87 31
so far as London, even for poor Isabella's sake; and who E I 11 91 2
"Ah! my dear," said he, "poor Miss Taylor--it is a E I 11 93 6
deny that Mrs. Weston, poor Mrs. Weston, does come and see E I 11 94 16
You quite forget poor Mr. Weston." E I 11 95 17
You and I, Emma, will venture to take the part of the poor E I 11 95 18
"He wrote a letter to poor Mrs. Weston, to congratulate E I 11 96 22
he was but two years old when he lost his poor mother! E I 11 96 24
"My poor dear Isabella," said he, fondly taking her hand, E I 12 100 18
Poor Perry is bilious, and he has not time to take care of E I 12 101 25
But poor Mrs. Bates had a bad cold about a month ago." E I 12 102 32
"Ah! my poor dear child, the truth is, that in London it E I 12 102 36
of that poor young man without the greatest compassion. E I 14 121 17
Poor little creatures, how unhappy she would have made E I 14 122 17
Poor Mr. Woodhouse was silent from consternation; but E I 15 126 9
He was afraid poor Isabella would not like it. E I 15 128 22
And there would be poor Emma in the carriage behind. E I 15 128 22
He might have doubled his presumption to me--but poor E I 16 134 2
"Here have I," said she, "actually talked poor Harriet E I 16 137 11
But now, poor girl, her peace is cut up for some time. E I 16 137 11
to Harriet, and all that poor Harriet would be suffering, E I 16 137 12
why do not you stay at home like poor Mr. Elton?" E I 16 138 18
19

over the destiny of poor Isabella;--which poor Isabella, E I 17 140 1
of poor Isabella;--which poor Isabella, passing her life E I 17 140 1
some time of what the poor must suffer in winter, and E II 1 155 1
good to the poor!" she found something else must be done. E II 1 155 1
"Jane caught a bad cold, poor thing! so long ago as the E II 1 161 29
with, 'bless me! poor Jane is ill!--which my mother, being E II 1 162 31
away from the death of poor fairfax, before his own return E II 2 163 4
bear to have the poor old vicarage without a mistress. E II 3 174 35
at such a state of mind in poor Harriet--such a conclusion E II 3 180 56
And now, poor girl! she was considerably worse from this E II 4 184 10
a poor old grandmother, who has barely enough to live on. E II 5 194 40
"Poor comfort!" said Emma, laughing. E II 6 202 33
Poor Mrs. Dixon! E II 6 202 33
to be intended as a compliment, was but poor comfort. E II 7 208 7
thing of it; and there is poor Jane Fairfax, who is E II 8 215 16
Poor girl! E II 8 223 63
So would poor little Harriet. E II 11 249 11
I am sure, neither your father nor Mrs. Weston (poor Miss E II 11 252 30
Poor little Emma! E II 11 253 38
I hope whenever poor Isabella's little ones have the E II 11 253 38
"Our poor ball must be quite given up." E II 12 259 16
Poor Harriet was in a flutter of spirits which required E II 13 267 9
not to be supposed that poor Harriet should not be E II 14 270 3
how peculiarly unlucky poor Mr. Elton was in being in the E II 14 271 5
voices; and nobody speaks like you and poor Miss Taylor. E II 14 279 54

your sanction to such vanity-baits for poor young ladies." E II 14 280 59
It was not to be doubted that poor Harriet's attachment E II 15 282 3
"Poor Jane Fairfax!"--thought Emma.-- E II 15 284 10
Poor Miss Bates may very likely have committed her niece E II 15 286 21
two drawing rooms, at the poor attempt at rout-cakes, and E II 16 290 3
less inevitable that poor little Harriet must be asked to E II 16 291 5
And so does poor Mrs. Weston"--with half a sigh and half a E II 16 297 47
"I have not been severe upon poor Mrs. Churchill. E II 18 309 33
"Knightley has taken pity on poor little Miss Smith!-- E III 2 328 42
43
But poor Harriet could not follow. E III 3 333 5
Poor Mr. Woodhouse trembled as he sat, and, as Emma had E III 3 336 12
"My poor Harriet! and have you actually found happiness in E III 4 340 23
over the departure of the "poor little boys," or in fondly E III 5 347 20
She is poor; she has sunk from the comfort's she was born E III 7 375 61
Poor old Mrs. Bates, civil and humble as usual, looked as E III 8 378 5
her tears)--but, poor dear soul! if you were to see what a E III 8 379 8
My poor mother does not know how to bear it. E III 8 382 27
Poor old John, I have a great regard for him; he was clerk E III 8 383 29
him; he was clerk to my poor father twenty-seven years; E III 8 383 29
years; and now, poor old man, he is bed-ridden, and very E III 8 383 29
And poor John's son came to talk to Mr. Elton about relief E III 8 383 29
Poor dear Jane was talking of it just now.-- E III 8 384 33
It ought to be a first object, as I am sure poor Miss E III 9 387 10
"Poor Mrs. Churchill! no doubt she had been suffering a E III 9 387 13
solemn, and said, "Ah! poor woman, who would have thought E III 9 388 13
"Indeed, the truth was, that poor dear Jane could not bear E III 9 390 18
On that subject poor Miss Bates was very unhappy, and very E III 9 391 19
Half a dozen natural children, perhaps--and poor Frank cut E III 10 393 18
about Miss Fairfax; and poor Harriet;--and for some time E III 10 395 36
While poor Mrs. Churchill lived, I suppose there could not E III 10 398 55
"Harriet, poor Harriet!"-- E III 11 402 1
Poor Harriet! to be a second time the dupe of her E III 11 402 1
But poor Harriet was such an engrossing charge! E III 11 403 2
so, she supposed, had poor Mrs. Weston felt when _she_ was E III 11 404 3
"Poor girl!" said Emma. E III 12 418 7
"Poor girl!" said Emma again. E III 12 419 9
It was all the service she could now render her poor E III 13 431 38
Poor Mr. Woodhouse little suspected what was plotting E III 14 434 3
This letter reached me on the very morning of my poor E III 14 442 8
and could say at last, poor man! with a deep sigh, that he E III 14 443 8
Think she must of the possible difference to the poor E III 15 449 35
She would have been too happy for poor Harriet; but every E III 15 450 37
was securing for herself, poor Harriet must, in mere E III 15 450 37
otherwise; but for the poor girl herself, it seemed a E III 15 450 37
after Box-Hill, when poor Jane had been in such distress E III 16 452 8
poor Miss Bates had before made so happily intelligible.-- E III 16 452 8
"Poor child!" cried Emma; "at that rate, what will become E III 17 461 4
And if poor little Anna Weston is to be spoiled, it will E III 17 462 8
I wish I may not sink into 'poor Emma' with him at once.-- E III 17 464 24
I remember one evening the poor boys saying, 'uncle seems E III 17 465 27
Poor man!--it was at first a considerable shock to him, E III 17 466 29
single; and told of poor Isabella, and poor Miss Taylor.-- E III 17 466 29
The difficulty of disposing of poor Mr. Woodhouse had been E III 17 467 31
"Poor Knightley! poor fellow!--sad business for him.-- E III 17 469 36
Poor Knightley!-- E III 17 469 36
Poor fellow!-- E III 17 469 36
suspecting me of pleading poor Martin's cause, which was E III 18 474 34
"Ah! poor Harriet!" E III 18 474 35
every day, or poor Mrs. Weston would be disappointed. E III 18 476 43
Have a little mercy on the poor men. P III 3 20 17
But poor Mrs. Clay, who, with all her merits, can never P III 5 35 14
I really think poor Mrs. Clay may be staying here in P III 5 35 14
They are as fine healthy children as ever were seen, poor P III 6 45 8
mamma; she is thinking so much of poor Richard! P III 6 50 27
like it, was the name of poor Richard's captain, at one P III 6 50 27
or where, but a great while before he died, poor fellow! P III 6 50 27
and her head is quite full of it, and of poor Richard! P III 6 50 27
for him, by calling him "poor Richard," been nothing P III 6 51 29
so long an interval, her poor son gone for ever, and all P III 6 51 32
the kindness he had shewn poor dick, and very high respect P III 6 52 33
stamped as it was by poor Dick's having been six months P III 6 52 33
child to banish, and the poor suffering one to attend and P III 7 53 3
by ourselves, with this poor sick child--and not a P III 7 56 10
from his poor little boy; talks of his being on so well! P III 7 56 10
and because I am the poor mother, I am not to be allowed P III 7 56 10
scolding and teazing a poor child when it is ill; and you P III 7 56 12
to be spending the whole evening away from the poor boy?" P III 7 56 13
pleased heaven to spare my poor son, I dare say he would P III 8 64 5
6
which would have done for poor old Asp, in half the time; P III 8 66 16
away to the Laconia, and there he met with our poor boy.-- P III 8 66 18
Wentworth where it was he first met with your poor brother. P III 8 66 18
be afraid of mentioning poor dick before me, for it would P III 8 66 20
Poor Harville, sister! P III 8 67 23
one of the girls; "mamma is thinking of poor Richard." P III 8 67 26
"Poor dear fellow!" continued Mrs. Musgrove; "he was grown P III 8 67 27
Pray, what would become of us poor sailors' wives, who P III 8 69 43
of domestic society, in leaving poor Mary for Lady Russell. P III 11 93 2
attached to woman than poor benwick had been to Fanny P III 11 96 12
done a good deed in making that poor fellow talk so much. P III 12 107 24
and never left the poor fellow for a week; that's what he P III 12 108 28
what he did, and nobody else could have saved poor James. P III 12 108 28
Benwick had resigned the poor corpse-like figure entirely P III 12 110 42
of a good example, and the poor of the best attention and P IV 1 125 17
of the sinner, for when poor Lady Elliot died herself, no P IV 4 149 12
She was a widow, and poor. P IV 5 152 4
of superiority, into a poor, infirm, helpless widow, P IV 5 153 6
to one or two very poor families in this neighbourhood. P IV 5 155 9
A poor widow, barely able to live, between thirty and P IV 5 158 19
not even have told how the poor Admiral's complexion P IV 6 162 6
feels a good deal on his "poor sister's account; but, P IV 6 165 8
"Poor old gentleman." P IV 6 166 12
She, poor soul, is tied by the leg. P IV 6 170 29
Poor old Sir Archibald! P IV 6 170 29
"Poor Frederick!" said he at last. P IV 6 173 49
I am a very poor Italian scholar." P IV 8 186 25
he was then the poor one; he had chambers in the temple, P IV 9 199 55
My poor Charles, who had the finest, most generous spirit P IV 9 199 55
Mark his professions to my poor husband. P IV 9 204 75
handsome woman, poor and plausible, and altogether such in P IV 9 206 88
have found himself to be poor, seemed to have had no P IV 9 209 95
Poor man! P IV 10 213 4
poor sister, sat to him, and was bringing it home for her. P IV 11 232 15
"poor Fanny! she would not have forgotten him so soon!" P IV 11 232 15
point, be they ever so poor, or ever so imprudent, or even P IV 12 248 1
the poor good for nothing--as I dare say you find, sir." S 1 368 1
excite the industry of the poor and diffuse comfort & S 1 368 1
much looked up to & had a poor cousin living with her, S 3 375 1
her brother was a poor man for his rank in society. S 3 377 1
supply you know, that poor old Andrew may not lose his S 4 382 1
this morning on poor Arthur's trying to suppress a cough. S 5 387 1
it _is_ unfortunate for poor Arthur, that, at his time of S 5 388 1
was _not_ for what I owe to poor Mr Hollis's memory, I S 6 393 1
Poor Mr Parker got no more credit from Lady D. than he had S 6 393 1
It wd be only encouraging our servants & the poor to fancy S 6 393 1
supplied at a fair rate--(poor Mr Hollis's Chamber-Horse, S 6 393 1
And I verily beleive if my poor dear Sir Harry had never S 6 394 1
from his character;--& poor Burns's known irregularities, S 7 397 1
I _only_ notice them, for poor dear Sir Harry's sake. S 7 399 1
Poor dear Sir Harry (between ourselves) thought at first S 7 399 1
And poor young man, he needs it bad enough;--for though I S 7 400 1
Poor Miss Brereton!-- S 7 402 1
This poor Sir Edward & his sister.--how far nature meant S 7 402 1
we came within sight of poor old Sanditon--and the attack S 9 407 1
at being so poor a creature that she cd not come with me. S 9 407 1
And as for poor Arthur, he wd not have been unwilling S 9 407 1
I have not much confidence in poor Arthur's skill for S 9 411 1
dinner, you wd have thought me a very poor creature.--" S 10 415 1
you had better mention the poor Mullins's situation, & S 12 423 1
& I almost promised the poor woman yesterday to get S 12 423 1
There is a poor woman in Worcestershire, whom some friends S 12 424 1
And then,--there is the family of the poor man who was S 12 424 1
She is so frightened, poor thing, that I promised to come S 12 424 1
Poor Mr Hollis!-- S 12 427 1

POOR-BASKET (1)
no work of your own, I can supply you from the poor-basket. MP I 7 71 34

POORER (1)
a poorer man than at first, and with a child to maintain. E I 2 16 4

POORLY (6)
which you would have been poorly supported by an affection, SS III 11 350 9
She was still very poorly, and Elizabeth would not quit PP I 8 37 21
It makes me very nervous and poorly, to be thwarted so in PP II 2 140 4
a warmth, a delight, which words could but poorly express. PP III 13 347 25
must expect to see her grown thin, and looking very poorly. E II 1 162 31
is bed-ridden, and very poorly with the rheumatic gout in E III 8 383 29

POP (2)
and, plied well with good things, would soon pop off." MP I 3 24 5
I know I do sometimes pop out a thing before I am aware. E III 5 346 16

POPE (5)
From Pope, she learnt to censure those who "bear NA I 1 15 4
dozen lines of Milton, Pope, and prior, with a paper from NA I 5 37 4
assurance of his admiring Pope no more than is proper. SS I 10 47 4
she finds Miss Pope a treasure. PP II 6 165 32
in imitation of Pope?-- 'blest leaf! whose aromatic gales MP I 17 161 15

POPES (1)
The quarrels of popes and kings, with wars or pestilences, NA I 14 108 22

POPLARS (1)
with tall Lombardy poplars, shut out the offices. SS III 6 302 7

POPLIN (1)
such a trimming as this to my white and silver poplin. E II 17 302 22

POPT (1)
a well-meaning creature, but no conjurer, popt it all out. SS III 1 258 7

POPULAR (5)
very popular & most admired preachers generally have.-- W 343 20
to degenerate from the popular qualities, or lose the PP I 16 81 41
gave way before their popular manners and more diffused MP II 10 273 8
You were very popular before you came, because you were Mr. E II 6 200 15
They were more completely popular. P III 6 47 14

POPULARITY (7)
turned the tide of his popularity; for he was discovered PP I 3 10 5
Her daughter enjoyed a most uncommon degree of popularity E I 3 21 4
and your popularity will stand upon your own virtues." E II 6 200 15
must be amply repaid in the splendour of popularity. E II 9 231 1
beloved--which gives Isabella all her popularity.-- E II 13 269 16
her rights, and all her popularity, as well as to all her P IV 5 159 25
The popularity of the parkers brought them some visitors S 7 394 1

POPULOUS (3)
large and populous village, in a situation not unpleasant. NA II 11 212 17
Highbury, the large and populous village almost amounting E I 1 7 10
been in a particularly populous, dancing state, had been E II 6 197 5

PORCH (1)
the shelter of the old porch, and had even passed on to NA II 5 161 25

PORE (2)
she would pore over it till she had made out every word. E II 1 157 10
sitting down together to pore over it, with the professed P III 8 64 7

PORING (2)
eyes; and perhaps may be poring over the affairs of the NA II 8 187 15
"He will sit poring over his book, and not know when a P IV 2 132 19

PORK (10)
that the remaining cold pork bones and mustard in MP II 11 282 2
and delicate--Hartfield pork is not like any other pork-- E II 3 171 16
17
is not like any other pork--but still it is pork--and, my E II 3 171 16
17
pork--but still it is pork--and, my dear Emma, unless one E II 3 171 16
17
Such a beautiful hind-quarter of pork! E II 3 172 24
"We consider our Hartfield pork," replied Mr. Woodhouse-- E II 3 173 30
31
than another, it is pork--a roast loin of pork"----- "as E II 3 173 30
31
very superior to all other pork, that Emma and I cannot E II 3 175 39
40
is pork--a roast loin of pork"----- "as to who, or what E II 3 175 39
40
Pork: when we dress the leg it will be another thing. E II 3 177 50

PORKER (1)
we have killed a porker, and Emma thinks of sending them a E II 3 171 16
17

PORRIDGE (1)
your porridge,"--and I shall keep mine to swell my song. PP I 6 24 22

PORT (5)
breathing port wine, who followed them into the room. PP I 16 76 3
no stomach can bear roast port--I think we had better send E II 3 171 16
17
to Patty again about the port--Jane was standing in the E II 3 173 27
want to be conveyed to one port or another, after our P III 8 69 43
to put into another port, he calculates how soon it be P 1 6 235 31

PORT-ADMIRAL (1)
on a visit to the port-admiral, nor the commissioner, nor MP III 10 400 7

PORTENTOUS (1)
with a most intelligent portentous countenance that beyond S 1 364 1

PORTER (2)
"Are you certain that no servant, no porter has left any SS II 4 165 26
A pint of porter with my cold beef at Marlborough was SS III 8 318 18

PORTERS (1)
I might as well have asked for porters and a hand-barrow." MP I 6 58 35

PORTFOLIO (1)
therefore produced the portfolio containing her various E I 6 44 19

PORTION (23)
I want her to play & sing with some portion of taste, & a LS 7 253 1
It's effect on Reginald justifies some portion of vanity, LS 25 293 3
he then bestowed an equal portion of his fraternal NA I 7 49 43
is the true heroine's portion; to a pillow strewed with NA I 11 90 65
charms, there is a portion of them too reasonable and too NA I 14 111 29
dissolution, of a large portion of the ancient building NA II 2 141 13
he led the way to it across a small portion of the park. NA II 7 178 20
portion must yet remain to be told in a letter from James. NA II 15 247 14
attachment must be the portion of Henry and Catherine, and NA II 16 250 4
habit of spending a large portion of the year at the SS II 3 153 1
the very little portion of my time that I had bestowed on SS III 8 323 40
Your portion is unhappily so small that it will in all PP I 19 108 19
with some portion of her notice when service is over. PP II 5 157 7
unable to ward off any portion of that universal contempt PP II 18 231 18
heard her read the daily portion of history; but he MP I 2 22 3
they had been across a portion of the park into the very MP I 10 103 4
for himself no small portion of vexation and regret-- MP III 17 468 2
She went on herself, to give that portion of time to an E II 5 186
had been creating in Harriet was then their own portion. E III 3 334
Some portion of respect for herself, however, in spite of E III 11 408 3
other with a considerable portion of apparent indifference P IV 7 176
portion only of what I had to look over when I lost him. P IV 9 202 6
7

strong sense of duty is no bad part of a woman's portion." P IV 11 246 80
PORTIONING (1)
who there would be, and portioning out the indispensable E II 11 247 3
PORTIONLESS (2)
She was as insignificant, and perhaps as portionless as NA II 11 208 1
to marry a woman as portionless even as Miss Taylor, and E I 2 16 5
PORTIONS (1)
divided out their proper portions to Mrs Darling, Miss S 11 420 1
PORTLY (1)
& continual accessions of portly chaperons, & strings of W 328 8
PORTMAN-SQUARE (1)
in a house in one of the streets near Portman-Square. SS II 3 153 1
PORTMANTEAU (1)
kicked away his son's portmanteau, and his daughter's band- MP III 7 379 19
PORTRAIT (8)
Catherine did not think the portrait a very inviting one, NA I 9 62 10
over the fire-place the portrait of some handsome warrior, NA II 5 158 17
A portrait--very like--of a departed wife, not valued by NA II 7 181 39
in consequence was to the portrait in her bed-chamber. NA II 9 191 3
painter Mr. Willoughby's portrait was drawn, and at what SS II 10 215 11
You think it a faithful portrait undoubtedly." PP I 18 91 16
She had soon fixed on the size and sort of portrait. E I 6 46 23
P. that the whole-length portrait of a stately gentleman, S 12 427 1
PORTRAITS (7)
of Eleanor's;--the only portraits of which she had been in NA II 9 191 3
Do let the portraits of your uncle and aunt Philips be PP I 10 52 57
In the gallery there were many family portraits, but they PP III 1 250 47
larger part were family portraits, no longer any thing to MP I 9 84 3
her various attempts at portraits, for not one of them had E I 6 44 19
Oh! could the originals of the portraits against the P III 5 40 44
The portraits themselves seemed to be staring in P III 5 40 44
PORTRAITURES (1)
They hold forth the most splendid Portraitures of high S 8 403 1
PORTRAYED (1)
care, were yet less what her fancy had portrayed. NA II 5 162 26
PORTSMOUTH (47)
They may easily get her from Portsmouth to town by the MP I 1 8 8
channel, and sent into Portsmouth, with the first boat MP II 6 232 12
when you get back to Portsmouth, if it is not very far off, MP II 7 245 32
"If I were at Portsmouth, I should be at it perhaps." MP II 7 249 50
"But you do not wish yourself at Portsmouth, William?" MP II 7 249 51
I shall have enough of Portsmouth, and of dancing too, MP II 7 249 52
The Portsmouth girls turn up their noses at any body who MP II 7 249 52
William was required to be at Portsmouth on the 24th; the MP II 8 253 7
he must have got into a Portsmouth coach; and though this MP II 9 266 21
So the uniform remained at Portsmouth, and Edmund MP III 6 368 8
to Portsmouth, and spend a little time with her own family. MP III 6 368 9
at Mansfield, was to become a slight evil at Portsmouth. MP III 6 370 12
The next step was to communicate with Portsmouth. MP III 6 371 17
that, though taken to Portsmouth for nothing, it would be MP III 6 373 24
Edmund's plans were affected by this Portsmouth journey, MP III 6 373 25
Portsmouth their correspondence would dwindle into nothing. MP III 7 376 4
were in the environs of Portsmouth while there was yet MP III 7 376 6
character of all the Portsmouth servants; of whom she MP III 7 385 38
Servants are come to such a pass, my dear, in Portsmouth, MP III 7 385 39
from their reaching Portsmouth; and during those days, she MP III 8 388 2
might have some pains, Portsmouth could have no pleasures. MP III 8 392 12
As for any society in Portsmouth, that could at all make MP III 9 395 3
should be come down to Portsmouth neither on a visit to MP III 10 400 7
or the employment of wealth, had brought him to Portsmouth. MP III 10 400 7
"Her daughters were very much confined--Portsmouth was a MP III 10 401 10
his only business in Portsmouth was to see her, that he MP III 10 406 21
over the badness of the Portsmouth servants, and wound up MP III 11 408 4
since her being in Portsmouth, and but for Mr. Crawford MP III 11 409 6
I think the confinement of Portsmouth unfavourable to. MP III 11 410 16
day to be hardened at Portsmouth; and though Sir Thomas, MP III 11 413 30
Henry has been down to Portsmouth to see you; that he had MP III 12 415 1
2
this said visit to Portsmouth, and these two said walks, MP III 12 415 2
My dear little creature, do not stay at Portsmouth to lose MP III 12 416 3
her own release from Portsmouth came, her happiness would MP III 12 419 9
You are happy in Portsmouth, I hope, but this must not be MP III 13 423 2
that she had no chance of leaving Portsmouth till after it. MP III 14 430 6
When she had been coming to Portsmouth, she had loved to MP III 14 431 8
Portsmouth was Portsmouth; Mansfield was home. MP III 14 431 8
what he said at Portsmouth, about our conveying you home, MP III 14 435 14
that they should be in Portsmouth that very day, and to MP III 15 437 2
I shall be at Portsmouth the morning after you receive MP III 15 442 23
To-morrow! to leave Portsmouth to-morrow! MP III 15 443 24
passed the barriers of Portsmouth, and how Susan's face MP III 15 445 32
after his return from Portsmouth, he might have been MP III 17 467 20
and the three children, round from Portsmouth to Plymouth. P III 8 69 39
letters, but the Grappler was under orders for Portsmouth. P III 12 108 28
and day till he got to Portsmouth, rowed off the the P III 12 108 28
OSITION (8)
maintained a similar position, and separating themselves NA I 10 71 8
a date so ancient, a position so awful, proved to be one NA II 9 193 6
contradicted almost every position her mother advanced. NA II 14 239 28
ever since in the same position on the pianoforte, for her SS I 7 35 8
"Your first position is false. PP II 1 136 23
She had changed her position, and with her eyes fixed MP III 1 314 16
advantages in its position & some accidental circumstances S 2 371 1
I see by the position of your foot, that you have used it S 9 411 1
SITIONS (1)
were taking different positions; but from every window PP III 1 246 5
SITIVE (32)
"I cannot be quite positive about that, my dear; I have NA I 9 69 50
to Mrs. Allen, and Mrs. Allen's opinion was more positive. NA I 11 82 1
Bath, that you gave him the most positive encouragement. NA II 3 144 10
smiles, the alteration became too positive to be past over. NA II 4 149 1
absence of General Tilney, with much positive cheerfulness. NA II 6 166 8
and overdrawn; but here was proof positive of the contrary. NA II 7 181 40
positive conviction of his actually wishing their marriage. NA II 14 230 2
direct as to demand a positive answer was addressed to her. NA II 14 233 9
accompanied an almost positive command to his son of doing NA II 15 245 12
subsist only under a positive engagement, could be SS I 22 134 53
has broken no positive engagement with my sister." SS II 8 196 19
No positive engagement indeed! after taking her all over SS II 8 196 20
and what followed was a positive assertion that every SS II 8 199 37
a right to be equally positive in their opinion, and to SS II 12 233 20
by the too warm, too positive assurances of Marianne, that SS III 2 270 1
satisfaction at the moment of removal, was more positive. SS III 6 302 5
broke through the first positive resolution of not SS III 14 374 6
every symptom, however positive, of the nearness of that W 346 21
feeling a doubt of my positive happiness had my fair PP I 20 114 32
he begged leave to be positive as to the truth of his PP I 23 126 3
the day before, and a positive engagement made of his PP III 2 266 18
that she required more positive kindness, and with that MP I 2 17 20
There was no positive ill-nature in Maria or Julia; and MP I 2 20 32
reply, "never, Fanny, so very determined and positive! MP III 4 347 19
he soon proceeded to a positive recommendation to Mrs. MP III 10 401 10
observation there was no positive merit, they shewed, E II 6 197 3
of indifference; they are generally a very positive curse." E II 16 293 19
it would have been too positive an interruption; and E II 17 304 30
Mrs. Weston; "an engagement--a positive engagement.-- E III 10 395 32
but Charles is so positive! P III 9 77 16
that he had received a positive dismissal from Henrietta, P III 10 82 2
not so shape into any positive act of duty or discretion, P IV 10 227 69
ITIVELY (22)
to Solomon, but I had positively forbidden Frederica's LS 22 281 3
declare positively it is quite shocking. NA I 10 75 23
should say one thing so positively, and mean another all NA II 11 211 15
as much as herself; and positively refusing Elinor's SS II 9 203 10
Elinor contradicted it, however, very positively; and by SS III 5 295 13
Against staying longer, however, Elizabeth was positively PP I 12 59 1
to say--she could not positively answer--but she did not PP I 15 71 3
remain, their having positively assured Mrs. Rushworth, MP I 8 78 23
he should hold himself positively engaged, he should break MP II 2 192 11
their situations; and positively declared, that he would MP III 2 327 5
for so long only as you positively say, in every letter to MP III 11 411 18
out right, she was even positively civil; but it was an E I 14 118 4
Three months, she says so, positively, as I am going to E II 1 159 20
The party did not break up without Emma's being positively E II 11 256 60
You and I must positively exert our authority." E II 16 295 32
but nothing more is positively known of the Tupmans, E II 18 310 34
At the same time, I will not positively answer for my E III 5 346 16
and triumph--and she positively refused to take her E III 6 359 37
Jane's answer; but she positively declared she would not E III 8 381 15
said she--'I positively must have you all come.'" E III 8 381 17
He positively said that it had been known to no being in E III 10 399 60
protesting still more positively that it was Mr. Elliot, P IV 10 222 37
POSSESS (16)
had I even known her to possess so much as she does, I LS 24 288 11
& with those lively feelings which I know you to possess. LS 25 292 3
should be the first to possess the skill of unlocking a NA II 7 173 2
cheerful than hers, or possess, in a greater degree, that SS I 2 8 2
which it was no merit to possess; and by that still ardent SS III 9 333 2
all this, she must possess a certain something in her air PP I 8 39 50
"All this she must possess," added Darcy, "and to all this PP I 8 39 51
that you possess the talent of flattering with delicacy. PP I 14 68 10
"I certainly have not the talent which some people possess, PP II 8 175 24
"I do not pretend to possess equal frankness with your PP III 14 354 33
is the only ornament I have ever had a desire to possess. MP II 9 262 8
and such temper, the highest claims a woman could possess." E I 8 63 44
which I knew her to possess; and the secrecy she had E III 14 442 8
enthusiasm and violent agitation seldom really possess. P IV 4 146 6
of fascination he must possess over Lady Russell's mind, P IV 7 179 28
as he knew himself to possess, & such talents as he did S 8 405 2
POSSESSED (17)
had Frederica possessed the penetration, the abilities, LS 24 288 11
of whose faces possessed nothing to interest, and with all NA I 2 21 10
Feelings rather natural than heroic possessed her; instead NA I 12 93 4
advice was so effectual, possessed a strength of SS I 1 6 11
she felt thoroughly possessed, and whom she expected to SS II 1 141 4
Poor creature! she is possessed with the notion of Tom W 319 2
possessed, of bringing on the renewal of his addresses. PP III 2 266 16
Had she possessed greater leisure for the service of her MP I 2 20 31
that whatever she possessed was designed for their family, MP I 3 30 57
they possessed its favour as well as its admiration. MP I 4 34 4
It had been a friend and companion such as few possessed, E I 1 6 6
nerves; she had not yet possessed the instrument long E II 10 240 6
she possessed, or a heart more disposed to accept of his. E III 13 431 39
her a little to the faults of those who possessed them. P III 2 11 2
well-looking, and possessed, in an acute mind and P III 5 34 12
Very long has it possessed a charm over my fancy; and, if P IV 8 188 36
or the perfect, unrivalled hold it possessed over his own. P IV 11 242 63
POSSESSES (5)
I can gather, Lady Susan possesses a degree of captivating LS 4 248 2
help feeling that she possesses an uncommon union of LS 6 251 1
discrimination in viewing them himself than he possesses. SS I 18 97 6
on conceit and impertinence, which your lady possesses." PP I 10 52 55
that in the degree she possesses them, they are not . E I 8 63 44
POSSESSING (4)
gentle address, and I believe possessing an amiable heart." SS I 10 51 27
settled, and of her possessing such a husband and such a PP II 7 168 1
good and great, as possessing worth, which no one but MP I 4 37 8
his possessing the shadow of a right to introduce himself. P IV 3 144 19
POSSESSION (50)
younger brother's having possession of the family estate. LS 5 249 1
Not that I would envy him their possession, nor would for LS 25 293 3
into the quiet possession of a place, however, when her NA I 10 75 25
so little elated by the possession of such a home; that NA II 2 141 12
at one end of the chest in undisputed possession! NA II 6 164 3
ready furnished, and she might have immediate possession. SS I 5 26 5
Elinor took immediate possession of the post of civility SS II 4 160 2
put in possession of a very comfortable apartment. SS II 4 160 3
hair which is in your possession." M. D. SS II 7 188 42
which left to me the possession of the family property,) SS II 9 208 28
continued without the possession of the toothpick-case, SS II 11 221 5
in possession of an estate which might have been his own? SS III 1 269 56
and Elinor was left in possession of knowledge which might SS III 2 276 26
important secret in her possession, than by anything else, SS III 4 291 46
possession of the living, surprised her a little at first. SS III 12 357 2
for after Edward was in possession of the living, but the SS III 14 374 6
He came into possession of it, when he was very young, & W 328 8
& for being now in possession of a very smart house in W 349 23
in possession of a good fortune, must be in want of a wife. PP I 1 3 1
that he is to take possession before Michaelmas, and some PP I 1 3 10
this time have been in possession of a most valuable PP I 16 79 23
my family, and may take possession of Longbourn estate PP I 19 107 16
Collins should be in possession of the Longbourn estate, PP I 22 122 3
the hour of possession; and whenever she spoke in a low PP I 23 130 16
established him at once in the possession of every virtue. PP II 13 206 4
No sooner in possession of it, than hurrying into the PP III 10 321 1
though in the certain possession of his warmest affection, PP III 17 378 46
Mrs. Norris took possession of the white house, the Grants MP I 3 31 58
and Fanny was then put in almost full possession of her. MP I 4 37 8
sisters, was soon in possession of his mind, and which he MP II 5 223 48
ornament in her possession, a very pretty amber cross MP II 8 254 8
rather part with and see in your possession than any other. MP II 8 260 22
Reflecting and doubting, and feeling that the possession MP II 8 260 25
I did not use to think her wanting in self possession, but MP III 9 393 1
riches which she was in possession of herself, her uncle MP III 9 396 7
established in the full possession of her desired; Susan MP III 9 396 7
established in the full possession of her so much prettier MP III 9 396 7
an exquisite possession a good picture of her would be! E I 6 43 12
13
indeed, to use your own words, be an exquisite possession." E I 6 44 16
soon afterwards took possession of a narrow footpath, a E I 10 88 33
and merit, was in possession of an independent fortune, of E II 4 181 4
which had taken strong possession of her mind, had ever E II 5 192 33
The Crofts were to have possession at Michaelmas, and as P III 5 33 5
The Crofts took possession with true naval alertness, and P III 6 48 17
under foot, is still in possession of all the happiness P III 10 88 26
up stairs, and given possession of her own bed, assistance, P III 12 111 50
and had hardly taken possession of her lodgings, before P IV 5 154 9
left her in the quiet possession of that room, it would P IV 11 238 45
having received possession of her apartment, found S 4 384 1
Trafalgar house & took possession of the drawing room very S 6 391 1
POSSESSIONS (7)
to advantage; where possessions are so extensive as those LS 30 300 2
Under a mistaken persuasion of her possessions and claims, NA II 15 244 11
books and other possessions, to form themselves a home. SS I 6 29 5
was related, and whose possessions he was to inherit; SS I 9 44 23
she had added to her possessions, and spent more of her MP I 16 151 1
be interested in all my possessions and pleasures, try to MP II 6 231 9
themselves in their new possessions, their grass, and P III 9 73 2
POSSESSOR (4)
But they learnt, on inquiry, that its possessor, an SS I 9 40 2
much prized by the possessor, and often without any PP I 10 49 27
late possessor, she was delighting both him and herself. PP II 2 143 20
apprehension of the state required in its possessor. P III 1 9 19
POSSIBILITIES (5)
"I am talking of possibilities, Charles." PP I 8 38 37

be among the apparent possibilities of any one most dear MP II 7 238 1
I only name possibilities. E I 5 38 15
the possibilities of such a case, was against Mr. Elliot. P IV 5 160 26
all the possibilities of their action on each other."-- S 10 418 1

POSSIBILITY (65)

a treasure, the possibility of false linings to the NA II 6 169 11
half a minute, till the possibility of the door's having NA II 7 173 4
brow, she felt secure from all possibility of wronging him. NA II 8 187 13
The possibility of some conciliatory message from the NA II 13 227 27
But with this approach to his name ended all possibility NA II 13 229 31
To the possibility of motives unanswerable in themselves, SS I 15 79 28
as might remove the possibility of fear for Marianne. SS I 20 114 43
possibility of mistake, be so good as to look at this face. SS I 22 131 35
animating object in view, the same possibility of hope. SS II 4 159 1
by suggesting the possibility of its being Miss Morton's SS II 12 232 14
The possibility of a relapse would of course, in some SS III 7 315 25
The possibility of Colonel Brandon's arriving and finding SS III 8 317 7
I assure you there is not a possibility of fear with my W 339 18
your own sex, as to doubt the possibility of all this?" PP I 8 40 53
The possibility of his having really endured such PP I 17 85 1
imaginary; and the possibility of her deserving her PP I 20 112 24
The possibility of Mr. Collins's fancying himself in love PP I 22 124 12 13
almost as far from possibility as that she could encourage PP I 22 124 12 13
and urged the possibility of mistakes--but by everybody PP II 1 138 31
to Elizabeth the possibility of his being partial to her, PP II 9 181 30
she exclaimed, "there could be no possibility of objection. PP II 10 186 40
that there may be the possibility of consulting him, I PP II 12 203 5
death-warrant of all possibility of common sense for the PP II 18 230 14
Brighton comprised every possibility of earthly happiness. PP II 18 232 22
The possibility of meeting Mr. Darcy, while viewing the PP II 19 240 16
and precluding the possibility of the other, was soon to PP III 8 312 16
The situation of the house excluded the possibility of MP I 9 85 4
the possibility of improvements with much animation. MP I 10 97 3
servants' hall, and the possibility of raising five couple MP I 12 117 11
them all, so as to leave me no possibility of refusing! MP I 12 119 26
could even suggest the possibility of the rehearsal being MP II 1 177 5
she was safe from the possibility of giving Crawford the MP II 3 201 23
without chance or possibility of obtaining--but they are MP II 4 214 45
tone, to avoid the possibility of being heard by Edmund, MP II 5 225 57
seemed to comprehend her greatest possibility of happiness. MP II 9 267 22
the possibility of her power over my heart ever ceasing." MP II 12 297 31
(every chance, every possibility of it, resting upon her MP III 3 336 7
must have felt the possibility of a man's not being MP III 4 353 45
She began to feel the possibility of his turning out well MP III 10 405 16
opened the letter, the possibility of Mr. and Miss MP III 15 437 2
There was no possibility of rest. MP III 15 441 20
it possibility--Miss Crawford's letter stampt it a fact. MP III 15 441 20
on the more than possibility of the two young friends MP III 17 471 29
The possibility of the young man's coming to Mrs. E I 8 67 56
was, there could be no possibility of the two friends E I 10 83 2
on the subject, for the first start of its possibility. E I 16 135 6
She was pondering, in the mean while, upon the possibility, E II 1 158 13
There was no resisting such news, no possibility of E II 5 188 8
be thinking of the possibility of their all calling here. E II 5 190 20
The good lady had not given me the possibility of escape E II 6 199 7
The bare possibility of it acted as a further irritation E II 7 208 7
made him doubt the possibility of her going to Mrs. E III 9 389 16
a hope, a chance, a possibility;--but scarcely are her E III 10 398 55
each other now, without the possibility of farther mistake. E III 11 406 19
Every possibility of good was before me, and the first of E III 14 437 8
"it is well, perhaps, that I have not had the possibility. E III 16 459 45 46
hearing of the possibility of Kellynch Hall being to let, P III 3 21 18
from wishing for the possibility of exchange, she would P III 5 41 45
more anxious for the possibility of Lady Russell and P III 11 93 3
of their space, at the possibility of that woman, who had P IV 3 138 5
behind, with no possibility of moving from one to the P IV 5 154 8
would be every possibility of your being happy together. P IV 5 159 23
within herself such a possibility of having been induced P IV 9 211 102
To lose the possibility of speaking two words to Captain P IV 11 238 47
sake, the possibility of scheming longer for Sir Walter. P IV 12 250 8

POSSIBLE (353)

& to be as quiet as possible,--& I have been so; my dear LS 2 244 1
me--I was as amiable as possible on the occasion--but all LS 5 249 1
We shall be as stupid as possible. LS 5 250 2
it is scarcely possible that two men should be so grossly LS 6 252 2
I wish her to find her situation as unpleasant as possible. LS 7 253 1
take all possible pains to prevent his marrying Catherine. LS 12 260 2
It is possible that her behaviour may arise only from LS 12 261 4
but herself I can affirm, would ever have thought possible. LS 14 263 1
He is if possible to prevail on Miss Summers to let LS 15 266 4
I wish it had been possible for me to fetch her instead of LS 17 271 6
her with me as much as possible, & have taken great pains LS 18 273 3
more obliged to you than it is possible for me to express. LS 21 279 1
snew at once, by every possible attention to her brother LS 42 311 2
These are points in which a doubt is equally possible. NA I 3 27 28
whom she received every possible encouragement to continue NA I 5 36 2
look at that creature, and suppose it possible if you can." NA I 7 46 9
"My dear Isabella, how was it possible for me to get at NA I 8 56 13
hid herself as much as possible from his view, and when he NA I 10 74 23
vexed, and meant to make her apology as soon as possible." NA I 12 94 10
be taken as soon as possible; and, setting aside the NA I 12 95 16
I have promised your sister to be with her, if possible." NA I 15 123 33
and even supposed it possible, that some people might NA II 1 131 15
but even laughed openly at Henry for finding it possible. NA II 1 131 15
anxious for her seeing as much of the country as possible." NA II 5 156 4
would make as little alteration as possible in her dress. NA II 5 162 28
Her habit therefore was thrown off with all possible haste, NA II 6 163 1
after moving it in every possible way for some instants NA II 6 168 10
Could it be possible, or did not her senses play her false? NA II 7 172 2
them up as nearly as possible in the same shape as before, NA II 7 173 3
is well to have as many holds upon happiness as possible. NA II 7 174 8
Could it be possible?-- NA II 8 186 13
had persevered in every possible vice, going on from crime NA II 9 190 2
slipped with the least possible noise through the folding NA II 9 193 6
having received every possible attention which could NA II 9 197 25
He loved her, I am persuaded, as well as it was possible NA II 9 197 27
herself as miserable as possible for about half an hour, NA II 10 199 1
could have supposed it possible in the beginning of her NA II 10 201 4
you to have any concern in, for how is it possible?" NA II 13 225 21
could not believe it possible that any injury or any NA II 13 226 25
where it was possible; but very little remained to be done. NA II 13 227 27
"you must let me hear from you as soon as possible. NA II 13 228 28
been such as was scarcely possible to reach his knowledge. NA II 14 230 3
soothed beyond any thing that she had believed possible. NA II 14 233 9
much of all this it was possible for Henry to communicate NA II 15 247 14
And what possible claim could the Miss Dashwoods, who were SS I 2 8 3
must ornament his goodness with every possible charm." SS I 3 18 20
to outweigh every possible advantage belonging to the SS I 4 23 20
that of running with all possible speed down the steep SS I 9 41 6
had ceased to be possible, by Marianne's perfect recovery. SS I 10 48 7
than she had thought it possible before, by the charms SS I 11 54 5
what I look forward to as her greatest possible advantage. SS I 11 56 13
My Elinor, is it possible to doubt their engagement? SS I 15 80 36
Supposing it possible that they are not engaged, what SS I 16 84 9
off, and driven as much as possible from the sight." SS I 16 88 31
a serious accent, "to be as unlike myself as is possible. SS I 19 103 6
behaviour, in every possible variety which the different SS I 19 104 12
possible to speak at one without being heard at the other. SS I 19 105 13
of England, under every possible variation of form, face, SS I 21 119 3
he had just filled the sheet to me as full as possible." SS I 22 134 52
so poignant and so fresh, it was possible for them to be. SS II 1 141 6
to see him as little as possible; she could not deny SS II 1 142 7
them both with all possible kindness, was solicitous on SS II 4 160 2
if concealment be possible, is all that remains." SS II 5 173 44
as a loss to her of any possible good but as an escape SS II 7 184 15
Pray call again as soon as possible, and explain the SS II 7 187 40
But I will not suppose this possible, and I hope very soon SS II 7 187 40
only to deceive, let it be told as soon as possible. SS II 7 188 42
"No, Marianne, in no possible way." SS II 7 190 57
believing it hardly possible that she could sit out the SS II 8 193 5
more truth in it than I could believe possible at first." SS II 8 198 33
Elinor encouraged her as much as possible to talk of what SS II 9 201 2
avoiding, where it was possible, the presence of Mrs. SS II 9 201 2
deprived her of the only possible alleviation of her SS II 10 214 6
Sir John could not have thought it possible. SS II 10 214 9
and promoting the marriage by every possible attention. SS II 11 228 51
wished to be as much as possible with Charlotte, she went SS II 14 246 2
Could you have believed such a thing possible?-- SS III 1 258 7
the notion of its being possible to end otherwise at last, SS III 1 260 9
borne it as much as possible without spreading it farther. SS III 1 263 27
is not fit--it is not possible that it should be so.-- SS III 1 263 27
and cried, "gracious God! can this be possible!" SS III 1 267 39
"I cannot suppose it possible that she should." SS III 2 272 11
to spread as little as possible intelligence that had in SS III 2 276 27
he did not suppose it possible that Delaford living could SS III 3 284 22
much dreaded as soon as possible, "without receiving our SS III 4 288 28
Can it be possible?" SS III 4 289 32
event, must be concealed from her as much as possible. SS III 5 296 20
circumspection for a possible opportunity of making myself SS III 8 321 34
I avoided the Middletons as much as possible, as well as SS III 8 326 55
Had I sat down to wish for any possible good to my family, SS III 9 336 10
that would appear to you possible; and perhaps, as long as SS III 11 350 9
Were it possible, she should say it must be Edward. SS III 12 358 8
Marianne had retreated as much as possible out of sight, SS III 12 359 13
I shall retreat in as much secrecy as possible to the most W 335 13
my uncle's memory is if possible endeared to me by such a W 352 26
Eager to be as little among them as possible, Emma was W 361 30
to know as little as possible of the defects of the person PP I 6 23 10
"Upon my word, Caroline, I should think it more possible PP I 8 38 38
directions that every possible attention might be paid to PP I 8 40 59
every possible attention while she remains with us." PP I 9 41 5
"Perhaps that is not possible for any one. PP I 11 57 22
to make them every possible amends,--but of this hereafter. PP I 13 63 12
always wish to give them as unstudied an air as possible." PP I 14 68 11
and Lydia, determined if possible to find out, led the way PP I 15 72 8
Mrs. Bennet as much as possible, saying not much to PP I 17 86 9
they may have the trouble of saying as little as possible." PP I 18 91 13
cannot be excused from making as comfortable as possible. PP I 18 101 71
soon and as quietly as possible, she sat down again, and PP I 19 104 7
might be as little as possible, when the melancholy event PP I 19 106 10
but Jane with all possible mildness declined interfering;-- PP I 20 112 23
She represented to her sister as forcibly as possible what PP I 21 120 29
that I shall avail myself of it as soon as possible." PP I 22 123 5
not have supposed it possible that when called into action, PP I 22 125 18
to take place as soon as possible, which he trusted would PP I 23 128 10
It was possible, and sometimes she thought it probable, PP II 2 142 16
for him, as well as a possible advantage to Jane, she PP II 3 149 27
exercise, and owned she encouraged it as much as possible. PP II 5 156 4
How was that possible? PP II 6 164 28
to go, and as much as possible prevented her husband from PP II 10 187 41
herself as much as possible against Mr. Darcy, chose for PP II 11 188 1
any possible way that would have tempted me to accept it." PP II 11 192 25 26
in the church, were it possible that he could ever be in a PP II 12 201 5
again, and was resolved to avoid it as long as possible. PP II 16 223 25
to be kept as much as possible to myself; and if I PP II 17 226 23
Oh! my dear father, can you suppose it possible that they PP II 18 231 18
herself as much as possible; advice, which there was every PP II 18 235 40
only of returning to the carriage as quickly as possible. PP III 1 254 57
as possible, every attempt at conversation on either side. PP III 3 269 8
where secresy was possible, except to Elizabeth; and from PP III 3 270 10
After making every possible enquiry on that side London, PP III 4 275 5
begging you all to come here, as soon as possible. PP III 4 275 5
Conceal the unhappy truth as long as it is possible. PP III 4 278 21
They were to be off as soon as possible. PP III 4 280 26
They travelled as expeditiously as possible; and sleeping PP III 5 285 20
"How was it possible that such an idea should enter our PP III 5 290 50
as Mr. Bennet thought it possible they might have gone to PP III 6 295 5
him to find out, if possible, from some of the young man's PP III 6 295 6
It was possible, however, that some of his companions in PP III 6 296 8
yourself as much as possible, to throw off your unworthy PP III 6 297 11
"It is possible!" cried Elizabeth, when she had finished. PP III 7 303 15
"Can it be possible that he will marry her?" PP III 7 303 15
and was determined, if possible, to find out the extent of PP III 8 308 2
was to have as little trouble in the business as possible. PP III 8 309 5
seem valid, exceeded all that she could believe possible. PP III 8 310 10
I had not believed it possible." PP III 13 349 45
suppose the truth of it possible, I instantly resolved on PP III 14 353 26
"You have insulted me, in every possible method. PP III 14 357 63
"have any possible claim on me, in the present instance. PP III 14 358 70
had looked forward to as possible, at some future time. PP III 15 360 1
uneasiness as to the possible consequence of her PP III 15 360 2
in any possible way, that would induce you to accept me." PP III 16 368 16
them as much as possible; and, in return, it belongs to me PP III 18 381 7
imagination in every possible flight which the subject PP III 18 382 21
and threaten her with all its possible ill consequences. MP I 1 4 1
The little visitor meanwhile was as unhappy as possible. MP I 2 13 4
with Maria and Julia, and being as merry as possible. MP I 2 17 20
escaping as quickly as possible, could soon with cheerful MP I 3 24 4
the dear departed--what possible comfort could I have in MP I 3 29 46
saving her from all possible fatigue or exertion in every MP I 4 34 1
most hearty concurrence was conveyed as soon as possible. MP I 4 40 14
Till now, I could not have supposed it possible to be MP I 5 49 32
thing done in the best style, and made as nice as possible. MP I 6 53 9
I would have every thing as complete as possible in the MP I 6 57 31
a relation dead, it is done in the fewest possible words. MP I 6 59 43
as great a gloom as possible over their dinner and dessert. MP I 7 70 30
It was hardly possible indeed that any thing else should MP I 8 75 2
He was determined to prevent it, if possible, though his MP I 13 124 13
them roused as soon as possible by the remonstrance which MP I 14 137 23
the part if it were possible," cried Tom, "but unluckily MP I 15 144 33
of such magnitude as must, if possible, be prevented. MP I 16 154 8
Could it be possible? MP I 16 156 28
his friend as soon as possible, and immediately gave Sir MP II 1 184 27
the subject as fast as possible, and turn the current of MP II 2 188 3
to care for, how was it possible for even her activity to MP II 2 194 20
She must escape from him and Mansfield as soon as possible, MP II 3 202 25
the house as fast as possible; and to poor Miss Crawford, MP II 4 205 3
pleasure, both present and future, as much as possible. MP II 5 219 27
very awkwardest of all possible numbers to sit down to MP II 5 220 30
in trying to make it possible for him to learn his part-- MP II 5 224 53
arrival, came as soon as possible; and scarcely ten days MP II 6 233 14
"My plan may not be the best possible; I had not many MP II 7 243 27
prevent the marriage, if possible; but I know you, I know MP II 12 296 29
My uncle ought to know it as soon as possible." MP II 13 300 7
Every thing might be possible rather than serious MP II 13 306 26
must avoid seeing him if possible; and being then in her MP III 1 311 2
any one, it is hardly possible that your affections-----" MP III 1 316 31
"If it were possible for me to do otherwise," said she MP III 1 320 43
was then as nearly as possible what it had been before; MP III 1 323 53
still have avoided, if possible, but which became MP III 2 331 19

he sank as quietly as possible into a corner, turned his MP III 3 341 31
might have as much hope to sustain them as possible. MP III 4 345 2
"Very possible. MP III 4 350 28
I think it very possible that they might, one or both, be MP III 4 350 30
She absented herself as little as possible from Lady MP III 5 357 4
It is not possible, but that you must have had some MP III 5 362 18
heart, and will love you as nearly for ever as possible. MP III 5 363 24
it would be hardly possible for her to avoid paying her MP III 6 373 24
the next step as soon as possible, or speculations upon MP III 7 375 2
any reference to her possible convenience; but she had MP III 7 382 28
I am sure he still means to impose on me if possible, and MP III 11 411 20
And had it been possible for her to return Mr. Crawford's MP III 12 419 9
treated as concisely as possible at the end of a long MP III 13 425 6
the Bertram property, than any other possible 'sir.' MP III 14 434 13
her think it scarcely possible for them to support life MP III 15 442 21
His great object was to be off as soon as possible. MP III 15 445 29
Could you have believed it possible?-- MP III 16 456 23
I had not supposed it possible, coming in such a state of MP III 16 457 30
now he could scarcely comprehend to have been possible. MP III 17 463 9
little excuse of love as possible, and without the MP III 17 468 21
it might not be a possible, an hopeful undertaking to MP III 17 470 25
blessing, and it was not possible that encouragement from MP III 17 471 28
But it was possible to part with her, because Susan MP III 17 472 31
the endeavour to make a small income go as far as possible. E I 3 21 4
that I do not think any possible good can arise from E I 5 40 24
own and Mr. Weston's on the subject, as much as possible. E I 5 41 31
made him discern a likeness almost before it was possible. E I 6 47 26
to keep her with them as much as possible just at present. E I 8 57 1
I wonder you should think it possible for me to have such E I 8 62 39
She was as happy as possible with the Martins in the E I 8 63 42
down, and then there can be no possible reflection on you." E I 9 77 42
After this speech he was gone as soon as possible. E I 9 82 84
wife, it was hardly possible that any natural defects in E I 11 92 5
She would keep the peace if possible; and there was E I 11 97 27
cooler manners rendered possible; and if his willing E I 12 100 16
a possible thing in preference to a division of the party. E I 13 108 2
to think as little as possible of Mr. Elton's oddities, or E I 14 117 2
imagined? can it be possible for this man to be beginning E I 14 118 4
through all the possible accumulations of drifted snow E I 15 127 13
resolved on being seriously accepted as soon as possible. E I 15 129 24
of character, indeed, which I had not supposed possible! E I 15 130 30
No intercourse with Harriet possible but by note; no E I 16 138 17
have as much time as possible for getting the better of E I 17 141 5
a friend as Miss Woodhouse would have thought it possible. E I 17 141 8
Nobody but you, Mr. Knightley, would imagine it possible E I 18 147 17
hurried on as fast as possible; but then, as she was E II 3 177 52
a glance forward at any possible treachery in his guest, E II 5 193 35
it over as quickly as possible, and making no other E II 7 205 1
not wish him to think it possible; the hours would be too E II 7 208 9
"You will make my excuses, my dear, as civilly as possible. E II 7 209 14
as little about it as possible, which she plainly read in E II 8 220 46
Good soul! she was as grateful as possible, you may be E II 8 223 63
He is as happy as possible by himself; with his farm, and E II 8 225 74
Another accidental meeting with the Martins was possible, E II 9 233 23
I must speak to him if possible, just to thank him. E II 10 243 31
"It may be possible to do without dancing entirely. E II 11 247 1
in what possible manner they could be disposed of. E II 11 248 9
of the business might be gone through as soon as possible. E II 14 270 2
possible; and Mr. Suckling is extremely fond of exploring. E II 14 274 28
bride--I ought to have paid my respects to her if possible. E II 14 280 56
She could not have believed it possible that the taste or E II 15 285 12
have wished, had she deemed it possible enough for wishing. E II 16 291 5
Emma found it hardly possible to prevent their making two E II 17 299 1
Nobody but yourself could imagine such a thing possible. E II 18 308 25
it strikes me as a possible thing, Emma, that Henry and E II 18 312 48
time, induced them to name as early a day as possible. E III 1 318 11
there as soon as possible after themselves, for the E III 2 319 2
He would not ask Harriet to dance if it were possible to E III 2 326 33
It was not possible that the occurrence should not be E III 3 335 10
I should not have thought it possible you could forget E III 4 338 12
to, she also found it possible to accept dear Miss E III 5 344 3
be, made him seize every possible moment for darting his E III 5 348 23
Every thing as natural and simple as possible. E III 6 355 20
resources, it is not possible for her to be always shut up E III 6 356 26
wish every thing to be as much to your taste as possible." E III 6 356 27
over to join them, if possible; a proof of approbation and E III 6 357 31
down, at the greatest possible distance from the slight E III 6 363 53
Emma, I had not thought it possible." E III 7 374 55
She is as low as possible. E III 8 379 8
much for Miss Fairfax's advantage and comfort as possible. E III 8 380 9
alleviation that is possible--I mean, as to the character E III 8 381 22
as without supposing it possible that she could be E III 8 383 30
should be as handsome as possible; and his wife sat E III 9 388 13
She saw in a moment all the possible good. E III 9 388 13
future were all that could yet be possible on Emma's side. E III 9 388 15
Do, if it be possible. E III 10 392 2
the painful truth, however, and as soon as possible. E III 11 403 2
"I should not have thought it possible," she began, "that E III 11 405 18
possible that I could be supposed to mean any other person. E III 11 405 18
not have thought it possible--but if you, who had been E III 11 406 18
When we talked about him, it was clear as possible." E III 11 406 20
had been the person; and now--it is possible -----." E III 11 407 26
Is not it possible, that when enquiring, as you thought, E III 11 410 36
to exert herself if possible, and that her claims were E III 11 414 50
to give me intelligence of the letter as soon as possible." E III 12 420 16
Emma resolved to be out of doors as soon as possible. E III 13 424 1
and the first possible cause for it, suggested by her E III 13 424 1
"How is it possible?" cried Emma, turning her flowing E III 13 425 8
immediate feeling was to avert the subject, if possible. E III 13 429 26
any possible atonement; how to appear least her enemy?-- E III 14 435 4
merely because I would be as angry with her as possible. E III 14 441 8
concluded as soon as possible, she now sent me, by a safe E III 14 442 8
Think she must of the possible difference to the poor E III 15 449 35
It was a palpable display, repeated on every possible E III 16 454 16
How--how has it been possible?" E III 18 471 19
But is it possible that you had no suspicion?-- E III 18 477 53
doubt of its being possible for her to be really cured of E III 19 481 1
sixteen, to all that was possible, of her mother's rights P III 1 5 8
It had not been possible for him to spend less; he had P III 1 9 19
it done with the least possible pain to him and Elizabeth. P III 2 12 3
be contemplated as a possible thing, because we know how P III 3 17 4
get into it as soon as possible;--knew he must pay for his P III 3 22 23
it might yet have been possible to withstand her father's P III 4 27 5
time of life, had been possible to the nice tone of her P III 4 28 7
and wanted to make it possible for her to stay behind, P III 5 33 6
though dreading the possible heats of September in all the P III 5 33 6
to his family from the intimacy, were more than possible. P III 5 34 12
"Oh! but they ought to call upon you as soon as possible. P III 5 40 43
and all her ideas in as much of Uppercross as possible. P III 6 43 3
It was certainly carried nearly as far as possible, for P III 6 46 12
as possible; but what was there for a father to do? P III 7 55 7
only one that could be possible; but he is a very good- P III 9 76 15
She occupied her mind as much as possible in such like P III 10 84 7
but it was not possible, that when within reach of Captain P III 10 84 7
into the smallest possible space to leave her a corner; P III 10 91 41
She wished it might be possible for her to avoid ever P III 11 93 3
the Harvilles seemed, if possible, augmented by the event P III 11 97 12
him all her attention as long as attention was possible. P III 12 109 31
surgeon was with them almost before it had seemed possible. P III 12 112 52
between those two, she could want no possible attendance P III 12 113 56
he would be as little incumbrance as possible to Captain P III 12 113 58
occasions of its being possible for her to go to the hall P IV 1 123 9
again, and as soon as possible after their return to P IV 2 129 1
much as she could, every possible supply from Uppercross P IV 2 129 2
It was possible that he might stop in his way home, to ask P IV 3 142 17
politely taken as possible, but her part must follow then. P IV 3 143 18
Anne could not have supposed it possible that her first P IV 3 144 24
all the advantages of the connexion as far as possible? P IV 4 150 17
might be hereafter, of a possible attachment on his side, P IV 5 159 22
would be the highest possible gratification to me.-- P IV 5 159 25
A few minutes, though a few as possible, were inevitably P IV 8 190 48
back to Bath as soon as possible, and of fixing himself P IV 9 207 90
It was just possible that she might have been persuaded by P IV 9 211 102
as much composure as possible; and after all, her greatest P IV 10 212 1
as much of her time as possible, invited for every day and P IV 10 220 31
how soon it be possible to get them there, pretending to P I 6 235 31
Any thing was possible, any thing might be defied rather P IV 11 237 41
return "hither, or follow your party, as soon as possible. P IV 11 237 43
Anxious to omit no possible precaution, Anne struggled, P IV 11 239 48
49
it unpacked to the last possible moment, that I might see P IV 11 240 58
It was possible that you might retain the feelings of the P IV 11 244 70
profession which is, if possible, more distinguished in P IV 12 252 12
family, & every possible attention was paid in the kindest S 2 370 1
to Sanditon as soon as possible--and healthy as they all S 2 373 1
their getting out into the world, as much as possible. S 2 374 1
could--to receive every possible pleasure which Sanditon S 2 374 1
account as prudently as possible, to defy the reputed S 3 378 1
my dear, in wishing our boys to be as hardy as possible."-- S 4 381 1
Your sister Diana seems almost as ill as possible, but S 5 388 1
see as much, & as quickly as possible, where all was new. S 6 389 1
to detach her as much as possible from the rest of the S 7 396 1
to hurry on & get into the house if possible before her. S 9 406 1
as extensively useful as possible, & where some degree of S 9 410 1
Is not it possible to prevail on you to dine with us?" was S 9 410 1

POSSIBLY (59)

Can you possibly suppose that I was aware of her LS 24 289 12
your praise that could possibly be; and the praise of such NA I 7 50 47
I refused him as long as I possibly could, but he would NA II 1 134 39
I refused him as long as I possibly could, but he would NA II 1 134 39
claim on my affection, which no other can possibly share." SS I 14 73 15
handsomest dimensions in the world could possibly afford." SS I 14 73 17
expression of good humour in it that could possibly be. SS I 19 106 22
call on you, if I could possibly find a spare half hour, SS II 11 221 9
I heard him say all this as plain as could possibly be. SS III 2 273 16
Delaford, as far as she possibly could, of his servants, SS III 5 293 2
neither she nor her child could be possibly impoverished. SS III 5 295 17
being uncertain, and possibly far distant, it had been for SS III 8 320 32
sort of a home Emma cd possibly have been used to in W 350 24
suffer more from it herself, than I can possibly do." W 352 26
In a moment afterwards--"that is if I can possibly get W 360 28
a young man ought likewise to be, if he possibly can. PP I 4 14 3
Mrs. Bennet sent them word that they could not possibly PP I 12 59 1
for then we might possibly get a settled family there. PP II 9 178 9
You may possibly wonder why all this was not told you last PP II 12 202 5
and possibly a mutual desire of never meeting again. PP II 18 235 39
But the horror of what might possibly happen, almost took PP III 5 292 64
an answer to her letter, as soon as she possibly could. PP III 10 321 1
"Can you possibly guess, Lizzy, who is meant by this?" PP III 15 362 15
as Mrs. Norris could not possibly keep to herself, put an MP I 1 4 1
or to lose one connection that might possibly assist her. MP I 1 4 2
more attention than her poor mother could possibly give? MP I 1 5 4
Indeed, I do not see that you could possibly place her any MP I 1 10 13
Did she, in short, want any thing he could possibly get MP I 2 15 10
Lady Bertram could not possibly spare her." MP I 8 76 5
that you cannot possibly engage in any thing of the sort MP II 7 244 30
I feel much more than I can possibly express. MP II 9 262 5
"My dear Henry, where can you possibly have been all this MP II 12 291 1
But how could you possibly suppose me against you? MP III 4 346 14
Crawford more than she possibly could; and Miss Crawford, MP III 5 359 10
that she could not possibly be spared from Mansfield Park MP III 6 373 23
approve, but this cannot possibly be permitted before the MP III 12 417 3
please; but I cannot possibly say 'poor Miss Taylor.' E I 1 10 29
very worst sort of companion that Emma could possibly have. E I 5 38 15
What can it possibly be? E I 9 72 17
which they could possibly wish for, without the smallest E I 11 92 3
I could not imagine how you could possibly do without her.- E I 11 93 7
which it might very possibly have done, for Mr. Woodhouse E I 13 115 39
of the visit could not possibly pass without bringing E I 14 119 6
to Miss Smith!--what could she possibly mean!"-- E I 15 130 26
"Where could you possibly hear it, Mr. Knightley? E II 3 173 27
But, Mr. Knightley, how could you possibly have heard it? E II 3 173 27
to think who could possibly have ordered it--but now, they E II 8 214 13
beyond his fortnight, which could not possibly be refused. E II 11 256 59
some old acquaintance--and how could she possibly guess? E II 14 278 49
And how could it possibly come into your head?" E III 5 350 35
hearing that they could not possibly come till the autumn. E III 6 352 1
very possibly arise from the impropriety of his conduct." E III 10 397 47
it the very best thing that Frank could possibly have done. E III 10 401 69
"I cannot possibly do without Anne," was Mary's reasoning; P III 5 33 7
"Dear me! what can you possibly have to do?" P III 5 38 33
the very best that could possibly be, and, after a little P IV 6 172 40
41
a youth who could not possibly claim it under many years; P IV 10 217 20
to doubt it as long as you possibly can, I am sure.--" S 10 415 1
or any complaint which Asses milk cd possibly releive. S 11 422 1

POST (41)

he wrote by the same post to Reginald, a long letter full LS 13 262 1
Lady Susan had received a line from him by that day's post LS 17 269 1
detriment of the post office revenue, be continued longer. LS 42 311 1
writing by every post, nor exacted her promise of NA I 2 19 3
post their ready consent to her visit to Gloucestershire. NA II 2 140 11
to be taken post by you, at your age, alone, unattended!" NA II 13 225 23
"She travelled all the way post by herself, and knew NA II 14 237 21
post, which contained a proposal particularly well timed. SS I 4 23 20
letters to and from the post for them, and would not be SS I 6 30 6
I shall then go post." SS I 13 65 42
out letters himself from the post, and carries them to it. SS I 16 84 6
possession of the post of civility which she had assigned SS II 4 160 2
to get that letter conveyed for her to the two-penny post. SS II 4 161 5
Elinor, "she will write to Combe by this day's post." SS II 5 167 6
leaning against one of its post, again took up SS II 7 190 55
56
came post all the way, and had a smart beau to attend us. SS II 10 218 24
Elinor a letter by the two-penny post from Lucy herself. SS III 2 277 29
am informed by this day's post, is his, if he think it SS III 3 282 19
the idea of two young women travelling post by themselves. PP II 14 211 13
the post came in without bringing a single line from him. PP III 6 294 1
most anxious part of each was when the post was expected. PP III 6 296 9
The horses were post; and neither the carriage, nor the PP III 14 351 1
"But cousin--will it go to the post?" MP I 2 16 16
nothing better than a post of such honourable MP I 4 35 5
might now and then lend them the poney he sent to the post. MP I 4 36 7
The place of all places, the envied seat, the post of MP I 8 80 29
the idea of travelling post with four horses and such a MP II 9 266 21
The post was late this morning, but there has not been MP II 13 299 5
Fanny, they were to travel post, when she saw Sir Thomas MP III 6 372 21
Write to me by return of post, judge of my anxiety, and do MP III 14 434 13
authorized to write an acquiescence by the morrow's post.-- E III 6 359 37
morning's post had conveyed the history of Jane Fairfax.-- E III 13 433 41
at the same time by the post, stating her extreme surprise E III 14 442 8
my own blunder, I raved at the blunders of the post.-- E III 14 443 8
musician to a more active post, played country dances to P III 6 47 15
My dear Admiral, that post!--we shall certainly take that P III 10 92 47

Admiral, that post!--we shall certainly take that post." P III 10 92 47
myself from the morning post & the Kentish Gazette, only S 1 366 1
gentleman's carriage with post horses standing at the door S 9 406 1
I answered Fanny's letter by the same post & pressed for S 9 408 1
Mr & Mrs P.-- & Charlotte had seen two post chaises S 10 414 1
POST CAPTAINS (1)
Post captains may be very good sort of men, but they do MP I 6 60 49
POST-BOY (2)
Swiftly therefore shall her post-boy drive through the NA II 14 232 7
on settling with the post-boy, inveighing against the W 349 24
POST-BOYS (1)
at the park to her brother, who is one of the post-boys. SS III 11 354 27
POST-CHAISE (3)
A heroine in a hack post-chaise, is such a blow upon NA II 14 232 7
we'd join him in a post-chaise; and he behaved very SS II 10 218 24
"What!" cried Julia; "go box'd up three in a post-chaise MP I 8 77 10
POST-CHAISES (1)
this lane in post-chaises, it might not be a bad S 1 366 1
POST-HORSES (2)
post-horses directly, she wrote a few lines to her mother. SS III 7 311 15
a couple of pair of post-horses were kept, more for the E II 6 197 5
POST-MASTERS (1)
been indebted to the post-masters for the names of the NA II 14 232 6
POST-OFFICE (8)
"I went only to the post-office," said she, "and reached E II 16 293 12
The post-office has a great charm at one period of our E II 16 293 16
all my affections, a post-office, I think, must always E II 16 294 22
Going to the post-office in the rain!-- E II 16 295 30
To the post-office indeed! E II 16 295 32
walk somewhere, and the post-office is an object; and upon E II 16 296 35
"The post-office is a wonderful establishment!" said she.-- E II 16 296 40
subjects:--the post-office--catching cold--fetching E II 17 299 1
POSTCHAISE (1)
"Who could it be?--it was certainly a postchaise.-- W 355 28
POSTED (1)
thousand pounds, and was posted into the Laconia, if I had P IV 11 247 82
POSTERITY (1)
handed down to posterity with all the eclat of a proverb." PP I 18 91 15
POSTILIONS (2)
chaise-and-four--postilions handsomely liveried, rising so NA II 5 156 4
changed horses, see the postilions, and try if any thing PP III 5 293 69
POSTING (3)
the exorbitant advance in posting, & pondering over a W 349 24
He was posting away as if upon life and death, and could MP I 10 101 30
three veiws of Miss Diana posting over the down after a S 10 413 1
POSTMAN'S (1)
The postman's knock within the neighbourhood was beginning MP III 9 398 10
POSTMARK (1)
It bore the London postmark, and came from Edmund. MP III 15 442 23
POSTPONE (1)
daughter, rather than postpone his own walk a few minutes. NA I 12 95 17
POSTPONED (1)
and therefore readily postponed seeing him, till after the PP III 10 323 2
POSTPONING (1)
her story directly, or postponing it till Marianne were in SS III 10 345 23
POSTS (3)
the windows guarded by posts and chain, the door W 322 2
Monday, trusting that many posts would not pass before I MP II 13 299 5
Two posts came in, and brought no refutation, public or MP III 15 442 22
POSTSCRIPT (5)
that a verbal postscript from himself wd be requisite.--" W 338 17
Tuesday; and in her postscript it was added, that if Mr. PP I 12 59 1
on the postscript of the last, with trembling energy.-- PP III 4 280 26
There was also a postscript to this effect. PP III 6 295 5
Edmund's letter had this postscript. MP III 14 430 4
POSTURE (6)
my mind was entirely satisfied with the posture of affairs. LS 22 281 4
body she moved from one posture to another, till growing SS II 7 191 65
her continual change of posture, and heard the frequent SS III 7 310 10 11
eye, the sickly skin, the posture of reclining weakness, SS III 10 340 2
to the former subject, posture, and voice, as soon as Lady MP I 13 126 23
every place, every posture, she perceived that she had E III 11 411 43
POT (1)
blinds, to arrange a flower pot on the Balcony, or look at S 11 422 1
POTATOES (1)
Dr. Grant; "these potatoes have as much the flavour of a MP I 6 54 12
POTENT (4)
potent intelligence, as to supersede the necessity of more. LS 35 305 1
Her sensibility was potent enough! SS I 16 83 1
of the said books grew so potent and stimulative, that MP III 9 398 9
the prime character, the potent, pervading hero of the S 8 403 1
POTIONS (1)
potions to be procured, like rhubarb, from every druggist. NA II 10 200 3
POULTERER (3)
"Commend me to the nurseryman and the poulterer." MP II 4 212 32
as glad of your nurseryman and poulterer as you could be. MP II 4 212 33
and the poulterer--or perhaps on their very account. MP II 4 213 35
POULTICE (1)
line, "to poultice chesnut mare,"--a farrier's bill! NA II 7 172 2
POULTRY (6)
of his servants, his carriage, his cows, and his poultry. SS III 5 293 2
instructed her as to the care of her cows and her poultry. PP II 6 163 15
Her home and her housekeeping, her parish and her poultry, PP II 15 216 7
after the welfare and poultry of her eldest daughter; Mrs. PP II 16 222 21
and poultry, was very much in want of some variety at home. MP I 4 41 15
I had been looking about me in the poultry yard, and was MP I 15 141 22
POULTRY-HOUSE (1)
Mrs. Weston's poultry-house was robbed one night of all E III 19 483 10
POULTRY-YARD (1)
in visiting her poultry-yard, where, in the disappointed SS III 6 303 10
POULTRY-YARDS (1)
Other poultry-yards in the neighbourhood also suffered.-- E III 19 483 10
POUNDS (97)
even putting an hundred pounds bank-bill into her hands, NA I 2 19 3
be bound to go two miles in it for fifty thousand pounds." NA I 9 65 28
I would undertake for five pounds to drive it to York and NA I 9 65 30
thousand pounds, and five hundred to buy wedding-clothes. NA I 9 68 46
of about four hundred pounds yearly value, was to be NA II 1 135 42
fifty pounds a year, I should not have a wish unsatisfied. NA II 1 136 48
ten or fifteen thousand pounds which her father could give NA II 15 245 12
poor, and that Catherine would have three thousand pounds. NA II 16 251 6
only seven thousand pounds in his own disposal; for the SS I 1 4 2
the three girls, he left them a thousand pounds a-piece. SS I 1 4 3
He survived his uncle no longer; and ten thousand pounds, SS I 1 4 4
of his sisters by the present of a thousand pounds a-piece. SS I 1 5 8
"Yes, he would give them three thousand pounds: it would SS I 1 5 8
Three thousand pounds! he could spare so considerable a SS I 1 5 8
To take three thousand pounds from the fortune of their SS I 2 8 3
but that something need not be three thousand pounds. SS I 2 9 7
Five hundred pounds would be a prodigious increase to SS I 2 9 10
I may afford to give them five hundred pounds a-piece. SS I 2 10 14
have above three thousand pounds on their mother's death-- SS I 2 10 14
They will have ten thousand pounds divided amongst them. SS I 2 10 15
together on the interest of ten thousand pounds." SS I 2 10 15
is better than parting with fifteen hundred pounds at once. SS I 2 10 18
a hundred, or even fifty pounds from our own expences." SS I 2 11 22
A present of fifty pounds, now and then, will prevent SS I 2 11 23
of seven thousand pounds, besides the thousand pounds SS I 2 12 24
besides the thousand pounds belonging to each of the girls, SS I 2 12 24
brings them in fifty pounds a-year a-piece, and, of course, SS I 2 12 24
couple of hundred pounds, Willoughby says, would make it SS I 13 69 76
"He has only two thousand pounds of his own; it would be SS II 2 147 7
"Fifty thousand pounds, my dear. SS II 8 194 10
Fifty thousand pounds! and by all accounts it wo'nt come SS II 8 194 10
likewise heard that Miss Grey has fifty thousand pounds? SS II 8 199 38
of the late Lord Morton, with thirty thousand pounds. SS II 11 224 28
into Fanny's hands to the amount of two hundred pounds. SS II 11 224 28
been within some thousand pounds of being obliged to sell SS II 12 233 18
His own two thousand pounds she protested should be his SS III 1 267 38
The interest of two thousand pounds--how can a man live on SS III 1 268 50
has thirty thousand pounds,) I cannot picture to myself a SS III 1 268 50
with thirty thousand pounds to her fortune, for Lucy SS III 2 272 16
nothing but two thousand pounds, and no hope of any thing SS III 2 273 16
upon a curacy of fifty pounds a-year, with the interest of SS III 2 276 28
of his two thousand pounds, and what little matter Mr. SS III 2 276 28
might have got I dare say--fourteen hundred pounds. SS III 5 295 12
regard, and who had only two thousand pounds in the world. SS III 13 367 22
Edward had two thousand pounds, and Elinor one, which, SS III 13 369 32
pounds a-year would supply them with the comforts of life. SS III 13 369 32
with thirty thousand pounds, while Miss Dashwood was only SS III 14 373 3
endowed with a thousand pounds a-year, not the smallest SS III 14 374 4
the ten thousand pounds, which had been given with Fanny. SS III 14 374 4
an only child, & will have at least ten thousand pounds."-- W 321 2
as Robert, who has got a good wife & six thousand pounds?" W 321 2
he had been clerk, with a fortune of six thousand pounds.-- W 348 23
had that six thousand pounds, & for being now in W 349 23
that the aunt could never have had six thousand pounds.-- W 350 24
pounds, there was a young man who wd have thought of her." W 353 26
of twenty thousand pounds, were in the habit of spending PP I 4 15 11
an hundred thousand pounds from his father, who had PP I 4 15 11
attorney in Meryton, and had left her four thousand pounds. PP I 7 28 1
had cost eight hundred pounds, she felt all the force of PP I 16 75 2
and that one thousand pounds in the 4 per cents. which PP I 19 106 10
The sudden acquisition of ten thousand pounds was the most PP II 3 149 28
pounds, you want to find out that he is mercenary." PP II 4 153 9
I suppose you would not ask above fifty thousand pounds." PP II 10 184 15
There was also a legacy of one thousand pounds. PP II 12 200 5
pounds would be a very insufficient support therein. PP II 12 200 5
receive it, and accepted in return three thousand pounds. PP II 12 201 5
which is thirty thousand pounds; but I cannot help PP II 12 202 5
as three thousand pounds, again was she forced to hesitate. PP II 13 205 3
Colonel Forster believed that more than a thousand pounds PP III 6 298 12
trust you so near it as East Bourne, for fifty pounds! PP III 6 300 30
of the five thousand pounds, secured among your children PP III 7 302 14
her, during your life, one hundred pounds per annum. PP III 7 302 14
he takes her with a farthing less than ten thousand pounds. PP III 7 304 31
"Ten thousand pounds! PP III 7 304 32
thousand pounds, or any thing like it, has been advanced. PP III 7 304 35
How could he spare half ten thousand pounds?" PP III 7 304 35
Five thousand pounds was settled by marriage articles on PP III 8 308 4
He would scarcely be ten pounds a-year the loser, by the PP III 8 309 4
more than a thousand pounds, another thousand in addition PP III 10 324 2
with only seven thousand pounds, had the good luck to. MP I 1 3 1
three thousand pounds short of any equitable claim to it. MP I 1 3 1
Mrs. Grant had ever had more than five thousand pounds." MP I 3 31 59
estate in Norfolk, the daughter twenty thousand pounds. MP I 4 40 15
a girl of twenty thousand pounds, with all the elegance MP I 4 42 17
Perhaps it might cost a whole twenty pounds.-- MP I 13 127 31
I would not have been out of the way for a thousand pounds. MP III 7 380 20
to him, though her twenty thousand pounds had been forty. MP III 16 453 15
intimate with, who have all twenty thousand pounds apiece." E I 8 66 53
of thirty thousand pounds, were not quite so easily E I 16 135 7
the very few hundred pounds which she inherited from her E II 2 164 5
for the sake of the future twelve thousand pounds. E II 2 169 16
had not made less than twenty thousand pounds by the war. P III 9 75 10
should have his for fifty pounds, arms and motto, name and P IV 9 202 66
with a few thousand pounds, and was posted into the P IV 11 247 82
Captain Wentworth, with five-and-twenty thousand pounds, P IV 12 248 1
share of ten thousand pounds which must be hers hereafter. P IV 12 248 1
original thirty thousand pounds among them, the legal S 3 376 1
POUR (4)
for she was impatient to pour forth her thanks to him for SS III 10 340 1
the jilting girl, and pour forth her compassion towards SS III 13 370 37
But we must stem the tide of malice, and pour into the PP III 5 289 42
had been afraid it would pour down every moment--but she E II 3 177 52
POURED (9)
She shall find that she has poured forth her tender tale LS 22 282 8
of the other; and remonstrances poured in from all three. NA I 13 100 19
visited Miss Tilney, and poured forth her joyful feelings. NA II 2 138 1
questions now eagerly poured forth;--the first three NA II 7 180 37
of a western sun gaily poured through two sash windows! NA II 9 193 6
Prescriptions poured in from all quarters, and as usual, SS III 6 306 17
To the civil enquiries which then poured in, and amongst PP I 8 35 1
had seized a sheet of paper, and poured out his feelings. P IV 11 241 60
It struck her however, as he poured out this rather weak S 10 417 1
POURING (2)
making tea, and Elizabeth pouring out the coffee, in so PP III 12 341 16
of attachment; who was pouring out his sense of her merits, MP III 2 328 6
POURTRAY (1)
not know her own poverty, for she had no lover to pourtray. NA I 1 16 10
POVERTY (23)
At present she did not know her own poverty, for she had NA I 1 16 10
"What a picture of intellectual poverty! NA I 10 79 55
Where people are really attached, poverty itself is wealth: NA I 15 119 20
equal, and he had himself often complained of his poverty. SS I 14 71 4
could struggle with any poverty for him; but I love him SS II 2 147 7
Having now said enough to make his poverty clear, and to SS II 11 226 41
to infer from it;--no poverty of any kind, except of SS II 12 233 18
after dinner, this poverty was particularly evident, for SS II 12 233 19
To avoid a comparative poverty, which her affection and SS III 8 321 32
to outweigh that dread of poverty, or get the better of SS III 8 323 40
Poverty is a great evil, but to a woman of education & W 318 2
"You have reduced him to his present state of poverty, PP II 11 192 21
him to his present state of poverty, comparative poverty. PP II 11 192 21
a distance from us all in poverty and neglect, would be MP I 1 7 6
Poverty is exactly what I have determined against. MP II 4 214 41
no difficulties behind, no drawback of poverty or parent. MP III 17 471 29
poor old maid; and it is poverty only which makes celibacy E I 10 85 19
Poverty certainly has not contracted her mind: I really E I 10 85 19
In the present instance, it was sickness and poverty E I 10 86 24 25
Beauty, sweetness, poverty & dependance, do not want the S 3 378 1
than any--a dependant on poverty--an additional burthen on S 3 379 1
Such poverty & dependance joined to such beauty & merit, S 6 391 1
with pride & her poverty with discontent, & who was S 7 394 1
POWDER (4)
husband) you have not put any fresh powder in your hair."-- W 353 26
I think there is powder enough in my hair for my wife & W 353 26
not time even to put a little fresh powder in my hair."-- W 357 28
hairs of a side, and nothing but a dab of powder at top.-- P III 3 19 16
POWDER'D (1)
The door will be opened by a man in livery with a powder'd W 322 2
POWDERING (1)
in my night cap and powdering gown, and give as much PP III 6 300 28
POWER (233)
that it were not in your power to receive me. Yr most LS 1 244 1
that it will not be in our power to keep our promise of LS 3 246 1
I have made him sensible of my power, & can now enjoy the LS 10 257 1
that it can be in my power to inflict, for her ill-offices, LS 10 258 2
deficient in the power of saying those delightful things LS 10 258 3
Her power over him must now be boundless, as she has LS 11 259 1
You know your own rights, & that it is out of my power to LS 12 261 4
which they are known to have the power of committing. LS 14 264 3

We must commit the event to an higher power. yours LS 15 267 8
in everything but the power of being with me. LS 16 269 3
of all this, for we know power of gratitude on such a LS 18 272 2
took from me the power of speaking with any clearness. LS 20 277 6
She shall have all the retribution in my power to make; if LS 24 290 13
for tho' he is still in my power, I have given up the very LS 25 294 6
domestic pleasure in my power to procure her, will, I LS 27 297 2
Do not think me unkind for such an exercise of my power, LS 30 299 1
his wife live with you, it may be in your power to hasten. LS 39 308 1
would ere long be in her power to take Frederica into the LS 42 312 5
In every power, of which taste is the foundation, NA I 3 28 34
put that out of her power; she could strike out nothing NA I 9 64 27
greater inclination than power to dispute; "and I hope you NA I 9 67 34
of choice, woman only the power of refusal; that in both, NA I 10 77 33
as she was, having no power of getting away, was obliged NA I 11 87 53
When once my affections are placed, it is not in the power NA I 13 98 2
was greatly obliged; but it was quite out of her power. NA I 13 103 28
at parting, I would always do the best for you in my power. NA I 13 104 36
Here Catherine secretly acknowledged the power of love; NA I 15 118 12
that every thing in their power shall be done to forward NA I 15 121 26
It was not in the power of all his gallantry to detain her NA I 15 124 47
The power of early habit only could account for it. NA II 2 141 12
"You shall certainly have the best in my power to give. NA II 3 143 3
whom it was in her power to compare him with!-- NA II 5 157 5
She had no power to move. NA II 9 194 6
It is a power little worth knowing however, since it can NA II 9 196 21
"It will not be in my power, Catherine." NA II 13 224 15
a nominal mistress of it, that my real power is nothing." NA II 13 225 19
torture to herself, she trusted would not be in his power. NA II 14 231 3
good sense has very little power; and Catherine's feelings NA II 14 239 28
that moment in his power to say any thing to the purpose. NA II 15 242 8
doing every thing in his power to attach her, Henry was NA II 15 245 12
as to leave to himself no power of providing for those who SS I 1 4 3
to do every thing in his power to make them comfortable. SS I 1 5 6
much there might prudently be in his power to do for them. SS I 1 5 6
situation more comfortable than it was in his power to do. SS I 2 9 6
of feeling and every exquisite power of enjoyment. SS I 7 35 9
by insinuations of her power over such a young man; and SS I 8 36 1
the power of regarding him after their entering the house. SS I 9 43 11
But it is not in my power to delay my journey for one day!" SS I 13 64 26
But it is so uncertain, when I may have it in my power to SS I 13 65 36
"I assure you it is not in my power." SS I 13 66 44
be immediately in their power; for though Willoughby was SS I 14 71 4
He had not the power of accepting it. SS I 15 78 24
She was without any power, because she was without any SS I 15 82 47
To do him justice, he did every thing in his power to SS I 21 125 34
It raises my influence much too high; the power of SS II 2 150 33
"It will not be in my power to accept their invitation if SS II 2 151 39
but it has never been in my power to return to Barton." SS II 4 162 12
day, or the sun gained any power over a cold, gloomy SS II 7 180 1
attention in her power; and she would have tried to sooth SS II 7 180 5
me of it, to have given me the power of clearing myself? SS II 7 190 56
from my brother, that the power of receiving it had been SS II 9 207 26
it would not be in her power to avoid Edward entirely, SS II 10 214 7
all the particulars in her power of the approaching SS II 10 215 11
"people have little, have very little in their power. SS II 11 227 48
was not in Mrs. Ferrars's power to distress her by it now;- SS II 12 232 16
no power to wound them, sat pointedly slighted by both. SS II 12 232 16
and it was in their power to reconcile her to it entirely. SS II 14 247 4
in my power, as my taking them out this evening shews. SS II 14 253 21
I would ask them with all my heart, if it was in my power. SS II 14 253 23
24

about me, which it could not be in my power to satisfy." SS III 1 262 23
would do all in her power to prevent his advancing in it." SS III 1 267 38
so, because it is totally out of our power to assist him." SS III 1 268 50
But as it is, it must be out of anybody's power to assist SS III 1 269 53
should it ever be in your power to recommend him to any SS III 2 277 30
chance it should be in my power to serve him farther, I SS III 3 284 23
return the same good will, than the power of expressing it. SS III 4 290 43
by every means in my power, to make myself pleasing to her, SS III 8 320 29
a very short time, had the power of creating any return. SS III 8 322 36
of guilt that almost took from me the power of dissembling. SS III 8 324 42
more fully, have given him every encouragement in my power. SS III 9 337 18
But it was neither in Elinor's power, nor in her wish, to SS III 11 349 2
you, has put it in his power to make his own choice; and SS III 13 366 18
by every argument in her power;--told him, that in Miss SS III 14 373 3
it will always be in your power to set her off to SS III 14 375 9
future use, without your having any power over it now.-- W 352 26
I was her own neice, & he left to herself the power & the W 352 26
providing for you, to your father, & without the power.-- W 352 26
was not immediately in her power to preserve him from her W 356 28
were pleased, nor in the power of being agreeable where PP I 4 15 11
The power of doing any thing with quickness is always much PP I 10 49 27
and said all in her power to heighten her confidence in it. PP I 18 96 56
It will be in my power to assure him that her ladyship was PP I 18 97 59
him again, put it out of her power to dance with others. PP I 18 102 73
as among the least of the advantages in my power to offer. PP I 19 106 10
hand, do all in my power to prevent your being otherwise. PP I 19 107 16
or that it will be in her power to persuade him that PP I 21 119 20
before, it was yet in his power to give her fresher PP II 2 142 19
it would be in her power to say something of the Bingleys. PP II 3 147 20
The power of displaying the grandeur of his patroness to PP II 6 160 1
would vanish, if she could suppose him to be in her power. PP II 9 181 30
he has at least great pleasure in the power of choice. PP II 10 183 9
I do not know any body who seems more to enjoy the power PP II 10 183 9
I did every thing in my power to separate my friend from PP II 11 191 15
power, and suspicion certainly not in your inclination. PP II 12 202 5
any apology to be in his power; and stedfastly was she PP II 13 204 1
She read, with an eagerness which hardly left her power of PP II 13 204 1
been in her power, she had never felt a wish of enquiring. PP II 13 206 4
Elizabeth, "but it is not in my power to accept it.-- PP II 14 211 7
complete, it will be in my power to take one of you as far PP II 14 211 10
our power to prevent your spending your time unpleasantly." PP II 15 215 2
having it in our power to introduce you to very superior PP II 15 215 4
To know that she had the power of revealing what would so PP II 15 217 17
How much of pleasure or pain it was in his power to bestow! PP III 1 251 48
of the trees gave the eye power to wander, were many PP III 1 253 57
suspected that every power of pleasing would fail her. PP III 2 260 1
that she should employ the power, which her fancy told her PP III 2 266 16
the power of finding her otherwise than lovely and amiable. PP III 3 270 12
has thrown herself into the power of--of Mr. Wickham. PP III 4 277 11
Her power was sinking; every thing must sink under such a PP III 4 278 19
Gardiner readily promised every assistance in his power.-- PP III 4 280 26
She has been doing every thing in her power by thinking PP III 5 284 10
her every assistance in my power, I am afraid I did not do PP III 5 292 64
do every thing in his power to satisfy us on this head. PP III 6 295 6
but is was not in her power to give any information of so PP III 6 295 7
was forced to put it out of her power, by running away. PP III 9 320 31
you," replied Elizabeth; "but it is wholly out of my power. PP III 11 333 29
I should dread your having the power of reading again. PP III 16 368 20
by every civility in my power, that I was not so mean as PP III 16 370 32
him, unless it was in her power to offer him any attention, PP III 17 378 46
Such relief, however, as it was in her power to afford, by PP III 19 387 8
should ever have it in her power to tell them, as she now MP I 1 4 2
power to take any share in the personal charge of her. MP I 1 9 10
I could be more useful; but you see I do all in my power. MP I 1 9 12
It may hereafter be in my power, or in your's (I hope it MP I 3 23 3
enjoyed the power of being proud of her sister's. MP I 4 42 17
it must be quite out of their power to spare a horse." MP I 6 58 38
the relief of shewing her power over him; she could only MP I 7 70 30
she had not had the power of riding, and very seriously MP I 7 74 58
fullest conviction, by the power of actual comparison, of MP I 12 114 1

determinateness and his power, seemed to make allies MP I 14 130 3
It was not in Miss Crawford's power to talk Fanny into any MP I 16 150 1
and directions in her power, trying to make an artificial MP I 18 166 4
which it must be so completely beyond my power to command. MP II 4 213 39
power," was looking at Edmund for his opinion and help.-- MP II 4 215 47
of enjoyment in their power, which no subsequent MP II 6 235 18
With such means in his power he had a right to be listened MP II 6 236 21
sure he will do every thing in his power to get you made. MP II 7 250 55
which he felt in his power, and the only preparation for MP II 8 256 13
not but admit the superior power of one pleasure over his MP II 9 262 11
was the advice of absolute power, and she had only to rise MP II 10 280 33
pleasant assurance of her power, from one who she thought MP II 11 289 33
the possibility of her power over my heart ever ceasing." MP II 12 297 31
She could not have supposed it in the power of any MP II 13 303 13
that it had been in her power, without material MP II 13 304 19
me, and quite out of my power to return his good opinion." MP III 1 314 17
"Out of your power to return his good opinion! what is all MP III 1 315 18
to exist, and whose power, even of being agreeable, she MP III 2 327 6
I have told him so, that it never will be in my power-----" MP III 2 330 15
knack, the happiest power of jumping and guessing, he MP III 3 337 10
by every thing in the power of her modest gentle nature, MP III 3 342 32
Miss Crawford's power was all returning. MP III 4 349 24
over whom habit had most power, and novelty least; and MP III 4 354 46
If I had the power of recalling any one week of my MP III 5 358 9
understand how your power over Henry is thought of there! MP III 5 360 16
was trying to please you, by every attention in his power. MP III 5 362 18
it in one's power to pay off the debts of one's sex! MP III 5 363 22
the effect of the loss of power and consequence, on his MP III 6 368 7
them, without any power of engaging their respect. MP III 8 389 4
Indeed, you shall not, it shall not be in your power, for MP III 11 411 18
wanting, but nothing of that nature was ever in my power.-- MP III 13 420 2
did not see, had little power over her fancy; and she MP III 13 427 12
Here, its power was only a glare, a stifling, sickly glare, MP III 15 439 9
He was doing all in his power to quiet every thing, with MP III 16 450 9
had exposure in her power, and, supported by her mistress, MP III 16 450 10
putting herself in the power of a servant;--it was the MP III 16 455 19
he had put himself in the power of feelings on her side, MP III 17 468 21
The real evils indeed of Emma's situation were the power E I 1 5 4
her father's sake, in the power; though, as far as she was E I 3 22 6
for good company, and power of appreciating what was E I 4 26 2
She was ready to tell every thing in her power, but on E I 4 27 3
thing within your own power, or there will be plenty of E I 4 30 22
after, of having the power of choosing from among many, E I 8 63 44
Man's boasted power and freedom, all are flown; Lord of E I 9 71 14
Man's boasted power and freedom, all are flown. E I 9 73 18
of further delay in her power, being overtaken by a child E I 10 88 33
It was no longer in Emma's power to superintend his E I 11 91 1
that is, upon the power of eating and drinking, and E I 11 96 26
and as little under the power of fancy and whim in your E I 12 98 4
and secured him the power of sending to inquire after E I 13 110 10
man's not having it in his power to do as much as that. E I 14 122 22
have the power of directly saying any thing to the purpose. E I 15 125 6
Not one of them had the power of removal, or of effecting E I 17 143 14
"I cannot believe that he has not the power of coming, if E I 18 145 8
meanly exerting their power to delay it, are in their E I 18 147 18
power as well as the wish of being universally agreeable. E I 18 150 31
I had no intention, I thought I had no power of staying E II 1 162 32
his own return to England put any thing in his power. E II 2 163 4
out of Colonel Campbell's power; for though his income, by E II 2 164 5
wish to do so; but it was not immediately in her power. E II 3 179 53
again, with any necessity, or even any power of speech. E II 3 180 58
its power of censure, by bows or smiles--Mr. Knightley. E II 7 206 4
She felt that she should like to have had the power of E II 7 208 7
all the amends in her power, by helping them to large E II 8 213 6
reason herself into the power of performance; and Emma E II 10 240 6
of it, and said every thing in her power to do it away. E II 11 249 12
temper excellent in its power of forbearance, patience, E II 15 289 40
have power to draw me out, in worse weather than to-day." E II 16 294 22
"for I shall do all in my power to make them happy, which E II 18 311 39
before she had the power of forming some opinion of Frank E III 1 315 3
a dread of her returning power, and a discreet resolution E III 1 316 5
but Emma could have had power to place there and persuade E III 5 347 18
But consider;--you need not be afraid of delegating power E III 6 354 14
Mr. Knightley had done all in his power for Mr. E III 6 361 43
you all the relief in my power, be assured that no such E III 10 396 39
The power of observation would be soon given--frightfully E III 12 416 2
my dear madam, is much beyond my power of doing justice to. E III 14 439 8
Quite out of my power.-- E III 16 455 20
He had condescended to mortgage as far as he had the power, P III 1 10 20
it was quite out of his power--and how glad again, when he P III 7 54 4
Her power with him was gone for ever. P III 7 61 37
Anne longed for the power of representing to them all what P III 10 82 1
the power of attempting an introduction at all desirable. P III 12 106 18
In such moments Anne had no power of saying to herself, " P IV 1 126 18
to be comforted, that power of turning readily from evil P IV 5 154 8
satisfied; and as to the power of addressing him she felt P IV 7 180 32
the consequence in their power, draw as many eyes, excite P IV 8 185 19
too much to leave her any power of observation; and she P IV 8 186 22
"I am not one of those who neglect the reigning power to P IV 10 224 48
power to send an intelligible sentence by Captain Harville. P IV 11 239 53
gravel-walk, where the power of conversation would make P IV 11 240 59
service to you & this lady in every way in their power."-- S 1 367 1
anything out of her own power--and when on Sir Harry's S 3 375 1
his hand wd be as liberal as his heart, had he the power.-- S 3 377 1

POWERFUL (17)

the powerful protection of a very magnificent concerto----- SS II 2 149 24
25

the influence of the Pemberley house, is a powerful motive. PP I 16 81 41
there was a tolerable powerful feeling towards her, which PP I 18 94 43
there was a very powerful motive for secrecy, in addition PP III 6 297 12
was always the most powerful disturber of every decision MP III 5 364 30
as, guided by William's powerful voice, they were rattled MP III 7 376 6
that letter might be too powerful, she thought it best to E I 7 52 18
19

in happy analogy, and of powerful operation; and if the E I 16 137 13
Miss Bates's powerful, argumentative mind might have E II 12 260 26
away, still remained powerful enough to prompt to what was E II 13 268 13
"She must have some motive, more powerful than appears, E II 15 285 15
Such confidence, powerful in its own warmth, and P III 4 27 3
Mrs. Musgrove in her powerful whisper, "though we could P IV 11 230 6
to consider what powerful supports would be his! P IV 11 244 72
had a future to look forward to, of powerful consolation. P IV 12 250 5
with such a powerful discharge of unexpected obligation. S 10 414 1
motive for action, some powerful object of animation for S 10 415 1

POWERFULLY (1)

increased, more powerfully than pleasantly, by her hearing SS II 12 230 7

POWERLESS (3)

with ill-timed and powerless warmth, was beginning to be MP III 8 390 8
as made her absolutely powerless--and in this state, and E III 3 333 5
if every other leaf were powerless, he could read his own P III 1 3 1

POWERS (52)

She will have occasion for all those attractive powers for LS 3 247 1
idea of those bewitching powers which can do so much-- LS 4 248 2
it) the conversation of a woman of high mental powers. LS 14 263 2
These powers received due admiration from Catherine, to NA I 4 33 7
in which the greatest powers of the mind are displayed, in NA I 5 38 4
and to distrust his powers of giving universal pleasure. NA I 9 66 32
to frighten away all her powers of performance; and, after NA II 14 235 14
were all her thinking powers swallowed up in the NA II 14 237 20
her agreeable; but her powers had received no aid from SS I 22 127 2
to her, its healing powers on a disappointed heart might SS II 8 198 29
which might feed her powers of reflection some time, SS III 2 276 26

But we are not all born, you know, with the same powers-- SS III 5 299 35
Their powers of conversation were considerable. PP I 11 54 1
Mary's powers were by no means fitted for such a display; PP I 18 100 68
of affording pleasure, unconnected with his general powers. PP II 2 142 19
regard which his social powers had gained him in the mess. PP II 13 206 4
his wife; but where other powers of entertainment are PP II 19 236 1
case, you send me full powers to act in your name, PP III 7 303 14
she will force you to do justice to your natural powers." MP I 3 27 33
she may exert all her powers of pleasing without suspicion. MP I 5 45 12
his powers, for he was no more equal to the Baron! MP I 13 122 2
vary the scene, and exercise our powers in something new. MP I 13 125 18
It requires great powers, great nicety, to give her MP I 14 135 15
her liveliness--and she has talents to value his powers. MP II 3 199 13
incomprehensible in the powers, the failures, the MP II 4 208 12
We are to be sure a miracle every way--but our powers of MP II 4 209 12
as ever; but she felt his powers; he was entertaining, and MP II 6 232 11
powers of planning judged of by the day at Sotherton. MP II 7 245 31
With such powers as his, however, and such a disposition MP III 3 335 6
a little disordered her powers of comparing and judging. MP III 6 369 10
When really touched by affliction, her active powers had MP III 16 448 2
she had devoted all her powers to attach and amuse her in E I 1 6 6
her own situation in life, her leisure, and powers. E I 3 24 10
education as your powers would seem to promise; but you E I 5 38 11
if left quite to his own powers, and yet it is not the E I 7 51 5
Where a man does his best with only moderate powers, he E I 13 111 17
could her higher powers of mind be unfelt by the parents. E II 2 165 7
to admiration of her powers; and they had to listen to the E II 2 168 15
She knew the limitations of her own powers too well to E II 8 227 86
were feebly given, the powers of the instrument were E II 10 241 7
The remaining five were left to their own powers, and Emma E II 18 311 36
her, and tried her own powers; but, almost before she E III 9 390 18
action, and inequality of powers; and it mortified her E III 9 391 21
abilities to be captivated by very inferior powers? E III 11 413 48
to teach, should not have their powers in exercise again. E III 17 461 1
to his wife; but not of powers, or conversation, or grace, P III 6 43 5
recommended her musical powers to the notice of Mr. and P III 6 47 15
of life, she will cherish all her present powers of mind." P III 10 88 26
suspect that her keener powers might not consider either P III 10 92 47
him at liberty to exert his most open powers of pleasing. P IV 5 159 22
her natural endowments & powers, to have been preparing S 3 379 1
clever young man,--and with great powers of pleasing.-- S 4 382 1

PR WEEK (1)
a proper house at 8g pr week for Mrs G.--; she had also S 10 414 1

PRACTICABILITY (1)
or at least the practicability of a permanent removal. MP III 17 469 23

PRACTICABLE (8)
might suggest a hint of what was practicable to Marianne. SS III 1 261 12
Is it practicable for any of the others to double it? MP I 15 144 36
she hoped to make it practicable for him to chuse his own E I 10 89 38
How can you imagine such conduct practicable?" E I 18 147 17
that it might be practicable to get an invitation for her E III 14 435 4
receiving hints to exert it, beyond what was practicable. P III 6 44 7
arrangement which was practicable, drew from him some P III 8 64 4
have been resolved on, and found practicable so soon. P IV 1 122 3

PRACTICAL (1)
My theoretical and his practical knowledge together, could MP III 4 348 21

PRACTICE (17)
essentially assisted by the practice of keeping a journal." NA I 3 27 28
general opinions and practice, that a doubt sometimes SS I 14 71 4
but I am afraid my practice is much more on your sister's. SS I 17 94 42
according to the usual practice of elegant females." PP I 19 108 19
in music is to be acquired, without constant practice. PP II 8 173 10
I have been a selfish being all my life, in practice, PP III 16 369 24
power to afford, by the practice of what might be called PP III 19 387 8
enough, but I shall not be ashamed to practice economy now. MP I 3 29 50
"A very praiseworthy practice," said Edmund, "but not MP I 9 92 41
your plan for Thornton Lacey will ever be put in practice. MP II 7 242 24
but never required to bring it into daily practice. MP III 17 463 8
I suppose there is not a man in such practice any where. E I 12 101 25
effects, as I have been long in the practice of doing." E I 14 120 11
inducement to keep me in practice; for married women, you E II 14 277 38
much better than his wife's, and his practice not so bad.-- P III 6 44 6
"Well, it would serve to cure him of an absurd practice of P IV 3 144 19
ill effect of a contrary practice, as had fallen within P IV 11 231 11

PRACTICES (3)
"Happy with a man of libertine practices!-- SS III 11 350 7
of half her economical practices;-- pursuing her own SS III 12 357 3
the allusions to former practices and pursuits, suggested P IV 5 161 27

PRACTISE (11)
was the greatest stretch of forbearance I could practise. LS 24 291 14
never condescend to practise, gained her own end, and SS II 1 145 23
as she did so, that she should in future practise much. SS III 10 342 7
amended, and that I can practise the civilities, the SS III 10 347 30
have been suffered to practise it, but beyond that --and SS III 11 350 9
expect to excel, if she does not practise a great deal." PP II 8 173 8
exercise their memories, practise their duets, and grow MP I 2 20 33
The politeness which she had been brought up to practise MP I 9 91 36
might have obliged them to practise during the meal.-- E II 8 213 6
The pain of being obliged to practise concealment towards E III 17 463 15
mystery, so hateful to her to practise, might soon be over. E III 18 475 42

PRACTISED (8)
I cannot help wondering at its being practised by him." SS I 15 79 29
the self-command she had practised since her first SS III 1 261 12
at all amiss, if she practised more, and could have the PP II 8 176 27 28
knowledge of what was practised here, was on the point of MP III 15 446 35
--the great man--the practised politician, who is to read E I 18 150 32
sat down and practised vigorously an hour and a half. E II 9 231 3
endurance to be practised by her, even towards some of E III 6 363 51
the constant deception practised on her father and P IV 10 215 13

PRACTISES (2)
She practises very constantly." PP II 8 173 9
really well, unless she practises more; and though Mrs. PP II 8 173 10

PRACTISING (5)
of the day there; practising it is called, but I seldom LS 17 271 7
fault-- because I would not take the trouble of practising. PP II 8 175 25
and was actually practising her steps about the drawing- MP II 10 272 4
had been thus practising on herself, and living under!-- E III 11 411 43
"She has had the advantage, you know, of practising on me," E III 17 461 2

PRAISE (132)
of more extraordinary praise, and yesterday he actually LS 8 255 2
Reginald has a good figure, & is not unworthy the praise LS 10 258 3
as I had heard in your praise before I knew you, I had no LS 20 277 6 7
& once had said something in praise of her person. LS 22 280 1
young men for this simple praise than a quality heroine NA I 2 24 28
decisive sentence of praise or condemnation on the face of NA I 7 48 32
She said the highest things in your praise that could NA I 7 50 47
possibly be; and the praise of such a girl as Miss Thorpe NA I 7 50 47
on James's part, in praise of Miss Thorpe, till they NA I 7 51 54
"Well, my dear," said Mrs. Thorpe, impatient for praise of NA I 8 58 25
short sentences in her praise, after Thorpe had procured NA I 9 62 7
while we praise Udolpho in whatever terms we like best. NA I 14 108 17
in the world, but swore off many sentences in his praise. NA I 15 121 27
not for the world would I pain it by open praise. NA II 2 139 7
of listening to her own praise; of being thanked at least, NA II 5 157 5
authority, she boldly burst forth in wonder and praise. NA II 7 177 19
and all minuteness of praise, all praise that had much NA II 8 182 2
minuteness of praise, all praise that had much meaning, NA II 8 182 2
to say so, and the coldness of her praise disappointed him. NA II 11 213 18
offended, Elinor, if my praise of him is not in every SS I 4 19 5 6
others, and with an energy which always adorned her praise. SS I 9 43 11
in the common cant of praise she was called a beautiful SS I 10 46 2
If their praise is censure, your censure may be praise, SS I 10 50 18
warm in their praise, might be allowed to be a tolerable SS I 12 62 28
rose with this animated praise, and he set off directly SS I 21 119 3
though, in pursuit of praise for her children, the most SS I 21 120 6
encouragement from their example nor from their praise. SS II 1 141 6
spoken highly in her praise, not merely from Lucy's SS II 1 142 7
and such ill-timed praise of another, at Elinor's expense, SS II 12 235 34 35
She listened to her praise of Lucy with only moving from SS III 1 265 33
Mrs. Jennings was very warm in her praise of Edward's SS III 2 270 1
it aloud with many comments of satisfaction and praise. SS III 2 278 31
and disposition with that praise which she knew them to SS III 3 283 20
than pity, and in its unobtrusiveness entitled to praise. SS III 10 342 7
gave her instantly that praise and support which her SS III 10 346 29
how to love Edward, nor praise Elinor enough, how to be SS III 13 363 6
as warm as herself, in praise of the fullness, brilliancy W 336 14
of dirt--spoke again in praise of Half-boots--begged that W 347 21
had been cautious in her praise of Mr. Bingley before, PP I 4 14 1
what the owner said in its praise, and took it immediately. PP I 4 16 13
was glad to purchase praise and gratitude by Scotch and PP I 6 25 24
"I deserve neither such praise nor such censure," cried PP I 8 37 24
Mr. Collins was eloquent in her praise. PP I 14 66 1
occasional digressions in praise of his own humble abode, PP I 16 75 3
for his sister and her praise of himself, if he were PP I 16 83 56
"Indeed, Mr. Collins, all praise of me will be unnecessary. PP I 19 107 16
Miss Darcy's praise occupied the chief of it. PP II 1 133 2
and threw back the praise on her sister's warm affection. PP II 1 135 10
bestowing her tribute of praise on the character of its PP II 2 143 20
comforts, and mentioned nothing which she could not praise. PP II 3 146 19
obliged to take her ladyship's praise into his own hands. PP II 6 167 42
Mr. Darcy spoke with affectionate praise of his sister's PP II 8 173 7
assented to his cousin's praise; but neither at that PP II 8 176 29
of the like censure, is praise no less generally bestowed PP II 12 198 5
This was praise, of all others most extraordinary, most PP III 1 248 31
What praise is more valuable than the praise of an PP III 1 250 48
and she fancied that praise of Pemberley from her, might PP III 1 254 57
borrowed feathers, and give the praise where it was due. PP III 10 324 2
You must write again very soon, and praise him a great PP III 18 382 21
But they were too much used to company and praise, to have MP I 2 12 3
read, and heightened its attraction by judicious praise. MP I 2 22 35
"You are too kind," said Fanny, colouring at such praise; " MP I 3 26 30
were too eager in their praise of the night and their MP I 7 71 31
been more used to deserve praise than to hear it;" when MP I 11 112 33
the long paragraph in praise of the private theatricals at MP I 13 121 1
sympathizing in praise of Fanny's kind offices. MP I 18 170 23
forced herself to add her praise to the compliments each MP I 18 170 24
She had a great deal to insinuate in her own praise as to MP II 2 188 3
of notice and praise as other women were of neglect. MP II 3 198 13
"It may seem impertinent in me to praise, but I must MP II 4 209 14
a few half sentences of praise; but when he did awake and MP II 9 262 11
he spoke of her beauty with very decided praise. MP II 10 272 1
few persons present that were not disposed to praise her. MP II 10 276 13
Her praise was warm, and he received it as she could wish, MP II 10 276 14
Her temper he had good reason to depend on and to praise. MP II 12 294 16
or to repeat half that the Admiral said in his praise. MP II 13 299 5
I deferred it all, till his praise should be proved the MP II 13 300 5
the praise of a friend, as this day does prove it. MP II 13 300 5
if a word of accordant praise could be extorted from her; MP III 3 338 16
Her praise had been given in her attention, that must MP III 3 338 16
which is entitled to the highest praise and honour. MP III 3 341 28
I wish you could have overheard her tribute of praise; I MP III 4 352 42
if they did not begin, in praise of the thrush, MP III 7 375 2
her fond exclamations in praise of its beauties and MP III 10 405 17
a profusion of love and praise towards the fortunate MP III 13 420 1
She spoke of you with high praise and warm affection; yet, MP III 16 455 23
blindness of her affection, and the excess of her praise. MP III 17 463 7
She then repeated some warm personal praise which she had E I 4 34 43
I love to look at her; and I will add this praise, that I E I 5 39 21
with more voluntary praise than Emma had ever heard before. E I 8 58 9
it is not every body who will bestow praise where they may. E I 8 58 13
and friend, without praise and without blindness; but E I 11 93 5
After a little more discourse in praise of gruel, with E I 12 101 19 20
deal to be said--much praise and many comments--undoubting E I 12 104 50
indeed is much beyond praise, and he is exactly what one E I 13 116 43
I am sure there is nobody's praise that could give us so E II 1 158 12
never been denied their praise; but the skin, which she E II 2 167 12
play; and the thanks and praise which necessarily followed E II 2 168 15
little discerning; --what signified her praise? E II 3 179 53
Her regard was receiving strength by invariable praise of E II 4 184 10
much had been said in his praise; he was a very good E II 5 190 22
her with so much handsome praise, so much warm admiration, E II 5 191 28
He did not advance a word of praise beyond what she knew E II 5 191 28
understand whom I might praise without any danger of being E II 5 192 32
in; and if Harriet's praise could have satisfied her, she E II 9 231 4
joined her in all her praise; and the pianoforte, with E II 10 241 7
so that Mrs. Elton's praise passed from one mouth to E II 15 281 2
her visitor with praise, encouragement, and offers of E II 15 288 39
I have heard so much in praise of Mr. Frank Churchill.-- E II 18 309 31
Every body seemed happy; and the praise of being a E III 2 326 33
so much alike; and his praise of Harriet, his concession E III 3 332 1
Emma's colour was heightened by this unjust praise; and E III 9 385 7
Harriet repeated expressions of approbation and praise E III 11 409 35
it; she might give just praise to Harriet, or, by E III 13 429 30
young woman might think him rather cool in her praise. E III 17 464 19
Knightley's, whose fond praise of her gave the subject E III 17 466 30
quietly to a little more praise than she deserved. E III 18 475 36
He is a man whom I cannot presume to praise." E III 18 478 59
not perfectly well spelt praise, as "a fine dashing fellow, P III 6 52 33
and come back warm in his praise, and he was engaged with P III 7 53 1
add his confirmation and praise, and hope there would be P III 7 54 5
in a tone of calmer praise, such as made Anne suspect that P III 10 92 47
Lyme before; his warm praise of him as an excellent young P III 11 96 12
watchfulness; but the praise of the fine mind did not P IV 4 145 2
Such personal praise might have struck her, especially as P IV 4 146 4
to be always interesting--praise, warm, just, and P IV 7 178 24
"She had seemed to recommend and praise him!" P IV 9 211 100
justified Mr P.'s praise that Charlotte thought she had S 6 391 1
usual phrases employed in praise of their sublimity, & S 7 396 1
me every way, with her praise of this, & her praise of S 7 399 1
this, & her praise of that; but I saw what she was about.-- S 7 399 1
Miss Beaufort's side, of praise & celebrity from all who S 11 421 1

PRAISED (15)
He was not in spirits however; he praised their house, SS I 17 90 1
What! are you never to hear yourself praised!-- SS II 13 244 40
God be praised!-- SS III 8 318 10
were examined and praised; and his commendation of every PP I 13 65 26
He carved, and ate, and praised with delighted alacrity; PP II 6 163 14
for and attended, and praised; and Fanny was at first in MP I 17 160 6
honoured, and Fanny was praised, and the connection was MP III 2 329 12
He talked of Harriet, and praised her so warmly, that she E I 6 42 1
I praised the fair lady too, and altogether sent him away E I 8 59 27
to be praised, but Jane Fairfax's is much beyond it." E II 9 232 8
The whole party walked about, and looked, and praised E III 2 320 5
He praised her for being without art or affection, for E III 11 409 35
They praised the morning; gloried in the sea; sympathized P III 12 102 1 2
have heard her formerly praised; wanted very much to be P IV 10 214 12
it, & planned & built, & praised & puffed, & raised it to S 2 371 1

PRAISES (6)

"Oh! yes, quite well; and so full of your praises, he did SS I 20 115 54
unconcern with which her praises were received, formed a PP I 10 47 2
an interval to utter the praises he asked for, every view PP II 5 156 4
no airs; while the praises attending such behaviour, MP I 4 35 4
he had overheard his own praises, and did not want to hear E III 2 324 22
After one of the many praises of the day, which were P III 10 84 7
8

PRAISEWORTHY (1)
"A very praiseworthy practice," said Edmund, "but not MP I 9 92 41
PRAISING (3)
like their own, and they had great pleasure in praising it. MP I 7 69 23
We shew Fanny what a good girl we think her by praising MP II 11 285 11
she was at that moment very happy to assist in praising. E I 12 104 45
PRATT (8)
"Yes; Mr. Pratt. SS I 22 130 26
Did you never hear him talk of Mr. Pratt?" SS I 22 130 26
in the house of Mr. Pratt was a foundation for the rest, SS III 1 139 1
what little matter Mr. Steele and Mr. Pratt can give her.-- SS III 2 276 28
from the care of Mr. Pratt, I think-- nay, I am sure, it SS III 13 362 5
When Denny, and Wickham, and Pratt, and two or three more PP II 16 221 17
Pray make my excuses to Pratt, for not keeping my PP III 5 291 60
Dr & Mrs Brown--Mr Richard Pratt.-- S 6 389 1
PRAY (102)
house, "I like this man; pray heaven no harm come of it!" LS 2 244 1
to Mr Vernon, & pray bring all my grand children, & your LS 40 309 1
Pray heaven! LS 41 310 2
"And pray, sir, what do you think of Miss Morland's gown?" NA I 3 28 41
Pray let me know if they are coming. NA I 6 43 35
quite frightened, "then pray let us turn back; they will NA I 9 65 29
"Pray, pray stop, Mr. Thorpe.-- NA I 11 87 53
Well, pray do not let any body here be a restraint on you. NA I 11 90 63
"Pray do.-- NA I 15 123 41
"But pray tell me what you mean." NA II 1 133 25
Pray undeceive him as soon as you can, and tell him I beg NA II 3 145 13
Pray advise him for his own sake, and for every body's NA II 4 150 4
Pray write to me soon, and direct to my own home. NA II 12 216 2
Such a contrast between him and your brother!--pray send NA II 12 217 2
Pray explain every thing to his satisfaction; or, if he NA II 12 217 2
"Oh! pray, Miss Margaret, let us know all about it," said SS I 12 61 21
Marianne coloured, and replied very hastily, "where pray?"- SS I 13 67 62
Now, pray do,--and come while the Westons are with us. SS I 20 113 29
Is it true, pray? for of course you must know, as you have SS I 20 115 50
"Do come now," said he--"pray come--you must come--I SS I 21 119 4
"but pray do not tell it, for it's a great secret." SS I 21 125 38
park to the cottage--"but, pray, are you personally SS I 22 128 3
But pray, Colonel, how came you to conjure out that I SS II 4 163 14
"Pray, pray be composed," cried Elinor, "and do not betray SS II 6 176 5
Pray, when are they to be married?" SS II 7 181 8
Pray call again as soon as possible, and explain the SS II 7 187 40
Pray, pray let me hear it." SS II 9 204 19
about it myself, but pray tell her I am quite happy to SS III 2 275 25
Pray assure him of it." SS III 3 283 19
"Pray be quick, sir"--said Elinor impatiently--"I have no SS III 8 317 8
If the morning's tolerable, pray do us the honour of W 347 21
How long has she been such a favourite?--and pray when am PP I 6 27 51
"Pray tell your sister that I long to see her." PP I 10 47 9
on the harp, and pray let her know that I am quite in PP I 10 48 15
said Miss Bingley;--"and pray what is the result?" PP I 11 57 26
Pray do not talk of that odious man. PP I 13 61 7
"What is Mr. Darcy to me, pray, that I should be afraid of PP I 18 99 65
"Pray do, my dear Miss Lucas," she added in a melancholy PP II 3 113 26
Pray, how violent was Mr. Bingley's love?" PP II 2 141 8
Pray go to see them, with Sir William and Maria. PP II 3 149 26
"Pray, my dear aunt, what is the difference in matrimonial PP II 4 153 9
out, "Oh, my dear Eliza! pray make haste and come into the PP II 5 158 11
12
Pray, what is your age?" PP II 6 166 36
Then pray speak aloud. PP II 8 173 6
said Lady Catherine; "and pray tell her from me, that she PP II 8 173 8
"Pray let me hear what you have to accuse him of," cried PP II 8 174 17
pray, what is the usual price of an earl's younger son? PP II 10 183 15
And pray what sort of guardians do you make? PP II 10 184 19
"And pray may I ask?" but checking himself, he added in a PP II 18 234 33
with sneering civility, "pray, Miss Eliza, are not the ---- PP III 3 269 8
9
Pray make my excuses to Pratt, for not keeping my PP III 5 291 60
Pray write instantly, and let me understand it--unless it PP III 9 320 33
Pray forgive me, if I have been very presuming, or a least PP III 10 325 2
Pray read on." PP III 15 363 21
And pray, Lizzy, what said Lady Catherine about this PP III 15 364 24
You do not know what he really is; then pray do not pain PP III 17 376 34
Oh, my dear Lizzy! pray apologise for my having disliked PP III 17 378 43
"Pray, is she out, or is she not?-- MP I 5 48 30
"Pray, Miss Price, are you such a great admirer of this Mr. MP I 10 102 41
and out--but pray let me know my fate in the meanwhile. MP I 15 143 27
"Oh! sister, pray do not ask her now; for Fanny is not one MP I 18 167 9
then called out, "Oh! cousin, stop a moment, pray stop." MP II 9 261 3
Pray what is Henry going for?" MP II 10 277 17
with much agitation, "don't, Mr. Crawford, pray don't. MP II 13 301 7
Pray write to her, if it be only a line." MP II 13 306 28
In vain was her "pray, sir, don't--pray, Mr. Crawford," MP III 3 342 34
Pray do not make any more matches." E I 1 12 40
"But, my dear, pray do not make any more matches, they are E I 1 13 45
Pray excuse me; but supposing any little inconvenience may E I 5 40 24
Pray, pray attempt it. E I 6 44 16
"Pray do. E I 7 50 3
Pray, dear Miss Woodhouse, tell me what I ought to do?" E I 7 52 16
"Pray, Mr. Knightley," said Emma, who had been smiling to E I 8 60 28
No--pray let her have time to look about her." E I 8 64 46
This is saying very plainly--'pray, Miss Smith, give me E I 9 72 15
"My dear Isabella,"--exclaimed her hastily--"pray do not E I 12 104 43
If it be not inconvenient to you, pray let us go in, that E II 6 200 14
'Aye, pray do,' said Mr. Frank Churchill, 'Miss E II 9 236 46
Pray take care, Mrs. Weston, there is a step at the E II 9 239 53
Pray take care, Miss Woodhouse, ours is rather a dark E II 9 239 53
Miss Smith, pray take care. E II 9 239 53
Pray come in; do come in. E II 10 243 33
Pray do not let them talk of it. E II 11 249 11
Pray make my excuses and adieus to her." E II 13 266 5
"Pray, Emma," said he, "may I ask in what lay the great E III 5 349 27
Pray be sincere, Knightley. E III 6 355 22
"Then pray stay at Richmond." E III 6 365 71
Come, sir, pray let me hear it." E III 7 371 31
"Yes, yes, pray pass me," added her husband, with a sort E III 7 372 38
"Pray say no more. E III 16 459 50
"No, I have not; I know nothing; pray tell me." E III 18 470 11
Pray, what would become of us poor sailors' wives, who P III 8 69 43
And, pray, who is Charles Hayter? P III 9 76 13
"Pray," said Captain Wentworth, immediately, "can you tell P III 12 105 11
Pray sir," (turning to the waiter), "did not you hear,-- P III 12 106 14
good father, Miss Elliot, pray give my compliments and Mrs. P IV 1 128 29
Pray say so, with my compliments. P IV 1 128 30
for an answer, "and pray what brings the Crofts to Bath?" P IV 6 165 10
After another short silence-- "pray," said Mrs. Smith, "is P IV 9 194 19
20
Pray be so good as to mention to the other gentlemen that P IV 11 239 49
on your accident--but pray never run into Peril again, in S 5 386 1
Oh! Oh! pray, let us have none of the Tribe at Sanditon. S 6 393 1
AYER (3)
assembling regularly for the purpose of prayer, is fine!" MP I 9 86 12
I am thinking how such a prayer ought to be read, and MP III 3 340 25
his soul, and trying by prayer and reflection to calm them. P III 12 112 54

PRAYER-BOOK (1)
about sending her a prayer-book; but no second sound had MP III 7 387 45
PRAYER-BOOKS (1)
and taken down two old prayer-books of her husband, with MP III 7 387 45
PRAYERS (8)
and say their prayers in the same chapel the next morning. NA I 4 34 7
imagery of Edward reading prayers in a white surplice, and SS III 5 298 33
Prayers were always read in it by the domestic chaplain, MP I 9 86 9
pleasure, and say their prayers here twice a day, while MP I 9 86 13
left Oxford long enough to forget what chapel prayers are." MP I 9 88 18
that is, he might read prayers and preach, without giving MP II 7 247 42
by the influence of fervent prayers for his happiness. MP II 9 264 17
delivered, is more uncommon even than prayers well read. MP III 3 341 28
PRE-ARRANGED (1)
and the service pre-arranged in his mind, he offered SS III 7 311 15
PRE-ARRANGEMENT (1)
what courts the pre-arrangement of other people, should so E I 9 74 25
PRE-ARRANGING (1)
with a mind anxiously pre-arranging its result, and a SS III 10 348 34
PRE-ASSURED (1)
to his sanguine and pre-assured mind to stand in the way MP II 13 302 9
PRE-DETERMINED (2)
pre-determined to dislike, acknowledge one's superiority. LS 7 254 3
employed was easily pre-determined by all;--for after SS III 13 361 1
PRE-EMINENCE (2)
eyes could not be very long in obtaining the pre-eminence. MP III 17 470 27
But Burns--I confess my Sence of his pre-eminence Miss H.-- S 7 397 1
PRE-EMINENT (1)
with happy ease, and pre-eminent in all the lively turns, MP II 7 240 9
PRE-EMINENTLY (2)
just to note down any sentence pre-eminently beautiful? MP II 5 227 65
The destination of the thrush must be now pre-eminently MP III 7 382 29
PRE-ENGAGED (1)
He knew not that he had a pre-engaged heart to attack. MP III 2 326 3
PRE-ENGAGEMENT (1)
A pre-engagement in Edgar's Buildings prevented his NA I 7 51 54
PRE-OCCUPIED (1)
They were totally pre-occupied. MP I 17 163 21
PREACH (8)
twice every Sunday and preach such very good sermons in so MP I 11 112 30
for though he may preach himself into a good humour every MP I 11 112 31
coming to Mansfield to hear you preach your first sermon. MP II 5 227 65
You must preach at Mansfield, you know, that Sir Thomas MP II 5 227 65
he might read prayers and preach, without giving up MP II 7 247 42
and more than half a mind to take orders and preach myself. MP III 3 341 28
I could not preach, but to the educated; to those who were MP III 3 341 30
of her coming to Lyme, to preach patience and resignation P III 11 101 26
PREACHED (1)
Miss Nash has put down all the tests he has ever preached E I 9 75 26
PREACHER (6)
Howard spoken of as the preacher, & as having given them W 343 20
hearing, supposing the preacher to have the sense to MP I 9 92 46
A fine preacher is followed and admired; but it is not in MP I 9 93 49
The preacher who can touch and affect such an MP III 3 341 28
I never listened to a distinguished preacher in my life, MP III 3 341 30
may be as a celebrated preacher in some great society of MP III 16 458 30
PREACHERS (3)
very popular & most admired preachers generally have.-- W 343 20
They are known to the largest part only as preachers. MP I 9 93 49
great moralists and preachers, she had been eloquent on a P III 11 101 26
PREACHES (1)
and clever, and often preaches good sermons, and is very MP I 11 111 28
PREACHING (6)
he had already had the honour of preaching before her. PP I 14 66 1
the time I was dressing, preaching and talking away just PP III 9 319 24
You must feel it; and the usual satisfaction of preaching PP III 11 333 29
but it is not in the preaching only that a good clergyman MP I 9 93 49
thought reading was reading, and preaching was preaching. MP III 3 339 23
And, I do not know that I should be fond of preaching MP III 3 341 30
PREARRANGED (1)
used, but found it all prearranged; and when she would MP II 8 253 7
PRECARIOUS (1)
hints of my father's precarious state of health, as common LS 11 259 1
PRECAUTION (4)
had taken the wise precaution of bringing with her their SS I 6 31 9
"But why should such precaution be used?-- SS III 5 296 19
travels with her own sheets; and excellent precaution. E II 18 306 12
Anxious to omit no possible precaution, Anne struggled, P IV 11 239 48
49
PRECAUTIONS (2)
Not all her precautions, however, could save her from MP I 3 28 38
make it;--impossible to feel cold with such precautions. E I 13 115 37
PRECEDE (5)
I am thankful that my last letter will precede this by so LS 24 291 18
in the thought of all that was to precede them. W 322 3
for such arrangements as must precede the wedding. MP II 3 202 27
of the going to London, which was to precede her return. MP III 14 430 6
which must briefly precede it--the joyful consent of her MP III 15 444 25
PRECEDED (7)
were immediately preceded by a lady, an acquaintance of NA I 8 54 4
sister-in-law, who had preceded them to the house of her SS II 14 249 9
the important party, preceded by the attentive master of W 329 9
of the servant who preceded it, were familiar to them. PP III 14 351 1
have preceded them, or at least should make any impression. MP III 15 438 4
Mr. Knightley's eyes had preceded Miss Bates's in a glance E III 5 346 17
of what had directly preceded the present moment, which P IV 11 241 59
PRECEDENCE (4)
Sir Walter Elliot must ever have the precedence. P III 3 24 36
apt not to give her the precedence that was her due, when P III 6 45 10
Nobody doubts her right to have precedence of mamma, but P III 6 46 10
given Mrs. Musgrove precedence; but then, she had received P IV 2 129 3
PRECEDENT (1)
A most dangerous precedent indeed!-- E II 18 305 6
PRECEDES (1)
character generally precedes her; and Highbury had long E II 14 276 35
PRECEDING (17)
the settled rain of the two preceding days had occasioned. SS I 9 40 3
Willoughby had spent the preceding evening with them, and SS I 12 60 8
what a more animated look had intimated the preceding one. SS I 18 96 1
warranted by anything preceding, and most severely SS II 7 188 43
every symptom more favourable than on the preceding visit. SS III 7 310 8
her observation the preceding evening had marked who the SS III 8 328 61
the regiment since the preceding Wednesday; several of the PP I 12 60 7
Easter was approaching, and the week preceding it, was to PP II 7 170 6
preceding day, opened to them a new idea on the business. PP III 2 260 1
There was not much in the question, nor in the preceding PP III 2 263 9
when, according to all preceding plans, she was to remove MP II 11 287 17
He had dined at the parsonage only the preceding day. MP III 4 349 24
his own loud voice preceding him, as with something of the MP III 7 379 19
in the course of the preceding month, there was no time to P III 5 33 5
She had died the preceding summer, while he was at sea. P III 11 96 12
Their conversation, the preceding evening, did not P III 12 107 23
In his preceding attempts to attach himself to Louisa P IV 11 242 63
PRECEPTS (1)
the mind by the highest precepts, and the strongest P III 11 101 24
PRECINCTS (1)
such ease in the very precincts of the Abbey, and driven NA II 5 161 25
PRECIOUS (28)
one moment of your precious time by sending her to Edward LS 7 252 1
hasten with the precious treasure into your own chamber, NA II 5 160 21
She seized, with an unsteady hand, the precious manuscript, NA II 6 169 11
Mrs. Jennings's entrance, escaped with the precious card. SS II 5 169 14

It was a valued, a precious trust to me; and gladly would SS II 9 208 28
In such moments of precious, of invaluable misery, she SS III 6 303 9
Precious as was the company of her daughter to her, she SS III 14 378 13
a moment of the time so precious; but as she reached the PP III 4 276 6
unable to waste such a precious occasion, she suddenly got PP III 13 345 12
13

can justify, if such precious remains of the earliest MP II 6 235 18
affection, and with some very precious sensations on her's. MP II 9 270 40
When Mansfield was considered, time was precious; and the MP III 15 445 29
"What a precious deposit!" said he with a tender sigh, as E I 6 49 43
and being the bearer of something exceedingly precious. E I 8 68 58
It seemed too precious an offering for any degree of E I 9 77 43
availing himself of the precious opportunity, declaring E I 15 129 24
"every day more precious and more delightful than the day E II 12 260 21
Emma read the words most precious treasures on the top. E III 4 338 9
thinking of a much more precious circumstance--of Mr. E III 11 406 24
lose none of their precious intercourse of friendship and E III 12 416 1
This one half hour had given to each the same precious E III 13 432 41
own; and a daily intercourse had become precious by habit. P III 5 36 19
A beloved home made over to others; all the precious rooms P III 6 47 16
pleasure of taking the precious volume into his own hands P III 8 66 22
Scenes had passed in Uppercross, which made it precious. P IV 1 123 8
had been; of having the precious name of "Lady Elliot" P IV 5 160 26
"Tell me not that I am too late, that such precious " P IV 11 237 42
& precious, as she paid in proportion to her fortune.-- S 11 421 1
PRECIPITANCE (3)
to a degree of precipitance which ill accords with the LS 30 300 1
so very laudable in a precipitance which must leave very PP I 10 49 27
precipitance merely to shew off before the ladies." PP I 10 49 28
PRECIPITATE (4)
that I am cautious of appearing forward and precipitate. PP I 13 65 25
you may incur, by a precipitate closure with this PP III 15 362 15
Crawford had been too precipitate. MP III 3 335 6
his hands; she was too precipitate by half a second, she P III 12 109 32
PRECIPITATION (1)
It was a foolish precipitation last Christmas, but the MP III 14 434 13
PRECISE (4)
had not before had any precise limits, was instantly SS II 14 254 26
We must not be over precise Edmund. MP I 15 141 22
"He had been so fortunate as to--I forget the precise E II 3 174 32
day, the precise day of the instrument's coming to hand. E II 10 241 12
PRECISELY (24)
in the world, & seems precisely in her proper place, at LS 26 295 1
and the affair was arranged precisely after my plan. SS II 14 252 18
that I ever precisely heard Mrs. Ferrars say it herself-- SS III 5 297 31
This was precisely what Emma had longed for; & she W 339 18
But these, I suppose, are precisely what you are without." PP I 11 57 21
appeared precisely the young man to deserve and attach her. MP I 4 39 10
The circumstance was precisely as this lady has MP I 5 49 35
It is the very room for a theatre, precisely the shape and MP I 13 125 14
poor, is precisely what I have no manner of concern with. MP II 4 213 41
The ground seems precisely formed for it. MP II 7 242 23
this is the very thing, precisely what I wished for! this MP II 9 262 8
The yeomanry are precisely the order of people with whom I E I 4 29 14
you yesterday he was precisely the the height of Mr. Perry. E II 3 174 39
there, consisting precisely of those whose society was E II 7 208 7
It was precisely what Emma would have wished, had she E II 16 291 5
This is precisely what I wanted. E II 17 304 27
Frank the whole spring--precisely the season of the year E II 18 308 30
man, and his manners are precisely what I like and approve- E III 2 321 15
Precisely such had the paragraph originally stood from the P III 1 3 2
two girls, that it was precisely what they did not wish, P III 10 83 4
"That is precisely what I was going to observe," cried Mrs. P IV 11 230 7
us the most) may be precisely such as cannot be brought P IV 11 234 30
himself; and that precisely as he became fully satisfied P IV 11 243 66
Mr. Elliot's manners had precisely pleased her in their P IV 12 249 3
PRECISENESS (1)
Miss Crawford found a sister without preciseness or MP I 4 41 17
PRECISION (4)
to a precision the most charming young man in the world. NA II 16 251 5
with more elegance than precision, stiled Willoughby, SS I 10 46 1
arrange with rather more precision the degree of PP I 10 50 38
could be supposed attractive, with spirit and precision. E II 13 265 5
PRECLUDE (2)
distinct, as almost to preclude the means of ever hearing MP I 1 4 2
and happiness must preclude false indulgence and physic." E II 18 311 39
PRECLUDED (2)
was its kind; but they precluded that pain which Lady P IV 1 125 17
village like Sanditon, precluded by its size from S 1 368 1
PRECLUDES (1)
reconciliation with her mother precludes every dearer hope. LS 24 291 16
PRECLUDING (1)
An union of a different tendency, and precluding the PP III 8 312 16
PRECONCEIVED (2)
moving, proved her as ready as her aunt had preconceived. E III 5 349 25
inch of back & shoulders beyond her preconceived idea. S 10 415 1
PRECONCERTED (1)
Anne, remembering the preconcerted visits, at all hours, P IV 10 216 17
PREDESTINED (1)
Thursday, predestined to hope and enjoyment, came; and MP II 9 265 21
PREDETERMINATION (1)
according to the predetermination of Mrs. Grant and her MP II 7 239 4
PREDICAMENT (3)
else who is in the same predicament," glancing half MP I 15 143 26
Miss Bates stood in the very worst predicament in the E I 3 21 4
for a gentleman in his predicament:--he might there be P III 2 14 10
PREDICT (4)
intimacy, and ventured to predict the accomplishment of PP II 1 133 2
to predict their marrying with almost equal advantage. MP I 1 3 1
it was what every body else must think of and predict. E I 4 35 44
and another might predict disagreements among their E III 17 468 36
PREDICTED (1)
a tete so much less painful than her fears had predicted. MP III 5 365 33
PREDICTION (1)
morning's prediction, how was it to be accounted for?-- NA II 6 170 12
PREDICTIONS (2)
disclaimed, and the gentleman's predictions were verified. NA II 1 133 29
the confidence, the predictions of the small band of true E III 19 484 12
PREDISPOSED (1)
as might warrant strong suspicion in a predisposed mind. MP III 5 362 17
PREDOMINANCE (1)
or at least, by the predominance of virtue, atone for PP II 13 206 4
PREDOMINATE (1)
wishes to predominate, she began to regret that he came. PP III 3 268 7
PREDOMINATED (1)
Sometimes Mr. Elton predominated, sometimes the Martins; E II 4 184 11
PREFACE (2)
countenance, & after some preface informed me in so many LS 22 281 4
writer again; but I will not delay you by a long preface.-- E III 14 436 7
PREFACED (1)
Her cousin prefaced his speech with a solemn bow, and PP I 18 98 61
PREFER (37)
another place in England open to me, I would prefer it. LS 2 246 1
I infinitely prefer the tender & liberal spirit of LS 16 269 3
heroic about her, should prefer cricket, base ball, riding NA I 1 15 3
I prefer light eyes, and as to complexion--do you know--I NA I 6 42 30
Which would she prefer? NA II 7 176 17
to know that he would prefer the church to every other SS II 2 149 25
If you prefer this room to the other, there is no reason W 334 13
I shall wear one tomorrow that I think you will prefer to W 353 26
any kind too well, not to prefer being below, at all risks, W 361 30
prefer a plain dish to a ragout, had nothing to say to her. PP I 8 35 2
"Do you prefer reading to cards?" said he; "that is rather PP I 8 37 22
that Charlotte should not prefer the dining parlour for PP II 7 168 1
whom she did not prefer, his coming would furnish one PP II 7 170 6
I should infinitely prefer a book." PP II 16 223 23
his remembrance, and prefer him to every other man, that PP II 17 227 26
She has the advantage in every feature, and I prefer her MP I 5 45 8
to have the sense to prefer Blair's to his own, do all MP I 9 92 46
Nobody wonders that they should prefer the line where MP I 11 109 18
that Tom Bertram would prefer a comedy, and his sisters MP I 13 124 13
doubting only whether to prefer Lord Duberly or Dr. MP I 14 131 6
They both declared they should prefer it to anything. MP III 7 379 15
was Lady Lascelles's, and prefer it to almost any I know MP III 9 394 1
however, I should still prefer you, because it strikes me, MP III 14 434 13
I would infinitely prefer any increase of the pain of MP III 16 458 30
learn to prefer soft light eyes to sparkling dark ones.-- MP III 17 470 27
If you prefer Mr. Martin to every other person; if you E I 7 53 21
whom Mr. Elton could prefer, she should think the luckiest E I 8 68 58
willing to prefer Cromer to south end as he could himself." E I 12 106 60
of spirits which would have made her prefer being silent. E II 18 311 36
the person whom you might prefer, would be too greatly E III 4 341 35
Come on a donkey, however, if you prefer it. E III 6 356 27
should prefer Henrietta to Louisa, or Louisa to Henrietta. P III 9 77 18
could be allowed to prefer another man, there was nothing P IV 6 167 21
I prefer walking." P IV 7 176 11
I wd rather see his partner indeed--I would prefer the S 1 365 1
& prudence obliged him to prefer the quietest sort of ruin S 8 405 2
obliged to you, replied Charlotte--but I prefer tea." S 10 417 1
PREFERABLE (5)
letter, it was at least preferable to giving the SS III 4 287 26
would have been far preferable to her, it would not have SS III 5 297 31
almost think any thing would have been preferable to this. MP I 17 160 6
the barouche-landau; it will be so very much preferable. E II 14 274 28
a simple dress is so infinitely preferable to finery. E II 17 302 22
PREFERENCE (38)
heart I feel little--scarcely any doubt of his preference. SS I 4 21 15
on that result of his preference of her, which her mother SS I 4 22 18
the continuance of his preference seemed very uncertain; SS I 18 96 1
attributed that preference of herself which soon became SS I 22 127 1
encouragement from a preference only given her, because SS II 13 238 2
a most unconquerable preference for his niece, yet had I SS III 13 362 5
they were never insulted by her real favour and preference. SS III 14 375 10
can be, but I still profess my preference of a white skin. W 357 28
But you are always giving her the preference." PP I 1 4 26
was yielding to the preference which she had begun to PP I 6 21 1
We can all begin freely--a slight preference is natural PP I 6 21 2
we stood--the sort of preference which was often given me." PP I 16 80 32
dances especially,--a preference which I trust my cousin PP I 17 87 13
in love, their preference of each other was plain enough PP II 2 142 18
by encouraging the preference which she believed she had PP II 13 207 6
Pleased with the preference of one, and offended by the PP II 13 208 8
and her preference secured at any time by their renewal. PP II 18 233 25
help giving him the preference even over Wickham, much as PP III 15 364 24
Mrs. Grant, I believe, suspects him of a preference for MP I 12 116 8
the conviction of his preference for Maria had been forced MP I 17 160 8
subject--his decided preference of a quiet family-party to MP II 2 190 6
retirement, her decided preference of a London life--what MP II 8 255 10
with anything like a preference, he had always believed it MP III 3 335 6
loved, and talk to him of his infant preference of herself. MP III 7 381 25
am convinced, that she is not without a decided preference. MP III 13 421 2
not to betray such a preference of her uncle's house: it MP III 14 431 8
a possible thing in preference to a division of the party. E I 13 108 2
to conceal than her own preference; Mr. Dixon, perhaps, E II 2 169 16
Mr. Dixon's preference of her music to her friend's, I can E II 8 217 33
no actual preference--remained a little longer doubtful. E II 8 228 93
the value of his preference, and the character of his E II 11 250 19
admiration, a conscious preference of herself; and this E II 12 262 38
But that it will be a fortunate preference is more than I E III 4 342 39
she feel any right of preference herself--she submitted, E III 9 390 19
her admiration and preference of Frank Churchill before E III 11 402 1
a compliment implied, a preference inferred, had been E III 11 409 35
that there was a preference--and a preference which I E III 13 426 16
a preference which I never believed him to deserve.-- E III 13 426 16
PREFERENCES (1)
Her feelings, her preferences had each known the happiness NA II 2 141 11
PREFERMENT (9)
amount of Mr. Morland's preferment, trebling his private NA II 15 245 12
on his getting that preferment, of which, at present, SS III 2 276 26
The preferment, which only two days before she had SS III 3 283 20
especially towards those to whom he owes his preferment. PP I 18 101 71
I have been in early preferment; and I trust I am resigned. PP I 20 114 32
lieu of the preferment, by which he could not be benefited. PP II 12 200 5
to procure him better preferment; but it must not be MP I 3 23 3
with the certainty of preferment, may be fairly suspected, MP I 11 109 20
I am no young lady on her preferment. E III 6 354 14
PREFERRED (30)
She was fond of all boys' plays, and greatly preferred NA I 1 13 1
but in her heart she preferred it to any place she had NA II 11 212 17
to Mrs. Dashwood, she preferred going directly to the SS I 5 26 6
I always preferred the church, as I still do. SS I 19 102 4
and beneficence has preferred me to the valuable rectory PP I 13 62 12
others, that Bingley preferred your eldest sister, to any PP II 12 197 5
to her support, and consequently preferred her husband's. PP III 1 256 61
and must, therefore, be preferred; and, indeed, his being MP I 5 47 27
of being really the one preferred, comforted her under it, MP I 10 105 52
was slighted, Maria was preferred; the smile of triumph MP I 14 133 12
thanking them, said, "he preferred remaining where he was MP II 1 177 5
though Fanny would have preferred a longer and a plainer MP II 8 258 17
Fanny, in those early days, had preferred her to Susan; MP III 7 386 40
to, or read to, Edmund was the companion he preferred. MP III 14 429 2
were what he preferred, and, unless he fancied himself at E I 3 20 1
that the idea of being preferred by him would have all the E I 4 35 45
character of the one preferred--and acknowledge herself E I 17 141 5
"One would rather have a stranger preferred than one's E II 6 202 33
he would have preferred the society of William Larkins. E II 12 258 6
Colonel Campbell rather preferred an olive. E III 2 323 19
girl--infinitely to be preferred by any man of sense and E III 2 331 55
she cried, satisfied to have no one preferred to herself.-- E III 6 355 18
very scarce--chili preferred--white wood finest flavour of E III 6 358 35
he was not wanted there, preferred being out of doors."-- E III 13 424 1
enough to dissuade him from it, and make Bath preferred. P III 2 14 10
Which of the two sisters was preferred by Captain P III 9 74 8
It suited Mary best to think Henrietta the one preferred, P III 9 75 12
of the Lake were to be preferred, and how ranked the P III 11 100 23
Anne Elliot, and to be preferred by her, to her own family P IV 5 158 19
Mrs G. had preferred a small, retired place, like Sanditon, S 11 421 1
PREFERRING (10)
always preferring those which she was forbidden to take.-- NA I 1 13 1
were exactly alike in preferring the country to every NA I 10 71 3
preferring salmon to cod, or boiled fowls to veal cutlets. SS II 4 160 2
"Oh! no doubt he is very sincere in preferring an income MP I 11 110 23
actual comparison, of her preferring his younger brother. MP I 12 114 1
of preferring her style to that of any printed author. MP III 12 419 7
and Anne, very much preferring the office of musician to a P III 6 47 15
Anne was most sincere in preferring a walk with Mr. Elliot. P IV 7 174 3
her to be preferring him, it would have been another thing. P IV 8 182 10
Bs--, though naturally preferring any thing to smallness & S 11 421 1
PREFERS (2)
Though Julia fancies she prefers tragedy, I would not MP I 14 134 12
Fairfax prefers devoting the time to you and Mrs. Bates?" E II 1 161 24
PREJUDICE (19)
by Charles Smith to the prejudice of Lady Susan, as I am LS 14 264 4
that some attempts were made to prejudice you against me. LS 20 277 6

7
and her determined prejudice against herself, to SS II 13 238 1
and liberality, to the prejudice of his banished brother, SS III 5 298 32
"And never allow yourself to be blinded by prejudice?" PP I 18 93 34
With a strong prejudice against every thing he might say, PP II 13 204 1
The general prejudice against Mr. Darcy is so violent, PP II 17 226 23
by the kind of family prejudice, to which he attributed PP III 1 249 37
it was a circumstance which must prejudice her against him. PP III 13 350 52
prejudice, the blindness of love, she ought to be believed. MP II 3 201 22
She is exactly the woman to do away every prejudice of MP II 12 293 10
You must not prejudice Fanny against him. MP II 12 296 28
was all the conquest of prejudice, which he was so ready MP III 14 436 16
Will not the old prejudice be too strong?" E I 12 104 44
Mrs. Weston gives me a decided prejudice in his favour." E I 18 150 35
she considered it as a prejudice and mistake, arising P III 2 14 11
matter might add another shade of prejudice against him. P IV 7 178 27
it secure us, to the prejudice of E. Bourne & Hastings."-- S 4 382 1
I to be filling my house to the prejudice of Sanditon?-- S 7 401 1
PREJUDICED (9)
to dislike me, & prejudiced against all my past actions. LS 10 257 1
to be particularly prejudiced against her; but it is more LS 12 261 4
my sister is unhappily prejudiced beyond the hope of LS 14 264 2
and Marianne, who, prejudiced against him for being SS I 10 50 13
not more undiscerning, than you are prejudiced and unjust." SS I 10 50 18
that she had been blind, partial, prejudiced, absurd. PP II 13 208 7
from yourself, but from prejudiced persons, whose opinions MP I 11 110 24
to evil. we are both prejudiced; you against, I for him; E I 18 150 33
"Prejudiced! I am not prejudiced." E I 18 150 34
PREJUDICES (8)
so amiable in the prejudices of a young mind, that one is SS I 11 56 12
consequence of the prejudices I had been encouraging. PP II 17 226 21
how gradually all her former prejudices had been removed. PP III 16 368 19
Her prejudices, I trust, are not so strong as they were. MP III 13 422 2
a recantation of past prejudices and errors, than saying E II 2 168 15
consistent--but she had prejudices on the side of ancestry; P III 2 11 2
The prejudices which had met her at first in some quarters, S 3 379 1
And their very connection prejudices him.-- S 7 402 1
PRELIMINARY (1)
having been a single preliminary difference to modify of P III 5 32 3
PRELUDE (2)
party into raptures by a prelude on the pianoforte, of her NA I 1 16 10
hear that it was but the prelude to something so MP I 16 150 1
PREMATURE (4)
such an unlooked-for premature arrival as a most untoward MP II 1 176 4
have no doubt, some time or other; only a little premature. E III 5 345 14
the intelligence to prove, in some measure, pr^mature. E III 18 473 27
smiling, said, "I have been a little premature, I perceive. P IV 9 195 26
27
PREMATURELY (2)
silver, broken perhaps prematurely by some strange NA II 6 163 2
to, and of becoming prematurely an object of disgust P III 3 19 16
PREMEDITATED (2)
been premeditated, and how deeply contrived by her!-- SS II 7 190 58
and cheating a person of their premeditated contempt. PP I 10 52 50
PREMEDITATION (1)
her distress at such premeditation, and her intreaty that PP III 13 345 13
PREMISES (8)
The premises are before you. NA II 4 152 26
ornamental part of the premises, consisting of a walk NA II 11 214 25
its more immediate premises; and the rest of the morning SS III 6 303 10
formed on mistaken premises, my behaviour to you at the PP III 16 367 12
an oak just beyond their premises, was forced, though not MP II 4 205 3
I think the house and premises may be made comfortable, MP II 7 242 24
considerable aspect and premises of the great house, about P III 5 36 20
before, as soon as the premises of the said house were S 1 364 1
PREPARATION (26)
The important affair, which many words of preparation NA I 15 124 48
They all rose up in preparation for a round game. SS II 1 144 10
for a better preparation for death; and that was given. SS II 9 207 26
as to the time, or the preparation necessary; but I SS III 4 291 50
every thing in preparation, the day almost fixed----- SS III 8 328 63
Preparation!--day!-- SS III 8 328 63
painful, started up in preparation for going, and said, " SS III 8 331 70
71
After a slight preparation for good news, the letter was PP III 7 305 43
It was Fanny's first ball, though without the preparation MP I 12 117 11
but neither play nor preparation were otherwise much MP I 15 142 24
thing, the sweep of every preparation would be sufficient. MP II 2 187 2
of every theatrical preparation at Mansfield, the removal MP II 2 194 21
even the delay of much preparation, would have been an MP II 3 202 26
interests of preparation were enjoyments in themselves. MP II 5 219 27
his power, and the only preparation for the ball which he MP II 8 256 13
while the tea was in preparation--and wished Rebecca would MP III 15 439 9
going to separate in preparation for the regular four E I 9 81 78
would undoubtedly rush upon her without preparation. E II 3 177 51
and the instrument in preparation;--and at the same moment E II 8 226 85
How often is happiness destroyed by preparation, foolish E II 12 259 17
destroyed by preparation, foolish preparation!-- E II 12 259 17
Now, however, it was absolutely to be; every preparation E III 1 318 11
to the bustle and preparation, the regular eating and E III 6 352 2
In two minutes after Charles's preparation, the others P III 7 59 25
She had the advantage of him, in the preparation of the P IV 7 175 6
two moments preparation for the sight of Captain Wentworth. P IV 11 239 55
PREPARATIONS (16)
with many particulars of preparations and other matters. SS II 8 199 37
woman of fortune, the preparations for her entertainment W 348 23
coming to dinner, preparations were made for his W 360 30
for the necessary preparations of settlements, new PP I 18 103 77
on his, side, by preparations for the reception of his PP II 2 139 1
Other preparations were also in hand. MP I 14 130 1
act nothing--and the preparations will be all so much MP I 15 141 22
In all the important preparations of the mind she was MP II 3 202 26
The preparations of new carriages and furniture might wait MP II 3 202 26
The preparations meanwhile went on, and Lady Bertram MP II 8 254 9
and make the necessary preparations for his removal on MP III 7 381 24
but the necessary preparations to wait for; and when he E II 4 182 6
The preparations must take their time, nothing could be E II 12 257 1
were useable, but no preparations could be ventured on, E III 6 353 6
in assisting their preparations, and sending them off at P IV 1 122 5
Their preparations, however, were stopped short. P IV 10 226 63
PREPARATORY (5)
and affectionate preparatory speeches for a while. MP I 4 34 2
felt very much obliged to you for your preparatory hint. E II 6 198 7
The preparatory interest of this dinner, however, was not E II 16 291 7
together for the purpose of preparatory inspection. E III 2 319 3
to put the horses to, preparatory to their now daily drive E III 18 475 38
PREPARE (30)
Prepare my dear madam, for the worst. LS 24 291 17
With such news to communicate, and such a visit to prepare NA I 15 124 47
with a most happy indifference to prepare herself for bed. NA II 6 167 10
No theatre, no rooms to prepare for. NA II 9 195 18
you--does our education prepare us for such atrocities? NA II 9 197 29
Prepare for your sister-in-law, Eleanor, and such a sister- NA II 10 206 31
impartial opinion, and prepare his objections on a fairer NA II 11 208 2
I must go and prepare a dinner for you to be sure." NA II 11 211 9
into Devonshire, to prepare the house for their mistress's SS I 5 26 6
to you, yet unable to prepare you for it in the least.-- SS III 1 263 29
had ever occurred to prepare him for what followed;--and SS III 13 364 13
The ladies were invited upstairs to prepare for dinner. W 351 25
If there had not been a Netherfield ball to prepare for PP I 17 88 15
"You shall hear then--but prepare yourself for something PP II 8 175 18
for the present, and prepare for another disappointment. PP II 19 237 3
her satisfaction, and prepare for such a visitor, when PP III 2 261 5
repeated the other, as she ran into her room to prepare. PP III 4 281 28
had received orders to prepare for the arrival of her PP III 11 331 13
altered in her, and must prepare ourselves for gross MP I 1 10 14
And you may say, if you please, that I shall prepare my MP I 6 59 41
with him, and help him prepare for the evening, without MP I 18 170 23
He was gone before any thing had been said to prepare him MP II 1 181 17
to harden and prepare herself against farther questioning. MP III 1 316 33
subject to his niece, to prepare her briefly for its being MP III 2 331 19
blessing of what was, and prepare her mind for what might MP III 14 432 10
The advantage of much sleep to prepare them for their MP III 15 444 27
She had hurried on before her guests to prepare her father E III 5 345 15
conversation that could prepare him at this time for my E III 17 465 27
a blessing indeed; and prepare for it all the immortality P IV 11 240 59
Sir Walter at last to prepare his pen with a very good P IV 12 248 2
PREPARED (72)
I was by no means prepared for such an event, nor can I LS 3 246 1
at least I was myself prepared for an improper degree of LS 6 251 1
triumphing over a mind prepared to dislike me, & LS 10 257 1
We are therefore prepared for her arrival, & expected them LS 17 269 1
warm wine and water, and prepared herself for bed, as to NA I 3 29 52
to begin his journey to London, prepared to set off. NA I 15 122 29
"And are you prepared to encounter all the horrors that a NA II 5 157 13
She remembered with what feelings she had prepared for a NA II 10 200 2
to the breakfast-parlour, where breakfast was prepared. NA II 13 227 27
the law in his family, prepared for no reluctance but of NA II 15 247 15
merit, or better prepared by habitual suffering, to NA II 16 251 5
The instrument was unlocked, every body prepared to be SS I 7 35 8
She was prepared to be wet through, fatigued, and SS I 13 63 1
with an F. and this prepared a future mine of raillery SS I 18 99 15
spite of all that had passed, was not prepared to witness. SS II 3 155 6
Elinor was not prepared for such a question, and having no SS II 5 172 40
she went or staid, prepared without one look of hope, or SS II 6 175 1
I was prepared to meet you with the pleasure which our SS II 7 187 42
she went or not: and she prepared quietly and mechanically SS II 14 249 7
hurrying importance as prepared her to hear something SS III 1 257 2
3
"Well," said Elinor, "it is a comfort to be prepared SS III 2 275 23
I saw that my own feelings had prepared my sufferings, and SS III 10 345 28
she hoped, with address; prepared her anxious listener SS III 10 347 33
two long tables were prepared, Ld Osborne was to be seen W 332 11
where the tables were prepared, & the neat upper maid was W 336 14
But I can assure the young ladies that I come prepared to PP I 13 65 25
another table with Mr. Bennet, and prepared for backgammon. PP I 14 69 17
tranquillity; and though prepared, as he told Elizabeth, PP I 15 71 6
She had dressed with more than usual care, and prepared in PP I 18 89 1
Elizabeth was prepared to see him in his glory; and she PP II 5 155 4
Elizabeth, however astonished, was at least more prepared PP III 1 254 57
From what he said of Miss Darcy, I was thoroughly prepared PP III 5 284 14
it is right to be prepared for the worst, there is no PP III 5 288 37
Lydia's last letter, she had prepared her for such a step. PP III 5 290 50
one of the benches, and prepared to be happy; for the PP III 10 321 1
room, where Edmund prepared her paper, and ruled her lines MP I 2 16 20
and Miss Crawford was prepared to find a great chasm in MP I 6 52 1
where a collation was prepared with abundance and elegance. MP I 9 84 1
Fanny's imagination had prepared her for something grander MP I 9 85 6
prepared, by general agreement, to return to the house. MP I 10 103 49
that displeasure, which Maria had been half prepared for. MP I 15 138 1
most palpitating heart, while the others prepared to begin. MP I 18 172 32
she was complete; being prepared for matrimony by an MP II 3 202 26
which way to look, or how to be prepared for the answer. MP II 7 250 60
and injuring the noble fire which the butler had prepared. MP II 10 272 4
for her aunt, and prepared her materials without knowing MP II 13 307 30
She is very angry with you, Fanny; you must be prepared MP III 4 352 40
he has, how was I to be prepared to meet him with any MP III 4 353 45
and his manners coarser, than she had been prepared for. MP III 8 389 3
As she opened and saw its length she prepared herself for MP III 13 420 1
must be spoken to, Susan prepared, every thing got ready. MP III 15 443 25
the last thing before he prepared for the happiness of E I 13 111 14
of a much darker night than he had been prepared for. E I 15 128 22
This she had been prepared for when she entered the house; E II 1 156 6
She had not been prepared to have Jane Fairfax succeed Mr. E II 1 156 6
Harriet had not been at home; but a note had been prepared E II 4 184 11
"Elegant, agreeable manners, I was prepared for," said he; E II 5 192 30
Their love of society, and their new dining-room, prepared E II 7 207 6
There was a seriousness in Harriet's manner which prepared E III 4 337 3
He saw a short word prepared for Emma, and given to her E III 5 348 22
in the Abbey, especially prepared for him by a fire all E III 6 357 33
his cabinets, had been prepared for his old friend, to E III 6 362 43
With all the spirits she could command, she prepared him E III 17 465 28
It was no more than the principals were prepared for; they E III 17 468 35
"You are prepared for the worst, I see--and very bad it is. E III 18 470 12
Emma gave a start, which did not seem like being prepared-- E III 18 470 13
good spirits; Sir Walter prepared with condescending bows P III 5 35 18
falling of the cliff prepared the ground for such a state, P III 11 95 9
her sister's being in any degree prepared for the news. P IV 6 165 9
of real penetration & prepared for some fuller remarks-- S 7 401 1
For objections of this nature, Charlotte was not prepared, S 7 401 1
having noticed & caressed them all,--she prepared to go.-- S 9 410 1
PREPARING (42)
were just preparing to walk out, and he being hurried for NA I 12 94 10
Her brother she found was preparing to set off with all NA I 15 119 14
preparing for happiness which it had not afforded. NA II 1 129 1
with Captain Tilney preparing to give them hands across. NA II 1 133 29
haste, and she was preparing to unpin the linen package, NA II 6 163 1
and yours preparing by rest for the future mischief." NA II 8 187 15
in relating it, she was preparing enjoyment of no every- NA II 14 233 8
saw the necessity of preparing Marianne for its discussion. SS III 1 260 10
And there is one thing more preparing against him, which SS III 1 269 53
Jennings immediately preparing to say, said--"well, my dear, SS III 4 286 10
11
However, I will not disturb you (seeing her preparing to SS III 4 287 20
her; and while he was preparing to go, Colonel Brandon SS III 7 308 5
no time to be lost on Emma's side in preparing for it.-- W 340 19
ill-will, and she was preparing to see him with a degree PP I 13 64 20
very little entreaty, preparing to oblige the company. PP I 18 100 68
was concerned, and preparing her to be surprised, she PP II 17 224 1
They had just been preparing to walk as the letters came PP III 4 273 2
directions to Haggerston for preparing a proper settlement. PP III 7 303 14
"Perhaps preparing for his marriage with Miss de Bourgh," PP III 10 328 17
She was preparing for her ninth lying-in, and after MP I 1 5 2
supposing Fanny was now preparing for her appearance as of MP I 15 147 57
apology, saw them preparing to go as she quitted the room MP II 1 177 6
nor resolution, was preparing to encounter her share of it MP II 2 193 17
unprompted, that Fanny, preparing for a ball, might be MP II 9 271 41
who were educating and preparing you for that mediocrity MP III 1 313 12
rising, she was preparing to obey, when Mrs. Norris called MP III 1 325 60
she and Susan were preparing to remove as usual up stairs, MP III 10 399 2
There was a rich amends, however, preparing for her. MP III 13 425 7
Then, a letter which she had been previously preparing for MP III 13 427 12
Sir Thomas was preparing to act upon this letter, without MP III 16 450 9
But you were preparing yourself to be an excellent wife E I 5 38 11
The preparing and the going abroad in such weather, with E I 13 113 25
she was immediately preparing to speak with exquisite E I 15 129 24
bustle of collecting and preparing to depart, and the E III 7 374 54
a connexion had she been preparing for Mr. Knightley--or E III 19 482 3
at the same moment preparing to come down, politely drew P III 12 104 6
He was preparing only to bow and pass on, but her gentle " P IV 8 181 1
and she had been hastily preparing to interest Anne's P IV 9 210 99
the various sources of mortification preparing for them! P IV 10 215 13
quitting that chair, in preparing to quit the room, she P IV 10 225 62
in the house, & she was preparing in all the anger & S 3 378 1

& powers, to have been preparing for a situation little S 3 379 1
PREPONDERATED (1)
of general happiness preponderated, and she could think of NA II 6 166 8
PREPOSSESSED (3)
as can persuade me of her being prepossessed in my favour. LS 5 249 1
were both strongly prepossessed that neither she nor her SS II 11 228 53
to give pleasure were prepossessed in her favour. PP III 2 262 7
PREPOSSESSING (5)
must be highly prepossessing, & I am sure she feels it so. LS 18 272 1
was more assuming, and his countenance less prepossessing. NA II 1 131 15
as her sister's, but they were much more prepossessing. SS I 19 106 22
a young man and woman of very prepossessing appearance. MP I 4 41 17
who are at all inferior, it is extremely prepossessing. E II 15 283 7
PREPOSSESSION (6)
If she suspected any prepossession elsewhere, it could not SS III 1 266 38
Marianne's unhappy prepossession for that worthless young SS III 9 336 14
not know of any prepossession;--her eldest daughter, she PP I 15 71 3
I have courted prepossession and ignorance, and driven PP II 13 208 8
of our nature, eager curiosity and warm prepossession. E I 7 56 46
by his own sentiments, by his early prepossession. P IV 9 192 2
PRESCIENCE (1)
nothing but a kind of prescience of what happiness I SS I 14 73 17
PRESCRIBED (4)
the cordials prescribed, saw her with satisfaction sink at SS III 7 310 9
the silence and quiet prescribed by every nurse around her. SS III 9 334 5
A warm climate may be prescribed for her. E III 6 365 62
She wanted it to be prescribed, and felt as a duty. P III 2 13 5
PRESCRIPTIONS (2)
Prescriptions poured in from all quarters, and as usual, SS III 6 306 17
physician;--and his prescriptions must be their rule"--and S 11 422 1
PRESENCE (48)
into her guardian's presence, tho' I did not know a LS 32 302 1
same timid look in the presence of her mother as LS 42 311 3
entreating the immediate presence of her friend on a NA I 15 116 1
A letter form my steward tells me that my presence is NA II 2 139 7
It was only in his presence that Catherine felt the NA II 6 166 8
of his presence, and to Catherine terror upon terror. NA II 9 191 4
Upon this trust she dared still to remain in his presence, NA II 9 192 4
therefore, in her presence, search for those proofs of the NA II 9 193 5
which the General's presence had imposed, and most NA II 13 220 1
In Eleanor's presence friendship and pride had equally NA II 13 226 25
so little did her presence add to the pleasure of the SS I 11 55 6
presence is necessary to gain your admittance at Whitwell." SS I 13 64 21
of her sister's presence; and when at last they were told SS II 6 175 1
Elinor was robbed of all presence of mind by such an SS II 6 176 7
it was possible, the presence of Mrs. Jennings, and in a SS II 9 201 2
Their presence always gave her pain, and she hardly knew SS II 10 217 20
She would not allow the presence of Lucy, nor the SS II 13 241 20
each other should be checked by Lucy's unwelcome presence. SS II 13 242 25
Their presence was a restraint both on her and on Lucy. SS II 14 247 4
of the three, by their presence; and it was in their power SS II 14 247 4
unrestrained even by the presence of a harp, and a SS II 14 250 11
his presence, his manners, his assistance, would lessen it. SS III 7 311 16
and her mother's presence in aid, it proceeded so smoothly SS III 10 340 1
her daughter, nor be permitted to appear in her presence. SS III 13 371 38
to her presence, and pronounced to be again her son. SS III 14 373 1
but his presence gave variety & secured good manners.-- W 359 28
Teaze calmness of temper and presence of mind! PP I 11 57 18
want of presence of mind; Charlotte tried to console her. PP I 18 90 5
In Darcy's presence she dared not mention Wickham's name; PP III 3 269 10
thought her presence might be serviceable to her nieces. PP III 6 294 3
But, perhaps he could not in her mother's presence be what PP III 11 335 40
not merely from the presence of such a mistress, but the PP III 19 388 12
were considered--her presence was wanted--she was sought MP I 17 160 6
His presence was beginning to be odious to her; and if MP II 2 194 19
with his family, the presence of a stranger superior to Mr. MP II 2 194 21
There was never much laughing in his presence; or, if MP II 3 197 3
be some advantage in his presence, since every addition to MP II 5 223 48
to commend in her presence, but upon her leaving the room MP II 10 272 1
resolution; but Susan's presence drove him quite into MP III 15 445 33
their spirits in his presence, as to make their real MP III 17 463 7
not, with the greatest presence of mind, caught hold of E II 1 160 23
which made their presence so acceptable; for though her E II 7 208 8
in your presence, that you may see how rational I am grown. E III 4 338 6
The strength, resolution, and presence of mind of the Mr. E III 19 484 10
of being oppressed by the presence of so many strangers. P III 11 99 22
presence of mind never varied, whose tongue never slipped. P IV 5 161 28
When you had the presence of mind to suggest that benwick P IV 8 182 6
presence must really be interfering with her prime object. P IV 10 213 10
PRESENT (460)
Vernon to receive me at present, I shall hope within a few LS 1 243 1
much into society for my present situation & state of mind; LS 1 243 1
At present nothing goes smoothly. LS 2 244 1
thought it better to lay aside the scheme for the present. LS 2 245 1
He desires me to tell you that the present open weather LS 8 254 1
especially as I am not at present in want of money, & LS 10 257 1
my brother's having no present intention of marrying Lady LS 15 266 1
present as she is in real distress, & with too much cause. LS 15 266 2
present, till some other situation can be found for her. LS 15 266 4
We have a very unexpected guest with us at present, my LS 20 275 1
& my girl, & continue to you all your present happiness." LS 20 278 7
alteration of his present plan; things have gone too far. LS 23 284 7
At present my thoughts are fluctuating between various LS 25 293 4
with Reginald, which at present in fact I have not, for LS 25 294 6
for them to meet at present; & yet if you do not allow him LS 26 295 3
to present, in having been scarcely ten months a widow. LS 29 299 3
for reflection on the present state of our affairs, & LS 30 300 1
intimately judge of my present feelings; but I am not so LS 34 304 2
Come to me immediately, & explain what is at present LS 35 305 1
myself & everything about me, than at the present hour. LS 39 307 1
At present it is not very likely. Yrs &c. Cath. Vernon. LS 41 310 5
At present she did not know her own poverty, for she had NA I 1 16 10
or even (as in the present case) of young men, are not NA I 7 44 1
In the present instance, she confessed and lamented her NA I 14 111 29
"No doubt;--but that is no explanation of the present." NA I 14 113 42
alone who know my heart can judge of my present happiness. NA I 15 117 6
has by no means chosen ill in fixing on the present hour." NA II 1 134 36
that makes me just at present a little out of spirits; I NA II 1 136 48
We perfectly understand the present vexation; and every NA II 1 136 49
of being with him for the present bounded her views: the NA II 2 138 1
bounded her views: the present was now comprised in NA II 2 138 1
had been ease and quiet to the present disappointment. NA II 2 138 1
Every thing honourable and soothing, every present NA II 2 140 8
making a part of the present dwelling although the rest NA II 2 141 13
being arch, thought the present a fine opportunity for NA II 3 143 2
was glad to rest altogether for present ease and comfort. NA II 3 148 29
however careless of his present comfort the woman might be NA II 4 149 1
But Captain Tilney had at present no intention of removing; NA II 4 150 1
"My brother's heart, as you term it, on the present NA II 4 151 24
The weather was at present favourable, and at this time of NA II 7 176 17
desire of making use of the present smiling weather.-- NA II 7 177 17
"A mother would have been always present. NA II 7 180 36
days, and in the stoves and hot closets of the present. NA II 8 183 3
the General's father, and the present erected in its place. NA II 8 184 4
to make her feel secure at least of life for the present. NA II 9 192 4
very much to be pitied at present; but we must not, in our NA II 10 206 38
to Northanger than at the present time, that she suffered NA II 11 208 2
Witness myself, at this present hour. NA II 11 210 7
The past, present, future, were all equally in gloom. NA II 11 212 16
and most thankfully feel their present release from it. NA II 13 220 1
her, enjoying every thing present, and fearing little in NA II 13 228 27
thing to startle and recall them to the present moment. NA II 13 228 27
Just at present it comes hard to poor James; but that will NA II 14 237 19
acquaintance that all her present happiness depended; and NA II 14 239 28
by parental authority in his present application. NA II 15 243 10
eventually secure; his present income was an income of NA II 16 249 2
at the disposal of its present proprietor, was NA II 16 251 6
Dashwood had one son: by his present lady, three daughters. SS I 1 3 2
of his sisters by the present of a thousand pounds a-piece. SS I 1 5 8
in addition to his present income, besides the remaining SS I 1 5 8
no opportunity, till the present, of shewing them with how SS I 1 6 9
A present of fifty pounds, now and then, will prevent SS I 2 11 23
Some little present of furniture too may be acceptable SS I 2 12 25
At present, I know him so well, that I think him really SS I 4 20 9
his home comfortable at present, nor to give him any SS I 4 22 18
than immediately amongst their present acquaintance. SS I 4 24 21
present, as it is too late in the year for improvements. SS I 6 29 4
and garden in which their's might at present be deficient. SS I 6 30 6
followed before the end of the day by a present of game. SS I 6 30 6
In the present case it took up ten minutes to determine SS I 6 31 9
His name, he replied, was Willoughby, and his present home SS I 9 42 10
When he was present she had no eyes for any one else. SS I 11 53 1
the charms which his society bestowed on her present home. SS I 11 54 5
she had accepted the present without hesitation, and told SS I 12 58 1
of her receiving such a present from a man so little, or SS I 12 58 3
on being obliged to forego the acceptance of his present. SS I 12 59 6
"My engagements at present," replied Willoughby confusedly, SS I 15 76 15
he dares not therefore at present confess to her his SS I 15 78 26
for Willoughby to be but little in Devonshire at present. SS I 15 79 31
over the present reverse for the chief of the morning. SS I 16 83 2
between the past and present was certain of giving. SS I 16 83 3
what is meant at present to be unacknowledged to any one. SS I 16 84 9
him by talking of their present residence, its SS I 16 89 42
the past rather than the present, she avoided every SS I 16 89 42
"What are Mrs. Ferrars's views for you at present, Edward?" SS I 17 90 2
On the present occasion, for the better entertainment of SS I 18 99 16
as soon as their present engagements at Exeter were over. SS I 21 118 2
Mrs. Ferrars is certainly nothing to me at present,--but SS I 22 129 11
Besides in the present case, I really thought some SS I 22 132 42
to suspect it in the present case, where no temptation SS II 1 139001
once have been, she could not believe it such at present. SS II 1 139 1
done nothing to merit her present unhappiness, and SS II 1 140 4
and the present incumbent not likely to live a great while. SS II 2 149 25
every impediment to the present scheme which occurred to SS II 3 156 9
"and do not betray what you feel to every body present. SS II 6 176 5
of contributing, at present, to her ease, she hurried away SS II 7 184 16
For the present, adieu. M. D. SS II 7 187 38
My feelings are at present in a state of dreadful SS II 7 188 42
about it when she is present; and the less that may ever SS II 8 195 17
a cholicky gout were, at present, of little importance to SS II 8 198 29
must not say comfort--not present comfort--but conviction, SS II 9 204 18
perhaps, judging from my present forlorn and cheerless SS II 9 205 24
past sorrows and present humiliations, was given in the SS II 10 216 15
Perhaps just at present he may be undecided; the smallness SS II 11 223 24
that Marianne was not present, to share the provocation. SS II 11 226 40
not to be told, they could do nothing at present but write. SS II 11 230 4
but as Harry only was present; it was all conjectural SS II 12 233 20
home, ornamented her present drawing room; and these SS II 12 234 26
The nature of her commendation, in the present case, SS II 13 244 41
In the present instance, this last-arrived lady allowed SS II 14 248 6
was she dismissed on the present occasion of her brother's SS II 14 249 9
I have brought myself at present to consider the matter, SS III 1 264 29
present case you know, the connection must be impossible. SS III 1 267 45
their sentiments on the present occasion, as far at least SS III 1 269 57
that she still fancied present exertion impossible, and SS III 2 270 2
of which, at present, there seemed not the smallest chance. SS III 2 276 26
to him then, as I sincerely wish I could be at present. SS III 3 284 23
but I shall not mention it at present to any body else." SS III 4 286 13
approbation of your behaviour on the present occasion." SS III 4 289 31
Dashwood's part, either present or future, would ever SS III 5 293 2
nothing about it at present, and I believe it will be best SS III 5 295 18
to be found at a much later hour than the present. SS III 7 311 14
eating much;--and the present refreshment, therefore, with SS III 7 315 27
a rich reward in store, for every present inconvenience. SS III 7 316 28
Willoughby, I advise you at present to return to Combe.-- SS III 8 318 16
17
of my time that I had bestowed on her, in my present visit. SS III 8 323 40
I had reason to believe myself secure of my present wife, SS III 8 323 40
of my heart, and of my present feelings, will draw from SS III 8 330 67
The past, the present, the future, Willoughby's visit, SS III 9 333 3
that would suit us quite as well as our present situation." SS III 9 338 24
At present, if I could be satisfied on one point, if I SS III 10 344 17
and softened only his protestations of present regard. SS III 10 347 33
"At present," continued Elinor, "he regrets what he had SS III 11 351 13
of every lesser one, and of all his present discontents." SS III 11 352 17
of his plans, nothing certain even of his present abode. SS III 11 352 21
so uncomfortable in the present case as he really did, so SS III 13 361 2
be said of the past, the present, and the future;--for SS III 13 363 9
In what state the affair stood at present between them, SS III 13 366 20
of Delaford--"which, at present," said he, "after thanks SS III 13 368 30
till he had revealed his present engagement; for the SS III 14 373 3
promised either for the present or in future, beyond the SS III 14 374 4
On the present occasion, as only two of Mr W.'s children W 315 1
was increased in the present instance by a general spirit W 337 16
to the ridicule of richer people in her present home.-- W 345 21
seasons; & in the present instance had had the additional W 355 28
the past & the present, the employment of mind, the W 361 31
and I am in no humour at present to give consequence to PP I 3 11 13
With a book he was regardless of time; and on the present PP I 3 12 15
Mr. Darcy, you must allow me to present this young lady to PP I 6 26 38
39
At present, indeed, they were well supplied both with news PP I 7 28 3
an invitation to remain at Netherfield for the present. PP I 7 33 45
At present, however, I consider myself as quite fixed here. PP I 9 42 8
At present I have not room to do them justice." PP I 10 48 16
to his ideas of right, than in any other person present. PP I 10 51 46
consult the wishes of the present party; I am much PP I 11 55 6
I flatter myself that my present overtures of good-will PP I 13 63 12
At present I will not say more, but perhaps when we are PP I 13 65 25
best of them were of the present party; but Mr. Wickham PP I 16 76 3
"I know little of the game, at present," said he, "but I PP I 16 76 7
by his account of their present quarters, and the very PP I 16 79 23
consequently that she is aunt to the present Mr. Darcy." PP I 16 83 53
a doubt of his being present had never occurred to her. PP I 18 89 1
That reply will do for the present.-- PP I 18 91 11
"Are you consulting your own feelings in the present case, PP I 18 91 14
"The present always occupies you in such scenes--does it?" PP I 18 93 31
my character at the present moment, as there is reason to PP I 18 94 41
you of cruelty at present, because I know it to be the PP I 19 108 16
17
on the present occasion; and secondly, of my room. PP I 20 112 22
must be waved for the present, the lady felt no PP I 22 121 2
Mr. Collins's present circumstances made it a most PP I 22 122 3
On being made acquainted with the present Mr. Darcy's PP II 2 143 20
At present I am not in love with Mr. Wickham; no, I PP II 3 144 7
passion, I should at present detest his very name, and PP II 3 150 29
His present pursuit could not make him forget that PP II 4 151 3
her family under less than half the present distance." PP II 9 179 22
But, perhaps his sister does as well for the present, and, PP II 10 184 17
occurrences, or any communication of present suffering. PP II 11 188 1
"You have reduced him to his present state of poverty, PP II 11 192 21
ordained, if I would present him to the living in question- PP II 12 201 5
the present should induce me to unfold to any human being. PP II 12 201 5
an account of the present fashions from Jane, who sat some PP II 16 222 21

Context	Work	Vol	Ch	Page	Line
At present I will say nothing about it."	PP	II	17	226	23
to her family as under the present circumstances."	PP	II	18	230	14
					15
of teaching her that her present pursuits are not to be	PP	II	18	231	18
to tens and to scores of them at present unknown.	PP	II	18	232	22
In his present behaviour to herself, moreover, she had a	PP	II	18	233	25
for the present, and prepare for another disappointment.	PP	II	19	237	3
and, according to the present plan, were to go no farther	PP	II	19	238	7
A small part of Derbyshire is all the present concern.	PP	II	19	240	12
present from my master; she comes here to-morrow with him."	PP	III	1	248	22
Is there nothing you could take, to give you present	PP	III	4	276	9
than there was at present reason to hope, and leaving his	PP	III	4	278	22
what their present feelings were, seemed unjustifiable.	PP	III	5	291	56
wholly disinclined at present, to leave London, and	PP	III	6	295	5
At present we have nothing to guide us.	PP	III	6	295	6
family, in your present distress, which must be of the	PP	III	6	296	11
The present unhappy state of the family, rendered any	PP	III	6	298	17
inconvenience to himself, as by the present arrangement.	PP	III	8	309	4
for his chief wish at present, was to have as little	PP	III	8	309	5
to inform him of our present arrangements, and to request	PP	III	8	313	19
She had scarcely needed her present observation to be	PP	III	9	318	19
persuade her to quit her present disgraceful situation,	PP	III	10	322	2
conditionally only, and at the will of the present patron."	PP	III	10	328	29
you as it seems to be at present; that you actually	PP	III	10	329	31
us of the present report; and I know I appeared distressed.	PP	III	11	331	16
					17
he meant to make any stay in the country at present.	PP	III	11	337	52
Were the same fair prospect to arise at present, as had	PP	III	11	337	54
or say half that remained to be said, for the present.	PP	III	13	347	25
sister; for while he was present, Jane had no attention to	PP	III	13	349	44
"That will make your ladyship's situation at present more	PP	III	14	356	49
"have any possible claim on me, in the present instance.	PP	III	14	358	70
with gratitude and pleasure, his present assurances.	PP	III	16	366	8
She soon learnt that they were indebted for their present	PP	III	16	367	9
I am not indebted for my present happiness to your eager	PP	III	18	381	14
than make her a generous present of some of their least	MP	I	2	14	7
to be when Fanny was present, she calmly observed to her, "	MP	I	3	24	7
It had never occurred to her, on the present occasion, but	MP	I	3	28	38
of others at their present most interesting time of life.	MP	I	3	32	62
mother, who at present lived with him, and to whom she	MP	I	4	39	10
it every where as a matter not to be talked of at present.	MP	I	4	39	12
With all due respect to such of the present company as	MP	I	5	46	20
Mary was satisfied with the parsonage as a present home,	MP	I	5	47	26
up from much gaming at present, by a promise to his father,	MP	I	5	48	28
That is the faulty part of the present system.	MP	I	5	49	32
"No wonder that Mr. Rushworth should think so at present,"	MP	I	6	53	5
us--that is, it was a present from Sir Thomas, but I saw	MP	I	6	54	11
and liveliness, to put the matter by for the present.	MP	I	6	57	32
but I do not at present foresee any occasion for writing."	MP	I	6	59	42
You would not find it equal to your present ideas.	MP	I	6	61	54
though the Admiral's present conduct might incline one to	MP	I	7	63	7
But I think her present home must do her good.	MP	I	7	64	9
the present; she liked to have him near her; it was enough.	MP	I	7	65	13
might be an evil even beyond the loss of present pleasure."	MP	I	9	84	1
On the present occasion, she addressed herself chiefly to	MP	I	9	85	3
"Suppose we turn down here for the present," said Mrs.	MP	I	9	90	33
key again; but still this did not remove the present evil.	MP	I	10	98	4
this present time the guest of my own brother, Dr. Grant.	MP	I	11	111	28
bad example, he would not look beyond the present moment.	MP	I	12	114	3
her an account of the present state of a sick horse, and	MP	I	12	118	22
not allow herself to be considered in the present case.	MP	I	14	133	10
it could be chosen in the present instance--that it could	MP	I	14	137	23
We do not want your present services.	MP	I	15	145	45
obliged to her for her present kindness; and when from	MP	I	15	147	57
of present upon present that she had received from them.	MP	I	16	153	3
disapprobation when the present state of his house should	MP	II	1	179	10
For the present the danger was over, and Fanny's sick	MP	II	1	181	17
first difficulties, and present promising state of affairs;	MP	II	1	184	27
conviction that where the present pleasure of those she	MP	II	2	190	8
the play after the present happy interruption, (with a	MP	II	2	192	11
till Sir Thomas were present; but the subject involving,	MP	II	5	217	11
pleasure, both present and future, as much as possible.	MP	II	5	219	27
be your approach--through what is at present the garden.	MP	II	7	242	23
she had been present than remembered any thing about her.	MP	II	7	251	62
and confusion, would have returned the present instantly.	MP	II	8	259	20
but being her brother's present, is not it fair to suppose	MP	II	9	263	13
For Fanny's present comfort it was concluded perhaps at	MP	II	9	270	40
generous present to her when dear Mrs. Rushworth married.	MP	II	10	272	3
in that house before, the present arrangement was almost	MP	II	10	276	12
few persons present that were not disposed to praise her.	MP	II	10	276	13
conform to the tranquillity of the present quiet week.	MP	II	11	283	7
not think him likely to marry at all--or not at present."	MP	II	11	289	36
is to marry early; but at present, as far as I can judge,	MP	III	1	317	34
The past, present, future, every thing was terrible.	MP	III	1	321	46
delicacy, ceased to urge to see you for the present."	MP	III	1	321	47
For the present you have only to tranquillize yourself.	MP	III	1	321	48
that she did know her own present feelings, convinced him	MP	III	2	326	1
at the past and present, wondering at what was yet to come,	MP	III	2	329	10
as to the frequency of his visits, at present or in future.	MP	III	2	329	12
last fortnight, and the present situation of matters at	MP	III	3	334	4
the influence of her present indifference, honouring her	MP	III	3	335	6
I speak rather of the past, however, than the present.--	MP	III	3	339	23
Is there any thing in my present intreaty that you do not	MP	III	3	342	36
in what you look and do, and excites my present curiosity.	MP	III	3	342	36
Do you suppose you are ever present to my imagination	MP	III	3	344	41
of having others present when they met, was Fanny's only	MP	III	5	356	4
she stood affected on the present occasion, and whether	MP	III	6	366	1
which he must consider as at present diseased.	MP	III	6	369	10
from Mansfield Park at present; that she was a great deal	MP	III	6	373	23
compared with the ceaseless tumult of her present abode.	MP	III	8	392	11
In her present exile from good society, and distance from	MP	III	9	393	1
There was no gratitude for affection past or present, to	MP	III	9	396	5
it would not be unbecoming in her to make such a present.	MP	III	9	396	7
there was rising in importance from his present schemes.	MP	III	10	404	15
he was convinced that her present residence could not be	MP	III	11	410	7
are my present plans, if plans I can be said to have.--	MP	III	13	420	2
My present state is miserably irksome.	MP	III	13	422	2
intended journey, for the present intelligence was of a	MP	III	13	426	9
and conduct, at the present moment, she saw so much to	MP	III	14	435	15
at present, and that she should be felt an incumbrance."	MP	III	14	436	15
"Dear Fanny, you know our present wretchedness.	MP	III	15	442	23
You may imagine something of my present state.	MP	III	15	443	23
His present state, Fanny could hardly bear to think of.	MP	III	16	451	13
in supposing that Edmund gave his father no present pain.	MP	III	16	452	15
on the present, no reliance on future improvement.	MP	III	17	471	28
The danger, however, was at present so unperceived, that	E	I	1	5	4
such a close of the present day, a note was brought from	E	I	3	22	7
style; and on the present evening had particular pleasure	E	I	3	25	15
her present comfort; for I cannot lament the acquaintance.	E	I	5	39	16
break her resolution, at present," said Mrs. Weston, "as	E	I	5	41	30
I do not recommend matrimony at present to Emma, though I	E	I	5	41	30
in the case at present, I will break my resolution now."	E	I	6	46	21
wives in the case at present indeed, as you observe.	E	I	6	46	22
propriety requires, will present themselves unbidden to	E	I	7	51	11
to keep her with them as much as possible just at present.	E	I	8	57	1
when there are only men present, I am convinced that he	E	I	8	66	53
eyes; but at present I only want to keep Harriet to myself.	E	I	8	66	54
which engaged Harriet at present, the only mental	E	I	9	69	3
the subject, did not at present recollect any thing of the	E	I	9	70	6
much smartened up by the present proprietor; and, such as	E	I	10	83	2
And I am not only, not going to be married, at present,	E	I	10	84	11
an image as you could present, Harriet; and if I thought I	E	I	10	84	16
In the present instance, it was sickness and poverty	E	I	10	86	24
					25
been the occasion of much present enjoyment to both, and	E	I	10	90	41
that I think you are any of you looking well at present."	E	I	12	103	38
call to mind exactly the present line of the path	E	I	12	106	61
gradually removed the present evil, and the immediate	E	I	12	107	62
did not belong to the present half hour; but the very	E	I	14	117	2
But at present there was nothing more to be said.	E	I	14	122	18
chamber again, for the present--to entreat her to promise	E	I	15	125	4
flakes were falling at present, but the clouds were	E	I	15	127	16
He was satisfied of there being no present danger in	E	I	15	128	17
					18
I have no thoughts of matrimony at present."	E	I	15	132	36
justify their all three being quite asunder at present.	E	I	16	138	16
cheerfulness, and all the present comfort of delay, there	E	I	16	139	20
For the present, he could not be spared, to his "very	E	I	18	144	1
It soon flies over the present failure, and begins to hope	E	I	18	144	2
The acquaintance at present had no charm for her.	E	I	18	144	4
in such a mark of respect to him on the present occasion.	E	I	18	146	16
put up for the present with Jane Fairfax, who could bring	E	II	2	166	10
it, at least for the present, said and with a sincerity	E	II	3	171	14
					15
During his present short stay, Emma had barely seen him;	E	II	4	182	7
his ways; at present she only felt they were agreeable.	E	II	5	192	33
as any reason for their not meaning to make the present.	E	II	8	215	14
rejoiced that such a present had been made; and there were	E	II	8	215	15
It is a handsome present."	E	II	8	216	20
but at present I do not see what there is to question.	E	II	8	216	27
that it must be the joint present of Mr. and Mrs. Dixon.	E	II	8	217	31
Depend upon it, we shall soon hear that it is a present	E	II	8	218	39
nothing, was enough for the happiness of the present hour.	E	II	8	219	44
Emma divined what every body present must be thinking.	E	II	8	220	47
to consider it a present from the Campbells, may it not be	E	II	8	226	79
"This present from the Campbells," said she--	E	II	8	228	91
possible, and, in her present state, would be dangerous.	E	II	9	233	23
seemed to give fresh pleasure to the present meeting.	E	II	9	233	25
Only three of us--besides dear Jane at present--and she	E	II	9	237	46
of restoring your spectacles, healed for the present."	E	II	10	242	15
present curiosity, or affording him any future amusement.	E	II	12	257	2
A very few minutes more, however, completed the present	E	II	12	261	35
was another point; but at present she could not doubt his	E	II	12	262	38
and her father's being present to engage Mr. Elton, she	E	II	14	272	16
to take the trouble of making any inquiries at present."	E	II	17	300	9
in not wishing any thing to be attempted at present for me.	E	II	17	301	19
a conclusion of their present acquaintance!--and yet, she	E	III	1	315	2
something to alter her present composed and tranquil state.	E	III	1	315	2
warm--her large new shawl--Mrs. Dixon's wedding present.--	E	III	2	322	19
She was not present when the suspicion first arose.	E	III	5	343	2
could enrich their intellectual stores at present.	E	III	6	352	1
her alliance with the present and future proprietor could	E	III	6	358	35
her that she would not at present engage in any thing,	E	III	6	359	37
and this picture of her present sufferings acted as a cure	E	III	8	379	9
into any engagement at present--and so she told Mrs. Elton	E	III	8	380	15
knows not whether it was his present or his daughter's."	E	III	8	384	33
At present, there was nothing to be done for Harriet; good	E	III	9	388	15
Her present home, he could not but observe, was	E	III	9	389	16
this boast, of my present perfect indifference," she	E	III	10	396	41
The present crisis, indeed, seemed to be brought on by	E	III	10	397	47
her feelings from any present solicitude on her account.	E	III	11	403	2
"For the present, the whole affair was to be completely a	E	III	11	403	2
that she would not, at present, come to Hartfield;	E	III	12	416	2
not to go at all at present, to be allowed merely to write	E	III	12	417	5
of the present and of the future state of the engagement.	E	III	12	418	5
with all the excuse that present circumstances may appear	E	III	12	419	8
But her present forebodings she feared would experience no	E	III	12	422	19
animation; "absolutely silent! at present I ask no more."	E	III	13	430	35
At present, I ask only to hear, once to hear your voice."	E	III	13	430	37
it had been no present hope--he had only, in the momentary	E	III	13	432	40
due; a separation for the present; an averting of the evil	E	III	14	435	4
becomes freed from its present restraints, that it did not	E	III	14	438	8
every present comfort before he endeavoured to gain it.--	E	III	15	445	11
I have another person's interest at present so much at	E	III	15	448	30
but she would have nothing to do with it at present.--	E	III	16	452	6
the resemblance of their present situations increasing	E	III	16	452	7
her; and Miss Bates being present, it passed, of course,	E	III	17	468	35
fullest exultation in the present and future; for, as to	E	III	19	481	2
of her own family, must ever present the remembrance of.	P	III	1	7	13
though she was at this present time, (the summer of 1814,)	P	III	1	8	17
present down to Anne, as had been the usual yearly custom.	P	III	1	9	19
and consideration under his present difficulties.	P	III	2	11	2
"that the present juncture is much in our favour.	P	III	3	17	1
Clay, for Mrs. Clay was present; her father had driven her	P	III	3	18	7
the Admiral, and had been present almost all the time they	P	III	3	22	24
She did not imagine that her father had at present an idea	P	III	5	34	12
floor, to which the present daughters of the house were	P	III	5	40	44
for a handsome present from his father; but here, as on	P	III	6	43	5
a great shame that such a present was not made, he always	P	III	6	43	5
former neighbour's present state, with proper interest.	P	III	6	49	22
of her name and rate, and present non-commissioned class,	P	III	8	66	22
present curacy, and obtaining that of Uppercross instead.	P	III	9	78	19
which Anne had not been present, Captain Wentworth walked	P	III	9	78	21
of life, she will cherish all her present powers of mind."	P	III	10	88	26
Captain Harville had taken his present house for half a	P	III	11	97	12
the richness of the present age, and gone through a brief	P	III	11	100	23
brought forward by their present view, and she gladly gave	P	III	12	109	31
him less willing upon the present occasion; he did it,	P	III	12	109	32
a favourite; and on the present occasion, receiving her in	P	IV	1	126	19
without any present intention of quitting it any more.--	P	IV	1	126	20
not to proceed far at present; for when it was returned,	P	IV	1	128	31
Captain Wentworth was gone, for the present, to see his	P	IV	2	134	31
too strict to suit the unfeudal tone of the present day!	P	IV	3	139	7
the investigation of his present keener time of life was	P	IV	3	140	11
And there was a Mrs. Wallis, at present only known to them	P	IV	3	141	13
must give him leave to present him to his youngest	P	IV	3	143	18
She could determine nothing at present.	P	IV	4	147	8
In London, perhaps, in your present quiet style of living,	P	IV	4	151	19
on her attention, of past kindness and present suffering.	P	IV	5	152	2
in her legs, had made her for the present a cripple.	P	IV	5	152	4
the restrictions of the present; neither sickness nor	P	IV	5	153	7
Mrs. Rooke is in at present, will furnish much either to	P	IV	5	156	12
					13
Mrs. Clay, who had been present while all this passed, now	P	IV	5	158	20
She distrusted the past, if not the present.	P	IV	5	160	27
Elizabeth, may we venture to present him and his wife in	P	IV	6	166	15
as Mary, from the present course of events, they served	P	IV	6	167	19
at present, and adding, "I am only waiting for Mr. Elliot.	P	IV	7	177	15
She could not understand his present feelings, whether he	P	IV	7	178	24
at present, perhaps, it was as well to be asunder.	P	IV	8	185	18
were all described, they were all present to me."	P	IV	8	187	32
The difference between his present air and what it had	P	IV	8	190	47
be the conclusion of the present suspense good or bad, her	P	IV	9	192	2
who interests you at this present time, more than all the	P	IV	9	194	16
Let me plead for my--present friend I cannot call him--but	P	IV	9	196	30
Though I fully believe that, at present, you have not the	P	IV	9	199	53
which I never could quite reconcile with present times.	P	IV	9	200	56
"At present, believe me, I have no need of your services, "	P	IV	9	203	72
His present attentions to your family are very sincere,	P	IV	9	204	80
can ever be secure, while she holds her present influence.	P	IV	9	208	92
bear the sight of his present smiles and mildness, or the	P	IV	10	214	11
on the strength of this present income, with almost a	P	IV	10	217	20
enough to understand the present state of Uppercross, and	P	IV	10	219	27
was given to the two present, and promised for the absent,	P	IV	10	220	29

of sitting with Lady Russell must give way for the present. P IV 10 220 30
each other, under their present circumstances, could only P IV 10 221 33
eager to make use of the present leisure for getting out, P IV 10 225 61
The present was that Captain Wentworth would move about P IV 10 226 64
so long exerted, that at present she felt unequal to more, P IV 10 227 68
the fatigues of the present, by a toilsome walk to Camden- P IV 10 227 69
would make the present hour a blessing indeed; and prepare P IV 11 240 59
had directly preceded the present moment, which were so P IV 11 241 59
give his daughter at present but a small part of the share P IV 12 248 1
the road does not seem at present in a favourable state S 1 365 1
injury on the fallen side as to be unfit for present use.-- S 1 370 1
(however upheld for the present by fortuitous aids of S 2 373 1
takes alarm at a trifling present expence, without S 3 376 1
Sir Edward, the present baronet, nephew to Sir Harry, S 3 377 1
me too plainly that in my present state, the sea air wd S 5 387 1
present number of Visitants & the chances of a good season. S 6 392 1
milk--& I have two Milch Asses at this present time.-- S 6 393 1
Susan never eats I grant you--& just at present I shall S 9 411 1
air wd probably in her present state, be the death of her, S 10 412 1
You have only to state the present afflicted situation of S 12 423 1
be in bed myself at this present time, for I am hardly S 12 424 1

PRESENTATION (9)
consequence of the presentation; for he did not suppose it SS III 3 284 22
"Very well--and for the next presentation to a living of SS III 5 295 12
really sold the presentation, is old enough to take it.-- SS III 5 295 12
his presentation at St. James's had made him courteous. PP I 5 18 1
me the next presentation of the best living in his gift. PP I 16 79 25
of the wonders of his presentation and knighthood; and his PP II 4 152 4
as her father had done to his presentation at St. James's. PP II 6 161 7
disposal of the next presentation necessary, and the MP I 3 23 2
On Mr. Norris's death, the presentation became the right MP I 3 24 5

PRESENTED (21)
a third, a fourth, and a fifth presented nothing new. NA II 7 172 2
their time as shortly presented themselves, or that they SS I 11 53 1
Buildings, Holborn, presented themselves again before SS II 10 217 19
toothpick-cases presented to his inspection, by remaining SS II 11 221 4
it, when another gentleman presented himself at her side. SS II 11 221 6
approbation, Fanny presented them to her mother, SS II 12 235 28
to address Emma, presented her a note, which he had the W 338 17
"Has she been presented? PP I 14 67 8
by this time have been presented to her, as her future PP II 14 210 2
and Mrs. Norris presented themselves at the top, just MP I 10 103 50
presented her with a very curious specimen of heath. MP I 10 103 50
nor the gamester, presented any thing that could satisfy MP I 14 130 3
and countenance, presented a very sweet mixture of E I 6 46 24
before her--he was presented to her, and she did not think E II 5 190 22
which must follow here, presented themselves, she could E III 12 415 1
Always to be presented with the date of her own birth, and P III 1 7 12
domestic happiness it presented, made it to her a P III 11 98 17
were there, the room presented as strong a contrast as P IV 2 134 28
had parted, and each presented a somewhat different person P IV 5 153 6
The answer soon presented itself. P IV 6 166 19
condition has since presented himself to raise even the P IV 12 250 6

PRESENTIMENT (2)
Impelled by an irresistible presentiment, you will eagerly NA II 5 160 21
She had felt an early presentiment that she should like MP I 5 47 27

PRESENTIMENTS (3)
A thousand alarming presentiments of evil to her beloved NA II 2 18 2
Catherine, meanwhile, undisturbed by presentiments of such NA II 1 131 15
help feeling dreadful presentiments; and as the long MP I 4 38 9

PRESENTING (5)
or purple velvet, presenting even a funereal appearance. NA II 5 158 15
Such as it is, however, my pleasure in presenting him to SS III 3 283 19
to do him the honour of presenting him to Miss Emma Watson, W 334 13
while Harriet is presenting such a delightful inferiority? E I 5 38 15
exciting no surprise, presenting no disparity, affording E III 11 413 48

PRESENTLY (47)
If we make haste, we shall pass by them presently, and I NA I 6 43 41
saw him presently address Mr. Tilney in a familiar whisper. NA I 10 80 59
something of her, and presently he took up her scissars SS I 12 60 13
and with a forced smile presently added, "it is I who may SS I 15 75 4
yet ready for breakfast; I shall be back again presently." SS I 18 96 3
came over her, for she presently added, "do you not think SS II 12 235 31
32
"I think, Elinor," she presently added, "we must employ SS II 13 243 31
he;--"I will go to her presently, for I am sure she will SS III 5 294 6
Her voice sunk with the word, but presently reviving she SS III 10 344 14
15
"And that," he presently added, "might perhaps be in his SS III 13 364 12
Far be it from me," he presently continued in a voice that PP I 20 114 32
ill-natured attack, she presently answered the question in PP III 3 269 10
"There goes good humour I am sure," said he presently. MP I 11 112 34
"I come from Dr. Grant's," said Edmund presently. MP II 9 268 28
"Yes," said Lady Bertram presently--"and it is a comfort MP II 11 285 12
continued Sir Thomas, presently, "you must have been some MP III 1 316 29
her vulnerable side, she presently answered-- "my dear MP III 2 333 24
25
"But, Fanny," he presently added, "in order to have a MP III 4 346 8
may perceive," said she presently, with a playful smile, " MP III 5 359 9
continued Mary, presently, "than when he had succeeded in MP III 5 363 26
He presently added, with a smile, "I do not pretend to fix E I 8 58 19
20
said Mr. Knightley presently, "though I have kept my E I 8 64 47
she called me back presently, and let me look too, which E I 9 75 26
"It is one thing," said she, presently--her cheeks in a E I 9 76 35
it into a ditch, was presently obliged to entreat them to E I 10 89 36
"Yes," said Mr. John Knightley presently, with some E I 13 112 18
"My report from Mrs. Goddard's," said she presently, "was E I 13 114 29
it was, but we shall see presently in Jane's letter--wrote E II 1 159 20
says, as you will hear presently; Mr. Dixon does not seem E II 1 160 23
"Emma," said Mr. Knightley presently, "I have a piece of E II 3 172 20
Miss Woodhouse?)--for presently she came forward--came E II 3 178 52
Presently the carriage stopt; she looked up; it was stopt E II 5 188 6
Presently Mr. Knightley looked back, and came and sat down E II 8 228 88
With a faint blush, she presently replied, "such E II 15 286 19
20
"I hope," said he presently, "I have not been severe upon E II 18 309 33
to exclaim; but she presently found that it was a family E III 2 319 3
Churchill to Mrs. Weston presently, "what became of Mr. E III 5 344 5
I dare say my daughter will be here presently, Miss E III 8 378 6
I am sure she will be here presently." E III 8 378 6
Emma was quite relieved, and could presently say, with a E III 13 425 10
11
But I will promise," she added presently, laughing and E III 17 463 14
"If not in our dispositions," she presently added, with a E III 18 478 69
The others will be here presently." P III 9 79 26
Presently. P IV 6 169 29
hurry to leave her; and presently with renewed spirit, P IV 8 181 3
4
"But," continued Anne, presently, "though there is no P IV 9 198 43
Presently, struck by a sudden thought, Charles said, P IV 11 240 55
56

PRESENTS (9)
things, and sending them presents of fish and game, and so SS I 2 12 24
distribute her presents and describe the newest fashions. PP II 2 139 3
we have ever had any thing from him, except a few presents. PP III 7 306 47
and the continual presents in money, which passed to her, PP III 8 309 4
he made her some very pretty presents, and laughed at her. MP I 2 17 22
I have such innumerable presents from him that it is quite MP II 8 259 22
it would make some difference in her presents too. MP II 13 304 19
Consider, she is sitting down--which naturally presents a E I 6 48 35
to do--small, trifling presents, of any thing uncommon-- E II 3 171 16

17

PRESERVATION (3)
My own folly has endangered me, my preservation I owe to LS 36 305 1
owed to the latter the preservation of her favourite PP III 11 335 42
it essential to the preservation of my regard; but, though PP III 16 368 21

PRESERVATIVE (2)
must be their pleasantest preservative from want. PP I 22 122 3
This preservative she had now obtained; and at the age of PP I 22 123 3

PRESERVE (18)
which he might easily preserve them, she concluded at last, NA I 9 66 31
and of not being able to preserve their good opinion, that, NA II 5 154 1
her, while she could preserve the good opinion and NA II 14 239 28
by that means to preserve myself from her farther notice; SS III 8 326 53
and so steady as to preserve her from that reproach which SS III 14 373 1
in her power to preserve him from her brother's claims, W 356 28
have led me before, to preserve my friend from what I PP II 12 198 5
meeting, most eager to preserve the acquaintance, and PP III 2 265 16
understanding would preserve her from falling an easy prey. PP III 4 279 24
a character to preserve, they will both be more prudent. PP III 8 313 19
as they grow up; how to preserve in the minds of my MP I 1 10 17
made it some effort with her to preserve her good manners. E I 14 118 4
have something occur to preserve him in her fancy, in all E II 4 184 10
a situation of such danger, without trying to preserve her. E III 5 349 26
had a character to preserve, and would not use her ill; P IV 5 154 9
remain in the room, preserve an air of calmness, and P IV 6 165 9
determined to preserve every document of former intimacy. P IV 9 203 70
at hand to preserve their interest by reasonable attention. S 3 377 1

PRESERVED (17)
they were seated, on having preserved her gown from injury. NA I 2 22 11
and truly rejoiced to be preserved by his advice from the NA I 13 105 41
To be sure, the pointed arch was preserved--the form of NA II 5 162 26
From this, she was preserved too by another cause, by NA II 14 231 5
Her eagerness to be gone from Norland was preserved from SS I 5 27 6
Middleton was happily preserved from the frightful SS II 1 143 10
of her thoughts preserved her in ignorance of every thing SS II 8 193 6
one greater obstacle preserved her from suffering under SS II 13 238 1
Mrs. Ferrars's creation, preserved her from all dependence SS II 13 238 1
Elizabeth preserved as steady a silence as either Mrs. PP I 18 103 75
"Let us be thankful that you are preserved from a state of PP I 23 130 23
She likes to have the distinction of rank preserved." PP II 6 161 6
might at least have preserved the respectability of his PP II 19 236 2
so much credit, that I preserved it some time; and I dare E I 5 37 7
the idea--and the proportions must be preserved, you know. E I 6 48 35
she must have been preserved from the abominable E III 12 421 17
Mr. Knightley might be preserved from sinking deeper in E III 16 458 44

PRESERVER (1)
A lady, without a family, was the very best preserver of P III 3 22 24

PRESERVES (3)
tarts and preserves, my cook contrives to get them all." MP I 6 54 13
You need not be afraid of unwholesome preserves here. E I 3 25 14
In the centre of some of the best preserves in the kingdom, P IV 10 217 20

PRESERVING (6)
the general talk of his preserving them in their Gothic NA II 5 162 26
best towards preserving that good opinion a little longer. MP II 1 186 35
method in the world of preserving peace at home and E I 18 148 24
opinion is most worth preserving, are not disgusted to E III 16 459 47
"Family connexions were always worth preserving, good P IV 4 149 12
preserving, though there may be nothing durable beneath. P IV 9 198 53

PRESIDE (2)
by no means unwilling to preside at his table, nor was Mrs. PP I 4 15 13
and preside, she had no sigh of that description to heave. P IV 1 126 18

PRESIDED (4)
tea-table where Elinor presided, and whispered--"the SS II 8 198 30
went with the lady who presided over it, to ramsgate; and PP II 12 201 5
Edmund, who had taken down the mare and presided at the MP I 7 66 15
The curtain over which she had presided with such talent MP II 2 195 22

PRESIDES (1)
(who, wherever she is, presides,) to say, that she desires E III 7 369 16

PRESIDING (4)
all her attention to Mrs. Norris, who was presiding there. MP I 15 145 42
presiding; Mr. Knightley's answer was the most distinct. E III 7 369 17
of Kellynch Hall, presiding and directing with a self- P III 1 6 12
and name, and home, presiding and blessing in the same P IV 5 160 25

PRESS (23)
Her anxiety on the subject made her press for an early LS 42 311 2
no similar triumphs to press on the unwilling and NA I 4 32 2
strains of the trash with which the press now groans. NA I 5 37 4
Isabella had only time to press her friend's hand and say, NA I 8 52 2
be welcome; for I will not press you to return here SS I 15 76 14
Lady Middleton too, though she did not press their mother, SS I 19 109 40
from Lucy, might not press very hard upon his patience; SS II 1 140 3
circumstances, to press for greater openness in Marianne. SS II 5 170 27
Elinor, for her sister's sake, could not press the subject SS II 8 196 21
from her at intervals to press Colonel Brandon's hand, SS III 9 334 4
dance for a few minutes, to press his friend to join it. PP I 3 11 7
did not think it right to press the subject, from the PP II 9 181 30
was really unwell, did not press her to go, and as much as PP II 10 187 41
I am not so selfish, however, as to press for it, if PP III 4 275 5
will not take it, let me press you ever so much," and Miss MP I 8 81 32
angry as he was, he would not press that article farther. MP III 1 319 40
I do not mean to press you, however. MP III 4 346 10
as well as her own, to press their coming over directly, E II 1 159 20
There was no occasion to press the matter farther. E II 8 219 43
I shall press you no more." E III 6 366 73
interview, that he did not press for it at all; and, on P IV 2 133 25
ventured to press again for what he had to communicate. P IV 6 170 30
it would have been useless to press the enquiry farther. P IV 6 173 48

PRESSED (47)
of being continually pressed against by people, the NA I 2 21 10
from the first not to go, if they pressed me ever so much." NA I 14 115 52
You have no idea how he pressed me. NA II 1 134 39
and even of that, if hard pressed, would have yielded the NA II 10 200 3
He really pressed them, with some earnestness, to consider SS I 2 8 1
He earnestly pressed her, after giving the particulars of SS I 4 23 20
with his family, and pressed them, so cordially to dine at SS I 6 30 6
and Margaret was eagerly pressed to say something more. SS I 12 61 20
cottage; he was earnestly pressed by Mrs. Dashwood to stay SS I 19 101 1
too, though she did not press their mother, pressed them. SS I 19 109 40
her hand, pressed it, and kissed it with grateful respect. SS II 9 206 25
else, but Lucy still pressed her to own that she had SS II 13 239 7
of her guests, that she pressed them very earnestly to SS III 3 280 7
She could not refuse to give him her's;--he pressed it SS III 8 331 74
Marianne pressed her hand and replied, "you are very good.- SS III 10 347 29
30
closely pressed her sister's, and tears covered her cheeks. SS III 10 348 33
I earnestly pressed his coming to us, and should not be SS III 12 358 6
She was very much pressed by Robert & Jane to return with W 362 32
Bingley and his sister pressed them to stay longer, she PP I 12 59 1
of elegant, little, hot pressed paper, well covered with a PP I 21 116 6
coming up, they were all pressed to go into the house and PP III 1 257 66
and Mary, properly pressed and persuaded, was not long in MP I 8 76 7
and was hoping to have it pressed on her by the rest. MP I 14 133 11
still feeling her hand pressed to Henry Crawford's heart, MP II 1 182 19
The hand which had so pressed her's to his heart!-- MP II 2 193 18
His mind, now disengaged from the cares which had pressed MP II 7 238 1
All that I heard was that his friend had pressed him to MP II 11 288 23
He pressed for an answer. MP II 13 301 7
And when farther pressed, had added, that in her opinion MP III 2 327 5
He pressed for the strictest forbearance and silence MP III 2 332 20
her, took her hand, and pressed it kindly; and at that MP III 3 335 5
I was most kindly pressed, and had nearly consented. MP III 4 354 50
He pressed her hand, looked at her, and was gone. MP III 11 412 29

and she found herself pressed to his heart with only these MP III 15 444 28
But he was pressed to stay for Mrs. Fraser's party; his MP III 17 467 20
Emma was so sorry to be pressed. E I 7 50 4
Emma felt her foot pressed by Mrs. Weston, and did not E II 15 287 29
father, pressed them all to go in and drink tea with him. E III 5 344 3
it--but he took her hand, pressed it, and certainly was on E III 9 386 7
at first, but on being pressed had yielded; and in the E III 12 418 5
been spared from every pain which pressed on her now.-- E III 12 421 17
arm drawn within his, and pressed against his heart, and E III 13 425 12
13
Her arm was pressed again, as he added, in a more broken E III 13 426 13
but then he had been pressed to come to the great house P III 7 58 22
which had been so pressed on her,--and she declined on her P IV 5 157 14
parkers knew that to be pressed into their house, & S 6 390 1
I answered Fanny's letter by the same post & pressed for S 9 408 1

PRESSING (30)
cannot help thinking his pressing invitation to her to LS 3 247 1
him; and had no more pressing solicitude than that of NA II 11 209 5
of Eleanor's manner in pressing her to stay, and Henry's NA II 13 221 6
The pressing anxieties of thought, which prevented her NA II 14 231 5
on her mother's silently pressing her hand with tender SS I 15 82 46
parted, gave her a pressing invitation to visit her there. SS III 6 301 2
and Colonel Brandon only pressing her hand with a look of SS III 7 312 17
she only wanted a little pressing to accept it, when Jane PP I 7 33 45
in spite of Miss Lydia's pressing entreaties that they PP I 15 73 10
Miss de Bourgh ate, pressing her to try some other dish, PP II 6 163 14
her husband from pressing her, but Mr. Collins could not PP II 10 187 41
honour, which were very pressing; and scrupled not to lay PP III 10 323 2
yet given over pressing Lady Bertram to be of the party. MP I 8 75 2
Agatha's narrative, and pressing her hand to his heart, MP II 1 175 2
of improvement in pressing her frequent calls. MP II 4 205 2
"Dearest Fanny!" cried Edmund, pressing her hand to his MP II 9 269 38
a little time, a little pressing, a little patience, and a MP III 1 320 44
"My dearest Fanny," cried Edmund, pressing her arm closer MP III 4 352 42
pressing, joyful cares attending this summons to herself. MP III 15 443 24
minutes against the earnest pressing of both the others. E I 6 44 19
in compliance with the pressing entreaties of some friends, E I 17 140 2
can be more kind or pressing than their joint invitation, E II 1 160 23
Cole, to add his very pressing entreaties; and as, in E II 8 227 85
These are the motives which I have been pressing on you. E II 13 268 12
It was a more pressing concern to show attention to Jane E III 9 389 16
papa and mamma's farther pressing invitations, to come and P III 7 54 4
such men as have hearts!" pressing his own with emotion. P IV 11 235 31
pressing them to make use of his house for both purposes.-- S 1 367 1
I know how little it suits you to be pressing matters upon S 12 425 1
was at first almost pressing on the road--till an angle S 12 426 1

PRESSINGLY (2)
Mrs. Bennet was most pressingly civil in her hope of PP I 18 103 76
all came from her--Mrs. Dixon had written most pressingly. E II 15 285 14

PRESSURE (2)
the resistless pressure of a long string of passing ladies. NA I 10 76 29
Emma returned her friend's pressure with interest; and was E II 15 287 31

PRESUME (20)
your opinion on that point is unchanged, I presume?" SS I 17 93 29
"Your examination of Mr. Darcy is over, I presume," said PP I 11 57 26
thing indeed, and I wonder how he could presume to do it. PP I 18 94 45
"Any Mr. Yates, I presume, is not far off." MP II 5 224 51
I cannot but presume on having been no unacceptable MP III 1 314 16
the ramparts, taking her first lesson, I presume, in love. MP III 12 415 2
Let no one presume to give the feelings of a young woman MP III 17 471 28
many houses that I should presume on so far; but in coming E II 5 190 25
hardly suppose they would presume to invite--neither E II 7 207 6
objects she could presume to expect; and when her eyes E II 9 233 24
for me to presume to take such a liberty with you. E II 15 288 35
as far as I can presume to determine any thing without the E II 16 296 36
"You have heard of a certain Frank Churchill, I presume," E II 18 305 3
that is, if I may presume to call myself an addition. E II 18 307 23
That is, I presume it to be so on her side, and I can E III 5 351 37
themselves, she could not presume to indulge them. E III 12 415 1
Not that I presume to insinuate, however, that some people E III 16 457 33
He is a man whom I cannot presume to praise." E III 18 478 59
wit, and then added, "I presume to observe, Sir Walter, P III 3 17 2
3
She is not so near her end, I presume, but that she may P IV 5 157 15

PRESUMED (14)
From the latter circumstance it may be presumed, that, NA II 1 131 15
but to a man and a soldier, she presumed not to censure it. SS II 9 211 39
Your daughter Elizabeth, it is presumed, will not long PP III 15 362 14
excepting one--to be presumed the parsonage, within a MP II 7 241 13
It had been, as he before presumed, too hasty a measure on MP III 5 356 1
It was presumed that Mr. Crawford was travelling back to MP III 12 415 1
2
by the very few who presumed ever to see imperfection in E II 1 155 2
seeing my son's hand, presumed to open it--though it was E II 18 305 5
"I never should have presumed to think of it at first," E III 11 411 39
I should not have presumed on such early measures, but E III 14 440 8
his daughter had ever presumed to hope for at the moment, E III 19 484 11
After a short pause, Mr. Shepherd presumed to say, "in all P III 3 18 9
10
Anne presumed, however, still to smile about it; and at P IV 4 147 7
clear brain she presumed, & talked a good deal by rote.-- S 7 398 1

PRESUMING (6)
presuming to make it, than have seen him at Stanton.-- W 347 22
Presuming, however, that this studied avoidance spoke PP III 2 264 11
Pray forgive me, if I have been very presuming, or a least PP III 10 325 2
could not help modestly presuming that her mother meant to MP III 7 385 38
be wished; but without presuming to look forward to a MP III 17 468 22
presuming, familiar, ignorant, and ill-bred. E II 15 281 1

PRESUMPTION (14)
the request, though its presumption would certainly appear NA II 2 139 7
circumstance, the strangest presumption against him. NA II 10 206 31
the chaise into an hackney coach is such a presumption! PP III 5 282 6
There was nothing of presumption or folly in Bingley, that PP III 13 346 21
This match, to which you have the presumption to aspire, PP III 14 354 40
would be a presumption; for which she had not words strong MP II 9 264 18
an early return, was a presumption which hardly any thing MP III 14 436 15
of his inconstancy and presumption; and with fewer E I 15 130 29
30
He might have doubled his presumption to me--but poor E I 16 134 2
fancy himself shewing no presumption in addressing her!-- E I 16 135 8
But she had made up her mind how to meet this presumption E II 7 207 7
not the presumption to suppose--indeed I am not so mad.-- E III 4 341 36
too great a presumption almost, to dare to think of him. E III 11 405 18
How Harriet could ever have had the presumption to raise E III 11 414 50

PRESUMPTIVE (2)
in this finale: "heir presumptive, William Walter Elliot, P III 1 3 3
4
The heir presumptive, the very William Walter Elliot, Esq. P III 1 7 13

PRESUMPTUOUS (1)
that she had been presumptuous and silly, and self- E III 19 481 2

PRETENCE (23)
get Reginald home again, under any plausible pretence. LS 11 259 1
& they had therefore no pretence for interference, though LS 22 281 3
I shall probably put off his arrival, under some pretence LS 29 299 2
before, and on a false pretence too, must have been wrong. NA I 13 101 25
unprovided with any pretence for further delay, beyond NA II 8 182 1
He came with a pretence at an apology from their sister-in- SS II 11 222 14
as to determine, under pretence of fetching Marianne, to SS II 13 241 23
himself came & under pretence of talking to Charles, stood W 331 11
across the street, under pretence of wanting something in PP I 15 72 8
the law was a mere pretence, and being now free from all PP II 12 201 5
any thing, to have the pretence of being asked, of being MP I 12 120 26
pretence of receiving the note, was coming towards her. MP II 13 307 32
think of any tolerable pretence for going in;--no servant E I 10 83 7
This would not do; she immediately stopped, under pretence E I 10 88 33
it--exactly like the pretence of being in love with her, E I 15 125 4
of accent, such boastful pretence of amazement, that she E I 15 130 26
27
As to the pretence of trying her native air, I look upon E II 8 217 32
want of spirit in the pretence of it;--and she was E II 18 307 17
less to bear, she has no fair pretence of family or blood. E II 18 310 33
Mr. Woodhouse must not, under the specious pretence of a E III 6 356 29
end of people's coming to him, on some pretence or other.-- E III 16 455 23
supply his aunt with a pretence for absenting herself; and P III 8 63 1
pretence on the lady's side of meaning to leave them. P IV 4 145 1

PRETEND (34)
I do not pretend to say that I was not very much pleased NA I 6 41 19
laughingly, "I do not pretend to determine what your NA II 3 146 18
I will not pretend to say that while she lived, she might NA II 9 197 27
pretend to be unconscious, nor endeavour to be calm. SS I 4 23 19
Because he believes many people pretend to more admiration SS I 18 97 6
"Don't pretend to deny it, because you know it is what SS I 20 115 46
"Nay, my dear, I'm sure I don't pretend to say that there SS I 21 123 28
it is rather too much to pretend to know him very well." SS I 21 126 40
Don't pretend to defend him. SS II 8 196 20
but I do not pretend to be any thing extraordinary now. PP I 1 4 20
"I cannot pretend to be sorry," said Wickham, after a PP I 16 78 16
"How near it may be to mine, I cannot pretend to say.-- PP I 18 91 16
"I do not pretend to regret any thing I shall leave in PP I 21 116 8
"If! do you then pretend to be ignorant of it? PP III 14 354 30
"I do not pretend to possess equal frankness with your PP III 14 354 33
You are not going to be Missish, I hope, and pretend to be PP III 15 364 22
I do not pretend to set people right, but I do see that MP I 5 50 36
I do not pretend to know which was most to blame in their MP I 7 63 7
I do not pretend to Emma's genius for foretelling and E I 5 38 15
Don't pretend to be in raptures about mine. E I 6 43 15
He presently added, with a smile, "I do not pretend to fix E I 8 58 19
20
itself, I will not pretend to say that I might not E I 8 65 48
at her, "that she did not pretend to understand what his E I 8 68 58
"My dearest Emma, do not pretend, with your sweet temper, E I 14 123 25
before we pretend to decide upon what her nephew can do. E I 18 146 15
I do not pretend to it. E II 3 176 44
I do not pretend to be a wit. E III 7 372 37
then replied, "I will not pretend not to understand you; E III 10 396 39
he thinks--Oh! I cannot pretend to remember it, but it was P IV 2 131 9
Anne had always felt that she would pretend what was P IV 3 137 3
increased; now could he pretend to say that ten years had P IV 3 141 12
can give; for I do not pretend to understand the language. P IV 8 186 25
included; but I will not pretend to repeat half that I P IV 9 202 66
book she would lend me, and pretend I have read it through. P IV 10 215 15

PRETENDED (13)
Here she pretended to cry. LS 24 288 12
view, and when he spoke to her pretended not to hear him. NA I 10 74 23
being for daily use, pretended only to comfort, &c.; NA II 5 162 27
We happened to sit by the Mitchells, and they pretended to NA II 12 217 2
and pretended to see them blush whether they did or not. SS I 7 34 5
up all the blinds, and pretended there was nobody in the PP II 16 222 22
see you again the dupe of Miss Bingley's pretended regard." PP III 13 350 48
ago, or perhaps he only pretended the call, for the sake MP III 9 393 1
dinner, and therefore pretended to be waited for elsewhere. MP III 11 411 19
the greater seduction I pretended not to say)--but the MP III 16 457 30
raise his eyes to her, pretended to be in love; but she E I 16 135 7
and, leaning there in pretended employment, try to subdue P IV 5 160 26
was perfectly audible while it pretended to be a whisper. P IV 11 230 5

PRETENDING (10)
the younger ones, by pretending to be as handsome as their NA I 4 34 8
disagreed--but without pretending to decide it, I may say W 346 21
be aware--" but Emma pretending to understand nothing W 360 29
Mary, though pretending not to hear, was somewhat PP I 18 101 70
with walking to the window and pretending not to hear. PP I 20 114 31
with Kitty; and, while pretending to admire her work, said PP III 17 375 28
"The truth is, ma'am," said Mrs. Grant, pretending to MP I 6 54 13
whist-players, who were pretending to feel an interest in E III 2 325 32
nothing else, though pretending to listen to the others?" E III 18 480 77
to get them there, pretending to deceive himself, and P I 6 235 31

PRETENDS (3)
Every body pretends to feel and tries to describe with the SS I 18 97 7
He pretends to advise me to make a Hospital of it. S 4 382 1
He pretends to laugh at my improvements. S 4 382 1

PRETENSION (6)
of vanity, of pretension, of levity--& she is altogether LS 8 255 2
had not all the decided pretension, the resolute NA I 8 55 11
"No"--said Darcy, "I have made no such pretension. PP I 11 58 28
"I do assure you, sir, that I have no pretension whatever PP I 19 108 20
mixture of pique and pretension, now spread over his air. E II 4 182 7
and all her airs of pert pretension and under-bred finery. E II 14 279 52

PRETENSIONS (15)
low must sink my pretensions to common sense, if I am LS 14 263 1
simple, forming no pretensions, and knowing no disguise." NA II 10 206 31
is disgusted with such pretensions, he affects greater SS I 18 97 6
The Colonel, though disclaiming all pretensions to SS II 12 234 28
by thus withdrawing my pretensions to your daughter's PP I 20 114 32
Wickham's resigning all pretensions to the living, of his PP II 13 205 3
The upstart pretensions of a young woman without family, PP III 14 356 50
You shewed me how insufficient were all my pretensions to PP III 16 369 24
that he had no pretensions; his heart was reserved for you. MP III 4 350 30
of Mr. Knightley's pretensions) with the skill of such an E I 8 67 57
which people of high pretensions to judgment are for ever E I 13 112 23
Hayter, whose pretensions she wished to see put an end to. P III 9 75 12
man at least, of better pretensions than myself: and I P IV 11 244 70
a quiet village of no pretensions; but some natural S 2 371 1
young woman with any pretensions to beauty, he was S 8 405 2

PRETEXT (1)
party under some trifling pretext of employment; and her SS I 15 75 1

PRETTIER (6)
recovered to think it prettier than any pleasure-ground NA II 11 214 25
To my fancy, a thousand times prettier than Barton Park, SS II 8 197 22
Bingley had never met with pleasanter people or prettier PP I 4 16 15
Miss Crawford thought she had never seen a prettier MP II 8 259 20
of her so much prettier herself, she should never want MP III 9 396 7
Prettier musings of high-wrought love and eternal P IV 9 192 3

PRETTIER-COLOURED (1)
I have bought some prettier-coloured satin to trim it with PP II 16 219 4

PRETTIEST (11)
Do you know, I saw the prettiest hat you can imagine, in a NA I 6 39 4
I fancy; Mr. Allen thinks her the prettiest girl in Bath." NA I 7 51 50
going to dance with the prettiest girl in the room; and NA I 10 75 26
that a curricle was the prettiest equipage in the world; NA II 5 156 5
and ornaments over it of the prettiest English china. NA II 5 162 26
It is the prettiest room I ever saw;--it is the prettiest NA II 11 214 21
It is the prettiest cottage!"-- NA II 11 214 23
is one of the modestest, prettiest behaved young men I SS II 2 148 22
to be thought one of the prettiest girls in the room, W 315 1
women in the room, and which he thought the prettiest? PP I 5 19 7
Henrietta was perhaps the prettiest, Louisa had the higher P III 9 74 8

PRETTILY (9)
"Very well indeed!--how prettily she writes!--aye, that SS III 2 278 32
That sentence is very prettily turned. SS III 2 278 32
to say that he did, and he said it very prettily. SS III 13 366 20
& did everything very prettily; but as to any W 355 28
It was of gold prettily worked; and though Fanny would MP II 8 258 17
heard, and she said so prettily, 'let sister Susan have my MP III 7 386 44
"So prettily done! E I 6 48 36

Nobody could have written so prettily, but you, Emma." E I 9 78 52
Walk home!--you are prettily shod for walking home, I dare E I 15 127 15
PRETTILY-SHAPED (1)
It was a prettily-shaped room, the windows reaching to the NA II 11 213 21
PRETTINESS (1)
dark eye, clear brown complexion, and general prettiness. MP I 5 44 1
PRETTINESSES (1)
windows, and other prettinesses, was quite as likely to P III 5 36 20
PRETTY (253)
She is really excessively pretty. LS 6 251 1
which are now necessary to finish a pretty woman. LS 7 253 1
She is very pretty, tho' not so handsome as her mother, LS 17 270 5
I must punish Frederica, & pretty severely too, for her LS 25 293 4
girl,--she is almost pretty to day," were words which NA I 1 15 2
To look almost pretty, is an acquisition of higher delight NA I 1 15 2
and, when in good looks, pretty--and her mind about as NA I 2 18 1
hearing, two gentlemen pronounced her to be a pretty girl. NA I 2 24 28
excellence is pretty fairly divided between the sexes." NA I 3 28 34
"It is very pretty, madam," said he, gravely examining it; NA I 3 28 42
and answered with all the pretty expressions she could NA I 4 33 6
"Yes, pretty well; but are they all horrid, are you sure NA I 6 40 11
thought her friend quite as pretty as she could do herself. NA I 7 44 4
of the kind, though I had pretty well determined on a NA I 7 46 11
Miss Tilney had a good figure, a pretty face, and a very NA I 8 55 11
Miss Tilney was in a very pretty spotted muslin, and I NA I 9 68 42
Do you think her pretty?" NA I 10 73 15
and he seemed to have got some very pretty cattle too." NA I 11 85 39
A pretty good thought of mine--hey?" NA I 13 100 15
But I have a notion, Miss Morland, you and I think pretty NA I 15 124 44
and as he is now pretty well, is in a hurry to get home." NA II 2 138 2
urge his suit, and say all manner of pretty things to you. NA II 3 144 10
consent came--and I am pretty sure that you and John were NA II 3 145 12
You know I carry my notions of friendship pretty high. NA II 3 146 20
If I could believe it--my spirit, you know, is pretty NA II 3 147 22
"Is it a pretty place?" asked Catherine. NA II 7 175 14
Catherine was ashamed to say how pretty she thought it, as NA II 11 212 17
You know I have a pretty good spirit of my own. NA II 12 217 2
Allen thought them very pretty kind of your people; and NA II 14 236 15
which, perhaps, they pretty equally knew was already NA II 15 243 9
Isabella, but likewise pretty well resolved upon marrying NA II 15 244 12
give her, would be a pretty addition to Mr. Allen's estate. NA II 15 245 12
happened pretty often, they always looked another way. NA II 16 250 3
and eighteen, is to do pretty well; and professing myself NA II 16 252 7
The Miss Dashwoods were young, pretty, and unaffected. SS I 7 33 3
unaffected was all that a pretty girl could want to make SS I 7 33 3
always anxious to get a good husband for every pretty girl. SS I 8 36 1
Miss Dashwood; he has a pretty little estate of his own in SS I 9 44 23
regular features, and a remarkably pretty figure. SS I 10 46 2
"for one morning I think you have done pretty well. SS I 10 47 4
There is one remarkably pretty sitting room up stairs; of SS I 13 69 76
Charlotte is very pretty, I can tell you. SS I 19 105 16
She was short and plump, had a very pretty face, and the SS I 19 106 22
"Now, palmer, you shall see a monstrous pretty girl." SS I 19 108 34
was at his house; but they say it is a sweet pretty place." SS I 20 111 14
it must be some other place that is so pretty I suppose." SS I 20 111 17
me word they are very pretty, and that one of them is SS I 20 115 50
you both excessively pretty, and so does Mr. Palmer too I SS I 20 116 58
Lucy is monstrous pretty, and so good humoured and SS I 21 119 4
beauty; her features were pretty, and she had a sharp SS I 21 120 6
"Edward's love for me," said Lucy, "has been pretty well SS II 2 147 10
"All this," thought Elinor, "is very pretty; but it can SS II 2 148 13
is quite as modest and pretty behaved as Miss Dashwood's." SS II 2 148 23
was caught by every thing pretty, expensive, or new; who SS II 4 165 24
the truth it was not very pretty of him not to give you SS II 5 171 36
and with your pretty face you will never want admirers. SS II 8 192 3
to me, that a man should use such a pretty girl so ill! SS II 8 194 8
comes and makes love to a pretty girl, and promises SS II 8 194 10
choose for herself; and a pretty choice she has made!-- SS II 8 195 14
stewponds, and a very pretty canal; and every thing, in SS II 8 197 22
"Oh, Oh!" cried Mrs. Jennings; "very pretty, indeed! and SS II 10 218 25
"Aye, aye; that is very pretty talking--but it won't do-- SS II 10 218 27
will slope down just before it, and be exceedingly pretty. SS II 11 226 39
Elinor had painted a very pretty pair of screens for her SS II 12 234 26
"Hum"--said Mrs. Ferrars--"very pretty,"--and without SS II 12 235 29
said, "they are very pretty, ma'am--an't they?" SS II 12 235 30
31

be able to meet, and meet pretty often, for Lady SS II 13 240 15
It is as pretty a letter as ever I saw, and does Lucy's SS III 2 278 32
recommended by so pretty a face, was engaging; her folly, SS III 6 304 13
She was pretty too--at least I thought so then, and I had SS III 13 362 5
You are very pretty, & it would be very hard that you W 320 2
doing pretty well, tho' it would be nothing for Penelope.-- W 322 2
about 30 years ago; I am pretty sure I danced with her in W 325 4
A new face & a very pretty one, could not be slighted--her W 328 9
She is so pretty!" as they were immediately in motion W 332 11
& as the partridges were pretty high, Dr Richards would W 344 20
attention;--there is a pretty steep flight of steps up to W 344 20
Margaret was not without beauty; she had a slight, pretty W 349 23
A pretty peice of work your Aunt Turner has made of it!-- W 351 26
and there are several of them you see uncommonly pretty." PP I 3 11 10
you, who is very pretty, and I dare say, very agreeable. PP I 3 11 12
five times as pretty as every other woman in the room. PP I 4 14 5
Miss Bennet he acknowledged to be pretty, but she smiled PP I 4 16 15
there were a great many pretty women in the room, and PP I 5 19 7
Mr. Darcy had at first scarcely allowed her to be pretty; PP I 6 23 12
of fine eyes in the face of a pretty woman can bestow." PP I 6 27 48
leave it; and when I am in town it is pretty much the same. PP I 9 43 22
However, he wrote some verses on her, and very pretty they PP I 9 44 31
falls in love with a pretty girl for a few weeks, and when PP II 2 140 6
to Mrs. Collins, was a very genteel, pretty kind of girl. PP II 6 163 15
pretty friend has moreover caught his fancy very much. PP II 8 172 3
will give you a very pretty notion of me, and teach you PP II 8 174 15
that she had somehow or other got pretty near the truth. PP II 10 184 20
I do not think it is very pretty; but I thought I might as PP II 16 219 3
of man; and of late it has been shifting about pretty much. PP II 17 225 10
her return, agitation was pretty well over; the agitations PP II 18 233 25
Elizabeth thought this was going pretty far; and she PP III 1 248 30
were shewn into a very pretty sitting-room, lately fitted PP III 1 249 43
and I believe you thought her rather pretty at one time." PP III 3 271 17
You know pretty well, I suppose, what has been done for PP III 10 324 2
He smiled, looked handsome, and said many pretty things. PP III 11 330 7
and her nieces are very pretty behaved girls, and not at PP III 12 342 28
the term, she found that it had been pretty much the case. PP III 16 370 39
in the world, as there are pretty women to deserve them. MP I 1 3 1
Suppose her a pretty girl, and seen by Tom or Edmund for MP I 1 7 6
was sweet, and when she spoke her countenance was pretty. MP I 2 12 2
he made her some very pretty presents, and laughed at her. MP I 2 17 22
plan; and it was pretty soon decided between them, that MP I 2 18 23
sitting-room with pretty furniture, and made a choice MP I 4 41 15
Mary Crawford was remarkably pretty; Henry, though not MP I 4 41 17
most allowably a sweet pretty girl, while they were the MP I 5 44 1
to have it so; a talking pretty young woman like Miss MP I 5 47 26
"And a very pretty story it is, and with more truth in it, MP I 5 50 36
"if I were you, I would have a very pretty shrubbery. MP I 6 55 16
but it being excessively pretty, it was soon found MP I 6 57 31
She entertains me; and she is so extremely pretty, that I MP I 7 63 2
A young woman, pretty, lively, with a harp as elegant as MP I 7 65 13
all that was new, and admiring all that was pretty. MP I 8 80 31
Miss Crawford was not slow to admire; she pretty well MP I 8 82 35
"The metropolis, I imagine, is a pretty fair sample of the MP I 9 93 48
"A pretty trick, upon my word! MP I 10 100 26
A pretty good day's amusement you have had!" MP I 10 105 53
"I think you have done pretty well yourself, ma'am. MP I 10 105 54
Yes, indeed, a very pretty match. MP I 12 118 18
Four thousand a year is a pretty estate, and he seems a MP I 12 118 20
"A pretty modest request upon my word!" he indignantly MP I 12 119 26
Cottager's wife is a very pretty part I assure you. MP I 14 134 12
I believe I might speak pretty sharp; and I dare say it MP I 15 142 22
man;--his sister a sweet, pretty, elegant, lively girl." MP II 1 186 30
"Your uncle thinks you very pretty, dear Fanny--and that MP II 3 197 8
had not been thought very pretty before; but the truth is, MP II 3 197 8
You must try not to mind growing up into a pretty woman." MP II 3 198 8
pretty piece--and your cousin Edmund's prime favourite. MP II 4 207 9
"This is pretty--very pretty," said Fanny, looking around MP II 4 208 12
Your gown seems very pretty. MP II 5 222 44
He will have a very pretty income to make ducks and drakes MP II 5 226 61
not plain looking girl, but she is now absolutely pretty. MP II 6 229 5
I have always thought her pretty--not strikingly pretty-- MP II 6 230 6
strikingly pretty--but 'pretty enough' as people say; a MP II 6 230 6
the view is really very pretty; I am sure it may be done. MP II 7 242 23
very pretty meadows they are, finely sprinkled with timber. MP II 7 242 23
I am a pretty good dancer in my way, but I dare say you MP II 7 250 59
in her possession, a very pretty amber cross which William MP II 8 254 8
it six times; it is very pretty--but I never think of it; MP II 8 260 22
Young, pretty, and gentle, however, she had no MP II 10 276 13
strength for more were pretty well at an end; and Sir MP II 10 279 22
very accomplished and pleasing, and one very pretty. MP II 11 288 28
for it would be a very pretty establishment for them. MP II 11 289 34
By convincing her that Fanny was very pretty, which she MP III 2 332 22
enough; to know him pretty thoroughly, is, perhaps, not MP III 3 338 14
party of females were pretty well composed, and the mother MP III 7 385 37
of another sister, a very pretty little girl, whom she had MP III 7 385 40
from London; write me a pretty one in reply to gladden MP III 9 394 1
do not stay at Portsmouth to lose your pretty looks. MP III 12 416 3
I hope they get on pretty well together. MP III 13 423 2
It was a sort of laugh, as she answered, 'a pretty good MP III 16 458 30
unhappy, till some other pretty girl could attract him MP III 17 464 12
me how I do, in a very pretty manner; and when you have E I 1 9 19
Being pretty well aware of what sort of joy you must both E I 1 10 27
You have drawn two pretty pictures--but I think there may E I 1 13 43
"Mr. Elton is a very pretty young man to be sure, and a E I 1 14 47
She was a very pretty girl, and her beauty happened to be E I 3 23 9
little Welch cow, a very pretty little Welch cow, indeed; E I 4 27 4
"You understand the force of influence pretty well, E I 4 31 24
"But there may be pretty good guessing. E I 4 33 38
Very well; I shall not attempt to deny Emma's being pretty. E I 5 39 17
"Pretty! say beautiful rather. E I 5 39 18
a pretty height and size; such a firm and upright figure. E I 5 39 20
hints, she was soon pretty confident of creating as much E I 6 42 1
Then here is my last"--unclosing a pretty sketch of a E I 6 45 21
its being in every way a pretty drawing at last, and of E I 6 47 27
"It is very pretty," said Mr. Woodhouse. E I 6 48 36
I come in for a pretty good share as a second. E I 6 49 44
He must have a pretty good opinion of himself." E I 7 54 29
said he; "but she is a pretty little creature, and I am E I 8 58 10
She is pretty, and she is good tempered, and that is all. E I 8 61 38
as you describe her, only pretty and good-natured, let me E I 8 63 44
marriage flow in so fast, though she is a very pretty girl. E I 8 64 47
as Harriet wrote a very pretty hand, it was likely to be E I 9 70 4
pretty gallant charade remains, fit for any collection. E I 9 77 42
a very pretty charade, and we have just copied it in." E I 9 78 50
It is such a pretty charade, my dear, that I can easily E I 9 78 52
have him called Henry, which I thought very pretty of her. E I 9 80 72
all remarkably clever; and they have so many pretty ways. E I 9 80 72
Mrs. John Knightley was a pretty, elegant little woman, of E I 11 92 4
But I hope she is pretty well, sir." E I 11 93 7
"Pretty well, my dear--I hope--pretty well.-- E I 11 94 8
does come and see us pretty often--but then--she is always E I 11 94 16
However, it was an exceeding good, pretty letter, and gave E I 11 96 24
and by not being a pretty young woman and a spoiled child. E I 12 99 10
"Why, pretty well; but not quite well. E I 12 101 25
"Why, pretty well, my dear, upon the whole. E I 12 102 32
however, is just such another pretty kind of young person. E I 12 104 47
48

every constitution, and pretty severe Philippics upon the E I 12 104 50
The misfortune of Harriet's cold had been pretty well gone E I 14 117 3
I should like to see two more here,--your pretty little E I 14 119 7
Her height was pretty, just such as almost everybody would E II 2 167 12
I like old friends; and Miss Jane Fairfax is a very pretty E II 3 171 12
a very pretty and a very well-behaved young lady indeed. E II 3 171 12
There were several very pretty houses in and about it.-- E II 5 191 27
that I was to find a pretty young woman in Mrs. Weston." E II 5 192 30
that you have spoken of her as a pretty young woman." E II 5 192 31
He was soon pretty well resigned. E II 7 209 9
to sit and smile and look pretty, and say nothing, was E II 8 219 44
they will say something pretty loud about you and me in E II 10 245 49
pretty indeed, or only rather pretty, or not pretty at all. E II 14 270 1
A pretty fortune; and she came in his way." E II 14 271 12
The grounds of Hartfield were small, but neat and pretty; E II 14 272 18
The advantages of Bath to the young are pretty generally E II 14 275 32
before, she seems a very pretty sort of young lady; and I E II 14 279 54
Her observation had been pretty correct. E II 15 281 1
said Jane, "they are pretty sure to be equal; however, I E II 17 301 19
Well, pretty good news, is not it? E II 17 304 27
help to persuade him into it, which was done pretty soon.-- E III 2 325 31
Within abundance of silver paper was a pretty little E III 4 338 9
and after a a pretty long speech from Miss Bates, which E III 5 344 3
walk, and the view which closed it extremely pretty.-- E III 6 360 38
very pretty trick you have been playing me, upon my word! E III 10 400 67
68

She promised, however, to think of it; and pretty nearly E III 15 449 34
"Very pretty, sir, upon my word; to send me on here, to be E III 16 457 36
A few years before, Anne Elliot had been a very pretty P III 1 6 10
Your interest, Sir Walter, is in pretty safe hands. P III 3 19 10
had, in the course of a pretty long conference, expressed P III 3 21 18
and Anne an extremely pretty girl, with gentleness, P III 4 26 1
merits, can never have been reckoned tolerably pretty! P III 5 35 14
She was now lying on the faded sofa of the pretty little P III 5 37 21
22

their faces were rather pretty, their spirits extremely P III 5 40 45
"upon my word, I shall be pretty well off, when you are P III 6 42 1
"I knew pretty well what she was, before that day;" said P III 8 65 16
"Pretty well, ma'am, in the fifteen years of my marriage; P III 8 70 52
whenever my uncle dies, he steps into very pretty property. P III 9 76 15
"Well, and I had heard of you as a very pretty girl; and P III 10 92 46
and fashioned very pretty shelves, for a tolerable P III 11 99 18
her very regular, very pretty features, having the bloom P III 12 104 6
she was said to be an excessively pretty woman, beautiful. P IV 3 141 13
He did not mean to say that there were no pretty women, P IV 3 141 13
shewed to Mr. Elliot the pretty features which he had by P IV 3 143 18
his mind, nor (she began pretty soon to suspect) to P IV 4 147 6
mere pretty, silly, expensive, fashionable woman, I P IV 5 156 13
Here are pretty girls enough, I am sure. P IV 6 173 49
"She is pretty, I think; Anne Elliot; very pretty, when P IV 7 177 21
Colonel Wallis has a very pretty silly wife, to whom he P IV 9 205 82
So much was pretty soon understood; but till Sir Walter P IV 10 216 18
it, and Henrietta was pretty near as bad; and so we P IV 11 230 6
heads to marry, they are pretty sure by perseverance to P IV 12 248 1
admit that she had been pretty completely wrong, and to P IV 12 249 3
the mistress of a very pretty landaulette; but she had a P IV 12 250 5
They had very pretty property--enough, had their family S 2 373 1
a careful mother, many a pretty daughter, might it secure S 4 382 1
without, & among so many pretty temptations, & with so S 6 390 1
Miss Denham's character was pretty well decided with S 7 396 1

fine speeches to every pretty girl, was but the inferior S 8 405 2
The world is pretty much divided between the weak of mind S 9 410 1

PRETTY-BEHAVED (1)
However, she seems a very obliging, pretty-behaved young E II 14 279 54

PRETTYISH (1)
there seemed to be a prettyish kind of a little wilderness PP III 14 352 16
17

PREVAIL (19)
He is if possible to prevail on Miss Summers to let LS 15 266 4
I told him he had taken a very unlikely way to prevail NA II 1 134 39
But Sir John could not prevail. SS I 21 119 5
and Mrs. Jennings could not prevail on him to stay long. SS II 4 163 20
that she could neither prevail on him to make the offer SS II 10 216 15
seeing either of them, to prevail on her sister, who had SS II 10 217 18
Nothing should prevail on him to give up his engagement. SS III 1 267 42
and though he could not prevail with her to dance with him PP I 18 102 73
promised, at parting, to prevail on Mr. Bennet to return PP III 6 294 2
they could not always prevail; and in the course of a long MP II 9 267 22
prevail so decidedly against the habits of the Churchills. E II 6 198 5
"You certainly will meet them if I can prevail; and I E III 6 355 19
She resolved to prevail on her to spend a day at Hartfield. E III 9 389 16
I was fortunate enough to prevail, before we parted at E III 14 437 8
of things, and the reports beginning to prevail.-- P IV 9 206 90
His eloquence however could not prevail. S 2 373 1
melancholy, just as satire or morality might prevail.-- S 7 396 1
Is not it possible to prevail on you to dine with us?" was S 9 410 1
Such a plea must prevail, he got the butter & spread away S 10 417 1

PREVAILED (42)
"Yes, my father can seldom be prevailed on to give the NA II 2 138 2
Can you, in short, be prevailed on to quit this scene of NA II 2 139 7
as soon as she could be prevailed on, a physician attended NA II 9 196 25
would have kept it; but the discretion of Elinor prevailed. SS I 5 26 5
country, Marianne was prevailed on to join her sisters in SS I 16 85 15
of every week, they were prevailed on to stay nearly two SS II 2 151 43
difficulty that Elinor prevailed on her, when she went to SS III 6 306 17
Mrs. Dashwood was prevailed on to accept the use of his SS III 10 341 4
but was prevailed on to come down & drink tea with them.-- W 354 28
however, could not be prevailed on to join in their PP I 9 46 39
a hope that she might be prevailed on to favour them again, PP I 18 100 68
girls, and Mary might have been prevailed on to accept him. PP I 22 124 11
the report which shortly prevailed in Meryton of his PP I 23 129 12
But do you think she would be prevailed on to go back with PP II 2 141 10
Charlotte, but was scarcely ever prevailed on to get out. PP II 7 168 2
in the world whom I could ever be prevailed on to marry." PP II 11 193 28
by the feelings which prevailed on his entering the room; PP III 3 268 7
that, could Wickham be prevailed on to marry his daughter, PP III 8 309 4
married, that he was prevailed on to think as they thought, PP III 8 314 22
as soon as they could be prevailed on to receive her, PP III 10 322 2
But when her mother was gone, Jane would not be prevailed PP III 13 344 10
Bingley instantly prevailed on Miss Bennet to avoid the PP III 14 351 1
that Darcy might yet be prevailed on to make his fortune. PP III 19 386 6
But at length, by Elizabeth's persuasion, he was prevailed PP III 19 388 12
happy star no longer prevailed, was obliged to keep by the MP I 9 90 36
to his mother, and then prevailed on my sister to pay the MP II 2 188 3
"Your sister perhaps may be prevailed on to spend the day MP II 5 219 22
It was time to have done with cards if sermons prevailed, MP II 7 248 48
other circumstances, but Fanny's happiness still prevailed. MP II 10 273 5
puzzle, and could not be prevailed on to add another word, MP III 3 341 27
when Rebecca had been prevailed on to carry away the tea- MP III 7 385 37
She was not to be prevailed on to leave Mr. Crawford. MP III 17 464 10
curiosity to see him prevailed, though the compliment was E I 2 17 8
The like reserve prevailed on other topics. E II 2 169 17
We are in great hopes that Miss Woodhouse may be prevailed E II 8 216 16
Well, Mrs. Weston, you have prevailed, I hope, and these E II 9 237 46
her; but he could not be prevailed on by all his father's E III 1 317 6
spirits one morning because she thought she had prevailed. E III 5 346 16
of pleasure and pain, that she knew not which prevailed. P III 10 91 42
He almost wished she had been prevailed on to come home P IV 1 121 2
or the gapes, as real or affected taste for it prevailed. P IV 8 189 45
who, when once she is prevailed on to undraw her purse, S 12 424 1

PREVAILING (15)
Not that I am an advocate for the prevailing fashion of LS 7 253 1
but you could have any chance of prevailing with her. LS 21 279 1
for her choice of the prevailing colour of the paper and NA II 11 214 25
There was a thought yet nearer, a more prevailing, more NA II 14 231 4
Sir John was delighted; for to a man, whose prevailing SS II 3 157 19
nothing but the most prevailing desire to keep out of your SS III 8 326 55
feared, that instead of prevailing on feelings so selfish SS III 11 351 9
Anxiety on Jane's behalf, was another prevailing concern, PP II 14 213 18
The satisfaction of prevailing on one of the most PP III 8 308 1
flow of conversation prevailing in which she was not MP II 5 223 48
towards her, a general prevailing desire of recommending MP II 10 276 14
in Hill-Street, and prevailing on the Admiral to exert MP II 13 300 7
the remainder by prevailing on you to accompany me down MP III 1 314 16
I have great hope of our prevailing. P III 2 12 4
The sad accident at Lyme was soon the prevailing topic; P IV 1 126 20

PREVAILS (2)
of spirit, which prevails so much in modern days, even in MP III 1 318 39
of hand-writing often prevails in a family; and where the E II 16 297 45

PREVALENCE (3)
by the prevalence of every thing opposite to them here. MP III 8 391 10
the occasional prevalence of the ridiculous over the good. E III 7 375 61
in a circle",--to the prevalence of which rototory motion, S 11 421 1

PREVALENT (2)
is so prevalent, that I confess I cannot help trembling. MP III 14 433 13
But colds were never so prevalent as they have been this E I 12 102 33

PREVENT (101)
take some pains to prevent my brother-in-law's marrying LS 5 249 1
Could matters have been so arranged as to prevent the LS 5 249 1
little better, to prevent my beleiving whatever she says. LS 6 251 1
I shall trouble you meanwhile to prevent his forming any LS 7 253 1
This project will serve at least to amuse me, & prevent my LS 7 254 3
could prevent a young man's being in love if he chose it. LS 10 258 2
take all possible pains to prevent his marrying Catherine. LS 12 260 2
of my power to prevent your inheriting the family estate. LS 12 261 4
my eyes so much as to prevent my reading it myself, so I LS 13 262 1
of yours, should not only prevent our meeting this LS 13 263 1
some pains are taken to prevent her being much with me. LS 17 270 6
When she first came, I was at some pains to prevent her LS 19 274 3
least delay his journey to Bath, if not wholly prevent it. LS 28 298 1
Do not accuse me; indeed, it was impossible to prevent it. LS 32 303 1
of forty surrounding families cannot prevent her. NA I 1 16 11
her so much as to prevent her looking very often towards NA I 8 55 10
be taken by government to prevent its coming to effect." NA I 14 112 34
their dinner in haste, to prevent being in the dark; and NA I 15 116 1
put her on her guard, and prevent all the pain which her NA II 3 148 28
if a small sacrifice of time and attention can prevent it. NA II 11 210 6
twenty other causes may prevent, I must go away directly, NA II 11 210 7
would not on any account prevent her accompanying him. NA II 15 243 9
A present of fifty pounds, now and then, will prevent SS I 2 11 23
from Norland as to prevent his being of any service to her SS I 5 25 4
was enough to prevent her making any inquiry of Marianne. SS I 14 71 4
would prevent the denial which her wishes might direct." SS I 16 84 9
every copy, I believe, to prevent their falling into SS I 17 92 25
prevent your whole youth from being wasted in discontent. SS I 19 103 7
to subdue it, and to prevent herself from appearing to SS I 19 104 9
As it was impossible however now to prevent their coming, SS I 21 118 2
pocket, she added, "to prevent the possibility of mistake, SS I 22 131 35
in her endeavour to prevent a visit, which she could not SS II 3 154 6
least it need not prevent my accepting her invitation. SS II 3 156 14
"At any rate," said Elinor, wishing to prevent Mrs. SS II 5 167 4
With difficulty however could she prevent her from SS II 6 177 15
reached just in time to prevent her from falling on the SS II 7 185 16
commonest kind must prevent such a hasty removal as that." SS II 7 191 63
scenes as must prevent her ever knowning a moment's rest. SS II 10 214 6
would do all in her power to prevent his advancing in it." SS III 1 267 38
was very urgent to prevent her sister's going at all; and SS III 5 294 3
like mine, any thing was to be done to prevent a rupture. SS III 8 328 63
something would occur to prevent his marrying Lucy; that SS III 12 357 1
would have been taken to prevent the marriage; and he SS III 13 371 38
dignity, and as served to prevent every suspicion of good- SS III 14 373 3
did she endeavour to prevent such a proof of complaisance,- PP I 18 100 68
hand, do all in my power to prevent your being otherwise. PP I 19 107 16
from Netherfield would prevent Mr. Bingley's being there; PP I 21 116 8
will be so numerous as to prevent your feeling the loss of PP I 21 117 11
attachment and nothing to prevent it, am I wrong, my PP I 21 118 14
her lover, she could not prevent its frequently recurring. PP I 23 129 13
He shall not be in love with me, if I can prevent it." PP II 3 144 5
"Aye, no doubt; but that is what a governess will prevent, PP II 6 165 32
else was brought; and to prevent its ever happening again, PP II 10 182 1
which had made him prevent his friend's marrying her PP II 11 193 31
shall not prevent me from unfolding his real character. PP II 12 200 5
for the father, would always prevent his exposing the son. PP II 13 207 5
our power to prevent your spending your time unpleasantly." PP II 15 215 2
This unfortunate affair will, I fear, prevent my sister's PP III 4 278 20
But, however, that shan't prevent my asking him to dine PP III 11 333 26
From what she had said of her resolution to prevent their PP III 15 360 2
"What is to prevent you?" MP I 3 26 27
To prevent its being expected, she had fixed on the MP I 3 28 38
"You need not hurry when the object is only to prevent my MP I 9 94 56
to be wrong, could not help making an effort to prevent it. MP I 10 99 21
only half a play--an act--a scene; what should prevent us? MP I 13 123 6
He was determined to prevent it, if possible, though his MP I 13 124 13
difference of opinion, to prevent their being very good MP I 17 162 19
prevent what her judgment must certainly have disapproved. MP II 2 188 3
deference for him, could prevent him from soon discerning MP II 3 200 19
work in such a state as to prevent her being missed. MP II 5 220 29
the very name, I would prevent the marriage, if possible; MP II 12 296 29
You have an understanding, which will prevent you from MP III 1 313 12
and she did not know how to prevent or put an end to it. MP III 11 409 5
and we cannot prevent ourselves from being greatly alarmed, MP III 13 426 11
in; but he brings no intelligence to prevent my sending it. MP III 14 435 14
with, and just in time to prevent their sitting down to MP III 15 445 31
vain, as earnestly tried to prevent any body's eating it. E I 2 19 14
decidedly, I think, as must prevent any second application. E I 8 65 48
yet been no weather to prevent the young ladies from E I 10 83 1
and Mrs. Weston do really prevent our missing her by any E I 11 94 14
not begin yesterday, and prevent this day's party, which E I 13 115 39
either could say could prevent some renewal of alarm at E I 15 128 22
The very want of such equality might prevent his E I 16 136 9
forward to prevent Harriet's being obliged to say a word. E II 1 156 5
of her, I cannot wish to prevent it, provided the weather E II 7 209 10
Miss Woodhouse, I hope nothing may happen to prevent the E II 12 258 5
And then, to prevent further outrage and indignation, E II 14 276 34
35
no degree of vanity can prevent her acknowledging her own E II 15 287 23
it hardly possible to prevent their making two distinct E II 17 299 1
No misfortune occurred, again to prevent the ball. E III 2 319 1
came, and went early, that nothing might prevent her. E III 8 377 2
first object to prevent her from suffering unnecessarily.-- E III 15 446 20
be, and that he could not prevent it--a very promising E III 19 483 9
"My feelings, you see, did not prevent my taking Mrs. P III 8 69 44
could prevent her from going to look for a better also. P III 10 86 21
to suspect) to prevent his thinking of a second choice. P IV 4 147 6
"Why, to be sure, ma'am," said she, "it would not prevent P IV 9 208 92
of Mr. Elliot's subtleties, in endeavouring to prevent it. P IV 10 215 13
to exist there as must prevent the marriage from being P IV 10 217 20
I think, all parents should prevent as far as they can." P IV 11 231 9
not have been able to prevent) her air was calm & grave.-- S 7 395 1

PREVENTED (84)
The long illness of her dear father prevented my paying LS 1 244 1
with you; & we are prevented that happiness by a LS 3 246 1
My having prevented it, may perhaps have given his wife an LS 5 250 1
of propriety which prevented Miss Summers from keeping the LS 19 274 2
not to have prevented your speaking to me on the subject. LS 24 286 7
skelton; when her friend prevented her, by saying,--for NA I 6 42 33
alley, they were prevented crossing by the approach of a NA I 7 44 1
for her question, but he prevented her by saying, "novels NA I 7 48 34
A pre-engagement in Edgar's Buildings prevented his NA I 7 51 54
of these requisites, prevented their doing more than going NA I 8 56 11
of the time prevented her buying a new one for the evening. NA I 10 73 22
lobby for a chair, he prevented the inquiry which had NA I 12 95 18
the party had not been prevented by her refusing to join NA I 14 115 55
Miss Tilney, however, prevented their wishing it otherwise; NA II 5 154 1
"And that prevented you;" said Henry, earnestly regarding NA II 9 195 16
He was prevented, however, from even looking his surprize NA II 10 203 8
have always been prevented by some silly trifler or other. NA II 12 216 2
The pressing anxieties of thought, which prevented her NA II 14 231 5
the fears which had prevented their mother and Elinor from SS I 9 41 4
Edward could have prevented from being immediately sprung. SS I 18 99 15
grief, it was at least prevented from unnecessary increase, SS I 19 104 10
want of instruction prevented their meeting in SS I 22 127 2
a flutter in them which prevented their giving much SS II 4 161 6
on her own, prevented their calling in Berkeley-Street. SS II 5 170 28
unhappiness, and was prevented even from wishing it SS II 5 174 47
his own misconduct, and prevented her from believing him SS II 6 178 17
Marianne's mind not only prevented her from remaining in SS II 7 180 5
Elinor was prevented from making any reply to this civil SS II 13 240 18
him to Mr. Pratt's, all this would have been prevented.' SS II 14 251 13
usual, had prevented her going to them within that time. SS III 2 270 3
did she find herself prevented by a settled rain from SS III 6 303 11
companion, and only prevented from being so always, by too SS III 6 304 15
Nothing but such a persuasion could have prevented his SS III 13 367 21
Mrs. Bennet was prevented replying by the entrance of the PP I 7 30 14
most pleasing, and they prevented her feeling herself so PP I 8 35 2
constitution, which has prevented her making that progress PP I 11 67 7
heart; but the delicacy of it prevented farther inquiry. PP I 16 78 21
of rain as prevented their walking to Meryton once. PP I 17 88 15
her mother's reproach prevented his feeling any regret. PP I 20 112 24
seen her for a twelvemonth, prevented their coming lower. PP II 4 152 5
When have you been prevented by want of money from going PP II 10 183 11
and as much as possible prevented her husband from PP II 10 187 41
The feelings which, you tell me, have long prevented the PP II 11 190 7
that had long prevented my forming any serious design. PP II 11 192 22
Ultimately have prevented the marriage, had it not been PP II 12 199 5
Regard for my sister's credit and feelings prevented any PP II 12 202 5
valueless, you cannot be prevented by the same cause from PP II 12 203 5
Mr. Gardiner would be prevented by business from setting PP II 19 238 7
This observation would not have prevented her from trying PP III 3 268 5
might have prevented it!--I who knew what he was. PP III 4 277 12
had alone prevented their exceeding their income. PP III 8 308 3
that if he had been prevented going, the wedding need not PP III 9 319 25
of his concern, at having been prevented by business. PP III 11 338 59
indifferent, would have prevented his coming down again!" PP III 13 350 49
in their marriage, to be prevented by a young woman of PP III 14 355 43
His diffidence had prevented his depending on his own PP III 16 371 45
the difference which prevented their being more apparent; MP I 2 21 34
which prevented her from being very ungracious. MP I 6 52 1
of seeing Mr. Rushworth prevented her thinking so much of MP I 10 101 33
By a look at her brother, she prevented any farther MP I 15 147 56
of such magnitude as must, if possible, be prevented. MP I 16 154 8
of unquietness, but prevented him even from seeing the MP II 1 184 27
for as she was not prevented from offering, nor you from MP II 9 263 14
of a housemaid prevented any further conversation. MP II 9 270 40

she would not have prevented it, was lamenting the change MP II 11 284 10
whose modesty had prevented her from understanding his MP III 2 326 3
Farther discussion was prevented by various bustles; first, MP III 7 379 19
before he declared himself prevented by a prior engagement. MP III 10 406 22
I will not be prevented, however, from making my own MP III 13 420 2
should rather be prevented than sought--all this together MP III 16 457 30
reserved manners which prevented his being generally E I 11 92 5
recollections of the other, prevented any renewal of it. E I 12 107 62
Many vain solicitudes would be prevented--many E II 4 182 8
often hoping, intending to come--but was always prevented. E III 1 316 6
attack of Mrs. Churchill that he was prevented coming.-- E III 6 361 41
She might have prevented the indulgence and increase of E III 11 402 1
was very conscious that she ought to have prevented them.-- E III 11 402 1
no tongue could express, prevented her marrying the E III 11 413 49
would have prevented the instrument's coming if she could." E III 15 446 18
mother's love, and mother's rights, it would be prevented. P III 4 27 3
wisdom might not have prevented, she was soon spared all P III 7 60 31
32
His lameness prevented him from taking much exercise; but P III 11 99 18
her sense of personal respect to her father prevented her. P IV 5 158 20
He had been prevented setting off for Thornberry, but I P IV 10 228 71

PREVENTING (12)
those endeavours at preventing their union, which have LS 14 264 2
it was implied in his preventing her admittance to his NA I 12 95 17
The General's evident desire of preventing such an NA II 8 186 6
her comfort by preventing her from setting off half an MP I 7 68 19
"I am convinced, madam," said Edmund, preventing Fanny, " MP I 15 141 17
I am of some use I hope in preventing waste and making the MP I 15 141 22
to her," cried Edmund, preventing his cousin's speaking, " MP II 5 217 2
too, would be the best way of preventing such things." MP III 15 440 13
and preventing his father's having any right to complain. E I 18 148 24
no preventing a laugh, sometimes in the very midst of them. E III 18 475 40
would go home with her; there was no preventing him. P IV 11 239 54
the day; whether, after preventing her from being the wife P IV 12 250 8

PREVENTION (1)
she felt some alarm from the dread of a second prevention. NA I 10 71 8

PREVENTS (2)
"Her indifferent state of health unhappily prevents her PP I 14 67 9
I assure you, Miss Anne, it prevents my wishing to see P III 6 45 8

PREVIOUS (27)
he known nothing of her previous to this personal LS 8 255 2
the house with so little previous formality, there was a SS I 9 43 11
to the many weeks of previous indisposition which SS III 7 313 21
Mrs. Dashwood by her own previous alarm; for so great was SS III 9 335 6
of the moment, or are the result of previous study?" PP I 14 68 10
intrusion, without any previous acquaintance with her, PP I 15 73 11
them so many previous months of suspense and vexation. PP III 13 347 28
But Tom's extravagance had, previous to that event, been MP I 3 23 2
pacify her, and make her overlook the previous affront? MP I 14 135 18
A fine blush having succeeded the previous paleness of her MP II 1 178 7
usual, and brought the previous self-inquiry of whether MP II 4 214 46
of there being some previous ill-opinion of him to be MP II 6 231 11
to suspect that his previous inquiries of Mrs. Norris, MP II 10 278 20
as it generally did upon a week's previous inactivity. MP III 11 409 6
the thoughtlessness and selfishness of his previous habits. MP III 17 462 4
and busy in her own previous conceptions and views to hear E I 13 110 10
been rather a pleasure, previous to the suspicions of this E I 15 129 23
she left her with every previous resolution confirmed of E I 17 142 10
him, in spite of every previous determination against it. E II 12 262 38
for in spite of her previous and fixed determination never E II 13 264 1
which he had had no previous suspicion of--and there was E III 10 399 57
which might have made every previous caution useless?-- E III 14 441 8
She was obliged, in spite of her previous determination to E III 15 444 1
Miss Bates was out, which accounted for the previous E III 16 453 11
which she wanted to carry, against previous inclination. P III 2 16 16
of attachment previous to Captain Wentworth's introduction. P III 9 73 4
the justness of his own previous opinion as to the P III 12 116 72

PREVIOUSLY (31)
to a young man previously attached to Mr Manwaring's LS 4 248 1
dearly purchased by all that you have previously suffered. LS 23 283 1
lesson, that to go previously engaged to a ball, does not NA I 8 55 10
his attentions, he had previously excited; and what had NA II 7 181 40
to be points on which I had been previously informed." SS I 10 51 22
John had been previously forming, were put in execution. SS I 11 53 1
any unreasonable abridgment, might be previously finished. SS II 3 157 15
with whom he had been previously talking, he felt the SS II 6 177 11
She was previously disposed, I believe, to doubt the SS III 8 323 40
had been for some time previously sitting--her rising SS III 11 349 3
Ignorant as you previously were of every thing concerning PP II 12 202 5
whom she had previously received the information of his PP II 13 206 4
own conduct, which had previously distressed her, and MP I 16 156 28
fancies she had been previously indulging on the strength MP II 7 248 47
his own arrangement, previously communicated to his wife MP II 7 251 65
a note which she was previously engaged in writing for MP II 12 296 31
He had previously made her the happiest of human beings, MP II 13 302 10
her spirits not being previously in the strongest state, MP III 5 365 35
surprise, that she had previously seen the upper servant, MP III 7 383 32
though she could not previously have believed herself MP III 10 399 4
Then, a letter which she had been previously preparing for MP III 13 427 12
Mr. Woodhouse, who had previously made up his mind to walk E I 8 57 2
She had previously determined how far she would proceed, E III 4 341 34
Each lady was previously well disposed for an agreement, P III 5 32 2
other house, where the Crofts had previously been calling. P III 6 49 25
Mrs. Musgrove should be previously alarmed by some share P III 12 114 64
and, previously, there had been a great deal of enjoyment. P IV 8 184 16
you might hear me previously spoken of in my own family." P IV 8 187 31
I did not know his wife previously, (her inferior P IV 9 200 57
They had previously known embarrassments enough to try the P IV 9 209 96
She had previously, in the anticipation of their marriage, P IV 9 210 99

PREY (3)
is luckily too poor to be an object of prey to any body. PP II 18 232 20
understanding would preserve her from falling an easy prey. PP III 4 279 24
We live at home, quiet, confined, and our feelings prey P IV 11 232 19

PREYED (1)
have been on herself, preyed altogether so much on her SS II 10 212 1

PRICE (119)
The price is immense, & much beyond what I can ever LS 2 246 1
the price and weigh the merits of a new muff and tippet. NA I 7 51 54
easy till she knew the price of every part of Marianne's SS II 14 249 8
fetch such a price!--what was the value of this?" SS III 5 294 10
pray, what is the usual price of an earl's younger son? PP II 10 183 15
of the rooms, and the price of the furniture, in vain. PP III 1 249 37
To save herself from useless remonstrance, Mrs. Price MP I 1 4 1
Mrs. Price in her turn was injured and angry; and an MP I 1 4 1
By the end of eleven years, however, Mrs. Price could no MP I 1 4 2
a more important advantage to Mrs. Price resulted from it. MP I 1 5 4
her wish, that poor Mrs. Price should be relieved from the MP I 1 5 4
really serviceable to Mrs. Price, and creditable to MP I 1 7 7
Mrs. Price seemed rather surprised that a girl should be MP I 1 11 19
Fanny Price was at this time just ten years old, and MP I 2 12 2
for the children of Mrs. Price; he assisted her liberally MP I 2 21 34
"I begin now to understand you all, except Miss Price," MP I 5 48 30
But now I must be satisfied about Miss Price. MP I 5 51 41
Miss Price is not out." MP I 5 51 43
"Miss Price has a brother at sea," said Edmund, "whose MP I 6 59 45
"My dear Miss Price," said Miss Crawford, as soon as she MP I 7 68 18
Miss Price, I give way to you with a very bad grace; but I MP I 7 68 20
She will have a companion in Fanny Price you know, so it MP I 8 76 3
the young lady too, Miss Price, who had never been at MP I 8 76 4
hall, of mentioning Miss Price as one who would probably MP I 8 79 23
Crawford, "you have quite convinced Miss Price already." MP I 9 93 51
Miss Price has found it so, though she did not know it." MP I 9 96 71
"Miss Price all alone!" and "my dear Fanny, how comes this? MP I 10 97 2
"Or if we are, Miss Price will be so good as to tell him, MP I 10 99 20
"Pray, Miss Price, are you such a great admirer of this Mr. MP I 10 102 41
"No, my dear Miss Price, and for reasons good. MP I 11 109 19
you a better fate Miss Price, than to be the wife of a man MP I 11 112 31
manner, "I fancy Miss Price has been more used to deserve MP I 11 112 33
"never mind, my dear Miss Price--this is a cross evening,-- MP I 15 147 56
My dear Miss Price, I beg your pardon, but I have made my MP I 18 168 15
"if Miss Price would be so good as to read the part." MP I 18 171 28
Price dripping with wet in the vestibule, was delightful. MP II 4 205 3
nothing frightful in such a picture, is there, Miss Price? MP II 4 210 21
But Miss Price and Mr. Edmund Bertram, I dare say, would MP II 4 215 49
Mrs. Grant's shewing civility to Miss Price, to Lady MP II 5 218 18
"Yes, they have been there--about a fortnight, Miss Price, MP II 5 224 50
in the letters to Mansfield Park; do you, Miss Price?-- MP II 5 224 52
"We are unlucky, Miss Price," he continued in a lower tone, MP II 5 225 57
I think, Miss Price, we would have indulged ourselves with MP II 5 225 57
Miss Price, will not you join me in encouraging your MP II 5 227 65
No, my plan it to make Fanny Price in love with me." MP II 6 229 3
"Fanny Price! MP II 6 229 4
"But I cannot be satisfied without Fanny Price, without MP II 6 229 5
But with William and Fanny Price, it was still a sentiment MP II 6 235 18
he had been a William price, distinguishing himself and MP II 6 236 22
and the arrival of William price, had much to do with it, MP II 7 238 1
thought that Mr. Crawford was the admirer of Fanny Price. MP II 7 238 2
her ladyship and Miss Price, and teach them, it was MP II 7 239 8
her dealings with William price, and securing his knave at MP II 7 242 25
Thomas, as you have perhaps heard me telling Miss Price. MP II 7 247 38
your sister dance, Mr. Price," said Henry Crawford, MP II 7 250 61
in company who does not like to have Miss Price spoken of." MP II 7 251 61
Miss Price, known only by name to half the people invited, MP II 9 266 22
Who could be happier than Miss Price? MP II 9 267 22
But Miss Price had not been brought up to the trade of MP II 9 267 22
the attic floor, when Miss Price came out of her room MP II 9 271 41
Is not there a something wanted, Miss Price, in our MP II 11 287 22
You don't speak, Fanny--Miss Price--you don't speak.-- MP II 11 289 34
be aware that I am quite determined to marry Fanny Price." MP II 12 291 4
Fanny Price--wonderful--quite wonderful!-- MP II 12 293 11
that his opinion of Fanny Price was scarcely beyond her MP II 12 294 18
never have selected Fanny Price as the girl most likely to MP II 12 294 19
"Henry, I think so highly of Fanny Price, that if I could MP II 12 296 29
in the world to make Fanny Price happy, or of ceasing to MP II 12 296 30
of ceasing to love Fanny Price, was of course the ground- MP II 12 296 30
the promotion of young price, and inclosing two more, one MP II 13 298 3
could not require William price to excite a greater MP II 13 300 5
been stumbling at Miss Price for at least the last six MP II 13 303 15
Baddeley, I am sure; Sir Thomas wants me, not Miss Price." MP III 1 325 60
"No, ma'am, it is Miss Price, I am certain of its being MP III 1 325 61
it is Miss Price, I am certain of its being Miss Price." MP III 1 325 61
to go with them--to go and see her poor dear Sister Price. MP III 6 372 21
seen her poor dear Sister Price for more than twenty years; MP III 6 372 21
her poor dear Sister Price would feel it very unkind of MP III 6 372 21
So, her poor dear Sister Price was left to all the MP III 6 373 24
the door of a small house now inhabited by Mr. Price. MP III 7 376 6
In they both came, and Mrs. Price having kindly kissed her MP III 7 378 13
and lastly in walked Mr. Price himself, his own loud voice MP III 7 379 19
had quite forgot her, Mr. Price now received his daughter; MP III 7 380 22
Mrs. Price, Rebecca, and Betsey, all went up to defend MP III 7 382 27
to the sally-port; and Mr. Price walked off at the same MP III 7 384 36
the tea-things, and Mrs. Price had walked about the room MP III 7 385 37
"Her year!" cried Mrs. Price; "I am sure I hope I shall be MP III 7 385 39
"Now, Susan," cried Mrs. Price in a complaining voice, " MP III 7 386 44
Mrs. Price was not unkind--but, instead of gaining on her MP III 8 389 4
Of her two sisters, Mrs. Price very much more resembled MP III 8 390 5
Mr. Price was out, which she regretted very much. MP III 10 400 6
They talked of William, a subject on which Mrs. Price MP III 10 400 7
recommendation to Mrs. Price and her daughters, to take MP III 10 401 10
Mrs. Price, it appeared, scarcely ever stirred out of MP III 10 401 10
Mrs. Price was greatly obliged, and very complying.-- MP III 10 401 10
man, a very different Mr. Price in his behaviour to this MP III 10 402 12
but for Mr. Crawford, Mr. Price would have turned thither MP III 10 402 13
a singular manner, had Mr. Price been allowed the entire MP III 10 403 14
or any crowd, when Mr. Price was only calling out, "come MP III 10 403 14
When Mr. Price and his friend had seen all that they MP III 10 406 21
cheerful looking Mrs. Price, coming abroad with a fine MP III 11 408 2
Mrs. Price took her weekly walk on the ramparts every fine MP III 11 408 4
miles off--not even Mrs. Price, beyond a brief question or MP III 13 428 14
Mrs. Price did quite as much for Lady Bertram, as Lady MP III 13 428 15
Bertram, as Lady Bertram would have done for Mrs. Price. MP III 13 428 15
poor dear Sister Price to have them so well provided for. MP III 13 428 15
Mr. Price cared too little about the report, to make her MP III 15 440 17
"Indeed, I hope it is not true," said Mrs. Price MP III 15 440 18
unkind, except Mrs. Price, could have overlooked, when the MP III 15 442 22
Mrs. Price talked of her poor sister for a few minutes-- MP III 15 444 26
As nothing was really left for the decision of Mrs. Price, MP III 15 444 27
and tenderness of Fanny Price, there would have been every MP III 17 467 19
were sold at a reasonable price, and where girls might be E I 3 21 5
finest flavour of all--price of strawberries in London-- E III 6 358 35
Bad things for a country;--sure to raise the price of S 1 368 1
mischeif by raising the price of things--and I have heard S 6 392 1
come among us to raise the price of our necessaries of S 6 392 1
"My dear madam, they can only raise the price of S 6 392 1
will be thinking of the price of butcher's meat in time-- S 6 393 1

PRIDE (113)
Where pride & stupidity unite, there can be no LS 4 248 2
my endeavour to humble the pride of these self-important LS 7 254 3
It would be the death of that honest pride with which I LS 12 261 4
him such an instance of pride; & am doubtful whether I LS 25 293 4
From pride, ignorance, or fashion, our foes are almost as NA I 5 37 4
was all pride, pride, insufferable haughtiness and pride! NA II 1 129 1
I know no harm of him; I do not suspect him of pride. NA II 1 130 9
not credit there being any pride in their hearts. the NA II 1 131 14
A distinction to which they had been born gave no pride. NA II 2 141 12
on which an humble man might have looked with pride.-- NA II 8 182 2
In Eleanor's presence friendship and pride had equally NA II 13 226 25
enough to melt Catherine's pride in a moment, and she NA II 13 229 30
of a deception which his pride could not pardon, and which NA II 15 244 11
and which a better pride would have been ashamed to own. NA II 15 244 11
agitation of gratified pride, and, as far as they alone NA II 16 249 1
smooth the descent of his pride, and by no means without NA II 16 251 6
It is a reasonable and laudable pride which resists such SS II 7 189 51
no," cried Marianne, "misery such as mine has no pride. SS II 7 189 52
the strong characters of pride and ill nature. she was not SS II 12 232 15
She had seen enough of her pride, her meanness, and her SS II 13 238 1
No pride, no hauteur, and your sister just the same--all SS II 13 239 6
Her flattery had already subdued the pride of Lady SS II 14 254 27
may think what a blow it was to all her vanity and pride. SS III 1 258 7
"It was necessary to my own pride. SS III 8 324 42
but did not suit her pride, & she wd rather have known W 347 22
that he is ate up with pride, and I dare say he had heard PP I 5 19 14
"His pride," said Miss Lucas, "does not offend me so much PP I 5 20 18
as pride often does, because there is an excuse for it. PP I 5 20 18
forgive his pride, if he had not mortified mine." PP I 5 20 19
"Pride," observed Mary, who piqued herself upon the PP I 5 20 20
Vanity and pride are different things, though the words PP I 5 20 20
Pride relates more to our opinion of ourselves, vanity to PP I 5 20 20
bad indeed, a mixture of pride and impertinence; she had PP I 8 35 3
"Such as vanity and pride." PP I 11 57 23
But pride--where there is a real superiority of mind, PP I 11 57 24
of mind, pride will be always under good regulation." PP I 11 57 24
of pride and obsequiousness, self-importance and humility. PP I 15 70 1
Every body is disgusted with his pride. PP I 16 78 15

I wonder that the very pride of this Mr. Darcy has not PP I 16 81 38
traced to pride;--and pride has often been his best friend. PP I 16 81 39
to me, there were stronger impulses even than pride." PP I 16 81 39
"Can such abominable pride as his, have ever done him good? PP I 16 81 40
Family pride, and filial pride, for his is very proud of PP I 16 81 41
He has also brotherly pride, which with some brotherly PP I 16 82 41
His pride never deserts him; but with the rich, he is PP I 16 82 48
and the rest from the pride of her nephew, who chuses that PP I 16 84 58
refuse him; and though his pride was hurt, he suffered in PP I 20 112 24
Mr. Collins was also in the same state of angry pride. PP I 21 115 2
all the importance of money, great connections, and pride." PP II 1 136 23
he was the cause, his pride and caprice were the cause of PP II 10 186 38
with Mr. Darcy, whose pride, she was convinced, would PP II 10 187 40
by this worst kind of pride, and partly by the wish of PP II 10 187 40
more eloquent on the subject of tenderness than of pride. PP II 11 189 5
overlooked, had not your pride been hurt by my honest PP II 11 192 22
But his pride, his abominable pride, his shameless avowal PP II 11 193 31
It was all pride and insolence. PP II 13 204 1
His pride, in that direction, may be of service, if not to PP II 18 234 38
Mrs. Reynolds, either from pride or attachment, had PP III 1 248 23
whom his pride had revolted, in his offer to herself. PP III 1 254 58
They had nothing to accuse him of but pride; pride he PP III 2 265 14
Such a change in a man of so much pride, excited not only PP III 2 266 16
expected most pleasure and pride in her company, for she PP III 8 313 20
He generously imputed the whole to his mistaken pride, and PP III 10 322 2
Every kind of pride must revolt from the connection. he PP III 10 326 3
the appetite and pride of one who had ten thousand a-year. PP III 11 338 60
principles, but left to follow them in pride and conceit. PP III 16 369 24
Indeed he has no improper pride. PP III 17 376 34
With what delighted pride she afterwards visited Mrs. PP III 19 385 1
from principle as well as pride, from a general wish of MP I 1 3 1
reflections on the pride of Sir Thomas, as Mrs. Norris MP I 1 4 1
longer afford to cherish pride or resentment, or to lose MP I 1 4 2
Maria was indeed the pride and delight of them all-- MP I 4 39 10
a flutter as vanity and pride could furnish, when they MP I 8 83 37
Maria, who wanted neither pride nor resolution, was MP II 2 193 17
all the comfort that pride and self-revenge could give. MP II 3 201 24
might not be accused of pride or indifference, or some MP II 8 258 17
whether it were dignity or pride, or tenderness or remorse, MP III 3 337 10
William was her pride; Betsey, her darling; and John, MP III 8 389 4
had been wont with such pride of heart to feel and say, MP III 16 448 1
of pride and importance, which the connection would offend. E I 2 15 2
man had made Highbury feel a sort of pride in him too. E I 2 17 7
"One should be sorry to see greater pride or refinement in E I 7 56 41
This is an attachment which a woman may well feel pride in E I 9 74 20
father, and nothing of the pride or reserve of Enscombe. E II 6 198 5
Of pride, indeed, there was, perhaps, scarcely enough; his E II 6 198 5
Emma had feelings, less of curiosity than of pride or E II 14 270 2
The rich brother-in-law near Bristol was the pride of the E II 14 272 17
and his place and his carriages were the pride of him. E II 14 272 17
that the taste or the pride of Miss Fairfax could endure E II 15 285 12
Mr. Churchill has pride; but his pride is nothing to his E II 18 309 33
gentlemanlike sort of pride that would harm nobody, and E II 18 309 33
and tiresome; but her pride is arrogance and insolence! E II 18 309 33
She felt all the honest pride and complacency which her E III 6 358 35
spirits, and the pride of the moment, laugh at her, humble E III 7 375 61
had softened away his pride, and he was, earlier than I E III 14 443 8
hoped "the young lady's pride would now be contented;" and E III 17 469 36
and whose strong family pride could see only in him, a P III 1 8 17
involving the loss of any indulgence of taste or pride. P III 1 10 21
pardonable pride, received it as a most unfortunate one. P III 4 26 2
never admitted by the pride of some, and the delicacy of P III 4 31 11
terms, there being no pride on one side, and no envy on P III 9 74 6
by her nonsense and her pride; the Elliot pride. P III 10 88 28
She has a great deal too much of the Elliot pride.-- P III 10 88 28
Louisa called the Elliot pride could not endure to make a P III 10 90 38
and family-honour, without pride or weakness; he lived P IV 4 146 6
wish that they had more pride; for "our cousins Lady P IV 4 148 11
I suppose (smiling) I have more pride than any of you; but P IV 4 151 18
myself otherwise, for our pride, if investigated, would P IV 4 151 21
having the same sort of pride, she was pleased with him P IV 4 151 22
(the attempts of angry pride), he protested that he had P IV 11 242 63
there begun to deplore the pride, the folly, the madness P IV 11 242 63
the blindness of his own pride, and the blunders of his P IV 11 243 69
felt her consequence with pride & her poverty with S 7 394 1

PRIDED (2)
cried.--"I, who have prided myself on my discernment!-- PP II 13 208 8
applications) prided himself on remaining single for his P III 1 5 8

PRIEST (1)
"undoubtedly understands the duty of a parish priest.-- MP II 7 248 46

PRIM (1)
But Mary Edwardes is rather prim & reserved; I do not W 321 2

PRIME (10)
in town, which was now a prime object, it became, by the MP I 4 38 10
pretty piece--and your cousin Edmund's prime favourite. MP II 4 207 9
a sentiment in all its prime and freshness, wounded by no MP II 6 235 18
seated at the table of prime intellectual state and MP II 7 239 8
to his son, for his prime motive in sending her away, had MP III 6 368 9
His charitable kindness had been rearing a prime comfort MP III 17 472 30
it became henceforth her prime object of interest; and E I 11 91 1
presence must really be interfering with her prime object. P IV 10 213 10
fail her; and while these prime supplies of good remained, P IV 12 252 12
machinations of the prime character, the potent, pervading S 8 403 1

PRIMITIVE (2)
from the strict line of Primitive obligations)--to hazard S 8 403 1
These are the novels which enlarge the Primitive S 8 404 1

PRINCES (1)
It is a name of heroism and renown--of kings, princes, and MP II 4 211 23

PRINCIPAL (50)
Oxford roads, and the principal inn of the city, that a NA I 7 44 1
Fidelity and complaisance are the principal duties of both; NA I 10 76 29
In the principal facts they have sources of intelligence NA I 14 109 23
she found herself the principal cause of the lecture; and NA II 5 154 2
what must be his principal, his only object of happiness. SS III 3 284 23
maid, who was one of the principal nurses, was recreating SS III 7 310 9
knew not on which child to bestow her principal attention. SS III 11 353 24
into the scrape, was the principal instrument of his SS III 14 375 10
acquainted with all the principal people in the room; he PP I 3 10 6
lived, and of which they were the principal inhabitants. PP I 3 12 15
the situation and the principal rooms, satisfied with what PP I 4 16 13
Bingley was the principal spokesman, and Miss Bennet the PP I 15 72 8
principal spokesman, and Miss Bennet the principal object. PP I 15 72 8
Miss Bingley the principal design and arrangement of them. PP II 10 186 38
that you have been the principal, if not the only means of PP II 11 191 12
and from these tastes had arisen his principal enjoyments. PP II 19 236 1
having seen all the principal wonders of the country; and PP II 19 240 12
The picture gallery, and two or three of the principal bed- PP III 1 250 46
His principal object must be, to discover the number of PP III 5 293 69
to enquire at all the principal hotels in town, as Mr. PP III 6 295 5
The principal purport of his letter was to inform them, PP III 8 312 18
not place herself as his principal inducement, she could, PP III 10 326 3
cousin cannot tell the principal rivers in Russia--or she MP I 2 18 23
and most of the principal events of their reigns!" MP I 2 18 25
to the spacious stone steps before the principal entrance. MP I 8 83 37
proceeded towards the principal stair-case, and taken them MP I 9 89 31
by Mr. Rushworth, whose principal business seemed to be to MP I 10 97 3
was coming at a quick pace down the principal walk. MP I 10 100 24
but every character first-rate, and three principal women. MP I 14 130 3
opinion, to being the principal lady in company, and to MP II 5 223 48
north--the entrance and principal rooms, I mean, must be MP II 7 242 23
that is, to the principal road through the village, must MP II 7 242 23
creeping slowly up the principal staircase, pursued by the MP II 10 280 33
of success in the principal, Sir Thomas was soon able to MP III 2 329 11
compliments rather more than I could endure as a principal. E I 6 49 44
Ford's was the principal woollen-draper, linen-draper, and E II 3 178 52
house, though the principal one of the sort, where a E II 6 197 5
myself that Mr. Dixon is a principal in the business." E II 8 218 41
a knowledge of their principal subjects:--the post-office-- E II 17 299 1
all the right of being principal talker, which a day spent E II 17 303 24
She is his principal correspondent, I assure you. E II 18 305 5
And now I come to the principal, the only important part E III 14 438 8
the arms and motto: "principal seat, Kellynch Hall, in the P III 1 3 3 4
inconvenient to the principal part of her family, and be P III 9 76 13
of the town, the principal street almost hurrying into the P III 11 95 9
Miss Elliot, surrounded by her cousins, and the principal P IV 8 186 23
me in Bath, my first and principal acquaintance on P IV 9 201 59
and Mr. Elliot--all the principal family connexions--on P IV 10 223 43
to himself, & the other principal land holder, the S 2 371 1
Diana was evidently the cheif of the family; principal S 10 414 1

PRINCIPALLY (28)
effect on her in that point to which it principally tended. SS I 5 25 3
on their side, Elinor principally attributed that SS I 22 127 1
any notion of what was principally meant by it, provoked SS II 12 235 34 35
same; and Mrs. Hurst, principally occupied in playing with PP I 11 54 3
which have principally offended Mr. Darcy; but he will PP I 18 95 50
points she principally dwelt during the rest of the day. PP I 21 127 5
the errors of her daughter must be principally owing. PP III 5 287 34
As it principally concerns yourself, you ought to know its PP III 15 362 10
though they arose principally from doubts of her sister's MP I 4 41 16
her at different times, principally by Tom; and she grew MP I 16 153 3
an intimacy resulting principally from Miss Crawford's MP II 4 207 11
prospect of a ball given principally for her gratification. MP II 8 254 8
differences, resulting principally from situation, no MP II 9 263 16
a long morning, spent principally with her two aunts, she MP II 9 267 22
This wish was levelled principally at Julia, who had just MP II 11 284 10
for the affection appears to me principally on their side. MP III 13 421 2
"Exactly so; that is what principally strikes me. E I 6 42 6
and pursuits, but principally of those of the elder, whose E I 12 100 16
christian name, and say whose music she principally played. E II 4 181 2
He thought principally of Mrs. Churchill's illness, and E II 12 259 11
which, though principally addressed to Mrs. Weston, he had E II 17 303 24
The belief of being prudent, and self-denying principally P III 4 28 5
in reading, though principally in poetry; and besides the P III 11 100 23
his subjects were principally such as were wont to be P IV 7 178 24
We were principally in town, living in very good style. P IV 9 199 55
lived with him, wd be principally remembered in her will. S 3 377 1
After having avoided London for many years, principally on S 3 378 1
that line of life, principally for the indulgence of an S 10 418 1

PRINCIPALS (4)
The principals being all agreed in this respect, it soon MP II 3 202 27
passed except the three principals, and especially for her E I 16 138 15
It was no more than the principals were prepared for; they E III 17 468 35
give, could be properly interesting only to the principals. P IV 11 230 5

PRINCIPLE (37)
But your mind is warped by an innate principle of general NA II 12 219 15
engrossed on the most affectionate principle by my mother. SS I 4 20 9
to act by her as every principle of honour and honesty SS II 1 142 7
Elinor avoided it upon principle, as tending to fix still SS III 2 270 1
own ease, was, in every particular, his ruling principle." SS III 11 351 11
She will be more hurt by it, and on the same principle SS III 13 366 19
change the meaning of principle and integrity, nor PP II 1 135 13
must expect him to keep or quit it on the same principle." PP II 9 178 9
The vicious propensities--the want of principle which he PP II 12 200 5
"No principle of either, would be violated by my marriage PP III 14 358 70
being all my life, in practice, though not in principle. PP III 16 369 24
Sir Thomas Bertram had interest, which, from principle as MP I 1 3 1
Under this infatuating principle, counteracted by no real MP I 1 8 9
of her own heart, that principle of right which had not MP I 9 91 36
had not affection or principle enough to make them MP I 17 162 19
She had all the heroism of principle, and was determined MP II 9 265 19
The principle was good in itself, but it may have been, MP III 1 313 12
how always known no principle to supply as a duty what the MP III 2 329 9
Accordingly, on this principle Sir Thomas took the first MP III 2 330 14
On this principle, he soon afterwards observed, "they go MP III 4 354 48
and no sufficient principle on either side, gave it MP III 15 441 20
Her's are faults of principle, Fanny, of blunted delicacy MP III 16 456 25
He feared that principle, active principle, had been MP III 17 463 8
the sterling good of principle and temper, and chiefly MP III 17 471 29
If he would act in this sort of manner, on principle, E I 18 147 18
And besides the operation of this, as a general principle, E II 15 286 23
the hill, there seemed a principle of separation, between E III 7 367 1
adherence to truth and principle, that disdain of trick E III 10 397 48
the steadiness and delicacy of principle that it wants. E III 15 448 30
of sensible people, by his acting like a man of principle. P III 2 12 4
This was the principle on which Anne wanted her father to P III 2 12 5
Henrietta from agitation seemed the governing principle. P III 12 116 70
on the principle of its being very ungenteel to be curious. P IV 3 144 19
and as a man of principle,--this was all clear enough. P IV 5 160 27
had any better principle to guide him than selfishness." P IV 9 208 93
the steadiness of principle and the obstinacy of self-will, P IV 11 242 63
baronet, who had not had principle or sense enough to P IV 12 248 1

PRINCIPLED (1)
the knowledge of her being well principled and religious. MP II 12 294 16

PRINCIPLES (32)
by a woman with whose principles he was so well acquainted, LS 11 259 2
in short but her principles; there I beleive she is not to LS 27 296 1
She had not been withstanding them on selfish principles NA I 13 101 25
Their tempers were mild, but their principles were steady, NA II 16 249 2
The excellence of his understanding and his principles can SS I 4 20 9
I am not acquainted with the minutia of her principles. SS I 11 56 16
I like a fine prospect, but not on picturesque principles. SS I 18 98 8
spoke of Edward's principles and disposition with that SS III 3 283 20
make his character and principles fixed;--and his SS III 9 338 20
Their resemblance in good principles and good sense, in SS III 13 370 36
I was given good principles, but left to follow them in PP III 16 369 24
the result of good principles; the effect, in short, of MP I 9 93 49
them, the proof of good principles, professional knowledge, MP II 6 236 21
feel the worth of good principles in a wife, thought he MP II 12 294 16
She longed to add, "but of his principles I have;" but her MP III 1 317 38
as a rock in her own principles, has a gentleness of MP III 4 351 32
cousin Edmund to direct her thoughts or fix her principles. MP III 9 397 8
and the purity of her principles added yet a keener MP III 13 428 13
Edmund's upright principles, unsuspicious temper, and MP III 15 442 21
purity of her mind, and the excellence of her principles. MP III 17 468 21
morality upon new principles and new systems--and where E I 3 21 5
in honour, by all her principles, admire it:--elegance, E II 2 167 12
Do not let any reflection fall on the principles or the E III 12 419 8
gave you understanding:--Miss Taylor gave you principles. E III 17 462 7
His good sense and good principles would delight you.-- E III 18 472 22
very seriously good principles, and placing her happiness E III 18 474 34
maintenance of the good principles and instruction which P III 1 5 6
were great, from the opposition of two leading principles. P III 2 11 2
There are on both sides good principles and good temper." P IV 8 182 7
nothing but discordant principles incapable of S 8 403 1
him derive only false principles from lessons of morality, S 8 404 1
impression on her heart, and to undermine her principles.-- S 8 405 2

PRINT (4)
commission for every new print of merit to be sent you-- SS I 17 92 25
the dimensions of a print, which she was going to copy for SS III 3 280 9
One was found to have too small a print for a child's eyes, MP III 7 387 45
contemplation of some print, and she not only might have P IV 6 169 25

PRINT-SHOPS (1)

day for booksellers, music-sellers, and print-shops! SS I 17 92 25
PRINTED (2)
of preferring her style to that of any printed author. MP III 12 419 7
the newspapers that are printed in one week throughout the S 1 366 1
PRINTER'S (1)
stood from the printer's hands; but Sir Walter had P III 1 3 2
PRINTSHOP (1)
He was standing by himself, at a printshop window, with P IV 6 169 25
PRIOR (13)
lines of Milton, Pope, and prior, with a paper from the NA I 5 37 4
just been reminded of a prior engagement, and must only NA I 13 98 1
There has been no prior engagement." NA I 13 98 2
having just recollected a prior engagement of going to NA I 13 100 15
and entreating him to make known her prior engagement. NA II 4 150 1
It is not to be supposed that any prior attachment on your SS II 11 224 24
very person herself, whose prior engagement ruined all my SS III 1 263 29
satisfaction in avowing her prior engagement.-- W 334 13
account, by mentioning her prior knowledge of it from PP I 23 126 4
proved to have been a prior acquaintance between him and PP II 12 201 5
I have almost grudged myself my own prior knowledge of MP II 13 299 5
before he declared himself prevented by a prior engagement. MP III 10 406 22
That was all prior to my coming to Bath. P IV 9 205 83
PRIORY (1)
to the old ruins of the Priory, and try to trace its SS III 10 343 9
PRISON (5)
as he passed to the prison of his wife; and, twice before NA II 8 188 19
it looked like a prison--quite a dismal old prison." MP I 6 53 2
"A prison, indeed! MP I 6 53 3
You will be to visit me in prison with a basket of MP I 14 135 17
in prison? I think I see you coming in with your basket." MP I 14 135 17
PRISONER (1)
freeze, she was for many days a most honourable prisoner. E I 16 138 17
PRIVACY (9)
She turned into the drawing-room for privacy, but Henry NA II 10 203 8
and sent away with a privacy which eluded all her SS II 5 167 7
speak to him with more privacy and more effect, was SS II 6 177 15
This is the end of all the privacy and propriety which was MP I 16 153 8
guided by him as to the privacy of the representation, was MP I 18 164 1
disinclination for privacy and retirement, her decided MP II 8 255 10
discussion; and the privacy of such a discussion was a MP II 8 256 14
contrived a minute's privacy for telling Fanny that his MP III 10 406 21
Privacy was certainly their object.-- S 12 426 1
PRIVATE (72)
her at one of the best private schools in town, where I LS 1 244 1
which confirms me in my own private explanation of it. LS 16 268 1
room, as she was anxious to speak with me in private. LS 20 276 5
him; & tho' a little private discourse with Lady Susan has LS 20 278 9
of which she shared, by private partnership with Morland, NA I 11 89 63
In a private consultation between Isabella and James, the NA I 13 97 1
as any private man in the county, has his profession." NA II 7 176 15
and in the General's private apartment, without NA II 8 183 2
preferment, trebling his private fortune, bestowing a rich NA II 15 245 12
its effect was the private intelligence, which he was at NA II 16 251 6
centered in domestic comfort and the quiet of private life. SS I 3 16 6
doors, and in winter his private balls were numerous SS I 7 32 2
The private balls at the park then began; and parties on SS I 11 53 1
of engaging Lucy in private, when Sir John called at the SS II 1 143 9
private balls and large dinners to proclaim its importance. SS II 2 151 43
disgusted with his mother, till they were more in private. SS II 13 243 34
immediate friends, the first private performers in England. SS II 14 250 10
to the misfortune of a private education; while he himself, SS II 14 250 12
private tuition, at the most critical time of his life? SS II 14 251 13
of speaking with her in private--a circumstance occurred-- SS III 8 321 34
opportunity of private conference between them occurred. SS III 9 335 7
to think it all over in private, to wish success to her SS III 9 339 27
only the daughter of a private gentleman, with no more SS III 14 373 3
in one of the first private seminaries in town, had a PP I 4 15 11
She had obtained private intelligence that Mr. Darcy did PP I 11 54 3
with their uncle, a private had been flogged, and it had PP I 12 60 7
Perhaps by and bye I may observe that private balls are PP I 18 91 11
private audience with her in the course of this morning?" PP I 19 104 1
2

Miss Lucas called soon after breakfast, and in a private PP I 22 124 11
the last resource, if her private enquiries as to the PP II 19 241 16
soon swallowed up every private care; and covering her PP III 4 278 20
Why must their marriage be private? PP III 5 283 8
beneath him, to lay his private actions open to the world. PP III 10 322 2
in her own private expences, she frequently sent them. PP III 19 387 8
any private fortune, and Miss Frances fared yet worse. MP I 1 3 1
It was only for the private use of the family. MP I 9 86 7
expected from the private devotions of such persons? MP I 9 87 16
capable of knowing his private character, and observing MP I 9 93 49
in praise of the private theatricals at Ecclesford, the MP I 13 121 1
In a general light, private theatricals are open to some MP I 13 125 17
it could be proposed and accepted in a private theatre! MP I 14 137 23
it exceedingly unfit for private representation, and that MP I 15 139 11
find, who thinks it very fit for private representation." MP I 15 140 12
each other in private on the jealous weakness to which MP I 17 158 1
not believe they had yet rehearsed it, even in private. MP I 18 167 13
his passage thither in a private vessel, instead of MP II 1 178 8
"I would rather find him private secretary to the first MP II 7 246 35
an opportunity for private discussion; and the privacy of MP II 8 256 14
She was talking at Fanny, and resenting this private walk MP III 1 324 57
Still, however, it was her private regale.-- MP III 14 431 8
came in, and brought no refutation, public or private. MP III 15 442 22
country--remote and private, where, shut up together with MP III 17 465 14
Granted;--for private enjoyment; and for private enjoyment E I 9 77 42
and respectable in his private character; but with E I 11 92 5
the daily happiness of private life depends, was one of E I 14 117 1
have been, but for her private perplexities, remarkably E I 16 139 20
me amends for the loss of any happiness in private life." E II 6 200 16
A private dance, without sitting down to supper, was E II 11 254 45
being a something of private liking, of private E III 5 344 2
of private liking, of private understanding even, between E III 5 344 2
none of it aloud, and agreed to none of it in private. E III 6 353 4
It was a private resolution of her's, not communicated to E III 10 397 51
then, for having consented to a private engagement?" E III 12 418 7
met with one or two private disappointments in very P III 1 5 8
To live no longer with the decencies even of a private P III 2 13 6
a little history of his private life, which rendered him P III 11 96 12
the elegant stupidity of private parties, in which they P IV 7 180 32
such testimonies, that no private correspondence could P IV 9 204 76
77

smiles reined in and spirits dancing in private rapture. P IV 11 240 59
those regular, steady, private families of thorough S 1 368 1
where, wanted something private, & wrote to ask the S 9 408 1
"From Mrs Charles Dupuis--said she.--some private hand."-- S 10 418 1
PRIVATEER (1)
the alarm of a French privateer was at the height, she MP II 1 180 10
PRIVATEERS (1)
her; and after taking privateers enough to be very P III 8 65 16
PRIVATELY (7)
When Robert first sought her acquaintance, and privately SS III 14 376 11
proud of marrying privately without his mother's consent. SS III 14 376 11
against her own, in privately urging Emma to go--"you do W 362 32
Elizabeth privately added, "and how much I shall have to PP II 15 217 14
for them to be married privately in town than to pursue PP III 4 275 5
to speak to Elizabeth privately of what Lydia had let fall; PP III 9 320 35
have been privately engaged to one another this long while. E III 11 404 8
PRIVATION (3)
They sat without a fire; but that was a privation familiar MP III 9 398 9
and happily through its little difficulties and privation. E I 2 18 11
Here, she must be leading a life of privation and penance; E II 8 217 32
PRIVATIONS (6)
privations and restrictions that may have been imposed. MP III 1 313 12
have suspected how many privations, besides that of MP III 11 412 30
of the privations inevitably belonging to a small one. E II 6 204 43
here month after month, under privations of every sort! E II 15 285 13
The picture which she had then drawn of the privations of E III 12 422 19
You have difficulties, and privations, and dangers enough P IV 11 233 23
PRIVILEGE (17)
deny me the privilege of disliking him as much as ever." SS I 10 52 28
Mrs. Smith has this morning exercised the privilege of SS I 15 75 6
He had abundantly earned the privilege of intimate SS II 10 216 15
feeling all the happy privilege of country liberty, of SS III 6 303 9
Edward was allowed to retain the privilege of first comer, SS III 13 369 34
had not taken the same privilege of coming, & accompanied W 347 22
of my encroaching on your privilege of universal good will. PP II 1 135 11
No one admitted to the privilege of hearing you, can think PP II 8 176 26
to refuse his daughter a privilege, without which her PP III 8 310 10
point of privilege and independence beyond all calculation. MP II 7 244 27
character and the privilege of true solicitude for him by MP II 9 265 18
without liking it, the privilege of exchanging any vacant E I 3 20 2
having somewhat of the privilege of speech that Emma's E I 5 40 24
of fine clothes, and the privilege of bashfulness, but the E II 14 271 5
or plea, or privilege, she must be wanting to assist and E II 15 282 4
have been used to do: a privilege rather endured than E III 7 374 55
56

All the privilege I claim for my own sex (it is not a very P IV 11 235 32
PRIVILEGED (10)
& think themselves privileged to refuse him their LS 12 260 1
unite them again in the fullness of privileged affection. NA II 16 250 3
with, as far as I thought myself privileged, for you. PP III 7 302 14
given any thing to be privileged to tell him, that his PP III 12 340 13
Mrs. Bennet was privileged to whisper it to Mrs. Philips, PP III 13 350 55
the kind authority of a privileged guardian into the house. MP III 4 355 55
We invalids think we are privileged people." E I 8 57 3
should not have thought myself privileged to inquire into. E III 7 370 20
and look and manner of the privileged relation and friend. P IV 7 177 16
There is someone in most families privileged by superior S 4 382 1
PRIVILEGES (3)
to a walk, would be a valuable addition to her privileges. E I 4 26 1
made up my mind as to the privileges to be annexed to it. P III 3 18 8
comforts and all the privileges which any home can give. P III 3 19 11
12

PRIVY (8)
with her own heart only privy to its folly; and she was on NA II 9 194 6
Henry and her own heart only were privy to the shocking NA II 14 230 3
She was privy, one evening, to the hopes of her aunt MP I 12 116 11
Had he been privy to her conversation with his son, he MP III 16 453 15
that the number of privy counsellors was not yet larger. E III 2 320 6
Mr. Knightley have been privy to all her attempts of E III 9 391 21
she was privy, and persuade them all to go to Lyme at once. P IV 1 122 5
I was privy to all the fors and againsts, I was the friend P IV 9 200 57
PRIZE (7)
or speculations upon prize money, which was to be MP III 7 375 2
what he and all that party would particularly prize. E II 10 241 8
I have it not--but I know how to prize and respect it.-- E II 13 269 16
to seek, to be the prize of a girl who would seek him?-- E III 11 413 48
At three and twenty to have drawn such a prize!-- E III 13 428 23
A prize indeed would Kellynch Hall be to him; rather the P III 3 17 2
him; rather the greatest prize of all, let him have taken P III 3 17 2
PRIZE-MONEY (1)
Fortune came, his prize-money as lieutenant being great,-- P III 11 96 12
PRIZED (4)
whose society she mostly prized--and, in addition to all NA II 2 141 11
quickness is always much prized by the possessor, and PP I 10 49 27
Two lines more prized had never fallen from the pen of the MP II 9 265 19
She prized the frank, the open-hearted, the eager P IV 5 161 28
PRIZES (1)
after prizes, to have attention for any one in particular. PP I 16 76 8
PRIZING (1)
Sick of ambitious and mercenary connections, prizing more MP III 17 471 29
PROBABILITIES (9)
Are no probabilities to be accepted, merely because they SS I 15 78 28
on every side by such probabilities and proofs, and SS II 1 139 1
other consideration of probabilities to make it natural SS II 1 142 7
events, determining probabilities, and reconciling herself PP II 13 209 12
times, persons, and probabilities, and you will feel that MP III 1 313 12
probabilities of a conclusion hereafter, like her sister's. MP III 16 452 13
exteriors and probabilities, Emma could only class it, as E I 10 83 6
manner; and all the probabilities of circumstance and E II 13 266 6
Charles, being somewhat more mindful of the probabilities P III 8 66 21
PROBABILITY (62)
such a visit is in all probability merely an affair of LS 3 246 1
The probability of their marrying is surely heightened. LS 24 291 17
she must alas! in all probability, be with Reginald--& LS 27 297 1
The world must judge from probability. LS 42 313 9
room; and though in all probability not an observation was NA I 10 72 8
and key, secured in all probability a cavity of importance. NA II 6 168 10
contain; a room in all probability never entered by him NA II 8 186 6
slept; and the probability that Mrs. Tilney yet lived, NA II 8 187 16
"you infer perhaps the probability of some negligence-- NA II 9 196 25
in fact, her fears in probability; and with a mind so NA II 13 227 26
she, "Elinor will in all probability be settled for life. SS I 3 17 15
the probability of wishing to throw ridicule on his age. SS I 8 37 3
Marianne was in all probability not merely giving way to SS I 15 77 20
the probability of many, and hope for the justice of all. SS I 15 82 45
And in all probability you will see your brother, and SS II 3 156 8
intentions were; in all probability he was already in town. SS II 4 159 1
Frosts will soon set in, and in all probability with SS II 5 167 3
for you, that in all probability when she dies you will SS II 11 226 42
far to outrun truth and probability, that on merely SS II 14 248 6
were effects that laid open the probability of greater. SS II 14 254 27
Elinor was quite of her opinion, as to the probability of SS III 4 292 58
cheerfulness, the probability of an entire recovery. SS III 7 314 23
at Barton; and in all probability,--for I hear it is a SS III 9 338 24
value as arising in all probability from the influence of PP I 6 21 1
a wet night, and on the probability of a rainy season, PP I 16 76 4
to understand that the probability of their marriage was PP I 17 88 14
no more; but though the probability of the statement was PP II 1 137 26
the probability of each statement--but with little success. PP II 13 205 3
Most earnestly did she labour to prove the probability of PP II 17 225 9
Mrs. Forster, and the probability of her being yet more PP II 18 230 14
they must in all probability have gained some news of them. PP III 6 295 4
could apply to, with a probability of gaining such a clue PP III 6 295 6
as to the greater probability of his coming there with his PP III 11 332 18
probability, would get her a creditable establishment. MP I 1 6 6
he might be, would, in all probability, die very soon. MP I 3 24 4
be, he mentioned its probability to his wife; and the MP I 3 24 7
They left England with the probability of being nearly a MP I 3 32 61
It would be the last--in all probability the last scene on MP II 1 182 22
and would, in all probability, be a continual supply of MP II 3 201 22
probability of your happiness together: do not imagine it. MP III 4 348 23
Her father's house would, in all probability, teach her MP III 6 369 10
Crawford's regard, the probability of his being very far MP III 12 419 9
enough to start the probability of its being merely to MP III 15 437 2
attachment, and strong probability of success; and who in MP III 16 452 15
been every probability of success and felicity for him. MP III 17 467 19
of existence with every probability of greater happiness E I 2 17 6
I felt, that as to fortune, in all probability he might do E I 8 61 38
Its probability and its eligibility have really so E I 9 74 20
There will be enough of them, in all probability, to E I 10 86 21
there had seemed every probability of her being E II 2 163 3

"And upon my word, they have an air of great probability. E II 8 217 33
"I am not speaking of its prudence; merely its probability. E II 8 224 71
"I see no probability in it, unless you have any better E II 8 224 72
What an air of probability sometimes runs through a dream! E III 5 345 14
pointed out to her the probability of its being some money E III 10 393 18
Smith; she must, in all probability, have been spared from E III 12 421 17
In all probability she was at this very time waited for E III 16 458 44
Either of them would, in all probability, make him an P III 9 77 18
In all probability he was already the richer of the two, P IV 3 140 11
his conduct as to the probability of the event he has been P IV 9 207 91
land holder, the probability of it's becoming a profitable S 2 371 1
six months--with the probability of another being then to S 3 379 1

PROBABLE (51)

could render probable, and must in the end make wretched. LS 12 261 3
But guided only by what was simple and probable, it had NA I 8 53 3
age, situation, and probable habits of life considered?-- NA II 1 132 20
"It is probable that she will neither love so well, nor NA II 4 151 16
your own sense of the probable, your own observation of NA II 9 197 29
His marrying Miss Thorpe is not probable. NA II 10 204 20
Morland, thinking it probable, as a secondary NA II 15 243 9
be the only doubt; what probable circumstance could work NA II 16 250 4
conjecture, and all seeming equally probable as they arose. SS I 14 70 3
She thought it probable that as they lived in the same SS I 20 114 43
of her, appeared very probable; it was plain that Edward SS II 1 142 7
might await her in its probable consequence, she could not SS II 6 179 18
feeling how more than probable it was that she was writing SS II 7 180 4
because I thought it probable that I might find you alone, SS II 9 204 18
foreseeing at first as a probable event, had brought SS II 10 213 4
there, and it is probable that Elinor was not without SS II 11 220 3
be some time--it is not probable that I should soon have SS III 4 288 27
it is most probable--that something might have been hit on. SS III 5 299 37
at her sister, the probable recurrence of many past scenes SS III 10 340 2
it is probable that her compassion would have been greater. SS III 11 349 2
languid remarks on the probable brilliancy of the ball, W 322 3
seemed to her the probable conclusion of almost all that W 348 23
She felt it to be the probable consequence of her PP I 18 102 74
should think exceedingly probable, stay quietly at home, PP I 22 124 9
It was possible, and sometimes she thought it probable, PP II 2 142 16
"I have never heard him say so; but it is probable that he PP II 9 177 8
to do, which was the more probable from the time of year. PP II 9 180 28
knowledge of your sister must make the latter probable.-- PP II 12 197 5
consequence, is perhaps probable;--but his regard did not PP II 12 199 5
from Miss Bennet, it is probable that it might add PP III 3 270 10
up with only having the probable credit of it, which went PP III 10 324 2
goodness too great to be probable, and at the same time PP III 10 326 3
as it seemed the only probable motive for her calling. PP III 14 352 15
promise, make <u>their</u> marriage at all more probable? PP III 14 357 61
Her opinion was sought as to the probable continuance of MP II 5 223 48
information as to the probable period of the Antwerp's MP II 6 232 13
Every thing natural, probable, reasonable was against it; MP II 13 305 26
each of them at times being held the most probable. MP III 10 399 1
it is probable that Mr. Yates would never have succeeded. MP III 17 466 18
and probable, for her to have much merit in planning it. E I 4 34 44
were added the highly probable circumstance of an E II 2 167 13
I felt how much more probable that it should be the E II 8 219 42
The more I think of it, the more probable it appears. E II 8 224 65
matter--which was most probable--still, in knowing her as E III 12 421 17
that could be probable or reasonable, entered her brain. E III 13 431 38
profession, all their probable fears, delays and P III 4 29 8
Captain Wentworth was to be regarded as the probable cause. P III 9 77 19
But it was more probable that he should be come to stay. P IV 7 178 26
it to be the most probable thing in the world to be wished P IV 9 197 36
at all for that friend's probable finances, but, on the P IV 9 209 95
her situation, for a change is not very probable there. P IV 12 250 6

PROBABLY (170)

should be to blame, & probably has sometimes judged it LS 17 272 8
dispute in which I might probably be as much to blame as LS 24 288 11
as to the rest, I shall probably put <u>that</u> project in LS 25 294 4
I shall probably put off his arrival, under some pretence LS 29 299 2
of Miss Morland, and probably aware that if adventures NA I 1 17 12
work, and how she will, probably, contribute to reduce NA I 2 19 7
of answering, as she probably would have done, had there NA I 7 50 44
it may be made--and probably with much greater, if the NA I 14 109 23
"Very probably. NA I 14 110 27
Bath with us, he will probably remain but a very short NA II 4 152 29
after your arrival, you will probably have a violent storm. NA II 5 159 19
accompany it, you will probably think you discern (for NA II 5 159 19
Catherine was probably the only one of the party who did NA II 7 175 12
of her daughter, and probably of her other children, at NA II 8 188 16
in the chamber, leading probably into dressing-closets; NA II 9 194 6
and shall probably be obliged to stay two or three days." NA II 11 209 5
Fullerton had its faults, but Woodston probably had none.-- NA II 11 212 16
To the former her raillery was probably, as far as it SS I 8 36 2
"This will probably be the case," he replied; "and yet SS I 11 56 12
The lady would probably have passed without suspicion, had SS I 11 57 17
on herself, if (as would probably be the case) she SS I 12 59 5
"Dear, dear Norland," said Elinor, "probably looks much as SS I 16 87 30
It has been, and is, and probably will always be a heavy SS I 19 102 4
connections, and probably inferior in fortune to herself. SS II 1 140 3
of Edward, which would probably flow from the excess of SS II 1 141 5
could dictate it, and, probably, on the very different SS II 7 184 16
"You have probably entirely forgotten a conversation--(it SS II 9 205 22
Recollecting, soon afterwards, that he was probably SS II 9 211 43
too encouraging herself, probably came over her, for she SS II 12 235 31
32
while he himself, though probably without any particular, SS II 14 250 12
with hesitation; which probably contributed to fix that SS III 4 290 36
recollection--that the case may probably be <u>this</u>. SS III 5 295 12
that Marianne might probably be to <u>her</u> what Charlotte was SS III 7 313 20
have probably heard the whole story long ago." SS III 8 321 34
probably he did not think it <u>would</u> --vex me horridly.-- SS III 8 330 69
always poor; and probably would soon have learnt to rank SS III 11 351 13
and Mrs. Dashwood probably found the same explanation. SS III 11 354 32
were probably going down to Mr. Pratt's, near Plymouth. SS III 11 355 39
a respectable one, and probably gained her consideration SS III 13 367 23
of thinking, would probably have been sufficient to unite SS III 13 370 36
& Mr Tom Musgrave; who probably imprisoned within his own W 329 9
"Never, probably.-- W 332 12
The stile of her last partner had probably led him to W 334 13
her sisters, & gave him probably the novel sensation of W 335 13
her, which may very probably have come to her knowledge."-- W 341 19
at a greater distance are probably doing at this moment.-- W 357 28
to health would probably remove her from Netherfield. PP I 9 41 2
quit Netherfield, I should probably be off in five minutes. PP I 9 42 8
next week,' you would probably do it, you would probably PP I 10 49 29
probably not go--and, at another word, might stay a month." PP I 10 49 29
four o'clock, and shall probably trespass on your PP I 13 63 12
after seeing, as you probably might, the very cold manner PP I 16 77 12
"and one, too, who had probably been his own companion PP I 16 80 36
"Probably not;--but Mr. Darcy can please where he chuses. PP I 16 82 48
people who have probably been concerned in the business?-- PP I 17 85 3
Elizabeth would wonder, and probably would blame her; and PP I 22 123 3
extremely well pleased, probably, to have the opportunity PP II 5 156 5
Our instrument is a capital one, probably superior to---- PP II 6 164 18
these strong objections probably were, her having one PP II 10 186 39
and respectability which he will probably never reach." PP II 10 187 40
which will probably soon drive away his regard for me. PP II 17 224 4
to spend a few days, was probably as great an object of PP II 19 239 7
For a few moments, indeed, she felt that he would probably PP III 1 254 57
of but pride; pride he probably had, and if not, it would PP III 2 265 14
"This is a most unfortunate affair; and will probably be PP III 5 289 42
her residence there will probably be of some duration." PP III 6 299 25
felt for her probably more than she felt for herself. PP III 9 315 1
With his notions of dignity he would probably feel that PP III 15 361 2
and who probably never looked at <u>you</u> in his life! PP III 15 363 18
was such as he had probably never felt before; and he PP III 16 366 8
We shall probably see much to wish altered in her, and MP I 1 10 14
Poor woman! she probably thought change of air might agree MP I 1 11 19
have felt, and probably with somewhat more exactness. MP I 2 16 20
memories, and your poor cousin has probably none at all. MP I 2 19 27
of her girls, she would probably have supposed it MP I 2 20 31
gratification that would probably have been forbidden by MP I 3 32 64
and there it has probably been these ten days, in spite of MP I 6 57 33
you can like to listen; probably much longer, for I dearly MP I 6 59 41
exercise, something was probably added in Edmund's MP I 7 66 15
all his coachmanship, probably knew nothing of the matter, MP I 7 67 16
The state of her spirits had probably had its share in her MP I 7 74 59
Probably, Miss Crawford will choose the barouche box MP I 8 78 15
Price as one who would probably be of the party, and had MP I 8 79 23
soon after my father's return--probably at Christmas." MP I 9 89 28
It would probably be the middle of November at least; the MP I 11 107 3
there was such a provision for me, probably did bias me. MP I 11 109 17
candidly, she would probably have made some important MP I 12 115 5
and Sir Thomas would probably have thought his MP I 13 121 1
but that though I shall probably do it very ill, I feel MP I 14 136 21
a stranger; and as she probably engaged in the part with MP I 16 154 14
unsuspected vexation was probably ready to burst on him. MP II 1 178 7
know, sir--the faster probably from <u>your</u> having so often MP II 1 184 26
Her feelings probably were not acute; he had never MP II 3 201 22
spirits; something unconnected with her was probably amiss. MP II 9 268 27
A weariness arising probably, in great measure, from the MP II 10 278 20
His errand you may probably conjecture." MP III 1 313 14
of discussion, explanation, and probably non-conviction. MP III 1 317 38
nobly settled, as will, probably, never occur to you again. MP III 1 318 39
"Sorry! yes, I hope you are sorry; and you will probably MP III 1 320 42
She had probably alienated love by the helplessness and MP III 6 371 17
Mr. Crawford probably could not regard his future father- MP III 10 402 12
good fortune, he would probably have feared to push his MP III 11 413 30
You are probably aware of this already.-- MP III 13 420 2
health, had probably induced his being conveyed thither MP III 13 427 13
agreeable manners, and probably of morals and discretion MP III 16 450 8
She seldom saw him--never alone--he probably avoided being MP III 16 453 16
take any pains to marry him, she would probably repent it. E I 4 30 18
with the wife, who will probably be some mere farmer's E I 4 31 24
nobody knows whom, with probably no settled provision at E I 8 61 38
it;--and here are we, probably with rather thinner E I 13 113 26
Going in dismal weather, to return probably in worse;-- E I 13 113 26
Mr. Perry has been with her, as you probably heard." E I 13 114 32
views; not being aware, probably, anymore than myself, of E I 15 132 36
There probably <u>was</u> something more to conceal than her own E II 2 169 16
Ambition, as well as love, had probably been mortified. E II 3 179 53
enough--to look plain, probably, by Harriet's side. E II 4 183 9
or to reason them away; probably a little of both--such E II 5 187 6
I smile because you smile, and shall probably suspect E II 8 216 27
She will probably have soon done, and then we shall go E II 9 234 31
The ladies here probably exchanged looks which meant, "men E II 11 253 43
She believed he was looking at her; probably reflecting on E II 12 261 32
friend of Mrs. Elton's, probably some vulgar, dashing E II 14 275 33
Offended, probably, by the little encouragement which her E II 15 281 3
Maple Grove will probably by my model more than it ought E II 15 283 9
Such a woman as Jane Fairfax probably never fell in Mrs. E II 15 287 23
you always at hand, I, probably, never shall again; and E II 16 294 22
I may probably be glad to dispose of myself. E II 17 300 9
would probably prolong rather than break up the party. E II 17 303 23
And Mrs. Churchill probably has not health or spirits like E II 18 307 21
concise than her's, and probably not much in the same E II 18 311 38
Absence, with the conviction probably of her indifference, E III 1 316 3
arrangement which would probably expose her even to the E III 6 353 3
Here,--probably this basket with pink ribbon. E III 6 355 20
Robert Martin had probably ceased to think of Harriet.-- E III 6 361 40
to; and, if she live to old age, must probably sink more. E III 7 375 61
probably find this day but the beginning of wretchedness. E III 11 411 43
But she probably had something of that in her thoughts, E III 12 419 12
They should lose her; and, probably, in great measure, her E III 12 422 20
more composure, "<u>you</u> probably have been less surprised E III 13 425 10
11
And old story, probably--a common case--and no more than E III 13 427 19
one sentiment having probably enlightened him as to the E III 13 432 41
sentiment having probably enlightened him as to the other. E III 13 432 41
it would probably have been better if Perry had seen it." E III 18 479 73
it <u>might</u>, that it probably <u>would</u>, turn out to be the very P III 6 52 33
that the cottage party, probably, would not like to leave P III 7 54 5
only in part, and probably not having Dick Musgrove at all P III 8 67 25
as to her son, he had probably been at some pains to get P III 8 67 28
easy--Charles Hayter, probably not at all better pleased P III 9 79 25
but it might, probably must, end in love with some. P III 10 82 1
He had, probably, never heard, and never thought of any P III 10 82 1
his usual companions had probably no concern in, she had P III 11 100 23
of the country, and probably might not be at home again P IV 1 128 31
period of his life (and probably not a short one) when he P IV 5 161 27
Byron; nay, that was probably learnt already; of course P IV 6 167 20
passed; neither of them, probably, much the wiser for what P IV 7 176 8
The circumstance, probably, which first opened your eyes P IV 9 201 63
very unlike him--led by him, and probably despised by him. P IV 9 209 95
to the fire-place; probably for the sake of walking away P IV 10 225 56
No man and woman would, probably. P IV 11 234 27
We each begin probably with a little bias towards our own P IV 11 234 30
Of all the family, Mary was probably the one most P IV 12 249 5
on that account--& probably very many more--and his own S 2 372 1
state, the sea air wd probably be the death of me.-- S 5 387 1
Two large families--one, for prospect house probably, the S 5 388 1
apart with him (which probably she might not have been S 7 395 1
Miss Lambe a young lady (probably a neice) under her care, S 9 409 1
our own lodgings, & probably the moment dinner is over, S 9 411 1
that the sea air wd probably in her present state, be the S 10 412 1
Miss D. probably felt a little awkward on being first S 11 420 1
shame & the blame, that probably when she had divided out S 11 420 1

PROBITY (1)

for the good conduct, the probity and honour of his friend, PP I 18 95 50

PROCEED (45)

I hope this does not proceed from anything wrong, & that I LS 20 278 11
But to her utter amazement she found that to proceed along NA I 2 21 9
a security worth having; and I shall proceed with courage. NA I 10 78 41
If we proceed to particulars, and engage in the never- NA I 14 107 11
"Well, proceed by all means. NA II 2 139 7
dressing-gown around you, proceed to examine this mystery. NA II 5 159 19
No, no, you will proceed into this small vaulted room, and NA II 5 160 21
mystery, to proceed in her dressing without further delay. NA II 6 164 3
over the titles of half a shelf, and was ready to proceed. NA II 8 182 2
But two advantages will proceed from this delay. SS I 4 22 17
the interruption to proceed less from any attention to her, SS I 12 62 27
of silent exertion enabled him to proceed with composure. SS II 9 207 25
They proceed from no misconduct, and can be no disgrace. SS II 9 210 32
no more apologies, but proceed to say that, thank God! SS III 2 277 29
30
Marianne would not let her proceed;--and Elinor, satisfied SS III 11 352 16
17
couple of nights, he was to proceed on his journey to town. SS III 13 372 46
"Will it not be advisable, before we proceed on this PP I 10 50 38
May I ask whether these pleasing attentions proceed from PP I 14 68 10
only suppose his visit to proceed from the difficulty of PP II 9 180 28
From what can it proceed? PP III 1 255 60
as the ceremony was over, they should proceed to Longbourn. PP III 8 314 22
The plan of the young couple was to proceed after a few MP II 3 203 31

not really require you to proceed upon my plan, though by MP II 7 243 27
as much encouragement to proceed as a well-judging your MP III 1 315 18
now in commission, their companions were ready to proceed. MP III 10 403 13
He has encouragement enough to proceed, without our E I 9 78 47
at the conviction, that she must proceed another step. E II 8 228 90
go quite right, did not proceed with all the rapidity E II 18 308 28
He did not believe it to proceed from any thing that care E III 1 317 6
Beyond it she would on no account proceed. E III 3 335 11
short hesitation, "I hope it does not proceed from----- E III 4 341 32
Should she proceed no farther?--should she let it pass, E III 4 341 34
She had previously determined how far she would proceed, E III 4 341 34
he was obliged to proceed so, for his proposal was caught E III 6 354 9
evident, though it could not often proceed beyond a look. E III 16 457 34
This, on his side, might merely proceed from her not being E III 17 463 15
be soon over too, she hesitated--she could not proceed. E III 19 483 9
allowing Mr. Shepherd to proceed in the treaty, and P III 3 24 35
He had intended, on first arriving, to proceed very soon P III 9 73 1
beginning to decline, she was not allowed to proceed. P III 10 91 41
began, was fated not to proceed far at present; for when P IV 1 128 31
marshal themselves, and proceed into the concert room; and P IV 8 185 19
and not daring to proceed as she might do in his absence. P IV 9 208 92
beyond it no wheels but cart wheels could safely proceed. S 1 364 1
into the turnpike road & proceed to Hailsham, & so home, S 1 367 1

PROCEEDED (70)
He is convinced that her attempt to run away, proceeded LS 17 271 7
see an old friend, they proceeded to make inquiries and NA I 4 32 2
In the meanwhile, they proceeded on their journey without NA I 11 88 54
Catherine, in deep mortification, proceeded on her way. NA I 12 92 3
that moment, and hurrying by him proceeded up stairs. NA I 13 102 25
Catherine, delighted by all that had passed, proceeded NA I 13 103 29
Thus wisely fortifying her mind, as she proceeded up NA II 6 167 9
ornament, they proceeded into the library, an apartment, NA II 8 182 2
nor cared for, they proceeded by quick communication to NA II 8 183 3
this must have proceeded from a sentiment of respect for NA II 9 196 23
the subject; and as he proceeded to give the particulars, NA II 15 244 11
Upon such intelligence the General had proceeded; for NA II 15 245 12
to his wishes, which proceeded not merely from interest, SS I 1 3 1
of his opinions, she proceeded to question him on the SS I 10 47 3
Surprised and alarmed they proceeded directly into the SS I 15 75 2
They then proceeded a few paces in silence. SS I 22 132 38
thing that was said, proceeded from Elinor, who was SS II 13 241 22
to Colonel Brandon, proceeded with his happiness to Lucy; SS III 5 293 1
She even proceeded so far as to be concerned to find that SS III 5 300 38
presence in aid, it proceeded so smoothly as to enable her SS III 10 340 1
Mr Edwards proceeded to relate every other little article W 323 3
the next morng; & had proceeded so far as to say--"the W 360 29
equal pleasure, and then proceeded to relate the PP I 20 110 1
on that head, he proceeded to inform them, with many PP I 23 128 10
merits, as they proceeded together up the great staircase. PP III 1 249 37
She then proceeded to enquire into the measures which her PP III 5 293 68
for her authority proceeded; but is was not in her power PP III 6 295 7
in you daughter, has proceeded from a faulty degree of PP III 6 297 11
well-doing, which had proceeded before, from all the PP III 8 309 6
They proceeded in silence along the gravel walk that led PP III 14 353 20
She heard the carriage drive away as she proceeded up PP III 14 358 74
was overcome, and he proceeded so far as to talk of giving PP III 19 387 9
Mrs. Rushworth proceeded next, under the conviction that MP I 8 76 7
in the cause, would have proceeded towards the principal MP I 9 89 31
married, Miss Crawford proceeded to inquire if she had MP I 15 147 57
part of the house, had proceeded some way, when the door MP I 18 172 33
carried this point, and Sir Thomas's narrative proceeded. MP II 1 180 12
was so indolent!"--proceeded from good breeding and good- MP II 7 238 2
Another deal proceeded, and Crawford began again about MP II 7 243 26
and kind attention, they proceeded in doors and upstairs, MP II 8 257 15
given her consent, proceeded to make the selection. MP II 8 258 17
They proceeded up stairs together, their rooms being on MP II 9 268 27
pause, proceeded in his account of Mr. Crawford's visit. MP III 1 313 15
and when Crawford proceeded to ask his opinion and give MP III 3 340 24
hundred others, Fanny proceeded in her journey, safely and MP III 7 376 5
was ever heard; all proceeded in a regular course of MP III 8 391 11
nothing, he soon proceeded to a positive recommendation to MP III 10 401 10
But as he proceeded in his story, these fears were over. MP III 16 454 18
Robert Martin would never have proceeded so far, if he had E I 8 63 42
of every part as she proceeded--and he was very much E I 9 78 51
said Emma, as they proceeded, "but then there will be an E I 10 83 5
by every body, he proceeded to say, with an air of grave E I 12 101 19
20
They joined company and proceeded together. E I 13 109 6
She then proceeded to say a good deal more than she felt, E I 18 145 5
she so very soon proceeded to ask them what they advised E II 7 208 8
Still, however, having proceeded so far, one is unwilling E II 11 250 18
them he would have proceeded to Miss Fairfax, but she was E II 17 304 30
The ball proceeded pleasantly. E III 2 326 33
she proceeded to give them all, it was of no consequence. E III 8 383 30
said she, as they proceeded--speaking more to assist Mr. E III 10 394 19
He proceeded a little farther, reading to himself; and E III 15 445 7
In all other respects, her visit began and proceeded very P III 6 46 12
to look on it at all, proceeded towards the Cobb, equally P III 11 96 10
the last, proceeded to make the proper adieus to the Cobb. P III 12 108 30
After clearing his throat, however, he proceeded thus, "I P IV 8 182 9
10
Whether he would have proceeded farther was left to Anne's P IV 10 225 61
The gentlemen had their own pursuits, the ladies proceeded P IV 10 227 68
stated;--it had not proceeded from any intention of S 2 371 1
after them as they proceeded--followed by an early S 7 395 1
some time before, she proceeded for Trafalgar house with S 9 406 1

PROCEEDING (24)
out of the house, & proceeding directly by the stage to LS 19 273 1
two gentlemen who were proceeding through the crowds, and NA I 7 44 1
her notice--and was proceeding to mention the costly NA II 5 162 27
you consider them as proceeding from a rapidity of thought PP I 10 48 27
her style, and which, proceeding from the serenity of a PP II 11 188 1
She was proceeding directly to her favourite walk, when PP II 12 195 1
which, though proceeding from shyness and the fear of PP III 3 267 3
bitterest kind, because proceeding from a cause which no PP III 6 296 11
She was then proceeding to all the particulars of calico, PP III 7 307 48
on a method of proceeding which would obviate the risk of MP I 4 37 8
it was the only way of proceeding with any advantage, in MP I 10 97 4
he was not proceeding beyond a very allowable curiosity. MP II 1 183 24
been much surprised, and much hurt, by such a proceeding. MP III 1 319 39
feelings of Mr. Crawford, as to any secrecy of proceeding. MP III 2 331 19
and judgment, all proceeding from the first cause, want of MP III 3 339 22
they must be planning, proceeding and hoping in E II 12 257 1
news he had heard, was proceeding to a family E II 17 303 24
shall always think it a very abominable sort of proceeding. E III 10 399 61
And, after proceeding a few steps, she added--"I stopped E III 13 429 32
her father to be proceeding, his friends to be urging him. P III 2 12 5
mechanically at work, proceeding for half an hour together, P III 8 72 58
she saw a great deal of most characteristic proceeding. P IV 10 216 19
and the other two proceeding together; and soon words P IV 11 240 59
them not to think of proceeding till the ancle had been S 1 367 1

PROCEEDINGS (9)
Mr Smith's account of her proceedings at Langford, where LS 11 259 1
to watch the proceedings of these alarming young men. NA I 6 43 34
have favoured the barbarous proceedings of her husband. NA II 8 188 17
their proceedings, and perhaps announce the marriage. PP III 5 287 33
of the eclat of their proceedings; and his brother, MP I 18 164 1
particulars of his proceedings and events, his arrivals MP II 1 178 8
proceedings, and argue him into a little more rationality. MP II 2 191 10
On the contrary, her plans and proceedings were more and E I 9 69 1
his proceedings, first on my affairs, and then on his own. E III 18 472 20

PROCEEDS (2)
proceeds from any thing but your own idleness and folly." MP II 6 230 6
He proceeds at his own risk. MP III 2 331 16

PROCESS (5)
tedious in the usual process of such a meeting. PP I 11 55 8
deal of pain in the process--so much to herself at this E II 5 187 4
being the commonest process of a not ill-disposed mind. E II 5 187 6
his family; the simplest process in the world of time upon P IV 4 147 7
his fortune, and by a rather quicker process than the law. P IV 9 200 59

PROCESSION (1)
The solemn procession, headed by Baddely, of tea-board, MP III 3 344 43

PROCLAIM (3)
private balls and large dinners to proclaim its importance. SS II 2 151 43
him but what I might proclaim to all the world; a sense of PP I 16 78 20
the acquaintance, and proclaim the value of the connection, P IV 2 135 35

PROCLAIMED (7)
had heard three proclaimed by all the clocks in the house, NA II 6 171 12
Happy the voice that proclaimed the discovery!-- NA II 14 233 8
which proclaimed its writer to be deep in hardened villany. SS II 7 183 14
the evening a proclaimed thing to all whom it concerned. MP II 8 254 8
She proclaimed her thoughts. MP III 6 372 21
as Harriet exultingly proclaimed it, there was a blush on E III 5 348 21
as right as this speech proclaimed; and its happy effect E III 10 400 69

PROCLAIMING (1)
would be more nice in proclaiming his suspicions of her SS I 21 125 36

PROCRASTINATING (1)
and as incapable of procrastinating any evil that was E II 12 261 35

PROCURE (18)
pleasure in my power to procure her, will, I trust, LS 27 297 2
he was at some pains to procure, that the Fullerton estate, NA II 16 251 6
at Whitwell, they might procure a tolerable composure of SS I 13 66 60
health of Marianne, to procure those inquiries which had SS II 5 171 38
it cost her some pains to procure that little;-- for the SS III 1 260 9
mode of treatment must procure, with a confidence which, SS III 7 312 19
Collins should be able to procure any woman's opinion, PP I 22 125 15
(I hope it will), to procure him better preferment; but it MP I 3 23 3
and at the same time procure for Fanny the immediate means MP I 4 37 8
wish to procure so agreeable a visitor for her sister?" MP II 5 218 17
could not help trying to procure a companion; and MP II 9 265 21
information could Emma procure as to what he truly was. E II 2 169 17
and resolve on going home by way of Randalls to procure it. E II 5 187 4
trouble of conquering any body's reserve to procure one. E II 6 203 41
Acquit me here, and procure for me, when it is allowable, E III 14 439 8
she recommended, and promised to procure and read them. P III 11 101 25
that she had something to procure at a shop, invited them P III 12 103 5
by far too much trouble taken to procure the acquaintance. P IV 4 150 18

PROCURED (22)
might, for the chance which had procured her such a friend. NA I 4 34 7
praise, after Thorpe had procured Mrs. Allen's admiration NA I 9 62 7
potions to be procured, like rhubarb, from every druggist. NA II 10 200 3
Her youth, civil manners and liberal pay, procured her all NA II 14 232 6
inhabitants he had now procured for his cottage at Barton. SS I 7 33 3
procured by some theft or contrivance unknown to herself. SS I 18 98 13
in the cause of society, procured her some other new SS I 21 118 1
A glass of wine, which Elinor procured for her directly, SS II 7 185 16
17
for years, and for the purpose had procured my exchange. SS II 9 206 24
which could not be procured at Barton, would be inevitable SS II 10 213 3
the ready wit that had procured it, wrote the next morning SS II 14 253 26
by the family in general, soon procured herself a book. SS III 6 304 12
since that time, procured me a nuncheon at Marlborough." SS III 8 318 20
rested was an opera, procured for her by Willoughby, SS III 10 342 7
returning to town, procured the forgiveness of Mrs. SS III 14 376 11
she was treated with, procured her in time the haughty SS III 14 377 11
and excellent acquaintance Meryton had procured them. PP I 16 79 23
towards her, which soon procured her pardon, and directed PP I 18 94 43
first coming to London, before they procured lodgings. PP III 6 295 5
At length, however, our kind friend procured the wished- PP III 10 322 2
the Mr. Crawford who had procured William's promotion! MP III 2 328 6
delayed, or he had yet procured no opportunity of seeing MP III 10 399 1

PROCURING (15)
that morning in hopes of procuring some addition to their SS I 7 33 4
The rest of Mrs. Palmer's sympathy was shewn in procuring SS II 10 215 11
much, however, towards procuring them seats at her table; SS II 12 231 9
And Lucy perhaps at first might think only of procuring SS III 13 364 12
former friends, than she had been in the way of procuring. PP II 2 142 19
you chose, or procuring any thing you had a fancy for?" PP II 10 183 11
The wish of procuring her regard, which she had assured PP III 8 311 13
Fanny, and no wish of procuring her pleasure at any time, MP I 8 79 23
Mr. Rushworth had no difficulty in procuring a divorce; MP III 17 464 12
and herself, in procuring him the proper invitation. E I 12 98 1
not she give him her influence in procuring it?" E I 15 125 4
intentions, from the procuring her a permanent situation E II 15 288 39
the difficulty of procuring exactly the desirable thing." E II 17 299 6
She had no difficulty in procuring Isabella's invitation; E III 16 451 3
And, as to procuring a dispensation, there could be no P III 12 102 2

PRODIGIES (1)
education, without any danger of coming back prodigies. E I 3 21 5

PRODIGIOUS (10)
to be a prodigious bargain by every lady who saw it. NA I 3 28 38
she had heard of the prodigious accumulation of dirt in NA I 11 86 50
Five hundred pounds would be a prodigious increase to SS I 2 9 10
"Norland is a prodigious beautiful place, is not it?" SS I 21 123 23
Now there's Mr. Rose at Exeter, a prodigious smart young SS I 21 123 28
"and I hear he is quite a beau, and prodigious handsome." SS I 21 125 35
Mr. Bingley, and takes a prodigious deal of care of him." PP II 10 184 23
But if I had more room, I should take a prodigious delight MP I 6 54 9
the expense of such an undertaking would be prodigious! MP I 13 127 31
to bring a prodigious influx;--nothing else was wanting. S 2 372 1

PRODIGIOUSLY (5)
The Dashwoods were so prodigiously delighted with the SS II 12 230 6
I am prodigiously proud of him. PP III 11 330 8
girls, and not at all handsome: I like them prodigiously." PP III 12 342 28
her calling here was prodigiously civil! for she only came, PP III 14 359 76
they thought her prodigiously stupid, and for the first MP I 2 18 23

PRODIGY (2)
be pleased with my son; but you must not expect a prodigy. E II 18 309 30
thought a fine young man, but do not expect a prodigy. E II 18 309 30

PRODUCE (42)
of every interesting conversation that Bath might produce. NA I 2 19 3
kind; not likely to produce animosities between the NA II 1 131 15
What this additional fortnight was to produce to her NA II 2 138 1
building such as 'what one reads about' may produce?-- NA II 5 157 13
considerable sum from the produce of an estate already SS I 1 4 4
It would not be likely to produce that dejection of mind SS I 4 22 18
"that I may defy many months to produce any good to me." SS I 19 103 8
at different times could produce;--with tenderness, pity, SS I 19 104 12
heard him would naturally produce; in the extasy of her SS II 4 161 7
in itself not apparently likely to produce evil to her. SS II 14 248 6
as the subject might naturally be supposed to produce. SS III 1 260 8
disappointed in his hopes of what the last would produce. SS III 7 313 21
conversation, was always wanted to produce this conviction. SS III 14 376 11
could produce, made her thankfully turn to a book.-- W 361 31
force or rapidity, and do not produce the same expression. PP II 8 175 25
what Lydia's infamy must produce, found additional anguish PP III 4 279 24
know nothing of the effects that such a step might produce. PP III 5 283 8
I defy even Sir William Lucas himself, to produce a more PP III 11 330 8
Elizabeth now expected that she would produce a letter for PP III 14 352 15
which it ought to produce, and her consciousness of misery MP I 2 13 4
the morrow might produce in continuation of the subject. MP I 16 150 1
than such an absence has a tendency to produce at first. MP II 3 197 3
the horse which he had fully intended it should produce. MP II 6 237 23
harangue might really produce on Mr. Crawford, it raised MP II 7 248 47

points would be the likeliest way to produce an extreme. MP III 4 349 23
supposing the first three or four days could produce any. MP III 6 366 2
It was an unsuitable connection, and did not produce much E I 2 15 3
air to produce a very white world in a very short time. E I 13 112 24
If it failed to produce equal exertion, it could not be an E I 18 148 20
Knightley, what a sensation his coming will produce? E I 18 149 29
a real friend, united to produce an offer from Colonel E II 2 163 4
attachment certainly must produce more of a struggle than E II 13 264 1
Had not Mrs. Weston any letter about her to produce?" E II 16 298 51
had my writing-desk, I am sure I could produce a specimen. E II 16 298 52
where inquiry would soon produce something--offices for E II 17 300 13
My liveliness and your solidity would produce perfection.-- E III 16 457 33
family-habits seemed to produce, of every thing being to P III 10 83 4
the general success and produce of the evening than Anne P IV 9 192 5
now another motive for being glad that I can produce it." P IV 9 203 70
I cannot produce written proof again, but I can give as P IV 9 204 80
implied it's right to produce a great impression--& seeing S 7 400 1
say among themselves, cd produce a happier catastrophe S 11 420 1

PRODUCED (90)

surprised at any effect produced on the heart of man by LS 8 255 2
was produced, & at best, the honour of victory is doubtful. LS 25 294 6
proudly would she have produced the book, and told its NA I 5 38 4
This compliment, delightful as it was, produced severe NA I 8 54 10
or reality, till Morland produced his watch, and NA I 9 67 33
in which her conduct produced such unpleasant reflections, NA II 7 173 5
failed, his own had often produced the perfection wanted. NA II 8 183 3
of beings equally hardened in guilt might not be produced. NA II 9 190 2
to mention the circumstance which had produced it. NA II 10 207 41
wind was high, and often produced strange and sudden NA II 13 227 26
on Sarah's side, which produced only a bow of NA II 15 243 9
years before his own, produced a great alteration in his SS I 1 3 1
violent emotion which it produced for a while; for when SS I 3 14 1
for that blind partiality to Edward which produced it. SS I 4 19 3
unavoidable, it had not produced the smallest effect on SS I 5 25 3
such as society produced, within a very narrow compass. SS I 7 32 1
produced occasional effusions of sorrow as lively as ever. SS I 16 83 4
Elinor pleasure, as it produced a reply from Marianne so SS I 16 85 14
among them, and every effect of solitude was produced. SS I 19 105 12
Dulness is as much produced within doors as without, by SS I 20 111 8
she believed, which produced his contemptuous treatment of SS I 20 112 28
the child's neck, produced from this pattern of gentleness, SS I 21 121 10
Elinor had expected; it produced not one novelty of SS II 1 143 10
our separation naturally produced, with the familiarity SS II 7 187 42
These assured him that his exertion had produced an SS II 10 216 15
she had been by what produced it; but Colonel Brandon's SS II 12 236 38
Jennings's happiness, produced a temporary alteration in SS II 14 246 2
Marianne, no effect was produced, but a look of SS II 14 247 4
and this misconstruction produced within a day or two SS II 14 248 6
necessarily produced between Elinor's conduct and her own. SS III 2 270 1
produced from Mrs. Jennings the following natural remark. SS III 2 276 27
A few moments' reflection, however, produced a very happy SS III 4 286 16
17
to-morrow would have produced, but for this unlucky SS III 7 308 4
The next day produced little or no alteration in the state SS III 7 308 5
for the sufferings produced by them, which made her think SS III 9 333 2
drew near the house had produced almost the conviction of SS III 9 334 4
The next morning produced no abatement in these happy SS III 10 342 8
hard labour of mind, he produced the remark of it's being W 345 21
knowledge of each other which such intercourse produced.-- W 348 23
It produced immediate complacency.-- W 353 26
Mr. Collins readily assented, and a book was produced; but PP I 14 68 13
other books were produced, and after some deliberation he PP I 14 68 13
be found at Longbourn, produced from her, amid very PP I 15 70 3
The morrow produced no abatement of Mrs. Bennet's ill PP I 21 115 2
in so amiable a light, which yesterday had produced. PP III 2 265 16
The next variation which their visit afforded was produced PP III 3 268 6
When the first transports of rage which had produced his PP III 8 309 5
which uncertainty had produced of what Mr. Darcy might PP III 10 326 3
The happiness which this reply produced, was such as he PP III 16 366 8
be serious, however, produced the desired effect; and she PP III 17 373 17
so many of her children, produced so happy an effect as to PP III 19 385 1
of their age, which produced as striking a difference MP I 2 13 4
and entertaining their young cousin, produced little union. MP I 2 14 7
The next meeting of the two Mansfield families produced MP I 8 79 28
of the debt which all these kind remembrances produced. MP I 16 153 3
retrospection and regret produced by it, by some inquiry MP II 6 236 23
Only think what grand things were produced there by our MP II 7 244 30
family which Sunday produced, she learnt that he had MP II 11 286 16
from the blush soon produced from such a look, only said, " MP II 11 290 38
which the finding herself in the east room again produced. MP III 5 357 6
being with William, soon produced their natural effect on MP III 7 375 1
with so fine a sound, produced altogether such a MP III 11 409 6
greasy than even Rebecca's hands had first produced it. MP III 15 439 9
The next morning produced a little more. MP III 15 446 34
almost to approve the evil which produced such a good. MP III 17 466 15
Emma wished to go to work directly, and therefore produced E I 6 44 19
The very day of Mr. Elton's going to London produced a E I 7 50 1
The very next day however produced some proof of E I 9 71 10
that if compassion has produced exertion and relief to the E I 10 87 30
and disposed of, produced a noise and confusion which his E I 11 92 3
The unhappiness produced by the knowledge of that E II 4 184 11
produced it was necessarily increasing Emma's dislike. E II 15 281 3
know whether the wet walk of this morning had produced any. E II 16 298 58
had produced this very natural and very desirable effect. E III 1 316 3
she must believe to be produced only by a consciousness of E III 11 413 47
And this belief produced another dread. E III 13 425 2
with her own heart produced the most solemn resolution of E III 14 435 4
contemplation of his worth which this comparison produced. E III 18 480 80
Such opposition, as these feelings produced, was more than P III 4 27 5
of Anne's side, produced a nearly a cure on Mary's. P III 5 39 40
the last of his wants, produced such a confusion of P III 9 80 34
and by the animation of eye which it had also produced. P III 12 104 6
always produced irritation in both, was beyond a doubt. P III 12 107 21
by the effect which a man of decent appearance produced. P IV 3 142 13
His enquiries, however, produced at length an account of P IV 3 144 22
added, "the day has produced some effects however--has had P IV 8 182 6
you may guess what it produced; the resolution of coming P IV 9 207 90
The absolute necessity of seeming like herself produced P IV 11 238 45
It produced a great & immediate change. S 10 416 1
of this tete a tete produced, Charlotte cd not but think S 12 426 1

PRODUCES (4)

such as a very imprudent marriage almost always produces. MP I 1 4 1
so much taller, and produces all these charms and graces! MP II 6 230 8
Vanity working on a weak head, produces every sort of E I 8 64 47
immediate resolution it produces: as soon as she found I E III 14 441 8

PRODUCING (14)

themselves, or producing coolness between their husbands. SS III 14 380 21
in the hope of its producing a better effect than any MP I 3 23 2
"So soon! my good friend," said Sir Thomas, producing his MP II 10 279 24
attentions of the lover producing a craving for their MP III 6 368 7
The blind fondness which was for ever producing evil MP III 9 396 5
and such hints producing nothing, he soon proceeded to a MP III 10 401 10
and many days to come, without producing any conclusion. MP III 12 417 4
all following and producing each other at hap-hazard. MP III 13 427 12
as time is for ever producing between the plans and MP III 17 471 29
had told her, though fearful of its producing Mr. Elton. E II 9 232 14
ever convincing without producing any effect, for ever E II 13 267 9
Emma was pleased with the thought; and producing the box, E III 5 347 20
mind, producing reserve and self-command, it would.-- E III 11 403 2
A day or two passed without producing any thing.-- P IV 7 179 32

PRODUCTION (3)

much greater, if the production of Mr. Hume or Mr. NA I 14 109 23
production which I know I can borrow of Colonel Brandon. SS III 10 343 9
production without finding food for a rambling fancy." MP II 4 209 16

PRODUCTIONS (1)

Although our productions have afforded more extensive and NA I 5 37 4

PRODUCTIVE (8)

Your applying however to Reginald can be productive only LS 24 287 7
that it might have been productive of much unpleasantness NA II 14 234 10
forward, and found productive of such countless jokes, SS I 21 125 36
an excursion would be productive of much amusement to both SS II 3 155 7
was by no means more productive of pleasure to her than to SS II 4 166 31
Their visits to Mrs. Philips were now productive of the PP I 7 28 4
agreeable, or at all productive of any thing useful with MP I 10 104 51
it was not more productive than such meetings usually are. E III 2 326 33

PROFESS (9)

the delight in a fine prospect which you profess to feel. SS I 18 97 8
your sister must allow me to feel no more than I profess. SS I 18 98 8
venture so far as to profess some concern for having ever SS III 13 372 42
"I wish Margt could have heard him profess his ignorance W 342 19
can be, but I still profess my preference of a white skin. W 357 28
Society has claims on us all; and I profess myself one of PP I 17 87 11
If they profess a disinclination for it, I only set it MP I 4 43 25
But are you so insensible as you profess yourself? MP III 5 362 16
hospitality--we do not profess to give dinners--few people P IV 10 219 29

PROFESSED (19)

thither; and tho' he professed himself quite undetermined, LS 27 297 4
leaving you, for whom I professed an unbounded affection, SS III 10 346 28
Emma thanked him--but professed herself very unwilling to W 339 18
found little, except the professed affection of the writer, PP II 1 133 2
The motive professed, was his conviction of its being PP III 10 321 2
was charming, except the professed lover of her daughter. PP III 13 345 18
Darcy professed a great curiosity to see the view from the PP III 17 375 25
in Frederick, he professed an equal willingness for that. MP I 14 132 8
to her professed opinions, sometimes a tinge of wrong. MP II 9 269 31
of his being less unreasonable than he professed himself. MP III 2 328 8
or any thing which professed, in long sentences of refined E I 3 21 5
He professed himself extremely anxious about her fair E I 15 124 3
the conviction he had professed that Mr. Elton would never E I 16 135 6
still more, and professed himself to have always felt the E II 5 191 26
and as agreeable as she professed herself, were very well E II 15 281 2
Emma and Harriet professed very high expectations of E III 6 357 31
a professed resolution of doing nothing for his daughter. P III 4 26 2
pore over it, with the professed view of finding out the P III 8 64 7
he talked well, professed good opinions, seemed to judge P IV 5 160 27

PROFESSEDLY (4)

could hardly be outdone by any creature professedly noisy. SS I 21 121 10
It was every day implied, but never professedly declared. SS II 7 186 34
was in fact as little valued, as it was professedly sought. SS II 14 246 2
Jane had come to Highbury professedly for three months; E II 15 285 14

PROFESSES (1)

She professes to keep her own counsel; she says, & truly W 318 2

PROFESSING (7)

to do pretty well; and professing myself moreover NA II 16 252 7
professing opinions which in fact are not your own." PP II 8 174 14
super-added objects of professing attention to the comfort MP I 6 55 17
Dr. Grant, professing an indisposition, for which he had MP I 18 171 26
A woman married only six months ago, a man professing MP III 15 441 20
the lover of Harriet, was professing himself her lover. E I 15 129 24
He defended himself; though professing that he would never P III 8 68 34

PROFESSION (61)

very partial to the profession;" and and something like a NA I 5 36 2
I should think any profession necessary for him; and NA II 7 176 15
as any private man in the county, has his profession." NA II 7 176 15
He is of no profession at all." SS I 12 61 24
for strangers, no profession, and no assurance, you may SS I 17 90 4
man if you had any profession to engage your time and give SS I 19 102 3
to engage me, no profession to give me employment, or SS I 19 102 4
We never could agree in our choice of a profession. SS I 19 102 4
for my having any profession at all, as I might be as SS I 19 103 4
church to every other profession; now my plan is that he SS II 2 149 25
were to enter into any profession with a view of better SS III 1 267 38
only in the rapturous profession of the lover, but in the SS III 13 361 3
Had my mother given me some active profession when I was SS III 13 362 5
instead of having any profession chosen for me, or being SS III 13 362 5
They are in the same profession, you know; only in PP I 10 53 57
The church ought to have been my profession--I was brought PP I 16 79 23
My father began life in the profession which your uncle, PP I 16 81 37
perfectly compatible with the profession of a clergyman.-- PP I 18 101 71
would be his profession, intended to provide for him in it. PP II 12 200 5
best manner that his profession might allow, and if he PP II 12 200 5
sake, he assisted him farther in his profession. PP III 19 387 9
but her husband's profession was such as no interest could MP I 1 3 1
in consequence of his profession, as made her gradually MP I 2 21 34
in speaking of his profession, and the foreign stations he MP I 6 60 47
felt grave, and only replied, "it is a noble profession." MP I 6 60 50
"Yes, the profession is well enough under two MP I 6 60 51
But, in short, it is not a favourite profession of mine. MP I 6 60 51
You must suppose me designed for some profession, and MP I 9 91 39
The profession, either navy or army, is its own MP I 11 109 19
in their choice of a profession, as heroism, and noise, MP I 11 110 22
we need not give up his profession for all that; because, MP I 11 111 30
that; because, whatever profession Dr. Grant had chose, he MP I 11 111 30
more active and worldly profession, where he would have MP I 11 111 30
is beyond the reach of almost every actress by profession. MP I 14 135 15
the man who chooses the profession itself, is, perhaps, MP I 15 145 41
a man might escape a profession and represent the county." MP I 17 161 13
profession to which he was now on the point of belonging. MP II 10 279 21
"Even in my profession"--said Edmund with a smile--"how MP III 3 339 23
information beyond his profession; he read only the MP III 8 389 3
because not rich enough, than because of my profession. MP III 13 422 2
man; rising in his profession, domestic, and respectable E I 11 92 5
Before she had committed herself by any public profession E II 2 168 15
you make so noble a profession of doing it, but I honestly E II 8 217 32
I have known a good deal of the profession; and besides P III 3 18 7
soon afterwards-- "the profession has its utility, but I P III 3 19 13
14
convinced, though every profession is necessary and P III 3 20 17
of a most uncertain profession, and no connexions to P III 4 26 3
farther rise in that profession; would be, indeed, a P III 4 26 3
He had been lucky in his profession, but spending freely, P III 4 27 4
anxiety attending his profession, all their probable fears, P III 4 29 8
His profession qualified him, his disposition led him, to P III 8 63 2
as it all was with his profession, the fruit of its P III 11 98 17
landlady, a nurse by profession, and who had always a home P IV 5 154 9
of life, and in his profession, he should not have many P IV 6 166 14
You have always a profession, pursuits, business of some P IV 11 232 19
and as high in his profession as merit and activity could P IV 12 248 1
His profession was all that could ever make her friends P IV 12 252 12
for belonging to that profession which is, if possible, P IV 12 252 12
not large fortune;--no profession--succeeding as eldest S 2 371 1
He is so delicate that he can engage in no profession.-- S 5 385 1
too sickly for any profession--& sit down at 1 & 20, on S 5 388 1

PROFESSIONAL (4)

into the hands of a professional man, Mr. Rushworth was MP I 6 61 58
of good principles, professional knowledge, energy, MP II 6 236 21
His professional engagements did not allow of his being E II 16 292 8
be so anxious for professional advice, so very little S 5 388 1

PROFESSIONALLY (1)

She has a large acquaintance, of course professionally, P IV 5 155 9

PROFESSIONS (28)

her display of Greif, & professions of regret, & general LS 3 247 1
am not apt to deal in professions, my dear Mrs Vernon, & I LS 20 277 6
7

Her professions of attachment were now as disgusting as NA II 12 218 3
him with the simple professions of unaffected benevolence; NA II 15 242 7
worded in a page full of empty professions to Mr. Morland. NA II 16 252 7
employments, professions, and trades as Columella's." SS I 19 103 5
having been more guarded in my professions of that esteem. SS II 7 183 13
desire of a release any professions of regret, SS II 7 183 14
the language, not the professions of Colonel Brandon, but SS III 9 336 13
two friends with many professions of pleasure; and PP I 11 54 1
The communication excited many professions of concern; and PP I 12 59 2
After a week spent in professions of love and schemes of PP II 2 139 1
and the inconsistency of his professions with his conduct. PP II 13 207 5
It would have spared her from explanations and professions PP III 17 376 30
Sir Thomas sent friendly advice and professions, Lady MP I 1 5 3
you know I am a woman of few words and professions. MP I 1 6 6
or rather of professions of a somewhat pointed character. MP II 7 246 36
considered him, in the professions of persevering, MP III 2 328 7
Mansfield, that all his professions and vows of unshaken MP III 4 345 2
from gratified in being the object of such professions." E I 15 130 30
His professions and his proposals did him no service. E I 16 135 7
letter, full of professions and falsehoods, and persuade E I 18 148 24
a parade of insincere professions; and that Mr. Knightley E II 6 197 4
her, and professions of Mrs. Elton's meditated activity. E II 17 299 1
To come among us with professions of openness and E III 10 399 61
But then, is not it the same with many other professions, P III 3 20 17
and even in the quieter professions, there is a toil and a P III 3 20 17
Mark his professions to my poor husband. P IV 9 204 75

PROFICIENCY (2)
by her mother; her proficiency in either was not NA I 1 14 1
spoke with affectionate praise of his sister's proficiency. PP II 8 173 7

PROFICIENT (2)
I had ever learnt, I should have been a great proficient. PP II 8 173 6
but I should be sorry to be examined by a real proficient." P IV 8 187 27

PROFILE (3)
lover's profile that she might be detected in the design. NA I 1 16 10
see only his expressive profile as he turned with a smile MP I 8 81 32
if by looking at Edmund's profile she could catch any of MP I 16 152 3

PROFILES (1)
a collection of family profiles thought unworthy of being MP I 16 152 2

PROFIT (12)
declining entirely to profit by such unexampled attention. LS 42 312 5
which brought her little profit, for they talked in NA I 14 110 28
she gained but little, her chief profit was in wonder. NA II 3 148 29
his wife, one only could profit by the kindness of their W 315 1
Pardon me for neglecting to profit by your advice, which PP I 18 97 61
said and listened to, without some profit to the speaker. MP III 3 344 44
they had never heard from any lips that could profit them. MP III 17 463 8
appearances, and thinking of nothing but profit and loss." E I 4 33 38
more of his master's profit than any thing; but Mrs. E II 9 239 51
I mean to make my profit of Mrs. Wallis, however. P IV 5 156 13
in proportion to their profit must be ours eventually in S 6 393 1
soon found that all her calculations of profit wd be vain. S 11 422 1

PROFITABLE (3)
made her a most attentive, profitable, thankful pupil. MP III 12 418 7
a lesson, a source of profitable humiliation to her own E II 4 182 7
of it's becoming a profitable speculation, they had S 2 371 1

PROFITED (1)
Elinor joyfully profited by the first of these proposals, SS II 1 145 23

PROFITING (1)
saw him instantly profiting by the release, to address SS III 13 363 8

PROFITS (2)
but, as the whole of the profits of his mercantile life E II 4 183 9
greater profits, and fortune in general had smiled on them. E II 7 207 6

PROFITTING (1)
myself the pleasure of profitting by your kind invitation LS 1 243 1

PROFLIGACY (2)
all these symptoms of profligacy at ten years old, she had NA I 1 14 1
The extravagance and general profligacy which he scrupled PP II 13 205 4

PROFLIGATE (1)
We both know that he has been profligate in every sense of PP III 5 284 12

PROFOUND (1)
This, however, was a profound secret; no to be breathed P III 2 15 13

PROFUSE (1)
Mrs. Bennet was profuse in her acknowledgments. PP I 9 42 6

PROFUSION (7)
The furniture was in all the profusion and elegance of NA II 5 162 26
chiding Elizth for the profusion on the table, & W 353 27
Your profusion makes me saving; and if you lament over him PP II 17 225 13
or more solemn than the profusion of mahogany, and the MP I 9 85 6
of happiness and a profusion of love and praise towards MP III 13 420 1
The laurels at Maple Grove are in the same profusion as E II 14 273 21
Such elegance and profusion!-- E III 2 330 45

PROGNOSTICATIONS (1)
all the officious prognostications of Mrs. Norris that she MP I 2 13 4

PROGNOSTICS (2)
for the most flattering prognostics of her future renown. LS 19 274 2
to the door with many cheerful prognostics of a bad day. PP I 7 31 28

PROGRESS (45)
I see plainly that she is uneasy at my progress in the LS 10 257 1
watched Miss Thorpe's progress down the street from the NA I 4 34 7
The progress of the friendship between Catherine and NA I 5 36 4
The progress of Catherine's unhappiness from the events of NA I 9 60 1
happiness of a progress through a long suite of lofty NA I 11 88 54
Delighted with her progress, and fearful of wearying her NA I 14 111 29
Her progress was not quick, for her thoughts and her eyes NA II 6 164 3
further soothed in her progress, by being told, that she NA II 8 183 2
During the progress of her disorder, Frederick and I (we NA II 9 197 25
time from watching her progress; and though no object on NA II 14 231 5
Mrs. Morland watched the progress of this relapse; and NA II 15 241 7
the progress of time which yet kept them in ignorance! SS III 7 315 26
could superintend the progress of the parsonage, and SS III 14 374 7
however its progress may be apparently obstructed, will do SS III 14 376 11
In their progress up the room, they paused almost W 329 9
him, was watching the progress of his letter, and PP I 10 47 1
in watching Mr. Darcy's progress through his book, as in PP I 11 54 4
her making that progress in many accomplishments, which PP I 11 67 7
and she watched her progress through the several stanzas PP I 18 100 68
direction; but their progress was slow, for Mr. Gardiner, PP III 1 254 57
in the course of their progress, her mind became so MP I 4 38 9
"It would be delightful to me to see the progress of it MP I 6 57 30
by her early progress, to make her unwilling to dismount. MP I 7 66 15
slow progress, and to feel the miseries of waiting. MP I 18 164 1
Sir Thomas himself was watching her progress down the MP II 10 276 13
I have (I flatter myself) made no inconsiderable progress MP II 12 292 6
of her complexion, the progress of her feelings, their MP II 13 298 3
have enlightened witnesses of the progress of his success. MP III 2 331 19
Edmund watched the progress of her attention, and was MP III 3 337 11
and sentiment, which the progress of time and variation of MP III 6 374 27
beginnings and progress of vegetation had delighted her.-- MP III 14 431 9
to stop him or make his progress slow; no doubts of her MP III 17 471 28
and had made more progress both in drawing and music than E I 6 44 19
pencil, to jump up and see the progress, and be charmed.-- E I 6 47 26
whole progress of the picture, which was rapid and happy. E I 6 47 30
of all hope, such a progress might be made towards a state E I 17 142 11
Cole of the rise and progress of the affair was so E II 4 181 4
amusing schemes for the progress and close of their E II 13 264 1
altered by time, by the progress of years," said John E II 16 294 23
like her's, once opening to suspicion, made rapid progress. E III 11 407 32
After this, he made some progress without any pause. E III 15 446 19
them better; felt their progress through the streets to be, P IV 2 135 34
All that sounded extravagant or irrational in the progress P IV 3 140 11
of her quiet, solitary progress up the town (and she felt P IV 11 238 47
as exhibit the progress of strong passion from the first S 8 403 1

PROGRESSIVELY (1)
of beauty, or my own choice, and acquired progressively. MP I 6 56 28

PROHIBITED (8)
the cherished, or the prohibited, county of Somerset, for SS III 6 302 6
make no inquiries on so prohibited a subject, but conclude SS III 11 353 21
Balls will be absolutely prohibited, unless you stand up PP III 6 300 30
and could allow yourself to think it not prohibited." MP I 10 99 18
"Prohibited! nonsense! I certainly can get out that way, MP I 10 99 19
not cruel custom prohibited its appearance except on duty. MP III 6 368 8
would be a subject prohibited entirely--he entered upon MP III 16 453 17
South end is prohibited, if you please. E I 12 101 23

PROHIBITION (1)
In such a point as this, your mother's prohibition ought LS 24 286 7

PROJECT (13)
spirit to resent a project which influenced me six years LS 5 249 1
This project will serve at least to amuse me, & prevent my LS 7 254 3
probably put that project in execution--for London will be LS 25 294 4
chuse papers, project shrubberies, and invent a sweep. SS III 14 374 7
There was no arguing upon such a project. PP I 18 102 73
she was, in fact, exceedingly delighted with the project. MP I 13 129 40
them in their darling project, and they congratulated each MP I 17 158 1
Your wicked project upon her peace turns out a clever MP II 12 295 19
It was a medicinal project upon his niece's understanding,. MP III 6 369 10
to school, Sam on some project of his own, and her father MP III 8 388 1
Emma's project of forgetting Mr. Elton for a while, made E I 14 118 4
was doing, of this very project of her's, which determined E III 10 398 51
and a project for going thither was the consequence. P III 11 94 6

PROJECTED (6)
it was agreed that the projected walk should be taken as NA I 12 95 16
In a doleful voice Mrs. Bennet thus began the projected PP I 20 114 31
dances of this little projected ball, to be given, not at E II 11 250 21
wait, and every projected party be still only talked of. E III 6 352 2
whose first views on the projected change had been for P III 2 14 10
when it had been first projected; more tender, more tried, P IV 11 240 59

PROJECTING (4)
no opportunity of projecting weddings among all the young SS I 8 36 1
with one hand, "on that projecting mound,--there I fell; SS III 10 344 12 13
more than the credit of projecting and arranging so MP I 1 8 9
Mrs. Clay had freckles, and a projecting tooth, and a P III 5 34 12

PROJECTION (1)
from their view at home by the projection of an hill. SS I 7 32 1

PROJECTOR (1)
of sensation as a Projector, the sisters were perhaps S 10 412 1

PROJECTS (4)
Do not you think these kind of projects objectionable?" NA I 13 104 31
I tell what horrid projects might not have been imputed? SS III 8 330 69
was full of ideas and projects, and, generally speaking, MP I 10 97 3
views, and plans, and projects you have;-- and as a friend E I 8 66 51

PROLOGUE (1)
It is a sort of prologue to the play, a motto to the E I 9 74 23

PROLONG (3)
urgent with me to prolong my stay, but their hospitable & LS 1 243 1
Mr Vernon's invitation to prolong his stay in Sussex that LS 8 254 1
would probably prolong rather than break up the party. E II 17 303 23

PROLONGATION (1)
by consenting to a prolongation of her stay, & in the LS 42 313 7

PROLONGED (2)
by no means displeased, prolonged the conversation on MP II 7 251 63
She was in gay spirits, and would have prolonged the E III 5 351 38

PROMINENT (4)
was obliged to be indebted to his more prominent attention. MP II 7 251 66
The dread of such a failure after all became the prominent E I 8 67 56
and therefore most prominent, was in her own cook at south E I 12 104 50
the happiest dream, was perhaps the most prominent feeling. E III 13 430 36

PROMISE (102)
in our power to keep our promise of spending the Christmas LS 3 246 1
be made to either, I can promise you a ready & chearful LS 12 261 3
from me a kind of promise never to invite you to my house. LS 26 296 4
here, for I consider my promise to Mr Johnson as LS 26 296 4
post, nor exacted her promise of transmitting the NA I 2 19 3
him, declined giving any absolute promise of sunshine. NA I 11 82 1
to have retracted a promise voluntarily made only five NA I 13 101 25
if she had broken her promise to them in order to do what NA I 13 105 41
my sister; breaking the promise I had made of reading it NA I 14 107 9
The needful was comprised in Mr. Morland's promise; his NA I 15 122 28
proposed to Miss Tilney the accomplishment of her promise. NA II 9 191 3
as they went of another promise, their first visit in NA II 9 191 3
A faithful promise!-- NA II 9 196 21
But a faithful promise--the fidelity of promising! NA II 9 196 21
sat down to fulfil her promise to Miss Tilney, whose trust NA II 14 235 14
too kind to exact any promise; and whenever Catherine NA II 16 250 3
When he gave his promise to his father, he meditated SS I 1 5 8
But as he required the promise, I could not do less than SS I 2 9 6
The promise, therefore, was given, and must be performed. SS I 2 9 6
I think, be amply discharging my promise to my father." SS I 2 11 23
her husband of the solemn promise on the part of his son SS I 3 14 2
the performance of his promise to his father was by this SS I 5 26 4
Now was the time when her son-in-law's promise to his SS I 5 27 6
securing their promise of dining at the park the next day. SS I 6 31 10
"Your promise makes me easy. SS I 14 74 19
The promise was readily given, and Willoughby's behaviour SS I 14 74 20
who concluded that a promise had been made by Willoughby SS I 15 75 1
He could only obtain a promise of their calling at the SS I 21 119 5
counter which seemed to promise the quickest succession; SS II 11 220 3
bound as she was by her promise of secrecy to Lucy, she SS II 13 234 47
complete enfranchisement from his promise to his father. SS II 14 252 20
My promise to Lucy, obliged me to be secret. SS III 1 262 23
from her whatever promise she required; and at her request, SS III 1 264 32
She performed her promise of being discreet, to admiration. SS III 1 265 33
Brandon to perform his promise of following her; and while SS III 7 308 5
he reminded me of an old promise about a pointer puppy. SS III 8 330 69
But her promise of relating it to her sister was SS III 9 335 5
she remembered that her promise to Willoughby was yet SS III 10 343 10
Miss Osborne has been so very kind as to promise to dance W 330 11
of Miss Osborne's second promise;--but tho' he contrived W 330 11
I was forced to say we were only going to church & promise W 350 24
"I believe, ma'am, I may safely promise you never to dance PP I 5 20 17
reminded him of his promise; adding, that it would be the PP I 9 45 36
gave him a voluntary promise of providing for me, I am PP I 16 81 37
A promise of secrecy was of course very dutifully given, PP I 22 123 3
each other, how can I promise to be wiser than so many of PP II 3 145 7
All that I can promise you, therefore, is not to be in a PP II 3 145 7
Promise me, therefore, to come to Hunsford." PP II 3 146 16
reminded Elizabeth of her promise concerning that PP II 3 149 28
an event of such happy promise as to make Elizabeth hope, PP II 19 238 6
He has the promise of an ensigncy in general ----'s PP III 8 312 19
"And will you promise me, never to enter into such an PP III 14 356 58
"I will make no promise of the kind." PP III 14 356 59
promise, make their marriage at all more probable? PP III 14 357 61
"If, therefore, an excuse for not keeping his promise, PP III 15 361 4
promise from her nephew, which she had refused to give. PP III 16 367 9
of promise, for I ought not to have mentioned the subject? PP III 18 381 13
stay with her, with the promise of balls and young men, PP III 19 385 4
a promise to his father, and of being Sir Thomas hereafter. MP I 5 48 28
After what passed at first, he would claim it as a promise. MP I 8 77 11
in the complaisance of the moment, to promise any thing. MP I 17 158 2
thing that could deserve or promise well. MP II 6 236 21
promise her greater happiness than she knows here." MP II 11 285 13
and which gave any promise of durability, was in a better MP III 9 395 4
honest man, to whom I have given half a promise already.-- MP III 11 412 20
was of a nature to promise occupation for the pen for many MP III 13 426 9

great acquisition in the promise of Fanny for a daughter, MP III 17 471 29
The event had every promise of happiness for her friend. E I 1 6 6
"I promise you to make none for myself, papa; but I must, E I 1 12 41
Some people even talked of a promise to his wife on her E I 1 12 41
your powers would seem to promise; but you were receiving E I 5 38 11
entreat her to promise him not to venture into such hazard E I 15 125 4
He could not be satisfied without a promise--would not she E I 15 125 4
to-day, and yet will not promise to avoid the danger of E I 15 125 5
destroy my comfort. you must promise me not to sit up." E II 7 211 21
and Mr. Woodhouse made us promise to have them done three E II 9 238 51
was pronounced to be altogether of the highest promise. E II 10 241 7
Better accommodations, he can promise them, and not a less E II 11 250 23
She has been so kind as to promise it. E II 12 261 36
They came from Birmingham, which is not a place to promise E II 18 310 34
Emma, to claim her former promise; and boasted himself an E III 2 325 31
It seemed as if every thing united to promise the most E III 3 335 10
will be a fortunate preference is more than I can promise. E III 4 342 39
to promise me many particulars that could not be given now. E III 10 398 53
the two of strongest promise to Harriet, were not without E III 11 410 35
I will not promise even to equal the elegant terseness of E III 17 463 14
But I will promise," she added presently, laughing and E III 17 463 14
will promise to call you once by your christian name. E III 17 463 14
It was a union of the highest promise of felicity in E III 17 468 31
afford, and should give Charles Hayter the promise of it. P III 9 78 19
must have a curate, and you had secured his promise. P III 9 78 20
but yield to such joint entreaties, and promise to stay. P IV 4 145 2
the more decided promise of a longer visit on the morrow. P IV 7 180 33
the next morning her promise of going to Mrs. Smith; P IV 9 192 1
"No, I did not promise. P IV 10 223 46
There was no promise." P IV 10 223 46
and in compliance with a promise to my poor sister, sat to P IV 11 232 15
Will you promise me to mention it, when you see them again? P IV 11 239 51
Do promise me." P IV 11 239 51
not that promise to be the very place?"-- S 1 364 1
He wanted to secure the promise of a visit--to get as many S 2 373 1
All that Mr Heywood himself could be persuaded to promise S 2 374 1

PROMISED (99)
only ten guineas, and promised her more when she wanted it. NA I 2 19 3
They promised to come at twelve, only it rained; but now, NA I 11 85 32
be disappointed of the promised walk, and especially NA I 11 88 54
Tilney to take their promised walk to-morrow; it was quite NA I 13 97 1
all a mistake--I never promised to go--I told them from NA I 13 102 25
my kind parents, and am promised that every thing in their NA I 15 121 26
"Yes; I have promised your sister to be with her, if NA I 15 123 33
"I am very sure," said she, "that my father has promised NA II 1 136 47
"And when they had gone over the house, he promised NA II 7 176 17
the house; and Eleanor promised to attend her there, NA II 8 186 7
The succeeding morning promised something better. NA II 9 191 3
Isabella promised so faithfully to write directly." NA II 9 195 20
"Promised so faithfully!-- NA II 9 196 21
But Isabella had promised and promised again; and when she NA II 10 201 5
again; and when she promised a thing, she was so NA II 10 201 5
longer visit had been promised--and could not but think NA II 13 221 2
at such a time, and he promised to do every thing in his SS I 1 5 6
shortly subdued; and she promised not to tempt her mother SS I 12 59 5
When their promised visit to the park and consequent SS I 21 120 6
promised me that nothing-----but how blindly I relate! SS II 9 205 24
Marianne had promised to be guided by her mother's opinion, SS II 10 214 6
anxiety which had once promised to attend such an SS II 12 230 6
them to deserve; and promised to undertake the commission SS III 3 283 20
whither her husband promised, at her earnest entreaty, to SS III 7 308 3
He promised to call again in the course of three or four SS III 7 313 19
But she had promised to hear him, and her curiosity no SS III 8 317 7
promised them all, the satisfaction of a sleepless night. SS III 13 363 6
utmost; nor was anything promised either for the present SS III 14 374 4
And I have promised to write him word who she dances with." W 320 2
and that Mrs. Long has promised to introduce him." PP I 2 6 4
her to return to bed, and promised her some draughts. PP I 7 33 44
Mr. Bingley with having promised on his first coming into PP I 9 45 35
interruption, and promised that it should not occur again, PP I 14 69 17
next day, and their aunt promised to make her husband call PP I 15 74 11
whom his father had promised to provide for.-- PP I 17 85 4
You promised me to insist upon her marrying him." PP I 20 112 21
The promised letter of thanks from Mr. Collins arrived on PP I 23 128 10
again, and promised their father another letter of thanks. PP II 2 139 1
to write to him, and almost promised to answer her letter. PP II 4 151 2
which Mr. Collins had promised; and, as he had likewise PP II 6 162 14
Elizabeth of having promised to play to him; and she sat PP II 8 173 12
there, and Mrs. Forster promised to have a little dance in PP II 16 221 17
place, bring all the satisfaction she had promised herself. PP II 19 237 3
When Lydia went away, she promised to write very often and PP II 19 238 5
Gardiner readily promised every assistance in his power.-- PP III 4 280 26
on, and their uncle promised, at parting, to prevail on Mr. PP III 6 294 2
to leave London, and promised to write again very soon. PP III 6 295 5
I promised them so faithfully! PP III 9 319 27
You forced me into visiting him last year, and promised if PP III 11 332 23
to town last winter, you promised to take a family dinner PP III 11 338 58
"Yes, he had promised he would, but he had told her to MP I 2 16 12
but his other children promised him nothing but good. MP I 2 20 33
their acquaintance soon promised as early an intimacy as MP I 5 44 1
promised well, and there was nothing to call him elsewhere. MP I 5 47 26
her desire, and had promised John groom to write to Mrs. MP I 7 73 53
him it was an ague, and promised him a charm for it; and MP I 10 103 50
pleasure in the promised ball, as Sir Thomas could desire. MP II 8 253 5
promised to remain some days longer with his friend! MP II 11 286 16
The promised departure was all that Fanny could think of MP III 2 331 17
their niece; she not only promised, but did observe it. MP III 2 332 20
I had almost promised it. MP III 4 354 48
Sir Thomas promised that it should be so. MP III 5 356 3
The promised visit from her "friend," as Edmund called MP III 5 356 4
had been promised to have done for him, entirely neglected. MP III 7 381 26
own, though mamma had promised her that Betsey should not MP III 7 386 42
The promised notification was hanging over her head. MP III 9 398 10
of hymen, and who had promised to become so brilliant a MP III 15 440 14
of it, that he had promised him conditionally to come. E I 9 81 78
which had been so long promised it--Mr. Frank Churchill-- E II 2 166 10
she, "that I absolutely promised Miss Bates last night, E II 9 234 26
"My brother and sister have promised us a visit in the E II 14 274 28
now the Campbells had promised their daughter to stay at E II 15 285 14
More and more frightened, she immediately promised them E III 3 334 6
She promised him again and again to come--much oftener E III 6 354 9
and Mr. Weston, unasked, promised to get Frank over to E III 6 357 31
promised her niece on no account to let Miss Woodhouse in. E III 9 390 18
I promised my wife to leave it all to her. E III 10 392 9
Emma had promised; but still Harriet must be excepted. E III 11 403 2
She promised to think of it, and advised him to think of E III 15 449 32
She promised, however, to think of it; and pretty nearly E III 15 449 34
of it; and pretty nearly promised, moreover, to think of E III 15 449 34
He promised to join me here, and pay his respects to you." E III 16 455 21
"He promised to come to me as soon as he could disengage E III 16 456 25
She promised Wright a receipt, and never sent it." E III 16 458 42
glad again, when he had promised in reply to papa and P III 7 54 4
And he had promised it in so pleasant a manner, as if he P III 7 54 4
but Captain Harville had promised them a visit in the P III 11 99 22
she recommended, and promised to procure and read them. P III 11 101 25
he had promised this and he had promised that, and the end P IV 2 130 5
promised this and he had promised that, and the end of it P IV 2 130 5
The Harvilles had promised to come with her and stay at P IV 2 134 31
She had once partly promised Mrs. Smith to spend the P IV 7 180 33
promised for the absent, Mary was as completely satisfied. P IV 10 220 29
be too abominable if you do! when you promised to go." P IV 10 223 45
She had promised to be with the Musgroves from breakfast P IV 11 229 1
He promised me the sight of a capital gun he is just going P IV 11 240 58
besides, the promised large families from Surry & S 6 389 1
is very great & I almost promised the poor woman yesterday S 12 423 1
She is so frightened, poor thing, that I promised to come S 12 424 1

PROMISES (14)
a handsome young man, who promises me some amusement. LS 7 254 3
by turns, on broken promises and broken arches, phaetons NA I 11 87 51
The embraces, tears, and promises of the parting fair ones NA II 4 153 31
to a pretty girl, and promises marriage, he has no SS II 8 194 10
to retort, but she remembered her promises, and forbore. SS III 1 267 41
and self-importance in his letter, which promises well. PP I 13 64 18
A scheme of which every part promises delight, can never PP II 19 237 4
He promises fairly, and I hope among different people, PP III 8 313 19
Mr. Knightley promises to give up his claim this Christmas- E I 9 79 63
it to be so, by his promises and messages; but if he E I 18 146 16
He did, on the condition of some promises on his side: such E II 7 211 22
in obtaining her promises of faith and correspondence. E III 14 437 8
of invitations and promises which may be imagined, they P III 12 108 30
those feelings and those promises which had once before P IV 11 240 59

PROMISING (27)
promising, till affairs have taken a more favourable turn. LS 30 301 4
But a faithful promise--the fidelity of promising! NA II 9 196 21
he had a younger brother who was more promising. SS I 3 16 6
I remember her promising to give you some. SS I 18 98 11
He had left her promising to return; he neither returned, SS II 9 209 30
down together in a most promising state of embarrassment.-- SS III 4 288 26
the rapid decease of a promising young brood, she found SS III 6 303 10
It was, moreover, such a promising thing for her younger PP I 18 99 63
"I never saw a more promising inclination. PP II 2 141 9
with advantage, so promising for happiness, Jane had been PP II 14 213 18
When I last saw her, she was not very promising. PP III 10 328 22
"This is not a very promising beginning," said Mrs. Norris MP I 2 13 5
that with all their promising talents and early MP I 2 19 30
any thing at all promising in their situation or conduct. MP I 2 21 34
he could, and by his promising to come; and he did come MP I 13 121 1
and present promising state of affairs; relating every MP II 1 184 27
few circumstances occurred which he thought more promising. MP III 3 336 8
her soon and often, and promising to be a good MP III 6 373 26
his niece in the most promising way of being starved, both MP III 11 413 30
as Mr. Elton's very promising attachment was likely to add. E I 6 47 27
This was all very promising; and, but for such an E II 7 206 2
their promising never to go beyond the shrubbery again. E III 3 336 12
Churchill had been promising a visit the last ten years. E III 9 388 15
very promising step of the mind on its way to resignation. E III 19 483 9
their entreaties for their all promising to dine with them. P III 11 97 15
Promising to be with them the whole of the following P IV 10 227 69
by nature, & promising to be the most chosen by man."-- S 1 368 1

PROMONTORIES (1)
be full of rocks and promontories, grey moss and brush SS I 18 97 4

PROMOTE (29)
whose welfare it is my first earthly duty to promote?" LS 24 289 12
will hereafter tend to promote the general distress of the NA I 2 19 7
and not likely to promote the good of either; for what NA II 3 145 16
it allowed him to promote the happiness of his children." NA II 10 205 30
pause, "would it be to promote his happiness, to enable NA II 10 205 30
almost at the moment, to promote the dismissal of NA II 15 248 16
who was always eager to promote their happiness as far as SS I 18 96 2
thing in his power to promote their unreserve, by making SS I 21 125 34
mother would be eager to promote--she could not expect to SS II 3 155 6
Had I remained in England, perhaps--but I meant to promote SS II 9 206 24
acquiescence would best promote it, she walked silently SS III 8 317 7
counsel as to the behaviour most likely to promote it. SS III 8 332 76
no scruples, if she can promote her own advantage.-- W 317 2
As a clergyman, moreover, I feel it my duty to promote and PP I 13 63 12
I think it would not be very likely to promote sisterly PP II 6 165 35
recommended it to me, to promote his advancement in the PP II 12 200 5
of his eagerness to promote the welfare of any of his PP III 8 312 18
a point of honour to promote her enjoyment to the utmost. MP I 8 82 35
promote the pleasure of the two so dear to her. MP I 17 161 9
father's claims, was to promote Harriet's comfort, and E I 17 142 10
Neither father nor mother could promote, and the daughter E II 2 164 6
His friends are eager to promote his happiness.-- E III 13 428 23
since it was a plan to promote the happiness of all--she E III 17 465 28
that his wishing to promote her father's getting more P IV 4 151 22
true parental hearts to promote their daughter's comfort. P IV 8 182 8
hand wd very materially promote the rise & prosperity of S 2 372 1
same, they were glad to promote their getting out into the S 2 374 1
or I wd promote their going down to you for a fortnight. S 5 387 1
me, & my being willing to promote a little Subscription S 12 423 1

PROMOTED (8)
"since leisure has not promoted your own happiness, that SS I 19 103 5
since eventually it promoted the interest of Elinor. SS III 13 370 35
which would now have promoted its continuance, and would PP III 4 279 23
had always wished and promoted the match; but it was a E I 1 6 6
If I had not promoted Mr. Weston's visits here and given E I 1 13 43
was so effectually promoted by Mr. and Mrs. Cole, that E II 8 229 98
She saw it all; and entering into her feelings, promoted E III 6 363 51
his failings, and promoted his real respectability for P III 1 4 6

PROMOTES (2)
He wants to marry her--her mother promotes the match--but LS 23 284 4
in young people, or promotes it more, than my father; and MP I 13 126 25

PROMOTING (12)
she was as eager in promoting the intercourse of the two NA I 5 36 3
and promoting the marriage by every possible attention. SS II 11 228 51
cherishing all her hopes, and promoting all her views! SS II 14 254 26
were to be taken for promoting its end, was all her SS III 2 276 27
happiness would lie in promoting their marriage; and since SS III 9 337 18
Mrs. Norris in promoting gaieties for her nieces, MP I 4 34 3
Mrs. Norris was most zealous in promoting the match, by MP I 4 39 10
he, "and you have been promoting her comfort by preventing MP I 7 68 19
mother must feel in promoting her children's enjoyment, MP II 11 285 10
I give her credit for promoting his going dutifully down MP III 14 435 13
have been the means of promoting it, by the sanction he E I 8 66 55
much they are occupied in promoting the good of others!-- S 5 388 1

PROMOTION (13)
companion, and in the promotion of whose enjoyment their NA II 5 154 1
In the promotion of this object she was zealously active, SS I 8 36 1
Miss Crawford civilly wished him an early promotion. MP I 6 60 47
valued blessing of promotion--who could give her direct MP II 6 234 18
William was kindly commended and his promotion hoped for. MP II 11 284 9
gone for, was but the promotion of gaiety; a day before it MP II 12 291 1
of congratulating you on your brother's promotion. MP II 13 298 2
he had undertaken, the promotion of young price, and MP II 13 298 3
on the first day of hearing of William's promotion. MP II 13 303 13
the Mr. Crawford who had procured William's promotion! MP III 2 328 6
William's promotion, with all its particulars, he was soon MP III 3 334 3
had been a year or two waiting for fortune and promotion. P III 11 96 12
lieutenant being great,--promotion, too, came at last; but P III 11 96 12

PROMPT (11)
tenderness which would prompt a visit like yours. NA II 9 196 23
therefore, was most prompt in inviting Mr. Collins to join PP I 15 71 6
Fanny was wanted only to prompt and observe them. MP I 18 170 24
To prompt them must be enough for her; and it was MP I 18 170 24
actually accepting the offer with much prompt satisfaction. MP I 13 110 12
their advice for her going was most prompt and successful. E II 7 208 8
powerful enough to prompt to what was right and support E II 13 268 13
could prompt such behaviour sunk them both very much.-- E II 15 281 3
Mr. Elton?" to which his prompt reply was, "most readily E III 2 327 34
the merriment it would prompt at his expense; the E III 11 413 48
all the worth and all the prompt welcome which met her in P IV 12 251 10

PROMPTED (13)
his fidelity, or influence the resolutions it prompted. NA II 15 247 15

and her own gratitude prompted; and every thing that SS I 10 46 1
which together prompted Colonel Brandon to this act, were SS III 3 283 20
were humanity out of the case, would have prompted him. SS III 9 337 17
whither my good stars prompted me to turn my horses heads-- W 338 18
a twelvemonth's abode in the family might have prompted. PP I 23 128 10
You need not be prompted to write with the appearance of E I 7 52 11
Emma only might be as nature prompted, and shew herself E I 14 117 1
True affection only could have prompted it." E II 10 242 21
which might have prompted her to entreat him to transfer E III 13 431 38
the disagreeable prompted by any body else, excused P III 2 11 1
which her own conscience prompted, she believed there P III 2 13 5
was done that Anne had prompted, but in vain; while P III 12 110 37
38

PROMPTER (4)
Rushworth, who was wanting a prompter through every speech. MP I 18 164 2
prompter, sometimes as spectator--was often very useful.-- MP I 18 165 3
and being able to follow the prompter through the rest. MP I 18 166 4
You were our audience and prompter. MP III 5 358 7
PROMPTING (1)
the contrary, had been prompting and encouraging expenses, P IV 9 209 95
PROMPTITUDE (2)
John to Elinor, of the promptitude with which he should SS III 6 301 1
to persuade them away with all her usual promptitude. E I 17 141 4
PROMPTLY (2)
departures, were most promptly delivered, as he sat by MP II 1 178 8
With due exceptions--woman feels for woman very promptly & S 3 378 1
PRONE (4)
nature is particularly prone to it, and that there are PP I 5 20 20
Human nature is so prone to fall into it! PP III 6 299 21
on my side which was prone to take disgust towards a girl E II 6 203 39
self-importance, was very prone to add to every other P III 5 37 21
PRONOUNCE (10)
mother; but yet I can pronounce her disposition to be LS 18 273 2
pronounce it with surprize within twenty minutes of five! NA II 5 162 27
the whole, I venture to pronounce that his mind is well- SS I 4 20 9
at Barton decisively to pronounce that Colonel Brandon was SS I 8 36 1
I can only pronounce him to be a sensible man, well-bred, SS I 10 51 27
how happy she would dare pronounce herself to be; though, PP II 3 146 19
and whose very name it was punishment to him to pronounce. PP III 10 326 3
attached to a connection with her, she dared not pronounce. PP III 15 360 2
"And now that I understand your question, I must pronounce E II 6 200 18
No, I can pronounce his name without the smallest distress. E II 16 297 48
PRONOUNCED (24)
hearing, two gentlemen pronounced her to be a pretty girl. NA I 2 24 28
I bought one for her the other day, and it was pronounced NA I 3 28 38
was, the stranger pronounced her's to be Thorpe; and Mrs. NA I 4 31 2
The terrified General pronounced the name of Allen with an NA II 15 246 13
almost driven me wild, pronounced with such impenetrable SS I 3 18 18
with one, idleness was pronounced on the whole to be the SS I 19 103 4
more stiffly than ever, pronounced in retort this bitter SS II 12 235 37
to her presence, and pronounced to be again her son. SS III 14 373 1
The gentlemen pronounced him to be a fine figure of a man, PP I 3 10 5
her and liked her, and pronounced her to be a sweet girl, PP I 4 17 16
Her manners were pronounced to be very bad indeed, a PP I 8 35 3
fact of his absence was pronounced by his friend Mr. Denny, PP I 18 89 1
2
as he did experience he pronounced to be of a most PP I 23 127 6
As she pronounced these words, Mr. Darcy changed colour; PP II 11 191 11
and stepping forward with eagerness, pronounced her name. PP II 12 195 2
parcels placed within, and it was pronounced to be ready. PP II 15 216 8
began; and each of them pronounced him to be infinitely PP III 1 257 67
The Bennets were speedily pronounced to be the luckiest PP III 13 350 56
over, and he was so far pronounced safe, as to make his MP III 14 429 1
was pronounced to be altogether of the highest promise. E II 10 241 7
down to supper, was pronounced an infamous fraud upon the E II 11 254 45
Emma blushed, and forbad its being pronounced in her E III 18 477 51
Giaour was to be pronounced, he shewed himself so P III 11 100 23
and though she might be pronounced to be altogether doing P IV 2 129 1
PRONOUNCING (5)
the necessity of pronouncing it, which can alone reconcile LS 30 301 4
in his manner of pronouncing it, and in his addressing her SS I 12 59 7
she started up, and pronouncing his name in a tone of SS II 6 176 7
to health, yet, by pronouncing her disorder to have a SS III 7 307 3
and drawing-room, and pronouncing them, after a short PP III 14 352 19
PRONOUNS (1)
We all know the difference between the pronouns he or she E II 15 286 23
PROOF (85)
What stronger proof of her dangerous abilities can be LS 8 255 1
cannot help being pleased with such a proof of attachment. LS 31 302 1
it after every fresh proof, which every morning brought, NA I 3 25 1
command; and, as the first proof of amity, she was soon NA I 4 33 6
proof of it to be given to their friends or themselves. NA I 5 36 4
to her, gave every proof on his side of equal satisfaction, NA I 7 44 4
that a clear blue sky was no longer a proof of a fine day. NA I 14 110 28
But here is a proof of what I was saying. NA II 3 144 6
Here was another proof. NA II 7 181 39
and overdrawn; but here was proof positive of the contrary. NA II 7 181 40
look, the full proof of that repining spirit to which she NA II 15 241 7
his feelings an inadequate proof of his resentment towards NA II 15 244 11
Willoughby, on his side, gave every proof of his pleasure SS I 10 48 7
"On the contrary, nothing can be a stronger proof of it, SS I 13 68 72
Jennings are to be the proof of impropriety in conduct, we SS I 13 68 74
"I want no proof of their affection," said Elinor; "but of SS I 15 79 33
But I require no such proof. SS I 15 80 42
proof of it which he constantly wore round his finger. SS I 19 102 2
she gave a very striking proof, by still loving and SS I 19 104 11
even, she could have no proof; for the assurances of her SS I 21 118 2
and that she was so, her very confidence was a proof. SS II 1 142 7
of one object, was such a proof, so strong, so full, of SS II 3 155 6
of her performance, in proof of her having spent seven SS II 4 160 3
share; and likewise as a proof of his high esteem for your SS III 4 289 31
up my shoulders in proof of its being so, and silencing SS III 8 326 53
The future must be my proof. SS III 10 347 30
to me by such a proof of tender respect for my aunt."-- W 352 26
to prevent such a proof of complaisance,--but in vain; PP I 18 100 68
"It is a proof of your own attachment to Hertfordshire. PP II 9 179 20
the more so, as she could bring no proof of its injustice. PP II 13 205 4
must sink under such a proof of family weakness, such an PP III 4 278 19
is no absolute proof that they are not gone to Scotland." PP III 5 282 5
His consenting to marry her is a proof, I will believe, PP III 7 305 37
to be proof against the temptation of immediate relief. PP III 10 323 2
many weeks, it would bring his passion to an early proof. MP I 5 48 29
proof as she has given, that her feelings are not strong." MP I 12 116 10
cry, or had given her some proof of affection which made MP I 16 152 2
proof and importance, was worth ages of doubt and anxiety. MP II 1 176 3
in them, the proof of good principles, professional MP II 6 236 21
To be urging her opinion against Sir Thomas's, was a proof MP II 10 275 11
had they been put to the proof; but as that very evening MP II 12 291 1
could not consider it as a proof of any thing more than MP III 7 383 31
used to think of as the proof of importance, or the MP III 10 400 7
She saw the proof of it in Miss Crawford, as well as in MP III 14 433 12
In proof, he repeats, and more eagerly, what he said at MP III 14 435 14
came back she had every proof that could be given in his MP III 17 461 2
give him the pleasantest proof of its being a great deal E I 2 17 6
was an irresistible proof of his great good sense, and a E I 2 18 10
The very next day however produced some proof of E I 9 71 10
you will soon receive the completest proof of it. E I 9 73 20
a proof of love, with Mr. Elton's seeing ready wit in her. E I 10 83 6
knowledge of taste, as one proof among others that he had E I 16 134 5
It is too unlikely, for me to believe it without proof." E I 18 145 8
his hat, being all in proof of how much he was in love! E II 4 184 10
proof of what degree of intimacy was chosen for the future. E II 4 185 13
as was an additional proof of his knowing how to please-- E II 5 191 28
and I remember one proof of her being thought to play well: E II 6 201 28
thought, in a man of known musical talent, was some proof." E II 6 201 28
"Proof, indeed!" said Emma, highly amused.-- E II 6 201 29
were the persons; and I thought it a very strong proof." E II 6 202 30
of the pianoforte--and proof only shall convince me that E II 8 226 84
Two months must bring it to the proof. E III 1 317 9
gratified by such a proof of intimacy, such a E III 6 354 9
join them, if possible; a proof of approbation and E III 6 357 31
Emma was gratified, to observe such a proof in her of E III 9 388 14
She had received a very recent proof of its impartiality.-- E III 12 415 1
At any rate, it would be a proof of attention and kindness E III 14 435 4
to give a woman any proof of affection which he knows she E III 15 446 18
and I think I can give you a proof that it must be so. E III 18 474 30
proof of his being a most responsible, eligible tenant. P III 3 21 18
must be brought to the proof; former times must P III 8 63 2
friendship; it was a proof of his own warm and amiable P III 10 91 42
This had been a proof of life, however, of service to her P III 12 112 51
a pleasure to her--as a proof of friendship, and of P III 12 117 75
became a sort of parting proof, its value did not lessen. P III 12 117 75
was a strong proof of his opinions on the subject. P IV 3 139 7
in short, by every proof of cousinly notice, and placing P IV 3 139 10
Here is complete proof." P IV 8 186 26
And yet you ought to have proof; for what is all this but P IV 9 202 66
what is all this but assertion? and you shall have proof." P IV 9 202 66
This is full proof undoubtedly, proof of every thing you P IV 9 204 77
I cannot produce written proof again, but I can give as P IV 9 204 80
is a difference of opinion which does not admit of proof. P IV 11 234 30
"Then sir, I can bring proof of your having a surgeon in S 1 366 1
proof of the increasing fashion of the place altogether. S 4 383 1
PROOFS (12)
confirmation strong, "as proofs of Holy Writ." NA I 1 16 7
search for those proofs of the General's cruelty, which NA II 9 193 5
were such sweet proofs of her importance with them, as NA II 13 221 6
and proofs, and contradicted by nothing but her own wishes. SS II 1 139 1
to withhold her pen, were proofs enough of her feeling how SS II 7 180 4
hazarded such unsolicited proofs of tenderness, not SS II 7 188 43
nor witness its proofs without sometimes wondering whether SS III 9 335 7
such bodily hardships, and given such proofs of mind. MP II 6 236 22
of the least agreeable proofs of his growing attachment. E I 6 42 1
considered as marks of acquiescence, or proofs of defiance. E II 5 192 33
and contained multiplied proofs to her who had seen them, E III 11 410 35
Alas! such delightful proofs of Hartfield's attraction, as E III 12 422 19
PROPELLED (1)
of what a man may be propelled to say, write or do, by the S 7 398 1
PROPENSITIES (5)
Such were her propensities--her abilities were quite as NA I 1 14 1
up to understand the propensities of a rattle, nor to know NA I 9 65 31
estimating the minuter propensities of his mind, his SS I 4 19 6
But of his minuter propensities as you call them, you have SS I 4 20 9
The vicious propensities--the want of principle which he PP II 12 200 5
PROPENSITY (6)
shewing the smallest propensity towards any unpleasant NA I 9 62 10
to censure in him but a propensity, in which he strongly SS I 10 48 9
Each faulty propensity in leading him to evil, had led him SS III 8 331 70
"And your defect is a propensity to hate every body." PP I 11 58 31
little company, in the propensity to talk or to be silent, MP III 4 349 23
her more than his propensity to dine with Mr. Cole. E II 8 213 5
PROPER (148)
circumstances it was proper to render her pecuniary LS 3 247 1
& seems precisely in her proper place, at Churchill with LS 26 295 1
Her manner, to be sure, was very kind & proper--& Mr LS 41 310 3
remiss, madam, in the proper attentions of a partner here; NA I 3 25 2
How proper Mr. Tilney might be as a dreamer or a lover, NA I 3 30 52
Miss Tilney expressing a proper sense of such goodness, NA I 8 55 10
or you will forget to be tired of it at the proper time.-- NA I 10 78 43
the simile, for it could hardly have been a proper one. NA I 13 101 24
it would not be both proper and kind in her to write to NA I 13 105 40
is known beforehand, proper measures will undoubtedly be NA I 14 112 34
object must occasion so serious a delay of proper repose. NA II 8 187 16
and treat her with proper attention; and could strive to SS I 1 7 13
assurance of his admiring Pope no more than is proper. SS I 10 47 4
It may be proper to conceal their engagement (if they are SS I 15 79 31
A proper establishment of servants, a carriage, perhaps SS I 17 91 14
as she did not think it proper that Marianne should be SS II 3 156 1
short time, on the answer it would be most proper to give. SS II 5 173 4
giddy from a long want of proper rest and food; for it was SS II 7 185 16
I saw her placed in comfortable lodgings, and under proper SS II 9 207 2
kept him from mixing in proper society, he candidly and SS II 14 250 1
in his proper situation, and would have wanted for nothing. SS III 1 269 5
which might have been Edward's, on proper conditions. SS III 1 269 5
restored to its proper state, its was not a subject on SS III 2 270
that was quite proper to let him be off if he would. SS III 2 278 3
to do so;--but supposed it to be the proper etiquette. SS III 3 281 9
Colonel write himself?--sure, he is the proper person." SS III 4 286 1
inclination, and forcing proper medicines on her at night, SS III 7 307
How soon he had walked himself into the proper resolution, SS III 13 361
good friends, as our near relationship now makes proper. SS III 13 365 1
occurred to the others, proper measures would have been SS III 13 371 3
I both think a letter of proper submission from him, SS III 13 371 3
"A letter of proper submission!" repeated he; "would they SS III 13 372 4
I know of no submission that is proper for me to make." SS III 13 372 4
the idea of a letter of proper submission; and therefore, SS III 13 372 4
After a proper resistance on the part of Mrs. Ferrars, SS III 14 373
greater solicitude to the proper security of her young W 327
was accordingly on the alert to gain her proper station. W 331 1
"Do you not think it would be a proper compliment to the PP I 6 26 3
"That is all very proper and civil, I am sure," said Mrs. PP I 14 66
whether he would think it proper to join in the evening's PP I 17 87 1
kingdom--provided that a proper humility of behaviour is PP I 18 97 6
6
With proper civilities the ladies then withdrew; all of PP I 22 124 1
of temper, that want of proper resolution which now made PP II 1 133
who marries him, cannot have a proper way of thinking. PP II 1 135 1
She will make him a very proper wife." PP II 5 158 1
it was performed in a proper manner, without any of those PP II 6 161 1
placing a screen in the proper direction before her eyes. PP II 6 162 1
The invitation was accepted of course, and at a proper PP II 8 172
answer, and with a proper air of indifference, that she PP II 19 241 1
directions to Haggerston for preparing a proper settlement. PP III 7 303 1
be her husband, might then have rested in its proper place. PP III 8 308
the neighbourhood for a proper situation for her daughter, PP III 8 310
would so shortly give the proper termination to the PP III 8 311 1
It was owing to him, to his reserve, and want of proper PP III 10 324
You thought me then devoid of every proper feeling, I am PP III 16 368 1
first, but my anger soon began to take a proper direction." PP III 16 369 2
example, she became, by proper attention and management, PP III 19 385
"as to the distinction proper to be made between the girls MP I 1 10 1
with proper masters, and could want nothing more. MP I 2 20 3
After dancing with each other at a proper number of balls, MP I 4 39 1
sometimes carried a little too far, it is all very proper. MP I 5 49 3
have been particularly proper and becoming in a brother to MP I 7 67 1
directly, if we had but a proper license, for here we are MP I 9 88 2
Mrs. Rushworth spoke with proper smiles and dignity of its MP I 9 88 2
accordingly, she was certain of the proper Frederick. MP I 14 132
eyes, and you will be a very proper, little old woman." MP I 15 146 5
the remembrance, and restored to its proper state. MP II 2 187
of explaining, with proper apologies for his father's MP II 2 191 1
It was a proper wedding. MP II 3 203 2
I understand you--and a very proper plan it is for a MP II 4 213 4
never respected when they step out of their proper sphere. MP II 5 220 3
no finery about you; nothing but what is perfectly proper. MP II 5 222 4

intent upon opening the proper doors could be called such. MP II 6 233 15
reception of it was so proper and modest, so calm and MP II 7 246 37
to know them by their proper name; but when he talked of MP II 12 294 16
now on a footing the most proper and hopeful, Sir Thomas MP III 2 330 14
of the voice, of proper modulation and emphasis, of MP III 3 339 22
It does him the highest honour; it shews his proper MP III 4 350 30
and send back proper messages, with cheerful looks. MP III 7 375 1
should have formed such proper opinions of what ought to MP III 9 397 8
kind and proper in the notice he took of Susan. MP III 10 406 21
Settle it as you like; say what is proper; I am sure you MP III 15 443 23
a most proper attention, that the visit should take place. E I 2 17 9
from pushing, shewing so proper and becoming a deference, E I 3 23 10
thing for her to be very much in love with a proper object. E I 5 41 29
given Harriet's fancy a proper direction and raised the E I 6 42 1
a pen in hand, his thoughts naturally find proper words. E I 7 51 5
A very proper compliment!--and then follows the E I 9 73 18
independence, a proper home--it will fix you in the centre E I 9 74 20
should so immediately shape itself into the proper form. E I 9 74 25
old maid! the proper sport of boys and girls; but a single E I 10 85 19
her, and a very proper, handsome letter it was. E I 11 96 22
"How very pleasing and proper of him!" cried the good- E I 11 96 25
and herself, in procuring him the proper invitation. E I 12 98 1
This was very proper; the sigh which accompanied it was E I 13 115 36
Emma spoke with a very proper degree of pleasure; and E I 14 119 8
the subject back into its proper course, there was no E I 15 125 4
sense would make it, in a proper manner--would do him more E I 18 147 18
party, and had seen only proper attention and pleasing E II 3 170 1
place the Martins under proper subordination in her fancy. E II 3 180 57
not the proper name--I should rather say Barnes, or Bates. E II 5 193 37
nothing could be more proper or pleasing than his whole E II 6 196 2
The want of proper families in the place, and the E II 6 198 5
body's returning into their proper place the next morning. E II 6 198 5
perhaps all that was proper; and I had told my father I E II 6 199 7
one other family, a proper unobjectionable country family, E II 8 214 13
Miss Woodhouse made the proper acquiescence; and finding E II 8 216 17
Emma best to lead, she gave a very proper compliance. E II 8 227 85
thing was rapidly clearing away, to give proper space. E II 8 229 98
pianoforte, with every proper discrimination, was E II 10 241 7
to mix in the world in a proper degree, without living in E II 14 275 30
always wish to pay every proper attention to a lady--and a E II 14 280 58
at exactly the proper hour, and in the proper order. E II 16 290 3
very proper attention, after the introduction had passed. E III 2 321 13
"And what are we to do for a proper partner for her?" said E III 2 325 30
and veneration, which are so proper, in me especially." E III 4 341 36
which she judged it proper to appear to censure; for she E III 5 348 22
"I did not know that proper names were allowed," pushed E III 5 349 23
so little credit for proper feeling, or esteemed so little E III 9 391 21
She was sensible that you had never received any proper E III 12 420 12
in a proper share of the happiness of the evening before. E III 14 435 5
level of what she deemed proper, I should have escaped the E III 14 440 8
was in every respect so proper, suitable, and E III 17 467 31
a proper match for Sir Walter Elliot's eldest daughter. P III 1 8 17
Anne said what was proper, and enquired after her husband. P III 5 37 25
were gradually giving the proper air of confusion by a P III 5 40 44
former neighbour's present state, with proper interest. P III 6 49 22
as she recollected it, proper notice to the other house, P III 7 53 3
She said all that was reasonable and proper on the P III 12 103 3
the last, proceeded to make the proper adieus to the Cobb. P III 12 108 30
if Anne will stay, no one so proper, so capable as Anne!" P III 12 114 61
would pretend what was proper on her arrival; but the P IV 3 137 3
It would excite no proper interest there. P IV 5 153 5
"Charles joins me in love, and every thing proper. P IV 6 164 7
disposed to take very kind and proper notice of him. P IV 9 200 58
might be recoverable by proper measures; and this property, P IV 9 210 98
After the waste of a few minutes in saying the proper P IV 10 226 64
and made her way to the proper apartment, she found . P IV 11 229 2
There could be only a most proper alacrity, a most P IV 11 240 59
withdraw; and no one of proper condition has since P IV 12 250 6
said every thing that was proper to recommend their S 1 370 1
at last secured a proper house at 8g pr week for Mrs G.--; S 10 414 1
as they could desire, or as he felt proper himself.-- S 10 417 1
she had divided out their proper portions to Mrs Darling, S 11 420 1
in Sanditon" to use a proper phrase, for every body must S 11 421 1
& a very well-bred bow & proper address to Miss Heywood on S 12 425 1
The fence was a proper park paling in excellent condition; S 12 426 1
in finding a proper spot for their stolen Interveiws.-- S 12 426 1

PROPERER (2)
to reason herself into a properer state; she should be MP III 6 370 12
properer person for shewing us how to do away difficulties. E II 11 255 55

PROPEREST (8)
make him understand what I mean, in the properest way. NA II 3 145 13
discovered that the properest thing to be done, was for MP I 8 75 1
to bring him home in the properest state of feeling the MP III 3 334 2
give his own as to the properest manner in which MP III 3 340 24
displayed none but the properest feelings, and this being E I 11 93 5
a mother's feelings, are a great deal the properest person. P III 7 57 16
benwick would be the properest person to fetch a surgeon, P IV 8 182 6
tempered woman, the properest wife in the world for a man S 2 372 1

PROPERLY (65)
her education will be properly attended to; but because LS 14 265 5
to make it clear that if properly treated by Lady Susan LS 18 273 3
properly called for, or when a confidence should be forced. NA I 5 36 2
Catherine cheerfully complied; and being properly equipped, NA I 12 91 3
When properly to relax is the trial of judgment; and, NA II 1 134 36
and numerous out-riders properly mounted, sunk a little NA II 5 156 4
cotton counterpane, properly folded, reposing at one end NA II 6 164 3
had passed, an apology might properly be received by her. NA II 13 227 27
Marianne's pianoforte was unpacked and properly disposed SS I 6 30 5
"You speak very properly. SS I 15 81 44
I was therefore entered at Oxford and have been properly SS I 19 103 4
excited, now less properly worded than if it had arisen SS III 3 284 24
be to express herself properly by letter, it was at least SS III 4 287 26
as particular as ever in having her properly attended to." W 350 24
Sr's opinion, to behave properly by them, but Eliz. & the W 360 30
"You judge very properly," said Mr. Bennet, "and it is PP I 14 68 10
their opinion, to be secure of judging properly at first." PP I 18 93 36
A clergyman like you must marry.-- chuse properly, chuse a PP I 19 105 10
The whole family in short were properly overjoyed on the PP I 22 122 3
Young women should always be properly guarded and attended, PP II 14 211 13
person whom he could so properly consult as your uncle, PP III 10 323 2
into a marriage which has not been properly sanctioned." PP III 15 363 22
By you, I was properly humbled. PP III 16 369 24
Give a girl an education, and introduce her properly into MP I 1 6 6
and too little understood to be properly attended to. MP I 2 14 6
which, properly directed, must be an education in itself. MP I 2 22 35
I would have every body marry if they can do it properly; MP I 4 43 27
and Mr. Crawford after properly depreciating his own MP I 6 61 58
Nothing of this would have happened had she been properly MP I 7 74 58
her sister; and Mary, properly pressed and persuaded, was MP I 8 76 7
to the chapel, which properly we ought to enter from above, MP I 9 85 5
so properly happy, so well suited, and so much the thing! MP I 12 118 16
She was properly punished. MP I 18 172 29
not be able to appear properly submissive and indifferent. MP II 5 218 12
You do not seem properly aware of her claims to notice. MP II 6 229 5
excited had been very properly lively, determining him on MP II 6 232 13
openly, so liberally, so properly, that Sir Thomas, MP III 1 314 16
But now, when he has made his overtures so properly, and MP III 1 315 18
received them very properly, (I have no accusation to make MP III 1 316 29
receiving his addresses properly, before the young man's MP III 5 356 3
It was pleasing to hear him speak so properly; here, he MP III 10 404 15
added that there must be a mind to be properly guided. MP III 14 430 2
when once married, and properly supported by her own MP III 16 457 29
that they had never been properly taught to govern their MP III 17 463 8
Your time has been properly and delicately spent, if you E I 1 12 42
Mr. Elton seemed very properly struck and delighted by the E I 6 46 22
You will express yourself very properly, I am sure. E I 7 51 11
"Aye, that's very just, indeed, that's very properly said. E I 9 78 52
And in this style he talked on for some time very properly, E I 15 124 3
The Coles expressed themselves so properly--there was so E II 7 208 9
of music; which was properly denied; and that he knew E II 8 227 86
dangerous; never properly aired, or fit to be inhabited. E II 11 251 26
time, nothing could be properly ready till the third week E II 12 257 1
very quietly and properly taken, Mrs. Elton was evidently E III 2 324 20
to be certain of being properly solicited by baronet-blood P III 1 7 12
While well, and happy, and properly attended to, she had P III 5 37 21
as soon as he could be properly tempted; actually looking P III 7 61 38
and the agony was, how to introduce themselves properly. P IV 4 148 10
seemed to judge properly and as a man of principle,--this P IV 5 160 27
I have equipped myself properly for Bath already, you see," P IV 7 177 14
on, and they were all properly arranged, she looked round P IV 8 186 22
give, could be properly interesting only to the principals. P IV 11 230 5
And I have now the charge of getting it properly set for P IV 11 232 15
receive and estimate him properly; nothing of P IV 12 251 10
Lady Denham can give, if she is properly attacked--& I S 12 424 1

PROPERTY (66)
Mr. Allen, who owned the chief of the property about NA I 1 17 12
formed, whether landed property were to be resigned, or NA I 15 122 28
It is a family living, Miss Morland; and the property in NA II 7 176 15
as considerable a landed property as any private man in NA II 7 176 15
the heir of the Tilney property had not grandeur and NA II 11 208 1
But whether such happiness were the lawful property of NA II 14 233 8
in the centre of their property, where, for many SS I 1 3 1
father's inheriting that property, could be but small. SS I 1 3 2
own, a gentleman of consequence and property in Devonshire. SS I 4 23 20
Mr. Willoughby had no property of his own in the country; SS I 9 44 23
family property,) she frequently visited me at Delaford. SS II 9 208 28
"Yes; he has very good property in Dorsetshire." SS II 11 223 17
my own property, that I felt it my duty to buy it. SS II 11 225 31
undoubted right to dispose of his own property as he chose. SS II 11 225 35
His property here, his place, his house, every thing in SS III 14 375 9
of a gentleman of property in Croydon, than the neice of W 349 24
likely to have any property for him to get direction of.-- W 349 24
rightful property of some one or other of their daughters. PP I 1 3 2
Mr. Bingley inherited property to the amount of nearly an PP I 4 15 11
Mr. Bennet's property consisted almost entirely in an PP I 7 28 1
of his viewing it all as his own future property. PP I 13 65 26
the heiress of Rosings, and of very extensive property." PP I 14 67 5
a man of very large property in Derbyshire, I understand." PP I 16 77 9
devoted all his time to the care of the Pemberley property. PP I 16 81 37
property, noble kindred, and extensive patronage. PP III 15 362 15
to Sir Thomas in the concerns of his West Indian property? MP I 1 5 2
as well as fact, the property of Edmund, Mrs. Norris could MP I 4 37 9
Miss Bertram's engagement made him in equity the property MP I 5 44 2
now all Mr. Rushworth's property on each side of the road," MP I 8 81 33
What is his property?" MP I 12 118 18
the property of Miss Crawford if she would accept it. MP I 14 133 10
I often think of Mr. Rushworth's property and independence, MP I 17 161 13
He is their lawful property, he fairly belongs to them. MP II 11 289 34
was to be mistress of property which she had been MP III 9 397 7
on the north, that I will be master of my own property. MP III 11 411 20
the Bertram property, than any other possible 'sir.' MP III 14 434 13
generations had been rising into gentility and property. E I 2 15 1
his share of the family property, it is, I dare say, all E I 4 30 20
to have some independent property; and she thought very E I 4 35 44
The landed property of Hartfield certainly was E I 16 136 9
mother, she became the property, the charge, the E II 2 163 3
I thought you had lost half your property, at least. E III 10 400 68
The Kellynch property was good, but not equal to Sir P III 1 9 19
and living on their own property, without the torment of P III 3 20 17
of a man, whose landed property and general importance, P III 4 28 7
A sick child is always the mother's property, her own P III 7 56 11
Mr. Hayter had some property of his own, but it was P III 9 74 5
whenever my uncle dies, he steps into very pretty property. P III 9 76 15
with that property, he will never be a contemptible man. P III 9 76 15
Good, freehold property. P III 9 76 15
of well-bound volumes, the property of Captain Benwick. P III 11 99 18
She had good reason to believe that some property of her P IV 9 210 98
measures; and this property, though not large, would be P IV 9 210 98
I cannot make her attend to the value of the property. P IV 10 218 22
recovering her husband's property in the West Indies; by P IV 12 251 11
family, holding landed property in the parish of Sanditon, S 1 368 1
as eldest son to the property which 2 or 3 generations had S 2 371 1
those of birthplace, property, and home,--it was his S 2 372 1
They had very pretty property--enough, had their family S 2 373 1
a man of considerable property in the country, of which a S 3 375 1
share of the accumulated property which they had certainly S 3 377 1
of them that have any real property, landed or funded.-- S 7 401 1
An income perhaps, but no property. S 7 401 1
It has always some property that is wholesome & S 10 415 1
cousin of her own had a property in, Mrs G. did never S 11 422 1
& every thing had a suitable air of property & order.-- S 12 427 1

PROPHECIES (1)
Mrs. Jennings's prophecies, though rather jumbled together, SS III 14 374 7

PROPHESIED (1)
Anne could do no more; but her heart prophesied some P IV 11 239 53

PROPHESIES (1)
her convictions, all her prophesies for the last six weeks. E I 17 141 5

PROPHESY (1)
be, I am inclined to hope you may always prophesy as well." MP I 3 27 36

PROPHETICALLY (1)
Mr. Knightley had spoken prophetically, when he once said, E III 11 402 1

PROPITIOUS (3)
consider as peculiarly propitious, would willingly have W 360 29
Her answer, therefore, was not propitious, at least not to PP I 12 59 1
which she did not seem propitious, and though trusting MP II 8 255 10

PROPORTION (20)
and no niggardly proportion was now dealt out to his fair SS I 21 124 33
that of the ladies in a proportion, which the case SS II 13 241 21
for it will be in proportion to their family and income." SS III 3 284 21
a regret, rather in proportion, as she soon acknowledged SS III 9 333 2
should always be in proportion to what is required." PP I 7 32 38
in displaying the good proportion of the room, its aspect PP II 5 155 4
rapturous air, the fine proportion and finished ornaments, PP II 6 161 10
His resentment was in proportion to the distress of his PP II 12 201 5
"Not, I should hope, of the proportion of virtue to vice MP I 9 93 49
composed in a good proportion of those who would talk and MP II 7 238 3
there are means in proportion, and would have every young MP III 1 317 34
there is a larger proportion who know a little of the MP III 3 340 23
will include a large proportion of the female world at MP III 13 425 6
her fortune bore no proportion to the family-estate--was E I 2 15 3
they had lived in proportion to their income, quietly, E II 7 207 6
but by much the larger proportion neither the one nor the E II 8 219 43
him with Jane, would yield its proportion of pleasure. E III 18 476 46
but the number of the plain was out of all proportion. P IV 3 141 13
must be insecure--& in proportion to their profit must be S 6 393 1
& precious, as she paid in proportion to her fortune.-- S 11 421 1

PROPORTIONABLY (3)
her opinion, she was proportionably more anxious to get LS 42 311 2
I have only to hope that they may be proportionably short. SS II 8 199 40
their acquaintance proportionably advanced, he contrived E II 5 191 28

PROPORTIONATE (2)
and with proportionate speed through the neighbourhood. PP III 8 309 6
always pay for its hopes by any proportionate depression. E I 18 144 2

PROPORTIONED (1)

people in general, she proportioned them to the number of	SS II 12 232 15
PROPORTIONS (5)	
But in what proportions it should be divided amongst the	PP III 8 308 4
the idea--and the proportions must be preserved, you know.	E I 6 48 35
Proportions, fore-shortening.--	E I 6 48 35
and mental sorrow have certainly no necessary proportions.	P III 8 68 30
of the mind, it should have its proportions and limits.	P III 12 116 72
PROPOSAL (44)	
by the General's proposal of her taking his place in his	NA II 5 156 4
his daughter, it was a proposal of too much happiness in	NA II 7 176 17
The proposal was his own.	NA II 7 177 18
conduct by the manner in which her proposal might be taken.	NA II 13 220 1
post, which contained a proposal particularly well timed.	SS I 4 23 20
her acceptance of his proposal; and then hastened to shew	SS I 4 24 20
"Did not Colonel Brandon know of Sir John's proposal to	SS I 20 117 63
Elinor, with great civility, declined the proposal.	SS II 10 219 40
Fanny was startled at the proposal.	SS II 14 253 20
did not find him very unwilling to accept your proposal?"	SS III 4 291 47
Emma felt distressed; she did not like the proposal--she	W 339 18
with their brother's proposal; and it was settled that Mr.	PP I 8 40 59
She would not listen therefore to her daughter's proposal	PP I 9 41 2
proposal accepted with as good a grace as she could.	PP I 17 87 14
Elizabeth was exceedingly pleased with this proposal, and	PP II 2 141 11
at any rate, was perfectly ready to accede to his proposal.	PP II 12 200 5
have hazarded such a proposal, if he had not been well	PP II 13 206 4
than any dislike of the proposal, and seeing in her	PP III 2 264 11
have no hesitation in acceding to the proposal before him.	PP III 8 308 4
such a weakness as a second proposal to the same woman?	PP III 12 341 19
at so convenient a proposal; yet was really vexed that her	PP III 17 374 21
to-morrow, and make the proposal; and, as soon as matters	MP I 1 7 8
for her sister's proposal of coming to her, a measure	MP I 4 41 15
was glad to put an end to his speech by a proposal of wine.	MP I 6 55 17
to him to enforce the proposal, added in a whisper--"we	MP I 12 119 23
she burst through his recital with the proposal of soup.	MP II 1 180 10
start back at first with a look of horror at the proposal.	MP II 8 258 15
The proposal was a very pleasant one to William himself,	MP II 9 266 21
on receiving a proposal of marriage at any time, which	MP III 1 319 39
was delighted to act on his proposal, for both your sakes."	MP III 5 362 20
She must absolutely decline the proposal.	MP III 14 436 15
Harriet was soon back again, and the proposal almost	E I 6 44 19
Mr. Martin, and contained a direct proposal of marriage.	E I 7 50 1
Yes, quite a proposal of marriage; and a very good letter,	E I 7 50 1
five minutes) the proposal of dancing--originating nobody	E II 8 229 98
I bring a new proposal on the subject:--a thought of my	E II 11 250 21
to proceed so, for his proposal was caught at with delight;	E III 6 354 9
the mere proposal of going out seemed to make her worse.--	E III 9 390 18
The change had perhaps been somewhat sudden;--her proposal	E III 13 431 38
consenting the next to a proposal which might have made	E III 14 441 8
This proposal of his, this plan of marrying and continuing	E III 15 450 36
It is Anne's own proposal, and so I shall go with you,	P III 7 57 18
she would feel scrupulous as to any proposal of ours.	P IV 6 166 16
by an early proposal to his sister--not merely for moving,	S 7 395 1
PROPOSALS (21)	
Sir James did make proposals to me for Frederica--but	LS 2 245 1
she did receive serious proposals from Sir James, but her	LS 14 265 4
with the most liberal proposals, he had, on being brought	NA II 15 246 12
Elinor joyfully profited by the first of these proposals,	SS II 1 145 23
I am very sensible of the honour of your proposals, but it	PP I 19 107 12
proposals, but to accept them is absolutely impossible.	PP I 19 109 20
parents, my proposals will not fail of being acceptable."	PP I 19 109 21
protesting against his proposals, but she dared not to	PP I 20 110 2
before she told her sister of Mr. Darcy's proposals.	PP II 15 217 17
could he know that the proposals which she had proudly	PP III 8 311 14
To Jane, he could be only a man whose proposals she had	PP III 11 334 36
seeing him there again the next day, to make his proposals.	PP III 12 343 29
with this gentleman's proposals, which, of course, you	PP III 15 362 15
of Fanny, make decided proposals for her, and intreat the	MP III 1 314 16
consider Crawford's proposals as most advantageous and	MP III 4 346 12
She took three days to consider of his proposals; and	MP III 5 361 16
His professions and his proposals did him no service.	E I 16 135 7
that, after making his proposals to her friend, he had the	E II 8 217 32
encouragement which her proposals of intimacy met with,	E II 15 281 3
declarations and proposals, or he in having them accepted.	P III 4 26 1
too much engrossed by proposals of carrying them away in	P III 6 49 25
PROPOSE (22)	
harsh a measure, merely propose to make it her own choice	LS 7 253 2
just then coming up to propose their returning home, she	NA II 3 147 28
judgment; he could not propose any thing improper for her;	NA II 5 156 5
Eleanor about it at once, propose going away, and be	NA II 13 220 1
that Willoughby should propose, or Marianne consent, to	SS I 13 68 66
"Have you any thing else to propose for my domestic	PP I 10 52 56
me into your house, I propose myself the satisfaction of	PP I 13 63 12
What could your ladyship propose by it?"	PP III 14 353 27
Nobody that wishes me well, I am sure, would propose it.	MP I 3 28 42
Mr. Rushworth then began to propose Mr. Crawford's doing	MP I 6 61 58
I wonder my son did not propose it."	MP I 12 117 13
It is an insult to propose it.	MP I 14 134 13
and I write, by his desire, to propose your returning home.	MP III 15 442 23
Bates, let me propose your venturing on one of these eggs.	E I 3 24 13
	14
written to Enscombe to propose staying a few days beyond	E II 11 256 59
And to propose that she and I should unite to form a	E II 14 279 52
She seemed to propose showing no agitation, or	E III 11 404 9
But I must not propose it yet.	E III 14 440 8
Elizabeth had nothing to propose of deeper efficacy.	P III 1 10 19
and then she was well enough to propose a little walk.	P III 5 39 40
I wish his friends would propose it to him.	P III 12 102 2
Should he ever propose to me (which I have very little	P IV 9 196 33
PROPOSED (53)	
of her situation, proposed walking, & we left the two	LS 20 276 4
Mrs Vernon encouraging the doubt, directly proposed her	LS 42 312 5
had just left, and of a proposed exchange of terriers	NA I 8 55 10
to go with her, it was proposed by the brother and sister	NA I 10 80 61
to avoid his displeasure, she proposed a compromise.	NA I 13 99 4
saying she should join Mrs. Allen, proposed their walking.	NA II 3 147 28
about the tea-house, proposed it as no unpleasant	NA II 7 179 27
The next day afforded no opportunity for the proposed	NA II 9 190 1
proposed to Miss Tilney the accomplishment of her promise.	NA II 9 191 3
She proposed it to him accordingly; but he did not catch	NA II 11 209 2
have had no good effect, proposed, as another expedient	NA II 14 236 18
same remedy was eagerly proposed for this unfortunate	SS I 21 121 10
Lady Middleton proposed a rubber of Casino to the others.	SS II 1 144 15
on Mrs. Palmer's, it was proposed by the latter that they	SS II 4 164 23
his fears in a moment, proposed to call in farther advice.	SS III 7 313 21
Miss Bingley was then sorry that she had proposed the	PP I 12 59 2
She had fully proposed being engaged by Wickham for those	PP I 17 87 14
tour of pleasure which they proposed taking in the summer.	PP II 4 154 21
see so much as they had proposed, or at least to see it	PP II 19 238 7
to be alone with Jane, proposed their all walking out.	PP III 16 365 1
on its being first proposed, so far from feeling slighted,	MP I 7 66 14
Mrs. Rushworth proposed that the chaise should be taken	MP I 9 84 2
speaking, whatever he proposed was immediately approved,	MP I 10 97 3
No piece could be proposed that did not supply somebody	MP I 14 131 3
For about the fifth time he then proposed the heir at law,	MP I 14 131 6
had been proposed before so likely to suit them all.	MP I 14 132 8
it could be proposed and accepted in a private theatre!	MP I 14 137 23
Edmund proposed, urged, entreated it--till the lady, not	MP I 18 170 24
family to themselves, proposed Mr. Yates's accompanying	MP II 1 177 5
manner than before, and proposed their going up into her	MP II 8 257 15
had been proposed, he would accept a place in his carriage.	MP II 9 265 21
once good-humouredly proposed, I hope I foresee two	MP III 10 405 19
it was very generally proposed, as a most proper attention,	E I 2 17 9
what they all proposed doing in the event of his marriage.	E I 8 59 27
I really never could think well of any body who proposed	E I 11 96 25
When the time proposed drew near, Mrs. Weston's fears were	E I 18 144 1
in--observing, as she proposed it to Harriet, that, as	E II 1 155 3
allow the visit to exceed the proposed quarter of an hour.	E II 5 186 2
Mrs. Weston proposed having no regular supper; merely	E II 11 254 45
hearing what was proposed, gave it his decided approbation.	E II 11 255 54
and their papa now proposed bringing them, and staying one	E II 16 292 7
a decision of action unusual to her, proposed a removal.--	E III 6 359 37
of her going to Mrs. Smallridge's at the time proposed.	E III 9 389 16
arrogance proposed to arrange everybody's destiny.	E III 11 412 47
her sister's side, Emma proposed it to her friend, and	E III 16 451 3
You cannot mean that he has even proposed to her again--	E III 18 471 17
be done, and had finally proposed these two branches of	P III 1 9 19
and as Sir Walter proposed removing to Bath in the course	P III 5 33 5
though that had been proposed at first; but then he had	P III 7 58 22
On its being proposed, Anne offered her services, as usual,	P III 8 71 56
and Captain Wentworth proposed, and Charles Musgrove	P III 12 114 64
was over, Charles had proposed coming with him, and Mrs.	P IV 10 216 19
what Mr. Musgrove had proposed the next, and what had	P IV 11 230 5
PROPOSER (1)	
of intimacy with the proposer--& yet fearful of	W 339 18
PROPOSES (2)	
and Edmund kindly proposes attending his brother	MP III 13 426 11
which Sir Thomas proposes should be done, and thinks best	MP III 13 426 11
PROPOSING (10)	
I shall never forget your goodnature in proposing it.	W 320 2
only one blunder, in proposing to stop at the milleners,	W 322 2
and was on the point of proposing it when Mrs. Grant spoke.	MP I 8 80 28
as to justify him in proposing to take his passage in the	MP I 11 107 2
Henry Crawford was just proposing, desirous at once of	MP I 18 168 14
been on the point of proposing the 22d herself, as by far	MP II 8 254 7
"that he was proposing to leave Highbury the following	E I 17 140 2
Weston that he had been proposing to Mrs. Elton, as her	E III 6 353 3
and Captain Wentworth proposing also to wait on her for a	P III 7 59 24
"He was just come from Eastbourne, proposing to spend two	S 12 425 1
PROPOSITION (8)	
proposition of its being the finest child in the world.	SS II 14 248 5
Emma scarcely knew how to answer such a proposition--& the	W 349 24
Her next proposition, of shewing the house to such of them	MP I 9 84 2
sort of self-evident proposition which many a clearer head	MP I 9 89 31
Mr. Elton looked all happiness at this proposition; and	E I 10 89 38
fully assented to his proposition of Mr. Frank Churchill	E I 14 119 8
His first proposition and request, that the dance begun at	E II 11 247 3
when there was a proposition for going into the library	S 7 398 1
PROPRIA PERSONA (1)	
any thing in propria persona, amazed at her own doings in	MP III 9 398 9
PROPRIETIES (2)	
appeared; and all the smiles and the proprieties passed.	E III 2 320 11
the horrible eligibilities and proprieties of the match!	P IV 11 244 72
PROPRIETOR (9)	
disposal of its present proprietor, was consequently open	NA II 16 251 6
not be seen, as the proprietor, who was then abroad, had	SS I 12 62 28
was, and who was its proprietor, when she had listened to	PP I 16 75 2
was the name of its proprietor, and with no little alarm,	PP II 19 241 17
to the fortune of their proprietor; but Elizabeth saw,	PP III 1 246 5
up by the present proprietor; and, such as it was, there	E I 10 83 2
the present and future proprietor could fairly warrant, as	E III 6 358 35
man, of middle age, the proprietor of the place, who	S 1 364 1
Mr Heywood, such was the name of the said proprietor,	S 1 365 1
PROPRIETORS (1)	
by three great proprietors, each more careful and jealous	P IV 10 217 20
PROPRIETY (61)	
tho' late, the path of propriety, occasioned her removal	LS 6 252 2
however at the parade of propriety which prevented Miss	LS 19 274 2
he remain here; you know my reasons--propriety & so forth.	LS 31 302 1
from a doubt of the propriety of accepting such an offer.	NA I 7 47 24
it might with propriety lead, nor to what rigours of	NA I 12 92 3
of propriety, only to enable her to be guilty of another?	NA I 13 105 41
to express neatness, propriety, and delicacy, or	NA I 14 108 16
our faults in the utmost propriety of diction, while we	NA I 14 108 17
felt no doubt of the propriety of an acquaintance which	NA II 2 140 11
appearance, propriety, to your family, to the world.	NA II 13 225 23
with propriety in the discharge of his ordinary duties.	SS I 1 5 7
first to reflect on the propriety of going, and her own	SS I 1 6 10
but he has an innate propriety and simplicity of taste,	SS I 4 19 2
to his father might with particular propriety be fulfilled.	SS I 5 27 6
gave more than usual propriety; it was that of running	SS I 9 41 6
the forms of worldly propriety, he displayed a want of	SS I 10 49 9
to suggest the propriety of some self-command to Marianne.	SS I 11 53 2
tendency of setting propriety at nought; and a better	SS I 11 56 13
Elinor then ventured to doubt the propriety of her	SS I 12 58 3
of an employment does not always evince its propriety."	SS I 13 68 71
each other in an insipid propriety of demeanour, and a	SS II 12 229 2
had suggested the propriety of their being really invited	SS II 14 252 20
Elinor would not argue upon the propriety of overcoming	SS III 3 280 6
time reflecting on the propriety or impropriety of	SS III 10 347 32
He reads extremely well, with great propriety & in a very	W 343 20
a degree of considerate propriety, totally unlike the half-	W 346 21
Mr. Darcy with grave propriety requested to be allowed the	PP I 6 26 40
without offering one argument in favour of its propriety."	PP I 10 50 34
sacrifice to propriety, not a pleasure to himself.	PP II 9 180 29
had to decide on the propriety of his friend's inclination,	PP II 10 185 36
of that total want of propriety so frequently, so almost	PP II 12 198 5
not have appeared with propriety in a different manner.--	PP II 14 212 13
ease, and with a propriety of behaviour equally free from	PP III 11 335 39
Are you lost to every feeling of propriety and delicacy?	PP III 14 355 43
in the main as to the propriety of doing every thing one	MP I 1 6 6
It did not suit his sense of propriety, and he was	MP I 6 57 32
her own sense of propriety could but just smooth over.	MP I 8 81 32
But dear Maria has such a strict sense of propriety, so	MP I 12 117 14
This is the end of all the privacy and propriety which was	MP I 16 153 8
soon agreed on the propriety of their walking quietly home	MP II 1 177 5
with true dowager propriety, to Bath--there to parade over	MP II 3 202 28
opinion as to the propriety of the invitation's being	MP II 5 217 9
must submit, as her own propriety of mind directed, in	MP II 5 223 48
The neatness and propriety of her dress was all that he	MP II 10 272 1
little to do with the propriety of her seeing her parents	MP III 6 368 9
regulation of subject, a propriety, an attempt towards	MP III 7 382 29
The elegance, propriety, regularity,harmony--and perhaps,	MP III 8 391 10
utmost politeness and propriety, at the same time with a	MP III 10 399 5
liberality, propriety, even delicacy of feeling.	E I 7 51 4
you are inflicting as propriety requires, will present	E I 7 51 11
take the lead, just as propriety may require, and to speak	E I 18 150 31
might have been said but for the restraints of propriety.--	E II 13 265 5
duty, and attention to propriety, an endeavour to avoid	E II 13 268 11
	12
than of pride or propriety, to make her resolve on not	E II 14 270 2
Their propriety, simplicity, and elegance, would make them	E II 14 278 47
her opinion as to the propriety and comfort of the rooms	E III 2 319 2
and by the readiness and propriety of his apologies, that	P III 12 104 7
any compromise of propriety on the side of the Elliots."	P IV 4 149 12
at that moment with propriety have spoken for himself!--	P IV 5 160 26
It was a struggle between propriety and vanity; but vanity	P IV 10 219 29
pleased her in their propriety and correctness, their	P IV 12 249 3
PROSAIC (1)	
with some of the prosaic decencies of life;--nor can you,	S 7 398 1
PROSE (6)	
have done more justice to simple and elegant prose,	SS I 3 18 19
and will be soon followed by matter-of-fact prose."	E I 9 74 23
desired a more spirited rejection of Mr. Martin's prose.	E I 9 76 36
thing very clever, be it prose or verse, original or	E III 7 370 23

a larger allowance of prose in his daily study; and on P III 11 101 24
histories are against you, all stories, prose and verse. P IV 11 234 27
PROSECUTION (1)
at least planning a vigorous prosecution of them in future. SS III 11 352 20
PROSING (2)
a well-meaning, civil, prosing, pompous woman, who thought MP I 8 75 2
satisfied--so smiling--so prosing --so undistinguishing E I 10 84 16
PROSINGS (1)
so well; but the quiet prosings of three such women made E I 3 22 6
PROSPECT (73)
Poor creature! the prospect from her window is not very LS 17 271 7
Our prospect is most delightful; & since matters have now LS 23 283 1
I wish there were a better prospect than now appears, of LS 41 310 5
sincerely did in the prospect of the connexion, it must be NA I 15 118 9
The prospect of four thousand a-year, in addition to his SS I 1 5 8
daughter-in-law in the prospect of her removal; a SS I 5 27 6
The prospect in front was more extensive; it commanded the SS I 6 29 3
had been raised, by his prospect of riches, was led before SS I 10 49 11
them, and examine a prospect which formed the distance of SS I 16 85 15
his attention to the prospect, "here is Barton valley. SS I 16 88 33
their house, admired its prospect, was attentive, and kind; SS I 17 90 1
the delight in a fine prospect which you profess to feel. SS I 18 97 8
I like a fine prospect, but not on picturesque principles. SS I 18 98 8
I could give up every prospect of more without a sigh. SS II 2 147 7
it would be an alarming prospect; but Edward's affection SS II 2 147 7
how blank was her own prospect, how cheerless her own SS II 4 159 1
the prospect of a very respectable establishment in life." SS II 11 223 18
Born to the prospect of such affluence! SS III 1 268 50
least for a time this fair prospect of busy tranquillity. SS III 10 343 10
to sooth his, with the prospect of Miss Osborne's second W 330 11
in memory & in prospect, but for the moment, she ceased to W 361 31
Mr. Bingley, and a charming prospect over that gravel walk. PP I 9 42 7
The prospect of such delights was very cheering, and they PP I 15 74 11
"It was the prospect of constant society, and good society, PP I 16 79 23
The prospect of the Netherfield ball was extremely PP I 17 86 10
and though every prospect of her own was destroyed for the PP I 18 90 4
terms on the happy prospect of their nearer connection. PP I 20 110 1
firmness that the prospect of their relationship was PP I 22 125 16
self-gratulation on the prospect of a connection between PP I 23 126 1
2
for her health, and the prospect of her northern tour was PP II 5 155 1
to be compared with the prospect of Rosings, afforded by PP II 5 156 4
But the gloom of Lydia's prospect was shortly cleared away; PP II 18 230 11
surveying it, went to a window to enjoy its prospect. PP III 1 246 5
Were the same fair prospect to arise at present, as had PP III 11 337 54
her delight in the prospect of their relationship. PP III 13 347 33
and without any near prospect of finishing his business. MP I 4 37 9
Sir Thomas, however, was truly happy in the prospect of an MP I 4 40 14
house, and it opens the prospect amazingly which makes me MP I 6 55 17
was again very happy in the prospect of hearing her play. MP I 6 60 52
little real comfort; her prospect always ended in Mr. MP I 8 81 32
the possibility of much prospect from any of the rooms, MP I 9 85 4
It was a gloomy prospect, and all that she could do was to MP I 11 107 3
prospect of acting the fool together with such unanimity. MP I 16 156 27
but if there were any prospect of a renewal of "Lovers' MP II 2 192 11
up, if she felt herself unhappy in the prospect of it. MP II 3 200 21
to leave her to fairest prospect of having only to listen MP II 5 223 48
prospect of a ball given principally for her gratification. MP II 8 254 8
change it made in the prospect of Julia's return, which MP II 11 284 10
sunk under the appalling prospect of discussion, MP III 1 317 38
remaining which made the prospect of it most sorrowful to MP III 6 367 4
seeing all this, by the prospect of another visitor, whose MP III 6 368 7
This was a prospect to be dwelt on with a fondness that MP III 6 370 11
motherly a joy in the prospect of seeing her child again, MP III 6 371 17
In space, light, furniture, and prospect, there was MP III 9 398 9
The prospect for her cousin grew worse and worse. MP III 12 417 4
with no prospect of a third to cheer a long evening. E I 1 6 5
in Highbury, that the prospect of the introduction had E I 3 25 15
With Tuesday came the agreeable prospect of seeing him E II 8 212 4
--his concern that she should have no happier prospect! E II 8 226 79
tolerate the prospect of being miserably crowded at supper. E II 11 254 44
One thing was wanting to make the prospect of the ball E II 12 257 1
we have the agreeable prospect of frequent visits from E II 18 308 30
all the old neglect of prospect, had scarcely a sight--and E III 6 358 35
gladly endured, in the prospect of the quiet drive home E III 7 374 54
all my heart, on the prospect of having one of the most E III 10 400 68
The prospect before her now, was threatening to a degree E III 12 422 19
of a similarity of prospect would certainly add to the E III 16 452 7
The sole grievance and alloy thus removed in the prospect E III 18 475 39
With the prospect of spending at least two months at P III 6 43 3
of his wishes, in his prospect of soon quitting his P III 9 78 19
To Anne, it chiefly wore the prospect of an hour of P IV 8 189 45
in crossing the down, a prospect house, a Bellevue Cottage, S 4 384 1
Two large families--one, for prospect house probably, the S 5 388 1
PROSPECTS (23)
at his own prospects, his uncertain behaviour towards SS II 1 139 1
my prospects; and told me, as I thought, with triumph.-- SS III 1 263 29
have my affections; our prospects are not very bright, to SS III 2 277 30
This paragraph was of some importance to the prospects and SS III 13 371 40
and his prospects of future wealth were exceedingly fair. PP I 22 122 3
Every park has its beauty and its prospects; and Elizabeth PP II 6 161 8
prosperity, and blasted the prospects of Mr. Wickham.-- PP II 12 196 5
to tear her from such prospects and such realities as PP II 18 232 23
Your prospects, however, are too fair to justify want of MP I 10 99 16
and destroying her prospects; and retired in proud resolve, MP II 3 201 23
was scarcely beyond her merits, rejoice in her prospects. MP II 12 294 18
to make his merit and prospects a kind of common concern. E I 2 17 7
to triumph in his happy prospects, and circulate the fame E II 4 181 2
His information and prospects as to Enscombe were neither E II 13 266 5
Emma saw how Mr. Weston understood these joyous prospects. E III 1 317 9
too strong for any fine prospects, or any cold collation, E III 7 367 1
to Jane Fairfax, whose prospects were closing, while E III 9 389 16
to me the happiest prospects, I should not have presumed E III 14 440 8
Yes, indeed, I quite understand--dearest Jane's prospects-- E III 16 455 20
prospects, beginning to own other eyes and other limbs! P III 6 47 16
I cannot believe his prospects so blighted for ever. P III 11 97 13
friends, the pleasant prospects of one should not be P IV 10 217 21
to the happiness of her prospects than what arose from the P IV 12 251 10
ROSPER (1)
Such half and half doings never prosper. MP I 5 51 41
ROSPERITY (18)
for our welfare and prosperity carries you too far." SS II 11 227 47
in the affair, and the prosperity which crowned it, SS III 14 376 11
of hard-hearted prosperity, low-minded conceit, & wrong- W 361 31
consequential feelings of early and unexpected prosperity. PP I 15 70 1
prosperity, and blasted the prospects of Mr. Wickham.-- PP II 12 196 5
happiness nor worldly prosperity, could be justly expected PP III 7 307 51
and selfish from prosperity and bad example, he would not MP I 12 114 3
not destroy her credit, her appearance, her prosperity too. MP II 3 202 25
all its appendages of prosperity and beauty, its rich E III 6 360 40
"You are sick of prosperity and indulgence. E III 6 365 63
"I sick of prosperity and indulgence!-- E III 6 365 64
and the elegance, the prosperity and the nothingness, of P III 1 9 18
earlier prosperity than could be reasonably calculated on. P III 4 29 8
though by what seemed prosperity in the shape of an early P IV 8 189 46
they should be so equal in their prosperity and comfort. P IV 10 217 21
defiance even to greater accessions of worldly prosperity. P IV 12 252 12
promote the rise & prosperity of the place--wd in fact S 2 372 1
cannot get rich without bringing prosperity to us.-- S 6 392 1
OSPEROUS (14)
in so prosperous a state as Marianne had believed it. SS I 4 22 18
Robert was carelessly kind, as became a prosperous man & a W 349 24
very different man from what he is to the less prosperous. PP I 16 82 48
for he was longing to publish his prosperous love. PP I 22 123 3
Every body around her was gay and busy, prosperous and MP I 17 159 6
She had been a beauty, and a prosperous beauty, all her MP III 2 332 22
it is to be hoped, more prosperous trial of the state--if MP III 17 464 12
All was safe and prosperous; and as the removal of one E II 12 257 2
I do not look upon myself as either prosperous or indulged. E III 6 365 64
and, were she prosperous, I could allow much for the E III 7 375 61
She would soon be well, and happy, and prosperous.-- E III 11 403 2
It is very difficult for the prosperous to be humble. E III 14 437 8
had seemed to foresee and to command his prosperous path. P III 4 29 8
in prosperous love, all that was most unlike Anne Elliot! P IV 1 123 7
PROSPEROUSLY (2)
It is an engagement in some respects not prosperously SS I 15 81 44
His business in Antigua had latterly been prosperously MP II 1 178 8
PROTECT (1)
from such wit, if age and infirmity will not protect him?" SS I 8 37 4
PROTECTED (5)
Miss Crawford had protected her only for the time; and if MP I 16 150 1
She was at liberty, she was busy, she was protected. MP III 3 344 43
one--she should be protected by him, and secured in every MP III 17 465 13
While either of them protected him and his, Hartfield was E III 19 484 10
While she remained, a bush or low rambling holly protected P III 10 88 27
PROTECTING (3)
Loving, guiding, protecting her, as he had been doing ever MP III 17 470 27
you, in protecting you from the gipsies, was spoken of." E III 11 406 21
On one side it seemed protecting kindness, on the other S 6 392 1
PROTECTION (17)
throw herself into the protection of a young man with whom LS 22 282 6
another, from whom can she expect protection and regard? NA I 5 37 4
wished for the protection of light after she were in bed." NA II 6 167 10
to descend and meet him under the protection of visitors. NA II 9 192 4
After courting you from the protection of real friends to NA II 13 225 19
the powerful protection of a very magnificent concerto----- SS II 2 149 24
25
us pleasure, or whose protection will give us consequence." SS II 3 156 12
to London under her protection, and as her guest, without SS II 4 159 1
her their personal protection and countenance, is such a PP III 7 305 36
My good qualities are under your protection, and you are PP III 18 381 7
authority and protection, or I think you might with little MP I 10 99 18
ran to her mother's protection, and Susan could only MP III 7 386 42
to leave Henry's protection, there will be much less MP III 16 457 29
The kindness and protection of Mrs. Elton!-- E II 15 284 10
of his son-in-law's protection, would have been under E III 19 483 10
her own table; to their protection she must trust, and P IV 11 237 41
42
established under his protection in London, it was evident P IV 12 250 7
PROTECTOR (1)
with William for the protector and companion of her MP III 6 369 11
PROTEGE (3)
"In defence of your protege you can even be saucy." SS I 10 50 19
"My protege, as you call him, is a sensible man; and sense SS I 10 51 20
of receiving in his protege, certainly a very different MP II 6 233 16
PROTEGEE (3)
for the comfort of her protegee, Mrs. Allen made her way NA I 2 21 9
which now obliged her protegee, after some months further MP I 4 40 15
the visit of her former protegee as a favour; but all that P IV 5 153 6
PROTEST (16)
and she could only protest over and over again, that no NA I 9 67 33
be believed, I solemnly protest that no syllable of such a NA II 3 144 11
And I protest, if I had any money to spare, I should buy a SS II 14 251 17
and I declare and protest to you I never was so shocked in SS III 5 299 35
Is there one among the sex, who would not protest against PP III 12 341 19
said Edmund, "that I absolutely protest against." MP I 13 128 32
"'tis Crawford's, Crawford's barouche, I protest! MP II 5 222 46
"You are right, Fanny, to protest against such an office, MP II 9 269 35
though Emma continued to protest against any assistance E I 7 55 35
I protest against having paid the smallest attention to E I 15 131 31
"Oh! no, indeed; I must protest against any such idea. E II 14 276 36
"here comes this dear old beau of mine, I protest!-- E II 17 302 21
22
affectedly) I must protest against that.-- E II 18 305 6
Mrs. Otway, I protest!--and good Mr. Otway, and Miss Otway E III 2 323 19
"Oh! for myself, I protest I must be excused," said Mrs. E III 7 371 37
I should loudly protest against the share of it which that E III 14 441 8
PROTESTATION (2)
full meaning of the protestation; and such a quick MP III 3 339 21
assured her, that this protestation had done her more good E III 10 396 42
PROTESTATIONS (5)
and softened only his protestations of present regard. SS III 10 347 33
all their first protestations; but Edmund said nothing.-- MP I 15 148 59
Here Fanny interposed however with anxious protestations MP II 7 239 8
It is not by protestations that I shall endeavour to MP III 3 343 41
could not help adding her warm protestations to theirs. P III 7 55 5
PROTESTED (21)
to Maria Manwaring; he protested that he had been only in LS 9 257 1
her hearing, he not only protested against every thought NA II 1 131 15
James had protested against writing to her till his return NA II 10 201 5
His own two thousand pounds she protested should be his SS III 1 267 38
Mr. Bennet protested against any description of finery. PP I 3 13 19
The boy protested that she should not; she continued to PP I 5 20 23
most important aspect he protested that he had never in PP I 14 66 1
and begging pardon, protested that he never read novels.-- PP I 14 68 13
This was agreed to, and Mrs. Philips protested that they PP I 15 74 11
He protested that Lady Catherine and her daughter, PP I 15 74 13
than politeness, protested he must be entirely mistaken, PP I 23 126 1
2
He protested that she should receive from him no mark of PP III 8 310 10
I have always protested against comedy, and this is comedy MP I 14 136 20
With the deepest blushes Fanny protested against such a MP II 8 259 21
Fanny protested her ignorance as steadily as her MP II 10 277 18
and having warmly protested against her suspicion as most E I 15 130 28
He protested that he had never thought seriously of E I 16 134 3
It is what I always protested against for my children. P IV 11 231 8
The chair was earnestly protested against; and Mrs. P IV 11 238 47
of angry pride), he protested that he had for ever felt it P IV 11 242 63
After having always protested against any such addition, S 3 377 1
PROTESTING (9)
at such a charge, protesting her innocence of every NA II 3 144 11
the table, & absolutely protesting against the entrance of W 353 27
doubt, and were both protesting that they knew many women PP I 8 40 55
Mr. and Mrs. Philips, protesting that he did not in the PP I 16 84 59
to encourage him by protesting against his proposals, but PP I 20 110 2
put it hastily away, protesting that she would not regard PP II 13 204 2
Emma amused herself by protesting that it was very E III 16 458 41
their uprightness; protesting that she was convinced of P III 11 99 19
family features, and protesting still more positively that P IV 10 222 37
PROTESTS (1)
"Mrs. Musgrove protests solemnly that she knew nothing of " P IV 6 165 8
PROTRACTED (3)
on the sweets of so protracted an autumn, they were forced MP II 4 208 11
protracted apologies and civil hesitations of the other. E I 8 57 2
It could be protracted no longer. E I 10 89 38
PROUD (55)
& according to Mr Smith's account, is equally dull & proud. LS 4 248 2
This Reginald has a proud spirit of his own!--a spirit, too, LS 25 292 1
his proud heart, without deigning to seek an explanation! LS 25 293 3
taking her hand with affection, "may be proud of." NA I 7 50 47
I am proud when I reflect on it, and I think it must NA I 14 107 9
no fortune, and I fancy she is an exceeding proud woman." SS I 22 132 39
But Mrs. Ferrars is a very headstrong proud woman, and in SS II 2 148 15
Elinor, Elinor, they who suffer little may be proud and SS II 7 189 52

flattery which Lucy was proud to think of and administer SS II 14 247 4
Fanny, rejoicing in her escape, and proud of the ready wit SS II 14 253 26
kindness, and my cousins would be proud to know her.-- SS III 2 277 30
He was proud of his conquest, proud of tricking Edward, SS III 14 376 11
proud of marrying privately without his mother's consent. SS III 14 376 11
but as playing cards with ly osborne, & looking proud.-- W 343 19
he was discovered to be proud, to be above his company, PP I 3 10 5
agreeable where they chose it; but proud and conceited. PP I 4 15 11
If I may so express it, he has a right to be proud." PP I 5 20 18
A person may be proud without being vain. PP I 5 20 20
came with his sisters, "I should not care how proud I was. PP I 5 20 21
"The indirect boast;--for you are really proud of your PP I 10 48 27
Lady Catherine was reckoned proud by many people he knew, PP I 14 66 1
too proud to be dishonest,--for dishonesty I must call it." PP I 16 81 38
Family pride, and filial pride, for his is very proud of PP I 16 81 41
But she is too much like her brother,--very, very proud.-- PP I 16 82 43
Darcy formerly spoken of as a very proud, ill-natured boy. PP II 2 143 20
in the affair; that proud and repulsive as were his PP II 13 207 6
Some people call him proud; but I am sure I never saw any PP III 1 249 38
people may call him proud, I have seen nothing of it." PP III 1 257 68
Miss Darcy was exceedingly proud; but the observation of a PP III 2 261 3
inferior, the belief of her being proud and reserved. PP III 3 267 3
prepared to see a proud, reserved, disagreeable girl. PP III 5 284 14
For herself she was humbled; but she was proud of him. PP III 10 327 3
Proud that in a cause of compassion and honour, he had PP III 10 327 3
I am prodigiously proud of him. PP III 11 330 8
That tall, proud man." PP III 11 334 34
We all know him to be a proud, unpleasant sort of man; but PP III 17 376 33
enjoyed the power of being proud of her sister's. MP I 4 42 17
prospects; and retired in proud resolve, determined only MP II 3 201 23
much complacency; he was proud of his niece, and without MP II 10 276 13
Betsey went with alacrity; proud to shew her abilities MP III 7 379 16
exert himself to subdue so proud a display of resentment; MP III 17 467 20
your merit?--what are you proud of?--you made a lucky E I 1 12 42
He saw his son every year in London, and was proud of him; E I 2 17 7
I am rather proud of little George. E I 6 45 21
We are very proud of the children, are not we, papa? E I 9 80 69
meant and believed him; proud, assuming, conceited; very E I 16 135 6
up by those who are proud, luxurious, and selfish, should E I 18 145 10
and selfish, should be proud, luxurious, and selfish too. E I 18 145 10
He seemed not merely happy with her, but proud. E II 15 281 2
His bright, proud eye spoke the happy conviction that he P III 7 62 40
be proud of between two walls, perhaps thirty feet asunder. P IV 3 138 5
"Well," said Anne, "I certainly am proud, too proud to P IV 4 151 20
You talk of being proud, I am called proud I know, and I P IV 4 151 21
But I was proud, too proud to ask again. P IV 11 247 84
a little parasol, which will make her as proud as can be. S 4 381 1

PROUD-LOOKING (1)

more than a little proud-looking woman of uncordial SS II 12 229 3

PROUDEST (2)

He was the proudest, most disagreeable man in the world, PP I 3 11 6
he would consider it as the proudest moment of his life." E I 9 82 83

PROUDLY (7)

of such a work, how proudly would she have produced the NA I 5 38 4
condemnation--instead of proudly resolving, in conscious NA I 12 93 4
Frederick too, who always wore his heart so proudly! who NA II 10 206 30
had been joyfully and proudly communicative;--and being at NA II 15 244 12
proposals which she had proudly spurned only four months PP III 8 311 14
The compliment was just returned, coldly and proudly; and, E I 15 132 37
And we sir--(speaking rather proudly) are not in the Weald. S 1 366 1

PROVE (52)

conduct at Langford, which prove that she does not confine LS 4 248 1
that Frederica vernon may prove more worthy than she has LS 14 265 5
I will prove myself a man, no less by the generosity of my NA I 14 112 36
weakness, it chanced to prove a source of fresh pain to SS II 9 202 4
you allow me to prove it, by relating some circumstances, SS II 9 204 18
but in the end may prove materially advantageous.-- SS II 11 226 42
was better, and tried to prove herself so, by engaging in SS III 7 307 1
else who was likely to prove an acquaintance in common. SS III 8 326 55
to misery, was likely to prove a source of unhappiness to SS III 8 331 70
is enough to prove him one of the worthiest of men." SS III 9 337 16
word; and I doubt not will prove a valuable acquaintance, PP I 13 63 13
it may prove so; for else they will be destitute enough. PP I 13 65 21
22
on this occasion to her sister, will prove what she felt. PP II 3 147 25
sister as to prove him capable of some amiable feeling. PP II 13 207 6
Most earnestly did she labour to prove the probability of PP II 17 225 9
its existence might prove, had at least outlived one day. PP III 2 263 10
And you are never to stir out of doors, till you can prove, PP III 6 300 30
This was enough to prove that her approbation need not be PP III 17 378 44
"I hope she will prove a well-disposed girl," continued MP I 1 10 13
"We cannot prove the contrary, to be sure--but I wish you MP I 11 112 31
you would never be able to prove that it was not Thornton MP II 7 241 15
among his parishioners and prove himself by constant MP II 7 248 42
We must hope his son may prove that he knows it too." MP II 7 248 46
What could more delightfully prove that the warmth of her MP II 12 294 16
the praise of a friend, as this day does prove it. MP II 13 300 5
Though their caution may prove eventually unnecessary, it MP III 1 313 12
She wished to prove to him that she did desire his comfort, MP III 1 322 50
as far as words could prove it, and in the language, tone, MP III 2 328 6
They shall prove, that as far as you can be deserved by MP III 3 343 41
You have proved yourself upright and disinterested, prove MP III 4 347 18
stated the case--you must prove yourself to be in your MP III 4 352 44
panting breaths seemed to prove--especially as they were MP III 7 383 31
went on, and who must prove a far more worthy companion MP III 10 403 15
London habits, would yet prove herself in the end too much MP III 12 417 4
That would only prove her affection not equal to MP III 13 422 2
it was to be hoped, would prove unfounded; but there was MP III 14 429 1
"This will prove a spirited beginning of your winter E I 15 126 7
8
comfort, and endeavour to prove her own affection in some E I 17 142 10
--and did, in truth, prove herself more resolutely in love E I 17 142 12
let us go in, that I may prove myself to belong to the E II 6 200 14
"Then it can be no argument to prove that he is in love. E II 8 226 80
prove to have an indifferent tone--what shall I say? E II 9 234 32
few steps were enough to prove in how gentlemanlike a E III 2 326 32
the subject in a manner to prove, that he now only wanted E III 10 400 69
My Emma, does not every thing serve to prove more and more E III 15 446 15
I only wanted to prove to you that Mrs. S. admits our E III 16 453 13
the intelligence to prove, in some measure, premature. E III 18 473 27
of their friends, and to prove that Mr. Elliot's had P IV 9 209 96
I will not allow books to prove any thing." P IV 11 234 28
"But how shall we prove any thing?" P IV 11 234 29
We never can expect to prove any thing upon such a point. P IV 11 234 30
best of the good--prove to be a Mrs Griffiths & her family. S 9 408 1

PROVED (87)

resolve to disallow, have been unanswerably proved to me. LS 36 305 1
at an inn, and that fortunately proved to be groundless. NA I 2 19 4
repeated so often, and proved so totally ineffectual, that NA I 2 21 9
hope which, when it proved to be fruitless, she felt to NA I 8 58 25
The silence of the lady proved it to be unanswerable. NA II 7 176 16
a position so awful, proved to be one end of what the NA II 9 193 6
motion of the lock proved that some hand must be on it. NA II 13 222 9
offers of accommodation, it proved to be exactly the case. NA II 13 229 31
two or three last weeks proved him to be neither; for NA II 15 246 12
The event proved her conjecture right, though it was SS II 9 204 17
opposition, though it proved perfectly different from what SS II 10 214 6
delicacy of his taste, proved to be beyond his politeness. SS II 11 220 3
The chance proved a lucky one, for a message from Mrs. SS II 13 238 3
Nothing has proved him unworthy; nor has any thing SS III 1 264 29
The event has proved, that I was a cunning fool, providing SS III 8 321 34
You have proved yourself, on the whole, less faulty than I SS III 8 329 66
You have proved your heart less wicked, much less wicked. SS III 8 329 66
looks and spirits proved her to be, as she repeatedly SS III 9 335 7
really amiable, as he has proved himself the contrary, SS III 9 338 22
had been wont to believe, or than it was now proved to be. SS III 11 355 46
since in every way been proved, it was not at the time an SS III 13 362 5
engagement, for she has proved that it fettered neither SS III 13 367 23
He proved a very useful addition to their table; without W 359 28
"You have only proved by this," cried Elizabeth, "that Mr. PP I 10 49 30
But, my dear sister, though the event has proved you right, PP II 3 148 26
Jane and herself, which proved that the former had, from PP II 4 152 6
when any dish on the table proved a novelty to them. PP II 6 163 14
so decisive a manner as proved that she was not used to PP II 6 163 15
at his stupidity, proved that he was generally different, PP II 9 180 29
on some passages which proved that Jane had not written in PP II 10 182 2
which proved him wholly unmoved by any feeling of remorse. PP II 11 191 13
though in a voice which proved it to be Mr. Darcy, she PP II 12 195 2
by design; for there proved to have been a prior PP II 12 201 5
But every line proved more clearly that the affair, which PP II 13 205 3
mediocrity of her fortune proved no longer the moderation PP II 13 207 6
His affection was proved to have been sincere, and his PP II 14 213 18
some kind of discourse, proved her to be more truly well PP III 3 267 4
of such an attempt, till it were proved against them? PP III 5 284 12
were proved beyond their greatest extent to be true! PP III 10 326 3
had been generally proved to be marked out for misfortune. PP III 13 350 56
and feel how right you proved to be, I am inclined to hope MP I 3 27 36
The new mare proved a treasure; with a very little trouble, MP I 4 37 8
The second meeting proved him not so very plain; he was MP I 5 44 2
proved the contrary, she never mentioned him. MP I 5 48 30
The door, however, proved not to be locked, and they were MP I 9 91 38
might be called, had been proved and perfected by Mr. MP I 13 121 1
would suit every body, proved to be no trifle; and the MP I 14 130 1
The gloom of her first anticipations was proved to have MP I 18 166 5
He proved, however, to be too late. MP II 6 232 13
conniving at, as each proved to the other by the MP II 6 233 15
When it was proved however to have done William no harm, MP II 6 237 23
her wants with a kindness which proved her a real friend. MP II 8 258 18
I deferred it all, till his praise should be proved the MP II 13 300 5
I had formed, and proved yourself of a character the very MP III 1 318 39
You have proved yourself upright and disinterested, prove MP III 4 347 18
the point attempted to be proved, she set herself very MP III 6 371 14
I am sure it will be all hushed up, and nothing proved by MP III 15 437 3
the difference could be such as she had now proved it. MP III 16 457 30
it take place, and be proved in the right, when so many E I 1 11 39
an amazing match, was proved to have much the worst of the E I 2 16 4
at all, and when that proved vain, as earnestly tried to E I 2 19 14
He proved to me that he could afford it; and that being E I 8 59 27
effects on my side of the argument have yet proved wrong. E I 12 99 11
So it proved;--for when happily released from Mr. Elton, E I 14 119 6
7
they meant to marry till it were proved against them. E II 5 193 35
Mr. John Knightley proved more talkative than his brother. E II 18 311 37
His dancing proved to be just what she had believed it, E III 2 328 41
no fortune, might be proved to have made Harriet's.-- E III 4 340 28
Jane's alertness in moving, proved her as ready as her E III 5 349 25
She was proved to have been universally mistaken; and she E III 11 413 47
of her daughter--who proved even too joyous to talk as E III 12 418 5
approaching winter, had proved erroneous; no friends had E III 12 422 19
"But it is proved by the smallness of the school, which I E III 16 456 32
She proved to be the daughter of a tradesman, rich enough E III 19 481 3
This meeting of the two parties proved highly satisfactory, P III 5 32 2
of the house; but it proved to be one much less calculated P III 9 79 25
was just coming up, and proved to be Admiral Croft's gig.-- P III 10 90 38
It was now proved that he belonged to the same inn as P III 12 104 7
short as it was, also proved again by the gentleman's P III 12 104 7
ladies, for it proved twice as fine as the first report. P III 12 111 49
but her illness had proved to her that her landlady had a P IV 5 154 9
admirably, has really proved an invaluable acquaintance.-- P IV 5 155 9
bitterness of Mrs. Smith, proved him to have been very P IV 9 208 94
gallant a line as ever, & proved that he had not been S 10 416 1
I dare say it would be proved to be the simplest thing in S 10 418 1
baronet, remained to be proved, but as to the animals, she S 11 422 1
And so it proved.-- S 12 425 1

PROVERB (3)

and her mother with a proverb; they were not in the habit NA I 9 65 31
handed down to posterity with all the eclat of a proverb." PP I 18 91 15
I was quite a proverb for it at Maple Grove. E II 14 274 30

PROVERBIAL (1)

The listener's proverbial fate was not absolutely hers; P III 10 89 34

PROVERBIALLY (1)

A most insalubrious air--roads proverbially detestable-- S 1 369 1

PROVERBS (1)

Songs and proverbs, all talk of woman's fickleness. P IV 11 234 27

PROVES (3)

It proves him unspoilt by his uncle. MP III 4 350 30
It proves him, in short, every thing that I had been used MP III 4 350 30
This proves that he can leave the Churchills." E I 18 146 12

PROVIDE (15)

In marriage, the man is supposed to provide for the NA I 10 77 35
sides, "his mother must provide for him sometime or other; SS I 22 133 46
but my father cannot provide for us, & it is very bad to W 317 2
He meant to provide for me amply, and thought he had done PP I 16 79 25
whom his father had promised to provide for.-- PP I 17 85 4
would be his profession, intended to provide for him in it. PP II 12 200 5
I had no other person to provide for, and I could not have PP II 12 201 5
Had there been a family to provide for, Mrs. Norris might MP I 1 8 9
them, would enable him better to provide for Fanny himself. MP I 3 30 57
We will provide ourselves with tablets and a pencil. MP II 5 227 65
who have brought him up, and are to provide for him!-- E I 18 147 17
To provide for her otherwise was out of Colonel Campbell's E II 2 164 5
else you may like to provide, it is to be all out of doors- E III 6 355 20
You provide for the family, you know, (with a smile at his E III 7 373 46
But they have a great many to provide for; and among the P III 8 65 11

PROVIDED (44)

Catherine will be amply provided for, & not like my LS 20 277 5
of information--for, provided that nothing like useful NA I 1 15 3
be gained from them, provided they were all story and no NA I 1 15 3
chaperon was provided with a dress of the newest fashion. NA I 2 20 8
her, it was agreed that, provided the weather were fair, NA I 13 97 1
solely on this living, he would not be ill provided for. NA II 7 176 15
Catherine might not be provided with money enough for the NA II 13 229 31
young man, was amply provided for by the fortune of his SS I 1 3 2
his wife that she was provided with an house, and should SS I 5 25 1
whom they were speedily provided from amongst those who SS I 5 26 5
arranged by her husband, provided every thing were SS I 11 55 6
For my part, I think they are vastly agreeable, provided SS I 21 123 28
They came from Exeter, well provided with admiration for SS I 21 124 33
for Edward, was already provided to enable him to marry;-- SS III 3 283 20
herself--& Charles being provided with his gloves & W 331 11
He might have provided decently for his widow, without W 352 26
but as he was now provided with a good house and the PP I 4 15 12
absence on a Sunday, provided that some other clergyman is PP I 13 63 12
as soon as he could, provided he chose with discretion; PP I 14 66 1
rank in the kingdom--provided that a proper humility of PP I 18 97 60
61
if we were at York, provided she can have her own way.-- PP I 20 113 28
Mrs. Bennet had so carefully provided for the PP II 2 142 18
and younger children would by that means be provided for. PP III 8 308 3
up must be adequately provided for, or there would be MP I 1 6 5
They are sure of being well provided for. MP I 3 30 53
Matrimony was her object, provided she could marry well, MP I 4 42 18
A young party is always provided with a shady lane. MP I 7 70 30
named, and agreed to, provided Mr. Crawford should be MP I 8 75 1

which Miss Crawford was provided, and such the object of MP II 8 258 15
wish to displace him--provided he does not try to displace MP III 11 412 20
provided it be only mercenary and ambitious enough. MP III 13 421 2
poor dear Sister Price to have them so well provided for. MP III 13 428 15
aunt Norris; and was so provided with happiness, so strong MP III 16 448 3
be agreeable to them, provided at least they have common E I 9 75 27
wish to prevent it, provided the weather be what it ought, E II 7 209 10
She had provided a plentiful dinner for them; she wished E II 8 213 6
Mrs. Weston sees no objection to it, provided you are E II 11 250 23
full two months longer, provided at least she were able to E III 5 343 1
and extremely well provided for, should have no thought of P III 1 5 8
cards with which she had provided herself, the "Miss P IV 10 226 64
inheritance, quite as well provided for as himself.-- S 2 371 1
the tray,--which seemed provided with almost as many S 10 416 1
the intermediate friend, provided her with this letter, S 10 419 1
for their releif, provided it meet with her approbation.--" S 12 423 1

PROVIDENCE (4)
merciful appointment of Providence that the heart which MP III 16 455 23
which seems to insult exertion and distrust Providence!-- P III 4 30 9
be the arrangement of Providence, that you should not be P III 12 106 17
the situation in which Providence had placed him, and who P IV 12 248 1

PROVIDING (11)
such a point of your providing nothing extraordinary:-- NA II 11 211 13
to himself no power of providing for those who were most SS I 1 4 3
The event has proved, that I was a cunning fool, providing SS III 8 321 34
to herself the power & the pleasure of providing for me."-- W 352 26
"But unluckily she has left the pleasure of providing for W 352 26
to Margaret which she was assiduous in providing him.-- W 356 28
a voluntary promise of providing for me, I am convinced PP I 16 81 37
one could by way of providing for a child one had in a MP I 1 6 6
It is, in fact, the only sure way of providing against the MP I 1 6 6
at first allow, and providing her with dry clothes; and MP II 4 206 3
Henry Crawford, to be providing for himself no small MP III 17 468 22

PROVINCE (2)
It has been so many years my province to give advice, that E I 5 40 24
Nursing does not belong to a man, it is not his province. P III 7 56 11

PROVING (15)
of feelings, which, in proving of what importance she was PP III 16 366 8
only afforded more frequent opportunities of proving them. MP I 2 21 34
at Mansfield, and on proving to be a hearty man of forty- MP I 3 24 5
himself useful, and proving his good-nature by any one? MP I 7 67 16
chair of the latter, who proving, however, to be close at MP I 12 119 22
entering the family, proving incompetent to suggest any MP I 16 150 1
such an opportunity of proving his regard for Admiral MP II 13 298 3
again his affection, proving, as far as words could prove MP III 2 328 6
I must hope, however, that time proving him (as I firmly MP III 4 348 21
that Miss Crawford, after proving herself cooled and MP III 12 417 4
The only way of proving it, however, will be to turn to E I 12 107 61
It was dreadfully mortifying; but Mr. Elton was proving E I 16 135 6
welcome piece of news, as proving that Mr. Elton could not E II 3 177 51
I can, satisfied with proving myself your friend by very E III 7 375 61
P.'s sprain proving too serious for him to move sooner.-- S 2 370 1

PROVISION (15)
and who most needed a provision, by any charge on the SS I 1 4 3
provision than 7000l. would support her in affluence. SS I 3 14 2
to be of the party, by way of provision for discourse. SS I 6 31 9
for the sake of the provision and security of a wife. SS I 8 38 10
was the only honourable provision for well-educated young PP I 22 122 3
sum, for the better provision of his children, and of his PP III 8 308 1
may arise, the provision of a gentlewoman, if no such MP I 1 7 7
of her support, and the obligation of her future provision. MP I 3 24 7
there was such a provision for me, probably did bias me. MP I 11 109 17
do it in the most complete uncertainty of any provision." MP I 11 109 20
and with such a secret provision of comfort within his own MP III 3 334 3
secure of a comfortable provision, and therefore cannot E I 1 11 38
provision at all, and certainly no respectable relations. E I 8 61 38
present, the only mental provision she was making for the E I 9 69 3
Miss Denham had a very small provision--& her brother was S 3 377 1

PROVISIONS (4)
amusement; cold provisions were to be taken, open SS I 12 62 28
prison with a basket of provisions; you will not refuse to MP I 14 135 17
in with a basket of provisions--though one might have MP I 14 136 18
to raise the price of provisions & make the poor good for S 1 368 1

PROVISO (1)
This was readily agreed to, with only a proviso of Miss NA I 10 80 61

PROVOCATION (7)
proceeded form no justifiable cause, & had no provocation. LS 17 271 7
that Marianne was not present, to share the provocation. SS II 11 226 40
was calm, not open to provocation, and he never wished to SS III 1 267 44
by no means without provocation, she feared the MP III 8 391 9
Former provocation re-appeared E II 2 168 15
Emma could not forgive her;--but as neither provocation E II 3 170 1
was a perpetual provocation to her there; and vexed her as P IV 4 146 5

PROVOCATIONS (1)
But I have other provocations. PP II 11 190 10

PROVOKE (13)
or any misfortune could provoke such ill-will against a NA II 13 226 25
could not shame, and seemed hardly to provoke them. SS I 11 54 3
to this, lest they might provoke each other to an SS II 2 150 35
But can we wonder that with such a husband to provoke SS II 9 206 24
of their future ennui, to provoke him to make that offer, SS III 3 280 9
She often tried to provoke Darcy into disliking her guest, PP I 10 52 54
only serve, after what had since passed, to provoke her. PP II 18 233 25
of the young couple, indeed, was enough to provoke him. PP III 9 315 4
for her sister's sake, to provoke him, she only said in PP III 10 329 33
34
in Bingley, that could provoke his ridicule, or disgust PP III 13 346 21
and not meant to provoke; and therefore she let it pass. E II 7 206 4
"but she does sometimes provoke me excessively, by her P III 10 88 28
of manners as might provoke a remonstrance on his side. P IV 10 214 11

PROVOKED (16)
I am indeed provoked at the artifice of this unprincipled LS 8 255 1
Never my dearest Alicia, was I so provoked in my life as LS 16 268 1
I am excessively provoked however at the parade of LS 19 274 2
At length he left me, as deeply provoked as myself, & he LS 22 282 7
Why he had done it, what could have provoked him to such a NA II 14 234 10
principally meant by it, provoked her immediately to say SS II 12 235 34
35
I am not conscious of having provoked the disappointment SS III 1 263 27
to Mr. Bingley, whose blind partiality provoked her. PP I 18 89 3
I was sometimes quite provoked, but then I recollected my PP III 10 325 2
distressed himself, or provoked his dear sister Elizabeth, PP III 11 330 1
Sir Thomas could not be provoked. MP II 1 180 11
Susan should have been provoked into disrespect and MP III 9 397 8
I could not help being provoked; for after all my pains, E I 6 45 21
she was too much provoked and and offended to have the E I 15 125 6
I doubted it more the next day on Box-Hill; when, provoked E III 14 441 8
The part which provoked her most, was that in all this P IV 7 179 31

PROVOKING (17)
The event of all this is very provoking. LS 2 245 1
How provoking it is my dear Catherine, that this unwelcome LS 13 263 1
This eclaircissement is rather provoking. LS 33 303 1
How very provoking! NA I 2 22 19
It was certainly very provoking. NA II 7 177 18
again and again how provoking it was to be so disappointed. SS I 13 66 52
"My dear," said he to his lady, "it is very provoking that SS I 20 111 19
"It is indeed for Mrs. Jennings; how provoking!" SS II 5 169 20
him, which immediately provoking Elizabeth to do it, she PP I 6 24 17
18
impolitic too--for it is provoking me to retaliate, and PP II 8 174 15
not let me smile, and are provoking me to it every moment." PP III 12 343 33
had taken in the affair, was provoking him exceedingly. E I 8 66 55
were sometimes provoking him to a rational remonstrance or E I 11 93 5
It was most provoking. E I 16 136 8
"And now we shall just miss them; too provoking!-- E II 5 187 6
vexation Mr. Knightley's provoking indifference about it. E II 12 257 2
"Only think! well, that must be infinitely provoking! E II 18 310 34

PROXY (3)
"what! always to be watched, in person or by proxy!" NA II 3 147 21
very shoe-roses for Netherfield were got by proxy. PP I 17 88 15
no proxy can be capable of satisfying to the same extent. MP II 7 247 42

PRUDENCE (26)
& general resolutions of prudence were sufficient to LS 3 247 1
Her prudence & economy are exemplary, her regard for Mr LS 14 265 5
opinion of Miss Thorpe's prudence, to suppose that she NA II 10 206 31
and ease, and suited the prudence of her eldest daughter, SS I 3 14 1
it from motives of prudence, for, except a trifling sum, SS I 3 15 5
common care, common prudence, were all sunk in Mrs. SS I 16 85 10
do, and on your prudence I have the strongest dependence. SS II 5 173 44
Few people of common prudence will do that; and whatever SS II 11 227 44
urge him to it for prudence sake, and would have parted SS III 2 277 30
concluding that prudence required dispatch, and that her SS III 8 317 7
that nothing else in common prudence remained for me to do. SS III 8 323 40
me, that selfishness is prudence, and insensibility of PP II 1 135 13
lurking behind, of which prudence forbad the disclosure. PP II 17 227 25
knew that she had not prudence enough to hold her tongue PP III 5 288 40
"Because honour, decorum, prudence, nay, interest, forbid PP III 14 355 45
was begun as a matter of prudence, soon grew into a matter MP I 1 8 9
No cold prudence for me. MP II 7 243 25
nothing on the side of prudence to stop him or make his MP III 17 471 28
that a reasonable prudence might originally suggest; and E I 8 67 57
of prudence, she was very sure did not belong to Mr. Elton. E I 8 67 57
be no more than common prudence to stay at home and take E I 13 110 9
have him, that vanity and prudence were equally contented. E II 4 181 4
"I am not speaking of its prudence; merely its probability. E II 8 224 71
She had been forced into prudence in her youth, she P III 4 30 9
What prudence had at first enjoined, was now rendered S 2 374 1
to his purse, & prudence obliged him to prefer the S 8 405 2

PRUDENT (21)
prudent advice of your parents has not been given in vain. LS 37 306 1
amiable, interesting: she was every thing but prudent. SS I 1 6 12
Elinor had always thought it would be more prudent for SS I 4 24 21
now, for he is a very prudent man, and to be sure must SS I 14 70 2
him too well to be so prudent as I ought to have been.-- SS I 22 130 28
"And what," said Mrs. Dashwood, "is my dear prudent Elinor SS II 3 156 11
she thought it most prudent and kind, after some SS II 5 174 45
be calm, could be even prudent, when the life of a child SS III 9 334 5
Mrs. Dashwood was prudent enough to remain at the cottage, SS III 14 380 20
respectability, and Charlotte's prudent, steady character. PP II 1 135 12
affairs, between the mercenary and the prudent motive? PP II 4 153 9
a character to preserve, they will both be more prudent. PP III 8 313 19
Her prudent mother, occupied by the same ideas, forbore to PP III 12 340 11
It was more pleasant than prudent. MP II 5 226 59
desire rather more unguardedly than was perfectly prudent. MP III 4 350 30
such obscurity--and most prudent men would be afraid of E I 8 64 47
Miss Fairfax; but it was most prudent to avoid speech. E II 8 220 48
Emma thought it most prudent to go with her. E II 9 233 23
The belief of being prudent, and self-denying principally P III 4 28 5
think, it would be more prudent to let me get you a chair." P IV 7 177 14
he had become a prudent man) and beginning to be rich, P IV 9 209 95

PRUDENTIAL (1)
She seems perfectly happy, however, and in a prudential PP II 9 178 15

PRUDENTLY (3)
much there might prudently be in his power to do for them. SS I 1 5 6
if he marry prudently, his wife may teach him. PP III 10 325 2
by her own account as prudently as possible, to defy the S 3 378 1

PRUDISH (1)
Is she prudish? MP II 6 230 7

PRY (1)
"I do not want to pry into other men's concerns. SS I 13 65 39

PSEUDO-PHILOSOPHY (2)
It were Hyper-criticism, it were Pseudo-philosophy to S 7 398 1
T'were Pseudo-philosophy to assert that we do not feel S 8 404 1

PSHA (2)
"Psha! my dear creature," she replied, "do not think me NA II 3 143 2
"Psha, nonsense!" was Isabella's answer in the same half NA II 3 147 22

PUBLIC (73)
a young lady into public, being as fond of going every NA I 2 20 8
and perfectly satisfied with her share of public attention. NA I 2 24 28
"Upon my honour," said James, "in these public assemblies, NA I 8 57 22
Now and then it is very well; but going to inns and public NA I 13 104 31
on to quit this scene of public triumph and oblige your NA II 2 139 7
But when Catherine saw her in public, admitting Captain NA II 4 149 1
have no more talents than inclination for a public life!" SS I 17 90 3
if Mrs. Dashwood should not like to go into public." SS I 20 110 4
will almost always appear in public with Lady Middleton." SS II 3 156 13
in it, make it unfit to become the public conversation. SS II 8 196 19
notice of it from the public papers, which she saw her SS II 10 217 16
from the advantage of a public school, was as well fitted SS II 14 250 12
of the advantage of a public school, she could not think SS II 14 251 14
But though confidence between them was, by this public SS III 2 270 1
to stay at home, than venture into so public a place. SS III 2 271 4
his engagement became public, and therefore not since his SS III 4 288 26
a more warm, though less public, assurance, from John to SS III 6 301 1
up, was to make her first public appearance in the W 315 1
village was on no very public road, & contained no W 354 28
last current report as to public news, & the general W 356 28
be able to impose on the public in such a case; but it is PP I 6 21 2
country for my part, except the shops and public places. PP I 9 43 21
affection had brought her into public at an early age. PP I 9 45 36
would have much to suffer when the affair became public. PP I 17 86 8
that private balls are much pleasanter than public ones.-- PP I 18 91 11
feelings prevented any public exposure, but I wrote to Mr. PP II 12 202 5
has not authorised me to make his communication public. PP II 17 226 23
To have his errors made public might ruin him for ever. PP II 17 227 24
exposed herself in some public place or other, and we can PP II 18 230 14
15
which must arise from the public notice of Lydia's PP II 18 231 16
much too full of lines under the words to be made public. PP II 19 238 5
to make our knowledge public; for of what use could it PP III 5 285 16
Lady Bertram did not go into public with her daughters. MP I 4 35 5
before they appear in public than afterwards." MP I 5 50 38
There certainly is impropriety in making them public." MP I 7 63 7
And with regard to their influencing public manners, Miss MP I 9 93 49
I always come to you to know what I am to think of public MP I 12 119 22
from her cousin Tom, so public and so persevered in, and MP I 16 150 1
After all his objections--objections so just and so public! MP I 16 156 28
create jealousy, and bring a public disturbance at last. MP I 17 163 19
and long standing and public as was the engagement, her MP II 3 200 20
Every public place was new to Maria, and Brighton is MP II 3 203 31
Such a match as Miss Bertram has made is a public blessing, MP II 4 210 21
whom one could not (in his public capacity) honour enough. MP III 3 341 28
in spite of all the too public opposition she foresaw to MP III 3 344 42
of whom was clerk in a public office in London, and the MP III 7 381 26
It was her public place; there she met her acquaintance, MP III 11 408 4
indeed a matter of certified guilt and public exposure. MP III 15 441 21
Two posts came in, and brought no refutation, public or MP III 15 442 22
Every thing was by that time public beyond a hope. MP III 16 450 10
That punishment, the public punishment of disgrace, should MP III 17 468 22
for having much of the public favour; and she had no E I 3 21 4
public eye, but perhaps you may not dislike looking at it." E I 9 71 11
which makes celibacy contemptible to a generous public! E I 10 85 19
Before she had committed herself by any public profession E II 2 168 15
I assure you the utmost stretch of public fame would not E II 6 200 16

would be the very person for you to go into public with." E II 14 275 32
her going into public under the auspices of a friend of E II 14 275 33
The public pays and must be served well." E II 16 297 43
and spread abroad what public news he had heard, was E II 17 303 24
public enough for safety, had led them into alarm.-- E III 3 333 5
looks, which I did not believe meant to be public." E III 5 350 36
upon an acquaintance formed only in a public place!-- E III 7 372 40
that Bath, or any public place, can give--it is all E III 7 372 40
needs no apology to the public, which is rather apt to be P III 1 5 8
in his making a bold public declaration, when he came in P III 7 55 7
variety which Lyme, as a public place, might offer; the P III 11 95 9
knowing her but in public, and when very young himself. P IV 3 140 11
defying public opinion in any point of worldly decorum. P IV 4 146 6
heat and animation of a public room was necessary to P IV 10 214 12
obliging compliance for public view; and smiles reined in P IV 11 240 59
blush for in the public manners of her father and sister. P IV 11 246 78
here, or even a Co--since Sanditon had been a public place. S 7 401 1

PUBLICATION (3)
part of that voluminous publication, of which either the NA I 5 38 4
dreadful than a new publication which is shortly to come NA I 14 113 39
engagement; for the publication of that circumstance, he SS III 14 373 3

PUBLICATIONS (2)
gets all the new publications, and has a very large P IV 4 146 5
Lady Russell quite bores one with her new publications. P IV 10 215 15

PUBLICITY (4)
We want no audience, no publicity. MP I 13 125 18
But if I can be the means of restraining the publicity of MP I 16 155 16
too precious an offering for any degree of publicity. E I 9 77 43
as of such general publicity and pervading interest; yet, P III 6 42 1

PUBLICLY (4)
He deserves to be publicly disgraced." PP I 16 80 28
openly acknowledged and publicly canvassed; and every body PP II 1 138 30
It will then be publicly seen, that on both sides, we meet PP III 12 339 6
taking the young man so publicly by the hand: "for they P III 1 8 16

PUBLISH (2)
for he was longing to publish his prosperous love. PP I 22 123 3
which his servants take care to publish where he goes. P III 12 106 16

PUBLISHES (1)
the man who collects and publishes in a volume some dozen NA I 5 37 4

PUBLISHING (1)
a white surplice, and publishing the banns of marriage SS III 5 298 33

PUCE-COLOURED (1)
evening, and wore her puce-coloured sarsenet; and she NA I 15 118 13

PUDDING (1)
roast mutton and rice pudding they were hastening home for. E I 13 109 6

PUDDINGS (1)
She was so little equal to Rebecca's puddings, and MP III 11 413 30

PUDDLE (1)
Frank knows a puddle of water when he sees it, and as to E II 5 195 48

PUDDLES (1)
stiles and springing over puddles with impatient activity, PP I 7 32 41

PUERILE (1)
You will never hear me advocating those puerile Emanations S 8 403 1

PUFF (1)
You will puff her up with such ideas of her own beauty, E I 8 64 47

PUFFED (2)
My feelings are not puffed about with every attempt to PP I 11 58 28
& built, & praised & puffed, & raised it to a something of S 2 371 1

PUG (7)
"I hope she will not tease my poor pug," said Lady Bertram; MP I 1 10 16
the sofa with herself and pug, and vain was even the sight MP I 2 13 4
thinking more of her pug than her children, but very MP I 2 19 31
Sitting and calling to pug, and trying to keep him from MP I 7 74 56
ladies, and the barking of pug in his mistress's arms. MP I 8 80 30
to put away her work, move pug from her side, and give all MP II 1 179 9
next time pug has a litter you shall have a puppy." MP III 2 333 28

PULL (3)
them, made his friend pull up, to know what was the matter. NA I 11 88 54
enough, I would instantly pull Combe down, and build it up SS I 14 72 11
I shall pull it to pieces as soon as I get home, and see PP II 16 219 3

PULLED (4)
to Catherine's dissatisfaction, pulled his brother away. NA II 1 132 16
of their entering, pulled the bell with violence, ordered " NA II 6 165 5
after dinner, who pulled her about, tore her clothes, and SS I 7 34 7
She saw their sashes untied, their hair pulled about their SS I 21 120 6

PULLING (4)
pulling him in to that cursed broken-winded jade's pace. NA I 11 88 56
the carpenter to work in pulling down what had been so MP II 2 190 9
without restraint, and pulling every thing about as she MP III 10 407 23
plaister that Frank Churchill had been pulling about!-- E III 4 339 15

PULMONARY (1)
nothing touching the pulmonary complaint, which was the E III 9 389 16

PULPIT (4)
I own, I do not like much action in the pulpit--I do not W 343 20
and cushions of the pulpit and family-seat were only MP I 9 86 9
One scarcely sees a clergyman out of his pulpit." MP I 9 93 46
There is something in the eloquence of the pulpit, when it MP III 3 341 28

PULSE (6)
flushed cheek, hollow eye, and quick pulse of a fever?" SS I 8 38 13
Her pulse was much stronger, and every symptom more SS III 7 310 8
and while attempting to sooth her, eagerly felt her pulse. SS III 7 311 14
amendment in her sister's pulse;--she waited, watched, and SS III 7 314 22
about her, a quick low pulse, &c. and she was sorry to E I 13 109 6
of the pulse being quickened again by injurious courtesy. E III 3 332 1

PULSES (1)
felt all over her, in all her pulses, and all her nerves. MP III 5 357 5

PULTENEY-STREET (15)
soon settled in comfortable lodgings in Pulteney-Street. NA I 2 19 6
till they reached Pulteney-Street, where he was welcomed NA I 7 51 54
Pulteney-Street reached the Upper-Rooms in very good time. NA I 8 52 1
This, on arriving on Pulteney-Street, took the direction NA I 9 60 1
till they stopped in Pulteney-Street again, induced her, NA I 9 66 32
to call for her in Pulteney-Street--and "remember--twelve NA I 10 80 61
They passed briskly down Pulteney-Street, and through NA I 11 86 51
We have been exactly an hour coming from Pulteney-Street, NA I 11 88 54
to Pulteney-Street without her speaking twenty words. NA I 11 89 61
proceeded gaily to Pulteney-Street; walking, as she NA I 13 103 29
Pulteney-Street, and obtained their sanction of his wishes. NA II 2 140 9
Edgar's Buildings or Pulteney-Street, her change of NA II 4 149 1
Catherine's stay in Pulteney-Street, and nothing passed NA II 4 153 31
almost have wished to return with him to Pulteney-Street. NA II 5 154 1
in returning down Pulteney-Street, she distinguished him P IV 7 178 28

PUMP-ROOM (24)
to be looked at; and the Pump-Room to be attended, where NA I 3 25 1
Catherine hastened to the Pump-Room the next day, secure NA I 4 31 1
a dozen turns in the Pump-Room, but required, when they NA I 4 34 7
Mr. Tilney was no fonder of the play than the Pump-Room. NA I 5 35 1
long enough in the Pump-Room to discover that the crowd NA I 5 35 2
His name was not in the Pump-Room book, and curiosity NA I 5 35 2
the two friends in the Pump-Room one morning, after an NA I 6 39 1
uneasy, as the gentlemen had just left the Pump-Room. NA I 6 43 36
to seek her for that purpose, in the Pump-Room at noon. NA I 9 60 1
In the Pump-Room, one so newly arrived in Bath must be met NA I 9 60 1
"Yes, I went to the Pump-Room as soon as you were gone, NA I 9 68 38
moment of going to the Pump-Room, she felt some alarm from NA I 10 71 8
off in good time for the Pump-Room, where the ordinary NA I 10 71 8
"He never comes to the Pump-Room, I suppose?" NA I 10 73 17
There will be very few people in the Pump-Room, if it NA I 11 83 13
her husband to the Pump-Room; he accordingly set off by NA I 11 84 17
than ever to be at the Pump-Room, that she might inform NA I 12 91 3
walked down to the Pump-Room, tasted the water, and laid NA I 15 116 1
as she walked along the Pump-Room one morning, by Mrs. NA II 3 143 1
to parade about the Pump-Room; and if she moved from her NA II 3 147 28
and walked out of the Pump-Room, leaving Isabella still NA II 3 147 28
to overhear in the Pump-Room, his behaviour was so NA II 4 149 1
He went into the Pump-Room afterwards; but I would not NA II 12 217 2
the Pump-Room, could not but have her moments of imagining. P IV 10 220 31

PUMP-YARD (2)
Half a minute conducted them through the Pump-Yard to the NA I 7 44 1
He turned back and walked with me to the Pump-Yard. P IV 10 228 71

PUN (2)
being contented with a pun, and her mother with a proverb; NA I 9 65 31
Now, do not be suspecting me of a pun, I entreat." MP I 6 60 49

PUNCH (1)
all have a bowl of punch, to make merry at her wedding." PP III 7 307 49

PUNCTUAL (9)
Why were not they more punctual? NA I 11 90 64
Mr. Harris was punctual in his second visit;--but he came SS III 7 313 21
Mr. Collins was punctual to his time, and was received PP I 13 64 21
Mr. Darcy was punctual in his return, and as Lydia PP III 10 325 2
Bingley was punctual to his appointment; and he and Mr. PP III 13 346 21
as good time as his own correctly punctual habits required. MP II 5 222 41
them, "and I shall be punctual, for there will be no kind MP II 10 280 31
Mr. Crawford had, as he foretold, been very punctual, and MP II 11 282 1
Every body was punctual, every body in their best looks. E I 1 11 35

PUNCTUALITY (5)
her that the strictest punctuality to the family hours NA II 5 162 27
stopped at the door, a punctuality not very agreeable to SS II 14 249 9
token of the coachman's punctuality, both Kitty and Lydia PP II 16 219 1
of their punctuality as sportsmen, were in very good time. PP III 12 340 11
and punctuality, were in favour of a pleasant party. E III 7 367 1

PUNCTUALLY (8)
Mr. Collins returned most punctually on the Monday PP I 23 129 15
Mrs. Gardiner's caution to Elizabeth was punctually and PP II 3 144 1
2
punctually repeated all his wife's offers of refreshment. PP II 5 155 3
forward at last most punctually with his eldest daughter E I 13 112 24
The quarter of an hour brought her punctually to the white E II 5 186 3
The day came, the party were punctually assembled, and Mr. E II 16 292 10
hour, and set off very punctually, it was so much past P III 11 95 8
She could not keep her appointment punctually, however; P IV 11 229 2

PUNCTURE (1)
Not a puncture, not a weak spot any where.-- P III 10 88 26

PUNISH (9)
whether I ought not to punish him, by dismissing him at LS 25 293 4
I must punish Frederica, & pretty severely too, for her LS 25 293 4
to Reginald; I must punish him for receiving it so LS 25 293 4
Leave Frederica therefore to punish herself for the plague LS 26 295 1
met by appointment, he to defend, I to punish his conduct. SS II 9 211 38
How shall we punish him for such a speech?" PP I 11 57 16
"We can all plague and punish one another. PP I 11 57 17
a least do not punish me so far, as to exclude me from p. PP III 10 325 2
I am not obliged to punish myself for *her* sins. MP I 10 101 32

PUNISHED (3)
But she *shall* be punished, she *shall* have him. LS 16 268 1
that I was sadly afraid your *brag* would be punished.-- W 343 19
She was properly punished. MP I 18 172 29

PUNISHMENT (22)
the severest punishment; & your resolution of quitting LS 25 292 3
and have suffered the punishment of an attachment, without SS III 1 264 29
forgave all his offences in compassion for his punishment. SS III 2 270 1
in leading him to evil, had led him likewise to punishment. SS III 8 331 70
has brought on herself a most appropriate punishment. SS III 13 366 18
without a pang; and his punishment was soon afterwards SS III 14 379 18
thus brought its own punishment, was sincere, need not be SS III 14 379 18
whom it would not be a punishment to me to stand up with." PP I 3 11 9
whom a ball would be rather a punishment than a pleasure." PP I 11 55 6
it would be the greater punishment to her partner to PP I 18 91 8
review of it; and as a punishment for him, as well as a PP II 3 149 27
and whose very name it was punishment to him to pronounce. PP III 10 326 3
carrying on there, some punishment to Maria for conduct so MP I 17 162 19
other's punishment, and then induce a voluntary separation. MP III 17 464 10
His punishment followed his conduct, as did a deeper MP III 17 464 12
as did a deeper punishment, the deeper guilt of his wife. MP III 17 464 12
supposed that their tempers became their mutual punishment. MP III 17 465 14
That punishment, the public punishment of disgrace, should MP III 17 468 22
this is a punishment beyond what you can have merited!-- E II 15 284 10
But after all the punishment that misconduct can bring, it E III 12 419 8
that she should have been in such a state of punishment." E III 15 446 20
to be placing her in such a state of unmerited punishment. E III 15 450 37

PUNY (2)
She spoke of her farther as somewhat delicate and puny, MP I 1 11 19
having fancied him a very puny, delicate-looking man, the S 10 413 1

PUPIL (3)
as a pupil; but he was almost always with us afterwards. SS I 22 130 28
made her a most attentive, profitable, thankful pupil. MP III 12 418 7
and Mrs. Weston's faithful pupil did not forget either at E II 5 189 19

PUPIL'S (1)
make his pupil's manners as unexceptionable as his own.-- W 335 13

PUPPIES (3)
of play with a litter of puppies just able to roll about, NA II 11 214 26
one of Folly's puppies! and this was the end of it!" SS II 10 215 9
You must know I have a vast dislike to puppies--quite a E III 2 321 15

PUPPY (5)
a large Newfoundland puppy and two or three terriers, was NA II 11 212 17
he reminded me of an old promise about a pointer puppy. SS III 8 330 69
next time pug has a litter you shall have a puppy." MP III 2 333 28
could not endure such a puppy when it came to the point." E I 18 150 32
An abominable puppy!-- E III 7 372 37

PUPPYISM (2)
features, and on the puppyism of his manner in deciding on SS II 11 221 4
truly the gentleman, without the least conceit or puppyism. E III 2 321 15

PURCHASE (22)
for, and that we often purchase them at a great NA II 11 210 7
dear Fanny; her life cannot be worth half that purchase." SS I 2 10 19
of any article of purchase, however it might equally SS II 4 165 24
And then I have made a little purchase within this half SS II 11 225 31
to purchase an estate, but did not live to do it.-- PP I 4 15 11
at Netherfield, and leave the next generation to purchase. PP I 4 15 12
concerto, was glad to purchase praise and gratitude by PP I 6 25 24
"But I would really advise you to make your purchase in PP I 8 38 35
possible to get Pemberley by purchase than by imitation." PP I 8 38 38
to give it up, as soon as any eligible purchase offers." PP II 9 178 10
that to be making such a purchase in his absence, and MP I 4 36 7
If not, you must purchase them. MP II 7 242 23
gold chain too, but the purchase had been beyond his means, MP II 8 254 8
the purchase necessary for the tranquillity of the house. MP III 9 397 7
to secure the purchase of a little estate adjoining E I 2 16 5
settling till he could purchase Randalls, and the sale of E I 2 16 6
be at all worth the purchase; and the whole of their drive E I 13 113 25
indulging himself in the purchase, hoping that some of our E II 8 216 16
always very long at a purchase; and while she was still E II 9 233 24
Mr. Suckling had completed the purchase before his death." E II 18 310 34
she could not afford to purchase the assistance of the law. P IV 9 210 98
There, with the hire of a harp for one, & the purchase of S 11 421 1

PURCHASE-MONEY (1)
with regard to the purchase-money, I might have been very SS II 11 225 33

PURCHASED (8)
dearly purchased by all that you have previously suffered. LS 23 283 1
But this was quite an old set, purchased two years ago. NA II 7 175 12
Importance may sometimes be purchased too dearly. PP II 3 150 29
of honour or credit could now be purchased for her. PP III 8 308 1
her own settled upon *her*, and his commission purchased. PP III 10 324 2
ornament which his money purchased three years ago, before MP II 8 259 20

ery glad to have purchased the mortification of having E II 8 219 44
ouse of Elliot, he had purchased independence by uniting P III 1 8 15
CHASES (6)
atherine too made some purchases herself, and when all NA I 2 20 8
s having likewise some purchases to make themselves; and SS II 4 164 23
bliged to make large purchases of linen, china, &c. to SS II 11 225 35
hen shewing her purchases: "look here, I have bought PP II 16 219 3
f Kitty's and Lydia's purchases, were seated in it. PP II 16 220 16
usy in some immediate purchases for the further good of S 6 390 1
CHASING (2)
ould have accrued to me from his purchasing vernon? LS 5 250 1
really must talk to him about purchasing a donkey. E III 6 356 26
E (10)
er friend's brother, so pure and uncoquettish were her NA I 7 47 18
ust and correct, and his taste delicate and pure. SS I 4 20 9
t ease, nor her satisfaction in their amusements so pure. SS I 11 54 6
inor feelings less pure, less pleasing, might have a SS III 3 283 20
im solely from the pure and disinterested desire of an PP I 22 122 2
really experienced that pure and elevating passion, I PP II 3 150 29
horsewoman; and to the pure genuine pleasure of the MP I 7 66 15
f the blessing of domestic happiness, and pure attachment. MP III 4 350 30
fine open sea, he says, and very pure air. E I 12 106 56
t was an impulse of pure, though unacknowledged P III 10 91 42
ELY (3)
y which she was almost purely governed, were rapidly MP I 15 147 56
I must suppose it to be purely for the pleasure of MP II 10 277 19
as not purely affectionate and disinterestedly anxious. MP III 13 427 12
ER (1)
ith a purer spirit did Fanny rejoice in the intelligence.- MP II 2 194 20
EST (2)
nd from the best, the purest of motives, might now be E II 2 168 13
haracters--the finest, purest sea breeze on the coast-- S 1 369 1
IFICATION (1)
t was almost enough to spread purification and perfume P IV 9 192 3
ITY (7)
hile her heart is all purity, her actions all innocence, NA I 8 53 2
he purity of her life, the formality of her notions, her SS III 8 323 40
o suspect the truth and purity of her own scruples, and MP I 16 153 3
ot misled her; for the purity of her intentions she could MP III 1 324 58
ot spare him; and the purity of her principles added yet MP III 13 428 13
urity of her mind, and the excellence of her principles. MP III 17 468 21
hat one, since the purity of her heart is not to be E III 13 428 23
PLE (4)
r purple velvet, presenting even a funereal appearance. NA II 5 158 15
wear nothing but purple now: I know I look hideous in it, NA II 12 218 2
ere only purple cloth; but this is not quite certain. MP I 9 86 9
nd return it into the purple and gold ridicule by her E III 16 453 12 13
PORT (8)
he purport of it frightened her so thoroughly that with a LS 19 273 1
ou can hardly doubt the purport of my discourse, however PP I 19 105 8
he principal purport of his letter was to inform them, PP III 8 312 18
urport of the message than on any thing else. MP I 13 129 39
ut she remembered the purport of her note, and was not MP III 1 311 1
oming as he did from such a purport fulfilled as had MP III 3 334 2
his is what I said--the purport of it--but, as you may MP III 16 458 30
f you feel in doubt as to the purport of your answer. E I 7 52 13
POSE (126)
t would surely be much more to the purpose to get LS 26 295 1
er for two years, on purpose to secure him, was defrauded LS 42 313 10
ou spend;--I will give you this little book on purpose." NA I 2 18 2
ood it is of you to come so far on purpose to see me." NA I 7 51 52
o seek her for that purpose, in the Pump-Room at noon. NA I 9 60 1
f he had sought her on purpose!--it did not appear to her NA I 10 75 24
ould not answer my purpose, it would not do for the field. NA I 10 76 28
ut to what purpose did she speak?-- NA I 11 87 53
ou were so kind as to look back on purpose." NA I 12 93 7
erson's courage that could sit down on purpose to do it." NA I 14 109 24
f all the rest, for the purpose of mere domestic economy; NA II 8 184 4
e more fitted for the purpose than that which yet bore NA II 8 188 17
orced to bend to one purpose by a mind which, before she NA II 10 199 2
he opened it; it was from Oxford; and to this purpose:-- " NA II 10 202 6 7
hat moment in his power to say any thing to the purpose. NA II 15 242 8
o give; but his first purpose was to explain himself, and NA II 15 243 9
ustained in his purpose by a conviction of its justice. NA II 15 247 15
ours before his usual time, on purpose to go to Whitwell." SS I 13 65 32
he shortness of his visit, the steadiness of his purpose SS I 19 102 2
ogether in one noisy purpose, immediately accepted the SS II 1 143 9
n writing to her mother, and sat down for that purpose. SS II 4 160 4
ame to town with me on purpose to buy wedding clothes? SS II 7 182 10
or years, and for the purpose had procured my exchange. SS II 9 206 24
o me the other day on purpose to ask my advice, and laid SS II 14 251 17
hursday and Friday, on purpose to get the better of it. SS III 2 273 16
ehind a chimney-board, on purpose to hear what we said." SS III 2 274 20
ven changed her seat, on purpose that she might not hear, SS III 3 281 9
as coming to you on purpose to inquire farther about it." SS III 5 294 8
eproachfully; "a note would have answered every purpose.-- SS III 8 324 41
iss Dashwood?--or have I said all this to no purpose?-- SS III 8 329 65
as free: and to what purpose that freedom would be SS III 13 361 1
ffence would serve no other purpose than to enrich Fanny. SS III 13 369 33
ff to be married, on purpose we suppose to make a shew SS III 13 370 37
im & given up a great deal of time to no purpose as yet.-- W 317 2
ith Robert and Jane on purpose to egg him on, by her W 319 2
That is nothing to the purpose.-- retorted the lady W 325 4
f a bedchamber, apparently on purpose to see them go by.-- W 327 7
no thought a comprehensive answer, most to the purpose.-- W 350 24
My overhearings were more to the purpose than yours, PP I 5 19 9
t all shake her purpose by his attempt at persuasion. PP I 6 26 40
aid Elizabeth, "my mother's purpose will be answered." PP I 7 31 27
t. steady to his purpose, he scarcely spoke ten words to PP I 12 60 4
e was then, he said, on his way to Longbourn on purpose PP I 15 72 8
n purpose to pass for a lady,--only think what fun! PP II 16 221 17
hey may be there, though for the purpose of concealment, PP III 5 282 7
urpose of concealment, for no more exceptionable purpose. PP III 5 282 7
nd went out myself on purpose to know the truth of it; PP III 11 331 15
he was going to the butcher's, she told me, on purpose to PP III 11 331 15
reakfast room for that purpose soon after tea; for as the PP III 13 346 21
ith her father had been short and to the purpose. PP III 13 347 30
f carrying my purpose; nor will I be dissuaded from it. PP III 14 355 48
hough Elizabeth would not, for the mere purpose of PP III 14 356 55 56
osings, for the sole purpose of breaking off her supposed PP III 15 360 1
Something very much to the purpose of course. PP III 15 362 14
ther struggles than what such a purpose must comprehend. PP III 16 370 33
My real purpose was to see you, and to judge, if I could, PP III 18 382 16
will send Nanny to London on purpose, and she may have a MP I 1 8 8
ertrams the next day on purpose to afford leisure for MP I 2 14 7
alculated for the purpose, and Fanny was then put in MP I 4 37 8
ery little purpose, as far as Mrs. Norris was concerned. MP I 4 38 9
ot saying much to the purpose, could talk of nothing else. MP I 6 52 1
wn quiet mare for the purpose of her first attempts, as MP I 7 66 14
oom, fitted up for the purpose of devotion--with nothing MP I 9 85 6
nd for how confined a purpose, compared with the old MP I 9 86 7
whole family assembling regularly for the purpose of MP I 9 86 12
he longed to be able to say something more to the purpose. MP I 10 102 37
urpose of her own feelings, if not of the conversation. MP I 11 111 27
t seems to join the billiard-room on purpose." MP I 13 125 14
aria felt her triumph, and pursued her purpose careless MP I 17 163 19
have made my way to you on purpose to entreat your help." MP I 18 168 15
nd your uncle say to see them used for such a purpose? MP I 18 169 21
o return for that purpose as soon as they could after MP I 18 171 25
disposition that was most favourable for the purpose. MP II 3 201 22
"That is not much to the purpose now; and as to my being MP II 4 214 45
walked down to the parsonage on purpose to bring her back. MP II 4 214 46
that could be said to any purpose, till Sir Thomas were MP II 5 217 11
I shall come on purpose to encourage a young beginner. MP II 5 227 65
the 22d herself, as by far the best day for the purpose. MP II 8 254 7
as more adapted for her purpose, she hoped in fixing on MP II 8 258 17
handsomer in its way, and for my purpose not half so fit. MP II 9 263 15
resolved to wear it--but it was too large for the purpose. MP II 9 271 40
to do, and as he returned to Mansfield on purpose to do. MP III 1 311 1
been very much to the purpose--was exceedingly happy to MP III 1 314 16
"I do not think you would answer the purpose at all." MP III 1 325 61
aware how much it concealed the sternness of her purpose. MP III 2 327 6
same purpose, to give them a knowledge of your character. MP III 4 354 46
William notes for the purpose, she was struck with the MP III 6 372 21
herself forced into a purpose of that kind, compelled into MP III 7 376 4
but no second sound had been heard of such a purpose. MP III 7 387 45
business, penned for the purpose of conveying necessary MP III 12 415 2
writing should answer the purpose of it, or that its MP III 17 467 20
of it, or that its purpose was unimportant--and staid. MP III 17 467 20
son into the parlour one night on purpose to sing to her. E I 4 28 6
"Perhaps you think I am come on purpose to quarrel with E I 5 36 5
vanity to a very good purpose, for she found her decidedly E I 6 42 1
his own civility, to leave Mr. Knightley for that purpose. E I 8 57 2
He came to the Abbey two evenings ago, on purpose to E I 8 59 27
He always speaks to the purpose; open, straight forward, E I 8 59 27
excellent charade indeed! and very much to the purpose. E I 9 72 15
"I never read one more to the purpose, certainly." E I 9 76 31
o'clock at night, on purpose to assure me that there was E I 11 95 19
have the power of directly saying any thing to the purpose. E I 15 125 6
his wife, fewer and quieter, but not less to the purpose. E II 5 188 8
away, and now the highest purpose for which it was ever E II 6 197 5
and lament that its original purpose should have ceased. E II 6 197 5
Good fires and carriages would be much more to the purpose E II 8 217 32
would deem it that James should put-to for such a purpose." E II 8 228 89
might be secured for the purpose; but it was at the other E II 11 254 44
"You will get nothing to the purpose from Miss Bates," E II 11 255 52
after themselves, for the purpose of taking her opinion as E III 2 319 2
together for the purpose of preparatory inspection. E III 2 319 3
Mrs. Weston, who seemed to have walked there on purpose to E III 6 357 33
I assure you: yes, indeed, on purpose to wait on you all." E III 16 456 23
that I should have had this hot walk to no purpose." E III 16 458 43
its being much to the purpose, that on quitting their box E III 18 472 20
"Nothing to the purpose," replied her brother. P III 8 69 38
and stopped for no other purpose than to say, that they P III 10 83 4
When people come in this manner on purpose to ask us, how P III 10 83 5
At first, they were capable of nothing more to the purpose P III 12 113 57 58
who got Anne near her on purpose to thank her most P IV 2 134 30
out on some obliging purpose of saving her sister trouble, P IV 10 215 14
particularly asked on purpose to meet Lady Dalrymple and P IV 10 223 43
family connexions--on purpose to be introduced to them? P IV 10 223 43
We were asked on purpose to be introduced. P IV 10 224 47
of overturning them on purpose (especially as the carriage S 1 364 1
She seemed placed with her on purpose to be ill-used. S 6 391 1
PURPOSED (1)
she was now very fully purposed to be the guest of neither MP II 12 295 24
PURPOSELY (17)
Twice did I leave them purposely together in the course of SS I 8 39 18
to Barton, whither he was purposely coming to visit them. SS I 16 86 22
You have perhaps been misinformed, or purposely deceived, SS II 7 188 42
seemed purposely made to humble her more, only amused her. SS II 12 232 16
"He comes from Mr. Pratt's purposely to see us. SS III 12 358 8
suspicion of his being purposely omitted for Mr. Darcy's PP I 18 89 1 2
It might seem as if she had purposely thrown herself in PP III 1 252 54
wishes, which may seem purposely to ask for your thanks. PP III 4 278 20
He had followed them purposely to town, he had taken on PP III 10 326 3
She then hastened away to her mother, who had purposely PP III 13 347 27
that I had known it, and purposely kept it from him. PP III 16 371 45
His absence had been extended beyond a fortnight purposely MP III 3 334 1
from Edmund, written purposely to give her a clearer idea MP III 14 429 1
latter, for some months purposely lengthened, ended very MP III 17 469 23
I purposely abstain from dates on this occasion, that MP III 17 470 26
seen them go by, and had purposely followed them; other E I 10 90 39
fair, and therefore purposely kept at a distance; but by E II 8 220 45
PURPOSES (5)
coquetry to subdue his judgement to her own purposes. LS 11 259 1
The purposes for which a few shapeless pantries and a NA II 8 184 4
now to all intents and purposes be considered as the SS III 5 297 29
temper; but for all the purposes of their acquaintance, he E II 11 250 19
pressing them to make use of his house for both purposes.-- S 1 367 1
PURSE (9)
but upon examining her purse, was convinced that but for NA II 13 229 31
perpetual demands upon his purse, which a man of any SS I 5 27 6
no otherwise than by netting a purse, or covering a skreen... PP I 8 39 46
kindness, her counsel and her patience, as from her purse. E I 10 86 24
money, and taking out her purse, gave them a shilling, and E III 3 334 6
her terror and her purse were too tempting, and she was E III 3 334 6
purse was open to him: I know that he often assisted him." P IV 9 199 55
was ill-suited to his purse, & prudence obliged him to S 8 405 2
on to undraw her purse, would as readily give 10Gs as 5.-- S 12 424 1
PURSES (3)
out some shillings in purses and spars; thence adjourned NA I 15 116 1
They all paint tables, cover skreens and net purses. PP I 8 39 45
"Aye--so I have heard--and because they have full purses, S 6 392 1
PURSUE (11)
was too intent on what he said, to pursue her employment.-- SS III 3 281 9
To be so bent on marriage--to pursue a man merely for the W 318 2
interest of her own to pursue, she turned her attention PP I 18 98 63
sleep, and pursue the usual course of their employments. PP II 18 229 1
privately in town than to pursue their first plan; and PP III 4 275 5
will not allow him to pursue any measure in the best and PP III 4 276 5
little would be gained by her attempting to pursue them. PP III 4 276 8
to pursue, while in town, for the recovery of his daughter. PP III 5 293 68
think it wiser to let him pursue his own way, and feel the MP II 2 191 10
She had resolution enough to pursue her own will in spite E I 2 15 3
that it was impossible to pursue the subject farther; and P IV 9 198 52
PURSUED (16)
when she was fortunately miss'd, pursued, & overtaken. LS 19 273 1
her, fearful of being pursued, yet determined to persevere. NA I 13 101 25
Margaret agreed, and they pursued their way against the SS I 9 41 6
The idea however started by her, was immediately pursued SS I 12 62 27
to her mother, she had pursued her own judgment rather SS III 7 310 8
The subject was pursued no farther, and the gentlemen soon PP II 7 171 12
It settled the matter; and they pursued the accustomed PP III 1 253 57
as any thing pursued by youth and zeal could hold out. MP I 14 130 2
Maria felt her triumph, and pursued her purpose careless MP I 17 163 19
pursued with "no, no, you must not part with the queen. MP II 7 244 28
the principal staircase, pursued by the ceaseless country- MP II 10 280 33
had no right to wonder at the line of conduct he pursued. MP III 2 331 17
to, pursued only by the sounds of her desultory good-will. E II 9 239 52
way--and never had she pursued it in more decided P III 2 16 16
to send for--the father pursued and informed--the mother P III 7 53 3
"And I do assure you, ma'am," pursued Mrs. Croft, "that P III 8 70 54
PURSUEING (1)
is busy in pursueing the plan of romance begun at Langford. LS 19 274 2
PURSUING (16)
yourself in Devonshire, pursuing fresh schemes, always gay, SS III 8 322 37
spirits; she therefore, pursuing the first subject, SS III 11 352 16 17
the cottage, and if not pursuing their usual studies with SS III 11 352 20

economical practices;-- pursuing her own interest in every SS III 12 357 3
Pursuing her way along the lane, she then began it. PP II 12 196 3
was eager in it, he meant to assist him in pursuing it. PP III 6 295 5
who was deliberately pursuing his way towards a small wood PP III 7 301 6
On pursuing the subject, he found that dear as all these MP I 2 15 12
and when Edmund, pursuing that idea, gave a hint of his MP I 17 158 2
And still pursuing the same cheerful thoughts, she soon MP III 2 333 28
Susan was only acting on the same truths, and pursuing the MP III 9 395 4
her thoughts from pursuing Edmund to London, whither, on MP III 9 398 10
effects of the shadows pursuing each other, on the ships MP III 11 409 6
woman, whom he had been pursuing with undoubted attachment, MP III 16 452 15
who was pursuing his triumph rather unfeelingly. E I 15 126 9
his the greatest zeal in pursuing it; for the lady was the E II 11 247 2

PURSUIT (24)

She arrived yesterday in pursuit of her husband; but LS 32 302 1
fast as they could walk, in pursuit of the two young men. NA I 6 43 44
to be, in danger from the pursuit of some one whom they NA I 10 74 23
"Here you are in pursuit only of amusement all day long." NA I 10 79 53
"But I do not want any such pursuit to get me out of doors. NA II 7 174 9
taste for your favourite pursuit which must be so SS I 4 22 17
a fond mother, though, in pursuit of praise for her SS I 21 120 6
feelings, in her pursuit of one object, was such a proof, SS II 3 155 6
yet had I then had any pursuit, any object to engage my SS III 13 362 5
was all in pursuit of Mr. Bingley, and under your orders." PP I 7 31 31
His present pursuit could not make him forget that PP II 4 151 3
half a day before they were in pursuit of the officers. PP II 16 223 25
morning with Elizabeth in pursuit of novelty and amusement. PP II 19 239 11
might suggest to be advisable for continuing their pursuit. PP III 6 298 13
drawn from the pursuit of accomplishments by Mrs. Bennet's PP III 19 386 5
enough for a determinate pursuit: and Fanny, though almost MP I 2 21 34
consolation in some pursuit, or some train of thought at MP I 16 151 2
steadily earnest in the pursuit of the blessing, and it MP III 17 471 28
and the only literary pursuit which engaged Harriet at E I 9 69 3
my friend Harriet--your pursuit of her, (pursuit, it E I 15 131 34
pursuit of her, (pursuit, it appeared,) gave me great E I 15 131 34
though in some points of pursuit or observation there was E II 6 197 3
suspect him of some double dealing in his pursuit of Emma. E III 5 343 2
far as man's determined pursuit of woman in defiance of S 8 404 1

PURSUITS (18)

and the ordinary pursuits which had given to Norland half SS I 9 40 1
What his pursuits, his talents and genius?" SS I 9 44 18
Whatever be his pursuits, his eagerness in them should SS I 9 45 28
be brought up to as many pursuits, employments, SS I 19 103 5
and more frivolous pursuits, had perhaps robbed her of SS II 1 140 2
of their mutual pursuits and cheerful society as the only SS III 10 343 8
her that her present pursuits are not to be the business PP II 18 231 18
and useful pursuits of all the young people as for her own. MP II 1 179 9
inclined to sedentary pursuits, or to information for MP III 12 418 7
any of the more homely pursuits in which his brothers were E I 2 15 1
The brothers talked of their own concerns and pursuits, E I 12 100 16
following their own pursuits, and living on their own P III 3 20 17
rationality, and elegance to his habits and pursuits. P III 6 43 5
and a decided taste for reading, and sedentary pursuits. P III 11 97 12
to former practices and pursuits, suggested suspicions not P IV 5 161 27
The gentlemen had their own pursuits, the ladies proceeded P IV 10 227 68
You have always a profession, pursuits, business of some P IV 11 232 19
divided between such pursuits as might attract admiration, S 11 421 1

PURVEY (1)

agreeable to the man; he is to purvey, and she is to smile. NA I 10 77 35

PURVIS LODGE (1)

from me; and as for Purvis Lodge, the attics are dreadful." PP III 8 310 8

PUSH (8)

Somebody gave me a push that has hurt it I am afraid." NA I 2 22 19
suppose;--and since you push me so hard, I must observe, MP I 11 111 28
I'll put you in and push you about; and you will do it MP I 15 146 50
She had made a sure push at Fanny's feelings here. MP III 5 364 27
the disposition that could push them to such length must MP III 8 391 9
probably have feared to push his experiment farther, lest MP III 11 413 30
of having made a push--of having thrown a die; and she E I 9 81 78
Once she contrived to push him away, but the boy had the P III 9 80 29

PUSHED (9)

Pushed back too, as if meant to be out of sight!-- NA II 6 163 2
fell on a roll of paper pushed back into the further part NA II 6 169 11
"And may I not, in my turn," said he, as he pushed back NA II 9 194 8
rushing out of the house, pushed the maid aside, and while MP III 7 377 7
by; but he rather pushed it towards me than towards you. E I 9 77 47
The word was discovered, and with a faint smile pushed E III 5 347 21
names were allowed," pushed away the letters with even an E III 5 349 23
of letters anxiously pushed towards her, and resolutely E III 5 349 25
had she closed it, with averted eyes, and pushed it away. P III 1 7 12

PUSHING (5)

There are his own two men pushing it back into its old MP II 5 222 46
talk--and yet so far from pushing, shewing so proper and E I 3 23 10
and pushing the paper towards Harriet--"it is for you. E I 9 71 12
13

Instead of pushing his fortune in the line marked out for P III 1 8 15
While Sir Walter and Elizabeth were assiduously pushing P IV 5 152 1

PUT (285)

which put one in good humour with oneself & all the world. LS 10 258 3
we left the two gentlemen together to put on our pelisses. LS 20 276 4
the rest, I shall probably put that project in execution-- LS 25 294 4
I shall probably put off his arrival, under some pretence LS 29 299 2
the best hand, her clothes put on with care, and both Mrs. NA I 2 20 8
They really put me quite out of countenance. NA I 6 43 33
her diffidence of herself put that out of her power; she NA I 9 64 27
now, for they were put by for her when her mother died." NA I 9 68 48
A good figure of a man; well put together.-- NA I 10 76 28
"that gentleman would have put me out of patience, had he NA I 10 76 29
world; and do not let us put it off--let us go to-morrow." NA I 10 80 61
I hope Mr. Allen will put on his great coat when he goes, NA I 11 83 13
he threw open the door--" put on your hat this moment-- NA I 11 84 18
We had much better put it off till another day, and turn NA I 11 88 54
"Go by all means, my dear; only put on a white gown; Miss NA I 12 91 2
to have it put off, made a point of her being denied. NA I 12 94 10
her, it would be nothing to put off a mere walk for one NA I 13 97 1
and must only beg to put off the walk till Tuesday." NA I 13 98 1
If they would only put off their scheme till Tuesday, NA I 13 99 4
If I had thought it right to put it off, I could have NA I 13 100 20
The speeches that are put into the heroes' mouths, their NA I 14 108 22
state of the nation, was put an end to by Catherine, who, NA I 14 111 29
Their conference was put an end to by the anxious young NA I 15 120 24
The entrance of her father put a stop to the civility, NA II 2 139 5
"Why do you put such things into my head? NA II 3 147 22
Catherine longed to give her a hint of it, to put her on NA II 3 148 28
His great coat, instead of being brought for him to put on NA II 5 155 4
"Miss Tilney, she was sure, would never put her into such NA II 5 160 23
How it came to be first put in this room I know not, but I NA II 6 165 4
to herself, and put on her bonnet in patient discontent. NA II 7 177 18
of an injured wife, before her room was put to rights. NA II 8 186 10
You are not to put yourself at all out of your way. NA II 11 210 6
Anne Mitchell had tried to put on a turban like mine, as I NA II 12 217 2
dignity was put to the trial--Eleanor brought no message. NA II 13 227 27
It is always good for young people to be put upon exerting NA II 14 234 12
of a few years could only put into Catherine's head what NA II 14 236 18
I put them on new the first time of our going to the Lower NA II 14 238 24
tore her clothes, and put an end to every kind of SS I 7 34 7
He put down his gun and ran to her assistance. SS I 9 42 8
John had been previously forming, were put in execution. SS I 11 53 1
a piece of white paper, and put it into his pocket-book." SS I 12 60 13
"It shall not be put off when we are so near it. SS I 13 64 25
"we might see whether it could be put off or not." SS I 13 64 27
and we must put off the party to Whitwell till you return." SS I 13 65 35
We will put it by, that when he comes again . . . . . SS I 16 85 12
They were obliged to put an end to such an expectation. SS I 20 110 3
and by changing the subject, put a stop to her entreaties. SS I 20 114 43
they were all cousins and must put up with one another. SS I 21 118 2
She put it into her hands as she spoke, and when Elinor SS I 22 132 26
Lucy, "has been pretty well put to the test, by our long, SS II 2 147 10
Lucy first put an end to it by saying in a lower tone, SS II 2 149 24
25
would be the wisest way to put an end to the business at SS II 2 149 29
30
advise you by all means to put an end to your engagement SS II 2 150 32
me, for I shan't put myself at all out of my way for you. SS II 3 153 2
I have no such scruples, and I am sure, I could put up SS II 3 156 14
put in possession of a very comfortable apartment. SS II 4 160 3
in joint affliction, she put all the letters into Elinor's SS II 7 182 12
as it might have been, before he chose to put an end to it. SS II 7 186 29
If we can but put Willoughby out of her head!" SS II 8 197 22
Elinor from her sister, he put an end to his visit, SS II 9 211 43
with us just now, she put bank-notes into Fanny's hands to SS II 11 224 28
was recovered enough to put an end to the bustle, and sit SS II 12 236 42
It was not Lucy's business to put herself forward, and the SS II 13 241 19
and conceit of the one, put her at all out of charity with SS II 14 250 12
Marianne's feelings had then broken in, and put an end to SS III 1 262 14
All that Mrs. Ferrars could say to make him put an end to SS III 1 266 38
Look, she made me this bow to my hat, and put in the SS III 2 272 12
the least mind for it, to put an end to the matter SS III 2 273 16
so I just run up stairs and put on a pair of silk SS III 2 274 16
his wish to put off so agreeable an office to another. SS III 3 283 20
I am sure it would put me quite out of patience!-- SS III 4 291 51
entrance of Mrs. John Dashwood put an end to the subject. SS III 5 300 38
myself most improperly to put off, from day to day, the SS III 8 321 34
copying such sentences as I was ashamed to put my name to. SS III 8 328 63
was forced to put them up, and could not even kiss them. SS III 8 329 63
may be the means-- it may put me on my guard--at least, it SS III 8 332 77
She shook her head, put the music aside, and after running SS III 10 342 7
It was put an end to by Mrs. Dashwood, who felt obliged to SS III 12 359 14
He put the letter into Elinor's hands. SS III 13 365 13
resentment against you, has put it in his power to make SS III 13 366 18
mrs edwards put on her very stiffest look at the sound.-- W 338 17
He was also obliged to put an end to his visit--for Mrs W 340 19
It put me out of patience.-- W 347 22
& stay till Christmas, if you don't put in your word."-- W 350 24
I hope I can put up with a small apartment for two or W 351 25
wait, said she, so I put on the first thing I met with.-- W 353 26
My dear Mr W.--(to her husband) you have not put any fresh W 353 26
To put an end to this altercation, & soften the evident W 353 26
We got here so late, that I had not time even to put a W 357 28
"I beg you would not put it into Lizzy's head to be vexed PP I 5 19 10
Upon this signal, the youngest of her daughters put PP I 9 45 35
Put them next to your great uncle the judge. PP I 10 53 57
of one stranger was soon put an end to by exclamations and PP I 15 73 11
satisfaction till supper put an end to cards; and gave the PP I 16 84 59
him again, put it out of her power to dance with others. PP I 18 102 73
for him, she means (most kindly!) to put me on my guard? PP I 21 118 15
unpleasant a situation, now put herself forward to confirm PP I 23 126 4
herself; and endeavoured to put a stop to the exclamations PP I 23 126 4
Miss Bingley's letter arrived, and put an end to doubt. PP II 1 133 1
I would advise you merely to put on whatever of your PP II 6 160 6
calm and concise--and soon put an end to by the entrance PP II 9 179 26
"Yes--if Darcy does not put it off again. PP II 10 183 8
utmost force of passion to put aside, in my own case; the PP II 12 198 5
of the last page or two, put it hastily away, protesting PP II 13 204 2
She put down the letter, weighed every circumstance with PP II 13 205 3
ill; and if I was her, I would not have put up with it. PP II 17 228 29
in their marriage put an end to all real affection for her. PP II 19 236 1
in rosing's park, when he put his letter into her hand! PP III 1 252 54
was now put an end to, by the approach of the whole party. PP III 5 286 32
I will put on my things in a moment. PP III 7 306 44
occasion; no one was to be put in competition with him. PP III 9 318 20
put it off, and then I should have gone quite distracted. PP III 9 319 24
If you'll believe me, I did not once put my foot out of PP III 9 319 25
not be put off, for Mr. Darcy might have done as well." PP III 9 319 25
On such encouragement to ask, Elizabeth was forced to put PP III 9 320 31
to his niece, was forced to put up with only having the PP III 10 324 2
I know; though it was not put in as it ought to be. PP III 11 336 49
and the little value he put on his own good qualities. PP III 13 350 51
So, do not put yourself to inconvenience." PP III 17 375 26
put an end to every intreaty and expectation of the kind. PP III 19 386 8
possibly keep to herself, put an end to all intercourse MP I 1 4 1
fetch her, however it may put me to inconvenience to have MP I 1 9 12
I suppose, sister, you will put the child in the little MP I 1 9 12
Nobody meant to be unkind, but nobody put themselves out MP I 2 14 6
"Dear mamma, only think, my cousin cannot put the map of MP I 2 18 23
the latter, when it did not put herself to inconvenience, MP I 2 19 31
and care, and put the cheerfullest spirits too the test. MP I 3 28 42
that my health and spirits put it quite out of the MP I 3 30 56
and Fanny was then put in almost full possession of her. MP I 4 37 8
and been obliged to put up with exactly the reverse! MP I 5 46 22
Mr. Norris's death, that we put in the apricot against the MP I 6 54 9
was glad to put an end to his speech by a proposal of wine. MP I 6 55 17
I should not put myself into the hands of an improver. MP I 6 56 28
and liveliness, to put the matter by for the present. MP I 6 57 32
you did tremble when Sir Thomas first had you put on!" MP I 7 69 22
"No; but they were to be put into the spare room to day; MP I 7 73 51
"Don't be affronted," said she laughing; "but it does put MP I 11 108 10
Bertrams, as ought to have put them both on their guard, MP I 12 114 3
If others have blundered, it is your place to put them MP I 15 140 13
There is no occasion to put them so very close together. MP I 15 141 22
I shall be Cottager, I'll put you in and push you about; MP I 15 146 50
Put yourself in Miss Crawford's place, Fanny. MP I 16 154 14
I can do nothing; I have put them in good humour by this MP I 16 155 16
been nobody to put him in the way of doing any thing yet." MP I 17 161 14
could put Mrs. Grant right the other day in twenty places. MP I 18 172 31
every question of his two sons almost before it was put. MP II 1 178 8
so sensibly animated as to put away her work, move pug MP II 1 179 9
what had been so lately put up in the billiard room, and MP II 2 190 9
on your person, you must put up with it, and trust to his MP II 3 197 6
"If you put such a question to her," cried Edmund, MP II 5 217 2
she was endeavouring to put her aunt's evening work in MP II 5 220 29
answer all that you could put in the course of an hour, MP II 7 241 15
your plan for Thornton Lacey will ever be put in practice. MP II 7 242 24
the servant to have just put round her shoulders, was MP II 7 251 66
the parcel he had just put into her hand, and seeing MP II 9 262 8
real and imaginary--and put them round her neck, and seen MP II 9 271 40
her, and her thoughts were put into another channel by his MP II 10 274 8
bad weather, had they been put to the proof; but as that MP II 12 291 1
reason to lament the hour that first put it into my head. MP II 12 295 20
and mother would be able to put him in the way of getting MP II 13 305 19
We had better put an end to this most mortifying MP III 1 318 39
of any consultation, put a decided negative on it. MP III 1 319 39
butler) but you are so very eager to put yourself forward. MP III 1 325 60
discouragement from herself would put an end to it in time. MP III 2 331 18
"Fanny has been reading to me, and only put the book down MP III 3 336 9
Nay, nay, I entreat you; for one moment put down your work. MP III 3 342 33
the whim of the moment--easily tempted--easily put aside. MP III 3 343 41
better time for the visit--but now I cannot put her off. MP III 5 359 12
it as meaning nothing, I put it down as simply being his MP III 5 362 21
and energy, and very determined, is easily put by. MP III 5 364 29
and see if Rebecca has put the water on; and tell her to MP III 7 379 15
"that's just where I should have put her myself. MP III 7 380 21
meal; Susan looking as she put the kettle on the fire and MP III 7 383 32
Such was the home which was to put Mansfield out of her MP III 8 391 10

ho would not rather put up with the misfortune of being MP III 10 402 11
nd she did not know how to prevent or put an end to it. MP III 11 409 5
nto Norfolk directly, and put every thing at once on such MP III 11 412 20
ut it is impossible to put an hundredth part of my great MP III 12 415 2
rom Edmund so long expected, was put into Fanny's hands. MP III 13 420 1
f one of the last epistolary uses she could put them to. MP III 13 425 6
put it to your conscience, whether 'Sir Edmund' would MP III 14 434 13
ickening knock, and a letter was again put into her hands. MP III 15 442 22
ith his daughter, to put an end to an intimacy which was MP III 16 450 8
aved them both, he had put himself in the power of MP III 17 468 21
r put Edmund Bertram sufficiently out of her head. MP III 17 469 24
ut James will not like to put the horses to for such a E I 1 8 17
They are to be put into Mr. Weston's stable, papa. E I 1 8 18
wanted them to put off the wedding." E I 1 10 26
orry to see any thing put on it; and while his E I 3 24 12
small half glass--put into a tumbler of water? E I 3 25 14
artfield will only put her out of conceit with all the E I 5 38 15
he acquaintance, should put an end to it, so long as it E I 5 40 24
his did not want much of being finished, when I put it E I 6 45 21
ut was really obliged to put an end to it, and request E I 6 46 24
uch to persuade him to put off his journey only one day; E I 8 68 58
usiness which he would not put off for any inducement in E I 8 68 58
f Highbury in general should be put under requisition. E I 9 70 7
iss Nash has put down all the tests he has ever preached E I 9 75 26
ave you thought, my dear, where you shall put her--and E I 9 79 56
y the bye, that is almost enough to put one out of E I 10 86 23
er inability to put herself to rights so as to be able to E I 10 89 36
nd that Frank's coming depends upon their being put off. E I 14 120 11
f they are not put off, he cannot stir. E I 14 120 11
ears, they always are put off when it comes to the point. E I 14 120 11
ven if this family, the Braithwaites, are put off, I am E I 14 122 21
was sure it could not be far off; but I had put my E II 1 157 10
ow I think you will be put to it to make out all that E II 1 157 10
is own return to England put any thing in his power. E II 2 163 4
he evil day was put off. E II 2 164 6
rank Churchill--must put up for the present with Jane E II 2 166 10
mma, at last, in order to put the Martins out of her head, E II 3 180 56
ad been a little put aside by Elizabeth Martin's calling E II 4 184 11
he farm, and she was to be put down, at the end of the E II 5 186 2
o obliging occasionally to put it to a better use than we E II 8 216 16
o not put it into his head. E II 8 225 74
he stept forward and put an end to all further singing. E II 8 229 98
or my mother had no use of her spectacles--could not put E II 9 236 46
o put up your horse at the crown, and come in." E II 10 244 42
word was put in for a second young Cox; and at last, Mr. E II 11 248 9
ith a bench round it, which put me so exactly in mind! E II 14 273 21
pon my word it is enough to put one in a fright. E II 14 277 40
id not allow of his being put off, but both father and E II 16 292 8
ately, but having answered the letter, had put it away. E II 16 298 51
iss Woodhouse, he will, of course, put forth his best." E II 16 298 55
must put on a few ornaments now, because it is expected E II 17 302 22
ut it up, put it up; we will have a good talk about it E II 17 304 27
efore hymen's saffron robe would be put on for us! E II 18 308 28
have no business to put myself forward." E III 2 320 10
rs. Weston begs you to put on your tippet. E III 2 328 45
ow well you put it on!--so gratified! E III 2 329 45
ooked them through, and put them all to rights, she was E III 3 332 3
treasure of it--so I put it by never to be used, and E III 4 338 12
And so you actually put this piece of court plaister by E III 4 339 15
eer, and he wanted to put it down; but when he took out E III 4 339 18
onvinced her that every thing need not be put off. E III 6 352 2
ule--gardeners never to be put out of their way-- E III 6 358 35
o then, I try to put it out of her thoughts, and say, E III 8 382 27
indness, and, in short, put an end to the miserable state E III 10 398 51
gainst it, and try to put difficulties in the way. E III 11 407 28
hen these effusions were put by, they had talked a good E III 12 418 5
ust put an end to, might be a little extraordinary!-- E III 13 431 38
s to put up with it, and seek no farther explanation. E III 13 431 38
er, and she must have put it off; but Mr. Knightley was E III 17 465 28
nightley came in, and distressing thoughts were put by. E III 18 470 1
reatment, because I never put up with any other; and, E III 18 474 29
ames's being gone out to put the horses to, preparatory E III 18 475 38
ady Russell's had no success at all--could not be put up P III 2 13 6
suppose, and they never put themselves out of their way." P III 5 38 29
t is a pity you cannot put your sister in the way of P III 6 44 8
he should put it off as long as she could." P III 6 48 17
he child's situation put the visit entirely aside, but P III 7 53 2
omething a little inferior I shall of course put up with, P III 7 62 41
ay for us, when you were put captain into that ship. P III 8 67 24
he attractions of Uppercross induced him to put this off. P III 9 73 1
ayter, whose pretensions she wished to see put an end to. P III 9 75 12
aptain Wentworth may soon put him quite out of her head, P III 9 76 16
ut Charles Hayter soon put an end to his attempts, by P III 9 79 27
ee what was going on, and put in his claim to any thing P III 9 79 28
ouisa certainly put more forward for his notice than her P III 10 84 7
he sweet scenes of autumn were for a while put by--unless P III 10 85 12
n determined I will:" he put out his hands; she was too P III 12 109 32
he was put down in Camden-Place; and Lady Russell then P IV 2 136 37
ady Russell's composed mind and polite manners were put P IV 4 146 5
great amusement; and she put me in the way of making P IV 5 155 9
ut surely, you may put off this old lady till to-morrow. P IV 5 157 15
ut I do not think I can put off my engagement, because it P IV 5 157 16
o ended the first part, which had been afterwards put P IV 6 164 8
he excused herself and put it off, with the more decided P IV 7 180 33
ime, more than all the rest of the world put together." P IV 9 194 16
f her life, and can answer any question you wish to put." P IV 9 200 57
ells me, that it is to be put into the marriage articles P IV 9 208 92
orry but that they could put on a decent air of welcome; P IV 10 216 18
o Mrs. Musgrove--put her quite out of her way. P IV 10 219 29
We had better put it off. P IV 10 224 51
ou see he cannot put the card out of his hand." P IV 10 227 66
erhaps, and obliged to put into another port, he P 1 6 235 31
or now I could at least put myself in the way of P IV 11 243 70
he had been too wary to put anything out of her own power- S 3 375 1
could soon put the necessary Irons in the fire.-- S 5 387 1
y early hours are not to put my neighbours to S 6 390 1
hey have Miss Clara's room to put to rights as well as my S 7 401 1
n vain may we put them into a literary Alembic;--we S 8 403 1
urn my Toasts--I never put them too near the fire at S 10 417 1
lmost as much butter as he put on, & then seize an odd S 10 417 1
he must put her shawl over her shoulders, & be running S 10 619 1
-OFF (1)
e, but that she thinks there will be another put-off. E I 14 120 11
-TO (1)
ould deem it that James should put-to for such a purpose." E II 8 228 89
NEY (3)
alued old friend in Putney, with a carriage at her NA I 15 122 28
hey live at Putney." NA II 10 205 28
all at Putney when next in town, might set all to rights. NA II 12 217 2
RID (3)
er disorder to have a putrid tendency, and allowing the SS III 7 307 3
ashwood was dying of a putrid fever at Cleveland-- a SS III 8 330 69
hope not of a putrid infectious sort. E I 13 109 7
RIFYING (1)
ffluvia of a ridge of putrifying sea weed, can end in S 1 369 1
S (4)
always puts me in mind of the country that Emily and NA I 14 106 4
is not a little matter that puts me out of temper." NA I 15 117 3
puts him quite out of heart." SS I 22 131 35
iss Emma Watson puts me very much in mind of her eldest W 324 3
TING (45)
ho coming to town & putting herself to an expence in LS 42 313 10

on his banker, or even putting an hundred pounds bank-bill NA I 2 19 3
delighted, which was putting herself rather out of her way; SS II 3 157 19
her sister's chair, and putting one arm round her neck, SS II 12 236 39
40

Elinor's heart could easily account for his not putting SS III 11 354 32
could have prevented his putting an end to an engagement, SS III 13 367 21
half opening the door & putting in her head, said "please W 346 21
And what was the use of my putting up your last new coat, W 353 26
Jane recollected herself soon, and putting the letter away, PP I 21 116 6
the apprehension was putting away her half-finished letter PP II 9 177 1
Putting away the letter immediately and forcing a smile, PP II 10 182 2
3
find some opportunity of putting this letter in your hands PP II 12 203 5
She saw the indelicacy of putting himself forward as he PP II 13 207 5
occurrence, as quietly putting an end to what might ere MP I 17 160 9
I think you may give me your help in putting it together.-- MP I 18 166 6
not to venture: he was putting on his wig--so I said, ' MP II 2 189 5
and intreat you not to be putting yourself forward, and MP II 5 221 32
to complete the gift by putting the necklace round her and MP II 8 258 17
with bringing them up and putting them out in the world! MP II 13 305 24
being at Twickenham--her putting herself in the power of a MP III 16 455 19
very often to recollect something worth their putting in. E I 9 70 5
of putting all the Mr. Westons aside as much as she can." E I 11 95 18
was no putting and end to his extreme solicitude about her. E I 15 125 4
be requisite, and always putting forward to prevent E II 1 156 5
therefore, in the hope of putting it by, she calmly said, " E II 12 261 30
31
I have some notion of putting such a trimming as this to E II 17 302 22
"My dearest Harriet!" cried Emma, putting her hand before E III 4 338 13
I ever have thought of putting by in cotton a piece of E III 4 339 15
she could have no doubt--putting every thing together-- E III 9 391 21
And putting up her hand to screen her words from Emma--"a E III 16 456 23
caution, under which she acted, in putting an end to it. P III 4 27 5
be always putting herself forward to take place of mamma. P III 6 46 10
be now no occasion for putting Captain Wentworth off, and P III 7 54 5
and the Admiral was putting his horse into motion again, P III 10 91 39
afterwards judiciously putting out her hand, they neither P III 10 92 48
her father and mother for putting it off till summer; and P III 11 94 7
"Putting all these very extraordinary circumstances P III 12 106 17
more; and yet perhaps by "putting the children away in the P III 12 113 56
putting us in mind of those we first had at North Yarmouth. P IV 6 170 29
Such a letter could not be read without putting Anne in a P IV 9 204 74
75
"You are a good soul," cried Captain Harville, putting his P IV 11 235 34
and Captain Wentworth, by putting her in the way of P IV 12 251 11
wrong here, said he--putting his hand to his ancle--but S 1 364 1
undertaken to cure, by putting out the fire, opening the S 10 413 1
the sum we wanted for putting them all out, yet if you can S 12 424 1
PUZZLE (10)
of many; but it did not puzzle Mrs. Allen, for after only NA I 8 59 34
elucidated by this speech, soon ceased to be a puzzle. NA I 13 102 26
or leave you to puzzle out an explanation as you can? NA I 14 112 36
to her reason, her judgment, it was completely a puzzle. SS III 13 364 10
I hear such different accounts of you as puzzle me PP I 18 93 40
Elizabeth with some warmth, "you puzzle me exceedingly. PP I 19 108 18
I only puzzle them, and oblige them to make civil speeches. MP I 15 144 36
She stopt, felt herself getting into a puzzle, and could MP III 3 341 27
Here is quite a separate puzzle." E II 15 285 15
I want to puzzle you again." E III 5 347 19
PUZZLED (14)
It puzzled her to account for all this. NA II 1 129 1
Sir John was rather puzzled. SS I 9 44 19
"I should be puzzled to spend a large fortune myself," SS I 17 92 23
expressions as had puzzled him before; and when their SS I 18 100 23
This speech at first puzzled Mrs. Jennings exceedingly. SS III 4 286 16
of eldest son, might have puzzled many people to find out; SS III 14 377 12
done to succeed to it, might have puzzled them still more. SS III 14 377 12
But no letter appeared, and she was completely puzzled. PP III 14 352 15
and Julia? or was she puzzled about any thing in her MP I 2 15 10
I am puzzled.-- MP I 5 48 30
to please, he grew puzzled; and Edmund was glad to put an MP I 6 55 17
to answer questions which puzzled her sister at seventeen. E I 5 37 9
She would not have been puzzled, had she dared fix on them. E II 8 218 41
for each other, or for any body else who would be puzzled. E III 5 347 20
PUZZLES (2)
That puzzles me.-- NA II 9 196 21
They owed to him their two or three politest puzzles; and E I 9 70 7
PUZZLING (3)
found it quite as puzzling when she awoke the next morning. MP I 16 150 1
while Harriet was puzzling over the paper in all the E I 9 72 15
his name so often, puzzling over past years, and at last P III 6 52 33
PYRAMIDS (1)
eat; and the beautiful pyramids of grapes, nectarines, and PP III 3 268 6
PYRENEES (2)
Of the Alps and Pyrenees, with their pine forests and NA II 10 200 3
Among the Alps and Pyrenees, perhaps, there were no mixed NA II 10 200 3

QR (3)
If we any of us want to bathe, we have not a qr of a mile S 4 381 1
Bs--, though it was 1/2 a qr of a mile round about, & S 11 422 1
conducting at the end of a qr of a mile through second S 12 426 1
QRS (1)
or veiw, only one mile & 3 qrs from the noblest expanse of S 4 380 1
QUACK (1)
for Medecine, especially quack Medecine, had given them an S 10 412 1
QUADRANGLE (4)
discover looked into a quadrangle, before Miss Tilney led NA II 5 162 28
and two sides of the quadrangle, rich in Gothic ornaments, NA II 7 177 19
the fourth side of the quadrangle having, on account of NA II 8 184 4
The side of the quadrangle, in which she supposed the NA II 8 188 19
QUADRILLE (5)
before, to make up her pool of quadrille in the evening. PP I 14 66 1
of assisting to form a quadrille table at Rosings, in the PP I 17 88 14
our pools at quadrille, while Mrs. Jenkinson was arranging PP I 19 105 10
Down to quadrille; and as Miss de Bourgh chose to play at PP II 6 166 41
old lady, almost past every thing but tea and quadrille. E I 3 21 4
QUAINT (1)
I admire all that quaint, old-fashioned politeness; it is E II 17 302 22
QUALIFICATION (3)
Every qualification is raised at times, by the SS II 10 215 13
his doubts of their qualification, and his zeal after MP I 12 115 4
common neglect of the qualification, the total inattention MP III 3 339 22
QUALIFICATIONS (3)
and generous qualifications, which had been rather more SS I 19 101 2
your modesty, economy, and other amiable qualifications." PP I 19 107 15
I do not know any better qualifications for a friend and MP I 3 26 29
QUALIFIED (17)
who is therefore well qualified to make the communication. LS 4 248 1
James accepted this tribute of gratitude, and qualified NA I 7 51 53
they are perfectly well qualified to torment readers of NA I 14 109 25
allow himself to be informed, they were qualified to give. NA II 16 251 6
of judgment, which qualified her, though only nineteen, to SS I 1 6 11
looks, wd give but a qualified admiration; & Mr E. not W 323 3
He was in fact excellently qualified to shine at a round W 359 28
I am not qualified to form one. PP I 16 77 14
find me in every respect ill qualified for the situation." PP I 19 107 14
but I am ill qualified to recommend myself to strangers." PP II 8 175 21
was now almost equally well qualified to shew the house. MP I 9 84 3
had she been otherwise qualified for criticism, her MP I 18 170 24
as useful as I can; but I am not qualified for an adviser. MP II 9 269 34
such an early age can be qualified for the care of E II 2 164 6
enough in herself to be qualified for a country life. E II 18 307 21
His profession qualified him, his disposition led him, to P III 8 63 2
had then written, nothing was to be retracted or qualified. P IV 11 241 61
QUALIFY (1)
And at last, as if resolved to qualify his opinion E II 5 192 29
QUALIFYING (1)
He was immediately qualifying himself to form an opinion, E III 2 321 13
QUALITIES (21)
her; she has her good qualities, but she has no faith, no W 317 2
Such amiable qualities must speak for themselves. PP I 3 11 6
from the popular qualities, or lose the influence of the PP I 16 81 41
of his valuable qualities, though at first unwillingly PP III 2 265 16
and the little value he put on his own good qualities. PP III 13 350 51
with energy all his good qualities, she did conquer her PP III 17 376 36
My good qualities are under your protection, and you are PP III 18 381 7
trying to make her good qualities understood, and to MP I 2 21 34
seemed, by her amiable qualities and accomplishments, the MP I 4 39 10
he has a thousand good qualities! and is so disposed to MP II 2 190 7
of her character (qualities which he believed most rare MP III 2 326 3
You have qualities which I had not before supposed to MP III 3 343 41
to my sisters' good qualities, I think it very possible MP III 4 350 30
She was willing to allow he might have more good qualities MP III 10 405 16
No, no; she has qualities which may be trusted; she will E I 5 40 22
his good and agreeable qualities, there was a sort of E I 9 82 84
Harriet Smith has some first-rate qualities, which Mrs. E III 2 331 55
for his having many, very many, good qualities; and-----" E III 10 397 49
though very eccentric, he had a thousand good qualities.-- E III 17 469 36
now very willing to grant you all Harriet's good qualities. E III 18 474 34
that, like all other qualities of the mind, it should have P III 12 116 72
QUALITY (9)
this simple praise than a quality heroine would have been NA I 2 24 28
it was to resolve on the quality of her wedding-gown. NA I 15 120 23
on the score of some quality or other, real or imaginary. PP I 5 20 20
quality, who has neither manner nor sense to recommend him. PP II 4 154 19
or accomplishment or good quality in the person, who have MP I 5 46 22
she could believe no good quality to exist, and whose MP III 2 327 6
and acts up to his resolutions--an inestimable quality. MP III 13 423 2
"It is a most repulsive quality, indeed," said he. E II 6 203 40
of very superior quality was speedily despatched to Miss E III 9 391 20
QUANTITIES (1)
up--quantities of matting--my dear Jane, indeed you must. E III 2 328 45
QUANTITY (9)
There is but such a quantity of merit between them; just PP II 17 225 10
grievances, nor of the quantity of butter and eggs that MP I 3 31 59
where a reasonable quantity of accomplishments were sold E I 3 21 5
of the first order, in form as well as quantity. E I 9 70 4
As to there being any quantity of snow fallen or likely to E I 15 126 11
William Larkins let me keep a larger quantity than usual E II 9 238 51
most distressing, by their sort rather than their quantity. P IV 2 135 33
lately arrived, & by the quantity of Luggage taking off, S 9 406 1
"With a reasonable quantity of butter spread over it, very S 10 417 1
QUARREL (28)
The quarrel between Lady Susan & Reginald is made up, & we LS 24 285 1
they have had a dreadful quarrel about it, & he is going. LS 24 286 7
And why should your ladyship at any rate quarrel with my LS 24 290 12
very article by which our quarrel was produced, & at best, LS 25 294 6
her quarrel with my brother, and then fly off himself?" NA II 12 218 6
that some unfortunate quarrel had taken place between him SS I 15 77 19
was such as a serious quarrel could most reasonably SS I 15 77 19
love for him was, a quarrel seemed almost impossible. SS I 15 77 19
between two women can never end without a quarrel. PP I 7 30 17
and till he did, it was useless to quarrel about him. PP I 17 88 14
did not quarrel with him for his wish of independence. PP II 3 149 28
Do not let us quarrel about the past. PP III 10 329 34
"We will not quarrel for the greater share of blame PP III 16 367 13
newspaper, watch the weather, and quarrel with his wife. MP I 11 110 23
"I think the man who could often quarrel with Fanny," said MP I 11 112 32
grew indifferent to the quarrel, or rather thought it a MP I 17 160 9
And as to my poor word 'success,' which you quarrel with, E I 1 13 43
"Perhaps you think I am come on purpose to quarrel with E I 5 36 5
Mr. Knightley might quarrel with her, but Emma could not E I 9 69 1
quarrel with her, but Emma could not quarrel with herself. E I 9 69 1
would be ready to quarrel with you for using such words. E II 5 192 31
for we never had a quarrel in our lives; but she was quite E II 9 238 51
Knightley not wanting to quarrel with her, how very happy E III 3 332 1
I would not quarrel with you for any liberties of manner. E III 7 375 61
but it was impossible to quarrel with words, whose E III 9 390 18
In short, my dear madam, it was a quarrel blameless on her E III 14 441 8
I must not quarrel with a spirit of forbearance which has E III 14 441 8
him agreable, & did not quarrel with the suspicion of his S 7 395 1
QUARRELING (1)
law, & I am sometimes quarreling with myself for suffering LS 30 300 2
QUARRELLED (9)
They must have quarrelled, & about Frederica too. LS 23 285 7
Can they have quarrelled? SS I 15 77 23
but Mrs. Bennet, who quarrelled with no compliments, PP I 13 65 21
22
with her? or had she quarrelled with Maria and Julia? or MP I 2 15 10
that they had ever quarrelled; and she hoped it might E I 12 98 2
And when he was gone, she almost quarrelled with me--no, I E II 9 238 51
I should not say quarrelled, for we never had a quarrel in E II 9 238 51
We quarrelled.-- E III 14 440 8
happy no longer; she quarrelled with her own seat,--was P III 10 86 21
QUARRELLING (16)
she & Reginald had been quarrelling, & looked with anxious LS 23 284 6
with me; and have been quarrelling with myself ever since, SS II 2 146 5
Nobody can tell how much I hate quarrelling. W 343 19
rather have quarrelling going on, than nothing at all."-- W 343 19
I have been quarrelling with you all the way we came, have W 350 24
Why could not he keep on quarrelling with you, as his PP I 13 62 10
will we begin quarrelling about its relative situation. PP II 4 154 23
for teazing and quarrelling with you as often as may be; PP III 18 381 7
bad enough to have him quarrelling about green goose from MP I 11 112 31
Grant, who are always quarrelling, and that poking old MP I 12 119 26
but her aunt was soon quarrelling with her: and when she MP III 1 323 53
You are always quarrelling about that knife. MP III 7 386 44
full basket, two curs quarrelling over a dirty bone, and a E II 9 233 24
Alas! there was soon no leisure for quarrelling with Mr. E II 12 258 7
of half his merits, and quarrelling with him because he E III 12 415 1
"There is no quarrelling with you.-- P IV 11 235 34
QUARRELS (2)
The quarrels of popes and kings, with wars or pestilences, NA I 14 108 22
of one of our quarrels about Emma, Mr. Knightley." E I 5 36 4
QUARRELSOME (4)
stubborn, scarcely ever quarrelsome, and very kind to the NA I 1 14 1
were disposed to be quarrelsome, discontented or too poor, PP II 7 169 4
I wish you would not be so quarrelsome. MP III 7 386 44
She could not be complying, she dreaded being quarrelsome; E I 13 114 27
QUARTER (80)
from a quarter, whence I had least reason to apprehend it. LS 22 281 4
the crowd in less than a quarter of an hour, and Catherine NA I 10 71 8
I shall not give it up till a quarter after twelve. NA I 11 83 15
After sitting with them a quarter of an hour, she rose to NA I 13 103 28
to think it a very long quarter of an hour, when they both NA II 1 132 16
He would follow them in a quarter of an hour. NA II 7 181 41
"It is only a quarter past four, (shewing his watch) and NA II 9 195 18
You will soon hear enough from another quarter to know NA II 10 202 7
"A quarter would be enough." NA II 11 209 4
a quarter before one on Wednesday, you may look for us." NA II 11 210 6
The two houses were only a quarter of a mile apart; and, NA II 14 236 19
to detain her, a quarter of an hour had elapsed ere she NA II 15 241 7
at the end of a quarter of an hour she had nothing to say. NA II 15 242 9
to the church, and only a quarter of a mile from the SS II 8 197 22
In this manner they had continued about a quarter of an SS II 9 203 11
and debating for a quarter of an hour over every toothpick- SS II 11 220 3
say to them; for of the quarter of an hour bestowed on SS II 12 229 3
she would not give, soon flowed from another quarter. SS II 12 229 4
in the course of a quarter of an hour's conversation; for, SS II 14 250 12
elsewhere, it could not be in that quarter. SS III 1 266 38
Hunter, more than once; I have my fears in that quarter. W 320 2
that he agreed to allow himself another quarter of an hour. W 357 28
of attention in that quarter as Elizabeth herself could be, PP I 11 56 12
he continued to apologise for about a quarter of an hour. PP I 13 65 26
an alteration; for in a quarter of an hour's tete-a-tete PP I 15 70 3
for their carriages a quarter of an hour after every body PP I 18 102 75
must mean an allusion to what might arise in that quarter. PP II 10 182 1
Mr. and Mrs. Gardiner were half a quarter of a mile behind. PP III 1 257 65
a quarter, than by supposing a partiality for their niece. PP III 2 260 1
After sitting in this manner a quarter of an hour, without PP III 3 268 5
father, from a different quarter, from Mr. Collins; which, PP III 6 296 10
it is not much above a quarter of a mile, I cannot think I MP I 7 73 53
"We have been exactly a quarter of an hour here," said. MP I 9 95 65
A quarter of an hour, twenty minutes, passed away, and MP I 10 97 1
was quite grieved to be losing even a quarter of an hour.-- MP I 12 117 11
room, undisturbed, for a quarter of an hour, when a gentle MP I 18 168 14
at this time, for any engagements but in one quarter. MP II 3 196 1
In this quarter, indeed, disappointment was impending over MP II 3 200 19
"Another quarter of an hour," said Miss Crawford, "and we MP II 4 207 7
are quite in a different quarter: and if I could have MP II 4 212 31
at the end of a quarter of an hour's silent consideration, MP II 11 285 10
any thing of a serious nature in such a quarter? MP II 13 306 26
In about a quarter of an hour her uncle returned; she was MP III 1 321 47
Intreaty should be from one quarter only. MP III 2 330 14
and that you will not hear so soon from any other quarter." MP III 6 373 26
Another quarter of an hour brought her a great deal more. MP III 7 381 26
saucer; and after another quarter of an hour of earnest MP III 7 384 36
Every thing in that quarter failed her, except William's MP III 8 388 2
which he may have laid down for the next quarter of a year. MP III 11 410 16
had just occurred in that quarter to draw the notice of MP III 15 438 4
deal to alarm him in that quarter, wrote to recommend Sir MP III 16 450 8
take Emma's advice and go out for a quarter of an hour. E I 8 57 3
a most unexceptionable quarter:--Robert Martin is the man. E I 8 59 25
much, something, he thought, might come from that quarter. E I 9 70 6
passed, and then, about a quarter of a mile down the lane E I 10 83 2
from the sea--a quarter of a mile off--very comfortable. E I 12 106 56
allow the visit to exceed the proposed quarter of an hour. E II 5 186 2
The quarter of an hour brought her punctually to the white E II 5 186 3
one quarter; --of course it must be from Col. Campbell. E II 8 214 13
That, from such a quarter, one might expect. E II 10 242 21
that the space which a quarter of an hour before had been E II 11 249 12
touch it seldom; for evil in that quarter was at hand. E II 13 267 8
Mr. Elton, she had a quarter of an hour of the lady's E II 14 272 16
attend to her; and the quarter of an hour quite convinced E II 14 272 16
Consider from how partial a quarter your information came. E II 14 276 36
was his staying only a quarter of an hour, and hurrying E III 1 316 4
Jane had not been gone a quarter of an hour, and they had E III 6 363 53
He was here only a quarter of an hour, and in a state of E III 10 397 47
tell you, he could stay with us but a quarter of an hour.-- E III 10 398 57
with satisfaction, than a quarter of an hour spent in Mrs. E III 12 417 4
changed into a softer quarter; the clouds were carried off; E III 13 424 1
the vicarage quarter, which was now graciously overcome.-- E III 16 455 20
obliged to separate before the end of the first quarter. E III 17 469 36
"Since the idea had been started in the very quarter which P III 2 13 7
company in attending the quarter sessions at Taunton; and P III 3 21 18
of the great house, about a quarter of a mile farther on. P III 5 36 20
of resting herself a quarter of an hour at Winthrop, as P III 10 86 17
that the difference of a quarter of an hour, it was found, P III 12 108 30
would be in that quarter of the mind which could not be P IV 10 212 1
by its effects in one quarter, that it became a matter of P IV 11 229 1
QUARTERED (3)
another regiment should be quartered in Meryton. PP II 19 238 6
Since the ----shire were first quartered in Meryton, PP III 5 283 10
in general ----'s regiment, now quartered in the north. PP III 8 312 19
QUARTERLY REVIEWS (1)
chit-chat, and Quarterly Reviews, till the return of the MP I 10 104 51
QUARTERS (14)
Two hours and three quarters will carry us to Woodston, I NA II 11 210 6
Prescriptions poured in from all quarters, and as usual, SS III 6 306 17
every night to his old quarters at the park; from whence SS III 13 369 34
remain the whole winter, and Meryton was the head quarters. PP I 7 28 3
account of their present quarters, and the very great PP I 16 79 23
they changed their quarters, either Jane or herself were PP III 19 387 8
I sat three quarters of an hour in the flower garden, MP I 7 72 42
of full three quarters of a yard), and was actually MP I 14 130 1
are his own two men pushing it back into its old quarters. MP II 3 222 46
sitting with them very nearly three quarters of an hour. E II 6 199 7
we soon shifted their quarters; and now I am quite snug, P IV 1 128 28
the rest of the family were again in their usual quarters. P IV 2 133 27
The prejudices which had met her at first in some quarters, S 3 379 1
the hotel must be his quarters--he was expecting to be S 12 425 1

QUARTO (1)
meet with, into a thin quarto of hot-pressed paper, made E I 9 69 3
QUEEN (7)
for that queen; no, no, a dozen is more than it is worth. MP II 7 243 27
pursued with "no, no, you must not part with the queen. MP II 7 244 28
Your sister does not part with the queen. MP II 7 244 28
and must be regarded as the queen of the evening. MP II 9 266 22
The king, the queen, Buckingham, wolsey, Cromwell, all MP III 3 337 10
she may, with moving the queen of a palace, though the MP III 9 394 1
Quite the queen of the evening!-- E III 2 329 45
QUEEN MAB (1)
in a more lasting home, Queen Mab shall receive you." SS I 12 59 6
QUEEN-SQUARES (1)
of your Queen-Squares for us!" or in the anxious P III 6 42 1
QUEER (6)
strangely harassed by a queer, half-witted man, who would NA I 3 26 22
I thought he began to look a little queer, so I turned it MP I 18 169 21
Is she queer?-- MP II 6 230 7
know, I begin to like that queer fashion already, though MP II 6 235 19
Now do not make yourself uneasy with any queer fancies, MP III 14 435 14
What queer fellows your fine painters must be, to think P IV 6 169 25
QUEERNESSES (1)
If you remember any queernesses, set them all to the right E III 14 439 8
QUELL (1)
up from Northampton to quell the insurgents, and the NA I 14 113 39
QUERULOUS (2)
invaded by her fretful displeasure, & querulous attacks.-- W 360 30
Mrs. Bennet was restored to her usual querulous serenity, PP II 19 238 6
QUERY (1)
"Query," said Mr. Crawford, looking round him, "whether we MP I 9 90 34
QUEST (16)
their business, whether in quest of pastry, millinery, or NA I 7 44 1
in her mother's arms, in quest of this medicine, and as SS I 21 122 10
there, quitted the room in quest of her; and Elinor was SS III 5 298 32
was at that moment in quest of a person to employ on the W 338 18
her eyes round the room in quest of some amusement; when PP I 11 55 5
6
up in the street in quest of the officers, and nothing PP I 15 72 7
which fronted the lane, in quest of this wonder; it was PP II 5 158 13
Elizabeth walked on in quest of the only face whose PP III 1 250 47
than she set off again in quest of her former acquaintance, PP III 1 259 76
her from Derbyshire in quest of her sister, had been PP III 16 370 33
They were always moving from place to place in quest of a PP III 19 387 8
about the country in quest of any body who can be MP I 16 155 22
and disturb every body in quest of two needlefulls of MP II 6 236 21
still living, walked in quest of her cottage from one end E II 6 197 3
but Miss Woodhouse was the very person she was in quest of. E III 6 362 43
party, some of them did decide on going in quest of tea. P IV 8 188 44
UESTION (172)
However you may chuse to question the allurements of a LS 6 251 1
You must not question me however my dear sister, too LS 24 289 12
take her assurance of it, on either side of the question? LS 42 313 9
This question answered, as it readily was, the stranger NA I 4 31 2
to vary the subject by a question which had been long NA I 7 48 32
to apologize for her question, but he prevented her by NA I 7 48 34
him--and he repeated his question, adding in explanation, " NA I 9 63 10
rain for Miss Tilney to venture, must yet be a question. NA I 11 83 16
sprang the following question, thoroughly artless in NA I 12 94 11
"I know you do; but that is not the question. NA I 13 104 33
mention it I beg; that is quite out of the question. NA II 1 130 13
question, to which Catherine listened with a beating heart. NA II 2 138 1
that night, she felt must be entirely out of the question. NA II 6 170 12
augmented with every question, whether answered or not. NA II 7 180 37
art of her own question, "hangs in your father's room?" NA II 7 180 38
to look or breathe, rushed forward to the one in question. NA II 9 193 6
Tuesday, therefore, we may say is out of the question. NA II 11 210 6
How can you ask the question?-- NA II 11 211 9
The room in question was of a commodious, well- NA II 11 213 21
that deserved the name of sleep, was out of the question. NA II 13 227 26
of her being gone, was a question of force and interest to NA II 14 231 4
to fetch the book in question, anxious to lose no time in NA II 15 241 7
Concerning the one in question therefore I have only to NA II 16 251 5
expectations: the question is, what you can afford to do." SS I 2 10 13
she proceeded to question him on the subject of books; her SS I 10 47 3
Willoughby was out of the question. SS I 11 55 7
to question your judgment than to doubt your inclination." SS I 15 76 14
so indulgent a mother, the question could not give offence. SS I 16 84 8
"I would not ask such a question for the world. SS I 16 84 9
all on your side of the question; but I am afraid my SS I 17 94 42
of these scenes, and to question him more minutely on the SS I 18 96 4
so heartily at the question, as to shew she understood it. SS I 19 108 35
In some surprise at the familiarity of this question, or SS I 21 123 22
"You will think my question an odd one, I dare say," said SS I 22 128 3
Elinor did think the question a very odd one, and her SS I 22 128 4
"Pardon me," replied Elinor, startled by the question; " SS I 22 133 45
for herself out of the question, with his integrity, his SS II 1 140 1
she was fearful that her question had implied much more SS II 4 162 13
Elinor was not prepared for such a question, and having no SS II 5 172 40
but I was convinced before I could ask the question. SS II 5 173 44
a joke, but so serious a question seems to imply more; and SS II 7 182 9
it is quite out of the question, the objections are SS II 11 224 24
I question whether Marianne now, will marry a man worth SS II 11 227 50
The first question on her side, which led to farther SS III 1 262 14
15
must be quite out of the question; yet why, after her late SS III 5 296 19
But however, all that is quite out of the question--not to SS III 5 297 31
Domestic happiness is out of the question. SS III 8 332 77
must be though no question was suffered to speak it, SS III 10 348 34
Mrs. Dashwood could think of no other question, and Thomas SS III 11 355 45
inexperienced in such a question, it might be strange that SS III 13 361 2
One question after this only remained undecided, between SS III 13 369 32
blush accompany the question, & there seemed something W 324 3
the question of, "have you been walking this morning?" W 345 21
and his answering immediately to the last question-- Oh! PP I 5 19 7
where nothing is in question but the desire of being well PP I 6 22 7
That is a question which Mr. Darcy only can answer." PP I 6 24 15
That is exactly the question which I expected you to ask. PP I 6 27 52
e repeated the question, with some surprise at her PP I 10 52 49
onversation; he merely answered her question, and read on. PP I 11 55 4
as not in her nature to question the veracity of a young PP I 17 85 1
aria thought speaking out of the question, and the PP II 6 163 14
I can answer your question," said Fitzwilliam, "without PP II 8 175 23
im to the living in question--of which he trusted there PP II 12 201 5
ffairs, and whose character she had no reason to question. PP II 13 206 4
most welcome negative followed the last question--and PP II 19 241 17
t length, however, the question was asked by her uncle; PP III 1 246 8
here was not much in the question, nor in the preceding PP III 2 263 9
nswered the question in a tolerably dis-engaged tone. PP III 3 269 10
heir visit did not continue long after the question and PP III 3 270 12
ut he found, in reply to this question, that Wickham PP III 10 323 2
nd Mrs. Gardiner did, a question which she could not PP III 11 335 43
That is a question which I hardly know how to answer. PP III 12 343 37
ave answered this question; she could not but say, after PP III 14 356 55
56
o this question his daughter replied only with a laugh; PP III 15 364 25
een walking to?" was a question which Elizabeth received PP III 17 372 1
ertain? forgive the question--are you quite certain that PP III 17 373 9
east as things then were, was quite out of the question. MP I 1 9 10
ut it quite out of the question--besides that, I really MP I 3 30 56
ou mean--but I will not undertake to answer the question. MP I 5 49 31
oftened voice; "but I question whether her headach might MP I 7 72 45
efore her; and her going now is quite out of the question. MP I 8 76 5
mrs. Rushworth submitted, and the question of surveying MP I 9 89 32
to Fanny's last question of whether she had seen any thing MP I 10 101 33
of an Agatha in the question, took on her to decide it, by MP I 14 132 8
She fell asleep before she could answer the question, and MP I 16 150 1
Mr. Rushworth's repeated question of, "shall I go too?-- MP II 1 176 3
every question of his two sons almost before it was put. MP II 1 178 8
"Whose stables do you use at Bath?" was the next question; MP II 2 193 17
"I did--and was in hopes the question would be followed up MP II 3 198 11
became no uncommon question, even without her being wanted MP II 4 205 1
This was not so very easy a question to answer, and MP II 4 214 44
"If you put such a question to her," cried Edmund, MP II 5 217 2
then addressed to her a question or observation, which she MP II 5 227 68
understanding the question, was at no loss for an answer. MP II 7 247 40
Fanny, in dismay at such an unprecedented question, did MP II 7 250 60
am sorry to say that I am unable to answer your question. MP II 7 250 60
The issue of all depended on one question. MP II 8 255 11
And this question, which he was continually repeating to MP II 8 255 11
in a very agitated manner, "thanks are out of the question. MP II 9 261 5
"That is the first question, you know," said Miss Crawford, MP II 11 288 28
than to answer such a question, though nothing be more MP II 12 292 8
Mrs. Norris being not at all inclined to question its MP II 13 305 23
that is quite out of the question--quite impossible. MP III 1 316 32
in fact, entirely on his father's side of the question. MP III 3 335 6
That is out of the question. MP III 3 344 41
Can it admit of a question? MP III 4 347 16
to have the question asked as your cousin fancies. MP III 5 362 18
The only question is how? MP III 13 422 2
Price, beyond a brief question or two if she saw her MP III 13 428 14
To be otherwise comforted was out of the question. MP III 16 449 5
been no young woman in question, had there been no young MP III 17 465 13
it comes to the question of dependence or independence!-- E I 1 10 29
Such a friend as Mrs. Weston was out of the question. E I 4 26 2
The next question was: "what sort of looking man is Mr. E I 4 29 10
11
an observer on such a question as herself, that he had E I 8 67 57
"I cannot make a question, or listen to a question about E I 9 74 23
the question: and I do not wish to see any such person. E I 10 84 13
child, and talk to and question her, was the most natural E I 10 88 33
Concession must be out of the question; but it was time to E I 12 98 2
"I hope he will be here to-morrow, for I have a question E I 12 101 27
make more than a simple question on that head; it hardly E I 13 108 3
any reviving question from her would have been awkward. E I 14 118 4
and had some question to ask, or some comfort to offer. E I 15 126 9
the other side of the question from her real opinion, and E I 18 145 5
might be a difficult question to answer; Mr. Knightley had E II 2 166 11
which no one could question----- "she is a sort of elegant E II 3 171 14
15
"Who shall answer that question?" cried Emma. E II 3 174 38
a question, however, which did not augur much. E II 5 189 17
"And now that I understand your question, I must pronounce E II 6 200 18
if the lady in question could sit down instead--never E II 6 201 28
between Miss Fairfax and me is quite out of the question. E II 6 203 41
Might not the evening end in a dance? had been a question E II 7 208 7
but at present I do not see what there is to question. E II 8 216 27
But the question is not, whether it would be a bad E II 8 226 79
"Quite out of the question, quite out of the question," he E II 8 228 90
suppers had not been in question; and a small card-room E II 11 254 44
was quite out of the question; and she was not perfectly E II 14 276 34
anxious friend--give Emma some hint, ask her some question. E III 5 349 26
A situation, a most desirable situation, was in question. E III 6 359 37
after a little reflection, venture the following question. E III 11 410 36
This was the knowledge of herself, on the first question E III 11 412 46
herself which was now in question; but there was a hope (E III 12 416 1
you well, my Emma?" was Mrs. Weston's parting question. E III 12 420 15
He stopped in his earnestness to look the question, and E III 13 430 34
guard the comfort of both to the utmost, was the question. E III 14 434 4
With respect to her father, it was a question soon E III 14 435 4
situation requiring such concealment, is another question. E III 14 437 8
on your side of the question; all the merit on mine. E III 17 464 24
by the others as having any interest in the question. P III 2 12 3
indecision, the great question of whither he should go, P III 2 13 8
treason to call it in question; but I am sure, without P III 6 45 9
she could, that the same brother must still be in question. P III 6 49 25
was hating herself for the folly which asked the question. P III 7 60 30
On one other question, which perhaps her utmost wisdom P III 7 60 31
32
to your aunt was in question;--and woe betide him, and her P III 10 87 26
on this interesting question, be the gainer, almost as P III 11 93 2
Anne did think on the question with perfect decision, and P III 12 108 29
occurred to him now, to question the justness of his own P III 12 116 72
of never asking a question at an inn, which he had adopted, P IV 3 144 19
and Elizabeth began to question also; but the difference P IV 3 144 22
However it might end, he was without any question their P IV 4 148 9
cousins again, was the question; and it was a question P IV 4 149 12
question; and it was a question which, in a more rational P IV 4 149 12
company, but she had not courage to ask the question. P IV 8 187 35
of her life, and can answer any question you wish to put." P IV 9 200 57
long before the term in question, the two families had P IV 10 217 20
question, of whether Captain Wentworth would come or not? P IV 10 227 69
sex?" and she answered the question, smiling also, "yes. P IV 11 232 19
"We shall never agree upon this question"--Captain P IV 11 233 24
But I too have been thinking over the past, and a question P IV 11 247 82
was quite out of the question, for they were all three S 9 407 1
& was consulted on the question; she wrote the same day to S 9 408 1
QUESTIONABLE (2)
might well be questionable; and he was not so irrational MP III 2 328 7
the very questionable enjoyments of this day of pleasure. E III 7 374 54
QUESTIONED (11)
Perhaps, if particularly questioned, she might just give NA II 10 203 9
eagerly questioned by his wife and five daughters at once. PP I 13 61 5
that Mr. Bingley, when questioned by Jane, had long ago PP II 13 207 6
"Yes; but when questioned by him Denny denied knowing any PP III 5 290 48
She questioned him as to the society in Yorkshire-- the E II 8 221 48
the world--but if I am questioned about it, I must E III 5 345 16
Her care and attention could not be questioned; they were, E III 9 389 16
therefore, and only questioned Miss Bates farther as to E III 9 390 19
and he was very much questioned, and especially by the two P III 8 64 4
When he questioned, Sir Walter and Elizabeth began to P IV 3 144 22
She wondered, and questioned him eagerly--but in vain. P IV 8 187 33
QUESTIONER (2)
"You are a very close questioner." NA II 4 151 20
"Most willingly, fair questioner.-- S 8 403 1
QUESTIONING (1)
to harden and prepare herself against farther questioning. MP III 1 316 33
QUESTIONS (56)
distressing her, to ask many questions as they travelled. LS 17 271 6
heart to ask questions; but I hope we shall soon know all. LS 40 308 1
Was it from dejection of spirits?"--were questions now NA II 7 180 37
her dread of further questions made her, for the first NA II 9 195 19
his beauty, and ask him questions which his mother SS I 6 31 9
was forced from him by questions, and distinguished Elinor SS I 16 87 23
&c. extorting from him occasional questions and remarks. SS I 16 89 42
in asking so many questions about Mrs. Ferrars, must seem SS I 22 129 16
to endure the questions and remarks of all these people. SS II 7 191 64
to speak, when her questions or remarks gave him anything W 331 11
Charles was now free enough to hazard a few questions in W 332 12
ways; with barefaced questions, ingenious suppositions, PP I 3 9 1
"May I ask to what these questions tend?" PP I 18 93 37
and asking me a thousand questions; and I find that the PP I 18 94 45
in such very direct questions on his return, as required PP I 22 123 3
Elizabeth asked questions in vain; Maria would tell her PP II 5 158 13
addressed a variety of questions to Maria and Elizabeth, PP II 6 163 15

Elizabeth felt all the impertinence of her questions, but PP II 6 164 15
escape all impertinent questions, when the door opened, PP II 9 177 1
some odd unconnected questions--about her pleasure in PP II 10 182 1
"These are home questions--and perhaps I cannot say that I PP II 10 183 12
behaved?" were questions with which she amused herself. PP II 14 210 2
Lady Catherine had many other questions to ask respecting PP II 14 212 16
communicativeness by his questions and remarks; Mrs. PP III 1 248 23
When they were all in the drawing room, the questions PP III 5 287 33
burning with curiosity; "we will ask you no questions." PP III 9 319 29
You may ask questions, which I shall not choose to answer." PP III 14 354 34
having asked one or two questions about the dinner, which MP I 7 71 31
would torment him with questions and remarks relative to MP II 1 184 25
in the room, asked some questions about it, which soon led MP II 4 206 5
will you have?" were questions immediately following with MP II 4 206 5
"I answer no such irrelevant and insidious questions; MP II 7 241 15
his voice, receive his questions, and even answer them MP II 11 284 8
But it is very foolish to ask questions about any young MP II 11 288 28
he had a variety of questions from Crawford as to his MP III 3 340 24
feelings and success; questions which being made--though MP III 3 340 24
he went on, re-urging the same questions as before. MP III 3 342 34
"Well," said Crawford, after a course of rapid questions MP III 3 343 41
see you, of the endless questions I shall have to answer! MP III 5 360 16
I ask no questions.-- MP III 13 420 2
Does Susan go?"--were questions following each other MP III 15 445 29
in her power, but on this subject questions were vain. E I 4 27 3
With this inspiriting notion, her questions increased in E I 4 28 6
to answer questions which puzzled her sister at seventeen. E I 5 37 9
length, by the eagerness of Harriet's wondering questions. E I 9 72 16
grave looks and short questions, he was soon led on to E I 12 98 2
perseverance in asking questions, and amused to think how E II 3 171 10
She will not even listen to your questions. E II 11 255 52
relative questions, all answered with patient politeness. E III 2 324 20
A young lady who faints, must be recovered; questions must E III 3 333 4
"Depend upon me--but ask no more questions. E III 10 392 6
She asked no more questions therefore, merely employed her E III 10 393 18
a subject, to ask questions, to speak more openly than E III 16 459 46
he; "asked more questions about the house, and terms, and P III 3 22 25
but still there were questions enough asked, to make it P IV 5 157 14
of calmness, and answer the common questions of the moment. P IV 6 165 9

QUICK (84)
Catherine and Isabella was quick as its beginning had been NA I 5 36 4
Come, Miss Morland, be quick, for the others are in a NA I 9 61 1
the stairs he was calling out to Miss Morland to be quick. NA I 11 84 18
friendship by strangers, does cut me to the quick, I own. NA I 13 98 2
Her progress was not quick, for her thoughts and her eyes NA II 6 164 3
Catherine's heart beat quick, but her courage did not fail NA II 6 169 11
was her search; her quick eyes directly fell on a roll of NA II 6 169 11
for, they proceeded by quick communication to the kitchen-- NA II 8 183 3
"And from these circumstances," he replied, (his quick eye NA II 9 196 25
"How quick you are!" cried Catherine: "you have guessed it, NA II 10 204 19
foreboding remark; but quick was the consolation of there NA II 16 249 1
She was remarkably quick in the discovery of attachments, SS I 8 36 1
flushed cheek, hollow eye, and quick pulse of a fever?" SS I 8 38 13
Willoughby was a young man of good abilities, quick SS I 10 48 7
and she had a sharp quick eye, and a smartness of air, SS I 21 120 6
replied Miss Steele, with quick exultation; "we came post SS II 10 218 24
in them the quick feelings, and needless alarm of a lover. SS III 6 305 16
sir--be quick--and if you can--less violent." SS III 8 317 5
"Pray be quick, sir"--said Elinor impatiently--"I have no SS III 8 317 8
"I hope there is."--said Mrs E. gravely, with a quick W 326 5
say to eliz: in a sharp quick accent, totally unlike the W 351 24
Mr. Bennet was so odd a mixture of quick parts, sarcastic PP I 1 5 34
field after field at a quick pace, jumping over stiles and PP I 7 32 41
open the door and with quick step pass her towards the PP I 20 110 1
equally surprised to find that he meditated a quick return. PP I 22 124 11
to recommend their being quick, as Lady Catherine very PP II 6 161 7
"And this," cried Darcy, as he walked with quick steps PP II 11 192 22
a visitor, when Bingley's quick step was heard on the PP III 2 261 5
in undertaking business, he was quick in its execution. PP III 8 309 5
Come be quick, be quick! where is your sash my dear?" PP III 13 344 9
body to be as forward and quick at learning as yourself." MP I 2 18 24
quick in carrying messages, and fetching what she wanted." MP I 2 20 31
He knew her to be clever, to have a quick apprehension as MP I 2 22 35
was coming at a quick pace down the principal walk. MP I 10 100 24
down to table, it was a quick succession of busy nothings MP I 10 104 52
and she walks too quick, and speaks too quick, and would MP I 14 134 12
and speaks too quick, and would not keep her countenance. MP I 14 134 12
that Tom Bertram spoke so quick he would be unintelligible, MP I 18 164 2
His manner seemed changed; his voice was quick from the MP II 1 178 7
Fanny's heart beat quick, and she felt quite unequal to MP II 4 210 20
the whole evening; and if quick enough to keep her from MP II 7 240 8
in all the lively turns, quick resources, and playful MP II 7 240 9
Fanny gave a quick negative, and tried to hide her MP II 7 244 28
Quick, quick. MP II 7 251 64
Then, her understanding was beyond every suspicion, quick MP II 12 294 16
protestation; and such a quick consciousness of compliment, MP III 3 339 21
of friendly interest and quick taste--without any touch of MP III 3 340 24
A quick looking girl of Susan's age was the very worst MP III 10 403 15
Sometimes how quick to feel! MP III 16 454 18
two, her feelings, though quick, were more controulable; MP III 17 466 17
Quick and decided in her ways, Emma lost no time in E I 4 26 1
quick eye sufficiently acquainted with Mr. Robert Martin. E I 4 31 27
She was always quick and assured: Isabella slow and E I 5 37 9
are too conscious and too quick, and appear to affix more E I 9 77 47
the usual smile, and her quick eye soon discerned in his E I 9 81 78
the child's pace was quick, and theirs rather slow; and E I 10 88 33
She was quick in feeling the little injuries to Isabella, E I 11 93 5
and seemed to ensure a quick dispatch of the roast mutton E I 13 109 5
deal of heat about her, a quick low pulse, &c. and she was E I 13 109 6
of her good sense and quick feelings: standing in a E I 18 149 26
as she always is, though she speaks rather too quick. E II 3 171 12
know--it is not much, but she does not hear quite quick. E II 3 175 39
think I am particularly quick at those sort of discoveries. E II 3 176 44
so glorious--the steps so quick, from the accidental E II 4 181 4
quick amendment; and so ended a most satisfactory meeting. E II 5 189 16
liveliness of his father's; he looked quick and sensible. E II 5 190 22
His quick eye she detected again and again glancing E II 5 193 34
She speaks a little too quick. E II 14 279 54
then exercise all her quick observation, and speedily E III 1 315 3
not the sort of fatigue--quick walking will refresh me.-- E III 6 363 50
together and on their way at a quick pace for Randall's. E III 10 392 7
Her heart beat quick on hearing Harriet's footstep and E III 11 404 3
Isabella, to be sure, was no very quick observer; yet if E III 17 463 16
She was a woman rather of sound than of quick abilities, P III 2 11 2
How quick come the reasons for approving what we like!-- P III 2 15 15
the speed which a clear head and quick taste could allow. P III 7 61 38
breathe very quick, and feel a hundred things in a moment. P IV 8 183 11
instant to give a look--one quick, conscious look at her. P IV 11 231 10
ideas, she had been too quick in suspecting them to P IV 12 249 3
suavity, she had been too quick in receiving them as the P IV 12 249 3
she must pay the tax of quick alarm for belonging to that P IV 12 252 12
of it's Abysses, it's quick vicissitudes, it's direful S 7 396 1
looks, that you are nmot used to such quick measures."-- S 9 410 1
The parkers, were no doubt a family of imagination & quick S 10 412 1

QUICK-CHANGING (1)
A large party in an hotel ensured a quick-changing, P IV 10 221 32

QUICK-SIGHTED (5)
observant or quick-sighted in general, but in such a case SS II 2 148 12
He, her father, a well-meaning, but not a quick-sighted SS II 9 209 28
That I should be cautious and quick-sighted, and feel many MP II 1 186 34
a littleness the being quick-sighted on such points, he MP II 7 238 1
body's happiness, quick-sighted to every body's merits; E I 3 21 4

QUICKEN (2)
power to superintend his happiness or quicken his measures. E I 11 91 1
delivered to her, and to quicken the pleasure and surprise, P IV 6 162 1

QUICKENED (5)
being Willoughby, quickened her pace and kept up with her. SS I 16 86 20
but the general pace was quickened, and they all MP II 4 215 47
attempt to speak; but quickened by one sovereign wish she MP II 9 261 3
had been hearing what quickened every feeling of affection. MP III 3 335 6
of the pulse being quickened again by injurious courtesy. E III 3 332 1

QUICKENING (2)
not be at ease; and quickening her pace when she got clear NA I 13 101 25
moment was quickening her perception of the horrible evil. MP III 15 440 19

QUICKER (10)
Heaven forbid it!--but why should I be quicker sighted LS 15 267 4
hopes of exciting his politeness to a quicker dispatch. SS II 11 220 3
It was lower and quicker than ever! and Marianne, still SS III 7 311 14
But if these soldiers are quicker than other people in a W 337 15
sermon, she could not help listening with a quicker ear.-- W 343 20
seized by Mr. Crawford's quicker hand, and she was obliged MP II 7 251 66
earlier, later, and quicker, that he might gain half a day. E II 5 190 23
complete Reformation, a quicker release from debt, a much P III 2 12 3
his fortune, and by a rather quicker process than the law. P IV 9 200 59
They were in Union-Street, when a quicker step behind, a P IV 11 239 55

QUICKEST (4)
seemed to promise the quickest succession; one gentleman SS II 11 220 3
full of news, Miss Bates knew not which to give quickest. E II 3 172 23
There was time only for the quickest arrangement of mind. E III 13 424 1
We must do whatever is to be done quickest, and I think E III 16 459 50

QUICKLY (31)
hare and many friends," as quickly as any girl in England. NA I 1 14 1
Never had any day passed so quickly! NA II 11 214 26
be the matter?" it was quickly decided by Eleanor to be NA II 13 222 7
they walked, Mrs. Morland quickly dispatched all that she NA II 14 236 19
Never had any week passed so quickly--he could hardly SS I 19 101 1
Long letters from her, quickly succeeding each other, SS II 10 213 2
"I guessed you would say so"--replied Lucy quickly--"but SS II 13 239 9
"I suppose, said Margt rather quickly to Emma, you & I are W 351 25
dispatched, and its contents as quickly complied with. PP I 9 41 1
was to meet them, they quickly perceived, in token of the PP II 16 219 1
only of returning to the carriage as quickly as possible. PP III 1 254 57
The good news quickly spread through the house; and with PP III 8 309 6
sorrow; but escaping as quickly as possible, could soon MP I 3 24 4
"Those who see quickly, will resolve quickly and act MP I 6 61 57
quickly, will resolve quickly and act quickly," said Julia. MP I 6 61 57
and this reflection quickly restored so much of her good MP II 8 253 4
ball, which would be very quickly followed by one of them, MP II 8 254 10
to appear satisfied, he quickly added, "no, no, I know MP III 1 316 32
all--" he began rather quickly, but checking himself, E II 6 202 38
by her passing it over as quickly as possible, and making E II 7 205 1
"Yes," said his brother quickly, "it is Randalls that does E II 18 312 47
He walked off to find his father, but was quickly back E III 2 325 29
the box, the table was quickly scattered over with E III 5 347 20
quickly in from the garden, and with a look of escape.-- E III 6 362 43
"Good or bad?" said she, quickly, looking up in his face. E III 18 470 3
in passing afterwards quickly from her own chamber to P III 12 104 7
"No," cried Anne quickly, "it cannot be Mr. Elliot, I P IV 10 222 35
side, as Mrs. Clay walked quickly off on the other; and P IV 10 222 39
of various kinds to recommend her quickly and permanently. P IV 12 251 10
see as much, & as quickly as possible, where all was new. S 6 389 1
countenance, added quickly--"he did not bequeath it to his S 7 400 1

QUICKNESS (18)
race; far from any quickness in catching, or bitterness in NA II 14 233 10
that I ever beheld--such quickness & spirit! he lets W 358 28
Lizzy has something more of quickness than her sisters." PP I 1 5 27
general; and with more quickness of observation and less PP I 4 15 11
The power of doing any thing with quickness is always much PP I 10 49 27
cried Julia with angry quickness;--"I am *not* to be Agatha, MP I 14 136 20
"Do you, ma'am?" cried he with quickness. MP III 3 339 20
With quickness in understanding the tempers of those she MP III 17 472 31
There is an openness, a quickness, almost a bluntness in E I 4 34 42
understanding or any quickness; and with this resemblance E I 11 92 4
He had all the clearness and quickness of mind which she E I 11 93 5
not help replying with quickness, "Mr. Elton, this is the E I 15 130 26
27
But, be it sweetness or be it stupidity in her --quickness E II 6 202 35
A little quickness of voice there is which rather hurts E II 14 279 54
They must begin with some quickness of sight and hand, and E II 16 296 43
She may not have surmised the whole, but her quickness E III 14 438 8
enough to familiarize the idea to his quickness of mind.-- E III 17 468 33
There is a quickness of perception in some, a nicety in P IV 12 249 4

QUIESCENT (1)
Lady Bertram was perfectly quiescent and contented, and MP II 8 253 6

QUIET (111)
months a widow, & to be as quiet as possible,--& I have LS 2 244 1
entreat you my dear sir to quiet your mind, & no longer LS 14 263 1
The air of a gentle-woman, a great deal of quiet, inactive NA I 2 20 8
to go on in the same quiet manner, without shewing the NA I 9 62 10
Scarcely had they worked themselves into the quiet NA I 10 75 25
and quiet!--so much better than going to the Lower Rooms. NA I 11 84 19
for the quiet and country air of an inn at Clifton. NA I 11 89 63
The past suspense of the morning had been ease and quiet NA II 2 138 1
tossed about in her bed, and envied every quiet sleeper. NA II 6 170 12
struck twelve, and all was quiet, she would, if not quite NA II 8 189 19
As such, however, they were treated by her with quiet SS I 2 8 1
All his wishes centered in domestic comfort and the quiet SS I 3 16 6
She saw only that he was quiet and unobtrusive, and she SS I 3 16 7
to you, by speaking, in so quiet a way, of my own feelings. SS I 4 21 15
not help smiling at the quiet archness of his manner, and, SS I 18 100 28
29
and quiet--never was there such a quiet little thing!" SS I 21 121 9
spirits; I cannot bear them if they are tame and quiet." SS I 21 122 19
think of tame and quiet children with any abhorrence." SS I 21 123 20
From this moment her mind was never quiet; the expectation SS II 5 169 15
Elinor paid her every quiet and unobtrusive attention in SS II 7 180 5
returned, she continued on the bed quiet and motionless. SS II 7 191 65
hoped, in a way to get some quiet rest before she left her. SS II 8 197 25
conversation, she was herself left to quiet reflection. SS III 2 271 5
She sighed for the air, the liberty, the quiet of the SS III 3 279 1
Her sleep, though not so quiet as Elinor wished to see it, SS III 7 310 9
more quiet--not more herself--remained in an heavy stupor. SS III 7 313 21
at six o'clock sink into a quiet, steady, and to all SS III 7 315 25
the silence and quiet prescribed by every nurse around her. SS III 9 334 5
be at all afraid to drive this quiet old creature, home. W 320 2
For now we have a quiet little whist club that meets three W 325 4
were transported from the quiet warmth of a snug parlour, W 327 7
Your sisters all know how quiet they are; they have none W 339 18
her visit would pass, the quiet tenor of their usual PP II 5 157 10
In this quiet way, the first fortnight of her visit soon PP II 7 169 6
leaving her to enjoy them in quiet, set off by themselves. PP III 4 273 2
The quiet, the retirement of such a life, would have PP III 10 328 28
pleased to find that she had said enough to keep him quiet. PP III 11 330 1
and, after half an hour's quiet reflection in her own room, PP III 17 377 41
Nor was her respect for him, though it made her more quiet, PP III 18 384 27
of it conveyed by her quiet passive manner, when she was MP I 2 15 9
of her eldest niece, as tolerably to quiet her nerves. MP I 4 38 9
sisters, a quiet mother, and an agreeable man himself-- MP I 5 48 28
In a quiet way, very little attended to, she paid her MP I 5 48 30
Girls should be quiet and modest. MP I 5 49 32
and the offer of his own quiet mare for the purpose of her MP I 7 66 14
all her feelings in a quiet congratulation, heard it with MP I 11 108 4
be in a very small and quiet way; and I think a theatre MP I 13 127 28
Fanny, who had been a quiet auditor of the whole, and who MP I 14 136 20

I am well aware that nothing else will quiet Tom." MP I 16 154 10
a quiet family-party to the bustle and confusion of acting. MP II 2 190 6
There is such a quiet simplicity in the plan of the walk!-- MP II 4 209 14
"Too quiet for you I believe." MP II 4 210 18
to listen in quiet, and of passing a very agreeable day. MP II 5 223 48
She was then merely a quiet, modest, not plain looking MP II 6 229 5
for her gliding about with quiet, light elegance, and in MP II 7 251 62
taken his resolution in quiet independence, the result of MP II 8 252 1
conform to the tranquillity of the present quiet week. MP II 11 283 7
will find Mansfield very quiet;--all the noisy ones gone, MP II 11 288 30
Innocent and quiet as you sit here, you cannot have an MP III 5 360 16
I was quiet, but I was not blind. MP III 5 363 21
but her happiness was of a quiet, deep, heart-swelling MP III 6 369 11
and the comparatively quiet state of the house, from Tom MP III 8 388 1
hand, and now and then the quiet observation of "my poor MP III 13 428 14
By her other aunt, Susan was received with quiet kindness. MP III 16 448 3
He was doing all in his power to quiet every thing, with MP III 16 450 9
What I advise is, that your father be quiet. MP III 16 457 29
tolerably domestic and quiet; and, at any rate, there was MP III 17 462 4
steady and quiet, and not living merely for himself. MP III 17 462 4
things so well; but the quiet prosings of three such women E I 3 22 6
them suspected; and the quiet transition which Mr. E I 5 41 31
have me draw her four children that she would not be quiet. E I 6 45 21
little woman, of gentle, quiet manners, and a disposition E I 11 92 4
The evening was quiet and conversible, as Mr. Woodhouse E I 12 100 15
son; but before she could quiet Mr. Elton, the subject was E I 14 118 4
of separating allowed her the relief of quiet reflection. E I 15 133 38
She wanted, rather, to be quiet, and out of temptation; E I 18 144 4
gratefully welcomed; the quiet neat old lady, who with her E II 1 155 4
a pleasant evening," said Mr. Woodhouse, in his quiet way. E II 3 171 12
He agreed to it, but with so quiet a "yes," as inclined E II 5 194 43
Mr. Weston must be quiet, and every thing deliberately E II 7 209 12
"You have sung quite enough for one evening--now, be quiet. E II 8 229 94
of; and we are a very quiet set of people, I believe; more E II 14 274 29
He gave me a quiet hint; I told him he was mistaken; he E II 15 288 38
acquaintance and a quiet girl, and he could talk to her. E II 16 292 10
to his wife's: his is a quiet, indolent, gentlemanlike E II 18 309 33
A very little quiet reflection was enough to satisfy Emma E III 1 315 1
spend some quiet interval in the young man's company. E III 2 319 2
as soon as Miss Bates was quiet, she found herself E III 2 323 20
and it was to be done in a quiet, unpretending, elegant E III 6 352 2
in the prospect of the quiet drive home which was to close E III 7 374 54
of air and scene, and quiet rational conversation, even E III 9 390 16
The quiet, heartfelt satisfaction of the old lady, and the E III 12 418 5
The "how d'ye do's," were quiet and constrained on each E III 13 424 1
With a great deal of quiet observation, and a knowledge, P III 5 34 12
told him to keep quiet, he was sure to begin kicking about. P III 7 56 12
umpire, was now added to the advantages of a quiet evening. P III 9 77 17
very strong feelings with quiet, serious, and retiring P III 11 97 12
to the others, tried to quiet Mary, to animate Charles, to P III 12 111 44
to do her good as a little quiet cheerfulness at home. P IV 2 134 30
could be so good for her as a little quiet cheerfulness. P IV 2 135 33
In London, perhaps, in your present quiet style of living, P IV 4 151 19
the greater space and quiet of Belmont, and as she was not P IV 6 170 30
or quiet attention, and the Admiral had it all his own way. P IV 6 173 48
We live at home, quiet, confined, and our feelings prey P IV 11 232 19
Wentworth's hitherto perfectly quiet division of the room. P IV 11 233 24
Would they only have gone away, and left her in the quiet P IV 11 238 45
in the course of her quiet, solitary progress up the town (P IV 11 238 47
towards the comparatively quiet and retired gravel-walk, P IV 11 240 59
It gives me no pain while I am quiet,--and as soon as S 1 367 1
A very few years ago, & it had been a quiet village of no S 2 371 1
children demanded a very quiet, settled, careful course of S 2 373 1

UIET-LOOKING (1)
A quiet-looking young man. MP I 15 148 59

UIETED (6)
have quieted her ambition to see him driving a barouche. SS I 3 16 6
had in some measure quieted it, and I had been growing a SS III 8 326 53
Lady Lucas quieted her fears a little by starting the idea PP I 3 10 4
Elizabeth's collected behaviour, however, soon quieted his PP III 3 270 11
She was an altered creature, quieted, stupified, MP III 16 448 2
How was such jealousy to be quieted? P IV 8 191 51

IETER (3)
by this, as her mother could be, though in a quieter way. PP I 3 12 15
his wife, fewer and quieter, but not less to the purpose. E II 5 188 8
off: and even in the quieter professions, there is a toil P III 3 20 17

IETEST (4)
and off they went in the quietest manner imaginable, NA I 9 62 10
and moreover the quietest five months I ever passed." MP II 4 210 17
They were out in the very quietest part of a watering- S 6 389 1
him to prefer the quietest sort of ruin & disgrace for the S 8 405 2

IETLY (54)
Everything however was going on calmly & quietly; & tho' I LS 22 281 4
Yet, I wish she had staid quietly at Langford. LS 33 303 1
Her plan for the morning thus settled, she sat quietly NA I 9 60 1
Catherine must excuse her, and must sit quietly down again. NA II 3 147 28
drove so well,--so quietly--without making any disturbance, NA II 5 157 5
she stepped quietly forward, and opened the door. NA II 13 223 9
gone, we shall go on so quietly and happily together with SS II 3 155 8
or not: and she prepared quietly and mechanically for SS II 14 249 7
Their party was small, and the hours passed quietly away. SS III 6 303 12
to each other, again quietly settled at the cottage, and SS III 11 352 20
The morng passed quietly away in discussing the merits of W 338 17
A week or ten days rolled quietly away after this visit, W 348 23
on finding sitting quietly employed after tea, that he was W 355 28
t over as soon and as quietly as possible, she sat down PP I 19 104 7
Elizabeth passed quietly out of the room, Jane and Kitty PP I 20 114 31
probable, stay quietly at home, and be satisfied that we PP I 22 124 9
Elizabeth quietly answered "undoubtedly;"--and after an PP I 22 125 18
quietly at Longbourn, and depend on my diligence and care. PP III 7 303 14
they will settle so quietly, and live in so rational a PP III 7 305 37
er mother, but remained quietly in the hall, till she and PP III 13 345 17
o return into the house, walked quietly into it herself. PP III 14 358 74
he evening passed quietly, unmarked by any thing PP III 17 372 2
dmund said no more to either lady; but going quietly to MP I 7 74 57
t a lucky occurrence, as quietly putting an end to what MP I 17 160 9
anny took the work very quietly without attempting any MP I 18 167 7
8
f their walking quietly home and leaving the family to MP II 1 177 5
hawl which Edmund was quietly taking from the servant to MP II 7 251 66
oon as she would listen quietly, could read his list of MP II 8 253 7
eemed then to be only quietly agreeable, she could not MP II 10 274 8
ery cordial adieus, pass quietly away; stopping at the MP II 10 280 33
he week which passed so quietly and peaceably at the MP II 11 285 15
e well tried, he sank as quietly as possible into a MP III 3 341 31
e done, however, but to submit quietly, and hope the best. MP III 5 356 3
earnt to think it no misfortune to be quietly employed. MP III 9 398 9
he could do nothing but glide in quietly and look at him; MP III 14 429 2
hey now walked on together quietly, till within view of E I 10 89 36
r. John Knightley here asked Emma quietly whether there E I 11 94 9
o their income, quietly, keeping little company, and that E II 7 207 6
hat a man who might have spent his evening quietly at E II 17 302 23
ook, compliments very quietly and properly taken, Mrs. E III 2 324 20
arriet distinct from the rest, quietly leading the way. E III 6 360 40
erself rather walking quietly about with any of the E III 7 374 54
Have I?" said he quietly, and looking at her; "of what E III 13 425 4
he checked herself, however, and submitted quietly to a E III 18 475 36
he child was to be kept in bed, and amused as quietly as P III 7 55 7
he cottage were sitting quietly at work, they were P III 10 83 3
d quietly obliged her to be assisted into the carriage. P III 10 91 41
hen she could command Mary's attention, Anne quietly P III 12 106 18
re contented to pass quietly and carefully down the P III 12 109 32
The plan had reached this point, when Anne, coming quietly P III 12 114 60
The first three or four days passed most quietly, with no P IV 1 125 14
and to retrace, as quietly as she could, the few steps of P IV 10 214 11
her own embarrassment, Anne did move quietly to the window. P IV 10 222 39
of the drawing room very quietly--without seeming to hear S 6 391 1

QUIETLY-CHEARFUL (1)
was a quietly-chearful, gentlemanlike air in Mr H. which W 333 13

QUIETLY-SOCIABLE (1)
As their quietly-sociable little meal concluded, Miss W 343 19

QUIETNESS (5)
It was performed with suitable quietness and uneventful NA I 2 19 4
his worth: and even that quietness of manner which SS I 3 16 13
in a quietness which the room had not known for many hours. SS I 21 122 10
I think he values the very quietness you speak of, and MP II 3 196 3
The quietness of the game made it particularly eligible E III 5 347 20

QUIT (44)
Can you, in short, be prevailed on to quit this scene of NA II 2 139 7
her uneasiness, or make her quit them in apprehension. NA II 4 153 31
quit her hold, and the lid closed with alarming violence. NA II 6 164 3
To quit the neighbourhood of Norland was no longer an evil; SS I 4 24 20
different people to quit the topic, it fell to the ground. SS I 12 62 27
Her unwillingness to quit her mother was her only SS II 3 158 21
park, and were to quit it only with the rest of the family. SS II 3 158 22
In a short time Elinor saw Willoughby quit the room by the SS II 6 178 15
Determined not to quit Marianne, though hopeless of SS II 7 184 16
as she had long been to quit it, could not, when it came SS III 6 301 4
in turning instantly to quit the room, and her hand was SS III 8 317 1
2
Mrs. Jennings could not quit Cleveland during the SS III 10 341 4
Elizabeth did not quit her room for a moment, nor were the PP I 7 33 44
She was still very poorly, and Elizabeth would not quit PP I 8 37 21
quit Netherfield, I should probably be off in five minutes. PP I 9 42 8
must expect him to keep or quit it on the same principle." PP II 9 178 9
him the next moment open the front door and quit the house. PP II 11 193 30
"if the Gouldings would quit it, or the great house at PP III 8 310 8
been to persuade her to quit her present disgraceful PP III 10 322 2
was still with him, but would quit town the next morning. PP III 10 323 2
People did say, you meant to quit the place entirely at PP III 11 336 49
to quit the sphere, in which you have been brought up." PP III 14 356 50
"The place, Fanny, is what you will not quit, though you MP I 3 27 35
is what you will not quit, though you quit the house. MP I 3 27 35
as great an escape to be quit of the intrusion of Charles MP I 17 158 2
I know that the apprehension of being forced to quit MP III 4 348 21
ended, and they were to quit Sir Thomas's carriage, she MP III 7 375 1
was certainly able to quit London whenever she chose.-- MP III 14 432 11
I quit such odious subjects as soon as I can, impatient to MP III 17 461 1
It ended in Mrs. Norris's resolving to quit Mansfield, and MP III 17 465 14
determination never to quit her father, never to marry, a E II 13 264 1
Such a man, to quit the tranquillity and independence of E II 17 303 23
She was immediately up, and wanting to quit the table; but E III 5 349 25
She could never quit him." E III 15 448 31
indifference to her when she was called on to quit them.-- P III 1 4 6
No, he would sooner quit Kellynch-Hall at once, than P III 2 13 6
"Quit Kellynch-Hall." P III 2 13 7
Sir Walter would quit Kellynch-Hall;--and after a very few P III 2 13 8
He was not only to quit his home, but to see it in the P III 2 15 13
struggle, however, Charles Hayter seemed to quit the field. P III 10 82 2
to be gone, she could not quit the mansion-house, or look P IV 1 123 8
She could not quit the room in peace without seeing P IV 8 189 45
chair, in preparing to quit the room, she would have found, P IV 10 225 62
induced by business to quit the high road, & attempt a S 1 363 1

QUITE (938)
Churchill, & therefore if quite convenient to you & Mrs LS 1 243 1
my children, but I am not quite weak enough to suppose a LS 3 247 1
Your friend Mr Smith's story however cannot be quite true, LS 6 252 2
expediency, tho' I am not quite determined on following it. LS 10 257 1
He is quite agreable enough however, to afford me LS 10 258 3
I really grow quite uneasy my dearest mother about LS 11 259 1
I meant moreover to have reminded him of our being quite LS 13 262 1
Poor fellow! he is quite distracted by jealousy, which I LS 16 269 3
his countenance with exultation, was quite out of patience. LS 17 270 3
as Lady Susan's--& she has quite the vernon cast of LS 17 270 5
not yet quite resolved on the manner of bringing it about. LS 19 275 4
I was quite cool, but he gave way to the most violent LS 22 282 7
so favourable a turn, I am quite sorry that I ever LS 23 283 1
Nay, I know not whether I ought to be quite tranquil now, LS 25 292 1
which might convince him that I was not quite happy. LS 25 292 3
tho' he professed himself quite undetermined, there there LS 27 297 4
I have told him that I am not quite well, & must be alone-- LS 31 302 1
him that I shall be quite wretched if he remain here; you LS 31 302 1
thought Frederica looked quite as well as she had done at LS 42 312 4
decided what might not have been decided quite so soon. LS 42 312 6
Such were her propensities--her abilities were quite as NA I 1 14 1
"Catherine grows quite a good-looking girl,--she is almost NA I 1 15 2
and her maid declared she looked quite as she should do. NA I 2 20 8
lively eye, and, if not quite handsome, was very near it. NA I 3 25 2
a hole already; I shall be quite sorry if it has, for this NA I 3 28 35
Mrs. Allen was quite struck by his genius. NA I 3 28 39
"I am quite of your opinion, sir," replied Mrs. Allen; " NA I 3 28 44
Mrs. Allen was now quite happy--quite satisfied with Bath. NA I 5 36 3
coquelicot ribbons instead of green; I quite longed for it. NA I 6 39 4
"Oh! yes, quite; what can it be?-- NA I 6 39 7
"Yes, quite sure; for a particular friend of mine, a Miss NA I 6 40 12
They really put me quite out of countenance. NA I 6 43 33
thought her friend quite as pretty as she could do herself. NA I 7 44 4
"That was very good-natured of you," said Catherine, quite NA I 7 47 16
"my dearest Catherine, I quite envy you; but I am afraid, NA I 7 48 30
who had been engaged quite as long as his sister, was very NA I 8 52 2
I tell him he is quite in luck to be sent here for his NA I 8 54 5
for his health last winter, and came away quite stout." NA I 8 54 7
I have been quite wretched without you." NA I 8 56 12
a degree, my dear Catherine, you would be quite amazed.-- NA I 8 56 14
Tell him, that it would quite shock you to see me do such NA I 8 58 23
I quite doat on her." NA I 9 62 8
"Good heavens!" cried Catherine, quite frightened, "then NA I 9 65 29
"Yes, I fancy they are, but I am not quite certain. NA I 9 68 48
"I cannot be quite positive about that, my dear; I have NA I 9 69 50
and that John Thorpe himself was quite disagreeable. NA I 9 69 51
I assure you, my brother is quite in love with you already; NA I 10 70 1
I really am quite wild with impatience. NA I 10 70 1
were so exactly the same, it was quite ridiculous! NA I 10 71 3
I felt so sure of his being quite gone away." NA I 10 73 11
I declare positively it is quite shocking. NA I 10 75 23
"Then I am quite at a loss. NA I 10 77 37
"Yes, quite--more so, indeed." NA I 10 78 42
James's coming (my eldest brother) is quite delightful-- NA I 10 79 56
"I do not quite despair yet. NA I 11 83 15
A gleam of sunshine took her quite by surprize; she looked NA I 11 83 16
She could not think the Tilneys had acted quite well by NA I 11 86 50
"You will quite break my heart. NA I 11 90 64
Miss Tilney to be at home, but was not quite certain. NA I 12 91 3
with a look which did not quite confirm his words, said he NA I 12 91 3
rendered every thing else of the kind "quite horrid." NA I 12 92 4
been quite wild to speak to you, and make my apologies. NA I 12 93 5
"Well done, General, said I, I am quite of your mind." NA I 12 96 22
walk to-morrow; it was quite determined, and she would not, NA I 13 97 1
shall think you quite unkind, if you still refuse." NA I 13 99 3
Even James was quite angry. NA I 13 100 19
suit her as well, it was quite ridiculous, quite absurd to NA I 13 100 19
ridiculous, quite absurd to make any further objection. NA I 13 100 19
entering the house, he was quite angry with the servant NA I 13 102 27
Catherine was greatly obliged; but it was quite out of her NA I 13 103 28

Text	Work	Vol.	Ch.	Page	Line
Here Catherine was quite lost.	NA	I	14	110	28
She was quite wild to go.	NA	I	14	115	52
"Thank you; but it is quite a matter of indifference to me.	NA	I	14	115	54
"that I quite doated on you the first moment I saw you.	NA	I	15	118	11
mention it I beg; that is quite out of the question.	NA	II	1	130	13
for a partner; but he is quite mistaken, for she would not	NA	II	1	132	17
given; but as it was not quite enough for Catherine's	NA	II	1	133	30
My spirits are quite jaded with listening to his nonsense:	NA	II	1	134	39
I had quite forgot it.	NA	II	3	144	6
"Nay, my sweetest Catherine, this is being quite absurd!	NA	II	3	144	10
a little common honesty is sometimes quite as becoming.	NA	II	3	144	10
me--but indeed it has been quite unintentional on my side,	NA	II	3	145	13
Catherine heard all this, and quite out of countenance	NA	II	3	147	28
She was quite pained by the severity of his father's	NA	II	5	154	2
But this was quite an old set, purchased two years ago.	NA	II	7	175	12
quite appalled by darkness, steal out and look once more.	NA	II	8	189	19
She was quite impatient to know how the Bath world went on,	NA	II	10	201	5
them, she seemed quite disappointed that it was not more.	NA	II	10	206	35
happy, and Catherine was quite delighted with the scheme.	NA	II	11	209	5
"I am sure it is quite unnecessary upon your sister's	NA	II	11	211	13
I really am quite ashamed of my idleness; but in this	NA	II	12	216	2
I am quite uneasy about your dear brother, not having	NA	II	12	216	2
Afterwards he got worse, and became quite my shadow.	NA	II	12	217	2
news of the latter--I am quite unhappy about him, he	NA	II	12	217	2
and they pretended to be quite surprized to see me out.	NA	II	12	217	2
that Henry loved her, and quite always that his father and	NA	II	13	221	6
often as sudden, if not quite so unseasonable, and	NA	II	13	222	7
"I am quite well.	NA	II	13	223	9
every fancy--a pleasure quite unlooked for by all but the	NA	II	14	233	8
but her spirits were quite worn down; and, to be silent	NA	II	14	235	13
"Catherine took us quite by surprize yesterday evening,"	NA	II	14	237	21
thought his expressions quite good enough to be	NA	II	14	237	22
You know you and I were quite forlorn at first."	NA	II	14	238	22
I have a notion you danced with him, but am not quite sure.	NA	II	14	238	26
Catherine, I am afraid you are growing quite a fine lady.	NA	II	15	240	2
I did not quite like, at breakfast, to hear you talk so	NA	II	15	241	4
Marianne's abilities were, in many respects, quite equal	SS	I	1	6	12
My mother was quite sick of it.	SS	I	2	11	20
your giving them more, it is quite absurd to think of it.	SS	I	2	12	24
Poor brandon! he is quite smitten already, and he is very	SS	I	9	45	32
"But indeed this is quite another thing.	SS	I	12	60	11
Marianne was quite angry with her for doubting it.	SS	I	13	68	67
was quite overcome, she burst into tears and left the room.	SS	I	15	82	46
quite overcome by the captivating manners of Mrs. Dashwood.	SS	I	17	90	1
"Quite the contrary," replied Elinor, looking expressively	SS	I	17	94	41
said he, "for we shall be quite alone--and to-morrow you	SS	I	18	99	17
She happened to be quite alone.	SS	I	19	105	13
a gentleman and lady, who were quite unknown to her.	SS	I	19	105	13
This was quite a new idea to Mrs. Dashwood, she had never	SS	I	19	107	27
times over, that it had been quite an agreeable surprise.	SS	I	19	107	28
they had not travelled quite so fast, nor made such a long	SS	I	19	107	29
I declare they are quite charming; I could look at them	SS	I	19	108	36
It was quite a sudden thing our coming at all, and I knew	SS	I	20	110	2
with a laugh, "I shall be quite disappointed if you do not.	SS	I	20	110	4
"Do you know that you are quite rude?"	SS	I	20	112	23
It will be quite delightful!----	SS	I	20	113	29
The Westons will be with us, and it will be quite	SS	I	20	113	33
with us that I never saw before, it is quite charming!	SS	I	20	113	33
you know," she continued--"he says it is quite shocking."	SS	I	20	113	37
It will be quite delightful, I declare!	SS	I	20	115	52
"Oh! yes, quite well; and so full of your praises, he did	SS	I	20	115	54
He is such a charming man, that it is quite a pity he	SS	I	20	115	56
I declare I quite doat upon them already, and indeed I am	SS	I	21	122	17
smart young man, quite a beau, clerk to Mr. Simpson you	SS	I	21	123	28
I suppose your brother was quite a beau, Miss Dashwood,	SS	I	21	124	28
"and I hear he is quite a beau, and prodigious handsome.	SS	I	21	125	35
and the other Miss Dashwoods, quite as his own sisters."--	SS	I	22	130	16
It puts him quite out of heart."	SS	I	22	131	35
"You are quite in the right;" replied Elinor calmly.	SS	I	22	132	38
I am sure I wonder my heart is not quite broke."	SS	I	22	133	42
to you, that I was afraid you would think him quite ill."	SS	I	22	133	46
be quite alone, except her mother and the two Miss Steeles.	SS	II	1	143	9
in your manner, that made me quite uncomfortable.	SS	II	2	146	5
is quite as modest and pretty behaved as Miss Dashwood's."	SS	II	2	148	23
I had quite depended upon meeting you there.	SS	II	2	151	40
me with your company, for I've quite set my heart upon it.	SS	II	3	153	2
"Mrs. Palmer appeared quite well, and I am commissioned to	SS	II	4	163	17
"Are you quite sure of it?" she replied.	SS	II	4	165	26
lit up, quite full of company, and insufferably hot.	SS	II	6	175	2
but as for Miss Marianne, she is quite an altered creature.	SS	II	7	181	8
it is quite grievous to see her look so ill and forlorn.	SS	II	7	181	8
and though I am quite at a loss to discover in what point	SS	II	7	183	13
Poor dear, it seems quite cruel to let her be alone.	SS	II	8	195	14
"Dear ma'am, this kindness is quite unnecessary, Marianne	SS	II	8	195	15
comforts and conveniences; quite shut in with great garden	SS	II	8	196	22
you said so--she does not consider it quite as you do?"	SS	II	8	200	41
"I should have been quite disappointed if I had not found	SS	II	10	217	21
of that kind, it is quite out of the question, the	SS	II	11	224	24
very unwell, has lost her colour, and is grown quite thin.	SS	II	11	227	48
that her mother had been quite rude enough,--for,	SS	II	12	235	30
					31
She could say no more; her spirits were quite overcome,	SS	II	12	236	41
handsome a few months ago; quite as handsome as Elinor.--	SS	II	12	237	43
Or at least, if she did not bring herself quite to rejoice	SS	II	13	238	1
should seem to say, she had quite took a fancy to me.	SS	II	13	239	4
You saw it all; and was not you quite struck with it?"	SS	II	13	239	4
nor could his conscience have quite the ease of Elinor's.	SS	II	13	241	21
When I got to Mr. Palmer's, I found Charlotte quite in a	SS	III	1	257	5
Marianne was quite subdued.--	SS	III	1	264	30
be weathered without our being any of us quite overcome.	SS	III	1	265	36
It was quite out of the benevolence of her heart, that she	SS	III	1	266	36
She was quite in an agony.	SS	III	1	266	38
she is quite come to, and we are as good friends as ever.	SS	III	2	272	12
I can tell you; and it's quite a shame for such ill-	SS	III	2	272	14
at all, it would be quite unkind to keep her on to the	SS	III	2	273	16
but pray tell her I am quite happy to hear she is not in	SS	III	2	275	25
dreadfully, we are both quite well now, and as happy as we	SS	III	2	277	29
					30
that was quite proper to let him be off if he would.	SS	III	2	278	32
was settled--"for they are quite resolved upon going home	SS	III	3	280	8
it all over in the evening, for we shall be quite alone.	SS	III	4	286	11
Elinor did not quite understand the beginning of Mrs.	SS	III	4	286	18
Mrs. Jennings was quite right in what she said.	SS	III	4	288	28
I am sure it would put me quite out of patience!--	SS	III	4	291	51
It seemed quite ridiculous.	SS	III	4	292	55
Elinor was quite of her opinion, as to the probability of	SS	III	4	292	58
that must be quite out of the question; yet why, after her	SS	III	5	296	19
But however, all that is quite out of the question--not to	SS	III	5	297	31
There is no doubt of your doing exceedingly well--quite as	SS	III	5	297	31
to drop in for ten minutes; and I saw quite enough of her.	SS	III	5	299	37
Elinor perceived with alarm that she was not quite herself,	SS	III	7	311	14
It came out quite unawares, quite undesignedly.	SS	III	9	336	12
Yet after a time I did say, for at first I was quite	SS	III	9	337	18
There, however, he is quite mistaken.	SS	III	9	338	20
Her daughter could not quite agree with her, but her	SS	III	9	338	23
that would suit us quite as well as our present situation."	SS	III	9	338	24
their usual studies with quite so much vigour as when they	SS	III	11	352	20
they were neither of them quite enough in love to think	SS	III	13	369	32
who, she was sure, had quite doted upon the worthless	SS	III	13	370	37
"A young man of very good fortune, quite independant, &	W			315	1
"You quite shock me by what you say of Penelope--said Emma.	W			316	2
Not that I can ever quite forgive Penelope."--	W			317	2
away on that account--the Shaws are quite on her side.--	W			318	2
The Edwards' have a noble house you see, & they live quite	W			322	2
It is quite as necessary to young ladies in their first."--	W			326	6
The two first dances were not quite over, when the	W			329	9
Ld Osborne was to be seen quite alone at the end of one,	W			332	11
"We had quite lost you--said Mrs E.--who followed her with	W			333	13
"No faith! my Lord, I have had quite enough of it.	W			335	13
& that as his road lay quite wide from r., it was	W			338	18
do so, our carriage is quite at your service, & Mary will	W			339	18
Beleive me--added he lowering his voice--you are quite	W			339	18
a ball, it is a thing quite out of rule I assure you--	W			340	18
"Yes, quite as full as ever, except the Osbornes.	W			340	19
Why--he is quite one of the great & grand ones;--did not	W			342	19
day; my old friends were quite surprised to see me amongst	W			344	20
we dine in--which do not quite agree with my gouty foot--&	W			344	20
quite as much impertinence in it's form as Goodbreeding.--	W			347	22
"Sweet little darling!--cried Margt--it quite broke my	W			350	24
Emma was quite distress'd by such behaviour;--& she did	W			351	24
I always wish to be treated quite "en famille" when I come	W			351	25
"So Emma, said he, you are quite the stranger at home.	W			351	26
I am quite at your service.	W			354	28
you at home, you must be quite at a loss to amuse him--why	W			354	28
She was quite vanquished, & the fashions of Osborne-Castle	W			358	28
calling his next meal a dinner, was quite insupportable.--	W			359	28
I cannot quite agree with you there.	PP	I	2	7	18
He was quite young, wonderfully handsome, extremely	PP	I	3	9	1
Mrs. Bennet was quite disconcerted.	PP	I	3	9	4
thought her quite beautiful, and danced with her twice.	PP	I	3	12	16
quite struck with Jane as she was going down the dance.	PP	I	3	13	16
"Oh! my dear," continued Mrs. Bennet, "I am quite	PP	I	3	13	18
I quite detest the man."	PP	I	3	13	20
man that it would be quite a misfortune to be liked by him.	PP	I	5	19	10
"Are you quite sure, ma'am?--is not there a little mistake?	PP	I	5	19	11
This is not quite enough to make her understand his	PP	I	6	22	7
but I did not feel quite certain that the air of London	PP	I	6	26	36
such society; and indeed I am quite of your opinion.	PP	I	6	27	47
Her dirty petticoat quite escaped my notice." "you	PP	I	8	36	7
and alone, quite alone! what could she mean by it?	PP	I	8	36	10
I hope it will soon be increased by seeing her quite well."	PP	I	8	37	25
Bingley was quite uncomfortable; his sisters declared that	PP	I	8	40	59
At present, however, I consider myself as quite fixed here.	PP	I	9	42	8
"I assure you there is quite as much of that going on in	PP	I	9	43	19
"You quite mistook Mr. Darcy.	PP	I	9	43	24
and never open their mouths, quite mistake the matter."	PP	I	9	44	27
I shall tell Colonel Forster it will be quite a shame if	PP	I	9	46	38
let her know that I am quite in raptures with her	PP	I	10	48	15
Your conduct would be quite as dependant on chance as that	PP	I	10	49	29
Miss Bingley's attention was quite as much engaged in	PP	I	11	54	4
At length, quite exhausted by the attempt to be amused	PP	I	11	55	4
as for the ball, it is quite a settled thing; and as soon	PP	I	11	55	7
I have great hopes of finding him quite the reverse.	PP	I	13	64	18
Mrs. Philips was quite awed by such an excess of good	PP	I	15	73	11
astonish--and perhaps you would not express it quite so	PP	I	16	77	14
"This is quite shocking!--	PP	I	16	80	28
I hear you are quite delighted with George Wickham!--	PP	I	18	94	44
					45
of his history, and is quite ignorant of the circumstances	PP	I	18	95	50
him that her ladyship was quite well yesterday se'nnight."	PP	I	18	97	59
her, quite disengaged, he never came near enough to speak.	PP	I	18	102	74
the man and the match were quite good enough for her, the	PP	I	18	103	77
"Sir, you quite misunderstand me," said Mrs. Bennet,	PP	I	20	111	5
his regard for her was quite imaginary; and the	PP	I	20	112	24
"your representation of all this, might make me quite easy.	PP	I	21	119	21
quite so gracious as it had been on his first introduction.	PP	I	23	129	15
He was growing quite inattentive to other people, and	PP	II	2	141	9
"And that is quite impossible; for he is now in the	PP	II	2	141	13
reputed disposition when quite a lad, which might agree	PP	II	2	143	20
know this anxiety to be quite needless, yet if she feels	PP	II	3	148	26
"We have not quite determined how far it shall carry us,"	PP	II	4	154	22
"La! my dear," said Maria quite shocked at the mistake, "	PP	II	5	158	15
She is quite a little creature.	PP	II	5	158	15
and her manner of living, quite frightened Maria Lucas,	PP	II	6	161	7
Elizabeth found herself quite equal to the scene, and	PP	II	6	162	11
Your mother must have been quite a slave to your education.	PP	II	6	164	28
to me, and the family are quite delighted with her.	PP	II	6	165	32
Lady Catherine seemed quite astonished at not receiving a	PP	II	6	166	38
It distressed her a little, and she was quite glad to find	PP	II	10	182	1
want of sense; and she was quite decided at last, that he	PP	II	10	187	40
"You have said quite enough, madam.	PP	II	11	193	29
paper, written quite through, in a very close hand.--	PP	II	12	196	3
Well, now let us be quite comfortable and snug, and talk	PP	II	16	221	17
Jane will be quite an old maid soon, I declare.	PP	II	16	221	17
"You are quite right.	PP	II	17	227	24
They look upon it quite as their own, I dare say, whenever	PP	II	17	228	33
ornaments as made her quite wild; that she had a new gown,	PP	II	19	238	5
quite consistent with his behaviour to our poor friend."	PP	III	1	249	40
astonishment was quite equal to what it had been at first,	PP	III	1	254	57
This was a stroke of civility for which she was quite	PP	III	1	254	58
She was quite amazed at her own discomposure; but amongst	PP	III	2	260	1
I am quite well.	PP	III	4	277	10
Mary and Kitty, thank heaven! are quite well."	PP	III	5	286	30
It is not quite a week since they left Brighton.	PP	III	5	288	37
I knew that his conduct had not been always quite right.	PP	III	5	290	50
mother was too happy, to be quite so obstinate as usual.	PP	III	7	307	48
said she, "it will be quite shocking to send her away!	PP	III	8	313	21
they then turned, was not quite so cordial. his	PP	III	9	315	4
Elizabeth had not before believed him quite equal to such	PP	III	9	316	5
put it off, and then I should have gone quite distracted.	PP	III	9	319	24
I quite forgot!	PP	III	9	319	27
I was sometimes quite provoked, but then I recollected my	PP	III	10	325	2
I shall never be quite happy till I have been all round	PP	III	10	325	2
Mrs. Bennet was quite in the fidgets.	PP	III	11	331	13
And so, is it quite certain he is coming?"	PP	III	11	331	14
with an interest, if not quite so tender, at least as	PP	III	11	334	36
They are gone down to Newcastle, a place quite northward,	PP	III	11	336	51
natured, and as unaffected, though not quite so chatty.	PP	III	11	337	56
"You are quite a visit in my debt, Mr. Bingley," she added,	PP	III	11	338	58
"And quite alone?	PP	III	12	341	23
reason, that she was quite disappointed at not seeing him	PP	III	12	343	29
are not, I hope, quite so easily changed as that implies."	PP	III	16	368	21
you quite certain that you can be happy with him?"	PP	III	17	373	9
And do you really love him quite well enough?	PP	III	17	373	11
Are you quite sure that you feel what you ought to do?"	PP	III	17	373	11
"Now I am quite happy," said she, "for you will be as	PP	III	17	374	18
her, saying, "I am quite sorry, Lizzy, that you should be	PP	III	17	375	25
					26
Mary or Kitty, send them in, for I am quite at leisure."	PP	III	17	377	40
Bennet sat quite still, and unable to utter a syllable.	PP	III	17	378	42
I shall like your husband quite as well as Jane's."	PP	III	17	379	48
by Mrs. Bennet's being quite unable to sit alone.	PP	III	19	386	5
have quite money enough to live upon without some help.	PP	III	19	386	7
Miss Ward and Miss Frances quite as handsome as Miss Maria,	MP	I	1	3	1
notions, which indeed are quite of a piece with your	MP	I	1	6	6
of directing, and she knew quite as well how to save her	MP	I	1	8	9
least as things then were, was quite out of the question.	MP	I	1	9	10
Mrs. Norris was quite at his service; and though she	MP	I	1	11	18
looks, and quite overcome by Mrs. Norris's admonitions.	MP	I	2	14	8
It is quite settled.	MP	I	3	25	20
"And I am quite convinced that your being with Mrs. Norris,	MP	I	3	27	37
for any thing, my spirits quite broke down, what could I	MP	I	3	28	42
"Then you will not mind living by yourself quite alone?"	MP	I	3	29	47
health and spirits put it quite out of the question--	MP	I	3	30	56

A fine lady in a country parsonage was quite out of place. MP I 3 31 59
He could not think Lady Bertram quite equal to supply his MP I 3 32 62
Fanny's relief, and her consciousness of it, were quite MP I 3 32 64
that they seemed to be quite free from it, and gave MP I 4 35 4
coming to her, a measure quite as welcome on one side, as MP I 4 41 15
"I have thought of something to make it quite complete. MP I 4 42 19
detestable--the Admiral's lessons have quite spoiled him." MP I 4 43 24
a week, she was quite ready to be fallen in love with. MP I 5 44 2
I beg your pardon, but I cannot quite believe you. MP I 5 46 23
time from reserve to quite the opposite--to confidence! MP I 5 49 32
I am quite in the dark. MP I 5 49 34
"Ah! you carry it off very well, but I cannot be quite so MP I 5 49 35
Mothers certainly have not yet got quite the right way of MP I 5 50 36
That is worse than any thing--quite disgusting!" MP I 5 50 39
it looked like a prison--quite a dismal old prison." MP I 6 53 2
It would be quite a burlesque. MP I 6 54 9
the parsonage; we made it quite a different place from MP I 6 54 9
Mr. Rushworth is quite right, I think, in meaning to give MP I 6 56 26
aunt and I went down to it quite in raptures; but it being MP I 6 57 31
it must be quite out of their power to spare a horse." MP I 6 58 38
was quite at his service in any way that could be useful. MP I 6 61 58
conversation that struck you Fanny, as not quite right?" MP I 7 63 3
I was quite astonished. MP I 7 63 4
of her brother, treating him, they say, quite like a son. MP I 7 63 4
It was shady enough in the alcove, but I declare I quite MP I 7 72 42
She has time enough before her; and her going now is quite MP I 8 76 5
No, my dear Edmund, that will not quite do." MP I 8 77 10
seemed to her a difficulty quite impossible to be got over. MP I 8 78 23
"Fanny will feel quite as grateful as the occasion MP I 8 79 26
down upon; but as we are quite among friends, I will take MP I 9 85 5
were only purple cloth; but this is not quite certain. MP I 9 86 9
are not ordained, Mr. Rushworth and Maria are quite ready." MP I 9 89 25
practice," said Edmund, "but not quite universal. MP I 9 92 41
been used to hear given, or than I can quite comprehend. MP I 9 92 46
"There," cried Miss Crawford, "you have quite convinced MP I 9 93 51
"I am afraid I am not quite so much the man of the world MP I 10 98 10
My feelings are not quite so evanescent, nor my memory of MP I 10 98 10
She felt that he had been very ill-used, and was quite MP I 10 101 33
this spot to the house, quite into the house; and when MP I 10 102 46
quite impatient, she resolved to go in search of them. MP I 10 103 49
already; but this was not quite sufficient to do away the MP I 10 103 49
She was quite shocked when I asked her whether wine was MP I 10 105 55
would quite force upon me; she would not take a denial. MP I 10 106 57
as she understood I lived quite alone, to have a few MP I 10 106 57
"My taking orders I assure you is quite as voluntary as MP I 11 108 13
and was welcomed thither quite as gladly by those whom he MP I 12 115 3
that a man, before he has quite made up his own mind, will MP I 12 116 10
was quite grieved to be losing even a quarter of an hour.-- MP I 12 117 11
Mrs. Norris continued, "it is quite delightful, ma'am, to MP I 12 118 16
Mrs. Rushworth, who saw nothing but her son, was quite at MP I 12 118 17
Your mother is quite anxious about it but cannot very well MP I 12 119 23
was yet an untasted pleasure, was quite alive at the idea. MP I 13 123 6
"Oh! quite enough," cried Mr. Yates, "with only just a MP I 13 123 8
seemed so decided, as to make Edmund quite uncomfortable. MP I 13 124 13
I have quite as great an interest in being careful of his MP I 13 127 29
the next morning, were quite as impatient of his advice, MP I 13 128 38
impatient of his advice, quite as unyielding to his MP I 13 128 38
quite as determined in the cause of pleasure, as Tom.-- MP I 13 128 38
comic, Tom Bertram, not quite alone, because it was MP I 14 130 3
She was acknowledged to be quite right, and the two parts MP I 14 132 8
I quite detest her. MP I 14 136 20
Say this with firmness, and it will be quite enough.-- MP I 15 140 15
Tom would be quite angry; and if we are so very nice, we MP I 15 141 21
and which altogether was quite overpowering to Fanny; and MP I 15 146 53
is about nothing,--I am quite ashamed of you, Fanny, to MP I 15 146 53
Her judgment may be quite as safely trusted.-- MP I 15 147 54
sea, and said that she had quite a curiosity to see him, MP I 15 147 57
found it quite as puzzling when she awoke the next morning. MP I 16 150 1
and for some time was quite deserted, except by Fanny, MP I 16 151 1
"To have it quite in their own family circle was what they MP I 17 158 2
"No, she is quite determined. MP I 17 159 4
Julia was a sufferer too, though not quite so blamelessly. MP I 17 160 7
a companion in uneasiness; quite as far from having no MP I 18 166 5
Mrs. Norris thought her quite as well off as the rest, was MP I 18 166 6
Lady Bertram seemed quite resigned to waiting.-- MP I 18 167 12
Fanny, quite surprised, endeavoured to show herself MP I 18 168 16
"Thank you--I am quite warm, very warm. MP I 18 168 17
She had been quite overlooked by her cousins; and as her MP II 1 176 4
She was quite oppressed. MP II 1 178 7
Sir Thomas did not quite understand this, and looked with MP II 1 186 32
said no more; but my heart quite ached for him at every MP II 2 189 5
thing you can imagine, I was quite in an agony about him. MP II 2 189 5
look up to you, that I am quite laughed at about it, for MP II 2 190 7
Sir Thomas had been quite indifferent to Mr. Crawford's MP II 2 194 21
Such language was so new to Fanny that it quite MP II 3 197 7
We shall be quite a small party at home. MP II 3 199 17
kindness, but he was quite mistaken in supposing she had MP II 3 200 21
quite so far as his judgment might have dictated to others. MP II 3 201 22
Her mind was quite determined and varied not. MP II 3 202 25
Mrs. Rushworth was quite ready to retire, and make way for MP II 3 202 28
to his lady, and Julia was quite as eager for novelty and MP II 3 204 32
Fanny's heart beat quick, and she felt quite unequal to MP II 4 210 20
I have my alarms, but they are quite in a different MP II 4 212 31
and finding herself quite unable to attend as she ought to MP II 4 214 46
I shall be here, so you may be quite easy about your aunt. MP II 5 220 30
agitation: "quite unnecessary!--a great deal too kind! MP II 5 221 38
39
This is quite a surprize, Fanny. MP II 5 223 46
With a significant smile, which made Fanny quite hate him, MP II 5 224 49
that in my opinion, every thing had gone quite far enough." MP II 5 225 58
Henry Crawford had quite made up his mind by the next MP II 6 229 1
quite a different creature from what she was in the autumn. MP II 6 229 5
said, "I do not quite know what to make of Miss Fanny. MP II 6 230 7
thankfully acknowledged--quite thankfully and warmly, for MP II 6 232 13
done with the stream; but I could not quite determine what. MP II 7 242 23
She is quite determined. MP II 7 244 28
William, you are quite out of luck; but the next time you MP II 7 245 32
There were points on which they did not quite agree, there MP II 8 255 10
and embarrassment quite diverting to her companion, she MP II 8 259 20
I have such innumerable presents from him that it is quite MP II 8 259 22
"I feel quite stupid. MP II 11 283 5
If we have been kind to her, she is now quite as necessary MP II 11 285 11
or some days longer, I am not quite sure which." MP II 11 288 23
And they are quite in the right, for it would be a very MP II 11 289 34
down from London again in quite, or more than quite, his MP II 12 291 1
in quite, or more than quite, his usual cheerfulness, she MP II 12 291 1
I am quite determined, Mary. MP II 12 291 4
No--you must be aware that I am quite determined to marry MP II 12 291 4
No, Mary, you are quite mistaken. MP II 12 293 10
Fanny Price--wonderful--quite wonderful!-- MP II 12 293 11
But you are quite right, you could not have chosen better. MP II 12 293 11
that you are doing quite right, and though I should never MP II 12 294 19
"Well, well, we do not think quite alike here. MP II 12 296 28
It quite delights me. MP II 12 297 32
would be quite distressing to her to see him again so soon. MP II 13 303 12
as usual; but it was quite impossible for her not to look MP II 13 303 13
Her comfort in that day's dinner was quite destroyed; she MP II 13 304 16
She had quite convinced herself of this before Sir Thomas MP II 13 306 26
The difficulty was in maintaining the conviction quite so MP II 13 306 26
Quite unpractised in such sort of note-writing, had there MP II 13 307 30
31
"Oh! I thank you, I have quite done, just done--it will be MP II 13 307 34

and in her agitation, had quite overlooked the deficiences MP III 1 312 5
speaking or looking up quite impossible, turned away his MP III 1 313 15
me, and quite out of my power to return his good opinion." MP III 1 314 17
tell her uncle that he was wrong--"you are quite mistaken. MP III 1 315 19
still more,--if I had been quite certain of his meaning MP III 1 315 19
I am half inclined to think, Fanny, that you do not quite MP III 1 316 29
that is quite out of the question--quite impossible. MP III 1 316 32
She was struck, quite struck, when on returning from her MP III 1 322 51
Fanny would have had quite as good a walk there, I assure MP III 1 323 56
that such a change was quite impossible, that the subject MP III 2 327 5
Lady Bertram was quite talkative. MP III 2 333 27
than Sir Thomas could quite echo, he was most earnest in MP III 3 335 6
or within a page or two, quite near enough to satisfy Lady MP III 3 336 10
Your ladyship is quite mistaken. MP III 3 339 20
You quite astonish me--I wonder how you can"----- MP III 3 342 35
they were quite mistaken who wished you to do otherwise. MP III 4 347 18
And she spoke with a warmth which quite astonished Edmund, MP III 4 347 19
that I consider it as quite impossible we should ever be MP III 4 348 22
You are quite enough alike. MP III 4 348 23
His avoiding her was quite at an end. MP III 4 349 24
your worth to her brother, quite as it deserved, and of MP III 4 351 36
feel it quite impossible to do any thing but love you." MP III 5 359 9
There never was anything quite like it." MP III 5 360 14
For as to secrecy, Henry is quite the hero of an old MP III 5 360 16
Quite unlike his usual self, he scarcely said any thing. MP III 5 365 35
be quite enough to support the spirits he was watching.-- MP III 6 368 7
in the dock-yard, too, which he quite longed to shew her. MP III 6 372 18
It was a correspondence which Fanny found quite as MP III 7 376 4
It takes me quite unawares. MP III 7 378 10
Campbell has been here, quite in a worry about you; and MP III 7 378 10
With an acknowledgement that he had quite forgot her, Mr. MP III 7 380 22
is quite a miracle if one keeps them more than half-a-year. MP III 7 385 39
Mansfield, had for a short time been quite afflicted.-- MP III 7 386 40
Fanny was quite shocked. MP III 7 386 43
Her heart and her time were already quite full; she had MP III 8 389 4
on them; they were quite untameable by any means of MP III 8 391 8
but she had not quite enough for the demands of yesterday. MP III 9 393 1
use, and Susan was entertained in a way quite new to her. MP III 10 404 15
the place, she felt it quite the voice of a friend when he MP III 10 405 17
that shrunk from it would soon be quite unpardonable. MP III 10 406 20
Not quite a month.-- MP III 11 410 9
ample allowance, I should think six weeks quite enough.-- MP III 11 410 16
owing to contrast, she was quite persuaded of his being MP III 11 413 32
his importance to her were quite what it had been before MP III 12 417 4
It is quite settled that the Grants go to Bath; they leave MP III 13 423 2
Thomas was quite unkind, both to her aunt and to herself.-- MP III 13 424 4
She is quite as likely to have led them astray. MP III 13 424 4
Poor Tom, I am quite grieved for him, and very much MP III 13 427 12
Mrs. Price did quite as much for Lady Bertram, as Lady MP III 13 428 15
I really am quite agitated on the subject. MP III 14 434 13
having breakfasted, and being quite ready in half an hour. MP III 15 445 29
much unusual activity, was quite and completely ready as MP III 15 445 31
Susan's presence drove him quite into himself, and his MP III 15 445 33
each with the person quite dependant on them, at this time, MP III 16 449 4
soon able to understand quite as much as she wished of the MP III 16 449 7
one of whose affectionate sympathy he was quite convinced. MP III 16 453 17
"Cruel!" said Fanny--"quite cruel! MP III 16 456 24
Fanny thought exactly the same; and they were also quite MP III 16 460 31
Here was comfort indeed! and quite as soon as Sir Thomas MP III 17 462 5
at the time when it was quite natural that it should be so, MP III 17 470 26
"Well! that is quite surprizing, for we have had a vast E I 1 10 26
person, and quite determined to continue the acquaintance. E I 3 23 9
a little more knowledge and elegance to be quite perfect. E I 3 23 10
The happiness of Miss Smith was quite equal to her E I 3 25 15
Altogether she was quite convinced of Harriet Smith's E I 4 26 2
It was quite a different sort of thing--a sentiment E I 4 26 2
indeed; one of them quite as large as Mrs. Goddard's E I 4 27 4
to give them up, for they are quite as well educated as me. E I 4 31 25
It was quite a chance, he said, that he had not gone round E I 4 32 29
that he quite forgot it, but he goes again to-morrow. E I 4 32 29
Mr. Elton's situation was most suitable, quite the E I 4 35 44
when he is not quite frightened enough about the children. E I 5 40 23
She was quite convinced of Mr. Elton's being in the E I 6 42 1
There is my sister; and really quite her own little E I 6 45 21
(Mrs. Weston and I were quite agreed in thinking it very E I 6 45 21
very satisfactory; she was quite enough pleased with the E I 6 47 27
Yes, quite a proposal of marriage; and a very good letter, E I 7 50 1
himself so well, if left quite to his own powers, and yet E I 7 51 5
one's mind ought to be quite made up--one should not be E I 7 52 20
by myself; and I have now quite determined, and really E I 7 53 22
23
regard for--but that is quite a different thing from--and E I 7 54 30
I am quite determined to refuse him. E I 7 55 34
As to anything superior for you, I suppose she is quite in E I 7 56 41
Mr. Perry could not quite understand him, but he was very E I 8 68 58
and heal.-- made her quite sorry to acknowledge that E I 9 70 7
it through again to be quite certain, and quite mistress E I 9 72 15
to be quite certain, and quite mistress of the lines, and E I 9 72 15
the parts, so as to feel quite sure that her friend were E I 9 77 43
or even quite all the meaning which may be affixed to it. E I 9 77 47
"Yes, papa, we have something to read you, something quite E I 9 78 50
charming, Harriet, is not quite enough to induce me to E I 10 84 10
11
And the distinction is not quite so much against the E I 10 85 19
You quite forget poor Mr. Weston." E I 11 95 17
"Why, pretty well; but not quite well. E I 12 101 25
"Oh! the good Bateses--I am quite ashamed of myself--but E I 12 102 31
I hope they are quite well. E I 12 102 31
or heavy--except when it has been quite an influenza." E I 12 102 33
free from any where, I am quite well myself; and if the E I 12 103 39
with many people, but indeed it is quite a mistake, sir.-- E I 12 105 55
have had lodgings there quite away from the sea--a quarter E I 12 106 56
she added soon afterwards--as if quite another subject. E I 13 110 8
"You do quite right," said she;--"we will make your E I 13 110 11
"I thank you; but I assure you you are quite mistaken. E I 13 112 23
"Quite seasonable; and extremely fortunate we may think E I 13 115 39
This is quite the season indeed for friendly meetings. E I 13 115 39
Harriet seemed quite forgotten in the expectation of a E I 13 115 42
parties of London, may not quite enter into our feelings." E I 13 116 43
He seemed by this connection between the families, quite E I 14 119 5
and my son--and then I should say we were quite complete. E I 14 119 7
Churchill and Miss Smith making their party quite complete. E I 14 119 8
The case, you see, is--(but this is quite between E I 14 120 11
had drank his tea he was quite ready to go home; and it E I 15 124 1
a bad sore throat; and Emma was quite in charity with him. E I 15 124 3
as for myself, I am not, I think, quite so must at a loss. E I 15 132 35
father, as to seem--if not quite ready to join him in a E I 15 132 38
thousand pounds, were not quite so easily obtained as he E I 16 135 7
She was quite concerned and ashamed, and resolved to do E I 16 137 10
There I was quite right. E I 16 137 11
justify their all three being quite asunder at present. E I 16 138 16
Her father was quite taken up with the surprize of so E I 17 141 4
Knightley; and exclaimed quite as much as was necessary, (E I 18 145 5
out, till they are quite as unmanageable as great ones. E I 18 147 19
were just now quite safe from any letter from Jane Fairfax. E II 1 155 3
honour!' said she; 'well, that is quite unexpected. E II 1 157 7
being aware, and so it was quite hid, but I had it in my E II 1 157 10
Jane was quite longing to go to Ireland, from his account E II 1 160 20
Colonel and Mrs. Campbell; quite depend upon it; nothing E II 1 160 23
Campbell think she does quite right, just what they should E II 1 161 25
air, as she has not been quite so well as usual lately." E II 1 161 25
unwell, than I burst out quite frightened with, 'bless me! E II 1 162 31

She had never been quite well since the time of their	E II 2 165 9
her conscience could not quite acquit her. but "she could	E II 2 166 11
My dear Miss Woodhouse--I come quite overpowered.	E II 3 172 24
"Well! that is quite----- I suppose there never was a	E II 3 173 29
a thousand thanks, and says you really quite oppress her."	E II 3 173 29
know--it is not much, but she does not hear quite quick.	E II 3 175 39
Colonel Campbell, you know, is quite our angel.	E II 3 175 39
And Mr. Dixon seems a very charming young man, quite	E II 3 175 39
I always say, we are quite blessed in our neighbours.--	E II 3 175 39
She seems quite recovered now.	E II 3 176 44
"Quite wrong, my dear aunt; there is no likeness at all."	E II 3 176 45
and they both went to quite the farther end of the shop;	E II 3 178 52
she came forward--came quite up to me, and asked me how I	E II 3 178 52
know, and as if he did not quite know what to do; and so	E II 3 179 52
for I should find the near way quite floated by this rain.	E II 3 179 52
as a mere trifle, and quite unworthy of being dwelt on.	E II 3 180 54
Her mind was quite sick of Mr. Elton and the Martins.	E II 5 187 4
Emma's spirits were mounted quite up to happiness; every	E II 5 189 16
merits, without seeming quite to forget that in the common	E II 5 192 29
to feel quite assured of himself till after another night.	E II 5 193 35
only going to the crown, quite on the other side of the	E II 5 195 47
"my good friend, this is quite unnecessary; Frank knows a	E II 5 195 48
If the talking aunt had taken me quite by surprise, it	E II 6 198 7
Intimacy between Miss Fairfax and me is quite out of the	E II 6 203 41
they know you do not dine out," was not quite sufficient.	E II 7 207 7
You will say that I am quite an invalid, and go no where,	E II 7 209 14
He was quite as undaunted and as lively as ever; and after	E II 8 212 2
	3
I am quite glad to see you."	E II 8 213 8
account, Jane herself was quite at a loss, quite	E II 8 214 13
was quite at a loss, quite bewildered to think who could	E II 8 214 13
It always has quite hurt me that Jane Fairfax, who plays	E II 8 215 16
It seemed quite a shame, especially considering how many	E II 8 215 16
I was saying this to Mr. Cole but yesterday, and he quite	E II 8 216 16
to know a little more, and this tells me quite enough.	E II 8 218 38
	39
I was quite surprized;--very glad, I am sure; but really	E II 8 223 63
glad, I am sure; but really quite surprized.	E II 8 223 63
tell you, would be quite enough to account for the horses.	E II 8 224 72
"Quite out of the question, quite out of the question," he	E II 8 228 90
"You have sung quite enough for one evening--now, be quiet.	E II 8 229 94
and there were two points on which she was not quite easy.	E II 9 231 2
to be quite certain that she ought to have held her tongue.	E II 9 231 2
I think you play quite as well as she does.	E II 9 231 7
"Well, I always shall think that you play quite as well as	E II 9 232 9
was amused enough; quite enough still to stand at the door.	E II 9 233 24
I should be quite in the way.	E II 9 234 30
Quite otherwise indeed, if I understood Miss Fairfax's	E II 9 234 33
"Aye, that will be much best," said Harriet, quite	E II 9 235 42
breakfast, you would be quite frightened if you saw it.	E II 9 237 46
But I was really quite shocked the other day--for Mr.	E II 9 238 51
in our lives; but she was quite distressed that I had	E II 9 238 51
he said, was quite displeased at their being all sent away.	E II 9 239 51
Miss Woodhouse, I am quite concerned, I am sure you hit	E II 9 239 53
was not quite firm; an unevenness in the floor, I believe.	E II 10 240 5
was quite ready to sit down to the pianoforte again.	E II 10 240 6
conjecture how soon I shall make this rivet quite firm.	E II 10 242 15
turning to Emma, said, "here is something quite new to me.	E II 10 242 20
	21
Quite delightful to have you all meet so!--	E II 10 243 31
Quite delightful; so many friends!"	E II 10 244 44
Yes, that will be quite enough for pleasure.	E II 11 248 4
Mrs. Weston, you would be quite laid up; do not let them	E II 11 249 11
Do not tell his father, but that young man is not quite	E II 11 249 11
you against him, but indeed he is not quite the thing!"	E II 11 249 11
was now endeavoured to be made out quite enough for ten.	E II 11 249 12
"No, no," said she, "you are quite unreasonable.	E II 11 249 17
Exquisite, quite exquisite!--	E II 11 250 18
of their acquaintance, he was quite amiable enough.	E II 11 250 19
for dancing has not been quite frightened away, I hope, by	E II 11 250 21
and then, being quite new, further representations were	E II 11 251 25
This Emma felt was aimed at her; and it made her quite	E II 12 258 4
that Mrs. Weston was quite mistaken in that surmise.	E II 12 258 6
Her father's feelings were quite distinct.	E II 12 259 11
"Our poor ball must be quite given up."	E II 12 259 16
think you can hardly be quite without suspicion"-----	E II 12 260 29
she calmly said, "you were quite in the right; it was most	E II 12 261 30
	31
He stopt again, rose again, and seemed quite embarrassed.--	E II 12 261 34
often thinking of him, and quite impatient for a letter,	E II 13 264 1
I am quite enough in love.	E II 13 264 2
to do otherwise, as my own mind is quite made up.	E II 13 265 4
do not look upon him to be quite the sort of man--I do not	E II 13 265 4
"I think her beautiful, quite beautiful."	E II 14 271 9
being married, you know, it is quite a different thing.	E II 14 271 15
and the quarter of an hour quite convinced her that Mrs.	E II 14 272 16
She was quite struck by the likeness!--	E II 14 272 18
struck by its beauty; but to me, it has been quite a home.	E II 14 273 19
I always say this is quite one of the evils of matrimony."	E II 14 273 19
"Oh! yes, I am quite aware of that.	E II 14 273 24
I was quite a proverb for it at Maple Grove.	E II 14 274 30
do agree, it is quite wonderful the relief they give.	E II 14 275 32
their going to Bath was quite out of the question; and she	E II 14 276 34
thing; but my resources made me quite independent.	E II 14 276 36
'But,' said I, 'to be quite honest, I do not think I can	E II 14 277 36
I use to be quite angry with Selina; but really I begin	E II 14 277 40
Mr. Weston seems an excellent creature--quite a first-rate	E II 14 278 44
But she is really quite the gentlewoman."	E II 14 278 46
Emma was quite at a loss.	E II 14 278 49
Knightley is quite the gentleman.	E II 14 278 50
I quite rave about Jane Fairfax.--	E II 15 282 5
My greatest danger, perhaps, in housekeeping, may be quite	E II 15 283 9
She was quite one of her worthies--the most amiable,	E II 15 284 12
"She is a riddle, quite a riddle!" said she.--	E II 15 285 13
Here is quite a separate puzzle."	E II 15 285 15
We really seem quite the fashion.	E II 16 290 2
She was not yet quite able to see him and his charming	E II 16 291 5
Mr. Woodhouse was quite at ease; and the seeing him so,	E II 16 292 9
She was quite determined not to utter a word that should	E II 16 298 59
"Here is April come!" said she, "I get quite anxious about	E II 17 299 2
When I am quite determined as to the time, I am not at all	E II 17 300 13
sale--not quite of human flesh--but of human intellect."	E II 17 300 13
You quite shock me; if you mean a fling at the slave-trade,	E II 17 300 14
the good Campbells will be quite on my side; with your	E II 17 301 18
who feels for me, but I am quite serious in wishing	E II 17 301 19
"And I am quite serious too, I assure you," replied Mrs.	E II 17 302 20
the idea of being over-trimmed--quite a horror of finery.	E II 17 302 22
But I am quite in the minority, I believe; few people seem	E II 17 302 22
Selina says it is quite horror to her--and I believe I	E II 18 306 12
as you may suspect--but this is quite between ourselves.	E II 18 307 18
have so many myself as to be quite independent of society."	E II 18 307 21
"When Frank left us," continued he, "it was quite	E II 18 308 27
because things did not go quite right, did not proceed	E II 18 308 28
one morning, I remember*, he came to me quite in despair."	E II 18 308 28
I have quite a horror of upstarts.	E II 18 310 34
The Enscombe family were not in town quite so soon as had	E III 1 315 3
If he was quite sincere, if he really tried to come, it	E III 1 316 6
He was quite delighted.	E III 1 317 10
You must know I have a vast dislike to puppies--quite a	E III 2 321 15
as to offer, but another time it will be quite unnecessary.	E III 2 321 17
Quite thick shoes.	E III 2 322 19
I hope you are quite well.	
	E III 2 322 19
Jane and I quite ready.	E III 2 323 19
Very well I thank you, quite well.	E III 2 323 19
This is meeting quite in fairy-land!--	E III 2 323 19
Quite wonderful how she does her hair!--	E III 2 323 19
Quite well, I am much obliged to you.	E III 2 323 19
I am quite roasted.	E III 2 328 42
She did not think he was quite so hardened as his wife,	43
Grandmamma was quite well, had a charming evening with Mr.	E III 2 329 45
Quite the queen of the evening!--	E III 2 329 45
the asparagus quite boiled enough, sent it all out again.	E III 2 329 45
to reach Hartfield, before her spirits were quite overcome.	E III 3 334 7
manner which prepared her, quite as much as her words, for	E III 4 337 3
As I am happily quite an altered creature in <u>one respect</u>,	E III 4 337 4
Emma was quite eager to see this superior treasure.	E III 4 339 17
"Yes, simpleton as I was!--but I am quite ashamed of it	E III 4 340 24
came to a sufficient explanation, and quite undesignedly.	E III 4 340 28
as ourselves--but it was quite a secret, known to nobody	E III 5 345 16
These delays and disappointments are quite odious.	E III 6 353 7
Quite a humourist.	E III 6 355 18
"That's quite unnecessary; I see Jane every day:--but as	E III 6 355 20
It is to be a morning scheme, you know, Knightley; quite a	E III 6 355 20
"Not quite.	E III 6 355 21
he was happily placed, quite at his ease, ready to talk	E III 6 357 33
"But it is too far, indeed it is, to be walking quite	E III 6 362 47
some hours--and he had quite given up every thought of	E III 6 363 53
back all the better--grown quite cool--and, with good	E III 6 364 59
You are quite mistaken.	E III 6 365 64
"You are not quite so miserable, though, as when you first	E III 6 365 65
I had quite determined to go away again."	E III 7 368 4
I will not say quite all.	E III 7 370 19
Exactly so, indeed--quite unheard of--but some ladies say	E III 7 370 22
<u>Perfection</u> should not have come quite so soon."	E III 7 371 36
round the fire; but quite out of place, in my opinion,	E III 7 372 37
An old married man--quite good for nothing.	E III 7 372 38
I am quite ready.	E III 7 374 53
sitting almost alone, and quite unattended to, in tranquil	E III 7 374 54
as if she did not quite understand what was going on.	E III 8 378 5
know one cannot feel any blessing quite as it may deserve.	E III 8 379 8
You were kept waiting at the door--I was quite ashamed--	E III 8 379 8
first heard of it, she was quite decided against accepting	E III 8 380 15
Quite a surprise to me!	E III 8 381 15
of woman's destiny, and quite unconscious on what her eyes	E III 8 384 32
	33
deranged--appetite quite gone--and though there were no	E III 9 389 16
and thanks, but is quite unequal to any exercise."	E III 9 390 16
	17
without success; Jane was quite unpersuadable; the mere	E III 9 390 18
that made him appear quite a different creature from any	E III 10 399 57
"I am quite easy on that head," replied Mrs. Weston.	E III 10 399 62
Emma looked at her, quite unable to speak.	E III 11 404 9
"Not quite," returned Emma, with forced calmness, "for all	E III 11 406 21
story of Jane Fairfax, that was quite sunk and lost.--	E III 11 408 33
and of his having indeed quite a different manner towards	E III 11 409 35
she had not quite done nothing--for she had done mischief.	E III 11 413 47
Emma was quite relieved, and could presently say, with a	E III 13 425 10
	11
"No"--replied Emma--quite confirmed by the depressed	E III 13 429 32
Her way was clear, though not quite smooth.--	E III 13 431 38
and figuratively, was quite necessary to reinstate her in	E III 14 435 5
We are quite well.--	E III 14 436 7
I did not quite like your looks on Tuesday, but it was an	E III 14 436 7
to be happier than I deserve, I quite of your opinion.--	E III 14 443 8
"I was not quite impartial in my judgment, emma:--but yet,	E III 15 445 13
have been quite without resentment under such a stroke.	E III 16 451 2
she was quite eager to have Harriet under her care.--	E III 16 451 3
Let us be discreet--quite on our good behaviour.--	E III 16 454 13
<u>My</u> representation, you see, has quite appeased her."	E III 16 454 13
<u>It</u> must be the same party, you know, quite the same party,	E III 16 455 18
Yes, indeed, I quite understand--dearest Jane's prospects--	E III 16 455 20
Quite out of my power.--	E III 16 455 20
Oh! yes, quite indispensable."	E III 16 456 23
to her; and it would be quite a pity that any one who so	E III 17 461 1
My interference was quite as likely to do harm as good.	E III 17 462 7
Isabella sent quite as good an account of her visitor as	E III 17 463 16
I believe I did not play with the children quite so much	E III 17 465 27
"You mistake me, you quite mistake me," she replied,	E III 18 471 17
You laugh at me about William Larkins; but I could quite	E III 18 473 22
my word, I believe you know her quite as well as I do.--	E III 18 473 26
Are you quite sure that you understand the terms on which	E III 18 474 29
"I am quite sure," he replied, speaking very distinctly, "	E III 18 474 30
"That appears quite wonderful.	E III 18 477 55
Have you quite forgotten?"	E III 18 478 62
"Not quite so miserable as to be insensible to mirth.	E III 18 478 67
evening before, from the infant's appearing not quite well.	E III 18 479 73
if not quite the luckiest, to yield only to herself.	E III 19 482 4
Elizabeth did not quite equal her father in personal	P III 1 6 12
She was fully satisfied of being still quite as handsome	P III 1 7 12
quite out of place, could hint of caution and reserve.	P III 2 15 15
drive to Kellynch: "but I quite agree with my father in	P III 3 18 7
I never saw quite so wretched an example of what a sea-	P III 3 20 16
The lawyer plods, quite care-worn; the physician is up at	P III 3 20 17
of their personableness when they cease to be quite young."	P III 3 20 17
be sure, but not much; and quite the gentleman in all this	P III 3 22 23
took out a gun, but never killed;--quite the gentleman.	P III 3 22 23
And moreover, Sir Walter, I found she was not quite	P III 3 22 25
Mr. Wentworth was nobody, I remember; quite unconnected;	P III 3 23 33
of the arrangement quite as keenly as Lady Russell.	P III 5 34 12
other prettinesses, was quite as likely to catch the	P III 5 36 20
not mind a word I say, and walter is growing quite as bad."	P III 5 38 27
It was quite unkind of you not to come on Thursday."	P III 5 38 31
They are quite different creatures with you!	P III 6 44 8
I believe Mrs. Charles is not quite pleased with my not	P III 6 45 8
Mrs. Charles quite swears by her, I know; but I just give	P III 6 45 9
She was quite easy on that head, and consequently full of	P III 6 49 18
	19
black idea; and Mary was quite ready to be affronted, when	P III 6 50 26
and her head is quite full of it, and of poor Richard!	P III 6 50 27
time by his family, though quite as much as he deserved;	P III 6 50 28
sorry when he said it was quite out of his power--and how	P III 7 54 4
And off they ran, quite as full of glee as of love, and	P III 7 54 4
This was quite a female case, and it would be highly	P III 7 55 7
just now that I would come, and he thought me quite right.	P III 7 55 8
of speaking, that he was quite determined on going, and	P III 7 55 9
am sure I ought if I can, quite as much as Charles, for	P III 7 57 16
I should not go, you may be sure, if I did not feel quite	P III 7 57 16
and fetch her; but she was quite unpersuadable; and this	P III 7 58 20
here I am, Sophia, quite ready to make a foolish match.	P III 7 61 38
	39
Quite worn out and broken up.	P III 8 64 9
"My dear Frederick, you are talking quite idly.	P III 8 69 43
Yes, indeed, Oh yes, I am quite of your opinion, Mrs.	P III 8 71 55
I am quite of your opinion.	P III 8 71 55
The answer was, "Oh! no, never; she has quite given up	P III 8 72 58
yet quite doubtful, as far as Anne's observation reached.	P III 9 74 8
Charles gave it for Louisa, Mary for Henrietta, but quite	P III 9 75 9
and thought it would be quite a misfortune to have the	P III 9 75 12
Wentworth may soon put him quite out of her head, and I	P III 9 76 16
many of them, should be quite fixed on engaging a curate;	P III 9 78 19
should make his curacy quite as good as he could afford,	P III 9 78 19
She was ashamed of herself, quite ashamed of being so	P III 9 81 34
they were gone by degrees quite out of sight and sound,	P III 10 86 21

ugh lane, before she was quite awake to what they said. P III 10 91 43
nsider either of them as quite worthy of her brother; " P III 10 92 47
ere she felt she had been stationed quite long enough. P III 11 93 4
ite unknowingly, within twenty miles of each other. P III 11 94 6
h! yes,--I am quite convinced that, with very few P III 12 102 2
deed I think it quite melancholy to have such excellent P III 12 102 2
not you think it is quite a mistaken point of P III 12 103 2
am afraid of her, as I have told you before, quite P III 12 103 4
t she would have felt quite ill-used by Anne's having P III 12 106 19
r husband would have quite walking enough by the time he P III 12 108 30
rtially revived, she was quite helpless; and in this P III 12 111 49
was all quite natural, however. P III 12 116 70
en the father and mother quite as composed as could be P III 12 117 76
miral Croft's manners were not quite of the tone to suit P IV 1 127 23
arters; and now I am quite snug, with my little shaving P IV 1 128 28
at we are settled here quite to our liking, and have no P IV 1 128 29
ooting, and he seemed quite delighted, and for my part, P IV 2 130 5
ot" and he had "been quite misunderstood,"--and he had P IV 2 130 5
Louisa improved, he had improved; and he was now quite P IV 2 133 25
t but feel that Uppercross was already quite alive again. P IV 2 134 28
tters; and sounds are quite innoxious, or most P IV 2 135 33
e family, and the family honours, he was quite indignant. P IV 3 138 7
e the circumstance in quite so favourable a light, she P IV 3 139 9
ne listened, but without quite understanding it. P IV 3 140 11
"a most charming woman, quite worthy of being known in P IV 3 141 13
h! no, that must have been quite accidental. P IV 3 142 15
was quite as good-looking as he had appeared at Lyme, P IV 3 143 18
ich he had adopted, when quite a young man, on the P IV 3 144 19
manners to make him quite the thing, are more absurd, I P IV 3 144 20
d not only been quite at her ladyship's service P IV 5 158 21
d reduced, seemed to have quite delighted Mr. Elliot. P IV 5 158 21
ite as well, if not "better, than her grand-children. P IV 6 163 7
harles heard it quite by chance: they have not had "the P IV 6 164 7
ndeed Mrs. Harville and I quite agree that we love her P IV 6 165 8
e Crofts knew quite as many people in Bath as they P IV 6 168 24
sirable for women, and quite enough to make it very P IV 7 174 2
r civility rendered her quite as anxious to be left to P IV 7 174 3
an she had ever observed before; he looked quite red. P IV 7 175 6
at point were settled, she could not be quite herself. P IV 7 178 24
s not tried, was quite impatient for the concert evening. P IV 7 180 32
could not leave it till Louisa's doing well was quite P IV 8 183 13
ject of Colonel Wallis's gallantry, was quite contented. P IV 8 186 23
the concert were quite happy enough to animate her P IV 9 192 5
. Elliot appeared to me quite as good as others, and P IV 9 199 55
ich I never could quite reconcile with present times. P IV 9 200 56
not unlikely to marry "again; he is quite fool enough. P IV 9 203 72
your family are very sincere, quite from the heart. P IV 9 204 80
does not come to me in quite so direct a line as that; P IV 9 204 82
uite delightful!" cried Mrs. Clay, not daring, however, P IV 10 213 6
acid look, and appear quite satisfied with the curtailed P IV 10 213 10
d quite painful to have him approach and speak to her. P IV 10 214 11
ite sincere, but now she saw insincerity in every thing. P IV 10 214 11
dy Russell quite bores one with her new publications. P IV 10 215 15
take place in a few months, quite as soon as Louisa's. P IV 10 217 20
hope your father and mother are quite happy with regard P IV 10 218 21
out, no laughing or dancing; it is quite different. P IV 10 218 24
Mrs. Musgrove--put her quite out of her way. P IV 10 219 29
if they believed themselves quite in the secret. P IV 10 222 37
are quite near relations, you know: and Mr. Elliot too, P IV 10 224 47
r for such kindness; and quite as much so, moreover, for P IV 10 224 52 53
ither arriving quite in time, nor the first to arrive. P IV 11 229 2
r Charles Hayter was quite wild about it, and Henrietta P IV 11 230 6
ot quite, a few lines more. P IV 11 234 26
rville, putting his hand on her arm quite affectionately. P IV 11 235 34
h! my dear, it is quite understood, I give you my word. P IV 11 239 50
ptain Harville holds himself quite engaged, I'll answer P IV 11 239 52
was now esteemed quite worthy to address the daughter P IV 12 248 1
f, on the other side of Battel--quite down in the Weald. S 1 366 1
ite the contrary I assure you.-- S 1 368 1
untenance that she is quite of my opinion & thinks it a S 1 370 1
heritance, quite as well provided for as himself.-- S 2 371 1
e has good natural sense, but quite uncultivated.-- S 3 376 1
e cannot look forward quite as I would have her--& takes S 3 376 1
are quite as well off for Gardenstuff as ever we were-- S 4 380 1
out with it, and fancy herself quite a little woman.-- S 4 381 1
ere--now the old house is quite left behind.-- S 4 381 1
ry, you will be quite sorry to hear how ill they have S 5 386 1
yn in vain, till we are quite convinced that they can do S 5 386 1
for getting to Sanditon myself, it is quite an S 5 387 1
ve quite such a servants hall full to feed, as I have.-- S 6 393 1
e felt that she had had quite enough of Sir Edw: for one S 7 398 1
nourable man, quite the gentleman of ancient family.-- S 7 400 1
is glorious sentiment seemed quite to remove suspicion. S 7 400 1
am not quite certain that I do.-- S 8 403 1
felt that he was formed to be a dangerous man--quite in S 8 405 2
r seduction was quite determined on. S 8 405 2
t "that was quite out of the question, for they were all S 9 407 1
ite unavoidable.-- S 9 407 1
rtain--quite certain.-- S 9 411 1
all the party continuing quite well, their brother & S 10 413 1
s astonished to find him quite as tall as his brother & S 10 413 1
ou are quite in the right, to doubt it as long as you S 10 415 1
o more do I--said he exceedingly pleased--we think quite S 10 417 1
the reports of each made that matter quite certain. S 10 419 1
S (2)
ederica shall be Sir James's wife before she quits my LS 39 308 1
must consider what Miss Fairfax quits, before we E II 15 286 17
TED (50)
quired, when they all quitted it together, that Miss NA I 4 34 7
thanked her for her fears, and said that he had quitted NA I 8 54 4
n, Catherine would have quitted Woodston with little NA II 11 215 28
itted the supper-room on the day of Henry's departure. NA II 13 222 7
tter, she would have quitted the house for ever, had not SS I 1 6 10
s just arrived, and quitted not his hold till he had SS I 9 42 8
e room she had just quitted, where they found only SS I 15 75 2
r speech, and instantly quitted the parlour to give way SS I 15 77 18
which Marianne had quitted the room was such as a SS I 15 77 19
ll a year after he had quitted as a pupil; but he was SS I 22 130 28
ey quitted it only with the removal of the tea-things. SS II 1 144 10
served Marianne as she quitted the room, with such SS II 4 162 8
ou shall; and, to be brief, when I quitted Barton last SS II 9 204 20
rianne's indignation burst forth as soon as he quitted SS III 1 269 58
s sister's being there, quitted the room in quest of her; SS III 5 298 32
the housekeeper, she quitted it again, stealing away SS III 6 302 8
in the others as they quitted the house, on an excursion SS III 6 303 10
thout saying a word, quitted the room, and walked out SS III 12 360 26
had quitted Oxford within four and twenty hours after SS III 13 366 20
four days, the two gentlemen quitted Barton together.-- SS III 13 372 46
s. Bennet was perfectly satisfied; and quitted the house PP I 18 103 77
d rising as she thus spoke, she would have quitted the PP I 19 108 16 17
on after it had been quitted by the Gardiners and Jane; PP II 3 145 11
u all quitted Netherfield last November, Mr. Darcy! PP II 9 177 3 4
therfield family had quitted the country, he had told PP II 13 207 5
d returned to it again before they quitted the gallery. PP III 1 250 47
he quitted the room, Elizabeth felt how improbable it PP III 4 279 23
d been formed before he quitted the inn, and that his PP III 16 370 33
go--saying, as she quitted the room, "if any young men PP III 17 377 40
thin the last three years, when she had quitted them.-- MP I 15 150 1
eparing to go as she quitted the room herself to perform MP II 1 177 6

fashionable world, having quitted her husband's roof in MP III 15 440 14
Mr. Crawford, who had quitted his uncle's house, as for a MP III 16 450 11
He quitted the militia and engaged in trade, having E I 2 16 5
recommendation, had I quitted Mr. Woodhouse's family and E I 5 37 10
comfort or advice, she quitted the cottage with an E I 10 86 24 25
Soon afterwards Mr. Elton quitted them, and she could not E I 13 111 14
When the gloves were bought and they had quitted the shop E II 6 201 26
Harriet, when they had quitted the house, and after E II 14 271 6
before they quitted the ball-room, she had strong hopes. E III 3 332 1
a lower tone, before he quitted the room,--"I have been as E III 10 394 25
Jane Fairfax had already quitted Highbury, and was E III 19 483 7
behind her when they quitted the house; and Louisa, by P III 11 99 19
full of astonishment and emotion to Anne, she quitted Lyme. P III 12 116 70
quitted the house but to be conveyed into the warm Bath.-- P IV 5 154 8
Perhaps he had quitted the field, had given Louisa up, had P IV 6 166 18
Your home, country, friends, all quitted. P IV 11 233 23
He soon quitted Bath; and on Mrs. Clay's quitting it P IV 12 250 7
on the cliff--but as they quitted the library they were S 6 390 1
exertion, always quitted the terrace, in his way to his S 11 422 1
QUITTING (37)
& your resolution of quitting Churchill is undoubtedly in LS 25 292 3
aside the misery of his quitting their box, she was, upon NA I 12 95 16
parlour; and, on Anne's quitting it to call her sister, NA I 15 116 1
determined upon quitting Bath by the end of another week. NA II 2 138 1
themselves, her quitting them now would not long be felt. NA II 5 154 1
settled long before her quitting Bath, and it seemed as if NA II 10 200 2
parlour; and on their quitting it to walk round the NA II 11 213 21
to the estate, their quitting his house might be looked on SS I 5 27 6
And Elinor, in quitting Norland and Edward, cried not as I SS I 8 39 18
the circumstances of his quitting that place, with the SS II 4 162 13
by choice ever since his quitting London, he had had no SS III 13 364 13
a small market town; and quitting them both, he had PP I 5 18 1
You will not think of quitting it in a hurry I hope, PP I 9 42 7
if you ever resolved on quitting Netherfield you should be PP I 10 49 27
Mr. Collins repeated his apologies in quitting the room, PP I 15 74 11
known fact that, on his quitting Derbyshire, he had left PP III 2 265 15
On his quitting the room, she sat down, unable to support PP III 4 276 9
that Mr. Wickham had resolved on quitting the militia. PP III 8 312 18
I should not consider myself as quitting that sphere. PP III 14 356 51
it new grace, and in quitting it he trusted would extend MP I 2 20 33
Mrs. Norris, on quitting the parsonage, removed first to MP I 3 23 1
Thomas to the effort of quitting the rest of his family, MP I 3 32 62
Bertram was on the very point of quitting it as he entered. MP II 13 298 1
It was three months, full three months, since her quitting MP III 15 446 35
feelings, promoted her quitting the house immediately, and E III 6 363 51
the most solemn resolution of never quitting her father.-- E III 14 435 4
The impossibility of her quitting her father, Mr. E III 15 448 31
She felt that, in quitting Donwell, he must be sacrificing E III 15 449 32
to the purpose, that on quitting their box at Astley's, my E III 18 472 20
in his prospect of soon quitting his present curacy, and P III 9 78 19
On quitting the Cobb, they all went indoors with their new P III 11 98 17
Anne had never entered Kellynch since her quitting Lady P IV 1 123 9
without any present intention of quitting it any more.-- P IV 1 126 20
of her heart in quitting that chair, in preparing to quit P IV 10 225 62
He soon quitted Bath; and on Mrs. Clay's quitting it P IV 12 250 7
His object in quitting the high road, to hunt for an S 2 371 1
He surprised her by quitting clara immediately on their S 7 396 1
QUIVERED (1)
Marianne's lips quivered, and she repeated the word " SS III 11 351 10
QUIVERING (5)
a moment, and with quivering lips just made it NA II 13 229 31
crimson'd cheeks, quivering lips, & eyes bent on the floor. W 330 11
it off, but a blush, a quivering lip, a tear in the eye, E II 16 294 24
hour:'--and the quivering lip, Emma, which uttered it, was E III 12 418 6
And with a quivering lip he wound up the whole by adding, " P IV 11 232 15
QUIZ (6)
and point out a quiz through the thickness of a crowd. NA I 4 33 7
that quiz of a hat, it makes you look like an old witch? NA I 7 49 43
"Do not you?--then let us walk about and quiz people. NA I 8 59 37
and at last he walked off to quiz his sisters by himself. NA I 8 59 38
up with somebody else, they will quiz me famously." NA I 10 75 26
But I will quiz you with a great deal of pleasure, if you MP I 5 49 34
QUIZZERS (1)
you the four greatest quizzers in the room; my two younger NA I 8 59 37
QUIZZES (1)
ladies; such as dress, balls, flirtations, and quizzes. NA I 4 33 7
QUIZZING (1)
You are quizzing me and Miss Anderson." MP I 5 49 33
QUOTA (1)
counsels, and add their quota of significant looks and NA I 15 120 25
QUOTATION (1)
Anne could not immediately fall into a quotation again. P III 10 85 12
QUOTATIONS (4)
memories with those quotations which are so serviceable NA I 1 15 3
such like musings and quotations; but it was not possible, P III 10 84 7
I could bring you fifty quotations in a moment on my side P IV 11 234 27
quotations, & the bewilderment of some of his sentences.-- S 7 396 1
QUOTED (1)
His celebrated passages are quoted by every body; they are MP III 3 338 14

R. DE COURCY (4)
you very soon, & am your affec. brother R. De Courcy. LS 4 249 2
mortify & distress me.-- I am &c. R. De Courcy. LS 14 265 6
they have never been able to gain. R. De Courcy. LS 34 304 2
on which their strength was founded. R. De Courcy. LS 36 306 2
RACE (5)
They were far from being an irritable race; far from any NA II 14 233 10
by wealthy connexions; a forward, bragging, scheming race. NA II 15 246 12
in trusting themselves with me, even on a race course.-- W 339 18
race of mankind, as was here collected in one individual. PP II 17 224 9
Not all that the whole Parker race could say among S 11 420 1
RACES (4)
about the horse which he had to run at the B---- races. MP I 5 48 28
These races were to call him away not long after their MP I 5 48 29
induce her to attend the races, and schemes were made for MP I 5 48 29
demanded, to tell of races and Weymouth, and parties and MP I 12 114 1
RACING (1)
for incredible sums; of racing matches, in which his NA I 9 66 31
RACK (2)
would have been the rack, and arrow-root from the E III 11 403 2
in the toast rack--and till it was all done, she heard S 10 416 1
RACKED (1)
not so dreadfully racked as your's seems to have been. PP III 10 321 2
RACKING (1)
Every other child must be racking his heart. MP III 16 452 14
RAGE (5)
and, when she heard it rage round a corner of the ancient NA II 6 166 9
I never saw Lucy in such a rage in my life. SS III 2 272 12
contempt which her rage of admiration will excite. PP II 18 231 18
When the first transports of rage which had produced his PP III 8 309 5
transparencies, made in a rage for transparencies, for the MP I 16 152 2
RAGED (1)
The storm still raged, and various were the noises, more NA II 6 170 12
RAGES (1)
around our house, simply rages & passes on--while down in S 4 381 1
RAGGED (2)
As he left the room, two rosy-faced boys, ragged and dirty, MP III 7 381 25
mother lamented over the ragged carpet as usual, while the MP III 15 439 9
RAGOUT (1)
prefer a plain dish to a ragout, had nothing to say to her. PP I 8 35 2
RAIL (1)
and she continued to rail bitterly against the cruelty of PP I 13 62 8
RAILLERY (8)
to know when delicate raillery was properly called for, or NA I 5 36 2
arise from such common-place raillery as Mrs. Jennings's. SS I 7 34 5
To the former her raillery was probably, as far as it SS I 8 36 2
fortunate rival; and the raillery which the other had SS I 10 49 12
subjects of raillery as delighted her husband and mother. SS I 12 62 27
a future mine of raillery against the devoted Elinor, SS I 18 99 15
hearing any other raillery on the subject, than what she SS II 14 247 4
"My dearest Jane--do not overpower me with your raillery.-- W 350 24
RAIN (61)
In the first place, I was so afraid it would rain this NA I 6 39 4
it did not rain, which Catherine was sure it would not. NA I 10 80 61
would generally turn to rain, but a cloudy one foretold NA I 11 82 1
a few specks of small rain upon the windows caught NA I 11 82 2
The rain continued--fast, though not heavy. NA I 11 83 14
rain for Miss Tilney to venture, must yet be a question. NA I 11 83 16
two hours ago if it had not been for this detestable rain. NA I 11 84 19
A sudden scud of rain driving full in her face, made it NA II 5 161 25
than a thick mizzling rain; and having given a good shake NA II 5 161 25
The wind roared down the chimney, the rain beat in NA II 6 168 10
the settled rain of the two preceding days had occasioned. SS I 9 40 3
their heads, and a driving rain set full in their face.-- SS I 9 41 6
still more interesting, in the midst of an heavy rain. SS I 9 42 10
he has threatened me with rain when I wanted it to be SS I 10 52 28
and much was said on the subject of rain by both of them. SS I 12 62 27
is as much produced within doors as without, by rain. SS I 20 111 8
At this time of year, and after such a series of rain, we SS II 5 167 3
by a settled rain from going out again after dinner. SS III 6 303 11
but an heavy and settled rain even she could not fancy dry SS III 6 303 11
morning of the same continued rain had reduced very low. SS III 6 304 14
The wind roared round the house, and the rain beat against SS III 7 316 28
it seems likely to rain; and then you must stay all night." PP I 7 30 21
The rain continued the whole evening without intermission; PP I 7 31 28
once, as if the credit of making it rain were all her own. PP I 7 31 29
of rain as prevented their walking to Meryton once. PP I 17 88 15
contemplating the dismal rain in a very desponding state MP II 4 205 3
for an hour while the rain continued, the blessing of MP II 4 206 3
establish her during the rain, her being in such cottage MP II 4 206 4
"And if it should rain, which I think exceedingly likely, MP II 5 221 34
doors by a series of rain and snow, with nothing to do and MP II 11 286 15
quite surprizing, for we have had a vast deal of rain here. E I 1 10 26
the weather; shall we have rain!" convinced her that he E I 5 41 31
every morning beginning in rain or snow, and every evening E I 16 138 17
upon its beginning to rain, Emma was obliged to expect E II 3 177 51
had been afraid it would rain--she had been afraid it E II 3 177 52
she came out it began to rain, and she did not know what E II 3 177 52
you know, because of the rain; but I did so wish myself E II 3 178 52
and said it did not rain, and I must go: and so off I set; E II 3 179 52
for I should find the near way quite floated by this rain. E II 3 179 52
his little boys, when it had been just beginning to rain. E II 16 293 10
said she, "and reached home before the rain was much. E II 16 293 12
"Not a walk in the rain, I should imagine." E II 16 293 13
"No, but it did not absolutely rain when I set out." E II 16 293 14
think letters are never worth going through the rain for." E II 16 293 16
Miss Fairfax, of your being out this morning in the rain. E II 16 294 24
25
By this time, the walk in the rain had reached Mrs. Elton, E II 16 295 29
Going to the post-office in the rain!-- E II 16 295 30
Somebody talked of rain.-- E III 2 321 14
No rain at all. E III 2 322 19
as the weather threatened rain; Mr. and Mrs. Weston and E III 5 344 3
A cold stormy rain set in, and nothing of July appeared E III 12 421 18
He had ridden home through the rain; and had walked up E III 13 433 41
day, a small thick rain almost blotting out the very few P IV 1 123 8
buildings, smoking in rain, without any wish of seeing P IV 2 135 34
It began to rain, not much, but enough to make shelter P IV 7 174 2
The rain was a mere trifle, and Anne was most sincere in P IV 7 174 3
But the rain was also a mere trifle to Mrs. Clay; she P IV 7 174 3
It was beginning to rain again, and altogether there was a P IV 7 176 10
her conviction, that the rain would come to nothing at P IV 7 177 15
of time, and before the rain increased; and in another P IV 7 177 16
she had grieved over the rain on her friends' account, and P IV 11 229 2
RAINED (11)
The clock struck twelve, and it still rained.-- NA I 11 83 14
They promised to come at twelve, only it rained; but now, NA I 11 85 32
moon was not up, and it rained a little, and Mr. Morland's NA I 15 116 1
the time the party broke up, it blew and rained violently. NA II 6 166 9
at this moment, "that it rained very hard," though she SS I 12 62 27
of year, and that it had rained every day for the last SS I 12 62 29
The morning was rather favourable, though it had rained SS I 13 63 2
Jane had not been gone long before it rained hard. PP I 7 31 28
It rained dreadfully hard for half an hour, while we were E I 1 10 26
to go to the outer door; she wanted to see if it rained. P IV 7 175 6
She would see if it rained. P IV 7 175 6
RAINING (2)
If it keeps raining, the streets will be very wet." NA I 11 82 9
that, if it still kept on raining another five minutes, NA I 11 83 14
RAINS (3)
few people in the Pump-Room, if it rains all the morning. NA I 11 83 13
We have had such incessant rains almost since October MP II 1 181 16
"But it rains." P IV 7 177 12
RAINY (2)
in the set; and if a rainy morning deprived them of other NA I 5 37 4
on the probability of a rainy season, made her feel that PP I 16 76 4
RAISE (45)
well, which is true must raise abhorrence against her, & LS 8 255 1
females, whose society can raise no other emotion than NA I 2 20 8
made her expect to raise no inconsiderable emotion in Mr. NA I 15 124 48
the day before, did raise some emotion in Mrs. Allen. NA I 15 125 48
To raise your spirits, moreover, she gives you reason to NA II 5 158 17
a circumstance to raise no common degree of astonishment. NA II 6 164 2
in the room in itself to raise curiosity, this must have NA II 9 196 23
well known spot ceased to raise the violent emotion which SS I 3 14 1
character;--but I will not raise objections against any SS I 15 81 43
"And who knows but you may raise a dance," said she. SS I 18 99 18
Mr. Palmer made her no answer, and did not even raise his SS I 19 107 25
which he delighted to raise, for he had at least as much SS I 21 125 37
been intended to raise myself at the expense of others." SS II 9 210 32
to gratify her vanity, and raise her self-importance, to SS III 5 297 32
though Elinor tried to raise her spirits, and make her SS III 7 308 4
raise any emotion--my feelings were very, very painful.-- SS III 8 325 50
too natural in itself to raise anything less tender than SS III 10 342 7
of accepted love to swell his heart, and raise his spirits. SS III 13 361 3
for Maria would scarcely raise her eyes from her book, and MP I 7 71 31
Yates, I think we must raise a little theatre at Mansfield, MP I 13 123 5
to her and endeavour to raise her spirits, in spite of MP I 15 147 56
the usual habits of all to raise any emotion in Mrs. MP II 7 238 3
You may raise it into a place. MP II 7 243 27
by changes that will only raise her character the more by MP II 9 269 38
He could not have devised any thing more likely to raise MP II 11 286 15
There was nothing to raise her spirits in the confined and MP III 7 387 47
sensations which are to raise ecstacy even in retrospect. MP III 12 415 1
2
much depressed to calm and raise; and her own imagination MP III 14 430 2
the very last sort of person to raise my curiosity. E I 4 29 14
"Be satisfied," said he, "I will not raise any outcry. E I 5 40 27
Nothing so easy as for a young lady to raise her E I 8 64 47
This, Harriet, is an alliance which can never raise a E I 9 74 20
led to such a branch of the subject as must raise them. E I 9 80 68
unavoidable absences, and raise her spirits by E I 13 109 6
He wanted to marry well, and having the arrogance to raise E I 16 135 7
do him more good, raise him higher, fix his interest E I 18 147 18
It's tendency would be to raise and refine her mind--and E III 4 342 40
men, nor names, nor places, that could raise a blush. E III 6 358 35
How Harriet could ever have had the presumption to raise E III 11 414 50
was not disappointed in the interest he hoped to raise. P IV 8 187 33
to raise even the unfounded hopes which sunk with him. P IV 12 250 6
Bad things for a country;--sure to raise the price of S 1 368 1
this last year, to raise that paltry Hamlet, lying, as it S 1 369 1
if they come among us to raise the price of our S 6 392 1
"My dear madam, they can only raise the price of S 6 392 1
RAISED (56)
his complexion was raised, & he spoke with great emotion. LS 23 283 3
emotion must appear to be raised by your reply, and NA I 3 26 8
left to the luxury of a raised, restless, and frightened NA I 7 51 54
his sudden reappearance raised in Catherine, passed away NA I 8 53 3
curiosity to be raised in the unprivileged younger sisters. NA I 15 120 25
by the interest he had raised, to be able to carry it NA II 5 160 23
some darker wood, and raised, about a foot from the ground, NA II 6 163 2
resist her efforts, she raised the lid a few inches; but NA II 6 164 3
once raised, but you may in time come to love a rose?" NA II 7 174 8
She raised her eyes towards him more fully than she had NA II 9 196 25
her spirits were gradually raised to a modest tranquillity. NA II 10 199 2
objection that might be raised against her character, NA II 11 208 1
of alarm, or misled by a raised imagination, she stepped NA II 13 223 9
of the Abbey before she raised her head; and the highest NA II 14 230 1
She had raised herself from the ground, but her foot had SS I 9 42 8
laugh which his gallantry raised against Marianne, SS I 9 43 11
their marriage had been raised, by his prospect of riches, SS I 10 49 11
filled the mind and raised the wonder of Mrs. Jennings for SS I 14 70 1
of both her sisters were raised to detain her, a third, SS I 16 86 20
the eldest of them they raised a curiosity to know the SS I 21 125 37
This event, while it raised the spirits of Elinor, SS II 5 169 15
three letters which now raised a much stronger curiosity SS II 7 186 37
Every qualification is raised at times, by the SS II 10 215 13
that his tythes should be raised to the utmost; and SS III 5 293 2
by the lingering frost, raised the laughter of Charlotte,-- SS III 6 303 10
Her apprehensions once raised, paid by the excess for all SS III 7 312 17
of an evening which had raised such splendid expectations. PP I 3 12 15
Mr. Bennet raised his eyes from his book as she entered, PP I 20 111 8
you find it likely to be raised by your coming to us again, PP I 22 124 9
than it had ever raised before; she remembered its warmth, PP III 1 251 48
favourite, as their attentions raised them in her opinion. PP III 4 280 25
impulse of curiosity, she raised her eyes to his face, she PP III 11 335 43
and to be thereby raised to the rank of a Baronet's lady, MP I 1 3 1
long have raised expectations in more than Mrs. Grant.-- MP I 17 160 9
his selfish vanity had raised in Maria and Julia Bertram. MP II 2 193 18
her judgment, when it was raised by pleasantry on people MP II 4 208 11
on Mr. Crawford, it raised some awkward sensations in two MP II 7 248 47
good; it rather sank than raised his comfort; and MP II 10 279 21
fortune, raised her, therefore, very much in her opinion. MP III 2 332 22
And I must say, that its being for you, has raised him MP III 4 350 30
At Mansfield, no sounds of contention, no raised voice, no MP III 8 391 11
and somebody had lately raised her from the condition of E I 3 22 8
a proper direction and raised the gratitude of her young E I 6 42 1
narrow footpath, a little raised on one side of the lane, E I 10 88 33
the alarm that had been raised could not be appeased so as E I 15 128 17
objection raised, except in one habitation, the vicarage.-- E III 17 468 36
No objection was raised on the father's side; the young E III 19 482 4
with him; and Louisa was raised up and supported more P III 12 110 37
38
talking with a very raised voice, but, from the clamour of P IV 2 134 29
Mr. Elliot, raised by his marriage to great affluence, and P IV 9 209 95
Surprise was the strongest emotion raised by their P IV 10 216 18
to move, his head was raised, pausing, listening, and he P IV 11 231 10
& praised & puffed, & raised it to a something of young S 2 371 1
But I should not like to have butcher's meat raised, S 6 393 1
sort of attachment which her personal charms had raised.-- S 8 405 2
tho' we really have raised the sum we wanted for putting S 12 424 1
RAISES (5)
than what is expected, and it raises no gratitude at all. SS I 2 11 22
It raises my influence much too high; the power of SS II 2 150 33
this, without being aware of the expectation she raises." SS II 11 227 46
"But she raises none in those most concerned. SS II 11 227 47
It raises my spleen more than any thing, to have the MP I 12 120 26
RAISING (16)
They display imagination without raising interest. NA I 14 109 23
enjoyed the advantage of raising the blushes and the SS I 8 36 1
its horrors, I have, by raising myself to affluence, lost SS III 8 321 32
from the danger of raising expectations which might only PP II 9 181 30
He was writing, and, without raising his head, coolly PP III 7 305 39
40
has legally hired, without raising all this speculation! PP III 11 332 19
and the possibility of raising five couple with the help MP I 12 117 11
her engagement as only raising her so much more above MP I 13 128 38
never took the trouble of raising her so much voice, was always MP II 5 218 12
By only raising my voice, and saying anything two or three E II 1 158 14
And (raising his voice still more) I do not see why Miss E II 10 245 49
end, be assured that your raising your thoughts to him, is E III 4 342 39
undue distinction, and raising men to honours which their P III 3 19 16
the view of supporting her hopes and raising her spirits. P III 12 116 70
the girls, at the risk of raising even an unpleasant P IV 11 242 65

not be doing mischeif by raising the price of things--and S 6 392 1
RALLIED (3)
Mrs. Gardiner then rallied her niece on Wickham's PP II 4 153 7
The dear Colonel rallied his spirits tolerably till just PP II 14 210 3
My spirits rallied with the morning, and I felt that I had P IV 11 245 76
RALLY (1)
He will rally again, and be happy with another." P III 11 97 13
RALLYING (1)
Miss Crawford rallying her spirits, and recovering her MP I 9 89 29
RAMBLE (3)
More than once did Elizabeth in her ramble within the park, PP II 10 182 1
"I am afraid I interrupt your solitary ramble, my dear PP III 10 327 5
came in, and their ramble did not appear to have been more MP I 10 104 51
RAMBLED (1)
She then ran gaily off, rejoicing as she rambled about, in PP I 10 53 66
RAMBLES (3)
"This lengthened absence, these solitary rambles, did not NA II 8 182 1
she had carefully avoided every companion in her rambles. SS I 16 85 15
the Palmers, in the indulgence of such solitary rambles. SS III 6 303 9
RAMBLING (4)
In her rambling and her idleness she might only be a NA II 15 240 1
production without finding food for a rambling fancy." MP II 4 209 16
a good deal of ground, rambling and irregular, with many E III 6 358 35
While she remained, a bush or low rambling holly protected P III 10 88 27
RAMPARTS (8)
To see and explore either the ramparts and keep of the one, NA II 2 141 11
no walk on the ramparts, no visit to the dock-yard, no MP III 8 388 2
them, and made one in the family party on the ramparts. MP III 11 408 3
Mrs. Price took her weekly walk on the ramparts every fine MP III 11 408 4
and dashing against the ramparts with so fine a sound, MP III 11 409 6
on the next day, on the ramparts; when the balmy air, the MP III 12 415 1
2
the ramparts, taking her first lesson, I presume, in love. MP III 12 415 2
He would walk round the ramparts, and join them with the MP III 15 445 29
RAMSGATE (4)
who presided over it, to ramsgate; and thither also went PP II 12 201 5
When my niece Georgiana went to ramsgate last summer, I PP II 14 211 13
"Except," thought Elizabeth, "when she goes to ramsgate." PP III 1 248 26
I went down to ramsgate for a week with a friend last MP I 5 51 40
RAN (54)
He then left me & ran upstairs. LS 23 284 5
immediately; I dared not look at him--& ran away directly. LS 24 286 5
no whisper of eager inquiry ran round the room, nor was NA I 2 23 27
Catherine then ran directly up stairs, and watched Miss NA I 4 34 7
good sort of fellow; he ran it a few weeks, till, I NA I 7 46 11
Catherine took the advice, and ran off to get ready. NA I 9 61 7
of the Crescent, she almost ran over the remaining ground NA I 13 101 25
I ran away in a great hurry to explain it.-- NA I 13 102 25
and in half a minute they ran down stairs together, in an NA II 6 165 5
Catherine's blood ran cold with the horrid suggestions NA II 8 186 13
disappeared with him, she ran for safety to her own room, NA II 9 192 4
and with tears of shame she ran off to her own room. NA II 9 198 30
Tears filled her eyes, and even ran down her cheeks as she NA II 10 203 8
He put down his gun and ran to her assistance. SS I 9 42 8
at her eyes; and without noticing them ran up stairs. SS I 15 75 2
of a death-like paleness, instantly ran out of the room. SS II 7 181 7
than before, directly ran over the contents of all. SS II 7 186 37
I ran away from you all as soon as I could; but not before SS III 8 327 55
"Last night, in Drury-Lane lobby, I ran against Sir John SS III 8 330 69
And with these words, he almost ran out of the room. SS III 8 332 84
horrible suspense, she ran immediately into the hall, and SS III 9 333 3
She almost ran out of the room, and as soon as the door SS III 12 360 26
ran away from a subject which was odious to her feelings.-- W 360 29
She then ran gaily off, rejoicing as she rambled about, in PP I 10 53 66
When the ladies removed after dinner, Elizabeth ran up to PP I 11 54 1
nothing more, and down they ran into the dining-room, PP II 5 158 13
"That is all settled;" repeated the other, as she ran into PP III 4 281 28
Jane ran to her uncle and aunt, and welcomed and thanked PP III 5 287 32
Away ran the girls, too eager to get in to have time for PP III 7 301 4
They ran through the vestibule into the breakfast room; PP III 7 301 4
5
the hall once more, and ran across the lawn after their PP III 7 301 6
her thoughts and her words ran wholly on those attendants PP III 8 310 7
the door was thrown open, and she ran into the room. PP III 9 315 3
She got up, and ran out of the room; and returned no more, PP III 9 317 9
In ran Mrs. Bennet to her daughter's room, in her dressing PP III 13 344 6
7
whispering a few words to her sister ran out of the room. PP III 13 346 22
one among them who ran more in her thoughts than the rest. MP I 2 15 12
Her curiosity was all awake, and she ran through it with MP I 14 137 23
gave orders and Mrs. Norris ran about, but all this gave MP II 8 254 9
Old Scholey ran in at breakfast time, to say she had MP III 7 380 20
get it away; but the child ran to her mother's protection, MP III 7 386 42
The two Abbotts and I ran into the front room and peeped E I 9 75 26
She ran away to indulge the inclination, leaving the E I 9 82 84
unchecked, ran eagerly through what she had to tell. E II 3 177 52
not know what to do; so she ran on directly. as fast as E II 3 177 52
And away he ran. E II 11 255 58
All this ran so glibly through her thoughts, that by the E II 14 279 53
In this style she ran on; never thoroughly stopped by any E II 17 302 21
22
Yes, my dear, I ran home, as I said I should, to help E III 2 329 45
on Harriet to follow her, ran up a steep bank, cleared a E III 3 333 5
And off they ran, quite as full of glee as of love, and P III 7 54 4
fell into a rut, nor ran foul of a dung-cart; and Anne, P III 10 92 48
her enjoyment, ran up the steps to be jumped down again. P III 12 109 32
the sea & the sea shore--& ran with energy through all the S 7 396 1
RANDALL'S (27)
but as he came from Randall's immediately to Hartfield, E III 1 315 3
Such was his own account at Randall's. E III 1 316 6
he had declared himself convinced of it, at Randall's. E III 1 316 6
nephew's letter to Randall's communicated a change of plan. E III 1 317 7
reached Randall's before dinner, and every thing was safe. E III 2 319 1
likely to Randall's; yes, I think it was to Randall's. E III 5 346 16
sent to Randall's to take Mr. Frank Churchill to Richmond. E III 8 383 29
of the servants at Randall's, was, that a messenger had E III 8 383 31
An express arrived at Randall's to announce the death of E III 9 387 11
Short letters from Frank were received at Randall's. E III 9 388 15
"can you come to Randall's at any time this morning?-- E III 10 392 1
2
together and on their way at a quick pace for Randall's. E III 10 392 7
If we walk fast, we shall soon be at Randall's." E III 10 393 17
They hurried on, and were speedily at Randall's.-- E III 10 394 25
Mrs. Weston felt when she was approaching Randall's. E III 11 404 3
The child to be born at Randall's must be a tie there even E III 12 422 20
was brought her from Randall's--a very thick letter;--she E III 14 436 6
when I first arrived at Randall's; you must consider me as E III 14 437 8
on my first visit to Randall's;--and here I am conscious E III 14 437 8
Remember how few minutes I was at Randall's, and in how E III 14 439 8
I was really gone from Randall's, she closed with the E III 14 441 8
first to announce it at home, and then at Randall's.-- E III 17 465 28
of its being known at Randall's, how soon it would be over E III 17 468 35
their now daily drive to Randall's; and she had, therefore, E III 18 475 38
being obliged to go to Randall's every day, or poor Mrs. E III 18 476 43
pay a visit at Randall's; he wants to be introduced to her. E III 18 477 57
argument; and on leaving Randall's, and falling naturally E III 18 480 80
RANDALLS (59)
Randalls is such a distance. E I 1 8 15
Randalls, because of his daughter's being housemaid there. E I 1 8 18
till he could purchase Randalls, and the sale of Randalls E I 2 16 6
and the sale of Randalls was long looked forward to: but E I 2 16 6
very easy distance of Randalls from Hartfield, so E I 2 18 11
when they left her at Randalls in the centre of every E I 2 18 12
Fortunately for him, Highbury, including Randalls in the E I 3 20 1
She had ventured once alone to Randalls, but it was not E I 4 26 1
a chance, he said, that he had not gone round by Randalls. E I 4 32 29
He thought we walked towards Randalls most days. E I 4 32 29
There were wishes at Randalls respecting Emma's destiny, E I 5 41 31
figure-pieces in her drawing-room, at Randalls?" E I 6 43 14
I could never hope to equal my own doings at Randalls. E I 8 66 54
Your marrying will be equal to the match at Randalls. E I 9 75 25
whether there were any doubts of the air of Randalls. E I 11 94 9
both, either at Randalls or here--and as you may suppose, E I 11 94 14
they must all dine at Randalls one day;--even Mr. E I 13 108 2
and found her doom already signed with regard to Randalls. E I 13 109 5
extricated him from Randalls, and secured him the power of E I 13 110 10
it was to afford at Randalls to see that it was cold, and E I 13 112 24
coolly, "I cannot wish to be snowed up a week at Randalls." E I 13 115 40
41
since their being at Randalls?--he felt much anxiety--he E I 15 124 3
able to keep them all at Randalls; and with the utmost E I 15 126 11
of being blocked up at Randalls, while her children were E I 15 127 13
Emma should remain at Randalls, while she and her husband E I 15 127 13
of any comfort for him while he continued at Randalls. E I 15 128 17
off his ill-humour at Randalls, that his amiableness never E I 16 139 20
with the hope of coming to Randalls at no distant period." E I 18 144 1
not coming, except as a disappointment at Randalls. E I 18 144 4
It is on her account that attention to Randalls is doubly E I 18 149 26
do you smile so?--where did you hear it?--at Randalls?" E II 3 172 21
He had time only to say, "no, not at Randalls; I have not E II 3 172 22
23
I have not been near Randalls," when the door was thrown E II 3 172 22
23
and resolve on going home by way of Randalls to procure it. E II 5 187 4
The refreshment of Randalls was absolutely necessary. E II 5 187 4
He had reached Randalls the evening before. E II 5 190 23
He was very much pleased with Randalls, thought it a most E II 5 191 26
to think of them all at Randalls any hour of the day, with E II 5 195 49
to invite--neither Donwell, nor Hartfield, nor Randalls. E II 7 207 6
Donwell and Randalls had received their invitation, and E II 7 207 7
She looked down the Randalls road. E II 9 233 25
was a little nearer Randalls than Ford's; and had all but E II 9 233 25
to Hartfield gates, before they set off for Randalls. E II 10 246 55
with his daughter at Randalls, was passed by the two young E II 11 247 2
ball, to be given, not at Randalls, but at the crown inn?" E II 11 250 21
them, and not a less grateful welcome than at Randalls. E II 11 250 23
Ten couple, in either of the Randalls rooms, would have E II 11 250 23
If they must dance, they had better dance at Randalls. E II 11 251 26
cold--so much less danger at the crown than at Randalls! E II 11 251 27
nobody would think of opening the windows at Randalls. E II 11 251 30
It will be as clean as Randalls by candle-light. E II 11 253 42
"This will not be your only visit to Randalls." E II 12 259 14
Certainly his being at Randalls had given great spirit to E II 12 262 38
was the chance of his coming to Randalls again this spring. E II 13 264 1
own imagination, fix a time for coming to Randalls again. E II 13 266 5
"We have been calling at Randalls," said she, "and found E II 14 278 44
The difference which Randalls, Randalls alone makes in E II 18 312 46
"Yes," said his brother quickly, "it is Randalls that does E II 18 312 47
"Very well--and as Randalls, I suppose, it not likely to E II 18 312 48
RANDALLS' (3)
time, the Randalls' party just sufficiently before them. E III 2 319 2
He was dining with the Randalls' family, and Jane, at the E III 5 343 2
The Randalls' party agreed to it immediately; and after a E III 5 344 3
RANDOM (4)
in which Henry talked at random, without sense or NA II 15 243 10
fair," said Emma in a whisper, "mine was a random guess. E II 10 241 10
last obliged to answer at random, before she could at all E III 12 420 14
you will be convinced that I am not speaking at random. S 1 366 1
RANG (2)
were married, the bells rang and every body smiled; and, NA II 16 252 7
Mrs. Bennet rang the bell, and Miss Elizabeth was summoned PP I 20 111 14
RANGE (11)
On one side it had a range of doors, and it was lighted on NA II 5 162 28
thing unusual, a double range of small drawers appeared in NA II 6 168 10
over this suspected range of cells, and the stair-case by NA II 8 188 17
range of my acquaintance, that are really accomplished." PP I 8 39 46
hills, with the long range of woods overspreading many, PP III 1 253 57
were over, it would be time for the wider range of London. MP II 3 203 31
to let her imagination range and work at Harriet's fortune, E I 9 69 3
visitings were among a range of great families, none very E II 8 221 48
can have had such a range; but what restrictions I might P III 3 18 8
to the solitary range of the house was the consequence. P IV 1 122 5
passed to their seats, her mind took a hasty range over it. P IV 8 185 21
RANGING (1)
while the girls were ranging over the town and making what SS II 9 209 28
RANK (44)
every neat house above the rank of a cottage, and at all NA II 11 212 17
a woman who had not either a great fortune or high rank." SS I 4 21 15
would soon have learnt to rank the innumerable comforts of SS III 11 351 13
have a woman of higher rank and larger fortune;--and SS III 14 373 3
50, she was very handsome, & had all the dignity of rank.-- W 329 9
associating with people of rank; and were therefore in PP I 4 15 11
For though elated by his rank, it did not render him PP I 5 18 1
behaviour in a person of rank--such affability and PP I 14 66 1
and that the most elevated rank, instead of giving her PP I 14 67 9
which he felt for his high rank, and his veneration for PP I 15 70 1
of her abilities from her rank and fortune, part from her PP I 16 84 58
dignity with the highest rank in the kingdom--provided PP I 18 97 60
61
silence and respect which her rank will inevitably excite. PP I 19 106 10
She likes to have the distinction of rank preserved." PP II 6 161 6
rank, she thought she could witness without trepidation. PP II 6 161 9
such as to make her visitors forget their inferior rank. PP II 6 162 11
there are not many in my rank of life who can afford to PP II 10 183 14
be thereby raised to the rank of a Baronet's lady, with MP I 1 3 1
Their rank, fortune, rights, and expectations, will always MP I 1 11 17
habitation which could rank as genteel among the buildings MP I 3 28 38
to support me in the rank of a gentlewoman, and enable me MP I 3 29 46
those feelings which you rank highly as temptation and MP I 11 110 22
stepping out of their rank and trying to appear above MP II 5 221 32
they did not by any means rank as misfortunes with her. E I 1 5 4
of young woman in the same rank as his own, with a little E I 4 30 18
but he is undoubtedly her inferior as to rank in society.-- E I 8 62 39
the gradations of rank below him, and be so blind to what E I 16 135 8
deal, to have had the Martins in a higher rank of life. E II 5 187 4
confusion of rank, bordered too much on inelegance of mind. E II 6 198 5
How very few of those men in a rank of life to address E III 17 467 31
His rank in society I would alter if I could; which is E III 18 472 22
High in the rank of her most serious and heartfelt E III 18 475 42
His good looks and his rank had one fair claim on his P III 1 4 6
she had a value for rank and consequence, which blinded P III 2 11 2
gained the other step in rank--and must now, by successive P III 4 29 8
of condition and rank more strongly than most people. P III 5 35 14
of them, after talking of rank, people of rank, and P III 6 46 10
talking of rank, people of rank, and jealousy of rank, P III 6 46 10
of rank, and jealousy of rank, said, "I have no scruple of P III 6 46 10
His value for rank and connexion she perceived to be P IV 4 148 10
Bath this winter, and as rank is rank, your being known to P IV 4 150 17
winter, and as rank is rank, your being known to be P IV 4 150 17
against her superiority of rank; and all this, assisted by P IV 12 248 2
her brother was a poor man for his rank in society. S 3 377 1
RANKED (5)
for plays was not to be ranked; but perhaps it was because NA I 12 92 4
visitor; of hearing it ranked as real friendship, and NA II 5 157 5

Marianne, let it not be ranked as the least considerable, SS III 14 380 21
it appear as if they ranked nothing beyond the happiness P III 3 23 34
to be preferred, and how ranked the Giaour and The Bride P III 11 100 23
RANKS (2)
of grandeur; "we know very little of the inferior ranks. MP I 6 60 49
circles, spheres, lines, ranks, every thing--and Mrs. E III 6 359 37
RANT (4)
I shall offer to pay him to-morrow; he will rant and storm PP III 17 377 39
every thing, as if I could rant and storm, or sigh, or cut MP I 13 123 6
had grudged every rant of Lord Ravenshaw's, and been MP I 14 132 8
She knew that Mr. Yates was in general thought to rant MP I 18 164 2
RANTING (3)
Let us have no ranting tragedies. MP I 14 131 3
there was some very good ranting ground in Frederick, he MP I 14 132 8
theatre, and opposed to a ranting young man, who appeared MP II 1 182 22
RANTS (2)
for, take away his rants, and the poor Baron has nothing. MP III 9 394 1
makes!--if his rents were but equal to his rants!-- MP III 9 394 1
RAP (6)
At about half past twelve, a remarkably loud rap drew her NA I 9 61 1
more than once by a rap at a neighbouring door, when a SS II 4 161 7
window, in hopes of distinguishing the long-expected rap. SS II 4 166 31
Her letter was scarcely finished, when a rap foretold a SS II 5 172 40
bear any sudden noise, was startled by a rap at the door. SS II 9 203 11
by the sound of as smart a rap as the end of a riding-whip W 344 21
RAPACIOUS (1)
her children, the most rapacious of human beings, is SS I 21 120 6
RAPACITY (1)
a victim to her mother's rapacity for whist players, and PP III 12 342 26
RAPID (22)
the very rapid increase of Lady Susan's influence. LS 11 259 1
the match, from seeing the rapid increase of her affection LS 22 280 1
So rapid had been her movements, that in spite of the NA I 13 102 25
took a rapid flight over its attendant felicities. NA I 15 122 28
as she was exceedingly rapid in the performance of every SS I 5 26 5
stolen by a fox, or in the rapid decease of a promising SS III 6 303 10
The rapid decay, the early death of a girl so young, so SS III 7 313 20
Here ceased the rapid flow of self-reproving spirit; and SS III 10 346 29
led soon afterwards, by rapid degrees, to the highest SS III 14 377 11
A lady's imagination is very rapid; it jumps from PP I 6 27 52
had he left them than her feelings found a rapid vent. PP I 23 126 5
Conjectures as to the meaning of it, rapid and wild, PP III 9 320 32
latterly been prosperously rapid, and he came directly MP II 1 178 8
"Well," said Crawford, after a course of rapid questions MP III 3 343 41
Miss Crawford now, at the rapid rate in which their MP III 9 393 1
whole progress of the picture, which was rapid and happy. E I 6 47 30
the felicities of rapid motion have once been, though E II 11 247 1
A mind like her's, once opening to suspicion, made rapid E III 11 407 32
worsting; and the rapid increase of the crow's foot about P III 1 6 11
moment (it was all done in rapid moments) Captain Benwick P III 12 110 42
rapid; for who would be glad to see her when she arrived? P IV 2 135 34
not comprehend a very rapid recovery from the awful P IV 4 147 8
RAPIDITY (17)
of the subject, his rapidity of expression, and her NA I 9 64 27
of his master for ever, if not his place, by her rapidity. NA I 13 103 27
formality, there was a rapidity of thought which SS I 9 43 11
then folded up, sealed and directed with eager rapidity. SS II 4 161 5
alarm, gave some explanation to such unexpected rapidity. SS III 7 316 29
Dashwood; and by his rapidity in seeking that fate, it is SS III 13 366 20
as proceeding from a rapidity of thought and carelessness PP I 10 48 27
In vain did Elizabeth endeavour to check the rapidity of PP I 18 99 64
They have not the same force or rapidity, and do not PP II 8 175 25
now smiled at the rapidity and ease with which an affair PP III 13 347 28
Mrs. Grant laughed at her for her rapidity." MP III 4 352 36
with such delightful rapidity--the first hour of E II 4 181 4
was coming; and in the rapidity of half a moment's thought, E II 5 188 8
not proceed with all the rapidity which suited his E II 18 308 28
been got through, even by the smart rapidity of a waiter. P III 12 105 13
care, and was off for the town with the utmost rapidity. P III 12 110 42
his letter with great rapidity, was indeed ready, and had P IV 11 236 39
RAPIDLY (19)
warm, and they passed so rapidly through every gradation NA I 5 36 4
the Abbey, and driven so rapidly along a smooth, level NA II 5 161 25
Her greedy eye glanced rapidly over a page. NA II 7 172 2
looked forward to their marriage as rapidly approaching. SS I 3 17 14
her alarm increased so rapidly, as to determine her on SS III 7 311 14
his constitution, and carry him off as rapidly as before. SS III 14 373 3
was now rapidly forming, with nearly equal complacency.-- W 331 11
The wheels rapidly approached;--in two minutes the general W 354 28
"My ideas flow so rapidly that I have not time to express PP I 10 48 23
increased at last very rapidly, as well as her affection PP I 12 60 5
purely governed, were rapidly restoring her to all the MP I 15 147 56
Susan go?"--were questions following each other rapidly. MP III 15 445 29
They might advance rapidly if they would, however; they E I 11 91 1
took the reproof, so rapidly did another subject succeed; E I 15 125 7
These feelings rapidly restored his comfort, while Mrs. E I 18 144 3
thing was rapidly clearing away, to give proper space. E II 8 229 98
Emma hoped it must rapidly work Harriet's cure; but the E II 15 281 3
They were rapidly forming words for each other, or for any E III 5 347 20
and when acquainted, rapidly and deeply in love. P III 4 26 1
RAPTURE (8)
with spirits elated to rapture, with Henry at her heart, NA II 2 140 11
could not witness the rapture of delightful expectation SS II 4 159 1
none, and dawdled away her time in rapture and indecision. SS II 4 165 24
The rapture of Lydia on this occasion, her adoration of PP II 18 230 12
and welcomed her with rapture; gave her hand with an PP III 9 315 3
tranquillize every care, and lift the heart to rapture! MP I 11 113 35
smiles reined in and spirits dancing in private rapture. P IV 11 240 59
Letitia's, of curiosity & rapture in all who came near her S 11 421 1
RAPTURES (23)
a whole party into raptures by a prelude on the pianoforte, NA I 1 16 10
of all the party, heard her without being in raptures. SS I 7 35 9
without hesitation, and told her sister of it in raptures. SS I 12 58 1
with the house, and in raptures with the furniture, and SS I 21 119 3
With her children they were in continual raptures, SS I 21 120 6
it was time for the raptures of Edward to cease; for SS II 13 242 23
he left the room, fatigued with the raptures of his wife. PP I 2 8 25
know that I am quite in raptures with her beautiful little PP I 10 48 15
"Will you give me leave to defer your raptures till I PP I 10 48 16
and mentioned with raptures, some plans of the latter with PP II 1 133 2
she could not be in such raptures as Mr. Collins expected PP II 6 161 8
had passed; and their raptures continued with little PP II 18 233 24
should hear the first raptures of her joy, than the first PP III 17 375 27
went down to it quite in raptures; but it being MP I 6 57 31
visit, and now her raptures might well be over, for Edmund MP II 9 262 11
Had Fanny been at all addicted to raptures, she must have MP III 6 369 11
Don't pretend to be in raptures about mine. E I 6 43 15
Keep your raptures for Harriet's face. E I 6 43 15
raptures, and defended it through every criticism. E I 6 47 30
received notice of it that morning, and was in raptures. E III 6 359 37
Emma was only saved from raptures and fondness, which at E III 11 411 42
The same story and the same raptures were repeated, when P III 7 54 5
burst forth into raptures of admiration and delight on the P III 11 99 19
RAPTUROUS (10)
Not one, however, started with rapturous wonder on NA I 2 23 27
was very far from that rapturous delight, which, in her SS I 4 19 3
and dwelt upon with so rapturous a delight, that any young SS I 10 47 3
them, looked neither rapturous nor gay, said little but SS I 16 87 23
and was not only in the rapturous profession of the lover, SS III 13 361 3
inform them, with many rapturous expressions, of his PP I 23 128 10
pointed out, with a rapturous air, the fine proportion and PP II 6 161 10
of Mr. Crawford was more rapturous than any thing which MP I 5 47 27
of the old lady, and the rapturous delight of her daughter- E III 12 418 5
impression--& seeing no rapturous astonishment in S 7 400 1
RAPTUROUSLY (3)
afterwards Marianne rapturously exclaimed, "it is he; it SS I 16 86 16 17
and admire what she admires as rapturously as herself?" SS I 17 95 49
"My dear, dear aunt," she rapturously cried, "what delight! PP II 4 154 23
RARE (6)
The chaise of a traveller being a rare sight in Fullerton, NA II 14 233 8
his sex might make it rare; for his heart had not the SS II 13 241 21
which he believed most rare indeed), was of a sort to MP III 2 326 3
A sermon, good in itself, is no rare thing. MP III 3 341 28
He has chosen his partner, indeed, with rare felicity. MP III 4 351 32
some few articles of a rare species of wood, excellently P III 11 98 17
RARELY (4)
general conduct, which in London can rarely be the case. MP I 9 93 49
with the past; a sombre family-party rarely enlivened. MP II 3 196 1
totally distinct, or very rarely mixing--and Emma only E I 12 100 15
so before, that the sea is very rarely of use to any body. E I 12 101 22
RARITY (1)
be mustered; but the rarity and the suddenness of it made E II 8 230 100
RASCAL (3)
he had done otherwise, I should have thought him a rascal. SS III 1 267 43
I have not been always a rascal, to obtain something like SS III 8 319 23
Oh, God!--what an hard-hearted rascal I was!" SS III 8 324 42
RASCALLY (1)
I owe such a grudge to myself for the stupid, rascally SS III 8 324 45
RASH (2)
her ideas of perfection, had been rash and unjustifiable. SS I 10 49 10
Her continual disagreements with her mother, her rash MP III 8 391 9
RASHLY (1)
censure, we must not rashly condemn those who living in LS 14 264 3
RASHNESS (1)
"Would Mr. Darcy then consider the rashness of your PP I 10 49 32
RAT-HUNTING (1)
We had a famous set-to at rat-hunting all the morning, in P IV 10 219 26
RATE (56)
with Mrs Manwaring; at any rate it must be exaggerated; it LS 6 252 2
And why should your ladyship at any rate quarrel with my LS 24 290 12
My removal therefore, which must at any rate take place LS 25 293 3
may be directed, & at any rate, I shall there be rewarded LS 25 294 4
At any rate I hope he will plague his wife more than ever. LS 32 303 2
But this will just give you a notion of the general rate NA I 9 64 24
much obliged to you at any rate for wishing us a pleasant NA I 12 93 7
At this rate, I shall not pity the writers of history any NA I 14 109 24
"At any rate, however, I am pleased that you have learnt NA II 7 174 10
How were people, at that rate, to be understood? NA II 11 211 15
Catherine, at any rate, heard enough to feel, that in NA II 15 247 14
mother laughing, "at this rate you must be in continual SS I 8 37 7
At any rate it would be most ungenerous. SS I 16 84 9
"At any rate," said Elinor, wishing to prevent Mrs. SS II 5 167 4
At any rate I shall expect you to-morrow. SS II 7 187 38
by officious condolence to rate good-breeding as more SS II 10 215 13
And at any rate, she lost nothing by continuing the SS III 13 367 23
condition of the land, and rate of the tythes, to Elinor SS III 13 368 31
who could satisfy them, and a ball was at any rate, a ball. PP I 17 86 10
at any rate, was perfectly ready to accede to his proposal. PP II 12 200 5
"Why, at that rate, you will have been here only six weeks. PP II 14 211 8
At any rate, she cannot grow many degrees worse, without PP II 18 232 20
at any rate, there seemed a gulf impassable between them. PP III 8 311 12
pleasant, indeed, at any rate; he was the sort of young MP I 5 47 28
She made me almost laugh; but I cannot rate so very highly MP I 7 64 10
"At any rate, it is safer to leave people to their own MP I 9 87 15
his knave at an exorbitant rate, exclaimed, "there, I will MP II 7 242 25
of your taste, but at any rate, I know you will be kind to MP II 9 261 2
But at any rate his staying away at a time, when, MP II 11 287 17
Crawford, delighted to get her to speak at any rate, was MP III 3 343 40
Crawford now, at the rapid rate in which their MP III 9 393 1
will clear it up--at any rate, that Henry is blameless, MP III 15 437 3
which must, at any rate, have been torn from me now. MP III 16 458 30
At this rate, you will soon reform every body at Mansfield MP III 16 458 30
and quiet; and, at any rate, there was comfort in finding MP III 17 462 4
At any rate, it must be better to have only one to please, E I 1 10 29
away at a very unusual rate; and the supper-table, which E I 3 24 11
"I cannot rate her beauty as you do," said he; "but she is E I 8 58 10
to look down on the common rate of social intercourse, and E I 11 97 27
falling in with the second rate and third rate of Highbury, E II 1 155 3
the second rate and third rate of Highbury, who were E II 1 155 3
and admired amid the usual rate of conversation; a few E II 8 219 43
good livelihood as a working-silversmith at this rate." E II 10 240 4
that he was sure at this rate it would be may before E II 18 308 28
while you can: at any rate do not let them carry you far, E III 4 342 39
The year will wear away at this rate, and nothing done. E III 6 354 7
on the morrow, or, at any rate, have the pleasure of being E III 6 361 42
At any rate, it would be a proof of attention and kindness E III 14 435 4
"Poor child!" cried Emma; "at that rate, what will become E III 17 461 4
However, at any rate, as I have a great deal more at stake P III 5 35 16
statement of her name and rate, and present non- P III 8 66 22
useful if wanted, at any rate, to enjoy the sight of a P III 12 111 49
I should have visited Admiral Croft, however, at any rate. P IV 6 162 5
At any rate, said I, it will be better than a long P IV 11 230 6
may be supplied at a fair rate--(poor Mr Hollis's Chamber- S 6 393 1
At any rate, she was seen all the following morng walking S 11 420 1
RATED (6)
His estate had been rated by Sir John at about six or SS I 14 71 4
the modesty with which he rated his own deserts, and the SS III 13 366 20
She rated his abilities much higher than any of the others; PP I 22 124 11
She rated her own claims to comfort as low even as Mrs. MP II 5 221 35
She rated Lady Russell's influence highly, and as to the P III 2 13 5
herself to be so highly rated by a sensible man, without P IV 5 159 21
RATES (1)
a man you of war; I speak, you know, of the higher rates. P III 8 70 54
RATHER (517)
but I must own myself rather romantic in that respect, & LS 2 245 1
There is something about him that rather interests me, a LS 7 254 3
I would rather work for my bread than marry him. LS 21 279 1
"Say rather that she has been unfortunate in her education. LS 24 288 11
This eclaircissement is rather provoking. LS 33 303 1
Sally, or rather Sarah, (for what young lady of common NA I 2 19 3
composure, which seemed rather consistent with the common NA I 2 19 3
from the crowd; it seemed rather to increase as they went NA I 2 21 9
He seemed to be about four or five and twenty, was rather NA I 3 25 2
"That is artful and deep, to be sure; but I had rather be NA I 3 29 49
brown skin, with dark eyes, and rather dark hair.'-- NA I 6 42 30
her at that time rather more than any thing else in the NA I 6 42 33
he might have thought her sufferings rather too acute. NA I 8 54 10
left, when it ended, with rather a strengthened belief of NA I 9 64 26
of his conversation, or rather talk, began and ended with NA I 9 66 31
one of the other sex rather than her own, a brother rather NA I 10 73 22
than her own, a brother rather than a great aunt might NA I 10 73 22
This disposition on your side is rather alarming. NA I 10 77 37
Allen, which took them rather early away, and her spirits NA I 10 81 61
I would much rather take a chair at any time." NA I 11 83 11
he will not, for he had rather do any thing in the world NA I 11 83 13
I had rather, ten thousand times rather get out now, and NA I 11 87 53
with pleasure; though rather than be disappointed of the NA I 11 88 54
walk, and especially rather than be thought ill of by the NA I 11 88 54
"It is all one to me," replied Thorpe rather angrily; and NA I 11 88 55
I would fifty times rather you should have them than NA I 11 90 64
Feelings rather natural than heroic possessed her; instead NA I 12 93 4
But I had ten thousand times rather have been with you; NA I 12 93 5
artless in itself, though rather distressing to the NA I 12 94 11

daughter, rather than postpone his own walk a few minutes. NA I 12 95 17
to by Catherine, who, in rather a solemn tone of voice, NA I 14 111 29
Her tenderness for her friend seemed rather the first NA II 4 153 31
of the building they inhabited, was rather distressing. NA II 7 174 5
And though the love of a hyacinth may be rather domestic, NA II 7 174 8
rather angrily back, demanding whither she were going?-- NA II 8 185 6
gallery, that she would rather be allowed to examine that NA II 8 185 5
rather wonder that Eleanor should not take it for her own. NA II 9 196 21
her, was that he paid her rather more attention than usual. NA II 10 199 1
"Aye, and sadly too--for I had much rather stay." NA II 11 211 11
it was eleven o'clock, rather a late hour at the Abbey, NA II 13 222 7
With these feelings, she rather dreaded than sought for NA II 14 232 6
house rather than remain fixed for any time in the parlour. NA II 15 240 1
felicity, was perhaps rather conducive to it, by improving NA II 16 252 7
He was not an ill-disposed young man, unless to be rather SS I 1 5 7
rather cold hearted, and rather selfish, is to be ill- SS I 1 5 7
"One had rather, on such occasions, do too much than too SS I 2 9 12
mother while she lives rather than for them--something of SS I 2 10 16
to, that he seemed rather to stand in need of more money SS I 5 27 6
talked a great deal, seemed very happy, and rather vulgar. SS I 7 34 5
She rather suspected it to be so, on the very first SS I 8 36 1
"I rather think you are mistaken, for when I was talking SS I 8 39 17
Sir John was rather puzzled. SS I 9 44 19
and his reserve appeared rather the result of some SS I 10 50 12
"Or rather, as I believe, she considers them impossible to SS I 11 56 10
To some few of the company, it appeared rather a bold SS I 12 62 29
The morning was rather favourable, though it had rained SS I 13 63 2
inconveniences and hardships rather than be otherwise. SS I 13 63 2
Elinor, it was rather ill-judged in me to go to Allenham; SS I 13 69 76
likely, for I have a notion she is always rather sickly. SS I 14 70 2
the spring, I would even rather lay it uselessly by than SS I 14 72 10
added, "it is I who may rather expect to be ill--for I am SS I 15 75 4
You had rather take evil upon credit than good. SS I 15 78 28
You had rather look out for misery for Marianne and guilt SS I 15 78 28
He looked rather distressed as he added, that he had been SS I 16 87 26
to him by the past rather than the present, she avoided SS I 16 89 42
"I do not doubt it," replied he, rather astonished at her SS I 18 100 30
which had been rather more painfully extorted from her, SS I 19 101 2
It was rather a wish of distinction she believed, which SS I 20 112 28
the little Middletons rather too much indulged; perhaps SS I 21 122 19
and who now said rather abruptly, "and how do you like SS I 21 123 21
Marianne; indeed it was rather his favourite joke of the SS I 21 125 36
it is rather too much to pretend to know him very well." SS I 21 126 40
it struck her as being rather ill-natured, and suggested SS I 21 126 41
I am sure I would rather do any thing in the world than be SS I 22 128 9
"I am rather of a jealous temper too by nature, and from SS II 2 147 12
which it may involve you, rather than run the risk of her SS II 2 148 14
"Then I rather suspect that my interest would do very SS II 2 149 28
which was putting herself rather out of her way; and as SS II 3 157 19
it was what she had rather expected all along; so angry at SS II 4 164 21
where the mind is perhaps rather unwilling to be convinced, SS II 5 173 44
He approached, and addressing himself rather to Elinor SS II 6 176 7
"By all the world, rather than by his own heart. SS II 7 189 50
I could rather believe every creature of my acquaintance SS II 7 189 50
world whom I would not rather suspect of evil than SS II 7 189 50
determined (though rather against the opinion of Sir John) SS II 10 215 14
and Miss Dashwood seemed rather to declare that the SS II 10 216 15
but such a one as seemed rather to demand than express SS II 11 221 5
see his sisters again; it rather gave them satisfaction; SS II 11 221 7
"Nothing at all, I should rather suppose; for she has only SS II 11 226 43
Miss Morton's mother, rather than her own, whom they were SS II 12 232 14
For their own comfort, they would much rather have SS II 14 246 2
situation, and it seemed rather surprising to him that SS II 14 251 16
That belonged rather to the hearer, for Marianne listened SS III 1 261 12
for herself which she rather wished to do away; and SS III 2 270 1
of meeting them, chose rather to stay at home, than SS III 2 271 4
who, though looking rather shy, expressed great SS III 2 271 5
The Miss Dashwoods had now been rather more than two SS III 3 279 1
"Oh! very well," said Mrs. Jennings rather disappointed. SS III 4 286 14
But, my dear, is not this rather out of character? SS III 4 286 17
"Colonel Brandon is so delicate a man, that he rather SS III 4 287 19
office, (breathing rather faster than usual as she spoke.) SS III 4 288 28
last, and as if it were rather an effort, he said, " SS III 4 290 36
37

him; on his, with rather an attempt to return the same SS III 4 290 43
pursued her own judgment rather than her friend's, in SS III 7 310 8
different kind, and led to anything rather than to gaiety. SS III 7 315 24
and saying, in a voice rather of command than supplication, SS III 8 317 1
2

a tenderness, a regret, rather in proportion, as she soon SS III 9 333 2
and wished any thing rather than Mrs. Willoughby's death. SS III 9 335 5
so warm a sympathy--or rather not thinking at all, I SS III 9 336 12
"Rather say your mother's imprudence, my child," said Mrs. SS III 11 352 15
By that time, Marianne was rather better, and her mother SS III 11 353 25
"I wrote to him, my love, last week, and rather expect to SS III 12 358 6
Edward, who had till then looked any where, rather than at SS III 12 360 26
with Edward had not rather been fulfilled, than that she SS III 13 371 38
Mrs. Jennings's prophecies, though rather jumbled together, SS III 14 374 7
and Marianne, and rather better pasturage for their cows. SS III 14 374 7
though rather more liberal than what John had expressed. SS III 14 378 13
I declare I had rather have her well-married than myself."- W 317 2
I would rather be teacher at a school (and I can think of W 318 2
"I would rather do any thing than be teacher at a school-- W 318 2
I suppose my aunt brought you up to be rather refined." W 318 2
But Mary Edwardes is rather prim & reserved; I do not W 321 2
his complexion has been rather too much exposed to all W 324 3
"Rather more so, my dear--replied he, because young ladies W 326 6
& tho' Miss Edwards was rather discomposed at the very W 326 7
& mother think it has given him rather an unsettled turn.-- W 328 8
a moment, saw her looking rather distressed, but by no W 328 8
Tho' rather distressed by such observation, Emma could not W 331 11
ball, were ratner flat, in comparison with the others.-- W 336 14
The note, which Emma was beginning to read rather before W 338 18
was rather afraid of the sort of carriage--. W 339 18
of as much;--for I am rather fond of dancing than not.-- W 340 19
could not say no, tho' it rather went against me to be W 341 19
to a certain point--his address rather--is pleasing.-- W 342 19
rather have quarrelling going on, than nothing at all."-- W 343 19
simplicity, such shameless truth rather bewildered him.-- W 346 21
suit her pride, & she wd rather have known that he wished W 347 22
slight, pretty figure, & rather wanted countenance than W 349 23
I do not much attend the balls, they are rather too mixed,- W 350 24
"I suppose, said Margt rather quickly to Emma, you & I are W 351 25
"Oh!--(in a soften'd voice, & rather mortified to find she W 351 25
"I do not mean to make you cry.--said robt rather softened- W 352 26
tempted to eat a bit, for it is rather a favourite dish." W 354 27
Were you not rather warm last Saturday about 9 or 10 W 358 28
at all risks, as she had rather talk of Croydon to Jane, W 361 30
He had rather hoped that all his wife's views on the PP I 3 12 15
They were rather handsome, had been educated in one of the PP I 4 15 11
he admired her--indeed I rather believe he did--I heard PP I 5 18 6
as it is, I would really rather not sit down before those PP I 6 24 22
"I had much rather go in the coach." PP I 7 30 24
has rather affected your admiration of her fine eyes." PP I 8 36 12
when it appeared to her rather right than pleasant that PP I 8 37 21
reading to cards?" said he; "that is rather singular." PP I 8 37 22
She is now about Miss Elizabeth Bennet's height, or rather PP I 8 38 41
I rather wonder now at your knowing any." PP I 8 39 52
I write rather slowly." PP I 10 47 6
subject, to arrange with rather more precision the degree PP I 10 50 38
he was rather offended; and therefore checked her laugh. PP I 10 51 40
Elizabeth, having rather expected to affront him, was PP I 10 52 52

whom a ball would be rather a punishment than a pleasure." PP I 11 55 6
any thing and everything, rather than his disappointing PP I 16 78 20
and clever; but I rather believe she derives part of her PP I 16 84 58
amusement; and she was rather surprised to find that he PP I 17 87 12
an impertinent freedom, rather than a compliment to his PP I 18 97 60
you any disservice, rather adds to your other perfections. PP I 19 105 8
"Upon my word, sir," cried Elizabeth, "your hope is rather PP I 19 107 14
I would rather be paid the compliment of being believed PP I 19 108 20
Risk any thing rather than her displeasure; and if you PP I 22 124 9
she called at Longbourn rather oftener than usual to say PP I 23 127 8
it was for the sake of what had been, rather than what was. PP II 3 146 19
might rather give contentment to her aunt than to herself. PP II 3 149 28
sign of repentance; and rather looked with wonder at her PP II 5 156 4
It was rather small, but well built and convenient; and PP II 5 157 5
I rather expected, from my knowledge of her affability, PP II 6 160 2
Elizabeth at first had rather wondered that Charlotte PP II 7 168 1
the effect of necessity rather than of choice--a sacrifice PP II 9 180 29
"You are rather disposed to call his interference PP II 10 185 35
Catherine's being rather displeased by her staying at home. PP II 10 187 41
I rather wished, than believed him to be sincere; but at PP II 12 200 5
and Lydia, in a voice rather louder than any other PP II 16 222 21
The separation between her and her family was rather noisy PP II 18 235 40
letters to Kitty, though rather longer, were much too full PP II 19 238 5
handsome as Wickham; or rather he has not Wickham's PP III 1 257 70
studied avoidance spoke rather a momentary embarrassment, PP III 2 264 11
alteration than her being rather tanned,--no miraculous PP III 3 271 14
and I believe you thought her rather pretty at one time." PP III 3 271 17
cordial. his countenance rather gained in austerity; and PP III 9 315 4
the strength of her love, rather than by his; and she PP III 9 318 19
To be sure London was rather thin, but however the little PP III 9 319 25
any satisfaction, she had rather be without a confidante. PP III 9 320 35
coolly, "will be rather a confirmation of it; if, indeed, PP III 14 354 29
that his letter was not rather addressed to herself; when PP III 15 362 11
12

It was necessary to laugh, when she would rather have PP III 15 364 25
to be laughed at, and it was rather too early to begin. PP III 16 371 46
agitated and confused, rather knew that she was happy, PP III 17 372 2
Oh, Lizzy! do any thing rather than marry without PP III 17 373 11
Kitty owned that she had rather stay at home. PP III 17 375 25
to you without rather wishing to give you pain than not. PP III 18 380 3
do not speak to Mr. Darcy about it, if you had rather not. PP III 19 386 7
As it happened that Elizabeth had much rather not, she PP III 19 386 8
and, poor as I am, would rather deny myself the MP I 1 7 8
Mrs. Price seemed rather surprised that a girl should be MP I 1 11 19
on the occasion with rather an injudicious particularity. MP I 2 12 3
believe you to be right rather than myself, and I am very MP I 3 27 34
do rather more--to lay by a little at the end of the year." MP I 3 30 50
"Why, you know Sir Thomas's means will be rather MP I 3 30 54
his place with them, or rather to perform what should have MP I 3 32 62
her deportment showed rather conscious superiority than MP I 6 52 1
I would rather have an inferior degree of beauty, or my MP I 6 56 28
I would rather abide by my own blunders than by his." MP I 6 56 28
rather grieved that I could not give the advantage to all. MP I 6 58 37
rather black upon me, when he found what I had been at." MP I 6 58 37
Fanny would rather have had Edmund tell the story, but his MP I 6 60 47
The harp arrived, and rather added to her beauty, wit, and MP I 7 64 12
and water for her, would rather go without it than not. MP I 7 65 14
Active and fearless, and, though rather small, strongly MP I 7 66 15
She began to think it rather hard upon the mare to have MP I 7 68 16
been out very often lately, and would rather stay at home. MP I 7 70 29
Mrs. Norris, in a rather softened voice; "but I question MP I 7 72 45
But I thought it would rather do her good after being MP I 7 73 55
This is rather a surprise to me." MP I 9 91 38
The manners I speak of, might rather be called conduct, MP I 9 93 49
And to tell you the truth," speaking rather lower, "I do MP I 10 98 7
"I am rather surprised," said she, "that Mr. Crawford MP I 12 115 5
it was rather a pity they should have been obliged to part. MP I 12 117 13
to come; and he did come rather earlier than had been MP I 13 121 1
We must rather adopt Mr. Crawford's views, and make the MP I 13 124 9
that I consider it rather as a motive; for the expectation MP I 13 126 18
She stopped--Henry Crawford looked rather foolish, and as MP I 14 136 18
to the quarrel, or rather thought it a lucky occurrence, MP I 17 160 9
"I rather wonder Julia is not in love with Henry," was her MP I 17 161 10
Or why had not she rather gone to her own room, as she had MP I 18 172 29
nothing till tea came--he would rather wait for tea. MP II 1 180 10
"But indeed I would rather have nothing but tea." MP II 1 180 11
as he sat down; "I found myself in it rather unexpectedly. MP II 1 184 25
to Sir Thomas, and at rather an early hour they were MP II 2 192 11
"I believe our evenings are rather returned to what they MP II 3 197 4
to the party must rather forward her favourite indulgence MP II 5 223 48
She could not wish him to stay, and would much rather not MP II 5 224 48
You would look rather blank, Henry, if your menus plaisirs MP II 5 226 62
which had a tendency rather to forward his views of MP II 6 232 12
The wish was rather eager than lasting. MP II 6 236 23
I must be satisfied with rather less ornament and beauty. MP II 7 242 24
"And Fanny had much rather it were William's," said Edmund, MP II 7 244 29
"I would rather find him private secretary to the first MP II 7 246 35
or rather of professions of a somewhat pointed character. MP II 7 246 36
her dancing had been, and rather took it for granted that MP II 7 251 62
and her maid was rather hurried in making up a new dress MP II 8 254 9
She would rather perhaps have been obliged to some other MP II 8 258 18
rather part with and see in your possession than any other. MP II 8 260 22
home again--with a change rather than a diminution of MP II 8 260 25
she would rather not part with it, when it is not wanted?" MP II 9 263 13
make that sacrifice rather than give pain to one who has MP II 9 263 16
am sure she is not serious--but I would rather not hear it. MP II 9 268 29
It was rather honour than happiness to Fanny, for the MP II 10 276 13
rather than insensible of pleasure in Henry's attentions. MP II 10 277 20
She would much rather not have been asked by him again so MP II 10 278 20
could do him good; it rather sank than raised his comfort; MP II 10 279 21
Thomas having seen her rather walk than dance down the MP II 10 279 22
and I cannot help being rather concerned at not seeing him MP II 11 287 22
But honestly now, do not you rather expect it than MP II 11 289 34
to give him something rather considerable; that is, for MP II 13 304 19
Every thing might be possible rather than serious MP II 13 306 26
Fanny would rather have been silent, but being obliged to MP III 1 312 11
She would rather die than own the truth, and she hoped by MP III 1 317 33
Any thing might be bearable rather than such reproaches. MP III 1 322 49
He considered her rather as one who had never thought on MP III 2 326 3
He rather derived spirits from it. MP III 2 327 4
sisters; and it would be rather gratifying to him to have MP III 2 331 19
have expected any thing rather than a look of satisfaction, MP III 3 334 2
always believed it to be rather the reverse, and could MP III 3 335 6
honouring her in rather stronger terms than Sir Thomas MP III 3 335 6
of a hint, he thought, was rather favourable than not. MP III 3 339 21
I speak rather of the past, however, than the present.-- MP III 3 339 23
looking at Fanny he saw rather a flush of vexation, he MP III 3 344 44
She assented to it all rather by look than word. MP III 4 346 7
I am myself convinced that it is rather a favourable MP III 4 349 23
desire rather more unguardedly than was perfectly prudent. MP III 4 350 30
"Say rather, that he has not thought at all upon serious MP III 4 350 32
not rather fixed on some woman of distinction, or fortune. MP III 4 351 36
It is anger to be talked of, rather than felt. MP III 4 352 42
because she was rather my most particular friend of the MP III 5 359 12
The first, at least, of these favours Fanny would rather MP III 5 364 33
let her go; obtaining it rather from submission, however, MP III 6 370 14
"To be sure, I had much rather she had stayed in harbour, MP III 7 378 12
Sam, loud and overbearing as he was, she rather regretted MP III 8 390 8
kingdoms, who would not rather put up with the misfortune MP III 10 402 11
It was her manner, however, rather than any infrequency of MP III 13 421 2
For though Lady Bertram rather shone in the epistolary MP III 13 425 6
It was evident that she would rather remain where she was. MP III 14 433 11

disappointment, she was rather in expectation, from her MP III 15 437 1
of losing her, rather than have to think of her as I do. MP III 16 456 25
of her brother, should rather be prevented than sought-- MP III 16 457 30
in finding his estate rather more, and his debts much less, MP III 17 462 4
were the power of having rather too much her own way, and E I 1 5 4
But if, which I rather imagine, your making the match, as E I 1 12 42
years' marriage, he was rather a poorer man than at first, E I 2 16 4
(though it seemed rather against the bias of inclination,) E I 2 19 14
very unwholesome made him rather sorry to see any thing E I 3 24 12
inferior creature--and rather wondering at yourself for E I 4 32 32
"There is no saying, indeed!" replied Harriet, rather E I 4 33 37
"Why, to own the truth, I am afraid you are rather thrown E I 5 38 13
"Oh! you would rather talk of her person than her mind, E I 5 39 17
"Pretty! say beautiful rather. E I 5 39 18
I am rather proud of little George. E I 6 45 21
But for Harriet's sake, or rather for my own, and as there E I 6 46 21
compliments rather more than I could endure as a principal. E I 6 49 44
I'd rather you would." E I 7 50 3
"Yes, indeed, a very good letter," replied Emma rather E I 7 51 5
She was rather low all the evening, but Emma could allow E I 7 55 36
to abbey-mill again," was said in rather a sorrowful tone. E I 7 55 37
Harriet's equal; and am rather surprized indeed that he E I 8 61 37
chose rather to take up her own line of the subject again. E I 8 63 43
to believe, that he had rather said what he wished E I 8 67 57
he might naturally be rather attentive than otherwise to E I 8 67 57
at last he recalled, and rather sentimentally recited, E I 9 70 7
by; but he rather pushed it towards me than towards you. E I 9 77 47
He looked rather doubtingly--rather confused; said E I 9 82 81
I would rather not be tempted. E I 10 84 13
was quick, and theirs rather slow; and she was the more E I 10 88 33
exciting of course rather more than the usual interest. E I 11 91 2
Mr. Weston is rather an easy, cheerful tempered man, than E I 11 96 26
Mr. Knightley was to dine with them--rather against the E I 12 98 1
and she hoped it might rather assist the restoration of E I 12 98 2
and if the children were rather pale before they went to E I 12 103 39
Mr. Woodhouse was rather agitated by such harsh E I 12 107 62
away, which she would rather feed and assist than not, she E I 13 110 8
are we, probably with rather thinner clothing than usual, E I 13 113 26
Smith was not better, by no means better, rather worse. E I 13 114 31
Emma was rather in dismay when only half a minute E I 13 115 36
and for my part, I would rather, under such circumstances, E I 13 116 43
for a while, made her rather sorry to find, when they had E I 14 118 4
that she knew the first meeting must be rather alarming.-- E I 14 121 14
who was pursuing his triumph rather unfeelingly. E I 15 126 9
it would have been rather a pleasure, previous to the E I 15 129 23
But now, she would rather it had not happened. E I 15 129 23
It was rather too late in the day to set about being E I 17 142 10
She wanted, rather, to be quiet, and out of temptation; E I 18 144 4
acting a part, perhaps rather more,) at the conduct of the E I 18 145 5
"I rather doubt that. E I 18 147 19
"Me!--not at all," replied Mr. Knightley, rather E I 18 149 28
imperfection in her, as rather negligent in that respect, E II 1 155 2
The very thing that we have always been rather afraid of; E II 1 160 23
to what is moderate rather than to what is superior, E II 2 165 7
Once, I felt the fire rather too much; but then I moved E II 3 171 12
as she always is, though she speaks rather too quick. E II 3 171 12
Well, I had always rather fancied it would be some young E II 3 176 44
Oh! Miss Woodhouse, I would rather done any thing than E II 3 179 52
Emma learned to be rather glad that there had been such a E II 3 180 58
of things it was to be rather supposed that Miss Taylor E II 5 192 29
not the proper name--I should rather say Barnes, or Bates. E II 5 193 37
on dancing; and Emma was rather surprized to see the E II 6 198 5
"Yes--(rather hesitatingly)--I believe I do." E II 6 201 22
"One would rather have a stranger preferred than one's E II 6 202 33
them all--" he began rather quickly, but checking himself, E II 6 202 38
I am sure, rather than run the risk of hurting Mr. and Mrs. E II 7 210 20
The party was rather large, as it included one other E II 8 214 13
"I rather wonder that it was never made before." E II 8 216 22
I rather believe you are giving me more credit for E II 8 216 27
in the awkwardness of a rather long interval between the E II 8 218 38
39
she had been used to despise the place rather too much. E II 8 220 48
in the same way; Emma rather gaining ground over the mind E II 8 226 85
I am sure I had much rather hear you. E II 9 231 7
"They told me something," said Harriet rather hesitatingly, E II 9 232 13
"Oh! but indeed I would much rather have it only in one. E II 9 235 40
Voices approached the shop--or rather one voice and two E II 9 235 43
Pray take care, Miss Woodhouse, ours is rather a dark E II 9 239 53
staircase--rather darker and narrower than one could wish. E II 9 239 53
"This is a pleasure," said he, in rather a low voice, " E II 10 240 3
and that he would rather oppose than lose the pleasure of E II 11 250 19
"Sir," said Mr. Woodhouse, rather warmly, "you are very E II 11 251 28
"Well--if you please," said Mrs. Weston rather hesitating, E II 11 255 51
as I can; but I would rather be at home, looking over E II 12 257 3
William Larkins's week's account; much rather, I confess.-- E II 12 257 3
I would much rather have been merry than wise." E II 12 260 18
Do not we rather surpass your expectations? E II 12 260 22
He laughed rather consciously; and though denying the E II 12 260 23
His feelings are warm, but I can imagine them rather E II 13 265 4
because for your own sake rather, I would wish it to be E II 13 268 11
12
forget what was due--or rather what would be kind by me." E II 13 268 12
pretty indeed, or only rather pretty, or not pretty at all. E II 14 270 1
she behaved very well, and was only rather pale and silent. E II 14 270 3
Her person was rather good; her face not unpretty; but E II 14 270 4
We are rather out of distance of the very striking E II 14 274 29
"Having understood as much, I was rather astonished to E II 14 278 46
A little quickness of voice there is which rather hurts E II 14 279 54
of her conversation, rather than return to the superior E II 15 285 13
imagined, would rather disgust than gratify Miss Fairfax. E II 15 286 19
20
Both felt rather anxious to hear him speak again; and E II 15 286 22
23
"She would rather not be in his company more than she E II 16 291 5
would not be displeased, she would rather stay at home." E II 16 291 5
A circumstance rather unlucky occurred. E II 16 292 7
"Thank you, but I would rather you did not mention the E II 17 300 11
Mr. Suckling was always rather a friend to the abolition." E II 17 300 14
I fancy I am rather a favourite; he took notice of my gown. E II 17 302 22
would probably prolong rather than break up the party. E II 17 303 23
her agitation, which she rather thought was considerable. E II 17 304 28
"I rather hope to satisfy you both," said Emma, "for I E II 18 311 39
she could not help rather anticipating something decisive. E III 1 315 2
It was not very long, though rather longer than Mr. Weston E III 1 315 3
perfect cure; and she was rather inclined to think it E III 1 316 5
Colonel Campbell rather preferred an olive. E III 2 323 19
beginning to feel myself rather an old married man, and E III 2 327 36
Is there nobody you would not rather?-- E III 2 329 45
and asparagus--so she was rather disappointed, but we E III 2 329 45
or rather surrounded, by the whole gang, demanding more. E III 3 334 6
that of the two I had rather not see him--and indeed I E III 4 337 6
Your resolution, or rather your expectation of never E III 4 341 35
I am a talker, you know; I am rather a talker; and now and E III 5 346 16
that ought to be treated rather as winter than summer. E III 5 347 19
She would rather busy herself about any thing than speak. E III 5 350 31
unwelcome interference, rather than her welfare; to E III 5 350 31
rather than the remembrance of neglect in such a cause. E III 5 350 31
circumstances--feelings rather of a totally different E III 5 350 37
"--Mrs. Weston, I suppose," interrupted Mrs. Elton, rather E III 6 354 16
I would rather walk.-- E III 6 362 48
rather because she felt less happy than she had expected. E III 7 368 3
your temper under your own command rather than mine." E III 7 369 11
ourselves, and it is rather too much to be talking E III 7 369 15
Let me hear any thing rather than what you are all E III 7 370 19
and wished herself rather walking quietly about with any E III 7 374 54
used to do: a privilege rather endured than allowed, E III 7 374 55
56
every body seemed rather fagged after the morning's party. E III 8 381 19
"Yes--rather--I have been thinking of it some little time." E III 9 385 4
might, perhaps, have rather offered it--but he took her E III 9 386 7
"From something that he said, my dear Emma, I rather E III 10 397 45
now you are come back, that will rather surprise you." E III 13 425 2
3
I was rather disappointed that I did not hear from her E III 14 442 8
"I would rather be talking to you," he replied; "but as it E III 15 444 5
which he knows she would rather dispense with; and he did E III 15 446 18
In such a party, Harriet would be rather a dead weight E III 15 450 37
'Upon my word, Mr. E., I often say, rather you than I.-- E III 16 455 23
William seemed rather out of humour. E III 16 458 43
thought of; but Emma was rather inclined to attribute it E III 17 463 15
young woman might think him rather cool in her praise. E III 17 464 19
rather in expectation of hearing something of the kind." E III 17 465 25
Hartfield, could daringly exclaim, "rather he than I!"-- E III 17 469 36
were in such a crowd, as to make Miss Smith rather uneasy." E III 18 472 20
and awful charge rather, to confide to the authority and P III 1 4 6
to the public, which is rather apt to be unreasonably P III 1 5 8
on Sir Walter, would rather have the disagreeable prompted P III 2 11 1
She was a woman rather of sound than of quick abilities, P III 2 11 2
and seemed to love her, rather because she would love her, P III 2 16 16
A prize indeed would Kellynch Hall be to him; rather the P III 3 17 2
alliance or fortune; or rather sunk by him into a state of P III 4 27 3
the autumn, entreated, or rather required her, for it was P III 5 33 7
who she is; and as I am rather better acquainted with her P III 5 35 14
I think it rather unnecessary in you to be advising me." P III 5 35 16
at all hours, that it was rather a surprise to her to find P III 5 36 21
Their dress had every advantage, their faces were rather P III 5 40 45
weeks, she had expected rather more curiosity and sympathy P III 6 42 1
cottage, to be interrupted by it, was rather an advantage. P III 6 46 12
brought her an accession rather of frightened, enquiring P III 7 53 3
have you go; but it seems rather hard that she should be P III 7 58 19
me, for it would be rather a pleasure to hear him talked P III 8 66 20
looked rather in suspense, and as if waiting for more. P III 8 67 25
It is rather from feeling how impossible it is, with all P III 8 68 35
She had rather play. P III 8 72 58
hearing her thanks, and rather sought to testify that her P III 9 80 34
considered Louisa to be rather the favourite, she could P III 10 82 1
separate us, and I would rather be overturned by him, than P III 10 85 9
she might be considered rather as leaving him behind, than P III 11 93 2
met at the great house at rather an early breakfast hour, P III 11 95 8
Anne's lot to be placed rather apart with Captain Benwick; P III 11 100 23
For, though shy, he did not seem reserved; it had rather P III 11 100 23
"Miss Elliot," said he, speaking rather low, "you have P III 12 107 24
Though it was rather desirable that Mr. and Mrs. Musgrove P III 12 114 64
tell how, and brought a rather improving account of Louisa. P IV 1 125 14
he must be rather a dressy man for his time of life.-- P IV 1 127 28
Anne, amused in spite of herself, was rather distressed P IV 1 128 29
said Mary, "I think he is rather my acquaintance, for I P IV 2 132 14
Mary spoke with animation of their meeting with, or rather P IV 2 132 22
most distressing, by their sort rather than their quantity. P IV 2 135 33
she felt that she would rather see Mr. Elliot again than P IV 2 136 36
time of life was another concern, and rather a fearful one. P IV 3 140 11
rather than generosity and fortitude, that one hears of. P IV 5 156 11
"Westgate-Buildings must have been rather surprised by the P IV 5 157 19
she did, when we were "rather surprised not to find P IV 6 164 8
but James benwick is rather too piano for me, and though P IV 6 172 39
that his cousin Anne's boots were rather the thickest. P IV 7 174 3
rather than words, was offering his services to her. P IV 7 176 10
"This," said she, "is nearly the sense, or rather the P IV 8 186 25
and shut in: but she would rather have caught his eye. P IV 8 188 42
a laundress and a waiter, rather more of the general P IV 9 192 5
his fortune, and by a rather quicker process than the law. P IV 9 200 59
This is all in confirmation, rather, of what we used to P IV 9 202 67
"Oh!" cried Elizabeth, "I have been rather too much used P IV 10 213 5
He answered rather hesitatingly, "yes, I believe I do-- P IV 10 218 24
I am sure she would rather not come--she cannot feel easy P IV 10 220 29
day and all day long, or rather claimed as a part of the P IV 10 220 31
meaning, of surprise rather than gratification, of polite P IV 10 226 65
of polite acknowledgment rather than acceptance. P IV 10 226 65
"I would rather have young people settle on a small income P IV 11 230 7
It is, perhaps, our fate rather than our merit. P IV 11 232 19
Any thing was possible, any thing might be defied rather P IV 11 237 41
Every moment rather brought fresh agitation. P IV 11 238 44
She is rather done for this morning, and must not go so P IV 11 240 58
up, who had been influenced by any one rather than by me. P IV 11 245 74
the way, his partner will just as well--or rather better--. S 1 365 1
I wd rather see his partner indeed--I would prefer the S 1 365 1
And we sir--(speaking rather proudly) are not in the Weald. S 1 366 1
the Travellor to think rather more as he had done at first S 1 367 1
He gets a better house by it--& I, a rather better S 4 380 1
I wd rather them run about in the sunshine than not. S 4 381 1
came from--or rather what wd Sidney say if he were here?-- S 5 385 1
must check herself--or rather she reflected that at two & S 6 390 1
tho' her manner was rather downright & abrupt, as of a S 6 391 1
& fluently touched;--rather commonplace perhaps--but doing S 7 396 1
looking rather than sickly; with an agreable face, & a S 9 407 1
I would be anything rather than not clear."-- S 9 409 1
I should recommend rather more of it to you than I suspect S 10 416 1
A large dish of rather weak cocoa every evening, agrees S 10 417 1
It struck her however, as he poured out this rather weak S 10 417 1
reply of "tis rather stronger than it should be tonight"-- S 10 417 1
"It sounds rather odd to be sure--answered Charlotte S 10 418 1
It could not but strike her rather unfavourably with S 12 426 1
it was furniture rather originally good & extremely well S 12 427 1

RATIFYING (1)
the imprudence by ratifying it, while there is so much LS 30 300 1

RATING (2)
I am sure his sisters, rating him as they do, must have MP III 4 353 45
There can be no want of gallantry, Admiral, in rating the P III 8 69 35

RATIONAL (50)
I am bewilder'd in my endeavours to form some rational LS 35 304 1
"Now I must give one smirk, and then we may be rational NA I 3 26 18
conceiving, as any rational creature would have done, that NA I 14 113 39
must be exactly of the true size for rational happiness. NA II 6 166 7
and made her reply less rational; for soon were all her NA II 14 237 20
think he deserved the compliment of rational opposition. SS II 14 252 19
too late to see this darling child, or to see her rational. SS III 7 312 18
her eyes on her with a rational, though languid, gaze. SS III 7 314 22
of such rational employment and virtuous self-controul. SS III 10 343 10
two rational creatures, yet with lovers it is different. SS III 13 363 9
It would surely be much more rational if conversation PP I 11 55 8
"Much more rational, my dear Caroline, I dare say but it PP I 11 56 9
just, sincere, rational, honourable, and perhaps agreeable, PP I 16 82 48
Elizabeth allowed that he had given a very rational PP I 16 84 59
as a rational creature speaking the truth from her heart." PP I 19 109 20
have spent ten minutes of every day in a rational manner." PP II 6 300 30
quietly, and live in so rational a manner, as may in time PP III 7 305 37
looking forward, neither rational happiness nor worldly PP III 7 307 51
not in rational expectation survive such a blow as this. PP III 8 311 13
It was a rational scheme to be sure! but from what the PP III 15 360 1
The greatest degree of rational consistency could not have MP I 9 96 76
or any endeavour at rational tranquillity for herself.-- MP I 17 160 8
She would endeavour to be rational, and to deserve the MP II 9 265 18
This is not like yourself, your rational self." MP III 4 347 19
heart, and the rational tranquillity of her ways.-- MP III 17 469 24

He could not meet her in conversation, rational or playful. E I 1 7 7
man, like weston, and a rational unaffected woman, like E I 1 13 44
better; and that as to a rational companion or useful E I 8 61 38
rational remonstrance or sharp retort equally ill bestowed. E I 11 93 5
With men he can be rational and unaffected, but when he E I 13 111 16
As he became rational, he ought to have roused himself and E I 18 148 22
daughter, in all the rational pleasures of an elegant E II 2 164 6
pleasures of life, of rational intercourse, equal society, E II 2 165 8
Harriet rational, Frank Churchill not too much in love, E III 3 332 1
in your presence, that you may see how rational I am grown. E III 4 338 6
more totally bare of rational satisfaction at the time, E III 8 377 1
air and scene, and quiet rational conversation, even for E III 9 390 16
of cheerful or of rational society within their reach? E III 12 422 20
would yet find her more rational, more acquainted with E III 12 423 21
and am now, I hope, rational enough to make the rest of my E III 14 440 8
He knows he is wrong, and has nothing rational to urge.-- E III 15 445 11
one real, rational difficulty to oppose or delay it. E III 17 468 31
and reflected, she could be fit for nothing rational. E III 18 475 37
was, generally speaking, rational and consistent--but she P III 2 11 2
women were all fine ladies, instead of rational creatures. P III 8 70 45
who were completely rational, was suffering most, Captain P III 12 110 43
which, in a more rational manner, neither Lady Russell nor P IV 4 149 12
Mr. Elliot was rational, discreet, polished,--but he was P IV 5 161 28
and insinuations highly rational against Mrs. Clay. P IV 7 178 24
much on this argument of rational dependance--"surely, if P IV 10 221 33
TIONALITY (3)
proceedings, and argue him into a little more rationality. MP II 2 191 10
t did not accord with the rationality of plan, the E II 7 205 1
rationality, and elegance to his habits and pursuits. P III 6 43 5
TIONALLY (13)
"But then you spend your time so much more rationally in NA I 10 79 49
years--years, which if rationally spent, give such SS II 1 140 2
n between them, was rationally treated as enormously SS III 13 371 38
f Hunsford and Rosings rationally softened; and Elizabeth PP II 3 147 19
o earnestly, yet so rationally and so mildly, to receive PP III 8 314 22
f felicity, to be rationally founded, because they had PP III 13 347 33
ould rationally be hoped in the dirty month of February. MP III 7 376 5
very thing was rationally and duly accomplished, and the MP III 15 444 27
here she spoke very rationally. MP III 16 455 21
hom he had rationally, as well as passionately loved. MP III 17 468 22
ationally to the varieties of her situation in life.-- E I 5 39 15
lton may talk sentimentally, but he will act rationally. E I 8 66 53
nd when it came to be rationally considered, a day in the P III 11 94 8
TLE (6)
ittle too much of the rattle perhaps, but a year or two LS 20 276 5
ver lived; a little of a rattle; but that will recommend NA I 7 50 45
he propensities of a rattle, nor to know to how many idle NA I 9 65 31
e is such a rattle!-- NA II 1 134 37
o with about as much delight as the rattle of the chaise. PP II 4 152 4
o my fancy, it is only because he does not rattle away PP III 1 249 38
TLED (1)
owerful voice, they were rattled into a narrow street, MP III 7 376 6
E (1)
quite rave about Jane Fairfax.-- E II 15 282 5
ED (2)
atherine could have raved at the hand which had swept NA II 8 184 4
y own blunder, I raved at the blunders of the post.-- E III 14 443 8
ENSHAW'S (1)
very fant of Lord Ravenshaw's, and been forced to re-rant MP I 14 132 8
ENSHAWS (1)
overs' Vows do for us as well as for the Ravenshaws? MP I 14 132 7
ING (1)
is dependence; and after raving a little about the E I 16 136 9
(1)
o the next to look at the raw efforts of those who have MP I 13 124 12
(1)
ay of common sense added some bitter emotions of shame. NA II 9 193 6
S (5)
ou, with only the feeble rays of a single lamp to take in NA II 5 158 15
ith the sun's first rays she was determined to peruse it. NA II 6 170 12
e excused himself however from attending them:--"the rays NA II 7 179 29
udiciously watched, some rays of light form the General's NA II 8 188 19
here; and the sun's rays falling strongly into the MP III 15 439 9
ADMITTED (1)
s you know, and re-admitted into the family; and there it P IV 9 207 90
ANIMATED (1)
is affection might be re-animated, and the influence of PP II 2 142 16
ANIMATION (1)
t was a most delightful re-animation of exhausted spirits. E II 5 188 8
APPEAR (1)
umour and cheerfulness began to re-appear at Longbourn. PP II 19 238 6
APPEARANCE (1)
onsiderably worse from this re-appearance of Mr. Elton. E II 4 184 10
APPEARED (5)
n a very few minutes she re-appeared, having scarcely NA I 9 62 7
f it till the butler re-appeared ten minutes afterwards, MP III 1 324 60
ormer provocation re-appeared E II 2 168 15
appy,) when the carriage re-appeared, and all was over. E II 5 187 4
ong before he re-appeared, attending the short, neat, E II 11 255 59
ARRANGE (1)
ver, and arrange, and re-arrange, Edmund could not, on MP II 8 256 13
ASSEMBLED (1)
ill they were all re-assembled in the drawing-room, when MP II 5 224 49
ASSURANCE (1)
er manners gave some re-assurance to Edward, and he had SS II 13 241 21
COMMENCING (1)
he performance was re-commencing, and she was forced to P IV 8 188 41
CONSIDER (1)
he sat down to re-consider the past, recal the words and SS III 4 291 45
CONSIDERING (1)
ariety of thought; re-considering events, determining PP II 13 209 12
DECLINED (1)
e re-urged--she re-declined; and he seemed then about to E I 9 81 79
80
ENTERED (2)
n this more placid state of things William re-entered, MP III 7 384 34
his conversation, she re-entered the house so happy as to P IV 11 245 77
ENTERING (1)
nd immediately on re-entering the breakfast room, NA II 7 175 13
ENTRANCE (1)
ire, longing for the re-entrance of her elder cousin, on MP I 12 116 11
ESTABLISH (2)
ime my intention to re-establish my circumstances by SS III 8 320 32
hat he has done, and anxious to re-establish a character. PP II 17 227 24
ESTABLISHED (4)
hoice, and re-established him completely in her favour. SS III 14 375 10
t re-established peace and kindness. MP I 1 5 3
erseverance had soon re-established the sort of familiar MP III 17 468 21
he visit was paid, their acquaintance re-established, P IV 5 153 6
ESTABLISHING (1)
s much too late for re-establishing harmony, as it MP I 10 104 51
KINDLED (2)
er sister re-kindled the admiration of her former lover. PP III 11 337 56
heir interest in each other more than re-kindled. P IV 5 153 6
PERUSING (1)
he was engaged one day as she walked, in re-perusing PP II 10 182 2
POSSESSED (1)
ere reclaimed and re-possessed, and another hour of P IV 8 189 45
RANT (1)
nd been forced to re-rant it all in his own room. MP I 14 132 8
READ (1)
ut when she read, and re-read with the closest attention, PP II 13 205 3

RE-SEATED (1)
Having introduced him, however, and being all re-seated, MP III 10 399 4
RE-SEEING (1)
disappointed in her hope of re-seeing her partner. NA I 5 35 2
RE-SETTLED (1)
after their being thus re-settled in Berkeley-Street, Mrs. SS III 1 257 2
3
RE-SETTLING (1)
In re-settling themselves, there were now many changes, P IV 8 189 46
RE-UNION (2)
And I do take leave, longing for a happy re-union, and MP III 5 364 30
happy, perhaps, in their re-union, than when it had been P IV 11 240 59
RE-URGE (1)
The two ladies continued to talk, to re-urge the same P IV 11 231 11
RE-URGED (1)
He re-urged--she re-declined; and he seemed then about to E I 9 81 79
80
RE-URGING (1)
he went on, re-urging the same questions as before. MP III 3 342 34
REACH (54)
true that I am vain enough to beleive it within my reach. LS 10 257 1
of common gentility will reach the age of sixteen without NA I 2 19 3
box which her eye could reach; but she looked in vain. NA I 5 35 1
to be within her daily reach, and she could not entirely NA II 2 141 11
long as the last echo can reach you--and when, with NA II 5 159 17
the left, in another long reach of gallery, when the NA II 8 185 6
herself at last within the reach of something worth her NA II 8 185 5
been such as was scarcely possible to reach his knowledge. NA II 14 230 3
had never happened to reach in any of their walks before. SS I 16 85 15
is to us, not to have it reach his mother; for she would SS I 22 132 39
only beyond the reach of Marianne, it was beyond her wish. SS II 6 176 6
The cruelty of Mrs. Jennings no language, within her reach SS II 9 202 8
unpleasant report should reach the young ladies under your SS III 1 258 5
spoken too low to reach her ear, hurried into the carriage. SS III 7 312 17
no sooner were they within reach of Emma, than Mrs B. W 333 13
Mrs. Bennet was beyond the reach of reason; and she PP I 13 62 8
in all families within the reach of my influence; and on PP I 13 63 12
neighbourhood in general, was beyond the Collinses' reach. PP II 7 169 5
she felt beyond the reach of Lady Catherine's curiosity. PP II 7 169 5
and respectability which he will probably never reach." PP II 10 187 40
her life, she will soon be beyond the reach of amendment. PP II 18 231 18
have been beyond the reach of his discrimination, for it PP III 1 252 54
fall of ground, or a finer reach of the woods to which PP III 1 253 55
such as no interest could reach; and before he had time to MP I 1 3 1
disposal, and to have every indulgence within their reach. MP I 3 32 64
or the imagination supplied what the eye could not reach. MP I 7 67 16
Her eye was eagerly taking in every thing within her reach; MP I 8 82 35
the whole morning to reach at last; and had been sitting MP I 10 103 49
affectionately, "must be beyond the reach of any sermons." MP I 11 112 32
Simplicity, indeed, is beyond the reach of almost every MP I 14 135 15
were all within her reach;--or if indisposed for MP I 16 151 2
She was beyond their reach; and if at last obliged to MP I 16 157 28
voice, not meant to reach far, and the subject dropped. MP II 7 246 35
is something in this which my comprehension does not reach. MP III 1 315 27
to for the truth, his sisters not being within my reach. MP III 14 434 1
3000
was happiness elsewhere which no description can reach. MP III 17 471 28
was much beyond her daily reach; and many a long October E I 1 7 9
while, nobody within her reach will be good enough for her. E I 8 64 47
on which she is beyond his reach, it is but too likely, E I 14 123 27
to reach Hartfield, before her spirits were quite overcome. E III 3 334 7
appearance, and was beyond the reach of Mr. Weston's hint. E III 5 345 15
behind him, which he could reach as he sat, "have your E III 5 347 19
of cheerful or of rational society within their reach? E III 12 422 20
reach, was therefore an object of first-rate importance. P III 2 16 17
the head at once, before they reach Admiral Baldwin's age." P III 3 20 16
She could not, however, reach such a degree of certainty, P III 6 49 25
possible, that when within reach of Captain Wentworth's P III 10 84 7
did not seem within her reach; and Anne-----but it would P IV 8 185 20
was not, her eye could not reach him; and the concert P IV 8 186 22
she had been before, much more within reach of a passer-by. P IV 8 189 46
How was the truth to reach him? P IV 8 191 51
He is totally beyond the reach of any sentiment of justice P IV 9 199 53
"I must speak to you by such means as are within my reach. P IV 11 237 42
a bad exchange, when we reach Trafalgar house--which by S 4 380 1
REACHED (108)
of Mr Vernon which had reached me in common with the world LS 36 305 1
She had reached the age of seventeen, without having seen NA I 1 16 10
of Miss Thorpe, till they reached Pulteney-Street, where NA I 7 51 54
Pulteney-Street reached the Upper-Rooms in very good time. NA I 8 52 1
She reached the house without any impediment, looked at NA I 12 91 3
She reached home without seeing any thing more of the NA I 13 103 29
They had reached the end of the gallery; and with tears of NA II 9 198 30
associations; and, having reached the ornamental part of NA II 11 214 25
They had just reached the head of the stairs, when it NA II 13 222 7
reached her home in safety, as the cause of his intrusion. NA II 15 241 7
himself, and before they reached Mr. Allen's grounds he NA II 15 243 9
After winding along it for more than a mile, they reached SS I 6 28 1
whole of the valley, and reached into the country beyond. SS I 6 29 3
as far as her ability reached; and missed no opportunity SS I 8 36 1
hurried along, and reached the bottom in safety. SS I 9 41 7
Fortunately for her, they had now reached the cottage, and SS I 22 135 56
They reached town by three o'clock the third day, glad to SS II 4 160 2
the bed, and whom she reached just in time to prevent her SS II 7 185 16
It is now three years ago, (she had just reached her SS II 9 208 28
"The first news that reached me of her," he continued, " SS II 9 209 30
and all that reached Elinor of their influence there, SS II 14 254 28
with such screams as reached your brother's ears, as he SS III 1 259 7
Her first communication had reached no farther than to SS III 1 262 14
the Colonel's inevitably reached her ear, in which he SS III 3 281 9
of it by the time he reached Bartlett's Buildings, that SS III 5 293 1
assurances which reached the ear, but could not enter the SS III 7 313 21
"When the first of her's reached me, (as it immediately SS III 8 325 50
Some vague report had reached her before of my attachment SS III 8 328 61
into the hall, and reached the outward door just in time SS III 9 333 3
its foundations as far as we are told they once reached. SS III 10 343 9
home; and till they reached the door of the cottage, SS III 10 348 34
and till her last letter reached him, he had always SS III 13 366 21
No rumour of Lucy's marriage had yet reached him;--he knew SS III 13 370 35
from them, Margaret had reached an age highly suitable for SS III 14 380 20
young guest than had yet reached him, he began with, "I W 325 4
injured a higher degree of excellence than she had reached. PP I 6 25 24
girls, reached Netherfield soon after the family breakfast. PP I 9 41 1
the two gentlemen turning back had reached the same spot. PP I 15 72 8
The idea soon reached to conviction, as she observed his PP I 17 88 14
I was right, therefore; my last letter had never reached PP II 3 147 23
on indifferent matters till they reached the parsonage. PP II 10 186 38
He had by that time reached it also, and holding out a PP II 12 195 2
leaving Hunsford, they reached Mr. Gardiner's house, where PP II 15 217 15
others, and when they had reached the carriage, Mr. and PP III 1 257 65
as their acquaintance reached, there was no fault to find. PP III 2 264 14
at Pemberley, for she had reached it only to a late PP III 2 266 17
Not a syllable had ever reached her of Miss Darcy's PP III 3 270 10
so precious; but as she reached the door, it was opened by PP III 4 276 6
on the road, reached Longbourn by dinner-time the next day. PP III 5 285 20
in thought, continued silent till they reached the house. PP III 7 304 33
A report of a most alarming nature, reached me two days PP III 14 353 26
report she concluded had reached Lady Catherine) had only PP III 15 360 1
he continued the conversation till they reached the house. PP III 16 371 46
As far as walking, talking, and contriving reached, she MP I 1 8 9
July, and Fanny had just reached her eighteenth year, when MP I 4 40 15
When we reached Albion Place they were out; we went after MP I 5 51 40

to conceal her vexation and anger, till she reached home. MP I 7 70 30
from Antigua, which soon afterwards reached Mansfield. MP I 11 107 1
worth playing before I reached Ecclesford; and though Lord MP I 13 122 2
To the theatre he went, and reached it just in time to MP II 1 182 22
the hall as soon as the noises of the arrival reached them. MP II 6 233 15
the lobby she had just reached Edmund himself, standing at MP II 9 267 24
Mrs. Chapman had just reached the attic floor, when Miss MP II 9 271 41
were over, or he had reached the beginning of the joyful MP II 13 302 9
"Yes, when I reached the house I found the two sisters MP III 4 352 38
stop any where, till they reached Newbury, where a MP III 7 376 5
of her death had at last reached Mansfield, had for a MP III 7 386 40
He had reached it late the night before, was come for a MP III 10 400 7
"A most scandalous, ill-natured rumour has just reached me, MP III 15 437 3
As no scandalous, ill-natured rumour had reached her, it MP III 15 438 4
Edmund's deep sighs often reached Fanny. MP III 15 445 33
They reached Mansfield on Thursday, and it was not till MP III 16 453 17
vain; and when he had reached such a point as this, she E I 12 106 59
being quarrelsome; her heroism reached only to silence. E I 13 114 27
a different account of Harriet from what had reached her. E I 13 114 28
had been there shewn than any she had reached herself. E I 16 135 6
duty; though she had now reached the age which her own E II 2 165 8
She went, however; and when they reached the farm, and she E II 5 186 2
He had reached Randalls the evening before. E II 5 190 23
"I went only to the post-office," said she, "and reached E II 16 293 12
By this time, the walk in the rain had reached Mrs. Elton, E II 16 295 29
before Mr. Woodhouse had reached her with his request to E II 16 298 56
57

reached Randall's before dinner, and every thing was safe. E III 2 319 1
which she reached; and without being long in reaching it.-- E III 11 412 46
They had reached the house. E III 13 429 30
This letter reached me on the very morning of my poor E III 14 442 8
No; do not pity me till I reached Highbury, and saw how E III 14 443 8
I reached Highbury at the time of the day when, from my E III 14 443 8
had such an end been reached, than Anne, who had been a P III 3 24 38
of sorrowful interest had reached its close; and time had P III 4 28 7
her bloom, only reached the dignity of being "a fine girl." P III 5 37 21
to lose him before he reached his twentieth year; that he P III 6 50 28
likewise; and when they reached the cottage, they were P III 6 51 32
yet quite doubtful, as far as Anne's observation reached. P III 9 74 8
when the party had all reached the gate of exit, the P III 10 90 38
enough by the time he reached home, determined the P III 12 108 30
The plan had reached this point, when Anne, coming quietly P III 12 114 60
there had of course reached him, though only twenty-four P IV 3 138 6
evident that no rumour of the news had yet reached them. P IV 6 168 22
and they had just reached this point when Anne, as she sat P IV 7 175 4
Before Sir Walter had reached this point, Anne's eyes had P IV 8 188 41
how any report of Captain Wentworth could have reached her. P IV 9 194 19
When she reached the White Hart, and made her way to the P IV 11 229 2
and those tones which had reached him while she talked P IV 11 241 60
I began to wonder the bustle should not have reached them.- S 1 370 1
on shore; but she had not reached the little lawn, when S 9 406 1
over by the time we reached the hotel--so that we got her S 9 407 1
It was a close, misty morng, & when they reached the brow S 12 425 1

REACHING (15)

Soon after their reaching the bottom of the set, Catherine NA I 10 80 59
It was a prettily-shaped room, the windows reaching to the NA II 11 213 21
lay before them; and on reaching that point, they stopped SS I 16 85 15
On reaching the spacious lobby above, they were shewn into PP III 1 249 43
the very day after her reaching Pemberley; and was PP III 2 260 1
On reaching the house, they were shewn through the hall PP III 3 267 2
On reaching the bottom of the steps to the terrace, Mrs. MP I 10 103 50
On reaching home, Fanny went immediately up stairs to MP II 9 261 1
four days from their reaching Portsmouth; and during those MP III 8 388 2
number of nursery-maids, all reaching Hartfield in safety. E I 11 91 3
They all united; and, on reaching Hartfield gates, Emma, E III 5 344 3
Emma, on reaching home, called the housekeeper directly, E III 9 391 20
which she reached; and without being long in reaching it.-- E III 11 412 46
now, compared with her state on first reaching Bath. P IV 5 154 9
She found, on reaching home, that she had, as she intended, P IV 10 212 2

READ (225)

father when he offered to read it to me, by which means he LS 13 262 1
He caught all your fears the moment he had read your LS 13 262 1
the first fifteen years of her life, that can or will read. LS 17 271 7
for a heroine; she read all such works as heroines must NA I 1 15 3
works as heroines must read to supply their memories with NA I 1 15 3
she brought herself to read them; and though there seemed NA I 1 16 10
and dirt, and shut themselves up, to read novels together. NA I 5 37 4
ever permitting them to be read by their own heroine, who, NA I 5 37 4
I often read novels--it is really well for a novel."-- NA I 5 37 4
finished Udolpho, we will read the Italian together; and I NA I 6 40 8
"I will read you their names directly; here they are, in NA I 6 40 10
creatures in the world, has read every one of them. NA I 6 40 12
to read, I feel as if nobody could make me miserable. NA I 6 41 19
"It is so odd to me, that you should never have read NA I 6 41 20
it was, "have you ever read Udolpho, Mr. Thorpe?" NA I 7 48 32
Oh, Lord! not I; I never read novels; I have something NA I 7 48 33
Jones, except The Monk; I read that t'other day; but as NA I 7 48 34
"I think you must like Udolpho, if you were to read it; it NA I 7 48 35
No, if I read any, it shall be Mrs. Radcliff's; her novels NA I 7 49 36
"I have never read it." NA I 7 49 41
Catherine knew all this very well; her great aunt had read NA I 10 73 22
"Oh! no, I only mean what I have read about. NA I 14 106 4
But you never read novels, I dare say?" NA I 14 106 4
not clever enough for you--gentlemen read better books." NA I 14 106 6
I have read all Mrs. Radcliffe's works, and most of them NA I 14 106 7
that you undertook to read it aloud to me, and that when I NA I 14 107 8
if they do--for they read nearly as many as women. NA I 14 107 11
I myself have read hundreds and hundreds. NA I 14 107 11
inquiry of 'have you read this?' and 'have you read that?' NA I 14 107 11
this?' and 'have you read that?' I shall soon leave you as NA I 14 107 11
"That is, I can read poetry and plays, and things of that NA I 14 108 20
I read it a little as a duty, but it tells me nothing that NA I 14 108 22
If a speech be well drawn up, I read it with pleasure, by NA I 14 109 23
If people like to read their books, it is all very well, NA I 14 109 24
difficulty of learning to read; and even you yourself, who NA I 14 110 27
for the sake of being able to read all the rest of it. NA I 14 110 27
But I confess, as soon as I read this letter, I thought it NA II 3 145 16
Well read in the art of concealing a treasure, the NA II 6 169 11
Yes, he certainly read in Miss Morland's eyes a judicious NA II 7 177 17
She had often read of such characters; characters, which NA II 7 181 40
from such as she had read about--from abbeys and castles, NA II 8 184 4
Catherine had read too much not to be perfectly aware of NA II 9 191 2
in which she had last read, remain to tell what nothing NA II 9 194 6
Catherine had not read three lines before her sudden NA II 10 202 8
"It is very true, however; you shall read James's letter NA II 10 205 21
"No, read it yourself," cried Catherine, whose second NA II 10 205 23
He gladly received the letter; and, having read it through, NA II 10 205 24
Miss Tilney, at Catherine's invitation, now read the NA II 10 205 25
The old gentleman died; his will was read, and like almost SS I 1 4 3
I loved him, to hear him read with so little sensibility. SS I 3 18 20
Her resolution was formed as she read. SS I 4 23 20
They read, they talked, they sang together; his musical SS I 10 48 8
were considerable; and he read with all the sensibility SS I 10 48 8
world; has been abroad; has read, and has a thinking mind. SS I 10 51 20
She read nothing but what they had been used to read SS I 16 83 3
the table and continued to read it as long as he staid. SS I 19 106 22
"No, none at all," he replied, and read on. SS I 19 108 33
She sometimes endeavoured for a few minutes to read; but SS II 4 166 31
appeared, and the note being given her, she read it aloud. SS II 5 170 28
turning eagerly to Willoughby's letter, read as follows: SS II 7 182 12
13

With what indignation such a letter as this must be read SS II 7 183 14
astonishment; then read it again and again; but every SS II 7 184 15
But the letter, when she was calm enough to read it, SS II 9 202 8
of Mrs. Jennings, who read it aloud with many comments of SS III 2 278 31
which she was unable to read, or in lying, weary and SS III 7 307 1
she opened the letter directly, and read its contents. SS III 8 328 61
She read what made her wretched. SS III 8 328 61
Elinor read and returned it without any comment. SS III 13 365 16
now arrived to be read with less emotion than mirth. SS III 13 370 37
The note, which Emma was beginning to read rather before W 338 18
Mr H. read like a scholar & a gentleman."-- W 344 20
She was at leisure, she could read & think,--tho' her W 361 31
I know, and read great books, and make extracts." PP I 2 7 18
By all that I have ever read, I am convinced that it is PP I 5 20 20
eagerly calling out, while her daughter read, "well, Jane, PP I 7 30 14
15

"It is from Miss Bingley," said Jane, and then read it PP I 7 30 16
"Well, my dear," said Mr. Bennet, when Elizabeth had read PP I 7 31 31
conversation; he merely answered her question, and read on. PP I 11 55 4
was over, glad to invite him to read aloud to the ladies. PP I 14 68 13
and begging pardon, protested that he never read novels.-- PP I 14 68 13
very monotonous solemnity, read three pages, she PP I 14 68 13
14

I am sure we never read the same, or not with the same PP I 18 93 28
Elizabeth instantly read her feelings, and at that moment PP I 18 95 48
countenance change as she read it, and saw her dwelling PP I 21 116 6
She then read the first sentence aloud, which comprised PP I 21 116 8
I will read it to you--"when my brother left us yesterday, PP I 21 117 10
11

I will read you the passage which particularly hurts me. PP I 21 117 14
that if encouraged to read and improve himself by such an PP I 22 124 11
when the letters were read, Elizabeth felt that Charlotte PP II 3 146 19
We were always encouraged to read, and had all the masters PP II 6 165 31
had not my character required it to be written and read. PP II 12 196 4
account of my actions and their motives has been read.-- PP II 12 196 5
Her feelings as she read were scarcely to be defined. PP II 13 204 1
She read, with an eagerness which hardly left her power of PP II 13 204 1
of Mr. Wickham, when she read with somewhat clearer PP II 13 204 2
But when she read, and re-read with the closest attention, PP II 13 205 3
Again she read on. PP II 13 205 3
a considerable while, she once more continued to read. PP II 13 206 4
had appeared very insufficient; and she read it again. PP II 13 208 9
"Lizzy, when you first read that letter, I am sure you PP II 17 226 18
the utmost impatience, read as follows: it had been PP III 4 274 4
absence, she accordingly read; and Elizabeth, who knew PP III 6 296 10
letters always were, looked over her, and read it likewise. PP III 6 296 10
from his pocket; "but perhaps you would like to read it." PP III 7 302 11
"Read it aloud," said their father, "for I hardly know PP III 7 302 13
Elizabeth read on; "I have seen them both. PP III 7 302 14
"May we take my uncle's letter to read to her?" PP III 7 305 41
preparation for good news, the letter was read aloud. PP III 7 305 43
As soon as Jane had read Mr. Gardiner's hope of Lydia's PP III 7 305 43
She read over her aunt's commendation of him again and PP III 10 327 3
Pray read on." PP III 15 363 21
Nay, when I read a letter of his, I cannot help giving him PP III 15 364 24
Fanny could read, work, and write, but she had been taught MP I 2 18 23
Miss Lee taught her French, and heard her read the daily MP I 2 22 35
read, and heightened its attraction by judicious praise. MP I 2 22 35
She talked to her, listened to her, read to her; and the MP I 4 35 6
Prayers were always read in it by the domestic chaplain, MP I 9 86 9
be slovenly and selfish--read the newspaper, watch the MP I 11 110 23
I cannot but suppose you will when you have read it MP I 15 140 11
Read only the first act aloud, to either your mother or MP I 15 140 12
There Miss Lee had lived, and there they had read and MP I 15 150 1
She had read, and read the scene again with many painful, MP I 18 167 13
read the part, for I can say very little of it." MP I 18 169 20
"If Miss Price would be so good as to read the part." MP I 18 171 28
"You have only to read the part," said Henry Crawford with MP I 18 172 30
to cry--and the service was impressively read by Dr. Grant. MP II 3 203 29
(or one should not read about them) as are never to be MP II 6 231 11
that is, he might read prayers and preach, without giving MP II 7 247 42
listen quietly, could read his list of the families to be MP II 8 253 7
to do, and happy, as she read it, to feel that the MP II 13 303 14
any good; for though she read in too much haste and MP II 13 304 16
She had read Miss Crawford's note only once; and how to MP II 13 307 30
been long used; her uncle read well--her cousins all-- MP III 3 337 10
with you," said he; "you read as if you knew it well." MP III 3 338 12
but to read him well aloud, is no every-day talent." MP III 3 338 14
to be read, and longing to have it to read myself----- MP III 3 340 25
delivered, is more uncommon even than prayers well read. MP III 3 341 28
I would spell it, read it, write it with any body. MP III 3 343 38
Fanny, who that heard him read, and saw you listen to MP III 4 348 23
never rest till she had read the chief of the letter to MP III 7 376 4
beyond his profession; he read only the newspaper and the MP III 8 389 3
Susan had read nothing, and Fanny longed to give her a MP III 9 398 9
his sister, opened and read by, on another account, MP III 12 415 1
2

This was a letter to be run through eagerly, to be read MP III 12 417 4
to, or read to, Edmund was the companion he preferred. MP III 14 429 2
She loved to fancy how she could have read to her aunt, MP III 14 432 10
Her father read his newspaper, and her mother lamented MP III 15 439 9
Fanny read to herself that "it was with infinite concern MP III 15 440 14
It had been the shock of conviction as she read. MP III 15 440 16
Miss Crawford's letter, which she had read so often as to MP III 15 441 19
He does not read?" E I 4 29 9
know--but I believe he has read a good deal--but not what E I 4 29 10
we went to cards, he would read something aloud out of the E I 4 29 10
And I know he has read the Vicar of Wakefield. E I 4 29 10
He never read the Romance of the Forest, nor the Children E I 4 29 10
it will be an inducement to her to read more herself. E I 5 36 6
They will read together. E I 5 36 6
"Emma has been meaning to read more ever since she was E I 5 37 7
of books that she meant to read regularly through--and E I 5 37 7
You never could persuade her to read half so much as you E I 5 37 7
"If he would be so good as to read to them, it would be a E I 6 46 25
"Will you read the letter!" cried Harriet. E I 7 50 3
She read, and was surprized. E I 7 50 4
caught the meaning, read it through again to be quite E I 9 72 15
I have read worse charades. E I 9 72 15
"For Miss ----, read Miss Smith. E I 9 73 18
Read it in comfort to yourself. E I 9 73 18
She read the concluding lines, and was all flutter and E I 9 73 19
it is, without exception, the best charade I ever read." E I 9 76 30
"I never read one more to the purpose, certainly." E I 9 76 31
You must let me read it to him." E I 9 77 45
"Yes, papa, we have something to read you, something quite E I 9 78 50
She read it to him, just as he liked to have any thing E I 9 78 51
he liked to have any thing read, slowly and distinctly, E I 9 78 51
If I draw less, I shall read more; if I give up music, I E I 10 85 21
Every letter from her is read forty times over; her E I 10 86 23
politician, who is to read every body's character, and E I 18 150 32
I am going to read to you,) and has never been well since. E II 1 161 29
to myself first, before I read them aloud to my mother, E II 1 162 31
However, when I read on, I found it was not near so bad as E II 1 162 31
He had just read elton's letter as I was shewn in, and E II 3 173 28
which she plainly read in the fair heroine's countenance. E II 8 220 46
When once it had been read, there was no doing any thing, E II 12 259 10
He looked at her, as if wanting to read her thoughts. E II 12 260 30
the perusal of it; and she read it with a degree of E II 13 265 5
"Read it, read it," said he, "it will give you pleasure; E II 17 303 25
only a few lines--will not take you long; read it to Emma." E II 17 303 25
Has Emma read it all? E II 17 304 27
It was not in his calmness that she read his comparative E III 1 316 4

She held the parcel towards her, and Emma read the words E III 4 338 9
time or other, to look at--or my tour to read--or my poem. E III 6 364 60
not, I know it will be read with candour and indulgence.-- E III 14 436 8
when Mr. Knightley came again, she desired him to read it. E III 15 444 2
shortly afterwards, "to speak my opinion aloud as I read. E III 15 445 8
When he came to Miss Woodhouse, he was obliged to read the E III 15 445 14 15
It was all read, however, steadily, attentively, and E III 15 447 21
'Nay, nay, read on.-- E III 15 447 23
'Say nothing, my dear Emma, while you oblige me to read-- E III 15 447 26
'I wish you would read it with a kinder spirit towards him. E III 15 447 27
Now I say, my dear, in our case, for lady, read ---- mum! E III 16 454 13
sensible man," replied Emma, when she had read the letter. E III 17 464 20
were powerless, he could read his own history with an P III 1 3 1
Now, how were his sentiments to be read? P III 7 60 30
the trouble, and once more read aloud the little statement P III 8 66 22
poet, worthy of being read, some attempt at description, P III 10 84 7
to hope he did not always read only poetry; and to say, P III 11 100 23
she recommended, and promised to procure and read them. P III 11 101 25
Give him a book, and he will read all day long." P IV 2 132 18
that they are well read; for they see it occasionally P IV 5 156 10
Such a letter could not be read without putting Anne in a P IV 9 204 74 75
book she would lend me, and pretend I have read it through. P IV 10 215 15
has done him no harm, for he has fought as well as read. P IV 10 219 26
but Anne could imagine she read there the consciousness of P IV 10 228 70
'I had not waited even these ten days, could I have read " P IV 11 237 42
Miss H., if you will give me leave, I will read Diana's S 5 386 1
He read.-- S 5 386 1
That man who can read them unmoved must have the nerves of S 7 396 1
'I have read several of Burn's poems with great delight, S 7 397 1
She had read it, in an anxious glance or two on his side-- S 7 398 1
We have many leisure hours, & read a great deal.-- S 8 403 1
spot had read more sentimental novels than agreed with him. S 8 404 1
were unjust to say that he read nothing else, or that his S 8 404 1
He read all the Essays, letters, Tours & criticisms of the S 8 404 1
And having read a few lines, exclaimed aloud "well, this S 10 418 1
She read the letter aloud for comfort.-- S 10 419 1

ADABLE (1)
surprize me; I thought it had not been readable. NA I 6 42 24

ADER (8)
of Mrs. Allen, that the reader may be able to judge, in NA I 2 19 7
"I am no novel reader--I seldom look into novels--do not NA I 5 37 4
and unprejudiced reader of Camilla gave way to the NA I 7 49 43
in review before the reader; the events of each day, its NA I 13 97 1
She is a great reader and has no pleasure in any thing PP I 8 37 23
a great reader, and I have pleasure in many things." PP I 8 37 24
for a walker than a reader, was extremely well pleased to PP I 15 71 6
Captain Harville was no reader; but he had contrived P III 11 99 18

ADER'S (2)
may be stated, for the reader's more certain information, NA I 2 18 1
I leave it to my reader's sagacity to determine how much NA II 15 247 14

ADERS (4)
or fashion, our foes are almost as many as our readers. NA I 5 37 4
well qualified to torment readers of the most advanced NA I 14 109 25
fear, to the bosom of my readers, who will see in the tell- NA II 16 250 4
unable as any other two readers, to think exactly alike of P III 12 107 23

ADIER (1)
Perhaps I am the readier to suspect, because, to tell you E III 18 478 67

ADIEST (2)
immediately following with the readiest good humour. MP II 4 206 5
same musician engaged, met with the readiest acquiescence. E II 11 247 3

ADILY (58)
this scheme, I cannot so readily credit what Lady Susan LS 17 271 7
this question answered, as it readily was, the stranger NA I 4 31 2
Catherine readily agreed. NA I 6 43 40
acquainted with her, and readily talked therefore whenever NA I 8 56 11
in commendation, but she readily echoed whatever he chose NA I 9 64 27
This was readily agreed to, with only a proviso of Miss NA I 10 80 61
quite well by her, in so readily giving up their NA I 11 86 50
Tilney's attentions as readily as they were offered, and NA II 4 149 1
soon her only wish, she readily agreed to her mother's NA II 14 235 13
shall be readily given to accommodate her as far as I can. SS I 2 12 25
The honour was readily granted, and he then departed, to SS I 9 42 10
The promise was readily given, and Willoughby's behaviour SS I 14 74 20
Mrs. Jennings and Elinor readily consented, as having SS II 4 164 23
admitted the excuse most readily, and Elinor, after seeing SS II 7 185 16
This lock of hair, which now he can so readily give up, SS II 7 189 46
The weather was remarkably fine, and she readily consented. SS II 11 223 15
from every charge but of imprudence, was readily offered. SS III 1 261 12
concurrence being readily gained, every thing relative to SS III 3 280 7
conversation, submitted readily to the silence and quiet SS III 9 334 5
of mine, & I shd most readily return to my father; & W 320 2
The advice was followed readily, for the feverish symptoms PP I 7 33 44
"To yield readily--easily--to the persuasion of a friend PP I 10 50 35
A regard for the requester would often make one readily PP I 10 50 37
answered most readily, "you are very kind, sir, I am sure; PP I 13 65 21 22
Mr. Collins readily assented, and a book was produced; but PP I 14 68 13
"I can readily believe," answered he gravely, "that report PP I 18 94 41
Bingley was all grateful pleasure, and he readily engaged PP I 18 103 76
William, in which she was readily joined by Jane, and by PP I 23 126 4
We accordingly went--and there I readily engaged in the PP II 12 198 5
towards Mr. Darcy, will readily comprehend how sincerely I PP II 18 234 37 38
again applied to, could readily answer, and with a proper PP II 19 241 17
little in the habit of giving invitations, readily obeyed. PP III 2 263 11
He readily assured her of his secrecy--again expressed his PP III 4 278 22
Gardiner readily promised every assistance in his power.-- PP III 4 280 26
"You may readily comprehend," she added, "what my PP III 9 320 33
your uncle, and therefore readily postponed seeing him, PP III 10 323 2
it,) your uncle would most readily have settled the whole. PP III 10 324 2
He readily agreed to it. PP III 11 336 48
It will be readily believed that Mrs. Norris did not write MP I 1 11 19
Northamptonshire, and as readily engaged to fetch her away MP I 4 41 16
How well she walks! and how readily she falls in with the MP I 11 112 34
Miss Crawford accepted the part very readily, and soon MP I 15 138 1
accede to it more readily than her own judgment authorised. MP III 5 364 33
the more readily to give them the honour of his company." E II 7 208 9
You may guess how readily he came into my wishes; and E II 8 223 63
by Miss Woodhouse, who readily continued her first E II 15 281 2
I can much more readily enter into the temptation of E II 15 288 39
was, "most readily Mrs. Weston, if you will dance with me." E III 2 327 34
as Mrs. Elton had very readily acceded to it, so it was to E III 6 353 3
They met readily and smiling, but with a consciousness E III 18 476 46
country, and her own dear country, readily agreed to stay. P III 5 33 9
Mrs. Musgrove had most readily made room for him;--they P III 8 68 29
It would have surprised Anne, if Louisa could have readily P III 10 88 27
that power of turning readily from evil to good, and of P IV 5 154 8
"No," said Anne, "I can readily believe all that of my P IV 9 196 33
she ought, and enter most readily into all the P IV 10 219 28
All that he understood of himself, he readily told, for he S 2 371 1
on to undraw her purse, would as readily give 10Gs as 5.-- S 12 424 1

ADINESS (20)
a want of pleasure and readiness in accepting my SS I 8 39 15
with the readiness of good-breeding and good nature." SS I 10 51 20
to convince Lucy, by her readiness to enter on the matter SS II 1 141 7
Aye, to be sure, he must be ordained in readiness; and I SS III 4 286 17
of only ten days, his readiness to converse with her, and SS III 6 305 16
obviated, for with a readiness that seemed to speak the SS III 7 311 15
of the living, but the readiness of the house, to which SS III 14 374 6
as to assure you of my readiness to make them every PP I 13 63 12
on his side by a happy readiness of conversation--a PP I 15 72 8
of conversation--a readiness at the same time perfectly PP I 15 72 8
directly with the readiness and ease of a well-bred man, PP II 7 171 10
I will do my best with the greatest readiness--but I must MP I 18 169 20
His readiness, however, in agreeing to dine at the MP II 7 228 2
be of it; and the readiness with which his invitation was MP II 10 280 32
well adapted for it by a readiness of mind, and an MP III 17 472 31
and a great readiness to be pleased with other people. E I 8 63 44
ease of manner, and a readiness to talk, which convinced E II 5 190 22
very lovely, and by the readiness and propriety of his P III 12 104 7
to express her perfect readiness for the play, if P IV 10 223 42 43
about her--a civility & readiness to be acquainted with S 6 391 1

READING (84)
so much as to prevent my reading it myself, so I could not LS 13 262 1
fond of books & spending the cheif of her time in reading. LS 18 273 3
on reading the note, this moment received from you. LS 35 304 1
"And what are you reading, Miss ----?" NA I 5 38 4
"Yes, I have been reading it ever since I woke; and I am NA I 6 39 5
I should like to spend my whole life in reading it. NA I 6 40 7
they are worth reading; some fun and nature in them." NA I 7 49 36
the promise I had made of reading it aloud, and keeping NA I 14 107 9
You are fond of that kind of reading?" NA I 14 108 17
Consider--if reading had not been taught, Mrs. Radcliffe NA I 14 110 27
of that sort of reading which she had there indulged. NA II 10 200 2
"Will you take the trouble of reading to us the passages NA II 10 205 22
with sincerity on it, and reading aloud the most material NA II 12 218 4
how tame was Edward's manner in reading to us last night! SS I 3 17 18
because they were fond of reading she fancied them SS II 14 246 3
imagery of Edward reading prayers in a white surplice, and SS III 5 298 33
Colonel Brandon would get farther than reading that night. SS III 6 303 12
I shall divide every moment between music and reading. SS III 10 343 9
But there are many works well worth reading, at the park; SS III 10 343 9
By reading only six hours a-day, I shall gain in the SS III 10 343 9
ideas which only reading could produce, made her W 361 31
"Do you prefer reading to cards?" said he; "that is rather PP I 8 37 22
in the improvement of her mind by extensive reading." PP I 8 39 51
his book, as in reading her own; and she was perpetually PP I 11 54 4
I declare after all there is no enjoyment like reading! PP I 11 55 4
to Mr. Darcy, and reading in her neighbours' looks their PP I 18 90 8
work in the garden, or in reading and writing, and looking PP II 7 168 1
Will you do me the honour of reading that letter?"-- PP II 12 195 2
Never, since reading Jane's second letter, had she PP III 4 279 24
cause of their summons, reading the two letters aloud, and PP III 4 280 26
and talking away just as if she was reading a sermon. PP III 9 319 24
I shall not sport with your impatience, by reading what he PP III 15 362 14
Did you, on reading it, give any credit to its contents?" PP III 16 368 18
I should dread your having the power of reading again. PP III 16 368 20
a few days before, on his reading Mr. Collins's letter; PP III 17 377 40
sense, and a fondness for reading, which, properly MP I 2 22 35
her judgment; he made reading useful by talking to her of MP I 2 22 35
when Mrs. Norris, as if reading in her two nieces' minds MP I 6 61 58
worth reading, to his sisters, when they are separated. MP I 7 64 10
You want to be reading. MP I 16 156 27
He went; but there was no reading, no china, no composure MP I 16 156 28
beyond all her hopes, and reading with the tenderest MP II 9 265 19
and as Sir Thomas was reading to himself, no sounds were MP II 11 283 6
"Fanny has been reading to me, and only put the book down MP III 3 336 9
was forced to listen; his reading was capital, and her MP III 3 337 10
was capital, and her pleasure in good reading extreme. MP III 3 337 10
To good reading, however, she had been long used; her MP III 3 337 10
but in Mr. Crawford's reading there was a variety of MP III 3 337 10
play might give, and his reading brought all his acting MP III 3 337 10
The subject of reading aloud was farther discussed. MP III 3 339 22
to the necessity of reading aloud, which had fallen within MP III 3 339 22
little the art of reading has been studied! how little a MP III 3 339 23
thought reading was reading, and preaching was preaching. MP III 3 339 23
slovenly style of reading can destroy; but it has also MP III 3 340 25
and repetitions, which require good reading not to be felt. MP III 3 340 25
she was thus forced into reading from the brother's pen, MP III 7 376 4
will not be worth your reading, for there will be no MP III 9 393 1
its daily terrors--and if reading could banish the idea MP III 9 398 10
The early habit of reading was wanting. MP III 12 419 7
done with expecting any course of steady reading from Emma. E I 5 37 7
It then occurred to her to employ him in reading. E I 6 46 24
for the permission of attending and reading to them again. E I 6 47 28
by a great deal of useful reading and conversation, had E I 9 69 3
you will not object to my reading the charade to him. E I 9 77 45
I was reading it to Mrs. Cole, and since she went away, I E II 1 157 10
she went away, I was reading it again to my mother, for it E II 1 157 10
as I am going to have the pleasure of reading to you. E II 1 159 20
I always make a point of reading Jane's letters through to E II 1 162 31
her first remark, on reading it, was that "of course it E II 7 208 8
is either reading to himself or settling his accounts." E II 18 312 50
must contain, and deprecated the necessity of reading it.-- E III 14 436 6
He proceeded a little farther, reading to himself; and E III 15 445 7
Mr. Knightley returned to his reading with greater E III 15 445 10
she had apparently been reading aloud to Miss Fairfax, and E III 16 453 12 13
reading her name in any other page of his favourite work. P III 1 6 10
and a decided taste for reading, and sedentary pursuits. P III 11 97 12
of considerable taste in reading, though principally in P III 11 100 23
His head is full of some books that he is reading upon P IV 2 131 9
thinking, feeling, reading Captain Benwick, seemed each of P IV 6 166 19
He is a clever man, a reading man--and I confess that I do P IV 8 182 10
elbow, reading verses, or whispering to her, all day long." P IV 10 218 24
His reading has done him no harm, for he has fought as P IV 10 219 26
reading one of her own novels, for want of employment.-- S 6 389 1
Though he owed many of his ideas to this sort of reading, S 8 404 1

READINGS (1)
readings and conversation with Susan were much suspended. MP III 12 418 5

READS (8)
She very often reads Sir Charles Grandison herself; but NA I 6 41 21
"But is it like what one reads of?" NA I 11 85 26
It not it a fine old place, just like what one reads about? NA II 5 157 12
building such as 'what one reads about' may produce?-- NA II 5 157 13
He reads extremely well, with great propriety & in a very W 343 20
"She often reads to me out of those books and she was in MP III 3 336 9
He reads the Agricultural Reports and some other books, E I 4 29 10
of the window seats--but he reads all them to himself. E I 4 29 10

READY (231)
I can promise you a ready & chearful consent; but it is my LS 12 261 3
You would have found in me a friend always ready to assist LS 24 286 6
letters, was very ready to oblige the whole party by LS 42 313 7
the morning were over, and ready to meet him with a smile:- NA I 4 31 1
both together, far more ready to give than to receive NA I 4 32 2
Catherine took the advice, and ran off to get ready. NA I 9 61 7
"you have been at least three hours getting ready. NA I 9 62 7
joined them, and asked Miss Tilney if she was ready to go. NA I 10 73 19
With what sparkling eyes and ready motion she granted his NA I 10 75 24
dignity injured by this ready condemnation--instead of NA I 12 93 4
mistake, why should you be so ready to take offence?" NA I 12 94 11
received by him with such ready, such solicitous NA I 13 102 27
she was almost as ready to admire, as what she did. NA I 14 114 49
post their ready consent to her visit to Gloucestershire. NA II 2 140 11
to her habit, she was ready to be shewn into the common NA II 5 161 25
for her friend's being ready, entered the room, and to the NA II 6 165 4
much better to find a fire ready lit, than to have to wait NA II 6 167 9
joyful haste, and she was ready to attend him in a moment. NA II 7 176 17
first three received a ready affirmative, the two others NA II 7 180 37
the room by their return, was at last ready to escort them. NA II 8 182 1
over the titles of half a shelf, and was ready to proceed. NA II 8 182 2

Eleanor was ready to oblige her; and Catherine reminding NA II 9 191 3
three terriers, was ready to receive and make much of them. NA II 11 212 17
I can be ready by seven. NA II 13 226 24
The carriage was soon announced to be ready; and Catherine, NA II 13 229 31
than till every thing were ready for her inhabiting it. SS I 5 25 1
ready furnished, and she might have immediate possession. SS I 5 26 5
and she had at this time ready money enough to supply all SS I 6 29 4
in other respects irreproachable, I am ready to confess it. SS I 10 52 28
yet ready for breakfast; I shall be back again presently." SS I 18 96 3
Lucy made room for her with ready attention, and the two SS II 1 145 23
carriage, and ready to enjoy all the luxury of a good fire. SS II 4 160 2
As dinner was not to be ready in less than two hours from SS II 4 160 4
is!"" and seemed almost ready to throw herself into his SS II 4 161 7
and having no answer ready, was obliged to adopt the SS II 5 172 40
I am perfectly ready to hear your justification of it. SS II 7 187 42
have believed it; and I was almost ready to sink as it was. SS II 8 192 3
remained on the bed, was ready to assist her into the SS II 8 193 5
he grows poor, and a richer girl is ready to have him. SS II 8 194 10
I warrant you, Miss Marianne would have been ready to wait SS II 8 194 10
and before breakfast was ready, they had gone through the SS II 9 201 2
Sir John was ready to like anybody, and though Mr. SS II 11 228 52
even genteel, she was as ready as Sir John to ask them to SS II 12 230 8
doing to her own care, and ready to give so exact, so SS II 14 247 5
carriage; which they were ready to enter five minutes SS II 14 249 9
You know I am always ready to pay them any attention in my SS II 14 253 21
Fanny, rejoicing in her escape, and proud of the ready wit SS II 14 253 26
Miss Dashwoods very ready to reassume their former share. SS III 1 257 1
The carriage was at the door ready to take my poor cousins SS III 1 259 7
You have got your answer ready." SS III 2 275 23
a speech, she was almost ready to cry out, "Lord! what SS III 3 281 11
I now do, if I am not as ready to be useful to him then, SS III 3 284 23
"Well, and how soon will he be ready?-- SS III 4 291 49
most grateful warmth, was ready to own all their SS III 5 293 2
As for Colonel Brandon, she was not only ready to worship SS III 5 293 2
her bed, Elinor was very ready to adopt Mrs. Jennings's SS III 7 307 2
with such active, such ready friendship, is enough to SS III 9 337 16
with him, I shall be as ready as yourself to think our SS III 9 337 17
till every thing was ready, and the ceremony took place in SS III 14 374 6
might be judged from the ready discharge of his duties in SS III 14 377 12
street, & he came ready to tell what ever might interest.-- W 323 3
Maam was instantly ready to attend his new acquaintance.-- W 331 11
you should be so ready to think your own children silly. PP I 7 29 8
"I am perfectly ready, I assure you, to keep my engagement; PP I 9 45 37
her ladyship, and be ever ready to perform those rites and PP I 13 62 12
Mr. Bennet indeed said little; but the ladies were ready PP I 13 64 21
Mr. Wickham did not play at whist, and with ready delight PP I 16 76 8
that he had been so ready to close with their kind wish of PP I 23 128 10
eligible match; and be ready to believe, for every body's PP II 1 135 12
We must not be so ready to fancy ourselves intentionally PP II 1 136 14
and felt persuaded of her sister's ready acquiescence. PP II 2 141 11
to relinquish her, she was ready to allow it a wise and PP II 5 150 26
acceptance of the invitation was most ready and grateful. PP II 4 154 23
was in her room getting ready for a walk, a sudden noise PP II 5 158 11
Elizabeth was ready to speak whenever there was an opening, PP II 6 163 14
her ladyship's carriage was ready to take them all home. PP II 8 176 30
at any rate, was perfectly ready to accede to his proposal. PP II 12 200 5
parcels placed within, and it was pronounced to be ready. PP II 15 216 8
I was ready to die of laughter. PP II 16 222 22
Bingley was ready, Georgiana was eager, and Darcy PP III 2 262 7
When first he entered the corps, she was ready enough to PP III 5 285 18
As she went up stairs to get ready, Mrs. Bennet followed PP III 17 375 25
26

Whatever I can do, as you well know, I am always ready MP I 1 7 8
a week, she was quite ready to be fallen in love with. MP I 5 44 2
worth pleasing, and were ready to be pleased, and were MP I 5 44 3
to be pleased, and were ready to be pleased; and he began MP I 5 44 3
nome, and Henry equally ready to lengthen his visit. MP I 5 47 26
easy in her manners, and as ready to talk as to listen. MP I 5 51 40
Mr. Rushworth was very ready to request the favour of Mr. MP I 6 61 58
in expressing their ready concurrence, excepting Edmund, MP I 6 62 59
she rode without her cousins, were ready to set forward. MP I 7 66 15
Fanny was ready and waiting, and Mrs. Norris was beginning MP I 7 67 15
Mrs. Norris was very ready with the only objection which MP I 8 78 23
and as every body was ready, there was nothing to be done MP I 8 80 29
are not ordained, Mr. Rushworth and Maria are quite ready." MP I 9 89 25
at the top, just ready for the wilderness, at the end of MP I 10 103 50
speeches to Mrs. Rushworth, was ready to lead the way. MP I 10 104 52
in preferring an income ready made, to the trouble of MP I 11 110 23
Henry Crawford was ready to take either. MP I 14 132 8
of the audience, they were ready, in the complaisance of MP I 17 158 2
ready to regret that some other play had not been chosen. MP I 18 164 1
unsuspected vexation was probably ready to burst on him. MP II 1 178 7
unusual degree; and he was ready to give every information MP II 1 178 8
Tom was the only one at all ready with an answer, but he MP II 1 185 30
I was ready to move heaven and earth to persuade my sister, MP II 2 189 3
Mrs. Rushworth was quite ready to retire, and make way for MP II 3 202 28
long enough arrived to be ready for dinner; and the smiles MP II 5 223 48
of her home, at Mansfield--ready to think of every member MP II 6 234 18
Mrs. Norris was ready with her suggestions as to the rooms MP II 8 253 7
on her side for such ready and kind attention, they MP II 8 257 15
away her appetite, she was ready to sink with shame, from MP II 13 304 16
just done--it will be ready in a moment--I am very much MP II 13 307 34
she was almost ready to faint at the sight of him. MP III 1 321 47
He was returning to Mansfield with spirits ready to feed MP III 3 334 1
was almost ready to wonder at his friend's perseverance.-- MP III 3 336 7
of compliment, such a ready comprehension of a hint, he MP III 3 339 21
Crawford's feelings, I am ready to acknowledge, have MP III 4 351 32
Her habits of ready submission, on the contrary, made her MP III 5 357 5
But the evil ready to burst on her, was at least delayed MP III 5 357 6
spared--(she being ready to give up all her own time to MP III 6 371 15
things, they will never be ready in time; for she may have MP III 7 378 10
your journey, or else I would have got something ready. MP III 7 378 14
Well, well, we are ready, whatever happens. MP III 7 380 20
off; every thing was ready, William took leave, and all of MP III 7 384 36
of getting Sam ready in time, was at leisure to think of MP III 7 385 37
shipped off at last, with more than half his linen ready MP III 8 390 7
of them, she was almost as ready to despair of being able MP III 8 391 9
now in commission, their companions were ready to proceed. MP III 10 403 13
her more fatigued or more ready to sit down; but he could MP III 10 403 15
time for, the others were ready to return; and in the MP III 10 406 21
capital inn afforded, was ready for their enjoyment, and MP III 11 412 29
thing noble, and I am ready to blame myself for a too MP III 13 421 2
of himself, as to be as ready as his physician to have a MP III 13 426 10
Susan was always ready to hear and to sympathize. MP III 13 428 14
which he was so ready to congratulate himself upon. MP III 14 436 16
this, and hope to find you ready to set off for Mansfield. MP III 15 442 23
must be spoken to, Susan prepared, every thing got ready. MP III 15 443 25
duly accomplished, and the girls were ready for the morrow. MP III 15 444 27
She was ready to sink, as she entered the parlour. MP III 15 444 28
When shall you be ready?-- MP III 15 445 29
having breakfasted, and being quite ready in half an hour. MP III 15 445 29
and completely ready as the carriage drove from the door. MP III 15 445 31
at Mansfield, and was ready to kiss and like her; and MP III 16 448 3
time, was all set out and ready, and moved forwards to the E I 3 24 11
She was ready to tell every thing in her power, but on E I 4 27 3
Harriet was very ready to speak of the share he had had in E I 4 28 6
in a lover; and he was ready at the smallest intermission E I 6 47 26
A man always imagines a woman to be ready for anybody who E I 8 60 33
They ready wit the word will soon supply, may its approval E I 9 71 14
Thy ready wit the word will soon supply E I 9 72 15
Humph--Harriet's ready wit! E I 9 72 15
a proof of love, with Mr. Elton's seeing ready wit in her. E I 10 83 6

into their troubles with ready sympathy, and always gave E I 10 86 24
"Oh! yes, sir," cried she with ready sympathy, "how you E I 11 93 7
"True, true," cried Mr. Knightley, with most ready E I 12 106 61
What a strange thing love is! he can see ready wit in E I 13 111 13
Mr. Woodhouse was soon ready for his tea; and when he had E I 15 124 1
drank his tea he was quite ready to go home; and it was as E I 15 124 1
subject, was ready to listen with most friendly smiles. E I 15 124 2
"I am ready, if the others are." E I 15 128 19
hoping--fearing--adoring--ready to die if she refused him; E I 15 129 24
as to seem--if not quite ready to join him in a basin of E I 15 132 38
To be sure, the charade, with its "ready wit"--but then, E I 16 134 4
she had gone to bed, more ready to see alleviations of the E I 16 138 14
you will always find me ready to make to your convenience; E I 18 146 16
ill of him. I should be as ready to acknowledge his merits E I 18 149 28
talking daughter, almost ready to overpower them with care E II 1 155 4
gave the arrangement their ready sanction, and said, that E II 2 166 10
and spencer on, just ready to come out--I was only gone E II 3 173 27
me how I did, and seemed ready to shake hands, if I would. E II 3 178 52
phrase, been so very ready to have him, that vanity and E II 4 181 4
to be congratulated--ready to be laughed at--and, with E II 4 182 5
the same regrets--to be ready to return to the same good E II 5 187 4
as Emma must suspect, as ready as the best of them to be E II 5 187 4
"Well, well, I am ready;"--and turning again to Emma, "but E II 5 189 13
would be ready to quarrel with you for using such words. E II 5 192 31
Mrs. Weston was very ready to say how attentive and E II 7 205 2
and there were enough ready to speak to allow Emma to E II 8 215 15
was quite ready to sit down to the pianoforte again. E II 10 240 6
That she was not immediately ready, Emma did suspect to E II 10 240 6
We were just in time; my mother just ready for us. E II 10 243 33
nothing could be properly ready till the third week were E II 12 257 1
Emma was ready for her visitor some time before he E II 12 259 12
Eltons' departure, and was ready to speak, she was very E II 14 279 53
Mrs. Elton, before she could be spoken to, was ready; and E II 16 298 56
57

He was in high spirits; as ready to talk and laugh as ever, E III 1 316 4
Jane and I quite ready. E III 2 322 19
"I am ready," said Emma, "whenever I am wanted." E III 2 331 58
Jane's alertness in moving, proved her as ready as her E III 5 349 25
Mr. Knightley was fortunate in every body's most ready E III 6 357 31
placed, quite at his ease, ready to talk with pleasure of E III 6 357 33
and her basket, was very ready to lead the way in E III 6 358 35
Mrs. Churchill's state, however, as many were ready to E III 6 361 41
I am quite ready. E III 7 374 53
I was ready to have gone with her, but this will do just E III 7 374 53
the carriage; it was ready; and, before she could speak E III 7 375 62
its all turning out well, and ready to hope that it may. E III 10 398 53
It struck her with dreadful force, and she was ready to E III 11 408 33
Harriet seemed ready to worship her friend for a sentence E III 11 411 42
had better go;"--with most ready encouragement from her E III 11 411 42
Emma was almost ready to sink under the agitation of this E III 13 430 36
But you will be ready to say, what was your hope in doing E III 14 437 8
with her, I am very ready to believe his character will E III 15 448 30
Emma's answer was ready at the first word. E III 15 448 31
Who was so useful to him, who so ready to write his E III 17 466 29
and Mrs. Weston was ready, on the first meeting, to E III 17 467 30
which her disposition was most ready to welcome as a duty. E III 18 475 42
which Emma had formerly been so ready to vouch for!-- E III 19 482 3
"Where shall we go?" said she, when they were ready. P III 5 39 41
idea; and Mary was quite ready to be affronted, when P III 6 50 26
I will go and tell Charles, and get ready directly. P III 7 57 16
Charles shewed himself at the window, all was ready, their P III 7 59 25
actually looking round, ready to fall in love with all the P III 7 61 38
here I am, Sophia, quite ready to make a foolish match. P III 7 61 38
39

The Musgroves could hardly be more ready to invite than he P III 9 73 2
were, therefore, exactly ready for this walk, and they P III 10 83 6
against any gate, was ready to do as Mary wished; but "no," P III 10 85 16
into the subject, as ready to do good by entering into the P III 12 103 3
breakfast was likely to be ready; but Louisa recollecting, P III 12 103 5
She expressed herself most willing, ready, happy to remain. P III 12 114 63
Captain Wentworth now hurried off to get every thing ready P III 12 115 65
as she told Anne, almost ready to exclaim, "can this be Mr. P IV 4 146 6
was convinced that he was ready to be acknowledged as an P IV 7 176 9
catch the music; like unfledged sparrows ready to be fed. P IV 9 193 6
Anne talked of being perfectly ready, and tried to look it; P IV 10 225 62
I am only ready whenever you are.-- P IV 11 234 27
that is, Harville, if you are ready, I am in half a minute. P IV 11 236 38
great rapidity, was indeed ready, and had even a hurried, P IV 11 236 39
dividing them, he was ready to say almost every thing else P IV 12 251 10
that road in a carriage--& ready offers of assistance. S 1 365 1
they were just equally ready for entering the house.-- S 9 406 1

READY-FURNISHED (2)

A ready-furnished house in a favourite spot was engaged, E III 1 317 7
what rent a ready-furnished house of that consequence P III 3 22 23

READY-MONIED (1)

disadvantage, giving ready-monied actual happiness for a NA II 11 210 7

READY-PREPARED (1)

of bread, brought up ready-prepared in the toast rack--and S 10 416 1

REAL (197)

till I better understand her real meaning in coming to us. LS 3 247 1
I have now my dear sir, written my real sentiments of Lady LS 14 265 6
present as she is in real distress, & with too much cause. LS 15 266 2
that the former has no real love for her daughter & has LS 17 270 5
& understand the real affection we feel for each other! LS 20 278 7
As soon as I can get her alone, I will discover the real LS 20 278 11
be her real sentiments, said nothing in opposition to mine. LS 22 280 1
the particulars & assure himself of her real wishes! LS 22 281 5
I have a real regard for him & was beyond expression LS 24 290 13
I will not dissemble what real pleasure his sight afforded LS 29 299 2
At the same time do not forget my real interest; say all LS 31 302 1
having inspired one real passion, and without having NA I 1 16 10
The men think us incapable of real friendship you know, NA I 6 40 14
aware that, as the real dignity of her situation could not NA I 8 53 2
Miss Morland with the real delicacy of a generous mind NA I 8 55 10
stilishness of Miss Thorpe's, had more real elegance. NA I 8 55 11
a clearer insight into his real opinion on the subject; NA I 9 66 31
that Mrs. Allen had no real intelligence to give, and that NA I 9 69 51
I would give any money for a real good hunter. NA I 10 76 28
With real interest and strong admiration did her eye now NA I 10 80 60
"But this was something of real consequence; and I do not NA I 13 105 37
But history, real solemn history, I cannot be interested NA I 14 108 20
formed into pictures, with all the eagerness of real taste. NA I 14 110 28
a source of some real agitation to the mind of Isabella. NA I 15 119 14
arrived, had worked herself into a state of real distress. NA I 15 121 26
upon it therefore, that real jealousy never can exist NA II 4 152 28
sleepless, have been the real cause of his rising late.-- NA II 5 155 3
real friendship, and described as creating real gratitude. NA II 5 157 5
The shock however being less real than the relief, offered NA II 7 179 29
real drawing-room, used only with company of consequence.-- NA II 8 182 2
writing, was free from any real anxiety about him; and had NA II 11 209 5
After courting you from the protection of real friends to NA II 13 225 19
a nominal mistress of it, that my real power is nothing." NA II 13 225 19
"I hope, I earnestly hope that to your real safety it will NA II 13 225 23
with the embarrassment of real sensibility began to NA II 15 241 7
You will gain a brother, a real, affectionate brother. SS I 3 17 17
And besides all this, I am afraid, mama, he has no real SS I 3 17 18
She tried to explain the real state of the case to her SS I 4 21 11
Elinor had given her real opinion to her sister. SS I 4 22 18
Their arrival seemed to afford him real satisfaction, and SS I 6 30 6
their comfort to be an object of real solicitude to him. SS I 6 30 6
But Sir John's satisfaction in society was much more real; SS I 7 32 2
therefore he had the real satisfaction of a good heart; SS I 7 33 3

Context	Work	Vol	Ch	Page	Line
Nothing but real indisposition could occasion this	SS	I	8	39	14
But Marianne abhorred all concealment where no real	SS	I	11	53	2
for if there had been any real impropriety in what I did,	SS	I	13	68	72
within itself, more real accommodation and comfort than	SS	I	14	73	17
so eligible of knowing the real state of the affair, and	SS	I	16	84	7
Beyond a competence, it can afford no real satisfaction,	SS	I	17	91	10
youngest, to her want of real elegance and artlessness,	SS	I	21	124	32
"No;" returned Elinor, cautious of giving her real opinion	SS	I	22	128	6
for the want of much real enjoyment from any of their	SS	II	5	168	11
an account of her real situation with respect to him.	SS	II	5	172	39
The real state of things between Willoughby and her sister	SS	II	5	173	45
a deliverance the most real, a blessing the most important.	SS	II	7	184	15
opened the door and walked in with a look of real concern.	SS	II	8	192	1
Their own good-nature must point out to them the real	SS	II	8	195	17
gain very little by the inforcement of the real truth.	SS	II	8	196	21
moment, to more than its real value; and she was sometimes	SS	II	10	215	13
an happy air of real conceit and affected indifference.	SS	II	11	221	5
only given her, because her real situation was unknown.	SS	II	13	238	2
great many people who had real taste for the performance,	SS	II	14	250	10
her acquainted with the real truth, and in endeavouring to	SS	III	1	260	10
to be its writer's real design, by placing it in the hands	SS	III	2	278	31
was inforced with so much real politeness by Mr. Palmer	SS	III	3	279	1
his real favourite, to make her suspect it herself.	SS	III	6	305	16
certainty and efficacy of sleep, and felt no real alarm.	SS	III	7	307	1
to go, as well from real humanity and good-nature, as from	SS	III	7	308	5
"Is this the real reason of your coming?"	SS	III	8	319	24
had involved him in a real attachment, which extravagance,	SS	III	8	331	70
more accordant with her real disposition, than the	SS	III	9	338	22
approbation of their real friends, their intimate	SS	III	13	369	32
they were never insulted by her real favour and preference.	SS	III	14	375	10
on the score of some quality or other, real or imaginary.	PP	I	5	20	20
can be of no real advantage to yourself or any one else?"	PP	I	10	49	27
Miss Bingley succeeded no less in the real object of her	PP	I	11	56	12
But pride--where there is a real superiority of mind,	PP	I	11	57	24
The master of the house heard with real sorrow that they	PP	I	12	59	3
Elizabeth sometimes with real earnestness and sometimes	PP	I	20	112	23
that Elizabeth was the real cause of all the mischief; and	PP	I	21	127	5
no real confidence could ever subsist between them again.	PP	I	23	127	9
half-hour's acquaintance, as to a real strong attachment.	PP	II	2	140	8
so well able to expose my real character, in a part of the	PP	II	8	174	15
and anxiety, but his countenance expressed real security.	PP	II	11	189	6
shall not prevent me from unfolding his real character.	PP	II	12	200	5
and his account of the real, the worst objections to the	PP	II	13	204	1
As to his real character, had information been in her	PP	II	13	206	4
leisure to observe the real state of her sister's spirits.	PP	II	17	227	26
will keep her out of any real mischief; and she is luckily	PP	II	18	232	20
in their marriage put an end to all real affection for her.	PP	II	19	236	1
thing around them, threw a real gloom over their domestic	PP	II	19	237	3
and more real elegance, than the furniture of Rosings.	PP	III	1	246	5
which had something of real regret, that it "was a very	PP	III	2	262	8
to him, she felt a real interest in his welfare; and she	PP	III	2	266	16
"When my eyes were opened to his real character.--Oh! had	PP	III	4	277	18
in excuse of my stay, but real, though unavailing, concern.	PP	III	4	278	20
upon such terms as for her to disclose the real truth!	PP	III	4	281	28
that there was no real occasion for such a seclusion from	PP	III	5	288	40
their plan, and would not give his real opinion about it.	PP	III	5	290	48
Does he know his real character?"	PP	III	5	291	53
would not marry Lydia, if he had not a real regard for her.	PP	III	7	304	35
I fancy, Lizzy, that obstinacy is the real defect of his	PP	III	10	324	2
"And this is your real opinion!	PP	III	14	358	71
"My real purpose was to see you, and to judge, if I could,	PP	III	18	382	16
fully resolved to be the real and consistent patron of the	MP	I	1	8	9
Under this infatuating principle, counteracted by no real	MP	I	1	8	9
of any real pleasure, that time of course never came.	MP	I	4	35	7
in his favour, a park, a real park five miles round, a	MP	I	5	48	28
there is no more real modesty in their behaviour before	MP	I	5	50	38
Bertram had very little real comfort; her prospect always	MP	I	8	81	32
"True, to see real acting, good hardened real acting; but	MP	I	13	124	12
Fanny into any real forgetfulness of what had passed.--	MP	I	16	150	1
Edmund, between his theatrical and his real part, between	MP	I	17	163	21
his daughters helped to conceal the want of real harmony.	MP	II	2	191	11
are aware that there is no real occasion for your going	MP	II	5	220	28
especially as there is no real squire's house to dispute	MP	II	7	244	27
her wants with a kindness which proved her a real friend.	MP	II	8	258	18
It was not a real animation! and she began to dress for it	MP	II	9	270	40
each other by every thing real and imaginary--and put them	MP	II	9	271	40
the explanation of the second necklace--the real chain.	MP	II	10	274	9
It had been real business, relative to the renewal of a	MP	III	10	404	15
It was a real indulgence to her to hear or to speak of	MP	III	10	405	17
style, in the language of real feeling and alarm; then,	MP	III	13	427	12
The real solicitude now awakened in the maternal bosom was	MP	III	13	427	13
With real affection, Fanny like mine, more might be	MP	III	14	434	13
Tell me the real truth, as you have it form the fountain	MP	III	14	434	13
her answer was conveying a real disappointment, she was	MP	III	15	437	1
to his knowledge of her real character, by some hint of	MP	III	16	459	31
presence, as to make their real disposition unknown to him,	MP	III	17	463	7
The real evils indeed of Emma's situation were the power	E	I	1	5	4
Real, long-standing regard brought the Westons and Mr.	E	I	3	20	2
and into vanity--but a real, honest, old-fashioned	E	I	3	21	5
and attentively, with the real good-will of a mind	E	I	3	24	11
mortified voice, "he is not so genteel as real gentlemen."	E	I	4	32	31
company of some, such very real gentlemen, that you must	E	I	4	32	32
He has too much real feeling to address any woman on the	E	I	8	63	42
comprehending, as it does, real, thorough sweetness of	E	I	8	63	44
in the centre of all your real friends, close to Hartfield	E	I	9	74	20
all but indifference, the real attachment which would have	E	I	12	99	14
To her, it was real enjoyment to be with the Westons.	E	I	14	117	1
an inconstancy, if real, the most contemptible and	E	I	15	125	4
There had been no real affection either in his language or	E	I	16	135	7
or fancy any tone of voice, less allied with real love.	E	I	16	135	7
as (supposing her real motive unperceived) might warrant a	E	I	16	136	9
of the question from her real opinion, and making use of	E	I	18	145	5
himself, was unworthy the real liberality of mind which	E	I	18	150	37
his own wish of being a real friend, united to produce an	E	II	2	163	4
There was no getting at her real opinion.	E	II	2	169	15
She seemed bent on giving no real insight into Mr. Dixon's	E	II	2	169	16
but not a syllable of real information could Emma procure	E	II	2	169	17
at her grandmother's, it must have been a real indulgence."	E	II	3	170	2
result of real feeling, and she could not but pity them.	E	II	3	179	53
her almost to doubt his real concurrence; and yet there	E	II	5	194	43
There must be ample room in it for every real comfort.	E	II	6	204	42
was so much real attention in the manner of it--so much	E	II	7	208	9
The conviction seemed real; he looked as if he felt it.	E	II	8	219	43
real injury to the children--a most mortifying change,	E	II	8	228	87
iss Bates, in her real anxiety for Jane, could hardly	E	II	8	229	98
f one talks at all;--your real workmen, I suppose, hold	E	II	10	242	15
ny real alarm for his aunt, to lessen his repugnance.	E	II	12	258	8
t was the language of real feelings towards Mrs. Weston;	E	II	13	265	5
Ah! there is nothing like staying at home, for real	E	II	14	274	30
ave always loved her with such real, generous affection."	E	II	15	285	13
r. Weston's ball was to be a real thing.	E	III	1	318	12
ot that Emma was gay and thoughtless from any real	E	III	7	368	3
eculiarly lucky!--for as to any real knowledge of a	E	III	7	372	40
here, indeed, lay real pleasure, for there she was giving	E	III	8	377	1
hich constituted the real misery of the business to her.	E	III	11	402	1
t was merely a blind to conceal his real situation with	E	III	13	427	19
musement in detecting the real cause of that violent	E	III	15	449	35
ne real, rational difficulty to oppose or delay it.	E	III	17	468	31
ailings, and promoted his real respectability for	P	III	1	4	6
igh with any people of real understanding, was nobody	P	III	1	5	8
ere insufficient for the real extent of the evil, the	P	III	1	10	19
im; and that a woman of real understanding might have	P	III	6	43	5
to, or encouraged by any just appreciation or real taste.	P	III	6	47	13
years longer in the world than her real eight and thirty.	P	III	6	48	18
The real circumstances of this pathetic piece of family	P	III	6	50	28
all that was real and unabsurd in the parent's feelings.	P	III	8	67	28
had the hope of being of real use to him in some	P	III	11	100	23
I well know the sight of beauty is a real gratification."	P	IV	4	145	1
There is so little real friendship in the world!--and	P	IV	5	156	11
supposing such attachment to be real, and returned.	P	IV	5	159	22
to me--but there is real beauty at lyme: and in short" (	P	IV	8	184	16
but I should be sorry to be examined by a real proficient."	P	IV	8	187	27
or the gapes, as real or affected taste for it prevailed.	P	IV	8	189	45
situations, would he ever learn her real sentiments?	P	IV	8	191	51
to be made acquainted with Mr. Elliot's real character.	P	IV	9	199	53
All his caution was spent in being secured of the real	P	IV	9	202	66
and memorandums of real importance had been destroyed.	P	IV	9	203	70
"Indeed, Mrs. Smith, we must not expect to get real	P	IV	9	205	85
all; and Mrs. Musgrove's real affection had been won by	P	IV	10	220	31
Charles, in his real concern and good-nature, would go	P	IV	11	239	54
receiving her first real comfort from the sight of several	S		1	364	1
We have all the grandeur of the storm, with less real	S		4	381	1
of them that have any real property, landed or funded.--	S		7	401	1
saw in it the evidence of real penetration & prepared for	S		7	401	1

REALISED (2)

Context	Work	Vol	Ch	Page	Line
the high sense of having realised a great acquisition in	MP	III	17	471	29
to impossible that he should have realised any thing yet."	E	I	4	30	20

REALITIES (1)

Context	Work	Vol	Ch	Page	Line
realities as these, what would have been her sensations?	PP	II	18	232	23

REALITY (11)

Context	Work	Vol	Ch	Page	Line
where she must in reality have been particularly happy.	LS		6	252	2
it founded on reason or reality, till Morland produced his	NA	I	9	67	33
then--how mournfully superior in reality and substance!	NA	II	13	227	26
alarm, where there is nothing to be alarmed at in reality."	SS	I	21	122	12
much slighter in reality, than she had been wont to	SS	III	11	355	46
reality of reason and truth, one of the happiest of men.	SS	III	13	361	3
new, and which had little reality in Fanny's feeling.	MP	II	4	207	11
You have given the name such reality of sweetness, that	MP	III	3	344	41
anticipation and then in reality, it became henceforth her	E	I	11	91	1
She thought it in reality a sad exchange for herself, to	E	II	16	292	8
was involved in the reality of Sir Walter's retrenching,	P	III	2	13	7

REALIZATION (1)

Context	Work	Vol	Ch	Page	Line
Impatient for the realization of all that he hoped at home,	NA	I	15	120	24

REALIZED (3)

Context	Work	Vol	Ch	Page	Line
hope to have all my expectations of pleasure realized.	PP	II	19	237	4
He had, by that time, realized an easy competence--enough	E	I	2	16	5
freely, what had come freely, had realized nothing.	P	III	4	27	4

REALLY (537)

Context	Work	Vol	Ch	Page	Line
a country village, for I am really going to Churchill.	LS		2	245	1
his heart, & make him really confide in her sincerity.	LS		3	247	1
I really have a regard for him, he is so easily imposed on!	LS		5	250	1
She is really excessively pretty.	LS		6	251	1
as he is, that it was really her choice to leave Langford	LS		6	252	2
of education, which I really wish to be attended to, while	LS		7	252	1
with her as I am sure he is, does really astonish me.	LS		8	255	2
of, & tho' no one can really deserve you my dearest Susan,	LS		9	256	1
I really grow quite uneasy my dearest mother about	LS		11	259	1
the Clarkes, & had really got as far as the length of two	LS		19	273	1
by wishing with a laugh, that he might be really one soon.	LS		20	278	10
it was impossible for me really to torment him, as Sir	LS		22	280	2
He beleived me more to blame than I really was; I	LS		24	290	13
of de courcy, I am really delighted with him, he is full	LS		38	307	3
Can it be true that they are really separated--& for ever?	LS		41	309	1
And Reginald really with you!	LS		41	309	1
"Really!" with affected astonishment.	NA	I	3	26	6
I often read novels--it is really well for a novel."--	NA	I	5	37	4
I am very sorry for it; but really I thought I was in very	NA	I	6	39	3
There is nothing I would not do for those who are really	NA	I	6	40	14
Where the heart is really attached, I know very well how	NA	I	6	41	16
They really put me quite out of countenance.	NA	I	6	43	33
so very much as if she really felt it, that had Thorpe,	NA	I	8	54	10
Allen for her opinion; "but really I did not expect you."	NA	I	9	61	4
"You do not really think, Mr. Thorpe," said Catherine,	NA	I	9	65	27
that he would not really suffer his sister and his friend	NA	I	9	66	31
You really have done your hair in a more heavenly style	NA	I	10	70	1
I really am quite wild with impatience.	NA	I	10	70	1
to every other place; really, our opinions were so exactly	NA	I	10	71	3
But I really had been engaged the whole day to Mr. Thorpe."	NA	I	10	72	11
"but I am really going to dance with your brother again.	NA	I	10	74	23
I really believe I shall always be talking of Bath, when I	NA	I	10	79	56
"What, is it really a castle, an old castle?"	NA	I	11	85	24
"But now really--are there towers and long galleries?"	NA	I	11	85	28
what her own conduct had really been, she took occasion to	NA	I	13	103	29
But I really thought before, young men despised novels	NA	I	14	107	10
But now really, do not you think Udolpho the nicest book	NA	I	14	107	12
Catherine spoke the pleasure she really felt on hearing	NA	I	14	115	51
Can you--can you really be in love with James?"	NA	I	15	117	7
Where people are really attached, poverty itself is wealth:	NA	I	15	119	20
I really believe John has the most constant heart."	NA	II	1	130	7
Do you really desire it?--	NA	II	1	133	26
to my brother, I really think Miss Thorpe has by no means	NA	II	1	134	36
wonder at your surprize; and I am really fatigued to death.	NA	II	1	134	37
opportunity for being really so; and therefore gaily said,	NA	II	3	143	2
Modesty, and all that, is very well in its way, but really	NA	II	3	144	10
But it cannot really happen to me.	NA	II	5	159	18
I am sure your housekeeper is not really Dorothy.--	NA	II	5	159	18
apprehension of really meeting with what he related.	NA	II	5	160	23
An Abbey!--yes, it was delightful to be really in an Abbey!	NA	II	5	161	26
felt for the first time that she was really in an Abbey.--	NA	II	6	166	9
there could be nothing really in it, there was something	NA	II	6	168	10
Now she has really got the man she likes, she may be	NA	II	10	206	33
business before him as it really was, enabling the General	NA	II	11	208	2
I really could not face my acquaintance if I staid away	NA	II	11	210	6
I really am quite ashamed of my idleness; but in this	NA	II	12	216	2
"Then you do not suppose he ever really cared about her?"	NA	II	12	219	8
of this single remark--"I really have not patience with	NA	II	14	237	22
And, "I really have not patience with the general," was	NA	II	14	238	22
to--"I really have not patience with the General!	NA	II	14	238	27
Her husband was really deserving of her; independent of	NA	II	16	251	5
so far from being really injurious to their felicity, was	NA	II	16	252	7
Norland estate was not so really important as to his	SS	I	1	3	2
He then really thought himself equal to it.	SS	I	1	5	8
He really pressed them, with some earnestness, to consider	SS	I	2	8	1
so much for his sisters, even if really/ his sisters!	SS	I	2	9	11
her penetration; but she really felt assured of his worth:	SS	I	3	16	13
that I shall never see a man whom I can really love.	SS	I	3	18	20
At present, I know him so well, that I think him really	SS	I	4	20	9
What his mother really is we cannot know; but, from	SS	I	4	21	15
"And you really are not engaged to him!" said she.	SS	I	4	22	17
But, whatever might really be its limits, it was enough,	SS	I	4	23	19
He seemed really anxious to accommodate them, and the	SS	I	4	23	20
He really felt conscientiously vexed on the occasion; for	SS	I	5	26	4
when his feelings began really to call for the ridicule so	SS	I	10	49	12
Elinor, though she felt really interested in the welfare	SS	I	14	71	3
her mind of their being really engaged, and this doubt was	SS	I	14	71	4
But are you really so attached to this place as to see no	SS	I	14	72	10
But you really do admit the justice of what I have said in	SS	I	15	79	30
Do you suppose him really indifferent to her?"	SS	I	15	80	38
always with animation--but she is not often really merry."	SS	I	17	93	35
or stupid than they really are, and I can hardly tell why,	SS	I	17	93	37
of nature than they really feel, and is disgusted with	SS	I	18	97	6
"I am convinced," said Edward, "that you really feel all	SS	I	18	97	8
Marianne spoke inconsiderately what she really felt--but	SS	I	18	98	12
But really, I never understood that you were at all	SS	I	22	128	10

upon your secrecy; and I really thought my behaviour in SS I 22 129 16
what you tell me, that really--I beg your pardon; but SS I 22 131 29
Besides in the present case, I really thought some SS I 22 132 42
to understand what Lucy really felt for Edward, whether SS II 1 141 7
within herself of being really beloved by Edward, it SS II 1 142 7
to Elinor: "and as you really like the work, perhaps you SS II 1 145 22
was only my own fancy, and that you do not really blame me. SS II 2 146 5
I do of yours; and I do really believe, that if you was to SS II 2 150 32
to say more than she really knew or believed. SS II 5 174 45
replied, "and have you really, ma'am, talked yourself into SS II 7 181 9
many nights since she had really slept; and now, when her SS II 7 185 16
almost convinced that he never was really attached to her. SS II 8 199 40
quick-sighted man, could really, I believe, give no SS II 9 209 28
John Dashwood was really far from being sorry to see his SS II 11 221 7
that really she had no leisure for going any where." SS II 11 222 14
"More than you think it really and intrinsically worth." SS II 11 225 32
relinquished, and he was really resolved on seeking an SS II 11 228 51
"Lady Middleton is really a most elegant woman! SS II 11 228 53
of Lucy, who, though really uncomfortable herself, hoped SS II 12 232 14
two mothers, though each really convinced that her own son SS II 12 234 21
22

in her behaviour as really should seem to say, she had SS II 13 239 4
"I am glad of it with all my heart, but really you did not SS II 13 239 13
by themselves: and she really did it, and that in the SS II 13 241 23
such witnesses he dared not say half what he really felt. SS II 13 242 25
And I really believe he has the most delicate conscience SS II 13 243 40
be tricked out of assurances, that are not really wanted." SS II 13 244 46
Elinor and Marianne, she did not really like them at all. SS II 14 246 3
gaucherie which he really believed kept him from mixing in SS II 14 250 12
propriety of their being really invited to become such, SS II 14 252 20
This was enough to make Lucy really and reasonably happy. SS II 14 254 26
expectation of its event really was; though she earnestly SS III 1 260 9
She was going to remove what she really believed to be her SS III 1 261 11
to his sisters that he really believed there was no SS III 1 269 57
What had really passed between them was to this effect. SS III 3 282 16
the Colonel been really making her an offer of his hand. SS III 3 283 20
with pleasure, if it were really his wish to put off so SS III 3 283 20
this narration of what really passed between Colonel SS III 3 284 24
"Really," said Elinor, "I know so little of these kind of SS III 4 291 50
of doing anything in the world for those she really valued. SS III 5 293 2
for which no one could really have less inclination, and SS III 5 294 3
it be true?--has he really given it to Edward?-- SS III 5 294 8
"Really!-- SS III 5 294 10
really sold the presentation, is old enough to take it.-- SS III 5 295 12
heart which made Elinor really love her, declared her SS III 7 308 3
really believed herself, that it would be a very short one. SS III 7 308 4
Her heart was really grieved. SS III 7 313 20
But is it true?--is it really true?" SS III 8 318 10
Well may it be doubted; for, had I really loved, could I SS III 8 320 32
any part of what had really passed between Mrs. Smith and SS III 8 324 42
The sight of your dear sister, however, was really SS III 8 324 42
Yet when I thought of her to-day as really dying, it was a SS III 8 327 55
Willoughby turned out as really amiable, as he has proved SS III 9 338 22
know, what it really is, I am sure it must be a good one." SS III 9 339 26
open such facts as were really due to his character, SS III 11 349 2
had not Elinor, who really wished to hear her sister's SS III 11 349 5
in a tone that implied--"do you really think him selfish?" SS III 11 351 10
countenance how much she really suffered, and in a moment SS III 11 353 24
really did, so much in need of encouragement and fresh air. SS III 13 361 2
more subjects than can really be in common between any two SS III 13 363 9
at the cottage, as he really wished not only to be better SS III 13 368 30
"And if they really do interest themselves," said Marianne, SS III 13 372 45
really believed, one of the happiest couple in the world. SS III 14 374 7
And wd you really give up the ball, that I might be able W 320 2
"And so, you really did not dance with Tom M. at all?-- W 342 19
least, a nobleman & a stranger, was really distressing.-- W 344 21
I am really frightened out of my wits with the number of W 354 27
"A month! have you really been gone a month! 'tis amazing W 356 28
I really did not consider how unfit I was to be here or I W 357 28
One cannot know what a man really is by the end of a PP I 2 7 16
heart enough to be really in love without encouragement. PP I 6 21 2
but as it is, I would really rather not sit down before PP I 6 24 22
Elizabeth, feeling really anxious, was determined to go to PP I 7 32 33
She really looked almost wild." PP I 8 35 4
"I have an excessive regard for Jane Bennet, she is really PP I 8 36 14
"But I would really advise you to make your purchase in PP I 8 38 35
range of my acquaintance, that are really accomplished." PP I 8 39 46
assistant, "no one can be really esteemed accomplished, PP I 8 39 50
"The indirect boast;--for you are really proud of your PP I 10 48 27
He really believed, that were it not for the inferiority PP I 10 52 52
you really serious in meditating a dance at Netherfield?-- PP I 11 55 5
6

I really cannot laugh at it. PP I 11 58 29
of pleasure, was really glad to see them; he had felt PP I 12 60 6
in the collection, but really talking to Mr. Bennet, with PP I 15 71 6
or a really new muslin in a shop window, could recal them. PP I 15 72 7
of having really done any thing to deserve to lose it. PP I 16 79 27
humour itself, and is, I really believe, truly amiable, be PP I 16 82 44
45

The possibility of his having really endured such PP I 17 85 1
favourite's guilt; but really considering his descent, one PP I 18 94 45
It was really a very handsome thought. PP I 16 98 62
And upon Elizabeth's seeming really, with vexed and PP I 19 104 6
"Really, Mr. Collins," cried Elizabeth with some warmth, " PP I 19 108 18
Collins; "but if she is really headstrong and foolish, I PP I 20 110 4
she saw nothing in it really to lament; it was not to be PP I 21 116 8
to meet her again. I really do not think Georgiana Darcy PP I 21 117 14
Mrs. Bennet was really in a most pitiable state. PP I 23 129 16
That he was really fond of Jane, she doubted no more than PP II 1 133 3
Bingley's regard had really died away, or were suppressed PP II 1 134 3
Your sweetness and disinterestedness are really angelic; I PP II 1 134 9
There are few people whom I really love, and still fewer PP II 1 135 11
should meet at all, unless he really comes to see her." PP II 2 141 12
saw--and if he becomes really attached to me--I believe it PP II 3 144 7
But really, and upon my honour, I will try to do what I PP II 3 145 9
persuade herself that he is really partial to Miss Darcy. PP II 3 148 26
seriously hoped he might really soon marry Mr. Darcy's PP II 3 149 27
much in love; for had I really experienced that pure and PP II 3 150 29
When Mr. Collins could be forgotten, there was really a PP II 5 157 5
the manners of the great really are, which my situation in PP II 6 160 3
But really, ma'am, I think it would be very hard upon PP II 6 165 35
sake, she made more favourable than it really was. PP II 6 166 42
Colonel Fitzwilliam seemed really glad to see them; any PP II 8 172 3
that she will never play really well, unless she practises PP II 8 173 10
"because you could not really believe me to entertain any PP II 8 174 14
He seldom appeared really animated. PP II 9 180 29
"Care of him!--yes, I really believe Darcy does take care PP II 10 184 24
Mrs. Collins, seeing that she was really unwell, did not PP II 10 187 41
concern in missing him; she really rejoiced at it. PP II 13 209 13
really be discreditable to you to let them go alone." PP II 14 212 13
It is really too distressing. PP II 17 225 12
it will not signify to anybody here, what he really is. PP II 17 226 23
really had no pleasure in fine carpets or satin curtains. PP II 19 240 14
that she had not really any dislike to the scheme. PP II 19 241 17
her master were really absent, but had not courage for it. PP III 1 246 8
to speak with calmness, if he really intended to meet them. PP III 1 254 57
his resentment had not made him think really ill of her. PP III 1 256 64
It was more than civil; it was really attentive; and there PP III 1 257 69
Mrs. Gardiner, "I really should not have thought that he PP III 1 258 74
My poor mother is really ill and keeps her room. PP III 4 275 5
drove from the town; "and really, upon serious PP III 5 282 1
"Do you really think so?" cried Elizabeth, brightening up PP III 5 282 2
It is really too great a violation of decency, honour, and PP III 5 282 3
But, really, I know not what to say. PP III 5 283 10
But Jane knows, as well as I do, what Wickham really is. PP III 5 284 12
"And do you really know all this?" cried Mrs. Gardiner, PP III 5 284 13
a doubt, I suppose, of their being really married?" PP III 5 290 49
"And they are really to be married!" cried Elizabeth, as PP III 7 304 34
the admiring multitude what connubial felicity really was. PP III 8 312 16
"No really," replied Elizabeth; "I think there cannot be PP III 9 318 23
But if you are really innocent and ignorant, I must be PP III 10 321 2
for she really did know where her friend was to be found. PP III 10 322 2
against the grain; and I really believe your letter this PP III 10 324 2
In spite of what her sister declared, and really believed PP III 11 332 20
and was really persuaded that she talked as much as ever. PP III 11 337 56
being a lover, Elizabeth really believed all his PP III 13 347 33
voice and manner plainly shewed how really happy he was. PP III 13 348 34
to town last November, he really loved me, and nothing but PP III 13 350 49
"Good heaven! can it be really so! PP III 17 373 9
And do you really love him quite well enough? PP III 17 373 11
a proposal; yet was really vexed that her mother should be PP III 17 374 21
of man; but this would be nothing if you really liked him." PP III 17 376 33
You do not know what he really is; then pray do not pain PP III 17 376 34
that Mr. Darcy was really the object of her choice, by PP III 17 376 36
And is it really true? PP III 17 378 43
Had you not been really amiable you would have hated me PP III 18 380 5
of accounting for it; and really, all things considered, I PP III 18 380 5
You supposed more than really existed. PP III 18 382 21
letter, that Charlotte, really rejoicing in the match, was PP III 18 383 26
Darcy, as well as Elizabeth, really loved them; and they PP III 19 388 13
in, and that to make it really serviceable to Mrs. Price, MP I 1 7 7
"Should her disposition be really bad," said Sir Thomas, " MP I 1 10 14
supposed the girls so nearly of an age as they really were. MP I 2 13 4
to leave her home is really against her, for, with all its MP I 2 13 5
"But, aunt, she is really so very ignorant!-- MP I 2 18 25
deal for any body she really interests herself about, and MP I 3 27 33
If I could suppose my aunt really to care for me, it would MP I 3 27 34
misled Sir Thomas to suppose it really intended for Fanny. MP I 3 28 38
of, or for any body to wish that really knows us both. MP I 3 28 42
question--besides that, I really should not have a bed to MP I 3 30 56
and she really grieved because she could not grieve. MP I 3 32 64
"But do you really? for Miss Bertram is in general thought MP I 5 45 7
I really know very little of Sotherton." MP I 6 56 18
any occasion, but really I cannot do every thing at once. MP I 7 73 53
and attention, that she really did not feel equal to it. MP I 8 78 23
Those cottages are really a disgrace. MP I 8 82 34
"Upon my word, it is really a pity that it should not take MP I 9 88 24
You really are fit for something better. MP I 9 93 53
"I am really not tired, which I almost wonder at; for we MP I 9 94 60
it might be done, if you really wished to be more at large, MP I 10 99 18
"Well," said he, "if you really think I had better go; it MP I 10 103 48
her conviction of being really the one preferred, MP I 10 105 52
to me, and though he is really a gentleman, and I dare say MP I 11 111 28
he is really thinking of, more than the woman herself. MP I 12 116 10
"I really believe," said he, "I could be fool enough at MP I 13 123 6
I and my company have really acted there must be some MP I 14 134 14
too strongly; and I really cannot undertake to harangue MP I 15 140 14
"I must really congratulate your ladyship," said she, "on MP I 15 143 26
almost every eye was upon her; "but I really cannot act." MP I 15 145 49
theatrical board, and the really good feelings by which MP I 15 147 56
ungenerous, it would be really wrong to expose her to it. MP I 16 154 14
it was not a matter which really involved her happiness, MP I 17 161 9
brother, instead of being really guided by him as to the MP I 18 164 1
a little, for really there is a speech or two----- MP I 18 168 17
as by his wife, who was really extremely happy to see him, MP II 1 179 9
own character, but was really as far from pleased with the MP II 1 183 23
but by looking as he really felt, most exceedingly pleased MP II 1 186 35
You must really begin to harden yourself to the idea of MP II 3 198 8
Mrs. Grant, really eager to get any change for her sister, MP II 4 205 2
"And really," added Edmund, "the day is so mild, that your MP II 4 212 29
her feel that she had really been much longer absent than MP II 4 214 46
formed after tea--formed really for the amusement of Dr. MP II 5 227 68
I do desire that you will not be making her really unhappy; MP II 6 230 8
and their young inmates really worth visiting; and though MP II 7 238 1
the view is really very pretty; I am sure it may be done. MP II 7 242 23
have suggested, (I do not really require you to proceed MP II 7 243 27
Whatever effect Sir Thomas's little harangue might really MP II 7 248 47
and consider it, as it really is, a token of the love of MP II 9 261 2
The necklace really looked very well; and Fanny left her MP II 9 271 40
It had really occurred to her, unprompted, that Fanny, MP II 9 271 41
When the carriages were really heard, when the guests MP II 10 273 7
when the guests began really to assemble, her own gaiety MP II 10 273 7
Not but that she was really pleased to have Fanny admired; MP II 10 277 15
talked of William, he was really not un-agreeable, and MP II 10 278 20
To Fanny's mind, Edmund's absence was really in its cause MP II 11 285 15
Well might his sister, believing as she really did that MP II 12 294 18
Have you really--was it by your desire--I beg your pardon, MP II 13 300 6
appear to think any thing really intended, she wrote thus, MP II 13 307 30
31

consideration, and for really examining your own MP III 1 318 39
Mr. Crawford; yet, if he really loved her, and were MP III 1 321 46
"I must be a brute indeed, if I can be really ungrateful!" MP III 1 322 52
afterwards,--and she really had known something like MP III 2 332 23
him to stay dinner; it was really a necessary compliment. MP III 3 335 7
"It was really like being at a play," said she.-- MP III 3 338 17
the pulpit, when it is really eloquence, which is MP III 3 341 28
They really go on Monday! and I was within a trifle of MP III 4 354 48
a while towards him--because he really seemed to feel.-- MP III 5 365 35
When he had really resolved on any measure, he could MP III 6 370 14
and in short could not really be wanted or missed. MP III 6 371 15
She was really glad to receive the letter when it did come. MP III 9 393 1
We seemed very glad to see each other, and I do really MP III 9 393 1
Good sense, like hers, will always act when really called MP III 10 399 4
She was sorry, really sorry; and yet, in spite of this and MP III 10 406 21
It was really March; but it was April in its mild air, MP III 11 409 6
expressed himself, and really seemed, might not it be MP III 11 414 32
How Miss Crawford really felt--how she meant to act, or MP III 12 417 4
She thought he was really good-tempered, and could fancy MP III 12 419 9
asserted that he is really in a decline, that the symptoms MP III 14 433 13
I really am quite agitated on the subject. MP III 14 434 13
It would really be gratifying to see them all again, and a MP III 14 435 14
She had begun to think he really loved her, and to fancy MP III 15 438 6
As nothing was really left for the decision of Mrs. Price, MP III 15 444 27
most attached to Maria, was really the greatest sufferer. MP III 16 448 1
When really touched by affliction, her active powers had MP III 16 448 2
under the idea of being really loved by a man who had long MP III 16 454 18
thoroughly up, could really close such a conversation. MP III 16 459 31
Yates, desirous of being really received into the family, MP III 17 462 4
early love; and now, on really knowing each other, their MP III 17 472 30
and name, did really belong, afforded her no equals. E I 1 7 10
she would not have him really suspect a circumstance as E I 1 11 33
"But, Mr. Knightley, she is really very sorry to lose poor E I 1 11 36
And he was really a very pleasing young man, a young man E I 4 35 45
Do you really think it a bad thing?--why so?" E I 5 36 2
will never lead any one really wrong; she will make so E I 5 40 22
"I know that you all love her really too well to be unjust E I 5 40 24
But really, I could almost venture, if Harriet would sit E I 6 43 13
There is my sister; and really quite her own little E I 6 45 21
my pains, and when I had really made a very good likeness E I 6 45 21
without offence; but was really obliged to put an end to E I 6 46 24
And he wrote as if he really loved her very much--but she E I 7 50 1
and really almost made up my mind--to refuse Mr. Martin. E I 7 53 22
23

However, I do really think Mr. Martin a very amiable young E I 7 54 30

You have cured her of her school-girl's giggle; she really E I 8 58 12
unconcerned, but was really feeling uncomfortable and E I 8 65 50
He was invited to contribute any really good enigmas, E I 9 70 7
Its probability and its eligibility have really so E I 9 74 20
Could it really be meant for me?" E I 9 74 22
do indeed--and really it is strange; it is out of the E I 9 74 25
"That Mr. Elton should really be in love with me,--me, of E I 9 75 26
I cannot really change for the better. E I 10 84 13
Poverty certainly has not contracted her mind: I really E I 10 85 19
the want of which is really the great evil to be avoided E I 10 85 21
"And really, I do not think the impression will soon be E I 10 87 27
I really am a most troublesome companion to you both, but E I 10 89 37
It did not often happen; for Mr. John Knightley had really E I 11 93 5
Mr. Weston is really as kind as herself. E I 11 94 14
Mr. and Mrs. Weston do really prevent our missing her by E I 11 94 14
I really never could think well of any body who proposed E I 11 96 25
Emma, who was not really at all frightened herself, E I 13 110 8
of her's, he had not really the least inclination to give E I 13 110 10
it was really estimable; but it should have lasted longer. E I 13 115 36
suggestion of "can it really be as my brother imagined? E I 14 118 4
with Isabella; and, she really believed, would scarcely E I 14 122 18
It really was so. E I 15 129 24
You cannot really, seriously, doubt it. E I 15 131 31
Mr. Elton should not be really in love with her, or so E I 16 138 15
and believed him to be really taking comfort in some E I 16 138 18
19
heart and understanding--really for the time convinced E I 17 142 9
state of spirits to care really about Mr. Frank E I 18 144 4
of other people: nothing really amiable about him." E I 18 149 26
and we have no chance of agreeing till he is really here." E I 18 150 33
first of all, I really must, in justice to Jane, apologise E II 1 157 10
My mother's are really very good indeed. E II 1 158 10
it really is full two years, you know, since she was here. E II 1 158 14
she saw in her the really accomplished young woman, which E II 2 166 11
clearness and delicacy which really needed no fuller bloom. E II 2 167 12
My dear sir, you really are too bountiful. E II 3 173 29
a thousand thanks, and says you really quite oppress her." E II 3 173 29
my dear Miss Woodhouse; but we really must take leave. E II 3 176 50
I shall not attempt calling on Mrs. Goddard, for I really E II 3 177 50
know; I dare say he is really nothing extraordinary:"-- E II 5 189 13
He did really look and speak as if in a state of no common E II 5 191 26
about any body, that I really think you may say what you E II 6 200 19
I wanted the opinion of some one who could really judge. E II 6 201 28
I was not very flattering to Miss Campbell; but she really E II 6 202 34
honour, if not of being really in love with her, of being E II 7 206 2
convinced her that it was really said only to relieve his E II 7 206 4
without seeming really at all ashamed of what he had done. E II 8 212 2
Now I shall really be very happy to walk into the same E II 8 214 10
I was telling Mr. Cole, I really was ashamed to look at E II 8 215 16
use than we can; and that really is the reason why the E II 8 216 16
"Were you really?-- E II 8 218 36
"I believe I have been very rude; but really Miss Fairfax E II 8 222 56
I was quite surprized;--very glad, I am sure; but really E II 8 223 63
really good-natured, useful, considerate, or benevolent. E II 8 223 64
and if Mr. Knightley really wished to marry, you would not E II 8 224 67
so, it is so; but if he really loves Jane Fairfax-----" E II 8 225 75
I really wish you to call with me. E II 9 234 34
Jane at present--and she really eats nothing--makes such a E II 9 237 46
But I was really quite shocked the other day--for Mr. E II 9 238 51
So I begged he would not--for really as to ours being gone, E II 9 238 51
"But really, I am half ashamed, and wish I had never taken E II 10 243 26
We really are so shocked! E II 10 245 52
Emma found it really time to be at home; the visit had E II 10 246 55
I really do not think there will." E II 11 248 6
He sat really lost in thought for the first few minutes; E II 12 259 12
13
when one is really interested in the absent!--she will E II 12 261 36
are really out of luck; you are very much out of luck!" E II 12 262 40
41
I do suspect that he is not really necessary to my E II 13 264 2
Miss Woodhouse, whom she really loved extremely, made her E II 13 268 13
She did not really like her. E II 14 270 4
as much affectedly, and as little really easy as could be. E II 14 271 5
She could really almost fancy herself at Maple Grove." E II 14 272 18
I really could not help exclaiming! E II 14 273 19
'I really cannot get this girl to move form the house. E II 14 274 30
I had been used to, I really could not give it a thought. E II 14 277 36
"I should hope not; but really when I look round among my E II 14 277 40
I use to be quite angry with Selina; but really I begin E II 14 277 40
But she is really quite the gentlewoman." E II 14 278 46
mentioned, that I was really impatient to see him; and I E II 14 278 50
wear off, for there really is nothing in the manners of E II 15 284 9
"Why really, dear Emma, I say that he is so very much E II 15 289 42
We really seem quite the fashion. E II 16 290 2
whom she really wanted to make the eighth, Jane Fairfax.-- E II 16 291 5
You really are a very sad girl, and do not know how to E II 16 295 32
know; and from us I really think, my dear Jane, you can E II 16 295 34
and all that it does so well, it is really astonishing!" E II 16 296 40
I really am ashamed of always leading the way." E II 16 298 57
"But have you really heard of nothing?" E II 17 299 4
Your inexperience really amuses me! E II 17 300 12
as well as play;--yes, I really believe you might, even E II 17 301 18
also, that nothing really unexceptionable may pass us." E II 17 302 20
"If she is really ill, why not go to Bath, Mr. Weston?-- E II 18 307 19
Her own attachment had really subsided into a mere nothing; E III 1 315 1
If he was quite sincere, if he really tried to come, it E III 1 316 6
That she was really ill was very certain; he had declared E III 1 316 6
Now, it would be really having Frank in their E III 1 317 10
Oh! Mr. Weston, you must really have had Aladdin's Lamp. E III 2 322 19
and you know we are not really so much brother and sister E III 2 331 62
"And had you really some at hand yourself?-- E III 4 339 14
because this is what did really once belong to him, which E III 4 339 16
"This was really his," said Harriet.-- E III 4 339 18
"Never! really, never!-- E III 5 345 11
I really was persuaded of Mrs. Weston's having mentioned E III 5 345 13
We really must wish you good night." E III 5 349 24
she was really ashamed of having ever imparted them. E III 5 350 28
I really must talk to him about purchasing a donkey. E III 6 356 26
for one's self--the only way of really enjoying them.-- E III 6 358 35
"Your gallantry is really unanswerable. E III 7 369 15
said Mrs. Elton; "I really cannot attempt--I am not at all E III 7 371 37
in my own way, but I really must be allowed to judge when E III 7 372 37
I am really tired of exploring so long on one spot. E III 7 372 39
I really cannot venture to name her salary to you, Miss E III 8 382 23
say of the good wishes which she really felt, took leave. E III 8 384 34
so much--but, except them, Jane would really see nobody." E III 9 390 18
Is she really not ill?" E III 10 392 5
Something really important seemed announced by his looks; E III 10 392 7
I have really for some time past, for at least these three E III 10 396 41
he certainly did--while he really belonged to another?-- E III 10 396 44
"And do you really believe the affair to have been E III 10 399 58
But you really frightened me. E III 10 400 68
Mr. Knightley should really--if he does not mind the E III 11 407 28
the idea of his feelings for her more than he really does." E III 11 411 40
41
she had never really cared for Frank Churchill at all! E III 11 412 45
really confused--"I am in a very extraordinary situation. E III 13 426 17
She could really say nothing.-- E III 13 430 35
Whether Miss Woodhouse began really to understand me E III 14 438 8
soon as she found I was really gone from Randall's, she E III 14 441 8
he is, beyond, a doubt, really attached to Miss Fairfax, E III 15 448 30
than now; and it really was too much to hope even of E III 15 450 38
Harriet really wished, and had wished some time, to E III 16 451 3
He really is engaged from morning to night.-- E III 16 455 23
I have nothing to do with William's wants, but it really E III 16 458 43
Martin," that she was really expecting the intelligence to E III 18 473 27
was really in danger of becoming too happy for security.-- E III 18 475 39
she too was really hearing him, though trying to seem deaf. E III 18 480 76
see Frank Churchill, and really regarding him as she did E III 18 480 80
possible for her to be really cured of her attachment to E III 19 481 1
to Mr. Knightley, and really able to accept another man E III 19 481 1
For one daughter, his eldest, he would really have given P III 1 5 8
event of Admiral Croft's really taking Kellynch-Hall, she P III 4 30 10
And as to my father, I really should not have thought that P III 5 35 14
I really think poor Mrs. Clay may be staying here in P III 5 35 14
on her account, I have really been so busy, have had so P III 5 38 32
I really am very ill--a great deal worse than I ever own." P III 6 44 7
I really think Charles might as well have told his father P III 7 57 14
The only time that I ever really suffered in body or mind, P III 8 71 54
it were really so, I should do just the same in her place. P III 10 85 9
Anne, really tired herself, was glad to sit down; and she P III 10 87 22
I really think they ought. P III 12 102 2
Anne, or Charles, who, really a very affectionate brother, P III 12 110 43
"She really left nothing for Mary to do. P IV 1 121 2
must call on Mrs. Croft; I really must call upon her soon. P IV 1 125 14
so very useful, had made really an agreeable fortnight. P IV 2 130 3
said, "now Mary, you know very well how it really was.-- P IV 2 130 6
I have really a curiosity to see the person who can give P IV 2 132 20
If he really sought to reconcile himself like a dutiful P IV 2 136 35
There might really have been a liking formerly, though P IV 3 140 11
Russell, in the wish of really comprehending what had P IV 3 144 22
enthusiasm and violent agitation seldom really possess. P IV 4 146 6
admirably, has really proved an invaluable acquaintance.-- P IV 5 155 9
could not be satisfied that she really knew his character. P IV 5 160 27
"We see nothing of them, and this is really an instance of P IV 6 164 7
not really Mrs. Croft, she must let him have his own way. P IV 6 170 30
comprehend so soon as she really did; but now she could P IV 6 170 32
feelings, whether he were really suffering much from P IV 7 178 24
It was really expected to be a good one, and Captain P IV 7 180 32
It is really very good of you to come and sit with me, P IV 9 194 18
greater right to influence him, than is really the case. P IV 9 195 25
"Can you really?" P IV 9 204 79
but I have heard nothing which really surprises me. P IV 9 207 91
I was really in pain for him; for your hard-hearted sister, P IV 10 213 4
for I would never really omit an opportunity of bringing P IV 10 213 5
When I found he was really going to his friends at P IV 10 213 9
presence must really be interfering with her prime object. P IV 10 213 10
She had some satisfaction in finding that he was really P IV 10 214 13
I really cannot be plaguing myself for ever with all new P IV 10 215 15
appearance; but Anne was really glad to see them; and the P IV 10 216 18
She was just in time to ascertain that it really was Mr. P IV 10 222 39
off for Thornberry, but I really forget by what--for I was P IV 10 228 71
than he really was, strongly enforced the invitation. P IV 11 231 12
flattered, to make him really happy on the occasion, was P IV 12 248 2
He held it indeed as certain, that no person cd be really S 2 373 1
of health) could be really in a state of secure & S 2 373 1
complaints--but it really is not so--or very little--they S 5 385 1
But there is really no affectation about them. S 5 385 1
Sidney laughs at him--but it really is no joke--tho' S 5 385 1
We wanted just to see you & make sure of your being really S 6 391 1
gravely answered "I really know nothing of the matter.-- S 7 398 1
nothing really incredible--and so it was settled.-- S 10 419 1
cried he, it is impossible you can be really at a loss. S 12 423 1
assizes at York, tho' we really have raised the sum we S 12 424 1
business,--therefore I really have not a moment to spare-- S 12 424 1
They were really ill-used.-- S 12 427 1
REANIMATE (1)
His affections seemed to reanimate towards them all, and SS I 17 90 1
REAP (2)
leave her to reap the fruits of her own heinous offence. PP III 6 297 11
to him, and was now to reap the consequence, which P III 10 90 37
REAPED (1)
Marianne, though without knowing it herself, reaped all SS II 10 214 8
REAPPEARANCE (1)
which his sudden reappearance raised in Catherine, passed NA I 8 53 3
REAPPEARED (1)
Hayter had but just reappeared, when Anne had to listen to P III 9 75 9
REAR (1)
which followed, added-- "he is rear Admiral of the white. P III 3 21 20
21
REARED (1)
acquaintance who had reared and supported a boy NA I 1 16 10
REARING (1)
His charitable kindness had been rearing a prime comfort MP III 17 472 30
REARS (1)
Of Rears, and vices, I saw enough. MP I 6 60 49
REASON (251)
& I have but too much reason to fear that the governess to LS 1 244 1
I arrived here in safety, & have no reason to complain of LS 5 249 1
acquaintance; but against reason, against conviction, to LS 8 255 2
I have reason to imagine that she did receive serious LS 14 265 4
Nothing satisfactory transpires as to her reason for LS 17 270 6
no time in demanding the reason of her behaviour, & soon LS 19 273 1
because I have reason to believe that some attempts were LS 20 277 6
7
from a quarter, whence I had least reason to apprehend it. LS 22 281 4
words, that he wished to reason with me on the impropriety LS 22 281 4
I trust however my dear mother, that we have no reason to LS 23 284 7
I have another reason for urging this. LS 26 295 2
while there is so much reason to fear the connection would LS 30 300 1
But the influence of reason is often acknowledged too late LS 30 300 2
to threaten her reason--how is she to be consoled? LS 36 306 1
Have I not reason to rejoice? LS 39 308 1
Allen had no particular reason to hope it would be NA I 4 31 2
uncommon steadiness of reason to resist the attraction of NA I 7 50 44
of it founded on reason or reality, till Morland produced NA I 9 67 33
Have I not reason to fear, that if the gentleman who spoke NA I 10 78 37
This was of course vehemently talked down as no reason at NA I 11 84 19
who, on hearing the reason of their speedy return, said, " NA I 11 89 62
who, she had reason to believe, were in a shop hard by. NA I 12 91 3
reason of such incivility; but perhaps I can do it as well. NA I 12 94 10
of the most advanced reason and mature time of life. NA I 14 109 25
Ten to one but he guesses the reason, and that is exactly NA II 1 131 13
To raise your spirits, moreover, she gives you reason to NA II 5 158 17
man had reason to believe himself loved, I was that man. NA II 10 202 7
"I wish I could reason like you, for his sake and my own. NA II 11 211 14
and any thing in reason--a bow thrown out, perhaps--though, NA II 11 213 19
Without any reason that could justify, any apology that NA II 13 226 25
of reason and the dictate of conscience could make it. NA II 15 247 15
You are endeavouring to disarm me by reason, and to SS I 10 51 28
subjection of reason to common-place and mistaken notions. SS I 11 53 2
Elinor's compassion for him increased, as she had reason SS I 11 55 8
what could be the reason of it; was sure there must be SS I 14 70 1
was independent, there was no reason to believe him rich. SS I 14 71 4
Is nothing due to the man whom we have all so much reason SS I 15 79 28
to love, and no reason in the world to think ill of? SS I 15 79 28
and I have every reason to hope I never shall. SS I 17 90 5
than I do, if you have any reason to expect such a match." SS I 20 114 45
gave them reason to hope that it would not be rejected.-- SS I 21 121 10
unable to divine the reason or object of such a SS I 22 129 15
that was reason enough for his not mentioning it." SS I 22 131 32
What other reason for the disclosure of the affair could SS II 1 142 7
be assured that you shall never have reason to repent it. SS II 2 146 6
or you are carrying your disinterestedness beyond reason." SS II 2 148 16

REASON/REASONABLE

The reason alleged was their determined resolution of not SS II 3 153 1
The Miss Dashwoods had no greater reason to be SS II 5 168 11
"Aye,aye," said Mrs. Jennings, "we know the reason of all SS II 5 171 36
and explain the reason of my having expected this in vain. SS II 7 187 40
"That a gentleman, whom I had reason to think--in short, SS II 8 199 35
right, is there not some reason to fear I may be wrong?" SS II 9 204 18
and there was every reason to fear that she had removed SS II 9 207 26
years I had every reason to be pleased with her situation. SS II 9 208 28
and this was the reason of my leaving Barton so suddenly, SS II 9 209 30
She had yet another reason for wishing her children to SS II 10 213 5
"A man of whom he had always had such reason to think well! SS II 10 214 9
And there can be no reason why you should not try for him. SS II 11 223 24
entirely on reason, and certainly not at all on truth. SS II 12 231 11
her to own that she had reason for her happiness; and SS II 13 239 7
there was no reason in the world why Mrs. Ferrars should SS II 13 239 9
recent meeting--and this she had every reason to expect. SS II 13 245 47
reason for alarm; I hope Mrs. Dashwood will do very well." SS III 1 258 5
There is no reason on earth why Mr. Edward and Lucy should SS III 1 259 7
had soon afterwards good reason to think her object gained; SS III 3 280 9
whom neither of the others had so much reason to dislike. SS III 5 294 3
I have good reason to think--indeed I have it from the SS III 5 297 31
Not that you have any reason to regret, my dear Elinor. SS III 5 297 31
He tried to reason himself out of fears, which the SS III 7 309 7
Her former apprehensions, now with greater reason restored, SS III 7 313 20
"Is this the real reason of your coming?" SS III 8 319 24
I will not reason here--now will I stop for you to SS III 8 321 34
I had reason to believe myself secure of my present wife, SS III 8 323 40
But you have not explained to me the particular reason of SS III 8 330 68
which ought not in reason to have weight; by that person SS III 9 333 2
Elinor was half inclined to ask her reason for thinking so, SS III 9 336 11
be checked by religion, by reason, by constant employment." SS III 10 347 30
many other circumstances, reason enough to be convinced SS III 11 350 9
recovered the use of her reason and voice as to be just SS III 11 353 25
experienced, so much reason as they had often had to be SS III 11 355 45
reality of reason and truth, one of the happiest of men. SS III 13 361 3
to her reason, her judgment, it was completely a puzzle. SS III 13 364 10
and he found fresh reason to rejoice in what he had done SS III 13 370 35
of her clemency, gave him reason for believing that had he SS III 14 379 18
"There was a reason for that--replied Miss W. changing W 316 2
Having no reason to be dissatisfied with her partner, W 329 9
that she had no better reason to give than that Miss W 332 12
If you prefer this room to the other, there is no reason W 334 13
simpler mind, or juster reason saved her from such W 345 21
should be guided by reason; and, in my opinion, exertion PP I 7 32 38
without waiting for arguments to reason one into it. PP I 10 50 37
I have reason to expect an addition to our family party." PP I 13 61 1
was beyond the reach of reason; and she continued to rail PP I 13 62 8
for his compliance, but could not wait for his reason. PP I 16 76 7
meet him, but I have no reason for avoiding him but what I PP I 16 78 20
moment, as there is reason to fear that the performance PP I 18 94 41
"I have no reason, I assure you," said he, "to be PP I 18 98 62
he trusted he had every reason to be satisfied, since the PP I 20 110 1
she added, "that Lizzy shall be brought to reason. PP I 20 110 3
that any attempt to reason with or sooth her would only PP I 20 113 29
almost secure, and with reason, for Charlotte had been PP I 22 121 1
You have no reason. PP II 1 134 7
of his bride, as he had reason to hope, that shortly after PP II 2 139 1
I do not at all comprehend her reason for wishing to be PP II 3 148 26
friend had an excellent reason for what she did, for Mr. PP II 7 168 1
"Shall we ask your cousin the reason of this?" said PP II 8 175 22
I have reason to think Bingley very much indebted to him. PP II 10 185 24
"And remember that I have not much reason for supposing it PP II 10 185 28
against your reason, and even against your character? PP II 11 190 10
"I have every reason in the world to think ill of you. PP II 11 191 12
inclination; by reason, by reflection, by every thing. PP II 11 192 22
impartial conviction, as truly as I wished it in reason.-- PP II 12 197 5
affairs, and whose character she had no reason to question. PP II 13 206 4
and driven reason away, where either were concerned. PP II 13 208 8
had not yet been able to reason away, was such a PP II 15 217 17
There was another reason too for her opposition. PP II 16 223 25
in taking so decided a dislike to him, without any reason. PP II 17 225 17
which there was every reason to believe would be attended PP II 18 235 40
But she had no reason to fear Mr. and Mrs. Gardiner's PP III 2 264 13
herself the reason, she had very little to say in reply. PP III 2 266 17
Colonel Forster gives us reason to expect him here soon. PP III 4 274 3
but too much reason to fear they are not gone to Scotland. PP III 4 274 3
than there was at present reason to hope, and leaving his PP III 4 278 22
no reason, I suppose, to believe them fond of each other." PP III 5 285 17
And it is the more to be lamented, because there is reason PP III 6 297 11
to be satisfied, from the reason of things, that their PP III 9 318 19
of this, was another reason for his resolving to follow us. PP III 10 322 2
The reason why all this was to be done by him alone, was PP III 10 324 2
to meet, frequently meet, reason with, persuade, and PP III 10 326 3
But he had given a reason for his interference, which PP III 10 326 3
He was not seated by her; perhaps that was the reason of PP III 11 335 43
were so far beyond reason, that she was quite disappointed PP III 12 343 29
Elizabeth made no attempt to reason with her mother, but PP III 13 345 17
surprise, there was reason to fear that her mother had PP III 13 346 22
Miss Bennet, to understand the reason of my journey hither. PP III 14 353 22
23

so; it must be so, while he retains the use of his reason. PP III 14 354 36
"Only this; that if he is so, you can have no reason to PP III 14 354 41
We have reason to imagine that his aunt, Lady Catherine de PP III 15 363 17
but, though we have both reason to think my opinions not PP III 16 368 21
The reason of this sudden removal was soon evident. PP III 18 383 26
family; but there is no reason to expect so great an evil. MP I 1 10 14
There is no reason in the world why you should not be MP I 3 26 29
kind pains you took to reason and persuade me out of my MP I 3 27 36
and myself, have taken to reason, coax, or trick him into MP I 4 42 21
"That would not be a very handsome reason for using Mr. MP I 8 77 13
"You can have no reason I imagine madam," said he, MP I 8 78 18
and there is some reason to think that the linings and MP I 9 86 9
understandings while they reason, feels the comfort of. MP I 11 107 3
be overcome, and I see no reason why a man should make a MP I 11 109 17
there might be some reason for the glance his father gave MP II 1 183 24
there had been no reason that she should; but Miss MP II 4 206 5
like to go; and I can see no reason why she should not." MP II 5 217 2
can see no reason why she should be denied the indulgence." MP II 5 219 18
of such a loan, and some alarms to reason away in Fanny. MP II 6 237 23
at Sotherton, to afford a reason, an occasion for such a MP II 8 252 2
Northampton, and she had reason to think Mr. Crawford MP II 8 256 14
by this happy mixture of reason and weakness, she was able, MP II 9 265 20
Sir Thomas approved of it for another reason. MP II 9 266 21
Edmund, she had too much reason to suppose, was at the MP II 9 267 22
Oh yes," cried Mrs. Norris, "she has good reason to look MP II 10 272 3
"And there is no reason to suppose," added Sir Thomas, " MP II 11 284 9
Her temper he had good reason to depend on and to praise. MP II 12 294 16
And she shall have no reason to lament the hour that first MP II 12 295 20
would have half the reason which my poor ill aunt had to MP II 12 296 29
For what reason?" MP III 1 315 25
any reason, child, to think ill of Mr. Crawford's temper?" MP III 1 317 36
have reason to be long sorry for this day's transactions." MP III 1 320 42
endeavour to reason yourself into a stronger frame of mind. MP III 1 321 48
on, she felt all the reason she had to bless the kindness MP III 1 323 53
be thankful for the right reason in her, which had saved MP III 1 324 59
He had every well-grounded reason for solid attachment; he MP III 2 326 3
were equally got over--and equally without apparent reason. MP III 6 367 4
she should be able to reason herself into a properer state; MP III 6 370 12
Sir Thomas had appealed to her reason, conscience, and MP III 6 371 15
She had reason to suppose herself not yet forgotten by Mr. MP III 7 375 4
that age of feeling and reason, which might suggest the MP III 8 390 8
on her own unassisted reason, should err in the method of MP III 9 395 4
Susan had in point of reason the advantage, and never was MP III 9 396 5
For her approbation, the particular reason of his going MP III 10 404 15
there was no reason why Fanny should not know the truth. MP III 14 429 1
her, that she had some reason to think lightly of the MP III 14 433 12
them to support life and reason under such disgrace; and MP III 15 442 21
and there was every reason to conclude her to be concealed MP III 16 450 11
rest, when they were in reason to think that one interview MP III 16 452 15
vanity was not of a strength to fight long against reason. MP III 16 459 31
and for ever repeated reason to rejoice in what he had MP III 17 473 31
tell you that I have good reason to believe your little E I 8 58 19
20

"I have reason to think," he replied, "that Harriet Smith E I 8 59 25
But I could not reason so to a man in love, and was E I 8 61 38
"Upon my word, Emma, to hear you abusing the reason you E I 8 64 45
without having any such reason to give for her long E I 8 67 56
"Leave out the two last lines, and there is no reason why E I 9 77 40
His ostensible reason, however, was to ask whether Mr. E I 9 81 78
"Yes," said he, smiling--"and reason good. E I 12 99 6
she could not wish to reason away, which she would rather E I 13 110 8
She had reason to believe her nearly recovered from her E I 17 141 5
There was always sufficient reason for such an attention; E II 1 155 2
That is the reason of her writing out of rule, as we call E II 1 159 18
her murmurs, or to reason them away; probably a little of E II 5 187 6
I have no reason to think ill of her--not the least-- E II 6 203 41
He had no reason to wish his hair longer, to conceal any E II 8 212 2
reason to wish the money unspent, to improve his spirits. E II 8 212 2
Emma had as much reason to be satisfied with the rest of E II 8 214 12
as any reason for their not meaning to make the present. E II 8 215 14
and that really is the reason why the instrument was E II 8 216 16
she knew she had no reason to complain, and was amused E II 9 233 24
is no reason to suppose the instrument is indifferent. E II 9 234 33
without emotion; she must reason herself into the power of E II 10 240 6
Mr. Perry might have reason to regret the alteration, but E II 11 251 27
There was no reason to suppose Mr. Elton thought at all E II 15 281 2
But for that reason, I should imagine the likeness must be E II 16 297 45
She had soon afterwards reason to believe that the E III 4 340 28
Mr. Knightley, who, for some reason best known to himself, E III 5 343 2
"Have you never at any time had reason to think that he E III 5 350 34
Mr. Knightley had another reason for avoiding a table in E III 6 356 29
can be no reason for your being exposed to danger now. E III 6 362 49
Though her nephew had had no particular reason to hasten E III 9 387 11
gave me reason to understand that you did care about him?" E III 11 405 13
Emma smiled, and felt that Mr. Weston had very good reason E III 12 417 5
She talked with a great deal of reason, and at least equal E III 12 420 14
reason to regret that I was not in the secret earlier." E III 13 426 15
that becomes the acknowledgment of more than your reason.-- E III 13 426 16
I have as much reason to be ashamed of confessing that I E III 13 426 17
reason for asking it, without resorting to invention.-- E III 16 451 3
I was!--for I had reason to believe her very lately more E III 18 473 24
(whom I have always had reason to believe as much in love E III 18 474 34
every day was giving her fresh reason for thinking so.-- E III 19 481 3
perhaps, as there was no reason to suppose it perpetuated P III 1 8 17
of his constancy, she had no reason to believe him married. P III 4 30 8
thought, have reason to reproach her for giving no warning. P III 5 34 12
and she did not see any reason why she was to be P III 6 45 10
"And I will tell you our reason," she added, "and all P III 6 50 27
there being no sufficient reason against it, he ought to P III 7 55 7
My being the mother is the very reason why my feelings P III 7 56 10
Soon, however, she began to reason with herself, and try P III 7 60 28
and though she had no reason to suppose his eye wandering P III 8 63 2
conjunctions, which reason will patronize in vain,--which P III 8 68 30
in a sort of whisper, "that must not be any reason, indeed. P IV 4 145 1
there was but too much reason to apprehend that the P IV 4 149 12
Yet, in spite of all this, Anne had reason to believe that P IV 5 154 8
as the Harvilles; and "what do you think was the reason? P IV 6 164 8
She saw no reason against their being happy. P IV 6 167 20
at it, I have a reason of my own for wondering at it." P IV 6 173 47
But I have no reason to suppose it so. P IV 8 182 10
I have no reason, from any thing that has fallen within my P IV 9 196 33
(which I have very little reason to imagine he has any P IV 9 196 33
She had good reason to believe that some property of her P IV 9 210 98
I had no reason to believe her of less authority now.-- P IV 11 245 74
He had strong reason to beleive that one family had been S 2 372 1
to the utmost Energies of reason half-dethroned,--where we S 8 403 1
"The reason of this hesitation, was her having no S 9 409 1

REASONABLE (75)

Wigmore Street, till she becomes a little more reasonable. LS 2 246 1
as to afford the most reasonable hope of her being LS 19 274 2
of Frederica's having a reasonable dislike to Sir James, I LS 24 290 13
reasonable, is too common to excite surprise or resentment. LS 30 300 2
easily assumed, and not less reasonable than any other.-- NA I 3 26 8
with the Tilneys in any reasonable time, had just passed NA I 10 75 24
a portion of them too reasonable and too well informed NA I 14 111 29
for as the time of reasonable expectation drew near, NA I 15 121 26
the occasion with the reasonable resentment of a sensible NA II 14 237 22
A more reasonable cause might be found in the dependent SS I 4 22 18
the others; and she was reasonable enough to allow that a SS I 7 35 9
her opinions on the reasonable basis of common sense and SS I 11 56 11
been able to form any reasonable apology for your SS II 7 187 42
It is a reasonable and laudable pride which resists such SS II 7 189 51
excellent disposition, was neither reasonable nor candid. SS II 9 201 4
which the case rendered reasonable, though his sex might SS II 13 241 21
But she shall forgive me again, and on more reasonable SS III 8 319 27
of a mind awakened to reasonable exertion; for no sooner SS III 10 342 7
disturb a solitude so reasonable as what she now sought; SS III 10 348 34
Lucy's marriage, the unceasing and reasonable wonder among SS III 13 364 10
The forgiveness at first, indeed, was reasonable, SS III 14 376 11
It was reasonable, however, to hope, that they would not PP II 4 152 6
In vain did Elizabeth attempt to make her reasonable, and PP II 18 230 14
might be so tolerably reasonable as not to mention an PP II 19 238 6
he could get; but at length was reduced to be reasonable. PP III 10 323 2
It was reasonable that he should feel he had been wrong; PP III 10 326 3
as reasonable and just, as what Jane felt for Bingley. PP III 11 334 36
the happiest, wisest, most reasonable end!" PP III 13 347 29
I expected to find a more reasonable young woman. PP III 14 356 60
I hoped to find you reasonable; but depend upon it I will PP III 14 358 71
before I was reasonable enough to allow their justice." PP III 16 367 14
had been more reasonable, her expressions more moderate! PP III 17 376 30
considered, I begin to think it perfectly reasonable. PP III 18 380 5
"How unlucky that you should have a reasonable answer to PP III 18 381 13
give, and that I should be so reasonable as to admit it! PP III 18 381 13
the other so evidently reasonable, that the Miss Bertrams, MP I 16 151 1
of her sister so reasonable as ought to have been their MP I 17 160 8
"You will find his consequence very just and reasonable MP I 17 162 16
It was imputed to very reasonable weariness, and she was MP I 18 170 24
Sir Thomas, with a very reasonable dependence perhaps on MP II 1 180 10
Her niece thought it perfectly reasonable. MP II 5 221 35
we have given with a reasonable hope of its contributing MP II 9 263 12
situation, no reasonable hindrance to a perfect friendship. MP II 9 263 16
Every thing natural, probable, reasonable was against it; MP II 13 305 26
they were--though very reasonable in themselves, with ill- MP III 8 390 8
I dare say I was not reasonable in carrying with me hopes MP III 13 420 2
a reasonable period from Edmund's marrying Mary. MP III 17 467 19
where a reasonable quantity of accomplishments were sold E I 3 21 5
were sold at a reasonable price, and where girls might be E I 3 21 5
John loves Emma with a reasonable and therefore not a E I 5 40 23
any hesitations that a reasonable prudence might E I 8 67 57
and more than a reasonable, becoming degree of prudence, E I 8 67 57
the time she judged it reasonable to have done with her E I 10 88 33
but it seemed to her reasonable that at Harriet's age, and E I 17 142 11
reasonable excuse for not hurrying on the wretched moment. E II 2 165 9
A reasonable visit paid, Mr. Weston began to move.-- E II 5 193 36

And there was time enough for Emma to form a reasonable E II 6 196 2
do, as our hours are so reasonable, and yet get home E II 7 209 10
a natural and reasonable admiration--but without E II 15 282 4
Yes, I am sure you are much too reasonable. E II 16 295 33
her nephew in the most reasonable dependence--and Mrs. E III 6 361 41
and regret, in a reasonable way, that he should be so late. E III 6 364 59
friends; and, in a reasonable time, curiosity to know E III 9 387 12
Miss Fairfax, it was reasonable to suppose, would soon E III 12 422 20
that could be probable or reasonable, entered her brain. E III 13 431 38
A great deal of very reasonable, very just displeasure I E III 14 443 8
had there been such; but her's were all reasonable. E III 15 446 20
She immediately felt how reasonable it was, that Mrs. P III 6 49 22
confined--though any reasonable woman may be perfectly P III 8 70 54
She said all that was reasonable and proper on the P III 12 103 3
consequently it was not reasonable to expect accommodation P IV 7 174 3
She hoped to be wise and reasonable in time; but alas! P IV 7 178 25
their family been of reasonable limits to have allowed S 2 373 1
at hand to preserve their interest by reasonable attention. S 3 377 1
"With a reasonable quantity of butter spread over it, very S 10 417 1

REASONABLENESS (4)
always debating on the reasonableness of it's emotions. LS 16 269 3
taste which marked the reasonableness of that attachment. NA I 6 39 1
Elinor felt all the reasonableness of the idea, and it SS III 7 314 21
of the degree of her own regard, nor of its reasonableness. PP I 6 22 7

REASONABLY (25)
All this sounds very reasonably. LS 15 267 7
be reasonably looked for in the course of a twelvemonth. LS 42 313 8
that she was most reasonably encouraged to expect another NA I 9 60 1
It did come, and exactly when it might be reasonably NA II 11 212 17
sanguine, and he might reasonably hope to live many years, SS I 1 4 4
only such as might be reasonably expected of you; for SS I 2 12 24
had reasonably forfeited by their shameless want of taste. SS I 7 35 9
quarrel could most reasonably account for, though when she SS I 15 77 19
might be as reasonably tried on herself as on her sister. SS II 8 198 29
make your situation pleasant, might be reasonably expected. SS II 11 222 11
This was enough to make Lucy really and reasonably happy. SS II 14 254 26
in general, not less reasonably excited, now less properly SS III 3 284 24
Beyond that, had you endeavoured, however reasonably, to SS III 11 351 9
Mrs. Ferrars at first reasonably endeavoured to dissuade SS III 14 373 3
the days till she might reasonably hope to hear again. PP I 23 128 10
of which his wife might reasonably be ashamed, which PP II 5 156 4
sister's absence, I may reasonably hope to have all my PP II 19 237 4
of her fate, may be reasonably looked up to, as one of the PP III 15 362 14
other home that may reasonably promise her greater MP II 11 285 13
from the Frasers that could be reasonably expected. MP III 13 420 2
knew herself, and could reasonably combine, she was soon MP III 16 449 7
no judgment, it may be reasonably supposed that their MP III 17 465 14
in its best, might reasonably please a young man who had E II 8 221 49
earlier prosperity than could be reasonably calculated on. P III 4 29 8
who might very reasonably wish for her original thirty S 3 376 1

EASONED (7)
till the very last, if I reasoned with her, she declared NA II 10 202 7
He still reasoned with her, but in vain. MP I 9 96 76
not have relinquished without pain; and thus he reasoned. MP II 3 201 22
had been silent--he had reasoned--she had ridiculed--and MP II 10 279 21
So reasoned Edmund, till his father made him the confident MP III 6 368 8
too great; but no, he reasoned and talked in vain; she P III 12 109 32
"Perhaps I ought to have reasoned thus," he replied, "but P IV 11 244 74

EASONING (7)
feel the truth of this reasoning, & will hereby learn to LS 14 265 4
Catherine had nothing to oppose against such reasoning; NA I 6 43 44
"Ah! Elinor," said John, "your reasoning is very good, but SS III 5 296 20
ridiculous, contained much good sense and solid reasoning. PP III 15 361 2
His displeasure against herself she trusted, reasoning MP III 16 452 14
Your reasoning carry my judgment along with them entirely. E II 8 219 42
"I cannot possibly do without Anne," was Mary's reasoning; P III 5 33 7
reasonings of family partiality, or a desire of revenge." NA II 12 219 15
Such were my reasonings, as, in a sort of desperate SS III 8 329 63
Such and such-like were the reasonings of Sir Thomas-- MP II 3 201 22
which required all the reasonings and soothings and E II 13 267 9
in view that her gentle reasonings should be employed in E III 17 465 28
Alas! with all her reasonings, she found, that to P III 7 60 29

EASONS (22)
I should be glad to hear your reasons for disbeleiving Mr LS 12 261 5
Poor woman! tho' I have reasons enough for my dislike, I LS 15 266 2
cannot have all my reasons for rejoicing in such an event. LS 20 277 5
accuse me of instability, without first hearing my reasons. LS 30 299 1
he remain here; you know my reasons--propriety & so forth. LS 31 302 1
not from a variety of reasons how to part with her LS 42 312 5
I have three unanswerable reasons for disliking Colonel SS I 10 52 28
The reasons for this alteration were at the same time SS I 12 59 6
Willoughby may undoubtedly have very sufficient reasons SS I 15 79 29
perhaps there may be reasons--I wish I might venture; but SS I 22 128 7
wish of renewing it; and this for more reasons than one. SS II 1 141 7
on her own account she had particular reasons to avoid. SS II 3 154 6
for me to state my reasons for marrying--and moreover for PP I 19 105 8
and he continued: "my reasons for marrying are, first, PP I 19 105 9
10
My reasons for believing it are briefly these:--it does PP I 19 108 19
"Did Mr. Darcy give you his reasons for this interference?" PP II 10 185 29
it is, for very cogent reasons, to remain in the secrecy PP III 9 320 33
"No, my dear Miss Price, and for reasons good. MP I 11 109 19
"What!"--cried Edmund, "if she knew your reasons!" MP I 15 141 20
These were her reasons--she had no better. E II 2 167 11
the offer, and for the reasons you mention; exactly as you E III 8 380 15
How quickly come the reasons for approving what we like!-- P III 2 15 15

ASSEMBLED (2)
soon after their being reassembled in the drawing-room, MP I 15 142 25
The whole party were but just reassembled in the drawing- E II 17 302 23

ASSUME (1)
Miss Dashwoods very ready to reassume their former share. SS III 1 257 1

ASSUMED (1)
Harville's countenance reassumed the serious, thoughtful P IV 11 232 12

ASSURE (1)
attentions of the General himself entirely reassure her. NA II 5 154 2

ECCA (16)
he kitchen, and see if Rebecca has put the water on; and MP III 7 379 15
cannot think what Rebecca has been about. MP III 7 379 17
oom; and I could not get Rebecca to give me any help." MP III 7 379 18
quabble between Sam and Rebecca, about the manner of MP III 7 379 19
f the second story, for his mother and for Rebecca. MP III 7 381 26
rs. Price, Rebecca, and Betsey, all went up to defend MP III 7 382 27
ll talking together, but Rebecca loudest, and the job was MP III 7 382 27
nd accordingly, when Rebecca had been prevailed on to MP III 7 385 37
etailing the faults of Rebecca, against whom Susan had MP III 7 385 38
o part with Rebecca, I should only get something worse. MP III 7 385 39
is rum and water, and Rebecca never where she ought to be. MP III 7 387 46
nto danger, or Rebecca pass by with a flower in her hat. MP III 11 408 2
reparation--and wished Rebecca would mend it; and Fanny MP III 15 439 9
f I have spoke once to Rebecca about that carpet, I am MP III 15 440 18
usan's clothes, because Rebecca took away all the boxes MP III 15 444 26
the good offices of Rebecca, every thing was rationally MP III 15 444 27

ECCA'S (5)
ould not avoid, from Rebecca's alertness in going to the MP III 10 399 2
ebecca's cookery and Rebecca's waiting, and Betsey's MP III 10 407 23
e was so little equal to Rebecca's puddings, and MP III 11 413 30
ebecca's puddings, and Rebecca's hashes, brought to table MP III 11 413 30
easy than even Rebecca's hands had first produced it. MP III 15 439 9

LLIOUS (1)
e, with her little rebellious heart & indelicate LS 22 282 6

KE (1)
very far from dreading a rebuke either from the archbishop, PP I 17 87 12

RECAL (7)
to re-consider the past, recal the words and endeavour to SS III 4 291 45
with great self-reproach, recal the tenderness which, for SS III 8 322 36
or a really new muslin in a shop window, could recal them. PP I 15 72 7
I can recal nothing worse. PP I 16 80 27
She had never been able to recal anything approaching to MP III 8 389 3
him to her mother, and recal her remembrance of the name, MP III 10 399 4
of the place, and recal the still greater within. E I 10 87 27

RECALL (9)
thing to startle and recall them to the present moment. NA II 13 228 27
or gay, I love to recall it--and you will never offend me SS I 17 92 26
again alone and able to recall the whole, she was inclined MP I 18 170 24
secured her fate beyond recall--that she had pledged MP II 3 201 23
not for the life of him recall what her dancing had been, MP II 7 251 62
I cannot recall all her words. MP III 16 454 18
She could not but recall the attempt with great E III 9 386 7
indeed!--(Harriet could not recall it without a blush.) E III 11 410 35
Nor can I exactly recall the beginning at this moment--but- S 7 397 1

RECALLED (11)
in the opposite box, recalled her to anxiety and distress. NA I 12 92 4
solicitous politeness as recalled Thorpe's information to NA I 13 102 27
dismissed her, it recalled her to the sense of what she NA II 6 164 3
Such a compliment recalled all Catherine's consciousness, NA II 11 214 25
He was recalled from wit to wisdom, not by any reproof of SS III 5 298 34
From a reverie of this kind she was recalled at the end of SS III 8 331 70
71
But the feelings of the past could not be recalled.-- SS III 11 349 1
her memory, and as she recalled his very words, it was PP II 13 205 3
minutes, was only recalled to a sense of her situation by PP III 4 278 20
She recalled her past kindness--the kindness, the E I 1 6 6
with which at last he recalled, and rather sentimentally E I 9 70 7

RECALLING (2)
breakfast, when, after recalling and commending what his MP II 8 252 1
If I had the power of recalling any one week of my MP III 5 358 9

RECANTATION (1)
or done more towards a recantation of past prejudices and E II 2 168 15

RECANTING (1)
Mr. Elliot, already recanting the sentiment she had so P IV 2 135 35

RECEDE (1)
not deceive yourself into a belief that I will ever recede. PP III 14 356 60

RECEDING (2)
to the sound of her receding footsteps as long as the last NA II 5 159 17
In the pause which succeeded, a sound like receding NA II 6 170 12

RECEIPT (11)
than hers, on the receipt of the letter--& is his LS 15 267 4
Early in February, within a fortnight from the receipt of SS II 10 216 16
months have been in the receipt of two thousand, five SS III 1 268 50
on this serenity, was the receipt of a letter from Croydon W 348 23
Come as soon as you can on the receipt of this. PP I 7 30 17
sister justified by the receipt of two letters from her at PP III 4 273 1
cows, and given her the receipt for a famous cream cheese; MP I 10 103 50
Within a few days from the receipt of Edmund's letter, MP III 13 425 7
8
what followed the receipt of the next letters from London. MP III 16 450 10
She promised Wright a receipt, and never sent it." E III 16 458 42
mark them excepting the receipt of a note or two from Lyme, P IV 1 125 14

RECEIVE (95)
to you & Mrs Vernon to receive me at present, I shall hope LS 1 243 1
were not in your power to receive me. Yr most obliged LS 1 244 1
we should at some future period be obliged to receive her. LS 3 246 1
Vernon on being about to receive into your family, the LS 4 248 1
& of course I cannot receive that pleasure from the length LS 8 255 1
I have reason to imagine that she did receive serious LS 14 265 4
her life, than a beauty from her cradle can ever receive. NA I 1 15 2
ready to give than to receive information, and each NA I 4 32 2
To receive so flattering an invitation! NA II 2 140 8
Being no longer able however to receive pleasure from the NA II 7 181 41
back in half a minute to receive a strict charge against NA II 7 181 41
three terriers, was ready to receive and make much of them. NA II 11 212 17
"No, Eleanor, if you are not allowed to receive a letter NA II 13 228 29
by habitual suffering, to receive and enjoy felicity. NA II 16 251 5
which his age could receive; and the cheerfulness of the SS I 1 3 1
She could consult with her brother, could receive her SS I 1 7 13
she never appeared to receive more enjoyment from them, SS I 11 55 6
all, build a stable to receive them, she had accepted the SS I 12 58 1
in a more lasting home, Queen Mab shall receive you." SS I 12 59 6
Middleton, "that I should receive this letter today, for SS I 13 64 19
middle of her story, to receive the rest of the party; SS I 19 106 21
that she was very soon to receive a visit from two girls SS I 21 118 2
she knew she could receive no assistance, while her self- SS II 1 141 6
would neither receive encouragement from their example nor SS II 1 141 6
she scarcely expected to receive any support in her SS II 3 154 6
equally ill-disposed to receive or communicate pleasure. SS II 5 171 30
I wish you may receive this in time to come here to-night, SS II 7 187 38
and I hope very soon to receive your personal assurance of SS II 7 187 40
that Marianne should not receive the first notice of it SS II 10 217 16
just in time to receive and support her as she entered it. SS III 9 333 3
behind Emma, to receive the Compts of some acquaintance, & W 329 9
off without being able to receive his uncle's suffrage.-- W 332 11
he had been used to receive from her sisters, & gave him W 335 13
was not unwilling to receive it, when she instantly drew PP I 6 26 38
"that Miss Bennet shall receive every possible attention PP I 9 41 5
"How delighted Miss Darcy will be to receive such a letter! PP I 10 47 3
not bring herself to receive them with pleasure before. PP I 12 59 1
If you should have no objection to receive me into your PP I 13 63 12
subject I shall hope to receive a more favourable answer PP I 19 108 16
17
I have been hoping to receive; and you may be very certain PP I 22 123 5
it, you will speedily receive from me a letter of thanks PP I 22 124 10
and not a note, not a line, did I receive in the mean time. PP II 3 148 26
Who could have imagined that we should receive an PP II 6 160 2
Her ladyship, with great condescension, arose to receive PP II 6 161 10
She found that she was to receive no other answer--and, PP II 9 177 6
7
she was convinced, would receive a deeper wound from the PP II 10 187 40
for the pain he was to receive; till, roused to resentment PP II 11 189 6
That she should receive an offer of marriage from Mr. PP II 11 193 31
receive it, and accepted in return three thousand pounds. PP II 12 201 5
But as Elizabeth could not receive comfort from any such PP II 17 228 30
He protested that she should receive from him no mark of PP III 8 310 10
and so mildly, to receive her and her husband at Longbourn, PP III 8 314 22
were assembled in the breakfast room, to receive them. PP III 9 315 2
her inquiries would receive any satisfaction, she had PP III 9 320 35
and had she been able to receive them into her house, they PP III 10 322 2
could be prevailed on to receive her, offering his PP III 10 322 2
and all money matters were then to receive the last finish. PP III 10 324 2
obligations to a person who could never receive a return. PP III 10 326 3
alluded, as to make her receive with gratitude and PP III 16 366 8
that I did not expect to receive more than my due." PP III 16 370 31
Though Darcy could never receive him at Pemberley, yet, PP III 19 387 9
could never receive kindness without wishing to return it. MP I 3 26 29
only just large enough to receive herself and her servants, MP I 3 28 38
Mr. Rushworth was at the door to receive his fair lady, MP I 9 84 1
to receive Mr. Rushworth's parting attentions as she ought. MP I 10 105 52
All this may be stamped on it; and that house receive such MP II 7 244 27
to receive ordination in the course of the Christmas week. MP II 8 255 10
from him; she might never receive another; it was MP II 9 265 19
that she ever should receive another so perfectly MP II 9 265 19
uncle, hear his voice, receive his questions, and even MP II 11 284 8
She was really glad to receive the letter when it did come. MP III 9 393 1
I shall be at Portsmouth the morning after you receive MP III 15 442 23

You are his object--and you will soon receive the	E I 9 73 20
Receive it on my judgment.	E I 9 74 23
Harriet turned away; but Emma could receive him with the	E I 9 81 78
to receive her assistance in the most comfortable manner.	E I 10 89 38
at last the drawing-room party did receive an augmentation.	E I 15 124 1
This lesson, she very much feared, they would receive only	E II 7 207 6
delighted to see her and receive her approbation, very	E II 11 253 40
think it as much her duty as Mrs. Weston's to receive them.	E III 2 322 18
Jane was resolved to receive no kindness form her.	E III 9 391 21
means Hartfield would receive the constant addition of	E III 17 465 28
counsel, they would never receive any of such certain	P III 4 29 8
was delighted to receive him; while a thousand feelings	P III 7 59 25
must return in time to receive their younger children for	P IV 2 129 1
The Musgroves came back to receive their happy boys and	P IV 2 133 27
the hope of seeing him receive the hand of her beloved	P IV 5 161 30
Anne did not receive the perfect conviction which the	P IV 6 173 48
Anne could command herself enough to receive that look,	P IV 11 239 55
but to have no family to receive and estimate him properly;	P IV 12 251 10
Excepting two journeys to London in the year, to receive	S 2 373 1
better if she could--to receive every possible pleasure	S 2 374 1
whom Lady D. had been induced to receive into her family.	S 3 377 1
Not a shilling do I receive from the denham estate.	S 7 400 1
having no house large enough to receive such a family.--	S 9 408 1
RECEIVED (265)	
girl of sixteen who has received so wretched an education	LS 3 247 1
I received your note my dear Alicia, just before I left	LS 5 249 1
at Langford, such as he received from a gentleman who knew	LS 8 255 1
My dear sir I have this moment received your letter,	LS 14 263 1
good opinion merits a better return than it has received.	LS 14 265 5
Lady Susan had received a line from him by that day's post	LS 17 269 1
the idea of the meeting, received her with perfect self-	LS 17 269 2
I have received yours, & have engaged the lodgings in	LS 28 298 2
I have received your letter; & tho' I do not attempt to	LS 30 299 1
Since we parted yesterday, I have received from	LS 34 304 1
I received my information in Mr Johnson's house, from Mrs	LS 34 304 1
on reading the note, this moment received from you.	LS 35 304 1
for the hospitality with which you were received into it!	LS 36 305 1
After some time they received an offer of tea from one of	NA I 2 23 22
These powers received due admiration from Catherine, to	NA I 4 33 7
friend, from whom she received every possible	NA I 5 36 2
was wholly unexpected, received her brother with the	NA I 7 44 4
from him she directly received the amends which were her	NA I 7 45 5
mother's heart, for she received him with the most	NA I 7 49 43
received from him the smiling tribute of recognition.	NA I 8 54 4
to her father, and received by him with such ready, such	NA I 13 102 27
party, received the delightful confession of an equal love.	NA I 15 117 8
she was most politely received by General Tilney, and	NA II 1 129 1
James Morland's second letter was then received, and the	NA II 1 135 42
James soon followed his letter, and was received with the	NA II 1 137 50
an offer, and that you received his advances in the	NA II 3 144 10
could think of it; he could not have received my last."	NA II 3 146 16
forth;--the first three received a ready affirmative, the	NA II 7 180 37
witness to her having received every possible attention	NA II 9 197 25
He gladly received the letter; and, having read it through,	NA II 10 205 24
the carriage again received them; and so gratifying had	NA II 11 215 28
my dearest Catherine, I received your two kind letters	NA II 12 216 1, 2
attentions you would have received but half what you ought.	NA II 13 224 18
had passed, an apology might properly be received by her.	NA II 13 227 27
She was received by the Allens with all the kindness which	NA II 14 237 21
by his appearance, received him with the simple	NA II 15 242 7
and whenever Catherine received a letter, as, at that time,	NA II 16 250 3
her loss, he invited and received into his house the	SS I 1 3 1
years, he had received from his niece and her daughters.	SS I 1 4 3
or received, was to her a source of immoveable disgust.	SS I 1 6 9
of good weather, they received an impression in its favour	SS I 6 28 2
received additional charms from his voice and expression.	SS I 9 42 9
received particular spirit from his exterior attractions.--	SS I 9 43 11
He was received by Mrs. Dashwood with more than politeness;	SS I 10 46 1
he ought, and you have received every assurance of his	SS I 10 47 4
I have just received my dispatches, and taken my farewel	SS I 15 76 6
He received the kindest welcome from her; and shyness,	SS I 17 90 1
than by those which we received from them a few weeks ago.	SS I 19 109 42
but her powers had received no aid from education, she was	SS I 22 127 2
happiness whenever she received a letter from Edward, it	SS II 2 151 42
Mrs. Jennings received the refusal with some surprize, and	SS II 3 153 1
Mrs. Jennings received the information with a great deal	SS II 3 157 19
hard to say whether she received most pleasure from	SS II 4 164 21
concern them both; she received no pleasure from any thing;	SS II 4 165 24
they received no mark of recognition on their entrance.	SS II 5 171 30
Have you not received my letters?	SS II 6 176 7
"But have you not received my notes?" cried Marianne in	SS II 6 177 10
only that Marianne had received a letter from Willoughby,	SS II 7 181 7
at not having received any answer to a note which I sent	SS II 7 187 39, 40
without knowing that she received warmth from one, or	SS II 7 190 55, 56
me," was all the notice that her sister received from her.	SS II 8 197 24
It was forwarded to me from Delaford, and I received it on	SS II 9 209 30
She received the news with resolute composure; made no	SS II 10 217 17
The ivory, the gold and the pearls, all received their	SS II 11 221 5
the Miss Dashwoods were, received his eager civilities	SS II 12 230 6
them; and after they had received the gratifying testimony	SS II 12 235 28
her toilette, which it received from Miss Steele in the	SS II 14 249 8
with both her friends, received a very warm invitation	SS III 3 279 1
in which Elinor received her brother's congratulations on	SS III 6 301 1
of his concerns, she now received intelligence from	SS III 6 305 16
"Remember," cried Willoughby, "from whom you received the	SS III 8 322 36
a letter that morning received from Mrs. Jennings declared	SS III 8 330 69
and how he was received, need not be particularly told.	SS III 13 361 3
the only letter I ever received from her, of which the	SS III 13 365 17
not a line has been received from him on the occasion.	SS III 13 371 38, 39
They settled in town, received very liberal assistance	SS III 14 377 11
girls were received, with now & then a fresh gentleman	W 328 8
From Miss Osborne & Miss Carr she received something like	W 336 13
"I received that note from the fair hands of Miss Watson	W 338 18
more surprise than he received, when instead of being	W 355 28
and from none received either attention or pleasure.	PP I 4 16 15
By Jane this attention was received with the greatest	PP I 6 21 1
"Yes, indeed, and received no inconsiderable pleasure from	PP I 6 25 30
She was received, however, very politely by them; and in	PP I 7 33 42
which she very early received from Mr. Bingley by a	PP I 9 41 1
which her praises were received, formed a curious dialogue,	PP I 10 47 2
Miss Bingley warmly resented the indignity he had received,	PP I 10 51 40
of her dear friend Jane, received some assistance from her	PP I 10 52 53
"About a month ago I received this letter, and about a	PP I 13 61 6
the subject, for having received ordination at Easter, I	PP I 13 62 12
weeks since they had received pleasure from the society of	PP I 13 64 20
Mr. Collins was punctual to his time, and was received	PP I 13 64 21
She received him with her very best politeness, which he	PP I 15 73 11
for she had not only received him with the utmost civility,	PP I 15 74 13
he received at the other table between Elizabeth and Lydia.	PP I 16 76 8
Mr. Darcy than he has received; and I am sorry to say that	PP I 18 95 50
"This account then is what he has received from Mr. Darcy.	PP I 18 96 53
Mr. Collins received and returned these felicitations with	PP I 20 110 1
Charlotte's first letters were received with a good deal	PP II 3 146 19
coming, when she found herself so affectionately received.	PP II 5 155 3
however, before they received any invitation thither, for	PP II 8 172 1
Her ladyship received them civilly, but it was plain that	PP II 8 172 2
Elizabeth received them with all the forbearance of	PP II 8 176 30
which it had hardly received on the first perusal.	PP II 11 188 1
recital which I received many months ago from Mr. Wickham.	PP II 11 191 17
that though she received his attentions with pleasure, she	PP II 12 197 5
designs on Miss Darcy, received some confirmation from	PP II 13 206 4
whom she had previously received the information of his	PP II 13 206 4
she had received, must make her feel the obliged.	PP II 15 215 3
for the kindness he had received at Longbourn in the	PP II 15 217 8
cleared away; for she received an invitation from Mrs.	PP II 18 230 11
on his approach, received his compliments with an	PP III 1 251 52
In this room they were received by Miss Darcy, who was	PP III 3 267 3
"By this time, my dearest sister, you have received my	PP III 4 274 5
dreadful news which I have just received from Longbourn."	PP III 4 277 10
conversation together, received them exactly as might be	PP III 5 287 34
on Tuesday, his wife received a letter from him; it told	PP III 6 295 5
which, as Jane had received directions to open all that	PP III 6 296 10
Mr. Gardiner did not write again, till he had received an	PP III 6 297 12
Elizabeth had received none since her return, that could	PP III 6 298 16
Elizabeth received her congratulations amongst the rest,	PP III 7 307 50
ago, would now have been gladly and gratefully received!	PP III 8 311 14
she must have received benefit of greater importance.	PP III 8 312 15
off for the north, received at first an absolute negative.	PP III 8 313 22
Mr. Wickham had received his commission before he left	PP III 9 318 17
"I have just received your letter, and shall devote this	PP III 10 321 2
that he had been received and noticed as he was.	PP III 10 324 2
The housekeeper at Netherfield had received orders to	PP III 11 331 13
increased; yet she received them with tolerable ease, and	PP III 11 335 39
He was received by Mrs. Bennet with a degree of civility,	PP III 11 335 41
offer no compensation, received soon afterwards material	PP III 11 337 56
that Bingley had received his sanction to be happy, had	PP III 12 340 12
she yet received pleasure from observing his behaviour.	PP III 12 340 13
high importance, received her with the utmost politeness.	PP III 14 351 4
He then said, "I have received a letter this morning that	PP III 15 362 9, 10
at hearing that you received the young couple into your	PP III 15 363 22
and the person who received it, are now so widely	PP III 16 368 23
question which Elizabeth received from Jane as soon as she	PP III 17 372 1
The congratulatory letter which Elizabeth received from	PP III 19 386 6
Her mind received knowledge which had never before fallen	PP III 19 388 11
which its woods had received, not merely from the presence	PP III 19 388 12
Sir Thomas and Lady Bertram received her very kindly, and	MP I 2 12 2
She had never received kindness from her aunt Norris, and	MP I 3 25 10
a favourable voyage, was received; though not before Mrs.	MP I 4 34 2
consent could be received; but in the mean while, as no	MP I 4 39 12
society of the village received an addition in the brother	MP I 4 40 15
up; and Mrs. Grant received in those whom she hoped to	MP I 4 41 17
assurances we have so often received to the contrary."	MP I 6 57 33
party, and had directly received a very sufficient	MP I 8 79 23
but this was scarcely received as an amendment; the young	MP I 9 84 2
but was very graciously received, and Julia's day was	MP I 10 105 52
and the carpenter had received his orders and taken his	MP I 14 130 1
help coming, and were received with the most grateful joy.	MP I 15 142 25
of present upon present that she had received from them.	MP I 16 153 3
from a young man's being received in this manner--	MP I 16 154 14
and that had she received even the greatest, she could	MP I 17 160 6
Sir Thomas received Mr. Yates with all the appearance of	MP II 1 183 23
sure I can answer for your being kindly received by both.	MP II 7 245 32
and I have only just now received it at Northampton.	MP II 9 261 2
which she had ever received from him; she might never	MP II 9 265 19
after, and should have received a partner only through a	MP II 10 274 8
Her praise was warm, and he received it as she could wish,	MP II 10 276 14
She will be disappointed if she received nothing from you.	MP II 13 306 28
far as I understand), received as much encouragement to	MP III 1 315 18
and though you always received them very properly, (I have	MP III 1 316 29
He then saw Mr. Crawford, and received his account.--	MP III 2 329 11
every encouragement received with grateful joy, and the	MP III 2 329 13
for having received such an offer, than for refusing it.	MP III 2 332 20
which Fanny had ever received from her aunt in the course	MP III 2 333 27
I received an impression which will never be got over."	MP III 4 349 25
received at the end of about ten years' happy marriage."	MP III 4 354 46
Had I received any letter from Mansfield, to tell me how	MP III 4 354 50
Oh! you received it just as it was meant.	MP III 5 362 18
her, Mr. Price now received his daughter; and, having	MP III 7 380 22
The only interruption which thoughts like these received	MP III 7 383 30
contentment as she received from introductions either to	MP III 9 395 3
The first solid consolation which Fanny received for the	MP III 9 395 4
they had received notice by express, a few hours before.	MP III 13 426 9
security, till she received a few lines from Edmund,	MP III 14 429 1
was received to revive old, and create some new sensations.	MP III 14 433 12
The horror of a mind like Fanny's, as it received the	MP III 15 440 19
catching his eye, received an affectionate smile, which	MP III 15 445 34
Lady Bertram nor Tom had received from her the smallest	MP III 16 448 2
By her other aunt, Susan was received with quiet kindness.	MP III 16 448 3
Street, Sir Thomas had received a letter from an old and	MP III 16 450 8
He had received a note from Lady Stornaway to beg him to	MP III 16 454 18
desirous of being really received into the family, was	MP III 17 462 4
had her received at home, and countenanced by them all.	MP III 17 464 13
He saw Mrs. Rushworth, was received by her with a coldness	MP III 17 467 20
He had received a good education, but on succeeding early	E I 2 15 1
mention of the handsome letter Mrs. Weston had received.	E I 2 18 9
are infinitely superior to what she received from nature."	E I 6 42 2
deposit!" said he with a tender sigh, as he received it.	E I 6 49 43
to think he must have received a different account of	E I 13 114 28
and the encouragement I received"----- "encouragement!--I	E I 15 132 35, 36
and understanding had received every advantage of	E II 2 164 6
For it is not five minutes since I received Mrs. Cole's	E II 3 173 27
They had received her doubtingly, if not coolly; and	E II 5 186 4
family from whom he had received such a blessing must be	E II 5 192 28
Donwell and Randalls had received their invitation, and	E II 7 207 7
She was received with a cordial respect which could not	E II 8 214 12
That very dear part of Emma, her fancy, received an	E II 8 214 13
congratulations were received, the blush of guilt which	E II 8 220 45
He had said that Jane Fairfax received attentions from Mrs.	E II 16 291 5
Mrs. Elton's looks also received the due share of censure.	E III 2 330 46
which made the information she received more valuable.	E III 4 340 28
The invitation was every where so well received, that it	E III 6 357 31
Mrs. Elton had received notice of it that morning, and was	E III 6 359 37
&c. and Emma received a smile which seemed to say, "these	E III 6 361 40
favour, as if his eyes received the truth from her's, and	E III 9 385 7
Short letters from Frank were received at Randall's,	E III 9 388 15
voice, whether Harriet could indeed have received any hint.	E III 11 404 5
of the notice she had received from him, a look, a speech,	E III 11 409 35
She had received a very recent proof of its impartiality.--	E III 12 415 1
She was sensible that you had never received any proper	E III 12 420 12
be received with gratitude; and the other--what was she?--	E III 12 421 17
was pained by the manner in which they had been received.	E III 13 424 1
had been all received as discouragement from herself.--	E III 13 430 38
He had despaired at one period; he had received such an	E III 13 431 38
articles of news he had received from Mr. Perry, and	E III 14 434 3
She received my attentions with an easy, friendly,	E III 14 438 8
We removed to Windsor; and two days afterwards I received	E III 14 442 8
was, that he should be received at Hartfield; that so long	E III 15 449 31
baby, and Mr. Woodhouse received the thanks for coming,	E III 18 476 44
The happiness of this most happy day, received its	E III 18 480 80
all the honour, and received none: Elizabeth would, one	P III 1 6 10
be transmitted whole and entire, as he had received it.	P III 1 10 20
She had never received from her more than outward	P III 2 16 16
received a hint of the Admiral from a London correspondent.	P III 3 21 18
pardonable pride, received it as a most unfortunate one.	P III 4 26 2
received any information of their short-lived engagement.--	P III 4 30 10
young 'squire, it had received the improvement of a farm-	P III 5 36 20
They were received with great cordiality.	P III 5 41 46
and mother had ever received from him during the whole of	P III 6 51 30

received in the back, as roused the most alarming ideas. P III 7 53 3
It was Mary's hope and belief, that he had received a P III 10 82 2
She received no other answer, than an artificial, P III 10 86 20
a severe wound which he received two years before, and P III 11 94 6
him in the passage, and received his very polite excuses, P III 12 106 19
The head had received a severe contusion, but he had seen P III 12 112 52
but then, she had received so very handsome an apology P IV 2 129 3
however, in the welcome she received, did her good. P IV 3 137 2
of solicitude to be received as a relation again, that P IV 3 138 6
an interval of so many years, to be well received by them. P IV 3 140 11
Anne drew a little back, while the others received his P IV 3 143 18
and entreated to be received as an acquaintance already. P IV 3 143 18
letter of condolence was received at Kellynch, and, P IV 4 149 12
of those who having only received "the best education in P IV 5 155 9
"I shall be surprised at least if you ever received a " P IV 6 164 8
to feel for him, would have received the same compliment. P IV 6 167 19
She had received ideas which disposed her to be courteous P IV 8 184 17
He had many years ago received such a description of Miss P IV 8 187 34
but scarcely had she received their sound, than her P IV 8 188 37
received the idea, or from whom she could have heard it. P IV 9 197 34
"Dear Smith, I have received yours. P IV 9 203 72
The scheme had received its first impulse by Captain P IV 10 216 19
she could not have received a more gratifying attention. P IV 10 220 29
in which it had been received, a manner of doubtful P IV 10 226 65
At Lyme, he had received lessons of more than one sort. P IV 11 242 62
His courtesies were received with good-breeding & S 1 365 1
was discovered to have received such injury on the fallen S 1 370 1
& friendliness was received as it ought--as there was not S 2 371 1
& attention she received from every body--found her good S 3 378 1
while Charlotte having received possession of her S 4 384 1
How clara received it, was less obvious--but she was S 7 395 1

RECEIVES (3)
because she does not accept the first offer she receives? E I 8 64 46
But (with a reproachful smile at Emma) she receives E II 15 286 18
for the refreshment the mind receives in doing it's duty.-- S 9 410 1

RECEIVING (78)
vernon milkiness; but on receiving the letter in which I LS 16 268 1
interference, & that on receiving her letter he had LS 22 281 5
receiving it so favourably, & for the rest of his conduct. LS 25 293 4
of his gig; and then receiving her friend's parting good NA I 9 62 7
for causes unknown, and receiving from the pitiless hands NA II 8 187 16
trifling circumstance receiving importance from an NA II 10 199 2
declared her to be receiving unpleasant news; and Henry, NA II 10 202 8
of her, and of receiving, in her behaviour to himself, the SS I 11 53 1
the propriety of her receiving such a present from a man SS I 12 58 3
I had the pleasure of receiving the information of your SS II 6 177 11
just had the honour of receiving your letter, for which I SS II 7 183 13
will be, Willoughby, on receiving this; and I think you SS II 7 186 38
that the power of receiving it had been made over some SS II 9 207 26
put an end to his visit, receiving from her again the same SS II 9 211 43
of Mrs. Dashwood on receiving and answering Elinor's SS II 10 212 2
life than she was on receiving Mrs. John Dashwood's card. SS II 12 231 9
in meeting them, and on receiving encouragement from the SS III 2 271 5
give Edward the pain of receiving an obligation from her, SS III 3 283 20
as possible, "without receiving our good wishes, even if SS III 4 288 28
altered looks, and in receiving the pale hand which she SS III 10 340 2
the improvements it was receiving, he was happily employed PP I 16 75 3
from Meryton; and, after receiving her answer, asked in an PP I 16 77 8
flattered by receiving the invitation from Mr. Bingley PP I 17 86 10
close; for Mary, on receiving amongst the thanks of the PP I 18 100 68
confusion here on receiving so direct a reproach; though, PP I 22 124 14
15
had the pleasure of receiving her brother and his wife, PP II 2 139 2
I spoke to him twice myself, without receiving an answer. PP II 2 141 9
nor was her manner of receiving them, such as to make her PP II 6 162 11
Lady Catherine seemed quite astonished at not receiving a PP II 6 166 38
"Be not alarmed, madam, on receiving this letter, by the PP II 12 196 4
to the living, of his receiving in lieu, so considerable a PP II 13 205 3
not leave the house without receiving her thanks for it. PP II 15 215 2
they had descended, receiving increased abruptness form PP III 1 246 5
Elizabeth was roused by receiving from her a cold enquiry PP III 3 268 5
When he was gone, they were certain at least of receiving PP III 6 294 2
I will not encourage the impudence of either, by receiving PP III 8 310 9
Elizabeth had the satisfaction of receiving an answer to PP III 10 321 1
for the first time after receiving his explanatory letter. PP III 11 334 36
Instead of receiving any such letter of excuse from his PP III 16 365 1
The joy which Miss Darcy expressed on receiving similar PP III 18 383 25
the addition it was ever receiving in the consideration of MP I 4 37 8
looked almost aghast under the new idea she was receiving. MP I 9 89 26
was doubtless receiving all the compliments it called for. MP I 14 136 21
tea, when the bustle of receiving Sir Thomas were over and MP II 1 177 5
had the pleasure of receiving in his protege, certainly a MP II 6 233 16
In every meeting there was a hope of receiving farther MP II 8 256 13
pretence of receiving the note, was coming towards her. MP II 13 307 32
will prevent you from receiving things only in part, and MP III 1 313 12
of my daughters, on receiving a proposal of marriage at MP III 1 319 39
and he found himself receiving a welcome, unquestionably MP III 3 334 1
persuaded herself into receiving his addresses properly, MP III 5 356 3
way, though with no advantage of manner in receiving her. MP III 7 377 9
letter from town after receiving this, than she had been MP III 12 418 5
and again; they were receiving frequent accounts from MP III 13 427 12
On receiving it, she could instantly decide on its MP III 15 437 2
of a young woman on receiving the assurance of that MP III 17 471 28
to promise; but you were receiving a very good education E I 5 38 11
wanted drawing out, and receiving a few, very few hints. E I 6 42 3
After receiving a very indifferent education she is left E I 8 62 42
he was in the habit of receiving, to emulate the "very E I 13 113 27
exciting or receiving unpleasant and most unsuitable ideas. E I 16 138 17
suffer in winter, and receiving no other answer than a E II 1 155 1
Her regard was receiving strength by invariable praise of E II 4 184 10
again; and Miss Smith receiving her summons, was with her E II 5 186 3
the compliments she was receiving on her voice and her E II 8 229 99
It was an awkward ceremony at any time to be receiving E II 14 271 5
formerly; but without receiving any benefit; and Mr. Perry, E II 14 275 31
He looked with smiling penetration; and, on receiving no E III 2 330 48
as she was for ever receiving from yourself and your E III 7 375 59
receiving, is what my conscience tells me ought not to be. E III 12 419 8
the happiest; she, in receiving his declarations and P III 4 26 1
receiving hints to exert it, beyond what was practicable. P III 6 44 7
her so; and Anne, in receiving her compliments on the P IV 1 124 10
on the present occasion, receiving her in that house, P IV 1 126 19
infirm, helpless widow, receiving the visit of her former P IV 5 153 6
had been too quick in receiving them as the certain result P IV 12 249 3
or suggest anything--& receiving her first real comfort S 1 364 1
who supported herself by receiving such great girls & S 11 420 1

RECENT (25)
now be clearer than the absurdity of her recent fancies. NA II 7 173 2
the effect of some recent alterations about the tea-house, NA II 7 179 27
by the failure of a very recent endeavour to accomplish a NA II 15 246 12
Her partiality for this gentleman was not of recent origin; NA II 16 251 5
or for spirits depressed by recent disappointment? SS I 15 78 28
recent meeting--and this she had every reason to expect. SS II 13 245 47
news and happiness by the recent arrival of a militia PP I 7 28 3
"And which of the two do you call my little recent piece PP I 10 48 26
two eldest, from their recent absence, were particularly PP I 15 73 11
With a glance she saw, that he had lost none of his recent PP III 1 254 57
Every thing was too recent for gaiety, but the evening PP III 17 377 41
than heretofore, by some recent losses on his West India MP I 3 24 7
to see other symptoms of recent habitation, and a general MP II 1 182 22
She gave the history of her recent visit, and now her MP II 9 262 11
Their being so new and so recent was all in their MP III 4 354 46
all her recent agitation, she hardly knew how to bear it. MP III 7 382 28
There was not only the debility of recent illness to MP III 14 430 2
all to the recent event, took her hand, and said in a low, MP III 15 446 34
favourable state which a recent disappointment gives, MP III 17 470 27
had to instance, the most recent, and therefore most E I 12 104 50
She had received a very recent proof of its impartiality.-- E III 12 415 1
Miss Fairfax's recent illness had offered a fair plea for E III 12 418 5
in much too strong and recent alarm to bear the thought; P III 7 55 5
To have been described long ago to a recent acquaintance, P IV 8 187 33
Her recent good offices by Anne had been enough in P IV 12 251 11

RECENTLY (11)
a notion that has recently struck me, your kind impression LS 18 272 1
that suspicion in his mind which had recently entered it. SS III 4 290 36
Emma Watson who was very recently returned to her family W 315 1
of a young man who had recently succeeded to one of the MP I 4 38 9
and that friend having recently had his grounds laid out MP I 6 52 1
"no" and the "yes" had been very recently in alternation. MP II 8 255 12
of being very recently closed, a volume of Shakespeare.-- MP III 3 336 9
the wife he had so very recently lost; and everybody E III 11 403 2
of all that had so recently passed on Harriet's side, so E III 18 473 27
you know, when they have recently escaped from severe pain, P IV 5 155 9
from Charles that, very recently, (since Mary's last P IV 10 217 20

RECENTLY-IMPROVED (1)
Henrietta was exactly in that state of recently-improved P IV 10 220 31

RECEPTION (31)
reason to complain of my reception from Mr Vernon; but I LS 5 249 1
the encouragement of his reception, to which every day SS I 10 48 7
them give way to the reception of more general opinions." SS I 11 56 12
of regard in her reception of him than even Elinor herself. SS I 16 87 23
coldness, reserve could not stand against such a reception. SS I 17 90 1
of his reception, and consious that he merited no kind one. SS III 12 359 11
he did not, upon the whole, expect a very cruel reception. SS III 13 366 20
After a cordial reception of Emma, he turned to his W 323 3
attack Mr. Darcy, whose reception of his advances she PP I 18 97 61
you," said he, "to be dissatisfied with my reception. PP I 18 98 62
His reception however was of the most flattering kind. PP I 22 121 1
fortnight, but his reception at Longbourn was not quite so PP I 23 129 15
by preparations for the reception of his bride, as he had PP II 2 139 1
Their reception at home was most kind. PP II 16 222 19
Georgiana's reception of them was very civil; but attended PP III 3 267 3
Their reception from Mr. Bennet, to whom they then turned, PP III 9 315 4
I came to you without a doubt of my reception. PP III 16 369 24
Mr. Rushworth was not forgotten; a most friendly reception MP II 1 179 8
address; and Fanny's reception of it was so proper and MP II 7 246 37
went on, after a civil reception, a short sentence about MP II 13 298 1
Her reception of him was of a sort which he could not have MP III 3 334 2
was altered; my first reception was so unlike what I had MP III 13 421 2
and her very kind reception of himself, as was an E II 5 191 28
silence in their first reception, and the warmest E III 12 418 5
as if no other reception of her were felt sufficient.-- E III 16 452 8
spread farther, and other persons' reception of it tried. E III 17 465 28
most bewitching in his reception there; the old were so P III 9 73 1
made but a mortifying reception of Anne; or must at least P III 12 115 68
She was sure of a pleasant reception; and her friend P IV 9 192 4
adapted for Clara's reception;--but the expense alas! of S 8 405 2
Nothing cd be kinder than her reception from both husband S 9 406 1

RECESS (2)
back in a deep recess on one side of the fire-place. NA II 6 163 1
delay from her literary recess, delighted to see Mr Parker S 6 390 1

RECIPE (1)
A large income is the best recipe for happiness I ever MP II 4 213 36

RECIPROCAL (3)
and felt no doubt of its being a reciprocal enjoyment. SS I 21 120 6
If the strength of your reciprocal attachment had failed, SS II 2 147 8
seems no harm in him:"--reciprocal compliments, which P III 5 32 4

RECITAL (9)
"Certainly;" replied I, deeply sighing at the recital of LS 24 287 10
afflictions, with a recital which may seem to have been SS II 9 210 32
She managed the recital, as she hoped, with address; SS III 10 347 33
Your character was unfolded in the recital which I PP II 11 191 17
So far each recital confirmed the other: but when she came PP II 13 205 3
She was not sorry, however, to have the recital of them PP II 15 216 7
she burst through his recital with the proposal of soup. MP II 1 180 10
in the slightest particular from the original recital. E III 3 336 13
and she listened to a recital which, if it did not P IV 9 208 94

RECITALS (1)
His recitals were amusing in themselves to Sir Thomas, but MP II 6 236 21

RECITED (1)
and rather sentimentally recited, that well-known charade, E I 9 70 7

RECITING (1)
reciting kind, I think he has always a decided taste. MP I 13 126 25

RECITOR (1)
was to understand the recitor, to know the young man by MP II 6 236 21

RECKON (8)
cousin, that I do not reckon the notice and kindness of PP I 19 106 10
distance, or reckon time, with feminine lawlessness. MP I 9 94 61
Once fairly in the dock-yard, he began to reckon upon some MP III 10 403 15
How will a conundrum reckon?" E III 7 371 29
"No, no," said Emma, "it will not reckon low. E III 7 371 31
"I do not reckon the Hayters as any body. P IV 6 163 7
& think we may safely reckon on securing you two large S 5 387 1
"I hope you will eat some of this toast, said he, I reckon S 10 417 1

RECKONED (14)
Morland, it would be reckoned a cheap thing by some people, NA I 7 47 19
Now, for instance, it was reckoned a remarkable thing at NA I 9 64 24
The estate at Delaford was never reckoned more than two SS I 14 70 2
but she is in general reckoned to draw extremely well." SS II 12 234 27
were not often reckoned very like her youngest brother.-- W 324 3
He is reckoned remarkably agreable I understand.--" W 328 8
I thought turner had been reckoned an extraordinary W 352 26
Lady Catherine was reckoned proud by many people he knew, PP I 14 66 1
in that house reckoned too small for anybody's comfort. MP III 7 387 47
better end, the effect of good luck, not to be reckoned on. MP III 17 464 12
for Highbury was reckoned a particularly healthy spot: she E I 3 22 5
He was reckoned very handsome; his person much admired in E I 4 35 45
"She believed he was reckoned a very fine young man." E II 2 169 17
merits, can never have been reckoned tolerably pretty! P III 5 35 14

RECKONER (1)
"You are a most accurate and honest reckoner. MP III 11 410 10

RECKONING (4)
seven hundred, without reckoning the water meadows; so MP I 6 55 17
had followed, of reckoning up exactly who there would be, E II 11 247 3
But a week must pass; only a week, in Anne's reckoning, P III 7 53 1
They were reckoning him as certain, but, with her, it was P IV 10 227 69

RECKONINGS (1)
two hours beyond the reckonings of the game--"and that MP II 11 283 6

RECKONS (2)
which, because they are removed, he now reckons as nothing. SS III 11 351 13
since he was 7 years old--but my father reckons us alike." W 324 3

RECLAIM (1)
I thought your sister's influence might yet reclaim him. SS II 9 210 32

RECLAIMED (1)
again, benches were reclaimed and re-possessed, and P IV 8 189 45

RECLINING (1)
skin, the posture of reclining weakness, and the warm SS III 10 340 2

RECOGNISE (2)
he cd not immediately recognise arranged with all the W 355 28
Anne was astonished to recognise the same hills and the P III 12 117 73

RECOGNISED (2)
She recognised the whole of Lucy in the message, and was SS III 11 355 39
he was known, would not have recognised it for Mr. Darcy. PP III 2 264 14

RECOGNISING (2)
Elizabeth immediately recognising the livery, guessed what PP III 2 260 1

mad idea of her recognising him so soon as she did herself. P IV 7 179 28
RECOGNITION (3)
received from him the smiling tribute of recognition. NA I 8 54 4
they received no mark of recognition on their entrance. SS II 5 171 30
was complete internal recognition on each side; she was P IV 7 176 9
RECOGNIZED (1)
Mrs. Allen immediately recognized the features of a former NA I 4 31 2
RECOLLECT (58)
I am forced to recollect how many successive springs her LS 6 251 1
the Manwarings, & when I recollect on the different mode LS 6 252 2
"Yes, she did; but I cannot recollect now. NA I 9 68 46
dare say--but for the life of me, I cannot recollect it.-- NA II 3 145 13
"My dear madam," said Lady Middleton, "recollect what you SS I 13 64 13
but seeming to recollect himself, said no more on the SS II 4 162 11
"Why to be sure," said he, seeming to recollect himself, " SS II 11 227 48
recollect that I am the last person in the world to do it. SS II 13 244 46
the room, he could not recollect; but determining to be on SS III 4 288 26
replied; "I did not recollect that I had omitted to give SS III 8 322 38
"He does not exactly recollect the circumstances, though PP I 18 96 54
We will know where we have gone--we will recollect what we PP II 4 154 23
for, if I recollect right, he went but the day before. PP II 9 177 4
She tried to recollect some instance of goodness, some PP II 13 206 4
and I particularly recollect your saying one night, after PP III 3 271 16
17
"I do not recollect that we did." PP III 10 328 25
I met her at Mrs. Holford's--and did not recollect her. MP I 5 50 35
I do not recollect it. MP I 6 56 18
How she had looked before, Fanny could not recollect, for MP I 12 117 15
As well as I can recollect, it was always much the same. MP II 3 197 3
But I cannot recollect that our evenings formerly were MP II 3 197 3
at the same time to recollect, that his mother had been MP II 4 214 46
"She could not recollect what it was that she had heard MP II 11 283 4
I told him--I cannot recollect my exact words--but I am MP III 1 315 19
The time of the play, is a time which I hate to recollect. MP III 4 349 26
to studying it, without seeming to recollect her existence. MP III 7 382 28
I hope she will recollect it, and be satisfied, as well MP III 9 394 1
very often to recollect something worth their putting in. E I 9 70 5
did not at present recollect any thing of the riddle kind; E I 9 70 6
conundrums that he might recollect; and she had the E I 9 70 7
can only recollect the first stanza; and there are several. E I 9 78 54
And that is all that I can recollect of it--but it is very E I 9 78 54
I wish I could recollect more of it. E I 9 79 56
"I declare I cannot recollect what I was talking of.-- E II 9 237 51
I did not immediately recollect. E II 11 255 58
to Maple Grove, he could recollect that there were ladies E III 2 321 16
Dear Jane, how shall we ever recollect half the dishes for E III 2 330 45
"Now," said Harriet, "you must recollect." E III 4 338 10
I cannot recollect.-- E III 4 340 20
It is very odd, but I cannot recollect.-- E III 4 340 20
no, now I recollect, now I have it; something happened E III 8 382 29
"Oh, dear," cried Harriet, "now I recollect what you mean; E III 11 406 24
before she could at all recollect what letter it was which E III 12 420 14
mad with joy: but when I recollect all the uneasiness I E III 14 439 8
to leave off abruptly, to recollect and compose myself.-- E III 14 440 8
Do not you recollect?-- E III 18 470 8
At this moment I cannot recollect his name, though I have P III 3 23 25
"My dear Mary, recollect what a comfortable account you P III 5 38 32
More than I can recollect in a moment: but I can tell you P III 5 38 34
to recollect himself, and feel how he ought to behave. P III 9 78 22
She left it to himself to recollect, that Mrs. Smith was P IV 5 158 20
he had not mentioned it, or she could not recollect it. P IV 7 178 26
Would she recollect him? P IV 7 178 26
in Bath, but could not recollect the exact number, and I P IV 7 179 30
She was obliged to recollect that her seeing the letter P IV 9 204 76
77
guide, perhaps, may recollect what you have seen him do." P IV 9 207 90
I recollect.-- P IV 10 222 34
"True," said Anne, "very true; I did not recollect; but P IV 11 233 21
RECOLLECTED (38)
for she soon recollected, in the first place, that she was NA I 12 92 4
say, that having just recollected a prior engagement of NA I 13 100 15
Isabella recollected herself. NA II 1 136 48
Catherine recollected herself, blushed deeply, and could NA II 9 194 8
My father has recollected an engagement that takes our NA II 13 224 13
I am only sorry it was not recollected sooner, that I NA II 13 225 22
Catherine away, when he recollected this engagement," said NA II 14 234 11
This hint was enough, Lucy recollected herself instantly SS II 1 144 12
"My dear," said she, entering, "I have just recollected SS II 8 197 27
When they stopped at the door, Mrs. Jennings recollected SS II 11 220 2
me, it will be better recollected and explained to-morrow." SS III 8 318 17
wondering whether her mother ever recollected Edward. SS III 9 335 7
He recollected himself, & came forward, delighted to find W 355 28
Jane recollected herself soon, and putting the letter away, PP I 21 116 6
But Elizabeth had now recollected herself, and making a PP I 22 125 16
at last, that she recollected having heard Mr. Fitzwilliam PP II 2 143 20
and till Elizabeth recollected that there might be other PP II 7 168 3
a word, he suddenly recollected himself, and took leave. PP III 1 252 53
At last she recollected that she had been travelling, and PP III 1 257 66
openly disdained, and recollected their last lively scene PP III 2 263 10
to meet, scarcely recollected her interest in the affair, PP III 3 270 11
Nothing of the past was recollected with pain; and Lydia PP III 9 316 6
However, I recollected afterwards, that if he had been PP III 9 319 25
I was sometimes quite provoked, but then I recollected my PP III 10 325 2
to imagine; till she recollected that his being the PP III 15 360 1
He then recollected her embarrassment a few days before, PP III 17 377 40
Her aunt Bertram had recollected her on this occasion, MP II 9 271 41
When she had spoken it, she recollected herself, and MP II 12 295 22
but the more she recollected and observed, the more deeply MP III 6 366 4
the Bates lodged, Emma recollected his intended visit the E II 6 198 6
Emma recollected, blushed, was sorry, but tried to laugh E III 7 374 57
Emma soon recollected, and understood him; and while she E III 18 480 76
Wentworth whom they recollected meeting, once or twice, P III 6 52 33
sending, as soon as she recollected it, proper notice to P III 7 53 3
She coloured deeply; and he recollected himself, and moved P III 12 114 63
I had not recollected it before, I declare,--but it must P IV 1 127 24
Captain Wentworth recollected him perfectly. P IV 7 177 16
Anne recollected with pleasure the next morning her P IV 9 192 1
RECOLLECTING (25)
home; because, (recollecting myself) I know my father LS 24 286 4
Catherine, recollecting herself, grew ashamed of her NA II 5 160 23
Stay-----there is one part-----" recollecting with a blush NA II 10 205 21
it has been in recollecting that he sometimes shewed a SS I 8 39 15
easily reconciled, by recollecting, that Edward Ferrars, SS II 3 157 15
Recollecting, soon afterwards, that he was probably SS II 9 211 43
to see them without recollecting a word of the matter; and SS II 10 215 14
Recollecting himself, however, he added, "that is, I mean SS II 11 224 24
After a few moments' chat, John Dashwood, recollecting SS III 5 298 32
and in this emergence recollecting when she had seen him PP II 9 177 3
4
"But," she continued, recollecting herself, "as we know PP II 10 186 36
Lady Catherine without recollecting, that had she chosen PP II 14 210 2
But no,"--recollecting herself,--"that could never be: my PP III 1 246 6
than politeness; then recollecting himself, "I will not PP III 4 276 7
which was which, and recollecting that he had once seen MP I 15 138 1
way--but our powers of recollecting and of forgetting, do MP II 4 209 12
"I understand," cried her uncle recollecting himself, and MP III 1 312 12
the same room, without recollecting what you once told me, MP III 13 423 2
Mr. Elton, you know, (recollecting herself,) is out of the E I 10 84 13
father; and on recollecting that an old woman who had E II 6 197 3
months ago, to lace up her boot, without recollecting. E II 14 270 3
Harriet should not be recollecting too; but she behaved E II 14 270 3
for finishing or recollecting what he had begun, Anne was P III 6 49 25
be ready; but Louisa recollecting, immediately afterwards, P III 12 103 5
to them!"--then recollecting herself, and not wishing to P IV 4 150 18
RECOLLECTION (68)
Upon recollection, however, I have a notion they are both NA I 9 68 48
arising, no sudden recollection, no unexpected summons, no NA I 14 106 1
by my having no recollection of it, that I never thought, NA II 3 145 13
brought to her recollection a countless variety of NA II 6 166 9
returned her recollection of the manuscript; and springing NA II 7 172 1
the General; and by a recollection of some most generous NA II 11 208 1
brightening at the recollection of what had first given NA II 14 238 23
but the tears which recollection called forth as they SS I 6 28 2
his emotion with the tender recollection of past regard. SS I 11 57 17
indulging the recollection of past enjoyment and crying SS I 16 83 2
Mrs. Palmer laughed heartily at the recollection of their SS I 19 107 28
the recollection of what civility demanded towards herself. SS II 4 162 8
It was a lucky recollection, all her good spirits were SS II 5 167 3
He stopt a moment for recollection, and then, with another SS II 9 205 21
partiality of tender recollection, there is a very strong SS II 9 205 23
24
gloom,--even now the recollection of what I suffered-----" SS II 9 206 24
They were relieved however, not by her own recollection, SS II 12 231 11
after a moment's recollection, to welcome him, with a look SS II 13 241 20
to that is added the recollection, that he might, but for SS III 1 268 50
I suppose, however--on recollection--that the case may SS III 5 295 12
for that want of recollection and elegance, which made her SS III 6 304 13
After a moment's recollection, therefore, concluding that SS III 8 317 7
said, after a moment's recollection, "Mr. Willoughby, you SS III 8 318 21
22
peculiar, some painful recollection, she grew silent and SS III 10 342 7
has given me leisure and calmness for serious recollection. SS III 10 345 28
after a few moments recollection, was not sorry for it. PP I 11 58 34
In comparing her recollection of Pemberley, with the PP II 2 143 20
Elizabeth smiled at the recollection of all that she had PP II 5 155 2
walk, when the recollection of Mr. Darcy's sometimes PP II 12 195 1
But no such recollection befriended her. PP II 13 206 4
soon brought to her recollection that Mr. Darcy's PP II 13 208 9
fatigue, and a recollection of her long absence, made her PP II 13 209 12
but with a moment's recollection and a returning smile, PP II 18 233 27
This was a lucky recollection--it saved her from something PP III 1 246 7
way to the charm of recollection; and she was too much PP III 1 258 76
denoted a recollection of Jane, not untinctured by PP III 2 262 8
The recollection of what I then said, of my conduct, my PP III 16 367 14
he needed a little recollection before he could say, "your MP I 9 87 16
we were; but I have not the least recollection at what. MP I 10 98 12
if struck by a sudden recollection, she exclaimed, "my MP I 15 143 27
Grant, with sudden recollection, turned to her and asked MP II 4 215 47
pain and pleasure retraced with the fondest recollection. MP II 6 234 18
the more by the recollection of the faults she once had. MP II 9 269 38
can, dismissing the recollection of every thing unpleasant. MP III 2 331 16
she blushed at the recollection of herself, when she saw MP III 4 347 19
after a pause of recollection and exertion, "that every MP III 4 353 45
The recollection of what had been done for William was MP III 5 364 30
and niece, in the recollection that she could not possibly MP III 6 373 23
of allusion, of recollection, so much of Mansfield in MP III 7 376 4
A moment's recollection enabled her to say, "Rushworth, MP III 15 439 10
to each other, was yet a dearer, tenderer recollection. E I 1 6 6
her happiness in the sight or the recollection of him. E I 17 143 13
I hate the recollection." E II 8 222 51
His recollection of Harriet, and the words which clothed E II 13 266 6
The very recollection of it, and all that I felt at the E III 4 342 38
be abhorred in recollection, than any she had ever passed. E III 8 377 1
and so strong was the recollection of all that had so E III 18 473 27
But he laughed so heartily at the recollection, that Emma E III 18 478 64
65
past, which seemed almost to deny any recollection of it. P III 4 30 10
this very day, with a recollection of the name of P III 6 51 31
be brought to the recollection of each; they could not but P III 8 63 2
She gave a moment's recollection, as they hurried along, P III 12 115 66
She felt it all behind her; all but the recollection that P IV 1 123 8
A sudden recollection seemed to occur, and to give him P IV 8 182 9
She was in need of a little interval for recollection." P IV 8 185 18
you, was not the recollection of what had been, the P IV 11 244 72
This is a recollection which ought to make me forgive P IV 11 247 84
recollection of having written or felt any such thing.-- S 10 412 1
RECOLLECTIONS (20)
grieved to the soul by a thousand tender recollections. PP I 16 78 20
recollections that might not unreasonably have alarmed her. PP I 18 89 1
indulge in all the delight of unpleasant recollections. PP II 14 212 16
When to these recollections was added the development of PP II 14 213 19
when some unlucky recollections obtruded, and she fancied PP III 1 254 57
and the various recollections connected with him gave her PP III 3 269 10
These recollections will not do at all. PP III 16 368 17
Painful recollections will intrude, which cannot, which PP III 16 369 24
to bury some of the recollections of Mansfield which were MP III 9 398 10
he had secured agreeable recollections for his own mind. MP III 10 404 15
at work with his recollections; and at the same time, as E I 9 70 7
recollections of the other, prevented any renewal of it. E I 12 107 62
The visit afforded her many pleasant recollections the E II 9 231 1
It was one of the agreeable recollections of the ball, E III 3 332 1
number of embarrassing recollections on each side. E III 18 476 46
you can bear such recollections, is astonishing to me!-- E III 18 480 78
79
With all these circumstances, recollections and feelings, P III 4 30 10
a faint blush at some recollections) "altogether my P IV 8 184 16
claimed; and Anne's recollections of the concert were P IV 9 192 5
recollections of their own future lives could bestow. P IV 11 240 59
RECOMMENCED (3)
him on the subject of muslins till the dancing recommenced. NA I 3 29 47
When the dancing recommenced, however, and Darcy PP I 18 90 8
Fanny's rides recommenced the very next day, and as it was MP I 8 75 1
RECOMMEND (60)
has not even manners to recommend her, & according to Mr LS 4 248 2
She is a stupid girl, & has nothing to recommend her. LS 7 252 1
I confess it does not particularly recommend itself to me. LS 16 269 3
which have only genius, wit, and taste to recommend them. NA I 5 37 4
a rattle; but that will recommend him to your sex I NA I 7 50 45
that his manners would recommend him to all her sex; but NA I 9 66 32
recommend parental tyranny, or reward filial disobedience. NA II 16 252 7
of the party which could recommend them as companions to SS I 7 34 7
ever be in your power to recommend him to any body that SS III 2 277 30
"They have none of them much to recommend them," replied PP I 1 5 27
in short, to recommend her, but being an excellent walker. PP I 8 35 3
4
young ladies who seek to recommend themselves to the other PP I 8 40 56
Let me recommend you, however, as a friend, not to give PP I 18 94 45
You will never recommend yourself to his friend by so PP I 18 99 66
delicate attentions to recommend himself to her, and that PP I 18 102 73
quality, who has neither manner nor sense to recommend him. PP II 4 154 19
different doors, to recommend their being quick, as Lady PP II 6 161 7
but I am ill qualified to recommend myself to strangers." PP II 8 175 21
world, is ill-qualified to recommend himself to strangers. PP II 8 175 22
was wounding, but was very unlikely to recommend his suit. PP II 11 189 5
so little suited to recommend them; but still more was she PP II 17 224 2
their duty to teach and recommend; and it will, I believe, MP I 9 93 49
friend, had not much to recommend him beyond habits of MP I 13 121 1
to recommend yourself, for we are a great deal together." MP II 6 231 10
to recommend her as a wife by shewing her persuadableness. MP II 10 281 34
you, with every thing to recommend him; not merely MP III 1 315 27
gentleness of character so well adapted to recommend them. MP III 4 351 32
that quarter, wrote to recommend Sir Thomas's coming to MP III 16 450 8
the meal, and help and recommend the minced chicken and E I 3 24 11
self-approbation, recommend, though he might constrain E I 3 24 13

14
I would not recommend an egg boiled by any body else--but E I 3 24 14
weston had asked me to recommend him a wife, I should E I 5 38 11
I do not recommend matrimony at present to Emma, though I E I 5 41 30
and good-humour to recommend them; and his mind has more E I 8 65 49
You must go to bed early, my dear--and I recommend a E I 12 100 18
Am I to believe that you have never sought to recommend E I 15 131 34
trade, or any thing to recommend him to notice but his E I 16 136 9
"Well, if he have nothing else to recommend him, he will E I 18 149 29
just what they should recommend; and indeed they E II 1 161 25
have so often heard Mr. Woodhouse recommend a baked apple. E II 9 237 46
on, I shall decidedly recommend their bringing the E II 14 274 28
Let me recommend Bath to you. E II 14 275 30
might be supposed to recommend the other, but from the E II 15 282 4
all that I have to recommend being comprised in, do not E II 18 311 38
Oh! do you recommend this side?-- E III 2 330 45
without feeling, and to recommend himself without E III 5 348 23
The manner, perhaps, may have as little to recommend them. E III 13 430 37
One set might recommend their all removing to Donwell, and E III 17 468 36
and only begged leave to recommend an implicit deference P III 2 11 1
and I should recommend Miss Elliot to be on her guard with P III 3 18 8
nothing but himself to recommend him, and no hopes of P III 4 26 3
of mind, she ventured to recommend a larger allowance of P III 11 101 24
than well; or I should recommend Gowland, the constant use P IV 4 146 3
would very generally recommend him, among all sensible P IV 4 147 7
Let me recommend Mr. Elliot. P IV 9 196 30
"She had seemed to recommend and praise him!" P IV 9 211 100
of various kinds to recommend her quickly and permanently. P IV 12 251 10
What in the name of common sense is to recommend Brinshore? S 1 369 1
thing that was proper to recommend their father's offers; S 1 370 1
exercise;--and I should recommend rather more of it to you S 10 416 1

RECOMMENDATION (31)
brought the double recommendation of being her brother's NA I 7 47 18
he was affected by a recommendation of such a nature at SS I 1 5 6
belonging to the place, was now its first recommendation. SS I 4 23 20
eldest left her no recommendation, and as Elinor was not SS I 21 124 32
must be recommendation enough to her husband." SS II 2 149 26
an accidental recommendation to look at Netherfield house. PP I 4 16 13
a merely conditional recommendation, and to assert that I PP I 16 79 27
particular advice and recommendation of the very noble PP I 19 105 10
Her brother's recommendation was enough to ensure her PP III 3 270 12
of attending to the recommendation of Sir Charles, that MP II 13 298 3
sufficient recommendation to you, had there been no other. MP III 1 316 27
It had every recommendation to him, and while honouring MP III 3 335 6
without a single recommendation, that Fanny could not help MP III 7 385 38
to a positive recommendation to Mrs. Price and her MP III 10 401 10
completed by every recommendation of growing worth, what MP III 17 470 27
spirit, were a recommendation to every body and a mine of E I 3 21 4
dependent on your recommendation, had I quitted Mr. E I 5 37 10
to have every recommendation of person and mind; to be E II 4 181 2
To complete every other recommendation, he had almost told E II 12 262 38
It ought to be no recommendation to you. E II 14 280 57
I must confess it is a recommendation to me. E II 15 283 7
of ill-health was a recommendation to her--and though not E III 16 451 3
Dick had been left ill at Gibraltar, with a recommendation P III 8 66 19
is reading upon your recommendation, and he wants to talk P IV 2 131 9
Mrs. Clay has been using it at my recommendation, and you P IV 4 146 3
His manners were an immediate recommendation; and on P IV 4 146 6
next Lady Elliot, through Mrs. Wallis's recommendation?" P IV 9 208 92
least, Charles Hayter might get a special recommendation. P IV 10 217 20
line settled at Sanditon, it wd be no recommendation to us. S 5 386 1
the same post & pressed for the recommendation of Sanditon. S 9 408 1
This is a letter of recommendation & introduction to me, S 10 419 1

RECOMMENDATIONS (11)
by the most impartial eye to have many recommendations. NA II 7 175 15
were self-evident recommendations: and having never heard NA II 16 249 1
They saw him often, and to his other recommendations was PP II 1 138 30
they are not trivial recommendations to the world in E I 8 63 44
one of the great recommendations of this change would be E II 11 251 27
And as to its recommendations to you, I fancy I need not E II 14 275 32
Her introductions and recommendations must all wait, and E III 6 352 2
She knew that he saw such recommendations in Harriet; he E III 11 409 35
of the two recommendations to Mr. Woodhouse's mind.-- E III 17 467 30
encounter of such lavish recommendations could not fail. P III 4 26 1
of business, and recommendations to shops; with intervals P IV 10 220 31

RECOMMENDATORY (1)
wishing to marry at all so early is recommendatory to me. MP II 13 317 34

RECOMMENDED (45)
This charming sentiment, recommended as much by sense as NA I 15 119 19
and to him Mr. Dashwood recommended, with all the strength SS I 1 5 5
Edward Ferrars was not recommended to their good opinion SS I 3 15 6
It was a contrast which recommended him most forcibly to SS I 3 16 7
thought which particularly recommended the action to her. SS I 9 43 11
recommended him to her affection beyond every thing else. SS I 10 48 7
They recommended the army. SS I 19 102 4
for which it was recommended, "how good you are! SS II 8 198 28
She recommended it to her daughters, therefore, by all SS II 10 213 3
The same manners however, which recommended Mrs. John SS II 12 229 3
So well had they recommended themselves to Lady Middleton, SS II 12 230 8
her kindness, recommended by so pretty a face, was SS III 6 304 13
young ladies were carefully recommended to lose no time.-- W 323 3
The dancing now recommended; Miss Carr being impatient to W 335 13
He recommended exercise in defiance of dirt--spoke again W 347 21
artificial sensibility was not recommended by the idea.-- W 351 25
be of any service, recommended an express to town for one PP I 8 40 59
easy manners recommended her, had increased into assurance. PP I 9 45 36
A fortunate chance had recommended him to Lady Catherine PP I 15 70 1
party, but his manners recommended him to every body. PP I 16 84 59
the other day, that I recommended another young person, PP II 6 165 32
which of course recommended him still more; and Elizabeth PP II 9 180 28
will he particularly recommended it to me, to promote his PP II 12 200 5
and aid, he so far recommended himself to Georgiana, whose PP II 12 201 5
and good spirits had recommended her and Lydia to each PP II 18 230 11
of history; but he recommended the books which charmed her MP I 2 22 35
Sir Thomas, after a moment's thought, recommended MP II 7 239 6
She walked out directly as her uncle recommended, and MP III 1 322 50
"I recommended the shrubbery to Fanny as the dryest place," MP III 1 323 55
to his father; and recommended there being nothing more MP III 5 356 2
his talents could not have recommended him at any time. E I 1 7 8
of his forgetting to inquire for the book you recommended. E I 4 33 40
be very safely recommended to take Mr. Elton as a model. E I 4 34 42
"Mr. Wingfield most strenuously recommended it, sir--or we E I 12 101 21
He recommended it for all the children, but particularly E I 12 101 21
Mrs. Churchill had been recommended to the medical skill E III 1 317 7
complaints, she recommended his taking some refreshment; E III 6 364 56
it is equally to be recommended as a clearer of ill-fame. E III 9 387 12
any thing:--Mr. Perry recommended nourishing food; but E III 9 391 19
a kindness which always recommended her musical powers to P III 6 47 15
strength, and when he recommended the advantage of resting P III 10 86 17
she recommended, and promised to procure and read them. P III 11 101 25
again, whose manners recommended him to every body, & they S 6 390 1
Sanditon had been recommended by Mrs Darling, & that the S 9 408 1
friends--and he recommended Sanditon;--without my S 9 412 1

RECOMMENDING (14)
company, and anxiously recommending the study of her NA II 13 220 1
service in recommending it to their lasting approbation. SS I 6 28 2
not the best method of recommending herself; but angry PP III 3 271 16
cause, could not avoid recommending moderation to her, as PP III 5 288 39
in to the others, and recommending her to their kindness. MP I 2 12 1
prevailing desire of recommending herself to him, took an MP II 10 276 14
may have weight in recommending the most solid truths; and, MP III 3 340 23
He was to be describing and recommending matrimony to me. MP III 5 358 9
of all, and above all, recommending to us a compliance, a MP III 16 457 30
variously urging and recommending, Mr. Knightley and Emma E I 15 128 17
18
recommending for him; and it might have a very good effect. E I 18 147 19
should not be strongly recommending each to the other. E III 3 335 10
your new penknife, and your recommending court plaister?-- E III 4 338 12
the finger, and my recommending court plaister, and saying E III 4 338 13

RECOMMENDS (1)
"Speculation I beleive, said Elizth--my sister recommends W 358 28

RECOMPOSED (1)
back to her chair, recomposed, and with the comfortable P IV 10 223 39

RECONCILE (15)
it, which can alone reconcile it to myself, will be LS 30 301 4
did not by any means reconcile her more to her lot; nor NA I 8 55 10
she knew not how to reconcile two such very different NA I 9 65 31
and it was in their power to reconcile her to it entirely. SS II 14 247 4
her father's incredulity, and reconcile him to the match. PP III 17 376 36
inclined to allow, to reconcile Fanny to the novelty of MP I 2 14 6
obliged to you for trying to reconcile me to what must be. MP I 3 27 34
were mad; but Fanny can reconcile me to any thing"--and MP II 6 235 19
if any son of mine could reconcile himself to doing less. MP II 7 247 42
side, tending to reconcile his wife to the arrangement. MP II 11 284 10
She might assist his resolution, or reconcile him to it; E III 13 429 30
"You need not be at any pains to reconcile me to the match. E III 18 473 24
an agreeable manner might not gradually reconcile one to." P III 5 35 15
If he really sought to reconcile himself like a dutiful P IV 2 136 35
which I never could quite reconcile with present times. P IV 9 200 56

RECONCILED (20)
To this determination she was the more easily reconciled, SS II 3 157 15
a few months must have reconciled me to it, or at least I SS II 9 206 24
arguments with which I reconciled myself to the expediency SS III 13 368 28
for their exercise, reconciled Mrs. Ferrars to his choice, SS III 14 375 10
It was a long time before she became at all reconciled to PP I 22 125 18
"I cannot be so easily reconciled to myself. PP III 16 367 14
persuaded me to be reconciled to things that I disliked at MP I 3 25 18
family, he soon grew reconciled to a distinction, which at MP I 3 30 57
its utility to his son, reconciled Sir Thomas to the MP I 3 32 62
of being far better reconciled to a country residence than MP II 4 210 20
21
discredit, could she be reconciled to the risk, or feel MP II 6 237 23
he was by no means yet reconciled to his own daughter's E I 1 7 10
grow reconciled to the idea, and I wish them very happy. E III 10 399 61
he was become perfectly reconciled, and not far from E III 10 401 69
Mr. Churchill could be reconciled to the engagement's E III 12 417 5
as not to mean to be reconciled in time; but I was the E III 14 441 8
anticipated, wholly reconciled and complying; and could E III 14 443 8
But it is done; we are reconciled, dearer, much dearer, E III 14 443 8
Mr. Woodhouse could not be soon reconciled; but the worst E III 17 466 30
your feelings are less reconciled to the change than mine. P IV 1 125 15
16

RECONCILIATION (17)
reconciliation with her mother precludes every dearer hope. LS 24 291 16
our reconciliation, or by marrying & teizing him for ever. LS 25 293 4
to accomplish a reconciliation between Morland and NA II 15 246 12
It determined him to attempt a reconciliation, though not SS III 13 371 40
"in bringing about a reconciliation, I shall think that SS III 13 372 45
and in seeking a reconciliation with the Longbourn family PP I 15 70 2
offence, and seek a reconciliation; and, after a little PP III 19 388 12
as could not but dispose them all to a reconciliation. MP I 1 4 2
supposed to have in her wish for a complete reconciliation. MP III 16 459 31
means of a sort of reconciliation; and Mr. and Mrs. E I 2 16 4
continue to feel all the value of such a reconciliation.-- E III 15 447 28
we have not once met since the day of reconciliation. E III 18 477 57
of friendship and reconciliation, which could never be P IV 1 123 8
first opportunity of reconciliation, to be restored to the P IV 3 139 7
the progress of the reconciliation might have no origin P IV 3 140 11
appeared, in Mr. Elliot's great desire of a reconciliation. P IV 4 147 7
efforts he made towards a reconciliation with my father. P IV 9 205 83

RECONCILING (3)
been dismissed--for in reconciling Reginald to me, I was LS 25 293 4
probabilities, and reconciling herself as well as she PP II 13 209 12
was lost, and in part reconciling him to himself; though MP III 17 462 6

RECONTRE (1)
within her memory; no recontre, no alarm of the kind;--and E III 3 335 10

RECORD (1)
It stood the record of many sensations of pain, once P IV 1 123 8

RECORDABLE (1)
Of very important, very recordable events, it was not more E III 2 326 33

RECORDS (1)
in former histories and records, which may be as much NA I 14 109 23

RECOURSE (4)
without having constant recourse to a journal?-- NA I 3 27 28
to which he had often recourse, about its being a d---- NA I 11 89 61
any reply, she had recourse, as soon as she was dressed, MP I 16 150 1
Then having recourse to her workbasket, in excuse for E III 18 471 19

RECOVER (27)
for poor James, I suppose he will hardly ever recover it." NA II 10 206 37
from which he did not recover till after Eleanor had NA II 16 250 4
But not so easily did Elinor recover from the alarm into SS I 12 62 27
Again he stopped to recover himself; and Elinor spoke her SS II 9 208 27
She could not yet recover from the surprise of what had PP II 12 195 1
and before he could recover himself enough to speak, she, PP III 4 276 6
"No, I thank you;" she replied, endeavouring to recover PP III 4 276 10
has been attempted, to recover her?" "my father is gone to PP III 4 277 15
As soon as they were gone, Elizabeth walked out to recover PP III 12 339 1
She began at length to recover, to fidget about in her PP III 17 378 42
It was long before Fanny could recover from the agitating MP II 6 233 17
becoming, she turned away for a moment to recover herself. MP III 5 358 9
and giving her time to recover, while he devoted himself MP III 10 399 5
to lessen more, or to recover itself, were subjects for MP III 12 417 4
He turned away to recover himself, and when he spoke again, MP III 15 444 29
she may recover her footing in society to a certain degree. MP III 16 457 29
and cool, and the other recover his temper and happiness E I 15 128 21
there is generally time to recover from it afterwards. E III 7 373 44
Emma might have time to recover--"you may well be amazed. E III 10 395 35
"Well," said she at last, trying to recover herself; "this E III 10 395 37
Emma understood him; and as soon as she could recover from E III 13 426 14
15
as she could not recover from, till enabled by the P III 9 80 34
long application of solitude and reflection to recover her. P III 9 81 34
She had much to recover from, before she could move. P III 10 89 34
She paused a moment to recover from the emotion of hearing P III 12 114 62
A man does not recover from such a devotion of the heart P IV 8 183 10
others, before she could recover calmness enough to return P IV 9 204 76
77

RECOVERABLE (1)
incumbrances, might be recoverable by proper measures; and P IV 9 210 98

RECOVERED (44)
& when Reginald has recovered his usual good spirits, (as LS 40 309 1
she was sufficiently recovered to think it prettier than NA II 11 214 25
in the triumph of recovered reputation, and all the NA II 14 232 7
When Marianne was recovered, the schemes of amusement at SS I 11 53 1
Marianne rose the next morning with recovered spirits and SS II 4 164 21
when her spirits were recovered, she debated for a short SS II 5 173 45
of instant exertion, he recovered himself again, and after SS II 6 177 11
"No; as soon as she recovered from her lying-in, for I SS II 9 211 42
In a few minutes, however, Marianne was recovered enough SS II 12 236 42
The ladies recovered themselves first. SS II 13 241 19
to-morrow would find her recovered; and the idea of what SS III 7 308 4
"Will you repeat to your sister when she is recovered, SS III 8 330 67
As soon as Mrs. Dashwood had recovered herself, to see SS III 9 334 5
"When the weather is settled, and I have recovered my SS III 10 343 9

Long before I was enough recovered to talk, I was SS III 10 345 28
disordered, had so far recovered the use of her reason and SS III 11 353 25
Emma had just recovered from her own perturbation in time W 326 5
and when your sister is recovered, you shall if you please PP I 9 45 37
Jane was already so much recovered as to intend leaving PP I 10 53 66
she was not enough recovered; but Jane was firm where she PP I 12 59 3
who was now enough recovered to echo whatever his son in PP II 6 163 14
June Kitty was so much recovered as to be able to enter PP II 19 238 6
Wickham, Georgiana also recovered in time, though not PP III 3 270 11
Anxious not to appear unhappy, she soon recovered herself: MP III 7 384 35
Fanny was just recovered enough to feel that she could not MP III 10 400 6
She had reason to believe her nearly recovered from her E I 17 141 5
should have completely recovered her usual strength, they E II 2 165 9
She seems quite recovered now. E II 3 176 44
A young lady who faints, must be recovered; questions must E III 3 333 4
as soon as she had recovered her senses and speech.-- E III 3 334 8
In the meanwhile the lame horse recovered so fast, that E III 6 357 32
She recovered her voice. E III 7 373 43
assure her that she had fully recovered his good opinion.-- E III 9 386 8
His air and voice recovered their usual briskness: he E III 10 400 69
our saucy little friend here is charmingly recovered?-- E III 16 454 16 17
But she is charmingly recovered.-- E III 16 455 20
As soon as Mrs. Weston was sufficiently recovered to admit E III 17 465 28
seen greater injuries recovered from: he was by no means P III 12 112 52
If Louisa recovered, it would all be well again. P IV 1 123 7
and as soon as she recovered, they were to be acquainted. P IV 3 141 13
that his friend had recovered, or from some other P IV 8 183 11
I hope you think Louisa perfectly recovered now?" P IV 10 218 23
believe I do--very much recovered; but she is altered: P IV 10 218 24
Such a letter was not to be soon recovered from. P IV 11 238 44

RECOVERIES (1)
Disorders & Recoveries so very much out of the common way, S 10 412 1

RECOVERING (25)
chests; and the General recovering his politeness as he NA II 6 165 6
however," said Elinor, recovering herself, and determined SS III 4 288 28
"We may treat it as a joke," said he at last, recovering SS III 5 298 35
For some moments her voice was lost; but recovering SS III 11 350 6
she had no wish of her recovering immediately, as her PP I 9 41 2
Recovering himself, however, shortly, he turned to his PP I 18 93 24 25
at the idea; but, recovering herself, said in a lively PP II 10 183 15
surprise; but shortly recovering himself, advanced towards PP III 1 251 51
assist Mr. Bennet in every endeavour for recovering Lydia. PP III 5 287 36
a step or two, but recovering herself in a moment, MP I 9 88 21
Miss Crawford rallying her spirits, and recovering her MP I 9 89 29
they had been gradually recovering much of their former MP II 3 203 32
There was no recovering the complexion from the moment MP III 9 394 1
There was no recovering Miss Taylor--nor much likelihood E I 2 19 14
Mrs. Churchill was recovering, and he dared not yet, even E II 13 266 5
herself, she just recovering from her mania for Mr. Elton. E III 3 335 10
his sake!" said Emma, recovering from her state of shame E III 4 339 15
His spirits had been greatly recovering lately, as might P IV 2 133 25
Louisa was now recovering apace. P IV 2 134 31
severe pain, or are recovering the blessing of health, and P IV 5 155 9
though considered to be recovering fast, was still at Lyme; P IV 6 162 1
other, and Louisa, just recovering from illness, had been P IV 6 167 19
She caught it instantaneously; and, recovering courage P IV 9 194 21
former acquaintance and recovering such a footing in the P IV 9 207 90
her in the way of recovering her husband's property in the P IV 12 251 11

RECOVERY (21)
the next morning, her recovery was not equal to their NA II 14 235 13
had ceased to be possible, by Marianne's perfect recovery. SS I 10 48 7
boldly of a speedy recovery, and Miss Dashwood was equally SS III 7 309 7
his felicitations on a recovery in her sister even SS III 7 314 22
cheerfulness, the probability of an entire recovery. SS III 7 314 23
that every symptom of recovery continued, and saw Marianne SS III 7 315 25
place her;--and in her recovery she had yet another source SS III 9 335 7
long enough to make her recovery slow; and with youth, SS III 10 340 1
gave me, I wonder at my recovery,-- wonder that the very SS III 10 345 28
great anxiety for the recovery of her dear friend Jane, PP I 10 52 53
recovery of her spirits, by all that affection could do. PP II 11 188 1
to pursue, while in town, for the recovery of his daughter. PP III 5 293 68
poor Mr. Bertram has a bad chance of ultimate recovery. MP III 14 433 13
conduct, and his recovery so much thrown back by it, that MP III 16 451 13
for the recovery of her health, than on any thing else. E II 2 166 10
her mind there was none, of what would follow her recovery. P IV 1 123 7
how long Miss Musgrove's recovery might yet be doubtful, P IV 1 126 21
recovery from the awful impression of its being dissolved. P IV 4 147 8
eventually one of those most concerned in her recovery." P IV 8 182 6
She, in the overflowing spirits of her recovery, repeats P IV 9 205 82
to leave Lyme, and await her complete recovery elsewhere. P IV 11 243 66

RECPT (1)
hazards the day after the recpt of your letter, though it S 5 386 1

RECREATING (1)
principal nurses, was recreating herself in the SS III 7 310 9

RECREATION (2)
of recreation and amusement as desirable for every body." PP I 17 87 11
Besides that would be all recreation and indulgence, MP II 6 229 3

RECTIFIED (2)
Here is some great misapprehension which must be rectified. MP III 1 312 10
to feel; but she began to hope they might be rectified. MP III 9 396 6

RECTIFY (2)
but a year or two will rectify that, & he is in other LS 20 276 5
fashions of London; could rectify the opinions of her new NA I 4 33 7

RECTITUDE (2)
want of delicacy, of rectitude, and integrity of mind, SS I 22 127 2
to her sister, of whose rectitude and delicacy she was PP I 23 128 9

RECTOR (4)
and his rights as a rector, made him altogether a mixture PP I 15 70 1
The rector of a parish has much to do.-- PP I 18 101 71
It was an encouragement of vice; and had I been the rector PP III 15 364 22
that Dr. Shirley, the rector, who for more than forty P III 9 78 19

RECTOR'S (1)
road, & contained no gentleman's family but the Rector's.-- W 354 28

RECTORY (3)
It is a rectory, but a small one; the late incumbent, I SS III 3 282 19
"This little rectory can do no more than make Mr. Ferrars SS III 3 284 23
me to the valuable rectory of this parish, where it shall PP I 13 62 12

RECUR (3)
a stranger it might not recur again--but the misery of E II 6 202 33
A thousand vexatious thoughts would recur. E II 14 270 3
and recur to old stories: and he was not without agitation. E III 1 316 4

RECURRED (2)
one subject always to be recurred to by the ladies in case SS I 6 31 9
to which she daily recurred, her solitary walks and silent SS I 16 83 4

RECURRENCE (5)
In this unceasing recurrence of doubts and inquiries, on NA II 14 231 5
sister, the probable recurrence of many past scenes of SS III 10 340 2
yet almost every recurrence of either had led to something MP I 16 152 2
subject again, by the recurrence of his very frequent E I 9 78 49
had to suffer from the recurrence of any such uncertainty. E III 19 481 1

RECURRENCES (1)
or dangerous recurrences to the past, and give the most E II 4 185 13

RECURRING (4)
Eleanor made no answer; and Catherine's thoughts recurring NA II 13 224 17
her lover, she could not prevent its frequently recurring. PP I 23 129 13
her being found there, recurring to her mind, the few PP III 1 252 52
of the room, and, by recurring to former days, supplied P III 11 100 23

RED (18)
eyes looked very red, & she was as much agitated as before. LS 17 270 2
cheeks would have been as red as your roses; I would not NA I 10 71 5
the cause, by turning very red, and saying in an angry SS I 12 61 17 18
her eyes were red, her countenance was not uncheerful. SS I 15 77 21
Her eyes were red and swollen; and it seemed as if her SS I 15 82 46
and expensive without a red coat on my back as with one, SS I 19 103 4
Mary was surrounded by red coats the whole eveng. W 337 15
I remember the time when I liked a red coat myself very PP I 7 29 12
Both changed colour, one looked white, the other red. PP I 15 73 8
among the cluster of red coats there assembled, a doubt of PP I 18 89 1
on seeing her with red eyes, set her down as a hypocrite. MP I 3 33 64
growing more and more red from excessive agitation, and MP I 15 146 53
with injury, and looking as red as she had been white MP II 1 175 2
"My dear Sir Thomas!" cried Mrs. Norris, red with anger, " MP II 5 221 36
She turned extremely red. MP III 16 458 30
Knightley actually looked red with surprize and E I 8 60 31 32
"The last time I saw her, she had a red nose, but I hope P IV 3 142 14
than she had ever observed before; he looked quite red. P IV 7 175 6

RED-GUM (2)
the world but the red-gum;' and nurse said just the same. SS III 1 257 5
in the world but the red-gum, and then Charlotte was easy. SS III 1 257 5

REDDEN (1)
Mrs. Norris, who had begun to redden, was appeased, and, MP I 6 55 14

REDDENED (1)
face; though her reddened and weather-beaten complexion, P III 6 48 18

REDDENING (2)
"Indeed!" cried Mrs. Norris, reddening. MP II 13 305 21
that emotion which was reddening Anne's cheeks and fixing P IV 8 182 9

REDDER (1)
senses, and with cheeks only a little redder than usual. NA I 8 53 3

REDEEM (2)
engaged with pleasure to redeem it by a visit at the SS III 10 341 4
total want of spirits when he did come might redeem him. E II 12 259 12

REDRESS (1)
Why did not you seek legal redress?" PP I 16 79 26

REDUCE (2)
probably, contribute to reduce poor Catherine to all the NA I 2 19 7
their embarrassments and reduce their expenditure, without P III 1 10 21

REDUCED (12)
had reduced her to open the door of the apartment herself. NA I 13 102 27
morning of the same continued rain had reduced very low. SS III 6 304 14
Their party was now farther reduced; for Mr. Palmer, SS III 7 308 5
always happy, she was reduced to the extremest indigence." SS III 8 322 37
"You have reduced him to his present state of poverty, PP II 11 192 21
be reduced to tricks and stratagems to find it out." PP III 9 320 34
he could get; but at length was reduced to be reasonable. PP III 10 323 2
despise, and where he was reduced to meet, frequently meet, PP III 10 326 3
as they formed their very reduced circle after dinner; and MP II 11 284 9
soothe her mind, and was reduced to so low and wan and MP III 15 442 22
in life, and was reduced to form a wish which she had P IV 4 148 11
and reduced, seemed to have quite delighted Mr. Elliot. P IV 5 158 21

REDUCTION (2)
without him, and for her reduction of income by the MP I 3 23 1
difference of style, the reduction of servants, which a P IV 10 219 29

REDUCTIONS (2)
be affected by these reductions; and that the true dignity P III 2 12 4
the whole list of Lady Russell's too gentle reductions. P III 2 13 5

REDUNDANCIES (1)
but it has also redundancies and repetitions, which MP III 3 340 25

REEL (2)
Bennet, to seize such an opportunity of dancing a reel?" PP I 10 51 47 48
to dance a reel at all--and now despise me if you dare." PP I 10 52 50

REESTABLISHED (1)
former good understanding was completely reestablished. P IV 3 138 6

REFER (5)
seek her good opinion and refer to her judgment, began to MP III 9 397 8
seem, I accept it, and refer myself to you as a friend.-- E III 13 429 33
For my temptation to think it a right, I refer every E III 14 437 8
He could refer Sir Walter to all who knew him; and, P IV 3 139 7
your advertisements refer to the other--which is Great S 1 366 1

REFERENCE (15)
I am gratified by your reference, & this is my advice; LS 26 295 1
judgment; and, without reference to my brother, I really NA II 1 134 36
as this necessary reference to Fullerton would allow. NA II 2 140 10
tempest, with an arch reference to the character of the NA II 7 174 5
her away without any reference to her own convenience, or NA II 13 226 25
he even confused her by his too significant reference! NA II 14 230 2
report, without any reference to any other account, the PP III 2 264 14
my happiness, without reference to you, or to any person PP III 14 358 68
engagement, with a due reference to the absent Sir Thomas, MP I 4 39 11
any reference to the ball, be kept for commoner occasions. MP II 9 263 16
the paper, without any reference to her possible MP III 7 382 28
Nothing could be done without a reference to Elizabeth; P III 3 24 37
been theirs, without reference to the actual results of P III 4 29 8
It was a reference to the future, which Anne, after a P IV 4 147 8
Yes, yes, if you please, no reference to examples in books. P IV 11 234 28

REFERENCES (1)
character--respectable references--wishing to form a S 1 366 1

REFERRED (3)
to the plan, and merely referred it to her mother's SS II 3 154 6
must be referred to the imagination of husbands and wives. SS III 13 366 20
and at last she was referred for the truth of every PP II 13 206 4

REFERRING (2)
withdrew, still referring her to the letter for comfort. SS II 9 202 8
Referring the education to her seemed to imply it. E III 7 373 51

REFINE (2)
"My dear Harriet, you must not refine too much upon this E I 9 77 47
It's tendency would be to raise and refine her mind--and E III 4 342 40

REFINED (8)
life, than with the refined susceptibilities, the tender NA I 2 19 3
approve it, they were not refined enough to make any NA II 16 249 2
I suppose my aunt brought you up to be rather refined." W 318 2
I can see in a great many things that you are very refined. W 318 2
There, I said you were very refined;--& that's an instance W 319 2
in long sentences of refined nonsense, to combine liberal E I 3 21 5
She will grow just refined enough to be uncomfortable with E I 5 38 15
If not wise or refined herself, she would have connected E II 14 272 17

REFINEMENT (8)
and delicacy, or refinement;--people were nice in their NA I 14 108 16
by the irritable refinement of her own mind, and the too SS II 9 201 4
the regulators of refinement and courtesy, the masters of MP I 9 93 49
and much less incumbered by refinement or self-distrust. MP II 6 234 17
"One should be sorry to see greater pride or refinement in E I 7 56 41
of female right and refinement than he could be; but yet E I 8 65 50
scruple of mine with multiplied strength and refinement.-- E III 14 440 8
All idle refinement!-- P III 8 69 37

REFINEMENTS (2)
when the romantic refinements of a young mind are obliged SS I 11 56 17
I consider it as one of the first refinements of polished PP I 6 25 26

REFLECT (21)
I am proud when I reflect on it, and I think it must NA I 14 107 9
girl induced her first to reflect on the propriety of SS I 1 6 10
she could not reflect without the deepest concern. SS II 6 179 18
I shall never reflect on my former acquaintance with your SS II 7 183 13
misapplied, she could not reflect on the mean-spirited SS II 12 233 16
In short, I do not mean to reflect upon the behaviour of SS III 1 268 45
and, of course, to reflect on her own with discontent. SS III 4 291 45
It is astonishing, when I reflect on what it was, and what SS III 8 320 29
enough recovered to talk. I was perfectly able to reflect. SS III 10 345 28
Emma did not think, or reflect;--she felt & acted--. W 330 11
that the performance would reflect no credit on either." PP I 18 94 41

Elizabeth was then left to reflect on what she had heard. PP I 22 125 18
affair, on which I do not reflect with satisfaction; it is PP II 12 199 5
And this consideration leads me moreover to reflect with PP III 6 297 11
want of new clothes must reflect on her daughter's PP III 8 310 10
with cheerful selfishness reflect, 1st, that he had not MP I 3 24 4
I do not mean to reflect upon the good intentions of E II 8 217 32
time to reflect, "now, how am I going to introduce him?-- E II 16 297 48
arranged every thing, before the others began to reflect. P III 12 113 56
It was so humiliating to reflect on the constant deception P IV 10 215 13
but, when I began to reflect that others might have felt P IV 11 242 65

REFLECTED (12)
She reflected on the affair for some time in much NA I 9 66 31
As she walked, she reflected on what had passed. NA I 13 101 25
"And ought it not," reflected Catherine, "to endear it to NA II 7 180 33
the chief of it, reflected that, though its good effects SS II 8 198 29
Her astonishment, as she reflected on what had passed, was PP II 11 193 31
nearest relations, and reflected how materially the credit PP II 13 209 11
anguish as she reflected on that wretched business. PP III 4 279 24
he appeared; but if this reflected at all upon his E II 12 259 12
As she reflected more, she seemed but to feel it more. E III 7 376 63
and reflected, she could be fit for nothing rational. E III 18 475 37
She watched--observed--reflected--and finally determined P IV 5 154 8
herself--or rather she reflected that at two & twenty S 6 390 1

REFLECTING (8)
Catherine was silently reflecting that now Henry must have NA II 14 239 28
But how she contrives it without reflecting on the SS I 11 56 11
Elinor, who had now been for some time reflecting on the SS III 10 347 32
her mother and sisters, reflecting on what she had heard, PP I 23 126 1
his own motives, and of reflecting to what the indulgence MP I 12 114 3
to this play, without reflecting on his friends at MP I 15 139 11
Reflecting and doubting, and feeling that the possession MP II 8 260 25
She believed he was looking at her; probably reflecting on E II 12 261 32

REFLECTION (78)
I had ample leisure for reflection on the present state of LS 30 300 1
no reflection, she had never any objection to books at all. NA I 1 15 3
to bestow even on the reflection of her own felicity, in NA I 7 51 54
she could not, upon reflection, imagine him aware of it. NA II 4 149 1
indulgence of grief and reflection, Catherine felt equal NA II 10 203 9
"No," said Catherine, after a moments' reflection, "I do NA II 10 207 39
This was the sad finale of every reflection:--and Captain NA II 11 211 16
swallowed up in the reflection of her own change of NA II 14 237 20
wretchedness in every reflection that could afford it, and SS I 1 7 13
him farther, by a reflection which Elinor chanced one day SS I 3 16 7
it as an unfeeling reflection on the Colonel's advanced SS I 8 36 2
and engross her memory, her reflection, and her fancy. SS I 19 105 12
but after a moment's reflection, she added with revived SS I 22 131 29
for her on serious reflection to suspect it in the present SS II 1 139001
more than once dropt a reflection on the inconstancy of SS II 14 247 4
conversation, she was herself left to quiet reflection. SS III 2 271 5
feed her powers of reflection some time, though she had SS III 2 276 26
A few moments' reflection, however, produced a very happy SS III 4 286 16
17
she trusted of serious reflection, must eventually lead SS III 10 341 6
and perceiving that as reflection did nothing, resolution SS III 10 347 32
Reflection had given calmness to her judgment, and sobered SS III 11 349 2
was hardly such as to make reflection very soothing. W 361 31
a young lady of deep reflection I know, and read great PP I 2 7 18
After a few minutes reflection, however, she continued, "I PP I 16 80 34
It was a subject, in short, on which reflection would be PP II 1 134 3
of noticing this civil reflection, but its meaning did not PP II 11 191 16
inclination; by reason, by reflection, by every thing. PP II 11 192 22
Reflection must be reserved for solitary hours; whenever PP II 14 212 16
To Elizabeth with a countenance of grave reflection, soon PP III 5 289 41
42
Bingley looked a little silly at this reflection, and said PP III 11 338 59
of her, was a wretched reflection, and she sat in misery PP III 17 375 28
half an hour's quiet reflection in her own room, she was PP III 17 377 41
She cried bitterly over this reflection when her uncle was MP I 3 33 64
this impropriety is a reflection itself upon Mrs. Crawford, MP I 7 63 8
This was a most unjust reflection, but Fanny could allow MP I 10 101 29
What a pity," he added, after an instant's reflection, " MP I 11 112 34
sinking under her aunt's unkind reflection and reproach. MP I 16 150 1
But reflection brought better feelings, and shewed her MP I 17 160 6
It is no reflection on you; it is no more than what the MP II 7 249 53
the evening, and this reflection quickly restored so much MP II 8 253 4
in a reverie of fond reflection, uttering only now and MP II 9 262 11
accustomed to serious reflection to know them by their MP II 12 294 16
but she could not help this reflection on the Admiral. MP II 12 296 29
by a reflection to fortify herself beyond betraying it. MP III 1 317 33
As a general reflection on Fanny, Sir Thomas thought MP III 1 323 57
After a moment's reflection, Mr. Crawford replied, "I know MP III 11 410 16
supply matter for much reflection, and to leave every MP III 12 417 4
be giving her time for reflection before she resolves on MP III 13 422 2
afraid of the result of reflection than of an immediate MP III 13 422 2
After a little reflection, he went on with a sort of MP III 16 455 19
said Mr. Knightley; "but I meant no reflection on any body. E I 1 11 34
down, and then there can be no possible reflection on you." E I 9 77 42
was her consoling reflection; "any thing interests between E I 10 89 35
Emma could not like what bordered on a reflection on Mr. E I 11 96 27
with an air of grave reflection, "it was an awkward E I 12 101 19
20
of separating allowed her the relief of quiet reflection. E I 15 133 38
you--and it will be a painful reflection to me for ever. E II 13 268 10
A very little quiet reflection was enough to satisfy Emma E III 1 315 1
Rousing from reflection, therefore, and subduing her E III 11 408 33
after a little reflection, venture the following question. E III 11 410 36
This was the conclusion of the first series of reflection. E III 11 412 46
had enjoyed it without reflection; and only in the dread E III 12 415 1
Do not let any reflection fall on the principles or the E III 12 419 8
food for unpleasant reflection, by increasing her esteem E III 12 420 17
wretchedness but the reflection never far distant from her E III 12 422 20
and, after steady reflection, thus-- "very bad--though it E III 15 445 14
15
convinced, that no reflection could alter his wishes or E III 15 449 32
felicities, was the reflection that all necessity of E III 18 475 42
long application of solitude and reflection to recover her. P III 9 81 34
on more serious reflection, that, like many other great P III 11 101 26
his soul, and trying by prayer and reflection to calm them. P III 12 112 54
(looking with serious reflection) "I should think he must P IV 1 127 28
taste, and sentimental reflection, was amusing, but she P IV 6 167 20
A moment's reflection shewed her the mistake she had been P IV 9 194 21
Half an hour's solitude and reflection might have P IV 11 238 44
till the leisure for reflection which followed it, he had P IV 11 242 63
to supply the cooler reflection which her own husband S 2 372 1
Among other points of moralising reflection which the S 12 426 1

REFLECTIONS (37)
How unpleasant, one would think, must his reflections be! LS 22 282 8
But not one of these grave reflections troubled the NA I 10 74 22
such unpleasant reflections, and found her way with all NA II 7 173 5
In the course of this morning's reflections, she came to a NA II 9 192 5
The very painful reflections to which this thought led, NA II 11 208 1
These reflections were long indulged undisturbed by any NA II 13 228 27
favour, which gave comfort to his last earthly reflections. SS I 3 14 2
Her imagination was busy, her reflections were pleasant, SS I 9 43 11
His reflections ended thus. SS III 5 297 30
of the idea, and it gave fresh misery to her reflections. SS III 7 314 21
to speak to--my own reflections so cheerful--when I looked SS III 8 325 45
secret reflections may be no more unpleasant than my own. SS III 10 345 24
such feelings as these reflections gave me, I wonder at my SS III 10 345 28
of her reflections, "is a very common failing I believe. PP I 5 20 20
her what lady had the credit of inspiring such reflections. PP I 6 27 49
50
the train of agreeable reflections which her observations PP I 18 98 63
Her reflections were in general satisfactory. PP I 22 122 3
was a solidity in his reflections which often struck her, PP I 22 124 11
the pain she gives me by her continual reflections on him. PP II 1 134 4
5
She continued in very agitating reflections till the sound PP II 11 194 32
such reflections as must make her unfit for conversation. PP II 13 209 12
She was roused from her seat, and her reflections, by some PP III 10 327 4
such very disrespectful reflections on the pride of Sir MP I 1 4 1
Her elder cousins mortified her by reflections on her size, MP I 2 14 8
Her own thoughts and reflections were habitually her best MP I 8 80 31
the wonder, the reflections, the reproach that must attend MP II 3 201 22
have hopes; and these reflections having passed across his MP III 1 320 44
These were reflections that required some time to soften; MP III 17 461 4
agitated by such harsh reflections on his friend Perry, to E I 12 107 62
her in most unmirthful reflections some time longer, and E I 16 137 12
made; and ending with reflections on the Churchills again, E I 18 145 5
I leave you to your own reflections." E III 2 330 51
secret severity in her reflections on the unmanageable E III 6 353 3
knee, indulging in such reflections as these, was one of E III 17 468 32
An hour's complete leisure for such reflections as these, P IV 1 123 8
But he must not be addressing his reflections to Anne P IV 3 144 21
some of her immediate reflections--& much worse than all S 11 420 1

REFORM (3)
turn off his servants, and make a thorough reform at once? SS II 8 194 10
err in the method of reform was not wonderful; and Fanny MP III 9 395 4
At this rate, you will soon reform every body at Mansfield MP III 16 458 30

REFORMATION (3)
at the time of the Reformation, of its having fallen into NA II 2 141 13
a more complete Reformation, a quicker release from debt, P III 2 12 3
persuading them to a complete, than to half a Reformation. P III 2 13 5

REFORMED (1)
would be reformed, and her son be at liberty to be happy. SS I 19 102 2

REFRAIN (15)
she could no longer refrain from the gentle reproof of, " NA II 15 240 2
Elinor had some difficulty here to refrain from observing, SS III 5 295 17
"very true, it will be wise in me to refrain from that. PP II 3 145 7
Darcy to leave her, or to refrain from saying, in a tone PP III 4 276 9
duties of my station, or refrain from declaring my PP III 15 363 22
income; nor could he refrain from often saying to himself, MP I 4 40 13
his niece--nor perhaps refrain (though unconsciously) from MP II 7 238 1
either to wear the cross, or to refrain from wearing it. MP II 8 257 15
Fanny, not able to refrain entirely from observing them, MP II 10 279 21
but not enough to refrain from unreasonable regrets at E I 2 15 3
resolution enough to refrain from making any answer at all. E I 13 113 27
He began with great earnestness to entreat her to refrain E I 15 125 4
you would not have him refrain on Henry's account, a boy E II 8 224 67
this, she was not able to refrain from a start, or a heavy E III 12 423 21
charities, and to refrain from new-furnishing the drawing- P III 1 9 19

REFRAINED (4)
undoubtedly would have refrained from the hint; but she PP III 3 269 10
Mary refrained from saying what she felt, that there could MP II 12 296 29
seat any longer, or have refrained from at least trying to MP III 3 344 42
character, and refrained from any allusion that might E III 9 388 14

REFRESH (5)
to refresh her spirits by a change of place and neighbour. MP II 7 248 48
"There is hardly any desiring to refresh such a memory as E I 5 37 9
look around her; eager to refresh and correct her memory E III 6 357 34
not the sort of fatigue--quick walking will refresh me.-- E III 6 363 50
civility, or to refresh the others, as she was well aware. P III 6 46 13

REFRESHED (2)
found her just awaking, refreshed by so long and sweet a SS III 9 333 3
Fanny's spirit was as much refreshed as her body; her head MP III 7 384 33

REFRESHING (6)
I assure you it is very refreshing after sitting so long PP I 11 56 11
ground, admitted a most refreshing view of the high woody PP III 3 267 2
for there is nothing so refreshing as a walk after a MP I 7 73 55
more refreshing-- only objection to gathering strawberries E III 6 358 35
The shade was most refreshing, and Emma found it the E III 6 361 40
The Admiral, after taking two or three refreshing turns P III 8 68 31
32

REFRESHMENT (14)
might be glad of some refreshment after so much exercise? NA II 8 185 5
much;--and the present refreshment, therefore, with such SS III 7 315 27
they thus adjourned for refreshment;--the Tearoom was a W 332 11
She danced next with an officer, and had the refreshment PP I 18 90 5
punctually repeated all his wife's offers of refreshment. PP II 5 155 3
and if she accepted any refreshment, seemed to do it only PP II 7 169 3
the house and take some refreshment; but this was declined, PP III 1 257 66
ladyship to take some refreshment; but Lady Catherine very PP III 14 352 16
17
They all felt the refreshment of it, and for some time MP I 9 91 38
and look upon verdure, is the most perfect refreshment." MP I 9 96 72
The refreshment of Randalls was absolutely necessary. E II 5 187 4
his taking some refreshment; he would find abundance of E III 6 364 56
been examined, & some refreshment taken, & very cordially S 1 367 1
for the refreshment the mind receives in doing it's duty.-- S 9 410 1

REFRESHMENTS (4)
five minutes to order refreshments to be in the room by NA II 8 182 1
that a tray full of refreshments was introduced by his NA II 11 213 20
open for tea and other refreshments; and let the supper be SS II 14 252 18
to carry round the refreshments at exactly the proper hour, E II 16 290 3

REFUGE (2)
refuge in her own room, that she might think with freedom. PP III 7 307 50
be obliged to take daily refuge in the dining of the park. MP I 4 38 9

REFUSAL (24)
woman only the power of refusal; that in both, it is an NA I 10 77 33
for one day longer, and they would not hear of a refusal. NA I 13 97 1
go, she should go, and they would not hear of a refusal. NA I 13 98 1
irritated by Catherine's refusal, and yet more by the NA II 15 246 12
Mrs. Jennings received the refusal with some surprize, and SS II 3 153 1
difficulty in getting a refusal accepted; as they thought W 362 32
the refusal is repeated a second or even a third time. PP I 19 107 13
I am perfectly serious in my refusal.-- PP I 19 107 14
not how to express my refusal in such a way as may PP I 19 108 18
your refusal of my addresses is merely words of course. PP I 19 108 19
be satisfied, since the refusal which his cousin had PP I 20 110 1
for a moment repent her refusal, or feel the slightest PP II 14 212 17
unhappiness which her sister's refusal must have given him. PP II 17 224 2
but her placid manner of refusal made Mrs. Rushworth still MP I 8 76 2
intermingled with her refusal so expressive of obligation MP III 2 328 7
The surprise of your refusal, Fanny, seems to have been MP III 4 352 44
Were it a decided thing, an actual refusal, I hope I MP III 13 422 2
it may be; and as to the refusal itself, I will not E I 8 65 48
seek her; for since her refusal of the brother, the E II 3 180 58
be giving her refusal less meaning than she could wish. E II 7 207 6
to have had the power of refusal; and afterwards, as the E II 7 208 7
Her resolution of refusal only grew more interesting by E II 13 266 6
Russell had lamented her refusal; for Charles Musgrove was P III 4 28 7
and distresses which this refusal had heaped on her, in P IV 9 209 96

REFUSALS (1)
considering her repeated refusals as flattering PP I 19 109 22

REFUSE (52)
My dear brother I can no longer refuse myself the LS 1 243 1
to refuse him their confidence & slight his advice. LS 12 260 1
it myself, so I could not refuse your father when he LS 13 262 1
not in his nature to refuse, when urged in such a manner?" LS 24 290 12
the dirt; come, you must go; you cannot refuse going now." NA I 11 86 42
would not seriously refuse such a trifling request to a NA I 13 98 2
shall think you quite unkind, if you still refuse." NA I 13 99 3
be given, they would not refuse to spare her to her friend. NA I 13 103 28
contest the point, nor refuse to have been as full of arch NA I 15 119 14

"Nay, since you make such a point of it, I can refuse you NA II 1 130 13
see Mr. Palmer expects you; so you cannot refuse to come." SS I 20 113 31
She could not refuse to give him her's;--he pressed it SS III 8 331 74
I should not refuse a man because he was not Purvis--. W 317 2
refuse Emma--said she--nor what you have to bear at home.-- W 362 32
You cannot refuse to dance, I am sure, when so much beauty PP I 6 26 38
motive his cousin could refuse him; and though his pride PP I 20 112 24
being his wife, I advise you by all means to refuse him." PP I 21 119 24
Elizabeth could not refuse, though she foresaw little PP II 3 146 17
resentment, as to refuse his daughter a privilege, without PP III 8 310 10
You refuse, then to oblige me. PP III 14 358 69
You refuse to obey the claims of duty, honour, and PP III 14 358 69
Did she call to refuse her consent?" PP III 15 364 24
never dare refuse any thing, which he condescended to ask. PP III 17 376 35
provisions; you will not refuse to visit me in prison? I MP I 14 135 17
unwilling at first, could refuse no longer--and Fanny was MP I 18 170 24
But, Crawford, though I refuse you as a tenant, come to me MP II 7 247 41
to love you, and she will never have the heart to refuse." MP II 12 293 15
silence, "that you mean to refuse Mr. Crawford?" MP III 1 315 21
"Refuse him?" MP III 1 315 23
"Refuse Mr. Crawford! MP III 1 315 25
happiness, you resolve to refuse him at once, without MP III 1 318 39
That you could refuse such a man as Henry Crawford, seems MP III 4 352 44
Oh, I am sure it is not in woman's nature to refuse such a MP III 5 363 22
was impossible for her to refuse the correspondence; it MP III 5 364 33
drawn that I could not refuse; but there is no making E I 6 45 21
"You think I ought to refuse him then," said Harriet, E I 7 52 12
"Ought to refuse him! E I 7 52 13
accept a man or not, she certainly ought to refuse him. E I 7 52 18 19
and really almost made up my mind--to refuse Mr. Martin. E I 7 53 22 23
I am quite determined to refuse him. E I 7 55 34
a man that a woman should ever refuse an offer of marriage. E I 8 60 33
Harriet Smith refuse Robert Martin? madness, if it is so; E I 8 60 34
You persuaded her to refuse him." E I 8 60 36
but still, he cannot refuse an invitation, he must dine E I 13 111 13
her-- and now we are such a nice party, she cannot refuse. E II 9 236 46
Oh! yes, I must be there; I could not refuse; and I will E II 12 257 3
came, that she could not refuse him, and must therefore E III 2 319 2
kind way as she did, and refuse to take Jane's answer; but E III 8 381 15
It is impossible to refuse what you ask in such a way. E III 10 392 5
sublimity of resolving to refuse him at once and for ever, E III 13 431 38
and that therefore, she persuaded Anne to refuse him." P III 10 89 33
Anne could not refuse; but never had she sacrificed to P IV 8 190 47

REFUSED (36)
Summers had absolutely refused to allow of Miss Vernon's LS 17 269 1
Why should I subject you to entreaties, which I refused to LS 24 289 12
I refused him as long as I possibly could, but he would NA II 1 134 39
I refused him as long as I possibly could, but he would NA II 1 134 39
He steadily refused to accompany his father into NA II 15 248 16
affair; and for some time she refused to submit to them. SS I 12 58 3
the cottage, absolutely refused on her own account; her SS I 19 108 40
of impatient suffering, she at first refused to do. SS II 8 197 25
"Very well--and this offer of marriage you have refused?" PP I 20 111 15
He made her an offer in this very room, and she refused PP II 2 140 4
a woman who had already refused him, as able to overcome a PP III 10 326 3
whose proposals she had refused, and whose merit she had PP III 11 334 36
"A man who has once been refused! PP III 12 341 19
promise from her nephew, which she had refused to give. PP III 16 367 9
Norris, and she carefully refused him every opportunity. MP II 13 306 27
I am refused, that, I think, will be the honest motive. MP III 13 422 2
writing nonsense--were I refused, I must bear it; and till MP III 13 422 2
Accepted or refused, his heart is wedded to her for ever.-- MP III 13 424 4
He did speak yesterday--that is, he wrote and was refused." E I 8 60 30
it is impossible; she has refused him, and so decidedly, I E I 8 65 48
She must abide by the evil of having refused him, whatever E I 8 65 48
to die if she refused him; but flattering himself that his E I 15 129 24
beyond his fortnight, which could not possibly be refused. E II 11 256 59
declaration on his side was that she refused him. E II 13 264 1
she positively refused to take her friend's negative, E III 6 359 37
The invitation was refused, and by a verbal message. E III 9 389 16
exercise, so peremptorily refused to go out with her in E III 9 391 21
Had she refused, I should have gone mad.-- E III 14 437 8
She absolutely refused to allow me, which I then thought E III 14 441 8
He had even refused one regular invitation to dinner; and P III 10 82 2
not have been pleased, if we had refused to join them. P III 10 83 5
Wentworth said, "do you mean that she refused him?" P III 10 89 29 30
wife's; they would not be refused; they compressed P III 10 91 41
in a manner not to be refused, to sit between them; and by P IV 8 189 46
course among us, that every man is refused--till he offers. P IV 9 195 30
a certainty that you had refused one man at least, of P IV 11 244 70

REFUSING (22)
To disobey her mother by refusing an unexceptionable offer LS 19 274 2
Here was I, in my eagerness to get on, refusing to wait NA I 14 107 9
been prevented by her refusing to join it, and very NA I 14 115 55
herself; and positively refusing Elinor's offered SS II 9 203 10
Marianne, not contented with absolutely refusing to go SS III 5 294 3
I wish you very happy and very rich, and by refusing your PP I 19 107 16
into your head to go on refusing every offer of marriage PP I 20 113 28
wishing to make her feel what she had lost in refusing him. PP II 5 155 4
I might have felt in refusing you, had you behaved in a PP II 11 192 23 24
You will hardly blame me for refusing to comply with this PP II 12 201 5
You do not blame me, however, for refusing him?" PP II 17 224 4
Supposing him to be attached to me, would my refusing to PP III 14 357 61
He could not but wonder at her refusing to do any thing MP I 3 30 57
them all, so as to leave me no possibility of refusing! MP I 12 119 26
Was she right in refusing what was so warmly asked, so MP I 16 153 3
His still refusing to tell her what he had gone for, was MP II 12 291 1
for having received such an offer, than for refusing it. MP III 2 332 20
as his father's, at her refusing Crawford, because, so far MP III 3 335 6
cannot, you have done exactly as you ought in refusing him. MP III 4 346 12
acquitted her conduct in refusing him, but this, though MP III 16 452 14
for refusing this invitation," was Emma's conclusion. E II 15 285 15
every hope;--she had begun by refusing to hear him.-- E III 13 431 38

REFUTATION (2)
Two posts came in, and brought no refutation, public or MP III 15 442 22
allow, when Anne's refutation of the supposed engagement P IV 9 210 99

REFUTE (2)
Mr. Wickham, I can only refute it by laying before you the PP II 12 199 5
But his character and general conduct must refute it. P IV 3 139 7

REFUTED (1)
had been eagerly refuted at the time, there were moments E II 2 166 11

REGAIN (6)
And off they went, to regain their former place. NA I 8 58 25
She might in time regain tranquillity; but he, what had he SS II 1 140 1
Kitty might in time regain her natural degree of sense, PP II 19 237 3
wants, made her eager to regain the friends she had so MP I 1 4 2
comfort, and sought to regain his favour; and he had given MP III 1 322 50
kept him from trying to regain her when thrown in his way. P IV 11 242 63

REGAINED (3)
she expected, she soon regained her composure, and calmly PP I 22 124 14 15
There was comfort also in Tom, who gradually regained his MP III 17 462 4
She regained the street--happy in this, that though much E II 1 162 33

REGAINING (1)
his health, without regaining the thoughtlessness and MP III 17 462 4

REGAL (1)
its rise and grandeur, regal visits and loyal efforts, MP I 9 85 3

REGALE (1)
Still, however, it was her private regale.-- MP III 14 431 8

REGALED (1)
by Mrs. Norris, who thus regaled in the credit of being MP I 2 12 1

REGALING (2)
other drawing-room, and regaling themselves with her P IV 10 216 18
up,--and she was now regaling in the delight of opening S 10 414 1

REGARD (227)
to gain any share of my regard; & I shall certainly LS 3 247 1
I really have a regard for him, he is so easily imposed on! LS 5 250 1
this affair extremely, & regard it as a very happy mixture LS 7 253 2
Her prudence & economy are exemplary, her regard for Mr LS 14 265 5
truly deserving of our regard, & when I have communicated LS 18 272 1
Contemptible as a regard founded only on compassion, must LS 22 280 1
He can have no true regard for me, or he would not have LS 22 282 6
I have a real regard for him, & was beyond expression LS 24 290 13
You know how sincerely I regard both husband & wife. I LS 30 301 5
She may whimper, & the Vernons may storm; I regard them LS 39 308 1
And may you always regard me as unalterably yours S. LS 39 308 2
another, from whom can she expect protection and regard? NA I 5 37 4
I have a great regard for him, I assure you: a gentleman- NA I 12 95 18
I am excessively concerned that he should have any regard NA II 3 145 13
the taste of ladies in regard to places as well as men. NA II 7 175 15
and that it might not cost her Henry's entire regard. NA II 10 199 2
with unreserve; on whose regard you can place dependence; NA II 10 207 38
I do not believe she had ever any regard either for James NA II 12 218 4
of such expressions with regard to Henry and herself, had NA II 14 230 2
her by his pointed regard--had he even confused her by his NA II 14 230 2
turned all his partial regard for their daughter into NA II 14 234 10
the persuasion of his regard for Elinor perhaps assisted SS I 3 16 13
She believed the regard to be mutual; but she required SS I 4 21 11
I am by no means assured of his regard for me. SS I 4 21 15
A doubt of her regard, supposing him to feel it, need not SS I 4 22 18
seemed the nature of his regard; and sometimes, for a few SS I 4 22 18
was no hindrance to the regard of Colonel Brandon. SS I 10 49 12
amends for the regard of Lady Middleton and her mother. SS I 10 50 18
Her admiration and regard, even her sisterly regard, was SS I 11 55 7
his emotion with the tender recollection of past regard. SS I 11 57 17
I am persuaded that Mrs. Smith suspects his regard for SS I 15 78 26
of regard in her reception of him than even Elinor herself. SS I 16 87 23
Now there is no one to regard them. SS I 16 88 31
Her joy and expressions of regard long outlived her wonder. SS I 17 90 1
She was not in a humour, however, to regard it as an SS I 18 98 13
disposed on the whole to regard his actions with all the SS I 19 101 2
of every mark of regard in look or word which fell from SS I 19 102 2
his suspicions of her regard for Edward, than he had been SS I 21 125 36
Had he feigned a regard for her which he did not feel? SS II 1 139 1
had been conscious of his regard for her at Norland; it SS II 1 139 1
her declaration of tender regard for him, and she SS II 1 141 7
and I hope out of some regard to me, your brother might be SS II 2 149 25
With regard to herself, it was now a matter of unconcern SS II 3 158 20
but at the same time her regard for Colonel Brandon SS II 4 162 8
time with much concern his continued regard for her sister. SS II 5 168 12
She feared it was a strengthening regard. SS II 5 169 12
Absence might have weakened his regard, and convenience SS II 6 179 17
it, but that such a regard had formerly existed she could SS II 6 179 17
her, nor in appearing to regard her, but in endeavouring SS II 7 181 6
believed you, that your regard for us all was insincere, SS II 7 188 42
Till yesterday, I believe, she never doubted his regard; SS II 8 199 40
My regard for her, for yourself, for your mother--will you SS II 9 204 18
but a very sincere regard--nothing but an earnest desire SS II 9 204 18
I had hoped that her regard for me would support her under SS II 9 205 24
My brother had no regard for her; his pleasures were not SS II 9 206 24
Regard for a former servant of my own, who had since SS II 9 207 26
than I gave: but with regard to the purchase-money, I SS II 11 225 33
altogether so great a regard for you, that in all SS II 11 226 42
convinced of your regard for her, and next to Edward's love, SS II 13 240 14 15
Happy had it been for her, if her regard for Edward had SS II 14 250 12
of any person whom you have a regard for, Mrs. Jennings. SS III 1 268 45
never be, he did not regard his mother's anger, while he SS III 2 277 30
to engage her regard, without a thought of returning it.-- SS III 8 320 32
She knew I had no regard for her when we married.-- SS III 8 329 65
"His regard for her, infinitely surpassing anything that SS III 9 336 14
and softened only his protestations of present regard. SS III 10 347 33
regard, and who had only two thousand pounds in the world. SS III 13 367 22
other, made that mutual regard inevitable and immediate, SS III 13 370 36
past affliction;--her regard and her society restored his SS III 14 379 17
retained that decided regard which interested him in SS III 14 379 19
two sisters, whose mutual regard was increasing with the W 348 23
If I can perceive her regard for him, he must be a PP I 6 22 3
of the degree of her own regard, nor of its reasonableness. PP I 6 22 7
of the party whom she could regard with any complacency. PP I 8 35 2
"I have an excessive regard for Jane Bennet, she is really PP I 8 36 14
A regard for the requester would often make one readily PP I 10 50 37
he did not in the least regard his losses at whist, PP I 16 84 59
unworthy of Mr. Bingley's regard; and yet, it was not in PP I 17 85 1
imprudent, and has deserved to lose Mr. Darcy's regard." PP I 18 95 50
entertained of Bingley's regard, and said all in her power PP I 18 96 56
of your feelings with regard to my family, and may take PP I 19 107 16
in no other way. his regard for her was quite imaginary; PP I 20 112 24
Jane must soon cease to regard it, in the enjoyment of his. PP I 21 116 8
every other mark of your regard during my stay in PP I 22 124 10
made her turn with fonder regard to her sister, of whose PP I 23 128 9
some plans of the latter with regard to new furniture. PP II 1 133 2
and yet whether Bingley's regard had really died away, or PP II 1 134 3
may feel something like regard and esteem for our cousin." PP II 1 135 12
that Charlotte had any regard for him, I should only think PP II 1 135 13
especially, there subsisted a very particular regard. PP II 2 139 2
with regard to this young man will influence her. PP II 2 141 12
been entirely deceived in Miss Bingley's regard for me. PP II 3 148 26
him with a most sincere regard; and she parted from him PP II 4 151 3
of woman whom one cannot regard with too much deference." PP II 5 157 9
acknowledgment of your regard, can have little difficulty PP II 11 190 7
any symptom of peculiar regard, and I remained convinced PP II 12 197 5
his affection with sincere, if not with equal regard.-- PP II 12 199 5
probable;--but his regard did not appear to me enough PP II 12 199 5
Regard for my sister's credit and feelings prevented any PP II 12 202 5
would not regard it, that she would never look in it again. PP II 13 204 2
regard which his social powers had gained him in the mess. PP II 13 206 4
either been deceived with regard to her fortune, or had PP II 13 207 6
Our situation with regard to Lady Catherine's family is PP II 15 215 4
which will probably soon drive away his regard for me. PP II 17 224 4
in love before, her regard had all the warmth of first PP II 17 227 26
she thought of his regard with a deeper sentiment of PP III 1 251 48
look appeared on either side that spoke particular regard. PP III 2 262 8
any indelicate display of regard, or any peculiarity of PP III 2 265 16
But if otherwise, if the regard springing from such PP III 4 279 24
would not marry Lydia, if he had not a real regard for her. PP III 7 304 35
This was one point, with regard to Lydia at least, which PP III 8 308 4
The wish of procuring her regard, which she had assured PP III 8 311 13
this for a girl whom he could neither regard nor esteem. PP III 10 326 3
see you again the dupe of Miss Bingley's pretended regard." PP III 13 350 48
Do you pay no regard to the wishes of his friends? PP III 14 355 43
"You have no regard, then for the honour and credit of my PP III 14 357 65
And with regard to the resentment of his family, or the PP III 14 358 70
to the preservation of my regard; but, though we have both PP III 16 368 21
the hundredth part of the regard I bear your own dear MP I 1 7 8
My own trouble, you know, I never regard. MP I 1 7 8
mother, as evincing least regard for her niece, he could MP I 4 37 8
"I pay very little regard," said Mrs. Grant, "to what any MP I 4 43 25
cried Mrs. Norris, "I am sure you need not regard it. MP I 6 53 9
And with regard to their influencing public manners, Miss MP I 9 93 49

of any thing useful with regard to the object of the day. MP I 10 104 51
imprudent, I think, with regard to Maria, whose situation MP I 13 125 17
without particular regard for either, without jealousy MP II 1 185 30
therefore he must regard her acquiescence in their wrong MP II 2 188 3
I caught a dreadful cold, but that I did not regard. MP II 2 190 5
of Edmund's too partial regard, to the unconcern of his MP II 2 194 20
you so long; and with regard to some others, I can MP II 3 198 13
She must know herself too secure of the regard of all the MP II 3 199 14
that she had--with great regard, with almost decided MP II 5 227 69
to regard all the connections of our family as his own." MP II 7 245 34
His conviction of her regard for him was sometimes very MP II 8 255 10
You are not sensible of the gain, for your regard for him MP II 12 296 27
of proving his regard for Admiral Crawford, and that the MP II 13 298 3
knew not what to say--how to class or how to regard it. MP II 13 302 10
paying my opinion or my regard the compliment of any MP III 1 319 39
Here was again a want of delicacy and regard for others MP III 2 328 9
not regard the connection as more desirable than he did. MP III 3 335 6
her situation with regard to Crawford should be mentioned MP III 4 345 1
of creating that regard which had not been created before. MP III 4 347 18
be answered for--I think I never shall return his regard." MP III 4 347 20
Mr. Crawford probably could not regard his future father- MP III 10 402 12
to return Mr. Crawford's regard, the probability of his MP III 12 419 9
If I did not believe that she had some regard for me, of MP III 13 421 2
His warm regard, his kind expressions, his confidential MP III 13 425 5
her correspondent was not of a sort to regard a slight one. MP III 15 438 6
But your's--your regard was new compared with----- MP III 15 446 34
vice, he could not but regard the step she had taken, as MP III 16 452 13
approbation and increased regard; and happy as all this MP III 17 461 2
regard for him would be foundation enough for wedded love. MP III 17 470 25
With such a regard for her, indeed, as his had long been, MP III 17 470 27
as his had long been, a regard founded on the most MP III 17 470 27
I have a great regard for you and Emma; but when it comes E I 1 10 29
a very good young man, and I have a great regard for him. E I 1 14 47
Real, long-standing regard brought the Westons and Mr. E I 3 20 2
considered with all the regard and respect which a E I 3 21 4
Mrs. Weston was the object of a regard, which had its E I 4 26 2
I shall always have a great regard for the Miss Martins, E I 4 31 25
She had no scruple with regard to him. E I 6 42 1
I must confess that I regard it as a most happy thought, E I 6 48 39
Do you mean with regard to this letter?" E I 7 51 7
hand, it was not mechanically twisted about without regard. E I 7 53 22
to him, and have a great regard for--but that is quite a E I 7 54 30
He knows I have a thorough regard for him and all his E I 8 59 27
and a strong habit of regard for every old acquaintance. E I 11 92 4
had really a great regard for his father-in-law, and E I 11 93 5
regard to these children, I observe we never disagree." E I 12 98 3
I have a great regard for Mr. Perry. E I 12 101 26
and found her doom already signed with regard to Randalls. E I 13 109 5
They are jealous even of his regard for his father E I 14 122 21
set all their claims on his gratitude and regard at nought. E I 18 148 19
Emma's brain with regard to Jane Fairfax, this charming Mr. E II 1 160 21
22
They continued together with unabated regard however, till E II 2 165 7
With regard to her not accompanying them to Ireland, her E II 2 166 10
Where I have a regard, I always think a person well- E II 3 176 49
Her regard was receiving strength by invariable praise of E II 4 184 10
of his uncle with warm regard, was fond of talking of him-- E II 7 205 2
He had a great regard for Mrs. Goddard; and Emma should E II 7 209 13
You will not regard being tired. E II 7 211 20
He has a great regard for the Bateses, you know, E II 8 224 72
My regard for Hartfield is most warm"----- E II 12 261 33
You may have done wrong with regard to Mr. Dixon, but this E II 15 284 10
Jane will be treated with such regard and kindness!-- E III 8 382 23
Poor old John, I have a great regard for him; he was clerk E III 8 383 29
He looked at her with a glow of regard. E III 9 385 7
have lavished every distinction of regard or sympathy. E III 9 389 16
thing she could offer of assistance or regard be repulsed. E III 11 403 2
Frank Churchill's having the least regard for Jane Fairfax. E III 11 405 11
nothing to forfeit the regard and interest which had been E III 11 408 33
his regard for her had not been infinitely the most dear. E III 11 412 45
herself, and be over-rating his regard for her.-- E III 12 416 1
regard, must, I think, be the happiest of mortals.-- E III 13 428 23
Emma Woodhouse, whom I regard with so much brotherly E III 14 439 8
return of her former regard for the writer, and the very E III 15 444 1
She had such a regard for Mr. Knightley, as to think he E III 17 467 31
And with regard to Anne's dislike of Bath, she considered P III 2 14 11
in the other; and, with regard to the gentlemen, there was P III 5 32 2
for besides having a regard for his cousin, Charles Hayter P III 9 76 14
With regard to Charles Hayter, she had delicacy which must P III 9 77 18
She had too old a regard for him to be so wholly estranged, P III 9 77 19
That he did not regard it as a desperate case--that he did P III 12 112 53
to stay; though, with regard to any attendance on Miss P III 12 113 56
the common claims of regard, for his sake; and she hoped P III 12 116 69
With regard to Captain Wentworth, though Anne hazarded no P IV 2 133 25
and manners, and with regard to education is not very nice. P IV 4 150 17
"I own that to be able to regard you as the future P IV 5 159 25
Nothing that I regard." P IV 7 177 13
I regard Louisa Musgrove as a very amiable, sweet-tempered P IV 8 182 10
merely by friendship and regard, but by the tenderness of P IV 8 185 21
Anne Elliot; and I do regard her as one who is too modest, P IV 8 187 28
she owed him gratitude and regard, perhaps compassion. P IV 9 192 2
in his conduct then with regard to my father and sister, P IV 9 200 56
"Yes; which I objected to, but he would not regard. P IV 9 202 66
in Camden-Place; but his regard for Mr. Elliot gave him an P IV 9 206 90
With a confidence in Mr. Elliot's regard, more creditable P IV 9 209 96
I hope your father and mother are quite happy with regard P IV 10 218 21
which made her full of regard and interest for every body P IV 10 220 31
Louisa at all, he must regard himself as bound to her, if P IV 11 243 66
and wrong, I mean with regard to myself; and I must P IV 11 246 79
80
had been mistaken with regard to both; that she had been P IV 12 249 3
appearance secured a very strong hold in Lady D.'s regard. S 3 379 1
great deal too active to regard the walk of a mile as any S 6 390 1
How it might answer with regard to the baronet, remained S 11 422 1
rather unfavourably with regard to clara;--but hers was a S 12 426 1

REGARDED (25)

herself to be earnestly regarded by a gentleman who stood NA I 10 80 59
probably, as far as it regarded only himself, perfectly SS I 8 36 2
man, and she regarded him with respect and compassion. SS I 10 50 12
and from the first had regarded her with a kindness which SS I 11 54 6
not an inch to its size, if my feelings are regarded." SS I 14 72 7
At last he turned round again, and regarded them both; she SS II 6 176 7
as far at least as it regarded Mrs. Ferrars's conduct, the SS III 1 269 57
made very light of, at least as far as regarded its size. SS III 3 283 20
windows; but Elinor, all happiness within, regarded it not. SS III 7 316 28
herself that her husband regarded the affair as she wished, PP I 20 112 20
As her successor in that house, she regarded her with PP I 23 130 16
benefits, and whom she regarded herself with an interest, PP III 11 334 36
She regarded her cousin as an example of every thing good MP I 4 37 8
and must be regarded as the queen of the evening. MP II 9 266 22
was the first of her girls whom she had ever much regarded. MP III 8 389 4
must not be regarded as of any consequence, if you feel MP III 11 411 16
going of both seemed regarded--and the ecstacy of Susan MP III 15 444 25
What was unwholesome to him, he regarded as unfit for any E I 2 19 14
This was Colonel Campbell, who had very highly regarded E II 2 163 4
It regarded a supper-room. E II 11 254 44
heir expectant had formerly been so tenaciously regarded. E III 15 449 35
was expressed, but apparently very little regarded. P III 1 8 16
Captain Wentworth was to be regarded as the probable cause. P III 9 77 19
result of the most correct opinions and well regarded mind. P IV 12 249 3
also give himself credit for. he regarded it as his duty.-- S 8 405 2

REGARDFUL (1)

more gentle, and regardful of others, than formerly. MP III 11 413 32

REGARDING (7)

"And that prevented you;" said Henry, earnestly regarding NA II 9 195 16
the power of regarding him after their entering the house. SS I 9 43 11
within herself, regarding her sister with uneasiness. SS II 4 165 29
regarding them at all, returned them to her daughter. SS II 12 235 29
far beyond the necessity of regarding little matters." PP I 16 83 50
to beg him to call; and regarding it as what was meant to MP III 16 454 18
Churchill, and really regarding him as she did with E III 18 480 80

REGARDLESS (5)

regardless of every thing but her own gratification. NA I 13 98 3
With a book he was regardless of time; and on the present PP I 3 12 15
The first mentioned was, that, regardless of the PP II 12 196 5
could have made her regardless of that greatest fault of E I 11 93 5
Always deceived in fact by his own wishes, and regardless E III 15 445 15

REGARDS (5)

him with her best regards to his father and mother, and NA I 15 125 48
Who regards me?" SS II 7 191 62
My mother desires her very best compliments and regards, E II 3 173 29
mean, as far as regards society, and all the habits and E III 13 428 23
"Kindest regards. P IV 10 215 16

REGD DE COURCY (1)

in your opinion of her. I am &c. Regd De Courcy. LS 12 261 6

REGIMENT (23)

will soon expire, and he must return to his regiment.-- NA II 4 152 29
He went away to his regiment two days ago, and I trust I NA II 12 217 2
was with my regiment in the East Indies) she should fall? SS II 9 206 24
arrival of a militia regiment in the neighbourhood; it was PP I 7 28 3
Much had been done, and much had been said in the regiment PP I 12 60 7
regiment of militia, and the monthly balls of Meryton." PP II 16 220 7
two days together when Colonel Millar's regiment went away. PP II 18 229 4
the Colonel of the regiment, to accompany her to Brighton. PP II 18 230 11
other cause for satisfaction in the loss of the regiment. PP II 19 237 3
another regiment should be quartered in Meryton. PP II 19 238 6
She had never perceived while the regiment was in PP III 4 280 25
Could he expect to be noticed again by the regiment, after PP III 5 282 1
way, and others of the regiment, who treated her with more PP III 5 285 18
man's intimates in the regiment, whether Wickham has any PP III 6 295 6
in general ----'s regiment, now quartered in the north. PP III 8 312 19
They will then join his regiment, unless they are first PP III 8 313 19
should be taken from a regiment where she was acquainted PP III 8 313 20
may not be so pleasant in general ----'s regiment." PP III 8 313 21
and he was to join his regiment at the end of a fortnight. PP III 9 318 17
He confessed himself obliged to leave the regiment, on PP III 10 323 2
because her husband's regiment happens to be so far off. PP III 11 331 12
His regiment is there; for I suppose you have heard of his PP III 11 337 51
The marriage of Lieut. Fairfax, of the ---- regiment of E II 2 163 2

REGIMENT'S (3)

The comfort to her, of the regiment's approaching removal, PP II 16 223 25
It was the last of the regiment's stay in Meryton, and all PP II 18 229 1
On the very last day of the regiment's remaining in PP II 18 233 26

REGIMENTALS (3)

in their eyes when opposed to the regimentals of an ensign. PP I 7 29 4
the other night at Sir William's in his regimentals." PP I 7 29 12
wanted only regimentals to make him completely charming. PP I 15 72 8

REGINALD (75)

Reginald has long wished I know to see this captivating LS 3 247 1
Well my dear Reginald, I have seen this dangerous creature, LS 6 250 1
& to persuade Reginald that she has scandalously belied me. LS 7 254 3
My dear mother You must not expect Reginald back again LS 8 254 1
excessive anxiety about Reginald would subject him to an LS 8 254 1
& which Reginald himself was entirely disposed to credit. LS 8 255 1
& if I did not know that Reginald is too much at home at LS 8 256 1
Sir Reginald is very infirm, & not likely to stand in your LS 8 256 3
Reginald has a good figure, & is not unworthy the praise LS 9 256 1
my dearest mother about Reginald, from witnessing the very LS 10 258 3
I wish you could get Reginald home again, under any LS 11 259 1
in love with her, which Reginald firmly beleived when he LS 11 259 1
very far was it, from originating in anxiety for Reginald. LS 11 259 2
Sir Reginald de courcy to his son. Parklands. LS 12 260 1
but I hope my dear Reginald that you will be superior to LS 12 260 1
my dear Reginald, of seeing you settled in the world. LS 12 261 3
I had intended to write to Reginald myself, as soon as my LS 13 262 1
vexed that Sir Reginald should know anything of a matter LS 13 262 1
by the same post to Reginald, a long letter full of it all, LS 13 262 1
Mr De Courcy to Sir Reginald. Churchill. LS 14 263 1
along the shrubbery with Reginald, calling forth all his LS 15 267 4
Reginald is so incensed against the poor silly girl! LS 15 267 7
Reginald is never easy unless we are by ourselves, & when LS 16 268 2
Manwaring is indeed beyond compare superior to Reginald-- LS 16 269 3
Poor Reginald was beyond measure concerned to see his fair LS 17 270 3
an hour together, in earnest conversation with Reginald. LS 17 271 7
Yet Reginald still thinks Lady Susan the best of mothers-- LS 17 271 7
Oh! Reginald, how is your judgement enslaved! LS 17 271 7
Reginald is only repeating after her ladyship. I am &c. LS 17 272 8
with a smile when Reginald says anything amusing; & let LS 18 272 1
She is actually falling in love with Reginald de courcy. LS 19 274 2
I am not yet certain that Reginald sees what she is about; LS 19 274 3
at the door; it was Reginald, who came by Lady Susan's LS 20 275 1
Reginald observed all that passed, in perfect silence. LS 20 276 3
As for Reginald, I beleive he does not know what to make LS 20 278 9
The girl, whose heart can distinguish Reginald de courcy, LS 20 278 11
of her affection for Reginald, & from not feeling LS 22 280 1
It is true that Reginald had not in any degree grown cool LS 22 280 1
Reginald came this morning into my dressing room, with a LS 22 281 4
you, as that Reginald should be returning to Parklands. LS 23 283 2
I concluded of course that she & Reginald had been LS 23 284 6
The quarrel between Lady Susan & Reginald is made up, & we LS 24 285 1
Reginald was all but gone; his horse was ordered, & almost LS 24 285 1
Your applying however to Reginald can be productive only LS 24 287 7
at seeing Reginald come out of Lady Susan's dressing room. LS 24 287 8
Reginald was glad to get away, & I went to Lady Susan; LS 24 287 10
If you think your daughter at all attached to Reginald, LS 24 290 12
This Reginald has a proud spirit of his own!--a spirit too, LS 25 292 1
It's effect on Reginald justifies some portion of vanity, LS 25 293 3
And yet this Reginald, whom a very few words from me LS 25 293 3
for her application to Reginald; I must punish him for LS 25 293 4
in reconciling Reginald to me, I was not able to save that LS 25 293 4
Her idle love for Reginald too; it is surely my duty to LS 25 294 5
being on good terms with Reginald, which at present in LS 25 294 6
letter my dear mother, will be brought you by Reginald. LS 27 296 1
be with Reginald--& that would be the greatest evil of all. LS 27 297 1
I could not help asking Reginald if he intended being in LS 27 297 4
of Reginald, to the infinite disadvantage of the latter. LS 29 299 2
when Reginald according to our agreement is to be in town. LS 29 299 2
on the caprice of Sir Reginald, will not suit the freedom LS 29 299 3
my acquaintance with Reginald as more than the commonest LS 29 299 4
My dear friend, That tormenting creature Reginald is LS 31 301 1
was out when both she & Reginald came, or I would have LS 32 302 1
Depend upon it, I can make my own story with Reginald. LS 33 303 1
Reginald will be a little enraged at first, but by LS 33 303 2
Reginald, you agitate me beyond expression. LS 35 304 1
Your husband I abhor--Reginald I despise--& I am secure of LS 39 307 1
brought myself to marry Reginald; & am equally determined LS 39 308 0
1000
for he is returned, Reginald is returned, not to ask our LS 40 308 1
It has been a sad heavy winter hitherto, without Reginald, LS 40 309 1
Frederica runs much in my thoughts, & when Reginald has LS 40 309 1
And Reginald really with you! LS 41 309 1
Reginald may not be in town again by that time! LS 41 310 2
No remembrance of Reginald, no consciousness of guilt, LS 42 311 2
aunt, till such time as Reginald de courcy could be talked, LS 42 313 8

REGINALD'S (7)
than this perversion of Reginald's judgement, which when LS 8 255 1
to see a young man of Reginald's sense duped by her at all. LS 8 256 4
& he is certainly less uneasy since Reginald's letter. LS 13 263 1
My dear mother I return you Reginald's letter, & LS 15 266 1
She may be Reginald's wife. LS 15 267 4
vexation of knowing of Reginald's being gone to town, for LS 40 308 1
Three months might have done it in general, but Reginald's LS 42 313 8
REGION (1)
be in any doubtful, or distant, or unapproachable region." MP II 11 289 32
REGRET (122)
Greif, & professions of regret, & general resolutions of LS 3 247 1
his visit, I should regret Mr Vernon's giving him any. LS 8 256 3
his regret at having ever beleived the contrary himself. LS 11 259 1
I never can sufficiently regret that I wrote to you at all. LS 24 285 1
Far from me be all complaint, & every sigh of regret. LS 36 305 1
state; divided between regret for the loss of one great NA I 11 86 50
concern, regret, and dependence on Catherine's honour.-- NA I 12 94 9
rest, there was nothing to regret for half an instant.-- NA I 15 116 2
only source of Isabella's regret; and when she saw her at NA II 1 137 50
point with you, we should leave it without a single regret. NA II 2 139 7
view of Bath without any regret, and met with every mile- NA II 5 155 4
that she could not regret her being led on, though so NA II 10 207 41
by the sweetest confidence in his regret and resentment. NA II 14 231 4
gratitude without servile regret, be guarded without NA II 14 235 14
The time may come when Harry will regret that so large a SS I 2 9 8
to regret you!--when learn to feel a home elsewhere!-- SS I 5 27 8
of the pleasure or the regret you occasion, and insensible SS I 5 27 8
teach her to think of Norland with less regret than ever. SS I 11 54 6
heartily in the general regret on so unfortunate an event; SS I 13 66 60
observed with regret that they were only eight altogether. SS I 20 111 18
and banish every regret which might lessen her SS II 4 159 1
whom, to Lady Middleton's regret, she had never dropped, SS II 5 168 11
four days, to make Elinor regret what she had done, in SS II 6 175 1
It is with great regret that I obey your commands of SS II 7 183 13
any professions of regret, acknowledged no breach of faith, SS II 7 183 14
he may harbour some regret, in the end he must become so. SS III 1 263 27
that he mentioned with regret, that the house was small SS III 3 283 20
Not that you have any reason to regret, my dear Elinor. SS III 5 297 31
would give her a moment's regret to be divided for ever, SS III 6 302 5
Her sorrow, her disappointment, her deep regret, when I SS III 8 324 42
with a tenderness, a regret, rather in proportion, as she SS III 9 333 2
"As for regret," said Marianne, "I have done with that, as SS III 10 344 17
his heart, and made him regret the connection which had SS III 11 351 9
And why does he regret it?-- SS III 11 351 13
"and I have nothing to regret--nothing but my own folly." SS III 11 352 14
had been a continual source of disquiet and regret to him. SS III 13 367 21
of Colonel Brandon with envy, and of Marianne with regret. SS III 14 379 18
her mother's reproach prevented his feeling any regret. PP I 20 112 24
to their aunt's where his regret and vexation, and the PP I 21 115 3
"I do not pretend to regret any thing I shall leave in PP I 21 116 8
with her brother's regret at not having had time to pay PP II 1 133 1
herself that she did not regret it; but she could no PP II 3 147 25
would make him abundantly regret what he had thrown away. PP II 3 149 27
I cannot say that I regret my comparative insignificance. PP II 3 150 29
He expressed no regret for what he had done which PP II 13 204 1
source of vexation and regret; and in the unhappy defects PP II 14 212 17
"Oh! no, my regret and compassion are all done away by PP II 17 225 13
connected with a little absurdity, are not worth a regret. PP II 18 231 17
one ceaseless source of regret in my sister's absence, I PP II 19 237 4
recollection--it saved her from something like regret. PP III 1 246 7
had something of real regret, that it "was a very long PP III 2 262 8
wishes to predominate, she began to regret that he came. PP III 3 268 7
Be that as it may, she saw him go with regret; and in this PP III 4 279 24
tears and lamentations of regret, invectives against the PP III 5 287 34
though mixed with regret, on finding how steadfastly both PP III 10 327 3
and hand, I shall soon cease to regret him at all." PP III 15 361 4
clever, and I shall only regret that you have not half-a- MP I 4 42 21
care, but with great regret that she was not stronger. MP I 9 96 76
topic than that of his regret at her secession from their MP I 15 142 24
her, with infinite regret, that he found it absolutely MP I 15 148 58
ready to regret that some other play had not been chosen. MP I 18 164 1
only a softened air and stronger expressions of regret. MP II 2 193 18
By all the others it was mentioned with regret, and his MP II 2 194 20
could he regret any thing but the exclusion of the Grants. MP II 3 196 2
regret which they had never done much to deserve! MP II 3 204 33
He was roused from the reverie of retrospection and regret MP II 6 236 23
she should leave her with regret; that she began to MP II 8 256 12
and truly tender regret, that they were not at home to MP II 10 275 12
If she had felt impatience and regret before--if she had MP II 11 286 17
It is the regret and disappointment of a sister, who MP III 4 352 40
Edmund did not discern any symptoms of regret, and thought MP III 6 366 2
that <u>she</u> could not regret it; for to her many other MP III 10 400 6
moment was passed, could regret that she had not forced MP III 10 406 20
moment, lead it to do what it may afterwards regret. MP III 13 423 2
"I cannot but say, I much regret your being from home at MP III 14 431 8
even these incitements to regret, were feeble, compared MP III 14 432 9
it is best for me--since it leaves me so little to regret. MP III 16 456 25
That, perhaps, it was best for me; I had less to regret in MP III 16 458 30
He was suffering from disappointment and regret, grieving MP III 17 461 3
portion of vexation and regret--vexation that must rise MP III 17 468 22
to self-reproach, and regret to wretchedness--in having so MP III 17 468 22
must have gone with some regret, from the scenes and MP III 17 469 24
thought, where the only regret was for a partial E I 2 18 10
and of moments only of regret; and her satisfaction--her E I 2 18 12
It crossed my mind immediately that you would not regret E I 8 61 38
Not regret her leaving Highbury for the sake of marrying a E I 8 62 39
Papa is only speaking his own regret." E I 11 94 10
I always regret excessively on dear Emma's account that E I 12 104 46
great mortification and regret; but still he looked E I 18 144 1
of curiosity, wonder and regret, pain and pleasure, as to E II 3 180 57
"Perhaps you may now begin to regret that you spent one E II 8 222 52
"No," said he, smiling, "that is no subject of regret at E II 8 222 53
The other circumstance of regret related also to Jane E II 9 231 3
She did unfeignedly and unequivocally regret the E II 9 231 3
Mr. Perry might have reason to regret the alteration, but E II 11 251 27
to judge of her honest regret in this woeful change; but E II 12 263 42
dinner, as could make me regret having asked <u>more</u> than E II 15 283 9
She did not regret it. E III 3 332 2
and regret, in a reasonable way, that he should be so late. E III 6 364 59
She spoke as she felt, with earnest regret and solicitude-- E III 8 380 9
Emma could not regret her having gone to Miss Bates, but E III 9 386 8
Neither would she regret that he should be going to E III 9 386 8
She had scarcely a stronger regret than for her past E III 9 389 16
herself, and leave her less to regret when it were gone. E III 12 423 21
reason to regret that I was not in the secret earlier." E III 13 426 15
He is no object of regret, indeed! and it will not be very E III 13 426 16
and sorrowful regret that had ever surrounded it.-- E III 14 435 4
"It is not now worth a regret," said Emma. E III 18 477 56
had been taken, and her regret that Mrs. Clay should still P IV 1 124 11
make enquiries, she must regret the imprudence, lament the P IV 1 124 12
And looked back, with fond regret, to the bustles of P IV 2 135 34
should see nothing to regret in the duties and dignity of P IV 3 138 5
something of hers, and regret that he should have lost P IV 3 143 19
His regret increased as he listened. P IV 3 144 19
regret and entreaty, to his right honourable cousin. P IV 4 149 13
No, it was not regret which made Anne's heart beat in P IV 6 167 21
was gone--he had disappeared: she felt a moment's regret. P IV 8 184 18
There was much to regret. P IV 9 192 2
her regret that she had said so much, simple as it was. P IV 10 222 36
Henrietta have known the regret and reluctance of her P IV 10 225 62
not give her a moment's regret; but to have no family to P IV 12 251 10
back window with something like the fondness of regret.-- S 4 380 1
REGRETS (22)
as invariable, as with regrets so poignant and so fresh, SS II 1 141 6
those regrets which the remembrance of me occasioned. SS II 9 206 24
service, might lessen her regrets, I would not have SS II 9 210 32
regrets, which <u>she</u> could wish her not to indulge! SS II 10 213 2
"At present," continued Elinor, "he regrets what he had SS III 11 351 13
Comparisons would occur--regrets would arise;--and her joy, SS III 13 363 7
usage, and most painful regrets at his being what he is. PP I 16 78 20
the indulgence of those regrets, which must have been PP II 17 227 26
him with fears and regrets in disposing of her, was a PP III 17 375 28
of their regrets and difficulties, left them and walked on. MP I 9 90 36
well known to me, as my wishes and regrets must be to you. MP III 2 330 16
nothing, would awaken very wholesome regrets in her mind.-- MP III 6 366 1
the evening, and be attacked by no regrets but her own. E I 1 9 20
refrain from unreasonable regrets at that brother's E I 2 15 3
allow for her amiable regrets, and sometimes relieved them E I 7 55 36
of happy regrets and fearful affection with his daughter. E I 12 100 17
praise of him, and her regrets kept alive, and feelings E II 4 184 10
consciousness, the same regrets--to be ready to return to E II 5 187 4
to give her some regrets and some apprehensions. P III 1 7 12
Her attachment and regrets had, for a long time, clouded P III 4 28 6
who, overcome by fond regrets, could not help saying, "Ah! P III 8 64 5
6
She desired her best love, with a thousand regrets at S 9 407 1
REGRETTED (24)
but repeatedly regretted the necessity of its concealment, NA I 15 125 48
She felt the unexpected compliment, and deeply regretted NA II 8 185 5
Tuesday, and very much regretted that I was not fortunate SS II 6 177 9
that she had very much regretted being from home, when he SS II 13 241 20
continual self-reproach, regretted most bitterly that she SS III 2 270 2
hearing, & she only regretted that he had not been able to W 335 13
who regretted very much her not being of the party.-- W 350 24
No one but Mrs. Bennet, regretted that their stay would be PP III 9 318 18
mother--<u>she</u>, indeed, regretted that his part was not more MP I 18 166 4
time, that her not loving him now was scarcely regretted. MP III 2 327 4
been so much to her, should not be more visibly regretted. MP III 6 366 3
Sam, loud and overbearing as he was, she rather regretted MP III 8 390 8
Mr. Price was out, which she regretted very much. MP III 10 400 6
I have since--sometimes--for a moment--regretted that I MP III 16 459 30
She was regretted by no one at Mansfield. MP III 17 466 16
few weeks, and very much regretted the impossibility he E I 17 140 2
go, if they did; and she regretted that her father's known E II 7 207 6
She bitterly regretted not having sought a closer E III 12 421 17
for Perry, and only regretted that she had not done it. E III 18 479 73
and less at Hartfield; which was not to be regretted.-- E III 19 482 5
of, and scarcely at all regretted, when the intelligence P III 6 50 28
of being deeply regretted in their old neighbourhood, P IV 3 137 3
having been wished for, regretted, and at the same time P IV 5 158 21
lost no friend by it, certainly nothing to be regretted. P IV 6 167 21
REGRETTING (19)
"I am at least very far from regretting it, my dear sister, LS 24 288 11
She spoke to Henry Tilney on the subject, regretting his NA II 4 150 1
Northanger earnestly regretting that any necessity should NA II 13 220 1
Mrs. Jennings, though regretting that she had not been SS II 8 198 29
sometimes at Elinor, regretting only that their delight in SS II 13 242 25
to exist but with me, regretting only <u>that</u> heart which had SS III 10 346 28
to join with him in regretting that Lucy's engagement with SS III 13 371 38
give a suspicion of his regretting the extent of his SS III 14 377 12
and though evidently regretting that her visitors were to PP II 15 216 7
If he is satisfied with only regretting me, when he might PP III 15 361 4
"The soil is good; and I never pass it without regretting, MP I 6 54 10
it deserved, and of her regretting that he had not rather MP III 4 351 36
you, regretting, as well she might, the loss of such a----. MP III 16 455 21
he could not help it, regretting Fanny, even at the moment, MP III 17 468 21
even at the moment, but regretting her infinitely more, MP III 17 468 21
Scarcely had he done regretting Mary Crawford, and MP III 17 470 25
could comprehend his regretting that Captain Wentworth P III 9 80 34
She stopped, regretting with a deep blush that she had P IV 9 197 34
However, when I found how excessively he was regretting P IV 10 213 5
REGT (1)
"One of his particular friends,"--"all in the same Regt W 337 15
REGULAR (45)
Our regular employments, our books & conversation, with LS 27 297 2
Every morning now brought its regular duties;--shops were NA I 3 25 1
To be tied down to the regular payment of such a sum, on SS I 2 11 21
for the building was regular, the roof was tiled, the SS I 6 28 2
Miss Dashwood had a delicate complexion, regular features, SS I 10 46 2
his home, and from the regular cheerfulness of his spirits, SS III 14 377 12
which he supposed a regular part of the business. PP I 19 104 1
correspondence was as regular and frequent as it had ever PP II 3 146 19
without steady and regular instruction, and nobody but a PP II 6 165 32
companions of her own age, and of a regular instructress." MP I 1 9 11
that Fanny should have a regular lady's horse of her own MP I 4 36 7
time, and is a large, regular, brick building--heavy, but MP I 6 56 26
"If Fanny would be more regular in her exercise, she would MP I 7 73 55
Every thing was now in a regular train; theatre, actors, MP I 18 164 1
The first regular rehearsal of the three first acts was MP I 18 171 25
It is a regular thing. MP II 11 288 28
the sound of a step in regular approach was heard--a heavy MP III 1 312 4
heard; all proceeded in a regular course of cheerful MP III 8 391 11
debarred from her usual, regular exercise; she had lost MP III 11 409 6
It would have all ended in a regular standing flirtation, MP III 16 456 23
blue eyes, light hair, regular features, and a look of E I 3 23 9
eye--and so brilliant! regular features, open countenance, E I 5 39 20
return to Hartfield, to make a regular visit of some days. E I 8 57 1
in preparation for the regular four o'clock dinner, the E I 9 81 78
ladies from tolerably regular exercise; and on the morrow, E I 10 83 1
they had been seen in a regular way by their Surry E I 11 91 2
it was not regular, but it was very pleasing beauty. E II 2 167 12
The regular and best families Emma could hardly suppose E II 7 207 6
stairs without having any regular narration to attend to, E II 9 239 52
Mrs. Weston proposed having no regular supper; merely E II 11 254 45
and have regular weekly meetings at your house, or ours. E II 14 277 38
kind," said Emma, "will soon be in so regular a train-----" E II 14 278 41
regular difficulty of deciding who should do it for him. E II 16 291 4
should have had such a regular connected dream about E III 5 345 14
and preparation, the regular eating and drinking, and pic- E III 6 352 2
on her side, of a regular, equal, kindly intercourse. E III 8 377 1
"Oh! no, it is a meeting at the crown, a regular meeting. E III 16 456 27
any, who can live in a regular way, in the country, P III 3 20 17
He had even refused one regular invitation to dinner; and P III 10 82 2
She was looking remarkably well; her very regular, very P III 12 104 6
necessity of having a regular nurse, and finances at that P IV 5 154 9
Charles's brain for a regular history of their coming, or P IV 10 216 18
It shall be a regular party--small, but most elegant." P IV 10 220 29
very best company, those regular, steady, private families S 1 368 1
for them:--daily, regular exercise;--and I should S 10 416 1
REGULARITY (6)
and put an end to all regularity of detail; and for some SS III 1 262 14
laid out with too much regularity, was darkness and shade, MP I 9 91 38
such a steadiness and regularity of conduct, such a high MP II 12 294 16
without contrivance or regularity; dissatisfied with her MP III 8 389 4
The elegance, propriety, regularity,harmony--and perhaps, MP III 8 391 10
"The regularity and dispatch of it! E II 16 296 40
REGULARLY (16)
true, as she corresponds regularly with Mrs Manwaring; at LS 6 252 2
descriptions, who come regularly every winter, lengthen NA I 10 78 45
liveried, rising so regularly in their stirrups, and NA II 5 156 4
any acquaintance grew, so regularly grew their fortune. NA II 15 245 12
Her ladyship's carriage is regularly ordered for us. PP II 5 157 7
butter and eggs that were regularly consumed in the house. MP I 3 31 59

and as the Miss Bertrams regularly wanted their horses
A whole family assembling regularly for the purpose of MP I 4 35 7
and no delays they regularly advanced, and were in the MP I 9 86 12
these accounts were as regularly transmitted to Fanny, in MP III 7 376 6
and all her alarms were regularly sent off to her husband; MP III 13 427 12
or in chat, she had been regularly losing ground in his MP III 16 451 13
that she meant to read regularly through--and very good MP III 17 465 15
regularly, their little minds would bend to his." E I 5 37 7
Frank Churchill comes as regularly into my mind!"---- E I 18 147 18
Elegantly tall, regularly handsome, with great delicacy of E II 14 279 52
REGULARS (2) S 6 391 1
It is Mr. Wickham's intention to go into the regulars; and,
the ----shire, and of his being gone into the regulars. PP III 8 312 19
REGULATE (4) PP III 11 337 51
angry; but resolving to regulate her behaviour to him by
on by the others, to regulate the game & determine some SS I 16 89 42
laity, and those which regulate the clergy; for give me W 359 28
PP I 18 97 60
61
is so or not, and to regulate your behaviour accordingly.
REGULATED (6) E I 13 112 22
But it shall be regulated, it shall be checked by religion,
every thing ought to be regulated in so small a family as SS III 10 347 30
Having regulated her thoughts and comforted her feelings PP II 6 163 15
with a voice as well regulated as she could--"and how do MP II 9 265 20
a friend to her son, and regulated by the wish of MP II 11 287 18
"It is certainly very well regulated." MP III 10 400 6
REGULATING (2) E II 16 296 41
her judgment, and regulating her notions, his worth would
be looked up to, as regulating the modes of life, in MP III 6 367 5
REGULATION (3) P III 2 13 7
of mind, pride will be always under good regulation."
of times and seasons, a regulation of subject, a propriety, PP I 11 57 24
been allowed the entire regulation of it, as the two girls, MP III 7 382 29
REGULATIONS (3) MP III 10 403 14
upon the last naval regulations, or settle the number of
If he will adopt these regulations, in seven years he will MP III 10 403 13
living on board, daily regulations, food, hours, &c.; and P III 2 12 4
REGULATORS (1) P III 8 64 4
of good breeding, the regulators of refinement and
REHEARSAL (14) MP I 9 93 49
To think only of the licence which every rehearsal must
so needlessly often the rehearsal of the first scene MP I 16 154 14
theatre, and attend the rehearsal of the first act--in MP I 18 164 2
after the first rehearsal or two, Fanny began to be their MP I 18 165 3
forward enough in their rehearsal to comprehend all his MP I 18 165 3
it, most unnecessary rehearsal of the first act, which MP I 18 166 4
The first regular rehearsal of the three first acts was MP I 18 166 14
from the morning's rehearsal, and little vexations seemed MP I 18 171 25
to be safest, instead of attending the rehearsal at all? MP I 18 171 25
the possibility of the rehearsal being renewed after tea, MP I 18 172 29
in the middle of a rehearsal when you arrived this evening. MP II 1 177 5
Sir Thomas gravely, "but without any other rehearsal."-- MP II 1 185 28
Your cousin came too; and we had a rehearsal. MP II 1 185 29
A delightful rehearsal. MP III 5 358 7
REHEARSALS (3) MP III 5 358 7
and dresses, rehearsals and jokes, was his never-failing
at leisure, I mean to look in at their rehearsals too. MP I 13 121 1
MP I 18 167 7
8
the whole course of his rehearsals, Tom Bertram entered at
REHEARSE (9) MP II 1 182 22
a great many of my own, before we rehearse together.--
seldom get any body to rehearse with him; his complaint MP I 15 149 61
I have brought my book, and if you would but rehearse it MP I 18 164 2
I came here to-day intending to rehearse it with Edmund-- MP I 18 168 17
You must rehearse it with me, that I may fancy you him, MP I 18 168 17
Fanny, to ask her to rehearse with him, and help him MP I 18 168 19
They must now rehearse together. MP I 18 170 23
They could not act, they could not rehearse with any MP I 18 170 24
I came to rehearse. MP I 18 171 28
REHEARSED (3) MP III 5 358 7
will be three acts rehearsed to-morrow evening, and that
if the three acts were rehearsed, Edmund and Miss Crawford MP I 18 167 10
She did not believe they had yet rehearsed it, even in MP I 18 167 12
REHEARSERS (1) MP I 18 167 13
by those indefatigable rehearsers, Agatha and Frederick.
REHEARSING (3) MP I 18 169 21
bless himself, for we are rehearsing all over the house.
my opinion it is very disagreeable to be always rehearsing. MP I 18 169 21
"The scene we were rehearsing was so very remarkable! MP II 1 186 33
REIGN (1) MP III 5 358 9
same melancholy, seemed to reign at Hartfield--but in the
REIGNED (1) E III 13 424 1
reigned in it with few interruptions throughout the year.
REIGNING (2) MP I 9 89 30
which elegance was the reigning character, and as such,
"I am not one of those who neglect the reigning power to E II 2 167 12
REIGNS (4) P IV 10 224 48
and most of the principal events of their reigns!"
he bends a slave, and woman, lovely woman, reigns, alone. MP I 2 18 25
And woman, lovely woman, reigns alone. E I 9 71 14
he bends a slave, and woman, lovely woman, reigns alone. E I 9 72 17
REINED (1) E I 9 73 18
smiles reined in and spirits dancing in private rapture.
REINS (3) P IV 11 240 59
which he had then held the reins, and the singular
no direction of the reins to take the right turning, & NA I 9 62 10
But by coolly giving the reins a better direction herself, W 322 2
REINSTATE (2) P III 10 92 48
He had to reinstate himself in all the wonted concerns of
was quite necessary to reinstate her in a proper share of MP II 2 190 9
REITERATED (1) E III 14 435 5
coincided with the reiterated observation of others, that
REJECT (4) W 329 9
side, and not lead you to reject the offered olive branch.
with young ladies to reject the addresses of the man whom PP I 13 63 12
custom of your sex to reject a man on the first PP I 19 107 13
PP I 19 108 16
17
if you do not absolutely reject it as false, you will, I
REJECTED (12) PP II 12 202 5
Cliff, she voluntarily rejected the whole city of Bath, as
whose steadier judgment rejected several houses as too NA I 14 111 29
gave them reason to hope that it would not be rejected.-- SS I 3 14 1
and Mr. Hurst soon found even his open petition rejected. SS I 21 121 10
so little endeavour at civility, I am thus rejected. PP I 11 54 3
indicated respectability, was not to be hastily rejected. PP II 11 190 9
be, rejected many as deficient in size and importance. PP III 2 264 14
was tender-hearted again towards the rejected Mr. Martin. PP III 8 310 7
He had gone away rejected and mortified--disappointed in a E I 7 56 42
But Harriet rejected the suspicion with spirit. E II 4 181 3
Like him, she had tried the scheme and rejected it; but E III 11 410 36
least better than being rejected as no good at all; and E III 15 449 32
REJECTING (3) P III 5 33 9
If therefore she actually persists in rejecting my suit,
of her manner in rejecting him, and all the unjust PP I 20 110 4
Mansfield for him, rejecting Sotherton and London, PP III 2 265 16
REJECTION (5) MP II 3 202 25
of a conscientious rejection, by engaging her faith before
are not serious in your rejection of me, I shall chuse to NA II 15 244 11
and all the unjust accusations accompanying her rejection. PP I 19 108 19
expect but a determined rejection? unless it were an PP III 2 265 16
Emma could not have desired a more spirited rejection of MP II 8 255 10
REJOICE (35) E I 9 76 36
before I left town, & rejoice to be assured that Mr
you Reginald's letter, & rejoice with all my heart that my LS 5 249 1
with your veiws, & I rejoice to find that the prudent LS 15 266 1
Have I not reason to rejoice? LS 37 306 1
and most heartily did she rejoice in the happier LS 39 308 1
I rejoice to say, that the young man whom, of all others, NA II 6 166 9
account, could not but rejoice in the kind caution with NA II 12 216 2
Or at least, if she did not bring herself quite to rejoice NA II 15 244 11
When Elinor had ceased to rejoice in the dryness of the SS II 13 238 1
he found fresh reason to rejoice in what he had done for SS III 12 359 14
"Yes, indeed; his friends may well rejoice in his having SS III 13 370 35
friend from your sister, or that I rejoice in my success. PP II 9 178 15
Could you expect me to rejoice in the inferiority of your PP II 11 191 15
to rejoice over her words, or to distrust their meaning. PP II 11 192 22
how sincerely I must rejoice that he is wise enough to PP II 18 234 35
PP II 18 234 37
38
(and let us rejoice over it) marks nothing bad at heart.
wretched as is his character, we are forced to rejoice!" PP III 4 273 3
Julia could rejoice that he was gone.-- PP III 7 304 34
With a purer spirit did Fanny rejoice in the intelligence.- MP II 2 194 19
disposed to wonder and rejoice in having carried her point MP II 2 194 20
Mary was in a state of mind to rejoice in a connection MP II 10 280 32
How they will rejoice! MP II 12 292 5
was scarcely beyond her merits, rejoice in her prospects. MP II 12 292 7
How they might be benefited, how they must rejoice in such MP II 12 294 18
ever repeated reason to rejoice in what he had done for MP III 1 318 39
herself whether to rejoice or be angry, ashamed or only MP III 17 473 31
consider it so, and sincerely did she rejoice in their joy. E II 3 180 56
every friend must rejoice in it; and the family from whom E II 5 188 8
but could most heartily rejoice in that light, cheerful, E II 5 192 28
Emma could not but rejoice to hear that she had a fault. E II 8 219 44
there was time also to rejoice that Harriet's secret had E II 15 288 37
Yet she soon began to rejoice that she had heard them. E III 13 431 38
With all my soul I wish them happy, and rejoice over every P III 7 61 35
animate her features, and make her rejoice to talk of it. P IV 8 182 8
state of Uppercross, and rejoice in its happiness; and P IV 9 192 5
REJOICED (26) P IV 10 219 27
own conduct, and truly rejoiced to be preserved by his
and was heartily rejoiced therefore at neither seeing nor NA I 13 105 41
of his own heart she rejoiced; and she reproached herself NA I 14 106 1
Marianne was rejoiced to find her sister so easily pleased. SS I 3 14 2
Elinor, rejoiced to be assured of his being in London, now SS I 4 20 8
had Lucy been more amiable, she ought to have rejoiced. SS II 5 169 14
invaluable misery, she rejoiced in tears of agony to be at SS II 13 238 1
She rejoiced in his being cleared from some part of his SS III 6 303 9
of her allusions to Mr. Wickham, and rejoiced in it. SS III 11 349 1
concern in missing him; she really rejoiced at it. PP I 18 102 74
she firmly believed and rejoiced in his domestic comforts. PP II 13 209 13
Mrs. Bennet rejoiced to see Jane in undiminished beauty; PP II 15 216 7
PP II 16 222 19
20
When Elizabeth had rejoiced over Wickham's departure, she
a stranger, I might have rejoiced in them as my own, and PP II 19 237 3
How rejoiced was Elizabeth that their own journey had not PP III 1 246 6
and would formerly have rejoiced in its termination. PP III 1 247 8
"Mr. Collins moreover adds," "I am truly rejoiced that my PP III 4 279 23
I need not say how rejoiced I shall be to hear there has PP III 15 363 22
Campbell, and equally rejoiced that such a present had MP III 14 433 13
She had never rejoiced at the sound before, nor ever E II 8 215 15
He saw the advantages of the match, and rejoiced in them E III 8 378 3
danger, and would have rejoiced to be certain of being E III 17 468 33
nineteen, she would have rejoiced to see her at twenty-two, P III 1 7 12
Kellynch-Hall, she rejoiced anew over the conviction which P III 4 28 7
Anne had very sincerely rejoiced in there being no means P III 4 30 10
rejoiced, her sigh had none of the ill-will of envy in it. P III 6 48 17
REJOICING (13) P IV 10 219 27
cannot have all my reasons for rejoicing in such an event. LS 20 277 5
They gaily ascended the downs, rejoicing in their own SS I 9 41 4
Fanny, rejoicing in her escape, and proud of the ready wit SS II 14 253 26
was all cheerfulness; rejoicing that in her letters to her SS III 7 310 8
She then ran gaily off, rejoicing as she rambled about, in PP I 10 53 66
In a moment they were all out of the chaise, rejoicing at PP II 5 155 3
doubted: and Elizabeth, rejoicing that such an effusion PP III 17 378 44
that Charlotte, really rejoicing in the match, was anxious PP III 18 383 26
He stept to the door, rejoicing at that moment in having MP II 1 182 22
she could help rejoicing from beginning to end, it was as MP III 15 444 26
cold," and walked on, rejoicing in having extricated him E I 13 110 10
of such a reprieve, the rejoicing, deep and silent, after P III 12 112 53
"Lady Dalrymple, Lady Dalrymple," was the rejoicing sound; P IV 8 184 17
REJOINDER (2)
was Mr. Shepherd's rejoinder, and "Oh! certainly," was his P III 3 19 13
14
Lady Russell let this pass, and only said in rejoinder, "I P IV 5 159 25
REJOINED (8)
"Oh! yes," rejoined the other, "Maria is gone.
"For my own part," she rejoined, "I must confess that I NA I 14 115 52
"There was no help for it certainly," rejoined Mrs. Norris, PP III 3 271 15
else, and soon afterwards rejoined the party at the fire. MP I 7 72 45
others;" rejoined Mr. Woodhouse, understanding but in part. MP I 15 144 36
not do such a thing again," eagerly rejoined Mrs. Elton. E I 1 13 45
"As to all that," rejoined Sir Walter coolly, "supposing I E II 16 295 34
The two ladies continued walking together till rejoined by P III 3 18 8
REKINDLING (1) S 8 403 1
light in the Wick Could give hope to the rekindling breath. NA II 6 170 12
RELAPSE (3)
Mrs. Morland watched the progress of this relapse; and
The possibility of a relapse would of course, in some NA II 15 241 7
She stopt to blush and laugh at her own relapse, and then SS III 7 315 25
RELAPSED (1) E I 16 137 12
Fanny was silent--and Miss Crawford relapsed into
RELAPSING (1) MP II 4 210 22
and every thing was relapsing much into its usual state.
RELATE (35) E II 2 168 15
that does not relate to the beloved object!
that such words could relate only to a circulating library, NA I 6 41 16
What could it contain?--to whom could it relate?--by what NA I 14 113 39
Henry, in having such things to relate of his father, was NA II 6 170 12
promised me that nothing-----but how blindly I relate! NA II 15 247 15
But I am sorry to relate what ensued. SS II 9 205 24
for you to relate, or for me to listen any longer. SS III 1 266 38
SS III 8 320 30
31
Relate only what in your conscience you think necessary
Mr Edwards proceeded to relate every other little article SS III 8 325 52
They could describe an entertainment with accuracy, relate W 323 3
and then proceeded to relate the particulars of their PP I 11 54 1
Mrs. Bennet had many grievances to relate, and much to PP I 20 110 1
Scarcely a syllable was uttered that did not relate to the PP II 2 139 3
the truth of what I shall relate, I can summon more than PP II 6 166 41
too! and having to relate such a thing to his sister! PP II 12 199 5
She dared not relate the other half of Mr. Darcy's letter, PP II 17 225 12
it is not worth while to relate; but his lies about the PP II 17 227 25
or to relate her own change of sentiment towards him. PP III 5 284 14
Oh! Lizzy, to know that what I have to relate will give PP III 11 334 36
through London, and relate her journey to Longbourn, its PP III 13 347 26
silence obliged her to relate her brother's situation; her PP III 16 367 9
that Mrs. Rushworth could relate of the family in former MP I 6 60 47
and saw nothing that did not immediately relate to it. MP I 9 85 3
by all that he could relate of his own horsemanship in MP I 17 163 21
to what his nephew could relate of the different modes of MP II 6 237 23
I know now to whom it must relate, and am in no hurry for MP II 7 251 63
he had in fact nothing to relate but his own sensations, MP II 12 293 11
as far as they relate to my dearest William. MP II 12 293 16
She could only perceive that it must relate to Wimpole MP II 13 307 31
MP III 15 438 4

What can be to be broke to me, that does not relate to one E III 10 393 14
It does relate to him, and I will tell you directly;" (E III 10 394 30
then said, appeared to me to relate to a different person. E III 11 406 21
relate all the particulars of so interesting an interview. E III 12 417 3
This is all that I can relate of the how, where, and when. E III 18 472 20
evening than Anne could relate; and who now asked in vain P IV 9 192 5

RELATED (48)
whose agonies while she related the past, seem'd to LS 36 306 1
of every day to be related as they ought to be, unless NA I 3 27 28
her daughters,--when she related their different NA I 4 32 2
in them by young men, to whom they are not even related?" NA I 13 104 33
apprehension of really meeting with what he related. NA II 5 160 23
Miss Dashwoods, who were related to him only by half blood, SS I 2 8 3
every kind of discourse except what related to themselves. SS I 7 34 7
Marianne's accident being related to him, he was eagerly SS I 9 43 12
Court, to whom he was related, and whose possessions he SS I 9 44 23
conformity of judgment in all that related to either. SS I 10 47 3
were at the same time related, and they were such as to SS I 12 59 6
Margaret related something to her the next day, which SS I 12 60 8
circumstance related by Mrs. Jennings was perfectly true. SS I 13 68 67
cousins, and they are my wife's, so you must be related." SS I 21 119 4
large fortune, they are related to you, and every civility, SS II 11 222 11
I offered immediately, as soon as my mother related the SS III 5 299 37
listener with caution; related simply and honestly the SS III 10 347 33
He related the dishes & told what he had ate himself. W 344 20
of the subject, and related, with much bitterness of PP I 3 13 19
As they walked home, Elizabeth related to Jane what she PP I 15 74 12
particulars that he has related of her ladyship, I suspect PP I 16 83 57
Elizabeth related to Jane the next day, what had passed PP I 17 85 1
with Elizabeth related the event of the day before. PP I 22 124 11
Mr. Darcy related the mistake which had occasioned his PP II 9 179 26
Nor am I ashamed of the feelings I related. PP II 11 192 22
For the truth of every thing here related, I can appeal PP II 12 202 5
perusal of all that related to Wickham, and commanded PP II 13 205 3
was exactly what he had related himself; and the kindness PP II 13 205 3
her to be surprised, she related to her the next morning PP II 17 224 1
She related the subject of the pictures, the dimensions of PP III 1 249 37
In confirmation of this, she related the particulars of PP III 1 258 75
As that was the case, neither Jane, to whom I related the PP III 5 285 16
and her daughter, to whom I have related the affair. PP III 6 297 11
have given the lie more effectually to what they related? PP III 15 363 18
of consequence, but as it related to her own and her son's MP I 8 75 2
Mrs. Norris related again her triumph over Dick Jackson, MP I 15 142 24
For Fanny, somewhat more was related than the accidental MP III 10 404 15
Those parts of the letter which related only to Mr. MP III 12 418 4
and that, as far as related to mind, it had been the MP III 16 457 30
not any one, to whom she related with such conviction of E I 14 117 1
The other circumstance of regret related also to Jane E II 9 231 3
had; and she made the most of it while her friend related. E III 12 417 5
of it aloud--all that related to her, with a smile; a look; E III 15 445 14
15
herself, in all that related to Kellynch; and it pleased P III 6 48 18
your being known to be related to them will have its use P IV 4 150 17
indeed, be known to be related to them!"--then P IV 4 150 18
If we were not related, it would not signify; but as P IV 6 166 16
been such as could not be related without anguish of P IV 9 209 96

RELATES (6)
Pride relates more to our opinion of ourselves, vanity to PP I 5 20 20
What I have to say relates to poor Lydia. PP III 4 273 3
What relates to yourself, is as follows. PP III 15 362 14
party, but as it relates to yourself, to your own comfort. MP I 8 78 18
"This is very true," said she, "at least as far as relates E II 16 291 6
"So far as that it relates to Mr. Frank Churchill, I do E III 10 394 29

RELATING (16)
of her biographer in relating it, she was preparing NA II 14 233 8
for his intrusion by relating its cause, in a manner so SS I 9 42 9
to her mother, relating all that had passed, her SS II 5 172 39
allow me to prove it, by relating some circumstances, SS II 9 204 18
very positively; and by relating that she had herself been SS III 5 295 13
But her promise of relating it to her sister was SS III 9 335 5
Mrs. Gardiner; and after relating the circumstances, she PP II 3 150 29
of the three others, or relating some anecdote of herself. PP II 6 166 41
under the necessity of relating feelings which may be PP II 12 197 5
every thing relating to their journey was speedily settled. PP III 4 280 26
of him had undergone, relating her absolute certainty that PP III 17 376 36
Oh! I believe I was relating to her some ridiculous MP I 10 99 12
state of affairs; relating every thing with so blind an MP II 1 184 27
upon the luxury of relating circumstances and sensations MP III 16 453 17
Mrs. Cole seemed to be relating something of her that was E II 8 214 13
irresistible; every line relating to herself was E III 15 444 1

RELATION (40)
he took the liberty of a relation, & concluded by wishing LS 20 278 10
to alarm her with a relation of its tricks, congratulated NA I 9 62 10
terms, belonging to a relation of her own, a gentleman of SS I 4 23 20
She is a relation of the Colonel's, my dear; a very near SS I 13 66 57
a relation of the Colonel's, my dear; a very near relation. SS I 13 66 57
he felt for us the attachment of the nearest relation? SS I 15 80 36
to be amused by the relation of all the news of the day. SS II 8 193 7
I was banished to the house of a relation far distant, and SS II 9 206 24
Elinor, affected by his relation, and still more by his SS II 9 206 25
I have fancied between her and my poor disgraced relation. SS II 9 208 28
I called her a distant relation; but I am well aware that SS II 9 208 28
as a friend and almost a relation, were his due, by the SS II 13 241 20
I come now to the relation of a misfortune, which about SS II 14 248 6
speak disrespectfully of any relation of yours, madam. SS III 1 267 44
45
for the house of a near relation of Mr. Palmer's, who SS III 7 308 3
imagine by some distant relation, whose interest it was to SS III 8 321 34
heirs male, on a distant relation; and their mother's PP I 7 28 1
a low voice whether her relation were very intimately PP I 16 83 51
there is now in the room a near relation of my patroness. PP I 18 96 57
of the house, and his relation of what the glazing PP II 6 161 8
just as likely to marry her, had she been his relation. PP II 8 176 29
clearer attention, a relation of events, which, if true, PP II 13 204 2
of Mr. Darcy and his relation, Colonel Fitzwilliam, I was PP III 5 284 16
It was not known that Wickham had a single relation, with PP III 6 297 12
It is a relation which you tell me is to give you great PP III 10 325 2
I am almost the nearest relation he has in the world, and PP III 14 354 38
intreaty of so near a relation might settle every doubt, PP III 15 361 3
the belief that such a relation must assist her endeavours PP III 16 367 9
towards their relation; but still they cannot be equals. MP I 1 11 17
a relation dead, it is done in the fewest possible words. MP I 6 59 43
Mrs. Rushworth began her relation. MP I 9 86 9
other her near relation--the whole family, both families MP III 15 441 20
Circumstances that might swell to half an hour's relation, E III 11 410 35
to justify himself by a relation of what had kept him away. P III 11 94 5
to be received as a relation again, that their former good P IV 3 138 6
to the footing of a relation and heir-presumptive, was a P IV 3 139 7
and look and manner of the privileged relation and friend. P IV 7 177 16
You must consider me only as Mr. Elliot's relation. P IV 9 195 25
of the young female relation, whom Lady D. had been S 3 377 1
to a lady, who has a relation lately settled at Clapham, S 9 412 1

RELATIONS (62)
even from their nearest relations, into affairs of the LS 12 260 1
relations to whom you are so much attached & are so dear. LS 25 292 3
a long train of noble relations in their several phaetons, NA II 14 232 7
of discovering to be her relations, and this was enough SS I 21 118 2
Their being her relations too made it so much the worse; SS I 21 118 2
his family, and all his relations, and no niggardly SS I 21 124 33
Not a soul of all my relations know of it but Anne, and I SS I 22 129 16
end of January to some relations who have been wanting us SS II 2 151 40
This lady was one of my nearest relations, an orphan from SS II 9 205 24
before their more grand relations in Conduit and Berkeley- SS II 10 217 19
As my mother-in-law's relations, I shall be happy to shew SS II 11 222 9
and every one of his relations on both sides, there was no SS II 14 248 5
own merit, than on the merit of his nearest relations! SS II 14 250 12
giving the same number of days to such near relations." SS II 14 253 22
"The unkindness of your own relations has made you SS III 4 289 33
Mr. Palmer and all his relations were at the devil, it SS III 8 317 4
my own conviction, our relations were all led away by it SS III 13 368 26
first settling by almost all their relations and friends. SS III 14 375 8
for she had many relations and old acquaintance to cut-- SS III 14 376 11
party of such very near relations as could have felt W 359 28
at the expense of their dear friend's vulgar relations. PP I 8 37 20
occasionally for a week or two, to visit his relations. PP I 14 66 1
of ridiculing her relations was bad enough, and she could PP I 18 102 72
intimate footing, her relations all wish the connection as PP I 21 118 14
You had better neglect your relations, than run the risk PP I 22 123 7
He took leave of his relations at Longbourn with as much PP II 2 139 1
things may come out, as will shock your relations to hear." PP II 8 174 15
To congratulate myself on the hope of relations, whose PP II 11 192 22
defects of your nearest relations, and your displeasure at PP II 12 198 5
the work of her nearest relations, and reflected how PP II 13 209 11
she had some relations for whom there was no need to blush. PP III 1 255 59
she had heard from his relations in Kent, his actions were PP III 1 258 75
of surprise to her relations, by acquainting them with the PP III 2 260 1
herself, but to the very relations whom he had openly PP III 2 263 10
or his dignified relations at Rosings, had she seen him so PP III 2 263 10
relations, with only one serious, parting, look, went away. PP III 4 278 22
whether Wickham has any relations or connections, who PP III 6 295 6
relations he had now living, better than any other person." PP III 6 295 6
She had never heard of his having had any relations, PP III 6 296 8
of discovery by Lydia's relations, for it had just PP III 6 297 12
have no scruple in abusing you to all your relations." PP III 16 367 11
So near a vicinity to her mother and Meryton relations was PP III 19 385 3
there was, at least, nothing to disgust her relations. MP I 2 12 2
that you are with relations and friends, who all love you, MP I 2 15 11
could resolve to hazard herself among her other relations. MP I 4 41 16
You have not much time before you; and your relations are MP II 4 213 40
Your cousins are not of a sort to forget their relations, MP II 7 245 32
him driven away by the vulgarity of her nearest relations. MP III 10 402 11
paper to her)--much good may such fine relations do you. MP III 15 439 13
on a visit to some relations of Sir Thomas; a removal MP III 16 450 8
What can equal the folly of our two relations?"-- MP III 16 454 18
provision at all, and certainly no respectable relations. E I 8 61 38
understanding, and warm-hearted, well meaning relations. E II 2 163 3
liberty with those kind relations to whom she was so very E II 2 166 10
he could apply for information of her relations or friends. E III 18 474 30
from the want of near relations and a settled home, P IV 5 152 2
and happiness again no relations to assist in the P IV 5 154 8
these, their nearest relations, were not arrived with any P IV 10 216 18
We are quite near relations, you know: and Mr. Elliot too, P IV 10 224 47
of having no relations to bestow on him which a man of P IV 12 251 10
be courted by; her own relations, who might very S 3 376 1
to every attempt of her relations to introduce this young S 3 377 1

RELATIONS' (2)
leaving her own and her relations' behaviour to the PP I 9 46 39
and secure of her relations' consent, there was still PP III 17 378 46

RELATIONSHIP (20)
her appearance and her relationship to Mr. Tilney, was NA I 8 56 11
she considered as no relationship at all, have on his SS I 2 8 3
Well, this is very astonishing!--no relationship!--no SS III 5 294 10
good friends, as our near relationship now makes proper. SS III 13 365 14
be justified by his relationship to the young ladies who PP I 15 73 11
of de Bourgh, and my relationship to your own, are PP I 19 108 19
the prospect of their relationship was highly grateful to PP I 22 125 16
who from our near relationship and constant intimacy, and PP II 12 202 5
and as she named their relationship to herself, she stole PP III 1 255 59
called upon, by our relationship, and my situation in life, PP III 6 296 11
so ill of him, in the very beginning of our relationship." PP III 7 304 31
added, an alliance and relationship of the nearest kind PP III 8 311 12
claimed their relationship, would have delighted them all. PP III 9 316 5
so natural as abhorrence against relationship with Wickham. PP III 10 326 3
her delight in the prospect of their relationship. PP III 13 347 33
he welcomed the relationship, alluded to the past, and P IV 3 143 18
that the Dalrymples considered the relationship as closed. P IV 4 149 12
solicitous to have the relationship acknowledged, which we P IV 4 151 18
to make use of the relationship which had been so pressed P IV 5 157 14
compatible with their relationship, and to retrace, as P IV 10 214 11

RELATIVE (22)
Every thing indeed relative to this important journey was NA I 2 19 3
maintained by them relative to their engagement, which in SS I 14 71 4
The slightest mention of any thing relative to Willoughby SS I 15 82 47
gained, every thing relative to their return was arranged SS III 3 280 7
will of course have much to do relative to his ordination." SS III 4 286 15
will we begin quarrelling about its relative situation. PP II 4 154 23
The far and the near must be relative, and depend on many PP II 9 179 22
On the contrary every particular relative to his sister, PP II 17 226 23
be so consistent with the relative situations of each. MP I 1 7 7
questions and remarks relative to it, and finally would MP II 1 184 25
He was to go to town, as soon as some business relative to MP III 6 367 4
It had been real business, relative to the renewal of a MP III 10 404 15
to do right, which their relative situations admitted; but MP III 17 465 13
relative to every body about me, I would marry to-morrow. E I 10 84 16
try to conceal any thing relative to the Churchills from E I 14 122 18
How has Wright done my hair?"--with many other relative E III 2 324 20
what she had been saying relative to Harriet had been all E III 13 430 38
From our relative situation, those attentions were her due, E III 14 438 8
one or two things relative to the marriage, which made a P IV 3 139 8
They were not much interested in any thing relative to P IV 5 157 14
relative to Mrs. Smith, in which his conduct was involved. P IV 9 211 103
be out again on business relative to them, for we hope to S 9 411 1

RELATIVES (1)
her finding their mutual relatives more disagreeable than SS II 13 243 34

RELATOR (1)
by the shrewdness of the relator, been constrained to NA II 15 246 12

RELATORS (1)
might have no origin but in the language of the relators. P IV 3 140 11

RELAX (1)
When properly to relax is the trial of judgment; and, NA II 1 134 36

RELAXATION (1)
relaxation of anger, or any material digression of thought. NA II 14 238 22

RELAXED (2)
aunt, but I have since relaxed, as I beleive I may depend LS 19 274 3
& Medecine, more relaxed in air, & more subdued in voice. S 10 413 1

RELAXING (1)
They were healing, softing, relaxing--fortifying & bracing- S 2 373 1

RELEASE (14)
In spite of this release, Frederica still looks unhappy, LS 24 291 16
compliments--it had been a release to get away from him. NA II 1 129 1
At last, however, the order of release was given; and much NA II 5 156 4
and most thankfully feel their present release from it. NA II 13 220 1
with his desire of a release any professions of regret, SS II 7 183 14
the circumstances of his release might appear to the whole SS III 13 361 1
enough thankful for his release without wounding his SS III 13 363 6
profiting by the release, to address herself and declare SS III 13 363 8
The moment of her release from him was exstacy. PP I 18 90 4
He would act for her and release her. MP II 3 200 21
to feel that when her own release from Portsmouth came, MP III 12 419 9
Now my dear madam, I will release you; but I could not E III 14 443 8
Reformation, a quicker release from debt, a much higher P III 2 12 3
Mrs P. was delighted at this release, & set off very happy S 12 425 1

RELEASED (11)
scene had passed, which released his suffering wife, and NA II 8 186 6

natural course of things, she must ere long be released. NA II 8 188 16
third day, glad to be released, after such a journey, from SS II 4 160 2
He was released without any reproach to himself, from an SS III 13 361 3
him honourably released from his former engagement, saw SS III 13 363 8
old, rushed into it just released from school, and coming MP III 7 381 25
He was released from the engagement to be mortified and MP III 17 464 12
So it proved;--for when happily released from Mr. Elton, E I 14 119 6
7
moment, and released Captain Wentworth as well as herself. P III 9 79 23
in the state of being released from him; some one was P III 9 80 33
till at once released from Louisa by the astonishing and P IV 11 243 69

RELEIF (6)
at 7 o'clock was some releif--& luckily Mr & Mrs Edwards W 326 7
I must own however that it is a releif to me, to find you W 343 19
We shall soon get releif.-- S 1 364 1
of our own wretched constitutions for any releif.-- S 5 386 1
in want of employment than of actual afflictions & releif. S 10 412 1
for their releif, provided it meet with her approbation.--" S 12 423 1

RELEIVE (2)
so enraged before, & must releive myself by writing to you, LS 22 280 1
or any complaint which Asses milk cd possibly releive. S 11 422 1

RELEIVED (1)
day for 10 days together releived her so little that we S 5 387 1

RELENT (1)
in your favour; that your own family might in time relent. SS III 13 367 23

RELENTED (1)
In two minutes, however, he relented in his own favour; E III 6 364 57

RELENTING (7)
I gave him hopes of Frederica's relenting, & told him a LS 9 257 1
there, an indication of relenting, which encouraged her to MP I 10 102 47
And with a relenting smile he added, "I come home to be MP II 1 185 29
began to think a little relenting, a little change of MP III 1 320 44
Mr. Knightley could not impute to Emma a more relenting E III 13 431 39
gentleman's side, and a relenting on the lady's, and that P III 10 89 36
and of some instances of relenting feeling, some P IV 1 123 8

RELIANCE (7)
Where was his reliance on my sense or goodness then; where LS 22 282 6
to his words, and perfect reliance on their truth. NA I 10 80 60
too with such reliance, such confidence in me!-- SS III 8 324 42
own he reliance, and of his judgment the highest opinion. PP I 4 16 14
a case, but his reliance on mine, made every thing easy. PP III 16 371 45
and though feeling no reliance on her, could not help PP III 18 383 24
on the present, no reliance on future improvement. MP III 17 471 28

RELICK (1)
except your saving this relick--I knew nothing of that E III 4 338 13

RELICS (1)
wife's words, and parted with the last relics of Marianne. SS III 8 329 63

RELIED (5)
she firmly relied on the liberality of his intentions. SS I 3 14 2
at Barton Park; and she relied so undoubtingly on Sir SS I 5 26 6
authority, but stating it to be such as might be relied on. PP III 1 258 75
Lady Elliot mainly relied for the best help and P III 1 5 6
she had always loved and relied on, could not, with such P III 4 27 5

RELIEF (66)
learning, to their mutual relief, that they should see NA I 4 34 7
The shock however being less real than the relief, offered NA II 7 179 29
It was some relief, however, that they were to return to NA II 8 183 2
Catherine's swelling heart needed relief. NA II 13 226 25
way to as a relief, but feeding and encouraging as a duty. SS I 15 77 20
opposition and unkindness, could be felt as a relief! SS II 1 140 3
On the contrary it was a relief to her, to be spared the SS II 1 141 5
that it was a very great relief to you, to acknowledge SS II 2 146 6
lead to her sister's relief, Elinor resolved to write the SS II 5 171 38
had obliged her to dispose of it for some immediate relief. SS II 9 207 26
I was called away to the relief of one, whom he had made SS II 9 209 30
the occasion was an happy relief to Elinor's spirits, SS II 10 215 12
Elinor could have given her immediate relief by suggesting SS II 12 232 14
but were together without the relief of any other person. SS II 13 241 19
Marianne found some relief in drawing up a statement of SS III 3 280 7
who seemed to feel a relief to himself, in leaving behind SS III 7 309 5
for some immediate relief, fancied that all relief might SS III 7 312 18
relief, fancied that all relief might soon be in vain, SS III 7 312 18
and talked of the relief which a fresh mode of treatment SS III 7 312 19
can I suppose it a relief to your own conscience." SS III 8 329 64
instantly gave the joyful relief;--and her mother, SS III 9 334 4
Marianne slowly continued-- "it is a great relief to me-- SS III 11 350 5
6
he could find no better relief to his feelings than by PP I 8 40 59
She owed her greatest relief to her friend Miss Lucas, who PP I 18 102 73
relief to them all, and especially to her friend. PP I 21 115 1
a little relief from home, may be as useful as anything." PP II 2 141 10
any thing was a welcome relief to him at Rosings; and Mrs. PP II 8 172 3
way to it as the greatest relief; and not a day went by PP II 14 212 16
take, to give you present relief?--a glass of wine;--shall PP III 4 276 9
Her eldest daughter endeavoured to give some relief to the PP III 7 306 45
to be proof against the temptation of immediate relief. PP III 10 323 2
soon afterwards material relief, from observing how much PP III 11 337 56
was gone, Jane constantly sought the same means of relief. PP III 13 349 44
for the sake of giving relief to my own feelings, care not PP III 16 365 2
3
Such relief, however, as it was in her power to afford, by PP III 19 387 8
Fanny's relief, and her consciousness of it, were quite MP I 3 32 64
and she had not even the relief of shewing her power over MP I 7 70 30
It must be a great relief to her," said Fanny, trying for MP I 16 155 23
absence was really in its cause and its tendency a relief. MP II 11 285 15
call you, to the infinite relief of a tongue that has been MP II 13 303 15
the sound of approaching relief, the very sound which she MP III 3 344 42
I had thought it might be a relief." MP III 4 346 10
for me to find any relief in talking of what I feel." MP III 4 346 11
such an interval would be felt a great relief to herself.-- MP III 9 393 1
nay, it seemed a relief to her worn mind to be at any MP III 10 401 9
and to her great relief discerned), her father was a very MP III 10 402 12
state of his own mind made him find relief only in motion. MP III 15 445 29
in exertions for the relief of his brother's, and Fanny MP III 16 449 4
with a view to his relief and benefit, no less than theirs. MP III 16 452 15
This has been the greatest relief, and now we will have MP III 16 459 30
the poor were as sure of relief from her personal E I 10 86 24
has produced exertion and relief to the sufferers, it has E I 10 87 30
To Isabella, the relief of such tidings was very great, E I 15 128 17
of separating allowed her the relief of quiet reflection. E I 15 133 38
do agree, it is quite wonderful the relief they give. E II 14 275 32
And poor John's son came to talk to Mr. Elton about relief E III 8 383 29
and to give you all the relief in my power, be assured E III 10 396 39
must be the greatest relief to her companion, pent up E III 12 418 5
It was a very great relief to Emma to find Harriet as E III 16 451 1
of all the relief which cheerful companions could give. P III 6 51 32
His kindness in stepping forward to her relief--the manner- P III 9 80 34
see her suffer, without the desire of giving her relief. P III 10 91 42
of the best attention and relief, that however sorry and P IV 1 125 17
Anne could perfectly comprehend the exquisite relief, and P IV 9 210 97
But this was the only point of relief. P IV 10 212 1
exceedingly anxious for relief--and her husband by this S 1 370 1

RELIEVE (15)
must, at such a moment, relieve the fulness of her heart. NA I 2 18 2
that she could not relieve the irksomeness of imprisonment NA I 2 21 10
relieve her anxiety, she had heard nothing of any of them. NA I 14 114 50
If you knew what a consolation it was to me to relieve my SS II 2 146 5
not occur to relieve my spirits at first--no, Marianne.-- SS III 1 264 29
whose attendance must relieve, and whose friendship might SS III 7 311 16
hospitality, to assist his tenants, and relieve the poor. PP I 16 81 41
Elizabeth, feeling it incumbent on her to relieve him from PP I 23 126 4
at hand to relieve you, if you tire of the great book. MP I 16 156 27
and from not daring to relieve herself by a single attempt MP II 7 248 47
not relieve herself by speaking of it to any human being. MP III 15 438 7
was really said only to relieve his own feelings, and not E II 7 206 4
As for Jane Fairfax, she might at least relieve her E III 11 403 2
him his own independence, relieve him from that state of E III 13 429 30
with; they might at least relieve Mrs. Harville from the P IV 1 122 5

RELIEVED (32)
Catherine, relieved for herself, felt uneasy for Isabella; NA I 13 105 40
wrong, felt greatly relieved by Mr. Allen's approbation of NA I 13 105 41
find how much her spirits were relieved by the separation. NA II 7 179 29
her spirits so very much relieved by this conversation, NA II 10 207 41
his heart was greatly relieved by such unlooked-for NA II 15 242 8
return; he neither returned, nor wrote, nor relieved her." SS II 9 209 30
They were relieved however, not by her own recollection, SS II 12 231 11
relieved her own feelings, and gave no intelligence to him. SS III 5 298 34
her mother would be relieved from the dreadful suspense in SS III 7 315 26
Her curiosity however was unexpectedly relieved. PP I 16 77 8
which was very little relieved by the long speeches of Mr. PP I 18 102 75
done; and the boys were relieved from their apprehension PP I 22 122 3
love-making relieved them from a great deal of his company. PP I 23 129 15
was much relieved by discerning such different feelings. PP III 2 261 4
her into, was shortly relieved, and her mind opened again PP III 11 331 13
looking at him, she was a little relieved by his smile. PP III 17 375 28
Elizabeth's mind was now relieved from a very heavy weight; PP III 17 377 41
Mrs. Price should be relieved from the charge and expense MP I 1 5 4
to himself to be relieved from the expense of her support, MP I 3 24 7
They were relieved by it from all restraint; and without MP I 3 32 64
followed could only be relieved by the influence of MP II 9 264 17
Mrs. Norris, however, relieved him. MP III 2 332 20
Her companions were relieved, but there was no good for MP III 16 448 2
To be relieved from her, therefore, was so great a MP III 17 466 15
the expense of the child, however, he was soon relieved. E I 2 16 4
regrets, and sometimes relieved them by speaking of her E I 7 55 36
"Mr. Weston will be almost as much relieved as myself," E III 10 396 43
and thoughts a little relieved, she had taken a few turns, E III 13 424 1
Emma was quite relieved, and could presently say, with a E III 13 425 10
11
while Mrs. Musgrove relieved her heart a little more; and P III 8 64 7
good Dr. Shirley's being relieved from the duty which he P III 9 78 19
In one point, her feelings were relieved by this knowledge P IV 10 212 1

RELIEVES (1)
The old lady relieves the high-flown benevolence of her MP I 14 134 12

RELIEVING (2)
I may perhaps do no good, but that of relieving my own LS 12 261 5
active, indispensable employment, for relieving sorrow. MP III 15 443 25

RELIGION (3)
But it shall be regulated, it shall be checked by religion, SS III 10 347 30
has the guardianship of religion and morals, and MP I 9 92 45
They had been instructed theoretically in their religion, MP III 17 463 8

RELIGIOUS (4)
death or a religious retirement closed their black career. NA II 9 190 2
the knowledge of her being well principled and religious. MP III 12 294 16
the strongest examples of moral and religious endurances. P III 11 101 24
his description of the religious Cottager, as opposed to S 1 370 1

RELINQUISH (1)
him a few struggles to relinquish her, she was ready to PP II 5 150 26

RELINQUISHED (4)
The Clifton scheme had been deferred, not relinquished, NA I 13 97 1
to himself to be relinquished, and he was really resolved SS II 11 228 51
It was an alliance which he could not have relinquished MP II 3 201 22
enjoyments of ease and leisure as must now be relinquished. E II 2 165 9

RELINQUISHING (2)
or relinquishing their comforts in a way not to be borne. P III 1 10 19
in understanding and relinquishing Mr. Elliot, and be P IV 12 249 3

RELINQUISHMENT (1)
feeling himself ill-used by so forced a relinquishment.-- P III 4 28 5

RELISH (4)
of Bath--and the honest relish of balls and plays, and NA I 10 79 57
of the children added a relish to his existence. SS I 1 3 1
best--though I do not much relish the finery I am to have." MP I 15 143 29
to restore him to the relish of his own smooth gruel. E I 12 105 51

RELISHED (2)
who might not have relished domestic felicity in so PP III 19 385 1
and very thoroughly relished the means it afforded her of MP I 4 35 5

RELUCTANCE (16)
family, prepared for no reluctance but of feeling, no NA II 15 247 15
submitted without any reluctance, for nothing had been SS II 2 151 41
wishes, with less reluctance than she had expected to feel. SS II 3 158 20
that she submitted to the change without much reluctance. PP III 19 386 5
not without some modest reluctance on her part, to come in. MP II 4 205 3
and having with modest reluctance given her consent, MP II 8 258 17
But Fanny shewed such reluctance, such misery, at the idea MP III 1 320 45
It was with reluctance that he suffered her to go, but MP III 2 328 8
with her extreme reluctance to bring the writer of it and MP III 14 435 15
No reluctance, no horror, no feminine--shall I say? no MP III 16 455 18
in overcoming the reluctance, in working himself into the MP III 17 467 19
Some scruples and some reluctance the widower-father may E I 2 16 4
I cannot bear to imagine any reluctance on his side; but I E I 14 122 21
her doubts, her reluctance, her discouragement, had been E III 13 430 38
known the regret and reluctance of her heart in quitting P IV 10 225 62
side, she found no reluctance to admit from subsequent S 6 391 1

RELUCTANT (7)
mother's ungracious and reluctant good wishes, and PP II 3 145 11
pleasantry, but could only force one most reluctant smile. PP III 15 363 19
were so shy and reluctant that he could not advance in any. MP II 5 226 59
of rapid questions and reluctant answers--"I am happier MP III 3 343 41
with his grave looks and reluctant conversation opposed to E II 16 292 8
This, though late and reluctant and ungracious, was yet P IV 8 181 2
Even, if your own feelings were reluctant or indifferent, P IV 11 244 72

RELUCTANTLY (4)
She listened reluctantly, and her replies were short. NA I 11 88 54
Reluctantly, and with much hesitation, did she then begin NA II 14 233 10
Eliza had confessed to me, though most reluctantly, the SS II 9 211 38
Anne had never submitted more reluctantly to the jealous P III 12 115 66

RELY (3)
I rely on your friendship for this. LS 39 308 0
1000
or whose counsel, in any difficulty, you could rely on. NA II 10 207 38
comprehend what I must feel, and I rely upon his goodness." PP III 4 276 5

RELYING (3)
Mr. and Mrs. Morland, relying on the discretion of the NA II 2 140 11
of their engagement, and relying as warmly as ever on his SS II 9 202 8
She now found that she had erred in relying on Elinor's SS III 11 355 46

REMAIN (80)
At Churchill however I must remain till I have something LS 2 246 1
myself that she will not remain long enough at school to LS 7 253 1
take her any where else, & she is not to remain here long. LS 15 267 5
Sir James invited himself with great composure to remain LS 20 278 10
he actually invited himself to remain here a few days. LS 22 280 1
the feelings of either to remain longer in the same house. LS 25 292 3
& nonsensical an idea to remain long on my mind, I do not LS 29 299 2
he remain here; you know my reasons--propriety & so forth. LS 31 302 1
breakfast, resolving to remain in the same place and the NA I 9 60 1
Sunday only now remain to be described, and close the week. NA I 13 97 1
with us, he will probably remain but a very short time, NA II 4 152 29
and, as they were to remain only one more week in Bath NA II 5 154 1
attempt, she could not remain many paces from the chest. NA II 6 164 3
Upon this trust she dared still to remain in his presence, NA II 9 192 4
remain to tell what nothing else was allowed to whisper? NA II 9 194 6
house rather than remain fixed for any time in the parlour. NA II 15 240 1
portion must yet remain to be told in a letter from James. NA II 15 247 14
But who will remain to enjoy you?" SS I 5 27 8

Depend upon it that whatever unemployed sum may remain, SS I 14 72 10
Tell me that not only your house will remain the same, but SS I 14 74 19
saw him, with amazement, remain the whole evening more SS II 8 200 43
wishing her children to remain where they were; a letter SS II 10 213 5
could remain to him in the loss of friends and fortune. SS III 2 270 1
urged him so strongly to remain, that he, who was SS III 7 309 5
I am not at leisure to remain with you longer.-- SS III 8 318 17
while I was obliged to remain in Devonshire, more SS III 8 319 29
Mrs. Dashwood, "even if I remain at Barton; and in all SS III 9 338 24
lines, and shall always remain, your sincere well- SS III 13 365 14
Mrs. Dashwood was prudent enough to remain at the cottage, SS III 14 380 20
remain the whole winter, and Meryton was the head quarters. PP I 7 28 3
an invitation to remain at Netherfield for the present. PP I 7 33 45
But Elizabeth, who had not the least inclination to remain PP I 10 53 64 65
I remain, dear sir, with respectful compliments to your PP I 13 63 12
Mr. Gardiner's house, where they were to remain a few days. PP II 15 217 15
Mrs. Gardiner and the children were to remain in PP III 6 294 3
His debts to be discharged, and something still to remain! PP III 7 304 30
Their visitors were not to remain above ten days with them. PP III 9 318 17
very cogent reasons, to remain in the secrecy which Lydia PP III 9 320 33
"Yes, she will remain there till Christmas." PP III 12 341 22
objection which could remain, their having positively MP I 8 78 23
glad to remain behind and gain a little breathing time. MP II 1 176 4
and very little will remain of the theatre to-morrow.-- MP II 2 193 13
and not bearing to remain with her in what might seem a MP II 5 221 38 39
whist table there would remain sufficient for a round game, MP II 7 239 4
of Henry, in engaging to remain where he was till January, MP II 8 256 12
promised to remain some days longer with his friend! MP II 11 286 16
With thanks for the honour of your note, I remain, MP II 13 307 31
she resolved there to remain, during the whole of his MP III 1 311 2
It was evident that she would rather remain where she was. MP III 14 433 11
chance of his marrying her, than if she remain with him. MP III 16 457 29
but as there must still remain a degree of uneasiness E I 13 110 8
father and Emma should remain at Randalls, while she and E I 15 127 13
Little Henry must remain the heir of Donwell. E II 8 228 87
allow their nephew to remain a day beyond his fortnight. E II 12 257 1
Happy those, who can remain at Highbury!" E II 12 260 21
Such talents as her's must not be suffered to remain E II 15 282 5
"To chuse to remain here month after month, under E II 15 285 13
For two or three months longer I shall remain where I am, E II 17 301 19
and exceedingly terrified, she had been obliged to remain. E III 3 333 5
for it, she was likely to remain there full two months E III 5 343 1
his daughter resolved to remain with him, that Mrs. Weston E III 6 361 42
to be added, what would remain of cheerful or of rational E III 12 422 20
she was invited to remain till they could bring her back. E III 17 464 16
deal better for her to remain single; and told of poor E III 17 466 29
at once, than remain in it on such disgraceful terms." P III 2 13 6
think that, every thing considered, she wished to remain. P III 5 33 6
that my wish would be to remain with Lady Russell to the P III 5 38 32
Musgrove cannot think it wrong, while I remain with him." P III 7 57 15
could not but resolve to remain where he was, and take all P III 9 73 1
She was obliged to kneel down by the sofa, and remain P III 9 79 25
cousinly little interview must remain a perfect secret. P III 12 106 19
That Louisa must remain where she was, however distressing P III 12 112 56
She, who had not been able to remain in Louisa's room, or P III 12 114 59
She expressed herself most willing, ready, happy to remain. P III 12 114 63
I have been thinking whether you had not better remain in P III 12 117 74
suited, and there remain till dear Louisa could be moved. P IV 1 122 5
still remain to suffer from the concussion hereafter!-- P IV 1 126 21
pity Henrietta did "not remain at Lyme as long as Louisa; P IV 6 163 7
effort that she could remain in the room, preserve an air P IV 6 165 9
as much alacrity as could remain, after having been S 9 406 1

REMAINDER (9)
to leave space for the remainder to walk about in some NA I 2 23 27
The remainder was shut off by knolls of old trees, or NA II 7 177 19
other, and so leave the remainder of that other for an SS I 6 29 4
The peace of the party for the remainder of that day, & W 360 30
he might not spend the remainder of his days at PP I 4 15 12
I may execute the remainder by prevailing on you to MP III 1 314 16
sacks were sold, it did not signify who ate the remainder. E II 9 239 51
It was a remainder of former sentiment; it was an impulse P III 10 91 42
The remainder of Anne's time at Uppercross, comprehending P IV 1 121 1

REMAINED (128)
For a minute or two I remained in the same spot, LS 23 284 5
Mrs. Thorpe and Mrs. Allen, between whom she now remained. NA I 8 52 2
about her, while she remained in the rooms, which speedily NA I 9 60 1
as long as both parties remained in the room; and though NA I 10 72 8
Blaize Castle remained her only comfort; towards that, she NA I 11 88 54
sat, but his father remained, and perhaps he might be now NA I 12 93 5
something of solicitude remained, from which sprang the NA I 12 94 11
He remained with them some time, and was only too NA I 12 95 16
secured, Catherine only remained to be apprized of it. NA I 13 97 1
voice while his father remained in the room; and even NA II 5 155 3
The place in the middle alone remained now unexplored; and NA II 6 169 11
back could have remained undiscovered in a room such as NA II 7 173 2
She remained there at least an hour, in the greatest NA II 9 192 4
in the next day, and remained in almost constant NA II 9 197 25
where it was possible; but very little remained to be done. NA II 13 227 27
exchanged while they remained up stairs, Catherine in busy NA II 13 227 27
Returning in silence to his seat, therefore, he remained NA II 15 242 8
forward; and Catherine remained at Fullerton to cry. NA II 16 250 3
was all that remained for his widow and daughters. SS I 1 4 4
Mrs. Dashwood remained at Norland several months; not from SS I 3 14 1
One consolation however remained for them, to which the SS I 9 41 6
no farther; and Marianne remained thoughtfully silent, SS I 18 98 10
Edward remained a week at the cottage; he was earnestly SS I 19 101 1
Marianne remained perfectly silent, though her countenance SS I 20 111 16
Elinor for a few moments remained silent. SS I 22 130 17
But indeed, while Elinor remained so well assured within SS II 1 142 7
them, and while they remained there, she was too well SS II 1 143 10
They had not remained in this manner long, before Elinor SS II 6 176 3
while Marianne still remained on the bed, was ready to SS II 8 193 5
Jennings's going away, remained fixed at the table where SS II 9 203 10
Had I remained in England, perhaps--but I meant to promote SS II 9 206 24
Stanhill effects that remained at Norland (and very SS II 11 225 35
would much rather have remained, at least all the morning, SS II 14 246 2
time of its taking place remained as absolutely uncertain, SS III 2 276 26
Nor could she leave the place in which Willoughby remained, SS III 6 302 4
of every day while she remained with the Palmers, in the SS III 6 303 9
as long as Marianne remained ill, and of endeavouring, by SS III 7 308 3
room, and Elinor remained alone with Marianne. SS III 7 310 9
more quiet--not more herself--remained in an heavy stupor. SS III 7 313 21
All that remained to be done, was to be speedy; and SS III 7 316 30
that nothing else in common prudence remained for me to do. SS III 8 323 40
carriage had died away, remained too much oppressed by a SS III 9 333 1
left by themselves, they remained long together in a SS III 11 355 46
a hope, while Edward remained single, that something would SS III 12 357 1
at Oxford, where he had remained by choice ever since his SS III 13 364 13
One question after this only remained undecided, between SS III 13 369 32
none, still remained some weeks longer unpardoned. SS III 14 376 11
Mr. Darcy walked off; and Elizabeth remained with no very PP I 3 12 14
diffuseness and warmth remained for Bingley's salutation. PP I 11 54 2
and nothing therefore remained to be done, but to think PP I 17 85 1
the conquest of all that remained unsubdued of his heart, PP I 18 89 1
deal while Sir William remained; but no sooner had he left PP I 23 126 5
situation remained the same, her peace equally wounded. PP II 1 134 3
request of the gentlemen remained at the instrument till PP II 8 176 30
peculiar regard, and I remained convinced from the PP II 12 197 5
indecision in which she remained, as to the extent of what PP II 15 217 17
some acquaintance still remained, they bent their steps, PP II 19 240 12
principal bed-rooms, were all that remained to be shewn. PP III 1 250 46
Of the lady's sensations they remained a little in doubt; PP III 2 262 6
While the contents of the first letter remained on her PP III 4 279 24
be idle, she would have remained certain that all PP III 4 281 29
at the inn, nothing remained to be done but to go; and PP III 4 281 29
talk on without interruption, while the servants remained. PP III 8 310 9
Since such were her feelings, it only remained, he thought, PP III 10 323 2
with her mother, but remained quietly in the hall, till PP III 13 345 17
or say half that remained to be said, for the present. PP III 13 347 25
Her carriage remained at the door, and Elizabeth saw that PP III 14 353 20
than he remained in any doubt of your sister's sentiments. PP III 16 371 45
Mr. Bingley and Jane remained at Netherfield only a PP III 19 385 3
Mary was the only daughter who remained at home; and she PP III 19 386 5
occupy every spring, and remained wholly in the country, MP I 2 20 33
with her as long as she remained single, was highly MP I 4 41 15
young eye what little remained to be done, and my own MP I 6 61 56
the supper tray yet remained, brought a glass of Madeira MP I 7 74 57
Fanny, and Miss Crawford remained in a cluster together. MP I 9 86 11
she remained without sight or sound of any companion. MP I 10 100 23
offer of Amelia to Miss Crawford; and Fanny remained alone. MP I 14 136 22
a few minutes, and still remained so sensibly animated as MP II 1 179 9
each other, she remained in tranquillity; and as a whist MP II 5 227 68
and her tranquillity remained undisturbed the rest of the MP II 5 227 68
use entirely so long as he remained in Northamptonshire. MP II 6 237 23
They remained together at the otherwise deserted card- MP II 7 249 49
He remained steadily inclined to gratify so amiable a MP II 8 252 1
and excepting what remained of her scruples, was MP II 8 258 18
He was gone as he spoke; and Fanny remained to MP II 9 264 17
Nothing remained of last night but remembrances, which she MP II 11 282 4
Fanny could not have remained insensible of his drift, had MP II 13 300 7
So the uniform remained at Portsmouth, and Edmund MP III 6 368 8
By the time Mrs. Price's answer arrived, there remained MP III 6 372 21
She had now seen all that were at home; there remained MP III 7 381 26
There had remained only a general impression of roughness MP III 8 389 3
returned so often, or remained so long between them, as MP III 12 419 8
Sir Thomas, however, remained yet a little longer in town, MP III 16 451 12
Well, she went on to say, that what remained now to be MP III 16 456 29
of success, though it remained for a later period to tell MP III 17 471 28
securities all that remained to him of domestic felicity, MP III 17 471 29
with her, because Susan remained to supply her place.-- MP III 17 472 31
They remained but a few minutes together, as Miss E I 4 32 28
Emma remained in a state of vexation too; but there was E I 8 67 56
It was not closed however, it still remained ajar; but by E I 10 89 38
but nothing now remained of it, save the melancholy E II 2 163 2
too young; and Jane remained with them, sharing, as E II 2 164 6
years ago, an uncle remained--in the law line--nothing E II 4 183 9
Emma remained very well pleased with this beginning of the E II 5 195 49
no actual preference--remained a little longer doubtful. E II 8 228 93
comforted away, still remained powerful enough to prompt E II 13 268 13
He remained at Hartfield after all the rest, his thoughts E III 5 349 26
all the time with him, remained, when all the others were E III 6 357 33
Mrs. Weston remained with Mr. Woodhouse. E III 7 367 1
Mr. Weston, his son, Emma, and Harriet, only remained; and E III 7 374 54
All that remained to be wished was, that the nephew should E III 9 388 13
As long as Mr. Knightley remained with them, Emma's fever E III 14 434 4
lines, to satisfy her, remained without any uneasiness.-- E III 14 442 8
and the smile partly remained as she turned towards him, E III 18 480 78 79
friends; and one remained a widower, the other a widow. P III 1 5 7
Admiral Croft, who still remained at Taunton, and fix a P III 3 24 35
The brow of the hill, where they remained, was a cheerful P III 10 86 21
While she remained, a bush or low rambling holly protected P III 10 88 27
But the remembrance of the appeal remained a pleasure to P III 12 117 75
Though Charles and Mary had remained at Lyme much longer P IV 2 129 1
Henrietta remained with Louisa; but all the rest of the P IV 2 133 27
collected, and all that remained, was to marshal P IV 8 185 19
She remained in her seat, and so did Lady Russell; but she P IV 8 189 44
Mrs. Harville, her children, and Captain Benwick, remained P IV 10 217 19
He had remained in Shropshire, lamenting the blindness of P IV 11 243 69
prime supplies of good remained, she might have bid P IV 12 252 12
or spraining his ancle, she remained equally useless.-- S 2 372 1
How it might answer with regard to the baronet, remained S 11 422 1

REMAINING (52)
I can have no veiw in remaining with Lady Susan than to LS 14 263 2
I am sure my dear sister, you will excuse my remaining LS 20 277 5
My remaining here cannot give that pleasure to Mr & Mrs LS 25 293 3
complied; and after remaining a few moments silent, was on NA I 6 42 33
remaining ground till she gained the top of Milsom-Street. NA I 13 101 25
and the servant still remaining at the open door, she used NA I 13 102 25
father's injunction of remaining wholly at Northanger in NA II 13 221 7
said by either during the time of their remaining together. NA II 13 229 31
own disposal; for the remaining moiety of his first wife's SS I 1 4 2
income, besides the remaining half of his own mother's SS I 1 5 8
to Mrs. Dashwood as remaining there till she could SS I 2 8 1
had made her resolve on remaining at Norland no longer SS I 5 25 3
absent, was perfectly satisfied with her remaining at home. SS I 15 75 1
I will not torment myself any longer by remaining among SS I 15 76 16
He had been blameable, highly blameable, in remaining at SS II 1 140 1
The remaining five were now to draw their cards. SS II 1 145 18
only prevented her from remaining in the room a moment SS II 7 180 5
to his inspection, by remaining unconscious of it all; for SS II 11 221 4
After that, I suppose, I was wrong in remaining so much in SS III 13 368 28
expecting,-- instead of remaining even for ever with her SS III 14 378 16
on her daughters remaining at Netherfield till the PP I 12 59 1
make a point of remaining close to her the whole evening. PP I 18 102 73
On the very last day of the regiment's remaining in PP II 18 233 26
But he found Lydia absolutely resolved on remaining where PP III 10 322 2
perhaps, believe, that remaining partiality for her, might PP III 10 326 3
breakfast, and always remaining till after supper; unless PP III 13 349 43
They both set off, and the conjectures of the remaining PP III 14 351 1
never spare time, but the remaining five set off together. PP III 16 365 1
good wishes of the two remaining ladies, and the barking MP I 8 80 30
The remaining three, Mrs. Rushworth, Mrs. Norris, and MP I 9 90 36
Edmund urged her remaining where she was with an MP I 9 96 76
said, "he preferred remaining where he was that he might MP II 1 177 5
unsheltered, remaining perhaps till in the midst of some MP II 4 208 11
state and dignity, the remaining six, under Miss MP II 7 239 8
enthusiasm, and that the remaining cold pork bones and MP II 11 282 2
were bad feelings still remaining which made the prospect MP III 6 367 4
to see William to the last hour of his remaining on land. MP III 6 369 11
her father and herself remaining; and he taking out a MP III 7 382 28
the sadly small party remaining at Mansfield, were cares MP III 13 427 12
could be satisfied with remaining in London at such a time- MP III 14 432 11
came to visit; and after remaining there as long as she E I 10 86 24 25
The remaining five were left to their own powers, and Emma E II 18 311 36
nothing to herself, but his remaining single all his life. E III 12 416 1
himself on remaining single for his dear daughter's sake. P III 1 5 8
the very last, the only remaining one of all that had P IV 1 123 6
By remaining in the neighbourhood, I am become inured to P IV 1 125 16
and a settled home, remaining another year at school, had P IV 5 152 2
free him from all the remaining restraints of widowhood, P IV 5 159 22
was to comprise all the remaining dues of the Musgroves. P IV 10 226 64
and I felt that I had still a motive for remaining here." P IV 11 245 76
D.'s invitation of remaining on the terrace with her.-- S 7 398 1
might be a mere trifle of reproach remaining for herself.-- S 11 420 1

REMAINS (26)
to be attended to, while she remains with Miss Summers. LS 7 252 1
between returning tenderness & the remains of displeasure. LS 25 293 3
to such an extremity while any other alternative remains. LS 38 306 1
rooms, exhibiting the remains of magnificent furniture, NA I 11 88 54
on one side perhaps the remains of a broken lute, on the NA II 5 158 17

blood, and in a third the remains of some instrument of	NA II 5 160 21
end were the imperfect remains of handles also of silver,	NA II 6 163 2
"It remains as it was, I suppose?" said she, in a tone of	NA II 8 186 7
The cottage remains."	NA II 11 214 24
if concealment be possible, is all that remains."	SS II 5 173 44
misery, over the small remains of a fire, which, till	SS II 8 197 23
before me, to be the remains of the lovely, blooming,	SS II 9 207 26
her and her child into the country, and there she remains."	SS II 9 211 42
every possible attention while she remains with us."	PP I 9 41 5
He must write his own sermons; and the time that remains	PP I 18 101 71
favour of matrimony; it remains to be told why my views	PP I 19 106 10
And now nothing remains for me but to assure you in the	PP I 19 106 10
shoes to encounter the remains of a white frost, turned	PP II 5 156 5
justify, if such precious remains of the earliest	MP II 6 235 18
ever be mentioned between them with any remains of liberty.	MP III 6 373 26
given to the sight, more yet remains for the imagination.	MP III 15 446 35
Mr. Knightley, at this little remains of office."	E I 5 40 24
pretty gallant charade remains, fit for any collection.	E I 9 77 42
Fairfax she caught the remains of a smile, when she saw	E II 10 243 22
remains of Mr. Woodhouse's fire, looking very deplorable.	E III 6 363 53
scarcely are her remains at rest in the family vault, than	E III 10 398 55
REMARK (31)	
her father and mother remark on her personal improvement.	NA I 1 15 2
you would have made some droll remark or other about it."	NA I 10 71 3
have made so improper a remark upon any account; and	NA I 10 71 6
"how handsome a family they are!" was her secret remark.	NA I 10 80 60
happiness, with a remark, on the gentleman's side, in	NA I 15 124 48
addition of this single remark--"I really have not	NA II 14 237 22
her mother's foreboding remark; but quick was the	NA II 16 249 1
for herself beyond the most common-place inquiry or remark.	SS I 6 31 8
neither objection nor remark, attempted no vindication of	SS II 10 212 1
This remark was not calculated to make Edward or Elinor	SS II 13 242 27
produced from Mrs. Jennings the following natural remark.	SS III 2 276 27
Marianne assented most feelingly to the remark; and her	SS III 11 352 18
Mrs. Dashwood feared to hazard any remark, and ventured	SS III 11 355 46
for me"--was Ld Osborne's remark, when his friend carried	W 335 13
of mind, he produced the remark of it's being a very fine	W 345 21
"Undoubtedly," replied Darcy, to whom this remark was	PP I 8 40 57
remark on the size of the room, or the number of couples."	PP I 18 91 9
nor in the preceding remark, but there was a look and a	PP III 2 263 9
"That is a fair remark."	MP I 7 64 9
than once, however, to remark on his good fortune in	MP II 1 178 8
As yet Sir Thomas had seen nothing to remark in Mr.	MP II 7 246 36
Emma's remark was-- "there it is.	E I 10 83 2
	3
of intercourse; former intimacy might sink without remark.	E II 4 182 8
for though her first remark, on reading it, was that "of	E II 7 208 8
There was no time for farther remark or explanation.	E III 5 347 18
"I perfectly agree with you, sir,"--was then his remark.	E III 15 446 20
and without the smallest remark; and, excepting one	E III 15 447 21
replied Sir Walter, "that's all I have to remark.	P III 3 17 2
but Sir Walter's remark was, soon afterwards-- "the	P III 3 19 13
	14
but very similar remark of Mr. and Mrs. Musgrove--"so,	P III 6 42 1
of solicitude or remark about them, in the mansion-house;	P III 9 75 9
REMARKABLE (31)	
face with a remarkable expression of pensive admiration!	LS 18 272 1
and, what is more remarkable, with a good constitution.	NA I 1 13 1
in either was not remarkable, and she shirked her lessons	NA I 1 14 1
It is remarkable, however, that she neither insisted on	NA I 2 19 3
Now, for instance, it was reckoned a remarkable thing at	NA I 9 64 24
within my small circle of friends is remarkable!	NA I 14 109 24
without perceiving any thing very remarkable in either.	NA II 5 160 21
it was certainly a very remarkable coincidence!	NA II 6 168 10
was still something remarkable, for she could now manage	NA II 7 173 4
so much wished for, struck Catherine as very remarkable.	NA II 7 181 41
"It would be something remarkable now," he continued, "	SS II 11 224 26
The events of the evening were not very remarkable.	SS II 14 250 10
In her person there was nothing remarkable; her manners	W 349 23
consideration for his comfort, appeared very remarkable.	PP I 14 66 1
Every time they met, it was more decided and remarkable.	PP II 2 141 9
pounds was the most remarkable charm of the young lady, to	PP II 3 149 28
there was nothing remarkable, and who was entirely engaged	PP II 6 162 12
There is in every thing a most remarkable resemblance of	PP II 15 216 6
nor of any of the remarkable places through which their	PP II 19 240 12
saw and admired every remarkable spot and point of view.	PP III 1 245 3
For so young a woman it is remarkable!	MP II 3 198 13
"The scene we were rehearsing was so very remarkable!	MP III 5 358 9
had certainly shewn no remarkable fondness for her	MP III 6 371 17
But it is very remarkable that she should always hear Jane	E II 1 158 14
Mrs. Dixon, I understand, has no remarkable degree of	E II 1 161 26
It is remarkable, that Emma, in the many, very many,	E III 15 449 35
"Nothing remarkable.	P III 5 39 39
The younger boy, a remarkable stout, forward child, of two	P III 9 79 28
not try to hear it; yet she caught little very remarkable.	P III 10 84 7
themselves, the remarkable situation of the town, the	P III 11 95 9
"It was very strange!--very remarkable!--very	S 10 419 1
REMARKABLY (42)	
At about half past twelve, a remarkably loud rap drew her	NA I 9 61 1
She was remarkably quick in the discovery of attachments,	SS I 8 36 1
regular features, and a remarkably pretty figure.	SS I 10 46 2
There is one remarkably pretty sitting room up stairs; of	SS I 13 69 76
The weather was remarkably fine, and she readily consented.	SS II 11 223 15
the boys were both remarkably tall for their age, and	SS II 12 234 24
but Marianne was remarkably handsome a few months ago;	SS II 12 237 43
quite independant, & remarkably agreable, an universal	W 315 1
He is reckoned remarkably agreable I understand.--"	W 328 8
With them he is remarkably agreeable."	PP I 5 19 13
I thought Miss Elizabeth Bennet looked remarkably well,	PP I 8 36 7
I mend pens remarkably well."	PP I 10 47 11
and the eye-lashes, so remarkably fine, might be copied."	PP I 10 53 58
She has the reputation of being remarkably sensible and	PP I 16 84 58
he has been always remarkably kind to him, though George	PP I 18 94 45
that he was a remarkably clever, good kind of young man.	PP I 18 101 71
at it, as Jane had written the direction remarkably ill.	PP III 4 273 1
the partridges were remarkably well done; and I suppose he	PP III 12 342 28
He sat with them above an hour, and was in remarkably good	PP III 13 344 1
feelings, and a temper remarkably easy and indolent, would	MP I 1 4 1
They were a remarkably fine family, the sons very well-	MP I 2 13 4
Mary Crawford was remarkably pretty; Henry, though not	MP I 4 41 17
and ours is such a remarkably large, fair sort, that what	MP I 6 54 13
of her appearance and her being in remarkably good looks.	MP II 10 272 1
thought not remarkably late,--he began to talk of going	MP II 13 306 28
You did look remarkably well.	MP III 2 333 28
There had been something remarkably amiable about her.	MP III 7 386 40
She was not struck by any thing remarkably clever in Miss	E I 3 23 10
"He is very plain, undoubtedly--remarkably plain:--but	E I 4 32 30
"Mr. Knightley's air is so remarkably good, that it is not	E I 4 33 34
of Mr. Elton's being a remarkably handsome man, with most	E I 6 42 1
They are all remarkably clever; and they have so many	E I 9 80 72
and a disposition remarkably amiable and affectionate;	E I 11 92 4
my children in:--but we are so remarkably airy!--	E I 12 103 37
private perplexities, remarkably comfortable, as such	E I 16 139 20
Jane Fairfax was very elegant, remarkably elegant; and she	E II 2 167 12
"Very nicely dressed, indeed; a remarkably elegant gown."	E II 14 271 10
Thank you, my mother is remarkably well.	E III 2 322 19
He had been remarkably handsome in his youth; and, at	P III 1 4 5
He was, at that time, a remarkably fine young man, with a	P III 4 26 1
She was looking remarkably well; her very regular, very	P III 12 104 6
He came into the room remarkably well, talked much--& very	S 7 394 1
REMARKED (2)	
might be remarked, he meant to make enquiries at Clapham.	PP III 5 293 69
but yet more to be remarked for his very good address &	S 7 394 1
REMARKS (34)	
I made no remarks however, for words would have been in	LS 24 287 10
little incommoded by the remarks and ejaculations of Mrs.	NA I 9 60 1
Mrs. Morland's common remarks about the weather and roads.	NA II 15 242 8
to some very impertinent remarks, do you not now begin to	SS I 13 68 73
"If the impertinent remarks of Mrs. Jennings are to be the	SS I 13 68 74
&c. extorting from him occasional questions and remarks.	SS I 16 89 42
Lucy was naturally clever; her remarks were often just and	SS I 22 127 2
to endure the questions and remarks of all these people.	SS II 7 191 64
into a reverie, which no remarks, no inquiries, no	SS III 12 360 26
some very, very languid remarks on the probable brilliancy	W 322 3
The discussion led to more intimate remarks, & Miss	W 324 3
when her questions or remarks gave him anything to say; &	W 331 11
in the course of the remarks & retrospections which now	W 336 14
half-awkward, half-fearless stile of his former remarks.--	W 346 21
behaviour to the remarks of the two ladies and Mr. Darcy;	PP I 9 46 39
by making a variety of remarks on the happiness that might	PP I 23 126 4
remarks might have been enough to drive happiness away.	PP I 23 127 8
Lady Catherine continued her remarks on Elizabeth's	PP II 8 176 30
by his questions and remarks; Mrs. Reynolds, either from	PP III 1 248 23
At length, however, the remarks of her companions on her	PP III 1 253 56
afraid of myself, but I dread other people's remarks."	PP III 11 332 17
and heard all her silly remarks with a forbearance and	PP III 13 345 18
own remarks to him, lest it should appear like ill-nature.	MP I 7 66 14
of the night and their remarks on the stars, to think	MP I 7 71 31
him with questions and remarks relative to it, and finally	MP II 1 184 25
own replies, and his own remarks to have been very much to	MP III 1 314 16
Fanny's explanations and remarks were a most important	MP III 12 419 7
remarks, and evidently making Mr. Rushworth uneasy.	MP III 16 450 8
day remarks, dull repetitions, old news, and heavy jokes.	E II 8 219 43
continually making severe remarks upon, in her absence;	P III 5 34 12
Her answers to the kindness and the remarks of her	P III 10 91 43
herself with common-place remarks, or quiet attention, and	P IV 6 173 48
prepared for some fuller remarks--but it was followed only	S 7 401 1
The rest was common enquiries & remarks, with kind notice	S 12 425 1
REMEDIED (1)	
at this time, or the evil would have been earlier remedied.	MP I 4 36 7
REMEDIES (2)	
to bed, to try one or two of the simplest of the remedies.	SS III 6 306 17
he, with all the common remedies for sprains & bruises--&	S 1 367 1
REMEDY (6)	
bruised temple, the same remedy was eagerly proposed for	SS I 21 121 10
They were hopeless of remedy.	PP II 14 213 17
to remedy an evil, which had been brought on by himself.	PP III 10 322 2
there might not be a remedy found for some of these evils.	MP III 7 385 40
it was not remedy for the absence of Mrs. Weston.	E I 3 22 6
when once at home, we have our remedy at hand you know.--	S 1 367 1
REMEMBER (165)	
I remember saying to myself as I drove to the house, "I	LS 2 244 1
sadly neglected however, & her mother ought to remember it.	LS 15 266 3
very person, as you may remember, whom it was said she had	LS 20 275 2
But remember what I tell you of Frederica; you must make	LS 23 284 4
If you remember, I left the room almost immediately.	LS 24 288 11
I charged her to write to me very often, & to remember	LS 41 310 4
I remember Miss Andrews could not get through the first	NA I 6 42 22
Every body acquainted with Bath may remember the	NA I 7 44 1
Aye, I remember, so it was; I was thinking of that other	NA I 7 49 38
Well, remember that it is not my fault, if we set all the	NA I 8 58 25
"Something was said about it, I remember," said Catherine,	NA I 9 61 4
Yes; I remember, I asked you while you were waiting in the	NA I 10 75 26
Pulteney-Street--and "remember--twelve o'clock," was her	NA I 10 80 61
not lay down again;--I remember finishing it in two days--	NA I 14 106 7
"Yes," added Miss Tilney, "and I remember that you	NA I 14 107 8
I remember I wore my yellow gown, with my hair done up in	NA I 15 118 11
"I remember too, Miss Andrews drank tea with us that	NA I 15 118 13
I do remember now being with you, and seeing him as well	NA II 3 145 13
She could remember dozens who had persevered in every	NA II 9 190 2
Remember the country and the age in which we live.	NA II 9 197 29
Remember that we are English, that we are Christians.	NA II 9 197 29
Henry, remember that Robinson is spoken to about it.	NA II 11 214 24
Tilney, who, as you may remember, was amazingly disposed	NA II 12 216 2
Do you remember that evening?"	NA II 14 238 24
I remember I had my favourite gown on."	NA II 14 238 26
"Remember, my love, that you are not seventeen.	SS I 3 18 21
it was too long ago for his young cousins to remember him.	SS I 6 30 6
"I remember last Christmas, at a little hop at the park,	SS I 9 44 25
manner to Margaret, "remember that whatever your	SS I 12 61 17
	18
"You must remember, my dear mother, that I have never	SS I 15 80 41
"Remember, Elinor," said she, "how very often Sir John	SS I 16 84 6
too far, Marianne-- remember I have no knowledge in the	SS I 18 96 4
I remember her promising to give you some.	SS I 18 98 11
But remember that the pain of parting from friends will be	SS I 19 103 7
of Lucy's veracity; "I remember he told us, that he had	SS I 22 134 49
I remember her aunt very well, Biddy Henshawe; she married	SS II 8 194 10
One thing, especially, I remember, because it served to	SS II 8 199 37
I cannot remember the time when I did not love Eliza; and	SS II 9 205 24
you must remember the place, where old Gibson used to live.	SS II 11 225 31
I remember Fanny used to say that she would marry sooner	SS II 11 227 50
Remember me kindly to her.	SS III 2 276 25
remember, as well Edward too, who I have told of it.	SS III 2 277 30
I remember her perfectly.	SS III 5 299 37
"Remember," cried Willoughby, "from whom you received the	SS III 8 322 36
to me for ever; and I remember how happy, how gay were my	SS III 8 324 42
Remember that you are married.	SS III 8 325 52
There was always a something,--if you remember,--in	SS III 9 338 20
Elinor could not remember it;--but her mother, without	SS III 9 338 21
	22
"I will remember her partners if I can--but you know they	W 320 2
"I think Miss Emma, I remember your aunt very well about	W 325 4
Ah! I remember--& she is gone to settle in Ireland.--	W 326 5
"No--perhaps not--but I remember my dear when you & I did	W 337 15
Remember, I say nothing of my disinterestedness.--	W 339 18
Remember we never eat suppers."--	W 351 25
"Remember, Eliza, that he does not know Jane's disposition	PP I 6 22 4
appetite; but you must remember that four evenings have	PP I 6 22 8
I remember the time when I liked a red coat myself very	PP I 7 29 12
"Lizzy," cried her mother, "remember where you are, and do	PP I 9 42 14
"Nay," cried Bingley, "this is too much, to remember at	PP I 10 49 28
representation, you must remember, Miss Bennet, that the	PP I 10 50 34
I do not remember her name among the ladies at court."	PP I 14 67 8
she continued, "I do remember his boasting one day, at	PP I 16 80 34
years, but I very well remember that I never liked her,	PP I 16 84 58
suddenly exclaiming, "I remember hearing you once say, Mr.	PP I 18 93 32
Remember that she is one of a large family; that as to	PP II 1 135 12
of him, she tried to remember something of that	PP II 2 143 20
"And remember that I have not much reason for supposing it	PP II 10 185 28
am certain, remember, with the design of soon returning.--	PP II 12 198 5
address; but she could remember no more substantial good	PP II 13 206 4
speak, she continued, "I remember, when we first knew her	PP III 3 271 16
	17
I can remember no symptom of affection on either side; and	PP III 5 285 18
that; I told you so from the first, you may remember."	PP III 10 329 30
You may remember what I told you on that point, when first	PP III 10 329 32
I remember, as soon as ever I saw him, when he first came	PP III 13 348 40
I can remember some expressions which might justly make	PP III 16 368 20
This is the last time I shall ever remember it myself."	PP III 17 373 7
to make her remember that she is not a Miss Bertram.	MP I 1 10 17
good girl; but you must remember that you are with	MP I 2 15 11
I cannot remember the time when I did not know a great	MP I 2 18 25
And remember that, if you are ever so forward and clever	MP I 2 19 27

Oh! cousin, if I am to go away, I shall remember your MP I 3 26 30
Ah! cousin, when I remember how much I used to dread MP I 3 27 36
Remember that, my dear brother. MP I 5 45 11
You young ones do not remember much about it, perhaps. MP I 6 54 9
two, but I forestall you; remember I have forestalled you." MP I 9 94 55
"But if you remember, before we left that first great path, MP I 9 95 63
I remember him. MP I 15 148 59
"Do you remember Hawkins Browne's 'Address to Tobacco,' in MP I 17 161 15
they ought, nobody would remember on which side they were MP I 18 165 2
Remember that, Fanny. MP II 5 220 30
Remember, where-ever you are, you must be the lowest and MP II 5 221 32
You remember the Gregorys; they are grown up amazing fine MP II 7 249 52
You should always remember the coachman and horses. MP II 7 251 64
impossible for me to value, or for him to remember half. MP II 8 259 22
I can remember that they were evidently fond of his MP III 4 350 30
Do you remember it? MP III 5 358 7
"How perfectly I remember my resolving to look for you up MP III 5 360 14
How well I remember what I was thinking of as I came along; MP III 5 360 14
I remember it perfectly." MP III 5 362 18
"I wonder he did not remember the book"--was all Harriet's E I 4 34 41
The list she drew up when only fourteen--I remember E I 5 37 7
never remember Emma's omitting to do any thing I wished." E I 5 37 8
thrown over my senses, must still see, hear, and remember. E I 5 37 9
I remember saying to myself, 'even Emma, with all her E I 8 62 38
could not remember them! but he hoped he should in time." E I 9 70 5
But I can remember nothing;--not even that particular E I 9 78 54
I remember it was written from Weymouth, and dated sept. E I 11 96 24
I remember that perfectly." E I 11 96 24
the precise words--one has no business to remember them. E II 3 174 32
my dear Jane, if you remember, I told you yesterday he was E II 3 174 39
I remember she said she was sorry we never met now; which E II 3 178 52
They all seemed to remember the day, the hour, the party, E II 5 187 4
remember you knew her at Weymouth, and a fine girl she is. E II 5 194 38
said Mrs. Weston smiling, "remember that I am here.-- E II 6 201 23
I have been used to hear her's admired; and I remember one E II 6 201 28
We must remember to let James know that the carriage will E II 7 210 14
Do not you remember what Mr. Perry said, so many years ago, E II 11 252 37
Do not you remember, Mrs. Weston, employing him to write E II 16 298 52
"So I remember to have heard. E II 18 307 23
one morning, I remember*, he came to me quite in despair." E II 18 308 28
Do not you remember his cutting his finger with your new E III 4 338 12
Remember it? E III 4 338 13
Ay, I remember it all now; all, except your saving this E III 4 338 13
"Do not you remember one morning?--no, I dare say you do E III 4 339 18
"I do remember it," cried Emma; "I perfectly remember it.-- E III 4 339 19
I perfectly remember it.-- E III 4 340 19
Mr. Elton was sitting here, I remember, much about where I E III 4 340 20
I remember it perfectly. E III 5 344 9
You must remember it now?" E III 5 345 9
Jane, don't you remember grandmamma's telling us of it E III 5 346 16
Perfectly remember Mrs. Perry's coming.-- E III 5 346 16
Remember." E III 7 373 50
are at all like what I remember to have been myself, I E III 8 382 24
before tea, because I remember thinking--Oh! no, now I E III 8 382 29
"My dear Harriet, I perfectly remember the substance of E III 11 406 23
to take leave of her, I remember that I was within a E III 14 438 8
I remember her telling me at the ball, that I owed Mrs. E III 14 439 8
If you remember any queernesses, set them all to the right E III 14 439 8
Remember how few minutes I was at Randall's, and in how E III 14 439 8
Do you remember the morning spent at Donwell?-- E III 14 440 8
We must look to her one fault, and remember that she had E III 15 446 20
You remember those lines--I forget the poem at this moment: E III 16 454 13
"I remember once calling you 'George,' in one of my E III 17 462 12
I remember one evening the poor boys saying, 'uncle seems E III 17 465 27
"I know you saw my letter, and think you may remember my E III 18 477 59
archly; "but do not I remember the time when you found E III 18 478 62
can mean, Shepherd; I remember no gentleman resident at P III 3 23 27
to consult me once, I remember, about a trespass of one of P III 3 23 28
You remember him, I am sure." P III 3 23 32
Mr. Wentworth was nobody, I remember; quite unconnected; P III 3 23 33
Bath in the winter; but remember, papa, if we do go, we P III 6 42 1
"Your first was the Asp, I remember; we will look for the P III 8 64 8
ever since you could remember, and which at last, on some P III 8 65 16
and you will please to remember, that he is the eldest son; P III 9 76 15
affliction, and you must remember, Captain Harville, that P III 12 108 25
I cannot pretend to remember it, but it was something very P IV 2 131 9
"I hope I shall remember, in future," said Lady Russell, P IV 2 135 32
will say; but "if you remember, I never thought him P IV 6 165 8
her. Miss Elliot, do you remember our walking together at P IV 11 232 15
Charles, if you see Captain Harville any where, remember P IV 11 239 52
If I was wrong in yielding to persuasion once, remember P IV 11 244 73
I remember seeing Mrs Hillier after one of those dreadful S 4 381 1
village!--nor did he remember any during the whole summer, S 4 383 1
"Do you remember, said he, Scott's beautiful lines on the S 7 396 1
I remember none at this moment, of the sea, in either of S 7 397 1

REMEMBERED (37)

How are your various dresses to be remembered, and the NA I 3 27 28
Morland, before she remembered that her eldest brother had NA I 4 33 5
the resentful sensation; she remembered her own ignorance. NA I 12 92 3
her hand; but Catherine remembered Henry's instructions, NA II 4 153 31
peculiar awe, she well remembered the doors of which the NA II 8 188 17
She remembered with what feelings she had prepared for a NA II 10 200 2
She remembered too, her own surprise at the time, at his SS I 22 134 49
Marianne was going to retort, but she remembered her SS III 1 267 41
and respectfully remembered to her, and to Sir John, and SS III 2 278 30
Her smile however changed to a sigh when she remembered SS III 10 343 10
Elinor remembered what Robert had told her in Harley- SS III 13 364 11
She perfectly remembered every thing that had passed in PP II 13 206 5
She remembered that he had boasted of having no fear of PP II 13 207 5
She remembered also, that till the Netherfield family had PP II 13 207 5
When she remembered the style of his address, she was PP II 14 212 17
all their grief; she remembered what she had herself PP II 18 229 3
remembered to have sometimes seen, when he looked at her. PP III 1 250 47
ever raised before; she remembered its warmth, and PP III 1 251 48
She is well, and begs to be dutifully remembered to you PP III 8 313 19
She remembered that he had yet to learn to be laught at, PP III 16 371 46
"Why, indeed, Fanny, I should hope to be remembered at MP I 3 26 31
if she were forgotten the poor mare should be remembered. MP I 7 68 16
she had been present than remembered any thing about her. MP II 7 251 62
will be nothing to be remembered by either you or me, that MP II 9 269 38
next morning; but she remembered the purport of her note, MP III 1 311 1
If Mr. Crawford remembered her message to her cousin, she MP III 12 418 5
being no otherwise remembered, than as he furnished a E I 9 69 2
saw, felt, anticipated, and remembered just as she ought. E I 9 74 21
She remembered what Mr. Knightley had once said to her E I 16 135 6
together than she had remembered; it was not regular, but E II 2 167 12
I remembered what I used to do myself. E II 5 190 24
Harriet was remembered only from being her friend. E II 13 266 5
No, except when she thought of her mother, and remembered P IV 1 126 18
Mr. Elliot, too, it must be remembered, had not been a P IV 4 147 8
She knew it well; and she remembered another person's look P IV 4 148 9
misery, and could never be remembered with indifference. P IV 5 152 2
lived with him, wd be principally remembered in her will. S 3 377 1

REMEMBERING (17)

eager expectation, and remembering how often she had been NA II 3 143 2
Lady Middleton luckily remembering that in a scene of SS I 21 121 10
perceive the necessity of her remembering them farther. SS II 11 227 46
Then, remembering Colonel Brandon, reproved herself, felt SS III 9 335 5
Miss E.'s cheek, & in remembering what Elizabeth had said W 326 5
leaving Kent, without remembering that his cousin was to PP II 11 188 2
remembering what Charlotte's opinion had always been.-- PP II 13 208 9
to appropriate it--for remembering that there was some MP I 14 132 8
at nothing beyond his remembering the catchword, and the MP I 18 166 4
over to you all the duty of remembering the original giver. MP II 8 259 19
he could not help remembering what he had seen; nor could E III 5 344 2
had haunted her when remembering how disappointed a heart E III 16 451 4
was no occasion for remembering Mary) and Anne, smiling P IV 3 143 18
remembering former partialities and talking over old times. P IV 5 153 6
Anne, remembering the preconcerted visits, at all hours, P IV 10 216 17
Never worth remembering. P IV 10 223 44
Miss P-- whom, remembering the three teeth drawn in one S 10 413 1

REMEMBERS (1)

all are delighted to see, and nobody remembers to talk to." SS I 10 50 14

REMEMBRANCE (45)

No remembrance of Reginald, no consciousness of guilt, LS 42 311 2
a most pleasing remembrance of all the heroines of her NA I 15 119 19
The remembrance of Mr. Allen's opinion, respecting young NA II 5 156 5
excited by this tender remembrance, shewed itself directly NA II 7 179 31
The painful remembrance of the folly it had helped to NA II 11 212 16
that she left "her kind remembrance for her absent friend." NA II 13 229 31
which the remembrance of his assistance created. SS I 10 46 2
affection, to the remembrance of every mark of regard in SS I 19 102 2
brought back to her remembrance, all the circumstances of SS II 4 162 13
He looked pleased by this remembrance, and added, "if I am SS II 9 205 23
24
those regrets which the remembrance of me occasioned. SS II 9 206 24
imprint on Elinor the remembrance of a person and face, of SS II 11 220 3
with complacency on the remembrance of Edward's generous SS III 6 305 15
Willoughby to her remembrance, and in spite of herself SS III 8 319 25
which the remembrance of Willoughby could be connected.-- SS III 10 342 7
How should I have lived in your remembrance!-- SS III 10 346 28
His remembrance can be overcome by no change of SS III 10 347 30
eliz: giving another sigh to the remembrance of Purvis.-- W 321 2
did she value his remembrance, and prefer him to every PP II 17 227 26
felicity, nor humbled by any remembrance of her misconduct. PP III 7 306 43
Think only of the past as its remembrance gives you PP III 11 369 23
the time, to make the remembrance when she was alone much MP I 16 150 1
had not an interesting remembrance connected with it.-- MP I 16 151 2
the remembrance, and restored to its proper state. MP II 2 187 2
but no embarrassing remembrance affected his spirits. MP II 5 224 48
The remembrance of all her earliest pleasures, and of what MP III 6 370 11
were brought to her remembrance every hour of the day, by MP III 8 391 10
heaved a sigh at the remembrance of all her books and MP III 9 398 9
after a few days, the remembrance of the said books grew MP III 9 398 9
mother, and recal her remembrance of the name, as that of " MP III 10 399 4
The remembrance of her first evening in that room, of her MP III 15 439 9
more than an indistinct remembrance of her caresses, and E I 1 5 2
it, save the melancholy remembrance of him dying in action E II 2 163 2
to her taste, or a remembrance of what she had said; and E II 13 266 5
rather than the remembrance of neglect in such a cause. E III 5 350 31
but pity; and the remembrance of the less just and less E III 8 379 9
piano forte; and the remembrance of all her former E III 8 384 34
of giving pain--no remembrance of Box-Hill seemed to exist. E III 15 447 21
should hold my speeches in such affectionate remembrance." E III 17 462 10
She had the remembrance of all this; she had the P III 1 7 12
of her own family, must ever present the remembrance of. P III 1 7 13
he could be unvisited by remembrance any more than herself. P III 8 63 2
But the remembrance of the appeal remained a pleasure to P III 12 117 75
his eyes, as if the remembrance were still too painful; P IV 8 182 6
is over, the remembrance of it often becomes a pleasure. P IV 8 183 16

REMEMBRANCER (1)

It is to be a family remembrancer. MP II 8 259 19

REMEMBRANCES (8)

by melancholy remembrances, she was impatient to be gone, SS I 3 14 1
of the debt which all these kind remembrances produced. MP I 16 153 3
Nothing remained of last night but remembrances, which she. MP II 11 282 4
to feed on melancholy remembrances, and tender MP III 3 334 1
She was in a reverie of sweet remembrances. MP III 5 358 8
she not left bitter remembrances behind her, there might MP III 17 466 15
you know, to keep any remembrances, after he was married. E III 4 340 24
a satisfaction, as no remembrances, even connected with Mr. E III 19 482 6

REMIND (8)

She wished by a gentle remonstrance, to remind Isabella of NA II 4 150 1
in some moments, occur to remind her of what anxiety was-- SS III 7 315 25
a good deal from curiosity, dared not remind him.-- W 359 28
At least, you should not remind your mother of inviting PP II 3 145 7
Darcy had been given, to remind her of her post. there was PP III 3 268 6
opinion, and perhaps to remind the latter of all the PP III 3 269 10
to remind her that all this might soon be over. E II 2 164 6
as many were ready to remind her, was liable to such E III 6 361 41

REMINDED (18)

I meant moreover to have reminded him of our being quite LS 13 262 1
that you had just been reminded of a prior engagement, and NA I 13 98 1
A continuance in a place where every thing reminded her of SS I 2 8 2
they were sometimes only reminded of her being amongst SS I 11 55 6
"I love to be reminded of the past, Edward--whether it be SS I 17 92 26
he reminded me of an old promise about a pointer puppy. SS III 8 330 69
the ball, and abruptly reminded him of his promise; adding, PP I 9 45 36
When tea was over, Mr. Hurst reminded his sister-in-law of PP I 11 54 3
Mrs. Gardiner about this time reminded Elizabeth of her PP II 3 149 28
When coffee was over, Colonel Fitzwilliam reminded PP II 8 173 12
more; and Elizabeth was reminded by her own satisfaction PP II 9 180 28
closed, when he suddenly reminded them, with some PP II 15 217 8
was almost always reminded by a something of the same MP I 7 66 14
suffered the less because reminded by it of the east-room. MP III 9 398 9
delightful to me, to be reminded of a place I am so E II 14 273 19
It reminded her of their first forlorn tete-a-tete, on the E III 12 422 19
She was reminded, more than once, of her having always E III 17 466 29
pleasant ridicule, which reminded Anne of the early days P III 8 64 4

REMINDING (6)

Eleanor was ready to oblige her; and Catherine reminding NA II 9 191 3
mansion, which, by reminding them a little of Norland, SS I 9 40 2
her every enjoyment, reminding her of what she was to PP II 4 151 3
that must be inevitably reminding him of its existence. MP II 2 194 21
Mr. Weston, I am much obliged to you for reminding me. E II 7 210 20
father's compassion, by reminding him, that so long as I E III 14 437 8

REMINDS (1)

My paper reminds me to conclude, and begging to be most SS III 2 278 30

REMISS (8)

have hitherto been very remiss, madam, in the proper NA I 3 25 2
could have made me so remiss; but now I could go and sit a MP I 6 62 58
Mr. Rushworth is never remiss. MP I 12 117 14
fear that she had been remiss herself in forwarding it; MP II 2 194 20
Not to wait upon a bride is very remiss. E II 14 280 54
She had been often remiss, her conscience told her so; E III 8 377 1
conscience told her so; remiss, perhaps, more in thought E III 8 377 1
all, I have often observed, extremely awkward and remiss.-- E III 16 458 42

REMISSNESS (2)

morning by Frederick's remissness in writing, was free NA II 11 209 5
account for any remissness of his sister's in writing, for MP III 9 393 1

REMNANT (4)

It was done completely; not a remnant of light in the Wick NA II 6 170 12
to each other without any remnant or shadow of reserve." MP III 5 364 30
contemplating the limited remnant of the earliest patent; P III 1 3 1
advantage of being the remnant of a connection which she S 3 377 1

REMONSTRANCE (12)

She wished by a gentle remonstrance, to remind Isabella of NA II 4 150 1
unkindness; but for remonstrance, either opportunity or NA II 4 150 1
But, however this remonstrance might have staggered or PP II 12 198 5
To save herself from useless remonstrance, Mrs. Price MP I 1 4 1
by the remonstrance which Edmund would certainly make. MP I 14 137 23
a remonstrance, a reproof, which he felt at his heart. MP II 1 184 27
He did not enter into any remonstrance with his other MP II 2 187 2
And without attempting any further remonstrance, she left MP II 6 231 11

rational remonstrance or sharp retort equally ill bestowed. E I 11 93 5
I cannot see you acting wrong, without a remonstrance. E III 7 374 56
of manners as might provoke a remonstrance on his side. P IV 10 214 11
to cut short, both his remonstrance to the driver & his S 1 364 1
REMONSTRANCES (3)
of the other; and remonstrances poured in from all three. NA I 13 100 19
though spurning the remonstrances of Susan, given as they MP III 8 390 8
Mrs. Elton, and her remonstrances now opened upon Jane. E II 16 295 29
REMONSTRATED (2)
Morland remonstrated, pleaded the authority of road-books, NA I 7 45 7
and Mr. Perry had remonstrated with him about it, and told E I 8 68 58
REMORSE (5)
feeling of humanity or remorse; till a violent death or a NA II 9 190 2
in the constancy of mine as ever, awakened all my remorse. SS III 8 325 53
which proved him wholly unmoved by any feeling of remorse. PP II 11 191 13
pride, or tenderness or remorse, or whatever were to be MP III 3 337 10
He had no sooner been free from the horror and remorse P IV 11 242 64
REMOTE (6)
young ladies away to some remote farm-house, must, at such NA I 2 18 2
as possible to the most remote corner of the house, where W 335 13
Nobody else could be interested in so remote an evil as MP III 13 428 14
them in another country--remote and private, where, shut MP III 17 465 14
The first remote sound to which she felt herself obliged E II 8 214 13
for considering it as too remote from the beach, he had S 4 383 1
REMOTENESS (1)
Their remoteness and unpunctuality, or their exorbitant MP II 4 213 35
REMOVAL (55)
propriety, occasioned her removal from a family where she LS 6 252 2
My removal therefore, which must at any rate take place LS 25 293 3
By a removal for some months from each other, we shall LS 30 301 4
but Frederica's removal from the risk of infection. LS 42 312 6
the trouble of urging a removal, which Lady Susan had LS 42 313 7
and Captain Tilney's removal would at least restore peace NA II 4 150 1
ease as to the necessity of any sudden removal of her own. NA II 11 208 2
The marriage of Eleanor Tilney, her removal from all the NA II 16 250 5
or expense of so sudden a removal, her beloved Elinor SS I 4 23 19
fancy, though it was a removal from the vicinity of SS I 4 24 21
in the prospect of her removal; a satisfaction which was SS I 5 27 6
They quitted it only with the removal of the tea-things. SS II 1 144 10
commonest kind must prevent such a hasty removal as that." SS II 7 191 63
He made no answer; and soon afterwards, by the removal of SS II 8 200 43
than herself for their removal, and only so much less bent SS III 3 279 1
Elinor's satisfaction at the moment of removal, was more SS III 6 302 5
of her immediate removal with her infant; and Mr. Palmer, SS III 7 307 3
confidence to attempt the removal of;--he listened to them SS III 7 311 15
without attempting a removal to Delaford; and fortunately SS III 14 380 20
My sister, I am sure, will not hear of her removal." PP I 9 41 4
the suddenness of their removal surprised her, she saw PP I 21 116 8
but that after their removal, it had been every where PP II 13 207 5
approaching removal, was indeed beyond expression. PP II 16 223 25
with me, in considering a removal from that corps as PP III 8 312 19
advantages of Wickham's removal from the ----shire, as PP III 8 313 20
The reason of this sudden removal was soon evident. PP III 18 383 26
soon after her removal, to be a sailor, was invited to MP I 2 21 34
had been her fears of a removal; and her spontaneous, MP I 3 31 58
The removal of the book-case from before the billiard room MP II 1 182 22
at Mansfield, the removal of every thing appertaining to MP II 2 194 21
That will be done, by the removal of the farm-yard, for MP II 7 243 27
But the removal of his alarm did his niece no service; as MP III 1 317 36
preparations for his removal on board directly, that he MP III 7 381 24
bear the removal without material inconvenience or injury. MP III 13 426 11
of Sir Thomas; a removal which her father and mother were MP III 16 450 8
Mrs. Norris's removal from Mansfield was the great MP III 17 465 15
or at least the practicability of a permanent removal. MP III 17 469 23
to all; and after Fanny's removal, succeeded so naturally MP III 17 472 31
Not one of them had the power of removal, or of effecting E I 17 143 14
All was safe and prosperous; and as the removal of one E II 12 257 2
that Mrs. Churchill's removal to London had been of no E III 1 316 6
to a certainty by this removal,--the ball at the crown. E III 1 318 11
a decision of action unusual to her, proposed a removal.-- E III 6 359 37
expected; and their first removal, on the departure of the E III 9 388 15
him, a look, a speech, a removal from one chair to another, E III 11 409 35
companion--and a removal that would leave Mrs. Clay behind, P III 2 16 17
growing so strong for a removal, that she was happy to P III 3 24 37
Accordingly their removal was made together, and Anne was P III 5 36 19
to learn that a removal from one set of people to another, P III 6 42 1
forward to an early removal to Kellynch, and beginning to P III 11 93 1
in anticipating her removal from Uppercross, where she P III 11 93 4
Her removal was impossible. P III 12 112 56
for the necessity of the removal, she could not but in P IV 1 125 17
might be able to bear the removal home; and her father and P IV 2 129 1
Susan had only superintended their final removal from the S 10 414 1
REMOVALS (5)
hurried walks and sudden removals from her own fire-side, MP II 2 188 3
in the course of those removals to which all midshipmen P III 6 51 30
changes, alienations, removals,--all, all must be P III 7 60 28
them; and by some other removals, and a little scheming of P IV 8 189 46
When they were all finally seated, after some removals to S 10 414 1
REMOVE (23)
for to remove far from that beloved spot was impossible. SS I 3 14 1
guest: and to remove for ever from that beloved place SS I 4 24 20
as might remove the possibility of fear for Marianne. SS I 20 114 43
She was going to remove what she really believed to be her SS III 1 261 11
The Palmers were to remove to Cleveland about the end of SS III 3 279 1
as to enable her to remove, within four days after the SS III 10 340 1
means, now remove the guilt of his conduct towards Eliza. SS III 11 349 1
to health would probably remove her from Netherfield. PP I 9 41 2
key again; but still this did not remove the present evil. MP I 10 98 4
has no faults but what a serious attachment would remove." MP I 12 116 8
her own perseverance to remove; she had begun to feel MP I 16 152 3
was at little pains to remove; and the chances of Mr. MP I 18 165 4
Mrs. Norris contrived to remove one article from his sight MP II 2 195 22
remove to London, meant something that she could not bear. MP II 11 287 17
Susan were preparing to remove as usual up stairs, they MP III 10 399 2
and medicine might not remove, or at least that she might E III 1 317 6
They were going to remove immediately to Richmond. E III 1 317 7
The next remove was to the house; they must all go in and E III 6 361 41
any cold collation, or any cheerful Mr. Weston, to remove. E III 7 367 1
induce Mr. Woodhouse to remove with her to Donwell; he had E III 15 448 31
by one or the other to remove their embarrassments and P III 1 10 21
Sir Walter and his family were to remove from the country. P III 2 15 15
This glorious sentiment seemed quite to remove suspicion. S 7 400 1
REMOVED (68)
might be immediately removed, as she had been detected in LS 15 266 2
The small pianoforte has been removed within these few LS 17 271 7
The spell is removed. LS 34 304 1
anxious to get Frederica removed from such a mother, & LS 42 311 2
kind--her manners just removed from the awkwardness and NA I 2 18 1
care and anxiety seemed removed, her spirits became almost NA I 15 121 26
its decaying state, been removed by the General's father, NA II 8 184 4
In having this cause of uneasiness so pleasantly removed, NA II 13 221 6
but till that one was removed, it must be impossible for NA II 16 249 1
His unexpected accession to title and fortune had removed NA II 16 251 5
No leaf will decay because we are removed, nor any branch SS I 5 27 8
any partiality arose, was removed when his feelings began SS I 10 49 12
find they correspond, every fear of mine will be removed." SS I 15 80 41
which, in my opinion, cannot be so easily removed." SS II 3 156 9
even from wishing it removed, by her anxiety for the very SS II 5 174 47
had removed from him only to sink deeper in a life of sin. SS II 9 207 26
fourteenth year,) that I removed her from school, to place SS II 9 208 28
her near her delivery, I removed her and her child into SS II 9 211 42
The Miss Steeles removed to Harley-Street, and all that SS II 14 254 28
"Yes, you have certainly removed something--a little.-- SS III 8 329 66
I did not know my danger till the danger was removed; but SS III 10 345 28
which, because they are removed, he now reckons as nothing. SS III 11 351 13
profession when I was removed at eighteen from the care of SS III 13 362 5
doubt, every solicitude removed, compared her situation SS III 13 363 8
be removed by another half hour's discourse with himself. SS III 14 376 11
When the tea-things were removed, Tom began to talk of his W 357 28
them both, he had removed with his family to a house about PP I 5 18 1
"Removed!" cried Bingley. PP I 9 41 4
When the ladies removed after dinner, Elizabeth ran up to PP I 11 54 1
change of room; and she removed at his desire to the other PP I 11 54 2
Catherine de Bourgh, I am removed far beyond the necessity PP I 16 83 50
and Mrs. Younge was of course removed from her charge. PP II 12 202 5
of her brain were removed, her other sister, from whose PP II 19 237 3
her alarms being now removed, she was at leisure to feel a PP II 19 241 17
heard an accent so far removed from hauteur or disdain of PP III 2 263 10
Eliza, are not the ----shire militia removed from Meryton? PP III 3 269 8 9
entering that place they removed into a hackney-coach and PP III 4 274 5
"When they all removed to Brighton, therefore, you had no PP III 5 285 17
When the tea-things were removed, and the card tables PP III 12 342 26
Two obstacles of the five being thus removed, Mrs. Bennet PP III 13 345 11
how gradually all her former prejudices had been removed. PP III 16 368 19
time when they should be removed from society so little PP III 18 384 27
a temper as Lydia, and, removed from the influence of PP III 19 385 4
Mrs. Norris, on quitting the parsonage, removed first to MP I 3 23 1
white house, I suppose, as soon as she is removed there." MP I 3 25 20
had suggested and removed at least two sets of MP I 14 130 1
very early in November removed herself, her maid, her MP II 3 202 28
The house is by no means bad, and when the yard is removed, MP II 7 242 22
scruples; and if they are removed, it must be by changes MP II 9 269 38
me!" said Lady Bertram, when the tea-things were removed. MP II 11 283 5
Tom's extreme impatience to be removed to Mansfield, and MP III 13 427 13
even Julia; for Julia had removed from Wimpole Street two MP III 16 450 8
On that event they removed to Mansfield, and the parsonage MP III 17 473 33
Her sister, though comparatively but little removed by E I 1 7 9
was the distress known to Mr. Elton, than it was removed. E I 6 49 40
his daughters gradually removed the present evil, and the E I 12 107 62
his fate, removed the chief of even Emma's vexation. E II 16 292 9
after the Churchills had removed to Richmond, a few lines E III 1 318 11
were by no means removed, she was really ashamed of having E III 5 350 28
desirable to have her removed just now for a time from E III 14 435 4
We removed to Windsor; and two days afterwards I received E III 14 442 8
The sole grievance and alloy thus removed in the prospect E III 18 475 39
Emma had instantly removed every fear of that nature, by E III 19 481 2
so respectably removed from the partialities and injustice P III 4 28 7
That brother had been long removed from the country--and P III 4 30 10
This invitation of Mary's removed all Lady Russell's P III 5 34 10
and subject, by being removed three miles from Kellynch: P III 6 46 12
day, when, being removed into lodgings & all the party S 10 413 1
REMOVES (2)
Lady Susan's conduct, & removes all the blame which has LS 14 264 3
When my mother removes into another house my services SS I 2 12 25
REMOVING (21)
from Sir James, but her removing from Langford immediately LS 14 265 4
Every five minutes, by removing some of the crowd, gave NA I 2 23 27
But Captain Tilney had at present no intention of removing; NA II 4 150 1
oppose her mother's intention of removing into Devonshire. SS I 4 24 21
his being of any service to her in removing her furniture. SS I 5 25 4
affair, and of instantly removing all mystery, that she SS I 16 84 7
the happiness of both by removing from her for years, and SS II 9 206 24
Before her removing from Norland, Elinor had painted a SS II 12 234 26
her what he meant to do himself towards removing them.-- SS III 6 305 16
her daughter's wishes began to talk of removing to Barton. SS III 10 340 4
"Oh! but their removing from the chaise into an hackney PP III 5 282 6
a gentleman and lady's removing from one carriage into PP III 5 293 69
to separate us, were the means of removing all my doubts. PP III 18 381 14
poor, so unpractised in removing evils, or bestowing MP III 9 396 7
and then left the sopha, removing to a seat by her sister, E I 15 125 6
Of their all removing to Donwell, Emma had already had her E III 15 449 32
One set might recommend their all removing to Donwell, and E III 17 468 36
as Sir Walter proposed removing to Bath in the course of P III 5 33 5
at Uppercross, that in removing thence she might be P III 11 93 2
home again before Lady Russell would be removing to Bath. P IV 1 128 31
had succeeded in removing her & her large income to his S 3 375 1
RENCONTRE (4)
course of their third rencontre that he was asking some PP II 10 182 1
On this rencontre they all returned to the house together, MP I 10 104 51
from the accidental rencontre, to the dinner at Mr. E II 4 181 4
she hoped the rencontre would do them no harm. E III 16 453 11
RENDER (15)
it was proper to render her pecuniary assistance, I cannot LS 3 247 1
could render probable, and must in the end make wretched. LS 12 261 3
of friendship, must render any future intercourse the LS 25 292 3
and hanging coppice render it so striking an object from NA I 14 106 1
the apothecary seemed to render absurd; but the many hours SS III 7 309 7
care could do to render her comfortable, was the office of SS III 10 341 6
For though elated by his rank, it did not render him PP I 5 18 1
may not be long enough to render it necessary, I shall now PP I 22 124 10
could so represent, as to render Mr. Darcy's conduct in it PP II 13 205 3
been so great, as to render a different disposal of the MP I 3 23 2
service it could render Fanny, might as well have been MP I 3 28 38
known to him, to render his introduction as the " MP II 1 183 23
known to him to render him culpable in authorising it, MP III 17 461 4
It was all the service she could now render her poor E III 13 431 38
she had rendered, or ever meant to render, to his wife. P IV 12 251 11
RENDERED (38)
the utmost submission, & rendered more tractable, more LS 25 293 3
rendered every thing else of the kind "quite horrid." NA I 12 92 4
every bitter feeling was rendered more severe by the NA II 14 230 1
His father was rendered easy by such an assurance, and Mr. SS I 1 5 6
affliction as rendered her careless of surrounding objects. SS I 3 16 7
father was by this arrangement rendered impracticable.-- SS I 5 26 4
her former style of life rendered many additions to the SS I 6 29 4
what her situation rendered necessary, took her up in his SS I 9 42 8
education might have rendered so respectable; but she saw, SS I 22 127 2
which the case rendered reasonable, though his sex might SS II 13 241 21
with her beloved child, rendered dearer to her than ever SS III 9 334 5
he began to find it was rendered uncommonly intelligent by PP I 6 23 12
of their actions, may be rendered ridiculous by a person PP I 11 57 20
might be rendered interesting by the skill of the speaker. PP I 16 76 4
Mrs. Gardiner, rendered suspicious by Elizabeth's warm PP II 2 142 18
She was not rendered formidable by silence; but whatever PP II 6 162 11
whose northern aspect rendered it delightful for summer. PP III 3 267 2
Rendered spiritless by the ill-success of all their PP III 6 298 13
The present unhappy state of the family, rendered any PP III 6 298 17
that his flight was rendered necessary by distress of PP III 9 318 19
His ease and cheerfulness rendered him a most agreeable PP III 13 345 18
Lady Catherine had been rendered so exceedingly angry by PP III 18 383 26
own circumstances were rendered less fair than heretofore, MP I 3 24 7
from the conviction, rendered her temper so bad, and her MP III 17 464 10
as his cooler manners rendered possible; and if his E I 12 100 16
The contrivances of modern days indeed have rendered a E I 13 115 37
Ever since the service he rendered Jane at Weymouth, when E II 1 160 23
The service he rendered you was enough to warm your heart." E III 4 342 37
I am sure the service Mr. Frank Churchill had rendered you, E III 11 406 21
the service he had rendered you, it was extremely natural:- E III 11 406 23
better sense would have rendered her, to the advice which E III 17 463 15
make a degrading match; but he might be rendered unhappy. P III 5 35 14
his private life, which rendered him perfectly interesting P III 11 96 12
in short, her civility rendered her quite as anxious to be P IV 7 174 3
behind her, which rendered every thing else trivial. P IV 8 188 37

in society, indeed, rendered that impossible) yet I knew P IV 9 200 57
she had rendered, or ever meant to render, to his wife. P IV 12 251 11
What prudence had at first enjoined, was now rendered S 2 374 1
RENDERING (5)
it her own choice by rendering her thoroughly LS 7 253 2
you, as rendering the conditions incapable of comparison." NA I 10 77 35
be contrived, without rendering the cottage at Barton SS III 14 378 13
lady, to whom he was now rendering himself agreeable; but PP II 3 149 28
and the sense of rendering justice, and was determining E II 2 167 13
RENDEZVOUS (1)
though less economical rendezvous being accordingly MP I 1 8 9
RENEW (3)
I am sure of Sir James at any time, & could make him renew LS 7 253 1
each other, she could only renew her former caution as to MP I 17 161 9
was too much affected to renew the subject--and when he P III 12 108 29
RENEWAL (16)
turn for comfort to the renewal of her confidence in SS I 19 102 2
With a renewal of tenderness, however, they repaired to PP I 8 37 21
She would not even wish for any renewal of his attentions. PP II 3 149 27
of those sentiments, or renewal of those offers, which PP II 12 196 4
expect it to contain a renewal of his offers, she had PP II 13 204 1
and her preference secured at any time by their renewal. PP II 18 233 25
possessed, of bringing on the renewal of his addresses. PP III 2 266 16
How could I ever be foolish enough to expect a renewal of PP III 12 341 19
such an instantaneous renewal of cheerfulness into the MP I 17 159 6
were any prospect of a renewal of "Lovers' Vows", he MP II 2 192 11
It had been real business, relative to the renewal of a MP III 10 404 15
for a renewal of such confidential intercourse as had been. MP III 16 453 16
recollections of the other, prevented any renewal of it. E I 12 107 62
say could prevent some renewal of alarm at the sight of E I 15 128 22
It must not be: and yet the danger of a renewal of the E II 4 185 12
They did not like each other, and no renewal of P III 11 93 3
RENEWED (29)
a few minutes' silence, renewed the conversation about his NA I 7 47 19
her acquaintance so renewed; and her mother, perceiving NA II 14 236 18
renewed, was sought for, was created again and again. SS I 1 7 13
It was broken by Lucy, who renewed the subject again by SS I 22 128 8
9
be renewed with yet greater satisfaction as sisters?-- PP I 21 117 9
in town, had there renewed a slight acquaintance. PP II 13 205 4
of an intercourse renewed after many years discontinuance. PP III 1 259 76
The fishing scheme had been renewed the day before, and a PP III 2 266 18
on that lady's side, the acquaintance would now be renewed. PP III 3 267 1
disappointment had been renewed on each of the mornings PP III 4 273 1
"If I were to decline the part," said Maria with renewed MP I 15 141 19
the part," said Henry Crawford with renewed entreaty. MP I 18 172 30
of the rehearsal being renewed after tea, when the bustle MP II 1 177 5
Miss Crawford however, with renewed animation, soon went MP II 4 210 20
21
every succeeding morrow renewed a tete-a-tete, which Sir MP II 6 234 17
opposition; and with renewed but less happy thanks MP II 8 260 23
to that room seemed all renewed, and she felt as if he MP III 1 312 4
them, came over her with renewed strength, and it seemed MP III 6 370 11
it was a sort of renewed separation from Mansfield; and MP III 11 413 31
when the acquaintance was renewed in town, and Mr. MP III 17 466 18
The confession completely renewed her first shame-- and E I 17 141 6
beds when to be renewed--gardeners thinking exactly E III 6 358 35
a more inviting accent, renewed the conversation; for as E III 11 408 33
Whether former feelings were to be renewed, must be P III 8 63 2
families renewed--very sad for herself and her children. P III 9 75 12
It was very desirable that the connexion should be renewed, P IV 4 149 12
For the first time, since their renewed acquaintance, she P IV 7 175 6
her; and presently with renewed spirit, with a little P IV 8 181 3
4
would you, in short, have renewed the engagement then?" P IV 11 247 82
RENEWING (7)
wish of renewing it; and this for more reasons than one. SS II 1 141 7
he soon testified of renewing those attentions which had PP II 18 233 25
Hertfordshire, anxiously renewing them at all the PP III 4 275 5
example than to be renewing old grievances, and that if E I 12 99 10
taking another turn, her renewing the conversation which E III 13 431 38
renewing an acquaintance of a very different description. P IV 5 152 1
a time, with the view of renewing his former acquaintance P IV 9 207 90
RENOUNCED (2)
or not, when I was renounced by my mother, and stood to SS III 13 367 22
Emma would have renounced their own home for Hartfield! E III 17 467 31
RENOWN (3)
for the most flattering prognostics of her future renown. LS 19 274 2
It is a name of heroism and renown--of kings, princes, and MP II 4 211 23
to a something of young renown--and Mr Parker could not S 2 371 1
RENOWNED (1)
for the object of his affections, to the more renowned.-- S 8 405 2
RENT (9)
got that frightful great rent in my best Mechlin so NA II 14 238 22
of such a sum, on every rent day, is by no means desirable: SS I 2 11 21
so simple a scale, and the rent so uncommonly moderate, as SS I 4 24 21
"The rent of this cottage is said to be low; but we have SS I 19 109 41
His scheme was to rent the house himself the following MP II 7 246 37
I shall let Everingham, and rent a place in this MP II 12 295 20
convenience;--knew what rent a ready-furnished house of P III 3 22 23
off in being permitted to rent it on the highest terms, he P III 3 24 35
The Crofts who rent Kellynch? P IV 6 162 3
RENTER (2)
doings in every way; to be a renter, a chuser of books! MP III 9 398 9
will be best known in Bath as the renter of Kellynch-Hall. P IV 6 166 15
RENTING (2)
knew by character, as renting a large farm of Mr. E I 3 23 10
for the advantage of renting it; making it appear as if P III 3 23 34
RENTS (3)
What a difference a vowel makes!--if his rents were but MP III 9 394 1
tenant in Somersetshire,--the Croft, who rents Kellynch." P IV 8 188 40
If they do not gain, our rents must be insecure--& in S 6 393 1
REPACK (1)
and all my trunks to repack, from not having understood in P III 5 38 34
REPAID (8)
There was a something, however, in his words which repaid NA II 1 133 29
to be repaid by-----but I must not trust myself with words. NA II 13 223 13
of Mrs. Jennings, I had repaid with ungrateful contempt. SS III 10 346 28
it amply repaid her for the little sacrifice of her time. PP I 22 121 1
How is half such a sum to be repaid?" PP III 7 304 32
of concentrating our folly, I shall be well repaid. MP I 16 155 16
must be amply repaid in the splendour of popularity. E II 9 231 1
and Anne was well repaid the first trouble of exertion. P III 11 100 23
REPAIR (7)
While they snugly repair to their own end of the house, NA II 5 158 15
It had not been built many years and was in good repair. SS I 6 28 2
"He spoke of its being out of repair." SS III 4 285 8
Why don't he repair it?-- SS III 4 286 9
likely may be out of repair; but to hear a man apologising, SS III 4 292 55
house of Rushworth did many a time repair to this chapel? MP I 9 87 15
Tired as she was, she must instantly repair to the hotel, S 10 419 1
REPAIRED (7)
As for Mr. Allen, he repaired directly to the card-room, NA I 2 20 9
directing the dogs had repaired the mistakes of the most NA I 9 66 31
In the drawing-room, whither she then repaired, she was SS II 8 197 26
In Meryton they parted; the two youngest repaired to the PP I 7 32 41
With a renewal of tenderness, however, they repaired to PP I 8 37 21
Mrs. Bennet, to whose apartment they all repaired, after a PP III 5 287 34
When they repaired to the dining-room, Elizabeth eagerly PP III 12 340 11
REPARATION (1)
injured, no reparation could be too much for her to make. SS III 1 265 32
REPARTEE (1)
on the borders of a repartee for half an hour together MP I 9 94 56
REPASSING (1)
In repassing through the small vaulted room, however, your NA II 5 160 21
REPAST (2)
to the same repast, but in circumstances how different! NA II 13 228 27
The cold repast was over, and the party were to go out E III 6 361 42
REPAYMENT (1)
His liberality had a rich repayment, and the general MP III 17 472 30
REPAYS (1)
But success more than repays.-- S 5 387 1
REPEAT (21)
be ridiculous in me to repeat the instances of great LS 12 260 2
Her mother was three months in teaching her only to repeat NA I 1 14 1
your conjectures may be, you have no right to repeat them." SS I 12 61 17
18
to repeat it over and over again as often as they liked. SS II 12 233 20
that--Oh, la! one can't repeat such kind of things you SS III 2 273 16
or I should not repeat it, for otherwise it would be very SS III 5 297 31
"Will you repeat to your sister when she is recovered, SS III 8 330 67
at the time, she had the same story to repeat every day. PP II 1 137 26
He did not repeat his persuasion of their not marrying-- PP III 5 290 48
"Could Colonel Forster repeat the particulars of Lydia's PP III 5 291 57
"Oh! do not repeat what I then said. PP III 16 368 17
How long ago it is, aunt, since we used to repeat the MP I 2 18 25
Fanny was too much surprised to do more than repeat her MP I 3 25 8
Mrs. Rushworth was gone to repeat her lesson to Mr. MP I 9 86 11
"I repeat again," added Sir Thomas, "that Thornton Lacey MP II 7 248 44
and she was obliged to repeat again and again that she was MP II 9 264 17
repeat what he had said, and more fully and more solemnly. MP II 12 291 5
or to repeat half that the Admiral said in his praise. MP II 13 299 5
I need not repeat what has passed. MP III 1 321 47
She was obliged to repeat and explain it, before it was E II 11 251 25
to repeat half that I used to hear him say on that subject. P IV 9 202 66
REPEATED (108)
wishes; but they were repeated so often, and proved so NA I 2 21 9
with Mrs. Allen, and she repeated it after every fresh NA I 3 25 1
was repeated by them all, two or three times over. NA I 4 32 5
which had passed twenty years before, be minutely repeated. NA I 4 34 9
Catherine did not understand him--and he repeated his NA I 9 63 10
"Tilney," he repeated, "hum--I do not know him. NA I 10 76 28
"Only go and call on Mrs. Allen!" he repeated. NA I 10 79 55
did not think it could ever be repeated too often. NA II 15 243 9
required no explanation to her, repeated, "Devonshire! SS I 5 25 1
them to the drawing room repeated to the young ladies the SS I 7 33 4
the neighbourhood, and repeated assurances of his carriage SS I 9 40 2
of fellow, I believe, as ever lived," repeated Sir John. SS I 9 44 25
She had already repeated her own history to Elinor three SS I 11 54 6
Colonel Brandon again repeated his sorrow at being the SS I 13 65 33
My visits to Mrs. Smith are never repeated within the SS I 15 76 10
"A fortnight!" she repeated, surprised at his being so SS I 16 87 25
"Hunters!" repeated Edward--"but why must you have hunters? SS I 17 91 16
"Ferrars!" repeated Miss Steele; "Mr. Ferrars is the happy SS I 21 126 39
"Did not you think him sadly out of spirits?" repeated SS I 22 134 50
of their engagement repeated again, she wanted more SS II 1 141 7
"A great coxcomb!" repeated Miss Steele, whose ear had SS II 2 148 20
some surprize, and repeated her invitation immediately. SS II 3 153 1
Mrs. Jennings repeated her assurance that Mrs. Dashwood SS II 3 154 6
"How odd indeed!" repeated Elinor within herself, SS II 4 165 29
Willoughby, frequently repeated, first caught my attention, SS II 8 199 37
When the particulars of this conversation were repeated by SS II 10 212 1
his visit; and with repeated assurances to his sisters SS III 1 269 57
"Opportunity!" repeated Mrs. Jennings--"Oh! as to that, SS III 4 285 5
Elinor repeated the particulars of it, as she had given SS III 5 298 33
He repeated the inquiry with yet greater eagerness. SS III 8 318 11
security I have repeated it to him more fully, have given SS III 9 337 18
Marianne sighed, and repeated--"I wish for no change." SS III 11 350 8
Marianne's lips quivered, and she repeated the word " SS III 11 351 10
"Mrs Robert ferrars!"--was repeated by Marianne and her SS III 12 360 22
She repeated it to Edward. SS III 13 364 11
"A letter of proper submission!" repeated he; "would they SS III 13 372 41
"Captain!--repeated Mrs E. the gentleman is in the army W 326 5
the Osbornes are coming"--was repeated round the room.-- W 329 9
to her neighbour with repeated & fervent acknowledgements W 331 11
"Capt. Hunter." was repeated, in a very humble tone--"hum!- W 337 15
of entertainment; he repeated the smart sayings of one W 359 28
As Margt would not allow a doubt to be repeated of W 360 30
"Miss Elizabeth Bennet!" repeated Miss Bingley. PP I 6 27 51
The sisters, on hearing this, repeated three or four times PP I 8 35 1
He repeated the question, with some surprise at her PP I 10 52 49
Mr. Collins repeated his apologies in quitting the room, PP I 15 74 11
have this pleasure often repeated, especially when a PP I 18 92 23
the refusal is repeated a second or even a third time. PP I 19 107 13
in considering her repeated refusals as flattering PP I 19 109 22
Gracechurch-Street, and repeated conversations occurring PP II 4 152 6
punctually repeated all his wife's offers of refreshment. PP II 5 155 3
The entertainment of dining at Rosings was repeated about PP II 7 169 5
"Can you deny that you have done it?" she repeated. PP II 11 191 14
"His misfortunes!" repeated Darcy contemptuously; "yes, PP II 11 191 20
"Already arisen!" repeated Mr. Bennet. PP II 18 231 17
usual sedateness; and he repeated his enquiries as to the PP III 1 252 52
mechanically to the repeated appeals of her uncle and aunt, PP III 1 253 55
Lydia at all, which was repeated to Colonel F. who PP III 4 274 5
"That is all settled;" repeated the other, as she ran into PP III 4 281 28
subject, by its repeated discussion, no other could detain PP III 5 285 19
asked, were of course repeated by the others, and they PP III 5 287 33
"Mr. Darcy!" repeated Elizabeth, in utter amazement. PP III 9 319 26
reply; and at length, by repeated assurances that Mr. PP III 17 376 36
"My uncle!" repeated Fanny with a frightened look. MP I 2 16 18
Lady Bertram repeated enough of this conversation to her MP I 3 30 57
The scheme was soon repeated to Henry. MP I 4 42 18
"Fanny!" repeated Mrs. Norris; "my dear Edmund, there is MP I 8 78 17
her, and doomed to the repeated details of his day's sport, MP I 12 115 4
Tom repeated his resolution of going to him early on the MP I 15 148 60
persevered--as Edmund repeated his wish, and with a look MP I 18 172 32
Mr. Rushworth's repeated question of, "shall I go too?-- MP II 1 176 3
it is what you must not depend upon ever being repeated. MP II 5 220 28
"Walk!" repeated Sir Thomas, in a tone of most MP II 5 221 37
With silent indignation, Fanny repeated to herself, "never MP II 5 225 56
of a coolness arise," he repeated, his voice sinking a MP II 9 264 16
Mr. Crawford," repeated twice over; and in vain did she MP III 3 342 34
Crawford's liveliness repeated to her at such a moment, MP III 4 354 47
on, Fanny, is not fit--is hardly fit to be repeated to you. MP III 16 454 18
collectedly or methodically as I have repeated it to you. MP III 16 458 30
and aid, Sir Thomas saw repeated, and for ever repeated MP III 17 473 31
repeated, and for ever repeated reason to rejoice in what MP III 17 473 31
She then repeated some warm personal praise which she had E I 4 34 43
This was obliged to be repeated before it could be E I 8 60 31
32
which she repeated immediately with great delight. E I 8 68 58
"Frank," and "my son," repeated several times over; and E I 14 118 4
And he repeated her words with such assurance of accent, E I 15 130 26
27
her own silly compliment repeated twice over before the E II 1 158 13
"Ever hear her!" repeated Emma. E II 6 201 27
two Miss Coxes five," had been repeated many times over. E II 11 248 4
"Something that would do!" repeated Mrs. Elton. E II 17 301 16
"Jane!"--repeated Frank Churchill, with a look of surprise E III 2 324 24
or verse, original or repeated--or two things moderately E III 7 370 23
exclaim, and require confirmation, repeated confirmation. E III 10 395 36
Composure with a witness! to look on, while repeated E III 10 397 46
Harriet repeated expressions of approbation and praise E III 11 409 35
"As a friend!"--repeated Mr. Knightley.-- E III 13 429 33

or ways of either, he repeated to them very comfortably E III 14 434 3
It was a palpable display, repeated on every possible E III 16 454 16
The same story and the same raptures were repeated, when P III 7 54 5
"It is over! it is over!" she repeated to herself again, P III 7 60 26
agony of the other; he repeated, with such tremulous P III 11 100 23
Many had looked on each other, and many had repeated the P III 12 105 13
"Yes, yes, to the inn," repeated Captain Wentworth, P III 12 111 48
"Mr. Elliot!" repeated Anne, looking up surprised. P IV 9 194 21
"The whole history!" repeated Anne, laughing. P IV 9 197 41
"Our coast too full"--repeated Mr P.-- S 1 369 1
long & often enjoyed the repeated defeats she had given to S 3 377 1
"Impossible" & "impossible", was repeated over & over S 10 419 1

REPEATEDLY (28)

concealment, but repeatedly regretted the necessity of its NA I 15 125 48
his figure so repeatedly, as to catch Miss Tilney's notice. NA II 8 187 13
both at home) saw her repeatedly; and from our own NA II 9 197 25
consent, and so repeatedly assured her that he had never NA II 11 208 2
He said so repeatedly; other things he said too, which SS I 19 101 1
said she repeatedly, with a strong emphasis on the word. SS II 10 217 21
her to be, as she repeatedly declared herself, one of the SS III 9 335 7
of his letter, and repeatedly calling off his attention by PP I 10 47 1
were to go so soon, and repeatedly tried to persuade Miss PP I 12 59 3
dishes at supper, and repeatedly fearing that he crouded PP I 16 84 59
since they had met, and repeatedly asked what she had been PP I 17 86 9
it inevitable, and even repeatedly to say in an ill- PP II 3 145 11
His eyes had been soon and repeatedly turned towards them PP II 8 172 3
4
She wished to discredit it entirely, repeatedly exclaiming, PP II 13 204 2
and talked with them both, Wickham repeatedly, Lydia once. PP III 10 321 2
I talked to her repeatedly in the most serious manner, PP III 10 325 2
her two cousins having repeatedly proved the contrary, she MP I 5 48 30
Miss Crawford, who had been repeatedly eyeing Dr. Grant MP II 5 226 60
the conversation; tried repeatedly before he could succeed; MP III 1 323 57
She had heard repeatedly from his sister within the three MP III 7 375 4
with us, you have been repeatedly in the company of some, E I 4 32 32
and his own brother and family have been there repeatedly." E I 12 105 55
having no instrument repeatedly; oftener than I should E II 8 226 81
has ceased to be, was repeatedly given in the very E III 2 326 33
She had been repeatedly very earnest in trying to get Anne P III 2 16 16
and Anne Elliot were repeatedly in the same circle. P III 8 63 1
Mr. Elliot had called repeatedly, had dined with them once, P IV 3 139 10
Wentworth, saw him repeatedly by daylight and eyed him P IV 12 248 2

REPEATING (19)

Reginald is only repeating after her ladyship. I am &c. LS 17 272 8
Tilney an opportunity of repeating the agreeable request NA I 8 58 25
'The lock of hair, (repeating it from the letter,) which SS II 7 190 56
of the carriage, and repeating his hope of being able to SS II 11 222 13
"How!" cried Elinor; "have you been repeating to me what SS III 2 274 19
Mrs. Bennet began repeating her thanks to Mr. Bingley for PP I 9 45 35
of being hurried into repeating something of Bingley, PP II 15 217 17
She then spoke of the letter, repeating the whole of its PP II 17 224 9
and continually was she repeating, "why is he so altered? PP III 1 255 60
Bingley could not help repeating to him some part of what PP III 3 270 12
suspicion, she was not distressed by his repeating it. PP III 15 364 25
To her he soon turned, repeating much of what he had MP II 2 193 18
And this question, which he was continually repeating to MP II 8 255 11
After repeating this, Edmund was so much affected, that MP III 16 457 30
by the idea, and was repeating, "no husbands and wives in E I 6 46 22
engage in any thing, repeating the same motives which she E III 6 359 37
of Captain Wentworth, repeating his name so often, P III 6 52 33
hedges, and from repeating to herself some few of the P III 10 84 7
but declined it all, repeating her conviction, that the P IV 7 177 15

REPEATS (3)

In proof, he repeats, and more eagerly, what he said at MP III 14 435 14
which he had better not, and he repeats it all to her. P IV 9 205 82
She, in the overflowing spirits of her recovery, repeats P IV 9 205 82

REPEL (1)

herself vigorously to repel the ill-natured attack, she PP III 3 269 10

REPELLANT (1)

him spoken of with cooling moderation or repellant truth. E I 17 143 15

REPELLED (1)

will intrude, which cannot, which ought not to be repelled. PP III 16 369 24

REPENT (14)

I am sometimes half disposed to repent that I did not let LS 5 249 1
her brother; but she could not repent her resistance. NA I 13 101 25
in too great a hurry, you will certainly live to repent it. NA II 3 146 20
and for many days successively, and he did not repent. SS I 1 5 8
be assured that you shall never have reason to repent it. SS II 2 146 6
Emma could not repent what she had done, so happy had it W 331 11
could she for a moment repent her refusal, or feel the PP II 14 212 17
I wish you may not repent it. "yours, &c." MP III 15 437 3
take any pains to marry him, she would probably repent it. E I 4 30 18
She did not repent what she had done; she still thought E I 8 65 50
She was sorry, but could not repent. E I 9 69 1
If I were to marry, I must expect to repent it." E I 10 84 13
She could not repent. E II 5 187 4
Emma did not repent her condescension in going to the E II 9 231 1

REPENTANCE (6)

should pass away and repentance succeed it? and she only NA II 13 227 27
did justice to his repentance, and softened only his SS III 10 347 33
That his repentance of misconduct, which thus brought its SS III 14 379 18
him by any sign of repentance; and rather looked with PP II 5 156 4
She felt the engagement to be a source of repentance and E III 14 442 8
She felt the engagement to be a source of repentance and E III 15 447 22

REPENTED (2)

I have more than once repented that I did not marry him LS 2 245 1
She was humbled, she was grieved; she repented, though she PP III 8 311 13

REPENTING (1)

acquaintance, and on knowing him better she was repenting. MP II 3 200 20

REPERUSAL (1)

as she supposed; and the reperusal of these letters, after P III 6 51 32

REPETITION (17)

wondered over the repetition of a disappointment, which NA II 10 201 6
attended the third repetition; and, after completing the NA II 14 238 22
going through a repetition of particulars with composure. SS II 1 142 7
continual repetition on Marianne, she could stay no longer. SS II 8 193 7
would be only to give a repetition of what her daughters SS II 10 212 2
warmth, nor to the repetition of any other part of the SS II 13 245 47
herself to the brief repetition of such simple particulars, SS III 2 276 27
long yawning at the repetition of delights which she saw PP I 18 100 68
of its containing any repetition of those sentiments, or PP II 12 196 4
this entreaty, or for resisting every repetition of it. PP II 12 201 5
continual repetition of, "Oh! no, that will never do. MP I 14 131 3
need not fear a repetition--it would be a subject MP III 16 453 17
on the desired repetition of entreaties and assurances,-- E I 6 49 41
foresaw nothing but a repetition of excuses and delays; E I 18 144 3
enough; and, with a repetition of every thing that she E III 8 384 34
repetition, and all the insolence of imaginary superiority. E III 14 442 8
given; time and continual repetition must do the rest.-- E III 17 466 30

REPETITIONS (3)

and repetitions, which require good reading not to be felt. MP III 3 340 25
irritated by ceaseless repetitions of Miss Hawkins's E II 4 184 10
day remarks, dull repetitions, old news, and heavy jokes. E II 8 219 43

REPINE (6)

Far be it from me to repine at his doing so; he had an SS II 11 225 35
But I will not repine. PP II 1 134 5
Mrs. Bennet still continued to wonder and repine at his PP II 1 137 26
One ought not repine;--but, to be sure, it would have been PP III 10 328 28
the she could, upon the whole, have no cause to repine." PP III 14 355 46
so far, than to repine at the counteraction which followed. MP II 10 280 32

REPINING (4)

the full proof of that repining spirit to which she had NA II 15 241 7
indolence and selfish repining, now at work in introducing SS III 10 343 10
continued in the parlour repining at her fate in terms as PP II 18 230 12
but on the third, her repining was over, and her sister PP III 4 273 1

REPININGS (1)

sister whose constant repinings at the dulness of every PP II 19 237 3

REPLACE (1)

Nothing could replace him, therefore, in her former esteem, SS III 11 349 1

REPLACED (1)

the collar-bone was soon replaced, and though Mr. Robinson P III 7 54 4

REPLACING (1)

at the book again, and replacing it on the table,) he E I 9 82 83

REPLETE (3)

in every respect, so replete with advantage, so promising PP II 14 213 18
which she believed more replete with good than any she E I 14 119 5
Impossible that any situation could be more replete with E III 8 380 13

REPLIED (420)

I replied that it was. LS 23 284 6
"My love, replied I, do not think it necessary to LS 24 286 4
"No, you shall not, replied I.-- LS 24 286 7
"No Catherine, replied I. LS 24 287 8
"Certainly;" replied I, deeply sighing at the recital of LS 24 287 10
"You did indeed, replied I very gravely, but I flattered LS 24 287 11
"Yes, my dear," replied Mrs. Allen, with perfect serenity, NA I 2 22 13
"Very agreeable indeed," she replied, vainly endeavouring NA I 2 23 24
"About a week, sir," replied Catherine, trying not to NA I 3 26 5
"I am quite of your opinion, sir," replied Mrs. Allen; " NA I 3 28 44
replied, "I like him very much; he seems very agreeable." NA I 7 50 44
"Indeed I am," she replied; "I love her exceedingly, and NA I 7 50 48
"Do just as you please, my dear," replied Mrs. Allen, with NA I 9 61 7
"Henry!" she replied with a smile. NA I 10 72 10
"No," replied her friend very placidly, "I know you never NA I 11 82 7
"It is all one to me," replied Thorpe rather angrily; and NA I 11 88 55
his countenance, and he replied in a tone which retained NA I 12 93 7
He replied by asking her to make room for him, and talking NA I 12 95 15
"I hope I am not less so now," she replied, very feelingly; NA I 13 100 11
and hastily replied, "indeed!--and of what nature?" NA I 14 112 30
Catherine replied only by a look of wondering ignorance. NA I 15 117 5
"Morland says exactly the same," replied Isabella; "and NA I 15 119 15
"Then why do you stay away so long?" replied Catherine-- NA I 15 123 37
Catherine, without hesitation, replied, that she was very NA II 1 132 16
"Psha! my dear creature," she replied, "do not think me NA II 3 143 2
"A great and increasing one," replied the other, in a low NA II 7 180 34
"How came I up that staircase!" he replied, greatly NA II 9 194 7
"And from these circumstances," he replied, (his quick eye NA II 9 196 25
affectionate a sister," replied Henry, warmly, "must be a NA II 10 204 14
"Indeed I am afraid she will," replied Henry; "I am afraid NA II 10 206 34
Eleanor only replied, "I cannot wonder at your feelings. NA II 13 228 30
"It was my father's last request to me," replied her SS I 2 9 4
"I would not wish to do any thing mean," he replied. SS I 2 9 12
"It is certainly an unpleasant thing," replied Mr. SS I 2 11 21
"Like him!" replied her mother with a smile. SS I 3 16 10
"No taste for drawing," replied Elinor; "why should you SS I 4 19 2
At length she replied: "do not be offended, Elinor, if my SS I 4 19 5
6
"I am sure," replied Elinor with a smile, "that his SS I 4 20 7
"It would be impossible, I know," replied Elinor, "to SS I 8 38 11
His name, he replied, was Willoughby, and his present home SS I 9 42 10
as if he did, and then replied, "aye, you will make SS I 9 45 31
32
"That he is patronized by you," replied Willoughby, "is SS I 10 50 17
so much in the mass," replied Elinor, "and so much on the SS I 10 51 27
"No," replied Elinor, "her opinions are all romantic." SS I 11 56 9
"This will probably be the case," he replied; "and yet SS I 11 56 12
"You have said so," replied Elinor, "almost every day SS I 12 60 10
"I never had any conjectures about it," replied Margaret; " SS I 12 61 19
"I have no doubt of it," replied Marianne. SS I 13 65 31
Marianne coloured, and replied very hastily, "where pray?"- SS I 13 67 62
"I am afraid," replied Elinor, "that the pleasantness of SS I 13 68 71
"I flatter myself," replied Elinor, "that even under the SS I 14 73 14
"You are a good woman," he warmly replied. SS I 14 74 19
"I hope not," he replied, trying to look cheerful; and SS I 15 75 4
He coloured as he replied, "you are very kind, but I have SS I 15 76 10
fixed on the ground he only replied, "you are too good." SS I 15 76 12
"My engagements at present," replied Willoughby confusedly, SS I 15 76 15
"I confess," replied Elinor, "that every circumstance SS I 15 80 37
"It is a beautiful country," he replied; "but these SS I 16 88 34
"Because," replied he, smiling, "among the rest of the SS I 16 88 36
Marianne coloured as she replied, "but most people do." SS I 17 92 17
"Why should you think so!" replied he, with a sigh. SS I 17 93 34
"I believe you are right," he replied, "and yet I have SS I 17 93 36
"Quite the contrary," replied Elinor, looking expressively SS I 17 94 41
her own worth too well for false shame," replied Edward. SS I 17 94 44
"I do not understand you," replied he, colouring. SS I 17 94 48
glance at Elinor, replied, "yes; it is my sister's hair. SS I 18 98 12
"I do not doubt it," replied he, rather astonished at her SS I 18 100 30
"I do assure you," he replied, "that I have long thought SS I 19 102 4
"I think," replied Edward, "that I may defy many months to SS I 19 103 8
"No, none at all," he replied, and read on. SS I 19 108 33
"Certainly,"--he replied with a sneer--"I came into SS I 20 113 30
"Oh! dear; yes; I know him extremely well," replied Mrs. SS I 20 114 44
"Upon my word," replied Elinor, "you know much more of the SS I 20 114 45
"I confess," replied Elinor, "that while I am at Barton SS I 21 123 20
manner in which it was spoken, Elinor replied that she was. SS I 21 123 22
"I think every one must admire it," replied Elinor, "who SS I 21 123 25
"Upon my word," replied Elinor, "I cannot tell you, for I SS I 21 124 29
"Indeed!" replied Lucy; "I wonder at that, for I thought SS I 22 128 5
"No;" replied Lucy, "not to Mr. Robert Ferrars--I never SS I 22 129 14
"I think I have," replied Elinor, with an exertion of SS I 22 130 27
"It is strange," replied Elinor in a most painful SS I 22 131 31
"You are quite in the right;" replied Elinor calmly. SS I 22 132 38
"Pardon me," replied Elinor, startled by the question; " SS I 22 133 45
"No," replied Elinor, most feelingly sensible of every SS I 22 134 49
herself instantly and replied, "indeed you are very much SS II 1 144 12
"And yet I do assure you," replied Lucy, her little sharp SS II 2 146 5
"I should be always happy," replied Elinor, "to shew any SS II 2 149 26
"Indeed you wrong me," replied Lucy with great solemnity; " SS II 2 150 32
Edward's future wife, and replied, "this compliment would SS II 2 150 33
"That is very true," replied her mother; "but of her SS II 3 156 13
"I am not going to write to my mother," replied Marianne SS II 4 160 5
"Yes," he replied, with some embarrassment, "almost ever SS II 4 162 12
He replied with his accustomary mildness to all her SS II 4 163 19
"Are you quite sure of it?" she replied. SS II 4 165 26
The man replied that none had. SS II 4 165 27
"Did you?" replied Elinor. SS II 5 171 32
He tried to smile as he replied, "your sister's engagement SS II 5 173 40
"No, Elinor," she replied, "ask nothing; you will soon SS II 7 180 3
trying to smile, replied, "and have you really, ma'am, SS II 7 181 9
"I only wish," replied her sister, "there were any thing I SS II 7 185 18
Elinor would not contend, and only replied, "whoever may SS II 7 189 51
"Dear ma'am," replied Elinor, smiling at the difference of SS II 8 198 28
"Perhaps, then," he hesitatingly replied, "what I heard SS II 8 198 33
"Yes," he replied gravely, "once I have. SS II 9 211 35
"Not in the stage, I assure you," replied Miss Steele, SS II 10 218 24
"No, indeed!" replied her cousin, with affected SS II 10 218 28
"Indeed I believe you," replied Elinor; "but I am very SS II 11 223 23
towards it," he gravely replied; "but however there is SS II 11 226 37
"I guessed you would say so"--replied Lucy quickly--"but SS II 13 239 9
But it seemed to satisfy Lucy, for she directly replied, " SS II 13 240 14
15
"Oh! don't think of me!" she replied, with spirited SS II 13 242 26
the sting; for she calmly replied, "not so, indeed; for, SS II 13 243 39
40

"Well may you wonder, Marianne," replied her brother, "at	SS III 1 267 40
He therefore replied, without any resentment, "I would by	SS III 1 267 44
	45
"The cruelty, the impolitic cruelty,"--he replied, with	SS III 3 282 19
into; and therefore only replied to its conclusion.	SS III 4 286 18
"Certainly, ma'am," replied Elinor, not hearing much of	SS III 4 287 23
"No," replied he, with sudden consciousness, "not to find	SS III 4 289 34
"Indeed," replied Elinor, "I believe that you will find	SS III 4 290 38
"I am not sorry to see you alone," he replied, "for I have	SS III 5 294 8
brother's tone, calmly replied, "the lady, I suppose, has	SS III 5 296 25
	26
time; to every inquiry replied that she was better, and	SS III 7 307 1
"Not yet," replied the other, concealing her terror, and	SS III 7 311 12
"No, sir," she replied with firmness, "I shall not stay.	SS III 8 317 3
"I understand you," he replied, with an expressive smile,	SS III 8 318 18
"I insist on your hearing the whole of it," he replied.	SS III 8 320 32
know it," he warmly replied; "I did not recollect that I	SS III 8 322 38
"I do not know what I told her," he replied, impatiently; "	SS III 8 324 45
"Well"--he replied--"once more good bye.	SS III 8 332 79
"I know it is"--replied her mother seriously, "or after	SS III 9 337 16
Marianne pressed her hand and replied, "you are very good.-	SS III 10 347 29
	30
"The whole of his behaviour," replied Elinor, "from the	SS III 11 351 11
In an hurried manner, he replied in the affirmative.	SS III 12 359 14
"At Longstaple!" he replied, with an air of surprise-- "no,	SS III 12 359 18
"There was a reason for that--replied Miss W. changing	W 316 2
"We must not all expect to be individually lucky replied	W 321 2
"I see the likeness between her & Miss Watson, replied Mr	W 324 3
"Rather more so, my dear--replied he, because young ladies	W 326 6
seat by the fire you know, Mr Musgrave." replied Mrs E.	W 327 7
"I do not think her handsome." replied Emma, to whom all	W 340 19
"If it were not a breach of confidence, replied Tom with	W 340 19
disposed to be pleased, he only replied--"phoo! phoo!--	W 348 22
"You are very good--replied her mother--& I assure you it	W 350 24
"Very much"--replied Emma, who thought a comprehensive	W 350 24
"My good creatures, replied Jane, use no ceremony with me,	W 351 25
me with money, replied Emma, & I am a woman too.--"	W 351 26
"You know, replied Emma struggling with her tears, my	W 352 26
"My dear, replied Eliz. the turkey is roasted, & it may	W 354 27
"I could not be earlier, he replied.	W 356 28
Mr. Bennet replied that he had not.	PP I 1 3 4
"My dear Mr. Bennet," replied his wife, "how can you be so	PP I 1 4 16
"They have none of them much to recommend them," replied	PP I 1 5 27
"I do not cough for my own amusement," replied Kitty	PP I 2 6 10
"He is also handsome," replied Elizabeth, "which a young	PP I 4 14 3
"That is very true," replied Elizabeth, "and I could	PP I 5 20 19
"It may perhaps be pleasant," replied Charlotte, "to be	PP I 6 21 2
"Your plan is a good one," replied Elizabeth, "where	PP I 6 22 7
Mr. Darcy replied with great intrepidity, "Miss Elizabeth	PP I 6 27 49
	50
"Not at all," he replied; "they were brightened by the	PP I 8 36 13
men of any consideration in the world," replied Darcy.	PP I 8 37 19
"It ought to be good," he replied. "it has been the work	PP I 8 38 30
"Undoubtedly," replied Darcy, to whom this remark was	PP I 8 40 57
"Whatever I do is done in a hurry," replied he; "and	PP I 9 42 8
"When I am in the country," he replied, "I never wish to	PP I 9 43 22
"I should like balls infinitely better," she replied, "if	PP I 11 55 8
"Certainly," replied Elizabeth--"there are such people,	PP I 11 57 21
"And yours, he replied with a smile, "is wilfully to	PP I 11 58 32
"Yes," replied Wickham;--"his estate there is a noble one.	PP I 16 77 10
"I will not trust myself on the subject," replied Wickham,	PP I 16 80 35
"It is wonderful,"--replied Wickham,--"for almost all his	PP I 16 81 39
"Lady Catherine de Bourgh," she replied, "has very lately	PP I 16 83 52
"I believe her to be both in a great degree," replied	PP I 16 84 58
He replied, and was again silent.	PP I 18 91 8
"Both," replied Elizabeth archly; "for I have always seen	PP I 18 91 15
your friendship," replied Elizabeth with emphasis, "and in	PP I 18 92 21
"Yes, always," she replied, without knowing what she said,	PP I 18 93 32
no means suspend any pleasure of yours," he coldly replied.	PP I 18 94 43
"I beg your pardon," replied Miss Bingley, turning away	PP I 18 95 47
"No," replied Jane, "I have not forgotten him; but I have	PP I 18 95 50
partner she had scarcely replied, before Mr. Collins came	PP I 18 96 56
when she ceased speaking, replied thus, "my dear Miss	PP I 18 97 60
	61
him time to speak, replied with an air of distant civility.	PP I 18 98 61
"I am not now to learn," replied Mr. Collins, with a a	PP I 19 107 13
Elizabeth replied that it was.	PP I 20 111 15
"My dear," replied her husband, "I have two small favours	PP I 20 112 22
and sometimes with playful gaiety replied to her attacks.	PP I 20 112 23
"My dear madam," replied he, "let us be for ever silent on	PP I 20 114 32
"If we thought alike of Miss Bingley," replied Jane, "your	PP I 21 119 21
"My dear madam," he replied, "this invitation is	PP I 22 123 5
"My dear sir," replied Mr. Collins, "I am particularly	PP I 22 123 8
replied, "why should you be surprised, my dear Eliza?--	PP I 22 124 14
	15
"I see what you are feeling," replied Charlotte,--"you	PP I 22 125 17
in speaking of both," replied Jane, "and I hope you will	PP II 1 136 14
him to chuse Miss Darcy," replied Jane; "but this may be	PP II 1 137 24
"I am the less surprised at what has happened," replied	PP II 6 160 3
"With three younger sisters grown up," replied Elizabeth	PP II 6 166 37
"I assure you, madam," he replied, "that she does not need	PP II 8 173 9
"I shall not say that you are mistaken," he replied, "	PP II 8 174 14
"I have been making the tour of the park," he replied, "as	PP II 10 183 4
"He likes to have his own way very well," replied Colonel	PP II 10 183 10
She directly replied, "you need not be frightened.	PP II 10 184 20
	21
"I might as well enquire," replied she, "why with so	PP II 11 190 10
With assumed tranquillity he then replied, "I have no wish	PP II 11 191 15
your kind invitation," replied Elizabeth, "but it is not	PP II 14 211 7
a more smiling solemnity replied, "it gives me the	PP II 15 215 3
	4
To this, Mary very gravely replied, "far be it from me, my	PP II 16 222 23
"Indeed," replied Elizabeth, "I am heartily sorry for him;	PP II 17 224 4
Miss Bennet paused a little and then replied, "surely	PP II 17 226 22
and a returning smile, replied, that he had formerly seen	PP II 18 233 27
while Mrs. Reynolds replied, that he was, adding, "but we	PP III 1 246 8
every body will say that knows him," replied the other.	PP III 1 248 30
in him to be sure," replied her aunt, "but it is confined	PP III 1 257 68
a little whimsical in his civilities," replied her uncle.	PP III 1 258 72
"Yes," replied Darcy, who could contain himself no longer,	PP III 3 271 18
"No, I thank you;" she replied, endeavouring to recover	PP III 4 276 10
"In the first place," replied Mr. Gardiner, "there is no	PP III 5 282 5
"It does seem, and it is most shocking indeed," replied	PP III 5 283 10
"I do, indeed," replied Elizabeth, colouring.	PP III 5 284 14
"Not yet," replied Jane.	PP III 5 286 24
"Oh! my dear brother," replied Mrs. Bennet, "that is	PP III 5 288 38
"Perhaps it would have been better;" replied her sister.	PP III 5 291 56
"He meant, I believe," replied Jane, "to go to Epsom, the	PP III 5 293 69
he must have endured, he replied, "say nothing of that.	PP III 6 299 19
"You must not be too severe upon yourself," replied	PP III 6 299 20
"I dislike it very much," he replied; "but it must be done.	PP III 7 303 22
"I comfort myself with thinking," replied Jane, "that he	PP III 7 304 35
"Their conduct has been such," replied Elizabeth, "as	PP III 7 305 38
raising his head, coolly replied, "just as you please."	PP III 7 305 39
	40
To Mr. Bennet's acknowledgments he briefly replied, with	PP III 8 312 18
"No really," replied Elizabeth; "I think there cannot be	PP III 9 318 23
"You certainly do," she replied with a smile; "but it does	PP III 10 327 6
She replied in the affirmative.	PP III 10 327 10
"Certainly," he replied, biting his lips.	PP III 10 328 15
"You may depend on it," replied the other, "for Mrs.	PP III 11 331 15
"I wish I could say any thing to comfort you," replied	PP III 11 333 29
"There is no saying, indeed!" replied Harriet, rather	E I 4 33 37
"I dare say," replied Mrs. Weston, smiling, "that I	E I 5 37 8
"I have not a fault to find with her person," he replied.	E I 5 39 21
"Do you think so?" replied he.	E I 6 48 32
"Yes, indeed, a very good letter," replied Emma rather	E I 7 51 5
"I have reason to think," he replied, "that Harriet Smith	E I 8 59 25
"Certainly," replied he, surprized, "I do not absolutely	E I 8 60 29
"Very well," replied Emma, "a most natural feeling; and	E I 9 77 45
"I have no hesitation in saying," replied Mr. Elton,	E I 9 82 83
Emma laughed, and replied, "my being charming, Harriet, is	E I 10 84 10
	11
"He has not been here yet," replied Emma.	E I 11 95 21
"A material difference then," she replied--"and no doubt	E I 12 99 7
"Mr. Elton's manners are not perfect," replied Emma; "but	E I 13 111 17
"Me!" she replied with a smile of astonishment, "are you	E I 13 112 19
"My first enjoyment," replied John Knightley, as they	E I 13 116 46
like doubt in the case," replied Emma; "but am disposed to	E I 14 120 12
"My Emma!" replied Mrs. Weston, smiling, "what is the	E I 14 121 16
knows Mrs. Churchill," replied Isabella: "and I am sure I	E I 14 121 17
one decides upon what he can do," replied Mrs. Weston.	E I 14 123 23
"Indeed!" replied he.	E I 15 127 15
state, she replied, "I am very much astonished, Mr. Elton.	E I 15 129 24
	25
replied, "it is impossible for me to doubt any longer.	E I 15 130 29
	30
"Me!--not at all," replied Mr. Knightley, rather	E I 18 149 28
You are so kind!" replied the happily deceived aunt, while	E II 1 157 10
"You are extremely kind," replied Miss Bates highly	E II 1 158 12
"We consider our Hartfield pork," replied Mr. Woodhouse--	E II 3 173 30
	31
"No--I have never seen Mr. Elton," she replied, starting	E II 3 174 37
"When I have seen Mr. Elton," replied Jane, "I dare say I	E II 3 175 43
"I hope I should know better," he replied" "no, depend	E II 5 192 32
"Yes, Oh! yes--he replied; I was just going to mention it.	E II 6 198 7
"Thank you for rousing me," he replied.	E II 8 222 56
he replied;--"but you must often wish it, I am sure."	E II 8 228 90
"Yes," he replied, and without the smallest apparent	E II 8 228 92
"I do not believe any such thing," replied Emma.--	E II 9 234 33
"I have not been working uninterruptedly," he replied, "I	E II 10 240 5
"Very true," he gravely replied; "it was very bad."	E II 11 249 15
"There is no denying it," he replied.	E II 11 249 18
"No, I fancy not," replied Mrs. Elton, with a most	E II 14 274 26
With a faint blush, she presently replied, "such	E II 15 286 19
	20
"Yes," he replied, "any body may know how highly I think	E II 15 287 25
Mr. John Knightley smiled, and replied, "that is to say,	E II 16 293 15
	16
"I have often thought them the worst of the two," replied	E II 16 293 21
of the slave-trade," replied Jane; "governess-trade, I	E II 17 300 15
"And I am quite serious too, I assure you," replied Mrs.	E II 17 302 20
"I did," replied Emma, "and they cannot forgive me."	E III 2 330 49
She hesitated a moment, and then replied, "with you, if	E III 2 331 60
"I shall be happier to burn it," replied Harriet.	E III 4 340 26
it should pass unnoticed or not, replied, "never marry!--	E III 4 341 29
	30
"No, sir," replied his son, laughing, "I seem to have had	E III 5 345 13
"The joke," he replied gravely, "seemed confined to you	E III 5 350 30
"You had better explore to Donwell," replied Mr. Knightley.	E III 6 354 8
"No,"--he calmly replied,--"there is but one married woman	E III 6 354 15
and Emma very feelingly replied, "that can be no reason	E III 6 362 49
"I say nothing of which I am ashamed," replied he, with	E III 7 369 16
"So very kind!" replied Miss Bates.	E III 8 380 10
"No, no,"--he gravely replied.--	E III 10 392 9
Emma pondered a moment, and then replied, "I will not	E III 10 396 39
"His sufferings," replied Emma drily, "do not appear to	E III 10 398 54
"I am quite easy on that head," replied Mrs. Weston.	E III 10 399 62
"La!" replied Kitty, "it looks just like that man that	PP III 11 334 34
Bingley replied that he did, and made his congratulations.	PP III 11 336 50
"You are a good girl;" he replied, "and I have great	PP III 13 348 38
"I suspected as much," replied Elizabeth.	PP III 13 349 46
Elizabeth replied very concisely that she was.	PP III 14 352 6
"Miss Bennet," replied her ladyship, in an angry tone, "	PP III 14 353 26
Lady Catherine hesitated for a moment, and then replied, "	PP III 14 354 42
	43
"These are heavy misfortunes," replied Elizabeth.	PP III 14 355 46
"Neither duty, nor honour, nor gratitude," replied	PP III 14 358 70
To this question his daughter replied only with a laugh;	PP III 15 364 25
"I am sorry, exceedingly sorry," replied Darcy, in a tone	PP III 16 365 4
"If you will thank me," he replied, "let it be for	PP III 16 366 6
Elizabeth coloured and laughed as she replied, "yes, you	PP III 16 367 11
"When I wrote that letter," replied Darcy, "I believed	PP III 16 368 22
"My object then," replied Darcy, "was to shew you, by	PP III 16 370 32
"It may do very well for the others," replied Mr. Bingley;	PP III 17 374 24
"I do, I do like him," she replied, with tears in her eyes,	PP III 17 376 34
"There is a great deal of truth in what you say," replied	MP I 1 7 7
Edmund, to whom this was chiefly addressed, replied, "I	MP I 5 49 31
"I do not know," replied Miss Crawford hesitatingly.	MP I 5 50 39
"No," replied Edmund, "I do not think she has ever been to	MP I 5 51 42
"The tree thrives well beyond a doubt, madam," replied Dr.	MP I 6 54 10
"You were imposed on, ma'am," replied Dr. Grant; "these	MP I 6 54 12
Edmund again felt grave, and only replied, "it is a noble	MP I 6 60 50
"No, not that I know of," replied Mrs. Norris; "she was	MP I 7 71 32
"I can hardly believe you," he replied; "I know your looks	MP I 7 72 38
her complexion, replied only, "if I had known this before,	MP I 9 89 29
After a moment's embarrassment the lady replied, "you are	MP I 10 98 8
"More easily amused," he replied, "consequently you know,"	MP I 10 99 14
"There is no sacrifice in the case," replied Edmund with a	MP I 11 108 11
"No," replied Fanny, "but we need not give up his	MP I 11 111 30
"Yes, ma'am, indeed"--replied the other, with a stately	MP I 12 117 13
"I should be most happy," replied he aloud, and jumping up	MP I 12 119 24
"If you are resolved on acting," replied the persevering	MP I 13 127 28
filled up, with us," replied Edmund, turning away to the	MP I 15 139 9
"You chose very wisely, I am sure," replied Miss Crawford,	MP I 15 144 30
"I shall not ask him," replied Tom, in a cold determined	MP I 15 144 35
"I should have no objection," she replied; "for though I	MP I 15 144 38
by no means tempt me," he replied, "for I should be sorry	MP I 15 145 41
"I am not going to urge her,"--replied Mrs. Norris sharply,	MP I 15 147 55
After a moment's thought, Miss Crawford calmly replied, "	MP I 15 148 59
"I dare say she is," replied Mary, coldly.	MP I 17 161 11
"My indulgence shall be given, sir," replied Sir Thomas	MP II 1 185 29
Sir Thomas looked again, and then replied with an	MP II 1 186 34
"Yes," replied Miss Crawford carelessly, "it does very	MP II 4 209 15
"To say the truth," replied Miss Crawford, "I am something	MP II 4 209 17
consideration of her, replied in a calmer, graver tone,	MP II 5 226 59
"The most interesting in the world," replied her brother--"	MP II 5 226 61
sister, and laughingly replied, "I cannot say there was	MP II 7 245 31
Sir Thomas, politely bowing, replied--"it is the only way,	MP II 7 247 39
"My daughters," replied Sir Thomas, gravely interposing, "	MP II 8 252 3
too when you wear that necklace," replied Miss Crawford.	MP II 8 259 19
"Well then," replied Miss Crawford more seriously but	MP II 8 259 22
"Well, then," replied Miss Crawford laughing, "I must	MP II 10 277 19
niece, and then gravely replied, "she will never leave us,	MP II 11 285 13
Mansfield parsonage, and replied but to invite her in the	MP II 12 295 22
"We have not been so silent all the time," replied his	MP III 3 336 9
"It will be a favourite I believe from this hour," replied	MP III 3 338 13
Fanny, at once agitated and dejected, replied, "if you	MP III 4 346 9
"My dear Fanny," replied Edmund, scarcely hearing her to	MP III 4 349 26
"I will not say," replied Fanny, "that I was not half	MP III 5 362 21
After a moment's reflection, Mr. Crawford replied, "I know	MP III 11 410 16
"I am perfectly serious,"--he replied,--"as you perfectly	MP III 11 411 18
As soon as I could speak, I replied that I had not	MP III 16 457 30
Her father fondly replied, "Ah! my dear, I wish you would	E I 1 12 40

"What news do you mean?" replied Emma, unable to guess, by E III 11 404 5
stoutly on the subject," replied Emma, smiling; "but you E III 11 405 13
"Yes," replied Harriet modestly, but not fearfully--"I E III 11 407 31
to say no more, he replied, "if you mean Miss Fairfax and E III 13 425 6
7
tender consideration, replied, "you are very kind--but you E III 13 426 14
15
"No"--replied Emma--quite confirmed by the depressed E III 13 429 32
"I would rather be talking to you," he replied; "but as it E III 15 444 5
"I hope he does," replied Mr. Knightley coolly, and E III 15 447 24
"Nothing can be actually settled yet, perhaps," replied E III 16 460 54
"That is," replied Mr. Knightley, "she will indulge her E III 17 461 3
Emma laughed, and replied: "but I had the assistance of E III 17 462 6
"He writes like a sensible man," replied Emma, when she E III 17 464 20
"There is one subject," he replied, "I hope but one, on E III 18 470 8
"You mistake me, you quite mistake me," she replied, E III 18 471 17
"You ought to know your friend best," replied Mr. E III 18 473 25
"I am quite sure," he replied, speaking very distinctly, " E III 18 474 30
"I am perfectly satisfied," replied Emma, with the E III 18 474 31
"I have always admired her complexion," replied Emma, E III 18 478 62
"Very beautiful, indeed," replied emma: and she spoke so E III 18 479 71
72
"He would be a very lucky man, Shepherd," replied Sir P III 3 17 2
'Forty,' replied Sir Basil, 'forty, and no more.' P III 3 20 16
"There is hardly any personal defect," replied Anne, " P III 5 35 15
"I am sorry to find you unwell," replied Anne. P III 5 37 23
"Well, you will soon be better now," replied Anne, P III 5 38 28
not the smallest objection on that account," replied Anne. P III 5 39 42
"I felt my luck, Admiral, I assure you;" replied Captain P III 8 65 13
"Nothing to the purpose," replied her brother. P III 8 69 38
"Upon my word it would," replied Mary. P III 9 75 11
and when Mary immediately replied, with some jealousy, at P III 10 83 4
"We had better not talk about it, my dear," replied Mrs. P III 10 92 45
Anne, far from wishing to cavil at the pleasure, replied, " P IV 5 155 10
"She sees nothing to blame in it," replied Anne; "on the P IV 5 157 18
"The last few hours were certainly very painful," replied P IV 8 183 16
in Camden-Place so long," replied he, "without knowing P IV 8 187 28
Anne replied, and spoke in defence of the performance so P IV 8 190 47
improved, and he replied again with almost a smile. P IV 8 190 47
"No!" he replied impressively, "there is nothing worth my P IV 8 190 50
"I have been a good deal acquainted with him," replied Mrs. P IV 9 194 22
slightest use to you," replied Anne; "but I suspect that P IV 9 195 25
"No," replied Anne, "nor next week, nor next, nor next. P IV 9 195 28
"It first came into my head," replied Mrs. Smith, "upon P IV 9 197 36
"Mr. Elliot," replied Mrs. Smith, "at that period of his P IV 9 200 59
"Lessening, I understand," replied Mrs. Smith. P IV 9 208 92
"Phoo? phoo!" replied Charles, "what's an evening party? P IV 10 223 44
"No," replied Anne, in a low feeling voice. P IV 11 232 16
"Your feelings may be the strongest," replied Anne, "but P IV 11 233 23
"I hardly know," replied Captain Wentworth, surprised. P IV 11 240 57
"You should have distinguished," replied Anne. P IV 11 244 73
"Perhaps I ought to have reasoned thus," he replied, "but P IV 11 244 74
at her, replied, as if in cool deliberation, "not yet. P IV 11 246 81
82
"The surgeon sir!--replied Mr Heywood--I am afraid you S 1 365 1
Mr H. looked very much astonished--& replied--"what sir! S 1 365 1
"Excuse me sir--replied the other. S 1 365 1
"Not down in the Weald I am sure sir, replied the S 1 366 1
"Yes--I have heard of sanditon. replied Mr H.-- S 1 368 1
"I do not at all know--replied his sister--have not the S 9 409 1
"I like the air too, as well as any body can; replied S 10 415 1
"Oh! I am very fond of exercise myself--he replied--& mean S 10 416 1
"I am much obliged to you, replied Charlotte--but I prefer S 10 417 1
"Keep you awake perhaps all night"--replied Charlotte, S 10 418 1
"I will do whatever you wish me, replied his wife--but you S 12 423 1

REPLIES (7)

her beauty, replies only that her eyes have no brilliancy. LS 17 271 7
Oh! it is only a novel!" replies the young lady; while she NA I 5 38 4
She listened reluctantly, and her replies were short. NA I 11 88 54
ease, which she felt very unable to equal in her replies. PP III 9 316 6
moreover, his own replies, and his own remarks to have MP III 1 314 16
"In not one of all my clever replies, my delicate E II 13 264 2
to the good old lady's replies, she saw her with a sort of E III 16 453 12
13

REPLY (100)

& when I lamented in reply the badness of her disposition, LS 8 255 2
to be raised by your reply, and surprize is more easily NA I 3 26 8
her to a very gracious reply, when John Thorpe came up to NA I 8 59 35
This declaration brought on a loud and overpowering reply, NA I 9 64 26
"My dear, you tumble my gown," was Mrs. Allen's reply. NA I 12 93 6
The cruel reply was passed on to the other, and he NA II 1 132 16
He made no reply, and was beginning to talk of something NA II 4 150 4
unworthy of such respect, and knew not how to reply to it. NA II 5 154 2
complaisance, and made her reply less rational; for soon NA II 14 237 20
her perplexity of words in reply, the meaning, which one NA II 15 242 9
pleasure, as it produced a reply from Marianne so SS I 16 85 14
She gave him a brief reply. SS I 18 100 23
Elinor made her a civil reply, and they walked on for a SS I 21 128 8
He made no reply; his complexion changed and all his SS II 6 177 11
Elinor was prevented from making any reply to this civil SS II 13 240 18
Miss Steele was going to reply on the same subject, but SS III 2 275 24
had done, however, her first reply was not very auspicious. SS III 3 279 2
What Elinor said in reply she could not distinguish, but SS III 3 281 9
sang-froid, and go away without making her any reply!-- SS III 3 282 15
of saying much in reply herself, and from the danger of SS III 5 297 32
He coloured, and stammered out an unintelligible reply. SS III 12 359 12
Emma's calm curtsey in reply must have struck him as very W 335 13
Tom made no reply.-- W 357 28
"With the greatest pleasure"--was his first reply. W 360 28
some very inapplicable reply, & jumping up, ran away from W 360 29
Mrs. Bennet deigned not to make any reply; but unable to PP I 2 6 7
After a song or two, and before she could reply to the PP I 6 25 23
Miss Bingley was not so entirely satisfied with this reply PP I 8 40 58
No one made any reply. PP I 11 55 5
a serious dispute must be the consequence of any reply. PP I 17 88 14
that she could hardly reply with tolerable civility to the PP I 18 89 3
That reply will do for the present.-- PP I 18 91 11
Elizabeth would make no reply, and immediately and in PP I 19 109 22
She would not give him time to reply, but hurrying PP I 20 111 6
Charlotte's reply was spared by the entrance of Jane and PP I 20 113 27
astonished to hear, in reply to her minute enquiries, that PP II 4 152 6
madam," said he, when no longer able to avoid a reply. PP II 8 173 5
all the reply which I am to have the honour of expecting! PP II 11 190 8
9
hand, said in reply, "do not make yourself uneasy, my love. PP II 18 231 19
20
she could reply, he added, "it is above eight months. PP III 2 262 8
herself the reason, she had very little to say in reply. PP III 2 266 17
in amazement, but was too much oppressed to make reply. PP III 5 289 44
But he found, in reply to this question, that Wickham PP III 10 323 2
him, she only said in reply, with a good-humoured smile, " PP III 10 329 33
34
ungracious, made no other reply to Elizabeth's salutation, PP III 14 351 3
The happiness which this reply produced, was such as he PP III 16 366 8
She had only to say in reply, that they had wandered about, PP III 17 372 1
earnest and solemn in her reply; and at length, by PP III 17 376 36
what Mr. Bennet sent to Mr. Collins, in reply to his last. PP III 18 383 22
of her character, in her reply to the letter which PP III 19 388 12
him with a reply to them all whether stated or not. MP I 1 6 5
fully explained; and, in reply to Lady Bertram's calm MP I 1 9 10
"My dear," their considerate aunt would reply; "it is very MP I 2 18 24
"Fanny must have a horse," was Edmund's only reply. MP I 4 36 7

But Miss Bertram thought it most becoming to reply: "the MP I 6 55 17
18
When Edmund, therefore, told her in reply, as he did when MP I 8 79 23
requires," was Edmund's only reply, and the subject dropt. MP I 8 79 26
"I am afraid I should do it very awkwardly," was his reply, MP I 9 88 22
amazement, was his only reply to Mr. Rushworth; and he MP I 15 139 5
incompetent to suggest any reply, she had recourse, as MP I 16 150 1
of calm approbation in reply to an eager appeal of Mr. MP II 1 183 24
"I believe you are right, Fanny," was his reply, after a MP II 3 197 4
glad to see the evergreens thrive!" said Fanny in reply. MP II 4 209 16
was Fanny's instinctive reply; though when she had turned MP II 5 219 26
which her uncle was most collectedly dictating in reply. MP II 6 232 12
and accordingly the reply to her reply, fixing a very MP II 6 233 14
the reply to her reply, fixing a very early day for his MP II 6 233 14
she does look very well," was Lady Bertram's placid reply. MP II 10 277 15
note only once; and how to reply to any thing so MP II 13 307 30
reply, "never, Fanny, so very determined and positive! MP III 4 347 19
"That may be, sister,"--was all Lady Bertram's reply--"I MP III 6 371 16
was wounded by her sister's speech and her mother's reply. MP III 7 386 43
write me a pretty one in reply to gladden Henry's eyes, MP III 9 394 1
I only said in reply, that from my heart I wished her well, MP III 16 458 30
It was most convenient to Emma not to make a direct reply E I 8 63 43
"Very much to the honour of both," was the handsome reply. E I 11 94 11
to be immediately able to reply: and two moments of E I 15 131 32
33
before he could make any reply, Mr. Woodhouse, whose E II 3 171 16
17
"Nonsensical girl!" was his reply, but not at all in anger. E II 8 214 11
Emma could get no more approving reply, than, "very well. E II 12 257 2
3
Emma made as slight a reply as she could; but it was fully E II 14 273 20
and therefore only said in reply, "when you have seen more E II 14 273 22
23
to which his prompt reply was, "most readily Mrs. Weston, E III 2 327 34
and he murmured, in reply, "very true, my love, very true. E III 7 370 21
to enable her to say in reply, "Harriet, I will only E III 11 411 40
41
having had the smallest reply to her last; and adding, E III 14 442 8
No; she heard nothing but the instant reply of, "beg her E III 16 452 8
Emma dared not attempt any immediate reply. E III 18 472 21
"Indeed!" was the reply, and with a look of surprise. P III 3 19 15
reasoning; and Elizabeth's reply was, "then I am sure Anne P III 5 33 7
when he had promised in reply to papa and mamma's farther P III 7 54 4
of the case, only nodded in reply, and walked away. P III 8 66 21
say,"--had been Anne's reply, in all the confusion that P III 9 79 23
Anne avoided a direct reply, but it was just the P III 12 107 21
and said as much in reply as her own feelings could P III 12 108 29
looked, and made only this cautious reply: "Elizabeth! P IV 4 147 7
She made no reply. P IV 5 158 20
Mrs. Smith made no reply; but when she was leaving her, P IV 7 180 35
"My dear," was Mrs. Smith's reply, "there was nothing else P IV 9 211 101
somewhat conscious reply of "tis rather stronger than it S 10 417 1

REPLYING (10)

She had great satisfaction in replying that she was going SS I 5 25 1
Mrs. Bennet was prevented replying by the entrance of the PP I 7 30 14
himself with coolly replying, that he perceived no other PP III 3 271 14
Then, perceiving in Elizabeth no inclination of replying, PP III 5 289 43
Fanny roused herself, and replying only in part, said, " MP III 5 359 11
The looking over his letter again, in replying to it, had E I 7 55 35
that she could not help replying with quickness, "Mr. E I 15 130 26
27
me over at any time, to save you the trouble of replying." P III 3 17 4
for Elizabeth was replying, in a sort of whisper, "that P IV 4 145 1
shrewd glance at her & replying--"yes, yes, he is very S 7 400 1

EPORT (51)

us how little the general report of any one ought to be LS 14 264 3
I expect my surveyor from Brockham with his report in the NA II 11 210 6
thing in spreading the report, and you will find that you SS II 7 182 11
fear any unpleasant report should reach the young ladies SS III 1 258 5
grave on Mr. Harris's report, and confirming Charlotte's SS III 7 307 3
Some vague report had reached her before of my attachment SS III 8 328 61
ago, the last current report as to public news, & the W 356 28
Her report was highly favourable. PP I 3 9 1
party for the ball; and a report soon followed that Mr. PP I 3 10 4
noble mien; and the report which was in general PP I 3 10 5
and amiable as they were represented by common report. PP I 15 70 2
"I can readily believe," answered he gravely, "that report PP I 18 94 41
tidings of him than the report which shortly prevailed in PP I 23 129 12
the whole winter; a report which highly incensed Mrs. PP I 23 129 12
"You may, in fact, carry a very favourable report of us PP II 15 216 6
and his servant's report, without any reference to any PP III 2 264 14
us of the present report; and I know I appeared distressed. PP III 11 331 16
17
A report of a most alarming nature, reached me two days PP III 14 353 26
"At once to insist upon having such a report universally PP III 14 354 28
of it; if, indeed, such a report is in existence." PP III 14 354 29
Do you not know that such a report is spread abroad?" PP III 14 354 30
sure! but from what the report of their engagement could PP III 15 360 1
with the Collinses, the report she concluded had reached PP III 15 360 1
I hope, and pretend to be affronted at an idle report. PP III 15 364 22
pray, Lizzy, what said Lady Catherine about this report? PP III 15 364 24
bringing some fresh report of it into the drawing-room. MP I 2 18 23
fair report of being very respectable, agreeable people. MP I 3 24 6
and then encouraged to report any evil of them, she was MP III 8 391 9
been any mistake, but the report is so prevalent, that I MP III 14 433 13
report should spread so far; but she hoped it might not. MP III 15 438 4
Mr. Price cared too little about the report, to make her MP III 15 440 17
of him; and his fond report of him as a very fine young E I 2 17 7
that he might carry some report of her to Hartfield--they E I 13 109 6
be able to give a better report; and he sighed and smiled E I 13 111 14
"My report from Mrs. Goddard's," said she presently, "was E I 13 114 29
morning will bring us both a more comfortable report. E I 13 114 34
after his brother's first report of the snow, came back E I 15 127 16
his concerns; and every report, therefore, every guess-- E II 4 184 10
day to supply a different report, and the situation of Mrs. E III 6 352 1
after breakfast, to report his proceedings, first on my E III 18 472 20
letter, which sent me the report, is passing under her eye- E III 18 480 77
By the report which he hastened over to Kellynch to make, P III 3 21 18
by report, to the Admiral, as a model of good breeding. P III 5 32 2
By this time the report of the accident had spread among P III 12 111 49
ladies, for it proved twice as fine as the first report. P III 12 111 49
Every report agreed in Captain Wentworth's appearing fixed P IV 1 122 4
will have nothing to report but of lace and finery.-- P IV 5 156 13
"I knew you by report long before you came to Bath. P IV 8 187 32
how any report of Captain Wentworth could have reached her. P IV 9 194 19
It was evident that the report concerning her had spread; P IV 10 222 37
even an unpleasant report, were there no other ill effects. P IV 11 242 65

REPORTED (1)

Reported fit for home service for a year or two,--and so I P III 8 64 9

REPORTING (1)

she never came without reporting some fresh instance of PP III 6 294 3

REPORTS (8)

from Lady Susan to contradict the late shocking reports. LS 13 262 1
a shame for such ill-natured reports to be spread abroad. SS III 2 272 14
tea, nor, from Betsey's reports from the kitchen, much MP III 7 381 24
He reads the Agricultural Reports and some other books, E I 4 29 10
paid without leading to reports:--but Mr. Weston had E III 12 417 5
of things, and the reports beginning to prevail.-- P IV 9 206 90
in the reports of each made that matter quite certain. S 10 419 1
All that had the appearance of incongruity in the reports S 11 420 1

EPOSE (16)

They were not long able, however, to enjoy the repose of NA I 2 21 10

way so agitated, repose must be absolutely impossible. NA II 6 170 12
she could have neither repose nor comfort; and with the NA II 6 170 12
object must occasion so serious a delay of proper repose. NA II 8 187 16
Sleep, or repose that deserved the name of sleep, was out NA II 13 227 26
of more than momentary repose, the hours passed away, and NA II 14 231 5
bed in more need of repose than when she lay down in it. SS I 16 83 1
The repose of the latter became more and more disturbed; SS III 7 310 10 11
much, that her hours of repose should not be broken in on. PP III 5 292 66
"Here's harmony!" said she, "here's repose! MP I 11 113 35
that the repose of his own family-circle is all he wants. MP II 3 196 3
from being the friend with whom it could find repose. MP II 10 278 20
far from amiable, and from affording any repose to herself. MP III 8 391 9
habits, the picture of repose and domestic happiness it P III 11 98 17
claims of Dr. Shirley to repose, as she ought; saw how P III 12 103 3
politeness could repose no longer, and the fainter self- P IV 1 125 14

REPOSING (1)
properly folded, reposing at one end of the chest in NA II 6 164 3

REPOSITORY (1)
of a charitable Repository at Burton on Trent.-- S 12 424 1

REPREHENSIBLE (5)
her more wrong and reprehensible, according to his ideas PP I 10 51 46
been at all reprehensible, I here beg leave to apologise." PP I 20 114 32
contempt of her own children, was so highly reprehensible. PP II 19 236 2
was apparently cherishing very reprehensible feelings. E II 10 243 22
I saw nothing reprehensible in what Mr. Elliot was doing. P IV 9 201 64

REPREHENSION (1)
hope, lay me open to reprehension, excepting on one point. E III 14 438 8

REPRESENT (13)
vanity induced him to represent the family as yet more NA II 15 244 12
children, he was able to represent the whole family to the NA II 15 245 12
they now were, she would represent in the strongest manner SS II 4 165 30
her own feelings, or to represent herself as suffering SS III 1 261 12
One person I was sure would represent me as sufficiently SS III 8 331 69
"Not as you represent it. PP I 6 22 8
left Hertfordshire, and represent to her the imprudence of PP II 2 142 18
any contrivance could so represent, as to render Mr. PP II 13 205 3
of the last who would wish to represent it on the stage." MP I 15 145 41
A man might represent the county with such an estate; a MP I 17 161 13
a man might escape a profession and represent the county." MP I 17 161 13
marry well are not so contemptible as you represent them. E I 8 63 44
other, not at all to represent Captain Benwick's manners P IV 6 172 40 41

REPRESENTATION (28)
This pathetic representation lasted the whole evening, & LS 17 270 3
representation, no studied appeal to their passions. NA II 14 237 21
relying on Elinor's representation of herself; and justly SS III 11 355 46
the truth of her representation, he was by no means SS III 14 373 3
according to your representation, you must remember, Miss PP I 10 50 34
"your representation of all this, might make me quite easy. PP I 21 119 21
displeasure at this representation of them, let it give PP II 12 198 5
might take a similar representation of the evils attached PP III 15 360 22
of such honourable representation, and very thoroughly MP I 4 35 5
the business; but no representation of his aunt's could MP I 4 39 13
within two days of representation, when the sudden death MP I 13 121 1
as unyielding to his representation, quite as determined MP I 13 128 38
improper for home representation--the situation of one, MP I 14 137 23
representation, and that I hope you will give it up.-- MP I 15 139 11
find, who thinks it very fit for private representation." MP I 15 140 12
them to confine the representation within a much smaller MP I 16 155 16
to the privacy of the representation, was giving an MP I 18 164 1
forward to their representation of it as a circumstance MP I 18 167 13
representation of younger sons who have little to live on. MP II 4 214 45
Upon my representation of what you were suffering, he MP III 1 321 47
Her representation of her cousin's state at this time, was MP III 14 436 16
of safety, her representation of the excellence of the E I 15 127 12
The truth of his representation there was no denying. E III 7 376 62
My representation, you see, has quite appeased her." E III 16 454 13
she imagined no bad representation of the general guidance P III 10 92 48
I know those who would be shocked by such a representation P IV 9 207 91
only the most perfect representation of whatever heroine S 6 391 1
period (under another representation) perfectly decided, & S 11 420 1

REPRESENTATIONS (7)
little the ungenerous representations of any one to the LS 10 257 1
justness of her own representations, Catherine was NA II 14 239 28
to think over the representations of her mother, to SS I 15 82 45
representations--& the visitors departed without her.-- W 362 32
after such representations from her aunt, cost her some MP II 5 222 40
representations were necessary to make it acceptable. E II 11 251 25
of friendship, any representations from one who had almost P III 4 27 3

REPRESENTATIVE (2)
as an only son & the representative of an ancient family, LS 12 260 1
Consider, my father's heir--the future representative of P IV 10 224 47

REPRESENTATIVES (2)
among the dashing representatives, or idle heir apparents, MP III 17 469 24
"Don't talk to me about heirs and representatives," cried P IV 10 224 48

REPRESENTED (20)
To our family, she has always been represented in softened LS 12 260 2
I am to thank my sister I suppose, for having represented LS 14 263 1
Udolpho, as her fancy represented Blaize Castle to be, was NA I 11 86 50
sister Anne, whom she represented as insupportably cross, NA I 15 116 2
It represented a very lovely woman, with a mild and NA II 9 191 3
be as fruitful in horrors as they were there represented. NA II 10 200 3
in this low connection, represented to him the certain SS III 1 266 38
working on others;--and represented it, therefore, as a SS III 3 280 6
I certainly should have represented it to Edward in a very SS III 5 300 37
and amiable as they were represented by common report. PP I 15 70 2
She represented to her sister as forcibly as possible what PP I 21 120 29
Lady Catherine to be exactly what he had represented. PP II 6 162 11
That had his actions been what Wickham represented them, PP II 13 208 6
She represented to him all the improprieties of Lydia's PP II 18 230 14
canvas, on which he was represented, and fixed his eyes PP III 1 251 48
His wife represented to him how absolutely necessary such PP III 11 332 24
circumstance was precisely as this lady has represented it. MP I 5 49 35
more difficult to be well represented than even Agatha. MP I 14 135 15
has been represented to me in the most affecting terms.-- S 12 424 1
of the room, little conspicuous, represented Mr Hollis.-- S 12 427 1

REPRESENTING (9)
for her mother, by representing the inconveniences which SS I 12 59 5
He concluded with representing to her the strength of that PP II 11 189 6
most serious manner, representing to her all the PP III 10 325 2
which the idea of representing Edmund was so strongly MP I 18 169 22
raise her spirits by representing how much Mr. Elton's E I 13 109 6
comfort herself, by representing that though he certainly E II 16 292 8
to Harriet, or, by representing to him his own E III 13 429 30
of High Sheriff, representing a borough in three P III 1 3 3 4
Anne longed for the power of representing to them all what P III 10 82 1

REPRESS (5)
she could not entirely repress a doubt, while she bore NA I 9 66 32
Unable of course to repress your curiosity in so NA II 5 159 19
disappointment, or repress the peevishness of her temper--. W 360 30
Elizabeth could not repress a smile at this, but she PP II 18 235 39
evil, by teaching them to repress their spirits in his MP III 17 463 7

REPRESSED (8)
My spirits are not so high as to need being repressed. LS 30 301 5
and some might have repressed it from motives of prudence, SS I 3 15 5
My feelings will not be repressed. PP II 11 189 4
and while she steadily repressed it, could not but feel PP II 18 233 25
manner repressed all the flow of their spirits before him. MP I 2 19 30
If Jane repressed her for a little time, she soon began E II 17 299 1
guilty of having encouraged what she might have repressed. E III 11 402 1

of rings & Broches repressed farther solicitation & paid S 6 390 1

REPRESSING (3)
in consequence of my repressing by the calm dignity of my LS 10 257 2
and the resolution of repressing such reflections as must PP II 13 209 12
and repressing imagination all the rest of her life. E I 17 142 10

REPRIEVE (1)
the ecstasy of such a reprieve, the rejoicing, deep and P III 12 112 53

REPRIMAND (4)
he was impelled, & by whom commissioned to reprimand me. LS 22 281 4
reprimand on the subject five or six times every day. SS I 21 118 2
it, by Lucy's sharp reprimand, which now, as on many SS II 10 219 42
sharp reprimand to Fanny; "I was out above an hour. MP I 7 72 42

REPRIMANDING (1)
whether helping, or reprimanding, or indulging them, MP III 8 389 4

REPROACH (52)
I reproach myself for having ever, tho' so innocently, LS 24 290 13
the injustice of general reproach; but the loss of his LS 30 300 3
Tell me that you submit to my arguments, & do not reproach LS 30 301 5
Catherine thought this reproach equally strange and unkind. NA I 13 98 3
health, which seemed to reproach her for her opinion of NA II 7 181 41
speak a mind at ease, or a conscience void of reproach."-- NA II 8 182 1
already did Catherine reproach herself with having parted NA II 14 235 14
once in ten minutes, this reproach would have been spared." SS I 10 48 5
for the esteem of the others, it is a reproach in itself. SS I 10 50 17
"Nay, Edward," said Marianne, "you need not reproach me. SS I 17 93 33
"Nay, Elinor, this reproach from you--you who have SS II 5 170 24
to express, I shall reproach myself for not having been SS II 7 183 13
and now she could reproach her only by the tears which SS II 9 202 8
passionate violence--a reproach, however, so entirely lost SS II 9 202 8
so, and silencing every reproach, overcoming every scruple, SS III 8 326 53
He was released without any reproach to himself, from an SS III 13 361 3
preserve her from, that reproach which she always seemed SS III 14 373 1
of incurring, the reproach of being too amiable, Edward SS III 14 373 1
reproach shall ever pass my lips when we are married." PP I 19 106 10
her mother's reproach prevented his feeling any regret. PP I 20 112 24
on receiving so direct a reproach; though, as it was no PP I 22 124 14 15
either to hope or fear, and nothing to reproach him with. PP II 1 134 7
yet merited reproach, her sense of shame was severe. PP II 13 208 10
Fixed there by the keenest of all anguish, self reproach, PP III 5 285 19
be so totally void of reproach, that the contentment PP III 16 369 24
sinking under her aunt's unkind reflection and reproach. MP I 16 150 1
was such as made her reproach herself for loving him so MP II 1 178 7
Such a look of reproach at Edmund from his father she MP II 1 185 27
the reflections, the reproach that must attend it, happy MP II 3 201 22
She might have to endure the reproach again and again; she MP III 1 321 46
austerity, without reproach, and she revived a little. MP III 1 321 47
spirit of reproach, exerted on a more momentous subject. MP III 1 323 53
arch, yet affectionate reproach, and taking her hand, MP III 5 357 6
which could be fancied a reproach on their account!-- MP III 6 370 11
and Susan could only reproach, which she did very warmly, MP III 7 386 42
that again--and no reproach seemed conveyed to the equally MP III 9 396 7
itself, giving it every reproach but the right, MP III 16 457 30
to a retirement and reproach, which could allow no second MP III 17 464 12
as to deserve such a reproach; but his temper was not his E I 11 92 5
pain to her friend, or reproach to herself, in the E II 4 184 11
a small mixture of reproach, with a great deal of kindness; E II 4 184 11
with a look of gentle reproach--"Ah! Miss Taylor, if you E II 7 209 10
Harriet, is the strongest reproach you can make me. E II 13 268 10
in her general conduct, be open to any severe reproach. E III 8 377 1
on her must rest all the reproach of having given it a E III 11 413 47
She had led her friend astray, and it would be a reproach E III 13 431 38
through every bitter reproach and sorrowful regret that E III 14 435 4
thought, have reason to reproach her for giving no warning. P III 5 34 12
in turn to Mary's reproach of "Charles spoils the children P III 6 44 6
It was too pleasing a blunder for a reproach. P IV 11 243 68
human nature, nothing to reproach myself with; and if I P IV 11 246 80
might be a mere trifle of reproach remaining for herself.-- S 11 420 1

REPROACHED (8)
She reproached her with having more affection for Miss NA I 13 98 2
she rejoiced; and she reproached herself for being unjust SS I 3 14 2
heart?--and I have reproached you for being happy!"-- SS III 1 262 20
glad to see me, and reproached me for giving her no notice PP II 3 147 23
Very frequently were they reproached for this PP II 18 229 1
She reproached herself, coloured and looked fearfully MP III 14 431 8
She had lived with him to be reproached as the ruin of all MP III 17 464 11
with it; as you have many a time reproached me with doing. E II 8 226 84

REPROACHES (9)
I cannot bear reproaches. LS 30 301 5
Her reproaches, however, were not spared. NA I 11 87 53
with supplications or reproaches, and her arm was still NA I 13 99 9
With strong concern, and with many reproaches for not SS III 7 313 20
his abuse of me to others, as in his reproaches to myself. PP II 12 201 5
reproaches!--he left her in a glow of gratitude. MP III 1 322 49
Any thing might be bearable rather than such reproaches. MP III 1 322 49
It was over, and she had escaped without reproaches and MP III 5 365 34
be supposed, without reproaches, or apparent sense of ill E III 16 451 2

REPROACHFUL (2)
reproachful; but on catching his were instantly withdrawn. MP II 7 244 31
But (with a reproachful smile at Emma) she receives E II 15 286 18

REPROACHFULLY (1)
reproachfully; "a note would have answered every purpose.-- SS III 8 324 41

REPROACHING (4)
have been reproaching them every day for incautiousness." SS I 15 79 32
of poor Elinor, who, reproaching herself for having SS III 7 312 18
small house, without reproaching herself for some little MP II 11 282 3
a moment overcome--then reproaching herself for having E III 7 376 62

REPROBATE (2)
whole of your family, far & near, must highly reprobate. LS 12 260 1
Miss Dashwood, can ever reprobate too much--I was acting SS III 8 320 32

REPROBATED (4)
occur to her even enough to be reprobated and forbidden? MP II 9 264 18
same Mr. Crawford whom whom she had so reprobated before. MP III 2 329 9
She reprobated her brother's folly in being drawn on by a MP III 16 454 18
it was the detection, not the offence which she reprobated. MP III 16 455 19

REPROBATES (1)
nice; and that she reprobates all inequality of condition P III 5 35 14

REPROBATING (2)
by her feelings in reprobating the ball, for she enjoyed E II 12 258 4
ever been before, in reprobating any such alliance for him, E III 13 431 38

REPROBATION (2)
without danger of reprobation, because chapel was missed, MP I 9 87 15
He was warm in his reprobation of Mr. Elton's conduct; it E III 2 330 46

REPROOF (20)
urge the necessity of reproof, if you see me too lenient." LS 15 267 6
severity of his father's reproof, which seemed NA II 5 154 2
refrain from the gentle reproof of, "my dear Catherine, I NA II 15 240 2
Sir John did not much understand this reproof; but he SS I 9 45 31 32
Mrs. Jennings, without attending to her daughter's reproof. SS I 13 64 14
He was recalled from wit to wisdom, not by any reproof of SS III 5 298 34
Thunderbolts and daggers!--what a reproof would she have SS III 8 325 50
Elinor stopped him with a reproof. SS III 8 332 78
Mr. Bingley," said Elizabeth, "must disarm reproof." PP I 10 48 24
could not but feel the reproof contained in his believing, PP II 18 233 25
to you at the time, had merited the severest reproof. PP III 16 367 12
Your reproof, so well applied, I shall never forget 'had PP III 16 367 14
a remonstrance, a reproof, which he felt at his heart. MP I 1 184 27
The reproof of an immediate conclusion of every thing, the MP II 2 187 2
Some very grave reproof, or at least the coldest MP II 7 250 60
by such an extremity of reproof, found herself sadly MP III 3 343 40
against her, and that a reproof was designed her for MP III 9 397 7

She had not time to know how Mr. Elton took the reproof, E I 15 125 7
You could not give me a greater reproof for the mistake I E II 13 268 10
not be done without a reproof to him, which would be E III 6 353 3
REPROOFS (3)
My reproofs at Hunsford could not work such a change as PP III 1 255 60
by letting you see that your reproofs had been attended to. PP III 16 370 32
She restrained herself, however, from any of the reproofs E II 14 276 34
REPROVE (1)
not, on this occasion, have found any thing to reprove. E III 9 391 21
REPROVED (3)
Then, remembering Colonel Brandon, reproved herself, felt SS III 9 335 5
back her thoughts, reproved herself, and grieved lest they MP III 7 377 10
She felt reproved. MP III 16 454 18
REPUGNANCE (2)
But there were other causes of repugnance;--causes which, PP II 12 198 5
any real alarm for his aunt, to lessen his repugnance. E II 12 258 8
REPUGNANT (1)
some time ceased to be repugnant to her feelings; and it PP III 2 265 16
REPULSE (1)
modest gentle nature, to repulse Mr. Crawford, and avoid MP III 3 342 32
REPULSED (3)
I was repulsed indeed! SS II 7 187 42
They repulsed every attempt of Mrs. Bennet at conversation, PP I 18 102 75
thing she could offer of assistance or regard be repulsed. E III 11 403 2
REPULSES (1)
persevere against a few repulses; and becoming soon too MP I 17 160 9
REPULSIVE (7)
was so particularly repulsive, that in comparison of it SS I 7 34 7
affair; that proud and repulsive as were his manners, she PP II 13 207 6
seen him so seldom, his reserve may be a little repulsive. MP II 3 199 13
her in more than a few repulsive looks, but she felt her MP III 16 448 3
which ought to have been repulsive, and have established MP III 17 467 20
"It is a most repulsive quality, indeed," said he. E II 6 203 40
Mary was not so repulsive and unsisterly as Elizabeth, nor P III 6 43 4
REPULSIVELY (1)
herself enough to receive that look, and not repulsively. P IV 11 239 55
REPUTABLE (1)
I dare say there is always some reputable tradesman's wife MP I 1 8 8
REPUTATION (8)
of establishing her reputation by following, tho' late, LS 6 252 2
It would have been trifling with my reputation, to allow LS 25 292 1
triumph of recovered reputation, and all the dignity of a NA II 14 232 7
in London, where the reputation of elegance was more SS II 5 170 29
She has the reputation of being remarkably sensible and PP I 16 84 58
endless ruin--that her reputation is no less brittle than PP III 5 289 43
the claims to reputation which her marriage had given her. PP III 19 387 8
or sorry to know her reputation for accomplishment often E I 6 44 19
REPUTE (1)
Mrs. Goddard's school was in high repute--and very E I 3 22 5
REPUTED (4)
The suddenness of her reputed illness; the absence of her NA II 8 188 16
of that gentleman's reputed disposition when quite a lad, PP II 2 143 20
to find that she was a reputed beauty; and I particularly PP III 3 271 16
17
as possible, to defy the reputed expensiveness of such a S 3 378 1
REQUEST (48)
placed her daughter, to request that Miss Vernon might be LS 15 266 2
few days at Lady Susan's request, into her dressing room, LS 17 271 7
written to him, to request his interference, & that on LS 22 281 5
& I make it my particular request that I may not in any LS 25 293 3
Here they were interrupted by a request from Mrs. Thorpe NA I 8 54 10
repeating the agreeable request which had already NA I 8 58 25
motion she granted his request, and with how pleasing a NA I 10 75 24
a trifling request to a friend who loved her so dearly. NA I 13 98 2
"I was just beginning to make the request, sir, as you NA II 2 139 6
I am almost ashamed to make the request, though its NA II 2 139 7
He was not ill inclined to obey this request, for, though NA II 15 242 8
"It was my father's last request to me," replied her SS I 2 9 4
My father certainly could mean nothing more by his request SS I 2 12 25
say very well, at their request went through the chief of SS I 7 35 8
waiting to have her request of admittance answered, opened SS II 8 192 1
at the particular request of the Middletons, spent the SS II 14 246 2
next morning to Lucy, to request her company and her SS II 14 253 26
she required; and at her request, Marianne engaged never SS III 1 264 32
When there, at her own particular request, for she was SS III 10 340 1
brought, by their united request, to consider his own SS III 10 341 4
At his and Mrs. Jennings's united request in return, Mrs. SS III 10 341 4
Emma curtsied, the gentleman bowed--made a hasty request W 333 13
and Irish airs, at the request of her younger sisters, who PP I 6 25 24
one readily yield to a request, without waiting for PP I 10 50 37
is to appertain to this request, as well as the degree of PP I 10 50 38
and after a polite request that Elizabeth would lead the PP I 10 51 45
that morning should be mentioned, and the request made. PP I 12 59 1
to attend them, at the request of Mr. Bennet, who was most PP I 15 71 6
replied her husband, "I have two small favours to request. PP I 20 112 22
of civility; and at the request of the gentlemen remained PP II 8 176 30
arrangements, and to request that he will satisfy the PP III 8 313 19
His daughter's request, for such it might be considered, PP III 8 313 22
letter to her aunt, to request an explanation of what PP III 9 320 32
entrance, though no request of introduction had been made. PP III 14 351 3
was very ready to request the favour of Mr. Crawford's MP I 6 61 58
The request had not been foreseen, and was very graciously MP I 10 105 52
"A pretty modest request upon my word!" he indignantly MP I 12 119 26
to Fanny; at the earnest request of Miss Crawford, Mrs. MP I 17 159 6
with a most earnest request to be allowed to sit between MP II 7 239 8
but that he should request to speak with you alone, be it MP III 1 321 48
a request too natural, a claim too just to be denied. MP III 1 321 48
This is my modest request and expectation, for you are so MP III 14 433 13
with her; a most welcome request: for Miss Smith was a E I 3 22 7
an end to it, and request him to place himself elsewhere. E I 6 46 24
His first proposition and request, that the dance begun at E II 11 247 3
had reached her with his request to be allowed to hand her E II 16 298 56
57
at his own particular request, been admitted to their P IV 3 139 8
stepped to Lady Dalrymple, to request her assistance. P IV 7 174 2
REQUESTED (10)
my dear Fanny; he only requested me, in general terms, to SS I 2 9 6
ringing the bell, requested the footman who answered it, SS II 4 161 5
work, particularly requested to look at them; and after SS II 12 235 28
Mr. Darcy with grave propriety requested to be allowed the PP I 6 26 40
In spite of this amendment, however, she requested to have PP I 9 41 1
before her, and being requested to chuse from among MP II 8 257 15
her own time to her as requested) and in short could not MP III 1 371 15
all my letters, and requested, that if I could not E III 14 442 8
she was continually requested, or at least receiving hints P III 6 44 7
study; and on being requested to particularize, mentioned P III 11 101 24
REQUESTER (1)
A regard for the requester would often make one readily PP I 10 50 37
REQUESTING (8)
once on the point of requesting from Mr. Thorpe a clearer NA I 9 66 31
was given, by Henry's requesting to know, if she thought NA II 1 132 16
the night before, and requesting the company of her mother SS II 5 170 28
by Tom Musgrave, who requesting Mrs E. aloud to do him the W 334 13
of requesting you to interpose your authority in my behalf. PP I 20 114 32
that I am not afraid of requesting it, though I have still PP III 4 275 5
among the most urgent in requesting to hear the glee again. MP I 11 113 42
from Mrs. Goddard, requesting, in most respectful terms, E I 3 22 7
REQUIRE (27)
could not require you to wait for his emancipation. LS 9 256 1
to convince me that they require a delicacy and LS 30 300 1
He has a right to require a woman of fortune in his LS 30 300 2
Why do you require particulars? LS 36 305 1
like herself could require; and stopping only to change NA II 14 232 6
I require so much! SS I 3 18 20
But I require no such proof. SS I 15 80 42
happy when I am so miserable--Oh! who can require it?" SS II 7 190 54
for his arrival, or even require Jane to confess that if PP I 23 129 14
There were two nephews of Lady Catherine to require them, PP II 7 170 7
go away, till you have given me the assurance I require." PP III 14 357 60
years old, of an age to require more attention than her MP I 1 5 4
for avoiding whatever her unreasonable aunts might require. MP I 7 74 58
Maria's situation might require particular caution and MP I 13 128 38
(I do not really require you to proceed upon my plan, MP II 7 243 27
Now I may say that even I could not require William price MP II 13 300 5
and repetitions, which require good reading not to be felt. MP III 3 340 25
would require a great deal, but she would finally accept. MP III 12 417 4
just as propriety may require, and to speak extremely well E I 18 150 31
circumstances, to require something more than human E II 2 165 9
I do not require you to adopt all my suspicions, though E II 8 217 32
these sort of things require a good deal of consideration. E II 11 252 32
and your friends would require for you, is no every day E II 17 300 12
exclaim, and require confirmation, repeated confirmation. E III 10 395 36
must be too well known to require definition; and I was E III 14 437 8
inconsistent, nothing to require more motives than P IV 4 147 7
return to Kellynch, and act as circumstances might require. P IV 11 243 66
REQUIRED (84)
than the subject required; said many things over and over LS 20 276 3
of his design, I calmly required an explanation, & begged LS 22 281 4
yet it required some consideration to be tranquilly happy. LS 23 284 5
in the Pump-Room, but required, when they all quitted it NA I 4 34 7
know exactly what is required and what can be borne; and NA II 4 152 28
business required and would keep him two or three days. NA II 7 175 13
afternoon service was required by the General in exercise NA II 9 190 1
own consequence always required that theirs should be NA II 15 245 12
many solitary hours were required to compose, had returned NA II 15 248 16
of other people she could act when occasion required it. SS I 1 6 9
But as he required the promise, I could not do less than SS I 2 9 6
He was not handsome, and his manners required intimacy to SS I 3 15 6
She believed the regard to be mutual; but she required SS I 4 21 11
required no explanation to her, repeated, "Devonshire! SS I 5 25 1
Colonel's advanced state of life which humanity required. SS I 7 35 9
Of their personal charms he had not required a second SS I 10 46 1
As it was, it required but a slight effort of fancy to SS I 11 57 17
especially, which required some trouble and time to subdue. SS I 19 104 9
of telling lies when politeness required it, always fell. SS I 21 122 14
know that any more was required; to be together was, in SS I 21 124 33
beloved by Edward, it required no other consideration of SS II 1 142 7
and she hoped it was not required of her for Willoughby's; SS II 8 196 21
her whatever promise she required; and at her request, SS III 1 264 32
I, as I thought my duty required, urge him to it for SS III 2 277 30
concluding that prudence required dispatch, and that her SS III 8 317 7
its offspring, necessity, had required to be sacrificed. SS III 8 331 70
since her illness required;--and they had advanced only so SS III 10 344 12
13
for the better, it required several hours to give SS III 13 363 8
call/, everybody was required to stand up--& Tom W 335 13
Her father, if ill, required little more than gentleness & W 361 30
should always be in proportion to what is required." PP I 7 32 38
to be civil also, and say what the occasion required. PP I 9 45 35
and burying his parishioners whenever it were required. PP I 13 64 16
no more this winter, my choice will never be required. PP I 21 120 27
on his return, as required some ingenuity to evade, and he PP I 22 123 3
that gentleman, and required information; and Elizabeth PP II 3 149 28
had not my character required it to be written and read. PP II 12 196 4
acknowledged to have required the utmost force of passion PP II 12 198 5
All that is required of you is, to assure to your daughter, PP III 7 302 14
pleasure, because it required an explanation that would PP III 10 324 2
was insufficient, when required to depend on his affection PP III 10 326 3
It required a longer time, however, than Mrs. Norris was MP I 2 14 6
but he now felt that she required more positive kindness, MP I 2 17 20
of conscious beauty required; his lengthened absence from MP I 12 114 2
so many best characters required, and above all, such a MP I 14 130 2
Mansfield, at any time required by the party; he was going MP II 2 192 11
at Mansfield, a chasm which required some time to fill up. MP II 3 204 33
as good time as his own correctly punctual habits required. MP II 5 222 41
in which she was not required to take any part--there was MP II 5 223 48
and being required either to draw a card for whist or not. MP II 7 239 4
required some minutes silence to be settled into composure. MP II 8 253 4
William was required to be at Portsmouth on the 24th; the MP II 8 253 7
in view, and nothing is required of you but to bear with MP III 2 331 16
endeavoured herself, nor required Fanny to advise her, to MP III 16 449 5
"And what," said Fanny, (believing herself required to MP III 16 455 20
These were reflections that required some time to soften; MP III 17 461 4
but never required to bring it into daily practice. MP III 17 463 8
His spirits required support. E I 1 7 10
she wanted--exactly the something which her home required. E I 4 26 2
care of, she might be required to sink herself for ever. E I 4 27 5
"You have given Miss Smith all that she required," said he; E I 6 42 2
solace or her own sins required more; and she was E II 1 155 1
Poor Harriet was in a flutter of spirits which required E II 13 267 9
Emma was not required, by any subsequent discovery, to E II 15 281 1
The persons to be invited, required little thought. E II 16 291 5
tender habits required almost every evening throughout the E III 5 351 38
Emma found that she must wait; and now it required little E III 10 393 18
to act exactly opposite to what she would have required. E III 10 398 55
Knightley--but justice required that she should not be E III 11 408 33
of love, as the subject required; concluding, however, E III 15 445 14
15
other words his life--required Hartfield to continue her E III 15 449 31
Lady Elliot, had never required indulgence afterwards.-- P III 1 4 6
apprehension of the state required in its possessor. P III 1 9 19
every consolation was required, for she had to encounter P III 4 28 5
entreated, or rather required her, for it was hardly P III 5 33 7
no intercourse but what the commonest civility required. P III 8 63 3
where residence was not required, lived at his father's P III 9 73 4
but so it was; and it required a long application of P III 9 81 34
nature of the country required, for going and returning. P III 11 94 8
of delay; yet the time required by the Uppercross horses P III 12 114 64
little of the trouble required, which it is very natural P IV 9 196 32
of every help which Mary required, from altering her P IV 10 220 31
driver on being first required to take that direction, had S 1 364 1
Sir Edward's required longer observation. S 7 396 1
REQUIRES (19)
delicacy about him which requires the fullest explanation LS 16 268 2
& the suddenness of it requires some apology to you my LS 20 276 5
are united, it requires uncommon steadiness of reason to NA I 7 50 44
business which requires my immediate attendance in town." SS I 13 64 19
of that festival which requires a more than ordinary share SS II 2 151 43
upon my notice, requires a very particular excuse.-- SS III 8 318 21
22
requires," was Edmund's only reply, and the subject dropt. MP I 8 79 26
It requires great powers, great nicety, to give her MP I 14 135 15
It requires a delicacy of feeling which they have not. MP I 14 135 15
It requires a gentlewoman--a Julia Bertram. MP I 14 135 15
"This requires explanation. MP III 1 316 31
She requires constant air and exercise. MP III 11 410 16
inflicting as propriety requires, will present themselves E I 7 51 11
be interested--but I believe it requires that with me. E II 3 175 43
The spring I always think requires more than common care. E II 16 295 33
be thinking of, and only requires something very E III 7 370 23
my own anxiety, or requires very solicitous explanation. E III 14 438 8
Walter's continuing in singleness requires explanation.-- P III 1 5 8
Good company requires only birth, education and manners, P IV 4 150 17
EQUIRING (14)

she was dressed, but requiring at once solitude and SS II 7 180 5
grounds, and that by requiring her longer continuance in SS II 10 214 6
therefore in requiring an explanation of his two motives. PP I 11 56 14
it a case of some delicacy, and requiring early attention. PP I 13 61 6
glance at Elizabeth, requiring no partner in his pleasure. PP I 14 68 12
Lady Catherine is far from requiring that elegance of PP II 6 160 6
of exertion, and requiring constant attendance; and though PP III 4 280 26
to it, that you find it requiring more exertion and MP I 15 140 15
she found every body requiring something they had not, and MP I 18 165 2
She will never submit to any thing requiring industry and E I 5 37 7
My right to place myself in a situation requiring such E III 14 437 8
placed in circumstances, requiring fortitude and strength P III 10 87 26
of a mile as any thing requiring rest, & talked of going S 6 390 1
young woman next to him, requiring in common politeness S 10 415 1

REQUISITE (10)
pointed out to be requisite to its complete SS II 14 252 20
to make requisite, was kept off by irritation of spirits. SS III 9 334 5
Very little apology cd. be requisite to the Edwardes, who W 320 2
that a verbal postscript from himself wd be requisite.--" W 338 17
of her friends, were requisite to check the indulgence of PP II 17 227 26
would give them exactly the requisite command of the house. MP I 10 97 4
if requisite, to do every thing for the good of the other. E I 12 99 14
But you have not an idea of what is requisite in E I 18 147 17
that could be requisite, and always putting forward to E II 1 156 5
of pointed neglect that could be further requisite.-- E III 3 332 1

REQUISITES (1)
of one or more of these requisites, prevented their doing NA I 8 56 11

REQUISITION (2)
not merely Tom, for the requisition was now backed by MP I 15 146 53
of Highbury in general should be put under requisition. E I 9 70 7

REQUISITIONS (1)
How Anne's more rigid requisitions might have been taken, P III 2 13 6

REQUITED (3)
The kindness of my uncle and aunt can never be requited. PP III 7 305 36
having so requited hospitality, so injured family peace, MP III 17 468 22
determined friend, fully requited the services which she P IV 12 251 11

RESCUE (3)
benevolence, that might rescue him from the attacks of Mr. PP II 13 206 4
very person was chancing to pass by to rescue her!-- E III 3 335 10
had been in seeing him come forward to your rescue.-- E III 11 406 23

RESCUED (1)
of the brow had rescued her countenance from the disgrace SS II 12 232 15

RESEARCH (1)
attendant on such a research; in which supplication had PP III 10 326 3

RESEARCHES (1)
blessed the researches of the fondest biographer. MP II 9 265 19

RESEATED (2)
Lucy directly drew her work table near her and reseated SS II 1 144 14
as soon as they were reseated in the carriage, "not to P IV 2 135 32

RESEMBLANCE (36)
and not often any resemblance of subject, for Mrs. Thorpe NA I 5 36 3
Taken in that light certainly, their resemblance is not NA I 10 77 33
bearing always an equal resemblance of mother and child. NA II 9 191 3
The resemblance between her and her mother was strikingly SS I 1 6 12
who were attracted by resemblance of disposition; and that SS I 3 15 5
no more adapted by resemblance of manner to be his friend, SS I 7 34 6
that however a general resemblance of disposition between SS I 10 49 12
strong resemblance between them, as well in mind as person. SS II 9 205 23
24

said he, by the resemblance I have fancied between her and SS II 9 208 28
"has been the unhappy resemblance between the fate of SS II 9 211 40
the most striking resemblance between this baby and every SS II 14 248 5
to make Marianne, by a resemblance in their situations, SS III 1 261 11
brought back by that resemblance between Marianne and SS III 10 340 2
"Our situations have borne little resemblance." SS III 10 345 27
Their resemblance in good principles and good sense, in SS III 13 370 36
There might be resemblance in countenance; & the W 324 3
My dear, do you perceive the least resemblance?"-- W 324 3
am very sure there is no resemblance between her & Sam."-- W 324 3
"This is no very striking resemblance of your own PP I 18 91 16
she soon found some resemblance of Mr. Darcy, she turned PP II 6 162 12
There is in every thing a most remarkable resemblance of PP II 15 216 6
A resemblance in good humour and good spirits had PP II 18 230 11
she beheld a striking resemblance of Mr. Darcy, with such PP III 1 250 47
Had his first appearance, or his resemblance to the PP III 1 251 52
as he looked at her, he was trying to trace a resemblance. PP III 2 262 8
That was the only point of resemblance between her and the MP I 8 80 31
is so much general resemblance in true generosity and MP II 9 263 16
I exclude extremes of course; and a very close resemblance MP III 4 349 23
It was the only point of resemblance. MP III 9 398 9
It appears to me a most perfect resemblance in every E I 6 48 32
and with this resemblance of her father, she inherited E I 11 92 4
in having no other resemblance to a child, than in a total E III 6 362 43
the event of the disclosure bear an equal resemblance!-- E III 11 404 3
longing to see her; the resemblance of their present E III 16 452 7
exactly forward--"but there I think ends the resemblance. P IV 8 182 8
An accidental resemblance of names & circumstances, S 10 419 1

RESEMBLE (2)
of the two--and that to resemble her would be more for her E I 17 142 9
to all that is felt by you, and by those who resemble you. P IV 11 235 32

RESEMBLED (6)
in what particular he resembled either, for of course SS I 6 31 9
behaviour, they strongly resembled each other in that SS I 7 32 1
in which he strongly resembled and peculiarly delighted SS I 10 48 9
temper and mind greatly resembled your sister, who thought SS I 11 57 17
Of her two sisters, Mrs. Price very much more resembled MP III 8 390 5
her mother's, which resembled the soft monotony of Lady MP III 8 392 11

RESEMBLING (3)
as resembling, in some measure, your sister Marianne." SS II 9 205 22
than equal any of the resembling scenes of the far-famed P III 11 95 9
eye;--her manners resembling her brother's in their ease & S 9 407 1

RESENT (15)
& vindictive spirit to resent a project which influenced LS 5 249 1
James or Isabella to resent her resistance any longer. NA I 14 115 55
thoughtlessness which Catherine could not but resent. NA II 4 149 1
They felt and they deplored--but they could not resent it; NA II 16 250 3
will, and should never resent her behaviour as any affront, PP I 14 69 17
his displeasure, "to resent the behaviour of your daughter. PP I 20 114 32
I have no such injuries to resent. PP II 18 231 18
I was not so mean as to resent the past; and I hoped to PP III 16 370 32
any body but you would resent that you had not been MP II 3 197 8
should resent any former supposed slight to Miss Bertram. MP III 13 423 2
they might resent, how naturally Harriet must suffer. E II 5 187 4
She had half a mind to resent; but an instant's E II 7 206 4
to another woman, before her face, and not resent it.-- E III 10 397 46
I have been forgiven by one who had still more to resent. E III 14 436 8
I was mad enough, however, to resent.-- E III 14 441 8

RESENTED (7)
warmly Miss Manwaring resented her lover's defection, LS 14 265 4
was chiefly resented from being disrespectful to her. NA II 5 154 2
him that he no longer resented his giving him the living SS III 13 368 30
Miss Bingley warmly resented the indignity he had received, PP I 10 51 40
have resented a comparison with the housekeeper's room. PP I 16 75 2
advice being given on such a point, without being resented. PP II 3 145 10
Sir Walter had resented it. P III 1 8 16

RESENTFUL (10)
If her manners have so great an influence on my resentful LS 6 251 2
of a man whose passions were so violent and resentful. LS 25 292 1
the resentful sensation; she remembered her own ignorance. NA I 12 92 3
so well concealed his resentful ire, as to make her feel NA II 9 192 4
address himself to an uncandid judge or a resentful heart. NA II 15 242 7
My temper would perhaps be called resentful.-- PP I 11 58 28
avoid her but by stiffness of manner and resentful silence. PP I 21 115 1
Miss Crawford, a little suspicious and resentful of a MP II 7 242 25
could not be severely resentful of any thing that injured MP II 13 301 7
"Unjust I may have been, weak and resentful I have been, " P IV 11 237 42

RESENTFULLY (3)
said her mother resentfully, "since we are not to visit." PP I 2 6 3
have nothing farther to say," she resentfully answered. PP III 14 357 63
resentfully to be true, than what he knew anything about. E I 8 67 57

RESENTING (4)
or bitterness in resenting affronts:--but here, when the NA II 14 233 10
She was talking at Fanny, and resenting this private walk MP III 1 324 57
Elizabeth, though resenting the suspicion, might yet be P III 5 35 17
Mary, resenting that she should be supposed not to know P IV 10 222 37

RESENTMENT (63)
Keep up his resentment therefore I charge you. LS 2 245 1
then; where the resentment which true love would have LS 22 282 6
He endeavoured, long endeavoured to soften my resentment, LS 22 282 7
world, & the severest resentment of her injured mother. LS 22 282 8
reasonable, is too common to excite surprise or resentment. LS 30 300 2
innocence, to shew her resentment towards him who could NA I 12 93 4
who in a voice of cold resentment said, "very well, then NA I 13 99 4
still exceeded her in resentment, Catherine, though she NA I 13 102 26
no displeasure, no resentment that you can feel I myself--- NA II 13 225 19
made her for a short time sensible only of resentment. NA II 13 228 27
by the sweetest confidence in his regret and resentment. NA II 14 231 4
it, extend an useless resentment, and perhaps involve the NA II 14 231 5
and honest without resentment--a letter which Eleanor NA II 14 235 14
with the reasonable resentment of a sensible friend; and NA II 14 237 22
resentment towards herself, and his contempt of her family. NA II 15 244 11
every appearance of resentment or displeasure, and treated SS I 16 89 42
Her resentment of such behaviour, her indignation at SS II 1 139 1
of contempt and resentment, on this impertinent SS II 11 221 4
for her sister, or any resentment against Edward. SS III 1 260 10
her distress, lessen her alarms, and combat her resentment. SS III 1 262 14
He therefore replied, without any resentment, "I would by SS III 1 267 44
45

my marriage, I had seen without surprise or resentment. SS III 8 330 69
The independence she settled on Robert, through resentment SS III 13 366 18
resentment, by his having slighted one of her daughters. PP I 3 11 6
"Implacable resentment is a shade in a character. PP I 11 58 29
that your resentment once created was unappeasable. PP I 18 93 32
solicitude for Wickham, resentment against his enemies, PP I 18 95 48
Elizabeth had hoped that his resentment might shorten his PP I 21 115 2
Nor did that day wear out her resentment. PP I 23 127 5
for her sister, and resentment against all the others. PP II 1 133 3
till, roused to resentment by his subsequent language, she PP II 11 189 6
to catch her words with no less resentment than surprise. PP II 11 190 8
pain on her, your resentment has not been unreasonable. PP II 12 197 5
His resentment was in proportion to the distress of his PP II 12 201 5
his resentment had not made him think really ill of her. PP III 1 256 64
point of inconceivable resentment, as to refuse his PP III 8 310 10
any symptom of resentment, or any unnecessary complaisance. PP III 11 335 39
And with regard to the resentment of his family, or the PP III 14 358 70
she dropt all her resentment; was fonder than ever of PP III 19 387 10
part of his aunt, her resentment gave way, either to her PP III 19 388 12
to cherish pride or resentment, or to lose one connection MP I 1 4 2
to do away any little resentment of the other two; and MP I 10 104 51
with some feelings of resentment and mortification, moved MP I 15 145 42
at a distance, was felt with resentment and mortification. MP II 5 227 69
suppose you will ever harbour resentment on that account.-- MP III 1 313 12
She could not but feel some resentment against Mr. MP III 1 321 46
Some resentment did arise at a perseverance so selfish and MP III 2 328 9
heart is made for love and kindness, not for resentment. MP III 4 352 42
a kin to resentment to be long guiding Fanny's soliloquies. MP III 13 424 5
so proud a display of resentment; it was anger on Fanny's MP III 17 467 20
this state of swelling resentment, and mutually deep E I 15 132 37
feelings, concealing resentment, and avoiding eclat, were E I 16 137 12
Resentment could not have been more plainly spoken than in E I 17 140 3
neither provocation nor resentment were discerned by Mr. E II 3 170 1
suspicions, and imagined capable of pitiful resentment. E II 16 290 4
endure, she spoke her resentment in a form of words E III 14 441 8
was a something of resentment, a something bordering on it E III 16 451 2
have been quite without resentment under such a stroke. E III 16 451 2
been a little show of resentment towards Jane, from the E III 16 455 20
it with high and unjust resentment, though perfectly P III 10 91 42
at least; that anger, resentment, avoidance, were no more; P IV 8 185 21
folly, the madness of resentment, which had kept him from P IV 11 242 63
unwise & unjustifiable resentment at the time of Mr. S 3 377 1

RESENTMENTS (1)
of his resentments, of his having an unforgiving temper. PP I 16 80 34

RESERVATION (1)
at home, with only the reservation of enough to make the MP III 7 375 2

RESERVE (42)
I have disconcerted him already by my calm reserve; & it LS 7 254 3
law's reserve, & listening to her husband's insipid talk. LS 10 258 3
only a little affected reserve:--"we were much obliged to NA I 12 93 7
To Catherine's simple feelings, this odd sort of reserve NA I 15 121 25
had yet something more in reserve, and the ten or fifteen NA II 15 245 12
Her manners were attaching and soon banished his reserve. SS I 3 16 13
she had neither shyness nor reserve in their discussion. SS I 10 47 3
She liked him--in spite of his gravity and reserve, she SS I 10 50 12
His manners, though serious, were mild; and his reserve SS I 10 50 12
to perceive that her reserve was a mere calmness of manner SS I 11 55 6
His coldness and reserve mortified her severely; she was SS I 16 89 42
coldness, reserve could not stand against such a reception. SS I 17 90 1
Elinor, distressed by this charge of reserve in herself, SS II 5 170 27
and as her vehemence made reserve impossible in Elinor, SS III 1 269 58
parts, sarcastic humour, reserve, and caprice, that the PP I 1 5 34
with his usual reserve, to Mrs. Collins; and whatever PP II 7 171 9
or unbending reserve as now, when no importance could. PP III 2 263 10
The particulars, I reserve till we meet. PP III 7 302 14
It was owing to him, to his reserve, and want of proper PP III 10 324 2
I doubt whether his reserve, or anybody's reserve, can be PP III 10 324 2
or anybody's reserve, can be answerable for the event. PP III 10 324 2
affectionate, and the reserve of his manner repressed all MP I 2 19 30
They sometimes pass in such very little time from reserve MP I 5 49 32
seen him so seldom, his reserve may be a little repulsive. MP II 3 199 13
a day or two of mutual reserve, he was induced by his MP III 4 345 1
had discretion enough to reserve the rest till they might MP III 5 357 6
to each other without any remnant or shadow of reserve." MP III 5 364 30
she could wish to overcome her own shyness and reserve. MP III 9 395 3
With a little reserve of manner, Emma continued: "you mean E I 7 52 14
15

was such coldness and reserve--such apparent indifference E II 2 166 11
The like reserve prevailed on other topics. E II 2 169 17
all that part of her reserve which ought to be overcome, E II 3 171 7
father, and nothing of the pride or reserve of Enscombe. E II 6 198 5
And then, her reserve--I never could attach myself to any E II 6 203 39
There is safety in reserve, but no attraction. E II 6 203 40
"Not till the reserve ceases towards oneself; and then the E II 6 203 41
trouble of conquering any body's reserve to procure one. E II 6 203 41
mind, producing reserve and self-command, it would.-- E III 11 403 2
we could enter without ceremony or reserve on the subject." E III 17 464 22
quite out of place, could hint of caution and reserve. P III 2 15 15
Wentworth, no shyness or reserve; they seemed all to know P III 7 58 22
However, Waterloo is in reserve--& if we have S 4 380 1

RESERVED (29)
well-bred, she was reserved, cold, and had nothing to say SS I 6 31 8
I ought to have been reserved, spiritless, dull, and SS I 10 48 5
"But you would still be reserved," said Marianne, "and SS I 17 94 45
Edward Stared--"reserved! SS I 17 94 46
Am I reserved, Marianne?" SS I 17 94 46

"Reserved!--how, in what manner? SS I 17 95 48
Do not you know that she calls every one reserved who does SS I 17 95 49
But Mary Edwardes is rather prim & reserved; I do not W 321 2
friendly woman, had a reserved air, & a great deal of W 322 3
He was at the same time haughty, reserved, and fastidious, PP I 4 16 14
Reflection must be reserved for solitary hours; whenever PP II 14 212 16
which the kindness of her aunt had reserved for them. PP II 15 217 16
inferior, the belief of her being proud and reserved. PP III 3 267 3
prepared to see a proud, reserved, disagreeable girl. PP III 5 284 14
But Lizzy, you have been very sly, very reserved with me. PP III 17 374 18
Elizabeth reserved to herself the application for her PP III 17 375 27
Fanny estranged from him, silent and reserved, was an MP III 4 345 4
that he had no pretensions; his heart was reserved for you. MP III 4 350 30
character; but with reserved manners which prevented his E I 11 92 5
She was disgustingly, was suspiciously reserved. E II 2 169 15
was most, she was more reserved on the subject of Weymouth E II 2 169 16
enough;" but she said only, "Miss Fairfax is reserved." E II 3 171 6
guessed, she is so very reserved, so very unwilling to E II 6 200 19
could attach myself to any one so completely reserved." E II 6 203 39
One cannot love a reserved person." E II 6 203 40
She is reserved, more reserved, I think, than she used to E II 15 289 40
For, though shy, he did not seem reserved; it had rather P III 11 100 23
Wentworth, in a reserved yet hurried sort of farewell. P IV 8 190 48
Miss D. was a fine young woman, but cold & reserved, S 7 394 1

RESERVEDNESS (1)
uncertain; and the reservedness of his manner towards her SS I 18 96 1

RESERVES (4)
I will have no reserves from you." PP I 21 117 14
that he had then no reserves, no scruples in sinking Mr. PP II 13 207 5
Jane could have no reserves from Elizabeth, where PP III 13 346 23
continued, "to have no reserves with you on this subject. E III 4 337 4

RESERVING (2)
had influenced her; only reserving for himself this MP III 16 459 31
be the day, Charles only reserving the advantage of still P IV 10 225 55

RESETTLED (1)
her as soon as she was resettled, was looking forward to P III 11 93 1

RESIDE (3)
"You reside in Devonshire, I think"--was his next SS II 14 251 15
to visit, or wish to reside; for not only was it SS III 6 301 2
who came consequently to reside at Mansfield, and on MP I 3 24 5

RESIDED (4)
in the country; that he resided there only while he was SS I 9 44 23
part of the town, she had resided every winter in a house SS II 3 153 1
the lady I have always resided with when in Bath, would be E II 14 275 32
nephew to Sir Harry, resided constantly at Denham Park; & S 3 377 1

RESIDENCE (37)
dangers of a six weeks' residence in Bath, it may be NA I 2 18 1
by Isabella since her residence in Bath; and she was now NA I 7 44 1
Their estate was large, and their residence was at Norland SS I 1 3 1
which half a year's residence in her family afforded; and SS I 3 14 3
the place of his own residence, from whence she might SS I 4 23 20
by admitting them to a residence within his own manor. SS I 7 33 3
His name was good, his residence was in their favourite SS I 9 43 11
talking of their present residence, its conveniences, &c. SS I 16 89 42
A three weeks' residence at Delaford, where, in his SS III 13 369 35
his business and to his residence in a small market town; PP I 5 18 1
by a lane from Rosings Park, her ladyship's residence." PP I 14 67 3
Mrs. Gardiner's former residence, and where she had lately PP II 19 240 12
her residence there will probably be of some duration." PP III 6 299 25
and ancient manorial residence of the family, with all its MP I 8 81 33
to a country residence than I had ever expected to be. MP II 4 210 20
21
the air of a gentleman's residence without any very heavy MP II 7 242 24
You talk of giving it the air of a gentleman's residence. MP II 7 243 27
the air of a gentleman's residence, so much the look of a MP II 7 243 27
"The air of a gentleman's residence, therefore, you cannot MP II 7 243 27
from being the mere gentleman's residence, it becomes, by MP II 7 244 27
improvement, the residence of a man of education, taste, MP II 7 244 27
"Certainly, sir, I have no idea but of residence. MP II 7 247 41
and occasional residence of a man of independent fortune-- MP II 7 248 47
A residence of eight or nine years in the abode of wealth MP III 6 369 10
that her present residence could not be comfortable, and, MP III 11 410 7
from considering her residence there as the motive. MP III 17 465 13
Mansfield, an excuse for residence in London, and an MP III 17 469 23
causes, from his long residence at Hartfield, and his good E I 3 20 1
and Col. Campbell's residence being in London, every E II 2 164 6
The pain of his continued residence in Highbury, however, E II 4 182 8
respect for it, as the residence of a family of such true E III 6 358 35
to a long, uneventful residence in one country circle, to P III 1 9 18
into a cottage for his residence; and Uppercross Cottage, P III 5 36 20
One of the least agreeable circumstances of her residence P III 6 44 7
the neighbourhood where residence was not required, lived P III 9 73 4
all directing him to a residence unexpensive, and by the P III 11 97 12
some respectable family determined on a long residence.-- S 9 406 1

RESIDENT (6)
Mr. Suckling, who has been eleven years a resident at E II 18 310 34
resident at Monkford since the time of old Governor Trent." P III 3 23 27
with Lady Russell, still resident in Kellynch, and Mary P III 4 31 12
young man, as a resident curate, and was even courteous P III 12 103 3
at the advantage of such resident curate's being married. P III 12 103 3
and dignity of the resident land-holder; should find so P IV 3 138 5

RESIDENTS (1)
any family but of the residents left--and, as there is P III 11 95 9

RESIDES (1)
her education, and who still resides with them. PP I 11 67 7

RESIDING (6)
very respectable woman, residing in Dorsetshire, who had SS II 9 208 28
up her plan of their residing in Hertfordshire, was a PP III 8 313 20
resources of ladies residing in the country without a MP I 4 41 15
of Mr. Knightley, and residing in the parish of Donwell-- E I 3 23 10
to Emma,) a lady residing in or near Highbury; a family of E II 5 193 37
with whom he had been residing, had received any P III 4 30 10

RESIDUE (1)
and on that he rested for the residue of their income. SS III 13 369 33

RESIGN (5)
I look upon the event as so far decided, that I resign LS 27 297 4
He meant to resign his commission immediately; and as to PP III 10 323 2
resign his to me, it was impossible to take it, you know. MP I 13 122 2
she thought she could resign herself to almost every thing. MP III 5 365 34
They sang together once more; and Emma would then resign E II 8 227 86

RESIGNATION (6)
Resignation to inevitable evils is the duty of us all; the PP I 20 114 32
often observed that resignation is never so perfect as PP I 20 114 32
very promising step of the mind on its way to resignation. E III 19 483 9
to preach patience and resignation to a young man whom she P III 11 101 26
this was not a case of fortitude or of resignation only.-- P IV 5 154 8
fortitude, patience, resignation--of all the conflicts and P IV 5 156 10

RESIGNED (15)
property were to be resigned, or funded money made over, NA I 15 122 28
yearly value, was to be resigned to his son as soon as he NA II 1 135 42
coming, Lady Middleton resigned herself to the idea of it, SS I 21 118 2
She resigned herself at first to all the misery of her SS II 9 206 24
I have been in early preferment; and I trust I am resigned. PP I 20 114 32
she was at length so far resigned as to think it PP II 3 145 11
He resigned all claim to assistance in the church, were it PP II 12 201 5
Lady Catherine seemed resigned. PP II 14 211 12
to make her reasonable, and Jane to make her resigned. PP II 18 230 14
her elder sister has resigned it, and the chosen partner PP III 15 362 14
account, was tolerably resigned to her having the use of MP I 16 151 1
Lady Bertram seemed quite resigned to waiting.-- MP I 18 167 12
He was soon pretty well resigned. E II 7 209 9
Mr. Woodhouse was resigned. E III 1 318 13
Captain Benwick had resigned the poor corpse-like figure P III 12 110 42

RESIGNING (3)
caprices of others--of resigning my own judgement in LS 39 308 1
herself frightened; so, resigning herself to her fate, and NA I 9 62 10
following of Wickham's resigning all pretensions to the PP II 13 205 3

RESIST (29)
doubt if I could resist even matrimony offered by him. LS 39 308 1
Lady Susan continued to resist, her resistance in the LS 42 312 5
steadiness of reason to resist the attraction of being NA I 7 50 44
in some small degree, to resist such high authority, and NA I 9 66 32
With difficulty, for something seemed to resist her NA II 6 164 3
offending Mrs. Smith, to resist the temptation of SS I 15 81 43
to resist the solicitations of his friends to do nothing. SS I 19 103 4
They thanked her; but were obliged to resist all her SS I 20 110 5
with Mrs. Jennings, was a temptation we could not resist. SS II 7 187 38
resist insult, or return mortification--but I cannot. SS II 7 189 52
it for ever, and at a third could resist it with energy. SS II 9 201 2
the obstinacy which could resist such arguments as these. SS III 1 267 40
was not in a state of mind to resist their influence. SS III 7 309 7
your sister, could not resist the temptation of telling me SS III 8 330 69
eliz, at last not able to resist hints, which her own W 359 28
She answered in the affirmative, and, unable to resist the PP I 18 92 18
how am I even to know that it would be wisdom to resist? PP II 3 145 7
young man to resist an opportunity of having a companion. PP III 9 318 19
occasionally, unable to resist the impulse of curiosity, PP III 11 335 43
which she could not resist, and she was left on the bench MP I 9 96 76
I resisted; it was the impulse of the moment to resist, MP III 16 459 30
Harriet could not long resist so delightful a persuasion. E I 9 73 19
was too ill and low to resist the authority which excluded E I 13 109 5
lady, and not liking to resist any advice of her's, he had E I 13 110 10
Emma could not resist. E III 7 370 25
My friend Robert would not resist. E III 18 472 20
to resist idle interference in such a trifle as this. P III 10 87 26
ever, was a charm which she could not immediately resist. P IV 5 160 26
This was an opportunity which Anne could not resist; she P IV 6 172 42

RESISTANCE (8)
to resist, her resistance in the course of a few days LS 42 312 5
her brother; but she could not repent her resistance. NA I 13 101 25
James or Isabella to resent her resistance any longer. NA I 14 115 55
Elinor made no resistance that was not easily overcome. SS III 7 311 15
After a proper resistance on the part of Mrs. Ferrars, SS III 14 373 1
Her resistance had not injured her with the gentleman, and PP I 6 27 44
45
after a little farther resistance on the part of his aunt, PP III 19 388 12
but offered no farther resistance; and they went together MP I 2 16 20

RESISTED (14)
would have led his fair partner away, but she resisted. NA I 8 57 21
She had resisted its approaches during the whole length of NA II 4 153 30
and tried to turn it; but it resisted her utmost strength. NA II 6 168 10
their kind hostess, who resisted them with all the SS III 3 279 1
"To have resisted such attractions, to have withstood such SS III 8 321 34
He had nothing to urge against it, but still resisted the SS III 13 372 45
visit were most steadily resisted, the coach conveyed him PP I 16 75 1
in a manner not to be resisted, made over to his use MP II 6 237 23
Fanny still resisted, and from her heart. MP II 8 258 17
She gave advice; advice too sound to be resisted by a good MP III 9 397 8
I resisted; it was the impulse of the moment to resist, MP III 16 459 30
Nature resisted it for a while. MP III 16 459 31
kinder and wiser to have resisted the temptation of any E II 2 165 9
for attack could not be resisted; and Harriet was soon E III 3 333 6

RESISTING (5)
way against the wind, resisting it with laughing delight SS I 9 41 6
There is no resisting a cockade my dear."-- W 326 5
this entreaty, or for resisting every repetition of it. PP II 12 201 5
There was no resisting so much apparent affection. MP III 5 365 33
There was no resisting such news, no possibility of E II 5 188 8

RESISTLESS (1)
the resistless pressure of a long string of passing ladies. NA I 10 76 29

RESOLUTE (11)
they were still resolute in meeting in defiance of wet and NA I 5 37 4
decided pretension, the resolute stilishness of Miss NA I 8 55 11
Her resolute effort threw back the lid, and gave to her NA II 6 164 3
children; and she was resolute in declining to visit any SS I 9 40 2
She received the news with resolute composure; made no SS II 10 217 17
around it with a look of resolute firmness, as if SS III 10 342 7
the same time the most resolute composure of countenance, PP I 14 68 12
have a horse," was the resolute declaration with which he MP I 4 36 7
to have just such resolute measures advised, as he meant P III 2 11 1
But so eager and so resolute! P III 12 116 71
much in favour of happiness, as a very resolute character. P III 12 116 72

RESOLUTELY (16)
the church-yard, and resolutely turning away her eyes, NA I 12 91 3
They both eagerly and resolutely declined her invitation. SS I 20 113 32
and she struggled so resolutely against the oppression of SS I 22 134 53
He was resolutely silent however; and, from a PP III 3 271 16
17
Jane resolutely kept her place at the table; but Elizabeth, PP III 11 333 31
but Lady Catherine very resolutely, and not very politely, PP III 14 352 16
17
but Sir Thomas resolutely declined all dinner; he would MP II 1 180 10
prove herself more resolutely in love than Emma had E I 17 142 12
say at once, simply and resolutely, to Mrs. Churchill--' E I 18 146 16
in his turn, for most resolutely and commandingly did he E II 10 244 34
35
would not have been so resolutely encountered but in full E II 16 298 58
towards her, and resolutely swept away by her unexamined. E III 5 349 25
"Harriet!" cried Emma, collecting herself resolutely--"let E III 11 406 19
her neck, and he was resolutely borne away, before she P III 9 80 33
she felt so tired, she resolutely answered, "Oh! no, P III 10 86 17
But now it was to be more resolutely undertaken, at a more S 12 423 1

RESOLUTION (111)
<to> me, that his resolution of going might be occasioned LS 24 287 11
Where my own resolution was taken, I could not wish for LS 24 289 12
His resolution of leaving Churchill is consistent with his LS 24 290 13
punishment; & your resolution of quitting Churchill is LS 25 292 3
For an hour or two, I was even stagger'd in my resolution LS 29 299 2
To assist us in such a resolution, I feel that absence LS 30 301 4
of Miss Thorpe, and her resolution of humbling the sex, NA I 6 43 44
and almost her first resolution, to seek her for that NA I 9 60 1
Catherine's resolution of endeavouring to meet Miss Tilney NA I 10 71 8
When Catherine knew this, her resolution was directly made. NA II 4 150 1
Her resolution was supported by Isabella's behaviour in NA II 4 153 31
she came to a resolution of making her next attempt on the NA II 9 192 5
several points, and her resolution formed, of always NA II 10 201 4
Eleanor seemed now impelled into resolution and speech. NA II 13 228 27
His resolution was soon formed. NA II 15 245 12
of Mrs. Ferrars's resolution that both her sons should SS I 4 23 19
Her resolution was formed as she read. SS I 4 23 20
she were to alter her resolution in favour of this gift, SS I 12 58 1
found that in her resolution to know where they had been, SS I 13 67 65
"But then at other times I have not resolution enough for SS I 22 133 44
The reason alleged was their determined resolution of not SS II 3 153 1
overcame all her resolution, and though she had promised SS II 9 205 24
"Is Mr. Edward Ferrars," said Elinor, with resolution, " SS II 11 224 27
was pacified by the resolution of inviting his sisters SS II 14 253 25
by something else, your resolution, your self-command, are, SS III 1 263 28
is a good one, and her resolution equal to any thing. SS III 1 265 36
"Yes," continued Elinor, gathering more resolution, as SS III 4 289 31
called on to act with resolution, immediately said to her, SS III 5 299 35
love her, declared her resolution of not stirring from SS III 7 308 3
followed the resolution of its performance; and as soon as SS III 7 311 14
At last, however, my resolution was taken, and I had SS III 8 321 34

to ruin all my resolution, and with it all my comfort. SS III 8 321 34
whether I could see her again, and keep to my resolution. SS III 8 323 40
My resolution was soon made, and at eight o'clock this SS III 8 331 69
But the resolution was made only to be broken. SS III 10 344 10
reflection did nothing, resolution must do all, soon found SS III 10 347 32
its result, and a resolution of reviving the subject again, SS III 10 348 34
had done; but while her resolution was unsubdued, and she SS III 11 352 19
Lucy; that some resolution of his own, some mediation of SS III 12 357 1
How soon he had walked himself into the proper resolution, SS III 13 361 3
the first positive resolution of not marrying till every SS III 14 374 6
had taken the sudden resolution of attending the W 338 18
was her only alternative. she declared her resolution. PP I 7 32 33
the other to change a resolution of no very great moment, PP I 10 50 37
her; and though her resolution was not to be shaken, her PP I 22 123 3
that want of proper resolution which now made him the PP II 1 133 3
feelings, and want of resolution, will do the business." PP II 1 136 17
Your father would depend on your resolution and good PP II 3 144 2
as usual, and the resolution of repressing such PP II 13 209 12
and unembarrassed;--a resolution the more necessary to be PP III 3 268 8
and came to town with the resolution of hunting for them. PP III 10 321 2
actually declared your resolution of never taking orders, PP III 10 329 31
Consoled by this resolution, she was the better able to PP III 11 333 27
of Mr. Darcy, and her resolution to be civil to him only PP III 11 334 36
Her resolution was for a short time involuntarily kept by PP III 12 339 5
with the determined resolution of carrying my purpose; nor PP III 14 355 48
From what she had said of her resolution to prevent their PP III 15 360 2
resolution; and perhaps he might be doing the same. PP III 16 365 1
Now was the moment for her resolution to be executed, and, PP III 16 365 2
3

soon learnt that his resolution of following her from PP III 16 370 33
My resolution of thanking you for your kindness to Lydia PP III 18 381 13
please them all, the resolution to act something or other, MP I 13 124 13
Tom repeated his resolution of going to him early on the MP I 15 148 60
neither pride nor resolution, was preparing to encounter MP II 2 193 17
welcome was his sudden resolution of coming to them for a MP II 5 223 48
over and taken his resolution in quiet independence, the MP II 8 252 1
shame, she spoke with a resolution which sprung from MP III 15 440 16
and the resolution of avoiding any farther allusion. MP III 15 444 29
in spite of every resolution; but Susan's presence drove MP III 15 445 33
She had resolution enough to pursue her own will in spite E I 2 15 3
tempt her to break her resolution, at present," said Mrs. E I 5 41 30
in the case at present, I will break my resolution now." E I 6 46 21
pales, when a sudden resolution, of at least getting E I 10 89 36
resolution enough to refrain from making any answer at all. E I 13 113 27
Now, it so happened that in spite of Emma's resolution of E I 14 118 5
"I admired your resolution very much, sir," said he, "in E I 15 126 10
her with every previous resolution confirmed of being E I 17 142 10
by manoeuvring and finessing, but by vigour and resolution. E I 18 146 16
a resolution to do right against the will of others. E I 18 148 22
But now she made the sudden resolution of not passing E II 1 155 3
not oppose such a resolution, though their feelings did. E II 2 165 9
still her resolution held of never marrying)--the honour, E II 7 206 2
Her resolution of refusal only grew more interesting by E II 13 266 6
However, my resolution is taken as to noticing Jane E II 15 284 9
There is great fear, great caution, great resolution E II 15 285 15
discreet resolution of not trusting himself with her long. E III 1 316 5
to show his liberty, and his resolution of maintaining it. E III 2 327 34
Emma's first resolution was to keep her father from the E III 3 335 12
I knew it was--but had not resolution enough to part with E III 4 340 24
This is a new resolution." E III 4 341 30
Your resolution, or rather your expectation of never E III 4 341 35
she had come to the resolution of accepting it.-- E III 8 381 15
It was a private resolution of her's, not communicated to E III 10 397 51
now,) gave Emma the resolution to sit and endure farther E III 11 408 33
be drawn, was in the resolution of her own better conduct, E III 12 423 21
She might assist his resolution, or reconcile him to it; E III 13 429 30
the most solemn resolution of never quitting her father.-- E III 14 435 4
Its effect upon her appears in the immediate resolution it E III 14 441 8
It was perfectly accordant with that resolution of E III 14 442 8
The strength, resolution, and presence of mind of the Mr. E III 19 484 10
a professed resolution of doing nothing for his daughter. P III 4 26 2
The resolution of doing so helped to form the comfort of P III 6 52 34
decidedly declaring his resolution of calling on his aunt, P III 10 86 17
mind, if she have not resolution enough to resist idle P III 10 87 26
of her fatigue, and his resolution to give her rest. P III 10 91 42
having formed the resolution to go, and besides the P III 11 94 7
Charles agreed; but declared his resolution of not going P III 12 113 58
would supply resolution, but here was something more; here P IV 5 154 8
what it produced; the resolution of coming back to Bath as P IV 9 207 90
breathed the same stern resolution of not engaging in a P IV 9 209 97
of heedlessness and the resolution of a collected mind. P IV 11 242 63

RESOLUTIONS (9)
of regret, & general resolutions of prudence were LS 3 247 1
Young men are often hasty in their resolutions--& not more LS 23 284 6
forming wise resolutions with the most violent dispatch. NA II 6 165 5
his fidelity, or influence the resolutions it prompted. NA II 15 247 15
and my own consequent resolutions, I had not been of age MP I 6 61 56
making all these good resolutions on the side of self- MP II 9 265 19
heighten all his wishes, and confirm all his resolutions. MP III 2 326 3
and acts up to his resolutions--an inestimable quality. MP III 13 423 2
and in her resolutions; and yet there was no preventing a E III 18 475 40

RESOLVE (32)
I cannot easily resolve on anything so serious as marriage, LS 10 257 1
Besides, if you take my advice, & resolve to marry de LS 26 295 3
of my spirit; & if I resolve to wait for that event, I LS 29 299 3
resolve to disallow, have been unanswerably proved to me. LS 36 305 1
it was to resolve on the quality of her wedding-gown. NA I 15 120 23
had made her resolve on remaining at Norland no longer SS I 5 25 3
of you,' I should resolve upon doing it immediately." SS II 2 150 32
therefore if I should resolve to quit Netherfield, I PP I 9 42 8
This is your final resolve! PP III 14 358 71
could resolve to hazard herself among her other relations. MP I 4 41 16
"Those who see quickly, will resolve quickly and act MP I 6 61 57
To do him justice, however, he did not resolve to MP I 14 132 8
and retired in proud resolve, determined only to behave MP II 3 201 23
seemed to want to be encouraged even by her to resolve on. MP II 5 223 48
effort, to resolve on wearing Miss Crawford's necklace too. MP II 9 271 40
for happiness, you resolve to refuse him at once, without MP III 1 318 39
any one, she did resolve to give occasional hints to Susan, MP III 9 396 6
her hastily resolve on avoiding such immediate horrors at MP III 17 466 18
made her resolve to restrain herself when she did speak. E I 15 129 24
and resolve on going home by way of Randalls to procure it. E II 5 187 4
in a humour to resolve that they should both come in time. E II 5 189 18
but resolve never to expose them to her neighbour again. E II 10 240 6
One cannot resolve upon them in a hurry. E II 11 252 32
or propriety, to make her resolve on not being the last to E II 14 270 2
Jane might very naturally resolve on seeing Mrs. Cole or E III 8 379 9
her, and to resolve that it need not and should not.-- E III 13 431 38
She could only resolve at last, that she would still avoid E III 14 435 4
one scheme more--nearly resolve, that it might be E III 14 435 4
What! actually resolve to break with him entirely!-- E III 15 447 22
She could only resolve to avoid such self-delusion in P III 6 42 2
that he could not but resolve to remain where he was, and P III 9 73 1
Some must resolve on being off for Uppercross instantly. P III 12 113 58

RESOLVED (130)
I have therefore resolved on placing her at one of the LS 1 244 1
from Wigmore Street, she resolved on getting out of the LS 19 273 1
not yet quite resolved on the manner of bringing it about. LS 19 275 4
I have for some time been more particularly resolved on LS 22 280 1
I was resolved to lose no time in clearing up these LS 24 288 11
I resolved to have an explanation before it were too late. LS 24 290 13
hope of success, was resolved to leave nothing unattempted LS 42 311 2
which Lady Susan had doubtless resolved on from the first. LS 42 313 7
about, that he was resolved to go and dance; so I thought NA I 8 58 30
resolved never to think so seriously on the subject again. NA II 4 153 30
ease on this point, she resolved to lose no time in NA II 6 163 1
hasp of the lock, she resolved at all hazards to satisfy NA II 6 164 3
what Henry had foretold, resolved instantly to peruse NA II 6 169 11
from an imagination resolved on alarm, and every thing NA II 10 199 2
She resolved on not answering Isabella's letter; and tried NA II 12 219 16
her mind, she very soon resolved to speak to Eleanor about NA II 13 220 1
the earliest hour, as if resolved to have her gone before NA II 13 226 25
but likewise pretty well resolved upon marrying Catherine NA II 15 244 12
which one of her sisters had resolved never to be taught. SS I 1 6 11
and resolved against ever admitting consolation in future. SS I 1 7 13
before; and he finally resolved, that it would be SS I 2 13 29
each for the sake of the others resolved to appear happy. SS I 6 28 2
lively nor young, seemed resolved to undervalue his merits. SS I 10 50 13
"Well, as you are resolved to go, I wish you a good SS I 13 65 43
You are resolved to think him blameable, because he took SS I 15 78 28
else, she internally resolved henceforward to catch every SS I 18 98 13
he seemed resolved to be gone when his enjoyment among his SS I 19 101 1
and while she was firmly resolved to act by her as every SS II 1 142 7
now, I am resolved to finish the basket after supper." SS II 1 144 12
politeness: and resolved within herself, that if her SS II 3 156 15
there; and Elinor was resolved not only upon gaining very SS II 4 159 1
sister's relief, Elinor resolved to write the next morning SS II 5 171 38
Tell me that it is all absolutely resolved on, that any SS II 5 173 44
him so much that she was resolved never to mention his SS II 10 215 10
at Gray's, it was resolved, that while her young friends SS II 11 220 2
and he was really resolved on seeking an intimacy with SS II 11 228 51
with Miss Morton was resolved on, or till her husband's SS II 12 229 4
after more, she had resolved from the first to pay a visit SS III 2 270 3
they are quite resolved upon going home from the Palmers;-- SS III 3 280 8
the utmost; and secretly resolved to avail herself, at SS III 5 293 2
luxurious solitude, she resolved to spend almost every SS III 6 303 9
she resolved to sit with her during the whole of it. SS III 7 310 9
Smith and myself--and I resolved therefore on calling at SS III 8 324 42
fully, so firmly resolved within myself on doing right! SS III 8 324 42
Willing therefore to delay the evil hour, she resolved to SS III 10 343 10
than on paper, it was resolved that, instead of writing to SS III 13 372 45
morning that if you ever resolved on quitting Netherfield PP I 10 49 27
In the desperation of her feelings she resolved on one PP I 11 56 10
11

was positively resolved--nor did she much expect it would PP I 12 59 1
He wisely resolved to be particularly careful that no sign PP I 12 60 4
She was resolved against any sort of conversation with him, PP I 18 89 3
dances, and at first was resolved not to break it; till PP I 18 91 8
Having resolved to do it without loss of time, as his PP I 19 104 1
of their having just resolved to follow their brother to PP I 21 116 8
She resolved to give her the information herself, and PP I 22 123 3
a little uneasy; and she resolved to speak to Elizabeth on PP II 2 142 18
perfectly resolved to continue the acquaintance no longer. PP II 3 148 26
for employment, she resolved soon after breakfast to PP II 12 195 1
we shortly resolved on joining him directly in London.-- PP II 12 198 5
me that, having finally resolved against taking orders, he PP II 12 200 5
and was now absolutely resolved on being ordained, if I PP II 12 201 5
she instantly resolved to be false, and his account of the PP II 13 204 1
At one time she had almost resolved on applying to him, PP II 13 206 4
She dreaded seeing Wickham again, and was resolved to PP II 16 223 25
and she finally resolved that it could be the last PP II 19 241 16
than before, and resolved to appear and to speak with PP III 1 254 57
and was consequently resolved not to be out of sight of PP III 2 260 1
No sooner did he appear, than Elizabeth wisely resolved to PP III 3 268 8
that Mr. Wickham had resolved on quitting the militia. PP III 8 312 18
But he found Lydia absolutely resolved on remaining where PP III 10 322 2
When all this was resolved on, he returned again to his PP III 10 324 2
nothing will ever be resolved on; so easy, that every PP III 13 348 38
it possible, I instantly resolved on setting off for this PP III 14 353 26
"You are then resolved to have him?" PP III 14 358 67
I am only resolved to act in that manner, which will, in PP III 14 358 68
During their walk, it was resolved that Mr. Bennet's PP III 17 375 27
I now give it to you, if you are resolved on having him. PP III 17 376 35
for Sir Thomas was fully resolved to be the real and MP I 1 8 9
this third he resolved to exchange for one that his cousin MP I 4 37 8
and very seriously resolved, however unwilling he must be MP I 7 74 58
quite impatient, she resolved to go in search of them. MP I 10 103 49
materially; but I was resolved to make no difficulties. MP I 13 122 2
"If you are resolved on acting," replied the persevering MP I 13 127 28
in to do what you had resolved against, and what you are MP I 16 155 15
Sir Thomas resolved to speak seriously to her. MP II 3 200 20
of him, or absolutely resolved on enduring his rival, her MP II 3 201 24
others, she had nearly resolved on going home immediately, MP II 4 214 46
I am sure it may all be resolved into a better style of MP II 6 230 6
so far as to be resolved (almost resolved) on bringing it MP II 8 255 10
to be resolved (almost resolved) on bringing it to a MP II 8 255 10
and seemed resolved either to take another or none at all. MP II 8 259 20
She had, to oblige Edmund, resolved to wear it--but it was MP II 9 271 40
her way up stairs, she resolved there to remain, during MP III 1 311 2
and hopeful, Sir Thomas resolved to abstain from all MP III 2 330 14
face, and immediately resolved to forbear all farther MP III 4 354 48
When he had really resolved on any measure, he could MP III 6 370 14
I had almost resolved on leaving London again directly.-- MP III 13 421 2
resolved on doing nothing till she returns to Mansfield. MP III 13 422 2
sacrifice to right; he resolved to defer his Norfolk MP III 17 467 20
his Norfolk journey, resolved that writing should answer MP III 17 467 20
Mary, though perfectly resolved against ever attaching MP III 17 469 24
resolved on being seriously accepted as soon as possible. E I 15 129 24
She was quite concerned and ashamed, and resolved to do E I 16 137 10
She now resolved to keep Harriet no longer in the dark. E I 17 141 5
letter, and had almost resolved on hurrying away directly E II 1 158 13
She had long resolved that one-and-twenty should be the E II 2 165 8
noviciate, she had resolved at one-and-twenty to complete E II 2 165 8
or more honourable than the sacrifices she had resolved on. E II 2 168 13
And at last, as if resolved to qualify his opinion E II 5 192 29
their going farther was resolved on, confessed his wish to E II 6 196 2
consulted, he seemed resolved that it should not interest E II 12 257 2
and Mr. Elton's seeming resolved to learn to like it too. E III 4 339 19
of hopes and chances, she was perfectly resolved.-- E III 4 341 34
angry spirit, and looked resolved to be engaged by no E III 5 349 23
more; and his daughter resolved to remain with him, that E III 6 361 42
Frank Churchill having resolved to go home directly, E III 8 383 31
have thought it!" and resolved, that his mourning should E III 9 388 13
She resolved to prevail on her to spend a day at Hartfield. E III 9 389 16
Jane was resolved to receive no kindness form her. E III 9 391 21
her work, and seeming resolved against looking up.) E III 10 394 30
In the meanwhile, she resolved against seeing Harriet.-- E III 12 416 2
She was resolved not to be convinced, as long as she could E III 12 416 2
Emma resolved to be out of doors as soon as possible. E III 13 424 1
She considered--resolved--and, trying to smile, began-- " E III 13 425 2
3

She had resolved to defer the disclosure till Mrs. Weston E III 16 452 6
She soon resolved, equally as a duty and a pleasure, to E III 16 452 7
employed in the cause, resolved first to announce it at E III 17 465 28
I am resolved to have some in an ornament for the head. E III 18 479 70
have been resolved on, and found practicable so soon. P IV 1 122 3
of her own, she resolved to hurry on & get into the house S 9 406 1

RESOLVES (1)
reflection before she resolves on her answer, and I am MP III 13 422 2

RESOLVING (22)
book after breakfast, resolving to remain in the same NA I 9 60 1
of proudly resolving, in conscious innocence, to shew her NA I 12 93 4
She listened--the sound had ceased; and resolving not to NA II 9 194 6
so cautiously; but resolving not to be again overcome by NA II 13 223 9

instantly left the room, resolving that, whatever might be SS I 4 23 19
and half angry; but resolving to regulate her behaviour to SS I 16 89 42
Elinor, resolving to exert herself, though fearing the SS III 12 359 16
17
she heard, and who was resolving to retail it all among PP I 16 75 3
satisfy myself without resolving to chuse a wife from PP I 19 106 10
Longbourn estate, and resolving to turn herself and her PP I 23 130 16
her return, and almost resolving to walk after her till PP II 13 209 13
overcome; and at length resolving to suppress every PP II 17 224 1
but she sat down, resolving within herself, to draw no PP III 9 316 5
of this, was another reason for his resolving to follow us. PP III 10 322 2
and Miss Bertram's resolving to go down to the parsonage MP I 14 136 22
"How perfectly I remember my resolving to look for you up MP III 5 360 14
It ended in Mrs. Norris's resolving to quit Mansfield, and MP III 17 465 14
visit to Ireland, and resolving to divide herself E II 2 168 13
Mrs. Elton gaily, "in resolving to be always on the watch, E II 17 302 20
more simple sublimity of resolving to refuse him at once E III 13 431 38
She closed with this offer, resolving to break with me E III 14 442 8
were gone too, suddenly resolving to walk to the end of P III 7 59 25

RESORT (3)
They had their great cousins, to be sure, to resort to for P IV 12 251 9
every thing, & the sure resort of the very best company, S 1 368 1
by nature for the resort of the invalid--the very spot S 1 369 1

RESORTED (3)
Our own library is too well known to me, to be resorted to SS III 10 343 9
in the room they were in resorted to again; and with such E II 11 249 12
measure should have been resorted to at all--wondered, P III 5 34 11

RESORTING (2)
of all the numbers resorting hither, except Sir James LS 2 244 1
reason for asking it, without resorting to invention.-- E III 16 451 3

RESOUNDED (1)
in his loudest tone, resounded through the building, NA II 9 191 4

RESOUNDING (1)
Such were the kind of lamentations resounding perpetually PP II 18 229 10

RESOURCE (4)
Forgive me my dear friend, it is my last resource. LS 2 246 1
being her constant resource when determined on pleasing.-- W 349 23
it could be the last resource, if her private enquiries as PP II 19 241 16
Her only resource was to get out of the subject as fast as MP II 2 188 3

RESOURCES (15)
humoured her children; and these were their only resources. SS I 7 32 1
run through the usual resources of ladies residing in the MP I 4 41 15
all Miss Crawford's resources, her accomplishments, her MP II 3 199 16
the lively turns, quick resources, and playful impudence MP II 7 240 9
a great many independent resources; and I do not perceive E I 10 85 21
Blessed with so many resources within myself, the world E II 14 276 36
To those who had no resources it was a different thing; E II 14 276 36
thing; but my resources made me quite independent. E II 14 276 36
caro sposo, and her resources, and all her airs of pert E II 14 279 52
A woman with fewer resources than I have, need not have E II 16 290 2
Or, perhaps she may not have resources enough in herself E II 18 307 21
I always say a woman cannot have too many resources--and I E II 18 307 21
Mrs. Elton's resources were inadequate to such an attack. E III 6 353 6
woman have ever so many resources, it is not possible for E III 6 356 26
completely; she had no resources for solitude; and P III 5 37 21

RESPECT (172)
in that respect, & that riches only, will not satisfy me. LS 2 245 1
place for her in every respect, as well from the elegant & LS 3 246 1
everybody ought to respect the delicacy of those feelings, LS 5 249 1
inspired him with greater respect for me than his sister's LS 7 254 3
neither to delicacy nor respect, & that he felt she would LS 8 255 1
Have I not explained everything to you with respect to LS 35 304 1
those, to whom I owe no duty, & for whom I feel no respect. LS 39 308 1
In one respect she was admirably fitted to introduce a NA I 2 20 8
entirely new; and the respect which they naturally NA I 4 33 7
I have no notion of treating men with such respect. NA I 6 43 43
"In one respect, there certainly is a difference. NA I 10 77 35
She felt utterly unworthy of such respect, and knew not NA II 5 154 2
they were not in every respect answered, for Catherine had NA II 9 191 3
It could be much better in every respect that Eleanor NA II 9 192 5
from a sentiment of respect for my mother's character, as NA II 9 196 23
With a look of much respect, he immediately rose, and NA II 15 241 7
their father's particular respect, had seen with NA II 15 245 12
His abilities in every respect improve as much upon SS I 4 20 9
attention; and she felt a respect for him on the occasion, SS I 7 35 9
in that respect as earnest, as his abilities were strong. SS I 10 49 10
man, and she regarded him with respect and compassion. SS I 10 50 12
in any degree claim the respect of abilities, excite the SS I 11 55 7
looks, his manner, his attentive and affectionate respect? SS I 15 80 36
Lady Middleton, and totally unlike her in every respect. SS I 19 106 22
than he had been with respect to Marianne; indeed it was SS I 21 125 36
at his total silence with respect even to their names. SS I 22 134 49
in any respect less happy at Longstaple than he used to be. SS II 2 147 12
If you could be supposed to be biassed in any respect by SS II 2 150 34
an account of her real situation with respect to him. SS II 5 172 39
her hand, pressed it, and kissed it with grateful respect. SS II 9 206 25
Concern for her unhappiness, and respect for her fortitude SS II 9 210 32
a kind of compassionate respect, and though she saw her SS II 10 212 1
relations, I shall be happy to shew them every respect. SS II 11 222 9
The land was so very desirable for me in every respect, so SS II 11 225 31
Marianne was in every respect materially better, and he SS III 7 314 23
Your wife has a claim to your politeness, to your respect, SS III 8 329 64
they equally love and respect him; and even my own SS III 9 337 17
grateful, so full of respect and kind wishes as seemed due SS III 10 341 5
not make my home in every respect comfortable, as I had no SS III 13 362 5
unpleasant feelings, with respect to her own family, had W 322 3
to me by such a proof of tender respect for my aunt."-- W 352 26
Margt had just respect enough for her Br & Sr's opinion, W 360 30
I have a high respect for your nerves. PP I 1 5 29
were therefore in every respect entitled to think well of PP I 4 15 11
In that respect his friend had greatly the advantage. PP I 4 16 14
than commerce; but with respect to any other leading PP I 6 22 9
myself with grateful respect towards her ladyship, and be PP I 13 62 12
was vacant; and the respect which he felt for her high PP I 15 70 1
may vary greatly with respect to me; and I could wish, PP I 18 94 41
his respect towards any body connected with the family." PP I 18 101 71
silence and respect which her rank will inevitably excite. PP I 19 106 10
find me in every respect ill qualified for the situation." PP I 19 107 14
My feelings in every respect forbid it. PP I 19 109 20
again, and was in every respect so altered a creature, PP II 3 148 26
of what he had done with respect to Jane, his unpardonable PP II 11 193 31
to condemn them.-- with respect to that other, more PP II 12 199 5
he had assured her that respect for the father, would PP II 13 207 5
his general character respect; but she could not approve PP II 14 212 17
so desirable in every respect, so replete with advantage, PP II 14 213 18
Respect, esteem, and confidence, had vanished for ever; PP II 19 236 1
Mrs. Reynolds's respect for Elizabeth seemed to increase PP III 1 247 13
With respect to Wickham, the travellers soon found that he PP III 2 265 15
The respect created by the conviction of his valuable PP III 2 265 16
But above all, above respect and esteem, there was a PP III 2 265 16
The world has been deceived in that respect; and I am PP III 7 302 14
Had he done his duty in that respect, Lydia need not have PP III 8 308 1
His behaviour to us has, in every respect, been as PP III 10 325 2
It would have suited me in every respect." PP III 10 328 26
Much as I respect them, I believe, I thought only of you." PP III 16 366 6
of seeing you unable to respect your partner in life. PP III 17 376 35
Nor was her respect for him, though it made her more quiet, PP III 18 384 27
He, who had always inspired in herself a respect which PP III 19 388 61
nor consider her, in any respect, so much my own, I should MP I 1 7 8
With all due respect to such of the present company as MP I 5 46 20
of the park; in that respect, unfavourable for improvement. MP I 6 56 26
Henry, who is in every other respect exactly what a MP I 6 59 43
her respect for her aunt's memory which misleads her here. MP I 7 63 7
but with respect," she added, "now, where is the avenue? MP I 8 82 35
of the cloth with more respect," and turned the subject. MP I 9 89 29
of it in every other respect, had she been sure that she MP I 12 115 5
of Amelia to be in every respect the property of Miss MP I 14 133 10
in every respect; but I can think of no other alternative. MP I 16 154 12
Grant was entitled to respect, which could never have MP I 17 160 6
six times as many; but we respect your pheasants, sir, I MP II 1 181 16
Its vicinity to my own room--but in every respect indeed MP II 1 184 25
own he could not hold Sir Thomas in greater respect.'" MP II 2 190 7
respect; and I only wish you would talk to him more.-- MP II 3 198 9
The principals being all agreed in this respect, it soon MP II 3 202 27
not envy you; I do not much think I shall even respect you. MP II 4 213 40
I have a much greater respect for those that are honest MP II 4 213 40
"Your degree of respect for honesty, rich or poor, is MP II 4 213 41
and he felt the highest respect for a lad who, before he MP II 6 236 22
In one respect it was better, as it gave him the means of MP II 6 237 23
There was no want of respect in the young man's address; MP II 7 246 37
with the respect and attention that are due to her.-- MP III 1 313 12
unpleasant to me in every respect, and that I begged him MP III 1 315 19
have thought it a gross violation of duty and respect. MP III 1 319 39
and beauty and wealth were all that excited her respect. MP III 2 332 22
greatest admiration and respect, and more than half a mind MP III 3 341 28
though in that respect, I think the difference between us MP III 4 349 25
the conjugal manners of Mansfield parsonage with respect. MP III 5 361 16
She soon learnt to think with respect of her own little MP III 7 387 47
respect, the very reverse of what she could have wished. MP III 8 388 3
She could not respect her parents, as she had hoped. MP III 8 389 3
them, without any power of engaging their respect. MP III 8 389 4
her at first with some respect in consideration of her MP III 9 395 3
her sister as an object of mingled compassion and respect. MP III 9 396 6
from the physician, with respect to some strong hectic MP III 14 429 1
Edmund had greatly the advantage of her in this respect. MP III 17 470 25
with all the regard and respect which a harmless old lady, E I 3 21 4
or frighten those who might hate her, into outward respect. E I 3 21 4
In that respect Mrs. Weston's loss had been important. E I 4 26 1
But in every respect as she saw more of her, she approved E I 4 26 1
Her next beginning was, "in one respect, perhaps, Mr. E I 4 34 41
42
She could not respect his eye, but his love and his E I 6 47 26
In what respect? E I 7 51 7
judged it best in every respect, safest and kindest, to E I 8 57 1
had a sort of habitual respect for his judgment in general, E I 8 65 50
slightly touched upon his respect for Miss Smith as her E I 15 130 28
error with respect to your views, till this moment. E I 15 131 34
any thing but grateful respect to her as Harriet's friend. E I 16 134 5
in such a mark of respect to him on the present occasion. E I 18 146 16
Respect would be added to affection. E I 18 147 18
Respect for right conduct is felt by every body. E I 18 147 18
rather negligent in that respect, and as not contributing E II 1 155 2
thing but compassion and respect; especially, if to every E II 2 167 13
and seemed to mean always to speak of her with respect. E II 7 205 2
this morning was in another respect particularly opportune. E II 7 206 5
She was received with a cordial respect which could not E II 8 214 12
and as, in every respect, it suited Emma best to lead, she E II 8 227 85
amusement, and much less compunction with respect to her.-- E II 10 243 22
affection, gratitude, and respect which was natural and E II 13 265 5
I have it not--but I know how to prize and respect it.-- E II 13 269 16
In one respect Mrs. Elton grew even worse than she had E II 15 281 3
treats her with all the respect which she has a claim to. E II 15 286 23
"In that respect how unlike dear Mrs. Elton, who wants to E II 15 288 39
how Selina feels with respect to sleeping at an inn, you E II 18 306 12
The difference in that respect of Richmond and London was E III 1 317 10
As I am happily quite an altered creature in one respect, E III 4 337 4
Emma felt an increasing respect for it, as the residence E III 6 358 35
And I hope she will be better off in one respect, and not E III 9 387 10
for her society, and testify respect and consideration. E III 9 389 16
of placidity, which I can neither comprehend nor respect." E III 10 397 46
of it, as a token of respect to the wife he had so very E III 11 403 2
Some portion of respect for herself, however, in spite of E III 11 408 33
She thought well of Frank in almost every respect; and, E III 12 420 14
In one respect he is the object of my envy." E III 13 428 25
With respect to her father, it was a question soon E III 14 435 4
With the greatest respect, and the warmest friendship, do E III 14 438 8
In one respect, my good fortune is undoubted, that of E III 14 443 8
would not find in any respect objectionable; it was, that E III 15 449 31
Emma; and it was in every respect so proper, suitable, and E III 17 467 31
a connexion, and in one respect, one point of the highest E III 17 467 31
into admiration and respect, by contemplating the limited P III 1 3 1
the constant object of his warmest respect and devotion. P III 1 4 5
to be on her guard with respect to her flower-garden. P III 3 18 8
poor dick, and very high respect for his character, P III 6 52 33
Mary had no feelings to make her respect her sister's in a P III 7 60 32
open look, in no respect lessening his personal advantages. P III 7 61 34
of his having, in every respect, a better curacy; of his P III 9 78 19
is so very clever; but I respect her amazingly, and wish P III 12 103 4
more than answered their expectations in every respect. P IV 3 137 4
her sense of personal respect to her father prevented her. P IV 5 158 20
It would have been very unpleasant to me in every respect. P IV 9 193 11
I consider him with great respect. P IV 9 196 33
a scruple was there on his side, with respect to her birth. P IV 9 202 66
But she was too ignorant and giddy for respect, and he had P IV 9 211 101
In every other respect, in looking around her, or P IV 10 212 1
Mr. Elliot looking up with so much respect!" P IV 10 231 5
or in some respect saying what should not be said." P IV 11 234 30
Many thanks my dear Tom for the kindness with respect to S 5 386 1
kindness, on the other grateful & affectionate respect.-- S 6 392 1

RESPECTABILITY (16)
Brandon seems a man of great worth and respectability. SS III 4 290 36
37
Consider Mr. Collins's respectability, and Charlotte's PP II 1 135 12
and respectability which he will probably never reach." PP II 10 187 40
Our importance, our respectability in the world, must be PP II 18 231 18
have preserved the respectability of his daughters, even PP II 19 236 2
indicated respectability, was not to be hastily rejected. PP III 2 264 14
him in situations of respectability, he would have been MP I 1 3 1
such an addition of respectability and influence, and very MP II 3 201 22
own family, people of respectability as they are, she may MP III 16 457 29
In respectability of character, there can be no doubt that E III 18 473 24
and promoted his real respectability for seventeen years; P III 1 4 6
old country family of respectability and large fortune, P III 1 6 10
Kellynch-Hall has a respectability in itself, which cannot P III 2 12 4
Their respectability was as dear to her as her own; and a P III 5 36 19
properly; nothing of respectability, of harmony, of good- P IV 12 251 10
had all the beauty & respectability which an abundance of S 12 426 1

RESPECTABLE (83)
whom that great word "respectable" is always given, & I am LS 2 245 1
or poor, and a very respectable man, though his name was NA I 1 13 1
and of a very respectable family in Gloucestershire. NA I 3 30 52
attended her, a very respectable man, and one in whom she NA II 9 196 25
whole family to the General in a most respectable light. NA II 15 245 12
they had lived in so respectable a manner, as to engage SS I 1 3 1
The son, a steady respectable young man, was amply SS I 1 3 2
been made still more respectable than he was:--he might SS I 1 5 7
discovered an ancient respectable looking mansion, which, SS I 9 40 2
you say, that he is a respectable young man, and one whose SS I 9 44 24
I consider him, on the contrary, as a very respectable man, SS I 10 51 25
They are a very respectable family, Mr. Ferrars; and SS I 16 88 40
might have rendered so respectable; but she saw, with less SS I 22 127 2
the care of a very respectable woman, residing in SS II 9 208 28
the prospect of a very respectable establishment in life." SS II 11 223 18
in securing so respectable and agreeable a neighbour, and SS III 3 283 20

Allow me to congratulate you on having so respectable and SS III 4 289 28
The connection was certainly a respectable one, and SS III 13 367 23
every thing in such respectable and excellent condition!-- SS III 14 375 9
They were of a respectable family in the north of England; PP I 4 15 11
a brother settled in London in a respectable line of trade. PP I 7 28 2
I knew it to be a most respectable, agreeable corps, and PP I 16 79 23
man of character, to respectable people, can have any evil PP I 17 87 13
Mr. Wickham is by no means a respectable young man. PP I 18 95 50
of elegance which consists in tormenting a respectable man. PP I 19 108 20
You wish to think all the world respectable, and are hurt PP II 1 135 11
To work in his garden was one of his most respectable PP II 5 156 4
"Lady Catherine is a very respectable, sensible woman PP II 5 157 8
Mr. Wickham is the son of a very respectable man, who had PP II 12 199 5
with you, and all your respectable family, in your present PP III 6 296 11
on the father's, from respectable, honourable, and ancient, PP III 14 356 50
I know that you could be neither happy nor respectable, PP III 17 376 35
objection, and a more respectable, though less economical MP I 1 8 9
would extend its respectable alliances; and the character MP I 2 20 33
fair report of being very respectable, agreeable people. MP I 3 24 6
but respectable looking, and has many good rooms. MP I 6 56 26
right is the steward's house; he is a very respectable man. MP I 8 82 34
It is not there, that respectable people of any MP I 9 93 49
sermons, and is very respectable, I see him to be an MP I 11 111 28
respectable author than in chattering in words of our own. MP I 13 125 18
been done in so many respectable families, and by so many MP I 13 128 38
as one might suppose a respectable old country family had MP II 7 243 27
and see only the respectable, elegant, modernized, and MP II 7 248 47
chosen so well, his constancy has a respectable stamp. MP III 2 330 14
respectable mother of nine children, on a small income. MP III 8 390 5
her influence do not make him cease to be respectable!"-- MP III 13 424 4
London very much at war with all respectable attachments. MP III 14 433 12
to Edmund had been respectable, the most respectable part MP III 14 433 12
respectable, the most respectable part of her character, MP III 14 433 12
Highbury, and born of a respectable family, which for the E I 2 15 1
"I have no doubt of his being a very respectable young man. E I 4 29 16
well-meaning, respectable young man, with any deficiency E I 4 35 44
Mr. Martin is a very respectable young man, but I cannot E I 8 61 37
provision at all, and certainly no respectable relations. E I 8 61 38
married to a respectable, intelligent gentleman-farmer!" E I 8 62 40
Let her marry Robert Martin, and she is safe, respectable, E I 8 64 47
Elton is a very good sort of man, and a very respectable E I 8 66 53
fortune, the respectable establishment, the rise in the E I 9 75 27
good fortune, is always respectable, and may be as E I 10 85 19
domestic, and respectable in his private character; but E I 11 92 5
could have made it more respectable in Emma's eyes--and E I 17 142 9
supplying the means of respectable subsistance hereafter. E II 2 164 5
The Coles were very respectable in their way, but they E II 7 207 6
do them, would be to give Jane such a respectable home." E II 8 225 77
delighted to see the respectable length of the set as it E III 2 325 32
as she viewed the respectable size and style of the E III 6 358 35
have made her happy and respectable in the line of life to E III 11 413 49
They were both so truly respectable in their happiness, so E III 12 418 5
She would be respectable and happy; and Emma admitted her E III 19 482 4
rise of the ancient and respectable family, in the usual P III 1 3 3
4
Mr. and Mrs. Musgrove's respectable forms in the usual P III 6 46 12
worthy of her brother; "and a very respectable family. P III 10 92 47
have some active, respectable young man, as a resident P III 12 103 3
Wallis, a highly respectable man, perfectly the gentleman, P IV 3 139 8
character--respectable references--wishing to form a S 1 366 1
The Heywoods were a thoroughly respectable family, & every S 2 370 1
home;--that he was of a respectable family, & easy though S 2 371 1
or respectable acquaintance to sons or daughters. S 2 374 1
it might have: many a respectable family, many a careful S 4 382 1
the other, a most respectable girls Boarding school, or S 5 387 1
nature meant them to be respectable I cannot tell,--but S 7 402 1
some respectable family determined on a long residence.-- S 9 406 1
was anxious for a respectable introduction--& Mrs C. S 10 419 1

RESPECTABLE-LOOKING (1)
The housekeeper came; a respectable-looking, elderly woman, PP III 1 246 5

RESPECTABLY (5)
with having so respectably settled her young charge, NA I 8 55 10
she had lived to see respectably married, and she had now SS I 8 36 1
Mrs E. was sitting respectably attired in one of the two W 323 3
girl; and I should be happy to see her respectably settled. E I 15 131 35
her at twenty-two, so respectably removed from the P III 4 28 7

RESPECTED (19)
of them more beloved and respected in their different NA I 4 32 2
example; by no means respected in their own neighbourhood, NA II 15 246 12
he was, in general, well respected; for he conducted SS I 1 5 7
Our respected father, as you well know, bequeathed all the SS II 11 225 35
and her character ought to have been respected by me. SS III 8 322 36
A sigh accompanied these words, which Emma respected in W 316 2
you that I have your respected mother's permission for PP I 19 105 8
Wherever you and Jane are known, you must be respected and PP II 18 231 20
She respected, she esteemed, she was grateful to him, she PP III 2 266 16
Her feelings ought to be respected. MP I 16 155 14
on people or subjects which she wished to be respected. MP II 4 208 11
more he would have been respected! for people are never MP II 5 220 30
never respected when they step out of their proper sphere. MP II 5 220 30
was peculiarly to be respected, and they went down their MP II 10 278 20
opinions of the man she loved and respected, as her own.-- MP III 6 367 6
of her father were so respected by Mrs. John Knightley, E I 11 92 3
He should have respected even unreasonable scruples, had E III 15 446 20
her nearly as well, and respected her a great deal more P III 6 43 4
to live, and they only deserved to be respected and loved. P III 11 99 19

RESPECTFUL (9)
addressing herself with respectful form, as much to Mrs. NA I 14 114 49
inquiries after their mother were respectful and attentive. SS II 11 221 7
from it; for her respectful humility, assiduous attentions, SS III 14 375 10
I remain, dear sir, with respectful compliments to your PP I 13 63 12
all that was respectful, grateful, confiding, and tender. MP I 4 37 8
respectful manners, and such as confirmed him his friend. MP II 6 233 16
requesting, in most respectful terms, to be allowed to E I 3 22 7
the want of respectful forbearance towards her father. E I 11 93 5
a peculiar degree of respectful compassion, was not very S 10 413 1

RESPECTFULLY (2)
be most gratefully and respectfully remembered to her, and SS III 2 278 30
He was on foot, and after looking very respectfully at her, E I 4 31 27

RESPECTING (16)
friend, for your advice respecting Mr De Courcy, which I LS 10 257 1
The remembrance of Mr. Allen's opinion, respecting young NA II 5 156 5
by still loving and respecting that sister, in spite of SS I 19 104 11
Mrs. Palmer's information respecting Willoughby was not SS I 20 116 59
conduct in an affair, respecting which she had never been SS II 3 155 6
was now finally settled respecting his marriage with Miss SS II 8 199 37
so liberally bestowed, respecting each circumstance, I PP II 12 196 5
Lady Catherine had many other questions to ask respecting PP II 14 212 16
She had always seen it with pain; but respecting his PP II 19 236 2
"He was certainly right in respecting such feeling; he was MP I 17 159 6
plans, and solicitudes respecting that long thought of, MP II 6 234 18
in general, considered respecting her, it would very much MP II 9 267 22
The forbearance of her family on a point, respecting which MP III 2 330 14
There were wishes at Randalls respecting Emma's destiny, E I 5 41 31
good an understanding respecting the Eltons, and that E III 3 332 1
to compare opinions respecting the place, but especially P IV 3 143 19

RESPECTIVE (7)
since their respective marriages, and that many years ago. NA I 4 31 2
To begin perfect happiness at the respective ages of NA II 16 252 7
respective homes, to meet, by appointment, on the road. SS III 6 301 3
of their respective houses; and what is to divide them? PP III 14 356 50
satisfaction of their respective families, and of the MP I 4 39 11
one another by every circumstance of your respective homes. E I 9 75 25
How, in all the peculiar disadvantages of their respective P IV 8 191 51

RESPECTS (31)
& he is in other respects so very eligible a match for LS 20 276 5
Edgar's Buildings, and pay their respects to Mrs. Thorpe. NA I 7 47 18
"But I say, Miss Morland, I shall come and pay my respects NA I 15 123 40
intention of paying his respects to them, and, with a NA II 15 242 9
Marianne's abilities were, in many respects, quite equal SS I 1 6 12
in other respects irreproachable, I am ready to confess it. SS I 10 52 28
It is an engagement in some respects not prosperously SS I 15 81 44
had been, tho' in some respects unpleasantly, W 336 14
in time for me to pay my respects to him, which I am now PP I 18 97 57
had time to pay his respects to his friends in PP II 1 133 1
morning he hastened to Rosings to pay his respects. PP II 7 170 7
her with his best respects to all her family, not PP II 15 217 8
wish to have your humble respects delivered to them, with PP II 15 217 9
have chosen so much more advantageously in many respects. PP III 13 349 47
sixteen in some respects too much like his sister at ten." MP I 3 33 64
by all means to pay his respects to Sir Thomas without MP II 1 176 3
that he might pay his respects to the old gentleman MP II 1 177 5
was anxious to pay his respects to Sir Thomas, and at MP II 2 192 11
to go over and pay your respects to them; and I could send MP II 7 245 32
proving himself, in many respects, the very reverse of E I 16 135 6
house, was to pay her respects to them as they sat E II 8 213 6
the last to pay her respects; and she made a point of E II 14 270 2
bride--I ought to have paid my respects to her if possible. E II 14 280 56
you be so anxious to pay your respects to a bride? E II 14 280 57
He promised to join me here, and pay his respects to you." E III 16 455 21
In all other respects, her visit began and proceeded very P III 6 46 12
"Mary is good-natured enough in many respects," said she; " P III 10 88 28
a point of paying his respects to Lady Russell, and sat P IV 2 134 29
lost such an opportunity of paying his respects to her. P IV 3 143 19
man, and in many respects I think highly of him," said P IV 5 159 24
"It will be more painful to me in some respects to be in P IV 9 208 93

RESPITE (2)
feeling a little respite of her weekly cares, and only MP III 11 408 2
to hope for a little respite of suffering;--she was now in E III 14 434 1

RESPONSES (1)
be pitied;" were the kind responses of listening sympathy. MP I 13 122 3

RESPONSIBILITY (1)
accent--"in such an office of high responsibility!" MP III 4 351 33

RESPONSIBLE (2)
for having a choice of tenants, very responsible tenants. P III 3 17 1
proof of his being a most responsible, eligible tenant. P III 3 21 18

REST (296)
me fixed at this place for the rest of the winter. LS 2 244 1
receiving it so favourably, & for the rest of his conduct. LS 25 293 4
my determination as to the rest, I shall probably put that LS 25 294 4
& the rest of his family, by making her marry Sir James. LS 26 295 1
is in the country for the rest of his life--& you know it is LS 38 306 1
information--amongst the rest, that -----"trifles NA I 1 16 7
in motion for tea, and they must squeeze out like the rest. NA I 2 21 10
rest, "how excessively like her brother Miss Morland is!" NA I 4 32 4
"Thank you; but will not your horse want rest?" NA I 7 47 26
"Rest! he has only come three-and-twenty miles to-day; all NA I 7 47 27
horses so much as rest; nothing knocks them up so soon. NA I 7 47 27
I believe: and how do you like the rest of the family?" NA I 7 50 45
of some, the growth of the rest, and other family matters, NA I 7 51 54
The rest of the evening she found very dull; Mr. Tilney NA I 8 59 38
the rest for a minute; but he will soon know his master. NA I 9 62 9
forgotten; and all the rest of his conversation, or rather NA I 9 66 31
the rest of the evening; so I charge you not to expect it. NA I 10 70 1
Isabella smiled incredulously, and talked the rest of the NA I 10 71 7
themselves from the rest of their party, they walked in NA I 10 71 8
If I could but have papa and mamma, and the rest of them NA I 10 79 56
good night's rest in the course of the next three months. NA I 11 90 65
honour of dining and spending the rest of the day with her. NA I 13 103 28
with Johnson and Blair all the rest of the way." NA I 14 108 14
for the sake of being able to read all the rest of it. NA I 14 110 27
rest, there was nothing to regret for half an instant.-- NA I 15 116 2
and with whom I like, and the devil take the rest, say I.-- NA I 15 123 44
house over my head, and what care I for all the rest? NA I 15 124 46
in good-nature yourself to all the rest of the world." NA II 1 133 28
for that period, the rest of her life was at such a NA II 2 138 1
all the rest, this roof was to be the roof of an Abbey!-- NA II 2 141 11
dwelling although the rest was decayed, or of its standing NA II 2 141 13
seeing him as well as the rest--but that we were ever NA II 3 145 13
was glad to rest altogether for present ease and comfort. NA II 3 148 29
his son's curricle for the rest of the journey:--"the day NA II 5 156 4
she is always lodged apart from the rest of the family. NA II 5 158 15
will retire to rest, and get a few hours' unquiet slumber. NA II 5 159 19
part of the hanging more violently agitated than the rest. NA II 5 159 19
looked at her, spent the rest of his time in scolding his NA II 6 165 6
to peruse every line before she attempted to rest. NA II 6 169 11
And the larger sheet, which had inclosed the rest, seemed NA II 7 172 2
and alarm, and robbed her of half her night's rest! NA II 7 172 2
the value of all the rest, for the purpose of mere NA II 8 184 4
of the house, than see all the finery of all the rest.-- NA II 8 185 5
see it, as well as all the rest of that side of the house; NA II 8 186 7
and yours preparing by rest for the future mischief." NA II 8 187 15
interest were the demands of his younger brother to rest? NA II 11 208 1
disengaged from the rest of it, stood the parsonage, a new- NA II 11 212 17
I believe if I could see you I should not mind the rest, NA II 12 216 2
but when a third night's rest had neither restored her NA II 15 240 2
Mr. John Dashwood had not the strong feelings of the rest SS I 1 5 6
Four bed-rooms and two garrets formed the rest of the SS I 6 28 2
of debating on the rest of the children, as Sir John would SS I 6 31 10
nothing to do but to marry all the rest of the world. SS I 8 36 1
Marianne herself had seen less of his person than the rest, SS I 9 43 11
share of his discourse to herself for the rest of his stay SS I 10 46 2
and all the rest of the party to get her a good hand. SS I 11 54 3
to be equally indifferent during the rest of their lives?" SS I 11 56 15
Among the rest there was one for Colonel Brandon;--he took SS I 13 63 3
which did not happen till after the return of all the rest. SS I 13 67 60
could give, and to the rest of the family it was the SS I 14 71 5
of ending there, where the rest of the day was spent by SS I 14 71 5
"Because," replied he, smiling, "among the rest of the SS I 16 88 36
"As moderate as those of the rest of the world, I believe. SS I 17 91 7
perceived her, he left the rest of the party to the SS I 19 105 13
her story, to receive the rest of the party; Lady SS I 19 106 21
I wanted her to stay at home and rest this morning, but SS I 19 107 29
He then made his bow and departed with the rest. SS I 19 108 39
The rest of the company soon dropt in. SS I 20 111 9
was a foundation for the rest, at once indisputable and SS II 1 139 1
upon, and we might trust to time and chance for the rest." SS II 2 149 25
to see him; but as to the rest of the family, it is a SS II 3 157 17
park, and were to quit it only with the rest of the family. SS II 3 158 22
I cannot rest--I shall not have a moment's peace till this SS II 6 177 13
from a long want of proper rest and food; for it was many SS II 7 185 16
if I can to go early to bed, for I am sure she wants rest." SS II 8 195 15
hoped, in a way to get some quiet rest before she left her. SS II 8 197 25
so much service to her as rest, if you will give me leave, SS II 8 198 28
Like half the rest of the world, if more than half there SS II 9 201 4
attendance, went out alone for the rest of the morning. SS II 9 203 10
her every day during the rest of her short life; I was SS II 9 207 26
the rest, for eight long months, was left to conjecture. SS II 9 209 28
acquit him than by all the rest; for it irritates her mind SS II 9 211 34
scenes as must prevent her ever knowning a moment's rest. SS II 10 214 6
The rest of Mrs. Palmer's sympathy was shewn in procuring SS II 10 215 11
burst out, and for the rest of the day, she was in a state SS II 10 217 17
and we spent the rest of the day with Mrs. Ferrars. SS II 11 221 9
and sit down among the rest; though her spirits retained SS II 12 236 42

and happy above all the rest, in the absence of Marianne, SS III 1 260 8
that little;-- for the rest of the party none at all. SS III 1 260 9
south-east, could fondly rest on the farthest ridge of SS III 6 302 8
premises; and the rest of the morning was easily whiled SS III 6 303 10
For the rest of his character and habits, they were marked, SS III 6 304 15
and his conceit, to rest with complacency on the SS III 6 305 15
of wildness than in the rest, where the trees were the SS III 6 305 17
throat, a good night's rest was to cure her entirely; and SS III 6 306 17
the apothecary, and to watch by her the rest of the night. SS III 7 312 17
conclusion to take some rest before her mother's arrival, SS III 7 315 27
might lead you, or the rest of the neighbourhood, to SS III 8 324 42
But the rest, which one night entirely sleepless, and many SS III 9 334 5
"His character, however," answered Elinor, "does not rest SS III 9 337 17
body alike strengthened by rest, she looked and spoke with SS III 10 343 8
of the other, as to lead by degrees to all the rest. SS III 13 364 11
His attendance was by this means secured, and the rest SS III 14 376 11
must talk to me all the rest of the day, without stopping, W 341 19
You must come to Croydon as well as the rest, & see what W 353 26
perhaps surpassing the rest; though when the first tumult PP I 2 7 23
The rest of the evening was spent in conjecturing how soon PP I 2 8 28
other lady, and spent the rest of the evening in walking PP I 3 11 6
hating each other for the rest of our lives, for a whole PP I 7 30 17
He leaves out half his words, and blots the rest." PP I 10 48 22
manner, and the rest from the pride of her nephew, who PP I 16 84 58
rest of the ladies their share of Mr. Wickham's attentions. PP I 16 84 59
To the rest of the family they paid little attention; PP I 17 86 9
story, and has learnt the rest from that friend himself, I PP I 18 96 55
The rest of the evening brought her little amusement. PP I 18 102 73
detached from the rest, and talked only to each other. PP I 18 103 75
were transferred for the rest of the day to Miss Lucas, PP I 21 115 1
an awkward pause, they returned to the rest of the family. PP I 22 125 18
points she principally dwelt during the rest of the day. PP I 21 127 5
Jane could attend to the rest of the letter, she found PP II 1 133 2
she must wait for her own visit there, to know the rest. PP II 3 147 19
to the rest, there is no occasion for any thing more. PP II 6 160 6
with thoughts that could rest on nothing, she walked on; PP II 13 205 3
thus self-attracted by the rest of her family;--and as she PP II 13 209 11
In the afternoon Lydia was urgent with the rest of the PP II 16 223 25
people as to the rest of his conduct, who will believe me? PP II 17 226 23
authorizing us to lock her up for the rest of her life." PP II 18 232 20
The rest of the evening passed with the appearance, on his PP II 18 235 39
the rest of the party with whom he had been travelling. PP III 1 256 61
of the rest, whether all her sisters were at Longbourn. PP III 2 262 9
You know him too well to doubt the rest. PP III 4 277 11
her aunt, and amongst the rest there were notes to be PP III 4 281 29
at heart, that I can get no rest by night nor by day. PP III 5 288 38
on knowing more than the rest of us, that in Lydia's last PP III 5 290 50
Elizabeth received her congratulations amongst the rest, PP III 7 307 50
and let my hand just rest upon the window frame, so that PP III 9 316 8
my dear Lizzy, you may rest perfectly assured, that your PP III 10 324 2
in a few moments after seated with the rest of the party. PP III 12 342 26
Lady Catherine would not come in again and rest herself. PP III 14 358 74
The surprise of the rest of the family, on hearing who PP III 15 361 5
The rest of his letter is only about his dear Charlotte's PP III 15 364 22
Were it known to the rest of my family, I should not have PP III 16 365 3
of course, I could not rest till I knew the particulars. PP III 16 366 5
to think meanly of all the rest of the world, to wish at PP III 16 369 24
informed woman for the rest of her life; though perhaps it PP III 19 385 1
one among them who ran more in her thoughts than the rest. MP I 2 15 12
to her brother, which delighted her beyond all the rest. MP I 2 16 20
Of the rest she saw nothing; nobody seemed to think of her MP I 2 21 34
Without any display of doing more than the rest, or any MP I 2 21 34
the effort of quitting the rest of his family, and of MP I 3 32 62
when they called away the rest of the family; and as Miss MP I 4 35 6
She dined at the parsonage, with the rest of you, which MP I 5 48 30
Mrs. Rushworth while the rest of you walked about and MP I 6 62 58
The rest of the way is such as it ought to be. MP I 8 82 34
While this was passing, the rest of the party being MP I 9 88 19
manners of a large congregation for the rest of the week? MP I 9 92 46
I imagine, is a pretty fair sample of the rest." MP I 9 93 48
not what they ought to be, so are the rest of the nation." MP I 9 93 49
all the rest of his days but eat, drink, and grow fat. MP I 11 110 23
of the inclination of the rest; and though nothing was MP I 13 124 13
Edmund, and I'll take care of the rest of the family." MP I 13 127 27
fine tragic parts in the rest of the Dramatis Personae. MP I 14 131 6
And as for the rest, they may be filled up by any body. MP I 14 132 7
and was hoping to have it pressed on her by the rest. MP I 14 133 11
your conduct must be law to the rest of the party." MP I 15 140 13
to harangue all the rest upon a subject of this kind.-- MP I 15 140 14
Learn part, and we will teach you all the rest. MP I 15 146 50
Let her choose for herself as well as the rest of us.-- MP I 15 147 54
her in a determined denial in spite of all the rest? MP I 16 153 3
before her as well as the rest; and so decided to her eye MP I 18 164 2
and being able to follow the prompter through the rest. MP I 18 166 4
quite as well off as the rest, was evident by the manner MP I 18 166 6
Her going roused the rest; and at the same moment, the two MP II 1 176 3
that was endured by the rest, by the right of a MP II 1 176 4
her attention and all the rest of her sofa to her husband. MP II 1 179 9
Then turning away towards any or all of the rest, he MP II 1 185 29
and was obliged to rest satisfied with the conviction that MP II 2 190 8
of the regard of all the rest of you," said Fanny with MP II 3 199 14
The rest might wait. MP II 3 202 26
more wonderful than the rest, I do think it is memory. MP II 4 208 12
to say that it had honour from all the rest of the party." MP II 5 225 53
remained undisturbed the rest of the evening, except when MP II 5 227 68
the coast clear of the rest of the family, said, with a MP II 6 229 1
never to see my cards; and Mr. Crawford does all the rest." MP II 7 240 12
of the rest, till some of the rest began to think of them. MP II 7 249 49
of the evening, which the rest of the family were looking MP II 8 256 13
more frequently placed before her eyes than the rest. MP II 8 258 17
have allowed him an hour's rest before he must have got MP II 9 266 21
and taking an arm of each, they followed with the rest. MP II 10 275 9
communications; the rest was only a languid "yes--yes-- MP II 11 283 4
A good night's rest improved her spirits. MP II 11 283 7
to whom it must relate, and am in no hurry for the rest. MP II 12 293 11
As soon as her eagerness could rest in silence, he was as MP II 12 293 16
thought he was wishing to speak to her unheard by the rest. MP II 13 306 27
The rest of your note I know means nothing; but I am so MP II 13 307 31
You will see him with the rest of us, in the same manner, MP III 2 331 16
Compared with me, all the rest were blameless. MP III 4 350 26
undertake the part, we must not be surprised at the rest." MP III 4 350 28
You will supply the rest; and a most fortunate man he is MP III 4 351 32
enough to reserve the rest till they might be secure of MP III 5 357 6
when once with her again, Fanny could not doubt the rest.-- MP III 6 367 4
for Edmund would never rest till she had read the chief of MP III 7 376 4
But here, one subject swallowed up all the rest. MP III 7 382 29
Ay, Sam's voice louder than all the rest! MP III 7 383 30
for though a good night's rest, a pleasant morning, the MP III 8 388 1
She is tender, and not used to rough it like the rest of MP III 8 388 2
Charles, occupied all the rest of her maternal solicitude, MP III 8 389 4
the stairs were never at rest, nothing was done without a MP III 8 392 11
been yet more ashamed of her father, than of all the rest. MP III 10 400 6
Fanny was most conveniently in want of rest. MP III 10 403 15
Fanny was out of spirits all the rest of the day. MP III 11 413 31
There was no possibility of rest. MP III 15 441 20
could not be kept from the rest of the family. MP III 16 450 10
in addition to all the rest, when they were in reason to MP III 16 452 15
to tolerable comfort, and to have done with all the rest. MP III 17 461 1
if she had spent all the rest of her life at Hartfield. E I 1 7 10
was no rest for his benevolent nerves till it was all gone. E I 2 19 14
and any one of them might do for any one of the rest. E I 6 45 21
at Mrs. Goddard's all the rest of her life--or, at least, (E I 8 64 47

poor creatures all the rest of the day; and yet, who can E I 10 87 25
the rest is empty sympathy, only distressing to ourselves." E I 10 87 30
Square is very different from almost all the rest. E I 12 103 37
of thinking that the rest of the visit could not possibly E I 14 119 6
estate, to which all the rest of Highbury belonged; but E I 16 136 9
should have stopped, and left the rest to time and chance. E I 16 137 11
never failed him during the rest of his stay at Hartfield. E I 16 139 20
and conversation during the rest of their lonely evening. E I 17 141 4
and repressing imagination all the rest of her life. E I 17 142 10
not another syllable of communication could rest with him. E II 3 172 23
as their visit included all the rest of the morning. E II 6 196 2
Emma had as much reason to be satisfied with the rest of E II 8 214 12
took their turn; and the rest of the dinner passed away; E II 8 219 43
The rest of the gentlemen being now in the room, Emma E II 8 222 54
at her brother's, and must be invited with the rest. E II 11 248 9
her; but she took the compliment, and forgave the rest. E II 11 250 19
the inclinations of the rest of the people as any body. E II 11 254 50
All the rest, in speculation at least, was perfectly E II 11 255 59
that all the rest of my time might be given to Hartfield. E II 12 261 32
33
joined to all the rest, made her think that she must be a E II 12 262 38
This appeal to her affections did more than all the rest. E II 13 268 13
"Yes; but we must not rest our claims on that distinction. E II 14 273 25
settled before the Campbells or I have any rest." E II 17 301 18
agreeable among the rest; and having satisfied the E II 17 303 24
moved away to make the rest of his friends happy by a E II 17 304 29
had threatened to ruin the rest of her evening, had been E III 3 332 1
were coming in during the rest of the day; and he had the E III 3 336 12
I deserve to be under a continual blush all the rest of my E III 4 339 13
superiority to all the rest of the world, with the E III 4 341 36
take his seat with the rest round the large modern E III 5 347 18
He remained at Hartfield after all the rest, his thoughts E III 5 349 26
The rest I leave to you. E III 6 355 18
Harriet distinct from the rest, quietly leading the way. E III 6 360 40
water, will make you nearly on a par with the rest of us." E III 6 365 65
The rest of the party were now returning, and all were E III 6 366 74
It did not seem to touch the rest of the party equally; E III 7 371 35
36
acquaintance, and rued it all the rest of his life!" E III 7 372 40
How it might be considered by the rest of the party, she E III 8 377 1
are her remains at rest in the family vault, than her E III 10 398 55
In addition to all the rest, there had been the shock of E III 10 399 57
to draw her from the rest to himself--and at first, he had E III 11 410 35
The rest of the day, the following night, were hardly E III 11 411 43
to take place, on her must rest all the reproach of having E III 11 413 47
The rest had been the work of the moment, the immediate E III 13 432 40
enough to make the rest of my letter what it ought to be.-- E III 14 440 8
given; time and continual repetition must do the rest.-- E III 17 466 30
All equality of alliance must rest with Elizabeth; for P III 1 6 10
all the rest of his family and acquaintance were growing. P III 1 6 11
and expected all the rest of the year; but he never came. P III 1 8 15
to come back sick and cross for the rest of the day."-- P III 6 44 8
The rest was all tranquillity; till just as they were P III 6 49 23
24
letters; all the rest had been mere applications for money. P III 6 51 30
when the child might be at rest for the night, and kindly P III 7 58 20
very superior in cultivation and manners to all the rest. P III 9 74 5
rest of the party waited for them at the top of the hill. P III 10 86 18
of her fatigue, and his resolution to give her rest. P III 10 91 42
He stood his chance for the rest--wrote up for leave of P III 12 108 28
But as to the rest;--as to the others;--if one stays to P III 12 114 61
Henrietta remained with Louisa; but all the rest of the P IV 2 133 27
had never seen any of the rest of the family, and the P IV 4 148 12
affairs, no health to make all the rest supportable. P IV 5 154 8
She goes into the warm Bath to-morrow, and for the rest of P IV 5 157 16
time, more than all the rest of the world put together." P IV 9 194 16
rest of my life, to be only yours "truly, "Wm. Elliot." P IV 9 203 73
all the rest of her astonishment in a convenient silence. P IV 10 213 8
and give them all the rest of the day; but her spirits had P IV 10 227 68
say nothing of all the rest of the field, men, women, S 1 364 1
accept such a home for the rest of her stay as their S 3 378 1
sister Susan's, are more distressing than all the rest.--" S 5 388 1
as any thing requiring rest, & talked of going home again S 6 390 1
much as possible from the rest of the party & to give her S 7 396 1
than all the rest--& very delicate health.-- S 9 409 1
Your ancle wants rest. S 9 411 1
to various disorders;--the rest of their sufferings was S 10 412 1
much worse than all the rest, must have been the sort of S 11 420 1
we shall both go to our rooms for the rest of the day."-- S 12 424 1
The rest was common enquiries & remarks, with kind notice S 12 425 1

RESTED (7)
on which her eye first rested was an opera, procured for SS III 10 342 7
and on that he rested for the residue of their income. SS III 13 369 33
be her husband, might then have rested in its proper place. PP III 8 308 1
"I shall soon be rested," said Fanny; "to sit in the shade MP I 9 96 72
Fanny said she was rested, and would have moved too, but MP I 9 96 76
and compassion--and then rested with lightened feelings on E III 9 388 13
rested, as it now almost wholly did, on Isabella's letters. E III 17 463 15

RESTING (3)
"I must move," said she, "resting fatigues me.-- MP I 9 96 73
every possibility of it, resting upon her embarrassment MP III 3 336 7
the advantage of resting herself a quarter of an hour at P III 10 86 17

RESTLESS (18)
the luxury of a raised, restless, and frightened NA I 7 51 54
You men have such restless curiosity! NA I 8 57 18
When does she try to avoid society, or appear restless and SS I 8 39 18
Restless and dissatisfied every where, her sister could SS II 4 165 24
while Marianne, too restless for employment, too anxious SS II 5 172 39
long together; and the restless state of Marianne's mind SS II 7 180 5
give her ease; and in restless pain of mind and body she SS II 7 191 65
A very restless and feverish night, however, disappointed SS III 7 307 2
more heavy, restless, and uncomfortable than before. SS III 7 310 9
without an effort, the restless, unquiet thoughtfulness in SS III 11 349 3
flew about the house in restless ecstacy, calling for PP II 18 230 12
and fatigued, restless and agitated, yet feeling, in spite MP II 10 280 33
four days more, she was in a most restless, anxious state. MP III 12 418 5
still greater evil of a restless, officious companion, too MP III 14 432 10
either in themselves or in any restless attendance on them. E I 11 92 3
her as anxious and restless about the Eltons as before.-- E II 13 267 9
the broodings of this restless agitation, to let Mrs. Clay P IV 10 228 70
a spirit of restless activity, & the glory of doing more S 10 412 1

RESTLESSLY (1)
Catherine was restlessly miserable; she could almost have NA I 12 93 4

RESTLESSNESS (4)
with Edmund; and what was the restlessness of Mrs. Norris? MP II 10 273 5
Vanity, extravagance, love of change, restlessness of E II 7 205 1
were evidently fluttered; there was restlessness about him. E III 1 316 4
there was a restlessness, which showed a mind not at ease. E III 2 320 7

RESTORATION (5)
Your restoration to peace will, I doubt not, speedily LS 37 306 1
immediately, as her restoration to health would probably PP I 9 41 2
They owed the restoration of Lydia, her character, every PP III 10 326 3
Their manner of living, even when the restoration of peace PP III 19 387 8
might rather assist the restoration of friendship, that E I 12 98 2

RESTORATIVE (2)
her mother was her only restorative to calmness; and at SS II 3 158 21
hurricane a bad restorative of the nerves, which Louisa's P IV 2 134 30

RESTORATIVES (2)
and the return of Harriet were very adequate restoratives. E I 8 67 56
assistance, cordials, restoratives were supplied by her P III 12 111 50

RESTORE (15)
to her faults, you will restore me to happiness; but if LS 12 261 6

however was not enough to restore her composure, till she NA I 13 101 25
would at least restore peace to every heart but his own. NA II 4 150 1
that a few days would restore her sister to health, yet, SS III 7 307 3
Nothing could restore him with a faith unbroken--a SS III 11 349 1
of the other two, and restore general good humour. MP I 10 104 51
day--for every day would restore the knowledge of MP II 13 308 36
of money might, perhaps, restore peace for ever on the MP III 9 396 7
as I can, impatient to restore every body, not greatly in MP III 17 461 1
not by a vain attempt to restore what never could be MP III 17 465 13
to restore him to the relish of his own smooth gruel. E I 12 105 51
look as she thought must restore him to his senses; and E I 15 125 6
save your health and credit, and restore your tranquility. E II 13 268 11
12
and to have forgotten to restore them, he had been obliged E III 3 334 7
she was forced to seem to restore her attention to the P IV 8 188 41
RESTORED (35)
My understanding is at length restored, & teaches me no LS 36 306 2
and a good appetite of her own, restored her to peace. NA II 6 165 6
the General was shortly restored to his complacency, and NA II 11 213 20
night's rest had neither restored her cheerfulness, NA II 15 240 2
If, indeed, it could ever be restored to our poor little SS I 2 9 7
look, voice, and manner, restored to all her usual SS II 3 158 20
recollection, all her good spirits were restored by it. SS II 5 167 3
the spirits of Elinor, restored to those of her sister, SS II 5 169 15
own room, where hartshorn restored her a little to herself. SS II 6 178 16
this public discovery, restored to its proper state, its SS III 2 270 1
Her former apprehensions, now with greater reason restored, SS III 7 313 20
Marianne restored to life, health, friends, and to her SS III 7 315 24
Marianne was restored to her from a danger in which, as SS III 9 335 7
which would then be restored, of their mutual pursuits and SS III 10 343 8
Margaret returned, and the family were again all restored SS III 11 352 20
regard and her society restored his mind to animation, and SS III 14 379 17
The boy in one moment restored to all his first delight-- W 331 11
immediately before them, restored Elizabeth to the PP I 8 35 1
Mrs. Bennet was restored to her usual querulous serenity, PP II 19 238 6
for an arrangement which restored him to his share of the MP I 8 80 28
the remembrance, and restored to its proper state. MP II 2 187 2
this period more nearly restored to what it had been in MP II 7 238 1
this reflection quickly restored so much of her good MP II 8 253 4
that, could I have restored her to what she had appeared MP III 16 458 30
what never could be restored, be affording his sanction to MP III 17 465 13
These feelings rapidly restored his comfort, while Mrs. E I 18 144 3
and ease were generally restored, Emma said, "the arrival E II 8 218 38
39
her attention could be restored as before, she saw Frank E II 8 222 54
Upon my word, Perry has restored her in a wonderful short E III 16 454 17
Highbury, and was restored to the comforts of her beloved E III 19 483 7
and freshness of youth restored by the fine wind which had P III 12 104 6
More than former happiness would be restored. P IV 1 123 7
of reconciliation, to be restored to the footing of a P IV 3 139 7
in herself; of being restored to Kellynch, calling it her P IV 5 160 26
again, in seeing Anne restored to the rights of seniority, P IV 12 250 5
RESTORING (7)
in restoring peace than I ever intended to submit too. LS 25 292 1
restoring her spirits, that they should call on Mrs. Allen. NA II 14 236 18
restoring Marianne's peace of mind, and confirming her own. SS III 6 302 5
Darcy's explanation, by restoring Bingley to all the little she PP II 14 213 18
governed, were rapidly restoring her to all the little she MP I 15 147 56
I have the pleasure, madam, (to Mrs. Bates,) of restoring E II 10 242 15
yet a gentleness, which seemed almost restoring the past.-- P III 12 114 63
RESTRAIN (12)
would be nothing to restrain you from conversing with him NA I 10 78 37
Her grateful and gratified heart could hardly restrain its NA II 2 140 8
a friend to advise or restrain her, (for my father lived SS II 9 206 24
of such folly, could not restrain her eyes from being SS III 5 298 34
never exert himself to restrain the wild giddiness of his PP II 14 213 17
could hardly restrain her astonishment from being visible. PP III 2 263 10
of Mrs. Rushworth, and restrain her impatient feet to that MP I 9 90 36
he oftener endeavours to restrain himself than he would if MP I 11 112 30
no natural timidity to restrain any consequent wishes, she MP III 17 472 31
To restrain him as much as might be, by her own manners, E I 15 129 24
made her resolve to restrain herself when she did speak. E I 15 129 24
Her looks and words had nothing to restrain them. E II 17 304 28
RESTRAINED (10)
Lady Susan; the same restrained manners, the same timid LS 42 311 3
and pride had equally restrained her tears, but no sooner NA II 13 226 25
politeness had hitherto restrained, now burst forth SS I 13 66 52
as if her tears were even then restrained with difficulty. SS I 15 82 46
But as no such delicacy restrained her mother, an hour PP I 23 129 14
must have restrained her from venturing at disapprobation. MP I 18 170 24
who neither taught nor restrained her children, whose MP III 8 390 6
mother and Betsey were restrained from some excesses of MP III 9 395 4
Emma restrained her indignation, and only turned from her E II 8 220 47
She restrained herself, however, from any of the reproofs E II 14 276 34
RESTRAINING (2)
all possibility of restraining her feelings; and, hiding NA II 13 229 31
But if I can be the means of restraining the publicity of MP I 16 155 16
RESTRAINT (33)
merely an impatience of restraint, & a desire of escaping LS 17 271 7
or more obliging manners, when acting without restraint. LS 18 273 3
Well, pray do not let any body here be a restraint on you. NA I 11 90 63
Miss Tilney she felt no restraint; and, with the interest NA II 5 155 4
in moments of languor or restraint, a sense of general NA II 6 166 8
sensible of the restraint which the General's presence had NA II 13 220 1
and to aim at the restraint of sentiments which were not SS I 11 53 2
wishes and his own, and without any restraint on his time. SS I 19 101 1
Their presence was a restraint both on her and on Lucy. SS II 14 247 4
to enjoy his own thoughts, & gape without restraint.-- W 332 11
Between Elizabeth and Charlotte there was a restraint PP I 23 127 9
being now free from all restraint, his life was a life of PP II 12 201 5
and disdain of all restraint which mark Lydia's character. PP II 18 231 18
spoke likewise restraint, said, "I am afraid you have been PP III 4 278 20
As to what restraint the apprehension of disgrace in the PP III 5 283 8
They were relieved by it from all restraint; and without MP I 3 32 64
was carried on without restraint, and no other attempt MP I 4 39 12
The obligation of attendance, the formality, the restraint, MP I 9 87 15
that ha-ha, give me a feeling of restraint and hardship. MP I 10 99 17
her so much more above restraint, and leaving her less MP I 13 128 38
no longer under any restraint, were giving vent to their MP II 1 176 4
her feelings under the restraint of society; for general MP II 2 193 18
She was less and less able to endure the restraint which MP II 3 202 25
by an hatred of home, restraint, and tranquillity; by the MP II 3 202 26
They were no sooner in the hall than all restraint of MP III 5 357 6
without fear or restraint, to feel herself the equal of MP III 6 370 11
eating at table without restraint, and pulling every thing MP III 10 407 23
friends without any restraint, without even Julia; for MP III 16 450 8
be greater severity and restraint--made her hastily MP III 17 466 18
painful sensation of restraint or alarm, soon grew as dear MP III 17 473 33
her to impose any restraint; and the shadow of authority E I 1 5 3
being being under such restraint, as not to be able to E I 14 122 22
any restraint beyond her own scanty rule of good-breeding. E II 15 288 39
RESTRAINTS (7)
Did I imitate your forbearance, or lessen your restraints, SS III 10 346 28
suddenly on a footing which must do away all restraints. MP I 16 154 14
might have been said but for the restraints of propriety.-- E II 13 265 5
restraints, that it did not take her wholly by surprise. E III 14 438 8
to burst their usual restraints; and having talked of P III 11 100 23
from all the remaining restraints of widowhood, and leave P IV 5 159 22
with all the restraints of her situation, could do nothing P IV 11 238 44
RESTRICTED (1)
they must be again restricted to the other topics with E III 6 352 1
RESTRICTION (1)
at my mother's disposal, without any restriction whatever. SS I 2 11 20
RESTRICTIONS (5)
privations and restrictions that may have been imposed. MP III 1 313 12
table,--contradictions and restrictions every where. P III 2 13 6
such a range; but what restrictions I might impose on the P III 3 18 8
in the world, nor the restrictions of the present; neither P IV 5 153 7
his lectures and restrictions on her designs on Sir Walter. P IV 10 228 70
RESULT (45)
but Catherine heard neither the particulars nor the result. NA I 7 48 32
The result of her observations was not agreeable. NA II 4 149 1
would be the natural result of the suspected engagement, NA II 11 209 5
She was far from depending on that result of his SS I 4 22 18
appeared rather the result of some oppression of spirits, SS I 10 50 12
It would be the natural result of your affection for her. SS I 16 84 8
Some inconvenience to your friends, indeed, might result SS I 19 102 3
Should the result of her observations be unfavourable, she SS II 4 159 1
anxious to observe the result of it herself, she resolved SS III 7 310 9
was the general result, to think even of her sister. SS III 9 333 1
mind, which, in being the result as she trusted of serious SS III 10 341 6
pre-arranging its result, and a resolution of reviving the SS III 10 348 34
in the doorway for the result, as Emma with some amusement W 334 13
the whole visit, and the result of it was, that the PP I 9 45 35
said Miss Bingley;--"and pray what is the result?" PP I 11 57 26
of the moment, or are the result of previous study?" PP I 14 68 10
their interview, with the result of which he trusted he PP I 20 110 1
when no importance could result from the success of his PP III 2 263 10
It was the natural result of the conduct of each party, MP I 1 4 1
of the manners which result from their influence. MP I 9 92 45
conduct, perhaps, the result of good principles; the MP I 9 93 49
all that time; and the result of the whole was to her MP I 10 103 49
to-morrow evening, I should not be afraid of the result. MP II 1 185 28
the candid result of conviction, "I believe you are right. MP II 5 226 59
quiet independence, the result of it appeared the next MP II 8 252 1
anxious feelings, many doubting hours as to the result. MP II 8 255 10
speak, to utter something like an inquiry as to the result. MP II 9 268 28
to her alone," was the result of such thoughts as these; MP III 4 345 5
He gave this opinion as the result of the conversation, to MP III 5 356 2
detection; and the result of these looks was, that though MP III 11 409 7
I am less afraid of the result of reflection than of an MP III 13 422 2
were made known to him only in their sad result. MP III 17 464 10
All that followed was the result of her imprudence; and he MP III 17 468 21
Emma waited the result with impatience, but not without E I 7 53 22
The result of his thoughts appeared at last in these words. E I 8 66 50
result of real feeling, and she could not but pity them. E II 3 179 53
The result of his reverie was, "no, Emma, I do not think E II 15 288 36
another happy result--the cure of Harriet's infatuation.-- E III 3 332 1
The result of this distress was, that, with a much more E III 19 484 11
imprudence, lament the result, and Captain Wentworth's P IV 1 124 12
many changes, the result of which was favourable for her. P IV 8 189 46
the result of immediate feeling--"it is a period, indeed! P IV 10 225 60
result, not the cause of a revival of his warm attachment. P IV 11 243 68
result of the most correct opinions and well regarded mind. P IV 12 249 3
These feelings were not the result of any spirit of S 6 391 1
RESULTED (3)
a more important advantage to Mrs. Price resulted from it. MP I 1 5 4
One advantage resulted from it to Fanny; at the earnest MP I 17 159 6
home to himself, whence resulted her brother's disposition E I 11 97 27
RESULTING (5)
own!--a spirit too, resulting from a fancied sense of LS 25 292 1
of washing-bills, resulting from a long visit at NA II 16 251 5
going away, an intimacy resulting principally from Miss MP II 4 207 11
few slight differences, resulting principally from MP II 9 263 16
first answer to herself, resulting, she supposed, from E III 16 455 19
RESULTS (3)
of never marrying, results from an idea that the person E III 4 341 35
reference to the actual results of their case, which, as P III 4 29 8
she was sensible that results the most serious to his P III 5 34 12
RESUME (3)
occur again, if he would resume his book; but Mr. Collins, PP I 14 69 17
due time, to go down and resume her usual employments near MP II 9 265 20
Her first return, was to resume her place in the modern P IV 1 123 9
RESUMED (14)
After a short pause, Catherine resumed with "then you do NA II 4 151 17
After a short pause he resumed the conversation by saying-- SS I 11 56 14
15
on each side, she resumed the conversation which had MP I 10 97 3
done all this before he resumed his seat as master of the MP II 2 190 9
something more, and she resumed her attentions to Susan, MP III 12 418 6
be mentioned at all,--he resumed the subject of his own E I 15 130 28
her own relapse, and then resumed a more serious, more E I 16 137 12
much obliged to you for the carriage," resumed Miss Bates. E II 10 244 37
be; every preparation was resumed, and very soon after the E III 1 318 11
"Here," resumed Harriet, turning to her box again, "here E III 4 339 16
"More than an attachment, indeed," resumed Mrs. Weston; " E III 10 395 32
"I do not wonder, Miss Woodhouse," she resumed, "that you E III 11 407 28
"I cannot make speeches, emma:"--he soon resumed; and in a E III 13 430 37
"I have some hope," resumed he, "of my uncle's being E III 18 477 57
RESUMING (5)
two gentlemen behind, on resuming their places, after PP III 1 255 61
there were any plan for resuming the play after the MP II 2 192 11
tell you directly;" (resuming her work, and seeming E III 10 394 30
replied Mr. Knightley coolly, and resuming the letter.-- E III 15 447 24
How absurd to be resuming the agitation which such an P III 7 60 28
RESUSCITATION (1)
and now, by the resuscitation of Edward, she had one again. SS III 14 373 2
RETAIL (1)
and who was resolving to retail it all among her PP I 16 75 3
RETAILED (1)
in another, by her retailed explanation, as had at first SS III 11 349 2
RETAILING (2)
& had a lively way of retailing a common-place, or saying W 359 28
her, and on the other, retailing them all to the younger PP II 16 222 21
RETAIN (5)
Edward was allowed to retain the privilege of first comer, SS III 13 369 34
thought it advisable to retain the right of visiting at PP III 19 387 10
loved, and now hoped to retain with her as long as she MP I 4 41 15
civilities he should ever retain a greatful sense-- and E I 17 140 2
It was possible that you might retain the feelings of the P IV 11 244 70
RETAINED (9)
replied in a tone which retained only a little affected NA I 12 93 7
By that her eye was instantly caught and long retained; NA II 9 190 1
rest; though her spirits retained the impression of what SS II 12 236 42
her loss--he always retained that decided regard which SS III 14 379 19
whose affectionate heart retained a strong impression of PP II 12 201 5
and her manners, she retained all the claims to reputation PP III 19 387 8
His daughters he felt, while they retained the name of MP I 2 20 33
kept his station and retained her sister's hand, her MP II 1 175 2
comfort they would have retained her wholly; but this E II 2 165 9
RETAINING (6)
be equally capable of retaining them, is less certain." PP I 18 92 20
partly by the wish of retaining Mr. Bingley for his sister. PP II 10 187 40
who chose, instead of retaining his niece, to bring his MP I 4 41 15
successful in sending away, than in retaining a companion. MP I 10 103 48
Henry Crawford's retaining her hand at such a moment, a MP II 1 176 3
the first shock, without retaining any influence to alarm. E II 3 180 58
RETAINS (1)
"It ought to be so; it must be so, while he retains the PP III 14 354 36
RETALIATE (1)
it is provoking me to retaliate, and such things may come PP II 8 174 15
RETARDED (1)
the engagement, and retarded the marriage, of Edward and SS II 13 238 1
RETARDING (1)

Jealousy of Mr. Elliot had been the retarding weight, the P IV 11 241 60

RETENTIVE (3)
The memory is sometimes so retentive, so serviceable, so MP II 4 209 12
are most acute and retentive--and that there could be no E I 16 138 15
she found, that to retentive feelings eight years may be P III 7 60 29

RETIRE (5)
will retire to rest, and get a few hours' unquiet slumber. NA II 5 159 19
To retire to bed, however, unsatisfied on such a point, NA II 6 168 10
The latter was not going to retire. NA II 8 187 15
Mrs. Rushworth was quite ready to retire, and make way for MP II 3 202 28
the sacrifice, and retire from all the pleasures of life, E II 2 165 8

RETIRED (19)
But I, who live in a small retired village in the country, NA I 10 78 46
to admit her; and as she retired down the street, could NA I 12 91 3
A cottage in some retired village would be extasy. NA I 15 120 20
They retired whispering together; and, though her delicate NA II 1 132 16
and retired to her own room to write letters and sleep. SS III 7 316 27
At five o'clock the two ladies retired to dress, and at PP I 8 35 1
Accordingly, when she retired at night, she asked the PP II 19 241 17
After tea, Mr. Bennet retired to the library, as was his PP III 13 344 11
her prospects; and retired in proud resolve, determined MP II 3 201 23
field, in the midst of a retired little village between MP II 7 241 13
It is a retired place. E II 18 307 20
I fine place, but very retired." E II 18 307 20
Nothing can stand more retired from the road than Maple E II 18 307 21
considerable stretch very retired; and when the young E III 3 333 5
sense than herself; retired enough for safety, and E III 19 482 4
their parents' inferior, retired, and unpolished way of P III 9 74 5
and still more its sweet retired bay, backed by dark P III 11 95 9
comparatively quiet and retired gravel-walk, where the P IV 11 240 59
Mrs G. had preferred a small, retired place, like Sanditon, S 11 421 1

RETIREMENT (18)
when I shall be admitted into your delightful retirement. LS 1 243 1
might for a time make her wish for retirement. LS 6 252 2
If my sister in the security of retirement, with as little LS 14 264 3
death or a religious retirement closed their black career. NA II 9 190 2
London than even in the retirement of Barton, where it SS II 10 213 4
her only pleasures in retirement and study, as afterwards SS III 14 378 16
a weak head, living in retirement, and the consequential PP I 15 70 1
The quiet, the retirement of such a life, would have PP III 10 328 28
of her as pining in the retirement of Mansfield for <u>him</u>, MP II 3 202 25
for privacy and retirement, her decided preference of a MP II 8 255 10
stronger feelings to a retirement and reproach, which MP III 17 464 12
a young man who had more retirement at home than he liked. E II 8 221 49
his fears lest the retirement of it should be disagreeable; E II 14 276 36
up--parties, balls, plays--for I had no fear of retirement. E II 14 276 36
now in such retirement, such obscurity, so thrown away.-- E II 15 283 7
out from every thing--in the most complete retirement.-- E II 18 307 21
of the country, and the retirement of Lyme in the winter, P III 11 97 12
thing to smallness & retirement, yet having in the course S 11 421 1

RETIRING (4)
only her retiring to dress half an hour earlier than usual. NA II 9 193 5
She was always so gentle and retiring, that her emotions MP III 6 366 1
the business; Sir Thomas retiring from it with some MP III 6 368 9
with quiet, serious, and retiring manners, and a decided P III 11 97 12

RETOOK (1)
soon after his going, she retook her chosen place near the MP I 6 52 1

RETORT (4)
than ever, pronounced in retort this bitter phillippic; " SS II 12 235 37
Marianne was going to retort, but she remembered her SS III 1 267 41
triumph on being able to retort on Mrs. Bennet the comfort PP I 23 127 8
rational remonstrance or sharp retort equally ill bestowed. E I 11 93 5

RETORTED (1)
"That is nothing to the purpose.-- retorted the lady W 325 4

RETRACE (2)
her, and seemingly to retrace all that had then passed, MP III 5 358 7
relationship, and to retrace, as quietly as she could, the P IV 10 214 11

RETRACED (1)
pain and pleasure retraced with the fondest recollection. MP II 6 234 18

RETRACT (7)
determined, and she would not, upon any account, retract. NA I 13 97 1
But that she <u>must</u> and <u>should</u> retract, was instantly the NA I 13 97 1
No, you must excuse me, I cannot retract my consent. MP I 15 141 21
discovery, to retract her ill opinion of Mrs. Elton. E II 15 281 1
in what way she had best retract, when Mr. Weston went on. E II 18 307 17
I hope you do not retract what you then said." E III 18 476 47
that it was too late to retract, and the whole six set P III 10 83 6

RETRACTED (2)
to Miss Tilney, to have retracted a promise voluntarily NA I 13 101 25
Of what he had then written, nothing was to be retracted P IV 11 241 61

RETRACTION (1)
to gain, no unworthy retraction of a tacit consent, no NA II 15 247 15

RETREAT (5)
but it was too late to retreat, and she was too young to NA I 9 62 10
To retreat was impossible. SS III 8 326 53
I shall retreat in as much secrecy as possible to the most W 335 13
midst of their noise, or retreat from it to the solitude MP I 17 159 6
no change in her wish of retreat, and she worked and MP I 18 168 14

RETREATED (7)
But while she did so, the gentleman retreated, and her NA I 10 80 59
and Eleanor had likewise retreated thither, and were at NA II 10 203 8
Marianne had retreated as much as possible out of sight, SS III 12 359 13
She retreated from the window, fearful of being seen; and PP III 2 260 2
As she leant on the sofa, to which she had retreated that MP I 7 74 59
with such vain artifice retreated three months ago, to E II 14 270 3
Mr. Elton had retreated into the cardroom, looking (Emma E III 2 328 42

RETREATING (6)
she was on the point of retreating as softly as she had NA II 9 194 6
"I will not trust to <u>that</u>," retreating to her own room. SS II 9 204 16
the end of one, as if retreating as far as he could from W 332 11
of its being Mr. Darcy, she was directly retreating. PP II 12 195 2
or other; often retreating towards her own chamber to cry; MP I 2 14 9
The sounds were retreating, and Anne distinguished no more. P III 10 89 34

RETREIVED (1)
Sanditon also, till their circumstances were retreived. S 11 421 1

RETRENCH (4)
I know I cannot live as I have done, but I must retrench MP I 3 29 50
even as to say, "can we retrench? does it occur to you P III 1 9 19
article in which we can retrench?"--and Elizabeth, to do P III 1 9 19
They must retrench; that did not admit of a doubt. P III 2 12 3

RETRENCHED (1)
long as your frugality retrenched only on your own comfort, SS III 11 350 9

RETRENCHING (1)
reality of Sir Walter's retrenching, and who was perfectly P III 2 13 7

RETRENCHMENT (1)
of retrenchment, which was at last submitted to Sir Walter. P III 2 12 3

RETRENCHMENTS (1)
the most comprehensive retrenchments could secure, and saw P III 2 12 5

RETRIBUTION (1)
She shall have all the retribution in my power to make; if LS 24 290 13

RETROSPECT (3)
sensations which are to raise ecstacy even in retrospect. MP III 12 415 1
2
than pain by this retrospect of what might have been--but MP III 16 455 21
It is, in fact, a most mortifying retrospect for me. E III 14 440 8

RETROSPECTION (1)
He was roused from the reverie of retrospection and regret MP II 6 236 23

RETROSPECTIONS (3)
& retrospections which now ensued, over the welcome soup.-- W 336 14
<u>Your</u> retrospections must be so totally void of reproach, PP III 16 369 24
indulge in those retrospections and acknowledgments, and P IV 11 241 59

RETROSPECTIVE (1)
and as she threw a retrospective glance over the whole of PP III 4 279 23

RETURN (305)
originally fixed for his return, is occasioned as much by LS 8 255 1
good opinion merits a better return than it has received. LS 14 265 5
My dear mother I return you Reginald's letter, & LS 15 266 1
out of the room & did not return for some time; when she LS 17 270 2
of <u>that</u> affection might not in the end awaken a return. LS 22 280 1
In about ten minutes after my return to the parlour, Lady LS 23 284 6
robbed of it's peace, in return for the hospitality with LS 36 305 1
tho' inviting her to return in one or two affectionate LS 42 313 7
her dear Catherine, and would therefore shortly return. NA I 5 36 2
to you just now were to return, or if any other gentleman NA I 10 78 37
threatening on each return that, if it still kept on NA I 11 83 14
reason of their speedy return, said, "I am glad your NA I 11 89 62
of rudeness in return it might justly make her amenable. NA I 12 92 3
the ordinary course of life can hardly afford a return. NA I 15 117 8
party, she found, on her return, without spending many NA II 1 129 1
and sent therefore by return of post their ready consent NA II 2 140 11
her preferences had each known the happiness of a return. NA II 2 141 11
"I certainly cannot return his affection, and as certainly NA II 3 145 15
His leave of absence will soon expire, and he must return NA II 4 152 29
almost have wished to return with him to Pulteney-Street. NA II 5 154 1
exhausted, you will return towards your own apartment. NA II 5 160 21
against taking her friend round the Abbey till his return. NA II 7 181 41
the room by their return, was at last ready to escort them. NA II 8 182 1
It was some relief, however, that they were to return to NA II 8 183 2
it over before Henry's return, who was expected on the NA II 9 193 5
"I did not expect to be able to return sooner, when I went NA II 9 195 12
as to return only to see her mother in her coffin." NA II 9 197 25
James had protested against writing to her till his return NA II 10 201 5
violence, forced to return; and the others withdrew, after NA II 10 203 8
As to-morrow is Sunday, Eleanor, I shall not return." NA II 11 211 14
they were to dine, and at six to set off on their return. NA II 11 214 26
anxiety as to the how or the when she might return to it. NA II 11 215 28
there, they would be too generous to hasten her return."-- NA II 13 221 2
His unlooked-for return was enough in itself to make NA II 13 223 13
Can you, when you return from this Lord's, come to NA II 13 224 14
conclusion; for to return in such a manner to Fullerton NA II 14 231 5
the cause, or collect the particulars of her sudden return. NA II 14 233 10
all this; and now, how altered a being did she return! NA II 14 237 20
She was assured of his affection; and that heart in return NA II 15 243 9
On his return from Woodston, two days before, he had been NA II 15 244 10
permitted his son to return to Northanger, and thence made NA II 16 252 7
when the money is once parted with, it never can return. SS I 2 9 7
And in return for an acknowledgment, which must give me SS I 10 52 28
"if you were to defer your journey till our return." SS I 13 64 28
and we must put off the party to Whitwell till you return." SS I 13 65 35
my power to return, that I dare not engage for it at all." SS I 13 65 36
them was seen till their return, which did not happen till SS I 13 67 60
which did not happen till after the return of all the rest. SS I 13 67 60
On their return from the park they found Willoughby's SS I 15 75 2
I will not press you to return here immediately, because SS I 15 76 14
minutes notice--gone too without intending to return!-- SS I 15 77 23
and did not return your kindness with any cordiality. SS I 15 81 43
But, in return, your sister must allow me to feel no more SS I 18 98 8
no little alarm on the return of Sir John, by hearing that SS I 21 118 2
give him my picture in return, which I am very much vexed SS I 22 132 37
but it has never been in my power to return to Barton." SS II 4 162 12
But" (with a little return of anxiety) "it cannot be SS II 5 167 3
Scarcely a word was spoken during their return to Berkeley- SS II 6 178 16
and while she waited the return of Mrs. Jennings, had SS II 6 178 16
followed by a return of the same excessive affliction. SS II 7 180 4
for which I beg to return my sincere acknowledgments. SS II 7 183 13
what they were, you will return my notes, and the lock of SS II 7 188 42
resist insult, or return mortification--but I cannot. SS II 7 189 52
Mrs. Jennings came immediately to their room on her return, SS II 8 192 1
which her sister could not make or return for herself. SS II 8 193 7
He had left her promising to return; he neither returned, SS II 9 209 30
for Marianne than an immediate return into Devonshire. SS II 10 214 7
to make a very gracious return to the overpowering delight SS II 10 217 20
their's, she should pay her visit and return for them. SS II 11 220 2
Edward tried to return her kindness as it deserved, but SS II 13 242 25
employ Edward to take care of us in our return to Barton. SS II 13 243 31
was dressed, and did not return till late in the evening; SS II 14 246 2
Is this the only return I can make you?-- SS III 1 264 31
very earnestly to return with her again from Cleveland. SS III 3 280 7
thing relative to their return was arranged as far as it SS III 3 280 7
return the same good will, than the power of expressing it. SS III 4 290 43
exactness the time in which she might look for his return. SS III 7 312 17
Willoughby, I advise you at present to return to Combe.-- SS III 8 318 16
17
a very short time, had the power of creating any return. SS III 8 322 36
"Did you tell her that you should soon return?" SS III 8 324 44
At his and Mrs. Jennings's united request in return, Mrs. SS III 10 341 4
pleasure of Margaret's return, and talking of the dear SS III 10 343 8
I have burnt all your letters, and will return your SS III 13 365 15
house, on every monthly return throughout the winter.-- W 314 1
& I shd most readily return to my father; & should not be W 320 2
entirely alone, it was her wish to return home to dinner.-- W 339 18
I cannot return the visit.-- W 348 22
to announce the speedy return of Margaret, & a visit of W 348 23
which made her dread her return; & the day which brought W 348 23
She was very much pressed by Robert & Jane to return with W 362 32
her ideas," he continued, "let us return to Mr. Bingley." PP I 2 7 20
how soon he would return Mr. Bennet's visit, and PP I 2 8 28
You had better return to your partner and enjoy her smiles, PP I 3 12 13
her to return to bed, and promised her some draughts. PP I 7 33 44
is supposed to desire his return to the house, and the PP I 10 50 34
Denny, concerning whose return from London Lydia came to PP I 15 72 8
hat--a salutation which Mr. Darcy just deigned to return. PP I 15 73 8
surprise at their sudden return home, which, as their own PP I 15 73 11
Mr. Collins on his return highly gratified Mrs. Bennet by PP I 15 74 13
of obliging her in return, by sitting down to whist. PP I 16 76 6
The two first dances, however, brought a return of PP I 18 90 4
waiting on her, after his return from London, whither he PP I 18 103 76
Soon after their return, a letter was delivered to Miss PP I 21 116 6
of the party will return into Hertfordshire this winter. PP I 21 117 10
return to Netherfield and answer every wish of her heart. PP I 21 120 29
to secure her from any return of Mr. Collins's addresses, PP I 22 121 1
direct questions on his return, as required some ingenuity PP I 22 123 3
wish for so speedy a return, immediately said, "but is PP I 22 123 6
7
equally surprised to find that he meditated a quick return. PP I 22 124 11
now been gone a week, and nothing was heard of his return. PP I 23 128 9
he hoped to be able to return on Monday fortnight; for PP I 23 128 10
Mr. Collins's return into Hertfordshire was no longer a PP I 23 128 11
shortly after his next return into Hertfordshire, the day PP II 2 139 1
Caroline did not return my visit till yesterday; and not a PP II 3 148 26
And when we <u>do</u> return, it shall not be like other PP II 4 154 23
He had before believed her to return his affection with PP II 12 199 5
receive it, and accepted in return three thousand pounds. PP II 12 201 5
made her at length return home; and she entered the house PP II 13 209 12
an hour, hoping for her return, and almost resolving to PP II 13 209 13
her daughter; and on his return, brought back, with great PP II 14 210 1
He wrote last week to hurry my return." PP II 14 211 9
herself obliged, on her return, to undo all the work of PP II 14 213 20
The first week of their return was soon gone. PP II 18 229 1
with him since her return, agitation was pretty well over; PP II 18 233 25
her niece with a smile, but Elizabeth could not return it. PP III 1 247 10
shock is over, shall I own that I long for your return? PP III 4 275 5
prevail on Mr. Bennet to return to Longbourn, as soon as PP III 6 294 2
intreaty that he would return to his family, and leave it PP III 6 298 13

Elizabeth had received none since her return, that could PP III 6 298 16
Two days after Mr. Bennet's return, as Jane and Elizabeth PP III 7 301 1
at ----, and they were to return in it, by dinner-time. PP III 9 315 1
situation, and return to her friends as soon as they could PP III 10 322 2
Mr. Darcy was punctual in his return, and as Lydia PP III 10 325 2
obligations to a person who could never receive a return. PP III 10 326 3
for London, but was to return home in ten days time. PP III 13 344 1
I must beg to return to the house." PP III 14 357 63
to return into the house, walked quietly into it herself. PP III 14 358 74
In that case he would return no more. PP III 15 361 3
call on him in her return through London, and relate her PP III 16 367 9
much as possible; and, in return, it belongs to me to find PP III 18 381 7
In return for such services she loved him better than any MP I 2 22 35
could never receive kindness without wishing to return it. MP I 3 26 29
was gone perhaps never to return! that she should see him MP I 3 33 64
return, and then Sir Thomas might settle it all himself. MP I 4 36 7
waiting till Sir Thomas's return in September, for when MP I 4 37 9
The return of winter engagements, however, was not without MP I 4 38 9
"If poor Sir Thomas were fated never to return, it would MP I 4 38 9
his return, which he was again looking eagerly forward to. MP I 4 40 14
September--just after my return from the West Indies--my MP I 5 51 40
airs against his return, in compassion to his feelings, as MP I 6 59 41
and then we could all return to a late dinner here, or MP I 6 62 58
Before his return Mrs. Grant and Miss Crawford came in. MP I 8 75 2
On his return to the breakfast-room, he found Mrs. Norris MP I 8 77 8
"Yes, I shall take orders soon after my father's return-- MP I 9 89 28
prepared, by general agreement, to return to the house. MP I 10 103 49
charm for it; and he, in return, had shewn her all his MP I 10 103 50
till the return of the others, and the arrival of dinner. MP I 10 104 51
November was the black month fixed for his return. MP I 11 107 2
a husband, and the return of the friend most solicitous MP I 11 107 3
on the subject of his return, and would hardly have found MP I 11 107 4
"Your father's return will be a very interesting event." MP I 11 108 6
land, offered sacrifices to the gods on their safe return." MP I 11 108 10
Sir Thomas was to return in November, and his eldest son MP I 12 114 1
and wishing him not to return; and a fortnight of MP I 12 114 3
a week till my father's return, and invite all the country. MP I 13 125 18
the expectation of his return must be a very anxious MP I 13 126 18
soon after Miss Bertram's return from the parsonage, Mr. MP I 15 138 1
Every thing seems to depend upon Sir Thomas's return." MP I 17 162 15
From this moment there was a return of his former jealousy, MP I 18 165 4
Crawfords were engaged to return for that purpose as soon MP I 18 171 25
little, and thinking his return a misfortune; and when, on MP II 1 178 7
alarm; but she was vexed by the manner of his return. MP II 1 179 10
Sir Thomas's return made a striking change in the ways of MP II 3 196 1
days, when there was no return, no letter, no message--no MP II 3 201 24
sir, I would not have delayed his return for a day. MP II 5 225 58
that it was impossible not to be civil to him in return. MP II 6 232 11
determining him on his return to town to apply for MP II 6 232 13
period of the Antwerp's return from the Mediterranean, &c.; MP II 6 232 13
The return of Henry Crawford, and the arrival of William MP II 7 238 1
return, and hoped to obtain his approbation of her doing. MP II 9 262 11
what she wished. "return the necklace! no, my dear Fanny, MP II 9 262 11
the prospect of Julia's return, which would otherwise have MP II 11 284 10
written home to defer his return, having promised to MP II 11 286 16
affection, soliciting a return, and, finally, in words so MP II 13 301 7
was engaged to return and dine there that very day. MP II 13 303 12
whereas the pain she hoped would return no more. MP II 13 308 36
me, and quite out of my power to return his good opinion." MP III 1 314 17
"Out of your power to return his good opinion! what is all MP III 1 315 18
opinion of you from the period of my return to England. MP III 1 318 39
perseverance secure a return, and at no great distance; MP III 2 327 4
Edmund had great things to hear on his return. MP III 3 334 1
on the score of Edmund's return, Sir Thomas felt himself MP III 3 335 7
you most devotedly, that has the best right to a return. MP III 3 344 41
and desirable, if you could return his affection. MP III 4 346 12
should wish you could return it; but that as you cannot, MP III 4 346 12
be answered for--I think I never shall return his regard." MP III 4 347 20
and then a return of affection might not be very distant. MP III 5 356 1
she could have hoped her return thither, to be as distant MP III 6 366 4
a craving for their return; and he was soon afterwards MP III 6 368 7
Every afternoon brought a return of their riotous games MP III 8 391 8
hours in London after his return from Norfolk, before he MP III 10 400 8
the others were ready to return; and in the course of MP III 10 406 21
cooled and staggered by a return to London habits, would MP III 12 417 4
And had it been possible for her to return Mr. Crawford's MP III 12 419 9
thither too early, as a return of fever came on, and for a MP III 13 427 13
At about the week's end from his return to Mansfield, MP III 14 429 1
It came, and she had yet heard nothing of her return-- MP III 14 430 6
of the going to London, which was to precede her return. MP III 14 430 6
or when I return to Mansfield, I shall do so and so."-- MP III 14 431 8
They might return to Mansfield when they chose; travelling MP III 14 432 11
Julia had offered to return if wanted--but this was all.-- MP III 14 432 11
Write to me by return of post, judge of my anxiety, and do MP III 14 434 13
even to offer an early return, was a presumption which MP III 14 436 15
she must suppose her return would be unwelcome at present, MP III 14 436 15
in return, was every thing that could be done for her. MP III 16 449 5
Very soon after the Rushworths' return to Wimpole Street, MP III 16 450 8
hope of Mrs. Rushworth's return, but was so much MP III 16 450 9
from the day of his return from Antigua: in every MP III 17 465 15
to Everingham after his return from Portsmouth, he might MP III 17 467 20
every thing due to her in return for the great goodness of E I 2 15 3
love, and in some doubt of a return; it would do her good. E I 5 41 29
a time, had gone home to return again to dinner: she E I 7 50 1
"you mean to return a favourable answer, I collect." E I 7 52 14
15

return to Hartfield, to make a regular visit of some days. E I 8 57 1
"I will tell you something, in return for what have told E I 8 60 30
and the return of Harriet were very adequate restoratives. E I 8 67 56
and not meaning to return till the morrow, though it was E I 8 68 58
soon after Mr. Elton's return, and being hung over the E I 9 69 2
But how shall I ever be able to return the paper, or say I E I 9 76 37
evening did not close without a little return of agitation. E I 12 104 50
Going in dismal weather, to return probably in worse;-- E I 13 113 26
to fall to impede their return, that was a mere joke; he E I 15 126 11
there it seemed as if her return only were wanted to make E I 15 132 38
return of day will hardly fail to bring return of spirits. E I 16 137 13
whole party set off, and return to his lamentations over E I 17 140 1
of her other complaint before the gentleman's return. E I 17 141 5
the time of Mr. Elton's return, as to allow them all to E I 17 142 11
If Mr. Elton, on his return, made his own indifference as E I 17 143 13
The Churchills might not have a word to say in return; but E I 18 147 19
his own return to England put any thing in his power. E II 2 163 4
When he did return, he sought out the child and took E II 2 163 4
return, and wishing to do more than she dared to confess. E II 4 184 11
judged it best for her to return Elizabeth Martin's visit. E II 4 185 11
regrets--to be ready to return to the same good E II 5 187 4
and set off, intending to return to dinner, but with no E II 7 205 1
return from him for a few minutes, and listen to Mr. Cole. E II 8 222 54
Before he could return to his chair, it was taken by Mrs. E II 8 222 58
about you and me in return; but I cannot stay to hear it." E II 10 245 49
from Mr. Churchill to urge his nephew's instant return. E II 12 258 7
head)--the uncertainty of when I may be able to return!-- E II 12 259 15
I doubt whether he will return the compliment, and E II 14 279 52
conversation, rather than return to the superior E II 15 285 13
In the course of the spring she must return their E II 16 290 3
He had done his duty and could return to his son. E II 18 308 26
"And, in return for your acknowledging so much, I will do E III 2 331 55
bank brought on such a return of it as made her absolutely E III 3 333 5
grandmother's; and as the return of the Campbells from E III 5 343 1
I shall go abroad for a couple of years--and when I return, E III 7 373 50
she hoped, might lead the way to a return of old feelings. E III 8 378 7
it was to be delayed till Colonel Campbell's return." E III 8 380 9
till Colonel Campbell's return, and nothing should induce E III 8 380 15
to find that she had engaged herself before their return?" E III 8 382 28
Richmond soon after the return of the party from box hill-- E III 8 383 31
had not lived above six-and-thirty hours after his return. E III 9 387 11
Miss Bates was obliged to return without success; Jane was E III 9 390 18
increased by Harriet's having some hope of a return? E III 11 408 32
Frank Churchill would return among them no more; and Miss E III 12 422 20
Yes, you see, you understand my feelings--and will return E III 13 430 37
unsuspicious of what they could have told him in return. E III 14 434 3
itself, by the natural return of her former regard for the E III 15 444 1
Mr. Weston was to call in the evening, and she must return E III 15 444 4
to Miss Fairfax, and return it into the purple and gold E III 16 453 12
13

return of the Campbells, he named the name of Dixon.-- E III 18 477 51
Let me return your congratulations.-- E III 18 477 59
He had a great deal to say in return, and very E III 18 480 80
Captain Wentworth made a very early return to Mr. P III 7 53 2
Her brother's return was the first comfort; he could take P III 7 54 4
and desired nothing in return but to be unobserved. P III 8 71 56
own, and some return of indisposition in little Charles. P III 9 77 17
The time now approached for Lady Russell's return; the day P III 11 93 1
to go in the morning and return at night, but to this Mr. P III 11 94 8
and gaze on a first return to the sea, who ever deserve to P III 11 96 10
had given of him, on his return from Lyme before; his warm P III 11 96 12
but without waiting the return, travelled night and day P III 12 108 28
them to their door, and then return and set off themselves. P III 12 108 30
of hope and fear, from a return of her own insensibility. P III 12 112 51
Charles was to return to Lyme the same afternoon, and his P IV 1 121 3
Her first return, was to resume her place in the modern P IV 1 123 9
their return to Uppercross, they drove over to the lodge.-- P IV 2 129 1
and mother, who must return in time to receive their P IV 2 129 1
herald; nor could Anne return from any stroll of solitary P IV 2 133 26
return the compliment entirely, which had embarrassed him. P IV 3 141 12
and it was only at intervals that he could return to Lyme. P IV 3 144 21
part of the town, and return alone to Camden-Place; and in P IV 6 168 25
and make enquiries in return, in spite of the formidable P IV 8 181 1
calmness enough to return the letter which she had been P IV 9 204 76
77

family, long before your return to it; and Colonel Wallis P IV 9 206 90
the very evening of his return; but from Thursday to P IV 10 214 13
of the family; and in return, she naturally fell into all P IV 10 220 31
She was earnestly begged to return and dine, and give them P IV 10 227 68
for his being determined not to be delayed in his return. P IV 10 228 71
"I must go, uncertain of my fate; but I shall return " P IV 11 237 43
return to Kellynch, and act as circumstances might require. P IV 11 243 66
of good-will to offer in return for all the worth and all P IV 12 251 10
stroll on the cliff gave way to an immediate return home.-- S 6 390 1

RETURNED (236)

My dear mother Mr Vernon returned on Thursday night, LS 17 269 1
Be that as it may however, Frederica is returned on my LS 19 274 2
"I should not have hazarded such an opinion, returned she, LS 24 287 11
As soon as I was tolerably composed, I returned to the LS 24 291 15
There is not a chance of her affection being returned. LS 24 291 16
gone to town, for he is returned, Reginald is returned, LS 40 308 1
is returned, Reginald is returned, not to ask our consent LS 40 308 1
already returned home--which I was very far from crediting. LS 41 310 2
Frederica returned to Churchill with her uncle & aunt, & LS 42 312 6
She returned it with pleasure, and then advancing still NA I 8 54 4
settled her young charge, returned to her party. NA I 8 55 10
Catherine found Mrs. Allen just returned from all the busy NA I 9 67 34
Miss Tilney met her with great civility, returned her NA I 10 72 8
This civility was duly returned; and they parted--on Miss NA I 10 73 21
and she instantly returned to the window to watch over and NA I 11 83 16
companion so; and they returned to Pulteney-Street without NA I 11 89 61
In a few minutes the servant returned, and with a look NA I 12 91 3
eyes were immediately returned to their former direction. NA I 12 93 4
much uneasiness, and returned home, pleased that the party NA I 14 115 55
an hour, when they both returned, and an explanation was NA II 1 132 16
subjects very different--returned in full force, and every NA II 5 161 24
of existence, returned her recollection of the manuscript; NA II 7 172 1
same shape as before, returned them to the same spot NA II 7 173 3
They returned to the hall, that the chief stair-case might NA II 8 184 5
the folly of too easily thinking his affection returned. NA II 10 202 7
with close attention, returned it saying, "well, if it is NA II 10 205 24
"You are mistaken, indeed," returned Eleanor, looking at NA II 13 223 13
feel, and look, when he returned on the morrow to NA II 14 231 4
"I am sorry for the young people," returned Mrs. Morland; " NA II 14 234 12
lady of seventeen, just returned from her first excursion NA II 14 235 13
Mrs. Allen again returned to--"I really have not patience NA II 14 238 27
hour had elapsed ere she returned down stairs with the NA II 15 241 7
required to compose, had returned almost instantly to NA II 15 248 16
Henry returned to what was now his only home, to watch NA II 16 250 3
"Certainly," returned Mrs. John Dashwood. SS I 2 12 26
her daughter, and that Elinor returned the partiality. SS I 3 15 5
and when the visit was returned by the Middletons dining SS I 8 36 1
In about five minutes he returned. SS I 13 63 7
When Sir John returned, he joined most heartily in the SS I 13 66 60
In about half an hour her mother returned, and though her SS I 15 77 21
"My judgment," he returned, "is all on your side of the SS I 17 94 42
His gravity and thoughtfulness returned on him in their SS I 17 95 50
Edward returned to them with fresh admiration of the SS I 18 96 4
at her some minutes, and then returned to his newspaper. SS I 19 108 35
She surprised Elinor very much as they returned into the SS I 20 113 40
The Palmers returned to Cleveland the next day, and the SS I 21 118 1
"No;" returned Elinor, cautious of giving her real opinion SS I 22 128 6
She returned it almost instantly, acknowledging the SS I 22 132 36
the Miss Steeles returned to the park, and Elinor was then SS I 22 135 56
"I am sorry for that," returned the other, while her eyes SS II 2 150 38
and when they afterwards returned to the drawing room, SS II 4 161 6
listening half a minute, returned into the room in all the SS II 4 161 7
It was late in the morning before they returned home; and SS II 4 165 25
thrown aside, and she returned to the more interesting SS II 4 166 31
at her sister when they returned was enough to inform her, SS II 5 169 16
"Me!" returned Elinor in come confusion; "indeed, Marianne, SS II 5 170 25
She complained of it as they returned to Berkeley-Street. SS II 5 171 35
"It cannot be generally known," returned Elinor, "for her SS II 5 173 41
all his embarrassment returned; but as if, on catching the SS II 6 177 11
seeing her safe off, returned to Marianne, whom she found SS II 7 185 16
returned, she continued on the bed quiet and motionless. SS II 7 191 65
acknowledgments, and returned her those civilities, which SS II 8 193 7
All her impatience to be at home again now returned; her SS II 9 203 9
after this unhappy period before I returned to England. SS II 9 207 26
He had left her promising to return; he neither returned, SS II 9 209 30
her lover; and when he returned to town, which was within SS II 9 211 38
We returned unwounded, and the meeting, therefore, never SS II 9 211 38
Twice was his card found on the table, when they returned SS II 12 230 5
regarding them at all, returned them to her daughter. SS II 12 235 29
her once or twice a day, returned from that period to her SS III 1 257 1
As soon as they returned to the carriage, Mrs. Jennings SS III 2 276 27
When Mrs. Jennings came home, though she returned from SS III 4 291 46
at Cleveland; and as she returned by a different circuit SS III 6 303 9
She returned just in time to join the others as they SS III 6 303 10
unable to sit up, and returned voluntarily to her bed, SS III 7 307 2
It was then about twelve o'clock, and she returned to her SS III 7 312 17
as he returned to his seat--"what does it signify?-- SS III 8 318 15
"I have," returned Elinor, colouring likewise, and SS III 8 322 35
to be happy, and afterwards returned to town to be gay.-- SS III 8 329 65
When at last she returned to the unconscious Marianne, she SS III 9 333 3
Margaret returned, and the family were again all restored SS III 11 352 20
Margaret and the maid, returned to Elinor, who, though SS III 11 353 25
to chuse any myself, I returned home to be completely idle; SS III 13 362 5

one another, we are just returned from the altar, and are SS III 13 365 14
Elinor read and returned it without any comment. SS III 13 365 16
from whence he usually returned in the morning, early SS III 13 369 34
who was very recently returned to her family from the care W 315 1
of obliging--& when they returned to the parlour where Mrs W 323 3
Mr Watson returned in the evening, not the worse for the W 343 19
W. to let nobody in, returned in half a minute, with a W 344 21
you are returned upon their hands without a sixpence." W 352 26
"But it is," returned she; "for Mrs. Long has just been PP I 1 3 5
In a few days Mr. Bingley returned Mr. Bennet's visit, and PP I 3 9 3
They returned therefore in good spirits to Longbourn, the PP I 3 12 15
The visit was returned in due form. PP I 6 21 1
When dinner was over, she returned directly to Jane, and PP I 8 35 3
departed, and Elizabeth returned instantly to Jane, PP I 9 46 39
Mr. Wickham, who had returned with him the day before from PP I 15 72 8
politeness, which he returned with as much more, PP I 15 73 11
before, and was not yet returned; adding, with a PP I 18 89 1
2
When those dances were over she returned to Charlotte PP I 18 90 5
Mr. Collins then returned to Elizabeth. PP I 18 98 61
Mr. Collins received and returned these felicitations with PP I 20 110 1
if Mr. Wickham were returned, and to lament over his PP I 21 115 3
Mr. Collins when he returned to Longbourn to dinner, to PP I 22 123 3
an awkward pause, they returned to the rest of the family. PP I 22 125 18
Mr. Collins returned most punctually on the Monday PP I 23 129 15
Lodge, and he sometimes returned to Longbourn only in time PP I 23 129 15
Mr. Collins returned into Hertfordshire soon after it had PP II 3 145 11
pain; but her spirits returned as she considered that Jane PP II 3 149 27
ladies drove on, and the others returned into the house. PP II 5 159 20
When the ladies returned to the drawing room, there was PP II 6 163 15
away, the whole family returned to their usual employments, PP II 7 168 1
when Mr. Collins returned the gentlemen accompanied him. PP II 7 170 7
of Charlotte and her sister, just returned from their walk. PP II 9 179 26
sentiments avowed, however unequally they may be returned. PP II 11 189 6
7
When the party broke up, Lydia returned with Mrs. Forster PP II 18 235 40
than that they were just returned from the library, where PP II 19 238 5
house, all her apprehensions of meeting its owner returned. PP III 1 245 4
and returned to it again before they quitted the gallery. PP III 1 250 47
had been seen, they returned down stairs, and taking leave PP III 1 251 49
she returned to his civil enquiries after her family. PP III 1 251 52
friends, and were just returned to the inn to dress PP III 2 260 1
When Darcy returned to the saloon, Miss Bingley could not PP III 3 270 12
their visit, as they returned, except what had PP III 3 271 20
And when I returned home, the ----shire was to leave PP III 5 285 16
over, he naturally returned to all his former indolence. PP III 8 309 5
She got up, and ran out of the room; and returned no more, PP III 9 317 9
"Well, mamma," said she, when they were all returned to PP III 9 317 11
When all this was resolved on, he returned again to his PP III 10 324 2
The colour which had been driven from her face, returned PP III 11 334 37
to take a family dinner with us, as soon as you returned. PP III 11 338 58
were out of sight, then returned into the drawing room. PP III 13 345 17
unless Mr. Darcy returned within the stated time. PP III 13 345 20
Bingley of course returned with him to dinner; and in the PP III 13 346 21
"You have a very small park here," returned Lady Catherine PP III 14 352 9
When he returned to understand how Fanny was situated, and MP I 4 36 7
sister," said he, as he returned from attending them to MP I 5 45 4
Mr. Rushworth was returned with his head full of the MP I 6 52 1
presided at the whole, returned with it in excellent time, MP I 7 66 15
Before half this was said, Fanny was returned to her seat MP I 7 71 35
They were just returned into the wilderness from the park, MP I 10 103 49
On this rencontre they all returned to the house together, MP I 10 104 51
of Mansfield, he gladly returned to it at the time MP I 12 115 3
Every thing returned into the same channel as before his MP I 12 115 4
The thought returned again and again. MP I 13 123 6
but her brother soon returned to business and Lovers' Vows, MP I 14 136 21
answer; the others soon returned, and Edmund found that to MP I 15 142 23
minutes, Miss Crawford returned to the party round the MP I 15 143 27
"The count has two and forty speeches," returned Mr. MP I 15 144 31
the three gentlemen returned to the drawing-room together, MP II 1 183 24
"I believe our evenings are rather returned to what they MP II 3 197 4
fox-chase; nor till he returned safe and well, without MP II 6 237 23
and confusion, would have returned the present instantly. MP II 8 259 20
the having any thing returned on our hands, which we have MP II 9 263 12
same hour that she had returned from the parsonage, and MP II 9 267 23
William's good fortune returned again upon her mind, and MP II 9 270 40
Had Henry returned, as he talked of doing, at the end of MP II 11 287 17
to do, and as he returned to Mansfield on purpose to do. MP III 1 311 1
In about a quarter of an hour her uncle returned; she was MP III 1 321 47
He then returned to his former station, and went on as if MP III 3 341 27
it due to herself, returned to Mr. Crawford, and said, "it MP III 4 349 25
The idea that returned the oftenest, was that Miss MP III 12 417 4
of lesser matters, none returned so often, or remained so MP III 12 419 8
I am returned to Mansfield in a less assured state than MP III 13 420 2
I have been returned since Saturday. MP III 13 420 2
know), and is not yet returned; and Julia is with the MP III 14 434 13
She was returned to Mansfield Park, she was useful, she MP III 17 461 2
When he returned from Richmond, he would have been glad to MP III 17 468 21
He had returned to a late dinner after some days absence, E I 1 9 21
little returned that he had never been there in his life. E I 2 17 8
Miss Bates, or when Mrs. and Miss Bates returned the visit. E I 2 17 9
A very gracious invitation was returned, and the evening E I 3 22 7
and was now just returned from a long visit in the country E I 3 23 8
again to dinner: she returned, and sooner than had been E I 7 50 1
from the table, she returned it----- "Oh! here's the E I 9 81 79
80
very last thing before I returned to dress, I was told E I 13 114 31
The compliment was just returned, coldly and proudly; and, E I 15 132 37
of the subject as they returned;-- but it burst out again E II 1 155 1
Emma saw its artifice, and returned to her first surmises. E II 2 169 16
Mr. Elton returned, a very happy man. E II 4 181 3
reward him, returned with Mrs. Weston to Mrs. Bates's door. E II 9 235 35
it was folded up and returned to Mrs. Weston, that it had E II 13 266 6
"I dare say," returned Harriet, sighing again, "I dare say E II 14 271 13
When the visit was returned, Emma made up her mind. E II 14 272 16
Her mind returned to Mrs. Elton's offences, and long, very E II 14 280 61
Emma returned her friend's pressure with interest; and was E II 15 287 31
When the ladies returned to the drawing-room after dinner, E II 17 299 1
He had returned to a late dinner, and walked to Hartfield E II 17 302 23
In a few minutes the carriage returned.-- E III 2 321 14
Frank Churchill returned to his station by Emma; and as E III 2 323 20
I do not by any means engage for its being returned. E III 4 342 39
Emma returned all her attention to her father, saying in E III 6 364 57
59
In half an hour the arrow-root was returned, with a E III 9 391 20
Emma's courage returned, and she walked on. E III 10 393 16
"You may well be amazed," returned Mrs. Weston, still E III 10 395 35
"Not quite," returned Emma, with forced calmness, "for all E III 11 406 21
in an airing, was now returned with much more to say, and E III 12 417 4
"I am afraid," returned Emma, sighing, "that I must often E III 12 419 11
It was the first intimation of his being returned from E III 13 424 1
"He is a most fortunate man!" returned Mr. Knightley, with E III 13 428 23
She was his own Emma, by hand and word, when they returned E III 13 433 42
on mine; and I returned the same evening to Richmond, E III 14 441 8
her, my own letters all returned!--and a few lines at the E III 14 442 8
Mr. Knightley returned to his reading with greater E III 15 445 10
he returned, that he should certainly be at home till one." E III 16 457 38
The smile was returned as Jane answered, "you are very E III 16 460 55
56
When the Campbells are returned, we shall meet them in E III 18 477 57
It was with a daughter of Mr. Shepherd, who had returned, P III 2 15 15
and was glad to be within when the visit was returned. P III 6 48 17

Wentworth, is just returned to England, or paid off, or P III 6 50 27
the Miss Musgroves had returned and finished their visit P III 7 60 31
32
Unintentionally she returned to that part of the room; he P III 8 72 58
59
a certain Charles Hayter returned among them, to be a good P III 9 73 3
newspaper; and Captain Wentworth returned to his window. P III 9 79 27
Just as they were setting off, the gentlemen returned. P III 10 83 6
a cheerful spot; Louisa returned, and Mary finding a P III 10 86 21
Charles and Henrietta returned, bringing, as may be P III 10 89 36
a little longer, they returned to the inn; and Anne in P III 12 104 7
hill as they could, they returned to the breakfast-table. P III 12 105 10
a few hours and then returned to Lyme--and without any P IV 1 126 20
present; for when it was returned, the Crofts announced P IV 1 128 31
with her and stay at Uppercross, whenever she returned. P IV 2 134 31
Sir Walter, Elizabeth and Mrs. Clay returned one morning P IV 5 156 14
supposing such attachment to be real, and returned. P IV 5 159 22
The visit of ceremony was paid and returned, and Louisa P IV 6 168 22
(for there was no cousin returned) were walking off; and P IV 7 176 10
The others returned, the room filled again, benches were P IV 8 189 45
Her distress returned, however, on perceiving smiles and P IV 10 222 37
and ease and animation returned to most of those they left, P IV 10 226 65
with Mrs. Musgrove, to keep her there till they returned. P IV 11 229 2
There they returned again into the past, more exquisitely P IV 11 240 59
her in Bath; that had returned, after a short suspension, P IV 11 241 60
Tell me if, when I returned to England in the year eight, P IV 11 247 82
Sir Harry's decease she returned again to her own house at S 3 375 1
Clara had returned with her--& by her good Sence & merit S 3 379 1

RETURNING (86)

you, as that Reginald should be returning to Parklands. LS 23 283 2
between returning tenderness & the remains of displeasure. LS 25 293 3
with you, that I may be in no danger of his returning here. LS 31 302 1
proposed her Neice's returning with them into the country. LS 42 312 5
theatre that evening, in returning the nods and smiles of NA I 5 35 1
up to propose their returning home, she joined her and NA II 3 147 28
Returning through the large and lofty hall, they ascended NA II 5 162 28
most urgent for returning with his daughter to the house. NA II 7 181 41
A heroine returning, at the close of her career, to her NA II 14 232 7
Returning in silence to his seat, therefore, he remained NA II 15 242 8
I have no idea of returning into Devonshire immediately. SS I 15 76 10
resist the temptation of returning here soon, and yet SS I 15 81 43
"Writing to each other," said Lucy, returning the letter SS I 22 135 54
necessity of their returning to fulfil them immediately, SS II 2 151 43
I obey your commands of returning the letters, with which SS II 7 183 13
to town," said Lucy, returning, after a cessation of SS II 10 218 30
Mrs. Jennings, on returning from her ordinary visit to Mrs. SS III 1 257 2
3
fix the time of her returning to that dear mother, whom SS III 3 280 6
And away she went; but returning again in a moment, "I SS III 4 287 21
22
apologising for not returning herself, had obliged him to SS III 4 287 25
to her, without any design of returning her affection." SS III 8 320 29
to engage her regard, without a thought of returning it.-- SS III 8 320 32
from thence returning to town, procured the forgiveness of SS III 14 376 11
not quite over, when the returning sound of carriages W 329 9
have met with some unexpected opportunity of returning."-- W 355 28
My kind friends will not hear of my returning home till I PP I 7 31 30
The idea of his returning no more Elizabeth treated with PP I 21 120 28
wonder and repine at his returning no more, and though a PP II 1 137 26
Miss Bingley said something of his never returning to PP II 3 149 26
has not much idea of ever returning to Netherfield again?" PP II 9 177 6
7
am certain, remember, with the design of soon returning.-- PP II 12 198 5
To persuade him against returning into Hertfordshire, when PP II 12 199 5
recollection and a returning smile, replied, that he had PP II 18 233 27
only of returning to the carriage as quickly as possible. PP III 1 254 57
neighbouring gentlemen, on his returning to Netherfield. PP III 11 332 24
But on returning to the drawing room, when her letter was PP III 13 346 22
Tom returning from them into the drawing-room, where MP I 13 125 14
Well, Edmund," he continued, returning to the former MP I 13 126 23
dread of her uncle was returning, and with it compassion MP II 1 176 4
into his own dear room, every agitation was returning. MP II 1 181 17
should make a point of returning to Mansfield, at any time MP II 2 192 11
being also obliged on returning down stairs, to be fixed MP II 4 206 3
thought, urged Fanny's returning with her in a much more MP II 8 257 15
not have thought of returning it; but being her brother's MP II 9 263 13
invariable; and to be returning them with what must have MP II 9 263 16
over the work, then returning to her seat to finish a note MP II 12 296 31
She was struck, quite struck, when on returning from her MP III 1 322 51
He was returning to Mansfield with spirits ready to feed MP III 3 334 1
Miss Crawford's power was all returning. MP III 4 349 24
capable of returning an affection as this seems to imply." MP III 4 353 45
To be sure, your uncle's returning that very evening! MP III 5 360 14
almost half her life, of returning for a couple of months MP III 6 369 11
arise about your returning to Mansfield--without waiting MP III 11 411 16
could not think of his returning to town, and being MP III 11 413 31
you are,) keep away, when you have the means of returning. MP III 14 435 14
and I write, by his desire, to propose your returning home. MP III 15 442 23
to her aunt Bertram, returning to every former office, MP III 16 449 4
A better written letter, Harriet, (returning it,) than I E I 7 51 5
by Mr. John Knightley returning from the daily visit to E I 13 109 6
no present danger in returning home, but no assurances E I 15 128 17
18
better, than Harriet's returning the visit; but in a way E II 4 185 13
body's returning into their proper place the next morning. E II 6 198 5
Cole's carriage horses returning from exercise, or a stray E II 9 233 24
Well, (returning into the room,) I have not been able to E II 10 245 52
He had met her before breakfast as he was returning from a E II 16 293 10
of the two, were to be returning with the same warmth of E III 1 315 1
implied a dread of her returning power, and a discreet E III 1 316 5
get away, the day would be spent in coming and returning. E III 1 318 10
and mortification she must be returning to her seat. E III 2 327 38
he had the pleasure of returning for answer, that they E III 3 336 12
he joined them; and, on returning, they fell in with a E III 5 344 3
The rest of the party were now returning, and all were E III 6 366 74
you any idea of Mr. Knightley's returning your affection?" E III 11 407 29
30
Now there would be pleasure in her returning.-- E III 18 475 41
he mentioned it no more; returning, with all his zeal, to P III 3 23 34
Then, returning to his former earnest tone: "my first wish P III 10 88 26
had taken their intended drive, and were returning home. P III 10 90 38
nature of the country required, for going and returning. P III 11 94 8
his intention of returning in the same carriage to Lyme; P III 12 117 76
again, and returning through the well-known apartments. P IV 1 125 17
There was one point which Anne, on returning to her family, P IV 4 145 1
in vain; but at last, in returning down Pulteney-Street, P IV 7 178 28
that he had a heart returning to her at least; that anger, P IV 8 185 21
were heard returning; the door opened; it was himself. P IV 11 236 40
moments, marked by returning hope or increasing P IV 11 244 71
day for them to be all returning from their Airings to S 4 384 1

RETURNS (9)

be in town, or whether she returns here again, I know not. LS 27 297 3
The ladies were not wanting in civil returns; & Robert W 357 28
last night my dear Emma & returns today, is more W 360 29
period, to enjoy many returns of the delightful PP I 21 116 8
"But if he returns no more this winter, my choice will PP I 21 120 27
if the Antigua estate is to make such poor returns." MP I 3 30 54
resolved on doing nothing till she returns to Mansfield. MP III 13 422 2
she returns to Wimpole-Street to-day, the old lady is come. MP III 14 435 14
what returns it will make her in a year or two. S 3 376 1

REV. MR. NORRIS (1)

attached to the Rev. Mr. Norris, a friend of her brother- MP I 1 3 1

REVEALED (7)
the whole truth were revealed, and now on this attack, SS II 3 157 17
secure, till he had revealed his present engagement; for SS III 14 373 3
With apprehensive caution therefore it was revealed, and SS III 14 373 3
of myself to know what could or ought to be revealed. PP II 12 202 5
To no creature had it been revealed, where secresy was PP III 3 270 10
in, when the mystery of her parentage came to be revealed. E I 8 64 47
the one revealed to her--her affection for Mr. Knightley.-- E III 11 412 46
REVEALING (1)
To know that she had the power of revealing what would so PP II 15 217 17
REVEALMENT (1)
when circumstances make the revealment of it eligible. SS I 16 84 9
REVEIW (1)
of our affairs, & every reveiw has served to convince me LS 30 300 1
REVEL (1)
boys were holding high revel; the whole completed by a P IV 2 134 29
REVELLED (1)
but internally her heart revelled in angry pleasure, in P IV 1 125 13
REVENGE (9)
deserving every sort of revenge that it can be in my power LS 10 258 2
would be a species of revenge to which I should hardly LS 12 261 4
reasonings of family partiality, or a desire of revenge." NA II 12 219 15
Lucy, eager to take some revenge on her, "you think young SS II 13 243 38
"Well!" said Mrs. Jennings, "that is her revenge. SS III 1 269 54
revenge, such injustice, such inhumanity as this!" PP I 16 80 33
His revenge would have been complete indeed. PP II 12 202 5
was now cool enough to dispense with any other revenge.-- MP II 2 194 19
Doubtless it was so; and she could take no revenge, for he P III 7 61 34
REVENGING (1)
hope of revenging himself on me, was a strong inducement. PP II 12 202 5
REVENUE (1)
detriment of the post office revenue, be continued longer. LS 42 311 1
REVERED (1)
I could not have forgotten my revered father's intentions. PP II 12 201 5
REVERENTIAL (1)
their Gothic form with reverential care, were yet less NA II 5 162 26
REVERIE (14)
A reverie succeeded this conviction--and when Isabella NA I 15 120 23
As she said this, she sunk into a reverie for a few SS I 16 88 33
From a reverie of this kind, as she sat at her drawing- SS I 19 105 13
From a reverie of this kind she was recalled at the end of SS III 8 331 70
71
rousing himself from a reverie at least equally painful, SS III 8 331 70
71
afterwards he fell into a reverie, which no remarks, no SS III 12 360 26
by Miss Bingley, "I can guess the subject of your reverie." PP I 6 27 44
45
He was roused from the reverie of retrospection and regret MP II 6 236 23
his opinion; he was in a reverie of fond reflection, MP II 9 262 11
She was in a reverie of sweet remembrances. MP III 5 358 8
"Why, Fanny, you are absolutely in a reverie! MP III 5 360 16
The result of his reverie was, "no, Emma, I do not think E II 15 288 36
Harriet, who had been standing in no unhappy reverie, was E III 11 408 34
from a little reverie, "to be coming and finding us here.-- P IV 1 127 24
REVERIES (2)
the charm of those reveries which his image did not fill. NA II 2 141 11
She had a few tender reveries now and then, which he could MP III 11 409 7
REVERSE (22)
in, would undergo so speedy, so melancholy a reverse! LS 24 285 1
she was the very reverse of all that she had been before. NA II 15 240 1
over the present reverse for the chief of the morning. SS I 16 83 2
Such behaviour as this, so exactly the reverse of her own, SS I 19 104 11
that you should then know how much I was the reverse!"-- SS III 1 262 21
of dinner by their sudden reverse, from eating much;--and SS III 7 315 27
more so under this sudden reverse;--he stood the picture W 330 11
I have great hopes of finding him quite the reverse. PP I 13 64 18
and been obliged to put up with exactly the reverse! MP I 5 46 22
and cheerful, the very reverse of what they found in the MP I 7 71 31
a state absolutely their reverse; there had been no MP II 9 270 40
of a character the very reverse of what I had supposed. MP III 1 318 39
it to be rather the reverse, and could imagine her to be MP III 3 335 6
respect, the very reverse of what she could have wished. MP III 8 388 3
in Mrs. Norris, by its reverse in himself, clearly saw MP III 17 463 7
But, Ah! united, what reverse we have! E I 9 71 14
But Ah! united (courtship, you know,) what reverse we have! E I 9 73 18
many respects, the very reverse of what she had meant and E I 16 135 6
for a woman to feel in confessing exactly the reverse.-- E III 13 426 17
in the event of such a reverse would be so much more to be P III 5 34 12
must be considered as the very reverse of frightful.-- P IV 8 182 6
I believe the reverse. P IV 11 233 22
REVERSED (1)
myself, I am sure I only wish our situations were reversed. NA I 15 119 18
REVERSES (1)
Like other great men under reverses," he added with a P IV 11 247 84
REVERSING (1)
of a tacit consent, no reversing decree of unjustifiable NA II 15 247 15
REVERSION (2)
deal to say; and the reversion of Mansfield Park, and a MP I 5 47 28
peace, which "may be a decent equivalent for the reversion. P IV 9 203 72
REVERT (2)
of the game as never to revert to what he had been saying W 359 28
no sooner had he begun to revert to her own home, than her MP I 2 15 10
REVERTED (5)
Thorpe's ideas then all reverted to the merits of his own NA I 9 64 27
that she reverted to it again as soon as Elinor appeared. SS III 4 291 46
Edmund reverted to the harp, and was again very happy in MP I 6 60 52
could not but be reverted to; the year of their engagement P III 8 63 2
and when Lady Russell reverted to their former hopes and P IV 1 124 11
REVERTING (2)
was on the point of reverting to what interested her at NA I 6 42 33
Elizabeth could not help reverting once more to the first, PP I 16 82 44
45
REVIEW (7)
have now passed in review before the reader; the events of NA I 13 97 1
humanity, in its fearful review of past scenes of guilt? NA II 8 187 13
more severe by the review of objects on which she had NA II 14 230 1
His character sunk on every review of it; and as a PP II 3 149 27
on what had passed, was increased by every review of it. PP II 11 193 31
ten years, I will take you to a review at the end of them." PP III 6 300 32
In a review of the two houses, as they appeared to her MP III 8 392 12
REVIEWERS (1)
Let us leave it to the reviewers to abuse such effusions NA I 5 37 4
REVIVAL (5)
acknowledge a temporary revival, tried to keep her young SS III 7 314 22
nor was there any revival of past occurrences, or any PP II 11 188 1
all well pleased with its revival, and an early day was MP I 8 75 1
at Kellynch, without a revival of former pain; and many a P III 4 30 10
result, not the cause of a revival of his warm attachment. P IV 11 243 68
REVIVE (7)
when her spirits began to revive, and her mind became SS I 3 14 1
such friends, however, and such flattery, he did revive. SS III 13 370 35
Elizabeth now began to revive. PP I 18 100 68
was received to revive old, and create some new sensations. MP III 14 433 12
to other subjects, and revive some interest in the usual MP III 16 449 6
before, was beginning to revive a little local agitation; E II 5 186 2
in Anne that she could fancy the mother to revive again. P III 1 6 9
REVIVED (18)
be revived again, or at least, be listened to again. LS 35 304 1
which she awoke perfectly revived, in excellent spirits, NA I 9 60 1
Catherine's spirits revived as they drove from the door; NA II 5 155 4
to see the house, soon revived the subject; and her father NA II 8 182 1
she added with revived security of Edward's honour and SS I 22 131 29
From this time that subject was never revived by Elinor, SS II 2 151 42
and when the subject was revived the next morning, and she PP II 19 241 17
of Bingley, in half an hour's visit, had revived. PP III 12 339 10
She was a little revived, however, by his bringing back PP III 12 341 20
21
in the drawing-room; it was revived in the dining-parlour. MP I 6 52 1
pianoforte, she suddenly revived it by turning round MP I 11 108 4
austerity, without reproach, and she revived a little. MP III 1 321 47
From this hour, the subject is never to be revived between MP III 2 330 16
having so many friends about them, revived him a little. E I 15 127 12
Mr. Elton's rights, however, gradually revived. E II 3 180 57
Woodhouse revived the former good old days of the room?-- E II 6 198 5
for, though partially revived, she was quite helpless; and P III 12 111 49
of "Lady Elliot" first revived in herself; of being P IV 5 160 26
REVIVING (5)
of others, while reviving her with lavender water. SS II 6 177 12
Her voice sunk with the word, but presently reviving she SS III 10 344 14
15
and a resolution of reviving the subject again, should SS III 10 348 34
dress--listening with reviving spirits to his cheerful MP III 7 384 35
any reviving question from her would have been awkward. E I 14 118 4
REVOLT (2)
Every kind of pride must revolt from the connection. he PP III 10 326 3
Her feelings were all in revolt. MP III 4 354 47
REVOLTED (3)
from which her heart revolted; & instead of adopting so LS 7 253 2
whom his pride had revolted, in his offer to herself. PP III 1 254 58
even when her heart revolted from it as impossible--when MP III 15 441 20
REVOLTING (2)
duplicity must ever be revolting, but I have heard nothing P IV 9 207 91
not so complicate nor so revolting as his; and Anne would P IV 10 215 13
REVOLTS (2)
Oh! no, no;--every feeling revolts. E II 8 225 72
Every thing that revolts other people, low company, paltry P IV 5 157 15
REVOLUTION (4)
What a revolution in her ideas! she, who had so longed to NA II 11 212 16
suffered no revolution from the marriage of her sisters. PP III 19 386 6
Here was another strange revolution of mind!-- MP III 9 393 1
The revolution which one instant had made in Anne, was P IV 11 237 41
REVOLVING (4)
In revolving these matters, while she undressed, it NA II 8 188 17
In revolving Lady Catherine's expressions, however, she PP III 15 360 2
Thirteen winters' revolving frosts had seen her opening P III 1 7 12
Elizabeth was, in fact, revolving a great measure. P IV 10 226 64
REWARD (25)
a sort of reward to behaviour deserving very differently. LS 15 267 5
length to have its just reward, for hardly had she been NA I 4 31 2
reward in the affection it makes every body feel for you. NA II 1 136 46
recommend parental tyranny, or reward filial disobedience. NA II 16 252 7
"Perhaps then you would bestow it as a reward on that SS I 17 93 29
With such a reward for her tears, the child was too wise SS I 21 121 10
His chief reward for the painful exertion of disclosing SS II 10 216 15
his mother's threats, for a woman who could not reward him. SS III 1 268 46
a rich reward in store, for every present inconvenience. SS III 7 316 28
than to his rival's, the reward of her sister was due, and SS III 9 335 5
reward in her bodily ease, and her calmness of spirits. SS III 10 341 6
Marianne, by general consent, was to be the reward of all. SS III 14 378 13
My reward is to be the indulgence of conveying you to W 339 18
to work upon these, and grounds that will well reward you. MP I 6 53 9
highly as temptation and reward to the soldier and sailor MP I 11 110 22
next morning, seemed the reward of his ingenuity in MP II 6 232 13
be a kindness, and even reward the owner with a smile when MP II 6 237 23
animate, and reward those duties might yet be unattainable. MP II 8 255 10
you by his steady affection, will give him his reward. MP III 4 348 21
Fanny must have been his reward--and a reward very MP III 17 467 19
been his reward--and a reward very voluntarily bestowed-- MP III 17 467 19
reward him, returned with Mrs. Weston to Mrs. Bates's door. E II 9 235 35
dancing, I believe, like virtue, must be its own reward. E II 12 258 3
She had never considered herself as entitled to reward for P IV 10 212 1
Smith, but here was a reward indeed springing from it!-- P IV 10 212 1
REWARDED (11)
I might have been rewarded for my exertions as I ought.-- LS 2 245 1
rate, I shall there be rewarded by your society & a little LS 25 294 4
hearts. the evening rewarded her confidence; she was met NA II 1 131 14
and her confidence was rewarded by finding even the former, SS II 12 229 1
thought herself amply rewarded for the sacrifice of the SS II 14 247 4
And now to be so rewarded! SS III 1 266 36
He was rewarded by a gracious answer, & a more liberal W 346 21
which was very ill rewarded at their close; for Mary, on PP I 18 100 68
Her impatience for this second letter was as well rewarded PP II 3 147 21
it would now be rewarded by her acceptance of his hand. PP II 11 189 6
And is he to be rewarded with that sweet young woman?-- E III 13 426 16
REWARDS (1)
I have valued myself on honourable toils and just rewards. P IV 11 247 84
REYNOLDS (9)
with alarm, while Mrs. Reynolds replied, that he was, PP III 1 246 8
"And that," said Mrs. Reynolds, pointing to another of the PP III 1 247 11
Mrs. Reynolds then directed their attention to one of miss PP III 1 247 20
and remarks; Mrs. Reynolds, either from pride or PP III 1 248 23
Mrs. Reynolds could interest her on no other point. PP III 1 249 37
Mrs. Reynolds anticipated Miss Darcy's delight, when she PP III 1 250 45
Mrs. Reynolds informed them, that it had been taken in his PP III 1 250 47
The commendation bestowed on him by Mrs. Reynolds was of PP III 1 250 48
Poor Reynolds, she was always very fond of me. PP III 10 327 11
RHAPSODIZING (1)
You will think me rhapsodizing; but when I am out of doors, MP II 4 209 16
RHAPSODY (1)
with high compliment & Rhapsody on the slightest S 8 405 2
RHEUMATIC (4)
day) of a slight rheumatic feel in one of his shoulders." SS I 8 38 11
and very poorly with the rheumatic gout in his joints--I E III 8 383 29
to contend with a severe rheumatic fever, which finally P IV 5 152 4
You are not rheumatic I suppose?--" S 10 415 1
RHEUMATISM (3)
"Did not you hear him complain of the rheumatism? and is SS I 8 37 6
box on account of the rheumatism which I had been MP II 2 189 5
It gives me the rheumatism.-- S 10 415 1
RHEUMATISMS (1)
with aches, cramps, rheumatisms, and every species of SS I 8 38 12
RHODOMONTADE (1)
misled by the rhodomontade of his friend to believe his NA II 15 246 12
RHUBARB (1)
potions to be procured, like rhubarb, from every druggist. NA II 10 200 3
RHYMING (1)
Crawford, and here is the rhyming butler for me--if nobody MP I 14 132 7
RIBBAND (1)
ribband or string, or any thing just to keep my boot on." E I 10 89 37
RIBBON (7)
indispensable yard of ribbon which must be bought without NA I 14 114 50
had nothing but a bit of ribbon to fasten it to; and MP II 8 254 8
figured; and that a blue ribbon, be it ever so beautiful, E II 9 235 35
But I shall want the ribbon directly--so it had better go E II 9 235 36
it had better go to Hartfield--at least the ribbon. E II 9 235 36
Here,--probably this basket with pink ribbon. E III 6 355 20
from altering her ribbon to settling her accounts, from P IV 10 220 31
RIBBONS (5)
coquelicot ribbons instead of green; I quite longed for it. NA I 6 39 4
But why should not I wear pink ribbons? SS III 2 272 12
I hear you have a charming collection of new ribbons from E II 9 237 48
of 1814,) wearing black ribbons for his wife, she could P III 1 8 17
the two, Miss B.'s white ribbons might not have fallen S 12 426 1
RICE (1)

roast mutton and rice pudding they were hastening home for. E I 13 109 6
RICH (87)
Charles is very rich I am sure; when a man has once got LS 5 250 2
Mrs. Thorpe was a widow, and not a very rich one; she was NA I 4 34 8
very abruptly, "old Allen is as rich as a Jew--is not he?" NA I 9 63 10
Yes, I believe, he is very rich." NA I 9 63 11
But they are very good king of people, and very rich. NA I 9 68 46
A very fine fellow; as rich as a Jew. NA I 12 96 20
rich in Gothic ornaments, stood forward for admiration. NA II 7 177 19
kitchen of the convent, rich in the massy walls and smoke NA II 8 183 3
its wood, and ornaments of rich carving might be pointed NA II 8 184 5
She was guilty only of being less rich than he had NA II 15 244 11
fortune, bestowing a rich aunt, and sinking half the NA II 15 245 12
of a man who had died very rich; and some might have SS I 3 15 5
It was a pleasant fertile spot, well wooded., and rich in SS I 6 28 1
It would be an excellent match, for he was rich and she SS I 8 36 1
Men are very safe with us, let them be ever so rich. SS I 9 44 24
was independent, there was no reason to believe him rich. SS I 14 71 4
is attainable, and were I rich enough, I would instantly SS I 14 72 11
the country, though still rich, was less wild and more SS I 16 85 15
"if my children were all to be rich without my help." SS I 17 92 23
comfortable and snug--with rich meadows and several neat SS I 18 97 4
Miss Dashwood, before he married, as he was so rich?" SS I 21 124 28
then--Miss Grey I think you called her--is very rich?" SS II 8 194 9
But the family are all rich together. SS II 8 194 10
to know him to be rich, to be equally civil to him. SS II 11 223 14
being rich, and how acceptable Mrs. Ferrars's kindness is." SS II 11 226 35
a rich reward in store, for every present inconvenience. SS III 7 316 28
Marianne, he might at once have been happy and rich. SS III 14 379 18
but I beleive it is a rich old Dr Harding, uncle to the W 317 2
"He is rich, is not he?"-- W 328 8
"If I were as rich as Mr. Darcy," cried a young Lucas who PP I 5 20 21
rich husband, or any husband, I dare say I should adopt it. PP I 6 22 7
His pride never deserts him; but with the rich, he is PP I 16 82 48
His being such a charming young man, and so rich, and PP I 18 99 63
them in the way of other rich men; and lastly, it was so PP I 18 99 63
I wish you very happy and very rich, and by refusing your PP I 19 107 16
We are not rich enough, or grand enough for them; and she PP I 21 119 20
many others, because he is rich, and many others are poor. PP II 10 183 10
Though Mr. Bennet was not imagined to be very rich, he PP III 10 323 2
He is rich, to be sure, and you may have more fine clothes PP III 17 376 31
Oh! my sweetest Lizzy! how rich and how great you will be! PP III 17 378 43
It is a great comfort to have you so rich, and when you PP III 19 386 7
by shrubs in the rich foliage of summer, was enough to MP I 7 65 13
floors, solid mahogany, rich damask, marble, gilding and MP I 9 84 3
"I mean to be too rich to lament or to feel any thing of MP II 4 213 36
"You intend to be very rich," said Edmund, with a look MP II 4 213 37
a much greater respect for those that are honest and rich." MP II 4 213 40
"Your degree of respect for honesty, rich or poor, is MP II 4 213 41
in the midst of all the rich ornaments which she supposed MP II 8 254 8
the way of a rich, superior, longworded, arbitrary uncle. MP II 12 297 35
accept him, for he was rich, and she had nothing; but he MP III 5 361 16
I could better bear to lose her, because not rich enough, MP III 13 422 2
There was a rich amends, however, preparing for her. MP III 13 425 7
His liberality had a rich repayment, and the general MP III 17 472 30
Emma Woodhouse, handsome, clever, and rich, with a E I 1 5 1
His own stomach could bear nothing rich, and he could E I 2 19 14
for a woman neither young, handsome, rich, nor married. E I 3 21 4
and good luck, he may be rich in time, it is next to E I 4 30 20
thrive and be a very rich man in time--and his being E I 4 34 40
Is not this room rich in specimens of your landscapes and E I 6 43 14
little minds belong to rich people in authority, I think E I 18 147 19
of Mr. Dixon, a young man, rich and agreeable, almost as E II 2 165 7
pleasure at Col. Campbell's being so rich and so liberal.-- E II 8 216 20
The rich brother-in-law near Bristol was the pride of the E II 14 272 17
to me to be with the rich; my mortifications, I think, E II 17 301 17
fruit--only too rich to be eaten much of--inferior to E III 6 358 35
prosperity and beauty, its rich pastures, spreading flocks, E III 6 360 40
She proved to be the daughter of a tradesman, rich enough E III 19 481 3
by uniting himself to a rich woman of inferior birth. P III 1 8 15
This peace will be turning all our rich navy officers P III 3 17 1
If a rich Admiral were to come in our way, Sir Walter-----" P III 3 17 1
But, he was confident that he should soon be rich;--full P III 4 27 4
could not doubt his being rich;--and, in favour of his P III 4 30 8
He was rich, and being turned on shore, fully intended to P III 7 61 38
a very rich gentleman, and would be a baronight some day." P III 12 106 15
rich, and excessively in love with his friend. P IV 3 139 9
man) and beginning to be rich, just as his friend ought to P IV 9 209 95
not large, would be enough to make her comparatively rich. P IV 9 210 98
She might have been absolutely rich and perfectly healthy, P IV 12 252 12
& that she was a very rich old lady, who had buried two S 3 375 1
Lady D. had been a rich Miss Brereton, born to wealth but S 3 375 1
well fenced & planted, & rich in the garden, orchard & S 4 379 1
two large families, one a rich West Indian from Surry, the S 5 387 1
Our Butchers & Bakers & Traders in general cannot get rich S 6 392 1
marry somebody of fortune too--she must get a rich husband. S 7 401 1
Thus it is, when rich people are Sordid."-- S 7 402 1
The rich Westindians, & the young ladies seminary had all S 11 420 1
In Miss Lambe, here was the very young lady, sickly & rich, S 11 422 1
RICHARD (11)
his name was Richard--and he had never been handsome. NA I 1 13 1
And besides that, my cousin Richard said himself, that SS III 2 272 16
Richard, and if he does, Colonel Forster will hire him. PP I 14 68 13
14
her darling; and John, Richard, Sam, Tom, and Charles, MP III 8 389 4
Where's dear Mr. Richard?-- E III 2 323 19
How do you do, Mr. Richard?-- E III 2 323 19
mamma; she is thinking so much of poor Richard! P III 6 50 27
and her head is quite full of it, and of poor Richard! P III 6 50 27
him, by calling him "poor Richard," been nothing better P III 6 51 29
one of the girls; "mamma is thinking of poor Richard." P III 8 67 26
Dr & Mrs Brown--Mr Richard Pratt.-- S 6 389 1
RICHARD III. (1)
from Shylock or Richard iii. down to the singing hero of a MP I 13 123 6
RICHARD'S (2)
I do not know when poor Richard's cravats would be done, NA II 15 240 2
it, was the name of poor Richard's captain, at one time, I P III 6 50 27
RICHARDSON'S (1)
appeared to tread in Richardson's steps, so far as man's S 8 404 1
RICHARDSONS (3)
pair of silk stockings, and came off with the Richardsons." SS III 2 274 16
"Oh, la! here come the Richardsons. SS III 2 275 25
exceptionable parts of Richardsons; & such authors as have S 8 404 1
RICHER (8)
not be sixpence the richer for it at the end of the year. SS I 2 11 23
he grows poor, and a richer girl is ready to have him. SS II 8 194 10
to the ridicule of richer people in her present home.-- W 345 21
It is for your children's good that I wish to be richer. MP I 3 30 52
In all probability he was already the richer of the two, P IV 3 140 11
gentlemen were richer, but he has no other fault to find. P IV 10 218 22
richer man than either Captain Benwick or Charles Hayter.-- P IV 12 249 5
Miss Lambe has an immense fortune--richer than all the S 9 409 1
RICHES (7)
in that respect, & that riches only, will not satisfy me. LS 2 245 1
to the enjoyment of riches, considers fortune as necessary LS 30 301 4
by his prospect of riches, was led before the end of a SS I 10 49 11
"May she always be poor; if she can employ her riches no SS I 14 72 9
the privilege of riches upon a poor dependent cousin, by SS I 15 75 6
ideas of the necessity of riches, which I was naturally SS III 8 323 40
was continually, and the riches which she was in MP III 9 396 7
RICHEST (1)
Mr. Martin may be the richest of the two, but he is E I 8 62 39

RICHLY (4)
"If it were merely a fine house richly furnished," said PP II 19 240 15
whom nature had so richly endowed?-- spoilt,spoilt!--" MP III 16 455 18
and agitation richly scattered--the lady had been so E II 4 181 4
which has been so richly extended towards myself; but, E III 14 441 8
RICHLY-ENDOWED (1)
Abbey having been a richly-endowed convent at the time of NA II 2 141 13
RICHMOND (17)
There are some charming little villas about Richmond." NA I 15 120 20
"Richmond!" cried Catherine.-- NA I 15 120 21
going down to Richmond for the whole time of her being at MP III 16 455 19
When he returned from Richmond, he would have been glad to MP III 17 468 21
They were going to remove immediately to Richmond. E III 1 317 7
The difference in that respect of Richmond and London was E III 1 317 10
but Richmond was the very distance for easy intercourse. E III 1 318 10
had removed to Richmond, a few lines from Frank, to say E III 1 318 11
and taken a road, the Richmond road, which, though E III 3 333 5
every moment from Richmond; and Mrs. Elton, in all her E III 6 358 35
"Then pray stay at Richmond." E III 6 365 71
Richmond was to take him back before the following evening. E III 6 366 76
sent to Randall's to take Mr. Frank Churchill to Richmond. E III 8 383 29
had come over from Richmond soon after the return of the E III 8 383 31
The following day brought news from Richmond to throw E III 9 387 11
which the late event at Richmond had brought forward. E III 10 393 18
the same evening to Richmond, though I might have staid E III 14 441 8
RICHNESS (1)
talked of poetry, the richness of the present age, and P III 11 100 23
RICKETTY (1)
It is the most devilish little ricketty business I ever NA I 9 65 28
RID (27)
that I am impatient to be rid of him, as Manwaring comes LS 31 302 1
"Well, I am amazingly glad I have got rid of them! NA I 6 43 39
"Yes, sometimes; but he has rid out this morning with my NA I 10 73 18
Impatient to get rid of those hateful evidences of her NA II 7 173 3
she added, desiring to get rid of the subject; "and storms NA II 7 174 5
occurred; and eager to get rid of such a weight on her NA II 13 220 1
and over every year, and there is no getting rid of it. SS I 2 10 20
her husband could not get rid of her; and exultingly said, SS I 20 112 26
had got upon his horse, and rid into the country some SS III 2 273 16
assistance from her desire of getting rid of Elizabeth. PP I 10 52 53
who was most anxious to get rid of him, and have his PP I 15 71 6
She had got rid of two of the secrets which had weighed on PP II 17 227 25
she had walked fast to get rid of him; and unwilling for PP III 10 329 33
34
Mrs. Bennet got rid of her two most deserving daughters. PP III 19 385 1
seeing him out of it, to be rid of the worst object MP II 2 194 21
I took uneasiness with me, and there was no getting rid of MP III 4 355 52
am sure I hope I shall be rid of her before she has staid MP III 7 385 39
kindness, and till she got rid of this idea, till it MP III 12 418 5
to get rid of them at the idlest haunts in the kingdom. E I 18 146 12
industriously getting rid of the subject as they returned;- E II 1 155 1
I must get rid of every thing.-- E III 4 340 26
which Emma could not get rid of, and which constituted the E III 11 402 1
every captain wishes to get rid of, been six months on P III 6 51 30
been at some pains to get rid of him; but it was too P III 8 67 28
had the pleasure of getting rid of Mr. Elliot; and she did P IV 8 189 44
to avoid and get rid of as he can--very natural, perhaps. P IV 9 196 32
"Give me joy: I have got rid of Sir Walter and Miss. P IV 9 203 72
RIDDEN (2)
horses and mules he had ridden, or his many narrow escapes MP II 6 237 23
He had ridden home through the rain; and had walked up E III 13 433 41
RIDDLE (3)
any thing of the riddle kind; but he had desired Perry to E I 9 70 6
even that particular riddle which you have heard me E I 9 78 54
"She is a riddle, quite a riddle!" said she.-- E II 15 285 13
RIDDLE-BOOK (1)
There go you and your riddle-book one of these days."-- E I 10 83 3
RIDDLES (2)
and transcribing all the riddles of every sort that she E I 9 69 3
"So many clever riddles as there used to be when he was E I 9 70 5
RIDE (35)
Consider how far you have to ride. NA I 15 120 24
You have had a very fine day for your ride." NA II 9 195 13
That is good news however; I will ride over to-morrow, and SS I 9 43 13
"Yes; and he was up again at eight to ride to covert." SS I 9 45 27
and keep a servant to ride it, and after all, build a SS I 12 58 1
she added, "and when it arrives, we will ride every day. SS I 12 58 2
"Ladies should ride in dirty weather.-- W 345 21
Do you ride?" W 345 21
to give a flat denial, and ride off as fast as I could." PP I 10 49 31
window, enter the paddock, and ride towards the house. PP III 11 333 30
Was it merely to ride to Longbourn and be embarrassed? or PP III 18 381 15
from, the same people to look at, the same horse to ride." MP I 3 27 35
by her aunts, "she might ride one of her cousins' horses MP I 4 35 7
one that his cousin might ride; he knew where such a one MP I 4 37 8
never can; and unluckily it is out of distance for a ride. MP I 6 56 23
an inclination to learn to ride, which the former caught MP I 7 66 14
half an hour before her ride were to begin; and Fanny, on MP I 7 66 14
"For there is more than time enough for my cousin to ride MP I 7 68 19
you will have a pleasant ride, and that I may have nothing MP I 7 68 20
"I was sure she would ride well," said Julia; "she has the MP I 7 69 24
Edmund asked Fanny whether she meant to ride the next day. MP I 7 69 26
"I shall not ride to-morrow, certainly," said Fanny; "I MP I 7 70 29
Fanny's comfort, and the ride to Mansfield common took MP I 7 70 30
persuaded, that when she does not ride, she ought to walk. MP I 7 73 55
and ride over to Stoke, and settle with one of them." MP I 15 148 58
"To walk and ride with me, to be sure." MP II 6 229 2
told you what happened to me yesterday in my ride home." MP II 7 240 13
Mansfield Park; he might ride over, every Sunday, to a MP II 7 247 42
is sure to ride through every week in his way to Kingston. E I 4 29 13
in executing it! he could ride to London at any time. E I 6 49 40
An hour's ride. E III 1 317 10
had he known how hot a ride he should have, and how late, E III 6 363 53
He must have had a wet ride.-- E III 13 424 1
anxiously hoping might not have taken cold from his ride.-- E III 14 434 3
Benwick seemed much more disposed to ride over to Kellynch. P IV 2 133 25
RIDER (2)
A very decent shot, and there is not a bolder rider in SS I 9 43 17
He did not believe there was a bolder rider in England! SS II 10 214 9
RIDES (5)
They took their cheerful rides in the fine mornings of MP I 4 36 7
She rides only for pleasure, you for health." MP I 7 70 29
Fanny's rides recommenced the very next day, and as it was MP I 8 75 1
country; and Fanny, whose rides had never been extensive, MP I 8 80 31
Pleasant rides?-- E II 5 191 27
RIDGE (3)
rest on the farthest ridge of hills in the horizon, and SS III 6 302 8
ground, and backed by a ridge of high woody hill;-- and in PP III 1 245 3
the constant effluvia of a ridge of putrifying sea weed, S 1 369 1
RIDICULE (16)
the probability of wishing to throw ridicule on his age. SS I 8 37 3
to call for the ridicule so justly annexed to sensibility. SS I 10 49 12
laughed at; but ridicule could not shame, and seemed SS I 11 54 3
But I doubt whether ridicule,--has Penelope much wit?"-- W 318 2
to the ridicule of richer people in her present home.-- W 345 21
I hope I never ridicule what is wise or good. PP I 11 57 21
which often expose a strong understanding to ridicule." PP I 11 57 22
the mention of his misfortunes with contempt and ridicule." PP II 11 192 21
would draw down the ridicule and censure of the ladies PP III 2 263 10
that could provoke his ridicule, or disgust him into PP III 13 346 21
the pains of tyranny, of ridicule, and neglect, yet almost MP I 16 152 2
by a single attempt at throwing ridicule on his cause. MP II 7 248 47

or of deriving it, except in subsequent ridicule. E III 8 378 3
gold ridicule by her side, saying, with significant nods, E III 16 453 12
13
from him some pleasant ridicule, which reminded Anne of P III 8 64 4
taste cannot tolerate,--which ridicule will seize. P III 8 68 30

RIDICULED (2)
her being ridiculed & despised by every man who sees her. LS 19 274 2
they had parted at last with mutual vexation. MP II 10 279 21

RIDICULING (2)
such an opportunity of ridiculing her relations was bad PP I 18 102 72
to him alone, and ridiculing the acting of the others. MP I 17 160 8

RIDICULOUS (25)
it would be ridiculous in me to repeat the instances of LS 12 260 2
There is a sort of ridiculous delicacy about him which LS 16 268 2
were so exactly the same, it was quite ridiculous! NA I 10 71 3
ridiculous, quite absurd to make any further objection. NA I 13 100 19
It is too ridiculous! SS I 8 37 4
It is so ridiculous!" SS I 19 107 26
It will be so ridiculous to see all his letters directed SS I 20 113 35
and sometimes almost ridiculous, made her those SS II 8 193 7
It seemed quite ridiculous. SS III 4 292 55
and Mary brown, he could conceive nothing more ridiculous. SS III 5 298 33
it was even a ridiculous one, but to her reason, her SS III 13 364 10
disposition, which delighted in any thing ridiculous. PP I 3 12 14
may be rendered ridiculous by a person whose first object PP I 11 57 20
flirt that ever made herself and her family ridiculous. PP II 18 231 18
ridiculous, contained much good sense and solid reasoning. PP III 15 361 2
It would be too ridiculous for me to attempt any thing MP I 6 53 9
Oh! I believe I was relating to her some ridiculous MP I 10 99 12
be sorry to make the character ridiculous by bad acting. MP I 15 145 41
set up for a fine actor, is very ridiculous in my opinion." MP I 18 165 3
house, making part of a ridiculous exhibition in the midst MP II 1 183 23
"Oh! no--I hope I shall not be ridiculous about it. E I 9 78 48
income, must be a ridiculous, disagreeable, old maid! the E I 10 85 19
what is ridiculous are most unfortunately blended in her." E III 7 375 60
the occasional prevalence of the ridiculous over the good. E III 7 375 61
help feeling it almost ridiculous, that she should have E III 11 403 3

RIDICULOUSNESS (1)
There is a ridiculousness about him that entertains me-- W 342 19

RIDING (19)
cricket, base ball, riding on horseback, and running about NA I 1 15 3
or sang, and whether she was fond of riding on horseback. NA I 8 56 11
which the boldness of his riding, though it had never NA I 9 66 31
one; it was a man on horseback riding towards them. SS I 16 86 16
that he was very fond of riding, & had a horse of his own W 331 11
and Darcy and Bingley were seen riding down the street. PP I 15 72 8
how much I used to dread riding, what terrors it gave me MP I 3 27 36
as good for your mind, as riding has been for your health-- MP I 3 27 37
importance of her riding on horseback, no measures were MP I 4 35 7
Miss Crawford's enjoyment of riding was such, that she did MP I 7 66 15
both on horseback, riding side by side, Dr. and Mrs. Grant, MP I 7 67 16
see a lady with such a good heart for riding!" said he. MP I 7 69 22
Bertrams; her delight in riding was like their own; her MP I 7 69 23
If she had been riding before, I should not have asked it MP I 7 73 55
had not had the power of riding, and very seriously MP I 7 74 58
fatigues her so soon, Miss Crawford, except riding." MP I 9 95 68
Tom go on in this way, riding about the country in quest MP I 16 155 22
by a Robert Martin's riding about the country to get E I 4 35 45
most rough usage, and riding out the heaviest weather." P IV 11 233 22

RIDING-WHIP (1)
a rap as the end of a riding-whip cd give--& tho' charged W 344 21

RIGHT (342)
that whatever I do must be right; & look with a degree of LS 16 269 3
been perfectly right in attributing it to my own letter. LS 19 273 1
She has no right to make you unhappy, & she shall not do LS 24 287 7
Besides I could have no right to interfere--Miss Vernon LS 24 287 9
mistaken, it is true, but I beleived myself to be right." LS 24 289 12
He has a right to require a woman of fortune in his LS 30 300 2
Morlands had little other right to the word, for they were NA I 1 13 1
That gentleman knows your name, and you have a right to NA I 10 80 59
She was right; in a few minutes he appeared, and, making NA I 12 93 5
I could have no right." NA I 12 95 14
"Well, nobody would have thought you had no right who saw NA I 12 95 15
But all in vain; Catherine felt herself to be in the right, NA I 13 98 2
If I am wrong, I am doing what I believe to be right." NA I 13 100 12
I must run after Miss Tilney directly and set her right." NA I 13 100 18
If I had thought it right to put it off, I could have NA I 13 100 20
Her conviction of being right however was not enough to NA I 13 101 25
which happened to be the right, she immediately found NA I 13 102 25
subsided) to doubt whether she had been perfectly right. NA I 13 103 29
It is not right; and I wonder Mrs. Thorpe should allow it. NA I 13 104 31
I know it is all very right and necessary, I have often NA I 14 109 24
has a right to do what they like with their own money." NA II 1 136 47
of their own affections, and I believe he is very right. NA II 3 147 20
not doing exactly what was right, and of not being able to NA II 5 154 1
She knew not that she had any right to be surprized, but NA II 5 161 25
and simple, thought it right to encourage the manufacture NA II 7 175 12
for being right, however disagreeable to her his going. NA II 11 211 15
Your kind offices will set all right:--he is the only man NA II 12 216 2
"It is very right that you should stand by your brother." NA II 12 219 14
Catherine said no more, and, with an endeavour to do right, NA II 15 241 7
had passed he had little right to expect a welcome at NA II 15 241 7
was assisted by that right understanding of Mr. Morland's NA II 16 251 6
No one could dispute her right to come; the house was her SS I 1 6 9
Had he been in his right senses, he could not have thought SS I 2 9 5
"I believe you are right, my love; it will be better that SS I 2 11 23
said Mr. Dashwood, "I believe you are perfectly right. SS I 2 12 25
of taste, which in general direct him perfectly right." SS I 4 19 2
as to leave her no right of objection on either point; and, SS I 4 24 21
Every thing he did, was right. SS I 11 54 3
your conjectures may be, you have no right to repeat them." SS I 12 61 17
18
Mrs. Jennings sat on Elinor's right hand; and they had not SS I 13 67 61
only person who can have a right to shew that house; and SS I 13 68 70
or a deviation from what I may think right and consistent." SS I 15 81 43
You are very right in supposing how my money would be SS I 17 92 26
"I believe you are right," he replied, "and yet I have SS I 17 93 36
"But I thought it was right, Elinor," said Marianne, "to SS I 17 93 38
"You are quite in the right;" replied Elinor calmly. SS I 22 132 38
It is very right that you should go to town; I would have SS II 3 156 8
But I have no right, and I could have no chance of SS II 5 173 44
The event proved her conjecture right, though it was SS II 9 204 17
right, is there not some reason to fear I may be wrong?" SS II 9 204 18
What I endured in so beholding her--but I have no right to SS II 9 207 26
it right that they should sometimes see their brother. SS II 10 213 5
undoubted right to dispose of his own property as he chose. SS II 11 225 35
and every body had a right to be equally positive in their SS II 12 233 20
Elinor set him right as to its situation, and it seemed SS II 14 251 16
the consciousness of doing right, that could remain to him SS III 2 270 1
if I understand the matter right, he has been entirely SS III 3 282 17
Mrs. Jennings was quite right in what she said. SS III 4 288 28
Did not I do right?-- SS III 4 291 47
herself that all continued right, left her there again to SS III 7 316 27
fully, so firmly resolved within myself on doing right! SS III 8 324 42
"This is not right, Mr. Willoughby.-- SS III 8 325 52
What Edward had done to forfeit the right of eldest son, SS III 14 377 12
of the reins to take the right turning, & making only one W 322 2
of pleasing, & shewing himself pleased in a right place.--" W 340 19
"You did very right; tho' I wonder at your forbearance, & W 341 19
cd never do anything right--& Emma, whom she seemed no W 360 30
If I may so express it, he has a right to be proud." PP I 5 20 18
right than pleasant that she should go down stairs herself. PP I 8 37 21
"Aye--that is because you have the right disposition. PP I 9 43 23
to his ideas of right, than in any other person present. PP I 10 51 46
but Jane was firm where she felt herself to be right. PP I 12 59 3
by the patronage of the right honourable Lady Catherine de PP I 13 62 12
But here he was set right by Mrs. Bennet, who assured him PP I 13 65 26
"I have no right to give my opinion." said Wickham, "as to PP I 16 77 14
to the right cause, and not to any disrespect for her." PP I 17 87 13
decide on what is right than a young lady like yourself." PP I 18 97 61
first, that I think it a right thing for every clergyman PP I 19 105 9
10
"That is right.-- PP I 21 119 22
I was right, therefore; my last letter had never reached PP II 3 147 23
But, my dear sister, though the event has proved you right, PP II 3 148 26
The last born has as good a right to the pleasures of PP II 6 165 35
Elizabeth had scarcely time to disclaim all right to the PP II 7 170 9
Darcy smiled and said, "you are perfectly right. PP II 8 176 26
for, if I recollect right, he went but the day before. PP II 9 177 4
cannot have a right to such very strong local attachment. PP II 9 179 23
Collins did not think it right to press the subject, from PP II 9 181 30
But I ought to beg his pardon, for I have no right to PP II 10 185 24
"I do not see what right Mr. Darcy had to decide on the PP II 10 185 36
a violation of every thing right could hardly have been PP II 13 208 6
from right herself, was entirely insensible of the evil. PP II 14 213 17
placing gowns in the only right way, that Maria thought PP II 14 213 20
"You are quite right. PP II 17 227 24
I have just as much right to be asked as she has, and more PP II 18 230 13
enough to assume even the appearance of what is right. PP II 18 234 37
38
her temper to be happy; and all was soon right again. PP II 19 239 8
added he, "though it is right to be prepared for the worst, PP III 5 288 37
I knew that his conduct had not been always quite right. PP III 5 290 50
I am sure, but I did not think it right for either of them. PP III 5 292 66
I will believe, that he is come to a right way of thinking. PP III 7 305 37
"Well," cried her mother, "it is all very right; who PP III 7 306 47
son and daughter, let us come to a right understanding. PP III 8 310 9
walk up to her mother's right hand, and hear her say to PP III 9 317 9
you have certainly no right to concern yourself in mine. PP III 14 357 61
As a child I was taught what was right, but I was not PP III 16 369 24
it advisable to retain the right of visiting at Pemberley, PP III 19 387 10
a general wish of doing right, and a desire of seeing all MP I 1 3 1
endeavours to choose exactly the right line of conduct." MP I 1 11 17
a strong desire of doing right; and he could perceive her MP I 2 16 20
On Mr. Norris's death, the presentation became the right MP I 3 24 5
ought to believe you to be right rather than myself, and I MP I 3 27 34
little while, and feel how right you proved to be, I am MP I 3 27 36
It was a connection exactly of the right sort; in the same MP I 4 40 14
set it down that they have not yet seen the right person." MP I 4 43 25
Mothers certainly have not yet got quite the right way of MP I 5 50 36
I do not pretend to set people right, but I do see that MP I 5 50 36
gallantly, "are doing a a great deal to set them right." MP I 5 50 37
Mr. Rushworth is quite right, I think, in meaning to give MP I 6 56 26
London--but this morning we heard of it in the right way. MP I 6 57 33
conversation that struck you Fanny, as not quite right?" MP I 7 63 3
She cannot have given her right notions of what was due to MP I 7 64 8
And what right had she to suppose, that you would not MP I 7 64 10
"The right of a lively mind, Fanny, seizing whatever may MP I 7 64 11
again, he should think it right to attend Mrs. Grant and MP I 7 65 14
To the right is the steward's house; he is a very MP I 8 82 34
heart, that principle of right which had not formed any MP I 9 91 36
for she had set him right as to his grandson's illness, MP I 10 103 50
unemployed, felt all the right of missing him much more. MP I 12 115 4
is employed, every thing will be right with Sir Thomas.-- MP I 13 127 31
Fanny seemed nearer being right than Edmund had supposed. MP I 14 130 1
She was acknowledged to be quite right, and the two parts MP I 14 132 8
is your place to put them right, and shew them what true MP I 15 140 13
to set them right must be his only satisfaction. MP I 15 142 23
Was she right in refusing what was so warmly asked, so MP I 16 153 3
She has a right to be felt for, because she evidently MP I 16 154 14
"He was certainly right in respecting such feeling; he was MP I 17 159 6
"Am I right?-- MP I 18 168 15
could put Mrs. Grant right the other day in twenty places. MP I 18 172 31
Will not it be right for me to go too?" but they were no MP II 1 176 3
by the rest, by the right of a disposition which not even MP II 1 176 4
He had the best right to be the talker; and the delight of MP II 1 178 8
"I believe you are right, Fanny," was his reply, after a MP II 3 197 4
"Miss Crawford was very right in what she said of you the MP II 3 198 13
own sister, I think I had a right to alarm you a little." MP II 4 212 30
he will consider it a right thing by Mrs. Grant, as well MP II 5 217 9
Fanny was perfectly right in giving only a conditional MP II 5 219 18
makes me think it right to give you a hint, Fanny, now MP II 5 221 32
the candid result of conviction, "I believe you are right. MP II 5 226 59
With such means in his power he had a right to be listened MP II 6 236 21
on a sort of knoll to my right--which church was MP II 7 241 13
as Mr. Rushworth's fine fortune gives them a right to be. MP II 7 245 32
and to deserve the right of judging of Miss Crawford's MP II 9 265 18
It will all end right. MP II 9 268 31
"You are right, Fanny, to protest against such an office, MP II 9 269 35
She acknowledged it to be right. MP II 9 271 40
And they are quite in the right, for it would be a very MP II 11 289 34
But you are quite right, you could not have chosen better. MP II 12 293 11
that you are doing quite right, and though I should never MP II 12 294 19
to his own house, and to claim the best right in her. MP II 12 295 22
Fanny and myself for we shall both have a right in you. MP II 12 295 23
"That's right; and in London, of course, a house of your MP II 12 295 27
Compared with you, who has a right to be happy? MP II 13 299 5
to turn her eyes to the right hand where he sat, she felt MP II 13 304 16
the right hand too, and there was pain in the connection. MP II 13 304 17
Am I right? MP III 1 317 34
some right to guide you--without even asking their advice. MP III 1 318 39
place, that she had done right, that her judgment had not MP III 1 324 58
and be thankful for the right reason in her, which had MP III 1 324 59
had no right to wonder at the line of conduct he pursued. MP III 2 331 17
I want to be set right. MP III 3 342 33
you most devotedly, that has the best right to a return. MP III 3 344 41
By that right I do and will deserve you; and when once MP III 3 344 41
Perhaps I have as yet no right--but by what other name can MP III 3 344 41
far as you have gone, Fanny, I think you perfectly right. MP III 4 347 16
time to attach yourself; but I think you perfectly right. MP III 4 347 16
right to every thing he may wish for, at the first moment. MP III 4 352 40
I had my doubts at the time about her being right, for he MP III 5 361 16
still feeling a right, by all his knowledge of human MP III 6 368 7
dignified musings, as a right and desirable measure; but MP III 6 368 9
it every way, and saw nothing but what was right. MP III 6 368 9
are very right, but I am sure I shall miss her very much." MP III 6 371 16
How right and comfortable it will all be!" MP III 6 372 20
in which he had a strong right of interest, being to MP III 7 377 8
What right had she to be of importance to her family? MP III 7 382 29
be dearest--they always had been--and he had every right. MP III 7 382 29
Nobody was in their right place, nothing was done as it MP III 8 388 3
Fanny was right enough in not expecting to hear from Miss MP III 9 393 1
the last, but she was not right in supposing that such an MP III 9 393 1
, on farther observation, admit no right of superiority. MP III 9 395 3
that much was wrong at home, and wanted to set it right. MP III 9 395 4
duped by a man who has no right of creditor to dupe me-- MP III 11 412 20
"I advise!--you know very well what is right." MP III 11 412 21
When you give me your opinion, I always know what is right. MP III 11 412 22
Your judgment is my rule of right." MP III 11 412 22
and doubtful notions of right; there was no occasion to MP III 14 436 15
it every reproach but the right, considering its ill MP III 16 457 30
of carrying with me the right of tenderness and esteem. MP III 16 458 30
was right; and such has been the end of our acquaintance! MP III 16 459 30
been expected, and for his sake been more near doing right. MP III 16 459 31

he had sacrificed the right to the expedient, and been MP III 17 461 4
every encouragement to do right, which their relative MP III 17 465 13
to make any sacrifice to right; he resolved to defer his MP III 17 467 20
the lock of the door the right way and never bangs it. E I 1 9 19
and be proved in the right, when so many people said Mr. E I 1 11 39
His mother is perfectly right not to be in a hurry. E I 4 30 18
I had no right to expect much, and I did not expect much; E I 4 32 30
where Emma errs once, she is in the right a hundred times." E I 5 40 22
that was a fault on the right side--after all this, came E I 6 45 21
Do you think I am right?" E I 7 53 23
"Perfectly, perfectly right, my dearest Harriet; you are E I 7 53 24
of such a point of female right and refinement than he E I 8 65 50
were right and her adversary's wrong, as Mr. Knightley. E I 8 67 56
"Being my friend's, I have no right to expose it in any E I 9 71 11
"Whatever you say is always right," cried Harriet, "and E I 9 74 22
gives love exactly the right direction, and sends it into E I 9 75 25
and always right in any man's eyes as I am in my father's." E I 10 84 15
Emma's sense of right however had decided it; and besides E I 12 98 1
give me a chance of being right, if we think differently. E I 12 99 9
As far as good intentions went, we were both right, and I E I 12 99 11
of turning it more to the right that it may not cut E I 12 106 61
"You do quite right," said she;--"we will make your E I 13 110 11
all would yet turn out right, she was even positively E I 14 118 4
to her, "we want only two more to be just the right number. E I 14 119 6
7
"Yes--I have some right to that knowledge; though I have E I 14 120 13
Have not I some right to complain? E I 15 125 5
assuming to himself the right of first interest in her; E I 15 125 6
feelings, she had little right to wonder that he, with E I 16 136 9
There I was quite right. E I 16 137 11
busy, might have been a model of right feminine happiness. E I 17 140 1
He would feel himself in the right; and the declaration -- E I 18 147 18
Respect for right conduct is felt by every body. E I 18 147 18
He may have as strong a sense of what would be right, as E I 18 148 19
a resolution to do right against the will of others. E I 18 148 22
and preventing his father's having any right to complain. E I 18 148 24
think she does quite right, just what they should E II 1 161 25
"That's right, my dear, very right. E II 3 172 19
and not only losing the right lady, but finding himself E II 4 181 3
just the right weather for him, fine, dry, settled weather. E II 5 188 7
and again into his room, to be sure that all is right." E II 5 189 20
What is right to be done cannot be done too soon. E II 5 194 40
It is always the lady's right to decide on the degree of E II 6 200 18
skill or right of judging of any body's performance.-- E II 6 201 28
"You are right. E II 6 202 34
a great deal decidedly right; he spoke of his uncle with E II 7 205 2
But you will do every thing right. E II 7 210 14
guessing exactly the right; but I am sure there must be a E II 8 217 32
dish was placed exactly right, and occupation and ease E II 8 218 38
39
It was hardly right; but it had been so strong an idea, E II 9 231 2
"Conjecture--aye, sometimes one conjectures right, and E II 10 242 15
Oh! you were perfectly right! E II 11 250 23
I felt how right you were the whole time, but was too E II 11 250 23
Not that James ever complains; but it is right to spare E II 11 252 35
That's right. E II 11 256 60
Oh! Miss Woodhouse, why are you always so right?" E II 12 259 17
"Indeed, I am very sorry to be right in this instance. E II 12 260 18
I was a right thing to do. E II 12 260 27
right; it was most natural to pay your visit, then"----- E II 12 261 30
31
her, that Harriet had a right to all her ingenuity and all E II 13 267 9
to what was right and support her in it very tolerably. E II 13 268 13
must allow him to have the right to look as little wise, E II 14 271 5
"You are right, Mrs. Weston," said Mr. Knightley warmly, " E II 15 286 18
talents, you have a right to move in the first circle. E II 17 301 18
as usual, and with all the right of being principal talker, E II 17 303 24
things did not go quite right, did not proceed with all E II 18 308 28
tenaciously setting her right if she varied in the E III 3 336 13
hill for the next,--the weather appearing exactly right. E III 6 357 32
I have a right to talk on such subjects, without being E III 6 361 40
The black mare was blameless; they were right who had E III 6 363 53
to say, that she waves her right of knowing exactly what E III 7 370 23
neither could she feel any right of preference herself-- E III 9 390 19
"You are right. E III 10 394 30
What right had he to come among us with affection and E III 10 396 44
What right had he to endeavour to please, as he certainly E III 10 396 44
of this one great deviation from the strict rule of right. E III 10 400 65
him that all was as right as this speech proclaimed; and E III 10 400 69
by the person, whose counsels had never led her right.-- E III 11 408 33
her doing right, which no other creature had at all shared. E III 12 415 1
I have been acting contrary to all my sense of right; and E III 12 419 8
kind--but you are mistaken--and I must set you right.-- E III 13 426 14
15
My right to place myself in a situation requiring such E III 14 437 8
For my temptation to think it a right, I refer every E III 14 437 8
If you remember any queernesses, set them all to the right E III 14 439 8
But she was always right. E III 14 440 8
I hope she is right.-- E III 14 443 8
it over very handsomely--but you were perfectly right." E III 15 445 12
right, he made a fuller pause to say, "this is very bad.-- E III 15 446 20
Mr. E. is knightley's right hand." E III 16 456 25
Jane answered, "you are very right; it has been thought of. E III 16 460 55
56
It was very natural for you to say, what right has he to E III 17 462 7
right that equal worth can give, to be happy together. E III 17 465 25
It was all right, all open, all equal. E III 17 468 31
thing, and every body, was right; and Mr. Shepherd's P III 5 32 3
It would be most right, and most wise, and, therefore, P III 5 33 6
So far all was perfectly right; but Lady Russell was P III 5 34 11
uses for his money, and a right to spend it as he liked. P III 6 43 5
Nobody doubts her right to have precedence of mamma, but P III 6 46 10
when Louisa made all right by saying, that she only came P III 6 50 26
just now that I would come, and he thought me quite right. P III 7 55 8
to Mary, said all that was right; said something to the P III 7 59 25
A large bulky figure has as good a right to be in deep P III 8 68 30
Such a number of women and children have no right to be P III 8 69 42
have made, she has no right to throw herself away. P III 9 75 13
I do not think any young woman has a right to make a P III 9 76 13
were sure all could not be right, and talked, with grave P III 10 82 2
do, and that I knew to be right, by the airs and P III 10 87 23
and feeling in herself the right of seniority of mind, she P III 11 101 24
and had the best right to stay in Henrietta's stead! P III 12 115 65
Mrs. Clay was right. P IV 3 142 17
his possessing the shadow of a right to introduce himself. P IV 3 144 19
regret and entreaty, to his right honourable cousin. P IV 4 149 13
by her) you have a better right to be fastidious than P IV 4 150 17
manners as consciously right as they were invariably P IV 5 153 6
She always takes the right time for applying. P IV 5 155 9
He certainly knew what was right, nor could she fix on any P IV 5 160 27
There, take my arm; that's right; I do not feel P IV 6 169 27
enough that they must wait till her brain was set to right. P IV 6 171 33
distinguished him on the right hand pavement at such a P IV 7 178 28
have lost the right moment for seeing whether he saw them. P IV 7 179 31
equal to everything which she believed right to be done. P IV 8 181 1
Anne's eyes had caught the right direction, and P IV 8 188 41
their acquaintance; of the right which he seemed to have P IV 9 192 2
greater right to influence him, than is really the case. P IV 9 195 25
you do not design to be cruel, when the right moment comes. P IV 9 195 30
However, I have determined; I think I am right; I think P IV 9 199 53
a little trouble in the right place might do it, and to P IV 9 210 98
However, I do not mean to say they have not a right to it. P IV 10 218 22

ways; and that I had no right to be trying whether I could P IV 11 242 65
to judge of the right and wrong, I mean with regard to P IV 11 246 79
80
I must believe that I was right, much as I suffered from P IV 11 246 79
80
it, that I was perfectly right in being guided by the P IV 11 246 79
80
But I mean, that I was right in submitting to her, and P IV 11 246 80
of mind, consciousness of right, and one independent P IV 12 248 1
believed her to have been right in originally dividing P IV 12 251 10
which they had certainly the best right to inherit.-- S 3 377 1
little that we thought it right to change our measures-- S 5 387 1
which implied it's right to produce a great impression--& S 7 400 1
That's right; all right & clean. S 9 408 1
in England who have so sad a right to that appellation!-- S 9 410 1
"You are quite in the right, to doubt it as long as you S 10 415 1
of my right side, before I had swallowed it 5 minutes.-- S 10 418 1
The use of my right side is entirely taken away for S 10 418 1
by those who have studied right sides & green tea S 10 418 1

RIGHT HON. LORD RAVENSHAW (1)
of the Right Hon. Lord Ravenshaw, in Cornwall, which would MP I 13 121 1

RIGHT-ANGLES (1)
a lane leading at right-angles from the broad, though E I 10 83 2

RIGHT-HAND (1)
"On the right-hand pavement--she must be almost out of NA I 11 87 53

RIGHT-MINDED (1)
Living constantly with right-minded and well-informed E II 2 164 6

RIGHT-MINDEDNESS (1)
had died all such right-mindedness, and from that period P III 1 9 19

RIGHTFUL (1)
rightful property of some one or other of their daughters. PP I 1 3 2

RIGHTLY (11)
from our not rightly understanding each other's meaning. LS 24 287 11
"If I understand you rightly, you had formed a surmise of NA II 9 197 29
deserving young woman--have I been rightly informed?-- SS III 3 282 17
of talents; talents which rightly used, might at least PP II 19 236 2
"Let me be rightly understood. PP III 14 354 40
Fanny is the only one who has judged rightly throughout, MP II 2 187 1
you to let me know how far I have been rightly informed. MP III 14 433 13
A man who felt rightly would say at once, simply and E I 18 146 16
the nephew, who had done rightly by his father, would do E I 18 147 18
by his father, would do rightly by them; for they know, as E I 18 147 18
"I was very often influenced rightly by you--oftener than E III 17 462 8

RIGHTS (26)
You know your own rights, & that it is out of my power to LS 12 261 4
notice of one, without injuring the rights of the other. NA I 10 76 29
of an injured wife, before her room was put to rights. NA II 8 186 10
call at Putney when next in town, might set all to rights. NA II 12 217 2
as a clergyman, and his rights as a rector, made him PP I 15 70 1
Their rank, fortune, rights, and expectations, will always MP I 1 11 17
with his situation and rights; he made her some very MP I 2 17 22
family, with all its rights of Court-Leet and Court-Baron. MP I 8 81 33
her now with rights that demanded different treatment. MP III 2 328 7
rights so as to be able to walk home in tolerable comfort. E I 10 89 36
Mr. Elton's rights, however, gradually revived. E II 3 180 57
infamous fraud upon the rights of men and women; and Mrs. E II 11 254 45
and put them all to rights, she was just turning to the E III 3 332 3
her nephew Henry, whose rights as heir expectant had E III 15 449 35
possible, of her mother's rights and consequence; and P III 1 5 8
Walter Elliot, Esq. whose rights had been so generously P III 1 7 13
taking care that no tenant has more than his just rights. P III 3 19 10
mother's love, and mother's rights, it would be prevented. P III 4 27 3
be able to set things to rights, that I have no very good P III 6 45 9
How was Anne to set all these matters to rights? P III 6 46 11
How to have this anxious business set to rights, and be P IV 4 149 12
succeeding to all her rights, and all her popularity, as P IV 5 159 25
Anne restored to the rights of seniority, and the mistress P IV 12 250 5
watchfulness which a son-in-law's rights would have given. P IV 12 250 7
in setting the Carge to rights & turning the horses round, S 1 367 1
They have Miss Clara's room to put to rights as well as my S 7 401 1

RIGID (1)
How Anne's more rigid requisitions might have been taken, P III 2 13 6

RIGOURS (1)
lead, nor to what rigours of rudeness in return it might NA I 12 92 3

RING (19)
before her, as to make a ring, with a plait of hair in the SS I 18 98 10
"I never saw you wear a ring before, Edward," she cried. SS I 18 98 11
I gave him a lock of my hair set in a ring when he was at SS I 22 135 54
Perhaps you might notice the ring when you saw him?" SS I 22 135 54
picture, the letter, the ring, formed altogether such a SS II 1 139 1
eyes--will you ring the bell for some working candles? SS II 1 144 13
Please to destroy my scrawls--but the ring with my hair SS III 13 365 15
point of asking leave to ring the bell & make enquiries, W 338 17
Lydia, my love, ring the bell. PP I 13 61 3
by a ring at the door, the certain signal of a visitor. PP II 9 177 1
Ring the bell, Kitty, for hill. PP III 7 306 44
see the ring, and then I bowed and smiled like any thing." PP III 9 316 8
after dinner to shew her ring and boast of being married, PP III 9 317 10
Fanny, ring the bell; I must have my dinner.-- MP I 15 140 16
would by no means go through the ring of the cross. MP II 9 270 40
"Shall I ring the bell?" E I 15 128 20
in some dreadful way, and not able to ring the bell! P III 5 37 24
will have the goodness to ring for Mary--stay, I am sure P IV 9 202 68
Charles, ring and order a chair. P IV 11 238 46

RINGING (3)
complete than Marianne, ringing the bell, requested the SS II 4 161 5
servants' dinner bell was ringing at the very moment over MP I 15 142 22
the actual approach--new carriage, bell ringing and all. E II 13 267 8

RINGS (5)
and a brilliant exhibition of hoop rings on her finger. NA I 15 122 28
The fine old, lofty drawing-room rings again. W 358 28
with her bracelets and rings, joined now and then in her PP I 11 54 3
we shall be able to send back some dozens of the rings.-- MP I 15 141 22
turned from the drawers of rings & Broches repressed S 6 390 1

RIOT (4)
have the goodness to satisfy me as to this dreadful riot." NA I 14 112 37
"Riot!--what riot?" NA I 14 112 38
"My dear Eleanor, the riot is only in your own brain. NA I 14 113 39
to whom, in all the riot of his gratifications, it was yet MP I 13 123 6

RIOTOUS (2)
Every afternoon brought a return of their riotous games MP III 8 391 8
and cold pies, where riotous boys were holding high revel; P IV 2 134 29

RIPENING (1)
They are ripening fast." E III 6 354 8

RISE (29)
A corner of it catching her eye as she lay, seemed to rise NA II 7 173 2
of force and interest to rise over every other, to be NA II 14 231 4
by his countenance gave rise to conjectures, which might SS I 11 57 17
so unfortunate as to give rise to a belief of more than I SS II 7 183 13
she found attempting to rise from the bed, and whom she SS II 7 185 16
had given rise to a general expectation of their marriage. PP II 12 197 5
library, she saw Mr. Darcy rise also and follow him, and PP III 17 375 28
in former times, its rise and grandeur, regal visits and MP I 9 85 3
with obscurity when it might rise to distinction." MP II 4 214 42
"But how may it rise?-- MP II 4 214 43
How may my honesty at least rise to any distinction?" MP II 4 214 43
Then she could gradually rise up to the genuine MP II 10 274 8
power, and she had only to rise and, with Mr. Crawford's MP II 10 280 33
her almost instantly rise and lead the way out of the room. MP III 5 357 5
regret--vexation that must rise sometimes to self-reproach, MP III 17 468 22
the rise in the world which must satisfy them." E I 9 75 27
and beginning to rise--"my father will be expecting us. E II 1 162 32

They might all have hoped to rise by Harriet's E II 3 179 53
to give Mrs. Cole of the rise and progress of the affair E II 4 181 4
to be the drudge of some attorney, and too stupid to rise. E II 4 183 9
and did sigh, could not but agree, and rise to take leave. E II 12 261 35
Then followed the history and rise of the ancient and P III 1 3 3 4
of being insulted by the rise of one whose father, his P III 3 19 16
to secure even his farther rise in that profession; would P III 4 26 3
If he should rise to any very great honours! P III 9 75 11
Anne was obliged to turn away, to rise, to walk to a P IV 5 160 26
to rise in cordiality, and do the honours of it very well. P IV 10 216 18
may have given rise to--allow me to tell you who we are. S 1 367 1
materially promote the rise & prosperity of the place--wd S 2 372 1

RISEN (4)
next morning, had she not risen from her bed in more need SS I 16 83 1
a tolerable fortune and risen to the honour of knighthood PP I 5 18 1
Fanny, with doubting feelings, had risen to meet him, but MP III 7 379 20
She would certainly have risen to their blessings if she P IV 10 219 27

RISES (3)
And there, beneath that farthest hill, which rises with SS I 16 88 33
My courage always rises with every attempt to intimidate PP II 8 174 13
My courage rises while I write. E III 14 437 8

RISING (51)
and the others rising up, Isabella had only time to press NA I 8 52 2
sheltered from the north and east by rising woods of oak. NA II 2 141 13
sleepless, have been the real cause of his rising late.-- NA II 5 155 3
handsomely liveried, rising so regularly in their stirrups, NA II 5 156 4
walls of grey stone, rising amidst a grove of ancient oaks, NA II 5 161 24
the room, and to the rising shame of having harboured for NA II 6 165 4
The night was stormy; the wind had been rising at NA II 6 166 9
A violent gust of wind, rising with sudden fury, added NA II 6 170 12
of sympathetic early rising did not advance her composure. NA II 7 175 11
and the steep woody hills rising behind to give it shelter, NA II 7 177 19
and Catherine, instantly rising, a long and affectionate NA II 13 229 31
to them, and, with a rising colour, asked her if she would NA II 15 242 9
And then rising, she went away to join Marianne, whom she SS II 8 197 23
He could say no more, and rising hastily walked for a few SS II 9 206 25
said he, soon afterwards, rising from his chair Elinor SS III 4 290 40 41
after persisting in rising, confessed herself unable to SS III 7 307 2
I mean never to be later in rising than six, and from that SS III 10 343 9
previously sitting--her rising colour, as she spoke--and SS III 11 349 3
in woman;--and many a rising beauty would be slighted by SS III 14 379 19
late; they are but just rising from dinner at midnight."-- W 325 4
On rising from tea, there was again a scramble for the W 333 13
They were soon gone again, rising from their seats with an PP I 17 86 9
And rising as she thus spoke, she would have quitted the PP I 19 108 16 17
It was a handsome modern building, well situated on rising PP II 5 156 4
standing well on rising ground, and backed by a ridge of PP III 1 245 3
any thing; and then rising up, said to Elizabeth, "Miss PP III 14 352 16 17
assured her that he was rising every hour in his esteem. PP III 17 379 47
Elizabeth's spirits soon rising to playfulness again, she PP III 18 380 1
all its demesnes, gently rising beyond the village road; MP I 7 67 16
village between gently rising hills; a small stream before MP II 7 241 13
"Oh! yes, sir," cried Fanny, rising eagerly from her seat MP II 10 279 28
"Oh! yes, certainly," cried Fanny, rising in haste, the MP II 13 306 29
Fanny obeyed, with eyes cast down and colour rising.-- MP III 1 313 13
conscious of it, when, rising from his chair, he said, " MP III 1 314 16
so heavy, so multiplied, so rising in dreadful gradation! MP III 1 319 40
her cheeks; but instantly rising, she was preparing to MP III 1 325 60
directly to Fanny--who, rising from her seat, looked at MP III 7 384 34
the gentlemen, noise rising upon noise, and bustle upon MP III 7 384 36
there was rising in importance from his present schemes. MP III 10 404 15
good conduct, and rising fame, and in the general well- MP III 17 473 31
generations had been rising into gentility and property. E I 2 15 1
"Good morning to you,"--said he, rising and walking off E I 8 66 55
The most satisfactory comparisons were rising in her mind. E I 9 76 34
and very clever man; rising in his profession, domestic, E I 11 92 5
and blushes rising in importance--with consciousness and E II 4 181 4
But his spirits were soon rising again, and with laughing E III 18 477 51
But soon afterwards, rising and pacing the room, he P III 3 18 5 6
saw her, and, instantly rising, said, with studied P III 8 72 58 59
who neglect the reigning power to bow to the rising sun. P IV 10 224 48
favourite--for a young & rising Bathing-Place, certainly S 1 368 1
At Trafalgar house, rising at a little distance behind the S 4 384 1

RISK (33)
angry it will make mama, but I must run the risk. LS 21 279 1
but Frederica's removal from the risk of infection. LS 42 312 6
subject, without any risk of being heard at the card-table. SS II 1 145 23
risk of her displeasure for a while by owning the truth?" SS II 2 148 14
to run the risk of his calling again in her absence. SS II 5 170 28
and to run the risk of a tete-a-tete with a woman, whom SS III 5 294 3
him, should overlook every thing but the risk of delay. SS III 12 357 2
who are so daring as to risk their happiness on the chance PP I 19 107 14
You had better neglect your relations, than run the risk PP I 22 123 7
Risk any thing rather than her displeasure; and if you PP I 22 124 9
to speak openly to her aunt, than to run such a risk. PP II 19 240 16
His temptation is not adequate to the risk." PP III 5 282 1
which would obviate the risk of his father's thinking he MP I 4 37 8
I am of a cautious temper, and unwilling to risk my MP I 4 43 23
the liberty, nor run the risk; and at last on a hint from MP I 8 75 1
sister, entreat him not to risk his tranquillity by too MP I 17 161 9
felt their error, than to run the risk of investigation. MP II 2 187 2
she be reconciled to the risk, or feel any of that MP II 6 237 23
He proceeds at his own risk. MP III 2 331 16
which could not be delayed without risk of evil. MP III 12 415 2
I am sure, rather than run the risk of hurting Mr. and Mrs. E II 7 210 20
in uncertainty--at the risk--in her opinion, the great E II 12 257 1
her opinion, the great risk, of its being all in vain. E II 12 257 1
letters, than run the risk of bringing on your cough again. E II 16 295 33
He owed it to her, to risk any thing that might be E III 5 350 31
transplantation would be a risk of her father's comfort, E III 15 448 31
with Sir Walter, nothing to risk by a state of variance. P IV 3 140 11
could be perpetrated without risk of his general character. P IV 9 199 53
labouring and toiling, exposed to every risk and hardship. P IV 11 233 23
of the girls, at the risk of raising even an unpleasant P IV 11 242 65
to persuasion exerted on the side of safety, not of risk. P IV 11 244 73
In marrying a man indifferent to me, all risk would P IV 11 244 73
leads him--(though at the risk of some Aberration from the S 8 403 1

RISKED (1)
others, and who scarcely risked an original thought of his MP I 10 97 3

RISKING (3)
easily attained, it was risking too much for the SS II 5 170 29
She felt that she had been risking her friend's happiness E III 11 402 1
that whether he were risking his fortune or spraining his S 2 372 1

RISKS (5)
For one letter, at all risks, all hazards, I must entreat. NA II 13 228 28
prefer being below, at all risks, as she had rather talk W 361 30
immediate horrors at all risks, it is probable that Mr. MP III 17 466 18
Let me entreat you to run no risks. E I 13 109 7
Miss Fairfax, you must not run such risks.-- E II 16 295 33

RITES (1)
ready to perform those rites and ceremonies which are PP I 13 62 12

RIVAL (8)
He might be jealous of her brother as a rival, but if more NA II 4 149 1
off to his more fortunate rival; and the raillery which SS I 10 49 12
by any inquiry after his rival; and at length by way of SS II 4 162 12
to Miss Darcy, who had been set up as a rival of Jane. PP III 2 262 8
resolved on enduring his rival, her answer might have been MP II 3 201 24
In Jane's eyes she had been a rival; and well might any E III 11 403 2
Edw: as standing without a rival, as having the fairest S 3 377 1
She was his rival in Lady D.'s favour, she was young, S 8 405 2

RIVAL'S (2)
thus much of her rival's intentions, and while she was SS II 1 142 7
far more than to his rival's, the reward of her sister was SS III 9 335 5

RIVALRY (2)
Rivalry, treachery between sisters!-- W 316 2
Since rivalry between the sisters had ceased, they had MP II 3 203 32

RIVALS (4)
and the two fair rivals were thus seated side by side at SS II 1 145 23
With such rivals for the notice of the fair, as Mr. PP I 16 76 5
even tragedians; and the rivals, the school for scandal, MP I 14 130 3
have made it credible that they were not decided rivals. P III 8 71 57

RIVER (10)
of the river, "without thinking of the south of France." NA I 14 106 2
on the whole scene, the river, the trees scattered on its PP III 1 246 5
As they walked across the lawn towards the river, PP III 1 251 50
They entered the woods, and bidding adieu to the river for PP III 1 253 57
the opposite side of the river, in the nearest direction; PP III 1 254 57
to the brink of the river for the better inspection of PP III 1 255 61
house, was engaged by the river, and had left him only on PP III 3 268 8
the river, seemed the finish of the pleasure grounds.-- E III 6 360 38
and the river making a close and handsome curve around it. E III 6 360 38
where no damps from the river were imagined even by him, E III 6 361 42

RIVERS (2)
Lakes, mountains, and rivers, shall not be jumbled PP II 4 154 23
cannot tell the principal rivers in Russia--or she never MP I 2 18 23

RIVERS-STREET (4)
Russell then drove to her own lodgings, in Rivers-Street. P IV 2 136 37
she began to talk of spending the morning in Rivers-Street. P IV 10 215 14
They all three called in Rivers-Street for a couple of P IV 10 220 30
still to defer her explanatory visit in Rivers-Street. P IV 11 229 1

RIVET (7)
world, fastening in the rivet of my mother's spectacles.-- E II 9 236 46
The rivet came out, you know, this morning.-- E II 9 236 46
Here is the rivet of your mistress's spectacles out. E II 9 236 46
'Oh!' said he, 'I do think I can fasten the rivet; I like E II 9 237 51
'Oh!' said he, 'I can fasten the rivet. E II 9 238 51
I wish I could conjecture how soon I shall make this rivet E II 10 242 15
never been in fault since; the rivet never came out again. E III 2 323 19

ROAD (77)
A famous clever animal for the road--only forty guineas. NA I 10 76 28
"Well, I saw him at that moment turn up the Lansdown road,- NA I 11 85 37
with the interest of a road entirely new to her, of an NA II 5 155 4
and every bend in the road was expected with solemn awe to NA II 5 161 24
along a smooth, level road of fine gravel, without NA II 5 161 25
This passage is at least as extraordinary a road from the NA II 9 195 8
Unfortunately, the road she now travelled was the same NA II 14 230 1
though no object on the road could engage a moment's NA II 14 231 5
spirits since last she had trodden that well-known road. NA II 14 237 20
They walked along the road through the valley, and chiefly SS I 16 85 15
a long stretch of the road which they had travelled on SS I 16 85 15
respective homes, to meet, by appointment, on the road. SS III 6 301 3
and closer wood walk, a road of Smith gravel winding round SS III 6 302 7
The Dashwoods were two days on the road, and Marianne bore SS III 10 341 6
before him, the nearest road to Barton, had had no leisure SS III 13 366 20
which that road did not hold the most intimate connection. SS III 13 366 20
that day, & that as his road lay quite wide from r., it W 338 18
"Your road through the village is infamous, eliz:; said he, W 349 24
road, & contained no gentleman's family but the Rector's.-- W 354 28
out of his road merely to call for ten minutes at Stanton. W 355 28
When they left the high road for the lane to Hunsford, PP II 5 155 2
The garden sloping to the road, the house standing in it, PP II 5 155 3
out of window in his own book room, which fronted the road. PP II 7 168 1
room, crossing the road, and immediately running into the PP II 7 170 7 8
"And what is fifty miles of good road? PP II 9 178 18
up the lane, which led her farther from the turnpike road. PP II 12 195 1
It was not in their direct road, nor more than a mile or PP II 19 240 12
the valley, into which the road with some abruptness wound. PP III 1 245 3
forward from the road, which led behind it to the stables. PP III 1 251 50
this is, that they were seen to continue the London road. PP III 4 275 5
seated in the carriage, and on the road to Longbourn. PP III 4 281 29
no traces of them were to be found on the Barnet road." PP III 5 282 6
on the road, reached Longbourn by dinner-time the next day. PP III 5 285 20
She is on her road somewhere, I dare say, and so passing PP III 14 359 76
ten miles of indifferent road, to pay a morning visit. MP I 4 39 10
rising beyond the village road; and in Dr. Grant's meadow MP I 7 67 16
Their road was through a pleasant country; and Fanny, MP I 8 80 31
there was any stretch of road behind them, or when he MP I 8 81 31
on each side of the road," without elation of heart; and MP I 8 81 33
"Now we shall have no more rough road, Miss Crawford, our MP I 8 82 34
much smaller circle than they are now in the high road for. MP I 16 155 16
that is, to the principal road through the village, must MP II 7 242 23
creature travelling the road; especially as there is no MP II 7 244 27
he had done so, on this road to happiness, there was MP III 17 471 28
very next day, as they were walking on the Donwell road. E I 4 31 27
He did not think we ever walked this road. E I 4 32 29
Elton was actually on his road to London, and not meaning E I 8 68 58
Their road to this detached cottage was down Vicarage-Lane, E I 10 83 2
good house, almost as close to the road as it could be. E I 10 83 2
side of the lane, leaving them together in the main road. E I 10 88 33
Another hour or two's snow can hardly make the road E I 15 126 10
He wished the road might be impassable, that he might be E I 15 126 11
and fancying the road to be now just passable for E I 15 127 13
way along the Highbury road--the snow was no where above E I 15 127 16
sleeping two nights on the road, and express very genuine E II 5 193 35
than from any run on the road; and his companions had not E II 6 197 5
She looked down the Randalls road. E II 9 233 25
Immediately they crossed the road and came forward to her; E II 9 233 25
that she means to sleep only two nights on the road.-- E II 18 306 11
Nothing can stand more retired from the road than Maple E II 18 307 21
out together, and taken a road, the Richmond road, which, E III 3 333 5
taken a road, the Richmond road, which, though apparently E III 3 333 5
to meet him by another road, a mile or two beyond Highbury- E III 3 334 7
made the road appear but half as long as on the day before. P III 12 117 73
I told him the distance and the road, and I told him of P IV 2 131 12
of your company the little way our road lies together. P IV 6 169 26
business to quit the high road, & attempt a very rough S 1 363 1
his masters own) if the road had not indisputably become S 1 364 1
that road in a carriage--& ready offers of assistance. S 1 365 1
loss of time; and as the road does not seem at present in S 1 365 1
steps into the turnpike road & proceed to Hailsham, & so S 1 367 1
We are on our road home from London;--my name perhaps-- S 1 368 1
His object in quitting the high road, to hunt for an S 2 371 1
hill, or a heavy bit of road, and to give the visiting S 3 375 1
room which commanded the road & all the paths across the S 7 395 1
The road to Sanditon h. was a broad, handsome, planted S 12 426 1
almost pressing on the road--till an angle here, & a curve S 12 426 1

ROAD-BOOKS (1)
Morland remonstrated, pleaded the authority of road-books, NA I 7 45 7

ROAD-HORSE (1)
Two of them were hunters; the third, a useful road-horse: MP I 4 37 8

ROADS (12)
great London and Oxford roads, and the principal inn of NA I 7 44 1
and where roads and newspapers lay every thing open? NA II 9 197 29
Mrs. Morland's common remarks about the weather and roads. NA II 15 242 8
of the weather and the roads, and had I spoken only once SS I 10 48 5
The house, furniture, neighbourhood, and roads, were all PP II 3 146 19
is not very fond of the roads between this and Sotherton; MP I 8 77 12

find no inconvenience from narrow roads on Wednesday."	MP I 8 77 13
the bearings of the roads, the difference of soil, the	MP I 8 80 31
and the roads almost impassable, but I did persuade her."	MP II 2 189 3
if you had seen the state of the roads that day!	MP II 2 189 5
A most insalubrious air--roads proverbially detestable--	S 1 369 1
in a new carriage & better roads, an occasional month at	S 2 373 1
ROARED (2)	
The wind roared down the chimney, the rain beat in	NA II 6 168 10
The wind roared round the house, and the rain beat against	SS III 7 316 28
ROARING (1)	
the whole completed by a roaring Christmas fire, which	P IV 2 134 29
ROAST (5)	
the entrance of the roast turkey--which formed the only	W 353 27
roast mutton and rice pudding they were hastening home for.	E I 13 109 6
smallest grease, and not roast it, for no stomach can bear	E II 3 171 16
	17
for no stomach can bear roast port--I think we had better	E II 3 171 16
	17
another, it is pork--a roast loin of pork"----- "as to who,	E II 3 175 39
	40
ROASTED (3)	
"My dear, replied Eliz. the turkey is roasted, & it may	W 354 27
The venison was roasted to a turn--and everybody said,	PP III 12 342 28
I am quite roasted.	E III 2 323 19
ROB (8)	
soon will) we will try to rob him of his heart once more,	LS 40 309 1
that any necessity should rob him even for an hour of Miss	NA II 13 220 1
How could he answer it to himself to rob his child, and	SS I 2 8 3
You would rob it of its simplicity by imaginary	SS I 14 73 17
But I will not stay to rob myself of all your	SS III 8 332 83
rob it of a few petrified spars without his perceiving me."	PP II 19 239 9
an explanation that would rob him of his borrowed feathers,	PP III 10 324 2
of Mr. Crawford's would rob her of many hours of his	MP II 9 266 21
ROBBED (8)	
the man, whose family you robbed of it's peace, in return	LS 36 305 1
and alarm, and robbed her of half her night's rest!	NA II 7 172 2
his lifting her up, had robbed her of the power of	SS I 9 43 11
pursuits, had perhaps robbed her of that simplicity, which	SS II 1 140 2
Elinor was robbed of all presence of mind by such an	SS II 6 176 7
a few weeks ago, had robbed her of one; the similar	SS III 14 373 2
You have robbed Edmund for ten, twenty, thirty years,	MP I 3 23 3
Mrs. Weston's poultry-house was robbed one night of all	E III 19 483 10
ROBBERS (1)	
Neither robbers nor tempests befriended them, nor one	NA I 2 19 4
ROBBING (3)	
be the selfish means of robbing him, perhaps, of all that	SS II 2 147 7
by an apprehension of its robbing Marianne of farther	SS III 9 334 5
service too, without robbing him of one personal grace!	P IV 7 179 28
ROBE (2)	
wore my sprigged muslin robe with blue trimmings--plain	NA I 3 26 22
before hymen's saffron robe would be put on for us!	E II 18 308 28
ROBERT (77)	
Are you acquainted with Mr. Robert Ferrars?	SS I 22 129 13
"No;" replied Lucy, "not to Mr. Robert Ferrars--I never	SS I 22 129 14
secure every thing to Robert, and the idea of that, for	SS II 2 148 15
"Do you know Mr. Robert Ferrars?" asked Elinor.	SS II 2 148 18
Mr. Dashwood introduced him to her as Mr. Robert Ferrars.	SS II 14 250 11
Why they were different, Robert explained to her himself	SS II 14 250 12
Why would you be persuaded by my uncle, sir Robert,	SS II 14 251 13
that estate upon Robert immediately, which might have been	SS III 1 269 53
same to Miss Morton whether she marry Edward or Robert."	SS III 5 296 28
"Certainly, there can be no difference; for Robert will	SS III 5 297 29
from her brother, by the entrance of Mr. Robert Ferrars.	SS III 5 297 32
her acquaintance with Robert, who, by the gay unconcern,	SS III 5 298 32
John; and their effect on Robert, though very different,	SS III 5 298 33
mean--my brother--you mean Mrs.-- Mrs. Robert Ferrars."	SS III 12 360 20
	21
"Mrs Robert ferrars!"--was repeated by Marianne and her	SS III 12 360 22
and by what attraction Robert could be drawn on to marry a	SS III 13 364 10
Elinor remembered what Robert had told her in Harley-	SS III 13 364 11
"That was exactly like Robert,"--was his immediate	SS III 13 364 12
The independence she settled on Robert, through resentment	SS III 13 366 18
"She will be more hurt by it, for Robert always was her	SS III 13 366 19
similar annihilation of Robert had left her for a	SS III 14 373 2
her eldest; for while Robert was inevitably endowed with a	SS III 14 374 4
That was due to the folly of Robert, and the cunning of	SS III 14 375 10
which had at first drawn Robert into the scrape, was the	SS III 14 375 10
When Robert first sought her acquaintance, and privately	SS III 14 376 11
gradually to talk only of Robert,--a subject on which he	SS III 14 376 11
comprehended only Robert; and Lucy, who had owed his	SS III 14 376 11
Lucy became as necessary to Mrs. Ferrars, as either Robert	SS III 14 376 11
disagreements between Robert and Lucy themselves, nothing	SS III 14 377 11
to find out; and what Robert had done to succeed to it,	SS III 14 377 11
to spend a month with Robert and Jane on purpose to egg	SS III 14 377 12
as Robert, who has got a good wife & six thousand pounds?"	W 319 2
Robert--but I cannot perceive any likeness to Mr Samuel."	W 321 2
three days from Mr & Mrs Robert Watson, who undertook to	W 324 3
Robert watson was an attorney at Croydon, in a good way of	W 348 23
Robert was carelessly kind, as became a prosperous man & a	W 348 23
"How charming Emma is!--" whispered Margt to Mrs Robert in	W 349 24
to Robert, who had equally irritated & greived her.--	W 350 24
Mrs Robert exactly as smart as she had been at her own	W 353 26
He shook hands with Robert, bowed & smiled to the ladies,	W 353 26
be understood, before Robert could let his attention be	W 355 28
Mrs Robert Smartly--but we think a month very little.	W 356 28
The ladies were not wanting in civil returns; & Robert	W 356 28
Croydon now, said Mrs Robert--we never think of any other.	W 357 28
Mrs Robert offered not another word in support of the game.	W 358 28
comprised the length of Robert & Jane's visit, was	W 358 28
She was very much pressed by Robert & Jane to return with	W 360 30
some of my plants which Robert will leave out because the	W 362 32
every body (at least Robert) by surprize, and I shall lose	MP II 4 212 31
quick eye sufficiently acquainted with Mr. Robert Martin.	MP II 4 212 31
I could not have visited Mrs. Robert Martin, of Abbey-Mill	E I 4 31 27
a most unexceptionable quarter:--Robert Martin is the man.	E I 7 53 24
I never heard better sense from any one than Robert Martin.	E I 8 59 25
Harriet Smith refuse Robert Martin? madness, if it is so;	E I 8 59 27
or education, to any connection higher than Robert Martin?	E I 8 60 34
She is superior to Mr. Robert Martin."	E I 8 61 38
Robert Martin would never have proceeded so far, if he had	E I 8 62 41
Let her marry Robert Martin, and she is safe, respectable,	E I 8 63 42
But as to my letting her marry Robert Martin, it is	E I 8 64 47
"Robert Martin has no great loss--if he can but think so;	E I 8 65 48
could be clearer; even a Robert Martin would have been	E I 8 66 51
without being suspected of introducing Robert Martin."--	E II 4 183 10
Robert Martin had probably ceased to think of Harriet.--	E III 6 361 40
Harriet Smith marries Robert Martin."	E III 6 361 40
Mr. Knightley; "I have it from Robert Martin himself.	E III 18 470 12
mean to say, that Harriet Smith has accepted Robert Martin.	E III 18 471 14
My friend Robert would not resist.	E III 18 471 17
Larkins; but I could quite as ill spare Robert Martin."	E III 18 472 20
air of Mr. Knightley and Robert Martin was, at this moment,	E III 18 473 22
better than to think of Robert Martin," that she was	E III 18 473 27
It would be a great pleasure to know Robert Martin.	E III 18 473 27
as it was!--that Robert Martin had thoroughly supplanted	E III 18 475 41
Harriet had always liked Robert Martin; and that his	E III 19 481 1
became acquainted with Robert Martin, who was now	E III 19 481 2
saw her hand bestowed on Robert Martin with so complete a	E III 19 482 4
Robert Martin and Harriet Smith, the latest couple engaged	E III 19 482 6
marriage of Mr. and Mrs. Robert Martin, to join the hands	E III 19 483 6
ROBERT MARTIN'S (4)	E III 19 484 11
gratified by a Robert Martin's riding about the country to	E I 4 35 45
"Robert Martin's manners have sense, sincerity, and good-	E I 8 65 49
However, I must say that Robert Martin's heart seemed for	E III 18 472 20
sake, and for Robert Martin's sake, (whom I have always	E III 18 474 34
ROBERT'S (8)	
a short pause, "of Robert's marrying Miss Morton."	SS III 5 296 24
She will hardly be less hurt, I suppose, by Robert's	SS III 13 366 18
Steele, she feared that Robert's offence would serve no	SS III 13 369 33
Robert's offence was unpardonable, but Lucy's was	SS III 13 371 38
my mother's pardon for Robert's ingratitude to her, and	SS III 13 372 41
in self-condemnation for Robert's offence, and gratitude	SS III 14 377 11
nothing ever appeared in Robert's style of living or of	SS III 14 377 12
friend of Robert's, who used to be with us a great deal.	W 316 2
ROBIN ADAIR (1)	
She is playing Robin Adair at this moment--his favourite."	E II 10 243 29
ROBINSON (5)	
Henry, remember that Robinson is spoken to about it.	NA II 11 214 24
it-- but I hardly know what--something about Mr. Robinson.	PP I 5 18 6
between him and Mr. Robinson; did not I mention it to you?	PP I 5 19 7
replaced, and though Mr. Robinson felt and felt, and	P III 7 54 4
to the spine, but Mr. Robinson found nothing to increase	P III 7 55 7
ROBUST (3)	
She is too tall and robust.	MP I 14 135 16
Man is more robust than woman, but he is not longer-lived;	P IV 11 233 23
very materially of not a robust family, was astonished to	S 10 413 1
ROCK (3)	
a woman, who firm as a rock in her own principles, has a	MP III 4 351 32
where fragments of low rock among the sands make it the	P III 11 95 9
in toiling up it's long ascent half rock, half sand.--	S 1 363 1
ROCKED (1)	
we had been literally rocked in our bed, and she did not	S 4 381 1
ROCKS (6)	
on horseback, that they were going as far as Wick Rocks."	NA I 11 86 46
believe it to be full of rocks and promontories, grey moss	SS I 18 97 4
What are men to rocks and mountains?	PP II 4 154 23
chasms between romantic rocks, where the scattered forest	P III 11 95 9
looking about them at the rocks and mountains, as if they	P IV 6 169 25
mud--no weeds--no slimey rocks--never was there a place	S 1 369 1
ROCKY (1)	
transition from a piece of rocky fragment and the withered	NA I 14 111 29
RODE (9)	
window, that he wore a blue coat and rode a black horse.	PP I 3 9 3
what passed, took leave and rode on with his friend.	PP I 15 73 9
she rode without her cousins, were ready to set forward.	MP I 7 66 15
I rode fifty yards up the lane between the church and the	MP II 7 242 23
walking together through the village, as he rode into it.--	MP III 3 334 1
very conscious and smiling, and rode off in great spirits.	E I 8 68 58
He rode down for a couple of hours; he could not yet do	E III 1 315 3
I saw you the other day as you rode through the town-----	E III 2 323 19
I walked and rode a great deal; and the more I saw, the	P IV 8 183 13
ROLL (8)	
they will only get a roll if it does break down; and there	NA I 9 65 30
to its foundation will roll round the neighbouring	NA II 5 159 19
compartment will open--a roll of paper appears:--you seize	NA II 5 160 21
eyes directly fell on a roll of paper pushed back into the	NA II 6 169 11
which had burst from the roll on its falling to the ground,	NA II 7 172 1
over in books, for the roll, seeming to consist entirely	NA II 7 172 1
of puppies just able to roll about, brought them to four	NA II 11 214 26
An enormous roll of green baize had arrived from	MP I 14 130 1
ROLLED (2)	
and that if people who rolled in money could not afford	NA I 11 89 61
A week or ten days rolled quietly away after this visit,	W 348 23
ROLLING (2)	
as rolling down the green slope at the back of the house.	NA I 1 14 1
to Miss Lucy Steele, in rolling her papers for her; and	SS II 1 145 19
ROLLS (1)	
has once got his name in a banking house he rolls in money.	LS 5 250 2
ROMAN (1)	
"Yes," added the other; "and of the Roman emperors as low	MP I 2 18 25
ROMANCE (8)	
is busy in pursueing the plan of romance begun at Langford.	LS 19 274 2
The visions of romance were over.	NA II 10 199 1
common life began soon to succeed to the alarms of romance.	NA II 10 201 5
It is a new circumstance in romance, I acknowledge, and	NA II 15 243 9
a good deal of Marianne's romance, without having much of	SS I 1 7 14
the hero of an old romance, and glories in his chains.	MP III 5 360 16
in her youth, she learned romance as she grew older--the	P III 4 30 9
the result of any spirit of romance in Charlotte herself.	S 6 391 1
ROMANCE OF THE FOREST (2)	
He never read the Romance of the Forest, nor the Children	E I 4 29 10
He has not been able to get the Romance of the Forest yet.	E I 4 32 29
ROMANCERS (1)	
that romancers may say, there is no doing without money.	NA II 3 146 16
ROMANCING (1)	
you see, I was not romancing so much as you supposed."	P IV 9 205 82
ROMANTIC (12)	
I must own myself rather romantic in that respect, & that	LS 2 245 1
it is surely my duty to discourage such romantic nonsense.	LS 25 294 5
you, by indulging that romantic tender-heartedness which	LS 26 295 1
Without suffering any romantic alarm, in the consideration	NA II 14 234 10
so keen, a generosity so romantic, that any offence of the	SS I 1 6 9
"No," replied Elinor, "her opinions are all romantic."	SS I 11 56 9
desire it,--for when the romantic refinements of a young	SS I 11 56 17
were all sunk in Mrs. Dashwood's romantic delicacy.	SS I 16 85 10
I am not romantic you know.	PP I 22 125 17
Romantic delicacy was certainly not to be expected from	MP III 2 331 17
temptations, had no romantic expectations of extraordinary	E I 10 86 24
its green chasms between romantic rocks, where the	P III 11 95 9
ROMANTICALLY (1)	
which was seen romantically situated among wood on a high	S 1 364 1
ROOF (12)	
times before, under that roof, in every Bath season, yet	NA I 10 72 8
for weeks under the same roof with the person whose	NA II 2 141 11
all the rest, this roof was to be the roof of an Abbey!--	NA II 2 141 11
building was regular, the roof was tiled, the window	SS I 6 28 2
Then, and then only, under such a roof, I might perhaps be	SS I 14 73 13
discovery that took place under our roof yesterday."	SS III 1 265 34
his mistress under his own roof; and to this Mrs. Grant	MP I 4 41 15
did yet mean to stay a few days longer under his roof.	MP II 2 191 10
When no longer under the same roof with Edmund, she	MP III 7 376 4
quitted her husband's roof in company with the well known	MP III 15 440 14
Wentworth under his own roof, and welcoming him to all	P III 7 53 1
they were all beneath his roof; and while Louisa, under	P III 12 111 50
ROOFS (1)	
single rooms, with as many roofs as windows--it is not	MP II 7 243 27
ROOKE (6)	
and nurse Rooke thoroughly understands when to speak.	P IV 5 155 9
Call it gossip if you will; but when nurse Rooke has half	P IV 5 155 9
situation my friend Mrs. Rooke is in at present, will	P IV 5 156 12
	13
"It was my friend, Mrs. Rooke--nurse Rooke, who, by the by,	P IV 9 197 40
On Monday evening my good friend Mrs. Rooke let me thus	P IV 9 205 82
but my sensible nurse Rooke sees the absurdity of it.--	P IV 9 208 92
ROOM (651)	
My dear Catherine, Unluckily I was confined to my room	LS 13 262 1
in my life as Frederica when she entered the room.	LS 17 269 1
took her out of the room & did not return for some time;	LS 17 270 2
request, into her dressing room, & Frederica spends great	LS 17 271 7
are plenty of books in the room, but it is not every girl	LS 17 271 7
very instructive, for that room overlooks the lawn you	LS 17 271 7
of sixteen we shall have room for the most flattering	LS 19 274 2
as ashes came running up, & rushed by me into her own room.	LS 20 275 1
In the breakfast room we found Lady Susan & a young man of	LS 20 275 2

Context	Work	Vol	Ch	Page	Line
when we entered the room, that I felt for her exceedingly.	LS		20	276	3
room, as she was anxious to speak with me in private.	LS		20	276	5
Reginald came this morning into my dressing room, with a	LS		22	281	4
parlour, when my brother called me out of the room.	LS		23	283	3
my return to the parlour, Lady Susan entered the room.	LS		23	284	6
She soon afterwards left the room.	LS		23	284	7
& sat with him in his room, talking over the whole matter.	LS		24	285	2
After breakfast however, as I was going to my own room I	LS		24	286	5
at seeing Reginald come out of Lady Susan's dressing room.	LS		24	287	8
You will find Mr Vernon in his own room."	LS		24	287	8
We went into my room.	LS		24	287	9
If you remember, I left the room almost immediately.	LS		24	288	11
Mr Johnson, while he waited in the drawing room for me.	LS		32	302	1
The season was full, the room crowded, and the two ladies	NA	I	2	20	9
that to proceed along the room was by no means the way to	NA	I	2	21	9
gained even the top of the room, their situation was just	NA	I	2	21	9
to dance, but she had not an acquaintance in the room.	NA	I	2	21	9
any thing I like so well in the whole room, I assure you."	NA	I	2	22	11
the room, nor was she once called a divinity by any body.	NA	I	2	23	27
"Perhaps you are not sitting in this room, and I am not	NA	I	3	27	28
was to be seen in the room at different periods of the	NA	I	4	31	1
clock, after parading the room till they were tired; "and	NA	I	4	31	1
Miss Thorpe, and take a turn with her about the room.	NA	I	4	33	6
sit down at the other end of the room, and enjoy ourselves.	NA	I	6	39	4
sake! let us move away from this end of the room.	NA	I	6	42	33
I am afraid, brother, you will not have room for a third."	NA	I	7	48	30
The time of the two parties uniting in the Octagon Room	NA	I	7	51	54
that part of the room where she had left Mr. Tilney.	NA	I	8	55	10
in the room more happy to oblige her than Catherine.	NA	I	8	55	10
Is he in the room?	NA	I	8	57	16
in the room; my two younger sisters and their partners.	NA	I	8	59	37
every new face, and almost every new bonnet in the room.	NA	I	10	71	8
saw just entering the room with Mrs. Hughes, and whom she	NA	I	10	72	8
parties remained in the room; and though in all	NA	I	10	72	8
I asked you as soon as I came into the room, and I was	NA	I	10	75	26
the prettiest girl in the room; and when they see you	NA	I	10	75	26
do not, I will kick them out of the room for blockheads.	NA	I	10	76	28
stand opposite each other in a long room for half an hour."	NA	I	10	77	32
the room besides him, that I have any acquaintance with."	NA	I	10	78	38
He replied by asking her to make room for him, and talking	NA	I	12	95	15
Isabella now entered the room with so eager a step, and a	NA	I	15	117	4
as they walked about the room arm in arm, Isabella thus	NA	II	1	134	37
was nobody else in the room he could bear to think of; and	NA	II	1	134	39
his father remained in the room; and even afterwards, so	NA	II	5	155	3
Morland would not have room to sit; and, so much was he	NA	II	5	155	4
the floor of a room without windows, doors, or furnitures.	NA	II	5	158	15
your hand, will pass through it into a small vaulted room."	NA	II	5	159	19
No, no, you will proceed into this small vaulted room, and	NA	II	5	160	21
In repassing through the small vaulted room, however, your	NA	II	5	160	21
as she looked round the room, whether any thing within her	NA	II	5	161	26
of the smallness of the room and simplicity of the	NA	II	5	162	27
and the air of the room altogether far from uncheerful.	NA	II	6	163	1
at the door of the room made her, starting, quit her hold,	NA	II	6	164	3
being ready, entered the room, and to the rising shame of	NA	II	6	165	4
How it came to be first put in this room I know not, but I	NA	II	6	165	4
The dining-parlour was a noble room, suitable in its	NA	II	6	165	6
by no means an ill-sized room; and further confessed, that,	NA	II	6	166	6
and she had never seen so large a room as this in her life.	NA	II	6	166	7
from her, to enter her room with a tolerably stout heart;	NA	II	6	167	9
She looked round the room.	NA	II	6	167	10
a parting glance round the room, she was struck by the	NA	II	6	168	10
Darkness impenetrable and immoveable filled the room.	NA	II	6	170	12
remained undiscovered in a room such as that, so modern,	NA	II	7	173	2
She got away as soon as she could from a room in which her	NA	II	7	173	5
re-entering the breakfast room, Catherine walked to a	NA	II	7	175	13
He left the room, and Catherine, with a disappointed,	NA	II	7	177	17
art of her own question, "hangs in your father's room?"	NA	II	7	180	38
the room by their return, was at last ready to escort them.	NA	II	8	182	1
anti-chamber, into a room magnificent both in size and	NA	II	8	182	2
through a dark little room, owning Henry's authority, and	NA	II	8	183	2
the gallery in which her room lay, and shortly entered one	NA	II	8	184	5
into what was my mother's room--the room in which she died-	NA	II	8	186	6
was my mother's room--the room in which she died-----"	NA	II	8	186	6
of such objects as that room must contain; a room in all	NA	II	8	186	6
that room must contain; a room in all probability never	NA	II	8	186	6
be watched from home, before that room could be entered.	NA	II	8	186	7
of an injured wife, before her room was put to rights.	NA	II	8	186	10
"My father," she whispered, "often walks about the room in	NA	II	8	187	13
she stole gently from her room to the corresponding window	NA	II	8	188	19
ran for safety to her own room, and, locking herself in,	NA	II	9	192	4
On tip-toe she entered; the room was before her; but it	NA	II	9	193	6
She could not be mistaken as to the room; but how grossly	NA	II	9	193	6
but to be safe in her own room, with her own heart only	NA	II	9	194	6
said Catherine, looking down, "to see your mother's room."	NA	II	9	195	9
"My mother's room!--	NA	II	9	195	10
My mother's room is very commodious, is it not?	NA	II	9	196	21
there is nothing in the room in itself to raise curiosity,	NA	II	9	196	23
and with tears of shame she ran off to her own room.	NA	II	9	198	30
The formidable Henry soon followed her into the room, and	NA	II	10	199	1
hurried away to her own room; but the house-maids were	NA	II	10	203	8
and great coated into the room where she and Eleanor were	NA	II	11	210	7
had very little idea of the room in which she was sitting.	NA	II	11	212	18
was the most comfortable room in the world; but she was	NA	II	11	213	18
The room in question was of a commodious, well-	NA	II	11	213	21
It was a prettily-shaped room, the windows reaching to the	NA	II	11	213	21
"Oh! why do not you fit up this room, Mr. Tilney?	NA	II	11	214	21
It is the prettiest room I ever saw;--it is the prettiest	NA	II	11	214	21
room I ever saw;--it is the prettiest room in the world!"	NA	II	11	214	21
to enter the room, and a still greater to speak when there.	NA	II	13	223	9
That room, in which her disturbed imagination had	NA	II	13	227	26
Soon after six Eleanor entered her room, eager to show	NA	II	13	227	27
When every thing was done they left the room, Catherine	NA	II	13	227	27
The contrast between this and her last breakfast in room,	NA	II	13	228	27
after Mr. Allen left the room, without any relaxation of	NA	II	14	238	22
hastily left the room to fetch the book in question,	NA	II	15	241	7
till, on entering the room, the first object she beheld	NA	II	15	241	7
Use those words again and I will leave the room this	SS	I	4	21	14
and instantly left the room, resolving that, whatever	SS	I	4	23	19
A room or two can easily be added; and if my friends find	SS	I	5	25	2
On each side of the entrance was a sitting room, about	SS	I	6	28	2
drawings were affixed to the walls of their sitting room.	SS	I	6	30	5
them to the drawing room repeated to the young ladies the	SS	I	7	33	4
Soon after this, upon Elinor's leaving the room, "mama,"	SS	I	8	38	14
not likely that the room would be wanted for some time."	SS	I	8	39	17
time did he most unaccountably follow me out of the room.	SS	I	8	39	18
and mama went out of the room, they were whispering and	SS	I	12	60	13
direction, changed colour, and immediately left the room.	SS	I	13	63	3
hope;" said Mrs. Jennings, as soon as he entered the room.	SS	I	13	63	8
a good morning, and attended by Sir John, left the room.	SS	I	13	66	51
There is one remarkably pretty sitting room up stairs; of	SS	I	13	69	76
It is a corner room, and has windows on two sides.	SS	I	13	69	76
have described every room in the house with equal delight.	SS	I	13	69	77
eager to pass through the room which has hitherto	SS	I	14	73	17
directly into the room she had just quitted, where they	SS	I	15	75	2
He then hastily took leave of them all and left the room.	SS	I	15	76	17
Marianne had quitted the room was such as a serious	SS	I	15	77	19
room and took her place at the table without saying a word.	SS	I	15	82	46
was quite overcome, she burst into tears and left the room.	SS	I	15	82	46
He entered the room with a look of self-consequence,	SS	I	19	106	22
"Well! what a delightful room this is!	SS	I	19	107	24
on different sides of the room; "but, however, I can't	SS	I	19	107	29
Mr. Palmer looked up on her entering the room, stared at	SS	I	19	108	35
was now caught by the drawings which hung round the room.	SS	I	19	108	35
soon forgot that there were any such things in the room.	SS	I	19	108	36
after again examining the room, that is was very low	SS	I	19	108	39
who just then entered the room--"you must help me persuade	SS	I	20	110	9
Sir John mean by not having a billiard room in his house?	SS	I	20	111	8
When they were seated in the dining room, Sir John	SS	I	20	111	18
She was carried out of the room therefore in her mother's	SS	I	21	122	10
in a quietness which the room had not known for many hours.	SS	I	21	122	10
an hour or two together in the same room almost every day.	SS	I	21	124	33
parlour and drawing room: to the latter, the children	SS	II	1	143	10
Lucy made room for her with ready attention, and the two	SS	II	1	145	23
that any body was in the room besides herself, was luckily	SS	II	1	145	23
returned to the drawing room, seemed anxiously listening	SS	II	4	161	6
in her own room, could see little of what was passing.	SS	II	4	161	7
minute, returned into the room in all the agitation which	SS	II	4	161	7
be borne with calmness, and she immediately left the room.	SS	II	4	162	8
as she quitted the room, with such astonishment and	SS	II	4	162	8
she came laughing into the room; so delighted to see them	SS	II	4	164	21
and forwards across the room, pausing for a moment	SS	II	4	166	31
nodded to Mrs. Jennings from the other side of the room.	SS	II	5	171	30
company of any kind, left the room before he entered it.	SS	II	5	172	40
She sat by the drawing room fire after tea, till the	SS	II	6	175	1
voice, and entered a room splendidly lit up, quite full of	SS	II	6	175	2
In a short time Elinor saw Willoughby quit the room by the	SS	II	6	178	15
own room, where hartshorn restored her a little to herself.	SS	II	6	178	16
her from remaining in the room a moment after she was	SS	II	7	180	5
of a death-like paleness, instantly ran out of the room.	SS	II	7	181	7
hurried away to their room, where, on opening the door,	SS	II	7	182	12
long she had been in the room, that when on hearing a	SS	II	7	184	16
Mrs. Jennings came immediately to their room on her return,	SS	II	8	192	1
She then went away, walking on tiptoe out of the room, as	SS	II	8	192	4
into the dining room as soon as they were summoned to it.	SS	II	8	193	5
her, she directly got up and hurried out of the room.	SS	II	8	193	7
is gone to her own room I suppose to moan by herself.	SS	II	8	195	14
I dare say will not leave her room again this evening.	SS	II	8	195	15
she expected, in her own room, leaning, in silent misery,	SS	II	8	197	23
of looking round the room for Marianne, Elinor immediately	SS	II	8	198	30
she walked across the room to the tea-table where Elinor	SS	II	8	198	30
were together in their own room after breakfast, which	SS	II	9	202	4
comfort, she entered their room, saying, "now, my dear, I	SS	II	9	202	5
					6
rushing eagerly into the room to inforce, at her feet, by	SS	II	9	202	7
"I will not trust to that," retreating to her own room.	SS	II	9	204	16
and rising hastily walked for a few minutes about the room.	SS	II	9	206	25
not well;" for Marianne had left the room on their arrival.	SS	II	10	219	37
people before them in the room, that there was not a	SS	II	11	220	3
The old walnut trees are all come down to make room for it.	SS	II	11	226	39
her present drawing room; and these screens, catching the	SS	II	12	234	26
other gentlemen into the room, were officiously handed by	SS	II	12	234	26
walk out of the room again, as to advance farther into it.	SS	II	13	240	19
She then left the room; and Elinor dared not follow her to	SS	II	13	244	47
would fix them at pleasure on any other object in the room.	SS	II	14	250	11
There is not a room in this cottage that will hold ten	SS	II	14	252	18
walked about the room, and said he did not know what to do.	SS	III	1	259	7
Marianne got up, and walked about the room.	SS	III	1	269	55
as soon as he quitted the room; and as her vehemence made	SS	III	1	269	58
was forced to go into the room and interrupt them, to ask	SS	III	2	274	16
"you were all in the same room together, were not you?"	SS	III	2	274	17
Marianne had left the room before the conversation began.	SS	III	4	286	12
on first coming into the room, he could not recollect; but	SS	III	4	288	26
"Fanny is in her own room, I suppose," said he;--"I will	SS	III	5	294	6
being there, quitted the room in quest of her; and Elinor	SS	III	5	298	32
who attended her into the room, and hung enamoured over	SS	III	5	300	38
room, and Elinor remained alone with Marianne.	SS	III	7	310	9
and retired to her own room to write letters and sleep.	SS	III	7	316	27
instantly to quit the room, and her hand was already on	SS	III	8	317	1
					2
He rose up, and walked across the room.	SS	III	8	318	14
And with these words, he almost ran out of the room.	SS	III	8	332	84
His emotion in entering the room, in seeing her altered	SS	III	10	340	2
Dashwood's assistance, supported her into the other room.	SS	III	11	353	25
His countenance, as he entered the room, was not too happy,	SS	III	12	359	11
She almost ran out of the room, and as soon as the door	SS	III	12	360	26
saying a word, quitted the room, and walked out towards	SS	III	12	360	26
girls in the room, there is a great deal in novelty.	W			315	1
she should, that "Mr Tomlinson's family were in the room."	W			327	7
The cold & empty appearance of the room & the demure air	W			328	8
& people the centre of the room, than she found herself	W			328	9
the Osbornes are coming"--was repeated round the room.--	W			329	9
imprisoned within his own room, had been listening in	W			329	9
In their progress up the room, they paused almost	W			329	9
seemed to speak him out of his element in a ball room.	W			329	10
Tearoom was a small room within the cardroom, & in passing	W			332	11
of being first out of the room, which happened to be	W			333	13
I shall find her in the tea room.	W			333	13
If you prefer this room to the other, there is no reason	W			334	13
the others were out of the room, to "beg her pardon", &	W			336	13
some of the last in the room--"here we are, back again I	W			336	14
she walked into the dining room, where the tables were	W			336	14
the same table in the same room, with only one change of	W			336	14
other people in a ball room, what are young ladies to do?"	W			337	15
flight of steps up to the room we dine in--which do not	W			344	20
Elizth always takes care to have a room to herself."--	W			351	25
just come from my father's room, he seems very indifferent.	W			352	26
the usual little sitting room, the door of the best	W			355	28
admitting me, in such dishabille into your drawing room.	W			357	28
he left the room, fatigued with the raptures of his wife.	PP	I	2	8	25
And when the party entered the assembly room, it	PP	I	3	10	4
drew the attention of the room by his fine, tall person,	PP	I	3	10	5
principal people in the room; he was lively and unreserved,	PP	I	3	10	6
the room, speaking occasionally to one of his own party.	PP	I	3	11	6
not another woman in the room, whom it would not be a	PP	I	3	11	9
room," said Mr. Darcy, looking at the eldest Miss Bennet.	PP	I	3	11	11
"Oh! my dear Mr. Bennet," as she entered the room, "we	PP	I	3	12	16
the only creature in the room that he asked a second time.	PP	I	3	12	16
five times as pretty as every other woman in the room.	PP	I	4	14	5
acquainted with all the room; and as to Miss Bennet, he	PP	I	4	16	15
women in the room, and which he thought the prettiest?	PP	I	5	19	7
officers joined eagerly in dancing at one end of the room.	PP	I	6	25	24
was very feverish and not well enough to leave her room.	PP	I	7	33	43
Elizabeth did not quit her room for a moment, nor were the	PP	I	7	33	44
began abusing her as soon as she was out of the room.	PP	I	8	35	3
remarkably well, when she came into the room this morning.	PP	I	8	36	7
they repaired to her room on leaving the dining-parlour,	PP	I	8	37	21
she could suit herself perfectly with those in the room.	PP	I	8	38	28
thereby at an end, Elizabeth soon afterwards left the room.	PP	I	8	40	55
the night in her sister's room, and in the morning had the	PP	I	9	41	1
You have a sweet room here, Mr. Bingley, and a charming	PP	I	9	42	7
At present I have not room to do them justice."	PP	I	10	48	16
yours till I am out of the room, I shall be very thankful;	PP	I	10	51	42
intend leaving her room for a couple of hours that evening.	PP	I	10	53	66
suffer from the change of room; and she removed at his	PP	I	11	54	2
cast her eyes round the room in quest of some amusement;	PP	I	11	55	5
					6
and soon afterwards got up and walked about the room.	PP	I	11	56	10
you to follow my example, and take a turn about the room.--	PP	I	11	56	11
to walk up and down the room together, with either of	PP	I	11	56	12
and conceit in every other room in the house, he was used	PP	I	15	71	6
Mr. Collins repeated his apologies in quitting the room,	PP	I	15	74	11
have resented a comparison with the housekeeper's room.	PP	I	16	75	2
Wickham walked into the room, Elizabeth felt that she had	PP	I	16	76	3
breathing port wine, who followed them into the room.	PP	I	16	76	3

Context	Text	Vol.	Ch.	Page	Line
remark on the size of the room, or the number of couples."	PP	I	18	91	9
that will amaze the whole room, and be handed down to	PP	I	18	91	15
to the other side of the room; but on perceiving Mr. Darcy	PP	I	18	92	22
people in the room who had less to say for themselves.--	PP	I	18	93	26
there is now in the room a near relation of my patroness.	PP	I	18	96	57
had been spoken so loud as to be heard by half the room.--	PP	I	18	101	71
and offer to introduce him to any young lady in the room.	PP	I	18	102	73
she would have quitted the room, had not Mr. Collins thus	PP	I	19	108	16
on the present occasion; and secondly, of my room.					17
Elizabeth passed quietly out of the room, Jane and Kitty	PP	I	20	112	22
to be in the same room, the same party with him for so	PP	I	20	114	31
When they had gained their own room, Jane taking out the	PP	I	21	115	4
	PP	I	21	116	6
He made her an offer in this very room, and she refused					7
affected herself, accompanied her out of the room.	PP	II	2	140	4
the good proportion of the room, its aspect and its	PP	II	3	145	11
of furniture in the room, from the sideboard to the fender,	PP	II	5	155	4
About the middle of the next day, as she was in her room	PP	II	5	156	4
an anti-chamber, to the room where Lady Catherine, her	PP	II	5	158	11
When the ladies returned to the drawing room, there was	PP	II	6	161	10
out of window in his own book room, which fronted the road.	PP	II	6	163	15
The room in which the ladies sat was backwards.	PP	II	7	168	1
use; it was a better sized room, and had a pleasanter	PP	II	7	168	1
From the drawing room they could distinguish nothing in	PP	II	7	168	1
that was passing in the room during these visits.	PP	II	7	168	2
Charlotte had seen them from her husband's room, crossing	PP	II	7	169	3
	PP	II	7	170	7
shortly afterwards the three gentlemen entered the room.					8
they joined the party in Lady Catherine's drawing room.	PP	II	7	170	9
to Darcy, much more than to any other person in the room.	PP	II	8	172	2
well entertained in that room before; and they conversed	PP	II	8	172	2
day, and play on the piano forte in Mrs. Jenkinson's room.	PP	II	8	172	3
"True; and nobody can ever be introduced in a ball room.	PP	II	8	173	10
surprise, Mr. Darcy, and Mr. Darcy only, entered the room.	PP	II	8	175	20
There, shut into her own room, as soon as their visitor	PP	II	9	177	1
her utter amazement, she saw Mr. Darcy walk into the room.	PP	II	10	186	38
a few moments, and then getting up walked about the room.	PP	II	11	188	3
with quick steps across the room, "is your opinion of me!	PP	II	11	189	3
And with these words he hastily left the room, and	PP	II	11	192	22
Charlotte's observation, and hurried her away to her room.	PP	II	11	193	30
there will be very good room for one of you--and indeed,	PP	II	11	194	32
obliged to walk about the room, while Elizabeth tried to	PP	II	14	211	10
Kitty and Lydia looking out of a dining room up stairs.	PP	II	15	216	5
It was a large, well-proportioned room, handsomely fitted	PP	II	16	219	1
This room was my late master's favourite room, and these	PP	III	1	246	5
In the next room is a new instrument just come down for	PP	III	1	247	18
who had taken a liking to the room, when last at Pemberley.	PP	III	1	248	22
Miss Darcy's delight, when she should enter the room.	PP	III	1	249	43
into a glen, allowed room only for the stream, and a	PP	III	1	250	45
she walked up and down the room, endeavouring to compose	PP	III	1	253	57
heard on the stairs, and in a moment he entered the room.	PP	III	2	260	2
In this room they were received by Miss Darcy, who was	PP	III	2	261	5
moment that some of the gentlemen would enter the room.	PP	III	3	267	3
on his entering the room; and then, though but a moment	PP	III	3	268	5
not watch his behaviour when he first came into the room.	PP	III	3	268	7
My poor mother is really ill and keeps her room.	PP	III	3	268	8
On his quitting the room, she sat down, unable to support	PP	III	4	275	5
walking up and down the room in earnest meditation; his	PP	III	4	276	9
As he quitted the room, Elizabeth felt how improbable it	PP	III	4	278	19
entered the room, the misery of her impatience was severe.	PP	III	4	279	23
repeated the other, as she ran into her room to prepare.	PP	III	4	280	26
When they were all in the drawing room, the questions	PP	III	4	281	28
They ran through the vestibule into the breakfast room;	PP	III	5	287	33
	PP	III	7	301	4
refuge in her own room, that she might think with freedom.					5
The family were assembled in the breakfast room, to	PP	III	7	307	50
the door was thrown open, and she ran into the room.	PP	III	9	315	2
looked eagerly round the room, took notice of some little	PP	III	9	315	3
She got up, and ran out of the room; and returned no more,	PP	III	9	315	4
the breakfast room, "and what do you think of my husband?	PP	III	9	317	9
ourselves, so there will be just room at table for him."	PP	III	9	317	11
On entering the room, he seemed to hesitate; but Jane	PP	III	11	333	26
Darcy had walked away to another part of the room.	PP	III	12	340	11
the room, as to make him play as unsuccessfully as herself.	PP	III	12	341	18
In ran Mrs. Bennet to her daughter's room, in her dressing	PP	III	12	342	26
	PP	III	13	344	6
my love, I want to speak to you," took her out of the room.					7
	PP	III	13	345	12
and I are going up stairs to sit in my dressing room."					13
were out of sight, then returned into the drawing room.	PP	III	13	345	16
went into the breakfast room for that purpose soon after	PP	III	13	345	17
But on returning to the drawing room, when her letter was	PP	III	13	346	21
whispering a few words to her sister ran out of the room.	PP	III	13	346	22
together in the dining room, their attention was suddenly	PP	III	13	346	22
She entered the room with an air more than usually	PP	III	14	351	1
"This must be a most inconvenient sitting room for the	PP	III	14	351	3
Elizabeth obeyed, and running into her own room for her	PP	III	14	352	11
said he, "I was going to look for you; come into my room."	PP	III	14	352	19
room, and from all the others when they sat down to table.	PP	III	15	361	7
Her father was walking about the room, looking grave and	PP	III	17	372	1
as she quitted the room, "if any young men come for Mary	PP	III	17	376	29
reflection in her own room, she was able to join the	PP	III	17	377	40
But before she had been three minutes in her own room, her	PP	III	17	377	41
said Mrs. Norris when Fanny had left the room.--	PP	III	17	378	44
Come with me into the breakfast room, we shall find every	MP	I	2	13	5
thing there, and be sure of having the room to ourselves."	MP	I	2	16	15
into the breakfast room, where Edmund prepared her paper,	MP	I	2	16	15
Fanny left the room with a very sorrowful heart; she could	MP	I	2	16	20
and allow a spare room for a friend, of which she made a	MP	I	3	25	17
to give her, for I must keep a spare room for a friend."	MP	I	3	28	38
little girl or two in the room--the governess being sick	MP	I	3	30	56
I felt that I must be the jest of the room at the time--	MP	I	5	50	35
But if I had more room, I should take a prodigious delight	MP	I	5	50	35
from the other end of the room, which was a very long one,	MP	I	6	54	9
"No; but they were to be put into the spare room to day;	MP	I	7	71	33
to lock the door of the room and bring away the key, so	MP	I	7	73	51
Edmund got up and walked about the room, saying, "and	MP	I	7	73	51
you; there can be no doubt of your having room for her."	MP	I	7	73	52
Julia, hastily leaving the room as she spoke, from a	MP	I	8	78	16
Every room on the west front looked across a lawn to the	MP	I	8	79	25
a mere, spacious, oblong room, fitted up for the purpose	MP	I	9	85	4
house, dawdling from one room to another--straining one's	MP	I	9	85	6
for Mr. Bertram was in the room again, and though feeling	MP	I	9	95	71
Any room in this house might suffice."	MP	I	12	118	22
hardly walk from this room to the next to look at the raw	MP	I	13	123	6
It is the very room for a theatre, precisely the shape and	MP	I	13	124	12
book-case in my father's room, is the very thing we could	MP	I	13	125	14
And my father's room will be an excellent green-room.	MP	I	13	125	14
not to be'd, in this very room, for his amusement!	MP	I	13	125	14
our sitting more in this room, and less in the breakfast-	MP	I	13	126	25
being moved from one side of the room to the other.--	MP	I	13	127	29
Tom walked out of the room as he said it, and Edmund was	MP	I	13	127	29
Henry Crawford entered the room, fresh from the parsonage,	MP	I	13	128	33
and been forced to re-rant it all in his own room.	MP	I	13	129	38
And so saying, she walked hastily out of the room, leaving	MP	I	14	132	8
to consult farther in the room now beginning to be called	MP	I	14	136	20
In a few minutes Mr. Bertram was called out of the room to	MP	I	14	136	22
the only speaker in the room, and to feel that almost	MP	I	15	139	11
had continued her sleeping room ever since her first	MP	I	15	145	49
The room had then become useless, and for some time was	MP	I	16	150	1
The east room as it had been called, ever since Maria	MP	I	16	151	1
seemed to imply that it was the best room in the house.	MP	I	16	151	1
see an object in that room which had not an interesting	MP	I	16	151	1
The room was most dear to her, and she would not have	MP	I	16	151	2
as she walked round the room her doubts were increasing.	MP	I	16	152	2
solitude of the east room, without being seen or missed.	MP	I	16	152	3
be always walking from one room to the other and doing the	MP	I	17	159	6
with her work to the east room, that she might have no	MP	I	18	166	6
and meditated in the east room, undisturbed, for a quarter	MP	I	18	168	14
Yes; this is the east room.	MP	I	18	168	14
herself mistress of the room by her civilities, and looked	MP	I	18	168	15
Yates is storming away in the dining room.	MP	I	18	168	16
Or why had not she rather gone to her own room, as she had	MP	I	18	169	21
way, when the door of the room was thrown open, and Julia	MP	I	18	172	29
she turned out of the room, saying "I need not be afraid	MP	I	18	172	33
to go as she quitted the room herself to perform the	MP	II	1	175	2
Instead of being sent for out of the room, and seeing him	MP	II	1	177	6
into his own dear room, every agitation was returning.	MP	II	1	180	10
candles burning in his room; and on casting his eye round	MP	II	1	181	17
The removal of the book-case from before the billiard room	MP	II	1	182	22
from the billiard room to astonish him still further.	MP	II	1	182	22
at the other end of the room; and never had he found	MP	II	1	182	22
ceiling and stucco of the room; and that when he inquired	MP	II	1	182	22
Its vicinity to my own room--but in every respect indeed	MP	II	1	183	24
going to him up in his room before we set off to advise	MP	II	1	184	25
put up in the billiard room, and given the scene painter	MP	II	2	189	5
only the floor of one room, ruined all the coachman's	MP	II	2	190	9
into the breakfast room, where were most of the family.	MP	II	2	190	9
observing a harp in the room, asked some questions about	MP	II	2	192	11
him sitting in that room again and again, perhaps in the	MP	II	4	206	5
slipped out of the room; for to hear herself the subject	MP	II	4	207	10
wide table too, which fills up the room so dreadfully!	MP	II	5	218	12
unanswerable dignity, and coming farther into the room.--	MP	II	5	220	30
her uncle out of the room, having staid behind him only	MP	II	5	221	37
	MP	II	5	221	38
seated in the drawing room, Sir Thomas saw them off in as					39
could fidget about the room, and disturb every body in	MP	II	5	222	41
their going up into her room, where they might have a	MP	II	6	236	21
favourite box in the east room which held all her smaller	MP	II	8	257	15
languidly towards her own room, and felt as incapable of	MP	II	9	261	1
from the parsonage, and found Edmund in the east room.--	MP	II	9	267	22
well; and Fanny left her room at last, comfortably	MP	II	9	267	23
Miss Price came out of her room completely dressed, and	MP	II	9	271	40
but upon her leaving the room again soon afterwards, he	MP	II	9	271	41
her aunts out of the room, Edmund, who was holding open	MP	II	10	272	1
party of ladies out of the room; and Mrs. Grant coming up	MP	II	10	272	4
their own place in the room, and have their share of a	MP	II	10	275	9
to move all the chaperons to a better part of the room.	MP	II	10	275	12
finest young man in the room; somebody had whispered	MP	II	10	277	16
sounds were heard in the room for the next two hours	MP	II	11	283	4
had made in that room, and all that part of the house.	MP	II	11	283	6
could not sit in the same room with her uncle, hear his	MP	II	11	283	6
But at last Lady Bertram left the room--and then almost	MP	II	11	284	8
to a servant in his way towards the room they were in.	MP	II	11	287	18
up and down the east room in the utmost confusion of	MP	II	13	302	9
shy and uncomfortable when their visitor entered the room.	MP	II	13	302	9
Mr. Crawford was not only in the room; he was soon close	MP	II	13	303	13
Mr. Crawford was in the room; for once or twice a look	MP	II	13	303	14
Sir Thomas was out of the room, or at all engaged with Mrs.	MP	II	13	306	26
approached the east room, she grew gradually composed,	MP	II	13	306	27
The terror of his former occasional visits to that room	MP	III	1	311	3
I understood that you had the use of this room by way of	MP	III	1	312	4
room, after breakfast, when Mr. Crawford was shewn in.--	MP	III	1	312	10
He is in my room, and hoping to see you there."	MP	III	1	313	14
up and walking about the room, with a frown, which Fanny	MP	III	1	314	16
and going into the east room again, the first thing which	MP	III	1	317	36
tea called out of the room; an occurrence too common to	MP	III	1	322	51
Thomas wishes to speak with you, ma'am, in his own room."	MP	III	1	324	60
seeing her in her uncle's room, none such might occur	MP	III	1	324	60
I had not been in the room five minutes, before she began,	MP	III	3	343	40
"Was Mrs. Grant in the room, then?"	MP	III	4	351	36
kept away form the east room, and took no solitary walk in	MP	III	4	352	37
her almost instantly rise and lead the way out of the room.	MP	III	5	357	4
which the finding herself in the east room again produced.	MP	III	5	357	5
The east room.	MP	III	5	357	6
Once only was I in this room before!"--and after stopping	MP	III	5	358	7
Here we were, just in this part of the room, here was your	MP	III	5	358	7
"I have had a little fit since I came into this room, as	MP	III	5	358	7
the east room, without having an idea whereabouts it was!	MP	III	5	359	9
and when he had left the room, she was better pleased that	MP	III	5	360	14
In the calmness of her own dressing room, in the impartial	MP	III	5	365	36
the idea of there being room for a third in the carriage,	MP	III	6	370	14
She had tears for every room in the house, much more for	MP	III	6	372	21
room; and I could not get Rebecca to give me any help."	MP	III	6	374	28
candle was brought, however, and he walked into the room.	MP	III	7	379	18
As he left the room, two rosy-faced boys, ragged and dirty,	MP	III	7	379	19
Within the room all was tranquil enough, for Susan having	MP	III	7	381	25
boys all burst into the room together and sat down, Fanny	MP	III	7	382	28
Price had walked about the room some time looking for a	MP	III	7	383	31
turning pale about, when Mr. Crawford walked into the room.	MP	III	7	385	37
I could not see him, and my eldest sister in the same room,	MP	III	10	399	3
the patient and the sick room in a juster and stronger	MP	III	13	423	2
The remembrance of her first evening in that room, of her	MP	III	14	429	2
came from the drawing room to meet her; came with no	MP	III	15	439	9
told--no one else in the room, except his mother, who,	MP	III	15	447	37
the lessons of affliction--and immediately left the room.	MP	III	16	453	17
Harriet was on the point of leaving the room, and only	MP	III	16	458	30
	E	I	6	43	10
Is not this room rich in specimens of your landscapes and					11
The two Abbotts and I ran into the front room and peeped	E	I	6	43	14
put her--and what room there will be for the children?"	E	I	9	75	26
"Oh! yes--she will have her own room, of course; the room	E	I	9	79	56
own room, of course; the room she always has;--and there	E	I	9	79	57
The room they were taken into was the one he chiefly	E	I	9	79	57
for him to chuse his own subject in the adjoining room.	E	I	10	89	38
that when he came into the room she had one of the	E	I	10	89	38
might in one of the carriages find room for Harriet also.	E	I	12	98	2
I did not mention a syllable of it in the other room.	E	I	13	108	3
now came into the room from examining the weather, and	E	I	14	120	11
who had left the room immediately after his brother's	E	I	15	125	7
left no room for the little zigzags of embarrassment.	E	I	15	127	16
Standing up in the middle of the room, I suppose, and	E	I	15	132	37
her father been out of the room, but speaking plain enough	E	I	18	147	17
open, and Miss Bates and Miss Fairfax walked into the room.	E	II	3	170	1
	E	II	3	172	22
In that very room she had been measured last September,					23
down stairs from her own room, "always over-careful for	E	II	5	187	4
and again into his room, to be sure that all is right."	E	II	5	189	20
the history of the large room visibly added; it had been	E	II	5	189	20
He saw no fault in the room, he would acknowledge none	E	II	6	197	5
Woodhouse revived the former good old days of the room?--	E	II	6	198	5
There must be ample room in it for every real comfort.	E	II	6	198	5
by no housekeeper's room, or a bad butler's pantry, but no	E	II	6	204	42
be more thought of than any other person's in the room.	E	II	6	204	43
really be very happy to walk into the same room with you."	E	II	7	210	19
as soon as she entered the room had been struck by the	E	II	8	214	10
The rest of the gentlemen being now in the room, Emma	E	II	8	214	13
the room at Miss Fairfax, who was sitting exactly opposite.	E	II	8	222	54
Mr. Weston came into the room, and I could get at him, I	E	II	8	222	54
a little bustle in the room shewed them that tea was over,	E	II	8	223	63
you all cold; but I can go into my mother's room you know.	E	II	8	226	85
Our little room so honoured!"	E	II	10	243	31
"No, no, your room is full enough.	E	II	10	243	31
	E	II	10	244	47

Well, (returning into the room,) I have not been able to E II 10 245 52
first in pacing out the room they were in to see what it E II 11 247 2
five; and for five couple there will be plenty of room." E II 11 248 4
one side, "but will there be good room for five couple?-- E II 11 248 5
6
of dancing only in the room they were in resorted to again; E II 11 249 12
"We allowed unnecessary room. E II 11 249 13
"I think there will be very tolerable room for ten couple." E II 11 249 15
16
to be dancing in a crowd--and a crowd in a little room!" E II 11 249 17
A crowd in a little room--Miss Woodhouse, you have the art E II 11 249 18
and he entered the room with such an agreeable smile as E II 11 250 20
A room at an inn was always damp and dangerous; never E II 11 251 26
He had never been in the room at the crown in his life-- E II 11 251 26
But I do not understand how the room at the crown can be E II 11 251 28
Another room of much better size might be secured for the E II 11 254 44
little room; but that was scouted as a wretched suggestion. E II 11 254 45
room, observed, "I do not think it is so very small. E II 11 254 45
46
could not be in the same room to which she had with such E II 14 270 3
was in being in the same room at once with the woman he E II 14 271 5
room, the entrance, and all that she could see or imagine. E II 14 272 18
That room was the very shape and size of the morning-room E II 14 272 18
at Maple Grove; her sister's favourite room."-- E II 14 272 18
"If we were in the other room," said Emma, "if I had my E II 16 298 52
other ladies out of the room, arm in arm, with an E II 16 298 59
Woodhouse came into the room; her vanity had then a change E II 17 302 21
22
of being highly interesting to every body in the room. E II 17 303 24
of what the whole room must have overheard already. E II 17 304 29
The room at the crown was to witness it;--but it would be E III 2 319 2
gentlemen, walked into the room; and Mrs. Elton seemed to E III 2 322 18
Good Mrs. Stokes would not know her own room again. E III 2 322 19
And I see very few pearls in the room except mine.-- E III 2 324 21
He came to the part of the room where the sitters-by were E III 2 327 34
what passed in this very room about court plaister, one of E III 4 338 12
was growing dusk, and the room was in confusion; and how E III 5 349 25
Place, Venice, when Frank Churchill entered the room. E III 6 363 53
and niece seemed both escaping into the adjoining room. E III 8 378 4
into her own room--I want her to lie down upon the bed. E III 8 379 8
but, however, she is not; she is walking about the room. E III 8 379 8
Mr. Elton was called out of the room before tea, old John E III 8 383 29
always to one room;--he could have wished it otherwise-- E III 9 389 16
"Well, my dear," said he, as they entered the room--"I E III 10 394 25
before he quitted the room,--"I have been as good as my E III 10 394 25
the room--"is not this the oddest news that ever was?" E III 11 404 4
with me; and when there was no other partner in the room. E III 11 406 24
about, she tried her own room, she tried the shrubbery--in E III 11 411 43
from walking about the room for a few seconds--and the E III 12 423 21
could he have entered the room, she must have shaken hands E III 15 444 1
to attend her out of the room, to go with her even down E III 16 459 45
46
In half a minute they were in the room. E III 18 476 46
But soon afterwards, rising and pacing the room, he P III 3 18 5
6
to the whole, left the room, to seek the comfort of cool P III 3 24 38
They are both so very large, and take up so much room! P III 5 39 39
at the other end of the room, beautifying a nosegay; then, P III 5 39 40
more room for the harp, which was bringing in the carriage. P III 6 50 26
She said nothing, therefore, till he was out of the room, P III 7 56 9
10
mark an easy footing: the room seemed full--full of P III 7 59 25
with the sportsmen: the room was cleared, and Anne might P III 7 59 25
They had been once more in the same room! P III 7 60 27
room for him;--they were divided only by Mrs. Musgrove. P III 8 68 29
refreshing turns about the room with his hands behind him, P III 8 68 31
32
Unintentionally she returned to that part of the room; he P III 8 72 58
59
soon as he was out of the room, "but it would be shocking P III 9 76 16
would have been out of the room the next moment, and P III 9 79 23
over her little patient to their cares, and leave the room. P III 9 80 34
Here is excellent room for three, I assure you. P III 10 91 40
down to his large fishing-net at one corner of the room. P III 11 99 18
talk on one side of the room, and, by recurring to former P III 11 100 23
The waiter came into the room soon afterwards. P III 12 105 10
of being in the same room with Louisa, was kept, by the P III 12 112 51
Captain Benwick must give up his room to them, and get a P III 12 113 56
away in the maids' room, or swinging a cot somewhere," P III 12 113 56
to think of not finding room for two or three besides, P III 12 113 56
She, who had not been able to remain in Louisa's room, or P III 12 114 59
quietly down from Louisa's room, could not but hear what P III 12 114 60
A bed on the floor in Louisa's room would be sufficient P III 12 114 63
A few months hence, and the room now so deserted, occupied P IV 1 123 7
place, for yours were always kept in the butler's room. P IV 1 127 26
so, I heard it myself, and you were in the other room.-- P IV 2 131 9
Wentworth were there, the room presented as strong a P IV 2 134 28
a happy glance round the room, that after all she had gone P IV 2 134 30
foot-boy could give, Mr. Elliot was ushered into the room. P IV 3 142 17
He had spent his whole solitary evening in the room P IV 3 144 19
in the room) in one point, I am sure, we must feel alike. P IV 4 151 21
it advisable to leave the room, and Anne could have said P IV 5 158 20
"But perhaps if she were to leave the room vacant we " P IV 6 163 7
she could remain in the room, preserve an air of calmness, P IV 6 165 9
In her own room she tried to comprehend it. P IV 6 166 18
took their station by one of the fires in the Octagon Room. P IV 8 181 1
the various noises of the room, the almost ceaseless slam P IV 8 183 11
arrive nearly at the same instant, advanced into the room. P IV 8 184 17
She was just in time to see him turn into the concert room. P IV 8 184 18
proceed into the concert room; and be of all the P IV 8 185 19
saw nothing, thought nothing of the brilliancy of the room. P IV 8 185 21
and she passed along the room without having a glimpse of P IV 8 186 22
be in the same part of the room, but he was not, her eye P IV 8 186 22
The others returned, the room filled again, benches were P IV 8 189 45
She could not quit the room in peace without seeing P IV 8 189 45
it had been in the Octagon Room was strikingly great.-- P IV 8 190 47
myself, but I heard Mr. Elliot say they were in the room." P IV 9 193 7
see Mr. Elliot enter the room; and quite painful to have P IV 10 214 11
and animation of a public room was necessary to kindle his P IV 10 214 12
"Mr. and Mrs. Charles Musgrove" were ushered into the room. P IV 10 216 17
hastened him away from the concert room, still governed. P IV 10 221 32
I know you love a play; and there is room for us all. P IV 10 223 41
in preparing to quit the room, she would have found, in P IV 10 225 62
The comfort, the freedom, the gaiety of the room was over, P IV 10 226 63
Two minutes after her entering the room, Captain Wentworth P IV 11 229 2
3
at the other end of the room from where the two ladies P IV 11 231 12
Wentworth's hitherto perfectly quiet division of the room. P IV 11 233 24
He had passed out of the room without a look! P IV 11 236 39
and instantly crossing the room to the writing table, and P IV 11 236 40
was again out of the room, almost before Mrs. Musgrove was P IV 11 236 40
quiet possession of that room, it would have been her cure; P IV 11 238 45
and she went to her room, and grew steadfast and fearless P IV 11 245 77
it, the hotel & billiard room--here began the descent to S 4 384 1
was sitting in her inner room, reading one of her own S 6 389 1
possession of the drawing room very quietly--without S 6 391 1
Mrs P.-- in the drawing room in time to see them all.-- S 7 394 1
He came into the room remarkably well, talked much--& very S 7 394 1
At last, from the low French windows of the drawing room S 7 395 1
They have Miss Clara's room to put to rights as well as my S 7 401 1
room, and she was soon introduced to Miss Diana Parker. S 9 406 1
in a small neat drawing room, with a beautiful veiw of the S 10 413 1
was all at the other end of the room by a brisk fire.-- S 10 413 1
own, was to have the best room in the lodgings, & was S 11 421 1
They were shewn into the usual sitting room, well- S 12 427 1
of the room, little conspicuous, represented Mr Hollis.-- S 12 427 1

ROOM'S (1)
or elegance of any room's fitting-up could be nothing to NA II 8 182 2

ROOMS (83)
when you come from the rooms at night; and I wish you NA I 2 18 2
evening came which was to usher her into the upper rooms. NA I 2 20 8
They made their appearance in the Lower Rooms; and here NA I 3 25 2
you have been at the upper rooms, the theatre, and the NA I 3 25 2
Have you yet honoured the upper rooms?" NA I 3 26 10
Friday, went to the Lower Rooms; wore my sprigged muslin NA I 3 26 22
at the upper nor Lower Rooms, at dressed or undressed NA I 5 35 2
while she remained in the rooms, which speedily brought on NA I 9 60 1
at the last party in my rooms, that upon an average we NA I 9 64 24
She entered the rooms on Thursday evening with feelings NA I 10 74 23
and quiet!--so much better than going to the Lower Rooms. NA I 11 84 19
we go up every staircase, and into every suite of rooms?" NA I 11 86 43
a long suite of lofty rooms, exhibiting the remains of NA I 11 88 54
Her satisfaction, too, in not being at the Lower Rooms, NA I 11 89 63
to me this evening; we shall meet them at the rooms." NA II 1 130 10
Why, as he had such rooms, he thought it would be simple NA II 6 166 7
might be more comfort in rooms of only half their size. NA II 6 166 7
hours in the Abbey, and had seen only a few of its rooms. NA II 7 176 17
kitchen, the six or seven rooms she had now seen NA II 8 183 2
they were to return to the rooms in common use, by passing NA II 8 183 2
your way into all the rooms in the house by yourself?" NA II 9 195 14
were coming here to these rooms--but only--(dropping her NA II 9 195 15
"Have you looked into all the rooms in that passage?" NA II 9 195 16
No theatre, no rooms to prepare for. NA II 9 195 18
world went on, and how the rooms were attended; and NA II 10 201 5
I have not been to the rooms this age, nor to the play, NA II 12 217 2
Rooms, you know, and I have worn them a great deal since. NA II 14 238 24
the disadvantage of better rooms and a broader staircase, SS I 14 73 14
fixing on the very rooms they were to live in hereafter!" SS II 8 196 20
knowledge has five sitting rooms on the ground-floor, and SS III 4 292 55
her in the old rooms at Bath, the year before I married--. W 325 4
and the principal rooms, satisfied with what the owner PP I 4 16 13
Lady Catherine's drawing rooms, and found that the chimney- PP I 16 75 2
that the sight of such rooms, so many servants, and so PP II 6 160 4
Our plain manner of living, our small rooms, and few PP II 15 215 2
As they passed into other rooms, these objects were taking PP III 1 246 5
The rooms were lofty and handsome, and their furniture PP III 1 246 5
With these rooms I might now have been familiarly PP III 1 246 6
of the rooms, and the price of the furniture, in vain. PP III 1 249 37
a short survey, to be decent looking rooms, walked on. PP III 14 352 19
The rooms were too large for her to move in with ease; MP I 2 14 9
but respectable looking, and has many good rooms. MP I 6 56 26
one or two intermediate rooms into the appointed dining- MP I 9 84 1
shewn through a number of rooms, all lofty, and many large, MP I 9 84 3
prospect from any of the rooms, and while Fanny and some MP I 9 85 4
Having visited many more rooms than could be supposed to MP I 9 85 5
taken them through all the rooms above, if her son had not MP I 9 89 31
entrance and principal rooms, I mean, must be on that side, MP II 7 242 23
It is not a scrambling collection of low single rooms, MP II 7 243 27
Mrs. Norris was ready with her suggestions as to the rooms MP II 8 253 7
They proceeded up stairs together, their rooms being on MP II 9 268 27
The smallness of the rooms above and below indeed, and the MP III 7 387 47
rooms and worse company than they might have had at home." E I 13 113 26
of there being but two spare rooms in the house. E I 15 126 11
me that dancing at the rooms at Bath was-----Mrs. Cole was E II 1 156 7
The doors of the two rooms were just opposite each other. E II 11 248 10
"Might not they use both rooms, and dance across the E II 11 248 10
away, I hope, by the terrors of my father's little rooms. E II 11 250 21
Ten couple, in either of the Randalls rooms, would have E II 11 250 23
If I could be sure of the rooms being thoroughly aired-- E II 11 252 35
fro, between the different rooms, some suggesting, some E II 11 256 60
And as to smaller-sized rooms than I had been used to, I E II 14 277 36
She was a little shocked at the want of two drawing rooms, E II 16 290 3
own terms, have as many rooms as you like, and mix in the E II 17 301 18
and comfort of the rooms before any other persons came, E III 2 319 2
of the most comfortable rooms in the Abbey, especially E III 6 357 33
with many comfortable and one or two handsome rooms.-- E III 6 358 35
to go into infected rooms, and expose his health and looks P III 3 20 17
A beloved home made over to others; all the precious rooms P III 6 47 16
at the hall;--those rooms had witnessed former meetings P III 11 93 3
place, might offer; the rooms were shut up, the lodgers P III 11 95 9
and melancholy looking rooms, and still descending, soon P III 11 96 10
new friends, and found rooms so small as none but those P III 11 98 17
The varieties in the fitting-up of the rooms, where the P III 11 98 17
saying to herself, "these rooms ought to belong only to us. P IV 1 126 18
Get up and go over all the rooms in the house if you like P IV 1 127 24
low company, paltry rooms, foul air, disgusting P IV 5 157 15
The theatre or the rooms, where he was most likely to be, P IV 7 180 32
of all their party, at the rooms in the evening; and as P IV 8 181 1
They have not seen two such drawing rooms before. P IV 10 220 29
time taken up all the morng, in dusting out bed rooms.-- S 7 401 1
but such as called for warm rooms & good nourishment.-- S 10 418 1
we shall both go to our rooms for the rest of the day."-- S 12 424 1

ROOMY (2)
carried on in appropriate divisions, commodious and roomy. NA II 8 184 4
is a solid walled, roomy, mansion-like looking house, such MP II 7 243 27

ROOTED (2)
He thinks Marianne's affection too deeply rooted for any SS III 9 338 20
which neither fashion nor extravagance had rooted up.-- E III 6 358 35

ROPE'S (1)
But my g-- if she belonged to me, I'd give her the rope's MP III 15 440 13

ROSE (38)
After sitting with them a quarter of an hour, she rose to NA I 13 103 28
for her brother, she rose up, and saying she should join NA II 3 147 28
over the bed, she rose directly, and folding them up as NA II 7 173 3
once raised, but you may in time come to love a rose?" NA II 7 174 8
Catherine's colour rose at the sight of it; and the NA II 13 228 27
With a look of much respect, he immediately rose, and NA II 15 241 7
High hills rose immediately behind, and at no great SS I 6 28 3
Elinor and her mother rose up in amazement at their SS I 9 42 9
When Lady Middleton rose to go away, Mr. Palmer rose also, SS I 19 108 37
Sir John's confidence in his own judgment rose with this SS I 21 119 3
Now there's Mr. Rose at Exeter, a prodigious smart young SS I 21 123 28
They all rose up in preparation for a round game. SS II 1 144 10
Marianne rose the next morning with recovered spirits and SS II 4 164 21
on her ceasing to speak, rose directly from his seat, and SS II 5 174 46
Colonel Brandon rose up and went to them without knowing SS II 12 236 41
to write to him, but then her spirit rose against that. SS III 2 273 16
He rose up, and walked across the room. SS III 8 318 14
impression she immediately rose, saying, "Mr. Willoughby, SS III 8 318 16
17
He rose from his seat and walked to the window, apparently SS III 12 360 22
23
visit; and when she rose to take leave, Elizabeth, ashamed PP II 3 145 11
when he ceased, the colour rose into her cheeks, and she PP II 11 189 6
7
When the gentlemen rose to go away, Mrs. Bennet was PP III 11 338 57
placed, the ladies all rose, and Elizabeth was then hoping PP III 12 342 26
had sat down, suddenly rose, and whispering a few words to PP III 13 346 22
And she rose as she spoke. PP III 14 357 64
Lady Catherine rose also, and they turned back. PP III 14 357 64
apparent suggestion, they rose into a canter; and to MP I 7 67 16
The whole party rose accordingly, and under Mrs. MP I 9 84 3
of a mile down the lane rose the vicarage; an old and not E I 10 83 2
and be so blind to what rose above, as to fancy himself E I 16 135 8

for her mother and herself; and Jane's offences rose again. E II 2 168 15
His son, too well bred to hear the hint, rose immediately E II 5 193 36
37
He stopt again, rose again, and seemed quite embarrassed.-- E II 12 261 34
placed and sheltered, rose the Abbey-Mill Farm, with E III 6 360 38
young man's spirits now rose to a pitch almost unpleasant. E III 7 374 54
She rose early, and wrote her letter to Harriet; an E III 14 435 5
pleasures; her spirits rose under their influence; and, P IV 2 135 33
His spirits rose with the very sight of the sea & he cd S 4 384 1

ROSEBUSH (1)
a dormouse, feeding a canary-bird, or watering a rosebush. NA I 1 13 1

ROSES (8)
as your roses; I would not have had you by for the world." NA I 10 71 5
roses, and very pleasant it was I assure you, but very hot. MP I 7 72 42
"Fanny has been cutting roses, has she?" MP I 7 72 43
walking as well as cutting roses; walking across the hot MP I 7 72 47
Bertram; "but when the roses were gathered, your aunt MP I 7 72 49
"But were there roses enough to oblige her to go twice?" MP I 7 73 50
being stooping among the roses; for there is nothing so MP I 7 73 55
"it was cutting the roses, and dawdling about in the MP I 7 73 55

ROSINGS (45)
She had also asked him twice to dine at Rosings, and had PP I 14 66 1
"She has one only daughter, the heiress of Rosings, and of PP I 14 67 5
breakfast parlour at Rosings; a comparison that did not at PP I 16 75 2
understood from him what Rosings was, and who was its PP I 16 75 2
table at Rosings, in the absence of more eligible visitors. PP I 17 88 14
It was Mr. Collins's picture of Hunsford and Rosings PP II 3 147 19
with the prospect of Rosings, afforded by an opening in PP II 5 156 4
We dine at Rosings twice every week, and are never allowed PP II 5 157 7
and the gaieties of their intercourse with Rosings. PP II 5 157 10
the whole party was asked to dine at Rosings the next day. PP II 5 159 20
us on Sunday to drink tea and spend the evening at Rosings. PP II 6 160 2
the whole day or next morning, but their visit to Rosings. PP II 6 160 4
to her introduction at Rosings, with as much apprehension, PP II 6 161 7
all that she had seen at Rosings, which, for Charlotte's PP II 6 166 42
Collins did not walk to Rosings, and not many in which his PP II 7 168 3
The entertainment of dining at Rosings was repeated about PP II 7 169 5
at Rosings, which in so small a circle must be important. PP II 7 170 6
new to look at in their Rosings parties, and she might be PP II 7 170 6
On the following morning he hastened to Rosings to pay his PP II 7 170 7
welcome relief to him at Rosings; and Mrs. Collins's PP II 8 172 3
told her, to come to Rosings every day, and play on the PP II 8 173 10
They then sat down, and when her enquiries after Rosings PP II 9 177 3
She watched him whenever they were at Rosings, and PP II 9 181 29
and that in speaking of Rosings and her not perfectly PP II 10 182 1
cousins to Rosings, where they were engaged to drink tea. PP II 10 187 41
It was some consolation to think that his visit to Rosings PP II 11 188 1
It was dated from Rosings, at eight o'clock in the morning, PP II 12 196 3
the two gentlemen from Rosings had each called during her PP II 13 209 13
The two gentlemen left Rosings the next morning; and Mr. PP II 14 210 1
the melancholy scene so lately gone through at Rosings. PP II 14 210 1
To Rosings he then hastened to console Lady Catherine, and PP II 14 210 1
Their first subject was the diminution of the Rosings PP II 14 210 3
His attachment to Rosings, certainly increases." PP II 14 210 3
Their engagements at Rosings were as frequent during the PP II 14 213 20
from our connection with Rosings, the frequent means of PP II 15 215 4
while they are sharers of our intimacy at Rosings." PP II 15 216 4
forgotten to leave any message for the ladies of Rosings. PP II 15 217 8
"We have dined nine times at Rosings, besides drinking tea PP II 15 217 13
both spent three weeks at Rosings, and asked him if he PP II 18 233 26
added, "how long did you say that he was at Rosings?" PP II 18 233 27
and more real elegance, than the furniture of Rosings. PP III 1 246 5
dignified relations at Rosings, had she seen him so PP III 2 263 10
and censure of the ladies both of Netherfield and Rosings. PP III 2 263 10
"It is nothing in comparison of Rosings, my lady, I dare PP III 14 352 10
of this journey from Rosings, for the sole purpose of PP III 15 360 1

ROSINGS PARK (2)
by a lane from Rosings Park, her ladyship's residence." PP I 14 67 3
The paling of Rosings Park was their boundary on one side. PP II 5 155 2

ROSY-FACED (1)
As he left the room, two rosy-faced boys, ragged and dirty, MP III 7 381 25

ROTE (2)
to the unconcern of his mother speaking entirely by rote. MP II 2 194 20
clear brain she presumed, & talked a good deal by rote.-- S 7 398 1

ROTOTORY (1)
the prevalence of which rototory motion, is perhaps to be S 11 421 1

ROUGE (1)
If she would only wear rouge, she would not be afraid of P IV 10 215 16

ROUGH (14)
walk amidst the rough coppice-wood which bordered it. PP III 1 253 57
"Now we shall have no more rough road, Miss Crawford, our MP I 8 82 34
and when we got into the rough lanes about Stoke, where MP II 2 189 5
Three years ago, this was nothing but a rough hedgerow MP II 4 208 12
he had been engaged, the rough horses and mules he had MP II 6 237 23
She is tender, and not used to rough it like the rest of MP III 8 388 2
I think their father is too rough with them very often." E I 9 81 72
"He appears rough to you," said Emma, "because you are so E I 9 81 73
him with other papas, you would not think him rough. E I 9 81 73
the colour of mahogany, rough and rugged to the last P III 3 19 16
along the rough, wild sort of channel, down the centre. P III 10 87 22
They had travelled half their way along the rough lane, P III 10 91 43
most rough usage, and riding out the heaviest weather." P IV 11 233 22
road, & attempt a very rough lane, were overturned in S 1 363 1

ROUGHNESS (2)
by ill humour of roughness; and there is not a shadow of MP I 7 64 11
There had remained only a general impression of roughness MP III 8 389 3

ROUND (177)
of eager inquiry ran round the room, nor was she once NA I 2 23 27
way are they gone?" said Isabella, turning hastily round. NA I 6 43 37
cried Isabella, turning round; "my dearest Catherine, I NA I 7 48 30
the shoulder, and turning round, perceived Mrs. Hughes NA I 8 55 10
"Look at that young lady with the white beads round her NA I 8 56 15
"Where can he be?" said Catherine, looking round; but she NA I 8 58 31
but she had not looked round long before he saw him NA I 8 58 31
round, you were gone!--this is a cursed shabby trick! NA I 10 75 26
by surprize; she looked round; the clouds were parting, NA I 11 83 16
Catherine looked round and saw Miss Tilney leaning on her NA I 11 87 53
in a moment out of sight round the corner of laura-place, NA I 11 87 53
much better put it off till another day, and turn round." NA I 11 88 54
she could almost have run round to the box in which he sat, NA I 12 93 4
and perhaps he might be now coming round to their box. NA I 12 93 5
They determined on walking round Beechen Cliff, that noble NA I 14 106 1
its foundation will roll round the neighbouring mountains-- NA II 5 159 19
she doubted, as she looked round the room, whether any NA II 5 161 26
when she heard it rage round a corner of the ancient NA II 6 166 9
She looked round the room. NA II 6 167 10
on giving a parting glance round the room, she was struck NA II 6 168 10
and she felt round each with anxious acuteness in vain. NA II 6 169 11
against taking her friend round the Abbey till his return. NA II 7 181 41
Upon looking round it then, she perceived in a moment that NA II 11 213 18
their quitting it to walk round the grounds, she was shewn, NA II 11 213 21
consisting of a walk round two sides of a meadow, on which NA II 11 214 25
they were all seated round the tea-table, which Mrs. NA II 14 233 9
minutes together, walking round the garden and orchard NA II 15 240 1
The furniture was all sent round by water. SS I 5 26 4
her children all the year round, while Sir John's SS I 7 32 1
with two pointers playing round him, was passing up the SS I 9 42 8
Marianne wore his picture round her neck; but it turned SS I 12 60 10
He turned round on their coming in, and his countenance SS I 15 75 2
her; and abruptly turning round, she was hurrying back, SS I 16 86 20
round with surprise to see and welcome Edward Ferrars. SS I 16 86 20
over and they had drawn round the fire; "are you still to SS I 17 90 2
round, was astonished to see Edward himself come out. SS I 18 96 2
round to her and said, in a whisper, "I have been guessing. SS I 18 100 23
proof of it which he constantly wore round his finger. SS I 19 102 2
of it, for they came all round by London upon account of SS I 19 107 29
was now caught by the drawings which hung round the room. SS I 19 108 35
newspaper, stretched himself, and looked at them all round. SS I 19 108 37
They all rose up in preparation for a round game. SS II 1 144 10
"Oh!" cried Miss Steele, looking significantly round at SS II 2 148 23
Marianne gave one glance round the apartment as she SS II 5 171 30
At last he turned round again, and regarded them both; she SS II 6 176 7
themselves, after it, round the common working table, when SS II 7 181 7
"Forgive me, forgive me," throwing her arms round her SS II 7 185 24
would have been ready to wait till matters came round. SS II 8 194 10
She hates whist I know; but is there no round game she SS II 8 195 14
by his manner of looking round the room for Marianne, SS II 8 198 30
excited, they were handed round for general inspection. SS II 12 234 28
chair, and putting one arm round her neck, and one cheek SS II 12 236 39
40
of Smith gravel winding round a plantation, led to the SS III 6 302 7
whiled away, in lounging round the kitchen garden, SS III 6 303 10
"But she must not go round by London," cried Marianne, in SS III 7 311 13
The wind roared round the house, and the rain beat against SS III 7 316 28
wine, when they were drawn round the fire to enjoy their W 324 4
the Osbornes are coming"--was repeated round the room.-- W 329 9
make a round game he may be tempted to sit down with us."-- W 354 28
Speculation is the only round game at Croydon now, but I W 354 28
the honours of visiting round the fire, & Miss Watson W 355 28
"What's your game?"--cried he, as they stood round the W 358 28
"It is the only round game played at Croydon now, said Mrs W 358 28
He was in fact excellently qualified to shine at a round W 359 28
"Which do you mean?" and turning round, he looked for a PP I 3 11 13
book, and cast her eyes round the room in quest of some PP I 11 55 5
6
has made white soup enough I shall send round my cards." PP I 11 55 7
up, the players gathered round the other table, and Mr. PP I 16 82 49
From his garden, Mr. Collins would have led them round his PP II 5 156 5
The party then gathered round the fire to hear lady PP II 6 166 42
because if it were to get round to the lady's family, it PP II 10 185 26
Mr. Gardiner expressed a wish of going round the whole PP III 1 253 57
smile, they were told, that it was ten miles round. PP III 1 253 57
and peaches, soon collected them round the table. PP III 3 268 6
sat down, looked eagerly round the room, took notice of PP III 9 315 4
I shall never be quite happy till I have been all round PP III 10 325 2
to look round, and happened to smile: it was decided. PP III 12 340 11
the ladies had crowded round the table, where Miss Bennet PP III 12 341 16
as they hastily turned round, and moved away from each PP III 13 346 22
round, she added, "I take no leave of you, Miss Bennet. PP III 14 358 72
73
We will go round the park every day. PP III 18 382 21
secured, and brought round by their aunt, served to MP I 4 35 4
a real park five miles round, a spacious modern-built MP I 5 48 28
The soup would be sent round in a most spiritless manner, MP I 6 52 1
"Query," said Mr. Crawford, looking round him, "whether we MP I 9 90 34
little difficulty pass round the edge of the gate, here, MP I 10 99 18
revived it by turning round towards the group and saying, " MP I 11 108 4
Edmund looked round at Mr. Rushworth too, but had nothing MP I 11 108 5
is to the family, employing the man all the year round!" MP I 15 142 22
After continuing in chat with the party round the fire a MP I 15 143 27
returned to the party round the table; and standing by MP I 15 143 27
table--(looking round)--it certainly will not be taken." MP I 15 144 38
While he spoke, Maria was looking apprehensively round at MP I 15 148 59
as she walked round the room her doubts were increasing. MP I 16 152 3
Sir Thomas was at that moment looking round him, and MP II 1 177 7
who at his suggestion now seated themselves round the fire. MP II 1 178 8
and on casting his eye round it, to see other symptoms of MP II 1 182 22
Sir Thomas, when they sat round the same table, which made MP II 2 191 10
turning from the cheerful round of such amusements to MP II 4 210 21
And round their enormous great wide table too, which fills MP II 5 220 30
you have the carriage come round?" she felt a degree of MP II 5 221 35
The coachman drove round to a minute; another minute MP II 5 222 41
the three others standing round him, shewed how welcome MP II 5 223 48
to the Admiral, he looked round at his sister as he sealed MP II 6 229 1
remain sufficient for a round game, and every body being MP II 7 239 4
Miss Crawford's direction, were arranged round the other. MP II 7 239 8
to the game; and the round table was altogether a very MP II 7 240 9
what now is, sweeping round from the lane I stood in to MP II 7 242 23
irregularly round the fire, and waiting the final break up. MP II 7 249 49
servant to bring and put round her shoulders, was seized MP II 7 251 66
necklace round her and making her see how well it looked. MP II 8 258 17
much flattered by seeing round your lovely throat an MP II 8 259 20
imaginary--and put them round her neck, and seen and felt MP II 9 271 40
a sofa very near, turned round before she began to dance, MP II 10 276 14
to feel when Friday came round again and brought no Edmund- MP II 11 286 16
and then threw her arms round his neck to sob out her MP III 7 384 34
He would walk round the ramparts, and join them with the MP III 15 445 29
her neat parlour hung round with fancy-work whenever she E I 3 22 5
"He had gone three miles round one day, in order to bring E I 4 28 6
It was quite a chance, he said, that he had not gone round E I 4 32 29
to all friends go round and round again; and if she does E I 10 86 23
all friends go round and round again; and if she does but E I 10 86 23
is very sad--but he is always wanted all round the country. E I 12 101 25
by the sudden whirling round of something or other among E II 1 160 23
The muffin last night--if it had been handed round once, I E II 3 170 4
I shall just go round by Mrs. Cole's; but I shall not stop E II 3 176 50
last, I fancy, he looked round and saw me; for instead of E II 3 178 52
I had much better go round by Mr. Cole's stables. for I E II 3 179 52
to Elizabeth, and I came round by the stables--I believe I E II 3 179 52
out; and when she turned round to Harriet, she saw E II 5 189 16
completely for travelling round to its object, he wound it E II 5 192 29
for an hour or two--first round the shrubberies of E II 6 196 2
distance from the numbers round the instrument, to listen. E II 8 227 87
of dawdling children round the baker's little bow-window E II 9 233 24
Jane did not look round. E II 10 241 9
with a bench round it, which put me so exactly in mind! E II 14 273 21
"I should hope not; but really when I look round among my E II 14 277 40
could furnish, to carry round the refreshments at exactly E II 16 290 3
I saw a vast deal of that in the neighbourhood round Maple E II 17 299 8
Such an immense plantation all round it! E II 18 307 21
Tea was carrying round, and Mr. Weston, having said all E II 18 310 35
a sort of half circle round the fire, to observe in their E III 2 320 5
She looked round for a moment; he had joined Mr. Knightley E III 2 328 38
for fear of its getting round to dear Miss Woodhouse, who E III 2 329 45
I would go any distance round to avoid him--but I do not E III 4 337 6
his seat with the rest round the large modern circular E III 5 347 18
She gave a slight glance round the table, and applied E III 5 347 21
as the others did, and collect round the strawberry beds.-- E III 6 358 35
Mr. Woodhouse, who had already taken his little round in E III 6 361 42
It can be round in five minutes." E III 6 362 47
shan't I?--(looking round with the most good-humoured E III 7 370 24
when one is sitting round the fire; but quite out of place, E III 7 372 37
who may have been carrying round, comparing and sitting in E III 10 399 61
and, while he was coming round, added, "now, dearest Emma, E III 10 400 65
Emma turned round to look at her in consternation, and E III 11 407 29
30
and all his family sought round the world for a perfect E III 13 428 23
They sat down to tea--the same party round the same table-- E III 14 434 2
and a pear-tree trained round its casements; but upon the P III 5 36 20
without an idea that they would be carried round to her. P III 7 61 36
tempted; actually looking round, ready to fall in love P III 7 61 38
and the three children, round from Portsmouth to Plymouth. P III 8 69 39
walk to the Cobb, skirting round the pleasant little bay, P III 11 95 9
Captain Wentworth looked round at her instantly in a way P III 12 104 6

curricle--but only coming round from the stable-yard to P III 12 105 8
with a happy glance round the room, that after all she had P IV 2 134 30
In fact, Anne could never see the crape round his hat, P IV 4 147 8
The country round Lyme is very fine. P IV 8 183 13
arranged, she looked round to see if he should happen to P IV 8 186 22
a touch on her shoulder obliged Anne to turn round.-- P IV 8 190 47
in the seats of grandeaur; round the orchestra, of course." P IV 9 193 10
old friends were seated round Mrs. Musgrove, and Charles P IV 10 221 32
listening, and he turned round the next instant to give a P IV 11 231 10
of mine, which you shot with one day, round Winthrop." P IV 11 240 58
& turning the horses round, the best thing we can do will S 1 367 1
a very young plantation round it, about an hundred yards S 4 384 1
She has been trying to get round me every way, with her S 7 399 1
round about, & added two steps to the ascent of the hill. S 11 422 1
ROUNDABOUT (1)
Is it necessary for me to use any roundabout phrase?-- E II 16 297 48
ROUNDLY (1)
of the matter, and had no voice at all, roundly asserted. E II 8 227 86
ROUSE (8)
and could strive to rouse her mother to similar exertion, SS I 1 7 13
was almost wishing to rouse her from so painful a slumber, SS III 7 310 10
11
power, nor in her wish, to rouse such feelings in another, SS III 11 349 2
may often rouse better feelings than are begun with. MP I 9 88 18
What shall we do to rouse them? E III 7 369 16
entering the parlour, she found those who must rouse her. E III 9 385 1
moment as calculated to rouse and fortify the mind by the P III 11 101 24
He caught the word; it seemed to rouse him at once, and P III 12 110 40
41
ROUSED (35)
From this state of humiliation, she was roused, at the end NA I 8 53 3
as this, she was suddenly roused by a touch on the NA I 8 55 10
As they entered Argyle-Buildings, however, she was roused NA I 11 87 51
where she was; till, roused by the voice of Isabella, she NA II 1 133 29
was the sound which first roused Catherine; and she opened NA II 7 172 1
Lady Middleton seemed to be roused to enjoyment only by SS I 7 34 7
of mind which was now roused and increased by the example SS I 10 48 7
drawing-table, she was roused one morning, soon after SS I 19 105 13
In this situation, Elinor, roused from sleep by her SS II 7 180 1
2
constancy, had only been roused by Elinor's application, SS II 9 202 8
This roused a general astonishment; and he had the PP I 13 61 5
While settling this point, she was suddenly roused by the PP II 11 188 3
he was to receive; till, roused to resentment by his PP II 11 189 6
on her absence of mind roused her, and she felt the PP III 1 253 56
voice, Elizabeth was roused by receiving from her a cold PP III 3 268 5
She was roused from her seat, and her reflections, by some PP III 10 327 4
I roused, and interested you, because I was so unlike them. PP III 18 380 5
She was again roused from disagreeable musings by sudden MP I 10 100 24
in the heavy tone of one half roused,--"I was not asleep." MP I 13 126 22
and longed to have them roused as soon as possible by the MP I 14 137 23
A tap at the door roused her in the midst of this attempt MP I 16 153 3
Her going roused the rest; and at the same moment, the two MP II 1 176 3
He was roused from the reverie of retrospection and regret MP II 6 236 23
Fanny roused herself, and replying only in part, said, " MP III 5 359 11
it; and Fanny was first roused by his calling out to her, MP III 15 439 9
As he became rational, he ought to have roused himself and E I 18 148 22
her eyes were fixed, till roused by Miss Bates's saying, " E III 8 384 32
33
there his faculties were roused into admiration and P III 1 3 1
received in the back, as roused the most alarming ideas. P III 7 53 3
From thus listening and thinking, she was roused by a P III 8 64 5
6
She roused herself to say, as they struck by order into P III 10 85 12
the servant in mourning roused Anne's curiosity, and the P III 12 105 9
She only roused herself from the broodings of this P IV 10 228 70
She roused herself and went to him. P IV 11 231 12
The passing admiration of Mr. Elliot had at least roused P IV 11 242 62
ROUSES (1)
striking, any thing that rouses the attention, without MP III 3 341 28
ROUSING (8)
for a few moments;--but rousing herself again, "now, SS I 16 88 33
Willoughby first rousing himself, broke it thus: "well, SS III 8 327 56
57
by Willoughby, who, rousing himself from a reverie at SS III 8 331 70
71
less than Lady Bertram's rousing thoroughly up, could MP III 16 459 31
"Thank you for rousing me," he replied. E II 8 222 56
few minutes; and when rousing himself, it was only to say, E II 12 259 12
13
Rousing from reflection, therefore, and subduing her E III 11 408 33
you," said he, suddenly rousing from a little reverie, "to P IV 1 127 24
ROUT-CAKES (1)
at the poor attempt at rout-cakes, and there being no ice E II 16 290 3
ROUTE (7)
her to it; so great had been her ignorance of her route. NA II 14 232 6
places through which their route thither lay; Oxford, PP II 19 240 12
In talking over their route the evening before, Mrs. PP II 19 240 12
the alarm, set off from B. intending to trace their route. PP III 4 274 5
Having been out some time, and taken a different route to MP I 8 75 2
command, as well as the route and the method of his E II 5 188 9
same time, to give his own route, understand something of P IV 3 143 19
ROUTINE (1)
meet again in the common routine of acquaintance, without E I 17 142 11
ROW (3)
whole row of young men who could be compared with him.-- E III 2 326 32
excepting one short row of smart-looking houses, called S 4 384 1
In this row were the best milliner's shop & the library--a S 4 384 1
ROWED (1)
till he got to Portsmouth, rowed off the the Grappler that P III 12 108 28
ROWS (3)
through the then thinning rows, spoke with like calm NA I 12 93 5
its abundance of timber in rows and avenues, which neither E III 6 358 35
rows of old thorns following its line almost every where.-- S 12 426 1
RUB (3)
"As to that," said he, "I must rub through the world as SS III 8 332 77
In spite of this little rub, however, Emma was smiling E III 2 325 32
Rub her hands, rub her temples; here are salts,--take them, P III 12 110 36
RUBBED (3)
obliged her to be seated, rubbed her temples with lavender- NA II 13 223 9
felt and felt, and rubbed, and looked grave, and spoke low P III 7 54 4
persevered in, (& I rubbed his ancle with my own hand for S 5 386 1
RUBBER (9)
Lady Middleton proposed a rubber of Casino to the others. SS II 1 144 15
in till another rubber, or will you take your chance now?" SS II 1 145 22
conclusion of the first rubber, and the confidential SS II 2 151 41
Lady Middleton, though in the middle of a rubber, on being SS II 6 178 16
he does; & very few people that play a fairer rubber.-- W 325 4
objection to join us in a rubber; shall you?"--then MP I 12 119 23
of the first rubber, to go to her and pay her compliments. MP II 7 240 10
at the end of the second rubber, and leaving Dr. Grant and MP II 7 246 36
friend on their account; her father was sure of his rubber. E I 9 81 79
RUBBERS (2)
But he had won 4 rubbers out of 5, & everything went well. W 336 14
their rubbers were made up,--so young as he looked!-- E III 2 325 32
RUBBISH (1)
The stream is as good as at first; the little rubbish it P IV 9 204 82
RUBS (1)
There will be little rubs and disappointments every where, MP I 5 46 23
RUDE (17)
They must think it so strange; so rude of me! to go by NA I 11 87 53
You must have thought me so rude; but indeed it was not my NA I 12 93 5
her think you intolerably rude to your sister, and a great NA I 14 113 40
"Do you know that you are quite rude?" SS I 20 112 23
heaven that she had never made so rude a speech. SS II 1 145 16
her mother had been quite rude enough,--for, colouring a SS II 12 235 30
31
and only occasionally rude to his wife and her mother; she SS III 6 304 15
Lady Lucas without being rude, and many months were gone PP I 23 127 5
"She is abominably rude to keep Charlotte out of doors in PP II 5 158 16
"Well, all I know is, that it will be abominably rude if PP III 11 332 26
She began then to be afraid of appearing rude and MP I 7 68 17
me as doing a very rude thing, I shall take Emma's advice E I 8 57 3
For her own sake she could not be rude; and for Harriet's, E I 14 118 4
without seeming very rude, of making her escape from Jane E II 1 158 13
"I believe I have been very rude; but really Miss Fairfax E II 8 222 56
be uncivil and give a very rude answer, but we have never E II 9 236 46
would be rude--but upon my word, Miss Woodhouse, you do E III 2 323 19
RUDENESS (6)
of rudeness in return it might justly make her amenable. NA I 12 92 3
led me into one act of rudeness by his mistake on Friday. NA I 13 101 20
for the abruptness, the rudeness, nay, the insolence of it. NA II 13 226 25
and some exaggeration, the shocking rudeness of Mr. Darcy. PP I 3 13 19
Mr. Darcy felt their rudeness and immediately said,-- " PP I 10 53 62
63
it had been unpardonable rudeness; and Mrs. Elton's looks E III 2 330 46
RUDER (1)
This is only doing it in a ruder way; and how do I know NA I 13 101 20
RUDIMENTS (1)
going through the first rudiments of an acquaintance, by NA I 8 56 11
RUED (1)
acquaintance, and rued it all the rest of his life!" E III 7 372 40
RUFFLE (1)
has now occurred to ruffle it in an uncommon degree; some NA II 13 225 21
RUFFLED (1)
almost every mind was ruffled; and the music which Sir MP II 2 191 11
RUG (1)
lengths of worsted for her rug, to see any thing at all; SS II 7 181 7
8
RUGGED (2)
ought to be irregular and rugged; and distant objects out SS I 18 97 4
of mahogany, rough and rugged to the last degree, all P III 3 19 16
RUIN (26)
in London could compensate for the ruin of her comfort. LS 27 296 1
Was at home; it lessened their gaiety, but did not ruin NA II 13 222 7
and why was he to ruin himself, and their poor little SS I 2 8 3
leagued together to ruin me in his opinion, than believe SS II 7 189 50
as she feared would ruin him for ever in her good opinion,- SS III 1 261 11
to ruin all my resolution, and with it all my comfort. SS III 8 321 34
the mind of Marianne, and ruin at least for a time this SS III 10 343 10
to stop the ruin which had begun before your marriage?-- SS III 11 350 9
It has been the ruin of my happiness. W 316 2
They will ruin your happiness. PP II 1 135 12
To have his errors made public might ruin him for ever. PP II 17 227 24
involves her in endless ruin--that her reputation is no PP III 5 289 43
assurance of her sister's ruin still more certain; and PP III 6 295 4
You are determined to ruin him in the opnion of all his PP III 14 358 69
part of Agatha, or it will be the ruin of all my solemnity. MP I 14 133 11
The ruin of the play was to them a certainty, they felt MP II 1 177 5
of mind, sighing over the ruin of all her plan of exercise MP II 4 205 3
Those vile sea-breezes are the ruin of beauty and health. MP III 12 416 3
She had lived with him to be reproached as the ruin of all MP III 17 464 11
minutes had threatened to ruin the rest of her evening, E III 3 332 1
that she is enough to ruin any servants she comes near. P III 6 45 9
led astray, he will not be misled by others to his ruin." P IV 9 196 32
cause of leading into ruin, he can neglect and desert P IV 9 199 53
and encouraging expenses, which could end only in ruin. P IV 9 209 95
a short suspension, to ruin the concert; and that had P IV 11 241 60
the quietest sort of ruin & disgrace for the object of his S 8 405 2
RUINED (12)
Its long, damp passages, its narrow cells and ruined NA II 2 141 11
I do not like ruined, tattered cottages. SS I 18 98 8
whose prior engagement ruined all my prospects; and told SS III 1 263 29
Poor Edward! he is ruined for ever. SS III 5 298 35
'I am ruined for ever in their opinion--said I to myself-- SS III 8 328 63
He had ruined for a while every hope of happiness for the PP II 10 186 38
of honour and humanity, ruined the immediate prosperity, PP II 12 196 5
the floor of one room, ruined all the coachman's sponges, MP II 2 190 9
Henry Crawford, ruined by early independence and bad MP III 17 467 19
cheer her father with the spirits only of ruined happiness. E III 12 422 19
seemed to have closed her heart or ruined her spirits. P IV 5 153 7
And the Smiths accordingly had been ruined. P IV 9 209 95
RUINING (3)
ruining her character, or turning her out of doors. NA I 2 19 7
his boasted interest and ruining his dearest hopes. NA II 15 245 12
who has been the means of ruining, perhaps for ever, the PP II 11 190 10
RUINS (3)
all nonsense; nothing ruins horses so much as rest; NA I 7 47 27
will often go to the old ruins of the Priory, and try to SS III 10 343 9
to trace in them the ruins of the face which had once P III 8 72 58
RULE (26)
"I should no more lay it down as a general rule that women NA I 3 28 34
I make it a rule never to mind what they say. NA I 6 42 26
amiss; and it is a rule with me, Miss Morland, never to NA II 11 210 6
The Osbornes are to be no rule for us. W 325 4
it is a thing quite out of rule I assure you--never heard W 340 18
"It is a rule with me, that a person who can write a long PP I 10 48 19
"Do you talk by rule then, while you are dancing?" PP I 18 91 12
it became, by the same rule of moral obligation, her MP I 4 38 10
not pleasant by any common rule, he talked no nonsense, he MP I 7 65 13
differing in the first rule and law of their existence. MP II 4 209 16
You are not to be judged by the same rule. MP III 1 319 39
This was almost the only rule of conduct, the only piece MP III 2 333 27
Your judgment is my rule of right." MP III 11 412 22
She had a rule to apply to, which settled every thing. MP III 14 436 15
alphabetically, and sometimes by some other rule. E I 5 37 7
lay it down as a general rule, Harriet, that if a woman E I 7 52 18
19
uncle did not lay down the rule of their taking turns, E I 9 81 75
That is the reason of her writing out of rule, as we call E II 1 159 18
any restraint beyond her own scanty rule of good-breeding. E II 15 288 39
Then she is no rule for Mrs. Churchill, who is as thorough E II 18 306 16
different--no general rule--gardeners never to be put out E III 6 358 35
of this one great deviation from the strict rule of right. E III 10 400 65
and let his behaviour be the rule of mine--and so I have. E III 11 411 39
One man's style must not be the rule of another's. E III 15 445 7
And on Mrs. Musgrove's side, it was,--"I make a rule of P III 6 45 9
must be their rule"--and except in favour of some Tonic S 11 422 1
RULED (1)
prepared her paper, and ruled her lines with all the good MP I 2 16 20
RULES (10)
observing the rules I have laid down for their discourse. LS 19 274 3
is a most improper thing, and entirely against the rules. NA I 8 57 21
to add--(aware that the rules of composition forbid the NA II 16 251 5
We can never suffer this--it is against the rules of the W 334 13
herself mistress of the rules of the game in three minutes, MP II 7 240 8
compose well; that is, the rules and trick of composition MP III 3 341 28
Mrs. Churchill rules at Enscombe, and is a very odd- E I 14 121 16
not be judged by general rules: she is so very E I 14 123 23
to lay down rules for it: you must let it go its own way. E I 14 123 25
thoughtless, gay set, without any strict rules of conduct. P IV 9 201 64
RULING (1)
own ease, was, in every particular, his ruling principle." SS III 11 351 11
RUM (1)

his rum and water, and Rebecca never where she ought to be. MP III 7 387 46
RUMBLE (1)
carriages, the heavy rumble of carts and drays, the P IV 2 135 33
RUMFORD (1)
was contracted to a Rumford, with slabs of plain though NA II 5 162 26
RUMINATION (1)
it, and that a silent rumination might suffice to restore E I 12 105 51
RUMOUR (7)
No rumour of Lucy's marriage had yet reached him;--he knew SS III 13 370 35
"A most scandalous, ill-natured rumour has just reached me, MP III 15 437 3
As no scandalous, ill-natured rumour had reached her, it MP III 15 438 4
There was a strange rumour in Highbury of all the little E I 2 19 15
whom he, on the rumour of considerable illness, had been E I 13 109 6
all our caution, some rumour of the truth should get P III 3 17 4
evident that no rumour of the news had yet reached them. P IV 6 168 22
RUMOURS (1)
if in consequence of any rumours getting abroad of your P III 3 17 4
RUN (75)
as she had been detected in an attempt to run away. LS 15 266 2
That horrid girl of mine has been trying to run away.-- LS 16 268 1
He is convinced that her attempt to run away, proceeded LS 17 271 7
angry it will make mama, but I must run the risk. LS 21 279 1
she could almost have run round to the box in which he sat, NA I 12 93 4
have stopped, I would have jumped out and run after you." NA I 12 94 8
I must run after Miss Tilney directly and set her right." NA I 13 100 18
expectation, she had there run backwards and forwards some NA II 14 237 20
You have had a long run of amusement, and now you must try NA II 15 240 2
voice, that "her head did not run upon Bath-----much." NA II 15 240 3
Has she run away because we are come? SS I 19 105 18
involve you, rather than run the risk of her displeasure SS II 2 148 14
to run the risk of his calling again in her absence. SS II 5 170 28
to leave Edward; so I just run up stairs and put on a pair SS III 2 274 16
less inclination, and to run the risk of a tete-a-tete SS III 5 294 3
families was confidently run over as sure of attending, & W 314 1
She had scarcely run her eye thro' the whole, before she W 338 18
"Then why was you in such a hurry to run away from her? W 350 24
where you are, and do not run on in the wild manner that PP I 9 42 14
life. but before I am run away with by my feelings on this PP I 19 105 8
his solemn composure, being run away with by his feelings, PP I 19 105 9
10
You had better neglect your relations, than run the risk PP I 22 123 7
But as it is--you must not let your fancy run away with PP II 3 144 2
to speak openly to her aunt, than to run such a risk. PP II 19 240 16
"I am not going to run away, papa," said Kitty, fretfully; PP III 6 300 29
Lizzy, my dear, run down to your father, and ask him how PP III 7 306 44
Kitty, run down and order the carriage. PP III 7 307 49
when Lydia had first run away, they had been generally PP III 13 350 56
they are about, and not run hastily into a marriage which PP III 15 363 22
Grant having by this time run through the usual resources MP I 4 41 15
about the horse which he had to run at the B---- races. MP I 5 48 28
governess being sick or run away, and the mother in and MP I 5 50 35
authorize the liberty, nor run the risk; and at last on a MP I 8 75 1
just a side wing or two run up, doors in flat, and three MP I 13 123 8
it must be scrupulousness run mad, that could see any MP I 13 128 38
All the best plays were run over in vain. MP I 14 130 3
Frederick and his knapsack would be obliged to run away." MP I 14 133 11
would be fair by the others to have every body run away." MP II 1 177 5
felt their error, than to run the risk of investigation. MP II 2 187 2
Do not run away the first moment of its holding up. MP II 4 207 7
were in the midst of a good run, and at some distance from MP II 7 240 13
friend was still run away with a little, by the enthusiasm MP III 4 353 46
on her side; she did not run into the match MP III 5 361 16
"Then, Betsey, my dear, run into the kitchen, and see if MP III 7 379 15
and be talked to, but to run about and make a noise; and MP III 7 381 25
if she saw her boys run into danger, or Rebecca pass by MP III 11 408 2
This was a letter to be run through eagerly, to be read MP III 12 417 4
of wholesome food, let them run about a great deal in the E I 3 22 5
Harriet, Harriet, do not deceive yourself; do not be run E I 7 53 21
were otherwise of a sort to run into great length, by the E I 9 72 16
The course of true love never did run smooth-- E I 9 75 25
the benefit of a country run, and seemed to ensure a quick E I 13 109 6
Let me entreat you to run no risks. E I 13 109 7
neighbourhood than from any run on the road; and his E II 6 197 5
I am sure, rather than run the risk of hurting Mr. and Mrs. E II 7 210 20
"You take up an idea, Mrs. Weston, and run away with it; E II 8 226 84
"My dear Miss Woodhouse," said the latter, "I am just run E II 9 235 44
Oh! then, said I, I must run across, I am sure Miss E II 9 236 46
will allow me just to run across and entreat her to come E II 9 236 46
Miss Fairfax, you must not run such risks.-- E II 16 295 33
letters, than run the risk of bringing on your cough again. E II 16 295 33
Do not run away with such an idea." E II 18 306 15
bounds yesterday, and run away from your own management; E III 7 369 11
but no flight of generosity run mad, opposing all that E III 13 431 38
and Henrietta, should just run down for a few minutes, to P III 10 86 18
dining-room, had nearly run against the very same P III 12 104 7
by Anne's having actually run against him in the passage, P III 12 106 19
I would as soon have been run up to the yard-arm. P III 12 108 28
You must not run away from us now. P IV 4 145 1
He was steady, observant, moderate, candid; never run away P IV 4 146 6
But it was a nice place for the children to run about in. S 4 380 1
I wd rather them run about in the sunshine than not. S 4 381 1
Having run his eye over the letter, he shook his head & S 5 385 1
accident--but pray never run into Peril again, in looking S 5 386 1
Activity run mad!"--had just passed through Charlotte's S 9 410 1
RUNG (3)
and as soon as she had rung up the maid to take her place SS III 7 311 14
And the bell was rung, and the carriages spoken for. E I 15 128 21
was on the steps & had rung, but the door was not opened, S 9 406 1
RUNNING (37)
satisfactory transpires as to her reason for running away. LS 17 270 6
every girl who has been running wild the first fifteen LS 17 271 7
from my authority by running away from Wigmore Street, she LS 19 273 1
as ashes came running up, & rushed by me into her own room. LS 20 275 1
riding on horseback, and running about the country at the NA I 1 15 3
think we have been running it from Tetbury, Miss Morland?" NA I 7 45 5
before John Thorpe came running up stairs, calling out, " NA I 9 61 1
most interesting part, by running away with the volume, NA I 14 107 9
of knowledge, by running over the titles of half a shelf, NA II 8 182 2
I am afraid I alarmed you by running so fast up those NA II 9 195 12
propriety; it was that of running with all possible speed SS I 9 41 6
door, Mrs. Palmer came running in at the other, looking as SS I 20 110 1
She shook her head, put the music aside, and after running SS III 10 342 7
do cure the younger girls of running after the officers.-- PP I 10 52 55
running away without telling us that you were coming out." PP I 10 53 61
Do not be afraid of my running into any excess, of my PP II 1 135 11
she heard somebody running up stairs in a violent hurry, PP II 5 158 11
the road, and immediately running into the other, told the PP II 7 170 7
8
where Jane, who came running down stairs from her mother's PP III 5 286 22
so much in the habit of running as Elizabeth, soon lagged PP III 7 301 7
8
was forced to put it out of her power, by running away. PP III 9 320 31
I will not spend my hours in running after my neighbours PP III 11 332 25
Elizabeth obeyed, and running into her own room for her PP III 14 352 19
"If Edmund were but in orders!" cried Julia, and running MP I 9 89 25
these letters, her eye running from one to the other, and MP II 13 299 4
and Harriet then came running to her with a smiling face, E I 4 32 28
"I am afraid we must be running away," said Emma, glancing E II 1 162 32
"Well my dear Jane, I believe we must be running away. E II 3 176 50
and Emma felt the tears running down her cheeks almost all E III 7 376 63
so much in the habit of running in and out of each other's P III 5 36 21
I must say it is very unfeeling of him, to be running away P III 7 56 10
not be satisfied without his running on to give notice. P III 7 59 24
He has been running after them, too, long enough, one P III 10 92 44
is altered: there is no running or jumping about, no P IV 10 218 24
As it is, he does what he can--& is running up a tasteful S 3 377 1
by a young whitby running off with 5 vols. under his arm S 8 403 1
She must put her shawl over her shoulders, & be running S 10 619 1
RUNS (5)
Frederica runs much in my thoughts, & when Reginald has LS 40 309 1
Your head runs too much upon Bath; but there is a time for NA II 15 240 2
I can,--or, perhaps, I may defer it, till Kitty runs away." PP III 6 300 28
One takes up a notion, and runs away with it. Mr. Dixon, E II 3 176 46
What an air of probability sometimes runs through a dream! E III 5 345 14
RUPTURE (6)
I am greived, tho' I cannot be astonished at your rupture LS 38 306 1
an immediate and irreconcileable rupture with him. SS II 6 179 18
"I am sorry to say, ma'am, in a most unhappy rupture:-- SS III 1 268 48
like mine, any thing was to be done to prevent a rupture. SS III 8 328 63
embarrassing evils of a rupture, the wonder, the MP II 3 201 22
rupture.) or in any novelty or enlargement of society.-- P III 4 28 7
RUSH (2)
would undoubtedly rush upon her without preparation. E II 3 177 51
a cold sleety April day rush out again into the world!-- E II 17 303 23
RUSHED (13)
as ashes came running up, & rushed by me into her own room. LS 20 275 1
at first, immediately rushed across her; and though there NA II 6 168 10
to look or breathe, rushed forward to the one in question. NA II 9 193 6
She rushed forwards towards the drawing-room,--she entered SS III 7 316 31
The colour now rushed into Elizabeth's cheeks in the PP III 15 362 11
12
The colour rushed into her cheeks as she spoke. MP II 9 269 37
She rushed out at an opposite door from the one her uncle MP II 13 302 9
be going on; a suspicion rushed over her mind which drove MP III 1 325 60
eight and nine years old, rushed into it just released MP III 7 381 25
The truth rushed on her; and how she could have spoken at MP III 15 440 16
of all that had rushed on her within the last few hours. E III 11 411 43
while a thousand feelings rushed on Anne, of which this P III 7 59 25
A few lines more however, and the colour rushed into her S 10 419 1
RUSHING (4)
by Willoughby himself, rushing eagerly into the room to SS II 9 202 7
of rushing into intimacy on so slight an acquaintance.-- W 322 3
where she was, instead of rushing out into the hall as MP II 6 233 15
of eleven years old, who rushing out of the house, pushed MP III 7 377 7
RUSHWORTH'S (33)
the expediency of Mr. Rushworth's marrying Miss Bertram. MP I 4 39 11
to himself, in Mr. Rushworth's company, "if this man had MP I 4 40 13
good humour, on Mr. Rushworth's account, who was partly MP I 7 70 30
herself on Mrs. Rushworth's account, because he had taken MP I 8 79 23
Mr. Rushworth's consequence was hers. MP I 8 81 33
it was now all Mr. Rushworth's property on each side of MP I 8 81 33
and under Mrs. Rushworth's guidance were shewn through a MP I 9 84 3
lessen, it ended in Mr. Rushworth's declaring outright MP I 10 98 4
the key and without Mr. Rushworth's authority and MP I 10 99 18
to receive Mr. Rushworth's parting attentions as she ought. MP I 10 105 52
I often think of Mr. Rushworth's property and independence, MP I 17 161 13
"I would not give much for Mr. Rushworth's chance, if MP I 17 162 17
and the chances of Mr. Rushworth's ever attaining to the MP I 18 165 4
stand, to contrive Mr. Rushworth's cloak without sending MP I 18 166 6
They walked off, utterly heedless of Mr. Rushworth's MP II 1 176 3
There was nothing disagreeable in Mr. Rushworth's MP II 1 179 8
had whisked away Mr. Rushworth's pink satin cloak as her MP II 1 179 10
Sir Thomas meant to be giving Mr. Rushworth's opinion in MP II 1 186 35
bringing Mr. Rushworth's admiration of Maria to any effect. MP II 2 188 3
There is nothing very striking in Mr. Rushworth's manners, MP II 2 190 6
Rushworth, not all Mr. Rushworth's deference for him, MP II 3 200 19
She had the highest esteem for Mr. Rushworth's character MP II 3 200 21
first pleasures of Mr. Rushworth's wife must be to fill MP II 4 210 21
Fanny, he said, "you were Mr. Rushworth's best friend. MP II 5 224 53
as Mr. Rushworth's fine fortune gives them a right to be. MP II 7 245 32
But Mrs. Rushworth's day of good looks will come; we cards MP III 9 394 1
be all hushed up, and nothing proved by Rushworth's folly. MP III 15 437 3
with the hope of Mrs. Rushworth's return, but was so much MP III 16 450 9
by the influence of Mr. Rushworth's mother, that the worst MP III 16 450 9
comfort arose on Mrs. Rushworth's side for the misery she MP III 17 461 4
best, and since Mrs. Rushworth's elopement, her temper had MP III 17 466 16
in town, and Mr. Rushworth's house became Crawford's MP III 17 466 18
for Mrs. Rushworth's credit than he felt it for his own.-- MP III 17 468 21
RUSHWORTH-FEELINGS (1)
She had Rushworth-feelings, and Crawford-feelings, and in MP I 8 81 33
RUSHWORTHS (5)
was in having formed the connection with the Rushworths. MP II 2 188 3
The Rushworths were the only addition to his own domestic MP II 3 196 1
eldest cousin and the Rushworths and Julia I am sure of MP III 5 364 32
He will see the Rushworths, which I own I am not sorry for- MP III 12 417 3
If the Rushworths were gone themselves to Mansfield, as MP III 15 438 4
RUSHWORTHS' (1)
Very soon after the Rushworths' return to Wimpole Street, MP III 16 450 8
RUSSIA (1)
the principal rivers in Russia--or she never heard of Asia MP I 2 18 23
RUSTIC (1)
and flower gardens, and rustic seats innumerable; but it MP I 6 57 31
RUSTICITIES (1)
The little rusticities and awkwardnesses which had at MP I 2 17 21
RUSTICITY (1)
without preciseness or rusticity--a sister's husband who MP I 4 41 17
RUT (1)
they neither fell into a rut, nor ran foul of a dung-cart; P III 10 92 48

S. V. (5)
I am sir, your most humble Servt F. S. V. LS 21 279 1
as Manwaring comes within half an hour. adeiu. S. V. LS 31 302 1
dinner, everything will be well again. adeiu. S. V. LS 33 303 2
I shall count every moment till your arrival. S. V. LS 35 305 1
of surviving my share in this disappointment. S. V. LS 37 306 1
S. VERNON (11)
me. Yr most obliged & affec: sister S. Vernon. LS 1 244 1
as soon as I arrive in town.-- yours ever, S. Vernon. LS 2 246 2
Adeiu. yours ever S. Vernon. LS 7 254 3
of my intentions very soon.-- yours &c. S. Vernon. LS 10 258 4
to themselves & the opinion of the world. S. Vernon. LS 16 269 3
therefore must wait a little. yours ever S. Vernon. LS 19 275 4
of her injured mother. Yrs affec:ly S. Vernon. LS 22 282 8
a short distance of you. Yr most attached S. Vernon. LS 25 294 7
am enchanted with my lodgings. Yrs ever, S. Vernon. LS 29 299 4
& wife. I am ever, faithfully yours S. Vernon. LS 30 301 5
may you always regard me as unalterably yours S. Vernon. LS 39 308 2
SACK (1)
He sends us a sack every year; and certainly there never E II 9 238 51
SACKS (1)
sacks were sold, it did not signify who ate the remainder. E II 9 239 51
SACKVILLE-STREET (1)
them to Gray's in Sackville-Street, where Elinor was SS II 11 220 1
SACRED (4)
I have been called an unkind mother, but it was the sacred LS 2 245 1
blame on the memory of one, whose name is sacred with me." LS 24 288 11
was to keep my heart as safe and sacred as my honour. SS III 13 368 28
I charge you by all that is sacred, not to attempt E III 10 393 12
SACRIFICE (43)
friendship, I am far from exacting so heavy a sacrifice. LS 7 252 1
for me to suffer such a sacrifice, as it must be, to leave LS 25 292 3
The sacrifice is not much; and to oblige such a friend--I NA I 13 99 3
A sacrifice was always noble; and if she had given way to NA I 13 103 29
me in wishing you to sacrifice all your happiness merely NA II 3 146 20
if a small sacrifice of time and attention can prevent it. NA II 11 210 6
But you may be assured that I would not sacrifice one SS I 14 72 10
amply rewarded for the sacrifice of the best place by the SS II 14 247 4
with no other sacrifice than that of time and conscience. SS III 14 376 11
Instead of falling a sacrifice to an irresistible passion, SS III 14 378 16
to beleive it no sacrifice on her sister's part.-- W 361 30
"What you ask," said Elizabeth, "is no sacrifice on my PP I 10 51 43
I think it no sacrifice to join occasionally in evening PP I 17 87 11
it amply repaid her for the little sacrifice of her time. PP I 22 121 1
friends, and led him to sacrifice his own happiness to the PP II 1 133 3
Had his own happiness, however, been the only sacrifice, PP II 1 133 3
she could not understand that sacrifice of so many hours. PP II 7 168 3
sacrifice to propriety, not a pleasure to himself. PP II 9 180 29
countenance, is such a sacrifice to her advantage, as PP III 7 305 36
obliging manners to the sacrifice of any real pleasure, MP I 4 35 7
"There is no sacrifice in the case," replied Edmund with a MP I 11 108 11
My other sacrifice of course you do not understand." MP I 11 108 12
It can be no sacrifice on their side, for it is highly MP I 14 133 10
and Easter, I suppose, will be the sum total of sacrifice." MP II 5 226 61
night, if it be a sacrifice--I am sure you will, upon MP II 9 263 16
consideration, make that sacrifice rather than give pain MP II 9 263 16
that even this slight sacrifice cannot be often demanded. MP III 2 331 16
He called it a sacrifice, and demanded it of her goodness MP III 6 371 15
therefore must certainly sacrifice every other pleasure to MP III 6 373 23
He too had a sacrifice to make to Mansfield Park, as well MP III 6 373 25
mind unused to make any sacrifice to right; he resolved to MP III 17 467 20
such weather, with the sacrifice of his children after E I 13 113 25
that while she makes no sacrifice for the comfort of the E I 14 123 24
Mrs. Churchill--'every sacrifice of mere pleasure you will E I 18 146 16
to complete the sacrifice, and retire from all the E II 2 165 8
making any use of the word sacrifice," said she.-- E II 13 264 2
negatives, is there any allusion to making a sacrifice. E II 13 264 2
and in Bath, it would have been a most serious sacrifice. E II 14 276 36
I hoped I was perfectly equal to any sacrifice of that E II 14 277 36
But the plan which had arisen on the sacrifice of this, he E III 15 449 31
No sacrifice on any side worth the name. E III 17 468 31
her to think that the sacrifice of one pair of horses P III 2 13 5
than she had been in the sacrifice of it; and this, she P III 4 29 8
SACRIFICED (10)
She must not be sacrificed to policy or ambition, she must LS 20 278 11
loved, could I have sacrificed my feelings to vanity, to SS III 8 320 32
what is more, could I have sacrificed her's?---- SS III 8 320 32
its offspring, necessity, had required to be sacrificed. SS III 8 331 70
have sacrificed every better feeling to worldly advantage. PP I 22 125 18
she had so carelessly sacrificed; and she addressed Lady MP I 1 4 2
the engagement, her happiness must not be sacrificed to it. MP II 3 200 20
that in so doing he had sacrificed the right to the MP III 17 461 4
Anne could not refuse; but never had she sacrificed to P IV 8 190 47
interest, and she had sacrificed, for the young man's sake, P IV 12 250 8
SACRIFICES (9)
land, offered sacrifices to the gods on their safe return." MP I 11 108 10
much exertion and many sacrifices to glance at in the form MP II 2 188 3
demanding such sacrifices of situation and employment on MP II 8 255 10
affection not equal to sacrifices, which, in fact, I am MP III 13 422 2
are sometimes to be pleased only by a good many sacrifices. E I 14 120 9
or more honourable than the sacrifices she had resolved on. E II 2 168 13
efforts, and all one's sacrifices, to make the P III 8 68 35
when a clergyman sacrifices his health for the sake of P III 12 103 2
the conflicts and all the sacrifices that ennoble us most. P IV 5 156 10
SACRIFICING (5)
of other people, in sacrificing general politeness to the SS I 10 49 9
of--poor Maria, in sacrificing such a situation, plunging MP III 16 454 18
I had less to regret in sacrificing a friendship--feelings- MP III 16 458 30
She felt that, in quitting Donwell, he must be sacrificing E III 15 449 32
But she could not be long ungrateful; he was sacrificing P IV 11 239 54
SAD (65)
We are now in a sad state; no house was ever more altered; LS 2 245 1
is a sad thing & of course highly afflicting to Lady Susan. LS 15 266 2
It has been a sad heavy winter hitherto, without Reginald, LS 40 309 1
This was the sad finale of every reflection:--and Captain NA II 11 211 16
Morland; "they must have a sad time of it; but as for any NA II 14 234 12
you always were a sad little shatter-brained creature; but NA II 14 234 12
"Catherine would make a sad heedless young house-keeper to NA II 16 249 1
"It might have been a very sad accident." SS I 21 122 11
Had not Elinor, in the sad countenance of her sister, seen SS II 8 193 7
But I am afraid I have been a very sad neighbour of late. W 334 13
You are a sad shabby girl.-- W 350 24
It will be a sad break-up when he dies. W 353 26
I am afraid I am a sad figure.-- W 353 26
You know what a sad visitor I make.-- W 356 28
is your opinion now of this sad business of Jane's? PP II 17 227 27
And since this sad affair has taken place, it is said, PP III 5 291 54
that my cousin Lydia's sad business has been so well PP III 15 363 22
This was a sad omen of what her mother's behaviour to the PP III 17 378 46
But he had ended his speech in a way to sink her in sad MP I 3 33 64
by these ideas, in the sad solitariness of her cottage, as MP I 4 38 9
been done, but for poor Mr. Norris's sad state of health. MP I 6 54 9
She alone was sad and insignificant; she had no share in MP I 17 159 6
Mrs. Grant's non-attendance was sad indeed. MP I 18 171 28
It was a sad anxious day; and the morrow, though differing MP II 2 192 11
She said nothing, however, but, "sad, sad girl! MP III 5 357 6
He has now and then been a sad flirt, and cared very MP III 5 363 22
Her heart was completely sad at parting. MP III 6 374 28
"Dear me!" continued the anxious mother, "what a sad fire MP III 7 379 17
confined--Portsmouth was a sad place--they did not often MP III 10 401 10
It was sad to Fanny to lose all the pleasures of spring. MP III 14 431 9
Let us talk over this sad business. MP III 16 454 18
were made known to him only in their sad result. MP III 17 464 10
Miss Taylor had done as sad a thing for herself as for E I 1 7 10
"Ah! poor Miss Taylor! 'tis a sad business." E I 1 10 28
poor Mr. Woodhouse's feelings were in sad warfare. E I 3 24 12
the sad change at Hartfield since she had been there last. E I 11 93 5
It is a sad change indeed.-- E I 11 93 7
But how sad it is that he should not live at home with his E I 11 96 25
is very sad--but he is always wanted all round the country. E I 12 101 25
no end of the sad consequences of your going to south end. E I 12 105 51
Such a sad loss to our party to-day!" E I 13 114 34
She might have been unconsciously sucking in the sad E II 2 168 13
on his journey, through the sad evils of sleeping two E II 5 193 35
Well, a little while ago it occurred to me how very sad it E II 8 223 63
"It would be a crowd--a sad crowd; and what could be worse E II 11 249 14
It was a sad change. E II 12 262 38
you know--there is a sad story against them, in general. E II 14 277 38
Ah! it shews what a sad invalid I am! E II 14 280 54
She thought it in reality a sad exchange for herself, to E II 16 292 8
You sad girl, how could you do such a thing?-- E II 16 295 30
You really are a very sad girl, and do not know how to E II 16 295 32
"Aye, we men are sad fellows. E II 18 305 7
Emma heard the sad truth with fortitude. E III 2 325 29
lame carriage-horse threw every thing into sad uncertainty. E III 6 353 6
It was a sad event--a great shock--with all her faults, E III 9 388 13
so very serious, so nearly sad, that Mr. Knightley, in E III 14 435 5
"Poor Knightley! poor fellow!--sad business for him.-- E III 17 469 36
influence so sweet and so sad of the autumnal months in P III 5 33 6
families renewed--very sad for herself and her children. P III 9 75 12
The sad accident at Lyme was soon the prevailing topic; P IV 1 126 20
As to the sad catastrophe itself, it could be canvassed P IV 1 126 21
all the particulars of past sad scenes, all the minutiae P IV 9 210 97
in the more, from the sad want of such blessings at home. P IV 10 220 31
his own sisters who were sad invalids, & whom he was very S 2 372 1
in England who have so sad a right to that appellation!-- S 9 410 1
SADDENED (4)
Fanny's heart was not absolutely the only saddened one MP I 17 160 7
spirits of many others saddened, it was all sameness and MP II 3 196 1
with a very saddened heart to grieve over the melancholy MP II 11 282 2
tenements of the village, without a saddened heart.-- P IV 1 123 8
SADDLE (1)
first leisure from the saddle of mutton, to say to her, " E I 14 119 6
7
SADLER'S (1)
the sadler's, and the child be appointed to meet her there. MP I 1 8 8
SADLY (18)
She has been sadly neglected however, & her mother ought LS 15 266 3
We are sadly off in the country; not but what we have very NA I 3 29 46
"Aye, and sadly too--for I had much rather stay." NA II 11 211 11
and you were sadly out of luck too in your Isabella. NA II 14 236 15
a year, and his brother left every thing sadly involved. SS I 14 70 2
"Did not you think him sadly out of spirits?" repeated SS I 22 134 50
My poor little girl would be sadly disappointed, I know, SS II 1 144 13
Miss W.--she was sadly disappointed in Tom Musgrave, who W 317 2
You talked so stoutly beforehand, that I was sadly afraid W 343 19
is lessening the honour of my cousin's triumph very sadly." PP II 10 186 37
Our poor mother is sadly grieved. PP III 4 274 3
of reproof, found herself sadly mistaken, and that it was MP III 3 343 40
Poor Janet has been sadly taken in; and yet there was MP III 5 361 16
Fanny shrunk back to her seat, with feelings sadly pained MP III 7 380 23
to attend him, and the sadly small party remaining at MP III 13 427 12
Poor Isabella!--she is sadly taken away from us all!-- and E I 9 79 58
on the watch, heard distinctly, and was sadly alarmed at. E II 1 162 31
Emma was sadly fearful that this second disappointment E III 11 403 2
SADNESS (6)
oppress her heart with sadness, and drown her in tears for NA I 2 18 2
but in her silence and sadness she was the very reverse of NA II 15 240 1
so heavy that no farther sadness could be gained; and this SS I 16 83 3
themselves, but of which sadness was the general result, SS III 9 333 1
So thought Fanny in good truth and sober sadness, as she MP III 2 329 10
Nay, in sober sadness, I believe I now love you all." MP III 5 358 9
SAFE (79)
Who would not have felt safe? LS 24 285 1
Oh, curse it! the carriage is safe enough, if a man knows NA I 9 65 30
safe, and therefore would alarm herself no longer. NA I 9 66 31
and now we may all go to-morrow with a safe conscience. NA I 13 100 13
But my secret I was always sure would be safe with you." NA I 15 118 13
Is he safe only in solitude?--or, is her heart constant to NA II 4 152 28
The Abbey would be always safe and dry.-- NA II 7 177 17
She was sick of exploring, and desired but to be safe in NA II 9 194 6
Till I know you to be safe at home, I shall not have an NA II 13 228 28
Let me have the satisfaction of knowing that you are safe NA II 13 228 28
There can be no doubt of my getting home safe." NA II 13 228 29
and equally safe did she believe her secret with each. NA II 14 230 3
matter now; Catherine is safe at home, and our comfort NA II 14 234 12
When is a man to be safe from such wit, if age and SS I 8 37 4
Men are very safe with us, let them be ever so rich. SS I 9 44 24
Your secret is safe with me; but pardon me if I express SS I 22 132 40
Elinor, after seeing her safe off, returned to Marianne, SS II 7 185 16
I thought we had been safe." SS II 9 203 12
"We are never safe from him." SS II 9 203 14
her to be at least equally safe in town as in the country, SS II 10 213 4
might have thought myself safe.' thought myself safe.' SS III 1 266 38
determining to be on the safe side, he made his apology in SS III 4 288 26
was to keep my heart as safe and sacred as my honour. SS III 13 368 28
are quite safe, the danger is only mine."-- W 339 18
attachment, that it is not safe to leave any to itself. PP I 6 21 2
convinced her that all was safe, her wit flowed long. PP I 6 27 54
You are safe from me." PP I 11 58 29
that it would not be safe for her--that she was not enough PP I 12 59 3
sister to announce their safe arrival in London; and when PP II 3 147 20
Wickham is safe." PP II 16 220 10
"And Mary king is safe!" added Elizabeth; "safe from a PP II 16 220 11
from that moment perfectly safe from all expectation, or MP I 3 30 57
The earliest intelligence of the travellers' safe arrival MP I 4 34 2
All is safe with a lady engaged; no harm can be done." MP I 5 45 12
I am assured that it is safe at Northampton; and there it MP I 6 57 33
Her cousin was safe on the other side, while these words MP I 10 100 22
land, offered sacrifices to the gods on their safe return." MP I 11 108 10
I was in safe hands. MP I 11 109 17
She was safe; but peace and safety were unconnected here. MP I 17 159 6
lady and I shall be very safe; you know how steady Stephen MP II 2 189 5
to Sotherton--that she was safe from the possibility of MP II 3 201 23
nor till he returned safe and well, without accident or MP II 6 237 23
as long as she could be safe from the notice of her aunt MP II 10 272 4
which however I can have little doubt,) you would be safe. MP II 12 293 15
You are on safe ground. MP III 2 331 16
She was safe in the breakfast-room, with her aunt, when MP III 5 357 5
mention of the Crawfords, safe from every look which could MP III 6 370 11
looks or his kindness, and safe from the perpetual MP III 6 370 12
he was so far pronounced safe, as to make his mother MP III 14 429 1
she was beloved; she was safe from Mr. Crawford, and when MP III 17 461 2
"But it is never safe to sit out of doors, my dear." E I 6 48 38
The business was finished, and Harriet safe. E I 7 55 36
Let her marry Robert Martin, and she is safe, respectable, E I 8 64 47
"will be to find myself safe at Hartfield again." E I 13 116 46
I dare say we shall be all safe at Hartfield before E I 15 126 10
convince him that it was safe to stay; and while the E I 15 128 17
18
it, and she was therefore safe from either exciting or E I 16 138 17
were just now quite safe from any letter from Jane Fairfax. E II 1 155 3
You will be perfectly safe, you know, among your friends." E II 7 211 20
see that every thing were safe in the house, as usual. E II 7 211 22

his interest was yet safe; and she led off the dance with E II 8 230 100
All was safe and prosperous; and as the removal of one E II 12 257 2
reached Randall's before dinner, and every thing was safe. E III 2 319 1
as to speaking ill of him, there I must have been safe." E III 10 399 64
been safe; none of this dreadful sequel would have been. E III 11 413 49
in short, I was somehow or other safe from him." E III 13 427 19
she now sent me, by a safe conveyance, all my letters, and E III 14 442 8
was all complete, and Harriet was safe in Brunswick Square. E III 16 451 3
defer the disclosure till Mrs. Weston were safe and well. E III 16 452 6
And I will own to you, (I am sure it will be safe), that E III 16 460 56
either of them protected him and his, Hartfield was safe.-- E III 19 484 10
if you chose to leave them, would be perfectly safe. P III 3 18 7
Your interest, Sir Walter, is in pretty safe hands. P III 3 19 10
am so glad when they are over, and he is safe back again." P III 8 71 55
Every thing was safe enough, and she smiled over the many P IV 1 128 32
is safe, and I shall give myself no more trouble about him. P IV 9 196 32
You are safe in all wordly matters, and safe in his P IV 9 196 32
herself, and felt safe till to-morrow, when she heard that P IV 10 212 2
her to wait till she might be safe from such a companion. P IV 10 215 14

SAFE-GUARD (1)
the constitutional safe-guard of a flannel waistcoat! SS III 14 378 15

SAFEGUARD (1)
continual, is the best safeguard of manners and conduct." MP III 4 349 23

SAFELY (49)
For this I shall impatiently wait; & meanwhile can safely LS 39 307 1
but they were now safely lodged in perfect bliss; and with NA II 2 140 11
the impatience of her curiosity might safely be indulged. NA II 6 164 3
now judged, she might safely, under the shelter of its SS II 1 145 23
I can safely say that he has never gave me one moment's SS II 2 147 10
Thomas Palmer, Esq. was safely delivered of a son and heir; SS II 14 246 1
Their journey was safely performed. SS III 6 302 6
all safely out of the house one morning, and left my name." SS III 8 326 53
speech and look, where minuteness could be safely indulged. SS III 10 348 34
could safely trust to the effect of time upon her health. SS III 11 352 19
I can safely say I owe you no ill-will, and am sure you SS III 13 365 14
carriage ceased moving--safely arrived;--& by the market W 322 2
"I believe, ma'am, I may safely promise you never to dance PP I 5 20 17
me out as she did; I can safely say, that every advance to PP II 3 148 26
Elizabeth could safely say that it was a great happiness PP II 15 216 7
Tom arrived safely, bringing an excellent account of his MP I 4 38 9
Her judgment may be quite as safely trusted.-- MP I 15 147 54
No, I can safely say, I have no pleasure so complete, so MP II 9 262 9
proceeded in her journey, safely and cheerfully, and as MP III 7 376 5
Taylor, may be safely left to manage their own concerns. E I 1 13 44
which Emma thought might be safely left to itself. E I 4 34 41
They might be more safely held up as a pattern. E I 4 34 42
On the contrary, I think a young man might be very safely E I 4 34 42
Where Miss Taylor failed to stimulate, I may safely affirm E I 5 37 7
It is not a state to be safely entered into with doubtful E I 7 52 19
The picture, elegantly framed, came safely to hand soon E I 9 69 2
Mr. Woodhouse had been safely seated long enough to give E I 14 117 3
Mr. Elton might never get safely to the end of it, and saw E I 17 141 4
Manners were all that could be safely judged of, under a E II 2 169 17
still I have no doubt that James will take you very safely. E II 7 210 14
when the table was again safely covered, when every corner E II 8 218 38
39

Married women, you know, may be safely authorized. E III 6 354 14
Mr. Woodhouse was safely conveyed in his carriage, with E III 6 357 33
It might be safely viewed with all its appendages of E III 6 360 40
and watched her safely off with the zeal of a friend. E III 6 363 51
Mr. Weston directed the whole, officiating safely between E III 7 367 1
"Well, my dear, and did you get there safely?-- E III 9 385 6
as if Emma could not safely have attached herself to any E III 17 467 31
in one of them; and I can safely say, that the happiest P III 8 70 54
be overturned by him, than driven safely by anybody else." P III 10 85 9
found herself safely deposited by them at the cottage. P III 10 92 48
of poetry, to be seldom safely enjoyed by those who P III 11 100 23
did it, however; she was safely down, and instantly, to P III 12 109 32
"She and the Harvilles came on Tuesday very safely, and in P IV 6 164 8
did; but now she could safely suggest the name of "Louisa." P IV 6 170 32
beyond it no wheels but cart wheels could safely proceed. S 1 364 1
the travellers were safely set down, & all was happiness & S 4 384 1
having; & think we may safely reckon on securing you two S 5 387 1
I did not think he cd safely venture,--for I am _sure_ there S 9 407 1

SAFER (10)
Catherine felt that nothing could have been safer; but NA I 15 119 14
"At any rate, it is safer to leave people to their own MP I 9 87 15
Fanny's interest seems in safer hands with you than with MP I 9 95 70
Fanny could have said a great deal, but it was safer to MP II 3 199 16
It will be safer to say 'no', perhaps.-- E I 7 53 20
the crown can be safer for you than your father's house." E II 11 251 28
approver, (a much safer character,) she was truly welcome. E II 11 256 60
Emma disappointed; but they would all be safer at home. E II 12 259 11
the sort; and it would be safer for both, to have the E III 4 341 34
It was a much safer place for a gentleman in his P III 2 14 10

SAFEST (5)
measure in the best and safest way, and Colonel Forster is PP III 4 276 5
to be safest, instead of attending the rehearsal at all? MP I 18 172 29
it best in every respect, safest and kindest, to keep her E I 8 57 1
what might be safest, had been a point of some doubtful E II 4 185 12
would make them the safest model for any young woman." E II 14 278 47

SAFETY (32)
I arrived here in safety, & have no reason to complain of LS 5 249 1
performed with suitable quietness and uneventful safety. NA I 2 19 4
With more care for the safety of her new gown than for the NA I 2 21 9
mild day of February, with the consciousness of safety. NA I 9 62 10
with him, she ran for safety to her own room, and, locking NA II 9 192 4
Eleanor their brother's safety, congratulating them with NA II 12 218 4
"I hope, I earnestly hope that to your real safety it will NA II 13 225 23
each found her greatest safety in silence, and few and NA II 13 227 27
that she could determine on with any confidence of safety. NA II 14 235 14
reached her home in safety, as the cause of his intrusion. NA II 15 241 7
hurried along, and reached the bottom in safety. SS I 9 41 7
my being acquainted with it could not add to its safety." SS I 22 132 40
visit, Marianne's safety, and her mother's expected SS III 9 333 3
that he had arrived in safety, and to give me his PP III 5 286 28
The little girl performed her long journey in safety, and MP I 2 12 1
by any alarm for his safety, or solicitude for his comfort, MP I 3 32 63
She was safe; but peace and safety were unconnected here. MP I 17 159 6
it in the aggregate for honesty or safety in particulars. MP I 18 170 24
Not that we would have endangered his safety by any MP II 5 225 57
pack it as to ensure its safety without much incommoding E I 6 49 42
number of nursery-maids, all reaching Hartfield in safety. E I 11 91 3
To her he looked for comfort; and her assurances of safety, E I 15 127 12
She determined to call upon them and seek safety in E II 1 155 2
There is safety in reserve, but no attraction. E II 6 203 40
public enough for safety, had led them into alarm.-- E III 3 333 5
to give assurance of her safety to Mrs. Goddard, and E III 3 334 8
have walked again in safety before their panic began, and E III 3 336 13
Mrs. Weston's friends were all made happy by her safety; E III 17 461 1
enough for safety, and occupied enough for cheerfulness. E III 19 482 4
think poor Mrs. Clay may be staying here in perfect safety. P III 5 35 14
with the feeling of safety, soon added, more composedly, " P IV 9 194 21
to persuasion exerted on the side of safety, not of risk. P IV 11 244 73

SAFFRON (1)
before hymen's saffron robe would be put on for us! E II 18 308 28

SAGACIOUSLY (1)
"Well, Miss Dashwood," said Mrs. Jennings, sagaciously SS III 4 285 1

SAGACITY (9)
her heart at ease by the sagacity of their "I know what;" NA I 15 121 25
I leave it to my reader's sagacity to determine how much NA II 15 247 14
Margaret's sagacity was not always displayed in a way so SS I 12 61 15
The selfish sagacity of the latter, which had at first SS III 14 375 10
your sagacity, to discover the name of your admirer. PP III 15 362 12
sure of her, and been delighted with his own sagacity. MP III 8 388 1
wonder in many a family circle, with great sagacity. E III 17 468 35
with a look of arch sagacity--"Miss Esther wants me to S 7 399 1
graces, the spirit, the sagacity, & the perseverance, of S 8 404 1

SAGES (1)
may be forgiven by older sages, for looking on the chance MP III 6 367 5

SAIL (2)
They contained a noble piece of water; a sail on which was SS I 12 62 28
to-morrow; but you cannot sail with this wind, if you are MP III 7 380 20

SAILED (3)
the last moment before he sailed, and perhaps find her MP III 6 372 18
of every day before they sailed, and even of getting her MP III 7 384 35
had changed, and he was sailed within four days from their MP III 8 388 2

SAILOR (10)
her removal, to be a sailor, was invited to spend a week MP I 2 21 34
that I am neither a lawyer, nor a soldier, nor a sailor." MP I 9 91 39
reward to the soldier and sailor in their choice of a MP I 11 110 22
unhappy by him as a sailor or soldier than as a clergyman. MP I 11 111 30
fondness of the young sailor, which led him to say, with MP II 6 235 19
in thinking a sailor might be a very desirable tenant. P III 3 18 7
favour, I assure you, be he sailor or soldier." P III 3 18 8
vigour most horribly; a sailor grows old sooner than any P III 3 19 16
to be the best-looking sailor he had ever met with, and P III 5 32 4
Should not this be enough for a sailor, who has had no P III 7 62 39

SAILOR'S (2)
which fall to every sailor's share--like bad weather and MP II 7 249 53
She gloried in being a sailor's wife, but she must pay the P IV 12 252 12

SAILORS (8)
Soldiers and sailors are always acceptable in society. MP I 11 109 19
Nobody can wonder that men are soldiers and sailors." MP I 11 109 19
Sailors work hard enough for their comforts, we must all P III 3 19 12
The sea is no beautifier, certainly; sailors do grow old P III 3 20 17
been accused of supposing sailors to be living on board P III 8 64 4
We sailors, Miss Elliot, cannot afford to make long P III 10 92 44
that she was convinced of sailors having more worth and P III 11 99 19
men walking about here, who, I am told, are sailors. P IV 6 166 16

SAILORS' (1)
Pray, what would become of us poor sailors' wives, who P III 8 69 43

SAILS (1)
or other among the sails, would have been dashed into the E II 1 160 23

SAINT (2)
ready to worship him as a saint, but was moreover truly SS III 5 293 2
and because _I_ was a libertine, _she_ must be a saint. SS III 8 322 36

SAKE (133)
comes to us, which I am glad of, for her sake & my own. LS 3 247 1
I take on my lap & sigh over for his dear uncle's sake. LS 5 250 2
Neither for your sake, for hers, nor for my own, could LS 24 289 12
sake! let us move away from this end of the room. NA I 6 42 33
Come along, my dearest Catherine, for heaven's sake, and NA I 8 58 25
Look about for heaven's sake! NA I 10 70 1
I only came for the sake of dancing with _you_, and I firmly NA I 10 75 26
I only go for the sake of driving you." NA I 13 99 7
for the sake of being able to read all the rest of it. NA I 14 110 27
For heaven's sake, waste no more time. NA I 15 120 24
Pray advise him for his own sake, and for every body's NA II 4 150 4
sake, and for every body's sake, to leave Bath directly, NA II 4 150 4
"I wish I could reason like you, for his sake and my own. NA II 11 211 14
"And only made believe to do so for mischief's sake?" NA II 12 219 10
and it was only for Eleanor's sake that she attempted it. NA II 13 225 22
his improvements for her sake, to whose share in them he NA II 16 250 3
Mr. Dashwood had wished for it more for the sake of his SS I 1 4 3
of it for her daughters' sake with satisfaction, though as SS I 3 14 2
For their brother's sake too, for the sake of his own SS I 3 14 2
each for the sake of the others resolved to appear happy. SS I 6 28 2
Marianne was vexed at it for her sister's sake, and turned SS I 7 34 5
for the sake of the provision and security of a wife. SS I 8 38 10
I have suffered for Edward's sake these last four years. SS I 22 133 42
could not be supposed to meet for the sake of conversation. SS II 1 142 8
They met for the sake of eating, drinking, and laughing SS II 1 143 8
idea of that, for Edward's sake, frightens away all my SS II 2 148 15
"And for your own sake too, or you are carrying your SS II 2 148 16
But I only go for the sake of seeing Edward. SS II 2 151 40
Tell me, Willoughby; for heaven's sake tell me, what is SS II 6 177 10
the window-seats for the sake of all the little light she SS II 7 180 1
you suffer; for her sake you must exert yourself." SS II 7 185 21
Willoughby's sake, would have been unwilling to believe. SS II 7 188 43
"But for my mother's sake and mine"----- SS II 7 190 53
I came only for Willoughby's sake--and now who cares for SS II 7 191 62
which, for the sake of every one concerned in it, make it SS II 8 196 19
Elinor, for her sister's sake, could not press the subject SS II 8 196 21
all my heart, it were _twice_ as much, for your sake." SS II 11 223 22
thankful for her _own sake_, that one greater obstacle SS II 13 238 1
anxious was she, _for_ his sake and her own, to do it well, SS II 13 241 20
And it was entirely for _her_ sake, and upon _her_ account, SS III 2 273 16
the sake of her own consequence, would chuse to have known. SS III 2 276 27
him to it for prudence sake, and would have parted for SS III 2 277 30
own sake, and as a friend of yours, I wish it still more. SS III 3 282 19
you for the sake of giving ten guineas to Mr. Ferrars!" SS III 4 291 53
"For God's sake tell me, is she out of danger, or is she SS III 8 318 12
the connection, for the sake of which he had, with little SS III 8 331 70
an unbounded affection, to be miserable for my sake." SS III 10 346 28
taking orders for the sake of two hundred and fifty at the SS III 14 374 4
a man merely for the sake of situation--is a sort of thing W 318 2
"Don't keep coughing so, Kitty, for heaven's sake! PP I 2 6 8
For God's sake, say no more of his partners. PP I 3 13 17
Elizabeth, for the sake of saying something that might PP I 9 43 26
"For heaven's sake, madam, speak lower.-- PP I 18 99 66
a gentlewoman for _my_ sake; and for your _own_, let her be an PP I 19 105 10
understand; and all for the sake of Mr. Collins too!-- PP I 23 130 24
believe, for every body's sake, that she may feel PP II 1 135 12
You shall not, for the sake of one individual, change the PP II 1 135 13
it was for the sake of what had been, rather than what was. PP II 3 146 19
a little change was not unwelcome for its own sake. PP II 4 151 1
For your sake," turning to Charlotte, "I am glad of it; PP II 6 164 16
sake, she made more favourable than it really was. PP II 6 166 42
to do it only for the sake of finding out that Mrs. PP II 7 169 3
chiefly for the sake of having somebody at his disposal. PP II 10 184 16
17

It cannot be for _me_, it cannot be for _my_ sake that his PP III 1 255 60
could make him for her sake, forego every chance of PP III 5 283 8
agreed in wishing, for the sake of their sister's feelings PP III 8 314 22
unwilling for her sister's sake, to provoke him, she only PP III 10 329 33
34

creature; and, for the sake of giving relief to my own PP III 16 365 2
3

so many mortifications, for the sake of discovering them." PP III 16 366 5
it: it is all for Jane's sake, you know; and there is no PP III 17 375 26
I wish I could say, for the sake of her family, that the PP III 19 385 1
sake, he assisted him farther in his profession. PP III 19 387 9
for our own children's sake, continue her in the family; MP I 1 10 14
If I could wish it for my own sake, I would not do so MP I 3 29 46
for William's sake, "they can write long letters." MP I 6 59 44
He was not a man to be endured but for his children's sake, MP II 2 191 10
and London, independence and splendour for _his_ sake. MP II 3 202 25
cross and to keep for her sake, saying every thing she MP II 8 258 15
For my own sake, I could wish there had been no ball just MP II 9 268 29
for the sake of securing her at that part of the evening. MP II 10 278 20
in addition, for the sake of at least hearing his name. MP II 11 287 17
sake, she could scarcely dare mention to their father. MP III 1 317 38
see how he is courted, and how I am courted for his sake! MP III 5 360 16

I wish Margaret were married, for my poor friend's sake, MP III 5 361 16
man in the blues, for the sake of that horrid Lord MP III 5 361 16
sake of being travelling at the same time that you were. MP III 9 393 1
the dashing young captains whom you disdain for his sake." MP III 9 394 1
for information's sake, she had so strong a desire of not MP III 12 418 7
He is anxious to get you there for my mother's sake. MP III 15 442 23
pain of parting, for the sake of carrying with me the MP III 16 458 30
been expected, and for his sake been more near doing right. MP III 16 459 31
was she, for her father's sake, in the power; though, as E I 3 22 6
But for Harriet's sake, or rather for my own, and as there E I 6 46 21
Highbury, for the sake of her being settled so well. E I 8 61 38
Not regret her leaving Highbury for the sake of marrying a E I 8 62 39
even for poor Isabella's sake; and who consequently was E I 11 91 2
cards entirely for the sake of comfortable talk with his E I 12 100 15
such a day as this, for the sake of coming to see him. E I 13 113 26
For her own sake she could not be rude; and for Harriet's, E I 14 118 4
for the sake of the future twelve thousand pounds. E II 2 169 16
For his own sake, I would not have him do so mad a thing." E II 8 225 72
talked of; and, for his sake, greater pleasure than ever E II 13 264 1
yourself Harriet for my sake; think less, talk less of Mr. E II 13 268 11
12
less of Mr. Elton for my sake; because for your own sake E II 13 268 11
12
sake; because for your own sake rather, I would wish it to E II 13 268 11
12
it to be done, for the sake of what is more important than E II 13 268 11
12
man's house, for the sake of being in mixed company till E II 17 302 23
court plaister by for his sake!" said Emma, recovering E III 4 339 15
into the hall for the sake of a few moments' free E III 6 362 43
Wish it she must, for his sake--be the consequence nothing E III 12 416 1
And if he were to be lost to them for Harriet's sake; if E III 12 422 20
father's sake--I know you will not allow yourself-----." E III 13 426 13
I have no motive for wishing him ill--and for her sake, E III 13 428 21
He had induced her to place herself, for his sake, in a E III 15 446 20
I have taken some pains for your sake, and for Robert E III 18 474 34
and for Robert Martin's sake, (whom I have always had E III 18 474 34
himself on remaining single for his dear daughter's sake. P III 1 5 8
He felt it all, so much for her sake.-- P III 8 67 23
this Mr. Musgrove, for the sake of his horses, would not P III 11 94 8
his health for the sake of duties, which may be just as P III 12 103 2
"Go to him, go to him," cried Anne, "for heaven's sake go P III 12 110 36
claims of regard, for his sake; and she hoped he would not P III 12 116 69
Her father and sister were glad to see her, for the sake P IV 3 137 2
offer one solution; it was, perhaps, for Elizabeth's sake. P IV 3 140 11
If I would not go for the sake of your father, I should P IV 10 224 48
should think it scandalous to go for the sake of his heir. P IV 10 224 48
probably for the sake of walking away from it soon P IV 10 225 56
to do for the sake of these treasures of his existence! P IV 11 235 31
sake, the possibility of scheming longer for Sir Walter. P IV 12 250 8
I only notice them, for poor dear Sir Harry's sake. S 7 399 1
This was said cheifly for the sake of saying something-- S 7 400 1
for Sir Edward's sake, & the sake of her Milch Asses. S 11 422 1
this corner house, for the sake of a glimpse of the Miss S 11 422 1
SAKES (7)
and for their sakes avoid a breach with their brother. SS I 1 6 10
marry him; guess what I must have felt for all your sakes. SS II 9 210 32
every day; but for your sakes, we would do any thing. PP I 2 8 26
and Jane, and for their sakes had patience with her. PP III 10 325 2
was delighted to act on his proposal, for both your sakes." MP III 5 362 20
single so long for our sakes, need be suspected now. P III 5 35 14
pleasure for their sakes, than mortification for her own. P III 6 47 13
SALARY (3)
And her salary!-- E III 8 382 23
I really cannot venture to name her salary to you, Miss E III 8 382 23
heard named as a salary on such occasions, dearly earned." E III 8 382 24
SALE (4)
especially as the sale took place exactly at the time of LS 5 249 1
charge on the estate, or by any sale of its valuable woods. SS I 1 4 3
purchase Randalls, and the sale of Randalls was long E I 2 16 6
sale--not quite of human flesh--but of human intellect." E II 17 300 13
SALEABLE (1)
that if baronetcies were saleable, any body should have P IV 9 202 66
SALINE (1)
Saline air & immersion will be the very thing.-- S 1 367 1
SALISBURY (4)
have very good shops in Salisbury, but it is so far to go;- NA I 3 29 46
Morland says that by sending it to-night to Salisbury, we NA I 15 120 22
be at Salisbury, and then I am only nine miles from home." NA II 13 224 17
Salisbury she had known to be her point on leaving NA II 14 232 6
SALLAD (1)
the sentinel on guard, and dressing a sallad and cucumber. PP II 16 219 1
SALLIED (1)
or too poor, she sallied forth into the village to settle PP II 7 169 4
SALLIES (1)
I am no match for your arch sallies.--" W 350 24
SALLOW (3)
She had a thin awkward figure, a sallow skin without NA I 1 13 1
you know--I like a sallow better than any other. NA I 6 42 30
Her complexion was sallow; and her features small, without SS II 12 232 15
SALLY (5)
her next sister, sally, could say it better than she did. NA I 1 14 1
Sally, or rather Sarah, (for what young lady of common NA I 2 19 3
there with a message from sally at the park to her brother, SS III 11 354 27
but I wish you would tell sally to mend a great slit in my PP III 5 292 60
"She had been into the kitchen," she said, "to hurry sally MP III 7 383 32
SALLY-PORT (1)
and Mr. Campbell to the sally-port; and Mr. Price walked MP III 7 384 36
SALMON (1)
preferring salmon to cod, or boiled fowls to veal cutlets. SS II 4 160 2
SALOON (3)
and let the supper be set out in the saloon.' SS II 14 252 18
through the hall into the saloon, whose northern aspect PP III 3 267 2
When Darcy returned to the saloon, Miss Bingley could not PP III 3 270 12
SALTED (1)
There will be the leg to be salted, you know, which is so E II 3 172 18
SALTING-PAN (1)
was so afraid that we had not any salting-pan large enough. E II 3 173 27
SALTS (5)
immediately gave her, her salts; and Sir John felt so SS II 12 236 41
mother stood with salts in her hand, expecting to be MP II 3 203 29
Rub her hands, rub her temples; here are salts,--take them, P III 12 110 36
that she sat with salts in her hand, took drops two or S 10 413 1
of the drops & the salts by means of one or the other. S 10 413 1
SALUTARY (1)
therefore, could not be salutary for her, and he was MP III 11 410 7
SALUTATION (7)
he, after the first salutation, "and she encouraged me to SS II 9 204 18
waiting neither for salutation nor inquiry, instantly gave SS III 9 334 4
diffuseness and warmth remained for Bingley's salutation. PP I 11 54 2
hat--a salutation which Mr. Darcy just deigned to return. PP I 15 73 8
the mere ceremonious salutation attending his entrance. PP III 12 340 14
reply to Elizabeth's salutation, than a slight inclination PP III 14 351 3
with a very civil salutation--much concern for the S 1 365 1
SALUTATIONS (2)
dear Fanny, how comes this?" were the first salutations. MP I 10 97 2
followed the first salutations; and Henry Crawford was MP I 15 143 26
SAM (19)
Here is a friend of mine, Sam Fletcher, has got one to NA I 10 76 28
but if she does you know, it is all over with poor Sam.-- W 320 2
Sam is only a surgeon you know.-- W 321 2
"Unless Sam feels on sure grounds with the lady herself, W 321 2
Mr Sam Watson is a very good sort of young man, & I dare W 324 3
am very sure there is no resemblance between her & Sam."-- W 324 3
tell me how you like them all, & what I am to say to Sam. W 341 19
But what am I to say to Sam?"-- W 341 19
She once mentioned Sam, & certainly with a little W 341 19
Poor Sam!-- W 342 19
was a squabble between Sam and Rebecca, about the manner MP III 7 379 19
by the superior noise of Sam, Tom, and Charles chasing MP III 7 382 27
Holla--you there--Sam--stop your confounded pipe, or I MP III 7 383 30
impossibility of getting Sam ready in time, was at leisure MP III 7 385 37
being gone to school, Sam on some project of his own, and MP III 8 388 1
darling; and John, Richard, Sam, Tom, and Charles, MP III 8 389 4
set about working for Sam immediately, and by working MP III 8 390 7
Sam, loud and overbearing as he was, she rather regretted MP III 8 390 8
of the Luggage, & helping old Sam uncord the trunks.-- S 9 407 1
SAM'S (3)
which made her think her brother Sam's a hopeless case.-- W 328 8
know what I am to do about Sam's things, they will never MP III 7 378 10
Ay, Sam's voice louder than all the rest! MP III 7 383 30
SAM. (1)
"Is Sam. attached to Miss Edwardes?"-- W 320 2
SAME (550)
so much--engaging at the same time & in the same house the LS 4 248 2
at the same time & in the same house the affections of two LS 4 248 2
since; he wrote by the same post to Reginald, a long LS 13 262 1
From the same to the same./ Churchill. LS 18 272 1
For a minute or two I remained in the same spot, LS 23 284 5
From the same to the same. Churchill. LS 24 285 1
however, & at the same time began to think that we had LS 24 290 13
the feelings of either to remain longer in the same house. LS 25 292 3
But at the same time, it is not for me to suffer such a LS 25 292 3
at pleasure; it was the same, when I wanted to join the LS 28 298 1
At the same time do not forget my real interest; say all LS 31 302 1
mine, it will unite us again in the same intimacy as ever. LS 39 307 1
Frederica was no more altered than Lady Susan; the same LS 42 311 3
restrained manners, the same timid look in the presence of LS 42 311 3
situation was just the same; they saw nothing of the NA I 2 21 9
every day wished for the same thing was at length to have NA I 4 31 2
and say their prayers in the same chapel the next morning. NA I 4 34 7
her air, and dressing in the same style, did very well. NA I 4 34 8
Now, had the same young lady been engaged with a volume of NA I 5 38 4
out a list of ten or twelve more of the same kind for you." NA I 6 40 8
"Good heaven! 'tis James!" was uttered at the same moment NA I 7 44 3
resolving to remain in the same place and the same NA I 9 60 1
in the same place and the same employment till the clock NA I 9 60 1
Isabella was going at the same time with James, was NA I 9 61 6
continued to go on in the same quiet manner, without NA I 9 62 10
drank in Oxford, and the same happy conviction of her NA I 9 64 26
different accounts of the same thing; for she had not been NA I 9 65 31
were so exactly the same, it was quite ridiculous! NA I 10 71 3
lady has at some time or other known the same agitation. NA I 10 74 23
I cannot look upon them at all in the same light, nor NA I 10 77 35
the same light, nor think the same duties belong to them." NA I 10 77 35
by the approach of the same two open carriages, containing NA I 11 84 17
carriages, containing the same three people that had NA I 11 84 17
I verily believe at the same instant; and we should have NA I 11 84 19
"Exactly--the very same." NA I 11 85 27
and John is just the same; he has amazing strong feelings. NA I 11 90 64
who was never in the same part of the house for ten NA I 12 95 17
entered it, continued the same kind of delicate flattery, NA I 12 96 23
The same arguments assailed her again; she must go, she NA I 13 98 1
language, and now he is taking the same liberty with you. NA I 14 107 14
"Morland says exactly the same," replied Isabella; "and NA I 15 119 15
then you know, we may try the truth of this same old song." NA I 15 123 34
And I am heartily glad to hear you say the same. NA I 15 124 44
was met by one with the same kindness, and by the other NA II 1 131 14
and by the other with the same attention as heretofore: NA II 1 131 14
to be for weeks under the same roof with the person whose NA II 2 141 11
of your brother never did alter; it was always the same. NA II 3 146 19
"Psha, nonsense!" was Isabella's answer in the same half NA II 3 147 22
"Is not it the same thing?" NA II 4 151 11
a foot from the ground, on a carved stand of the same. NA II 6 163 2
of the lid, was a mysterious cypher, in the same metal. NA II 6 163 2
unfasten the door, the same difficulty occurring in the NA II 6 169 11
She seized another sheet, and saw the same articles with NA II 7 172 2
Two others, penned by the same hand, marked an expenditure NA II 7 172 2
nearly as possible in the same shape as before, returned NA II 7 173 3
returned them to the same spot within the cabinet, with a NA II 7 173 3
kitchen-garden in the same aspect; the walls surrounding NA II 7 175 15
wished he could do the same, for he never entered his, NA II 7 178 23
one on the same plan, but superior in length and breadth. NA II 8 184 5
on the point of doing the same by the first door to the NA II 8 185 6
The name of "Eleanor" at the same moment, in his loudest NA II 9 191 4
not all, you know, the same tenderness of disposition--and NA II 9 197 27
for me to be in the same house with Captain Tilney." NA II 10 204 17
supported by Henry, at the same time that a tray full of NA II 11 213 20
to the same repast, but in circumstances how different! NA II 13 228 27
Unfortunately, the road she now travelled was the same NA II 14 230 1
Woodston, saved her at the same time from watching her NA II 14 231 5
It is all the same to me what I eat." NA II 15 241 5
He must enter into all my feelings; the same books, the SS I 3 17 18
the same books, the same music must charm us both. SS I 3 17 18
her uneasy; and at the same time, (which was still more SS I 4 23 19
for the houses were in the same parish, could, by any SS I 4 23 20
ye well-known trees!--but you will continue the same.-- SS I 5 27 8
No; you will continue the same; unconscious of the SS I 5 27 8
the concern which the same subject had drawn from him the SS I 7 33 4
had lain ever since in the same position on the pianoforte, SS I 7 35 8
The same books, the same passages were idolized by each-- SS I 10 47 3
Willoughby thought the same; and their behaviour, at all SS I 11 53 2
Towards her husband and mother she was the same as to them; SS I 11 55 6
spirits were always the same; and though she did not SS I 11 55 6
called at the cottage, the same day, Elinor heard her SS I 12 59 6
The reasons for this alteration were at the same time SS I 12 59 6
he added in the same low voice--"but, Marianne, the horse SS I 12 59 6
party; but at the same time declared it to be unavoidable. SS I 13 65 33
"Yes," cried he in the same eager tone, "with all and SS I 14 73 13
Tell me that not only your house will remain the same, but SS I 14 74 19
in the same county with Elinor without seeing her before. SS I 16 87 25
"Perhaps," said Elinor, smiling, "we may come to the same SS I 17 91 11
distinguished her by the same affection which once she had SS I 18 96 1
them, originated in the same fettered inclination, the SS I 19 102 2
same inevitable necessity of temporising with his mother. SS I 19 102 2
came down stairs at the same time, and they all sat down SS I 19 106 21
She thought it probable that as they lived in the same SS I 20 114 43
pinching one of the same lady's fingers, she fondly SS I 21 121 8
for a bruised temple, the same remedy was eagerly proposed SS I 21 121 10
an hour or two together in the same room almost every day. SS I 21 124 33
We cannot mean the same Mr. Ferrars." SS I 22 131 29
I am afraid it is just the same with him now; for he SS I 22 134 52
of education, while the same period of time, spent on her SS II 1 140 2
her own end, and pleased Lady Middleton at the same time. SS II 1 145 23
seated side by side at the same table, and with the utmost SS II 1 145 23
the utmost harmony engaged in forwarding the same work. SS II 1 145 23
he is undoubtedly supported by the same trust in your's. SS II 2 147 8
situation to have the same animating object in view, the SS II 4 159 1
animating object in view, the same possibility of hope. SS II 4 159 1
In a few moments Marianne did the same. SS II 4 160 4
Elinor was disappointed too; but at the same time her SS II 4 162 8
her own, though at the same time she would never have SS II 4 164 21
but who saw at the same time with much concern his SS II 5 168 12
It was not the first time of her feeling the same kind of SS II 5 172 40

might be, and at the same time wished to shield her SS II 5 174 45
her; and then continued his discourse with the same lady. SS II 6 176 3
followed by a return of the same excessive affliction. SS II 7 180 4
but what any one would have written in the same situation. SS II 7 188 43
said Elinor; "but unfortunately he did not feel the same." SS II 7 188 45
"He did feel the same, Elinor--for weeks and weeks he felt SS II 7 188 46
Mrs. Jennings was not struck by the same thought; for, SS II 8 198 30
the next morning to the same consciousness of misery in SS II 9 201 1
again and again; with the same steady conviction and SS II 9 201 2
on Elinor's side, the same impetuous feelings and varying SS II 9 201 2
She expected from other people the same opinions and SS II 9 202 4
The same warmth of heart, the same eagerness of fancy and SS II 9 205 24
Our ages were nearly the same, and from our earliest years SS II 9 205 24
debt; and there, in the same house, under a similar SS II 9 207 26
Their fates, their fortunes cannot be the same; and had SS II 9 208 28
other girls of about the same time of life; and for two SS II 9 208 28
from her again the same grateful acknowledgments, and SS II 9 211 43
Elinor wished that the same forbearance could have SS II 10 214 8
have a brother and I a sister settling at the same time. SS II 11 224 26
The same manners however, which recommended Mrs. John SS II 12 229 3
the servant at the same time--"there is nobody here but SS II 12 231 13
second son William, who were nearly of the same age. SS II 12 233 19
her at the same time, that they were done by Miss Dashwood. SS II 12 235 28
No pride, no hauteur, and your sister just the same--all SS II 13 239 6
every other baby of the same age; nor could he even be SS II 14 248 5
giving the same number of days to such near relations." SS II 14 253 22
another year; at the same time, however, slyly suspecting SS II 14 253 25
the world but the red-gum;' and nurse said just the same. SS III 1 257 5
of a passion!--and Mr. Donavan thinks just the same. SS III 1 259 7
A few minutes more spent in the same kind of effusion, SS III 1 269 57
"you were all in the same room together, were not you?" SS III 2 274 17
And I am sure Lucy would have done just the same by me; SS III 2 274 20
Miss Steele was going to reply on the same subject, but SS III 2 275 24
us, and Lady Middleton the same; and if any thing should SS III 2 275 25
but however, at the same time, gratefully acknowledge many SS III 2 277 30
But at the same time, she could not help thinking that no SS III 3 283 20
a manner; though at the same time, I should have been SS III 4 288 27
action, but she was at the same time so unwilling to SS III 4 290 36
return the same good will, than the power of expressing it. SS III 4 290 43
So far was she, at the same time, from any backwardness to SS III 5 293 2
same to Miss Morton whether she marry Edward or Robert." SS III 5 296 28
But we are not all born, you know, with the same powers-- SS III 5 299 35
born, you know, with the same powers--the same address.-- SS III 5 299 35
every other place of the same degree of importance, it had SS III 6 302 7
morning of the same continued rain had reduced very low. SS III 6 304 14
her situation continued, with little variation, the same. SS III 7 309 7
cried Marianne, in the same hurried manner, "I shall never SS III 7 311 13
"Has she!"--he cried, in the same eager tone.-- SS III 8 319 27
I do not mean to justify myself, but at the same time SS III 8 322 36
To know that Marianne was in town was--in the same SS III 8 325 50
before me, as I travelled, in the same look and hue." SS III 8 327 55
carried about me in the same pocket-book, which was now SS III 8 329 63
as Willoughby--but at the same time, there is something SS III 9 338 20
though smiling to see the same eager fancy which had been SS III 10 343 10
had intuitively taken the same direction, was shocked to SS III 11 353 24
and Mrs. Dashwood probably found the same explanation. SS III 11 354 32
eyes were fixed on him with the same impatient wonder. SS III 12 360 22
She will be more hurt by it, and on the same principle SS III 13 366 19
Tom Musgrave should be named with him in the same day."-- W 316 2
the whole time at the same table in the same room, with W 336 14
at the same table in the same room, with only one change W 336 14
"One of his particular friends,"--"all in the same Regt W 337 15
not--but I remember my dear when you & I did the same."-- W 337 15
written down, I bring your sister's orders for the same.--" W 339 18
the same time without any theatrical grimace or violence.-- W 343 20
Howard had not taken the same privilege of coming, & W 347 22
with himself for the same, & for having married the only W 348 23
dreaded the meeting, & at the same time longed for it.-- W 356 28
He was at the same time haughty, reserved, and fastidious, PP I 4 16 14
If a woman conceals her affection with the same skill from PP I 6 21 2
Mrs. Hurst thought the same, and added, "she has nothing, PP I 8 35 3
4

who arrived about the same time, think it at all advisable. PP I 9 41 2
leave it; and when I am in town it is pretty much the same. PP I 9 43 22
"There has been many a one, I fancy, overcome in the same PP I 9 44 32
They are in the same profession, you know; only in PP I 10 53 57
Darcy took up a book; Miss Bingley did the same; and Mrs. PP I 11 54 3
maintaining at the same time the most resolute composure PP I 14 68 12
the two gentlemen turning back had reached the same spot. PP I 15 72 8
readiness at the same time perfectly correct and PP I 15 72 8
same house with him, and I think him very disagreeable." PP I 16 77 13
"We were born in the same parish, within the same park, PP I 16 81 37
together; inmates of the same house, sharing the same PP I 16 81 37
the same amusements, objects of the same parental care. PP I 16 81 37
There are undoubtedly many who could not say the same, but PP I 16 83 50
I am sure we never read the same, or not with the same PP I 18 93 28
by your account to be the same," said Elizabeth angrily; " PP I 18 95 46
to make inquiries on the same subject of Bingley. PP I 18 95 48
humility of behaviour is at the same time maintained. PP I 18 97 60
61

Her mother's thoughts she plainly saw were bent the same PP I 18 98 63
Her mother would talk of her views in the same PP I 18 100 67
who came to tell the same news, and no sooner had they PP I 20 113 26
Mr. Collins was also in the same state of angry pride. PP I 21 115 2
Darcy;--that to be in the same room, the same party with PP I 21 115 4
be in the same room, the same party with him for so many PP I 21 115 4
cannot be so, and at the same time convinced that when PP I 21 117 10
11

evade, and he was at the same time exercising great self- PP I 22 123 3
situation remained the same, her peace equally wounded. PP II 1 134 3
at the time, she had the same story to repeat every day. PP II 1 137 26
not living in the same house with her brother, she might PP II 2 142 17
with me, but if the same circumstances were to happen PP II 3 148 26
They have not the same force or rapidity, and do not PP II 8 175 25
force or rapidity, and do not produce the same expression. PP II 8 175 25
must expect him to keep or quit it on the same principle." PP II 9 178 9
He answered her in the same style, and the subject dropped. PP II 10 184 16
Elizabeth awoke the next morning to the same thoughts and PP II 12 195 1
a young man of nearly the same age with himself, and who PP II 12 200 5
cannot be prevented by the same cause from confiding in my PP II 12 203 5
Jane, and must, at the same time, so highly gratify PP II 15 217 17
his answers were at the same time so vague and equivocal, PP II 16 223 26
from exciting in her the same feelings as in her mother PP II 18 230 14
the same, and she left him disappointed and sorry. PP II 18 232 21
only by her mother, who might have felt nearly the same. PP II 18 232 23
It was drawn at the same time as the other--about eight PP III 1 247 11
offering at the same time to supply him with fishing PP III 1 255 60
for dining with the same family, when the sound of a PP III 2 260 1
with the same good-humoured ease that he had ever done. PP III 2 261 5
indulgence, though, at the same time, for the consolation PP III 6 297 11
to London, at the same time that Mr. Bennet came from it. PP III 6 298 15
Another day I will do the same; I will sit in my library, PP III 6 300 28
depended; but at the same time, there was no one, whose PP III 8 311 12
to be probable, and at the same time dreaded to be just, PP III 10 326 3
her mother, "but at the same time, Mr. Bingley, it is very PP III 11 336 51
Were the same fair prospect to arise at present, as had PP III 11 337 54
would be hastening to the same vexatious conclusion. PP III 11 337 54
Her prudent mother, occupied by the same ideas, forbore to PP III 12 340 11
such a weakness as a second proposal to the same woman? PP III 12 341 19
The same anxiety to get them by themselves, was visible PP III 13 344 11
was gone, Jane constantly sought the same means of relief. PP III 13 349 44
to do the same by all her neighbours in Meryton. PP III 13 350 55

They are descended on the maternal side, from the same PP III 14 356 50
satisfied it, with the same kind of supposition, which had PP III 15 361 5
of which we have been advertised by the same authority. PP III 15 362 14
resolution; and perhaps he might be doing the same. PP III 16 365 1
and it will be just the same to Miss Lee, whether she has MP I 1 9 12
his eldest son with the same conviction, in the hope of MP I 3 23 2
But you must come up and tack on my patterns all the same." MP I 3 25 9
as a child; but it was the same with us all, or nearly so. MP I 3 26 25
You will have the same walks to frequent, the same library MP I 3 27 35
from, the same people to look at, the same horse to ride." MP I 3 27 35
distinction, which at the same time that it was MP I 3 30 57
ever be admitted to the same, and listened therefore MP I 4 35 6
Mrs. Norris could not see it in the same light. MP I 4 36 7
done too much, and at the same time procure for Fanny the MP I 4 37 8
object, it became, by the same rule of moral obligation, MP I 4 38 10
It was a connection exactly of the right sort; in the same MP I 4 40 14
the same country, and the same interest; and his most MP I 4 40 14
A girl not out, has always the same sort of dress; a close MP I 5 49 32
out, give themselves the same airs and take the same MP I 5 50 39
same liberties as if they were, which I have seen done. MP I 5 50 39
They looked just the same; both well dressed, with veils MP I 5 51 40
his own place in the same way; and though not saying much MP I 6 52 1
having always intended the same himself, with the super- MP I 6 55 17
same nature whenever she was in her company; but so it was. MP I 7 66 14
are as good, and she has the same energy of character. MP I 7 69 25
broke at the same moment from them both, more than once. MP I 8 81 31
I must go and look through that iron gate at the same view, MP I 9 96 73
same path which she had trod herself, and were before her. MP I 10 97 1
At the same moment Mr. Crawford approaching Julia, said, " MP I 10 105 52
"It is the same sort of thing," said Fanny, after a short MP I 11 109 18
Every thing returned into the same channel as before his MP I 12 115 4
given a choice, and at the same time addressed in such a MP I 12 120 26
ten days together in the same society, and the friendship, MP I 13 121 1
The same evening afforded him an opportunity of trying his MP I 13 124 14
Can we be wrong if Mary Crawford feels the same?" MP I 13 129 39
kept back, inclined the same way; but his determinateness MP I 14 130 3
effort was ended by the same speaker, who taking up one of MP I 14 132 7
"I was just going to say the very same thing," said Mrs. MP I 15 141 22
body else who is in the same predicament," glancing half MP I 15 143 26
spoke together to tell the same melancholy truth--that MP I 15 143 28
Do not you see it in the same light?" MP I 16 154 8
their interest were the same, the sisters, under such a MP I 17 162 19
not one of those who can talk and work at the same time.-- MP I 18 167 9
was come on the very same business that had brought Miss MP I 18 169 23
Her going roused the rest; and at the same moment, the two MP II 1 176 3
Maria joined them with the same intent, just then the MP II 1 176 3
"Still the same anxiety for every body's comfort, my dear MP II 1 180 11
to find our sentiments on this subject so much the same. MP II 1 186 34
To be a second time disappointed in the same way was an MP II 2 191 10
when they sat round the same table, which made Mr. Yates MP II 2 191 10
As well as I can recollect, it was always much the same. MP II 3 197 3
be meeting again in the same sort of way, allowing for the MP II 3 199 14
before the middle of the same month the ceremony had taken MP II 3 202 28
door to Sotherton, was the same chaise which Mr. Rushworth MP II 3 203 29
it less amazing, that the same soil and the same sun MP II 4 209 16
that the same soil and the same sun should nurture plants MP II 4 209 16
and Edmund began at the same time to recollect, that his MP II 4 214 46
Has not Miss Crawford a gown something the same?" MP II 5 222 44
Here he was again on the same ground where all had passed MP II 5 224 49
she could see in him the same William as before, and talk MP II 6 233 17
Children of the same family, the same blood, with the same MP II 6 235 18
Children of the same family, the same blood, with the same MP II 6 235 18
Gibraltar, appeared in the same trim, I thought they were MP II 6 235 19
addressed himself on the same subject to Sir Thomas, in a MP II 7 247 37
no proxy can be capable of satisfying to the same extent. MP II 7 247 42
with thinking just the same, and with having been on the MP II 8 254 7
near Peterborough in same situation as himself, and they MP II 8 255 10
looking forward to the same event in situations more at MP II 9 266 22
it had been about the same hour that she had returned from MP II 9 267 23
stairs together, their rooms being on the same floor above. MP II 9 268 27
been terrible; but at the same time there was a MP II 10 274 8
in great measure, from the same feelings which he had MP II 10 278 20
she could not sit in the same room with her uncle, hear MP II 11 284 8
almost another week of the same small party in the same MP II 12 291 1
same small party in the same bad weather, had they been MP II 12 291 1
he had expressed the same sentiment with a little MP II 12 292 8
You are not to be judged by the same rule. MP III 1 319 39
which saved her from the same spirit of reproach, exerted MP III 1 323 53
so lately expressing the same sentiments himself, and he MP III 1 323 57
Here was again a something of the same Mr. Crawford whom MP III 2 329 9
You will see him with the rest of us, in the same manner, MP III 2 331 16
And still pursuing the same cheerful thoughts, she soon MP III 2 333 28
try to move away--in the same low eager voice, and the MP III 3 342 34
low eager voice, and the same close neighbourhood, he went MP III 3 342 34
he went on, re-urging the same questions as before. MP III 3 342 34
same purpose, to give them a knowledge of your character. MP III 4 354 46
to be attended to in the same way, that a friendship and MP III 5 364 29
When no longer under the same roof with Edmund, she MP III 7 376 4
at the same time to carry back his neighbour's newspaper. MP III 7 384 36
eyes, meaning to screen it at the same time from Susan's. MP III 7 386 40
sake of being travelling at the same time that you were. MP III 9 393 1
Susan was only acting on the same truths, and pursuing the MP III 9 395 4
truths, and pursuing the same system, which her own MP III 9 395 4
and propriety, at the same time with a degree of MP III 10 399 5
They often stopt with the same sentiment and taste, MP III 11 409 7
to Susan, and again awakened the same interest in them. MP III 12 418 6
the idea, that we have the same friend, and that whatever MP III 13 420 2
I could not see him, and my eldest sister in the same room, MP III 13 423 2
to Fanny, in the same diffuse style, and the same medley MP III 13 427 12
diffuse style, and the same medley of trusts, hopes, and MP III 13 427 12
to her than to find her aunt using the same language.-- MP III 14 431 8
of a week, she had still the same feeling when it did come. MP III 15 437 1
the house again at the same moment, just in time to spend MP III 15 445 31
His having been in the same neighbourhood, Fanny already MP III 16 450 8
sent express from the same friend, to break to him the MP III 16 450 9
that he felt the same, her own conviction was insufficient. MP III 16 453 16
tax her kindness in the same way again--she need not fear MP III 16 453 17
Fanny thought exactly the same; and they were also quite MP III 16 460 31
had been used to; but the same happiness of disposition MP III 17 469 24
he would like to have the same kind office done for him! E I 1 13 46
including Randalls in the same parish, and Donwell Abbey E I 3 20 1
never believe that in the same situation she should not E I 4 27 3
sort of young woman in the same rank as his own, with a E I 4 30 18
low connections; at the same time not of any family that E I 4 35 44
admiration of her two companions would have been the same. E I 6 44 20
The same civilities and courtesies, the same success and E I 6 47 30
recollections; and at the same time, as she could perceive, E I 9 70 7
Approve my charade and my intentions in the same glance.' E I 9 72 15
to have you settled in the same country and circle which E I 9 75 27
of you different creatures; you do not look like the same. E I 12 103 38
and the answer had been, "much the same--not better." E I 13 114 28
bringing forward the same information again, or the E I 14 119 6
"One ought to use the same caution, perhaps, in judging of E I 14 123 23
Had the same behaviour continued, Miss Smith might have E I 15 132 36
Their being fixed, so absolutely fixed, in the same place, E I 17 143 14
Every body is so surprized; and every body says the same E II 1 159 18
their ages were the same, every body had supposed they E II 2 166 11
Mr. Frank Churchill had been at Weymouth at the same time. E II 2 169 17
"No," said Mr. Knightley, nearly at the same time; "you E II 3 170 5
At the same time, nobody could wonder if Mr. Elton should E II 3 176 44
She did not do any of it in the same way that she used; I E II 3 178 52
the occasion--to feel the same consciousness, the same E II 5 187 4

same consciousness, the same regrets--to be ready to E II 5 187 4
be ready to return to the same good understanding; and E II 5 187 4
Emma wondered whether the same suspicion of what might be E II 5 192 33
but if left to him, he should always chuse the same. E II 6 196 1
she trusted to its bearing the same construction with him. E II 6 196 1
heard many people say the same--but yet he must confess, E II 6 199 10
Were you often in the same society?" E II 6 199 13
in town; and at Weymouth we were very much in the same set. E II 6 200 20
we should arrive at the same moment! for, if we had met E II 8 213 9
Now I shall really be very happy to walk into the same E II 8 214 10
he said, he was beginning to have no longer the same wish. E II 8 221 49
They combated the point some time longer in the same way; E II 8 226 85
preparation;--and at the same moment Mr. Cole approaching E II 8 226 85
Miss Woodhouse looks as if she could almost say the same. E II 9 234 30
so liberal as he had been already; and Jane said the same. E II 9 238 51
However, the very same evening William Larkins came over E II 9 239 51
basket of apples, the same sort of apples, a bushel at E II 9 239 51
Mrs. Weston had been speaking to her at the same moment. E II 10 241 9
the others, as if it had passed within the same apartment." E II 10 243 32
finished there--that the same party should be collected, E II 11 247 3
same musician engaged, met with the readiest acquiescence. E II 11 247 3
And Mr. Weston at the same time, walking briskly with long E II 11 254 47
48

to, without being able to make their opinions the same. E II 13 267 9
again, could not be in the same room to which she had with E II 14 270 3
Elton was in being in the same room at once with the woman E II 14 271 5
was; placed exactly in the same part of the house. E II 14 273 19
The laurels at Maple Grove are in the same profusion as E II 14 273 21
and stand very much in the same way--just across the lawn; E II 14 273 21
are always pleased with any thing in the same style." E II 14 273 21
And the same may be said of Mrs. Jeffereys-- Clara E II 14 277 40
Of the same age--and always knowing her--I ought to have E II 16 291 6
John Knightley, "that the same sort of hand-writing often E II 16 297 45
and where the same master teaches, it is natural enough. E II 16 297 45
heard her saying in the same half-whisper to Jane, "here E II 17 302 21
22

Does Mrs. Churchill do the same?" E II 18 306 12
At the same time it is fair to observe, that I am one of E II 18 309 31
probably not much in the same spirit; all that I have to E II 18 311 38
to be returning with the same warmth of sentiment which he E III 1 315 1
of his feeling the same tenderness in the same degree. E III 1 316 3
to come early with the same distinguishing earnestness, on E III 2 319 3
earnestness, on the same errand, that it seemed as if half E III 2 319 3
conduct, discretion, and indiscretion, told the same story. E III 5 343 2
At the same time, I will not positively answer for my E III 5 346 16
not spoken a word--"I was just going to say the same thing. E III 5 349 24
the same motives which she had been heard to urge before.-- E III 6 359 37
"It comes to the same thing. E III 7 369 12
her that there was not the same cheerful volubility as E III 8 378 7
with both, and in the very same neighbourhood:--lives only E III 8 380 13
Elton at the same moment came congratulating me upon it! E III 8 382 29
called at Hartfield, the same morning, it appeared that E III 9 389 16
of course, the same origin, must be equally under cure.-- E III 11 403 2
she should have the very same distressing and delicate E III 11 403 3
as her own heart, was before her in the same few minutes. E III 11 408 33
She had often observed the change, to almost the same E III 11 409 35
Let him but continue the same Mr. Knightley to her and her E III 12 416 1
to her and her father, the same Mr. Knightley to all the E III 12 416 1
The weather continued much the same all the following E III 13 424 1
following morning; and the same loneliness, and the same E III 13 424 1
same loneliness, and the same melancholy, seemed to reign E III 13 424 1
This one half hour had given to each the same precious E III 13 432 41
each the same degree of ignorance, jealousy, or distrust.-- E III 13 432 41
Churchill, from about the same period, one sentiment E III 13 432 41
the other, from about the same period, one sentiment E III 13 432 41
They sat down to tea--the same party round the same table-- E III 14 434 2
had her eyes fallen on the same shrubs in the lawn, and E III 14 434 2
observed the same beautiful effect of the western sun!-- E III 14 434 2
afterwards to go over the same ground again with him, E III 14 435 5
mine; and I returned the same evening to Richmond, though E III 14 441 8
a few lines at the same time by the post, stating her E III 14 442 8
What say you both to our collecting the same party, and E III 16 455 18
It must be the same party, you know, quite the same party, E III 16 455 18
I wish our opinions were the same. E III 18 471 16
by him to join their party the same evening to Astley's. E III 18 471 20
wanted him to go on in the same style; but his mind was E III 18 478 60
61

have been some amusement to myself in the same situation. E III 18 478 67
but by the operation of the same system in another way.-- E III 19 483 10
It was so with Elizabeth; still the same handsome Miss P III 1 6 11
The undesirableness of any other house in the same P III 2 15 13
a degree, I know it is the same with them all: they are P III 3 20 16
But then, is not it the same with many other professions, P III 3 20 17
An Admiral speaks his own consequence, and, at the same P III 3 24 36
and Anne walked up at the same time, in a sort of desolate P III 5 35 18
though, at the same time, Anne could believe, with Lady P III 6 43 5
she could, that the same brother must still be in question. P III 6 49 25
turn out to be the very same Captain Wentworth whom they P III 6 52 33
she was all but calling there in the same half hour!-- P III 7 53 2
The same story and the same raptures were repeated, when P III 7 54 5
same view of escaping introduction when they were to meet. P III 7 59 23
They had been once more in the same room! P III 7 60 27
She had seen the same Frederick Wentworth. P III 7 61 34
and Anne Elliot were repeatedly in the same circle. P III 8 63 1
There must be the same immediate association of thought, P III 8 63 2
When he talked, she heard the same voice, and discerned P III 8 64 4
she heard the same voice, and discerned the same mind. P III 8 64 4
better men than himself applying for her at the same time. P III 8 65 12
when I had still the same luck in the Mediterranean." P III 8 67 23
They were actually on the same sofa, for Mrs. Musgrove had P III 8 68 29
it were really so, I should do just the same in her place. P III 10 85 9
"Had you?" cried he, catching the same tone; "I honour you! P III 10 85 11
She turned through the same gate,--but could not see them.- P III 10 87 21
carriage advancing in the same direction, which had been P III 10 90 38
It would place her in the same village with Captain P III 11 93 2
would have to frequent the same church, and there must be P III 11 93 2
seemed however to have the same good feelings; and nothing P III 11 97 15
the sitting down to the same table with him now, and the P III 11 99 21
beach, a gentleman at the same moment preparing to come P III 12 104 6
same gentleman, as he came out of an adjoining apartment. P III 12 104 7
It was now proved that he belonged to the same inn as P III 12 104 7
In the very same inn with us! P III 12 105 14
At the same time, however, it was a secret gratification P III 12 106 19
Captain Benwick obeyed, and Charles at the same moment, P III 12 110 37
38

incapable of being in the same room with Louisa, was kept, P III 12 112 51
it was decided; and Henrietta at first declared the same. P III 12 113 59
which the same spots had witnessed earlier in the morning. P III 12 115 66
Anne was astonished to recognise the same hills and the P III 12 117 73
to recognise the same hills and the same objects so soon. P III 12 117 73
of returning in the same carriage to Lyme; and when the P III 12 117 76
Louisa was much the same. P IV 1 121 2
Charles was to return to Lyme the same afternoon, and his P IV 1 121 3
her intelligence from the same hour of yester morn, that P IV 1 126 20
sensible eye, but, at the same time, "must lament his P IV 3 141 12
It was the same, the very same man, with no difference but P IV 3 142 18
They were not the same, but they were, perhaps, equally P IV 3 143 18
to be guests in the same inn at the same time, to give his P IV 3 143 19
in the same inn at the same time, to give his own route, P IV 3 143 19
at a distance telling the same tale, before Mr. Elliot or P IV 3 144 23
In the course of the same morning, Anne and her father P IV 4 145 3
same time, there had been an unlucky omission at Kellynch. P IV 4 148 12

would have the same object, I have no doubt, though the P IV 4 151 21
in their having the same sort of pride, she was pleased P IV 4 151 22
Lady Dalrymple for the same evening, and Anne was already P IV 5 156 14
the same time honoured for staying away in such a cause.-- P IV 5 158 21
and blessing in the same spot, and only superior to her in P IV 5 160 25
The same image of Mr. Elliot speaking for himself, brought P IV 5 160 26
had been living in the same small family party; since P IV 6 167 19
and instead of drawing the same conclusion as Mary, from P IV 6 167 19
to feel for him, would have received the same compliment. P IV 6 167 19
blows through one of the cupboards just in the same way." P IV 6 170 29
for this young lady, this same Miss Musgrove, instead of P IV 6 171 33
walking the same way, but there was no mistaking him. P IV 7 179 28
arrive nearly at the same instant, advanced into the room. P IV 8 184 17
should happen to be in the same part of the room, but he P IV 8 186 22
Ninety-nine out of a hundred would do the same. P IV 9 196 32
all your acquaintance have disposed of you in the same way. P IV 9 197 36
It must have been about the same time that he became known P IV 9 200 56
which all breathed the same stern resolution of not P IV 9 209 97
under a cold civility, the same hard-hearted indifference P IV 9 209 97
every man to have the same objects and pleasures as myself. P IV 10 218 26
from his looks, that the same unfortunate persuasion, P IV 10 221 32
Charles and Mary still talked on in the same style; he, P IV 10 224 50
and, wherever she looked, saw symptoms of the same. P IV 10 226 63
and a great deal in the same style of open-hearted P IV 11 230 5
all over her, and at the same moment that her eyes P IV 11 231 10
The two ladies continued to talk, to re-urge the same P IV 11 231 11
replied Anne, "but the same spirit of analogy will P IV 11 233 23
answer for it; and Captain Wentworth the same, I dare say." P IV 11 239 52
might have felt the same--her own family, nay, perhaps P IV 11 242 65
interest, which the same consciousness sought to conceal;-- P IV 11 246 78
But very far from wishing their children to do the same, S 2 374 1
At the same time last year, (late in July) there had not S 4 383 1
day's health is;--& at the same time, they are such S 5 385 1
from the influence of the same conscious importance or a S 7 399 1
still talking on in the same way, allowed her thoughts to S 7 402 1
He has persuaded her to engage in the same speculation--& S 7 402 1
is the same, he fancies she feels like him in others.-- S 7 402 1
Charlotte--our taste in novels is not at all the same." S 8 404 1
of the day--& with the same ill-luck which made him derive S 8 404 1
she wrote the same day to Fanny Noyce and mentioned it to S 9 408 1
I answered Fanny's letter by the same post & pressed for S 9 408 1
I had the pleasure of hearing soon afterwards by the same S 9 408 1
I sounded Susan--the same thought had occurred to her.-- S 9 409 1
left Chichester at the same hour today--& here we are.--" S 9 409 1
stream--and at the same moment, his sisters both crying S 10 417 1
That both should have the same name.-- S 10 418 1
But it cannot be the same.-- S 10 419 1
Impossible that it should be the same."-- S 10 419 1
Surry & the family from Camberwell were one & the same.-- S 11 420 1
the journey, was the very same Mrs G. whose plans were at S 11 420 1
G. whose plans were at the same period (under another S 11 420 1

SAMENESS (6)
can never find greater sameness in such a place as this, NA I 10 78 46
But certainly there is much more sameness in a country NA I 10 79 48
on this head, feared the sameness of every day's society NA II 11 209 5
her, an affectation and a sameness to disgust and weary. PP II 18 233 25
saddened, it was all sameness and gloom, compared with the MP II 3 196 1
agitations to vary, the sameness and the elegance, the P III 1 9 18

SAMPLE (2)
"The metropolis, I imagine, is a pretty fair sample of the MP I 9 93 48
these young ladies a sample of true conjugal obedience-- E III 16 457 36

SAMPLER (1)
were a good little girl working your sampler at home!" NA I 14 107 11

SANCTION (10)
Pulteney-Street, and obtained their sanction of his wishes. NA II 2 140 9
his son, steady as the sanction of reason and the dictate NA II 15 247 15
it must be impossible for them to sanction the engagement. NA II 16 249 1
Bingley had received his sanction to be happy, had she not PP III 12 340 12
for her, and intreat the sanction of the uncle, who seemed MP III 1 314 16
be affording his sanction to vice, or in seeking to lessen MP III 17 465 13
of promoting it, by the sanction he had given; and the E I 8 66 55
arrangement their ready sanction, and said, that they E II 2 166 10
your sanction to such vanity-baits for poor young ladies." E II 14 280 59
Without his sanction I could not hope to be listened to E III 14 443 8

SANCTIONED (4)
to judge how far he was sanctioned by parental authority NA II 15 243 10
extravagance however sanctioned--& tho' complacently W 323 3
am persuaded that when sanctioned by the express authority PP I 19 109 21
into a marriage which has not been properly sanctioned." PP III 15 363 22

SAND (2)
in toiling up it's long ascent half rock, half sand.-- S 1 363 1
bathing--fine hard sand--deep water 10 yards from the S 1 369 1

SANDCROFT HILL (1)
And when we got to the bottom of Sandcroft Hill, what do MP II 2 189 5

SANDERSONS (1)
The Parrys and Sandersons luckily are coming to-night you SS II 8 192 3

SANDITON (66)
Mr Parker of Sanditon; this lady, my wife Mrs Parker.-- S 1 368 1
in the parish of Sanditon, may be unknown at this distance S 1 368 1
from the coast--but Sanditon itself--everybody has heard S 1 368 1
has heard of Sanditon,--the favourite--for a young & S 1 368 1
to a small village like Sanditon, precluded by its size S 1 368 1
No sir, I assure you, Sanditon is not a place-----" S 1 368 1
Such a place as Sanditon sir, I may say was wanted, was S 1 369 1
the subject of Sanditon, a complete enthusiast.-- S 2 371 1
Sanditon,--the success of Sanditon as a small, fashionable S 2 371 1
some medical man at Sanditon, which the nature of the S 2 371 1
last year from trying Sanditon on that account--& probably S 2 372 1
very anxious to get to Sanditon this summer, could hardly S 2 372 1
Sanditon was a second wife & 4 children to him--hardly S 2 372 1
to follow him to Sanditon as soon as possible--and healthy S 2 373 1
possible pleasure which Sanditon could be made to supply S 2 374 1
could send everyone to Sanditon, who asked his advice, & S 2 374 1
The great lady of Sanditon, was Lady Denham; & in their S 3 375 1
in speculation, Sanditon itself could not be talked of S 3 375 1
parish of Sanditon, with manor & mansion house made a part. S 3 375 1
in the neighbourhood of Sanditon had succeeded in removing S 3 375 1
to her own house at Sanditon, she was said to have made S 3 375 1
into the improvement of Sanditon with a spirit truly S 3 376 1
"He is a warm friend to Sanditon--said Mr Parker--& his S 3 377 1
lady as a companion at Sanditon house, she had brought S 3 377 1
to Clara's admission at Sanditon, as no bad S 3 378 1
of their Sanditon Breezes, that loveliness was complete. S 3 379 1
brings us to Sanditon--modern Sanditon--a beautiful spot.-- S 4 380 1
I wish we may get him to Sanditon. S 4 382 1
church & neat village of Sanditon, which stood at the foot S 4 382 1
woods & enclosures of Sanditon house and whose height S 4 383 1
expected such a sight at a Shoemaker's in old Sanditon!-- S 4 383 1
In ascending, they passed the Lodge-Gates of Sanditon S 5 385 1
chance of seeing them at Sanditon I am sorry to say.-- S 5 386 1
line settled at Sanditon, it wd be no recommendation to us. S 5 387 1
As for getting to Sanditon myself, it is quite an S 5 387 1
Most sincerely do we wish you a good season at Sanditon, & S 5 388 1
So anxious for Sanditon! S 6 392 1
The conversation turned entirely upon Sanditon, its S 6 393 1
Sanditon house as I do;--it is not for my own pleasure.-- S 6 393 1
Oh! pray, let us have none of the Tribe at Sanditon. S 7 394 1
who having been at Sanditon h-- drove on to pay their S 7 399 1
me at Sanditon house, as I did last summer--but I shan't.-- S 7 401 1
here, or even a Co--since Sanditon had been a public place. S 7 401 1
& stay at Sanditon house, she will find herself mistaken.-- S 7 401 1
I to be filling my house to the prejudice of Sanditon?-- S 7 401 1

One day soon after Charlotte's arrival at Sanditon, she S 9 406 1
sight of poor old Sanditon--and the attack was not very S 9 407 1
the same post & pressed for the recommendation of Sanditon. S 9 408 1
link of connection that Sanditon had been recommended by S 9 408 1
to Mrs D. more doubtingly on the subject of Sanditon.-- S 9 409 1
that the largest house at Sanditon cannot be too large. S 9 409 1
family coming to Sanditon, said Mr P. as he walked with S 9 411 1
he recommended Sanditon;--without my appearing however-- S 9 412 1
her, and now she was at Sanditon, intending to make some S 10 412 1
Mrs G.-- being a stranger at Sanditon, was anxious for a S 10 419 1
had all entered Sanditon in those two hack chaises. S 11 420 1
to Sanditon, but the others all happened to be absent.-- S 11 421 1
Mrs G. had preferred a small, retired place, like Sanditon, S 11 421 1
Sanditon also, till their circumstances were retreived. S 11 421 1
in which they moved in Sanditon" to use a proper phrase, S 11 421 1
of all the visitors at Sanditon, & on one side, whatever S 11 422 1
Charlotte had been 10 days at Sanditon without seeing S 12 423 1
Sanditon without seeing Sanditon house, every attempt at S 12 423 1
friend & her little girl, on this walk to Sanditon house.-- S 12 425 1
as it might happen, at Sanditon--but the hotel must be his S 12 425 1
The road to Sanditon h. was a broad, handsome, planted S 12 426 1
SANDITON-HOUSE (1)
time, we can always buy what we want at Sanditon-House.-- S 4 380 1
SANDS (7)
of low rock among the sands make it the happiest spot for P III 11 95 9
They went to the sands, to watch the flowing of the tide, P III 12 102 1
one end of the sands to the other, without saying a word. P IV 2 132 16
Airings to dinner--but the sands & the terrace always S 4 384 1
He longed to be on the sands, the cliffs, at his own house, S 4 384 1
& tranquillity on the terrace, the cliffs, & the sands.-- S 6 389 1
as she ascended from the sands to the terrace, a S 9 406 1
SANDWICH (1)
once set going, even the sandwich tray, and Dr. Grant MP I 7 65 13
SANDWICHES (1)
regular supper; merely sandwiches, &c. set out in the E II 11 254 45
SANDY-HAIRED (2)
figure, though sandy-haired) without observing that every P IV 3 142 13
as Colonel Wallis, and certainly was not sandy-haired. P IV 3 142 13
SANG (7)
or sang, and whether she was fond of riding on horseback. NA I 8 56 11
so attentively while she sang to them; and when the visit SS I 8 36 1
They read, they talked, they sang together; his musical SS I 10 48 8
Mrs. Hurst sang with her sister, and while they were thus PP I 10 51 46
She played and sang;--and drew in almost every style; but E I 6 44 19
They sang together once more; and Emma would then resign E II 8 227 86
Frank Churchill sang again. E II 8 227 87
SANG-FROID (1)
sang-froid, and go away without making her any reply!-- SS III 3 282 15
SANGUINE (31)
General Tilney was not less sanguine, having already NA II 2 140 9
temper was cheerful and sanguine, and he might reasonably SS I 1 4 4
a greater degree, that sanguine expectation of happiness SS I 2 8 2
Dashwood was equally sanguine; but the expectation of the SS III 7 309 7
Her sister, however, still sanguine, was willing to SS III 7 310 9
however, you have not yet made him equally sanguine." SS III 9 338 19
as sure of attending, & sanguine hopes were entertained W 314 1
The sanguine hope of good, however, which the benevolence PP III 5 287 33
though she was not very sanguine in expecting it, the PP III 6 296 8
should offer as you are so sanguine in expecting." MP I 1 7 7
and puny, but but was sanguine in the hope of her being MP I 1 11 19
imagined; as well as the sanguine views and spirits of the MP I 2 21 34
"I am not very sanguine as to our play"--said Miss MP I 15 149 61
was often under the influence of much less sanguine views. MP II 9 267 22
alone seemed to his sanguine and pre-assured mind to stand MP II 13 302 9
note, and was not less sanguine, as to its effect, than MP III 1 311 1
operating on an active, sanguine spirit, of more warmth MP III 2 326 2
the determined views and sanguine perseverance of the MP III 2 329 11
earnest in hoping, and sanguine in believing, that it MP III 3 335 6
On her father, her confidence had not been sanguine, but MP III 8 389 3
would convey to the sanguine mind of her correspondent, MP III 14 436 16
I cannot be so sanguine as Mr. Weston. E I 14 121 14
on his coming, and I wish Mr. Weston were less sanguine." E I 14 122 21
for Mr. Elton's sanguine state of mind, he tried to take E I 15 131 32
33
much more sober: but a sanguine temper, though for ever E I 18 144 2
in a very sanguine hope, after a series of what had E II 4 181 3
I would not have you too sanguine; though, however it may E III 4 342 39
Mr. Weston's sanguine temper was a blessing on all his E III 15 445 11
His sanguine temper, and fearlessness of mind, operated P III 4 27 4
All his sanguine expectations, all his confidence had been P III 4 29 8
easy to please;--of a sanguine turn of mind, with more S 2 372 1
SANGUINELY (1)
had due notice, and he sanguinely hoped that neither dear E III 1 318 13
SANK (6)
Her spirits sank under the glow of theirs, and she felt MP I 18 170 24
do him good; it rather sank than raised his comfort; and MP II 10 279 21
were to be well tried, he sank as quietly as possible into MP III 3 341 31
had risen to meet him, but sank down again on finding MP III 7 379 20
beloved place, the hearts of both sisters sank a little. MP III 15 446 35
Her spirits sank. P IV 10 227 65
SARAH (7)
Sally, or rather Sarah, (for what young lady of common NA I 2 19 3
Her father, mother, Sarah, George, and Harriet, all NA II 14 233 9
and wonder; though Sarah indeed still indulged in the NA II 14 234 10
this engagement," said Sarah, "but why not do it civilly?" NA II 14 234 11
Here, Sarah, come to Miss Bennet this moment, and help her PP III 13 344 7
Vague wishes of getting Sarah thither, had occurred before P IV 1 122 3
I wish Sarah was here to doctor you, but I am no doctor P IV 11 238 46
SARAH'S (1)
sir," was information on Sarah's side, which produced only NA II 15 243 9
SARCASTIC (4)
Her manner had been neither sententious nor sarcastic, but W 346 21
Mr. Bennet was so odd a mixture of quick parts, sarcastic PP I 1 5 34
before, observed in a sarcastic manner, and with a glance, MP I 15 148 60
moment, added, with only sarcastic dryness, "if Mr. Perry E I 12 106 60
SARCASTICALLY (1)
the room, he observed sarcastically, "there are few among P III 3 18 5
6
SARSENET (1)
wore her puce-coloured sarsenet; and she looked so NA I 15 118 13
SASH (3)
of a western sun gaily poured through two sash windows! NA II 9 193 6
Come be quick, be quick! where is your sash my dear?" PP III 13 344 9
and throw up a sash, without its being suspected. E II 11 252 31
SASHED (2)
at the two superior sashed windows which were open to look E II 6 197 5
sashed windows below, and casements above, in Highbury. E III 14 437 8
SASHES (2)
She saw their sashes untied, their hair pulled about their SS I 21 120 6
that she had but two sashes, and had never learnt French; MP I 2 14 7
SAT (193)
The poor girl sat all this time without opening her lips; LS 20 276 3
& sat with him in his room, talking over the whole matter. LS 24 285 2
said Mrs. Allen, as they sat down near the great clock, NA I 4 31 1
of the place where they sat; he seemed to be moving that NA I 8 53 3
Allen's bosom, Catherine sat erect, in the perfect use of NA I 8 53 3
Her plan for the morning thus settled, she sat quietly NA I 9 60 1
and, therefore, while she sat at her work, if she lost her NA I 9 60 1
she sat peaceably down, and saw Thorpe sit down by her. NA I 9 62 10
as Catherine and Isabella sat together, there was then an NA I 10 70 1
in which he sat, and forced him to hear her explanation. NA I 12 93 4
seen where he had hitherto sat, but his father remained, NA I 12 93 5
have been miserable if I had sat down the whole evening. NA II 1 134 39
"This is my favourite place," said she, as they sat down NA II 3 143 1
And then his hat sat so well, and the innumerable capes of NA II 5 157 5
with which he spoke, and sat pale and breathless, in a NA II 6 165 6
filled her eyes, and even ran down her cheeks as she sat. NA II 10 203 8
Catherine sat down, breathless and speechless. NA II 13 225 19
Henry had been there, Henry had sat by her and helped her. NA II 13 228 27
from her companion, who sat as deep in thought as herself; NA II 13 228 27
As soon as breakfast was over, she sat down to fulfil her NA II 14 235 14
Mrs. Jennings sat on Elinor's right hand; and they had not SS I 13 67 61
Elinor," said she, as she sat down to work, "and with how SS I 15 77 22
been oftenest joined, and sat at the instrument gazing on SS I 16 83 3
sat down to table indignant against all selfish parents. SS I 17 90 1
fullest extent--and he sat for some time silent and dull. SS I 17 95 50
Elinor sat down to her drawing-table as soon as he was out SS I 19 104 10
From a reverie of this kind, as she sat at her drawing- SS I 19 105 13
the same time, and they all sat down to look at one SS I 19 106 21
had done before; and Elinor sat down to the card table SS II 2 151 41
She sat in silence almost all the way, wrapt in her own SS II 4 160 2
in writing to her mother, and sat down for that purpose. SS II 4 160 4
sat down to the breakfast table with a happy countenance. SS II 5 167 3
was not there--and she sat down, equally ill-disposed to SS II 5 171 30
other, or sat down by the fire in melancholy meditation. SS II 5 172 39
to tell her, sat for some time without saying a word. SS II 5 172 40
She sat by the drawing room fire after tea, till the SS II 6 175 1
doing less, Lady Middleton sat down to Casino, and as SS II 6 175 2
She sat in an agony of impatience, which affected every SS II 6 176 6
to hold up her head, and sat in such a general tremour as SS II 7 181 7
any foundation for it, then sat down to write her mother SS II 9 203 10
she sat at least seven minutes and a half in silence. SS II 12 229 3
no power to wound them, sat pointedly slighted by both. SS II 12 232 16
Again they all sat down, and for a moment or two all were SS II 13 242 25
too much or too little, and sat deliberating over her SS III 4 287 24
He too was much distressed, and they sat down together in SS III 4 288 26
For a short time he sat deep in thought, after Elinor had SS III 4 290 36
37
And with this pleasing anticipation, she sat down to re- SS III 4 291 45
than the fatigue of having sat up to have her bed made; SS III 7 310 9
and the servant who sat up with her, for she would not SS III 7 312 17
it, she walked silently towards the table, and sat down. SS III 8 317 7
Had I sat down to wish for any possible good to my family, SS III 9 336 10
from their notice, sat earnestly gazing through the window. SS III 10 342 7
She moved away and sat down. SS III 12 358 8
to be open, she sat down again and talked of the weather. SS III 12 359 12
by all but Elinor, who sat with her head leaning over her SS III 12 360 24
This only need be said;--that when they all sat down to SS III 13 361 3
days before Lucy called and sat a couple of hours with me. SS III 13 370 37
contemplating her, he then sat in silence for some minutes W 346 21
visit, and sat about ten minutes with him in his library. PP I 3 9 3
Mrs. Long told me last night that he sat close to her for PP I 5 19 10
Hurst, by whom Elizabeth sat, he was an indolent man, who PP I 8 35 2
dining-parlour, and sat with her till summoned to coffee. PP I 8 37 21
He then sat down by her, and talked scarcely to any one PP I 11 54 2
When they sat down to supper, therefore, she considered it PP I 18 98 63
of it was overheard by Mr. Darcy, who sat opposite to them. PP I 18 99 64
as quietly as possible, she sat down again, and tried to PP I 19 104 7
almost out of her senses, sat on the edge of her chair, PP II 6 162 11
Lady Catherine, Sir William, and Mr. and Mrs. Collins sat PP II 6 166 41
The room in which the ladies sat was backwards. PP II 7 168 1
his own apartment, had they sat in one equally lively; and PP II 7 168 1
Collins, sat for some time without speaking to any body. PP II 7 171 10
play to him; and she sat down directly to the instrument. PP II 8 173 12
They then sat down, and when her enquiries after Rosings PP II 9 177 3
It could not be for society, as he frequently sat there PP II 9 180 29
Eliza, she sat herself seriously to work to find it out.-- PP II 9 180 29
He sat down for a few moments, and then getting up walked PP II 11 189 3
from actual weakness sat down and cried for half an hour. PP II 11 193 31
some news for you," said Lydia, as they sat down to table. PP II 16 220 8
fashions from Jane, who sat some way below her, and on the PP II 16 222 21
On his quitting the room, she sat down, unable to support PP III 4 276 9
and when at length they all sat down, looked eagerly round PP III 9 315 4
to such assurance; but she sat down, resolving within PP III 9 316 5
to be interrupted, she sat down on one of the benches, and PP III 10 321 1
saw Mr. Darcy with him, and sat down again by her sister. PP III 11 333 31
She sat intently at work, striving to be composed, and PP III 11 335 39
civility would allow, and sat down again to her work, with PP III 11 335 40
He sat with them above an hour, and was in remarkably good PP III 13 344 1
thus removed, Mrs. Bennet sat looking and winking at PP III 13 345 11
She then sat still five minutes longer; but unable to PP III 13 345 12
13
as well as the other had sat down, suddenly rose, and PP III 13 346 22
of the head, and sat down without saying a word. PP III 14 351 3
Mrs. Bennet assured her that they never sat there after PP III 14 352 12
13
her father to the fire place, and they both sat down. PP III 15 362 9
aunt, of which her daughter sat in momentary dread, PP III 16 365 1
room, and from all the others when they sat down to table. PP III 17 372 1
reflection, and she sat in misery till Mr. Darcy appeared PP III 17 375 28
Bennet sat quite still, and unable to utter a syllable. PP III 17 378 42
and may; and Fanny either sat at home the whole day with MP I 4 36 7
I sat there an hour one morning waiting for anderson, with MP I 5 50 35
nature it was most astonishing to see how well she sat. MP I 7 67 16
I sat three quarters of an hour in the flower garden, MP I 7 72 42
her and the lady who sat by her; in every thing but a MP I 8 80 31
was a comfortable-sized bench, on which they all sat down. MP I 9 95 67
The sort of dread in which Fanny now sat of seeing Mr. MP I 10 101 33
And he sat down with a most gloomy countenance by Fanny. MP I 10 101 36
away to the fire where sat his mother, aunt, and Fanny, MP I 15 139 9
She either sat in gloomy silence, wrapt in such gravity as MP I 17 160 8
promptly delivered, as he sat by Lady Bertram and looked MP II 1 178 8
"I come from your theatre," said he composedly, as he sat MP II 1 184 25
many of his friends as they sat, the change of countenance, MP II 1 184 27
in Sir Thomas, when they sat round the same table, which MP II 2 191 10
in the very spot where she sat now, listening with MP II 4 207 10
towards them, and he sat silently observing them for a few MP II 7 249 49
Sir Thomas said no more; but when they sat down to table MP II 10 272 4
From that time, Mr. Crawford sat down likewise. MP II 10 279 22
She sat and cried con amore as her uncle intended, but it MP II 11 282 2
to the right hand where he sat, she felt that his were MP II 13 304 16
She thought Lady Bertram sat longer than ever, and began MP II 13 304 18
the fireplace, where sat the others, he had nothing to do MP II 13 307 35
She sat some time in a good deal of agitation, listening, MP III 1 311 3
Sir Thomas came towards the table where she sat in MP III 1 318 39
and sober sadness, as she sat musing over that too great MP III 2 329 10
They sat so much longer than usual in the dining parlour, MP III 3 334 5
He came to her, sat down by her, took her hand, and MP III 3 335 5
from her hand while she sat motionless over it--and at MP III 3 337 11
After this speech, the two girls sat many minutes silent, MP III 5 360 13
Mr. Crawford; and she sat thinking deeply of it till Mary, MP III 5 364 30
Henry Crawford came and sat some time with them; and her MP III 5 365 35
harbour, that I might have sat a few hours with you in MP III 7 378 12
as she sat in bewildered, broken, sorrowful contemplation. MP III 7 382 28
into the room together and sat down, Fanny could not MP III 7 383 31
As she now sat looking at Betsey, she could not but think MP III 7 385 40
without a clatter, nobody sat still, and nobody could MP III 8 392 11
They sat without a fire; but that was a privation familiar MP III 9 398 9
while the young people sat down upon some timbers in the MP III 10 403 15
She sat in a blaze of oppressive heat, in a cloud of MP III 15 439 9
that Emma first sat in mournful thought of any continuance. E I 1 6 5
As she sat one morning, looking forward to exactly such a E I 3 22 7
of her, if she would have sat longer, but she was in such E I 6 45 21
While she was gone, Mr. Knightley called, and sat some E I 8 57 2

likewise, sat down again, seemingly inclined for more chat. E I 8 58 9
then passing it to Harriet, sat happily smiling, and E I 9 72 15
He sat musing a little while, and then said, "but I do not E I 9 80 65
66
Emma sat with her as long as she could, to attend her in E I 13 109 6
her mind, while he not only sat at her elbow, but was E I 14 118 4
The hair was curled, and the maid sent away, and Emma sat E I 16 134 1
away, and Emma sat sat down to think and be miserable.-- E I 16 134 1
In short, she sat, during the first visit, looking at Jane E II 2 167 13
Cole told Mrs. Cole of it, she sat down and wrote to me. E II 3 173 27
respects to them as they sat together after dinner; and E II 8 213 6
There she sat--and who would have guessed how many tears E II 8 219 44
side of the circle, where sat Miss Woodhouse; and till he E II 8 220 47
Presently Mr. Knightley looked back, and came and sat down E II 8 228 88
sat down and practised vigorously an hour and a half. E II 9 231 3
He sat by her at dinner. E II 9 233 21
He sat really lost in thought for the first few minutes; E II 12 259 12
13
A few awkward moments passed, and he sat down again; and E II 12 261 32
33
of him so much, and, as she sat drawing or working, E II 13 264 1
The two ladies looked over it together; and he sat smiling E II 17 303 26
After tea, Mr. and Mrs. Weston, and Mr. Elton sat down E II 18 311 36
Poor Mr. Woodhouse trembled as he sat, and, as Emma had E III 3 336 12
which he could reach as he sat, "have your nephews taken E III 5 347 19
introduced, and who now sat happily occupied in lamenting, E III 5 347 20
He sat a little while in doubt. E III 5 350 31
was intolerable--and he sat down, at the greatest possible E III 6 363 53
When they all sat down it was better; to her taste a great E III 7 367 3
the other nothing--and she sat musing on the difference of E III 8 384 32
33
as possible; and his wife sat sighing and moralizing over E III 9 388 13
Her voice was lost; and she sat down, waiting in great E III 11 405 16
Emma's eyes were instantly withdrawn; and she sat silently E III 11 407 32
second, was his having sat talking with her nearly half an E III 11 410 35
own head and heart!--she sat still, she walked about, she E III 11 411 43
They sat down to tea--the same party round the same table-- E III 14 434 2
to be said; and having all sat down again, there was for E III 18 476 46
of Anne, while the Admiral sat by Mary, and made himself P III 6 48 17
fill with tears as she sat at the instrument, she was P III 8 71 56
being over, and he had sat down to try to make out an air P III 8 72 58
Mary sat down for a moment, but it would not do; she was P III 10 87 21
every thing else was done, sat down to his large fishing- P III 11 99 18
of him afterwards, as he sat near a table, leaning over it P III 12 112 54
to Lady Russell, and sat down close to her for ten minutes, P IV 2 134 29
Her making a fourth, when they sat down to dinner, was P IV 3 137 2
He sat down with them, and improved their conversation P IV 3 143 19
point when Anne, as she sat near the window, descried, P IV 7 175 4
She sat an hour with me on Monday evening, and gave me the P IV 9 197 40
poor sister, sat to him, and was bringing it home for her. P IV 11 232 15
Was not the very sight of the friend who sat behind you, P IV 11 244 72
& Sir Edw: as they sat, could not but observe Lady D. & S 7 395 1
His soul was the altar in which lovely woman sat enshrined, S 7 397 1
Diana--& excepting that she sat with salts in her hand, S 10 413 1
own account, had not once sat down during the space of S 10 414 1
declining it, and he sat down again with much satisfaction. S 10 415 1
completely to the fire, sat coddling and cooking it to his S 10 416 1
SATED (1)
were an amusement to his sated mind; and finding nothing MP I 12 115 3
SATIN (9)
the colour of the satin; and all minuteness of praise, all NA II 8 182 2
some prettier-coloured satin to trim it with fresh, I PP II 16 219 4
really had no pleasure in fine carpets or satin curtains. PP II 19 240 14
a blue dress, and a pink satin cloak, and afterwards am to MP I 15 138 3
know myself in a blue dress, and a pink satin cloak." MP I 15 139 10
sending for any more satin; and now I think you may give MP I 18 166 6
away Mr. Rushworth's pink satin cloak as her brother-in- MP II 1 179 10
"Very little white satin, very few lace veils; a most E III 19 484 12
and the ladies in the blue satin have seen what was going P III 5 40 44
SATIRE (2)
"Bravo!--an excellent satire on modern language." NA II 1 133 24
melancholy, just as satire or morality might prevail.-- S 7 396 1
SATIRICAL (3)
she fancied them satirical: perhaps without exactly SS II 14 246 3
what it was to be satirical; but that did not signify. SS II 14 246 3
He has a very satirical eye, and if I do not begin by PP I 6 24 16
SATISFACTION (152)
on his side of equal satisfaction, which he could have NA I 7 44 4
Woman is fine for her own satisfaction alone. NA I 10 74 22
Her satisfaction, too, in not being at the Lower Rooms, NA I 11 89 63
Catherine listened with heartfelt satisfaction. NA I 15 116 2
embraced half the inhabitants of Bath with satisfaction. NA I 15 121 27
Because I am to hope for the satisfaction of seeing you at NA II 11 210 7
Pray explain every thing to his satisfaction; or, if he NA II 12 217 2
Let me have the satisfaction of knowing that you are safe NA II 13 228 28
to give general satisfaction among all her acquaintance. NA II 16 250 5
daughters' sake with satisfaction, though as for herself SS I 3 14 2
She had great satisfaction in replying that she was going SS I 5 25 1
by the evident satisfaction of her daughter-in-law in the SS I 5 27 6
of her removal; a satisfaction which was but feebly SS I 5 27 6
Their arrival seemed to afford him real satisfaction, and SS I 6 30 6
the satisfaction of sending them his newspaper every day. SS I 6 30 6
But Sir John's satisfaction in society was much more real; SS I 7 32 2
he had the real satisfaction of a good heart; and in SS I 7 33 3
he had all the satisfaction of a sportsman; for a SS I 7 33 3
him for her own satisfaction, were now actually excited by SS I 10 49 12
If it will be any satisfaction to you, however, to be told, SS I 10 52 28
Her heart was not so much at ease, nor her satisfaction in SS I 11 54 6
I felt an immediate satisfaction and interest in the event, SS I 14 73 17
satisfaction of seeing him soon become more like himself. SS I 17 90 1
Beyond a competence, it can afford no real satisfaction, SS I 17 91 10
His visit afforded her but a very partial satisfaction, SS I 18 96 1
Mrs. Jennings had the satisfaction of discovering to be SS I 21 118 2
could have no lasting satisfaction in the company of a SS I 22 127 2
might lessen her satisfaction in the happiness of Marianne. SS II 4 159 1
It was a great satisfaction to Elinor that Mrs. Jennings, SS II 4 161 7
who often derived more satisfaction from conversing with SS II 5 168 12
and though expressing satisfaction at finding Miss SS II 5 172 40
though she saw with satisfaction the effect of it, in her SS II 10 212 1
it rather gave them satisfaction; and his inquiries after SS II 11 221 7
It was a great satisfaction to us to hear it, I assure you. SS II 11 222 11
It is a match that must give universal satisfaction. SS II 11 224 24
You shan't talk me out of my satisfaction. SS II 13 239 9
abode in Mr. Pratt's family, with any satisfaction. SS II 14 251 14
shy, expressed great satisfaction in meeting them, and on SS III 2 271 5
it aloud with many comments of satisfaction and praise. SS III 2 278 31
of surprise and satisfaction was over, "and very likely SS III 4 292 55
can have the smallest satisfaction in knowing that her son SS III 5 296 19
Elinor's satisfaction at the moment of removal, was more SS III 6 302 5
saw her with satisfaction sink at last into a slumber, SS III 7 310 9
All within Elinor's breast was satisfaction, silent and SS III 7 315 24
promised them all, the satisfaction of a sleepless night. SS III 13 363 6
Mrs. Dashwood's satisfaction, and to give her the dignity SS III 13 369 34
satisfaction in avowing her prior engagement.-- W 334 13
I propose myself the satisfaction of waiting on you and PP I 13 63 12
together with mutual satisfaction till supper put an end PP I 16 84 59
be renewed with yet greater satisfaction as sisters?-- PP I 21 117 9
Charlotte assured her friend of her satisfaction in being PP I 22 121 1
between them to the satisfaction of both; and as they PP I 22 121 2
with the greatest satisfaction, spoke of him in terms of PP II 7 170 6
reminded by her own satisfaction in being with him, as PP II 9 180 28
I do not reflect with satisfaction; it is that I PP II 12 199 5
back, with great satisfaction, a message from her ladyship, PP II 14 210 1
indeed?" cried Elizabeth, with the greatest satisfaction. PP II 16 219 5
other cause for satisfaction in the loss of the regiment. PP II 19 237 3
place, bring all the satisfaction she had promised herself. PP II 19 237 3
time to express her satisfaction, and prepare for such a PP III 2 261 5
half hour with some satisfaction, though while it was PP III 2 264 12
was left to all the satisfaction of having forced him to PP III 3 271 19
She is up stairs, and will have great satisfaction in PP III 5 286 30
reflect with augmented satisfaction on a certain event of PP III 6 297 11
not express so much satisfaction as her children expected, PP III 6 298 13
such as, upon the whole, I hope will give you satisfaction. PP III 7 302 14
The satisfaction of prevailing on one of the most PP III 8 308 1
And their mother had the satisfaction of knowing, that she PP III 8 314 22
any satisfaction, she had rather be without a confidante. PP III 9 320 35
Elizabeth had the satisfaction of receiving an answer to PP III 10 321 1
You must feel it; and the usual satisfaction of preaching PP III 11 333 29
to them all; the satisfaction of Miss Bennet's mind gave a PP III 13 348 34
though with little satisfaction, till the door was thrown PP III 14 351 1
Elizabeth had the satisfaction of seeing her father taking PP III 17 379 47
thought with greater satisfaction of their benevolent plan; MP I 2 18 23
sensible of the truest satisfaction in hearing of any MP I 2 21 34
of living with her aunt with any thing like satisfaction. MP I 3 25 17
it would give me great satisfaction to be able to do MP I 3 30 50
satisfaction in the main among their new acquaintance. MP I 3 31 59
into, much to the satisfaction of their respective MP I 4 39 11
thing to his entire satisfaction, and leaving Antigua MP I 4 40 14
her pain, and her own satisfaction in seeing Sotherton MP I 8 79 27
more engaging, and they talked with mutual satisfaction. MP I 9 96 76
will be some satisfaction in looking on now, and I think MP I 12 117 13
all serenity and satisfaction, and Julia well knew that on MP I 14 135 18
to set them right must be his only satisfaction. MP I 15 142 23
they could not rehearse with any satisfaction without her. MP I 18 171 28
looked with heartfelt satisfaction on the faces around him- MP II 1 178 8
It gives me sincere satisfaction. MP II 1 186 34
him to the hall door, were given with genuine satisfaction. MP II 2 194 21
which he had been hearing of with great satisfaction. MP II 4 211 25
of with the warmest satisfaction, as so particularly MP II 4 216 50
details with full satisfaction--seeing in them, the proof MP II 6 236 21
you can make on the subject, to your entire satisfaction. MP II 7 250 61
Could we be all assembled, our satisfaction would MP II 8 252 3
a favour or shewn a kindness more to his satisfaction. MP II 8 253 5
did not bring much satisfaction, she now walked home again- MP II 8 260 25
rise up to the genuine satisfaction of having a partner, a MP II 10 274 8
But still his attentions made no part of her satisfaction. MP II 10 278 20
I have the infinite satisfaction of congratulating you on MP II 13 298 2
satisfaction than I gave Maria's to Mr. Rushworth." MP III 1 319 39
was all that Fanny could think of with much satisfaction. MP III 2 331 17
of satisfaction, and words of simple, pleasant meaning. MP III 3 334 2
of the head to the satisfaction of her ardent lover; and MP III 3 341 31
of with some feelings of satisfaction, and views of good over MP III 6 368 9
her the smallest satisfaction; she saw nobody in whose MP III 9 395 3
with her--the general satisfaction with which the going of MP III 15 444 25
My Fanny indeed at this very time, I have the satisfaction MP III 17 461 2
a sorrow so founded on satisfaction, so tending to ease, MP III 17 461 3
pondered with genuine satisfaction on the more than MP III 17 471 29
and there was some satisfaction in considering with what E I 1 6 6
of regret; and her satisfaction--her more than E I 2 18 12
more than satisfaction--her cheerful enjoyment was so just E I 2 18 12
increased, so did their satisfaction in each other. E I 4 26 1
looked with most unfeigned satisfaction at her companion. E I 4 31 27
the same success and satisfaction, took place on the E I 6 47 30
Even your satisfaction I made sure of. E I 8 61 38
absence, she felt a satisfaction which settled her with E I 8 67 56
her at first great satisfaction, and then a little E I 12 98 2
3
actually accepting the offer with much prompt satisfaction. E I 13 110 12
got to the end of his satisfaction that James should come E I 14 117 3
there was a sort of satisfaction in seeing him behave so E II 3 179 52
twenty miles off would administer most satisfaction. E II 4 182 7
heard anything that has given me more satisfaction!-- E II 8 215 16
I assure you it has been the greatest satisfaction, E II 14 276 36
not given with equal satisfaction, and on many accounts E II 16 291 5
have the greatest satisfaction in seeing you at Hartfield." E II 16 294 27
fit that you should have the satisfaction of knowing it. E III 4 337 4
with a satisfaction which silenced, Mr. Knightley. E III 5 351 38
bare of rational satisfaction at the time, and more to be E III 8 377 1
could not but recall the attempt with great satisfaction. E III 9 386 7
much more to say with satisfaction, than a quarter of an E III 12 417 4
The quiet, heartfelt satisfaction of the old lady, and the E III 12 418 5
It would be a secret satisfaction; but the consciousness E III 16 452 7
her safety; and if the satisfaction of her well-doing E III 17 461 1
There, the surprise was not softened by any satisfaction. E III 17 469 36
the news with the warmest interest and satisfaction.-- E III 18 477 59
with so complete a satisfaction, as no remembrances, even E III 19 482 6
and to the very great satisfaction of Lady Russell, whose P III 2 14 10
to her very great satisfaction, she heard some other P III 9 79 25
It was the highest satisfaction to her, to believe Captain P III 10 82 1
and she had the satisfaction of knowing herself extremely P IV 1 121 1
fears, and spoke her satisfaction in the house in Camden- P IV 1 124 11
Elizabeth were settled there, much to their satisfaction. P IV 3 137 1
Her satisfaction in Mr. Elliot outweighed all the plague P IV 4 147 6
Their mutual friend answered for the satisfaction which a P IV 5 153 5
in Gay-Street, perfectly to Sir Walter's satisfaction. P IV 6 168 23
"But for my satisfaction; if you will have the goodness to P IV 9 202 68
She had some satisfaction in finding that he was really P IV 10 214 13
in a tone of great satisfaction--& with a look of arch S 7 399 1
declining it, and he sat down again with much satisfaction. S 10 415 1
cooking it to his own satisfaction & toasting some slices S 10 416 1
SATISFACTIONS (3)
was spent in the satisfactions of an intercourse renewed PP III 1 259 76
And the morning wore away in satisfactions very sweet, if MP I 17 159 6
of some of its highest satisfactions; and she looked E III 3 332 1
SATISFACTORILY (4)
To her the conference closed as satisfactorily as to him. MP II 3 201 23
Having so satisfactorily settled the conviction her note MP III 1 311 2
and her children were answered most satisfactorily. E I 1 9 21
They can do nothing satisfactorily without you." E II 11 253 39
SATISFACTORY (29)
Your account of Sir James is most satisfactory, & I mean LS 10 258 4
it; I wish it was more satisfactory, but it seems written LS 13 262 1
Nothing satisfactory transpires as to her reason for LS 17 270 6
shake of the head, your meditations are not satisfactory." NA I 3 29 47
would be more satisfactory if made without any companion. NA II 9 192 5
always displayed in a way so satisfactory to her sister. SS I 12 61 15
I have explained it to myself in the most satisfactory way; SS I 15 78 26
method of understanding the affair as satisfactory as this. SS I 15 78 26
This conviction, though not entirely satisfactory, gave SS II 4 161 5
all that had passed, satisfactory, convincing; and SS II 9 202 7
But now I can carry her a most satisfactory account of SS II 11 228 53
a very interesting and satisfactory paragraph, at least to SS II 14 246 1
her husband any satisfactory description of Mr. Bingley. PP I 3 9 1
forgotten him; but I have nothing satisfactory to tell you. PP I 18 95 50
Her reflections were in general satisfactory. PP I 22 122 3
farther, it was satisfactory; it was gratifying to know PP III 1 256 64
without gaining any satisfactory information; and that he PP III 6 295 5
of so satisfactory a nature, as the compliment deserved. PP III 6 295 7
for your long, kind satisfactory, detail of particulars; PP III 18 382 21
The meeting was very satisfactory on each side. MP I 4 41 17
she had made a most satisfactory acquaintance, for she had MP I 10 103 50
the most assured and satisfactory, I may execute the MP III 1 314 16
in a much more satisfactory style; and on the present E I 3 25 15
The sitting was altogether very satisfactory; she was E I 6 47 27

The most satisfactory comparisons were rising in her mind. E I 9 76 34
quick amendment; and so ended a most satisfactory meeting. E II 5 189 16
of the ball completely satisfactory to Emma--its being E II 12 257 1
for a sentence so satisfactory; and Emma was only saved E III 11 411 42
This meeting of the two parties proved highly satisfactory, P III 5 32 2

SATISFIED (213)

not equally satisfied with the behaviour of his lady. LS 5 249 1
I wish I could be as well satisfied as he is, that it was LS 6 252 2
disadvantage, & is never satisfied till he thinks he has LS 16 268 2
of my merit, is satisfied that whatever I do must be right; LS 16 269 3
my mind was entirely satisfied with the posture of affairs. LS 22 281 4
Here I concluded, & I hope you will be satisfied with my LS 25 293 3
I am satisfied--& will trouble you no more when these few LS 37 306 1
more at ease, or better satisfied with myself & everything LS 39 307 1
I am now satisfied that I never could have brought myself LS 39 308 0
1000

and perfectly satisfied with her share of public attention. NA I 2 24 28
charge he was on inquiry satisfied; for he had early in NA I 3 30 52
Their increasing attachment was not to be satisfied with NA I 4 34 7
Mrs. Allen was now quite happy--quite satisfied with Bath. NA I 5 36 3
could be; never satisfied with the day unless she spent NA I 5 36 3
James and Isabella led the way; and so well satisfied was NA I 7 47 18
away as soon as he had satisfied the demands of the other. NA I 7 51 54
and Mrs. Hughes, satisfied with having so respectably NA I 8 55 10
But be satisfied, for you are not to know any thing at all NA I 8 57 18
Catherine satisfied his curiosity. NA I 10 76 28
could go with them, and every body might then be satisfied. NA I 13 99 4
satisfied of her having a great deal of natural taste. NA I 14 111 29
If I can but be near you, I shall be satisfied. NA I 15 120 22
felt equally well satisfied, and heartily congratulated NA II 1 135 43
When the General had satisfied his own curiosity, in a NA II 8 182 2
"I trust," said the General, with a most satisfied smile," NA II 11 214 22
As long as she was happy, they would always be satisfied." NA II 13 221 2
was upon the whole well satisfied; for though her former SS I 6 29 4
mother, were perfectly satisfied with having two entire SS I 7 34 4
a compact of convenience, and the world would be satisfied. SS I 8 38 10
absent, was perfectly satisfied with her remaining at home. SS I 15 75 1
"I am perfectly satisfied of both." SS I 15 79 34
whenever she wanted them, which at least satisfied herself. SS I 16 84 5
controuled, and Elinor, satisfied with gaining one point, SS I 16 85 15
You must be satisfied with such admiration as I can SS I 18 97 4
felt as well satisfied as Marianne; the only difference in SS I 18 98 13
But Sir John would not be satisfied--the carriage should SS I 19 109 40
well-informed mind, be satisfied with a wife like her-- SS II 1 140 1
and I shall be satisfied, in being able to satisfy you. SS II 7 188 42
minutes earlier, was satisfied with the compromise; and SS II 8 198 29
Elinor's curiosity to see Mrs. Ferrars was satisfied.-- SS II 13 238 1
herself, was perfectly satisfied, and soon talked of SS II 13 243 32
But Charlotte, she would not be satisfied, so Mr. Donavan SS III 1 257 5
Mrs. Jennings, perhaps satisfied with the partial SS III 7 314 23
and opened a window-shutter, to be satisfied of the truth. SS III 7 316 29
"If that is all, you may be satisfied already,--for SS III 8 319 26
satisfied with myself, delighted with every body! SS III 8 324 42
at stake, and Marianne, satisfied in knowing her mother SS III 9 334 5
for thinking so, because satisfied that none founded on an SS III 9 336 11
At present, if I could be satisfied on one point, if I SS III 10 344 17
am now perfectly satisfied, I wish for no change. SS III 11 350 6
Marianne would not let her proceed;--and Elinor, satisfied SS III 11 352 16
17

waited at table, he had satisfied the inquiries of his SS III 11 353 22
23

& Mr E. not less satisfied with Mary, paid some W 323 3
of the day, without stopping, or I shall not be satisfied. W 341 19
I wish everybody were as easily satisfied as you--but poor W 343 19
way of business; very satisfied with himself for the same, W 348 23
"Do be satisfied with being fine yourself, & leave your W 353 26
and the principal rooms, satisfied with what the owner PP I 4 16 13
Miss Bingley was not so entirely satisfied with this reply PP I 8 40 58
miserable; but being satisfied on seeing her that her PP I 9 41 2
was satisfied, and soon afterwards ordered her carriage. PP I 9 45 35
Lydia declared herself satisfied. PP I 9 45 38
she was satisfied with the occurrences of the evening.-- PP I 18 95 48
I am perfectly satisfied. PP I 18 96 53
Mrs. Bennet was perfectly satisfied; and quitted the house PP I 18 103 77
In making me the offer, you must have satisfied the PP I 19 107 16
had every reason to be satisfied, since the refusal which PP I 20 110 1
been glad to be equally satisfied that her daughter had PP I 20 110 2
by a little curiosity, satisfied herself with walking to PP I 20 114 31
home, and be satisfied that we shall take no offence." PP I 22 124 9
over, I hope you will be satisfied with what I have done. PP I 22 125 17
I think to be wisest; and now, I hope you are satisfied." PP II 3 145 9
and her vanity was satisfied with believing that she would PP II 3 149 28
was more and more satisfied with coming, when she found PP II 5 155 3
satisfied her; his style was not penitent, but haughty. PP II 13 204 1
Take your choice, but you must be satisfied with only one. PP II 17 225 10
But it was her business to be satisfied--and certainly her PP II 19 239 8
On this point she was soon satisfied; and two or three PP III 2 262 8
Let them triumph over us at a distance, and be satisfied." PP III 5 293 67
observation to be satisfied, from the reason of things, PP III 9 318 19
hurried into her brain; but she was satisfied with none. PP III 9 320 32
and then I must endeavour to be satisfied with ignorance." PP III 9 320 33
you how little I was satisfied with her behaviour while PP III 10 325 2
Mr. Wickham was so perfectly satisfied with this PP III 11 330 1
"It must make you better satisfied that your other four PP III 11 330 11
her better satisfied with their visitors, than Elizabeth. PP III 12 339 5
I am perfectly satisfied from what his manners now are, PP III 12 343 32
Miss Bennet, I insist on being satisfied. PP III 14 354 34
If he is satisfied with only regretting me, when he might PP III 15 361 4
but they obligingly satisfied it, with the same kind of PP III 15 361 5
soon satisfied Jane by her solemn assurances of attachment. PP III 17 373 17
which could not be satisfied till she had written a long MP I 1 4 1
She is satisfied with herself. MP I 5 45 12
Mary was satisfied with the parsonage as a present home, MP I 5 47 26
But now I must be satisfied about Miss Price. MP I 5 51 41
the nine not tolerably satisfied with their lot, was now MP I 9 91 36
but she had just satisfied herself that it was not those MP I 10 97 1
heard it with an attention not so easily satisfied. MP I 11 108 4
Those who have not more, must be satisfied with what they MP I 12 118 20
"I believe we must be satisfied with less," said Maria. MP I 13 124 9
moderation myself in being satisfied with the old butler. MP I 14 134 14
stopt her in the middle, but Edmund was satisfied. MP I 16 156 26
So far from being all satisfied and all enjoying, she MP I 18 165 2
Every body was satisfied--and she was left to the tremors MP I 18 172 32
and was obliged to rest satisfied with the conviction that MP II 2 190 8
Sir Thomas was satisfied; too glad to be satisfied perhaps MP II 3 201 22
You ought to be satisfied with her two cousins." MP II 6 229 4
"But I cannot be satisfied without Fanny Price, without MP II 6 229 5
I must be satisfied with rather less ornament and beauty. MP II 7 242 24
will find yourself not satisfied with much less than it is MP II 7 243 27
Mrs. Norris was obliged to be satisfied with thinking just MP II 8 254 7
Miss Crawford's eyes which she could not be satisfied with. MP II 8 260 23
last, comfortably satisfied with herself and all about her. MP II 9 271 40
observing them, had seen enough to be tolerably satisfied. MP II 10 279 21
and habit--one so easily satisfied, the other so unused to MP II 11 285 15
"Well, well, I am satisfied. MP II 12 293 11
staircase, till she had satisfied herself of his being MP II 13 302 12
at least to appear satisfied, he quickly added, "no, no, I MP III 1 316 32
cannot expect him to be satisfied with less; and you only MP III 1 320 44
The gentleman was not so easily satisfied. MP III 2 326 1
Satisfied that the cause was now on a footing the most MP III 2 330 14
they were both better satisfied, though your warm-hearted MP III 4 353 46
be conjectured of her sentiments, and he was satisfied.-- MP III 5 356 1
Would they but love her, she should be satisfied. MP III 7 377 9
The instinct of nature was soon satisfied, and Mrs. MP III 8 389 4
I hope she will recollect it, and be satisfied, as well MP III 9 394 1
conveyed to the equally satisfied mother, which Fanny had MP III 9 396 7
seemed very well satisfied in going about together and MP III 10 403 15
I am not satisfied about Maddison.-- MP III 11 411 20
I am more and more satisfied with all that I see and hear MP III 13 423 2
It astonished her that Tom's sisters could be satisfied MP III 14 432 11
Henry's messages; be satisfied, that the spirit of each MP III 14 435 14
and Susan was more than satisfied, for she came perfectly MP III 16 448 3
Could he have been satisfied with the conquest of one MP III 17 467 19
were engaged; and had satisfied an active cheerful mind E I 2 15 1
She had been satisfied to hear and believe just what Mrs. E I 4 27 3
She had already satisfied herself that he thought Harriet E I 4 35 45
"Be satisfied," said he, "I will not raise any outcry. E I 5 40 27
and teach her to be satisfied with nothing less than a man E I 8 64 47
She did not always feel so absolutely satisfied with E I 8 67 56
Emma was soon perfectly satisfied of Mr. Martin's being no E I 9 69 2
Bates! so silly--so satisfied--so smiling--so prosing --so E I 10 84 16
now you have Emma's account, I hope you will be satisfied." E I 11 94 15
other that I could be satisfied to have my children in:-- E I 12 103 37
Be satisfied with doctoring and coddling yourself and the E I 12 104 43
vision, was very well satisfied with his muttering E I 13 110 10
coolly said, "I shall not be satisfied, unless he comes." E I 14 123 26
and be as well satisfied with him as before, and on his E I 15 124 2
He could not be satisfied without a promise--would not she E I 15 125 4
He was satisfied of there being no present danger in E I 15 128 17
18

Oh! that I had been satisfied with persuading her not to E I 16 137 11
have her father so well satisfied with his being all alone E I 16 138 18
19

But when satisfied on all these points, and their E II 5 191 28
on seeing them together, she became perfectly satisfied. E II 6 196 2
to attend, were mentioned; but he was not satisfied. E II 6 198 5
Emma had as much reason to be satisfied with the rest of E II 8 214 12
they were both perfectly satisfied that it could be from E II 8 214 13
At first, while I suppose you satisfied that Col. Campbell E II 8 219 42
we have all been so well satisfied to consider it a E II 8 226 79
have satisfied her, she might soon have been comforted. E II 9 231 4
said Harriet, quite satisfied, "I should not at all like E II 9 235 42
Weston sees no objection to it, provided you are satisfied. E II 11 250 23
Now you must be satisfied--our own dear Mrs. Weston, who E II 11 252 37
curiosity could not be satisfied by a bride in a pew, and E II 14 270 1
woman, extremely well satisfied with herself, and thinking E II 14 272 16
not," replied Mrs. Elton, with a most satisfied smile. E II 14 274 26
herself, were very well satisfied; so that Mrs. Elton's E II 15 281 2
first; and she was not satisfied with expressing a natural E II 15 282 4
Emma, in the meanwhile, could not be satisfied without a E II 16 290 4
the rest; and having satisfied the inquiries of his wife E II 17 303 24
to talk, was very well satisfied with what she did say, E II 17 304 29
would scarcely be satisfied without their promising never E III 3 336 12
"Ah! you are an odd creature!" she cried, satisfied to E III 6 355 18
that as soon as she was satisfied of her father's comfort, E III 6 357 34
you truths while I can, satisfied with proving myself your E III 7 375 61
"dear Jane would not be satisfied without its being sent E III 9 391 20
I must love him; and now that I am satisfied on one point, E III 10 398 53
at ease, and incline him to be satisfied with the match. E III 10 400 65
Satisfied that it was so, and feeling it her due, she had E III 12 415 1
at all, she believed she should be perfectly satisfied.-- E III 12 416 1
"You do not appear so well satisfied with his letter as I E III 15 448 29
them, is so perfectly satisfied, so delighted even-----" E III 16 459 48
He went to Highbury the next morning, and satisfied E III 17 468 35
must consider it as what satisfied your friend; and I will E III 18 472 22
"I am perfectly satisfied," replied Emma, with the E III 18 474 31
she became perfectly satisfied--unaccountable as it was!-- E III 19 481 1
She was fully satisfied of being still quite as handsome P III 1 7 12
though Lady Russell, as satisfied as ever with her own P III 4 29 7
especially, as she had satisfied herself in the very first P III 6 48 18
not be satisfied without his running on to give notice. P III 7 59 24
"I was as well satisfied with my appointment as you can P III 8 65 13
can get Captain Wentworth, I shall be very well satisfied." P III 9 76 15
she knew it would have satisfied neither husband nor wife; P III 10 82 1
a stile, was very well satisfied so long as the others all P III 10 86 21
She did: he was satisfied, and said no more. P III 12 117 75
She is not satisfied. P IV 4 150 17
could not be satisfied that she really knew his character. P IV 5 160 27
She, therefore, satisfied herself with common-place P IV 6 173 48
fancied she should be satisfied; and as to the power of P IV 7 180 32
even then very little satisfied with Mr. Elliot, I was P IV 9 203 70
in believing it; but I have never been satisfied. P IV 9 207 91
look, and appear quite satisfied with the curtailed P IV 10 213 10
the change; and so well satisfied with the journey in her P IV 10 219 28
And this satisfied Elizabeth: and when the invitation was P IV 10 220 29
promised for the absent, Mary was as completely satisfied. P IV 10 220 29
Her jealous eye was satisfied in one particular. P IV 10 226 64
as he became fully satisfied of his not caring for Louisa P IV 11 243 66
if she was equally satisfied with her situation, for a P IV 12 250 6
Anne, satisfied at a very early period of Lady Russell's P IV 12 251 10
done--& cook will be satisfied--which will be a great S 4 381 2
Mr P. could not be satisfied without an early visit to the S 6 389 1
were constrained to be satisfied with Sanditon also, till S 11 421 1
Miss Beauforts were soon satisfied with "the circle in S 11 421 1

SATISFIES (2)

honest flirtation which satisfies most people, but aspires LS 4 248 1
at once bewitches his senses and satisfies his judgment. E I 8 64 46

SATISFY (56)

in that respect, & that riches only, will not satisfy me. LS 2 245 1
I say all I can however to satisfy your father, & he is LS 13 263 1
are you now at leisure to satisfy me in these particulars? NA I 3 25 2
And this address seemed to satisfy all the fondest wishes NA I 7 49 43
"And is that likely to satisfy me, do you think?" NA I 8 57 19
have the goodness to satisfy me as to this dreadful riot." NA I 14 112 37
to be sure that a much smaller income would satisfy me. NA II 1 136 48
A moment's glance was enough to satisfy Catherine that her NA II 6 163 1
all hazards to satisfy herself at least as to its contents. NA II 6 164 3
Catherine was delighted enough even to satisfy the General. NA II 11 213 21
To satisfy me, those characters must be united. SS I 3 17 18
But Marianne could no more satisfy him as to the colour of SS I 9 44 21
seeing a man who could satisfy her ideas of perfection, SS I 10 49 10
you can----it will not satisfy you, I know; but you shall SS I 15 78 26
for famous you must be to satisfy all your family; and SS I 17 90 4
and I shall be satisfied, in being able to satisfy you. SS II 7 188 42
But it seemed to satisfy Lucy, for she directly replied, " SS II 13 240 14
15

about me, which it could not be in my power to satisfy." SS III 1 262 23
into the sick chamber, to satisfy herself that all SS III 7 316 27
who could satisfy them, and a ball was at any rate, a ball. PP I 17 86 10
longer,) I could not satisfy myself without resolving to PP I 19 106 10
"Thank you, sir, but a less agreeable man would satisfy me. PP II 1 138 28
to hear and satisfy his enquiries after all her family. PP II 5 155 3
could by no means satisfy Mr. Collins, and he was very PP II 6 167 42
many enquiries, which Jane was equally eager to satisfy. PP III 5 289 45
do every thing in his power to satisfy us on this head. PP III 6 295 6
to request that he will satisfy the various creditors of PP III 8 313 19
table; but Elizabeth, to satisfy her mother, went to the PP III 11 333 31
such anxious designs, or satisfy the appetite and pride of PP III 11 338 60
in terms warm enough to satisfy her feelings, though she PP III 13 348 34
every thing that could satisfy his anxiety. MP I 2 20 33
lest Mansfield should not satisfy the habits of a young MP I 4 41 15
Nothing would satisfy that good old Mrs. Whitaker, but my MP I 10 105 55
any thing that could satisfy even tragedians; and the MP I 14 130 3
satisfy him, and a short parley of compliment ensued. MP I 14 132 8

Context	Text	Vol.	Ch.	Page	Line
called out of the room to satisfy some doubts of the	MP	I	15	139	11
He will satisfy you.	MP	II	3	197	6
Fanny, still unable to satisfy herself, as to what she	MP	II	8	256	14
had not words strong enough to satisfy her own humility.	MP	II	9	264	18
tranquillity as might satisfy any looker-on, that Sir	MP	II	10	278	20
two, quite near enough to satisfy Lady Bertram, who	MP	III	3	336	10
by a different conduct; nothing else will satisfy them.	MP	III	4	352	44
any one who could satisfy the better taste she had	MP	III	17	469	24
the rise in the world which must satisfy them."	E	I	9	75	27
They seem to satisfy every body else."	E	I	18	149	25
"I suspect they do not satisfy Mrs. Weston.	E	I	18	149	26
They hardly can satisfy a woman of her good sense and	E	I	18	149	26
She saw that Enscombe could not satisfy, and that Highbury,	E	II	8	221	49
you are; but it will not satisfy your friends to have you	E	II	17	301	16
"I rather hope to satisfy you both," said Emma, "for I	E	II	18	311	39
A very little quiet reflection was enough to satisfy Emma	E	III	1	315	1
a liveliness that did not satisfy himself; but what	E	III	1	316	4
lines, to satisfy her, remained without any uneasiness.--	E	III	14	442	8
sofa, and remain there to satisfy her patient; and thus	P	III	9	79	25
In speaking of the Harvilles, he seemed unable to satisfy	P	IV	1	121	2
I can satisfy you, perhaps, on points which you would	P	IV	9	200	57
SATISFYING (8)					
eyeing the hair and of satisfying herself, beyond all	SS	I	18	98	13
not very desirous of satisfying, what seemed impertinent	SS	I	22	128	6
to all her inquiries, but without satisfying her in any.	SS	II	4	163	19
calming every fear, satisfying every inquiry of her	SS	III	7	315	25
suddenly ill;--but satisfying them instantly on that head,	PP	III	4	280	26
no proxy can be capable of satisfying to the same extent.	MP	II	7	247	42
he had true pleasure in satisfying; and when Crawford	MP	III	3	340	24
door--and accordingly satisfying myself with a breif	S		1	367	1
SATTIN (2)					
attired in one of the two Sattin gowns which went thro'	W			323	3
The party passed on--Mrs E's Sattin gown swept along the	W			327	8
SATURDAY (37)					
Monday, Tuesday, Wednesday, Thursday, Friday and Saturday	NA	I	13	97	1
We leave Bath, as she has perhaps told you, on Saturday	NA	II	2	139	7
the greatest part on Saturday--and we were coming here to	NA	II	9	195	15
From Saturday to Wednesday, however, they were now to be	NA	II	11	211	16
him to leave them on Saturday for a couple of nights.	NA	II	13	221	7
nothing of coming till Saturday night; for General Tilney,	NA	II	14	237	21
and Saturday, and did not know what was become with him.	SS	III	2	272	16
Were you not rather warm last Saturday about 9 or 10	W			358	28
through the whole of Saturday, and though they were at one	PP	I	12	60	4
hospitality till the Saturday se'night following, which I	PP	I	13	63	12
sent for him only the Saturday before, to make up her pool	PP	I	14	66	1
My aunt told me so herself on Saturday.	PP	I	14	68	14
Saturday, Sunday and Monday, endurable to Kitty and Lydia.	PP	I	17	88	15
only to the following Saturday, and having no feelings of	PP	I	19	104	1
and it was but the very Saturday night before I left	PP	I	19	105	10
He was always to have gone on Saturday, and to Saturday he	PP	I	21	115	2
from his amiable Charlotte by the arrival of Saturday.	PP	II	2	139	1
"Do you certainly leave Kent on Saturday?" said she.	PP	II	10	183	7
I must be in town next Saturday."	PP	II	14	211	7
On Saturday morning Elizabeth and Mr. Collins met for	PP	II	15	215	1
They were off Saturday night about twelve, as is	PP	III	4	274	3
father at home on the following day, which was Saturday.	PP	III	6	298	13
Soon after you left me on Saturday, I was fortunate enough	PP	III	7	302	14
On Saturday he came again.	PP	III	10	323	2
about green goose from Monday morning till Saturday night."	MP	I	11	112	31
brought no Edmund--when Saturday came and still no Edmund--	MP	II	11	286	16
appearance was not the better from its being Saturday.	MP	III	10	401	11
to the dock-yard last Saturday, and one still more to be	MP	III	12	415	1
					2
I have been returned since Saturday.	MP	III	13	420	2
Yes, Friday or Saturday; she cannot say which, because	E	II	1	159	18
Oh, yes, Friday or Saturday next.	E	II	1	159	18
"And so she is to come to us next Friday or Saturday, and	E	II	1	161	31
told me--that Mr. Martin dined with them last Saturday."	E	II	9	232	15
From Monday next to Saturday, I assure you we have not a	E	II	16	290	2
done; most likely they will be there to-morrow or Saturday.	E	II	17	304	27
at Hartfield yesterday, and spoke of it as for Saturday."	E	III	16	456	28
from Thursday to Saturday evening his absence was certain.	P	IV	10	214	13
SATURDAY'S (1)					
sigh at the approach of Saturday's constant half holiday.	MP	III	8	391	8
SAUCER (1)					
tea-maker's, a cup and saucer; and after another quarter	MP	III	7	384	36
SAUCERS (1)					
cleaned, the cups and saucers wiped in streaks, the milk a	MP	III	15	439	9
SAUCINESS (2)					
interests me, a sort of sauciness, of familiarity which I	LS		7	254	3
and then a little sauciness, she could not help saying, as	E	I	12	98	2
					3
SAUCY (7)					
"In defence of your protege you can even be saucy."	SS	I	10	50	19
every saucy speech she had ever directed towards him.	PP	III	10	327	3
that had passed, a saucy playful smile, seeming to invite,	MP	III	16	459	30
she only gave herself a saucy conscious smile about it,	E	III	15	449	35
our saucy little friend here is charmingly recovered?--	E	III	16	454	16
					17
to me, with one of your saucy looks--'Mr. Knightley, I am	E	III	17	462	9
Sidney is a saucy fellow, Miss H.--	S		5	385	1
SAUNTER (2)					
A saunter into other meadows, and through part of the	NA	II	11	214	26
strength for a two hours' saunter of this kind, coming as	MP	III	11	409	6
SAUNTERED (2)					
an hour, Mr. Palmer sauntered towards the Miss Dashwoods	SS	II	5	171	30
She went however, and they sauntered about together many	MP	II	4	208	11
SAUNTERING (2)					
soon afterwards, on seeing Mr. Elton sauntering about.	E	III	2	326	33
them, seeing neither sauntering politicians, bustling	P	IV	11	241	59
SAVAGE (1)					
Every savage can dance."	PP	I	6	25	27
SAVE (30)					
of knowing that we have done our utmost to save him.	LS		15	267	8
interference;" said I, wishing to save her the explanation.	LS		24	286	5
to me, I was not able to save that ill-fated young man--&	LS		25	293	4
She tried to eat, as well to save herself from the pain of	NA	II	13	228	27
Eager to save her mother from every unnecessary moment's	SS	III	9	333	3
in Derbyshire could then save him from having a most	PP	I	3	10	5
you, and will save all the best of the covies for you."	PP	III	11	337	53
It will save me a world of trouble and economy.	PP	III	17	377	39
To save herself from useless remonstrance, Mrs. Price	MP	I	1	4	1
well how to save her own as to spend that of her friends.	MP	I	1	8	9
Not all her precautions, however, could save her from	MP	I	3	28	38
It would save me many a heart-ache."	MP	I	5	47	24
it would supply, to save Sir Thomas from anger on finding	MP	II	1	183	23
as might save him the trouble of ever coming back again.	MP	II	2	192	11
the end of the hour, and save her from the shame of having	MP	II	4	206	4
her, she must have a constitution which nothing could save.	MP	II	6	231	9
almost any thing that might save her from her aunt Norris.	MP	III	1	322	50
that all her anxiety to save her brother-in-law's money	MP	III	6	372	21
now remained of it, save the melancholy remembrance of him	E	II	2	163	2
herself, to save her from hearing it abruptly from others.	E	II	3	177	51
save your health and credit, and restore your tranquility.	E	II	13	268	11
					12
I want you to save yourself from greater pain.	E	II	13	268	12
in her service, and save herself from being hurried into a	E	III	5	343	1
He would save himself from witnessing again such permitted,	E	III	13	432	41
me over at any time, to save you the trouble of replying."	P	III	3	17	4
Mr. ----; a Mr. (save, perhaps, some half dozen in the	P	III	3	24	36
into his own hands to save them the trouble, and once more	P	III	8	66	22
tired; it would save her full a mile, and they were going	P	III	10	90	38
still adverse to any man save one; her judgment, on a	P	IV	5	160	26
how determined he was to save himself from being cut out	P	IV	12	250	7
SAVED (32)					
moment that you can be saved from feeling a joy which	LS		24	291	18
Catherine was saved the embarrassment of attempting an	NA	II	7	175	11
neighbourhood of Woodston, saved her at the same time from	NA	II	14	231	5
with which Henry had saved her from the necessity of a	NA	II	15	244	11
plate, and linen was saved, and is now left to your mother.	SS	I	2	12	26
by a woman who never saved in her life, they were wise	SS	I	6	29	5
to them, and to be saved likewise from hearing that	SS	II	1	141	5
her temper; but she was saved the trouble of checking it,	SS	II	10	219	42
By one measure I might have saved myself.	SS	III	8	323	40
Emma was saved the trouble of apologizing, by their being	W			334	13
mind, or juster reason saved her from such mortification--	W			345	21
himself on having lately saved a friend from the	PP	II	10	185	28
This was a lucky recollection--it saved her from something	PP	III	1	246	7
There--I have saved you the trouble of accounting for it;	PP	III	18	380	5
Norris might never have saved her money; but having no	MP	I	1	8	9
might as well have saved him the trouble; that it would	MP	I	7	67	16
I wish you had saved yourself this walk home."	MP	I	7	68	19
bless the kindness which saved her from the same spirit of	MP	III	1	323	53
I could very ill spare the time, and you might have saved	MP	III	1	323	54
in her, which had saved him from its evil consequences.	MP	III	1	324	59
To all, she must have saved some trouble of head or hand;	MP	III	14	432	10
saved her, and how many messages she might have carried.	MP	III	14	432	10
in anger, might have saved them both, he had put himself	MP	III	17	468	21
a severe camp-fever, as he believed had saved his life.	E	II	2	163	4
at least very near it, and saved only be her own	E	II	7	206	2
"And then, he saved her life.	E	II	8	217	34
My being saved from pain is a very secondary consideration.	E	II	13	268	12
and Emma was only saved from raptures and fondness, which	E	III	11	411	42
advice which would have saved her from the worst of all	E	III	17	463	15
acquaintance; but still, saved as we all are by some	P	III	5	41	45
what he did, and nobody else could have saved poor James.	P	III	12	108	28
and happened to be saved; why, one can hardly imagine.	P	IV	9	203	70
SAVES (2)					
and whatever she saves, she will be able to dispose of."	SS	II	11	227	44
It saves trouble, and is a something to get me out.	E	II	16	293	12
SAVING (18)					
"Oh! Lord, it would be the saving of thousands.	NA	I	9	64	22
acceptance, with only the saving clause of papa and	NA	II	2	140	8
had some difficulty in saving her own new writing-desk	NA	II	5	155	4
Your profusion makes me saving; and if you lament over him	PP	II	17	225	13
If she is half as sharp as her mother, she is saving	PP	II	17	228	31
been despaired of, but it was then too late to be saving.	PP	III	8	308	3
the servants, and equally saving her from all possible	MP	I	4	34	1
by Mrs. Norris (with a saving, by her good management, of	MP	I	14	130	1
nobody thanked her, and saving, with delighted integrity,	MP	I	17	163	21
a most considerable saving had always arisen, and more	MP	II	2	188	3
It might not be saving them much, but it was something,	MP	II	2	189	5
estimation, your marrying early may be the saving of you.	MP	II	12	296	27
Mrs. Norris seemed as much delighted with the saving it	MP	II	13	304	19
Ay, I remember it all now; all, except your saving this	E	III	4	338	13
it must be saving her from the danger of degradation.	E	III	4	342	40
she was as desirous of saving Sir Walter's feelings, as	P	III	2	11	2
some obliging purpose of saving her sister trouble, which	P	IV	10	215	14
Only conceive sir, the advantage of saving a whole mile,	S		1	369	1
SAVINGS (1)					
could be made from the savings of an income of five	SS	I	6	29	5
SAVOURS (1)					
"Take care, Lizzy; that speech savours strongly of	PP	II	4	154	20
SAW (551)					
Mr Vernon declares that he never saw deeper distress than	LS		15	267	4
They came while we were at tea, & I never saw any creature	LS		17	269	1
We saw no more of her daughter.	LS		17	270	2
is untractable, but I never saw a face less indicative of	LS		17	270	5
I never saw a girl of her age, bid fairer to be the sport	LS		19	274	2
We all three went down altogether, & I saw my brother	LS		20	275	2
Instantly saw that something was the matter; his	LS		23	283	3
I met her on the stairs & saw that she was crying.	LS		24	285	2
my entire beleif before I saw you, but which you by the	LS		36	305	1
was just the same; they saw nothing of the dancers but the	NA	I	2	21	9
They saw nothing of Mr. Allen; and after looking about	NA	I	2	22	10
to be a prodigious bargain by every lady who saw it.	NA	I	3	28	38
Do you know, I saw the prettiest hat you can imagine, in a	NA	I	6	39	4
we parted yesterday, I saw a young man looking at you so	NA	I	6	41	16
stuff it must be before I saw it: as soon as I heard she	NA	I	7	49	40
I never saw any thing half so beautiful!	NA	I	8	57	16
long before he saw him leading a young lady to the dance.	NA	I	8	58	31
carriage in the street, or saw a speck upon her gown, she	NA	I	9	60	1
she sat peaceably down, and saw Thorpe sit down by her.	NA	I	9	62	10
Mrs. Hughes saw all the clothes after they came from the	NA	I	9	68	46
young man in the world; she saw him this morning you know:	NA	I	10	70	1
whom she most joyfully saw just entering the room with Mrs.	NA	I	10	72	8
was engaged the other evening, when he saw me sitting down.	NA	I	10	72	11
beginning, and she saw nothing of the Tilneys.	NA	I	10	74	23
saw him presently address Mr. Tilney in a familiar whisper.	NA	I	10	80	59
experience, she scarcely saw any thing during the evening.	NA	I	10	81	61
turned into Broad-Street, I saw them--does he not drive a	NA	I	11	85	33
"Yes, I know he does; I saw him.	NA	I	11	85	35
"Well, I saw him at that moment turn up the Lansdown road,-	NA	I	11	85	37
"And well they might, for I never saw so much dirt in my	NA	I	11	85	41
Catherine looked round and saw Miss Tilney leaning on her	NA	I	11	87	53
She saw them both looking back at her.	NA	I	11	87	53
How could you say, that you saw them driving up the	NA	I	11	87	53
How could you say, you saw them driving out in a phaeton?"	NA	I	11	87	53
but issuing from the door, she saw Miss Tilney herself.	NA	I	12	91	3
as soon as ever I saw you; now, Mrs. Allen, did not-----	NA	I	12	94	8
morning when I called; I saw her walk out of the house the	NA	I	12	94	9
"Well, nobody would have thought you had no right who saw	NA	I	12	95	15
"that I quite doated on you the first moment I saw you.	NA	I	15	118	11
him, I thought I never saw any body so handsome before."	NA	I	15	118	11
She saw herself at the end of a few weeks, the gaze and	NA	I	15	122	28
I suppose he saw Isabella sitting down, and fancied she	NA	II	1	132	17
Isabella, she looked up and saw her with Captain Tilney	NA	II	1	133	29
such a smart young fellow, I saw every eye was upon us."	NA	II	1	134	39
regret; and when she saw her at their next interview as	NA	II	1	137	50
In the course of the morning which saw this business	NA	II	2	138	1
When she saw her indeed surrounded only by their immediate	NA	II	4	149	1
But when Catherine saw her in public, admitting Captain	NA	II	4	149	1
She saw him grave and uneasy; and however careless of his	NA	II	4	149	1
she was to breakfast, and saw her seated with the kindest	NA	II	5	154	1
eye of Catherine, who saw little more than its	NA	II	6	165	6
behind each curtain, saw nothing on either low window seat	NA	II	6	167	10
She now plainly saw that she must not expect a manuscript	NA	II	7	172	1
She seized another sheet, and saw the same articles with	NA	II	7	172	2
but I never could, till I saw them the other day in Milsom-	NA	II	7	174	7
she should not know what was picturesque when she saw it.	NA	II	7	177	18
the Abbey, as she saw it for the first time from the lawn.	NA	II	7	177	19
Allen; and, when Catherine saw what was necessary here,	NA	II	8	184	4
And, when she saw him in the evening, while she worked	NA	II	8	187	13
She saw a large, well-proportioned apartment, an handsome	NA	II	9	193	6
"Have you had any letter form Bath since I saw you?"	NA	II	9	195	19
The world, I believe, never saw a better woman.	NA	II	9	196	23
(we were both at home) saw her repeatedly; and from our	NA	II	9	197	25
She saw that the infatuation had been created, the	NA	II	10	200	2
letter, saw plainly that it ended no better than it began.	NA	II	10	202	8
It is the prettiest room I ever saw;--it is the prettiest	NA	II	11	214	21
He is the greatest coxcomb I ever saw, and amazingly	NA	II	12	217	2
Eleanor saw that she wished to be alone; and believing it	NA	II	13	226	24
I do not suppose, Mrs. Morland, you ever saw a better-bred	NA	II	14	238	26
Elinor saw, with concern, the excess of her sister's	SS	I	1	7	13

Context	Text	Vol	Ch	Page	Line
She saw only that he was quiet and unobtrusive, and she	SS	I	3	16	7
Mrs. John Dashwood saw the packages depart with a sigh:	SS	I	5	26	4
got the nicest little black bitch of a pointer I ever saw.	SS	I	9	44	20
became collected, when she saw that to the perfect good-	SS	I	10	46	2
in Marianne's; and Elinor saw nothing to censure in him	SS	I	10	48	9
She saw it with concern; for what could a silent man of	SS	I	10	50	12
Willoughby when she saw him next, that it must be declined.	SS	I	12	59	5
name alone, she instantly saw an intimacy so decided, a	SS	I	12	59	7
I am almost sure it is, for I saw him cut it off.	SS	I	12	60	13
They saw him step into his carriage, and in a minute it	SS	I	15	76	17
They saw nothing of Marianne till dinner time, when she	SS	I	15	82	46
Marianne saw and listened with increasing surprise.	SS	I	16	87	23
Elinor saw, with great uneasiness, the low spirits of her	SS	I	18	96	1
"I never saw you wear a ring before, Edward," she cried.	SS	I	18	98	11
really felt--but when she saw how much she had pained	SS	I	18	98	12
Edward saw enough to comprehend, not only the meaning of	SS	I	18	100	23
window, and she saw a large party walking up to the door.	SS	I	19	105	13
I never saw anything so charming!	SS	I	19	107	24
"As vile a spot as I ever saw in my life," said Mr. Palmer.	SS	I	20	111	15
with us that I never saw before, it is quite charming!	SS	I	20	113	33
She began by inquiring if they saw much of Mr. Willoughby	SS	I	20	114	43
Mama saw him here once before;--but I was with my uncle at	SS	I	20	114	44
kind of sense, when she saw with what constant and	SS	I	21	120	6
She saw with maternal complacency all the impertinent	SS	I	21	120	6
She saw their sashes untied, their hair pulled about their	SS	I	21	120	6
I never saw such fine children in my life.--	SS	I	21	122	17
replied Elinor, "who ever saw the place; though it is not	SS	I	21	123	25
Elinor saw, and pitied her for, the neglect of abilities	SS	I	22	127	2
so respectable; but she saw, with less tenderness of	SS	I	22	127	2
Robert Ferrars--I never saw him in my life; but," fixing	SS	I	22	129	14
she spoke, and when Elinor saw the painting, whatever	SS	I	22	132	26
I saw you, I felt almost as if you was an old acquaintance.	SS	I	22	132	42
Elinor saw that is was his hand, and she could doubt no	SS	I	22	134	53
Perhaps you might notice the ring when you saw him?"	SS	I	22	135	54
"Not at all--I never saw him; but I fancy he is very	SS	II	2	148	19
behaved young men I ever saw; but as for Lucy, she is such	SS	II	2	148	22
understood her sister, and saw to what indifference to	SS	II	3	154	6
town or not, and when she saw her mother so thoroughly	SS	II	3	158	20
She instantly saw that it was not unnoticed by him, that	SS	II	4	162	8
about it, yet while she saw Marianne in spirits, she could	SS	II	5	167	7
Marianne persevered, and saw every night in the brightness	SS	II	5	168	10
daily occurrence, but who saw at the same time with much	SS	II	5	168	12
Elinor watched his countenance and saw its expression	SS	II	6	177	8
In a short time Elinor saw Willoughby quit the room by the	SS	II	6	178	15
Elinor, who saw as plainly by this, as if she had seen the	SS	II	7	181	7
That good lady, however, saw only that Marianne had	SS	II	7	181	7
saw a young woman so desperately in love in my life!	SS	II	7	181	7
					8
on opening the door, she saw Marianne stretched on the bed,	SS	II	7	182	12
Their good friend saw that Marianne was unhappy, and felt	SS	II	8	193	7
You saw I did not all dinner time.	SS	II	8	196	18
to compliance, and Elinor saw her lay her aching head on	SS	II	8	197	25
head on the pillow, and saw her, as she hoped, in a way to	SS	II	8	197	25
of hope and happiness, saw him, with amazement, remain the	SS	II	8	200	43
him thither, and who saw that solicitude in his disturbed	SS	II	9	204	17
He saw her concern, and coming to her, took her hand,	SS	II	9	206	25
I saw her placed in comfortable lodgings, and under proper	SS	II	9	207	26
I saw her there whenever I could, and after the death of	SS	II	9	208	28
to her mind, though she saw with satisfaction the effect	SS	II	10	212	1
respect, and though she saw her spirits less violently	SS	II	10	212	1
tell everybody she saw, how good-for-nothing he was."	SS	II	10	215	10
papers, which she saw her eagerly examining every morning.	SS	II	10	217	16
day, when she saw him crossing the street to the house.	SS	II	10	218	26
as any I ever saw; and as likely to attract the men.	SS	II	11	227	50
while Lady Middleton saw enough of fashion in his	SS	II	11	228	52
You saw it all; and was not you quite struck with it?"	SS	II	13	239	4
I saw a vast deal more.	SS	II	13	239	6
But Marianne, who saw his agitation, and could easily	SS	II	13	243	32
most incapable of being selfish, of any body I ever saw.	SS	II	13	244	40
and general curiosity; she saw every thing, and asked	SS	II	14	249	8
I immediately saw that there could be no difficulty in it,	SS	II	14	252	18
He saw the necessity of inviting the Miss Steeles	SS	II	14	253	25
and as soon as ever he saw the child, he said just as we	SS	III	1	257	5
saw the necessity of preparing Marianne for its discussion.	SS	III	1	260	10
She saw nothing of the Willoughbys, nothing of Edward, and	SS	III	2	271	5
I never saw Lucy in such a rage in my life.	SS	III	2	272	12
on Wednesday, and we saw nothing of him not all Thursday,	SS	III	2	272	16
It is as pretty a letter as ever I saw, and does Lucy's	SS	III	2	278	32
would be at, for it is as good a one as ever I saw."	SS	III	4	285	7
to drop in for ten minutes; and I saw quite enough of her.	SS	III	5	299	37
It gave her no surprise that she saw nothing of Mrs.	SS	III	7	309	6
the cordials prescribed, saw her with satisfaction sink at	SS	III	7	310	9
anxiety was--but when she saw, on her frequent and minute	SS	III	7	315	25
of recovery continued, and saw Marianne at six o'clock	SS	III	7	315	25
She instantly saw that her ears had not deceived her.	SS	III	7	316	29
drawing-room,--she entered it,--and saw only Willoughby.	SS	III	7	316	31
declared; for I went, I saw her, and saw her miserable,	SS	III	8	323	40
for I went, I saw her, and saw her miserable, and left her	SS	III	8	323	40
"Yes, I saw every note that passed."	SS	III	8	325	49
she would appear to those, who saw her last in this world.	SS	III	8	327	55
You saw what she said.	SS	III	8	328	61
John Middleton, and when he saw who I was--for the first	SS	III	8	330	69
Elinor's delight, as she saw what each felt in the meeting,	SS	III	9	334	5
not conceal his distress; I saw that it equalled my own,	SS	III	9	336	12
to very different effect, saw nothing in the Colonel's	SS	III	10	340	3
fortitude to conceal, now saw with a joy, which no other	SS	III	10	341	6
nor blame; and when she saw, as she assisted Marianne from	SS	III	10	342	7
she had been crying, she saw only an emotion too natural	SS	III	10	342	7
mound,--there I fell; and there I first saw Willoughby."	SS	III	10	344	12
					13
I considered the past; I saw in my own behaviour since the	SS	III	10	345	28
I saw that my own feelings had prepared my sufferings, and	SS	III	10	345	28
Whenever I looked towards the past, I saw some duty	SS	III	10	346	28
Elinor, according to her expectation, saw on the two or	SS	III	11	352	19
fixed her eyes upon Elinor, saw her turning pale, and fell	SS	III	11	353	24
The servant, who saw only that Miss Marianne was taken ill,	SS	III	11	353	25
But she soon saw how likely it was that Lucy, in her self-	SS	III	12	357	2
She saw them in an instant in their parsonage-house; saw	SS	III	12	357	3
In Edward--she knew not what she saw, nor what she wished	SS	III	12	357	4
She saw her mother and Marianne change colour; saw them	SS	III	12	358	9
where, rather than at her, saw her hurry away, and perhaps	SS	III	12	360	26
hurry away, and perhaps saw--or even heard, her emotion;	SS	III	12	360	26
so lately it had been,--saw him honourably released from	SS	III	13	363	8
from his former engagement, saw him instantly profiting by	SS	III	13	363	8
watch her at such a moment, saw her looking rather	W			328	8
soon afterwards she saw the smartest officer of the sett,	W			330	11
It seems but the day before yesterday that I saw them all	W			334	13
Some saw no fault, & some no beauty--.	W			337	17
to expect it; for I never saw him before in my life.--	W			344	20
She saw that her sister in law despised her immediately.--	W			350	24
as careless as her son, if she saw me in this condition."--	W			357	28
whose beauty he had heard much; but he saw only the father.	PP	I	3	9	3
I never in my life saw any thing more elegant than their	PP	I	3	13	18
lively; and I never saw such happy manners!--so much ease,	PP	I	4	14	2
"I certainly saw Mr. Darcy speaking to her."	PP	I	5	19	11
but Elizabeth still saw superciliousness in their	PP	I	6	21	1
She danced four dances with him at Meryton; she saw him	PP	I	6	22	7
"You saw me dance at Meryton, I believe, sir."	PP	I	6	25	29
saw how much affection and solicitude they shewed for Jane.	PP	I	7	33	44
"Yes, and her petticoat; I hope you saw her petticoat, six	PP	I	8	36	6
"I never saw such a woman.	PP	I	8	40	54
I never saw such capacity, and taste, and application, and	PP	I	8	40	54
Miss Bingley saw, or suspected enough to be jealous; and	PP	I	10	52	53
Elizabeth, at work in the opposite corner, saw it all with	PP	I	11	54	2
a person whom I never saw in the whole course of my life."	PP	I	13	61	4
"No; he never saw him till the other morning at Meryton."	PP	I	18	96	52
as if hearing it all, and saw in the motion of his lips	PP	I	18	98	61
She saw her in idea settled in that very house in all the	PP	I	18	98	63
Her mother's thoughts she plainly saw were bent the same	PP	I	18	98	63
of delights which she saw no likelihood of sharing, was	PP	I	18	100	68
She looked at his two sisters, and saw them making signs	PP	I	18	100	68
of conference, no sooner saw Elizabeth open the door and	PP	I	20	110	1
flowing hand; and Elizabeth saw her sister's countenance	PP	I	21	116	6
and saw her dwelling intently on some particular passages.	PP	I	21	116	6
removal surprised her, she saw nothing in it really to	PP	I	21	116	8
a conviction that if they saw him depart, they could not	PP	I	22	121	1
which ceased when he saw her no more; but though the	PP	II	1	137	26
They saw him often, and to his other recommendations was	PP	II	1	138	30
They had all been very ill-used since she last saw her	PP	II	2	139	3
"I never saw a more promising inclination.	PP	II	2	141	9
Without supposing them, from what she saw, to be very	PP	II	2	142	18
most agreeable man I ever saw--and if he becomes really	PP	II	3	144	7
with Mr. Darcy, that they they scarcely ever saw him.	PP	II	3	147	23
Four weeks passed away, and Jane saw nothing of him.	PP	II	3	147	25
She saw instantly that her cousin's manners were not	PP	II	5	155	3
Mr. Collins no sooner saw the two girls than he began to	PP	II	5	159	20
prospects; and Elizabeth saw much to be pleased with,	PP	II	6	161	8
aspect; but she soon saw that her friend had an excellent	PP	II	7	168	1
Elizabeth saw what he was doing, and at the first	PP	II	8	174	12
					13
in comparing them, she saw there was less captivating	PP	II	9	180	28
saw on looking up that Colonel Fitzwilliam was meeting her.	PP	II	10	182	2
her utter amazement, she saw Mr. Darcy walk into the room.	PP	II	11	188	3
She paused, and saw with no slight indignation that he was	PP	II	11	191	13
She saw him start at this, but he said nothing, and she	PP	II	11	192	25
					26
I had not been long in Hertfordshire, before I saw, in	PP	II	12	197	5
She saw the indelicacy of putting himself forward as he	PP	II	13	207	5
I never saw such a long chin in my life.	PP	II	16	220	10
Elizabeth saw directly that her father had not the	PP	II	16	223	26
But I cannot find out that Jane saw any thing of him in	PP	II	17	227	27
Mr. Bennet saw that her whole heart was in the subject;	PP	II	18	231	19
					20
She saw with the creative eye of fancy, the streets of	PP	II	18	232	22
She saw herself the object of attention, to tens and to	PP	II	18	232	22
She saw all the glories of the camp; its tents stretched	PP	II	18	232	22
to complete the view, she saw herself seated beneath a	PP	II	18	232	22
"And you saw him frequently?"	PP	II	18	234	29
She saw that he wanted to engage her on the old subject of	PP	II	18	235	39
saw and admired every remarkable spot and point of view.	PP	III	1	245	3
proprietor; but Elizabeth saw, with admiration of his	PP	III	1	246	5
She approached, and saw the likeness of Mr. Wickham	PP	III	1	247	9
Some people call him proud; but I am sure I never saw any	PP	III	1	249	38
the other two that they now saw Mr. Darcy, the gardener's	PP	III	1	251	52
With a glance she saw, that he had lost none of his recent	PP	III	1	254	57
off, Elizabeth saw him walking slowly towards the house.	PP	III	1	257	66
them to a window, and they saw a gentleman and lady in a	PP	III	2	260	1
to compose herself, saw such looks of enquiring surprise	PP	III	2	260	2
did catch a glimpse, she saw an expression of general	PP	III	2	263	10
When she saw him thus seeking the acquaintance, and	PP	III	2	263	10
been a disgrace; when she saw him thus civil, not only to	PP	III	2	263	10
They saw much to interest, but nothing to justify enquiry.	PP	III	2	264	13
Elizabeth soon saw that she was herself closely watched by	PP	III	3	268	5
easily kept, because she saw that the suspicions of the	PP	III	3	268	8
more to talk; and Elizabeth saw that he was anxious for	PP	III	3	269	8
Miss Bingley saw all this likewise; and, in the imprudence	PP	III	3	269	8
					9
saw any one so much altered as she is since the winter.	PP	III	3	270	13
as to my father, I never in my life saw him so affected.	PP	III	4	275	5
Be that as it may, she saw him go with regret; and in this	PP	III	4	279	24
An hour, however, saw the whole completed; and Mr.	PP	III	4	281	29
Till I was in Kent, and saw so much both of Mr. Darcy and	PP	III	5	284	16
"I never saw any one so shocked.	PP	III	5	292	62
behind the house, they saw the housekeeper coming towards	PP	III	7	301	1
Mr. Bennet and his daughters saw all the advantages of	PP	III	8	313	20
she, who never heard nor saw any thing of which she chose	PP	III	9	316	8
He saw Wickham, and afterwards insisted on seeing Lydia.	PP	III	10	322	2
They met again on Sunday and then I saw him too.	PP	III	10	324	2
And you saw the old housekeeper, I suppose?	PP	III	10	327	11
When I last saw her, she was not very promising.	PP	III	10	328	22
as soon as they were out of the house, "as ever I saw.	PP	III	11	330	8
in Meryton last night; I saw her passing by, and went out	PP	III	11	331	15
together, she said, "I saw you look at me to day, Lizzy,	PP	III	11	331	16
					17
in Hertfordshire, she saw him from her dressing-room	PP	III	11	333	30
saw Mr. Darcy with him, and sat down again by her sister.	PP	III	11	333	31
short period saw him looking both pleased and embarrassed.	PP	III	11	335	41
The dinner was as well dressed as any I ever saw.	PP	III	12	342	28
a turn--and everybody said, they never saw so fat a haunch.	PP	III	12	342	28
And, my dear Jane, I never saw you look in greater beauty.	PP	III	12	342	28
letter was finished, she saw, to her infinite surprise,	PP	III	13	346	22
I remember, as soon as ever I saw him, when he first came	PP	III	13	348	40
I saw them the night before last."	PP	III	14	352	14
Her carriage remained at the door, and Elizabeth saw that	PP	III	14	353	20
Maria; and as Elizabeth saw no occasion for making it a	PP	III	16	365	2
to the library, she saw Mr. Darcy rise also and follow him,	PP	III	17	375	28
dearly bought, when she saw Mr. Darcy exposed to all the	PP	III	18	384	26
her affection, she now saw the object of open pleasantry.	PP	III	19	388	61
so dull, she must add, she saw no harm in the poor little	MP	I	2	20	31
womanly; and their father saw them becoming in person,	MP	I	2	20	33
Of the rest she saw nothing; nobody seemed to think of her	MP	I	2	21	34
Her brother was not handsome; no, when they first saw him,	MP	I	5	44	2
I never saw a place so altered in my life.	MP	I	6	53	2
I never saw a place that wanted so much improvement in my	MP	I	6	53	4
from Sir Thomas, but I saw the bill, and I know it cost	MP	I	6	54	11
Of Rears, and vices, I saw enough.	MP	I	6	60	49
I am glad you saw it all as I did."	MP	I	7	64	11
meadow she immediately saw the group--Edmund and Miss	MP	I	7	67	16
had hold of her hand; she saw it, or the imagination	MP	I	7	67	16
of mind, of feeling; she saw nature, inanimate nature,	MP	I	8	81	31
that first great path, we saw directly to the end of it.	MP	I	9	95	63
We looked down the whole vista, and saw it closed by iron	MP	I	9	94	63
opinion; and he directly saw a knoll not half a mile off,	MP	I	10	97	4
"Yes, yes, we saw him.	MP	I	10	101	30
Mrs. Rushworth, who saw nothing but her son, was quite at	MP	I	12	118	17
She saw a glance at Maria, which confirmed the injury to	MP	I	14	133	12
and saw his look, and felt what his sensations must be.	MP	I	15	139	4
all the advantage of what I saw at Ecclesford; and it is	MP	I	15	139	6
Fanny saw and pitied much of this in Julia; but there was	MP	I	17	163	20
Tom was engrossed by the concerns of his theatre, and saw	MP	I	17	163	21
and sister's apology, saw them preparing to go as she	MP	II	1	177	6
her eyes to his face, she saw that he was grown thinner	MP	II	1	178	7
I never saw Mansfield wood so full of pheasants in my life	MP	II	1	181	16
from notice herself, saw all that was passing before her.	MP	II	1	185	27
Sir Thomas saw all the impropriety of such a scheme among	MP	II	2	187	2
Sir Thomas soon appeared, and Maria saw with delight and	MP	II	2	192	11
I went up for my shawl I saw them from the staircase	MP	II	4	211	28
in the intimacy which he saw with so much pleasure	MP	II	4	216	50
likely, for I never saw it more threatening for a wet	MP	II	5	221	34
drawing room, Sir Thomas saw them off in as good time as	MP	II	5	222	41
a new gown, and you never saw her so well dressed before.	MP	II	6	230	6
me to any thing"--and saw, with lively admiration, the	MP	II	6	235	19
continued Edmund, "and how did you like what you saw?"	MP	II	7	241	20
in order to look about me; and saw how it might all be.	MP	II	7	242	23

terrible nuisance, I never saw a house of the kind which MP II 7 243 27
She saw decision in his looks, and her surprize and MP II 8 253 4
were what they had ever been, but he saw them no longer. MP II 9 264 17
Starting and looking up she saw across the lobby she had MP II 9 267 24
To the former she was an interesting object, and he saw MP II 10 272 1
Fanny saw that she was approved; and the consciousness of MP II 10 272 4
she did not like, and she saw his eye glancing for a MP II 10 274 8
Miss Crawford saw much of Sir Thomas's thoughts as he MP II 10 276 14
She was happy whenever she looked at William, and saw how MP II 10 278 20
confusion, for her brother saw her only as the supposed MP II 12 295 22
He saw her lips formed into a no, though the sound was MP III 1 316 32
he looked at his niece, and saw the state of feature and MP III 1 320 45
She saw nothing more of her uncle, nor of her aunt Norris, MP III 1 323 53
He then saw Mr. Crawford, and received his account.-- MP III 2 329 11
Meanwhile, he saw enough of Fanny's embarrassment to make MP III 3 335 6
He was very willing to hope that Crawford saw clearer; and MP III 3 336 7
I once saw Henry the 8th acted.-- MP III 3 338 13
Edmund saw it all, and saw Fanny so determined not to see MP III 3 339 21
I saw your lips move. MP III 3 340 25
on looking at Fanny he saw rather a flush of vexation, he MP III 3 344 44
of herself, when she saw his look, and heard him reply, " MP III 4 347 19
that heard him read, and saw you listen to Shakespeare the MP III 4 348 23
I then saw him behaving, as it appeared to me, so very MP III 4 349 25
"As a by-stander," said Fanny, "perhaps I saw more than MP III 4 350 27
"It is above a week since I saw Miss Crawford." MP III 4 352 39
Edmund saw weariness and distress in her face, and MP III 4 354 48
Still, however, Fanny, was oppressed and wearied; he saw MP III 4 355 55
Edmund considered it every way, and saw nothing but what MP III 6 368 9
to travel post, when she saw Sir Thomas actually give MP III 6 372 21
The next morning saw them off again at an early hour; and MP III 7 376 6
I saw her. MP III 7 377 7
be invited on; but when she saw there was no other door, MP III 7 377 10
smallest satisfaction; she saw nobody in whose favour she MP III 9 395 3
Susan saw that much was wrong at home, and wanted to set MP III 9 395 4
submission and forbearance, saw also with sympathetic MP III 9 397 8
and only discomposed if she saw her boys run into danger, MP III 11 408 2
As she opened and saw its length she prepared herself for MP III 13 420 1
I was three weeks in London, and saw her (for London) very MP III 13 420 2
The last time I saw Crawford was at Mrs. Fraser's party. MP III 13 423 2
I saw him draw back surprised, and I was sorry that Mr. MP III 13 423 2
question or two if she saw her daughter with a letter in MP III 13 428 14
She saw the proof of it in Miss Crawford, as well as in MP III 14 433 12
Mrs. R. knows a decline is apprehended; he saw her this MP III 14 435 14
at the present moment, she saw so much to condemn; the MP III 14 435 15
be a witness--but that he saw nothing--of the tranquil MP III 15 445 31
important points; and she saw, therefore, in all its MP III 16 449 5
She saw that it was. MP III 16 451 13
She seldom saw him--never alone--he probably avoided being MP III 16 453 16
She saw it only as folly, and that folly stamped only by MP III 16 455 19
I saw her change countenance. MP III 16 458 30
I imagined I saw a mixture of many feelings--a great, MP III 16 458 30
He saw how ill he had judged, in expecting to counteract MP III 17 463 7
reverse in himself, clearly saw that he had but increased MP III 17 463 7
He saw Mrs. Rushworth, was received by her with a coldness MP III 17 467 20
and aid, Sir Thomas saw repeated, and for ever repeated MP III 17 473 31
He saw his son every year in London, and was proud of him; E I 2 17 7
Mr. Woodhouse saw the letter, and he says he never saw E I 2 18 9
every domestic comfort, or saw her go away in the evening E I 2 18 12
But in every respect as she saw more of her, she approved E I 4 26 1
of this speech, and saw no alarming symptoms of love. E I 4 31 26
Every body who saw it was pleased, but Mr. Elton was in E I 6 47 30
I never saw such a likeness in my life. E I 6 48 32
I never saw such a likeness. E I 6 48 39
I can hardly imagine the young man whom I saw talking with E I 7 51 5
"I saw her answer, nothing could be clearer." E I 8 60 35
"You saw her answer! you wrote her answer too. E I 8 60 36
Mr. Knightley saw no such passion, and of course thought E I 8 67 57
of its effects; but she saw too much of it, to feel a E I 8 67 57
I never saw any thing so hard. E I 9 72 17
saw, felt, anticipated, and remembered just as she ought. E I 9 74 21
When I look back to the first time I saw him! E I 9 75 26
sigh; and as Emma saw his spirits affected by the idea of E I 9 80 68
I never saw Mrs. Weston better in my life--never looking E I 11 94 10
saw a man more intent on being agreeable than Mr. Elton. E I 13 111 15
16
Emma soon saw that her companion was not in the happiest E I 13 113 25
Emma saw Mrs. Weston's surprize, and felt that it must be E I 15 125 6
for of course you saw there would be snow very soon. E I 15 126 10
end of it, and saw nothing extraordinary in his language. E I 17 141 4
Emma felt that, till she saw her in the way of cure, there E I 17 143 15
I do not know that I ever saw anybody more surprized. E II 1 157 7
told her it was because she saw in her the really E II 2 166 11
by fancy, that she never saw Jane Fairfax the first time E II 2 167 12
of person or of mind, she saw so little in Highbury. there, E II 2 167 12
Emma saw its artifice, and returned to her first surmises. E II 2 169 16
Emma saw his anxiety, and wishing to appease it, at least E II 3 171 14
15
Mr. Knightley soon saw that he had lost his moment, and E II 3 172 23
Well, Mr. Knightley, and so you actually saw the letter; E II 3 174 31
32
I was sitting near the door--Elizabeth saw me directly; E II 3 178 52
I am sure she saw me, but she looked away directly, and E II 3 178 52
fancy, he looked round and saw me; for instead of going on E II 3 178 52
Emma saw him only once; but two or three times every day E II 4 184 10
was always among those who saw no fault in Mr. Elton, and E II 4 184 10
Emma could imagine she saw a touch of the arm at this E II 5 188 11
round to Harriet, she saw something like a look of spring, E II 5 189 16
She opened the parlour door, and saw two gentlemen sitting E II 5 190 21
we passed her house--I saw Miss Bates at the window. E II 5 194 38
You saw her with the Campbells when she was the equal of E II 5 194 40
He saw no fault in the room, he would acknowledge none E II 6 198 5
good-looking houses as he saw around him, could not E II 6 198 5
A very successful visit:--I saw all the three ladies; and E II 6 198 7
much she saw to like in his disposition altogether. E II 7 205 2
"I dare say you would; but I, simple I, saw nothing but E II 8 218 37
Campbell was the giver, I saw it only as paternal kindness, E II 8 219 42
introduced, and she saw the blush of consciousness with E II 8 220 45
She saw that Enscombe could not satisfy, and that Highbury, E II 8 221 49
be restored as before, she saw Frank Churchill looking E II 8 222 54
I never saw any thing so outree!-- E II 8 222 56
He was gone immediately; and Emma soon saw him standing E II 8 222 57
And as I looked at her, though I never saw her appear to E II 8 223 63
I saw she had execution, but I did not know she had any E II 9 232 11
breakfast, you would be quite frightened if you saw it. E II 9 237 46
finest looking home-baked apples I ever saw in my life.' E II 9 238 51
of a smile, when she saw that with all the deep blush of E II 10 243 22
Miss Woodhouse and Mr. Frank Churchill; I never saw any E II 10 245 48
It was some days before she saw Jane Fairfax, to judge of E II 12 263 42
and the next half hour saw her as anxious and restless E II 13 267 9
"considering we never saw her before, she seems a very E II 14 279 54
I saw Jane Fairfax and conversed with her, with admiration E II 15 289 40
"I never saw any gentleman's handwriting"--Emma began, E II 16 297 48
writes one of the best gentlemen's hands I ever saw." E II 16 297 49
I saw a vast deal of that in the neighbourhood round Maple E II 17 299 8
Emma saw how Mr. Weston understood these joyous prospects. E III 1 317 9
I saw her as I came in; she was standing in the entrance. E III 2 322 19
I saw you the other day as you rode through the town----- E III 2 323 19
Emma saw it. E III 2 327 34
and by only turning her head a little she saw it all. E III 2 327 34
I never saw any thing equal to the comfort and style-- E III 2 329 45
the cotton, Emma saw only a small piece of court plaister. E III 4 338 9
Emma then looked up, and immediately saw how it was; and E III 4 341 29
30
saw him coming--his noble look--and my wretchedness before. E III 4 342 38
"myself creating what I saw," brought him yet stronger E III 5 344 2
From Frank Churchill's face, where he thought he saw E III 5 346 17
He saw a short word prepared for Emma, and given to her E III 5 348 22
He saw that Emma had soon made it out, and found it highly E III 5 348 22
it, and it was not long before he saw it to be Dixon. E III 5 348 23
Mr. Knightley thought he saw another collection of letters E III 5 349 25
I saw the word, and am curious to know how it could be so E III 5 349 27
"I have lately imagined that I saw symptoms of attachment E III 5 350 36
what he saw, for he was slow, constant, and methodical.-- E III 6 362 43
She saw it all; and entering into her feelings, promoted E III 6 363 51
"I saw you first in February. E III 7 369 16
I saw you first in February." E III 7 369 16
Her eyes were towards Donwell as she walked, but she saw E III 8 378 2
whose judgement never fails her, saw farther than I did. E III 8 380 15
She saw in a moment all the possible good. E III 9 388 13
She saw it all with a clearness which had never blessed E III 11 408 33
She knew that he saw such recommendations in Harriet; he E III 11 409 35
She saw that there never had been a time when she did not E III 11 412 45
She saw, that in persuading herself, in fancying, in E III 11 412 45
taken a few turns, when she saw Mr. Knightley passing E III 13 424 1
and my father as great extenuation of what you saw amiss. E III 14 439 8
all about it, and instantly saw what she had been doing. E III 14 442 8
No; do not pity me till I reached Highbury, and saw how E III 14 443 8
Do not pity me till I saw her wan, sick looks.-- E III 14 443 8
Emma saw symptoms of it immediately in the expression of E III 16 453 12
13
old lady's replies, she saw her with a sort of anxious E III 16 453 12
13
Elton, but to Miss Woodhouse, as the latter plainly saw. E III 16 457 34
the affair to her; but she saw in it only increase of E III 17 467 31
He saw the advantages of the match, and rejoiced in them E III 17 468 33
"I know you saw my letter, and think you may remember my E III 18 477 59
Harriet to church, and saw her hand bestowed on Robert E III 19 482 6
Perhaps, indeed, at that time she scarcely saw Mr. Elton, E III 19 482 6
could secure, and saw no dignity in any thing short of it. P III 2 12 5
I never saw quite so wretched an example of what a sea- P III 3 20 16
for Anne; but Lady Russell saw it very differently.-- P III 4 27 3
She saw in it but an aggravation of the evil. P III 4 27 4
for an agreement, and saw nothing, therefore, but good P III 5 32 2
You saw how hysterical I was yesterday." P III 7 56 10
when it is ill; and you saw, this morning, that if I told P III 7 56 12
that part of the room; he saw her, and, instantly rising, P III 8 72 58
59
an eldest son, and he saw things as an eldest son himself. P III 9 76 14
She saw how her own character was considered by Captain P III 10 89 34
Wentworth long, when they saw him coming after them, with P III 11 96 11
to repose, as she ought; saw how very desirable it was P III 12 103 3
"The last time I saw her, she had a red nose, but I hope P IV 3 142 14
forgotten, and instantly saw, with amusement at his little P IV 3 143 18
Colonel Wallis said it, and Lady Russell saw it; but it P IV 4 147 6
acquaintance in Bath; she saw nobody equal to him; and it P IV 4 148 9
Anne saw the misery of such feelings. P IV 5 156 12
She saw that there had been bad habits; that Sunday- P IV 5 161 27
Lady Russell saw either less or more than her young friend, P IV 5 161 30
her young friend, for she saw nothing to excite distrust. P IV 5 161 30
She saw no reason against their being happy. P IV 6 167 20
Anne saw them wherever she went. P IV 6 168 24
and the very next time Anne walked out, she saw him. P IV 7 174 1
For a few minutes she saw nothing before her. P IV 7 175 5
She saw that he saw Elizabeth, that Elizabeth saw him, P IV 7 176 9
have lost the right moment for seeing whether he saw them. P IV 7 179 31
I walked and rode a great deal; and the more I saw, the P IV 8 183 13
again by Captain Wentworth, she saw that he was gone. P IV 8 184 18
Anne saw nothing, thought nothing of the brilliancy of the P IV 8 185 21
She saw him not far off. P IV 8 189 47
He saw her too; yet he looked grave, and seemed irresolute, P IV 8 189 47
towards the bench, as if he saw a place on it well worth P IV 8 190 47
"Oh! you saw enough for your own amusement.-- P IV 9 193 12
I saw nothing reprehensible in what Mr. Elliot was doing. P IV 9 201 64
He saw you then at Lyme, and liked you so well as to be P IV 9 206 88
forward, she saw more to distrust and to apprehend. P IV 10 212 1
I never saw any body in my life spell harder for an P IV 10 213 4
quite sincere, but now she saw insincerity in every thing. P IV 10 214 11
She saw Mrs. Clay fairly off, therefore, before she began P IV 10 215 14
she saw a great deal of most characteristic proceeding. P IV 10 216 19
I saw them turn the corner from Bath-Street just now. P IV 10 222 34
The careless expression was life to Anne, who saw that P IV 10 224 49
and, wherever she looked, saw symptoms of the same. P IV 10 226 63
She knew him; she saw disdain in his eye, and could not P IV 10 226 65
Anne caught his eye, saw his cheeks glow, and his mouth P IV 10 227 67
"I was six weeks with Edward," said he, "and saw him happy. P IV 11 243 67
I saw you with the very person who had guided you in that P IV 11 243 74
On the contrary, when he saw more of Captain Wentworth, P IV 12 248 2
more of Captain Wentworth, saw him repeatedly by daylight P IV 12 248 2
good Sence with even liberality which he saw in Lady D.-- S 3 378 1
house, & saw the top of the house itself among its groves. S 4 383 1
above twice--and never saw the face of a doctor in all my S 6 394 1
this, & her praise of that; but I saw what she was about.-- S 7 399 1
I saw through it all.-- S 7 399 1
Charlotte directly saw that it was laying her open to S 7 400 1
She spoke this so seriously that Charlotte instantly saw S 7 401 1
Clara saw through him, & had not the least intention of S 8 405 2
the little lawn, when she saw a lady walking nimbly behind S 9 406 1
I knew Miss Heywood the moment I saw her before me on the S 9 407 1
contain herself as she saw him watching his sisters, while S 10 417 1
out what sort of carriage it was, which they saw coming up. S 12 425 1
stepping to the pales, she saw indeed--& very decidedly, S 12 426 1

SAYINGS (1)
he repeated the smart sayings of one lady, detailed the W 359 28

SCALE (4)
John, was on so simple a scale, and the rent so uncommonly SS I 4 24 21
Miss Darcy was tall, and on a larger scale than Elizabeth; PP III 2 261 4
such collections on a very grand scale are not uncommon. E I 9 69 4
was not the very first distinction in the scale of vanity. E III 2 319 4

SCALLOPED (1)
the minced chicken and scalloped oysters with an urgency E I 3 24 11

SCAMPERED (1)
the servant having now scampered up, the gentlemen jumped NA I 7 44 3

SCAMPERING (1)
Why must she be scampering about the country, because her PP I 8 36 5

SCANDAL (1)
rivals, the school for scandal, wheel of fortune, heir at MP I 14 130 3

SCANDALOUS (9)
is now he is persuaded only a scandalous invention. LS 11 259 1
so easily beleived the scandalous tales invented by LS 14 264 4
The confusion there is scandalous. NA I 14 113 39
His behaviour to myself has been scandalous; but I verily PP I 16 78 20
never failed to contradict as a most scandalous falsehood. PP I 23 129 12
Though I know it must be a scandalous falsehood; though I PP III 14 353 26
"A most scandalous, ill-natured rumour has just reached me, MP III 15 437 3
As no scandalous, ill-natured rumour had reached her, it MP III 15 438 4
should think it scandalous to go for the sake of his heir. P IV 10 224 48

SCANDALOUSLY (1)
& to persuade Reginald that she has scandalously belied me. LS 7 254 3

SCANTILY-FURNISHED (1)
in the confined and scantily-furnished chamber that she MP III 7 387 47

SCANTY (5)
"is this fair? is this just? are my ideas so scanty? SS I 10 47 5
make any part of the scanty communication which passed W 321 2
what she ought to the stock of their scanty comforts. E II 1 155 2

any restraint beyond her own scanty rule of good-breeding. E II 15 288 39
ball of credit which a scanty neighbourhood afforded; and P III 1 7 12

SCARBOROUGH (1)

The others have been gone on to Scarborough, these three PP III 12 342 24

SCARCE (5)

be got at market this morning, it is so uncommonly scarce." NA I 9 68 38
He danced only four dances, though gentlemen were scarce; PP II 8 175 18
eatable--hautboys very scarce--chili preferred--white wood E III 6 358 35
"I have scarce had the pleasure of seeing you, Miss E III 16 454 18
But Heiresses are monstrous scarce! S 7 401 1

SCARCELY (189)

family are at war, & Manwaring scarcely dares speak to me. LS 2 245 1
be exaggerated; it is scarcely possible that two men LS 6 252 2
Miss Manwaring's lover was scarcely better founded. LS 14 264 4
He scarcely dares even allow her to be handsome, & when I LS 17 271 7
with whom she had scarcely ever exchanged two words before. LS 22 282 6
I am so much agitated by delight that I can scarcely hold LS 23 283 2
She is besides afraid of me; she scarcely loves me. LS 24 288 11
I had scarcely concluded my last, when Wilson brought me LS 25 292 1
of at Bath, that I can scarcely command myself at all. LS 28 298 2
I arrived last night about five, & had scarcely swallowed LS 29 299 2
to present, in having been scarcely ten months a widow. LS 29 299 3
After such a discovery as this, you will scarcely affect LS 36 306 2
was seldom stubborn, scarcely ever quarrelsome, and very NA I 1 14 1
and her daughters had scarcely begun the history of their NA I 4 33 5
but in which there was scarcely ever any exchange of NA I 5 36 3
on such works, and scarcely ever permitting them to be NA I 5 37 4
The two dances were scarcely concluded before Catherine NA I 8 56 12
haste to the window, and scarcely had she time to inform NA I 9 61 1
In a very few minutes she re-appeared, having scarcely NA I 9 62 7
Scarcely had they worked themselves into the quiet NA I 10 75 25
experience, she scarcely saw any thing during the evening. NA I 10 81 61
talked in phrases which conveyed scarcely any idea to her. NA I 14 110 28
to say or to hear; and scarcely had she felt a five NA II 3 143 1
opinion of him; but she scarcely heard his voice while his NA II 5 155 3
children's spirits, and scarcely any thing was said but by NA II 5 156 4
chapel of St. Anthony, scarcely two miles off--could you NA II 5 159 21
your own chamber, but scarcely have you been able to NA II 5 160 21
way into a chamber, and scarcely staying to hope she would NA II 5 162 28
marked an expenditure scarcely more interesting, in NA II 7 172 2
She was all impatience to see the house, and had scarcely NA II 7 177 18
her indiscriminating eye scarcely discerned the colour of NA II 8 182 2
of the court, she could scarcely believe it, or overcome NA II 8 183 2
him, yet she could scarcely hope to have escaped his eye; NA II 9 192 4
broken heart, and could scarcely give an intelligible NA II 10 199 1
o'clock, when Catherine scarcely thought it could be three. NA II 11 214 26
Scarcely, however, had she convicted her fancy of error, NA II 13 222 9
the minds of both, scarcely another word was said by NA II 13 229 31
been such as was scarcely possible to reach his knowledge. NA II 14 230 3
and explanation; but scarcely, within the time, could they NA II 14 233 10
unutterable happiness, scarcely opened her lips, dismissed NA II 15 243 10
up his wife, she had scarcely sinned against his character, NA II 15 247 14
It taught him that he had been scarcely more misled by by NA II 16 251 6
"My love, it will be scarcely a separation. SS I 3 17 17
Music seems scarcely to attract him, and though he admires SS I 3 17 18
with so much composure, she seemed scarcely to notice it. SS I 3 18 18
In my heart I feel little--scarcely any doubt of his SS I 4 21 15
They were scarcely ever without some friends staying with SS I 7 32 1
twisted in the fall, and she was scarcely able to stand. SS I 9 42 8
stand together and scarcely spoke a word to any body else. SS I 11 54 3
He was confused, seemed scarcely sensible of pleasure in SS I 16 87 23
from whom however she scarcely expected to receive any SS II 3 154 6
other people, you will scarcely have any thing at all, and SS II 3 156 13
her own meditations, and scarcely ever voluntarily SS II 4 160 2
She could scarcely eat any dinner, and when they SS II 4 161 6
of abode, for although scarcely settled in town, Sir John SS II 5 170 29
Her letter was scarcely finished, when a rap foretold a SS II 5 172 40
Scarcely a word was spoken during their return to Berkeley- SS II 6 178 16
which at first was scarcely less violent than Marianne's. SS II 7 182 12
a conduct which can scarcely be called less than insulting; SS II 7 187 42
They had scarcely been two minutes by themselves, before SS III 5 298 33
But as it was, such a notion had scarcely ever entered her SS III 6 305 16
she continued till noon, scarcely stirring from her SS III 7 313 21
The Colonel too!--perhaps scarcely less an object of pity!- SS III 7 315 26
me--(may I say it?) was scarcely less warm than her's; and SS III 8 322 36
of duty or friendship; scarcely allowing sorrow to exist SS III 10 346 28
Scarcely had she so determined it, when the figure of a SS III 12 358 8
chairs, it might have seemed a matter scarcely perceived.-- W 336 14
She had scarcely run her eye thro' the whole, before she W 338 18
Emma scarcely knew how to answer such a proposition--& the W 349 24
Mr. Darcy had at first scarcely allowed her to be pretty; PP I 6 23 12
Breakfast was scarcely over when a servant from PP I 7 31 29
30
by Mr. Darcy, her sister scarcely less so; and as for Mr. PP I 8 35 2
I scarcely know any one who cannot do all this, and I am PP I 8 39 45
He then sat down by her, and talked scarcely to any one PP I 11 54 2
to his purpose, he scarcely spoke ten words to her, PP I 12 60 4
During dinner, Mr. Bennet scarcely spoke at all; but when PP I 14 66 1
The latter part of this address was scarcely heard by PP I 18 92 24
her last partner she had scarcely replied, before Mr. PP I 18 96 56
Mrs. Hurst and her sister scarcely opened their mouths PP I 18 102 75
He scarcely ever spoke to her, and the assiduous PP I 21 115 1
the truth, we are scarcely less eager to meet her again. I PP I 21 117 14
Bingley's name was scarcely ever mentioned between them. PP II 1 137 25
with Mr. Darcy, that they they scarcely ever saw him. PP II 3 147 23
walk and cross walk, and scarcely allowing them an PP II 5 156 4
I have scarcely any hesitation in saying that she will PP II 5 157 7
Scarcely any thing was talked of the whole day or next PP II 6 160 4
Scarcely a syllable was uttered that did not relate to the PP II 6 166 41
Charlotte, but was scarcely ever prevailed on to get out. PP II 7 168 2
Elizabeth had scarcely time to disclaim all right to the PP II 7 170 9
disposed towards every one, had been scarcely ever clouded. PP II 11 188 1
a young man who had scarcely any other dependence than on PP II 12 196 5
had been given, was scarcely the work of a moment.-- PP II 12 199 5
Her feelings as she read were scarcely to be defined. PP II 13 204 1
the whole letter, though scarcely knowing any thing of the PP II 13 204 2
and careless, would scarcely give them a hearing. PP II 14 213 17
the mortification of Kitty, are scarcely to be described. PP II 18 230 12
While she spoke, Wickham looked as if scarcely knowing PP II 18 234 35
astonished and confused, scarcely dared lift her eyes to PP III 1 251 52
To Mr. and Mrs. Gardiner he was scarcely a less PP III 2 261 6
she wished or feared it most, she could scarcely determine. PP III 3 268 5
them, and that there was scarcely an eye which did not PP III 3 268 8
Her brother, whose eye she feared to meet, scarcely PP III 3 270 11
for consideration, and scarcely knowing what she felt, PP III 4 274 4
He seemed scarcely to hear her, and was walking up and PP III 4 278 19
He would scarcely be ten pounds a-year the loser, by the PP III 8 309 4
which her marriage would scarcely seem valid, exceeded all PP III 8 310 10
gained in austerity; and he scarcely opened his lips. PP III 9 315 4
She had scarcely needed her present observation to be PP III 9 318 19
not answer without confusion, said scarcely any thing. PP III 11 335 43
to whom he spoke, had scarcely patience enough to help PP III 12 341 18
He scarcely needed an invitation to stay supper; and PP III 13 345 19
"It taught me to hope," said he, "as I had scarcely ever PP III 16 367 10
You know not, you can scarcely conceive, how they have PP III 16 367 14
You could scarcely escape discredit and misery. PP III 17 376 35
her brother-in-law, with scarcely any private fortune, and MP I 1 3 1
and could scarcely speak to be heard, or without crying. MP I 2 13 4
her comfort; she could scarcely swallow two mouthfuls MP I 2 13 4
Mansfield Park, and was scarcely ever seen in her offices. MP I 3 31 59
Mrs. Grant knew nothing, she had scarcely seen them since. MP I 4 40 15
of our apricot is; he is scarcely ever indulged with one, MP I 6 54 13
The houses, though scarcely half a mile apart, were not MP I 7 67 16
there, for Maria would scarcely raise her eyes from her MP I 7 71 31
taken also; but this was scarcely received as an amendment; MP I 9 84 2
One scarcely sees a clergyman out of his pulpit." MP I 9 93 46
"You scarcely touch me," said he. MP I 9 94 59
hear the others, and who scarcely risked an original MP I 10 97 3
At first he scarcely said any thing; his looks only MP I 10 101 33
though Julia, who had scarcely opened her lips before, MP I 15 148 60
would do, she could scarcely see an object in that room MP I 16 151 2
especially, but he had scarcely more than time to feel MP II 1 182 22
good opinion, and saying scarcely any thing, he did his MP II 1 186 35
She had scarcely ever been at the parsonage since the MP II 4 206 5
at Sotherton, she had scarcely ever dined out before; and MP II 5 219 27
as soon as possible; and scarcely ten days had passed MP II 6 233 14
was scarcely beyond her merits, rejoice in her prospects. MP II 12 294 18
The conclusion was scarcely intelligible from increasing MP II 13 307 32
Young as you are, and having seen scarcely any one, it is MP III 1 316 31
sake, she could scarcely dare mention to their father. MP III 1 317 38
time, that her not loving him now was scarcely regretted. MP III 2 327 4
"My dear Fanny," replied Edmund, scarcely hearing her to MP III 4 349 26
Quite unlike his usual self, he scarcely said any thing. MP III 5 365 35
Fanny believed there was scarcely a second feeling in MP III 6 367 5
have scarcely an enquiry made after Mansfield! MP III 7 382 29
and loudness; and now he scarcely ever noticed her, but to MP III 8 389 3
an hour, having spent scarcely twenty-four hours in London MP III 10 400 8
Mrs. Price, it appeared, scarcely ever stirred out of MP III 10 401 10
and I believe, there is scarcely a young lady in the MP III 10 402 11
which, in fact, I am scarcely justified in asking; and if MP III 13 422 2
They scarcely spoke. MP III 13 423 2
and so it continued, with scarcely any change till Easter. MP III 14 430 5
made her think it scarcely possible for them to support MP III 15 442 21
She had, indeed, scarcely the shadow of a hope to soothe MP III 15 442 22
Fanny had scarcely passed the solemn-looking servants, MP III 15 447 37
now he could scarcely comprehend to have been possible. MP III 17 463 9
Scarcely had he done regretting Mary Crawford, and MP III 17 470 25
which she has scarcely allowed herself to entertain a hope. MP III 17 471 28
to company, there was scarcely an evening in the week in E I 3 20 1
There can scarcely be a doubt that her father is a E I 8 62 41
really believed, would scarcely try to conceal any thing E I 14 122 18
He joined them immediately, and with scarcely an E I 15 124 1
great, and they were scarcely less acceptable to Emma on E I 15 128 17
and the night; but scarcely had she begun, scarcely had E I 15 129 24
scarcely had she begun, scarcely had they passed the sweep- E I 15 129 24
was such as to make them scarcely secondary to Donwell E I 16 136 9
and Mr. Weston had scarcely finished his explanation of E II 5 190 21
Of pride, indeed, there was, perhaps, scarcely enough; his E II 6 198 5
We scarcely got home in time. E II 16 293 11
my word, I have scarcely ever had a bad morning before." E II 16 296 35
Emma had foreseen, would scarcely be satisfied without E III 3 336 12
neglect of prospect, had scarcely a sight--and its E III 6 358 35
dispersed way, scarcely any three together, they E III 6 360 38
She had scarcely a stronger regret than for her past E III 9 389 16
Emma scarcely heard what was said.-- E III 10 395 36
his nephew--gave his consent with scarcely a difficulty. E III 10 398 55
a possibility;--but scarcely are her remains at rest in E III 10 398 55
do it, and have scarcely a doubt of its happy effect.-- E III 14 436 7
Perhaps, indeed, at that time she scarcely saw Mr. Elton, E III 19 482 6
it is a time of life at which scarcely any charm is lost. P III 1 6 11
Lady Russell, indeed, had scarcely any influence with P III 2 16 16
seldom heard of, and scarcely at all regretted, when the P III 6 50 28
ships, that it had made scarcely any impression at the P III 6 51 31
lodgers almost all gone, scarcely any family but of the P III 11 95 9
As to the wretched party left behind, it could scarcely be P III 12 110 43
She thought it could scarcely escape him to feel, that a P III 12 116 72
She could scarcely imagine a more cheerless situation in P IV 5 153 8
Such she believed were his words; but scarcely had she P IV 8 188 37
But, upon my word, I am scarcely sensible of his P IV 10 213 7
and of yesterday and to-day there could scarcely be an end. P IV 11 241 59
eager eye which hoped to see scarcely any empty houses.-- S 4 384 1

SCARCITY (1)

Elizabeth Bennet had been obliged, by the scarcity of PP I 3 11 7

SCARE (1)

either low window seat to scare her, and on placing a hand NA II 6 167 10

SCARE-CROWS (1)

Such scare-crows as the streets were full of! P IV 3 142 13

SCARLET (4)

cousin should come in a scarlet coat, and it was now some PP I 13 64 20
gay, and dazzling with scarlet; and to complete the view, PP II 18 232 22
singing hero of a farce in his scarlet coat and cocked hat. MP I 13 123 6
me that there was no scarlet fever at Cobham, I have been E I 11 95 19

SCATTER (1)

But then, they who scatter their money so freely, never S 6 392 1

SCATTERED (12)

eagerly collected every scattered sheet which had burst NA II 7 172 1
detestable papers then scattered over the bed, she rose NA II 7 173 3
and several neat farm houses scattered here and there. SS I 18 97 4
the river, the trees scattered on its banks, and the PP III 1 246 5
chesnuts which were scattered over the intermediate lawn. PP III 3 267 2
rest of the party being scattered about the chapel, Julia MP I 9 88 19
and agitation richly scattered--the lady had been so E II 4 181 4
the table was quickly scattered over with alphabets, which E III 5 347 20
over the gardens in a scattered, dispersed way, scarcely E III 6 360 38
rocks, where the scattered forest trees and orchards of P III 11 95 9
from different people scattered here and there, while many P IV 9 203 70
a letter from under the scattered paper, placed it before P IV 11 236 40

SCENE (65)

Can you, in short, be prevailed on to quit this scene of NA II 2 139 7
by him since the dreadful scene had passed, which released NA II 8 186 6
she supposed the guilty scene to be acting, being, NA II 8 188 19
indulged, every meal a scene of ease and good-humour, NA II 13 220 1
again the scene of agitated spirits and unquiet slumbers. NA II 13 227 26
Amongst the objects in the scene, they soon discovered an SS I 16 86 16
remembering that in a scene of similar distress last week, SS I 21 121 10
So up he flew directly, and a terrible scene took place, SS III 1 259 7
Mrs. Ferrars too--in short it has been a scene of such SS III 1 265 36
An heavy scene however awaited me, before I could leave SS III 8 323 40
which became the solemn scene, said to Miss Edwardes, "the W 327 8
Mr. Bennet, in equal silence, was enjoying the scene. PP I 18 103 75
The next day opened a new scene at Longbourn. PP I 19 104 1
Change of scene might be of service--and perhaps a little PP II 2 141 10
to describe any particular scene, will we begin PP II 4 154 23
Mr. Collins expected the scene to inspire, and was but PP II 6 161 8
Elizabeth found herself quite equal to the scene, and PP II 6 162 11
the melancholy scene so lately gone through at Rosings. PP II 14 210 1
of varying the humble home scene, I think we may flatter PP II 15 215 4
the chief of the scene between Mr. Darcy and herself. PP II 17 224 1
To the little town of Lambton, the scene of Mrs. PP II 19 240 12
she looked on the whole scene, the river, the trees PP III 1 246 5
they pointed out, she distinguished no part of the scene. PP III 1 253 55
the general air of the scene; it was a spot less adorned PP III 1 253 57
were now approaching the scene of her former pleasures, PP III 1 258 76
their last lively scene in Hunsford parsonage, the PP III 2 263 10
It was exactly a scene, and exactly among people, where he PP III 9 320 32
The season, the scene, the air, were all favourable to MP I 7 65 13
You have a very smiling scene before you." MP I 10 99 16
looking out on a twilight scene, while the Miss Bertrams, MP I 11 108 4
like her's towards the scene without, where all that was MP I 11 112 35
more out of themselves by contemplating such a scene." MP I 11 113 35
Be it only half a play--an act--a scene; what should MP I 13 123 6
vary the scene, and exercise our powers in something new. MP I 13 125 18
still discovering such a scene, she very kindly took his MP I 15 138 1
him, that Anhalt's last scene with the Baron admitted a MP I 17 158 2

dress, their favourite scene, their friends and MP I 17 159 6
Entirely against his judgment, a scene painter arrived MP I 18 164 1
Tom himself began to fret over the scene painter's slow MP I 18 164 1
the rehearsal of the first scene between her and Mr. MP I 18 164 2
third act would bring a scene between them which MP I 18 167 12
She had read, and read the scene again with many painful, MP I 18 167 13
had got through half the scene, when a tap at the door MP I 18 169 22
At last the scene was over, and Fanny forced herself to MP I 18 170 24
It would be the last--in all probability the last scene on MP II 1 182 22
room, and given the scene painter his dismissal, long MP II 2 190 9
The scene painter was gone, having spoilt only the floor MP II 2 190 9
the back ground of the scene, and longing to be with him. MP II 10 273 7
more," to view the happy scene, and take a last look at MP II 10 280 33
for the occupation and the scene which the tea things MP III 3 335 5
at will, on the best scene, or the best speeches of each; MP III 3 337 10
scene before her than ever that spot had yet witnessed. MP III 5 357 6
"The scene we were rehearsing was so very remarkable! MP III 5 358 9
very curious, that we should have such a scene to play! MP III 5 358 9
whose house was the scene of mismanagement and discomfort MP III 8 390 6
with an impression of the scene as made her say to Harriet, E I 10 86 24 25

She meant to be very happy, in spite of the scene being E II 8 213 5
The scene enlarged; two persons appeared; Mrs. Weston and E II 9 233 25
give her change of air and scene, and quiet rational E III 9 390 16
had been a gratifying, yet almost an affecting, scene. E III 12 418 5
the nothingness, of her scene of life--such the feelings P III 1 9 18
not sorry to have the scene of it in the country, and her P III 5 33 9
for such a state, where a scene so wonderful and so lovely P III 11 95 9
length an account of the scene she had been engaged in P IV 3 144 22
in an hotel ensured a quick-changing, unsettled scene. P IV 10 221 32

SCENERY (4)
admiration of landscape scenery is become a mere jargon. SS I 18 97 7
"Oh! for the Ecclesford theatre and scenery to try MP I 13 123 6
Many parts of our best plays are independent of scenery." MP I 13 124 9
help, to ascertain what scenery would be necessary--while MP I 14 136 21

SCENES (32)
the space of two entire scenes, did she thus watch Henry NA I 12 92 4
was never withdrawn from the stage during two whole scenes. NA I 12 92 4
into scenes, where pleasures of every kind had met her. NA II 2 141 11
scenes of horror being acted within the solemn edifice. NA II 5 161 25
situations and horrid scenes, which such buildings had NA II 6 166 9
of a walk through scenes so fallen, had the General NA II 8 184 4
humanity, in its fearful review of past scenes of guilt? NA II 8 187 13
as all mention of Bath scenes were avoided, she thought NA II 13 222 8
own admiration of these scenes, and to question him more SS I 18 96 4
scenes as must prevent her ever knowning a moment's rest. SS II 10 214 6
recurrence of many past scenes of misery to his mind, SS III 10 340 2
As they approached Barton, indeed, and entered on scenes, SS III 10 342 7
"The present always occupies you in such scenes--does it?" PP I 18 93 31
that scenes might arise unpleasant to more than myself." PP I 21 115 4
of these distressing scenes; but now as the first shock is PP III 4 275 5
known, or warm her imagination with scenes of the past. MP I 9 85 3
flat, and three or four scenes to be let down; nothing MP I 13 123 8
of knowing half the scenes by heart already, he did now MP I 14 132 8
You have only two scenes, and as I shall be Cottager, I'll MP I 15 146 50
to comprehend all his scenes, but the others aspired at MP I 18 166 4
the last week, to get up a few scenes, a mere trifle. MP II 1 181 16
terrific scenes, which such a period, at sea, must supply. MP II 6 235 19
a couple of months to the scenes of her infancy, with MP III 6 369 11
him, and the lovely scenes of home must be shut out. MP III 15 447 35
some regret, from the scenes and people she had been used MP III 17 469 24
"however, it is impossible for me to behind the scenes. E II 6 202 38
The sweet scenes of autumn were for a while put by--unless P III 10 85 12
The scenes in its neighbourhood, Charmouth, with its high P III 11 95 9
any of the resembling scenes of the far-famed Isle of P III 11 95 9
Scenes had passed in Uppercross, which made it precious. P IV 1 123 8
particulars of past sad scenes, all the minutiae of P IV 9 210 97
least roused him, and the scenes of the Cobb, and at P IV 11 242 62

SCEPTICISM (1)
But Emma still shook her head in steady scepticism. E II 10 244 36

SCHEME (94)
thought it better to lay aside the scheme for the present. LS 2 245 1
she was detected in this scheme, I cannot so readily LS 17 271 7
from a fear of your interrupting the diabolical scheme? LS 24 289 12
You are to thank your brother and me for the scheme; it NA I 11 84 19
It was a strange, wild scheme." NA I 11 89 62
The Clifton scheme had been deferred, not relinquished, NA I 13 97 1
If they would only put off their scheme till Tuesday, NA I 13 99 4
a brother angry, and a scheme of great happiness to both NA I 13 103 29
Allen the half-settled scheme of her brother and the NA I 13 103 29
the most delightful scheme in the world; that nobody could NA I 15 116 1
"a famous good thing this marrying scheme, upon my soul! NA I 15 122 30
happy, and Catherine was quite delighted with the scheme. NA II 11 209 5
"I will honestly tell you of one scheme which has lately SS II 2 149 25
to such a scheme, if her elder sister would come into it. SS II 3 154 3
impediment to the present scheme which occurred to you, SS II 3 156 9
Poor Elinor!--here was a new scheme for getting her to SS III 9 339 25
introducing excess into a scheme of such rational SS III 10 343 10
no leisure to form any scheme of conduct, with which that SS III 13 366 20
"That would be a good scheme," said Elizabeth, "if you PP I 7 30 22
Elizabeth tried hard to dissuade him from such a scheme; PP I 18 97 60
Such was Miss Lucas's scheme; and appearances were so PP I 22 121 1
There was novelty in the scheme, and as, with such a PP II 4 151 1
No scheme could have been more agreeable to Elizabeth, and PP II 4 154 23
It would be such a delicious scheme, and I dare say would PP II 16 219 6
scheme, indeed, and completely do for us at once. PP II 16 220 7
body went on; but Elizabeth steadily opposed the scheme. PP II 16 223 25
found that the Brighton scheme, of which Lydia had given PP II 16 223 26
in the scheme, every part of it would have been perfect. PP II 19 237 3
A scheme of which every part promises delight, can never PP II 19 237 4
that she had not really any dislike to the scheme. PP II 19 241 17
The fishing scheme had been renewed the day before, and a PP III 2 266 18
her to, it was not on her side a scheme of infamy. PP III 5 292 61
should consent to such a scheme, and, had she consulted PP III 8 314 22
Not one party, or scheme, or any thing. PP III 9 319 25
no means entered into her scheme of their all going to PP III 11 330 2
It was a rational scheme to be sure! but from what the PP III 15 360 1
pleasures of so benevolent a scheme were already enjoyed. MP I 1 8 9
The scheme was soon repeated to Henry. MP I 4 42 18
much; but then, if one scheme of happiness fails, human MP I 5 46 23
A successful scheme of this sort generally brings on MP I 7 70 30
The Sotherton scheme was mentioned of course. MP I 8 75 2
I could not, when the scheme was first mentioned the other MP I 8 77 9
partiality for her own scheme because it was her own, than MP I 8 79 23
had destroyed the scheme and dispersed the performers. MP I 13 121 1
If they persist in the scheme they will find something--I MP I 13 128 35
The scheme advanced. MP I 13 129 40
to herself; it was a scheme--a trick; she was slighted, MP I 14 133 12
be so essential to a scheme on which some of those to whom MP I 16 153 3
This acting scheme gets worse and worse you see. MP I 16 153 8
After being known to oppose the scheme from the beginning, MP I 16 154 12
say he did not like the scheme in general, and must MP I 17 158 1
been easy in joining a scheme which, considering only her MP I 17 160 6
total destruction of the scheme to be inevitably at hand; MP II 1 177 5
of the whole acting scheme, defending his own share in it MP II 2 187 1
Sir Thomas saw all the impropriety of such a scheme among MP II 2 187 2
object connected with the scheme, and the last that must MP II 2 194 21
of interest in a scheme for extending his stay at MP II 5 223 48
Henry Crawford was in the first glow of another scheme MP II 7 246 37
His scheme was to rent the house himself the following MP II 7 246 37
uncle too well to consult him on any matrimonial scheme. MP II 12 292 9
him the confident of a scheme which placed Fanny's chance MP III 6 368 8
This scheme was that she should accompany her brother back MP III 6 368 9
Every flattering scheme of being of consequence to her MP III 8 389 4
I should like the scheme, and we would make a little MP III 12 416 3
in every pleasure, every scheme of her's;--one to whom she E I 1 6 6
"to meet in a charitable scheme; this will bring a great E I 10 87 32
nobody that she could wish to scheme about for her. E II 2 168 14
It was a good scheme; but on driving to the door they E II 5 187 5
is more like a young woman's scheme than an elderly man's. E II 8 217 29
It seemed the best scheme; and yet it was not so good but E II 11 248 10
given up, and the first scheme of dancing only in the room E II 11 249 12
agreeable smile as certified the continuance of the scheme. E II 11 250 20
She will enjoy the scheme, I am sure; and I do not know a E II 11 255 55
of a scheme for his subsequent consolation and happiness. E II 13 266 6
There could be no harm in a scheme, a mere passive scheme. E III 3 335 11
It is to be a morning scheme, you know, Knightley; quite a E III 6 355 20
of your attention to me in the whole of this scheme. E III 6 356 28
the scheme as a particular compliment to themselves.-- E III 6 357 31
final arrangement for the next day's scheme, they parted. E III 6 366 74
Such another scheme, composed of so many ill-assorted E III 7 374 54
The wretchedness of a scheme to box hill was in Emma's E III 8 377 1
But is not this a sudden scheme?" E III 9 385 3
and--indulging in one scheme more--nearly resolve, that it E III 14 435 4
A boyish scheme, indeed!-- E III 15 446 18
Like him, she had tried the scheme and rejected it; but E III 15 449 32
of it, with the intention of finding it a very good scheme. E III 15 449 34
her, in marking out the scheme of retrenchment, which was P III 2 12 3
scheme, which had been happily engrafted on the beginning. P III 2 15 13
The first heedless scheme had been to go in the morning P III 11 94 8
and a much better scheme followed and was acted upon. P IV 1 121 3
A scheme, worthy of Mrs. Wallis's understanding, by all P IV 9 208 92
The scheme had received its first impulse by Captain P IV 10 216 19
jesting, maintaining the scheme for the play; and she, P IV 10 224 50
in town, but conclude his scheme to the I. of Wight has S 5 387 1

SCHEMED (1)
minute, Emma felt the glory of having schemed successfully. E I 10 90 39

SCHEMES (31)
disturbance of all my schemes, & that too from a quarter, LS 22 281 4
my thoughts are fluctuating between various schemes. LS 25 293 4
in excellent spirits, with fresh hopes and fresh schemes. NA I 9 60 1
These schemes are not at all the thing. NA I 13 104 31
and in schemes of sisterly happiness the hours flew along. NA I 15 120 25
When Marianne was recovered, the schemes of amusement at SS I 11 53 1
schemes, and absent himself from Devonshire for a while. SS I 15 78 26
and while his continual schemes for their meeting were SS I 21 124 33
new engagements, and new schemes, in which she could have SS III 6 302 4
pursuing fresh schemes, always gay, always happy, she was SS III 8 322 37
those kind of schemes, and cheating a person of their PP I 10 52 50
After a week spent in professions of love and schemes of PP II 2 139 1
In her kind schemes for Elizabeth, she sometimes planned PP II 9 181 31
Other schemes too came into her hand. PP III 7 307 48
way to all the happy schemes, which the good humour, and PP III 12 339 10
Mrs. Bennet's schemes for this day were ineffectual. PP III 13 345 18
she could not be wanted to counteract her mother's schemes. PP III 13 346 21
their pleasures and schemes were sometimes of a nature to MP I 2 17 21
to attend the races, and schemes were made for a large MP I 5 48 29
sympathizing in praise of Fanny's kind offices. MP I 18 170 23
she would be employed, schemes for an action with some MP III 7 375 2
there was rising in importance from his present schemes. MP III 10 404 15
begun to influence his schemes; but as it was not the E I 2 16 6
and forming all these schemes in the in-betweens, that the E I 3 24 11
passed by the two young people in schemes on the subject. E II 11 247 2
a thousand amusing schemes for the progress and close of E II 13 264 1
to stay at home than engage in schemes of pleasure." E II 14 274 29
In this state of schemes, and hopes, and connivance, June E III 5 343 1
Such schemes as these are nothing without numbers. E III 6 353 4
There she had listened to Henrietta's schemes for Dr. P III 12 115 66
build my own selfish schemes on Mr. Elliot's good fortune." P IV 9 195 27

SCHEMING (5)
by wealthy connexions; a forward, bragging, scheming race. NA II 15 246 12
Elizabeth; "but without scheming to do wrong, or to make PP II 1 136 17
though infinitely above scheming or contriving for any the MP II 7 238 1
removals, and a little scheming of her own, Anne was P IV 8 189 46
sake, the possibility of scheming longer for Sir Walter. P IV 12 250 8

SCHOLAR (7)
was so hopeful a scholar, that when they gained the top of NA I 14 111 29
Mr H. read like a scholar & a gentleman."-- W 344 20
and I dare say a good scholar and clever, and often MP I 11 111 28
"I had a very apt scholar. MP I 11 113 38
from the condition of scholar to that of parlour-boarder. E I 3 22 8
who had chosen to be a scholar and a gentleman, and who P III 9 74 5
I am a very poor Italian scholar." P IV 8 186 25

SCHOLEY (2)
But old Scholey was saying just now, that he thought you MP III 7 380 20
Old Scholey ran in at breakfast time, to say she had MP III 7 380 20

SCHOOL (47)
Miss Vernon is to be placed at a school in town before her LS 3 247 1
long enough at school to understand anything thoroughly. LS 7 253 1
a good foundation, for school must be very humiliating to LS 7 253 1
another school, unless we can get her married immediately. LS 16 268 1
Frederica continued at school, it had better not be known LS 20 277 5
too old ever to submit to school confinement, and have LS 20 277 5
seen me then above twice, for it was before I left school. SS I 20 117 64
spent seven years at a great school in town to some effect. SS II 4 160 3
home; and my little Eliza was therefore placed at school. SS II 9 208 28
that I removed her from school, to place her under the SS II 9 208 28
the advantage of a public school, was as well fitted to SS II 14 250 12
the advantage of a public school, she could not think of SS II 14 251 14
I would rather be teacher at a school (and I can think of W 318 2
"I would rather do any thing than be teacher at a school-- W 318 2
I have been at school, Emma, & know what a life they lead; W 318 2
My father supported him at school, and afterwards at PP II 12 200 5
About a year ago, she was taken from school, and an PP II 12 201 5
You have been in a bad school for matrimony, in hill MP I 5 46 21
and the rivals, the school for scandal, wheel of fortune, MP I 14 130 3
it just released from school, and coming eagerly to see MP III 7 381 25
and Charles being gone to school, Sam on some project of MP III 8 388 1
had been brought up in a school of luxury and epicurism. MP III 10 407 23
Mrs. Goddard was the mistress of a school--not of a E I 3 21 5
Mrs. Goddard's school was in high repute--and very E I 3 22 5
back, at Mrs. Goddard's school, and somebody had lately E I 3 22 8
to some young ladies who had been at school there with her. E I 3 23 8
and the affairs of the school in general, formed naturally E I 4 27 4
pride or refinement in the teacher of a school, Harriet. E I 7 56 41
She is known only as parlour-boarder at a common school. E I 8 61 38
and great girls in the school; and it must be at Hartfield E I 17 143 15
had been formed in a bad school, pert and familiar; that E II 14 272 16
"But it is proved by the smallness of the school, which I E III 16 456 32
only school, and not more than five-and-twenty children." E III 16 456 32
been three years at school there, after her mother's death, P III 2 14 11
sister, Mary, had been at school while it all occurred-- P III 4 31 11
who had brought from a school at Exeter all the usual P III 5 40 45
"I do not exactly know, for Henrietta and I were at school P III 10 89 33
master Harry, sent to school after his brothers, was now P IV 1 121 3
happy boys and girls from school, bringing with them Mrs. P IV 2 133 27
home, before her brothers and sisters went to school again. P IV 2 134 31
Anne had gone unhappy to school, grieving for the loss of P IV 5 152 2
remaining another year at school, had been useful and good P IV 5 152 2
Miss Hamilton had left school, had married not long P IV 5 152 3
girls Boarding school, or academy, from Camberwell.-- S 5 387 1
A West Indy family & a school. S 6 392 1
Well Mr Parker--and the other is a Boarding school, a S 6 393 1
is a Boarding school, a French Boarding school, is it?-- S 6 393 1

SCHOOL-BOY'S (1)
not suppose any school-boy's bosom to feel more keenly. MP III 14 431 7
SCHOOL-BOYS (1)
My father wished us, as school-boys, to speak well, but he MP I 13 127 26
SCHOOL-FELLOW (2)
features of a former school-fellow and intimate, whom she NA I 4 31 2
of there being an old school-fellow in Bath, who had the P IV 5 152 2
SCHOOL-FELLOWS (1)
and Mrs. Hughes were school-fellows; and Miss Drummond had NA I 9 68 46
SCHOOL-GIRL'S (1)
You have cured her of her school-girl's giggle; she really E I 8 58 12
SCHOOL-MASTER (1)
perticular about the school-master," were bent on P III 6 52 33
SCHOOL-ROOM (4)
cousins, whether in the school-room, the drawing-room, or MP I 2 14 8
It had been their school-room; so called till the Miss MP I 16 150 1
There--very good school-room chairs, not made for a MP I 18 169 21
Wax-candles in the school-room! E II 17 300 8
SCHOOL-SYSTEM (1)
to it, in the ordinary school-system for boys, the MP III 3 339 22
SCHOOLFELLOW (3)
was engaged to spend the evening with an old schoolfellow." P IV 5 157 14
what this old schoolfellow was; and Elizabeth was P IV 5 157 14
Her kind, compassionate visits to this old schoolfellow, P IV 5 158 21
SCHOOLS (1)
one of the best private schools in town, where I shall LS 1 244 1
SCIENCE (2)
that you are an adept in the science yourself, Mr. Darcy." PP I 6 25 28
Alembic;--we distil nothing which can add to science.-- S 8 403 1
SCIENCES (1)
all the language arts & sciences; it is throwing time away; LS 7 253 1
SCIENTIFIC (1)
gay, attention for the scientific, and patience for the P IV 8 186 24
SCIENTIFICALLY (1)
sides & green tea scientifically & thoroughly understand S 10 418 1
SCISSARS (4)
presently he took up her scissars and cut off a long lock SS I 12 60 13
and their knives and scissars stolen away, and felt no SS I 21 120 6
to do; took up a pair of scissars that lay there, and SS III 12 360 22
23
have borrowed a pair of scissars the night before of Miss E III 3 334 7
SCISSORS (1)
when one drops one's scissors, or any thing that happens. P IV 2 132 19
SCOLD (10)
I scold them all amazingly about it." NA I 6 40 12
"Scold them! NA I 6 40 13
Do you scold them for not admiring her?" NA I 6 40 13
I should scold her myself, if she were capable of wishing SS I 10 48 6
Elinor scolded him, harshly as ladies always scold the SS III 13 368 25
their complaints, and scold them into harmony and plenty. PP II 7 169 4
Norris was beginning to scold her for not being gone, and MP I 7 67 15
"Well," said Miss Crawford, "and do not you scold us for MP II 4 211 26
She might scold herself for the weakness, but there was no MP III 10 400 6
with it, and he only said, "I shall not scold you. E III 2 330 50
51
SCOLDED (11)
I scolded him for making love to Maria Manwaring; he LS 9 257 1
and when he scolded or abused her, she was highly diverted. SS I 20 112 26
hardly; for your sister scolded like any fury, and soon SS III 1 259 7
Elinor scolded him, harshly as ladies always scold the SS III 13 368 25
Her mother only scolded her for being nonsensical. PP I 18 99 64
Fanny sighed alone at the window till scolded away by Mrs. MP I 11 113 43
"Perhaps I might have scolded," said Edmund, "if either of MP II 4 211 28
I have often scolded him for it, but it is his only fault; MP III 5 363 22
and Miss Nash came and scolded us away, and staid to look E I 9 75 26
You have scolded me too much for match-making, for me to E II 15 288 35
She was lost; and when she had scolded back her senses, P IV 7 175 5
SCOLDING (10)
I have been scolding him to such a degree, my dear NA I 8 56 14
the rest of his time in scolding his daughter, for so NA II 6 165 6
the morning in the kitchen herself directing & scolding.-- W 360 30
to contain herself, began scolding one of her daughters. PP I 2 6 7
see Elizabeth without scolding her, a month passed away PP I 23 127 5
Mrs. Norris began scolding. MP I 7 71 33
I do not know when I shall have done scolding you," and MP III 5 357 6
comfortable; for as to scolding you, Fanny, which I came MP III 5 359 9
for the weakness, but there was no scolding it away. MP III 10 400 6
for I cannot be always scolding and teazing a poor child P III 7 56 12
SCOPE (1)
in all matters within the scope of your understanding, but PP I 18 97 60
61
SCORE (12)
ever, tho' so innocently, made her unhappy on that score. LS 24 290 13
all that she felt on the score of James's disappointment. NA II 14 236 19
moment of parting, her grief on that score was excessive. SS II 3 158 21
on the score of some quality or other, real or imaginary. PP I 5 20 20
being alarmed on the score of the gentleman's conduct; but PP I 21 120 30
to you last spring! is nothing due to me on that score? PP III 14 355 47
apparent, that on the score of some family objections on PP III 15 363 22
nothing to suffer on that score; for as her being out was MP II 4 206 4
said, and Sir Thomas was easy on the score of the cousins. MP III 1 317 36
Crawford called the next day, and on the score of Edmund's MP III 3 335 7
Mr. Woodhouse opposed it earnestly, on the score of health. E II 11 248 10
sure our thanks are due to you, Mrs. Weston, on that score. E III 2 322 19
SCORES (3)
she was sharing with the scores of other young ladies NA I 8 53 2
to tens and to scores of them at present unknown. PP II 18 232 22
Crawford, who had seen scores of great houses, and cared MP I 9 85 3
SCORN (2)
but I scorn to accept a hand while the heart was another's. SS III 13 365 14
in general would have too much sense to join in the scorn." PP III 14 358 70
SCORNED (3)
not without its use; she scorned the causeless fears of an NA II 6 167 10
of the nearest kind with the man whom he so justly scorned. PP III 8 311 12
There had been a time when he would have scorned her as a E III 6 360 40
SCORNFUL (1)
perhaps, more in thought than fact; scornful, ungracious. E III 8 377 1
SCORNFULLY (1)
To have his love used so scornfully! for they say he is SS III 1 259 7
SCORNING (1)
villain upon earth, scorning, hating me in her latest SS III 8 330 69
SCORNS (1)
The Admiral hates trouble, and scorns asking favours; and MP III 5 364 29
SCOTCH (3)
a thick grove of old Scotch firs; and Catherine, struck by NA II 7 179 29
praise and gratitude by Scotch and Irish airs, at the PP I 6 25 24
the charm by a lively Scotch air; and soon afterwards Mr. PP I 10 51 47
48
SCOTLAND (11)
were within a few hours of eloping together for Scotland. SS II 9 206 24
that she was gone off to Scotland with one of his officers; PP III 4 273 3
but too much reason to fear they are not gone to Scotland. PP III 4 274 3
but not beyond; they are certainly not gone to Scotland." PP III 4 277 14
Why should they not go on to Scotland, if that had been PP III 5 282 4
is no absolute proof that they are not gone to Scotland." PP III 5 282 5
less expeditiously, married in London, than in Scotland." PP III 5 282 7
their not being gone to Scotland: when that apprehension PP III 5 290 46
when if they had gone to Scotland, which she had never PP III 6 295 4
elopement; she is gone to Scotland with Yates. MP III 15 442 23
have a bailiff from Scotland, to look after his new estate. E I 12 104 44
SCOTT (5)
You know what he thinks of Cowper and Scott; you are SS I 10 47 4
Thomson, Cowper, Scott-- she would buy them all over and SS I 17 92 25
talking as before of Mr. Scott and Lord Byron, and still P III 12 107 23
to be an enthusiast for Scott and Lord Byron; nay, that P IV 6 167 20
If Scott has a fault, it is the want of passion.-- S 7 397 1
SCOTT'S (2)
"Do you remember, said he, Scott's beautiful lines on the S 7 396 1
at this moment, of the sea, in either of Scott's poems."-- S 7 397 1
SCOTTISH (1)
No signs that a 'Scottish monarch sleeps below.'" MP I 9 86 6
SCOUNDREL (3)
Such a scoundrel of a fellow! such a deceitful dog! SS II 10 215 9
My business was to declare myself a scoundrel, and whether SS III 8 328 63
warmest friendship--indignation--abominable scoundrel!"-- E III 13 426 13
SCOUTED (1)
little room; but that was scouted as a wretched suggestion. E II 11 254 45
SCRAMBLE (3)
On rising from tea, there was again a scramble for the W 333 13
to be out of the way and scramble themselves into a little E I 3 21 5
an early age, and scramble into any hand they can get. E II 16 297 45
SCRAMBLED (2)
And she immediately scrambled across the fence, and walked MP I 10 101 33
& the gentleman having scrambled out & helped out his S 1 364 1
SCRAMBLING (2)
countries, of the scrambling parties in which he had been MP II 6 237 23
It is not a scrambling collection of low single rooms, MP II 7 243 27
SCRAP (1)
she seized the scrap of paper on which Edmund had begun MP II 9 265 19
SCRAPE (9)
on her he bestowed a whole scrape and half a short bow. NA I 7 45 5
you and I are very well off to be out of the scrape.-- NA I 14 115 50
drawn Robert into the scrape, was the principal instrument SS III 14 375 10
of a ball but the first scrape of one violin, blessed the W 327 7
young man to get into a scrape of that sort, and from PP II 10 185 28
got into a dreadful scrape last year from the want of them. MP I 5 51 40
"I wish you may not get into a scrape, Harriet, whenever E I 4 30 22
It was the scrape which he had drawn her into on Harriet's E III 11 402 1
wife) I am very sorry to have brought you into this scrape. S 1 367 1
SCRAPED (1)
while he scrupulously scraped off almost as much butter as S 10 417 1
SCRAPES (1)
but you always contrive to keep out of these scrapes." MP I 10 100 28
SCRAPS (1)
To know him in bits and scraps, is common enough; to know MP III 3 338 14
SCRATCH (1)
for this unfortunate scratch, and a slight intermission of SS I 21 121 10
SCRATCHED (1)
when he comes home find all the varnish scratched off." MP I 8 77 12
SCRATCHING (2)
head dress slightly scratching the child's neck, produced SS I 21 121 10
of the narrow lanes scratching his carriage, and you know MP I 8 77 12
SCRAWL (1)
three lines of scrawl from the Dowager Viscountess. P IV 4 149 13
SCRAWLS (1)
Please to destroy my scrawls--but the ring with my hair SS III 13 365 15
SCREAM (1)
frightened, gave a great scream, and calling on Harriet to E III 3 333 5
SCREAMED (3)
She still screamed and sobbed lustily, kicked her two SS I 21 121 10
her face with her handkerchief, almost screamed with agony. SS II 7 182 12
"She is dead! she is dead!" screamed Mary, catching hold P III 12 109 34
SCREAMS (3)
gentleness, such violent screams, as could hardly be SS I 21 121 10
a slight intermission of screams in the young lady on SS I 21 121 10
immediately, with such screams as reached your brother's SS III 1 259 7
SCREEN (8)
She walked eagerly on as she spoke; and Elinor, to screen SS I 16 86 20
see her faint, tried to screen her from the observation of SS II 6 177 12
the acacia, and a thick screen of them altogether, SS III 6 302 7
placing a screen in the proper direction before her eyes. PP II 6 162 12
eyes, meaning to screen it at the same time from Susan's. MP III 7 386 40
And putting up her hand to screen her words from Emma--"a E III 16 456 23
To pacify Mary, and perhaps screen her own embarrassment, P IV 10 222 39
of his person as a screen, & was very thankful for every S 10 415 1
SCREENED (8)
the valley, but it was screened from their view at home by SS I 7 32 1
in the cardroom somewhat screened by a door, she heard Ld W 333 13
so well placed and well screened as to deserve to be in MP I 5 48 28
end of the sofa, and, screened from notice herself, saw MP II 1 185 27
was also to dine there, screened her a little from view. MP II 13 303 14
glad to have the light screened from her aching head, as MP III 7 382 28
Sitting forwards, however, and screened by her bonnet, MP III 15 445 32
as very completely screened, Captain Wentworth should be P III 8 68 29
SCREENS (4)
a very pretty pair of screens for her sister-in-law, which SS II 12 234 26
drawing room; and these screens, catching the eye of John SS II 12 234 26
warmly admired the screens, as he would have done any SS II 12 234 28
And so saying, she took the screens out of her sister-in- SS II 12 235 36
SCREWED (2)
like a civil answer--she screwed up her mouth, and turned MP I 5 50 35
for enormous pay might be screwed out of health and into E I 3 21 5
SCRUPLE (32)
had no scruple in owning herself greatly surprized by it. NA I 13 102 26
she called herself without scruple the happiest of mortals. NA I 15 121 26
Your sister need not have any scruple even of visiting her, SS II 11 228 53
to be so, she made no scruple of turning away her eyes SS II 14 250 11
overcoming every scruple, by secretly saying now and then, SS III 8 326 53
which he had, with little scruple, left her sister to SS III 8 331 70
on her character, had no scruple in believing her capable SS III 13 366 21
none of them the smallest scruple in trusting themselves W 339 18
that he entertained no scruple whatever on that head, and PP I 17 87 12
for she did not scruple to call out, "what is that you are PP II 8 172 3
4
But I shall not scruple to assert, that the serenity of PP II 12 197 5
have no scruple in abusing you to all your relations." PP III 16 367 11
as Miss Maria, did not scruple to predict their marrying MP I 1 3 1
He did not scruple to add, that her being at home for a MP III 6 372 19
She might scruple to make use of the words, but she must MP III 8 390 6
She had no scruple with regard to him. E I 6 42 1
My only scruple in advising the match was on his account, E I 8 61 38
Without scruple--without apology--without much apparent E I 15 129 24
delight, she had less scruple in the amusement, and much E II 10 243 22
I do not scruple to say that she plays extremely well. E II 15 282 5
you can have no scruple to accept such an accommodation." E II 16 295 34
Don't scruple. E III 6 355 18
Why he should feel such a scruple, why he should change E III 9 386 7
nay, which he did not scruple to feel, having never E III 13 433 41
scruple of mine with multiplied strength and refinement.-- E III 14 440 8
to all, and had no scruple in urging him to the utmost.-- E III 17 467 31
to dictate, he had no scruple," he said, "in confessing P III 2 13 7
of rank, said, "I have no scruple of observing to you, how P III 6 46 10
Your sister being with you, my love, I have no scruple at P III 7 55 8
a scruple was there on his side, with respect to her birth. P IV 9 202 66
Because if you are, I shall have no scruple in asking you P IV 11 240 58
And I can have no scruple on Diana's account--for her S 5 386 1
SCRUPLED (4)
of Mrs. Jennings, who scrupled not to attribute the SS III 7 313 21
The extravagance and general profligacy which he scrupled PP II 13 205 4
were very pressing; and scrupled not to lay all the ill- PP III 10 323 2
been spared; and she scrupled to point out her own remarks MP I 7 66 14
SCRUPLES (32)
I have no such scruples, and I am sure, I could put up SS II 3 156 14
no scruples, if she can promote her own advantage.-- W 317 2

had some filial scruples on that head, as you will hear." PP I 13 62 11
and all Mr. Collins's scruples of leaving Mr. and Mrs. PP I 16 75 1
honest confession of the scruples that had long prevented PP II 11 192 22
had then no reserves, no scruples in sinking Mr. Darcy's PP II 13 207 5
I have no fears, and no scruples. MP I 13 126 18
and purity of her own scruples, and as she looked around MP I 16 153 3
and feel many scruples which my children do not feel, is MP II 1 186 34
"I can have no scruples now. MP II 6 231 10
and with only some scruples to obviate in Sir Thomas, who MP II 6 237 23
think of to obviate the scruples which were making Fanny MP II 8 258 15
what remained of her scruples, was exceedingly pleased MP II 8 258 18
be ashamed of my own scruples; and if they are removed, it MP II 9 269 38
had there been time for scruples and fears as to style, MP II 13 307 30
31
properly, and honourably--what are your scruples now?" MP III 1 315 18
His objections, the scruples of his integrity, seemed all MP III 6 367 4
She persisted in placing his scruples to her account, MP III 17 465 13
Some scruples and some reluctance the widower-father may E I 2 16 4
to the early hours and civil scruples of their guests. E I 3 24 11
made; and she had no scruples which could stand many E I 6 44 19
both, though against the scruples of his own civility, to E I 8 57 2
By your account, he does seem to have had some scruples. E I 8 61 37
and I should have no scruples of staying as late as Mrs. E II 7 211 21
"There might be scruples of delicacy, my dear Emma. E II 8 226 83
"Trouble! aye, I know your scruples. E II 17 300 10
But Harriet was less humble, had fewer scruples than E III 11 414 50
He should have respected even unreasonable scruples, had E III 15 446 20
he had no farther scruples as to her being left to dine P III 7 58 20
They would not listen to scruples: he was obeyed; they P III 12 111 50
The Harvilles silenced all scruples; and, as much as they P III 12 112 56
for it--a very few civil scruples were enough--especially S 1 370 1

SCRUPLING (1)
worse than absurdity, of scrupling to engage my faith SS III 8 321 34

SCRUPULOUS (16)
Besides, the most scrupulous point of honour could not LS 9 256 1
a thing, she was so scrupulous in performing it! this made NA II 10 201 5
in the world; the most scrupulous in performing every SS II 13 243 40
"You are over scrupulous surely. PP I 1 4 25
Agatha, began to be scrupulous on Miss Crawford's account. MP I 14 133 8
need not be so scrupulous as I might feel necessary. MP I 15 141 21
lady had, with a most scrupulous fear of being late, been MP II 5 222 41
only by a less scrupulous opinion, and more noisy abuse of MP II 6 234 18
so angry, and so little scrupulous of what she said; and MP III 5 356 4
"So scrupulous for others," he continued, "and yet so E I 15 125 5
drawback from her scrupulous conscience, she must be, I E III 12 420 13
scrupulous and cautious: I thought her even cold. E III 14 440 8
"Oh! you are too scrupulous, indeed you are," cried Emma, E III 16 459 48
He is so very strict and scrupulous in his notions; over- P III 12 103 2
she would feel scrupulous as to any proposal of ours. P IV 6 166 16
particularly careful & scrupulous on all those matters S 9 409 1

SCRUPULOUSLY (2)
to make him scrupulously guard against exciting it a MP III 3 335 6
his sisters, while he scrupulously scraped off almost as S 10 417 1

SCRUPULOUSNESS (1)
and it must be scrupulousness run mad, that could see any MP I 13 128 38

SCRUTINIES (1)
The impertinence of these kind of scrutinies, moreover, SS II 14 249 8

SCRUTINY (1)
from the evening's scrutiny, that though she received his PP II 12 197 5

SCUD (1)
A sudden scud of rain driving full in her face, made it NA II 5 161 25

SCULLERY (1)
and a comfortless scullery were deemed sufficient at NA II 8 184 4

SE'NIGHT (1)
till the Saturday se'night following, which I can do PP I 13 63 12

SE'NNIGHT (3)
Bath, as she has perhaps told you, on Saturday se'nnight. NA II 2 139 7
him that her ladyship was quite well yesterday se'nnight." PP I 18 97 59
and could not get away till that very day se'nnight." E I 13 115 39

SEA (73)
and William at sea,--and all of them more beloved and NA I 4 32 2
with his sister in Northamptonshire, before he went to sea. MP I 2 21 34
"Miss Price has a brother at sea," said Edmund, "whose MP I 6 59 45
"At sea, has she?-- MP I 6 60 46
lately from her brother at sea, and said that she had MP I 15 147 57
drawn before he went to sea again--she could not help MP I 15 147 57
terrific scenes, which such a period, at sea, must supply. MP II 6 235 19
variety of danger, which sea and war together could offer. MP II 6 236 21
I wonder any body can ever go to sea." MP II 6 236 21
He longed to have been at sea, and seen and done and MP II 6 236 22
ever-varying hues of the sea now at high water, dancing in MP III 11 409 6
balmy air, the sparkling sea, and your sweet looks and MP III 12 415 1
2
if within ten miles of the sea, which the Admiral of MP III 12 416 3
Lord of the earth and sea, he bends a slave, and woman, E I 9 71 14
Lord of the earth and sea, he bends a slave, and woman, E I 9 73 18
I never had much opinion of the sea air." E I 12 101 20
in little Bella's throat,--both sea air and bathing." E I 12 101 21
"Ah! my dear, but Perry had many doubts about the sea E I 12 101 22
so before, that the sea is very rarely of use to any body. E I 12 101 22
an unsafe subject, "I must beg you not to talk of the sea. E I 12 101 23
you went to the sea this autumn, instead of coming here." E I 12 105 51
52
"And, moreover, if you must go to the sea, it had better E I 12 105 54
A fine open sea, he says, and very pure air. E I 12 106 56
from the sea--a quarter of a mile off--very comfortable. E I 12 106 56
have been dashed into the sea at once, and actually was E II 1 160 23
The sea is no beautifier, certainly; sailors do grow old P III 3 20 17
been almost as much at sea as her husband, made her seem P III 6 48 18
that he had been sent to sea, because he was stupid and P III 6 50 28
He had been several years at sea, and had, in the course P III 6 51 30
happened before I went to sea in the year six," occurred P III 8 63 2
a few hundred men to sea, in a ship not fit to be employed. P III 8 65 11
It was a great object with me, at that time, to be at sea,- P III 8 65 13
all the time I was at sea in her; and after taking P III 8 65 16
going to sea, but never knew what sickness was afterwards. P III 8 71 54
done was unquestionably to walk directly down to the sea. P III 11 95 9
found themselves on the sea shore, and lingering only, as P III 11 96 10
on a first return to the sea, who ever deserve to look on P III 11 96 10
She had died the preceding summer, while he was at sea. P III 11 96 12
unexpensive, and by the sea; and the grandeur of the P III 11 97 12
agreed to stroll down to the sea before breakfast.-- P III 12 102 1
They praised the morning; gloried in the sea; sympathized P III 12 102 1
2
that being by the sea, always makes him feel young again. P III 12 102 2
it a pity that he does not live entirely by the sea. P III 12 102 2
the week before; no danger of her being sent to sea again. P III 12 108 28
A little of our own bracing sea air will soon set me on my S 1 367 1
Depend upon it my dear, it is exactly a case for the sea. S 1 367 1
or other starting up by the sea, & growing the fashion.-- S 1 368 1
finest, purest sea breeze on the coast--acknowledged to be S 1 369 1
sea weed, can end in nothing but their own disappointment. S 1 369 1
that every one of them wd be benefited by the sea.-- S 2 373 1
without spending at least 6 weeks by the sea every year.-- S 2 373 1
The sea air & sea bathing together were nearly infallible, S 2 373 1
Nobody could catch cold by the sea, nobody wanted appetite S 2 373 1
the sea, nobody wanted spirits, nobody wanted strength.-- S 2 373 1
If the sea breeze failed, the Sea-bath was the certain S 2 373 1
bathing disagreed, the sea breeze alone was evidently S 2 373 1
Dip within 2 miles of the sea, they passed close by a S 4 379 1
more obliquely towards the sea, gave a passage to an S 4 383 1
who came from London for sea sir after the hooping cough, S 4 383 1
His spirits rose with the very sight of the sea & he cd S 4 384 1
to the sea, dancing & sparkling in sunshine & freshness.-- S 4 384 1
state, the sea air wd probably be the death of me.-- S 5 387 1
There is the sea & the downs & my Milch-Asses--& I have S 6 393 1
& feeling, to talk of the sea & the sea shore--& ran with S 7 396 1
to talk of the sea & the sea shore--& ran with energy S 7 396 1
remember, said he, Scott's beautiful lines on the sea?-- S 7 396 1
I remember none at this moment, of the sea, in either of S 7 397 1
If people want to be by the sea, why dont they take S 7 402 1
Mrs G. meant to go to the sea, for her young people's S 9 408 1
by her feelings, that the sea air wd probably in her S 10 412 1
a beautiful veiw of the sea if they had chosen it,-- but S 10 413 1
removals to look at the sea & the hotel, Charlotte's place S 10 414 1
"We shd not have one at home, said he, but the sea air is S 10 415 1

SEA-AIR (1)
with very few exceptions, the sea-air always does good. P III 12 102 2

SEA-BATH (1)
If the sea breeze failed, the Sea-bath was the certain S 2 373 1

SEA-BATHING (3)
"A little sea-bathing would set me up for ever." PP II 18 229 8
autumn had given to sea-bathing for the children, and it E I 11 91 2
he holds it to be the best of all the sea-bathing places. E I 12 105 56

SEA-BREEZES (1)
Those vile sea-breezes are the ruin of beauty and health. MP III 12 416 3

SEA-FARING (1)
an example of what a sea-faring life can do; but to a P III 3 20 16

SEA-SIDE (1)
absence in a tour to the sea-side, which was the plan.-- E III 19 483 8

SEAL (2)
I am come here to bespeak Fanny a seal. SS II 11 222 9
cousin William, and sent him half a guinea under the seal. MP I 2 16 20

SEALED (4)
then folded up, sealed and directed with eager rapidity. SS II 4 161 5
round at his sister as he sealed and threw the letter from MP II 6 229 1
This letter, however, was written, and sealed, and sent. E I 7 55 36
Mrs. Croft left them, and Captain Wentworth having sealed P IV 11 236 39

SEAMANSHIP (1)
commence his career of seamanship in her at this very time. MP III 7 377 8

SEAMS (1)
There are but three seams, you may do them in a trice.-- MP I 18 166 6

SEARCH (10)
He was no where to be met with; every search for him was NA I 5 35 2
After a very short search, you will discover a division in NA II 5 159 19
its folding doors, and search into every drawer;--but for NA II 5 160 21
then added the shame of being caught in so idle a search. NA II 6 165 4
as hitherto, was her search; her quick eyes directly fell NA II 6 169 11
in her presence, search for those proofs of the General's NA II 9 193 5
her; but the search was as fruitless as it was melancholy. SS II 9 207 26
every eye was in search of the parsonage, and every PP II 5 155 2
something to direct his search, which was more than we had; PP III 10 322 2
quite impatient, she resolved to go in search of them. MP I 10 103 49

SEARCHED (3)
accounted for if their cause be fairly searched out. NA I 1 16 10
ears, their work-bags searched, and their knives and SS I 21 120 6
which was now searched by madam with the most ingratiating SS III 8 329 63

SEARCHING (1)
She was busily searching through the neighbourhood for a PP III 8 310 7

SEAS (5)
second brings, behold him there, the monarch of the seas! E I 9 71 14
Behold him there, the monarch of the seas! E I 9 72 17
second brings; behold him there, the monarch of the seas! E I 9 73 18
the Admiral (captain Croft then) was in the north seas. P III 8 71 54
Lord Byron's "dark blue seas" could not fail of being P III 12 109 31

SEASON (40)
I never found the season so dreary before, but this happy LS 40 309 1
The season was full, the room crowded, and the two ladies NA I 2 20 9
Sunday throughout the season, they hastened away to the NA I 5 35 2
that roof, in every Bath season, yet the merit of their NA I 10 72 8
to get a house in Leicestershire, against the next season. NA I 10 76 28
fish and game, and so forth, whenever they are in season. SS I 2 12 24
It was very early in September; the season was fine, and SS I 6 28 2
This was the season of happiness to Marianne. SS I 11 54 5
What feelings have they, the season, the air altogether SS I 16 88 31
the dryness of the season, a very awful pause took place. SS III 12 359 14
Charming season for hunting." W 357 28
probability of a rainy season, made her feel that the PP I 16 76 4
the gaieties which that season generally brings, and that PP I 21 117 11
all the finest fruits in season; but this did not take PP III 3 268 6
all this took from the season of courtship much of its PP III 18 384 27
Fanny had no share in the festivities of the season; but MP I 4 35 6
The season, the scene, the air, were all favourable to MP I 7 65 13
The season and duties which brought Mr. Bertram back to MP I 12 114 3
with a week's calm in the Atlantic at that season." MP II 5 225 57
use of it in the hunting season, (as he was then telling MP II 7 246 37
upon one amusement or one season of the year: he had set MP II 7 246 37
influence in this season of love, had already done so MP III 6 367 5
morning, and at the season of the year a fine morning so MP III 10 401 10
the advance of that season which cannot, in spite of its MP III 14 432 9
make the approaching season no hindrance to their spending E I 2 18 11
Perry does not call it altogether a sickly season." E I 12 102 34
the truth is, that in London it is always a sickly season. E I 12 102 36
This is quite the season indeed for friendly meetings. E I 13 115 39
come in their chaise, I think, at that season of the year. E II 14 274 28
spring--precisely the season of the year which one should E II 18 308 30
extant of autumn, that season of peculiar and P III 10 84 7
and tenderness, that season which has drawn form every P III 10 84 7
little bay, which in the season is animated with bathing P III 11 95 9
a candidate for, before the end even of this season." S 3 377 1
In a good season we shd have more applications than we S 4 380 1
He anticipated an amazing season.-- S 4 383 1
Most sincerely do we wish you a good season at Sanditon, & S 5 387 1
be said to lead off the season, were followed by nothing S 6 389 1
to the success of the season, was busy in some immediate S 6 390 1
present number of Visitants & the chances of a good season. S 6 392 1

SEASON'D (1)
parents and guardians"--and a "capital season'd hunter." MP III 3 341 31

SEASONABLE (2)
listening to him, was a seasonable relief to them all, and PP I 21 115 1
"Quite seasonable; and extremely fortunate we may think E I 13 115 39

SEASONS (3)
In seasons of cheerfulness, no temper could be more SS I 2 8 2
visits at extraordinary seasons; & in the present instance W 355 28
of times and seasons, a regulation of subject, a propriety, MP III 7 382 29

SEAT (70)
"Curricle-hung you see; seat, trunk, sword-case, splashing- NA I 7 46 13
inviting her to a secret conference, led the way to a seat. NA II 3 143 1
He approached immediately, and took the seat to which her NA II 3 147 21
and if she moved from her seat she should miss her sisters, NA II 3 147 28
The middle seat of the chaise was not drawn out, though NA II 5 155 4
on either low window seat to scare her, and on placing a NA II 6 167 10
Returning in silence to his seat, therefore, he remained NA II 15 242 8
I could hardly keep my seat. SS I 3 18 18
rose directly from his seat, and after saying in a voice SS II 5 174 46
once stirring from her seat, or altering her attitude, SS II 6 175 1
they were to go to Combe Magna, his seat in Somersetshire. SS II 8 199 37
he instantly changed his seat to one close by Lucy Steele, SS II 12 236 41
and had even changed her seat, on purpose that she might SS III 3 281 9
as he returned to his seat--"What does it signify?"-- SS III 8 318 15
and therefore took a seat as far from him as she could, SS III 12 359 13
He rose from his seat and walked to the window, apparently SS III 12 360 22
23
seat by the fire you know, Mr Musgrave." replied Mrs E. W 327 7

& look in the window seat behind her for the gloves which W 336 13
very low bow, and take his seat without saying a word; and PP II 6 162 11
foretold, he took his seat at the bottom of the table, by PP II 6 162 14
darting from her seat as she finished the letter, in PP III 4 276 6
day, she again took her seat at the head of her table, and PP III 8 310 7
She was roused from her seat, and her reflections, by some PP III 10 327 4
such misery of shame, that she could hardly keep her seat. PP III 11 337 52
Before half this was said, Fanny was returned to her seat MP I 7 71 35
I believe it would be generally thought the favourite seat. MP I 8 78 15
The place of all places, the envied seat, the post of MP I 8 80 29
the latter took her seat within, in gloom and MP I 8 80 30
I wish you had my seat, but I dare say you will not take MP I 8 81 32
the next time we come to a seat, if it is not disagreeable MP I 9 94 57
Edmund left the seat likewise. MP I 9 96 74
she is afraid of the evening air in so exposed a seat." MP I 10 105 52
you?"--then leaving her seat, and coming to him to enforce MP I 12 119 23
at Ecclesford, the seat of the Right Hon. Lord Ravenshaw, MP I 13 121 1
"Oh! we do not want to disturb you from your seat. MP I 15 145 45
She had found a seat, where in excessive trembling she was MP II 1 176 4
this before he resumed his seat as master of the house at MP II 2 190 9
"Fanny," said he directly, leaving his seat and his pen, MP II 9 261 2
rising eagerly from her seat to be nearer her uncle, "I MP II 10 279 28
then returning to her seat to finish a note which she was MP II 12 296 31
and led her back to her seat, and was in the middle of his MP II 13 301 7
Fanny could hardly have kept her seat any longer, or have MP III 3 344 42
Fanny shrunk back to her seat, with feelings sadly pained MP III 7 380 23
rising from her seat, looked at him for a moment in MP III 7 384 34
in the yard, or found a seat on board a vessel in the MP III 10 403 15
the seat of Mr. Knightley, comprehended many such. E I 3 20 1
was civilly offering a seat in his carriage, if the E I 13 110 12
to a seat by her sister, and giving her all her attention. E I 15 125 6
and till he could find a seat by her, would not sit at all. E II 8 220 47
except that he had found a seat by Miss Fairfax, followed E II 8 227 85
Suckling's seat"--a comparison of Hartfield to Maple Grove. E II 14 272 18
we shall sometimes find a seat for her in the barouche- E II 15 284 9
The kind-hearted, gentle Mrs. Weston had left her seat to E III 2 327 34
and mortification she must be returning to her seat. E III 2 327 38
Knightley must take his seat with the rest round the large E III 5 347 18
arms and motto: "principal seat, Kellynch Hall, in the P III 1 3 3
4
So, there was I, crowded into the back seat with Henrietta P III 5 39 39
madam, this is your seat;" and though she immediately drew P III 8 72 58
59
Mary finding a comfortable seat for herself, on the step P III 10 86 21
quarrelled with her own seat,--was sure Louisa had got a P III 10 86 21
Anne found a nice seat for her, on a dry sunny bank, under P III 10 87 21
Louisa had found a better seat somewhere else, and she P III 10 87 21
in, they kindly offered a seat to any lady who might be P III 10 90 38
of the household, and taking his seat, to drive off. P III 12 105 9
He looked, as he spoke, to the seat which Mrs. Clay had P IV 4 151 22
She left her seat, she would go, one half of her should P IV 7 175 6
of his friend Colonel Wallis, as to have a seat by her. P IV 8 186 23
She remained in her seat, and so did Lady Russell; but she P IV 8 189 44
Captain Wentworth left his seat, and walked to the fire- P IV 10 225 56
none of it, now left his seat, and moved to a window; and P IV 11 231 12

SEATED (60)

as soon <as> we were seated, took her out of the room & LS 17 270 2
they were seated, on having preserved her gown from injury. NA I 2 22 11
but when they were seated at tea, she found him as NA I 3 25 2
for hardly had she been seated ten minutes before a lady NA I 4 31 2
minutes after they were seated; and James, who had been NA I 8 52 2
to breakfast, and saw her seated with the kindest welcome NA II 5 154 1
till they were happily seated at the dinner-table, when NA II 6 165 6
notice when they were seated at table; and, luckily, it NA II 7 175 12
obliged her to be seated, rubbed her temples with lavender- NA II 13 223 9
curiosity, they were all seated round the tea-table, which NA II 14 233 9
his hold till he had seated her in a chair in the parlour. SS I 9 42 8
which always attended her, invited him to be seated. SS I 9 42 10
they had not been long seated, before she leant behind her SS I 13 67 61
and happy, was hardly seated before her admiration of the SS I 19 106 23
else, though they were seated on different sides of the SS I 19 107 29
When they were seated in the dining room, Sir John SS I 20 111 18
She was seated in her mother's lap, covered with kisses, SS I 21 121 10
two fair rivals were thus seated side by side at the same SS II 1 145 23
the other; and Marianne, seated at the foot of the bed, SS II 7 190 55
56
as soon as he was seated, "of the very shocking discovery SS III 1 265 34
party only were formally seated, while three or four W 327 8
she knew not how, seated amongst the osborne set; & she W 330 11
seeing her father comfortably seated in his arm chair.-- W 354 28
Mr. Darcy was writing, and Miss Bingley, seated near him, PP I 10 47 1
politely and more earnestly negatived, she seated herself. PP I 10 51 45
He had not been long seated before he complimented Mrs. PP I 13 64 21
behaviour as any affront, seated himself at another table PP I 14 69 17
woman by whom he finally seated himself; and the agreeable PP I 16 76 4
an opening, but she was seated between Charlotte and Miss PP II 6 163 14
He now seated himself by her, and talked so agreeably of PP II 8 172 3
of Kitty's and Lydia's purchases, were seated in it. PP II 16 220 16
the view, she saw herself seated beneath a tent, tenderly PP II 18 232 22
and on their being seated, a pause, awkward as such pauses PP III 3 267 4
latter, had they not been seated at an inconvenient PP III 3 268 5
seated in the carriage, and on the road to Longbourn. PP III 4 281 29
of grave reflection, soon after they were seated at table, PP III 5 289 41
42
He was not seated by her; perhaps that was the reason of PP III 11 335 43
in a few moments after seated with the rest of the party. PP III 12 342 26
in the drawing-room, seated themselves in committee at a MP I 15 142 25
Henry Crawford was soon seated with the other three at the MP I 15 143 26
who at his suggestion now seated themselves round the fire. MP II 1 178 8
late, been many minutes seated in the drawing room, Sir MP II 5 222 41
Dr. and Mrs. Grant, being seated at the table of prime MP II 7 239 8
They had not been long seated and composed when Mr. E I 11 93 5
Mr. Woodhouse had been safely seated long enough to give E I 14 117 3
from Mr. Elton, and seated by Mr. Weston, at dinner, he E I 14 119 6
7
with scarcely an invitation, seated himself between them. E I 15 124 1
who with her knitting was seated in the warmest corner, E II 1 155 4
at dinner she found him seated by her--and, as she firmly E II 8 214 12
With mixed feelings, she seated herself at a little E II 8 227 87
Mrs. Weston, capital in her country-dances, was seated, E II 8 229 98
He contrived that she should be seated by him; and was E II 10 240 6
The very first subject after being seated was Maple Grove, E II 14 272 18
till her being seated at table and taking up her spoon. E III 2 328 44
seated and busy, and still Frank Churchill did not come. E III 6 361 41
steady old friends were seated round Mrs. Musgrove, and P IV 10 221 32
the terrace, & there, seated on one of the two green S 7 395 1
When they were all finally seated, after some removals to S 10 414 1
of the mist; Miss B-- seated, not far before her, at the S 12 426 1
along;--Miss Brereton seated, apparently very composedly-- S 12 426 1

SEATING (6)

"I am so glad to see you!" said she, seating herself SS I 20 110 2
Elinor drew near, but without saying a word; and seating SS II 7 182 12
Then seating herself with a gentleman on each side, she MP I 10 97 3
Fanny, and seating himself with a look of great vexation. MP I 15 139 9
"They do not want me at all," said she, seating herself. MP I 15 144 36
end to his attempts, by seating himself near the table, P III 9 79 27

SEATS (14)

they should easily find seats and be able to watch the NA I 2 21 9
Tilney with seats, as they had agreed to join their party. NA I 8 54 10
towards procuring them seats at her table; but as Lady SS II 12 231 9
concern they took their seats--Ld. Osborne near Emma, & W 345 21
Musgrave?--" said Emma, as they were taking their seats.-- W 358 28
they had all taken their seats, Mr. Collins was at leisure PP I 16 75 2
They were soon gone again, rising from their seats with an PP I 17 86 9
engravings of gentlemen's seats in the kingdom, and MP I 5 48 28
seats innumerable; but it must be all done without my care. MP I 6 57 31
in this weather, when we may have seats in a barouche! MP I 8 77 10
of the window seats--but he reads all them to himself. E I 4 29 10
Seats tolerably in the shade were found; and now Emma was E III 6 359 37
passed to their seats, her mind took a hasty range over it. P IV 8 185 21
in the seats of grandeaur; round the orchestra, of course." P IV 9 193 10

SECESSION (1)

of his regret at her secession from their company, and Mr. MP I 15 142 24

SECLUDE (2)

not bear to have her seclude herself from any chance of SS II 1 143 9
at another she would seclude herself from it for ever, and SS II 9 201 2

SECLUDED (3)

been secluded from the world, in some distant farm house. PP III 8 309 6
you, who have lived so secluded a life; and I could E II 14 275 32
very elegant & very secluded; with the hope on Miss S 11 421 1

SECLUSION (8)

Elinor, who greatly disapproved such continual seclusion. SS I 16 85 15
real occasion for such a seclusion from the family, they PP III 5 288 40
part of my future days will be spent in utter seclusion. MP I 3 29 48
comfortable, as such seclusion exactly suited her brother, E I 16 139 20
on the side of dignified seclusion, must be amply repaid E II 9 231 1
or spirits like Selina to enjoy that sort of seclusion. E II 18 307 21
have found us out at last, have you, in our seclusion?-- E III 2 324 22
23
to the bustles of Uppercross and the seclusion of Kellynch. P IV 2 135 34

SECLUSIONS (1)

favourable spot for the seclusions of the Miss Beauforts. S 11 422 1

SECOND (147)

indelicacy of so early a second marriage, must subject me LS 30 300 3
Whether Lady Susan was, or was not happy in her second LS 42 313 9
Miss Thorpe in the second, before John Thorpe came running NA I 9 61 1
she felt some alarm from the dread of a second prevention. NA I 10 71 8
Allen was called on to second him, and the two others NA I 11 84 19
the second, that it was a play she wanted very much to see. NA I 12 92 4
Setting her own inclination apart, to have failed a second NA I 13 101 25
He talked of fore-grounds, distances, and second distances- NA I 14 111 29
Bond-Street overtook the second Miss Thorpe, as she was NA I 14 114 50
first five minutes; the second unfolded thus much in NA I 15 116 1
James Morland's second letter was then received, and the NA II 1 135 42
to decline it; but her second was of greater deference for NA II 5 156 5
But on the second, or at farthest the third night after NA II 5 159 19
not waste a moment upon a second attempt, she could not NA II 6 164 3
each folding door, the second being secured only by bolts NA II 6 168 10
With less alarm and greater eagerness she seized a second, NA II 6 169 11
This second instance of his anxiety to delay what she so NA II 7 181 41
To involve her in the danger of a second detection, to NA II 9 192 5
"No, read it yourself," cried Catherine, whose second NA II 10 205 23
A second engagement must give way to a first. NA II 13 224 14
Of their personal charms he had not required a second SS I 10 46 1
picturesque beauty, and second marriages, and then you can SS I 10 47 4
I understand, does not approve of second attachments." SS I 11 55 8
her objections against a second attachment? or is it SS I 11 56 14
15
any instance of a second attachment's being pardonable." SS I 11 56 16
And soon afterwards, on the second boy's violently SS I 21 121 8
inform her, that Willoughby had paid no second visit there. SS II 5 169 16
Her second note, which had been written on the morning SS II 7 187 39
40
second son William, who were nearly of the same age. SS II 12 233 19
they might not expect to go out with her a second time? SS II 14 248 6
Edward seemed a second Willoughby; and acknowledging as SS III 1 261 13
Gardens, though it was only the second week in March. SS III 2 271 4
The second day brought them into the cherished, or the SS III 6 302 6
Mr. Harris was punctual in his second visit;--but he came SS III 7 313 21
But when the second moment had passed, when she found SS III 13 363 8
while acknowledging a second engagement, almost as SS III 13 372 44
This is the second time within this twelvemonth that she W 319 2
will dispose a great many people to attend the second.-- W 323 3
I hope she is likely to be happy in her second choice." W 325 4
"Elderly ladies should be careful how they make a second W 326 6
to elderly ladies, or to a second choice added his wife. W 326 6
of Miss Osborne's second promise;--but tho' he contrived W 330 11
Observing his second daughter employed in trimming a hat, PP I 2 6 1
2
the only creature in the room that he asked a second time. PP I 3 12 16
much flattered by his asking me to dance a second time. PP I 4 14 4
"Yes;--but he seemed to like his second better." PP I 5 18 5
chosen because it was the second volume of his, she gave a PP I 11 55 4
second, I can admire you much better as I sit by the fire." PP I 11 56 15
After a pause of some minutes she addressed him a second PP I 18 91 8
9
with the length of his second speech, and at the end of it PP I 18 98 61
He took the hint, and when Mary had finished her second PP I 18 100 68
69
the refusal is repeated a second or even a third time. PP I 19 107 13
their happiness on the chance of being asked a second time. PP I 19 107 14
trouble in achieving a second; in which there is certainly PP I 21 119 20
Her impatience for this second letter was as well rewarded PP II 3 147 21
She was to accompany Sir William and his second daughter. PP II 4 151 1
he welcomed them a second time with ostentatious formality PP II 5 155 3
And you only the second.-- PP II 6 165 34
How it could occur a second time therefore was very odd!-- PP II 10 182 1
Widely different was the effect of a second perusal.-- PP II 13 208 9
It was the second week in may, in which the three young PP II 16 219 1
The second began. PP II 18 229 1
Never, since reading Jane's second letter, had she PP III 4 279 24
But, on second thoughts, perhaps Lizzy could tell us, what PP III 6 295 6
such a weakness as a second proposal to the same woman? PP III 12 341 19
Mr. Bennet missed his second daughter exceedingly; his PP III 19 385 2
Crawford, the children of her mother by a second marriage. MP I 4 40 15
The second meeting proved him not so very plain; he was MP I 5 44 2
is wrong, we make a second better; we find comfort MP I 5 46 23
The second day's trial was not so guiltless. MP I 7 66 15
ever since she came back from your house the second time." MP I 7 72 46
and were drawing a second time to the door in the middle MP I 9 91 37
or a grandfather to leave a fortune to the second son." MP I 9 92 40
wine was allowed at the second table, and she has turned MP I 10 105 55
the second time--"we shall see some happy faces again now." MP I 12 117 12
To be a second time disappointed in the same way was an MP II 2 191 10
of thread or a second hand shirt button in the midst of MP II 6 236 21
up at the end of the second rubber, and leaving Dr. Grant MP II 7 246 36
They were now on the second floor, and the appearance of a MP II 9 270 40
And though there was no second glance to disturb her, MP II 10 274 8
the explanation of the second necklace--the real chain. MP II 10 274 9
Soon after the second breakfast, Edmund bad them good bye MP II 11 282 4
on both the first and second day, as they formed their MP II 11 284 9
good health; but on the second it led to something farther. MP II 11 284 9
feeling; but my second, which you shall have as sincerely, MP II 12 292 7
Price's commission as second lieutenant of H. M. Sloop MP II 13 298 3
it a second time, by any word, or look, or movement. MP III 3 335 6
Fanny believed there was scarcely a second feeling in MP III 6 367 5
of the second story, for his mother and for Rebecca. MP III 7 381 26
but no second sound had been heard of such a purpose. MP III 7 387 45
again; and though no second letter arrived for the space MP III 15 437 1
The next day came and brought no second letter. MP III 15 438 8
There was no second letter to explain away the first, from MP III 15 442 22
to Oxford; but the second was over at a much earlier hour. MP III 15 446 35
he might set forward on a second, and it is to be hoped, MP III 17 464 12
which could allow no second spring of hope or character. MP III 17 464 12

Her beauty and acquirements had held but a second place. MP III 17 466 17
first marriage; but his second must shew him how E I 2 17 6
After these came a second set; among the most come-at-able E I 3 20 3
I come in for a pretty good share as a second. E I 6 49 44
decidedly, I think, as must prevent any second application. E I 8 65 48
denote, which my second is destin'd to feel and my whole E I 9 70 7
Another view of man, my second brings, behold him there, E I 9 71 14
Another view of man, my second brings; behold him there, E I 9 73 18
"Yes, papa, it is written out in our second page. E I 9 79 55
John, the second, is named after his father. E I 9 80 72
The cold, however, was severe; and by the time the second E I 13 112 24
doubt of seeing him here about the second week in January." E I 14 120 9
and followed into the second carriage by Mr. Elton, that E I 15 128 23
Her second duty now, inferior only to her father's claims, E I 17 142 10
of falling in with the second rate and third rate of E II 1 155 3
could hardly believe it to be only their second meeting. E II 6 203 42
style of living, second only to the family at Hartfield. E II 7 207 6
second, slightly but correctly taken by Frank Churchill. E II 8 227 86
Towards the end of Jane's second song, her voice grew E II 8 229 93
The strength of the song falls on the second." E II 11 229 95
A word was put in for a second young Cox; and at last, Mr. E II 11 248 9
Such as Mrs. Elton appeared to her on this second E II 15 281 1
Mrs. Churchill will not be second to any lady in the land E II 18 306 13
No second meeting had there yet been between him and Emma. E III 2 319 2
Emma must submit to stand second to Mrs. Elton, though she E III 2 325 31
Before this second looking over was begun, however, Emma E III 6 362 43
Poor Harriet! to be a second time the dupe of her E III 11 402 1
Emma was sadly fearful that this second disappointment E III 11 403 2
about farming:--the second, was his having sat talking E III 11 410 35
circumstance (as second causes) to direct the human fate? E III 11 413 48
A second allusion, indeed, gave less pain.-- E III 19 483 9
Elliot, Esq., great grandson of the second Sir Walter." P III 1 3 3
4
have no thought of a second marriage, needs no apology to P III 1 5 8
No second attachment, the only thoroughly natural, happy, P III 4 28 7
general importance, were second, in that country, only to P III 4 28 7
and the second blessing was the arrival of the apothecary. P III 7 54 4
as themselves; and this second meeting, short as it was, P III 12 104 7
having met with him the second time; luckily Mary did not P III 12 106 19
too precipitate by half a second, she fell on the pavement P III 12 109 32
was to be blessed with a second spring of youth and beauty. P IV 1 124 10
He had called in Camden-Place; had called a second time, a P IV 2 135 35
to suspect) to prevent his thinking of a second choice. P IV 4 147 6
In the course of a second visit she talked with great P IV 5 153 8
"I have not had a creature call on me since the second " P IV 6 163 7
never insult me with my second W. again, "meaning, for the P IV 9 203 73
strenuous opposer of Sir Walter's making a second match. P IV 9 208 92
But she was a very good woman, and if her second object P IV 12 249 4
Sanditon was a second wife & 4 children to him--hardly S 2 372 1
They are more likely to want a second.-- S 9 410 1
"Upon second thoughts Mary, said her husband, I will not S 12 425 1
of a qr of a mile through second gates into the grounds, S 12 426 1

SECOND-HAND (2)
To be guided by second-hand conjecture is pitiful. NA II 4 152 26
the second-hand intelligence of their neighbour Lady Lucas. PP I 3 9 1

SECOND-SIZED (1)
By his description, a good deal like the second-sized P IV 11 240 58

SECONDARY (6)
Miss Tilney was earnest, though gentle, in her secondary NA II 2 140 10
it probable, as a secondary consideration in his wish of NA II 15 243 9
and failures with their secondary causes, the want of MP III 3 339 22
as to make them scarcely secondary to Donwell Abbey itself, E I 16 136 9
My being saved from pain is a very secondary consideration. E II 13 268 12
the Musgroves, were now become but of secondary interest. P IV 1 124 11

SECONDED (4)
entreaty was warmly seconded by Mr. Palmer, who seemed to SS III 7 309 5
social temper more than half seconded, gave the invitation. W 359 28
had it not been seconded by the assurance which I PP II 12 199 5
seconded a sudden wish of her's, to have Harriet's picture. E I 6 43 8

SECONDING (1)
up the parlour window, and loudly seconding the invitation. PP I 15 73 10

SECONDLY (9)
the appearance of her carriage--and secondly, in herself. NA II 14 233 8
Secondly, that I am convinced it will add very greatly to PP I 19 105 10
on the present occasion; and secondly, of my room. PP I 20 112 22
the whole of the matter; secondly, she was very sure that PP I 23 127 5
she was willing to hope, secondly, that her uncle's MP III 1 324 58
it herself; and which, secondly, when constrained at last MP III 2 326 1
as a settled, and secondly, as a good one--well aware of E III 17 467 30
her mother's death, and, secondly, from her happening to P III 2 14 11
never dreamt of; and secondly, as it cuts up a man's youth P III 3 19 16

SECONDS (3)
could not be borne many seconds, she opened the door, SS II 4 161 7
He stood for a few seconds, in silent amazement.-- W 355 28
about the room for a few seconds--and the only source E III 12 423 21

SECRECY (30)
But for this strange kind of secrecy maintained by them SS I 14 71 4
Secrecy may be advisable; but still I cannot help SS I 15 79 29
to justify doubt; no secrecy has been attempted; all has SS I 15 80 42
distance; and even secrecy, as far as it can be observed, SS I 15 81 44
We have already agreed that secrecy may be necessary, and SS I 16 84 6
in the world upon your secrecy; and I really thought my SS I 22 129 16
I had not supposed any secrecy intended, as they openly SS II 5 173 42
obstinate and ill-judged secrecy, she would tell nothing, SS II 9 209 28
and the appearance of secrecy must still be kept up. SS II 13 241 19
she was by her promise of secrecy to Lucy, she could give SS II 13 244 47
The secrecy with which every thing had been carried on SS III 13 371 38
I shall retreat in as much secrecy as possible to the most W 335 13
A promise of secrecy was of course very dutifully given, PP I 22 123 3
Having said thus much, I feel no doubt of your secrecy. PP II 12 201 5
He readily assured her of his secrecy--again expressed his PP III 4 278 22
"But why all this secrecy? PP III 5 283 8
very powerful motive for secrecy, in addition to his fear PP III 6 297 12
There were few people on whose secrecy she would have more PP III 8 311 12
were compatible with the secrecy which had been intended. PP III 9 320 32
reasons, to remain in the secrecy which Lydia seems to PP III 9 320 33
Elizabeth told her the motives of her secrecy. PP III 17 374 19
no other attempt made at secrecy, than Mrs. Norris's MP I 4 39 12
has a little spirit of secrecy, and independence, and MP III 1 323 56
feelings of Mr. Crawford, as to any secrecy of proceeding. MP III 2 331 19
For as to secrecy, Henry is quite the hero of an old MP III 5 360 16
Miss Crawford need not have urged secrecy with so much MP III 15 438 7
Secrecy could not have been more desirable for Mrs. MP III 17 468 21
If he had been anxious for secrecy, he would not have left E I 9 77 47
her to possess; and the secrecy she had maintained, as to E III 14 442 8
had I broken the bond of secrecy and told you every thing." E III 18 477 55

SECRESY (4)
To no creature had it been revealed, where secresy was PP III 3 270 10
great deal under such a system of secresy and concealment." E III 10 398 53
to have been carrying on with such perfect secresy?-- E III 10 399 58
An injunction of secresy had been among Mr. Weston's E III 11 403 2

SECRET (78)
is no secret to your friends, & to warn you against her. LS 12 261 5
so admirably adapted for secret discourses and unlimited NA I 9 60 1
"how handsome a family they are!" was her secret remark. NA I 10 80 60
But my secret I was always sure would be safe with you." NA I 15 118 13
mystery of an affected secret, on the other of undefined NA I 15 121 25
The disclosure however of the great secret of James's NA I 15 125 48
so far as to indulge in a secret "perhaps," but in general NA II 2 138 1
inviting her to a secret conference, led the way to a seat. NA II 3 143 1
that there is a secret subterraneous communication between NA II 5 159 21
At last, however, by touching a secret spring, an inner NA II 5 160 21
communicating by some secret means with those cells, might NA II 8 188 17
and equally safe did she believe her secret with each. NA II 14 230 3
an evident wonder and a secret admiration which equally SS I 9 42 9
"Oh! Elinor," she cried, "I have such a secret to tell you SS I 12 60 9
in themselves, though unavoidably secret for a while? SS I 15 79 28
"but pray do not tell it, for it's a great secret." SS I 21 125 38
meant to be a great secret, and I am sure has been SS I 22 129 16
Our first care has been to keep the matter secret.-- SS I 22 131 32
faithfully keeping this secret, because you must know of SS I 22 132 39
Your secret is safe with me; but pardon me if I express SS I 22 132 40
Elinor was mourning in secret over obstacles which must SS II 1 141 4
with a secret, so confessedly and evidently important. SS II 1 142 7
to let you into the secret, for you are a party concerned. SS II 2 149 25
was no longer to be a secret--it would take place even SS II 8 199 37
Well, and so this was kept a great secret, for fear of Mrs. SS III 1 258 7
My promise to Lucy, obliged me to be secret. SS III 1 262 23
And to have entered into a secret engagement with a young SS III 1 267 45
occupied by the important secret in her possession, than SS III 4 291 46
to her own heart from a secret acknowledgment of past SS III 10 341 5
secret reflections may be no more unpleasant than my own. SS III 10 345 24
her, and made her his secret standard of perfection in SS III 14 379 19
& he was obliged to keep his friend's secret.-- W 340 19
Their lodgings were not long a secret, and at length they PP I 7 28 4
confidence and have secret affairs to discuss, or because PP I 11 56 15
"Oh, Jane had we been less secret, had we told what we PP III 5 291 55
It was to be such a secret!" PP III 9 319 27
"If it was to be secret," said Jane, "say not another word PP III 9 319 28
affairs in the Longbourn family could not be long a secret. PP III 13 350 55
of; and with such a secret provision of comfort within his MP III 3 334 3
him, he hoped to be expressing Fanny's secret feelings too. MP III 3 337 11
Her secret was still her own; and while that was the case, MP III 5 365 34
was Fanny's secret declaration, as she finished this. MP III 13 424 3
in the indulgence of her secret meditations; and nothing MP III 14 431 8
Fanny was not in the secret of her uncle's feelings, Sir MP III 16 453 15
Sir Thomas not in the secret of Miss Crawford's character. MP III 16 453 15
but as you make no secret of your love of match-making, it E I 8 66 51
she felt too much in the secret herself, to think the E II 8 220 45
there had been a smile of secret delight, she had less E II 10 243 22
it was quite a secret, known to nobody else, and only E III 5 345 16
a heavy arrear due of secret severity in her reflections E III 6 353 3
in secret-- "I am glad I have done being in love with him. E III 6 364 57
59
Mr. Weston in keeping his secret, than with any other view. E III 10 394 19
at Weymouth, and kept a secret from everybody. E III 10 395 35
and such a league in secret to judge us all!-- E III 10 399 61
present, the whole affair was to be completely a secret. E III 11 403 2
He told me it was to be a great secret; and, therefore, I E III 11 404 6
believed herself in the secret of everybody's feelings; E III 11 412 47
reason to regret that I was not in the secret earlier." E III 13 426 15
to rejoice that Harriet's secret had not escaped her, and E III 13 431 38
me as having a secret which was to be kept at all hazards. E III 14 437 8
the creation to stoop in charity to a secret engagement.-- E III 14 437 8
Fancying you to have fathomed his secret. E III 15 445 15
It would be a secret satisfaction; but the consciousness E III 16 452 7
acquainted with what was still a secret to other people. E III 16 453 12
till my dear father is in the secret, and hear his opinion. E III 17 464 24
"It is to be a secret, I conclude," said he. E III 17 468 34
"These matters are always a secret, till it is found out E III 17 468 34
This, however, was a profound secret; no to be breathed P III 2 15 13
could not be kept a secret,)--accidentally hearing of the P III 3 21 18
secret of Sir Walter's estimate of the dues of a tenant. P III 3 23 34
of her own friends in the secret of the past, which seemed P III 4 30 10
too much in the secret of the complaints of each house. P III 6 44 7
This was his only secret exception, when he said to his P III 7 61 38
39
At the same time, however, it was a secret gratification P III 12 106 19
cousinly little interview must remain a perfect secret. P III 12 106 19
as if they believed themselves quite in the secret. P IV 10 222 37
harassing herself in secret with the never-ending question, P IV 10 227 69
extreme difficulty which secret lovers must have in S 12 426 1

SECRETARY (2)
"I would rather find him private secretary to the first MP II 7 246 35
two more, one from the secretary of the first Lord to a MP II 13 298 3

SECRETED (1)
the suspicion of there being many chambers secreted. NA II 8 183 2

SECRETLY (10)
Here Catherine secretly acknowledged the power of love; NA I 15 118 12
hope and expect it; and secretly to congratulate herself SS I 10 49 11
he could be all the time secretly engaged to another SS III 1 266 38
to the utmost; and secretly resolved to avail herself, at SS III 5 293 2
every scruple, by secretly saying now and then, 'I shall SS III 8 326 53
of the man whom they secretly mean to accept, when he PP I 19 107 13
not help secretly advising her father not to let her go. PP II 18 230 14
to talk; Elizabeth was secretly forming a desperate PP III 16 365 1
And secretly she added to herself, "Lord bless me! when E III 4 339 15
"Engaged since October,--secretly engaged.-- E III 10 395 38

SECRETS (6)
Come, come, let's have no secrets among friends." SS II 4 163 18
Sharpe and I had so many secrets together, she never made SS III 2 274 20
Do not trust her with any secrets of your own, take W 317 2
She had got rid of two of the secrets which had weighed on PP II 17 227 25
There are secrets in all families, you know)--the case is, E I 14 120 11
let me thus much into the secrets of Marlborough-Buildings. P IV 9 205 82

SECURE (81)
whose hearts I shall be very eager to secure an interest. LS 1 243 1
not feeling perfectly secure that a knowledge of that LS 22 280 1
Your husband I abhor--Reginald I despise--& I am secure of LS 39 307 1
it, but after all that I have seen, how can one be secure? LS 41 309 1
two years, on purpose to secure him, was defrauded of her LS 42 313 10
Pump-Room the next day, secure within herself of seeing Mr. NA I 4 31 1
carried her point and was secure of her walk, she began (NA I 13 103 29
She knew enough to feel secure of an honourable and speedy NA I 15 122 28
The utmost care could not always secure the most valuable NA II 7 178 21
brow, she felt secure from all possibility of wronging him. NA II 8 187 13
to make her feel secure at least of life for the present. NA II 9 192 4
need of my being played off to make her secure of Tilney. NA II 10 202 7
settlements, eventually secure; his present income was an NA II 16 249 2
They think themselves secure, you do no more than what is SS I 2 11 22
be secure of their approbation before her answer were sent. SS I 4 24 20
It was enough to secure his good opinion; for to be SS I 7 33 3
Your mother will secure to you, in time, that independence SS I 19 103 7
it, would very likely secure every thing to Robert, and SS II 2 148 15
Elinor felt secure of its announcing Willoughby's approach, SS II 4 161 7
Dashwood was careful to secure Colonel Brandon, who, SS II 12 230 6
as soon as he could secure his attention,--"she has not SS II 12 236 43
I had reason to believe myself secure of my present wife, SS III 8 323 40
His own merits must soon secure it." SS III 9 337 18
sister's health were more secure, before she appointed it. SS III 10 343 10
care, in her haste to secure him, should overlook every SS III 12 357 2
of his existence secure, till he had revealed his present SS III 14 373 3
When she is secure of him, there will be leisure for PP I 6 22 6
their opinion, to be secure of judging properly at first." PP I 18 93 36
She endeavoured to secure Jane in her interest, but Jane PP I 20 112 23
My object has been to secure an amiable companion for PP I 20 114 32
of an event which will secure the happiness of so many?" PP I 21 118 14
was nothing less, than to secure her from any return of Mr. PP I 22 121 1
for though feeling almost secure, and with reason, for PP I 22 121 1
and if he is attached to me, no other woman can secure it." PP II 1 136 22
I wonder he does not marry, to secure a lasting PP II 10 184 17
remained, he thought, to secure and expedite a marriage, PP III 10 323 2
But she would not be secure. PP III 11 334 37
warmest affection, and secure of her relations' consent, PP III 17 378 46

to ourselves, we must secure to the child, or consider MP I 1 7 7
ourselves engaged to secure to her hereafter, as MP I 1 7 7
put themselves out of their way to secure her comfort. MP I 2 14 6
account, she was glad to secure any pleasure for her MP I 8 76 7
obliging the others, to secure it, the matter was settled MP I 8 80 29
She must know herself too secure of the regard of all the MP II 3 199 14
must attend it, happy to secure a marriage which would MP II 3 201 22
It certainly may secure all the myrtle and turkey part of MP II 4 213 36
only did not pay her for what she had given to secure it. MP II 7 243 26
To be secure of a partner at first, was a most essential MP II 10 274 8
her disposition would secure her all your own immediately. MP II 12 293 15
must with perseverance secure a return, and at no great MP III 2 327 4
secure, she was in every way an object of painful alarm. MP III 5 356 4
they might be secure of having four walls to themselves. MP III 5 357 6
Though tolerably secure of not seeing Mr. Crawford again, MP III 11 413 31
That Miss Crawford should endeavour to secure a meeting MP III 12 418 4
to secure herself from being again too much attracted. MP III 17 466 18
place and any society, secure her a great deal to enjoy, MP III 17 469 24
must appear as secure as earthly happiness can be.-- MP III 17 473 32
important to her to be secure of a comfortable provision, E I 1 11 38
competence--enough to secure the purchase of a little E I 2 16 5
Now I am secure of you for ever." E I 7 53 24
and will hazard nothing till he believes himself secure." E I 10 90 40
should be very glad to be secure of undergoing the anxiety E I 14 121 14
off from some advantages, it will secure him many others." E I 18 148 23
secure you some of the best society in the place. E II 14 275 32
Her situation should secure your compassion. E III 7 375 61
Could she be secure of that, indeed, of his never marrying E III 12 416 1
could secure, and saw no dignity in any thing short of it. P III 2 12 5
and no connexions to secure even his farther rise in that P III 4 26 3
which they were going to secure, was very unwilling to P III 5 33 6
began to wish that she could feel secure even for a week. P III 7 53 1
They secure an introduction. P IV 6 162 5
can ever be secure, while she holds her present influence. P IV 9 208 92
had once before seemed to secure every thing, but which P IV 11 240 59
He wanted to secure the promise of a visit--to get as many S 2 373 1
be really in a state of secure & permanent health without S 2 373 1
with Sir Edward, and to secure for herself & her family S 3 377 1
it secure us, to the prejudice of E. Bourne & Hastings."-- S 4 382 1
to secure for you--the West Indians, & the seminary.--" S 9 408 1
Whitby to secure them a house?--but neither pleased me.-- S 9 409 1
he only eat enough to secure the coats of his stomach;--& S 10 417 1
themselves so perfectly secure from observation!--the S 12 427 1

SECURED (48)

secured, Catherine only remained to be apprized of it. NA I 13 97 1
suspense, and every thing secured when it was determined NA II 2 138 1
The affection of Isabella was to be secured to her in a NA II 2 141 11
to be secured by her seeing nothing of Captain Tilney? NA II 4 152 28
door being only secured by massy bars and a padlock, you NA II 5 159 19
strength, that, unless secured by supernatural means, the NA II 6 164 3
door, the second being secured only by bolts of less NA II 6 168 10
and key, secured in all probability a cavity of importance. NA II 6 168 10
would part with one gentleman before the other was secured. NA II 10 206 31
wife's fortune was also secured to her child, and he had SS I 1 4 2
of four years old, it was secured, in such a way, as to SS I 1 4 3
Dashwood would have been secured by any act of attention SS I 9 42 9
a look of approbation as secured the largest share of his SS I 10 46 2
But at length she was secured by the exertions of Elinor, SS I 16 85 15
after his arrival, he had secured his lady, engaged her SS III 13 361 3
With an income sufficient to their wants thus secured to SS III 14 374 6
His attendance was by this means secured, and the rest SS III 14 376 11
"It might have been secured to your future use, without W 352 26
She had thus secured him from her sisters--but it was not W 356 28
but his presence gave variety & secured good manners.-- W 359 28
hope to be in future secured, when the following account PP II 12 196 5
and her preference secured at any time by their renewal. PP II 18 233 25
the five thousand pounds, secured among your children PP III 7 302 14
Jane's happiness, and his own, would be speedily secured. PP III 12 340 13
attending such behaviour, secured, and brought round by MP I 4 35 4
instrument; one morning secured an invitation for the next, MP I 7 64 12
She was in a state of mind to be glad that she had secured MP II 3 201 23
a voluntary partner secured against the dancing began. MP II 10 274 8
he had secured agreeable recollections for his own mind. MP III 10 404 15
be protected by him, and secured in every comfort, and MP III 17 465 13
man; his own temper had secured him from that, even in his E I 2 17 6
of congratulation which her marriage had already secured. E I 2 18 10
him from Randalls, and secured him the power of sending to E I 13 110 10
for the happiness she secured to his father, and her very E II 5 191 28
Her father's comfort was amply secured, Mrs. Bates as well E II 8 213 6
to Emma, had secured her hand, and led her up to the top. E II 8 229 98
Another room of much better size might be secured for the E II 11 254 44
Emma's being positively secured for the two first dances E II 11 256 60
and happy she is to have secured such a situation. E III 8 379 8
and confidence, and her peace would be fully secured.-- E III 12 416 1
the first of blessings secured, in obtaining her promises E III 14 437 8
must have a curate, and you had secured his promise. P III 9 78 20
All his caution was spent in being secured of the real P IV 9 202 66
I have been to the theatre, and secured a box for to- P IV 10 223 41
instead of depriving her of one friend, secured her two. P IV 12 251 11
appearance secured a very strong hold in Lady D.'s regard. S 3 379 1
difficulties at last secured a proper house at 8g pr week S 10 414 1
G. to Miss Diana Parker, secured them immediately an S 11 421 1

SECURELY (3)

He is more securely her's than ever. LS 24 291 17
as securely as if it had been her own chamber at Fullerton. NA II 6 167 9
Maria could now speak so securely of her happiness with MP II 3 201 22

SECURES (2)

A very little trouble on your side secures him. SS II 11 223 24
A large party secures its own amusement. E III 6 353 4

SECURING (12)

securing their promise of dining at the park the next day. SS I 6 31 10
of his own advantage in securing so respectable and SS III 3 283 20
obstructed, will do in securing every advantage of fortune, SS III 14 376 11
with William price, and securing his knave at an early MP II 7 242 25
leisure which followed securing the odd trick by Sir MP II 7 245 32
for the sake of securing her at that part of the evening. MP II 10 278 20
of considering her as a friend and securing her affection. E II 6 196 2
too anxious for securing any thing to like to yield. E II 11 250 23
The delightful family-party which Emma was securing for E III 15 450 37
After securing accommodations, and ordering a dinner at P III 11 95 9
the man who was securing the happiness of her other child. P IV 12 249 4
we may safely reckon on securing you two large families, S 5 387 1

SECURITIES (1)

bind by the strongest securities all that remained to him MP III 17 471 29

SECURITY (26)

If my sister in the security of retirement, with as little LS 14 264 3
"And is that to be my only security? alas, alas!" NA I 10 78 39
"Now you have given me a security worth having; and I NA I 10 78 41
three lines, and in one moment all was joyful security. NA I 15 121 26
varieties of suspense, security, and disappointment; but NA II 2 140 11
there was surely some security for the existence even of a NA II 10 200 3
With what cheerful ease, what happy, though false security, NA II 13 228 27
for the sake of the provision and security of a wife. SS I 8 38 10
she added with revived security of Edward's honour and SS I 22 131 29
Elinor's security sunk; but her self-command did not sink SS I 22 131 33
for all her former security; and the servant who sat up SS III 7 312 17
since our delightful security I have repeated it to him SS III 9 337 18
elevated at once to that security with another, which he SS III 13 361 3
solicitude to the proper security of her young Charges' W 327 7
and insensibility of danger, security for happiness." PP II 1 135 13
and anxiety, but his countenance expressed real security. PP II 11 189 6
only security for her husband's not being killed in a duel. PP III 6 294 2
evenings, her perfect security in such a tete-a-tete from MP I 4 35 6
With all the security which love of another and disesteem MP II 6 231 11
This seems as if nothing were a security for matrimonial MP III 5 361 16
Fanny shared her aunt's security, till she received a few MP III 14 429 1
she; "that is the only security for its freshness; and E I 9 71 8
Two days of joyful security were immediately followed by E II 12 258 7
was really in danger of becoming too happy for security.-- E III 18 475 39
the hope of more, of security, stability, and improvement. E III 19 482 4
the very security of his affection, wherewith to pity her. P IV 10 225 62

SEDATE (3)

Eleanor's countenance was dejected, yet sedate; and its NA II 9 191 4
Jane looked a little paler than usual, but more sedate PP III 11 335 39
degree of sedate civility entreated her to study it. E III 5 348 23

SEDATENESS (2)

several hours to give sedateness to her spirits, or any SS III 13 363 8
had none of its usual sedateness; and he repeated his PP III 1 252 52

SEDENTARY (3)

Catherine's disposition was not naturally sedentary, nor NA II 15 240 1
much less inclined to sedentary pursuits, or to MP III 12 418 7
and a decided taste for reading, and sedentary pursuits. P III 11 97 12

SEDUCE (1)

serious designs; it was clara whom he meant to seduce.-- S 8 405 2

SEDUCED (3)

and innocence he had seduced, in a situation of the utmost SS II 9 209 30
Emma was very willing now to acquit her of having seduced E II 2 168 13
least intention of being seduced--but she bore with him S 8 405 2

SEDUCER (1)

I could not trace her beyond her first seducer, and there SS II 9 207 26

SEDUCTION (4)

loss of his heart; his seduction and desertion of Miss SS II 10 212 1
seduction, had been extended into every tradesman's family. PP III 6 294 4
whom lay the greater seduction I pretended not to say)-- MP III 16 457 30
Her seduction was quite determined on. S 8 405 2

SEDUCTIVE (1)

Sir Edw:'s great object in life was to be seductive.-- S 8 405 2

SEDULOUSLY (2)

too sedulously divided in word and deed on every occasion. SS II 12 229 4
Harvilles, whom she was sedulously guarding from the P IV 2 134 29

SEE (1062)

I am determined you see, not to be denied admittance at LS 1 244 1
Reginald has long wished I know to see this captivating LS 3 247 1
I long to see her, & shall certainly accept your kind LS 4 248 2
I hope to see her the wife of Sir James within a LS 7 253 1
& it is impossible to say when you may see him in Kent. LS 8 254 1
to see a young man of Reginald's sense duped by her at all. LS 8 256 4
I see plainly that she is uneasy at my progress in the LS 10 257 1
It is impossible to see the intimacy between them, so very LS 11 259 1
I should blush to see him, to hear of him, to think of him. LS 12 261 4
as I think you will like to see it; I wish it was more LS 13 262 1
it was easy to see that her veiws extended to marriage. LS 14 264 4
urge the necessity of reproof, if you see me too lenient." LS 15 267 6
Poor Reginald was beyond measure concerned to see his fair LS 17 270 3
her's; & from what I now see of the behaviour of each to LS 17 270 5
she is shy, & I think I can see that some pains are taken LS 17 270 6
on one side, where she may see her mother walking for an LS 17 271 7
my brother, I so very often see her eyes fixed on his face LS 18 272 1
such kind intentions, could see the terms on which we now LS 20 278 7
but I see nothing in it more like encouragement. LS 20 278 11
which I was pleased to see not unmixed with jealousy; but LS 22 280 2
I have not yet tranquillized myself enough to see LS 22 282 8
with earnestness--I do not know when you will see me again. LS 23 284 4
you must make it your business to see justice done her. LS 23 284 4
myself) I know my father wants very much to see him. LS 24 286 4
I see how closely she observes him & Lady Susan. LS 24 291 16
while I spoke, to see the struggle between returning LS 25 293 3
if you do not allow him to see you here, I cannot answer LS 26 295 3
She is going to town, to see her particular friend, Mrs LS 27 296 1
It is impossible to say when I shall be able to see you. LS 28 298 2
I see you as you are. LS 34 304 1
& your dear neice is included of course; I long to see her. LS 40 309 1
any doubt of the fact--but merely to see how she looked. LS 41 310 1
I took care to see her alone, that I might say all this, & LS 41 310 4
her second choice--I do not see how it can ever be LS 42 313 9
have six children more--to see them growing up around her, NA I 1 13 1
Mrs. Morland was a very good woman, and wished to see her NA I 1 15 3
Here are no tea things for us, you see." NA I 2 22 18
"I see what you think of me," said he gravely--"I shall NA I 3 26 20
about, and nobody wanted to see; and he only was absent. NA I 4 31 1
what a pleasure it was to see an old friend, they NA I 4 32 2
will be so delighted to see you: the tallest is Isabella, NA I 4 32 3
relief, that they should see each other across the theatre NA I 4 34 7
"It is very true, upon my honour, but I see how it is; you NA I 6 41 16
about Mr. Tilney, for perhaps I may never see him again." NA I 6 41 17
"Not see him again! NA I 6 41 18
You said you should like to see it." NA I 6 43 39
you ever see an animal so made for speed in your life?" NA I 7 46 9
look at his loins; only see how he moves; that horse NA I 7 46 11
"Curricle-hung you see; seat, trunk, sword-case, splashing- NA I 7 46 13
you see complete; the iron-work as good as new, or better. NA I 7 46 13
her, when they withdrew to see the new hat, that John NA I 7 50 44
young woman I could wish to see you attached to; she has NA I 7 50 47
"Because I thought I should soon see you myself. NA I 7 50 49
good it is of you to come so far on purpose to see me." NA I 7 51 52
that way, but he did not see her, and therefore the smile NA I 8 53 3
"I am very happy to see you again, sir, indeed; I was NA I 8 54 4
longed to point out that gentleman, she could see nothing. NA I 8 55 10
I could not even see where you were." NA I 8 56 13
Do go and see for her, Mr. Morland, said I--but all in NA I 8 56 14
I die to see him. NA I 8 57 16
of all Isabella's impatient desire to see Mr. Tilney. NA I 8 57 21
Tell him, that it would quite shock you to see me do such NA I 8 58 23
Did you ever see such a little tittuppy thing in your life? NA I 9 65 28
"Did you see any body else of our acquaintance?" NA I 9 68 39
Oh! what would not I give to see him! NA I 10 70 1
I assure you, I can hardly exist till I see him." NA I 10 70 1
"No," said Catherine, "he is not here; I cannot see him NA I 10 70 2
a moment's silence, "how surprized I was to see him again. NA I 10 72 11
in the room; and when they see you standing up with NA I 10 75 26
I walk about here, and so I do there;--but here I see a NA I 10 79 54
said, "I see that you guess what I have just been asked. NA I 10 80 59
in England--worth going fifty miles at any time to see." NA I 11 85 23
"Then I should like to see it; but I cannot-----I cannot NA I 11 85 30
"I should like to see the castle; but may we go all over NA I 11 86 43
she might not be obliged to see her beloved Isabella and NA I 12 91 3
the second, that it was a play she wanted very much to see. NA I 12 92 4
she was; for she would not see me this morning when I NA I 12 94 9
been wishing ever since to see you, to explain the reason NA I 12 94 10
Thorpe, however, would see her to her chair, and, till she NA I 12 96 23
"I cannot help being jealous, Catherine, when I see myself NA I 13 98 2
for my own peace; and to see myself supplanted in your NA I 13 98 2
I cannot bear to see it." NA I 13 104 34
You see, Miss Morland, the injustice of your suspicions. NA I 14 107 9
that she soon began to see beauty in every thing admired NA I 14 111 29
I cannot bear to see you linger so. NA I 15 120 24
My father and mother will be very glad to see you." NA I 15 123 41
hope, Miss Morland, you will not be sorry to see me." NA I 15 123 42
There are very few people I am sorry to see. NA I 15 123 43
We shall be very glad to see you at Fullerton, whenever it NA I 15 124 47
"Well, I shall see how they behave to me this evening; we NA II 1 130 10
said Mrs. Thorpe, "we perfectly see into your heart. NA II 1 136 49
our mode of living, as you see, is plain and unpretending; NA II 2 139 7
To see and explore either the ramparts and keep of the one, NA II 2 141 11

Context	Work	Vol	Ch	Page	Line
It must be all and completely a mistake--for I did not see	NA	II	3	145	11
Ah! here he comes; never mind, he will not see us, I am	NA	II	3	147	20
about without any thing to see, next followed--and her	NA	II	5	156	4
They all attended in the hall to see him mount his horse,	NA	II	7	175	13
Even Frederick, my eldest son, you see, who will perhaps	NA	II	7	176	15
She was all impatience to see the house, and had scarcely	NA	II	7	177	18
her friend's curiosity to see the house, soon revived the	NA	II	8	182	1
of the house, than see all the finery of all the rest.--	NA	II	8	185	5
wish of being permitted to see it, as well as all the rest	NA	II	8	186	7
window in the gallery, to see if it appeared; but all	NA	II	8	188	19
"I have been," said Catherine, looking down, "to see your	NA	II	9	195	9
"No, I only wanted to see-----	NA	II	9	195	17
as to return only to see her mother in her coffin."	NA	II	9	197	25
I left her and Bath yesterday, never to see either again.	NA	II	10	202	7
from her, perhaps never to see her again, I do not feel so	NA	II	10	207	39
Let me see; Monday will be a busy day with you, we will	NA	II	11	210	6
I believe if I could see you I should not mind the rest,	NA	II	12	216	2
and they pretended to be quite surprized to see me out.	NA	II	12	217	2
I see what she has been about.	NA	II	12	218	4
I see that she has had designs on Captain Tilney, which	NA	II	12	218	6
should be so glad to see him, and have so much to say, for	NA	II	13	222	8
enough in this house to see that I am but a nominal	NA	II	13	225	19
now left her with "I shall see you in the morning."	NA	II	13	226	24
the morning, that he might not be obliged even to see her.	NA	II	13	226	25
if Henry should chance to see, was an undertaking to	NA	II	14	235	14
before I left Bath, that one can hardly see where it was.	NA	II	14	238	22
of you; for ten to one whether you ever see him again.	NA	II	15	240	4
"You may see the house from this window, sir," was	NA	II	15	243	9
of my readers, who will see in the tell-tale compression	NA	II	16	250	4
longed to see him distinguished--as--they hardly knew what.	SS	I	3	15	6
to see him connected with some of the great men of the day.	SS	I	3	16	6
have quieted her ambition to see him driving a barouche.	SS	I	3	16	6
that I shall never see a man whom I can really love.	SS	I	3	18	20
see imperfection in his face, than I now do in his heart."	SS	I	4	21	10
"It is but a cottage," she continued, "but I hope to see	SS	I	5	25	2
see me, I am sure I will find none in accommodating them."	SS	I	5	25	2
of our friends as I hope to see often collected here; and	SS	I	6	29	4
I shall see how much I am before-hand with the world in	SS	I	6	29	4
They were of course very anxious to see a person on whom	SS	I	6	31	8
They would see, he said, only one gentleman there besides	SS	I	7	33	4
and pretended to see them blush whether they did or not.	SS	I	7	34	5
her eyes towards Elinor to see how she bore these attacks,	SS	I	7	34	5
of whom she had lived to see respectably married, and she	SS	I	8	36	1
Mrs. Jennings had been anxious to see Colonel Brandon well	SS	I	8	36	1
"Aye, aye, I see how it will be," said Sir John, "I see	SS	I	9	45	29
But I see what you mean.	SS	I	10	48	5
all are delighted to see, and nobody remembers to talk to."	SS	I	10	50	14
see him myself without taking pains to converse with him."	SS	I	10	50	16
mind, that one is sorry to see them give way to the	SS	I	11	56	12
on the following day to see a very fine place about twelve	SS	I	12	62	28
"we might see whether it could be put off or not."	SS	I	13	64	27
"I hope we shall see you at Barton," added her ladyship, "	SS	I	13	65	35
It is a very large one I know, and when I come to see you,	SS	I	13	67	64
we did not go there, or that we did not see the house?	SS	I	13	68	68
I did not see it to advantage, for nothing could be more	SS	I	13	69	76
"I could see it in his face.	SS	I	14	70	2
But are you really so attached to this place as to see no	SS	I	14	72	10
"Shall we see you to-morrow to dinner?" said Mrs. Dashwood	SS	I	14	74	21
that he wanted, Elinor; I could plainly see that.	SS	I	15	78	24
If you were to see them at the altar, you would suppose	SS	I	15	80	42
round with surprise to see and welcome Edward Ferrars.	SS	I	16	86	20
How have I delighted, as I walked, to see them driven in	SS	I	16	87	31
Did you ever see their equals?	SS	I	16	88	33
You may see one end of the house.	SS	I	16	88	33
rest of the objects before me, I see a very dirty lane."	SS	I	16	88	36
It is not likely that I should now see or hear anything to	SS	I	17	93	30
"Marianne is as stedfast as ever, you see," said Elinor, "	SS	I	17	93	31
round, was astonished to see Edward himself come out.	SS	I	18	96	2
"I am going into the village to see my horses," said he, "	SS	I	18	96	3
You may see her if you look this way."	SS	I	19	105	16
I see her instrument is open."	SS	I	19	105	18
I have brought my other son and daughter to see you.	SS	I	19	106	20
"You may believe how glad we all were to see them," added	SS	I	19	107	29
would come with us; she longed so much to see you all!"	SS	I	19	107	29
"Now, palmer, you shall see a monstrous pretty girl."	SS	I	19	108	34
But they had no curiosity to see how Mr. and Mrs. Palmer	SS	I	19	108	40
"I am so glad to see you!" said she, seating herself	SS	I	20	110	2
"There now"--said his lady, "you see Mr. Palmer expects	SS	I	20	113	31
It will be so ridiculous to see all his letters directed	SS	I	20	113	35
"There now; you see how droll he is.	SS	I	20	113	39
You can't think how much I longed to see you!	SS	I	20	116	60
her some other new acquaintance to see and observe.	SS	I	21	118	1
And they both long to see you of all things, for they have	SS	I	21	119	4
and for my part, I love to see children full of life and	SS	I	21	122	19
But I can't bear to see them dirty and nasty.	SS	I	21	123	28
to see in every carriage which drove near their house.	SS	II	1	141	4
affection for Edward and to see him as little as possible;	SS	II	1	142	7
And in all probability you will see your brother, and	SS	II	3	156	8
and shall always be glad to see him; but as to the rest of	SS	II	3	157	17
in her own room, could see little of what was passing.	SS	II	4	161	7
"I am monstrous glad to see you--sorry I could not come	SS	II	4	163	14
to tell you, that you will certainly see her to-morrow."	SS	II	4	163	17
young ladies with me, you see--that is, you see but one of	SS	II	4	163	18
see but one of them now, but there is another somewhere.	SS	II	4	163	18
the room; so delighted to see them all, that it was hard	SS	II	4	164	21
"Mr. Palmer will be so happy to see you," said she; "what	SS	II	4	164	22
It grieved her to see the earnestness with which he often	SS	II	5	169	12
though he could not but see her; and then continued his	SS	II	6	176	3
Elinor turned involuntarily to Marianne, to see whether it	SS	II	6	176	3
expecting every moment to see her faint, tried to screen	SS	II	6	177	12
Tell him I must see him again--must speak to him instantly.	SS	II	6	177	13
of worsted for her rug, to see any thing at all; and	SS	II	7	181	7
					8
it is quite grievous to see her look so ill and forlorn.	SS	II	7	181	8
Did not I see them together in Devonshire every day, and	SS	II	7	182	10
she went to the window to see who could be coming so	SS	II	7	184	16
And can you believe me to be so, while I see you so	SS	II	7	185	23
"I can have no pleasure while I see you in this state."	SS	II	7	186	27
"And you will never see me otherwise.	SS	II	7	186	28
from you, and still more to see you, every hour of the day.	SS	II	7	187	40
as soon as she was gone, "how it grieves me to see her!	SS	II	8	194	8
Did you ever see her? a smart, stilish girl they say, but	SS	II	8	194	10
But I shall see them to-morrow."	SS	II	8	195	16
the house, you may see all the carriages that pass along.	SS	II	8	197	22
expected, nor wished to see her there, and, in short, that	SS	II	8	198	30
and whispered--"the Colonel looks as grave as ever you see.	SS	II	8	198	30
and who expected to see the effect of Miss Dashwood's	SS	II	8	200	43
might have been all that you will live to see the other be.	SS	II	9	208	28
To suffer you all to be so deceived; to see your sister--	SS	II	9	210	32
her was not entirely such as the former had hoped to see.	SS	II	10	212	1
irritated than before, she did not see her less wretched.	SS	II	10	212	1
it right that they should sometimes see their brother.	SS	II	10	213	5
vent, was able not only to see the Miss Dashwoods from the	SS	II	10	215	14
emotion, but very soon to see them without recollecting a	SS	II	10	215	14
Elinor only was sorry to see them.	SS	II	10	217	20
talking--but it won't do-- the doctor is the man, I see."	SS	II	10	218	27
"I am sorry we cannot see your sister, Miss Dashwood,"	SS	II	10	219	37
I think she might see us; and I am sure we would not speak	SS	II	10	219	39
Miss Steele, "we can just as well go and see her."	SS	II	10	219	41
John Dashwood was really far from being sorry to see his	SS	II	11	221	7
obliged to take Harry to see the wild beasts at Exeter	SS	II	11	221	9
John Dashwood very soon, and bring her sisters to see her.	SS	II	11	223	14
have too much sense not to see all that.	SS	II	11	224	24
are all truly anxious to see you well settled; Fanny	SS	II	11	224	24
on being unable to see Edward, though he had arrived in	SS	II	11	230	4
though she could now see her with perfect indifference as	SS	II	12	230	6
given by his sister; and to see him for the first time	SS	II	12	231	10
In a moment I shall see the person that all my happiness	SS	II	12	232	13
She could not but smile to see the graciousness of both	SS	II	12	232	16
Fanny still more, did not see the necessity of enforcing	SS	II	12	234	25
I do not know whether you ever happened to see any of her	SS	II	12	234	27
not bear to see a sister slighted in the smallest point.	SS	II	12	236	38
Now you see it is all gone."	SS	II	12	237	43
Elinor's curiosity to see Mrs. Ferrars was satisfied.--	SS	II	13	238	1
Did you see nothing but only civility?--	SS	II	13	239	6
say more than once, they should always be glad to see me.--	SS	II	13	240	15
that she was happy to see him, and that she had very much	SS	II	13	241	20
Elinor is well, you see.	SS	II	13	242	26
"Could she not see that we wanted her gone!--how teazing	SS	II	13	244	44
It is but natural that he should like to see her as well	SS	II	13	244	45
So that, in fact, you see, if people do but know how to	SS	II	14	252	18
"I do not see how it can be done," said she, "without	SS	II	14	253	21
Her husband, but with great humility, did not see the	SS	II	14	253	22
I never happened to see them together, or I am sure I	SS	III	1	258	7
to her;--and even to see Edward himself, if chance should	SS	III	1	264	32
be his all; she would never see him again; and so far	SS	III	1	267	38
at my house; and so I would tell him if I could see him.	SS	III	1	268	51
continued John, "than to see his younger brother in	SS	III	1	269	56
You see I cannot leave Mrs. Clarke."	SS	III	2	271	6
arm--"for I wanted to see you of all things in the world."	SS	III	2	271	8
I must see what I can give them towards furnishing their	SS	III	2	277	28
to see them, and love to Miss Marianne, I am, &c. &c.	SS	III	2	278	30
She calls me dear Mrs. Jennings, you see.	SS	III	2	278	32
Yes, yes, I will go and see her, sure enough.	SS	III	2	278	32
whom she so much wished to see, in a more eligible, more	SS	III	3	280	6
"When I see him again," said Elinor to herself, as the	SS	III	4	291	44
door shut him out, "I shall see him the husband of Lucy."	SS	III	4	291	44
not even her curiosity to see how she looked after the	SS	III	5	294	3
would by very glad to see her, invited her to come in.	SS	III	5	294	4
"I am not sorry to see you alone," he replied, "for I have	SS	III	5	294	8
Poor fellow!--to see him in a circle of strangers!--to be	SS	III	5	299	35
marry this young woman, I never will see him again.'	SS	III	5	299	35
own family, Elinor could see its influence on her mind, in	SS	III	5	300	38
leave town, as she hoped to see more of them;--an exertion	SS	III	5	300	38
which he should come to see her at Delaford, was all that	SS	III	6	301	1
mind the persuasion that he should see Marianne no more.	SS	III	7	309	7
Her sleep, though not so quiet as Elinor wished to see it,	SS	III	7	310	9
manner, "I shall never see her, if she goes by London."	SS	III	7	311	13
too late to see this darling child, or to see her rational.	SS	III	7	312	18
To see Marianne, I felt would be dreadful, and I even	SS	III	8	323	40
whether I could see her again, and keep to my resolution.	SS	III	8	323	40
her miserable--and left her hoping never to see her again."	SS	III	8	323	40
As soon as Mrs. Dashwood had recovered herself, to see	SS	III	9	334	5
We will walk to the farm at the edge of the down, and see	SS	III	10	343	9
as this; though smiling to see the same eager fancy which	SS	III	10	343	10
"I wish to assure you both," said she, "that I see every	SS	III	11	349	4
"I see Mr. Ferrars myself, ma'am, this morning in Exeter,	SS	III	11	354	27
by the chaise, and so I see directly it was the youngest	SS	III	11	354	27
had not time to come on and see you, but they was in a	SS	III	11	354	27
when they come back, they'd make sure to come and see you."	SS	III	11	354	27
"Yes, ma'am, I just see him leaning back in it, but he did	SS	III	11	354	31
"Did you see them off, before you came away?"	SS	III	11	355	41
saw, nor what she wished to see;--happy or unhappy,--	SS	III	12	357	4
and rather expect to see, than to hear from him again.	SS	III	12	358	6
to see him walk in to-day or to-morrow, or any day."	SS	III	12	358	6
"He comes from Mr. Pratt's purposely to see us.	SS	III	12	358	8
that I could make no comparisons, and see no defects.	SS	III	13	362	5
has great curiosity to see, but thought I would first	SS	III	13	365	14
much thrown together, and see little of anybody else--and	SS	III	14	375	9
But though Mrs. Ferrars did come to see them, and always	SS	III	14	375	10
her valued friend; and to see Marianne settled at the	SS	III	14	378	13
to the friend she goes to see;--& she has taken a vast	W			317	2
But I can see in a great many things that you are very	W			318	2
Well, we shall see how irresistable Mr Tom Musgrave & I	W			319	2
You may see the church tower over the hedge, & the White	W			321	2
The Edwards' have a noble house you see, & they live quite	W			322	2
sister, & sometimes I see a look of Miss Penelope--& once	W			324	3
"I see the likeness between her & Miss Watson, replied Mr	W			324	3
own perturbation in time to see a blush on Miss E.'s cheek,	W			326	5
of a bedchamber, apparently on purpose to see them go by.--	W			327	7
are determined to be in good time I see, as usual.--	W			327	7
"But you may come to Wickstead & see mama, & she can take	W			332	12
It is a pity you should not see them."--	W			333	12
"Let us see you soon at the castle; & bring me word how	W			335	13
I should have been better pleased to see her dancing with	W			337	15
or waiting to see how the young lady's inclination lay.	W			339	18
tricks;--but I did long to see you, & it was a clever way	W			341	19
But I see nothing else to admire in him.--	W			342	19
were quite surprised to see me amongst them--& I must say	W			344	20
I mention this, in hopes of Yr being drawn out to see	W			347	21
to bring her home & wished to see their sister Emma.--	W			348	23
She was now so "delighted to see dear, dear Emma" that she	W			349	24
"en famille" when I come to see you--& now I do hope you	W			351	25
You must come to Croydon as well as the rest, & see what	W			353	26
formed the only exception to "you see your dinner".--	W			353	27
And I was so excessively impatient to see Emma;--I dreaded	W			356	28
Did you ever see anything more perfectly beautiful?--	W			357	28
cards--I wish you could see him overdraw himself on both	W			358	28
"Do you see much of the parsonage family at the castle, Mr	W			358	28
I see you are dieing to know.--	W			358	28
not engage--you will not think of me unless you see me."--	W			360	28
in a chaise and four to see the place, and was so much	PP	I	1	3	10
"I see no occasion for that.	PP	I	1	4	19
"But, my dear, you must indeed go and see Mr. Bingley when	PP	I	1	4	22
I dare say Mr. Bingley will be very glad to see you; and I	PP	I	1	4	25
"But I hope you will get over it, and live to see many	PP	I	1	5	31
"If I can but see one of my daughters happily settled at	PP	I	3	9	2
I hate to see you standing about by yourself in this	PP	I	3	11	8
and there are several of them you see uncommonly pretty."	PP	I	3	11	10
I was so vexed to see him stand up with her; but, however,	PP	I	3	13	16
You never see a fault in any body.	PP	I	4	14	7
to see you at it I should take away your bottle directly."	PP	I	5	20	22
and as they always see each other in large mixed parties,	PP	I	6	22	6
I shall certainly let him know that I see what he is about.	PP	I	6	24	16
I would go and see her, if I could have the carriage."	PP	I	7	32	32
"I shall be very fit to see Jane--which is all I want."	PP	I	7	32	35
we may see something of Captain Carter before he goes."	PP	I	7	32	40
not wish to see your sister make such an exhibition."	PP	I	8	36	7
"How I long to see her again!	PP	I	8	38	42
"I cannot see that London has any great advantage over the	PP	I	9	43	21
sure, Jane--one does not often see any body better looking.	PP	I	9	44	31
"Pray tell your sister that I long to see her."	PP	I	10	47	9
I shall see her in January.	PP	I	10	48	17
"I see your design, Bingley," said his friend.--	PP	I	10	51	41
it would always give her to see her either at Longbourn or	PP	I	12	60	5
was really glad to see them; he had felt their importance	PP	I	12	60	6
Well, I am sure I shall be extremely glad to see Mr.	PP	I	13	61	3
I am impatient to see him."	PP	I	13	64	18
and she was preparing to see him with a degree of	PP	I	13	64	20
and Elizabeth happening to see the countenance of both as	PP	I	15	73	8
Mrs. Philips was always glad to see her nieces, and the	PP	I	15	73	11
if she had not happened to see Mr. Jones's shop boy in the	PP	I	15	73	11
The two ladies were delighted to see their dear friend	PP	I	17	86	9
I see nothing in it but your own wilful ignorance and the	PP	I	18	95	48

It vexed her to see him expose himself to such a man. PP I 18 98 61
She looked at Jane, to see how she bore it; but Jane was PP I 18 100 68
which gave them time to see how heartily they were wished PP I 18 102 75
she should undoubtedly see her daughter settled at PP I 18 103 77
"Yes, or I will never see her again." PP I 20 111 18
Your mother will never see you again if you do not marry PP I 20 112 19
Mr. Collins, and I will never see you again if you do." PP I 20 112 19
be able to see your friends before they leave the country. PP I 21 117 9
"Mr. Darcy is impatient to see his sister, and to confess PP I 21 117 14
too early on the morrow to see any of the family, the PP I 22 123 4
how happy they should be to see him at Longbourn again, PP I 22 123 4
"I see what you are feeling," replied Charlotte,--"you PP I 22 125 17
A week elapsed before she could see Elizabeth without PP I 23 127 5
Whenever Charlotte came to see them she concluded her to PP I 23 130 16
for her, and live to see her take my place in it!" PP I 23 130 17
The more I see of the world, the more am I dissatisfied PP II 1 135 11
should meet at all, unless he really comes to see her." PP II 2 141 12
I see the imprudence of it.-- PP II 3 144 7
you unhappy; but since we see every day that where there PP II 3 145 7
Will you come and see me?" PP II 3 146 14
"but she was very glad to see me, and reproached me for PP II 3 147 23
I wish I could see her. PP II 3 147 23
I dare say I shall soon see them here." PP II 3 147 23
not a word of wishing to see me again, and was in every PP II 3 148 26
Pray go to see them, with Sir William and Maria. PP II 3 149 26
Elizabeth was watchful enough to see it all, but she could PP II 3 149 28
but she could see it and write of it without material pain. PP II 3 149 28
face, was pleased to see it healthful and lovely as ever. PP II 4 152 5
Elizabeth was prepared to see him in his glory; and she PP II 5 155 4
and of letting them see her civility towards himself and PP II 6 160 1
glad of it; but otherwise I see no occasion for entailing PP II 6 164 16
to find that they did not see more of her cousin by the PP II 7 168 1
Have you never happened to see her there?" PP II 7 171 11
had; but she wished to see whether he would betray any PP II 7 171 12
Colonel Fitzwilliam seemed really glad to see them; any PP II 8 172 3
appear interested in their concerns, as I often see done." PP II 8 175 24
in the masterly manner which I see so many women's do. PP II 8 175 25
Elizabeth looked at Darcy to see how cordially he assented PP II 8 176 29
surprise to Mr. Bingley to see you all after him so soon; PP II 9 177 4
"I do not see what right Mr. Darcy had to decide on the PP II 10 185 36
to her unwillingness to see Mr. Darcy, it determined her PP II 10 187 41
As he said this, she could easily see that he had no doubt PP II 11 189 6
But the person who advanced, was now near enough to see PP II 12 195 2
extinguished for him to see her without some danger.-- PP II 12 199 5
She could see him instantly before her, in every charm of PP II 13 206 4
Elizabeth could not see Lady Catherine without PP II 14 210 2
or feel the slightest inclination ever to see him again. PP II 14 212 17
and the little we see of the world, must make Hunsford PP II 15 215 2
You see on what a footing we are. PP II 15 216 4
You see how continually we are engaged there. PP II 15 216 4
I shall pull it to pieces as soon as I get home, and see PP II 16 219 3
Mrs. Bennet rejoiced to see Jane in undiminished beauty; PP II 16 222 19
20
to walk to Meryton and see how every body went on; but PP II 16 223 25
"I cannot see why Mrs. Forster should not ask me as well PP II 18 230 13
Come, let me see the list of the pitiful fellows who have PP II 18 231 17
Elizabeth was now to see Mr. Wickham for the last time. PP II 18 233 25
for them to go so far, and see so much as they had PP II 19 238 7
proposed, or at least to see it with the leisure and PP II 19 238 7
It was impossible for her to see the word without thinking PP II 19 239 9
Gardiner expressed an inclination to see the place again. PP II 19 240 12
"My love, should not you like to see a place of which you PP II 19 240 13
great deal of curiosity to see the house herself; and when PP II 19 241 17
On applying to see the place, they were admitted into the PP III 1 245 4
you will see a finer, larger picture of him than this. PP III 1 247 18
"If your master would marry, you might see more of him." PP III 1 248 27
on the other side, allowed them to see him before they met. PP III 1 254 57
stole a sly look at him, to see how he bore it; and was PP III 1 255 59
With astonishment did Elizabeth see, that her new PP III 2 261 3
They had long wished to see him. PP III 2 261 6
"I must confess that I never could see any beauty in her. PP III 3 271 15
was that they should ever see each other again on such PP III 4 279 23
She was wild to be at home--to hear, to see, to be upon PP III 4 280 26
His most particular friend, you see by Jane's account, was PP III 5 283 8
"But you see that Jane," said her aunt, "does not think so PP III 5 284 11
prepared to see a proud, reserved, disagreeable girl. PP III 5 284 14
He brought it with him for us to see." PP III 5 291 58
as this, one cannot see too little of one's neighbours. PP III 5 293 67
they last changed horses, see the postilions, and try if PP III 5 293 69
that they might expect to see their father at home on the PP III 6 298 13
I shall see her again!-- PP III 7 306 44
How I long to see her! and to see dear Wickham too! PP III 7 306 44
see the ring, and then I bowed and smiled like any thing." PP III 9 316 8
She then joined them soon enough to see Lydia, with PP III 9 317 9
She longed to see Mrs. Phillips, the Lucasses, and all PP III 9 317 10
You and papa, and my sisters, must come down and see us. PP III 9 317 13
said, "I was surprised to see Darcy in town last month. PP III 10 328 15
16
Did you see him while you were at Lambton? PP III 10 328 18
"This is the consequence you see, madam, of marrying a PP III 11 330 11
you know, and I am sure I never want to see him again. PP III 11 331 14
that he comes alone; because we shall see the less of him. PP III 11 332 17
if I went to see him, he should marry one of my daughters. PP III 11 332 23
see Mr. Bingley in consequence of it, before they did. PP III 11 333 27
"It would be nothing; I could see him with perfect PP III 11 333 28
"Let me first see how he behaves," said she; "it will then PP III 11 335 38
Did you see it?" PP III 11 336 49
Let me never see either one or the other again!" PP III 11 337 56
I have not forgot, you see; and I assure you, I was very PP III 11 338 58
They did not see the gentlemen again till Tuesday; and Mrs. PP III 12 339 10
eagerly watched to see whether Bingley would take the PP III 12 340 11
discourse, but she could see how seldom they spoke to each PP III 12 340 13
But when they see, as I trust they will, that their PP III 13 349 47
It would vex me, indeed, to see you again the dupe of Miss PP III 13 350 48
If I could but see you as happy! PP III 13 350 53
"Your coming to Longbourn, to see me and my family," said PP III 14 354 29
Lady Catherine might see him in her way through town; and PP III 15 361 3
"Mr. Darcy, you see, is the man! PP III 15 363 18
Mr. Darcy, who never looks at any woman but to see a PP III 15 363 18
by letting you see that your reproofs had been attended to. PP III 16 370 32
Darcy professed a great curiosity to see the view from the PP III 17 375 25
"My real purpose was to see you, and to judge, if I could, PP III 18 382 16
My avowed one, or what I avowed to myself, was to see PP III 18 382 16
of the sisters was exactly what Darcy had hoped to see. PP III 19 387 11
of him, or her curiosity to see how his wife conducted PP III 19 388 12
Is not she a sister's child? and could I bear to see her MP I 1 7 8
I only wish I could be more useful; but you see I do all MP I 1 9 12
Indeed, I do not see that you could possibly place her any MP I 1 10 13
We shall probably see much to wish altered in her, and MP I 1 10 14
I should wish to see them very good friends, and would, on MP I 1 11 17
was William whom she talked of most and wanted most to see. MP I 2 15 12
Fanny sighed, and said, "I cannot see things as you do; MP I 3 27 34
return! that she should see him go without a tear!--it was MP I 3 33 64
that he hoped she might see William again in the course of MP I 3 33 64
Mrs. Norris could not see it in the same light. MP I 4 36 7
be peculiarly consoling to see their dear Maria well MP I 4 38 9
Edmund was the only one of the family who could see a MP I 4 39 13
"There, Mrs. Grant, you see how he dwells on one word, and MP I 4 43 24
She did not want to see or understand. MP I 5 44 3
I could see it in her eyes, when he was mentioned. MP I 5 45 14
Look where I will, I see that it is so; and I feel that it MP I 5 46 20
Depend upon it, you see but half. MP I 5 46 23
You see the evil, but you do not see the consolation. MP I 5 46 23
One does not like to see a girl of eighteen or nineteen so MP I 5 49 32
"I believe I have; but this is hardly fair; I see what you MP I 5 49 33
I did not see her again for a twelvemonth. MP I 5 50 35
I do not pretend to set people right, but I do see that MP I 5 50 36
"I wish you could see Compton," said he, "it is the most MP I 6 53 2
You see the house in the most surprising manner. MP I 6 53 2
"I should like to see Sotherton before it is cut down, to MP I 6 56 22
before it is cut down, to see the place as it is now, in MP I 6 56 22
Whenever I do see it, you will tell me how it has been MP I 6 56 24
"It would be delightful to me to see the progress of it MP I 6 57 30
of it, you must see the importance of getting in the grass. MP I 6 58 38
What would not I give to see it again!" MP I 6 61 53
"Those who see quickly, will resolve quickly and act MP I 6 61 57
with Miss Crawford, and not see more of the sort of fault MP I 7 66 14
nature it was most astonishing to see how well she sat. MP I 7 67 16
"It is a pleasure to see a lady with such a good heart for MP I 7 69 22
"I never see one sit a horse better. MP I 7 69 22
yet, and it was a pity she should not see the place." MP I 8 76 4
body must be wanting to see Sotherton, to include Miss MP I 8 76 7
Fanny has a great desire to see Sotherton. MP I 8 78 21
and merriment; and to see only his expressive profile as MP I 8 81 32
she wished they could all see it, &c." but her only offer MP I 8 81 32
It is not ugly, you see, at this end; there is some fine MP I 8 82 34
You may see something of it here--something of the more MP I 8 83 36
"This chapel was fitted up as you see it, in James the MP I 9 86 9
her, "I do not like to see Miss Bertram so near the altar." MP I 9 88 20
I see walls of great pleasure. MP I 9 90 34
One does not see much of this influence and importance in MP I 9 92 46
at the same view, without being able to see it so well." MP I 9 96 73
"It is an immense distance," said she; "I see that with a MP I 9 96 75
ever see Sotherton again with so much pleasure as I do now. MP I 10 98 7
a man of the world not to see with the eyes of the world. MP I 10 98 8
I was glad to see you so well entertained. MP I 10 98 11
I cannot see them any where," looking eagerly into the MP I 10 100 26
go any further," said he sullenly; "I see nothing of them. MP I 10 101 35
For my part, I can see nothing in him." MP I 10 102 41
when the mist cleared away, she should see nothing else. MP I 11 107 3
to be overcome, and I see no reason why a man should make MP I 11 109 17
is very respectable, I see him to be an indolent selfish MP I 11 111 28
of self-indulgence; and to see your sister suffering from MP I 11 111 29
I wish I could see Cassiopeia." MP I 11 113 39
Sotherton, she could never see Mr. Crawford with either MP I 12 115 5
the second time--"we shall see some happy faces again now." MP I 12 117 12
quite delightful, ma'am, to see young people so properly MP I 12 118 16
Do you see no symptoms there?" MP I 12 118 17
If you look at them, you may see they are so many couple MP I 12 119 22
I was surprised to see Sir Henry such a stick. MP I 13 122 2
than you do, or can have gone much farther to see one." MP I 13 124 11
"True, to see real acting, good hardened real acting; but MP I 13 124 12
You must see the difference yourself. MP I 13 127 26
Don't imagine that nobody in this house can see or judge MP I 13 128 31
run mad, that could see any thing to censure in a plan MP I 13 128 38
in prison? I think I see you coming in with your basket." MP I 14 135 17
your mother or aunt, and see how you can approve it.-- MP I 15 140 12
"We see things very differently," cried Maria--"I am MP I 15 140 12
be made, of course, I can see nothing objectionable in it; MP I 15 140 12
sure--but I still think you see things too strongly; and I MP I 15 140 14
out, when who should I see but Dick Jackson making up to MP I 15 141 22
You see she does not like to act.-- MP I 15 147 54
had quite a curiosity to see him, and imagined him a very MP I 15 147 57
a man as you will see any where, so I will take my horse MP I 15 148 58
do, she could scarcely see an object in that room which MP I 16 151 2
doubting spirit--to see if by looking at Edmund's profile MP I 16 152 3
This acting scheme gets worse and worse you see. MP I 16 153 8
Do not you see it in the same light?" MP I 16 154 8
I see your judgment is not with me. MP I 16 154 14
"I am sorry for Miss Crawford; but I am more sorry to see MP I 16 155 15
"They will not have much cause of triumph, when they see MP I 16 155 16
She was not pleased to see Julia excluded from the play, MP I 17 161 9
reasonable when you see him in his family, I assure you. MP I 17 162 16
and Julia could never see Maria distinguished by Henry MP I 17 163 19
between ourselves, to see such an undersized, little, mean- MP I 18 165 3
she was longing and dreading to see how they would perform. MP I 18 167 12
What would your governess and your uncle say to see them MP I 18 169 21
she could notice this, and see that, in spite of the shock MP II 1 175 2
Why do not I see my little Fanny?", and on perceiving her, MP II 1 177 7
really extremely happy to see him, and whose feelings were MP II 1 179 9
It was so agreeable to her to see him again, and hear him MP II 1 179 9
his eye round it, to see other symptoms of recent MP II 1 182 22
expression, began to see more clearly than he had ever MP II 1 183 24
Edmund's first object the next morning was to see his MP II 2 187 1
To see them straining away! MP II 2 189 5
of his Mansfield life, to see his steward and his bailiff-- MP II 2 190 9
She had been expecting to see him the whole morning--and MP II 2 192 11
Mr. Yates had staid to see the destruction of every MP II 2 194 21
serious month, and I can see that Mrs. Grant is very MP II 3 199 15
of something fresh to see and think of was thus extended MP II 4 206 3
said Miss Crawford, "and we shall see how it will be. MP II 4 207 7
"South or north, I know a black cloud when I see it; and MP II 4 207 9
"I am so glad to see the evergreens thrive!" said Fanny in MP II 4 209 16
xiv; and may declare that I see no wonder in this MP II 4 209 17
in town and I come to see you, I dare say I shall find you MP II 4 213 35
like to go; and I can see no reason why she should not." MP II 5 217 2
can see no reason why she should be denied the indulgence." MP II 5 219 18
No, I see no finery about you; nothing but what is MP II 5 222 44
I shall be very glad to see him." MP II 5 223 46
I see him now;--his toil and his despair. MP II 5 224 53
sorry to see you trying at it, than almost any other man." MP II 5 227 66
You see her every day, and therefore do not notice it, but MP II 6 229 5
had vanished, and she could see in him the same William as MP II 6 233 17
I am never to see my cards; and Mr. Crawford does all the MP II 7 240 12
due time in the very place which I had a curiosity to see. MP II 7 241 13
of.--(excuse me, your ladyship must not see your cards. MP II 7 243 27
let me see, Mary; Lady Bertram bids a dozen for that MP II 7 243 27
to drive about the grounds, and see his genius take fire. MP II 7 244 30
I see things very differently now. MP II 7 245 31
daughters would be happy to see their cousins any where; MP II 7 245 34
it would be, not to see Edmund every day; and the other, MP II 7 248 47
sink the clergyman, and see only the respectable, elegant, MP II 7 248 47
"I should like to go to a ball with you and see you dance. MP II 7 250 59
I should like to see you dance, and I'd dance with you if MP II 7 250 59
a gentlewoman when we do see her, which perhaps we may MP II 7 250 60
Do not you see your aunt is going? MP II 7 251 64
body else who might wish to see Fanny dance, and to give MP II 8 252 1
It would give me pleasure to see you both dance. MP II 8 252 1
"You see what a collection I have," said she, "more by MP II 8 258 16
necklace round her and making her see how well it looked. MP II 8 258 17
rather part with and see in your possession than any other. MP II 8 260 22
deal with Mr. Crawford, to see William enjoy himself, and MP II 9 267 22
You see how it is; and could tell me, perhaps better than MP II 9 268 31
it was delightful to see the effort so successfully made. MP II 10 273 6
She must watch the general arrangements and see how every MP II 10 275 10
not see that--I should not know one from the other." MP II 11 283 4
Maria might be very glad to see her at Sotherton now and MP II 11 285 14
"He did not, the only time he went to see Mr. Owen before." MP II 11 287 21
as if wanting to hear or see more, and then laughingly MP II 11 289 32
I may be discovered by those who want to see me. MP II 11 289 32
To see her with her brother! MP II 12 294 16
in his face, "how glad I am to see you so much in love! MP II 12 297 32
They will now see what sort of woman it is that can attach MP II 12 297 33
And they will now see their cousin treated as she ought to MP II 12 297 33

Context	Work	Vol	Ch	Page	Line
You will, perhaps, like to see them."	MP	II	13	298	2
To see the expression of her eyes, the change of her	MP	II	13	298	3
would be quite distressing to her to see him again so soon.	MP	II	13	303	12
not but be astonished to see Mr. Crawford, as she	MP	III	1	311	2
He is in my room, and hoping to see you there."	MP	III	1	314	16
she might hear it, or see it, or know it to exist for ever	MP	III	1	321	46
delicacy, ceased to urge to see you for the present."	MP	III	1	321	47
Even to see Mr. Crawford would be less overpowering.	MP	III	1	322	49
whom she had hated to see or to speak to, in whom she	MP	III	2	327	6
You will see him with the rest of us, in the same manner,	MP	III	2	331	16
her only to see her displeasure, and not to hear it.	MP	III	2	332	21
he could not have hoped for, had he expected to see her.	MP	III	3	334	2
Both gentlemen had a glance at Fanny, to see if a word of	MP	III	3	338	16
so determined not to see it, as to make it clear that the	MP	III	3	339	21
and grieved to the heart to see Edmund's arrangements, was	MP	III	3	342	32
I see nothing alarming in the word.	MP	III	3	343	38
But we shall see.--	MP	III	3	343	41
in love with Julia, but I could never see anything of it.	MP	III	4	350	30
You will see her, however, before she goes.	MP	III	4	352	40
She was determined to see Fanny alone, and therefore said	MP	III	5	357	5
I think I see him now, trying to be as demure and composed	MP	III	5	358	9
Poor Sir Thomas, who was glad to see you?	MP	III	5	358	9
I shall see no one half so amiable where I am going.	MP	III	5	359	10
If you were to see how he is courted, and how I am courted	MP	III	5	360	16
see you, of the endless questions I shall have to answer!	MP	III	5	360	16
but of that, I shall see nothing with the Frasers.	MP	III	5	361	16
No, no, I see you are not."	MP	III	5	362	16
I could not but see that Mr. Crawford allowed himself in	MP	III	5	363	21
I wish we could see him."	MP	III	5	364	29
"I shall see your cousin in town soon; he talks of being	MP	III	5	364	32
see him again till he were the husband of some other woman.	MP	III	5	365	35
human nature, to expect to see the effect of the loss of	MP	III	6	368	7
to see William to the last hour of his remaining on land.	MP	III	6	369	11
And besides, he wanted her so very much to see the thrush	MP	III	6	372	18
to go with them--to go and see her poor dear Sister Price.	MP	III	6	372	21
about five--both glad to see her in their way, though with	MP	III	7	377	9
"Oh! my dear William, how glad I am to see you.	MP	III	7	378	10
"Then, Betsey, my dear, run into the kitchen, and see if	MP	III	7	379	15
Glad to see you.	MP	III	7	380	20
Sharp is the word, you see.	MP	III	7	380	20
here in the morning to see the thrush go out of harbour.	MP	III	7	380	20
leading her forward;--"it is so dark you do not see her."	MP	III	7	380	21
and coming eagerly to see their sister, and tell that the	MP	III	7	381	25
and even of getting her to Spithead to see the sloop.	MP	III	7	384	35
intreaty, determined to see their brother and Mr. Campbell	MP	III	7	384	36
home yesterday, and we were glad to see each other again.	MP	III	9	393	1
We seemed very glad to see each other, and I do really	MP	III	9	393	1
in Portsmouth was to see her, that he was come down for a	MP	III	10	406	21
To have had him join their family dinner-party and see all	MP	III	10	407	23
"My love to your sister, if you please; and when you see	MP	III	11	412	27
been down to Portsmouth to see you; that he had a	MP	III	12	415	1
					2
He will see the Rushworths, which I own I am not sorry for-	MP	III	12	417	3
Had she been different when I did see her, I should have	MP	III	13	421	2
I am more and more satisfied with all that I see and hear	MP	III	13	423	2
I could not see him, and my eldest sister in the same room,	MP	III	13	423	2
very mortifying to her to see it fall to the share of her	MP	III	13	425	6
The sufferings which Lady Bertram did not see, had little	MP	III	13	427	12
I am so shocked to see him, that I do not know what to do.	MP	III	13	427	12
Fanny, Fanny, I see you smile, and look cunning, but upon	MP	III	14	434	13
very moment, he is wild to see you, and occupied only in	MP	III	14	435	14
It would really be gratifying to see them all again, and a	MP	III	14	435	14
Now she could see her own mistake as to who were gone--or	MP	III	15	441	19
You will see me early, by the mail. your's, &c."	MP	III	15	443	23
on the event, she could see it only in one light, as	MP	III	16	449	6
He had been invited to see her.	MP	III	16	454	18
"I heard you were in town," said she--"I wanted to see you.	MP	III	16	454	18
said she, 'such a woman as he will never see again.	MP	III	16	455	21
he would have been glad to see Mrs. Rushworth no more.--	MP	III	17	468	21
every day was to see her there, or to get her away from it.	MP	III	17	472	30
"How often we shall be going to see them and they coming	E	I	1	8	14
shall be going to see them and they coming to see us!--	E	I	1	8	14
Whenever I see her, she always curtseys and asks me how I	E	I	1	9	19
Taylor to have somebody about her that she is used to see.	E	I	1	9	19
Whenever James goes over to see his daughter you know, she	E	I	1	9	19
of the few people who could see faults in Emma Woodhouse,	E	I	1	11	33
and a lively curiosity to see him prevailed, though the	E	I	2	17	8
He liked very much to have his friends come and see him;	E	I	3	20	1
She was delighted to see her father look comfortable, and	E	I	3	22	6
made him rather sorry to see any thing put on it; and	E	I	3	24	12
small, you see--one of our small eggs will not hurt you.	E	I	3	24	14
But, did you never see him?	E	I	4	29	13
I want to see you permanently well connected--and to that	E	I	4	31	24
I see the difference plain enough.	E	I	4	33	33
You might not see one in a hundred, with gentlemen so	E	I	4	33	34
You must see the difference."	E	I	4	33	35
But on the other hand, as Emma wants to see her better	E	I	5	36	6
thrown over my senses, must still see, hear, and remember.	E	I	5	37	9
Where shall we see a better daughter, or a kinder sister,	E	I	5	39	22
I should like to see Emma in love, and in some doubt of a	E	I	5	41	29
Mrs. Weston again, and again, and again, you see.	E	I	6	45	21
strong a likeness of his cockade as you would wish to see.	E	I	6	45	21
pencil, to jump up and see the progress, and be charmed.--	E	I	6	47	26
"One should be sorry to see greater pride or refinement in	E	I	7	56	41
If they are anxious to see you happily married, here is a	E	I	9	75	27
"Ah! it is no difficulty to see who you take after!	E	I	9	78	53
					54
she will be when she comes, not to see Miss Taylor here!"	E	I	9	79	58
then said, "but I do not see why poor Isabella should be	E	I	9	80	65
					66
and she imagined he was come to see how it might turn up.	E	I	9	81	78
doubt that, could he see his little effusion honoured as I	E	I	9	82	83
effusion honoured as I see it, (looking at the book again,	E	I	9	82	83
and her curiosity to see it was so extreme, that,	E	I	10	83	6
"I must see somebody very superior to any one I have seen	E	I	10	84	13
the question: and I do not wish to see any such person.	E	I	10	84	13
She could never see a fault in any of them.	E	I	11	92	4
"And do you see her, sir, tolerably often?" asked Isabella	E	I	11	94	12
Mrs. Weston, does come and see us pretty often--but then--	E	I	11	94	16
As for Isabella, she has been married long enough to see	E	I	11	95	18
He will be so pleased to see my little ones."	E	I	12	101	26
They are always so pleased to see my children.--	E	I	12	102	31
I shall see you at the Abbey to-morrow morning I hope, and	E	I	12	107	61
Why does not Perry see her?"	E	I	13	109	7
to hear him impartially, or see him with clear vision, was	E	I	13	110	10
What a strange thing love is! he can see ready wit in	E	I	13	111	13
to see that it was cold, and too well wrapt up to feel it.	E	I	13	112	24
such a day as this, for the sake of coming to see him.	E	I	13	113	26
Ha! snows a little I see."	E	I	13	115	37
that James should come and see his daughter, when the	E	I	14	117	3
had a great curiosity to see him, a decided intention of	E	I	14	119	5
I should like to see two more here,--your pretty little	E	I	14	119	7
The case, you see, is--(but this is quite between	E	I	14	120	11
A few minutes more, and Emma hoped to see one troublesome	E	I	15	128	21
girl; and I should be happy to see her respectably settled.	E	I	15	131	35
gone to bed, more ready to see alleviations of the evil	E	I	16	138	14
children, was obliged to see the whole party set off, and	E	I	17	140	1
If Frank Churchill had wanted to see his father, he would	E	I	18	145	10
convenience; but I must go and see my father immediately.	E	I	18	146	16
few who presumed ever to see imperfection in her, as	E	II	1	155	2
put my huswife upon it, you see, without being aware, and	E	II	1	157	10
letter--only two pages you see--hardly two--and in general	E	II	1	157	10
good as they were, she can see amazingly well still, thank	E	II	1	157	10
had very strong eyes to see as you do--and so much fine	E	II	1	158	10
"My mother's deafness is very trifling you see--just	E	II	1	158	14
to see her friends at Highbury, as they can be to see her.	E	II	1	159	18
The case is, you see, that the Campbells are going to	E	II	1	159	20
her father and mother to come over and see her directly.	E	II	1	159	20
but she is so impatient to see them again--for till she	E	II	1	159	20
which it was, but we shall see presently in Jane's letter--	E	II	1	159	20
But you see, every thing turns out for the best.	E	II	1	160	23
must expect to see her grown thin, and looking very poorly.	E	II	1	162	31
for dinner, as well as to see exhibitions of new caps and	E	II	2	168	15
I do not see it."	E	II	3	171	8
So I said I would go down and see, and Jane said, 'shall I	E	II	3	173	27
We were always glad to see him at Hartfield."	E	II	3	174	34
wonder that you have such a curiosity to see him."	E	II	3	174	35
What is before me, I see.	E	II	3	176	44
she would just step in and see how it went on; and though	E	II	3	177	52
way that she used; I could see she was altered; but	E	II	3	178	52
to hear his voice, or see his shoulder, just to have	E	II	4	184	10
We have been sitting with your father--glad to see him so	E	II	5	188	7
Frank comes to-morrow--I had a letter this morning--we see	E	II	5	188	7
comfort but your own; I see you now in all your little	E	II	5	189	20
"You cannot see too much perfection in Mrs. Weston for my	E	II	5	192	31
She must see more of him to understand his ways; at	E	II	5	192	33
you will to-day. you will see her to advantage; see her	E	II	5	194	44
will see her to advantage; see her and hear her--no, I am	E	II	5	194	44
They will be extremely glad to see you, I am sure, and one	E	II	5	195	45
She was wanting to see him again, and especially to see	E	II	6	196	2
was rather surprized to see the constitution of the weston	E	II	6	198	5
"Did you see her often at Weymouth?	E	II	6	199	13
"He should be happy to see Mrs. Goddard.	E	II	7	209	13
see that every thing were safe in the house, as usual.	E	II	7	211	22
door; and was pleased to see that it was Mr. Knightley's;	E	II	8	213	7
I am quite glad to see you."	E	II	8	213	8
but at present I do not see what there is to question.	E	II	8	216	27
And now I can see it in no other light than as an offering	E	II	8	219	42
I see nobody else looking like her!--	E	II	8	222	56
Yes, I will--I declare I will--and you shall see how she	E	II	8	222	56
See the consequence of keeping you company!--	E	II	8	224	65
"I see no probability in it, unless you have any better	E	II	8	224	72
a little disparity of age, I can see nothing unsuitable."	E	II	8	225	73
I see no sign of attachment--I believe nothing of the	E	II	8	226	84
She could see nothing but evil in it.	E	II	8	227	87
taste, to look about, and see what became of Mr. Knightley.	E	II	8	229	99
seeing nothing, and can see nothing that does not answer.	E	II	9	233	24
But then, Mrs. Goddard will want to see it.--	E	II	9	235	36
will be so very happy to see her-- and now we are such a	E	II	9	236	46
I did not see you before.	E	II	9	237	48
I am always glad to see him.	E	II	9	239	51
You see we have been wedging one leg with paper.	E	II	10	240	5
"I do not see much sign of it.	E	II	10	243	29
They will be so very happy to see you."	E	II	10	244	46
Did you ever see such dancing?--	E	II	10	245	48
And (raising his voice still more) I do not see why Miss	E	II	10	245	49
the room they were in to see what it could be made to hold-	E	II	11	247	2
"Yes; if you and Mr. Woodhouse see no objection, and I	E	II	11	250	23
morning, we may talk it over, and see what can be done."	E	II	11	252	32
There were Mr. and Mrs. Weston; delighted to see her and	E	II	11	253	40
Look! in places you see it is dreadfully dirty; and the	E	II	11	253	41
You will see nothing of it by candle-light.	E	II	11	253	42
We never see any thing of it on our club-nights."	E	II	11	253	42
I see no advantage in consulting Miss Bates."	E	II	11	255	52
She could then see more and judge better.	E	II	14	272	16
room, the entrance, and all that she could see or imagine.	E	II	14	272	18
naturally wishes them to see as much as possible; and Mr.	E	II	14	274	28
"Well," said Mrs. Elton, laughing, "we shall see."	E	II	14	278	42
I was really impatient to see him; and I must do my caro	E	II	14	278	50
"I see how it is," said she.	E	II	16	290	2
"I see what a life I am to lead among you.	E	II	16	290	2
She was not yet quite able to see him and his charming	E	II	16	291	5
Mrs. Bragge's is the one I would most wish to see you in."	E	II	17	300	8
Mr. Woodhouse was almost as glad to see him now, as he	E	II	17	302	23
see him now, as he would have been sorry to see him before.	E	II	17	302	23
"Well, he is coming, you see; good news, I think.	E	II	17	303	27
In town next week, you see--at the latest, I dare say; for	E	II	17	304	27
see him again, which makes this day's news doubly welcome.	E	II	18	308	27
would happen in our favour; and so it has, you see.	E	II	18	308	27
They all walked about together, to see that every thing	E	III	2	319	3
"I have a great curiosity to see Mrs. Elton, I have heard	E	III	2	320	8
"I will see that there are umbrellas, sir," said Frank to	E	III	2	321	14
Jane, Jane, look--did you ever see any thing?	E	III	2	322	19
And I see very few pearls in the room except mine.--	E	III	2	324	21
We shall see if our styles suit.--	E	III	2	324	21
enjoyment, delighted to see the respectable length of the	E	III	2	325	32
whom I should be very glad to see dancing--Miss Smith."	E	III	2	327	37
and she were enabled to see that Mr. Elton was not the	E	III	3	332	1
She was not to see Frank Churchill this morning.	E	III	3	332	2
had never less expected to see together--Frank Churchill,	E	III	3	332	3
He dared not stay longer than to see her well; these	E	III	3	334	8
I can see nothing at all extraordinary in him now.--	E	III	4	337	6
of the two I had rather not see him--and indeed I would go	E	III	4	337	6
in your presence, that you may see how rational I am grown.	E	III	4	338	6
Emma was quite eager to see this superior treasure.	E	III	4	339	17
them both behind the fire, and I wish you to see me do it."	E	III	4	340	22
Knightley so placed as to see them all; and it was his	E	III	5	341	21
and it was his object to see as much as he could, with as	E	III	5	341	21
He could not see her in a situation of such danger,	E	III	5	349	26
Emma had never been to box hill; she wished to see what	E	III	6	352	2
"That's quite unnecessary; I see Jane every day:--but as	E	III	6	355	20
Nothing can be more simple, you see.	E	III	6	355	20
He should like to see the old house again exceedingly, and	E	III	6	356	30
He could not see any objection at all to his, and Emma's,	E	III	6	357	30
the he should be glad to see him; and Mr. Weston engaged	E	III	6	357	31
She wished to see the whole extent."--	E	III	6	359	37
It was an odd tete-a-tete; but she was glad to see it.--	E	III	6	360	40
would have been sorry to see Harriet in a spot so	E	III	6	360	40
were to go out once more to see what had not yet been seen,	E	III	6	361	42
to think of him--but she was very glad to see him.	E	III	6	363	53
Yes, I see what she means, (turning to Mr. Knightley,) and	E	III	7	371	28
He looked around, as if to see that no one were near, and	E	III	7	374	55
					56
I cannot see you acting wrong, without a remonstrance.	E	III	7	374	56
It was not unlikely, she thought, that she might see Mr.	E	III	8	377	2
dear soul! if you were to see what a headach she has.	E	III	8	379	8
is Miss Woodhouse: I am sure you will like to see her.'--	E	III	8	379	8
'I can see nobody,' said she; and up she got, and would go	E	III	8	379	8
steady friend, when she might not bear to see herself.	E	III	8	379	9
his joints--I must go and see him to-day; and so will Jane,	E	III	8	383	29
"ay, I see what you are thinking of, the piano forte.	E	III	8	384	32
					33
dear Jane could not bear to see anybody--anybody at all--	E	III	9	390	18
so much--but, except them, Jane would really see nobody."	E	III	9	390	18
Mrs. Weston wants to see you.	E	III	10	392	2
She must see you."	E	III	10	392	2
come to you, but she must see you alone, and that you know-	E	III	10	392	4
You will not see him.	E	III	10	394	20
You (blushing as she spoke) who can see into everybody's	E	III	11	404	10
hoped, that when able to see them together again, she	E	III	12	416	2
She should see them hence-forward with the closest	E	III	12	416	2
You are determined, I see, to have no curiosity.--	E	III	13	429	27
Yes, you see, you understand my feelings--and will return	E	III	13	430	37
truth of the whole; to see that Harriet's hopes had been	E	III	13	430	38

He had come, in his anxiety to see how she bore Frank E III 13 432 40
directly after dinner, to see how this sweetest and best E III 13 433 41
See me, then, under these circumstances, arriving on my E III 14 437 8
You will look back and see that I did not come till Miss E III 14 437 8
If I could but see her again!-- E III 14 440 8
Now, however, I see nothing in it but a very natural and E III 14 441 8
She ought to go--and she was longing to see her; the E III 16 452 7
You see how delightfully she writes. E III 16 454 13
My representation, you see, has quite appeased her." E III 16 454 13
wanted to see Knightley to-day on that very account.-- E III 16 457 40
that I should see Knightley to day; and it becomes a E III 16 458 43
Theodore, and we shall now see her own little adelaide E III 17 461 2
"Here is his answer, if you like to see it." E III 17 464 17
often; he should be glad to see him every day;--but they E III 17 466 29
him every day;--but they did see him every day as it was.-- E III 17 466 29
I see it in your countenance. E III 18 470 5
"You are prepared for the worst, I see--and very bad it is. E III 18 470 12
Harriet will make a much longer history when you see her.-- E III 18 472 20
Then, he said, he would endeavour to see her in the course E III 18 474 30
Emma was extremely glad to see him--but there was a degree E III 18 476 46
I am particularly glad to see and shake hands with you-- E III 18 476 48
You see how my father and Mrs. Weston doat upon her." E III 18 477 50
words were, "did you ever see such a skin?--such E III 18 478 60
61
out, "how delighted I am to see you again! and to see you E III 18 479 71
72
you again! and to see you in such excellent looks!-- E III 18 479 71
72
I see it in her cheek, her smile, her vain attempt to E III 18 480 77
Do not you see that, at this instant, the very passage of E III 18 480 77
pleased as she had been to see Frank Churchill, and really E III 18 480 80
She could not bear to see him suffering, to know him E III 19 483 9
else; for he could plainly see how old all the rest of his P III 1 6 11
date of her own birth, and see no marriage follow but that P III 1 7 12
strong family pride could see only in him, a proper match P III 1 8 17
measures advised, as he meant to see finally adopted. P III 2 11 1
He was not only to quit his home, but to see it in the P III 2 15 13
forming an intimacy, which she wished to see interrupted. P III 2 15 15
should be sorry to see any friend of mine belonging to it." P III 3 19 13
14
she would have rejoiced to see her at twenty-two, so P III 4 28 7
I began to think I should never see you. P III 5 37 22
"You will see them yet, perhaps, before the morning is P III 5 38 30
call at the great house before they have been to see you?" P III 5 39 41
believe if Charles were to see me dying, he would not P III 6 44 7
is always wanting to see them, for she humours and P III 6 44 8
I assure you, Miss Anne, it prevents my wishing to see P III 6 45 8
the watch; because, if you see any thing amiss, you need P III 6 45 9
families; and she did not see any reason why she was to be P III 6 45 10
She wished, however, to see the Crofts, and was glad to be P III 6 48 17
something, and is coming to see them almost directly; and P III 6 50 27
You would not like to leave him yourself, but you see I P III 7 55 8
"Yes; you see his papa can, and why should not I?-- P III 7 56 14
Had he wished ever to see her again, he need not have P III 7 58 21
For an old built sloop, you would not see her equal. P III 8 65 12
to the Asp, to see what an old thing they had given you." P III 8 65 16
I hate to hear of women on board, or to see them on board; P III 8 69 35
"My feelings, you see, did not prevent my taking Mrs. P III 8 69 44
to another war, we shall see him do as you and I, and a P III 8 70 46
Hayter, whose pretensions she wished to see put an end to. P III 9 75 12
I wish you had been there to see her behaviour. P III 9 77 16
She hoped, on turning her head, to see the master of the P III 9 79 25
straight to the sofa to see what was going on, and put in P III 9 79 28
down for a few minutes, to see their aunt and cousins, P III 10 86 18
She turned through the same gate,--but could not see them.- P III 10 87 21
I see that more than a mere dutiful morning-visit to your P III 10 87 26
yours is the character of decision and firmness, I see. P III 10 88 26
see her suffer, without the desire of giving her relief. P III 10 91 42
and were Lady Russell to see them together, she might P III 11 93 3
to see him had determined him to go immediately to Lyme. P III 11 94 6
that an earnest desire to see Lyme themselves, and a P III 11 94 6
The young people were all wild to see Lyme. P III 11 94 7
it must be, who does not see charms in the immediate P III 11 95 9
I, at this moment, see something like Anne Elliot again." P III 12 104 6
In mourning, you see, just as our Mr. Elliot must be. P III 12 105 14
"There! you see!" cried Mary, in an ecstacy, "just as I P III 12 106 16
eyes from one sister, to see the other in a state as P III 12 110 43
then, I shall be very happy to see Captain Benwick." P IV 2 132 15
that she would very soon see no deficiency in his manner." P IV 2 132 17
I have really a curiosity to see the person who can give P IV 2 132 20
is a man," said Lady Russell, "whom I have no wish to see. P IV 2 133 23
without wondering whether she might see him or hear of him. P IV 2 133 26
Captain Wentworth was gone, for the present, to see his P IV 2 134 31
rapid; for who would be glad to see her when she arrived? P IV 2 135 34
to Mary, of his being "a man whom she had no wish to see." P IV 2 135 35
She had a great wish to see him. P IV 2 135 35
felt that she would rather see Mr. Elliot again than not, P IV 2 136 36
Her father and sister were glad to see her, for the sake P IV 3 137 2
in his change; should see nothing to regret in the duties P IV 3 138 5
though Elizabeth could not see the circumstance in quite P IV 3 139 9
"He longed to see her. P IV 3 141 13
see Mrs. Clay stealing, a glance at Elizabeth and herself. P IV 4 145 2
at my recommendation, and you see what it has done for her. P IV 4 146 3
You see how it has carried away her freckles." P IV 4 146 3
that Lady Russell should see nothing suspicious or P IV 4 147 7
In fact, Anne could never see the crape round his hat, P IV 4 147 8
lively a wish to see again, and to see more of, as herself. P IV 4 148 9
are well read; for they see it occasionally under every P IV 5 156 10
end, I presume, but that she may hope to see another day. P IV 5 157 15
Elliot--to look forward and see you occupying your dear P IV 5 159 25
had appeared completely to see what Mrs. Clay was about, P IV 5 161 29
"We see nothing of them, and this is really an instance of P IV 6 164 7
him attached to "Louisa; I never could see any thing of it. P IV 6 165 8
"And this is the end, you see, of Captain Benwick's being " P IV 6 165 8
She longed to see the Crofts, but when the meeting took P IV 6 168 22
failed to think of them, and never failed to see them. P IV 6 168 24
or equally delighted to see the Admiral's hearty shake of P IV 6 168 24
Here I am, you see, staring at a picture. P IV 6 169 25
Did you ever see the like? P IV 6 169 25
Brigden stares to see anybody with me but my wife. P IV 6 169 29
If you look across the street, you will see Admiral Brand P IV 6 170 29
went off to Plymouth, and then he went off to see Edward. P IV 6 171 33
to go to the outer door; she wanted to see if it rained. P IV 7 175 6
She would see if it rained. P IV 7 175 6
for Bath already, you see," (pointing to a new umbrella) " P IV 7 177 14
He came in with eagerness, appeared to see and think only P IV 7 177 16
Lady Russell would in all likelihood see him somewhere.-- P IV 7 178 26
see no curtains hereabouts that answer their description." P IV 7 179 30
side glance to see a slight curtsey from Elizabeth herself. P IV 8 181 2
"I should very much like to see Lyme again," said Anne. P IV 8 183 14
She was just in time to see him turn into the concert room. P IV 8 184 18
and look, had been such as she could see in only one light. P IV 8 185 21
she looked round to see if he should happen to be in the P IV 8 186 22
"Yes, yes, I see you are. P IV 8 186 26
I see you know nothing of the matter. P IV 8 186 26
I did not see them myself, but I heard Mr. Elliot say they P IV 9 193 7
I see it in your eye. P IV 9 194 14
I perfectly see how the hours passed--that you had always P IV 9 194 14
Anne half smiled and said, "do you see that in my eye?" P IV 9 194 15
see you, and was delighted to be in the way to let you in. P IV 9 197 40
When I talked of a whole history therefore, you see, I was P IV 9 205 82
Did he see you last summer or autumn, 'somewhere down in P IV 9 205 86

To Anne herself it was most distressing to see Mr. Elliot P IV 10 214 11
but Anne was really glad to see them; and the others were P IV 10 216 18
in Bath, whom she wanted to see; it was thought a good P IV 10 217 19
Charles and Mary, to go and see her and Henrietta directly. P IV 10 220 29
to the White Hart, to see again the friends and companions P IV 10 220 30
asked us to dinner, I think, if he had wanted to see us. P IV 10 223 44
You see he cannot put the card out of his hand." P IV 10 227 66
away, that she might neither see nor hear more to vex her. P IV 10 227 67
of his soul when he does see them again; when, coming back P 1 6 235 31
card too, though I did not see it--and you are disengaged, P IV 11 236 36
They could then see that she looked very ill--were shocked P IV 11 238 45
that we hope to see your whole party this evening. P IV 11 239 49
and Captain Wentworth, that we hope to see them both." P IV 11 239 49
Will you promise me to mention it, when you see them again? P IV 11 239 51
You will see them both again this morning, I dare say P IV 11 239 51
Charles, if you see Captain Harville any where, remember P IV 11 239 52
see it; and if I do not turn back now, I have no chance. P IV 11 240 58
He never even believed himself to see her equal. P IV 11 241 61
"To see you," cried he, "in the midst of those who could P IV 11 244 72
not be my well-wishers, to see your cousin close by you, P IV 11 244 72
in this belief; and yet--I was determined to see you again. P IV 11 245 76
sensible and well-judging, her first was to see Anne happy. P IV 12 249 4
I wd rather see his partner indeed--I would prefer the S 1 365 1
I need not ask whether I see the house; (looking towards S 1 365 1
with exultation to his wife)--you see how it is. S 1 370 1
like to it--but I want to see something applied to your S 1 370 1
Now sir, let us see how you can be best conveyed into the S 1 370 1
That is--we think differently, we now & then, see things S 3 376 1
When you see us in contact, you will judge for yourself."-- S 3 376 1
eager eye which hoped to see scarcely any empty houses.-- S 4 384 1
I by myself, can see nothing in it but what is either very S 5 387 1
see as much, & as quickly as possible, where all was new. S 6 389 1
recess, delighted to see Mr Parker again, whose manners S 6 390 1
We wanted just to see you & make sure of your being really S 6 391 1
of the morng had given her a great curiosity to see. S 6 391 1
address, Charlotte could see in her only the most perfect S 6 391 1
She cd see nothing worse in Lady Denham, than the sort of S 6 392 1
Aye--that young lady smiles I see;--I dare say she thinks S 6 393 1
Mrs P.-- in the drawing room in time to see them all.-- S 7 394 1
He is too kind hearted to see clearly.-- S 7 402 1
I can see no good in her.-- S 7 402 1
half-dethroned,--where we see the strong spark of woman's S 8 403 1
But my dear Mary, send for the children;--I long to see S 9 407 1
how is Arthur?--& why do not we see him here with you?"-- S 9 407 1
My dear Tom I am so glad to see you walk so well. S 9 408 1
Only a short chain, you see, between us, & not a link S 9 408 1
You see how it was all managed. S 9 408 1
what to make of me.-- I see by your looks, that you are S 9 410 1
it was "and when shall we see you again? and how can we be S 9 410 1
I see by the position of your foot, that you have used it S 9 411 1
the eveng, & delighted to see you at any time, but as soon S 9 411 1
She had had considerable curiosity to see Mr Arthur Parker; S 10 413 1
the terrace, & you will often see me at Trafalgar house."-- S 10 416 1
You would see me all in a Bath by the time I got there!-- S 10 416 1
you see, there is not a corner but what is well browned.-- S 10 417 1
than he ought; --but you see Mary, how impossible it is S 12 424 1
back in his own house & see the best place by the fire S 12 427 1

SEE-SAW (2)

And old man playing at see-saw! NA I 7 49 40
at see-saw and learning Latin; upon my soul there is not." NA I 7 49 42

SEEING (314)

I wanted her to be delighted at seeing me--I was as LS 5 249 1
my dear Reginald, of seeing you settled in the world. LS 12 261 3
some pains to prevent her seeing much of her aunt, but I LS 19 274 3
perceive that she had no particular pleasure in seeing him. LS 20 276 3
daughter that he could exist no longer without seeing her. LS 20 276 5
on the match, from seeing the rapid increase of her LS 22 280 1
What delight will be yours in seeing him again, in seeing LS 23 285 7
At that moment, how great was my astonishment at seeing LS 24 287 8
His confusion on seeing me was very evident. LS 24 287 8
in spite of Mr Johnson, to make opportunities of seeing me. LS 26 295 3
I despise--& I am secure of never seeing either again. LS 39 307 1
without Reginald, & seeing nobody from Churchill; I never LS 40 309 1
& I am full of hopes of seeing their hands joined at no LS 40 309 1
and seeing every thing herself as any young lady could be. NA I 2 20 8
secure within herself of seeing Mr. Tilney there before NA I 4 31 1
the pleasure of seeing you, but is not your name Allen?" NA I 4 31 2
weather were answered by seeing a beautiful morning, she NA I 5 35 1
there will be no danger of our seeing them at all." NA I 6 43 42
a pleasanter feeling, by seeing, not Mr. Thorpe, but Mr. NA I 8 53 3
morning after his having had the pleasure of seeing her. NA I 8 54 4
whose desire of seeing Miss Tilney again could at that NA I 9 61 6
"When Henry had the pleasure of seeing you before, he was NA I 10 73 12
"That never occurred to me; and of course, not seeing him NA I 10 73 13
"I hope I shall have the pleasure of seeing you again soon, NA I 10 73 19
of seeing her there, but no one appeared at them. NA I 12 91 3
the excursion itself, by seeing Blaize Castle; no, she had NA I 13 101 25
She reached home without seeing any thing more of the NA I 13 103 29
therefore at neither seeing nor hearing any thing of them. NA I 14 106 1
as I am in the habit of seeing almost every day of my life NA I 14 109 26
her as before; instead of seeing Henry Tilney to greater NA II 1 129 1
the pleasure of sometimes seeing Henry Tilney, made but a NA II 2 138 1
in my hope of seeing the Marquis of Longtown and General NA II 2 139 7
her seeing Isabella for more than a few minutes together. NA II 3 143 1
I do remember now being with you, and seeing him as well NA II 3 145 13
to be secured by her seeing nothing of Captain Tilney? NA II 4 152 28
fears of her seeing nothing to her taste--though never in NA II 5 154 2
anxious for her seeing as much of the country as possible." NA II 5 156 4
she was heartily weary of seeing and wondering, he NA II 7 179 27
No summons however arrived; and at last, on seeing a NA II 9 192 4
Because I am to hope for the satisfaction of seeing you at NA II 11 210 7
and the pleasure of seeing her, leaving them at first NA II 14 233 9
Her parents seeing nothing in her ill-looks and agitation, NA II 14 235 13
of this relapse; and seeing, in her daughter's absent and NA II 15 241 7
he has great pleasure in seeing the performances of other SS I 4 19 2
was fine, and from first seeing the place under the SS I 6 28 2
was not in the habit of seeing much occupation at home, SS I 9 40 1
and a half, of ever seeing a man who could satisfy her SS I 10 49 10
"Is there no chance of my seeing you and your sisters in SS I 13 66 46
walking over Mrs. Smith's grounds, or in seeing her house. SS I 13 68 74
sensible of pleasure in seeing them, looked neither SS I 16 87 23
in the same county with Elinor without seeing her before. SS I 16 87 25
Mrs. Dashwood was surprised only for a moment at seeing SS I 17 90 1
satisfaction of seeing him soon become more like himself. SS I 17 90 1
As Elinor was certain of seeing her in a couple of minutes, SS I 19 105 17
the evening before, on seeing their friends, without SS I 19 107 28
the hand, and expressed great delight in seeing them again. SS I 20 110 1
Every thing in such suspense and uncertainty; and seeing SS I 22 133 42
than a fortnight with us, and seeing me so much affected.-- SS I 22 134 52
But I only go for the sake of seeing Edward. SS II 2 151 40
nothing but grief and disappointment in seeing him. SS II 4 162 8
speak of his pleasure at seeing them in London, making the SS II 4 162 11
Mrs. Jennings from seeing her sister's thoughts as clearly SS II 5 167 4
quiet; the expectation of seeing him every hour of the day, SS II 5 169 15
express his surprise on seeing them in town, though SS II 5 171 30
and Elinor, after seeing her safe off, returned to SS II 7 185 16
my dear sister, by seeing how nobly the consciousness of SS II 7 189 51
The triumph of seeing me so may be open to all the world. SS II 7 189 52
what I must have felt on seeing your sister as fond of him SS II 9 210 32
From all danger of seeing Willoughby again, her mother SS II 10 213 4
could be no danger of her seeing either of them, to SS II 10 217 18
to miss the pleasure of seeing you; but she has been very SS II 10 219 38

The expectation of seeing her, however, was enough to make SS II 12 230 6
of seeing Elinor alone, to tell her how happy she was. SS II 13 238 2
You know how I dreaded the thoughts of seeing her;--but SS II 13 239 4
Her pleasure in seeing him was like every other of her SS II 13 242 23
not keep herself from seeing that Elinor changed colour, SS III 3 281 9
However, I will not disturb you (seeing her preparing to SS III 4 287 20
to leave London without seeing you and your sister; SS III 4 288 27
though she returned from seeing people whom she had never SS III 4 291 46
have the least objection in the world to seeing you.-- SS III 5 294 6
His heart was softened in seeing mine suffer; and so much SS III 8 330 69
her, my Elinor, ever since the first moment of seeing her." SS III 9 336 12
His emotion in entering the room, in seeing her altered SS III 10 340 2
seeing her mother's servant, on hearing Lucy's message! SS III 12 357 2
"How comes it, that we have not the pleasure of seeing W 334 13
was appeased, on seeing Mr Howard come forward and claim W 335 13
be pleased with the opportunity of seeing your sister."-- W 339 18
seeing her father comfortably seated in his arm chair.-- W 354 28
He could not help seeing that you were about five times as PP I 4 14 5
after a pause, on seeing Bingley join the group;--"and I PP I 6 25 28
deny me the happiness of seeing you; and though this PP I 6 26 41
Carter, and her hope of seeing him in the course of the PP I 7 29 7
They insist also on my seeing Mr. Jones--therefore do not PP I 7 31 30
she had the comfort of seeing her asleep, and when it PP I 8 37 21
I hope it will soon be increased by seeing her quite well." PP I 8 37 25
but being satisfied on seeing her that her illness was not PP I 9 41 2
ran up to her sister, and seeing her well guarded from PP I 11 54 1
seeing them all in due time well disposed of in marriage. PP I 13 64 21
His plan did not vary on seeing them.-- PP I 15 70 3
that she had neither been seeing him before, nor thinking PP I 16 76 3
such an assertion, after seeing, as you probably might, PP I 16 77 12
If he wishes to avoid seeing me, he must go. PP I 16 78 20
with Mr. Wickham, and of seeing a confirmation of every PP I 17 86 10
had the mortification of seeing Mary, after very little PP I 18 100 68
civil in her hope of seeing the whole family soon at PP I 18 103 76
when I have the honour of seeing her again I shall speak PP I 19 107 15
opportunity now of seeing her on the most intimate footing, PP I 21 118 14
and had soon the pleasure of seeing its happy effect. PP I 21 120 29
with their kind wish of seeing him again at Longbourn, PP I 23 128 10
you will be convinced of it, by seeing them happy together. PP II 1 136 14
being withheld from seeing Jane, she felt a solicitude on PP II 2 142 16
spend a morning with her, without any danger of seeing him. PP II 2 142 17
Jane had been a week in town, without either seeing or PP II 3 147 21
Absence had increased her desire of seeing Charlotte again, PP II 4 151 1
will have the honour of seeing Lady Catherine de Bourgh on PP II 5 157 6
7

she might be amused in seeing how hopeless Miss Bingley's PP II 7 170 6
The first time of my ever seeing him in Hertfordshire, you PP II 8 175 18
Mrs. Collins, seeing that she was really unwell, did not PP II 10 187 41
who had opportunities of seeing him in unguarded moments, PP II 12 200 5
of having no fear of seeing Mr. Darcy--that Mr. Darcy PP II 13 207 5
She dreaded seeing Wickham again, and was resolved to PP II 16 223 25
compassion are all done away by seeing you so full of both. PP II 17 225 13
she had set her heart on seeing the lakes; and still PP II 19 239 8
and was obliged to assume a disinclination for seeing it. PP II 19 240 14
Whether he had felt more of pain or of pleasure in seeing PP III 1 253 55
with which he expressed himself, on seeing her again. PP III 2 261 5
In seeing Bingley, her thoughts naturally flew to her PP III 2 262 8
had had the pleasure of seeing her;" and, before she could PP III 2 262 8
expressing their wish of seeing Mr. and Mrs. Gardiner, and PP III 2 263 11
of the proposal, and seeing in her husband, who was fond PP III 2 264 11
in the certainty of seeing Elizabeth again, having still a PP III 2 264 12
not always wise; and in seeing him at last look somewhat PP III 3 271 16
having the pleasure of seeing you at Pemberley to day." PP III 4 278 20
stairs, and will have great satisfaction in seeing you all. PP III 5 286 30
desirous of seeing you all, before she leaves the south. PP III 8 313 19
He saw Wickham, and afterwards insisted on seeing Lydia. PP III 10 322 2
seeing him, till after the departure of the former. PP III 10 323 2
invitation could be sent; hopeless of seeing him before. PP III 11 333 30
attend her sister, in seeing him almost for the first time PP III 11 334 36
views were overthrown, by seeing him fall a victim to her PP III 12 342 26
seeing him there again the next day, to make his proposals. PP III 12 343 29
at all able to account for the honour of seeing you here." PP III 14 353 25
seeing too little, she might have fancied too much. PP III 15 364 25
But I believe I must date it from my first seeing his PP III 17 373 16
and follow him, and her agitation on seeing it was extreme. PP III 17 375 28
My child, let me not have the grief of seeing you unable PP III 17 376 35
Elizabeth had the satisfaction of seeing her father taking PP III 17 379 47
right, and a desire of seeing all that were connected with MP I 1 3 1
kindly, and Sir Thomas seeing how much she needed MP I 2 12 2
on seeing her with red eyes, set her down as a hypocrite. MP I 3 33 64
dressing-closet without seeing one farm yard, nor walk in MP I 6 58 37
little tranquillized, by seeing the party in the meadow MP I 7 68 17
not lightened by seeing, as she looked back, that the MP I 7 69 21
she will have opportunities in plenty of seeing Sotherton. MP I 8 76 5
in seeing Sotherton would be nothing without him. MP I 8 79 27
been doing this morning--seeing a great house, dawdling MP I 9 95 71
of disappointment, cried out on seeing her, "hey-day! MP I 10 100 24
The sort of dread in which Fanny now sat of seeing Mr. MP I 10 101 33
without the means of seeing what clergymen are, being at MP I 11 111 28
Fanny agreed to it, and had the pleasure of seeing him MP I 11 112 35
had the mortification of seeing him advance too, moving MP I 11 113 42
been sure that she was seeing clearly, and judging MP I 12 115 5
give you an opportunity of seeing all the actors at once." MP I 18 167 10
Instead of being sent for out of the room, and seeing him MP II 1 180 10
prevented him even from seeing the expression of the face MP II 1 184 27
own eyes were fixed--from seeing Sir Thomas's dark brow MP II 1 184 27
and Sir Thomas hoped, in seeing him out of it, to be rid MP II 2 194 21
and trust to his seeing as much beauty of mind in time." MP II 3 197 6
than he was aware of; but seeing that she was distressed, MP II 3 198 9
she could dispense with seeing her husband a leading, MP II 3 201 22
and of every chance of seeing a single creature beyond MP II 4 205 3
no wonder in this shrubbery equal to seeing myself in it. MP II 4 209 17
It was the first time of his seeing them together since MP II 4 211 25
certain of seeing or hearing something there to pain me?" MP II 5 219 26
much in her thoughts on seeing him; but no embarrassing MP II 5 224 48
the letter from him, and seeing the coast clear of the MP II 6 229 1
have seen him and be seeing him perhaps daily, his direct MP II 6 233 14
with full satisfaction--seeing in them, the proof of good MP II 6 236 21
"I have had the pleasure of seeing your sister dance, Mr. MP II 7 250 61
But I believe (seeing Fanny look distressed) it must be at MP II 7 250 61
William's desire of seeing Fanny dance, made more than a MP II 8 252 1
be too much flattered by seeing round your lovely throat MP II 8 259 20
put into her hand, and seeing before her, in all the MP II 9 262 8
After seeing William to the last moment, Fanny walked back MP II 11 282 2
rather concerned at not seeing him again before I go to MP II 11 287 22
me such an opportunity of seeing you alone: I have been MP II 13 298 2
himself, as I knew he would after seeing your brother. MP II 13 299 5
her, but she must avoid seeing him if possible; and being MP III 1 311 2
of the lover; and when seeing such confidence of success MP III 2 329 11
I have engaged for your seeing him whenever he calls, as MP III 2 331 16
to suffer in seeing him on the stage with Miss Bertram. MP III 3 337 10
amused and gratified by seeing how she gradually slackened MP III 3 337 11
None such had occurred since his seeing her in her uncle's MP III 3 343 40
Fanny--nay--(seeing her draw back displeased) forgive me. MP III 3 344 41
depended upon her seeing every thing in so just a light. MP III 4 351 35
36

You are sure therefore of seeing your friend either to- MP III 4 354 48
being the last time of seeing you; for I do not know how MP III 5 359 9
and my looking in and seeing you here, sitting at this MP III 5 360 14
astonishment when he opened the door at seeing me here! MP III 5 360 14
and indubitably seeing all this, by the prospect of MP III 6 368 7
Fanny had any chance of seeing it, all its own freshness, MP III 6 368 8

placed Fanny's chance of seeing the 2d lieutenant of H. M. MP III 6 368 8
with the propriety of her seeing her parents again, and MP III 6 368 9
duty of Fanny's sometimes seeing her family, he did induce MP III 6 370 14
a joy in the prospect of seeing her child again, as to MP III 6 371 17
nurse, and now felt a particular pleasure in seeing again. MP III 7 381 25
she had begun almost to despair of seeing that evening. MP III 7 383 32
morning, the hope of soon seeing William again, and the MP III 8 388 1
by one, who, while seeing all the obligation and MP III 9 397 8
no opportunity of seeing Miss Crawford alone--or, he was MP III 10 399 1
of going over to the island, nor of seeing the dock-yard. MP III 10 400 7
thought himself lucky in seeing Mary for even half an hour, MP III 10 400 8
happiness, and his in seeing her, must be so much greater. MP III 11 410 7
Though tolerably secure of not seeing Mr. Crawford again, MP III 11 413 31
circle she had been just seeing him, nor how much might be MP III 11 413 32
and seeing the inside of St. George's, Hanover-Square. MP III 12 416 3
be unlovely, and seeing its increasing beauties, from the MP III 14 432 9
The idea of immediately seeing him, with the knowledge of MP III 15 444 28
I should be surprized if, after seeing them, you could be E I 4 32 32
I have been seeing their intimacy with the greatest E I 5 36 4
she had the pleasure of seeing him most intently at work E I 9 70 7
and at Harriet, and then seeing the book open on the table, E I 9 82 81
a proof of love, with Mr. Elton's seeing ready wit in her. E I 10 83 6
"Oh! papa, we have missed seeing them but one entire day E I 11 94 14
But now I have no doubt of seeing him here about the E I 14 120 9
I am as confident of seeing Frank here before the middle E I 14 120 11
by no means so sure of seeing Mr. Frank Churchill, in my E I 14 121 16
though her dependence on seeing the young man had been so E I 18 144 2
We never were so long without seeing her before, and as I E II 1 158 14
and her own wish of seeing Ireland, Miss Fairfax prefers E II 1 161 24
You, who have been hearing and seeing so much of late on E II 3 175 42
in seeing him behave so pleasantly and so kindly. E II 3 179 52
have been thankful to be assured of never seeing him again. E II 4 182 7
But on seeing them together, she became perfectly E II 6 196 2
lively as ever; and after seeing him, Emma thus moralized E II 8 212 2
3

With Tuesday came the agreeable prospect of seeing him E II 8 212 4
be, who were now seeing them together for the first time. E II 8 212 4
To be in company, nicely dressed herself and seeing others E II 8 219 44
I have no pleasure in seeing my friends, unless I can E II 8 222 53
Mrs. Weston, she had been seeing nothing, except that he E II 8 227 85
A mind lively and at ease, can do with seeing nothing, and E II 9 233 24
able to shew a most happy countenance on seeing Emma again. E II 10 240 2
Pleasure in seeing dancing!--not I, indeed--I never look E II 12 257 3
idea, the expectation of seeing him which every morning E II 12 262 38
pleasure than ever in seeing Mr. and Mrs. Weston; she was E II 13 264 1
Woodhouse, I do not think I shall mind seeing them again. E II 14 271 15
Mr. Woodhouse was quite at ease; and the seeing him so, E II 16 292 9
have the greatest satisfaction in seeing you at Hartfield." E II 16 294 27
both have great pleasure in seeing him at the vicarage." E II 18 305 4
I met the letters in my way this morning, and seeing my E II 18 305 5
There could be no doubt of his great pleasure in seeing E III 1 316 3
whole difference of seeing him always and seeing him never. E III 1 317 10
So afraid you might have a headach!--seeing you pass by so E III 2 322 19
But Emma's wonder lessened soon afterwards, on seeing Mr. E III 2 326 33
She was evidently displeased; looked up, and seeing E III 5 349 23
body found so well worth seeing, and she and Mr. Weston E III 6 352 2
He said nothing worth hearing--looked without seeing-- E III 7 367 2
It is only by seeing women in their own homes, among their E III 7 372 40
She will be extremely sorry to miss seeing you, Miss E III 8 379 8
very naturally resolve on seeing Mrs. Cole or any other E III 8 379 9
would not go away without seeing you, but I have no time E III 9 385 1
2

had been in seeing him come forward to your rescue.-- E III 11 406 23
In the meanwhile, she resolved against seeing Harriet.-- E III 12 416 2
"I have scarce had the pleasure of seeing you, Miss E III 16 454 18
But I am not afraid of your seeing what he writes." E III 17 464 19
our agreeable surprise in seeing him arrive this morning. E III 18 476 45
she had long felt, of seeing Frank Churchill once more, E III 18 476 46
once more, and of seeing him with Jane, would yield its E III 18 476 46
the pleasure of sometimes seeing the lawns and groves of P III 2 14 9
Admiral and Mrs. Croft's seeing Kellynch-Hall, Anne found P III 5 32 1
sorry that she had missed the opportunity of seeing them. P III 5 32 1
have her advantage in seeing how unknown, or unconsidered P III 6 42 1
go twice into my nursery without seeing something of them. P III 6 45 9
to shew his gratitude, by seeing Captain Wentworth under P III 7 53 1
pleasure of seeing them set off together in high spirits. P III 7 58 20
He wished to avoid seeing her. P III 7 59 23
very altered manners, and of seeing Captain Wentworth. P III 9 74 4
Mr. and Mrs. Musgrove, either from seeing little, or from P III 9 74 9
under the constant dependance of seeing him to-morrow. P III 10 82 2
Henrietta, conscious and ashamed, and seeing no cousin P III 10 85 16
the first time of my seeing you, and our sitting down P III 10 92 44
for her to avoid ever seeing Captain Wentworth at the hall; P III 11 93 3
not leave much time for seeing a new place, after P III 11 94 8
on seeing Louisa and Captain Wentworth coming towards them. P III 12 103 5
"Oh course," said Mary, "you will mention our seeing Mr. P III 12 107 20
Kellynch-Hall, or of seeing him in company with her friend. P IV 1 128 32
being so very well worth seeing, for as he has a taste for P IV 2 131 12
for I have been seeing him every day this last fortnight." P IV 2 132 14
rain, without any wish of seeing them better; felt their P IV 2 135 34
Hers is a line for seeing human nature; and she has a fund P IV 5 155 9
feeling than the hope of seeing him receive the hand of P IV 5 161 30
of seeing her sister turn away with unalterable coldness. P IV 7 176 9
have lost the right moment for seeing whether he saw them. P IV 7 179 31
She could not quit the room in peace without seeing P IV 8 189 45
say for seeing, because I appear to have seen very little." P IV 9 193 11
with all the semblance of seeing nothing beyond; and Anne, P IV 9 197 34
Anne, seeing her friend to be earnestly bent on it, did as P IV 9 202 69
She was obliged to recollect that her seeing the letter P IV 9 204 76
77

as she intended, escaped seeing Mr. Elliot; that he had P IV 10 212 2
that had happened, or my seeing him could never have gone P IV 10 228 71
twelve hours sooner, and seeing them arrive at last, as if P 1 6 235 31
every group around them, seeing neither sauntering P IV 11 241 59
into contact again, in seeing Anne restored to the rights P IV 12 250 5
She had soon the mortification of seeing Mr. Elliot P IV 12 250 6
her, acting for her, and seeing her through all the petty P IV 12 251 11
I remember seeing Mrs Hillier after one of those dreadful S 4 381 1
chance of seeing them at Sanditon I am sorry to say.-- S 5 385 1
a great impression--& seeing no rapturous astonishment in S 7 400 1
she had the pleasure of seeing just as she ascended from S 9 406 1
& Morgan's looks on seeing her, were a moment's S 9 406 1
deal of surprise but still more pleasure in seeing her.-- S 9 406 1
As to seeing me again today--I cannot answer for it; the S 9 411 1
Charlotte had been 10 days at Sanditon without seeing S 12 423 1
I will take an opportunity of seeing Lady D. myself.-- S 12 425 1

SEEK (34)
She is poor, & may naturally seek an alliance which may be LS 12 261 4
his proud heart, without deigning to seek an explanation! LS 25 293 3
I must endeavour to seek amusement abroad, & fortunately LS 30 301 5
she must seek them abroad, invited her to go with them. NA I 1 17 12
to seek her for that purpose, in the Pump-Room at noon. NA I 9 60 1
him with you, we had better not seek after the cause." NA II 12 219 7
window of the cottage to seek the exquisite enjoyment of SS I 9 40 3
"I certainly did not seek your confidence," said Elinor; SS I 22 132 40
arrive, was of course to seek for her; but the search was SS II 9 207 26
without seeming to seek, he did not turn away from the W 356 28
She was therefore obliged to seek another branch of the PP I 3 13 19
of those young ladies who seek to recommend themselves to PP I 8 40 56
Why did not you seek legal redress?" PP I 16 79 26
error, and seek to clear one, without involving the other. PP II 17 225 9
But Mr. Bennet was not of a disposition to seek comfort PP II 19 236 1

her to seek the other less interesting mode of attachment. PP III 4 279 24
"If he wants our society, let him seek it. PP III 11 332 25
overlook the offence, and seek a reconciliation; and, PP III 19 388 12
was already at work, while a play was still to seek. MP I 14 130 1
she might seek directly all that solitude could do for her. MP II 2 193 18
mind became cool enough to seek all the comfort that pride MP II 3 201 24
to wear, determined to seek the counsel of the more MP II 8 256 14
himself still impelled to seek her again, she had MP II 10 279 21
fully she was inclined to seek her good opinion and refer MP III 9 397 8
to seek and his own situation to improve as he could. E I 2 16 4
She determined to call upon them and seek safety in E II 1 155 2
or the condescension to seek her; for since her refusal of E II 3 180 58
Was it new for one, perhaps too busy to seek, to be the E III 11 413 48
to seek, to be the prize of a girl who would seek him?-- E III 11 413 48
as to put up with it, and seek no farther explanation. E III 13 431 38
whole, left the room, to seek the comfort of cool air for P III 3 24 38
the stranger's eye will seek; and a very strange stranger P III 11 95 9
did not disincline him to seek her again; and they walked P III 12 107 23
taking as much pains to seek the acquaintance, and P IV 2 135 35

SEEKING (27)

she was so far from seeking to attract their notice, that NA I 7 47 18
to him all the trouble of seeking an explanation, and to NA I 12 93 4
could not warrant; seeking to better themselves by wealthy NA II 15 246 12
They gave themselves up wholly to their sorrow, seeking SS I 1 7 13
fix her sorrow, by seeking silence, solitude, and idleness. SS I 19 104 9
If in the supposition of his seeking to marry herself, his SS II 1 140 3
he was really resolved on seeking an intimacy with that SS II 11 228 51
farther, without seeking after more, she had resolved from SS III 2 270 3
Vanity, while seeking its own guilty triumph at the SS III 8 331 70
of the information without the exertion of seeking it. SS III 11 353 25
and by his rapidity in seeking that fate, it is to be SS III 13 366 20
intended to marry; and in seeking a reconciliation with PP I 15 70 2
a smile, at his being now seeking the acquaintance of some PP III 1 254 58
When she saw him thus seeking the acquaintance, and PP III 2 263 10
they were on the point of seeking him up stairs with their PP III 7 301 4
5
produced his activity in seeking her were over, he PP III 8 309 5
You may depend upon my seeking no further." PP III 9 319 28
and voluntarily seeking her was almost equal to what she PP III 11 334 36
among other means, by seeking an intimacy with the MP I 4 39 10
He too had his book, and was seeking Fanny, to ask her to MP I 18 170 23
but the chief object in seeking them, was to understand MP II 6 236 21
attached to you, and seeking your hand in the most MP III 1 319 39
sanction to vice, or in seeking to lessen its disgrace, by MP III 17 465 13
not get at her, without seeking her, where hitherto they E II 3 180 58
he had persevered in seeking it, making allowance for the P III 1 7 14
themselves, and seeking his acquaintance, as soon as they P III 6 52 33
good company always worth seeking; Lady Dalrymple had P IV 4 149 12

SEEM (133)

seem to have the sort of temper to make severity necessary. LS 17 270 4
Sir James may seem to have drawn an harder lot than mere LS 42 313 10
we came here--we seem forcing ourselves into their party." NA I 2 22 14
Mr. Tilney was polite enough to seem interested in what NA I 3 29 47
They seem very agreeable people. NA I 9 68 42
These Tilneys seem to swallow up every thing else." NA I 13 98 2
who do not altogether seem particularly friendly to very NA I 14 110 27
"I do not say so; but he did not seem in good spirits." NA II 1 130 4
It was wonderful that her friends should seem so little NA II 2 141 12
Peals of thunder so loud as to seem to shake the edifice NA II 5 159 19
But she would not make up her fire; that would seem NA II 6 167 10
Perhaps it may seem odd, that with only two younger NA II 7 176 15
And, upon my word, there are some things that seem very NA II 10 206 35
of the dinner did not seem to create the smallest NA II 11 214 27
it might seem an intrusion if she staid much longer. NA II 13 220 1
of such a message, I seem guilty myself of all its insult; NA II 13 225 19
my decay; and it must seem to you a miracle that my life SS I 8 37 7
To me it would seem only a commercial exchange, in which SS I 8 38 10
for some time, he should seem to act an ungenerous, a SS I 15 81 43
shy, that I often seem negligent, when I am only kept back SS I 17 94 42
hills are steep, the woods seem full of fine timber, and SS I 18 97 4
Ferrars, must seem so odd, that it ought to be explained. SS I 22 129 16
Your case is a very unfortunate one; you seem to me to be SS II 2 146 6
We seem so beset with difficulties on every side, that SS II 2 149 30
I always pity them when they do; they seem to take it so SS II 5 167 1
The clouds seem parting too, the sun will be out in a SS II 5 168 9
I seem to have been distressing you for nothing. SS II 9 208 28
with a recital which may seem to have been intended to SS II 9 210 32
Mr. Dashwood did not seem to know much about horses, he SS II 11 228 52
should seem to say, she had quite took a fancy to me. SS II 13 239 4
why Mrs. Ferrars should seem to like me, if she did not, SS II 13 239 9
"Are you ill, Miss Dashwood?--you seem low--you don't SS II 13 239 11
seem strong, feel all her own disappointment over again. SS III 1 261 11
This delay on the Colonel's side, however, did not seem to SS III 3 281 13
14
"But Colonel Brandon does not seem to have any idea of the SS III 4 292 56
And though, perhaps, Marianne may not seem exactly the SS III 14 375 9
It must seem odd enough to you to be here.-- W 351 26
To be sure that did seem as if he admired her--indeed I PP I 5 18 6
Well, that was very decided in deed--that does seem as if-- PP I 5 19 8
"Why, indeed, he does seem to have had some filial PP I 13 62 11
fearing lest it might seem disrespectful to his memory for PP I 13 62 12
said Mary, "his letter does not seem defective. PP I 13 64 19
herself; and yet it should seem by her manner of talking, PP II 3 148 26
But when Elizabeth told of his silence, it did not seem PP II 9 180 28
We seem to have been designed for each other." PP II 15 216 6
were to go, she did not seem to ask for compassion. PP II 15 216 7
Nor did he seem much more at ease; when he spoke, his PP III 1 252 52
It might seem as if she had purposely thrown herself in PP III 1 252 54
To Kitty, however, it does not seem so wholly unexpected. PP III 4 273 3
wishes, which may seem purposely to ask for your thanks. PP III 4 278 20
"It does seem, and it is most shocking indeed," replied PP III 5 283 10
Can she be ignorant of what you and Jane seem so well to PP III 5 284 15
seem valid, exceeded all that she could believe possible. PP III 8 310 10
She did not seem to have a thought of fear. MP I 7 69 22
Your brother's taste, and your sisters', seem very MP I 13 128 34
Julia did seem inclined to admit that Maria's situation MP I 13 128 38
and comedy, that there did seem as little chance of a MP I 14 130 2
said to him, "you do not seem afraid of not keeping your MP I 14 136 18
longer behind it might seem disrespectful, when this point MP II 1 177 6
They seem to belong to us--they seem to be part of MP II 3 196 2
seem out of spirits, and Tom is certainly not at his ease. MP II 3 196 2
and of forgetting, do seem peculiarly past finding out." MP II 4 209 12
"It may seem impertinent in me to praise, but I must MP II 4 209 14
with her in what might seem a state of triumph, she MP II 5 221 38
39
You do not seem properly aware of her claims to notice. MP II 6 229 5
in which she did not seem propitious, and though trusting MP II 8 255 10
companions makes her seem, gives to her conversation, to MP II 9 269 31
expression of indifference seem almost an effort of self- MP III 2 327 6
an effort of self-denial; seem at least, to be giving MP III 2 327 6
And my friend does not manage him well; she does not seem MP III 5 361 16
"I do not know how it is," said he, "but we seem to want MP III 6 372 20
deal more, and who did seem so thoroughly without a single MP III 7 385 38
They seem very comfortable as they are, and if she were to E I 4 30 18
and situation in life seem to allow it; but if any young E I 4 34 42
as your powers would seem to promise; but you were E I 5 38 11
Isabella does not seem more my sister; has never excited a E I 5 40 27
"There does, indeed, seem as little to tempt her to break E I 5 41 30
By your account, he does seem to have had some scruples. E I 8 61 37
There does seem to be a something in the air of Hartfield E I 9 75 25
"You seem to me to have forgotten Mrs. and Miss Bates," E I 12 102 30
up his mind, and does not seem to feel the cold himself, I E I 13 110 9
of her father, as to seem--if not quite ready to join him E I 15 132 38
They seem to satisfy every body else." E I 18 149 25
"You seem determined to think ill of him." E I 18 149 27
Dixon does not seem in the least backward in any attention. E II 1 160 23
on; and though she did not seem to stay half a moment E II 3 177 52
said she; "but you seem to have behaved extremely well; E II 3 180 55
of Mrs. Cole's did not seem to contradict, that when he E II 4 182 6
to Miss Campbell; but she really did not seem to feel it." E II 6 202 34
William did not seem to mind it himself, he was so pleased E II 9 239 51
You seem but just come--so very obliging of you." E II 10 245 54
She does seem a charming young woman, just what he E II 14 272 15
both at home; and very pleasant people they seem to be. E II 14 278 44
But upon my honour, there seem no limits to the E II 15 284 10
We really seem quite the fashion. E II 16 290 2
But I am quite in the minority, I believe; few people seem E II 17 302 22
You seem shut out from every thing--in the most complete E II 18 307 21
she let it pass, and seem to suspect nothing?-- E III 4 341 34
He is your superior, no doubt, and there do seem E III 4 342 39
"No, sir," replied his son, laughing, "I seem to have had E III 5 345 13
It did not seem to touch the rest of the party equally; E III 7 371 35
36
This does not seem much like joy, indeed, in me--(E III 8 378 8
But now I seem to feel that I may deserve him; and that if E III 11 411 39
and a heavy sigh) I seem to have been doomed to blindness." E III 13 425 11
Emma, I accept your offer--extraordinary as it may seem, I E III 13 429 33
He does seem to have suffered in finding her ill.-- E III 15 447 28
Things did not seem--that is, there seemed a little cloud E III 16 454 18
They seem not able to do any thing without him.-- E III 16 455 23
Emma gave a start, which did not seem like being prepared-- E III 18 470 13
she too was really hearing him, though trying to seem deaf. E III 18 480 76
as her husband, made her seem to have lived some years P III 6 48 18
such happiness might seem; as for herself, she was left P III 7 58 20
liked him,--and Henrietta did seem to like him." P III 9 74 6
Captain Wentworth did not seem admitted to perfect P III 10 89 36
did not seem fit for the mirth of the party in general. P III 11 100 22
For, though shy, he did not seem reserved; it had rather P III 11 100 23
our family, they seem shut out from all the world. P III 12 102 2
have no doubt, though the kind may seem a little different. P IV 4 151 21
"The Admiral does not seem very ill, and I sincerely hope " P IV 6 164 8
It did certainly seem, last autumn, as if there was an P IV 6 172 42
to wish for which did not seem within her reach; and Anne-- P IV 8 185 20
and she was forced to seem to restore her attention to the P IV 8 188 41
from Mrs. Wallis herself, which did not seem bad authority. P IV 9 197 40
Your father and mother seem so totally free from all those P IV 10 218 23
He did not seem to want to be near enough for conversation. P IV 10 221 32
They seem deep in talk. P IV 10 222 34
You seem to have forgot all about Lyme." P IV 10 222 38
and as the road does not seem at present in a favourable S 1 365 1
The Hilliers did not seem to feel the storms last winter S 4 381 1
our bed, and she did not seem at all aware of the wind S 4 381 1
I dare say, but their measures seem to touch on extremes.-- S 5 388 1
But I seem to be spinning out my story to an endless S 9 408 1
It should seem that they must either be very busy for the S 10 412 1

SEEM'D (1)

she related the past, seem'd to threaten her reason--how LS 36 306 1

SEEMED (600)

little devil before; she seemed to have all the vernon LS 16 268 1
Even Lady Susan seemed a little disconcerted by this LS 20 278 10
& the whole business seemed most comfortably arranged. LS 22 281 3
He seemed astonished at the summons, and looked as if half LS 25 292 2
She was in excellent spirits, & seemed eager to shew at LS 42 311 2
the course of a few days seemed somewhat less formidable. LS 42 312 5
not less unpropitious for heroism seemed her mind. NA I 1 13 1
them; and though there seemed no chance of her throwing a NA I 1 16 10
and composure, which seemed rather consistent with the NA I 2 19 3
from the crowd; it seemed rather to increase as they went NA I 2 21 9
He seemed to be about four or five and twenty, was rather NA I 3 25 2
The name seemed to strike them all; and, after speaking to NA I 4 32 4
face and ungraceful form, seemed fearful of being too NA I 7 45 5
And this address seemed to satisfy all the fondest wishes NA I 7 49 43
place where they sat; he seemed to be moving that way, but NA I 8 53 3
affectedly open; and she seemed capable of being young, NA I 8 56 11
the original subject seemed entirely forgotten; and though NA I 8 57 21
She seemed to have missed by so little the very object she NA I 8 59 35
By him the whole matter seemed entirely forgotten; and all NA I 9 66 31
You would have told us that we seemed born for each other. NA I 10 71 5
"Did upon my soul; knew him again directly, and he seemed NA I 11 85 39
of spirits; but Isabella seemed to find a pool of commerce, NA I 11 89 63
his innocence, it seemed likely that William would lose NA I 13 103 27
It seemed as if a good view were no longer to be taken NA I 14 110 28
with every thing, and who seemed only to want Mr. NA I 15 120 25
this odd sort of reserve seemed neither kindly meant, nor NA I 15 121 25
all care and anxiety seemed removed, her spirits became NA I 15 121 26
about, hummed a tune, and seemed wholly self-occupied. NA I 15 122 29
of the day, she seemed hardly so intimate with her as NA II 1 129 1
seemed to be his only care to entertain and make me happy." NA II 1 130 8
Her whole happiness seemed at stake, while the affair was NA II 2 138 1
Every thing seemed to co-operate for her advantage. NA II 2 140 11
of an hour, had seemed too nearly impossible for desire. NA II 2 141 11
It seemed to her that Captain Tilney was falling in love NA II 3 148 28
Isabella seemed an altered creature. NA II 4 149 1
a rival, but if more had seemed implied, the fault must NA II 4 149 1
Her tenderness for her friend seemed rather the first NA II 4 153 31
Nay, perverse as it seemed, she doubted whether she might NA II 5 154 2
father's reproof, which seemed disproportionate to the NA II 5 154 2
though so charming a man, seemed always a check upon his NA II 5 156 4
The breeze had not seemed to waft the sighs of the NA II 5 161 25
This seemed the word of separation, and Catherine found NA II 5 162 27
With difficulty, for something seemed to resist her NA II 6 164 3
her gown, her toilette seemed so nearly finished, that the NA II 6 164 3
The window curtains seemed in motion. NA II 6 167 10
every thing seemed to speak the awfulness of her situation. NA II 6 168 10
but now every blast seemed fraught with awful intelligence. NA II 6 170 12
The very curtains of her bed seemed at one moment in NA II 6 171 12
Hollow murmurs seemed to creep along the gallery, and more NA II 6 171 12
and modern characters, seemed all that was before her! NA II 7 172 2
And the larger sheet, which had inclosed the rest, seemed NA II 7 172 2
A corner of it catching her eye as she lay, seemed to rise NA II 7 173 2
gratitude; and it seemed as if his own estimation of NA II 7 178 19
The walls seemed countless in number, endless in length; a NA II 7 178 21
a village of hot-houses seemed to arise among them, and a NA II 7 178 21
for her health, which seemed to reproach her for her NA II 7 181 41
and passed through, and seemed on the point of doing the NA II 8 185 6
distance down stairs, seemed to point out:--"I was going NA II 8 186 6
even enter the church, seemed wonderful to Catherine. NA II 9 190 2
seemed always at hand when least wanted,) much worse!-- NA II 9 194 6
hastily opened; some one seemed with swift steps to ascend NA II 9 194 6
He seemed to be looking in her countenance for that NA II 9 194 8
Her folly, which now seemed even criminal, was all exposed NA II 10 199 1
her quitting Bath, and it seemed as if the whole might be NA II 10 200 2
them, she seemed quite disappointed that it was not more. NA II 10 206 35
it, as the General seemed to think an apology necessary NA II 11 212 17
unhappy about him, he seemed so uncomfortable when he went NA II 12 217 2
of the stairs, when it seemed, as far as the thickness of NA II 13 222 7
door made her start; it seemed as if some one was touching NA II 13 222 9
Though evidently intending to come in, it seemed an effort NA II 13 223 9
Eleanor seemed now impelled into resolution and speech. NA II 13 228 27
Such an agreeable, worthy man as he seemed to be! NA II 14 238 26
was voluntary; and it seemed as if she could even walk NA II 15 240 1
turn her from the house seemed the best, though to his NA II 15 244 11
almost equal openness,) seemed sufficient vouchers for his NA II 15 245 12
Yet she bore it with so much composure, she seemed SS I 3 18 18

Context	Work	Vol	Ch	Page	Line
the more doubtful seemed the nature of his regard; and	SS	I	4	22	18
He seemed really anxious to accommodate them, and the	SS	I	4	23	20
exposed to, that he seemed rather to stand in need of more	SS	I	5	27	6
Their arrival seemed to afford him real satisfaction, and	SS	I	6	30	6
talked a great deal, seemed very happy, and rather vulgar.	SS	I	7	34	5
Colonel Brandon, the friend of Sir John, seemed no more	SS	I	7	34	6
Lady Middleton seemed to be roused to enjoyment only by	SS	I	7	34	7
lively nor young, seemed resolved to undervalue his merits.	SS	I	10	50	13
could not shame, and seemed hardly to provoke them.	SS	I	11	54	3
fast as could be, and he seemed to be begging something of	SS	I	12	60	13
They both seemed delighted with their drive, but said only	SS	I	13	67	60
Elinor could hardly believe this to be true, as it seemed	SS	I	13	68	66
The cottage seemed to be considered and loved by him as	SS	I	14	71	5
the country, his heart seemed more than usually open to	SS	I	14	72	6
love for him was, a quarrel seemed almost impossible.	SS	I	15	77	19
that at first seemed strange to me as well as to you."	SS	I	15	78	24
Her eyes were red and swollen; and it seemed as if her	SS	I	15	82	46
No letter from Willoughby came; and none seemed expected	SS	I	16	84	5
He was confused, seemed scarcely sensible of pleasure in	SS	I	16	87	23
His affections seemed to reanimate towards them all, and	SS	I	17	90	1
of his preference seemed very uncertain; and the	SS	I	18	96	1
on self-mortification, he seemed resolved to be gone when	SS	I	19	101	1
to Marianne, than her own had seemed faulty to her.	SS	I	19	104	11
their entreaties, all seemed equally anxious to avoid a	SS	I	19	109	40
by Miss Steele, who seemed very much disposed for	SS	I	21	123	21
said Lucy, who seemed to think some apology necessary for	SS	I	21	123	24
what seemed impertinent curiosity--"I know nothing of her."	SS	I	22	128	6
for a while; but it seemed to have deprived himself of all	SS	II	1	140	1
from his mother had seemed great, how much greater were	SS	II	1	140	3
and cheerfulness which seemed to infer that she could	SS	II	1	144	14
full of meaning, "there seemed to me to be a coldness and	SS	II	2	146	5
one lady than another, or seemed in any respect less happy	SS	II	2	147	12
of which she seemed so thoroughly aware that he was weary.	SS	II	2	151	41
one of the three, who seemed to consider the separation as	SS	II	3	158	21
seemed anxiously listening to the sound of every carriage.	SS	II	4	161	6
indeed it is!"" and seemed almost ready to throw herself	SS	II	4	161	7
The disappointment of the evening before seemed forgotten	SS	II	4	164	21
But Marianne seemed hardly to hear her, and on Mrs.	SS	II	5	169	14
He could not then avoid it, but her touch seemed painful	SS	II	6	177	8
She was soon undressed and in bed, and as she seemed	SS	II	6	178	16
was weary of it, seemed equally clear; for however	SS	II	6	178	17
that embarrassment which seemed to speak a consciousness	SS	II	6	178	17
embitter such an evil seemed uniting to heighten the	SS	II	6	179	18
The latter, though unable to speak, seemed to feel all the	SS	II	7	182	12
added in a voice which seemed to distrust itself, "and	SS	II	8	199	39
My behaviour must have seemed strange to you then; but now	SS	II	9	210	32
of Willoughby, and seemed to shew by her tears that she	SS	II	10	212	1
Colonel and Miss Dashwood seemed rather to declare that	SS	II	10	216	15
end of the counter which seemed to promise the quickest	SS	II	11	220	3
but such a one as seemed rather to demand than express	SS	II	11	221	5
ever was, and you all seemed to enjoy it beyond any thing.	SS	II	11	222	11
with a curiosity which seemed to say, that he only wanted	SS	II	11	223	14
seemed purposely made to humble her more, only amused her.	SS	II	12	232	16
behaviour to her sister, seemed, to her, to foretel such	SS	II	12	236	39
					40
make the attention which seemed only paid her because she	SS	II	13	238	2
But it seemed to satisfy Lucy, for she directly replied, "	SS	II	13	240	14
					15
They all looked exceedingly foolish; and Edward seemed to	SS	II	13	240	19
Lucy, with a demure and settled air, seemed determined to	SS	II	13	241	22
Elinor was very angry, but Marianne seemed entirely	SS	II	13	243	39
					40
Elinor set him right as to its situation, and it seemed	SS	II	14	251	16
Mrs. Dashwood seemed actually working for her, herself;	SS	II	14	254	26
so short an acquaintance, seemed to declare that the good	SS	II	14	254	27
and looked grave, and seemed to know something or other,	SS	III	1	258	5
Edward seemed a second Willoughby; and acknowledging as	SS	III	1	261	13
Marianne seemed much struck.--	SS	III	1	262	24
my misery, who have seemed to be only suffering for me!--	SS	III	1	264	31
They all looked their assent; it seemed too awful a moment	SS	III	1	265	35
over again, he said, it seemed to him as if, now he had no	SS	III	2	273	16
of which, at present, there seemed not the smallest chance.	SS	III	2	276	26
he seemed to be apologizing for the badness of his house.	SS	III	3	281	9
it likewise, still seemed so desirous of its being given	SS	III	3	283	20
so uncheerful, as seemed to say, that he might hereafter	SS	III	4	290	39
It seemed quite ridiculous.	SS	III	4	292	55
over her accents, seemed to distinguish every thing that	SS	III	5	300	38
It amused her to observe that all her friends seemed	SS	III	6	301	2
by Mr. Palmer, who seemed to feel a relief to himself, in	SS	III	7	309	5
of the apothecary seemed to render absurd; but the many	SS	III	7	309	7
for with a readiness that seemed to speak the occasion,	SS	III	7	311	15
an attitude of deep meditation, and seemed not to hear her.	SS	III	8	317	9
and of such manners, seemed no otherwise intelligible; and	SS	III	8	318	16
					17
the most wearing anxiety seemed to make requisite, was	SS	III	9	334	5
and kind wishes as seemed due to her own heart from a	SS	III	10	341	5
he seemed anxious that she should engross at least half.	SS	III	10	341	5
Every body seemed injured by me.	SS	III	10	346	28
Thomas's intelligence seemed over.	SS	III	11	355	40
very handsome young lady--and she seemed vastly contented."	SS	III	11	355	44
He coloured, seemed perplexed, looked doubtingly, and	SS	III	12	360	20
					21
In such a situation as that, where there seemed nothing to	SS	III	13	367	22
knowledge of each other seemed to make their happiness	SS	III	13	369	32
reproach which she always seemed fearful of incurring, the	SS	III	14	373	1
seemed the only person surprised at her not giving more.	SS	III	14	374	5
Some people say that he has never seemed to like any girl	W			316	1
civility--& the papers, seemed very naturally to have	W			322	3
the question, & there seemed something still more	W			324	3
fair creature seemed glad to escape into the card-room.--	W			328	8
up a favourite air, which seemed to call the young men to	W			328	9
seemed to speak him out of his element in a ball room.	W			329	10
The two dances seemed very short, & she had her partner's	W			335	13
chairs, it might have seemed a matter scarcely perceived.--	W			336	14
There seemed no vacancy anywhere--& everybody danced with	W			340	19
He seemed so eager to fetch you, that I could not say no,	W			341	19
declared it seemed only two days since he had seen her.--"	W			342	19
had nothing but fried beef, how good it has all seemed.--	W			343	19
me great attention, & seemed to feel for me as an invalid.-	W			344	20
the party to Stanton seemed to her the probable conclusion	W			348	23
right--& Emma, whom she seemed no longer to think about,	W			360	30
can, you know; and he seemed quite struck with Jane as she	PP	I	3	13	16
"Yes;--but he seemed to like his second better."	PP	I	5	18	5
her;--but she said he seemed very angry at being spoke to."	PP	I	5	19	12
But that gentleman," looking at Darcy, "seemed to think	PP	I	9	43	23
of the whole party on the subject, seemed to justify her.	PP	I	11	54	3
to talk, and Mr. Collins seemed neither in need of	PP	I	13	64	21
observing that he seemed very fortunate in his patroness.	PP	I	14	66	1
Her ladyship seemed pleased with the idea, and you may	PP	I	14	67	9
her charming daughter seemed born to be a duchess, and	PP	I	14	67	9
the officers, Mr. Collins seemed likely to sink into	PP	I	16	76	5
At first there seemed danger of Lydia's engrossing him	PP	I	16	76	8
Darcy made no answer, and seemed desirous of changing the	PP	I	18	92	22
allusion to his friend seemed to strike him forcibly, and	PP	I	18	92	24
and Mr. Darcy's contempt seemed abundantly increasing with	PP	I	18	98	61
Mr. Darcy seemed much pleased with the attention. he	PP	I	18	98	62
It was an animating subject, and Mrs. Bennet seemed	PP	I	18	99	63
could encourage him, seemed almost as far from possibility	PP	I	22	124	12
					13
for it clearly, there seemed little chance of her ever	PP	II	1	137	26
She wrote cheerfully, seemed surrounded with comforts, and	PP	II	3	146	19
But though every thing seemed neat and comfortable, she	PP	II	5	156	4
a sudden noise below seemed to speak the whole house in	PP	II	5	158	11
But Lady Catherine seemed gratified by their excessive	PP	II	6	163	14
Lady Catherine seemed quite astonished at not receiving a	PP	II	6	166	38
accepted any refreshment, seemed to do it only for the	PP	II	7	169	3
path, which no one seemed to value but herself, and where	PP	II	7	169	5
highest admiration, and seemed almost angry to find that	PP	II	7	170	6
Colonel Fitzwilliam seemed really glad to see them; any	PP	II	8	172	3
He seemed astonished too on finding her alone, and	PP	II	9	177	2
were made, seemed in danger of sinking into total silence.	PP	II	9	177	3
and when he did speak, it seemed the effect of necessity	PP	II	9	180	29
in it, and sometimes it seemed nothing but absence of mind.	PP	II	9	181	29
It seemed like wilful ill-nature, or a voluntary penance,	PP	II	10	182	1
the house, he seemed to expect that whenever she came into	PP	II	10	182	1
His words seemed to imply it.	PP	II	10	182	1
on with a warmth which seemed due to the consequence he	PP	II	11	189	5
eyes fixed on her face, seemed to catch her words with no	PP	II	11	190	8
All connection between us seemed now dissolved.	PP	II	12	201	5
just at last; but Darcy seemed to feel it most acutely,	PP	II	14	210	3
Lady Catherine seemed resigned.	PP	II	14	211	12
Mrs. Reynolds's respect for Elizabeth seemed to increase	PP	III	1	247	13
He absolutely started, and for a moment seemed immoveable	PP	III	1	251	51
At length, every idea seemed to fail him; and, after	PP	III	1	252	53
her uncle and aunt, and seemed to direct her eyes to such	PP	III	1	253	55
She wanted to talk, but there seemed an embargo on every	PP	III	1	257	66
though as it passed it seemed long, was not long enough to	PP	III	2	265	16
as his greatest enemy, seemed, on this accidental meeting,	PP	III	2	265	16
seemed to have fixed them on her more, and more cheerfully.	PP	III	3	270	11
But afterwards she seemed to improve on you, and I believe	PP	III	3	271	17
He seemed scarcely to hear her, and was walking up and	PP	III	4	278	19
her uncle's interference seemed of the utmost importance,	PP	III	4	280	26
attention he has ever seemed to give to what was going	PP	III	5	283	8
what their present feelings were, seemed unjustifiable.	PP	III	5	291	56
All Meryton seemed striving to blacken the man, who, but	PP	III	6	294	4
He added, that Mr. Bennet seemed wholly disinclined at	PP	III	6	295	5
at any rate, there seemed a gulf impassable between them.	PP	III	8	311	12
She wanted to hear of him, when there seemed the least	PP	III	8	311	13
They seemed each of them to have the happiest memories in	PP	III	9	316	6
his conduct in the noblest light, seemed most improbable.	PP	III	9	320	32
five minutes seemed to be giving her more of his attention.	PP	III	11	337	56
On entering the room, he seemed to hesitate; but Jane	PP	III	12	340	11
"The party seemed so well selected, so suitable one with	PP	III	12	343	30
as it seemed the only probable motive for her calling.	PP	III	14	352	15
"Miss Bennet, there seemed to be a prettyish kind of a	PP	III	14	352	16
					17
Lady Catherine seemed pleased.	PP	III	14	356	57
do, which had often seemed likely, the advice and intreaty	PP	III	15	361	3
had all done for her, she seemed to be wanting to do more:	MP	I	1	5	4
Mrs. Price seemed rather surprised that a girl should be	MP	I	1	11	19
disposition, and seemed likely to give them little trouble.	MP	I	2	18	23
Of the rest she saw nothing; nobody seemed to think of her	MP	I	2	21	34
a visit, nobody at home seemed to want her; but William	MP	I	2	21	34
seemed likely to disappoint Mr. Bertram's calculations.	MP	I	3	24	5
to them, he had never seemed the friend of their pleasures,	MP	I	3	32	64
Their vanity was in such good order, that they seemed to	MP	I	4	35	4
its ill effects, there seemed with him but one thing to be	MP	I	4	36	7
his income was unsettled, seemed to her very unjustifiable.	MP	I	4	36	7
Sir Thomas's sending away his son, seemed to her so like a	MP	I	4	38	9
ever seen, Miss Bertram seemed, by her amiable qualities	MP	I	4	39	10
the rest of you, which seemed like being out; and yet she	MP	I	5	48	30
To want a horse and cart in the country seemed impossible,	MP	I	6	58	37
of Miss Crawford, but he seemed to think it enough that	MP	I	7	66	14
small, strongly made, she seemed formed for a horsewoman;	MP	I	7	66	15
attended to, seemed almost determined to say no more.	MP	I	7	71	31
seemed to her a difficulty quite impossible to be got over.	MP	I	8	78	23
all seemed to feel that they had been there long enough.	MP	I	9	89	30
No objection was made, but for some time there seemed no	MP	I	9	90	36
Crawford and Fanny, who seemed as naturally to unite, and	MP	I	9	90	36
seemed likely to assist them, and be back in a few minutes.	MP	I	9	96	76
whose principal business seemed to be to hear the others,	MP	I	10	97	3
"You seemed to enjoy your drive here very much this	MP	I	10	98	11
She seemed to have the little wood all to herself.	MP	I	10	100	23
had taken place at last seemed, to Fanny's observation, to	MP	I	10	104	51
his complacency seemed confirmed by the arrangement.	MP	I	10	105	52
of the others, and which seemed to say that Julia was Mr.	MP	I	12	116	11
seemed so decided, as to make Edmund quite uncomfortable.	MP	I	13	124	13
Fanny seemed nearer being right than Edmund had supposed.	MP	I	14	130	1
and his power, seemed to make allies unnecessary; and	MP	I	14	130	3
seemed to govern them all, and wondering how it would end.	MP	I	14	131	4
the tallest, seemed to fit him peculiarly for the Baron.	MP	I	14	132	8
and standing by them, seemed to interest herself in their	MP	I	15	143	27
seemed to imply that it was the best room in the house.	MP	I	16	151	1
corners of the mouth, and seemed to think it as great an	MP	I	17	158	2
Miss Crawford came with looks of gaiety which seemed an	MP	I	17	159	6
Lady Bertram seemed quite resigned to waiting.--	MP	I	18	167	12
There seemed a general diffusion of cheerfulness on the	MP	I	18	171	25
and little vexations seemed every where smoothed away.	MP	I	18	171	25
His manner seemed changed; his voice was quick from the	MP	II	1	178	7
had been awful in his dignity seemed lost in tenderness.	MP	II	1	178	7
His immediate communications were exhausted, and it seemed	MP	II	1	180	13
minutes seemed to mark him the most at home of the two.	MP	II	1	183	23
He seemed to feel exactly as one could wish."	MP	II	2	190	6
the other day--that you seemed almost as fearful of notice	MP	II	3	198	13
and a listener who seemed so much obliged, so full of	MP	II	4	207	6
Fanny went to her every two or three days; it seemed a	MP	II	4	208	11
A look of consciousness as he spoke, and what seemed a	MP	II	4	214	46
in a very ill humour, and seemed intent only on lessening	MP	II	5	219	27
seemed to want to be encouraged even by her to resolve on.	MP	II	5	223	48
with Dr. Grant, which seemed entirely to engross them, and	MP	II	5	224	49
He seemed determined to be answered; and Fanny, averting	MP	II	5	225	58
When we talked of her last night, you none of you seemed	MP	II	6	229	5
news, the next morning, seemed the reward of his ingenuity	MP	II	6	232	13
"because Sir Thomas seemed so ill inclined! and Lady	MP	II	7	238	2
and sister; but that seemed forgotten by Mrs. Norris, who	MP	II	7	251	65
to call on her, and as it seemed to her, that her friend,	MP	II	8	257	15
and seemed resolved either to take another or none at all.	MP	II	8	259	20
seemed to comprehend her greatest possibility of happiness.	MP	II	9	267	22
upon her mind, and seemed of greater value than at first.	MP	II	9	270	40
again, her good fortune seemed complete, for upon trial	MP	II	9	270	40
of ease and enjoyment seemed diffused, and they all stood	MP	II	10	273	6
her, though his object seemed then to be only quietly	MP	II	10	274	8
beauty, as Mrs. Norris seemed to do, to her	MP	II	10	276	13
when her modesty alone seemed to his sanguine and pre-	MP	II	13	302	9
Mrs. Norris seemed as much delighted with the saving it	MP	II	13	304	19
her superiors--who seemed so little open to serious	MP	II	13	305	26
every body, and seemed to find no one essential to him?--	MP	II	13	305	26
for once or twice a look seemed forced on her which she	MP	II	13	306	26
At last--it seemed an at last to Fanny's nervousness,	MP	II	13	306	28
the house, there seemed little danger of her being wanted.	MP	III	1	311	2
visits to that room seemed all renewed, and she felt as if	MP	III	1	312	4
mediocrity of condition which seemed to be your lot.--	MP	III	1	313	12
of the uncle, who seemed to stand in the place of her	MP	III	1	314	16
Mr. Crawford's choice seemed to justify," said Sir Thomas,	MP	III	13	317	34
A fire! it seemed too much; just at that time to be giving	MP	III	1	322	51
She seemed determined to be interested by nothing else.	MP	III	3	337	10
which, at the beginning, seemed to occupy her totally; how	MP	III	3	337	11
know yourself as well as you seemed to do at that moment."	MP	III	3	343	39
But though the conference had seemed full long to him, and	MP	III	3	344	44
because he was taking, what seemed, very idle notice of me.	MP	III	4	353	45
her hand, seemed hardly able to help beginning directly.	MP	III	5	357	6
a while towards him--because he really seemed to feel.--	MP	III	5	365	35
His objections, the scruples of his integrity, seemed all	MP	III	6	367	4
renewed strength, and it seemed as if to be at home again,	MP	III	6	370	11

soon, seemed very much inclined to forget her again. MP III 7 380 22
faces and panting breaths seemed to prove--especially as MP III 7 383 31
We seemed very glad to see each other, and I do really MP III 9 393 1
again--and no reproach seemed conveyed to the equally MP III 9 396 7
circumstance; nay, it seemed a relief to her worn mind to MP III 10 401 9
a time the two officers seemed very well satisfied in MP III 10 403 15
glad to have him gone, it seemed as if she was now MP III 11 413 31
himself, and really seemed, might not it be fairly MP III 11 414 32
go into Northamptonshire, seemed almost to blame her for MP III 12 419 8
seemed to seize the frame on the departure of the fever. MP III 14 429 1
which hardly any thing would have seemed to justify. MP III 14 436 15
Edmund would be forgiven for being a clergyman, it seemed, MP III 14 436 16
Fanny seemed to herself never to have been shocked before. MP III 15 441 20
a glow, and for a time, seemed to distance every pain, and MP III 15 443 24
which the going of both seemed regarded--and the ecstacy MP III 15 444 25
never do enough for one who seemed so much to want her. MP III 16 449 4
Mrs. Norris, whose attachment seemed to augment with the MP III 17 464 13
much the worse, as there seemed no chance of its ceasing MP III 17 465 15
she seemed a part of himself, that must be borne for ever. MP III 17 465 15
and happy disposition, seemed to unite some of the best E I 1 5 1
Mr. Weston, who had been a widower so long, and who seemed E I 1 12 41
acknowledge, (though it seemed rather against the bias of E I 2 19 14
Mr. Elton seemed very properly struck and delighted by the E I 6 46 22
he seemed mostly fearful of not being incommoded enough. E I 6 49 42
It seemed too precious an offering for any degree of E I 9 77 43
He re-urged--she re-declined; and he seemed then about to E I 9 81 79
80
higher ties, a warmer love might have seemed impossible. E I 11 92 4
under a calmness that seemed all but indifference, the E I 12 99 14
It seemed to him a very ill-judged measure." E I 12 106 58
of a country run, and seemed to ensure a quick dispatch of E I 13 109 6
increasing coldness, he seemed to have no idea of E I 13 112 24
Harriet seemed quite forgotten in the expectation of a E I 13 115 42
so little knowledge as seemed terribly like a would-be E I 14 118 4
He seemed by this connection between the families, quite E I 14 119 5
But at last there seemed a perverse turn; it seemed all at E I 15 124 4
and the three-quarters of a mile would have seemed but one. E I 15 129 23
James; and there it seemed as if her return only were E I 15 132 38
clearly they had seemed to point at Harriet. E I 16 134 4
to be attaching, seemed on Harriet's side, not her own. E I 17 141 8
in particular; but it seemed to her reasonable that at E I 17 142 11
and aunt, there had seemed every probability of her being E II 2 163 3
and varying spirits, seemed, under the most favourable E II 2 165 9
seemed to point out the likeliest evil of the two. E II 2 167 12
she was going to live, it seemed impossible to feel any E II 2 167 13
Wrapt up in a cloak of politeness, she seemed determined E II 2 169 15
She seemed bent on giving no real insight into Mr. Dixon's E II 2 169 16
He seemed to me very well off as he was. E II 3 174 34
me how I did, and seemed ready to shake hands, if I would. E II 3 178 52
altered; but however, she seemed to try to be very E II 3 178 52
The young man's conduct, and his sister's, seemed the E II 3 179 53
On that article, truth seemed attainable. E II 4 183 9
And all the grandeur of the connection seemed dependent on E II 4 183 9
of, how much he seemed attached?--his air as he walked by E II 4 184 10
They all seemed to remember the day, the hour, the party, E II 5 187 4
James and his horses seemed not half so sluggish as before. E II 5 189 16
apprehension of any; it seemed as if he could not think so E II 5 193 35
to whom and to Highbury he seemed to take very cordially. E II 6 196 1
He seemed to have all the life and spirit, cheerful E II 6 198 5
seemed to like to hear one if he could hear the other. E II 6 201 28
His ideas seemed more moderate--his feelings warmer. E II 6 203 42
A sudden freak seemed to have seized him at breakfast, and E II 7 205 1
and seemed to mean always to speak of her with respect. E II 7 205 2
Mrs. Cole seemed to be relating something of her that was E II 8 214 13
It seemed quite a shame, especially considering how many E II 8 215 16
The conviction seemed real; he looked as if he felt it. E II 8 219 43
seemed to give fresh pleasure to the present meeting. E II 9 233 25
So began Miss Bates; and Mr. Knightley seemed determined E II 10 244 34
35
It seemed the best scheme; and yet it was not so good but E II 11 248 10
his being consulted, he seemed resolved that it should not E II 12 257 2
It seemed like the forerunner of something absolutely E II 12 260 30
He stopt again, rose again, and seemed quite embarrassed.-- E II 12 261 34
Mrs. Elton seemed most favourably impressed by the size of E II 14 272 18
He seemed not merely happy with her, but proud. E II 15 281 2
attentions and tolerate Mrs. Elton as she seemed to do. E II 15 285 12
He seemed hardly to hear her; he was thoughtful--and in a E II 15 287 33
34
and Mr. John Knightley seemed early to devote himself to E II 16 292 10
A pleasant "thank you" seemed meant to laugh it off, but a E II 16 294 24
well; for Mr. Knightley seemed little disposed for E II 18 311 36
Mr. Knightley seemed to be trying not to smile; and E II 18 312 51
and laugh as ever, and seemed delighted to speak of his E III 1 316 4
Lively as he was, it seemed a liveliness that did not E III 1 316 4
nor his hurrying away, seemed like a perfect cure; and she E III 1 316 5
of this arrangement, and seemed most fully to appreciate E III 1 317 8
Frank Churchill seemed to have been on the watch; and E III 2 319 3
the same errand, that it seemed as if half the company E III 2 319 3
the room; and Mrs. Elton seemed to think it as much her E III 2 322 18
Emma could hardly understand him; he seemed in an odd E III 2 325 29
He seemed often observing her. E III 2 326 32
They seemed more like cheerful, easy friends, than lovers. E III 2 326 32
Every body seemed happy; and the praise of being a E III 2 326 33
and Harriet would have seemed almost too lucky, if it had E III 2 328 41
It seemed as if her eyes were suddenly opened, and she E III 3 332 1
It seemed as if every thing united to promise the most E III 3 335 10
The last night's ball seemed lost in the gipsies. E III 3 336 12
admirer of Miss Woodhouse, seemed somewhat out of place. E III 5 343 2
of catching her eye--he seemed watching her intently--in E III 5 346 17
Tea passed pleasantly, and nobody seemed in a hurry to E III 5 347 18
one seemed so much disposed to employ as their two selves. E III 5 347 20
Disingenuousness and double-dealing seemed to meet him at E III 5 348 21
This gallant young man, who seemed to love without feeling, E III 5 348 23
Jane Fairfax's perception seemed to accompany his; her E III 5 348 23
"The joke," he replied gravely, "seemed confined to you E III 5 350 30
Emma's confusion, and the acknowledged intimacy, seemed to E III 5 350 31
Churchill, whose health seemed every day to supply a E III 6 352 1
Donwell was famous for its strawberry-beds, which seemed a E III 6 354 9
so well received, that it seemed as if, like Mrs. Elton, E III 6 357 31
Mrs. Weston, who seemed to have walked there on purpose to E III 6 357 33
The pertinacity of her friend seemed more than she could E III 6 359 37
the river, seemed the finish of the pleasure grounds.-- E III 6 360 38
with high pillars, which seemed intended, in their E III 6 360 38
Now they seemed in pleasant conversation. E III 6 360 40
a smile which seemed to say, "these are my own concerns. E III 6 361 40
the exercise and variety which her spirits seemed to need. E III 6 361 42
sometimes alone!"--seemed to burst from an over-charged E III 6 363 51
He was not in his best spirits, but seemed trying to E III 6 364 59
It seemed at first an accidental division, but it never E III 7 367 1
spent on the hill, there seemed a principle of separation, E III 7 367 1
To amuse her, and be agreeable in her eyes, seemed all E III 7 368 3
Referring the education to her seemed to imply it. E III 7 373 51
As she reflected more, she seemed but to feel it more. E III 7 376 63
There was only Harriet, who seemed not in spirits herself, E III 7 376 63
The aunt and niece seemed both escaping into the adjoining E III 8 378 4
The touch seemed immediate. E III 8 378 7
every body seemed rather fagged after the morning's party. E III 8 381 19
say that any of them seemed very much to have enjoyed it. E III 8 381 19
It seemed as if there were an instantaneous impression in E III 9 385 7
now he seemed more sudden than usual in his disappearance. E III 9 386 7
Her health seemed for the moment completely deranged-- E III 9 389 16
Her spirits seemed overcome. E III 9 389 16

the mere proposal of going out seemed to make her worse.-- E III 9 390 18
Her heart was grieved for a state which seemed but the E III 9 391 21
Something really important seemed announced by his looks; E III 10 392 7
The present crisis, indeed, seemed to be brought on by E III 10 397 47
spoke in a manner which seemed to promise me many E III 10 398 53
She seemed to propose showing no agitation, or E III 11 404 9
He seemed to want to be acquainted with her. E III 11 409 35
He seemed to be almost asking her, whether her affections E III 11 410 35
Harriet seemed ready to worship her friend for a sentence E III 11 411 42
her inferiority, whether of mind or situation, seemed E III 11 414 50
She had seemed more sensible of Mr. Elton's being to stoop E III 11 414 50
in marrying her, than she now seemed of Mr. Knightley's.-- E III 11 414 50
and the same melancholy, seemed to reign at Hartfield--but E III 13 424 1
They seemed to be within half a sentence of Harriet, and E III 13 429 26
We seemed to understand each other. E III 14 438 8
For the world would not she have seemed to threaten me.-- E III 14 442 8
of giving pain--no remembrance of Box-Hill seemed to exist. E III 15 447 21
His evils seemed to lessen, her own advantages to increase, E III 15 450 36
every blessing of her own seemed to involve and advance E III 15 450 37
the poor girl herself, it seemed a peculiarly cruel E III 15 450 37
It might be only her own consciousness; but it seemed as E III 16 451 2
Things did not seem--that is, there seemed a little cloud E III 16 454 18
It seemed an unnecessary caution; Jane was wanting to give E III 16 457 34
Mr. Elton was so hot and tired, that all this wit seemed E III 16 457 37
William seemed rather out of humour. E III 16 458 43
fortunate, that now it seemed as if Emma could not safely E III 17 467 31
However, I must say that Robert Martin's heart seemed for E III 18 472 20
for, though the child seemed well now, very well E III 18 479 73
her pain and confusion seemed to die away with the words, E III 19 481 2
ought to be, and must be, seemed already beginning, and in E III 19 482 5
both father and daughter seemed to expect that something P III 1 10 21
consulted Anne, who never seemed considered by the others P III 2 12 3
with Elizabeth, and seemed to love her, rather because she P III 2 16 16
It seemed as if Mr. Shepherd, in this anxiety to bespeak P III 3 21 18
"And a very well-spoken, genteel, shrewd lady, she seemed P III 3 22 25
Admiral himself, and seemed more conversant with business. P III 3 22 25
His genius and ardour had seemed to foresee and to command P III 4 29 8
past, which seemed almost to deny any recollection of it. P III 4 30 10
She spoke, and seemed only to offend. P III 5 34 13
The portraits themselves seemed to be staring in P III 5 40 44
Nothing seemed amiss on the side of the great house family, P III 5 41 46
He had very good spirits, which never seemed much affected P III 6 43 5
connected with her son, seemed one of those extraordinary P III 6 51 31
shyness or reserve; they seemed all to know each other P III 7 58 22
house instead, and he seemed afraid of being in Mrs. P III 7 58 22
an easy footing: the room seemed full--full of persons and P III 7 59 25
and Mrs. Croft, who seemed particularly attached and happy, P III 8 63 3
two Miss Musgroves, who seemed hardly to have any eyes but P III 8 64 4
It was a merry, joyous party, and no one seemed in higher P III 8 71 57
and Louisa, they both seemed so entirely occupied by him, P III 8 71 57
near them, seemed to leave every thing to take its chance. P III 9 74 9
It had then seemed the object nearest her heart, that Dr. P III 9 78 19
attention to give, and seemed to have forgotten all the P III 9 78 19
Charles Hayter seemed aware of being slighted, and yet P III 10 82 1
After a short struggle, however, Charles Hayter seemed to P III 10 82 2
which the family-habits seemed to produce, of every thing P III 10 83 4
her sister aside, seemed to be arguing the matter warmly. P III 10 85 16
She seemed to be in the middle of some eager speech. P III 10 87 22
And Henrietta seemed entirely to have made up hers to call P III 10 87 23
This little circumstance seemed the completion of all that P III 10 91 42
and not even Louisa seemed to feel that they had parted P III 11 96 11
him and the Harvilles seemed, if possible, augmented by P III 11 97 12
than her husband, seemed however to have the same good P III 11 97 15
as an excuse; but they seemed almost hurt that Captain P III 11 98 15
seemed to furnish him with constant employment within. P III 11 99 18
Captain Benwick listened attentively, and seemed grateful P III 11 101 25
of brightness, which seemed to say, "that man is struck P III 12 104 6
He seemed about thirty, and, though not handsome, had an P III 12 105 7
accomplish, or as his seemed able to bear, for he was too P III 12 108 29
by Captain Benwick, who seemed to cling to them to the P III 12 108 30
He caught the word; it seemed to rouse him at once, and P III 12 110 40
41
Both seemed to look to her for directions. P III 12 111 44
The surgeon was with them almost before it had seemed P III 12 112 52
yet a gentleness, which seemed almost restoring the past.-- P III 12 114 63
One thing more, and all seemed arranged. P III 12 114 64
seen Mr. Elliot; a moment seemed all that could now be P III 12 115 66
and, united as they all seemed by the distress of the day, P III 12 115 67
To spare Henrietta from agitation seemed the governing P III 12 116 70
In speaking of the Harvilles, he seemed unable to satisfy P IV 1 121 2
who at twenty-three had seemed to understand somewhat of P IV 1 125 13
day; and in short, it seemed to have been only a stranger P IV 2 129 2
him some shooting, and he seemed quite delighted, and for P IV 2 130 5
and, on the contrary, seemed to have a plan of going away P IV 2 133 25
Benwick seemed much more disposed to ride over to Kellynch. P IV 2 133 25
Christmas fire, which seemed determined to be heard, in P IV 2 134 29
Sir Walter seemed to admit it as complete apology, and P IV 3 139 9
was encouraging the idea, seemed apparent by a glance or P IV 3 140 11
a defect which time seemed to have increased; now could he P IV 3 141 12
or any of them seemed to feel that he had been there long. P IV 3 144 23
any particularity of attention seemed almost impossible. P IV 4 147 8
him about Lyme, which he seemed to have as lively a wish P IV 4 148 9
seemed to have closed her heart or ruined her spirits. P IV 5 153 7
and reduced, seemed to have quite delighted Mr. Elliot. P IV 5 158 21
professed good opinions, seemed to judge properly and as a P IV 5 160 27
reading Captain Benwick, seemed each of them every thing P IV 6 166 19
who had listened and seemed to feel for him, would have P IV 6 167 19
the gout, and Mrs. Croft seemed to go shares with him in P IV 6 168 24
but he did not; he seemed in no hurry to leave her; and P IV 8 181 3
4
A sudden recollection seemed to occur, and to give him P IV 8 182 9
an opinion which he had seemed solicitous to give, his P IV 8 185 21
As her eyes fell on him, his seemed to be withdrawn from P IV 8 188 41
She seemed as if she had been one moment too late; and as P IV 8 188 41
effect; though by what seemed prosperity in the shape of P IV 8 189 46
He saw her too; yet he looked grave, and seemed irresolute, P IV 8 189 47
of the right which he seemed to have to interest her, by P IV 9 192 2
reception; and her friend seemed this morning particularly P IV 9 192 4
to her for coming, seemed hardly to have expected her, P IV 9 192 4
It seemed to announce a different sort of man." P IV 9 200 56
found himself to be poor, seemed to have had no concern at P IV 9 209 95
"She had seemed to recommend and praise him!" P IV 9 211 100
be added to their party, seemed the destruction of every P IV 10 215 13
and Mrs. Harville had seemed to like the idea of it very P IV 10 216 19
or two, every thing seemed to be in suspense, or at an end. P IV 10 216 19
spacious as it was, seemed more than half filled: a party P IV 10 221 32
which seemed to ensure that it would now spread farther. P IV 10 222 37
Miss Elliot, whose entrance seemed to give a general chill. P IV 10 226 63
to mention it; and it seemed to her that there was guilt P IV 10 228 70
yet, as Captain Harville seemed thoughtful and not P IV 11 230 5
thoughtful expression which seemed its natural character. P IV 11 232 12
which had once before seemed to secure every thing, but P IV 11 240 59
That evening seemed to be made up of exquisite moments. P IV 11 244 71
invalid--the very spot which thousands seemed in need of.-- S 1 369 1
bathing place was the object, for which he seemed to live. S 2 371 1
& lucky cousins, who seemed always to have a spy on her, S 3 378 1
straw hats & pendant lace seemed left to their fate both S 6 389 1
the good will, she seemed to feel;--and as for Miss S 6 391 1
She seemed placed with her on purpose to be ill-used. S 6 391 1
& merit, seemed to leave no choice in the business.-- S 6 391 1
On one side it seemed protecting kindness, on the other S 6 392 1
She wanted to have the place fill faster, & seemed to have S 6 392 1

Stationing himself close by her, he seemed to mean to S 7 396- 1
He seemed very sentimental, very full of some feelings or S 7 398 1
This glorious sentiment seemed quite to remove suspicion. S 7 400 1
Lodging-Taking, but he seemed to like the commission.--" S 9 411 1
out of the common way, seemed more like the amusement of S 10 412 1
He took his own cocoa from the tray,--which seemed S 10 416 1
No part of it however seemed to trouble her long. S 11 420 1
& which a narrow path seemed to skirt along;--Miss S 12 426 1

SEEMING (43)

& good humour, & seeming more as if she were to marry him LS 41 309 1
in books, for the roll, seeming to consist entirely of NA II 7 172 1
After an evening, the little variety and seeming length of NA II 8 187 15
conjecture, and all seeming equally probable as they arose. SS I 14 70 3
He heard her with the most earnest attention, but seeming SS II 4 162 11
He looked at them slightly, without seeming to know who SS II 5 171 30
her appearance, and seeming equally indifferent whether SS II 6 175 1
"Why to be sure," said he, seeming to recollect himself, " SS II 11 227 48
continued Miss W. without seeming to hear her, I was very W 316 2
eyes in time, to avoid seeming to hear her young companion W 332 11
fortunate another time--& seeming unwilling to leave her, W 334 13
inclination for speech seeming to increase with the W 347 21
without seeming to seek, he did not turn away from the W 356 28
though without seeming to have any intention of speaking, PP I 6 24 17 18
In another minute Mr. Bingley, but without seeming to have PP I 15 73 9
And upon Elizabeth's seeming really, with vexed and PP I 19 104 6
her, and sleep seeming to be her likeliest friend, she was MP I 2 13 4
she left it at night, as seeming as desirably sensible of MP I 2 14 9
in Fanny's age, seeming not merely to do away any former MP I 3 24 7
up into seeming piety, but with heads full of something MP I 9 87 15
gate and stood there, without seeming to know what to do. MP I 10 101 33
the good news; and though seeming to have no concern in MP I 11 108 4
up the play, and with seeming carelessness was turning MP I 14 133 11
should be gone by without seeming to advance that point. MP II 2 191 11
speaking a word, or seeming at all interested in the MP II 3 198 12
unfixed, and without seeming much aware of it himself. MP II 3 200 19
poor Mr. Rushworth, not seeming to care how he exposed or MP III 4 349 25
to studying it, without seeming to recollect her existence. MP III 7 382 28
a saucy playful smile, seeming to invite, in order to MP III 16 459 30
and becoming a deference, seeming so pleasantly grateful E I 3 23 10
Emma was half ashamed of her friend for seeming so pleased E I 7 50 1
raving a little about the seeming incongruity of gentle E I 16 136 9
the possibility, without seeming very rude, of making her E II 1 158 13
Taylor's merits, without seeming quite to forget that in E II 5 192 29
without seeming really at all ashamed of what he had done. E II 8 212 2
And he smiled with such seeming pleasure at the conviction, E II 8 228 90
and Mr. Elton's seeming resolved to learn to like it too. E III 4 339 19
at all, and his horse seeming to have got a cold, Tom had E III 8 383 31
her work, and seeming resolved against looking up.) E III 10 394 30
slight acquaintance, seeming to acknowledge such as she P III 7 59 23
to a window; and Anne seeming to watch him, though it was P IV 11 231 12
The absolute necessity of seeming like herself produced P IV 11 238 45
very quietly--without seeming to hear a word of Mrs P.'s S 6 391 1

SEEMINGLY (8)

betray her into any observations seemingly unhandsome. MP II 3 199 16
to look about her, and seemingly to retrace all that had MP III 5 358 7
maid-servant, seemingly in waiting for them at the door, MP III 7 377 7
likewise, sat down again, seemingly inclined for more chat. E I 8 58 9
and parting with her seemingly with ceremonious civility. E II 5 186 3
Apologies for her seemingly ungracious silence in their E III 12 418 5
them nothing but that seemingly perfect good understanding P III 5 41 45
& bracing-- seemingly just as was wanted--sometimes one, S 2 373 1

SEEMS (128)

He is lively & seems clever, & when I have inspired him LS 7 254 3
more satisfactory, but it seems written with such a LS 13 262 1
but as her situation seems to have been unexceptionable, LS 15 266 2
& justly enough, as it seems a sort of reward to behaviour LS 15 267 5
of that heart which seems always debating on the LS 16 269 3
keeping the girl; & it seems so extraordinary a peice of LS 19 274 2
But the conquest it seems was not designed for herself, or LS 20 276 2
discover the real truth, but she seems to wish to avoid me. LS 20 278 11
All things considered therefore, it seems encumbent on me LS 25 294 5
you credit in the world, & seems precisely in her proper LS 26 295 1
of conversation with him--seems a most extraordinary NA I 3 27 26
by a thousand pens,--there seems almost a general wish of NA I 5 37 4
replied, "I like him very much; he seems very agreeable." NA I 7 50 44
wanted you to know her; and she seems very fond of you. NA I 7 50 47
He seems a good kind of old fellow enough, and has lived NA I 9 63 18
Well, my dear Catherine, the case seems to be, that you NA II 3 145 14
which just at this moment seems important; but which I can NA II 13 225 21
Music seems scarcely to attract him, and though he admires SS I 3 17 18
There are moments when the extent of it seems doubtful; SS I 4 21 15
His setting off in such a hurry seems very like it. SS I 14 70 2
It seems but the work of a moment. SS I 15 77 23
"Certainly;" said Elinor, "he seems very agreeable." SS I 20 114 41
He seems an excellent man; and I think him uncommonly SS I 20 115 55
There seems to me a very decided difference. SS II 5 168 9
"So my daughter Middleton told me, for it seems Sir John SS II 5 171 38
to-day," or "your sister seems out of spirits," he had SS II 5 172 40
but so serious a question seems to imply more; and I must SS II 7 182 9
Lord! nothing seems to do her any good. SS II 8 194 8
Poor dear, it seems quite cruel to let her be alone. SS II 8 195 14
This seems to have been a day of general elucidation, for SS II 8 199 36
in some points, there seems a hardness of heart about him." SS II 8 200 40
He seems a most gentlemanlike man; and I think, Elinor, I SS II 11 223 18
"She seems a most valuable woman indeed.-- SS II 11 226 42
short of the matter, by all I can learn, seems to be this. SS III 1 258 7
Mr. Edward Ferrars, it seems, has been engaged above this SS III 1 258 7
What I am now doing indeed, seems nothing at all, since it SS III 3 284 23
Brandon seems a man of great worth and respectability. SS III 4 290 36 37
For it seems all to depend upon that." SS III 4 291 49
to Plymouth; for Lucy it seems borrowed all her money SS III 13 370 37
for as Colonel Brandon seems a great deal at home, nobody SS III 14 375 9
"He seems to have most engaging manners!--said Emma.-- W 319 2
with the lady herself, it seems a pity to me that he W 321 2
It seems but the day before yesterday that I saw them all W 334 13
On the contrary, he seems very vain, very conceited, W 342 19
just come from my father's room, he seems very indifferent. W 352 26
it seems likely to rain; and then you must stay all night." PP I 7 30 21
It seems to me to shew an abominable sort of conceited PP I 8 36 10
"She seems a very pleasant young woman," said Bingley. PP I 9 44 30
"He seems to be a most conscientious and polite young man, PP I 13 63 13
how can Mr. Bingley, who seems good humour itself, and is, PP I 16 82 44 45
It seems an hopeless business." PP I 20 111 11
"It seems likely to have been a desirable match for Jane," PP II 2 140 6
"But there seems indelicacy in directing his attentions PP II 4 153 14
He took the hint, and soon began with, "this seems a very PP II 9 178 12
She seems perfectly happy, however, and in a prudential PP II 9 178 15
I do not know any body who seems more to enjoy the power PP II 10 183 9
a few minutes silence, "it seems but a day or two since we PP II 15 217 11
She had known, it seems, of their being in love with each PP III 5 290 50
"since I went away; it seems but a fortnight I declare; PP III 9 316 7
in the secrecy which Lydia seems to think necessary; and PP III 9 320 33
not so dreadfully racked as your's seems to have been. PP III 10 321 2
There is a lady, it seems, a Mrs. Younge, who was some PP III 10 322 2
But slyness seems the fashion. PP III 10 325 2
so palatable to you as it seems to be at present; that you PP III 10 329 31
One seems so forlorn without them." PP III 11 330 10
seems, and there they are to stay, I do not know how long. PP III 11 336 51
daughter, of which it seems he has been told, by some of PP III 15 362 14
Bath seems full, and every thing as usual. MP I 6 59 43
"It seems very odd," said Maria, "that you should be MP I 8 79 24
Fanny's interest seems in safer hands with you than with MP I 9 95 70
judges of time, and every half a minute seems like five." MP I 10 102 46
Your lap seems full of good things, and here is a basket MP I 10 105 54
Four thousand a year is a pretty estate, and he seems a MP I 12 118 20
It seems to join the billiard-room on purpose." MP I 13 125 14
Every thing seems to depend upon Sir Thomas's return." MP I 17 162 15
Lady Bertram seems more of a cipher now than when he is at MP I 17 162 16
hurry Baddeley a little, he seems behind hand to-night." MP II 1 180 12
There seems something more speakingly incomprehensible in MP II 4 208 12
princes, and knights; and seems to breathe the spirit of MP II 4 211 23
Your gown seems very pretty. MP II 5 222 44
The ground seems precisely formed for it. MP II 7 242 23
and sisters--never seems to have had a moment's share in MP III 1 318 39
The surprise of your refusal, Fanny, seems to have been MP III 4 352 44
That you could refuse such a man as Henry Crawford, seems MP III 4 352 44
capable of returning an affection as this seems to imply." MP III 4 353 45
This seems as if nothing were a security for matrimonial MP III 5 361 16
She seems in high spirits, and very happy. MP III 12 416 2
Julia seems to enjoy London exceedingly. MP III 13 423 2
any body; but your aunt seems to feel out of luck that MP III 13 424 2
Now it seems nothing, yet it is an heavy aggravation. MP III 15 442 23
"We were all disposed to wonder--but it seems to have been MP III 16 455 23
He seems to me, to be grown particularly gentle of late. E I 4 34 42
The only thing I do not thoroughly like is, that she seems E I 6 48 36
Her visit to abbey-mill, this summer, seems to have done E I 8 59 25
they cannot stay longer--but it seems a case of necessity. E I 9 79 63
seems to have a great deal of good-will towards you." E I 13 112 18
"Yes--it seems to depend upon nothing but the ill-humour E I 14 121 15
And Mr. Dixon seems a very charming young man, quite E II 3 175 39
She seems quite recovered now. E II 3 176 44
But Jane, it seems, had a letter from them very lately, E II 8 215 14
But you observed nothing of course, for it seems to be a E II 8 218 36
He seems every thing the fondest parent could. . . . E II 9 238 51
It seems the only improvement that could be. E II 11 251 24
Mr. Weston seems an excellent creature--quite a first-rate E II 14 278 44
never saw her before, she seems a very pretty sort of E II 14 279 54
However, she seems a very obliging, pretty-behaved young E II 14 279 54
Well, I am sure, Mr. Churchill--only it seems too good-- E III 2 330 45
"It seems like madness! E III 4 337 6
and me; and, therefore, it seems as if such a thing even E III 11 407 28
be very glad to look it over," said he, "but it seems long. E III 15 444 3
"but as it seems a matter of justice, it shall be done." E III 15 444 5
He seems perfectly unprepared for that." E III 17 465 26
the poor boys saying, 'uncle seems always tired now.'" E III 17 465 27
It seems an impossibility!-- E III 18 471 17
which seems to insult exertion and distrust Providence!-- P III 4 30 9
Thames on fire, but there seems no harm in him:"-- P III 6 32 4
harp, for it seems to amuse her more than the piano-forte. P III 6 50 27
to have you go; but it seems rather hard that she should P III 7 58 19
seems designed to counterbalance almost every other want. P IV 5 154 8
but "Mrs. Musgrove seems to like them quite as well, if P IV 6 163 7
It seems, on the contrary, to have been a perfectly P IV 8 183 10
replied Mrs. Smith, gravely, "but it seems worn out now. P IV 9 194 22
He seems to have a calm, decided temper, not at all open P IV 9 196 33
Even the smooth surface of family-union seems worth P IV 9 198 53
hard-hearted sister, Miss Anne, seems bent on cruelty." P IV 10 213 4
"It seems to have as many comforts about it as Willingden," S 4 379 1
Your sister Diana seems almost as ill as possible, but S 5 388 1
Sometimes indeed a flash of feeling seems to irradiate him- S 7 397 1

SEEN (421)

Well my dear Reginald, I have seen this dangerous creature, LS 6 250 1
that I have seldom seen so lovely a woman as Lady Susan. LS 6 251 1
I have seen Sir James,--he came to town for a few days LS 9 256 1
I am more angry with her than ever since I have seen her LS 17 270 4
times that he had seen Mrs Johnson a few evenings before. LS 20 276 3
you well know, I never wished him to be seen at Churchill. LS 22 280 1
It is a great while since I have seen my father & mother. LS 23 283 4
to look for Frederica, whom I had not seen since breakfast. LS 24 285 2
it, but after all that I have seen, how can one be secure? LS 41 309 1
I asked her whether she had seen my brother since his LS 41 310 1
No one who had ever seen Catherine Morland in her infancy, NA I 1 13 1
She had reached the age of seventeen, without having seen NA I 1 16 10
For my part I have not seen any thing I like so well in NA I 2 22 11
She was now seen by many young men who had not been near NA I 2 23 27
and had the company only seen her three years before, they NA I 2 24 27
Every creature in Bath, except himself, was to be seen in NA I 4 31 1
and intimate, whom she had seen only once since their NA I 4 31 2
not a genteel face to be seen, which every body discovers NA I 5 35 2
"You have seen Mrs. Thorpe then?" NA I 9 68 37
a variety of things to be seen and done all day long, NA I 10 78 46
declared he had never seen two men so much alike in his NA I 11 87 53
Tilney was no longer to be seen where he had hitherto sat, NA I 12 93 5
manner, whether she had seen him talking with General NA I 12 95 18
to spell, if you had ever seen how stupid they can be for NA I 14 109 26
you by describing my anxiety; you have seen enough of it. NA I 15 118 13
wished she could have seen him before he went, as she NA I 15 125 48
seen before, and who now evidently belonged to their party. NA II 1 131 15
and she had never seen so large a room as this in her life. NA II 6 166 7
since that time; he had seen some beautiful specimens when NA II 7 175 12
hours in the Abbey, and had seen only a few of its rooms. NA II 7 176 17
Catherine had seen nothing to compare with it; and her NA II 7 177 19
words, that she had never seen any gardens at all equal to NA II 7 178 21
or seven rooms she had now seen surrounded three sides of NA II 8 183 2
From the dining-room of which, though already seen, and NA II 8 183 3
seen, and always to be seen at five o'clock, the General NA II 8 183 3
And what was there more to be seen?-- NA II 8 185 6
Had not Miss Morland already seen all that could be worth NA II 8 185 6
Catherine, who, having seen, in a momentary glance beyond NA II 8 185 7
Is there any thing extraordinary to be seen there?" NA II 9 195 10
They had seldom seen him eat so heartily at any table but NA II 11 215 27
very greatly discomposed; I have seldom seen him more so. NA II 13 225 21
Three months ago had seen her all this; and now, how NA II 14 237 20
she beheld was a young man whom she had never seen before. NA II 15 241 7
particular respect, had seen with astonishment the NA II 15 245 12
day for the Abbey, where his performances have been seen. NA II 15 247 13
be in doubt, who has seen him often enough to engage him SS I 4 20 9
I have seen a great deal of him, have studied his SS I 4 20 9
Marianne herself had seen less of his person than the rest, SS I 9 43 11
But she had seen enough of him to join in all admiration SS I 9 43 11
an eagerness which could hardly be seen without delight. SS I 10 46 2
He has seen a great deal of the world; has been abroad; SS I 10 51 20
in perfect unison with what she had heard and seen herself. SS I 12 61 14
interest it could not be seen, as the proprietor, who was SS I 12 62 28
nothing more of them was seen till their return, which did SS I 13 67 60
You must have seen the difference as well as I. SS I 15 77 23
He had just parted from my sister, had seen her leave him SS I 15 81 43
transporting sensations have I formerly seen them fall! SS I 16 87 31
They are seen only as a nuisance, swept hastily off, and SS I 16 88 31
to the village, he had seen many parts of the valley to SS I 18 96 4
spoke to him indeed; but I have seen him for ever in town. SS I 20 114 44
However, I dare say we should have seen a great deal of SS I 20 114 44
He had not seen me then above twice, for it was before I SS I 20 117 64
girls whom she had never seen in her life, and of whose SS I 21 118 2
do but meet him of a morning, he is not fit to be seen.-- SS I 21 123 28
Elinor had not seen them more than twice, before the SS I 21 125 34
"Though we have seen him once or twice at my uncle's, it SS I 21 126 40
it, as she answered that she had never seen Mrs. Ferrars. SS I 22 128 4
for I thought you must have seen her at Norland sometimes. SS I 22 128 5
Dashwood, you must have seen enough of him to be sensible SS I 22 130 28
I dare say you have seen enough of Edward to know that he SS II 2 149 25

Context	Work	Vol.	Ch.	Page	Line
if he had been in London ever since she had seen him last.	SS	II	4	162	12
to go, for still she had seen nothing of Willoughby; and	SS	II	5	170	28
former, whom they had not seen before since their arrival	SS	II	5	171	30
Marianne, who had seen him from the window, and who hated	SS	II	5	172	40
me in to-day, accidentally seen a letter in his hand,	SS	II	5	173	44
Elinor, who saw as plainly by this, as if she had seen the	SS	II	7	181	7
Had you seen his look, his manner, had you heard his voice	SS	II	7	189	46
Had not Elinor, in the sad countenance of her sister, seen	SS	II	8	193	7
"ever seen Mr. Willoughby since you left him at Barton?"	SS	II	9	211	34
before her, such as she had always seen him there.	SS	II	10	213	3
and at what warehouse Miss Grey's clothes might be seen.	SS	II	10	215	11
She had seen enough of her pride, her meanness, and her	SS	II	13	238	1
free;--and she had seen enough to be thankful for her <u>own</u>	SS	II	13	238	1
"I am sure I should have seen it in a moment, if Mrs.	SS	II	13	240	17
I have seen Mr. Ferrars two or three times in Harley-	SS	III	3	282	19
a short time, but I have seen enough of him to wish him	SS	III	3	282	19
She had not seen him before since his engagement became	SS	III	4	288	26
people whom she had never seen before, and of whom	SS	III	4	291	46
she had never seen him in such spirits before in her life.	SS	III	5	293	1
"Have you ever seen the lady?"	SS	III	5	299	36
fancy that from their summits Combe Magna might be seen.	SS	III	6	302	8
Elinor had seen so little of Mr. Palmer, and in that	SS	III	6	304	15
and in that little had seen so much variety in his address	SS	III	6	304	15
I had seen Marianne's sweet face as white as death.--	SS	III	8	327	55
That he had cut me ever since my marriage, I had seen	SS	III	8	330	69
a hope!--could he have seen her happy with another--	SS	III	9	336	14
She, who had seen her week after week so constantly	SS	III	10	341	6
You, who had seen all the fretful selfishness of my latter	SS	III	10	346	28
so <u>then</u>, and I had seen so little of other women, that I	SS	III	13	362	5
"For worlds would not I have had a letter of her's seen by	SS	III	13	365	17
his woods!--I have not seen such timber any where in	SS	III	14	375	9
I would not be the means of keeping you from being seen.--	W			320	2
Emma had seen the Edwardses only one morng at Stanton,	W			322	3
said Emma, for I have not seen him since he was 7 years	W			324	3
Ld Osborne was to be seen quite alone at the end of one,	W			332	11
As Tom Musgrave was seen no more, we may suppose his plan	W			336	14
declared it seemed only two days since he had seen her.--"	W			342	19
presuming to make it, than have seen him at Stanton.--	W			347	22
Have you seen the one I gave Margaret?"--	W			353	26
"I do beg & entreat that no turkey may be seen today.	W			354	27
You have seen Miss Osborne?--she is my model for a truly	W			357	28
Mrs. Bennet had seen her eldest daughter much admired by	PP	I	3	12	15
Darcy, on the contrary, had seen a collection of people in	PP	I	4	16	15
You will not be fit to be seen when you get there."	PP	I	7	32	34
but to be so easily seen through I am afraid is pitiful."	PP	I	9	42	12
and Elizabeth had never seen them so agreeable as they	PP	I	11	54	1
but <u>he</u> had never seen any thing but affability in her.	PP	I	14	66	1
man, whom they had never seen before, of most	PP	I	15	72	8
and Darcy and Bingley were seen riding down the street.	PP	I	15	72	8
to Jane what she had seen pass between the two gentlemen;	PP	I	15	74	12
her daughter, he had never seen a more elegant woman; for	PP	I	15	74	13
manners, and sees him only as he chuses to be seen."	PP	I	16	78	16
with all that he had yet seen, and speaking of the latter	PP	I	16	78	22
Wickham; "I have not seen her for many years, but I very	PP	I	16	84	58
Lucas, whom she had not seen for a week, she was soon able	PP	I	18	90	4
"Both," replied Elizabeth archly; "for I have always seen	PP	I	18	91	15
Such very superior dancing is not often seen.	PP	I	18	92	23
No one who has ever seen you together, can doubt his	PP	I	21	119	20
Could she have seen half as much love in Mr. Darcy for	PP	I	21	119	20
Mrs. Gardiner had seen Pemberley, and known the late Mr.	PP	II	2	143	20
She wrote again when the visit was paid, and she had seen	PP	II	3	147	23
seen her for a twelvemonth, prevented their coming lower.	PP	II	4	152	5
we have gone--we <u>will</u> recollect what we have seen.	PP	II	4	154	23
for enjoyment; for she had seen her sister looking so well	PP	II	5	155	1
such a sight to be seen! I will not tell you what it is.	PP	II	5	158	11
					12
of all that she had seen at Rosings, which, for	PP	II	6	166	42
had already been frequently seen by Miss Lucas and herself.	PP	II	7	170	6
Charlotte had seen them from her husband's room, crossing	PP	II	7	170	7
					8
For the last week they had seen very little of either lady	PP	II	8	172	1
the time, but Mr. Darcy they had only seen at church.	PP	II	8	172	1
"of conversing easily with those I have never seen before.	PP	II	8	175	24
<u>when</u> she had seen him last in Hertfordshire, and feeling	PP	II	9	177	3
					4
I had often seen him in love before.--	PP	II	12	197	5
of intimacy with his ways, seen any thing that betrayed	PP	II	13	207	6
Have you seen any pleasant men?	PP	II	16	221	17
that he had formerly seen him often; and after observing	PP	II	18	233	27
She had always seen it with pain; but respecting his	PP	II	19	236	2
them, and where she had seen such beautiful ornaments as	PP	II	19	238	5
In that county, there was enough to be seen, to occupy the	PP	II	19	239	7
their steps, after having seen all the principal wonders	PP	II	19	240	12
She had never seen a place for which nature had done more,	PP	III	1	245	3
but from every window there were beauties to be seen.	PP	III	1	246	5
"Oh! yes--the handsomest young lady that ever was seen;	PP	III	1	248	22
remembered to have sometimes seen, when he looked at her.	PP	III	1	250	47
inspection had been seen, they returned down stairs, and	PP	III	1	251	49
Never in her life had she seen his manners so little	PP	III	1	252	54
not tell, but he certainly had not seen her with composure.	PP	III	1	253	55
people may call him proud, <u>I</u> have seen nothing of it."	PP	III	1	257	68
that she had never seen him so pleasant as this morning.	PP	III	1	258	71
"From what we have seen of him," continued Mrs. Gardiner, "	PP	III	1	258	74
She retreated from the window, fearful of being seen; and	PP	III	2	260	2
at Rosings, had she seen him so desirous to please, so	PP	III	2	263	10
The looks and behaviour of every body they had seen were	PP	III	3	272	20
All that is known after this is, that they were seen to	PP	III	4	275	5
any success, no such people had been seen to pass through.	PP	III	4	275	5
her clothes, till she has seen me, for she does not know	PP	III	5	288	38
They must have seen them together for ever."	PP	III	5	290	45
Had Colonel Forster seen Denny himself?"	PP	III	5	290	47
It is enough to know they are discovered, I have seen them	PP	III	7	302	14
Elizabeth read on; "I have seen them both.	PP	III	7	302	14
were, and that he had seen and talked with them both,	PP	III	10	321	2
But Mr. Gardiner could not be seen, and Mr. Darcy found,	PP	III	10	323	2
our uncle and aunt, that you have actually seen Pemberley."	PP	III	10	327	9
Had she not seen him in Derbyshire, she might have	PP	III	11	332	18
more disturbed, more unequal, than she had often seen them.	PP	III	11	332	20
in Hertfordshire, than as she had seen him at Pemberley.	PP	III	11	335	40
Bingley, she had likewise seen for an instant, and in that	PP	III	11	335	41
I suppose you have heard of it; indeed, you must have seen	PP	III	11	336	49
It will then be publicly seen, that on both sides, we meet	PP	III	12	339	6
to be happy, had she not seen his eyes likewise turned	PP	III	12	340	12
great spirits; she had seen enough of Bingley's behaviour	PP	III	12	343	29
and less eccentric than the other had ever seen him.	PP	III	13	346	21
Oh! he is the handsomest young man that ever was seen!"	PP	III	13	349	41
tell him of their having seen his aunt, of which her	PP	III	16	365	1
his eye, she might have seen how well the expression of	PP	III	16	366	8
but I believe in about half an hour after I had seen you."	PP	III	16	370	32
It is a nice long walk, and Mr. Darcy has never seen the	PP	III	17	374	23
Suppose her a pretty girl, and seen by Tom or Edmund for	MP	I	1	7	6
Mansfield Park, and was scarcely ever seen in her offices.	MP	I	3	31	59
young ladies she had ever seen, Miss Bertram seemed, by	MP	I	4	39	10
Mrs. Grant knew nothing, she had scarcely seen them since.	MP	I	4	40	15
marry well, and having seen Mr. Bertram in town, she knew	MP	I	4	42	18
set it down that they have not yet seen the right person."	MP	I	4	43	25
young men were not often seen together even in London, and	MP	I	5	47	27
when one has seen her hardly able to speak the year before.	MP	I	5	49	32
same liberties as if they were, which I <u>have</u> seen done.	MP	I	5	50	39
It was seen by some farmer, and he told <u>the</u> miller, and	MP	I	6	57	33
that she might not be seen, the pain of her mind had been	MP	I	7	74	59
extremely happy to have seen the young lady too, Miss	MP	I	8	76	4
for Miss Crawford, who had seen scores of great houses,	MP	I	9	85	3
"The Miss Bertrams have never seen the wilderness yet."	MP	I	9	90	35
it be acquired where they are so seldom seen themselves?	MP	I	9	92	46
line, for we have never seen the end of it yet, since we	MP	I	9	94	62
beyond a wish that they had seen his friend Smith's place.	MP	I	10	97	3
almost all that she had seen and heard, astonished at Miss	MP	I	10	100	23
notice, only asked her if she had not seen Mr. Rushworth.	MP	I	10	101	29
whether she had seen any thing of Miss Crawford and Edmund.	MP	I	10	101	33
Though <u>I</u> have not seen much of the domestic lives of	MP	I	11	110	25
seen by too many to leave any deficiency of information."	MP	I	11	110	25
never seen much symptom of it, but I wish it may be so.	MP	I	12	116	8
acted, for she had never seen even half a play, but every	MP	I	14	131	4
I have seen good actresses fail in the part.	MP	I	14	135	15
that he had once seen the play in London, and had thought	MP	I	15	138	1
Have I ever seen either of the gentlemen?--	MP	I	15	148	59
After all that she had heard him say, and seen him look,	MP	I	16	156	28
She had seen her influence in every speech, and was	MP	I	16	156	28
solitude of the east room, without being seen or missed.	MP	I	17	159	6
to confess having never seen any of the impropriety which	MP	II	2	188	3
"My dear Sir Thomas, if you had seen the state of the	MP	II	2	189	5
course of his life, had he seen one of that class, so	MP	II	2	191	10
But they had seen no one from the parsonage--not a	MP	II	2	192	11
seen him so seldom, his reserve may be a little repulsive.	MP	II	3	199	13
spot, must already have seen him and be seeing him perhaps	MP	II	6	233	14
Young as he was, William had already seen a great deal.	MP	II	6	236	21
He longed to have been at sea, and seen and done and	MP	II	6	236	22
never played the game nor seen it played in her life; and	MP	II	7	239	8
a gentleman's house to be seen excepting one--to be	MP	II	7	241	13
Have you ever seen the place?"	MP	II	7	244	27
As yet Sir Thomas had seen nothing to remark in Mr.	MP	II	7	246	36
I have never seen Fanny dance since she was a little girl;	MP	II	7	250	60
True enough, he had once seen Fanny dance; and it was	MP	II	7	251	62
He had seen her eyes sparkle as she spoke of the dear	MP	II	8	256	12
Miss Crawford thought she had never seen a prettier	MP	II	8	259	20
She had long seen it.	MP	II	8	260	24
them round her neck, and seen and felt how full of William	MP	II	9	271	40
observing them, had seen enough to be tolerably satisfied.	MP	II	10	279	21
end; and Sir Thomas having seen her rather walk than dance	MP	II	10	279	22
the ball, but her aunt had seen so little of what passed,	MP	II	11	282	4
I should like to have seen him once more, I confess.	MP	II	11	287	22
Indeed how can one care for those one has never seen?--	MP	II	11	288	30
He had often seen it tried.	MP	II	12	294	16
she has ever yet been herself, or ever seen any body else.	MP	II	12	295	20
To have seen you grow like the Admiral in word or deed,	MP	II	12	296	27
"Had you seen her this morning, Mary," he continued, "	MP	II	12	296	31
Had you seen her so, Mary, you would not have implied the	MP	II	12	297	31
a piece with what she had seen before; and she would not	MP	II	13	301	7
her so again: he must have seen how unwelcome it was to	MP	II	13	302	11
in a man, who had seen so many, and been admired by so	MP	II	13	305	26
I have seen too much of Mr. Crawford not to understand his	MP	II	13	307	31
Young as you are, and having seen scarcely any one, it is	MP	III	1	316	31
<u>He</u>, indeed, I have lately thought has seen the woman he	MP	III	1	317	34
"well, Fanny, I have seen Mr. Crawford again, and learn	MP	III	2	330	14
was to be seen by Edmund again, she felt dreadfully guilty.	MP	III	3	334	5
I wish you could have seen her countenance, when she said	MP	III	4	352	42
which Fanny had never seen in her before, and now thought	MP	III	5	358	9
You must have seen that he was trying to please you, by	MP	III	5	362	18
to her; she had not seen her poor dear Sister Price for	MP	III	6	372	21
She had now seen all that were at home; there remained	MP	III	7	381	26
But though she had <u>seen</u> all the members of the family, she	MP	III	7	381	26
that she had previously seen the upper servant, brought in	MP	III	7	383	32
Could Sir Thomas have seen all his niece's feelings, when	MP	III	8	388	1
Could he have seen only half that she felt before the end	MP	III	8	388	1
during those days, she had seen him only twice, in a short	MP	III	8	388	2
At last, after various attempts at meeting, I have seen	MP	III	9	393	1
She felt that she had never seen so agreeable a man in her	MP	III	10	400	7
few days; that he had not seen him, himself, but that he	MP	III	10	400	8
as such, though he had seen the dock-yard again and again;	MP	III	10	402	13
tenants, whom he had never seen before; he had begun	MP	III	10	404	15
When Mr. Price and his friend had seen all that they	MP	III	10	406	21
improved since she had seen him; he was much more gentle,	MP	III	10	406	21
Mansfield; she had never seen him so agreeable--so <u>near</u>	MP	III	10	406	21
The family were now seen to advantage.	MP	III	11	408	2
for nothing more was seen of him at Mr. Price's; and two	MP	III	12	415	1
					2
I will say, then, that we have seen him two or three times,	MP	III	12	416	2
He had seen Miss Crawford.	MP	III	16	454	18
Not a tear, and hardly a long face to be seen.	E	I	1	11	35
his wife, who had never seen him, and who were full of	E	I	2	15	2
the little Perrys being seen with a slice of Mrs. Weston's	E	I	2	19	15
goose: the finest goose Mrs. Goddard had ever seen.	E	I	4	28	8
"That may be--and I may have seen him fifty times, but	E	I	4	29	14
I have seen a great many lists of her drawing up at	E	I	5	37	7
seen a face or figure more pleasing to me than her's.	E	I	5	39	19
But I have no idea that she has yet ever seen a man she	E	I	5	41	29
my visiting here I have seen people--and if one comes to	E	I	7	54	30
I can imagine, that before she had seen anybody superior,	E	I	8	65	48
and altogether, having seen nobody better (that must have	E	I	8	65	48
child, and Miss Nash had seen him, and he had told Miss	E	I	8	68	58
"I must see somebody very superior to any one I have seen	E	I	10	84	13
That is, I know you must have seen her a hundred times--	E	I	10	86	22
told Harriet that he had seen them go by, and had	E	I	10	90	39
months since they had been seen in a regular way by their	E	I	11	91	2
Surry connections, or seen at all by Mr. Woodhouse, who	E	I	11	91	2
excepting one, have we seen either Mr. Weston or Mrs.	E	I	11	94	14
It makes me envious and miserable;--I who have never seen	E	I	12	101	23
that you had seen Mr. Wingfield before you left home."	E	I	12	103	42
is so long since I have seen her, except now and then for	E	I	12	104	46
Has Perry seen her?	E	I	13	109	7
such hazard till he had seen Mr. Perry and learnt his	E	I	15	125	4
Every body must have seen the snow coming on. I admired	E	I	15	126	10
He had seen the coachmen, and they both agreed with him in	E	I	15	128	16
insinuating)--I am sure you have seen and understood me."	E	I	15	131	31
I have seen you only as the admirer of my friend.	E	I	15	132	36
Who could have seen through such thick-headed nonsense?	E	I	16	134	4
been of the party, and had seen only proper attention and	E	II	3	170	1
Jane, you have never seen Mr. Elton!--no wonder that you	E	II	3	174	35
"No--I have never seen Mr. Elton," she replied, starting	E	II	3	174	37
"When I have seen Mr. Elton," replied Jane, "I dare say I	E	II	3	175	43
During his present short stay, Emma had barely seen him;	E	II	4	182	7
Bath, was to be seen under the operation of being lifted	E	II	5	186	1
She had seen only Mrs. Martin and the two girls.	E	II	5	186	4
He had never seen so lovely a face, and was delighted with	E	II	8	220	47
my friends, unless I can believe myself fit to be seen.	E	II	8	222	53
Mrs. Elton was first seen at church: but though devotion	E	II	14	270	1
in reply, "when you have seen more of this country, I am	E	II	14	273	22
					23
In my Bath life, I have seen such instances of it!	E	II	14	275	32
the other day, I had never seen him before; and of course,	E	II	14	278	50
Knightley!--never seen him in her life before, and call	E	II	14	279	52
John had seen more drops than they could count long before.	E	II	16	293	15
					16
She had heard and seen it all; and felt some curiosity to	E	II	16	298	58
"But you have not seen so much of the world as I have.	E	II	17	299	8
"He had seen a group of old acquaintance in the street as	E	III	1	316	4
I have never seen either Mr. or Mrs. Elton.	E	III	2	320	10
I have seen nothing like it since--well, where shall we	E	III	2	330	45
even a mathematician have seen what she did, have	E	III	3	335	9
at the Eltons'; and he had seen a look, more than a single	E	III	5	343	2
remembering what he had seen; nor could he avoid	E	III	5	344	2
full of what he had seen; so full, that when the candles	E	III	5	349	26
English verdure, English culture, English comfort, seen	E	III	6	360	39

see what had not yet been seen, the old Abbey fish-ponds; E III 6 361 42
"I shall never be easy till I have seen some of these E III 6 364 60
She had never seen Frank Churchill so silent and stupid. E III 7 367 2
I thought I had seen you first in February." E III 7 369 14
You, whom she had known from an infant, whom she had seen E III 7 375 61
ostler had stood out and seen it pass by, the boy going a E III 8 383 31
best counteract this unwillingness to be seen or assisted. E III 9 390 18
Emma wished she could have seen her, and tried her own E III 9 390 18
When Emma afterwards heard that Jane Fairfax had been seen E III 9 391 21
could he even have seen into her heart, he would not, on E III 9 391 21
creature from any thing I had ever seen him before.-- E III 10 399 57
proofs to her who had seen them, had passed undiscerned by E III 11 410 35
Emma's feelings: "Oh God! that I had never seen her!" E III 11 411 42
Could he have seen the heart, he would have cared very E III 14 434 3
Mr. Knightley, had seen so much to blame in his conduct. E III 15 444 2
Emma had never seen her look so well, so lovely, so E III 16 453 8
Oh! if you had seen her, as I did, when she was at the E III 16 454 17
"Yes, yes--but I am amused that he should have seen so far E III 17 465 27
You must have seen that I did. E III 18 474 34
it would probably have been better if Perry had seen it." E III 18 479 73
Thirteen years had seen her mistress of Kellynch Hall, P III 1 6 12
Thirteen winters' revolving frosts had seen her opening P III 1 7 12
The following spring he was seen again in town, found P III 1 8 15
"for they must have been seen together," he observed, " P III 1 8 16
Anne had been too little from home, too little seen. P III 2 15 12
and every weather, till they are not fit to be seen. P III 3 20 16
He had seen Mrs. Croft, too; she was at Taunton with the P III 3 22 24
so well by sight; seen him a hundred times; came to P III 3 23 28
at Taunton, and fix a day for the house being seen. P III 3 24 35
It would be difficult to say which had seen highest P III 4 26 1
A few months had seen the beginning and the end of their P III 4 28 6
not be ashamed of being seen with him any where; and the P III 5 32 4
I have not seen a creature the whole morning!" P III 5 37 22
I have not seen him since seven o'clock. P III 5 37 25
I assure you, I have not seen a soul this whole long P III 5 37 25
I have not seen one of them to-day, except Mr. Musgrove, P III 5 38 29
in the blue satin have seen what was going on, have been P III 5 40 44
They are as fine healthy children as ever were seen, poor P III 6 45 8
She had seen him. P III 7 60 27
She had seen the same Frederick Wentworth. P III 7 61 34
to her, and had never seen a woman since whom he thought P III 7 61 37
old pelisse, which you had seen lent about among half your P III 8 65 16
Charles "had never seen a pleasanter man in his life; and P III 9 75 10
things should have been seen by Anne; but she had staid at P III 9 77 17
For herself--she feared to move, lest she should be seen. P III 10 88 27
man whom she had never seen before; nor could she help P III 11 101 26
of the curricle was to be seen issuing from the door P III 12 105 9
to herself to have seen her cousin, and to know that the P III 12 106 19
Captain Benwick had been seen flying by their house, with P III 12 111 50
The head had received a severe contusion, but he had seen P III 12 112 52
farther on, she had first seen Mr. Elliot; a moment seemed P III 12 115 66
was over, and he had seen the father and mother quite as P III 12 117 76
up all the children, and seen the very last, the lingering P IV 1 121 3
He had not seen Louisa; and was so extremely fearful of P IV 2 133 25
as could be wished, to the last state she had seen it in. P IV 2 134 28
which they had either seen or heard of; and the P IV 3 137 4
and he had no objection to being seen with him any where." P IV 3 141 12
As yet, you have seen nothing of Bath. P IV 4 145 1
Anne had never seen her father and sister before in P IV 4 148 11
viscount, but had never seen any of the rest of the family, P IV 4 148 12
She had seen too much of the world, to expect sudden or P IV 5 154 9
We have seen nothing of him since November. P IV 6 171 33
carriage, which was seen waiting at a little distance; she, P IV 7 174 2
she knew was unfit to be seen), she was yet perfectly P IV 7 179 28
he said, "I have hardly seen you since our day at Lyme. P IV 8 181 3
4
by Lady Russell's countenance that she had seen him. P IV 8 189 44
She never misses, I know; and you must have seen her. P IV 9 193 10
say for seeing, because I appear to have seen very little." P IV 9 193 11
"I have not seen Mr. Elliot these three years," was Mrs. P IV 9 198 52
and twenty years in the world, "and have seen none like it. P IV 9 203 72
He had seen you indeed, before he came to Bath and admired P IV 9 205 86
guide, perhaps, may recollect what you have seen him do." P IV 9 207 90
not be afraid of being seen; but last time I called, I P IV 10 215 16
They have not seen two such drawing rooms before. P IV 10 220 29
Charles, having civilly seen them off, and then made a P IV 10 223 40
41
know that she had been seen with Mr. Elliot three hours P IV 10 228 70
"Have you not seen this? P IV 11 237 42
There, he had seen every thing to exalt in his estimation P IV 11 242 63
of a cottage, which was seen romantically situated among S 1 364 1
maid servants, were now seen issueing from the house)-- S 1 370 1
white were actually to be seen with their books & camp S 4 383 1
not taken place, or we should have seen him in his way.-- S 5 387 1
elderly man might be seen, who was forced to move early & S 6 389 1
had never seen one neither, he wd have been alive now.-- S 6 394 1
He had very early seen the necessity of the case, & had S 8 405 2
welcome the sister he had seen from the Drawg room, and S 9 406 1
Miss Heywood must have seen our carriage standing at the S 9 407 1
lady whom she had never seen, & who had never employed her. S 10 413 1
Mr & Mrs P.-- & Charlotte had seen two post chaises S 10 414 1
The Miss Ps-- & Arthur had also seen something;--they S 10 414 1
If you had seen me today before dinner, you wd have S 10 415 1
At any rate, she was seen all the following morng walking S 11 420 1
Yet here, she had seen them. S 12 427 1

SEES (28)

her being ridiculed & despised by every man who sees her. LS 19 274 2
I am not yet certain that Reginald sees what she is about; LS 19 274 3
It sees through every thing." NA I 15 117 4
dare say when Mr. Morland sees you, my dear child--but do NA II 1 136 46
"Perhaps he must, if he sees enough of her. PP I 6 22 6
she sees them now very often standing in Clarke's library." PP I 7 30 13
I do not believe she often sees such at home." PP I 13 61 2
manners, and sees him only as he chuses to be seen." PP I 16 78 16
Miss Bingley sees that her brother is in love with you, PP I 21 118 18
What a meeting for her, when she first sees my aunt!" PP III 7 305 36
"Oh! yes, very glad, if your aunt sees no objection." MP I 8 78 22
One scarcely sees a clergyman out of his pulpit." MP I 9 93 46
to be in the army, and nobody sees any thing wrong in that. MP I 11 109 18
merely beyond what one sees, because one never sees any MP III 3 344 41
sees, because one never sees any thing like it--but beyond MP III 3 344 41
It is he who sees and worships your merit the strongest, MP III 3 344 41
He sees difficulties no where; and his pleasantness and MP III 4 348 23
a year or two, and sees others made commanders before him? MP III 6 368 8
so very ill-looking as I did, at least one sees many worse. MP III 12 416 2
a puddle of water when he sees it, and as to Mrs. Bates's, E II 5 195 48
Mrs. Weston sees no objection to it, provided you are E II 11 250 23
Every body who sees it is struck by its beauty; but to me, E II 14 273 19
"She sees nothing to blame in it," replied Anne; "on the P IV 5 157 18
Look, he sees us; he kisses his hand to you; he takes you P IV 6 170 29
"More air than one often sees in Bath.-- P IV 8 188 39
"He thinks Mrs. Clay afraid of him, aware that he sees P IV 9 208 92
but my sensible nurse Rooke sees the absurdity of it.-- P IV 9 208 92
One sees clearly enough by all this, the sort of woman Mrs S 9 409 1

SEISURE (1)

Mrs. Jennings had determined very early in the seisure SS III 7 309 7

SEIZE (10)

letter from her mother, or seize upon any other odd piece NA I 1 14 1
of paper appears:--you seize it--it contains many sheets NA II 5 160 21
the girls at last to seize the advantage of an outer door, NA II 7 179 27
Bennet, to seize such an opportunity of dancing a reel?" PP I 10 51 47
48
which were too apt to seize her mind if her fingers only MP III 9 398 10
seemed to seize the frame on the departure of the fever. MP III 14 429 1
for any thing?--why not seize the pleasure at once?-- E II 12 259 17
word might be, made him seize every possible moment for E III 5 348 23
taste cannot tolerate,--which ridicule will seize. P III 8 68 30
as he put on, & then seize an odd moment for adding a S 10 417 1

SEIZED (19)

found her arm gently seized by her faithful Isabella, who NA I 8 56 12
caution on a chair, she seized the key with a very NA II 6 168 10
With less alarm and greater eagerness she seized a second, NA II 6 169 11
She seized, with an unsteady hand, the precious manuscript, NA II 6 169 11
She seized another sheet, and saw the same articles with NA II 7 172 2
Astonishment and doubt first seized them; and a shortly NA II 9 193 6
the desperation which had seized her at sixteen and a half, SS I 10 49 10
this letter, instantly seized the other, and opening it PP III 4 274 4
cup himself; and she seized the opportunity of saying, "is PP III 12 341 20
21
round her shoulders, was seized by Mr. Crawford's quicker MP II 7 251 66
of self-government, she seized the scrap of paper on which MP II 9 265 19
carriage, and suddenly seized with a strong inclination to MP III 6 372 21
subject cut up--her hand seized--her attention demanded, E I 15 129 24
Miss Bates turned to her again and seized her attention. E II 1 158 13
A sudden freak seemed to have seized him at breakfast, and E II 7 205 1
Mr. Weston instantly seized the opportunity of going on. E II 18 308 29
her fervor as she seized and clung to his arm, with a E III 3 335 11
Suppose I were to be seized of a sudden in some dreadful P III 5 37 24
had seized a sheet of paper, and poured out his feelings. P IV 11 241 60

SEIZING (3)

growing greater; and seizing, with trembling hands, the NA II 6 164 3
She could not bear such suspense; and hastily seizing a PP III 9 320 32
"The right of a lively mind, Fanny, seizing whatever may MP I 7 64 11

SEIZURE (4)

"My mother's illness," he continued, "the seizure which NA II 9 196 25
illness in her; a nervous seizure, which had lasted some E III 6 363 53
A sudden seizure of a different nature from any thing E III 9 387 11
attendance at hand, in case of his having another seizure. P III 12 102 2

SELDOM (52)

were mistaken, for I have seldom spent three months more LS 2 244 1
that I have seldom seen so lovely a woman as Lady Susan. LS 6 251 1
called, but I seldom hear any noise when I pass that way. LS 17 271 7
nor a bad temper; was seldom stubborn, scarcely ever NA I 1 14 1
"I am no novel reader--I seldom look into novels--do not NA I 5 37 4
people, who seldom aimed at wit of any kind; her father, NA I 9 65 31
"Yes, my father can seldom be prevailed on to give the NA II 2 138 2
without you, for people seldom know what they would be at, NA II 3 146 20
They had seldom seen him eat so heartily at any table but NA II 11 215 27
very greatly discomposed; I have seldom seen him more so. NA II 13 225 21
him so seldom--we can hardly meet above twice a-year. SS I 22 133 42
entered on by Lucy, who seldom missed an opportunity of SS II 2 151 42
to please them, had seldom been happier in her life than SS II 12 231 9
her mother, an hour seldom passed in which she did not PP I 23 129 14
no more, and though a day seldom passed in which Elizabeth PP II 1 137 26
young people are seldom withheld by immediate want of PP II 3 145 7
He seldom appeared really animated. PP II 9 180 29
Happy spirits which had seldom been depressed before, were PP II 14 213 19
She seldom listened to any body for more than half a PP II 16 223 24
for Mr. Gardiner, though seldom able to indulge the taste, PP III 1 254 57
or irregularity, she seldom went away without leaving them PP III 6 294 3
but she could see how seldom they spoke to each other, and PP III 12 340 13
had seldom known a pause in its alarms or embarrassments. MP I 4 35 6
My mother seldom goes into company herself, and dines no MP I 5 51 42
Dr. Grant and Mrs. Norris were seldom good friends; their MP I 6 55 14
it be acquired where they are so seldom seen themselves? MP I 9 92 46
without observation, and seldom without wonder or censure; MP I 12 115 5
true delicacy which one seldom meets with now-a-days, Mrs. MP I 12 117 14
She knew, also, that poor Mr. Rushworth could seldom get MP I 18 164 2
seen him so seldom, his reserve may be a little repulsive. MP II 3 199 13
sisters, of whom she very seldom heard--who was interested MP II 6 234 18
and her feelings could seldom withstand the melancholy MP III 5 359 10
He wondered that Fanny spoke so seldom of her, and had so MP III 6 366 3
seldom, with her large family, find time for a walk.-- MP III 10 401 10
She seldom saw him--never alone--he probably avoided being MP III 16 453 16
but I confess that I have seldom seen a face or figure E I 5 39 19
to attach her; and she goes so seldom from home." E I 5 41 29
on them for ever, and therefore she seldom went near them. E II 1 155 3
touch it seldom; for evil in that quarter was at hand. E II 13 267 8
"So seldom that any negligence or blunder appears! E II 16 296 42
So seldom that a letter, among the thousands that are E II 16 296 42
who know how very, very seldom I am ever two hours from E II 18 312 50
delightful ball, which is seldom bestowed till after a E III 2 326 33
Never had she been more surprised, seldom more delighted, E III 2 328 40
Miss Fairfax, who had seldom spoken before, except among E III 7 372 41
Seldom, very seldom, does complete truth belong to any E III 13 431 39
to any human disclosure; seldom can it happen that E III 13 431 39
Harriet was very seldom mentioned between them. E III 17 463 15
seldom leaves a man's looks to the natural effect of time. P III 3 20 17
as much as he deserved; seldom heard of, and scarcely at P III 6 50 28
of poetry, to be seldom safely enjoyed by those who P III 11 100 23
enthusiasm and violent agitation seldom really possess. P IV 4 146 6

SELECT (2)

too mixed,--but our parties are very select & good.-- W 350 24
are select, they are perhaps the most agreeable of any. E I 13 116 43

SELECTED (6)

It now first struck her, that she was selected from among PP I 17 88 14
in finding herself thus selected as the object of such PP II 18 233 25
"The party seemed so well selected, so suitable one with PP III 12 343 30
consistent patron of the selected child, and Mrs. Norris MP I 1 8 9
whom her dear son had selected;--and very early in MP II 3 202 28
I should never have selected Fanny Price as the girl most MP II 12 294 19

SELECTING (3)

ere long occur of selecting one--though not for himself. NA II 7 175 12
with the design of selecting a wife, as I certainly did." PP I 19 105 8
her place;--but in selecting the one, Lady D. had shewn S 3 379 1

SELECTION (3)

given her consent, proceeded to make the selection. MP II 8 258 17
Russell, than in this selection of Mrs. Clay; turning from P III 2 16 16
My sister wanted my counsel in the selection of some books. S 8 403 1

SELF (22)

She wished Isabella had talked more like her usual self, NA II 3 148 28
no real satisfaction, as far as mere self is concerned." SS I 17 91 10
short, but your own dear self, mama, and Edward, may have SS II 7 189 50
the necessity of his absence had been self imposed. PP I 21 115 3
But self, though it would intrude, could not engross her. PP III 4 278 20
Fixed there by the keenest of all anguish, self reproach, PP III 5 285 19
when her own fair self was before him, leaning on her MP III 3 334 1
This is not like yourself, your rational self." MP III 4 347 19
Quite unlike his usual self, he scarcely said any thing. MP III 5 365 35
to her, independently--she believed independently of self. MP III 6 367 4
I did not use to think her wanting in self possession, but MP III 9 393 1
no half concealment, no self deception on the present, no MP III 17 471 28
in general, like her usual self, she took care to express E I 18 144 4
the certainty of his own self, reached Randall's before E III 2 319 1
Delightful to gather for one's self--the only way of E III 6 358 35
such a developement of self, such a burst of threatening E III 11 409 34
summon enough of her usual self to be the attentive lady E III 14 434 2
but by her silent, pensive self, might be filled again P IV 1 123 7
You are your mother's self in countenance and disposition; P IV 5 160 25
What wild imaginations one forms, where dear self is P IV 9 201 63
you know, and (since self will intrude) who can say that P IV 9 208 92
My own self. P IV 11 247 82

SELF-AMUSEMENT (1)

an indulgence of self-amusement to be detected by any who P III 8 67 28

SELF-APPROBATION (3)
could, with thorough self-approbation, recommend, though E I 3 24 13
14
He walked off in more complete self-approbation than he E I 8 67 56
of a few broken sentences of self-approbation & success.-- S 10 416 1
SELF-ASSURED (1)
to that of a self-assured man, especially where the beauty NA I 7 48 32
SELF-ATTRACTED (1)
which had been thus self-attracted by the rest of her PP II 13 209 11
SELF-COMMAND (19)
her with perfect self-command, & without betraying the LS 17 269 2
Even now her self-command is invariable. SS I 8 39 18
to suggest the propriety of some self-command to Marianne. SS I 11 53 2
The business of self-command she settled very easily;-- SS I 19 104 11
Elinor's security sunk; but her self-command did not sink SS I 22 131 33
assistance, while her self-command would neither receive SS II 1 141 6
her self-command to make it appear that she did not. SS II 10 217 22
otherwise than as the self-command she had practised since SS III 1 261 12
your resolution, your self-command, are, perhaps, a little SS III 1 263 28
said Mrs. Bennet with civil self-command to Miss Lucas. PP I 5 18 4
that higher species of self-command, that just MP I 9 91 36
and demanded it of her goodness and self-command as such. MP III 6 371 15
showed the wish of self-command, and the resolution of MP III 15 444 29
my comfort, a habit of self-command in you, a E II 13 268 11
12
I intended you to say so, but I meant self-command. E III 7 369 11
I can have no self-command without a motive. E III 7 369 12
extremely well on the occasion, with great self-command. E III 9 388 14
mind, producing reserve and self-command, it would.-- E III 11 403 2
some credit for the self-command with which he attended to P III 8 68 29
SELF-COMPLACENCY (2)
unconcern, the happy self-complacency of his manner while SS III 5 298 32
cherish a feeling of self-complacency on the score of some PP I 5 20 20
SELF-CONCEIT (2)
counteracted by the self-conceit of a weak head, living in PP I 15 70 1
wilfulness of temper, self-conceit, and every tendency to MP III 1 318 39
SELF-CONDEMNATION (3)
on her fan; and a self-condemnation for her folly, in NA I 10 75 24
and messages, in self-condemnation for Robert's offence, SS III 14 377 11
under some degree of self-condemnation or undefined alarm, MP II 1 175 1
SELF-CONQUEST (1)
but the belief of his self-conquest brought nothing PP III 4 278 19
SELF-CONSEQUENCE (6)
He entered the room with a look of self-consequence, SS I 19 106 22
a sort of natural self-consequence, which the attentions PP I 9 45 36
please, so free from self-consequence, or unbending PP III 2 263 10
of delightful self-consequence; and misinterpreting MP II 10 277 17
not given her so very hurtful a degree of self-consequence. MP III 17 466 17
to give Harriet notions of self-consequence but herself?-- E III 11 414 50
SELF-CONTENTMENT (1)
talked on with much self-contentment, totally unsuspicious E III 14 434 3
SELF-CONTROUL (2)
of such rational employment and virtuous self-controul. SS III 10 343 10
patience, self-controul; but it wants openness. E II 15 289 40
SELF-CREATED (1)
been all a voluntary, self-created delusion, each trifling NA II 10 199 2
SELF-DECEIT (1)
could by the easiest self-deceit persuade herself that she MP II 4 205 2
SELF-DECEIVED (1)
and silly, and self-deceived, before, her pain and E III 19 481 2
SELF-DECEPTION (1)
To such perseverance in wilful self-deception Elizabeth PP I 19 109 22
SELF-DEFENDING (1)
in a fearless, self-defending tone, which startled Fanny. MP III 7 379 18
SELF-DELUSION (1)
She could only resolve to avoid such self-delusion in P III 6 42 2
SELF-DENIAL (8)
that self-denial is a word hardly understood by him. SS III 11 350 9
time exercising great self-denial, for he was longing to PP I 22 123 3
you know, must be inured to self-denial and dependence." PP II 10 183 10
Now, seriously, what have you ever known of self-denial PP II 10 183 11
almost an effort of self-denial; seem at least, to be MP III 2 327 6
and of the necessity of self-denial and humility, he MP III 17 463 8
for whatever unwilling self-denial his care of their E II 8 213 6
to the severe degree of self-denial, which her own P III 2 13 5
SELF-DENIALS (1)
than the exertions and self-denials of the one, which her MP III 8 390 5
SELF-DENYING (5)
without me, ma'am," said Fanny in a self-denying tone----- MP II 5 217 4
how little self-denying his life had (apparently) been. MP III 13 428 13
considering with what self-denying, generous friendship E I 1 6 6
The belief of being prudent, and self-denying principally P III 4 28 5
ardent, disinterested, self-denying attachment, of heroism, P IV 5 156 10
SELF-DESTINED (1)
of himself, if he were already self-destined to another. PP I 16 83 56
SELF-DESTRUCTION (1)
Had I died,--it would have been self-destruction. SS III 10 345 28
SELF-DISTRUST (1)
and much less incumbered by refinement or self-distrust. MP II 6 234 17
SELF-DOCTORING (1)
be no judge of what the habit of self-doctoring may do.--" S 5 388 1
SELF-ENGROSSED (2)
Her mind was entirely self-engrossed. MP III 5 358 8
surprised him--so totally self-engrossed had he been.-- S 10 416 1
SELF-EVIDENT (4)
His pleasing manners and good sense were self-evident NA II 16 249 1
the most simple and self-evident sensations, while in the SS III 10 340 3
conduct, nor more self-evident than the motive of it. SS III 13 367 24
"For if," said he, with the sort of self-evident MP I 9 89 31
SELF-EXAMINATION (1)
were moments of self-examination in which her conscience E II 2 166 11
SELF-GOVERNMENT (1)
on the side of self-government, she seized the scrap of MP II 9 265 19
SELF-GRATULATION (2)
the first points of self-gratulation; and then it was such PP I 18 99 63
With many compliments to them, and much self-gratulation PP I 23 126 1
2
SELF-IMPORTANCE (7)
vanity, and raise her self-importance, to agitate her SS III 5 297 32
and yet the self-importance of all these people!-- PP I 6 27 47
There is a mixture of servility and self-importance in his PP I 13 64 18
of pride and obsequiousness, self-importance and humility. PP I 15 70 1
a tone, as marked her self-importance, and brought Mr. PP II 6 162 11
share of the Elliot self-importance, was very prone to add P III 5 37 21
"There is at times said he--a little self-importance--but S 3 376 1
SELF-IMPORTANT (2)
the pride of these self-important De Courcies still lower, LS 7 254 3
they met again.-- self-important, presuming, familiar, E II 15 281 1
SELF-IMPOSED (1)
due to his uncle, his engagements were all self-imposed.-- MP II 2 193 18
SELF-INDULGENCE (2)
very faulty habit of self-indulgence; and to see your MP I 11 111 29
(for with all his self-indulgence he had become a prudent P IV 9 209 95
SELF-INQUIRY (1)
brought the previous self-inquiry of whether she should MP II 4 214 46
SELF-INTEREST (3)
would have given, for self-interest alone could induce a SS II 2 151 41
unceasing attention to self-interest, however its progress SS III 14 376 11
self-interest to blind him, should have mistaken her's. E I 16 136 9
SELF-KNOWLEDGE (1)
acquirements of self-knowledge, generosity, and humility. MP I 2 19 30
SELF-MORTIFICATION (1)
were bent only on self-mortification, he seemed resolved SS I 19 101 1
SELF-OCCUPIED (2)
about, hummed a tune, and seemed wholly self-occupied. NA I 15 122 29
the gentlemen might each be too much self-occupied to hear. P IV 11 230 5
SELF-POSSESSION (2)
and directing with a self-possession and decision which P III 1 6 12
that he had too much self-possession, and she too little. P III 11 93 3
SELF-PROVIDENT (1)
was that Lucy, in her self-provident care, in her haste to SS III 12 357 2
SELF-PROVOCATION (1)
with less self-provocation, and greater fortitude. SS III 11 356 46
SELF-REPROACH (6)
by self-reproach, which must attend her through life. SS II 9 210 32
the pain of continual self-reproach, regretted most SS III 2 270 2
I often, with great self-reproach, recal the tenderness SS III 8 322 36
estate whenever it falls, without any self-reproach. PP I 19 107 16
known before; and the self-reproach arising from the MP III 17 462 4
must rise sometimes to self-reproach, and regret to MP III 17 468 22
SELF-REPROVING (1)
Here ceased the rapid flow of self-reproving spirit; and SS III 10 346 29
SELF-RESPECT (1)
self-respect and happy ardour, instead of what he was! MP II 6 236 22
SELF-REVENGE (1)
all the comfort that pride and self-revenge could give. MP II 3 201 24
SELF-SATISFACTION (1)
With a triumphant smile of self-satisfaction, the general NA II 7 178 23
SELF-SATISFIED (2)
He came back gay and self-satisfied, eager and busy, E II 4 181 3
with a shrewd eye, & self-satisfied air--but not an S 6 391 1
SELF-SUFFICIENCY (1)
a self-sufficiency without fashion, which is intolerable." PP III 3 271 15
SELF-THREATENINGS (1)
and the fainter self-threatenings of the past, became in a P IV 1 125 14
SELF-WILL (1)
and the obstinacy of self-will, between the darings of P IV 11 242 63
SELF-WILLED (4)
advice; and Lydia, self-willed and careless, would PP II 14 213 17
to Fanny than such self-willed, unmanageable days often MP II 9 265 21
Self-willed, obstinate, selfish, and ungrateful. MP III 1 319 40
gallantry was a little self-willed, and that he would E II 11 250 19
SELFISH (47)
she did, from the most selfish motives, take all possible LS 12 260 2
Isabella appeared to her ungenerous and selfish, NA I 13 98 3
She had not been withstanding them on selfish principles NA I 13 101 25
And could we carry our selfish point with you, we should NA II 2 139 7
cold hearted, and rather selfish, is to be ill-disposed: SS I 1 5 7
caricature of himself;-- more narrow-minded and selfish. SS I 1 5 7
sat down to table indignant against all selfish parents. SS I 17 90 1
with a wife like her--illiterate, artful, and selfish? SS II 1 140 1
him too well to be the selfish means of robbing him, SS II 2 147 7
then learn to avoid every selfish comparison, and banish SS II 4 159 1
most incapable of being selfish, of any body I ever saw. SS II 13 244 40
in that horrid state of selfish vanity, I did not know the SS III 8 320 32
and vanity had made him cold-hearted and selfish. SS III 8 331 70
of languid indolence and selfish repining, now at work in SS III 10 343 10
prevailing on feelings so selfish to consent to it, you SS III 11 351 9
she repeated the word "selfish?" in a tone that implied--" SS III 11 351 10
in a tone that implied--"do you really think him selfish?" SS III 11 351 10
The selfish sagacity of the latter, which had at first SS III 14 375 10
Beleive me Emma, I am not so selfish as that comes to. W 320 2
She is a selfish, hypocritical woman, and I have no PP I 2 6 5
your conceit, and your selfish disdain of the feelings of PP II 11 193 28
I am not so selfish, however, as to press for it, if PP III 4 275 5
Unfeeling, selfish girl! PP III 14 357 65
"Mr. Darcy, I am a very selfish creature; and, for the PP III 16 365 2
I have been a selfish being all my life, in practice, PP III 16 369 24
almost taught me to be selfish and overbearing, to care PP III 16 369 24
but to be slovenly and selfish--read the newspaper, watch MP I 11 110 23
see him to be an indolent selfish bon vivant, which must MP I 11 111 28
but, thoughtless and selfish from prosperity and bad MP I 12 114 3
was driven to it by the force of selfish inclinations only. MP I 17 158 1
his selfish vanity had raised in Maria and Julia Bertram. MP II 2 193 18
made his own habits of selfish indulgence appear in MP II 6 236 22
in idle cares and selfish solicitudes unconnected with him. MP II 11 282 2
Self-willed, obstinate, selfish, and ungrateful. MP III 1 319 40
Selfish and ungrateful! to have appeared so to him! MP III 1 321 46
all, perhaps all, would think her selfish and ungrateful. MP III 1 321 46
Some resentment did arise at a perseverance so selfish and MP III 2 328 9
disappointments of selfish passion, can excite little pity. MP III 17 464 12
eloped with any worse feelings than those of selfish alarm. MP III 17 467 18
to address any woman on the hap-hazard of selfish passion. E I 8 63 42
and selfish, should be proud, luxurious, and selfish too. E I 18 145 10
engagement, with no selfish view, no view at all, but of E III 13 432 40
not have been induced by any selfish views to go on.-- E III 14 438 8
all the discredit of the selfish arrangements which shut P III 2 16 16
But it was not a merely selfish caution, under which she P III 4 27 5
all selfish vanity, of the other all generous attachment. P IV 8 185 20
build my own selfish schemes on Mr. Elliot's good fortune." P IV 9 195 27
SELFISHLY (1)
Selfishly dear as she had long been to Lady Bertram, she MP III 17 472 31
SELFISHNESS (29)
which have been attributed to selfishness in Lady Susan. LS 14 264 2
There was a kind of cold hearted selfishness on both sides, SS II 12 229 2
of his epicurism, his selfishness, and his conceit, to SS III 6 305 15
with a meanness, selfishness, cruelty--which no indignant, SS III 8 320 32
man!--and without selfishness--without encouraging a hope!- SS III 9 336 14
You, who had seen all the fretful selfishness of my latter SS III 10 346 28
to the end of the affair, has been grounded on selfishness. SS III 11 351 11
It was selfishness which first made him sport with your SS III 11 351 11
yourself or me, that selfishness is prudence, and PP II 1 135 13
soon with cheerful selfishness reflect, 1st, that he had MP I 3 24 4
Selfishness must always be forgiven you know, because MP I 7 68 18
did, between the selfishness of another person and his own. MP I 12 119 25
unamused to observe the selfishness which, more or less MP I 14 131 4
Was it not ill-nature--selfishness--and a fear of exposing MP I 16 153 3
Jealousy and bitterness had been suspended: selfishness MP II 1 175 2
that bordered on selfishness in her affection for Edmund. MP II 9 264 18
She could just find selfishness enough to wonder whether MP III 13 427 12
good luck, and to her selfishness and vanity it would be MP III 14 430 3
been governed by motives of selfishness and worldly wisdom. MP III 17 461 4
the thoughtlessness and selfishness of his previous habits. MP III 17 462 4
his habits of gentle selfishness and of being never able E I 1 7 10
be selfishness:--what must be at last, had better be soon. E II 2 165 9
and all the selfishness of imaginary complaints. E III 9 387 12
from the injustice and selfishness of angry feelings, she E III 11 403 2
with by spirits or by selfishness, which fancied itself P IV 4 146 6
a sick chamber; it is selfishness and impatience rather P IV 5 156 11
The manoeuvres of selfishness and duplicity must ever be P IV 9 207 91
had any better principle to guide him than selfishness." P IV 9 208 93
Mrs. Clay's selfishness was not so complicate nor so P IV 10 215 13
SELINA (9)
Many a time has Selina said, when she has been going to E II 14 274 30
Selina has entirely given up music--never touches the E II 14 277 40
I use to be quite angry with Selina; but really I begin E II 14 277 40
you, if you knew how Selina feels with respect to sleeping E II 18 306 12
Selina says it is quite horror to her--and I believe I E II 18 306 12
Selina is no fine lady, I assure you. E II 18 306 15
or spirits like Selina to enjoy that sort of seclusion. E II 18 307 21
Selina, who is mild almost to a fault, bore with them much E III 2 321 15
Selina would stare when she heard of it."-- E III 19 484 12
SELINA'S (1)

Selina's choice--handsome, I think, but I do not know	E II 17 302 22
SELL (10)	
when we were obliged to sell it, but it was a trying	LS 5 249 1
I would not sell my horse for a hundred.	NA I 7 47 21
Sam Fletcher, has got one to sell that would suit any body.	NA I 10 76 28
carriage, she agreed to sell that likewise at the earnest	SS I 5 26 5
Why don't he, in such a case, sell his horses, let his	SS II 8 194 10
pounds of being obliged to sell out at a loss, nothing	SS II 12 233 18
Now indeed it would be too late to sell it, but a man of	SS III 5 295 12
heart; I will buy Pemberley itself if Darcy will sell it."	PP I 8 38 36
I dare say they sell gloves."	E II 6 200 14
as he had the power, but he would never condescend to sell.	P III 1 10 20
SELVES (5)	
manner, where their two selves only were concerned, was	PP III 2 265 16
unnecessary by their four selves, still was not it too	E II 11 254 44
one seemed so much disposed to employ as their two selves.	E III 5 347 20
been known to no being in the world but their two selves."	E III 10 399 60
Henrietta, and Captain Harville, beside their two selves.	P IV 10 216 19
SEMBLANCE (3)	
without the semblance of the most common-place flirtation.	LS 10 258 2
and with all the semblance of seeing nothing beyond; and	P IV 9 197 34
exercise & spirits in a semblance of health) could be	S 2 373 1
SEMI-CIRCULAR (1)	
stone house, with its semi-circular sweep and green gates,	NA II 11 212 17
SEMI-METALS (1)	
Semi-metals, Planets, and distinguished philosophers."	MP I 2 18 25
SEMINARIES (1)	
of the first private seminaries in town, had a fortune of	PP I 4 15 11
SEMINARY (7)	
of a school--not of a seminary, or an establishment, or	E I 3 21 5
to secure for you--the West Indians, & the seminary.--"	S 9 408 1
Camberwell seminary; have we a good chance of them?"	S 9 411 1
who actually attends the seminary and gives lessons on	S 9 412 1
Could it be the Camberwell seminary?--	S 10 414 1
that two hack chaises could never contain a seminary.--	S 10 414 1
The rich Westindians, & the young ladies seminary had all	S 11 420 1
SENCE (3)	
good Sence with even liberality which he saw in Lady D.--	S 3 378 1
Clara had returned with her--& by her good Sence & merit	S 3 379 1
But Burns--I confess my Sence of his pre-eminence Miss H.--	S 7 397 1
SEND (99)	
I will send you a line, as soon as I arrive in town.--	LS 2 246 2
He means to send for his horses immediately, & it is	LS 8 254 1
her, & persuading her to send Sir James away, I shall be	LS 21 279 1
pen, but am determined to send you a few lines by James,	LS 23 283 2
I am going to send James forward with my hunters	LS 23 283 4
Send him away immediately.	LS 23 284 4
Send me your opinion on all these matters, my dear Alicia,	LS 25 294 7
can have influence enough to send him back to his wife.	LS 26 295 3
Would she be pleased to send up her name?	NA I 12 91 3
Such a contrast between him and your brother!--pray send	NA II 12 217 2
The General will send a servant with me, I dare say, half	NA II 13 224 17
"He intends to send his groom into Somersetshire	SS I 12 58 2
you were so good as to send me," turned hastily away with	SS II 6 177 11
of a gentleman, as to send a letter so impudently cruel: a	SS II 7 183 14
she would like, I would send all over the town for it.	SS II 8 194 8
where they are forced to send three miles for their meat,	SS II 8 197 22
frightened that he would send for Mr. Donavan, and Mr.	SS III 1 259 7
be done, and at last she determined to send for Edward.	SS III 1 266 38
and to be sure they did send us home in their own chariot,	SS III 2 275 22
seemed determined to send her to Delaford;-a place, in	SS III 6 301 2
most acceptably; for to send to Colonel away while his	SS III 7 309 5
I cannot get him out of my head, but you must send for him	SS III 13 371 37
unless the Edwardses wd send her which was hardly to be	W 338 18
sister might be allow'd to send Emma the name of her	W 347 21
You and the girls may go, or you may send them by	PP I 1 4 19
to see you; and I will send a few lines by you to assure	PP I 1 4 25
you were sure that they would not offer to send her home."	PP I 7 30 22
"Is this a hint to me, Lizzy," said her father, "to send	PP I 7 32 36
pleasure of being able to send a tolerable answer to the	PP I 9 41 1
has made white soup enough I shall send round my cards."	PP I 11 55 7
her that they were not to send any more draughts to	PP I 15 73 11
and Elizabeth had such to send as might rather give	PP II 3 149 28
"Mrs. Collins, you must send a servant with them.	PP II 13 211 13
You must contrive to send somebody.	PP II 13 211 13
You must send John with the young ladies, Mrs. Collins.	PP II 14 212 13
"My uncle is to send a servant for us."	PP II 14 212 14
You need not send them word at Longbourn of my going, if	PP III 5 291 60
I shall send for my clothes when I get to Longbourn; but I	PP III 5 292 60
pleasing intelligence to send, but even of that they would	PP III 6 294 1
and then he had nothing of a pleasant nature to send.	PP III 6 297 12
"My dear brother, "at last I am able to send you some	PP III 7 302 14
I shall send this by express, that no time may be lost in	PP III 7 302 14
If, as I conclude will be the case, you send me full	PP III 7 303 14
Send back your answer as soon as you can, and be careful	PP III 7 303 14
but was too angry with Lydia, to send any message to her.	PP III 8 309 5
said she, "it will be quite shocking to send her away!	PP III 8 313 21
I send no compliments to your mother.	PP III 14 358 73
Mary or Kitty, send them in, for I am quite at leisure."	PP III 17 377 40
"I think we cannot do better," said she, "let us send for	MP I 1 5 4
I will send Nanny to London on purpose, and she may have a	MP I 1 8 8
It will not be necessary to send you to your father's	MP I 15 140 11
we shall be able to send back some dozens of the rings.--	MP I 15 141 22
mother had chanced to send him of a message to father, and	MP I 15 141 22
we will send him off, though he is Henry, for a time."	MP I 17 162 18
to them; and I could send a little parcel by you that I	MP II 7 245 32
smiles this afternoon, and send him back to me even	MP II 13 303 15
moment, and saying, "have you nothing to send to Mary?	MP II 13 306 28
and send back proper messages, with cheerful looks.	MP III 7 375 1
William trying in vain to send Betsey down again, or keep	MP III 7 382 27
when he comes back--and send me an account of all the	MP III 9 394 1
send her brothers in the evening for biscuits and buns.	MP III 11 413 30
If he wanted, he would send for her; and even to offer an	MP III 14 436 15
was so very kind as to send Mrs. Goddard a beautiful goose:	E I 4 28 8
again; and if she does but send her aunt the pattern of a	E I 10 86 23
So very good of them to send her the whole way!	E II 1 159 18
we had better send the leg--do not you think so, my dear?"	E II 3 171 16 17
"Should I send it to Mrs. Goddard's, ma'am?" asked Mrs.	E II 9 235 36
No, you shall send it to Hartfield, if you please.	E II 9 235 36
Then, if you please, you shall send it all to Mrs.	E II 9 235 40
'I am sure you must be,' said he, 'and I will send you	E II 9 238 51
I will send you some more, before they get good for	E II 9 238 51
"Mrs. Cole has servants to send.	E II 10 244 41
little ones have the measles, she will send for Perry."	E II 11 253 38
I should be extremely displeased if Wright were to send us	E II 15 283 9
"And if you find them troublesome, you must send them home	E II 18 311 40
And if they are, I only beg you to send them home."	E II 18 312 48
What a pleasure it is to send one's carriage for a friend!-	E III 2 321 17
Have you any thing to send or say, besides the 'love,'	E III 9 385 2
allowed me to send it, had any choice been given her.--	E III 14 439 8
command her's, so as to send them to Highbury within a	E III 14 442 8
at home, to wait in the passage, and send up her name.--	E III 16 452 8
"Very pretty, sir, upon my word; to send me on here, to be	E III 16 457 36
of some papers which I was wanting to send to John.--	E III 18 471 20
"She should always send for Perry, if the child appeared	E III 18 479 73
She could not be too soon alarmed, nor send for Perry too	E III 18 479 73
at once--the apothecary to send for--the father pursued	P III 7 53 3
Anne will send for me if any thing is the matter."	P III 7 55 8
And she could send us word every hour how he was.	P III 7 56 14
You can send for us, you know, at a moment's notice, if	P III 7 57 16
and grow coarse, I would send her a new hat and pelisse."	P IV 3 142 16
"I kept my letter open, that I might send you word how "	P IV 6 164 8
"Very well," said Elizabeth, "I have nothing to send but	P IV 10 215 15
power to send an intelligible sentence by Captain Harville.	P IV 11 239 53
gun he is just going to send off; said he would keep it	P IV 11 240 58
you to send off one of these good people for the surgeon."	S 1 365 1
promise was, that he could send everyone to Sanditon, who	S 2 374 1
Send me more particulars in your next.--	S 5 386 1
we are doing our utmost to send you company worth having;	S 5 387 1
But my dear Mary, send for the children;--I long to see	S 9 407 1
SENDING (45)	
of your precious time by sending her to Edward St,	LS 7 252 1
who is the means of sending my brother home; because, (	LS 24 286 4
liberty I have taken in sending to you, said I; but as I	LS 25 292 3
engagement, without sending her any message of excuse.	NA I 11 86 50
Morland says that by sending it to-night to Salisbury, we	NA I 15 120 22
John Dashwood, without sending any notice of her intention	SS I 1 5 9
to move their things, and sending them presents of fish	SS I 2 12 24
her mother from sending her letter of acquiescence.	SS I 4 24 21
the satisfaction of sending them his newspaper every day.	SS I 6 30 6
poor dependent cousin, by sending me on business to London.	SS I 15 75 6
It will only be sending Betty by the coach, and I hope I	SS II 3 153 2
great inconvenience of sending her carriage for the Miss	SS II 14 248 6
as myself, instead of sending him to Mr. Pratt's, all this	SS II 14 251 13
Jennings's advice, of sending for the Palmers' apothecary.	SS III 7 307 2
She knew not that she had been the means of sending the	SS III 7 309 6
as to determine her on sending instantly for Mr. Harris,	SS III 7 311 14
She was on the point of sending again for Mr. Harris, or	SS III 7 312 19
Your Cloathes I would undertake to find means of sending	W 320 2
information, was as sincere as her brother's in sending it.	PP III 18 383 25
determined him on sending home his son, and waiting the	MP I 4 38 9
Sir Thomas's sending away his son, seemed to her so like a	MP I 4 38 9
She found herself more successful in sending away, than in	MP I 10 103 48
Rushworth's cloak without sending for any more satin; and	MP I 18 166 6
stay at Mansfield, and sending for his hunters from	MP II 5 223 48
with her own kindness in sending Chapman to her, that she	MP II 10 277 15
In thus sending her away, Sir Thomas perhaps might not be	MP II 10 281 34
let my brother go without sending you a few lines of	MP II 13 303 15
for his prime motive in sending her away, had very little	MP III 6 368 9
at Mansfield Park, about sending her a prayer-book; but no	MP III 7 387 45
for coming himself, or sending your aunt's maid for you,	MP III 11 410 16
in; but he brings no intelligence to prevent my sending it.	MP III 14 435 14
unknown to him, and sending them for all their indulgences	MP III 17 463 7
evening had particular pleasure in sending them away happy.	E I 3 25 15
sending to inquire after Harriet every hour of the evening.	E I 13 110 10
and Emma thinks of sending them a loin or a leg; it is	E II 3 171 16 17
bear that he should be sending us more, so liberal as he	E II 9 238 51
"To think of your sending us all your store apples.	E II 10 245 52
she had been within half a minute of sending for Mr. Perry.	E III 18 479 73
very much for thinking of sending for Perry, and only	E III 18 479 73
Mary's declaration was, "I hate sending the children to	P III 6 44 8
and soothe;--besides sending, as soon as she recollected	P III 7 53 3
now and then, with sending a few hundred men to sea, in a	P III 8 65 11
farther advantage of sending an account of Louisa's night.	P III 12 114 64
their preparations, and sending them off at an early hour,	P IV 1 122 5
I have done very little besides sending away some of the	P IV 1 127 28
SENDS (6)	
the business which she sends him off to transact, is	SS I 15 78 26
cottage, I hear, and mama sends me word they are very	SS I 20 115 50
Mr. Darcy sends you all the love in the world, that he can	PP III 18 383 21
and sends it into the very channel where it ought to flow.	E I 9 75 25
My aunt always sends me off when she is shopping.	E II 9 234 30
He sends us a sack every year; and certainly there never	E II 9 238 51
SENIOR (1)	
The maid-servant of Mrs. Rushworth, senior, threatened	MP III 16 450 9
SENIORITY (3)	
of what was due to seniority; and for the first evening	PP I 15 70 3
in herself the right of seniority of mind, she ventured to	P III 11 101 24
to the rights of seniority, and the mistress of a very	P IV 12 250 5
SENSATION (27)	
the resentful sensation; she remembered her own ignorance.	NA I 12 92 3
love, must have long outlived every sensation of the kind.	SS I 8 37 4
him probably the novel sensation of doubting his own	W 335 13
mind, a more gentle sensation towards the original, than	PP III 1 250 48
over every ungracious sensation she had ever encouraged,	PP III 10 327 3
Elizabeth with a triumphant sensation, looked towards his	PP III 12 340 12
There can hardly be a more unpleasant sensation than the	MP II 9 263 12
his two dearest, before the words gave her any sensation.	MP II 9 264 17
She must have a sensation of being honoured, and whether	MP III 2 328 7
sensation, and unvarying cheerfulness all dinner-time.	MP III 3 334 3
have an idea of the sensation that you will be occasioning,	MP III 5 360 16
with every dearest sensation, that there are few who might	MP III 17 461 3
but with some painful sensation of restraint or alarm,	MP III 17 473 33
every sort of sensation that declining life can need.	E I 10 86 21
Cannot you imagine, Mr. Knightley, what a sensation his	E I 18 149 29
that was too general a sensation for any thing of peculiar	E II 8 218 37
"This sensation of listlessness, weariness, stupidity,	E II 12 262 39
ashamed of every sensation but the one revealed to her--	E III 11 412 46
disinterested in every sensation; thought so much of Jane;	E III 12 418 5
Never had the exquisite sight, smell, sensation of nature,	E III 13 424 1
but this was no new sensation: excepting one short period	P III 6 47 13
except from some natural sensation of curiosity, he had no	P III 7 61 37
her from the stiles; the sensation was delightful to her.	P III 12 109 32
Still, however, she had the sensation of there being	P IV 3 140 11
full sensation, Charles, Mary, and Henrietta all came in.	P IV 11 238 44
for his superfluity of sensation as a Projector, the	S 10 412 1
have been the sort of sensation of being less clear-	S 11 420 1
SENSATIONS (55)	
It would indeed give me most painful sensations to know	LS 1 244 1
talent of affecting sensations foreign to my heart; &	LS 20 277 6 7
conveyed from her sight without very uneasy sensations.	NA II 1 132 16
to the tempest with sensations of awe; and, when she heard	NA II 6 166 9
acknowledged with awful sensations this striking	NA II 6 169 11
mother and Elinor from sharing such delightful sensations.	SS I 9 41 4
"Oh!" cried Marianne, "with what transporting sensations	SS I 16 87 31
to fill her heart with sensations of exquisite comfort,	SS III 7 315 24
simple and self-evident sensations, while in the actions	SS III 10 340 3
are my sensations in finding myself once more at Stanton.	W 356 28
her with most painful sensations; and she watched her	PP I 18 100 68
realities as these, what would have been her sensations?	PP II 18 232 23
Of the lady's sensations they remained a little in doubt;	PP III 2 262 6
The division of gratifying sensations ought not, in strict	MP I 1 8 9
and saw his look, and felt what his sensations must be.	MP I 15 139 4
and the delight of his sensations in being again in his	MP II 1 178 8
and what were the sensations of her children upon hearing	MP II 1 180 13
and with many awkward sensations he did his best.	MP II 1 183 23
for such unsatisfactory sensations on each side; and Sir	MP II 1 183 24
Her sensations were indefinable, and so were they a few	MP II 2 192 11
it raised some awkward sensations in two of the others,	MP II 7 248 47
affection, and with some very precious sensations on her's.	MP II 9 270 40
and filling her with sensations of delightful self-	MP II 10 277 17
own sensations, nothing to dwell on but Fanny's charms.--	MP II 12 293 16
she had created sensations which his heart had never known	MP II 13 301 7
her so many painful sensations on the first day of hearing	MP II 13 303 13
spite of some amiable sensations, and much personal	MP III 6 367 5
sensations which are to raise ecstacy even in retrospect.	MP III 12 415 1 2
Such sensations, however, were too near a kin to	MP III 13 424 5
was received to revive old, and create some new sensations.	MP III 14 433 12
circumstances and sensations of the first interest to	MP III 16 453 17
With such sensations, Mr. Elton's civilities were	E I 14 119 6

this--which of all her unpleasant sensations was uppermost. E I 15 131 32
to open to sensations of softened pain and brighter hope. E I 16 137 13
herself into all the sensations of curiosity, wonder and E II 3 180 57
Miss Fairfax's sensations from you, or from any body else. E II 6 202 37
sensations, and think she had undervalued their strength. E II 13 265 5
Harriet's cure; but the sensations which could prompt such E II 15 281 3
Let his behaviour be the guide of your sensations. E III 4 342 39
just and less gentle sensations of the past, obliged her E III 8 379 9
even what your sensations had been in seeing him come E III 11 406 23
difference in Emma's sensations; but she could not think E III 16 452 5
sensations into a very, very earnest shake of the hand. E III 16 453 10
the exquisite delight of her sensations may be imagined. E III 18 475 39
there any unwelcome sensations, arising from domestic P III 1 3 1
Such were Elizabeth elliot's sentiments and sensations; P III 1 9 18
was left with as many sensations of comfort, as were, P III 7 58 20
Her sensations on the discovery made her perfectly P III 9 80 34
It stood the record of many sensations of pain, once P IV 1 123 8
agreeable sensations which her friend meant to create. P IV 5 159 21
of the moment, with exquisite, though agitated sensations. P IV 8 184 17
was considered with sensations unqualified, unperplexed.-- P IV 10 212 1
found, in all her own sensations for her cousin, in the P IV 10 225 62
My sensations tell me so already."-- S 1 367 1
our sensations--"like Angel's visits, few & far between." S 7 397 1

SENSE (222)

to see a young man of Reginald's sense duped by her at all. LS 8 256 4
I do not wish to work on your fears, but on your sense & LS 12 261 4
my pretensions to common sense, if I am suspected of LS 14 263 1
Every person of sense however will know how to value & LS 14 265 5
her of ill-nature & sometimes to lament her want of sense. LS 17 272 8
first, & to have all the sense & all the wit of the LS 19 274 3
Where was his reliance on my sense or goodness then; where LS 22 282 6
grateful for so favourable a sign of my daughter's sense. LS 24 288 11
you alone should be ignorant of your daughter's sense." LS 24 288 11
sense of superior integrity which is peculiarly insolent. LS 25 292 1
sense of their kindness, & her pleasure in their society. LS 42 311 2
Lady Susan was unable to express her sense of such LS 42 312 5
Her mother was a woman of useful plain sense, with a good NA I 1 13 1
to; she has so much good sense, and is so thoroughly NA I 7 50 47
Tilney expressing a proper sense of such goodness, Miss NA I 8 55 10
Her manners shewed good sense and good breeding; they were NA I 8 56 11
brother had so much sense; I am glad you are come back. NA I 11 89 62
This charming sentiment, recommended as much by sense as NA I 15 119 19
it recalled her to the sense of what she ought to be doing, NA II 6 164 3
of languor or restraint, a sense of general happiness NA II 6 166 8
not wholly dead to every sense of humanity, in its fearful NA II 8 187 13
ray of common sense added some bitter emotions of shame. NA II 9 193 6
Consult your own understanding, your own sense of the NA II 9 197 29
with the greatest good sense, she had nothing to do but to NA II 10 201 4
has chosen a wife with less sense than his family expected. NA II 10 205 24
There was a great deal of good sense in all this; but NA II 14 239 28
human mind in which good sense has very little power; and NA II 14 239 28
talked at random, without sense or connection, and NA II 15 243 10
His pleasing manners and good sense were self-evident NA II 16 249 1
of it; that in no sense of the word were they necessitous NA II 16 251 6
her mind there was a sense of honour so keen, a generosity SS I 1 6 9
without having much of her sense, she did not, at thirteen, SS I 1 7 14
is not in every thing equal to your sense of his merits. SS I 4 19 5
6
the highest opinion in the world of his goodness and sense. SS I 4 19 6
"Of his sense and his goodness," continued Elinor, "no one SS I 4 20 9
know no moderation, and leave him no sense of fatigue." SS I 9 45 28
to assure him of the sense, elegance, mutual affection, SS I 10 46 1
"My protege, as you call him, is a sensible man; and sense SS I 10 51 20
mere calmness of manner with which sense had nothing to do. SS I 11 55 6
reasonable basis of common sense and observation; and then SS I 11 56 11
child much less; because a sense of duty would prevent the SS I 16 84 9
but in vain; common sense, common care, common prudence, SS I 16 85 10
"Shyness is only the effect of a sense of inferiority in SS I 17 94 44
what was worn and hackneyed out of all sense and meaning." SS I 18 97 7
an air of more fashion and sense than his wife, but of SS I 19 106 22
credit for some kind of sense, when she saw with what SS I 21 120 6
She was stronger alone, and her own good sense so well SS II 1 141 6
last able to express some sense of her kindness, by saying, SS II 7 185 16
17
it in the strictest sense, by watching over her education SS II 9 208 28
Lady Middleton expressed her sense of the affair about SS II 10 215 14
have too much sense not to see all that. SS II 11 224 24
being agreeable--want of sense, either natural or improved- SS II 12 233 18
They had too much sense to be desirable companions to the SS II 14 246 3
Lucy does not want sense, and that is the foundation on SS III 1 263 27
late to sell it, but a man of Colonel Brandon's sense!-- SS III 5 295 12
but Elinor had no sense of fatigue, no capability of sleep SS III 7 315 27
and common sense might have told her how to find it out." SS III 8 322 38
I approached her with a sense of guilt that almost took SS III 8 324 42
Your sense of honour and honesty would have led you, I SS III 11 350 9
was taken ill, had sense enough to call one of the maids, SS III 11 353 25
Their resemblance in good principles and good sense, in SS III 13 370 36
cause, & increased her sense of the awkwardness of rushing W 322 3
Miss E.--the shew of good sense, a modest unpretending W 323 3
sense of inferiority, she felt no particular shame.-- W 345 21
But as he wanted neither sense nor a good disposition, he W 346 21
"My uncle's sense is not at all impeached in my opinion, W 352 26
silence; &, being a man of sense and education, was if W 361 30
With your good sense, to be so honestly blind to the PP I 4 14 9
such girls to have the sense of their father and mother.-- PP I 7 29 12
almost all its sense, by the absence of Jane and Elizabeth. PP I 12 60 6
"There is some sense in what he says about the girls PP I 13 63 14
to all the world; a sense of very great ill usage, and PP I 16 78 20
can be placed on the appearance of either merit or sense. PP II 1 135 11
You have sense, and we all expect you to use it. PP II 3 144 2
being deficient in something herself--sense or feeling." PP II 4 153 16
quality, who has neither manner nor sense to recommend him. PP II 4 154 19
"Shall we ask him why a man of sense and education, and PP II 8 175 22
than from their want of sense; and she was quite decided PP II 10 187 40
gave her a keener sense of her sister's sufferings. PP II 11 188 1
His sense of her inferiority--of its being a degradation-- PP II 11 189 5
mode to express a sense of obligation for the sentiments PP II 11 189 6
7
it is honourable to the sense and disposition of both.-- PP II 12 198 5
to give, which a just sense of shame would not conceal. PP II 13 204 1
incapable of attending to the sense of one before her eyes. PP II 13 204 1
yet merited reproach, her sense of shame was severe. PP II 13 208 10
good opinion, heightened the sense of what Jane had lost. PP II 14 213 18
has yet expressed her sense of your kindness in coming to PP II 15 215 2
man, that all her good sense, and all her attention to the PP II 17 227 26
Elizabeth tried to be diverted by them; but all sense of PP II 18 229 10
all possibility of common sense for the latter; and PP II 18 230 14
her natural degree of sense, since the disturbers of her PP II 19 237 3
and whose steady sense and sweetness of temper exactly PP II 19 239 10
her brother, but there was sense and good humour in her PP III 2 261 4
was only recalled to a sense of her situation by the voice PP III 4 278 20
her eyes, "that a sister's sense of decency and virtue in PP III 5 283 10
We both know that he has been profligate in every sense of PP III 5 284 12
nuptials, than to any sense of shame at her eloping and PP III 8 310 10
Jane's delicate sense of honour would not allow her to PP III 9 320 35
Her mother's ungraciousness, made the sense of what they PP III 12 340 13
in general would have too much sense to join in the scorn." PP III 14 358 70
ridiculous, contained much good sense and solid reasoning. PP III 15 361 2
think meanly of their sense and worth compared with my own. PP III 16 369 24
to do credit to her sense; and she could no more bear that PP III 17 375 27
of Edmund, his strong good sense and uprightness of mind, MP I 2 20 33
as well as good sense, and a fondness for reading, which, MP I 2 22 35

You have good sense, and a sweet temper, and I am sure you MP I 3 26 29
He was a heavy young man, with not more than common sense; MP I 4 38 10
He did not want them to die of love; but with sense and MP I 5 45 3
She has the age and sense of a woman, but the outs and not MP I 5 49 31
It did not suit his sense of propriety, and he was MP I 6 57 32
her own sense of propriety could but just smooth over. MP I 8 81 32
the preacher to have the sense to prefer Blair's to his MP I 9 92 46
Crawford has too much sense to stay here if he found MP I 12 116 10
But dear Maria has such a strict sense of propriety, so MP I 12 117 14
His sense of decorum is strict." MP I 13 127 26
which their own sense of superiority could demand, were MP I 16 151 1
gales dispense to Templars modesty, to parsons sense.' MP I 17 161 15
looks dispense to children affluence, to Rushworth sense. MP I 17 161 15
though irrational hope, with a strong sense of ill-usage. MP I 17 162 19
tending to increase his sense of the insignificance of all MP I 18 164 1
like her, without any sense of obligation for being sought MP II 4 208 11
against common sense, that a woman could be plagued with. MP II 4 212 30
He might not have sense enough himself to estimate the MP II 5 225 53
A great deal of good sense followed on Sir Thomas's side, MP II 11 284 10
Henry Crawford had too much sense not to feel the worth of MP II 12 294 16
it is that can attach me, that can attach a man of sense. MP II 12 297 33
Here is a young man of sense, of character, of temper, of MP III 1 319 39
who was pouring out his sense of her merits, describing MP III 2 328 6
is totally distinct from giving his sense as you gave it. MP III 3 338 14
who has about as much sense, Fanny, as Mr. Rushworth, but MP III 5 361 16
her company that could lessen her sense of such feelings. MP III 8 390 6
If tenderness could be ever supposed wanting, good sense MP III 8 392 11
Good sense, like hers, will always act when really called MP III 10 399 4
the support of their own bad sense to her too lively mind. MP III 13 421 2
have trusted to her sense of what was due to her cousin. MP III 15 438 7
Sir Thomas's parental solicitude, and high sense of honour MP III 15 442 21
truths, half a sense of shame--but habit, habit carried it. MP III 16 458 30
with no want of sense, or good companions, was durable in MP III 17 462 4
Sir Thomas, deadening his sense of what was lost, and in MP III 17 462 6
and tempers, by that sense of duty which can alone suffice. MP III 17 462 8
her sense, and wonderfully borne with her manners before. MP III 17 465 15
fairly consider a man of sense like Henry Crawford, to be MP III 17 468 22
What must be his sense of it now, therefore? MP III 17 471 28
application, the high sense of having realised a great MP III 17 471 29
proof of his great good sense, and a most welcome addition E I 2 18 10
would have been, and had sense and energy and spirits that E I 2 18 11
that she must have good sense and deserve encouragement. E I 3 23 10
and is therefore in one sense as much above my notice as E I 4 29 14
The longer she considered it, the greater was her sense of E I 4 35 44
"I either depend more upon Emma's good sense than you do, E I 5 39 16
It was short, but expressed good sense, warm attachment, E I 7 51 4
I never heard better sense from any one than Robert Martin. E I 8 59 27
for he is as much her superior in sense as in situation. E I 8 61 38
What! think a farmer, (and with all his sense and all his E I 8 62 39
birth, though in a legal sense she may be called nobody, E I 8 62 41
she may be called nobody, it will not hold in common sense. E I 8 62 41
She had no sense of superiority then. E I 8 63 42
She is not a clever girl, but she has better sense than E I 8 63 44
Better be without sense, than misapply it as you do." E I 8 64 45
Men of sense, whatever you may chuse to say, do not want E I 8 64 47
"Robert Martin's manners have sense, sincerity, and good- E I 8 65 49
at least they have common sense; and we are not to be E I 9 75 27
a glow--"to have very good sense in a common way, like E I 9 76 35
the candour and common sense of the world as appears at E I 10 85 19
and generally a strong sense of what was due to him; but E I 11 93 5
Emma's sense of right however had decided it; and besides E I 12 98 1
ever retain a greatful sense-- and had Mr. Woodhouse any E I 17 140 2
of course, as a man of sense would make it, in a proper E I 18 147 18
He may have as strong a sense of what would be right, as E I 18 148 19
"Then, it would not be so strong a sense. E I 18 148 20
They hardly can satisfy a woman of her good sense and E I 18 149 26
My dear Emma, your own good sense could not endure such a E I 18 150 32
The good sense of Colonel and Mrs. Campbell could not E II 2 165 9
twofold complacency; the sense of pleasure and the sense E II 2 167 13
sense of pleasure and the sense of rendering justice, and E II 2 167 13
man had only his own good sense to depend on; and when she E II 14 271 5
intimacy than her own good sense would have dictated, in E II 15 286 21
enjoyment and very high sense of the distinction which her E III 2 328 41
any man of sense and taste to such a woman as Mrs. Elton. E III 2 331 55
communicated, which is sense, is, that they are as far E III 5 350 37
hems with a commiseration and good sense, true and steady. E III 9 388 13
Common sense would have directed her to tell Harriet, that E III 11 402 1
"But, with common sense," she added, "I am afraid I have E III 11 402 1
very warmly as to your sense of that service, and E III 11 406 23
appearance, and a strong sense of justice by Harriet--(E III 11 408 33
I have been acting contrary to all my sense of right; and E III 12 419 8
and her sense of past injustice towards Miss Fairfax. E III 12 420 17
Your own excellent sense--your exertions for your father's E III 13 426 13
for any woman of sense to endure, she spoke her resentment E III 14 441 8
to Jane Fairfax's sense of right, he made a fuller pause E III 15 446 20
What a view this gives of her sense of his behaviour!-- E III 15 447 22
was never struck with any sense of injury to her nephew E III 15 449 35
reproaches, or apparent sense of ill usage; and yet Emma E III 16 451 2
unchecked by that sense of injustice, of guilt, of E III 16 451 4
I doubt whether my own sense would have corrected me E III 17 462 6
service which his better sense would have rendered her, to E III 17 463 15
His good sense and good principles would delight you.-- E III 18 472 22
him all the appearance of sense and worth which could bid E III 19 482 4
her, and who had better sense than herself; retired enough E III 19 482 4
He was very uneasy; and but for the sense of his son-in- E III 19 483 10
whose known good sense he fully expected to have just such P III 2 11 1
She was of strict integrity herself, with a delicate sense P III 2 11 2
to them, as any body of sense and honesty could well be. P III 2 11 2
Charles Musgrove was civil and agreeable; in sense and P III 6 43 5
was undoubtedly a gentleman, and had an air of good sense. P III 12 106 19
unable to satisfy his own sense of their kindness, P IV 1 121 2
The intervals of sense and consciousness were believed to P IV 1 122 4
all this, joined to the sense of being so very useful, had P IV 2 130 3
Anne found in Mrs. Smith the good sense and agreeable P IV 5 153 7
and she has a fund of good sense and observation which, as P IV 5 155 9
her sense of personal respect to her father prevented her. P IV 5 158 20
"This," said she, "is nearly the sense, or rather the P IV 8 186 25
words, for certainly the sense of an Italian love-song P IV 8 186 25
Mr. Elliot has sense to understand the value of such a P IV 9 196 32
strong sense of duty is no bad part of a woman's portion." P IV 11 246 80
had not had principle or sense enough to maintain himself P IV 12 248 1
to bestow on him which a man of sense could value. P IV 12 251 10
What in the name of common sense is to recommend Brinshore? S 1 369 1
She has good natural sense, but quite uncultivated.-- S 3 376 1
more endebted to her sense of justice than he had allowed S 3 376 1
uniformly with great good sense, & evidently gaining by S 3 378 1
which it cannot impugn the sense or be any Dereliction of S 8 404 1

SENSELESS (2)

One of my senseless tricks!-- E III 4 339 13
They were too much like joy, senseless joy! P IV 6 168 21

SENSES (22)

This brother of yours would persuade me out of my senses, NA I 7 46 9
senses, and with cheeks only a little redder than usual. NA I 8 53 3
Could it be possible, or did not her senses play her false? NA II 7 172 2
"I could hardly believe my senses, when I heard it;--and NA II 13 225 19
Had he been in his right senses, he could not have thought SS I 2 9 5
think nobody else has any senses; but it is no such thing, SS II 7 182 10
If I had had my senses about me I might have called in SS II 8 195 16
that nobody in their senses could expect Mr. Ferrars to SS III 2 272 16
almost out of her senses, sat on the edge of her chair, PP II 6 162 11
Every girl in, or near Meryton, was out of her senses PP III 5 285 18
"I mean, that no man in his senses, would marry Lydia on PP III 7 304 29

Are you out of your senses, to be accepting this man? PP III 17 376 29
as any body in their senses would have done, instead of MP II 5 220 30
heart was so full and her senses still so that she could MP II 13 300 7
yourself to be in your senses as soon as you can, by a MP III 4 352 44
thrown over my senses, must still see, hear, and remember. E I 5 37 9
at once bewitches his senses and satisfies his judgment. E I 8 64 46
must restore him to his senses; and then left the sopha, E I 15 125 6
as soon as she had recovered her senses and speech.-- E III 3 334 8
the conviction, lost her senses too, and would have fallen P III 12 109 34
Shocked as Captain Harville was, he brought senses and P III 12 111 50
She was lost; and when she had scolded back her senses, P IV 7 175 5

SENSIBILITIES (2)
whose sensibilities are not of a nature to comprehend ours. LS 30 301 4
Her sensibilities, I suspect, are strong--and her temper E II 15 289 40

SENSIBILITY (31)
myself with the great sensibility to one in particular, a LS 5 250 2
could call forth her sensibility; without having inspired NA I 1 16 10
though her delicate sensibility did not take immediate NA II 1 132 16
embarrassment of real sensibility began to apologise for NA II 15 241 7
excess of her sister's sensibility; but by Mrs. Dashwood SS I 1 7 13
I loved him, to hear him read with so little sensibility. SS I 3 18 20
he read with all the sensibility and spirit which Edward SS I 10 48 8
to call for the ridicule so justly annexed to sensibility. SS I 10 49 12
Her sensibility was potent enough! SS I 16 83 1
a strong sensibility, and the graces of a polished manner. SS II 9 201 4
impulse of affectionate sensibility, she moved, after a SS II 12 236 39
40
not by any reproof of her's, but by his own sensibility. SS III 5 298 34
suffered agonies of sensibility--and he considered the SS III 13 371 38
artificial sensibility was not recommended by the idea.-- W 351 25
air and manner, not often united with great sensibility. PP II 13 208 9
to make her betray a sensibility which might injure her in PP III 3 269 10
by great sensibility of her situation, and great timidity. MP I 2 16 20
and more than all, the sensibility which he, unsuspicious MP I 8 79 27
two-fold--for the sensibility which beautified her MP II 6 235 20
had herself been treated, as from sensibility for her son. MP III 16 450 10
more acute sensibility to fine sounds than to my feelings. E II 6 202 31
to his arm, with a sensibility amused and delighted; and E III 3 335 11
And the more sensibility you betray of their just horrors, E III 6 363 52
in a tone of great sensibility, speaking low, "time, my E III 13 425 12
13
Emma agreed to it, and with a blush of sensibility on E III 15 446 16
with a look of true sensibility, "there is a likeness in E III 18 478 69
and yet, with a sensibility to what was amiable and lovely, P IV 4 146 6
of fourteen, of strong sensibility and not high spirits, P IV 5 152 2
that she was betraying the least sensibility of the two. P IV 7 175 6
Glowing and lovely in sensibility and happiness, and more P IV 11 245 78
emotions they excite in the mind of sensibility.-- S 7 396 1

SENSIBLE (133)
I have made him sensible of my power, & can now enjoy the LS 10 257 1
You must be sensible that as an only son & the LS 12 260 1
my dear sister must be sensible, to treat my daughter with LS 15 267 6
I want to make him sensible of all this, for we know power LS 18 272 2
the choice of a sensible, intelligent man, like Mr. Allen. NA I 2 20 8
others, which a sensible person would always wish to avoid. NA I 14 110 28
She began first to be sensible of this, and to sigh for NA II 3 143 1
my honour, I never was sensible of them for a moment-- NA II 3 144 11
she had never been sensible of any; but spoken in haste, NA II 3 148 29
made her peculiarly sensible of Henry's importance among NA II 8 187 15
made her thoroughly sensible of the restraint which the NA II 13 220 1
made her for a short time sensible only of resentment. NA II 13 228 27
resentment of a sensible friend; and Mrs. Allen thought NA II 14 237 22
She was sensible and clever; but eager in every thing; her SS I 1 6 12
sensible, and his address was particularly gentlemanlike. SS I 7 34 6
"My protege, as you call him, is a sensible man; and sense SS I 10 51 20
I can only pronounce him to be a sensible man, well-bred, SS I 10 51 27
did, I should have been sensible of it at the time, for we SS I 13 68 72
I am not sensible of having done any thing wrong in SS I 13 68 74
He was confused, seemed scarcely sensible of pleasure in SS I 16 87 23
common for any sensible man to be lastingly hurt by it.-- SS I 20 112 28
a very plain and not a sensible face, nothing to admire; SS I 21 120 6
seen enough of him to be sensible he is very capable of SS I 22 130 28
"No," replied Elinor, most feelingly sensible of every SS I 22 134 49
incapable of attaching a sensible man, that she could not SS III 1 261 13
He is undoubtedly a sensible man, and in his manners SS III 4 290 37
E.--, very strongly--but I am not sensible of the others.-- W 324 3
topics he had a sensible, unaffected, way of expressing W 335 13
of life, was fully sensible of all that must be open to W 345 21
had been reckoned an extraordinary sensible, clever man.-- W 352 26
Mary wished to say something very sensible, but knew not PP I 2 7 19
ought to be," said she, "sensible, good humoured, lively; PP I 4 14 2
The eldest of them, a sensible, intelligent young woman, PP I 5 18 2
are silly I must hope to be always sensible of it." PP I 7 29 9
his felicity; sensible that if such an idea had been PP I 12 60 4
Can he be a sensible man, sir?" PP I 13 64 17
"I am very sensible, madam, of the hardship to my fair PP I 13 65 25
Mr. Collins was not a sensible man, and the deficiency of PP I 15 70 1
She has the reputation of being remarkably sensible and PP I 16 84 58
making her also sensible that it would be wisest to get it PP I 19 104 7
I am very sensible of the honour of your proposals, but it PP I 19 107 12
to this effusion, sensible that any attempt to reason with PP I 20 113 29
which he had been so sensible of himself, were transferred PP I 21 115 1
the smallest degree less sensible of your merit than when PP I 21 119 20
Mr. Collins to be sure was neither sensible nor agreeable; PP I 22 122 3
used to think tolerably sensible, was as foolish as his PP I 23 127 6
involved in it, as she thought he must be sensible himself. PP II 1 133 3
Mr. Gardiner was a sensible, gentlemanlike man, greatly PP II 2 139 2
"You are too sensible a girl, Lizzy, to fall in love PP II 3 144 2
"Lady Catherine is a very respectable, sensible woman PP II 5 157 8
She was perfectly sensible that he never had; but she PP II 7 171 12
with one of the very few sensible women who would have PP II 9 178 15
discovered; and, alike sensible that no time was to be PP II 12 198 5
partake; and she was sensible that nothing less than a PP II 17 227 25
Colonel Forster is a sensible man, and will keep her out PP II 18 232 20
before Elizabeth was sensible of any of it; and, though PP III 1 253 55
and they soon became sensible, that the authority of a PP III 2 264 14
She was even sensible of some pleasure, though mixed with PP III 10 327 3
and sensible young man, without having a wish beyond it. PP III 12 343 32
If you were sensible of your own good, you would not wish PP III 14 356 50
effect as to make her a sensible, amiable, well informed PP III 19 385 1
and they were both ever sensible of the warmest gratitude PP III 19 388 13
Mrs. Norris, "and be sensible of her uncommon good fortune MP I 1 10 13
as seeming as desirably sensible of her peculiar good MP I 2 14 9
from her family, was sensible of the truest satisfaction MP I 2 21 34
My aunt is acting like a sensible woman in wishing for you. MP I 3 26 23
one more sensible of the disadvantages she has been under. MP I 7 64 9
and consideration make me more sensible of my own neglect. MP I 9 95 70
A man--a sensible man like Dr. Grant, cannot be in the MP I 11 112 30
with you; and I am sensible of the importance of having an MP II 1 186 34
I could wish my father were more sensible of their very MP II 3 196 2
her engagement, or was sensible of any change of opinion MP II 3 200 21
you none of you seemed sensible of the wonderful MP II 6 229 5
You are not sensible of the gain, for your regard for him MP II 12 296 27
will not do for a man who has been used to sensible women. MP III 4 355 54
As to your brother's behaviour, certainly I was sensible MP III 5 362 21
I had been sensible of it some little time, perhaps two or MP III 5 362 21
Susan had an open, sensible countenance; she was like MP III 7 384 33
Much of all this, Fanny could not but be sensible of. MP III 8 390 6
attached father, and a sensible man;--his loud tones did MP III 10 402 12
acquaintance, been often sensible of some difference in MP III 16 457 30
Mr. Knightley, a sensible man about seven or eight-and- E I 1 9 21
and he looked like a sensible young man, but his person E I 4 31 27
found her decidedly more sensible than before of Mr. E I 6 42 1
No doubt he is a sensible man, and I suppose may have a E I 7 51 5
She is not a sensible girl, nor a girl of any information. E I 8 61 38
and may be as sensible and pleasant as anybody else. E I 10 85 19
of the very great inequality which you are so sensible of. E I 15 132 36
of gruel--perfectly sensible of its being exceedingly E I 15 132 38
"Depend upon it, Emma, a sensible man would find no E I 18 147 18
"Did he appear a sensible young man; a young man of E II 2 169 17
liveliness of his father's; he looked quick and sensible. E II 5 190 22
if they are done by sensible people in an impudent way. E II 8 212 2
3
a set of gentlemen-like, sensible men; and spoke so E II 8 220 48
When she became sensible of this, it struck her that she E II 13 264 1
And for a wife--a sensible man's wife--it is invaluable. E II 13 269 16
My daughter and I are both highly sensible of your E II 16 294 27
"Certainly; you must be sensible that the last half year E II 18 311 44
Yes, believe me, Knightley, I am fully sensible of your E III 6 356 28
kind and sensible--much cleverer than dining out.-- E III 6 357 30
Harriet had begun to be sensible of his talking to her E III 11 409 35
She had seemed more sensible of Mr. Elton's being to stoop E III 11 414 50
She was sensible that you had never received any proper E III 12 420 12
"He writes like a sensible man," replied Emma, when she E III 17 464 20
sensible of Mr. Knightley's high superiority of character. E III 18 480 80
Lady Elliot had been an excellent woman, sensible and P III 1 4 6
She had, however, one very intimate friend, a sensible, P III 1 5 6
of sensible people, by his acting like a man of principle. P III 2 12 4
the country--and being a sensible man, and, moreover, a P III 4 30 10
character, she was sensible that results the most serious P III 5 34 12
Captain Harville was a tall, dark man, with a sensible, P III 11 97 14
When they came to converse, she was soon sensible of some P IV 1 124 11
by a couple of steady, sensible women, whose judgments had P IV 1 126 21
A sensible man! and he had looked like a very sensible man, P IV 3 140 11
very sensible man, why should it be an object to him? P IV 3 140 11
good shaped face, his sensible eye, but, at the same time, P IV 3 141 12
There could be no doubt of his being a sensible man. P IV 3 143 19
was all the operation of a sensible, discerning mind. P IV 3 143 19
recommend him, among all sensible people, to be on good P IV 4 147 7
She is a shrewd, intelligent, sensible woman. P IV 5 155 9
be so highly rated by a sensible man, without many of P IV 5 159 21
That he was a sensible man, an agreeable man,--that he P IV 5 160 27
the woman who had been sensible of Captain Wentworth's P IV 6 167 21
fully sensible of his being less at ease than formerly. P IV 7 176 8
to be in himself a sensible, careful, discerning sort of P IV 9 205 82
your father enough to be sensible of it, though he did not P IV 9 206 90
but my sensible nurse Rooke sees the absurdity of it.-- P IV 9 208 92
And yet, he is sensible, he is agreeable, and with such a P IV 9 211 101
But, upon my word, I am scarcely sensible of his P IV 10 213 7
mind, became gradually sensible that he was inviting her P IV 11 231 12
sensible and well-judging, her first was to see Anne happy. P IV 12 249 4
her mind could well be sensible of, under circumstances of P IV 12 251 10
foot--& soon becoming sensible of it, was obliged in a few S 1 364 1

SENSIBLY (10)
& I own it would have sensibly hurt me, if my acquaintance LS 24 290 13
and I feel the goodness of Colonel Brandon most sensibly. SS III 4 285 2
for having spoken so sensibly, and observed in a half- PP I 18 101 71
on the occasion as sensibly and as warmly as a man PP III 16 366 8
and still remained so sensibly animated as to put away her MP II 1 179 9
than ever; the want of it at Mansfield more sensibly felt. MP II 3 202 25
forbearing manner, were sensibly felt; and when she MP III 2 331 17
in the visit to London, sensibly open to all the injustice P III 2 16 16
and whenever she spoke at all, it was very sensibly. P IV 11 230 5
"Aye my dear--that's very sensibly said cried Lady D--and S 7 401 1

SENSITIVE (1)
Her conscience, her sensitive conscience, would have felt SS III 11 350 7

SENT (142)
I have sent Charles to town to make matters up if he can, LS 16 268 1
colouring violently, Mama has sent for me, & I must go." LS 20 275 1
Little did I imagine my dear mother, when I sent off my LS 24 285 1
After I had sent off my letter to you, I went to Mr Vernon LS 24 285 2
I sent Wilson to say that I desired to speak with him LS 25 292 2
came, or I would have sent him away at all events; but she LS 32 302 1
for you, & if I had not sent off my letter this morning, LS 40 308 1
I tell him he is quite in luck to be sent here for his NA I 8 54 5
Told her you had sent me to say, that having just NA I 13 100 15
Maria was without ceremony sent away, and Isabella, NA I 15 117 4
under their eye, and sent therefore by return of post NA II 2 140 11
This ill-timed intruder was Miss Tilney's maid, sent by NA II 6 164 3
for her observation which sent his daughter to the bell. NA II 8 187 15
She sent you to look at it, I suppose?" NA II 9 196 21
His son was sent for, as soon as his danger was known, and SS I 1 5 5
be secure of their approbation before her answer were sent. SS I 4 24 20
The furniture was all sent round by water. SS I 5 26 4
The man and one of the maids were sent off immediately SS I 5 26 6
Lady Middleton had sent a very civil message by him, SS I 6 30 7
I do think he must have been sent for about money matters, SS I 14 70 2
May be his sister is worse at Avignon, and has sent for SS I 14 70 2
new print of merit to be sent you--and as for Marianne, I SS I 17 92 25
carriage should be sent for them and they must come. SS I 19 109 40
But if she did, the letter was written and sent away with SS II 5 167 7
The first, which was what her sister had sent him on their SS II 7 186 37
any answer to a note which I sent you above a week ago. SS II 7 187 39
40
If you had only sent him to Westminster as well as myself, SS II 14 251 13
so Mr. Donavan was sent for; and luckily he happened to be SS III 1 257 5
is told of it, for she was sent for as soon as ever my SS III 1 259 7
came out, how he had been sent for Wednesday to Harley- SS III 2 273 16
"Well, my dear," she cried, "I sent you up the young man. SS III 4 291 47
I sent no answer to Marianne, intending by that means to SS III 8 326 53
which Elinor had sent her, was led away by the exuberance SS III 9 335 7
Their man-servant had been sent one morning to Exeter on SS III 11 353 22
23
Marianne had already sent to say that she should eat SS III 11 355 45
Richards would have them sent away to the other end of the W 344 20
To find yourself, instead of heiress of 8 or 9000 L, sent W 352 26
Bingley urged Mr. Jones's being sent for immediately; PP I 8 40 59
that Mr. Jones should be sent for early in the morning, if PP I 8 40 59
requested to have a note sent to Longbourn, desiring her PP I 9 41 1
carriage might be sent for them in the course of the day. PP I 12 59 1
Mrs. Bennet sent them word that they could not possibly PP I 12 59 1
dine at Rosings, and had sent for him only the Saturday PP I 14 66 1
"I have sent for you on an affair of importance. PP I 20 111 15
Lucas himself appeared, sent by his daughter to announce PP I 23 126 1
Jane had sent Caroline an early answer to her letter, and PP I 23 128 10
After sitting a few minutes, they were all sent to one of PP II 6 162 13
The express was sent off directly. PP III 4 274 3
"John told us Mr. Darcy was here when you sent for us;-- PP III 8 280 26
his brother, therefore, he sent his permission for them to PP III 8 314 22
The carriage was sent to meet them at ----, and they were PP III 9 315 1
as soon as it was, the express was sent off to Longbourn. PP III 10 324 2
But it ended in nothing, and I will not be sent on a PP III 11 332 23
invitation could be sent; hopeless of seeing him before. PP III 11 333 30
what Mr. Bennet sent to Mr. Collins, in reply to his last. PP III 18 383 22
in her own private expences, she frequently sent them. PP III 19 387 8
its arrangement, she sent him language so very abusive, PP III 19 388 12
of Woolwich? or how could a boy be sent out to the east? MP I 1 5 2
Sir Thomas sent friendly advice and professions, Lady MP I 1 5 3
cousin William, and sent him half a guinea under the seal. MP I 2 16 20
might now and then lend them the poney he sent to the post. MP I 4 36 7
The soup would be sent round in a most spiritless manner, MP I 6 52 1
"The truth is, that our inquiries were too direct; we sent MP I 6 57 33
a small sketch of a ship sent four years ago from the MP I 16 152 2
He fancied it tough--sent away his plate--and has been MP I 18 171 27

delay, sent him after the others with delighted haste. MP II 1 176 3
Instead of being sent for out of the room, and seeing him MP II 1 180 10
The painter was sent off yesterday, and very little will MP II 2 193 13
Some members of their society sent away and the spirits of MP II 3 196 1
Fanny, having been sent into the village on some errand by MP II 4 205 3
can, and not be expecting the carriage to be sent for you. MP II 5 221 34
to Mansfield, and having sent for his hunters and written MP II 6 229 1
ship came up channel, and sent into Portsmouth, with the MP II 6 232 12
Invitations were sent with dispatch, and many a young lady MP II 8 254 8
to the ball, and when sent off with a parting worry to MP II 9 267 22
herself, she actually sent her own maid to assist her; too MP II 9 271 41
I sent Chapman to her." MP II 10 272 2
I sent Chapman to her." MP II 10 277 15
He would have sent you a description of every thing and MP II 11 288 24
his visit, unless actually sent for; and as Mrs. Norris MP III 1 311 2
and fearing to be sent for every moment; but as no MP III 1 311 3
I am very glad I sent Chapman to you. MP III 2 333 28
now, that he thought you would be sent first to the Texel. MP III 7 380 20
But you should not have taken it out, my dear, when I sent MP III 7 386 44
London; that she had sent her best and kindest love, but MP III 10 400 8
I ought to have sent you an account of your cousin's first MP III 12 416 2
Could I have sent a few happy lines, they should not have MP III 13 420 2
To be going so soon, sent for so kindly, sent for as a MP III 15 443 24
was followed by another, sent express from the same friend, MP III 16 450 9
her alarms were regularly sent off to her husband; and MP III 16 451 13
and where girls might be sent to be out of the way and E I 3 21 5
This letter, however, was written, and sealed, and sent. E I 7 55 36
I praised the fair lady too, and altogether sent him away E I 8 59 27
attention; and Emma having sent the child on, was E I 10 88 33
he had ever sent us off altogether, in such good case. E I 12 103 39
She had sent while dressing, and the answer had been, " E I 13 114 28
The hair was curled, and the maid sent away, and Emma sat E I 16 134 1
"My dear papa, I sent the whole hind-quarter. E II 3 172 18
at breakfast, and he had sent for a chaise and set off, E II 7 205 1
pianoforte that has been sent by somebody--though we have E II 8 226 79
it sent to Hartfield, and take it home with me at night. E II 9 235 40
should not at all like to have it sent to Mrs. Goddard's." E II 9 235 42
Then the baked apples came home, Mrs. Wallis sent them by E II 9 236 46
he said, was quite displeased at their being all sent away. E II 9 239 51
him, or that he may have sent only a general direction, an E II 10 241 12
This was all sent with the instrument. E II 10 242 21
Would Jane but go, means were to be found, servants sent, E II 15 285 14
Let them be sent to Donwell. E II 18 312 49
The carriage was sent for them now. E III 2 320 13
Mrs. Elton had most kindly sent Jane a note, or we should E III 2 322 19
the asparagus quite boiled enough, sent it all out again. E III 2 329 45
phrase--and to having it sent off in a letter to Maple E III 7 368 3
I had an acrostic once sent to me upon my own name, which E III 7 372 37
sent to Randall's to take Mr. Frank Churchill to Richmond. E III 8 383 29
and that Mr. Churchill had sent his nephew a few lines, E III 8 383 31
got a cold, Tom had been sent off immediately for the E III 8 383 31
without its being sent back; it was a thing she could not E III 9 391 20
answer, instead of being sent with all the many other E III 14 442 8
soon as possible, she now sent me, by a safe conveyance, E III 14 442 8
Very odd! very unaccountable! after the note I sent him E III 16 457 38
She promised Wright a receipt, and never sent it." E III 16 458 42
Isabella sent quite as good an account of her visitor as E III 17 463 16
of her own letter, which sent me the report, is passing E III 18 480 77
"You sent me such a good account of yourself on Thursday!" P III 5 37 23
what a comfortable account you sent me of yourself! P III 5 38 32
year; that he had been sent to sea, because he was stupid P III 6 50 28
a year or two,--and so I was sent off to the West Indies." P III 8 64 9
dog, who had spoilt their sport, and sent them back early. P III 10 83 6
I was at Plymouth, dreading to hear of him; he sent in P III 12 108 28
the week before; no danger of her being sent to sea again. P III 12 108 28
carriage and horses to be sent home the next morning early, P III 12 114 64
A chaise was sent for from Crewkherne, and Charles P IV 1 121 3
long-petted master Harry, sent to school after his P IV 1 121 3
No letter of condolence had been sent to Ireland. P IV 4 149 12
She was sent back, however, in a moment by the entrance of P IV 7 175 6
I sent him away with smiles. P IV 10 213 9
the boat that he has sent them off in, as long as it is in P IV 11 234 31
I sent him an account of my accident from Willingden, & S 5 385 1
Ten fees, one after another, did the man take who sent him S 6 394 1
Now, if we could get a young heiress to be sent here for S 7 401 1
coat & sent him off to the terrace, to take us lodgings.-- S 9 407 1
But my dear Miss Heywood, we are sent into this world to S 9 410 1

SENTENCE (38)

Cruel as this sentence may appear, the necessity of LS 30 301 4
than a short decisive sentence of praise or condemnation NA I 7 48 32
This was the last sentence by which he could weary NA I 10 76 29
every look and sentence as friendly as she could desire. NA I 13 102 26
something was, a short sentence of Miss Tilney's, as they NA II 8 186 6
could listen to; another sentence might have endangered NA II 14 237 20
and in the whole of the sentence, in his manner of SS I 12 59 7
over every sentence, exclaimed-----"it is too much! SS II 7 190 55
56
That sentence is very prettily turned. SS III 2 278 32
after hearing such a sentence, the Colonel should be able SS III 3 282 15
Such was the sentence which, when misunderstood, so justly SS III 3 284 24
I tried--but could not frame a sentence. SS III 8 327 55
She said little, but every sentence aimed at cheerfulness, SS III 10 342 7
there had been this sentence:--"we know nothing of our SS III 11 353 21
She then read the first sentence aloud, which comprised PP I 21 116 8
"What think you of this sentence, my dear Lizzy?-- said PP I 21 118 15
The very first sentence conveyed the assurance of their PP II 1 133 1
Elizabeth noticed every sentence conveying the idea of PP II 11 188 1
of knowing what the next sentence might bring, was PP II 13 204 1
herself so far as to examine the meaning of every sentence. PP II 13 205 3
She studied every sentence: and her feelings towards its PP II 14 212 17
they last parted, every sentence that he uttered was PP III 1 252 52
every expression, every sentence of her uncle, which PP III 1 255 59
sentence, when there was least danger of its being heard. PP III 3 267 4
and every following sentence added to its exuberance. PP III 7 305 43
Every sentence of kindness was a fresh source of happiness PP III 13 347 25
had not waited for that sentence to be thinking of Edmund, MP II 4 207 10
half a look, and half a sentence, that she had no MP II 4 215 47
just to note down any sentence pre-eminently beautiful? MP II 5 227 65
civil reception, a short sentence about being waited for, MP II 13 298 1
speak one intelligible sentence, she had introduced the MP III 16 454 18
had been inflicting deeper wounds in almost every sentence. MP III 16 457 30
it was in fact given in the formation of every sentence. E I 7 55 35
And then fly off, through half a sentence, to her mother's E II 8 225 78
Harriet seemed ready to worship her friend for a sentence E III 11 411 42
They seemed to be within half a sentence of Harriet, and E III 13 429 26
She could not immediately have uttered another sentence; P IV 11 235 33
power to send an intelligible sentence by Captain Harville. P IV 11 239 53

SENTENCES (15)

get through a few short sentences in her praise, after NA I 9 62 7
in the world, but swore off many sentences in his praise. NA I 15 121 27
few and trivial were the sentences exchanged while they NA II 13 227 27
copying such sentences as I was ashamed to put my name to. SS III 8 328 63
look at herself, and whisper a few sentences to each other. SS III 12 358 9
tried to unite civility and truth in a few short sentences. PP II 15 216 5
now and then a few half sentences of praise; but when he MP II 9 262 11
home so long again"--were most delightful sentences to her. MP III 14 431 8
which professed, in long sentences of refined nonsense, to E I 3 21 5
and sighed out his half sentences of admiration just as he E I 9 69 2
it in a few brief sentences: thus----- "your father will E I 15 128 17
18
strong attachment,--sentences begun which he could not P IV 8 185 21
quotations, & the bewilderment of some of his sentences.-- S 7 396 1
sentences from the style of our most approved writers.-- S 8 404 1
of a few broken sentences of self-approbation & success.-- S 10 416 1

SENTENTIOUS (1)

Her manner had been neither sententious nor sarcastic, but W 346 21

SENTIMENT (49)

I have subdued him entirely by sentiment & serious LS 10 258 2
This sentiment had been uttered so often in vain, that Mrs. NA I 4 31 2
dispute, but their sentiment was conveyed in such NA I 10 72 8
This charming sentiment, recommended as much by sense as NA I 15 119 19
who can tell, the sentiment once raised, but you may in NA II 7 174 8
have proceeded from a sentiment of respect for my mother's NA II 9 196 23
is such a blow upon sentiment, as no attempt at grandeur NA II 14 232 7
"I can feel no sentiment of approbation inferior to love." SS I 3 16 10
would not sacrifice one sentiment of local attachment of SS I 14 72 10
Nothing but a thorough change of sentiment could account SS II 6 178 17
seventeen, and with no sentiment superior to strong esteem SS III 14 378 15
with much sentiment, as they were sitting together.-- W 349 24
and on which there could be no difference of sentiment. PP I 18 96 56
did not invite them by any participation of sentiment.-- PP II 12 197 5
the coarseness of the sentiment was little other than her PP II 16 220 15
his regard with a deeper sentiment of gratitude than it PP III 1 251 48
change of sentiment will be neither improbable nor faulty. PP III 4 279 24
No sentiment of shame gave a damp to her triumph. PP III 8 310 7
as able to overcome a sentiment so natural as abhorrence PP III 10 326 3
or to relate her own change of sentiment towards him. PP III 11 334 36
the air, were all favourable to tenderness and sentiment. MP I 7 65 13
But with William and Fanny Price, it was still a sentiment MP II 6 235 18
had expressed the same sentiment with a little variation MP II 12 292 8
sentiment and feeling, and seriousness on serious subjects. MP III 3 340 24
but she did not deserve Edmund by any other sentiment. MP III 6 367 5
changes of opinion and sentiment, which the progress of MP III 6 374 27
They often stopt with the same sentiment and taste, MP III 11 409 7
summons came, but no sentiment dwelt long with her, that MP III 13 427 12
Where was either sentiment now? MP III 14 433 12
It was quite a different sort of thing--a sentiment E I 4 26 2
was a great deal of sentiment in his manner of naming E I 13 111 14
and his voice was the voice of sentiment as he answered. E I 13 114 30
as if he fully understood and honoured such a sentiment. E II 6 201 25
the sentiment, Emma was convinced that it had been so. E II 12 260 23
happy months there!(with a little sigh of sentiment). E II 14 273 19
Emma doubted the truth of this sentiment. E II 14 273 22
with the same warmth of sentiment which he had taken away, E III 1 315 1
any of that heroism of sentiment which might have prompted E III 13 431 38
the same period, one sentiment having probably enlightened E III 13 432 41
sentiment having probably enlightened him as to the other. E III 13 432 41
it in the voice, or the turn of sentiment and expression. P III 6 48 17
than tenderness and sentiment; and while the agitations of P III 8 68 29
It was a remainder of former sentiment; it was an impulse P III 10 91 42
already recanting the sentiment she had so lately P IV 2 135 35
He is totally beyond the reach of any sentiment of justice P IV 9 199 53
I have now, as far as such a sentiment is allowable in P IV 11 246 80
with an air of deep sentiment)--nor can any woman be a S 7 398 1
Certainly, there was no strain of doubtful sentiment, nor S 7 399 1
This glorious sentiment seemed quite to remove suspicion. S 7 400 1

SENTIMENTAL (4)

They were always engaged in some sentimental discussion or NA I 10 72 8
of literary taste, and sentimental reflection, was amusing, P IV 6 167 20
He seemed very sentimental, very full of some feelings or S 7 398 1
spot had read more sentimental novels than agreed with him. S 8 404 1

SENTIMENTALLY (2)

Elton may talk sentimentally, but he will act rationally. E I 8 66 53
recalled, and rather sentimentally recited, that well- E I 9 70 7

SENTIMENTS (55)

I will not disguise my sentiments on this change from you LS 8 254 1
I honestly tell you my sentiments & intentions. LS 12 261 4
I have now my dear sir, written my real sentiments of Lady LS 14 265 6
be her real sentiments, said nothing in opposition to mine. LS 22 280 1
to occasion so extraordinary a change in your sentiments. LS 35 304 1
nice in their dress, in their sentiments, or their choice. NA I 14 108 16
and disinterested sentiments on the subject of money, NA II 11 208 1
once do justice to her sentiments and her situation, NA II 14 235 14
him, have studied his sentiments and heard his opinion on SS I 4 20 9
doubtful; and till his sentiments are fully known, you SS I 4 21 15
Another meeting will suffice to explain his sentiments on SS I 10 47 4
to believe that the sentiments which Mrs. Jennings had SS I 10 49 12
aim at the restraint of sentiments which were not in SS I 11 53 2
a total change of sentiments--no, no, do not desire it,-- SS I 11 56 17
you to adopt their sentiments or conform to their judgment SS I 17 94 39
by an easy and frank communication of her sentiments. SS I 22 127 1
If your sentiments are no longer what they were, you will SS II 7 188 42
unanimous in their sentiments on the present occasion, as SS III 1 269 57
I had hoped that our sentiments coincided in every PP I 7 29 11
sentiments avowed, however unequally they may be returned. PP II 11 189 6
7
any repetition of those sentiments, or renewal of those PP II 12 196 4
that, regardless of the sentiments of either, I had PP II 12 196 5
But whatever may be the sentiments which Mr. Wickham has PP II 12 200 5
have delivered his sentiments in a manner so little suited PP II 17 224 2
this place, that I might make my sentiments known to you." PP III 14 353 26
You know my sentiments." PP III 14 358 66
to understand, that her sentiments had undergone so PP III 16 366 8
than he remained in any doubt of your sister's sentiments. PP III 16 371 45
Her sentiments towards him were compounded of all that was MP I 4 37 8
to find our sentiments on this subject so much the same. MP II 1 186 34
leave to learn his sentiments merely through his conduct. MP II 2 187 3
I know what her sentiments have always been. MP III 1 313 12
misconception of your sentiments, which, unfortunately for MP III 1 320 44
expressing the same sentiments himself, and he tried to MP III 1 323 57
anxious to know her sentiments--but I had not been in the MP III 4 351 36
be conjectured of her sentiments, and he was satisfied.-- MP III 5 356 1
the sentiments and expressions which were torturing me. MP III 13 421 2
that his daughter's sentiments had been sufficiently known MP III 17 461 4
and unaffected, and the sentiments it conveyed very much E I 7 50 4
Vigorous, decided, with sentiments to a certain point, not E I 7 51 5
opportunity, declaring sentiments which must be already E I 15 129 24
any danger of betraying sentiments or increasing them. E I 17 142 11
the material part, its sentiments, she yet found, when it E II 13 266 6
sitting in judgment on sentiments and words that were E III 10 399 61
prevented the indulgence and increase of such sentiments. E III 11 402 1
Such were Elizabeth elliot's sentiments and sensations; P III 1 9 18
acquainted with her sentiments than you can be, I can P III 5 35 14
Now, how were his sentiments to be read? P III 7 60 30
thoroughly into her sentiments, and was most happy to P IV 5 153 5
answer for the true sentiments of a clever, cautious man, P IV 5 161 27
situations, would he ever learn her real sentiments? P IV 8 191 51
by his own sentiments, by his early prepossession. P IV 9 192 2
mildness, or the sound of his artificial good sentiments. P IV 10 214 11
at last by those sentiments and those tones which had P IV 11 241 60
if her sentiments for him were what the Harvilles supposed. P IV 11 243 66

SENTINEL (1)

the sentinel on guard, and dressing a sallad and cucumber. PP II 16 219 1

SEPARATE (32)

"I have never yet known what it was to separate esteem and SS I 3 16 12
To separate Edward and Elinor was as far from being her SS I 5 25 3
and when obliged to separate for a couple of dances, were SS I 11 54 3
they might most easily separate themselves from the others; SS II 1 142 8
"And what arts did he use to separate them?" PP II 10 185 31
in the measures taken to separate Mr. Bingley and Jane, PP II 10 186 38
thing in my power to separate my friend from your sister, PP II 11 191 15
affect his endeavour to separate him from Miss Bennet, it PP III 3 270 10
their separate apartments, to make their appearance before. PP III 5 289 41
Lady Catherine's unjustifiable endeavours to separate us, PP III 18 381 14

in committee at a separate table, with the play open MP I 15 142 25
interest, cooled by no separate attachment, and feeling MP II 6 235 18
in spite of its separate lawn and shrubberies and name, E I 1 7 10
Harriet submitted, though her mind could hardly separate E I 9 77 43
the girls were going to separate in preparation for the E I 9 81 78
Anxious to separate herself from them as far as she could, E I 10 88 33
"I cannot separate Miss Fairfax and her complexion." E II 6 199 12
that, though he had his separate engagements, it was not E II 8 221 48
Here is quite a separate puzzle." E II 15 285 15
be set out with their separate candles and unbroken packs E II 16 290 3
Nothing should separate her from her father. E III 12 416 1
the full weight of their separate claims; and how to guard E III 14 434 4
increased the desirableness of their being separate.-- E III 16 451 2
obliged to separate before the end of the first quarter. E III 17 469 36
than she found in the separate, but very similar remark of P III 6 42 1
him, nothing should ever separate us, and I would rather P III 10 85 9
Materials were all at hand, on a separate table; he went P IV 11 229 4
"Yes," said he, "very true; here we separate, but Harville P IV 11 236 38
to form a separate establishment--you will find it at full S 1 366 1
than are often met with, either separate or together.-- S 5 385 1
library--but she cd not separate the idea of a complete S 6 391 1
am not poetic enough to separate a man's poetry entirely S 7 397 1

SEPARATED (17)
It must be to her advantage to be separated from her LS 3 247 1
Can it be true that they are really separated--& for ever? LS 41 309 1
I did we should certainly be separated the whole evening." NA I 8 52 2
She was separated from all her party, and away from all NA I 8 55 10
convinced that they were separated for ever, and spurning NA II 15 246 12
many weeks we had been separated, she was as constant in SS III 8 325 53
to keep out of your sight, could have separated us so long. SS III 8 326 55
her think of him as now separated for ever from her family SS III 9 333 2
"The garden in which stands my humble abode, is separated PP I 14 67 3
They had not long separated when Miss Bingley came towards PP I 18 94 44 45
Before they were separated by the conclusion of the play, PP II 4 154 21
though almost totally separated from her family, was MP I 2 21 34
worth reading, to his sisters, when they are separated. MP I 7 64 10
They must be separated; but there was a great deal of pain E II 5 187 4
They separated too much into parties. E III 7 367 1
but it contained, when separated from all the feebleness E III 11 409 34
The party separated. P IV 10 227 68

SEPARATELY (4)
and pleasures have been separately stated, and the pangs NA I 13 97 1
"but of her society, separately from that of other people, SS II 3 156 13
the morning, sometimes separately, sometimes together, and PP II 9 180 28
and Edmund had been separately conniving at, as each MP II 6 233 15

SEPARATES (1)
weeks, and when accident separates them, so easily forgets PP II 2 140 6

SEPARATING (5)
way be instrumental in separating a family so LS 25 293 3
a similar position, and separating themselves from the NA I 10 71 8
brother, in the hope of separating them for ever, she NA II 1 132 16
When the ladies were separating for the toilette, he said PP II 6 160 5 6
of separating allowed her the relief of quiet reflection. E I 15 133 38

SEPARATION (46)
as I am on the point of separation from my own daughter. LS 1 244 1
this dreadful separation from you & all whom I love. LS 7 254 3
fear the separation takes place too late to do us any good. LS 27 296 1
by urging a lengthened separation; & of insensibility to LS 30 301 4
necessity of an immediate & eternal separation from you. LS 34 304 1
some of the parties & separation between the others, could LS 42 311 1
from this terrific separation must oppress her heart with NA I 2 18 2
which the first separation of a heroine from her family NA I 2 19 3
This seemed the word of separation, and Catherine found NA II 5 162 27
find how much her spirits were relieved by the separation. NA II 7 179 29
"My love, it will be scarcely a separation. SS I 3 17 17
But whatever might be the particulars of their separation, SS I 15 77 20
me, and our continual separation, I was enough inclined SS II 2 147 12
that would accrue to them all, from this separation. SS II 3 155 7
to consider the separation as any thing short of eternal. SS II 3 158 21
of Marianne in a final separation from Willoughby--in an SS II 6 179 18
and confirm their separation for ever, she was not aware SS II 7 183 14
the pleasure which our separation naturally produced, with SS II 7 187 42
The day of separation and departure arrived; and Marianne, SS III 10 341 5
On Sunday, after morning service, the separation, so PP I 12 60 5
she had been doing with herself since their separation. PP I 17 86 9
may lessen the pain of separation by a very frequent and PP I 21 116 8
The pain of separation, however, might be alleviated on PP II 2 139 1
depravity, to which the separation of two young persons, PP II 12 196 5
The separation between her and her family was rather noisy PP II 18 235 40
forced to submit to a separation, which, as her husband by PP III 11 330 2
in those hours of separation that must sometimes occur. PP III 13 349 44
and the separation from every body she had been used to. MP I 2 14 6
gradually admit that the separation might have some use. MP I 2 21 34
family, after such a separation, made him communicative MP II 1 178 8
hope of advantage from separation--her mind became cool MP II 3 201 24
tightened for the moment by the very idea of separation. MP III 4 347 21
voluntarily to say of her concern at this separation. MP III 6 366 3
heal every pain that had since grown out of the separation. MP III 6 370 11
and because he could not endure a longer total separation. MP III 10 406 21
was a sort of renewed separation from Mansfield; and she MP III 11 413 31
been before the last separation--whether if lessened it MP III 12 417 4
other's punishment, and then induce a voluntary separation. MP III 17 464 10
was for a partial separation from friends, whose E I 2 18 10
If a separation of two months should not have cooled him, E III 1 315 1
seemed a principle of separation, between the other E III 7 367 1
every thing was due; a separation for the present; an E III 14 435 4
"There is nothing so bad as a separation. P III 8 71 55
loved, feeling her separation from home, and suffering as P IV 5 152 2
her more from other men, than their final separation. P IV 9 192 2
Six years of separation and suffering might have been P IV 11 247 84

SEPARATIONS (3)
"is the only comfort we have in such long separations. SS I 22 135 54
and no friend to early separations of any sort; but at E I 15 124 1
separations necessary, to keep with her brother and sister. P III 10 84 7

SEPT. 6 (1)
"Gracechurch-Street, Sept. 6. PP III 10 321 2

SEPTEMBER (21)
It was very early in September; the season was fine, and SS I 6 28 2
She was as handsome a girl last September, as any I ever SS II 11 227 50
the first of September, than any body else in the country. PP III 9 318 20
He would be at home in September, and where would be the MP I 4 37 7
where would be the harm of only waiting till September? MP I 4 37 7
Sir Thomas's return in September, for when September came, MP I 4 37 9
in September, for when September came, Sir Thomas was MP I 4 37 9
week with a friend last September--just after my return MP I 5 51 40
take his passage in the September packet, and he MP I 11 107 2
The approach of September brought tidings of Mr. Bertram MP I 12 114 1
could not do without him in the beginning of September. MP I 12 114 3
particular kindness last September twelvemonth in writing E I 11 95 19
Mr. Weston, "ever since September: every letter has been E I 14 119 9
he would have contrived it between September and January. E I 18 145 10
In that very room she had been measured last September, E II 5 187 4
Before the end of September, Emma attended Harriet to E III 19 482 6
the possible heats of September in all the white glare of P III 5 33 6
She could not think of much else on the 29th of September; P III 6 48 16
since her quitting Lady Russell's house, in September. P IV 1 123 9
Walter as long ago as September, (in short when they first P IV 9 206 88
It was but July however, & August & September were the S 6 389 1

SEQUEL (4)
over the dreadful sequel of this event, which Elizabeth PP III 5 290 45
been safe; none of this dreadful sequel would have been. E III 11 413 49
grew older--the natural sequel of an unnatural beginning. P III 4 30 9
The sequel explained it. P IV 10 226 64

SEQUESTRATION (1)
years under a sort of sequestration for the payment of its P IV 9 210 98

SERENITY (8)
"Yes, my dear," replied Mrs. Allen, with perfect serenity, NA I 2 22 13
The first circumstance to break in on this serenity, was W 348 23
proceeding from the serenity of a mind at ease with itself, PP II 11 188 1
But I shall not scruple to assert, that the serenity of PP II 12 197 5
Mrs. Bennet was restored to her usual querulous serenity, PP II 19 238 6
was as pleasant as the serenity of nature could make it; MP I 10 106 58
Maria looked all serenity and satisfaction, and Julia well MP I 14 135 18
She longed for the serenity they might gradually introduce; E III 13 424 1

SERIES (9)
inforced change--from a series of unfortunate SS I 11 57 17
At this time of year, and after such a series of rain, we SS II 5 167 3
autumn, nothing but a series of imprudence towards myself, SS III 10 345 28
a partner only through a series of inquiry, and bustle, MP II 10 274 8
within doors by a series of rain and snow, with nothing to MP II 11 286 15
sanguine hope, after a series of what had appeared to him E II 4 181 3
such a series of dissipation for me, I cannot imagine. E II 18 312 50
It was through a series of strange blunders!" E III 2 331 54
This was the conclusion of the first series of reflection. E III 11 412 46

SERIOUS (155)
she has anything more serious in veiw, but it mortifies me LS 8 256 4
I cannot easily resolve on anything so serious as marriage, LS 10 257 1
I have subdued him entirely by sentiment & serious LS 10 258 2
is one so much more serious, that the difference of even LS 12 260 2
I have reason to imagine that she did receive serious LS 14 265 4
the subject be ever so serious that he may be conversing LS 18 272 1
But I have little heart to jest; in truth, I am serious LS 35 305 1
Be more serious." NA I 14 114 46
"We shall get nothing more serious from him now, Miss NA I 14 114 48
object must occasion so serious a delay of proper repose. NA II 8 187 16
upon serious consideration, to be not perfectly amiable. NA II 10 200 3
had been the only cause of giving her a serious thought. NA II 15 243 9
An annuity is a very serious business; it comes over and SS I 2 10 20
than she considered their serious attachment as certain, SS I 3 17 14
His manners, though serious, were mild; and his reserve SS I 10 50 12
as to leave them little leisure for serious employment. SS I 11 53 1
One moment she feared that no serious design had ever been SS I 15 77 19
the room was such as a serious quarrel could most SS I 15 77 19
or conform to their judgment in serious matters?" SS I 17 94 39
"They will be brought up," said he, in a serious accent, " SS I 19 103 6
I confess, at so serious an inquiry into her character." SS I 22 128 10
was impossible for her on serious reflection to suspect it SS II 1 139001
the necessity of some serious inquiry into the affair. SS II 4 165 30
I thought it had been only a joke, but so serious a SS II 7 182 9
the whole evening more serious and thoughtful than usual. SS II 8 200 43
Norland Common, now carrying on, is a most serious drain. SS II 11 225 31
her figure, and serious, even to sourness, in her aspect. SS II 12 232 14
who came with a most serious aspect to talk over the SS III 1 265 33
head, gave her a look so serious, so earnest, so SS III 4 290 39
moment--"but upon my soul, it is a most serious business. SS III 5 298 35
Marianne's complaint more serious than Elinor, now looked SS III 7 307 3
"I mean"--said he, with serious energy--"if I can, to make SS III 8 319 23
result as she trusted of serious reflection, must SS III 10 341 6
and am determined to enter on a course of serious study. SS III 10 343 9
It has given me leisure and calmness for serious SS III 10 345 28
but he is a great flirt & never means anything serious." W 315 1
he never means anything serious, & when he had trifled W 317 2
"Nay, if you are so serious about it, I shall consider the PP I 6 27 53
you really serious in meditating a dance at Netherfield?-- PP I 11 55 5 6
a serious stamp, though written solely for their benefit. PP I 14 69 15 16
a serious dispute must be the consequence of any reply. PP I 17 88 14
were directed with a very serious expression towards PP I 18 92 24
I am perfectly serious in my refusal.-- PP I 19 107 14
conclude that you are not serious in your rejection of me, PP I 19 108 19
"My dear aunt, this is being serious indeed." PP II 3 144 2
"Yes, and I hope to engage you to be serious likewise." PP II 3 144 4
"Elizabeth, you are not serious now." PP II 3 144 6
that had long prevented my forming any serious design. PP II 11 192 22
had any apprehension of his feeling a serious attachment.-- PP II 12 197 5
and more serious tone, "that he is improved in essentials." PP II 18 234 33
of a most unexpected and serious nature; but I am afraid PP III 4 273 3
relations, with only one serious, parting, look, went away. PP III 4 278 22
town; "and really, upon serious consideration, I am much PP III 5 282 1
been taught to think on serious subjects; and for the last PP III 5 283 10
But at least it shews, that <u>she</u> was serious in the object PP III 5 292 61
Kitty, who took all these threats in a serious light, PP III 6 300 31
I talked to her repeatedly in the most serious manner, PP III 10 325 2
He looked serious as usual; and she thought, more as he PP III 11 335 40
"My dearest sister, now <u>be</u> be serious. PP III 17 373 15
Another intreaty that she would be serious, however, PP III 17 373 17
or had you intended any more serious consequence?" PP III 18 381 15
He debated and hesitated;--it was a serious charge;--a MP I 1 6 5
as a matter of very serious moment; but as it is, I hope MP I 1 10 14
mirth, and moments of serious conference, may be imagined; MP I 2 21 34
lively mind can hardly be serious even on serious subjects. MP I 9 87 16
replied Edmund with a serious smile, and glancing at the MP I 11 108 11
He has no faults but what a serious attachment would MP I 12 116 8
"You are not serious, Tom, in meaning to act?" said Edmund MP I 13 125 15
"Not serious! never more so, I assure you. MP I 13 125 16
nor Julia had ever had a serious thought of each other, MP I 17 161 9
She hailed it as an earnest of the most serious MP II 1 176 3
of your acting having assumed so serious a character. MP II 1 184 25
And it does not appear to me that we are more serious than MP II 3 196 3
November is a still more serious month, and I can see that MP II 3 199 15
which, to Fanny's eye, had a great deal of serious meaning. MP II 4 213 37
No, Miss Crawford," he added, in a more serious tone, " MP II 4 214 45
It was plain that he could have so serious views, no true MP II 5 228 69
of such a serious character as to make the ball, which MP II 8 254 10
to the excitement or expression of serious feelings. MP II 8 256 13
She is not serious. MP II 9 268 29
I think, I hope, I am sure she is not serious--but I would MP II 9 268 29
I have almost given up every serious idea of her; but I MP II 9 270 38
in a flutter that forbad its fixing on any thing serious. MP II 10 275 10
her, and then looked too serious and said too decidedly--" MP II 10 275 11
too little accustomed to serious reflection to know them MP II 12 294 16
knowing how to suppose him serious, she could hardly stand. MP II 13 301 7
She would not have him be serious, and yet what could MP II 13 302 10
attachment and even to <u>appear</u> to believe it serious. MP II 13 304 16
There was wretchedness <u>in the</u> idea of its being serious; MP II 13 304 16
<u>against</u> their being serious, but his words and manner. MP II 13 305 26
<u>How could she</u> have excited serious attachment in a man, MP II 13 305 26
seemed so <u>little</u> open to serious impressions, even where MP II 13 306 26
any thing of a serious nature in such a quarter? MP II 13 306 26
Every thing might be possible rather than serious MP II 13 306 26
serious attachment or serious approbation of it toward her. MP III 3 340 24
sentiment and feeling, and seriousness on serious subjects. MP III 4 348 23
He is lively, you are serious; but so much the better; his MP III 4 350 31
that he does not think as he ought, on serious subjects." MP III 4 350 32
"Say rather, that he has not thought at all upon serious MP III 5 362 21
as from wishing him to have any serious thoughts of me. MP III 9 394 1
but I do not know that he has any serious encouragement. MP III 11 411 18
"I am perfectly serious,"--he replied,--"as you perfectly MP III 16 454 18
She had met him, he said, with a serious--certainty a MP III 16 454 18
a serious--certainty a serious--even an agitated air; but MP III 16 454 18
that there would be no serious difficulty on Harriet's E I 4 31 26

should not be hesitating--it is a very serious thing.-- E I 7 52 20
"A very serious sort, I assure you;" still smiling. E I 8 59 22
"Very serious! E I 8 59 23
and allusions had been dropt, but nothing serious. E I 10 90 39
Accordingly, with a mixture of the serious and the playful, E I 15 129 24
25
ought to be serious, a trick of what ought to be simple. E I 16 137 10
and then resumed a more serious, more dispiriting E I 16 137 12
Mr. Frank Churchill still declined it, looking as serious E II 5 195 48
of something absolutely serious, which she did not wish. E II 12 260 30
and in Bath, it would have been a most serious sacrifice. E II 14 276 36
things, of course, without any idea of a serious meaning. E II 15 288 35
"Ah! you are not serious now. E II 16 293 22
equal; however, I am very serious in not wishing any thing E II 17 301 19
serious in wishing nothing to be done till the summer. E II 17 301 19
"And I am quite serious too, I assure you," replied Mrs. E II 17 302 20
full eighteen to Manchester-Street--was a serious obstacle. E III 1 318 10
"Not your vain spirit, but your serious spirit.-- E III 2 330 53
Harriet say in a very serious tone, "I shall never marry." E III 4 340 28
and obstacles of a very serious nature; but yet, Harriet, E III 4 342 39
I am serious, Miss Woodhouse, whatever your penetrating E III 6 365 62
You are not serious? E III 10 395 34
one or two such very serious points to consider, as made E III 14 434 4
which left her so very serious, so nearly sad, that Mr. E III 14 435 5
therefore, of very serious inconvenience that I should E III 16 458 43
she, with a sort of serious smile--"much less, perhaps, E III 17 464 22
the whole, there was no serious objection raised, except E III 17 468 36
Serious she was, very serious in her thankfulness, and in E III 18 475 40
High in the rank of her most serious and heartfelt E III 18 475 42
speak with serious feeling of his gratitude and happiness. E III 18 476 49
on the subject, and gave it much serious consideration. P III 2 11 2
We must be serious and decided--for, after all, the person P III 2 12 4
that results the most serious to his family from the P III 5 34 12
serious anxiety which they afterwards felt on his account. P III 7 53 2
"Are you serious?" cried Mary, her eyes brightening. P III 7 57 16
perfectly collected and serious; and almost instantly P III 8 67 28
spoken with such serious warmth!--she could imagine what P III 10 88 27
feelings with quiet, serious, and retiring manners, and a P III 11 97 12
she help fearing, on more serious reflection, that, like P III 11 101 26
Elliot" (looking with serious reflection) "I should think P IV 1 127 28
one; her judgment, on a serious consideration of the P IV 5 160 26
at least, careless on all serious matters; and, though he P IV 5 161 27
with an expression half serious, half arch, "well, I P IV 7 180 35
the same style; he, half serious and half jesting, P IV 10 224 50
play; and she, invariably serious, most warmly opposing it, P IV 10 224 50
countenance reassumed the serious, thoughtful expression P IV 11 232 12
An interval of meditation, serious and grateful, was the P IV 11 245 77
feeling could excite any serious anxiety, was Lady Russell. P IV 12 249 3
P.'s sprain proving too serious for him to move sooner.-- S 2 370 1
& are subject to a variety of very serious disorders.-- S 5 385 1
serious designs; it was clara whom he meant to seduce.-- S 8 405 2

SERIOUSLY (69)
an alarm which might seriously affect his health & spirits. LS 8 254 1
Nay, I cannot blame you--(speaking more seriously)--your NA I 6 41 16
"Shall you indeed!" said Catherine very seriously, "that NA I 7 48 28
Catherine would not seriously refuse such a trifling NA I 13 98 2
resolved never to think so seriously on the subject again. NA II 4 153 30
"Oh! not seriously!" NA II 11 211 10
Her intimacy there had made him seriously determine on her NA II 15 245 12
expect in the man who could seriously attach my sister. SS I 3 17 18
"Indeed, ma'am," said Elinor, very seriously, "you are SS II 7 182 11
effect; but had I not seriously, and from my heart SS II 9 210 32
Elinor tried very seriously to convince him that there was SS II 11 228 51
"not so, indeed; for, seriously speaking, I am very sure SS II 13 243 39
40
She began, however, seriously to turn her thoughts towards SS III 3 279 1
"I know it is"--replied her mother seriously, "or after SS III 9 337 16
Musgrave's being more seriously in love with her, than he W 319 2
himself, while his wife seriously commended Mr. Collins PP I 18 101 71
But, my dearest Jane, you cannot seriously imagine that PP I 21 119 20
what she saw, to be very seriously in love, their PP II 2 142 18
Seriously, I would have you be on your guard. PP II 3 144 2
advantage to Jane, she seriously hoped he might really PP II 3 149 27
She had not at first thought very seriously of going PP II 4 151 1
Eliza, she sat herself seriously to work to find it out.-- PP II 9 180 29
Now, seriously, what have you ever known of self-denial PP II 10 183 11
He was seriously concerned, that a cause of so little PP III 8 308 2
Seriously, however, she felt tolerably persuaded that all PP III 13 346 20
I am most seriously displeased." PP III 14 358 73
Elizabeth again, and more seriously assured her of its PP III 17 373 8
I want to talk very seriously. PP III 17 373 15
Sure Sir Thomas could not seriously expect such a thing! MP I 3 28 42
therefore, she did not forget to think of it seriously. MP I 4 42 18
of riding, and very seriously resolved, however unwilling MP I 7 74 58
"You take up a thing so seriously! as if we were going to MP I 13 125 18
we will talk to him seriously, and make him know his own MP I 17 162 18
and only added more seriously, "your uncle is disposed to MP II 3 198 9
Sir Thomas resolved to speak seriously to her. MP II 3 200 20
improved, so polite, so seriously and blamelessly polite, MP II 6 232 11
"Well then," replied Miss Crawford more seriously but MP II 8 259 22
speaking low and seriously, "you know what all this means. MP II 9 268 31
was now growing seriously near, and she so little MP II 10 274 8
When did you begin to think seriously about her?" MP II 12 292 7
of his meaning any thing seriously, but I did not like to MP III 1 315 19
other, as he was now beginning seriously to consider them. MP III 3 335 6
And I do seriously and truly believe that he is attached MP III 5 363 24
They were all very seriously frightened. MP III 13 427 13
resolved on being seriously accepted as soon as possible. E I 15 129 24
You cannot really, seriously, doubt it. E I 15 131 31
Smith?--that you have never thought seriously of her?" E I 15 131 34
I think seriously of Miss Smith?--Miss Smith is a very E I 15 131 35
He protested that he had never thought seriously of E I 16 134 3
And, seriously, Miss Fairfax is naturally so pale, as E II 6 199 9
Five couple are nothing, when one thinks seriously about E II 11 248 8
If Mr. Knightley did not begin seriously, he was obliged E III 6 354 9
Emma seriously hoped she would. E III 8 378 7
She had never been admitted before to be seriously ill. E III 9 387 12
"Upon my honour," said he very seriously, "it does not. E III 10 393 15
Can you seriously ask me, Harriet, whether I imagined him E III 11 404 11
happy now," said Emma, seriously, "which, in spite of E III 12 420 13
concluding, however, seriously, and, after steady E III 15 445 14
15
very good notions, very seriously good principles, and E III 18 474 34
his head, and whispering seriously) that my uncle means to E III 18 479 70
of female alarm, set seriously to think what could be done, P III 1 9 19
seriously described the woman he should wish to meet with. P III 7 62 40
I assure you;" replied Captain Wentworth, seriously.-- P III 8 65 13
Elliot?" and could not seriously picture to herself a more P IV 4 146 6
who forget to think seriously till it is almost too late." P IV 5 156 11
At nineteen, you know, one does not think very seriously, P IV 9 199 55
I had not thought seriously on this subject before. P IV 11 242 65
Seriously, a very indifferent account.-- S 5 386 1
She spoke this so seriously that Charlotte instantly saw S 7 401 1

SERIOUSNESS (5)
something in it's mild seriousness, as well as in the W 346 21
seriousness, "she is too good for him--much too good." MP II 5 224 53
sentiment and feeling, and seriousness on serious subjects. MP III 3 340 24
There was a seriousness in Harriet's manner which prepared E III 4 337 3
a trick, nothing that called for seriousness on my side. E III 13 427 19

SERLE (3)
Serle understands boiling an egg better than any body. E I 3 24 14
thoroughly boiled, just as Serle boils our's, and eaten E II 3 172 19
sit up for her; and that Serle and the butler should see E II 7 211 22

SERMON (10)
sermon, she could not help listening with a quicker ear.-- W 343 20
and talking away just as if she was reading a sermon. PP III 9 319 24
menus plaisirs; and a sermon at Christmas and Easter, I MP II 5 226 61
coming to Mansfield to hear you preach your first sermon. MP II 5 227 65
lessons than a weekly sermon can convey, and that if he MP II 7 248 42
"A sermon, well delivered, is more uncommon even than MP III 3 341 28
A sermon, good in itself, is no rare thing. MP III 3 341 28
A thoroughly good sermon, thoroughly well delivered, is a MP III 3 341 28
hearing an affecting sermon, had cried herself to sleep-- MP III 16 453 17
Was it part of your last sermon? MP III 16 458 30

SERMON-MAKING (1)
there was a time, when sermon-making was not so palatable PP III 10 329 31

SERMONS (9)
and after some deliberation he chose Fordyce's sermons. PP I 14 68 13
He must write his own sermons; and the time that remains PP I 18 101 71
"How should you have liked making sermons?" PP III 10 328 27
How can two sermons a week, even supposing them worth MP I 9 92 46
and often preaches good sermons, and is very respectable, MP I 11 111 28
and preach such very good sermons in so good a manner as MP I 11 112 30
depends upon his own sermons; for though he may preach MP I 11 112 31
affectionately, "must be beyond the reach of any sermons." MP I 11 112 32
It was time to have done with cards if sermons prevailed, MP II 7 248 48

SERPENTINE (1)
We have taken such a very serpentine course; and the wood MP I 9 94 62

SERVANT (78)
wormed out of Manwaring's servant that he had visited you LS 32 302 1
on his haunches, and the servant having now scampered up, NA I 7 44 3
the servant had just mounted the carriage and was driving NA I 7 46 9
door, in the first only a servant, her brother driving NA I 9 61 1
Every thing being then arranged, the servant who stood at NA I 9 62 10
In a few minutes the servant returned, and with a look NA I 12 91 3
view of them; and the servant still remaining at the open NA I 13 102 25
I would not stay for the servant." NA I 13 102 25
was quite angry with the servant whose neglect had reduced NA I 13 102 27
old servant frightening one by coming in with a faggot! NA II 6 167 9
by the negligence of a servant in the place whence she had NA II 7 172 2
To be found there, even by a servant, would be unpleasant; NA II 9 194 6
was introduced by his servant, the General was shortly NA II 11 213 20
The General will send a servant with me, I dare say, half NA II 13 224 17
here at seven o'clock, and no servant will be offered you." NA II 13 224 18
gentleman whose negligent servant left behind him that NA II 16 251 5
must buy another for the servant, and keep a servant to SS I 12 58 1
the servant, and keep a servant to ride it, and after all, SS I 12 58 1
As to an additional servant, the expence would be a trifle; SS I 12 58 3
Willoughby's curricle and servant in waiting at the SS I 15 75 2
He dismounted, and giving his horse to his servant, walked SS I 16 86 22
"Are you certain that no servant, no porter has left any SS II 4 165 26
if I had not, when the servant let me in to-day, SS II 5 173 44
eagerly caught from the servant, and, turning of a death- SS II 7 181 7
I am, dear madam, your most obedient humble servant, John SS II 7 183 13
Regard for a former servant of my own, who had since SS II 9 207 26
of Mrs. Jennings's servant, who came to tell her that his SS II 11 222 12
they all followed the servant at the same time--"there is SS II 12 231 13
and their mother's servant might easily come there to SS III 3 280 6
the whole way by a servant of Mrs. Jennings, were to have SS III 7 308 4
he went to hurry off his servant with a message to Mr. SS III 7 311 15
former security; and the servant who sat up with her, for SS III 7 312 17
I heard it from the servant. SS III 8 318 10
The servant, who saw only that Miss Marianne was taken ill, SS III 11 353 25
seeing her mother's servant, on hearing Lucy's message! SS III 12 357 2
from Netherfield, and the servant waited for an answer. PP I 7 30 14
Breakfast was scarcely over when a servant from PP I 7 31 29
30
Elizabeth most thankfully consented, and a servant was PP I 7 34 45
"Mrs. Collins, you must send a servant with them. PP II 14 211 13
"My uncle is to send a servant for us." PP II 14 212 14
more valuable than the praise of an intelligent servant? PP III 1 250 48
that in the eye of a servant comprehends every virtue." PP III 1 258 74
that the authority of a servant who had known him since he PP III 2 264 14
door, it was opened by a servant, and Mr. Darcy appeared. PP III 4 276 6
let me, or let the servant, go after Mr. and Mrs. Gardiner. PP III 4 276 7
Calling back the servant, therefore, she commissioned him, PP III 4 276 8
"Oh! Jane," cried Elizabeth, "was there a servant PP III 5 292 63
of her sister, as the servant was approaching the door. PP III 11 335 39
on; so easy, that every servant will cheat you; and so PP III 13 348 38
of the servant who preceded it, were familiar to them. PP III 14 351 1
too direct; we sent a servant, we went ourselves: this MP I 6 57 33
always arisen, and more than one bad servant been detected. MP II 2 188 3
A civil servant she had withstood; but when Dr. Grant MP II 4 205 3
quietly taking from the servant to bring and put round her MP II 7 251 66
waited for, and a "let Sir Thomas know," to the servant. MP II 13 298 1
to a servant in his way towards the room they were in. MP II 13 302 9
previously seen the upper servant, brought in every thing MP III 7 383 32
The servant of Mrs. Rushworth, the mother, had exposure in MP III 16 450 10
herself in the power of a servant;--it was the detection MP III 16 455 19
she will make a very good servant; she is a civil, pretty- E I 1 9 19
I am sure she will be an excellent servant; and it will be E I 1 9 19
for going in;--no servant that I want to inquire about of E I 10 83 7
to an old servant who was married, and settled in Donwell. E II 5 186 2
an arrangement, so needlessly troublesome to your servant. E II 16 296 37
Let my father's servant go with you.-- E III 6 362 47
near the two inns as they came back, should be his servant. P III 12 104 7
It was driven by a servant in mourning." P III 12 105 8
it with his own, the servant in mourning roused Anne's P III 12 105 9
servant say whether he belonged to the Kellynch family?" P III 12 106 14
the livery too; if the servant had not been in mourning, P III 12 106 16
of a servant, and of course almost excluded from society. P IV 5 152 4
which there was only one servant in the house to afford, P IV 5 154 8
impatient, now drew up; the servant came in to announce it. P IV 7 176 10
unattended but by the servant, (for there was no cousin P IV 7 176 10
to the servant as they entered, to bring tea directly. S 6 391 1
the lawn;--and when the servant appeared, they were just S 9 406 1
the entrance of the servant with the tea things, as a very S 10 416 1
Mr Sidney Parker driving his servant in a very neat S 12 425 1

SERVANT'S (6)
her brother's, nor the servant's; she would believe no NA I 9 67 33
being thrown open, the servant's announcing Mr. Ferrars, SS II 13 240 18
They were interrupted by the servant's coming in to SS III 4 286 10
11
Mrs. Dashwood, whose eyes, as she answered the servant's SS III 11 353 24
own feelings, and his servant's report, without any PP III 2 264 14
alarm, supposing, by the servant's account, that their PP III 4 280 26

SERVANTS (68)
to the care of servants or a governess very little better, LS 6 251 1
be confusion, for it is impossible to be sure of servants. LS 31 302 1
The number of servants continually appearing, did not NA II 8 184 4
noises convinced her that the servants must still be up. NA II 8 189 19
Murder was not tolerated, servants were not slaves, and NA II 10 200 3
to old superannuated servants by my father's will, and it SS I 2 10 20
horses, and hardly any servants; they will keep no company, SS I 2 12 24
Her wisdom too limited the number of their servants to SS I 5 26 5
They were cheered by the joy of the servants on their SS I 6 28 2
A proper establishment of servants, a carriage, perhaps SS I 17 91 14
turn off his servants, and make a thorough reform at once? SS II 8 194 10
The dinner was a grand one, the servants were numerous, SS II 12 233 18
of his servants, his carriage, his cows, and his poultry. SS III 5 293 2
The servants, I suppose, forgot to tell you that Mr. SS III 8 317 3
servants are to be in the house by the end of next week." PP I 1 3 10
For my part, Mr. Bingley, I always keep servants that can PP I 9 44 29
at all; but when the servants were withdrawn, he thought PP I 14 66 1

of such rooms, so many servants, and so splendid a dinner PP II 6 160 4
they followed the servants through an anti-chamber, to the PP II 6 161 10
and there were all the servants, and all the articles of PP II 6 162 14
made a point of her having two men servants go with her.-- PP II 14 211 13
There is not one of his tenants or servants but what will PP III 1 249 38
by the entrance of servants with cold meat, cake, and a PP III 3 268 6
her tongue before the servants, while they waited at table, PP III 5 288 40
nuptials, fine muslins, new carriages, and servants. PP III 8 310 7
talk on without interruption, while the servants remained. PP III 8 310 9
Mrs. Bennet, through the assistance of servants, contrived PP III 11 333 30
receive herself and her servants, and allow a spare room MP I 3 28 38
settling with the servants, and equally saving her from MP I 4 34 1
no witnesses, unless the servants chiefly intent upon MP II 6 233 15
from the passing of the servants behind her chair, and to MP II 7 238 3
did her sister Bertram manage about her servants? MP III 7 385 38
herself to get tolerable servants?"--soon led her mind MP III 7 385 38
of all the Portsmouth servants; of whom she believed her MP III 7 385 38
Servants are come to such a pass, my dear, in Portsmouth, MP III 7 385 39
her time was given chiefly to her house and her servants. MP III 8 389 4
dissatisfied with her servants, without skill to make them MP III 8 389 4
left to be with the servants at her pleasure, and then MP III 8 391 9
Whatever was wanted, was halloo'd for, and the servants MP III 8 392 11
of the Portsmouth servants, and wound up her spirits for MP III 11 408 4
sickness and solitude, and the attendance only of servants. MP III 13 426 10
Fanny had scarcely passed the solemn-looking servants, MP III 15 447 37
horses and four servants taken out for nothing but to E I 13 113 26
comprehending income, servants, and furniture, was E II 4 184 10
one of my servants shall go with you to shew you the way." E II 5 195 45
They added to their house, to their number of servants, to E II 7 207 6
"Mrs. Cole has servants to send. E II 10 244 41
Would Jane but go, means were to be found, servants sent, E II 15 285 14
directions to the servants had been forgotten, and spread E II 17 303 24
and all the youth and servants in the place were soon in E III 3 336 12
and ladies, with their servants and furniture, I think is E III 6 355 21
The appearance of the servants looking out for them to E III 7 374 54
and the knowledge of the servants at Randall's, was, that E III 8 383 31
could be so very eccentric;--and his servants forgot it. E III 16 458 42
happen with the Donwell servants, who are all, I have E III 16 458 42
among their servants; but yet, upon the whole, there was E III 17 468 36
Journeys, London, servants, horses, table,--contradictions P III 2 13 6
"Mrs. Musgrove thinks all her servants so steady, that it P III 6 45 9
that she is enough to ruin any servants she comes near. P III 6 45 9
keep from hysterics--the servants to control--the youngest P III 7 53 3
or any servants to wait, or any knife and fork to use. P III 8 64 4
Depend upon it, that is a circumstance which his servants P III 12 106 16
style, the reduction of servants, which a dinner must P IV 10 219 29
maid servants, were now seen issueing from the house)-- S 1 370 1
have quite such a servants hall full to feed, as I have.-- S 6 393 1
those are best off, that have fewest servants.-- S 6 393 1
It wd be only encouraging our servants & the poor to fancy S 6 393 1
The house was large & handsome; two servants appeared, to S 12 427 1

SERVANTS' (3)
a violin player in the servants' hall, and the possibility MP I 12 117 11
Jackson making up to the servants' hall door with two bits MP I 15 141 22
I knew what all this meant, for the servants' dinner bell MP I 15 142 22

SERVE (13)
This project will serve at least to amuse me, & prevent my LS 7 254 3
He will carry this note himself, which is to serve as an LS 31 302 1
and accomodation that can serve to make your situation SS II 11 222 11
should be in my power to serve him farther, I must think SS III 3 284 23
offence would serve no other purpose than to enrich Fanny. SS III 13 369 33
only serve, after what had since passed, to provoke her. PP III 18 233 25
But wishes were vain; or at best could serve only to amuse PP III 4 281 29
where their friends can serve them best, or suspects them MP I 11 109 18
thing will serve as introduction to what is near the heart. E I 10 89 35
Any nonsense will serve. E III 7 369 16
My Emma, does not every thing serve to prove more and more E III 15 446 15
"Well, it would serve to cure him of an absurd practice of P IV 3 144 19
of helpless Invalides whom I might essentially serve.-- S 9 409 1

SERVED (12)
& every reveiw has served to convince me that they require LS 30 300 1
so; but perhaps this has served to make her character NA II 12 218 4
but every perusal only served to increase her abhorrence SS II 7 184 15
One thing, especially, I remember, because it served to SS II 8 199 37
a kind of notice which served to imprint on Elinor the SS II 11 220 3
her own dignity, and as served to prevent every suspicion SS III 14 373 3
served to strengthen them in believing they had no faults. MP I 4 35 4
gallant again as occasion served, or Miss Crawford MP I 12 114 1
word miserable, which served to introduce it, Sir Thomas MP III 1 320 44
The public pays and must be served well." E II 16 297 43
course of events, they served only to confirm the idea of P IV 6 167 19
history & her character served to lighten the tediousness S 3 375 1

SERVICE (78)
As soon as divine service was over, the Thorpes and Allens NA I 5 35 2
to like the place, from finding it of service to him." NA I 8 54 6
He was equally at her service.-- NA II 7 176 17
morning and afternoon service was required by the General NA II 9 190 1
his being of any service to her in removing her furniture. SS I 5 25 4
service in recommending it to their lasting approbation. SS I 6 28 2
being always at their service, the independence of Mrs. SS I 9 40 2
extorted from her, for Willoughby's service, by her mother. SS I 19 101 2
will be of so much service to her as rest, if you will SS II 8 198 28
believed it might be of service, might lessen her regrets, SS II 9 210 32
was always at Elinor's service, so very much disliked Mrs. SS III 5 294 3
the occasion, and the service pre-arranged in his mind, he SS III 7 311 15
best compliments and service, and how sorry they was they SS III 11 354 27
carriage is quite at your service, & Mary will be pleased W 339 18
I am quite at your service. W 354 28
advice could be of any service, recommended an express to PP I 8 40 59
On Sunday, after morning service, the separation, so PP I 12 60 5
Mr. Wickham's society was of material service in PP II 1 138 30
Change of scene might be of service--and perhaps a little PP II 2 141 10
with some portion of her notice when service is over. PP II 5 157 7
my father to be of service to him, and on George Wickham, PP II 12 199 5
His pride, in that direction, may be of service, if not to PP II 18 234 38
disabled for active service, but not the less equal to MP I 1 4 2
Mrs. Norris was quite at his service; and though she MP I 1 11 18
Had she possessed greater leisure for the service of her MP I 2 20 31
for any very appropriate service it could render Fanny, MP I 3 28 38
In the King's service of course." MP I 6 60 46
was quite at his service in any way that could be useful. MP I 6 61 58
The greater length of the service, however, I admit to be MP I 9 88 18
might be spent in their service; she was, in fact, MP I 13 129 40
to cry--and the service was impressively read by Dr. Grant. MP II 3 203 29
and go through divine service; he might be the clergyman MP II 7 247 42
introduction to Admiral Crawford might be of service. MP II 9 266 21
for that stupid woman's service, and all this with such MP II 12 296 31
But the removal of his alarm did his niece no service; as MP III 1 317 36
Edmund had already gone through the service once since his MP III 3 340 24
passages in the service should be delivered, shewing it to MP III 3 340 24
now; he hoped to be of service to her, he thought he must MP III 4 345 4
of service to her, whom else had she to open her heart to? MP III 4 345 4
How was I to have an attachment at his service, as soon as MP III 4 353 45
(the thrush was certainly the finest sloop in the service). MP III 6 372 18
knowledge of Susan, and a hope of being of service to her. MP III 9 395 4
after morning service and staying till dinner-time. MP III 11 408 4
I am at your service and Henry's, at an hour's notice. MP III 12 416 3
and this is the only way I have of doing him a service." E I 1 13 46
almost always at the service of an invitation from E I 3 20 3
Either bathing has been of the greatest service to her, or E I 12 102 28
His professions and his proposals did him no service. E I 16 135 7
ground did her further service, for any thing was welcome E I 16 138 16
Ever since the service he rendered Jane at Weymouth, when E II 1 160 23
It did her no service however. E II 2 169 16
carriage would be at her service before it took us home; E II 8 223 63
and offers of service; that she will not be continually E II 15 288 39
no service to the wilful or nervous part of her disorder. E III 1 316 6
The service he rendered you was enough to warm your heart." E III 4 342 37
"Service! Oh! it was such an inexpressible obligation!-- E III 4 342 38
Elton's activity in her service, and save herself from E III 5 343 1
one of those who have witty things at every body's service. E III 7 372 37
might be of the greatest service--and every thing that E III 9 390 18
I am sure the service Mr. Frank Churchill had rendered you, E III 11 406 21
that considering the service he had rendered you, it was E III 11 406 23
as to your sense of that service, and mentioning even what E III 11 406 23
generosity; that was the service which made me begin to E III 11 406 24
It was all the service she could now render her poor E III 13 431 38
I hope it does him some service with you." E III 15 448 29
just to one important service which his better sense would E III 17 463 15
very bad wrong things, and such as did me no service.-- E III 18 477 55
Soldiers, in active service, are not at all better off: P III 3 20 17
of the Crofts did them no service with Sir Walter, he P III 3 23 34
Hardly fit for service then.-- P III 8 64 9
Reported fit for home service for a year or two,--and so I P III 8 64 9
been of the greatest service to Dr. Shirley, after his P III 12 102 2
This had been a proof of life, however, of service to her P III 12 112 51
quite at her ladyship's service themselves, but had P IV 5 158 21
service too, without robbing him of one personal grace! P IV 7 179 28
He can be of essential service to me; and if you would P IV 9 195 24
I shall be at your service in half a minute." P IV 11 236 38
service to you & this lady in every way in their power."-- S 1 367 1

SERVICEABLE (8)
quotations which are so serviceable and so soothing in the NA I 15 1 3
could be no longer serviceable, hastened to contradict all NA II 15 246 12
thought her presence might be serviceable to her nieces. PP III 6 294 3
that to make it really serviceable to Mrs. Price, and MP I 1 7 7
he had expected to be so essentially serviceable to her. MP I 3 31 58
The memory is sometimes so retentive, so serviceable, so MP II 4 209 12
It had been serviceable in deadening the first shock, E II 3 180 58
the subject in the most serviceable light--first, as a E III 17 467 30

SERVICES (14)
When my mother removes into another house my services SS I 2 12 25
The gentleman offered his services, and perceiving that SS I 9 42 8
with us, and offered her services, or any of her daughters, PP III 5 292 66
In return for such services she loved him better than any MP I 2 22 35
with the greatest alacrity offer his services for the part. MP I 14 132 8
and the conversation incessant, "we want your services." MP I 15 145 43
We do not want your present services. MP I 15 145 45
be influenced by Fanny's services, and gentle persuasions; MP III 8 390 8
a fresh occasion for Emma's services towards her friend. E I 7 50 1
On its being proposed, Anne offered her services, as usual, P III 8 71 56
rather than words, was offering his services to her. P IV 7 176 10
"At present, believe me, I have no need of your services," P IV 9 203 72
fully requited the services which she had rendered, or P IV 12 251 11
the hotel, to investigate the truth & offer her services.-- S 10 419 1

SERVILE (1)
convey gratitude without servile regret, be guarded NA II 14 235 14

SERVILELY (1)
"Yes, but I had only the credit of servilely copying such SS III 8 328 63

SERVILITY (2)
There is a mixture of servility and self-importance in his PP I 13 64 18
are obliged to be mean in their servility to her.-- S 7 402 1

SERVING (5)
am glad to find that you do not depend on her serving you." PP I 2 6 6
a stifling, sickly glare, serving but to bring forward MP III 15 439 9
of Susan herself, was all serving to support her spirits. MP III 15 444 25
how mentioned in Dugdale--serving the office of High P III 1 3 3
4

Diana, you are unequal'd in serving your friends & doing S 9 409 1

SERVT (1)
I am sir, your most humble Servt F. S. V. LS 21 279 1

SESSIONS (1)
in attending the quarter sessions at Taunton; and indeed, P III 3 21 18

SET (271)
of my life, chose to set herself so violently against the LS 2 245 1
assurances as to marriage &c., do not set my heart at ease. LS 13 262 1
Mr Vernon set off for town as soon as she had determined LS 15 266 4
Frederica had set herself violently against marrying Sir LS 24 288 11
those friends (a very bad set I doubt not) she must have LS 27 296 1
Then forming his features into a set smile, and affectedly NA I 3 26 4
and attornies might be set forth, and conversations, which NA I 4 34 9
not to be divided in the set; and if a rainy morning NA I 5 37 4
just as I wanted to set off; it looked very showery, and NA I 6 39 4
of humbling the sex, they set off immediately as fast as NA I 6 43 44
an hour with the Thorpes, set off to walk together to Mr. NA I 7 50 44
haste, of admiring the set of her gown, and envying the NA I 8 52 1
induce her to join the set before her dear Catherine could NA I 8 52 2
What could induce you to come into this set, when you knew NA I 8 56 12
Well, remember that it is not my fault, if we set all the NA I 8 58 25
there was a very beautiful set of pearls that Mr. Drummond NA I 9 68 48
them, and they all three set off in good time for the Pump- NA I 10 71 8
heart she went with him to the set, may be easily imagined. NA I 10 75 24
Soon after their reaching the bottom of the set, Catherine NA I 10 80 59
Pump-Room; he accordingly set off by himself, and NA I 11 84 17
We set out a great deal too late. NA I 11 88 54
of whom had particularly set her heart upon going, and the NA I 13 97 1
to set off very early, in order to be at home in good time. NA I 13 97 1
I must run after Miss Tilney directly and set her right." NA I 13 100 18
girl have been already set forth by the capital pen of a NA I 14 111 29
"They set off at eight this morning," said Miss Anne, "and NA I 14 115 50
Her brother she found was preparing to set off with all NA I 15 119 14
breathe his parting sigh before he set off for Wiltshire. NA I 15 120 24
Anne and Maria soon set her heart at ease by the sagacity NA I 15 121 25
to begin his journey to London, prepared to set off. NA I 15 122 29
that of having b a short set to dance down enjoyed her NA II 1 131 15
the three females, and they set off at the sober pace in NA II 5 155 4
The elegance of the breakfast set forced itself on NA II 7 175 12
But this was quite an old set, purchased two years ago. NA II 7 175 12
of that kind, might have been tempted to order a new set. NA II 7 175 12
They set forward; and, with a grandeur of air, a dignified NA II 8 182 2
They are a set of very worthy men. NA II 11 210 6
At four they were to dine, and at six to set off on their NA II 11 214 26
Your kind offices will set all right:--he is the only man NA II 12 216 2
would not be ungenerous, or set you against those you NA II 12 216 2
call at Putney when next in town, might set all to rights. NA II 12 217 2
visit would at least set her heart at ease for a time, and NA II 15 242 8
the world but himself, he set out the next day for the NA II 15 247 13
"Yes; and the set of breakfast china is twice as handsome SS I 2 13 28
household, before she set off for the west; and this, as SS I 5 26 5
off from their hills; and the two girls set off together. SS I 9 41 3
their heads, and a driving rain set full in their face.-- SS I 9 41 6
They set off. SS I 9 41 7
hills, and could never be found when the others set off. SS I 16 85 15
"and yet I have always set her down as a lively girl." SS I 17 93 36
to be true, so from that moment I set it down as certain. SS I 20 115 52
animated praise, and he set off directly for the cottage SS I 21 119 3
But I am determined to set for it the very first SS I 22 132 37
I gave him a lock of my hair set in a ring when he was at SS I 22 135 54
partiality could set aside, his ill-treatment of herself.-- SS II 1 139 1
breaking the ice; you have set my heart at ease by it; for SS II 2 146 3
me with your company, for I've quite set my heart upon it. SS II 3 153 2
So I would advise you two, to set off for town, when you SS II 3 154 3
Frosts will soon set in, and in all probability with SS II 5 167 3
style of living, and set of acquaintance, than with her SS II 5 168 11

much about horses, he soon set him down as a very good-	SS II 11 228 52
desire, Lady Middleton set her down in Berkeley-Street on	SS II 13 238 2
Elinor set him right as to its situation, and it seemed	SS II 14 251 16
and let the supper be set out in the saloon.'	SS II 14 252 18
people do but know how to set about it, every comfort may	SS II 14 252 18
no business of other people to set it down for certain."	SS III 2 272 14
no good comes of it, will set down upon a curacy of fifty	SS III 2 276 28
This set the matter beyond a doubt.	SS III 3 281 9
The consequence was, that Elinor set out by herself to pay	SS III 5 294 3
and Berkeley-Street set out from their respective homes,	SS III 6 301 3
Mr. Harris's arrival, she set off, with her little boy and	SS III 7 308 3
cousin, Mrs. Smith, was to set me free; yet the event	SS III 8 320 32
had already determined to set out for Cleveland on that	SS III 9 335 6
The sisters set out at a pace, slow as the feebleness of	SS III 10 344 12
	13
always be in your power to set her off to advantage, and	SS III 14 375 9
husband; I trusted her, she set him against me, with a	W 316 2
seated amongst the osborne set; & she was immediately	W 330 11
another minute was led by Col. Beresford to begin the set.	W 330 11
them on, they joined the set which was now rapidly forming,	W 331 11
of a carriage driving up to the door set her heart at ease.	W 338 17
I suppose your set was not a very full one."--	W 340 19
wits, to have had anything to do with the osborne's set."--	W 342 19
"Well, I only beg you will not set your neighbours against	W 350 24
"Indeed you should not have set out so late."--	W 356 28
the old card table being set out, & the fish & counters	W 357 28
there, my dear, to have given him one of your set downs.	PP I 3 13 20
their company, and the three young ladies set off together.	PP I 7 32 39
But here he was set right by Mrs. Bennet, who assured him	PP I 13 65 26
creditable, gentlemanlike set, and the best of them were	PP I 16 76 3
Elizabeth made no answer, and took her place in the set,	PP I 18 90 8
meaning to pass through the set to the other side of the	PP I 18 92 22
even at the moment, he set about it in a very orderly	PP I 19 104 1
myself) to set the example of matrimony in his parish.	PP I 19 105 9
	10
and instantly set out to meet him accidentally in the lane.	PP I 22 121 1
I only want to think you perfect, and you set yourself	PP II 1 135 11
The wedding took place; the bride and bridegroom set off	PP II 3 146 19
the three young ladies set out together from Gracechurch-	PP II 16 219 1
displayed a table set out with such cold meat as an inn	PP II 16 219 2
"A little sea-bathing would set me up for ever."	PP II 18 229 8
from whence they were to set out early the next morning.	PP II 18 235 40
Elizabeth was excessively disappointed; she had set her	PP II 19 239 8
The Gardiners staid only one night at Longbourn, and set	PP II 19 239 11
no sooner dined than she set off again in quest of her	PP III 1 259 76
to Miss Darcy, who had been set up as a rival of Jane.	PP III 2 262 8
leaving her to enjoy them in quiet, set off by themselves.	PP III 4 273 2
the alarm, set off from B. intending to trace their route.	PP III 4 274 5
the coachman had before set down his fare, he determined	PP III 5 293 69
Mr. Gardiner had waited only for the letters before he set	PP III 6 294 1
family again, before she set off for the north, received	PP III 8 313 22
back again in ten minutes time, and then we all set out.	PP III 9 319 25
They both set off, and the conjectures of the remaining	PP III 14 351 1
Lady Catherine) had only set that down, as almost certain	PP III 15 360 1
never spare time, but the remaining five set off together.	PP III 16 365 1
But whether she were violently set against the match, or	PP III 17 375 27
beginning; but what could set you off in the first place?"	PP III 18 380 1
on seeing her with red eyes, set her down as a hypocrite.	MP I 3 33 64
If they profess a disinclination for it, I only set it	MP I 4 43 25
I do not pretend to set people right, but I do see that	MP I 5 50 36
gallantly, "are doing a a great deal to set them right."	MP I 5 50 37
Mr. Bertram set off for ----, and Miss Crawford was	MP I 6 52 1
account when love is once set going, even the sandwich	MP I 7 65 13
she rode without her cousins, were ready to set forward.	MP I 7 66 15
lifted on her's, and they set off across another part of	MP I 7 69 21
He must not head mobs, or set the ton in dress.	MP I 9 92 45
He set off accordingly.	MP I 10 98 4
acquaintance, for she had set him right as to his	MP I 10 103 50
I shall get the dairy maid to set them under the first	MP I 10 106 57
with very few of a set of men you condemn so conclusively.	MP I 11 110 24
Mr. Rushworth has set a good example, and such things are	MP I 12 118 16
been bred to the trade,--a set of gentlemen and ladies,	MP I 13 124 12
we could have desired, if we had set down to wish for it.	MP I 13 125 14
wife; and I am sure I set her the example of moderation	MP I 14 134 14
You must set the example.--	MP I 15 140 13
to set them right must be his only satisfaction.	MP I 15 142 23
she owed the greatest complaisance, had set their hearts?	MP I 16 153 3
set up for a fine actor, is very ridiculous in my opinion."	MP I 18 165 3
up in his room before we set off to advise him not to	MP II 2 189 5
at dinner, he had also set the carpenter to work in	MP II 2 190 9
Mr. Rushworth had set off early with the great news for	MP II 2 192 11
appear as if I wanted to set myself off at their expense,	MP II 3 198 12
and you must not set forward while it is so threatening.	MP II 4 207 9
and therefore, if you do set about a flirtation with her,	MP II 6 230 6
air as to make its owner be set down as the great land-	MP II 7 244 27
season of the year: he had set his heart upon having a	MP II 7 246 37
dance down the shortening set, breathless and with her	MP II 10 279 22
Did she think of being up before you set off?"	MP II 10 279 27
whom the Admiral had set to work in the business, the	MP II 13 298 3
own children's merits set off by the depreciation of her.	MP III 1 323 57
It was over, however, at last; and the evening set in with	MP III 1 324 58
It was enough to set his heart in a glow, and to bring him	MP III 3 334 2
I want to be set right.	MP III 3 342 33
one object of curiosity and one set of words to another.	MP III 3 343 40
I think it ought not to be set down as certain, that a man	MP III 4 353 45
"but you are only going from one set of friends to another.	MP III 5 359 11
set herself very steadily against admitting any such thing.	MP III 6 371 14
You will set things going in a better way, I am sure.	MP III 6 372 20
tea, and Susan immediately set about making it, as if	MP III 7 383 33
its comforts, and therefore set about working for Sam	MP III 8 390 7
from one belonging to the set where her heart lived,	MP III 9 393 1
Susan saw that much was wrong at home, and wanted to set	MP III 9 395 4
from Norfolk, before he set off again; that her cousin	MP III 10 400 8
They were then to set forward for the dock-yard at once,	MP III 10 403 14
this, and hope to find you ready to set off for Mansfield.	MP III 15 442 23
combination of blessings as set her heart in a glow, and	MP III 15 443 24
Sir Thomas set off; Edmund would go with him; and the	MP III 16 450 10
Such was his opinion of the set into which she had thrown	MP III 16 452 13
again, and he might set forward on a second, and it is to	MP III 17 464 12
Having once set out, and felt that he had done so, on this	MP III 17 471 28
After these came a second set; among the most come-at-able	E I 3 20 3
watch the due time, was all set out and ready, and moved	E I 3 24 11
such a picture of another set of beings, and enjoying the	E I 4 27 4
However, I do not mean to set up my opinion against your's-	E I 4 31 25
were to set about copying him, he would not be sufferable.	E I 4 34 42
no distaste for her own set, nor any ambition beyond it.	E I 8 63 42
"If I had set my heart on Mr. Elton's marrying Harriet, it	E I 8 66 54
Tell your aunt, little Emma, that she ought to set you a	E I 12 99 10
their own especial set, were the only persons invited to	E I 13 108 4
of shrinking from it, and set forward at last most	E I 13 112 24
while she and her husband set forward instantly through	E I 15 127 13
be able to get along, if we set off directly; and if we do	E I 15 127 14
who was immediately set as much at ease on the subject as	E I 15 128 17
she could hardly devise any set of expressions, or fancy	E I 16 135 7
to see the whole party set off, and return to his	E I 17 140 1
It was rather too late in the day to set about being	E I 17 142 10
with those who have always set him the example of it.	E I 18 145 10
I shall, therefore, set off to-morrow.'--	E I 18 146 16
set all their claims on his gratitude and regard at nought.	E I 18 148 19
"She had set out from Mrs. Goddard's half an hour ago--	E II 3 177 52
"And so, there she had set, without an idea of any thing	E II 3 178 52
and I must go: and so off I set; and I had not got three	E II 3 179 52
to wait for; and when he set out for Bath again, there was	E II 4 182 6
in town; and at Weymouth we were very much in the same set.	E II 6 200 20
always was, by her aunt and grandmother, and all their set.	E II 6 203 39
had sent for a chaise and set off, intending to return to	E II 7 205 1
he found them in general a set of gentlemen-like, sensible	E II 8 220 48
And here are a new set of Irish melodies.	E II 10 242 21
to Hartfield gates, before they set off for Randalls.	E II 10 246 55
must be a very heavy set that does not ask for more.	E II 11 247 1
I do not mean to set you against him, but indeed he is not	E II 11 249 11
young people set off together without delay for the crown.	E II 11 253 40
merely sandwiches, &c. set out in the little room; but	E II 11 254 45
and must entreat him to set off for Enscombe without delay.	E II 12 258 7
notions were drawn from one set of people, and one style	E II 14 272 16
from her easy conceit, had been the best of her own set.	E II 14 272 17
of; and we are a very quiet set of people, I believe; more	E II 14 274 29
If we set the example, many will follow it as far as they	E II 15 283 9
her card tables should be set out with their separate	E II 16 290 3
"No, but it did not absolutely rain when I set out."	E II 16 293 14
business in London, should set off again, and walk half-a-	E II 17 302 23
respectable length of the set as it was forming, and to	E III 2 325 32
When she was half way up the set, the whole group were	E III 2 327 34
caught her;-- Mr. Knightley leading Harriet to the set!--	E III 2 328 40
I set off without saying a word, just as I told you.	E III 2 329 45
Come Emma, set your companions the example.	E III 2 331 57
of there being such a set of people in the neighbourhood	E III 3 334 8
to Mr. Knightley, he set off, with all the grateful	E III 3 334 8
Is Perry going to set up his carriage, Frank?	E III 5 345 12
"Well--as you please; only don't have a great set out.	E III 6 355 22
own homes, among their own set, just as they always are,	E III 7 372 40
look every thing that may set his heart at ease, and	E III 10 400 65
Woodhouse, you will not set yourself against it, and try	E III 11 407 28
Mrs. Weston had set off to pay the visit in a good deal of	E III 12 417 5
A cold stormy rain set in, and nothing of July appeared	E III 12 421 18
kind--but you are mistaken--and I must set you right.--	E III 13 426 14
	15
If you remember any queernesses, set them all to the right	E III 14 439 8
But I want to set your heart at ease as to Mrs. S.--	E III 16 454 13
the baby would soon have outgrown its first set of caps.	E III 17 468 32
One set might recommend their all removing to Donwell, and	E III 17 468 36
In the gayest and happiest spirits she set forward with	E III 18 476 43
They are to be new set.	E III 18 479 70
Has he set up his carriage?"	E III 18 480 75
ardour of female alarm, set seriously to think what could	P III 1 9 19
tenants as any set of people one should meet with.	P III 3 17 4
equal claim with any other set of men, for all the	P III 3 19 11
	12
the utmost: I know no other set of men but what lose	P III 3 20 17
Mr. Shepherd's clerks were set to work, without there	P III 5 32 3
The baronet will never set the Thames on fire, but there	P III 5 32 4
set off handsome features, but can never alter plain ones.	P III 5 35 16
made together, and Anne was set down at Uppercross Cottage,	P III 5 36 19
that a removal from one set of people to another, though	P III 6 42 1
because you may be able to set things to rights, that I	P III 6 45 9
How was Anne to set all these matters to rights?	P III 6 46 11
pleasure of seeing them set off together in high spirits.	P III 7 58 20
them to distinguish the very set who may be least missed."	P III 8 65 11
affliction, as the most graceful set of limbs in the world.	P III 8 68 30
retract, and the whole six set toward together in the	P III 10 83 6
early breakfast hour, and set off very punctually, it was	P III 11 95 8
and warmth than any other set of men in England; that they	P III 11 99 19
them to their door, and then return and set off themselves.	P III 12 108 30
attending to his wife, they set forward, treading back	P III 12 111 49
to be wrong; and they had set off immediately, informed	P III 12 111 50
but so it must be, and they set off for the town, Charles	P III 12 115 66
must be a most delightful set of people--longed to be with	P IV 3 144 19
than those of any other set of beings in the world.	P IV 3 144 20
How to have this anxious business set to rights, and be	P IV 4 149 12
they will move in the first set in Bath this winter, and	P IV 4 150 17
She had been the only one of the set absent; for Sir	P IV 5 158 21
enough that they must wait till her brain was set to right.	P IV 6 171 33
or of penance was to be set out, another hour of music was	P IV 8 189 45
thoughtless, gay set, without any strict rules of conduct.	P IV 9 201 64
And I have now the charge of getting it properly set for	P IV 11 232 15
set off with him, with no feeling but gratitude apparent.	P IV 11 239 54
wrong, and to take up a new set of opinions and of hopes.	P IV 12 249 3
A little of our own bracing sea air will soon set me on my	S 1 367 1
as the carriage being now set up, was discovered to have	S 1 370 1
I encouraged him to set up--& am afraid he does not do	S 4 382 1
the travellers were safely set down, & all was happiness &	S 4 384 1
She had not a wink of sleep either the night before we set	S 9 407 1
such a totally distinct set of people as were concerned in	S 10 419 1
for her, I beleive we must set a Subscription on foot--&	S 12 423 1
Mrs P. was delighted at this release, & set off very happy	S 12 425 1

SET-TO (1)

We had a famous set-to at rat-hunting all the morning, in	P IV 10 219 26

SETS (5)

They were in different sets.	NA I 8 55 10
After another pause, "nothing sets off a neat ankle more	W 345 21
and removed at least two sets of difficulties, and having	MP I 14 130 1
excusable in one who sets up as I do for understanding.	E III 13 427 19
bequeath, & three distinct sets of people to be courted by;	S 3 376 1

SETT (1)

smartest officer of the sett, walking off to the orchestra	W 330 11

SETTING (43)

my horse should dance about a little at first setting off.	NA I 9 62 9
a few minutes after her setting off; that, when he told	NA I 11 89 62
as soon as possible; and, setting aside the misery of his	NA I 12 95 16
Setting her own inclination apart, to have failed a second	NA I 13 101 25
now, perhaps, they were all setting off for Hereford.	NA II 14 239 28
You will be setting your cap at him now, and never think	SS I 9 45 29
wit is intended; and 'setting one's cap at a man,' or '	SS I 9 45 30
and he is very well worth setting your cap at, I can tell	SS I 9 45 32
Her systems have all the unfortunate tendency of setting	SS I 11 56 13
His setting off in such a hurry seems very like it.	SS I 14 70 2
The setting always casts a different shade on it you know."	SS I 18 98 12
time, and they were just setting themselves, after it,	SS II 7 181 7
with the Dashwoods and setting aside the jealousies and	SS III 14 377 11
With nothing to do but to expect the hour of setting off,	W 326 7
used to in Shropshire, & setting it as certain that the	W 350 24
Mr. Gardiner would be prevented by business from setting	PP II 19 238 7
I instantly resolved on setting off for this place, that I	PP III 14 353 26
by preventing her from setting off half an hour sooner;	MP I 7 68 19
end of it will be frost setting in all at once, taking	MP II 4 212 31
of the parsonage, just setting out to call on her, and as	MP II 8 257 15
for you up stairs; and setting off to find my way to the	MP III 5 360 14
the moment came for setting off; every thing was ready,	MP III 7 384 36
The prices were just setting off for church the next day	MP III 11 408 1
Just before their setting out from Oxford, while Susan was	MP III 15 446 34
a child from the cottage, setting out, according to orders,	E I 10 88 33
clothing than usual, setting forward voluntarily, without	E I 13 113 26
that he can;--here are we setting forward to spend five	E I 13 113 26
snow, and every evening setting in to freeze, she was for	E I 16 138 17
might be found out; and setting aside the 10,0001. it did	E II 4 183 9
the very morning of his setting off for Bath again, Emma,	E II 4 185 11
and still tenaciously setting her right if she varied in	E III 3 336 13
became of Mr. Perry's plan of setting up his carriage?"	E III 5 344 5
Perry's setting up his carriage! and his wife's persuading	E III 5 345 14
She and Mary were actually setting forward for the great	P III 7 53 2
say that they were just setting off, that he was come for	P III 7 59 24
Just as they were setting off, the gentlemen returned.	P III 10 83 6
first instant of their all setting forward for Uppercross.	P III 10 89 36
They ought to be setting off for Uppercross by one, and in	P III 12 107 22

coming away with us and setting off again afterwards to P IV 2 131 12
(always obliging) just setting off for Union-Street on a P IV 7 175 5
He had been prevented setting off for Thornberry, but I P IV 10 228 71
people have succeeded in setting the Carge to rights & S 1 367 1
were setting off,--a joyful sight--& full of speculation.-- S 10 414 1

SETTLE (53)

the connection, he will settle in the country for the rest LS 38 306 1
I detest: I would not settle in London for the universe. NA I 15 119 20
"You must settle near Fullerton. NA I 15 120 21
to settle, though somewhat embarrassed in speaking of. NA II 13 229 31
them whenever they leave Norland and settle in a new home." SS I 2 9 6
more prudent for them to settle at some distance from SS I 4 24 21
A few years however will settle her opinions on the SS I 11 56 11
about me a little, and settle my matters; for it is a long SS II 4 163 14
I have had Cartwright to settle with--Lord, I have been as SS II 4 163 14
settle on him a thousand a-year, if the match takes place. SS II 11 224 28
told him that she would settle on him the Norfolk estate, SS III 1 266 38
kind of spirit, to settle that estate upon Robert SS III 1 269 53
style of life would venture to settle on--and he said so. SS III 3 284 22
that one or two interviews would settle the matter. SS III 14 376 11
Ah! I remember--& she is gone to settle in Ireland.-- W 326 5
and we shall very soon settle it with her, I am sure." PP I 20 111 5
forth into the village to settle their differences, PP II 7 169 4
to settle on my niece, in addition to her own fortune. PP III 7 302 14
flatter myself they will settle so quietly, and live in so PP III 7 305 37
We will settle with your father about the money afterwards; PP III 7 306 47
She could settle it in no way that gave her pleasure. PP III 12 339 3
so near a relation might settle every doubt, and determine PP III 15 361 3
return, and then Sir Thomas might settle it all himself. MP I 4 36 7
persuade her brother to settle with her at his own country- MP I 4 41 16
I should dearly love to settle you both in this country, MP I 4 42 19
settle it your own way, I am sure I do not care about it." MP I 8 79 23
and ride over to Stoke, and settle with one of them." MP I 15 148 58
Leave him to settle that." MP II 5 221 32
Birthright and habit must settle the business. MP II 5 226 63
"Ha!" cried Mary, "settle in Northamptonshire! MP II 12 295 21
Mrs. Norris was left to settle the matter by herself; and MP III 6 373 23
naval regulations, or settle the number of three deckers MP III 10 403 13
if Sir Thomas cannot settle every thing for coming himself, MP III 11 410 16
Settle it as you like; say what is proper; I am sure you MP III 15 443 23
That is too young to settle. E I 4 30 18
That is a point which you must settle with your own E I 7 52 17
be imprudent in him to settle so early; whether I thought E I 8 59 27
letter over again, and settle how long he had been gone, E II 1 156 5
"He is very young to settle," was Mr. Woodhouse's E II 3 174 34
Well, I am glad she is gone to settle in Ireland." E II 6 202 33
to settle early in life, and to marry, from worthy motives. E II 6 204 43
were then to be paid, to settle whether she were very E II 14 270 1
to name the day, and settle with Mr. Weston as to pigeon- E III 6 353 6
"These are difficulties which you must settle for yourself. E III 6 366 73
I shall talk about it to him; he will settle for me; he E III 8 384 33
How to settle the claims of Enscombe and Hartfield had E III 17 467 31
attachment to herself, to settle close by her, in the P III 1 5 6
fortune, was wishing to settle in his own country, and had P III 3 21 18
do you think they will settle in?" and this, without much P III 6 42 1
shore, fully intended to settle as soon as he could be P III 7 61 38
time to settle the point of civility between the other two. P IV 7 174 3
others were obliged to settle it for them; Miss Elliot P IV 7 174 3
"I would rather have young people settle on a small income P IV 11 230 7

SETTLED (223)

my dear Reginald, of seeing you settled in the world. LS 12 261 3
Whether it would have done any good, can never be settled LS 13 262 1
has gone wrong--but it is now all happily settled. LS 24 287 9
They were soon settled in comfortable lodgings in Pulteney- NA I 2 19 6
But, my dearest Catherine, have you settled what to wear NA I 6 42 24
settled her young charge, returned to her party. NA I 8 55 10
Her plan for the morning thus settled, she sat quietly NA I 9 60 1
and it was finally settled between them without any NA I 9 64 27
Tilney--but that is a settled thing--even your modesty NA I 10 70 1
She had that moment settled with Miss Tilney to take their NA I 13 97 1
look, said, "well, I have settled the matter, and now we NA I 13 100 13
When every thing was settled, when Miss Tilney herself NA I 13 100 19
The affair thus happily settled, she was introduced by NA I 13 102 27
I thought it was all settled." NA II 1 130 12
Isabella on having every thing so pleasantly settled. NA II 1 135 43
a few minutes as nearly settled, as this necessary NA II 2 140 10
She had just settled this point, when the end of the path NA II 7 181 41
created, the mischief settled long before her quitting NA II 10 200 2
And it was directly settled that, till she had, her NA II 13 221 6
After what has so lately passed, so lately been settled NA II 13 223 13
"Ah, Catherine! were it settled so, it would be somewhat NA II 13 224 18
I leave it to be settled by whomsoever it may concern, NA II 16 252 7
The family of Dashwood had been long settled in Sussex. SS I 1 3 1
she, "Elinor will in all probability be settled for life. SS I 3 17 15
hoped that she would not be settled far from Norland. SS I 5 25 1
every thing was so far settled in their future abode as to SS I 5 27 7
day till they were better settled at home, that, though SS I 6 30 6
The Dashwoods were now settled at Barton with tolerable SS I 9 40 1
the settled rain of the two preceding days had occasioned. SS I 9 40 3
"I wish it would be so easily settled. SS I 13 64 26
It was settled that there should be a dance in the evening, SS I 13 67 61
and it ended in an absence of mind still more settled. SS I 18 99 14
The business of self-command she settled very easily;-- SS I 19 104 11
she was not without a settled habitation of her own. SS II 3 153 1
settled that the invitation should be fully accepted. SS II 3 157 19
for although scarcely settled in town, Sir John had SS II 5 170 29
Is every thing finally settled? SS II 5 173 44
thing was now finally settled respecting his marriage with SS II 8 199 37
Her mind did become settled, but it was settled in a SS II 10 212 1
And so you are most comfortably settled in your little SS II 11 222 11
anxious to see you well settled; Fanny particularly, for SS II 11 224 24
"It is not actually settled, but there is such a thing in SS II 11 224 28
Lucy, with a demure and settled air, seemed determined to SS II 13 241 22
But I had just settled within myself to ask the Miss SS II 14 253 24
their leaving her was settled--"for they are quite SS III 3 280 8
After this had been settled, Colonel Brandon began to talk SS III 3 283 20
And how came he not to have settled that matter before SS III 5 295 12
He had just settled this point with great composure, when SS III 5 300 38
by a settled rain from going out again after dinner. SS III 6 303 11
from it; but an heavy and settled rain even she could not SS III 6 303 11
But everything was then just settled between Miss Grey and SS III 8 326 53
and had so far settled her journey before his arrival, SS III 9 335 6
"When the weather is settled, and I have recovered my SS III 10 343 9
each other, again quietly settled at the cottage, and if SS III 11 352 20
They would soon, she supposed, be settled at Delaford.-- SS III 12 357 3
The independence she settled on Robert, through resentment SS III 13 366 18
They settled in town, received very liberal assistance SS III 14 377 11
and to see Marianne settled at the mansion-house was SS III 14 378 13
This matter was settled, & they went to dinner.-- W 324 4
I always said she ought to have settled something on you, W 351 26
at all, the affair was so settled, as soon as she could be W 361 30
"If I can but see one of my daughters happily settled at PP I 3 9 2
and never settled at Netherfield as he ought to be. PP I 3 10 4
it, I shall consider the matter as absolutely settled. PP I 6 27 53
a brother settled in London in a respectable line of trade. PP I 7 28 2
girl, and I wish with all my heart she were well settled. PP I 8 36 14
proposal; and it was settled that Mr. Jones should be sent PP I 8 40 59
the ball, it is quite a settled thing; and as soon as PP I 11 55 7
and at length it was settled that their original design of PP I 12 59 1
Things are settled so oddly." PP I 13 65 22
and for the first evening she was his settled choice. PP I 15 70 3
She saw her in idea settled in that very house in all the PP I 18 98 63
see her daughter settled at Netherfield, in the course of PP I 18 103 77
matter may be considered, therefore, as finally settled." PP I 19 107 16
allow, every thing was settled between them to the PP I 22 121 2
of their being all settled in London for the winter, and PP II 1 133 1
was finally settled according to Charlotte's first sketch. PP II 4 151 1
A lively imagination soon settled it all. PP II 5 158 10
and as Mrs. Collins had settled it with her husband that PP II 6 161 10
being most comfortably settled, and of her possessing such PP II 7 168 1
for then we might possibly get a settled family there. PP II 9 178 9
"It must be very agreeable to her to be settled within so PP II 9 178 16
"I should never have said Mrs. Collins was settled near PP II 9 179 19
"I do not mean to say that a woman may not be settled too PP II 9 179 22
The business was therefore soon settled. PP II 12 201 5
She was now, on being settled at home, at leisure to PP II 17 227 26
It settled the matter; and they pursued the accustomed PP III 1 253 57
Elizabeth had settled it that Mr. Darcy would bring his PP III 2 260 1
It had been settled in the evening, between the aunt and PP III 2 266 17
every thing relating to their journey was speedily settled. PP III 4 280 26
That is all settled." PP III 4 281 27
"That is all settled;" repeated the other, as she ran into PP III 4 281 28
Gardiner meanwhile having settled his account at the inn, PP III 4 281 29
And even when it was settled that Lydia should go with Mrs. PP III 5 285 16
to be at home, it was settled that she and her children PP III 6 298 15
"and how much is settled on his side on our sister, we PP III 7 305 36
Five thousand pounds was settled by marriage articles on PP III 8 308 4
which was now to be settled, and Mr. Bennet could have no PP III 8 308 4
Lydia's being settled in the north, just when she had PP III 8 313 20
them to come; and it was settled, that as soon as the PP III 8 314 22
And it was settled that we should all be there by eleven PP III 9 318 24
Every thing being settled between them, Mr. Darcy's next PP III 10 323 2
It was not all settled before Monday: as soon as it was, PP III 10 324 2
it,) your uncle would most readily have settled the whole. PP III 10 324 2
her own settled upon her, and his commission purchased. PP III 10 324 2
an affair was finally settled, that had given them so many PP III 13 347 28
great pleasure in thinking you will be so happily settled. PP III 13 348 38
It is settled between us already, that we are to be the PP III 17 373 10
as soon as matters are settled, I will engage to get the MP I 1 7 8
thing was considered as settled, and the pleasures of so MP I 1 8 9
It is quite settled. MP I 3 25 20
I thought you had settled it with Sir Thomas?" MP I 3 28 41
"Oh! that will soon be settled. MP I 3 30 55
Grant's being so well settled in life without being MP I 3 31 60
of you walked about and settled things, and then we could MP I 6 62 58
soon after her being settled at Mansfield from the example MP I 7 66 14
to learn what had been settled for Wednesday, to attend MP I 8 77 7
secure it, the matter was settled by Mrs. Grant's saying, MP I 8 80 29
of that sort, you know, can be settled without you." MP I 10 102 47
"It is not a settled thing, ma'am, yet.-- MP I 12 118 21
and though nothing was settled but that Tom Bertram would MP I 13 124 13
was turning over the first act, soon settled the business. MP I 14 133 11
Thus much was settled before Edmund, who had been out all MP I 15 138 2
It is too far settled; every body would be so disappointed. MP I 15 141 21
still a great deal to be settled; and the spirits of MP I 15 142 25
"Well, how do you go on?" and "what have you settled?" and MP I 15 143 26
when this point was settled, and being commissioned with MP II 1 177 6
we may; and when you are settled in town and I come to see MP II 4 213 35
independence, it was soon settled that if nothing were MP II 4 215 47
"Well, Fanny, it is all happily settled, and without the MP II 5 219 25
and teach them, it was settled; and Sir Thomas, Mrs. MP II 7 239 8
My dear Sir Thomas, we have settled it that the carriage MP II 7 251 64
Norris, who must fancy that she settled it all herself. MP II 7 251 65
required some minutes silence to be settled into composure. MP II 8 253 4
about the day, it appeared that the day was settled too. MP II 8 253 7
The ball was now a settled thing, and before the evening a MP II 8 254 8
first day of its being settled, within the first hour of MP II 8 256 12
The dress being settled in all its grander parts,--"but MP II 8 257 15
say she hoped it might be settled otherwise; in vain MP II 10 275 11
Owens settled at Thornton Lacey; how should you like it? MP II 11 289 34
But till it is absolutely settled--settled beyond all MP II 12 293 10
Having so satisfactorily settled the conviction her note MP III 1 311 2
income, settled as soon after four and twenty as he can. MP III 1 317 34
simple acknowledgment of settled dislike on her side, MP III 1 318 38
an opportunity of being settled in life, eligibly, MP III 1 318 39
nobly settled, as will, probably, never occur to you again. MP III 1 318 39
I mean when you are settled there. MP III 3 339 19
I wish I had settled with Mrs. Fraser not to go to her MP III 5 359 12
"You know you had but just settled that my sister Fanny MP III 7 379 18
I have no hope of ever being settled; and if I was to part MP III 7 385 39
by this time it is all settled," passed internally, MP III 10 401 9
It is quite settled that the Grants go to Bath; they leave MP III 13 423 2
"Why is not it settled?-- MP III 13 424 4
She had a rule to apply to, which settled every thing. MP III 14 436 15
It was settled that he should order the carriage to the MP III 15 445 29
by matrimony, being settled in London, only sixteen miles E I 1 7 9
You know we have settled all that already. E I 1 8 18
time of life to be settled in a home of her own, and how E I 1 11 38
Harriet Smith's intimacy at Hartfield was soon a settled E I 4 26 1
assurances,--and a very few minutes settled the business. E I 6 49 41
but it was then to be settled that she should return to E I 8 57 1
whom, with probably no settled provision at all, and E I 8 61 38
Highbury, for the sake of her being settled so well. E I 8 61 38
felt a satisfaction which settled her with her own mind, E I 8 67 56
they wish to have you settled in the same country and E I 9 75 27
she was eager to have it settled, that her father and Emma E I 15 127 13
Mr. Knightley and Emma settled it in a few brief sentences: E I 15 128 17
18

girl; and I should be happy to see her respectably settled. E I 15 131 35
He must know that the Woodhouses had been settled for E I 16 136 9
bed at last with nothing settled but the conviction of her E I 16 137 12
settled, while Jane Fairfax had yet her bread to earn. E II 2 165 7
By his style, I should imagine it just settled." E II 3 174 32
to an old servant who was married, and settled in Donwell. E II 5 186 2
just the right weather for him, fine, dry, settled weather. E II 5 188 7
This was the occurrence:--the Coles had been settled some E II 7 207 6
and it being briefly settled among themselves how E II 7 208 9
At last it was all settled, even to the destination of the E II 9 235 35
settled at any time between Mrs. Weston and Mrs. Stokes.-- E II 11 255 59
difficulties therefore, consider that point as settled." E II 16 296 36
settled before the Campbells or I have any rest." E II 17 301 18
People of the name of Tupman, very lately settled there, E II 18 310 34
was arranging himself for settled conversation, while E III 2 328 38
It was settled that they should go to box hill. E III 6 352 2
and at last Donwell was settled for one day, and box hill E III 6 357 32
yesterday evening it was all settled that Jane should go. E III 8 381 15
I did not know a word of it till it was all settled." E III 8 381 15
It was settled so, upon the hill, while we were walking E III 8 381 17
indeed, my dear, to hear she is to be comfortably settled. E III 9 387 10
"This was settled last night, and Frank was off with the E III 10 398 57
They would be married, and settled either at or near E III 12 422 20
When it was thus settled on her sister's side, Emma E III 16 451 3
"Nothing can be actually settled yet, perhaps," replied E III 16 460 54
our living with Mr. Churchill at Enscombe, it is settled. E III 16 460 56
light--first, as a settled, and secondly, as a good one-- E III 17 467 30
how it had been first settled in Cheshire; how mentioned P III 1 3 3
4

whither he should go, was settled, and the first outline P III 2 13 8
father's house, and settled so permanently near herself. P III 4 28 7
it was consequently soon settled that Anne should not go P III 5 34 10
and visit the brother settled in that country, but the P III 9 73 1
and consultations, it was settled between Charles and his P III 10 86 18
If it were war, now, he would have settled it long ago.-- P III 10 92 44
Captain Harville's being settled with his family at Lyme P III 11 94 6

of an old pier of unknown date, were the Harvilles settled. P III 11 96 10
them, and get a bed elsewhere--and the whole was settled. P III 12 113 56
"Then it is settled, Musgrove," cried Captain Wentworth, " P III 12 114 61
and say that we are settled here quite to our liking, and P IV 1 128 29
I thought it was all settled; when behold! on Tuesday P IV 2 130 5
Elizabeth were settled there, much to their satisfaction. P IV 3 137 1
of Sir Walter's being settled there had of course reached P IV 3 138 6
of near relations and a settled home, remaining another P IV 5 152 2
Musgrove; for it was all settled between "him and her P IV 6 164 8
that point were settled, she could not be quite herself. P IV 7 178 24
But hardly were they so settled, when the door opened P IV 8 181 1
allowed to think it all settled, and build my own selfish P IV 9 195 27
of the sort you are thinking of will be settled any week. P IV 9 195 28
She was their earliest visitor in their settled life; and P IV 12 251 11
demanded a very quiet, settled, careful course of life--& S 2 373 1
He lives too much in the world to be settled; that is his S 4 382 1
line settled at Sanditon, it wd be no recommendation to us. S 5 386 1
Charlotte was settled with Mrs P.-- in the drawing room in S 7 394 1
lodgings or other & be settled after breakfast tomorrow.-- S 9 411 1
who has a relation lately settled at Clapham, who actually S 9 412 1
nothing really incredible--and so it was settled.-- S 10 419 1
SETTLEMENT (2)
to your daughter, by settlement, her equal share of the PP III 7 302 14
directions to Haggerston for preparing a proper settlement. PP III 7 303 14
SETTLEMENTS (2)
son was, by marriage settlements, eventually secure; his NA II 16 249 2
preparations of settlements, new carriages and wedding PP I 18 103 77
SETTLES (2)
But so it always is with me; the first moment settles NA I 15 118 11
with which every body settles the abundance of those who MP II 5 226 62
SETTLING (19)
of a good heart; and in settling a family of females only SS I 7 33 3
have a brother and I a sister settling at the same time. SS II 11 224 26
They were visited on their first settling by almost all SS III 14 375 8
brother; more intent on settling with the post-boy, W 349 24
"Is that his design in settling here?" PP I 1 4 17
against the cruelty of settling an estate away from a PP I 13 62 8
While settling this point, she was suddenly roused by the PP II 11 188 3
of settling well, without farther expense to any body. MP I 1 6 6
writing to the attorney, settling with the servants, and MP I 4 34 1
He wrote in April, and had strong hopes of settling every MP I 4 40 14
After settling her at Thornton Lacey with every kind MP III 17 472 30
determination of never settling till he could purchase E I 2 16 6
you have been settling that I should marry Jane Fairfax." E II 15 287 33
34
is either reading to himself or settling his accounts." E II 18 312 50
not to be uneasy, and settling it with her father, that E III 10 392 7
lose neither consequence nor enjoyment by settling there. P III 2 14 10
fever, which finally settling in her legs, had made her P IV 5 152 4
altering her ribbon to settling her accounts, from finding P IV 10 220 31
P. had the pleasure of settling her new friends, & S 11 422 1
SEVE (1)
the clay of Staffordshire, as from that of Dresden or Seve. NA II 7 175 12
SEVEN (53)
very little more than seven miles; and, I suppose, we have NA I 11 88 54
of the kitchen, the six or seven rooms she had now seen NA II 8 183 2
of the sky between six and seven o'clock, or by the yet NA II 9 190 1
here at seven o'clock, and no servant will be offered you." NA II 13 224 18
I can be ready by seven. NA II 13 226 24
alarm, and between six and seven o'clock in the evening NA II 14 232 6
Their mother had nothing, and their father only seven SS I 1 4 2
live on the interest of seven thousand pounds, besides the SS I 2 12 24
Lady Middleton was not more than six or seven and twenty; SS I 6 31 8
a woman who is single at seven and twenty, I should not SS I 8 38 9
"A woman of seven and twenty," said Marianne, after SS I 8 38 10
you that a woman of seven and twenty could feel for a man SS I 8 38 11
Seven years would be insufficient to make some people SS I 12 59 4
each other, and seven days are more than enough for others. SS I 12 59 4
Sir John at about six or seven hundred a year; but he SS I 14 71 4
spent seven years at a great school in town to some effect. SS II 4 160 3
she sat at least seven minutes and a half in silence. SS II 12 229 3
away, in about seven days from the time of their arrival. SS III 7 309 6
At seven o'clock, leaving Marianne still sweetly asleep, SS III 7 315 27
and poor Nancy had not seven shillings in the world;--so I SS III 13 370 37
I had seven tables last week in my drawingroom. W 350 24
twelve ladies and seven gentlemen with him to the assembly. PP I 3 10 4
of Huntingdon, with only seven thousand pounds, had the MP I 1 3 1
seven years hence, and I dare say there would be mischief. MP I 1 7 6
it cost seven shillings, and was charged as a moor park." MP I 6 54 11
Now, at Sotherton, we have a good seven hundred, without MP I 6 55 17
For the first seven miles Miss Bertram had very little MP I 8 81 32
here so long before, full seven weeks; for I had MP I 12 115 5
I apprehend he will not have less than seven hundred a MP II 5 226 61
Seven hundred a year is a fine thing for a younger brother; MP II 5 226 61
menus plaisirs were to be limited to seven hundred a year." MP II 5 226 62
will have seven hundred a year, and nothing to do for it." MP II 5 226 63
through a period of seven years, and the uncle who had MP II 6 233 14
the one he had equipped seven years ago, but a young man MP II 6 233 16
and in the course of seven years had known every variety MP II 6 236 21
I shall let a seven years' lease of Everingham. MP II 12 295 20
Seven weeks of the two months were very nearly gone, when MP III 13 420 1
intercourse of the last seven years, the equal footing and E I 1 6 6
Mr. Knightley, a sensible man about seven or eight-and- E I 1 9 21
six days out of seven, and has always business at Ford's. E II 6 200 14
Seven miles were travelled in expectation of enjoyment, E III 7 367 1
nonsense for the entertainment of seven silent people." E III 7 369 15
Here are seven of you, besides myself, (who, she is E III 7 370 23
If he will adopt these regulations, in seven years he will P III 2 12 4
More than seven years were gone since this little history P III 4 28 7
alluded to,--but Anne, at seven and twenty, thought very P III 4 29 8
I have not seen him since seven o'clock. P III 5 37 25
not say whether it was seven or eight years ago,--was a P III 6 52 33
new place, after deducting seven hours, as the nature of P III 11 94 8
it must be remembered, had not been a widower seven months. P IV 4 147 8
elegant little woman of seven and twenty, with every P IV 5 153 6
expected him, but for his known engagement seven miles off. P IV 10 216 17
the space of seven hours, confessed herself a little tired. S 10 414 1
SEVEN-AND-TWENTY (1)
Depend upon it, a man of six or seven-and-twenty can take E I 1 14 48
SEVENTEEN (18)
But from fifteen to seventeen she was in training for a NA I 1 15 3
She had reached the age of seventeen, without having seen NA I 1 16 10
and uninformed as the female mind at seventeen usually is. NA I 2 18 1
of a young lady of seventeen, just returned from her first NA II 14 235 13
"Remember, my love, that you are not seventeen. SS I 3 18 21
"Perhaps," said Elinor, "thirty-five and seventeen had SS I 8 37 9
At seventeen, she was lost to me for ever. SS II 9 205 24
between thirty-six and seventeen, brought him to Barton in SS III 13 369 35
so late in life as at seventeen, and with no sentiment SS III 14 378 15
part of the sons, who at seventeen and sixteen, and tall MP I 2 12 3
of seventeen will always think fair with a child of ten. MP I 2 17 22
"Yes, I know there is, till I am seventeen. MP I 2 19 28
Miss Smith was a girl of seventeen whom Emma knew very E I 3 22 7
to answer questions which puzzled her sister at seventeen. E I 5 37 9
And is she, at seventeen, just entering into life, just E I 8 64 46
real respectability for seventeen years; and though not P III 1 4 6
himself; it was only seventeen miles from Uppercross; P III 11 94 7
And at Lyme too,--only seventeen miles off,--he would be P III 12 103 2
SEVENTH (1)
of Thornton Lacey every seventh day, for three or four MP II 7 247 42
SEVENTY (3)
there; but a journey of seventy miles, to be taken post by NA II 13 225 23
this will not do seventy miles from London--but this MP I 6 57 33
had been thinking of as seventy miles off, and as farther, MP III 3 334 1
SEVENTY-SIX (1)
two hundred and seventy-six pages in each, with a NA I 14 113 39
SEVERAL (79)
days last week, & called several times in Edward Street. LS 9 256 1
fix herself in town for several months, she could not be LS 41 310 3
at her attentively for several minutes, addressed her with NA I 4 31 2
A silence of several minutes succeeded their first short NA I 9 63 10
I took him down several times you know in my way." NA II 1 135 41
and through this into several others, without perceiving NA II 5 160 21
out, and observing several doors, that were neither opened NA II 8 183 2
fancies than all their several disappointments had done. NA II 10 199 1
Her mind made up on these several points, and her NA II 10 201 4
noble relations in their several phaetons, and three NA II 14 232 7
Mrs. Dashwood remained at Norland several months; not from SS I 3 14 1
judgment rejected several houses as too large for their SS I 3 14 1
Edward had been staying several weeks in the house before SS I 3 16 7
He had been to several families that morning in hopes of SS I 7 33 4
It was several days before Willoughby's name was mentioned SS I 16 85 11
12
and several neat farm houses scattered here and there. SS I 18 97 4
Mrs. Palmer was several years younger than Lady Middleton, SS I 19 106 22
have been wanting us to visit them these several years! SS II 2 151 40
After a pause of several minutes, their silence was broken, SS II 5 172 40
kissed her affectionately several times, and then gave way SS II 7 182 12
she has had a nervous complaint on her for several weeks." SS II 11 227 49
for she loitered away several minutes on the landing-place, SS II 13 241 23
meaning, and conversed with her there for several minutes. SS III 3 280 9
the better, it required several hours to give sedateness SS III 13 363 8
to cut--and he drew several plans for magnificent cottages; SS III 14 376 11
and there are several of them you see uncommonly pretty." PP I 3 11 10
They had several children. PP I 5 18 2
to the entreaties of several that she would sing again, PP I 6 25 23
the preceding Wednesday; several of the officers had dined PP I 12 60 7
he is unacquainted with several parts of the story, and PP I 18 96 55
her progress through the several stanzas with an PP I 18 100 68
as I have already said, may not be for several years. PP I 19 106 10
Mrs. Gardiner, who was several years younger than Mrs. PP II 2 139 2
say, one of her ladyship's carriages, for she has several." PP II 5 157 7
I have told Miss Bennet several times, that she will never PP II 8 173 10
After a silence of several minutes he came towards her in PP II 11 189 3
4
amongst several other miniatures, over the mantle-piece. PP III 1 247 9
She stood several minutes before the picture in earnest PP III 1 250 47
and, after a pause of several minutes, was only recalled PP III 4 278 20
as had marked their several meetings in Derbyshire; and as PP III 4 279 23
And there are several of the young men, too, that she PP III 8 313 21
Mr. Darcy called, and was shut up with him several hours. PP III 10 321 2
They met several times, for there was much to be discussed. PP III 10 323 2
We passed each other several times. PP III 10 328 16
her daughter made Mrs. Bennet very dull for several days. PP III 11 330 9
down in a day or two, to shoot there for several weeks. PP III 11 331 13
But now several minutes elapsed, without bringing the PP III 11 335 43
After walking several miles in a leisurely manner, and too PP III 16 370 35
doing several things that Sir Thomas and I used to talk of. MP I 6 54 9
to chuse from among several gold chains and necklaces. MP II 8 257 15
not being in town by several days so soon as I expected; MP II 9 261 2
He talked therefore for several minutes without Fanny's MP III 1 314 16
not by dint of several minutes of supplication and waiting. MP III 3 341 27
And there were several improvements in the dock-yard, too, MP III 6 372 18
under different degrees of danger, lasted several weeks. MP III 14 432 11
Somebody had placed her, several years back, at Mrs. E I 3 22 8
likenesses, and attempted several of my friends, and was E I 6 43 13
can only recollect the first stanza; and there are several. E I 9 78 54
and "my son," repeated several times over; and from a few E I 14 118 4
had been settled for several generations at Hartfield, the E I 16 136 9
There were several very pretty houses in and about it.-- E II 5 191 27
passing on, he stopt for several minutes at the two E II 6 197 5
to see her well; these several delays left him not another E III 3 334 8
after an interval of several years, felt with anger by P III 1 8 17
he has been stationed there, I believe, several years." P III 3 21 21
her from Kellynch for several weeks, she was unable to P III 5 33 6
I have been several times in the garden with Mackenzie, P III 5 38 34
He had been several years at sea, and had, in the course P III 6 51 30
Anne had called several times on her friend, before the P IV 5 156 14
It had been begun several days back. P IV 6 162 6
There are several odd-looking men walking about here, who, P IV 6 166 16
They had been thrown together several weeks; they had been P IV 6 167 19
now asked in vain for several particulars of the company. P IV 9 192 5
sight of several persons now coming to their assistance. S 1 364 1
"I have read several of Burn's poems with great delight, S 7 397 1
from one, out of the several Phials already at home on the S 10 413 1
before breakfast--& take several turns upon the terrace, & S 10 416 1
my right side is entirely taken away for several hours!" S 10 418 1
She had several more under her care than the three who S 11 421 1
SEVERE (60)
He is very severe against me indeed, & yet I hope I have LS 15 266 2
Lady Susan is surely too severe, because Frederica does LS 17 270 4
Mrs. Morland will be naturally supposed to be most severe. NA I 2 18 2
This compliment, delightful as it was, produced severe NA I 8 54 10
friendly to very severe, very intense application, may NA I 14 110 27
each morning became more severe: but, on the tenth, when NA II 10 201 6
feeling was rendered more severe by the review of objects NA II 14 230 1
Mr. Dashwood's disappointment was, at first, severe; but SS I 1 4 4
and on those still more severe which might await her in SS II 6 179 18
"Her sufferings have been very severe. SS II 8 199 40
far, and the blow was a severe one--but had her marriage SS II 9 206 24
to be inflicting a severe disappointment when she told her SS II 12 231 11
made every ailment more severe; for on that day they were SS III 7 308 4
"Upon my word, you are severe upon my friend!-- W 340 19
"You are severe on us." PP I 6 24 20
"Are you so severe upon your own sex, as to doubt the PP I 8 40 53
upon it, he means to be severe on us, and our surest way PP I 11 56 13
yet merited reproach, her sense of shame was severe. PP II 13 208 10
entered the room, the misery of her impatience was severe. PP III 4 280 26
that can alleviate so severe a misfortune; or that may PP III 6 296 11
"You must not be too severe upon yourself," replied PP III 6 299 20
in Hertfordshire, was a severe disappointment; and besides, PP III 8 313 20
the despondence that sunk her little heart was severe. MP I 2 14 8
a correspondent, makes her think you too severe upon us." MP I 6 59 45
was an instance of very severe ill-luck; and his MP II 2 191 10
supported her, but the agony of her mind was severe.-- MP II 2 193 18
unhandsome in us to be severe on Mrs. Rushworth, for I MP II 4 210 21
the severe one of shame for the home in which he found her. MP III 10 400 6
"Indeed, Harriet, it would have been a severe pang to lose E I 7 54 27
could sometimes act an ungracious, or say a severe thing. E I 11 93 5
constitution, and pretty severe Philippics upon the many E I 12 104 50
The cold, however, was severe; and by the time the second E I 13 112 24
charm away a sore throat; it is a most severe cold indeed. E I 13 114 32
penance of communication; and a severe one it was.-- E I 17 141 5
a severe camp-fever, as he believed had saved his life. E II 2 163 4
Liable as you have been to severe colds, indeed you ought E II 16 295 33
"I hope," said he presently, "I have not been severe upon E II 18 309 33
in her general conduct, be open to any severe reproach. E III 8 377 1
"It must be a severe trial to them all. E III 8 380 9
she was suffering under severe headachs, and a nervous E III 9 389 16
Don't let us be severe, don't let us be in a hurry to E III 10 398 53
second disappointment would be more severe than the first. E III 11 403 2
which this one article marked, gave her severe pain. E III 11 410 35
that there was no being severe; and could he have entered E III 15 444 1
We will not be severe." E III 15 445 7

my happiness to you, would not it be severe on them?" E III 17 461 5
highly, and as to the severe degree of self-denial, which P III 2 13 5
"Nay, Sir Walter," cried Mrs. Clay, "this is being severe P III 3 20 17
he was continually making severe remarks upon, in her P III 5 34 12
in good health since a severe wound which he received two P III 11 94 6
The head had received a severe contusion, but he had seen P III 12 112 52
sensations of pain, once severe, but now softened; and of P IV 1 123 8
have their own pain, and severe was its kind; but they P IV 1 125 17
sort to contend with a severe rheumatic fever, which P IV 5 152 4
bed, and suffering under severe and constant pain; and all P IV 5 154 9
recently escaped from severe pain, or are recovering the P IV 5 155 9
was; and Elizabeth was disdainful, and Sir Walter severe. P IV 5 157 14
The interruption had been short, though severe; and ease P IV 10 226 65
From that period his penance had become severe. P IV 11 242 64
me suffering under a more severe attack than usual of my S 5 386 1

SEVERED (1)
such a friendship as theirs should be severed unfairly. P IV 6 166 18

SEVERELY (13)
I blame myself severely for having so easily beleived the LS 14 264 4
I must punish Frederica, & pretty severely too, for her LS 25 293 4
I am the last person in the world to judge you severely. NA II 3 146 18
I felt for my sister most severely. SS I 3 17 18
His coldness and reserve mortified her severely; she was SS I 16 89 42
Marianne severely censured herself for what she had said; SS I 18 99 14
preceding, and most severely condemned by the event, when SS II 7 188 43
her good manners were severely taxed to conceal her MP I 7 70 30
upon no account. it would be mortifying her severely. MP II 9 262 11
attempt to describe; how severely mortified, how cruelly MP II 13 299 5
behalf, she could not be severely resentful of any thing MP II 13 301 7
to censure severely the faults of conduct to which it led. MP III 9 395 4
light, and severely aggravated the folly of her choice. MP III 16 452 13

SEVEREST (4)
the whole world, & the severest resentment of her injured LS 22 282 8
future intercourse the severest punishment; & your LS 25 292 3
to you at the time, had merited the severest reproof. PP III 16 367 12
But her uncle's anger gave her the severest pain of all. MP III 1 321 46

SEVERITY (13)
my daughter with some severity while she is here;--a most LS 15 267 6
seem to have the sort of temper to make severity necessary. LS 17 270 4
other, the invariable severity of Lady Susan, & the silent LS 17 270 5
was a spoilt child; the severity which it has since been LS 24 288 11
She was quite pained by the severity of his father's NA II 5 154 2
will soon set in, and in all probability with severity. SS II 5 167 3
not to attribute the severity and danger of this attack, SS III 7 313 21
But from the severity of that blame which was last night PP II 12 196 5
aunt had been continually contrasted with his own severity. MP III 17 463 7
herself would be greater severity and restraint--made her MP III 17 466 18
arrear due of secret severity in her reflections on the E III 6 353 3
The severity of the fall was broken by their slow pace & S 1 364 1
was a situation which must not be judged with severity.-- S 12 426 1

SEVERUS (1)
Roman emperors as low as Severus; besides a great deal of MP I 2 18 25

SEWELL'S (1)
"but which way did you turn after passing Sewell's farm?" MP II 7 241 14

SEX (37)
attachments & detesting the sex, might be reasonably LS 42 313 8
resolution of humbling the sex, they set off immediately NA I 6 43 44
where the beauty of her own sex is concerned, ventured at NA I 7 48 32
will recommend him to your sex I believe: and how do you NA I 7 50 45
recommend him to all her sex; but in spite of this, the NA I 9 66 32
from which one of the other sex rather than her own, a NA I 10 73 22
more trifling part of the sex, imbecility in females is a NA I 14 111 29
I have no patience with such of my sex as disdain to let NA I 14 112 36
is always desirable in your sex, as a means of getting you NA II 7 174 8
were such attentions; but I knew the fickle sex too well. NA II 12 217 2
esteems only those of his sex who are sportsmen likewise, SS I 7 33 3
like many others of his sex, that through some SS I 20 112 28
the dignity of her own sex, and spoken her decided censure SS II 10 215 14
reasonable, though his sex might make it rare; for his SS II 13 241 21
opinion among his sex, of all infants being alike; and SS II 14 248 5
understanding to half her sex; and time and habit will SS III 1 263 27
with no traits at all unusual in his sex and time of life. SS III 6 304 15
"Are you so severe upon your own sex, as to doubt the PP I 8 40 53
themselves to the other sex, by undervaluing their own; PP I 8 40 56
to the handsomest of her sex; because there is that in her PP I 14 67 7
established custom of your sex to reject a man on the PP I 19 108 16
17
in her behaviour towards the undeserving of the other sex." PP III 5 289 43
generous, she doubted not, as the most generous of his sex. PP III 8 311 14
Is there one among the sex, who would not protest against PP III 12 341 19
hundred of either sex, who is not taken in when they marry. MP I 5 46 20
of very much surpassing her sex in general by her early MP I 7 66 15
her sex, at least, let him be ever so generally agreeable. MP III 4 353 45
it in one's power to pay off the debts of one's sex! MP III 5 363 22
no young person of either sex belonging to him, to be MP III 17 465 13
of one of her own sex, after being used to it all her life. E I 5 36 6
I am very much mistaken if your sex in general would not E I 8 63 44
not breathe a compliment to the sex should pass his lips. E I 9 70 7
I always take the part of my own sex. E II 18 306 12
happened to hundreds of my sex before; and yet it may not E III 13 427 19
sex?" and she answered the question, smiling also, "yes. P IV 11 232 19
little bias towards our own sex, and upon that bias build P IV 11 234 30
All the privilege I claim for my own sex (it is not a very P IV 11 235 32

SEXES (1)
excellence is pretty fairly divided between the sexes." NA I 3 28 34

SHA'NT (2)
Michaelmas; and I am sure I sha'nt go if Lucy an't there." SS III 4 292 57
I am sure I sha'nt get a wink of sleep all night. PP III 13 348 40

SHABBINESS (1)
and a something of shabbiness or impropriety will be most NA I 10 74 22

SHABBY (7)
round, you were gone!--this is a cursed shabby trick! NA I 10 75 26
You are a sad shabby girl.-- W 350 24
worn and faded, so comfortless, so slatternly, so shabby. MP III 11 408 2
it, and told him how shabby it was in him, their best E I 8 68 58
it all extremely shabby, and very inferior to her own.-- E III 19 484 12
been gradually growing shabby, under the influence of four P III 5 37 21
22
Shabby fellows, both of them! P IV 6 170 29

SHADE (19)
of any change in those who walk under your shade!-- SS I 5 27 8
The setting always casts a different shade on it you know." SS I 18 98 12
beyond all doubt, that it was exactly the shade of her own. SS I 18 98 13
"Implacable resentment is a shade in a character. PP I 11 58 29
A deeper shade of hauteur overspread his features, but he PP I 18 92 19
for Mrs. Crawford, without throwing a shade on the Admiral. MP I 7 63 7
was darkness and shade, and natural beauty, compared with MP I 9 91 38
"I shall soon be rested," said Fanny; "to sit in the shade MP I 9 96 72
night, and the contrast of the deep shade of the woods. MP I 11 112 35
are so essential to the shade of a departed ball, she MP II 11 283 7
We must allow for the effect of shade, you know." E I 6 48 32
be all out of doors--a table spread in the shade, you know. E III 6 355 20
had another reason for avoiding a table in the shade. E III 6 356 29
bear it no longer--must go and sit in the shade." E III 6 358 35
Seats tolerably in the shade were found; and now Emma was E III 6 359 37
another to the delicious shade of a broad short avenue of E III 6 360 38
The shade was most refreshing, and Emma found it the E III 6 361 40
matter might add another shade of prejudice against him. P IV 7 178 27
"My dear, we shall have shade enough on the hill & more S 4 381 1

SHADED (2)
and standing back, well shaded and sheltered, and looking MP I 9 95 67
a sudden turn, and deeply shaded by elms on each side, it E III 3 333 5

SHADES (3)
perspectives--lights and shades;--and Catherine was so NA I 14 111 29
than he could describe to her the shades of his mind. SS I 9 44 21
Are the shades of Pemberley to be thus polluted?" PP III 14 357 62

SHADOW (11)
Afterwards he got worse, and became quite my shadow. NA II 12 217 2
a shadow of either, but in using the words so improperly. MP I 3 26 29
and there is not a shadow of either in the countenance or MP I 7 64 11
I would not have the shadow of a coolness between the two MP II 9 263 16
I would not have the shadow of a coolness arise," he MP II 9 264 16
to each other without any remnant or shadow of reserve." MP III 5 364 30
There is not a shadow of wavering. MP III 13 423 2
She had, indeed, scarcely the shadow of a hope to soothe MP III 15 442 22
any restraint; and the shadow of authority being now long E I 1 5 3
He had caught both substance and shadow--both fortune and E II 4 182 5
his possessing the shadow of a right to introduce himself. P IV 3 144 19

SHADOWS (1)
a sky, the effects of the shadows pursuing each other, on MP III 11 409 6

SHADY (4)
was hot, there were shady lanes wherever they wanted to go. MP I 7 70 30
A young party is always provided with a shady lane. MP I 7 70 30
It was shady enough in the alcove, but I declare I quite MP I 7 72 42
So shady in summer!" S 4 381 1

SHAKE (28)
shake of the head, your meditations are not satisfactory." NA I 3 29 47
and lengthened shake of hands, after learning, to their NA I 4 34 7
he, giving her a hearty shake of the hand: "where did you NA I 7 49 43
Upon my soul, you might shake it to pieces yourself with a NA I 9 65 28
Peals of thunder so loud as to seem to shake the edifice NA II 5 159 19
and having given a good shake to her habit, she was ready NA II 5 161 25
the eye, but could not shake the doubts of the well-read NA II 8 182 2
unjustifiable anger, could shake his fidelity, or NA II 15 247 15
Will you not shake hands with me?" SS II 6 176 7
Elizabeth was determined; nor did Sir William at all shake PP I 6 26 40
said she, endeavouring to shake off her gravity. PP I 18 93 38
He had said enough to shake the experience of eighteen. MP II 9 270 39
into explaining away that shake of the head to the MP III 3 341 31
"What did that shake of the head mean?" said he. MP III 3 342 33
What did that shake of the head mean?" MP III 3 342 33
With a friendly shake of his son's hand, and an eager MP III 7 379 20
with a melancholy shake of the head and a sigh, called his E I 11 93 5
Come, shake hands with me." E I 12 99 13
me how I did, and seemed ready to shake hands, if I would. E II 3 178 52
A very friendly shake of the hand, a very earnest "good E II 12 261 37
which made her at first shake her head over her own E II 13 265 5
and with a smile, and shake of the head, which spoke much, E III 9 385 7
with a smile; a look; a shake of the head; a word or two E III 15 445 14
15
sensations into a very, very earnest shake of the hand. E III 16 453 10
I am particularly glad to see and shake hands with you-- E III 18 476 48
busy as she was about Charles, she could not shake him off. P III 9 79 29
implied; and though with a shake of the head, and sighs P III 11 101 25
see the Admiral's hearty shake of the hand when he P IV 6 168 24

SHAKEN (14)
over, she wished that she had shaken hands with him too. SS III 12 359 12
shaken, her feelings must be hurt by such disapprobation. PP I 22 123 3
opinion could never be shaken, and for whose happiness she PP I 23 128 9
well, I trust; though her spirits are greatly shaken. PP III 5 286 30
many words; and having shaken hands with Edmund, meant to MP II 2 187 2
on youth, it had not shaken his determination of never E I 2 16 6
the evening, and actually shaken hands with her at last! E I 3 25 15
and shaken off all that was unworthy in their authority. E I 18 148 22
Churchill was a little shaken the following day, by E II 7 205 1
she must have shaken hands with him as heartily as ever. E III 15 444 1
you and I should make, if we could be shaken together. E III 16 456 33
must have so greatly shaken; but Mrs. Musgrove, who got P IV 2 134 30
He had grumbled & shaken his shoulders so much indeed, and S 1 364 1
neither of them at first felt more than shaken & bruised. S 1 364 1

SHAKES (1)
My cousin, Anne, shakes her head. P IV 4 150 17

SHAKESPEARE (9)
And from Shakespeare she gained a great store of NA I 1 16 7
taking up a volume of Shakespeare, exclaimed, "we have SS I 16 85 11
12
of being very recently closed, a volume of Shakespeare.-- MP III 3 336 9
of Shakespeare in my hand before, since I was fifteen.-- MP III 3 338 13
But Shakespeare one gets acquainted with without knowing MP III 3 338 13
"No doubt, one is familiar with Shakespeare in a degree," MP III 3 338 14
open, and we all talk Shakespeare, use his similies, and MP III 3 338 14
and saw you listen to Shakespeare the other night, will MP III 4 348 23
A Hartfield edition of Shakespeare would have a long note E I 9 75 25

SHAKING (11)
Good bye, he added shaking my hand with earnestness--I do LS 23 284 4
"Ah!" cried Mrs. Bennet, shaking her head, "then she is PP I 14 67 6
he was silent; till, shaking off his embarrassment, he PP II 18 234 37
38
was looking grave and shaking his head at the windows. MP I 9 85 4
swell of a cold gust shaking down the last few yellow MP II 4 208 11
Another short fit of abstraction followed--when, shaking MP III 5 360 15
"Ah!" said Mr. Woodhouse, shaking his head and fixing his E I 12 105 51
"Ah!--(shaking his head)--the uncertainty of when I may be E II 12 259 15
"I not aware!" said Jane, shaking her head; "dear Mrs. E II 17 299 7
"Me!" cried Emma, shaking her head.-- E III 18 474 35
They are parting, they are shaking hands. P IV 10 222 38

SHALLOW (1)
Such a strain of shallow artifice could not impose even NA II 12 218 3

SHAME (50)
her book with affected indifference, or momentary shame.-- NA I 5 38 4
took to herself all the shame of misconduct, or at least NA I 12 93 4
A misplaced shame. NA I 14 110 28
room, and to the rising shame of having harboured for some NA II 6 165 4
then added the shame of being caught in so idle a search. NA II 6 165 4
ray of common sense added some bitter emotions of shame. NA II 9 193 6
and with tears of shame she ran off to her own room. NA II 9 198 30
could not shame, and seemed hardly to provoke them. SS I 11 54 3
For shame, Willoughby. SS I 15 76 11
"Elinor, for shame!" said Marianne; "money can only give SS I 17 91 10
"She knows her own worth too well for false shame," SS I 17 94 44
"For shame, for shame, Miss Dashwood! how can you talk so! SS II 7 182 10
a shame for such ill-natured reports to be spread abroad. SS III 2 272 14
Oh for shame!-- SS III 2 274 18
sense of inferiority, she felt no particular shame.-- W 345 21
I shall tell Colonel Forster it will be quite a shame if PP I 9 46 38
of it, gave her all the shame and misery which a PP I 18 90 4
Elizabeth blushed and blushed again with shame and PP I 18 100 67
to give, which a just sense of shame would not conceal. PP II 13 204 1
yet merited reproach, her sense of shame was severe. PP II 13 208 10
by them; but all sense of pleasure was lost in shame. PP II 18 229 10
She was overpowered by shame and vexation. PP III 1 252 54
No sentiment of shame gave a damp to her triumph. PP III 8 310 7
than to any sense of shame at her eloping and living with PP III 8 310 10
such misery of shame, that she could hardly keep her seat. PP III 11 337 52
pains to overcome her shame in being so surprised, and MP I 2 15 10
Tom listened with some shame and some sorrow; but escaping MP I 3 24 4
"Oh! for shame!" cried Mrs. Norris. MP I 6 53 3
and save her from the shame of having Dr. Grant's carriage MP II 4 206 4
"Oh! shame, shame!-- MP II 7 249 53
she was ready to sink with shame, from the dread of Mr. MP II 13 304 16
fresh shame; and she did feel almost ashamed of herself, MP III 1 316 28
the severe one of shame for the home in which he found her. MP III 10 400 6
shame him from persisting any longer in addressing herself. MP III 15 438 5
She spoke from the instinctive wish of delaying shame, she MP III 15 440 16

with all the feelings of shame and wretchedness which MP III 16 454 18
truths, half a sense of shame--but habit, habit carried it. MP III 16 458 30
that it would be a shame to have him single any longer-- E I 1 13 46
The confession completely renewed her first shame-- and E I 17 141 6
It seemed quite a shame, especially considering how many E II 8 215 16
"For shame, Emma! E II 8 225 78
Leave shame to her. E II 10 243 27
of shame and feeling divided between wonder and amusement. E III 4 339 15
appear to censure; for she said, "nonsense! for shame!" E III 5 348 22
can never think of it," she cried, "without extreme shame." E III 18 477 52
"The shame," he answered, "is all mine, or ought to be. E III 18 477 53
Mary thought it a great shame that such a present was not P III 6 43 5
not of Frederick; and with shame at her own forgetfulness, P III 6 49 22
"For shame! for shame!--this is too much of flattery. P IV 8 187 29
There were so many to share in the shame & the blame, that S 11 420 1

SHAMEFACED (1)
Do not be so shamefaced. MP I 15 146 52

SHAMEFUL (10)
for society, and it is shameful to have you exiled from it. LS 26 295 1
it is a shameful length of time since I was at Stanton.-- W 335 13
the most shameful thing in the world if he did not keep it. PP I 9 45 36
Mr. Darcy's shameful boast of what misery he had been able PP II 11 188 1
him go without a tear!--it was a shameful insensibility." MP I 3 33 64
shameful towards herself, as well as towards Mr. Rushworth. MP I 17 162 19
indulgence appear in shameful contrast; and he wished he MP II 6 236 22
evil to himself; a very shameful and degrading connection. E II 8 225 78
which was all that was meant--and it is very shameful.-- E II 16 291 6
conduct on my side, such shameful, insolent neglect of her, E III 14 441 8

SHAMEFULLY (4)
What in a situation like mine, but a most shamefully SS III 10 345 20
I behaved shamefully. E III 14 440 8
Frank Churchill's confession of having behaved shamefully E III 15 446 19
"You did behave very shamefully. E III 15 446 20

SHAMELESS (3)
had reasonably forfeited by their shameless want of taste. SS I 7 35 9
simplicity, such shameless truth rather bewildered him.-- W 346 21
But his pride, his abominable pride, his shameless avowal PP II 11 193 31

SHAN'T (9)
me, for I shan't put myself at all out of my way for you. SS II 3 153 2
You shan't talk me out of my satisfaction. SS II 13 239 9
However, I shan't say anything against them to _you_; and to SS III 2 275 22
No Emma, whoever stays at home this winter, it _shan't_ be W 320 2
"You may have it in my dear, but I assure you I shan't W 354 27
But, however, that shan't prevent my asking him to dine PP III 11 333 26
whisper, "the men shan't come and part us, I am determined. PP III 12 341 16
17
as ever I open my mouth, shan't I?--(looking round with E III 7 370 24
me at Sanditon house, as I did last summer--but I shan't.-- S 7 399 1

SHAPE (14)
as possible in the same shape as before, returned them to NA II 7 173 3
drawing forth, in the shape of some fragmented journal, NA II 9 193 5
the sight of Japan in any shape: but even _she_ could allow, NA II 10 201 4
and till its size, shape, and ornaments were determined, SS II 11 220 3
but their colour and shape, and the eye-lashes, so PP I 10 53 58
or that came in the shape of a lover to any of them. PP III 17 378 42
It is the very room for a theatre, precisely the shape and MP I 13 125 14
Sorrow came--a gentle sorrow--but not at all in the shape E I 1 6 5
is a peculiarity in the shape of the eye and the lines E I 6 44 15
"Exactly so--the shape of the eye and the lines about the E I 6 44 16
should so immediately shape itself into the proper form. E I 9 74 25
That room was the very shape and size of the morning-room E II 14 272 18
seemed prosperity in the shape of an early abdication in P IV 8 189 46
which she could not so shape into any positive act of duty P IV 10 227 69

SHAPED (1)
and fashion, his good shaped face, his sensible eye, but; P IV 3 141 12

SHAPELESS (2)
The purposes for which a few shapeless pantries and a NA II 8 184 4
their lives in such a shapeless old cockleshell as that. P IV 6 169 25

SHAPING (1)
Sir Thomas had been amusing himself with shaping a very MP II 8 253 7

SHARE (113)
is celebrated, to gain any share of my regard; & I shall LS 3 247 1
& I do not in general share his feelings, I never can LS 26 296 5
of surviving _my_ share in this disappointment. S. V. LS 37 306 1
and perfectly satisfied with her share of public attention. NA I 2 24 28
gave her very little share in the notice of either. NA I 10 71 8
him almost an equal share with James in her notice and NA II 4 149 1
I hope he has not had any material share in bringing on Mr. NA II 10 204 20
in which you were wont to share at Bath, the very idea of NA II 10 207 38
author must share in the glory she so liberally bestows.-- NA II 14 232 7
for her sake, to whose share in them he looked anxiously NA II 16 250 3
But they would have been improved by some share of his SS I 6 31 8
share of his discourse to herself for the rest of his stay SS I 10 46 2
kindness which ensured her a large share of her discourse. SS I 11 54 6
of the others, by any share in their conversation, that SS I 11 55 6
You shall share its use with me. SS I 12 58 2
claim on my affection, which no other can possibly share." SS I 14 73 15
by, without claiming a share in what was passing. SS I 21 121 6
the work exceedingly, if she would allow me a share in it." SS II 1 145 19
a more than ordinary share of private balls and large SS II 2 151 43
the croud, and take their share of the heat and SS II 6 175 2
that Marianne was not present, to share the provocation. SS II 11 226 40
her, not one fell to the share of Miss Dashwood, whom she SS II 12 232 15
Some kindness as fell to the share of nobody but me!-- SS II 13 239 6
for the first time, some share in the expectations of Lucy; SS II 14 254 27
Miss Dashwoods very ready to reassume their former share. SS III 1 257 1
pleasing, might have a share in that emotion, her esteem SS III 3 283 20
and all your friends must share; and likewise as a proof SS III 4 289 31
Truth obliged her to acknowledge some small share in the SS III 4 290 36
she could have no share, without shedding many tears. SS III 6 302 4
helpmate, desirous to share in all her fatigues, and often SS III 7 308 3
no other could equally share, an apparent composure of SS III 10 341 6
to me; you will share my affections entirely between you. SS III 10 347 30
it, or had declined any share in a measure which carried W 347 22
I certainly _have_ had my share of beauty, but I do not PP I 1 4 20
afterwards to have their share of vexation; and it is PP I 6 23 10
tired of a conversation in which she had no share.-- PP I 11 58 33
rest of the ladies their share of Mr. Wickham's attentions. PP I 16 84 59
they should not have their share of society and amusement PP II 6 165 35
I must have my share in the conversation, if you are PP II 8 173 6
so as to avoid any share of the like censure, is praise no PP II 12 198 5
to be upon the spot, to share with Jane in the cares that PP III 4 280 26
herself; but she had her share of business as well as her PP III 4 281 29
by settlement, her equal share of the five thousand pounds, PP III 7 302 14
"I thank you for my share of the favour," said Elizabeth; " PP III 9 317 16
determine whether pleasure or pain bore the greatest share. PP III 10 326 3
"We will not quarrel for the greater share of blame PP III 16 367 13
But now she would no longer conceal from her, his share in PP III 17 374 19
power to take any share in the personal charge of her. MP I 1 9 10
home, and sustained their share in the introduction very MP I 2 12 3
sister-in-law to claim her share in their niece, the MP I 3 24 7
Fanny had no share in the festivities of the season; but MP I 4 35 6
The state of her spirits had probably had its share in her MP I 7 74 59
was not long in accepting her share of the civility. MP I 8 76 7
which restored him to his share of the party; and Mrs. MP I 8 80 28
She alone was sad and insignificant; she had no share in MP I 17 159 6
and then gladly take her share in any thing that brought MP I 17 161 9
Fanny did not share her aunt's composure; she thought of MP I 18 167 12
scheme, defending his own share in it as far only as he MP II 2 187 1
to encounter her share of it with tolerable calmness. MP II 2 193 17
fall to every sailor's share--like bad weather and hard MP II 7 249 53
but the wife who was to share, and animate, and reward MP II 8 255 10
of happiness as if she had been allowed no share in it. MP II 9 267 22
the room, and have their share of a pleasure which would MP II 10 275 12
night but remembrances, which she had nobody to share in. MP II 11 282 4
one in the house should share with you in the first MP II 13 298 2
had a moment's share in your thoughts on this occasion. MP III 1 318 39
a larger share than any one among so many could deserve. MP III 6 371 17
chamber that she was to share with Susan. MP III 7 387 47
Fanny longed to give her a share in her own first MP III 9 398 9
and letting Susan have her share of entertainment, with MP III 10 404 15
Nature had given them no inconsiderable share of beauty, MP III 11 408 2
her to see it fall to the share of her thankless son, and MP III 13 425 6
May God support you under _your_ share. MP III 15 442 23
attributing an undue share of the change, attributing _all_ MP III 15 446 34
Edmund could not share it. MP III 15 447 35
own peculiar and bitter share of this family affliction, MP III 16 453 16
by some hint of what share his brother's state of health MP III 16 459 31
measure attend _his_ share of the offence, is, we know, not MP III 17 468 22
Harriet was very ready to speak of the share he had had in E I 4 28 6
father died, whatever his share of the family property, it E I 4 30 20
I come in for a pretty good share as a second. E I 6 49 44
the tender and the sublime of pleasure to Harriet's share. E I 9 82 84
that any one should share with him in Isabella's first day. E I 12 98 1
She had not even a share in his opening compliments.-- E I 17 140 3
to have her share of surprize, introduction, and pleasure. E II 5 190 21
They were called on to share in the awkwardness of a E II 8 218 38
39
No, if he had believed me at all to share his feelings, he E II 13 265 4
unreserve, and her own share in the story, under a E II 15 282 3
Mrs. Elton's looks also received the due share of censure. E III 2 330 46
and gone through his share of this essential attention E III 12 417 4
in a proper share of the happiness of the evening before. E III 14 435 5
against the share of it which that woman has known.-- E III 14 441 8
had his five minutes share of it; but five minutes were E III 17 468 33
with a few months ended Anne's share of suffering from it. P III 4 28 6
believed, had the usual share, had even more than a usual P III 4 29 8
had even more than a usual share of all such solicitudes P III 4 29 8
inheriting a considerable share of the Elliot self- P III 5 37 21
she had sometimes more share than she wished, being P III 6 43 5
Mrs. Croft fell to the share of Anne, while the Admiral P III 6 48 17
Elizabeth's particular share in it she suspected; and that P III 12 107 21
previously alarmed by some share of delay; yet the time P III 12 114 64
Anne did not share these feelings. P IV 2 135 34
This was Sir Walter and Elizabeth's share of interest in P IV 6 166 17
of the past; yes, some share of the tenderness of the past. P IV 8 185 21
I assure you Mr. Elliot had not the share which you have P IV 9 197 33
share of ten thousand pounds which must be hers hereafter. P IV 12 248 1
in a very gentlemanlike share of luxuries & change--enough S 2 373 1
country, of which a large share of the parish of Sanditon, S 3 375 1
herself & her family that share of the accumulated S 3 377 1
us, which had so large a share in bringing on your S 5 386 1
indignation had the larger & the increasing share.-- S 7 402 1
anybody else, had their share in every exertion of S 10 412 1
There were so many to share in the shame & the blame, that S 11 420 1

SHARED (12)
in the fate of which she shared, by private partnership NA I 11 89 63
"No; my feelings are not often shared, not often SS I 16 88 33
and her mother equally shared, been overcome or overlooked; SS II 4 159 1
He shared it, however, in a silence even greater than her SS III 9 334 4
ladyship after a while shared the feeling, was more openly PP II 8 172 3
4
Their affectionate mother shared all their grief; she PP II 18 229 3
"Mary and Kitty have been very kind, and would have shared PP III 5 292 66
She shared in their attendance on Mrs. Bennet, and was a PP III 6 294 3
These shared her heart; her time was given chiefly to her MP III 8 389 4
nothing less, and Fanny shared her aunt's security, till MP III 14 429 1
If it were to be shared with the woman he loved, he could E II 6 204 42
her doing right, which no other creature had at all shared. E III 12 415 1

SHARER (1)
the sad poison, while a sharer of his conversation with E II 2 168 13

SHARERS (2)
must immediately be made sharers in their felicity; and NA I 15 121 27
while they are sharers of our intimacy at Rosings." PP II 15 216 4

SHARES (2)
Mrs. Croft seemed to go shares with him in every thing, P IV 6 168 24
It is very fit they should have daughter's shares; and I P IV 10 218 22

SHARING (11)
not be known, she was sharing with the scores of other NA I 8 53 2
mother and Elinor from sharing such delightful sensations. SS I 9 41 4
and sharing the kindness which they wanted to monopolize. SS II 14 246 3
of his sharing with herself in the bliss of the moment. SS III 9 334 4
so warmly insisted on sharing my fate, whatever it might SS III 13 367 22
of the same house, sharing the same amusements, objects of PP I 16 81 37
sharing, was left to the comforts of cold ham and chicken. PP I 18 100 68
her incapable of suitably sharing the distress even of MP III 15 443 24
Jane remained with them, sharing, as another daughter, in E II 2 164 6
of Jane Fairfax, and only sharing with others in a general E II 15 284 11
Anne, that instead of sharing in Mrs. Musgrove's kind P III 8 67 28

SHARK (3)
Or a trident? or a mermaid? or a shark? E I 9 73 17
Oh, no! shark is only one syllable. E I 9 73 17
us a charade made by a friend upon a mermaid or a shark? E I 9 73 18

SHARKS (1)
"Mermaids and sharks! E I 9 73 18

SHARP (18)
were pretty, and she had a sharp quick eye, and a SS I 21 120 6
"And yet I do assure you," replied Lucy, her little sharp SS II 2 146 5
of checking it, by Lucy's sharp reprimand, which now, as SS II 10 219 42
say to eliz: in a sharp quick accent, totally unlike the W 351 24
If she is half as sharp as her mother, she is saving PP II 17 228 31
They have a sharp, shrewish look, which I do not like at PP III 3 271 15
manner of Miss Crawford, nothing sharp, or loud, or coarse. MP I 7 64 11
sharp reprimand to Fanny; "I was out above an hour. MP I 7 72 42
I might speak pretty sharp; and I dare say it will cure MP I 15 142 22
you would have had a good sharp east wind blowing on you MP II 4 212 31
It was only better than Mrs. Norris's sharp answers would MP II 11 283 4
Sharp is the word, you see. MP III 7 380 20
care of yourselves--keep a sharp look out," he would give MP III 10 403 14
misbehave, can give them a sharp word now and then; but he E I 9 81 73
rational remonstrance or sharp retort equally ill bestowed. E I 11 93 5
It had been a frosty morning, to be sure, a sharp frost, P IV 3 142 13
"If I thought it would not tempt her to go out in sharp P IV 3 142 16
I hope they have a good sharp governess to look after them. S 6 393 1

SHARPEN (1)
yet to inspirit her play, sharpen her avarice, and harden MP II 7 240 8

SHARPENED (2)
general behaviour, was sharpened into particular PP I 3 11 6
the former was so sharpened by immediate disappointment, PP I 18 89 3

SHARPLY (2)
"I am not going to urge her,"--replied Mrs. Norris sharply, MP I 15 147 55
& cut his horses so sharply, that he might have been open S 1 364 1

SHATTER-BRAINED (1)
were a sad little shatter-brained creature; but now you NA II 14 234 12

SHAVING (1)
snug, with my little shaving glass in one corner, and P IV 1 128 28

SHAWL (12)
"for when I went up for my shawl I saw them from the MP II 4 211 28
disappointment--for the shawl which Edmund was quietly MP II 7 251 66
Fanny, William must not forget my shawl, if he goes to the MP II 13 305 25
he may go to the East Indies, that I may have my shawl. MP II 13 305 25
was snow on the ground, and she was sitting in a shawl. MP III 1 312 6
doors, with only a little shawl over her shoulders--and it E I 6 48 36
I made her take her shawl--for the evenings are not warm-- E III 2 322 19

warm--her large new shawl--Mrs. Dixon's wedding present.-- E III 2 322 19
but she was indeed behind, and too busy with her shawl. E III 5 346 17
She was afterwards looking for her shawl--Frank Churchill E III 5 349 25
back in the corner, with a shawl over her face, giving the P III 12 117 73
She must put her shawl over her shoulders, & be running S 10 619 1
SHAWLS (1)
I think I will have two shawls, Fanny." MP II 13 305 25
SHAWS (1)
away on that account--the Shaws are quite on her side.-- W 318 2
SHD (13)
company than of mine, & I shd most readily return to my W 320 2
I am sure I shd never have forgiven the person who kept me W 320 2
did not suit Capt. O'brien that I shd be of the party."-- W 326 5
"Would he give robt the meeting, they shd be very happy." W 359 28
In a good season we shd have more applications than we S 4 380 1
such very good hands, I shd have been with you at all S 5 386 1
I know you think it a great pity they shd give him such a S 5 388 1
of life he shd be encouraged to give way to indisposition. S 5 388 1
Why, what shd we do with a doctor here? S 6 393 1
two on his side--but why he shd talk so much nonsense, S 7 398 1
He only told me, & that but once, that he shd wish his S 7 400 1
You shd not move again after dinner." S 9 411 1
"We shd not have one at home, said he, but the sea air is S 10 415 1
SHE'LL (1)
I fancy she'll come back 'Miss Penelope' as she went.--" W 351 24
SHEATH (1)
both them and their sheath by cutting the latter to pieces SS III 12 360 22
23
SHED (5)
Many were the tears shed by them in their last adieus to a SS I 5 27 8
park; as to a stable, the merest shed would be sufficient. SS I 12 58 3
on it, and at first shed no tears; but after a short time SS II 10 217 17
Kitty was the only one who shed tears; but she did weep PP II 18 235 40
Till she had shed many tears over this deception, Fanny MP II 9 264 17
SHEDDING (4)
Lady Susan who had been shedding tears before & shewing LS 17 269 2
she could have no share, without shedding many tears. SS III 6 302 4
her friend;--and there, shedding tears of joy, though SS III 9 334 4
have guessed how many tears she had been lately shedding? E II 8 219 44
SHEDS (1)
In some countries we know the tree that sheds its leaf is MP II 4 209 16
SHEEP (2)
with his farm, and his sheep, and his library, and all the E II 8 225 74
their grass, and their sheep, and dawdling about in a way P III 9 73 2
SHEEP-SKIN (1)
device; said he, "the use of a sheep-skin for carriages. E I 13 115 36
SHEER (1)
and the Cleopatra, just to the eastward of the sheer hulk." MP III 7 380 20
SHEET (9)
collected every scattered sheet which had burst from the NA II 7 172 1
She seized another sheet, and saw the same articles with NA II 7 172 2
And the larger sheet, which had inclosed the rest, seemed NA II 7 172 2
He was tired, I dare say, for he had just filled the sheet SS I 22 134 52
The envelope contained a sheet of elegant, little, hot PP I 21 116 6
and hastily seizing a sheet of paper, wrote a short letter PP III 9 320 32
But it ought to be done, and if you will give me a sheet PP III 18 382 18
Bella, from one end of the sheet to the other, and any one E I 6 45 21
had seized a sheet of paper, and poured out his feelings. P IV 11 241 60
SHEETS (5)
it--it contains many sheets of manuscript--you hasten with NA II 5 160 21
of small disjointed sheets, was altogether but of trifling NA II 7 172 1
envelope containing two sheets of letter paper, written PP II 12 196 3
light than all Lady Bertram's sheets of paper could do. MP III 14 429 2
She always travels with her own sheets; and excellent E II 18 306 12
SHELF (2)
over the titles of half a shelf, and was ready to proceed. NA II 8 182 2
box which you will find on the upper shelf of the closet." P IV 9 202 68
SHELLS (1)
medals, cameos, corals, shells, and every other family E III 6 362 43
SHELTER (9)
carriage, was beneath the shelter of the old porch, and NA II 5 161 25
rising behind to give it shelter, were beautiful even in NA II 7 177 19
turn back, for no shelter was nearer than their own house. SS I 9 41 6
might safely, under the shelter of its noise, introduce SS II 1 145 23
endeavouring to find shelter under the branches and MP II 4 205 3
As soon as a general buz gave him shelter, he added, in a MP II 7 245 31
and keep all under shelter that he can;--here are we E I 13 113 26
as fast as she could, and took shelter at Ford's."-- E II 3 177 52
It began to rain, not much, but enough to make shelter P IV 7 174 2
SHELTERED (7)
sheltered from the north and east by rising woods of oak. NA II 2 141 13
where there was a nice sheltered path, which no one seemed PP II 7 169 5
The walk being here less sheltered than on the other side, PP III 1 254 57
back, well shaded and sheltered, and looking over a ha-ha MP I 9 95 67
situation, low and sheltered--its ample gardens stretching E III 6 358 35
favourably placed and sheltered, rose the Abbey-Mill Farm, E III 6 360 38
Charlotte, as in a sheltered Dip within 2 miles of the sea, S 4 379 1
SHELVES (3)
some herself,--some shelves in the closets up stairs." PP I 14 66 1
and fashioned very pretty shelves, for a tolerable P III 11 99 18
vol:s they had left behind them on Mrs Whitby's shelves.-- S 6 391 1
SHEPHERD (28)
hints of Mr. Shepherd, his agent, from his thoughts. P III 1 9 19
Their two confidential friends, Mr. Shepherd, who lived in P III 1 10 21
Mr. Shepherd, a civil, cautious lawyer, who, whatever P III 2 11 1
The hint was immediately taken up by Mr. Shepherd, whose P III 2 13 7
more of London, but Mr. Shepherd felt that he could not be P III 2 14 10
Mr. Shepherd had once mentioned the word, "advertise;"-- P III 2 15 14
It was with a daughter of Mr. Shepherd, who had returned, P III 2 15 15
Sir Walter," said Mr. Shepherd one morning at Kellynch P III 3 17 1
"He would be a very lucky man, Shepherd," replied Sir P III 3 17 2
let him have taken ever so many before--hey, Shepherd?" P III 3 17 2
Mr. Shepherd laughed, as he knew he must, at this wit, and P III 3 17 2
3
has its tax--I, John Shepherd, might conceal any family- P III 3 17 4
After a short pause, Mr. Shepherd presumed to say, "in all P III 3 18 9
10
so jealous for his own, as John Shepherd will be for him." P III 3 19 10
It seemed as if Mr. Shepherd, in this anxiety to bespeak P III 3 21 18
as he had foretold, Mr. Shepherd observed, Sir Walter's P III 3 21 18
feel; and given Mr. Shepherd, in his explicit account of P III 3 21 18
Mr. Shepherd answered for his being of a gentleman's P III 3 21 20
21
Mr. Shepherd hastened to assure him, that Admiral Croft P III 3 22 23
Mr. Shepherd was eloquent on the subject; pointing out all P III 3 22 24
A house was never taken good care of, Mr. Shepherd P III 3 22 24
"I have no conception whom you can mean, Shepherd; I P III 3 23 27
Mr. Shepherd was all gratitude. P III 3 23 31
As Mr. Shepherd perceived that this connexion of the P III 3 23 34
talked into allowing Mr. Shepherd to proceed in the treaty, P III 3 24 35
Mr. Shepherd was completely empowered to act; and no P III 3 24 38
have done, and that Mr. Shepherd thinks it the greatest P IV 1 127 28
Shepherd lives at one end, & three old women at the other." S 1 366 1
SHEPHERD'S (5)
He had his shepherd's son into the parlour one night on E I 4 28 6
What Miss Anne says, is very true," was Mr. Shepherd's P III 3 19 13
14
understanding his (Mr. Shepherd's) connection with the P III 3 21 18
behaviour by Mr. Shepherd's assurances of his being known, P III 5 32 2
was right; and Mr. Shepherd's clerks were set to work, P III 5 32 3
SHEW (81)
been necessary for me to shew, has entirely alienated her LS 24 288 11
She was in excellent spirits, & seemed eager to shew at LS 42 311 2
you know, and I am determined to shew them the difference. NA I 6 40 14
pass by them presently, and I am dying to shew you my hat." NA I 6 43 41
and therefore, to shew the independence of Miss Thorpe, NA I 6 43 44
Come along with me, and I will shew you the four greatest NA I 8 59 37
in conscious innocence, to shew her resentment towards him NA I 12 93 4
on the General's side to shew her over the Abbey? NA II 7 177 18
I shall be happy to shew it to you;--it is very like."-- NA II 7 181 39
I must shew it you some day or other. NA II 14 238 22
her if she would have the goodness to shew him the way. NA II 15 242 9
and then hastened to shew both letters to her daughters, SS I 4 24 20
as ever; and she wished to shew Mrs. John Dashwood by this SS I 5 25 3
who can have a right to shew that house; and as we went in SS I 13 68 70
wanted particularly to shew me the place; and it is a SS I 13 69 76
But I was willing to shew you that I had not forgot our SS I 17 92 25
so heartily at the question, as to shew she understood it. SS I 19 108 35
towards others, made every shew of attention and deference SS I 22 127 2
"I should be always happy," replied Elinor, "to shew any SS II 2 149 26
to shew by her tears that she felt it to be impossible. SS II 10 212 1
As my mother-in-law's relations, I shall be happy to shew SS II 11 222 9
to shew, and the master's ability to support it. SS II 12 233 18
busily helping Charlotte shew her child to the housekeeper, SS III 6 302 8
in town?-- that infamous letter--did she shew it you?" SS III 8 325 48
society it will be only to shew that my spirit is humbled, SS III 10 347 30
we suppose to make a shew with, and poor Nancy had not SS III 13 370 37
Emma found in Miss E.--the shew of good sense, a modest W 323 3
I assure you--I shall not shew myself here again when I W 335 13
as on every occasion of shew, her manner was all affection W 349 23
It seems to me to shew an abominable sort of conceited PP I 8 36 10
precipitance merely to shew off before the ladies." PP I 10 49 28
that she should be able to shew her married daughter in PP III 8 314 22
she went after dinner to shew her ring and boast of being PP III 9 317 10
never yet had courage to shew Mrs. Gardiner's letter, or PP III 11 334 36
"Go, my dear," cried her mother, "and shew her ladyship PP III 14 352 18
"My object then," replied Darcy, "was to shew you, by PP III 16 370 32
came to be civil, and to shew her civility especially, in MP I 8 75 1
was now almost equally well qualified to shew the house. MP I 9 84 3
to put them right, and shew them what true delicacy is.-- MP I 15 140 13
could hardly be said to shew any sign of alarm; but she MP II 1 179 10
We shew Fanny what a good girl we think her by praising MP II 11 285 11
would not allow herself to shew half the displeasure she MP II 13 301 7
If, as I am willing to suppose, you wish to shew me any MP III 1 321 48
with his niece, and to shew no open interference. MP III 2 330 14
by Crawford, and might shew that desire rather more MP III 4 350 30
Even Dr. Grant does shew a thorough confidence in my MP III 5 361 16
made, to shew his happiness and describe his uniform. MP III 6 368 7
He came; and he would have been delighted to shew his MP III 6 368 8
in the dock-yard, too, which he quite longed to shew her. MP III 6 372 18
Betsey went with alacrity; proud to shew her abilities MP III 7 379 16
A day or two might shew the difference. MP III 7 382 29
got there, my love?" said Fanny, "come and shew it to me." MP III 7 386 41
make a little circuit, and shew you Everingham in our way, MP III 12 416 3
But if you want to shew him any attention, my dear, ask E I 1 14 47
but his second must shew him how delightful a well-judging E I 2 17 6
Emma only might be as nature prompted, and shew herself E I 14 117 1
Cole does not know how to shew her kindness enough; and I E II 1 157 7
shew off in higher style her own very superior performance. E II 2 168 15
that she could not now shew greater kindness than in E II 3 177 52
one of my servants shall go with you to shew you the way." E II 5 195 45
of Jane Fairfax--and is always glad to shew them attention. E II 8 224 72
able to shew a most happy countenance on seeing Emma again. E II 10 240 2
just enough touched on to shew how keenly it was felt, and E II 13 265 5
would be most happy to shew you any attentions, and would E II 14 275 32
which they dared not shew in open disrespect to her, found E II 15 282 3
than yourself, can shew her any other attention than"---- E II 15 283 8
would soon shew them how every thing ought to be arranged. E II 16 290 3
But I will shew her greater attention than I have done." E II 16 291 6
"Well, well, I have that note; and can shew it after E II 16 298 54
simplicity of dress,--shew and finery are every thing. E II 17 302 22
was extremely anxious to shew his approbation to Miss E III 12 417 5
might have had a hint to shew themselves: and Anne walked P III 5 35 18
so impatient was he to shew his gratitude, by seeing P III 7 53 1
down, and instantly, to shew her enjoyment, ran up the P III 12 109 32
connection, as he had formerly taken pains to shew neglect. P IV 2 135 35
he was a dozen years ago, and I will shew him as he is now. P IV 9 204 80
friend, in being able to shew such pleasure as she did, in P IV 10 213 10
smile--if you were to shew me all the newspapers that are S 1 366 1
on;--and a smaller shew of company on the hill--fewer S 4 384 1
account--for her letters shew her exactly as she is, the S 5 386 1
with grandeur--such as shew her in the Sublimities of S 8 403 1
SHEWED (53)
declares that Miss Vernon shewed no sign of obstinacy or LS 17 271 7
deeply provoked as myself, & he shewed his anger more. LS 22 282 7
Her manners shewed good sense and good breeding; they were NA I 8 56 11
But for this Isabella shewed no inclination. NA II 3 147 28
this tender remembrance, shewed itself directly in her NA II 7 179 31
"Oh! no; she shewed me over the greatest part on Saturday-- NA II 9 195 15
that he sometimes shewed a want of pleasure and readiness SS I 8 39 15
in, and his countenance shewed that he strongly partook of SS I 15 75 2
by Marianne, who shewed more warmth of regard in her SS I 16 87 23
moment; and the countenance of each shewed that it was so. SS II 13 240 19
and with a voice which shewed her to feel what she said, " SS III 3 281 13
14
as she spoke--and her unsteady voice, plainly shewed. SS III 11 349 3
saw how much affection and solicitude they shewed for Jane. PP I 7 33 44
But to be sure, the good lady who shewed us the house, did PP III 1 258 74
While she spoke, an involuntary glance shewed her Darcy PP III 3 269 10
with an alacrity which shewed no doubt of their happiness. PP III 9 315 3
a cheerful look, which shewed her better satisfied with PP III 12 339 5
during dinner time, as shewed an admiration of her, which, PP III 12 340 13
voice and manner plainly shewed how really happy he was. PP III 13 348 34
You shewed me how insufficient were all my pretensions to PP III 16 369 24
was trying to suppress shewed how well it was understood, MP I 14 133 12
and shewed his feelings only by a determined gravity. MP I 15 148 60
But reflection brought better feelings, and shewed her MP I 17 160 6
performance, and who shewed herself not wanting in taste. MP II 4 207 6
standing round him, shewed how welcome was his sudden MP II 5 223 48
William and Fanny soon shewed themselves; and Sir Thomas MP II 6 233 16
and shewed even a warmth of heart which did him credit. MP II 10 278 20
occasion; it shewed a discretion highly to be commended. MP III 1 315 18
But Fanny shewed such reluctance, such misery, at the idea MP III 1 320 45
Susan shewed that she had delicacy; pleased as she was to MP III 9 397 7
A very few lines from Edmund shewed her the patient and MP III 14 429 2
was elegant and clever, shewed that there was no want of E I 4 26 2
did meet, his grave looks shewed that she was not forgiven. E I 9 69 1
She shewed it to me. E I 11 96 22
healthy, glowing faces shewed all the benefit of a country E I 13 109 6
She got her to Hartfield, and shewed her the most E I 17 142 10
no positive merit, they shewed, altogether, a good-will E II 6 197 3
about, and that he shewed a very amiable inclination to E II 6 204 43
little bustle in the room shewed them that tea was over, E II 8 226 85
Which you know shewed him to be so very . . . . E II 9 237 51
Mr. Knightley, however, shewed no triumphant happiness. E II 12 262 40
in a manner which shewed him not pleased, soon afterwards E II 15 287 33
34
a tear in the eye, shewed that it was felt beyond a laugh. E II 16 294 24
Charles Musgrove, indeed, afterwards shewed more of P III 7 55 6
Charles shewed himself at the window, all was ready, their P III 7 59 25
and natural grace, as shewed the kindest consideration for P III 8 67 28
But this was one of the points on which the lady shewed P III 10 86 17
was to be pronounced, he shewed himself so intimately P III 11 100 23
at her instantly in a way which shewed his noticing of it. P III 12 104 6

with a countenance which shewed something to be wrong; and	P III 12 111 50
blushing, very becomingly shewed to Mr. Elliot the pretty	P IV 3 143 18
A moment's reflection shewed her the mistake she had been	P IV 9 194 21
hurried, agitated air, which shewed impatience to be gone.	P IV 11 236 39
SHEWETH (1)	
difference to modify of all that "this indenture sheweth."	P III 5 32 3
SHEWEY (2)	
tolerable complexions, shewey figures, an upright decided	S 11 421 1
well kept, than new or shewey--and as Lady D. was not	S 12 427 1
SHEWING (33)	
Lady Susan who had been shedding tears before & shewing	LS 17 269 2
quiet manner, without shewing the smallest propensity	NA I 9 62 10
"It is only a quarter past four, (shewing his watch) and	NA II 9 195 18
till the present, of shewing them with how little	SS I 1 6 9
first admiration, by shewing that though perfectly well-	SS I 6 31 8
In shewing kindness to his cousins therefore he had the	SS I 7 33 3
her pocket and carelessly shewing the direction to Elinor.	SS I 22 134 52
openly shewing that I was very unhappy."--	SS III 1 264 29
Thank you, my dear, for shewing it me.	SS III 2 278 32
shewing that where I have most injured I can least forgive.	SS III 8 332 83
of pleasing, & shewing himself pleased in a right place.--"	W 340 19
You will not, I hope, consider me as shewing any	PP I 20 114 32
the opportunity of shewing it without her husband's help.	PP II 5 156 5
him out in his gig, and shewing him the country; but when	PP II 7 168 1
Then shewing her purchases: "look here, I have bought	PP II 16 219 3
spent in this manner, in shewing the Crawfords the country,	MP I 7 70 30
not even the relief of shewing her power over him; she	MP I 7 70 30
Her next proposition, of shewing the house to such of them	MP I 9 84 2
off at their expense, by shewing a curiosity and pleasure	MP II 3 198 12
Mrs. Grant's shewing civility to Miss Price, to Lady	MP II 5 218 18
as they had been before, shewing they could yet be	MP II 10 274 9
to recommend her as a wife by shewing her persuadableness.	MP II 10 281 34
should be delivered, shewing it to be a subject on which	MP III 3 340 24
the agreeable triumph of shewing her activity and	MP III 7 383 32
yet so far from pushing, shewing so proper and becoming a	E I 3 23 10
"At this moment, perhaps, Mr. Elton is shewing your	E I 7 56 44
Her wish of shewing you attention could not be doubted,	E I 11 94 15
fancy himself shewing no presumption in addressing her!--	E I 16 135 8
thinks of nothing but shewing off his own voice.	E II 8 229 97
But still she had inclination enough for shewing people	E II 11 247 2
properer person for shewing us how to do away difficulties.	E II 11 255 55
His looks shewing him not pained, but pleased with this	P III 11 101 24
see her, for the sake of shewing her the house and	P IV 3 137 2
SHEWN (50)	
Her solid affection for her child is shewn by placing her	LS 14 265 5
habit, she was ready to be shewn into the common drawing-	NA II 5 161 25
before of her being shewn over the house, and he now	NA II 7 176 17
She was here shewn successively into three large bed-	NA II 8 185 5
fatal morning, shewn something like affection for her.--	NA II 10 199 1
round the grounds, she was shewn, first into a smaller	NA II 11 213 21
She only wished that it were less openly shewn; and once	SS I 11 53 2
Why else should he have shewn such unwillingness to accept	SS I 15 78 23
us with less affection than his usual behaviour has shewn.	SS I 15 78 28
the greatest act of friendship that can be shewn Marianne.	SS II 9 204 19
The rest of Mrs. Palmer's sympathy was shewn in procuring	SS II 10 215 11
When the note was shewn to Elinor, as it was within ten	SS II 14 254 27
had been shewn, so much confidence had been placed!	SS III 1 265 36
to Fanny, and by her shewn to her mother, might not be	SS III 13 371 39
Emma was shewn to a very comfortable apartment, & as soon	W 323 3
when instead of being shewn into the usual little sitting	W 355 28
She was shewn into the breakfast-parlour, where all but	PP I 7 32 42
You have shewn him off now much more than he did himself."	PP I 10 49 30
which she believed she had most incautiously shewn.	PP II 13 207 6
On reaching the spacious lobby above, they were shewn into	PP III 1 249 43
principal bed-rooms, were all that remained to be shewn.	PP III 1 250 46
On reaching the house, they were shewn through the hall	PP III 3 267 2
There were many other views to the shewn, and though the	MP I 7 70 30
Rushworth's guidance were shewn through a number of rooms,	MP I 9 84 3
it; and he, in return, had shewn her all his choicest	MP I 10 103 50
I must admire the taste Mrs. Grant has shewn in all this.	MP II 4 209 14
His father had never conferred a favour or shewn a	MP II 8 253 5
Why should she lose a pleasure which she has shewn herself	MP II 9 263 12
room, after breakfast, when Mr. Crawford was shewn in.--	MP III 1 313 14
part of my commission, and shewn you every thing placed on	MP III 1 314 16
my behaviour must have shewn, formed a very favourable	MP III 1 318 39
But you have now shewn me that you can be wilful and	MP III 1 318 39
You have shewn yourself very, very different from any	MP III 1 318 39
been Miss Crawford, still shewn a mind led astray and	MP III 6 367 5
"mamma" who had certainly shewn no remarkable fondness for	MP III 6 371 17
had been there shewn than any she had reached herself.	E I 16 135 6
And I think she wrote us word that she had shewn them some	E II 1 160 20
He had just read elton's letter as I was shewn in, and	E II 3 173 28
He begged to be shewn the house which his father had lived	E II 6 197 3
such feelings as were now shewn, it could not be fairly	E II 6 197 4
and thirteen springs shewn their blossoms, as she	P III 1 7 12
Mr. Elliot had attempted no apology, and shewn himself as	P III 1 8 16
for the kindness he had shewn poor dick, and very high	P III 6 52 33
him; and worse, she had shewn a feebleness of character in	P III 7 61 36
Mary had shewn herself disobliging to him, and was now to	P III 10 90 37
Miss Hamilton, now Mrs. Smith, had shewn her kindness in	P IV 5 152 2
I have shewn you Mr. Elliot, as he was a dozen years ago,	P IV 9 204 80
Anne was shewn some letters of his on the occasion,	P IV 9 209 97
the one, Lady D. had shewn the good art of her character--	S 3 379 1
They were shewn into the usual sitting room, well-	S 12 427 1
SHEWS (13)	
very surprising--& yet it shews an illiberal & vindictive	LS 5 249 1
in my power, as my taking them out this evening shews.	SS II 14 253 21
The father is decidedly against him, the mother shews him	W 341 19
She danced twice with Capt. Hunter, & I think shews him in	W 341 19
to inspire devotion, & shews a much better taste.--	W 344 20
"It shews an affection for her sister that is very	PP I 8 36 11
It only shews her being deficient in something herself--	PP II 4 153 16
But at least it shews, that she was serious in the object	PP III 5 292 61
considering the event, shews some greatness of mind."	PP III 6 299 26
It does him the highest honour; it shews his proper	MP III 4 350 30
I honour that part of the attention particularly; it shews	E II 10 242 21
Ah! it shews what a sad invalid I am!	E II 14 280 54
But it shews you the man.	P IV 9 204 75
SHIELD (2)	
the same time wished to shield her conduct from censure,	SS II 5 174 45
Elizabeth did all she could, to shield him from the	PP III 18 384 27
SHIFT (7)	
were inevitably left to shift for themselves; and it was	NA I 1 15 3
helpless creature, but can shift very well for herself."	NA II 14 237 21
to the matter directly, and leave him to shift for himself.	SS III 2 273 16
No, no, let me shift for myself; and, perhaps, if I have	PP III 13 350 54
in Mrs. Goddard's hands to shift as she can;--to move, in	E I 8 62 42
with the help of a boarder, just made a shift to live!--	E II 14 275 33
You and I are to be left to shift by ourselves, with this	P III 7 56 10
SHIFTED (2)	
But here there was nothing to be shifted off in a wild	E III 17 468 31
So I got Sophy to lend me a hand, and we soon shifted	P IV 1 128 28
SHIFTING (2)	
of man; and of late it has been shifting about pretty much.	PP II 17 225 10
with a good tricking, shifting after-piece, and a figure-	MP I 13 124 10
SHIFTS (1)	
than all that a line of shifts and expedients can ever do.	E I 18 147 18
SHILLING (6)	
She, the heiress of a large fortune, he without a shilling!	LS 26 296 5
of her commanding a shilling--her writing desk, and her	MP I 16 151 2
if she had only a shilling in the world, she would be very	E I 10 85 19
her purse, gave them a shilling, and begged them not to	E III 3 334 6
on one of her heels, as large as a three shilling piece.	P IV 6 170 29
Not a shilling do I receive from the denham estate.	S 7 400 1
SHILLINGS (8)	
favourite gown, though it cost but nine shillings a yard."	NA I 3 28 35
I gave but five shillings a yard for it, and a true Indian	NA I 3 28 38
water, and laid out some shillings in purses and spars;	NA I 15 116 1
and paid ten or twelve shillings more than we did."	SS II 10 218 24
poor Nancy had not seven shillings in the world;--so I was	SS III 13 370 37
in such circumstances as to make five shillings any object.	PP I 16 83 50
it cost seven shillings, and was charged as a moor park."	MP I 6 54 11
be answered for) to spend even 5 shillings at Brinshore.--	S 2 374 1
SHINE (3)	
He was in fact excellently qualified to shine at a round	W 359 28
which he expected him to shine, by observing that he	PP I 14 66 1
that she meant to shine and be very superior, but with	E II 14 272 16
SHINES (1)	
Yes, certainly, the sun shines and the park looks very	MP I 10 99 17
SHINING (5)	
a broad staircase of shining oak, which, after many	NA II 5 162 28
of fifty years back, with shining floors, solid mahogany,	MP I 9 84 3
He is not a shining character, but he has a thousand good	MP II 2 190 7
her husband a leading, shining character, there would	MP II 3 201 22
with a small carpet and shining floor, to which the	P III 5 40 44
SHINS (1)	
still kicking each other's shins, and hallooing out at	MP III 7 383 31
SHIP (12)	
person. ship she valued beyond that of any other person.	PP I 22 123 3
wall, a small sketch of a ship sent four years ago from	MP I 16 152 2
lines, written as the ship came up channel, and sent into	MP II 6 232 12
or his being in such a ship. but the interest then excited	MP II 6 232 13
his early examination of ship news, the next morning,	MP II 6 232 13
That is ship;--plain as can be.--	E I 9 73 18
that he should soon have a ship, and soon be on a station	P III 4 27 4
a few hundred men to sea, in a ship not fit to be employed.	P III 8 65 11
day for us, when you were put captain into that ship.	P III 8 67 24
any ladies on board a ship of his, excepting for a ball,	P III 8 68 34
see them on board; and no ship, under my command, shall	P III 8 69 35
happiest part of my life has been spent on board a ship.	P III 8 70 54
SHIPPED (1)	
shipped off at last, with more than half his linen ready	MP III 8 390 7
SHIPS (4)	
each other, on the ships at Spithead and the island beyond,	MP III 11 409 6
as to the names of men or ships, that it had made scarcely	P III 6 51 31
out the ships which Captain Wentworth had commanded.	P III 8 64 7
ships I have lived in; and they have been five altogether."	P III 8 69 37
SHIPWRECK (1)	
nephew's account of a shipwreck or an engagement, every	MP II 6 236 21
SHIPWRECKED (1)	
Your peace will not be shipwrecked as mine has been.	P IV 9 196 32
SHIRKED (1)	
and she shirked her lessons in both whenever she could.	NA I 1 14 1
SHIRT (2)	
of thread or a second hand shirt button in the midst of	MP II 6 236 21
some time looking for a shirt sleeve, which Betsey at last	MP III 7 385 37
SHIRTS (1)	
Shirts, stockings, cravats and waistcoats faced her in	NA II 7 172 2
SHIVERING (3)	
than to have to wait shivering in the cold till all the	NA II 6 167 9
But a day spent in sitting shivering over the fire with a	SS III 7 307 1
but to convey five idle, shivering creatures into colder	E I 13 113 26
SHOCK (25)	
Tell him, that it would quite shock you to see me do such	NA I 8 58 23
The shock however being less real than the relief, offered	NA II 7 179 29
But, in such a cause, his anger though it must shock,	NA II 15 247 15
and herself, that the shock might be the less when the	SS II 3 157 17
It was too great a shock to be borne with calmness, and	SS II 4 162 8
The shock which her marriage had given me," he continued,	SS II 9 206 24
her!--as far as the shock of such a summons could be	SS III 7 311 16
The shock of Colonel Brandon's errand at Barton had been	SS III 9 335 6
"You quite shock me by what you say of Penelope--said Emma.	W 316 2
things may come out, as will shock your relations to hear."	PP II 8 174 15
shock is over, shall I own that I long for your return?	PP III 4 275 5
still agitated by the shock of such an attack from her	MP I 16 150 1
see that, in spite of the shock of her words, he still	MP II 1 175 2
It had been the shock of conviction as she read.	MP III 15 440 16
Tom's complaints had been greatly heightened by the shock	MP III 16 451 13
It had been serviceable in deadening the first shock,	E II 3 180 58
And though the consequent shock and alarm was very great	E II 8 218 37
You quite shock me; if you mean a fling at the slave-trade,	E II 17 300 14
It was a sad event--a great shock--with all her faults,	E III 9 388 13
In addition to all the rest, there had been the shock of	E III 10 399 57
Imagine the shock; imagine how, till I had actually	E III 14 443 8
Poor man!--it was at first a considerable shock to him,	E III 17 466 29
the effect of the suddenness of your alarm--of the shock.	P III 7 56 11
I am afraid you must have suffered from the shock, and the	P IV 8 181 4
Anne could not immediately get over the shock and	P IV 9 204 76
SHOCKED (36)	
He turned away; and Catherine was shocked to find how much	NA II 7 179 29
Elinor, though greatly shocked, still felt unable to	SS I 22 130 22
She was mortified, shocked, confounded.	SS I 22 135 55
Astonished and shocked at so unlover-like a speech, she	SS III 3 281 11
was so shocked in my life, as when it all burst forth.	SS III 5 299 35
immediately,--I was most uncommonly shocked indeed!--	SS III 5 299 35
I was too much shocked to be able to pass myself off as	SS III 8 330 69
the same direction, was shocked to perceive by Elinor's	SS III 11 353 24
"La! my dear," said Maria quite shocked at the mistake, "	PP II 5 158 15
charge, exceedingly shocked her; the more so, as she could	PP II 13 205 4
Elizabeth was shocked to think that, however incapable of	PP II 16 220 15
"I do not know when I have been more shocked," said she.	PP II 17 225 12
"I am grieved, indeed," cried Darcy; "grieved--shocked.	PP III 4 277 13
"I never saw any one so shocked.	PP III 5 292 62
Elizabeth was disgusted, and even Miss Bennet was shocked.	PP III 9 315 4
"Miss Bennet I am shocked and astonished.	PP III 14 356 60
She was quite shocked when I asked her whether wine was	MP I 10 105 55
by heart," said Fanny, shocked to find herself at that	MP I 15 145 49
I am shocked whenever I think that Maria could be capable	MP III 4 350 28
Fanny was quite shocked.	MP III 7 386 43
I am so shocked to see him, that I do not know what to do.	MP III 13 427 12
Fanny seemed to herself never to have been shocked before.	MP III 15 441 20
she was amazed and shocked; but it could not occupy her,	MP III 15 443 24
the subject in a manner which he owned had shocked him.	MP III 16 454 18
But I was really quite shocked the other day--for Mr.	E II 9 238 51
And so Patty told me, and I was excessively shocked indeed!	E II 9 239 51
of consequence--so shocked!--Jane and I are both so	E II 10 245 50
and I are both so shocked about the apples!"	E II 10 245 50
We really are so shocked!	E II 10 245 52
She was a little shocked at the want of two drawing rooms,	E II 16 290 3
How shocked had he been by her behaviour to Miss Bates!	E III 12 415 1
Shocked as Captain Harville was, he brought senses and	P III 12 111 50
I know those who would be shocked by such a representation	P IV 9 207 91
They could then see that she looked very ill--were shocked	P IV 11 238 45
I was startled and shocked.	P IV 11 242 65
Walter and Elizabeth were shocked and mortified by the	P IV 12 251 9
SHOCKING (35)	
from Lady Susan to contradict the late shocking reports.	LS 13 262 1
"It would have been very shocking to have it torn," said	NA I 2 22 11
I declare positively it is quite shocking.	NA I 10 75 23
It was amazingly shocking to be sure; but the Tilneys were	NA I 11 90 64
very shocking indeed, will soon come out in London."	NA I 14 111 29
Shocking as was the idea, it was at least better than a	NA II 8 188 16
said Catherine, "it would have been very shocking!"-----	NA II 9 197 28
Henry and her own heart only were privy to the shocking	NA II 14 230 3

We will not say how near, for fear of shocking the young SS I 13 66 57
would be a shocking thing, as we go away again to-morrow. SS I 20 110 2
you know," she continued--"he says it is quite shocking." SS I 20 113 37
a shocking thing to disappoint dear Annamaria after all." SS II 1 145 20
death, which is a melancholy and shocking extremity?-- SS II 2 148 14
Elinor, who knew that such grief, shocking as it was to SS II 7 182 12
13
by saying, "it is very shocking indeed!" and by the means SS II 10 215 14
in a whisper, a brief account of the whole shocking affair. SS II 12 236 41
was seated, "of the very shocking discovery that took SS III 1 265 34
and some exaggeration, the shocking rudeness of Mr. Darcy. PP I 3 13 19
they were grieved, how shocking it was to have a bad cold, PP I 8 35 1
"Oh! shocking!" cried Miss Bingley. PP I 11 56 16
"This is quite shocking!-- PP I 16 80 28
"It does seem, and it is most shocking indeed," replied PP III 5 283 10
said she, "it will be quite shocking to send her away! PP III 8 313 21
my word for it, it is a shocking trick for a young person MP I 7 71 34
grievances; and the shocking character of all the MP III 7 385 38
Mrs. Price plaintively, "it would be so very shocking!-- MP III 15 440 18
The event was so shocking, that there were moments even MP III 15 441 20
I am afraid you must have had a shocking walk." E I 1 10 22
There is something so shocking in a child's being taken E I 11 96 25
amiable as to make it shocking to disappoint him--that E I 16 138 15
nothing--makes such a shocking breakfast, you would be E II 9 237 46
as for the ball, it was shocking to have dear Emma E II 12 259 11
Shocking plan, living together. E III 17 469 36
Charles would be a very shocking match for Henrietta, and P III 9 76 15
room, "but it would be shocking to have Henrietta marry P III 9 76 16

SHOCKS (1)
a sort of thing that shocks me; I cannot understand it. W 318 2

SHOD (1)
Walk home!--you are prettily shod for walking home, I dare E I 15 127 15

SHOE (2)
found to have flung a shoe, Henry Crawford had been MP II 7 240 13
There was no blue shoe when we passed this way a month ago. S 4 383 1

SHOE-ROSES (1)
very shoe-roses for Netherfield were got by proxy. PP I 17 88 15

SHOE-STRING (1)
in letters, hair-powder, shoe-string and breeches-ball. NA II 7 172 2

SHOEMAKER (1)
Emma the name of her shoemaker--& concluded with saying, " W 347 21

SHOEMAKER'S (1)
Who wd have expected such a sight at a Shoemaker's in old S 4 383 1

SHOES (10)
trimmings--plain black shoes--appeared to much advantage; NA I 3 26 22
gown, the colour of her shoes, and the arrangement of her SS II 14 249 8
of sitting in her wet shoes and stockings--given Marianne SS III 6 305 17
but the ladies not having shoes to encounter the remains PP I 5 156 5
teeth, and how you do your hair, and who makes your shoes. MP III 5 360 16
Look at my shoes. E I 1 10 25
the way. I could change my shoes, you know, the moment I E I 15 127 14
solicitude for their shoes, anxious inquiries after Mr. E II 1 155 4
Quite thick shoes. E III 2 322 19
Blue shoes, & nankin boots!-- S 4 383 1

SHONE (2)
From them however the eight parts of speech shone out most NA I 15 120 24
For though Lady Bertram rather shone in the epistolary MP III 13 425 6

SHOOK (38)
she shook her head)--or it may be of something still less NA II 9 196 25
He shook his head. SS I 13 64 24
when we parted, he almost shook me by the hand while he SS III 8 330 69
She shook her head, put the music aside, and after running SS III 10 342 7
Elinor smiled, and shook her head. SS III 13 368 29
Emma shook her head in acquiescence.-- W 317 2
acquaintance, & Charles shook her by the hand & wished her W 335 13
He shook hands with Robert, bowed & smiled to the ladies, W 355 28
most tenderly, she even shook hands with the former.-- PP I 12 60 5
Wickham only shook his head. PP I 16 78 17
He shook his head.-- PP I 16 82 43
She shook her head. PP I 18 93 40
Jane shook her head. PP I 21 118 19
Elizabeth shook her head over this letter. PP II 3 147 24
upon their marriage; he shook his head when I expressed my PP III 4 275 5
Darcy shook his head in silent acquiesence. PP III 4 277 17
She looked at Jane, and smiled, and shook her head by PP III 11 331 13
They shook hands with great cordiality; and then till her PP III 13 347 33
her so expressively, and shook hands with such warmth, as PP III 17 374 22
Edmund smiled and shook his head. MP I 13 126 20
With something of consciousness he shook his head at his MP II 7 245 31
which she now and then shook back, and in the midst of all MP II 12 296 31
Here Fanny, who could not but listen, involuntarily shook MP III 3 341 31
"You shook your head at my acknowledging that I should not MP III 3 343 38
She immediately shook her head at Fanny with arch, yet MP III 5 357 6
Fanny shook her head. MP III 5 363 23
Mr. Knightley shook his head at her. E I 1 12 40
be very friendly, and we shook hands, and stood talking E II 3 178 52
He shook his head and laughed.-- E II 6 199 12
He shook his head with a smile, and looked as if he had E II 10 241 11
But Emma still shook her head in steady scepticism. E II 10 244 36
He shook his head; but there was a smile of indulgence E III 2 330 50
51
Even Mr. Weston shook his head, and looked solemn, and E III 9 388 13
their usual briskness: he shook her heartily and E III 10 400 69
with Mrs. Smith, she shook it off, and soon added in a P IV 5 156 12
13
She only smiled, blushed, and gently shook her head. P IV 5 159 22
looked earnestly, smiled, shook her head, and exclaimed, " P IV 9 195 29
30
Having run his eye over the letter, he shook his head & S 5 385 1

SHOOT (6)
task "to teach the young idea how to shoot." NA I 1 15 6
get here in time--but I shoot with Ld Osborne, & therefore W 360 28
down in a day or two, to shoot there for several weeks. PP III 11 331 13
and shoot as many as you please, on Mr. Bennet's manor. PP III 11 337 53
for his coming next morning to shoot with her husband. PP III 13 345 19
he was coming the very next morning to shoot with Charles. P III 7 58 22

SHOOTING (10)
foretold the winner; of shooting parties, in which he had NA I 9 66 31
I had no notion but he would go a shooting, or something PP III 17 374 20
in the intervals of shooting and sleeping, to have MP I 12 114 3
have another fine fancy suit by way of a shooting dress.-- MP I 15 138 3
enjoyment, was out snipe shooting; Edmund, she had too MP II 9 267 22
"Oh! Charles is out shooting. P III 5 37 25
when he came in from shooting, of his meaning to dress P III 7 55 7
Wentworth being gone a shooting together, as the sisters P III 10 83 3
to give him some shooting, and he seemed quite delighted, P IV 2 130 5
of doing something, as shooting was over, Charles had P IV 10 216 19

SHOOTING-JACKET (1)
all manly dresses a shooting-jacket was the most becoming. SS I 9 43 11

SHOP (32)
hat you can imagine, in a shop window in Milsom-Street NA I 6 39 4
who, she had reason to believe, were in a shop hard by. NA I 12 91 3
I turned directly into a shop that he might not speak to NA II 12 217 2
inquiry; and in whatever shop the party were engaged, her SS II 4 164 24
"In a stationer's shop in Pall Mall, where I had business. SS II 8 199 37
for I staid in the shop till they were gone, was a Mrs. SS II 8 199 37
toothpick-case in the shop, were finally arranged by his SS II 11 220 3
around her, in Mr. Gray's shop, as in her own bed-room. SS II 11 221 4
to make a very creditable appearance in Mr. Gray's shop. SS II 11 221 7
I have entered many a shop to avoid your sight, as the SS III 8 326 55
to their aunt and to a milliner's shop just over the way. PP I 7 28 3
or a really new muslin in a shop window, could recal them. PP I 15 72 7
something in an opposite shop, and fortunately had just PP I 15 72 8
to see Mr. Jones's shop boy in the street, who had told PP I 15 73 11
money, for we have just spent ours at the shop out there." PP II 16 219 3
much much uglier in the shop; and when I have bought some PP II 16 219 4
and the butcher's son-in-law left word at the shop." MP I 6 57 33
entirely, and planted up to shut out the blacksmith's shop. MP II 7 242 23
and haberdasher's shop united; the shop first in size and E II 3 178 52
united; the shop first in size and fashion in the place.-- E II 3 178 52
end of the shop; and I kept sitting near the door!-- E II 3 178 52
this must be the very shop that every body attends every E II 6 199 14
When the gloves were bought and they had quitted the shop E II 6 201 26
travelling homewards from shop with her full basket, two E II 9 233 24
Voices approached the shop--or rather one voice and two E II 9 235 43
at last move out of the shop, with no further delay from E II 9 237 47
48
a shop, invited them all to go back with her into the town. P III 12 103 5
once, as he had stood in a shop in Bond-Street, he had P IV 3 141 13
I can never get by this shop without stopping. P IV 6 169 25
the little crowd in the shop understand that Lady P IV 7 176 10
the corner of the baker's shop, the sound of a harp might S 4 383 1
In this row were the best milliner's shop & the library--a S 4 384 1

SHOPPING (2)
and shopping, and the evening at one of the theatres. PP II 4 152 5
My aunt always sends me off when she is shopping. E II 9 234 30

SHOPS (10)
Every morning now brought its regular duties;--shops were NA I 3 25 1
a charming place, sir; there are so many good shops here.-- NA I 3 29 46
but what we have very good shops in Salisbury, but it is NA I 3 29 46
and at all the little chandler's shops which they passed. NA II 11 212 17
all accompany her to some shops where she had business SS II 4 164 23
country for my part, except the shops and public places. PP I 9 43 21
be allowed to go to the shops they came out expressly to MP III 10 403 13
and variety, by the streets, the shops, and the children.-- E III 14 435 4
and recommendations to shops; with intervals of every help P IV 10 220 31
The shops were deserted--the straw hats & pendant lace S 6 389 1

SHORE (11)
been often taken on shore by the favour of his captain, MP II 6 236 21
cheerful hopes of being on shore some part of every day MP III 7 384 35
stupid and unmanageable on shore; that he had been very P III 6 50 28
He was rich, and being turned on shore, fully intended to P III 7 61 38
themselves on the sea shore, and lingering only, as all P III 11 96 10
in with all the grandeur which so flat a shore admitted. P III 12 102 1
The peace turned him on shore at the very moment, and he P IV 11 233 20
water 10 yards from the shore--no mud--no weeds--no slimey S 1 369 1
them be nearer the shore for fear of their tumbling in.-- S 4 383 1
talk of the sea & the sea shore--& ran with energy through S 7 396 1
wind blowing directly on shore; but she had not reached S 9 406 1

SHORT (337)
jealous; so jealous in short, & so enraged against me, LS 2 245 1
In short, I am persuaded that his continuing here beyond LS 8 255 1
at her disappointment, & in short were very agreable. LS 9 257 1
kind of confidence, and in short are likely to be engaged LS 10 258 2
of a clever woman for a short period, & of yeilding LS 12 261 6
Susan than to enjoy for a short time (as you have yourself LS 14 263 2
In short when a person is always to deceive, it is LS 17 272 8
In short, I found that she had in the first place actually LS 22 281 5
indifferent subjects for a short time, said to me, "I find LS 23 284 6
In short Catherine, everything has gone wrong--but it is LS 24 287 9
a short distance of you. Yr most attached S. Vernon. LS 25 294 7
& for everything in short but her principles; there I LS 27 296 1
There she fell miserably short of the true heroic height. NA I 1 16 10
been for a short time forgotten, was introduced likewise. NA I 4 32 4
Yet he had not mentioned that his stay would be so short! NA I 5 35 2
"It is only Cecilia, or Camilla, or Belinda;" or, in short, NA I 5 38 4
But this detestation, though so just, was of short NA I 7 44 2
on her he bestowed a whole scrape and half a short bow. NA I 7 45 5
to nothing more than a short decisive sentence of praise NA I 7 48 32
Mrs. Allen; and after a short silence, she added, "he is a NA I 8 58 32
at that moment bear a short delay in favour of a drive, NA I 9 61 6
to get through a few short sentences in her praise, after NA I 9 62 7
A silence of several minutes succeeded their first short NA I 9 63 10
After a short pause, "it comes on faster and faster!" said NA I 11 82 8
She listened reluctantly, and her replies were short. NA I 11 88 54
grown cold and indifferent, in short, towards herself. NA I 13 98 2
Catherine was sorry, but could do no more; and a short NA I 13 99 4
The general pause which succeeded his short disquisition NA I 14 111 29
The letter, whence sprang all this felicity, was short, NA I 15 122 28
me to death I dare say; but I shall cut him very short. NA II 1 130 13
except that of having b a short set to dance down enjoyed NA II 1 131 15
Can you, in short, be prevailed on to quit this scene of NA II 2 139 7
After a short pause, Catherine resumed with "then you do NA II 4 151 17
but a very short time, perhaps only a few days behind us. NA II 4 152 29
A very short trial convinced her that a curricle was the NA II 5 156 5
After a very short search, you will discover a division in NA II 5 159 19
out his watch, he stopped short to pronounce it with NA II 5 162 27
In short, she could not sleep till she had examined it. NA II 6 168 10
in some way or other, by its falling short of his plan. NA II 7 178 23
what the something was, a short sentence of Miss Tilney's, NA II 8 186 6
Her illness was sudden and short; and, before I arrived it NA II 8 186 12
Catherine said nothing--after a short silence, during NA II 9 196 23
On the third day, in short as soon as she could be NA II 9 196 25
Henry's address, short as it had been, had more thoroughly NA II 10 199 1
But now--in short, she made herself as miserable as NA II 10 199 1
change of countenance, and short exclamations of sorrowing NA II 10 202 8
Catherine took her place at the table, and, after a short NA II 10 203 9
"But," said Eleanor, after a short pause, "would it be to NA II 10 205 30
made her for a short time sensible only of resentment. NA II 13 228 27
Short, however, was that time. NA II 13 229 31
In the joyfulness of family love every thing for a short NA II 14 233 9
Catherine could not answer; and, after a short trial of NA II 14 238 27
After a short silence--"I hope, my Catherine, you are not NA II 15 240 4
the meaning, which one short syllable would have given, NA II 15 242 9
A very short visit to Mrs. Allen, in which Henry talked at NA II 15 243 10
was but one obstacle, in short, to be mentioned; but till NA II 16 249 1
declared; believe them, in short, to be such as his merit, SS I 4 21 15
After a short pause he resumed the conversation by saying-- SS I 11 56 14
15
After a short silence which succeeded the first surprise SS I 16 87 24
though the space was so short between the door and the SS I 19 105 13
She was short and plump, had a very pretty face, and the SS I 19 106 22
A short pause succeeded this speech, which was first SS I 21 123 21
been its dupe, for a short time made her feel only for SS II 1 139 1
to trust her on so short a personal acquaintance, with a SS II 1 142 7
"But what," said she after a short silence, "are your SS II 2 148 14
to consider the separation as any thing short of eternal. SS II 3 158 21
at her own situation, so short had their acquaintance with SS II 4 159 1
A short, a very short time however must now decide what SS II 4 159 1
After a short pause, "you have no confidence in me, SS II 5 169 23
that any attempt, that in short concealment, if SS II 5 173 44
short time, on the answer it would be most proper to give. SS II 5 173 45
In a short time Elinor saw Willoughby quit the room by the SS II 6 178 15
she be--or any one, in short, but your own dear self, mama, SS II 7 189 50
After a short silence on both sides, Mrs. Jennings, with SS II 8 196 21
canal; and every thing, in short, that one could wish for: SS II 8 197 22
to see her there, and, in short, that he was already aware SS II 8 198 30
"That a gentleman, whom I had reason to think--in short, SS II 8 199 35
I have only to hope that they may be proportionably short. SS II 8 199 40
A short account of myself, I believe, will be necessary, SS II 9 205 20
will be necessary, and it shall be a short one. SS II 9 205 20
of her short life; I was with her in her last moments." SS II 9 207 26
In short, I could learn nothing but that she was gone; all SS II 9 209 28
Have you," she continued, after a short silence, "ever SS II 9 211 34

Context	Work	Vol	Ch	Page	Line
shed no tears; but after a short time they would burst out,	SS	II	10	217	17
on your side--in short, you know as to an attachment of	SS	II	11	224	24
In short, it is a kind of thing that"--lowering his voice	SS	II	11	224	24
Her's has been a very short one!	SS	II	11	227	50
a very short time, by twice calling in Berkeley-Street.	SS	II	12	230	5
build one myself, within a short distance of London, where	SS	II	14	251	17
kindness, vouchsafed on so short an acquaintance, seemed	SS	II	14	254	27
So then it all came out; and the long and the short of the	SS	III	1	258	7
Mrs. Ferrars too--in short it has been a scene of such	SS	III	1	265	36
In short, I do not mean to reflect upon the behaviour of	SS	III	1	268	45
left her own party for a short time, to join their's.	SS	III	2	271	5
intimately acquainted in a short time, but I have seen	SS	III	3	282	19
It was an office in short, from which, unwilling to give	SS	III	3	283	20
in short, as might establish all your views of happiness."	SS	III	4	289	28
For a short time he sat deep in thought, after Elinor had	SS	III	4	290	36
					37
"We think now"--said Mr. Dashwood, after a short pause, "	SS	III	5	296	24
Elinor said no more, and John was also for a short time	SS	III	5	297	30
have it from her--that in short, whatever objections there	SS	III	5	297	31
I cannot help thinking, in short, that means might have	SS	III	5	300	37
One other short call in Harley-Street, in which Elinor	SS	III	6	301	1
really believed herself, that it would be a very short one.	SS	III	7	308	4
a very short time, had the power of creating any return.	SS	III	8	322	36
In short, it ended in a total breach.	SS	III	8	323	40
The next morning brought another short note from Marianne--	SS	III	8	327	55
A short pause of mutual thoughtfulness succeeded.	SS	III	8	327	56
And in short--what do you think of my wife's style of	SS	III	8	328	61
Short was the time, however, in which that fear could	SS	III	9	333	3
and so forth;--in short, you may as well give her a chance-	SS	III	14	375	9
equal to his own; and in short, it became speedily evident	SS	III	14	376	11
her sister after a short pause went on--"you will	W			316	2
In passing along a short gallery to the Assembly-Room,	W			327	7
The two dances seemed very short, & she had her partner's	W			335	13
ball we had last night!--he cried, after a short pause.	W			340	19
That's the long & the short of the business.	W			352	26
rather softened--& after a short silence, by way of	W			352	26
when they were alone for a short time the next morng; &	W			360	29
of the gentle voice beyond her calculation short.	W			360	30
Within a short walk of Longbourn lived a family with whom	PP	I	5	18	1
in short, to recommend her, but being an excellent walker.	PP	I	8	35	3
					4
A short pause followed this speech, and Mrs. Hurst began	PP	I	8	36	13
for the short time she could stay below with a book.	PP	I	8	37	21
it in a hurry I hope, though you have but a short lease."	PP	I	9	42	7
to say; and after a short silence Mrs. Bennet began	PP	I	9	45	35
instance, fame had fallen short of the truth; and added,	PP	I	13	64	21
said Wickham, after a short interruption, "that he or that	PP	I	16	78	16
by extravagance, imprudence, in short any thing or nothing.	PP	I	16	79	27
It is, in short, impossible for us to conjecture the	PP	I	17	85	2
standing within a very short distance of her, quite	PP	I	18	102	74
whither he was obliged to go the next day for a short time.	PP	I	18	103	76
that she could not use the short pause he allowed in any	PP	I	19	105	9
					10
"It is unlucky," said she, after a short pause, "that you	PP	I	21	117	9
In as short a time as Mr. Collins's long speeches would	PP	I	22	121	2
The whole family in short were properly overjoyed on the	PP	I	22	122	3
It was a subject, in short, on which reflection would be	PP	II	1	134	3
In short, my dear aunt, I should be very sorry to be the	PP	II	3	145	7
In short, I will do my best."	PP	II	3	145	7
a peep at Jane; and, in short, as the time drew near, she	PP	II	4	151	1
small gate, which led by a short gravel walk to the house,	PP	II	5	155	3
other answer--and, after a short pause, added, "I think I	PP	II	9	177	6
					7
A short dialogue on the subject of the country ensued, on	PP	II	9	179	26
done, however, and I hope will be of short duration.	PP	II	11	190	7
but the emotion was short, and he listened without	PP	II	11	191	11
tried to unite civility and truth in a few short sentences.	PP	II	15	216	5
letters were always long expected, and always very short.	PP	II	19	238	5
and as that left too short a period for them to go so far,	PP	II	19	238	7
After a short silence, the lady first spoke.	PP	III	1	256	61
sometimes did venture a short sentence, when there was	PP	III	3	267	4
Though Lydia's short letter to Mrs. F. gave them to	PP	III	4	274	5
Then, after a short silence, he continued, "Lizzy, I bear	PP	III	6	299	26
In a short time, I shall have a daughter married.	PP	III	7	306	47
their stay would be so short; and she made the most of the	PP	III	9	318	18
a sheet of paper, wrote a short letter to her aunt, to	PP	III	9	320	32
short period saw him looking both pleased and embarrassed.	PP	III	11	335	41
Her resolution was for a short time involuntarily kept by	PP	III	12	339	5
Mrs. Bennet, in short, was in very great spirits; she had	PP	III	12	343	29
with her father had been short and to the purpose.	PP	III	13	347	30
park here," returned Lady Catherine after a short silence.	PP	III	14	352	9
a short survey, to be decent looking rooms, walked on.	PP	III	14	352	19
event, let me now add a short hint on the subject of	PP	III	15	362	14
After a short pause, her companion added, "you are too	PP	III	16	366	7
three thousand pounds short of any equitable claim to it.	MP	I	1	3	1
After a short pause, Sir Thomas added with dignity, "yes,	MP	I	1	9	11
Did she, in short, want any thing he could possibly get	MP	I	2	15	10
herself to decide on so short an acquaintance, Mr.	MP	I	4	39	10
After a short interruption, Mr. Rushworth began again.	MP	I	6	55	15
But, in short, it is not a favourite profession of mine.	MP	I	6	60	51
"Yes, except as to his writing her such short letters.	MP	I	7	64	10
have her for a longer time--for a whole morning in short.	MP	I	7	69	28
to unite, and who after a short participation of their	MP	I	9	90	36
At length, after a short pause, Miss Crawford began with, "	MP	I	9	91	38
"Very true; but, in short, it had not occurred to me.	MP	I	9	92	40
principles; the effect, in short, of those doctrines which	MP	I	9	93	49
This was followed by a short silence.	MP	I	10	98	11
"It is the same sort of thing," said Fanny, after a short	MP	I	11	109	18
either, and just stopping short of the consistence, the	MP	I	12	115	4
After a short pause, however, the subject still continued,	MP	I	13	124	13
satisfy him, and a short parley of compliment ensued.	MP	I	14	132	8
A short silence followed.	MP	I	14	133	11
A short silence succeeded her leaving them; but her	MP	I	14	136	21
Crawford, after a short pause, "at this want of an Anhalt.	MP	I	15	144	32
after a short pause--"for he is a clergyman you know."	MP	I	15	144	40
Every body had a part either too long or too short;--	MP	I	18	165	2
little short of a declaration of love be made by the lady.	MP	I	18	167	12
it then became openly acknowledged, was a very short one.--	MP	II	2	193	18
right, Fanny," was his reply, after a short consideration.	MP	II	3	197	4
Fanny--and that is the long and the short of the matter.	MP	II	3	197	8
Mr. Rushworth had perhaps been accepted on too short an	MP	II	3	200	20
said Sir Thomas, after a short deliberation; "nor, were	MP	II	5	218	18
answers were as short and indifferent as civility allowed.	MP	II	5	223	48
I found myself in short in Thornton Lacey."	MP	II	7	241	13
a decision within a very short time, as soon as the	MP	II	8	255	10
After a short consideration, Sir Thomas asked Crawford to	MP	II	10	280	32
very punctual, and short and pleasant had been the meal.	MP	II	11	282	1
it was very short; indeed I am sure it was but a few lines.	MP	II	11	288	23
"My dearest Henry," cried Mary, stopping short, and	MP	II	12	297	32
after a civil reception, a short sentence about being	MP	II	13	298	1
till he, stopping short as he entered, said, with much	MP	III	1	312	5
The conference was neither so short, nor so conclusive, as	MP	III	2	326	1
her to love him in a very short time, that her not loving	MP	III	2	327	4
minutes, fixed on him in short till the attraction drew	MP	III	3	337	11
my cousin Maria, which--in short, at the time of the play,	MP	III	4	349	25
It proves him, in short, every thing that I had been used	MP	III	4	350	30
Another short fit of abstraction followed--when, shaking	MP	III	5	360	15
Oh! that I could transport you for a short time into our	MP	III	5	360	16
and in short could not really be wanted or missed.	MP	III	6	371	15
mother's answer, though short, was so kind, a few simple	MP	III	6	371	17
Mansfield, had for a short time been quite afflicted.--	MP	III	7	386	40
a short and hurried way, when he had come ashore on duty.	MP	III	8	388	2
by aunt Norris, they were short, they were trifling, they	MP	III	8	392	11
the mind is any thing short of perfect decision, an	MP	III	13	423	2
It was a letter, in short, which she would not but have	MP	III	13	425	5
The two ladies, even in the short time they had been	MP	III	16	450	10
was the detection in short--Oh! Fanny, it was the	MP	III	16	455	19
feelings--a great, though short struggle--half a wish of	MP	III	16	458	30
who had fallen little short of a mother in affection.	E	I	1	5	2
She was short, plump and fair, with a fine bloom, blue	E	I	3	23	9
for his long walk, or his short, as the year varied; and	E	I	4	26	1
a different--which in short gives exactly the idea--and	E	I	6	48	35
It was short, but expressed good sense, warm attachment,	E	I	7	51	4
forced to add, "is it a good letter? or is it too short?"	E	I	7	51	4
"Oh! no;--and it is but a short letter too."	E	I	7	54	32
him, was offering by his short, decided answers, an	E	I	8	57	2
thought her too young: in short, whether I approved his	E	I	8	59	27
as she can;--to move, in short, in Mrs. Goddard's line, to	E	I	8	62	42
Such things in general cannot be too short."	E	I	9	76	33
just what you must, in a short way; and another, to write	E	I	9	76	35
too, and that, in short, they would both be soon after her.	E	I	10	88	33
She then broke the lace off short, and dexterously	E	I	10	89	36
apprehensively happy in forestalling this too short visit.	E	I	11	91	2
short might be hoped to pass away in unsullied cordiality.	E	I	11	93	5
began with grave looks and short questions, he was soon	E	I	12	98	2
"A man cannot be more so," was his short, full answer.	E	I	12	99	12
John Knightley, in this short visit to Hartfield, going	E	I	13	108	1
was a delightful visit;--perfect, in being much too short.	E	I	13	108	1
air to produce a very white world in a very short time.	E	I	13	112	24
such circumstances, fall short by two than exceed by two.	E	I	13	116	43
his aunt's spirits and pleasure; in short, upon her temper.	E	I	14	121	16
In short, I can feel no dependence on his coming, and I	E	I	14	122	21
having some effect, and in short, very much resolved on	E	I	15	129	24
attentions, meaning (in short), to marry him!--should	E	I	16	135	8
for her writing so short a letter--only two pages you see--	E	II	1	157	10
In short, she sat, during the first visit, looking at Jane	E	II	2	167	13
letter; well"----- "it was short, merely to announce--but	E	II	3	174	31
					32
young man--but'---- in short, I do not think I am	E	II	3	176	44
The shower was heavy, but short; and it had not been over	E	II	3	177	52
sweetly disposed--had in short, to use a most intelligible	E	II	4	181	4
During his present short stay, Emma had barely seen him;	E	II	4	182	7
marrying)--the honour, in short, of being marked out for	E	II	7	206	2
a most wretched discovery," said he, after a short pause.--	E	II	8	221	51
And, in short, from knowing his usual ways, I am very much	E	II	8	223	63
In short, I have made a match between Mr. Knightley and	E	II	8	224	65
of cutting the matter short, she believed it to indicate	E	II	8	228	88
He cut her short with, "I am going to Kingston.	E	II	10	244	38
					39
Long before he re-appeared, attending the short, neat,	E	II	11	255	59
"In short," said he, "perhaps, Miss Woodhouse-----I think	E	II	12	260	29
Short had been the notice--short their meeting; he was	E	II	12	261	37
Every consideration of the subject, in short, makes me	E	II	13	265	4
The visit was of course short; and there was so much	E	II	14	270	3
This letter tells us--it is a short letter--written in a	E	II	18	305	7
place than Enscombe--in short, to spend in London; so that	E	II	18	308	30
made the best of her way by a short cut back to Highbury.	E	III	3	333	5
After another short hesitation, "I hope it does not	E	III	4	341	32
He saw a short word prepared for Emma, and given to her	E	III	5	348	22
and splendour it fell short only of them: it was with a	E	III	6	359	37
delicious shade of a broad short avenue of limes, which	E	III	6	360	38
the subject; and with a short final arrangement for the	E	III	6	366	74
Short of that, it is all guess and luck--and will	E	III	7	372	40
How many a man has committed himself on a short	E	III	7	372	40
general state, had carried her off after a short struggle.	E	III	9	387	11
Short letters from Frank were received at Randall's,	E	III	9	388	15
The answer was only in this short note: "Miss Fairfax's	E	III	9	390	16
					17
In short, my dear Emma, there is no occasion to be so	E	III	10	393	17
on his kindness, and, in short, put an end to the	E	III	10	398	51
Frank Churchill had once, for a short period, occupied?--	E	III	11	412	45
of her own heart--and, in short, that she had never really	E	III	11	412	45
They had gone, in short--and very great had been the	E	III	12	418	5
him very pleasant--and, in short, for (with a sigh) let me	E	III	13	427	19
in short, I was somehow or other safe from him."	E	III	13	427	19
would ask; but a very short parley with her own heart	E	III	14	435	4
In short, my dear madam, it was a quarrel blameless on her	E	III	14	441	8
to her at ---- : in short, the full direction to Mr.	E	III	14	442	8
Upon my word, Perry has restored her in a wonderful short	E	III	16	454	17
But, unfortunately--in short, if your compassion does not	E	III	16	459	47
could secure, and saw no dignity in any thing short of it.	P	III	2	12	5
Lady Russell was fond of Bath in short, and disposed to	P	III	2	14	12
After a short pause, Mr. Shepherd presumed to say, "in all	P	III	3	18	9
					10
A short period of exquisite felicity followed, and but a	P	III	4	26	2
of exquisite felicity followed, and but a short one.--	P	III	4	26	2
sensation: excepting one short period of her life, she had	P	III	6	47	13
He was cut short by the eager attacks of the little boys,	P	III	6	49	25
And, in short, he had looked and said every thing with	P	III	7	54	4
catch it; a heart, in short, for any pleasing young woman	P	III	7	61	38
A short absence from home had left his fair one unguarded	P	III	9	74	4
In short, you know, Dr. Shirley must have a curate, and	P	III	9	78	20
After a short struggle, however, Charles Hayter seemed to	P	III	10	82	2
short, her look and manner declared, that go she would not.	P	III	10	86	17
by no means bad; and, in short, Louisa, who was the most	P	III	11	94	7
and this second meeting, short as it was, also proved	P	III	12	104	7
And, in short, she said more than her husband could long	P	III	12	115	65
her own children; and in short they were so happy in the	P	IV	1	122	5
dinner every day; and in short, it seemed to have been	P	IV	2	129	2
stopped her short in the midst of the Elliot countenance.	P	IV	2	133	24
to them, concluded a short recapitulation of what she had	P	IV	2	134	30
in general; delighted, in short, by every proof of	P	IV	3	139	10
She gave him a short account of her party, and business at	P	IV	3	143	19
She believed, in short, what Anne did not believe.	P	IV	5	160	26
life (and probably not a short one) when he had been, at	P	IV	5	161	27
than Miss Anne's; and, in short, her civility rendered her	P	IV	7	174	3
After a short interval, however, he came towards her and	P	IV	7	176	8
for him, of her being in short intently observing him.	P	IV	7	179	28
evening with her; but in a short hurried call she excused	P	IV	7	180	33
beauty at lyme: and in short" (with a faint blush at some	P	IV	8	184	16
better singing; and, in short, must confess that he should	P	IV	8	190	47
already heard, through the short cut of a laundress and a	P	IV	9	192	5
After another short silence-- "pray," said Mrs. Smith, "is	P	IV	9	194	19
					20
"I beg your pardon for the short answers I have been	P	IV	9	198	52
					53
long ago as September, (in short when they first came	P	IV	9	206	88
and her sister; and, in short, it ended in being his	P	IV	10	217	19
Elizabeth was, for a short time, suffering a good deal.	P	IV	10	219	29
her had spread; and a short pause succeeded, which seemed	P	IV	10	222	37
Their preparations, however, were stopped short.	P	IV	10	226	63
The interruption had been short, though severe; and ease	P	IV	10	226	65
that had returned, after a short suspension, to ruin the	P	IV	11	241	60
He found too late, in short, that he had entangled himself;	P	IV	11	243	66
consciousness cut short; with Admiral and Mrs. Croft,	P	IV	11	246	78
It was in one of these short meetings, each apparently	P	IV	11	246	79
					80
would you, in short, have renewed the engagement then?"	P	IV	11	247	82
a natural penetration, in short, which no experience in	P	IV	12	249	4
in a few moments to cut short, both his remonstrance to	S		1	364	1
which always attend a short stay there--one is never able	S		1	367	1
The acquaintance, thus oddly begun, was neither short nor	S		2	370	1
building, excepting one short row of smart-looking houses,	S		4	384	1
But--after a short pause--if Miss Esther thinks to talk me	S		7	401	1

Only a short chain, you see, between us, & not a link S 9 408 1
SHORT-LIVED (1)
received any information of their short-lived engagement.-- P III 4 30 10
SHORTEN (5)
not on my account shorten your visit here, even an hour. LS 25 292 3
by all means not to shorten their visit to Mrs. Jennings; SS II 10 213 3
Elizabeth had hoped that his resentment might shorten his PP I 21 115 2
Mr. Maddox, that I shall shorten some of his speeches, and MP I 15 149 61
and occupation of mind to shorten it, that Emma would not E II 14 270 3
SHORTENED (1)
that admitted being shortened;--besides pointing out the MP I 15 138 1
SHORTENING (1)
than dance down the shortening set, breathless and with MP II 10 279 22
SHORTER (3)
they would have been yet shorter, had he not been NA I 15 120 24
found herself, in a shorter space of time than she could PP III 4 281 29
for variety; but Anne had never found an evening shorter. P IV 11 245 78
SHORTLY (43)
waited on Lady Susan, shortly after her arrival in town; & LS 42 311 2
Every body was shortly in motion for tea, and they must NA I 2 21 10
her dear Catherine, and would therefore shortly return. NA I 5 36 2
that there was shortly no fresh proof of it to be given to NA I 5 36 4
lands and government, he shortly found himself arrived at NA I 14 111 29
new publication which is shortly to come out, in three NA I 14 113 39
Shortly after breakfast Henry left them for Woodston, NA II 7 175 13
which her room lay, and shortly entered one on the same NA II 8 184 5
Astonishment and doubt first seized them; and a shortly NA II 9 193 6
and done, nothing could shortly be clearer, than that it NA II 10 199 2
"I have one favour to beg," said Catherine, shortly NA II 10 204 15
servant, the General was shortly restored to his NA II 11 213 20
But Mrs. Dashwood began shortly to give over every hope of SS I 5 27 6
to occupy their time as shortly presented themselves, or SS I 11 53 1
Marianne was shortly subdued; and she promised not to SS I 12 59 5
all in the parting, which shortly took place, and left an SS I 19 104 9
He shortly afterwards drew a chair close to her's, and, SS II 8 198 31
Lucy came very shortly to claim Elinor's compassion on SS II 11 230 4
best; he will be ordained shortly, and should it ever be SS III 2 277 30
Mr Musgrave was shortly afterwards announced;--& mrs W 338 17
Recovering himself, however, shortly, he turned to his PP I 18 93 24
25
him than the report which shortly prevailed in Meryton of PP I 23 129 12
had reason to hope, that shortly after his next return PP II 2 139 1
shortly afterwards the three gentlemen entered the room. PP II 7 170 9
we shortly resolved on joining him directly in London.-- PP II 12 198 5
and all surprise was shortly lost in other feelings. PP II 17 224 2
But the gloom of Lydia's prospect was shortly cleared away; PP II 18 230 11
from surprise; but shortly recovering himself, advanced PP III 1 251 51
and cambric, and would shortly have dictated some very PP III 7 307 48
her marriage would so shortly give the proper termination PP III 8 311 11
But it was a hope shortly checked by other considerations, PP III 10 326 3
event threw her into, was shortly relieved, and her mind PP III 11 331 13
when the two gentlemen shortly afterwards joined them. MP II 5 226 64
Shortly afterwards, Sir Thomas was again interfering a MP II 10 280 33
not lift up her eyes, he shortly afterwards, and in a MP III 1 317 36
to bring him to Mansfield shortly, which Sir Thomas MP III 13 426 11
Shortly afterwards Miss Bates, passing near the window, E II 10 243 30
little doubt of hearing of something to suit her shortly.-- E II 15 284 9
as those sort of visits conveyed, might shortly be over. E III 12 422 19
"It will be natural for me," he added shortly afterwards, " E III 15 445 8
she shortly afterwards began, "since the party to Box-Hill. E III 16 454 18
Croft, with whom he shortly afterwards fell into company P III 3 21 18
"I think very differently," answered Elizabeth, shortly; " P III 5 35 16
SHORTNESS (7)
and nothing but the shortness of the time prevented her NA I 10 73 22
irritation of nerves and shortness of breath--no NA I 13 102 25
The shortness of his visit, the steadiness of his purpose SS I 19 102 2
increase with the shortness of the term for indulgence.-- W 347 21
at last appear; but the shortness of her stay, and yet PP II 3 147 25
allowance for the shortness of the notice, to collect MP II 8 253 7
The style of the visit, and the shortness of it, were then E II 5 187 4
SHOT (6)
without having one good shot) than all his companions NA I 9 66 31
He hunted and shot, and she humoured her children; and SS I 7 32 1
A very decent shot, and there is not a bolder rider in SS I 9 43 17
And then, Fanny, the glory of fixing one who has been shot MP III 5 363 22
sort of excuse; "he never shot" and he had "been quite P IV 2 130 5
of mine, which you shot with one day, round Winthrop." P IV 11 240 58
SHOULDER (5)
roused by a touch on the shoulder, and turning round, NA I 8 55 10
One shoulder of mutton, you know, drives another down. SS II 8 197 22
her face on Elinor's shoulder, she burst into tears.-- SS II 12 236 41
his voice, or see his shoulder, just to have something E II 4 184 10
a touch on her shoulder obliged Anne to turn round.-- P IV 8 190 47
SHOULDERS (12)
Isabella shrugged her shoulders and smiled, the only NA II 1 133 30
day) of a slight rheumatic feel in one of his shoulders." SS I 8 38 11
shrugging up my shoulders in proof of its being so, and SS III 8 326 53
of her young Charges' shoulders & throats, led the way up W 327 7
If he did shrug his shoulders, it was not till Sir William PP III 18 384 26
bring and put round her shoulders, was seized by Mr. MP I 7 251 66
her shoulders--and it makes one think she must catch cold." E I 6 48 36
then shrugged his shoulders, and said, "I could not have E II 17 303 23
bulky forms and stooping shoulders of the elderly men, was E III 2 326 32
He had grumbled & shaken his shoulders so much indeed, and S 1 364 1
inch of back & shoulders beyond her preconceived idea. S 10 415 1
She must put her shawl over her shoulders, & be running S 10 619 1
SHOW (17)
Soon after six Eleanor entered her room, eager to show NA II 13 227 27
In nine cases out of ten, a woman had better show more PP I 6 22 2
It would show great want of feeling on my father's account, MP I 13 125 17
tears were beginning to show themselves, immediately said MP I 15 147 56
Fanny, quite surprised, endeavoured to show herself MP I 18 168 16
to show his liberty, and his resolution of maintaining it. E III 2 327 34
I have nothing more to show you, or to say--except that I E III 4 340 22
Would not Mr. Knightley show them the gardens--all the E III 6 359 37
to him, and now he would show them all to Emma;--fortunate E III 6 362 43
The greatest kindness you can show me, will be to let me E III 6 363 50
hand eager to show a difference; but it was just too late. E III 7 376 62
It was a more pressing concern to show attention to Jane E III 9 389 16
at Highbury, who wished to show her kindness--and with E III 9 389 16
She wanted to be of use to her; wanted to show a value for E III 9 389 16
They show her to the greatest advantage. E III 12 420 13
She said enough to show there need not be despair--and to E III 13 431 38
there had been a little show of resentment towards Jane, E III 16 455 20
SHOWED (9)
far from clever, she showed a tractable disposition, and MP I 2 18 23
to whom they showed the greatest fondness of the two. MP I 4 40 15
and though her deportment showed rather conscious MP I 6 52 1
faltered, his manner showed the wish of self-command, and MP III 15 444 29
there was a restlessness, which showed a mind not at ease. E III 2 320 7
Mr. and Mrs. Elton, indeed, showed no unwillingness to mix, E III 7 367 1
anger, though a slight blush showed that it could pain her. E III 7 371 27
tremulous inequality showed indisposition so plainly, and E III 9 390 18
and with a blush which showed me how it was all connected, E III 12 419 12
SHOWER (3)
was overtaken by a heavy shower close to the parsonage, MP II 4 205 3
home directly-- I would not have you out in a shower!-- E II 3 176 50
The shower was heavy, but short; and it had not been over E II 3 177 52
SHOWERS (1)
to see them driven in showers about me by the wind! SS I 16 87 31
SHOWERY (3)
very showery, and that would have thrown me into agonies! NA I 6 39 4
the partial sunshine of a showery sky, and unable longer SS I 9 40 3
and accomplished as often as a showery October would allow. SS I 11 53 1
SHOWING (4)
The Grants showing a disposition to be friendly and MP I 3 31 59
"Those who are showing the world what female manners MP I 5 50 37
Mrs. Weston had been showing them all to him, and now he E III 6 362 43
She seemed to propose showing no agitation, or E III 11 404 9
SHOWN (6)
The lower part of the house had been now entirely shown, MP I 9 89 31
You have shown that you can dance, and you know we are not E III 2 331 62
had shown how deeply she was suffering from consciousness. E III 12 418 5
the great kindness you had shown her during her illness; E III 12 419 12
the kindness you have ever shown me, and ten thousand for E III 14 443 8
Emma was gratified, and would soon have shown no want of E III 16 453 10
SHOWS (4)
Fanny," said he, "which shows you to be a very good girl; MP I 2 15 11
indeed, and shows a great want of genius and emulation. MP I 2 19 29
Well, Frank, your dream certainly shows that Highbury is E III 5 345 14
You were both talking of other things; of business, shows E III 18 473 26
SHRANK (1)
every feeling within her shrank, she could not, would not, MP I 18 170 24
SHREWD (5)
by the beauty, or the shrewd look of the youngest, to her SS I 21 124 32
"And a very well-spoken, genteel, shrewd lady, she seemed P III 3 22 25
She is a shrewd, intelligent, sensible woman. P IV 5 155 9
in her motions, with a shrewd eye, & self-satisfied air-- S 6 391 1
by Lady D's giving a shrewd glance at her & replying--"yes, S 7 400 1
SHREWDNESS (1)
to the point by the shrewdness of the relator, been NA II 15 246 12
SHREWISH (1)
They have a sharp, shrewish look, which I do not like at PP III 3 271 15
SHRINK (6)
miles off--could you shrink from so simple an adventure? NA II 5 159 21
It was no wonder that the General should shrink from the NA II 8 186 6
a connection she could not wonder that he should shrink. PP III 8 311 13
she would shrink unnecessarily from the office of a friend. P III 12 116 69
Anne did not shrink from it; on the contrary, she truly P IV 1 125 15
16
Russell's account, to shrink from conversation with P IV 8 189 44
SHRINKING (6)
mortification--& tho' shrinking under a general sense of W 345 21
timid and shy, and shrinking from notice; but her air, MP I 2 12 2
"My opinion!" she cried, shrinking from such a compliment, MP I 16 153 7
Then, she was shrinking again into herself, and blushing MP III 3 337 11
cried Fanny in a shrinking accent--"in such an office of MP III 4 351 33
to have no idea of shrinking from it, and set forward at E I 13 112 24
SHROPSHIRE (5)
How should I know in Shropshire, what is passing of that W 320 2
have been used to in Shropshire, & setting it as certain W 350 24
proceed very soon into Shropshire, and visit the brother P III 9 73 1
gone, for the present, to see his brother in Shropshire. P IV 2 134 31
He had remained in Shropshire, lamenting the blindness of P IV 11 243 69
SHRUB (1)
a shrub in it higher than the green bench in the corner. NA II 11 214 25
SHRUBBERIES (9)
of accompanying her into the shrubberies and garden." NA II 7 176 17
She was tired of the woods and the shrubberies--always so NA II 11 212 16
through the winding shrubberies, now just beginning to be SS III 6 302 8
chuse papers, project shrubberies, and invent a sweep. SS III 14 374 7
in the country, shrubberies and flower gardens, and rustic MP I 6 57 31
its separate lawn and shrubberies and name, did really E I 1 7 10
the shrubberies of Hartfield, and afterwards in Highbury. E II 6 196 2
of! the gardens and shrubberies would be kept in almost as P III 3 18 7
I am not fond of the idea of my shrubberies being always P III 3 18 8
SHRUBBERY (29)
by strolling along the shrubbery with Reginald, calling LS 15 267 4
is tolerable, we pace the shrubbery for hours together. LS 16 268 2
lawn you know with the shrubbery on one side, where she LS 17 271 7
it had its open shrubbery, and closer wood walk, a road of SS III 6 302 7
on the dry gravel of the shrubbery, but all over the SS III 6 305 17
end of the town with a shrubbery & sweep in the country.-- W 322 2
walking together in the shrubbery the next day, "you will PP I 10 52 55
The two young ladies were summoned from the shrubbery PP I 17 86 9
walking together in the shrubbery behind the house, they PP III 7 301 1
an intrusion, and walk away with him into the shrubbery. PP III 14 351 1
the drawing-room, or the shrubbery, was equally forlorn, MP I 2 14 8
"if I were you, I would have a very pretty shrubbery. MP I 6 55 16
One likes to get out into a shrubbery in fine weather." MP I 6 55 16
yard, nor walk in the shrubbery without passing another, I MP I 6 58 37
hour in Mrs. Grant's shrubbery, the weather being MP II 4 208 11
this shrubbery I am more struck with its growth and beauty. MP II 4 208 12
ever aspired to a shrubbery or any thing of the kind." MP II 4 209 15
no wonder in this shrubbery equal to seeing myself in it. MP II 4 209 17
you will have the shrubbery to yourself, and will be the MP III 1 322 48
you have walked in the shrubbery, or gone to my house." MP III 1 323 54
"I recommended the shrubbery to Fanny as the dryest place," MP III 1 323 55
walking alone in the shrubbery, he instantly joined her. MP III 4 345 5
the shrubbery, in her caution to avoid any sudden attack. MP III 5 357 4
Her father never went beyond the shrubbery, where two E I 4 26 1
their promising never to go beyond the shrubbery again. E III 3 336 12
own room, she tried the shrubbery--in every place, every E III 11 411 43
father, she lost no time in hurrying into the shrubbery.-- E III 13 424 1
He had followed her into the shrubbery with no idea of E III 13 432 40
You can slip in from the shrubbery at any time. P IV 1 127 26
SHRUBS (4)
lawn, surrounded by shrubs in the rich foliage of summer, MP I 7 65 13
immediately to turf and shrubs, and all the sweets of MP I 9 89 32
but in the trees and shrubs, which the wind was despoiling, E III 12 421 18
eyes fallen on the same shrubs in the lawn, and observed E III 14 434 2
SHRUG (1)
If he did shrug his shoulders, it was not till Sir William PP III 18 384 26
SHRUGGED (2)
Isabella shrugged her shoulders and smiled, the only NA II 1 133 30
John Knightley looked at him with amazement, then shrugged E II 17 303 23
SHRUGGING (1)
trifling, business, shrugging up my shoulders in proof of SS III 8 326 53
SHRUNK (4)
Fanny shrunk back to her seat, with feelings sadly pained MP III 7 380 23
and yielding temper would have shrunk from asserting. MP III 9 395 4
that shrunk from it would soon be quite unpardonable. MP III 10 406 20
I should myself have shrunk from any thing so hasty, and E III 14 440 8
SHUDDER (1)
shudder at the idea of the misery which must have followed. P IV 9 211 102
SHUDDERED (2)
She shuddered, tossed about in her bed, and envied every NA II 6 170 12
of what she had shuddered over in books, for the roll, NA II 7 172 1
SHUDDERING (1)
letter, and after shuddering over every sentence, SS II 7 190 55
56
SHUDDERINGS (2)
She passed only from feelings of sickness to shudderings MP III 15 441 20
Anne's shudderings were to herself, alone: but the Miss P III 8 66 17
SHUFFLING (1)
Ferrars herself, by her shuffling excuses, seemed the only SS III 14 374 5
SHUT (51)
He is now shut up in his apartment, whither I heard him go, LS 22 282 8
events; but she was shut up with Mr Johnson, while he LS 32 302 1
and dirt, and shut themselves up, to read novels together. NA I 5 37 4
The remainder was shut off by knolls of old trees, or NA II 7 177 19
Mrs. Tilney yet lived, shut up for causes unknown, and NA II 8 187 16
should not say I shut myself up because Tilney was gone. NA II 12 217 2
Her avocations above having shut out all noise but what NA II 15 241 7

of the valleys beneath shut up their superior beauties; SS I 9 40 3
and conveniences; quite shut in with great garden walls SS II 8 196 22
No, no; they were shut up in the drawing-room together, SS III 2 274 18
door shut him out, "I shall see him the husband of Lucy." SS III 4 291 44
Poor Edward!--he has done for himself completely--shut SS III 5 299 35
with tall Lombardy poplars, shut out the offices. SS III 6 302 7
I to myself-- I am shut out for ever from their society, SS III 8 328 63
to open a door which was never shut, made their appearance. W 329 9
father you have, girls," said she, when the door was shut. PP I 2 8 26
There, shut into her own room, as soon as their visitor PP II 10 186 38
was then allowed to be shut, and the carriage drove off. PP II 15 217 10
Mr. Darcy called, and was shut up with him several hours. PP III 10 321 2
He then shut the door, and coming up to her, claimed the PP III 13 347 33
to shut out the churchyard, just as Dr. Grant has done. MP I 6 54 9
had turned from him and shut the door, she could not help MP II 5 219 26
entirely, and planted up to shut out the blacksmith's shop. MP II 7 242 23
of a future thornton, to shut out the church, sink the MP II 7 248 47
cares to shut out every other care, or almost every other,. MP III 13 427 12
own amusements cut up, as to shut their eyes to the truth. MP III 14 434 13
him, and the lovely scenes of home must be shut out. MP III 15 447 35
have attended to her, were shut up, or wholly occupied MP III 16 449 4
who could get hold of and shut him up, the case would MP III 16 450 11
the certainty of having shut himself out for ever from MP III 16 456 29
and private, where, shut up together with little society, MP III 17 465 14
door was to be lawfully shut on them, and that they were E I 15 128 23
must now be shut up in London, untouched by any body." E II 8 216 24
the speech, and the door had soon shut out Frank Churchill. E II 12 261 37
the contrary, when people shut themselves up entirely from E II 14 275 30
I believe I was half an hour this morning shut up with my E II 14 278 40
You seem shut out from every thing--in the most complete E II 18 307 21
for her to be always shut up at home;--and very long walks, E III 6 356 26
and, before the door had shut them out, she heard Miss E III 8 378 4
and Knightley are shut up together in deep consultation.-- E III 16 456 25
selfish arrangements which shut her out, and on many P III 2 16 16
in him, who could be of no use at home, to shut himself up. P III 7 55 7
If I were to shut myself up for ever with the child, I P III 7 57 18
offer; the rooms were shut up, the lodgers almost all gone, P III 11 95 9
our family, they seem shut out from all the world. P III 12 102 2
It is bad for him, I know, to be shut up as he is; but P III 12 107 24
away from them all, and shut ourselves into our lodgings, P IV 6 170 29
and shut in: but she would rather have caught his eye. P IV 8 188 42
If one happens only to shut the door a little hard, she P IV 10 218 24
they left, as the door shut them out, but not to Anne. P IV 10 226 65
I shut my eyes, and would not understand you, or do you P IV 11 247 84

SHUTS (2)
which every body who shuts their eyes while they look, or MP I 11 107 3
which shuts out noisy pleasures, should much exceed theirs. MP II 1 186 34

SHUTTER (1)
shutter, felt the strongest conviction of the wind's force. NA II 6 167 10

SHUTTERS (2)
the divisions of the shutters; and she stept boldly NA II 6 167 10
was tiled, the window shutters were not painted green, nor SS I 6 28 2

SHUTTING (2)
of either murdering or shutting up his wife, she had NA II 15 247 14
Without shutting herself up from her family, or leaving SS I 19 104 12

SHY (18)
Frederica is too shy I think, & too much in awe of me, to LS 16 268 2
with my neice; she is shy, & I think I can see that some LS 17 270 6
Frederica looked so shy, so confused, when we entered the LS 20 276 3
does justice to herself; her manners are shy & childish. LS 24 288 11
breeding; they were neither shy, nor affectedly open; and NA I 8 56 11
shy before company as he could make noise enough at home. SS I 6 31 9
I never wish to offend, but I am so foolishly shy, that I SS I 17 94 42
were perfectly easy and graceful, I should not be shy." SS I 17 94 44
who, though looking rather shy, expressed great SS III 2 271 5
minutes convinced her, that she was only exceedingly shy. PP III 2 261 3
What made you so shy of me, when you first called, and PP III 18 381 7
exceedingly timid and shy, and shrinking from notice; but MP I 2 12 2
were so shy and reluctant that he could not advance in any. MP II 5 226 59
shy and uncomfortable when their visitor entered the room. MP II 13 303 13
inconveniently shy, not unwilling to talk--and yet so far E I 3 23 10
He was shy, and disposed to abstraction; but the engaging P III 11 100 23
For, though shy, he did not seem reserved; it had rather P III 11 100 23
had imagined, or he was too shy; and after giving him a P IV 2 133 26

SHYLOCK (1)
ever was written, from Shylock or Richard iii. down to the MP I 13 123 6

SHYNESS (14)
from the awkwardness and shyness of a girl; her person NA I 2 18 1
but when his natural shyness was overcome, his behaviour SS I 3 15 6
only by that shyness which too often keeps him silent. SS I 4 20 9
she had neither shyness nor reserve in their discussion. SS I 10 47 3
He received the kindest welcome from her; and shyness, SS I 17 90 1
"Marianne has not shyness to excuse any inattention of SS I 17 94 43
"Shyness is only the effect of a sense of inferiority in SS I 17 94 44
drawing-room, and whose shyness, as they had not seen her PP II 4 152 5
though proceeding from shyness and the fear of doing wrong, PP III 3 267 3
any thing like natural shyness, and their confidence MP I 2 12 3
her by noticing her shyness; Miss Lee wondered at her MP I 2 14 8
There must be a sort of shyness. MP II 3 197 3
she could wish to overcome her own shyness and reserve. MP III 9 395 3
in Captain Wentworth, no shyness or reserve; they seemed P III 7 58 22

SICILY (1)
had brought her from Sicily, was the greatest distress of MP II 8 254 8

SICK (44)
I tell Mr. Allen, when he talks of being sick of it, that NA I 8 54 5
Do you know I get so immoderately sick of Bath; your NA I 10 70 3
She was sick of exploring, and desired but to be safe in NA II 9 194 6
My mother was quite sick of it. SS I 2 11 20
constant confinement of a sick chamber, merely because he SS I 8 38 11
her up stairs into the sick chamber, to satisfy herself SS III 7 316 27
accommodation of her sick child; and the Colonel, at the SS III 10 341 4
"I am sick of Mr. Bingley," cried his wife. PP I 2 7 21
attention might be paid to the sick lady and her sister. PP I 8 40 59
I am sick of them all. PP II 4 154 19
way, if Kitty had not been sick; and when we got to the PP II 16 222 22
the rest, and then, sick of this folly, took refuge in her PP III 7 307 50
The fact is, that you were sick of civility, of deference, PP III 18 380 5
room--the governess being sick or run away, and the mother MP I 5 50 35
of the present state of a sick horse, and the opinion of MP I 12 118 22
am sure you must be sick of all our noise and difficulties. MP I 15 143 26
For the present the danger was over, and Fanny's sick MP II 1 181 17
but of one errand, which turned her too sick for speech.-- MP II 9 268 28
jellies to nurse a sick maid, there was peace and good MP II 11 283 4
wished her to be heartily sick of home before her visit MP III 6 369 9
her the patient and the sick room in a juster and stronger MP III 14 429 2
Even in the sick chamber, the fortunate Mary was not MP III 14 430 4
Sick of ambitious and mercenary connections, prizing more MP III 17 471 29
Mr. Perry had been to Mrs. Goddard's to attend a sick E I 8 68 58
a poor sick family, who lived a little way out of Highbury. E I 10 83 1
One is sick of the very name of Jane Fairfax. E I 10 86 23
refrain from visiting the sick chamber again, for the E I 15 125 4
Her mind was quite sick of Mr. Elton and the Martins. E II 5 187 4
Emma grew sick at the sound. E II 13 267 8
sick of England--and would leave it to-morrow, if I could." E III 6 365 62
"You are sick of prosperity and indulgence." E III 6 365 63
"I sick of prosperity and indulgence!-- E III 6 365 64
Do not pity me till I saw her wan, sick looks.-- E III 14 443 8
to come back sick and cross for the rest of the day."-- P III 6 44 8
ourselves, with this poor sick child--and not a creature P III 7 56 10
A sick child is always the mother's property, her own P III 7 56 11
be left at home by herself, to nurse our sick child." P III 7 58 19
not let him teaze his sick brother, he began to fasten P III 9 79 29
They were sick with horror while he examined; but he was P III 12 112 52
A sick chamber may often furnish the worth of volumes." P IV 5 156 10
strength that appears in a sick chamber; it is selfishness P IV 5 156 11
to this old schoolfellow, sick and reduced, seemed to have P IV 5 158 21
a state of stagnation, sick of knowing nothing, and P IV 7 180 32
"I am sick of it. P IV 9 203 73

SICK-ROOM (1)
of any more use in the sick-room than Charles, for I P III 7 56 12

SICKENING (1)
sickening knock, and a letter was again put into her hands. MP III 15 442 22

SICKENS (1)
My heart sickens within me. LS 24 291 14

SICKLY (19)
likely, for I have a notion she is always rather sickly. SS I 14 70 2
the melancholy and sickly figure before me, to be the SS II 9 207 26
to have been old and sickly, and likely to vacate it soon-- SS III 5 295 12
by the hollow eye, the sickly skin, the posture of SS III 10 340 2
to himself, for he was sickly & had lost his wife, one W 315 1
spare him, & just now it is a sickly time at Guilford--" W 321 2
She is unfortunately of a sickly constitution, which has PP I 11 67 7
"She looks sickly and cross.-- PP II 5 158 18
Miss de Bourgh was pale and sickly; her features, though PP II 6 162 12
Unless the elder brother is very sickly, I suppose you PP II 10 184 15
Here, its power was only a glare, a stifling, sickly glare, MP III 15 439 9
Perry does not call it altogether a sickly season." E I 12 102 34
Mr. Wingfield considers it very sickly except-----" E I 12 102 35
the truth is, that in London it is always a sickly season. E I 12 102 36
not allow it to have a sickly hue in general; and there E II 6 199 10
That she is old and sickly.-- P IV 5 157 15
be fancying himself too sickly for any profession--& sit S 5 388 1
looking rather than sickly; with an agreable face, & a S 9 407 1
In Miss Lambe, here was the very young lady, sickly & rich, S 11 422 1

SICKNESS (9)
felt immediately such a sickness at heart as made her SS II 7 181 7
her lips became whiter than even sickness had left them. SS III 10 347 33
sickness and solitude, and the attendance only of servants. MP III 13 426 10
She passed only from feelings of sickness to shudderings MP III 15 441 20
In the present instance, it was sickness and poverty E I 10 86 24
25
bursts, perseverance and weariness, health and sickness. E III 14 437 8
going to sea, but never knew what sickness was afterwards. P III 8 71 54
of the present; neither sickness nor sorrow seemed to have P IV 5 153 7
I think differently now; time and sickness, and sorrow, P IV 9 201 64

SIDE (354)
On my side, you may be sure of it's never being more, for LS 10 258 2
of great misconduct on her side, so very generally known. LS 12 260 2
with the shrubbery on one side, where she may see her LS 17 271 7
on your father's side of your marrying to advantage; where LS 30 300 2
take her assurance of it, on either side of the question? LS 42 313 9
a fear on Mrs. Allen's side, of having once left her clogs NA I 2 19 4
however, kept close at her side, and linked her arm too NA I 2 21 9
should not think the superiority was always on our side." NA I 3 27 29
parted, on the lady's side at least, with a strong NA I 3 29 52
the chief of it by the side of Mrs. Thorpe, in what they NA I 5 36 3
on one side or other by carriages, horsemen, or carts. NA I 7 44 1
gave every proof on his side of equal satisfaction, which NA I 7 44 4
to James on the other side of her, turned again to his NA I 8 52 2
sister's now being by his side; and therefore, instead of NA I 8 53 3
close to her on the other side, "I shall not speak another NA I 10 70 1
immediately took her usual place by the side of her friend. NA I 10 71 8
parted--on Miss Tilney's side with some knowledge of her NA I 10 73 21
This disposition on your side is rather alarming. NA I 10 77 37
as they walked along the side of the river, "without NA I 14 106 2
No difficulty was made on Mrs. Allen's side--and the only NA I 14 114 49
family ingenuity; on one side in the mystery of an NA I 15 121 25
If there is a good fortune on one side, there can be no NA I 15 124 47
remark, on the gentleman's side, in favour of Isabella's NA I 15 124 48
our side to make Northanger Abbey not wholly disagreeable." NA II 2 139 7
morning, by Mrs. Allen's side, without any thing to say or NA II 3 143 1
"As to any attentions on his side, I do declare, upon my NA II 3 144 11
whatever might pass on his side, you must be convinced, by NA II 3 145 13
on my side, I never had the smallest idea of it. NA II 3 145 13
or drawers, but on one side perhaps the remains of a NA II 5 158 17
On one side it had a range of doors, and it was lighted on NA II 5 162 28
was lighted on the other side by windows which Catherine NA II 5 162 28
back in a deep recess on one side of the fire-place. NA II 6 163 1
Could there be any unwillingness on the General's side to NA II 7 177 18
of the Abbey; the fourth side of the quadrangle having, on NA II 8 184 4
as all the rest of that side of the house; and Eleanor NA II 8 186 7
and the stair-case by the side of those apartments of NA II 8 188 17
The side of the quadrangle, in which she supposed the NA II 8 188 19
And how strange an infatuation on Frederick's side! NA II 10 205 30
The last two days he was always by the side of Charlotte NA II 12 217 2
how thankfully on my side!--as to your continuing here as NA II 13 223 13
was information on Sarah's side, which produced only a bow NA II 15 243 9
an attachment on either side; but as nothing, after all, NA II 16 249 1
maternal affection on the side of the former, the two SS I 3 14 3
No difficulty arose on either side in the agreement; and SS I 5 26 5
On each side of the entrance was a sitting room, about SS I 6 28 2
no great distance on each side; some of which were open SS I 6 28 3
for he was on the wrong side of five and thirty; but SS I 7 34 6
speed down the steep side of the hill which led SS I 9 41 6
Willoughby, on his side, gave every proof of his pleasure SS I 10 48 7
such as to make further entreaty on his side impossible. SS I 12 59 6
On one side you look across the bowling-green, behind the SS I 13 69 76
side of Marianne, and by his favourite pointer at her feet. SS I 14 71 5
ever been formed on his side; and the next that some SS I 15 77 19
Has there been any inconsistency on his side to create SS I 15 81 42
On Edward's side, more particularly, there was a SS I 16 87 23
"My judgment," he returned, "is all on your side of the SS I 17 94 42
As for the navy, it had fashion on its side, but I was too SS I 19 103 4
John was entirely on the side of the Miss Steeles, their SS I 21 124 33
at intimacy on their side, Elinor principally attributed SS I 22 127 1
side glance at her companion to observe its effect on her. SS I 22 129 12
as it was too on every side by such probabilities and SS II 1 139 1
of time, spent on her side in inferior society and more SS II 1 140 2
rivals were thus seated side by side at the same table, SS II 1 145 23
were thus seated side by side at the same table, and with SS II 1 145 23
We seem so beset with difficulties on every side, that SS II 2 149 30
with you, unless it were on the side of your wishes." SS II 2 150 31
had been said on either side, to make them dislike each SS II 2 151 41
affection on her side would have given, for self-interest SS II 2 151 41
and Mrs. Jennings on her side treated them both with all SS II 4 160 2
little interest on either side, they continued to talk, SS II 4 162 12
on Mrs. Jennings's side, and in laughter without cause on SS II 4 164 23
nodded to Mrs. Jennings from the other side of the room. SS II 5 171 30
Every additional day of unhappy confidence, on your side, SS II 7 186 29
certainty on either side will be ease to what I now suffer. SS II 7 188 42
But when there is plenty of money on one side, and next to SS II 8 194 8
on Colonel Brandon's side, as might have become a man in SS II 8 200 43
counsel on Elinor's side, the same impetuous feelings and SS II 9 201 2
No, not if it were to be by the side of Barton covert, and SS II 10 214 9
it, when another gentleman presented himself at her side. SS II 11 221 6
A very little trouble on your side secures him. SS II 11 223 24
prior attachment on your side--in short, you know as to an SS II 11 224 24
her opinion on William's side, by which she offended Mrs. SS II 12 234 25
The first question on her side, which led to farther SS III 1 262 14
15
This delay on the Colonel's side, however, did not seem to SS III 3 281 13
14
to be on the safe side, he made his apology in form as SS III 4 288 26
assurance on her side of her unceasing good wishes for his SS III 4 290 43

to ascend--a hill, whose side was covered with the woods & S 4 382 1
conduct on Lady Denham's side, she found no reluctance to S 6 391 1
On one side it seemed protecting kindness, on the other S 6 392 1
She had read it, in an anxious glance or two on his side-- S 7 398 1
of my right side, before I had swallowed it 5 minutes.-- S 10 418 1
The use of my right side is entirely taken away for S 10 418 1
hope on Miss Beaufort's side, of praise & celebrity from S 11 421 1
at Sanditon, & on one side, whatever might be going on at S 11 422 1
in the field on the other side;--it was something which S 12 426 1
apparently very composedly--& Sir E. D. by her side.-- S 12 426 1

SIDE-BOARD (1)
couple, with two violins, and a mere side-board collation. SS II 5 170 29

SIDE-DOORS (1)
was the loss of half a day's work about those side-doors.-- MP I 15 141 22

SIDE-GLANCE (1)
was a side-glance of great meaning at Jane.) E III 16 454 17

SIDE-GLASS (1)
And letting down the side-glass to distinguish, "'tis MP II 5 222 46

SIDE-SCREENS (1)
and second distances--side-screens and perspectives-- NA I 14 111 29

SIDE-TABLE (1)
at the side-table for cold meat which was not there. NA II 11 214 27

SIDEBOARD (2)
in the room, from the sideboard to the fender, to give an PP II 5 156 4
as his Harry stand at our sideboard for any consideration. E III 16 458 42

SIDES (20)
The whole building enclosed a large court; and two sides NA II 7 177 19
now seen surrounded three sides of the court, she could NA II 8 183 2
connected the different sides;--and she was further NA II 8 183 2
of a walk round two sides of a meadow, on which Henry's NA II 11 214 25
It is a corner room, and has windows on two sides. SS I 13 69 76
were seated on different sides of the room; "but, however, SS I 19 107 29
minutes silence on both sides, "his mother must provide SS I 22 133 46
After a short silence on both sides, Mrs. Jennings, with SS II 8 196 21
A very desirable connection on both sides, and I have not SS II 11 224 28
Abundance of civilities passed on all sides. SS II 11 228 52
There was a kind of cold hearted selfishness on both sides, SS II 12 229 2
assertion on both sides, and every body had a right to be SS II 12 233 20
of his relations on both sides, there was no convincing SS II 14 248 5
On both sides it was only assertion. PP II 13 205 3
So imprudent a match on both sides!-- PP III 4 273 3
It will then be publicly seen, that on both sides, we meet PP III 12 339 6
Their fortune on both sides is splendid. PP III 14 356 50
Four sides of paper were insufficient to contain all her PP III 18 383 25
There are on both sides good principles and good temper." P IV 8 182 7
who have studied right sides & green tea scientifically & S 10 418 1

SIDING (1)
This was the first time of her brother's openly siding NA I 13 99 4

SIDMOUTH (1)
in last night from Sidmouth,--dare say you heard the P III 12 105 12

SIDNEY (15)
What is it, your brother Sidney says about it's being a S 4 381 1
Sidney says any thing you know. S 4 382 1
In ours, it is Sidney; who is a very clever young man,-- S 4 382 1
Such a young man as Sidney, with his neat equipage & S 4 382 1
"Not a line from Sidney!--said he.-- S 4 382 1
came from--or rather what wd Sidney say if he were here?-- S 5 385 1
Sidney is a saucy fellow, Miss H.-- S 5 385 1
Sidney laughs at him--but it really is no joke--tho' S 5 385 1
really is no joke--tho' Sidney often makes me laugh at S 5 385 1
I have heard nothing of Sidney since your being together S 5 385 1
Though I dare say Sidney might find something extremely S 5 387 1
eagerly called out, "T'is uncle Sidney mama, it is indeed." S 5 387 1
Mr Sidney Parker driving his servant in a very neat S 12 425 1
friendly meeting between Sidney & his sister in law, who S 12 425 1
Sidney Parker was about 7 or 8 & 20, very good-looking, S 12 425 1

SIDNEY'S (2)
I got that man a hare from one of Sidney's friends--and he S 9 412 1
in the credit which Sidney's arrival wd give to the place. S 12 426 1

SIGH (52)
I take on my lap & sigh over for his dear uncle's sake. LS 5 250 2
Far from me be all complaint, & every sigh of regret. LS 36 305 1
and and something like a sigh escaped her as she said it. NA I 5 36 2
breathe his parting sigh before he set off for Wiltshire. NA I 15 120 24
She began first to be sensible of this, and to sigh for NA II 3 143 1
fond of this spot," said her companion, with a sigh. NA II 7 179 30
Mrs. John Dashwood saw the packages depart with a sigh: SS I 5 26 4
"Why should you think so!" replied he, with a sigh. SS I 17 93 34
of going away without a sigh--declared his time to be SS I 19 101 1
I could give up every prospect of more without a sigh. SS II 2 147 7
Elinor hardly knew whether to smile or sigh at this SS II 2 147 11
At length Lucy exclaimed with a deep sigh, "I believe it SS II 2 149 29
30
for recollection, and then, with another sigh, went on. SS II 9 205 21
"Do not talk to me of my wife," said he with an heavy sigh. SS III 8 329 65
cheerfulness, and though a sigh sometimes escaped her, it SS III 10 342 7
Her smile however changed to a sigh when she remembered SS III 10 343 10
Marianne at last with a sigh, "when I wish his secret SS III 10 345 24
A sigh accompanied these words, which Emma respected in W 316 2
eliz: giving another sigh to the remembrance of Purvis.-- W 321 2
"A great many indeed," said her companion with a sigh. PP II 15 217 12
A small sigh escaped Fanny here, and she did not know how MP I 10 102 44
I could rant and storm, or sigh, or cut capers in any MP I 13 123 6
Fanny with half a sigh, "to have any such apprehension. MP II 3 199 14
sigh at the approach of Saturday's constant half holiday. MP III 8 391 8
and she often heaved a sigh at the remembrance of all her MP III 9 398 9
It was a melancholy change; and Emma could not but sigh E I 1 7 10
true, my dear, indeed," said Mr. Woodhouse with a sigh. E I 1 10 31
giving a gentle sigh, and saying: "Ah! poor Miss Taylor. E I 2 19 12
13
"What a precious deposit!" said he with a tender sigh, as E I 6 49 43
says himself; but he does sigh and languish, and study for E I 6 49 44
After a little thinking, and a very tender sigh, he added, E I 9 78 53
54
only give a submissive sigh; and as Emma saw his spirits E I 9 80 68
shake of the head and a sigh, called his daughter's E I 11 93 5
This was very proper; the sigh which accompanied it was E I 13 115 36
She heard him sigh. E II 12 261 32
was natural for him to feel that he had cause to sigh. E II 12 261 32
and did sigh, could not but agree, and rise to take leave. E II 12 261 35
(with a gentle sigh,) what do you think of her?-- E II 14 271 6
happy months there!(with a little sigh of sentiment). E II 14 273 19
And so does poor Mrs. Weston"--with half a sigh and half a E II 16 297 47
from a start, or a heavy sigh, or even from walking about E III 12 423 21
and a heavy sigh) I seem to have been doomed to blindness." E III 13 425 11
in short, for (with a sigh) let me swell out the causes E III 13 427 19
poor man! with a deep sigh, that he wished I might find as E III 14 443 8
grove, said, with a gentle sigh, "a few months more, and P III 3 24 38
a sigh were necessary to dispel the agitation of the idea. P III 4 30 10
"Ay, true enough," (with a deep sigh) "only June." P III 12 108 26
and preside, she had no sigh of that description to heave. P IV 1 126 18
She might not wonder, but she must sigh that her father P IV 3 138 5
of a town; and she must sigh, and smile, and wonder too, P IV 3 138 5
rejoiced, her sigh had none of the ill-will of envy in it. P IV 10 219 27
But (with a bit of a sigh) he is gone, & we must not find S 7 399 1

SIGHED (14)
"No walk for me to-day," sighed Catherine;--"but perhaps NA I 11 82 4
Catherine sighed. NA II 14 234 12
Elinor sighed over the fancied necessity of this; but to a SS II 9 211 39
Marianne sighed out her similar apprehension; and Elinor's SS III 1 268 46
She sighed for the air, the liberty, the quiet of the SS III 3 279 1
Marianne sighed, and repeated--"I wish for no change." SS III 11 350 8
and varieties, sighed at the perverseness of those PP III 4 279 23
Fanny sighed, and said, "I cannot see things as you do; MP I 3 27 34
Fanny sighed alone at the window till scolded away by Mrs. MP I 11 113 43
got up to look at it, and sighed out his half sentences of E I 9 69 2
a better report; and he sighed and smiled himself off in a E I 13 111 14
"Yes," sighed Anne, "we shall, indeed, be known to be P IV 4 150 18
Anne sighed and blushed and smiled, in pity and disdain, P IV 7 179 31
happiness; and though she sighed as she rejoiced, her sigh P IV 10 219 27

SIGHING (12)
"Certainly;" replied I, deeply sighing at the recital of LS 24 287 10
"No," said Miss Tilney, sighing; "I was unfortunately from NA II 8 186 12
"No, I thank you," (sighing as she spoke,) "they are all NA II 10 203 10
On such a subject," sighing heavily, "I can have little SS II 9 205 20
Mr. Yates was particularly pleased; he had been sighing MP I 14 132 8
desponding state of mind, sighing over the ruin of all her MP II 4 205 3
And it was spoken with a sort of sighing animation, which E I 6 43 8
without our sighing out our souls over this charade." E I 9 78 47
"I dare say," returned Harriet, sighing again, "I dare say E II 14 271 13
and his wife sat sighing and moralizing over her broad E III 9 388 13
"I am afraid," returned Emma, sighing, "that I must often E III 12 419 11
her, and Mrs. Smith, sighing over it as she unlocked it, P IV 9 202 69
70

SIGHINGS (1)
to her large fat sighings over the destiny of a son, whom P III 8 68 29

SIGHS (4)
The breeze had not seemed to waft the sighs of the NA II 5 161 25
Edmund's deep sighs often reached Fanny. MP III 15 445 33
Sighs and fine words had been given in abundance; but she E I 16 135 7
a shake of the head, and sighs which declared his little P III 11 101 25

SIGHT (136)
I will not dissemble what real pleasure his sight afforded LS 29 299 2
countenance that one cannot help loving him at first sight. LS 38 307 3
It was a splendid sight, and she began, for the first time NA I 2 21 9
anxious to avoid his sight, lest he should engage her NA I 10 74 23
How I hate the sight of an umbrella!" NA I 11 82 10
right-hand pavement--she must be almost out of sight now." NA I 11 87 53
were in a moment out of sight round the corner of Laura- NA I 11 87 53
past only by avoiding his sight, or flirting with somebody NA I 12 93 4
at such a sight, could not help saying, "nay, Catherine. NA I 13 98 3
conveyed from her sight without very uneasy sensations. NA II 1 132 16
not looked so well pleased at the sight of Captain Tilney. NA II 3 148 28
her impatience for a sight of the Abbey--for some time NA II 5 161 24
The sight of it made her start; and, forgetting every NA II 6 163 1
2
I did not expect such a sight as this!-- NA II 6 163 2
Pushed back too, as if meant to be out of sight!-- NA II 6 163 2
If the evidence of sight might be trusted, she held a NA II 7 172 2
should shrink from the sight of such objects as that room NA II 8 186 6
her imagination beyond the sight of a very elegant NA II 9 190 1
she did not love the sight of Japan in any shape: but even NA II 10 201 4
Poor Thorpe is in town: I dread the sight of him; his NA II 10 202 7
Catherine's colour rose at the sight of it; and the NA II 13 228 27
The chaise of a traveller being a rare sight in Fullerton, NA II 14 233 8
eagerness, was a sight to awaken the best feelings of NA II 14 233 9
to move when the sight of every well known spot ceased to SS I 3 14 1
At first sight, his address is certainly not striking; and SS I 4 20 9
and they were soon out of sight; and nothing more of them SS I 13 67 60
into his carriage, and in a minute it was out of sight. SS I 15 76 17
off, and driven as much as possible from the sight." SS I 16 88 31
and distant objects out of sight, which ought only to be SS I 18 97 4
till breakfast time, avoiding the sight of every body. SS II 7 180 5
The sight of you, Edward, is the only comfort it has SS II 13 242 29
said about them, and I took care to keep mine out of sight. SS III 2 275 22
Elinor, staring back with a look of horror at the sight of SS III 8 317 1
2
The sight of your dear sister, however, was really SS III 8 324 42
I have entered many a shop to avoid your sight, as the SS III 8 326 55
to keep out of your sight, could have separated us so long. SS III 8 326 55
It was a horrid sight!-- SS III 8 327 55
to accustom herself to the sight of every object with SS III 10 342 7
Marianne had retreated as much as possible out of sight, SS III 12 359 13
yet enjoy, as she wished, the sight and society of both. SS III 13 363 6
and living almost within sight of each other, they could SS III 14 380 21
He had entertained hopes of being admitted to a sight of PP I 3 9 3
and received no inconsiderable pleasure from the sight. PP I 6 25 30
suddenly arrested by the sight of the stranger, and PP I 15 73 8
The sight of Miss Lucas was odious to her. PP I 23 129 16
out of the chaise, rejoicing at the sight of each other. PP II 5 155 3
such a sight to be seen! I will not tell you what it is. PP II 5 158 11
12
were to expect, that the sight of such rooms, so many PP II 6 160 4
again into the plantation, and was soon out of sight. PP II 12 195 2
his appearance, that it was impossible to avoid his sight. PP III 1 251 51
had been at first, by the sight of Mr. Darcy approaching PP III 1 254 57
to be out of sight of the inn the whole of that morning. PP III 2 260 1
The little Gardiners, attracted by the sight of a chaise, PP III 5 286 21
Why did the Forsters ever let her go out of their sight? PP III 5 287 35
but else I must say that I hate the very sight of him." PP III 11 334 35
were out of sight, then returned into the drawing room. PP III 13 345 17
to admit them in your sight, or allow their names to be PP III 15 364 22
shoulders, it was not till Sir William was out of sight. PP III 18 384 26
pug, and vain was even the sight of a gooseberry tart MP I 2 13 4
apart, were not within sight of each other; but by walking MP I 7 67 16
here in a moment you know--we shall not be out of sight." MP I 10 99 19
she remained without sight or sound of any companion. MP I 10 100 23
were strengthened by the sight of present upon present MP I 16 153 3
Her eyes brightened at the sight of Edmund. MP I 16 153 3
to herself, and of avoiding the sight of Mr. Rushworth. MP I 18 168 14
Mrs. Norris contrived to remove one article from his sight MP II 2 195 22
at the front door, and the sight of Miss Price dripping MP II 4 205 3
"She was checked by the sight of her uncle much nearer to MP II 7 250 56
Such a sight having never occurred before, was almost as MP II 9 261 1
was much subdued; the sight of so many strangers threw her MP II 10 273 7
she was almost ready to faint at the sight of him. MP III 1 321 47
farther softened by the sight of such emotion, hung about MP III 5 359 10
It was a beautiful sight. MP III 7 377 7
But by g--, you lost a fine sight by not being here in the MP III 7 380 20
She could have none, so long lost sight of! MP III 7 382 29
The sight of Betsey brought the image of little Mary back MP III 7 386 40
Warmed by the sight of such a friend to her son, and MP III 10 400 6
for being now used to the sight of him in his suffering, MP III 14 429 1
given to the sight, more yet remains for the imagination. MP III 15 446 35
the more irritated by the sight of the person whom, in the MP III 16 448 2
Emma knew very well by sight and had long felt an interest E I 3 22 7
him--but he knows you very well indeed--I mean by sight." E I 4 29 15
No sooner was she out of sight, than Emma exclaimed, "what E I 6 43 12
13
as to leave with us; thank you for the sight of it. E I 9 81 79
80
Elton was immediately in sight; and so near as to give E I 10 87 29
30
half hour; but the very sight of Mrs. Weston, her smile, E I 14 117 2
renewal of alarm at the sight of the snow which had E I 15 128 22
These were very cheering thoughts; and the sight of a E I 16 138 16
her first shame-- and the sight of Harriet's tears made E I 17 141 6
her happiness in the sight or the recollection of him. E I 17 143 13
Highbury entire, which the sight of him would have made; E I 18 145 5
pleasing at all; and his sight was so inseparably E II 4 182 7
to the front door, the sight of every thing which had E II 5 186 2
There was instant pleasure in the sight of them, and still E II 5 188 6
7
had been struck by the sight of a pianoforte--a very E II 8 214 13

But the sight of Mr. Knightley among the most attentive, E II 8 227 87
his life--did not know the people who kept it by sight.-- E II 11 251 26
I do not know her, even by sight." E II 11 252 35
They must begin with some quickness of sight and hand, and E II 16 296 43
In another moment a happier sight caught her;-- Mr. E III 2 328 40
others, and buried from sight, she should have looked on E III 5 348 21
prospect, had scarcely a sight--and its abundance of E III 6 358 35
With some there was great joy at the sight of Frank E III 6 366 74
the carriages was a joyful sight; and even the bustle of E III 7 374 54
Never had the exquisite sight, smell, sensation of nature, E III 13 424 1
"had I been offered the sight of one of this gentleman's E III 15 444 6
the gentleman so well by sight; seen him a hundred times; P III 3 23 28
done so well without the sight of Mr. and Mrs. Musgrove's P III 6 46 12
all better pleased by the sight of Captain Wentworth, than P III 9 79 25
than Captain Wentworth had been by the sight of Anne. P III 9 79 25
by degrees quite out of sight and sound, Mary was happy no P III 10 86 21
which spring from the sight of all the ingenious P III 11 98 17
at any rate, to enjoy the sight of a dead young lady, nay, P III 12 111 49
forgotten by her; nor the sight of him afterwards, as he P III 12 112 54
She had lately lost sight even of her father and sister P IV 1 124 11
It was evident how little the women were used to the sight P IV 3 142 13
To your fine mind, I well know the sight of beauty is a P IV 4 145 1
The sight of Mrs. Clay in such favour, and of Anne so P IV 4 146 5
Captain Wentworth must be out of sight. P IV 7 175 6
He was more obviously struck and confused by the sight of P IV 7 175 6
As soon as they were out of sight, the ladies of Captain P IV 7 177 17
language, to translate at sight these inverted, transposed, P IV 8 186 26
space at hand, when Captain Wentworth was again in sight. P IV 8 189 47
It was impossible but that Mrs. Clay must hate the sight P IV 10 213 10
she could hardly bear the sight of his present smiles and P IV 10 214 11
in, as long as it is in sight, and then turns away and P IV 11 234 31
two moments preparation for the sight of Captain Wentworth. P IV 11 239 55
He promised me the sight of a capital gun he is just going P IV 11 240 58
Was not the very sight of the friend who sat behind you, P IV 11 244 72
sight of several persons now coming to their assistance. S 1 364 1
Who wd have expected such a sight at a Shoemaker's in old S 4 383 1
His spirits rose with the very sight of the sea & he cd S 4 384 1
& which their groom was leading about still in her sight.-- S 7 394 1
till we came within sight of poor old Sanditon--and the S 9 407 1
were setting off,--a joyful sight--& full of speculation.-- S 10 414 1
reflection which the sight of this tete a tete produced, S 12 426 1

SIGHTED (1)
Heaven forbid it!--but why should I be quicker sighted LS 15 267 4

SIGHTS (4)
balls and plays, and every-day sights, is past with them." NA I 10 79 57
away, "these are the sights, Harriet, to do one good. E I 10 86 24
25
day, which only made such cruel sights the longer visible. E III 12 421 18
Such sights & sounds were highly Blissful to Mr P.-- S 4 383 1

SIGN (13)
that Miss Vernon shewed no sign of obstinacy or LS 17 271 7
grateful for so favourable a sign of my daughter's sense. LS 24 288 11
With an hasty exclamation of misery, and a sign to her SS II 8 193 7
unbiassed opinion, by an eager sign, engaged her silence. SS III 11 349 5
He wisely resolved to be particularly careful that no sign PP I 12 60 4
able to gratify him by any sign of repentance; and rather PP II 5 156 4
when I write to them, and sign my name Lydia Wickham. PP III 5 291 60
hardly be said to shew any sign of alarm; but she was MP II 1 179 10
There is no sign of displeasure, or even of hearing her. MP III 14 431 8
I see no sign of attachment--I believe nothing of the E II 8 226 84
"I do not see much sign of it. E II 10 243 29
It is a sign I was not there to take care of you." E II 16 295 30
and there cannot be a surer sign of nervousness.--" S 10 416 1

SIGNAL (5)
which was the constant signal for Mrs Edwards to order W 327 7
& no sooner had the signal been given, by the Orchestra's W 328 9
Upon this signal, the youngest of her daughters put PP I 9 45 35
by a ring at the door, the certain signal of a visitor. PP II 9 177 1
No hurry for a signal at all.-- P IV 11 234 27

SIGNED (3)
chance, if Henry stept in before the articles were signed." MP I 17 162 17
went on; and it was signed 'F. C. Weston Churchill.'-- E I 11 96 24
and found her doom already signed with regard to Randalls. E I 13 109 5

SIGNIFICANCE (1)
look of his own arch significance as he named her; but yet P IV 7 176 8

SIGNIFICANCY (1)
with so much significancy and so many nods and winks, as SS I 21 125 36

SIGNIFICANT (10)
and add their quota of significant looks and mysterious NA I 15 120 25
he even confused her by his too significant reference! NA II 14 230 2
learned from some very significant looks, how far their SS I 18 99 15
adding, with a significant smile, "I do not imagine his PP I 18 89 1
2
By many significant looks and silent entreaties, did she PP I 18 100 68
place till after many a significant look and smile from PP III 3 268 6
With a significant smile, which made Fanny quite hate him, MP II 5 224 49
dances and said, with a significant look, "perhaps you can MP II 10 277 17
also, but even encouraging him by significant glances.-- E III 2 327 34
gold ridicule by her side, saying, with significant nods, E III 16 453 12
13

SIGNIFICANTLY (6)
for you know (nodding significantly and pointing to her SS I 19 107 29
"Oh!" cried Miss Steele, looking significantly round at SS II 2 148 23
Between ourselves, Edmund," nodding significantly at his MP I 7 73 55
at an end (looking significantly at his father). MP II 2 193 13
said, looking so very significantly at her, "that she did E I 8 68 58
again:"--and nodding significantly--"there must be some E II 16 295 34

SIGNIFIED (2)
say; and it would not have signified whether he did or no. E I 18 149 26
little discerning; --what signified her praise? E II 3 179 53

SIGNIFIES (1)
Bertrams, "and for a theatre, what signifies a theatre? MP I 13 123 6

SIGNIFY (29)
"But it does not signify if they do;" said Catherine, very NA I 6 42 25
"Signify! NA I 6 42 26
What can it signify to you, what we are talking of? NA I 8 57 20
"Oh! that will not signify; I never mind dirt." NA I 11 82 6
But it does not signify, the nights are moonlight, and we NA I 11 84 19
It was dirty, indeed, but what did that signify? NA I 11 90 64
It does not signify talking. NA I 13 101 22
The difference of fortune can be nothing to signify." NA I 15 119 17
heart I know it would signify nothing; but we must not NA I 15 119 18
fortune at all: but that will not signify in your family.-- NA II 10 205 30
down to a middling one for one day could not signify." NA II 11 211 13
Well, it don't signify talking, but when a young man, be SS II 8 194 10
out at small cost, and then what does it signify? SS II 8 196 22
Cleveland; but it did not signify, for it was a great deal SS II 10 215 10
what it was to be satirical; but that did not signify. SS II 14 246 3
as he returned to his seat--"what does it signify?-- SS III 8 318 15
all that was--well, it does not signify; it is over now.-- SS III 8 327 55
And after all, what did it signify to my character in the SS III 8 328 63
have looked so awkward;--just the tray did not signify.--" W 347 22
Besides, it will not much signify what one wears this PP II 16 219 4
it will not signify to anybody here, what he really is. PP II 17 226 23
some time or other, and it did not much signify when. PP III 10 323 2
"Oh! it does not signify. MP I 6 56 24
and it will not much signify if nobody hears a word you MP I 15 145 47
I consider the ball as ill-timed;--what does it signify? MP II 9 268 31
sacks were sold, it did not signify who ate the remainder. E II 9 239 51
"What does all that signify? E II 11 253 42
Nothing to signify. E III 2 322 19
If we were not related, it would not signify; but as P IV 6 166 16

SIGNS (4)
all flattered Elinor with signs of amendment, and Marianne SS III 7 314 22
She looked at his two sisters, and saw them making signs PP I 18 100 68
No signs that a 'Scottish monarch sleeps below.'" MP I 9 86 6
door, and that there were signs of habitation before her, MP III 7 377 10

SILENCE (151)
Reginald observed all that passed, in perfect silence. LS 20 276 3
then was your intention when you insisted on her silence?" LS 24 289 12
said "not much indeed;"--but I left her almost in silence. LS 24 291 14
and, after a few minutes' silence, renewed the NA I 7 47 19
silence, she added, "he is a very agreeable young man." NA I 8 58 32
A silence of several minutes succeeded their first short NA I 9 63 10
a moment's silence, "how surprized I was to see him again. NA I 10 72 11
do no more; and a short silence ensued, which was broken NA I 13 99 4
and from politics, it was an easy step to silence. NA I 14 111 29
He made no answer; but after a minute's silence burst out NA I 15 122 30
He listened to his father in silence, and attempted not NA II 5 155 3
The silence of the lady proved it to be unanswerable. NA II 7 176 16
Catherine said nothing--after a short silence, during NA II 9 196 23
table, and, after a short silence, Eleanor said, "no bad NA II 10 203 9
Sometimes it appeared to them as if his silence would be NA II 11 209 5
her greatest safety in silence, and few and trivial were NA II 13 227 27
of herself; but in her silence and sadness she was the NA II 15 240 1
After a short silence--"I hope, my Catherine, you are not NA II 15 240 4
Returning in silence to his seat, therefore, he remained NA II 15 242 8
After a couple of minutes unbroken silence, Henry, turning NA II 15 242 9
His eyes were fixed on Marianne, and, after a silence of SS I 11 55 8
It was engrossed by the extraordinary silence of her SS I 14 71 3
As this silence continued, every day made it appear more SS I 14 71 3
that one is the total silence of both on the subject, and SS I 15 80 37
tried to find in it a motive sufficient for their silence. SS I 16 84 7
valley, and chiefly in silence, for Marianne's mind could SS I 16 85 15
After a short silence which succeeded the first surprise SS I 16 87 24
and, after a moment's silence, said, "Oh! Edward! SS I 18 100 28
29
fix her sorrow, by seeking silence, solitude, and idleness. SS I 19 104 9
reply, and they walked on for a few minutes in silence. SS I 21 128 8
They then proceeded a few paces in silence. SS I 22 132 38
"To be sure," continued Lucy, after a few minutes silence SS I 22 133 46
at his total silence with respect even to their names. SS I 22 134 49
"But what," said she after a short silence, "are your SS II 2 148 14
A mutual silence took place for some time. SS II 2 149 24
She sat in silence almost all the way, wrapt in her own SS II 4 160 2
After a pause of several minutes, their silence was broken, SS II 5 172 40
longer witness this torrent of unresisted grief in silence. SS II 7 185 20
After a short silence on both sides, Mrs. Jennings, with SS II 8 196 21
and in a determined silence when obliged to endure it. SS II 9 201 2
Have you," she continued, after a short silence, "ever SS II 9 211 34
over her sorrows in silence, gave more pain to her sister SS II 10 212 1
she sat at least seven minutes and a half in silence. SS II 12 229 3
Then, if I had not been bound to silence, perhaps nothing SS III 1 264 29
Elinor, while she waited in silence, and immovable gravity, SS III 5 298 34
He shared it, however, in a silence even greater than her SS III 9 334 4
the silence and quiet prescribed by every nurse around her. SS III 9 334 5
health;--and they crept on for a few minutes in silence. SS III 10 345 23
unbiassed opinion, by an eager sign, engaged her silence. SS III 11 349 5
together in a similarity of thoughtfulness and silence. SS III 11 355 46
They all waited in silence for the appearance of their SS III 12 359 10
far from him as she could, and maintained a strict silence. SS III 12 359 13
which Emma respected in silence--but her sister after a W 316 2
gratitude, & for a few minutes they jogged on in silence.-- W 320 2
that broke at intervals a silence of half an hour before W 322 3
her, he then sat in silence for some minutes longer, while W 346 21
softened--& after a short silence, by way of changing the W 352 26
more than gentleness & silence; &, being a man of sense W 361 30
Elizabeth listened in silence, but was not convinced; PP I 4 15 11
to say; and after a short silence Mrs. Bennet began PP I 9 45 35
"You dislike an argument, and want to silence this." PP I 10 51 41
repeated the question, with some surprise at her silence. PP I 10 52 49
intended to play, and the silence of the whole party on PP I 11 54 3
to imagine that their silence was to last through the two PP I 18 91 8
other dance and parted in silence; on each side PP I 18 94 43
Mr. Bennet, in equal silence, was enjoying the scene. PP I 18 103 75
Elizabeth preserved as steady a silence as either Mrs. PP I 18 103 75
silence and respect which her rank will inevitably excite. PP I 19 106 10
and immediately and in silence withdrew; determined, if he PP I 19 109 22
Her daughters listened in silence to this effusion, PP I 20 113 29
avoid her but by stiffness of manner and resentful silence. PP I 21 115 1
She was not rendered formidable by silence; but whatever PP II 6 162 11
settle their differences, silence their complaints, and PP II 7 169 4
were made, seemed in danger of sinking into total silence. PP II 9 177 3
But when Elizabeth told of his silence, it did not seem PP II 9 180 28
To interrupt a silence which might make him fancy her PP II 10 184 16
17
After a silence of several minutes he came towards her in PP II 11 189 3
4
after a few minutes silence, "it seems but a day or two PP II 15 217 11
engrossed by her own feelings, followed them in silence. PP III 1 252 54
After a short silence, the lady first spoke. PP III 1 256 61
They now walked on in silence; each of them deep in PP III 1 256 65
At such a time, much might have been said, and silence was PP III 1 257 66
of his concern, and observe her in compassionate silence. PP III 4 277 11
Then, after a short silence, he continued, "Lizzy, I bear PP III 6 299 26
of his silence; but it had not been so in Derbyshire. PP III 11 335 43
He stood by her, however, for some minutes, in silence; PP III 12 342 25
or disgust him into silence; and he was more communicative, PP III 13 346 21
After sitting for a moment in silence, she said very PP III 14 351 4
5
park here," returned Lady Catherine after a short silence. PP III 14 352 9
They proceeded in silence along the gravel walk that led PP III 14 353 20
Hear me in silence. PP III 14 356 50
word from you will silence me on this subject for ever." PP III 16 366 7
She was disheartened by Lady Bertram's silence, awed by MP I 2 14 8
story, but his determined silence obliged her to relate MP I 6 60 47
The chapel was soon afterwards left to the silence and MP I 9 89 30
A general silence succeeded. MP I 9 94 57
This was followed by a short silence. MP I 10 98 11
After an interval of silence, "I think they might as well MP I 10 102 38
A short silence followed. MP I 14 133 11
A short silence succeeded her leaving them; but her MP I 14 136 21
She either sat in gloomy silence, wrapt in such gravity as MP I 17 160 8
but her diligence and her silence concealed a very absent, MP I 18 168 14
where nothing was wanted but tranquillity and silence. MP II 1 180 10
"And I longed to do it--but there was such a dead silence! MP II 3 198 12
to the steady sobriety and orderly silence of the other. MP II 7 240 9
required some minutes silence to be settled into composure. MP II 8 253 4
Let us have the luxury of silence." MP II 10 278 20
As soon as her eagerness could rest in silence, he was as MP II 12 293 16
They will be angry," he added, after a moment's silence, MP II 12 297 33
silence, "that you mean to refuse Mr. Crawford?" MP III 1 315 21
In spite of his intended silence, Sir Thomas found himself MP III 2 331 19
He pressed for the strictest forbearance and silence MP III 2 332 20
Fanny, who had hoped to silence him by such an extremity MP III 3 343 40
some fifty yards in mutual silence and abstraction. MP III 4 351 35
always more inclined to silence when feeling most strongly. MP III 6 369 11
to be drawn from his silence, between which her mind was MP III 10 399 1
persuaded myself that you would understand my silence.-- MP III 13 420 2
silence, and behave as if you could forgive me directly. MP III 14 433 13
For a little while Emma persevered in her silence; but E I 7 52 18
19
Some minutes passed in this unpleasant silence, with only E I 8 65 50
After a mutual silence of some minutes, Harriet thus began E I 10 84 8

9
After a few minutes of entire silence between them, John E I 13 111 15
16
being quarrelsome; her heroism reached only to silence. E I 13 114 27
reply: and two moments of silence being ample E I 15 131 32
33
allow me to interpret this interesting silence. E I 15 131 32
33
not consider their their silence as any reason for their E II 8 215 14
her indignation, and only turned from her in silence. E II 8 220 47
and after a few minutes silence, he said, "another thing E II 15 286 22
23
her, he looked at in silence--wanting only to observe E II 16 292 10
it, till after a minute's silence she heard Harriet say in E III 4 340 28
mother-in-law's guarded silence; it was all in unison; E III 5 343 2
Apologies for her seemingly ungracious silence in their E III 12 418 5
Yet she could not bear this silence. E III 13 425 2
He listened in perfect silence. E III 13 427 18
injunction to caution and silence, as for the time crushed E III 13 431 38
last; and adding, that as silence on such a point could E III 14 442 8
Her silence disturbed him; and after observing her a E III 18 472 21
22
and, whether in speech or silence, conniving at the E III 18 476 43
great coldness, great silence, and a professed resolution P III 4 26 2
relief--the manner--the silence in which it had passed-- P III 9 80 34
And there was silence between them for a little while. P III 10 85 11
Her spirits wanted the solitude and silence which only P III 10 89 35
with a face as pallid as her own, in an agony of silence. P III 12 109 34
and there had been total silence among them for some time, P III 12 117 73
"I make no apology for my silence, because I know how " P IV 6 162 7
After another short silence-- "pray," said Mrs. Smith, "is P IV 9 194 19
20
all the rest of her astonishment in a convenient silence. P IV 10 213 8
composure, determined silence, or insipid talk, to meet P IV 10 226 63
the following words: "I can listen no longer in silence. P IV 11 237 41
42
to be kept from silence by the efforts of others, to Miss S 7 396 1
She kept her countenance & she kept a civil silence. S 7 402 1

SILENCED (17)
consciousness, and silenced her directly; and, though NA II 11 214 25
Lucy was silenced. SS II 10 219 36
appearance comfortable, sleep, she silenced every doubt. SS III 7 315 25
Ld Osborne was silenced. W 346 21
Elizabeth hoped she had silenced him; but he soon PP III 10 328 15
16
of propriety, and he was silenced, till induced by further MP I 6 57 32
This could not be denied, and Fanny was silenced. MP I 10 102 41
And Edmund silenced, was obliged to acknowledge that the MP I 13 129 39
Miss Crawford was silenced; and with some feelings of MP I 15 145 42
and as nearly being silenced as ever she had been in her MP II 2 188 3
It silenced her. MP III 2 333 27
Fanny was doubly silenced here; though when the moment was MP III 10 406 20
and, supported by her mistress, was not to be silenced. MP III 16 450 10
Emma was silenced. E II 14 274 27
"Well," said she, "and you soon silenced Mr. Cole, I E II 15 288 37
with a satisfaction which silenced, Mr. Knightley. E III 5 351 38
The Harvilles silenced all scruples; and, as much as they P III 12 112 56

SILENCING (2)
the gentleman, and a silencing nod from her mother; for NA II 15 243 9
of its being so, and silencing every reproach, overcoming SS III 8 326 53

SILENT (133)
of Lady Susan, & the silent dejection of Frederica, I am LS 17 270 5
will excuse my remaining silent on it so long, & agree LS 20 277 5
remaining a few moments silent, was on the point of NA I 6 42 33
could never be entirely silent; and, therefore, while she NA I 9 60 1
Catherine's silent appeal to her friend, meanwhile, was NA I 9 61 6
Isabella was silent. NA II 3 145 13
Miss Tilney continuing silent, she ventured to say, "her NA II 7 180 33
for an hour together in silent thoughtfulness, with NA II 8 187 13
and listened for its continuance; but all was silent. NA II 13 222 9
express her concern by silent attention; obliged her to be NA II 13 223 9
worn down; and, to be silent and alone becoming soon her NA II 14 235 13
only by that shyness which too often keeps him silent. SS I 4 20 9
He was silent and grave. SS I 7 34 6
She could not be silent when such points were introduced, SS I 10 47 3
She saw it with concern; for what could a silent man of SS I 10 50 12
more agreeable than her mother, only in being more silent. SS I 11 54 6
For a few moments every one was silent. SS I 15 76 13
her solitary walks and silent meditations, still produced SS I 16 83 4
fullest extent--and he sat for some time silent and dull. SS I 17 95 50
silent, till a new object suddenly engaged her attention. SS I 18 98 10
Marianne remained perfectly silent, though her countenance SS I 20 111 16
Marianne was silent; it was impossible for her to say what SS I 21 122 14
She turned towards Lucy in silent amazement, unable to SS I 22 129 15
Elinor for a few moments remained silent. SS I 22 130 17
She was silent.-- SS I 22 131 33
Lucy looked at Elinor again, and was silent. SS II 2 148 17
They were again silent for many minutes. SS II 2 149 29
Every thing was silent; this could not be borne many SS II 4 161 7
more thoughtful and silent than he had been before, and SS II 4 163 20
a letter then?" said Elinor, unable to be longer silent. SS II 5 169 21
He listened to her with silent attention, and on her SS II 5 174 46
Marianne was in a silent agony, too much oppressed even SS II 6 178 16
for a few moments with silent anxiety, said, in a tone of SS II 7 180 1
2
Again they were both silent. SS II 7 190 55
her own room, leaning, in silent misery, over the small SS II 8 197 23
A few minutes more of silent exertion enabled him to SS II 9 207 25
a moment or two all were silent; while Marianne was SS II 13 242 25
able to be silent, "he has acted like an honest man! SS III 1 267 43
her desire, confined herself to this silent ejaculation. SS III 3 281 11
Elinor was silent. SS III 5 296 23
said no more, and John was also for a short time silent.-- SS III 5 297 30
listened to them in silent despondence;-- but her SS III 7 311 15
for some time kept her silent, even to her friend--to SS III 7 314 22
All within Elinor's breast was satisfaction, silent and SS III 7 315 24
They were both silent for a few moments. SS III 8 324 43
pained, surprised and not surprised, was silent attention. SS III 9 336 9
recollection, she grew silent and thoughtful, and turning SS III 10 342 7
Perhaps, however, he is kept silent by his fear of SS III 13 371 39
offered--Mrs E. continued silent, either not understanding W 339 18
Mrs E. was silent no longer. W 339 18
He stood for a few seconds, in silent amazement.-- W 355 28
Mr. Darcy stood near them in silent indignation at such a PP I 6 25 25
He was silent. PP I 10 48 14
need of encouragement, nor inclined to be silent himself. PP I 13 64 21
went, for neither Lydia nor Mr. Collins were once silent. PP I 16 84 59
He replied, and was again silent. PP I 18 91 8
But now we may be silent." PP I 18 91 11
It would look odd to be entirely silent for half an hour PP I 18 91 13
He made no answer, and they were again silent till they PP I 18 93 18
By many significant looks and silent entreaties, did she PP I 18 100 68
not determine whether the silent contempt of the gentleman, PP I 18 102 72
On that head, therefore, I shall be uniformly silent; and PP I 19 106 10
Mr. Collins was not left long to the silent contemplation PP I 20 110 1
"My dear madam," replied he, "let us be for ever silent on PP I 20 114 32
which kept them mutually silent on the subject; and PP I 23 127 9
the chief of all this, heard it in silent indignation. PP II 1 133 3
She stared, coloured, doubted, and was silent. PP II 11 189 5
on this point it will be as well to be silent. PP II 15 216 6
for a few minutes he was silent; till, shaking off his PP II 18 234 37
38
He was resolutely silent however; and, from a PP III 3 271 16
17
Darcy shook his head in silent acquiesence. PP III 4 277 17
in thought, continued silent till they reached the house. PP III 7 304 33
engaged, that she did not always know when she was silent. PP III 11 338 56
"Why, if he came only to be silent, grave, and indifferent, PP III 12 339 2
If he no longer cares for me, why silent? PP III 12 339 4
lovers talked and laughed, the unacknowledged were silent. PP III 17 372 2
"Because you were grave and silent, and gave me no PP III 18 381 8
speaking it was altogether a silent drive to those within. MP I 10 106 58
Mr. Rushworth could be silent no longer. MP II 1 186 31
You are one of those who are too silent in the evening MP II 3 198 9
Fanny was silent--and Miss Crawford relapsed into MP II 4 210 22
established, it was a silent walk--for having finished MP II 4 216 50
of being suffered to sit silent and unattended to. MP II 5 223 48
With silent indignation, Fanny repeated to herself, "never MP II 5 225 56
He was surprized; but after a few moments silent MP II 5 226 59
They had talked--and they had been silent--he had reasoned- MP II 10 279 21
of a quarter of an hour's silent consideration, MP II 11 285 10
She was more silent than ever. MP II 13 304 17
Fanny would rather have been silent, but being obliged to MP III 1 312 11
"We have not been so silent all the time," replied his MP III 3 336 9
Fanny estranged from him, silent and reserved, was an MP III 4 345 4
to talk or to be silent, to be grave or to be gay. MP III 4 349 23
After this speech, the two girls sat many minutes silent, MP III 5 360 13
Fanny was silent; but not from being convinced that there MP III 7 385 40
The journey was likely to be a silent one. MP III 15 445 33
You do not wish me to be silent?--if you do, give me but a MP III 16 455 21
Fanny, watching him with silent, but most tender concern, MP III 16 457 30
themselves; of walking; of speaking; of being silent. E I 4 33 34
Harriet was silent. E I 7 52 14
talk of it, and that a silent rumination might suffice to E I 12 105 51
Poor Mr. Woodhouse was silent from consternation; but E I 15 126 9
Emma said, "you are silent, Miss Fairfax--but I hope you E II 3 175 41
42
for the moment, he was silent; but Emma heard him almost E II 7 206 4
I am sure he was particularly silent when Mrs. Cole told E II 8 226 83
He was silent. E II 12 261 32
she behaved very well, and was only rather pale and silent. E II 14 270 3
She is very timid and silent. E II 15 283 7
almost always either talking together or silent together. E II 17 299 1
and might have been silent, who had been in more than one E II 17 303 23
of spirits which would have made her prefer being silent. E II 18 311 36
if she were totally silent, it might only drive Harriet E III 4 341 34
Harriet kissed her hand in silent and submissive gratitude. E III 4 342 40
She had never seen Frank Churchill so silent and stupid. E III 7 367 2
nonsense for the entertainment of seven silent people." E III 7 369 15
and very willing to be silent; and Emma felt the tears E III 7 376 63
For a moment he was silent; and then added, in a tone much E III 10 394 23
24
He was silent. E III 13 425 2
silent; and, as far as she could judge, deep in thought. E III 13 427 20
"You are silent," he cried, with great animation; " E III 13 430 35
animation; "absolutely silent! at present I ask no more." E III 13 430 35
After the first chat of pleasure he was silent; and then, E III 18 470 1
2
I have been silent from surprise merely, excessive E III 18 473 24
Anne fully submitted, in silent, deep mortification. P III 7 60 34
saying, "I hope the little boy is better," was silent. P III 9 79 24
were silent; till Henrietta suddenly began again, with, P III 12 102 1
2
the rejoicing, deep and silent, after a few fervent P III 12 112 53
occupied but by her silent, pensive self, might be filled P IV 1 123 7
connecting them with the silent admiration of her cousin, P IV 1 124 10
She persisted in a very determined, though very silent, P IV 2 135 34
off, but knew not why; and delicacy had kept him silent. P IV 3 138 7
Twelve years had changed Anne from the blooming, silent, P IV 5 153 6
They were both silent--Mrs. Smith very thoughtful. P IV 9 198 52
where she might be sure of being as silent as she chose. P IV 10 227 68

SILENTLY (13)
Catherine was silently reflecting that now Henry must have NA II 14 239 28
time, on her mother's silently pressing her hand with SS I 15 82 46
"And now," silently conjectured Elinor, "she will write to SS II 5 167 6
at all; and she was silently grieving over the imprudence SS II 7 188 43
it, she walked silently towards the table, and sat down. SS III 8 317 7
Her thoughts were silently fixed on the irreparable injury SS III 8 331 70
The ladies were silently firm, & the gentleman found W 340 18
Elizabeth silently attended her. PP I 7 33 43
after looking at her for a moment, turned silently away. PP I 9 43 20
the view from the mount, and Elizabeth silently consented. PP III 17 375 25
towards them, and he sat silently observing them for a few MP II 7 249 49
silently at work as if there was nothing else to care for. MP III 3 336 8
Emma's eyes were instantly withdrawn; and she sat silently E III 11 407 32

SILK (3)
My dear, do not you think these silk gloves were very well? NA II 14 238 24
pair of silk stockings, and came off with the Richardsons." SS III 2 274 16
girls, cutting up silk and gold paper; and on the other P IV 2 134 29

SILKS (1)
a landscape in coloured silks of her performance, in proof SS II 4 160 3

SILLIEST (1)
you must be two of the silliest girls in the country. PP I 7 29 5
6

SILLY (39)
He is as silly as ever.-- yours faithfully Alicia. LS 9 257 1
Reginald is so incensed against the poor silly girl! LS 15 267 7
sir, I always thought him silly & impertinent & LS 21 279 1
Silly woman, to expect constancy from so charming a man! LS 26 296 5
But she was always silly; intolerably so, in marrying him LS 26 296 5
Silly woman! what does she expect by such manoeuvres? LS 33 303 1
have always been prevented by some silly trifler or other. NA II 12 216 2
was the husband of a very silly woman,--but she knew that SS I 20 112 28
he is very unlike his brother--silly and a great coxcomb." SS II 2 148 19
replied he; "they are all silly and ignorant like other PP I 1 5 27
you should be so ready to think your own children silly. PP I 7 29 8
"If my children are silly I must hope to be always PP I 7 29 9
"How can you be so silly," cried her mother, "as to think PP I 7 32 34
pompous, narrow-minded, silly man; you know he is, as well PP II 1 135 13
having a couple of--or I may say, three very silly sisters. PP II 18 231 20
But don't imagine it was from any silly cause. PP III 11 331 17
Bingley looked a little silly at this reflection, and said PP III 11 338 59
and then was enraged against herself for being so silly! PP III 12 341 18
mother, and heard all her silly remarks with a forbearance PP III 13 345 18
How could I be so silly as to wish it! PP III 18 382 21
she still was occasionally nervous and invariably silly. PP III 19 385 1
The boy looked very silly and turned away without offering MP I 15 142 22
silly things, and break up one's family circle grievously." E I 1 13 45
whatever you may chuse to say, do not want silly wives. E I 8 64 47
be like Miss Bates! so silly--so satisfied--so smiling--so E I 10 84 16
too good natured and too silly to suit me; but, in general, E I 10 85 19
And Emma had the advantage of hearing her own silly E II 1 158 13
"hum! just the trifling, silly fellow I took him for." E II 7 206 4
to be so, but certainly silly things do cease to be silly E II 8 212 2
3
things do cease to be silly if they are done by sensible E II 8 212 2
3
Mr. Knightley, he is not a trifling, silly young man. E II 8 212 3
No, I am perfectly sure that he is not trifling or silly." E II 8 212 3
said, a few downright silly, but by much the larger E II 8 219 43
had been presumptuous and silly, and self-deceived, before, E III 19 481 2
to the authority and guidance of a conceited, silly father. P III 1 4 6
fait as to the newest modes of being trifling and silly. P IV 5 155 9
mere pretty, silly, expensive, fashionable woman, I P IV 5 156 13

Wallis has a very pretty silly wife, to whom he tells P IV 9 205 82
She began to think him downright silly.-- S 7 398 1

SILVER (10)
splashing-board, lamps, silver moulding, all you see NA I 7 46 13
The lock was silver, though tarnished from age; at each NA II 6 163 2
of handles also of silver, broken perhaps prematurely by NA II 6 163 2
It was a silver knife. MP III 7 386 42
the sore subject of the silver knife, canvassed as it now MP III 9 396 7
It was made, however, at last; a silver knife was bought MP III 9 396 7
much upon silver forks, napkins, and finger classes. MP III 15 446 35
such a trimming as this to my white and silver poplin. E II 17 302 22
Within abundance of silver paper was a pretty little E III 4 338 9
struck "eleven with its silver sounds," and the watchman P IV 3 144 23

SIMILAR (23)
were, Mrs. Allen had no similar information to give, no NA I 4 32 2
information to give, no similar triumphs to press on the NA I 4 32 2
attendance, maintained a similar position, and separating NA I 10 71 8
similar exertion, and encourage her to similar forbearance. SS I 1 7 13
by Marianne, on a similar occasion, to augment and fix her SS I 19 104 9
that in a scene of similar distress last week, some SS I 21 121 10
than in many cases of a similar kind, for it has been SS II 8 196 19
under a similar confinement, was my unfortunate sister. SS II 9 207 26
Marianne sighed out her similar apprehension; and Elinor's SS III 1 268 46
robbed her of one; the similar annihilation of Robert had SS III 14 373 2
to each other, or ever so similar before-hand, it does not PP I 6 23 10
endured on a similar occasion, five and twenty years ago. PP II 18 229 3
And will you give yourself the trouble of carrying similar PP III 8 313 19
how he might take a similar representation of the evils PP III 15 360 2
The joy which Miss Darcy expressed on receiving similar PP III 18 383 25
Miss Crawford was not entirely free from similar MP I 4 41 16
and a situation of similar affluence and do-nothing-ness MP III 8 390 5
and others succeeded of similar moment, and passed away E I 12 104 50
and passed away with similar harmony; but the evening did E I 12 104 50
she feared would experience no similar contradiction. E III 12 422 19
were any young person, in similar circumstances, to apply P III 4 29 8
in the separate, but very similar remark of Mr. and Mrs. P III 6 42 1
so open, no tastes so similar, no feelings so in unison, P III 8 63 3

SIMILARITY (7)
You totally disallow any similarity in the obligations; NA I 10 77 37
together in a similarity of thoughtfulness and silence. SS III 11 355 46
always seen a great similarity in the turn of our minds.-- PP I 18 91 15
similarity of feeling and taste between her and himself. PP III 13 347 33
on a point of some similarity, and could not help MP I 12 116 11
the consciousness of a similarity of prospect would E III 16 452 7
any circumstance of tolerable similarity, give such advice. P IV 11 246 80

SIMILE (2)
Thorpe never finished the simile, for it could hardly have NA I 13 101 24
I want an appropriate simile;--as far as your friend Emily NA I 14 107 11

SIMILIES (1)
Shakespeare, use his similies, and describe with his MP III 3 338 14

SIMPATHY (1)
even to affect simpathy, that she cd say nothing.-- S 7 401 1

SIMPER (1)
other, with a stately simper--"there will be some MP I 12 117 13

SIMPERED (2)
So upon that, he smirked, and simpered, and looked grave, SS III 1 258 5
Kitty simpered and smiled, and hoped her turn was coming PP III 13 348 34

SIMPERING (2)
with a simpering air, "have you been long in Bath, madam?" NA I 3 26 4
"There now," said Miss Steele, affectedly simpering, " SS II 10 218 26

SIMPERS (1)
He simpers, and smirks, and makes love to us all. PP III 11 330 8

SIMPLE (69)
two young men for this simple praise than a quality NA I 2 24 28
But guided only by what was simple and probable, it had NA I 8 53 3
made the matter perfectly simple by assuring her that it NA I 9 62 10
To Catherine's simple feelings, this odd sort-of reserve NA I 15 121 25
My notion of things is simple enough. NA I 15 124 46
miles off--could you shrink from so simple an adventure? NA II 5 159 21
he thought it would be simple not to make use of them; but, NA II 6 166 7
it to be neat and simple, thought it right to encourage NA II 7 175 12
simple, forming no pretensions, and knowing no disguise." NA II 10 206 31
Tilney, and that is very simple of you; for ten to one NA II 15 240 4
received him with the simple professions of unaffected NA II 15 242 7
"He would certainly have done more justice to simple and SS I 3 18 19
The house, too, as described by Sir John, was on so simple SS I 4 24 21
But there was one method so direct, so simple, and in her SS I 16 84 7
Here too, Miss Dashwood's commendation, being only simple SS I 21 122 16
the simple and common expedient, of asking what he meant? SS II 5 172 40
to acknowledge the simple proposition of its being the SS II 14 248 5
Her narration was clear and simple; and though it could SS III 1 261 12
brief repetition of such simple particulars, as she felt SS III 2 276 27
"A very simple one--to be of use to Mr. Ferrars." SS III 5 295 15
generous temper, simple taste, and diffident feelings. SS III 6 305 15
be expressed; in a more simple one--perhaps too simple to SS III 8 325 50
simple one--perhaps too simple to raise any emotion--my SS III 8 325 50
what arose from the most simple and self-evident SS III 10 340 3
to declare only the simple truth, and lay open such facts SS III 11 349 2
His errand at Barton, in fact, was a simple one. SS III 13 361 2
"I was simple enough to think, that because my faith was SS III 13 368 28
of Mrs. Ferrars, by the simple expedient of asking it, SS III 14 376 11
forwards with an honest & simple thank you Maam was W 331 11
A simple delivery is much better calculated to inspire W 344 20
They crossed it by a simple bridge, in character with the PP III 1 253 57
were unbending, his attentions tranquil and simple. MP I 7 65 13
To Fanny herself it appeared a very simple and natural MP II 4 206 5
Simple as such an engagement might appear in other eyes, MP II 5 219 27
he listened to his clear, simple, spirited details with MP II 6 236 21
simple and neat, she could not help bursting forth again. MP II 9 262 8
honourable, so good, the simple acknowledgment of settled MP III 1 318 38
of satisfaction, and words of simple, pleasant meaning. MP III 3 334 2
short, was so kind, a few simple lines expressed so MP III 6 371 17
me;--but it would be simple to be duped by a man who has MP III 11 412 20
dupe me--and worse than simple to let him give me a hard- MP III 11 412 20
Would not it be worse than simple? MP III 11 412 20
and she turned in to her more simple one immediately. MP III 11 412 29
to confine herself to the simple, indubitable family- MP III 15 441 21
Simple girl!-- MP III 16 455 23
young and too simple to have acquired any thing herself. E I 8 61 38
able to make more than a simple question on that head; it E I 13 108 3
ought to be serious, a trick of what ought to be simple. E I 16 137 10
If it were love, it might be simple, single, successless E II 2 168 13
"I dare say you would; but I, simple I, saw nothing but E II 8 218 37
give him credit for more simple, disinterested benevolence E II 8 224 65
Fairfax--and even for simple dancing itself, without any E II 11 247 2
a simple dress is so infinitely preferable to finery. E II 17 302 22
morning scheme, you know, Knightley; quite a simple thing. E III 6 355 20
Nothing can be more simple, you see. E III 6 355 20
Every thing as natural and simple as possible. E III 6 355 20
My idea of the simple and the natural will be to have the E III 6 355 21
It was with him, of so simple, yet so dignified a nature.-- E III 9 386 7
This is the simple truth." E III 10 396 41
affection, for having simple, honest, generous, feelings.-- E III 11 409 35
the two--or even the more simple sublimity of resolving to E III 13 431 38
"It is a very simple story. E III 18 471 20
well as to give him that simple acknowledgment of P IV 8 181 2
her regret that she had said so much, simple as it was. P IV 10 222 36
If indeed a simple sprain, as you denominate it, nothing S 5 386 1
equipage than the simple gig in which they travelled, & S 7 394 1
than the simple enquiry of--"Sir Edward & Miss Denham?"-- S 7 399 1
afterwards by the same simple link of connection that S 9 408 1
Nothing can be more simple. S 12 423 1

SIMPLE-MINDED (1)
day to set about being simple-minded and ignorant; but she E I 17 142 10

SIMPLER (2)
He went; and, it being at any time a much simpler NA II 11 211 15
knew very little;--her simpler mind, or juster reason W 345 21

SIMPLEST (5)
to bed, to try one or two of the simplest of the remedies. SS III 6 306 17
him beyond what the simplest claims of conscious beauty MP I 12 114 2
but it will be on the simplest plan;--a green curtain and MP I 13 127 31
head of his family; the simplest process in the world of P IV 4 147 7
be proved to be the simplest thing in the world, by those S 10 418 1

SIMPLETON (12)
were not the greatest simpleton on earth, I might have LS 2 245 1
a simpleton who has it either by nature or affectation. LS 19 274 3
the woman; but she is by no means a simpleton in general." NA I 14 113 39
"do not think me such a simpleton as to be always wanting NA II 3 143 2
lecture and been a great simpleton herself, till they were NA II 6 165 6
him, he must be a simpleton indeed not to discover it too." PP I 6 22 3
in a whisper not to be a simpleton and allow her fancy for PP I 18 90 8
She is not such a simpleton. PP I 21 119 20
who, I shall think you a simpleton, for there is but one PP III 5 291 60
"then she is a greater simpleton than I ever believed her. E I 8 60 31 32
"Yes, simpleton as I was!--but I am quite ashamed of it E III 4 340 24
she was the greatest simpleton in the world, the most P IV 7 175 5

SIMPLICITY (23)
their being spoken with simplicity and truth, and without NA I 10 72 8
of the room and simplicity of the furniture, where every NA II 5 162 27
with all the honest simplicity with which she felt it. NA II 11 213 21
an innate propriety and simplicity of taste, which in SS I 4 19 2
You would rob it of its simplicity by imaginary SS I 14 73 17
robbed her of that simplicity, which might once have given SS II 1 140 2
their manly unstudied simplicity is much more accordant SS III 9 338 22
simplicity, such shameless truth rather bewildered him.-- W 346 21
give her playfulness and simplicity without extravagance. MP I 14 135 15
Simplicity, indeed, is beyond the reach of almost every MP I 14 135 15
There is such a quiet simplicity in the plan of the walk!-- MP II 4 209 14
I endeavoured to consult the simplicity of your taste, but MP II 9 261 2
The simplicity and cheerfulness of her nature, her E I 3 21 4
enjoying the youthful simplicity which could speak with so E I 4 27 4
Emma was in the humour to value simplicity and modesty to E I 17 141 8
her face and the warm simplicity of her manner; and all E II 13 266 6
Their propriety, simplicity, and elegance, would make them E II 14 278 47
was in the first style of guileless simplicity and warmth. E II 15 284 12
taste is all for simplicity; a simple dress is so E II 17 302 22
simplicity of dress,--shew and finery are every thing. E II 17 302 22
The nature and the simplicity of gentlemen and ladies, E III 6 355 21
of openness and simplicity; and such a league in secret to E III 10 399 61
His goodness of heart and simplicity of character were P IV 1 127 23

SIMPLY (8)
feelings, and less simply engrossed by her own, that her NA I 7 44 4
at Mr. Palmer's acting so simply, with good abilities, and SS I 21 118 1
with caution; related simply and honestly the chief points SS III 10 347 33
will not think the worse of you for being simply dressed. PP II 6 161 6
nothing, I put it down as simply being his way, and was as MP III 5 362 21
A man who felt rightly would say at once, simply and E I 18 146 16
I cannot expect that simply growing older should make me E II 16 293 17 18
it around our house, simply rages & passes on--while down S 4 381 1

SIN (4)
had removed from him only to sink deeper in a life of sin. SS II 9 207 26
treat as a trifle this sin of the first magnitude, who MP III 15 441 19
in the continuance of the sin, on the chance of a marriage MP III 16 457 30
She even wept over the idea of it, as a sin of thought. E III 14 435 4

SINCE (371)
friendship for us since her husband's death, that we LS 3 246 1
artful and ungenerous since our marriage was first in LS 3 247 1
entirely; since he will be stubborn, he must be tricked. LS 5 249 1
business out of his head since; he wrote by the same post LS 13 262 1
& he is certainly less uneasy since Reginald's letter. LS 13 263 1
one ought to be credited, since no character however LS 14 264 3
I am more angry with her than ever since I have seen her LS 17 270 4
of her aunt, but I have since relaxed, as I beleive I may LS 19 274 3
for herself, or she has since transferred it to her LS 20 276 2
with Lady Susan has since had it's effect, he is still LS 20 278 9
Our prospect is most delightful; & since matters have now LS 23 283 1
It is a great while since I have seen my father & mother. LS 23 283 4
to look for Frederica, whom I had not seen since breakfast. LS 24 285 2
the severity which it has since been necessary for me to LS 24 288 11
of her look & manner since Sir James has been dismissed-- LS 25 293 4
had visited you every day since your being in town, & had LS 32 302 1
Since we parted yesterday, I have received from LS 34 304 1
But since it must be so, I am obliged to declare that all LS 36 305 1
during the life & since the death of Mr Vernon which had LS 36 305 1
That you have corresponded with him ever since your LS 36 305 1
This is the most joyful hour he has ever given us, since LS 40 309 1
I asked her whether she had seen my brother since his LS 41 310 1
it is a long time since I had the pleasure of seeing you, NA I 4 31 2
since their respective marriages, and that many years ago. NA I 4 31 2
great, as well it might, since they had been contented to NA I 4 31 2
how time had slipped away since they were last together, NA I 4 32 2
"Yes, I have been reading it ever since I woke; and I am NA I 6 39 5
times a day, by Isabella since her residence in Bath; and NA I 7 44 1
decent one come out since Tom Jones, except The Monk; I NA I 7 48 34
It was ages since she had had a moment's conversation with NA I 9 67 33
I firmly believe you were engaged to me ever since Monday. NA I 10 75 26
She had never taken a country walk since her arrival in NA I 10 80 61
she had been wishing ever since to see you, to explain the NA I 12 94 10
foreseen by them both ever since her brother's arrival; NA I 15 124 48
"Nay, since you make such a point of it, I can refuse you NA II 1 130 13
Once or twice indeed, since James's engagement had taught NA II 2 138 1
"Since they can consent to part with you," said he, "we NA II 2 140 9
"Since that is the case, I am sure I shall not tease you NA II 3 145 16
She has been in love with him ever since they first met, NA II 4 151 13
an apartment never used since some cousin or kin died in NA II 5 158 15
a point, would be vain, since sleep must be impossible NA II 6 168 10
The manufacture was much improved since that time; he had NA II 7 175 12
"though I never loved it then, as I have loved it since. NA II 7 179 32
never entered by him since the dreadful scene had passed, NA II 8 186 6
"Have you had any letter form Bath since I saw you?" NA II 9 195 19
It is a power little worth knowing however, since it can NA II 9 196 21
to you almost every day since you left Bath, but have NA II 12 216 2
Since you went away, I have had no pleasure in it--the NA II 12 216 2
not having heard from him since he went to Oxford; and am NA II 12 216 2
almost gone since his arrival, and Eleanor did not come up. NA II 13 222 8
It was not four-and-twenty hours ago since they had met NA II 13 228 27
spirits since last she had trodden that well-known road. NA II 14 237 20
It was not three months ago since, wild with joyful NA II 14 237 20
Rooms, you know, and I have worn them a great deal since. NA II 14 238 24
for the first time since her mother's entrance, asked her, NA II 15 242 9
first over-rated, had ever since his introduction to NA II 15 245 12
who had since spent the greatest part of his time there. SS I 3 15 4
Since he had neglected to do it on first coming to the SS I 5 27 6
perhaps had lain ever since in the same position on the SS I 7 35 8
Brandon well married, ever since her connection with Sir SS I 8 36 1
had been able to afford, since the loss of their father. SS I 9 40 1
Elinor, "almost every day since they first met on high- SS I 12 60 10
many happy hours have been since spent by us together, you SS I 14 73 17
entered at Oxford and have been properly idle ever since." SS I 19 103 4
be," said Mrs. Dashwood, "since leisure has not promoted SS I 19 103 5
Only think, mama, how it is improved since I was here last! SS I 19 107 24
"Yes, a great while; ever since my sister married.-- SS I 20 116 62

a conquest of a very smart beau since she came to Barton. SS I 21 125 34
and more conjectural; and since Edward's visit, they had SS I 21 125 36
I shall go to the piano-forte; I have not touched it since SS II 1 144 15
with myself ever since, for having took such a liberty as SS II 2 146 5
long, very long absence since we were first engaged, and SS II 2 147 10
Since the death of her husband, who had traded with SS II 3 153 1
if he had been in London ever since she had seen him last. SS II 4 162 12
"almost ever since; I have been once or twice to Delaford SS II 4 162 12
for it is a long while since I have been at home, and you SS II 4 163 14
I have been as busy as a bee ever since dinner! SS II 4 163 14
But Colonel, where have you been to since we parted? SS II 4 163 18
"Has no letter been left here for me since we went out?" SS II 4 165 26
they had not seen before since their arrival in town, as SS II 5 171 30
food; for it was many days since she had any appetite, and SS II 7 185 16
appetite, and many nights since she had really slept; and SS II 7 185 16
You must be very much altered indeed since we parted, if SS II 7 187 40
of her for Willoughby's; since though Marianne might lose SS II 8 196 21
been since informed, is the name of Miss Grey's guardian." SS II 8 199 37
Regard for a former servant of my own, who had since SS II 9 207 26
I had allowed her, (imprudently, as it has since turned SS II 9 208 28
"ever seen Mr. Willoughby since you left him at Barton?" SS II 9 211 34
in town as in the country, since his acquaintance must now SS II 10 213 4
never yet left the house since the blow first fell, to go SS II 10 217 18
she had practised since her first knowledge of Edward's SS III 1 261 12
his manners towards them since her sister had been known SS III 3 279 1
What I am now doing indeed, seems nothing at all, since it SS III 3 284 23
I have not heard of any thing to please me so well since SS III 4 287 20
She had not seen him before since his engagement became SS III 4 288 26
public, and therefore not since his knowing her to be SS III 4 288 26
It was now above a week since John Dashwood had called in SS III 5 293 3
in Berkeley-Street, and as since that time no notice had SS III 5 293 3
away unseen by Willoughby since his marriage, and she SS III 6 302 5
"Had I known as much half an hour ago--but since I am here" SS III 8 318 15
since that time, procured me a nuncheon at Marlborough." SS III 8 318 20
Every year since my coming of age, or even before, I SS III 8 320 32
That he had cut me ever since my marriage, I had seen SS III 8 330 69
He has loved her, my Elinor, ever since the first moment SS III 9 336 12
their marriage; and since our arrival, since our SS III 9 337 18
and since our arrival, since our delightful security I SS III 9 337 18
exercise hitherto untried since her illness required;--and SS III 10 344 12
13

fancied him, since the story of that unfortunate girl"----- SS III 10 344 17
I considered the past; I saw in my own behaviour since the SS III 10 345 28
She had heard nothing of him since her leaving London, SS III 11 352 21
She smiled, and said how she had changed her name since SS III 11 354 29
was, foolish as it has since in every way been proved, it SS III 13 362 5
remained by choice ever since his quitting London, he had SS III 13 364 13
I believe I may say that since the first half year of our SS III 13 365 17
But Elinor had no such dependence; for since Edward would SS III 13 369 33
having, for the first time since her living at Barton, SS III 13 369 34
since eventually it promoted the interest of Elinor. SS III 13 370 35
no close carriage; & ever since there had been balls in W 314 1
to like any girl so well since, tho' he is always behaving W 316 1
And since then, she has been trying to make some match at W 317 2
I have observed it ever since you came home, & I am afraid W 318 2
Since you have been at home, I have been so busy with my W 321 2
since he was 7 years old--but my father reckons us alike." W 324 3
I suppose she is grown somewhat older since that time.-- W 325 4
it is a shameful length of time since I was at Stanton.-- W 335 14
declared it seemed only two days since he had seen her.--" W 342 19
you heard from Pen. since she went to Chichester?-- W 351 24
"It will be no use to us, if twenty such should come since PP I 1 5 32
said her mother resentfully, "since we are not to visit." PP I 2 6 3
by the world in general, since Jane united with great PP I 6 21 1
house, and has since dined in company with him four times. PP I 6 22 7
"Is Miss Darcy much grown since the spring?" said Miss PP I 8 38 40
Lucas had been at Longbourn since her coming away. PP I 9 43 26
been said in the regiment since the preceding Wednesday; PP I 12 60 7
me much uneasiness, and since I have had the misfortune to PP I 13 62 12
and it was now some weeks since they had received pleasure PP I 13 64 20
since, with the smallest degree of unreasonable admiration. PP I 16 76 3
Since her father's death, her home has been London, where PP I 16 82 43
again, called it an age since they had met, and repeatedly PP I 17 86 9
she had been doing with herself since their separation. PP I 17 86 9
able one I dare say, but since he is unacquainted with PP I 18 96 55
nature on your father, since I am well aware that it could PP I 19 106 10
reason to be satisfied, since the refusal which his cousin PP I 20 110 1
You could not have started a more happy idea, since you PP I 21 119 22
comparatively diffident since the adventure of Wednesday. PP I 22 121 1
They had all been very ill-used since she last saw her PP II 2 139 3
had been little there since the death of Darcy's father, PP II 2 142 19
any of you unhappy; but since we see every day that where PP II 3 145 7
which Jane had written to her since her being in Kent. PP II 11 188 1
As for myself, it is many, many years since I first began PP II 12 200 5
"it seems but a day or two since we first came!--and yet PP II 15 217 11
us hear what has happened to you all, since you went away. PP II 16 221 17
Having been frequently in company with him since her PP II 18 233 25
only serve, after what had since passed, to provoke her. PP II 18 233 25
natural degree of sense, since the disturbers of her brain PP II 19 237 3
and I have known him ever since he was four years old." PP III 1 248 30
Amazed at the alteration in his manner since they last PP III 1 252 52
Since her being at Lambton, she had heard that Miss Darcy PP III 2 261 3
it "was a very long time since he had had the pleasure of PP III 2 262 8
We have not met since the 26th of November, when we were PP III 2 262 8
servant who had known him since he was four years old, and PP III 2 264 14
saw any one so much altered as she is since the winter. PP III 3 270 13
her, for it is many months since I have considered her as PP III 3 271 18
"Since writing the above, dearest Lizzy, something has PP III 4 273 3
Never, since reading Jane's second letter, had she PP III 4 279 24
Since the ----shire were first quartered in Meryton, PP III 4 279 26
It is not quite a week since they left Brighton. PP III 5 283 10
And since this sad affair has taken place, it is said, PP III 5 288 37
His former acquaintance had been numerous; but since he PP III 5 291 54
Elizabeth had received none since her return, that could PP III 6 297 12
It was a fortnight since Mrs. Bennet had been down stairs, PP III 6 298 16
object of her wishes, since Jane was sixteen, was now on PP III 8 310 7
fears for her sister; for since her marriage would so PP III 8 310 7
laugh, that it was a great while since she had been there. PP III 8 311 11
"Only think of its being three months," she cried, "since PP III 9 315 4
and has since maintained herself by letting lodgings. PP III 9 316 7
Since such were her feelings, it only remained, he thought, PP III 10 322 2
It was many months since she had mentioned his name to PP III 10 323 2
PP III 11 331 16
17

"It is a long time, Mr. Bingley, since you went away," PP III 11 336 47
have happened in the neighbourhood, since you went away. PP III 11 336 49
which I cannot wonder at, since he might have chosen so PP III 13 349 47
Ever since I have known it, I have been most anxious to PP III 16 365 3
so material a change, since the period to which he alluded, PP III 16 366 8
since then, we have both, I hope, improved in civility." PP III 16 367 13
calm and cool, but I am since convinced that it was PP III 16 368 22
to make the confession to him which I have since made." PP III 18 382 16
How long ago it is, aunt, since we used to repeat the MP I 2 18 25
I suppose you have had as little to vex you, since you MP I 3 25 12
years which have passed since you parted, have not been MP I 3 33 64
Mrs. Grant knew nothing, she had scarcely seen them since. MP I 4 40 15
Mansfield, for the first time since the Crawfords' arrival. MP I 6 52 1
that the Admiral had since been spared; and she scrupled MP I 7 66 14
"Since a little before dinner. MP I 7 72 39
ever since she came back from your house the second time." MP I 7 72 46
her subsequent absence from home, had since lain dormant. MP I 8 75 1
Mr. Rushworth has made it since he succeeded to the estate. MP I 8 82 34
the end of it yet, since we left the first great path." MP I 9 94 62

winding in and out ever since we came into it; and MP I 9 95 64
a famous cream cheese; and since Julia's leaving them, MP I 10 103 50
I can hardly suppose;--and since you push me so hard, I MP I 11 111 28
It is a great while since we have had any star-gazing." MP I 11 113 41
any thing to dislike; but since the day at Sotherton, she MP I 12 115 5
her sleeping room ever since her first entering the family, MP I 16 150 1
The east room as it had been called, ever since Maria MP I 16 151 1
"He has been ill ever since; he did not eat any of the MP I 18 171 27
away his plate--and has been suffering ever since." MP I 18 171 27
old gentleman handsomely since he was come; and besides, MP II 1 177 5
We have had such incessant rains almost since October MP II 1 181 16
I have hardly taken out a gun since the 3d. MP II 1 181 16
days, but there has been no attempting any thing since. MP II 1 181 16
which I had been doctoring him for, ever since Michaelmas. MP II 2 189 5
Four-and-twenty hours had never passed before, since MP II 2 192 11
that she has passed in the country since her infancy. MP II 3 199 15
any change of opinion or inclination since her forming it. MP II 3 200 21
Since rivalry between the sisters had ceased, they had MP II 3 203 32
entered twice a year since Mr. Norris's death, she became MP II 4 205 2
her having never yet heard it since its being in Mansfield. MP II 4 206 5
She had scarcely ever been at the parsonage since the MP II 4 206 5
It was the first time of his seeing them together since MP II 4 211 25
But as I conclude that she must wish to go, since all MP II 5 219 18
advantage in his presence, since every addition to the MP II 5 223 48
She must be grown two inches, at least, since October." MP II 6 230 5
ten days had passed since Fanny had been in the agitation MP II 6 233 14
I have never seen Fanny dance since she was a little girl; MP II 7 250 60
He had since heard her express herself differently--with MP II 8 256 12
a diminution of cares since her treading that path before. MP II 8 260 25
Since the first joy from Mr. Crawford's note to William MP II 9 270 40
morning, but there has not been since, a moment's delay. MP II 13 299 5
said she, "which I have since, to my very great MP III 1 323 54
of Shakespeare in my hand before, since I was fifteen.-- MP III 3 338 13
Edmund had already gone through the service once since his MP III 3 340 24
None such had occurred since his seeing her in her uncle's MP III 3 343 40
long while since we have had a comfortable walk together." MP III 4 346 6
"It is above a week since I saw Miss Crawford." MP III 4 352 39
"I have had a little fit since I came into this room, as MP III 5 359 9
heal every pain that had since grown out of the separation. MP III 6 370 11
weeks which had passed since their leaving Mansfield, and MP III 7 375 4
Charles had been born since Fanny's going away, but Tom MP III 7 381 25
A week was gone since Edmund might be supposed in town, MP III 10 399 1
two of his acquaintance, since his arrival, but had no MP III 10 400 7
him altogether improved since she had seen him; he was MP III 10 406 21
lost ground as to health since her being in Portsmouth, MP III 11 409 6
It is only four weeks tomorrow since I left Mansfield." MP III 11 410 9
I have been returned since Saturday. MP III 13 420 2
It was so long since Fanny had had any letter from her, MP III 14 433 12
It was weeks since she had heard any thing of Miss MP III 14 433 12
some strong indiscretion, since her correspondent was not MP III 15 438 6
difference of the country since February; but, when they MP III 15 446 35
It was three months, full three months, since her quitting MP III 15 446 35
Perhaps it is best for me--since it leaves me so little to MP III 16 456 25
I have since--sometimes--for a moment--regretted that I MP III 16 459 30
those she loved best, and since Mrs. Rushworth's elopement, MP III 17 466 16
as he had been doing ever since her being ten years old, MP III 17 470 27
Ever since the day (about four years ago) that Miss Taylor E I 1 12 41
It was now some time since Miss Taylor had begun to E I 2 16 6
as the year varied; and since Mrs. Weston's marriage her E I 4 26 1
"I think, Harriet, since your acquaintance with us, you E I 4 32 32
"Emma has been meaning to read more ever since she was E I 5 37 7
thought so then;--but since we have parted, I can never E I 5 37 8
And ever since she was twelve, Emma has been mistress of E I 5 37 9
of Harriet's manner, since her introduction at Hartfield, E I 6 42 1
I must confess that since my visiting here I have seen E I 7 54 30
considered (especially since your making so much of her) E I 8 59 27
my wishes on the subject have been ever since I knew you. E I 9 73 20
tests he has ever preached from since he came to Highbury. E I 9 75 26
"I do not know, my dear--but it is so long since she was E I 9 79 58
since last Easter, and then only for a few days.-- E I 9 79 58
know it is longer since they were with him, than with us." E I 9 79 63
Till this year, every long vacation since their marriage E I 11 91 2
was therefore many months since they had been seen in a E I 11 91 2
the sad change at Hartfield since she had been there last. E I 11 93 5
missed seeing them but one entire day since they married. E I 11 94 14
day last Easter--and ever since his particular kindness E I 11 95 19
long it is, how terribly long since you were here! E I 12 100 18
which we have been applying at times ever since August." E I 12 102 28
Knightley--"it is so long since I have seen her, except E I 12 104 46
She had frequently thought--especially since his father's E I 14 119 5
Mr. Weston, "ever since September: every letter has been E I 14 119 9
"Did she know?--had she heard anything about her, since E I 15 124 3
and Mr. Cole had heard from Mr. Elton since his going away. E II 1 156 5
I was reading it to Mrs. Cole, and since she went away, I E II 1 157 10
just under my huswife--and since you are so kind as to E II 1 157 10
it really is full two years, you know, since she was here. E II 1 158 14
Ever since the service he rendered Jane at Weymouth, when E II 1 160 23
--But ever since we had the history of that day, I have E II 1 161 23
I am going to read to you,) and has never been well since. E II 1 161 29
She had never been quite well since the time of their E II 2 165 9
For it is not five minutes since I received Mrs. Cole's E II 3 173 27
And as it is some months since Miss Campbell married, the E II 3 175 43
to seek her; for since her refusal of the brother, the E II 3 180 58
A week had not passed since Miss Hawkins's name was first E II 4 181 2
We have never been there above once since the new approach E II 7 210 14
They had been meeting almost every day since his arrival. E II 12 262 38
Since her last conversation with Mrs. Weston and Mr. E II 16 291 5
A man who had been in motion since eight o'clock in the E II 17 303 23
of a gentleman; but ever since her being turned into a E II 18 310 33
never been in fault since; the rivet never came out again. E III 2 323 19
I have seen nothing like it since--well, where shall we E III 2 330 45
It was so long since Emma had been at the Abbey, that as E III 6 357 34
She has talked of it since. E III 7 375 59
There has been a solemn engagement between them ever since E III 10 395 35
"Engaged since October,--secretly engaged.-- E III 10 395 38
in his behaviour ever since those two decisive dances.-- E III 11 409 35
'I will not say, that since I entered into the engagement E III 12 418 6
Of all the sources of evil surrounding the former, since E III 12 421 17
error; and yet, perhaps, since my manners gave such an E III 13 426 17
but one--and that one, since the purity of her heart is E III 13 428 23
of her having since detected me, at least in some degree.-- E III 14 438 8
Since I began this letter, which will be longer than I E III 14 439 8
Ever since I left you this morning, Emma, my mind has been E III 15 448 30
not been into the house since the morning after Box-Hill, E III 16 452 8
she shortly afterwards began, "since the party to Box-Hill. E III 16 454 18
in love with you ever since you were thirteen at least." E III 17 462 7
to be consulted; but, since that business had been over, E III 17 463 16
with no difficulty, since it was a plan to promote the E III 17 465 28
"You are materially changed since we talked on this E III 18 474 32
Till this morning, we have not once met since the day of E III 18 477 57
claim on his attachment; since to them he must have owed a P III 1 4 6
Thirteen years had passed away since Lady Elliot's death, P III 1 5 7
"Since the idea had been started in the very quarter which P III 2 13 7
as I was going to observe, since applications will P III 3 17 4
been in the East Indies since; he has been stationed there, P III 3 21 21
resident at Monkford since the time of old Governor Trent." P III 3 23 27
More than seven years were gone since this little history P III 4 28 7
I have not seen him since seven o'clock. P III 5 37 25
with the other family, since there was neither superior P III 6 46 12
her life, she had never, since the age of fourteen, never P III 6 47 13
the age of fourteen, never since the loss of her dear P III 6 47 13
Since he actually was expected in the country, she must P III 6 52 33

for I have not dined at the other house since Tuesday." P III 7 57 18
almost eight years had passed, since all had been given up. P III 7 60 28
and had never seen a woman since whom he thought her equal; P III 7 61 37
your acquaintance, ever since you could remember, and P III 8 65 16
Captain Harville had never been in good health since a P III 11 94 6
must have passed away since the first partial falling of P III 11 95 9
since entering Lyme) drew half the party to the window. P III 12 105 8
hour already gone since they ought to have been off,--the P III 12 113 57
Anne had never entered Kellynch since her quitting Lady P IV 1 123 9
yesterday--(the first time since the accident) had brought P IV 1 126 20
in very good health, and very good looks since Michaelmas." P IV 3 142 15
It was now some years since Anne had begun to learn that P IV 4 147 7
letters of ceremony, ever since the death of that said P IV 4 148 12
Twelve years were gone since they had parted, and each P IV 5 153 6
It was three weeks since she had heard at all. P IV 6 162 1
"I have not had a creature call on me since the second " P IV 6 163 7
same small family party; since Henrietta's coming away, P IV 6 167 19
gone down to Edward's, and there he has been ever since. P IV 6 171 33
We have seen nothing of him since November. P IV 6 171 33
For the first time, since their renewed acquaintance, she P IV 7 175 6
he said, "I have hardly seen you since our day at Lyme. P IV 8 181 3
4
You can have been acquainted with it only since I came to P IV 8 187 31
It is a great while since we met." P IV 9 194 22
been staying there ever since; that she is a clever, P IV 9 206 88
But since he must be absent some time or other, I do not P IV 9 208 92
matrimony you know, and (since self will intrude) who can P IV 9 208 92
no attempt of that nature, since he did not even know her P IV 9 210 99
that, very recently, (since Mary's last letter to herself) P IV 10 217 20
part so well, that I have liked him the better ever since." P IV 10 219 26
been full of it too ever since I entered the house, and P IV 10 228 71
One day only had passed since Anne's conversation with Mrs. P IV 11 229 1
living with us, in our little family-circle, ever since." P IV 11 233 20
of proper condition has since presented himself to raise P IV 12 250 6
having lived here ever since I was born, man & boy 57 S 1 366 1
She was as thoroughly amiable as she was lovely--& since S 3 379 1
I have heard nothing of Sidney since your being together S 5 387 1
But since you are so very neighbourly, I beleive Miss S 6 394 1
here, or even a Co--since Sanditon had been a public place. S 7 401 1
Matters are altered with me since last summer you know--. S 7 401 1
& such authors as have since appeared to tread in S 8 404 1
is concerned, had since occupied the greater part of his S 8 404 1
It was not a week, since Miss Diana Parker had been told S 10 412 1

SINCERE (39)

and in a voice of most sincere concern she echoed Miss NA II 2 138 1
as from wishing it to be sincere; for she had not NA II 3 148 29
and she thought with sincere compassion of his approaching NA II 4 149 1
His value of her was sincere; and, if not permanently, he NA II 9 197 27
My own joy on the occasion is very sincere. NA II 16 251 5
I have been open and sincere where I ought to have been SS I 10 48 5
happy in marriage, which sincere affection on her side SS II 2 151 41
for which I beg to return my sincere acknowledgments. SS II 7 183 13
My esteem for your whole family is very sincere; but if I SS II 7 183 13
nothing but a very sincere regard--nothing but an earnest SS II 9 204 18
As Marianne's affection for her mother was sincere, it SS III 3 280 6
her sympathy in her sufferings was very sincere. SS III 7 313 20
and in spite of herself made her think him sincere. SS III 8 319 25
much more warm, as more sincere or constant--which ever we SS III 9 336 14
her joy, though sincere as her love for her sister, was of SS III 13 363 7
sincere well-wisher, friend, and sister, Lucy Ferrars. SS III 13 365 14
its own punishment, was sincere, need not be doubted;--nor SS III 14 379 18
is liberal-minded, just, sincere, rational, honourable, PP I 16 82 48
rather be paid the compliment of being believed sincere. PP I 19 108 20
her to him with a most sincere regard; and she parted from PP II 4 151 3
his affection with sincere, if not with equal regard.-- PP II 12 199 5
I rather wished, than believed him to be sincere; but at PP II 12 200 5
His affection was proved to have been sincere, and his PP II 14 213 18
"Having thus offered you the sincere congratulations of PP III 15 362 14
Now be sincere; did you admire me for my impertinence?" PP III 18 380 3
information, was as sincere as her brother's in sending it. PP III 18 383 25
At such a moment, the arrival of her friend was a sincere PP III 18 384 26
"Oh! no doubt he is very sincere in preferring an income MP I 11 110 23
It gives me sincere satisfaction. MP II 1 186 34
her to be open and sincere, and assured her that every MP II 3 200 21
I have a very sincere interest in Emma. E I 5 40 27
If he was quite sincere, if he really tried to come, it E III 1 316 6
Pray be sincere, Knightley. E III 6 355 22
and in a tone of such sincere, decided, intelligible E III 13 430 37
which she could not give any sincere explanation of. E III 15 446 16
were sincere, in their exclamations of pity and horror. P III 8 66 17
The rain was a mere trifle, and Anne was most sincere in P IV 7 174 3
His present attentions to your family are very sincere, P IV 9 204 80
quite sincere, but now she saw insincerity in every thing. P IV 10 214 11

SINCERELY (47)

How sincerely do I greive that she ever entered this house! LS 11 259 2
her heart I am persuaded, she sincerely wishes him gone. LS 20 278 10
You know how sincerely I regard both husband & wife. I LS 30 301 5
no defying destiny. Yr sincerely attached Alicia. LS 38 307 3
amiable disposition, and sincerely attached to her, gave NA I 7 44 4
congratulated herself sincerely on being under the care of NA I 9 62 10
Delighting, however, as Catherine sincerely did in the NA I 15 118 9
though Henry was now sincerely attached to her, though he NA II 15 243 9
Marianne felt for her most sincerely; but she did more SS I 12 61 17
18
"I love Willoughby, sincerely love him; and suspicion of SS I 15 81 43
very capable of making a woman sincerely attached to him." SS I 22 130 28
"I thank you, ma'am, sincerely thank you," said Marianne, SS II 3 154 5
him most sincerely, could she feel less than herself! SS III 1 261 13
I feel for him sincerely." SS III 1 269 56
to him then, as I sincerely wish I could be at present. SS III 3 284 23
Yes, I found myself, by insensible degrees, sincerely fond SS III 8 321 34
Sincerely wish you happy in your choice, and it shall not SS III 13 365 14
I sincerely hope your Christmas in Hertfordshire may PP I 21 117 11
good wishes, and sincerely affected herself, accompanied PP II 3 145 11
measure for both, and could very sincerely wish him happy. PP II 5 150 26
her sister how sincerely she had been valued by his friend. PP II 17 227 25
readily comprehend how sincerely I must rejoice that he is PP II 18 234 37
38
I am sincerely grieved for him and Mrs. F. but no one can PP III 4 275 5
Mrs. Collins and myself sincerely sympathise with you, and PP III 6 296 11
Your's, very sincerely, "M. Gardiner. PP III 10 325 2
"Yours sincerely, &c. PP III 18 383 23
Your's sincerely.' MP I 6 59 43
a very bad grace; but I sincerely hope you will have a MP I 7 68 20
But now, sincerely, do not you find the place altogether MP I 10 98 6
for a decision; and I do sincerely give you joy, madam, as MP I 15 143 26
by him, she was more sincerely impatient to go away at the MP II 4 207 10
find Mr. Rushworth most sincerely disposed to regard all MP II 7 245 34
which you shall have as sincerely, is that I approve your MP II 12 292 7
up a newspaper, very sincerely wishing that dear little MP III 3 341 31
I confess myself sincerely anxious that you may. MP III 4 351 34
I trust and hope, and sincerely wish you may never be MP III 14 431 8
Very sincerely did Emma wish to do so; but it was not E II 3 179 53
consider it so, and sincerely did she rejoice in their joy. E II 5 188 8
Emma was most sincerely interested. E III 8 379 9
regret and solicitude--sincerely wishing that the E III 8 380 9
one material point, I am sincerely anxious for its all E III 10 398 53
them to be very mutually and very sincerely attached." E III 13 428 22
the brightest smiles, "and most sincerely wish them happy." E III 18 474 31
Anne had very sincerely rejoiced in there being no means P III 6 48 17
"The Admiral does not seem very ill, and I sincerely hope " P IV 6 164 8
He sincerely hoped it.-- S 3 377 1

Most sincerely do we wish you a good season at Sanditon, & S 5 387 1

SINCEREST (1)

kindness and sympathy without the sincerest gratitude." MP II 9 270 38

SINCERITY (28)

his heart, & make him really confide in her sincerity. LS 3 247 1
perfect sincerity, "indeed, Catherine, I love you dearly." NA I 7 51 53
congratulating them with sincerity on it, and reading NA II 12 218 4
She doubted the sincerity of this assurance no more than SS I 3 14 2
Park with unaffected sincerity; and as he attended them to SS I 7 33 4
whether there were any sincerity in her declaration of SS II 1 141 7
Believe me," and Elinor spoke it with the truest sincerity, SS II 2 146 4
her, and with great sincerity, that she did pity her,--to SS II 12 232 14
partiality, but more sincerity, were equally earnest in SS II 12 234 23
"Then," cried Mrs. Jennings with blunt sincerity, no SS III 1 267 43
Such a noble mind!--such openness, such sincerity!-- no SS III 9 337 14
"I have not a doubt of Mr. Bingley's sincerity," said PP I 18 96 55
the case, and with equal sincerity could add that she PP II 15 216 7
Elizabeth's congratulations were given with a sincerity, a PP III 13 347 25
My character has ever been celebrated for its sincerity PP III 14 353 26
There was a charm, perhaps, in his sincerity, his MP I 7 65 13
wanting sincerity or good intentions in the choice of his." MP I 11 110 22
of feeling, from the sincerity of Edmund's too partial MP II 2 194 20
with the earnestness of sincerity; yet this was not enough, MP III 2 327 5
"Robert Martin's manners have sense, sincerity, and good- E I 8 65 49
present, said and with a sincerity which no one could E II 3 171 14
15
truth and sincerity in all our dealings with each other?" E III 15 446 15
"I honour his sincerity. E III 17 464 20
her own cause, and the sincerity of her manner being soon P III 7 58 20
And all this was said with a truth and sincerity of P III 12 113 56
more depend upon the sincerity of those who sometimes P IV 5 161 28
It was a heartiness, and a warmth, and a sincerity which P IV 10 220 31
I have not faith in the sincerity of the affections of a S 7 398 1

SINEWS (1)

The play of your Sinews a very little affected:--barely S 9 408 1

SING (17)

I want her to play & sing with some portion of taste, & a LS 7 253 1
that they sing better duets, or draw better landscapes. NA I 3 28 34
"May we?--but I never sing. NA I 15 123 35
to sing a particular song which Marianne had just finished. SS I 7 35 9
me to play and sing before any body and every body!-- PP I 6 24 22
of several that she would sing again, she was eagerly PP I 6 25 23
fortunate as to be able to sing, I should have great PP I 18 101 71
Do you play and sing, Miss Bennet?" PP II 6 164 16
Do your sisters play and sing?" PP II 6 164 18
one on the harp--and all sing--or would sing if they were MP II 11 288 28
all sing--or would sing if they were taught--or sing all MP II 11 288 28
if they were taught--or sing all the better for not being MP II 11 288 28
son into the parlour one night on purpose to sing to her. E I 4 28 6
He could sing a little himself. E I 4 28 6
mad, to let your niece sing herself hoarse in this manner? E II 8 229 97
I am very sure; but you sing as well as play;--yes, I E II 17 301 18
when he has got a wife, he will sing a different tune. P III 8 70 46

SINGERS (1)

he was close by the singers, among the most urgent in MP I 11 113 42

SINGING (15)

Italian, German, music, singing, drawing &c. will gain a LS 7 253 1
pianoforte alternately singing and crying; her voice often SS I 16 83 3
A woman must have a thorough knowledge of music, singing, PP I 8 39 50
for when supper was over, singing was talked of, and she PP I 18 100 68
his interference, lest Mary should be singing all night. PP I 18 100 68
singing hero of a farce in his scarlet coat and cocked hat. MP I 13 123 6
How they are singing out! MP III 7 383 30
She was very fond of singing. E I 4 28 6
she stept forward and put an end to all further singing. E II 8 229 98
regret the inferiority of her own playing and singing. E II 9 231 3
And I hate Italian singing.-- E II 9 232 11
She was in dancing, singing, exclaiming spirits; and till E III 18 475 37
the talking, laughing, and singing of their daughters. P III 6 46 12
There had been music, singing, talking, laughing, all that P III 7 58 22
had expected better singing; and, in short, must confess P IV 8 190 47

SINGLE (67)

with Charles & kept him single, I should have been very LS 5 249 1
Believe me, the single word of Langford is not of such LS 35 305 1
Catherine, "not to have a single acquaintance here!" NA I 2 22 12
There was not a single point in which we differed; I would NA I 10 71 3
point with you, we should leave it without a single regret. NA II 2 139 7
only the feeble rays of a single lamp to take in its size-- NA II 5 158 15
you that you will not have a single domestic within call. NA II 5 158 17
with the addition of this single remark--"I really have NA II 14 237 22
alone were concerned, had not a single objection to start. NA II 16 249 1
The late owner of this estate was a single man, who lived SS I 1 3 1
to be a woman who is single at seven and twenty, I should SS I 8 38 9
indeed! and the doctor is a single man, I warrant you." SS II 10 218 25
in the idea of a single and constant attachment, and all SS III 1 263 27
to speak of it to a single creature; knowing that it would SS III 1 263 29
could the utmost of your single management do to stop the SS III 11 350 9
while Edward remained single, that something would occur SS III 12 357 1
would be better for her to marry you than be single." SS III 13 367 23
he is married to another woman, while I am still single.-- W 316 2
I could do very well single for my own part--a little W 317 2
It is a truth universally acknowledged, that a single man PP I 1 3 1
"Is he married or single?" PP I 1 3 13
"Oh! single, my dear, to be sure! PP I 1 3 14
A single man of large fortune; four or five thousand a PP I 1 3 14
Mr. and Mrs. Bennet for a single evening during his visit PP I 16 75 1
depended less on any single event, or any particular PP I 17 86 10
to be able to consign her single daughters to the care of PP I 18 99 63
that whether married or single, he must always be her PP II 4 151 3
the post came in without bringing a single line from him. PP III 6 294 1
It was not known that Wickham had a single relation, with PP III 6 297 12
make you better satisfied that your other four are single." PP III 11 330 11
a single vacancy near her, which would admit of a chair. PP III 12 341 16
Kept back as she was by every body else, his single MP I 2 22 35
as long as she remained single, was highly agreeable; and MP I 4 41 15
a single entertaining story about "my friend such a one." MP I 6 52 1
every chance of seeing a single creature beyond themselves MP II 4 205 3
It is not a scrambling collection of low single rooms, MP II 7 243 27
by a single attempt at throwing ridicule on his cause. MP II 7 248 47
so thoroughly without a single recommendation, that Fanny MP III 7 385 38
the open air, and there was not a single oath to be heard. MP III 10 402 12
imaginary convenience of any single being in the family. MP III 11 410 16
a single evening in the year alone if he did not like it. E I 1 12 41
be a shame to have him single any longer--and I thought E I 1 13 46
pain, of Emma's losing a single pleasure, or suffering an E I 2 18 11
She lived with her single daughter in a very small way, E I 3 21 4
something or other, was a single man; that there was no E I 4 27 5
says he need not eat a single meal by himself if he does E I 9 75 26
A single woman, with a very narrow income, must be a E I 10 85 19
of boys and girls; but a single woman, of good fortune, is E I 10 85 19
to the taste of everybody, though single and though poor. E I 10 85 19
in many men, especially single men, such an inclination-- E I 13 111 13
But, as it is, the disappointment is single, and, I trust, E I 15 132 36
or motives, whether single, or double, or treble, gave the E II 2 166 10
If it were love, it might be simple, single, successless E II 2 168 13
He could now, without the drawback of a single unpleasant E II 5 193 35
chiefly among the single men, had already taken place. E II 7 207 6
seen a look, more than a single look, at Miss Fairfax, E III 5 343 7
nothing to herself, but his remaining single all his life. E III 12 416 1
single; and told of poor Isabella, and poor Miss Taylor.-- E III 17 466 29
himself on remaining single for his dear daughter's sake. P III 1 5 8
man, and, moreover, a single man at the time, she had a P III 4 30 10

there having been a single preliminary difference to P III 5 32 3
single so long for our sakes, need be suspected now. P III 5 35 14
You were single. P IV 11 243 70
of keeping Sir Walter single by the watchfulness which a P IV 12 250 7
and 2 sisters--all single & all independant--the eldest of S 2 371 1
there had not been a single Lodger in the village!--nor S 4 383 1
half at least--(for while single, the gentleman may S 7 394 1

SINGLE-MINDED (1)
An unpretending, single-minded, artless girl--infinitely E III 2 331 55

SINGLED (2)
Almost as soon as I entered the house I singled you out as PP I 19 105 8
"Oh! Lizzy, why am I thus singled from my family, and PP III 13 350 53

SINGLENESS (1)
Walter's continuing in singleness requires explanation.-- P III 1 5 8

SINGLING (1)
She was very wrong in singling me out as she did; I can PP II 3 148 26

SINGLY (2)
so well, nor flirt so well, as she might do either singly. NA II 4 151 16
I think for her labour singly, to finish it this evening. SS II 1 145 19

SINGS (1)
She plays and sings all day long. PP III 1 248 22

SINGULAR (7)
held the reins, and the singular discernment and dexterity NA I 9 62 10
tis singular is not it?" W 356 28
reading to cards?" said he; "that is rather singular." PP I 8 37 22
"I have found out," said he, "by a singular accident, that PP I 18 96 57
Crawford's opinion) in a singular manner, had Mr. Price MP III 10 403 14
"Your feelings are singular. E I 18 149 25
There will be nothing singular in his case; and it is P III 2 12 4

SINGULARITY (1)
in his case; and it is singularity which often makes the P III 2 12 4

SINGULARLY (2)
concealed?--and how singularly strange that it should fall NA II 6 170 12
peculiarly eligible, so singularly fortunate, that now it E III 17 467 31

SINK (29)
her; & equally low must sink my pretensions to common LS 14 263 1
him & Lady Susan to sink the latter lower than ever in her LS 42 311 2
However, when you sink into this abyss again, you will NA I 10 79 55
Will not your heart sink within you?" NA II 5 158 15
to make Catherine's heart sink, and for a few moments she NA II 13 223 13
Elinor's security sunk; but her self-command did not sink SS I 22 131 33
have believed it; and I was almost ready to sink as it was. SS II 8 192 3
had removed from him only to sink deeper in a life of sin. SS II 9 207 26
saw her with satisfaction sink at last into a slumber, SS III 7 310 9
Marianne at six o'clock sink into a quiet, steady, and to SS III 7 315 25
Collins seemed likely to sink into insignificance to the PP I 16 76 5
and I flatter myself it will not sink me in your esteem. PP I 19 106 10
Her power was sinking; every thing must sink under such a PP III 4 278 19
But he had ended his speech in a way to sink her in sad MP I 3 33 64
sound delightfully; but sink it under the chill, the MP II 4 211 24
to shut out the church, sink the clergyman, and see only MP II 7 248 47
coming to distress her brother, and sink her to the ground. MP II 7 250 60
appetite, she was ready to sink with shame, from the dread MP III 13 304 16
She was ready to sink, as she entered the parlour. MP III 15 444 28
care of, she might be required to sink herself for ever. E I 4 27 5
to, what she was going to sink from, how she was going to E II 2 167 13
of intercourse; former intimacy might sink without remark. E II 4 182 8
to; and, if she live to old age, must probably sink more. E III 7 375 61
narration, a substance to sink her spirit--especially with E III 11 409 34
It was horrible to Emma to think how it must sink him in E III 11 413 48
Emma was almost ready to sink under the agitation of this E III 13 430 36
I wish I may not sink into 'poor Emma' with him at once.-- E III 17 464 24
The intimacy between her and Emma must sink; their E III 19 482 5
"You sink your voice, but I can distinguish the tones of " P IV 11 237 42

SINKING (20)
I trust I am in no danger of sinking in your opinion." LS 24 290 13
a rich aunt, and sinking half the children, he was able to NA II 15 245 12
were made, seemed in danger of sinking into total silence. PP II 9 177 3
reserves, no scruples in sinking Mr. Darcy's character, PP II 13 207 5
Her power was sinking; every thing must sink under such a PP III 4 278 19
sinking under her aunt's unkind reflection and reproach. MP I 16 150 1
but every other heart was sinking under some degree of MP II 1 175 1
he repeated, his voice sinking a little, "between the two MP II 9 264 16
that the loss of it, the sinking again into nothing, would MP III 6 366 1
His opinion of her had been sinking from the day of his MP III 17 465 15
abroad--of his widow sinking under consumption and grief E II 2 163 2
sinking from it into the common course of Hartfield days. E II 12 262 38
and Harriet immediately sinking into a chair fainted away. E III 3 333 3
I wish I had attended to it--but--(with a sinking voice E III 13 425 11
might be preserved from sinking deeper in aggression E III 16 458 44
"Ah! by the bye,"--then sinking his voice, and looking E III 18 477 58
59
moment, Henrietta, sinking under the conviction, lost her P III 12 109 34
Anne entered it with a sinking heart, anticipating an P IV 3 137 2
her hands and eyes, and sinking all the rest of her P IV 10 213 8
she must trust, and sinking into the chair which he had P IV 11 237 41
42

SINNED (3)
sinned against his character, or magnified his cruelty. NA II 15 247 14
of those who had sinned, or of those who were sorrowing-- MP III 15 444 26
While you considered me as having sinned against Emma E III 14 439 8

SINNER (1)
The neglect had been visited on the head of the sinner, P IV 4 149 12

SINS (3)
I am not obliged to punish myself for her sins. MP I 10 101 32
She could not think that Harriet's solace or her own sins E II 1 155 1
Oh! my sins, my sins!-- E III 4 339 13

SIPPED (1)
And then he would have changed the subject, and sipped his MP II 1 184 25

SIR (220)
My dear sir I have this moment received your letter, LS 14 263 1
& I entreat you my dear sir to quiet your mind, & no LS 14 263 1
You will, I am sure my dear sir, feel the truth of this LS 14 265 4
I have now my dear sir, written my real sentiments of Lady LS 14 265 6
Sir, I hope you will excuse this liberty, I am forced LS 21 279 1
a sudden fancy I assure you sir, I always thought him LS 21 279 1
I am sir, your most humble Servt F. S. V. LS 21 279 1
"I beg your pardon sir, for the liberty I have taken in LS 25 292 3
"You need not give yourself that trouble, sir." NA I 3 25 3
"About a week, sir," replied Catherine, trying not to NA I 3 26 5
"Why should you be surprized, sir?" NA I 3 26 7
"Never, sir." NA I 3 26 9
"Yes, sir, I was there last Monday." NA I 3 26 11
"Yes, sir, I was at the play on Tuesday." NA I 3 26 13
"Yes, sir, on Wednesday." NA I 3 26 15
"Do you understand muslins, sir?" NA I 3 28 37
You must be a great comfort to your sister, sir." NA I 3 28 39
"And pray, sir, what do you think of Miss Morland's gown?" NA I 3 28 41
"I am quite of your opinion, sir," replied Mrs. Allen; " NA I 3 28 44
"Bath is a charming place, sir; there are so many good NA I 3 29 46
"I am very happy to see you again, sir, indeed; I was NA I 8 54 4
"Well, sir, and I dare say you are not sorry to be back NA I 8 54 5
"Thank you, sir. NA I 8 54 7
"Yes, sir--and Dr. Skinner and his family were here three NA I 8 54 9
"I was just beginning to make the request, sir, as you NA II 2 139 6
"And when do you think, sir, I may look forward to this NA II 11 209 5
"You may see the house from this window, sir," was NA II 15 243 9
Why would you be persuaded by my uncle, sir Robert, SS II 14 251 13
"Well, sir," said Mrs. Jennings, "and how did it end?" SS III 1 268 47
"No, sir," she replied with firmness, "I shall not stay. SS III 8 317 3
"With me!"--in the utmost amazement--"well, sir--be quick-- SS III 8 317 5
"Pray be quick, sir"--said Elinor impatiently--"I have no SS III 8 317 8
"Well, sir, and what said Mrs. Smith?" SS III 8 323 39
"Well, sir," said Elinor, who, though pitying him, grew SS III 8 325 47
"Dear sir, being very sure I have long SS III 13 365 14
"I dare say he would sir--& I wish with all my heart he W 325 4
"I hope so, I beleive so, sir--said Emma in some agitation. W 325 5
"About 2 years sir." W 325 5
"I was not so ungrateful sir, said Emma warmly, as to wish W 326 5
"I shall be very happy to dance with you sir, if you like W 330 11
"I am not going to dance with Master Blake sir." W 334 13
"And what had you for dinner sir?"--said his eldest W 344 20
"Certainly, sir;--and it has the advantage also of being PP I 6 25 27
"You saw me dance at Meryton, I believe, sir." PP I 6 25 29
"Never, sir." PP I 6 25 31
"indeed, sir, I have not the least intention of dancing.-- PP I 6 26 38
"Indeed I have, sir," was her answer. PP I 9 41 3
Dear sir, the disagreement subsisting between PP I 13 62 12
I remain, dear sir, with respectful compliments to your PP I 13 63 12
Can he be a sensible man, sir?" PP I 13 64 17
"you are very kind, sir, I am sure; and I wish with all my PP I 13 65 21
22
"Ah! sir, I do indeed. PP I 13 65 24
Does she live near you, sir?" PP I 14 67 2
"I think you said she was a widow, sir? has she any family? PP I 14 67 4
"I have been most highly gratified indeed, my dear sir. PP I 18 92 23
I appeal to Mr. Darcy:--but let me not interrupt you, sir.- PP I 18 92 23
"You are too hasty, sir," she cried. PP I 19 106 12
"Upon my word, sir," cried Elizabeth, "your hope is rather PP I 19 107 14
"I do assure you, sir, that I have no pretension whatever PP I 19 108 20
"Sir, you quite misunderstand me," said Mrs. Bennet, PP I 20 111 5
"I have, sir." PP I 20 111 16
of Lady Catherine's disapprobation here, my good sir?-- PP I 22 123 6
7
"My dear sir," replied Mr. Collins, "I am particularly PP I 22 123 8
"Believe me, my dear sir, my gratitude is warmly excited PP I 22 124 10
"Thank you, sir, but a less agreeable man would satisfy me. PP II 1 138 28
"Not so much as I could wish, sir; but I dare say he may PP III 1 248 25
"Yes, sir; but I do not know when that will be. PP III 1 248 28
"Yes, sir, I know I am. PP III 1 249 33
"My dear sir, "I feel myself called upon, by our PP III 6 296 11
Be assured, my dear sir, that Mrs. Collins and myself PP III 6 296 11
Let me advise you then, my dear sir, to console yourself PP III 6 297 11
"I am, dear sir, &c. &c, PP III 6 297 11
"Money! my uncle!" cried Jane, "what do you mean, sir?" PP III 7 304 28
"Dear sir, PP III 18 383 23
perfection, sir," addressing herself then to Dr. Grant. MP I 6 54 9
"Sir, it is a moor park, we bought it as a moor park, and MP I 6 54 11
You will hear enough of it to-morrow, sir. MP II 1 181 16
pheasants, sir, I assure you, as much as you could desire. MP II 1 181 16
I hope you will take a day's sport there yourself, sir, MP II 1 181 16
always spread you know, sir--the faster probably from your MP II 1 184 26
"My indulgence shall be given, sir," replied Sir Thomas MP II 1 185 29
and Lord Edmund or sir Edmund sound delightfully; but sink MP II 4 211 24
"Yes, sir," was Fanny's humble answer, given with the MP II 5 221 38
39
sir, I would not have delayed his return for a day. MP II 5 225 58
No, no, sir, hands off--hands off. MP II 7 244 28
is the only way, sir, in which I could not wish you MP II 7 247 39
"Certainly, sir, I have no idea but of residence. MP II 7 247 41
now close to them--"is not Fanny a very good dancer, sir?" MP II 7 250 59
were engaged; and the "yes, sir, to Mr. Crawford," was MP II 10 275 11
"Oh! yes, sir," cried Fanny, rising eagerly from her seat MP II 10 279 28
"I am not cold, sir--I never sit here long at this time of MP III 1 312 7
"No, sir." MP III 1 312 9
no, sir, I cannot, indeed I cannot go down to him. MP III 1 314 17
"You are mistaken, sir,"--cried Fanny, forced by the MP III 1 315 19
"Yes, sir." MP III 1 315 22
"Yes, sir." MP III 1 315 24
"I--I cannot like him, sir, well enough to marry him." MP III 1 315 26
"Oh! yes, sir, indeed I do. MP III 1 316 30
"Yes, sir." MP III 1 317 35
"No, sir." MP III 1 317 37
"Indeed, sir," said Fanny, "I am very sorry that Mr. MP III 2 330 15
"Sir, you do me honour;" was Crawford's answer, with a bow MP III 3 338 15
In vain was her "pray, sir, don't--pray, Mr. Crawford," MP III 3 342 34
"How can you, sir? MP III 3 342 35
"Perhaps, sir," said Fanny, wearied at last into speaking-- MP III 3 343 39
into speaking--"perhaps, sir, I thought it was a pity you MP III 3 343 39
"I will speak to her, sir; I will take the first MP III 4 345 5
please sir, and one of the officers has been here to"----- MP III 7 377 7
But here is my sister, sir, here is Fanny;" turning and MP III 7 380 21
the Bertram property, than any other possible 'sir.' MP III 14 434 13
moment's recollection enabled her to say, "Rushworth, sir." MP III 15 439 10
"Yes, sir." MP III 15 439 12
"It is a mistake, sir," said Fanny instantly; "it must be MP III 15 440 15
"Not at all, sir. E I 1 10 23
"Dirty, sir! E I 1 10 25
"We should not like her so well as we do, sir, if we could E I 1 11 38
"With a great deal of pleasure, sir, at any time," said Mr. E I 1 14 48
"You, sir, may say any thing," cried Mr. Elton; "but I E I 6 48 39
"My dear sir, do not make a stranger of me." E I 8 57 4
"You cannot do better, sir." E I 8 57 6
"Thank you, sir, thank you; I am going this moment myself; E I 8 58 8
"I dare say they are, sir. E I 9 80 71
"Oh! yes, sir," cried she with ready sympathy, "how you E I 11 93 7
But I hope she is pretty well, sir." E I 11 93 7
"And do you see her, sir, tolerably often?" asked Isabella E I 11 94 12
"Mr. Wingfield most strenuously recommended it, sir--or we E I 12 101 21
"Oh! good Mr. Perry--how is he, sir?" E I 12 101 24
"Oh! my dear sir, her throat is so much better that I have E I 12 102 28
How are they, sir?" E I 12 102 31
must not confound us with London in general, my dear sir. E I 12 103 37
"I am sorry to hear you say so, sir; but I assure you, E I 12 103 39
"What is the matter, sir?-- E I 12 103 41
"But why should you be sorry, sir?-- E I 12 105 53
with many people, but indeed it is quite a mistake, sir.-- E I 12 105 55
"But, my dear sir, the difference of the journey;--only E I 12 106 57
"I know nothing of the large parties of London, sir--I E I 13 116 44
Well, sir, the time must come when you will be paid for E I 13 116 45
prove a spirited beginning of your winter engagements, sir. E I 15 126 7
8
"I admired your resolution very much, sir," said he, "in E I 15 126 10
Believe me, sir, I am far, very far, from gratified in E I 15 130 30
"No, sir," cried Emma, "it confesses no such thing. E I 15 131 34
you have been entirely mistaken in supposing it. E I 15 132 35
36
I do not know a more luxurious state, sir, than sitting at E II 3 170 2
"True, sir; and Emma, because she had Miss Fairfax." E II 3 171 13
"Oh! my dear sir, how are you this morning? E II 3 172 24
My dear sir, you really are too bountiful. E II 3 173 29
than"----- "Oh! my dear sir, as my mother says, our E II 3 173 30
31
I say, sir," turning to Mr. Woodhouse, "I think there are E II 3 175 39
My dear sir, if there is one thing my mother loves better E II 3 175 39
40
Good morning to you, my dear sir. E II 3 177 50
going farther on business, sir, I will take the E II 5 193 36
37
"You are acquainted with Miss Jane Fairfax, sir, are you?" E II 5 194 45
"My dear sir, upon no account in the world; my father can E II 5 195 46
"Well, sir," cried Mr. Weston, "as I took Miss Taylor away, E II 7 209 11
"But my dear sir," cried Mr. Weston, "if Emma comes away E II 7 210 17
the Coles, I am sure, sir; friendly, good sort of people E II 7 210 19

"I was going to observe, sir," said Frank Churchill, "that E II 11 251 27
"Sir," said Mr. Woodhouse, rather warmly, "you are very E II 11 251 28
"From the very circumstance of its being large, sir. E II 11 251 29
bodies, which (as you well know, sir) does the mischief." E II 11 251 29
"Ah! sir--but a thoughtless young person will sometimes E II 11 252 31
"Have you indeed, sir?-- bless me! I never could have E II 11 252 32
"But, unfortunately, sir, my time is so limited-----" E II 11 252 33
"I can answer for every thing of that nature, sir, because E II 11 252 36
to wrap Miss Emma up, you need not have any fears, sir.' E II 11 252 37
"Both sir! E II 11 255 56
"Oh! I beg your pardon, sir. E II 11 255 58
"I dare say your apologies were accepted, sir. E II 14 280 55
"Yes, sir, I did indeed; and I am very much obliged by E II 16 294 26
"I will see that there are umbrellas, sir," said Frank to E III 2 321 14
A little tea if you please, sir, by and bye,--no hurry--Oh! E III 2 323 19
My dear sir, you are too obliging.-- E III 2 329 45
Sir, you are most kind. E III 2 329 45
"No, sir," replied his son, laughing, "I seem to have had E III 5 345 13
My dear sir, you are too obliging. E III 5 349 24
"Low, I am afraid, sir, very low," answered his son;--"but E III 7 371 30
Come, sir, pray let me hear it." E III 7 371 31
"I perfectly agree with you, sir,"--was then his remark. E III 15 446 20
"Very pretty, sir, upon my word; to send me on here, to be E III 16 457 36
"And I am sure, sir," said Mrs. Musgrove, "it was a lucky P III 8 67 24
Sir Frederick and Lady Wentworth! P III 9 75 11
"Yes, sir, a Mr. Elliot; a gentleman of large fortune,-- P III 12 105 12
say you heard the carriage, sir, while you were at dinner; P III 12 105 12
Pray sir," (turning to the waiter), "did not you hear,-- P III 12 106 14
"Another time, sir, I thank you, not now." P IV 1 127 25
"No, sir, she is not one and thirty; but I do not think I P IV 5 157 16
"A letter from Uppercross Cottage, sir." P IV 6 162 4
"Did you say that you had something to tell me, sir?" P IV 6 169 28
Indeed you are mistaken there, sir. P IV 6 171 38
are extremely obliging sir, & I take you at your word.-- S 1 365 1
"The surgeon sir!--replied Mr Heywood--I am afraid you S 1 365 1
"Nay sir, if he is not in the way, his partner will just S 1 365 1
Mr H. looked very much astonished--& replied--"what sir! S 1 365 1
"Excuse me sir--replied the other. S 1 365 1
"Yes sir, this is certainly Willingden." S 1 366 1
"Then sir, I can bring proof of your having a surgeon in S 1 366 1
Here sir--(taking out his pocket book--) if you will do me S 1 366 1
You will find it an advertisement sir, of the dissolution S 1 366 1
length sir"--offering him the two little oblong extracts.-- S 1 366 1
"Sir--said Mr Heywood with a good humoured smile--if you S 1 366 1
But as to that cottage, I can assure you sir that it is in S 1 366 1
looked them over, added--"I beleive I can explain it sir.-- S 1 366 1
And we sir--(speaking rather proudly) are not in the Weald. S 1 366 1
"Not down in the Weald I am sure sir, replied the S 1 366 1
Well sir--I dare say it is as you say, & I have made an S 1 367 1
we accept your hospitality sir,--& in order to do away S 1 367 1
the poor good for nothing--as I dare say you find, sir." S 1 368 1
"Not at all sir, not at all--cried Mr Parker eagerly. S 1 368 1
No sir, I assure you, Sanditon is not a place-----" S 1 368 1
to any place in particular sir, answered Mr H.-- S 1 368 1
Such a place as Sanditon sir, I may say was wanted, was S 1 369 1
Only conceive sir, the advantage of saving a whole mile, S 1 369 1
But Brinshore sir, which I dare say you have in your eye-- S 1 369 1
Depend upon it sir, that this is a most faithful S 1 369 1
"Sir, I never heard it spoken of in my life before, said S 1 369 1
Why, in truth sir, I fancy we may apply to Brinshore, that S 1 370 1
"With all my heart sir--apply any verses you like to it-- S 1 370 1
Now sir, let us see how you can be best conveyed into the S 1 370 1
came from London for sea sir after the hooping cough, and S 4 383 1
"Lord! my dear sir, she cried, how could you think of such S 6 393 1

SIR ARCHIBALD (2)
There comes old Sir Archibald drew and his grandson. P IV 6 170 29
Poor old Sir Archibald! P IV 6 170 29

SIR BASIL (2)
'Old fellow'! cried Sir Basil, 'it is Admiral Baldwin. P III 3 20 16
'Forty,' replied Sir Basil, 'forty, and no more.' P III 3 20 16

SIR BASIL MORLEY (1)
a friend of mine who was standing near, (Sir Basil Morley.) P III 3 20 16

SIR CHARLES (2)
recommendation of Sir Charles, that Sir Charles was much MP II 13 298 3
Sir Charles, that Sir Charles was much delighted in having MP II 13 298 3

SIR CHARLES GRANDISON (2)
She very often reads Sir Charles Grandison herself; but NA I 6 41 21
"Sir Charles Grandison! NA I 6 41 22

SIR E. D. (1)
apparently very composedly--& Sir E. D. by her side.-- S 12 426 1

SIR EDMUND (1)
I put it to your conscience, whether 'Sir Edmund' would MP III 14 434 13

SIR EDW: (12)
Mr P. had considered Sir Edw: as standing without a rival, S 3 377 1
the down, Charlotte & Sir Edw: as they sat, could not but S 7 395 1
Edw: was gone, of how agreeable he had actually been.-- S 7 395 1
one end of the bench, & Sir Edw: & Miss B. at the other.-- S 7 395 1
"Oh! no no--exclaimed Sir Edw: in an extasy. S 7 398 1
had quite enough of Sir Edw: for one morng, & very gladly S 7 398 1
The others all left them, Sir Edw: with looks of very S 7 399 1
Sir Edw: has no Payments to make me. S 7 400 1
And Sir Edw: is a very steady man in the main, & has got S 7 400 1
Sir Edward's gig--and Sir Edw: approaching Charlotte, said S 8 403 1
The truth was the Sir Edw: whom circumstances had confined S 8 404 1
discouragement indeed would not have affected Sir Edw:--. S 8 405 2

SIR EDW: DENHAM (2)
Mr & Mrs P---- Sir Edw: Denham & Miss Denham, whose names S 6 389 1
"Sir Edw: Denham, said Charlotte, with such personal S 7 400 1

SIR EDW:'S (3)
a slight change in Sir Edw:'s countenance--with an anxious S 7 395 1
Charlotte's first glance told her that Sir Edw:'s air was S 7 395 1
Sir Edw:'s great object in life was to be seductive.-- S 8 405 2

SIR EDWARD (8)
Sir Edward, the present baronet, nephew to Sir Harry, S 3 377 1
vie in favour with Sir Edward, & to secure for herself & S 3 377 1
lips of a handsome Sir Edward,--and she cd not but think S 7 396 1
than the simple enquiry of--"Sir Edward & Miss Denham?"-- S 7 399 1
she got well, have her fall in love with Sir Edward!"-- S 7 401 1
This poor Sir Edward & his sister.--how far nature meant S 7 402 1
all his absurdities & all his atrocities with Sir Edward. S 8 404 1
The very name of Sir Edward he thought, carried some S 8 405 2

SIR EDWARD'S (3)
Sir Edward's required longer observation. S 7 396 1
under his arm to Sir Edward's gig--and Sir Edw: S 8 403 1
for Sir Edward's sake, & the sake of her Milch Asses. S 11 422 1

SIR EDWD (4)
Sir Edwd was much her superior in air & manner;--certainly S 7 394 1
And when he died, I gave Sir Edwd his gold watch.--" S 7 400 1
I have been a very liberal friend to Sir Edwd. S 7 400 1
will think so--for Sir Edwd must marry for money.-- S 7 400 1

SIR EDWD DENHAM (1)
them, Sir Edwd Denham & his sister, who having been at S 7 394 1

SIR H. D. (1)
the best place by the fire constantly occupied by Sir H. D. S 12 427 1

SIR H. DENHAM (1)
the picture of Sir H. Denham--and that one among many S 12 427 1

SIR HARRY (3)
Sir Edward, the present baronet, nephew to Sir Harry, S 3 377 1
And I verily beleive if my poor dear Sir Harry had never S 6 394 1
Poor dear Sir Harry (between ourselves) thought at first S 7 399 1

SIR HARRY DENHAM (1)
The late Sir Harry denham, of Denham Park in the S 3 375 1

SIR HARRY DENHAM'S (1)
least in favour & Sir Harry Denham's the most.-- S 3 376 1

SIR HARRY'S (2)
power--and when on Sir Harry's decease she returned again S 3 375 1
I only notice them, for poor dear Sir Harry's sake. S 7 399 1

SIR HENRY (3)
Sir Henry thought the duke not equal to Frederick, but MP I 13 122 2
but that was because Sir Henry wanted the part himself; MP I 13 122 2
I was surprised to see Sir Henry such a stick. MP I 13 122 2

SIR HENRY RUSSELL'S (1)
"Sir Henry Russell's widow, indeed, has no honours to P IV 5 158 19

SIR JAMES (38)
Sir James did make proposals to me for Frederica--but LS 2 245 1
Sir James is gone, Maria highly incensed, and Mrs LS 2 245 1
I hope to see her the wife of Sir James within a LS 7 253 1
I am sure of Sir James at any time, & could make him renew LS 7 253 1
I have seen Sir James,--he came to town for a few days LS 9 256 1
Your account of Sir James is most satisfactory, & I mean LS 10 258 4
proposals from Sir James, but her removing from Langford LS 14 265 4
my intentions about Sir James, she actually attempted to LS 16 268 1
"Oh! cried she, he is come, Sir James is come--& what am I LS 20 275 1
to her daughter, for Sir James is now desperately in love LS 20 276 2
Sir James talked a good deal, & made many civil excuses to LS 20 276 3
Sir James is a young man of an amiable disposition, & LS 20 276 5
her union with Sir James was not very distant, I had LS 20 277 5
When Sir James first came, he appeared all astonishment & LS 20 278 9
Sir James invited himself with great composure to remain LS 20 278 10
Her behaviour before Sir James certainly speaks the LS 20 278 11
her to send Sir James away, I shall be more obliged to you LS 21 279 1
behaving civilly to Sir James, & gave her to understand LS 22 280 1
and at first observed Sir James with an attention which I LS 22 280 2
to torment him, as Sir James tho' extremely gallant to me, LS 22 280 2
They could none of them help perceiving that Sir James was LS 22 281 3
herself, Sir James, & me, which gave him great uneasiness. LS 22 281 4
I was sitting about half an hour ago with Sir James in the LS 23 283 3
I know that Frederica is made wretched by Sir James' LS 23 284 4
James is gone, Lady Susan vanquished, & Frederica at peace. LS 23 285 8
was so unhappy about Sir James that I could not help--I LS 24 286 5
had set herself violently against marrying Sir James"----- LS 24 288 11
Frederica has an excellent understanding, and Sir James LS 24 288 11
Sir James is certainly under par--(his boyish manners make LS 24 288 11
Did not you know that she disliked Sir James?" LS 24 289 12
her objecting to Sir James could not less deserve to be LS 24 290 12
reasonable dislike to Sir James, I shall instantly inform LS 24 290 13
look & manner since Sir James has been dismissed--for in LS 25 293 4
my daughter & Sir James, after having so long intended it. LS 25 294 5
to take her to town, & marry her immediately to Sir James. LS 25 294 5
& the rest of his family, by making her marry Sir James. LS 26 295 1
Persecution on the subject of Sir James was entirely at an LS 42 312 3
Sir James may seem to have drawn an harder lot than mere LS 42 313 10

SIR JAMES MARTIN (10)
hither, except Sir James Martin, on whom I bestowed a LS 2 244 1
Sir James Martin had been drawn in by that young lady to LS 14 264 4
by the name of Sir James Martin, the very person, as you LS 20 275 2
her, a better fate than to be Sir James Martin's wife. LS 20 278 11
I am very miserable about Sir James Martin, & have no LS 21 279 1
Who should come on Tuesday but Sir James Martin? LS 22 280 1
of allowing Sir James Martin to address my daughter, LS 22 281 4
One point only is gained; Sir James Martin is dismissed. LS 24 285 1
will have Sir James Martin before she leaves London again. LS 38 307 3
Lady Susan announced her being married to Sir James Martin. LS 42 312 6

SIR JAMES'S (4)
in my life than by Sir James's arrival, & the suddenness LS 20 276 5
the hours of Sir James's stay, my mind was entirely LS 22 281 4
Sir James's carriage was at the door, & he, merry as usual, LS 24 291 15
Frederica shall be Sir James's wife before she quits my LS 39 308 1

SIR JOHN (91)
The house, too, as described by Sir John, was on so simple SS I 4 24 21
Conversation however was not wanted, for Sir John was very SS I 6 31 9
of the children, as Sir John would not leave the house SS I 6 31 10
Sir John was a sportsman, Lady Middleton a mother. SS I 7 32 1
John, and gave exercise to the good-breeding of his wife. SS I 7 32 1
door of the house by Sir John, who welcomed them to Barton SS I 7 33 4
Colonel Brandon, the friend of Sir John, seemed no more SS I 7 34 6
mirth of Sir John and his mother-in-law was interesting. SS I 7 34 7
Sir John was loud in his admiration at the end of every SS I 7 35 9
her connection with Sir John first brought him to her SS I 8 36 1
Sir John called on them as soon as the next interval of SS I 9 43 12
"Willoughby!" cried Sir John; "what, is he in the country? SS I 9 43 13
Sir John was rather puzzled. SS I 9 44 19
On this point Sir John could give more certain SS I 9 44 23
of fellow, I believe, as ever lived," repeated Sir John. SS I 9 44 25
"Aye, aye, I see how it will be," said Sir John, "I see SS I 9 45 29
"That is an expression, Sir John," said Marianne, warmly, " SS I 9 45 30
Sir John did not much understand this reproof; but he SS I 9 45 31
32
Sir John had dropt hints of past injuries and SS I 10 50 12
John had been previously forming, were put in execution. SS I 11 53 1
highly beautiful, and Sir John, who was particularly warm SS I 12 62 28
"What is the matter with brandon?" said Sir John. SS I 13 63 4
"We must go," said Sir John.-- SS I 13 64 25
said Sir John, "when once you are determined on any thing. SS I 13 65 32
"Oh! he must and shall come back," cried Sir John. SS I 13 65 37
"Aye, so do, Sir John," cried Mrs. Jennings, "and then SS I 13 65 38
do not go to town on horseback, do you?" added Sir John. SS I 13 65 41
He wished her a good morning, and attended by Sir John, SS I 13 66 51
When Sir John returned, he joined most heartily in the SS I 13 66 60
to table, which Sir John observed with great contentment. SS I 13 67 61
His estate had been rated by Sir John at about six or SS I 14 71 4
"Remember, Elinor," said she, "how very often Sir John SS I 16 84 6
by any of her family; Sir John and Mrs. Jennings, indeed, SS I 16 85 11
12
they were visited by Sir John and Mrs. Jennings, who, SS I 18 99 15
With the assistance of his mother-in-law, Sir John was not SS I 18 99 15
Sir John never came to the Dashwoods without either SS I 18 99 16
"I wish with all my soul," cried Sir John, "that SS I 18 100 21
Amongst them were Sir John and Lady Middleton and Mrs. SS I 19 105 13
She was sitting near the window, and as soon as Sir John SS I 19 105 13
again; so I said to Sir John, I do think I hear a carriage; SS I 19 106 20
21
through the passage into the parlour, attended by Sir John. SS I 19 106 21
"Here comes Marianne," cried Sir John. SS I 19 108 34
Sir John had been very urgent with them all to spend the SS I 19 108 40
But Sir John would not be satisfied--the carriage should SS I 19 109 40
What the devil does Sir John mean by not having a billiard SS I 20 111 8
Sir John is as stupid as the weather." SS I 20 111 8
"I am afraid, Miss Marianne," said Sir John, "you have not SS I 20 111 10
When they were seated in the dining room, Sir John SS I 20 111 18
"Did not I tell you, Sir John, when you spoke to me about SS I 20 111 20
"You and I, Sir John," said Mrs. Jennings, "should not SS I 20 111 21
Sir John and Lady Middleton wished it very much. SS I 20 116 62
for me, otherwise Sir John would have mentioned it to the SS I 20 116 62
this was enough for Sir John to invite them directly to SS I 21 118 2
alarm on the return of Sir John, by hearing that she was SS I 21 118 2
Sir John wanted the whole family to walk to the park SS I 21 119 3
But Sir John could not prevail. SS I 21 119 5
"And Sir John too," cried the elder sister, "what a SS I 21 122 15
"We have heard Sir John admire it excessively," said Lucy, SS I 21 123 24
inevitable lot, for as Sir John was entirely on the side SS I 21 124 33
Sir John could do no more; but he did not know that any SS I 21 124 33
Elinor could not suppose that Sir John would be more nice SS I 21 125 36
But Sir John did not sport long with the curiosity which SS I 21 125 37

when alluded to, or even openly mentioned by Sir John. SS I 21 126 41
was mentioned by Sir John, lest she should out with it all. SS I 22 133 42
Such a thought would never enter either Sir John or Lady SS II 1 143 8
Lucy in private, when Sir John called at the cottage one SS II 1 143 9
Their favour increased, they could not be spared; Sir John SS II 2 151 43
"I have a notion," said Sir John, "that Miss Marianne SS II 3 154 3
Sir John was delighted; for to a man, whose prevailing SS II 3 157 19
following morning, "Sir John will not like leaving Barton SS II 5 167 1
John and Lady Middleton in town by the end of next week." SS II 5 167 4
settled in town, Sir John had contrived to collect around SS II 5 170 29
"So my daughter Middleton told me, for it seems Sir John SS II 5 171 38
Lord! how concerned Sir John and my daughters will be when SS II 8 195 16
Mrs. Palmer and Sir John against ever naming Mr. SS II 8 195 17
No more would Sir John nor my daughters, for they are all SS II 8 196 18
Mrs. Jennings, nor Sir John, nor even Mrs. Palmer herself, SS II 10 214 8
Sir John could not have thought it possible. SS II 10 214 9
against the opinion of Sir John) that as Mrs. Willoughby SS II 10 215 14
and introduce him to Sir John and Lady Middleton. SS II 11 223 15
at home, and Sir John came in before their visit ended. SS II 11 228 52
Sir John was ready to like anybody, and though Mr. SS II 11 228 52
she was as ready as Sir John to ask them to spend a week SS II 12 230 8
her, her salts; and Sir John felt so desperately enraged SS II 12 236 41
to oblige her, that if Sir John dined from home, she might SS II 14 247 4
Sir John, who called on them more than once, brought home SS II 14 254 28
a good word for us to Sir John, or Mr. Palmer, or any SS III 2 277 30
to her, and to Sir John, and Lady Middleton, and the dear SS III 2 278 30
I blundered on Sir John, I believe, the first day of his SS III 8 326 55
myself off as insensible even to the undiscerning Sir John. SS III 8 330 69
and fortunately for Sir John and Mrs. Jennings, when SS III 14 380 20

SIR JOHN MIDDLETON (5)

She instantly wrote Sir John Middleton her acknowledgment SS I 4 24 20
Sir John Middleton was a good looking man about forty. SS I 6 30 6
Sir John Middleton, who called on them every day for the SS I 9 40 1
the use of Sir John Middleton, his family, and all his SS I 21 124 33
ran against Sir John Middleton, and when he saw who I was-- SS III 8 330 69

SIR JOHN MIDDLETON'S (1)

brought Sir John middleton's first letter to Norland, SS I 5 27 7

SIR JOHN'S (15)

so undoubtingly on Sir John's description of the house, as SS I 5 26 6
The former was for Sir John's gratification, the latter SS I 7 32 1
year round, while Sir John's independent employments were SS I 7 32 1
But Sir John's satisfaction in society was much more real; SS I 7 32 2
for, in spite of Sir John's urgent entreaties that they SS I 9 40 2
a kindness which Sir John's account of him and her own SS I 10 46 1
correspondence were to pass through Sir John's hands." SS I 16 84 6
He was a particular friend of Sir John's. SS I 20 116 62
"Did not Colonel Brandon know of Sir John's proposal to SS I 20 117 63
and wife, before Sir John's and Mrs. Jennings's active SS I 21 118 1
Sir John's confidence in his own judgment rose with this SS I 21 119 3
And even Sir John's joking intelligence must have had some SS II 1 142 7
Business on Sir John's part, and a violent cold on her own, SS II 5 170 28
She joined them sometimes at Sir John's, and sometimes at SS II 14 247 5
on; we will walk to Sir John's new plantations at Barton- SS III 10 343 9

SIR LEWIS DE BOURGH (3)

widow of Sir Lewis de Bourgh, whose bounty and beneficence PP I 13 62 12
glazing altogether had originally cost Sir Lewis de Bourgh. PP II 6 161 8
It was not thought necessary in Sir Lewis de Bourgh's PP II 6 164 16

SIR REGINALD (5)

Sir Reginald is very infirm, & not likely to stand in your LS 9 256 1
Sir Reginald de courcy to his son. Parklands. LS 12 260 1
vexed that Sir Reginald should know anything of a matter LS 13 262 1
Mr De Courcy to Sir Reginald. Churchill. LS 14 263 1
on the caprice of Sir Reginald, will not suit the freedom LS 29 299 3

SIR THOMAS (281)

not contemptible, Sir Thomas being happily able to give MP I 1 3 1
on the pride of Sir Thomas, as Mrs. Norris could not MP I 1 4 1
it very wonderful to Sir Thomas, that Mrs. Norris should MP I 1 4 2
to Sir Thomas in the concerns of his West Indian property? MP I 1 5 2
No situation would be beneath him--or what did Sir Thomas MP I 1 5 2
Sir Thomas sent friendly advice and professions, Lady MP I 1 5 3
Sir Thomas could not give so instantaneous and unqualified MP I 1 6 5
"My dear Sir Thomas, I perfectly comprehend you, and do MP I 1 6 6
A niece of our's, Sir Thomas, I may say, or, at least of MP I 1 6 6
you say," replied Sir Thomas, "and far be it from me to MP I 1 7 7
My dear Sir Thomas, with all my faults I have a warm heart: MP I 1 7 8
Except to the attack on Nanny's cousin, Sir Thomas no MP I 1 8 9
have been equal; for Sir Thomas was fully resolved to be MP I 1 8 9
Sir Thomas heard, with some surprise, that it would be MP I 1 9 10
After a short pause, Sir Thomas added with dignity, "yes, MP I 1 9 11
"Should her disposition be really bad," said Sir Thomas, " MP I 1 10 14
Norris," observed Sir Thomas, "as to the distinction MP I 1 10 17
Sir Thomas and Lady Bertram received her very kindly, and MP I 2 12 2
her very kindly, and Sir Thomas seeing how much she needed MP I 2 12 2
In vain were the well-meant condescensions of Sir Thomas, MP I 2 13 4
As her appearance and spirits improved, Sir Thomas and Mrs. MP I 2 18 23
Sir Thomas did not know what was wanting, because, though MP I 2 19 30
by Sir Thomas, and in smaller concerns by her sister. MP I 2 19 31
the country, leaving Sir Thomas to attend his duty in MP I 2 20 33
children suggested, Sir Thomas did not forget to do what MP I 2 21 34
The time was now come when Sir Thomas expected his sister- MP I 3 24 7
misled Sir Thomas to suppose it really intended for Fanny. MP I 3 28 38
I thought you had settled it with Sir Thomas?" MP I 3 28 41
I never spoke a syllable about it to Sir Thomas, nor he to MP I 3 28 42
Sure Sir Thomas could not seriously expect such a thing! MP I 3 28 42
Sir Thomas is too much my friend. MP I 3 28 42
How came Sir Thomas to speak to you about it?" MP I 3 28 42
Sir Thomas says you will have six hundred a year." MP I 3 29 49
Sir Thomas will take care of that." MP I 3 30 53
Sir Thomas has been writing about it, I know." MP I 3 30 55
family--and so if Sir Thomas should ever speak again about MP I 3 30 56
Sir Thomas found it expedient to go to Antigua himself, MP I 3 32 61
his son, reconciled Sir Thomas to the effort of quitting MP I 3 32 62
been forbidden by Sir Thomas, they felt themselves MP I 3 32 64
"Sir Thomas, who had done so much for her and her brothers, MP I 3 33 64
She was sure Sir Thomas had never intended it; and she MP I 4 36 7
return, and then Sir Thomas might settle it all himself. MP I 4 36 7
when September came, Sir Thomas was still abroad, and MP I 4 37 9
"If poor Sir Thomas were fated never to return, it would MP I 4 38 9
to the absent Sir Thomas, was entered into, much to the MP I 4 39 11
Sir Thomas, however, was truly happy in the prospect of an MP I 4 40 14
a promise to his father, and of being Sir Thomas hereafter. MP I 5 48 28
But if dear Sir Thomas were here, he could tell you what MP I 6 54 9
doing several things that Sir Thomas and I used to talk of. MP I 6 54 9
was a present from Sir Thomas, but I saw the bill, and I MP I 6 54 11
Lord bless me! how you did tremble when Sir Thomas first MP I 7 69 22
when he comes home find all the varnish scratched off." MP I 8 77 12
Sir Thomas wrote of it with as much decision as experience MP I 11 107 2
Sir Thomas would have been deeply mortified by a suspicion MP I 11 107 4
Sir Thomas was to return in November, and his eldest son MP I 12 114 1
Mansfield Park, the Sir Thomas complete, which he was to MP I 12 114 2
independence; and Sir Thomas would probably have thought MP I 13 121 1
is employed, every thing will be right with Sir Thomas.-- MP I 13 127 31
"Sir Thomas would not like it.-- MP I 15 140 16
preventing Fanny, "that Sir Thomas would not like it." MP I 15 141 17
When Sir Thomas comes, I dare say he will be in for some MP I 17 161 14
"Sir Thomas is to achieve mighty things when he comes home, MP I 17 161 15
there to the absent Sir Thomas, to have leisure for MP I 17 163 21
Could Sir Thomas look in upon us just now, he would bless MP I 18 169 21
Sir Thomas in the house? MP II 1 175 1
pay his respects to Sir Thomas without delay, sent him MP II 1 176 3
mercy wishing poor Sir Thomas had been twice as long on MP II 1 176 4
bustle of receiving Sir Thomas were over and he might be MP II 1 177 5
Sir Thomas was at that moment looking round him, and MP II 1 177 7
Sir Thomas was indeed the life of the party, who at his MP II 1 178 8
appearance, and Sir Thomas was liking him already. MP II 1 179 8
through the house, Sir Thomas, with a very reasonable MP II 1 180 10
Would Sir Thomas have consented to eat, she might have MP II 1 180 10
of dispatch; but Sir Thomas resolutely declined all dinner; MP II 1 180 10
"Sure, my dear Sir Thomas, a basin of soup would be a much MP II 1 180 10
Sir Thomas could not be provoked. MP II 1 180 11
people have been amusing themselves lately, Sir Thomas? MP II 1 180 13
brought in, and Sir Thomas, getting up, said that he found MP II 1 181 17
Sir Thomas had been a good deal surprised to find candles MP II 1 182 22
At the very moment of Yates perceiving Sir Thomas, and MP II 1 182 22
Sir Thomas received Mr. Yates with all the appearance of MP II 1 183 23
supply, to save Sir Thomas from anger on finding himself MP II 1 183 23
on each side; and Sir Thomas, having exerted himself so MP II 1 183 24
with an increase of gravity which was not lost on all. MP II 1 183 24
Sir Thomas listened most politely, but found much to MP II 1 184 25
and immediately gave Sir Thomas an account of what they MP II 1 184 27
"To own the truth, Sir Thomas, we were in the middle of a MP II 1 185 28
"My indulgence shall be given, sir," replied Sir Thomas MP II 1 185 29
Sir Thomas did not quite understand this, and looked with MP II 1 186 32
Sir Thomas looked again, and then replied with an MP II 1 186 34
Sir Thomas meant to be giving Mr. Rushworth's opinion in MP II 1 186 35
Sir Thomas saw all the impropriety of such a scheme among MP II 2 187 2
was so glaring to Sir Thomas, and would not have admitted MP II 2 188 3
"My dear Sir Thomas, if you had seen the state of the MP II 2 189 5
own he could not hold Sir Thomas in greater respect.'" MP II 2 190 7
Sir Thomas gave up the point, foiled by her evasions, MP II 2 190 8
dissatisfied; and Sir Thomas was in hopes that another day MP II 2 190 9
was a something in Sir Thomas, when they sat round the MP II 2 191 10
moral, so infamously tyrannical as Sir Thomas. MP II 2 191 10
and the music which Sir Thomas called for from his MP II 2 191 11
pay his respects to Sir Thomas, and at rather an early MP II 2 192 11
Sir Thomas soon appeared, and Maria saw with delight and MP II 2 192 11
courteous glance at Sir Thomas,) because in that case, he MP II 2 192 11
In his departure Sir Thomas felt the chief interest; MP II 2 194 21
Sir Thomas had been quite indifferent to Mr. Crawford's MP II 2 194 21
character; and Sir Thomas hoped, in seeing him out of it, MP II 2 194 21
Sir Thomas drawing back from intimacies in general, was MP II 3 196 1
evil to follow--the impression it must leave on Sir Thomas. MP II 3 199 18
was impending over Sir Thomas. not all his good-will for MP II 3 200 19
Sir Thomas resolved to speak seriously to her. MP II 3 200 20
With solemn kindness Sir Thomas addressed her; told her MP II 3 200 21
Sir Thomas was satisfied; too glad to be satisfied perhaps MP II 3 201 22
Such and such-like were the reasonings of Sir Thomas-- MP II 3 201 22
Had Sir Thomas applied to his daughter within the first MP II 3 201 24
Sir Thomas felt as an anxious father must feel, and was MP II 3 203 30
I will ask Sir Thomas, as soon as he comes in, whether I MP II 5 217 8
to any purpose, till Sir Thomas were present; but the MP II 5 217 11
Thomas, stop a moment--I have something to say to you." MP II 5 217 11
was always heard and attended to; and Sir Thomas came back. MP II 5 218 12
"Well," said Sir Thomas, as if waiting more to accomplish MP II 5 218 13
"She will be late," said Sir Thomas, taking out his watch, MP II 5 218 15
"Nothing can be more natural," said Sir Thomas, after a MP II 5 218 18
"But can I do without her, Sir Thomas?" MP II 5 219 19
and invitation from Sir Thomas, was in a very ill humour, MP II 5 219 27
could; and when Sir Thomas, soon afterwards, just opening MP II 5 221 35
"My dear Sir Thomas!" cried Mrs. Norris, red with anger, " MP II 5 221 36
"Walk!" repeated Sir Thomas, in a tone of most MP II 5 221 37
in the drawing room, Sir Thomas saw them off in as good MP II 5 222 41
You must preach at Mansfield, you know, that Sir Thomas MP II 5 227 65
This was exactly what Sir Thomas and Edmund had been MP II 6 233 15
William and Fanny soon shewed themselves; and Sir Thomas MP II 6 233 16
a tete-a-tete, which Sir Thomas could not but observe with MP II 6 234 17
His recitals were amusing in themselves to Sir Thomas, but MP II 6 236 21
to obviate in Sir Thomas, who knew better than his nephew MP II 6 237 23
while, "because Sir Thomas seemed so ill inclined! and MP II 7 238 2
Luckily Sir Thomas was at hand. MP II 7 239 4
"What shall I do, Sir Thomas?-- MP II 7 239 5
Sir Thomas, after a moment's thought, recommended MP II 7 239 6
it was settled; and Sir Thomas, Mrs. Norris, and Dr. and MP II 7 239 8
Twice had Sir Thomas inquired into the enjoyment and MP II 7 240 10
As yet Sir Thomas had seen nothing to remark in Mr. MP II 7 246 36
Sir Thomas heard and was not offended. MP II 7 246 37
Thomas, in a more every day tone, but still with feeling. MP II 7 247 37
"I want to be your neighbour, Sir Thomas, as you have MP II 7 247 38
Sir Thomas, politely bowing, replied--"it is the only way, MP II 7 247 39
"We shall be the losers," continued Sir Thomas. MP II 7 247 42
"I repeat again," added Sir Thomas, "that Thornton Lacey MP II 7 248 44
"Sir Thomas," said Edmund, "undoubtedly understands the MP II 7 248 46
considering Sir Thomas, with decided ill-will, as the MP II 7 248 47
by Sir Thomas, who was standing in chat with Dr. Grant. MP II 7 249 49
of her dancing; and Sir Thomas, by no means displeased, MP II 7 251 63
My dear Sir Thomas, we have settled it that the carriage MP II 7 251 64
Sir Thomas could not dissent, as it had been his own MP II 7 251 65
The hope of an opportunity, which Sir Thomas had then MP II 8 252 1
"Ah! my dear Sir Thomas," interrupted Mrs. Norris, "I knew MP II 8 252 2
"My daughters," replied Sir Thomas, gravely interposing, " MP II 8 252 3
pleasure in the promised ball, as Sir Thomas could desire. MP II 8 253 5
Sir Thomas engaged for its giving her very little trouble, MP II 8 253 6
Sir Thomas had been amusing himself with shaping a very MP II 8 253 7
a new dress for her; Sir Thomas gave orders and Mrs. MP II 8 254 9
Sir Thomas approved of it for another reason. MP II 9 266 21
Only think, my dear Sir Thomas, what extraordinary MP II 10 272 3
Sir Thomas said no more; but when they sat down to table MP II 10 272 4
manners of neither Sir Thomas nor Lady Bertram were of a MP II 10 273 7
In a few minutes Sir Thomas came to her, and asked if she MP II 10 275 11
Mr. Crawford was not far off; Sir Thomas brought him to MP II 10 275 11
in vain however;--Sir Thomas smiled, tried to encourage MP II 10 275 11
Sir Thomas himself was watching her progress down the MP II 10 276 13
giving hints to Sir Thomas, and trying to move all the MP II 10 277 16
Thomas had been bringing up no wife for his younger son. MP II 10 278 20
well at an end; and Sir Thomas having seen her rather walk MP II 10 279 22
"So soon! my good friend," said Sir Thomas, producing his MP II 10 279 24
After a short consideration, Sir Thomas asked Crawford to MP II 10 280 32
Shortly afterwards, Sir Thomas was again interfering a MP II 10 280 33
In thus sending her away, Sir Thomas perhaps might not be MP II 10 281 34
to her, she had forgot to ask Sir Thomas what it could be." MP II 11 283 4
bed-time; and as Sir Thomas was reading to himself, no MP II 11 283 6
"And there is no reason to suppose," added Sir Thomas, " MP II 11 284 9
with Maria; and as Sir Thomas thought it best for each MP II 11 284 10
observed, "Sir Thomas, I have been thinking--and I am very MP II 11 285 10
Sir Thomas immediately improved this compliment by adding, MP II 11 285 11
Sir Thomas paused, half smiled, glanced at his niece, and MP II 11 285 13
"And that is not very likely to be, Sir Thomas. MP II 11 285 14
Who could write chat to Sir Thomas? MP II 11 288 24
to her; and so is Sir Thomas in his way, but it is the way MP II 12 297 35
What can Sir Thomas and Edmund together do, what do they MP II 12 297 35
waited for, and a "let Sir Thomas know," to the servant. MP II 13 298 1
She had burst away from him, and at that moment Sir Thomas MP II 13 302 9
Sir Thomas was as joyful as she could desire, and very MP II 13 303 12
any thing; and when Sir Thomas good humouredly observed, MP II 13 304 16
saving it would be to Sir Thomas, as with any part of it. MP II 13 304 19
"Sir Thomas told me 10l. would be enough." MP II 13 305 22
every year, to say nothing of what I do for them." MP II 13 305 24
and you know it makes very little difference to Sir Thomas. MP II 13 305 25
She had quite convinced herself of this before Sir Thomas MP II 13 306 26
intervals, whenever Sir Thomas was out of the room, or at MP II 13 306 27
It was indeed Sir Thomas, who opened the door, and asked MP III 1 312 4
After a moment's pause, Sir Thomas, trying to suppress a MP III 1 313 13
so properly, that Sir Thomas, feeling, moreover, his own MP III 1 314 16
which astonished Sir Thomas; but what was his increase of MP III 1 314 17

"I do not catch your meaning," said Sir Thomas, sitting MP III 1 315 18
"Am I to understand," said Sir Thomas, after a few MP III 1 315 21
"This is very strange!" said Sir Thomas, in a voice of MP III 1 315 27
"You must have been aware," continued Sir Thomas, MP III 1 316 29
Sir Thomas looked at her with deeper surprise. MP III 1 316 31
to justify," said Sir Thomas, beginning again, and very MP II 13 317 34
It was gently, but it was calmly said, and Sir Thomas was MP III 1 317 36
Sir Thomas came towards the table where she sat in MP III 1 318 39
to introduce it, Sir Thomas began to think a little MP III 1 320 44
enough to persevere--Sir Thomas began to have hopes; and MP III 1 320 44
down to him, that Sir Thomas, after a little consideration, MP III 1 320 45
She wondered that Sir Thomas could have leisure to think MP III 1 322 51
Sir Thomas had given orders for it. MP III 1 322 51
shrubbery to Fanny as the dryest place," said Sir Thomas. MP III 1 323 55
but you do not know how dry the path is to my house. MP III 1 323 56
As a general reflection on Fanny, Sir Thomas thought MP III 1 323 57
Thomas wishes to speak with you, ma'am, in his own room." MP III 1 324 60
What should Sir Thomas want you for? MP III 1 325 60
You mean me, Baddeley, I am sure; Sir Thomas wants me, not MP III 1 325 60
He had all the disposition to persevere that Sir Thomas MP III 2 326 1
Sir Thomas was obliged or obliged himself to wait till the MP III 2 329 11
Sir Thomas was soon able to depend on it himself. MP III 2 329 11
proper and hopeful, Sir Thomas resolved to abstain from MP III 2 330 14
Accordingly, on this principle Sir Thomas took the first MP III 2 330 14
"My dear," interrupted Sir Thomas, "there is no occasion MP III 2 330 16
In spite of his intended silence, Sir Thomas found himself MP III 2 331 19
When Sir Thomas understood this, he felt the necessity of MP III 2 332 19
Sir Thomas, indeed, was, by this time, not very far from MP III 2 332 19
Sir Thomas gave her more credit for discretion on the MP III 2 332 21
I must just speak of it once, I told Sir Thomas I must MP III 2 333 23
Sir Thomas said so. MP III 2 333 28
I shall tell Sir Thomas that I am sure it was done that MP III 2 333 28
unprepared, but Sir Thomas could not regard the connection MP III 3 335 6
stronger terms than Sir Thomas could quite echo, he was MP III 3 335 6
of Edmund's return, Sir Thomas felt himself more than MP III 3 335 7
"I wish Sir Thomas had been here." MP III 3 338 17
departure; and Sir Thomas thought it might be as well to MP III 4 345 2
Sir Thomas was most cordially anxious for the perfection MP III 4 345 3
Sir Thomas promised that it should be so. MP III 5 356 3
Poor Sir Thomas, who was glad to see you? MP III 5 358 9
Thomas, though I certainly did hate him for many a week. MP III 5 358 9
tolerably soon; and Sir Thomas, I dare say, in the course MP III 5 364 32
Sir Thomas, meanwhile, went on with his own hopes, and his MP III 6 368 7
It had occurred to Sir Thomas, in one of his dignified MP III 6 368 9
This was enough to determine Sir Thomas; and a decisive " MP III 6 368 9
of the business; Sir Thomas retiring from it with some MP III 6 368 9
the hardest for Sir Thomas to accomplish, and what only he MP III 6 370 13
thought Fanny ought to go, and therefore that she must. MP III 6 370 14
Sir Thomas had appealed to her reason, conscience, and MP III 6 371 15
post, when she saw Sir Thomas actually give William notes MP III 6 372 21
too necessary to Sir Thomas and Lady Bertram for her to be MP III 6 373 23
Could Sir Thomas have seen all his niece's feelings, when MP III 8 388 1
week after week, if Sir Thomas cannot settle every thing MP III 11 410 16
and though Sir Thomas, had he known all, might have MP III 11 413 30
Thomas was quite unkind, both to her aunt and to herself.-- MP III 13 424 4
invalid, whose state Sir Thomas fears may be very critical; MP III 13 426 11
happy to add, that Sir Thomas will not leave me on this MP III 13 426 11
shortly, which Sir Thomas proposes should be done, and MP III 13 426 11
and so is Sir Thomas; and how glad I should be, if you MP III 13 427 12
But Sir Thomas hopes he will be better to-morrow, and says MP III 13 427 12
His aunt worried him by her cares, and Sir Thomas knew not MP III 14 429 2
Poor Sir Thomas will feel it dreadfully. MP III 14 434 13
I don't know what Sir Thomas may think of such matters; he MP III 15 439 13
but, guided by Sir Thomas, she thought justly on all MP III 16 449 5
letters to and from Sir Thomas, and what she already knew MP III 16 449 7
to some relations of Sir Thomas; a removal which her MP III 16 450 8
to Wimpole Street, Sir Thomas had received a letter from MP III 16 450 8
Sir Thomas was preparing to act upon this letter, without MP III 16 450 9
Sir Thomas set off; Edmund would go with him; and the MP III 16 450 10
Sir Thomas, however, remained yet a little longer in town, MP III 16 451 12
to herself, would be poor consolation to Sir Thomas. MP III 16 452 14
others excited; but Sir Thomas was considering his MP III 16 452 15
Sir Thomas not in the secret of Miss Crawford's character. MP III 16 453 15
Let Sir Thomas trust to his honour and compassion, and it MP III 16 457 29
Crawford, and when Sir Thomas came back she had every MP III 17 461 2
Sir Thomas, poor Sir Thomas, a parent, and conscious of MP III 17 461 4
Here was comfort indeed! and quite as soon as Sir Thomas MP III 17 462 5
their alleviation to Sir Thomas, deadening his sense of MP III 17 462 6
Sir Thomas would not hear of it, and Mrs. Norris's anger MP III 17 465 13
account, though Sir Thomas very solemnly assured her, that MP III 17 465 13
countenance and aid, Sir Thomas saw repeated, and for ever MP III 17 473 31

SIR THOMAS BERTRAM (6)
to captivate Sir Thomas Bertram, of Mansfield Park, in the MP I 1 3 1
Sir Thomas Bertram had interest, which, from principle as MP I 1 3 1
apology to Sir Thomas Bertram, was such an exhibition, MP II 1 182 22
Sir Thomas Bertram's son is somebody; and now, he is in MP II 11 289 34
She is niece to Sir Thomas Bertram; that will be enough MP II 12 293 11
My own sister as a wife, Sir Thomas Bertram as a husband, MP III 5 361 16

SIR THOMAS'S (41)
silence, awed by Sir Thomas's grave looks, and quite MP I 2 14 8
a small house of Sir Thomas's in the village, and consoled MP I 3 23 1
somewhat easier to Sir Thomas's conscience, he could not MP I 3 23 2
"Why, you know Sir Thomas's means will be rather MP I 3 30 54
the others, when Sir Thomas's assurances of their both MP I 4 34 2
him to wait till Sir Thomas's return, and then Sir Thomas MP I 4 36 7
not waiting till Sir Thomas's return in September, for MP I 4 37 9
Sir Thomas's sending away his son, seemed to her so like a MP I 4 38 9
It was some months before Sir Thomas's consent could be MP I 4 39 12
I cannot but think of dear Sir Thomas's delight. MP I 12 118 16
his persuasion of Sir Thomas's disapprobation of the whole, MP I 16 153 3
Every thing seems to depend upon Sir Thomas's return." MP I 17 162 15
of her claims on Sir Thomas's affection was much too MP II 1 176 4
by many fears of Sir Thomas's disapprobation when the MP II 1 179 10
She carried this point, and Sir Thomas's narrative MP II 1 180 12
to catch Sir Thomas's meaning, or diffidence, or delicacy, MP II 1 184 25
fixed--from seeing Sir Thomas's dark brow contract as he MP II 1 184 27
Sir Thomas's look implied, "on your judgment, Edmund, I MP II 1 185 27
pleased with Sir Thomas's good opinion, and saying MP II 1 186 35
the current of Sir Thomas's ideas into a happier channel. MP II 2 188 3
Mr. Yates was beginning now to understand Sir Thomas's MP II 2 191 10
Sir Thomas's return made a striking change in the ways of MP II 3 196 1
And Sir Thomas's wishing just at first to be only with his MP II 3 199 14
was still owing to Sir Thomas's more than toleration of MP II 7 238 1
the odd trick by Sir Thomas's capital play and her own, MP II 7 245 32
she was stopped by Sir Thomas's saying with authority, "I MP II 7 245 34
Whatever effect Sir Thomas's little harangue might really MP II 7 248 47
To be urging her opinion against Sir Thomas's, was a proof MP II 10 275 11
She was attractive, she was modest, she was Sir Thomas's MP II 10 276 13
Miss Crawford saw much of Sir Thomas's thoughts as he MP II 10 276 14
"We miss our two young men," was Sir Thomas's observation MP II 11 284 9
A great deal of good sense followed on Sir Thomas's side, MP II 11 284 10
feelings, before Sir Thomas's politeness and apologies MP II 13 302 9
as these; and upon Sir Thomas's information of her being MP III 4 345 5
Mr. Crawford gone, Sir Thomas's next object was, that he MP III 6 366 1
they were to quit Sir Thomas's carriage, she was able to MP III 7 375 1
circumstance of Sir Thomas's being in Parliament, got into MP III 13 425 6
Sir Thomas's parental solicitude, and high sense of honour MP III 15 442 21
wrote to recommend Sir Thomas's coming to London himself, MP III 16 450 8
was the great supplementary comfort of Sir Thomas's life. MP III 17 465 15
It was a match which Sir Thomas's wishes had even MP III 17 471 29

SIR WALTER (100)
printer's hands; but Sir Walter had improved it by adding, P III 1 3 2
Elliot, Esq., great grandson of the second Sir Walter." P III 1 3 3
4
This friend, and Sir Walter, did not marry, whatever might P III 1 5 7
Be it known then, that Sir Walter, like a good father, (P III 1 5 8
years ago; and Sir Walter might be excused, therefore, in P III 1 6 11
Lady Elliot's death Sir Walter had sought the acquaintance, P III 1 7 14
Sir Walter had resented it. P III 1 8 16
by the family, as Sir Walter considered him unworthy of it: P III 1 8 16
the whole of which Sir Walter found himself obliged to P III 1 10 19
There was only a small part of his estate that Sir Walter P III 1 10 20
hold or his views on Sir Walter, would rather have the P III 2 11 1
all its due; and Sir Walter, independent of his claims as P III 2 11 2
was, as being Sir Walter, in her apprehension entitled to P III 2 11 2
of retrenchment, which was at last submitted to Sir Walter. P III 2 12 3
It did not appear to him that Sir Walter could materially P III 2 13 7
In any other place, Sir Walter might judge for himself; P III 2 13 7
Sir Walter would quit Kellynch-Hall;--and after a very few P III 2 13 8
Sir Walter had at first thought more of London, but Mr. P III 2 14 10
had been for Bath, Sir Walter and Elizabeth were induced P III 2 14 10
It would be too much to expect Sir Walter to descend into P III 2 14 11
neighbourhood for Sir Walter, was certainly much P III 2 15 13
Sir Walter could not have borne the degradation of being P III 2 15 14
approach it again; Sir Walter spurned the idea of its P III 2 15 14
Sir Walter and his family were to remove from the country. P III 2 15 15
"I must take leave to observe, Sir Walter," said Mr. P III 3 17 1
Could not be a better time, Sir Walter, for having a P III 3 17 1
If a rich Admiral were to come in our way, Sir Walter-----" P III 3 17 1
replied Sir Walter, "that's all I have to remark. P III 3 17 2
presume to observe, Sir Walter, that, in the way of P III 3 17 2
3
Therefore, Sir Walter, what I would take leave to suggest P III 3 17 4
Sir Walter only nodded. P III 3 18 5
These valuable pictures of yours, Sir Walter, if you chose P III 3 18 7
"As to all that," rejoined Sir Walter coolly, "supposing I P III 3 18 8
Your interest, Sir Walter, is in pretty safe hands. P III 3 19 10
"Nay, Sir Walter," cried Mrs. Clay, "this is being severe P III 3 20 17
"Then I take it for granted," observed Sir Walter, "that P III 3 22 22
been surprised if Sir Walter had asked more;--had inquired P III 3 22 23
And moreover, Sir Walter, I found she was not quite P III 3 22 25
He had the curacy of Monkford, you know, Sir Walter, some P III 3 23 32
them no service with Sir Walter, he mentioned it no more; P III 3 23 34
It succeeded, however; and though Sir Walter must ever P III 3 24 35
Sir Walter was not very wise; but still he had experience P III 3 24 36
Sir Walter, on being applied to, without actually P III 4 26 2
not but influence Sir Walter, who had besides been P III 5 32 2
Sir Walter, without hesitation, declared the Admiral to be P III 5 32 4
Michaelmas, and as Sir Walter proposed removing to Bath in P III 5 33 5
to go to Bath with Sir Walter and Elizabeth, as a most P III 5 34 11
was to draw Sir Walter, Miss Elliot, and Mrs. Clay to Bath. P III 5 35 18
The party drove off in very good spirits; Sir Walter P III 5 35 18
Miss Anne, Sir Walter and your sister are gone; and what P III 6 42 1
You will tell Sir Walter what we have done, and that Mr. P IV 1 127 28
Sir Walter had taken a very good house in Camden-Place, a P IV 3 137 1
He could refer Sir Walter to all who knew him; and, P IV 3 139 7
an ill-looking man, Sir Walter added) who was living in P IV 3 139 8
tempted Elliot, and Sir Walter was, moreover, assured of P IV 3 139 9
Sir Walter seemed to admit it as complete apology, and P IV 3 139 9
with Sir Walter, nothing to risk by a state of variance. P IV 3 140 11
They were describing him themselves; Sir Walter especially. P IV 3 141 12
Mr. Elliot appeared to think that he (Sir Walter) was P IV 3 141 12
last parted;" but Sir Walter had "not been able to return P IV 3 141 12
Sir Walter thought much of Mrs. Wallis; she was said to be P IV 3 141 13
Modest Sir Walter! P IV 3 142 13
"How is Mary looking?" said Sir Walter, in the height of P IV 3 142 14
Sir Walter talked of his youngest daughter; "Mr. Elliot P IV 3 143 18
When he questioned, Sir Walter and Elizabeth began to P IV 3 144 22
Sir Walter had once been in company with the late viscount, P IV 4 148 12
Sir Walter, however, would choose his own means, and at P IV 4 149 13
While Sir Walter and Elizabeth were assiduously pushing P IV 5 152 1
Sir Walter, Elizabeth and Mrs. Clay returned one morning P IV 5 156 14
was; and Elizabeth was disdainful, and Sir Walter severe. P IV 5 157 14
drawn up near its pavement!" observed Sir Walter.-- P IV 5 157 19
the set absent; for Sir Walter and Elizabeth had not only P IV 5 158 21
"What is this?" cried Sir Walter. P IV 6 162 3
Sir Walter wanted to know whether the Crofts travelled P IV 6 165 9
"Gout and decrepitude!" said Sir Walter. P IV 6 166 12
"I suspect," said Sir Walter coolly, "that Admiral Croft P IV 6 166 15
This was Sir Walter and Elizabeth's share of interest in P IV 6 166 17
Sir Walter, his two daughters, and Mrs. Clay, were the P IV 8 181 1
Sir Walter and his two ladies stepped forward to meet her. P IV 8 184 17
"A well-looking man," said Sir Walter, "a very well- P IV 8 188 38
Before Sir Walter had reached this point, Anne's eyes had P IV 8 188 41
"He had been introduced to Sir Walter and your sister P IV 9 200 57
"Give me joy: I have got rid of Sir Walter and Miss. P IV 9 203 72
with Miss Elliot and Sir Walter as long ago as September, P IV 9 206 88
added another motive) to watch Sir Walter and Mrs. Clay. P IV 9 207 90
an opportunity of bringing him and Sir Walter together. P IV 10 213 5
as much to Sir Walter as she would have done otherwise. P IV 10 213 10
"And mine," added Sir Walter. P IV 10 215 16
in that house, Sir Walter and Elizabeth were able to rise P IV 10 216 18
So much was pretty soon understood; but till Sir Walter P IV 10 216 18
was thrown open for Sir Walter and Miss Elliot, whose P IV 10 226 63
The card was pointedly given, and Sir Walter and Elizabeth P IV 10 226 64
his lectures and restrictions on her designs on Sir Walter. P IV 10 228 70
Sir Walter made no objection, and Elizabeth did nothing P IV 12 248 1
Sir Walter indeed, though he had no affection for Anne, P IV 12 248 2
name, enabled Sir Walter at last to prepare his pen with a P IV 12 248 2
best hope of keeping Sir Walter single by the watchfulness P IV 12 250 7
sake, the possibility of scheming longer for Sir Walter. P IV 12 250 8
being the wife of Sir Walter, he may not be wheedled and P IV 12 250 8
It cannot be doubted that Sir Walter and Elizabeth were P IV 12 251 9

SIR WALTER ELLIOT (11)
Sir Walter Elliot, of Kellynch-Hall, in Somersetshire, was P III 1 3 1
and the Sir Walter Elliot, who united these gifts, was the P III 1 4 5
but what Sir Walter Elliot was imperiously called on to do; P III 1 9 19
dignity of Sir Walter Elliot will be very far from P III 2 12 4
me, but Sir Walter Elliot has eyes upon him which it may P III 3 17 4
I venture to hint, that Sir Walter Elliot cannot be half P III 3 19 10
tenants of Sir Walter Elliot: an extraordinary taste, P III 3 23 34
In all their dealings and intercourse, Sir Walter Elliot P III 3 24 36
Heir to Sir Walter Elliot!-- P III 12 106 16
but in Bath, Sir Walter Elliot and his family will always P IV 4 151 19
and dignity which ought to belong to Sir Walter Elliot. P IV 4 151 21

SIR WALTER ELLIOT'S (2)
Elliot's character; vanity of person and of situation. P III 1 4 5
a proper match for Sir Walter Elliot's eldest daughter. P III 1 8 17

SIR WALTER'S (18)
of Somerset," and Sir Walter's hand-writing again in this P III 1 3 3
4
Walter's continuing in singleness requires explanation.-- P III 1 5 8
apprehension of the state required in its possessor. P III 1 9 19
desirous of saving Sir Walter's feelings, as solicitous P III 2 11 2
in the reality of Sir Walter's retrenching, and who was P III 2 13 7
and to Sir Walter's feelings they must have been dreadful. P III 2 14 11
stronger heads than Sir Walter's have found too much.-- P III 2 15 13
daughter's; but Sir Walter's remark was, soon afterwards-- P III 3 19 13
14
anxiety to bespeak Sir Walter's goodwill towards a naval P III 3 21 18
Shepherd observed, Sir Walter's concerns could not be kept P III 3 21 18
"And who is Admiral Croft?" was Sir Walter's cold P III 3 21 19
secret of Sir Walter's estimate of the dues of a tenant. P III 3 23 34
country, only to Sir Walter's, and of good character and P III 4 28 7

intelligence of Sir Walter's being settled there had of — P IV 3 138 6
illness of Sir Walter's at the same time, there had been — P IV 4 148 12
in Gay-Street, perfectly to Sir Walter's satisfaction. — P IV 6 168 23
general idea among Sir Walter's acquaintance, of her — P IV 9 206 88
strenuous opposer of Sir Walter's making a second match. — P IV 9 208 92

SIR WILLIAM (30)

Sir William and Lady Lucas are determined to go, merely on — PP I 1 4 24
Sir William had been delighted with him. — PP I 3 9 1
Lucas was his neighbour, till Sir William thus began. — PP I 6 25 25
Sir William only smiled. — PP I 6 25 28
discomposure to Sir William, "indeed, sir, I have not the — PP I 6 26 38
Elizabeth was determined; nor did Sir William at all shake — PP I 6 26 40
What an agreeable man Sir William is, Mr. Bingley--is not — PP I 9 44 27
Sir William could not have interrupted any two people in — PP I 18 93 26
Sir William and Lady Lucas were speedily applied to for — PP I 22 122 3
likely to live; and Sir William gave it as his decided — PP I 22 122 3
Sir William, how can you tell such a story?-- — PP I 23 126 2
congratulations to Sir William, in which she was readily — PP I 23 126 4
a great deal while Sir William remained; but no sooner had — PP I 23 126 5
she could speak to Sir William or Lady Lucas without being — PP I 23 127 5
Pray go to see them, with Sir William and Maria. — PP II 3 149 26
She was to accompany Sir William and his second daughter. — PP II 4 151 1
back; and while Sir William accompanied him, Charlotte — PP II 5 156 5
the ladies; and Sir William, to Elizabeth's high diversion, — PP II 5 158 19
happened," replied Sir William, "from that knowledge of — PP II 6 160 3
and even Sir William did not look perfectly calm.-- — PP II 6 161 9
In spite of having been at St. James's, Sir William was so — PP II 6 162 11
by him, and then by Sir William, who was now enough — PP II 6 163 14
Lady Catherine, Sir William, and Mr. and Mrs. Collins sat — PP II 6 166 41
Sir William did not say much. — PP II 6 166 41
Sir William staid only a week at Hunsford; but his visit — PP II 7 168 1
While Sir William was with them, Mr. Collins devoted his — PP II 7 168 1
for the loss of Sir William, and there being only one card — PP II 7 169 5
If he did shrug his shoulders, it was not till Sir William — PP III 18 384 26
He cannot bear the idea of not being Sir William. — P IV 9 207 90
caressed at last into making her the wife of Sir William. — P IV 12 250 8

SIR WILLIAM LUCAS (7)

Sir William Lucas had been formerly in trade in Meryton, — PP I 5 18 1
Lucas was his neighbour, till Sir William thus began. — PP I 6 25 25
At that moment Sir William Lucas appeared close to them, — PP I 18 92 22
it, when Sir William Lucas himself appeared, sent by his — PP I 23 126 1
Sir William Lucas, and his daughter Maria, a good humoured — PP II 4 152 4
I defy even Sir William Lucas himself, to produce a more — PP III 11 330 8
He could even listen to Sir William Lucas, when he — PP III 18 384 26

SIR WILLIAM LUCAS'S (3)

It was at Sir William Lucas's, where a large party were — PP I 6 24 13
by Sir William Lucas's accidental information, that — PP II 12 197 5
I assure you it is much larger than Sir William Lucas's." — PP III 14 352 10

SIR WILLIAM'S (6)

the other night at Sir William's in his regimentals." — PP I 7 29 12
by Darcy; but Sir William's allusion to his friend seemed — PP I 18 92 24
and said, "Sir William's interruption has made me forget — PP I 18 93 24 25

treatment; but Sir William's good breeding carried him — PP I 23 126 3
absurdities, but she had known Sir William's too long. — PP II 4 152 4
side, and as many bows on Sir William's, they departed. — PP II 6 166 42

SIRNAME (1)

forty, with little to live on, and no sirname of dignity. — P IV 5 158 20

SISTER (763)

a sister whom I have so long desired to be acquainted with. — LS 1 243 1
me. Yr most obliged & affec: sister S. Vernon. — LS 1 244 1
My dear sister I congratulate you & Mr Vernon on being — LS 4 248 1
Manwaring's sister, deprived an amiable girl of her lover. — LS 4 248 1
I mean to win my sister in law's heart through her — LS 5 250 2
wife & sister, & lamentations on the cruelty of his fate. — LS 5 250 3
His sister too, is I hope convinced how little the — LS 10 257 1
that the advice of a sister could prevent a young man's — LS 10 258 2
to overcome my sister in law's reserve, & listening to her — LS 10 258 3
I am to thank my sister I suppose, for having represented — LS 14 263 1
justice to us all; but my sister is unhappily prejudiced — LS 14 264 2
to the disadvantage of my sister, as to persuade her that — LS 14 264 3
If my sister in the security of retirement, with as little — LS 14 264 3
said she, as you my dear sister must be sensible, to treat — LS 15 267 6
to you my dear sister, tho' to me as a mother, it is — LS 20 276 5
I am sure my dear sister, you will excuse my remaining — LS 20 277 5
sister I beleive wanted only opportunity for doing so. — LS 22 281 3
"I am at least very far from regretting it, my dear sister, — LS 24 288 11
"Of what use my dear sister, could be any application to — LS 24 289 12
You must not question me however my dear sister, too — LS 24 289 12
Escuse me, my dearest sister, for thus trespassing on your — LS 24 290 13
a chance of obtaining her sister in law's consent to it. — LS 42 311 2
to her brother and sister, her sense of their kindness, & — LS 42 311 2
her next sister, sally, could say it better than she did. — NA I 1 14 1
this time the intimate friend and confidante of her sister. — NA I 2 19 3
and my sister has often trusted me in the choice of a gown. — NA I 3 28 38
You must be a great comfort to your sister, sir." — NA I 3 28 39
I have heard my sister say so forty times, when she has — NA I 3 28 45
her any where for his sister!" was repeated by them all, — NA I 4 32 5
be as handsome as their sister, imitating her air, and — NA I 4 34 8
quite as long as his sister, was very importunate with — NA I 8 52 2
up without your dear sister for all the world; for if I — NA I 8 52 2
her, turned again to his sister and whispered, "my dear — NA I 8 52 2
guessed to be his sister; thus unthinkingly throwing away — NA I 8 53 3
never mentioned a wife, and he had acknowledged a sister. — NA I 8 53 3
her friend from James--"it is Mr. Tilney's sister." — NA I 8 56 15
"There," cried Isabella, "you hear what your sister says, — NA I 8 58 25
not really suffer his sister and his friend to be exposed — NA I 9 66 31
having missed such a meeting with both brother and sister. — NA I 9 69 51
by the brother and sister they they should join in a walk, — NA I 10 80 61
can hear of; but here is your sister says she will not go." — NA I 11 84 21
late to go on to-day; your sister thinks so as well as I. — NA I 11 88 54
Did not they tell me that Mr. Tilney and his sister were — NA I 12 93 5
Tilney, why were you less generous than your sister? — NA I 12 94 11
only five minutes for my sister; breaking the promise I — NA I 14 107 9
Morland, he is treating you exactly as he does his sister. — NA I 14 107 14
"While, in fact," cried his sister, "it ought only to be — NA I 14 108 17
by the capital pen of a sister author;--and to her — NA I 14 111 29
And you, Miss Morland--my stupid sister has mistaken all — NA I 14 113 39
The fears of the sister have added to the weakness of the — NA I 14 113 39
intolerably rude to your sister, and a great brute in your — NA I 14 113 40
quitting it to call her sister, Catherine took the — NA I 15 116 1
effusion of pity for her sister Anne, whom she represented — NA I 15 116 2
The happiness of having such a sister was their first — NA I 15 118 8
"Yes; I have promised your sister to be with her, if — NA I 15 123 33
of either of brother or sister; and she did not credit — NA II 1 131 14
affection of Isabella was to be secured to her in a sister. — NA II 2 141 11
did not make amends for this thoughtlessness in his sister. — NA II 3 148 29
His sister, he said, was uncomfortably circumstanced--she — NA II 5 157 5
"Your sister taught me; I cannot tell how. — NA II 7 174 7
Has my sister a pleasant mode of instruction?" — NA II 7 174 10
firmness, "I have no sister, you know--and though Henry-- — NA II 7 180 34
"To have so kind-hearted, so affectionate a sister," — NA II 10 204 14
The brother and sister looked at each other. — NA II 10 205 30
His brother and sister knew not what to think. — NA II 11 209 5
that his father and sister loved and even wished her to — NA II 13 221 6
old, who expected a brother or sister in every carriage. — NA II 14 233 8
Far from comprehending him or his sister in their father's — NA II 15 242 7
had a constant companion and housekeeper in his sister. — SS I 1 3 1
Margaret, the other sister, was a good-humoured well- — SS I 1 7 14
wishes of his mother and sister, who longed to see him — SS I 3 15 6
day to make on the difference between him and his sister. — SS I 3 16 7
expect in the man who could seriously attach my sister. — SS I 3 17 18
I felt for my sister most severely. — SS I 3 17 18
mistake, she honoured her sister for that blind partiality — SS I 4 19 3
She would not wound the feelings of her sister on any — SS I 4 19 5
Marianne was rejoiced to find her sister so easily pleased. — SS I 4 20 8
tried to explain the real state of the case to her sister. — SS I 4 21 11
Elinor had given her real opinion to her sister. — SS I 4 22 18
which her mother and sister still considered as certain. — SS I 4 22 18
when perceived by his sister, to make her uneasy; and at — SS I 4 23 19
my younger sister in spite of all this tumbling down hills. — SS I 9 44 23
peculiarly delighted her sister, of saying too much what — SS I 10 48 9
actually excited by her sister; and that however a general — SS I 10 49 12
consolation for the total indifference of her sister. — SS I 11 55 7
with a faint smile, "your sister, I understand, does not — SS I 11 55 8
by saying-- "does your sister make no distinction in her — SS I 11 56 14 15

greatly resembled your sister, who thought and judged like — SS I 11 57 17
a piece of news to her sister, which in spite of all that — SS I 12 58 1
without hesitation, and told her sister of it in raptures. — SS I 12 58 1
and in his addressing her sister by her christian name — SS I 12 59 7
to her eldest sister, when they were next by themselves. — SS I 12 60 8
always displayed in a way so satisfactory to her sister. — SS I 12 61 15
her sister, and saying, "I must not tell, may I, Elinor?" — SS I 12 61 15
I hope it is not to say that your sister is worse." — SS I 13 63 10
thought, she came to her sister again, and said with great — SS I 13 69 76
May be his sister is worse at Avignon, and has sent for — SS I 14 70 2
silence of her sister and Willoughby on the subject, which — SS I 14 71 3
place between him and her sister;--the distress in which — SS I 15 77 19
Has he been acting a part in his behaviour to your sister — SS I 15 80 38
He had just parted from my sister, had seen her leave him — SS I 15 81 43
between Edward and her sister was but a continuation of — SS I 16 87 23
"Marianne," cried her sister, "how can you say so? — SS I 16 88 40
Elinor smiled again, to hear her sister describing so — SS I 17 91 15
"You have not been able then to bring your sister over to — SS I 17 94 40
know my sister well enough to understand what she means? — SS I 17 95 49
But, in return, your sister must allow me to feel no more — SS I 18 98 8
with amazement at Edward, with compassion at her sister. — SS I 18 98 9
as a free gift from her sister, Elinor was conscious must — SS I 18 98 13
had she known how little offence it had given her sister. — SS I 18 99 14
that sister, in spite of this mortifying conviction. — SS I 19 104 11
Only look, sister, how delightful every thing is! — SS I 19 107 24
"I have got such a favour to ask of you and your sister. — SS I 20 112 29
I know why you inquire about him, very well; your sister — SS I 20 114 44
talking of my brother and sister, and one thing and — SS I 20 115 50
Mama says he was in love with your sister too.-- — SS I 20 115 56
wherever he goes, and so you may tell your sister. — SS I 20 116 58
And I am so glad your sister is going to be well married! — SS I 20 116 60
"Yes, a great while; ever since my sister married.-- — SS I 20 116 62
"And Sir John too," cried the elder sister, "what a — SS I 21 122 15
think some apology necessary for the freedom of her sister. — SS I 21 123 24
looking ashamed of her sister, "that there are not as many — SS I 21 123 27
"Lord! Anne," cried her sister, "you can talk of nothing — SS I 21 124 31
It was there our acquaintance begun, for my sister and me — SS I 22 130 28
"No, sister," cried Lucy, "you are mistaken there, our — SS II 2 148 21
Lucy bit her lip, and looked angrily at her sister. — SS II 2 149 24
To be sure, your brother and sister will ask you to come — SS II 2 151 38
varying complexion of her sister, and the animated look — SS II 3 153 1
to such a scheme, if her elder sister would come into it. — SS II 3 154 3
who now understood her sister, and saw to what — SS II 3 154 6
herself, that if her sister persisted in going, she would — SS II 3 156 15
with the plan, and her sister exhilarated by it in look, — SS II 3 158 20
his behaviour to her sister with such zealous attention, — SS II 4 159 1
to open the eyes of her sister; should it be otherwise, — SS II 4 159 1
exclamation of delight exclusively addressed to her sister. — SS II 4 160 2
much pleasure to her sister, and this agitation increased — SS II 4 161 6
a man so partial to her sister should perceive that she — SS II 4 162 8
"Is your sister ill?" said he. — SS II 4 162 9
Restless and dissatisfied every where, her sister could — SS II 4 165 24
within herself, regarding her sister with uneasiness. — SS II 4 165 29
time with much concern his continued regard for her sister. — SS II 5 168 12
her sister, all, and more than all, their former agitation. — SS II 5 169 15
a moment's glance at her sister when they returned was — SS II 5 169 16
in persuading her sister to go, for still she had seen — SS II 5 170 28
her sister was concerned, impatiently expected its opening. — SS II 5 172 40
the observation of "your sister looks unwell to-day," or " — SS II 5 172 40
unwell to-day," or "your sister seems out of spirits," he — SS II 5 172 40
avowal of his love for her sister, affected her very much. — SS II 5 173 45
The real state of things between Willoughby and her sister — SS II 5 173 45
of emotion, "to your sister I wish all imaginable — SS II 5 174 46
him instantly, had not her sister caught hold of her. — SS II 6 176 3
But the feelings of her sister were instantly expressed. — SS II 6 176 7
She instantly begged her sister would entreat Lady — SS II 6 178 15
of being alone, her sister then left her, and while she — SS II 6 178 16
the affections of her sister from the first, without any — SS II 6 178 17
did not I know that your sister came to town with me on — SS II 7 182 10
immediate distress of her sister, forgot that she had — SS II 7 184 16
Mrs. Jennings, on account of her sister being indisposed. — SS II 7 184 16
"I only wish," replied her sister, "there were any thing I — SS II 7 185 18
The first, which was what her sister had sent him on their — SS II 7 186 37
triumph, my dear sister, by seeing how nobly the — SS II 7 189 51
and more hysterical, her sister could with difficulty keep — SS II 7 191 65
Marianne, to the surprise of her sister, determined on — SS II 8 192 5
she ate more and was calmer than her sister had expected. — SS II 8 193 6
which her sister could not make or return for herself. — SS II 8 193 7
Had not Elinor, in the sad countenance of her sister, seen — SS II 8 193 7
misery, and a sign to her sister not to follow her, she — SS II 8 193 7
What now," after pausing a moment--"your poor sister is — SS II 8 195 14
slightest allusion to what has passed, before my sister. — SS II 8 195 17
of; and as for your sister, I am sure I would not mention — SS II 8 196 18
has broken no positive engagement with my sister." — SS II 8 196 19
It will be all to one a better match for your sister. — SS II 8 196 22
me," was all the notice that her sister received from her. — SS II 8 197 24
tasted, so I have brought a glass of it for your sister. — SS II 8 197 27
Do take it to your sister." — SS II 8 198 27
might be as reasonably tried on herself as on her sister. — SS II 8 198 29
her of his good information, inquired after her sister. — SS II 8 198 31
to distrust itself, "and your sister--how did she -----" — SS II 8 199 39
But your sister does not--I think you said so--she does — SS II 8 200 41
injustice to which her sister was often led in her opinion — SS II 9 201 4
could not forgive her sister for esteeming him so lightly. — SS II 9 204 17
as resembling, in some measure, your sister Marianne." — SS II 9 205 22
as the attachment of your sister to Mr. Willoughby, and it — SS II 9 205 24
under a similar confinement, was my unfortunate sister. — SS II 9 207 26
"Your sister, I hope, cannot be offended," said he, by the — SS II 9 208 28
been less gay or less happy in the smiles of your sister? — SS II 9 209 30
have felt on seeing your sister as fond of him as ever, — SS II 9 210 32
To suffer you all to be so deceived; to see your sister-- — SS II 9 210 32
dividing Elinor from her sister, he put an end to his — SS II 9 211 43
by Miss Dashwood to her sister, as they very soon were, — SS II 10 212 1
gave more pain to her sister than could have been — SS II 10 212 1
would bring good to her sister; and Elinor, on the other — SS II 10 214 7
Her carefulness in guarding her sister from ever hearing — SS II 10 214 8
painful office of informing her sister that he was married. — SS II 10 216 16
them, to prevail on her sister, who had never yet left the — SS II 10 217 18
pity to have went away before your brother and sister came. — SS II 10 217 21
with your brother and sister, Miss Dashwood, when they — SS II 10 218 30
"I am sorry we cannot see your sister, Miss Dashwood," — SS II 10 219 37
My sister will be equally sorry to miss the pleasure of — SS II 10 219 38
Her sister was perhaps laid down upon the bed, or in her — SS II 10 219 40
sister, was of advantage in governing those of the other. — SS II 10 219 42
have a brother and I a sister settling at the same time. — SS II 11 224 26
to Fanny," said he, as he walked back with his sister. — SS II 11 228 53
Your sister need not have any scruple even of visiting her, — SS II 11 228 53

not elegant, and her sister not even genteel, she was as SS II 12 230 8
to a party given by his sister; and to see him for the SS II 12 231 10
"These are done by my eldest sister," said he; "and you, SS II 12 234 27
not bear to see a sister slighted in the smallest point. SS II 12 236 38
general behaviour to her sister, seemed, to her, to SS II 12 236 39
40

such good health as her sister,--she is very nervous,--she SS II 12 236 43
No pride, no hauteur, and your sister just the same--all SS II 13 239 6
Mrs. Ferrars is a charming woman, and so is your sister. SS II 13 239 9
half his time with his sister--besides, Lady Middleton and SS II 13 240 15
Mrs. Ferrars and your sister were both so good to say more SS II 13 240 15
I am sure if ever you tell your sister what I think of her, SS II 13 240 15
encouragement to hope that she should tell her sister. SS II 13 240 16
most high-minded fortitude, before she went to her sister. SS II 13 241 23
and a voice that expressed the affection of a sister. SS II 13 242 23
of pity for her sister to Elinor, and more than once dropt SS II 14 247 4
brother and sister, to a small musical party at her house. SS II 14 248 6
the ill-humour of his mother and sister would have begun. SS II 14 250 12
in music than his eldest sister, his mind was equally at SS II 14 252 20
she nor your brother or sister suspected a word of the SS III 1 258 7
so, away she went to your sister, who was sitting all SS III 1 258 7
very hardly; for your sister scolded like any fury, and SS III 1 259 7
I declare, I have no patience with your sister; and I hope, SS III 1 259 7
left the house, for your sister was sure she would be in SS III 1 259 7
has a sister out of place, that would fit them exactly." SS III 1 260 7
for her sister, or any resentment against Edward. SS III 1 260 10
I have had to contend against the unkindness of his sister, SS III 1 264 29
Such advances towards heroism in her sister, made Elinor SS III 1 265 33
"Your sister," he continued, "has suffered dreadfully. SS III 1 265 36
but not as her sister had hoped, to urge her to exertion SS III 2 270 2
How could you behave so unfairly by your sister?" SS III 2 274 19
And your brother and sister were not very kind! SS III 2 275 22
in a fright for fear your sister should ask us for the SS III 2 275 22
to take you and your sister away, and Mrs. Jennings should SS III 2 275 25
Betty's sister would never do for them now." SS III 2 277 28
towards them since her sister had been known to be unhappy, SS III 3 279 1
besides, you must long to tell your sister all about it." SS III 4 286 11
"I have just been thinking of Betty's sister, my dear. SS III 4 287 21
22

seeing you and your sister; especially as it will most SS III 4 288 27
"Of one thing, my dear sister," kindly taking her hand, SS III 5 297 31
find that Elinor and her sister were so soon to leave town, SS III 5 300 38
grateful for bringing her sister away unseen by Willoughby SS III 6 302 5
in his address to her sister and herself, that she knew SS III 6 304 15
days would restore her sister to health, yet, by SS III 7 307 3
was above with her sister, &c. she urged him so strongly SS III 7 309 5
Her sister, however, still sanguine, was willing to SS III 7 310 9
more disturbed; and her sister, who watched with SS III 7 310 10
11

to take her place by her sister, she hastened down to the SS III 7 311 14
The distress of her sister too, particularly a favourite, SS III 7 313 20
bent over her sister to watch--she hardly knew for what. SS III 7 314 22
on a recovery in her sister even surpassing his SS III 7 314 22
She continued by the side of her sister with little SS III 7 315 25
not to be kept away from her sister an unnecessary instant. SS III 7 315 27
Jennings's maid with her sister, she hurried down stairs. SS III 7 316 30
"Your sister," said he, with abruptness, a moment SS III 8 318 10
something like forgiveness from Ma--from your sister." SS III 8 319 23
for my behaviour to your sister, or what diabolical motive SS III 8 319 29
To attach myself to your sister, therefore, was not a SS III 8 320 32
The sight of your dear sister, however, was really SS III 8 324 42
that you and your sister were to be there, I should have SS III 8 327 55
With my head and heart full of your sister, I was forced SS III 8 327 55
Your sister is certainly better, certainly out of danger?" SS III 8 327 57
Your sister wrote to me again, you know the very next SS III 8 328 61
speak in this way, either of Mrs. Willoughby or my sister. SS III 8 329 64
"Will you repeat to your sister when she is recovered, SS III 8 330 67
me, and concern for your sister, could not resist the SS III 8 330 69
What I felt on hearing that your sister was dying--and SS III 8 330 69
little scruple, left her sister to misery, was likely to SS III 8 331 70
was the general result, to think even of her sister. SS III 9 333 1
made her only fearful of betraying herself to her sister. SS III 9 333 3
But her promise of relating it to her sister was SS III 9 335 5
the reward of her sister was due, and wished any thing SS III 9 335 5
is exactly the very one to make your sister happy. SS III 9 338 20
as he looked at her sister, the probable recurrence of SS III 10 340 2
"How then," asked her sister, "would you account for his SS III 10 345 21
should I have left you, my nurse, my friend, my sister!-- SS III 10 346 28
withdrew from her sister and walked slowly up stairs. SS III 10 348 34
cheerful and easy, her sister could safely trust to the SS III 11 352 19
as her love for her sister, was of a kind to give her SS III 13 363 7
sincere well-wisher, friend, and sister, Lucy ferrars. SS III 13 365 14
In a sister it is bad enough, but in a wife!--how I have SS III 13 365 17
line to Oxford, that his sister and I both think a letter SS III 13 371 39
in the manner pointed out by their brother and sister. SS III 13 371 40
"I will not say that I am disappointed, my dear sister," SS III 14 375 9
& her eldest sister, whose delight in a ball was not W 315 1
thus instructed & cautioned her inexperienc'd sister.-- W 315 1
"Dear sister, I beg your pardon, if I have unthinkingly W 316 2
in silence--but her sister after a short pause went on--" W 316 2
Could a sister do such a thing?-- W 316 2
do any thing than be teacher at a school--said her sister. W 318 2
in mind of her eldest sister, & sometimes I see a look of W 324 3
he had two brothers & a sister, that they & their mama all W 331 11
Among these was Mr Howard--his sister leaning on his arm-- W 333 13
"My eldest sister is the only one at home--& she could not W 334 13
of bringing from her sister; but to which he must observe W 338 17
be pleased with the opportunity of seeing your sister."-- W 339 18
that his sister might be allow'd to send Emma the name of W 347 21
to bring her home & wished to see their sister Emma.-- W 348 23
On meeting her long-absent sister, as on every occasion of W 349 23
than on welcoming a sister, who was no longer likely to W 349 24
She saw that her sister in law despised her immediately.-- W 350 24
was better to look at her sister in law's finery than W 353 26
evident vexation of her sister in law, Emma (tho' in no W 353 26
My kind brother & sister brought me home this very morng.-- W 356 28
she supposed her sister in law's feelings at that moment.-- W 357 28
"Speculation I beleive, said Elizth--my sister recommends W 358 28
intirely from her sister, she was half the morning in the W 360 30
expressed to her sister how very much she admired him. PP I 4 14 1
of temper than her sister, and with a judgment too PP I 4 15 11
Mrs. Hurst and her sister allowed it to be so--but still PP I 4 17 16
hardly excepting even her sister, and could not like them; PP I 6 21 1
Bingley likes your sister undoubtedly; but he may never do PP I 6 22 2
attentions to her sister, Elizabeth was far from PP I 6 23 12
at the instrument by her sister Mary, who having, in PP I 6 25 23
She had a sister married to a Mr. Phillips, who had been a PP I 7 28 2
Her enquiries after her sister were not very favourably PP I 7 33 43
Miss Bingley was engrossed by Mr. Darcy, her sister PP I 8 35 2
about the country, because her sister had a cold? PP I 8 36 5
not wish to see your sister make such an exhibition." PP I 8 36 7
"It shews an affection for her sister that is very PP I 8 36 11
"That is capital," added her sister, and they both laughed PP I 8 37 17
it, and making her sister the excuse, said she would amuse PP I 8 37 21
"In nursing your sister I am sure you have pleasure," said PP I 8 37 25
Mr. Bingley and his eldest sister, to observe the game. PP I 8 38 39
Elizabeth joined them again only to say that her sister PP I 8 40 59
attention might be paid to the sick lady and her sister. PP I 8 40 59
My sister, I am sure, will not hear of her removal." PP I 9 41 4
His sister was less delicate, and directed her eye towards PP I 9 43 26
and forced his younger sister to be civil also, and say PP I 9 45 35
engagement; and when your sister is recovered, you shall PP I 9 45 37

calling off his attention by messages to his sister. PP I 10 47 1
"Pray tell your sister that I long to see her." PP I 10 47 9
"Tell your sister I am delighted to hear of her PP I 10 48 15
Mrs. Hurst sang with her sister, and while they were thus PP I 10 51 46
Elizabeth ran up to her sister, and seeing her well PP I 11 54 1
Her sister made not the smallest objection, and the piano PP I 11 58 34
if Mr. Bingley and his sister pressed them to stay longer, PP I 12 59 1
of one sister much exceeded her affection for the other. PP I 12 59 2
was not forgotten; every sister except Mary agreed to go PP I 15 71 6
she could no more explain such behaviour than her sister. PP I 15 74 12
careful guardian of his sister; and you will hear him PP I 16 82 41
her affection for his sister and her praise of himself, if PP I 16 83 56
(glancing at her sister and Bingley,) shall take place. PP I 18 92 23
Your sister has been talking to me about him, and asking PP I 18 94 45
She then sought her eldest sister, who had undertaken to PP I 18 95 48
almost entirely on her sister and Mr. Bingley, and the PP I 18 98 63
to the care of their sister, that she might not be obliged PP I 18 99 63
it for Bingley and her sister that some of the exhibition PP I 18 101 72
Mrs. Hurst and her sister scarcely opened their mouths PP I 18 102 75
"Mr. Darcy is impatient to see his sister, and to confess PP I 21 117 14
we dare to entertain of her being hereafter our sister. PP I 21 117 14
nor wishes me to be her sister; that she is perfectly PP I 21 118 15
"But, my dear sister, can I be happy, even supposing the PP I 21 119 23
She represented to her sister as forcibly as possible what PP I 21 120 29
with fonder regard to her sister, of whose rectitude and PP I 23 128 9
Her heart was divided between concern for her sister, and PP II 1 133 3
Elizabeth looked at her sister with incredulous solicitude, PP II 1 134 6
What sister would think herself at liberty to do it, PP II 1 137 24
"So, Lizzy," said he one day, "your sister is crossed in PP II 1 137 27
superior to his sister as well by nature as education. PP II 2 139 2
had all been very ill-used since she last saw her sister. PP II 2 139 3
But, Lizzy! Oh, sister! it is very hard to think that she PP II 2 140 4
The lucases are very artful people indeed, sister. PP II 2 140 4
with her, made her sister a slight answer, and in PP II 2 140 5
But does not Jane correspond with the sister? PP II 2 141 14
sister, that they did not once sit down to a family dinner. PP II 2 142 18
Jane had already written a few lines to her sister to PP II 3 147 20
The letter which she wrote on this occasion to her sister, PP II 3 147 25
But, my dear sister, though the event has proved you right, PP II 3 148 26
dear as he is to his sister, whatever anxiety she may feel PP II 3 148 26
that Jane would no longer be duped, by the sister at least. PP II 3 149 27
soon marry Mr. Darcy's sister, as, by Wickham's account, PP II 3 149 27
Their first subject was her sister; and she was more PP II 4 152 6
for she had seen her sister looking so well as to banish PP II 5 155 1
him, Charlotte took her sister and friend over the house, PP II 5 156 5
will include you and my sister Maria in every invitation PP II 5 157 7
"my eldest sister has been in town these three months. PP II 7 171 10
11

But I will not be alarmed though your sister does play so PP II 8 174 13
of Charlotte and her sister, just returned from their walk. PP II 9 179 26
But, perhaps his sister does as well for the present, and, PP II 10 184 17
partly by the wish of retaining Mr. Bingley for his sister. PP II 10 187 40
perhaps for ever, the happiness of a most beloved sister?" PP II 11 190 10
friend from your sister, or that I rejoice in my success. PP II 11 191 15
his friend's marrying her sister, and which must appear at PP II 11 193 31
Mr. Bingley from your sister,--and the other, that I had, PP II 12 196 5
eldest sister, to any other young woman in the country.-- PP II 12 197 5
attentions to your sister had given rise to a general PP II 12 197 5
Your sister I also watched.-- PP II 12 197 5
Your superior knowledge of your sister must make the PP II 12 197 5
on you and your eldest sister, than it is honourable to PP II 12 198 5
My sister, who is more than ten years my junior, was left PP II 12 201 5
sister as to prove him capable of some amiable feeling. PP II 13 207 6
generous candour of my sister, and gratified my vanity, in PP II 13 208 8
The compliment to herself and her sister, was not unfelt. PP II 13 209 11
before she told her sister of Mr. Darcy's proposals. PP II 15 217 17
of Bingley, which might only grieve her sister farther. PP II 15 217 17
it from me, my dear sister, to depreciate such pleasures. PP II 16 222 23
particular in which her sister was concerned, and PP II 17 224 1
too! and having to relate such a thing to his sister! PP II 17 225 12
On the contrary every particular relative to his sister, PP II 17 226 23
her sister how sincerely she had been valued by his friend. PP II 17 227 25
I told my sister Philips so the other day. PP II 17 227 27
Had she known that her sister sought to tear her from such PP II 18 232 23
home she had a mother and sister whose constant repinings PP II 19 237 3
were removed, her other sister, from whose disposition PP II 19 237 3
correspondence with her sister, there was still less to be PP II 19 238 5
great pleasure in talking of her master and his sister. PP III 1 248 23
"Whatever can give his sister any pleasure, is sure to be PP III 1 250 45
sister to your acquaintance during your stay at Lambton?" PP III 1 256 63
His wish of introducing his sister to her, was a PP III 1 257 65
all, of his wishing her to be acquainted with his sister. PP III 1 259 77
Mr. Darcy would bring his sister to visit her, the very PP III 2 260 1
naturally flew to her sister; and Oh! how ardently did she PP III 2 262 8
between them that could justify the hopes of his sister. PP III 2 262 8
Mr. Darcy called on his sister to join him in expressing PP III 2 263 11
hearing her speak of her sister, was pleased; and on this PP III 2 264 12
of her friends, and bent on making her known to his sister. PP III 2 265 16
he was anxious for his sister and herself to get PP III 3 269 8
looking at her, and his sister overcome with confusion, PP III 3 269 10
to him some part of what she had been saying to his sister. PP III 3 270 12
They talked of his sister, his friends, his house, his PP III 3 272 20
was over, and her sister justified by the receipt of two PP III 4 273 1
"By this time, my dearest sister, you have received my PP III 4 274 5
My youngest sister has left all her friends--has eloped;-- PP III 4 277 11
I was to judge as your eldest sister does of the matter. PP III 5 282 1
Her sister, however, assured her, of her being perfectly PP III 5 286 32
Though her brother and sister were persuaded that there PP III 5 288 40
the loss of her favourite sister, or the anger which she PP III 5 289 41
"Perhaps it would have been better;" replied her sister. PP III 5 291 56
great consolation of his sister, who considered it as the PP III 6 294 2
lagged behind, while her sister, panting for breath, came PP III 7 301 7
8

of yourself and my sister; and, moreover, to enter into an PP III 7 302 14
then, as we have thought him;" said her sister. PP III 7 303 16
on his side on our sister, we shall exactly know what Mr. PP III 7 305 36
I will write to my sister Gardiner about them directly. PP III 7 306 44
and tell the good, good news to my sister Phillips. PP III 7 307 49
justly expected for her sister; in looking back to what PP III 7 307 51
with their fears for her sister; for since her marriage PP III 8 311 11
was wretched in the thought of what her sister must endure. PP III 9 315 1
She turned from sister to sister, demanding their PP III 9 315 4
her say to her eldest sister, "Ah! Jane, I take your place PP III 9 317 9
had found out where your sister and Mr. Wickham were, and PP III 10 321 2
Mr. Darcy asked him why he had not married your sister at PP III 10 323 2
ramble, my dear sister?" said he, as he joined her. PP III 10 327 5
And so, my dear sister, I find from our uncle and aunt, PP III 10 327 9
"Yes; he introduced us to his sister." PP III 10 328 19
"come, Mr. Wickham, we are brother and sister, you know. PP III 10 329 33
34

or provoked his dear sister Elizabeth, by introducing the PP III 11 330 1
"Well, well, and so Mr. Bingley is coming down, sister," (PP III 11 331 14
You know, sister, we agreed long ago never to mention a PP III 11 331 14
In spite of what her sister declared, and really believed PP III 11 332 20
to be sorry that he comes at all," said Jane to her sister. PP III 11 333 27
28

saw Mr. Darcy with him, and sat down again by her sister. PP III 11 333 31
which must attend her sister, in seeing him almost for the PP III 11 334 36
of her sister, as the servant was approaching the door. PP III 11 335 39
She enquired after his sister, but could do no more. PP III 11 336 46
her sister re-kindled the admiration of her former lover. PP III 11 337 56
by the approach of her sister, who joined her with a PP III 12 339 5

their former parties, had belonged to him, by her sister. PP III 12 340 11
His behaviour to her sister was such, during dinner time, PP III 12 340 13
of saying, "is your sister at Pemberley still?" PP III 12 341 20
21
"You are very cruel," said her sister, "you will not let PP III 12 343 33
On opening the door, she perceived her sister and Bingley PP III 13 346 22
whispering a few words to her sister ran out of the room. PP III 13 346 22
But she would not allow herself to stay with her sister, PP III 13 346 22
"Where is your sister?" said he hastily, as he opened the PP III 13 347 25
to her, claimed the good wishes and affection of a sister. PP III 13 347 31
and then till her sister came down, she had to listen to PP III 13 347 33
for conversation with her sister; for while he was present, PP III 13 347 33
I was told, that not only your sister was on the point of PP III 13 349 44
And is such a girl to be my nephew's sister? PP III 14 353 26
and her being the sister of Jane, was enough, at a time PP III 14 357 62
of her sister must bring them more frequently together. PP III 15 360 1
Bennet, after her elder sister has resigned it, and the PP III 15 360 1
you for your unexampled kindness to my poor sister. PP III 15 362 14
in quest of her sister, had been formed before he quitted PP III 16 365 3
as I had done, that your sister was indifferent to him; PP III 16 370 33
you told him that my sister loved him, or merely from my PP III 16 371 40
I could not allow myself to conceal that your sister had PP III 16 371 42
"My dearest sister, now be be serious. PP III 16 371 45
was to see whether your sister were still partial to PP III 17 373 15
and all her earnest desire of being loved by her sister. PP III 18 382 16
Philips, as well as her sister, stood in too much awe of PP III 18 383 25
allow in a sister more than ten years younger than himself. PP III 18 384 27
of Lady Bertram's sister; but her husband's profession was PP III 19 388 11
with merely giving up her sister, and thinking no more of MP I 1 3 1
which comprehended each sister in its bitterness, and MP I 1 4 1
could not get her poor sister and her family out of her MP I 1 4 1
angel, and she will never be more to either than a sister." MP I 1 5 4
I will write to my poor sister to-morrow, and make the MP I 1 7 6
no real affection for her sister, it was impossible for MP I 1 7 8
being the most liberal-minded sister and aunt in the world. MP I 1 8 9
shall the child come to first, sister, to you or to us?" MP I 1 8 9
I suppose, sister, you will put the child in the little MP I 1 9 10
that Mrs. Norris did not write to her sister in vain. MP I 1 9 12
by Sir Thomas, and in smaller concerns by her sister. MP I 1 11 19
with his sister in Northamptonshire, before he went to sea. MP I 2 19 31
Fanny, you are going to leave us, and live with my sister. MP I 2 21 34
You have been five years with us, and my sister always MP I 3 24 7
Mrs. Norris,-- "I think, sister, we need not keep Miss Lee MP I 3 25 9
MP I 3 28 38
39
"Dear sister!
"I hope, sister, things are not so very bad with you MP I 3 29 46
I fear he must find his sister at sixteen in some respects MP I 3 29 49
sixteen in some respects too much like his sister at ten." MP I 3 33 64
in those of her sister, and Mrs. Grant's wasteful doings MP I 3 33 64
was made over to her sister, who desired nothing better MP I 4 34 3
He could allow his sister to be the best judge of her own MP I 4 35 5
in the brother and sister of Mrs. Grant, a Mr. and Miss MP I 4 40 13
As children, their sister had been always very fond of MP I 4 40 15
The arrival, therefore, of a sister whom she had always MP I 4 40 15
could not accommodate his sister in an article of such MP I 4 41 15
Miss Crawford found a sister without preciseness or MP I 4 41 16
"My dear sister," said Mary, "if you can persuade him into MP I 4 41 17
"I like your Miss Bertrams exceedingly, sister," said he, MP I 4 42 21
"Well done, sister! MP I 5 45 4
about two years ago, his sister was not out, and I could MP I 5 47 24
Though I have no younger sister, I feel for her. MP I 5 50 35
you know, sister, and Fanny will stay at home with you." MP I 5 51 41
attend Mrs. Grant and her sister to their home, while Mr. MP I 6 62 58
For a few minutes, the brother and sister were too eager MP I 7 65 14
whether her headach might not be caught then, sister. MP I 7 71 31
"The fatigue would be too much for my sister, a great deal MP I 7 72 45
You must excuse my sister on this occasion, and accept of MP I 8 76 3
any pleasure for her sister; and Mary, properly pressed MP I 8 76 3
in Mr. Crawford and her sister sitting side by side full MP I 8 76 7
attention to her sister, by saying, "do look at Mr. MP I 8 81 32
mother, and expose her sister to the whispered gallantries MP I 9 88 19
Miss Bertram, displeased with her sister, led the way, and MP I 9 88 24
Your sister loves to laugh." MP I 9 89 30
was just the sort that my sister would be delighted with. MP I 10 99 12
My poor sister was forced to stay and bear it." MP I 10 105 55
and to see your sister suffering from it, must be MP I 11 111 28
in her jealousy of her sister, the absolute necessity of MP I 11 111 29
Each sister believed herself the favourite. MP I 12 114 3
Mr. Crawford with either sister without observation, and MP I 12 115 4
answer, "and I dare say it gives his sister pleasure. MP I 12 115 5
will distinguish the sister or intimate friend of the MP I 12 116 6
Each sister could echo the wish; and Henry Crawford, to MP I 12 116 10
My sister desires her love, and hopes to be admitted into MP I 13 123 6
Julia, meaning like her sister to be Agatha, began to be MP I 13 129 38
and me, but here is nothing for your sister, Mr. Crawford." MP I 14 133 8
of; he was very sure his sister had no wish of acting, but MP I 14 133 9
Each sister looked anxious; for each felt the best claim MP I 14 133 10
Your sister do that! MP I 14 133 11
thing of it fit for your sister, and we must not suffer MP I 14 134 13
She looked suspiciously at her sister; Maria's countenance MP I 14 134 15
at the table, while his sister made her way to Lady MP I 14 135 18
with a jealousy of her sister so reasonable as ought to MP I 15 143 26
caution as to the elder sister, entreat him not to risk MP I 17 160 8
The sister with whom she was used to be on easy terms, was MP I 17 161 9
"one cannot wonder, sister, that Fanny should be delighted; MP I 17 162 19
MP I 18 167 7
8
"Oh! sister, pray do not ask her now; for Fanny is not one MP I 18 167 9
was by no means to be compared in happiness to her sister. MP II 1 179 10
man;--his sister a sweet, pretty, elegant, lively girl." MP II 1 186 30
and then prevailed on my sister to pay the first visit, I MP II 2 188 3
I was ready to move heaven and earth to persuade my sister, MP II 2 189 3
and his friend's youngest sister, he believed he should MP II 2 191 10
at that moment that Tom had to speak and not his sister. MP II 2 193 13
Henry Crawford gone, she could even pity her sister. MP II 2 194 19
Mrs. Grant, really eager to get any change for her sister, MP II 4 205 2
"My sister and Mr. Bertram--I am so glad your eldest MP II 4 211 22
but you, Mrs. Grant, my sister, my own sister, I think I MP II 4 212 30
own sister, I think I had a right to alarm you a little." MP II 4 212 30
wish to procure so agreeable a visitor for her sister?" MP II 5 218 17
"nor, were there no sister in the case, could any thing in MP II 5 218 18
"She always makes tea, you know, when my sister is not MP II 5 219 21
"Your sister perhaps may be prevailed on to spend the day MP II 5 219 22
between the brother and sister about Bath, so much between MP II 5 223 48
of them with more particularity to his other sister. MP II 5 224 49
His sister tried to laugh off her feelings by saying, " MP II 5 226 62
he looked round at his sister as he sealed and threw the MP II 6 229 1
be instantly given to the sister, who had been his best MP II 6 233 14
of Mrs. Grant and her sister, that after making up the MP II 7 239 4
Your sister does not part with the queen. MP II 7 244 28
he shook his head at his sister, and laughingly replied, " MP II 7 245 31
"I have had the pleasure of seeing your sister dance, Mr. MP II 7 250 61
to his wife and sister; but that seemed forgotten by Mrs. MP II 7 251 65
to Mrs. Grant and her sister, whose acknowledged taste MP II 8 256 14
The sister is not to be in your mind without bringing the MP II 8 259 19
as a sister, was careless as a woman and a friend. MP II 8 260 24
and your sister is not used to these sort of hours." MP II 10 279 24
for there will be no kind sister to get up for me." MP II 10 280 31
an hour; and when his sister, who had been waiting for him MP II 12 291 1
three times over, his sister eagerly interrupted him with, MP II 12 292 8
Well might his sister, believing as she really did that MP II 12 294 18
Fanny will be so truly your sister!" MP II 12 295 23
the guest of neither brother nor sister many months longer. MP II 12 295 24

Knowing as I do what your feelings as a sister are, I MP II 13 298 2
He had a note to deliver from his sister. MP II 13 303 14
"Very true, sister, as you say. MP II 13 305 25
And further, how could it be supposed that his sister, MP II 13 306 26
desired;--go and take his sister with him, as he was to do, MP III 1 311 1
His sister, moreover, is your intimate friend, and he has MP III 1 316 27
of Henry Crawford and his sister walking together through MP III 3 334 1
It is the regret and disappointment of a sister, who MP III 4 352 40
"Yes, she was agreeing exactly with her sister. MP III 4 352 44
As a sister, so partial and so angry, and so little MP III 5 356 4
my excellent sister, yourself, and the Bertrams in general. MP III 5 359 12
And when I have done with her, I must go to her sister, MP III 5 359 12
thorough confidence in my sister, and a certain MP III 5 361 16
My own sister as a wife, Sir Thomas Bertram as a husband, MP III 5 361 16
What chiefly surprised Edmund was, that Crawford's sister, MP III 6 366 3
Alas! it was this sister, this friend and companion, who MP III 6 366 4
"That may be, sister,"--was all Lady Bertram's reply--"I MP III 6 371 16
William was almost as happy in the plan as his sister. MP III 6 371 18
Of pleasant talk between the brother and sister, there was MP III 7 375 2
She had heard repeatedly from his sister within the three MP III 7 375 4
proud to shew her abilities before her fine new sister. MP III 7 379 16
"You know you had but just settled that my sister Fanny MP III 7 379 18
But here is my sister, sir, here is Fanny;" turning and MP III 7 380 21
eagerly to see their sister, and tell that the thrush was MP III 7 381 25
fire and glanced at her sister, as if divided between the MP III 7 383 32
was sure her sister must want something after her journey." MP III 7 383 32
did her sister Bertram manage about her servants? MP III 7 385 38
particularly of another sister, a very pretty little girl, MP III 7 385 40
was her own knife; little sister Mary had left it to her MP III 7 386 42
said so prettily, 'let sister Susan have my knife, mamma, MP III 7 386 44
in honour of sister, she was off, leaving all below in MP III 7 387 46
Their sister soon despaired of making the smallest MP III 8 391 8
of 'Fanny,' and spoke of her as a sister should.-- MP III 9 394 1
her sister as an object of mingled compassion and respect. MP III 9 396 6
half an hour with his sister, the evening before his MP III 10 400 8
to sit down; but he could have wished her sister away. MP III 10 403 15
him to say something more of his sister and Edmund. MP III 10 406 20
being Lady Bertram's sister as she was but too apt to look. MP III 11 408 2
and will only let my sister know it, give her only the MP III 11 411 16
"My love to your sister, if you please; and when you see MP III 11 412 27
following letter from his sister, opened and read by her, MP III 12 415 1
2
especially to a fair sister of your's, a fine girl of MP III 12 415 2
He acknowledged no such inducement, and his sister ought MP III 12 418 4
and she paid her sister the compliment of preferring her MP III 12 419 7
for home than her elder sister; and as Fanny grew MP III 12 419 9
especially than her sister, Lady Stornaway, and is the MP III 13 421 2
upright conduct as a sister, she appears a very different MP III 13 421 2
I could not see him, and my eldest sister in the same room, MP III 13 423 2
poor sister Bertram must be in a great deal of trouble." MP III 13 428 14
might never hear from his sister any more this spring, MP III 14 433 12
his sister still said that he cared for nobody else. MP III 15 438 6
Mrs. Price talked of her poor sister for a few minutes-- MP III 15 444 26
"my Fanny--my only sister--my only comfort now." MP III 15 444 28
The being left with her sister and nephew, and all the MP III 16 448 2
she felt her, as Fanny's sister, to have a claim at MP III 16 448 3
in the offence of his sister and friend, cut off by it as MP III 16 452 15
which Crawford's sister ought to have known, he had gone MP III 16 454 18
by her brother and my sister--(with whom lay the greater MP III 16 457 30
Equally in brother and sister deceived! MP III 16 459 30
Her sister, though comparatively but little removed by E I 1 7 9
to answer questions which puzzled her sister at seventeen. E I 5 37 9
Where shall we see a better daughter, or a kinder sister, E I 5 39 22
alarmed, and might be made unhappy about her sister." E I 5 40 26
Isabella does not seem more my sister; has never excited a E I 5 40 27
There is my sister; and really quite her own little E I 6 45 21
sister very well married, and it is only a linen-draper." E I 7 55 40
company as she can while my brother and sister are here. E I 9 80 69
all the children of a sister I love so much, to care about. E I 10 85 21
to her father and sister that, but for these higher ties, E I 11 92 4
flattering to Isabella's sister, but they were only those E I 11 93 5
again to her father and sister, she had nothing worse to E I 12 104 45
what she had done every evening with her father and sister. E I 13 108 1
to a seat by her sister, and giving her all her attention. E I 15 125 6
dependent on the elder sister, who was very well married, E II 4 183 9
My brother and sister will be enchanted with this place. E II 14 273 21
"My brother and sister have promised us a visit in the E II 14 274 28
particularly to my brother and sister when they come to us. E II 15 284 9
have it believed that her sister was not a fine lady; E II 18 307 17
my brother and sister from the airs they give themselves! E II 18 310 34
so much brother and sister as to make it at all improper." E III 2 331 62
"Brother and sister! no, indeed." E III 2 331 63
Elton, as her brother and sister had failed her, that the E III 6 353 3
to the amiable solicitude of the sister and the aunt. E III 15 449 35
the patronage of your sister and Mrs. Bragge; the only E III 16 456 32
The party was to be our brother and sister, Henry, John-- E III 18 471 20
with either father or sister: her word had no weight; her P III 1 5 8
but that of a youngest sister, made the book an evil; and P III 1 7 12
society of so deserving a sister to bestow her affection P III 2 16 16
that is to say, she is sister to a gentleman who did live P III 3 22 25
she told me so herself: sister to the gentleman who lived P III 3 22 25
look on the part of her sister;--but Lady Russell, whom P III 4 27 5
mind in her younger sister; and Lady Russell had lamented P III 4 28 7
that Captain Wentworth's sister was likely to live at P III 4 30 10
The sister, Mrs. Croft, had then been out of England, P III 4 31 11
station, and her own sister, Mary, had been at school P III 4 31 11
herself from trying to make it perceptible to her sister. P III 5 34 12
Though better endowed than the elder sister, Mary had not P III 5 37 21
They ought to feel what is due to you as my sister. P III 5 40 43
Anne, Sir Walter and your sister are gone; and what part P III 6 42 1
Known to have some influence with her sister, she was P III 6 44 7
It is a pity you cannot put your sister in the way of P III 6 44 8
"it was you, and not your sister, I find, that my brother P III 6 49 18
19
Your sister being with you, my love, I have no scruple at P III 7 55 8
Her brother and sister came back delighted with their new P III 7 58 22
when he said to his sister, in answer to her suppositions, P III 7 61 38
39
Poor Harville, sister! P III 8 67 23
This brought his sister upon him. P III 8 69 36
"But you, yourself, brought Mrs. Harville, her sister, her P III 8 69 39
brother and sister, as to which was the one liked best. P III 9 75 9
the happiness of either sister, or impeaching his own P III 9 77 18
"They are up stairs with my sister--they will be down in a P III 9 79 23
in turning back with her sister, and lessening the P III 10 83 4
separations necessary, to keep with her brother and sister. P III 10 84 7
certainly put more forward for his notice than her sister. P III 10 84 7
"what glorious weather for the Admiral and my sister! P III 10 84 7
8
I assure you--but my sister makes nothing of it--she would P III 10 84 8
her sister aside, seemed to be arguing the matter warmly. P III 10 85 16
Your sister is an amiable creature; but yours is the P III 10 88 26
the hedge in a moment to say something to his sister.-- P III 10 91 39
He had been engaged to Captain Harville's sister, and was P III 11 96 12
turn his eyes from one sister, to see the other in a state P III 12 110 43
of service to her sister; and Henrietta, though perfectly P III 12 112 51
his sister in such a state, he neither ought, nor would. P III 12 113 58
"that you stay, and that I take care of your sister home. P III 12 114 61
Louisa, while she was her sister, and had the best right P III 12 115 65
care of his sister, and Captain Benwick attending to her. P III 12 115 66
the substitution of one sister for the other--the change P III 12 115 68
She had lately lost sight even of her father and sister P IV 1 124 11

SISTER/SISTERS

Her father and sister were glad to see her, for the sake P IV 3 137 2
Could Anne wonder that her father and sister were happy? P IV 3 138 5
his compliments, and her sister his apologies for calling P IV 3 143 18
fine mind did not appear to excite a thought in her sister. P IV 4 145 2
Anne had never seen her father and sister before in P IV 4 148 11
in her nurse, as a sister of her landlady, a nurse by P IV 5 154 9
His sister had a letter from him yesterday, in which he P IV 6 172 41
of seeing her sister turn away with unalterable coldness. P IV 7 176 9
say so, but I confess I admire her more than her sister." P IV 7 177 21
of the formidable father and sister in the back ground. P IV 8 181 1
His sister married my tenant in Somersetshire,--the Croft, P IV 8 188 40
the same time that he became known to my father and sister. P IV 9 200 56
regard to my father and sister, and afterwards in the P IV 9 200 56
"He had been introduced to Sir Walter and your sister P IV 9 200 57
that your father and sister, in their civilities and P IV 9 201 59
I should be continually hearing of your father and sister. P IV 9 201 59
over her father and sister, and had all the distress of P IV 10 212 1
I was really in pain for him; for your hard-hearted sister, P IV 10 213 4
purpose of saving her sister trouble, which determined her P IV 10 215 14
for herself and her sister; and, in short, it ended in P IV 10 217 19
She had no demands on her father or sister, and her P IV 10 219 28
to meet the heartless elegance of her father and sister. P IV 10 226 63
what had occurred to my sister hayter, and what the young P IV 11 230 5
poor sister, sat to him, and was bringing it home for her. P IV 11 232 15
blush for in the public manners of her father and sister. P IV 11 246 78
of brother and sister; with Lady Russell, attempts at P IV 11 246 78
It was creditable to have a sister married, and she might P IV 12 249 5
autumn; and as her own sister must be better than her P IV 12 249 5
It would be well for the eldest sister if she was equally P IV 12 250 6
doubt, that he & his sister Miss D-- who lived with him, S 3 377 1
Your sister Diana seems almost as ill as possible, but S 5 388 1
sister Susan's, are more distressing than all the rest.--" S 5 388 1
Sir Edwd Denham & his sister, who having been at Sanditon S 7 394 1
an early proposal to his sister--not merely for moving, S 7 395 1
a young gentleman & his sister--and so, my dear, the next S 7 402 1
This poor Sir Edward & his sister.--how far nature meant S 7 402 1
My sister wanted my counsel in the selection of some books. S 8 403 1
the hall to welcome the sister he had seen from the Drawg S 9 406 1
Here Mr P. drew his chair still nearer to his sister, & S 9 408 1
"I do not at all know--replied his sister--have not the S 9 409 1
& I know what Invalides both you & your sister are." S 9 410 1
& sister & herself were entreated to drink tea with them.-- S 10 413 1
was not very unlike her sister in person or manner--tho' S 10 413 1
His application thus withdrawn, his sister could say no S 12 425 1
between Sidney & his sister in law, who was most kindly S 12 425 1

SISTER PRICE (6)
Now, here are my Sister Price's children;--take them all MP II 13 305 24
to go with them--to go and see her poor dear Sister Price. MP III 6 372 21
seen her poor dear Sister Price for more than twenty years; MP III 6 372 21
her poor dear Sister Price would feel it very unkind of MP III 6 372 21
So, her poor dear Sister Price was left to all the MP III 6 373 24
poor dear Sister Price to have them so well provided for. MP III 13 428 15

SISTER'S (144)
respect for me than his sister's kind offices have LS 7 254 3
her wish of obtaining my sister's good opinion merits a LS 14 265 5
conclusion of his sister's now being by his side; and NA I 8 53 3
that need be said of his sister's concern, regret, and NA I 12 94 9
thanked at least, on his sister's account, for her NA II 5 157 5
"I am sure it is quite unnecessary upon your sister's NA II 11 211 13
Thorpe's interest in the family, by his sister's NA II 15 245 12
Elinor saw, with concern, the excess of her sister's SS I 1 7 13
soon after his sister's establishment at Norland, and who SS I 3 15 4
grave, Marianne; do you disapprove your sister's choice?" SS I 3 17 17
Marianne was vexed at it for her sister's sake, and turned SS I 7 34 5
Her form, though not so correct as her sister's, in having SS I 10 46 2
She knew her sister's temper. SS I 12 59 5
of their separation, her sister's affliction was SS I 15 77 20
as he must be of your sister's love, should leave her, and SS I 15 80 36
You cannot doubt your sister's wishes. SS I 15 81 42
considering her sister's youth, and urged the matter SS I 16 85 10
on him, and in her sister's happiness forgot for a time SS I 16 86 21
but I am afraid my practice is much more on your sister's. SS I 17 94 42
glance at Elinor, replied, "yes; it is my sister's hair. SS I 18 98 12
That her sister's affections were calm, she dared not deny, SS I 19 104 11
Her manners were by no means so elegant as her sister's, SS I 19 106 22
wished her joy on her sister's having been so lucky as to SS I 21 125 34
generally made an amendment to all her sister's assertions. SS I 21 126 40
afraid of his sister's suspecting any thing, that was SS I 22 131 32
which she could decently attribute her sister's behaviour. SS II 4 162 10
Jennings from seeing her sister's thoughts as clearly as SS II 5 167 4
that might lead to her sister's relief, Elinor resolved to SS II 5 171 38
He tried to smile as he replied, "your sister's engagement SS II 5 173 40
hand, directed to Mr. Willoughby in your sister's writing. SS II 5 173 44
and insensible of her sister's presence; and when at last SS II 6 175 1
persuasion of my sister's being engaged to Mr. Willoughby? SS II 7 181 9
her arms round her sister's neck; "I know you feel for me; SS II 7 185 24
Elinor, for her sister's sake, could not press the subject SS II 8 196 21
Her sister's earnest, though gentle persuasion, however, SS II 8 197 25
obtained her sister's consent to wait for that knowledge. SS II 9 203 9
conviction, lasting conviction to your sister's mind. SS II 9 204 18
I thought your sister's influence might yet reclaim him. SS II 9 210 32
after particulars, or any anxiety for her sister's health. SS II 10 215 12
discussion of her sister's disappointment, by the friendly SS II 10 216 15
After some opposition, Marianne yielded to her sister's SS II 11 220 1
her husband was all in a fright at his sister's audacity. SS II 12 236 38
after a moment, to her sister's chair, and putting one arm SS II 12 236 39
40

her company and her sister's, for some days, in Harley- SS II 14 253 26
your care as to their sister's indisposition, I think it SS III 1 258 5
believed to be her sister's chief consolation,--to give SS III 1 261 11
urgent to prevent her sister's going at all; and Mrs. SS III 5 294 3
yet uninformed of his sister's being there, quitted the SS III 5 298 32
only astonished at her sister's composure, who, though SS III 7 307 1
much uneasiness on her sister's account, would be to SS III 7 309 5
and she returned to her sister's apartment to wait for the SS III 7 312 17
her conviction of her sister's danger would not allow her SS III 7 313 20
stirring from her sister's bed, her thoughts wandering SS III 7 313 21
slight amendment in her sister's pulse;--she waited, SS III 7 314 22
Your sister's lovely person and interesting manners could SS III 8 319 29
"Your sister's marriage." SS III 8 332 81
sister's health were more secure, before she appointed it. SS III 10 343 10
closely pressed her sister's, and tears covered her cheeks. SS III 10 348 33
wished to hear her sister's unbiassed opinion, by an eager SS III 11 349 5
that might weaken her sister's spirits; she therefore, SS III 11 352 16
17

Tho' they are not written down, I bring your sister's W 339 18
"Your sister's complexion, said he at last, is as fine as W 357 28
to beleive it no sacrifice on her sister's part.-- W 361 30
Elizabeth passed the chief of the night in her sister's PP I 9 41 1
than her sister's, "what you have learnt about Mr. Wickham. PP I 18 95 49
account as well as his sister's, Mr. Wickham is by no PP I 18 95 50
and Elizabeth saw her sister's countenance change as she PP I 21 116 6
much as his own, and a sister's partiality is not PP I 21 118 14
he thought best; but her sister's was involved in it, as PP II 1 133 3
by the difference, her sister's situation remained the PP II 1 134 3
and threw back the praise on her sister's warm affection. PP II 1 135 10
and felt persuaded of her sister's ready acquiescence. PP II 2 141 11
could discover to Mr. Bingley her sister's being in town. PP II 3 147 24
Mr. Darcy spoke with affectionate praise of his sister's PP II 8 173 7
gave her a keener sense of her sister's sufferings. PP II 11 188 1
the serenity of your sister's countenance and air was such, PP II 12 197 5
I hesitated not in giving, of your sister's indifference. PP II 12 199 5
so far as to conceal from him your sister's being in town. PP II 12 199 5
If I have wounded your sister's feelings, it was PP II 12 199 5
Regard for my sister's credit and feelings prevented any PP II 12 202 5
Mr. Wickham's chief object was unquestionably my sister's PP II 12 202 5
His belief of her sister's insensibility, she instantly PP II 13 204 1
unsuspicious of her sister's attachment;--and she could PP II 13 208 9
unhappiness which her sister's refusal must have given him. PP II 17 224 2
leisure to observe the real state of her sister's spirits. PP II 17 227 26
Wholly inattentive to her sister's feelings, Lydia flew PP II 18 230 12
source of regret in my sister's absence, I may reasonably PP II 19 237 4
This unfortunate affair will, I fear, prevent my sister's PP III 4 278 20
in her eyes, "that a sister's sense of decency and virtue PP III 5 283 10
I felt a little uneasy--a little fearful of my sister's PP III 5 290 50
former assurance of her sister's ruin still more certain; PP III 6 295 4
of a sister's frailty would have mortified her so much. PP III 8 311 12
for the sake of their sister's feelings and consequence, PP III 8 314 22
Their sister's wedding day arrived; and Jane and Elizabeth PP III 9 315 1
Mr. Darcy had been at her sister's wedding. PP III 9 320 32
doing to forward her sister's match, which she had feared PP III 10 326 3
and unwilling for her sister's sake, to provoke him, she PP III 10 329 33
34

of all his sister's falsehood and contrivance! the PP III 13 347 29
"It must have been his sister's doing. PP III 13 349 47
particulars of your youngest sister's infamous elopement. PP III 14 357 62
than he remained in any doubt of your sister's sentiments. PP III 16 371 45
Is not she a sister's child? and could I bear to see her MP I 1 7 8
was indebted for her sister's proposal of coming to her, a MP I 4 41 15
from doubts of her sister's style of living and tone of MP I 4 41 16
or rusticity--a sister's husband who looked the gentleman, MP I 4 41 17
enjoyed the power of being proud of her sister's. MP I 4 42 17
at her sister's early care, or the choice it had fallen on. MP I 4 42 18
Does she dine out every where, as well as at my sister's?" MP I 5 51 41
events; your sister's marriage, and your taking orders." MP I 11 108 8
Yes, Mr. Charles Maddox dined at my sister's one day, did MP I 15 148 59
station and retained her sister's hand, her wounded heart MP II 1 175 2
with the brother and sister's apology, saw them preparing MP II 1 177 6
the park to support her sister's spirits, and drinking the MP II 3 203 30
views never entered his sister's imagination; and she MP II 12 291 5
heart lamented that his sister's feelings should be so MP III 7 375 3
of carrying up his sister's trunk, which he would manage MP III 7 379 19
was wounded by her sister's speech and her mother's reply. MP III 7 386 43
any remissness of his sister's in writing, for there has MP III 9 393 1
she yet feared that her sister's judgment had been against MP III 9 397 7
I am considering your sister's health," said he, MP III 11 410 16
so much to condemn; the sister's feelings--the brother's MP III 14 435 15
by the shock of his sister's conduct, and his recovery so MP III 16 451 13
probabilities of a conclusion hereafter, like her sister's. MP III 16 452 13
do not mean to defend Henry at your sister's expence.' MP III 16 454 18
him; and, had not her sister's conduct burst forth as it MP III 17 466 18
the true kindness of her sister's heart, and the rational MP III 17 469 24
in consequence of her sister's marriage, been mistress of E I 1 5 2
The coming of her sister's family was so very near at hand, E I 11 91 1
The young man's conduct, and his sister's, seemed the E II 3 179 53
at Maple Grove; her sister's favourite room."-- E II 14 272 18
boys; but you have your sister's letter, and every thing E II 18 311 37
38

When it was thus settled on her sister's side, Emma E III 16 451 3
hints broadest which were meant for her sister's benefit. P III 6 46 11
Mary had no feelings to make her respect her sister's in a P III 7 60 32
Camden-Place, or her own sister's intimacy with Mrs. Clay. P IV 1 124 11
into her father and sister's solicitudes on a subject P IV 4 148 10
a good deal on his "poor sister's account; but, however, P IV 6 165 8
Mary need not have feared her sister's being in any degree P IV 6 165 9
between it and her sister's; the origin of one all selfish P IV 8 183 20
My account states, that your sister's friend, the lady now P IV 9 206 88
did not even ask her own sister's family, though they were P IV 10 219 29
"We had your sister's card yesterday, and I understood P IV 11 236 36
disregarding his sister's motion to go, & persisting in S 7 395 1
My sister's complaints & mine are happily not often of a S 9 410 1

SISTER-IN-LAW (16)
I must torment my sister-in-law for the insolent triumph LS 25 293 4
Prepare for your sister-in-law, Eleanor, and such a sister- NA II 10 206 31
and such a sister-in-law as you must delight in!-- NA II 10 206 31
"Such a sister-in-law, Henry, I should delight in," said NA II 10 206 32
could receive her sister-in-law on her arrival, and treat SS I 1 7 13
feel much delighted with the idea of such a sister-in-law. SS I 22 129 13
and brother of your sister-in-law, Mrs. John Dashwood, is" SS I 22 131 30
an apology from their sister-in-law, for not coming too; SS II 11 222 14
of screens for her sister-in-law, which being now just SS II 12 234 26
agreeable to their sister-in-law, who had preceded them to SS II 14 249 9
love with her, that my sister-in-law was sure he would PP I 9 44 31
When tea was over, Mr. Hurst reminded his sister-in-law of PP I 11 54 3
Thomas expected his sister-in-law to claim her share in MP I 3 24 7
with his fair sister-in-law, could not spare his wife. MP I 18 171 26
his own wife and sister-in-law acquainted with the MP III 2 332 19
He was not a great favourite with his fair sister-in-law. E I 11 93 5

SISTER-IN-LAW'S (5)
What! your sister-in-law's brother, Miss Dashwood? a very SS I 21 126 39
with your sister-in-law's mother, Mrs. Ferrars?" SS I 22 128 3
her acquaintance with her sister-in-law's family." SS II 3 157 16
screens out of her sister-in-law's hands, to admire them SS II 12 235 36
he had mistaken his sister-in-law's views; and she was MP I 3 30 57

SISTERLY (9)
Mrs Vernon that her sisterly cautions have been bestowed LS 7 254 3
shall tranquillize the sisterly fears of Mrs Vernon, who, LS 30 301 4
and in schemes of sisterly happiness the hours flew along. NA I 15 120 25
Her admiration and regard, even her sisterly regard, was SS I 11 55 7
I think it would not be very likely to promote sisterly PP II 6 165 35
lessened by the strong sisterly partiality which made any PP II 17 224 2
bosoms of each other, the balm of sisterly consolation. PP III 5 289 42
to do; and it had a sound of most sisterly cordiality." MP III 4 352 42
her that her warm and sisterly regard for him would be MP III 17 470 25

SISTERS (238)
as to their families, sisters, and cousins, talking both NA I 4 32 2
drive my sisters about; that would be a good joke, faith! NA I 7 48 31
On his two younger sisters he then bestowed an equal NA I 7 49 43
concerning brothers and sisters, the situation of some, NA I 7 51 54
in the room; my two younger sisters and their partners. NA I 8 59 37
and at last he walked off to quiz his sisters by himself. NA I 8 59 38
"But why cannot Mr. Thorpe drive one of his other sisters? NA I 13 99 6
to Bath to drive my sisters about, and look like a fool. NA I 13 99 7
you once were the kindest, best-tempered of my sisters." NA I 13 99 10
curiosity to be raised in the unprivileged younger sisters. NA I 15 120 25
Are your sisters coming?" NA II 3 143 3
And, you know, we shall still be sisters." NA II 3 145 13
a blush) "there are more ways than one of being sisters.-- NA II 3 145 14
seat she should miss her sisters, she was expecting her NA II 3 147 28
she was expecting her sisters every moment; so that her NA II 3 147 28
Mr. and Mrs. Morland--your brothers and sisters--I hope NA II 10 203 9
important as to his sisters; for their fortune, SS I 1 3 2
command, the interest of his mother-in-law and sisters. SS I 1 5 5
of his sisters by the present of a thousand pounds a-piece. SS I 1 5 8
which one of her sisters had resolved never to be taught. SS I 1 6 11
to equal her sisters at a more advanced period of life. SS I 1 7 14
approve of what her husband intended to do for his sisters. SS I 2 8 3
Harry, by giving away all his money to his half sisters? SS I 2 8 3
Your sisters will marry, and it will be gone for ever. SS I 2 9 7
so much for his sisters, even if really/ his sisters! SS I 2 9 11
My sisters would feel the good effects of it as well as SS I 2 10 16
His attentive behaviour to herself and his sisters SS I 3 14 2
"Is there no chance of my seeing you and your sisters in SS I 13 66 46
moment to her mother and sisters, and forbidding all SS I 16 83 1

prevailed on to join her sisters in their usual walk, SS I 16 85 15
If her sisters intended to walk on the downs, she directly SS I 16 85 15
the voices of both her sisters were raised to detain her, SS I 16 86 20
and sisters were spared much solicitude on her account. SS I 19 104 10
absence of her mother and sisters, at least by the nature SS I 19 105 12
And where are your sisters? SS I 19 106 20
pleased with you and your sisters I can tell you, and you SS I 20 114 42
and the other Miss Dashwoods, quite as his own sisters."-- SS I 22 130 16
Her mother, sisters, Fanny, all had been conscious of his SS II 1 139 1
every suspicion of the truth from her mother and sisters. SS II 1 140 4
the appearance of the sisters, that Elinor was mourning in SS II 1 141 4
Thus a circumstance occurred, while the sisters were SS II 9 202 4
being sorry to see his sisters again; it rather gave them SS II 11 221 7
John Dashwood very soon, and bring her sisters to see her. SS II 11 223 14
ear-rings for each of his sisters, in his next visit at SS II 11 226 41
done nothing for his sisters himself, to be exceedingly SS II 11 228 51
the woman with whom her sisters were staying, by no means SS II 12 229 1
who met her husband's sisters without any affection, and SS II 12 229 3
There sisters and Mrs. Jennings were invited likewise, and SS II 12 230 6
It so happened that while her two sisters with Mrs. SS II 14 248 6
them to be Mr. Dashwood's sisters, she immediately SS II 14 248 6
mistake, in supposing his sisters their guests, had SS II 14 252 20
We can ask your sisters some other year, you know; but the SS II 14 253 24
of inviting his sisters another year; at the same time, SS II 14 253 25
way, 'that we had asked your sisters instead of them.'" SS III 1 266 36
assurances to his sisters that he really believed there SS III 1 269 57
of the brother and sisters in town;--and a faint SS III 6 301 1
The sisters set out at a pace, slow as the feebleness of SS III 10 344 12
13
uneasiness as both her sisters had lately experienced, so SS III 11 355 45
being in love with two sisters, and two sisters fond of SS III 13 370 36
with two sisters, and two sisters fond of each other, made SS III 13 370 36
and sisters spent much more than half their time with her. SS III 14 378 13
considerable, that though sisters, and living almost SS III 14 380 21
Rivalry, treachery between sisters!-- W 316 2
I had hoped to find all my sisters at home; to be able to W 318 2
If she is like her sisters, she will only want to be W 333 13
the pleasure of seeing your sisters here this evening?-- W 334 13
used to receive from her sisters, & gave him probably the W 335 13
Your sisters all know how quiet they are; they have none W 339 18
The sisters looked on each other with astonishment, when W 347 22
intercourse of the two sisters, whose mutual regard was W 348 23
It was an expectation to fill the thoughts of the sisters W 348 23
An absence of 14 years had made all her brothers & sisters W 348 23
there is powder enough in my hair for my wife & sisters.--" W 353 26
She had thus secured him from her sisters--but it was not W 356 28
a meeting with Miss Emma Watson,--or any of her sisters." W 356 28
Lizzy has something more of quickness than her sisters." PP I 1 5 27
six with him from London, his five sisters and a cousin. PP I 3 10 4
sisters, the husband of the eldest, and another young man. PP I 3 10 4
His sisters were fine women, with an air of decided PP I 3 10 5
Your sisters are engaged, and there is not another woman PP I 3 11 9
But there is one of her sisters sitting down just behind PP I 3 11 12
her twice, and she had been distinguished by his sisters. PP I 3 12 15
He is so excessively handsome! and his sisters are PP I 3 13 18
And so, you like this man's sisters too, do you? PP I 4 15 9
His sisters were very anxious for his having an estate of PP I 4 15 13
came with his sisters, "I should not care how proud I was. PP I 5 20 21
and the younger sisters not worth speaking to, a wish of PP I 6 21 1
request of her younger sisters, who with some of the PP I 6 25 24
Her sisters were uneasy for her, but her mother was PP I 7 31 28
When breakfast was over, they were joined by the sisters; PP I 7 33 44
The sisters, on hearing this, repeated three or four times PP I 8 35 1
To this speech Bingley made no answer; but his sisters PP I 8 37 20
immediately; while his sisters, convinced that no country PP I 8 40 59
Bingley was quite uncomfortable; his sisters declared that PP I 8 40 59
from the two elegant ladies who waited on his sisters. PP I 9 41 1
In consequence of an agreement between the sisters, PP I 12 59 1
Lydia was bid by her two eldest sisters to hold her tongue; PP I 14 69 15
16
and Lady Anne Darcy were sisters; consequently that she is PP I 16 83 53
Mr. Bingley and his sisters came to give their personal PP I 17 86 9
selected from among her sisters as worthy of being the PP I 17 88 14
if she and her sisters did not very often walk to Meryton. PP I 18 93 18
of endeavouring even to like Bingley's two sisters. PP I 18 98 63
to think how fond the two sisters were of Jane, and to be PP I 18 99 63
She looked at his two sisters, and saw them making signs PP I 18 100 68
That his two sisters and Mr. Darcy, however, should have PP I 18 102 72
Mr. Bingley and his sisters on the elegance of their PP I 18 102 75
be renewed with yet greater satisfaction as sisters?-- PP I 21 117 9
in accepting a man whose sisters and friends are all PP I 21 119 23
of disobliging his two sisters is more than equivalent to PP I 21 119 24
Elizabeth was sitting with her mother and sisters, PP I 23 126 1
of her mother and sisters, by the earnestness of her PP I 23 126 4
that his sisters would be successful in keeping him away. PP I 23 129 13
The united efforts of his two unfeeling sisters and of his PP I 23 129 13
"You persist, then, in supposing his sisters influence him. PP II 1 136 20
what I should feel in thinking ill of him or his sisters. PP II 1 137 24
and such uncompanionable sisters, home could not be PP II 4 151 1
She asked her at different times, how many sisters she had, PP II 6 163 15
Do your sisters play and sing?" PP II 6 164 18
Are any of your younger sisters out, Miss Bennet?" PP II 6 165 32
Your younger sisters must be very young?" PP II 6 165 34
be very hard upon younger sisters, that they should not PP II 6 165 35
"With three younger sisters grown up," replied Elizabeth PP II 6 166 37
He and his sisters were well, I hope, when you left London. PP II 9 177 4
younger sisters, and occasionally even by your father.-- PP II 12 198 5
After welcoming their sisters, they triumphantly displayed PP II 16 219 2
And when her sisters abused it as ugly, she added, with PP II 16 219 4
their sisters will not be often involved in the disgrace?" PP II 18 231 18
having a couple of--or I may say, three very silly sisters. PP II 18 231 20
adieus of her sisters were uttered without being heard. PP II 18 235 40
an acquaintance with you,--Mr. Bingley and his sisters." PP III 1 256 61
of the rest, whether all her sisters were at Longbourn. PP III 2 262 9
prohibited, unless you stand up with one of your sisters. PP III 6 300 30
which her sisters would not have alluded to for the world. PP III 9 316 6
I am sure my sisters must all envy me. PP III 9 317 11
You and papa, and my sisters, must come down and see us. PP III 9 317 13
leave one or two of my sisters behind you; and I dare say PP III 9 317 15
with her two elder sisters, she said to Elizabeth, "Lizzy, PP III 9 318 21
22
My sisters may write to me. PP III 11 330 6
Both sisters were uncomfortable enough. PP III 11 334 36
not be prevailed on to go down without one of her sisters. PP III 13 344 10
Not a word passed between the sisters concerning Bingley; PP III 13 345 20
Her younger sisters soon began to make interest with her PP III 13 349 41
"And that I suppose is one of your sisters." PP III 14 352 7
The darling wish of his sisters was then gratified; he PP III 19 385 3
spent the chief of time with her two elder sisters. PP III 19 385 4
suffered no revolution from the marriage of her sisters. PP III 19 386 6
of the sisters was exactly what Darcy had hoped to see. PP III 19 387 11
She had two sisters to be benefited by her elevation; and MP I 1 3 1
an absolute breach between the sisters had taken place. MP I 1 3 1
but the children of my sisters?--and I am sure Mr. Norris MP I 1 6 6
they would be, always together like brothers and sisters? MP I 1 6 6
idea of the brothers and sisters among whom she had always MP I 2 14 8
and you shall tell me all about your brothers and sisters." MP I 2 15 11
as all these brothers and sisters generally were, there MP I 2 15 12
He was, in fact, the most agreeable young man the sisters MP I 5 44 2
new furnished--pleasant sisters, a quiet mother, and an MP I 5 48 28
father and mother and sisters were there, all new to me. MP I 5 51 40
worth reading, to his sisters, when they are separated. MP I 7 64 10
Mr. Crawford driving his sisters; and as every body was MP I 8 80 29
The sisters, handsome, clever, and encouraging, were an MP I 12 115 3
prefer a comedy, and his sisters and Henry Crawford a MP I 13 124 13
shall speak to my sisters, and try to dissuade them, and MP I 13 128 35
with either Tom or my sisters that could be of any use; MP I 13 128 37
His sisters, to whom he had an opportunity of speaking the MP I 13 128 38
only brothers and sisters, and intimate friends, and which MP I 13 128 38
said he, "as Agatha does to one or other of my sisters. MP I 14 133 10
brother and sisters as if hardly doubting a contradiction. MP I 15 139 5
"I imagine both sisters are." MP I 17 161 11
were the same, the sisters, under such a trial as this, MP I 17 162 19
great attention to my mother and sisters while he was away. MP II 3 196 2
among ourselves; my sisters seem out of spirits, and Tom MP II 3 196 2
Since rivalry between the sisters had ceased, they had MP II 3 203 32
The two sisters were so kind to her and so pleasant, that MP II 4 206 4
She used to ask your sisters now and then, but she never MP II 5 217 3
warmly urged by the two sisters, was soon in possession of MP II 5 223 48
and mother, brothers and sisters, of whom she very seldom MP II 6 234 18
His friend Mr. Owen had sisters--he might find them MP II 11 286 17
ladies--about any three sisters just grown up; for one MP II 11 288 28
brothers and sisters--never seems to have had a moment's MP III 1 318 39
the future with both his sisters; and it would be rather MP III 2 331 19
"Yes, when I reached the house I found the two sisters MP III 4 352 38
all the claims which his sisters think he has, how was I MP III 4 353 45
I am sure his sisters, rating him as they do, must have MP III 4 353 45
His sisters should consider me as well as him. MP III 4 353 45
Who says we shall not be sisters? MP III 5 359 10
parents and brothers, and sisters, from whom she had been MP III 6 369 11
and there were her two sisters, Susan, a well-grown fine MP III 7 377 9
Of her two sisters, Mrs. Price very much more resembled MP III 8 390 5
I look upon her intimacy with those two sisters, as the MP III 13 421 2
It astonished her that Tom's sisters could be satisfied MP III 14 432 11
to for the truth, his sisters not being within my reach. MP III 14 434 1
3000
beloved place, the hearts of both sisters sank a little. MP III 15 446 35
Between them it was more the intimacy of sisters. E I 1 5 3
His mother and sisters were very fond of him. E I 4 28 6
his wife-- for though his sisters, from a superior E I 4 30 22
by your intimacy with the sisters, to be acquainted with E I 4 31 24
for her from one of his sisters, and gone away; and on E I 7 50 1
I think one of his sisters must have helped him. E I 7 51 5
of what his mother and sisters would think and say, and E I 7 55 35
"I wonder what they are all doing--whether his sisters E I 7 56 43
picture to his mother and sisters, telling how much more E I 7 56 44
of young ladies that his sisters are intimate with, who E I 8 66 53
of the brother, the sisters had never been at Mrs. E II 3 180 58
and sisters, when invited to come, would be ingratitude. E II 4 185 12
father of Anne and her sisters, was, as being Sir Walter, P III 2 11 2
In person, she was inferior to both sisters, and had, even P III 5 37 21
she had known so little herself with either of her sisters. P III 5 41 45
not at home, but the two sisters were together; and as it P III 6 48 17
He had, in fact, though his sisters were now doing all P III 6 51 29
for his dogs, that his sisters were following with captain P III 7 59 24
captain Wentworth, his sisters meaning to visit Mary and P III 7 59 24
Mrs. Musgrove and Mrs. Hayter were sisters. P III 9 74 5
Which of the two sisters was preferred by Captain P III 9 74 8
it would be a capital match for either of his sisters." P III 9 75 10
shooting together, as the sisters in the cottage were P III 10 83 3
at the window by the sisters from the mansion-house. P III 10 83 3
Charles and his two sisters, that he, and Henrietta, P III 10 86 18
home, before her brothers and sisters went to school again. P IV 2 134 31
happen: and that of two sisters, who both deserve equally P IV 10 217 21
better than her husband's sisters, it was very agreeable P IV 12 249 5
her in his brothers and sisters, was a source of as lively P IV 12 251 10
he had 2 brothers and 2 sisters--all single & all S 2 371 1
many more--and his own sisters who were sad invalids, & S 2 372 1
wife, Childn, brothers & sisters--& generally kind-hearted; S 2 372 1
& new Broches, for her sisters & herself at the library, S 2 374 1
I & all my brothers & sisters were born & bred--& where my S 4 379 1
But here is a letter from one of my sisters. S 5 385 1
I told you my sisters were excellent women, miss h----." S 5 388 1
considering the state in which both sisters appear to be.-- S 5 388 1
"Your sisters know what they are about, I dare say, but S 5 388 1
sisters, for the object which had taken him to Willingden. S 6 393 1
as a Projector, the sisters were perhaps driven to S 10 412 1
My sisters think me bilious, but I doubt it.--" S 10 415 1
at the same moment, his sisters both crying out--"Oh! S 10 417 1
conversation on dry toast, & hear no more of his sisters.-- S 10 417 1
without a struggle; his sisters accusing him of eating a S 10 417 1
she saw him watching his sisters, while he scrupulously S 10 417 1
different from his sisters--by no means so spiritualized.-- S 10 418 1

SISTERS' (7)

more vacant than their sisters', and when nothing better PP I 7 28 3
His sisters' uneasiness had been equally excited with my PP II 12 198 5
comparisons between her sisters' beauty and her own, it PP III 19 386 5
he went away, or to my sisters' pianoforte being moved MP I 13 127 29
Your brother's taste, and your sisters', seem very MP I 13 128 34
And Fanny, though I hope I do justice to my sisters' good MP III 4 350 30
of imagination in my two sisters' complaints--but it S 5 385 1

SISTERS-IN-LAW (1)

sisters-in-law were degraded to the condition of visitors. SS I 2 8 1

SIT (141)

situation, were obliged to sit down at the end of a table, NA I 2 22 10
But I think we had better sit still, for one gets so NA I 2 22 19
friend, and was forced to sit and appear to listen to all NA I 4 32 2
But now, let us go and sit down at the other end of the NA I 6 39 4
belonging to it, did not sit near her, and James and NA I 8 59 38
she sat peaceably down, and saw Thorpe sit down by her. NA I 9 62 10
person's courage that could sit down on purpose to do it." NA I 14 109 24
Let us sit down and talk in comfort. NA I 15 117 6
disengaged; but I would have given the world to sit still." NA II 1 134 37
my dear Morland, making him sit down upon an income hardly NA II 1 135 45
Catherine must excuse her, and must sit quietly down again. NA II 3 147 28
would not have room to sit; and, so much was he influenced NA II 5 155 4
and yet that he could sit so boldly collected within its NA II 9 190 2
"Well, if it was my house, I should never sit any where NA II 11 214 23
We happened to sit by the Mitchells, and they pretended to NA II 12 217 2
She could neither sit still, nor employ herself for ten NA II 15 240 1
and asked Marianne to sit down to it; and thus amidst the SS I 12 62 27
you will be glad of a little company to sit with you. SS I 19 106 20
Elinor and Marianne should sit so composedly by, without SS I 21 121 6
possible that she could sit out the dinner, said no more; SS II 8 193 5
for if you only go and sit up in an old yew arbour behind SS II 8 197 22
All that could be done was, to sit down at the end of the SS II 11 220 3
an end to the bustle, and sit down among the rest; though SS II 12 236 42
he had courage enough to sit down; but his embarrassment SS II 13 241 21
Lord! we shall sit and gape at one another as dull as two SS III 3 280 8
confessed herself unable to sit up, and returned SS III 7 307 2
she resolved to sit with her during the whole of it. SS III 7 310 9
"Sit down, and I will be both." SS III 8 317 6
Mrs. Dashwood would sit up with her all night, and Elinor, SS III 9 334 5
Elinor could sit it no longer. SS III 12 360 26
when they were going to sit up late, which lengthened the W 326 7
Emma--"there's Lord osborne--let you & I go & sit by him.-- W 332 11
"No, no, said Emma laughing you must sit with my friends." W 332 11
they would make me sit near the fire, & as the partridges W 344 20
make a round game he may be tempted to sit down with us."-- W 354 28
that if he staid he must sit down to supper in less than W 359 28
they were obliged to sit down without their guest.-- W 360 30
Margt's perverseness, than sit with only her father, who W 361 30
scarcity of gentlemen, to sit down for two dances; and PP I 3 11 7
I would really rather not sit down before those who must PP I 6 24 22

second, I can admire you much better as I sit by the fire." PP I 11 56 15
"I know very well, madam," said he, "that when persons sit PP I 16 83 50
sister, that they did not once sit down to a family dinner. PP II 2 142 18
Elizabeth then contrived to sit by her aunt. PP II 4 152 6
Another day I will do the same; I will sit in my library, PP III 6 300 28
Wickham, who happened to sit near Elizabeth, began PP III 9 316 6
by the same ideas, forbore to invite him to sit by herself. PP III 12 340 11
"Kitty and I are going up stairs to sit in my dressing PP III 13 345 16
others were all going to sit down to cards, she could not PP III 13 346 21
"Let us sit down. PP III 14 355 48
chair, get up, sit down again, wonder, and bless herself. PP III 17 378 42
"And if I had not a letter to write myself, I might sit by PP III 18 382 19
by Mrs. Bennet's being quite unable to sit alone. PP III 19 386 5
Bertram smile and make her sit on the sofa with herself MP I 2 13 4
but now I could go and sit a few hours with Mrs. Rushworth MP I 6 62 58
"I never see one sit a horse better. MP I 7 69 22
Why cannot you come and sit here, and employ yourself as MP I 7 71 34
be better that one should sit with Henry, and as you were MP I 8 80 29
to you, I should be glad to sit down for a little while." MP I 9 94 57
"I shall soon be rested," said Fanny; "to sit in the shade MP I 9 96 72
well spare time to sit down herself, because of her fringe. MP I 12 119 23
left to sit down and stir the fire in thoughtful vexation. MP I 13 128 33
nonsense of acting, and sit comfortably down to your table. MP I 16 156 27
fitted for little girls to sit and kick their feet against MP I 18 169 21
visit, I am as certain as I sit here, that nothing would MP II 2 188 3
he was hardly able to sit the box on account of the MP II 2 189 5
and I could not bear to sit at my ease, and be dragged up MP II 2 189 5
venturing sometimes even to sit down on one of the benches MP II 4 208 11
of all possible numbers to sit down to table; and I cannot MP II 5 220 30
of being suffered to sit silent and unattended to. MP II 5 223 48
request to be allowed to sit between her ladyship and Miss MP II 7 239 8
I am not born to sit still and do nothing. MP II 7 243 25
to sit on her sofa without any inconvenience from them. MP II 8 254 9
(with a smile that did not sit easy) she says it is to be MP II 9 268 29
thankful that she could not sit in the same room with her MP II 11 284 8
opinions, or learnt to sit over your dinner, as if it were MP II 12 295 27
gradually composed, could sit down, and be able to employ MP III 1 311 3
"I am not cold, sir--I never sit here long at this time of MP III 1 312 7
It is highly unfit for you to sit--be it only half an hour MP III 1 312 10
Sit down, my dear. MP III 1 313 12
leaving his poor niece to sit and cry over what had passed, MP III 1 320 45
the felicity of having a fire to sit over and think of it. MP III 2 329 10
it is over now; so let us sit down and be comfortable; for MP III 5 359 9
Innocent and quiet as you sit here, you cannot have an MP III 5 360 16
It is as true as that I sit here. MP III 5 362 21
saying, "I should like to sit talking with you here all MP III 5 364 30
her cry at being allowed to sit up only one hour MP III 7 387 46
to sit down; but he could have wished her sister away. MP III 10 403 15
she had then only to sit and think of what she had lost. E I 1 6 5
which she had been used to sit and watch the due time, was E I 3 24 11
Harriet?" said she: "did you ever sit for your picture?" E I 6 43 9
But really, I could almost venture, if Harriet would sit E I 6 43 13
"But I am afraid, Mr. Elton, Harriet will not like to sit. E I 6 44 17
She would sit whenever I asked her. E I 6 45 21
a great deal of trouble in persuading him to sit at all. E I 6 46 21
Harriet was to sit again the next day; and Mr. Elton, just E I 6 47 28
"But it is never safe to sit out of doors, my dear." E I 6 48 38
is any thing to say, to sit down and write a letter, and E I 9 76 35
He can sit down and write a fine flourishing letter, full E I 18 148 24
and had been so good as to sit an hour with them, and she E II 1 155 4
Cole was so kind as to sit some time with us, talking of E II 1 156 7
His extreme attention to my mother--wanting her to sit in E II 3 175 39
ask that other woman to sit down to the instrument, if the E II 6 201 28
the lady in question could sit down instead--never seemed E II 6 201 28
destroy my comfort. you must promise me not to sit up." E II 7 211 21
that her own maid should sit up for her; and that Serle E II 7 211 22
others nicely dressed, to sit and smile and look pretty, E II 8 219 44
and till he could find a seat by her, would not sit at all. E II 8 220 47
favour of you to come and sit down with us a little while, E II 9 235 44
was quite ready to sit down to the pianoforte again. E II 10 240 6
this disinclination to sit down and employ myself, this E II 12 262 39
I can sit and admire him now without any great misery. E II 14 271 15
You would not come in and sit with us in this comfortable E II 15 288 35
The kind-hearted, polite old man might then sit down and E II 16 295 28
it since--well, where shall we sit? where shall we sit? E III 2 330 45
Where I sit is of no consequence. E III 2 330 45
strawberries ourselves, and sit under trees;--and whatever E III 6 355 20
go very well; and he could sit still with Mrs. Weston, E III 6 356 30
body to come and sit down, and not to heat themselves.-- E III 6 357 33
on purpose to be tired, and sit all the time with him, E III 6 357 33
bear it no longer--must go and sit in the shade." E III 6 358 35
"You will soon be cooler, if you sit still." said Emma. E III 6 364 54
I shall sit by you. E III 6 365 66
Do you sit where you like? E III 8 378 6
gave Emma the resolution to sit and endure farther with E III 11 408 33
She could soon sit upright on the sofa, and began to hope P III 5 39 40
However, we may as well go and sit with them a little P III 5 40 43
To the great house accordingly they went, to sit the full P III 5 40 44
and no fond parents to sit by and fancy themselves P III 6 46 13
negative, he was not to be induced to sit down again. P III 8 72 58
59
Will not you sit down? P III 9 79 26
Anne, really tired herself, was glad to sit down; and she P III 10 87 22
If we were all like you, I believe we might sit four.-- P III 10 91 40
where she had been used to sit and preside, she had no P IV 1 126 18
They had left Louisa beginning to sit up; but her head, P IV 2 129 1
"He will sit poring over his book, and not know when a P IV 2 132 19
not to be refused, to sit between them; and by some other P IV 8 189 46
It is really very good of you to come and sit with me, P IV 9 194 18
She had only to submit, sit down, be outwardly composed, P IV 11 229 2
to his wife & himself--& sit down on the bank, unable to S 1 364 1
for any profession--& sit down at 1 & 20, on the interest S 5 388 1

SITS (3)
And Mr. Musgrove always sits forward. P III 5 39 39
and arrange in her air! and she sits so upright! P IV 10 215 15
in the water; and benwick sits at her elbow, reading P IV 10 218 24

SITTERS-BY (1)
He came to the part of the room where the sitters-by were E III 2 327 34

SITTING (160)
I heard a carriage at the door as I was sitting with my LS 20 275 1
I was sitting about half an hour ago with Sir James in the LS 23 283 3
"Perhaps you are not sitting in this room, and I am not NA I 3 27 28
are not sitting in this room, and I am not sitting by you. NA I 3 27 28
her own age, who was sitting by her, and had been looking NA I 4 31 2
the two Morlands, after sitting an hour with the Thorpes, NA I 7 50 44
still sitting down all the discredit of wanting a partner. NA I 8 53 2
address on Catherine's entering the box and sitting by her. NA I 10 70 1
was engaged the other evening, when he saw me sitting down. NA I 10 72 11
After sitting with them a quarter of an hour, she rose to NA I 13 103 28
I suppose he saw Isabella sitting down, and fancied she NA II 1 132 17
leaving Isabella still sitting with Captain Tilney. NA II 3 147 28
she and Eleanor were sitting, and said, "I am come, young NA II 11 210 7
dinner at home, that sitting down to a middling one for NA II 11 211 13
had very little idea of the room in which she was sitting. NA II 11 212 18
On each side of the entrance was a sitting room, about SS I 6 28 2
drawings were affixed to the walls of their sitting room. SS I 6 30 5
from eight o'clock till four, without once sitting down." SS I 9 44 25
might have experienced in sitting at home;--and so little SS I 11 55 6
the park, when they were sitting down together by mutual SS I 11 55 8
they had the pleasure of sitting down nearly twenty to SS I 13 67 61
There is one remarkably pretty sitting room up stairs; of SS I 13 69 76
She was sitting by Edward, and in taking his tea from Mrs. SS I 18 98 10
in a low voice, to miss Dashwood, by whom he was sitting. SS I 18 100 22
She was sitting near the window, and as soon as Sir John SS I 19 105 13
And then sitting down again, she very soon forgot that SS I 19 108 36
to, which consists of sitting an hour or two together in SS I 21 124 33
After sitting with them a few minutes, the Miss Steeles SS I 22 135 56
where Elinor was sitting by herself, with an air of such SS III 1 257 2
3
to your sister, who was sitting all alone at her carpet- SS III 1 258 7
brother's ears, as he was sitting in his own dressing-room SS III 1 259 7
to my knowledge has five sitting rooms on the ground-floor, SS III 4 292 55
greater imprudence of sitting in her wet shoes and SS III 6 305 17
But a day spent in sitting shivering over the fire with a SS III 7 307 1
He was sitting in an attitude of deep meditation, and SS III 8 317 9
for some time previously sitting--her rising colour, as SS III 11 349 3
parlour where Mrs E. was sitting respectably attired in W 323 3
when as she was sitting in the cardroom somewhat screened W 333 13
with much sentiment, as they were sitting together.-- W 349 24
he depended on finding sitting quietly employed after tea, W 355 28
into the usual little sitting room, the door of the best W 355 28
the fire, & Miss Watson sitting at the best Pembroke table, W 355 28
with the alternative of sitting above, with her father, & W 361 30
But there is one of her sisters sitting down just behind PP I 3 11 12
After sitting a little while with Jane, on Miss Bingley's PP I 9 41 2
I assure you it is very refreshing after sitting so long PP I 11 56 11
of obliging her in return, by sitting down to whist. PP I 16 76 6
Elizabeth was sitting with her mother and sisters, PP I 23 126 1
After sitting long enough to admire every article of PP II 5 156 4
Catherine, her daughter, and Mrs. Jenkinson were sitting.-- PP II 6 161 10
After sitting a few minutes, they were all sent to one of PP II 6 162 13
than one young lady was sitting down in want of a partner. PP II 8 175 18
Elizabeth was sitting by herself the next morning, and PP II 9 177 1
on Miss Bennet, and after sitting a few minutes longer PP II 9 179 26
Fitzwilliam had been sitting with them at least an hour, PP II 13 209 13
by Miss Darcy, who was sitting there with Mrs. Hurst and PP III 3 267 3
After sitting in this manner a quarter of an hour, without PP III 3 268 5
One morning, soon after their arrival, as she was sitting PP III 9 318 21
22
up the card party, and was sitting up stairs with Kitty. PP III 13 347 27
of the family were sitting together in the dining room, PP III 14 351 1
After sitting for a moment in silence, she said very PP III 14 351 4
5
"This must be a most inconvenient sitting room for the PP III 14 352 11
the table where she was sitting with Kitty; and, while PP III 17 375 28
youngest of the sons, sitting crying on the attic stairs. MP I 2 15 9
And sitting down by her, was at great pains to overcome MP I 2 15 10
She was a woman who spent her days in sitting nicely MP I 2 19 31
Fanny, who was sitting on the other side of Edmund, MP I 6 56 19
20
found in the three ladies sitting there, for Maria would MP I 7 71 31
Sitting and calling to pug, and trying to keep him from MP I 7 74 56
Crawford and her sister sitting side by side full of MP I 8 81 32
After sitting a little while, Miss Crawford was up again. MP I 9 96 73
while you were sitting here so composed and so happy! MP I 10 100 28
at last; and had been sitting down under one of the trees. MP I 10 103 49
from the time of their sitting down to table, it was a MP I 10 104 52
were dancing, and she sitting, most unwillingly, among the MP I 12 116 11
he would object to our sitting more in this room, and less MP I 13 127 29
"Me!" cried Fanny, sitting down again with a most MP I 15 145 46
from the play, and sitting by disregarded; but as it was MP I 17 161 9
I think we are a great deal better employed, sitting MP II 1 186 33
And while my cousins were sitting by without speaking a MP II 3 198 12
idea, and she fancied him sitting in that room again and MP II 4 207 10
her as they were thus sitting together one day: "every MP II 4 208 12
especially when I am sitting out of doors, I am very apt MP II 4 209 16
half their lecture upon sitting down out of doors at this MP II 4 211 24
What do you think we have been sitting down for but to be MP II 4 211 26
either of you had been sitting down alone; but while you MP II 4 211 28
"They cannot have been sitting long," cried Mrs. Grant, " MP II 4 211 28
day is so mild, that your sitting down for a few minutes MP II 4 212 29
Five, only five to be sitting around that table! MP II 5 221 30
at her side, gave his orders for her sitting down entirely. MP II 10 279 22
It might occur to him, that Mr. Crawford had been sitting MP II 10 281 34
It must be sitting up so late last night. MP II 11 283 5
say that he had been sitting with Lady Bertram and Fanny. MP II 12 291 1
"Sitting with them an hour and half!" exclaimed Mary. MP II 12 291 2
There was snow off the ground, and she was sitting in a MP III 1 312 6
"I do not catch your meaning," said Sir Thomas, sitting MP III 1 315 18
his mother and Fanny were sitting as intently and silently MP III 3 336 8
drawing in a chair, and sitting down close by her, that it MP III 3 341 31
in and seeing you here, sitting at this table at work; and MP III 5 360 14
After sitting some time longer, a candle was obtained; but, MP III 7 381 24
By sitting together up stairs, they avoided a great deal MP III 9 398 9
in time to prevent their sitting down to the breakfast MP III 15 445 31
Sitting forwards, however, and screened by her bonnet, MP III 15 445 32
Sitting with her on Sunday evening--a wet Sunday evening-- MP III 16 453 17
After wandering about and sitting under trees with Fanny MP III 17 462 5
father--but the idea of sitting for his picture made him E I 6 45 21
The sitting began; and Harriet, smiling and blushing, and E I 6 46 24
The sitting was altogether very satisfactory; she was E I 6 47 27
Consider, she is sitting down--which naturally presents a E I 6 48 35
is, that she seems to be sitting out of doors, with only a E I 6 48 36
her; and to have him sitting just opposite to her in angry E I 8 65 50
To be sitting long after dinner, was a confinement that he E I 14 122 18
Mrs. Weston and Emma were sitting together on a sopha. E I 15 124 1
"Yes; all the advantages of sitting still when he ought to E I 18 148 24
I do not know a more luxurious state, sir, than sitting at E II 3 170 2
I was sitting near the door--Elizabeth saw me directly; E II 3 178 52
end of the shop; and I kept sitting near the door!-- E II 3 178 52
by the house--the very sitting of his hat, being all in E II 4 184 10
We have been sitting with your father--glad to see him so E II 5 188 7
She opened the parlour door, and saw two gentlemen sitting E II 5 190 21
He had been sitting with her, it appeared, most E II 6 196 1
sitting with them very nearly three quarters of an hour. E II 6 199 7
I am only afraid of your sitting up for me. E II 7 211 21
I am afraid you will be sitting up by yourself, instead of E II 7 211 21
Been impatient to leave the dining-room--hated sitting E II 8 220 48
the room at Miss Fairfax, who was sitting exactly opposite. E II 8 222 54
who was still sitting at it, to play something more. E II 10 242 16
A private dance, without sitting down to supper, was E II 11 254 45
She heard of her walking with the Eltons, sitting with the E II 15 285 12
usual stipulation of not sitting at the bottom of the E II 16 291 4
only young lady sitting down;--and so equal had been E III 2 326 33
in her hand, and after sitting down and hesitating, thus E III 4 337 1
2
Well--(sitting down again) go on--what else?" E III 4 339 13
Mr. Elton was sitting here, I remember, much about where I E III 4 340 20
that to have any of them sitting down out of doors to eat E III 6 356 29
at Christmas, when one is sitting round the fire; but E III 7 372 37
any of the others, or sitting almost alone, and quite E III 7 374 54
during her absence, and were sitting with her father.-- E III 9 385 1
He had been sitting with them half an hour, she found. E III 9 386 8
round, comparing and sitting in judgment on sentiments and E III 10 399 61
Here have I been sitting this hour, giving these young E III 16 457 36
been at Uppercross); and sitting down together to pore P III 8 64 7
and Mrs. Musgrove were sitting, took a place by the latter, P III 8 67 28
in the cottage were sitting quietly at work, they were P III 10 83 3
do her more harm than any sitting down could do her good;"- P III 10 86 17
sitting down together in our lodgings at North Yarmouth?" P III 10 92 44
the flow of the tide, for sitting in unwearied P III 11 95 9
could ever be, that the sitting down to the same table P III 11 99 21
My dear cousin, (sitting down by her) you have a better P IV 4 150 17
Colonel Wallis declined sitting down again, and Mr. Elliot P IV 8 189 46

Her plan of sitting with Lady Russell must give way for P IV 10 220 30
where the two ladies were sitting, and though nearer to P IV 11 231 12
business of dinner or of sitting after dinner was going on S 6 389 1
Whitby at the library was sitting in her inner room, S 6 389 1
very favourably; for tho' sitting thus apart with him (S 7 395 1
change from Miss Denham sitting in cold grandeur in Mrs S 7 396 1
could,--& boasted much of sitting by the fire till he had S 10 414 1
was by Arthur, who was sitting next to the fire with a S 10 414 1
They were sitting so near each other & appeared so closely S 12 426 1
They were shewn into the usual sitting room, well- S 12 427 1

SITTING-ROOM (6)

entered their common sitting-room, than Marianne turned SS III 10 342 7
into a very pretty sitting-room, lately fitted up with PP III 1 249 43
filled her favourite sitting-room with pretty furniture, MP I 4 41 15
of the common sitting-room, he got up to look at it, and E I 9 69 2
The appearance of the little sitting-room as they entered, E II 10 240 1
Elton's voice from the sitting-room had not checked her, E III 16 453 10

SITUATED (15)

Marianne, "we could not be more unfortunately situated." SS I 16 88 39
Pleased to find herself more comfortably situated in that SS II 5 168 11
Cleveland was a spacious, modern-built house, situated on SS III 6 302 7
what, as you were then situated, could never be." SS III 13 368 26
It was a handsome modern building, well situated on rising PP II 5 156 4
are most delightfully situated through my means; and it PP II 6 165 32
Elizabeth found from her aunt, that Pemberley was situated. PP II 19 240 12
by Pemberley house, situated on the opposite side of the PP III 1 245 3
When he returned to understand how Fanny was situated, and MP I 4 36 7
So long divided, and so differently situated, the ties of MP III 13 428 15
and well situated as it was, with a melancholy aspect. MP III 15 447 36
must not hope to be ever situated as you are, in the midst E II 16 293 17
18
they were likely to be situated in such a part of Bath as P IV 6 165 9
Situated as we are with Lady Dalrymple, cousins, we ought P IV 6 166 16
was seen romantically situated among wood on a high S 1 364 1

SITUATION (267)

society for my present situation & state of mind; & I LS 1 243 1
living did not suit her situation or feelings, I might LS 6 252 2
I wish her to find her situation as unpleasant as possible. LS 7 253 1
not appear; but as her situation seems to have been LS 15 266 2
present, till some other situation can be found for her. LS 15 266 4
At length Lady Susan, weary I believe of her situation, LS 20 276 4
in unison with our situation & with those lively feelings LS 25 292 3
you have considered our situation in the light in which I LS 30 301 4
happier times, when your situation is as independant as LS 39 307 1
easy till I can go to town & judge of her situation myself. LS 41 310 4
Her situation in life, the character of her father and NA I 1 13 1
as she can?) must from situation be at this time the NA I 2 19 3
top of the room, their situation was just the same; they NA I 2 21 9
vain for a more eligible situation, were obliged to sit NA I 2 22 10
and sisters, the situation of some, the growth of the rest, NA I 7 51 54
the real dignity of her situation could not be known, she NA I 8 53 2
doubt the happiness of a situation which confining her NA I 10 71 8
to make known his situation and ask consent; and here was NA I 15 119 14
person's feelings, age, situation, and probable habits of NA II 1 132 20
remind Isabella of her situation, and make her aware of NA II 4 150 1
This was placing her in a very uncomfortable situation, NA II 5 155 2
which, though in a situation conspicuous enough, had never NA II 6 168 10
every thing seemed to speak the awfulness of her situation. NA II 6 168 10
about her, or which her situation in life could command. NA II 9 197 25
I do not envy his situation, either as a lover or a son." NA II 10 205 24
large and populous village, in a situation not unpleasant. NA II 11 212 17
the solitude of her situation, the darkness of her chamber, NA II 13 227 26
her sentiments and her situation, convey gratitude without NA II 14 235 14
Henry and Eleanor, perceiving nothing in her situation NA II 15 245 12
only by inferiority of situation from addressing her. NA II 16 251 5
woman in Mrs. Dashwood's situation, with only common SS I 1 6 9
situation more comfortable than it was in his power to do. SS I 2 9 6
But she could hear of no situation that at once answered SS I 3 14 1
situation which forbad the indulgence of his affection. SS I 4 22 18
she might think necessary, if the situation pleased her. SS I 4 23 20
The situation of Barton, in a county so far distant from SS I 4 23 20
She explained the situation. SS I 5 25 1
The situation of the house was good. SS I 6 28 3
those, whose situation might be considered, in comparison SS I 7 33 3
declined what her situation rendered necessary, took her SS I 9 42 8
its situation, and grieving that no one should live in it. SS I 14 73 17
from his dependent situation, to give into her schemes, SS I 15 78 26
But all this may be explained by such a situation of his SS I 15 81 43
Had he been in a situation to act independently and marry SS I 15 81 44
itself, in a much higher situation than the cottage, SS I 18 96 4
pointing to her daughter) it was wrong in her situation. SS I 19 107 29
in such an uncomfortable situation as I am; but however SS I 22 128 9
"No; considering our situation, it was not strange. SS I 22 131 32
you, to acknowledge your situation to me, and be assured SS II 2 146 6
your situation would have been pitiable indeed." SS II 2 147 8
wondering at her own situation, so short had their SS II 4 159 1
solicitude of Marianne's situation to have the same SS II 4 159 1
Impatient in this situation to be doing something that SS II 5 171 38
an account of her real situation with respect to him. SS II 5 172 39
Her own situation gained in the comparison; for while she SS II 6 179 18
In this situation, Elinor, roused from sleep by her SS II 7 180 1
2
but what any one would have written in the same situation. SS II 7 188 43
last the misery of her situation, for she experienced SS II 9 205 24
to all the misery of her situation; and happy had it been SS II 9 206 24
was--yes, in such a situation it was my greatest comfort. SS II 9 207 26
years I had every reason to be pleased with her situation. SS II 9 208 28
he had seduced, in a situation of the utmost distress, SS II 9 209 30
wretched and hopeless situation of this poor girl, and SS II 9 210 32
make your situation pleasant, might be reasonably expected. SS II 11 222 11
only given her, because her real situation was unknown. SS II 13 238 2
minute a detail of her situation, as only Miss Steele had SS II 14 247 5
Elinor set him right as to its situation, and it seemed SS II 14 251 16
I cannot conceive a situation more deplorable. SS III 1 268 50
in his proper situation, and would have wanted for nothing. SS III 1 269 53
"You forget," said Elinor, gently, "that its situation is SS III 3 279 4
passed--for the cruel situation in which the unjustifiable SS III 4 289 31
in every change of situation that might befal him; on his, SS III 4 290 43
her situation continued, with little variation, the same. SS III 7 309 7
I acknowledge that her situation and her character ought SS III 8 322 36
If you can pity me, Miss Dashwood, pity my situation as it SS III 8 327 55
to me, and in a situation like mine, any thing was to be SS III 8 328 63
that would suit us quite as well as our present situation." SS III 9 338 24
What in a situation like mine, but a most shamefully SS III 10 345 20
know, when aware of your situation, to attempt all the SS III 11 350 9
distressed by Marianne's situation, knew not on which SS III 11 353 24
on a change in his situation, so wonderful and so sudden;-- SS III 12 360 26
His situation indeed was more than commonly joyful. SS III 13 361 3
removed, compared her situation with what so lately it had SS III 13 363 8
In such a situation as that, where there seemed nothing to SS III 13 367 22
merely for the sake of situation--is a sort of thing that W 318 2
are above my situation, I must endeavour to conceal them.-- W 318 2
ever felt what was due to a woman, in Emma's situation.-- W 346 21
read & think,--tho' her situation was hardly such as to W 361 31
of their own kindness & situation, to suppose to offer W 362 32
was pleased with the situation and the principal rooms, PP I 4 16 13
though ample for her situation in life, could but ill PP I 7 28 1
to visit Jane, and form her own judgment of her situation. PP I 9 41 1
glad to improve myself, for in my situation of life-----" PP I 16 76 7
find me in every respect ill qualified for the situation." PP I 19 107 14
highly desirable. my situation in life, my connections PP I 19 108 19
wife to a man in my situation, who naturally looks for PP I 20 110 4
I cannot consider your situation with much compassion." PP I 21 120 26
connections, and situation in life, I am convinced that my PP I 22 125 17
him from so unpleasant a situation, now put herself PP I 23 126 4
situation remained the same, her peace equally wounded. PP II 1 134 3
allowance enough for difference of situation and temper. PP II 1 135 12
will we begin quarrelling about its relative situation. PP II 4 154 23
are, which my situation in life has allowed me to acquire. PP II 6 160 3
admired her, and his situation in life was most eligible; PP II 9 181 31
The situation of your mother's family, though PP II 12 198 5
he could ever be in a situation to receive it, and PP II 12 201 5
guarded and attended, according to their situation in life. PP II 14 211 13
How grievous then was the thought that, of a situation so PP II 14 213 18
Our situation with regard to Lady Catherine's family is PP II 15 215 4
and assurance, by a situation of such double danger as a PP II 19 237 3
superseded by Lydia's situation, hastily exclaimed, "I beg PP III 4 276 6
to a sense of her situation by the voice of her companion, PP III 4 278 20
our relationship, and my situation in life, to condole PP III 6 296 11
Poor Lydia's situation must, at best, be bad enough; but PP III 7 307 51
for a proper situation for her daughter, and, without PP III 8 310 7
her present disgraceful situation, and return to her PP III 10 322 2
future situation, he could conjecture very little about it. PP III 10 323 2
and his situation must have been benefited by marriage. PP III 10 323 2
She knew how little such a situation would give pleasure PP III 12 340 12
Their situation was awkward enough; but her's she thought PP III 13 346 22
The situation of affairs in the Longbourn family could not PP III 13 350 55
attached to her situation, the she could, upon the whole, PP III 14 355 46
"That will make your ladyship's situation at present more PP III 14 356 49
situation, and his expectation of a young olive-branch. PP III 15 364 22
and anxiety of his situation, now forced herself to speak; PP III 16 366 8
in the family when her situation became known; she was PP III 17 372 2
cheap situation, and always spending more than they ought. PP III 19 387 8
No situation would be beneath him--or what did Sir Thomas MP I 1 5 2
by great sensibility of her situation, and great timidity. MP I 2 16 20
was consistent with his situation and rights; he made her MP I 2 17 22
any thing at all promising in their situation or conduct. MP I 2 21 34
change in Mrs. Norris's situation, and the improvement in MP I 3 24 7
"Every thing--my situation--my foolishness and awkwardness. MP I 3 26 28
My situation is as much altered as my income. MP I 3 30 50
too lowly of her own situation to imagine she should ever MP I 4 35 6
more be made to his person than to his situation in life. MP I 4 42 18
her situation--Mr. Crawford must take care of himself." MP I 5 44 3
Miss Crawford soon felt, that he and his situation might MP I 5 48 28
to relate her brother's situation; her voice was animated MP I 6 60 47
fine timber, but the situation of the house is dreadful. MP I 8 82 34
The situation of the house excluded the possibility of MP I 9 85 4
But I cannot call that situation nothing, which has the MP I 9 92 45
Young folks in their situation should be excused complying MP I 12 117 13
regard to Maria, whose situation is a very delicate one, MP I 13 125 17
to admit that Maria's situation might require particular MP I 13 128 38
home representation--the situation of one, and language of MP I 14 137 23
"I do not like my situation; this place is too hot for me"- MP I 15 147 56
and ingratitude of her situation, had been too distressing MP I 16 150 1
any alarm for Maria's situation, or any endeavour at MP I 17 160 8
obtain them, and could better bear a subordinate situation. MP II 3 204 32
your relations are in no situation to do any thing for you, MP II 4 213 40
in a situation which he must know she would never stoop to. MP II 5 228 69
herself in the critical situation of being applied to for MP II 7 239 4
the value of such a situation in point of privilege and MP II 7 244 27
Peterborough in same situation as himself, and they were MP II 8 255 10
such sacrifices of situation and employment on his side as MP II 8 255 10
situation, no reasonable hindrance to a perfect friendship. MP II 9 263 16
him; not merely situation in life, fortune, and character, MP III 1 315 27
a situation which her fancy had never taken into account. MP III 2 326 3
His situation was new and animating. MP III 2 327 4
situation of matters at Mansfield were known to him. MP III 3 334 4
to chuse whether her situation with regard to Crawford MP III 4 345 1
In my situation, it would have been the extreme of vanity MP III 4 353 45
to Mrs. Fraser in consequence of his situation with you. MP III 5 360 16
Lady Bertram's; and a situation of similar affluence and MP III 8 390 5
idea of his brother's situation, and acquaint her with the MP III 14 429 1
him the almost desperate situation in which affairs then MP III 16 450 9
in sacrificing such a situation, plunging into such MP III 16 454 18
can exceed the misery of such a mind in such a situation? MP III 17 464 11
The real evils indeed of Emma's situation were the power E I 1 5 4
to seek and his own situation to improve as he could. E I 2 16 4
was more equal to her situation than most girls would have E I 2 18 11
Her situation was altogether the subject of hours of E I 2 18 12
her own situation in life, her leisure, and powers. E I 3 24 10
situation she should not have discovered the truth. E I 4 27 3
his figure and look, and situation in life seem to allow E I 4 34 42
Mr. Elton's situation was most suitable, quite the E I 4 35 44
and wanted another situation; I do not think you would E I 5 37 10
rationally to the varieties of her situation in life.-- E I 5 39 15
Any other situation would have been much less in character. E I 6 48 39
for he is as much her superior in sense as in situation. E I 8 61 38
You and Mr. Elton are by situation called together; you E I 9 75 25
It had no advantage of situation; but had been very much E I 10 83 2
sure I should be a fool to change such a situation as mine. E I 10 84 15
body else, to give up a situation which she believed more E I 14 119 5
him to notice but his situation and his civility.-- E I 16 136 9
conduct, without an intimate knowledge of their situation. E I 18 146 15
in Mr. Frank Churchill's situation, you would be able to E I 18 147 19
"Oh! the difference of situation and habit! E I 18 148 21
When she took in her history, indeed, her situation, as E II 2 167 13
very small, admired the situation, the walk to Highbury, E II 5 191 26
"You know Miss Fairfax's situation in life, I conclude; E II 6 201 21
to say when you speak of Miss Fairfax's situation in life. E II 6 201 23
I perfectly understand your situation, however, Miss E II 14 275 30
And her situation is so calculated to affect one!-- E II 15 282 5
with Miss Fairfax's situation and understand what her home E II 15 283 6
shall be constantly on the watch for an eligible situation. E II 15 284 9
her a permanent situation to the including her in those E II 15 288 39
which makes the difference, it is not age, but situation. E II 16 294 22
to imply the change of situation which time usually brings. E II 16 294 23
she had yet heard of any situation likely to suit her, and E II 17 299 1
A situation such as you deserve, and your friends would E II 17 300 12
inferior, commonplace situation, in a family not moving in E II 17 301 16
the comfort of such a situation together," said Jane, E II 17 301 19
be too greatly your superior in situation to think of you. E III 4 341 35
being hurried into a delightful situation against her will. E III 5 343 1
He could not see her in a situation of such danger, E III 5 349 26
report, and the situation of Mrs. Weston, whose happiness E III 6 352 1
becoming, characteristic situation, low and sheltered--its E III 6 358 35
A situation, a most desirable situation, was in question. E III 6 359 37
wit to a woman of her character, age, and situation?-- E III 7 374 56
Were she your equal in situation--but, Emma, consider how E III 7 375 61
Her situation should secure your compassion. E III 7 375 61
fortunate--such a situation, I suppose, as no young woman E III 8 379 8
and happy she is to have secured such a situation. E III 8 379 8
Impossible that any situation could be more replete with E III 8 380 13
of Mrs. Suckling's situation, she had come to the E III 8 381 15
but yet, this is such a situation as she cannot feel E III 8 382 29
to talk over Jane Fairfax's situation with Mr. Knightley.-- E III 9 386 8
I hope it is a dry situation, and that her health will be E III 9 387 10
And how much may be said in her situation for even that E III 10 400 65
of herself, it is in a situation like Jane Fairfax's.-- E III 10 400 66
Her inferiority, whether of mind or situation, seemed E III 11 414 50
really confused--"I am in a very extraordinary situation. E III 13 426 17
It was merely a blind to conceal his real situation with E III 13 427 19
favour,--equality of situation--I mean, as far as regards E III 13 428 23
the exact nature of my situation when I first arrived at E III 14 437 8
My right to place myself in a situation requiring such E III 14 437 8

From our relative situation, those attentions were her due, E III 14 438 8
for his sake, in a situation of extreme difficulty and E III 15 446 20
His situation is an evil--but you must consider it as what E III 18 472 22
have been some amusement to myself in the same situation. E III 18 478 67
Elliot's character; vanity of person and of situation. P III 1 4 5
From situation, Mrs. Clay was, in Lady Russell's estimate, P III 2 16 17
in the Admiral's situation in life, which was just high P III 3 24 36
for each party's perfectly knowing their situation. P III 5 34 13
we must be in a good situation--none of your Queen-Squares P III 6 42 1
The child's situation put the visit entirely aside, but P III 7 53 2
the remarkable situation of the town, the principal street P III 11 95 9
this allusion to his situation, she was emboldened to go P III 11 101 24
what was best to be done, as to their general situation. P III 12 112 56
entitled by birth and situation to be in love with an P IV 2 130 7
a lofty, dignified situation, such as becomes a man of P IV 3 137 1
high ideas of their own situation in life, and was reduced P IV 4 148 11
account brought her situation forward in a more decided P IV 5 152 3
She could scarcely imagine a more cheerless situation in P IV 5 153 8
"I do not suppose the situation my friend Mrs. Rooke is in P IV 5 156 12
13
you such as she was, in situation, and name, and home, P IV 5 160 25
It had been in situation. P IV 6 166 19
A man like him, in his situation! P IV 8 183 10
Such was her situation, with a vacant space at hand, when P IV 8 189 47
her, by every thing in situation, by his own sentiments, P IV 9 192 2
(her inferior situation in society, indeed, rendered that P IV 9 200 57
may have for his own situation in life now, as a young man P IV 9 202 66
and altogether such in situation and manner, as to give a P IV 9 206 88
sufferings of her situation, had been such as could not be P IV 9 209 96
of her situation, could do nothing towards tranquillity. P IV 11 238 44
maintain himself in the situation in which Providence had P IV 12 248 1
her situation, for a change is not very probable there. P IV 12 250 6
moment, & learning her situation, persuaded her to accept S 3 378 1
for a situation little better than a nursery maid.-- S 3 379 1
it--& I, a rather better situation!--one other hill brings S 4 380 1
Her situation with Lady Denham so very much in favour of S 6 391 1
Her situation in every way called for it. S 8 405 2
the poor Mullins's situation, & sound her ladyship as to a S 12 423 1
You have only to state the present afflicted situation of S 12 423 1
was a situation which must not be judged with severity.-- S 12 426 1

SITUATION'S (1)
assured her aunt of her situation's being uncomfortable, & LS 42 311 3

SITUATIONS (27)
related their different situations and views,--that John NA I 4 32 2
As for myself, I am sure I only wish our situations were NA I 15 119 18
variety of dreadful situations and horrid scenes, which NA II 6 166 9
on a fairer ground than inequality of situations. NA II 11 208 2
but there are some situations of the human mind in which NA II 14 239 28
of his cousins' situations in the most delicate SS I 21 125 34
and from our different situations in life, from his being SS II 2 147 12
"Nor I," answered Marianne with energy, "our situations SS II 5 170 26
had the nature of our situations allowed it; but I had no SS II 9 208 28
a resemblance in their situations, which to her fancy SS III 1 261 11
"Our situations have borne little resemblance." SS III 10 345 27
& few situations made him appear to greater advantage. W 359 28
connected with him in situations of respectability, he MP I 1 3 1
be so consistent with the relative situations of each. MP I 1 7 7
"You have undoubtedly--and there are situations in which MP I 10 99 16
difference in our situations--that she need not be so MP I 15 141 21
to the same event in situations more at ease, but under MP II 9 266 22
unfriendly in their situations; and positively declared, MP III 2 327 5
which their relative situations admitted; but farther than MP III 17 465 13
is requisite in situations directly opposite to your own. E I 18 147 17
who are in interesting situations, that a young person, E II 4 181 1
to conduct herself in critical situations, than I can be." E II 6 203 38
it as far as they can; though all have not our situations. E II 15 283 9
candidates there always are for the first situations. E II 17 299 8
situations increasing every other motive of good will. E III 16 452 7
situations, would he ever learn her real sentiments? P IV 8 191 51
made a baronet, she would not change situations with Anne. P IV 12 250 5

SIX (94)
me six years ago, & which never succeeded at last. LS 5 249 1
Frederica's visit was nominally for six weeks; but her LS 42 313 7
lived on--lived to have six children more--to see them NA I 1 13 1
and dangers of a six weeks' residence in Bath, it may be NA I 2 18 1
You ought to be tired at the end of six weeks." NA I 10 78 43
I should be tired, if I were to stay here six months." NA I 10 78 44
'For six weeks, I allow Bath is pleasant enough; but NA I 10 78 45
winter, lengthen their six weeks into ten or twelve, and NA I 10 78 45
of the kitchen, the six or seven rooms she had now seen NA II 8 183 2
light of the sky between six and seven o'clock, or by the NA II 9 190 1
At four they were to dine, and at six to set off on their NA II 11 214 26
at six o'clock, the General having taken his coffee, the NA II 11 215 28
Soon after six Eleanor entered her room, eager to show NA II 13 227 27
or alarm, and between six and seven o'clock in the evening NA II 14 232 6
children, a boy and girl of six and four years old, who NA II 14 233 8
farther than their maintenance for six months at Norland. SS I 5 27 6
Lady Middleton was not more than six or seven and twenty; SS I 6 31 8
a fine little boy about six years old, by which means SS I 6 31 9
"You would not be six hours later," said Willoughby, "if SS I 13 64 28
it wanted it very much, when I was there six years ago." SS I 13 67 64
His estate had been rated by Sir John at about six or SS I 14 71 4
Her husband was a grave looking young man of five or six SS I 19 106 22
reprimand on the subject five or six times every day. SS I 21 118 2
At last, however, and after I had been six months in SS II 9 207 26
expected by all to comprise at least five or six weeks. SS II 10 213 3
man worth more than five or six hundred a-year, at the SS II 11 227 50
and saw Marianne at six o'clock sink into a quiet, steady, SS III 7 315 25
I mean never to be later in rising than six, and from that SS III 10 343 9
By reading only six hours a-day, I shall gain in the SS III 10 343 9
he came into this country, six years ago; and very great W 316 1
as Robert, who has got a good wife & six thousand pounds?" W 321 2
he had been clerk, with a fortune of six thousand pounds.-- W 348 23
herself for having had that six thousand pounds, & for W 349 23
that the aunt could never have had six thousand pounds.-- W 350 24
six with him from London, his five sisters and a cousin. PP I 3 10 4
young Colonel, with five or six thousand a year, should PP I 7 29 12
and at half past six Elizabeth was summoned to dinner. PP I 8 35 1
"Yes, and her petticoat; I hope you saw her petticoat, six PP I 8 36 6
"I am no longer surprised at your knowing only six PP I 8 39 52
A thousand things may arise in six months!" PP I 21 120 27
"Why, at that rate, you will have been here only six weeks. PP II 14 211 8
She had spent six weeks with great enjoyment; and the PP II 15 215 3
tent, tenderly flirting with at least six officers at once. PP II 18 232 22
The children, two girls of six and eight years old, and PP II 19 239 10
Sir Thomas says you will have six hundred a year." MP I 3 29 49
been noticed for the next six months, and Miss Sneyd, I MP I 5 51 40
Very different from you, miss, when you first began, six MP I 7 69 22
she might have listened six weeks before with some MP I 12 114 1
I could name at this moment at least six young men within MP I 15 148 58
least six young men within six miles of us, who are wild MP I 15 148 58
Easton, and we brought home six brace between us, and MP II 1 181 16
and might each have killed six times as many; but we MP II 1 181 16
has taken place in her looks within the last six weeks. MP II 6 229 5
and dignity, the remaining six, under Miss Crawford's MP II 7 239 8
not suppose I have worn it six times; it is very pretty-- MP II 8 260 22
a last look at the five or six determined couple, who were MP II 10 280 33
for at least the last six weeks--I cannot let my brother MP II 13 303 15
Those five or six days more at Lessingby might have been MP III 4 354 48
six, and hoped you would be here in time to go with him." MP III 7 377 7
be off for Spithead by six, so you had better go with him. MP III 7 380 20
Maxwell, only six weeks before she was taken for death. MP III 7 387 44
and wound up her spirits for the six days ensuing. MP III 11 408 4
Two months is an ample allowance, I should think six weeks MP III 11 410 16
evening there; and from six o'clock to half past nine, MP III 11 413 32
A woman married only six months ago, a man professing MP III 15 441 20
Depend upon it, a man of six or seven-and-twenty can take E I 1 14 48
Six years hence, if he could meet with a good sort of E I 4 30 18
"Six years hence! dear Miss Woodhouse, he would be thirty E I 4 30 19
being asked for it five or six times, allowing them to E I 7 56 44
her convictions, all her prophesies for the last six weeks. E I 17 141 5
she had thankfully passed six weeks not six months ago?-- E II 5 187 4
He comes to Highbury himself, he says, six days out of E II 6 200 14
a boy of six years old, who knows nothing of the matter?" E II 8 224 67
Mr. Cole gave me a hint of it six weeks ago." E II 15 287 28
your walk, for you were not six yards from your own door E II 16 293 15
16
wishes to get rid of, been six months on board Captain P III 6 51 30
by poor Dick's having been six months under his care, and P III 6 52 33
"that was in the year six;" "that happened before I went P III 8 63 2
I went to sea in the year six," occurred in the course of P III 8 63 2
We had been six hours in the sound, when a gale came on, P III 8 66 16
instead of going six miles another way; of his having, in P III 9 78 19
to retract, and the whole six set toward together in the P III 10 83 6
curiosity, and the whole six were collected to look, by P III 12 105 9
at the great house very well, for a month "or six weeks. P IV 6 163 7
in six months, or even in twelve, but a long engagement!" P IV 11 231 8
"I was six weeks with Edward," said he, "and saw him happy. P IV 11 243 67
Six years of separation and suffering might have been P IV 11 247 84
The invitation was to one, for six months--with the S 3 379 1
The six months had long been over--& not a syllable was S 3 379 1
ancle with my own hand for six hours without intermission)- S 5 386 1
She has been suffering much from the headache and six S 5 387 1
They'll stay their six weeks.-- S 6 393 1
Our dinner is not ordered till six--& by that time I hope S 9 411 1
the inevitable expence of six new dresses each for a three S 11 421 1

SIX-AND-THIRTY (1)
had not lived above six-and-thirty hours after his return. E III 9 387 11

SIX-AND-TWENTY (1)
which, at the age of six-and-twenty, with no want of sense, MP III 17 462 4

SIXPENCE (5)
not be sixpence the richer for it at the end of the year. SS I 2 11 23
sent back a weight upon your family, without a sixpence.-- W 352 26
you are returned upon their hands without a sixpence." W 352 26
done for them, because Wickham has not sixpence of his own. PP III 7 305 36
very likely to give away sixpence of it; and nobody is E I 10 85 19

SIXPENCES (1)
she could, and win or lose a few sixpences by his fireside. E I 3 22 5

SIXTEEN (28)
her mother; & a girl of sixteen who has received so LS 3 247 1
Frederica must be as much as sixteen, & ought to know LS 15 266 3
at the tender age of sixteen we shall have room for the LS 19 274 2
will reach the age of sixteen without altering her name as NA I 2 19 3
was a sitting room, about sixteen feet square; and beyond SS I 6 28 2
which had seized her at sixteen and a half, of ever seeing SS I 10 49 10
She is a handsome girl, about fifteen or sixteen, and I PP I 16 82 43
"Yes, my youngest is not sixteen. PP II 6 165 35
Her character will be fixed, and she will, at sixteen, be PP II 18 231 18
though little more than sixteen, her figure was formed, PP III 2 261 4
She will be married at sixteen!-- PP III 7 306 44
And she was only sixteen last June. PP III 7 306 47
wishes, since Jane was sixteen, was now on the point of PP III 8 310 7
who at seventeen and sixteen, and tall of their age, had MP I 2 12 3
sixteen in some respects too much like his sister at ten." MP I 3 33 64
since Maria Bertram was sixteen, was now considered MP I 16 151 1
none to compare with him, and we were a party of sixteen. MP III 12 416 2
Sixteen years had Miss Taylor been in Mr. Woodhouses's E I 1 5 3
the affection of sixteen years--how she had taught and how E I 1 6 6
settled in London, only sixteen miles off, was much beyond E I 1 7 9
alarms were needless; the sixteen miles being happily E I 11 91 3
I was sixteen years old when you were born." E I 12 99 6
"I have still the advantage of you by sixteen years' E I 12 99 10
There was certainly no harm in his travelling sixteen E II 7 205 1
Sixteen miles--nay, eighteen--it must be full eighteen to E III 1 318 10
moment before, as unquestionably sixteen miles distant.-- E III 13 424 1
Three girls, the two eldest sixteen and fourteen, was an P III 1 4 6
Elizabeth had succeeded, at sixteen, to all that was P III 1 5 8

SIXTH (2)
The Allens had now entered on the sixth week of their stay NA II 2 138 1
and the two sixth with Lizzy, and the boulanger-----" PP I 3 13 16

SIXTY (3)
bid me sixty at once; Morland was with me at the time." NA I 7 47 19
having only one minute in sixty to bestow even on the NA I 7 51 54
'Sixty', said I, 'or perhaps sixty-two'. P III 3 20 16

SIXTY-FIVE (1)
Sixty-five miles farther than from Maple Grove to London. E II 18 306 10

SIXTY-TWO (1)
'Sixty', said I, 'or perhaps sixty-two'. P III 3 20 16

SIZE (38)
lamp to take in its size--its walls hung with tapestry NA II 5 158 15
might be more comfort in rooms of only half their size. NA II 6 166 7
must be exactly of the true size for rational happiness. NA II 6 166 7
size, and much less than she supposed it to be at first. NA II 7 172 1
a room magnificent both in size and furniture--the real NA II 8 182 2
of the country, and the size of the village; but in her NA II 11 212 17
well-proportioned size, and handsomely fitted up as a NA II 11 213 21
With the size and furniture of the house Mrs. Dashwood was SS I 6 29 4
of a nice comfortable size for constant use, and with SS I 13 69 76
not an inch to its size, if my feelings are regarded." SS I 14 72 7
I warrant you she is a fine size by this time." SS II 4 163 16
for himself, and till its size, shape, and ornaments were SS II 11 220 3
made very light of, at least as far as regarded its size. SS III 3 283 20
it caught mine-- and its size, the elegance of the paper, SS III 8 328 61
comparative height and size; for that will have more PP I 10 50 39
so much struck with the size and furniture of the PP I 16 75 2
remark on the size of the room, or the number of couples." PP I 18 91 9
be, rejected many as deficient in size and importance. PP III 8 310 7
Her elder cousins mortified her by reflections on her size, MP I 2 14 8
the fiftieth part of the size of Sotherton, I should be MP I 6 53 9
size displayed, and all were glad to be doing something. MP I 9 84 2
and neighbourhood are of a size capable of knowing his MP I 9 93 49
a pretty height and size; such a firm and upright figure. E I 5 39 20
they might decide together on the best size for Harriet. E I 6 44 19
of a gentleman in small size, whole-length--"my last and E I 6 45 21
She had soon fixed on the size and sort of portrait. E I 6 46 23
particularly graceful; her size a most becoming medium, E II 2 167 12
united; the shop first in size and fashion in the place.-- E II 3 178 52
were attached to its size, he could be no judge of the E II 6 204 43
their exactly equal size, that it was a little the largest. E II 11 247 2
Another room of much better size might be secured for the E II 11 254 44
Mrs. Elton seemed most favourably impressed by the size of E II 14 272 18
That room was the very shape and size of the morning-room E II 14 272 18
she viewed the respectable size and style of the building, E III 6 358 35
Mrs. Musgrove was of a comfortable substantial size, P III 8 68 29
Personal size and mental sorrow have certainly no P III 8 68 30
Sanditon, precluded by its size from experiencing any of S 1 368 1
What is the size of their family?--" S 9 409 1

SIZED (3)
been used to much better sized apartments at Mr. Allen's?" NA II 6 166 6
use; it was a better sized room, and had a pleasanter PP II 7 168 1
in the very moderate sized apartment, which was every E II 1 155 4

SKELETON (3)
I know it must be a skeleton, I am sure it is Laurentina's NA I 6 39 7
must be a skeleton, I am sure it is Laurentina's skeleton. NA I 6 39 7

I am sure there must be Laurentina's skeleton behind it." NA I 6 41 19
SKETCH (10)
enough even to attempt a sketch of her lover's profile NA I 1 16 10
hopes, by this vigorous sketch of their future ennui, to SS III 3 280 9
her; she turned away her head from every sketch of him. SS III 12 357 4
Miss Bennet, that you were not to sketch my character at PP I 18 94 41
was finally settled according to Charlotte's first sketch. PP II 4 151 1
You have given us an amusing sketch, and human nature MP I 9 87 16
against the wall, a small sketch of a ship sent four years MP I 16 152 2
Here is my sketch of the fourth, who was a baby. E I 6 45 21
Then here is my last"--unclosing a pretty sketch of a E I 6 45 21
pleased with the first day's sketch to wish to go on. E I 6 47 27
SKETCHED (1)
came near her while she sketched--and to both, the S 11 421 1
SKETCHES (2)
You will have my sketches, some time or other, to look at-- E III 6 364 60
"That may be--but not by sketches in Swisserland. E III 6 365 61
SKIES (1)
Allen not having his own skies and barometer about him, NA I 11 82 1
SKILFUL (2)
Skilful has been the hand." E I 6 43 6
in London, and had been skilful enough to dissuade him P III 2 14 10
SKILL (14)
in which his foresight and skill in directing the dogs had NA I 9 66 31
the first to possess the skill of unlocking a cabinet, the NA II 7 173 2
but he eluded the skill of them all; and they were at last PP I 3 9 1
If a woman conceals her affection with the same skill from PP I 6 21 2
might be rendered interesting by the skill of the speaker. PP I 16 76 4
concerned, or would have hesitated to try their skill. MP I 13 122 2
with her servants, without skill to make them better, and MP III 8 389 4
She was not much deceived as to her own skill either as an E I 6 44 19
of the beauty of one, the skill of the other, and the E I 6 47 27
pretensions) with the skill of such an observer on such a E I 8 67 57
"I thought he meant to try his skill, by his manner of E I 9 76 29
skill or right of judging of any body's performance.-- E II 6 201 28
Mrs. Churchill had been recommended to the medical skill E III 1 317 7
I have not much confidence in poor Arthur's skill for S 9 411 1
SKIN (14)
She had a thin awkward figure, a sallow skin without NA I 1 13 1
brown skin, with dark eyes, and rather dark hair.'-- NA I 6 42 30
Her skin was very brown, but from its transparency, her SS I 10 46 2
Her breath, her skin, her lips, all flattered Elinor with SS III 7 314 22
the hollow eye, the sickly skin, the posture of reclining SS III 10 340 2
Her skin was very brown, but clear, smooth and glowing--; W 328 9
With some her brown skin was the annihilation of every W 337 17
can be, but I still profess my preference of a white skin. W 357 28
but in that soft skin of her's, so frequently tinged with MP II 6 229 5
gives her such a soft skin and makes her so much taller, MP II 6 230 8
their praise; but the skin, which she had been used to E II 2 167 12
and delicacy in her skin which gave peculiar elegance to E II 6 199 10
"did you ever see such a skin?--such smoothness! such E III 18 478 60
skin, her complexion, greatly improved--clearer, fresher. P IV 4 145 61 3
SKINNERS (3)
The Skinners were here last year--I wish they were here NA I 2 22 17
I have been saying how glad I should be if the Skinners NA I 2 23 25
and mother, and her kind compliments to all the Skinners. NA I 15 125 48
SKINS (1)
dressed them in their cleanest skins and best attire. MP III 11 408 2
SKIPPING (1)
Amelia should be a small, light, girlish, skipping figure. MP I 14 135 16
SKIRT (1)
a narrow path seemed to skirt along;--Miss Brereton seated, S 12 426 1
SKIRTING (1)
the walk to the Cobb, skirting round the pleasant little P III 11 95 9
SKREEN (1)
no otherwise than by netting a purse, or covering a skreen. PP I 8 39 46
SKREENS (1)
They all paint tables, cover skreens and net purses. PP I 8 39 45
SKULKER (1)
John himself was no skulker in joy. NA I 15 121 27
SKY (9)
from its amendment, the sky began voluntarily to clear. NA I 11 83 16
that a clear blue sky was no longer a proof of a fine day. NA I 14 110 28
by the fading light of the sky between six and seven NA II 9 190 1
sunshine of a showery sky, and unable longer to bear the SS I 9 40 3
at every glimpse of blue sky; and when they caught in SS I 9 41 4
dispersing across the sky, and the sun frequently appeared. SS I 13 63 2
of the sky and imagining an alteration in the air. SS II 5 168 8
the influence of such a sky, the effects of the shadows MP III 11 409 6
their way down, and the sky had the appearance of being so E I 13 112 24
SLABS (1)
to a Rumford, with slabs of plain though handsome marble, NA II 5 162 26
SLACKEN (1)
though determined not to slacken as a correspondent, it PP II 3 146 19
SLACKENED (2)
seeing how she gradually slackened in the needle-work, MP III 3 337 11
passing it without a slackened pace and observing eyes.-- E I 10 83 2
SLAM (1)
room, the almost ceaseless slam of the door, and ceaseless P IV 8 183 11
SLAMMED (1)
her, and slammed the parlour door till her temples ached. MP III 7 381 25
SLANDER (1)
however upright, can escape the malevolence of slander. LS 14 264 3
SLAP (1)
This is like giving ourselves a slap, to be sure! and it E II 8 215 16
SLATTERN (1)
parent, a dawdle, a slattern, who neither taught nor MP III 8 390 6
SLATTERNLY (1)
worn and faded, so comfortless, so slatternly, so shabby. MP III 11 408 2
SLAVE (6)
which now made him the slave of his designing friends, and PP II 1 133 3
Your mother must have been quite a slave to your education. PP II 6 164 28
Did not you hear me ask him about the slave trade last MP II 3 198 10
too much, Miss Crawford was not the slave of opportunity. MP III 5 357 5
he bends a slave, and woman, lovely woman, reigns, alone. E I 9 71 14
Lord of the earth and sea, he bends a slave, and woman, E I 9 73 18
SLAVE-TRADE (2)
You quite shock me; if you mean a fling at the slave-trade, E II 17 300 14
"I did not mean, I was not thinking of the slave-trade," E II 17 300 15
SLAVERY (1)
I had no idea that the law had been so great a slavery. E I 13 116 45
SLAVES (1)
Murder was not tolerated, servants were not slaves, and NA II 10 200 3
SLAVING (1)
I have been slaving myself till I can hardly stand, to MP I 18 166 6
SLEEK (1)
They went in; and while the sleek, well-tied parcels of " E II 6 200 16
SLEEP (29)
fell into a sound sleep which lasted nine hours, and from NA I 9 60 1
her; I could not sleep a wink all night for thinking of it. NA I 15 118 13
In short, she could not sleep till she had examined it. NA II 6 168 10
would be vain, since sleep must be impossible with the NA II 6 168 10
To close her eyes in sleep that night, she felt must be NA II 6 170 12
Sleep, or repose that deserved the name of sleep, was out NA II 13 227 26
sleep at all the first night after parting from Willoughby. SS I 16 83 1
In this situation, Elinor, roused from sleep by her SS II 7 180 1 2
From a night of more sleep than she had expected, Marianne SS II 9 201 1
certainty and efficacy of sleep, and felt no real alarm. SS III 7 307 1
Her sleep, though not so quiet as Elinor wished to see it, SS III 7 310 9
appearance comfortable, sleep, she silenced every doubt. SS III 7 315 25
fatigue, no capability of sleep at that moment about her, SS III 7 315 27
and retired to her own room to write letters and sleep. SS III 7 316 27
by so long and sweet a sleep to the extent of her hopes. SS III 9 333 3
Marianne of farther sleep;--but Mrs. Dashwood could be SS III 9 334 5
the latter to dress dine & sleep at their house, on every W 314 1
to stretch himself on one of the sophas and go to sleep. PP I 11 54 3
sleep, and pursue the usual course of their employments. PP II 18 229 1
I am sure I sha'nt get a wink of sleep all night. PP III 13 348 40
tears interrupted her, and sleep seeming to be her MP I 2 13 4
ended every day's sorrows by sobbing herself to sleep. MP I 2 14 9
Sleep as long as you can and never mind me." MP II 10 279 25
The advantage of much sleep to prepare them for their MP III 15 444 27
had cried herself to sleep--it was impossible not to speak; MP III 16 453 17
Her father composed himself to sleep after dinner, as E I 1 6 5
that she means to sleep only two nights on the road.-- E II 18 306 11
having cried herself to sleep; when, as they were going up P III 12 117 73
She had not a wink of sleep either the night before we set S 9 407 1
SLEEPER (1)
tossed about in her bed, and envied every quiet sleeper. NA II 6 170 12
SLEEPING (11)
(at least in his absence) your not sleeping in the house. LS 26 296 4
and neither poison nor sleeping potions to be procured, NA II 10 200 3
They travelled as expeditiously as possible; and sleeping PP III 5 285 20
of shooting and sleeping, to have convinced the gentleman MP I 12 114 3
The little white attic, which had continued her sleeping MP I 16 150 1
Sleeping or waking, my head has been full of this matter MP I 16 156 27
I took him, as he was sleeping on the sofa, and it is as E I 6 45 21
eating and drinking, and sleeping and playing, which they E I 11 92 3
through the sad evils of sleeping two nights on the road, E II 5 193 35
feels with respect to sleeping at an inn, you would not E II 18 306 12
had engrossed them, sleeping or waking, the last twenty- E III 12 417 3
SLEEPLESS (9)
And now I may dismiss my heroine to the sleepless couch, NA I 11 90 65
Oh! Catherine, the many sleepless nights I have had on NA I 15 118 13
sleepless, have been the real cause of his rising late.-- NA II 1 155 3
Hour after hour passed away in sleepless pain and delirium SS III 7 312 17
But the rest, which one night entirely sleepless, and many SS III 9 334 5
promised them all, the satisfaction of a sleepless night. SS III 13 363 6
It would have spared her, she thought, one sleepless night PP III 6 299 17
without a pause of misery, the night was totally sleepless. MP III 15 441 20
in the course of the sleepless night, which was the tax E III 14 434 4
SLEEPLESSNESS (1)
storms and sleeplessness are nothing when they are over. NA II 7 174 5
SLEEPS (1)
No signs that a 'Scottish monarch sleeps below.'" MP I 9 86 6
SLEEPY (1)
"Eleven!--and I am not at all sleepy. W 332 12
SLEETY (1)
a cold sleety April day rush out again into the world!-- E II 17 303 23
SLEEVE (2)
take this pin out of my sleeve; I am afraid it has torn a NA I 3 28 35
time looking for a shirt sleeve, which Betsey at last MP III 7 385 37
SLEEVES (2)
I think it does not look amiss; the sleeves were entirely NA I 10 70 3
I am very glad to hear what you tell us, of long sleeves." PP II 2 140 4
SLENDER (2)
the agitations of Anne's slender form, and pensive face, P III 8 68 29
30, of middling height & slender;--delicate looking rather S 9 407 1
SLEPT (9)
that Miss Tilney slept only two doors from her, to enter NA II 6 167 9
only while the household slept; and the probability that NA II 8 187 16
doubt of their being soon slept away; and though, when NA II 14 235 13
since she had really slept; and now, when her mind was no SS II 7 185 16
Marianne slept through every blast, and the travellers-- SS III 7 316 28
Miss Bennet had slept ill, and though up, was very PP I 7 33 43
her, and which had all slept while she listened to him, MP I 16 156 28
forward stains and dirt that might otherwise have slept. MP III 15 439 9
Harriet slept at Hartfield that night. E I 8 57 1
SLICE (3)
Perrys being seen with a slice of Mrs. Weston's wedding- E I 2 19 15
breakfast, and how small a slice of mutton for dinner, as E II 2 168 15
Another slice of cold meat, another draught of Madeira and E III 6 365 65
SLICES (2)
by helping them to large slices of cake and full glasses E II 8 213 6
& toasting some slices of bread, brought up ready-prepared S 10 416 1
SLIDING (1)
Nerves fit for sliding pannels and tapestry?" NA II 5 158 13
SLIGHT (72)
to refuse him their confidence & slight his advice. LS 12 260 1
deserves, however he may slight her, a better fate than to LS 20 278 11
it was no more than in a slight slumber, or a morning doze NA I 3 29 52
They took a slight survey of all; and Catherine was NA II 8 184 4
and Eleanor Tilney, some slight imperfection might NA II 10 200 3
in another moment a slight motion of the lock proved that NA II 13 222 9
neglect or unkindness of slight acquaintance like the NA II 14 239 28
It was upon the behaviour of these very slight NA II 14 239 28
day) of a slight rheumatic feel in one of his shoulders." SS I 8 38 11
As it was, it required but a slight effort of fancy to SS I 11 57 17
scratch, and a slight intermission of screams in the young SS I 21 121 10
hastily away with a slight bow and joined his friend. SS II 6 177 11
and to decide on it by slight appearances, one's happiness SS II 14 248 6
him, Miss Dashwood, from your slight acquaintance.-- SS III 5 299 35
though affecting to slight it; and idled away the mornings SS III 6 304 15
hope she could perceive a slight amendment in her sister's SS III 7 314 22
she hoped no coolness, no slight, would appear in their SS III 12 358 9
long enough, he began to slight her for Margaret, & poor W 317 2
of rushing into intimacy on so slight an acquaintance.-- W 322 3
Margaret was not without beauty; she had a slight, pretty W 349 23
We can all begin freely--a slight preference is natural PP I 6 21 2
But if it be only a slight, thin sort of inclination, I am PP I 9 44 34
Mr. Hurst also made her a slight bow, and said he was " PP I 11 54 2
"I should take him, even on my slight acquaintance, to be PP I 16 78 17
him to talk, she made some slight observation on the dance. PP I 18 91 8
of it he only made him a slight bow, and moved another way. PP I 18 98 61
at least, it is slight, it is nothing in comparison of PP II 1 137 24
her, made her sister a slight answer, and in compassion to PP II 2 140 5
in it; she made a slight, formal, apology, for not calling PP II 3 148 26
after having addressed a slight observation on the house PP II 7 171 10
She paused, and saw with no slight indignation that he was PP II 11 191 13
And then, with a slight bow, turned again into the PP II 12 195 2
in town, had there renewed a slight acquaintance. PP II 13 205 4
but she answered only by a slight inclination of the head. PP II 18 235 39
Elizabeth answered only by a slight bow. PP III 1 256 62
Kitty is slight and delicate, and Mary studies so much, PP III 5 292 66
would marry Lydia on so slight a temptation as one hundred PP III 7 304 29
After a slight preparation for good news, the letter was PP III 7 305 43
salutation, than a slight inclination of the head, and sat PP III 14 351 3
The slight had been most determined. MP I 14 135 18
assurance of sympathy than what a slight bow conveyed. MP II 1 184 25
as to make the few slight differences, resulting MP II 9 263 16
when, through the slight communication with the other MP II 11 286 16
He leaves Northamptonshire so soon, that even this slight MP III 2 331 16
at Mansfield, was to become a slight evil at Portsmouth. MP III 6 370 12
at his new hat, and some slight, but essential alteration MP III 7 381 26
There had been at one moment a slight murmur in the MP III 7 387 45
should resent any former supposed slight to Miss Bertram. MP III 13 423 2
her correspondent was not of a sort to regard a slight one. MP III 15 438 6
Emma, though I mean no slight to the state I assure you." E I 5 41 30
Her good-nature, too, is not so very slight a claim, E I 8 63 44
The lane made a slight bend; and when that bend was passed, E I 10 87 29 30
first attempt on their side to make him slight his father. E I 18 148 22

away directly under some slight excuse, when Miss Bates E II 1 158 13
fat and thin, though a slight appearance of ill-health E II 2 167 12
If you do not call early it will be a slight." E II 5 194 40
must laugh at; but that one would not wish to slight. E II 12 260 27
Emma made as slight a reply as she could; but it was fully E II 14 273 20
ill did Mrs. Elton engross Jane Fairfax and slight herself. E II 17 299 1
She was stopped by a slight fit of coughing, and Mr. E II 18 308 29
The mistake had been slight. E III 2 320 13
a steep bank, cleared a slight hedge at the top, and made E III 3 333 5
She gave a slight glance round the table, and applied E III 5 347 21
distance from the slight remains of Mr. Woodhouse's fire, E III 6 363 53
anger, though a slight blush showed that it could pain her. E III 7 371 27
was a hope (at times a slight one, at times much stronger,) E III 12 416 1
as might suit a former slight acquaintance, seeming to P III 7 59 23
side glance to see a slight curtsey from Elizabeth herself. P IV 8 181 2
broken up for a time; but slight was the penance compared P IV 8 184 17
life, he should slight my father's acquaintance as he did. P IV 9 200 58
beginning to say, when a slight noise called their P IV 11 233 24
there was instantly a slight change in Sir Edw:'s S 7 395 1

SLIGHTED (22)
I should not have a doubt of it, were she slighted for any LS 27 297 2
To feel herself slighted by them was very painful. NA I 11 86 50
slighted for strangers, I, who love you so excessively! NA I 13 98 2
the more because he was slighted by Willoughby and SS I 10 50 13
no power to wound them, sat pointedly slighted by both. SS II 12 232 16
not bear to see a sister slighted in the smallest point. SS II 12 236 38
a rising beauty would be slighted by him in after-days as SS III 14 379 19
A new face & a very pretty one, could not be slighted--her W 328 9
resentment, by his having slighted one of her daughters. PP I 3 11 6
consequence to young ladies who are slighted by other men. PP I 3 11 13
You will be censured, slighted, and despised, by every one PP III 14 355 45
so far from feeling slighted, was almost overpowered with MP I 7 66 14
scheme--a trick; she was slighted, Maria was preferred; MP I 14 133 12
the conviction of being slighted was over, she had been MP III 17 466 18
poor James think himself slighted upon any account; and I E I 1 9 19
to have his charade slighted, much better than his passion. E I 9 77 42
Frank's mother would never have been slighted as she was E II 18 309 33
could now imagine why her own attentions had been slighted. E III 11 403 2
to deserve to be slighted by the person, whose counsels E III 11 408 33
you were the person slighted, you will forgive me E III 14 437 8
Charles Hayter seemed aware of being slighted, and yet P III 10 82 1
and which she had felt slighted, and been compelled to P IV 1 124 11

SLIGHTER (1)
so well understood, much slighter in reality, than she had SS III 11 355 46

SLIGHTEST (23)
in never alluding in the slightest way to what had passed, NA II 10 201 4
The slightest mention of any thing relative to Willoughby SS I 15 82 47
if there had been the slightest alteration in his SS II 2 147 12
slightest allusion to what has passed, before my sister. SS II 8 195 17
or feel the slightest inclination ever to see him again. PP II 14 212 17
"Not the slightest. PP III 5 285 18
He had never had the slightest suspicion. PP III 16 371 40
all expectation, or the slightest allusion to it from him. MP I 3 30 57
mount him without the slightest inconvenience to himself, MP II 6 237 23
he would not distress her by the slightest allusion. MP III 7 375 3
without involving the slightest alteration of the MP III 11 410 16
it, give her only the slightest hint, she and I will MP III 11 411 16
keenly felt to be a subject of the slightest communication. MP III 16 453 16
in the slightest particular from the original recital. E III 3 336 13
I never had the slightest suspicion, till within the last E III 11 405 11
evil, without the slightest perception of anything E III 14 434 3
for her to have the slightest inclination for thinking of E III 14 436 6
the slightest degree disordered, were it only for a moment. E III 18 479 73
from offering the slightest hint, and only begged leave to P III 2 11 1
any manner; forbad the slightest hint being dropped of his P III 2 15 14
to be of even the slightest use to you," replied Anne; " P IV 9 195 25
& Rhapsody on the slightest acquaintance; but it was clara S 8 405 2
appearing to have the slightest recollection of having S 10 412 1

SLIGHTING (6)
with his wife, his slighting me has an awkward look. LS 2 245 1
of the novelist, and of slighting the performances which NA I 5 37 4
was engaged, and in slighting too easily the forms of SS I 10 49 9
in the world; and as to slighting Mr. Weston, that E I 11 95 19
negligent or perverse, slighting his advice, or even E III 12 415 1
to reward for not slighting an old friend like Mrs. Smith, P IV 10 212 1

SLIGHTINGLY (5)
Now, if I were to hear any body speak slightingly of you, NA I 6 40 14
To treat her with unkindness, to speak of her slightingly SS III 8 329 64
If I wished to think slightingly of any body's children, PP I 7 29 8
deserve to have her understanding spoken of so slightingly. E I 8 63 44
of them all, most slightingly and contemptuously of the P III 1 8 17

SLIGHTLY (18)
her due; for while he slightly and carelessly touched the NA I 7 45 5
last, the General, after slightly naming a few of the NA II 8 185 5
of self-consequence, slightly bowed to the ladies, without SS I 19 106 22
Her love made no answer; and after slightly bowing to the SS I 20 110 7
ladyship's head dress slightly scratching the child's neck, SS I 21 121 10
He looked at them slightly, without seeming to know who SS II 5 171 30
and after slightly addressing him, said no more. SS II 13 241 19
"You doubt me," cried Jane, slightly colouring; "indeed PP II 1 134 7
Her heart had been but slightly touched, and her vanity PP II 3 149 28
to inspire, and was but slightly affected by his PP II 6 161 8
Elizabeth, after slightly surveying it, went to a window PP III 1 246 5
the help of a young man very slightly known to any of us. MP I 16 153 8
him--who thought so slightly, so carelessly, so MP II 13 305 26
Crawford and herself, touched her in comparison, slightly. MP III 12 418 4
as most injurious, and slightly touched upon his respect E I 15 130 28
second, slightly but correctly taken by Frank Churchill. E II 8 227 86
have once been, though slightly, felt--it must be a very E II 11 247 1
He had enquired after her, she found, slightly, as might P III 7 59 23

SLILY (1)
half fearfully, half slily, beyond Fanny to Edmund. MP I 15 143 26

SLIMEY (1)
mud--no weeds--no slimey rocks--never was there a place S 1 369 1

SLIP (1)
You can slip in from the shrubbery at any time. P IV 1 127 26

SLIPPED (7)
observing how time had slipped away since they were last NA I 4 32 2
At length, however, having slipped one arm into her gown, NA II 6 164 3
It was no time for thought; she hurried on, slipped with NA II 9 193 6
Her story began; and Fanny immediately slipped out of the MP II 5 218 12
to say she had slipped her moorings and was coming out. MP III 7 380 20
presence of mind never varied, whose tongue never slipped. P IV 5 161 28
not, at any time lately, slipped down, and got a blow on P IV 11 238 47

SLIPPERY (1)
which ended the narrow, slippery path through the cottage E I 10 87 27

SLIPPING (1)
gown--you will be in danger of slipping into the ha-ha. MP I 10 99 21

SLIT (1)
slit in my worked muslin gown, before they are packed up. PP III 5 292 60

SLOOP (6)
second lieutenant of H. M. Sloop Thrush, being made out, MP II 13 298 3
(the thrush was certainly the finest sloop in the service). MP III 6 372 18
and even of getting her to Spithead to see the sloop. MP III 7 384 35
Never was a better sloop than the Asp in her day.-- P III 8 65 12
For an old built sloop, you would not see her equal. P III 8 65 12
lost in only a sloop, nobody would have thought about me." P III 8 66 16

SLOPE (3)
as rolling down the green slope at the back of the house. NA I 1 14 1
will slope down just before it, and be exceedingly pretty. SS II 11 226 39
The considerable slope, at nearly the foot of which the E III 6 360 38

SLOPED (1)
foot of the bank which sloped down from the outside of the S 12 426 1

SLOPING (3)
a spacious, modern-built house, situated on a sloping lawn. SS III 6 302 7
The garden sloping to the road, the house standing in it, PP II 5 155 3
it the best aspect in the world--sloping to the south-east. MP II 7 242 23

SLOVENLY (2)
A clergyman has nothing to do but to be slovenly and MP I 11 110 23
not even a careless, slovenly style of reading can destroy; MP III 3 340 25

SLOW (22)
of pity!--Oh!--how slow was the progress of time which yet SS III 7 315 26
to make her recovery slow; and with youth, natural SS III 10 340 1
The sisters set out at a pace, slow as the feebleness of SS III 10 344 12 13
continual smiles & a very slow articulation being her W 349 23
but their progress was slow, for Mr. Gardiner, though PP III 1 254 57
Whilst wandering on in this slow manner, they were again PP III 1 254 57
Miss Crawford was not slow to admire; she pretty well MP I 8 82 35
feet to that lady's slow pace, while her aunt, having MP I 9 90 36
A watch is always too fast or too slow. MP I 9 95 66
Tom himself began to fret over the scene painter's slow MP I 18 164 1
Her days were spent in a kind of slow bustle; always busy MP III 8 389 4
Tom's amendment was alarmingly slow. MP III 14 430 5
him or make his progress slow; no doubts of her deserving, MP III 17 471 28
She was always quick and assured: Isabella slow and E I 5 37 9
Knightley, but I am a very slow walker, and my pace would E I 8 58 7
quick, and theirs rather slow; and she was the more E I 10 88 33
a charge to go very slow and wait for the other carriage. E I 15 128 22
what he saw, for he was slow, constant, and methodical.-- E III 6 362 43
chance, circumstance, slow effects, sudden bursts, E III 14 437 8
the toil of keeping up a slow and unsatisfactory P III 12 107 21
very slow degrees came at last near enough to speak to her. P IV 8 189 47
The severity of the fall was broken by their slow pace & S 1 364 1

SLOWLY (24)
Mr. Tilney and his companion, who continued, though slowly, NA I 8 54 4
on her brother's arm, walking slowly down the street. NA I 11 87 53
heart-rendering tidings, Catherine walked slowly up stairs. NA I 11 89 62
worked with her friend, slowly pacing the drawing-room for NA II 8 187 13
They walked slowly up the gallery. NA II 9 195 19
Her dying so suddenly," (slowly, and with hesitation it NA II 9 196 24
withdrew from her sister and walked slowly up stairs. SS III 10 348 34
Marianne slowly continued-- "it is a great relief to me-- SS III 11 350 5 6
who continued, though slowly, to mend; and in the evening PP I 10 47 1
I write rather slowly." PP I 10 47 6
Yet time and her aunt moved slowly--and her patience and PP III 1 257 66
off, Elizabeth saw him walking slowly towards the house. PP III 1 257 66
patiently while he was slowly turning over the leaves with MP I 15 138 1
"No," said Fanny, slowly, "not immediately--but-----" MP I 16 154 13
As she walked slowly up stairs she thought of yesterday; MP II 9 267 23
work--and then, creeping slowly up the principal staircase, MP II 10 280 33
Your cousin Edmund moves slowly; detained, perchance, by MP III 9 394 1
replied Emma rather slowly--"so good a letter, Harriet, E I 7 51 5
to have any thing read, slowly and distinctly, and two or E I 9 78 51
it, and as they walked on slowly together in conversation E I 13 109 6
coming up towards me too--slowly you know, and as if he E II 3 179 52
by no means moving slowly, could hardly be out of hearing. E III 2 321 14
She was then able to walk, though but slowly, and was E III 3 334 6
And there, as they slowly paced the gradual ascent, P IV 11 241 59

SLOWNESS (1)
and politeness, and slowness of speech would allow, and MP II 10 276 14

SLUGGISH (1)
James and his horses seemed not half so sluggish as before. E II 5 189 16

SLUMBER (5)
no more than in a slight slumber, or a morning doze at NA I 3 29 52
will retire to rest, and get a few hours' unquiet slumber. NA II 5 159 19
ashes were supposed to slumber, were she to behold the NA II 9 190 2
sink at last into a slumber, from which she expected the SS III 7 310 9
her from so painful a slumber, when Marianne, suddenly SS III 7 310 10 11

SLUMBERING (1)
her usual employment, slumbering on one side of the fire, E II 10 240 1

SLUMBERS (1)
again the scene of agitated spirits and unquiet slumbers. NA II 13 227 26

SLY (14)
the world; you are such a sly thing, I am sure you would NA I 10 71 3
Sly creature!-- NA I 15 117 6
"Oh! don't be so sly before us," said Mrs. Palmer; "for we SS I 20 111 12
as for Lucy, she is such a sly little creature, there is SS II 2 148 22
Because you are so sly about it yourself, you think nobody SS II 7 182 10
was ever carried on so sly; for it was but two days before SS III 13 370 37
Why Jane--you never dropt a word of this; you sly thing! PP I 13 61 3
to herself, she stole a sly look at him, to see how he PP III 1 255 59
I thought him very sly;--he hardly ever mentioned your PP III 10 325 2
But Lizzy, you have been very sly, very reserved with me. PP III 17 374 18
with the doctor," making a sly face as he spoke towards MP I 12 119 22
Here was a sly glance at Emma. E II 3 174 32
for Emma, and given to her with a look sly and demure. E III 5 348 22
"Oh! now you are looking very sly. E III 6 354 14

SLYLY (1)
at the same time, however, slyly suspecting that another SS II 14 253 25

SLYNESS (3)
morning with admirable slyness, and hasten to Lucas Lodge PP I 22 121 1
But slyness seems the fashion. PP III 10 325 2
presently, with some slyness, "he seems to have a great E I 13 112 18

SMACKED (1)
But Mr. Thorpe only laughed, smacked his whip, encouraged NA I 11 87 53

SMALL (170)
even twelve years becomes in comparison of small account. LS 12 260 2
The small pianoforte has been removed within these few LS 17 271 7
continued, with only one small digression on James's part, NA I 7 51 54
induced her, in some small degree, to resist such high NA I 9 66 32
But I, who live in a small retired village in the country, NA I 10 78 46
At about eleven o'clock however, a few specks of small NA I 11 82 2
So many instances within my small circle of friends is NA I 14 109 24
my fortune will be so small; they never can consent to it. NA I 15 119 15
Four hundred is but a small income to begin on indeed, but NA II 1 135 44
Tilney, made but a small part of Catherine's speculation. NA II 2 138 1
your hand, will pass through it into a small vaulted room." NA II 5 159 19
No, no, you will proceed into this small vaulted room, and NA II 5 160 21
In repassing through the small vaulted room, however, your NA II 5 160 21
unusual, a double range of small drawers appeared in view, NA II 6 168 10
them; and in the centre, a small door, closed also with a NA II 6 168 10
to consist entirely of small disjointed sheets, was NA II 7 172 1
he led the way to it across a small portion of the park. NA II 7 178 20
"Mr. Allen had only one small hot-house, which Mrs. Allen NA II 7 178 25
if a small sacrifice of time and attention can prevent it. NA II 11 210 6
We are considering it as a mere parsonage, small and NA II 11 213 19
father's inheriting that property, could be but small. SS I 1 3 2
out for a comfortable small house for them, helping them SS I 2 12 24
It was the offer of a small house, on very easy terms, SS I 4 23 20
A small green court was the whole of its demesne in front; SS I 6 28 1
As a house, Barton cottage, though small, was comfortable SS I 6 28 2
In comparison of Norland, it was poor and small indeed!-- SS I 6 28 2
said she, "it is too small for our family, but we will SS I 6 29 4
These parlours are both too small for such parties of our SS I 6 29 4
or her fortune small, I can suppose that she might bring SS I 8 38 10
tender compassion, her small degree of fortitude was quite SS I 15 82 46
in his favour, however small, was pleasing to her. SS I 20 116 59
Then taking a small miniature from her pocket, she added, " SS I 22 131 35
However small Elinor's general dependance on Lucy's SS II 1 139001
I have been always used to a very small income, and could SS II 2 147 7
Lady Middleton had given a small dance of eight or nine SS II 5 170 29

out at small cost, and then what does it signify? SS II 8 196 22
in silent misery, over the small remains of a fire, which, SS II 8 197 23
Her complexion was sallow; and her features small, without SS II 12 232 15
brother and sister, to a small musical party at her house. SS II 14 248 6
to be disobedient, and how small was the consolation, SS III 2 270 1
It is a rectory, but a small one; the late incumbent, I SS III 3 282 19
regret, that the house was small and indifferent;-- an SS III 3 283 20
Truth obliged her to acknowledge some small share in the SS III 4 290 36
"Aye, aye, the parsonage is but a small one," said she, SS III 4 292 55
clergyman, and living in a small parsonage-house, diverted SS III 5 298 33
Their party was small, and the hours passed quietly away. SS III 6 303 12
certainly must be some small house or cottage close by, SS III 9 338 24
His demands and your inexperience together on a small, SS III 11 350 9
together on a small, very small income, must have brought SS III 11 350 9
& the demure air of the small cluster of females at one W 328 8
Tearoom was a small room within the cardroom, & in passing W 332 11
but it cannot turn a small income into a large one."-- W 346 21
I hope I can put up with a small apartment for two or W 351 25
and to his residence in a small market town; and quitting PP I 5 18 1
father should have left so small a collection of books.-- PP I 8 38 29
supposed himself in the small summer breakfast parlour at PP I 16 75 2
up high, but able to make a small income go a good way. PP I 19 105 10
Your portion is unhappily so small that it will in all PP I 19 108 19
"My dear," replied her husband, "I have two small favours PP I 20 112 22
young women of small fortune, and however uncertain of PP I 22 122 3
carriage stopped at the small gate, which led by a short PP II 5 155 3
It was rather small, but well built and convenient; and PP II 5 157 5
Who would have thought she could be so thin and small!" PP II 5 158 15
Maria's astonishment, at her being so thin, and so small. PP II 6 162 12
to be regulated in so small a family as her's, and PP II 6 163 15
at Rosings, which in so small a circle must be important. PP II 7 170 6
But it is of small importance." PP II 11 190 9
Our plain manner of living, our small rooms, and few PP II 15 215 2
A small part of Derbyshire is all the present concern. PP II 19 240 12
it meant, and imparted no small degree of surprise to her PP III 2 260 1
of a small market-town, where the family did not visit. PP III 2 265 14
his way towards a small wood on one side of the paddock. PP III 7 301 6
A small sum could not do all this." PP III 7 304 30
That they should marry, small as is their chance of PP III 7 304 34
One day's delay she observed, would be of small importance; PP III 7 307 48
"You have a very small park here," returned Lady Catherine PP III 14 352 9
good liquor, and a very small income to supply their wants, MP I 1 4 2
She was small of her age, with no glow of complexion, nor MP I 2 12 2
park, and afterwards to a small house of Sir Thomas's in MP I 3 23 1
the difference to be so small, she could not think of MP I 3 25 17
and that might be of some small use to you with their MP I 6 62 58
gaieties of small talk, he began to be agreeable to her. MP I 7 65 13
Active and fearless, and, though rather small, strongly MP I 7 66 15
the field, which was not small, at a foot's pace; then, at MP I 7 67 16
A small sigh escaped Fanny here, and she did not know how MP I 10 102 44
hope it will be in a very small and quiet way; and I think MP I 13 127 28
Amelia should be a small, light, girlish, skipping figure. MP I 14 135 16
than one, but exciting small compassion in any except MP I 14 136 20
pinned against the wall, a small sketch of a ship sent MP I 16 152 2
Conversation with any of them occupied but a small part of MP II 2 190 9
We shall be quite a small party at home. MP II 3 199 17
Price, without making a small hole in Fanny Price's heart. MP II 6 229 5
gently rising hills; a small stream before me to be forded, MP II 7 241 13
and inexperienced, with small means of choice and no MP II 8 254 8
And as she spoke she was undoing a small parcel, which MP II 8 257 15
She was answered by having a small trinket-box placed MP II 8 257 15
cheerlessness of her own small house, without reproaching MP II 11 282 3
another week of the same small party in the same bad MP II 12 291 1
His hopes from both gentleman and lady suffered a small MP III 1 320 45
the morning; and when the small, diminished party met at MP III 6 374 29
the door of a small house now inhabited by Mr. Price. MP III 7 376 6
She was then taken into a parlour, so small that her first MP III 7 377 10
drawer in the kitchen, the small party of females were MP III 7 385 37
While considering her with these ideas, Betsey, at a small MP III 7 386 40
One was found to have too small a print for a child's eyes, MP III 7 387 45
in that house reckoned too small for anybody's comfort. MP III 7 387 47
respectable mother of nine children, on a small income. MP III 8 390 5
It had very early occurred to her, that a small sum of MP III 9 396 7
fourth may be added, some small hunting-box in the MP III 10 405 19
We shall greatly Miss Edmund in our small circle, but I MP III 13 426 11
attend him, and the sadly small party remaining at MP III 13 427 12
My influence, which is not small, shall all go that way; MP III 16 457 29
providing for himself no small portion of vexation and MP III 17 468 22
early in life to a small independence, had become E I 2 15 1
He had still a small house in Highbury, where most of his E I 2 16 5
She lived with her single daughter in a very small way, E I 3 21 4
the endeavour to make a small income go as far as possible. E I 3 21 4
Such another small basin of this gruel as his own, was all E I 3 24 13
14
small, you see--one of our small eggs will not hurt you. E I 3 24 14
A small half glass--put into a tumbler of water? E I 3 25 14
sketch of a gentleman in small size, whole-length--"my E I 6 45 21
true; and it would be a small consolation to her, for the E I 7 54 33
live perforce in a very small, and generally very inferior, E I 10 85 19
of society;--it will be a small party, but where small E I 13 116 43
a small party, but where small parties are select, they E I 13 116 43
And it is no small credit, in my opinion, to him, that he E I 14 121 13
ate for breakfast, and how small a slice of mutton for E II 2 168 15
one can venture to do--small, trifling presents, of any E II 3 171 16
17
loin or a leg; it is very small and delicate--Hartfield E II 3 171 16
17
the very style to touch; a small mixture of reproach, with E II 4 184 11
Small heart had Harriet for visiting. E II 5 186 1
allow it even to be very small, admired the situation, the E II 5 191 26
of the privations inevitably belonging to a small one. E II 6 204 43
and a small card-room adjoining, was the only addition. E II 11 254 44
still was not it too small for any comfortable supper? E II 11 254 44
room, observed, "I do not think it is so very small. E II 11 254 45
46
The grounds of Hartfield were small, but neat and pretty; E II 14 272 18
"It is too small--wants strength. E II 16 297 50
suddenly perceived at a small distance before them, on a E III 3 333 5
one morning to Emma with a small parcel in her hand, and E III 4 337 1
2
the cotton, Emma saw only a small piece of court plaister. E III 4 338 9
"Your parish there was small," said Jane. E III 16 456 30
the predictions of the small band of true friends who E III 19 484 12
There was only a small part of his estate that Sir Walter P III 1 10 20
A small house in their own neighbourhood, where they might P III 2 14 9
to descend into a small house in his own neighbourhood. P III 2 14 11
and, at the same time, can never make a baronet look small. P III 3 24 36
her taste, in the small limits of the society around them. P III 4 28 7
square parlour, with a small carpet and shining floor, to P III 5 40 44
Captain Wentworth, in a small paragraph at one corner of P III 8 66 16
account; for in a small house, near the foot of an old P III 11 96 10
and found rooms so small as none but those who invite from P III 11 98 17
on a dark November day, a small thick rain almost blotting P IV 1 123 8
been living in the same small family party; since P IV 6 167 19
and bringing me the small inlaid box which you will find P IV 9 202 68
to him, to my husband, a small portion only of what I had P IV 9 202 69
70
It shall be a regular party--small, but most elegant." P IV 10 220 29
"I would rather have young people settle on a small income P IV 11 230 7
a small miniature painting, "do you know who that is?" P IV 11 232 13
numerous for intimacy, too small for variety; but Anne had P IV 11 245 78
daughter at present but a small part of the share of ten P IV 12 248 1
Bourne--but not to a small village like Sanditon, S 1 368 1
Sanditon,--the success of Sanditon as a small, fashionable S 2 371 1
small circle; & they were older in habits than in age.-- S 2 373 1
Miss Denham had a very small provision--& her brother was S 3 377 1
division, in a small cluster of Fisherman's houses.-- S 4 383 1
building, standing in a small lawn with a very young S 4 384 1
for the eveng in a small neat drawing room, with a S 10 413 1
Mrs G. had preferred a small, retired place, like Sanditon, S 11 421 1
A little novelty has a great effect in so small a place; S 11 422 1

SMALL-SIZED (1)

to use, instead of the small-sized Pembroke, on which two E III 5 347 18

SMALLER (11)

to be sure that a much smaller income would satisfy me. NA II 1 136 48
was shewn, first into a smaller apartment, belonging NA II 11 213 21
was persuaded that a much smaller provision than 7000l. SS I 3 14 2
"A family cannot well be maintained on a smaller. SS I 17 91 14
by Sir Thomas, and in smaller concerns by her sister. MP I 2 19 31
much smaller circle than they are now in the high road for. MP I 16 155 16
room which held all her smaller treasures; but on opening MP II 9 261 1
They were indeed a smaller party than she had ever known MP II 11 284 8
too large, and he cut it smaller, and kept playing some E III 4 338 12
This discovery laid many smaller matters open. E III 11 403 2
had calculated on;--and a smaller shew of company on the S 4 384 1

SMALLER-SIZED (1)

And as to smaller-sized rooms than I had been used to, I E II 14 277 36

SMALLEST (109)

I have not detected the smallest impropriety in it,-- LS 8 255 2
brother would be in the smallest danger of being LS 11 259 2
without shewing the smallest propensity towards any NA I 9 62 10
the smallest consciousness of having explained them. NA I 10 73 21
that the smallest income in nature would be enough for me. NA I 15 119 20
on my side, I never had the smallest idea of it. NA II 3 145 13
been fixed without the smallest apprehension of really NA II 5 160 23
To an imagination which had hoped for the smallest NA II 5 162 26
that Catherine felt the smallest fatigue from her journey; NA II 6 166 8
it; not however with the smallest expectation of finding NA II 6 168 10
from the first had the smallest idea of finding any thing NA II 6 169 11
she should never have felt the smallest curiosity about it. NA II 7 173 3
itself could not in the smallest degree affect her doubts NA II 9 190 2
not seem to create the smallest astonishment in the NA II 11 214 27
considered without the smallest emotion; and though the NA II 13 227 26
girl whom we had not the smallest acquaintance with, and NA II 14 236 19
that they had the smallest idea of the false calculations NA II 15 245 12
it had not produced the smallest effect on her in that SS I 5 25 3
it, with whom Marianne had not the smallest acquaintance. SS I 13 68 66
Lady Middleton without the smallest surprise or distrust. SS I 21 120 6
still, for there is not the smallest alteration in him." SS I 21 124 29
And I am sure I should not have the smallest fear of SS I 22 128 9
say he never dropped the smallest hint of it to you or any SS I 22 129 16
the first without the smallest emotion, but very soon to SS II 10 215 14
Brandon has not the smallest wish of marrying me." SS II 11 223 23
that there could be the smallest difference in the world SS II 12 234 24
not bear to see a sister slighted in the smallest point. SS II 12 236 38
without expecting the smallest amusement from any, and SS II 14 249 7
without betraying the smallest increase of dislike to her;- SS III 1 264 32
from affording him the smallest assistance, that if he SS III 1 267 38
of which, at present, there seemed not the smallest chance. SS III 2 276 26
Ferrars can have the smallest satisfaction in knowing that SS III 5 296 19
never again have the smallest incitement to move; and if I SS III 10 347 30
Not the smallest suspicion, therefore, had ever occurred SS III 13 364 13
for whom she had not the smallest regard, and who had only SS III 13 367 22
pounds a-year, not the smallest objection was made against SS III 14 374 4
as soon as the smallest opening was given for their SS III 14 375 10
"No indeed, I had not the smallest suspicion of it. W 317 2
have none of them the smallest scruple in trusting W 339 18
in whom he had felt the smallest interest, and from none PP I 4 16 15
"I have not the smallest objection to explaining them," PP I 11 56 15
Her sister made not the smallest objection, and the piano PP I 11 58 34
she made not the smallest objection to his joining in the PP I 14 66 1
since, with the smallest degree of unreasonable admiration. PP I 16 76 3
Miss Darcy, he is in the smallest degree less sensible of PP I 21 119 20
"But he paid her not the smallest attention, till her PP II 4 153 12
her father had not the smallest intention of yielding; but PP II 16 223 26
I have not the smallest hope. PP III 4 277 16
There will not be the smallest occasion for your coming to PP III 7 303 14
I had not the smallest idea of their being ever felt in PP III 16 368 15
in my girls the smallest degree of arrogance towards their MP I 1 11 17
daughters, Lady Bertram paid not the smallest attention. MP I 2 19 31
Mrs. Norris had not the smallest intention of taking her. MP I 3 28 38
she had fixed on the smallest habitation which could rank MP I 3 28 38
"But there will not be the smallest difficulty in filling MP I 15 148 58
of them, nobody had the smallest idea of that except his MP I 18 166 4
as I had not the smallest suspicion of your acting having MP II 1 184 25
in supposing she had the smallest desire of breaking MP II 3 200 21
life, or could have the smallest insight into the MP II 3 203 30
You have not the smallest chance of moving me. MP II 4 212 31
and without the smallest hesitation on your uncle's side. MP II 5 219 25
need not make the smallest difference in your accepting it, MP II 8 259 22
Your being so far unlike, Fanny, does not in the smallest MP III 4 348 23
Their sister soon despaired of making the smallest MP III 8 391 8
to afford her the smallest satisfaction; she saw nobody in MP III 9 395 3
He must soon give her up, and cease to have the smallest MP III 10 402 11
directly, without the smallest consideration for his MP III 10 402 13
from her the smallest support or attempt at support. MP III 16 448 2
the smallest inconstancy of mind towards her cousin.-- MP III 17 468 21
and he was ready at the smallest intermission of the E I 6 47 26
While you were in the smallest degree wavering, I said E I 7 53 24
side; and had not the smallest doubt (nor have I now) that E I 8 61 38
he should be in the smallest degree necessary at Hartfield. E I 9 81 78
I do--I have not the smallest doubt that, could he see his E I 9 82 83
wish for, without the smallest delay, the children were E I 11 92 3
I have not the smallest doubt of the issue. E I 14 120 11
for there not being the smallest difficulty in their E I 15 127 16
I protest against having paid the smallest attention to E I 15 131 31
are fried, without the smallest grease, and not roast it, E II 3 171 16
17
that there would be the smallest difficulty in every E II 6 198 5
I am excessively fond of music, but without the smallest E II 6 201 28
"Yes," he replied, and without the smallest apparent E II 8 228 92
Oh! no, upon my word I have not the smallest wish for your E II 15 288 35
No, I can pronounce his name without the smallest distress. E II 16 297 48
Weston, he had not the smallest doubt of being highly E II 17 303 24
It is not in the smallest degree connected with any human E III 10 393 15
at not having had the smallest reply to her last; and E III 14 442 8
and without the smallest remark; and, excepting one E III 15 447 21
"I never had the smallest, I assure you." E III 18 477 54
likely to make the smallest difficulty about terms;--only P III 3 22 23
of others, to the smallest knowledge of it afterwards. P III 4 31 11
"I have not the smallest objection on that account," P III 5 39 42
never had the smallest temptation to say, "very true." P III 6 44 6
that there was not the smallest symptom of any knowledge P III 6 48 18
ailed me, and I never met with the smallest inconvenience." P III 8 71 54
There was not the smallest appearance of solicitude or P III 9 75 9
themselves into the smallest possible space to leave her a P III 10 91 41
certainly without the smallest suspicion of his possessing P IV 3 144 19
and having not the smallest wish for a total change, she P IV 8 183 11
12
you have not the smallest intention of accepting him, P IV 9 199 53
he can neglect and desert without the smallest compunction. P IV 9 199 53
now, as a young man he had not the smallest value for it. P IV 9 202 66
"I had not the smallest intention of asking him," said P IV 10 213 3
on Mary's account) would not be the smallest impediment. P IV 10 224 52

53
of Brinshore--not in the smallest degree exaggerated--& if S 1 369 1
& the Land's end, & without the smallest advantage from it. S 4 380 1
Oh! I have not the smallest doubt of our being a great S 4 381 1
man, the smallest very materially of not a robust family, S 10 413 1
Mrs G. would not allow Miss L. to have the smallest S 11 422 1

SMALLNESS (9)
began to talk of the smallness of the room and simplicity NA II 5 162 27
He hoped they would all excuse the smallness of the party, SS I 7 33 4
Perhaps just at present he may be undecided; the smallness SS II 11 223 24
"The smallness of the house," said she, "I cannot imagine SS III 3 284 21
as the white attic;--the smallness of the one making the MP I 16 151 1
The smallness of the house, and thinness of the walls, MP III 7 382 28
The smallness of the rooms above and below indeed, and the MP III 7 387 47
"But it is proved by the smallness of the school, which I E III 16 456 32
preferring any thing to smallness & retirement, yet having S 11 421 1

SMALLRIDGE (6)
"To a Mrs. Smallridge--charming woman--most superior--to E III 8 380 13
Mrs. Bragge's; but Mrs. Smallridge is intimate with both, E III 8 380 13
Mrs. Smallridge, a most delightful woman!-- E III 8 382 23
Mrs. Smallridge is in a great hurry. E III 8 382 27
"Mrs. Smallridge, too! E III 10 397 50
"'Smallridge!'-- E III 15 447 24

SMART (29)
she grew clean as she grew smart; she had now the pleasure NA I 1 15 2
Thorpe, pointing at three smart looking females, who, arm NA I 4 32 3
such a smart young fellow, I saw every eye was upon us." NA II 1 134 39
at being unable to get any smart young men to meet them. SS I 7 33 4
But that was not smart enough for my family. SS I 19 102 4
That was a great deal too smart for me. SS I 19 102 4
Their dress was very smart, their manners very civil, they SS I 21 119 3
"And had you a great many smart beaux there? SS I 21 123 26
I'm sure there's a vast many smart beaux in Exeter; but SS I 21 123 28
how could I tell what smart beaux there might be about SS I 21 123 28
agreeable, provided they dress smart, and behave civil. SS I 21 123 28
Now there's Mr. Rose at Exeter, a prodigious smart young SS I 21 123 28
a conquest of a very smart beau since she came to Barton. SS I 21 125 34
even now, under the first smart of the heavy blow, command SS II 1 140 4
Did you ever see her? a smart, stilish girl they say, but SS II 8 194 10
came post all the way, and had a smart beau to attend us. SS II 10 218 24
word she looked vastly smart, and she dared to say would SS II 14 249 8
at once a desire of smart appearance, with the utmost SS III 12 357 3
door, by the sound of as smart a rap as the end of a W 344 21
in possession of a very smart house in Croydon, where she W 349 23
I hope the old woman will smart for it." W 352 26
Mrs Robert exactly as smart as she had been at her own W 353 26
& he beheld a circle of smart people whom he cd not W 355 28
he repeated the smart sayings of one lady, detailed the W 359 28
at my heart; and if a smart young Colonel, with five or PP I 7 29 12
nothing less than a very smart bonnet indeed, or a really PP I 15 72 7
a smart place as that--poor scrubbery midshipman as I am." MP II 7 245 33
been got through, even by the smart rapidity of a waiter. P III 12 105 13
all her glossy curls & smart trinkets to wait on her.-- S 6 390 1

SMART-LOOKING (2)
turn up the Lansdown road,--driving a smart-looking girl." NA I 11 85 37
one short row of smart-looking houses, called the terrace, S 4 384 1

SMARTENED (2)
but had been very much smartened up by the present E I 10 83 2
of the best of them were smartened up with a white curtain S 4 383 1

SMARTEST (2)
afterwards she saw the smartest officer of the sett, W 330 11
to nothing, the smartest & most fashionable man of the two. W 347 22

SMARTING (1)
feelings which I had been smarting under year after year. P IV 11 245 74

SMARTLY (1)
Mrs Robert Smartly--but we think a month very little. W 356 28

SMARTLY-DRESSED (1)
& strings of smartly-dressed girls were received, with now W 328 8

SMARTNESS (1)
a sharp quick eye, and a smartness of air, which though it SS I 21 120 6

SMELL (2)
by his language and his smell of spirits; and he talked on MP III 7 380 23
Never had the exquisite sight, smell, sensation of nature, E III 13 424 1

SMELLS (2)
confinement, bad air, bad smells, substituted for liberty, MP III 14 432 9
I should not be helped so soon, but it smells most E III 2 330 45

SMILE (175)
always brightens with a smile when Reginald says anything LS 18 272 1
"Did not I tell you, said she with a smile, that your LS 24 287 11
Then forming his features into a set smile, and affectedly NA I 3 26 4
ready to meet him with a smile:--but no smile was demanded- NA I 4 31 1
no smile was demanded--Mr. Tilney did not appear. NA I 4 31 1
ideas by a squeeze of the hand or a smile of affection. NA I 8 52 1
see her, and therefore the smile and the blush, which his NA I 8 53 3
than one smile, one squeeze, and one "dearest Catherine." NA I 8 59 38
"Henry!" she replied with a smile. NA I 10 72 10
agreeable to the man; he is to purvey, and she is to smile. NA I 10 77 35
fearful of Isabella's smile) "I expect Miss Tilney and her NA I 11 85 32
such a bow! no smile, no continued observance attended it; NA I 12 93 4
more cordial, more natural smile into his countenance, and NA I 12 93 7
With a yet sweeter smile, he said every thing that need be NA I 12 94 9
"Government," said Henry, endeavouring not to smile, " NA I 14 112 35
With a triumphant smile of self-satisfaction, the general NA II 7 178 23
with him, listen to him, and even to smile when he smiled. NA II 7 181 41
of his meditations, he could still smile with them. NA II 8 182 1
Henry, I should delight in," said Eleanor, with a smile. NA II 10 206 32
"I trust," said the General, with a most satisfied smile, " NA II 11 214 22
"Like him!" replied her mother with a smile. SS I 3 16 10
"I am sure," replied Elinor with a smile, "that his SS I 4 20 7
with a good humoured smile, "that Mr. Willoughby will be SS I 9 44 24
were all good; her smile was sweet and attractive, and in SS I 10 46 2
he said with a faint smile, "your sister, I understand, SS I 11 55 8
and with a forced smile presently added, "it is I who may SS I 15 75 4
This was broken by Willoughby, who said with a faint smile, SS I 15 76 16
who could have gained a smile from her; but she dispersed SS I 16 86 21
she dispersed her tears to smile on him, and in her SS I 16 86 21
But (with a smile) you would be materially benefited in SS I 19 102 3
She came in with a smile, smiled all the time of her visit, SS I 19 106 22
"I should guess so," said Elinor with a smile, "from what SS I 21 122 18
Elinor hardly knew whether to smile or sigh at this SS II 2 147 11
"No;" answered Elinor, with a smile, which concealed very SS II 2 150 31
He tried to smile as he replied, "your sister's engagement SS II 5 173 40
and, therefore, trying to smile, replied, "and have you SS II 7 181 9
Elinor could only smile. SS II 11 225 34
She could not but smile to see the graciousness of both SS II 12 232 16
after them I suppose," said Elinor, with a faint smile. SS III 4 285 6
"I understand you," he replied, with an expressive smile, SS III 8 318 18
instead of an inquiry, she passed it off with a smile. SS III 9 336 11
her, it never passed away without the atonement of a smile. SS III 10 342 7
Her smile however changed to a sigh when she remembered SS III 10 343 10
with a lively eye, a sweet smile, & an open countenance, W 328 9
I am sorry, (with a witty smile) we have not been able to W 350 24
her eye towards Mr. Darcy with a very expressive smile. PP I 9 43 26
Elizabeth turned away to hide a smile. PP I 11 57 25
"And yours, he replied with a smile, "is wilfully to PP I 11 58 32
This information made Elizabeth smile, as she thought of PP I 16 83 56
adding, with a significant smile, "I do not imagine his PP I 18 89 1
2
Jane met her with a smile of such sweet complacency, a PP I 18 95 48
Elizabeth could not but smile at such a conclusion of such PP I 20 112 20
with a conscious smile; "very true, it will be wise in me PP II 3 145 7
turned to him with an arch smile, and said, "you mean to PP II 8 174 12

13
As he spoke there was a sort of smile, which Elizabeth PP II 9 179 21
Putting away the letter immediately and forcing a smile, PP II 10 182 2
3
He even looked at her with a smile of affected incredulity. PP II 11 191 13
smile, of what her ladyship's indignation would have been. PP II 14 210 2
It was some time, however, before a smile could be PP II 17 225 11
and a returning smile, replied, that he had formerly seen PP II 18 233 27
Elizabeth could not repress a smile at this, but she PP II 18 235 39
Mrs. Gardiner looked at her niece with a smile, but PP III 1 247 10
of Mr. Darcy, with such a smile over the face, as she PP III 1 250 47
With a triumphant smile, they were told, that it was ten PP III 1 253 57
could hardly suppress a smile, at his being now seeking PP III 1 254 58
a significant look and smile from Mrs. Annesley to Miss PP III 3 268 6
and thanked them both, with alternate smile and tears. PP III 5 287 32
hand with an affectionate smile to Wickham, who followed PP III 9 315 3
"You certainly do," she replied with a smile; "but it does PP III 10 327 6
with a good-humoured smile, "come, Mr. Wickham, we are PP III 10 329 33
34
an additional glow, and a smile of delight added lustre to PP III 11 334 37
to look round, and happened to smile: it was decided. PP III 12 340 11
not let me smile, and are provoking me to it every moment." PP III 12 343 33
pleasantry, but could only force one most reluctant smile. PP III 15 363 19
looking at him, she was a little relieved by his smile. PP III 17 375 28
aid of a good-humoured smile, became immediately the less MP I 2 12 2
in vain did Lady Bertram smile and make her sit on the MP I 2 13 4
see how he dwells on one word, and only look at his smile. MP I 4 43 24
You may smile--but it is so I assure you--and except that MP I 5 49 32
to Mrs. Norris, with a smile; "but depend upon it, MP I 6 53 5
as he turned with a smile to Julia, or to catch the laugh MP I 8 81 32
improvements," said Miss Crawford; with a smile, to Edmund. MP I 9 86 10
said she with an arch smile; "I am just as much surprised MP I 9 93 53
She would only smile and assert. MP I 9 96 76
Edmund with a serious smile, and glancing at the piano- MP I 11 108 11
Maria was preferred; the smile of triumph which Maria was MP I 14 133 12
by interference, gave her only an encouraging smile. MP I 15 146 53
with a most persuasive smile, that neither he nor Julia MP I 17 161 9
And with a relenting smile he added, "I come home to be MP II 1 185 29
replied with an approving smile, "I am happy to find our MP II 1 186 34
It was impossible for many of the others not to smile. MP II 1 186 35
said Edmund, with the kind smile of an affectionate MP II 5 222 42
With a significant smile, which made Fanny quite hate him, MP II 5 224 49
the family, said, with a smile, "and how do you think I MP II 6 229 1
Her eyes should be darker, but she has a sweet smile; but MP II 6 230 6
Her brother gave only a smile to this accusation, and soon MP II 6 230 7
reward the owner with a smile when the animal was one MP II 6 237 23
engaged to me; but (with a smile that did not sit easy) MP II 9 268 29
at her necklace--with a smile--she thought there was a MP II 10 274 8
there was a smile--which made her blush and feel wretched. MP II 10 274 8
wondered she did not smile, and thought her over-anxious, MP II 10 277 20
be something; so, you may smile upon him with your MP II 13 303 15
pause, Sir Thomas, trying to suppress a smile, went on. MP III 1 313 13
And there was a half smile with the words which meant, "I MP III 1 325 61
And he looked at Fanny with an expressive smile, which MP III 3 339 20
"Even in my profession"--said Edmund with a smile--"how MP III 3 339 23
In spite of herself, she could not help half a smile, but MP III 3 343 37
But (with an affectionate smile), let him succeed at last, MP III 4 347 18
Fanny could with difficulty give the smile that was here MP III 4 354 47
presently, with a playful smile, "but it is over now; so MP III 5 359 9
Fanny could not avoid a faint smile, but had nothing to MP III 5 363 25
it, and with the happiest smile over his face, walked up MP III 7 384 34
Fanny, Fanny, I see you smile, and look cunning, but upon MP III 14 434 13
received an affectionate smile, which comforted her; but MP III 15 445 34
'Mr. Bertram,' said she, with a smile--but it was a smile MP III 16 459 30
with a smile--but it was a smile ill-suited to the MP III 16 459 30
passed, a saucy playful smile, seeming to invite, in order MP III 16 459 30
He presently added, with a smile, "I do not pretend to fix E I 8 58 19
20
receive him with the usual smile, and her quick eye soon E I 9 81 78
this moment; never had his smile been stronger, nor his E I 13 111 12
"Me!" she replied with a smile of astonishment, "are you E I 13 112 19
Mr. Elton must smile less, and Mr. John Knightley more, to E I 14 117 1
sight of Mrs. Weston, her smile, her touch, her voice was E I 14 117 2
What is it?--why do you smile so?--where did you hear it?-- E II 3 172 21
said Mr. Knightley, with a smile which implied a E II 3 173 26
something like a look of spring, a tender smile even there. E II 5 189 16
"Why do you smile?" said she. "nay, why do you?" E II 8 216 18
"Me!--I suppose I smile for pleasure at Col. Campbell's E II 8 216 20
I smile because you smile, and shall probably suspect E II 8 216 27
nicely dressed, to sit and smile and look pretty, and say E II 8 219 44
But (with a smile) if Col. Campbell should have employed a E II 9 234 32
with a smile at Emma, "the person has not chosen ill. E II 10 241 8
He shook his head with a smile, and looked as if he had E II 10 241 11
caught the remains of a smile, when she saw that with all E II 10 243 22
there had been a smile of secret delight, she had less E II 10 243 22
agreeable smile as certified the continuance of the scheme. E II 11 250 20
not," replied Mrs. Elton, with a most satisfied smile. E II 14 274 26
But (with a reproachful smile at Emma) she receives E II 15 286 18
Mrs. Weston"--with half a sigh and half a smile at her. E II 16 297 47
Mr. Knightley seemed to be trying not to smile; and E II 18 312 51
Then changing from a frown to a smile--"no, do not tell me- E III 2 325 28
Whenever she caught his eye, she forced him to smile; but E III 2 326 32
He shook his head; but there was a smile of indulgence E III 2 330 50
51
The word was discovered, and with a faint smile pushed E III 5 347 21
a smile which seemed to say, "these are my own concerns. E III 6 361 40
You provide for the family, you know, (with a smile at his E III 7 373 46
unjust praise; and with a smile, and shake of the head, E III 9 385 7
She considered--resolved--and, trying to smile, began-- " E III 13 425 2
3
himself; and then, with a smile, observed, "humph!--a fine E III 15 445 7
related to her, with a smile; a look; a shake of the head; E III 15 445 14
15
herself a saucy conscious smile about it, and found E III 15 449 35
The smile was returned as Jane answered, "you are very E III 16 460 55
56
with a sort of serious smile--"much less, perhaps, than he E III 17 464 22
You are trying not to smile." E III 18 470 5
my dear Emma, that you will not smile when you hear it." E III 18 470 6
He wanted her to look up and smile; and having now brought E III 18 473 23
24
not to smile too broadly--she did--cheerfully answering, E III 18 473 23
24
I see it in her cheek, her smile, her vain attempt to E III 18 480 77
Jane was forced to smile completely, for a moment; and the E III 18 480 78
79
and the smile partly remained as she turned E III 18 480 78
79
for a moment; and the smile partly remained as she turned
Anne suppressed a smile, and listened kindly, while Mrs. P III 8 64 7
an artificial, assenting smile, followed by a contemptuous P III 10 86 20
and she must sigh, and smile, and wonder too, as Elizabeth P IV 3 138 5
Anne presumed, however, still to smile about it; and at P IV 4 147 7
because she had a smile and a civil answer for every body. P IV 4 150 14
and Captain Benwick too, without even half a smile. P IV 6 168 22
Anne looked down to hide her smile. P IV 6 172 44
spirit, with a little smile, a little glow, he said, "I P IV 8 181 3
4
improved, and he replied again with almost a smile. P IV 8 190 47
a courteous, comprehensive smile to all; and one smile and P IV 10 226 64
smile and one card more decidedly for Captain Wentworth. P IV 10 226 64
He looked at her with a smile, and a little motion of the P IV 11 231 12
a smile, "I must endeavour to subdue my mind to my fortune. P IV 11 247 84

up at her with a smile)--it cd not have happened, you know, S 1 364 1
"Sir--said Mr Heywood with a good humoured smile--if you S 1 366 1

SMILED (70)

and lady who only smiled on each other; and point out a NA I 4 33 7
Isabella smiled incredulously, and talked the rest of the NA I 10 71 7
Henry smiled, and said, "how very little trouble it can NA II 1 132 18
Isabella shrugged her shoulders and smiled, the only NA II 1 133 30
Henry smiled and said, "I am sure my brother would not NA II 4 150 4
He smiled, and said, "you have formed a very favourable NA II 5 157 11
with him, listen to him, and even to smile when he smiled. NA II 7 181 41
Henry only smiled. NA II 11 211 13
bells rang and every body smiled; and, as this took place NA II 16 252 7
Elinor smiled again, to hear her sister describing so SS I 17 91 15
She came in with a smile, smiled all the time of her visit, SS I 19 106 22
except when she laughed, and smiled when she went away. SS I 19 106 22
Mrs. Dashwood smiled and said nothing. SS II 3 157 18
But while she smiled at a graciousness so misapplied, she SS II 12 233 16
She smiled, and said how she had changed her name since SS III 11 354 29
Elinor smiled, and shook her head. SS III 13 368 29
He shook hands with Robert, bowed & smiled to the ladies, W 355 28
Miss Bennet he acknowledged to be pretty, but she smiled PP I 4 16 15
Sir William only smiled. PP I 6 25 28
Darcy only smiled; and the general pause which ensued made PP I 9 45 35
Mr. Darcy smiled; but Elizabeth thought she could perceive PP I 10 51 40
She smiled, but made no answer. PP I 10 52 49
by a summons to dinner; and the girls smiled on each other. PP I 13 65 26
He smiled, and assured her that whatever she wished him to PP I 18 91 10
Many smiled; but no one looked more amused than Mr. Bennet PP I 18 101 71
Elizabeth smiled at the recollection of all that she had PP II 5 155 2
Darcy smiled and said, "you are perfectly right. PP II 8 176 26
which were kindly smiled on by the mother and daughter. PP II 14 210 4
Mr. and Mrs. Gardiner smiled. PP III 1 248 29
see the ring, and then I bowed and smiled like any thing." PP III 9 316 8
He smiled, looked handsome, and said many pretty things. PP III 11 330 7
She looked at Jane, and smiled, and shook her head by PP III 11 331 13
Elizabeth smiled. PP III 12 343 31
Elizabeth, who was left by herself, now smiled at the PP III 13 347 28
Kitty simpered and smiled, and hoped her turn was coming PP III 13 348 34
would he only have smiled upon her and called her "my dear MP I 3 33 64
He smiled as he answered, "I am afraid the avenue stands a MP I 6 56 21
as an amendment; the young ladies neither smiled nor spoke. MP I 9 84 2
Mr. Crawford smiled his acquiescence, and stepping forward MP I 9 88 20
Edmund smiled and shook his head. MP I 13 126 20
Miss Crawford smiled her perfect approbation; and hastened MP II 8 258 17
vain however;--Sir Thomas smiled, tried to encourage her, MP II 10 275 11
Sir Thomas paused, half smiled, glanced at his niece, and MP II 11 285 13
Emma smiled and chatted as cheerfully as she could, to E I 1 8 10
11
and Harriet blushed and smiled, and said she had always E I 4 34 43
Harriet blushed and smiled, and said something about E I 7 56 42
Harriet smiled again, and her smiles grew stronger. E I 7 56 47
Emma only nodded, and smiled.-- E I 9 78 53
report; and he sighed and smiled himself off in a way that E I 13 111 14
Emma smiled and answered--"my visit was of use to the E I 13 114 32
journey; and she listened, and smiled, and congratulated. E II 5 188 9
young man--one who smiled so often and bowed so well; but E II 7 206 4
greater profits, and fortune in general had smiled on them. E II 7 207 6
And he smiled with such seeming pleasure at the conviction, E II 8 228 90
Mr. John Knightley smiled, and replied, "that is to say, E II 16 293 15
16
intended her by such a hope, smiled most graciously. E II 18 305 2
She smiled her acceptance; and nothing less than a summons E III 6 366 76
Emma smiled, and felt that Mr. Weston had very good reason E III 12 417 5
Emma would not have smiled for the world, and only said, " E III 16 456 26
Emma hung about him affectionately, and smiled, and said E III 17 466 29
Anne smiled more than once to herself during this speech, P III 12 103 3
and talked in vain; she smiled and said, "I am determined P III 12 109 32
Every thing was safe enough, and she smiled over the many P IV 1 128 32
Anne smiled and said, "my idea of good company, Mr. Elliot, P IV 4 150 15
16
She only smiled, blushed, and gently shook her head. P IV 5 159 22
Anne sighed and blushed and smiled, in pity and disdain, P IV 7 179 31
Anne half smiled and said, "do you see that in my eye?" P IV 9 194 15
Mrs. Smith looked at her again, looked earnestly, smiled, P IV 9 195 29
30
Captain Harville smiled, as much as to say, "do you claim P IV 11 232 19
Anne smiled, and let it pass. P IV 11 243 68

SMILES (57)

in returning the nods and smiles of Miss Thorpe, though NA I 5 35 1
together again; so, with smiles of most exquisite misery, NA I 9 67 33
Isabella's countenance was once more all smiles and good- NA I 13 100 16
smiles, the alteration became too positive to be past over. NA II 4 149 1
Miss Tilney's manners and Henry's smiles soon did away NA II 5 154 2
the General's complacent smiles, and a good appetite of NA II 6 165 6
Would he have been less gay or less happy in the smiles of SS II 9 209 30
to no outward demonstrations of joy, no words, no smiles. SS III 7 315 24
feelings & more natural smiles than they had taken away.-- W 323 3
all gentleness; continual smiles & a very slow W 349 23
tho' Margaret's modest smiles imported that she meant to W 355 28
You had better return to your partner and enjoy her smiles, PP I 3 12 13
amid very complaisant smiles and general encouragement, a PP I 15 70 3
the insolent smiles of the ladies, were more intolerable. PP I 18 102 72
the house, amidst the nods and smiles of the whole party. PP II 5 155 3
and gave most gracious smiles, especially when any dish on PP II 6 163 14
in spite of the smiles which overspread her face whenever PP III 3 269 8
Smiles decked the face of Mrs. Bennet, as the carriage PP III 9 315 2
what they ought his smiles and his easy address, while he PP III 9 316 5
I am happier even than Jane; she only smiles, I laugh. PP III 18 383 21
wine drank without any smiles, or agreeable trifling, and MP I 6 52 1
till induced by further smiles and liveliness, to put the MP I 6 57 32
spoke with proper smiles and dignity of its being a most MP I 9 88 24
There were not fewer smiles at the parsonage than at the MP I 17 159 6
ready for dinner; and the smiles and pleased looks of the MP II 5 223 48
I only want her to look kindly on me, to give me smiles as MP II 6 231 9
Crawford, whose eyes and smiles were immediately and more MP II 10 274 9
paid her with as many smiles and courteous words as she MP II 10 277 16
Last night it had been hope and smiles, bustle and motion, MP II 11 283 6
him with your sweetest smiles this afternoon, and send him MP II 13 303 15
face wore its broadest smiles, may be easily conceived. MP III 15 445 32
and screened by her bonnet, those smiles were unseen. MP III 15 445 32
off by the woman whose smiles had been so wholly at his MP III 17 467 20
to him in all her smiles, and all her ways, as Mary MP III 17 470 25
turned away her head, divided between tears and smiles. E I 1 11 37
drawing-room and the smiles of his lovely daughter, was in E I 3 20 2
Harriet smiled again, and her smiles grew stronger. E I 7 56 47
subject, was ready to listen with most friendly smiles. E I 15 124 2
party at Mrs. Brown's--smiles and blushes rising in E II 4 181 4
with cordial, fearless smiles, now addressing all the E II 4 182 5
its power of censure, by bows or smiles--Mr. Knightley. E II 7 206 4
Smiles of intelligence passed between her and the E II 8 220 48
Mr. and Mrs. Elton appeared; and all the smiles and the E III 2 320 11
elegance of her dress, and her smiles of graciousness. E III 2 320 13
to be attended to, and with happy smiles must hurry away. E III 2 321 16
while smiles of high glee passed between him and his wife. E III 2 328 38
down the middle, and was in a continual course of smiles. E III 2 328 41
opinion, to foresee the smiles, the sneers, the merriment E III 11 413 48
the brightest smiles, "and most sincerely wish them happy." E III 18 474 31
A little beauty, and a few smiles, and a few compliments P III 7 62 39
from the view of the last smiles of the year upon the P III 10 84 7
but her courtesies and smiles were more a matter of course. P IV 3 137 3
I sent him away with smiles. P IV 10 213 9
the sight of his present smiles and mildness, or the sound P IV 10 214 11
Her distress returned, however, on perceiving smiles and P IV 10 222 37
smiles reined in and spirits dancing in private rapture. P IV 11 240 59
Aye--that young lady smiles I see;--I dare say she thinks S 6 393 1

SMILING (85)

-----"like patience on a monument "smiling at grief." NA I 1 16 9
her friend with the most smiling and affectionate haste, NA I 8 52 1
received from him the smiling tribute of recognition. NA I 8 54 4
"Indeed he is, Mrs. Allen," said Mrs. Thorpe, smiling NA I 8 58 33
of the General, whose smiling compliments announced a NA II 7 175 11
desire of making use of the present smiling weather.-- NA II 7 177 17
honoured, turned with a smiling countenance to Catherine, NA II 8 185 5
Yet, though smiling within herself at the mistake, she SS I 4 19 3
"Because," replied he, smiling, "among the rest of the SS I 16 88 36
"Perhaps," said Elinor, smiling, "we may come to the same SS I 17 91 11
yet she could not help smiling at the quiet archness of SS I 18 100 28
29
"We can mean no other," cried Lucy smiling. SS I 22 131 30
Elinor could not help smiling at this display of SS II 3 156 15
"Dear ma'am," replied Elinor, smiling at the difference of SS II 8 198 28
and countenance gaily smiling, from the persuasion of SS II 9 202 5
6
though she could not forbear smiling at the form of it. SS III 1 268 52
Jennings, sagaciously smiling, as soon as the gentleman SS III 4 285 1
Elinor, smiling at the grave and decisive importance of SS III 5 296 25
26
so nobly as this; though smiling to see the same eager SS III 10 343 10
heart to be the only cold one?"--said Emma smiling. W 316 2
"Mr. Darcy is all politeness," said Elizabeth, smiling. PP I 6 26 42
"What think you of books?" said he, smiling. PP I 18 93 27
a countenance no less smiling than her sister's, "what you PP I 18 95 49
"How can you talk so?"--said Jane faintly smiling,-- "you PP I 21 119 25
Elizabeth could hardly help smiling, as she assured her PP II 6 164 29
smiling, "your ladyship can hardly expect me to own it." PP II 6 166 37
not talk to me of his own arts," said Fitzwilliam smiling. PP II 10 185 32
Mr. Collins was gratified; and with a more smiling PP II 15 215 3
4
"How can you be smiling so, Lizzy?" PP II 18 229 2
Elizabeth could not help smiling at his easy manner of PP III 16 371 41
replied, "consequently you know," smiling, "better company. MP I 10 99 14
You have a very smiling scene before you." MP I 10 99 16
words were spoken, and smiling with all the good-humour of MP I 10 100 22
deficiency of information, or (smiling) of something else. MP I 11 110 26
"Why should you dare say that? (smiling)-- MP II 3 197 6
be," said Mrs. Grant, smiling--"the turkey--and I assure MP II 4 215 48
rather it were William's," said Edmund, smiling at her. MP II 7 244 29
"If this is all you have to say, Fanny," smiling and MP II 9 262 6
Now, every thing was smiling. MP II 9 270 40
Mary, stopping short, and smiling in his face, "how glad I MP II 12 297 32
running to her with a smiling face, and in a flutter of E I 4 32 28
"I dare say," replied Mrs. Weston, smiling, "that I E I 5 37 8
"Yes," said he, smiling. E I 5 38 11
The sitting began; and Harriet, smiling and blushing, and E I 6 46 24
"Not for the world," said Emma, smiling graciously, "would E I 7 53 21
"A very serious sort, I assure you;" still smiling. E I 8 59 22
"Pray, Mr. Knightley," said Emma, who had been smiling to E I 8 60 28
very conscious and smiling, and rode off in great spirits. E I 8 68 58
"take it," said Emma, smiling, and pushing the paper E I 9 71 12
13
to Harriet, sat happily smiling, and saying to herself, E I 9 72 15
silly--so satisfied--so smiling--so prosing --so E I 10 84 16
Well, (smiling,) I hope it may be allowed that if E I 10 87 30
"Yes," said he, smiling--"and reason good. E I 12 99 6
Elton, spruce, black, and smiling, was with them instantly. E I 13 114 28
"My Emma!" replied Mrs. Weston, smiling, "what is the E I 14 121 16
directly, to say, with smiling interest----- "have you E II 1 157 8
9
"I am happy you approved," said Emma, smiling; "but I hope E II 3 170 3
said Mrs. Weston smiling, "remember that I am here.-- E II 6 201 23
"No," said he, smiling, "that is no subject of regret at E II 8 222 53
"Well," said Mrs. Weston, smiling, "you give him credit E II 8 224 65
"We cannot suppose," said Emma, smiling, "that Mr. Elton E II 14 277 37
explanation," continued he, smiling, "they are paid for it. E II 16 296 43
The two ladies looked over it together; and he sat smiling E II 17 303 26
In spite of this little rub, however, Emma was smiling E III 2 325 32
He looked with smiling penetration; and, on receiving no E III 2 330 48
She met Mr. Weston on his entrance, with a smiling E III 10 400 67
68
subject," replied Emma, smiling; "but you do not mean to E III 11 405 13
Emma, smiling--"but, excuse me, it must be thought of." E III 16 460 54
He paused a moment, again smiling, with his eyes fixed on E III 18 470 8
with smiling but determined decision, "and been accepted." E III 18 471 18
They met readily and smiling, but with a consciousness E III 18 476 46
well what she was, before that day;" said he, smiling. P III 8 65 16
Mrs. Clay was very pleasant, and very smiling; but her P IV 3 137 3
Mary) and Anne, smiling and blushing, very becomingly P IV 3 143 18
I suppose (smiling) I have more pride than any of you; but P IV 4 151 18
but in a moment half smiling again, added, "the day has P IV 8 182 6
smiling, said, "I have been a little premature, I perceive. P IV 9 195 26
27
"I can explain this too," cried Mrs. Smith, smiling. P IV 9 204 78
or an explanation of some smiling hints of particular P IV 10 216 18
sex?" and she answered the question, smiling also, "yes. P IV 11 232 19
I am in very good anchorage here," (smiling at Anne) "well P IV 11 234 27
by you, conversing and smiling, and feel all the horrible P IV 11 244 72
Now Mary, (smiling at his wife)--before I open it, what S 5 385 1
listening & talking with smiling attention or solicitous S 7 396 1
him, will go smirking & smiling about & paying girls S 7 400 1

SMILINGLY (3)

"I am not afraid of you," said he, smilingly. PP II 8 174 16
Her aunt asked her, smilingly, how she liked it. PP III 1 247 9
an awkward moment, Emma smilingly said, "you must make my E I 9 82 81
82

SMIRK (1)

"Now I must give one smirk, and then we may be rational NA I 3 26 18

SMIRKED (2)

So upon that, he smirked, and simpered, and looked grave, SS III 1 258 5
I only smirked and bowed, and said the word 'happy.' P IV 10 223 46

SMIRKING (1)

A handsome young fellow like him, will go smirking & S 7 400 1

SMIRKS (1)

He simpers, and smirks, and makes love to us all. PP III 11 330 8

SMITH (163)

I learnt all this from a Mr Smith now in this LS 4 248 1
tales invented by Charles Smith to the prejudice of Lady LS 14 264 4
not the young lady he danced with on Monday a Miss Smith?" NA I 10 73 13
enter the house while Mrs. Smith was in it, with whom SS I 13 68 66
"Yes, Marianne, but I would not go while Mrs. Smith was SS I 13 68 69
I should hear from Mrs. Smith, when I next came into the SS I 14 73 17
Mrs. Smith has this morning exercised the privilege of SS I 15 75 6
But Mrs. Smith must be obliged;--and her business will not SS I 15 76 9
My visits to Mrs. Smith are never repeated within the SS I 15 76 10
"And is Mrs. Smith your only friend? SS I 15 76 11
might be pleasing to Mrs. Smith; and on this head I shall SS I 15 76 14
I am persuaded that Mrs. Smith suspects his regard for SS I 15 78 26
engaged) from Mrs. Smith--and if that is the case, it must SS I 15 79 31
a fear of offending Mrs. Smith, to resist the temptation SS I 15 81 43
of marriage between John Smith and Mary brown, he could SS III 5 298 33
wood walk, a road of Smith gravel winding round a SS III 6 302 7
of my old cousin, Mrs. Smith, was to set me free; yet the SS III 8 320 32
"Mrs. Smith had somehow or other been informed, I imagine SS III 8 321 34
"Well, sir, and what said Mrs. Smith?" SS III 8 323 39
really passed between Mrs. Smith and myself--and I SS III 8 324 42

forgiveness of Mrs. Smith, who, by stating his marriage SS III 14 379 18
I told Smith I did not know where I was. MP I 6 53 2
As he has done so well by Smith, I think I had better have MP I 6 53 8
"Smith has not much above a hundred acres altogether in MP I 6 55 17
be allowed to bring Miss Smith with her; a most welcome E I 3 22 7
welcome request: for Miss Smith was a girl of seventeen E I 3 22 7
Harriet Smith was the natural daughter of somebody. E I 3 22 8
The happiness of Miss Smith was quite equal to her E I 3 25 15
pleasant; and a Harriet Smith, therefore, one whom she E I 4 26 1
Emma and Harriet Smith, but I think it a bad thing." E I 5 36 1
I can imagine your objection to Harriet Smith. E I 5 36 6
I may safely affirm that Harriet Smith will do nothing.-- E I 5 37 7
But Harriet Smith--I have not half done about Harriet E I 5 38 15
Harriet Smith--I have not half done about Harriet Smith. E I 5 38 15
Harriet Smith, or my dread of its doing them both harm." E I 5 39 21
"You have given Miss Smith all that she required," said he; E I 6 42 2
"The expression of the eye is most correct, but Miss Smith E I 6 47 31
the placing of Miss Smith out of doors; and the tree is E I 6 48 39
"I have reason to think," he replied, "that Harriet Smith E I 8 59 25
Harriet Smith refuse Robert Martin? madness, if it is so; E I 8 60 34
You have been no friend to Harriet Smith, Emma. E I 8 63 42
Miss Harriet Smith may not find offers of marriage flow in E I 8 64 47
at least, (for Harriet Smith is a girl who will marry E I 8 64 47
more true gentility than Harriet Smith could understand." E I 8 65 49
stopt a moment-- "or Miss Smith could inspire him." E I 9 71 9
This is saying very plainly--'pray, Miss Smith, give me E I 9 72 15
"For Miss ----, read Miss Smith. E I 9 73 18
"our little friend Harriet Smith, however, is just such E I 12 104 47
48
Smith was not better, by no means better, rather worse. E I 13 114 31
pretty little friend, Miss Smith, and my son--and then I E I 14 119 7
Churchill and Miss Smith making their party quite complete. E I 14 119 8
message to Miss Smith I shall be happy to deliver; but no E I 15 130 25
"Miss Smith!--message to Miss Smith!--what could she E I 15 130 26
upon his respect for Miss Smith as her friend,--but E I 15 130 28
his wonder that Miss Smith should be mentioned at all,--he E I 15 130 28
the last month, to Miss Smith--such attentions as I have E I 15 130 30
Miss Smith!-- E I 15 130 31
I never thought of Miss Smith in the whole course of my E I 15 130 31
sorry--but, Miss Smith, indeed!--Oh! Miss Woodhouse! who E I 15 130 31
who can think of Miss Smith, when Miss Woodhouse is near! E I 15 130 31
Smith?--that you have never thought seriously of her?" E I 15 131 34
I think seriously of Miss Smith?--Miss Smith is a very E I 15 131 35
alliance, as to be addressing myself to Miss Smith!-- E I 15 132 35
Had the same behaviour continued, Miss Smith might have E I 15 132 36
Miss Smith would do them the favour to eat a piece too." E II 1 155 4
How does Miss Smith do? E II 3 176 44
caring nothing for Miss Woodhouse, and defying Miss Smith. E II 4 181 3
white gate again; and Miss Smith receiving her summons, E II 5 186 3
that she thought Miss Smith was grown, had brought on a E II 5 186 4
Miss Fairfax, and Miss Smith; but already, at dinner, they E II 8 214 13
She introduced him to her friend, Miss Smith, and, at E II 8 220 47
us your opinion of our new instrument; you and Miss Smith. E II 9 235 44
How do you do, Miss Smith?-- E II 9 236 44
Miss Smith, pray take care. E II 9 239 53
Miss Smith, the step at the turning." E II 9 239 53
Miss Woodhouse and Miss Smith; so kind as to call to hear E II 10 244 42
"You and Miss Smith, and Miss Fairfax, will be three, and E II 11 248 4
You and Miss Smith, and Miss Fairfax, will be three, and E II 11 248 4
He did not omit being sometimes directly before Miss Smith, E III 2 327 34
whom I should be very glad to see dancing--Miss Smith." E III 2 327 37
"Miss Smith!--Oh!--I had not observed.-- E III 2 327 37
"Knightley has taken pity on poor little Miss Smith!-- E III 2 328 42
43
Harriet Smith has some first-rate qualities, which Mrs. E III 2 331 55
Miss Smith, and Miss Bickerton, another parlour boarder at E III 3 333 5
after), as well as Miss Smith, were coming in during the E III 3 336 12
persuaded--Miss Smith, you walk as if you were tired. E III 5 345 11
Now, an attachment to Harriet Smith would have nothing to E III 9 388 13
said, "Emma, you have been no friend to Harriet Smith."-- E III 11 402 1
Mr. Knightley and Harriet Smith!-- E III 11 413 48
Mr. Knightley and Harriet Smith!-- E III 11 413 48
Harriet Smith might think herself not unworthy of being E III 12 415 1
instead of in Harriet Smith; she must, in all probability, E III 12 421 17
with Harriet Smith; but it was too tender a subject.-- E III 17 463 15
Harriet Smith." E III 18 470 8
Harriet Smith marries Robert Martin." E III 18 470 12
You cannot mean to say, that Harriet Smith has accepted E III 18 471 17
to be our brother and sister, Henry, John--and Miss Smith. E III 18 471 20
and he followed with Miss Smith and Henry; and that at one E III 18 472 20
were in such a crowd, as to make Miss Smith rather uneasy." E III 18 472 20
Robert Martin and Harriet Smith, the latest couple engaged E III 19 483 6
Miss Hamilton, now Mrs. Smith, had shewn her kindness in P IV 5 152 2
give Mrs. Smith, and Anne therefore lost no time in going. P IV 5 153 5
Anne found in Mrs. Smith the good sense and agreeable P IV 5 153 7
There had been a time, Mrs. Smith told her, when her P IV 5 154 9
"And she," said Mrs. Smith, "besides nursing me most P IV 5 155 9
"Yes," said Mrs. Smith more doubtingly, "sometimes it may, P IV 5 156 11
It was but a passing emotion however with Mrs. Smith, she P IV 5 156 12
13
A Mrs. Smith. P IV 5 157 15
A widow Mrs. Smith,--and who was her husband? P IV 5 157 15
has generally taken me, when I have called on Mrs. Smith." P IV 5 157 18
A widow Mrs. Smith, lodging in Westgate-Buildings!-- P IV 5 158 19
and forty--a mere Mrs. Smith, an every day Mrs. Smith, of P IV 5 158 19
Smith, an every day Mrs. Smith, of all people and all P IV 5 158 19
Mrs. Smith, such a name!" P IV 5 158 19
She left it to himself to recollect, that Mrs. Smith was P IV 5 158 20
She had once partly promised Mrs. Smith to spend the P IV 7 180 33
Mrs. Smith gave a most good-humoured acquiescence. P IV 7 180 33
Mrs. Smith made no reply; but when she was leaving her, P IV 7 180 35
promise of going to Mrs. Smith; meaning that it should P IV 9 192 1
such an enquirer as Mrs. Smith, who had already heard, P IV 9 192 5
or notoriety in Bath was well known by name to Mrs. Smith. P IV 9 193 5
"And such being the case," continued Mrs. Smith, after a P IV 9 194 18
After another short silence-- "pray," said Mrs. Smith, "is P IV 9 194 19
20
replied Mrs. Smith, gravely, "but it seems worn out now. P IV 9 194 22
"To confess the truth," said Mrs. Smith, assuming her P IV 9 195 24
Mrs. Smith gave her a penetrating glance, and then, P IV 9 195 26
27
Mrs. Smith looked at her again, looked earnestly, smiled, P IV 9 195 29
30
"My dear Mrs. Smith, Mr. Elliot's wife has not been dead P IV 9 196 31
objections," cried Mrs. Smith, archly, "Mr. Elliot is safe, P IV 9 196 32
Will not this manner of speaking of him, Mrs. Smith, P IV 9 196 33
Mrs. Smith would hardly have believed so soon in Mr. P IV 9 197 34
impatient to know why Mrs. Smith should have fancied she P IV 9 197 34
"It first came into my head," replied Mrs. Smith, "upon P IV 9 197 36
Mrs. Smith said nothing. P IV 9 198 42
They were both silent--Mrs. Smith very thoughtful. P IV 9 198 52
"I know it all, I know it all," cried Mrs. Smith. P IV 9 200 57
"Mr. Elliot," replied Mrs. Smith, "at that period of his P IV 9 200 59
Mrs. Smith hesitated a little here. P IV 9 201 64
"Indeed, my dear Mrs. Smith, I want none," cried Anne. P IV 9 202 67
The box was brought and placed before her, and Mrs. Smith, P IV 9 202 69
70
This was the letter, directed to "Charles Smith, Esq. of P IV 9 203 71
"Dear Smith, I have received yours. P IV 9 203 72
Anne in a glow; and Mrs. Smith, observing the high colour P IV 9 204 74
75
"I can explain this too," cried Mrs. Smith, smiling. P IV 9 204 78
"My dear Mrs. Smith, your authority is deficient. P IV 9 205 83
"Indeed, Mrs. Smith, we must not expect to get real P IV 9 205 85
"Well," continued Mrs. Smith triumphantly, "grant my P IV 9 206 88
Here Mrs. Smith paused a moment; but Anne had not a word P IV 9 206 89
90
"Lessening, I understand," replied Mrs. Smith. P IV 9 208 92
Mrs. Smith had been carried away from her first direction, P IV 9 208 94
bitterness of Mrs. Smith, proved him to have been very P IV 9 208 94
Mrs. Smith did not want to take blame to herself, and was P IV 9 209 95
him, she could discern Mr. Smith to have been a man of P IV 9 209 95
than his judgment, Mr. Smith had appointed him the P IV 9 209 96
applications from Mrs. Smith, which all breathed the same P IV 9 209 97
relative to Mrs. Smith, in which his conduct was involved. P IV 9 211 103
Smith, but here was a reward indeed springing from it!-- P IV 10 212 1
Mrs. Smith had been able to tell her what no one else P IV 10 212 1
cruel conduct towards Mrs. Smith, she could hardly bear P IV 10 214 11
conversation with Mrs. Smith; but a keener interest had P IV 11 229 1
the world to add to his list, Lady Russell and Mrs. Smith. P IV 12 251 10
favour; and as for Mrs. Smith, she had claims of various P IV 12 251 10
Lieut: Smith r.N. capt: little,--Limehouse.-- S 6 389 1

SMITH'S (24)
& according to Mr Smith's account, is equally dull & proud. LS 4 248 2
Your friend Mr Smith's story however cannot be quite true, LS 6 252 2
Mr Smith's account of her proceedings at Langford, where LS 11 259 1
for disbeleiving Mr Smith's intelligence; you had no doubt LS 12 261 5
walking over Mrs. Smith's grounds, or in seeing her house. SS I 13 68 74
"Smith's place is the admiration of all the country; and MP I 6 55 15
beyond a wish that they had seen his friend Smith's place. MP I 10 97 3
remarkably clever in Miss Smith's conversation, but she E I 3 23 10
Harriet Smith's intimacy at Hartfield was soon a settled E I 4 26 1
Altogether she was quite convinced of Harriet Smith's E I 4 26 2
can arise from Harriet Smith's intimacy being made a E I 5 40 24
of her part, and lessen the irksomeness of Miss Smith's." E I 6 46 25
one exactly the idea of such a height as Miss Smith's. E I 6 48 35
The naivete of Miss Smith's manners--and altogether--Oh, E I 6 48 39
What are Harriet Smith's claims, either of birth, nature E I 8 61 38
"I do not offer it for Miss Smith's collection," said he. E I 9 71 11
I have ventured to write it into Miss Smith's collection. E I 9 82 80
were certain that Miss Smith's disorder had no infection? E I 15 125 4
her as near to Mrs. Smith's lodgings in Westgate-Buildings, P IV 5 153 5
a more cheerless situation in itself than Mrs. Smith's. P IV 5 153 8
three years," was Mrs. Smith's answer, given so gravely P IV 9 198 52
some surprise at Mrs. Smith's having spoken of him so P IV 9 211 100
"My dear," was Mrs. Smith's reply, "there was nothing else P IV 9 211 101
Mrs. Smith's enjoyments were not spoiled by this P IV 12 252 12

SMITHS (3)
"When Miss Smiths and Mr. Eltons get acquainted--they do E I 9 74 25
One of the five thousand Mr. Smiths whose names are to be P IV 5 157 15
And the Smiths accordingly had been ruined. P IV 9 209 95

SMITTEN (1)
Poor brandon! he is quite smitten already, and he is very SS I 9 45 32

SMOKE (2)
in the massy walls and smoke of former days, and in the NA II 8 183 3
orchard in blossom, and light column of smoke ascending.-- E III 6 360 40

SMOKES (2)
"With dark narrow stairs, and a kitchen that smokes, I SS I 14 72 12
The breakfast-room chimney smokes a little, I grant you, P IV 1 128 30

SMOKING (1)
the extensive buildings, smoking in rain, without any wish P IV 2 135 34

SMOOTH (15)
driven so rapidly along a smooth, level road of fine NA II 5 161 25
shrubberies--always so smooth and so dry; and the Abbey in NA II 11 212 16
it greatly contributed to smooth the descent of his pride, NA II 16 251 6
Elinor, endeavouring to smooth away the offence; "and I do SS II 1 145 17
Her skin was very brown, but clear, smooth and glowing--; W 328 9
her own sense of propriety could but just smooth over. MP I 8 81 32
The course of true love never did run smooth-- E I 9 75 25
by a basin of nice smooth gruel, thin, but not too thin. E I 12 104 50
to restore him to the relish of his own smooth gruel. E I 12 105 51
grown and good-looking, with smooth, plausible manners." E I 18 149 28
the rest, in speculation at least, was perfectly smooth. E II 11 255 59
palliate imprudence, or smooth objections; and by the time E III 10 401 69
Her way was clear, though not quite smooth.-- E III 13 431 38
We none of us expect to be in smooth water all our days." P III 8 70 45
Even the smooth surface of family-union seems worth P IV 9 198 53

SMOOTHED (3)
and little vexations seemed every where smoothed away. MP I 18 171 25
encouragements, and smoothed many little matters, it might E I 1 13 43
would be prevented--many awkwardnesses smoothed by it. E II 4 182 8

SMOOTHLY (4)
At present nothing goes smoothly. LS 2 244 1
in aid, it proceeded so smoothly as to enable her to SS III 10 340 1
Every thing, however, went on smoothly, and was finally PP II 4 151 1
the other half might not be so very smoothly wooed. MP II 8 255 10

SMOOTHNESS (4)
The evening passed with external smoothness, though almost MP II 2 191 11
It was all general approbation and smoothness; nothing E II 2 169 16
I can only say that there was smoothness outwardly. E II 6 202 38
see such a skin?--such smoothness! such delicacy!--and yet E III 18 478 60
61

SMOTHER (1)
and been compelled to smother among the Musgroves, were P IV 1 124 11

SNAPPISH (1)
poor Margt is very snappish, & Penelope owns she had W 343 19

SNATCHED (1)
Anne Elliot, so young; known to so few, to be snatched off P III 4 27 3

SNATCHING (1)
hope of discovering, and snatching her from farther vice, MP III 16 451 12

SNEAKED (1)
to curtsey, or some footman in dishabille sneaked off. NA II 8 184 4

SNEER (2)
"Certainly,"--he replied with a sneer--"I came into SS I 20 113 30
pardon," replied Miss Bingley, turning away with a sneer. PP I 18 95 47

SNEERED (1)
and the maid-servants sneered at her clothes; and when to MP I 2 14 8

SNEERING (3)
of saying, with sneering civility, "pray, Miss Eliza, are PP III 3 269 8
9
They were sneering and negligent. E II 15 281 3
husband, with a sort of sneering consciousness; "I have E III 7 372 38

SNEERS (1)
foresee the smiles, the sneers, the merriment it would E III 11 413 48

SNEYD (5)
West Indies--my friend Sneyd--you have heard me speak of MP I 5 51 40
have heard me speak of Sneyd, Edmund; his father and MP I 5 51 40
I made my bow in form, and as Mrs. Sneyd was surrounded by MP I 5 51 40
months, and Miss Sneyd, I believe, has never forgiven me. MP I 5 51 40
Poor Miss Sneyd! MP I 5 51 41

SNIPE (1)
enjoyment, was out snipe shooting; Edmund, she had too MP II 9 267 22

SNOW (19)
where what with frost and snow upon beds of stones, it was MP II 2 189 5
and snow, with nothing to do and no variety to hope for. MP II 11 286 15
There was snow on the ground, and she was sitting in a MP III 1 312 6
feels so very much like snow, that if it were to any other E I 13 110 9
in motion, a few flakes of snow were finding their way E I 13 112 24
much snow on the ground; but now it is of no consequence. E I 13 115 39
ground being covered with snow, and of its still snowing E I 15 125 7
and horses to be making their way through a storm of snow." E I 15 126 8
for of course you saw there would be snow very soon. E I 15 126 10
Every body must have seen the snow coming on. I admired E I 15 126 10
Another hour or two's snow can hardly make the road E I 15 126 10

As to there being any quantity of snow fallen or likely to	E I 15 126 11
accumulations of drifted snow that might impede them.	E I 15 127 13
first report of the snow, came back again, and told them	E I 15 127 16
the Highbury road--the snow was no where above half an	E I 15 127 16
alarm at the sight of the snow which had actually fallen,	E I 15 128 22
sight of a great deal of snow on the ground did her	E I 16 138 16
The ground covered with snow, and the atmosphere in that	E I 16 138 17
beginning in rain or snow, and every evening setting in to	E I 16 138 17
SNOWED (2)	
I was snowed up at a friend's house once for a week.	E I 13 115 39
coolly, "I cannot wish to be snowed up a week at Randalls."	E I 13 115 40
	41
SNOWING (3)	
Actually snowing at this moment!--	E I 13 113 26
snow, and of its still snowing fast, with a strong	E I 15 125 7
he had known it to be snowing some time, but had not said	E I 15 126 11
SNOWS (1)	
Ha! snows a little I see."	E I 13 115 37
SNUFFED (2)	
its ancient date might occasion, she hastily snuffed it.	NA II 6 169 12
Alas! it was snuffed and extinguished in one.	NA II 6 170 12
SNUG (13)	
and garret above, will make it a very snug little cottage.	SS I 6 29 4
looks comfortable and snug--with rich meadows and several	SS I 18 97 4
I have more pleasure in a snug farm-house than a watch-	SS I 18 98 8
Lord! how snug they might live in such another cottage as	SS III 1 260 7
from the quiet warmth of a snug parlour, to the bustle,	W 327 7
I shall order a Barrel of oysters, & be famously snug."	W 335 13
I think a snug chat infinitely better.	W 354 28
Well, now let us be quite comfortable and snug, and talk	PP II 16 221 17
and nothing in the world could be more snug and pleasant."	MP I 9 88 24
and now I am quite snug, with my little shaving glass in	P IV 1 128 28
Yes, yes, we will have a snug walk together; and I have	P IV 6 169 27
in our chairs, and are as snug as if we were at Kellynch,	P IV 6 170 29
two others are nice little snug houses, very fit for a	S 7 402 1
SNUG-LOOKING (1)	
"And whose very snug-looking place is this?"--said	S 4 379 1
SNUGLY (1)	
While they snugly repair to their own end of the house,	NA II 5 158 15
SOB (1)	
neck to sob out her various emotions of pain and pleasure.	MP III 7 384 34
SOBBED (1)	
She still screamed and sobbed lustily, kicked her two	SS I 21 121 10
SOBBING (1)	
ended every day's sorrows by sobbing herself to sleep.	MP I 2 14 9
SOBER (13)	
The morrow brought a very sober looking morning; the sun	NA I 11 82 1
He is not in a sober mood.	NA I 14 114 48
and they set off at the sober pace in which the handsome,	NA II 5 155 4
in her more calm and sober judgment she had determined on,-	SS III 14 378 16
These were anxious considerations; enough to sober her	MP II 8 254 8
dances together with such sober tranquillity as might	MP II 10 278 20
So thought Fanny in good truth and sober sadness, as she	MP III 2 329 10
Nay, in sober sadness, I believe I now love you all."	MP III 5 358 9
bring her mind into a sober state, and incline her to a	MP III 6 369 9
She will grow sober by degrees.--	MP III 9 394 1
or exercise it on sober facts; and the only literary	E I 9 69 3
in his own house, to get sober and cool, and the other	E I 15 128 21
man had been so much more sober: but a sanguine temper,	E I 18 144 2
SOBER-MINDED (2)	
No, she was a very sober-minded young lady, sufficiently	S 6 391 1
Sober-minded as she was, she thought him agreable, & did	S 7 395 1
SOBERED (1)	
Reflection had given calmness to her judgment, and sobered	SS III 11 349 2
SOBERER (1)	
as he could then, in a soberer moment, feel his motives to	MP II 2 187 1
SOBERING (2)	
of the future, the sobering suggestions of her own good	E II 2 164 6
They were of sobering tendency; they allayed agitation;	P III 7 61 35
SOBERNESS (1)	
the house in all the soberness of its general character;	MP II 2 194 21
SOBRIETY (2)	
happy conviction of her brother's comparative sobriety.	NA I 9 64 26
to the steady sobriety and orderly silence of the other.	MP II 7 240 9
SOBS (5)	
sleep by her agitation and sobs, first perceived her; and	SS II 7 180 1
	2
indeed," before her voice was entirely lost in sobs.	SS II 7 185 19
increased sobs explained to him where the grievance lay.	MP I 2 15 10
her uncle with struggling sobs, because she had displeased	MP III 6 374 28
hung over Louisa with sobs of grief, and could only turn	P III 12 110 43
SOCIABLE (2)	
their living in the most sociable terms with his family,	SS I 6 30 6
to be friendly and sociable gave great satisfaction in the	MP I 3 31 59
SOCIAL (13)	
country like this, where social and literary intercourse	NA II 9 197 29
I know nobody who likes a game of cards in a social way,	W 325 4
social temper more than half seconded, gave the invitation.	W 359 28
regard which his social powers had gained him in the mess.	PP II 13 206 4
in Norfolk to equal the social pleasures of Mansfield, he	MP I 12 115 3
As animated, as diversified, as social--but with	MP III 10 405 18
active cheerful mind and social temper by entering into	E I 2 15 1
to the wishes of his own friendly and social disposition.	E I 2 16 5
his being a disengaged and social man makes it all easy.	E I 11 94 15
social intercourse, and those to whom it was important.--	E I 11 97 27
cheerful feelings, and social inclinations of his father,	E II 6 198 5
of the first blessings of social life was just enough	E II 13 265 5
that every little social commonwealth should dictate its	P III 6 43 3
SOCIETIES (2)	
it as one of the first refinements of polished societies."	PP I 6 25 26
vogue amongst the less polished societies of the world.--	PP I 6 25 27
SOCIETY (163)	
lead them too much into society for my present situation &	LS 1 243 1
society must; & my visit has already perhaps been too long.	LS 25 293 3
there be rewarded by your society & a little dissipation	LS 25 294 4
for society, and it is shameful to have you exiled from it.	LS 26 295 1
be able to chuse our own society, & have true enjoyment.	LS 26 296 4
sense of their kindness, & her pleasure in their society.	LS 42 311 2
class of females, whose society can raise no other emotion	NA I 2 20 8
with the person whose society she mostly prized--and, in	NA II 2 141 11
Society is becoming irksome; and as for the amusements in	NA II 10 207 38
sameness of every day's society and employments would	NA II 11 209 5
and truly loved her society, I must confess that his	NA II 15 243 9
In the society of his nephew and niece, and their children,	SS I 1 3 1
such as society produced, within a very narrow compass.	SS I 7 32 1
But Sir John's satisfaction in society was much more real;	SS I 7 32 2
When does she try to avoid society, or appear restless and	SS I 8 39 18
overcame the wish of society for her children; and she was	SS I 9 40 2
His society became gradually her most exquisite enjoyment.	SS I 10 48 8
the charms which his society bestowed on her present home.	SS I 11 54 5
whose society it is impossible for me now to enjoy."	SS I 15 76 16
zeal in the cause of society, procured her some other new	SS I 21 118 1
on her side in inferior society and more frivolous	SS II 1 140 2
she is not a woman whose society can afford us pleasure,	SS II 3 156 12
her mother; "but of her society, separately from that of	SS II 3 156 13
society, no amusement, till my father's point was gained.	SS II 9 206 24
and doomed her to such society and such scenes as must	SS II 10 214 6
him from mixing in proper society, he candidly and	SS II 14 250 12
for ever from all decent society!--but, as I directly said	SS III 5 299 35
her affection and her society would have deprived of all	SS III 8 321 32
inclined to feel, and expensive society had increased.	SS III 8 323 40
out for ever from their society, they already think me an	SS III 8 328 63
and cheerful society as the only happiness worth a wish.	SS III 10 343 8
and if I do mix in other society it will be only to shew	SS III 10 347 30
yet enjoy, as she wished, the sight and society of both.	SS III 13 363 6
regard and her society restored his mind to animation, and	SS III 14 379 17
that he fled from society, or contracted an habitual gloom	SS III 14 379 18
"I assure you we have very good society at Croydon.--	W 350 24
mortifications of unequal society, & family discord--from	W 361 31
The change in her home society, & stile of life in	W 361 31
I am fond of superior society; but I did not feel quite	PP I 6 26 36
such society; and indeed I am quite of your opinion.	PP I 6 27 47
you move in a very confined and unvarying society."	PP I 9 43 17
pleasure from the society of a man in any other colour.	PP I 13 64 20
to his joining in the society of the neighbourhood, nor to	PP I 14 66 1
assisted by education or society; the greatest part of his	PP I 15 70 1
the neighbourhood, the society, appearing highly pleased	PP I 16 78 22
"It was the prospect of constant society, and good society,	PP I 16 79 23
"It was the prospect of constant society, and good society,	PP I 16 79 23
Society, I own, is necessary to me.	PP I 16 79 23
Jane pictured to herself a happy evening in the society of	PP I 17 86 10
Society has claims on us all; and I profess myself one of	PP I 17 87 11
except your society, my dearest friend; but we will hope	PP I 21 116 8
as to the loss of their society, she was persuaded that	PP I 21 116 8
nor agreeable; his society was irksome, and his attachment	PP I 22 122 3
the view of enjoying her society that he had been so ready	PP I 23 128 10
Mr. Wickham's society was of material service in	PP II 1 138 30
the case, unknown to the society of Hertfordshire; her	PP II 1 138 31
not have their share of society and amusement because the	PP II 6 165 35
he had pleasure in their society, a persuasion which of	PP II 9 180 28
It could not be for society, as he frequently sat there	PP II 9 180 29
My father was not only fond of this young man's society,	PP II 12 200 5
to invite him to Pemberley, or admit his society in town.	PP II 12 201 5
you to very superior society, and from our connection with	PP II 15 215 4
to leave her to such society!--but she had chosen it with	PP II 15 216 7
husband, who was fond of society, a perfect willingness to	PP III 2 264 11
"If he wants our society, let him seek it.	PP III 11 332 25
Their society can afford no pleasure, that will atone for	PP III 11 337 55
should be removed from society so little pleasing to	PP III 18 384 27
In society so superior to what she had generally known,	PP III 19 385 4
From the farther disadvantage of Lydia's society she was	PP III 19 385 4
be introduced into the society of this country under such	MP I 1 6 6
her of mixing in society without having horses to hire.	MP I 4 35 5
eighteenth year, when the society of the village received	MP I 4 40 15
of living and tone of society; and it was not till after	MP I 4 41 16
abode, or limitation of society, Henry Crawford had,	MP I 4 41 16
is always pleasant society to an indolent, stay-at-home	MP I 5 47 26
a great chasm in their society, and to miss him decidedly	MP I 6 52 1
and importance in society, and how can it be acquired	MP I 9 92 46
Soldiers and sailors are always acceptable in society.	MP I 11 109 19
days together in the same society, and the friendship, if	MP I 13 121 1
under the restraint of society; for general civilities	MP II 2 193 18
Some members of their society sent away and the spirits of	MP II 3 196 1
If he knew them better, he would value their society as it	MP II 3 196 2
and would improve in good society; and if Maria could now	MP II 3 201 22
the first society in the neighbourhood--looked-up to	MP II 4 210 21
She felt the want of his society every day, almost every	MP II 11 285 15
evidently fond of his society; and with such encouragement,	MP III 4 350 30
But I am spoilt, Fanny, for common female society.	MP III 4 355 54
In her present exile from good society, and distance from	MP III 9 393 1
As for any society in Portsmouth, that could at all make	MP III 9 395 3
Such a man could come from no place, no society, without	MP III 10 404 15
"what a society will be comprised in those houses!	MP III 10 405 19
would be to give up the society of some of those most dear	MP III 13 422 2
and a little addition of society might be of infinite use	MP III 14 435 14
she may recover her footing in society to a certain degree.	MP III 16 457 29
preacher in some great society of Methodists; or as a	MP III 16 458 30
to be endangered by the society, or hurt by the character	MP III 17 465 13
up together with little society, on one side no affection,	MP III 17 465 14
not one of the barriers, which society gives to virtue.	MP III 17 468 22
must in any place and any society, secure her a great deal	MP III 17 469 24
to fill the house and give her pleasant society again.	E I 1 7 9
and the pleasures of society, the next eighteen or twenty	E I 2 16 5
Mr. Woodhouse was fond of society in his own way.	E I 3 20 1
for the elegancies and society of Mr. Woodhouse's drawing-	E I 3 20 2
on the inferior society of Highbury and its connections.	E I 3 23 10
good society; she would form her opinions and her manners.	E I 3 23 10
established in good society, as to be independent even of	E I 4 31 24
a woman feels in the society of one of her own sex, after	E I 5 36 6
You would have thrown yourself out of all good society.	E I 7 54 27
You confined to the society of the illiterate and vulgar	E I 7 54 29
making so much of her) as in a line of society above him.	E I 8 59 27
but he is undoubtedly her inferior as to rank in society.--	E I 8 62 39
to introduce her into what you would call good society.	E I 8 62 42
very inferior, society, may well be illiberal and cross.	E I 10 85 19
upon what is called society for his comforts, that is,	E I 11 96 26
and so fond of society;--it will be a small party, but	E I 13 116 43
always lived in the best society, that with all the	E I 16 134 5
taking comfort in some society or other, it was very	E I 16 138 18
	19
of removal, or of effecting any material change of society.	E I 17 143 14
to their confined society in Surry; the pleasure of	E I 18 145 5
pleasures of an elegant society, and a judicious mixture	E II 2 164 6
intercourse, equal society, peace and hope, to penance and	E II 2 165 8
think there are few places with such society as Highbury.	E II 3 175 39
Highbury, perhaps, afforded society enough?--	E II 5 191 27
Was it a musical society?"	E II 5 191 27
Were you often in the same society?"	E II 6 199 13
Their love of society, and their new dining-room, prepared	E II 7 207 6
precisely of those whose society was dearest to her,	E II 7 208 7
She questioned him as to the society in Yorkshire-- the	E II 8 221 48
he would have preferred the society of William Larkins.	E II 12 258 6
a loss to their little society from his absence as to	E II 12 261 37
and that her society would certainly do Mr. Elton no good.	E II 14 272 16
up entirely from society, it is a very bad thing; and that	E II 14 275 30
secure you some of the best society in the place.	E II 14 275 32
to me, to hear what a musical society I am got into.	E II 14 276 36
used to a very musical society, both at Maple Grove and in	E II 14 276 36
think I can live without something of a musical society.	E II 14 277 36
being a very musical society in Highbury; and I hope you	E II 14 277 37
in society as Mrs. Elton's consequence only could surpass.	E II 15 281 1
such society and friendship as the vicarage had to offer.	E II 15 285 12
have so many myself as to be quite independent of society."	E II 18 307 21
He will find an addition to the society of Highbury when	E II 18 307 23
and your father, when her society must be so irksome."	E III 7 375 59
for her society, and testify respect and consideration.	E III 9 389 16
of cheerful or of rational society within their reach?	E III 12 422 20
as finding in Harriet's society all that she wanted; if	E III 12 422 20
mean, as far as regards society, and all the habits and	E III 13 428 23
His rank in society I would alter if I could; which is	E III 18 472 22
Lord be more delighted with the place he held in society.	P III 1 4 5
still have Lady Russell's society, still be near Mary, and	P III 2 14 9
A larger society would improve them.	P III 2 15 12
Clay; turning from the society of so deserving a sister to	P III 2 16 16
rupture.) or in any novelty or enlargement of society.--	P III 4 28 7
her taste, in the small limits of the society around them.	P III 4 28 7
who has had no society among women to make him nice?"	P III 7 62 39
in the first class of society in the country, the young	P III 9 74 5
of domestic society, in leaving poor Mary for Lady Russell.	P III 11 93 2
Will it not be wiser to accept the society of these good	P IV 4 150 17
We must feel that every addition to your father's society,	P IV 4 151 21
of a servant, and of course almost excluded from society.	P IV 5 152 4
inferior situation in society, indeed, rendered that	P IV 9 200 57
the common wants of society--for she had many thousands a	S 3 376 1

her brother was a poor man for his rank in society. S 3 377 1
to his own veiws of society) to approach with high S 8 405 2
SOCKET (1)
expires in the socket, and leaves you in total darkness." NA II 5 160 21
SODDEN (1)
no other look of an Invalide, than a sodden complexion.-- S 10 413 1
SOFA (24)
weary and languid, on a sofa, did not speak much in favour SS III 7 307 1
and make her sit on the sofa with herself and pug, and MP I 2 13 4
nicely dressed on a sofa, doing some long piece of MP I 2 19 31
was a very long one, told them that she was on the sofa. MP I 7 71 33
Fanny, to be idling away all the evening upon a sofa. MP I 7 71 34
trick for a young person to be always lolling upon a sofa; MP I 7 71 34
Fanny is as little upon the sofa as any body in the house." MP I 7 71 35
As she leant on the sofa, to which she had retreated that MP I 7 74 59
Lady Bertram was on the sofa at a little distance, and MP I 13 125 14
Lady Bertram, sunk back in one corner of the sofa, the MP I 13 126 19
her attention and all the rest of her sofa to her husband. MP II 1 179 9
her aunt's end of the sofa, and, screened from notice MP II 1 185 27
to sit on her sofa without any inconvenience from them. MP II 8 254 9
Mary, perceiving her on a sofa very near, turned round MP II 10 276 14
I took him, as he was sleeping on the sofa, and it is as E I 6 45 21
The corner of the sofa is very good. E I 6 45 21
She was now lying on the faded sofa of the pretty little P III 5 37 21
22

She could soon sit upright on the sofa, and began to hope P III 5 39 40
coming up to the sofa, on which she and Mrs. Musgrove were P III 8 67 28
They were actually on the same sofa, for Mrs. Musgrove had P III 8 68 29
and the little invalid Charles, who was lying on the sofa. P III 9 78 21
She was obliged to kneel down by the sofa, and remain P III 9 79 25
and went straight to the sofa to see what was going on, P III 9 79 28
Bile & hardly able to crawl from my bed to the sofa.-- S 5 386 1
SOFAS (1)
time as they could with sofas, and chit-chat, and MP I 10 104 51
SOFT (20)
be indistinct through the soft medium of a lazy atmosphere. SS I 18 97 4
But at last a soft, genial morning appeared; such as might SS III 10 344 11
At last however he was at liberty to hear Margaret's soft W 356 28
countenance; but in that soft skin of her's, so frequently MP II 6 229 5
gives her such a soft skin and makes her so much taller, MP II 6 230 8
which resembled the soft monotony of Lady Bertram's, only MP III 8 392 11
in its mild air, brisk soft wind, and bright sun, MP III 11 409 6
learn to prefer soft light eyes to sparkling dark ones.-- MP III 17 470 27
gives, those soft light eyes could not be very long in MP III 17 470 27
Those soft blue eyes and all those natural graces should E I 3 23 10
She was so busy in admiring those soft blue eyes, in E I 3 24 11
An egg boiled very soft is not unwholesome. E I 3 24 14
will soon supply, may its approval beam in that soft eye! E I 9 71 14
May its approval beam in that soft eye! E I 9 72 15
Soft, is the very word for her eye--of all epithets, the E I 9 72 15
Your soft eyes shall chuse their own time for beaming. E I 9 76 38
I think you will agree with me, (turning with a soft air E I 13 116 43
wit"--but then, the "soft eyes"--in fact it suited neither; E I 16 134 4
for that soft sort of manner does not do him justice." P IV 6 171 37
delicacy of complexion & soft blue eyes, a sweetly modest S 6 391 1
SOFT-HEARTED (1)
was a good-tempered, soft-hearted girl, not likely to be E III 18 473 25
SOFTEN (11)
were sufficient to soften his heart, & make him really LS 3 247 1
He endeavoured, long endeavoured to soften my resentment, LS 22 282 7
to soften it, and they always conversed with confidence. SS II 10 216 15
could not deny, and vain was every endeavour to soften it. SS III 8 323 40
To put an end to this altercation, & soften the evident W 353 26
These were reflections that required some time to soften; MP III 17 461 4
that affliction to soften and heal.-- made her quite E I 9 70 7
She could do little more than listen patiently, soften P III 6 46 11
Here was a great deal to soften the business. P IV 3 139 9
& soften Lady D--who wd enlarge her mind & open her hand.-- S 3 379 1
Without a little butter to soften it, it hurts the coats S 10 417 1
SOFTEN'D (1)
"Oh!--(in a soften'd voice, & rather mortified to find she W 351 25
SOFTENED (43)
To our family, she has always been represented in softened LS 12 260 2
and half fearing to be softened by what I might say. LS 25 292 2
a very few words from me softened at once into the utmost LS 25 293 3
her features were softened by plumpness and colour, her NA I 1 14 2
acquaintance with her, softened down every feeling of awe, NA I 4 33 7
At one moment she was softened, at another irritated; NA I 13 99 9
of her inferiors were softened, must always be gratifying, NA II 8 184 4
Whether the torments of absence were softened by a NA II 16 250 3
Marianne was softened in a moment. SS I 10 48 6
was more likely to be softened than she had thought it SS I 11 54 5
however, soon softened her to compliance, and Elinor saw SS II 8 197 25
"You did then," said Elinor, a little softened, "believe SS III 8 321 33
conversation, was now softened again;--yet she felt it her SS III 8 325 51
His heart was softened in seeing mine suffer; and so much SS III 8 330 69
at Barton had been much softened to Mrs. Dashwood by her SS III 9 335 6
and softened only his protestations of present regard. SS III 10 347 33
thing had been expressly softened at the time, to spare SS III 11 355 46
cry.--said robt rather softened--& after a short silence, W 352 26
be a little softened by his manner of expressing himself." PP I 13 62 9
In a softened tone she declared herself not at all PP I 13 65 26
and Rosings rationally softened; and Elizabeth perceived PP II 3 147 19
its warmth, and softened its impropriety of expression. PP III 1 251 48
be for my sake that his manners are thus softened. PP III 1 255 60
his mind might have been softened, his manners improved, PP III 8 312 15
Mrs. Norris, in a rather softened voice; "but I question MP I 7 72 45
anxious entreaty, which softened her a little; but while MP I 14 135 15
only a softened air and stronger expressions of regret. MP II 2 193 18
message--no symptom of a softened heart--no hope of MP II 3 201 24
You think with me, I hope--(turning with a softened voice MP II 7 244 27
He might have softened his father; but all, perhaps all, MP III 1 321 46
and addressing her in a softened voice; and upon her MP III 3 340 25
Crawford, yet farther softened by the sight of such MP III 5 359 10
state, her heart was softened for a while towards him-- MP III 5 365 35
She was soon more softened and sorrowful.-- MP III 13 425 5
such a state of mind, so softened, so devoted, as made it MP III 16 454 18
to open to sensations of softened pain and brighter hope. E I 16 137 13
Upon the whole, Emma left her with such softened, E II 2 168 14
among them not to be softened, from its power of censure, E II 7 206 4
the late event had softened away his pride, and he was, E III 14 443 8
There, the surprise was not softened by any satisfaction. E III 17 469 36
She had humoured, or softened, or concealed his failings, P III 1 4 6
its close; and time had softened down much, perhaps nearly P III 4 28 7
once severe, but now softened; and of some instances of P IV 1 123 8
SOFTENER (1)
What a softener of the heart was this persuasion! SS II 1 140 1
SOFTENING (3)
smile, and affectedly softening his voice, he added, with NA I 3 26 4
The boy had, with the additional softening claim of a E I 2 16 4
to it, had such a softening tendency, that it was E I 7 55 35
SOFTER (3)
me that his manners are softer than they used to be. E I 4 34 42
softer than upright justice and clear-sighted good will.-- E III 12 415 1
the wind changed into a softer quarter; the clouds were E III 13 424 1
SOFTEST (1)
was well lined with the softest cotton; but, excepting the E III 4 338 9
SOFTING (1)
They were healing, softing, relaxing--fortifying & bracing- S 2 373 1
SOFTLY (3)
point of retreating as softly as she had entered, when the NA II 9 194 6
"No, I do not," said Fanny softly--hoping she did not err MP II 11 290 37
"Now he has got my letter," said she softly. E I 7 56 43
SOFTNESS (5)
was less captivating softness in Colonel Fitzwilliam's PP II 9 180 28
Her diffidence, gratitude, and softness, made every MP III 2 327 6
Harriet, by additional softness, but it strikes me that E I 4 34 42
general; and there was a softness and delicacy in her skin E II 6 199 10
at Weymouth; and the softness of the upper notes I am sure E II 10 241 8
SOIL (5)
"The soil is good; and I never pass it without regretting, MP I 6 54 10
roads, the difference of soil, the state of the harvest, MP I 8 80 31
"My uncle's gardener always says the soil here is better MP II 4 209 16
amazing, that the same soil and the same sun should MP II 4 209 16
the place--& as for the soil--it is so cold & ungrateful S 1 369 1
SOLACE (3)
her daughters married; its solace was visiting and news. PP I 1 5 34
It is his companion all this evening, his solace, his E I 7 56 46
She could not think that Harriet's solace or her own sins E II 1 155 1
SOLACED (1)
They solaced their wretchedness, however, by duets after PP I 8 40 59
SOLD (10)
people, for I might have sold it for ten guineas more the NA I 7 47 19
bought for a trifle and sold for incredible sums; of NA I 9 66 31
furniture of Stanhill was sold, all the china, plate, and SS I 2 12 26
by her husband, had been sold soon after his death, and an SS I 5 26 5
I might have sold it again the next day, for more than I SS II 11 225 33
banker's hands, I must have sold out to very great loss." SS II 11 225 33
really sold the presentation, is old enough to take it.-- SS III 5 295 12
of accomplishments were sold at a reasonable price, and E I 3 21 5
to think his master had sold so many; for William, you E II 9 239 51
sacks were sold, it did not signify who ate the remainder. E II 9 239 51
SOLDIER (5)
but to a man and a soldier, she presumed not to censure it. SS II 9 211 39
that I am neither a lawyer, nor a soldier, nor a sailor." MP I 9 91 39
and reward to the soldier and sailor in their choice of a MP I 11 110 22
unhappy by him as a sailor or soldier than as a clergyman. MP I 11 111 30
favour, I assure you, be he sailor or soldier." P III 3 18 8
SOLDIERS (5)
But if these soldiers are quicker than other people in a W 337 15
Brighton, and a whole campful of soldiers, to us, who have PP II 16 220 7
Soldiers and sailors are always acceptable in society. MP I 11 109 19
Nobody can wonder that men are soldiers and sailors." MP I 11 109 19
Soldiers, in active service, are not at all better off: P III 3 20 17
SOLE (11)
Her assurance, however, standing sole as it did, was not NA I 12 93 7
should be left to the sole guidance of her own judgment, SS II 3 156 15
My object--my wish--my sole wish in desiring it--I hope, I SS II 9 204 18
is under his sole care, he may do what he likes with her." PP II 10 184 17
should be forwarded at the sole expence of his brother-in- PP III 8 308 2
from Rosings, for the sole purpose of breaking off her PP III 15 360 1
My sole dependence was on you; and I am sure nobody else PP III 17 372 5
"I can only say that my sole desire is to be of use to MP I 3 30 56
with the sole view of marking my adoration of yourself. E I 15 131 31
the former, with being the sole and original author of the E III 11 402 1
The sole grievance and alloy thus removed in the prospect E III 18 475 39
SOLELY (10)
agreeableness belongs solely to each other for that time. NA I 10 76 29
Did Henry's income depend solely on this living, he would NA II 7 176 15
I shall now live solely for my family. SS III 10 347 30
occupy himself solely in being civil to all the world. PP I 5 18 1
a serious stamp, though written solely for their benefit. PP I 14 69 15
16

Lucas, who accepted him solely from the pure and PP I 22 122 2
the consequence of views solely and hatefully mercenary; PP II 13 207 6
in a low voice directed solely at Fanny, "I should be MP II 7 245 31
evening amusements were solely in the elegant stupidity of P IV 7 180 32
It had been my doing--solely mine. P IV 8 183 13
SOLEMN (27)
convinced by my full & solemn assurance that your fears LS 14 265 6
But history, real solemn history, I cannot be interested NA I 14 108 20
who, in rather a solemn tone of voice, uttered these words, NA I 14 111 29
road was expected with solemn awe to afford a glimpse of NA II 5 161 24
scenes of horror being acted within the solemn edifice. NA II 5 161 25
attending her entrance within walls so solemn!-- NA II 6 166 9
by her husband of the solemn promise on the part of his SS I 3 14 2
Mr. Dashwood's strains were more solemn. SS III 13 371 38
whisper which became the solemn scene, said to Miss W 327 8
Mr. Collins, awkward and solemn, apologising instead of PP I 18 90 4
Her cousin prefaced his speech with a solemn bow, and PP I 18 98 61
The idea of Mr. Collins, with all his solemn composure, PP I 19 105 9
10

soon satisfied Jane by her solemn assurances of attachment. PP III 17 373 17
Elizabeth, still more affected, was earnest and solemn in PP III 17 376 36
ten days, in spite of the solemn assurances we have so MP I 6 57 33
more striking or more solemn than the profusion of MP I 9 85 6
where all that was solemn and soothing, and lovely, MP I 11 112 35
through; he is solemn and pathetic enough I am sure. MP I 14 134 14
from appearing a formal, solemn lecturer; and the man who MP I 15 145 41
With solemn kindness Sir Thomas addressed her; told her MP II 3 200 21
Is she solemn?-- MP II 6 230 7
The solemn procession, headed by Baddely, of tea-board, MP III 3 344 43
All manner of solemn nonsense was talked on the subject, E I 1 12 41
Do not let us be too solemn on the business. E I 9 78 47
Even Mr. Weston shook his head, and looked solemn, and E III 9 388 13
There has been a solemn engagement between them ever since E III 10 395 35
the most solemn resolution of never quitting her father.-- E III 14 435 4
SOLEMN-LOOKING (1)
Fanny had scarcely passed the solemn-looking servants, MP III 15 447 37
SOLEMNITY (17)
earnestness, such solemnity of expression! & yet I cannot LS 20 278 8
with a very unusual solemnity of countenance, & after some LS 22 281 4
could no longer command solemnity either of subject or NA II 5 160 23
solemnity of any kind, struck her as odd and inconsistent. NA II 5 161 25
"Indeed you wrong me," replied Lucy with great solemnity; " SS II 2 150 32
"You have heard, I suppose," said he with great solemnity, SS III 1 265 34
her hand with a look of solemnity, and a few words spoken SS III 7 312 17
The subject elevated him to more than usual solemnity of PP I 14 66 1
with very monotonous solemnity, read three pages, she PP I 14 68 13
14

and written with all the solemnity of gratitude which a PP I 23 128 10
Longbourn with as much solemnity as before; wished his PP II 2 139 1
and with a more smiling solemnity replied, "it gives me PP II 15 215 3
4

part of Agatha, or it will be the ruin of all my solemnity. MP I 14 133 11
"Dr. Grant is ill," said she, with mock solemnity. MP I 18 171 27
His father's looks of solemnity and amazement on this his MP II 1 182 22
and such an ill-judged solemnity of leave-taking in his E I 17 140 3
This nut," he continued, with playful solemnity,--"while P III 10 88 26
SOLEMNLY (7)
wish to be believed, I solemnly protest that no syllable NA II 3 144 11
"Many, many circumstances," said Elinor, solemnly. SS II 7 186 25
"I felt myself," she added, "to be as solemnly engaged to SS II 7 188 44
repeat what he had said, and more fully and more solemnly. MP II 12 291 5
though Sir Thomas very solemnly assured her, that had MP III 17 465 13
is no saying, indeed!" replied Harriet, rather solemnly. E I 4 33 37
"Mrs. Musgrove protests solemnly that she knew nothing of " P IV 6 165 8
SOLICIT (3)
That the General should come forward to solicit the NA II 16 249 2
Elizabeth, when I solicit for the honour of a private PP I 19 104 1
2

addition to his own domestic circle which he could solicit. MP II 3 196 1
SOLICITATION (6)
it; but, upon my word, you owe nothing to my solicitation." SS III 4 289 35

men; and though such a solicitation must be waved for the — PP I 22 121 2
there, beginning by chance, were continued by solicitation. — MP II 4 205 2
without solicitation, or plea, or privilege, she must be — E II 15 282 4
be gratified by more solicitation; but the charm was — P IV 10 214 12
farther solicitation & paid for what she bought.-- — S 6 390 1

SOLICITATIONS (2)
His anxiety for her comfort--his continual solicitations — NA II 5 154 2
to resist the solicitations of his friends to do nothing. — SS I 19 103 4

SOLICITED (10)
he never wished to inspire, nor solicited the avowal of. — LS 22 282 6
and again solicited to dance, by Mr. Tilney himself. — NA I 10 75 24
To have her company so warmly solicited! — NA II 2 140 8
that heart in return was solicited, which, perhaps, they — NA II 15 243 9
acquaintance in Bath, solicited her company at Northanger, — NA II 15 244 11
The honour of dancing with her, was solicited without loss — W 334 13
"They would have solicited the honour earlier, but had — E II 7 208 9
of being properly solicited by baronet-blood within the — P III 1 7 12
his being spontaneously solicited by some most — P III 2 15 14
She had been solicited, when about two-and-twenty, to — P III 4 28 7

SOLICITING (5)
this opportunity of soliciting yours, Miss Elizabeth, for — PP I 17 87 13
were concerned, was soliciting the good opinion of her — PP III 2 265 16
quite unequal to surmising or soliciting any thing more. — MP II 4 210 20
his affection, soliciting a return, and, finally, in words — MP II 13 301 7
When Mr & Mrs Parker therefore ceased from soliciting a — S 2 374 1

SOLICITOR (1)
Mr Beard--Solicitor, Grays Inn.-- — S 6 389 1

SOLICITOUS (13)
conversation she was solicitous only for the welfare & — LS 42 312 3
with such ready, such solicitous politeness as recalled — NA I 13 102 27
possible kindness, was solicitous on every occasion for — SS II 4 160 2
affection, the most solicitous care could do to render her — SS III 10 341 6
of the friend most solicitous for her happiness, would — MP I 11 107 3
and so particularly solicitous for the comfort of her — E I 15 132 38
civility in solicitous inquiries after Mr. Frank — E II 5 193 35
and the most solicitous for accommodation and appearance. — E II 11 247 2
my own anxiety, or requires very solicitous explanation. — E III 14 438 8
Walter's feelings, as solicitous for the credit of the — P III 2 11 2
that we should be so solicitous to have the relationship — P IV 4 151 18
which he had seemed solicitous to give, his wonder at — P IV 8 185 21
smiling attention or solicitous eagerness, was very — S 7 396 1

SOLICITOUSLY (1)
and solicitously addressing her upon every occasion. — E I 14 118 4

SOLICITUDE (71)
her with so much tender solicitude that I, who — LS 17 270 3
excessive solicitude about it often destroys its own aim. — NA I 10 73 22
yet a something of solicitude remained, from which sprang — NA I 12 94 11
Henry, "in this amiable solicitude for your brother's — NA II 4 152 28
himself--without any solicitude about it,--he did believe — NA II 7 178 21
had no more pressing solicitude than that of making Miss — NA II 11 209 5
her only just so much solicitude as the human mind can — NA II 13 221 6
and hung over her with affectionate solicitude. — NA II 13 223 9
their comfort to be an object of real solicitude to him. — SS I 6 30 6
amongst them by her solicitude about her troublesome boys. — SS I 11 55 6
and sisters were spared much solicitude on her account. — SS I 19 104 10
her surprise and solicitude--"may I ask if your engagement — SS I 22 130 17 18
she would engage in the solicitude of Marianne's situation — SS II 4 159 1
who was convinced that solicitude for Marianne brought him — SS II 9 204 17
and who saw that solicitude in his disturbed and — SS II 9 204 17
to express her anxious solicitude for Marianne, and — SS II 10 213 2
upon her caprice, or any solicitude for her good opinion. — SS II 13 238 1
not to create in them a solicitude about me, which it — SS III 1 262 23
his looks of anxious solicitude on Marianne's feeling, in — SS III 6 305 16
fixed in such speaking solicitude on my face!--and Sophia, — SS III 8 327 55
every doubt, every solicitude removed, compared her — SS III 13 363 8
with yet greater solicitude to the proper security of her — W 327 7
From being the first object of hope & solicitude of an — W 361 31
saw how much affection and solicitude they shewed for Jane. — PP I 7 33 44
the much superior solicitude of Mr. Bingley's, she could — PP I 8 35 1
and at that moment solicitude for Wickham, resentment — PP I 18 95 48
Elizabeth looked at her sister with incredulous solicitude, — PP II 1 134 6
seeing Jane, she felt a solicitude on the subject which — PP II 2 142 16
coincide, there was a solicitude, an interest which she — PP II 4 151 3
comprehend all her fears and solicitude on the subject. — PP III 5 288 40
with her affectionate solicitude; or allow her to hear it — PP III 13 347 26
needful solicitude, which there were no children to supply. — MP I 1 8 9
for his safety, or solicitude for his comfort, being one — MP I 3 32 63
superiority than any solicitude to oblige him, the mention — MP I 6 52 1
the steadiness, the solicitude, and the warmth which might — MP I 12 115 4
him--with solicitude on Edmund's account indescribable. — MP II 1 176 4
There was employment, hope, solicitude, bustle, for every — MP II 5 225 55
was a point of painful solicitude; and the almost solitary — MP II 8 254 8
Fanny, being more than half ashamed of her own solicitude. — MP II 8 256 14
the privilege of true solicitude for him by a sound — MP II 9 265 18
such a glow of what his solicitude had been, and used such — MP II 13 300 7
began with very natural solicitude to feel for their — MP III 7 378 13
solicitude, alternately her worries and her comforts. — MP III 8 389 4
The real solicitude now awakened in the maternal bosom was — MP III 13 427 13
added yet a keener solicitude, when she considered how — MP III 13 428 13
Sir Thomas's parental solicitude, and high sense of honour — MP III 15 442 21
Fanny watched him with never-failing solicitude, and — MP III 15 445 34
in spite of maternal solicitude for the immediate — E I 11 92 3
was no putting and end to his extreme solicitude about her. — E I 15 125 4
thanks for their visit, solicitude for their shoes, — E II 1 155 4
as the removal of one solicitude generally makes way for — E II 12 257 2
I am very much obliged by your kind solicitude about me." — E II 16 294 26
Jane's solicitude about fetching her own letters had not — E II 16 298 58
who came out, in her solicitude after her son-in-law, to — E III 6 359 36
to depart, and the solicitude of Mrs. Elton to have her — E III 7 374 54
She spoke as she felt, with earnest regret and solicitude-- — E III 8 380 9
towards the departed, solicitude for the surviving friends; — E III 9 387 12
her feelings from any present solicitude on her account. — E III 11 403 2
was there so much fond solicitude, so much keen anxiety — E III 13 433 41
to the amiable solicitude of the sister and the aunt. — E III 15 449 35
But now, another occupation and solicitude of mind was — P III 1 9 19
Hall, and extreme solicitude for the advantage of renting — P III 3 23 34
There was not the smallest appearance of solicitude or — P III 9 75 9
all the former doubt and solicitude of the negociation. — P III 9 78 19
These points formed her chief solicitude in anticipating — P III 11 93 4
the appearance of equal solicitude, on topics which had by — P IV 1 124 11
such great openness of solicitude to be received as a — P IV 3 138 6
could exceed his solicitude and care, and though his — P IV 7 178 24
solicitude never appeased for five minutes together. — P IV 10 227 69
amusement now;--it was solicitude & enjoyment, as she — S 3 378 1
Mrs G.'s cheif solicitude wd be for the accomodation & — S 10 419 1

SOLICITUDES (5)
and fears, plans, and solicitudes respecting that long — MP II 6 234 18
in idle cares and selfish solicitudes unconnected with him. — MP II 11 282 2
Many vain solicitudes would be prevented--many — E II 4 182 8
usual share of all such solicitudes and suspense been — P III 4 29 8
her father and sister's solicitudes on a subject which she — P IV 4 148 10

SOLID (12)
Her solid affection for her child is shewn by placing her — LS 14 265 5
gave him every degree of solid comfort which his age could — SS I 1 3 1
was good, and his education had given it solid improvement. — SS I 3 15 6
You know enough of him to do justice to his solid worth. — SS I 4 20 9
ridiculous, contained much good sense and solid reasoning. — PP III 15 361 2
back, with shining floors, solid mahogany, rich damask, — MP I 9 84 3
square farm-house--it is a solid walled, roomy, mansion- — MP II 7 243 27
He had every well-grounded reason for solid attachment; he — MP III 2 326 3
in recommending the most solid truths; and, besides, there — MP III 3 340 23
The first solid consolation which Fanny received for the — MP III 9 395 4
He was not very solid; but there was a hope of his — MP III 17 462 4
with him she found the solid so fully supporting the — P IV 4 146 6

SOLIDITY (3)
piqued herself upon the solidity of her reflections, "is a — PP I 5 20 20
the others; there was a solidity in his reflections which — PP I 22 124 11
My liveliness and your solidity would produce perfection.-- — E III 16 457 33

SOLIDLY (1)
kind I well know to be more solidly attaching to Marianne. — SS III 9 338 21 22

SOLILOQUIES (1)
a kin to resentment to be long guiding Fanny's soliloquies. — MP III 13 424 5

SOLILOQUY (3)
Now for my soliloquy." — MP I 18 169 21
in soliloquy; "heaven defend me from being ungrateful!" — MP III 1 322 52
she, in mental soliloquy, while walking down stairs from — E II 5 189 20

SOLITARILY (1)
She came solitarily down the gravel walk-- a Miss Martin — E II 5 186 3

SOLITARINESS (3)
either dreading its length, or feeling its solitariness. — NA II 14 230 1
ideas, in the sad solitariness of her cottage, as to be — MP I 4 38 9
and to escape the solitariness and the melancholy of so — P III 5 36 19

SOLITARY (25)
for, it is impossible for me not to be often solitary." — NA II 7 180 34
"This lengthened absence, these solitary rambles, did not — NA II 8 182 1
Henry, in an agitation of mind which many solitary hours — NA II 15 248 16
she daily recurred, her solitary walks and silent — SS I 16 83 4
the Palmers, in the indulgence of such solitary rambles. — SS III 6 303 9
immediately afterwards took his solitary way to Delaford. — SS III 10 341 5
at Hunsford, her love of solitary walks, and her opinion — PP II 10 182 1
Reflection must be reserved for solitary hours; whenever — PP II 14 212 16
a day went by without a solitary walk, in which she might — PP II 14 212 16
"I am afraid I interrupt your solitary ramble, my dear — PP III 10 327 5
They were two solitary sufferers, or connected only by — MP I 17 163 20
and the almost solitary ornament in her possession, a very — MP II 8 254 8
She could not live any longer in such solitary — MP II 11 287 17
east room, and took no solitary walk in the shrubbery, in — MP III 5 357 4
The solitary candle was held between himself and the paper, — MP III 7 382 28
They had been all solitary, helpless, and forlorn alike; — MP III 16 448 2
so convenient for even solitary female walking, and in Mr. — E I 2 18 11
for the dangers of a a solitary drive from Vicarage-Lane-- — E I 15 132 38
and her being left in solitary grandeur, even supposing — E II 7 208 7
to the solitary range of the house was the consequence. — P IV 1 122 5
from any stroll of solitary indulgence in her father's — P IV 2 133 26
He had spent his whole solitary evening in the room — P IV 3 144 19
the course of her quiet, solitary progress up the town (— P IV 11 238 47
lodging;--here & there a solitary elderly man might be — S 6 389 1
might not afford some solitary house adapted for Clara's — S 8 405 2

SOLITUDE (31)
have been left in total solitude, & I can hardly tell — LS 27 296 1
Is he safe only in solitude?--or, is her heart constant to — NA II 4 152 28
with the friends of his solitude, a large Newfoundland — NA II 11 212 17
and natural evil, the solitude of her situation, the — NA II 13 227 26
heroine to her home in solitude and disgrace; and no sweet — NA II 14 232 7
parlour to give way in solitude to the concern and alarm — SS I 15 77 18
fix her sorrow, by seeking silence, solitude, and idleness. — SS I 19 104 9
the house in determined solitude to avoid them, or lying — SS I 19 104 12
among them, and every effect of solitude was produced. — SS I 19 105 12
from the frightful solitude which had threatened her. — SS II 1 143 10
but requiring at once solitude and continual change of — SS II 7 180 5
in free and luxurious solitude, she resolved to spend — SS III 6 303 9
Elinor would not attempt to disturb a solitude so — SS III 10 348 34
of oysters, in dreary solitude--or gladly assisting the — W 336 14
Mr. Collins, meanwhile, was meditating in solitude on what — PP I 20 112 24
closed, Elizabeth in the solitude of her chamber had to — PP II 5 157 10
"Dear Lady Bertram! what am I fit for but solitude? — MP I 3 29 48
Fanny was again left to her solitude, and with no increase — MP I 10 100 23
The first use she made of her solitude was to take up the — MP I 14 137 23
solitude of the east room, without being seen or missed. — MP I 17 159 6
she might seek directly all that solitude could do for her. — MP II 2 193 18
Now it was languor, and all but solitude. — MP II 11 283 6
sickness and solitude, and the attendance only of servants. — MP III 13 426 10
her from the evil of solitude, or the still greater evil — MP III 14 432 10
in great danger of suffering from intellectual solitude. — E I 1 6 7
evening of his own blank solitude for the elegancies and — E I 3 20 2
walked home to the coolness and solitude of Donwell Abbey. — E III 5 351 38
she had no resources for solitude; and inheriting a — P III 5 37 21
long application of solitude and reflection to recover her. — P III 9 81 34
Her spirits wanted the solitude and silence which only — P III 10 89 35
Half an hour's solitude and reflection might have — P IV 11 238 44

SOLOMON (1)
that Sir James was no Solomon, but I had positively — LS 22 281 3

SOLUTION (1)
She could only offer one solution; it was, perhaps, for — P IV 3 140 11

SOMBRE (2)
"Woodston will make but a sombre appearance to-day." — NA II 7 175 13
with the past; a sombre family-party rarely enlivened. — MP II 3 196 1

SOME-WHERE (1)
Some-where about the grounds, walking with a young man, — PP III 14 352 8

SOMEHOW (15)
Somehow or other I never happened to be staying at Barton — SS I 20 114 44
at ease by it; for I was somehow or other afraid I had — SS II 2 146 3
a thing, somehow or other he will soon find an opportunity. — SS III 4 285 5
"Mrs. Smith had somehow or other been informed, I imagine — SS III 8 321 34
I dare say he had heard somehow that Mrs. Long does not — PP I 5 19 14
that she had somehow or other got pretty near the truth. — PP II 10 184 20
fatigue; and as it was somehow or other ascertained, or — MP III 10 402 13
they had been there long--somehow or other--there was no — MP III 11 409 5
must advance somehow or other whether they would or no. — E I 11 91 1
makes enjoyment of them somehow or other, depending, I — E I 11 96 26
You had, somehow or other, broken bounds yesterday, and — E III 7 369 11
was quite ashamed--but somehow there was a little bustle-- — E III 8 379 8
in short, I was somehow or other safe from him." — E III 13 427 19
the child; and therefore, somehow, they hardly knew how, — P III 7 58 22
I am sure you have, somehow or other, imbibed such a — P IV 9 195 25

SOMEONE (1)
There is someone in most families privileged by superior — S 4 382 1

SOMERSET (3)
prohibited, county of Somerset, for as such was it dwelt — SS III 6 302 6
in the county of Somerset,"--and by inserting most — P III 1 3 2
Hall, in the county of Somerset," and Sir Walter's hand- — P III 1 3 3 4

SOMERSETSHIRE (12)
estate of his own in Somersetshire besides; and if I were — SS I 9 44 23
on his estate in Somersetshire, and which was exactly — SS I 12 58 1
"He intends to send his groom into Somersetshire — SS I 12 58 2
a great deal of him in Somersetshire, if it had not — SS I 20 114 44
much known in your part of Somersetshire?" said Elinor. — SS I 20 116 57
they were to go to Combe Magna, his seat in Somersetshire. — SS II 8 199 37
"But it is in Somersetshire.-- — SS III 3 279 5
I cannot go into Somersetshire.-- — SS III 3 279 5
Sir Walter Elliot, of Kellynch-Hall, in Somersetshire, was — P III 1 3 1
Croft was a native of Somersetshire, who having acquired a — P III 3 21 18
had come into Somersetshire, in the summer of 1806; and — P III 4 26 1
His sister married my tenant in Somersetshire,--the Croft, — P IV 8 188 40

SOMETHING (564)
At Churchill however I must remain till I have something — LS 2 246 1
if not accompanied by something more substantial. — LS 3 247 1
There is something about him that rather interests me, a — LS 7 254 3
it is more likely that she should aim at something farther. — LS 12 261 4
If Mrs Vernon would allow something to my affection for — LS 14 264 2
Lady Susan had heard something so materially to the — LS 14 264 3

You will be eager I know to hear something farther of LS 19 273 1
But something must be done for this poor girl, if her LS 20 278 11
She said something of her misery, but that was all. LS 22 280 1
& once had said something in praise of her person. LS 22 280 1
Instantly saw that something was the matter; his LS 23 283 3
not help--I have done something very wrong I know--but you LS 24 286 5
I honestly own that there is something to conceal. LS 24 289 12
I found therefore that something must be done, for I did LS 25 292 1
There is something agreable in feelings so easily worked LS 25 293 3
there there was a something in his look and voice as he LS 27 297 4
Something must and will happen to throw a hero in her way. NA I 1 17 11
Still they moved on--something better was yet in view; and NA I 2 21 9
Here there was something less of crowd than below; and NA I 2 21 9
Catherine began to feel something of disappointment--she NA I 2 21 10
Nature may have done something, but I am sure it must be NA I 3 27 28
and and something like a sigh escaped her as she said it. NA I 5 36 2
confess there is something amazingly insipid about her. NA I 6 41 16
Something between both, I think. NA I 6 42 29
Oh, Lord! not I; I never read novels; I have something NA I 7 48 33
or you may happen to hear something not very agreeable." NA I 8 57 20
"Something was said about it, I remember," said Catherine, NA I 9 61 4
It was looked upon as something out of the common way. NA I 9 64 24
without personal conceit, might be something uncommon.-- NA I 10 72 8
for the former, and a something of shabbiness or NA I 10 74 22
I shall never be in want of something to talk of again to NA I 10 79 56
of its being excited by something wrong in her appearance, NA I 10 80 59
Thorpe then said something in the loud, incoherent way to NA I 11 89 61
this information, yet a something of solicitude remained, NA I 12 94 11
Tilney; and she felt something more than surprize, when NA I 12 95 17
"But this was something of real consequence; and I do not NA I 13 105 37
"I have heard that something very shocking indeed, will NA I 14 111 29
She thought it would be something very fine. NA I 14 115 52
There was a something, however, in his words which repaid NA II 1 133 29
of confusion; and that something occupied her mind so much, NA II 1 133 29
have come down with something more, for I am sure he must NA II 1 136 46
"But I thought, Isabella, you had something in particular NA II 3 144 5
You have both of you something to be sure, but it is not a NA II 3 146 16
A something of languid indifference, or of that boasted NA II 4 149 1
He made no reply, and was beginning to talk of something NA II 4 150 4
but there was a something in this mode of approach which NA II 5 161 25
With difficulty, for something seemed to resist her NA II 6 164 3
really in it, there was something whimsical, it was NA II 6 168 10
open however, was still something remarkable, for she NA II 7 173 4
In this there was surely something mysterious, and she NA II 7 173 4
Something had been said the evening before of her being NA II 7 176 17
attentive pause with which she waited for something more. NA II 7 179 31
And besides, handsome as he was, there was a something in NA II 7 180 37
last within the reach of something worth her notice; and NA II 8 185 5
Something was certainly to be concealed; her fancy, though NA II 8 186 6
her here; and what the something was, a short sentence of NA II 8 186 6
There must be some deeper cause: something was to be done NA II 8 187 16
The succeeding morning promised something better. NA II 9 191 3
head)--or it may be of something still less pardonable." NA II 9 196 25
fatal morning, shewn something like affection for her.-- NA II 10 199 1
"It contained something worse than any body could suppose!- NA II 10 204 13
leave you so soon, but something has happened that would NA II 10 204 17
suspect the truth, and something, in which Miss Thorpe's NA II 10 204 18
parsonage, something like Fullerton, but better: Fullerton NA II 11 212 16
away, with a cold, or something that affected his spirits. NA II 12 217 2
above, am afraid he took something in my conduct amiss. NA II 12 217 2
middle of a speech about something very different, to NA II 13 220 2
error, when the noise of something moving close to her NA II 13 222 9
thoughts recurring to something more directly interesting, NA II 13 224 17
His temper is not happy, and something has now occurred to NA II 13 225 21
upon it, it is something not at all worth understanding." NA II 14 234 10
speculations, he had yet something more in reserve, and NA II 15 245 12
Something must be done for them whenever they leave SS I 2 9 6
"Well, then, <u>let</u> something be done for them; but <u>that</u> SS I 2 9 7
but <u>that</u> something need not be three thousand pounds. SS I 2 9 7
be more advisable to do something for their mother while SS I 2 10 16
than for them--something of the annuity kind I mean.-- SS I 2 10 16
They will be much more able to give <u>you</u> something." SS I 2 12 24
of young man--there is a something wanting--his figure is SS I 3 17 18
indifference, spoke a something almost as unpromising. SS I 4 22 18
long enough to detract something from their first SS I 6 31 8
Confess, Marianne, is not there something interesting to SS I 8 38 13
"and yet there is something so amiable in the prejudices SS I 11 56 12
Margaret related something to her the next day, which SS I 12 60 8
he seemed to be begging something of her, and presently he SS I 12 60 13
and Margaret was eagerly pressed to say something more. SS I 12 61 20
"It must be something extraordinary that could make SS I 13 63 6
I suppose it is something he is ashamed of." SS I 13 65 39
together, they must do something by way of being happy; SS I 13 66 60
"Something very melancholy must be the matter, I am sure," SS I 14 70 2
Something more than what he owned to us must have happened. SS I 15 77 23
But suspicion of something unpleasant is the inevitable SS I 15 79 29
endeavoured to support something like discourse with him SS I 16 89 42
"No, Edward, I should have something else to do with it." SS I 17 93 28
by instantly talking of something else, she internally SS I 18 98 13
founded only on a something or a nothing between Mr. SS I 18 100 30
with something so droll--all about any thing in the world." SS I 20 113 39
married mens' being beaux--they have something else to do." SS I 21 124 30
fancying herself to know something to his disadvantage.-- SS I 21 126 41
Lucy, hoping to discover something in her countenance; SS I 22 132 41
two, to the number of inhabitants in London, was something. SS II 3 157 19
length by way of saying something, she asked if he had SS II 4 162 12
I forget what it was now, but it was something so droll!" SS II 4 164 22
something very droll on hearing that they were to come. SS II 5 171 30
Impatient in this situation to be doing something that SS II 5 171 38
or of inquiring, something particular about her. SS II 5 172 40
it will always find something to support its doubts, if I SS II 5 173 44
I think you will feel something more than surprise, when SS II 7 186 38
purposely deceived, in something concerning me, which may SS II 7 188 42
with a wine-glass, full of something, in her hand. SS II 8 197 26
I bring you something that I am sure will do you good." SS II 9 202 5
6

"You have something to tell me of Mr. Willoughby, that SS II 9 204 19
were all cousins, or something like it, and she should SS II 11 223 14
"It would be something remarkable now," he continued, " SS II 11 224 26
now," he continued, "something droll, if Fanny should have SS II 11 224 26
There was something in her style of beauty, to please them SS II 11 227 50
are something in Miss Morton's style of painting, ma'am?-- SS II 12 235 31
32

must allow that there is something very trying to a young SS II 12 236 43
Elinor wished to talk of something else, but Lucy still SS II 13 239 7
Poor Edward muttered something, but what it was, nobody SS II 13 243 32
and soon talked of something else. "we spent such a day, SS II 13 243 32
towards her arose from something more than merely malice SS II 14 254 27
as prepared her to hear something wonderful; and giving SS III 1 257 2
3

"Something so strange! SS III 1 257 5
and seemed to know something or other, and at last he said SS III 1 258 5
easily to be made up by something else, your resolution, SS III 1 263 28
glad to have it all, you know, or something of the kind. SS III 2 273 16
Elinor tried to talk of something else; but Miss Steele SS III 2 275 21
I have something of consequence to inform you of, which I SS III 4 288 28
But, my dear, we must touch up the Colonel to do something SS III 4 292 55
it is most probable--that something might have been hit on. SS III 5 299 37
on her mind, in the something like confusion of SS III 5 300 38
of them, where there was something more of wildness than SS III 6 305 17
But he judged it unnecessary; he had still something more SS III 7 313 21
something like forgiveness from Ma--from your sister." SS III 8 319 23

"Yes, you have certainly removed something--a little.-- SS III 8 329 66
"And you <u>do</u> think something better of me than you did?"-- SS16 331 75
me on my guard--at least, it will be something to live for. SS III 8 332 77
there is something much more pleasing in his countenance.-- SS III 9 338 20
There was always a something,--if you remember,--in SS III 9 338 20
must arise from something more than his affection for SS III 10 340 2
to think that something more than gratitude already dawned. SS III 10 340 3
remained single, that something would occur to prevent his SS III 12 357 1
from the impatience of her mind to have something going on. SS III 12 358 5
This was gaining something, something to look forward to. SS III 12 358 7
"No, but she might suppose that something would occur in SS III 13 367 23
certain--and they only wanted something to live upon. SS III 13 369 32
great; Miss Osborne perhaps, or something in that stile.--" W 319 2
naturally to have caught something of the stile of the W 322 3
question, & there seemed something still more suspicious W 324 3
that point; & Mr Edwards now turned to something else.-- W 325 4
From Miss Osborne & Miss Carr she received something like W 336 13
friend, he muttered something of doing himself the honour W 344 21
but there was a something in it's mild seriousness, as W 346 21
I always said she ought to have settled something on you, W 351 26
"I was thinking of it's being something to amuse my father, W 354 28
there is always something lively going on at Croydon, you W 362 32
Lizzy has something more of quickness than her sisters." PP I 1 5 27
Mary wished to say something very sensible, but knew not PP I 2 7 19
he <u>did</u>--I heard something about it-- but I hardly know PP I 5 18 6
it-- but I hardly know what--something about Mr. Robinson. PP I 5 18 6
Every day added something to their knowledge of the PP I 7 28 4
we may see something of Captain Carter before he goes." PP I 7 32 40
manners there was something better than politeness; there PP I 7 33 42
must possess a certain something in her air and manner of PP I 8 39 50
this she must yet add something more substantial, in the PP I 8 39 51
there is something new to be observed in them for ever." PP I 9 43 18
Elizabeth, for the sake of saying something that might PP I 9 43 26
He has always something to say to every body.-- PP I 9 44 27
because there was a something about her more wrong and PP I 10 51 46
to check that little something, bordering on conceit and PP I 10 52 55
something to say to him before he had advanced many steps. PP I 11 54 2
manner; but there is something insufferably tedious in the PP I 11 55 8
have tried long ago to do something or other about it." PP I 13 61 7
There is something very pompous in his stile.-- PP I 13 64 17
pretence of wanting something in an opposite shop, and PP I 15 72 8
Something he supposed might be attributed to his PP I 15 74 13
agreeable,--allowing something for fortune and figure." PP I 16 82 48
gallantry, from the idea it suggested of something more.-- PP I 17 87 14
"it is <u>your</u> turn to say something now, Mr. Darcy.-- PP I 18 91 8
9

unless we expect to say something that will amaze the PP I 18 91 15
in a ball-room; my head is always full of something else." PP I 18 93 30
is heightened into something still more interesting, from PP I 21 117 14
may feel something like regard and esteem for our cousin." PP II 1 135 12
You alluded to something else. PP II 1 136 14
What do it, unless there were something very objectionable? PP II 1 137 24
It is something to think of, and gives her a sort of PP II 1 137 27
she tried to remember something of that gentleman's PP II 2 143 20
it would be in her power to say something of the Bingleys. PP II 3 147 20
Miss Bingley said something of his never returning to PP II 3 149 26
men must have something to live on, as well as the plain." PP II 3 150 29
He knows of my being in town, I am certain, from something PP II 3 148 26
It only shews her being deficient in something herself-- PP II 4 153 16
"You shall hear then--but prepare yourself for something PP II 8 175 18
therefore, to think of something, and in this emergence PP II 9 177 3
4

From something that he told me in our journey hither, I PP II 10 185 24
hurried into repeating something of Bingley, which might PP II 15 217 17
And <u>that</u> made the men suspect something, and then they PP II 16 221 17
a man without now and then stumbling on something witty." PP II 17 226 17
But there was still something lurking behind, of which PP II 17 227 25
There was a something in her countenance which made him PP II 18 234 35
36

"But it is fortunate," thought she, "that I have something PP II 19 237 4
felt, that to be mistress of Pemberly might be something! PP III 1 245 3
This was a lucky recollection--it saved her from something PP III 1 246 7
"There <u>is</u> something a little stately in him to be sure," PP III 1 257 68
On the contrary, there is something pleasing about his PP III 1 258 74
And there is something of dignity in his countenance, that PP III 1 258 74
Elizabeth here felt herself called on to say something in PP III 1 258 75
and in a tone which had something of real regret, that it " PP III 2 262 8
that it might add something to his lively concern for the PP III 3 270 10
"Since writing the above, dearest Lizzy, something has PP III 4 273 3
going to Gretna Green, something was dropped by Denny PP III 4 274 5
you have been spared something of these distressing scenes; PP III 4 275 5
though I have still something more to ask of the former. PP III 4 275 5
Darcy, in wretched suspense, could only say something PP III 4 277 11
again, till he had something of importance to mention." PP III 5 286 28
the business, had given something more of fretfulness than PP III 5 289 41
it, the application was a something to look forward to. PP III 6 296 8
His debts to be discharged, and something still to remain! PP III 7 304 30
Though our kind uncle has done something towards clearing PP III 7 304 35
I was so afraid you know that something would happen to PP III 9 319 24
them; but he had something to direct his search, which was PP III 10 322 2
have been able to do something for him, and his situation PP III 10 323 2
"It must be something particular, to take him there at PP III 10 328 17
Yes, there was something in <u>that</u>; I told you so from the PP III 10 329 30
reflection, and said something of his concern, at having PP III 11 338 59
them to enter into something more of conversation, than PP III 12 340 14
"Something very much to the purpose of course. PP III 15 362 14
I had no notion but he would go a shooting, or something PP III 17 374 20
consent, there was still something to be wished for. PP III 17 378 46
finding something to fear in every person and place. MP I 2 14 8
in constant terror of something or other; often retreating MP I 2 14 9
"Cousin," said she, "something is going to happen which I MP I 3 25 18
from being suspected of something better; or, perhaps, her MP I 3 28 38
"And now," added Mrs. Grant, "I have thought of something MP I 4 42 19
"I must try to do something with it," said Mr. Rushworth, " MP I 6 53 6
We were always doing something, as it was. MP I 6 54 9
and tried to make out something complimentary; but between MP I 6 55 17
was something clever to be said at the close of every air. MP I 7 64 12
always reminded by a something of the same nature whenever MP I 7 66 14
of the exercise, something was probably added in Edmund's MP I 7 66 15
and instructions, and something more in the conviction of MP I 7 66 15
It would be something so very unceremonious, so bordering MP I 8 78 23
and even Fanny had something to say in admiration, and MP I 8 82 35
You may see something of it here--something of the more MP I 8 83 36
size displayed, and all were glad to be doing something. MP I 9 84 2
Fanny's imagination had prepared her for something grander MP I 9 85 6
There is something in a chapel and chaplain so much in MP I 9 86 12
but with heads full of something very different-- MP I 9 87 15
find something to employ us here, before we go farther? MP I 9 90 34
and <u>being</u> one, must do something for myself." MP I 9 92 41
You really are fit for something better. MP I 9 93 53
"Now you are going to say something about law being the MP I 9 94 55
And she longed to be able to say something more to the MP I 10 102 37
Miss Bertram had made up her mind to something different, MP I 10 105 52
and here is a basket of something between us, which has MP I 10 105 54
a bad passage or <u>something</u>; that favouring <u>something</u> which MP I 11 107 3
that favouring <u>something</u> which every body <u>who</u> shuts their MP I 11 107 3
deficiency of information, or (smiling) of something else. MP I 11 110 26
about, that I thought something would certainly occur when MP I 12 115 5
the Ecclesford theatre and scenery to try something with." MP I 13 123 6
Let us be doing something. MP I 13 123 6
the resolution to act something or other, seemed so MP I 13 124 13
vary the scene, and exercise our powers in something new. MP I 13 125 18

Context	Text	Vol.	Ch.	Page	Line
Something of a theatre we must have undoubtedly, but it	MP	I	13	127	31
If they persist in the scheme they will find something--I	MP	I	13	128	35
could have wished that something might be acted, for she	MP	I	14	131	4
Something must be fixed on.	MP	I	14	131	5
No matter what, so that something is chosen.	MP	I	14	131	5
more credit in making something of it; and if she is so	MP	I	14	134	14
That's something, is not it?--	MP	I	15	139	10
I forgot to tell Tom of something that happened to me this	MP	I	15	141	22
Miss Crawford talked of something else, and soon	MP	I	15	144	36
was but the prelude to something so infinitely worse, to	MP	I	16	150	1
of either had led to something consolatory; her aunt	MP	I	16	152	2
"If you have such a suspicion, something must be done, and	MP	I	17	162	18
every body requiring something they had not, and giving	MP	I	18	165	2
Agatha, there is something so maternal in her manner, so	MP	I	18	169	21
stepped forward, feeling the necessity of doing something.	MP	II	1	176	3
Still Mrs. Norris was at intervals urging something	MP	II	1	180	10
We have just been trying, by way of doing something, and	MP	II	1	181	16
Edmund was the first to speak: "something must be done,"	MP	II	1	181	17
					18
It might not be saving them much, but it was something,	MP	II	2	189	5
home; but there was a something in Sir Thomas, when they	MP	II	2	191	10
Anybody but myself would have made something more of it,	MP	II	3	197	8
forbearance, and she began to talk of something else.	MP	II	3	199	16
I am sorry for them all, and would give something that	MP	II	3	200	19
the blessing of something fresh to see and think of was	MP	II	4	206	3
And besides, I want to play something more to you--a very	MP	II	4	207	9
Crawford's desire of something new, and which had little	MP	II	4	207	11
There seems something more speakingly incomprehensible in	MP	II	4	208	12
"To say the truth," replied Miss Crawford, "I am something	MP	II	4	209	17
There is something in the sound of Mr. Edmund Bertram so	MP	II	4	211	22
These are something like grievances, and make me think the	MP	II	4	212	31
Honesty, in the something between, in the middle state of	MP	II	4	214	41
Thomas, stop a moment--I have something to say to you."	MP	II	5	217	11
It began, on Lady Bertram's part, with, "I have something	MP	II	5	218	12
certain of seeing or hearing something there to pain me?"	MP	II	5	219	26
ought to look upon it as something extraordinary: for I	MP	II	5	220	28
Has not Miss Crawford a gown something the same?"	MP	II	5	222	44
that there would be a something to do and to suffer for it,	MP	II	5	226	64
It would be something to be loved by such a girl, to	MP	II	6	235	20
Then the stream--something must be done with the stream;	MP	II	7	242	23
so much the look of a something above a mere parsonage	MP	II	7	243	27
With something of consciousness he shook his head at his	MP	II	7	245	31
his heart upon having a something there that he could come	MP	II	7	246	37
of, and each found it necessary to talk of something else.	MP	II	7	250	56
He is always giving me something or other.	MP	II	8	259	22
was attentive--he was something like what he had been to	MP	II	8	260	24
something in his hand, "I beg your pardon for being here.	MP	II	9	261	2
them with what must have something the air of ingratitude,	MP	II	9	263	16
He did not appear in spirits; something unconnected with	MP	II	9	268	27
speak, to utter something like an inquiry as to the result.	MP	II	9	268	28
herself occasionally called on to endure something worse.	MP	II	10	273	7
him to her, saying something which discovered to Fanny,	MP	II	10	275	11
of stepping aside to say something agreeable of Fanny.	MP	II	10	276	14
somebody had whispered something to her, she had forgot to	MP	II	11	283	4
Fanny, you must do something to keep me awake.	MP	II	11	283	5
good health; but on the second it led to something farther.	MP	II	11	284	9
remove to London, meant something that she could not bear.	MP	II	11	287	17
for her to get to Fanny and try to learn something more.	MP	II	11	287	17
Is not there a something wanted, Miss Price, in our	MP	II	11	287	22
in our language--a something between compliments and--and	MP	II	11	287	22
all the better for not being taught--or something like it."	MP	II	11	288	28
something planned as a pleasant surprize to herself.	MP	II	12	291	1
my consent will be something; so, you may smile upon him	MP	II	13	303	15
was afraid there was a something in his voice and manner	MP	II	13	304	16
that time, to give him something rather considerable; that	MP	II	13	304	19
"I am glad you gave him something considerable," said Lady	MP	II	13	305	20
said that it meant something very earnest, very pointed.	MP	II	13	306	26
them in abundance; but something must be instantly written,	MP	II	13	307	30
					31
loved best, from saying something in which the words "my	MP	III	1	312	11
"There is something in this which my comprehension does	MP	III	1	315	27
inclination, might have something to do with it; and to	MP	III	1	320	44
out--but there is a something about Fanny, I have often	MP	III	1	323	56
Here was again a something of the same Mr. Crawford whom	MP	III	2	329	9
she really had known something like impatience, to be	MP	III	2	332	23
woman breathing, without something more to warm his	MP	III	3	336	7
There is something in the eloquence of the pulpit, when it	MP	III	3	341	28
He had always something to intreat the explanation of.	MP	III	3	343	40
have a comfortable walk, something more is necessary than	MP	III	4	346	8
I know you have something on your mind.	MP	III	4	346	8
there is something in him which I object to still more.	MP	III	4	349	25
the world, Mary on something of less philosophic tendency.	MP	III	5	360	13
being so; for there was something in your look that	MP	III	5	362	21
and then musing on something else, suddenly called her	MP	III	5	364	30
only a passage-room to something better, and she stood for	MP	III	7	377	10
your journey, or else I would have got something ready.	MP	III	7	378	14
preceding him, as with something of the oath kind he	MP	III	7	379	19
He was in distress for something that he had left there,	MP	III	7	381	26
The next opening of the door brought something more	MP	III	7	383	32
was sure her sister must want something after her journey."	MP	III	7	383	32
Something like tranquillity might now be hoped for, and	MP	III	7	385	37
to part with Rebecca, I should only get something worse.	MP	III	7	385	39
There had been something remarkably amiable about her.	MP	III	7	386	40
was holding out something to catch her eyes, meaning to	MP	III	7	386	40
and giving her something more to love and be interested in.	MP	III	9	397	7
the idea for even half an hour, it was something gained.	MP	III	9	398	10
without importing something to amuse; his journeys and his	MP	III	10	404	15
off, by his adding a something too pointed of his hoping	MP	III	10	404	15
as well to talk of something else, and turned to Mansfield.	MP	III	10	405	17
him to say something more of his sister and Edmund.	MP	III	10	406	20
offend, and there was something particularly kind and	MP	III	10	406	21
At length, a something like composure succeeded.	MP	III	12	418	6
Time did something, her own exertions something more, and	MP	III	12	418	6
There is something soothing in the idea, that we have the	MP	III	13	420	2
any; she must have something to write about, even to her	MP	III	13	425	6
and only conjecture that something very imprudent had just	MP	III	15	438	4
his affection for her something more than common--and his	MP	III	15	438	6
were all of a piece with something very bad; and if there	MP	III	15	441	19
You may imagine something of my present state.	MP	III	15	443	23
Then, however, it all came on again, or something very	MP	III	16	459	31
Something must have been wanting within, or time would	MP	III	17	463	8
His affection had already done something.	MP	III	17	467	19
a third--a something between the do-nothing and the do-all.	E	I	1	13	43
she wanted--exactly the something which her home required.	E	I	4	26	2
good-nature in doing something or other, was a single man;	E	I	4	27	5
to cards, he would read something aloud out of the Elegant	E	I	4	29	10
hurried look, announcing something extraordinary to have	E	I	7	50	1
Harriet blushed and smiled, and said something about	E	I	7	56	42
"Something has happened to delay her; some visitors	E	I	8	58	16
friend will soon hear of something to her advantage."	E	I	8	58	19
					20
"I will tell you something, in return for what have told	E	I	8	60	30
Miss Nash had been telling her something, which she	E	I	8	68	58
in the world; and something about a very enviable	E	I	8	68	58
and being the bearer of something exceedingly precious.	E	I	8	68	58
very often to recollect something worth their putting in.	E	I	9	70	5
much, something, he thought, might come from that quarter.	E	I	9	70	6
when they did arrive at something more like conversation,	E	I	9	74	21
There does seem to be a something in the air of Hartfield	E	I	9	75	25
"Yes, papa, we have something to read you, something quite	E	I	9	78	50
confused; said something about "honour;"--glanced at Emma	E	I	9	82	81
"This would soon have led to something better of course,"	E	I	10	89	35
made her again find something very much amiss about her	E	I	10	89	36
There is something so shocking in a child's being taken	E	I	11	96	25
possible; and there was something honourable and valuable	E	I	11	97	27
an effort; especially as something was going on amongst	E	I	14	118	4
marrying, there was something in the name, in the idea of	E	I	14	118	5
Something new for your coachman and horses to be making	E	I	15	126	8
but every body else had something to say; every body was	E	I	15	126	9
Emma immediately talk of something else, though she could	E	I	18	150	36
good to the poor!" she found something else must be done.	E	II	1	155	1
breath; and Emma said something very civil about the	E	II	1	158	11
sudden whirling round of something or other among the	E	II	1	160	23
to require something more than human perfection of body	E	II	2	165	9
There probably was something more to conceal than her own	E	II	2	169	16
just to have something occur to preserve him in her fancy,	E	II	4	184	10
and though there was something in it which her own heart	E	II	4	185	14
could not approve --something of ingratitude, merely	E	II	4	185	14
something like a look of spring, a tender smile even there.	E	II	5	189	16
I must buy something at Ford's.	E	II	6	200	14
to me, you were saying something at the very moment of	E	II	6	200	16
suspicions of there there being something to conceal."	E	II	6	203	41
which must be doing something, good or bad; heedlessness	E	II	7	205	1
Something occurred while they were at Hartfield, to make	E	II	7	206	5
that she would take something to eat; that her own maid	E	II	7	211	22
Mrs. Cole seemed to be relating something of her that was	E	II	8	214	13
in engaging Jane Fairfax now, it might augur something.	E	II	8	229	99
"They told me something," said Harriet rather hesitatingly,	E	II	9	232	13
first thing I did, but something or other hindered me all	E	II	9	236	46
of a word--Miss Fairfax said something about conjecturing.	E	II	10	242	15
who was still sitting at it, to play something more.	E	II	10	242	16
for a moment, coloured deeply, and played something else.	E	II	10	242	20
turning to Emma, said, "here is something quite new to me.	E	II	10	242	20
					21
Mrs. Cole was saying the other day she wanted something	E	II	10	244	40
gratitude, they will say something pretty loud about you	E	II	10	245	49
"Oh! Mr. Knightley, one moment more; something of	E	II	10	245	50
by are usually thinking of something very different."	E	II	12	258	3
It seemed like the forerunner of something absolutely	E	II	12	260	30
manner said, "it was something to feel that all the rest	E	II	12	261	32
					33
and never without a something of pleasing connection,	E	II	13	266	5
think I can live without something of a musical society.	E	II	14	277	36
Something of that nature would be particularly desirable	E	II	14	277	38
And she appears so truly good--there is something so	E	II	14	278	44
must exert ourselves and endeavour to do something for her.	E	II	15	282	5
little doubt of hearing of something to suit her shortly.--	E	II	15	284	9
feel the influence of a something beyond common civility	E	II	15	286	23
with each other--a something more early implanted.	E	II	15	286	23
It saves trouble, and is a something to get me out.	E	II	16	293	12
would soon produce something--offices for the sale--not	E	II	17	300	13
doubt of very soon meeting with something that would do."	E	II	17	301	15
"Something that would do!" repeated Mrs. Elton.	E	II	17	301	16
something favourable would turn up--but nobody believed me.	E	II	18	308	27
always felt that something would happen in our favour; and	E	II	18	308	27
I always say there is something direful in the sound: but	E	II	18	310	34
she could not help rather anticipating something decisive.	E	III	1	315	2
something to alter her present composed and tranquil state.	E	III	1	315	2
There was one, however, which Emma thought something of.--	E	III	2	326	33
A moment sufficed to convince her that something	E	III	3	333	3
are at leisure--I have something that I should like to	E	III	4	337	1
					2
as much as her words, for something more than ordinary.	E	III	4	337	3
her box again, "here is something still more valuable, I	E	III	4	339	16
Mr. Knightley had been telling him something about brewing	E	III	4	339	18
of there being a something of private liking, of private	E	III	5	344	2
though it was something which she judged it proper to	E	III	5	348	22
and muttering something about spruce beer, walked off.	E	III	6	364	57
I shall do something to expose myself."	E	III	6	365	60
It is not Swisserland, but it will be something for a	E	III	6	365	67
of, and only requires something very entertaining from	E	III	7	370	23
now I have it; something happened before tea, but not that.	E	III	8	382	29
Emma felt that her own note had deserved something better;	E	III	9	390	18
Something really important seemed announced by his looks;	E	III	10	392	7
Something has happened in Brunswick Square.	E	III	10	393	10
some money concern--something just come to light, of a	E	III	10	393	18
of the family,--something which the late event at Richmond	E	III	10	393	18
Something of a very unpleasant nature, I find, has	E	III	10	394	27
"From something that he said, my dear Emma, I rather	E	III	10	397	45
but I was thinking of something very different at the time.	E	III	11	406	24
But she probably had something of that in her thoughts,	E	III	12	419	12
She made her plan; she would speak of something totally	E	III	13	429	26
					27
can it happen that something is not a little disguised, or	E	III	13	431	39
state of mind, to something so like perfect happiness,	E	III	13	432	40
And now, let me talk to you of something else.	E	III	15	448	30
Emma fancied there was a something of resentment, a	E	III	16	451	2
of resentment, a something bordering on it in her style,	E	III	16	451	2
injustice, of guilt, of something most painful, which had	E	III	16	451	4
And when Mrs. Bates was saying something to Emma,	E	III	16	454	17
But yet I think there was something wanting.	E	III	16	454	18
I long to make apologies, excuses, to urge something for	E	III	16	459	47
leave'--something which, you knew, I did not approve.	E	III	17	462	9
I want you to call me something else, but I do not know	E	III	17	462	11
rather in expectation of hearing something of the kind."	E	III	17	465	25
prepared him first for something strange, and then, in few	E	III	17	465	28
with, "I have something to tell you, Emma; some news."	E	III	18	470	1
					2
and she felt afraid of something, though she knew not what.	E	III	18	470	9
seemed to expect that something should be struck out by	P	III	1	10	21
something very opposite from her inclination fixed on.	P	III	2	14	9
set of men but what lose something of their personableness	P	III	3	20	17
might have asked yet for something more, while Anne was	P	III	4	28	7
Something occurred, however, to give her a different duty.	P	III	5	33	7
go twice into my nursery without seeing something of them.	P	III	6	45	9
England, or paid off, or something, and is coming to see	P	III	6	50	27
gone, that Wentworth, or something very like it, was the	P	III	6	50	27
all that was right; said something to the Miss Musgroves,	P	III	7	59	25
Frederick Wentworth had used such words, or something like	P	III	7	61	36
Something a little inferior I shall of course put up with,	P	III	7	62	41
I wanted to be doing something."	P	III	8	65	13
the Spicers, of getting something from the Bishop in the	P	III	9	76	15
her to come and do something for him, she would have been	P	III	9	79	23
the hedge in a moment to say something to his sister.--	P	III	10	91	39
The something might be guessed by its effects.	P	III	10	91	39
worked up, and with something curious and valuable from	P	III	11	98	17
it to her a something more, or less, than gratification.	P	III	11	98	17
afterwards, that she had something to procure at a shop,	P	III	12	103	5
I, at this moment, see something like Anne Elliot again."	P	III	12	104	6
but I think he had something of the Elliot countenance.	P	III	12	106	16
merits of either, till something occasioned an almost	P	III	12	107	23
when he spoke again, it was of something totally different.	P	III	12	108	29
comparatively collected, and eager to be doing something.	P	III	12	111	48
countenance which shewed something to be wrong; and they	P	III	12	111	50
them; he has found out something or other in one of them	P	IV	2	131	9
remember it, but it was something very fine--I overheard	P	IV	2	131	9
Lady Russell began talking of something else.	P	IV	2	132	22
sensation of there being something more than immediately	P	IV	3	140	11
own route, understand something of hers, and regret that	P	IV	3	143	19
Lady Russell confessed that she had expected something	P	IV	4	150	15
resolution, but here was something more; here was that	P	IV	5	154	8
to have something that makes one know one's species better.	P	IV	5	155	9
"I have something to communicate that will astonish you "	P	IV	6	164	8
together; and I have something to tell you as we go along.	P	IV	6	169	27

SOMETHING/SOMEWHAT

"Did you say that you had something to tell me, sir?" P IV 6 169 28
"well, now you shall hear something that will surprise you. P IV 6 170 30
31
be out, if they were all Sophys, or something of that sort. P IV 6 171 33
But even then, there was something odd in their way of P IV 6 171 33
There is something about Frederick more to our taste." P IV 6 172 39
It was agitation, pain, pleasure, a something between P IV 7 175 6
It had cost her something to encounter Lady Russell's P IV 7 178 27
deficient in understanding; but benwick is something more. P IV 8 182 10
he, "without knowing something of Miss Anne Elliot; and I P IV 8 187 28
She felt that something must be the matter. P IV 8 190 47
you had always something agreeable to listen to. P IV 9 194 14
of him, but there was a something in his conduct then with P IV 9 200 56
"This accounts for something which Mr. Elliot said last P IV 9 201 63
His chance of the Kellynch estate was something, but all P IV 9 202 66
There is always something offensive in the details of P IV 9 207 91
occurred, that something might be done in her favour by P IV 9 210 99
Something so formal and arrange in her air! and she sits P IV 10 215 15
ago; and by way of doing something, as shooting was over, P IV 10 216 19
almost a certainty of something more permanent long before P IV 10 217 20
mother, I have done something for you that you will like. P IV 10 223 40
41
"come to me, I have something to say;" and the unaffected, P IV 11 231 12
which had not something to say upon woman's inconstancy. P IV 11 234 27
"I am every instant hearing something which overpowers me. P IV 11 237 42
a quicker step behind, a something of familiar sound, gave P IV 11 239 55
It is something for a woman to be assured, in her eight- P IV 11 243 68
of happiness, I could exert myself, I could do something. P IV 11 243 70
She had something to suffer perhaps when they came into P IV 12 250 5
do something for his own interest and his own enjoyment. P IV 12 250 7
to stand--"there is something wrong here, said he--putting S 1 364 1
to it--but I want to see something applied to your leg--& S 1 370 1
puffed, & raised it to a something of young renown--and Mr S 2 371 1
back window with something like the fondness of regret.-- S 4 380 1
often wanted, to have something or other forgotten most S 4 382 1
Well, I think I have done something in my day.-- S 4 383 1
Though I dare say Sidney might find something extremely S 5 387 1
we wanted--but--here is something at hand, pleasanter S 5 389 1
This was said cheifly for the sake of saying something-- S 7 400 1
wish to strike out something new, to exceed those who had S 8 405 2
as to the where, wanted something private, & wrote to ask S 9 408 1
The Miss Ps-- & Arthur had also seen something;--they S 10 414 1
soon found that he had caught something from them.-- S 10 418 1
woman yesterday to get something done for her, I beleive S 12 423 1
over the pales of something white & Womanish in the field S 12 426 1
the other side;--it was something which immediately S 12 426 1

SOMETIME (2)
must provide for him sometime or other; but poor Edward is SS I 22 133 46
Sometime hence it will be all found out, and then we may PP II 17 226 23

SOMETIMES (197)
I am sometimes half disposed to repent that I did not let LS 5 249 1
deal to say, but he is sometimes impertinent & troublesome. LS 16 268 2
Sometimes he is sure that she is deficient in LS 17 271 8
to blame, & probably has sometimes judged it expedient to LS 17 272 8
her of ill-nature & sometimes to lament her want of sense. LS 17 272 8
daughter in law, & I am sometimes quarreling with myself LS 30 300 2
confess herself to have sometimes an anxious doubt of LS 42 312 4
she was taught; and sometimes not even then, for she was NA I 1 14 1
had now the pleasure of sometimes hearing her father and NA I 1 15 2
"I have sometimes thought," said Catherine, doubtingly, " NA I 3 27 29
The men take notice of that sometimes you know." NA I 6 42 25
"Yes, sometimes; but he has rid out this morning with my NA I 10 73 18
not a word was said, sometimes she was again attacked with NA I 13 99 9
think with pleasure that he might be sometimes depended on. NA I 13 102 27
instruct might sometimes be used as synonimous words." NA I 14 109 26
themselves sometimes down to the comprehension of yours. NA I 14 112 36
His manner might sometimes surprize, but his meaning must NA I 14 114 49
beyond the pleasure of sometimes seeing Henry Tilney, made NA II 2 138 1
a little common honesty is sometimes quite as becoming. NA II 3 144 10
her that his mistakes could sometimes be very egregious. NA II 3 148 29
My brother is a lively, and perhaps sometimes a NA II 4 152 26
of her father, was sometimes without any companion at all. NA II 5 157 5
it might sometimes be of use in holding hats and bonnets. NA II 6 165 4
Catherine sometimes started at the boldness of her own NA II 8 188 18
of her own surmises, and sometimes hoped or feared that NA II 8 188 18
Sometimes it appeared to them as if his silence would be NA II 11 209 5
conviction that a loss may be sometimes a gain. NA II 13 220 1
and soothing; it sometimes suggested the dread of his calm NA II 14 231 4
of his regard; and sometimes, for a few painful minutes, SS I 4 22 18
in recollecting that he sometimes shewed a want of SS I 8 39 15
that they were sometimes only reminded of her being SS I 11 55 6
practice, that a doubt sometimes entered her mind of their SS I 14 71 4
But sometimes they are."-- SS I 16 88 33
eager in all she does--sometimes talks a great deal and SS I 17 93 35
Sometimes one is guided by what they say of themselves, SS I 17 93 37
I detest jargon of every kind, and sometimes I have kept SS I 18 97 7
Disappointed, however, and vexed as she was, and sometimes SS I 19 101 2
not hear me." said she, laughing, "he never does sometimes. SS I 19 107 26
Sometimes he won't speak to me for half a day together, SS I 20 113 39
for I thought you must have seen her at Norland sometimes. SS I 22 128 5
"Sometimes," continues Lucy, after wiping her eyes, "I SS I 22 133 44
She sometimes endeavoured for a few minutes to read; but SS II 4 166 31
Sometimes I thought it had been--but it never was." SS II 7 186 34
often distressing, and sometimes almost ridiculous, made SS II 8 193 7
Sometimes she could believe Willoughby to be as SS II 9 201 2
I had no hope of interfering with success; and sometimes I SS II 9 210 32
it right that they should sometimes see their brother. SS II 10 213 5
real value; and she was sometimes worried down by SS II 10 215 13
eye with which Marianne sometimes observed him, and the SS II 10 216 15
speaking tenderness, sometimes at Edward and sometimes at SS II 13 242 25
sometimes at Edward and sometimes at Elinor, regretting SS II 13 242 25
She joined them sometimes at Sir John's, and sometimes at SS II 14 247 5
I declare sometimes I do not know which way to look before SS III 2 272 12
its proofs without sometimes wondering whether her mother SS III 9 335 7
and though a sigh sometimes escaped her, it never passed SS III 10 342 7
wicked as my fears have sometimes fancied him, since the SS III 10 344 17
Sometimes I think she does like him. W 321 2
of her eldest sister, & sometimes I see a look of Miss W 324 3
It has been excessively admired;--but sometimes I think W 353 26
I always say cards are very well sometimes, to break a W 354 28
Ly osborne sometimes declares she cannot hear herself W 358 28
with no wit himself, cd sometimes make use of the wit of W 359 28
Mr. Bingley intended it likewise, and sometimes made PP I 4 15 12
but it is sometimes a disadvantage to be so very guarded. PP I 6 21 2
ladies sometimes condescend to employ for captivation. PP I 8 40 57
sometimes convey no ideas at all to my correspondents." PP I 10 48 23
It is often only carelessness of opinion, and sometimes an PP I 10 48 25
the time, and though I sometimes amuse myself with PP I 14 68 11
and I may perhaps have sometimes spoken my opinion of him, PP I 16 80 27
"Sometimes. PP I 18 91 13
their favour; and that sometimes the refusal is repeated a PP I 19 107 13
Elizabeth sometimes with real earnestness and sometimes PP I 20 112 23
and sometimes with playful gaiety replied to her attacks. PP I 20 112 23
diffidence of affection sometimes overcame the hope, that PP I 21 120 29
at Lucas Lodge, and he sometimes returned to Longbourn PP I 23 129 15
It was possible, and sometimes she thought it probable, PP II 2 142 16
Importance may sometimes be purchased too dearly. PP II 3 150 29
the walks to Meryton, sometimes dirty and sometimes cold, PP II 4 151 1
and sometimes cold, did January and February pass away. PP II 4 151 1
They called at various times of the morning, sometimes PP II 9 180 28
sometimes separately, sometimes together, and now and then PP II 9 180 28
in it, and sometimes it seemed nothing but absence of mind. PP II 9 181 29
In her kind schemes for Elizabeth, she sometimes planned PP II 9 181 31
Young ladies of her age, are sometimes a little difficult PP II 10 184 19
of Mr. Darcy's sometimes coming there stopped her, and PP II 12 195 1
she found, what has been sometimes found before, that an PP II 19 237 3
remembered to have sometimes seen, when he looked at her. PP III 1 250 47
I could hardly help laughing aloud sometimes. PP III 1 258 74
Sometimes she could fancy, that he talked less than on PP III 2 262 8
to join in it; and sometimes did venture a short sentence, PP III 3 267 4
for her eyes, which have sometimes been called so fine, I PP III 3 271 15
Sometimes one officer, sometimes another had been her PP III 4 280 25
I was sometimes quite provoked, but then I recollected my PP III 10 325 2
"Yet it is hard," she sometimes thought, "that this poor PP III 11 332 19
in those hours of separation that must sometimes occur. PP III 13 349 44
mother would take it; sometimes doubting whether all his PP III 17 375 27
their meetings she must sometimes think the pleasure PP III 18 384 26
and schemes were sometimes of a nature to make a third MP I 2 17 21
sometimes carried a little too far, it is all very proper. MP I 5 49 32
They sometimes pass in such very little time from reserve MP I 5 49 32
Mr. Bertram, I dare say you have sometimes met with such MP I 5 49 32
I admit to be sometimes too hard a stretch upon the mind. MP I 9 88 18
cautiously, "I could sometimes almost think that he MP I 12 116 9
the terms in which she sometimes spoke of the indulgence, MP I 16 151 1
though there had been sometimes much of suffering to her-- MP I 16 152 2
only audience, and--sometimes as prompter, sometimes as MP I 18 165 3
prompter, sometimes as spectator--was often very useful.-- MP I 18 165 3
You have a look of his sometimes." MP I 18 169 19
for her; and it was sometimes more than enough; for she MP I 18 170 24
stake, her kindness did sometimes overpower her judgment. MP II 2 190 8
We are sometimes a little in want of animation among MP II 3 196 2
of year; and venturing sometimes even to sit down on one MP II 4 208 11
The memory is sometimes so retentive, so serviceable, so MP II 4 209 12
We may sometimes take greater liberties in November than MP II 4 212 29
Fraternal love, sometimes almost every thing, is at others MP II 6 235 18
unmoved, or without sometimes lifting her eyes from her MP II 6 236 21
To her, the cares were sometimes almost beyond the MP II 8 254 8
His conviction of her regard for him was sometimes very MP II 8 255 10
oftenest answered with a "yes," had sometimes its "no." MP II 8 255 11
to her professed opinions, sometimes a tinge of wrong. MP II 9 269 31
They have injured the finest mind!--for sometimes, Fanny, MP II 9 269 33
in his manner--and sometimes, when he talked of William, MP II 10 278 20
of man that though he sometimes loves where it is not, he MP II 12 294 16
I am aware that there has been sometimes, in some points, MP III 1 313 12
I do think that Mr. Rushworth was sometimes very jealous." MP III 4 350 27
on the duty of Fanny's sometimes seeing her family, he did MP III 6 370 14
the little irritations, sometimes introduced by aunt MP III 8 392 11
and then, which he could sometimes take advantage of, to MP III 11 409 7
Could she be detached from them!--and sometimes I do not MP III 13 421 2
I have sometimes thought of going to London again after MP III 13 422 2
again after Easter, and sometimes resolved on doing MP III 13 422 2
solicitude, and sometimes catching his eye, received an MP III 15 445 34
the unreserve which had sometimes been too much for her MP III 16 453 16
Sometimes how quick to feel! MP III 16 454 18
I have since--sometimes--for a moment--regretted that I MP III 16 459 30
that must rise sometimes to self-reproach, and regret to MP III 17 468 22
"I am afraid I am sometimes very fanciful and troublesome." E I 1 10 31
she knew her father, was sometimes taken by surprize at E I 2 18 12
But sometimes of an evening, before we went to cards, he E I 4 29 10
alphabetically, and sometimes by some other rule. E I 5 37 7
One hears sometimes of a child being 'the picture of E I 5 39 20
her amiable regrets, and sometimes relieved them by E I 7 55 36
sometimes by bringing forward the idea of Mr. Elton. E I 7 55 36
pleasing; and capable of being sometimes out of humour. E I 11 92 5
could sometimes act an ungracious, or say a severe thing. E I 11 93 5
all in her eyes which he sometimes fell into, the want of E I 11 93 5
and fidgettiness were sometimes provoking him to a E I 11 93 5
As to men and women, our opinions are sometimes very E I 12 98 3
are sometimes to be pleased only by a good many sacrifices. E I 14 120 9
true elegance was sometimes wanting; but, till this very E I 16 134 5
"Yes, sometimes he can." E I 18 146 13
sometimes with music and sometimes with conversation. E II 3 170 2
Sometimes Mr. Elton predominated, sometimes the Martins; E II 4 184 11
would be cross sometimes, and as long as so many sacks E II 9 239 51
"Conjecture--aye, sometimes one conjectures right, and E II 10 242 15
one conjectures right, and sometimes one conjectures wrong. E II 10 242 15
"Ah! sir--but a thoughtless young person will sometimes E II 11 252 31
Perhaps I may sometimes have felt that Harriet would not E II 13 268 12
spirits, which, I understand, are sometimes much depressed. E II 14 275 32
and I dare say we shall sometimes find a seat for her in E II 15 284 9
hear how my brother, Mr. Suckling, sometimes flies about. E II 18 306 10
Emma, that Henry and John may be sometimes in the way. E II 18 312 48
them; and we used sometimes to say very cutting things! E III 2 321 15
He did not omit being sometimes directly before Miss Smith, E III 2 327 34
What an air of probability sometimes runs through a dream! E III 5 345 14
it--I am sure I have sometimes the oddest dreams in the E III 5 345 16
I know I do sometimes pop out a thing before I am aware. E III 5 346 16
the comfort of being sometimes alone!"--seemed to burst E III 6 363 51
circumstances do sometimes occur both to men and women, I E III 7 373 44
Sometimes, indeed, I have thought you were half suspecting E III 18 474 34
no preventing a laugh, sometimes in the very midst of them. E III 18 475 40
They will sometimes obtrude--but how you can court them!" E III 18 480 79
It sometimes happens, that a woman is handsomer at twenty- P III 1 6 11
have the pleasure of sometimes seeing the lawns and groves P III 2 14 9
point of it;--said he sometimes took out a gun, but never P III 3 22 23
her unreasonableness sometimes to Anne's admiration; and, P III 6 43 5
(in which she had sometimes more share than she wished, P III 6 43 5
Bless me, how troublesome they are sometimes!-- P III 6 45 8
The party at the great house was sometimes increased by P III 6 47 14
extraordinary bursts of mind which do sometimes occur. P III 6 51 31
though her eyes would sometimes fill with tears as she sat P III 8 71 56
had sometimes the air of being divided between them. P III 10 82 1
young men are, sometimes, to be met with, strolling about P III 10 85 13
said she; "but she does sometimes provoke me excessively, P III 10 88 28
persuadable temper might sometimes be as much in favour of P III 12 116 72
He has walked with me, sometimes, from one end of the P IV 2 132 16
excellent friend could sometimes think differently; and it P IV 4 147 7
"Yes," said Mrs. Smith more doubtingly, "sometimes it may, P IV 5 156 11
sincerity of those who sometimes looked or said a careless P IV 5 161 28
Anne sometimes fancied she discerned him at a distance, P IV 8 189 45
a sudden idea, "you sometimes spoke of me to Mr. Elliot?" P IV 9 201 60
which her own husband sometimes needed, & so entirely S 2 372 1
just as was wanted--sometimes one, sometimes the other.-- S 2 373 1
it too far sometimes--& so do you my love, you know.-- S 5 388 1
the gentleman may sometimes be thought the better half, of S 7 394 1
Sometimes indeed a flash of feeling seems to irradiate him- S 7 397 1
My young folks, as I call them sometimes, for I take them S 7 399 1

SOMEWHAT (33)
I gave them somewhat awkwardly I beleive; for in fact, the LS 20 277 6
the course of a few days seemed somewhat less formidable. LS 42 312 5
"This is a somewhat heavy call upon your brother's NA II 7 175 13
"Ah, Catherine! were it settled so, it would be somewhat NA II 13 224 18
to settle, though somewhat embarrassed in speaking of. NA II 13 229 31
of the two, as being somewhat newer and more conjectural; SS I 21 125 36
alone, as if he had somewhat in particular to tell her, SS II 5 172 40
excess of suffering had somewhat spent itself, and then SS II 7 182 12
13
I suppose she is grown somewhat older since that time.-- W 325 4
sitting in the cardroom somewhat screened by a door, she W 333 13
The ladies were somewhat more fortunate, for they had the PP I 3 9 3
Mary, though pretending not to hear, was somewhat PP I 18 101 70
begins to lose somewhat on its value in our estimation. PP I 20 114 32
when she read with somewhat clearer attention, a relation PP II 13 204 2
was now heightened into somewhat of a friendlier nature, PP III 2 265 16

somewhat nettled, she had all the success she expected. PP III 3 271 16
that she had given somewhat of a trial to the latter PP III 4 279 24
have borne the dread of Lydia's infamy somewhat better. PP III 6 298 17
She spoke of her farther as somewhat delicate and puny, MP I 1 11 19
have felt, and probably with somewhat more exactness. MP I 2 16 20
had made the arrangement somewhat easier to Sir Thomas's MP I 3 23 2
that Mr. Crawford was somewhat distinguishing his niece-- MP II 7 238 1
or rather of professions of a somewhat pointed character. MP II 7 246 36
For Fanny, somewhat more was related than the accidental MP III 10 404 15
Time would undoubtedly abate somewhat of his sufferings, MP III 16 460 31
you know, as having somewhat of the privilege of speech E I 5 40 24
admirer of Miss Woodhouse, seemed somewhat out of place. E III 5 343 2
heart, and to describe somewhat of the continual endurance E III 6 363 51
The change had perhaps been somewhat sudden;--her proposal E III 13 431 38
Charles, being somewhat more mindful of the probabilities P III 8 66 21
had seemed to understand somewhat of the value of an Anne P IV 1 125 13
somewhat different person from what the other had imagined. P IV 5 153 6
eveng"--, with Arthur's somewhat conscious reply of "tis S 10 417 1

SOMEWHERE (21)

this country, & lodging somewhere near me incog.--but I LS 16 269 3
One's eyes must be somewhere, and you know what a foolish NA II 3 143 4
she felt confident of somewhere drawing forth, in the NA II 9 193 5
see but one of them now, but there is another somewhere. SS II 4 163 18
Sir John met him somewhere in the street this morning." SS II 5 171 38
"Yes; and they have another, who lives somewhere near PP I 8 36 16
He must go somewhere, but he did not know where, and he PP III 10 323 2
She is on her road somewhere, I dare say, and so passing PP III 14 359 76
better; we find comfort somewhere--and those evil-minded MP I 5 46 23
disposed them all for going somewhere else the day after. MP I 7 70 30
to you for a few minutes somewhere;" words that Fanny felt MP III 5 357 5
her to be concealed somewhere with Mr. Crawford, who had MP III 16 450 11
She was always having a glimpse of him somewhere or other. E II 4 184 10
is great fear, great caution, great resolution somewhere.-- E II 15 285 15
as I can, I must walk somewhere, and the post-office is an E II 16 296 35
to tempt the lady, who only wanted to be going somewhere. E III 6 354 9
had got a much better somewhere,--and nothing could P III 10 86 21
somewhere else, and she would go on, till she overtook her. P III 10 87 21
room, or swinging a cot somewhere," they could hardly bear P III 12 113 56
Lady Russell would in all likelihood see him somewhere.-- P IV 7 178 26
Did he see you last summer or autumn, 'somewhere down in P IV 9 205 86

SON (186)

Sir Reginald de courcy to his son. Parklands. LS 12 260 1
You must be sensible that as an only son & the LS 12 260 1
have hitherto considered my son, I should blush to see him, LS 12 261 4
of having divided the son from his parents, would make me, LS 30 300 3
dutiful and affectionate son, as they met Mrs. Thorpe, who NA I 7 49 43
of her son, "I hope you have had an agreeable partner." NA I 8 58 25
"I dare say she thought I was speaking of her son." NA I 8 59 34
"And is Mr. Tilney, my partner, the only son?" NA I 9 69 49
upon my soul!--stout, active,--looks as young as his son. NA I 12 95 18
the drawing-room with General Tilney, his son and daughter. NA I 13 102 25
Mrs. Thorpe and her son, who were acquainted with every NA I 15 120 25
embraced her daughter, her son, her visitor, and could NA I 15 121 27
was to be resigned to his son as soon as he should be old NA II 1 135 42
appearance of his eldest son, nor by the displeasure he NA II 5 154 2
out in the curricle in which he was to accompany his son. NA II 5 155 4
myself about ten years ago, for the benefit of my son. NA II 7 175 15
Even Frederick, my eldest son, you see, who will perhaps NA II 7 176 15
I do not envy his situation, either as a lover or a son." NA II 10 205 24
His son and daughter's observations were of a different NA II 11 214 27
of the wishes of his son, Catherine would have quitted NA II 11 215 28
The General, perceiving his son one night at the theatre NA II 15 244 12
in the countenance of his son; and thankful for Mr. NA II 15 245 12
positive command to his son of doing every thing in his NA II 15 245 12
brook the opposition of his son, steady as the sanction of NA II 15 247 15
Of a very considerable fortune, his son was, by marriage NA II 16 249 2
marriage, permitted his son to return to Northanger, and NA II 16 252 7
By a former marriage, Mr. Henry Dashwood had one son: by SS I 1 3 2
The son, a steady respectable young man, was amply SS I 1 3 2
than for himself or his son:--but to his son, and his SS I 1 4 3
or his son:--but to his son, and his son's son, a child of SS I 1 4 3
to his son, and his son's son, a child of four years old, SS I 1 4 3
His son was sent for, as soon as his danger was known, and SS I 1 5 5
promise on the part of his son in their favour, which gave SS I 1 5 5
Ferrars was the eldest son of a man who had died very rich; SS I 3 14 2
it was the affectionate attention of a son and a brother, SS I 3 15 5
excuse for every thing strange on the part of her son. SS I 14 71 5
would be reformed, and her son be at liberty to be happy. SS I 19 101 2
I have brought my other son and daughter to see you. SS I 19 102 2
"Mr. Edward Ferrars, the eldest son of Mrs. Ferrars of SS I 19 106 20
Is her son determined to submit to this, and to all the SS I 22 131 30
wife, when I consider whose son he is, I cannot bear to SS II 2 148 14
second son William, who were nearly of the same age. SS II 3 156 8
convinced that their own son was the tallest, politely SS II 12 233 19
SS II 12 234 21
22
was safely delivered of a son and heir; a very interesting SS II 14 246 1
to do very well by her son, and though Lucy has next to SS III 1 259 7
under her uncle's care, the son of a woman especially of SS III 1 267 45
But I don't think mine would be, to make one son SS III 1 269 54
know what she may be doing--what she may drive her son to. SS III 3 282 19
in knowing that her son has money enough to live upon,-- SS III 5 296 19
has done with her son, she has cast him off for ever, and SS III 5 296 19
Mrs. Ferrars can never forget that Edward is her son." SS III 5 296 20
be considered as the eldest son;--and as to any thing else, SS III 5 297 29
actually been bribing one son with a thousand a-year, to SS III 13 366 18
be induced to forgive her son, his wife should never be SS III 13 371 38
to her presence, and pronounced to be again her son. SS III 14 373 1
Edward was not her only son, he was by no means her eldest; SS III 14 374 4
What Edward had done to forfeit the right of eldest son, SS III 14 377 12
They consisted of Ly. Osborne, her son Ld Osborne, her W 329 9
who lived with him, her son a fine boy of 10 years old, & W 329 9
as careless as her son, if she saw me in this condition."-- W 357 28
Darcy liked me less, his son might have borne with me PP I 16 80 32
was the son of old Wickham, the late Mr. Darcy's steward. PP I 18 94 45
worse than of being the son of Mr. Darcy's steward, and of PP I 18 95 46
to echo whatever his son in law said, in a manner which PP II 6 163 14
Fitzwilliam, the younger son of his uncle, Lord ---- and PP II 7 170 7
I speak feelingly. a younger son, you know, must be inured PP II 10 183 10
"In my opinion, the younger son of an earl can know very PP II 10 183 11
pray, what is the usual price of an earl's younger son? PP II 10 183 15
Mr. Wickham is the son of a very respectable man, who had PP II 12 199 5
for the father, would always prevent his exposing the son. PP II 13 207 5
of a young gentleman, the son of her late master's steward, PP III 1 247 9
"Yes, ma'am, that he was indeed; and his son will be just PP III 1 249 36
of his concerns, with the son of his patron, were PP III 2 265 15
perfectly useless; for, of course, they were to have a son. PP III 8 308 3
This son was to join in cutting off the entail, as soon as PP III 8 308 3
the world, but yet the son was to come; and Mrs. Bennet, PP III 8 308 3
son and daughter, let us come to a right understanding. PP III 8 310 9
Is her husband, is the son of his late father's steward, PP III 14 357 62
Unfortunately an only son, (for many years an only child) PP III 16 369 24
eldest son, who feels born only for expense and enjoyment. MP I 2 17 22
His eldest son was careless and extravagant, and had MP I 2 20 33
tried to impress his eldest son with the same conviction, MP I 3 23 2
and he took his eldest son with him in the hope of MP I 3 32 61
hope of its utility to his son, reconciled Sir Thomas to MP I 3 32 62
Lady Bertram did; she entirely agreed with her son as to MP I 4 36 7
home his son, and waiting the final arrangement by himself. MP I 4 38 9
Sir Thomas's sending away his son, seemed to her so like a MP I 4 38 9
very desirous that her son should marry, and declared that MP I 4 39 10
The son had a good estate in Norfolk, the daughter twenty MP I 4 40 15
on Tom Bertram; the eldest son of a baronet was not too MP I 4 42 17

of her brother, treating him, they say, quite like a son. MP I 7 63 4
son, and the poor fellow was waiting for me half an hour. MP I 7 73 53
lieu of her son, and Dr. Grant was to join them at dinner. MP I 8 79 28
all the rooms above, if her son had not interposed with a MP I 9 89 31
"James," said Mrs. Rushworth to her son, "I believe the MP I 9 90 35
or a grandfather to leave a fortune to the second son." MP I 9 92 40
with the housekeeper, but the son I can get away from." MP I 10 101 32
a short pause, "as for the son of an Admiral to go into MP I 11 109 18
to go into the navy, or the son of a general to be in the MP I 11 109 18
Sir Thomas was to return in November, and his eldest son MP I 12 114 1
I wonder my son did not propose it." MP I 12 117 13
Mrs. Rushworth, who saw nothing but her son, was quite at MP I 12 118 17
and being the younger son of a Lord with a tolerable MP I 13 121 1
particular friends of his son, exceedingly unwelcome; and MP II 1 183 23
a time, as strongly as his son had ever supposed he must; MP II 2 187 2
'if Mr. Rushworth were a son of your own he could not hold MP II 2 190 7
young woman whom her dear son had selected;--and very MP II 3 202 28
for your not influencing your son against such a tenant?" MP II 7 247 38
if any son of mine could reconcile himself to doing less. MP II 7 247 42
We must hope his son may prove that he knows it too." MP II 7 248 46
Thomas had been bringing up no wife for his younger son. MP II 10 278 20
Sir Thomas Bertram's son is somebody; and now, he is in MP II 11 289 34
little likely my own eldest son, your cousin, Mr. Bertram, MP III 1 317 34
could love, which, I am convinced, my eldest son has not. MP III 1 317 34
for, less willing than his son to trust to the future, he MP III 5 356 3
he absolutely made up his mind, he consulted his son. MP III 6 368 9
he had communicated to his son, for his prime motive in MP III 6 368 9
Her son answered cheerfully, telling her that every thing MP III 7 378 11
he talked on only to his son, and only of the thrush, MP III 7 380 23
Warmed by the sight of such a friend to her son, and MP III 10 400 6
the share of her thankless son, and treated as concisely MP III 13 425 6
illness of her eldest son, of which they had received MP III 13 426 9
not one who was not more useful at times to her son. MP III 14 429 2
vanity it would be good luck to have Edmund the only son. MP III 14 430 3
She supposed he could not yet leave his son, but it was a MP III 14 430 6
had herself been treated, as from sensibility for her son. MP III 16 450 10
or of less weight with her son, who was always guided by MP III 16 450 11
Had he been privy to her conversation with his son, he MP III 16 453 15
No happiness of son or niece could make her wish the MP III 17 472 31
and others of the son and the uncle not letting him. E I 1 12 41
He saw his son every year in London, and was proud of him; E I 2 17 7
a mother and daughter, a son and son's wife, who all lived E I 4 27 5
He had his shepherd's son into the parlour one night on E I 4 28 6
for any body to be a better son; and therefore she was E I 4 28 6
from the wantonness of comfort, or his son may plague him." E I 5 38 13
He is an excellent young man, both as son and brother. E I 8 59 27
and is glad to catch at the old writing master's son." E I 8 64 47
if he could, but as his son and daughter's carriage and E I 13 108 3
some information about his son; she heard the words "my E I 14 118 4
she heard the words "my son," and "Frank," and "my son," E I 14 118 4
son," and "Frank," and "my son," repeated several times E I 14 118 4
an early visit from his son; but before she could quiet Mr. E I 14 118 4
and my son--and then I should say we were quite complete. E I 14 119 7
"And so you do not consider this visit from your son as by E I 14 122 20
19
to folly, though in his own son; but he is very likely to E I 18 148 23
Enscombe, which allowed his son to answer for having an E II 5 188 9
gentlemen sitting with her father--Mr. Weston and his son. E II 5 190 21
His son, too well bred to hear the hint, rose immediately E II 5 193 36
37
The son looked convinced. E II 5 194 41
in order to hear that his son was very handsome, knew E II 6 196 2
you were Mr. Weston's son--but lay out half-a-guinea at E II 6 200 15
both husband and wife; the son approached her with a E II 8 214 12
pleasure of introducing my son to you," said Mr. Weston. E II 18 305 1
know him to be my son, though he does not bear my name." E II 18 305 3
He had done his duty and could return to his son. E II 18 308 26
I hope you will be pleased with my son; but you must not E II 18 309 30
I give you notice that as I find your son, so I shall E II 18 309 31
him by her opinion of his son; and so briskly did she E III 2 321 14
While she talked of his son, Mr. Weston's attention was E III 2 321 16
son, Miss Bates and her niece, who had accidentally met. E III 5 344 3
"No, sir," replied his son, laughing, "I seem to have had E III 5 345 13
"Low, I am afraid, sir, very low," answered his son;--"but E III 7 371 30
Mr. Weston, his son, Emma, and Harriet, only remained; and E III 7 374 54
before tea, old John Abdy's son wanted to speak with him. E III 8 383 29
And poor John's son came to talk to Mr. Elton about relief E III 8 383 29
"Has your son been with you, then?" E III 10 394 21
He was the son of Mr. Weston--he was continually here--I E III 13 427 19
of being your husband's son, and the advantage of E III 14 437 8
obliged and affectionate son, F. C. Weston Churchill. E III 14 443 8
a still-born son, nov. 5, 1789; mary, born nov. 20, 1791." P III 1 3 1
Dec. 16, 1810, Charles, son and heir of Charles Musgrove, P III 1 3 2
Musgrove was the eldest son of a man, whose landed P III 4 28 7
very troublesome, hopeless son; and the good fortune to P III 6 50 28
as connected with her son, seemed one of those P III 6 51 31
long an interval, her poor son gone for ever, and all the P III 6 51 32
heaven to spare my poor son, I dare say he would have been P III 8 64 5
6
kind wishes, as to her son, he had probably been at some P III 8 67 28
in a low voice, about her son, doing it with so much P III 8 67 28
over the destiny of a son, whom alive nobody had cared for. P III 8 68 29
Uppercross; this eldest son of course excepted, who had P III 9 74 5
an eldest son, and he saw things as an eldest son himself. P III 9 76 14
that he is the eldest son; whenever my uncle dies, he P III 9 76 15
"Exactly like father and son! P IV 10 213 6
Dear Miss Elliot, may I not say father and son?" P IV 10 213 6
as eldest son to the property which 2 or 3 generations had S 2 371 1
that old Stringer & his son have a higher claim. S 4 381 1

SON'S (11)

father and mother would never oppose their son's wishes.-- NA I 15 119 14
taking his place in his son's curricle for the rest of the NA II 5 156 4
to his son, and his son's son, a child of four years old, SS I 1 4 3
in addition to his eldest son's extravagance, it became MP I 3 24 7
related to her own and her son's concerns, had not yet MP I 8 75 2
kind he kicked away his son's portmanteau, and his MP III 7 379 19
With a friendly shake of his son's hand, and an eager MP III 7 379 20
and daughter, a son and son's wife, who all lived together; E I 4 27 5
morning, and seeing my son's hand, presumed to open it-- E II 18 305 5
Mr. Weston might be his son's superior.-- E III 2 325 32
lined on their eldest son's coming of age 10 years ago.-- S 2 373 1

SON-IN-LAW (10)

of announcing to her son-in-law and his wife that she was SS I 5 25 1
were; a letter from her son-in-law had told her that he SS II 10 213 5
Lucas himself, to produce a more valuable son-in-law." PP III 11 330 8
as I value the impudence and hypocrisy of my son-in-law. PP III 15 364 24
awe of her intended son-in-law, that she ventured not to PP III 17 378 46
and the butcher's son-in-law left word at the shop." MP I 6 57 33
He had expected a very different son-in-law; and beginning MP II 3 200 20
turn attention from his son-in-law, who was pursuing his E I 15 126 9
Mrs. Weston and her son-in-law; they were walking into E II 9 233 25
solicitude after her son-in-law, to inquire if he were E III 6 359 36

SON-IN-LAW'S (3)

Now was the time when her son-in-law's promise to his SS I 5 27 6
for the sense of his son-in-law's protection, would have E III 19 483 10
watchfulness which a son-in-law's rights would have given. P IV 12 250 7

SONG (19)

Did you ever hear the old song, 'going to one wedding NA I 15 122 32
then you know, we may try the truth of this same old song." NA I 15 123 34
at the end of every song, and as loud in his conversation SS I 7 35 9
his conversation with the others while every song lasted. SS I 7 35 9
to sing a particular song which Marianne had just finished. SS I 7 35 9

She played over every favourite song that she had been SS I 16 83 3
your porridge,"--and I shall keep mine to swell my song. PP I 6 24 22
After a song or two, and before she could reply to the PP I 6 25 23
exhibiting was delightful to her, and she began her song. PP I 18 100 68
song, said aloud, "that will do extremely well, child. PP I 18 100 68
69
Lady Catherine listened to half a song, and then talked, PP II 8 174 12
figure-dance, and a horn-pipe, and a song between the acts. MP I 13 124 10
One accompaniment to her song took her agreeably by E II 8 227 86
Her pardon was duly begged at the close of the song, and E II 8 227 86
Towards the end of Jane's second song, her voice grew E II 8 229 93
Another song, however, was soon begged for. E II 8 229 95
The strength of the song falls on the second." E II 11 229 95
song, she explained the words of the song to Mr. Elliot.-- P IV 8 186 24
"Is not this song worth staying for?" said Anne, suddenly P IV 8 190 49
SONGS (5)
through the chief of the songs which Lady Middleton had SS I 7 35 8
After playing some Italian songs, Miss Bingley varied the PP I 10 51 47
48
found, besides the two songs which she had lent Elizabeth E I 7 50 1
with all the tenderest songs of the one poet, and all the P III 11 100 23
Songs and proverbs, all talk of woman's fickleness. P IV 11 234 27
SONNET (2)
that one good sonnet will starve it entirely away." PP I 9 44 34
by--unless some tender sonnet, fraught with he apt analogy P III 10 85 12
SONNETS (2)
she could not write sonnets, she brought herself to read NA I 1 16 10
have been for fifteen sonnets in celebration of her charms, NA I 2 24 28
SONS (18)
She had three sons before Catherine was born; and instead NA I 1 13 1
on the talents of her sons, and the beauty of her NA I 4 32 2
resolution that both her sons should marry well, and of SS I 4 23 19
own happiness, that your sons will be brought up to as SS I 19 103 5
could not learn whether her sons were to be of the party. SS II 12 230 6
For many years of her life she had had two sons; but the SS III 14 373 2
Younger sons cannot marry where they like." PP II 10 183 12
He thought of his own four children--of his two sons--of MP I 1 6 5
You are thinking of your sons--but do not you know that of MP I 1 6 6
least on the part of the sons, who at seventeen and MP I 2 12 3
They were a remarkably fine family, the sons very well- MP I 2 13 4
youngest of the sons, sitting crying on the attic stairs. MP I 2 15 9
and disposal of her sons as they became old enough for a MP I 2 21 34
every question of his two sons almost before it was put. MP II 1 178 8
representation of younger sons who have little to live on. MP II 4 214 45
She was fond of her sons, especially of William, but MP III 8 389 4
with either of Isabella's sons; but she was convinced that E III 17 461 1
or respectable acquaintance to sons or daughters. S 2 374 1
SONS-IN-LAW (2)
gained two such sons-in-law as Edward and Willoughby. SS I 10 49 11
"I admire all my three sons-in-law highly," said he. PP III 17 379 48
SOON (1135)
I shall soon have occasion for all my fortitude, as I am LS 1 244 1
I will send you a line, as soon as I arrive in town.-- LS 2 246 2
Susan, & we shall depend on his joining our party soon. LS 3 247 1
I shall be with you very soon, & am your affec. LS 4 249 2
I hope you will soon be able to form your own judgement. LS 6 250 1
of my intentions very soon.-- yours &c. S. Vernon. LS 10 258 4
between them, so very soon established, without some alarm, LS 11 259 1
I had intended to write to Reginald myself, as soon as my LS 13 262 1
Mr Vernon set off for town as soon as she had determined LS 15 266 4
bursting into tears as soon <as> we were seated, took her LS 17 270 2
reason of her behaviour, & soon found myself to have been LS 19 273 1
be wanted left the nursery soon afterwards & was half way LS 20 275 1
I led her thither accordingly, & as soon as the door was LS 20 276 5
by wishing with a laugh, that he might be really one soon. LS 20 278 10
As soon as I can get her alone, I will discover the real LS 20 278 11
gallant to me, very soon made the whole party understand LS 22 280 2
She shall not soon forget the occurrences of this day. LS 22 282 8
She soon afterwards left the room. LS 23 284 7
As soon as I was tolerably composed, I returned to the LS 24 291 15
door, & he, merry as usual, soon afterwards took his leave. LS 24 291 15
at any rate take place soon, may with perfect convenience LS 25 293 3
I have also an idea of being soon in town, & whatever may LS 25 294 4
misery enough; & come yourself to town, as soon as you can. LS 26 295 1
in town this winter, as soon as I found that her LS 27 297 4
If he leaves you soon for London, everything will be LS 27 297 4
or other, that you were soon to be in London, & LS 28 298 1
Let me hear from you as soon as you arrive, & in LS 28 298 2
Let me hear from you soon, very soon. LS 30 301 5
with him alone, as soon as he knew him to be in the house. LS 32 303 1
that your intercourse even by letter must soon be given up. LS 38 306 1
heart to ask questions; but I hope we shall soon know all. LS 40 308 1
& entreaty that you would come to us as soon as you can. LS 40 309 1
spirits, (as I trust he soon will) we will try to rob him LS 40 309 1
her neice, for the former soon perceived by the stile of LS 42 311 1
soon found some accomodating business to call him thither. LS 42 311 2
decided what might not have been decided quite so soon. LS 42 312 6
They were soon settled in comfortable lodgings in Pulteney- NA I 2 19 6
Mrs. Allen congratulated herself, as soon as they were NA I 2 22 11
"Thank you; for now we shall soon be acquainted, as I am NA I 3 29 51
which her keen eye soon made, that the lace on Mrs. NA I 4 32 2
proof of amity, she was soon invited to accept an arm of NA I 4 33 6
As soon as divine service was over, the Thorpes and Allens NA I 5 35 2
orders about the horses, soon joined them, and from him NA I 7 45 5
horses so much as rest; nothing knocks them up so soon. NA I 7 47 27
and looked it over, but I soon found it would not do; NA I 7 49 40
be before I saw it: as soon as I heard she has married an NA I 7 49 40
"Because I thought I should soon see you myself. NA I 7 50 49
away as soon as he had satisfied the demands of the other. NA I 7 51 54
John Thorpe came up to her soon afterwards, and said, " NA I 8 59 35
turned away, but not too soon to hear her friend exclaim NA I 9 62 8
the rest for a minute; but he will soon know his master. NA I 9 62 9
"Yes, I went to the Pump-Room as soon as you were gone, NA I 9 68 38
We soon found out that our tastes were exactly alike in NA I 10 71 3
"I hope I shall have the pleasure of seeing you again soon, NA I 10 73 19
As soon as they were joined by the Thorpes, Catherine's NA I 10 74 23
I asked you as soon as I came into the room, and I was NA I 10 75 26
Soon after their reaching the bottom of the set, Catherine NA I 10 80 59
John Thorpe was soon with them, and his voice was with NA I 11 84 18
and dine there; and, as soon as dinner is over, if there NA I 11 84 19
now, as it is so fine, I dare say they will be here soon." NA I 11 85 32
pleasure, and the hope of soon enjoying another, almost NA I 11 86 50
trot; the Tilneys, who had soon ceased to look after her, NA I 11 87 53
said he soon afterwards, "we might have done it very well. NA I 11 88 56
long continuance: for she soon recollected, in the first NA I 12 92 4
as soon as ever I saw you; now, Mrs. Allen, did not----- NA I 12 94 8
vexed, and meant to make her apology as soon as possible." NA I 12 94 10
walk should be taken as soon as possible; and, setting NA I 12 95 16
In that interval the plan was completed, and as soon as NA I 13 97 1
elucidated by this speech, soon ceased to be a puzzle. NA I 13 102 26
soon leave you as far behind me as--what shall I say?-- NA I 14 107 11
had better change it as soon as you can, or we shall be NA I 14 108 14
The Tilneys were soon engaged in another on which she had NA I 14 110 28
were so clear that she soon began to see beauty in every NA I 14 111 29
very shocking indeed, will soon come out in London." NA I 14 111 29
and though it ended too soon, its conclusion was NA I 14 114 49
From her, she soon learned that the party to Clifton had NA I 14 115 50
This bold surmise, however, she soon learnt comprehended NA I 15 117 8
Anne and Maria soon set her heart at ease by the sagacity NA I 15 121 25
be resigned to his son as soon as he should be old enough NA II 1 135 42
James soon followed his letter, and was received with the NA II 1 137 50
To have her acquaintance with the Tilneys end so soon, was NA II 2 138 1
James will soon be here." NA II 3 143 2
Pray undeceive him as soon as you can, and tell him I beg NA II 3 145 13
But I confess, as soon as I read this letter, I thought it NA II 3 145 16
fixing her eye on him as she spoke, soon caught his notice. NA II 3 147 21
His leave of absence will soon expire, and he must return NA II 4 152 29
Miss Tilney's manners and Henry's smiles soon did away NA II 5 154 2
She got away as soon as she could from a room in which her NA II 7 173 5
almost as plainly, as he soon forced her to tell him in NA II 7 178 21
Soon after her death I obtained it for my own, and hung it NA II 7 181 39
surrounding objects, she soon began to walk with lassitude; NA II 7 181 41
to see the house, soon revived the subject; and her father NA II 8 182 1
On the third day, in short as soon as she could be NA II 9 196 25
The formidable Henry soon followed her into the room, and NA II 10 199 1
The anxieties of common life began soon to succeed to the NA II 10 201 5
You will soon hear enough from another quarter to know NA II 10 202 7
Let me soon hear from you, dear Catherine; you are my only NA II 10 202 7
As soon as she dared leave the table she hurried away to NA II 10 203 8
You will soon know why." NA II 10 204 13
very sorry to leave you so soon, but something has NA II 10 204 17
than Henry's, she was very soon obliged to give him credit NA II 11 211 15
Pray write to me soon, and direct to my own home. NA II 12 216 2
"It will soon be as if you never had," said Henry. NA II 12 218 5
Soon after this, the General found himself obliged to go NA II 13 220 1
been for a dread of its soon becoming expedient to leave NA II 13 220 1
on her mind, she very soon resolved to speak to Eleanor NA II 13 220 1
to start forth her obligation of going away very soon. NA II 13 220 2
with firmness, but with eyes still cast down, soon went on. NA II 13 223 13
I am very, very sorry we are to part-- so soon, and so NA II 13 224 14
aloud, "Monday--so soon as Monday;--and you all go. NA II 13 224 17
the way--and then I shall soon be at Salisbury, and then I NA II 13 224 17
Soon after six Eleanor entered her room, eager to show NA II 13 227 27
"you must let me hear from you as soon as possible. NA II 13 228 28
The carriage was soon announced to be ready; and Catherine, NA II 13 229 31
whose pale and jaded looks soon caught her notice, before NA II 14 233 9
silent and alone becoming soon her only wish, she readily NA II 14 235 13
any doubt of their being soon slept away; and though, when NA II 14 235 13
As soon as breakfast was over, she sat down to fulfil her NA II 14 235 14
as the letter was finished; "soon made and soon ended.-- NA II 14 236 15
reply less rational; for soon were all her thinking powers NA II 14 237 20
"Very true: we soon met with Mrs. Thorpe, and then we NA II 14 238 24
her feelings soon hardened into even a triumphant delight. NA II 15 244 11
under their care, and--as soon as his acquaintance allowed NA II 15 245 12
His resolution was soon formed. NA II 15 245 12
being beloved, they soon learnt to consider it with only NA II 16 249 1
circumstances which, as soon as the General would allow NA II 16 251 6
On the strength of this, the General, soon after Eleanor's NA II 16 252 7
The event which it authorized soon followed: Henry and NA II 16 252 7
By his own marriage, likewise, which happened soon SS I 1 3 2
His son was sent for, as soon as his danger was known, and SS I 1 5 5
be almost completely fitted up as soon as she takes it." SS I 2 13 26
to their acquaintance soon after his sister's SS I 3 15 4
Her manners were attaching and soon banished his reserve. SS I 3 16 13
"I shall very soon think him handsome, Elinor, if I do not SS I 4 20 10
"Yet it certainly soon will happen. SS I 4 22 17
I shall not lose you so soon, and Edward will have greater SS I 4 22 17
of every thing that interested her, was soon done.-- SS I 5 26 5
her husband, had been sold soon after his death, and an SS I 5 26 5
forth as they entered the house were soon dried away. SS I 6 28 2
In such employments as these they were interrupted soon SS I 6 30 6
on Mrs. Dashwood as soon as she could be assured that her SS I 6 30 7
An opportunity was soon to be given to the Dashwoods of SS I 6 31 10
of discernment enabled her soon after her arrival at SS I 8 36 1
Soon after this, upon Elinor's leaving the room, "mama," SS I 8 38 14
"Had you any idea of his coming so soon?" said Mrs. SS I 8 39 15
favourite village, and she soon found out that of all SS I 9 43 11
Sir John called on them as soon as the next interval of SS I 9 43 12
"Well, Marianne," said Elinor, as soon as he had left them, SS I 10 47 4
You will soon have exhausted each favourite topic. SS I 10 47 4
I am sure she will be married to Mr. Willoughby very soon." SS I 12 60 9
I am sure they will be married very soon, for he has got a SS I 12 60 11
hope;" said Mrs. Jennings, as soon as he entered the room. SS I 13 63 8
added her ladyship, "as soon as you can conveniently leave SS I 13 65 35
He drove through the park very fast, and they were soon SS I 13 67 60
As soon as they left the dining-room, Elinor enquired of SS I 13 68 67
than they were, and they may soon be entirely done away. SS I 15 80 41
of returning here soon, and yet aware that by declining SS I 15 81 43
Amongst the objects in the scene, they soon discovered an SS I 16 86 16
I knew how soon he would come." SS I 16 86 19
They were soon within thirty yards of the gentleman. SS I 16 86 20
satisfaction of seeing him soon become more like himself. SS I 17 90 1
observed Elinor, "and your difficulties will soon vanish." SS I 17 92 24
as far as she could, soon left them to themselves. SS I 18 96 2
Elinor sat down to her drawing-table as soon as he was out SS I 19 104 10
was roused one morning, soon after Edward's leaving them, SS I 19 105 13
She was sitting near the window, and as soon as Sir John SS I 19 105 13
Mrs. Jennings asked her, as soon as she appeared, if she SS I 19 108 35
And then sitting down again, she very soon forgot that SS I 19 108 36
"Why should they ask us?" said Marianne, as soon as they SS I 19 109 41
however we shall meet again in town very soon, I hope." SS I 20 110 2
The rest of the company soon dropt in. SS I 20 111 9
"Oh! my dear Miss Dashwood," said Mrs. Palmer soon SS I 20 112 29
as soon as their present engagements at Exeter were over. SS I 21 118 2
hearing that she was very soon to receive a visit from two SS I 21 118 2
Their manners were particularly civil, and Elinor soon SS I 21 120 6
And soon afterwards, on the second boy's violently SS I 21 121 8
"Poor little creature!" said Miss Steele, as soon as they SS I 21 122 11
And to be better acquainted therefore, Elinor soon found SS I 21 124 33
And I hope you may have as good luck yourself soon,--but SS I 21 125 35
of herself which soon became evident in the manners of SS I 22 127 1
the time may come--how soon it will come must depend upon SS I 22 129 11
a great while; and as soon as I saw you, I felt almost as SS I 22 132 42
herself; but other ideas, other considerations soon arose. SS II 1 139 1
Lucy on the subject, she soon felt an earnest wish of SS II 1 141 7
he should take orders as soon as he can, and then through SS II 2 149 25
Elinor was soon called to the card-table by the conclusion SS II 2 151 41
caution, and dismissed as soon as civility would allow; SS II 2 151 42
Mrs. Jennings soon came in. SS II 4 163 14
The former left them soon after tea to fulfil her evening SS II 4 166 31
to read; but the book was soon thrown aside, and she SS II 4 166 31
Frosts will soon set in, and in all probability with SS II 5 167 3
Mrs. Jennings soon appeared, and the note being given her, SS II 5 170 28
of destination, and as soon as the string of carriages SS II 6 175 2
She soon caught his eye, and he immediately bowed, but SS II 6 176 3
"Go to him, Elinor," she cried, as soon as she could speak, SS II 6 177 13
they departed as soon as the carriage could be found. SS II 6 178 16
She was soon undressed and in bed, and as she seemed SS II 6 178 16
"No, Elinor," she replied, "ask nothing; you will soon SS II 7 180 3
continuing her talk, as soon as Marianne disappeared, she SS II 7 181 7
8
Pray call again as soon as possible, and explain the SS II 7 187 40
But I will not suppose this possible, and I hope very soon SS II 7 187 40
only to deceive, let it be told as soon as possible. SS II 7 188 42
He is to me married very soon--a good-for-nothing fellow! SS II 8 192 3
into the dining room as soon as they were summoned to it. SS II 8 193 5
As soon, however, as the consciousness of all this was SS II 8 193 7
"Poor soul!" cried Mrs. Jennings, as soon as she was gone, SS II 8 194 8
Well, I shall spirit up the Colonel as soon as I can. SS II 8 197 22
persuasion, however, soon softened her to compliance, and SS II 8 197 25
she then repaired, she was soon joined by Mrs. Jennings, SS II 8 197 26
by the same thought; for, soon after his entrance, she SS II 8 198 30
the man still more:--as soon as the ceremony was over, SS II 8 199 37
He made no answer; and soon afterwards, by the removal of SS II 8 200 43

Context	Work	Vol	Ch	Page	Line
will suffer much, I am sure she will soon become easier.	SS	II	9	211	34
"No; as soon as she recovered from her lying-in, for I	SS	II	9	211	42
Recollecting, soon afterwards, that he was probably	SS	II	9	211	43
her sister, as they very soon were, the effect on her was	SS	II	10	212	1
She could soon tell at what coachmaker's the new carriage	SS	II	10	215	11
smallest emotion, but very soon to see them without	SS	II	10	215	14
fortune, to leave her card with her as soon as she married.	SS	II	10	215	14
conveyed to herself, as soon as it was known that the	SS	II	10	217	16
The Willoughbys left town as soon as they were married;	SS	II	10	217	18
John Dashwood very soon, and bring her sisters to see her.	SS	II	11	223	14
Brandon's coming in soon after himself, he eyed him with a	SS	II	11	223	14
As soon as they were out of the house, his enquiries began.	SS	II	11	223	15
other day, as soon as we came to town, aware that money	SS	II	11	224	28
know much about horses, he soon set him down as a very	SS	II	11	228	52
she would not give, soon flowed from another quarter.	SS	II	12	229	4
give them--a dinner; and soon after their acquaintance	SS	II	12	230	6
anticipated the party, was soon afterwards increased, more	SS	II	12	230	7
to the Miss Steeles, as soon as the Dashwoods' invitation	SS	II	12	230	8
Brandon in a low voice, as soon as he could secure his	SS	II	12	236	43
Palmer soon after she arrived, carried Mrs. Jennings away.	SS	II	13	238	3
"My dear friend," cried Lucy as soon as they were by	SS	II	13	238	4
though she soon perceived them to be narrowly watching her.	SS	II	13	241	20
Her exertions did not stop her; for she soon afterwards	SS	II	13	241	23
perfectly satisfied, and soon talked of something else. "	SS	II	13	243	32
to Edward, that he very soon got up to go away.	SS	II	13	244	41
"Going so soon!" said Marianne; "my dear Edward, this must	SS	II	13	244	42
had his visit lasted two hours, soon afterwards went away.	SS	II	13	244	43
thither every morning as soon as she was dressed, and did	SS	II	14	246	2
She perceived him soon afterwards looking at herself, and	SS	II	14	250	11
Harley-Street, as soon as Lady Middleton could spare them.	SS	II	14	253	26
over directly, and as soon as ever he saw the child, he	SS	III	1	257	5
like any fury, and soon drove her into a fainting fit.	SS	III	1	259	7
for she was sent for as soon as ever my cousins left the	SS	III	1	259	7
no other subject, Elinor soon saw the necessity of	SS	III	1	260	10
with great solemnity, as soon as he was seated, "of the	SS	III	1	265	34
Marianne's indignation burst forth as soon as he quitted	SS	III	1	269	58
and Marianne's courage soon failed her, in trying to	SS	III	2	270	1
inquiry to her cousins as soon as she could; and nothing	SS	III	2	270	3
An intimate acquaintance of Mrs. Jennings joined them soon	SS	III	2	271	5
to say, and therefore soon judged it expedient to find her	SS	III	2	272	13
by what passed, that as soon as he had went away from his	SS	III	2	273	16
"Edward talks of going to Oxford soon," said she, "but now	SS	III	2	275	22
as soon as he can light upon a Bishop, he will be ordained.	SS	III	2	275	22
As soon as they returned to the carriage, Mrs. Jennings	SS	III	2	276	27
As soon as Elinor had finished it, she performed what she	SS	III	2	278	31
it;--and if so, she had soon afterwards good reason to	SS	III	3	280	9
calm voice, "I am afraid it cannot take place very soon."	SS	III	3	281	9
					10
breaking up the conference soon afterwards, and moving	SS	III	3	281	13
					14
least, I am afraid it cannot take place very soon.--"	SS	III	3	284	23
sagaciously smiling, as soon as the gentleman had	SS	III	4	285	1
not foresee that the opportunity would so very soon occur."	SS	III	4	285	4
a thing, somehow or other he will soon find an opportunity.	SS	III	4	285	5
as soon as he could say any thing, after taking a chair.	SS	III	4	288	26
that I should soon have the pleasure of meeting you again.	SS	III	4	288	27
she so much dreaded as soon as possible, "without	SS	III	4	288	28
James's-Street," said he, soon afterwards, rising from his	SS	III	4	290	40
					41
that she reverted to it again as soon as Elinor appeared.	SS	III	4	291	46
"Well, and how soon will he be ready?--	SS	III	4	291	49
might have got I dare say--fourteen hundred pounds.	SS	III	5	295	12
I offered immediately, as soon as my mother related the	SS	III	5	299	37
and her sister were so soon to leave town, as she hoped to	SS	III	5	300	38
was to join them at Cleveland soon after their arrival.	SS	III	6	301	3
by the family in general, soon procured herself a book.	SS	III	6	304	12
of its performance; and as soon as she had rung up the	SS	III	7	311	14
that all relief might soon be in vain, that every thing	SS	III	7	312	18
with unfeigned joy, and soon with unequivocal cheerfulness,	SS	III	7	314	23
and I had determined, as soon as I could engage her alone,	SS	III	8	321	34
The struggle was great--but it ended too soon.	SS	III	8	323	40
"Did you tell her that you should soon return?"	SS	III	8	324	44
I ran away from you all as soon as I could; but not before	SS	III	8	327	55
My resolution was soon made, and at eight o'clock this	SS	III	8	331	69
in proportion, as she soon acknowledged within herself--to	SS	III	9	333	2
As soon as Mrs. Dashwood had recovered herself, to see	SS	III	9	334	5
It was thus imparted to her, as soon as any opportunity of	SS	III	9	335	7
His own merits must soon secure it."	SS	III	9	337	18
known to others; and she soon discovered in his melancholy	SS	III	10	340	2
and Colonel Brandon was soon brought, by their united	SS	III	10	341	4
As for Willoughby--to say that I shall soon or that I	SS	III	10	347	30
must do all, soon found herself leading to the fact.	SS	III	10	347	32
As soon as they entered the house, Marianne with a kiss of	SS	III	10	348	34
poor; and probably would soon have learnt to rank the	SS	III	11	351	13
They will soon be back again, and then they'd be sure and	SS	III	11	354	38
now alike needless, were soon afterwards dismissed.	SS	III	11	355	45
That he should be married so soon, before (as she imagined)	SS	III	12	357	2
But she soon saw how likely it was that Lucy, in her self-	SS	III	12	357	2
They would soon, she supposed, be settled at Delaford.--	SS	III	12	357	3
She almost ran out of the room, and as soon as the door	SS	III	12	360	26
How soon he had walked himself into the proper resolution,	SS	III	13	361	3
resolution, however, how soon an opportunity of exercising	SS	III	13	361	3
as soon as he had learnt to consider it with desire.	SS	III	13	361	3
few months, I should very soon have outgrown the fancied	SS	III	13	362	5
and endless flatteries, as soon as the smallest opening	SS	III	14	375	10
he erred;--for though Lucy soon gave him hopes that his	SS	III	14	376	11
other, and in which she soon betrayed an interest even	SS	III	14	376	11
its graciousness, and led soon afterwards, by rapid	SS	III	14	377	11
and his punishment was soon afterwards complete in the	SS	III	14	379	18
his visits & soon after marrying somebody else.--	W			316	2
I suppose I shall know him as soon as I enter the ball-	W			319	2
should drive me over, as soon as I had made tea for him; &	W			319	2
Emma was soon left to know what they could be, by eliz.'s	W			322	3
Emma was shewn to a very comfortable apartment, & as soon	W			323	3
neighbours ensued--& as soon as they were all duely placed	W			327	8
at one end of it began soon to give way; the inspiriting	W			328	8
ver lively consultation--& soon afterwards she saw the	W			330	11
"Let us see you soon at the castle; & bring me word how	W			335	13
dear Miss Edwards--how soon it is at an end!--	W			336	14
Emma, said Miss W., as soon as they were alone, you must	W			341	19
once they had the inclination, the means wd soon follow."--	W			345	21
settled something on you, as soon as her husband died."	W			351	26
affair was so settled, as soon as she could be persuaded	W			361	30
and therefore you must visit him as soon as he comes."	PP	I	1	4	18
The rest of the evening was spent in conjecturing how soon	PP	I	2	8	28
An invitation to dinner was soon afterwards dispatched;	PP	I	3	9	4
he could have in town so soon after his arrival in	PP	I	3	10	4
for the ball; and a report soon followed that Mr. Bingley	PP	I	3	10	4
but his friend Mr. Darcy soon drew the attention of the	PP	I	3	10	5
Mr. Bingley had soon made himself acquainted with all the	PP	I	3	10	6
he soon found that he had a very different story to hear.	PP	I	3	12	15
no stiffness, he had soon felt acquainted with all the	PP	I	4	16	15
The ladies of Longbourn soon waited on those of	PP	I	6	21	1
being impertinent myself, I shall soon grow afraid of him."	PP	I	6	24	16
On his approaching them soon afterwards, though without	PP	I	6	24	17
					18
"It will be her turn soon to be teazed," said Miss Lucas.	PP	I	6	24	21
Come as soon as you can on the receipt of this.	PP	I	7	30	17
began abusing her as soon as she was out of the room.	PP	I	8	35	3
I hope it will soon be increased by seeing her quite well."	PP	I	8	37	25
for her book; and soon laying it wholly aside, she drew	PP	I	8	38	39
As all conversation was thereby at an end, Elizabeth soon	PP	I	8	40	55
girls, reached Netherfield soon after the family breakfast.	PP	I	9	41	1
was satisfied, and soon afterwards ordered her carriage.	PP	I	9	45	35
a lively Scotch air; and soon afterwards Mr. Darcy,	PP	I	10	51	47
					48
and Mr. Hurst soon found even his open petition rejected.	PP	I	11	54	3
a settled thing; and as soon as Nicholls has made white	PP	I	11	55	7
Miss Bingley made no answer; and soon afterwards got up	PP	I	11	56	10
them," said he, as soon as she allowed him to speak.	PP	I	11	56	15
I cannot forget the follies and vices of others so soon as	PP	I	11	58	28
that they were to go so soon, and repeatedly tried to	PP	I	12	59	3
may turn you all out of this house as soon as he pleases."	PP	I	13	61	6
She had even condescended to advise him to marry as soon	PP	I	14	66	1
on her to hint, was likely to be very soon engaged."	PP	I	15	71	3
soon done--done while Mrs. Bennet was stirring the fire.	PP	I	15	71	4
and trusted that she might soon have two daughters married;	PP	I	15	71	5
But the attention of every lady was soon caught by a young	PP	I	15	72	8
of one stranger was soon put an end to by exclamations and	PP	I	15	73	11
among her neighbours as soon as she could. to the girls,	PP	I	16	75	3
of lottery tickets, she soon grew too much interested in	PP	I	16	76	8
The whist party soon afterwards breaking up, the players	PP	I	16	82	49
They were soon gone again, rising from their seats with an	PP	I	17	86	9
The idea soon reached to conviction, as she observed his	PP	I	17	88	14
seen for a week, she was soon able to make a voluntary	PP	I	18	90	4
far from the subject, as soon afterwards appeared by her	PP	I	18	93	32
feeling towards her, which soon procured her pardon, and	PP	I	18	94	43
that Jane would be soon married to Mr. Bingley.--	PP	I	18	98	63
that Lady Lucas might soon be equally fortunate, though	PP	I	18	99	63
of seeing the whole family soon at Longbourn; and	PP	I	18	103	76
younger girls together, soon after breakfast, he addressed	PP	I	19	104	1
					2
wisest to get it over as soon and as quietly as possible,	PP	I	19	104	7
Mrs. Bennet and Kitty walked off, and as soon as they were	PP	I	19	105	7
Almost as soon as I entered the house I singled you out as	PP	I	19	105	8
Find such a woman as soon as you can, bring her to	PP	I	19	106	10
I will go directly to Mr. Bennet, and we shall very soon	PP	I	20	111	5
I shall be glad to have the library to myself as soon as	PP	I	20	112	22
Soon after their return, a letter was delivered to Miss	PP	I	21	116	6
Jane recollected herself soon, and putting the letter away,	PP	I	21	116	6
Jane must soon cease to regard it, in the enjoyment of his.	PP	I	21	116	8
and had soon the pleasure of seeing its happy effect.	PP	I	21	120	29
that Mr. Bingley would be soon down again and soon dining	PP	I	21	120	30
be soon down again and soon dining at Longbourn, and the	PP	I	21	120	30
if he had not been to leave Hertfordshire so very soon.	PP	I	22	121	1
cared not how soon that establishment were gained.	PP	I	22	122	2
that I shall avail myself of it as soon as possible."	PP	I	22	123	5
Miss Lucas called soon after breakfast, and in a private	PP	I	22	124	11
than she expected, she soon regained her composure, and	PP	I	22	124	14
					15
wished it to take place as soon as possible, which he	PP	I	23	128	10
out of the house, as soon as Mr. Bennet were dead.	PP	I	23	130	16
Elizabeth, to whom Jane very soon communicated the chief	PP	II	1	133	3
With a stronger voice she soon added, "I have this comfort	PP	II	1	134	8
Mr. Collins returned into Hertfordshire soon after it had	PP	II	3	145	11
Elizabeth soon heard from her friend; and their	PP	II	3	146	19
I dare say I shall soon see them here."	PP	II	3	147	23
Let me hear from you very soon.	PP	II	3	149	26
hoped he might really soon marry Mr. Darcy's sister, as,	PP	II	3	149	27
but Charlotte, she soon found, was depending on the plan,	PP	II	4	151	1
his attentions towards her, so soon after this event."	PP	II	4	153	14
into the house; and as soon as they were in the parlour,	PP	II	5	155	3
A lively imagination soon settled it all.	PP	II	5	158	10
it should be given so soon, was such an instance of Lady	PP	II	6	160	1
and deportment she soon found some resemblance of Mr.	PP	II	6	162	12
As soon as they had driven from the door, Elizabeth was	PP	II	6	166	42
Collins, and he was very soon obliged to take her	PP	II	6	167	42
pleasanter aspect; but she soon saw that her friend had an	PP	II	7	168	1
Elizabeth soon perceived that though this great lady was	PP	II	7	169	4
In this quiet way, the first fortnight of her visit soon	PP	II	7	169	6
Elizabeth had heard soon after her arrival, that Mr. Darcy	PP	II	7	170	6
His arrival was soon known at the parsonage, for Mr.	PP	II	7	170	7
Mr. Darcy would never have come so soon to wait upon me."	PP	II	7	170	8
The subject was pursued no farther, and the gentlemen soon	PP	II	7	171	12
His eyes had been soon and repeatedly turned towards them	PP	II	8	172	3
					4
see you all after him so soon; for, if I recollect right,	PP	II	9	177	4
to give it up, as soon as any eligible purchase offers."	PP	II	9	178	10
He took the hint, and soon began with, "this seems a very	PP	II	9	178	12
side calm and concise--and soon put an end to by the	PP	II	9	179	26
meaning of this!" said Charlotte, as soon as he was gone.	PP	II	9	179	27
with what had passed, she soon afterwards said, "I imagine	PP	II	10	184	16
					17
There, shut into her own room, as soon as their visitor	PP	II	10	186	38
But this idea was soon banished, and her spirits were very	PP	II	11	188	3
had not attempted to deny, soon overcame the pity which	PP	II	11	193	31
employment, she resolved soon after breakfast to indulge	PP	II	12	195	1
side, and she soon passed one of the gates into the ground.	PP	II	12	195	1
again into the plantation, and was soon out of sight.	PP	II	12	195	2
of both, cannot be too soon forgotten; and the effort	PP	II	12	196	4
am certain, remember, with the design of soon returning.--	PP	II	12	198	5
coincidence of feeling was soon discovered; and, alike	PP	II	12	198	5
family living might be his as soon as it became vacant.	PP	II	12	200	5
The business was therefore soon settled.	PP	II	12	201	5
were in a line which soon brought to her recollection that	PP	II	13	208	9
like to go home again so soon, she added, "but if that is	PP	II	14	211	5
					6
There can be no occasion for your going so soon.	PP	II	14	211	8
Mr. Darcy's letter, she was in a fair way of soon knowing	PP	II	14	212	17
I shall pull it to pieces as soon as I get home, and see	PP	II	16	219	3
As soon as all had ate, and the elder ones paid, the	PP	II	16	220	16
Jane will be quite an old maid soon, I declare.	PP	II	16	221	17
and then they soon found out what was the matter."	PP	II	16	221	17
Miss Bennet's astonishment was soon lessened by the strong	PP	II	17	224	2
which will probably soon drive away his regard for me.	PP	II	17	224	4
Wickham will soon be gone; and therefore it will not	PP	II	17	226	23
"Well, Lizzy," continued her mother soon afterwards, "and	PP	II	17	228	31
The first week of their return was soon gone.	PP	II	18	229	1
her life, she will soon be beyond the reach of amendment.	PP	II	18	231	18
for the inclination he soon testified of renewing those	PP	II	18	233	25
With an air of indifference he soon afterwards added, "how	PP	II	18	233	27
her temper to be happy; and all was soon right again.	PP	II	19	239	8
of her master, soon led again to the subject; and she	PP	III	1	249	37
The conversation soon turned upon fishing, and she heard	PP	III	1	255	60
They soon outstripped the others, and when they had	PP	III	1	257	65
guarded, enquiry; and they soon drew from those enquiries	PP	III	2	261	6
On this point she was soon satisfied; and two or three	PP	III	2	262	8
the housekeeper; and they soon became sensible, that the	PP	III	2	264	14
With respect to Wickham, the travellers soon found that he	PP	III	2	265	15
Mr. Gardiner left them soon after breakfast.	PP	III	2	266	18
Elizabeth soon saw that she was herself closely watched by	PP	III	3	268	5
and peaches, soon collected them round the table.	PP	III	3	268	6
Elizabeth's collected behaviour, however, soon quieted his	PP	III	3	270	11
a beauty!--I should as soon call her mother a wit.'	PP	III	3	271	16
					17
Colonel Forster gives us reason to expect him here soon.	PP	III	4	274	3
begging you all to come here, as soon as possible.	PP	III	4	275	5
Elizabeth soon observed, and instantly understood it.	PP	III	4	278	19
was bringing on them all, soon swallowed up every private	PP	III	4	278	20
Elizabeth was soon lost to every thing else; and, after a	PP	III	4	278	20
They were to be off as soon as possible.	PP	III	4	280	26
and they soon found that Jane had no intelligence to give.	PP	III	5	287	33
As soon as I get to town, I shall go to my brother, and	PP	III	5	288	37
In the dining-room they were soon joined by Mary and Kitty,	PP	III	5	289	41

To Elizabeth with a countenance of grave reflection, soon PP III 5 289 41
42
at your surprise tomorrow morning, as soon as I am missed. PP III 5 291 60
to return to Longbourn, as soon as he could, to the great PP III 6 294 2
to leave London, and promised to write again very soon. PP III 6 295 5
It will pass away soon enough." PP III 6 299 21
of running as Elizabeth, soon lagged behind, while her PP III 7 301 7
8
Soon after you left me on Saturday, I was fortunate enough PP III 7 302 14
Send back your answer as soon as you can, and be careful PP III 7 303 14
I shall write again as soon as any thing more is PP III 7 303 14
"No; but it must be done soon." PP III 7 303 18
cried Elizabeth, as soon as they were by themselves. PP III 7 304 34
As soon as Jane had read Mr. Gardiner's hope of Lydia's PP III 7 305 43
hope of Lydia's being soon married, her joy burst forth, PP III 7 305 43
"I will go to Meryton," said she, "as soon as I am dressed, PP III 7 307 49
and to discharge the obligation as soon as he could. PP III 8 308 2
This son was to join in cutting off the entail, as soon as PP III 8 308 3
His letter was soon dispatched; for though dilatory in PP III 8 309 5
Mr. Bennet was firm: it soon led to another; and Mrs. PP III 8 310 10
of the other, was soon to be formed in their family. PP III 8 312 16
Mr. Gardiner soon wrote again to his brother. PP III 8 312 18
do so," he added, "as soon as his marriage was fixed on. PP III 8 312 19
husband at Longbourn, as soon as they were married, that PP III 8 314 22
it was settled, that as soon as the ceremony was over, PP III 8 314 22
She then joined them soon enough to see Lydia, with PP III 9 317 9
One morning, soon after their arrival, as she was sitting PP III 9 318 21
22
an answer to her letter, as soon as she possibly could. PP III 10 321 1
to her for intelligence of him, as soon as he got to town. PP III 10 322 2
return to her friends as soon as they could be prevailed PP III 10 322 2
It was not all settled before Monday: as soon as it was, PP III 10 324 2
considerations, and she soon felt that even her vanity was PP III 10 326 3
Elizabeth hoped she had silenced him; but he soon PP III 10 328 15
16
of my duty, and the exertion would soon have been nothing. PP III 10 328 28
The day of his and Lydia's departure soon came, and Mrs. PP III 11 330 2
"He is as fine a fellow," said Mr. Bennet, as soon as they PP III 11 330 8
If that had been nearer, she would not have gone so soon." PP III 11 331 12
to Elizabeth; but now, as soon as they were alone together, PP III 11 331 16
17
"As soon as ever Mr. Bingley comes, my dear," said Mrs. PP III 11 332 22
We must have Mrs. Long and the Gouldings soon. PP III 11 333 26
no compensation, received soon afterwards material relief, PP III 11 337 56
to take a family dinner with us, as soon as you returned. PP III 11 338 58
As soon as they were gone, Elizabeth walked out to recover PP III 12 339 1
was then hoping to be soon joined by him, when all her PP III 12 342 26
"Well girls," said she, as soon as they were left to PP III 12 342 28
"We will be down as soon as we can," said Jane; "but I PP III 13 344 8
you know;" said her mother as soon as she was in the hall. PP III 13 345 16
room for that purpose soon after tea; for as the others PP III 13 346 21
simpered and smiled, and hoped her turn was coming soon. PP III 13 348 34
for the night; but as soon as he was gone, he turned to PP III 13 348 35
36
I remember, as soon as ever I saw him, when he first came PP III 13 348 40
Her younger sisters soon began to make interest with her PP III 13 349 41
man, who I believe will soon become a part of the family." PP III 14 352 8
As soon as they entered the copse, Lady Catherine began in PP III 14 353 22
23
in all likelihood, be soon afterwards united to my nephew, PP III 14 353 26
and hand, I shall soon cease to regret him at all." PP III 15 361 4
young couple into your house as soon as they were married. PP III 15 363 22
Bingley and Jane, however, soon allowed the others to PP III 16 365 1
She soon learnt that they were indebted for their present PP III 16 367 9
"Did it," said he, "did it soon make you think better of PP III 16 368 18
I was angry perhaps at first, but my anger soon began to PP III 16 369 28
How soon any other wishes introduced themselves I can PP III 16 370 32
of that interruption, she soon learnt that his resolution PP III 16 370 33
When I went away, I felt that it would soon happen." PP III 16 370 38
received from Jane as soon as she entered the room, and PP III 17 372 1
soon satisfied Jane by her solemn assurances of attachment. PP III 17 373 17
As soon as they entered, Bingley looked at her so PP III 17 374 22
good information; and he soon afterwards said aloud, "Mr. PP III 17 374 22
In the evening soon after Mr. Bennet withdrew to the PP III 17 375 28
such an effusion was heard only by herself, soon went away. PP III 17 378 44
with him; and Mr. Bennet soon assured her that he was PP III 17 379 47
Elizabeth's spirits soon rising to playfulness again, she PP III 18 380 1
You must write again very soon, and praise him a great PP III 18 382 21
Elizabeth will soon be the wife of Mr. Darcy. PP III 18 383 23
The reason of this sudden removal was soon evident. PP III 18 383 26
His affection for her soon sunk into indifference; her's PP III 19 387 8
make the proposal; and, as soon as matters are settled, I MP I 1 7 8
as a matter of prudence, soon grew into a matter of choice, MP I 1 8 9
want of it, they were soon able to take a full survey of MP I 2 12 3
The fatigue too, of so long a journey, became soon no MP I 2 13 4
plan; and it was pretty soon decided between them, that MP I 2 18 23
but William determining, soon after her removal, to be a MP I 2 21 34
quickly as possible, could soon with cheerful selfishness MP I 3 24 4
he might be, would, in all probability, die very soon. MP I 3 24 4
and, plied well with good things, would soon pop off." MP I 3 24 5
As soon as she met with Edmund, she told him her distress. MP I 3 25 17
white house, I suppose, as soon as she is removed there." MP I 3 25 20
Lady Bertram soon brought the matter to a certainty, by MP I 3 28 38
39
"Oh! that will soon be settled. MP I 3 30 55
for their family, he soon grew reconciled to a distinction, MP I 3 30 57
Fanny soon learnt how unnecessary had been her fears of a MP I 3 31 58
They had their faults, and Mrs. Norris soon found them out. MP I 3 31 59
invite him to Mansfield as soon as the squadron to which MP I 3 33 64
and Lady Bertram was soon astonished to find how very well MP I 4 34 1
made up his mind, the whole business was soon completed. MP I 4 37 8
and being inclined to marry, soon fancied himself in love. MP I 4 38 10
most hearty concurrence was conveyed as soon as possible. MP I 4 40 14
her own marriage had been soon followed by the death of MP I 4 40 15
The scheme was soon repeated to Henry. MP I 4 42 18
body should marry as soon as they can do it to advantage." MP I 4 43 27
and their acquaintance soon promised as early an intimacy MP I 5 44 1
was so well made, that one soon forgot he was plain; and MP I 5 44 2
Miss Crawford soon felt, that he and his situation might MP I 5 48 28
together at the park soon after his going, she retook her MP I 6 52 1
excessively pretty, it was soon found necessary to be MP I 6 57 31
instrument, and hoped to be soon allowed to hear her. MP I 6 59 40
have a listener, and every thing was soon in a fair train. MP I 7 64 12
which the former caught soon after her being settled at MP I 7 66 14
Her feelings for one and the other were soon a little MP I 7 68 17
"My dear Miss Price," said Miss Crawford, as soon as she MP I 7 68 18
in her exercise, she would not be knocked up so soon. MP I 7 73 55
losses both of health and pleasure would be soon made good. MP I 8 75 1
Wednesday was fine, and soon after breakfast the barouche MP I 8 80 29
never been extensive, was soon beyond her knowledge, and MP I 8 80 31
"Yes, I shall take orders soon after my father's return-- MP I 9 89 28
The chapel was soon afterwards left to the silence and MP I 9 89 30
Mr. Crawford was soon followed by Miss Bertram and Mr. MP I 9 90 36
Every sort of exercise fatigues her so soon, Miss Crawford, MP I 9 95 68
"I shall soon be rested," said Fanny; "to sit in the shade MP I 9 96 72
to the knoll, they were soon beyond her eye; and for some MP I 10 100 23
had tempted them very soon after their leaving her, and MP I 10 103 49
Dinner was soon followed by tea and coffee, a ten miles' MP I 10 104 52
from Antigua, which soon afterwards reached Mansfield. MP I 11 107 1
and of having his eyes soon turned like her's towards the MP I 11 112 35
should come back again so soon, after being here so long MP I 12 115 5
"My dear Tom," cried his aunt soon afterwards, "as you are MP I 12 119 23
posture, and voice, as soon as Lady Bertram began to nod MP I 13 126 23
was turning over the first act, soon settled the business. MP I 14 133 11
them; but her brother soon returned to business and MP I 14 136 21
to have them roused as soon as possible by the MP I 14 137 23
Miss Crawford accepted the part very readily, and soon MP I 15 138 1
Anhalt a very stupid fellow, he soon decided for the count. MP I 15 138 1
by Mr. Yates, and followed soon afterwards by Mr. MP I 15 139 11
Nobody was at the trouble of an answer; the others soon MP I 15 142 23
had soon talked away all that could be said of either. MP I 15 142 24
Tom, Maria, and Mr. Yates, soon after their being MP I 15 142 25
and Henry Crawford was soon seated with the other three at MP I 15 143 26
Miss Crawford talked of something else, and soon MP I 15 144 36
she had recourse, as soon as she was dressed, to another MP I 16 150 1
exceedingly; and as soon as I am gone, you will empty your MP I 16 156 27
amongst them, as she soon began to acknowledge herself.-- MP I 17 160 7
few repulses; and becoming soon too busy with his play to MP I 17 160 9
"I dare say he will be in Parliament soon. MP I 17 161 14
must be done, and as soon as the play is all over, we will MP I 17 162 18
had soon all the terror of other complaints from him.-- MP I 18 164 2
so am I still;-- and as soon as I am a little more at MP I 18 167 7
8
return for that purpose as soon as they could after dinner; MP I 18 171 25
All were alert and impatient; the ladies moved soon, the MP I 18 171 25
moved soon, the gentlemen soon followed them, and with the MP I 18 171 25
hand to his heart, and as soon as she could notice this, MP II 1 175 2
The Crawfords laughed at the idea; and having soon agreed MP II 1 177 5
Too soon did she find herself at the drawing-room door, MP II 1 177 7
"The all will be soon told," cried Tom hastily, and with MP II 1 181 16
you will take a day's sport there yourself, sir, soon." MP II 1 181 16
subsided; but when tea was soon afterwards brought in, and MP II 1 181 17
Mr. Yates took the subject from his friend as soon as MP II 1 184 27
been forgotten himself as soon as he could, after the MP II 2 187 2
But, however, I soon found it would not do; he was bent MP II 2 189 5
Sir Thomas soon appeared, and Maria saw with delight and MP II 2 192 11
To her he soon turned, repeating much of what he had MP II 2 193 18
for general civilities soon called his notice from her, MP II 2 193 18
could prevent him from soon discerning some part of the MP II 3 200 19
She must escape from him and Mansfield as soon as possible, MP II 3 202 25
The principals being all agreed in this respect, it soon MP II 3 202 27
questions about it, which soon led to an acknowledgment of MP II 4 206 5
And following the latter train of thought, she soon MP II 4 208 12
Miss Crawford however, with renewed animation, soon went MP II 4 210 20
21
independence, it was soon settled that if nothing were MP II 4 215 47
I will ask Sir Thomas, as soon as he comes in, whether I MP II 5 217 8
The good news soon followed her. MP II 5 219 24
and when Sir Thomas, soon afterwards, just opening the MP II 5 221 35
I ought to wear it as soon as I could, and that I might MP II 5 222 43
She was soon aware of this herself; for though she must MP II 5 223 48
by the two sisters, was soon in possession of his mind, MP II 5 223 48
instructions about the living he is to step into so soon. MP II 5 226 61
The assurance of Edmund's being so soon to take orders, MP II 5 227 69
Her brother gave only a smile to this accusation, and soon MP II 6 230 7
her very soon to dislike him less than formerly. MP II 6 231 11
This dear William would soon be amongst them. MP II 6 233 14
for his arrival, came as soon as possible; and scarcely MP II 6 233 14
the hall as soon as the noises of the arrival reached them. MP II 6 233 15
William and Fanny soon shewed themselves; and Sir Thomas MP II 6 233 16
was decided on almost as soon as whist; and Lady Bertram MP II 7 239 4
as whist; and Lady Bertram soon found herself in the MP II 7 239 4
As soon as a general buz gave him shelter, he added, in a MP II 7 245 31
as I trust you may soon have more convenient opportunities MP II 7 245 34
that thornton was so soon and so completely to be his home, MP II 7 248 47
"Yes, very;--only I am soon tired." MP II 7 250 58
There was comfort, however, soon at hand. MP II 8 253 4
of the business; and as soon as she would listen quietly, MP II 8 253 7
a very short time, as soon as the variety of business MP II 8 255 10
Miss Crawford was soon to leave Mansfield, and on this MP II 8 255 12
upstairs, and were soon deep in the interesting subject. MP II 8 257 15
in town by several days so soon as I expected; and I have MP II 9 261 2
days often volunteer, for soon after breakfast a very MP II 9 265 21
believed he had soon ceased to think of her countenance. MP II 9 268 27
her leaving the room again soon afterwards, he spoke of MP II 10 272 1
From a variety of causes she was happy, and she was soon MP II 10 272 4
The gentlemen joined them; and soon after began the sweet MP II 10 273 6
The stiffness of the meeting soon gave way before their MP II 10 273 8
niece, and she was soon said to be admired by Mr. Crawford. MP II 10 276 13
than his Lady Did, soon afterwards, when Mary, perceiving MP II 10 276 14
asked by him again so very soon, and she wished she had MP II 10 278 20
fan as if for life:--"how soon she is knocked up! MP II 10 279 23
How can you be tired so soon?" MP II 10 279 23
"So soon! my good friend," said Sir Thomas, producing his MP II 10 279 24
The ball was over--and the breakfast was soon over too; MP II 11 282 1
Soon after the second breakfast, Edmund bad them good bye MP II 11 282 4
He would soon be always gone; and she was thankful that MP II 11 284 8
I am looking for Henry every day, and as soon as he comes MP II 11 287 22
"The Miss Owens," said she soon afterwards--"suppose you MP II 11 289 34
spirit from the blush soon produced from such a look, only MP II 11 290 38
"Lucky, lucky girl!" cried Mary as soon as she could speak- MP II 12 292 7
As soon as her eagerness could rest in silence, he was as MP II 12 293 16
My uncle ought to know it as soon as possible." MP II 13 300 7
would be quite distressing to her to see him again so soon. MP II 13 303 12
Mr. Crawford was not only in the room; he was soon close MP II 13 303 14
income, settled as soon after four and twenty as he can. MP III 1 317 34
a trifle again; but she soon found, from the voluntary MP III 1 322 51
any; but her aunt was soon quarrelling with her: and when MP III 1 323 53
thing would soon be as if no such subject had existed. MP III 1 324 59
London would soon bring its cure. MP III 1 324 59
In London he would soon learn to wonder at his infatuation, MP III 1 324 59
of hopes, her uncle was soon after tea called out of the MP III 1 324 60
Sir Thomas was soon able to depend on it himself. MP III 2 329 11
He leaves Northamptonshire so soon, that even this slight MP III 2 331 16
"Well, Fanny," said she, as soon as they were alone MP III 2 332 23
And still pursuing the same cheerful thoughts, she soon MP III 2 333 28
William's promotion, with all its particulars, he was soon MP III 3 334 3
who assured him, as soon as he mentioned the name of MP III 3 336 10
said her ladyship soon afterwards--"and I will tell you MP III 3 338 19
be won by them nearly so soon, without the assistance of MP III 3 340 24
to be in your senses as soon as you can, by a different MP III 4 352 44
How was I to have an attachment at his service, as soon as MP III 4 353 45
imagine a woman so very soon capable of returning an MP III 4 353 45
On this principle, he soon afterwards observed, "they go MP III 4 354 48
said to her tolerably soon, in a low voice, "I must speak MP III 5 357 5
"I shall see your cousin in town soon; he talks of being MP III 5 364 32
of being there tolerably soon; and Sir Thomas, I dare say, MP III 5 364 32
He was to go to town, as soon as some business relative to MP III 6 367 4
their return; and he was soon afterwards able to account MP III 6 368 7
soon be what mother and daughter ought to be to each other. MP III 6 371 17
evening to write to her soon and often, and promising to MP III 6 373 26
and that you will not hear so soon from any other quarter." MP III 6 373 26
of being with William, soon produced their natural effect MP III 7 375 1
himself the next step as soon as possible, or speculations MP III 7 375 2
own inconvenience, in being obliged to hurry away so soon. MP III 7 378 11
Perhaps you would like some tea, as soon as it can be got." MP III 7 379 14
and tell her to bring in the tea-things as soon as she can. MP III 7 379 15
soon, seemed very much inclined to forget her again. MP III 7 380 22
a noise; and both boys had soon burst away from her, and MP III 7 381 25
William was soon calling out from the landing-place of the MP III 7 381 26
the others, there were soon only her father and herself MP III 7 382 28
heart were soon the better for such well-timed kindness. MP III 7 384 33
Anxious not to appear unhappy, she soon recovered herself: MP III 7 384 35
get tolerable servants?"--soon led her mind away from MP III 7 385 38

She soon learnt to think with respect of her own little	MP III 7 387 47
morning, the hope of soon seeing William again, and the	MP III 8 388 1
of being of consequence to her soon fell to the ground.	MP III 8 389 4
The instinct of nature was soon satisfied, and Mrs.	MP III 8 389 4
Their sister soon despaired of making the smallest	MP III 8 391 8
a Baronet's family, were soon offended by what they termed	MP III 9 395 3
not wonderful; and Fanny soon became more disposed to	MP III 9 395 4
Her greatest wonder on the subject soon became--not that	MP III 9 397 8
producing nothing, he soon proceeded to a positive	MP III 10 401 10
It was soon pain upon pain, confusion upon confusion; for	MP III 10 401 11
He must soon give her up, and cease to have the smallest	MP III 10 402 11
Fanny, as they were very soon joined by a brother lounger	MP III 10 403 15
too pointed of his hoping soon to have an assistant, a	MP III 10 404 15
that shrunk from it would soon be quite unpardonable.	MP III 10 406 20
Nay, had she been without his arm, she would soon have	MP III 11 409 6
beauty of the weather, would soon have been knocked up now.	MP III 11 409 6
I have half an idea of going into Norfolk again soon.	MP III 11 411 20
good as to say that--I suppose I shall soon hear from him."	MP III 11 412 27
desires her best love, and hopes to hear from you soon.	MP III 13 423 2
She was soon more softened and sorrowful.--	MP III 13 425 5
to her niece, and being so soon to lose all the benefit of	MP III 13 425 6
Instead of being soon well enough to follow his friends,	MP III 13 426 10
the poor sufferer will soon be able to bear the removal	MP III 13 426 11
distressing circumstances, I will write again very soon."	MP III 13 426 11
now awakened in the maternal bosom was not soon over.	MP III 13 427 13
of course he would soon be well again; Lady Bertram could	MP III 14 429 1
The end of April was coming on; it would soon be almost	MP III 14 430 6
"Forgive me, my dear Fanny, as soon as you can, for my	MP III 14 433 13
To be going so soon, sent for so kindly, sent for as a	MP III 15 443 24
His great object was to be off as soon as possible.	MP III 15 445 29
combine, she was soon able to understand quite as much as	MP III 16 449 7
Very soon after the Rushworths' return to Wimpole Street,	MP III 16 450 8
At last, "now, Fanny," said he, "I shall soon have done.	MP III 16 457 30
As soon as I could speak, I replied that I had not	MP III 16 457 30
At this rate, you will soon reform every body at Mansfield	MP III 16 458 30
hoped that she might soon learn to think more justly, and	MP III 16 458 30
I quit such odious subjects as soon as I can, impatient to	MP III 17 461 1
Here was comfort indeed! and quite as soon as Sir Thomas	MP III 17 462 5
she had been tolerably soon in a fair way of not thinking	MP III 17 466 18
animated perseverance had soon re-established the sort of	MP III 17 468 21
consequent wishes, she was soon welcome, and useful to all;	MP III 17 472 31
of restraint or alarm, soon grew as dear to her heart, and	MP III 17 473 33
unreserve which had soon followed Isabella's marriage on	E I 1 6 6
begin, we must go and pay our wedding-visit very soon."	E I 1 8 14
From the expense of the child, however, he was soon	E I 2 16 4
whole charge of the little Frank soon after her decease.	E I 2 16 4
Harriet Smith's intimacy at Hartfield was soon a settled	E I 4 26 1
he is determined to get them now as soon as ever he can."	E I 4 29 10
they talked together, soon made her quick eye sufficiently	E I 4 31 27
spirits, which Miss Woodhouse hoped very soon to compose.	E I 4 32 28
"But I," he soon added, "who have had no such charm thrown	E I 5 37 9
which Mr. Knightley soon afterwards made to "what does	E I 5 41 31
agreeable hints, she was soon pretty confident of creating	E I 6 42 1
Harriet was soon back again, and the proposal almost	E I 6 44 19
She had soon fixed on the size and sort of portrait.	E I 6 46 23
Harriet had been at Hartfield, as usual, soon after	E I 7 50 1
She had heard, as soon as she got back to Mrs. Goddard's,	E I 7 50 1
friend will soon hear of something to her advantage."	E I 8 58 19
	20
"that Harriet Smith will soon have an offer of marriage,	E I 8 59 25
The picture, elegantly framed, came safely to hand soon	E I 9 69 2
Emma was soon perfectly satisfied of Mr. Martin's being no	E I 9 69 2
They ready wit the word will soon supply, may its approval	E I 9 71 14
Thy ready wit the word will soon supply	E I 9 72 15
Things must come to a crisis soon now."	E I 9 72 15
You are his object--and you will soon receive the	E I 9 73 20
and will be soon followed by matter-of-fact prose."	E I 9 74 23
Mr. Woodhouse came in, and very soon led to the subject	E I 9 78 49
should be obliged to go back so soon, though he does.	E I 9 80 65
	66
smile, and her quick eye soon discerned in his the	E I 9 81 78
After this speech he was gone as soon as possible.	E I 9 82 84
Emma could not think it too soon; for with all his good	E I 9 82 84
yet, who can say how soon it may all vanish from my mind?"	E I 10 87 25
"And really, I do not think the impression will soon be	E I 10 87 27
as far as she could, she soon afterwards took possession	E I 10 88 33
too, and that, in short, they would both be soon after her.	E I 10 88 33
"This would soon have led to something better of course,"	E I 10 89 35
"There was a strong expectation of his coming soon after	E I 11 95 21
short questions, he was soon led on to talk of them all in	E I 12 98 2
I hope he will be calling soon.	E I 12 101 26
she added soon afterwards--as if quite another subject.	E I 13 110 8
Soon afterwards Mr. Elton quitted them, and she could not	E I 13 111 14
Emma soon saw that her companion was not in the happiest	E I 13 113 25
it, to Mrs. Weston, very soon after their moving into the	E I 14 121 14
Mr. Woodhouse very soon followed them into the drawing-	E I 14 122 18
Mr. Woodhouse was soon ready for his tea; and when he had	E I 15 124 1
for of course you saw there would be snow very soon.	E I 15 126 10
and there was every appearance of its being soon over.	E I 15 127 16
resolved on being seriously accepted as soon as possible.	E I 15 129 24
soon try for miss somebody else with twenty, or with ten.	E I 16 135 7
The weather soon improved enough for those to move who	E I 17 140 1
It soon flies over the present failure, and begins to hope	E I 18 144 2
talking of Jane; for as soon as she came in, she began	E II 1 156 7
"Are you expecting Miss Fairfax here soon?"	E II 1 158 15
If Jane does not get well soon, we will call in Mr. Perry.	E II 1 162 31
under consumption and grief soon afterwards--and this girl.	E II 2 163 2
to remind her that all this might soon be over.	E II 2 164 6
and agreeable, almost as soon as they were acquainted; and	E II 2 165 7
be selfishness:--what must be at last, had better be soon.	E II 2 165 9
connections by soon beginning her career of laborious duty.	E II 2 168 13
"A very pleasant evening," he began, as soon as Mr.	E II 3 170 2
"I always told you she was--a little; but you will soon	E II 3 171 7
Mr. Knightley soon saw that he had lost his moment, and	E II 3 172 23
"Mr. Elton going to be married!" said Emma, as soon as she	E II 3 174 33
stay half a moment there, soon after she came out it began	E II 3 177 52
hour before, its interest soon increased; and before their	E II 3 180 57
had been so very soon followed by distinguishing notice;	E II 4 181 4
and call for her again so soon, as to allow no time for	E II 4 185 13
Harriet could not very soon give an intelligible account.	E II 5 186 4
at this time, that she soon felt the necessity of a little	E II 5 187 4
"I shall soon bring him over to Hartfield," said he, at	E II 5 188 10
the elder at least must soon be coming out; and when she	E II 5 189 16
I am sure they will bring him soon."	E II 5 190 20
acquainted with her, and that acquainted they soon must be.	E II 5 190 22
What is right to be done cannot be done too soon.	E II 5 194 40
be declined," she so very soon proceeded to ask them what	E II 7 208 8
He was soon pretty well resigned.	E II 7 209 9
With this treatment, Mr. Woodhouse was soon composed	E II 7 209 13
"Oh! no, my love; but you will soon be tired.	E II 7 210 16
herself; of guessing how soon it might be necessary for	E II 8 212 4
on Miss Bates, and as soon as she entered the room had	E II 8 214 13
Depend upon it, we shall soon hear that it is a present	E II 8 218 39
They were soon joined by some of the gentlemen; and the	E II 8 220 47
He was gone immediately; and Emma soon saw him standing	E II 8 222 57
I could not bear the idea of it; so, as soon as Mr. Weston	E II 8 223 63
among the most attentive, soon drew away half Emma's mind;	E II 8 227 87
Another song, however, was soon begged for.	E II 8 229 95
young-lady-performers; but soon (within five minutes) the	E II 8 229 98
And left a name behind her that would not soon die away.	E II 9 231 1
have satisfied her, she might soon have been comforted.	E II 9 231 4
She will probably have soon done, and then we shall go	E II 9 234 31
Soon afterwards he began again, "how much your friends in	E II 10 241 11
	12
I wish I could conjecture how soon I shall make this rivet	E II 10 242 15
But soon it came to be on one side, "but will there be	E II 11 248 5
	6
It soon appeared that he came to announce an improvement.	E II 11 250 20
Alas! there was soon no leisure for quarrelling with Mr.	E II 12 258 7
him; and that he might be expected at Hartfield very soon."	E II 12 258 9
Mr. Woodhouse soon followed; and the necessity of exertion	E II 12 261 34
the speech, and the door had soon shut out Frank Churchill.	E II 12 261 37
He would soon be among them again; Mr. Elton and his bride.	E II 13 267 8
of the business might be gone through as soon as possible.	E II 14 270 2
"But every thing of that kind," said Emma, "will soon be	E II 14 278 41
The change on Mrs. Elton's side soon afterwards appeared,	E II 15 284 11
and with an arch look, but soon stopping--it was better,	E II 15 287 26
shewed him not pleased, soon afterwards said, "so you have	E II 15 287 33
	34
And soon afterwards, "Jane Fairfax is a very charming	E II 15 288 36
"Well," said she, "and you soon silenced Mr. Cole, I	E II 15 288 37
"Yes, very soon.	E II 15 288 38
in so fast that she had soon the pleasure of apprehending	E II 16 290 1
would soon shew them how every thing ought to be arranged.	E II 16 290 3
If Jane repressed her for a little time, she soon began	E II 17 299 1
June will soon be here."	E II 17 299 2
where inquiry would soon produce something--offices for	E II 17 300 13
doubt of very soon meeting with something that would do."	E II 17 301 15
dinner, and walked to Hartfield as soon as it was over.	E II 17 302 23
I always told you he would be here again soon, did not I?--	E II 17 304 27
with what she did say, and soon moved away to make the	E II 17 304 29
"I hope I shall soon have the pleasure of introducing my	E II 18 305 1
he would be here again soon, I was sure something	E II 18 308 27
that he wanted, soon took the opportunity of walking away.	E II 18 310 35
He was to leave them early the next day; and he soon began	E II 18 311 37
	38
She was soon convinced that it was not for herself she was	E III 1 315 1
The Enscombe family were not in town quite so soon as had	E III 1 315 3
been imagined, but he was at Highbury very soon afterwards.	E III 1 315 3
It soon appeared that London was not the place for her.	E III 1 317 7
It had not been forgotten before, but it had been soon	E III 1 318 11
was resumed, and very soon after the Churchills had	E III 1 318 11
for her arriving there as soon as possible after	E III 2 319 2
if half the company might soon be collected together for	E III 2 319 3
"I think she must be here soon," said he.	E III 2 320 8
every body's words, were soon lost under the incessant	E III 2 322 18
And Jane declares--well!--(as soon as she was within the	E III 2 322 19
station by Emma; and as soon as Miss Bates was quiet, she	E III 2 323 20
help to persuade him into it, which was done pretty soon.--	E III 2 325 31
But Emma's wonder lessened soon afterwards, on seeing Mr.	E III 2 326 33
said much, as soon as she could catch his eye again.	E III 2 328 40
I should not be helped so soon, but it smells most	E III 2 330 45
were all three soon in the hall, and Harriet immediately	E III 3 333 3
resisted; and Harriet was soon assailed by half a dozen	E III 3 333 6
as soon as she had recovered her senses and speech.--	E III 3 334 8
but she soon felt that concealment must be impossible.	E III 3 335 12
in the place were soon in the happiness of frightful news.	E III 3 336 12
the whole history dwindled soon into a matter of little	E III 3 336 13
was so little lead that he soon cut it all away, and it	E III 4 339 18
But I kept my eye on it; and, as soon as I dared, caught	E III 4 339 18
She had soon afterwards reason to believe that the	E III 4 340 28
You mentioned it as what was certainly to be very soon.	E III 5 344 9
He saw that Emma had soon made it out, and found it highly	E III 5 348 22
throughout the year, he soon afterwards took a hasty leave,	E III 5 351 38
been at the Abbey, that as soon as she was satisfied of	E III 6 357 34
Little expecting to meet Miss Woodhouse so soon, there was	E III 6 362 43
alone!--I, who may so soon have to guard others!"	E III 6 362 48
"You will soon be cooler, if you sit still." said Emma.	E III 6 364 54
"As soon as I am cooler I shall go back again.	E III 6 364 55
You will all be going soon I suppose; the whole party	E III 6 364 55
Emma listened, and looked, and soon perceived that Frank	E III 6 364 56
I should not like a man who is so soon discomposed by a	E III 6 364 58
"As soon as my aunt gets well, I shall go abroad," said he.	E III 6 364 60
persuasion, this morning, that I shall soon be abroad.	E III 6 365 62
the party were now returning, and all were soon collected.	E III 6 366 74
I shall be sure to say three dull things as soon as ever I	E III 7 370 24
Perfection should not have come quite so soon."	E III 7 371 36
"Happy couple!" said Frank Churchill, as soon as they were	E III 7 372 40
bowed in submission; and soon afterwards said, in a lively	E III 7 373 45
	46
We shall soon overtake her.	E III 7 374 53
She continued to look back, but in vain; and soon, with	E III 7 376 62
pleased to wait a moment, and then ushered her in too soon.	E III 8 378 4
But Miss Bates soon came--"very happy and obliged"--but	E III 8 378 7
has written her letters, she says she shall soon be well.	E III 8 379 8
"Very soon, very soon indeed; that's the worst of it.	E III 8 382 27
come over from Richmond soon after the return of the party	E III 8 383 31
little pleasing, that she soon allowed herself to believe	E III 8 384 34
she and Mr. Weston were soon out of the house together and	E III 10 392 7
Do not be impatient, Emma; it will all come out too soon."	E III 10 393 9
If we walk fast, we shall soon be at Randall's."	E III 10 393 17
her own fancy, and that soon pointed out to her the	E III 10 393 18
have brought her, and now I hope you will soon be better.	E III 10 394 25
"I am to hear from him soon," continued Mrs. Weston.	E III 10 398 53
"He told me at parting, that he should soon write; and he	E III 10 398 53
She would soon be well, and happy, and prosperous.--	E III 11 403 2
the painful truth, however, and as soon as possible.	E III 11 403 2
But as soon as she (Miss Woodhouse) appeared likely to	E III 11 410 35
The power of observation would be soon given--frightfully	E III 12 416 2
soon it appeared when her thoughts were in one course.	E III 12 416 2
Emma's attention; it was soon gone to Brunswick Square or	E III 12 420 14
know, but I hope it will soon come," she was obliged to	E III 12 420 14
Be sure to give me intelligence of the letter as soon as	E III 12 420 16
soon after tea, and dissipated every melancholy fancy.	E III 12 422 19
to suppose, would soon cease to belong to Highbury.	E III 12 422 20
Emma resolved to be out of doors as soon as possible.	E III 13 424 1
on Mr. Perry's coming in soon after dinner, with a	E III 13 424 1
steadier tone, he concluded with, "he will soon be gone.	E III 13 426 13
They will soon be in Yorkshire.	E III 13 426 13
Emma understood him; and as soon as she could recover from	E III 13 426 14
	15
"I cannot make speeches, emma:"--he soon resumed; and in a	E III 13 430 37
With respect to her father, it was a question soon	E III 14 435 4
did not arrive at all too soon; and half an hour stolen	E III 14 435 5
You will soon, I earnestly hope, know her thoroughly	E III 14 439 8
I know you will soon call on her; she is living in dread	E III 14 439 8
resolution it produces: as soon as she found I was really	E III 14 441 8
Have patience with me, I shall soon have done.--	E III 14 442 8
arrangement concluded as soon as possible, she now sent me,	E III 14 442 8
As soon as she came to her own name, it was irresistible;	E III 15 444 1
He did so, but very soon stopt again to say, "the piano-	E III 15 446 18
I shall soon have done.	E III 15 447 26
to Miss Fairfax, and will soon, it may be hoped, have the	E III 15 448 30
She soon resolved, equally as a duty and a pleasure, to	E III 16 452 7
Emma was gratified, and would soon have shown no want of	E III 16 453 10
She soon believed herself to penetrate Mrs. Elton's	E III 16 453 12
Soon after this Miss Bates came in, and Emma could not	E III 16 455 19
"He promised to come to me as soon as he could disengage	E III 16 456 25
who can say, you know, how soon it may be wanted?"	E III 16 457 36
As soon as Mrs. Weston was sufficiently recovered to admit	E III 17 465 28
Mr. Woodhouse could not be soon reconciled; but the worst	E III 17 466 30
of welcome; and he was soon used to be talked to by each,	E III 17 466 30
the baby would soon have outgrown its first set of caps.	E III 17 468 32
the wonder of it was very soon nothing; and by the end of	E III 17 468 33

known at Randall's, how soon it would be over Highbury; E III 17 468 35
Their conversation was soon afterwards closed by the E III 18 475 37
of concealment from Mr. Knightley would soon be over. E III 18 475 42
mystery, so hateful to her to practise, might soon be over. E III 18 475 42
But his spirits were soon rising again, and with laughing E III 18 477 51
She could not be too soon alarmed, nor send for Perry too E III 18 479 73
Emma soon recollected, and understood him; and while she E III 18 480 76
be soon over too, she hesitated--she could not proceed. E III 19 483 9
She had, while a very young girl, as soon as she had known P III 1 7 14
He had not been known to them as a boy, but soon after P III 1 7 14
found himself obliged to confess to her soon afterwards. P III 1 10 19
But soon afterwards, rising and pacing the room, he P III 3 18 5
6
Sir Walter's remark was, soon afterwards-- "the profession P III 3 19 13
14
I have often observed it; they soon lose the look of youth. P III 3 20 17
and to get into it as soon as possible;--knew he must pay P III 3 22 23
I shall forget my own name soon, I suppose. P III 3 23 28
Troubles soon arose. P III 4 26 2
But, he was confident that he should soon be rich;--full P III 4 27 4
he knew that he should soon have a ship, and soon be on a P III 4 27 4
soon have a ship, and soon be on a station that would lead P III 4 27 4
in one visit to Bath soon after the rupture.) or in any P III 4 28 7
He had, very soon after their engagement ceased, got P III 4 29 8
park, "I thought we should soon come to a deal, my dear, P III 5 32 4
have her hurried away so soon, and wanted to make it P III 5 33 6
and it was consequently soon settled that Anne should not P III 5 34 10
"Well, you will soon be better now," replied Anne, P III 5 38 28
She could soon sit upright on the sofa, and began to hope P III 5 39 40
"Oh! but they ought to call upon you as soon as possible. P III 5 40 43
Mrs. Croft's here soon; I dare say you know him by name." P III 6 49 23
24
acquaintance, as soon as they could hear of his arrival. P III 6 52 33
they must meet; and soon she began to wish that she could P III 7 53 1
sending, as soon as she recollected it, proper notice to P III 7 53 3
now the collar-bone was soon replaced, and though Mr. P III 7 54 4
room, but as soon as there was only Anne to hear, "so! P III 7 56 9
10
of her manner being soon sufficient to convince him, where P III 7 58 20
this was the most consoling, that it would soon be over. P III 7 59 25
And it was soon over. P III 7 59 25
Soon, however, she began to reason with herself, and try P III 7 60 28
have prevented, she was soon spared all suspense; for P III 7 60 31
32
Yet she soon began to rejoice that she had heard them. P III 7 61 35
intended to settle as soon as he could be properly tempted; P III 7 61 38
They were soon dining in company together at Mr. P III 8 63 1
Lucky fellow to get any thing so soon, with no more P III 8 65 12
If a man has not a wife, he soon wants to be afloat again." P III 8 65 14
He had intended, on first arriving, to proceed very soon P III 9 73 1
It was soon Uppercross with him almost every day. P III 9 73 2
cried Mary to Anne, as soon as he was out of the room, " P III 9 76 16
that Captain Wentworth may soon put him quite out of her P III 9 76 16
feelings, the alteration could not be understood too soon. P III 9 77 18
wishes, in his prospect of soon quitting his present P III 9 78 19
One morning, very soon after the dinner at the Musgroves, P III 9 78 21
but Charles Hayter soon put an end to his attempts, by P III 9 79 27
the conviction soon forced on her by the noise he was P III 9 80 34
Anne had soon been in company with all the four together P III 10 82 1
and Winthrop, and soon commanded a full view of the latter, P III 10 85 13
to sit down; and she very soon heard Captain Wentworth and P III 10 87 22
As soon as she could, she went after Mary, and having P III 10 89 35
Elliot were to hear how soon we came to an understanding, P III 10 92 45
engaged to join her as soon as she was resettled, was P III 11 93 1
and still descending, soon found themselves on the sea P III 11 96 10
herself; but it was soon lost in the pleasanter feelings P III 11 98 17
gentleness of her manners, soon had their effect; and Anne P III 11 100 23
The waiter came into the room soon afterwards. P III 12 105 10
Anne found Captain Benwick getting near her, as soon as P III 12 107 23
"And not known to him, perhaps, so soon." P III 12 108 27
I would as soon have been run up to the yard-arm. P III 12 108 28
so inclined, and Louisa soon grew so determined, that the P III 12 108 30
It was soon drawn per force another way. P III 12 109 31
Louisa had once opened her eyes, but soon closed them P III 12 112 51
She, however, was soon persuaded to think differently. P III 12 114 59
on his part, and to be soon followed by the two ladies. P III 12 115 65
to recognise the same hills and the same objects so soon. P III 12 117 73
have been resolved on, and found practicable so soon. P IV 1 122 3
She had little difficulty; it was soon determined that P IV 1 122 5
When they came to converse, she was soon sensible of some P IV 1 124 11
must call on Mrs. Croft; I really must call upon her soon. P IV 1 125 14
The sad accident at Lyme was soon the prevailing topic; P IV 1 126 20
So I got Sophy to lend me a hand, and we soon shifted P IV 1 128 28
be at home again, and as soon as possible after their P IV 2 129 1
"And that you are very likely to do very soon, I can tell P IV 2 131 12
from his manner that you will have him calling here soon. P IV 2 131 12
that she would very soon see no deficiency in his manner." P IV 2 132 17
said Lady Russell, as soon as they were reseated in the P IV 2 135 32
They were evidently in excellent spirits, and she was soon P IV 3 137 3
and as soon as she recovered, they were to be acquainted. P IV 3 141 13
As soon as he could, he began to talk to her of Lyme, P IV 3 143 19
alone; he knew it; he was soon diffused again among the P IV 3 144 21
been engaged in there, soon after his leaving the place. P IV 3 144 22
nor (she began pretty soon to suspect) to prevent his P IV 4 147 6
in the meeting had soon passed away, and left only the P IV 5 153 6
As soon as I could use my hands, she taught me to knit, P IV 5 155 9
she shook it off, and soon added in a different tone, "I P IV 5 156 12
13
The answer soon presented itself. P IV 6 166 19
fervour to begin with, and they would soon grow more alike. P IV 6 167 20
Ah! the peace has come too soon for that younker. P IV 6 170 29
As soon as they were fairly ascending Belmont, he began, " P IV 6 170 30
31
Anne had been ashamed to appear to comprehend so soon as P IV 6 170 32
He soon joined them again, successful, of course; Lady P IV 7 174 2
As soon as they were out of sight, the ladies of Captain P IV 7 177 17
mad idea of her recognising him so soon as she did herself. P IV 7 179 28
I had been too deeply concerned in the mischief to be soon P IV 8 183 13
Upon Lady Russell's appearance soon afterwards, the whole P IV 8 185 19
the feeling of safety, soon added, more composedly, "are P IV 9 194 21
and he is not a man, I think, to be known intimately soon. P IV 9 196 33
Mrs. Smith would hardly have believed so soon in Mr. P IV 9 197 34
You will soon be able to judge of the general credit due, P IV 9 205 86
of coming back to Bath as soon as possible, and of fixing P IV 9 207 90
to the game to be soon overcome by a gentleman's hints. P IV 10 213 5
And you may say, that I mean to call upon her soon. P IV 10 215 16
air of welcome; and as soon as it became clear that these, P IV 10 216 18
So much was pretty soon understood; but till Sir Walter P IV 10 216 18
to take place in a few months, quite as soon as Louisa's. P IV 10 217 20
common friends must be soon bringing them together again. P IV 10 221 32
It was soon generally agreed that Tuesday should be the P IV 10 225 55
of walking away from it soon afterwards, and taking a P IV 10 225 56
but would be back again soon, and that the strictest P IV 11 229 2
"poor Fanny! she would not have forgotten him so soon!" P IV 11 232 15
We certainly do not forget you, so soon as you forget us. P IV 11 232 19
continual occupation and change soon weaken impressions." P IV 11 232 19
the world does all this so soon for men, (which, however, P IV 11 232 20
port, he calculates how soon it be possible to get them P 1 6 235 31
but Harville and I shall soon be after you, that is, P IV 11 236 38
return "hither, or follow your party, as soon as possible. P IV 11 237 43
Such a letter was not to be soon recovered from. P IV 11 238 44
proceeding together; and soon words enough had passed P IV 11 240 59
Lady Dalrymple and Miss Carteret; they would soon be P IV 11 246 78
I trust to being in charity with her soon. P IV 11 247 82
She had soon the mortification of seeing Mr. Elliot P IV 12 250 6
He soon quitted Bath; and on Mrs. Clay's quitting it P IV 12 250 7
quitting it likewise soon afterwards, and being next heard P IV 12 250 7
worse than before, as soon as the premises of the said S 1 364 1
sprained his foot--& soon becoming sensible of it, was S 1 364 1
We shall soon get releif.-- S 1 364 1
It gives me no pain while I am quiet,--and as soon as S 1 367 1
A little of our own bracing sea air will soon set me on my S 1 367 1
excessively absurd, & must soon find themselves the dupes S 1 369 1
A thing of this kind soon makes a stir in a lonely place S 1 370 1
Mr Parker's character & history were soon unfolded. S 2 371 1
follow him to Sanditon as soon as possible--and healthy as S 2 373 1
open down where the new Buildgs might soon be looked for. S 4 382 1
I could soon put the necessary Irons in the fire.-- S 5 387 1
The party were very soon moving after dinner. S 6 389 1
good of every body, as soon as Miss Whitby could be S 6 390 1
to be placed--& she soon perceived that he had a fine S 7 394 1
She was very soon in his company again. S 7 395 1
delight, said Charlotte as soon as she had time to speak, S 7 397 1
could supply her)--and as soon as she got well, have her S 7 401 1
Lady D. soon added, with great glee--"and besides all this S 7 401 1
One day soon after Charlotte's arrival at Sanditon, she S 9 406 1
room, and she was soon introduced to Miss Diana Parker. S 9 406 1
I had the pleasure of hearing soon afterwards by the same S 9 408 1
you at any time, but as soon as I get back I shall hear S 9 411 1
Camberwell will be here to a certainty, & very soon.-- S 9 411 1
In one particular however, she soon found that he had S 10 418 1
Soon after tea, a letter was brought to Miss D. P-- from S 10 418 1
the Miss Beauforts were soon satisfied with "the circle in S 11 421 1
soon found that all her calculations of profit wd be vain. S 11 422 1
if she wished it--and as soon as that is over, I must S 12 424 1
a very neat carriage was soon opposite to them, & they all S 12 425 1
one of these, Charlotte as soon as they entered the S 12 426 1

SOONER (70)

I may therefore expect it will sooner subside; & perhaps LS 22 282 7
voice was with them yet sooner, for on the stairs he was NA I 11 84 18
No sooner had she expressed her delight in Mr. Allen's NA II 2 138 1
"I did not expect to be able to return sooner, when I went NA II 9 195 12
assistance to her; and sooner than she could have supposed NA II 10 201 4
a thousand apologies to make for not answering them sooner. NA II 12 216 1
2
I am only sorry it was not recollected sooner, that I NA II 13 225 22
And if we are to part, a few hours sooner or later, you NA II 13 226 24
no sooner was she gone than they burst forth in torrents. NA II 13 226 25
No sooner was his father's funeral over, than Mrs. John SS I 1 5 9
No sooner did she perceive any symptom of love in his SS I 3 17 14
No sooner was her answer dispatched, than Mrs. Dashwood SS I 5 25 1
They were no sooner in the passage than Marianne came SS I 15 75 2
in the direction, and no sooner was it complete than SS II 4 161 5
returned home; and no sooner had they entered the house SS II 4 165 25
things, the better, the sooner 'tis blown over and forgot. SS II 8 196 18
I remember Fanny used to say that she would marry sooner SS II 11 227 50
exertion; for no sooner had they entered their common SS III 10 342 7
knowing, as sooner or later I must have known, all this.-- SS III 11 350 6
and on the same principle will forgive him much sooner." SS III 13 366 19
had better meet every night, & break up two hours sooner." W 325 4
party to another, & no sooner had the signal been given, W 328 9
leaning on his arm--& no sooner were they within reach of W 333 13
But no sooner had he made it clear to himself and his PP I 6 23 12
How much sooner one tires of any thing than of a book!-- PP I 11 55 4
the end of conference, no sooner saw Elizabeth open the PP I 20 110 1
the same news, and no sooner had they entered the PP I 20 113 26
even from Wickham; and no sooner had he and his companion PP I 21 116 6
out a year or two sooner than they might otherwise have PP I 22 122 3
William remained; but no sooner had he left them than her PP I 23 126 5
Lizzy; you would have laughed yourself out of it sooner. PP II 2 141 10
Mr. Collins no sooner saw the two girls than he began to PP II 5 159 20
Had they been only ten minutes sooner, they should have PP III 1 252 54
walk, they had no sooner dined than she set off again in PP III 1 259 76
No sooner did he appear, than Elizabeth wisely resolved to PP III 3 268 8
No sooner in possession of it, than hurrying into the PP III 10 321 1
in love, &c.;--but no sooner had he deliberately begun to MP I 1 6 5
still persevered, and no sooner had he begun to revert to MP I 2 15 10
uncle died a few years sooner, it would have been duly MP I 3 23 2
setting off half an hour sooner; clouds are now coming up, MP I 7 68 19
Edmund, observing her; "why would not you speak sooner? MP I 9 95 68
too?" but they were no sooner through the door than Henry MP II 1 176 3
All are supplanted sooner or later. MP II 10 277 17
could not get away sooner--Fanny looked so lovely!-- MP II 12 291 4
"This comfort you might have had sooner, Fanny, had you MP III 4 346 14
They were no sooner in the hall than all restraint of MP III 5 357 6
No sooner was she out of sight, than Emma exclaimed, "what E I 6 43 12
13
But no sooner was the distress known to Mr. Elton, than it E I 6 49 40
dinner: she returned, and sooner than had been talked of, E I 7 50 1
myself; and I think the sooner *you* go the better. E I 8 58 8
takes place; and the sooner it *could* be over, the better." E I 14 122 20
considerably longer with them than if he had come sooner. E I 18 144 2
my usual caution; but no sooner did I come to the mention E II 1 162 31
"The sooner every party breaks up, the better." E II 7 210 18
He is to be in town next week, if not sooner. E II 18 305 5
of wrong, for that visit might have been sooner paid. E III 14 437 8
sure you were that he might have come sooner if he would. E III 15 445 12
London, and she had no sooner an opportunity of being one E III 19 481 1
No, he would sooner quit Kellynch-Hall at once, than P III 2 13 6
sooner than any other man; I have observed it all my life. P III 3 19 16
empowered to act; and no sooner had such an end been P III 3 24 38
I could not very conveniently have left Kellynch sooner." P III 5 38 32
for them twelve hours sooner, and seeing them arrive at P 1 6 235 31
heaven had given them wings, by many hours sooner still! P 1 6 235 31
"Dare not say that man forgets sooner than woman, that " P IV 11 237 42
He had no sooner been free from the horror and remorse P IV 11 242 64
of Louisa's accident, no sooner begun to feel himself P IV 11 242 64
ought to make me forgive every one sooner than myself. P IV 11 247 84
P.'s sprain proving too serious for him to move sooner.-- S 2 370 1
on foot--& therefore the sooner the better,--& Lady S 12 423 1

SOOTH (7)

she would have tried to sooth and tranquillize her still SS II 7 180 5
that could be done was to sooth her distress, lessen her SS III 1 262 14
and while attempting to sooth her, eagerly felt her pulse. SS III 7 311 14
and whose friendship might sooth her!--as far as the shock SS III 7 311 16
and Elinor, impatient to sooth, though too honest to SS III 10 346 29
His mother, stifling her own mortification, tried to sooth W 330 11
with or sooth her would only increase the irritation. PP I 20 113 29

SOOTHE (5)

Julia wavered: but was he only trying to soothe and pacify MP I 14 135 18
the letter--there was nothing in that to soothe irritation. MP III 13 424 4
She had, indeed, scarcely the shadow of a hope to soothe MP III 15 442 22
she allowed him an opening, to soothe or to counsel her.-- E III 13 432 40
one to attend and soothe;--besides sending, as soon as she P III 7 53 3

SOOTHED (5)

she was further soothed in her progress, by being told, NA II 8 183 2
soothed beyond any thing that she had believed possible. NA II 14 233 9
It soothed, but it could not console her for the contempt PP II 13 209 11
With that, she soothed herself and amused her friend. MP I 5 227 68
might, Fanny's immediate feelings were infinitely soothed. MP III 10 402 12

SOOTHING (14)

so soothing in the vicissitudes of their eventful lives. NA I 1 15 3
and dinner, incapable of soothing Mrs. Allen's fears on NA I 7 51 54
Every thing honourable and soothing, every present NA II 2 140 8

The evening wore away with no abatement of this soothing NA II 10 199 2
irritating and soothing; it sometimes suggested the dread NA II 14 231 4
picture so soothing!--Oh! it was a blessed journey!" SS III 8 325 45
to a soothing friend--not an application to a parent. SS III 9 337 18
her instantly with soothing tenderness, had not Elinor, SS III 11 349 5
was hardly such as to make reflection very soothing. W 361 31
all that was solemn and soothing, and lovely, appeared in MP I 11 112 35
There is something soothing in the idea, that we have the MP III 13 420 2
expressions;--but the soothing attentions of his daughters E I 12 107 62
soothing to him, had in all likelihood been given also. E II 15 282 3
a little additional soothing, in the Admiral's situation P III 3 24 36

SOOTHINGS (2)

and all their united soothings were ineffectual till Lady SS I 21 121 10
all the reasonings and soothings and attentions of every E II 13 267 9

SOPHA (4)

Mrs. Weston and Emma were sitting together on a sopha. E I 15 124 1
senses; and then left the sopha, removing to a seat by her E I 15 125 6
has not been able to leave the sopha for a week together. E II 18 306 11
no open window, but the sopha & the table, & the S 10 413 1

SOPHAS (1)

to stretch himself on one of the sophas and go to sleep. PP I 11 54 3

SOPHIA (5)

I was saying so to Emily and Sophia when you over took us." NA I 14 115 54
of an Emily and a Sophia to console her, she bade her NA I 14 115 55
on my face!--and Sophia, jealous as the devil on the other SS III 8 327 55
here I am, Sophia, quite ready to make a foolish match. P III 7 61 38
39
"All merged in my friendship, Sophia. P III 8 69 40

SOPHIA'S (1)

It happened to catch Sophia's eye before it caught mine-- SS III 8 328 61

SOPHY (6)

Sophy," said the Admiral;--"but there is no saying which. P III 10 92 44
So I got Sophy to lend me a hand, and we soon shifted P IV 1 128 28
Sophy cannot bear them. P IV 6 170 29
Even Sophy could not understand it. P IV 6 171 33
it is all our partiality, Sophy and I cannot help thinking P IV 6 172 39
Sophy must write, and beg him to come to Bath. P IV 6 173 49

SOPHYS (1)

I should never be out, if they were all Sophys, or P IV 6 171 33

SORDID (1)

Thus it is, when rich people are Sordid."-- S 7 402 1

SORE (9)

her limbs, a cough, and a sore throat, a good night's rest SS III 6 306 17
Her heart was sore and angry, and she was capable only of MP I 17 162 19
peace for ever on the sore subject of the silver knife, MP III 9 396 7
charm away a sore throat; it is a most severe cold indeed. E I 13 114 32
a bad sore throat; and Emma was quite in charity with him. E I 15 124 3
afraid of its being a bad sore throat on her account, than E I 15 124 4
the danger of catching an ulcerated sore throat herself! E I 15 125 5
It was but a very few days before I had my sore throat-- E III 4 338 12
while Anne could be of none, was a very sore aggravation. P III 5 34 11

SORE-FOOTED (1)

fears, soup and negus, sore-footed and fatigued, restless MP II 10 280 33

SORE-THROAT (3)

She was very feverish and had a bad sore-throat: Mrs. E I 13 109 5
as he exclaimed, "a sore-throat!--I hope not infectious. E I 13 109 6
7
butcher says there is a "bad sore-throat very much about. P IV 6 164 8

SORE-THROATS (2)

bad sore-throats, and had often alarmed her with them."-- E I 13 109 6
"I dare say I shall catch it; and my sore-throats, you " P IV 6 164 8

SORELY (2)

credit of it, which went sorely against the grain; and I PP III 10 324 2
deadened at the moment, must, she knew, be sorely felt. MP III 16 451 15

SORETHROAT (1)

to me--and excepting a sorethroat and head-ache there is PP I 7 31 30

SORROW (28)

denial, she expressed her sorrow on the occasion so very NA I 8 54 10
But this, with the look of sorrow accompanying it, was NA II 13 229 30
They gave themselves up wholly to their sorrow, seeking SS I 1 7 13
But in sorrow she must be equally carried away by her SS I 2 8 2
Colonel Brandon again repeated his sorrow at being the SS I 13 65 33
of that violent sorrow which Marianne was in all SS I 15 77 20
produced occasional effusions of sorrow as lively as ever. SS I 16 83 4
fix her sorrow, by seeking silence, solitude, and idleness. SS I 19 104 9
Oh! how easy for those who have no sorrow of their own to SS II 7 185 22
to any impression of sorrow or of joy on his account--she SS III 5 296 19
Her sorrow, her disappointment, her deep regret, when I SS III 8 324 42
scarcely allowing sorrow to exist but with me, regretting SS III 10 346 28
The master of the house heard with real sorrow that they PP I 12 59 3
expressed his sorrow for her distress, wished it a happier PP III 4 278 22
I must have been involved in all your sorrow and disgrace. PP III 6 297 11
briefly expressing her sorrow for what he must have PP III 6 299 19
Tom listened with some shame and some sorrow; but escaping MP I 3 24 4
occasion; not for their sorrow, but for their want of it. MP I 3 32 64
be neither wickedness nor sorrow in the world; and there MP I 11 113 35
"What do they bring but disappointment and sorrow?-- MP III 13 424 3
active, indispensable employment, for relieving sorrow. MP III 15 443 25
sorry; but it was with a sorrow so founded on satisfaction, MP III 17 461 3
Sorrow came--a gentle sorrow--but not at all in the shape E I 1 6 5
with the appearance of sorrow for his disappointment." E I 7 52 11
Every body had a degree of gravity and sorrow; tenderness E III 9 387 12
Personal size and mental sorrow have certainly no P III 8 68 30
neither sickness nor sorrow seemed to have closed her P IV 5 153 7
I think differently now; time and sickness, and sorrow, P IV 9 201 64

SORROWFUL (12)

from the table with a sorrowful countenance, which SS II 4 165 25
Fanny left the room with a very sorrowful heart; she could MP I 3 25 17
laughing answer, was sorrowful food for Fanny's MP II 4 214 46
the prospect of it most sorrowful to her, independently-- MP III 6 367 4
as she sat in bewildered, broken, sorrowful contemplation. MP III 7 382 28
She was soon more softened and sorrowful.-- MP III 13 425 5
being wished joy of so sorrowful an event; and the wedding- E I 2 19 14
to abbey-mill again," was said in rather a sorrowful tone. E I 7 55 37
to thank Mrs. Weston, look sorrowful, and have done. E II 8 230 101
upon his impatience, his sorrowful look and total want of E II 12 259 12
and sorrowful regret that had ever surrounded it.-- E III 14 435 4
this little history of sorrowful interest had reached its P III 4 28 7

SORROWFULLY (4)

I declare--said Emma sorrowfully, as she walked into the W 336 14
"I mean," she cried, sorrowfully, correcting herself, " MP III 4 347 20
year, as Fanny had most sorrowfully considered, on first MP III 14 430 6
She was most sorrowfully indignant; ashamed of every E III 11 412 46

SORROWING (3)

short exclamations of sorrowing wonder, declared her to be NA II 10 202 8
or of those who were sorrowing--if she could help MP III 15 444 26
"he had not, perhaps, a more sorrowing heart than I have. P III 11 97 13

SORROWS (11)

towards herself and her sorrows; so very little did they NA I 11 90 64
thing; her sorrows, her joys, could have no moderation. SS I 1 6 12
jennings's entering into her sorrows with any compassion. SS II 9 201 2
and brooding over her sorrows in silence, gave more pain SS II 10 212 1
of disclosing past sorrows and present humiliations, was SS II 10 216 15
I, and only I, knew your heart and its sorrows; yet, to SS III 10 346 28
They each felt his sorrows, and their own obligations, and SS III 14 378 13
friend, she was taken to finish her sorrows in bed. MP I 2 13 4
and when to these sorrows was added the idea of the MP I 2 14 8
ended every day's sorrows by sobbing herself to sleep. MP I 2 14 9
I must struggle through my sorrows and difficulties as I MP I 3 29 46

SORRY (231)

My dear mother I am very sorry to tell you that it LS 3 246 1
I am sorry it is so, for what is this but deceit? LS 6 251 1
I am sorry to have incurred his displeasure, but can LS 15 266 2
I am not sorry for, as I know no better support of love. LS 16 269 3
a turn, I am quite sorry that I ever imparted my LS 23 283 1
I am sorry to leave you, but I must go. LS 23 283 4
I wish we could bring dear Frederica too, but I am sorry LS 41 310 3
I am so sorry she has not had a partner!" NA I 2 23 25
already; I shall be quite sorry if it has, for this is a NA I 3 28 35
I am very sorry for it; but really I thought I was in very NA I 6 39 3
"Well, sir, and I dare say you are not sorry to be back NA I 8 54 5
Tilney's, was not sorry to be called away by Mr. Allen. NA I 12 96 23
Catherine looked grave, was very sorry, but could not go. NA I 13 97 1
Catherine was sorry, but could do no more; and a short NA I 13 99 4
Catherine submitted; and though sorry to think that NA I 13 105 41
hope, Miss Morland, you will not be sorry to see me." NA I 15 123 42
There are very few people I am sorry to see. NA I 15 123 43
"I am very sorry for it," said Catherine dejectedly, "if I NA II 2 139 3
I am sorry for it; I am sorry they find any thing so NA II 3 147 26
Mr. and Mrs. Allen were sorry to lose their young friend, NA II 5 154 1
"How sorry you must be for that!" NA II 5 157 8
"I am always sorry to leave Eleanor." NA II 5 157 9
"I am sorry," said Henry, closing the book he had just NA II 10 204 12
"Yes; I am sure I should be very sorry to leave you so NA II 10 204 17
I am very sorry for Mr. Morland--sorry that any one you NA II 10 204 20
if it is to be so, I can only say that I am sorry for it. NA II 10 205 24
I am very, very sorry we are to part-- so soon, and so NA II 13 224 14
"I am sure," said she, "I am very sorry if I have offended NA II 13 225 22
I am only sorry it was not recollected sooner, that I NA II 13 225 22
"I am sorry for the young people," returned Mrs. Morland; " NA II 14 234 12
I am sorry it happens so, for Mrs. Allen thought them very NA II 14 236 15
"We are sorry for him," said she; "but otherwise there is NA II 14 236 19
Elinor started at this declaration, and was sorry for the SS I 4 21 11
and again how exceedingly sorry he was that she had taken SS I 5 25 4
a young mind, that one is sorry to see them give way to SS I 11 56 12
"I am particularly sorry, ma'am," said he, addressing Lady SS I 13 64 19
Mrs Dashwood was sorry for what she had said; but it gave SS I 16 85 14
I am so sorry we cannot stay longer; however we shall meet SS I 20 110 2
I suppose you were very sorry to leave Sussex." SS I 21 123 21
I am sorry you do not happen to know Mrs. Ferrars." SS I 22 128 9
"I am sorry I do not," said Elinor, in great astonishment, SS I 22 128 10
"I am sorry for that," returned the other, while her eyes SS II 2 150 38
monstrous glad to see you--sorry I could not come before-- SS II 4 163 14
Miss Marianne, too--which you will not be sorry to hear. SS II 4 163 18
Mrs. Ellison would not be sorry to have Miss Grey married, SS II 8 194 12
Elinor only was sorry to see them. SS II 10 217 20
"I am sorry we cannot see your sister, Miss Dashwood," SS II 10 219 37
"I am sorry she is not well;" for Marianne had left the SS II 10 219 37
My sister will be equally sorry to miss the pleasure of SS II 10 219 38
John Dashwood was really far from being sorry to see his SS II 11 221 7
her brother; and was not sorry to be spared the necessity SS II 11 222 12
"I am sorry for that. SS II 11 227 50
I should be so sorry to have you ill; you, that have been SS II 13 239 13
But I am sorry to relate what ensued. SS III 1 266 38
"I am sorry to say, ma'am, in a most unhappy rupture:-- SS III 1 268 48
and Elinor was not sorry that by her continuing with them, SS III 2 271 5
I am sorry I did not know it before; for I certainly would SS III 2 274 19
Good bye; I am sorry Miss Marianne was not here. SS III 2 276 25
I am sorry to say that my patronage ends with this; and my SS III 3 284 23
should have been extremely sorry to leave London without SS III 4 288 27
"I am not sorry to see you alone," he replied, "for I have SS III 5 294 8
I am extremely sorry for it--for I know him to be a very SS III 5 298 35
and in her heart was not sorry that she could like him no SS III 6 305 15
like him no more;--not sorry to be driven by the SS III 6 305 15
guilt;--she was sorry for him;--she wished him happy. SS III 11 349 1
and service, and how sorry they was they had not time to SS III 11 354 27
"I am sorry for her anxieties, said Emma,--but I do not W 318 2
"I am sorry it happens so--she added, turning good- W 346 21
months together.--& I am sorry, (with a witty smile) we W 350 24
was not ill used) "I am sorry I am not to have the W 351 25
"I am sorry to hear that; but why did not you tell me so PP I 2 7 22
after a few moments recollection, was not sorry for it. PP I 11 58 34
Miss Bingley was then sorry that she had proposed the PP I 12 59 2
"I cannot pretend to be sorry," said Wickham, after a PP I 16 78 16
"I am sorry you think so; but if that be the case, there PP I 18 93 29
he has received; and I am sorry to say that by his account PP I 18 95 50
and Elizabeth sorry for her, and sorry for her father's PP I 18 101 70
sorry for her, and sorry for her father's speech, was PP I 18 101 70
I am sorry to say it of them, but so it is. PP II 2 140 4
"I am sorry it went off. PP II 2 140 6
Poor Jane! I am sorry for her, because, with her PP II 2 141 10
In short, my dear aunt, I should be very sorry to be the PP II 3 145 7
drew near, she would have been very sorry for any delay. PP II 4 151 1
I should be sorry to think our friend mercenary." PP II 4 153 8
I should be sorry, you know, to think ill of a young man PP II 4 153 18
I am sorry to pain you--but so it was. PP II 8 175 18
instant, she was at first sorry for the pain he was to PP II 11 189 6
I am sorry to have occasioned pain to any one. PP II 11 190 7
be offensive to your's, I can only say that I am sorry.-- PP II 12 197 5
They were excessively sorry to go! PP II 14 210 3
She was not sorry, however, to have the recital of them PP II 15 216 7
She was sorry that Mr. Darcy should have delivered his PP II 17 224 2
"Indeed," replied Elizabeth, "I am heartily sorry for him; PP II 17 224 4
He is now perhaps sorry for what he has done, and anxious PP II 17 227 24
heart, and then he will be sorry for what he has done." PP II 17 228 29
the same, and she left him disappointed and sorry. PP II 18 232 21
was not sorry to be spared the necessity of saying much. PP III 3 268 5
I am very, very sorry. PP III 4 273 3
I should be sorry to think so ill of him, in the very PP III 7 304 31
Elizabeth was now most heartily sorry that she had from PP III 8 311 11
"I should be sorry indeed, if it were. PP III 10 327 7
As the day of his arrival drew near, "I begin to be sorry PP III 11 333 27
28
"I am sorry, exceedingly sorry," replied Darcy, in a tone PP III 16 365 4
her, saying, "I am quite sorry, Lizzy, that you should be PP III 17 375 25
26
Mrs. Norris was sorry to say, that the little girl's MP I 1 9 10
do not know that her being sorry to leave her home is MP I 2 13 5
"You are sorry to leave mamma, my dear little Fanny," said MP I 2 15 11
"I shall be very sorry to go away," said she, with a MP I 3 25 11
Edmund was sorry to hear Miss Crawford, whom he was much MP I 6 57 32
She would be extremely sorry to interfere with you. MP I 7 70 29
to Lady Bertram's staying at home, could only be sorry. MP I 8 76 4
feelings, for she was sorry for almost all that she had MP I 10 100 23
"I am very sorry," said she; "it is very unlucky." MP I 10 102 37
It was very vexatious, and she was heartily sorry for it; MP I 12 114 2
I was sorry for him that he should have so mistaken his MP I 13 122 2
in the Baron, and was not sorry to withdraw; and to make MP I 13 123 5
"I am sorry for it," was his answer--"but in this matter MP I 15 140 13
went well--I shall be sorry to be an inconvenience--but as MP I 15 144 38
be sorry to make the character ridiculous by bad acting. MP I 15 145 41
"I am sorry for Miss Crawford; but I am more sorry to see MP I 16 155 15
He could immediately say with easy fluency, "I am sorry MP II 2 193 13
I am sorry for them all, and would give something that MP II 3 200 19
sorry to see you trying at it, than almost any other man." MP II 5 227 66
at Fanny, "I should be sorry to have my powers of planning MP II 7 245 31
But, on the contrary, it was no worse than, "I am sorry to MP II 7 250 60
Fanny struggled for speech, and said, "I am very sorry MP II 9 268 30
me any thing now, which hereafter you may be sorry for. MP II 9 269 36
before--if she had been sorry for what she said, and MP II 11 286 17
This is so much my opinion, that I am sorry to think how MP III 1 317 34
"I am very sorry," said she inarticulately through her MP III 1 319 41
inarticulately through her tears, "I am very sorry indeed." MP III 1 319 41
"Sorry! yes, I hope you are sorry; and you will probably MP III 1 320 42

have reason to be long sorry for this day's transactions."	MP III 1 320 42
"Indeed, sir," said Fanny, "I am very sorry that Mr.	MP III 2 330 15
Edmund was not sorry to be admitted again among the number	MP III 3 344 44
I may be sorry, I may be surprised--though hardly that,	MP III 4 347 16
You must be sorry for your own indifference."	MP III 4 348 21
She was sorry, really sorry; and yet, in spite of this and	MP III 10 406 21
He will see the Rushworths, which I own I am not sorry for-	MP III 12 417 3
I saw him draw back surprised, and I was sorry that Mr.	MP III 13 423 2
She talks of you almost every hour, and I am sorry to find	MP III 13 423 2
She was only sorry for the parties concerned and for	MP III 15 438 4
almost sorry that the subject had been entered on at all.	MP III 16 457 30
She knew it was so, and was sorry; but it was with a	MP III 17 461 3
"But, Mr. Knightley, she is really very sorry to lose poor	E I 1 11 36
made him rather sorry to see any thing put on it; and	E I 3 24 12
and should be very sorry to give them up, for they are	E I 4 31 25
Emma was not sorry to have such an opportunity of survey;	E I 4 31 27
"I should have been sorry, Mr. Knightley, to be dependent	E I 5 37 10
have others deceived, or sorry to know her reputation for	E I 6 44 19
Emma was so sorry to be pressed.	E I 7 50 4
"One should be sorry to see greater pride or refinement in	E I 7 56 41
She was sorry, but could not repent.	E I 9 69 1
heal.-- made her quite sorry to acknowledge that they	E I 9 70 7
from us all!-- and how sorry she will be when she comes,	E I 9 79 58
Indeed I am very sorry.--	E I 12 89 13
"How sorry I am!	E I 12 102 33
"I am sorry to hear you say so, sir; but I assure you,	E I 12 103 39
"I am sorry to find, my love, that my father does not	E I 12 103 42
"I shall always be very sorry that you went to the sea	E I 12 105 51
	52
"But why should you be sorry, sir?--	E I 12 105 53
low pulse, &c. and she was sorry to find from Mrs. Goddard	E I 13 109 6
a while, made her rather sorry to find, when they had all	E I 14 118 4
"I am sorry there should be any thing like doubt in the	E I 14 120 12
I am sorry for it.	E I 14 122 20
misled her, and I am very sorry--extremely sorry--but,	E I 15 130 31
am very sorry--extremely sorry--but, Miss Smith, indeed!--	E I 15 130 31
As to myself, I am very sorry that you should have been	E I 15 131 34
I am exceedingly sorry: but it is well that the mistake	E I 15 132 36
For half an hour Mr. Weston was surprized and sorry; but	E I 18 144 2
Emma was sorry;--to have to pay civilities to a person she	E II 2 166 11
suffered long; but she was sorry for Harriet: Harriet must	E II 3 177 51
I remember she said she was sorry we never met now; which	E II 3 178 52
Of course, he must be sorry to lose her--they must be all	E II 3 179 53
he must be sorry to lose her--they must be all sorry.	E II 3 179 53
I am sorry Mr. and Mrs. Cole should have done it.	E II 7 209 10
I should be extremely sorry to be giving them any pain.	E II 7 210 20
"Well, I am so sorry!--	E II 10 245 48
Mrs. Weston was sorry for such a charge.	E II 11 249 12
"Indeed, I am very sorry to be right in this instance.	E II 12 260 18
was gone; and Emma felt so sorry to part, and foresaw so	E II 12 261 37
to be afraid of being too sorry, and feeling it too much.	E II 12 261 37
He could not say that he was sorry on his own account; his	E II 12 262 40
	41
very steadily, that he was sorry for the disappointment of	E II 12 262 40
	41
I should be sorry to be more."	E II 13 264 2
They are very important--and sorry I am that you cannot	E II 13 268 12
urbanity, said, "I am very sorry to hear, Miss Fairfax, of	E II 16 294 24
	25
myself, and should be sorry to have any made by my friends.	E II 17 300 13
see him now, as he would have been sorry to see him before.	E II 17 302 23
If she is ill I should be sorry to do her injustice; but	E II 18 309 33
You will not be sorry to find yourself at home."	E III 5 345 11
it will not do--very sorry to check you in your first	E III 5 350 37
There had been a time also when Emma would have been sorry	E III 6 360 40
glad to be enlivened, not sorry to be flattered, was gay	E III 7 368 3
Emma recollected, blushed, was sorry, but tried to laugh	E III 7 374 57
She will be extremely sorry to miss seeing you, Miss	E III 8 379 8
keep you waiting--and extremely sorry and ashamed we were.	E III 8 379 8
"Her friends must all be sorry to lose her; and will not	E III 8 382 28
and Mrs. Campbell be sorry to find that she had engaged	E III 8 382 28
She was sorry, very sorry.	E III 9 391 21
I am sorry for her.	E III 13 426 13
suffered, and was very sorry--and he was so grateful to	E III 15 444 1
But she was not at all sorry that she had abused the	E III 17 469 36
She was not sorry.	E III 18 475 37
should be sorry to see any friend of mine belonging to it."	P III 3 19 13
	14
sorry that she had missed the opportunity of seeing them.	P III 5 32 1
a duty, and certainly not sorry to have the scene of it in	P III 5 33 9
Lady Russell was extremely sorry that such a measure	P III 5 34 11
"I am sorry to find you unwell," replied Anne.	P III 5 37 23
him to stay dinner--how sorry when he said it was quite	P III 7 54 4
Wentworth off, and only be sorry to think that the cottage	P III 7 54 5
I assure you, Captain Wentworth, we are very sorry he ever	P III 8 67 27
and relief, that however sorry and ashamed for the	P IV 1 125 17
She was not sorry for the excuse.	P IV 5 157 14
"I am sorry to say that I am very far from well; and "	P IV 6 164 8
I should be very sorry that such a friendship as has	P IV 6 173 46
was obliged, and not sorry to be obliged, to hurry away.	P IV 7 180 36
but I should be sorry to be examined by a real proficient."	P IV 8 187 27
must confess that he should not be sorry when it was over.	P IV 8 190 47
and the others were not so sorry but that they could put	P IV 10 216 18
Anne will not be sorry to join us, I am sure.	P IV 10 223 41
I am not sorry, indeed, to make it over to another.	P IV 11 232 15
I know you will not be sorry to be off.	P IV 11 236 38
But I am afraid; and I should be so very sorry!	P IV 11 239 51
I am sorry to have the appearance of contradicting you--	S 1 365 1
My dear--(to his wife) I am very sorry to have brought you	S 1 367 1
is not much above 20, I am sorry to say, is almost as	S 5 385 1
chance of seeing them at Sanditon I am sorry to say.--	S 5 385 1
Mary, you will be quite sorry to hear how ill they have	S 5 386 1
I am very sorry you met with your accident, but upon my	S 6 393 1
"I am sorry to hear it, indeed; but if this is the case I	S 12 424 1
SORT (325)	
confine herself to that sort of honest flirtation which	LS 4 248 1
rather interests me, a sort of sauciness, of familiarity	LS 7 254 3
Mrs Vernon's consciousness of deserving every sort of	LS 10 258 2
Were you not blinded by a sort of fascination, it would be	LS 12 260 2
a sort of reward to behaviour deserving very differently.	LS 15 267 5
There is a sort of ridiculous delicacy about him which	LS 16 268 2
This is one sort of love--but I confess it does not	LS 16 269 3
seem to have the sort of temper to make severity necessary.	LS 17 270 4
wonder--of a most agreable sort indeed; yet it required	LS 23 284 5
This sort of mysteriousness, which is always so becoming	NA I 5 35 2
of mine, a very good sort of fellow; he ran it a few weeks,	NA I 7 46 11
do; indeed I guessed what sort of stuff it must be before	NA I 7 49 40
drive it; a thing of that sort in good hands will last	NA I 9 65 30
"Not those who bring such fresh feelings of every sort to	NA I 10 79 57
you: a gentleman-like, good sort of fellow as ever lived."	NA I 12 95 18
plays, and things of that sort, and do not dislike travels.	NA I 14 108 20
To Catherine's simple feelings, this odd sort of reserve	NA I 15 121 25
the evening was spent in a sort of war of wit, a display	NA I 15 121 25
any amibition of that sort himself--without any solicitude	NA II 7 178 21
of that sort of reading which she had there indulged.	NA II 10 200 2
"Her mother is a very good sort of woman," was Catherine's	NA II 10 205 26
been her defects of that sort, her mother could not but	NA II 15 240 1
"And what sort of a young man is he?"	SS I 9 43 16
"He is as good a sort of fellow, I believe, as ever lived,"	SS I 9 44 25
Then perhaps you cannot tell me what sort of a woman she	SS I 22 128 5
You will be under the care of a motherly good sort of	SS II 3 156 8
The sort of desperate calmness with which this was said,	SS II 7 180 4
I knew him to be a very good sort of man, and I thought	SS II 9 209 28
way, she has given you a sort of claim on her future	SS II 11 227 46
sort of way, I should have gave it all up in despair.	SS II 13 240 17
Such were my reasonings, as, in a sort of desperate	SS III 8 329 63
a sort of thing that shocks me; I cannot understand it.	W 318 2
Mr Sam Watson is a very good sort of young man, & I dare	W 324 3
to say; & she learnt, by a sort of inevitable enquiry that	W 331 11
was rather afraid of the sort of carriage--.	W 339 18
his coming was a sort of notice which might please her	W 347 22
Mrs R. W. was indeed wondering what sort of a home Emma cd	W 350 24
"That's odd sort of talking!--	W 352 26
"You may imagine, said Margt in a sort of whisper what are	W 356 28
Do you not comprehend the sort of feeling?"--	W 356 28
& Howard's a very gentleman-like good sort of fellow!--	W 358 28
It seems to me to shew an abominable sort of conceited	PP I 8 36 10
and the lucases are very good sort of girls, I assure you.	PP I 9 44 29
But if it be only a slight, thin sort of inclination, I am	PP I 9 44 34
She had high animal spirits, and a sort of natural self-	PP I 9 45 36
you meant it to be a sort of panegyric, of compliment to	PP I 10 49 27
and Lydia had information for them of a different sort.	PP I 12 60 7
And what sort of young lady is she? is she handsome?"	PP I 14 67 6
her ladyship, and it is a sort of attention which I	PP I 14 67 9
But the fact is, that we are very different sort of men,	PP I 16 80 27
He had not a temper to bear the sort of competition in	PP I 16 80 32
we stood--the sort of preference which was often given me."	PP I 16 80 32
"What sort of a girl is Miss Darcy?"	PP I 16 82 42
She was resolved against any sort of conversation with him,	PP I 18 89 3
How wonderfully these sort of things occur!	PP I 18 96 57
his feelings were not of a sort to be much distressed by	PP I 18 101 72
her be an active, useful sort of person, not brought up	PP I 19 105 10
to be of a most agreeable sort; for it gratified him, he	PP I 23 127 6
It is something to think of, and gives her a sort of	PP II 1 137 27
her, that these sort of inconstancies are very frequent."	PP II 2 140 6
the least unwilling to think her a very good sort of girl.	PP II 3 150 29
"But, my dear Elizabeth," she added, "what sort of girl is	PP II 4 153 8
"If you will only tell me what sort of girl Miss King is,	PP II 4 153 10
what I say. she is the sort of woman whom one cannot	PP II 5 157 9
As he spoke there was a sort of smile, which Elizabeth	PP II 9 179 21
And pray what sort of guardians do you make?	PP II 10 184 19
get into a scrape of that sort, and from knowing them to	PP II 10 185 28
But disguise of every sort is my abhorrence.	PP II 11 192 22
of a gentleman within the sort of grove which edged the	PP II 12 195 2
together, and given her a sort of intimacy with his ways,	PP II 13 207 6
I have the greatest dislike in the world to that sort of	PP II 13 211 13
family is indeed the sort of extraordinary advantage and	PP II 15 215 4
enough to make one good sort of man; and of late it has	PP II 17 225 10
And what sort of table do they keep?	PP II 17 228 31
I only fear that the sort of cautiousness, to which you, I	PP II 18 234 38
This is not the sort of happiness which a man would in	PP II 19 236 1
impression on her was of a sort to be encouraged, as by no	PP III 2 266 16
We all know him to be a proud, unpleasant sort of man; but	PP III 17 376 33
the part of Tom, than that sort of merriment which a young	MP I 2 17 22
that no benefit of that sort would have been beyond his	MP I 3 23 3
But "no, he was a short-neck'd, apoplectic sort of fellow,	MP I 3 24 5
wanting in comforts of any sort, had never borne a bad	MP I 3 31 59
Lady Bertram listened without much interest to this sort	MP I 3 31 60
any former pleasure of the sort; and the addition it was	MP I 4 37 8
It was a connection exactly of the right sort; in the same	MP I 4 40 14
him into any thing of the sort, it will be a fresh matter	MP I 4 42 21
"Why as to that--Mr. Rushworth is a very good sort of	MP I 5 45 13
at any rate; he was the sort of young man to be generally	MP I 5 47 28
A girl not out, has always the same sort of dress; a close	MP I 5 49 32
a remarkably large, fair sort, that what with early tarts	MP I 6 54 13
or any body of that sort, would certainly have the avenue	MP I 6 55 17
Post captains may be very good sort of men, but they do	MP I 6 60 49
"You are fond of the sort of thing?" said Julia.	MP I 6 61 55
and not see more of the sort of fault which he had already	MP I 7 66 14
A successful scheme of this sort generally brings on	MP I 7 70 30
observing that "it was a sort of building which she could	MP I 8 82 35
"For if," said he, with the sort of self-evident	MP I 9 89 31
Every sort of exercise fatigues her so soon, Miss Crawford,	MP I 9 95 68
The sort of dread in which Fanny now sat of seeing Mr.	MP I 10 101 33
of that sort, you know, can be settled without you."	MP I 10 102 47
minutes, nor to banish the sort of curiosity she felt, to	MP I 10 103 49
was just the sort that my sister would be delighted with.	MP I 10 105 55
living creatures of that sort; and so to be sure it will.	MP I 10 106 57
"It is the same sort of thing," said Fanny, after a short	MP I 11 109 18
But it is not to be a display of that sort.	MP I 13 125 18
trifling part, but the sort of thing I should not dislike,	MP I 14 132 7
"I should not have thought it the sort of play to be so	MP I 15 139 9
always said so,--just the sort of people to get all they	MP I 15 142 22
in a trifle of this sort,--so kind as they are to you!--	MP I 15 146 53
so often encouraged the sort of thing in us formerly.	MP II 1 184 26
Mr. Rushworth is the sort of amiable modest young man who	MP II 2 188 3
differing in the sort of evil, did by no means bring less.	MP II 2 192 11
they are in fact exactly the sort of people he would like.	MP II 3 196 2
There must be a sort of shyness.	MP II 3 197 3
meeting again in the same sort of way, allowing for the	MP II 3 199 14
Such was the origin of the sort of intimacy which took	MP II 4 207 11
carelessly, "it does very well for a place of this sort.	MP II 4 209 15
I am very apt to get into this sort of wondering strain.	MP II 4 209 16
to be too rich to lament or to feel any thing of the sort.	MP II 4 213 36
Fanny never dines there, you know, in this sort of way.	MP II 5 217 1
going into company in this sort of way, or ever dining out	MP II 5 220 28
as people say; a sort of beauty that grows on one.	MP II 6 230 6
a church standing on a sort of knoll to my right--which	MP II 7 241 13
of the sort at Thornton Lacey, without accepting his help.	MP II 7 244 30
Your cousins are not of a sort to forget their relations,	MP II 7 245 32
a time when you will have nothing of that sort to endure.	MP II 7 249 53
It is the sort of subject on which it had better never be	MP II 9 269 35
and your sister is not used to these sort of hours."	MP II 10 279 24
too, and completing the sort of general break-up of a	MP II 11 286 15
the sort of friendly acquaintance we have had together?--	MP II 11 287 22
They will now see what sort of woman it is that can attach	MP II 12 297 33
This is a sort of talking which is very unpleasant to me.	MP II 13 301 7
Quite unpractised in such sort of note-writing, had there	MP II 13 307 30
	31
to any thing of the sort, that I hope you will excuse my	MP II 13 307 31
the pleasure was not of a sort to die with the day--for	MP II 13 308 36
her could distress him long; his mind was not of that sort.	MP III 1 324 59
While Fanny's mind was engaged in these sort of hopes, her	MP III 1 324 60
rare indeed), was of a sort to heighten all his wishes,	MP III 2 326 3
in a perseverance of this sort, against discouragement.	MP III 2 330 14
as you might have done, had nothing of this sort occurred.	MP III 2 331 16
it made her feel a sort of credit in calling her niece.	MP III 2 332 22
Her reception of him was of a sort which he could not have	MP III 3 334 2
distinguished preacher in my life, without a sort of envy.	MP III 3 341 30
You must have some feeling of that sort.	MP III 4 348 21
deep, heart-swelling sort; and though never a great talker,	MP III 6 369 11
to be cured, this was a sort of cure that would be almost	MP III 10 402 11
by everybody; it was a sort of renewed separation from	MP III 11 413 31
his entering into a plan of that sort, most pleasantly.	MP III 12 419 9
It was a sort of playing at being frightened.	MP III 13 427 12
I looked upon him as the sort of person to be made a fuss	MP III 14 433 13
her correspondent was not of a sort to regard a slight one.	MP III 15 438 6
At first, it was a sort of stupefaction; but every moment	MP III 15 440 19
her perceptions and her pleasures were of the keenest sort.	MP III 15 446 35
After a little reflection, he went on with a sort of	MP III 16 455 19
It was a sort of laugh, as she answered, 'a pretty good	MP III 16 458 30
but still it was a sort of thing which he never could get	MP III 16 460 31
soon re-established the sort of familiar intercourse--of	MP III 17 468 21
Being pretty well aware of what sort of joy you must both	E I 1 10 27

though she had one sort of spirit, she had not the best. E I 2 15 3
been the means of a sort of reconciliation; and Mr. and E I 2 16 4
man had made Highbury feel a sort of pride in him too. E I 2 17 7
happened to be of a sort which Emma particularly admired. E I 3 23 9
though very good sort of people, must be doing her harm. E I 3 23 10
It was quite a different sort of thing--a sentiment E I 4 26 2
The next question was: "what sort of looking man is Mr. E I 4 29 10
11

is the very last sort of person to raise my curiosity. E I 4 29 14
Six years hence, if he could meet with a good sort of E I 4 30 18
decided, commanding sort of manner--though it suits him E I 4 34 42
I think her the very worst sort of companion that Emma E I 5 38 15
And it was spoken with a sort of sighing animation, which E I 6 43 8
She had soon fixed on the size and sort of portrait. E I 6 46 23
Yes, I understand the sort of mind. E I 7 51 5
"Indeed! how so? of what sort?" E I 8 59 21
"A very serious sort, I assure you;" still smiling. E I 8 59 22
Mr. Knightley was a sort of general friend and advisor, E I 8 59 24
in her, to her having that sort of disposition, which, in E I 8 61 38
Vanity working on a weak head, produces every sort of E I 8 64 47
be; but yet she had a sort of habitual respect for his E I 8 65 50
Elton is a very good sort of man, and a very respectable E I 8 66 53
an attachment as her youth and sort of mind admitted. E I 9 69 2
all the riddles of every sort that she could meet with, E I 9 69 3
which were otherwise of a sort to run into great length, E I 9 72 16
It is a sort of prologue to the play, a motto to the E I 9 74 23
"It is a sort of thing which nobody could have expected. E I 9 74 24
He loves any thing of the sort, and especially any thing E I 9 77 45
qualities, there was a sort of parade in his speeches E I 9 82 84
every sort of sensation that declining life can need. E I 10 86 21
I hope not of a putrid infectious sort. E I 13 109 7
to a certain degree, and a sort of pleasure in the idea of E I 14 119 5
early separations of any sort; but at last the drawing- E I 15 124 1
Mr. Weston, with triumph of a different sort, was E I 15 126 11
home; and it is not the sort of thing that gives me cold." E I 15 127 14
"Then, my dear Isabella, it is the most extraordinary sort E I 15 127 15
Smith is a very good sort of girl; and I should be happy E I 15 131 35
and humiliation, of some sort or other; but, compared with E I 16 134 1
being but a sort of notch in the Donwell Abbey estate, to E I 16 136 9
not be of that superior sort in which the feelings are E I 16 138 15
an inclination of that sort unrequited, that she could not E I 17 142 12
If he would act in this sort of manner, on principle, E I 18 147 18
Can you think your friend behind-hand in these sort of E I 18 149 26
Fairfax is a very pretty sort of young lady, a very pretty E II 3 171 12
question----- "she is a sort of elegant creature that one E II 3 171 14
15

think I am particularly quick at those sort of discoveries. E II 3 176 44
I mean in person--tall, and with that sort of look--and E II 3 176 44
yet, you know, there was a sort of satisfaction in seeing E II 3 179 52
be looking around with a sort of fearful curiosity, which E II 5 186 2
the sort of meeting, and the sort of pain it was creating. E II 5 186 4
to have always felt the sort of interest in the country E II 5 191 26
in him of all such sort of penetration or suspicion, was a E II 5 193 35
must be a very distinct sort of elegance for the E II 5 194 43
the principal one of the sort, where a couple of pair of E II 6 197 5
and were very good sort of people--friendly, liberal, and E II 7 207 6
to their expenses of every sort; and by this time were, in E II 7 207 6
sure, sir; friendly, good sort of people as ever lived, E II 7 210 19
say, but with you it is a sort of bravado, an air of E II 8 213 10
about Enscombe, and the sort; and could make out from his E II 8 221 48
sort of thing that so few men would think of. E II 8 223 63
Mr. Knightley to do the sort of thing--to do any thing E II 8 223 64
As a sort of touchstone, however, she began to speak of E II 8 228 88
I like a job of that sort excessively.' E II 9 238 51
The apples themselves are the very finest sort for baking, E II 9 238 51
basket of apples, the same sort of apples, a bushel at E II 9 239 51
all the apples of that sort his master had; he had brought E II 9 239 51
if you suppose Mr. Perry to be that sort of character. E II 11 251 28
these sort of things require a good deal of consideration. E II 11 252 32
He said, from the first, it was a very good sort--which E II 11 253 38
upon him to be quite the sort of man--I do not altogether E II 13 265 4
of confirming us in that sort of true disinterested E II 13 267 7
When people come into a beautiful country of this sort, E II 14 274 28
beauties which attract the sort of parties you speak of; E II 14 274 29
she seems a very pretty sort of young lady; and I dare say E II 14 279 54
I have no idea of that sort of thing. E II 15 283 9
here month after month, under privations of every sort! E II 15 285 13
"She must be under some sort of penance, inflicted either E II 15 285 15
One says those sort of things, of course, without any idea E II 15 288 35
Knightley, "that the same sort of hand-writing often E II 16 297 45
or spirits like Selina to enjoy that sort of seclusion. E II 18 307 21
of our meetings, the sort of constant expectation there E II 18 309 30
indolent, gentlemanlike sort of pride that would harm E II 18 309 33
disgust of people of that sort; for there is a family in E II 18 310 34
else to do, formed a sort of half circle round the fire, E III 2 320 5
Nothing of the sort had ever occurred before to any young E III 3 335 10
should like to tell you--a sort of confession to make--and E III 4 337 1
2

on any application of the sort; and it would be safer for E III 4 341 34
knew it was exactly the sort of visiting that would be E III 5 344 3
This is a sort of dull-looking evening, that ought to be E III 5 347 19
by the more animated sort, which Mr. Weston had E III 5 347 20
There is to be no form or parade--a sort of gipsy party.-- E III 6 355 20
In a country life I conceive it to be a sort of necessary; E III 6 356 26
Under that peculiar sort of dry, blunt manner, I know you E III 6 356 28
Morning decidedly the best time--never tired--every sort E III 6 358 35
not the sort of fatigue--quick walking will refresh me.-- E III 6 363 50
"It is a sort of thing," cried Mrs. Elton emphatically, " E III 7 370 20
said, "this explains the sort of clever thing that is E III 7 371 35
36

cannot attempt--I am not at all fond of the sort of thing. E III 7 371 37
added her husband, with a sort of sneering consciousness; " E III 7 372 38
and every thing of that sort, but still he cannot keep his E III 8 383 29
more pitiable from this sort of irritation of spirits. E III 9 391 21
But I shall always think it a very abominable sort of E III 10 399 61
that he could have that sort of affection for herself E III 12 416 1
as those sort of visits conveyed, might shortly be over. E III 12 422 19
I am not in want of that sort of compassion. E III 13 426 15
then, he might have deemed him a very good sort of fellow. E III 13 433 42
sort of intimacy into which we were immediately thrown.-- E III 14 438 8
I felt that it would be of a different sort.-- E III 14 443 8
she saw her with a sort of anxious parade of mystery fold E III 16 453 12
13

she, with a sort of serious smile--"much less, perhaps, E III 17 464 22
must change into a calmer sort of goodwill; and, E III 19 482 5
up at the same time, in a sort of desolate tranquillity, P III 5 35 18
almost every house in the parish, as a sort of take-leave. P III 5 39 34
Mr. and Mrs. Musgrove were a very good sort of people; P III 5 40 45
suspicion of Mrs. Croft's side, to give a bias of any sort. P III 6 48 18
eight years ago,--was a new sort of trial to Anne's nerves. P III 6 52 33
I have not nerves for the sort of thing." P III 7 56 12
Where was this superfine, extraordinary sort of gallantry P III 8 69 39
a very good-natured, good sort of a fellow; and whenever P III 9 76 15
he will make a different sort of place of it, and live in P III 9 76 15
live in a very different sort of way; and with that P III 9 76 15
and admired again the sort of necessity which the family- P III 10 83 4
After a little succession of these sort of debates and P III 10 86 18
along the rough, wild sort of channel, down the centre. P III 10 87 22
He considered his disposition as of the sort which must P III 11 97 12
was to be their sort of intercourse, she could not foresee. P III 12 116 70
became a sort of parting proof, its value did not lessen. P III 12 117 75
A new sort of way this, for a young fellow to be making P IV 1 126 22

he made a very awkward sort of excuse; "he never shot" and P IV 2 130 5
he has a taste for those sort of things, I thought that P IV 2 131 12
He is just Lady Russell's sort. P IV 2 132 18
most distressing, by their sort rather than their quantity. P IV 2 135 33
in a sort of whisper, "that must not be any reason, indeed. P IV 4 145 1
in their having the same sort of pride, she was pleased P IV 4 151 22
She had had difficulties of every sort to contend with a P IV 5 152 4
be out, if they were all Sophys, or something of that sort. P IV 6 171 33
for that soft sort of manner does not do him justice." P IV 6 171 37
or even wounded, by a circumstance of this sort." P IV 6 173 46
There was consciousness of some sort or other. P IV 7 176 8
an incessant and fearful sort of watch for him in vain; P IV 7 178 28
She could thoroughly comprehend the sort of fascination he P IV 7 179 28
Wentworth, in a reserved yet hurried sort of farewell. P IV 8 190 48
There is a sort of domestic enjoyment to be known even in P IV 9 193 12
I assure you that nothing of the sort you are thinking of P IV 9 195 28
It seemed to announce a different sort of man." P IV 9 200 56
careful, discerning sort of character; but Colonel Wallis P IV 9 205 82
for many years under a sort of sequestration for the P IV 9 210 98
I have no pleasure in the sort of meeting, and should be P IV 10 224 53
pursuits, business of some sort or other, to take you back P IV 11 232 19
who thought only of one sort of illness, having assured P IV 11 238 47
At Lyme, he had received lessons of more than one sort. P IV 11 242 62
It is a sort of pain, too, which is new to me. P IV 11 247 84
impression which the sort of wild goose-chace you find me S 1 367 1
diffuse comfort & improvement among them of every sort.-- S 1 368 1
am afraid this is the only sort of acquaintance I shall S 5 386 1
She cd see nothing worse in Lady Denham, than the sort of S 6 392 1
say she thinks me an odd sort of a creature,--but she will S 6 393 1
But if you will describe the sort of novels which you do S 8 403 1
Though he owed many of his ideas to this sort of reading, S 8 404 1
sort of attachment which her personal charms had raised.-- S 8 405 2
him to prefer the quietest sort of ruin & disgrace for the S 8 405 2
One sees clearly enough by all this, the sort of woman Mrs S 9 409 1
he began even to make a sort of apology for having a fire. S 10 415 1
Miss P. drinking one sort of Herb-Tea & Miss Diana another, S 10 416 1
rest, must have been the sort of sensation of being less S 11 420 1
of this kind--it is a sort of tax upon all that come--yet S 12 423 1
I look upon her to be the sort of person who, when once S 12 424 1
out what sort of carriage it was, which they saw coming up. S 12 425 1

SORTS (2)

on the different sorts of friendship in the world, Mary on MP III 5 360 13
These the finest beds and finest sorts.-- E III 6 358 35

SOTHERTON (52)

I declare when I got back to Sotherton yesterday, it MP I 6 53 2
"but depend upon it, Sotherton will have every improvement MP I 6 53 5
part of the size of Sotherton, I should be always planting MP I 6 53 9
other subjects took place of the improvements of Sotherton. MP I 6 55 14
Now, at Sotherton, we have a good seven hundred, without MP I 6 55 17
have the avenue at Sotherton down; the avenue that leads MP I 6 55 17
I really know very little of Sotherton." MP I 6 56 18
"I should like to see Sotherton before it is cut down, to MP I 6 56 22
"I collect," said Miss Crawford, "that Sotherton is an old MP I 6 56 25
honour of coming over to Sotherton, and taking a bed there; MP I 6 61 58
dinner here, or dine at Sotherton just as might be most MP I 6 62 58
of the plan for visiting Sotherton, which had been started MP I 8 75 1
The Sotherton scheme was mentioned of course. MP I 8 75 2
Sotherton is the only place that could giver her a wish to MP I 8 76 3
who had never been at Sotherton yet, and it was a pity she MP I 8 76 4
she will have opportunities in plenty of seeing Sotherton. MP I 8 76 5
must be wanting to see Sotherton, to include Miss Crawford MP I 8 76 7
roads between this and Sotherton; he always complains MP I 8 77 12
Fanny has a great desire to see Sotherton. MP I 8 78 21
in seeing Sotherton would be nothing without him. MP I 8 79 27
When they came within the influence of Sotherton MP I 8 81 33
vicinity of Sotherton, the former had considerable effect. MP I 8 81 33
"those woods belonged to Sotherton," she could not MP I 8 81 33
ever see Sotherton again with so much pleasure as I do now. MP I 10 98 7
If other people think Sotherton improved, I have no doubt MP I 10 98 8
half pleased that Sotherton should be so complimented. MP I 10 106 56
The day at Sotherton, with all its imperfections, afforded MP I 11 107 1
but since the day at Sotherton, she could never see Mr. MP I 12 115 5
I think she likes Sotherton too well to be inconstant." MP I 17 162 16
But her chief strength lay in Sotherton. MP II 2 188 3
You know the distance to Sotherton; it was in the middle MP II 2 189 3
with the great news for Sotherton; and she had fondly MP II 2 192 11
"To-morrow, I think, my uncle dines at Sotherton, and you MP II 3 199 17
and the nearness of Sotherton to Mansfield must naturally MP II 3 201 22
pledged herself anew to Sotherton--that she was safe from MP II 3 201 23
for him, rejecting Sotherton and London, independence and MP II 3 202 25
over the wonders of Sotherton in her evening-parties-- MP II 3 202 28
had taken place, which gave Sotherton another mistress. MP II 3 202 28
from the church door to Sotherton, was the same chaise MP II 3 203 29
I expect we shall be all very much at Sotherton another MP II 4 210 21
for excepting the day at Sotherton, she had scarcely ever MP II 5 219 27
Only think how useful he was at Sotherton! MP II 7 244 30
there was much done at Sotherton; but it is a hot day, MP II 7 245 31
powers of planning judged of by the day at Sotherton. MP II 7 245 31
Sotherton was a word to catch Mrs. Norris, and being just MP II 7 245 32
hands, she called out in high good-humour, "Sotherton! MP II 7 245 32
Mrs. Rushworth at Sotherton, to afford a reason, an MP II 8 252 2
Maria might be very glad to see her at Sotherton now and MP II 11 285 14
Sotherton arose from difference of disposition and habit-- MP II 11 285 15
in the grounds of Sotherton, or the theatre at Mansfield MP III 2 328 7
"Mansfield, Sotherton, Thornton Lacey," he continued, " MP III 10 405 19
in yearly meetings at Sotherton and Everingham.' MP III 16 456 23

SOTHERTON COURT (3)

the mention of Sotherton Court, and the ideas attached to MP I 6 52 1
Sotherton Court is the noblest old place in the world." MP I 6 53 3
Such a place as Sotherton Court deserves every thing that MP I 6 53 9

SOUGHT (43)

Mr. Tilney, as if he had sought her on purpose!--it did NA I 10 75 24
jumped hastily in, and sought some suspension of agony by NA II 6 170 12
With these feelings, she rather dreaded than sought for NA II 14 232 6
renewed, was sought for, was created again and again. SS I 1 7 13
the whole day, neither sought nor avoided the mention of SS I 19 104 10
was in fact as little valued, as it was professedly sought. SS II 14 246 2
as what she now sought; and with a mind anxiously pre- SS III 10 348 34
When Robert first sought her acquaintance, and privately SS III 14 376 11
married,--and who still sought the constitutional safe- SS III 14 378 15
No aunt, no officers, no news could be sought after;--the PP I 17 88 15
She then sought her eldest sister, who had undertaken to PP I 18 95 48
have judged better, had I sought an introduction, but I am PP II 8 175 21
Had she known that her sister sought to tear her from such PP II 18 232 23
was gone, Jane constantly sought the same means of relief. PP III 13 349 44
was wanted--she was sought for and attended, and praised; MP I 17 160 6
long allowed and even sought his attentions, with a MP I 17 160 8
both, to have any comfort in having been sought by either. MP I 18 170 24
wife and children, had sought no confidant but the butler, MP II 1 180 10
of obligation for being sought after now when nobody else MP II 4 208 11
Her opinion was sought as to the probable continuance of MP II 5 223 48
have been the last to be sought after, and should have MP II 10 274 8
her hand being so eagerly sought after, that her MP II 10 278 20
way of the happiness he sought, was a cruel necessity.-- MP II 13 302 9
Maria is nobly married--but had Mr. Crawford sought MP III 1 319 39
desire his comfort, and sought to regain his favour; and MP III 1 322 50
of talent too, that he sought her for her gentleness, and MP III 2 328 6
To know Fanny to be sought in marriage by a man of fortune, MP III 2 332 22
you might have had sooner, Fanny, had you sought it. MP III 4 346 14
the misfortune of being sought by a clever, agreeable man, MP III 10 402 11
rather be prevented than sought--all this together most MP III 16 457 30
of being admired and sought after, of having the power of E I 8 63 44

Am I to believe that you have never sought to recommend E I 15 131 34
When he did return, he sought out the child and took E II 2 163 4
She bitterly regretted not having sought a closer E III 12 421 17
had he and all his family sought round the world for a E III 13 428 23
death Sir Walter had sought the acquaintance, and though P III 1 7 14
her thanks, and rather sought to testify that her P III 9 80 34
If he really sought to reconcile himself like a dutiful P IV 2 136 35
Their acquaintance was exceedingly sought after. P IV 3 137 4
She had sought him. P IV 3 139 9
I could never doubt that you would be loved and sought by P IV 11 244 70
the same consciousness sought to conceal;--and with P IV 11 246 78
mile or two of a Willingden, I sought no farther . . . S 1 367 1

SOUL (56)

He is devoted to me, heart & soul. LS 31 302 1
"Ten o'clock! it was eleven, upon my soul! NA I 7 46 9
at see-saw and learning Latin; upon my soul there is not." NA I 7 49 42
Upon my soul, you might shake it to pieces yourself with a NA I 9 65 28
"Did upon my soul; knew him again directly, and he seemed NA I 11 85 39
upon my soul!--stout, active,--looks as young as his son. NA I 12 95 18
"I have, upon my soul. NA I 13 100 15
by the generosity of my soul than the clearness of my head. NA I 14 112 36
for there is not a soul at Clifton at this time of year. NA I 14 115 50
"a famous good thing this marrying scheme, upon my soul! NA I 15 122 30
have such--upon my soul I do not know any body like you." NA I 15 123 38
"Upon my soul," said he, "I do not know much about him as SS I 9 44 20
I know her greatness of soul, there would not be music SS I 17 92 25
"I wish with all my soul," cried Sir John, "that SS I 18 100 21
Not a soul of all my relations know of it but Anne, and I SS I 22 129 16
said Miss Steele-- "dear little soul, how I do love her!" SS II 1 145 21
which filled the whole soul and beamed in the eyes of SS II 4 159 1
it,) I was once as dear to him as my own soul could wish. SS II 7 188 46
I wish with all my soul his wife may plague his heart out. SS II 8 192 3
"Poor soul!" cried Mrs. Jennings, as soon as she was gone, SS II 8 194 8
Poor soul! SS II 8 195 16
"Upon my soul," he added, "I believe it is nothing more; SS II 14 251 13
Poor soul! SS III 1 259 7
Poor soul! SS III 2 278 32
moment--"but upon my soul, it is a most serious business. SS III 5 298 35
enough!--but, upon my soul, I believe he has as good a SS III 5 299 35
"Upon my soul it is,"--was his answer, with a warmth which SS III 8 319 25
"But, upon my soul, I did not know it," he warmly replied; SS III 8 322 38
Now, however, his good-natured, honest, stupid soul, full SS III 8 330 69
Not a soul suspected anything of the matter, not even SS III 13 370 37
not even Nancy, who, poor soul! came crying to me the day SS III 13 370 37
grieved to the soul by a thousand tender recollections. PP I 16 78 20
Not a soul knew of it, but Col. and Mrs. Forster, and PP II 16 221 17
For the life and soul of me, I cannot admire him;--and MP I 18 165 3
No, I will not do her any harm dear little soul! MP II 6 231 9
I know it to be playfulness, it grieves me to the soul." MP II 9 269 31
your choice from my soul, and foresee your happiness as MP II 12 292 7
From my soul I do not think she would marry you without MP II 12 293 15
Poor little soul! she could but just speak to be heard, MP III 7 386 44
conveying you home, and I join him in it with all my soul. MP III 14 435 14
Good soul! she was as grateful as possible, you may be E II 8 223 63
day to this, I never mentioned it to a soul that I know of. E III 5 346 16
dear soul! if you were to see what a headach she has. E III 8 379 8
I assure you, I have not seen a soul this whole long P III 5 37 25
his soul, and trying by prayer and reflection to calm them. P III 12 112 54
all his understanding and soul; and I am sure from his P IV 2 131 12
She, poor soul, is tied by the leg. P IV 6 170 29
With all my soul I wish them happy, and rejoice over every P IV 8 182 8
listening with his whole soul; and that the last words P IV 10 224 49
And then, if I could convey to you the glow of his soul P 1 6 235 31
"You are a good soul," cried Captain Harville, putting his P IV 11 235 34
"You pierce my soul. P IV 11 237 42
Wordsworth has the true soul of it--Campbell in his S 7 397 1
His soul was the altar in which lovely woman sat enshrined, S 7 397 1
to expect from the soul of high toned genius, the S 7 398 1
elicit such fire in the soul of man as leads him--(though S 8 403 1

SOULS (2)

Poor souls! SS II 5 167 1
without our sighing out our souls over this charade." E I 9 78 47

SOUND (82)

immediately fell into a sound sleep which lasted nine NA I 9 60 1
There is not a sound piece of iron about it. NA I 9 65 28
Perhaps the abilities of women are neither sound nor acute- NA I 14 112 36
off--you listen to the sound of her receding footsteps as NA II 5 159 17
In the pause which succeeded, a sound like receding NA II 6 170 12
once her blood was chilled by the sound of distant moans. NA II 6 171 12
the next day, was the sound which first roused Catherine; NA II 7 172 1
with no sullen sound that could alarm a human being. NA II 9 193 6
she had entered, when the sound of footsteps, she could NA II 9 194 6
She listened--the sound had ceased; and resolving not to NA II 9 194 6
seemed anxiously listening to the sound of every carriage. SS II 4 161 6
some time even after the sound of his carriage had died SS III 9 333 1
called down stairs by the sound of another carriage.-- SS III 9 333 3
as a good mind and a sound understanding must consider it; SS III 11 350 9
though fearing the sound of her own voice, now said, "is SS III 12 359 16
17
wide staircase, while no sound of a ball but the first W 327 7
give way; the inspiriting sound of other carriages was W 328 8
over, when the returning sound of carriages after a long W 329 9
to the sound of the music, for the last half hour. W 329 9
enquiries, when the light sound of a carriage driving up W 338 17
mrs edwards put on her very stiffest look at the sound.-- W 338 17
to the front door, by the sound of as smart a rap as the W 344 21
A sound like a distant carriage was at this moment caught; W 354 28
It was an unusual sound in Stanton at any time of the day, W 354 28
"You make me laugh, Charlotte; but it is not sound. PP I 6 23 11
You know it is not sound, and that you would never act in PP I 6 23 11
very agreeably, when the sound of horses drew their notice, PP I 15 72 8
was suddenly roused by the sound of the door bell, and her PP II 11 188 3
She continued in very agitating reflections till the sound PP II 11 194 32
the same family, when the sound of a carriage drew them to PP III 2 260 1
without bringing the sound of his voice; and when PP III 11 335 43
to the window, by the sound of a carriage; and they PP III 14 351 1
a tete-a-tete from any sound of unkindness, was MP I 4 35 6
a doubt, for the sound of merriment ascended even to her. MP I 7 67 16
It was a sound which did not make her cheerful; she MP I 7 67 16
the corner, and listened till all sound of them had ceased. MP I 9 96 76
she remained without sight or sound of any companion. MP I 10 100 23
more caught her ear; the sound approached, and a few more MP I 10 103 49
wore away in satisfactions very sweet, if not very sound. MP I 17 159 6
twenty-four hours; the sound of a little bustle at the MP II 4 205 3
There is something in the sound of Mr. Edmund Bertram so MP II 4 211 22
"To me, the sound of mr. Bertram is so cold and nothing- MP II 4 211 23
Edmund or sir Edmund sound delightfully; but sink it under MP II 4 211 24
to say so, when the sound of the great clock at Mansfield MP II 4 214 46
sound of the carriage which was to bring her a brother. MP II 6 233 14
for him by a sound intellect and an honest heart. MP II 9 265 18
but the comfort of the sound was impaired by his turning MP II 13 306 28
when suddenly the sound of a step in regular approach was MP III 1 312 4
He saw her lips formed into a no, though the sound was MP III 1 316 32
trying to bury every sound of the business from himself in MP III 3 341 31
had it not been for the sound of approaching relief, the MP III 3 344 42
relief, the very sound which she had been long watching MP III 3 344 42
to do; and it had a sound of most sisterly cordiality." MP III 4 352 42
but no second sound had been heard of such a purpose. MP III 7 387 45
She gave advice; advice too sound to be resisted by a good MP III 9 397 8
ramparts with so fine a sound, produced altogether such a MP III 11 409 6
not avoid a little start, and a little blush, at the sound. E II 3 173 25
pleasure was conveyed in sound--for Mr. Weston immediately E II 5 188 6
7
The first remote sound to which she felt herself obliged E II 8 214 13
Emma grew sick at the sound. E II 13 267 8
I always say there is something direful in the sound: but E II 18 310 34
not hear the sound of at first, without great surprise. E III 2 319 3
he was watching for the sound of other carriages,-- E III 2 320 7
She had never rejoiced at the sound before, nor ever E III 8 378 3
dreadful penance, by the sound of her father's footsteps. E III 11 411 42
no want of words, if the sound of Mrs. Elton's voice from E III 16 453 10
and, from habit, it has not so very formal a sound.-- E III 17 462 11
side, so fresh the sound of those words, spoken with such E III 18 473 27
She was a woman rather of sound than of quick abilities, P III 2 11 2
"I have let my house to Admiral Croft," would sound P III 3 24 36
We had been six hours in the sound, when a gale came on, P III 8 66 16
quite out of sight and sound, Mary was happy no longer; P III 10 86 21
They had nearly done breakfast, when the sound of a P III 12 105 8
was enough to make the sound of Lady Russell's carriage P IV 1 123 8
"Lady Dalrymple, Lady Dalrymple," was the rejoicing sound; P IV 8 184 17
Elliot," said he, "has long had an interesting sound to me. P IV 8 188 36
had she received their sound, than her attention was P IV 8 188 37
mildness, or the sound of his artificial good sentiments. P IV 10 214 11
a something of familiar sound, gave her two moments P IV 11 239 55
of the baker's shop, the sound of a harp might be heard S 4 383 1
all who walked within the sound of her instrument, & on S 11 421 1
& sound her ladyship as to a Subscription for them. S 12 423 1

SOUNDED (4)

When first sounded on the subject, he was so miserable, E III 19 483 9
All that sounded extravagant or irrational in the progress P IV 3 140 11
cousins, the Dalrymples," sounded in her ears all day long. P IV 4 148 11
I sounded Susan--the same thought had occurred to her.-- S 9 409 1

SOUNDS (28)

All this sounds very reasonably. LS 15 267 7
her ears now and then; and how welcome were the sounds! NA I 1 15 2
"Yes, to be sure, as you state it, all this sounds very NA I 10 77 34
Yes, these were characteristic sounds;--they brought to NA II 6 166 9
frequent but inarticulate sounds of complaint which passed SS III 7 310 10
11
Such were the last audible sounds of Miss Watson's voice, W 321 2
How well it sounds. PP III 7 306 47
sounds of opening doors and passing footsteps. MP II 1 175 1
this, before there were sounds from the billiard room to MP II 1 182 22
"It sounds like it," said Edmund; "but which way did you MP II 7 241 14
reading to himself, no sounds were heard in the room for MP II 11 283 6
At Mansfield, no sounds of contention, no raised voice, no MP III 8 391 11
more acute sensibility to fine sounds than to my feelings. E II 6 202 31
to which the sweet sounds of the united voices gave only E II 8 227 87
to, pursued only by the sounds of her desultory good-will. E II 9 239 52
'Lady Wentworth' sounds very well. P III 9 75 11
The sounds were retreating, and Anne distinguished no more. P III 10 89 34
as in other matters; and sounds are quite innoxious, or P IV 2 135 33
"eleven with its silver sounds," and the watchman was P IV 3 144 23
was caught by other sounds immediately behind her, which P IV 8 188 37
After the usual period of suspense, the usual sounds of P IV 10 216 17
while still hearing the sounds he had uttered, she was P IV 10 225 61
Alarming sounds were heard; other visitors approached, and P IV 10 226 63
sounds, which yet she did not think he could have caught. P IV 11 233 24
Such sights & sounds were highly Blissful to Mr P.-- S 4 383 1
That sounds well. S 6 392 1
It sounds almost incredible--but it has happened to me so S 10 418 1
"It sounds rather odd to be sure--answered Charlotte S 10 418 1

SOUP (11)

the York hotel, ate some soup, and bespoke an early dinner, NA I 15 116 1
home perhaps--but you are sure of some comfortable soup.-- W 315 1
& retrospections which now ensued, over the welcome soup.-- W 336 14
has made white soup enough I shall send round my cards." PP I 11 55 7
The soup was fifty times better than what we had at the PP III 12 342 28
The soup would be sent round in a most spiritless manner, MP I 6 52 1
she burst through his recital with the proposal of soup. MP II 1 180 10
"Sure, my dear Sir Thomas, a basin of soup would be a much MP II 1 180 10
Do have a basin of soup." MP II 1 180 10
with hopes and fears, soup and negus, sore-footed and MP II 10 280 33
Soup too! E III 2 330 45

SOUR (3)

was, though Mrs. Bennet's sour looks and ill-natured PP I 23 127 8
has a tendency to contract the mind, and sour the temper. E I 10 85 19
had been no happiness to sour his mind, nor (she began P IV 4 147 6

SOURCE (35)

of another the true source of her debasement, is one of NA I 8 53 2
evening concluded, a new source of felicity arose to her. NA I 10 80 61
a source of some real agitation to the mind of Isabella. NA I 15 119 14
the marriage was the only source of Isabella's regret; and NA II 1 137 50
You have gained a new source of enjoyment, and it is well NA II 7 174 8
Yet how different now the source of her inquietude from NA II 13 227 26
or received, was to her a source of immoveable disgust. SS I 1 6 9
it chanced to prove a source of fresh pain to herself, SS II 9 202 4
was likely to prove a source of unhappiness to himself of SS III 8 331 70
she had yet another source of joy unthought of by Elinor. SS III 9 335 7
an inquiry of thomas, as to the source of his intelligence. SS III 11 353 25
had been a continual source of disquiet and regret to him. SS III 13 367 21
of character, as the source of her clemency, gave him SS III 14 379 18
opened to his nieces a source of felicity unknown before. PP I 7 28 4
of her northern tour was a constant source of delight. PP II 5 155 1
In her own past behaviour, there was a constant source of PP II 14 212 17
moreover, she had a fresh source of displeasure, for the PP II 18 233 25
But here, by carrying with me one ceaseless source of PP II 19 237 4
Every sentence of kindness was a fresh source of happiness PP III 13 347 25
addition to every other source of happiness, were within PP III 19 385 3
other, was a perpetual source of irritation, which her own MP I 8 81 32
though as far as ever from understanding their source. MP II 2 191 10
the joy, he found in it a source of most gratifying MP III 3 334 3
satisfied, and Mrs. Price's attachment had no other source. MP III 8 389 4
The deed thoroughly answered; a source of domestic MP III 9 397 7
who was not at this time a source of misery to him. MP III 16 451 13
welcome addition to every source and every expression of E I 2 18 10
to it, so long as it is a source of pleasure to herself. E I 5 40 24
as a penance, a lesson, a source of profitable humiliation E II 4 182 7
He was considering her as the source of all the happiness E III 1 317 9
few seconds--and the only source whence any thing like E III 12 423 21
She felt the engagement to be a source of repentance and E III 14 442 8
She felt the engagement to be a source of repentance and E III 15 447 22
I am sure it was a source of high entertainment to you, to E III 18 478 67
and sisters, was a source of as lively pain as her mind P IV 12 251 10

SOURCES (12)

In the principal facts they have sources of intelligence NA I 14 109 23
there from a variety of sources; she would perhaps expect SS II 3 157 16
young brood, she found fresh sources of merriment. SS III 6 303 10
springing from such sources is unreasonable or unnatural, PP III 4 279 24
But Elizabeth had sources of uneasiness which could not be PP III 11 334 36
have such extraordinary sources of happiness necessarily PP III 14 355 46
it; for to her many other sources of uneasiness was added MP III 10 400 6
She had sources of delight that must force their way. MP III 17 461 2
place dependence on such sources of good, Edmund was MP III 17 462 5
their fortune, from other sources, was such as to make E I 16 136 9
Of all the sources of evil surrounding the former, since E III 12 421 17
the various sources of mortification preparing for them! P IV 10 215 13

SOURED (1)

His temper might perhaps be a little soured by finding, SS I 20 112 28

SOURNESS (1)

her figure, and serious, even to sourness, in her aspect. SS II 12 232 14

SOUTH (18)

least in Tuscany and the south of France!--the night that NA I 11 83 15
of the river, "without thinking of the south of France." NA I 14 106 2

Switzerland, and the south of France, might be as fruitful NA II 10 200 3
desirous of seeing you all, before she leaves the south. PP III 8 313 19
This weather is all from the south." MP II 4 207 8
"South or north, I know a black cloud when I see it; and MP II 4 207 9
will not be tricked on the south side of Everingham, any MP III 11 411 20
spending the autumn at south end instead of coming here. E I 12 101 19
20
South end is prohibited, if you please. E I 12 101 23
was in her own cook at south end, a young woman hired for E I 12 104 50
no end of the sad consequences of your going to south end. E I 12 105 51
go to the sea, it had better not have been to south end. E I 12 105 54
South end is an unhealthy place. E I 12 105 54
Perry was surprized to hear you had fixed upon south end." E I 12 105 54
willing to prefer Cromer to south end as he could himself." E I 12 106 60
James Stevenson, Esq. of south park, Elizabeth, daughter P III 1 3 1
of James stvenson, esq. of south park, in the county of P III 1 3 1
of ocean between the south foreland & the Land's end, & S 4 380 1

SOUTH WALES (1)
desirable estate in South Wales"--"to parents and MP III 3 341 31

SOUTH-EAST (2)
tract of country to the south-east, could fondly rest on SS III 6 302 8
it the best aspect in the world--sloping to the south-east. MP II 7 242 23

SOUTH-EASTERLY (1)
tide, which a fine south-easterly breeze was bringing in P III 12 102 1

SOUTH-WESTERLY (1)
gales of an high south-westerly wind, they pitied the SS I 9 41 4

SOUTHEAST (1)
The house stands among fine meadows facing the southeast, NA II 7 175 15

SOUTHERLY (1)
The wind I fancy must be Southerly." S 7 398 1

SOUTHWARD (1)
they are all to move southward without loss of time." E II 18 305 7

SOVEREIGN (2)
but quickened by one sovereign wish she then called out, " MP II 9 261 3
or do, by the sovereign impulses of illimitable ardour." S 7 398 1

SPACE (23)
Lady Susan has certainly contrived in the space of a LS 8 255 1
was over--enough to leave space for the remainder to walk NA I 2 23 27
agreeableness for the space of an evening, and all our NA I 10 76 29
opposite box; and, for the space of two entire scenes, did NA I 12 92 4
speak to him, though the space was so short between the SS I 19 105 13
no space in a cottage; but this is all a mistake. SS II 14 252 18
herself, in a shorter space of time than she could have PP III 4 281 29
as she thought for that space of time, that his affection PP III 11 334 37
You have space to work upon these, and grounds that will MP I 6 53 9
the billiard-room for the space of a week without playing MP I 13 127 29
from the deficiency of space and accomodation in her MP I 16 151 1
In space, light, furniture, and prospect, there was MP III 9 398 9
letter arrived for the space of a week, she had still the MP III 15 437 1
thing was rapidly clearing away, to give proper space. E II 8 229 98
out the indispensable division of space to every couple. E II 11 247 3
Churchill's part, that the space which a quarter of an E II 11 249 12
could be worse than dancing without space to turn in?" E II 11 249 14
where there was ample space for all, they were thus P III 10 90 37
into the smallest possible space to leave her a corner; P III 10 91 41
other, boasting of their space, at the possibility of that P IV 3 138 5
had gained the greater space and quiet of Belmont, and as P IV 6 170 30
Such was her situation, with a vacant space at hand, when P IV 8 189 47
the space of seven hours, confessed herself a little tired. S 10 414 1

SPACES (1)
there were vacant spaces--& through one of these, S 12 426 1

SPACIOUS (10)
within this, their spacious theatre; and, when the genius NA II 8 183 3
enjoyed in a cottage as in the most spacious dwelling." SS II 14 252 18
Cleveland was a spacious, modern-built house, situated on SS III 6 302 7
On reaching the spacious lobby above, they were shewn into PP III 1 249 43
park five miles round, a spacious modern-built house, so MP I 5 48 28
to the spacious stone steps before the principal entrance. MP I 8 83 37
grander than a mere, spacious, oblong room, fitted up for MP I 9 85 6
another apartment, more spacious and more meet for walking MP I 16 150 1
necessary to my happiness, nor were spacious apartments. E II 14 277 36
when their dining-room, spacious as it was, seemed more P IV 10 221 32

SPACIOUSNESS (1)
than its spaciousness and the number of their attendants. NA II 6 165 6

SPANISH (1)
of the beautiful oaks and Spanish chesnuts which were PP III 3 267 2

SPARE (56)
Can you spare me for an hour or two? shall I go?" NA I 9 61 6
be given, they would not refuse to spare her to her friend. NA I 13 103 28
Eleanor had wished to spare her form so painful a notion, NA II 13 226 25
instantly determined to spare no pains in weakening his NA II 15 245 12
Three thousand pounds! he could spare so considerable a SS I 1 5 8
It may be very inconvenient some years to spare a hundred, SS I 2 11 22
a new grate for the spare bedchamber, she observed that SS I 8 39 17
Lord, I am sure your mother can spare you very well, and I SS II 3 153 2
that Mrs. Dashwood could spare them perfectly well; and SS II 3 154 6
"What a charming thing it is that Mrs. Dashwood can spare SS II 10 218 34
if I could possibly find a spare half hour, but one has SS II 11 221 9
And I protest, if I had any money to spare, I should buy a SS II 14 251 17
Harley-Street, as soon as Lady Middleton could spare them. SS II 14 253 26
me, I was glad to spare them from knowing how much I felt. SS III 1 263 27
sir"--said Elinor impatiently--"I have no time to spare." SS III 8 317 8
softened at the time, to spare her from an increase of SS III 11 355 46
spare him, & just now it is a sickly time at Guilford--" W 321 2
You know what inducements I had to bring me home,--spare W 350 24
Elizth as she opened the door of the spare bedchamber.-- W 351 25
"But, my dear, your father cannot spare the horses, I am PP I 7 30 25
them to stay longer, she could spare them very well.-- PP I 12 59 1
Mrs. Bennet could certainly spare you for another PP II 14 211 8
"Oh! your father of course may spare you, if your mother PP II 14 211 10
How could he spare half ten thousand pounds?" PP III 7 304 35
never spare time, but the remaining five set off together. PP III 16 365 1
you all the love in the world, that he can spare from me. PP III 18 383 21
I am not one of those that spare their own trouble; and MP I 1 9 12
her servants, and allow a spare room for a friend, of MP I 3 28 38
to give her, for I must keep a spare room for a friend." MP I 3 30 56
it must be quite out of their power to spare a horse." MP I 6 58 38
"No; but they were to be put into the spare room to day; MP I 7 73 51
Lady Bertram could not possibly spare her." MP I 8 76 5
spare time to tell us his errand, and where you all were." MP I 10 101 30
set them under the first spare hen, and if they come to MP I 10 106 57
well spare time to sit down herself, because of her fringe. MP I 12 119 23
with his fair sister-in-law, could not spare his wife. MP I 18 171 26
I cannot spare her, and I am sure she does not want to go.- MP II 5 217 1
"Edmund wants her to go. but how can I spare her?" MP II 5 218 14
I could very ill spare the time, and you might have saved MP III 1 323 54
feel that she could not spare him; and the purity of her MP III 13 428 13
coming now, depends upon her being willing to spare him." E I 14 121 16
of there being but two spare rooms in the house. E I 15 126 11
to come; but his uncle and aunt will not spare him." E I 18 145 7
no horses, having little spare money and a great deal of E II 8 213 7
Not that James ever complains; but it is right to spare E II 11 252 35
"Not five minutes to spare even for your friends Miss E II 12 260 26
these words--"I had not a spare moment on Tuesday, as you E II 13 266 5
his uncle and aunt would spare him again?' and so forth--I E II 18 308 27
in writing, and spare no arguments to induce him to come. E III 6 357 31
no time to spare, and therefore must now be gone directly. E III 9 385 1
2
decision;--how to spare her from any unnecessary pain; how E III 14 435 4
Larkins; but I could quite as ill spare Robert Martin." E III 18 473 22
it had pleased heaven to spare my poor son, I dare say he P III 8 64 5
6
To spare Henrietta from agitation seemed the governing P III 12 116 70
"Our neighbourhood cannot spare such a pleasant family. P IV 6 164 8
have not a moment to spare--besides that (between S 12 424 1

SPARE-ROOM (2)
of a spare-room for a friend was now never forgotten. MP I 3 28 38
of the importance of a spare-room, might have misled Sir MP I 3 28 38

SPARE-ROOMS (1)
particular point;--the spare-rooms at the parsonage had MP I 3 28 38

SPARED (48)
you might have been spared the vexation of knowing of LS 40 308 1
that she might have spared herself all the trouble of LS 42 313 7
but the latter was spared the misery of her friend's NA I 9 67 33
Her reproaches, however, were not spared. NA I 11 87 53
she should have been spared the distressing idea of a NA I 13 103 29
but she could gladly be spared a contest, where victory NA I 14 106 1
One moment surely might be spared; and, so desperate NA II 6 164 3
would willingly have been spared the mortification of a NA II 8 184 4
once in ten minutes, this reproach would have been spared." SS I 10 48 5
and sisters were spared much solicitude on her account. SS I 19 104 10
of their time as could be spared from the importunate SS I 21 120 6
On the contrary it was a relief to her, to be spared the SS II 1 141 5
Their favour increased, they could not be spared; Sir John SS II 2 151 43
will be spared, as you my dear madam will easily believe." SS II 8 195 17
you know it already, as surely you must, I may be spared." SS II 8 199 35
Marianne was spared from the troublesome feelings of SS II 11 221 4
and was not sorry to be spared the necessity of answering SS II 11 222 12
have been very glad to be spared herself;--but Colonel SS III 3 283 20
was therefore glad to be spared from the necessity of SS III 5 297 32
Charlotte's reply was spared by the entrance of Jane and PP I 20 113 27
any other way, than as it spared me the concern which I PP II 11 192 23
24
should have been spared, had not my character required it PP II 12 196 4
was not sorry to be spared the necessity of saying much. PP III 3 268 5
I am truly glad, dearest Lizzy, that you have been spared PP III 4 275 5
It would have spared her, she thought, one sleepless night PP III 6 299 17
and Elizabeth was spared from much teazing on the subject. PP III 15 361 5
It would have spared her from explanations and professions PP III 17 376 30
might as well have been spared, for Mrs. Norris had not MP I 3 28 38
Admiral had since been spared; and she scrupled to point MP I 7 66 14
kind indeed, and I am glad to have her spared." . . . . MP I 16 156 25
would of course be spared all thought and exertion, and it MP II 8 253 4
happy in having William spared from the fatigue of such a MP II 9 266 21
To be spared from her aunt Norris's interminable MP III 1 322 49
Fanny could be very well spared--(she being ready to give MP III 6 371 15
she could not possibly be spared from Mansfield Park at MP III 6 373 23
is, he cannot any how be spared till after the 14th, for MP III 12 417 3
Susan could never be spared. MP III 17 472 31
Emma spared no exertions to maintain this happier flow of E I 1 9 20
too necessary at Hartfield, to be spared to abbey-mill." E I 7 55 38
For the present, he could not be spared, to his "very E I 18 144 1
of any delay, and spared her from a taste of such E II 2 165 9
I could very ill be spared--but such a point had been made E III 6 364 55
There was little sympathy to be spared for any body else. E III 11 403 2
been spared from every pain which pressed on her now.-- E III 12 421 17
prevented, she was soon spared all suspense; for after the P III 7 60 31
32
The husband had died just in time to be spared the full P IV 9 209 96
to yourself might have spared you much or all of this." P IV 11 245 75
years of separation and suffering might have been spared. P IV 11 247 84

SPARING (3)
I think nobody can justly accuse me of sparing myself upon MP I 7 73 53
make any difficulty of sparing her, and therefore gave his MP II 4 215 47
to her aunt Bertram for sparing her, and that she was MP II 5 220 29

SPARINGLY (1)
the very feelings which ought to taste it but sparingly. P III 11 100 23

SPARK (1)
we see the strong spark of woman's Captivations elicit S 8 403 1

SPARKLE (1)
He had seen her eyes sparkle as she spoke of the dear MP II 8 256 12

SPARKLED (2)
Mrs. Bennet's eyes sparkled with pleasure, and she was PP I 7 30 14
15
Mrs. Bennet's eyes sparkled.-- PP I 13 61 3

SPARKLING (10)
With what sparkling eyes and ready motion she granted his NA I 10 75 24
Tilney, listening with sparkling eyes to every thing he NA II 1 131 15
"Did he indeed?" cried Marianne, with sparkling eyes, "and SS I 9 45 26
"Oh that they would!" cried Marianne, her eyes sparkling SS I 17 92 19
happy, her eyes were sparkling with pleasure, and she was MP I 12 117 15
when the balmy air, the sparkling sea, and your sweet MP III 12 415 1
2
learn to prefer soft light eyes to sparkling dark ones.-- MP III 17 470 27
though his own sparkling eyes at the moment were speaking E II 5 189 13
His lady greeted him with some of her sparkling vivacity. E III 16 457 35
to the sea, dancing & sparkling in sunshine & freshness.-- S 4 384 1

SPARKS (2)
for Miss Godby told Miss Sparks, that nobody in their SS III 2 272 16
had nothing at all; and I had it from Miss Sparks myself. SS III 2 272 16

SPARROWS (1)
catch the music; like unfledged sparrows ready to be fed. P IV 9 193 6

SPARS (2)
shillings in purses and spars; thence adjourned to eat ice NA I 15 116 1
rob it of a few petrified spars without his perceiving me." PP II 19 239 9

SPASM (1)
affection, it cost her only a spasm in her throat.-- SS III 1 265 33

SPASMODIC (1)
of my old greivance, Spasmodic Bile & hardly able to crawl S 5 386 1

SPASMS (1)
all over me, such spasms in my side, and pains in my head, PP III 5 288 38

SPEAK (411)
family are at war, & Manwaring scarcely dares speak to me. LS 2 245 1
to be handsome, & when I speak of her beauty, replies only LS 17 271 7
room, as she was anxious to speak with me in private. LS 20 276 5
Be assured that I speak from the fullest conviction of the LS 23 284 4
me never to speak to you or my uncle about it,--&--" LS 24 286 5
Will you let me speak to you a moment?" LS 24 287 8
Lady Susan I beleive wishes to speak to you about it, if LS 24 287 9
I sent Wilson to say that I desired to speak with him LS 25 292 2
to marry you, & would speak with him alone, as soon as he LS 32 303 1
to do there, or any body to speak to, except each other. NA I 2 22 10
Now, if I were to hear any body speak slightingly of you, NA I 6 40 14
gone into the card-room to speak to a friend, and nothing, NA I 8 52 2
and this lady stopping to speak to her, they, as belonging NA I 8 54 4
time with James, was therefore obliged to speak plainer. NA I 9 61 6
Do let us turn back, Mr. Thorpe; stop and speak to my NA I 9 65 29
"Did you indeed? and did they speak to you?" NA I 9 68 41
other side, "I shall not speak another word to you all the NA I 10 70 1
But to what purpose did she speak?-- NA I 11 87 53
been quite wild to speak to you, and make my apologies. NA I 12 93 5
She had left them for a few minutes to speak to Miss NA I 13 97 1
of saying that she must speak with Miss Tilney that moment, NA I 13 102 25
speak of, they are embellishments, and I like them as such. NA I 14 109 23
"You speak with astonishing composure! NA I 14 112 34
Maria desired no greater pleasure than to speak of it; and NA I 15 116 1
Hardly even to speak to her!" NA II 1 130 1
"Me?--yes; I cannot speak well enough to be unintelligible. NA II 1 133 23
some time, forgetting to speak or to listen, and almost NA II 1 133 29
daughter time to speak, "has been forming a very bold wish. NA II 2 139 7
I would not speak disrespectfully of a brother of your's, NA II 3 145 13
John desired me to speak to you on the subject, and NA II 3 145 16
Sure, if your father were to speak to him, he would go." NA II 4 152 27
every thing seemed to speak the awfulness of her situation. NA II 6 168 10

Context	Work	Vol.	Ch.	Page	Line
"What say you, Eleanor?--speak your opinion, for ladies	NA	II	7	175	15
anxious face, began to speak of her unwillingness that he	NA	II	7	177	17
speak a mind at ease, or a conscience void of reproach."--	NA	II	8	182	1
What could more plainly speak the gloomy workings of a	NA	II	8	187	13
any friend to whom you can speak with unreserve; on whose	NA	II	10	207	38
he might not speak to me;--I would not even look at him.	NA	II	12	217	2
she very soon resolved to speak to Eleanor about it at	NA	II	13	220	1
She trusted he would never speak of Miss Thorpe; and	NA	II	13	222	8
to enter the room, and a still greater to speak when there.	NA	II	13	223	9
to collect herself and speak with firmness, but with eyes	NA	II	13	223	13
It was with pain that Catherine could speak at all; and it	NA	II	13	225	22
To the General, of course, he would not dare to speak; but	NA	II	14	231	4
legacied hereafter; and to speak of her therefore as the	NA	II	15	245	12
I speak from experience.	SS	I	11	57	17
Mrs. Dashwood was too much astonished to speak, and	SS	I	15	76	16
He did not speak, he did not behave like himself.	SS	I	15	77	23
this morning;--he did not speak like himself, and did not	SS	I	15	81	43
"You speak very properly.	SS	I	15	81	44
all, could neither eat nor speak, and after some time, on	SS	I	15	82	46
to open the casement to speak to him, though the space was	SS	I	19	105	13
possible to speak at one without being heard at the other.	SS	I	19	105	13
Sometimes he won't speak to me for half a day together,	SS	I	20	113	39
length forcing herself to speak, and to speak cautiously,	SS	I	22	130	17 18
herself to speak, and to speak cautiously, she said with a	SS	I	22	130	17 18
I shall speak a good word for you to all the young men,	SS	II	3	154	2
and began directly to speak of his pleasure at seeing them	SS	II	4	162	11
and on her ceasing to speak, rose directly from his seat,	SS	II	5	174	46
but without attempting to speak to her, or to approach	SS	II	6	176	3
why does he not look at me? why cannot I speak to him?"	SS	II	6	176	4
"Go to him, Elinor," she cried, as soon as she could speak,	SS	II	6	177	13
Tell him I must see him again--must speak to him instantly.	SS	II	6	177	13
composure, till she might speak to him with more privacy	SS	II	6	177	15
which seemed to speak a consciousness of his own	SS	II	6	178	17
nervous irritability, not to speak to her for the world.	SS	II	7	180	5
Elinor, though never less disposed to speak than at that	SS	II	7	181	9
The latter, though unable to speak, seemed to feel all the	SS	II	7	182	12
dared not trust herself to speak, lest she might wound	SS	II	7	184	15
Had she tried to speak, or had she been conscious of half	SS	II	8	193	6
relation, and still more by his distress, could not speak.	SS	II	9	206	25
could not bring herself to speak of what she felt even to	SS	II	10	212	1
He would not speak another word to him, meet him where he	SS	II	10	214	9
she was obliged, or could oblige herself to speak to him.	SS	II	10	216	15
might see <u>us</u>; and I am sure we would not speak a word."	SS	II	10	219	39
for her?-- it is Elinor of whom <u>we</u> think and speak."	SS	II	12	235	34 35
seem low--you don't speak;--sure you an't well."	SS	II	13	239	11
sister what I think of her, you cannot speak too high."	SS	II	13	240	15
Edward was the first to speak, and it was to notice	SS	II	13	242	25
she felt very well able to speak of the affair without	SS	III	1	260	8
Now, I can think and speak of it with little emotion.	SS	III	1	263	27
being at liberty to speak of it to a single creature;	SS	III	1	263	29
Marianne engaged never to speak of the affair to any one	SS	III	1	264	32
speak disrespectfully of any relation of yours, madam.	SS	III	1	267	44 45
I have not time to speak to Mrs. Jennings about it myself,	SS	III	2	275	25
too, trust she will speak a good word for us to Sir John,	SS	III	2	277	30
and wanted to speak with him on very particular business.	SS	III	4	287	25
he, "that you wished to speak with me, at least I	SS	III	4	288	27
after Elinor had ceased to speak;--at last, and as if it	SS	III	4	290	36 37
before he began to speak of Edward; for he too had heard	SS	III	5	298	33
on a sofa, did not speak much in favour of her amendment;	SS	III	7	307	1
a readiness that seemed to speak the occasion, and the	SS	III	7	311	15
and though trying to speak comfort to Elinor, her	SS	III	7	313	20
Elinor would not speak.	SS	III	8	318	11
tediously--no creature to speak to--my own reflections so	SS	III	8	325	45
speak in this way, either of Mrs. Willoughby or my sister.	SS	III	8	329	64
To treat her with unkindness, to speak of her slightingly	SS	III	8	329	64
As bluntly as he could speak it, therefore, he told me	SS	III	8	330	69
though still unable to speak, embraced Elinor again and	SS	III	9	334	4
she had neither courage to speak of, nor fortitude to	SS	III	10	341	6
question was suffered to speak it, talked of nothing but	SS	III	10	348	34
began voluntarily to speak of him again;--but that it was	SS	III	11	349	3
She would have given the world to be able to speak--and to	SS	III	12	358	9
though Elinor could not speak, even <u>her</u> eyes were fixed on	SS	III	12	360	22
Marianne could speak <u>her</u> happiness only by tears.	SS	III	13	363	7
she had herself heard <u>him</u> speak without any admiration,--a	SS	III	13	364	10
"I think I have heard you speak of him before, said Emma.	W			315	1
large party, & then he will not speak to any body else.--"	W			319	2
seemed to speak him out of his element in a ball room.	W			329	10
was not unwilling to speak, when her questions or remarks	W			331	11
to me, to find you can speak as you do, of Tom Musgrave;	W			343	19
Emma" that she could hardly speak a word in a minute.--	W			349	24
"Do not speak disrespectfully of her--she was very good to	W			352	26
osborne sometimes declares she cannot hear herself speak.--	W			358	28
Such amiable qualities must speak for themselves.	PP	I	3	11	6
I never heard you speak ill of a human being in my life."	PP	I	4	14	7
in censuring any one; but I always speak what I think."	PP	I	4	14	8
She longed to speak, but could think of nothing to say;	PP	I	9	45	35
exactly explain the matter, Darcy must speak for himself."	PP	I	10	50	33
them," said he, as soon as she allowed him to speak.	PP	I	11	56	15
"The person of whom I speak, is a gentleman and a stranger.	PP	I	13	61	3
I must speak to hill, this moment."	PP	I	13	61	3
speak of the day before, was now high in her good graces.	PP	I	15	71	5
Mr. Wickham began to speak on more general topics, Meryton,	PP	I	16	78	22
It gives me pain to speak ill of a Darcy.	PP	I	16	82	43
though she did not often speak unnecessarily to Mr.	PP	I	17	87	12
One must speak a little, you know.	PP	I	18	91	13
disposition, unwilling to speak, unless we expect to say	PP	I	18	91	15
him time to speak, replied with an air of distant civility.	PP	I	18	98	61
"For heaven's sake, madam, speak lower.--	PP	I	18	99	66
her, quite disengaged, he never came near enough to speak.	PP	I	18	102	74
seeing her again I shall speak in the highest terms of	PP	I	19	107	15
Can I speak plainer?	PP	I	19	109	20
I will speak to her about it myself directly.	PP	I	20	110	3
"Speak to Lizzy about it yourself.	PP	I	20	111	12
know, that I should never speak to you again, and you will	PP	I	20	113	28
away before she could speak to Sir William or Lady Lucas	PP	I	23	127	5
A day or two passed before Jane had courage to speak of	PP	II	1	134	4 5
world respectable, and are hurt if I speak ill of any body.	PP	II	1	135	11
and she resolved to speak to Elizabeth on the subject	PP	II	2	142	18
to know how she would speak of her new home, how she would	PP	II	3	146	19
noise below seemed to speak the whole house in confusion;	PP	II	5	158	11
Elizabeth was ready to speak whenever there was an opening,	PP	II	6	163	14
Then pray speak aloud.	PP	II	8	173	6
his lips; and when he did speak, it seemed the effect of	PP	II	9	180	29
I speak feelingly. a younger son, you know, must be inured	PP	II	10	183	10
she tried to the utmost to speak with composure when she	PP	II	11	192	23 24
she had often heard him speak so affectionately of his	PP	II	13	207	6
You know I always speak my mind, and I cannot bear the	PP	II	14	211	13
And with no one to speak to, of what I felt, no Jane to	PP	II	17	226	19
For my part, I am determined never to speak of it again to	PP	II	17	227	27
Excuse me--for I must speak plainly.	PP	II	18	231	18
to speak openly to her aunt, than to run such a risk.	PP	II	19	240	16
That he should even speak to her was amazing!--but to	PP	III	1	252	54
to speak with such civility, to enquire after her family!	PP	III	1	252	54
to speak with calmness, if he really intended to meet them.	PP	III	1	254	57
into a wish of hearing her speak of her sister, was	PP	III	2	264	12
and that she could not speak a word, especially to Miss	PP	III	3	268	5
in time, though not enough to be able to speak any more.	PP	III	3	270	11
of making him speak, she continued, "I remember, when we	PP	III	3	271	16 17
recover himself enough to speak, she, in whose mind every	PP	III	4	276	6
to it, and for a few minutes could not speak another word.	PP	III	4	277	11
"I must confess that he did not speak so well of Wickham	PP	III	5	291	54
He could not speak a word for full ten minutes.	PP	III	5	292	62
some time before his daughters had courage to speak of it.	PP	III	6	299	18
would not allow her to speak to Elizabeth privately of	PP	III	9	320	35
His character was to speak for itself.	PP	III	10	322	2
I am sure (and I do not speak it to be thanked, therefore	PP	III	10	324	2
but himself; and to him she had hardly courage to speak.	PP	III	11	336	45
my love, I want to speak to you," took her out of the room.	PP	III	13	345	12 13
and called out, "Lizzy, my dear, I want to speak with you."	PP	III	13	345	13 14
Mrs. Bennet could not give her consent, or speak her	PP	III	13	348	34
"Yes, madam," said Mrs. Bennet, delighted to speak to a	PP	III	14	352	8
now forced herself to speak; and immediately, though not	PP	III	16	366	8
"Did you speak from your own observation," said she, "when	PP	III	16	371	42
I speak nothing but the truth.	PP	III	17	372	5
that she ventured not to speak to him, unless it was in	PP	III	17	378	46
in too much awe of him to speak with the familiarity which	PP	III	18	384	27
yet, whenever she <u>did</u> speak, she must be vulgar.	PP	III	18	384	27
But, however, do <u>not</u> speak to Mr. Darcy about it, if you	PP	III	19	386	7
and could scarcely speak to be heard, or without crying.	MP	I	2	13	4
in being so surprised, and persuade her to speak openly.	MP	I	2	15	10
You speak as if you were going two hundred miles off,	MP	I	3	26	31
but with <u>her</u> you will be forced to speak for yourself."	MP	I	3	27	31
How came <u>Sir</u> Thomas to speak to you about it?"	MP	I	3	29	42
if Sir Thomas should ever speak again about my taking	MP	I	3	30	56
Mrs. Norris could not speak with any temper of such	MP	I	3	31	59
could be less called on to speak their opinion than Fanny.	MP	I	5	48	30
when one has seen her hardly able to speak the year before.	MP	I	5	49	32
was not <u>out</u>, and I could not get her to speak to me.	MP	I	5	50	35
Sneyd--<u>you</u> have heard me speak of Sneyd, Edmund; his	MP	I	5	51	40
was much disposed to admire, speak so freely of her uncle.	MP	I	6	57	32
so I told my maid to speak for one directly; and as I	MP	I	6	58	37
feelings created, made it easier to swallow than to speak.	MP	I	7	74	57
as he is not here to speak for himself, I will answer for	MP	I	8	76	3
heightened by having Edmund to speak to of what she felt.	MP	I	8	80	31
Miss Bertram could now speak with decided information of	MP	I	8	83	37
his own, do all that you speak of? govern the conduct and	MP	I	9	92	46
The <u>manners</u> I speak of, might rather be called <u>conduct</u>,	MP	I	9	93	49
we <u>have</u> walked a mile in it, I must speak within compass."	MP	I	9	95	64
Edmund, observing her; "why would not you speak sooner?	MP	I	9	95	68
"I speak what appears to me the general opinion; and where	MP	I	11	110	25
We only speak of it among friends.	MP	I	12	118	21
My father wished us, as school-boys, to speak well, but he	MP	I	13	127	26
find something--I shall speak to my sisters, and try to	MP	I	13	128	35
command herself enough to speak, her brother gave his	MP	I	14	133	12
"I cannot before Mr. Yates speak what I feel as to this	MP	I	15	139	11
for I believe I might speak pretty sharp; and I dare say	MP	I	15	142	22
Edmund was too angry to speak; but Miss Crawford looking	MP	I	15	147	56
"We have but to speak the word; we may pick and choose.--	MP	I	15	148	58
"Can I speak with you, Fanny for a few minutes?" said he.	MP	I	16	153	4
Julia was the first to move and speak again.	MP	II	1	175	2
"Well then, Lady Bertram, suppose you speak for tea	MP	II	1	180	12
Edmund was the first to speak: "something must be done,"	MP	II	1	181	17 18
himself so far as to speak a few words of calm approbation	MP	II	1	183	24
in love or acting, could speak very handsomely of both.	MP	II	1	185	30
It was well at that moment that Tom had to speak and not	MP	II	2	193	13
I think he values the very quietness you speak of, and	MP	II	3	196	3
Sir Thomas resolved to speak seriously to her.	MP	II	3	200	20
and if Maria could now speak so securely of her happiness	MP	II	3	201	22
Dr. Grant was in the vestibule, and as they stopt to speak	MP	II	4	215	47
Edmund found himself obliged to speak and fill up the	MP	II	5	218	16
found herself expected to speak, could only say that she	MP	II	5	220	29
of astonishment which made it impossible for her to speak.	MP	II	5	221	35
to stay, and would much rather not have him speak to her.	MP	II	5	224	48
I could hardly get her to speak.	MP	II	6	230	7
speak to <u>me</u>, because Lucy is courted by a lieutenant."	MP	II	7	249	52
different ways, look and speak as much grateful pleasure	MP	II	8	253	5
thither; he had heard her speak of the pleasure of such a	MP	II	8	256	12
to yourself; but I can now speak my business, which is	MP	II	9	261	2
pleasure, could attempt to speak; but quickened by one	MP	II	9	261	3
She had never heard him speak so openly before, and though	MP	II	9	264	17
speak, to utter something like an inquiry as to the result.	MP	II	9	268	28
forced to be spoken to, and to curtsey, and speak again.	MP	II	10	273	7
and who was beginning to speak on the subject, when Fanny,	MP	II	10	274	9
Fanny would hardly even speak her agreement.	MP	II	10	278	20
Fanny felt obliged to speak.	MP	II	11	289	31
Now Fanny could not bring herself to speak, and Miss	MP	II	11	289	33
You don't speak, Fanny--Miss Price--you don't speak.--	MP	II	11	289	34
Mary as soon as she could speak--"what a match for her!	MP	II	12	292	7
Fanny could not speak, but he did not want her to speak.	MP	II	13	298	3
distressed, and for some moments unable to speak.	MP	II	13	301	7
She thought he was wishing to speak to her unheard by the	MP	II	13	306	27
coming up to speak to her whatever might be the subject.--	MP	III	1	312	4
but being obliged to speak, she could not forbear, in	MP	III	1	312	11
I must speak to you for a few minutes, but I will not	MP	III	1	313	12
She had no one to take her part, to counsel, or speak for	MP	III	1	321	46
that he should request to speak with you alone, be it only	MP	III	1	321	48
Thomas wishes to speak with you, ma'am, in his own room."	MP	III	1	324	60
she had hated to see or to speak to, in whom she could	MP	III	2	327	6
I must just speak of it <u>once</u>, I told Sir Thomas I must	MP	III	2	333	23
I speak rather of the past, however, than the present.--	MP	III	3	339	23
Did you speak?" stepping eagerly to Fanny, and addressing	MP	III	3	340	25
saying, "no," he added, "are you sure you did not speak?	MP	III	3	340	25
It is more difficult to speak well than to compose well;	MP	III	3	341	28
Crawford, delighted to get her to speak at any rate, was	MP	III	3	343	40
My conduct shall speak for me--absence, distance, time	MP	III	3	343	41
speak for me--absence, distance, time shall speak for me.--	MP	III	3	343	41
again among the number of those who might speak and hear.	MP	III	3	344	44
"I will speak to her, sir; I will take the first	MP	III	4	345	5
and unfeelingly, I may speak of it now because it is all	MP	III	4	349	25
"And Mrs. Grant, did she say--did she speak--was she there	MP	III	4	352	43
in a low voice, "I must speak to you for a few minutes	MP	III	5	357	5
Yet, Fanny, do not imagine I would now speak	MP	III	5	358	9
them, and could never speak of Miss Crawford without pain.	MP	III	6	367	6
suddenly opened, she could speak more largely to William	MP	III	6	369	11
Edmund, she could neither speak, nor look, nor think, when	MP	III	6	374	28
Poor little soul! she could but just speak to be heard,	MP	III	7	386	44
It was pleasing to hear him speak so properly; here, he	MP	III	10	404	15
It was a real indulgence to her to hear or to speak of	MP	III	10	405	17
It was a subject which she must learn to speak of, and the	MP	III	10	406	20
I know you cannot speak or write a falsehood,--so long	MP	III	11	411	18
The woman who could speak of him, and speak only of his	MP	III	12	417	4
If he would now speak to her with the unreserve which had	MP	III	16	453	16
was impossible not to speak; and so, with the usual	MP	III	16	453	17
before he had been able to speak one intelligible sentence,	MP	III	16	454	18
herself required to speak), "what could you say?"	MP	III	16	455	20
At such a moment to give way to gaiety and to speak with	MP	III	16	456	24
others speak, as she imagined every body else would speak.	MP	III	16	456	25
It was long before he could speak again.	MP	III	16	457	30
As soon as I could speak, I replied that I had not	MP	III	16	457	30
She tried to speak carelessly; but she was not so careless	MP	III	16	458	30
Fanny, now at liberty to speak openly, felt more than	MP	III	16	459	31
to whom she could speak every thought as it arose, and who	E	I	1	6	6
marrying, nor could ever speak of her but with compassion,	E	I	1	7	10

simplicity which could speak with so much exultation of E I 4 27 4
Harriet was very ready to speak of the share he had had in E I 4 28 6
"how do you know that Mr. Martin did not speak yesterday?" E I 8 60 28
He did speak yesterday--that is, he wrote and was refused." E I 8 60 30
I have heard him speak with great animation of a large E I 8 66 53
He certainly might have heard Mr. Elton speak with more E I 8 67 57
She could not speak. E I 9 73 19
But she was not wanted to speak. E I 9 73 19
who did not know him, to speak to him, at Michaelmas! E I 9 75 26
Papa, if you speak in that melancholy way, you will be E I 11 94 14
Did you speak to me?" cried Mr. John Knightley, hearing E I 12 103 41
though she could not speak of her loss without many tears. E I 13 109 5
I speak as a friend, Emma. E I 13 112 22
afterwards he began to speak of other things, and in a E I 13 115 36
But I never allow myself to speak ill of her, on Frank's E I 14 120 13
She should then have heard more: Mrs. Weston would speak E I 14 122 18
immediately preparing to speak with exquisite calmness and E I 15 129 24
made her resolve to restrain herself when she did speak. E I 15 129 24
not speak either to me, or of Harriet, in such a manner. E I 15 130 26
27
Frank Churchill; we shall think and speak of nobody else." E I 18 149 29
to speak extremely well on each; that is my idea of him." E I 18 150 31
that he should like to speak of his own place while he was E II 1 159 20
was only gone down to speak to Patty again about the port-- E II 3 173 27
to be married!" said Emma, as soon as she could speak. E II 3 174 33
he was persuading her to speak to me --(do you think he E II 3 178 52
by Mr. and Mrs. Weston, who were standing to speak to her. E II 5 188 6
He did really look and speak as if in a state of no common E II 5 191 26
"I have heard her speak of the acquaintance," said Emma, " E II 5 194 42
Then I will speak the truth, and nothing suits me so well. E II 6 200 20
to say when you speak of Miss Fairfax's situation in life. E II 6 201 23
and seemed to mean always to speak of her with respect. E II 7 205 2
there were enough ready to speak to allow Emma to think E II 8 215 15
She did not wish to speak of the pianoforte, she felt too E II 8 220 45
I have heard him speak, and so must you, so very highly of E II 8 226 79
As a sort of touchstone, however, she began to speak of E II 8 228 88
Emma took the opportunity of whispering, "you speak too E II 10 243 23
24
I must speak to him if possible, just to thank him. E II 10 243 31
How often have I heard you speak of it as such a E II 11 252 37
men and women; and Mrs. Weston must not speak of it again. E II 11 254 45
He felt the going away almost too much to speak of it. E II 12 259 12
Forcing herself to speak, therefore, in the hope of E II 12 261 30
31
the sort of parties you speak of; and we are a very quiet E II 14 274 29
to speak, she was very tolerably capable of attending. E II 14 279 53
I know enough of music to speak decidedly on that point. E II 15 282 5
Both felt rather anxious to hear him speak again; and E II 15 286 22
23
I shall speak to Mr. E. E II 16 295 34
were warm and open; but Emma could not speak so fluently. E II 17 304 28
She is very fond of Frank, and therefore I would not speak E II 18 307 18
for me to speak of her with the forbearance I could wish. E II 18 309 33
and seemed delighted to speak of his former visit, and E III 1 316 4
Must go and speak to Dr. and Mrs. Hughes for a moment.-- E III 2 323 19
but we agreed we would not speak of it to any body, for E III 2 329 45
to him, and hardly able to speak, had just strength enough E III 3 334 7
Emma was a good deal surprised; but begged her to speak. E III 4 337 3
I give you this caution now, because I shall never speak E III 4 342 39
two minutes, "if I must speak on this subject, there is no E III 5 345 16
He had hoped she would speak again, but she did not. E III 5 350 31
She would rather busy herself about any thing than speak. E III 5 350 31
Yet he would speak. E III 5 350 31
She did look vexed, she did speak pointedly--and at last, E III 6 359 37
You order me, whether you speak or not. E III 7 369 12
allowed to judge when to speak and when to hold my tongue. E III 7 372 37
"Emma, I must once more speak to you as I have been used E III 7 374 55
56
and, before she could speak again, he had handed her in. E III 7 375 62
She had not been able to speak; and, on entering the E III 7 376 62
Happily it was not necessary to speak. E III 7 376 63
before tea, old John Abdy's son wanted to speak with him. E III 8 383 29
five minutes, and wanted particularly to speak with her."-- E III 10 392 1
It will do you good to speak of your distress, whatever it E III 10 394 27
He came to speak to his father on a subject,--to announce E III 10 395 30
Emma could not speak the name of Dixon without a little E III 10 399 59
Emma looked at her, quite unable to speak. E III 11 404 9
"I am delighted to hear you speak so stoutly on the E III 11 405 13
She could not speak another word.-- E III 11 405 16
did speak, it was in a voice nearly as agitated as Emma's. E III 11 405 17
Emma could not speak. E III 11 407 27
She had hardly been able to speak a word, and every look E III 12 418 5
She then began to speak of you, and of the great kindness E III 12 419 12
Perhaps he wanted to speak to her, of his attachment to E III 13 425 2
She wished him to speak, but he would not. E III 13 427 18
He has only to speak.-- E III 13 428 23
"You speak as if you envied him." E III 13 428 24
She made her plan; she would speak of something totally E III 13 429 26
27
"Oh! then, don't speak it, don't speak it," she eagerly E III 13 429 28
But if you have any wish to speak openly to me as a friend, E III 13 429 32
I must speak to my uncle. E III 14 443 8
shortly afterwards, "to speak my opinion aloud as I read. E III 15 445 8
Weston and Cole will be there too; but one is apt to speak E III 16 456 27
which I have heard you speak of, as under the patronage of E III 16 456 32
speak more openly than might have been strictly correct.-- E III 16 459 46
She was forced to speak, and to speak cheerfully too. E III 17 465 28
Only let me be told when I may speak out.-- E III 17 468 34
speaking to Harriet; and certainly did not speak in vain.-- E III 18 472 20
To speak, she was sure would be to betray a most E III 18 472 21
speak with serious feeling of his gratitude and happiness. E III 18 476 49
might have disdained to speak to, and of becoming P III 3 19 16
One would imagine you had never heard my father speak of P III 5 35 14
I am so ill I can hardly speak. P III 5 37 22
found it most difficult to cease to speak to one another. P III 8 63 3
Her feelings made her speak low; and Captain Wentworth, P III 8 67 25
a man you of war; I speak, you know, of the higher rates. P III 8 70 54
Do not you hear your aunt speak? P III 9 80 31
They were now able to speak to each other, and consult. P III 12 112 56
They must speak of the accident at Lyme. P IV 1 124 12
She could not speak the name, and look straight forward to P IV 1 124 12
but especially wanting to speak of the circumstance of P IV 3 143 19
and when Anne ventured to speak her opinion of them to Mr. P IV 4 150 15
and nurse Rooke thoroughly understands when to speak. P IV 5 155 9
At last, it became necessary to speak of her.-- P IV 5 156 14
She would not speak to Anne with half the certainty she P IV 5 159 22
very much together, got to speak to each other with a P IV 7 176 8
"Now, how would she speak of him?" P IV 7 179 29
very slow degrees came at last near enough to speak to her. P IV 8 189 47
as an old friend, do give me a hint as to when I may speak. P IV 9 195 27
Facts shall speak. P IV 9 199 55
with him, but I heard him speak of them for ever. P IV 9 200 57
speak the truth of him, than if he had been your husband. P IV 9 211 101
and quite painful to have him approach and speak to her. P IV 10 214 11
I speak, you know, only of such men as have hearts!" P IV 11 235 31
"I must speak to you by such means as are within my reach. P IV 11 237 42
in the Octagon-Room to speak to him, the moment of Mr. P IV 11 244 71
here come my girls to speak for themselves & their mother. S 1 370 1
She can only speak in a whisper--and fainted away twice S 5 387 1
as soon as she had time to speak, but I am not poetic S 7 397 1
mood, you might as well speak in favour of another charity S 12 424 1
I will not trouble you to speak about the Mullins's.-- S 12 425 1

SPEAKER (6)
might be rendered interesting by the skill of the speaker. PP I 16 76 4
was ended by the same speaker, who taking up one of the MP I 14 132 7
at that moment the only speaker in the room, and to feel MP I 15 145 49
this, and looked with some surprize at the speaker. MP II 1 186 32
said and listened to, without some profit to the speaker. MP III 3 344 44
always guided by the last speaker, by the person who could MP III 16 450 11

SPEAKING (182)
took from me the power of speaking with any clearness. LS 20 277 6
for I am forbidden ever speaking to my uncle or aunt on LS 21 279 1
But before I leave you, he continued, speaking in a lower LS 23 283 4
not to have prevented your speaking to me on the subject. LS 24 286 7
You had forbidden her speaking to Mr Vernon or to me on LS 24 289 12
that I had forbidden her speaking to you on the subject, LS 24 289 12
for an hour, looking at every body and speaking to no one. NA I 3 25 1
There was little leisure for speaking while they danced; NA I 3 25 2
The name seemed to strike them all; and, after speaking to NA I 4 32 4
Nay, I cannot blame you--(speaking more seriously)--your NA I 6 41 16
"I dare say she thought I was speaking of her son." NA I 8 59 34
the avowed necessity of speaking to Miss Tilney, whom she NA I 10 72 8
to Pulteney-Street without her speaking twenty words. NA I 11 89 61
Early the next day, a note from Isabella, speaking peace NA I 15 116 1
unguarded in speaking of my partiality for the church!-- NA I 15 118 13
a few minutes; and then speaking through her tears, she NA II 10 204 11
to settle, though somewhat embarrassed in speaking of. NA II 13 229 31
Thorpe, most happy to be on speaking terms with a man of NA II 15 244 12
the warmth she had been betrayed into, in speaking of him. SS I 4 21 11
to you, by speaking, in so quiet a way, of my own feelings. SS I 4 21 15
Must it not have been so, Marianne?" speaking to her in a SS I 14 73 17
to the ladies, without speaking a word, and, after briefly SS I 19 106 22
towards Elinor, and speaking in a low voice as if she SS I 19 107 29
She did her best when thus called on, by speaking of Lady SS I 21 122 14
to relieve my heart by speaking to you of what I am always SS II 2 146 5
believed herself to be speaking their united inclinations. SS II 3 153 1
ever voluntarily speaking, except when any object of SS II 4 160 2
the impossibility of speaking to him again that evening, SS II 6 178 15
when he called, in her speaking to him, even voluntarily SS II 10 212 1
to him, even voluntarily speaking, with a kind of SS II 10 212 1
looking with the most speaking tenderness, sometimes at SS II 13 242 25
indeed; for, seriously speaking, I am very sure that SS II 13 243 39
40
looking at herself, and speaking familiarly to her brother; SS II 14 250 11
"Well, but Miss Dashwood," speaking triumphantly, "people SS III 2 272 14
"I only mean, that I suppose from your manner of speaking, SS III 5 296 28
taking her hand, and speaking in an awful whisper--"I may SS III 5 297 31
since I am here"--speaking with a forced vivacity as he SS III 8 318 15
have an opportunity of speaking with her in private--a SS III 8 321 34
eyes fixed in such speaking solicitude on my face!--and SS III 8 327 55
"Were you speaking to me?"--said Emma, who had caught her W 356 28
the room, speaking occasionally to one of his own party. PP I 3 11 6
"I certainly saw Mr. Darcy speaking to her." PP I 5 19 11
sisters not worth speaking to, a wish of being better PP I 6 21 1
to have any intention of speaking, Miss Lucas defied her PP I 6 24 17
18
I am not particularly speaking of such a case as you have PP I 10 50 37
"I wonder," said he, at the next opportunity of speaking, " PP I 16 78 18
he had yet seen, and speaking of the latter especially, PP I 16 78 22
had it pleased the gentleman we were speaking of just now." PP I 16 79 23
of whom they had been speaking; Mr. Bingley and his PP I 17 86 9
wholly surmount even in speaking to Mr. Bingley, whose PP I 18 89 3
They stood for some time without speaking a word; and she PP I 18 91 8
"I do not think we were speaking at all. PP I 18 93 26
and when she ceased speaking, replied thus, "my dear Miss PP I 18 97 60
61
Mr. Collins, however, was not discouraged from speaking PP I 18 98 61
do myself the honour of speaking to you next on this PP I 19 108 16
17
as a rational creature speaking the truth from her heart." PP I 19 109 20
"I must think your language too strong in speaking of both, PP II 1 136 14
opportunity of speaking to her alone; after honestly PP II 3 144 1
2
it; and, therefore, I am not afraid of speaking openly. PP II 3 144 2
Maria thought speaking out of the question, and the PP II 6 163 14
Lady Catherine was generally speaking--stating the PP II 6 166 41
Collins, sat for some time without speaking to any body. PP II 7 171 10
by her nephews, speaking to them, especially to Darcy, PP II 8 172 2
"We are speaking of music, madam," said he, when no longer PP II 8 173 5
my share in the conversation, if you are speaking of music. PP II 8 173 6
happiness; and that in speaking of Rosings and her not PP II 10 182 1
strong expressions in speaking of Wickham to Mr. Darcy, PP II 17 226 20
But the misfortune of speaking with bitterness, is a most PP II 17 226 21
us, and (comparatively speaking) a stranger to our family, PP III 9 320 33
It drew from her, however, the exertion of speaking, which PP III 11 337 52
then pray do not pain me by speaking of him in such terms." PP III 17 376 34
"Well, my dear," said he, when she ceased speaking, "I PP III 17 377 37
You were disgusted with the women who were always speaking PP III 18 380 5
half so much trouble, or speaking one word where he spoke MP I 2 12 2
the state; but, however, speaking from my own observation, MP I 5 46 22
Manners as well as appearance are, generally speaking, so MP I 5 49 32
We were speaking of them the other day, you know. MP I 5 49 35
voice was animated in speaking of his profession, and the MP I 6 60 47
feminine, except in the instances we have been speaking of. MP I 7 64 11
Edmund was fond of speaking to her of Miss Crawford, but MP I 7 66 14
was close to her, he was speaking to her, he was evidently MP I 7 67 16
Her own gentle voice speaking from the other end of the MP I 7 71 33
"You are speaking of London, I am speaking of the nation MP I 9 93 47
projects, and, generally speaking, whatever he proposed MP I 10 97 3
And to tell you the truth," speaking rather lower, "I do MP I 10 98 7
speaking it was altogether a silent drive to those within. MP I 10 106 58
You are speaking what you have been told at your uncle's MP I 11 110 24
pleasure, and she was speaking with great animation, for MP I 12 117 15
His sisters, to whom he had an opportunity of speaking the MP I 13 128 38
on the latter, and speaking a language, a remonstrance, a MP II 1 184 27
to the unconcern of his mother speaking entirely by rote. MP II 2 194 20
And while my cousins were sitting by without speaking a MP II 3 198 12
her happiness with him, speaking certainly without the MP II 3 201 22
preventing his cousin's speaking, "Fanny will immediately MP II 5 217 2
speaking low and seriously, "you know what all this means. MP II 9 268 31
him by her manner of speaking of the profession to which MP II 10 279 21
speaking of the clergy, and that should not have been. MP II 11 286 15
midst of all this, still speaking at intervals to me, or MP II 12 296 31
"Edmund--true, I believe he is (generally speaking) kind MP II 12 297 35
Sir Thomas was heard speaking to a servant in his way MP II 13 302 9
Fanny, meanwhile, speaking only when she could not help it, MP II 13 305 26
degree that made either speaking or looking up quite MP III 1 313 15
at this very time, by speaking the disinterestedness and MP III 2 326 3
Did you think me speaking improperly?--lightly, MP III 3 342 33
"Perhaps, sir," said Fanny, wearied at last into speaking-- MP III 3 343 39
the first opportunity of speaking to her alone," was the MP III 4 345 5
He had been speaking of her cheerfully from the hour of MP III 4 349 24
pleased by her manner of speaking of it yesterday, MP III 4 351 35
36
Crawford looking and speaking with much less particularity MP III 5 357 5
the warmest eulogium, in speaking of her uncle as all that MP III 10 405 17
not relieve herself by speaking of it to any human being. MP III 15 438 7
She was speaking only, as she had been used to hear others MP III 16 456 25
themselves; of walking; of speaking; of being silent. E I 4 33 34
We were speaking of it only yesterday, and agreeing how E I 5 36 6
relieved them by speaking of her own affection, sometimes E I 7 55 36
He began speaking of Harriet, and speaking of her with E I 8 58 9
Mr. Elton was speaking with animation, Harriet listening E I 10 88 33
Papa is only speaking his own regret." E I 11 94 10

He was always agreeable and obliging, and speaking E I 16 139 20
the room, I suppose, and speaking as loud as he could!-- E I 18 147 17
had succeeded, and after speaking some time of what the E II 1 155 1
but speaking plain enough to be very intelligible to Emma. E II 3 170 1
Mr. Dixon, you say, is not, strictly speaking, handsome." E II 3 176 46
at the moment were speaking a very different conviction. E II 5 189 13
his mother-in-law, and speaking of her with so much E II 5 191 28
Miss Woodhouse, you were speaking to me, you were saying E II 6 200 16
lady we were speaking of, play?" said Frank Churchill. E II 6 201 26
They had been speaking of it as they walked about Highbury E II 7 208 7
She had an opportunity now of speaking her approbation E II 8 213 7
We were speaking the other day, you know, of his being so E II 8 217 31
for while Miss Bates was speaking, a suspicion darted into E II 8 224 65
"I am not speaking of its prudence; merely its probability. E II 8 224 71
Mrs. Weston had been speaking to her at the same moment. E II 10 241 9
That young man (speaking lower) is very thoughtless. E II 11 249 11
I honestly said as much to Mr. E. when he was speaking of E II 14 276 36
When he was speaking of it in that way, I honestly said E II 14 276 36
Upon her speaking her wonder aloud on that part of the E II 15 285 16
"You are speaking of letters of business; mine are letters E II 16 293 20
answering, she began speaking again to Mr. John Knightley. E II 16 296 39
Am I unequal to speaking his name at once before all these E II 16 297 48
Miss Smith, or speaking to those who were close to her.-- E III 2 327 34
Emma had no opportunity of speaking to Mr. Knightley till E III 2 330 46
From Harriet's manner of speaking of the circumstance E III 3 332 1
you that I have been speaking truth, I am now going to E III 4 337 6
between the gentleman and lady we have been speaking of?" E III 5 350 32
"You were speaking," said he, gravely. E III 7 373 43
she, as they proceeded--speaking more to assist Mr. Weston E III 10 394 19
as to speaking ill of him, there I must have been safe." E III 10 399 64
Are you speaking of--Mr. Knightley?" E III 11 406 19
of great sensibility, speaking low, "time, my dearest Emma, E III 13 425 12
13
to the person we are speaking of, as it might be natural E III 13 426 17
a guess, Mrs. Elton, speaking louder, said, "yes, here I E III 16 455 20
21
I went over the fields too--(speaking in a tone of great E III 16 457 40
Indeed, Miss Woodhouse, (speaking more collectedly,) with E III 16 459 47
She was still looking in him with the most speaking E III 18 471 15
speaking to Harriet; and certainly did not speak in vain.-- E III 18 472 20
"I am quite sure," he replied, speaking very distinctly, " E III 18 474 30
before; and, generally speaking, if there had been neither P III 1 6 11
She had a cultivated mind, and was, generally speaking, P III 2 11 2
should be thinking and speaking of Edward, and not of P III 6 49 22
Mary knew, from Charles's manner of speaking, that he was P III 7 55 9
They were speaking as they drew near. P III 10 87 22
"Miss Elliot," said he, speaking rather low, "you have P III 12 107 24
he, turning to her and speaking with a glow, and yet a P III 12 114 63
In speaking of the Harvilles, he seemed unable to satisfy P IV 1 121 2
countenance improved by speaking, and his manners were so P IV 3 143 18
cousin, (he continued, speaking lower, though there was no P IV 4 151 21
of trial, but generally speaking it is its weakness and P IV 5 156 11
unfortunately" (speaking low and tremulously) "there are P IV 5 156 11
The same image of Mr. Elliot speaking for himself, brought P IV 5 160 26
While they were speaking, a whispering between her father P IV 8 181 2
feeling the necessity of speaking, and having not the P IV 8 183 11
12
"Perhaps," said Mr. Elliot, speaking low, "I have had a P IV 8 187 30
Her father and Lady Dalrymple were speaking. P IV 8 188 37
He began by speaking of the concert, gravely; more like P IV 8 190 47
Will not this manner of speaking of him, Mrs. Smith, P IV 9 196 33
To lose the possibility of speaking two words to Captain P IV 11 238 47
you will be convinced that I am not speaking at random. S 1 366 1
And we sir--(speaking rather proudly) are not in the Weald. S 1 366 1
we were speaking of--"Oh! woman in our hours of ease"--. S 7 397 1
loveliest Miss Heywood--(speaking with an air of deep S 7 398 1
You will not dislike speaking to her about it, Mary?"-- S 12 423 1

SPEAKINGLY (1)
There seems something more speakingly incomprehensible in MP II 4 208 12

SPEAKS (23)
She speaks of her with so much tenderness & anxiety, LS 6 251 1
in her look when she speaks either to her uncle or me, for LS 17 270 5
Her behaviour before Sir James certainly speaks the LS 20 278 11
"whom every body speaks well of, and nobody cares about; SS I 10 50 14
favour; and indeed, it speaks altogether so great a regard SS II 14 226 42
"Miss Bingley told me," said Jane, "that he never speaks PP I 5 19 13
"Mr. Collins," said she, "speaks highly both of Lady PP I 16 83 57
there is something pleasing about his mouth when he speaks. PP III 1 258 74
She speaks of her brother with a very pleasing affection." MP I 7 64 9
and speaks too quick, and would not keep her countenance. MP I 14 134 12
She does not think evil, but she speaks it--speaks it in MP II 9 269 31
Even now, she speaks with pleasure of being in Mansfield MP III 13 422 2
He always speaks to the purpose; open, straight forward, E I 8 59 27
Jane speaks so distinct! E II 1 158 14
as she always is, though she speaks rather too quick. E II 3 171 12
She speaks a little too quick. E II 14 279 54
voices; and nobody speaks like you and poor Miss Taylor. E II 14 279 54
does not talk to Miss Fairfax as she speaks of her. E II 15 286 22
23
I wonder how she speaks of the Coles--what she calls them! E II 15 288 39
This, you know, speaks a great degree of weakness--but now E II 18 306 11
But (lowering her voice)--nobody speaks except ourselves, E III 7 369 15
An Admiral speaks his own consequence, and, at the same P III 3 24 36
not know when a person speaks to him, or when one drops P IV 2 132 19

SPECIAL (3)
And a special licence. PP III 17 378 45
You must and shall be married by a special licence. PP III 17 378 45
least, Charles Hayter might get a special recommendation. P IV 10 217 20

SPECIES (7)
my life, would be a species of revenge to which I should LS 12 261 4
world, no species of composition has been so much decried. NA I 5 37 4
rheumatisms, and every species of ailment that can afflict SS I 8 38 12
his hearty approbation however on their species of house. SS II 14 251 16
the want of that higher species of self-command, that just MP I 9 91 36
few articles of a rare species of wood, excellently worked P III 11 98 17
to have something that makes one know one's species better. P IV 5 155 9

SPECIMEN (4)
nine days, is given as a specimen of their very warm NA I 6 39 1
presented her with a very curious specimen of heath. MP I 10 103 50
This specimen, written in haste as it was, had not a fault; MP II 9 265 19
had my writing-desk, I am sure I could produce a specimen. E II 16 298 52

SPECIMENS (3)
had seen some beautiful specimens when last in town, and NA II 7 175 12
At Hartfield you have had very good specimens of well E I 4 32 32
Is not this room rich in specimens of your landscapes and E I 6 43 14

SPECIOUS (1)
Mr. Woodhouse must not, under the specious pretence of a E III 6 356 29

SPECK (2)
in the street, or saw a speck upon her gown, she must NA I 9 60 1
Not a speck on them." E I 1 10 25

SPECKS (2)
At about eleven o'clock however, a few specks of small NA I 11 82 2
acknowledge some actual specks in the character of their NA II 10 200 3

SPECTACLES (9)
well still, thank God! with the help of spectacles. E II 1 157 10
world, fastening in the rivet of my mother's spectacles.-- E II 9 236 46
For my mother had no use of her spectacles--could not put E II 9 236 46
ought to have two pair of spectacles; they should indeed. E II 9 236 46
Here is the rivet of your mistress's spectacles out. E II 9 236 46
Oh! my mother's spectacles. E II 9 237 51
occupied about her spectacles, and Jane Fairfax, standing E II 10 240 1
of restoring your spectacles, healed for the present." E II 10 242 15
tell you my mother's spectacles have never been in fault E III 2 323 19

SPECTATOR (3)
with a paper from the spectator, and a chapter from Sterne, NA I 5 37 4
with a volume of the spectator, instead of such a work, NA I 5 38 4
prompter, sometimes as spectator--was often very useful.-- MP I 18 165 3

SPECULATE (1)
were more disposed to speculate and wonder; and Captain P III 9 75 9

SPECULATING (1)
of two or three speculating people about Brinshore, this S 1 369 1

SPECULATION (25)
Tilney, made but a small part of Catherine's speculation. NA II 2 138 1
was consequently open to every greedy speculation. NA II 16 251 6
of speculation, her wonder was otherwise disposed of. SS I 14 71 3
Speculation is the only round game at Croydon now, but I W 354 28
"Speculation I beleive, said Elizth--my sister recommends W 358 28
I have had some pleasant hours at speculation in my time-- W 358 28
I think it is a much better game than speculation. W 358 28
I cannot say I am very fond of speculation." W 358 28
has legally hired, without raising all this speculation! PP III 11 332 19
they always are, speculation was decided on almost as soon MP II 7 239 4
Whist and speculation; which will amuse me most?" MP II 7 239 5
Thomas, after a moment's thought, recommended speculation. MP II 7 239 6
answer--"then speculation if you please, Mrs. Grant. MP II 7 239 7
All the agreeable of her speculation was over for that MP II 7 248 48
and a very interesting speculation in what possible manner E II 11 248 9
All the rest, in speculation at least, was perfectly E II 11 255 59
be on fire with speculation and foresight!--especially E III 3 335 9
It was also a very early speculation with Emma. E III 9 388 13
to be shifted off in a wild speculation on the future. E III 17 468 31
it might not be a bad speculation for a surgeon to get a S 1 366 1
becoming a profitable speculation, they had engaged in it, S 2 371 1
was his lottery, his speculation & his Hobby Horse; his S 2 372 1
being his colleague in speculation, Sanditon itself could S 3 375 1
He has persuaded her to engage in the same speculation--& S 7 402 1
were setting off,--a joyful sight--& full of speculation.-- S 10 414 1

SPECULATIONS (3)
curiosity, and his own speculations, he had yet something NA II 15 245 12
soon as possible, or speculations upon prize money, which MP III 7 375 2
whatever feelings or speculations concerning him might P IV 11 243 66

SPECULATIVE (1)
Her mother too, in whose mind not one speculative thought SS I 10 49 11

SPED (1)
for observing how he sped with Fanny, and what degree of MP III 3 336 7

SPEECH (82)
He then told me, mixing in his speech a few insolent LS 22 281 4
I concluded, & I hope you will be satisfied with my speech. LS 25 293 3
o'clock," was her parting speech to her new friend. NA I 10 80 61
elucidated by this speech, soon ceased to be a puzzle. NA I 13 102 26
If a speech be well drawn up, I read it with pleasure, by NA I 14 109 23
From them however the eight parts of speech shone out most NA I 15 120 24
whole length of a speech, but it now carried her captive. NA II 4 153 30
Catherine had no leisure for speech, being at once NA II 6 165 5
Catherine did not hear enough of this speech to understand NA II 11 213 20
being in the middle of a speech about something very NA II 13 220 2
Eleanor seemed now impelled into resolution and speech. NA II 13 228 27
Mrs. Dashwood felt too much for speech, and instantly SS I 15 77 18
A short pause succeeded this speech, which was first SS I 21 123 21
heaven that she had never made so rude a speech. SS II 1 145 16
this speech, and Lucy was still the first to end it. SS II 2 150 35
Elinor's thanks followed this speech with grateful SS II 9 211 33
their assent; it seemed too awful a moment for speech. SS III 1 265 35
Astonished and shocked at so unlover-like a speech, she SS III 3 281 11
This speech at first puzzled Mrs. Jennings exceedingly. SS III 4 286 16
of Mrs. Jennings's speech; neither did she think it worth SS III 4 286 18
speech and look, where minuteness could be safely indulged. SS III 10 348 34
time, his inclination for speech seeming to increase with W 347 21
A short pause followed this speech, and Mrs. Hurst began PP I 8 36 13
To this speech Bingley made no answer; but his sisters PP I 8 37 20
How shall we punish him for such a speech?" PP I 11 57 16
Her cousin prefaced his speech with a solemn bow, and PP I 18 98 61
the length of his second speech, and at the end of it he PP I 18 98 61
father's speech, was afraid her anxiety had done no good.-- PP I 18 101 70
And with a bow to Mr. Darcy, he concluded his speech, PP I 18 101 71
you," said he, when she had finished her speech. PP I 20 111 9
"Take care, Lizzy; that speech savours strongly of PP II 4 154 20
ran the girls, too eager to get in to have time for speech. PP III 7 301 4
every saucy speech she had ever directed towards him. PP III 10 327 3
"That is the most unforgiving speech," said Elizabeth, " PP III 13 350 48
But he had ended his speech in a way to sink her in sad MP I 3 33 64
was glad to put an end to his speech by a proposal of wine. MP I 6 55 17
Mrs. Grant hearing the latter part of this speech, MP I 6 61 58
but felt too angry for speech; and he needed a little MP I 9 87 16
merest common-place--not a tolerable speech in the whole. MP I 14 134 13
hand, and curtailed every speech that admitted being MP I 15 138 1
for him as she heard this speech, and saw his look, and MP I 15 139 4
She had seen her influence in every speech, and was MP I 16 156 28
Rushworth, who was wanting a prompter through every speech. MP I 18 164 2
and the first line of his speech, and being able to follow MP I 18 166 4
a little, for really there is a speech or two----- MP I 18 168 17
There, look at that speech, and that, and that. MP I 18 168 19
to any one; and when her speech was over, she trembled and MP II 5 225 59
but of one errand, which turned her too sick for speech.-- MP II 9 268 28
Fanny struggled for speech, and said, "I am very sorry MP II 9 268 30
and slowness of speech would allow, and certainly MP II 10 276 14
the middle of a very fine speech of that man's--what's his MP III 3 336 9
"Let me have the pleasure of finishing that speech to your MP III 3 336 10
name of Cardinal Wolsey, that he had got the very speech.-- MP III 3 336 10
After this speech, the two girls sat many minutes silent, MP III 5 360 13
was wounded by her sister's speech and her mother's reply. MP III 7 386 43
but it was with agonies, which did not admit of speech. MP III 16 453 16
Emma watched her through the fluctuations of this speech, E I 4 31 26
of the privilege of speech that Emma's mother might have E I 5 40 24
a great part of this speech, "how do you know that Mr. E I 8 60 28
The speech was more to Emma than to Harriet, which Emma E I 9 71 12
After this speech he was gone as soon as possible. E I 9 82 84
Mr. Frank Churchill to be making such a speech as that to E I 18 147 17
again, with any necessity, or even any power of speech. E II 3 180 58
she saw a touch of the arm at this speech, from his wife. E II 5 188 11
Miss Fairfax; but it was most prudent to avoid speech. E II 8 220 48
the speech, and the door had soon shut out Frank Churchill. E II 12 261 37
and had not finished her speech under many minutes after E III 2 322 18
though too distant for speech, her countenance said much, E III 2 328 40
as soon as she had recovered her senses and speech.-- E III 3 334 8
and after a pretty long speech from Miss Bates, which E III 5 344 3
all was as right as this speech proclaimed; and its happy E III 10 400 69
from him, a look, a speech, a removal from one chair to E III 11 409 35
The bitter feelings occasioned by this speech, the many E III 11 411 40
41
he said, but he could hardly ever get the speech of him. E III 16 458 43
he said; and, whether in speech or silence, conniving at E III 18 476 43
Wentworth's face at this speech, a certain glance of his P III 8 67 28
and there was one speech of Louisa's which struck her. P III 10 84 7
She seemed to be in the middle of some eager speech. P III 10 87 22
readily answered such a speech--words of such interest, P III 10 88 27
Anne smiled more than once to herself during this speech, P III 12 103 3
Mr. Elliot's speech too distressed her. P IV 8 188 43
to let her finish her speech, "there is nothing I so P IV 11 230 8

SPEECHES (30)
The speeches that are put into the heroes' mouths, their NA I 14 108 22
the world, I hated fine speeches and compliments;--and so-- NA II 1 134 39
relieved by the long speeches of Mr. Collins, who was PP I 18 102 75
In as short a time as Mr. Collins's long speeches would PP I 22 121 2

the coach, and with many speeches of thankfulness on Mr. PP II 6 166 42
and affectionate preparatory speeches for a while. MP I 4 34 2
speeches to Mrs. Rushworth, was ready to lead the way. MP I 10 104 52
let her take Cottager's speeches instead of Cottager's MP I 14 134 14
speeches, I would undertake him with all my heart." MP I 14 134 14
"I come in three times, and have two and forty speeches. MP I 15 139 10
"The count has two and forty speeches," returned Mr. MP I 15 144 31
I only puzzle them, and oblige them to make civil speeches. MP I 15 144 36
not above half a dozen speeches altogether, and it will MP I 15 145 47
"If you are afraid of half a dozen speeches," cried Mr. MP I 15 145 48
shorten some of his speeches, and a great many of my own, MP I 15 149 61
and Mr. Rushworth undertook to count his speeches. MP I 17 158 2
of the feelings it excited in some speeches for Maria.-- MP I 18 165 3
knowledge of his two and forty speeches became much less. MP I 18 165 4
"Poor Rushworth and his two-and-forty speeches!" continued MP II 5 224 53
to make two-and-forty speeches to her"--adding, with a MP II 5 224 53
And these were her longest speeches and clearest MP II 11 283 4
best scene, or the best speeches of each; and whether it MP III 3 337 10
composed as Anhalt ought, through the two long speeches. MP III 5 358 9
lines from himself, warm and determined like his speeches. MP III 7 375 4
in his speeches which was very apt to incline her to laugh. E I 9 82 84
I wish you had heard his gallant speeches to me at dinner. E II 17 302 22
"I cannot make speeches, emma:"--he soon resumed; and in a E III 13 430 37
No wonder you should hold my speeches in such affectionate E III 17 462 10
Anne did not wish for more of such looks and speeches. P III 8 72 60
the fair, to make fine speeches to every pretty girl, was S 8 405 2

SPEECHLESS (4)

Catherine sat down, breathless and speechless. NA II 13 225 19
motionless as she was speechless, and grieved to the heart MP III 3 342 32
at him for a moment in speechless admiration, and then MP III 7 384 34
sensations on the discovery made her perfectly speechless. P III 9 80 34

SPEED (12)

you ever see an animal so made for speed in your life?" NA I 7 46 9
to set off with all speed to Fullerton, to make known his NA I 15 119 14
and four, which will drive off with incredible speed. NA II 1 131 15
and found her way with all speed to the breakfast-parlour, NA II 7 173 5
running with all possible speed down the steep side of the SS I 9 41 6
and with proportionate speed through the neighbourhood. PP III 8 309 6
the judicious law of her own brain laid down with speed.-- E III 4 341 34
with what appeared unusual speed, they were half way down E III 7 376 62
It darted through her, with the speed of an arrow, that Mr. E III 11 408 32
the speed which a clear head and quick taste could allow. P III 7 61 38
Their actual speed, heightened by some dread of the P III 12 117 73
Was not it Mrs. Speed, as usual, or the maid? P IV 9 197 39

SPEEDIEST (1)

I thought it my duty to give the speediest intelligence of PP III 15 363 22

SPEEDILY (24)

Your restoration to peace will, I doubt not, speedily LS 37 306 1
to her his devoirs were speedily paid, with a mixture of NA I 7 44 4
in the rooms, which speedily brought on considerable NA I 9 60 1
speedily be furnished: it waits only for a lady's taste!" NA II 11 214 22
almost impossible, might speedily take place, to unite NA II 16 250 3
She speedily comprehended all his merits; the persuasion SS I 3 16 13
man, with whom they were speedily provided from amongst SS I 5 26 5
They speedily discovered that their enjoyment of dancing SS I 10 47 3
The whole story would have been speedily formed under her SS I 11 57 17
acknowledged, nor too speedily made use of; and the visit SS II 14 254 26
or impropriety of speedily hazarding her narration, SS III 10 347 32
and in short, it became speedily evident to both, that he SS III 14 376 11
Sir William and Lady Lucas were speedily applied to for PP I 22 122 3
depend upon it, you will speedily receive from me a letter PP I 22 124 10
every thing relating to their journey was speedily settled. PP III 4 280 26
Jane's happiness, and his own, would be speedily secured. PP III 12 340 13
belief that all must speedily be concluded, unless Mr. PP III 13 345 20
The Bennets were speedily pronounced to be the luckiest PP III 13 350 56
You must answer it of course--and speedily." E I 7 51 9
quick observation, and speedily determine how he was E III 1 315 3
superior quality was speedily despatched to Miss Bates E III 9 391 20
They hurried on, and were speedily at Randall's.-- E III 10 394 25
not hear from her again speedily; but I made excuses for E III 14 442 8
he was expected, and speedily, but the Musgroves, in their P III 6 52 33

SPEEDY (19)

far from expecting so speedy a distinction, tho' I always LS 3 246 1
in, would undergo so speedy, so melancholy a reverse! LS 24 285 1
But the hindrance thrown in the way of a very speedy NA I 8 56 11
the reason of their speedy return, said, "I am glad your NA I 11 89 62
She knew enough to feel secure of an honourable and speedy NA I 15 122 28
of Sunday groups, and speedy shall be her descent from it. NA II 14 232 7
of the valley, she was as speedy in climbing the hills, SS I 16 85 15
might have been more speedy, had she known how little SS I 18 99 14
that her success was speedy, and for the time complete. SS I 22 134 53
still talked boldly of a speedy recovery, and Miss SS III 7 309 7
All that remained to be done, was to be speedy; and SS III 7 316 30
not find a more willing or speedy messenger than myself--. W 338 18
Croydon to announce the speedy return of Margaret, & a W 348 23
by no means wish for so speedy a return, immediately said, PP I 22 123 6
7
of speedy payment, for which I have pledged myself. PP III 8 313 19
leave of not just then, and how, to a very speedy issue. MP II 4 214 46
like Fanny; but there was speedy comfort in the determined MP III 2 329 11
After being long fed with hopes of a speedy visit form Mr. E III 6 352 1
A speedy cure must not be hoped, but every thing was going P IV 1 121 2

SPELL (4)

The spell is removed. LS 34 304 1
and then learning to spell, if you had ever seen how NA I 14 109 26
I would spell it, read it, write it with any body. MP III 3 343 38
I never saw any body in my life spell harder for an P IV 10 213 4

SPELT (1)

though not perfectly well spelt praise, as "a fine dashing P III 6 52 33

SPENCER (1)

I had got my bonnet and spencer on, just ready to come out- E II 3 173 27

SPEND (76)

on leaving them, & shall spend I hope a comfortable day LS 2 245 1
Allow him to spend the evening with you, that I may be in LS 31 302 1
you spend;--I will give you this little book on purpose." NA I 2 18 2
I should like to spend my whole life in reading it. NA I 6 40 7
"But then you spend your time so much more rationally in NA I 10 79 49
I hope you spend your time pleasantly, but am afraid you NA II 12 216 2
home, because there you must spend the most of your time. NA II 15 241 4
I am sure I cannot imagine how they will spend half of it; SS I 2 12 24
has more money than he can spend, more time than he knows SS I 10 51 25
"I should be puzzled to spend a large fortune myself," SS I 17 92 23
Sir John had been very urgent with them all to spend the SS I 19 108 40
Will you come and spend some time at Cleveland this SS I 20 112 29
as Sir John to ask them to spend a week or two in Conduit- SS II 12 230 8
dined from home, she might spend a whole day without SS II 14 247 4
and how much she had every year to spend upon herself. SS II 14 249 8
Lady Middleton, for they spend every day with her; SS II 14 253 21
myself to ask the Miss Steeles to spend a few days with us. SS II 14 253 24
solitude, she resolved to spend almost every hour of every SS III 6 303 9
that she has gone to spend a month with Robert and Jane on W 319 2
whether he might not spend the remainder of his days at PP I 4 15 12
"how pleasant it is to spend an evening in this way! PP I 11 55 4
confusion, Charlotte Lucas came to spend the day with them. PP I 20 112 25
obliged to spend his vacant hours in a comfortless hotel. PP I 21 117 10
11
who came as usual to spend the Christmas at Longbourn. PP II 2 139 2
spend a morning with her, without any danger of seeing him. PP II 2 142 17
Oh! what hours of transport we shall spend! PP II 4 154 23
us on Sunday to drink tea and spend the evening at Rosings. PP II 6 160 2
that he may spend very little of his time there in future. PP II 9 177 8
Kitty and me were to spend the day there, and Mrs. Forster PP II 16 221 17
and where they were now to spend a few days, was probably PP II 19 239 7
sir; but I dare say he may spend half his time here; and PP III 1 248 25
I will not spend my hours in running after my neighbours PP III 11 332 25
well how to save her own as to spend that of her friends. MP I 1 8 9
a sailor, was invited to spend a week with his sister in MP I 2 21 34
He had come, intending to spend only a few days with them, MP I 5 47 26
Twickenham for us all to spend our summers in; and my aunt MP I 6 57 31
She was a little surprised that he could spend so many MP I 7 66 14
Miss Crawford, on walking up with her brother to spend the MP I 11 108 4
I can even suppose it pleasant to spend half the year in MP II 4 210 21
"Your sister perhaps may be prevailed on to spend the day MP II 5 219 22
to Portsmouth, and spend a little time with her own family. MP III 6 368 9
By degrees the girls came to spend the chief of the MP III 9 398 9
moment, just in time to spend a few minutes with the MP III 15 445 31
Weston need not spend a single evening in the year alone E I 1 12 41
are we setting forward to spend five dull hours in another E I 13 113 26
be able to spend a week with his father, if he likes it." E I 14 122 22
friends, he had engaged to spend a few weeks, and very E I 17 140 2
absence to Highbury; to spend, perhaps, her last months of E II 2 166 10
Part of every winter she had been used to spend in Bath; E II 4 183 9
Woodhouse was persuaded to spend with his daughter at E II 11 247 2
He may spend the evening with his dear William Larkins now E II 12 262 39
"I must spend some time with them; I am sure they will E II 17 300 9
or has ordered herself, to spend in some warmer place than E II 18 308 30
Enscombe--in short, to spend in London; so that we have E II 18 308 30
Mrs. Bates was engaged to spend the evening at Hartfield, E III 1 318 13
spend some quiet interval in the young man's company. E III 2 319 2
as he very often did, to spend his evening at Hartfield. E III 5 344 3
'You must all spend your evening with us,' said she--'I E III 8 381 17
I am going to London, to spend a few days with John and E III 9 385 2
She resolved to prevail on her to spend a day at Hartfield. E III 9 389 16
Miss Fairfax has been persuaded to spend the day with us.-- E III 18 476 45
It had not been possible for him to spend less; he had P III 1 9 19
to the lodge, where she was to spend the first week. P III 5 35 18
uses for his money, and a right to spend it as he liked. P III 6 43 5
The folks of great house were to spend the evening of this P III 6 50 26
that they should have to spend the evening by themselves, P III 6 50 26
felt that she could not spend her last morning at P IV 1 122 5
engaged, to spend that evening in Westgate-Buildings. P IV 5 156 14
was engaged to spend the evening with an old schoolfellow." P IV 5 157 14
She had once partly promised Mrs. Smith to spend the P IV 7 180 33
Having long had as much money as he could spend, nothing P IV 9 206 90
to Camden-Place, there to spend the evening chiefly in P IV 10 227 69
be answered for) to spend even 5 shillings at Brinshore.-- S 2 374 1
"No people spend more freely, I beleive, than W. Indians." S 6 392 1
her & her brother to spend a week with me at Sanditon S 7 399 1
"He was just come from Eastbourne, proposing to spend two S 12 425 1

SPENDING (32)

when we last parted, of spending some weeks with you at LS 1 243 1
to keep our promise of spending the Christmas with you; & LS 3 246 1
fond of books & spending the cheif of her time in reading. LS 18 273 3
honour of dining and spending the rest of the day with her. NA I 13 103 28
on her return, without spending many hours in the NA II 1 129 1
Though Mrs. Jennings was in the habit of spending a large SS I 3 153 1
were in the habit of spending more than they ought, and of PP I 4 15 11
The improvement of spending a night in London was added in PP II 4 151 1
our power to prevent your spending your time unpleasantly." PP II 15 215 2
life, that, instead of spending his whole income, he had PP III 8 308 1
cheap situation, and always spending more than they ought. PP III 19 387 8
make the fortune, and there be discretion in spending it. MP I 6 60 51
It was evident that they had been spending their time MP I 10 103 49
them and spending the evening at the parsonage. MP II 1 177 5
duties of the day, by spending it at the park to support MP II 3 203 30
home, that I should be spending month after month here, as MP II 4 210 17
were now spending from two to three thousand a year in." MP II 7 243 27
forward with the hope of spending much, very much of his MP III 10 405 18
Mrs. R. has been spending Easter with the Aylmers at MP III 14 434 13
because he has been spending a few days at Richmond. he MP III 14 435 14
to their spending half the evenings in the week together. E I 2 18 11
For some weeks past she had been spending more than half E I 8 57 1
spending the autumn at south end instead of coming here. E I 12 101 19
20
near at hand, and spending the whole evening away from him. E II 7 208 9
sitting with the Eltons, spending a day with the Eltons! E II 15 285 12
and Lady Russell's spending some part of every winter P III 2 14 10
He had been lucky in his profession, but spending freely, P III 4 27 4
With the prospect of spending at least two months at P III 6 43 3
"But, could you be comfortable yourself, to be spending P III 7 56 13
she began to talk of spending the morning in Rivers-Street. P IV 10 215 14
without spending at least 6 weeks by the sea every year.-- S 2 373 1
her to be spending all her money the very first evening. S 6 390 1

SPENDS (2)

room, & Frederica spends great part of the day there; LS 17 271 7
I dare say, and Edward spends half his time with his SS II 13 240 15

SPENDTHRIFT (1)

daughter of a foolish, spendthrift baronet, who had not P IV 12 248 1

SPENT (127)

for I have seldom spent three months more agreably than LS 2 244 1
springs her ladyship spent in town, while her daughter was LS 6 251 1
which would be otherwise spent in endeavouring to overcome LS 10 258 3
talent, as the cheif of my time is spent in conversation. LS 16 268 2
or four days had been spent in learning what was mostly NA I 2 20 8
of Thorpe; and that he had spent the last week of the NA I 4 33 5
with the day unless she spent the chief of it by the side NA I 5 36 3
They all spent the evening together at Thorpe's. NA I 11 89 63
what;" and the evening was spent in a sort of war of wit, NA I 15 121 25
"But that you certainly did, for you spent the whole NA II 3 145 12
The Thorpes spent the last evening of Catherine's stay in NA II 4 153 31
father's, and some of my time is necessarily spent there." NA II 5 157 7
as he looked at her, spent the rest of his time in NA II 6 165 6
The fire therefore died away, and Catherine, having spent NA II 6 168 10
An hour passed away before the General came in, spent, on NA II 8 182 1
The day which she had spent at that place had been one of NA II 14 230 2
children, the old gentleman's days were comfortably spent. SS I 1 3 1
who had since spent the greatest part of his time there. SS I 3 15 4
Willoughby had spent the preceding evening with them, and SS I 12 60 8
I know where you spent the morning." SS I 13 67 61
had gone to Allenham, and spent a considerable time there SS I 13 67 65
I never spent a pleasanter morning in my life." SS I 13 68 70
more of his hours were spent there than at Allenham; and SS I 14 71 5
the rest of the day was spent by himself at the side of SS I 14 71 5
hours have been since spent by us together, you would SS I 14 73 17
She spent whole hours at the pianoforte alternately SS I 16 83 3
how my money would be spent --some of it, at least--my SS I 17 92 26
politeness made on it, was spent in admiration of whatever SS I 21 120 6
which if rationally spent, give such improvement to the SS II 1 140 2
the same period of time, spent on her side in inferior SS II 1 140 2
spent seven years at a great school in town to some effect. SS II 4 160 3
After an hour or two spent in what her mother called SS II 4 164 23
than to Elinor, for it was spent in all the anxiety of SS II 4 166 31
The morning was chiefly spent in leaving cards at the SS II 5 168 8
After some time spent in saying little and doing less, SS II 6 175 2
and after some time thus spent in joint affliction, she SS II 7 182 12
of suffering had somewhat spent itself, and then turning SS II 7 182 12
13
so many hours have been spent in convincing myself that I SS II 9 204 18
and we spent the rest of the day with Mrs. Ferrars. SS II 11 221 9
"we spent such a day, Edward, in Harley-Street yesterday! SS II 13 243 32
Middletons, spent the whole of every day in Conduit-Street. SS II 14 246 2
"They had already spent a week in this manner in Conduit- SS II 14 253 22
A few minutes more spent in the same kind of effusion, SS III 1 269 57
dear Mrs. Jennings, I spent two happy hours with him SS III 2 277 30

But a day spent in sitting shivering over the fire with a SS III 7 307 1
only ten minutes I have spent out of my chaise since that SS III 8 318 20
of my life were what I spent with her, when I felt my SS III 8 321 34
go the next morning--was spent by me in deliberating on SS III 8 323 40
welcome; and accordingly I spent the greatest part of my SS III 13 362 5
though a very few hours spent in the hard labour of SS III 13 363 9
themselves, for having spent so much time with them at SS III 13 368 25
visit were consequently spent in hearing and in wondering. SS III 13 370 35
The first month after their marriage was spent with their SS III 14 374 7
and sisters spent much more than half their time with her. SS III 14 378 13
The rest of the evening was spent in conjecturing how soon PP I 2 8 28
to any other lady, and spent the rest of the evening in PP I 3 11 6
spent together--and four evenings may do a great deal." PP I 6 22 8
Mrs. Hurst and Miss Bingley had spent some hours of the PP I 10 47 1
The first half hour was spent in piling up the fire, lest PP I 11 54 2
of his life having been spent under the guidance of an PP I 15 70 1
warmly,-- "I have spent four days in the same house with PP I 16 77 13
The chief of every day was spent by him at Lucas Lodge, PP I 23 129 15
After a week spent in professions of love and schemes of PP II 2 139 1
her marriage, she had spent a considerable time in that PP II 2 142 19
The evening was spent chiefly in talking over PP II 5 157 10
and upon the whole she spent her time comfortably enough; PP II 7 169 5
the very last evening was spent there; and her ladyship PP II 14 213 20
She had spent six weeks with great enjoyment; and the PP II 15 215 3
money, for we have just spent ours at the shop out there." PP II 16 219 3
Mr. Darcy's having both spent three weeks at Rosings, and PP II 18 233 26
and the evening was spent in the satisfactions of an PP III 1 259 76
mornings that had now been spent there; but on the third, PP III 4 273 1
have spent ten minutes of every day in a rational manner." PP III 6 300 30
Bennet spent the morning together, as had been agreed on. PP III 13 346 21
All was acknowledged, and half the night spent in PP III 17 374 19
Kitty, to her very material advantage, spent the chief of PP III 19 385 4
She was a woman who spent her days in sitting nicely MP I 2 19 31
part of my future days will be spent in utter seclusion. MP I 3 29 48
you parted, have not been spent on your side entirely MP I 3 33 64
Tome Bertram had of late spent so little of his time at MP I 4 34 1
Four fine mornings successively were spent in this manner, MP I 7 70 30
After some minutes spent in this way, Miss Bertram MP I 10 97 4
Weymouth, where they had spent ten days together in the MP I 13 121 1
think our time very well spent, and so I am sure will he.-- MP I 13 126 18
that every hour might be spent in their service; she was, MP I 13 129 40
to her possessions, and spent more of her time there; and MP I 16 151 1
had been irreproachably spent during his absence; she had MP II 1 179 9
it all and all, I never spent so happy a summer.-- MP II 4 210 19
of his year might be spent, and he might find himself MP II 7 246 37
course of a long morning, spent principally with her two MP II 9 267 22
"You spent your time pleasantly there." MP III 4 355 51
but a few days more to be spent at Mansfield; and for part MP III 6 372 21
Her days were spent in a kind of slow bustle; always busy MP III 8 389 4
eye, and hear that he had spent half an hour with his MP III 10 400 8
even half an hour, having spent scarcely twenty-four hours MP III 10 400 8
if he was not with them, spent the long, long evening MP III 11 413 32
grounds as she could, and spent her days very happily in MP III 16 449 4
if she had spent all the rest of her life at Hartfield. E I 1 7 10
Your time has been properly and delicately spent, if you E I 1 12 42
of his leisure days were spent; and between useful E I 2 16 5
feel that every evening so spent, was indeed one of the E I 3 22 6
a good deal; she had spent two very happy months with them, E I 4 27 4
24th of December) had been spent by Harriet at Hartfield, E I 13 108 5
the vicarage was spent by him in expressing his discontent. E I 13 113 25
more on a few months spent in her native air, for the E II 2 166 10
Jane had spent an evening at Hartfield with her E II 2 168 15
"Perhaps you may now begin to regret that you spent one E II 8 222 52
I have spent so many happy months there!(with a little E II 14 273 19
That a man who might have spent his evening quietly at E II 17 302 23
talker, which a day spent any where form home confers, was E II 17 303 24
Were he ever able to get away, the day would be spent in E III 1 318 10
or two spent at Donwell, be tempted away to his misery. E III 6 356 29
two whole hours that were spent on the hill, there seemed E III 7 367 1
"You spent the evening with Mrs. Elton?" E III 8 381 16
than a quarter of an hour spent in Mrs. Bates's parlour, E III 12 417 4
a few weeks spent in London must give her some amusement.-- E III 14 435 4
happy fortnight which I spent with you, did not, I hope, E III 14 438 8
Do you remember the morning spent at Donwell?-- E III 14 440 8
winter which she had afterwards spent there with herself. P III 2 14 11
morning, and hardly ever spent an evening asunder; but she P III 6 46 12
of the first evening they spent together: and though his P III 8 63 2
happiest part of my life has been spent on board a ship. P III 8 70 54
This was against her; but, on the other hand, he spent so P III 11 93 2
only two days, was spent entirely at the mansion-house, P IV 1 121 1
He had spent his whole solitary evening in the room P IV 3 144 19
All his caution was spent in being secured of the real P IV 9 202 66
Mr & Mrs P. spent a great part of the eveng at the hotel; S 10 413 1

SPHERE (4)
to quit the sphere, in which you have been brought up." PP III 14 356 50
I should not consider myself as quitting that sphere. PP III 14 356 51
never respected when they step out of their proper sphere. MP II 5 220 30
The sphere in which she moves is much above his.-- E I 8 62 39

SPHERES (1)
Delightful, charming, superior, first circles, spheres, E III 6 359 37

SPICERS (1)
fair chance, through the Spicers, of getting something P III 9 76 15

SPIES (1)
neighbourhood of voluntary spies, and where roads and NA II 9 197 29

SPIKES (1)
yourself against those spikes--you will tear your gown-- MP I 10 99 21

SPINE (1)
had been done to the spine, but Mr. Robinson found nothing P III 7 55 7

SPINNET (2)
the old forlorn spinnet; so, at eight years old she began. NA I 1 14 1
old spinnet in the world, to amuse herself with.-- E II 8 215 16

SPINNING (1)
But I seem to be spinning out my story to an endless S 9 408 1

SPIRE (1)
spire which would announce her within twenty miles of home. NA II 14 232 6

SPIRIT (124)
an illiberal & vindictive spirit to resent a project which LS 5 249 1
There is exquisite pleasure in subduing an insolent spirit, LS 7 254 3
I infinitely prefer the tender & liberal spirit of LS 16 269 3
& without betraying the least tenderness of spirit. LS 17 269 2
to the letter & not the spirit of mama's commands, but if LS 21 279 1
This Reginald has a proud spirit of his own!--a spirit too, LS 25 292 1
suit the freedom of my spirit; & if I resolve to wait for LS 29 299 3
He talked with fluency and spirit--and there was an NA I 3 25 2
admired the graceful spirit of her walk, the fashionable NA I 4 34 7
treat them with spirit, and make them keep their distance." NA I 6 42 26
called on to admire the spirit and freedom with which his NA I 9 64 27
exactly with the spirit of her dancing, and making her one NA I 13 103 28
a matter in which her disinterested spirit took no concern. NA I 15 122 28
If I could believe it--my spirit, you know, is pretty NA II 3 147 22
With this spirit she sprang forward, and her confidence NA II 6 164 3
You know I have a pretty good spirit of my own. NA II 12 217 2
of what had first given spirit to her existence there. NA II 14 238 23
proof of that repining spirit to which she had now begun NA II 15 241 7
But you have such a generous spirit!" SS I 2 9 11
His eyes want all that spirit, that fire, which at once SS I 3 17 18
and written in the true spirit of friendly accommodation. SS I 4 23 20
of Mrs. Dashwood's spirit overcame the wish of society for SS I 9 40 2
received particular spirit from his exterior attractions.-- SS I 9 43 11
with sparkling eyes, "and with elegance, with spirit?" SS I 9 45 26
dark, there was a life, a spirit, an eagerness which could SS I 10 46 2
and spirit which Edward had unfortunately wanted. SS I 10 48 8
Marianne, "that he has neither genius, taste, nor spirit. SS I 10 51 26
Well, I shall spirit up the Colonel as soon as I can. SS II 8 197 22
to make over for ever; but Mrs. Ferrars has a noble spirit. SS II 11 224 28
a very natural kind of spirit, to settle that estate upon SS III 1 269 53
"Can any thing be more galling to the spirit of a man," SS III 1 269 56
Once Lucy thought to write to him, but then her spirit SS III 2 273 16
getting her to Delaford!--but her spirit was stubborn. SS III 9 339 25
spoke with more genuine spirit, anticipating the pleasure SS III 10 343 8
Here ceased the rapid flow of self-reproving spirit; and SS III 10 346 29
be only to shew that my spirit is humbled, my heart SS III 10 347 30
fullness, brilliancy & spirit of the meeting. tho' as he W 336 14
instance by a general spirit of curiosity on Emma's W 337 16
everybody danced with spirit to the very last."-- W 340 19
beheld--such quickness & spirit! he lets nobody dream over W 358 28
He played with spirit, & had a great deal to say & tho' W 359 28
from being the life & spirit of a house, where all had W 361 31
She told the story however with great spirit among her PP I 3 12 14
with much bitterness of spirit and some exaggeration, the PP I 3 13 19
with humour, and laugh at their acquaintance with spirit. PP I 11 54 1
their parts with more spirit, or finer success; and happy PP I 18 101 72
conversed with so much spirit and flow, as to draw the PP II 8 172 3
the true Darcy spirit, she may like to have her own way." PP II 10 184 19
being actuated by one spirit, every thing relating to PP III 4 280 26
lost but little of their spirit in this change of PP III 8 309 6
that it was written in a dreadful bitterness of spirit." PP III 16 368 22
but Mrs. Norris had a spirit of activity, which could not MP I 1 4 1
benevolence of her husband with a good deal of spirit. MP I 14 134 12
on an agitated, doubting spirit--to see if by looking at MP I 16 152 3
a warm temper and a high spirit were likely to endure MP I 17 162 19
by the increasing spirit of Edmund's manner, had once MP I 18 170 24
She knelt in spirit to her uncle, and her bosom swelled to MP II 1 185 27
Her spirit supported her, but the agony of her mind was MP II 2 193 18
With a purer spirit did Fanny rejoice in the intelligence.- MP II 2 194 20
consequence, bustle and the world, for a wounded spirit. MP II 3 202 25
to breathe the spirit of chivalry and warm affections. MP II 4 211 23
an interest, such an animation, such a spirit diffused! MP II 5 225 55
"there, I will stake my last like a woman of spirit. MP II 7 242 25
carriage, when a general spirit of ease and enjoyment MP II 10 273 6
But though her wishes were overthrown there was no spirit MP II 10 280 32
and gathering greater spirit from the blush soon produced MP II 11 290 38
to that independence of spirit, which prevails so much in MP III 1 318 39
spirit of reproach, exerted on a more momentous subject. MP III 1 323 53
certainly has a little spirit of secrecy, and independence, MP III 1 323 56
on an active, sanguine spirit, of more warmth than MP III 2 326 2
the language, tone, and spirit of a man of talent too, MP III 2 328 6
There is now a spirit of improvement abroad; but among MP III 3 339 23
any touch of that spirit of banter or air of levity which MP III 3 340 24
of manner, that spirit and ingenuousness, which are so MP III 4 351 36
His sturdy spirit to bend as it did! MP III 5 358 9
There is a spirit of irritation, which, to say nothing MP III 5 361 16
Fanny's spirit was as much refreshed as her body; her head MP III 7 384 33
the spirit of each and every one is unalterable affection." MP III 14 435 14
The high spirit and strong passions of Mrs. Rushworth MP III 17 464 10
In this spirit he began the attack; and by animated MP III 17 468 21
though she had one sort of spirit, she had not the best. E I 2 15 3
contented and grateful spirit, were a recommendation to E I 3 21 4
With an alacrity beyond the common impulse of a spirit E I 3 24 11
and the tree is touched with such inimitable spirit! E I 6 48 39
He has the tenderest spirit of gallantry towards us all!-- E I 9 77 45
your spirit; and I dare say we shall get home very well. E I 15 126 10
had a great deal of the spirit and liveliness of his E II 5 190 22
He seemed to have all the life and spirit, cheerful E II 6 198 5
well; but there was one spirit among them not to be E II 7 206 4
wanted neither taste nor spirit in the little things which E II 8 227 86
his answer was in the spirit of cutting the matter short, E II 8 228 88
she led off the dance with genuine spirit and enjoyment. E II 8 230 100
Certainly his being at Randalls had given great spirit to E II 12 262 38
two weeks--indescribable spirit; the idea, the expectation E II 12 262 38
could be supposed attractive, with spirit and precision. E II 13 265 5
perhaps there was want of spirit in the pretence of it;-- E II 18 307 17
I think it is the state of mind which gives most spirit E II 18 309 30
not much in the same spirit; all that I have to recommend E II 18 311 38
Does my vain spirit ever tell me I am wrong?" E III 2 330 52
"Not your vain spirit, but your serious spirit.-- E III 2 330 53
with even an angry spirit, and looked resolved to be E III 5 349 23
a substance to sink her spirit--especially with the E III 11 409 34
But Harriet rejected the suspicion with spirit. E III 11 410 36
that, however inferior in spirit and gaiety might be the E III 12 423 21
I must not quarrel with a spirit of forbearance which has E III 14 441 8
"I wish you would read it with a kinder spirit towards him. E III 15 447 27
deal of intelligence, spirit and brilliancy; and Anne an P III 4 26 1
infuse as much of your own spirit into her, as you can. P III 10 88 26
A submissive spirit might be patient, a strong P IV 5 154 8
I should never augur want of spirit from Captain Benwick's P IV 6 171 38
She had only meant to oppose the too-common idea of spirit P IV 6 172 40
41
I hope his letter does not breathe the spirit of an ill- P IV 6 172 42
man to whine and complain; he has too much spirit for that. P IV 6 172 45
presently with renewed spirit, with a little smile, a P IV 8 181 3
4
she sacrificed to politeness with a more suffering spirit. P IV 8 190 47
My poor Charles, who had the finest, most generous spirit P IV 9 199 55
spirit, or listened to without corresponding indignation. P IV 9 209 96
Anne, "but the same spirit of analogy will authorise me to P IV 11 233 23
of Sanditon with a spirit truly admirable--though now & S 3 376 1
than cottages, but the spirit of the day had been caught, S 4 383 1
These feelings were not the result of any spirit of S 6 391 1
woman sat enshrined, his spirit truly breathed the S 7 397 1
head, the graces, the spirit, the sagacity, & the S 8 404 1
amiable feelings--but a spirit of restless activity, & the S 10 412 1

SPIRITED (8)
the spirited determination of disliking her at all events. SS II 12 232 15
"Oh! don't think of me!" she replied, with spirited SS II 13 242 26
they all joined in a very spirited critique upon the party. SS III 1 269 58
Her eldest was a boy of ten years old, a fine spirited MP I 1 5 2
to his clear, simple, spirited details with full MP II 6 236 21
the most; her style was spirited; but had there been much E I 6 44 20
Emma could not have desired a more spirited rejection of E I 9 76 36
"This will prove a spirited beginning of your winter E I 15 126 7
8

SPIRITLESS (5)
Oh! mama, how spiritless, how tame was Edward's manner in SS I 3 17 18
to have been reserved, spiritless, dull, and deceitful:-- SS I 10 48 5
Rendered spiritless by the ill-success of all their PP III 6 298 13
But the spiritless condition which this event threw her PP III 11 331 13
The soup would be sent round in a most spiritless manner, MP I 6 52 1

SPIRITS (349)
an alarm which might seriously affect his health & spirits. LS 8 254 1
of him to keep up our spirits these long winter evenings. LS 13 262 1
perturbation of spirits I was then in, would undergo so LS 24 285 1
My spirits are not so high as to need being repressed. LS 30 301 5
recovered his usual good spirits, (as I trust he soon will) LS 40 309 1
She was in excellent spirits, & seemed eager to shew at LS 42 311 2
who in great spirits exclaimed--"at last I have got you. NA I 8 56 12
John has charming spirits, has not he?" NA I 8 58 27
in excellent spirits, with fresh hopes and fresh schemes. NA I 9 60 1
He is full of spirits, playful as can be, but there is no NA I 9 62 9
early away, and her spirits danced within her, as she NA I 10 81 61
Catherine was disturbed and out of spirits; but Isabella NA I 11 89 63
(as the flutter of her spirits subsided) to doubt whether NA I 13 103 29
to support her spirits, and while away the many tedious NA I 15 121 26
seemed removed, her spirits became almost too high for NA I 15 121 26

Context	Work	Vol.	Ch.	Page	Line
of spirits, or for her want of enjoyment in his company.	NA	II	1	129	1
"I do not say so; but he did not seem in good spirits."	NA	II	1	130	4
My spirits are quite jaded with listening to his nonsense:	NA	II	1	134	39
present a little out of spirits; I hate money; and if our	NA	II	1	136	48
perfect bliss; and with spirits elated to rapture, with	NA	II	2	140	11
things should be allowed for in youth and high spirits.	NA	II	3	146	18
James was in excellent spirits, and Isabella most	NA	II	4	153	31
so much were his spirits affected, she could distinguish	NA	II	5	155	3
Catherine's spirits revived as they drove from the door;	NA	II	5	155	4
check upon his children's spirits, and scarcely any thing	NA	II	5	156	4
To raise your spirits, moreover, she gives you reason to	NA	II	5	158	17
when, with fainting spirits, you attempt to fasten your	NA	II	5	159	17
stout heart; and her spirits were immediately assisted by	NA	II	6	167	9
find how much her spirits were relieved by the separation.	NA	II	7	179	29
Was it from dejection of spirits?"--were questions now	NA	II	7	180	37
And the anxiousness of her spirits directed her eyes	NA	II	8	187	13
her spirits were gradually raised to a modest tranquillity.	NA	II	10	199	2
of her distress, her spirits became absolutely comfortable	NA	II	10	201	4
Catherine, by some chance or other, found her spirits so	NA	II	10	207	41
and Eleanor's spirits always affected by Henry's absence!	NA	II	11	212	16
and Catherine to all her usual ease of spirits.	NA	II	11	213	20
away, with a cold, or something that affected his spirits.	NA	II	12	217	2
Catherine's spirits however were tranquillized but for an	NA	II	13	223	9
again the scene of agitated spirits and unquiet slumbers.	NA	II	13	227	26
no sweet elation of spirits can lead me into minuteness.	NA	II	14	232	7
own amendment, but her spirits were quite worn down; and,	NA	II	14	235	13
restoring her spirits, that they should call on Mrs. Allen.	NA	II	14	236	18
spirits since last she had trodden that well-known road.	NA	II	14	237	20
Her loss of spirits was a yet greater alteration.	NA	II	15	240	1
for a while; for when her spirits began to revive, and her	SS	I	3	14	1
There was, at times, a want of spirits about him which, if	SS	I	4	22	18
In this state of her spirits, a letter was delivered to	SS	I	4	23	20
supported the good spirits of Sir John, and gave exercise	SS	I	7	32	1
But when this passed away, when her spirits became	SS	I	10	46	2
lively spirits, and open, affectionate manners.	SS	I	10	48	7
of spirits, than of any natural gloominess of temper.	SS	I	10	50	12
Her insipidity was invariable, for even her spirits were	SS	I	11	55	6
They were all in high spirits and good humour, eager to be	SS	I	13	63	2
or for spirits depressed by recent disappointment?	SS	I	15	78	28
This violent oppression of spirits continued the whole	SS	I	15	82	47
He was not in spirits however; he praised their house,	SS	I	17	90	1
was attentive, and kind; but still he was not in spirits.	SS	I	17	90	1
Elinor saw, with great uneasiness, the low spirits of her	SS	I	18	96	1
His spirits, during the last two or three days, though	SS	I	19	101	1
His want of spirits, of openness, and of consistency, were	SS	I	19	102	2
is all an effusion of immediate want of spirits, Edward.	SS	I	19	103	7
different state of her spirits at different times could	SS	I	19	104	12
"John is in such spirits to-day!" said she, on his taking	SS	I	21	121	7
spirits; I cannot bear them if they are tame and quiet."	SS	I	21	122	19
from the state of her spirits, to be pleased with the Miss	SS	I	22	127	1
of spirits, which increased with her increase of emotion.	SS	I	22	130	27
"Did not you think him sadly out of spirits?" repeated	SS	I	22	134	50
the same with him now; for he writes in wretched spirits.	SS	I	22	134	52
we met, or any lowness of spirits that I could not account	SS	II	2	147	12
would have no charms for me; I have not spirits for it."	SS	II	2	151	40
perturbation of her spirits and her impatience to be gone.	SS	II	3	158	21
Her spirits still continued very high, but there was a	SS	II	4	161	6
talked of head-aches, low spirits, and over fatigues; and	SS	II	4	162	10
out of spirits, and the thoughts of both engaged elsewhere.	SS	II	4	162	12
Marianne rose the next morning with recovered spirits and	SS	II	4	164	21
It was a lucky recollection, all her good spirits were	SS	II	5	167	3
in spirits, she could not be very uncomfortable herself.	SS	II	5	167	7
And Marianne was in spirits; happy in the mildness of the	SS	II	5	168	7
and his spirits were certainly worse than when at Barton.	SS	II	5	169	12
This event, while it raised the spirits of Elinor,	SS	II	5	169	15
"your sister seems out of spirits," he had appeared on the	SS	II	5	172	40
and even when her spirits were recovered, she debated for	SS	II	5	173	45
as Marianne was not in spirits for moving about, she and	SS	II	6	175	2
Mrs. Jennings laughed again, but Elinor had not spirits to	SS	II	7	182	12
own innocence and good intentions supports your spirits.	SS	II	7	189	51
warmth of heart, the same eagerness of fancy and spirits.	SS	II	9	205	24
and though she saw her spirits less violently irritated	SS	II	10	212	1
altogether so much on her spirits, that she could not	SS	II	10	212	1
happy relief to Elinor's spirits, oppressed as they often	SS	II	10	215	12
of elegance--want of spirits--or want of temper.	SS	II	12	233	18
She could say no more; her spirits were quite overcome,	SS	II	12	236	41
the rest; though her spirits retained the impression of	SS	II	12	236	42
She wondered that Lucy's spirits could be so very much	SS	II	13	238	2
always came in excellent spirits, full of delight and	SS	II	14	247	5
not occur to relieve my spirits at first--no, Marianne.--	SS	III	1	264	29
she had never seen him in such spirits before in her life.	SS	III	5	293	1
Her own happiness, and her own spirits, were at least very	SS	III	5	293	2
Elinor tried to raise her spirits, and make her believe,	SS	III	7	308	4
to another, and her spirits oppressed to the utmost by the	SS	III	7	313	21
inquiry of her enfeebled spirits, supplying every succour,	SS	III	7	315	25
happy, how gay were my spirits, as I walked from the	SS	III	8	324	42
into an agitation of spirits which kept off every	SS	III	9	333	3
to make requisite, was kept off by irritation of spirits.	SS	III	9	334	5
Mrs. Dashwood's looks and spirits proved her to be, as she	SS	III	9	335	7
"To judge from the Colonel's spirits, however, you have	SS	III	9	338	19
reward in her bodily ease, and her calmness of spirits.	SS	III	10	341	6
might weaken her sister's spirits; she therefore, pursuing	SS	III	11	352	16
					17
of accepted love to swell his heart, and raise his spirits.	SS	III	13	361	3
was of a kind to give her neither spirits nor language.	SS	III	13	363	7
to her spirits, or any degree of tranquility to her heart.	SS	III	13	363	8
cheerfulness of his spirits, he might be supposed no less	SS	III	14	377	12
to animation, and his spirits to cheerfulness; and that	SS	III	14	379	17
"Yes--she has great spirits, & never cares what she says."-	W			318	2
to her, & tho' her spirits were by no means insensible to	W			322	3
spirits, her head full of Osbornes, Blakes & Howards.--	W			337	15
Mr Musgrave in high spirits at his own importance, on the	W			345	21
in law, Emma (tho' in no spirits to make such nonsense	W			353	26
such as might have plunged weak spirits in despondence.--	W			362	31
They returned therefore in good spirits to Longbourn, the	PP	I	3	12	15
She had high animal spirits, and a sort of natural self-	PP	I	9	45	36
took leave of the whole party in the liveliest spirits.	PP	I	12	60	5
was very cheering, and they parted in mutual good spirits.	PP	I	15	74	11
I have been a disappointed man, and my spirits will not	PP	I	16	79	23
Elizabeth's spirits were so high on the occasion, that	PP	I	17	87	12
prepared in the highest spirits for the conquest of all	PP	I	18	89	1
not dwell long on her spirits; and having told all her	PP	I	18	90	4
"I did not think Caroline in spirits," were her words, "	PP	II	3	147	23
This letter gave Elizabeth some pain; but her spirits	PP	II	3	149	27
to support her spirits, there were periods of dejection.	PP	II	4	152	6
to Elizabeth; and her spirits were in a state for	PP	II	5	155	1
Jane had not written in spirits, when, instead of being	PP	II	10	182	2
recovery of her spirits, by all that affection could do.	PP	II	11	188	1
of the door bell, and her spirits were a little fluttered	PP	II	11	188	3
But this idea was soon banished, and her spirits were very	PP	II	11	188	3
and in as tolerable spirits as could be expected, after	PP	II	14	210	1
The dear Colonel rallied his spirits tolerably till just	PP	II	14	210	3
that Miss Bennet out of spirits, and immediately	PP	II	14	211	5
					6
Happy spirits which had seldom been depressed before, were	PP	II	14	213	19
of studying her spirits, amidst the various engagements	PP	II	15	217	16
leisure to observe the real state of her sister's spirits.	PP	II	17	227	26
A resemblance in good humour and good spirits had	PP	II	18	230	11
of checking her exuberant spirits, and of teaching her	PP	II	18	231	18
turned in at the lodge, her spirits were in a high flutter.	PP	III	1	245	1
"My mother is tolerably well, I trust; though her spirits	PP	III	5	286	30
hurry to be gone, and his spirits so greatly discomposed,	PP	III	5	293	69
for the lowness of her spirits unnecessary; nothing,	PP	III	6	298	17
at the head of her table, and in spirits oppressively high.	PP	III	8	310	7
Her ease and good spirits increased.	PP	III	9	317	10
into a flutter of spirits, in which it was difficult to	PP	III	10	326	3
could easily perceive that her spirits were affected by it.	PP	III	11	332	20
walked out to recover her spirits; or in other words, to	PP	III	12	339	1
It gave her all the animation that her spirits could boast;	PP	III	12	340	13
Mrs. Bennet, in short, was in very great spirits; she had	PP	III	12	343	29
them above an hour, and was in remarkably good spirits.	PP	III	13	344	1
The discomposure of spirits, which this extraordinary	PP	III	15	360	1
I never meant to deceive you, but my spirits might often	PP	III	16	369	27
Elizabeth's spirits soon rising to playfulness again, she	PP	III	18	380	1
without depressing her spirits too far, to make her	MP	I	1	10	17
cousin Edmund gave her better spirits with every body else.	MP	I	2	17	21
He was just entering into life, full of spirits, and with	MP	I	2	17	22
As her appearance and spirits improved, Sir Thomas and Mrs.	MP	I	2	18	23
manner repressed all the flow of their spirits before him.	MP	I	2	19	30
as the sanguine views and spirits of the boy even to the	MP	I	2	21	34
unfit for any thing, my spirits quite broke down, what	MP	I	3	28	42
and care, and put the cheerfullest spirits too the test.	MP	I	3	28	42
and nursing him, my spirits still worse, all my peace in	MP	I	3	29	46
say, that my health and spirits put it quite out of the	MP	I	3	30	56
easy manners, excellent spirits, a large acquaintance, and	MP	I	5	47	28
With such warm feelings and lively spirits it must be	MP	I	7	63	7
"Yes," added Maria, "and her spirits are as good, and she	MP	I	7	69	25
The state of her spirits had probably had its share in her	MP	I	7	74	59
Mrs. Norris was in high spirits about it, and Mrs.	MP	I	8	75	2
to have it so, and the young ladies were in spirits again.	MP	I	8	80	28
it was in the highest spirits; "her view of the country	MP	I	8	81	32
her opinion, and her spirits were in as happy a flutter as	MP	I	8	83	37
Miss Crawford rallying her spirits, and recovering her	MP	I	9	89	29
in which very high spirits would denote insensibility.	MP	I	10	99	16
however, are too fair to justify want of spirits.	MP	I	10	99	16
Their spirits were in general exhausted--and to determine	MP	I	10	106	58
and keeping up her spirits for the next few weeks, I shall	MP	I	13	126	18
to be settled; and the spirits of evening giving fresh	MP	I	15	142	25
her spirits, in spite of being out of spirits herself.--	MP	I	15	147	56
so persevered in, and her spirits sinking under her aunt's	MP	I	16	150	1
Her spirits sank under the glow of theirs, and she felt	MP	I	18	170	24
the end, Edmund was in spirits from the morning's	MP	I	18	171	25
in the elation of her spirits Lady Bertram became	MP	II	1	180	13
Some members of their society sent away and the spirits of	MP	II	3	196	1
seem out of spirits, and Tom is certainly not at his ease.	MP	II	3	196	2
her accomplishments, her spirits, her importance, her	MP	II	3	199	16
to support her sister's spirits, and drinking the health	MP	II	3	203	30
carry on her spirits to the period of dressing and dinner.	MP	II	4	206	3
but no embarrassing remembrance affected his spirits.	MP	II	5	224	48
a love which his stronger spirits, and bolder temper, made	MP	II	6	234	17
With spirits, courage, and curiosity up to any thing,	MP	II	6	237	23
He was in high spirits, doing every thing with happy ease,	MP	II	7	240	9
to refresh her spirits by a change of place and neighbour.	MP	II	7	248	48
enough to sober her spirits even under the prospect of a	MP	II	8	254	8
the usual observances without any apparent want of spirits.	MP	II	9	265	20
Fanny's spirits lived on it half the morning, deriving	MP	II	9	266	21
He did not appear in spirits; something unconnected with	MP	II	9	268	27
in a state so nearly approaching high spirits in her life.	MP	II	10	272	4
partner was in excellent spirits and tried to impart them	MP	II	10	276	13
but not from any flow of spirits on his side or any such	MP	II	10	278	20
Miss Crawford had been in gay spirits when they first	MP	II	10	279	21
A good night's rest improved her spirits.	MP	II	11	283	7
she thought must know; and her spirits were clouded again.	MP	II	11	289	33
she walked home again in spirits which might have defied	MP	II	12	291	1
wrote thus, in great trembling both of spirits and hand:	MP	II	13	307	30
					31
to-morrow, or whenever your spirits are composed enough.	MP	III	1	321	48
try to compose her spirits, and strengthen her mind.	MP	III	1	322	50
and more cheerfulness of spirits than she could have hoped	MP	III	1	324	58
He rather derived spirits from it.	MP	III	2	327	4
He was returning to Mansfield with spirits ready to feed	MP	III	3	334	1
Her spirits were low.	MP	III	4	346	7
but so much the better; his spirits will support yours.	MP	III	4	348	23
unlike in the flow of the spirits, in the manners, in the	MP	III	4	349	23
infinitely too great; his spirits often oppress me--but	MP	III	4	349	25
time with them; and her spirits not being previously in	MP	III	5	365	35
whether there were any difference in her spirits or not.	MP	III	6	366	1
on his niece's spirits, and the past attentions of the	MP	III	6	368	7
be quite enough to support the spirits he was watching.--	MP	III	6	368	7
natural effect on Fanny's spirits, when Mansfield Park was	MP	III	7	375	1
language and his smell of spirits; and he talked on only	MP	III	7	380	23
with reviving spirits to his cheerful hopes of being on	MP	III	7	384	35
There was nothing to raise her spirits in the confined and	MP	III	7	387	47
means of address which she had spirits or time to attempt.	MP	III	8	391	8
and wound up her spirits for the six days ensuing.	MP	III	11	408	4
Fanny was out of spirits all the rest of the day.	MP	III	11	413	31
She seems in high spirits, and very happy.	MP	III	12	416	2
She was in high spirits, and surrounded by those who were	MP	III	13	421	2
nerves much affected, spirits much depressed to calm and	MP	III	14	430	2
at this distressing time, so very trying to my spirits.--	MP	III	14	431	8
it only in supporting the spirits of her aunt Bertram,	MP	III	14	432	10
of Susan herself, was all serving to support her spirits.	MP	III	15	444	25
visited their agitated spirits, one all happiness, the	MP	III	15	444	27
She had not spirits to notice her in more than a few	MP	III	16	448	3
then melancholy state of spirits, of his perfect	MP	III	17	461	2
had given him pain before--improvement in his spirits.	MP	III	17	462	5
them to repress their spirits in his presence, as to make	MP	III	17	463	7
His spirits required support.	E	I	1	7	10
had sense and energy and spirits that might be hoped would	E	I	2	18	11
spirits, which Miss Woodhouse hoped very soon to compose.	E	I	4	32	28
and in very good spirits, and without having any such	E	I	8	67	56
very conscious and smiling, and rode off in great spirits.	E	I	8	68	58
sigh; and as Emma saw his spirits affected by the idea of	E	I	9	80	68
absences, and raise her spirits by representing how much	E	I	13	109	6
astonished now at Mr. Elton's spirits for other feelings.	E	I	13	115	42
It depends entirely upon his aunt's spirits and pleasure;	E	I	14	121	16
Mr. Elton, in very good spirits, was one of the first to	E	I	15	124	1
Emma, in good spirits too, from the amusement afforded her	E	I	15	124	2
elevate his spirits, not at all to confuse his intellects.	E	I	15	130	28
irritation of spirits, she was then conveyed to Hartfield.	E	I	15	132	37
return of day will hardly fail to bring return of spirits.	E	I	16	137	13
alarms, and Emma was in spirits to persuade them away with	E	I	17	141	4
Emma was not at this time in a state of spirits to care	E	I	18	144	4
frame and varying spirits, seemed, under the most	E	II	2	165	9
It was a most delightful re-animation of exhausted spirits.	E	II	5	188	8
Emma's spirits were mounted quite up to happiness; every	E	II	5	189	16
It was but an effusion of lively spirits.	E	II	6	198	5
further irritation on her spirits; and her being left in	E	II	7	208	7
reason to wish the money unspent, to improve his spirits.	E	II	8	212	2
were not in health or spirits for going; that they made a	E	II	8	221	48
total want of spirits when he did come might redeem him.	E	II	12	259	12
how he was, how were his spirits, how was his aunt, and	E	II	13	264	1
Poor Harriet was in a flutter of spirits which required	E	II	13	267	9
spirits, which, I understand, are sometimes much depressed.	E	II	14	275	32
than usual--a glow both of complexion and spirits.	E	II	16	298	58
And Mrs. Churchill probably has not health or spirits like	E	II	18	307	21
of spirits which would have made her prefer being silent.	E	II	18	311	36
He was in high spirits; as ready to talk and laugh as ever,	E	III	1	316	4
He was not calm; his spirits were evidently fluttered;	E	III	1	316	4
neither his agitated spirits, nor his hurrying away,	E	III	1	316	5
Emma heard that Frank wrote in the highest spirits of this	E	III	1	317	8
turning to the house with spirits freshened up for the	E	III	3	332	3
to reach Hartfield, before her spirits were quite overcome.	E	III	3	334	7
spirits one morning because she thought she had prevailed.	E	III	5	346	16

She was in gay spirits, and would have prolonged the E III 5 351 38
the exercise and variety which her spirits seemed to need. E III 6 361 42
we all know at times what it is to be wearied in spirits. E III 6 363 50
He was not in his best spirits, but seemed trying to E III 6 364 59
There was a languor, a want of spirits, a want of union, E III 7 367 1
young man's spirits now rose to a pitch almost unpleasant. E III 7 374 54
you now, in thoughtless spirits, and the pride of the E III 7 375 61
There was only Harriet, who seemed not in spirits herself, E III 7 376 63
Her spirits seemed overcome. E III 9 389 16
sort of irritation of spirits, inconsistency of action, E III 9 391 21
and its happy effect on his spirits was immediate. E III 10 400 69
done, for his temper and spirits--his delightful spirits, E III 12 419 12
spirits--his delightful spirits, and that gaiety, that E III 12 419 12
cheer her father with the spirits only of ruined happiness. E III 12 422 19
There, with spirits freshened, and thoughts a little E III 13 424 1
But never in such a state of spirits, never in anything E III 14 434 2
If I had followed her judgment, and subdued my spirits to E III 14 440 8
of this holiday of spirits in calling on Miss Fairfax.-- E III 16 452 7
like herself, in happy spirits; it was being in Miss E III 16 453 12
I am in a fine flow of spirits, an't I? E III 16 454 13
is, there seemed a little cloud upon the spirits of some.-- E III 16 454 18
had thought her out of spirits, which appeared perfectly E III 17 463 16
I am not conscious of any difference in my spirits or E III 17 465 27
With all the spirits she could command, she prepared him E III 17 465 28
She was in dancing, singing, exclaiming spirits; and till E III 18 475 37
In the gayest and happiest spirits she set forward with E III 18 476 43
But his spirits were soon rising again, and with laughing E III 18 477 51
be not in perfectly good spirits the only winter which she P III 2 14 11
fact, a change which must do both health and spirits good. P III 2 14 12
Her spirits were not high. P III 2 15 12
loss of bloom and spirits had been their lasting effect. P III 4 28 6
The party drove off in very good spirits; Sir Walter P III 5 35 18
Her friend was not in better spirits than herself. P III 5 36 19
unwell and out of spirits, was almost a matter of course. P III 5 36 21
good humour and excellent spirits; but any indisposition P III 5 37 21
were rather pretty, their spirits extremely good, their P III 5 40 45
He had very good spirits, which never seemed much affected P III 6 43 5
Her own spirits improved by change of place and subject, P III 6 46 12
papa and mamma are out of spirits this evening, especially P III 6 50 27
I will tell you why she is out of spirits. P III 6 50 27
had affected her spirits exceedingly, and thrown her into P III 6 51 32
pleasure of seeing them set off together in high spirits. P III 7 58 20
and no one seemed in higher spirits than Captain Wentworth. P III 8 71 57
Louisa had the higher spirits; and she knew not now, P III 9 74 8
Their time and strength, and spirits, were, therefore, P III 10 83 6
Her spirits wanted the solitude and silence which only P III 10 89 35
that Anne felt her spirits not likely to be benefited by P III 11 98 16
He ventured among them again, however, though his spirits P III 11 100 22
the view of supporting her hopes and raising her spirits. P III 12 116 70
distressed state of spirits, would have been difficulties. P IV 1 121 1
His spirits had been greatly recovering lately, as might P IV 2 133 25
the winter pleasures; her spirits rose under their P IV 2 135 33
They were evidently in excellent spirits, and she was soon P IV 3 137 3
never run away with by spirits or by selfishness, which P IV 4 146 6
sensibility and not high spirits, must suffer at such a P IV 5 152 2
seemed to have closed her heart or ruined her spirits. P IV 5 153 7
Mrs. Smith told her, when her spirits had nearly failed. P IV 5 154 9
suffering in health or spirits, and he talked of P IV 7 176 8
was yet better than nothing, and her spirits improved. P IV 8 181 2
involved in--the stretch of mind, the wear of spirits!-- P IV 8 183 15
feelings for the tender, spirits for the gay, attention P IV 8 186 24
She, in the overflowing spirits of her recovery, repeats P IV 9 205 82
Mary was in excellent spirits, enjoying the gaiety and the P IV 10 219 28
Her spirits sank. P IV 10 227 65
rest of the day; but her spirits had been so long exerted, P IV 10 227 68
smiles reined in and spirits dancing in private rapture. P IV 11 240 59
My spirits rallied with the morning, and I felt that I had P IV 11 245 76
Her spring of felicity was in the glow of her spirits, as P IV 12 252 12
aids of exercise & spirits in a semblance of health) could S 2 373 1
the sea, nobody wanted spirits, nobody wanted strength.-- S 2 373 1
by superior abilities or spirits to say anything.-- S 4 382 1
His spirits rose with the very sight of the sea & he cd S 4 384 1
to come & keep up her spirits, & go in the Machine with S 12 424 1

SPIRITUALIZED (1)
different from his sisters--by no means so spiritualized.-- S 10 418 1

SPITE (150)
Charles Vernon; and yet in spite of his generous LS 12 260 2
defection, determined, in spite of Mr and Mrs Manwaring's LS 14 265 4
In spite of this release, Frederica still looks unhappy, LS 24 291 16
in spite of Mr Johnson, to make opportunities of seeing me. LS 26 295 3
spite of incapacity or distaste, allowed her to leave off. NA I 1 14 1
In spite of Udolpho and the dress-maker, however, the NA I 8 52 1
him to all her sex; but in spite of this, the extreme NA I 9 66 32
of their walk; and, in spite of what she had heard of the NA I 11 86 50
flattery, in spite of her entreating him to have done. NA I 12 96 23
So rapid had been her movements, that in spite of the NA I 13 102 25
going to Clifton the next day, in spite of what had passed. NA I 13 105 40
little agreeable; and, in spite of their father's great NA II 1 129 1
civilities to her--in spite of his thanks, invitations, NA II 1 129 1
disappointment; for, in spite of what she had believed NA II 4 149 1
doing, and forced her, in spite of her anxious desire to NA II 6 164 3
of the feelings which, in spite of all his attentions, he NA II 7 181 40
upon the General; and in spite of all her virtuous NA II 7 181 41
She contemplated it, however, in spite of this drawback, NA II 9 191 3
I knew their spite:--at one time they could not be civil NA II 12 217 2
afforded; and perhaps in spite of every consideration of SS I 3 14 3
It is evident, in spite of his frequent attention to her SS I 3 17 18
His appearance however was not unpleasing, in spite of his SS I 7 34 6
were not many; for, in spite of Sir John's urgent SS I 9 40 2
pencil and their book, in spite of Marianne's declaration SS I 9 41 3
my younger sister in spite of all this tumbling down hills. SS I 9 44 23
spite of all this tumbling about and spraining of ancles." SS I 9 45 32
spite of all that he and Marianne could say in its support. SS I 10 49 9
She liked him--in spite of his gravity and reserve, she SS I 10 50 12
to her sister, which in spite of all that she knew before SS I 12 58 1
to hear, "I have found you out in spite of all your tricks. SS I 13 67 61
"are you still to be a great orator in spite of yourself?" SS I 17 90 2
said Elinor, "in spite of the insufficiency of wealth." SS I 17 92 20
Yet he must leave them at the end of a week, in spite of SS I 19 101 1
that sister, in spite of this mortifying conviction. SS I 19 104 11
in spite of her constant endeavour to appear to advantage. SS I 22 127 2
Elinor blushed in spite of herself. SS II 2 149 24
of their going; and in spite of their numerous and long SS II 2 151 43
engagements in Exeter, in spite of the absolute necessity SS II 2 151 43
spite of all that had passed, was not prepared to witness. SS II 3 155 6
overlooked; and Elinor, in spite of every occasional doubt SS II 4 159 1
can so easily give, will fix him, in spite of himself. SS II 11 223 24
In spite of the improvements and additions which were SS II 12 233 18
the Norland estate, and in spite of its owner having once SS II 12 233 18
with all my heart, it will be a match in spite of her. SS III 1 259 7
that she did, in spite of the almost impossibility of SS III 7 316 29
and in spite of herself made her think him sincere. SS III 8 319 25
as in former days, that in spite of the many, many weeks SS III 8 325 53
while her voice, in spite of herself, betrayed her SS III 8 329 64
of men, Willoughby, in spite of all his faults, excited a SS III 9 333 2
She now found, that in spite of herself, she had always SS III 12 357 1
it is to be supposed, in spite of the jealousy with which SS III 13 366 20
of Colonel Brandon, in spite of the modesty with which he SS III 13 366 20
In spite of his being allowed once more to live, however, SS III 14 373 3
For Marianne, however--in spite of his incivility in SS III 14 379 19
friendship, in spite of a great opposition of character,-- PP I 4 16 14
light and pleasing; and in spite of his asserting that her PP I 6 23 12
In spite of this amendment, however, she requested to have PP I 9 41 1
in spite of all Miss Bingley's witticisms on fine eyes. PP I 9 46 39
then made their bows, in spite of Miss Lydia's pressing PP I 15 73 10
would come in, and even in spite of Mrs. Philips' throwing PP I 15 73 10
misleads him, and that in spite of her being his patroness, PP I 16 83 57
consideration that in spite of your manifold attractions, PP I 19 108 19
Not yet, however, in spite of her disappointment in her PP I 20 112 23
But in spite of the certainty in which Elizabeth affected PP II 2 142 16
In spite of having been at St. James's, Sir William was so PP II 6 162 11
In spite of her deeply-rooted dislike, she could not be PP II 11 189 6
that attachment which, in spite of all his endeavours, he PP II 11 189 6
as to wish to marry her in spite of all the objections PP II 11 193 31
as in Miss Bingley's, in spite of the smiles which PP III 3 269 8
But in spite of all this fine talking, my dear Lizzy, you PP III 10 324 2
In spite of what her sister declared, and really believed PP III 11 332 20
Jane's perfections; and in spite of his being a lover, PP III 13 347 33
Yet in spite of all these temptations, let me warn my PP III 15 362 15
hated me for it; but in spite of the pains you took to PP III 18 380 5
unknown to her; and in spite of every thing, was not PP III 19 386 6
a little longer; and in spite of her youth and her manners, PP III 19 387 8
on them at Pemberley, in spite of that pollution which its PP III 19 388 12
in her affections, for in spite of the acknowledged MP I 4 35 7
Crawford very plain, in spite of her two cousins having MP I 5 48 30
been these ten days, in spite of the solemn assurances we MP I 6 57 33
at the window with her, in spite of the expected glee; and MP I 11 112 35
in spite of every thing, could hardly help laughing at.-- MP I 12 119 22
Maria blushed in spite of herself as she answered, "I take MP I 15 139 8
was not yet overcome, in spite of all that Edmund could do. MP I 15 145 44
her spirits, in spite of being out of spirits herself.-- MP I 15 147 56
her in a determined denial in spite of all the rest? MP I 16 153 3
of the first act--in spite of the feelings it excited in MP I 18 165 3
this, and see that, in spite of the shock of her words, he MP II 1 175 2
find you with yours, in spite of the nurseryman and the MP II 4 213 35
In spite of this conviction, however, she was glad. MP II 5 219 27
of mind directed, in spite of her aunt Norris's opinion, MP II 5 223 48
such a man as Crawford, in spite of there being some MP II 6 231 11
feeling as he did, that in spite of all Dr. Grant's very MP II 7 246 37
he could enter into, in spite of all that was passing MP II 8 256 13
It was a stab, in spite of every long-standing expectation; MP II 9 264 17
he stood, and having, in spite of all his wrongs towards MP II 10 276 14
in spite of every thing, that a ball was indeed delightful. MP II 10 280 33
The surprize was now complete; for in spite of whatever MP II 12 291 5
Another burst of tears; but in spite of that burst, and in MP III 1 320 44
of that burst, and in spite of that great black word MP III 1 320 44
In spite of his intended silence, Sir Thomas found himself MP III 2 331 19
In spite of herself, she could not help half a smile, but MP III 3 343 37
trying to get away in spite of all the too public MP III 3 344 42
In their very last conversation, Miss Crawford, in spite MP III 6 367 5
was vain, and that in spite of her wishes and hints for a MP III 6 372 21
the three boys, in spite of their mother's intreaty, MP III 7 384 36
She was sorry, really sorry; and yet, in spite of this and MP III 10 406 21
season which cannot, in spite of its capriciousness, be MP III 14 432 9
Henry is blameless, and in spite of a moment's etourderie. MP III 15 437 3
heart must have opened in spite of every resolution; but MP III 15 445 33
of knowing, must have been happy in spite of every thing. MP III 17 461 2
She must have been a happy creature in spite of all that MP III 17 461 2
to which Hartfield, in spite of its separate lawn and E I 1 7 10
She had resolution enough to pursue her own will in spite E I 2 15 3
to tell herself, in spite of Mr. Knightley's pretensions) E I 8 67 57
John Knightley, that in spite of maternal solicitude for E I 11 92 3
mind to the visit, that in spite of the increasing E I 13 112 24
Now, it so happened that in spite of Emma's resolution of E I 14 118 5
"But, in spite of all her friend's urgency, and her own E II 1 161 24
She meant to be very happy, in spite of the scene being E II 8 213 5
off, Emma found time, in spite of the compliments she was E II 8 229 99
hope of discovering, in spite of all that Mr. Weston could E II 11 247 2
stay in Surry; for, in spite of Mr. Weston's confidence, E II 12 257 1
him, in spite of every previous determination against it. E II 12 262 38
very much in love; for in spite of her previous and fixed E II 13 264 1
in spite of the very natural wish of a little change." E II 15 286 21
In spite of this little rub, however, Emma was smiling E III 2 325 32
In spite of the answer, therefore, she ordered the E III 9 390 18
to give her credit for, in spite of this one great E III 10 400 65
In spite of her vexation, she could not help feeling it E III 11 403 3
Some portion of respect for herself, however, in spite of E III 11 408 33
In spite of all her faults, she knew she was dear to him; E III 12 415 1
seriously, "which, in spite of every little drawback from E III 12 420 13
faultless in spite of all her faults, bore the discovery. E III 13 433 41
She was obliged, in spite of her previous determination to E III 15 444 1
But, in spite of these deficiencies, the wishes, the hopes, E III 19 484 12
there more than once, in spite of all that Lady Russell, P III 2 15 15
a deal, my dear, in spite of what they told us at Taunton. P III 5 32 4
Anne, amused in spite of herself, was rather distressed P IV 1 128 29
to be heard, in spite of all the noise of the others. P IV 2 134 29
Yet, in spite of all this, Anne had reason to believe that P IV 5 154 8
made Anne's heart beat in spite of herself, and brought P IV 6 167 21
enquiries in return, in spite of the formidable father and P IV 8 181 1
farther; and Anne, who, in spite of the agitated voice in P IV 8 183 11
had been uttered, and in spite of all the various noises P IV 8 183 11
In spite of the mischief of his attentions, she owed him P IV 9 192 2
Lady Russell, in spite of all her former transgressions, P IV 12 251 10
that it is in fact--(in spite of its spruce air at this S 1 366 1
often makes me laugh at them all in spite of myself.-- S 5 385 1
very decidedly, in spite of the mist; Miss B-- seated, not S 12 426 1

SPITEFUL (1)
before, from all the spiteful old ladies in Meryton, lost PP III 8 309 6

SPITHEAD (9)
Antwerp, at anchor, in Spithead; and when Crawford walked MP II 6 232 12
And now you must be off for Spithead too. MP III 7 378 10
Whereabouts does the thrush lay at Spithead! MP III 7 378 12
be off for Spithead by six, so you had better go with him. MP III 7 380 20
and there she lays at Spithead, and anybody in England MP III 7 380 20
It's the best birth at Spithead. MP III 7 380 21
and even of getting her to Spithead to see the sloop. MP III 7 384 35
the harbour, the Spithead, and the Motherbank; he swore MP III 8 389 3
other, on the ships at Spithead and the island beyond, MP III 11 409 6

SPLASHED (2)
You are splashed getting in and getting out; and the wind NA I 13 104 32
As they splashed along the dirty lane Miss Watson thus W 315 1

SPLASHING-BOARD (1)
trunk, sword-case, splashing-board, lamps, silver moulding, NA I 7 46 13

SPLEEN (3)
Adieu to disappointment and spleen. PP II 4 154 23
It raises my spleen more than any thing, to have the MP I 12 120 26
Emma shall be an angel, and I will keep my spleen to E I 5 40 23

SPLENDID (6)
It was a splendid sight, and she began, for the first time NA I 2 21 9
of an evening which had raised such splendid expectations. PP I 3 12 15
and so splendid a dinner might not wholly overpower them. PP II 6 160 4
Their fortune on both sides is splendid. PP III 14 356 50
property, noble kindred, and extensive patronage. PP III 15 362 15
They hold forth the most splendid Portraitures of high S 8 403 1

SPLENDIDLY (1)
and entered a room splendidly lit up, quite full of SS II 6 175 2

SPLENDOR (1)
fine; with less of splendor, and more real elegance, than PP III 1 246 5

SPLENDOUR (5)
neither by amusement nor splendour, for our mode of living, NA II 2 139 7
playing in beautiful splendour on its high Gothic windows. NA II 5 161 24
and London, independence and splendour for his sake. MP II 3 202 25
must be amply repaid in the splendour of popularity. E II 9 231 1
but in felicity and splendour it fell short only of them: E III 6 359 37

SPOIL (7)
That is the way to spoil them." NA I 6 43 43
Lady Middleton had the advantage of being able to spoil SS I 7 32 1
said, "and yet this house you would spoil, Mrs. Dashwood? SS I 14 73 17
& truly enough, that "too many cooks spoil the broth".-- W 318 2
would be that Betsey would spoil it, and get it for her MP III 7 386 42
comprised in, do not spoil them, and do not physic them." E II 18 311 38
it would be enough to spoil her; for she tells me, they P III 6 45 9
SPOILED (6)
detestable--the Admiral's lessons have quite spoiled him." MP I 4 43 24
Emma is spoiled by being the cleverest of her family. E I 5 37 9
and by not being a pretty young woman and a spoiled child. E I 12 99 10
his notions, less of the spoiled child of fortune, E II 6 203 42
And if poor little Anna Weston is to be spoiled, it will E III 17 462 8
Mrs. Smith's enjoyments were not spoiled by this P IV 12 252 12
SPOILING (1)
lay there, and while spoiling both them and their sheath SS III 12 360 22
23
SPOILS (1)
reproach of "Charles spoils the children so that I cannot P III 6 44 6
SPOILT (16)
During her poor father's life she was a spoilt child; the LS 24 288 11
girls that have been spoilt for home by great acquaintance- NA II 15 241 6
than in making a fillagree basket for a spoilt child. SS II 1 144 14
The picturesque would be spoilt by admitting a fourth. PP I 10 53 65
an only child) I was spoilt by my parents, who though good PP III 16 369 24
that Mrs. Grant spoilt every thing by laughing, that MP I 18 164 2
The scene painter was gone, having spoilt only the floor MP II 2 190 9
But I am spoilt, Fanny, for common female society. MP III 4 355 54
Betsey too, a spoilt child, trained up to think the MP III 8 391 9
away all the boxes and spoilt them, was much more in her MP III 15 444 26
whom nature had so richly endowed?-- spoilt,spoilt!--" MP III 16 455 18
darling of that very aunt, less flattered, and less spoilt. MP III 17 466 17
I am losing all my bitterness against spoilt children, my E III 17 461 5
But to be sure, in general they are so spoilt! P III 6 44 8
If he were a little spoilt by such universal, such eager P III 8 71 57
They had taken out a young dog, who had spoilt their sport, P III 10 83 6
SPOKE (246)
He has told me so in a warmth of manner which spoke his LS 11 259 1
She hardly spoke to her, & on Frederica's bursting into LS 17 270 2
convinced of it, from the manner in which he spoke of her. LS 22 282 6
his complexion was raised, & he spoke with great emotion. LS 23 283 3
"You therefore spoke to my brother, to engage his LS 24 286 5
confusion increasing as he spoke, that I have been acting LS 24 287 9
of his countenance while I spoke, to see the struggle LS 25 293 3
look and voice as he spoke, which contradicted his words. LS 27 297 4
only time that any body spoke to them during the evening, NA I 2 23 22
advancing still nearer, he spoke both to her and Mrs. NA I 8 54 4
Catherine, delighted at so happy an escape, spoke her NA I 9 62 10
view, and when he spoke to her pretended not to hear him. NA I 10 74 23
Have I not reason to fear, that if the gentleman who spoke NA I 10 78 37
environs were familiar, spoke of them in terms which made NA I 10 80 61
"I cannot go, because"-----(looking down as she spoke, NA I 11 85 32
the then thinning rows, spoke with like calm politeness to NA I 12 93 5
Catherine spoke the pleasure she really felt on hearing NA I 14 115 51
when Isabella spoke again, it was to resolve on the NA I 15 120 23
spoke her astonishment in very plain terms to her partner. NA II 1 133 30
fixing her eye on him as she spoke, soon caught his notice. NA II 3 147 21
She spoke to Henry Tilney on the subject, regretting his NA II 4 150 1
Catherine trembled at the emphasis with which he spoke, NA II 6 165 6
Of the former, she spoke aloud her admiration; and the NA II 6 166 6
features which spoke his not having behaved well to her. NA II 7 180 37
sedate; and its composure spoke her enured to all the NA II 9 191 4
"No, I thank you," (sighing as she spoke,) "they are all NA II 10 203 10
indifference, spoke a something almost as unpromising. SS I 4 22 18
stand together and scarcely spoke a word to any body else. SS I 11 54 3
Mrs. Dashwood first spoke. SS I 15 76 13
for them, if they spoke at all, to keep clear of every SS I 15 82 47
She walked eagerly on as she spoke; and Elinor, to screen SS I 16 86 20
Marianne spoke inconsiderately what she really felt--but SS I 18 98 12
house and environs--never spoke of going away without a SS I 19 101 1
"Did not I tell you, Sir John, when you spoke to me about SS I 20 111 20
spoke to him indeed; but I have seen him for ever in town. SS I 20 114 44
Elinor attentively as she spoke; "but perhaps there may be SS I 22 128 7
She put it into her hands as she spoke, and when Elinor SS I 22 132 26
Lucy spoke first. SS I 22 132 38
Believe me," and Elinor spoke it with the truest sincerity, SS II 2 146 4
the animated look which spoke no indifference to the plan, SS II 3 153 1
and walking to the window as she spoke, to examine the day. SS II 5 167 2
After a moment's pause, he spoke with calmness. SS II 6 177 8
no longer than while she spoke, and was immediately SS II 7 180 4
Again he stopped to recover himself; and Elinor spoke her SS II 9 208 27
nor even Mrs. Palmer herself, ever spoke of him before her. SS II 10 214 8
with tears as she spoke, "don't think of my health. SS II 13 242 26
She paused--no one spoke. SS II 13 243 30
Good gracious! (giggling as she spoke) I'd lay my life I SS III 2 275 22
She thanked him for it with all her heart, spoke of SS III 3 283 20
"He spoke of its being out of repair." SS III 4 285 8
office, (breathing rather faster than usual as she spoke.) SS III 4 288 28
give her, that she spoke of her friendship for them both SS III 5 293 2
on him with a look that spoke all the contempt it excited. SS III 5 298 34
But though she never spoke of it out of her own family, SS III 5 300 38
of his eye as he spoke, convincing Elinor, that whatever SS III 8 318 21
22
Elinor first spoke. SS III 8 324 43
was--for the first time these two months--he spoke to me.-- SS III 8 330 69
hand, with a look which spoke at once her gratitude, and SS III 9 334 4
by rest, she looked and spoke with more genuine spirit, SS III 10 343 8
as she spoke--and her unsteady voice, plainly shewed. SS III 11 349 3
the latter to pieces as he spoke, said, in an hurried SS III 12 360 22
23
Elizabeth first spoke.-- W 320 2
Howard who belonged to it spoke to his nephew; & Emma on W 332 11
He recommended exercise in defiance of dirt--spoke again W 347 21
soft address, as she spoke her fears of his having had a W 356 28
Mr. Bennet; and, as he spoke, he left the room, fatigued PP I 2 8 25
The manner in which they spoke of the Meryton assembly was PP I 4 16 15
her;--but she said he seemed very angry at being spoke to." PP I 5 19 12
his purpose, he scarcely spoke ten words to her, through PP I 12 60 4
During dinner, Mr. Bennet scarcely spoke at all; but when PP I 14 66 1
At length Darcy spoke, and in a constrained manner said, PP I 18 92 19
20
And rising as she thus spoke, she would have quitted the PP I 19 108 16
17
He scarcely ever spoke to her, and the assiduous PP I 21 115 1
and whenever she spoke in a low voice to Mr. Collins, was PP I 23 130 16
When alone with Elizabeth afterwards, she spoke more on PP II 2 140 6
I spoke to him twice myself, without receiving an answer. PP II 2 141 9
She had heard nothing of Lady Catherine that spoke her PP II 6 161 9
insignificant; and she spoke very little, except in a low PP II 6 162 12
the greatest satisfaction, spoke of him in terms of the PP II 7 170 6
Mr. Darcy spoke with affectionate praise of his sister's PP II 8 173 7
As he spoke there was a sort of smile, which Elizabeth PP II 9 179 21
As she spoke, she observed him looking at her earnestly, PP II 10 184 20
He spoke well, but there were feelings besides those of PP II 11 189 5
He spoke of apprehension and anxiety, but his countenance PP II 11 189 6
He spoke of it as a certain event, of which the time alone PP II 12 197 5
thing that spoke him of irreligious or immoral habits. PP II 13 207 6
She then spoke of the letter, repeating the whole of its PP II 17 224 9
While she spoke, Wickham looked as if scarcely knowing PP II 18 234 35
towards the party, and spoke to Elizabeth, if not in terms PP III 1 251 51
Nor did he seem much more at ease; when he spoke, his PP III 1 252 52
a way, as plainly spoke the distraction of his thoughts. PP III 1 252 52
After a short silence, the lady first spoke. PP III 1 256 61
of her manner as she spoke, joined to the circumstance PP III 2 260 1
her family, and looked and spoke with the same good- PP III 2 261 5
No look appeared on either side that spoke particular PP III 2 262 8
Presuming, however, that this studied avoidance spoke PP III 2 264 11
her face whenever she spoke to one of its objects; for PP III 3 269 8
While she spoke, an involuntary glance shewed her Darcy PP III 3 269 10
At length, she spoke again. PP III 4 277 11
a manner, which though it spoke compassion, spoke likewise PP III 4 278 20
it spoke compassion, spoke likewise restraint, said, "I am PP III 4 278 20
heard in what manner he spoke of the man, who had behaved PP III 5 284 14
could see how seldom they spoke to each other, and how PP III 12 340 13
every one to whom he spoke, had scarcely patience enough PP III 12 341 18
Jane instantly gave a look at Elizabeth, which spoke her PP III 13 345 13
And she rose as she spoke. PP III 14 357 64
She coloured as she spoke; but neither that, nor any thing PP III 17 372 1
the uncivil, and I never spoke to you without rather PP III 18 380 3
Bertram in a letter which spoke so much contrition and MP I 1 4 2
She spoke of her farther as somewhat delicate and puny, MP I 1 11 19
was sweet, and when she spoke her countenance was pretty. MP I 2 12 2
speaking one word where he spoke ten, by the mere aid of a MP I 2 12 2
I never spoke a syllable about it to Sir Thomas, nor he to MP I 3 28 42
know," turning to Miss Bertram particularly as he spoke. MP I 6 55 17
Edmund spoke of the harp as his favourite instrument, and MP I 6 59 40
leaving the room as she spoke, from a consciousness that MP I 8 79 25
and was on the point of proposing it when Mrs. Grant spoke. MP I 8 80 28
delight, and whenever she spoke to them, it was in the MP I 8 81 32
as an amendment; the young ladies neither smiled nor spoke. MP I 9 84 2
while Mrs. Rushworth spoke with proper smiles and dignity MP I 9 88 24
Miss Crawford's countenance, as Julia spoke, might have MP I 9 89 26
She took it, however, as she spoke, and the gratification MP I 9 94 59
As she spoke, and it was with expression, she walked to MP I 10 99 17
Fanny spoke her feelings. MP I 11 113 35
making a sly face as he spoke towards the chair of the MP I 12 119 22
For a moment no one spoke; and then many spoke together to MP I 15 143 28
While he spoke, Maria was looking apprehensively round at MP I 15 148 59
in which she sometimes spoke of the indulgence, seemed to MP I 16 151 1
Crawford, that Tom Bertram spoke so quick he would be MP I 18 164 2
for her appearance spoke sufficiently on that point. MP II 1 178 7
being evidently fair, spoke what she felt must be done. MP II 4 207 6
eyes brightened as she spoke--"take it all and all, I MP II 4 210 19
A look of consciousness as he spoke, and what seemed a MP II 4 214 46
engagement, which Edmund spoke of with the warmest MP II 4 216 50
her own cheeks in a glow of indignation as she spoke.) MP II 7 249 53
You spoke of the balls at Northampton. MP II 8 252 1
He had seen her eyes sparkle as she spoke of the dear MP II 8 256 12
And as she spoke she was undoing a small parcel, which MP II 8 257 15
He was gone as he spoke; and Fanny remained to MP II 9 264 17
The colour rushed into her cheeks as she spoke. MP II 9 269 37
he spoke of her beauty with very decided praise. MP II 10 272 1
that though her uncle spoke the contrary, she could not MP II 10 275 11
been his business; and he spoke with such a glow of what MP II 13 300 7
whenever Mr. Crawford spoke to her, and he spoke to her MP II 13 304 16
spoke to her, and he spoke to her much too often; and she MP II 13 304 16
to convince him--he spoke to me on this subject yesterday-- MP III 1 314 17
I know he spoke to you yesterday, and (as far as I MP III 1 315 18
He spoke calmly, however, without austerity, without MP III 1 321 47
her countenance, as she spoke, had extraordinary animation- MP III 2 332 23
And she spoke with a warmth which quite astonished Edmund, MP III 4 347 19
She spoke of you, Fanny, just as she ought. MP III 4 351 36
And I observed that she always spoke of you as 'Fanny,' MP III 4 352 42
She first spoke again. MP III 5 360 13
He wondered that Fanny spoke so seldom of her, and had so MP III 6 366 3
still, and nobody could command attention when they spoke. MP III 8 392 11
from the moment that I spoke of 'Fanny,' and spoke of her MP III 9 394 1
of 'Fanny,' and spoke of her as a sister should.-- MP III 9 394 1
They scarcely spoke. MP III 13 423 2
She spoke from the instinctive wish of delaying shame, she MP III 15 440 16
of delaying shame, she spoke with a resolution which MP III 15 440 16
for she spoke what she did not, could not believe herself. MP III 15 440 16
If I have spoke once to Rebecca about that carpet, I am MP III 15 440 18
I have spoke at least a dozen times; have not I, Betsey?-- MP III 15 440 18
He turned away to recover himself, and when he spoke again, MP III 15 444 29
"I could not answer, but I believe my looks spoke. MP III 16 454 18
There she spoke very rationally. MP III 16 455 21
She spoke of you with high praise and warm affection; yet, MP III 16 455 23
She spoke of it, Fanny, with a steadier voice than I can." MP III 16 456 29
the manner in which she spoke of the crime itself, giving MP III 16 457 30
She believed every body spoke well of him. E I 4 28 6
time to pass before he spoke to the lady, and as he does E I 8 60 27
Emma spoke for her. E I 9 73 19
a good deal while he spoke, "I have no hesitation in E I 9 82 83
in the world to whom she spoke with such unreserve, as to E I 14 117 1
Emma spoke with a very proper degree of pleasure; and E I 14 119 8
to do; and so he came and spoke, and I answered--and I E II 3 179 52
Some of the object of his curiosity spoke very amiable E II 6 197 3
deal decidedly right; he spoke of his uncle with warm E II 7 205 2
Mrs. Cole had many to agree with her; every body who spoke E II 8 215 15
sensible men; and spoke so handsomely of Highbury E II 8 220 48
and I could get at him, I spoke to him about the carriage. E II 8 223 63
obliged, and went down and spoke to William Larkins and E II 9 239 51
She was in the adjoining chamber while she still spoke, E II 10 243 32
and the window was open, and Mr. Knightley spoke loud. E II 10 245 54
sitters-by were collected, spoke to some, and walked about E III 2 327 34
very like her;--she spoke some of her feelings, by E III 2 328 42
43
have kept--I know that very well (blushing as she spoke).-- E III 4 337 6
She was decided, and thus spoke-- "Harriet, I will not E III 4 341 34
35
The gentlemen spoke of his horse. E III 5 344 4
She spoke with a confidence which staggered, with a E III 5 351 38
She spoke with great agitation; and Emma very feelingly E III 6 362 49
before, except among her own confederates, spoke now. E III 7 372 41
She spoke as she felt, with earnest regret and solicitude-- E III 8 380 9
It was after tea that Jane spoke to Mrs. Elton." E III 8 383 29
the head, which spoke much, she looked at Mr. Knightley.-- E III 9 385 7
It spoke such perfect amity.-- E III 9 386 7
They spoke, therefore, of Mrs. Churchill's death with E III 9 388 14
should soon write; and he spoke in a manner which seemed E III 10 398 53
You (blushing as she spoke) who can see into everybody's E III 11 404 10
She thought he neither looked nor spoke cheerfully; and E III 13 424 1
towards him; for while she spoke, it occurred to her that E III 13 425 8
which he still spoke--"I should like to take another turn. E III 13 429 32
While he spoke, Emma's mind was most busy, and, with all E III 13 430 38
She spoke then, on being so entreated.-- E III 13 431 38
A few words which dropped from him yesterday spoke his E III 14 438 8
of sense to endure, she spoke her resentment in a form of E III 14 441 8
I spoke; circumstances were in my favour; the late event E III 14 443 8
Mr. Knightley was at Hartfield yesterday, and spoke of it E III 16 456 28
Emma spoke her pity so very kindly, that, with a sudden E III 18 477 58
59
"Very beautiful, indeed," replied emma: and she spoke so E III 18 479 71
72
"Perry!" said he to Emma, and trying, as he spoke, to E III 18 479 75
Here Anne spoke,-- "the navy, I think, who have done much P III 3 19 11
12
She spoke, and seemed only to offend. P III 5 34 13
who just stopped and spoke through the window, but without P III 5 38 29
in an unhappy mood, thus spoke Mary;--"I do believe if P III 6 44 7
Mr. Wentworth of whom she spoke, that she had said nothing P III 6 49 22
and looked grave, and spoke low words both to the father P III 7 54 4

His bright, proud eye spoke the happy conviction that he P III 7 62 40
towards her while he spoke, Anne felt the utter P III 8 63 2
Once, too, he spoke to her. P III 8 72 58
She spoke to him--ordered, intreated, and insisted in vain. P III 9 80 29
and the fresh-made path spoke the farmer, counteracting P III 10 85 13
Before they were beyond her hearing, however, Louisa spoke P III 10 88 27
when he spoke again, it was of something totally different. P III 12 108 29
from: he was by no means hopeless; he spoke cheerfully. P III 12 112 52
towards her; and when he spoke at all, always with the P III 12 116 70
hopes and fears, and spoke her satisfaction in the house P IV 1 124 11
Mary spoke with animation of their meeting with, or rather P IV 2 132 22
she knew, must be made for the ideas of those who spoke. P IV 3 140 11
but Mr. Elliot spoke of her as "a most charming woman, P IV 3 141 13
He spoke and looked so much in earnest, that Anne was not P IV 4 145 2
He looked, as he spoke, to the seat which Mrs. Clay had P IV 4 151 22
He spoke to her, and then turned away. P IV 7 175 7
interval, however, he came towards her and spoke again. P IV 7 176 8
him, and making yet a little advance, she instantly spoke. P IV 8 181 1
Anne replied, and spoke in defence of the performance so P IV 8 190 47
Anne, conscious while she spoke, that there had in fact P IV 9 193 13
"I think you spoke of having known Mr. Elliot many years?" P IV 9 198 45
a sudden idea, "you sometimes spoke of me to Mr. Elliot?" P IV 9 201 60
While her father spoke, there was a knock at the door. P IV 10 216 17
"As she spoke, she felt that Captain Wentworth was looking P IV 10 222 36
and whenever she spoke at all, it was very sensibly. P IV 11 230 5
He took the peices of paper as he spoke--& having looked S 1 366 1
Mr Parker spoke warmly of Clara Brereton, & the interest S 3 378 1
She spoke this so seriously that Charlotte instantly saw S 7 401 1
Mr. P. spoke too mildly of her.-- S 7 402 1

SPOKEN (120)

I hear the young man well spoken of, & tho' no one can LS 9 256 1
the merit of their being spoken with simplicity and truth, NA I 10 72 8
in not being at the Lower Rooms, was spoken more than once. NA I 11 89 63
to put it off, I could have spoken to Miss Tilney myself. NA I 13 100 20
composure, till she had spoken to Miss Tilney she could NA I 13 101 25
Though spoken low, she could distinguish, "what! always to NA II 3 147 21
been sensible of any; but spoken in haste, and would never NA II 3 148 29
with hesitation it was spoken,) "and you--none of you NA II 9 196 24
Henry, remember that Robinson is spoken to about it. NA II 11 214 24
name had not yet been spoken by either, she paused a NA II 13 229 31
Henry and herself, had so spoken and so looked as to give NA II 14 230 2
and the roads, and had I spoken only once in ten minutes, SS I 10 48 5
"I have not wanted syllables where actions have spoken so SS I 15 79 36
of the world; and who has ever spoken to his disadvantage? SS I 15 81 44
manner in which it was spoken, Elinor replied that she was. SS I 21 123 22
The manner in which Miss Steele had spoken of Edward, SS I 21 126 41
that Edward had always spoken highly in her praise, not SS II 1 142 7
Scarcely a word was spoken during their return to Berkeley- SS II 6 178 16
of her own sex, and spoken her decided censure of what was SS II 10 215 14
of her feelings, strong in itself, and strongly spoken. SS II 13 242 23
I have always heard him spoken of as such, and your SS III 4 290 37
spoken too low to reach her ear, hurried into the carriage. SS III 7 312 17
the change was openly spoken in such a genuine, flowing, SS III 13 361 3
chusing herself had been spoken of in Mrs. Ferrars's SS III 13 369 33
in fortune and birth, was spoken of as an intruder, she SS III 14 377 11
when she heard Mr Howard spoken of as the preacher, & as W 343 20
in which it was spoken, she could not attempt to equal. W 349 24
never heard a young lady spoken of for the first time, PP I 8 39 45
She had always spoken to him as she would to any other PP I 14 66 1
You will not find him more favourably spoken of by any one. PP I 16 78 15
spoken my opinion of him, and to him, too freely. PP I 16 80 27
had been spoken so loud as to be heard by half the room.-- PP I 18 101 71
Mr. Collins for having spoken so sensibly, and observed in PP I 18 101 71
openly or artfully spoken, could influence a young man so PP I 21 120 28
Darcy formerly spoken of as a very proud, ill-natured boy. PP II 2 143 20
It was spoken of again while they were at dinner, when Mr. PP II 5 157 6
7

whatever she said, was spoken in so authoritative a tone, PP II 6 162 11
This was spoken jestingly, but it appeared to her so just PP II 10 186 38
"But you blame me for having spoken so warmly of Wickham." PP II 17 224 6
spoken with such gentleness as on this unexpected meeting. PP III 1 252 54
could not err, and he had spoken in such terms of PP III 3 270 12
When first he came in, he had spoken to her but little; PP III 11 337 56
I wonder when you would have spoken, if I had not asked PP III 18 381 13
the little girl who was spoken of in the drawing-room when MP I 2 14 9
"Oh! yes, she ought not to have spoken of her uncle as she MP I 7 63 4
this before, I would have spoken of the cloth with more MP I 9 89 29
I am a very matter of fact, plain spoken being, and may MP I 9 94 56
while these words were spoken, and smiling with all the MP I 10 100 22
Pleasantly, courteously it was spoken; but the manner was MP I 14 133 12
her aunt Bertram had spoken for her, or Miss Lee had been MP I 16 152 2
But I could not be easy till I had spoken to you, and come MP I 16 156 27
in making them was spoken of with a glow of admiration. MP I 17 159 6
not a word was spoken for half a minute; each with an MP II 1 175 1
to hear these words spoken in angry agitation: "quite MP II 5 221 38
39

She heard them spoken of by him only in a general way, MP II 5 224 49
She had never spoken so much at once to him in her life MP II 5 225 59
in company who does not like to have Miss Price spoken of." MP II 7 251 61
forced to be spoken to, and to curtsey, and speak again. MP II 10 273 7
She wished she had not spoken so warmly in their last MP II 11 286 15
When she had spoken it, she recollected herself, and MP II 12 295 22
spoken of their journey as what would take place ere long. MP III 1 311 1
best looks of the two, at least after you were spoken of. MP III 9 394 1
might be looked at and spoken to; and she was tolerably MP III 10 400 8
Edmund had not yet spoken. MP III 12 417 4
and alarm; then, she wrote as she might have spoken. MP III 13 427 12
The truth rushed on her; and how she could have spoken at MP III 15 440 16
must be spoken to, Susan prepared, every thing got ready. MP III 15 443 25
as you may imagine, not spoken so collectedly or MP III 16 458 30
all Harriet's answer, and spoken with a degree of grave E I 4 34 41
think you would have spoken a good word for me to any body. E I 5 37 10
And it was spoken with a sort of sighing animation, which E I 6 43 8
does not appear to have spoken yesterday, it is not E I 8 60 27
deserve to have her understanding spoken of so slightingly. E I 8 63 44
as herself, that he had spoken it hastily and in anger, E I 8 67 57
His good friend Perry too, whom he had spoken to on the E I 9 70 6
were wanting an embrocation, I would have spoken to-----" E I 12 102 29
But hardly had she so spoken, when she found her brother E I 13 110 12
And the bell was rung, and the carriages spoken for. E I 15 128 21
Resentment could not have been more plainly spoken than in E I 17 140 3
him spoken of with cooling moderation or repellant truth. E I 17 143 15
All this spoken extremely fast obliged Miss Bates to stop E II 1 158 11
either marries or dies, is sure of being kindly spoken of. E II 4 181 1
spoken with some anxiety, and meant only for her. E II 5 189 15
Don't let her imagine that you have spoken of her as a E II 5 192 31
Mrs. Elton, before she could be spoken to, was ready; and E II 16 298 56
57

Mrs. Elton was spoken of. E III 2 320 8
insensible, he had spoken of her terror, her naivete, her E III 3 335 11
not spoken a word--"I was just going to say the same thing. E III 5 349 24
"I cannot name a day," said he, "till I have spoken to E III 6 354 11
and only strawberries, could now be thought or spoken of.-- E III 6 358 35
Miss Fairfax, who had seldom spoken before, except among E III 7 372 41
years, was now spoken of with compassionate allowances. E III 9 387 12
each other spoken of in a way not perfectly agreeable!" E III 10 399 61
under any blunder, have spoken ill of her; and as to E III 10 399 64
Mr. Knightley had spoken prophetically, when he once said, E III 11 402 1
you, in protecting you from the gipsies, was spoken of." E III 11 406 21
the sound of those words, spoken with such emphasis, "no, E III 18 473 27
they had been informed, spoken most disrespectfully of P III 1 8 17
In each letter he had spoken well of his captain; but yet, P III 6 51 31
and, in the first moment of appeal, had spoken as he felt. P III 7 61 36
knew that he must have spoken of her;--she was hardly P III 8 72 58
It was spoken with enthusiasm. P III 10 85 10
of such interest, spoken with such serious warmth!--she P III 10 88 27
recover from the emotion of hearing herself so spoken of. P III 12 114 62
exertions, and had spoken of those exertions as great.-- P IV 1 126 20
then "Miss Elliot" was spoken of in the highest terms!-- P IV 2 131 9
Upon the hint of having spoken disrespectfully or P IV 3 138 7
Lady Russell had heard her spoken of as a charming woman. P IV 4 149 12
at that moment with propriety have spoken for himself!-- P IV 5 160 26
He had spoken to her with some degree of openness of Mrs. P IV 5 161 29
She had hardly spoken the words, when Mr. Elliot walked in. P IV 7 177 16
you might hear me previously spoken of in my own family." P IV 8 187 31
Anne could think of no one so likely to have spoken with P IV 8 187 35
But I never heard it spoken of till two days ago." P IV 9 197 36
"And has it indeed been spoken of?" P IV 9 197 37
at Mrs. Smith's having spoken of him so favourably in the P IV 9 211 100
She had spoken it; but she trembled when it was done, P IV 10 225 54
Nature had marked it out--had spoken in most intelligible S 1 369 1
if you have heard it differently spoken of-----" S 1 369 1
"Sir, I never heard it spoken of in my life before, said S 1 369 1

SPOKESMAN (1)

Bingley was the principal spokesman, and Miss Bennet the PP I 15 72 8

SPONGES (1)

ruined all the coachman's sponges, and made five of the MP II 2 190 9

SPONSORS (1)

their countenance as sponsors to the expected child, she MP I 1 5 2

SPONTANEOUS (5)

draw from her a more spontaneous, more natural, more SS III 8 330 67
of a removal; and her spontaneous, untaught felicity on MP I 3 31 58
was gone, this was the spontaneous burst of Emma's E III 11 411 42
cottage, she had this spontaneous information from mary: " P III 7 60 31
32

have been a perfectly spontaneous, untaught feeling on his P IV 8 183 10

SPONTANEOUSLY (3)

mentioned Frederica spontaneously & unnecessarily, & once LS 22 280 1
silent consideration, spontaneously observed, "Sir Thomas, MP II 11 285 10
of his being spontaneously solicited by some most P III 2 15 14

SPOON (1)

till her being seated at table and taking up her spoon. E III 2 328 44

SPORT (17)

I never saw a girl of her age, bid fairer to be the sport LS 19 274 2
to her some famous day's sport, with the fox-hounds, in NA I 9 66 31
But Sir John did not sport long with the curiosity which SS I 21 125 37
It was selfishness which first made him sport with your SS III 11 351 11
might have been allowed to sport with it in what ever PP II 1 133 3
parts of the stream where there was usually most sport. PP III 1 255 60
I shall not sport with your impatience, by reading what he PP III 15 362 14
For what do we live, but to make sport for our neighbours, PP III 15 364 22
be the favourite holiday sport of the moment, making MP I 2 14 7
details of his day's sport, good or bad, his boast of his MP I 12 115 4
Tolerable sport the first three days, but there has been MP II 1 181 16
I hope you will take a day's sport there yourself, sir, MP II 1 181 16
Why, the sport is but just begun. MP II 10 279 23
old maid! the proper sport of boys and girls; but a single E I 10 85 19
This was a device, I suppose, to sport with my curiosity, E III 10 400 68
As it was, he did nothing with much zeal, but sport; and P III 6 43 5
They had taken out a young dog, who had spoilt their sport, P III 10 83 6

SPORTING (4)

as to have been sporting with the affections of her sister SS II 6 178 17
horses and dogs, and in sporting of every kind, he found SS III 14 379 18
was sporting with from Camden-Place to Westgate-Buildings. P IV 9 192 3
ought," he observed, "Charles is too cool about sporting. P IV 10 217 20

SPORTIVE (2)

her doubts and anxieties were merely sportive irritations. NA II 13 221 6
at her lively, sportive manner of talking to her brother. PP III 19 387 11

SPORTS (3)

All field sports were over. PP II 9 180 28
"I cannot think well of a man who sports with any woman's MP III 5 363 23
fireside enlivened by the sports and the nonsense, the E III 17 461 1

SPORTSMAN (3)

Sir John was a sportsman, Lady Middleton a mother. SS I 7 32 1
the satisfaction of a sportsman; for a sportsman, though SS I 7 33 3
of a sportsman; for a sportsman, though he esteems only SS I 7 33 3

SPORTSMEN (5)

those of his sex who are sportsmen likewise, is not often SS I 7 33 3
'tis a said thing for sportsmen to lose a day's pleasure. SS II 5 167 1
This weather will keep many sportsmen in the country." SS II 5 167 2
of their punctuality as sportsmen, were in very good time. PP III 12 340 11
of the village with the sportsmen: the room was cleared, P III 7 59 25

SPOT (54)

I take town in my way to that insupportable spot, a LS 2 245 1
For a minute or two I remained in the same spot, LS 23 284 5
returned them to the same spot within the cabinet, with a NA II 7 173 3
"I am particularly fond of this spot," said her companion, NA II 7 179 30
His endowments of this spot alone might at any time have NA II 8 183 3
have passed near the very spot of this unfortunate woman's NA II 8 188 17
She beheld what fixed her to the spot and agitated every NA II 9 193 6
sight of every well known spot ceased to raise the violent SS I 3 14 1
for to remove far from that beloved spot was impossible. SS I 3 14 1
this spot, from whence perhaps I may view you no more!-- SS I 5 27 8
It was a pleasant fertile spot, well wooded., and rich in SS I 6 28 1
from the cottage, from a spot which they had never SS I 16 85 15
"As vile a spot as I ever saw in my life," said Mr. Palmer. SS I 20 111 15
parted for ever on the spot, would he consent to it; but SS III 2 277 30
with so little pain on the spot!--shall we ever talk on SS III 10 344 14
15

thing as they liked on the spot;--could chuse papers, SS III 14 374 7
the two gentlemen turning back had reached the same spot. PP I 15 72 8
saw and admired every remarkable spot and point of view. PP III 1 245 3
Her thoughts were all fixed on that one spot of Pemberley PP III 1 253 55
air of the scene; it was a spot less adorned than any they PP III 1 253 57
to see, to be upon the spot, to share with Jane in the PP III 4 280 26
from all those who were not immediately on the spot. PP III 8 311 11
"I cannot fix on the hour, or the spot, or the look, or PP III 18 380 2
Crawford's opinion on the spot, and that might be of some MP I 6 62 58
into the park, and make towards the spot where she stood. MP I 7 68 17
It was a good spot for fault-finding. MP I 9 90 36
you know, from this spot to the house, quite into the MP I 10 102 46
she had ever done on the spot--and before the middle of MP II 3 202 28
again, perhaps in the very spot where she sat now, MP II 4 207 10
from living on the spot, must already have seen him and be MP II 6 233 14
scene before her than ever that spot had yet witnessed. MP III 5 357 6
a particularly healthy spot: she had an ample house and E I 3 22 5
had led her to the very spot where, at that moment, a E II 5 186 1
be persuaded to join them and give your advice on the spot. E II 11 253 39
A ready-furnished house in a favourite spot was engaged, E III 1 317 7
sorry to see Harriet in a spot so favourable for the Abbey- E III 6 360 40
I am really tired of exploring so long on one spot. E III 7 372 39
Would not he like to have him always on the spot?-- E III 17 466 29
remained, was a cheerful spot; Louisa returned, and Mary P III 10 86 21
had no doubt of their still being--in some spot or other. P III 10 87 21
Not a puncture, not a weak spot any where.-- P III 10 88 26
sands make it the happiest spot for watching the flow of P III 11 95 9
informed and directed, as they passed, towards the spot. P III 12 111 50
and blessing in the same spot, and only superior to her in P IV 5 160 25
from Harville, written upon the spot, from Uppercross. P IV 6 172 41
succeeding to the very spot where he had leaned and P IV 11 237 41
42

certainly the favourite spot of all that are to be found S 1 368 1
invalid--the very spot which thousands seemed in need of.-- S 1 369 1
brings us to Sanditon--modern Sanditon--a beautiful spot.-- S 4 380 1

Trafalgar house, on the most elevated spot on the down was S 4 384 1
was therefore the favourite spot for beauty & fashion.-- S 4 384 1
spot had read more sentimental novels than agreed with him. S 8 404 1
favourable spot for the seclusions of the Miss Beauforts. S 11 422 1
in finding a proper spot for their stolen Interveiws.-- S 12 426 1

SPOTLESS (1)
There, such as were not as spotless as an angel, might NA II 10 200 3

SPOTS (6)
higher grounds; whence, in spots where the opening of the PP III 1 253 57
spots in its environs, to think of any thing else. PP III 1 258 76
It stands in one of the lowest spots of the park; in that MP I 6 56 26
the country, and doing the honours of its finest spots. MP I 7 70 30
I like these glossy spots. MP II 5 222 44
which the same spots had witnessed earlier in the morning. P III 12 115 66

SPOTTED (4)
Miss Tilney was in a very pretty spotted muslin, and I NA I 9 68 42
debating between her spotted and her tamboured muslin, and NA I 10 73 22
the spotted, the sprigged, the mull or the jackonet. NA I 10 74 22
La! if you have not got your spotted muslin on!-- SS III 2 276 25

SPOUTING (1)
any thing of the acting, spouting, reciting kind, I think MP I 13 126 25

SPRAIN (2)
P.'s sprain proving too serious for him to move sooner.-- S 2 370 1
If indeed a simple sprain, as you denominate it, nothing S 5 386 1

SPRAINED (4)
pleasant, and the pain of a sprained ancle was disregarded. SS I 9 43 11
Oh! that he had sprained his ancle in the first dance!" PP I 3 13 17
of the extrication sprained his foot--& soon becoming S 1 364 1
when her coachman sprained his foot as he was cleaning the S 5 386 1

SPRAINING (3)
spite of all this tumbling about and spraining of ancles." SS I 9 45 32
from any intention of spraining his ancle or doing himself S 2 371 1
or spraining his ancle, she remained equally useless.-- S 2 372 1

SPRAINS (1)
the common remedies for sprains & bruises--& I will answer S 1 367 1

SPRANG (6)
From these circumstances sprang the instant conclusion of NA I 8 53 3
remained, from which sprang the following question, NA I 12 94 11
The letter, whence sprang all this felicity, was short, NA I 15 122 28
With this spirit she sprang forward, and her confidence NA II 6 164 3
horrid suggestions which naturally sprang from these words. NA II 8 186 13
she, as she sprang down with his help; "I am very strong. MP I 7 68 20

SPREAD (32)
The brightest glow was instantly spread over Isabella's NA I 15 121 26
have spread a new grace and inspired a warmer interest. NA II 4 149 1
to put on directly, was spread out in the curricle in NA II 5 155 4
fire--nor be obliged to spread our beds on the floor of a NA II 5 158 15
a shame for such ill-natured reports to be spread abroad. SS III 2 272 14
but as Elinor wished to spread as little as possible SS III 2 276 27
"Indeed I can, both hands; & spread to their widest extent. W 343 19
no other way than as a piece of news to spread at Meryton. PP I 23 127 7
The good news quickly spread through the house; and with PP III 8 309 6
Do you not know that such a report is spread abroad?" PP III 14 354 30
him first, and having to spread the happy news through the MP II 1 180 10
from Ecclesford, and it spread as those things always MP II 1 184 26
as those things always spread you know, sir--the faster MP II 1 184 26
help make the toast, and spread the bread and butter--or MP III 7 383 32
it to spread over the largest part of a page of her own.-- MP III 13 425 6
the least credit to it, should it spread into the country. MP III 15 437 3
report should spread so far; but she hoped it might not. MP III 15 438 4
mixture of pique and pretension, now spread over his air. E II 4 182 7
had been forgotten, and spread abroad what public news he E II 17 303 24
be all out of doors--a table spread in the shade, you know. E III 6 355 20
will be to have the table spread in the dining-room. E III 6 355 21
The time was coming when the news must be spread farther, E III 17 465 28
The news was universally a surprise wherever it spread; E III 17 468 33
the whole blunder is spread before her--that she can E III 18 480 77
I wish Frederick would spread a little more canvas, and P III 10 92 46
By this time the report of the accident had spread among P III 12 111 49
It was almost enough to spread purification and perfume P IV 9 192 3
It was evident that the report concerning her had spread; P IV 10 222 37
which seemed to ensure that it would now spread farther. P IV 10 222 37
"With a reasonable quantity of butter spread over it, very S 10 417 1
you directly--& afterwards I will spread some for myself.-- S 10 417 1
Such a plea must prevail, he got the butter & spread away S 10 417 1

SPREADING (9)
Indeed, you are doing a very unkind thing in spreading the SS II 7 182 11
borne it as much as possible without spreading it farther. SS III 1 263 27
have had enough to do in spreading that knowledge farther, SS III 2 270 3
be the means of spreading misery farther in the family.-- SS III 13 371 38
She had no fear of its spreading farther, through his PP III 8 311 12
being made out, was spreading general joy through a wide MP II 13 298 3
There is no occasion for spreading the disappointment; say MP III 1 322 48
its rich pastures, spreading flocks, orchard in blossom, E III 6 360 40
I will have the pleasure of spreading some for you S 10 417 1

SPRIGGED (3)
the Lower Rooms; wore my sprigged muslin robe with blue NA I 3 26 22
the spotted, the sprigged, the mull or the jackonet. NA I 10 74 22
first came, not to buy that sprigged muslin, but you would. NA I 13 105 36

SPRING (54)
At last, however, by touching a secret spring, an inner NA II 5 160 21
But suites of apartments did not spring up with her wishes. NA II 8 183 2
attention which could spring from the affection of those NA II 9 197 25
could could spring from a consideration of the building. NA II 11 212 16
The spring fashions are partly down; and the hats the most NA II 12 216 2
Perhaps in the spring, if I have plenty of money, as I SS I 6 29 4
the spring, and we will plan our improvements accordingly." SS I 6 29 4
the cottage in the spring, he warmly opposed every SS I 14 72 6
up my accounts in the spring, I would even rather lay it SS I 14 72 10
exertion;--they did not spring up of themselves; --they SS III 1 264 29
"Is Miss Darcy much grown since the spring?" said Miss PP I 8 38 40
Your mother should have taken you to town every spring for PP II 6 164 24
he was totally ignorant of my being in town last spring! PP III 13 349 45
to you last spring! is nothing due to me on that score? PP III 14 355 47
loved him, or merely from my information last spring?" PP III 16 371 42
been used to occupy every spring, and remained wholly in MP I 2 20 33
The ensuing spring deprived her of her valued friend the MP I 4 35 7
It was only the spring twelvemonth before Mr. Norris's MP I 6 54 9
in many an early spring, and late autumn morning, to such MP I 16 151 2
intimacy which must spring from his being admitted among MP I 16 153 8
and spring, when her own taste could have fairer play. MP II 3 202 26
of your improved plan that may occur to you this spring." MP II 7 247 41
once or twice in the spring, after being anxiously MP III 3 341 30
say, in the course of the spring; and your eldest cousin MP III 5 364 32
It was sad to Fanny to lose all the pleasures of spring. MP III 14 431 9
his sister any more this spring, when the following letter MP III 14 433 12
which could allow no second spring of hope or character. MP III 17 464 12
for wheat, turnips, or spring corn, was entered into with E I 12 100 16
something like a look of spring, a tender smile even there. E II 5 189 16
should not be able to have another apple-tart this spring. E II 9 239 51
and aunt go to town this spring--but I am afraid--they did E II 12 259 15
last spring--I am afraid it is a custom gone for ever." E II 12 259 15
was the chance of his coming to Randalls again this spring. E II 13 264 1
us a visit in the spring, or summer at farthest," E II 14 274 28
In the course of the spring she must return their E II 16 290 3
of some weeks in the spring, and their papa now proposed E II 16 292 7
The spring I always think requires more than common care. E II 16 295 33
from Frank the whole spring--precisely the season of the E II 18 308 30
She felt as if the spring would not pass without bringing E III 1 315 2
was such an idea last spring; for Mrs. Perry herself E III 5 345 16
Here have we been, the whole winter and spring, completely E III 10 399 61
and in one of their spring excursions to London, when P III 1 7 14
The following spring he was seen again in town, found P III 1 8 15
He had given her some hints of it the last spring in town; P III 1 9 19
One day last spring, in town, I was in company with two P III 3 19 16
later at Lisbon, last spring, Frederick, you would have P III 8 68 31 32
hope, and spring, all gone together, blessed her memory. P III 10 85 12
and meaning to have spring again, they gained the summit P III 10 85 13
pleasanter feelings which spring from the sight of all the P III 11 98 17
to Dr. Shirley, after his illness, last spring twelvemonth. P III 12 102 2
was to be blessed with a second spring of youth and beauty. P IV 1 124 10
the constant use of Gowland, during the spring months. P IV 4 146 3
Her spring of felicity was in the glow of her spirits, as P IV 12 252 12
in the course of the spring been involved in the S 11 421 1

SPRINGING (5)
the Abbey walls, was springing, with Henry's assistance, NA II 5 161 25
of the manuscript; and springing from the bed in the very NA II 7 172 1
jumping over stiles and springing over puddles with PP I 7 32 41
But if otherwise, if the regard springing from such PP III 4 279 24
Smith, but here there was a reward indeed springing from it!-- P IV 10 212 1

SPRINGS (4)
how many successive springs her ladyship spent in town, LS 6 251 1
excellence of the springs, gave the motion of the carriage. NA I 9 64 27
the moral, if our comfort springs from a breach of promise, PP III 18 381 13
afforded; and thirteen springs shewn their blossoms, as P III 1 7 12

SPRINKLED (1)
very pretty meadows they are, finely sprinkled with timber. MP II 7 242 23

SPRUCE (6)
Elton, spruce, black, and smiling, was with them instantly. E I 13 114 28
a memorandum in his pocket-book; it was about spruce beer. E III 4 339 18
something about brewing spruce beer, and he wanted to put E III 4 339 18
Talking about spruce beer.-- E III 4 339 19
and muttering something about spruce beer, walked off. E III 6 364 57
in fact--(in spite of its spruce air at this distance--) S 1 366 1

SPRUNG (11)
admiration which equally sprung from his appearance, he SS I 9 42 9
Edward could have prevented from being immediately sprung. SS I 18 99 15
folly from which it sprung, nor observe the studied SS II 12 233 16
A thousand inquiries sprung up from her heart, but she SS III 10 347 33
was an inquiry which sprung from the impatience of her SS III 12 358 5
by the entrance of the lady from whom they sprung. PP II 15 216 7
her pleasure sprung, was beyond all her words to express. MP I 4 37 8
His mind was fagged, and her happiness sprung from being MP II 10 278 20
very ball had in great measure sprung, were well founded. MP II 10 280 32
with a resolution which sprung from despair, for she spoke MP III 15 440 16
from whatever it sprung; and in the event of Admiral P III 4 30 10

SPUNGING (2)
"What else have you been spunging?" said Maria, half MP I 10 106 56
"Spunging, my dear! MP I 10 106 57

SPUNGING-HOUSE (1)
me to visit him in a spunging-house, where he was confined SS II 9 207 26

SPUR (2)
It is such a spur to one's genius, such an opening for wit PP II 17 225 17
not it time for you to write to Fanny?' to spur me on. MP III 9 393 1

SPURN (1)
full as clever, and would spurn anybody's assistance." E III 6 356 25

SPURNED (3)
much as the idea of both might now be spurned by her. SS II 10 213 3
which she had proudly spurned only four months ago, would PP III 8 311 14
it again; Sir Walter spurned the idea of its being offered P III 2 15 14

SPURNING (2)
separated for ever, and spurning a friendship which could NA II 15 246 12
in the town; and though spurning the remonstrances of MP III 8 390 8

SPY (2)
but she felt her as a spy, and an intruder, and an MP III 16 448 3
who seemed always to have a spy on her, introduced S 3 378 1

SQUABBLE (1)
paid--then there was a squabble between Sam and Rebecca, MP III 7 379 19

SQUABBLES (1)
her mother, her rash squabbles with Tom and Charles, and MP III 8 391 9

SQUABLING (1)
Family squabling is the greatest evil of all, and we had MP I 13 128 37

SQUADRON (1)
Mansfield as soon as the squadron to which he belonged MP I 3 33 64

SQUARE (14)
square; and beyond them were the offices and the stairs. SS I 6 28 2
vulgar compactness of a square farm-house--it is a solid MP II 7 243 27
near Bedford Square; but I forgot their name and street. MP III 14 434 13
The neighbourhood of Brunswick Square is very different E I 12 103 37
Mr. Wingfield thinks the vicinity of Brunswick Square E I 12 103 37
grand, but a large-sized square pianoforte; and the E II 8 214 13
be going to Brunswick Square, for she knew how much his E III 9 386 8
Something has happened in Brunswick Square. E III 10 393 10
how many of my dearest friends are now in Brunswick Square. E III 10 393 12
soon gone to Brunswick Square or to Donwell; she forgot to E III 12 420 14
children in Brunswick Square; and she only waited for E III 13 429 26 27
to get an invitation for her to Brunswick Square.-- E III 14 435 4
was all complete, and Harriet was safe in Brunswick Square. E III 16 451 3
hour in the old-fashioned square parlour, with a small P III 5 40 44

SQUARENESS (1)
Mrs. Croft, though neither tall nor fat, had a squareness, P III 6 48 18

SQUEAMISH (1)
Such squeamish youths as cannot bear to be connected with PP II 18 231 17

SQUEEZE (3)
in motion for tea, and they must squeeze out like the rest. NA I 2 21 10
ideas by a squeeze of the hand or a smile of affection. NA I 8 52 1
than one smile, one squeeze, and one "dearest Catherine." NA I 8 59 38

SQUEEZED (1)
and the two ladies squeezed in as well as they could. NA I 2 20 9

SQUIRE (1)
Her father had no ward, and the squire of the parish no NA I 1 16 10

SQUIRE'S (1)
as there is no real squire's house to dispute the point; a MP II 7 244 27

ST. ANTHONY (1)
and the chapel of St. Anthony, scarcely two miles off-- NA II 5 159 21

ST. AUBIN (1)
that poor St. Aubin died!--such beautiful weather!" NA I 11 83 15

ST. CLEMENT'S (1)
We were married, you know, at St. Clement's, because PP III 9 318 24

ST. DOMINGO (1)
of the action off St. Domingo, and not immediately P III 4 26 1

ST. GEORGE'S (2)
men assembling in St. George's fields; the bank attacked, NA I 14 113 39
and seeing the inside of St. George's, Hanover-Square. MP III 12 416 3

ST. JAMES'S (6)
his presentation at St. James's had made him courteous. PP I 5 18 1
Do you often dance at St. James's?" PP I 6 25 30
and his wife should make their appearance at St. James's. PP I 22 122 3
as her father had done to his presentation at St. James's. PP II 6 161 7
In spite of having been at St. James's, Sir William was so PP II 6 162 11
frequently at St. James's, with very decent composure. PP III 18 384 26

ST. JAMES'S-STREET (1)
"Colonel Brandon, I think, lodges in St. James's-Street," SS III 4 290 40 41

ST. MARK'S (1)
Place, Venice, when Frank Churchill entered the room. E III 6 363 53

ST. PAUL'S (1)
of Westminster or St. Paul's, and I should be as glad of MP II 4 212 33

STAB (2)
was a stab;--for it told of his own convictions and views. MP II 9 264 17
It was a stab, in spite of every long-standing expectation; MP II 9 264 17

STABBED (1)

without her having stabbed Jane Fairfax's peace in a E III 12 421 17
STABILITY (3)
so dishonourable to the stability of her lover, she could PP I 23 129 13
a very sudden trial of our stability in good thoughts. E I 10 87 29
30
the hope of more, of security, stability, and improvement. E III 19 482 4
STABLE (7)
and after all, build a stable to receive them, she had SS I 12 58 1
park; as to a stable, the merest shed would be sufficient. SS I 12 58 3
the great expense of his stable at a time when a large MP I 4 36 7
the apricot against the stable wall, which is now grown MP I 6 54 9
fitted for a beginner that either stable could furnish. MP I 7 66 14
"They are to be put into Mr. Weston's stable, papa. E I 1 8 18
They will be so near their own stable." E II 11 252 34
STABLE-YARD (3)
"Because it is my nearest way from the stable-yard to my NA II 9 194 7
they passed close by the stable-yard and coach-house.-- MP II 5 222 45
coming round from the stable-yard to the front door-- P III 12 105 8
STABLE-YARDS (1)
and enclosed behind by stable-yards, no uniformity of NA II 8 184 4
STABLES (7)
as that staircase can be from the stables to mine." NA II 9 195 8
with a visit to the stables to examine some improvements, NA II 11 214 26
forward from the road, which led behind it to the stables. PP III 1 251 50
to walk into his stables and his gardens, and nearest MP II 2 190 9
"Whose stables do you use at Bath?" was the next question; MP II 2 193 17
and we will add to the stables on your own improved plan, MP II 7 247 41
and I came round by the stables--I believe I did--but I E II 3 179 52
STAFFORDSHIRE (4)
a great deal too kind to her, when he was in Staffordshire. LS 3 246 1
daughter was left in Staffordshire to the care of servants LS 6 251 1
She meant I suppose to go to the Clarkes in Staffordshire, LS 16 268 1
the clay of Staffordshire, as from that of Dresden or Seve. NA II 7 175 12
STAGE (22)
proceeding directly by the stage to her friends the LS 19 273 1
performances of the London stage, which she knew, on NA I 12 92 4
The stage could no longer excite genuine merriment--no NA I 12 92 4
was never withdrawn from the stage during two whole scenes. NA I 12 92 4
a moment's attention, she found no stage of it tedious. NA II 14 231 5
but after the first stage she had been indebted to the NA II 14 232 6
That she was, to all appearance, in the last stage of a SS II 9 207 26
"Not in the stage, I assure you," replied Miss Steele, SS II 10 218 24
The coach, therefore, took them the first stage of their PP III 6 298 15
of the last who would wish to represent it on the stage." MP I 15 145 41
at hand for you to bring forward to the front of the stage. MP I 18 169 21
it, found himself on the stage of a theatre, and opposed MP II 1 182 22
first appearance on any stage, and the gradual MP II 1 182 22
on that stage; but he was sure there could not be a finer. MP II 1 182 22
stage, and explaining very particularly what he had done. MP II 13 300 7
to suffer in seeing him on the stage with Miss Bertram. MP III 3 337 10
it shall be," closed that stage of the business; Sir MP III 6 368 9
and Fanny were talked of as already advanced one stage. MP III 6 374 29
by the time their first stage was ended, and they were to MP III 7 375 1
Cottage, in the first stage of Lady Russell's journey. P III 5 36 19
How the long stage would pass; how it was to affect their P III 12 116 70
And before she was beyond the first stage of full P IV 11 238 44
STAGES (1)
from Bath, to be now divided into two equal stages. NA II 5 155 4
STAGGER (2)
What can you now have heard to stagger your esteem for me? LS 35 304 1
feeling--till he began to stagger her by the number of his S 7 396 1
STAGGER'D (1)
For an hour or two, I was even stagger'd in my resolution LS 29 299 2
STAGGERED (3)
But, however this remonstrance might have staggered or PP II 12 198 5
herself cooled and staggered by a return to London habits. MP III 12 417 4
She spoke with a confidence which staggered, with a E III 5 351 38
STAGGERING (1)
Captain Wentworth, staggering against the wall for his P III 12 110 37
38
STAGNANT (1)
as it does between a stagnant marsh, a bleak moor & the S 1 369 1
STAGNATION (2)
could be ventured on, and it was all melancholy stagnation. E III 6 353 6
of such a state of stagnation, sick of knowing nothing, P IV 7 180 32
STAID (45)
& if she had not staid three months there before she LS 6 252 2
Yet, I wish she had staid quietly at Langford. LS 33 303 1
She staid nearly two hours, was as affectionate & agreable LS 41 309 1
of patience, had he staid with you half a minute longer. NA I 10 76 29
I really could not face my acquaintance if I staid away NA II 11 210 6
it might seem an intrusion if she staid much longer. NA II 13 220 1
the table and continued to read it as long as he staid. SS I 19 106 22
whether she went or staid, prepared without one look of SS II 6 175 1
The communicative lady I learnt, on inquiry, for I staid SS II 8 199 37
or other; and how he had staid about at an inn all SS III 2 273 16
I thought it had been for the 2 dances after, if we staid W 337 14
dinner hour at Stanton, staid with them only a few minutes, W 341 19
he well knew, that if he staid he must sit down to supper W 359 28
The Gardiners staid a week at Longbourn; and what with the PP II 2 142 18
Sir William staid only a week at Hunsford; but his visit PP II 7 168 1
The Gardiners staid only one night at Longbourn, and set PP II 19 239 11
Their visitors staid with them above half an hour, and PP III 2 263 11
her uncle and aunt, she staid with them only long enough PP III 2 264 12
behaviour while she staid with us, if I had not perceived, PP III 10 325 2
both of them frequently staid so long, that even Bingley's PP III 19 387 9
You had better have staid with us." MP I 10 97 2
"I think they might as well have staid for me," said he. MP I 10 102 38
"I should not have had to follow her if she had staid." MP I 10 102 40
and to feel that if she staid longer behind it might seem MP II 1 177 6
Mr. Yates had staid to see the destruction of every MP II 2 194 21
all whether she went or staid?--but if her uncle were to MP II 5 218 12
out of the room, having staid behind him only long enough MP II 5 221 38
39
He staid of course, and Edmund had then ample opportunity MP III 3 336 7
has staid a year, for that will not be up till November. MP III 7 385 39
of it, or that its purpose was unimportant--and staid. MP III 17 467 20
highly acceptable to those who went, and those who staid. MP III 17 469 23
and scolded us away, and staid to look through herself; E I 9 75 26
While he staid, the Martins were forgotten; and on the E II 4 185 11
If he had come at Christmas he could not have staid three E II 5 188 7
you had not married, you would have staid at home with me." E II 7 209 10
as long as he had staid, however, it had been pleasant E II 8 220 48
But I thought he would have staid now, and it would have E II 10 245 52
it--almost wished he had staid at home--nothing killed him E III 6 363 53
He had staid on, however, vigorously, day after day--till E III 13 433 41
though I might have staid with you till the next morning, E III 14 441 8
seen by Anne; but she had staid at home, under the mixed P III 9 77 17
a junction, she would have staid at home; but, from some P III 10 83 6
the exact steps of, had staid a few hours and then P IV 1 126 20
He staid an hour with them. P IV 3 144 23
They staid at home, that their children might get out;-- S 2 374 1
STAIN (2)
The stain of illegitimacy, unbleached by nobility or E III 19 482 3
by nobility or wealth, would have been a stain indeed. E III 19 482 3
STAINS (2)
Varnish and gilding hide many stains. MP III 14 434 13
forward stains and dirt that might otherwise have slept. MP III 15 439 9
STAIR-CASE (5)
They returned to the hall, that the chief stair-case might NA II 8 184 5
symptoms of a winding stair-case, believed herself at last NA II 8 185 5
range of cells, and the stair-case by the side of those NA II 8 188 17
Down that stair-case she had perhaps been conveyed in a NA II 8 188 17
towards the principal stair-case, and taken them through MP I 9 89 31
STAIRCASE (20)
we go up every staircase, and into every suite of rooms?" NA I 11 86 43
up a different staircase, and along many gloomy passages, NA II 5 158 15
they ascended a broad staircase of shining oak, which, NA II 5 162 28
staircase, and in a few moments it gave Henry to her view. NA II 9 194 6
"how came you here?--how came you up that staircase?" NA II 9 194 6
"How came I up that staircase!" he replied, greatly NA II 9 194 7
as that staircase can be from the stables to mine." NA II 9 195 8
rooms and a broader staircase, you will hereafter find SS I 14 73 14
by the door towards the staircase, and telling Marianne SS II 6 178 15
led the way up the wide staircase, while no sound of a W 327 7
pass her towards the staircase, than she entered the PP I 20 110 1
merits, as they proceeded together up the great staircase. PP III 1 249 37
from the staircase window, and then they were walking." MP II 4 211 28
himself, standing at the head of a different staircase. MP II 9 267 24
slowly up the principal staircase, pursued by the MP II 10 280 33
the head of the great staircase, till she had satisfied MP III 13 302 12
passage and staircase, struck her beyond her imagination. MP III 7 387 47
staircase--rather darker and narrower than one could wish. E II 9 239 53
"And the staircase--you know, as I came in, I observed how E II 14 273 19
how very like the staircase was; placed exactly in the E II 14 273 19
STAIRS (97)
& was half way down stairs, when Frederica as pale as LS 20 275 1
I met her on the stairs & saw that she was crying. LS 24 285 2
Catherine then ran directly up stairs, and watched Miss NA I 4 34 7
up stairs, calling out, "well, Miss Morland, here I am. NA I 9 61 1
parting good wishes, they both hurried down stairs. NA I 9 62 7
the stairs he was calling out to Miss Morland to be quick. NA I 11 84 18
heart-rendering tidings, Catherine walked slowly up stairs. NA I 11 89 62
that moment, and hurrying by him proceeded up stairs. NA I 13 102 25
gallant as they went down stairs, admiring the elasticity NA I 13 103 28
a minute they ran down stairs together, in an alarm not NA II 6 165 5
mind, as she proceeded up stairs, she was enabled, NA II 6 167 9
at some distance down stairs, seemed to point out:--"I was NA II 8 186 6
swift steps to ascend the stairs, by the head of which she NA II 9 194 6
am afraid I alarmed you by running so fast up those stairs. NA II 9 195 12
They had just reached the head of the stairs, when it NA II 13 222 7
while they remained up stairs, Catherine in busy agitation NA II 13 227 27
in one of the books up stairs upon much such a subject, NA II 15 241 6
down stairs with the volume from which so much was hoped. NA II 15 241 7
square; and beyond them were the offices and the stairs. SS I 6 28 2
I could wish the stairs were handsome. SS I 6 29 4
There is one remarkably pretty sitting room up stairs; of SS I 13 69 76
"With dark narrow stairs, and a kitchen that smokes, I SS I 14 72 12
at her eyes; and without noticing them ran up stairs. SS I 15 75 2
But before she was half way up stairs she heard the SS I 18 96 2
and Margaret came down stairs at the same time, and they SS I 19 106 21
a few steps towards the stairs, and after listening half a SS II 4 161 7
Marianne flew eagerly up stairs, and when Elinor followed, SS II 4 165 25
alighted, ascended the stairs, heard their names announced SS II 6 175 2
On ascending the stairs, the Miss Dashwoods found so many SS II 11 220 3
Mr. Dashwood attended them down stairs, was introduced to SS II 11 222 13
as they walked up the stairs together--for the Middletons SS II 12 231 13
own dressing-room down stairs, thinking about writing a SS III 1 259 7
Edward; so I just run up stairs and put on a pair of silk SS III 2 274 16
They walked up stairs into the drawing-room,-- SS III 5 294 4
Mrs. Jennings therefore attending her up stairs into the SS III 7 316 27
Jennings's maid with her sister, she hurried down stairs. SS III 7 316 30
called down stairs by the sound of another carriage.-- SS III 9 333 3
withdrew from her sister and walked slowly up stairs. SS III 10 348 34
well enough to be down stairs;--with much concern they W 345 21
right than pleasant that she should go down stairs herself. PP I 8 37 21
some herself,--some shelves in the closets up stairs." PP I 14 66 1
Come, Kitty, I want you up stairs." PP I 19 104 4
a glance from Jane invited her to follow her up stairs. PP I 21 116 6
As they went down stairs together, Charlotte said, "I PP II 3 146 11
12
On the stairs were a troop of little boys and girls, whose PP II 4 152 5
up stairs in a violent hurry, and calling loudly after her. PP II 5 158 11
Kitty and Lydia looking out of a dining room up stairs. PP II 16 219 1
but in the gallery up stairs you will see a finer, larger PP III 1 247 18
seen, they returned down stairs, and taking leave of the PP III 1 251 49
heard on the stairs, and in a moment he entered the room. PP III 2 261 5
stairs from her mother's apartment, immediately met her. PP III 5 286 22
She is up stairs, and will have great satisfaction in PP III 5 286 30
point of seeking him up stairs with their mother, when PP III 7 301 4
5
from his writing table, and they went up stairs together. PP III 7 305 43
It was a fortnight since Mrs. Bennet had been down stairs, PP III 8 310 7
either of us, for she went up stairs half an hour ago." PP III 13 344 8
was his custom, and Mary went up stairs to her instrument. PP III 13 344 11
"Kitty and I are going up stairs to sit in my dressing PP III 13 345 16
up the card party, and was sitting up stairs with Kitty. PP III 13 347 27
"With my mother up stairs. PP III 13 347 32
room for her parasol, attended her noble guest down stairs. PP III 14 352 19
heard the carriage drive away as she proceeded up stairs. PP III 14 358 74
The next morning, as she was going down stairs, she was PP III 15 361 6
As she went up stairs to get ready, Mrs. Bennet followed PP III 17 375 25
26
youngest of the sons, sitting crying on the attic stairs. MP I 2 15 9
I heard him as I came up stairs, and the theatre is MP I 18 169 21
obliged on returning down stairs, to be fixed in their MP II 4 206 3
in the lobby, on the stairs, for the first sound of the MP II 6 233 14
On reaching home, Fanny went immediately up stairs to MP II 9 261 1
As she walked slowly up stairs she thought of yesterday; MP II 9 267 23
They proceeded up stairs together, their rooms being on MP II 9 268 27
being then in her way up stairs, she resolved there to MP III 1 311 2
you to accompany me down stairs, where--though I cannot MP III 1 314 16
You must now come down stairs with me. MP III 1 320 44
Fanny naturally turned up stairs, and took her guest to MP III 5 357 6
to look for you up stairs; and setting off to find my way MP III 5 360 14
"I was up stairs, mamma, moving my things;" said Susan, in MP III 7 379 18
other up and down stairs, and tumbling about and hallooing. MP III 7 382 27
The doors were in constant banging, the stairs were never MP III 8 392 11
By sitting together up stairs, they avoided a great deal MP III 9 398 9
chief of the morning up stairs, at first only in working MP III 9 398 9
to remove as usual up stairs, they were stopt by the knock MP III 10 399 2
"He is just come, my dear Fanny, and is taken up stairs; MP III 13 427 12
many walks up and down stairs she might have saved her, MP III 14 432 10
while walking down stairs from her own room, "always over- E II 5 189 20
her visitors walked up stairs without having any regular E II 9 239 52
after all; and not the least draught from the stairs." E II 11 254 48
Tea was made down stairs, biscuits and baked apples and E III 2 329 45
nor walked up the stairs, with any wish of giving pleasure, E III 8 378 3
were on the stairs, we did not know any body was coming. E III 8 379 8
Emma was called down stairs to Mr. Weston, who "could not E III 10 392 1
she was met on the stairs by Jane herself, coming eagerly E III 16 452 8
to go with her even down stairs; it gave her an E III 16 459 45
46
as Anne followed her up stairs, she was in time for the P III 7 57 17
18
"They are up stairs with my sister--they will be down in a P III 9 79 23
not like a long walk!" said Mary, as she went up stairs. P III 10 83 5
was conveyed up stairs, and given possession of her own P III 12 111 50
STAKE (10)
there is everything at stake; your own happiness, that of LS 12 260 1
Her whole happiness seemed at stake, while the affair was NA II 2 138 1
the life of a child was at stake, and Marianne, satisfied SS III 9 334 5
stake, her kindness did sometimes overpower her judgment. MP II 2 190 8
"there, I will stake my last like a woman of spirit. MP II 7 242 25

you imagine me so where your happiness was at stake." MP III 4 347 14
a large and (he believed) industrious family was at stake. MP III 10 404 15
"Ah! my dear," as Perry says, "where health is at stake, E I 12 106 58
cause to him, for my suspense while all was at stake?-- E III 14 443 8
However, at any rate, as I have a great deal more at stake P III 5 35 16
STALE (1)
common-place, threadbare, stale in the comparison, E III 11 413 48
STALL (1)
form hopes, succeeded to a stall in Westminster, which, as MP III 17 469 23
STAMMERED (1)
He coloured, and stammered out an unintelligible reply. SS III 12 359 12
STAMMERING (1)
and while stammering out her great obligation, and her--" MP II 4 215 47
STAMP (5)
says it is always the case with minds of a certain stamp." NA II 3 144 4
a serious stamp, though written solely for their benefit. PP I 14 69 15
16
endowments of a higher stamp, for he had easy manners, MP I 5 47 28
chosen so well, his constancy has a respectable stamp. MP III 2 330 14
to succeed with one of her stamp, and therefore I hope we MP III 16 457 29
STAMPED (4)
All this may be stamped on it; and that house receive such MP II 7 244 27
She saw it only as folly, and that folly stamped only by MP III 16 455 19
for his character, stamped as it was by poor Dick's having P III 6 52 33
highly, which must have stamped him well in the esteem of P III 11 96 12
STAMPT (1)
it possibility--Miss Crawford's letter stampt it a fact. MP III 15 441 20
STAND (84)
Sir Reginald is very infirm, & not likely to stand in your LS 9 256 1
be any application to you, however the affair might stand? LS 24 289 12
with Isabella to stand up; but John was gone into the card- NA I 8 52 2
said she, "I would not stand up without your dear sister NA I 8 52 2
You know I never stand upon ceremony with such people." NA I 8 56 14
my dearest Catherine, for heaven's sake, and stand by me." NA I 8 58 25
you and I are to stand up and jig it together again." NA I 8 59 35
People that dance, only stand opposite each other in a NA I 10 77 32
I think you cannot stand out any longer now. NA I 13 99 3
then I found there would be no peace if I did not stand up. NA II 1 134 39
on to give more encouragement than one wishes to stand by. NA II 3 146 18
Can you stand such a ceremony as this? NA II 5 158 15
But so low did the building stand, that she found herself NA II 5 161 24
a foot from the ground, on a carved stand of the same. NA II 6 163 2
"It is very right that you should stand by your brother." NA II 12 219 14
"And if you would stand by your's, you would not be much NA II 12 219 15
that he seemed rather to stand in need of more money SS I 5 27 6
twisted in the fall, and she was scarcely able to stand. SS I 9 42 8
stand together and scarcely spoke a word to any body else. SS I 11 54 3
coldness, reserve could not stand against such a reception. SS I 17 90 1
said Mrs. Jennings, "should not stand upon such ceremony." SS I 20 111 21
her, and she could hardly stand; but exertion was SS I 22 134 53
white, and unable to stand, sunk into her chair, and SS II 6 177 12
that she should not stand upon ceremony, for they were all SS II 11 223 14
I declare I can hardly stand. SS II 12 232 13
"you think young men never stand upon engagements, if they SS II 13 243 38
He would stand to it, cost him what it might." SS III 1 267 42
I want to dance with her--& I will come & stand by you."-- W 333 13
everybody was required to stand up--& Tom Musgrave's W 335 13
hard thing for a woman to stand against the flattering W 343 19
Long and her neices must stand their chance; and therefore, PP I 2 7 16
whom it would not be a punishment to me to stand up with." PP I 3 11 9
I was so vexed to see him stand up with her; but, however, PP I 3 13 16
Allowing the case, however, to stand according to your PP I 10 50 34
in being allowed to stand opposite to Mr. Darcy, and PP I 18 90 8
In vain did she entreat him to stand up with somebody else, PP I 18 102 73
but that he should stand his ground; yet he had avoided PP II 13 207 5
impossible to find out the stand and number of the coach. PP III 5 293 69
Balls will be absolutely prohibited, unless you stand up PP III 6 300 30
But, if I were you, I would stand by the nephew. PP III 18 383 23
"Oh! dear--let him stand his chance and be taken in. MP I 5 46 18
"if you want to dance, Fanny, I will stand up with you."-- MP I 12 118 22
I can stand it no longer, and I think, I may say, that MP I 13 125 14
I could not stand your countenance dressed up in woe and MP I 14 133 11
I have been slaving myself till I can hardly stand, to MP I 18 166 6
Whatever might be its effect, however, she must stand the MP I 18 170 24
In every thing else the etiquette of the day might stand MP II 3 203 29
knowing how to suppose him serious, she could hardly stand. MP II 13 301 7
and pre-assured mind to stand in the way of the happiness MP II 13 302 9
the uncle, who seemed to stand in the place of her parents; MP III 1 314 16
and learn from him exactly how matters stand between you. MP III 2 330 14
he came home, not to stand and be talked to, but to run MP III 7 381 25
give her the rope's end as long a I could stand over her. MP III 15 440 13
no scruples which could stand many minutes against the E I 6 44 19
of three or four years old stand still you know; nor can E I 6 45 21
They will come and stand by my chair, and say, 'grandpapa, E I 9 80 72
and your popularity will stand upon your own virtues." E II 6 200 15
was amused enough; quite enough still to stand at the door. E II 9 233 24
to make her instrument stand steadily, it was not quite E II 10 240 5
couple are not enough to make it worth while to stand up. E II 11 248 7
8
Ten couple may stand here very well." E II 11 249 13
my father--and altogether--I might stand here very well." E II 11 250 18
of composure as could stand against the actual approach-- E II 13 267 8
profusion as here, and stand very much in the same way-- E II 14 273 21
I always stand up for women--and I assure you, if you knew E II 18 306 12
Nothing can stand more retired from the road than Maple E II 18 307 21
Emma must submit to stand second to Mrs. Elton, though she E III 2 325 31
any time to stand up with an old friend like Mrs. Gilbert." E III 2 327 36
Stop, stop, let us stand a little back, Mrs. Elton is E III 2 329 45
It used to stand here. E III 5 347 19
It is the very last thing I would stand the brunt of just E III 7 369 19
when Mr. Elton would not stand up with me; and when there E III 11 406 24
as his Harry stand at our sideboard for any consideration. E III 16 458 42
short, if your compassion does not stand my friend-----" E III 16 459 47
She could not stand it. P III 12 117 74
But now, do not stand upon ceremony.-- P IV 1 127 24
hardly one woman in a thousand could stand the test of. P IV 3 142 13
of the straight line to stand near her, and make enquiries P IV 8 181 1
did not think it fair to stand out any longer; for Charles P IV 11 230 6
on the bank, unable to stand--"there is something wrong S 1 364 1
heir, things do not stand between us in the way they S 7 400 1
He don't stand uppermost, beleive me.-- S 7 400 1
for I am hardly able to stand--and when the Leaches have S 12 424 1
used; to be obliged to stand back in his own house & see S 12 427 1
STANDARD (4)
and made her his secret standard of perfection in woman;-- SS III 14 379 19
that Mr. Elton is the standard of perfection in Highbury, E II 3 174 38
with manners that were held a standard of good-breeding. P III 2 11 2
it was good of a lower standard, for what could be offered P III 12 103 3
STANDARDS (1)
Bertram as a husband, are my standards of perfection. MP III 5 361 16
STANDER-BY (1)
a great deal more suffered than a stander-by can judge of." MP III 5 363 23
STANDERS-BY (1)
There he was, among the standers-by, where he ought not to E III 2 325 32
STANDING (84)
Tilney still continuing standing before them; and after a NA I 8 54 10
into while they were standing up, of the horses and dogs NA I 8 55 10
and when they see you standing up with somebody else, they NA I 10 75 26
Her assurance, however, standing sole as it did, was not NA I 12 93 7
it in two days--my hair standing on end the whole time." NA I 14 106 7
was decayed, or of its standing low in a valley, sheltered NA II 2 141 13
on a large high chest, standing back in a deep recess on NA II 6 163 1
composure to become a standing joke with Mrs. Jennings. SS I 12 61 16
I ask if your engagement is of long standing?" SS I 22 130 17
18
perceived Willoughby, standing within a few yards of them, SS II 6 176 3
one gentleman only was standing there, and it is probable SS II 11 220 3
as there is now standing in Delaford Hanger!-- SS III 14 375 9
dress & boots, who was standing in the doorway of a W 327 7
little boy, as he was standing before his mother, W 330 11
& 30, to a lady who was standing near her, when you know W 330 11
party of young men were standing engaged in ver lively W 330 11
time, Mr. Darcy had been standing near enough for her to PP I 3 11 7
I hate to see you standing about by yourself in this PP I 3 11 8
she sees them now very often standing in Clarke's library." PP I 7 30 13
whole party were still standing and talking together very PP I 15 72 8
notice; though often standing within a very short distance PP I 18 102 74
Mr. Bingley and Jane were standing together, a little PP I 18 103 75
The garden sloping to the road, the house standing in it, PP II 5 155 3
Mr. Collins and Charlotte were both standing at the gate PP II 5 158 19
It was a large, handsome, stone building, standing well on PP III 1 245 3
to fail him; and, after standing a few moments without PP III 1 252 53
Mrs. Gardiner was standing a little behind; and on her PP III 1 254 58
sight of a chaise, were standing on the steps of the house, PP III 5 286 21
her sister and Bingley standing together over the hearth, PP III 13 346 22
with two or three grooms, standing about and looking on. MP I 7 67 16
There is nothing so likely to give it as standing and MP I 7 72 45
Mr. Rushworth and Maria, standing side by side, exactly as MP I 9 88 19
had been talking of; and standing back, well shaded and MP I 9 95 67
Fanny thought she discerned in his standing there, an MP I 10 102 47
as Miss Crawford was standing at an open window with MP I 11 108 4
If I had not luckily thought of standing up with you, I MP I 12 120 26
where Edmund was standing thoughtfully by the fire, while MP I 13 125 14
round the table; and standing by them, seemed to interest MP I 15 143 27
Advantageous as would be the alliance, and long standing MP II 3 200 20
of the three others standing round him, shewed how welcome MP II 5 223 48
to be forded, a church standing on a sort of knoll to my MP II 7 241 13
by Sir Thomas, who was standing in chat with Dr. Grant. MP II 7 249 49
himself, standing at the head of a different staircase. MP II 9 267 24
only talkers, but they, standing by the fire, talked over MP III 3 339 22
inn, the other two were standing by the fire; and Edmund, MP III 15 446 34
It would have all ended in a regular standing flirtation, MP III 16 456 23
credit to them both--a standing memorial of the beauty of E I 6 47 27
The lovers were standing together at one of the windows. E I 10 90 39
Standing up in the middle of the room, I suppose, and E I 18 147 17
and quick feelings: standing in a mother's place, but E I 18 149 26
about the port--Jane was standing in the passage-- were E II 3 173 27
by Mr. and Mrs. Weston, who were standing to speak to her. E II 5 188 6
He was gone immediately; and Emma soon saw him standing E II 8 222 57
standing with her back to them, intent on her pianoforte. E II 10 240 1
It would be dreadful to be standing so close! E II 11 249 17
She is a standing lesson of how to be happy. E II 11 255 55
Those who are standing by are usually thinking of E II 12 258 3
Frank was standing by her, but not steadily; there was a E III 2 320 7
I saw her as I came in; she was standing in the entrance. E III 2 322 19
Upon my word, this is charming to be standing about among E III 2 323 19
Miss Fairfax, who were standing a little way behind her.-- E III 2 323 20
that his wife, who was standing immediately above her, was E III 2 327 34
Stop; Mr. Knightley was standing just here, was not he?-- E III 4 340 19
I have an idea he was standing just here." E III 4 340 19
complaint, which was the standing apprehension of the E III 9 389 16
"Break it to me," cried Emma, standing still with terror.-- E III 10 393 10
Harriet, who was standing at some distance, and with face E III 11 405 17
Harriet was standing at one of the windows. E III 11 407 29
Harriet, who had been standing in no unhappy reverie, was E III 11 408 34
a friend of mine who was standing near, (Sir Basil Morley.) P III 3 20 16
"I should never think of standing on such ceremony with P III 5 40 42
an indifferent house, standing low, and hemmed in by the P III 10 85 14
He was standing by himself, at a printshop window, with P IV 7 169 25
Anne was startled and confused, but after standing in a P IV 7 180 36
standing among a cluster of men at a little distance. P IV 8 188 41
standing under the colonnade, and a gentleman with her. P IV 10 222 34
the writing table, and standing with his back towards Mrs. P IV 11 236 40
but to have them all standing or waiting around her was P IV 11 238 45
considered Sir Edw: as standing without a rival, as having S 3 377 1
light elegant building, standing in a small lawn with a S 4 384 1
amusement enough in standing at her ample Venetian window, S 4 384 1
with post horses standing at the door of the hotel, as S 9 406 1
Miss Heywood must have seen our carriage standing at the S 9 407 1
I am very fond of standing at an open window when there is S 10 415 1
STANDS (8)
there your husband stands my friend, & the kindest, most LS 2 245 1
The house stands among fine meadows facing the southeast, NA II 7 175 15
"The garden in which stands my humble abode, is separated PP I 14 67 3
of whose good opinion and judgment he stands much in awe. PP II 18 234 38
He smiled as he answered, "I am afraid the avenue stands a MP I 6 56 21
It stands in one of the lowest spots of the park; in that MP I 6 56 26
It just stands for a gentleman, and that's all. MP II 4 211 23
say, has been telling you exactly how the matter stands." E I 14 121 14
STANHILL (3)
though the furniture of Stanhill was sold, all the china, SS I 2 12 26
He had formerly visited at Stanhill, but it was too long SS I 6 30 6
know, bequeathed all the Stanhill effects that remained at SS II 11 225 35
STANTON (15)
could take her away, from Stanton just as you were coming W 317 2
Emma had seen the Edwardses only one morng at Stanton, W 322 3
it is a shameful length of time since I was at Stanton.-- W 335 13
met her in the village of Stanton, whither my good stars W 338 18
indulgence of conveying you to Stanton in my curricle.-- W 339 18
as it was dinner hour at Stanton, staid with them only a W 341 19
will throw off at Stanton wood on Wednesday at 9 o'clock.-- W 347 21
Who would have thought of Ld Osborne's coming to Stanton.-- W 347 22
presuming to make it, than have seen him at Stanton.-- W 347 22
of the sisters at Stanton, & to busy the hours of one of W 348 23
brought the party to Stanton seemed to her the probable W 348 23
How do you like Stanton?"-- W 350 24
It was an unusual sound in Stanton at any time of the day, W 354 28
out of his road merely to call for ten minutes at Stanton. W 355 28
are my sensations in finding myself once more at Stanton. W 356 28
STANWIX LODGE (1)
rent a place in this neighbourhood--perhaps Stanwix Lodge. MP II 12 295 20
STANZA (1)
can only recollect the first stanza; and there are several. E I 9 78 54
STANZAS (1)
through the several stanzas with an impatience which was PP I 18 100 68
STAR (1)
for Julia, whose happy star no longer prevailed, was MP I 9 90 36
STAR-GAZING (1)
It is a great while since we have had any star-gazing." MP I 11 113 41
STARCHED (1)
The young Mrs. Eleanors and Mrs. Bridgets--starched up MP I 9 87 15
STARE (4)
"Oh! yes; and as like him as she can stare. SS I 13 66 59
It gained her a broad stare from Miss Osborne & Miss Carr W 331 11
A stare or two at Fanny, as William helped her out of the MP III 7 377 8
Selina would stare when she heard of it."-- E III 19 484 12
STARED (10)
The ladies stared. NA I 14 112 36
Edward Stared--"reserved! SS I 17 94 46
Mr. Palmer looked up on her entering the room, stared at SS I 19 108 35
The girls stared at their father. PP I 2 7 17
Kitty stared at him and Lydia exclaimed.-- other books PP I 14 68 13
Many stared.-- PP I 18 101 71
She stared, coloured, doubted, and was silent. PP II 11 189 5

Elizabeth almost stared at her.-- PP III 1 249 34
She came up to me, claimed me as an acquaintance, stared MP I 5 50 35
to Mr. Smallridge's, near Bristol, stared me in the face. E III 14 442 8

STARES (2)
three or four very broad stares; a kind of notice which SS II 11 220 3
Brigden stares to see anybody with me but my wife. P IV 6 169 29

STARING (5)
young men who have been staring at me this half hour. NA I 6 43 33
Elinor, staring back with a look of horror at the sight of SS III 8 317 1
2
The portraits themselves seemed to be staring in P III 5 40 44
Here I am, you see, staring at a picture. P IV 6 169 25
than three lodging papers staring me in the face at this S 7 402 1

STARLING (1)
I cannot get out, as the starling said." MP I 10 99 17

STARS (3)
Stanton, whither my good stars prompted me to turn my W 338 18
and their remarks on the stars, to think beyond themselves; MP I 7 71 31
Mrs. Goddard's, her evil stars had led her to the very E II 5 186 1

START (21)
Consider how many years I have had the start of you. NA I 14 107 11
His first address made Catherine start. NA II 3 147 21
The sight of it made her start; and, forgetting every NA II 6 163 1
2
to start forth her obligation of going away very soon. NA II 13 220 2
close to her door made her start; it seemed as if some one NA II 13 222 9
alone were concerned, had not a single objection to start. NA II 16 249 1
Marianne gave a violent start, fixed her eyes upon Elinor, SS III 11 353 24
She saw him start at this, but he said nothing, and she PP III 11 192 25
26
Her pale face and impetuous manner made him start, and PP III 4 276 6
nor did her aunt Norris's voice make her start very much. MP I 2 17 21
perhaps the very best start he had ever given in the whole MP II 1 182 22
start back at first with a look of horror at the proposal. MP II 8 258 15
There was a look, a start, an exclamation, on hearing this, MP III 1 314 17
two moments were enough to start the probability of its MP III 15 437 2
on the subject, for the first start of its possibility. E I 16 135 6
not avoid a little start, and a little blush, at the sound. E II 3 173 25
so soon, there was a start at first; but Miss Woodhouse E III 6 362 43
not able to refrain from a start, or a heavy sigh, or even E III 12 423 21
Emma gave a start, which did not seem like being prepared-- E III 18 470 13
amusement at his little start of surprise, that he had not P IV 3 143 18
Her start was perceptible only to herself; but she P IV 7 175 5

STARTED (24)
Not one, however, started with rapturous wonder on NA I 2 23 27
She started at its import. NA II 7 172 2
Catherine sometimes started at the boldness of her own NA II 8 188 18
Elinor started at this declaration, and was sorry for the SS I 4 21 11
The idea however started by her, was immediately pursued SS I 12 62 27
the subject was first started to enter it--and, at length, SS I 19 103 4
started as if she had forgotten that any one was expected. SS II 6 175 1
regarded them both; she started up, and pronouncing his SS II 6 176 7
little difficulty, over the imaginary evil she had started. SS III 3 280 6
noise in the house, started hastily up, and with feverish SS III 7 310 10
11
at least equally painful, started up in preparation for SS III 8 331 70
71
his guest, and therefore started a subject in which he PP I 14 66 1
circulating library,) he started back, and begging pardon, PP I 14 68 13
You could not have started a more happy idea, since you PP I 21 119 22
He absolutely started, and for a moment seemed immoveable PP III 1 251 51
Mrs. Norris almost started. MP I 3 28 40
Sotherton, which had been started a fortnight before, and MP I 8 75 1
She started no difficulties that were not talked down in MP I 13 129 40
Mr. Dixon, which she had so naturally started to herself. E II 2 167 13
He started. E II 8 222 56
till other subjects were started, that, though may, a fire E III 2 320 5
"Since the idea had been started in the very quarter which P III 2 13 7
their usual composure: he started, and could only say, "I P III 9 78 22
back one daughter with them, no difficulties were started. S 2 374 1

STARTING (8)
of the room made her, starting, quit her hold, and the lid NA II 6 164 3
approach, and Marianne starting up moved towards the door. SS II 4 161 7
Lady Lucas quieted her fears a little by starting the idea PP I 3 10 4
Starting, the lady instinctively moved a step or two, but MP I 9 88 21
Starting and looking up she saw across the lobby she had MP II 9 267 24
within half a minute of starting the idea, that Sir Thomas MP III 13 424 4
"No--I have never seen Mr. Elton," she replied, starting E II 3 174 37
or other starting up by the sea, & growing the fashion.-- S 1 368 1

STARTLE (2)
thing to startle and recall them to the present moment. NA II 13 228 27
"My expressions startle you. P IV 9 199 55

STARTLED (17)
chiefly addressed, was startled, and hastily replied, " NA I 14 112 30
the wind, which struck at intervals on her startled ear. NA II 6 170 12
I was startled, I confess, by the alteration in his SS I 15 81 43
"Pardon me," replied Elinor, startled by the question; " SS I 22 133 45
bear any sudden noise, was startled by a rap at the door. SS II 9 203 11
Elinor, startled by his manner, looked at him anxiously, SS II 9 211 36
37
Fanny was startled at the proposal. SS II 14 253 20
This information, however, startled Mrs. Bennet;--she PP I 20 110 2
village, when she was startled by a ring at the door, the PP II 9 177 1
day; and the other, startled from the agreeable fancies MP II 7 248 47
in a fearless, self-defending tone, which startled Fanny. MP III 7 379 18
when Mr. Knightley startled her, by saying, "you will not E III 13 429 26
27
Lady Russell was almost startled by the wrong of one part P III 5 34 11
Anne was startled and confused, but after standing in a P IV 7 180 36
he had uttered, she was startled to other subjects by P IV 10 225 61
down, but Anne was startled at finding him nearer than she P IV 11 233 24
I was startled and shocked. P IV 11 242 65

STARTS (3)
and after the first starts and exclamations, not a word MP II 1 175 1
out at sudden starts immediately under their father's eye. MP III 7 383 31
door a little hard, she starts and wriggles like a young P IV 10 218 24

STARVE (1)
that one good sonnet will starve it entirely away." PP I 9 44 34

STARVED (5)
He must be starved, you know;--that is certain; absolutely SS III 5 300 37
starved, you know;--that is certain; absolutely starved." SS III 5 300 37
we have got, and I dare say you are both starved with cold. MP III 7 379 17
promising way of being starved, both mind and body, into a MP III 11 413 30
no means so fond of being starved as they could desire, or S 10 417 1

STATE (238)
for my present situation & state of mind; & I impatiently LS 1 243 1
We are now in a sad state; no house was ever more altered; LS 2 245 1
of my father's precarious state of health, as common LS 11 259 1
might not hesitate; but a state of dependance on the LS 29 299 3
reflection on the present state of our affairs, & every LS 30 300 1
Very little assistance to the state could be derived from LS 42 311 1
and the particular state of your complexion, and curl of NA I 3 27 28
From this state of humiliation, she was roused, at the end NA I 8 53 3
"Yes, to be sure, as you state it, all this sounds very NA I 10 77 34
state are not so strict as your partner might wish? NA I 10 77 37
were in a very unsettled state; divided between regret for NA I 11 86 50
nature in a civilized state can deny; but in behalf of our NA I 14 109 25
short disquisition on the state of the nation, was put an NA I 14 111 29
state of confidence and curiosity, to Edgar's Buildings.-- NA I 15 116 1
arrived, had worked herself into a state of real distress. NA I 15 121 26
often deceived in, as the state of their own affections, NA II 3 147 20
announced a happy state of mind, but whose gentle hint of NA II 7 175 11
on account of its decaying state, been removed by the NA II 8 184 4
been conveyed in a state of well-prepared insensibility! NA II 8 188 17
deeply commiserating the state of her poor friend, and NA II 9 192 4
The anxiety, which in this state of their attachment must NA II 16 250 4
She tried to explain the real state of the case to her SS I 4 21 11
in so prosperous a state as Marianne had believed it. SS I 4 22 18
In this state of her spirits, a letter was delivered to SS I 4 23 20
Colonel's advanced state of life which humanity required. SS I 7 35 9
of knowing the real state of the affair, and of instantly SS I 16 84 7
every body at times, whatever be their education or state. SS I 19 103 7
which the different state of her spirits at different SS I 19 104 12
ill-disposed, from the state of her spirits, to be pleased SS I 22 127 1
Plymouth, his melancholy state of mind, his SS II 1 139 1
but melancholy was the state of the person, by whom the SS II 1 140 3
how cheerless her own state of mind in the comparison, and SS II 4 159 1
The real state of things between Willoughby and her sister SS II 5 173 45
together; and the restless state of Marianne's mind not SS II 7 180 5
"I can have no pleasure while I see you in this state." SS II 7 186 27
My feelings are at present in a state of dreadful SS II 7 188 42
of the day, she was in a state hardly less pitiable than SS II 10 217 17
reached no farther than to state the fact of the SS III 1 262 14
restored to its proper state, its was not a subject on SS III 2 270 1
down together in a most promising state of embarrassment.-- SS III 4 288 26
The next day produced little or no alteration in the state SS III 7 308 5
was not in a state of mind to resist their influence. SS III 7 309 7
hopeless; and in this state she continued till noon, SS III 7 313 21
me, even in that horrid state of selfish vanity, I did not SS III 8 320 32
over her work, in a state of such agitation as made her SS III 12 360 24
In what state the affair stood at present between them, SS III 13 366 20
degrees, to the highest state of affection and influence. SS III 14 377 11
His daughter felt the advantage of this gratified state of W 336 14
plea of Mr Watson's infirm state of health.-- W 348 22
with her tears, my uncle's melancholy state of health.-- W 352 26
"Her indifferent state of health unhappily prevents her PP I 14 67 9
have been in a pitiable state at this time, for from the PP I 17 88 15
be advisable for me to state my reasons for marrying--and PP I 19 105 8
who naturally looks for happiness in the marriage state. PP I 20 110 4
Mr. Collins was also in the same state of angry pride. PP I 21 115 2
as most people can boast on entering the marriage state." PP I 22 125 17
Mrs. Bennet was really in a most pitiable state. PP I 23 129 16
"Let us be thankful that you are preserved from a state of PP I 23 130 23
and her spirits were in a state for enjoyment; for she had PP II 5 155 1
me, Mr. Darcy, by coming in all this state to hear me? PP II 8 174 12
13
"You have reduced him to his present state of poverty, PP II 11 192 21
In this perturbed state of mind, with thoughts that could PP II 13 205 3
have conquered, but the state of indecision in which she PP II 15 217 17
leisure to observe the real state of her sister's spirits. PP II 17 227 26
mind or manners were in a state of improvement, but that PP II 18 234 35
36
Tell him what a dreadful state I am in,--that I am PP III 5 288 38
And in the wretched state of his own finances, there was a PP III 6 297 12
The present unhappy state of the family, rendered any PP III 6 298 17
Bingley; and the unsettled state of her own feelings had PP III 17 374 19
he deliberately begun to state his objections, than Mrs. MP I 1 6 5
Poor Mr. Norris's indifferent state of health made it an MP I 1 9 10
If you consider my unhappy state, how can she be any MP I 3 29 46
Such was the state of affairs in the month of July, and MP I 4 40 15
Nobody can think more highly of the matrimonial state than MP I 4 43 23
Crawford on feeling no disinclination to the state herself. MP I 4 43 26
"My poor aunt had certainly little cause to love the state; MP I 5 46 22
been done, but for poor Mr. Norris's sad state of health. MP I 6 54 9
it is now, in its old state; but I do not suppose I shall." MP I 6 56 22
The state of her spirits had probably had its share in her MP I 7 74 59
difference of soil, the state of the harvest, the cottages, MP I 8 80 31
their lot, was now in a state of complete penance, and as MP I 9 91 36
A clergyman cannot be high in state or fashion. MP I 9 92 45
an account of the present state of a sick horse, and the MP I 12 118 22
as well as its unfinished state admitted, were waiting MP I 18 171 25
when the present state of his house should be known, for MP II 1 179 10
and present promising state of affairs; relating every MP II 1 184 27
the remembrance, and restored to its proper state. MP II 2 187 2
"My dear Sir Thomas, if you had seen the state of the MP II 2 189 5
was the most favourable state they could be in. MP II 3 200 20
She was in a state of mind to be glad that she had secured MP II 3 201 23
rain in a very desponding state of mind, sighing over the MP II 4 205 3
Honesty, in the something between, in the middle state of MP II 4 214 41
work in such a state as to prevent her being missed. MP II 5 220 29
her in what might seem a state of triumph, she followed MP II 5 221 38
39
as if he had never known Mansfield in any other state. MP II 5 224 49
of prime intellectual state and dignity, the remaining six, MP II 7 239 8
and very little of her state could be known till Mrs. MP II 7 240 10
away, she had been in a state absolutely their reverse; MP II 9 270 40
She had hardly ever been in a state so nearly approaching MP II 10 272 4
she looked back to the state of things in the autumn, to MP II 10 276 12
effort into its everyday state, and easily conform to the MP II 11 283 7
Mary was in a state of mind to rejoice in a connection MP II 12 292 5
mind might be in such a state, as a little time, a little MP III 1 320 44
at his niece, and saw the state of feature and complexion MP III 1 320 45
him home in the properest state of feeling the full value MP III 3 334 2
reserved, was an unnatural state of things; a state which MP III 4 345 4
state of things; a state which he must break through, and MP III 4 345 4
'When two sympathetic hearts meet in the marriage state, MP III 5 358 9
in the strongest state, her heart was softened for a while MP III 5 365 35
her mind into a sober state, and incline her to a juster MP III 6 369 9
herself into a properer state; she should be able to think MP III 6 370 12
In this more placid state of things William re-entered, MP III 7 384 34
the comparatively quiet state of the house, from Tom and MP III 8 388 1
so they parted--Fanny in a state of actual felicity from MP III 10 406 22
four days more, she was in a most restless, anxious state. MP III 12 418 5
I am returned to Mansfield in a less assured state than MP III 13 420 2
My present state is miserably irksome. MP III 13 422 2
the poor invalid, whose state Sir Thomas fears may be very MP III 13 426 11
invalid in a less alarming state than might be apprehended, MP III 13 426 11
and for a week he was in a more alarming state than ever. MP III 13 427 13
in his suffering, helpless state, and hearing only the MP III 14 429 1
Such was the state of Mansfield, and so it continued, with MP III 14 430 5
days had been passing in a state of penance, which she MP III 14 430 6
I want to know the state of things at Mansfield Park, and MP III 14 433 13
Her representation of her cousin's state at this time, was MP III 14 436 16
for human nature, not in a state of utter barbarism, to be MP III 15 441 20
You may imagine something of my present state. MP III 15 443 23
state of his own mind made him find relief only in motion. MP III 15 445 29
were in that delightful state, when farther beauty is MP III 15 446 35
others had been left in a state of wretchedness, inferior MP III 16 450 10
His present state, Fanny could hardly bear to think of. MP III 16 451 13
This must be his state. MP III 16 453 16
had gone to her in such a state of mind, so softened, so MP III 16 454 18
possible, coming in such a state of mind into that house, MP III 16 457 30
what share his brother's state of health might be supposed MP III 16 459 31
in his then melancholy state of spirits, of his perfect MP III 17 461 2
prosperous trial of the state--if duped, to be duped at MP III 17 464 12
her temper had been in a state of such irritation, as to MP III 17 466 16
exactly in that favourable state which a recent MP III 17 470 27
Emma, though I mean no slight to the state I assure you." E I 5 41 30
It is not a state to be safely entered into with doubtful E I 7 52 19
just opposite to her in angry state, was very disagreeable. E I 8 65 50
Emma remained in a state of vexation too; but there was E I 8 67 56
but now, it is clear; the state of his mind is as clear E I 9 73 20
depressed when he knew her state; and left her at last E I 13 109 6
people, but in a state that admitted no delay, she was E I 15 127 13

state, she replied, "I am very much astonished, Mr. Elton. E I 15 129 24
25
for Mr. Elton's sanguine state of mind, he tried to take E I 15 131 32
33
supplication; and in this state of swelling resentment, E I 15 132 37
in that unsettled state between frost and thaw, which is E I 16 138 17
might be made towards a state of composure by the time of E I 17 142 11
Emma was not at this time in a state of spirits to care E I 18 144 4
and every thing was relapsing much into its usual state. E II 2 168 15
I do not know a more luxurious state, sir, than sitting at E II 3 170 2
The information was as you state, that he was going to be E II 3 174 32
or only amused, at such a state of mind in poor Harriet-- E II 3 180 56
He did really look and speak as if in a state of no common E II 5 191 26
populous, dancing state, had been occasionally used as E II 6 197 5
possible, and, in her present state, would be dangerous. E II 9 233 23
suspect to arise from the state of her nerves; she had not E II 10 240 6
been in a very suffering state (so said her husband) when E II 12 258 7
had not attained such a state of composure as could stand E II 13 267 8
father's state of health must be a great drawback. E II 14 275 30
Not merely when a state of warfare with one young lady E II 15 282 4
I think it is the state of mind which gives most spirit E II 18 309 30
something to alter her present composed and tranquil state. E III 1 315 2
a weaker state of health than she had been half a year ago. E III 1 317 6
had not been for the cruel state of things before, and for E III 2 328 41
powerless--and in this state, and exceedingly terrified, E III 3 333 5
In this state Frank Churchill had found her, she trembling E III 3 334 7
And knowing, as she did, the favourable state of mind of E III 3 335 10
She had an unhappy state of health in general for the E III 3 336 12
Emma, recovering from her state of shame and feeling E III 4 339 15
In this state of schemes, and hopes, and connivance, June E III 5 343 1
Mrs. Churchill's state, however, as many were ready to E III 6 361 41
that Frank Churchill's state might be best defined by the E III 6 364 56
general state, had carried her off after a short struggle. E III 9 387 11
that was immediately important of their state and plans. E III 9 388 15
Her heart was grieved for a state which seemed but the E III 9 391 21
He was here only a quarter of an hour, and in a state of E III 10 397 47
state of concealment that had been carrying on so long." E III 10 398 51
as you thought, into the state of your affections, he E III 11 410 36
of the present and of the future state of the engagement. E III 12 418 5
'The consequence,' said she, 'has been a state of E III 12 419 8
relieve him from that state of indecision, which must be E III 13 429 30
a thoroughly distressed state of mind, to something so E III 13 432 40
But never in such a state of spirits, never in anything E III 14 434 2
difficulties in the then state of Enscombe must be too E III 14 437 8
how bewildered, how mad a state: and I am not much better E III 14 439 8
as much happiness in the marriage state as he had done.-- E III 14 443 8
that she should have been in such a state of punishment." E III 15 446 20
to be placing her in such a state of unmerited punishment. E III 15 450 37
Oh! no; cautious as a minister of state. E III 16 454 15
Her mind was in a state of flutter and wonder, which made E III 18 475 37
In this state of suspense they were befriended, not by any E III 19 483 10
apprehension of the state required in its possessor. P III 1 9 19
He was a married man, and without children; the very state P III 3 22 24
state of most wearing, anxious, youth-killing dependance! P III 4 27 3
independence, to enter a state for which she held her to P III 4 29 7
The Musgroves, like their houses, were in a state of P III 5 40 45
state of imaginary agitation, when she came back. P III 6 48 17
former neighbour's present state, with proper interest. P III 6 49 22
from their nephew's state, as to give the information of P III 7 54 4
child's being in no such state as could make it P III 7 59 24
for the little boy's state could no longer supply his aunt P III 8 63 1
In another moment, however, she found herself in the state P III 9 80 33
the ground for such a state, where a scene so wonderful P III 11 95 9
exactly adapted to Captain Benwick's state of mind. P III 11 97 12
to see the other in a state as insensible, or to witness P III 12 110 43
his sister in such a state, he neither ought, nor would. P III 12 113 58
distressed state of spirits, would have been difficulties. P IV 1 121 1
as could be wished, to the last state she had seen it in. P IV 2 134 28
and Lady Russell was in a state of very agreeable P IV 2 135 35
with Sir Walter, nothing to risk by a state of variance. P IV 3 140 11
With all the state which a butler and foot-boy could give, P IV 3 142 17
now, compared with her state on first reaching Bath. P IV 5 154 9
state, and Captain Benwick was not inconsolable. P IV 6 167 19
Anne, wearied of such a state of stagnation, sick of P IV 7 180 32
Anne's mind was in a most favourable state for the P IV 8 186 24
that the wretched state of his affairs was fully known. P IV 9 209 96
at the composure of her friend's usual state of mind. P IV 9 210 97
personal exertion by her state of bodily weakness, and P IV 9 210 98
to understand the present state of Uppercross, and rejoice P IV 10 219 27
Henrietta was exactly in that state of recently-improved P IV 10 220 31
"Here," said he, "ended the worst of my state; for now I P IV 11 243 70
and followed in turn, is but a state of half enjoyment. P IV 12 251 9
at present in a favourable state for my getting up to his S 1 365 1
could be really in a state of secure & permanent health S 2 373 1
calling for her bill, that she might judge of her state.-- S 3 378 1
is known of the state of the air, below the tops of the S 4 381 1
shall we guess as to the state of health of those it came S 5 385 1
state, the sea air wd probably be the death of me.-- S 5 387 1
considering the state in which both sisters appear to be.-- S 5 388 1
her in a more capable state of judging, when Sir Edw: was S 7 395 1
This was the state of the case when I wrote to you;--but S 9 409 1
wd probably in her present state, be the death of her, and S 10 412 1
deal of fancy in such an extraordinary state of health.-- S 10 412 1
You have only to state the present afflicted situation of S 12 423 1

STATED (9)

in Bath, it may be stated, for the reader's more certain NA I 2 18 1
have been separately stated, and the pangs of Sunday only NA I 13 97 1
From such particulars, stated on such authority, Elinor SS I 12 61 14
These causes must be stated, though briefly.-- PP II 12 198 5
unless Mr. Darcy returned within the stated time. PP III 13 345 20
him with a reply to them all whether stated or not. MP I 1 6 5
understanding be it stated, that he did not by any means MP II 4 211 25
in good truth, as they stated the case--you must prove MP III 4 352 44
surgeon, was also plainly stated;--it had not proceeded S 2 371 1

STATELINESS (1)

virtue, and the mere stateliness of money and rank, she PP II 6 161 9

STATELY (5)

His air was grave and stately, and his manners were very PP I 13 64 21
entered with an air more stately than usual, and on PP I 20 113 29
30
"There is something a little stately in him to be sure," PP III 1 257 68
"Yes, ma'am, indeed"--replied the other, with a stately MP I 12 117 13
portrait of a stately gentleman, which placed over the S 12 427 1

STATEMENT (7)

often consisting in the statement of improbable NA I 5 38 4
relief in drawing up a statement of the hours, that were SS III 3 280 7
the probability of the statement was admitted at the time, PP II 1 137 26
the probability of each statement--but with little success. PP II 13 205 3
and give him a fair statement of the whole acting scheme, MP II 2 187 1
I much think your statement by no means fair. E I 8 62 39
read aloud the little statement of her name and rate, and P III 8 66 22

STATEMENTS (1)

by his bewildering statements, she could not acknowledge MP III 6 370 14

STATES (2)

My account states, that your sister's friend, the lady now P IV 9 206 88
with all new poems and states of the nation that come out. P IV 10 215 15

STATING

welcome at Fullerton, and stating his impatience to be NA II 15 241 7
of Mrs. Smith, who, by stating his marriage with a woman SS III 14 379 18
Lady Catherine was generally speaking--stating the PP II 6 166 41
be her excuse; and after stating her imprudence, I am PP II 12 202 5
authority, but stating it to be such as might be relied on. PP III 1 258 75
Mr. Crawford to William stating, that as he found himself MP II 9 265 21
same time by the post, stating her extreme surprise at not E III 14 442 8

STATION (18)

The Miss Steeles kept their station at the park, and were SS II 3 158 22
if not enough in love to station himself near any fair W 328 8
was accordingly on the alert to gain her proper station. W 331 11
station between his cousin Elizabeth and Mrs. Philips.-- PP I 16 82 49
I must not, however, neglect the duties of my station, or PP III 15 363 22
Tintern Abbey held its station between a cave in Italy, MP I 16 152 2
words, he still kept his station and retained her sister's MP II 1 175 2
He then returned to his former station, and went on as if MP III 3 341 27
your claim to that station by every thing within your own E I 4 30 22
to hold a very honourable station over the mantlepiece. E I 6 46 23
Frank Churchill returned to his station by Emma; and as E III 2 323 20
be on a station that would lead to every thing he wanted. P III 4 27 4
her husband on a foreign station, and her own sister, Mary, P III 4 31 11
with her to their former station, by the stile, felt some P III 10 89 35
took their station by one of the fires in the Octagon Room. P IV 8 181 1
she generally was in her station at a window overlooking P IV 10 220 31
and taking a station, with less bare-faced design, by Anne. P IV 10 225 56
to go, & persisting in his station & his discourse.-- S 7 395 1

STATIONARY (3)

Susan became the stationary niece--delighted to be so!-- MP III 17 472 31
She has now been a longer time stationary there, than she E II 18 307 20
obliged them to be stationary and healthy at Willingden. S 2 373 1

STATIONED (7)

near the card-table, and stationed herself between Mr. PP I 8 38 39
high diversion, was stationed in the door-way, in earnest PP II 5 158 19
towards the piano forte, stationed himself so as to PP II 8 174 12
Oxford, while Susan was stationed at a window, in eager MP III 15 446 34
he has been stationed there, I believe, several years." P III 3 21 21
where she felt she had been stationed quite long enough. P III 11 93 4
and four in waiting, stationed for their convenience in P III 12 115 68

STATIONER'S (1)

"In a stationer's shop in Pall Mall, where I had business. SS II 8 199 37

STATIONING (2)

She gave him credit for stationing himself where he might E I 6 46 24
Stationing himself close by her, he seemed to mean to S 7 396 1

STATIONS (2)

in their different stations than any other three beings NA I 4 32 2
and the foreign stations he had been on, but she could not MP I 6 60 47

STAUNCH (1)

When I am a wife, I mean to be just as staunch myself; and MP I 5 47 24

STAY (210)

with me to prolong my stay, but their hospitable & LS 1 243 1
stay in Sussex that they may have some hunting together. LS 8 254 1
during her whole stay in Wigmore St till she was detected LS 17 271 7
the hours of Sir James's stay, my mind was entirely LS 22 281 4
to a prolongation of her stay, & in the course of two LS 42 313 7
Yet he had not mentioned that his stay would be so short! NA I 5 35 2
Here is Morland and I come to stay a few days with you, so NA I 7 49 43
"I do not think I should be tired, if I were to stay here NA I 10 78 44
go away at last because they can afford to stay no longer." NA I 10 78 45
I would not stay for the servant." NA I 13 102 25
and I was obliged to stay till you had finished it." NA I 14 107 8
"Then why do you stay away so long?" replied Catherine-- NA I 15 123 37
The Allens had now entered on the sixth week of their stay NA II 2 138 1
in Mr. Allen's lengthened stay, than Miss Tilney told her NA II 2 138 1
"Does he?--then why does he stay here?" NA II 4 150 3
The Thorpes spent the last evening of Catherine's stay in NA II 4 153 31
If I stay till evening my candle may go out." NA II 6 163 2
Stay-----there is one part-----" recollecting with a blush NA II 10 205 21
and shall probably be obliged to stay two or three days." NA II 11 209 5
"Aye, and sadly too--for I had much rather stay." NA II 11 211 11
For my own pleasure, I could stay with you as long again."- NA II 13 221 6
manner in pressing her to stay, and Henry's gratified look NA II 13 221 6
on being told that her stay was determined, were such NA II 13 221 6
her afterwards to stay, and for their sakes avoid a breach SS I 1 6 10
share of his discourse to herself for the rest of his stay SS I 10 46 2
already a cold, was persuaded by Elinor to stay at home. SS I 12 62 29
by Mrs. Dashwood to stay longer; but as if he were bent SS I 19 101 1
I wanted her to stay at home and rest this morning, but SS I 19 107 29
I am so sorry we cannot stay longer; however we shall meet SS I 20 110 2
by their mother to stay behind, the four young ladies were SS I 21 122 10
not being able to stay more than a fortnight with us, and SS I 22 134 52
they were prevailed on to stay nearly two months at the SS II 2 151 43
and Mrs. Jennings could not prevail on him to stay long. SS II 4 163 20
home, as she was too miserable to stay a minute longer. SS II 6 178 15
"Yes; why should I stay here? SS II 7 191 62
two, perhaps; but I cannot stay here long, I cannot stay SS II 7 191 64
stay here long, I cannot stay to endure the questions and SS II 7 191 64
continual repetition on Marianne, she could stay no longer. SS II 8 193 7
that though their longer stay would therefore militate SS II 10 214 7
at Barton, that you should not stay above a month. SS II 10 217 21
"I suppose you will go and stay with your brother and SS II 10 218 30
her persuasion that Lucy could not stay much longer. SS II 13 244 43
Mrs. Dashwood declared they should not stay a minute SS III 1 259 7
her to let them stay till they had packed up their clothes. SS III 1 259 7
to stay at home, than venture into so public a place. SS III 2 271 4
I had a vast deal more to say to you, but I must not stay SS III 2 275 25
to come and stay with her for as long a time as she likes. SS III 2 275 25
for any change of weather during their stay at Cleveland. SS III 6 303 11
him at once that his stay at Cleveland was necessary to SS III 7 309 5
for half an hour--for ten minutes--I entreat you to stay." SS III 8 317 1
2
sir," she replied with firmness, "I shall not stay. SS III 8 317 3
But I will not stay to rob myself of all your SS III 8 332 83
during the Dashwoods' stay, and Colonel Brandon was soon SS III 10 341 4
If Mr E. does not lose his money at cards, you will stay W 315 1
do you stay in this heavenly place?--till sunrise?"-- W 335 13
"It is making it too much of a fatigue I think, to stay so W 340 19
Perhaps Emma may be tempted to go back with us, & stay W 350 24
& it may just as well come in, as stay in the kitchen. W 354 27
Even Emma was pleased that he would stay, for she was W 357 28
vex you more than you think for, if you stay at home.--" W 362 32
it seems likely to rain; and then you must stay all night." PP I 7 30 21
family with her stay, and bring back a supply of clothes. PP I 7 34 45
for the short time she could stay below with a book. PP I 8 37 21
'Bingley, you had better stay till next week,' you would PP I 10 49 29
probably not go--and, at another word, might stay a month." PP I 10 49 29
them, laughingly answered, "no, no; stay where you are.-- PP I 10 53 64
65
them to stay longer, she could spare them very well.-- PP I 12 59 1
said of wishing them to stay at least till the following PP I 12 59 2
I desire you will stay where you are."-- PP I 19 104 6
gone on Saturday, and to Saturday he still meant to stay. PP I 21 115 2
exceedingly probable, stay quietly at home, and be PP I 22 124 9
of your regard during my stay in Hertfordshire. as for my PP I 22 124 10
Charlotte did not stay much longer, and Elizabeth was then PP I 22 125 18
but the shortness of her stay, and yet more, the PP II 3 147 25
invitation with which she honours us during your stay here. PP II 5 157 7
to your mother to beg that you may stay a little longer. PP II 14 211 5
6
I expected you to stay two months. PP II 14 211 8
And if you will stay another month complete, it will be in PP II 14 211 10
the last week of her stay, as they had been at first. the PP II 14 213 20
She is gone down to her uncle at Liverpool; gone to stay. PP II 16 220 10
It was the last of the regiment's stay in Meryton, and all PP II 18 229 1
left Longbourn, and of her stay in Derbyshire, so often, PP III 1 252 52
sister to your acquaintance during your stay at Lambton?" PP III 1 256 63
in excuse of my stay, but real, though unavailing, concern. PP III 4 278 20
away; and was so good as to stay till Thursday with me. PP III 5 292 66

to town again; therefore, stay quietly at Longbourn, and PP III 7 303 14
Stay, stay, I will go myself. PP III 7 306 44
No one but Mrs. Bennet, regretted that their stay would be PP III 9 318 18
Happy shall I be, when his stay at Netherfield is over!" PP III 11 333 28
seems, and there they are to stay, I do not know how long. PP III 11 336 51
he meant to make any stay in the country at present. PP III 11 337 52
Mrs Bennet had been strongly inclined to ask them to stay PP III 11 338 60
He scarcely needed an invitation to stay supper; and PP III 13 345 19
But she would not allow herself to stay with her sister, PP III 13 347 25
Kitty owned that she had rather stay at home. PP III 17 375 25
invited her to come and stay with her, with the promise of PP III 19 385 4
Stay with us and we will cure you." MP I 5 47 25
without wanting to be cured, were very willing to stay. MP I 5 47 26
you know, sister, and Fanny will stay at home with you." MP I 6 62 58
you are next inclined to stay at home, I think Miss MP I 7 69 28
been out very often lately, and would rather stay at home. MP I 7 70 29
"would you have her stay within such a fine day as this? MP I 7 72 41
"You can, if I stay at home with you, as I mean to do." MP I 8 78 20
is no necessity for my going, and I mean to stay at home. MP I 8 78 21
that she ought to offer to stay at home herself. MP I 8 79 25
"They desired me to stay--my cousin Maria charged me to to MP I 10 101 34
My poor sister was forced to stay and bear it." MP I 11 111 28
"We will stay till this is finished, Fanny," said he, MP I 11 113 42
Crawford has too much sense to stay here if he found MP I 12 116 10
But do not stay here to be cold." MP I 16 156 27
any thing; she might go or stay, she might be in the midst MP I 17 159 6
"You had better stay till the curtain is hung," interposed MP I 18 167 11
Allow me to stay here a little while, and do have the MP I 18 168 17
did yet mean to stay a few days longer under his roof. MP II 2 191 10
voluntarily intending to stay away; for, excepting what MP II 2 193 18
You must stay and hear your cousin's favourite." MP II 4 207 9
And as to coming away at night, you are to stay just as MP II 5 221 32
a scheme for extending his stay at Mansfield, and sending MP II 5 223 48
She could not wish him to stay, and would much rather not MP II 5 224 48
apparently as willing to stay and be happy without the MP II 5 224 49
His stay became indefinite. MP II 6 236 20
I wish they would stay at home." MP II 11 284 9
"Perhaps he will always stay longer than he talks of. MP II 11 287 20
him to stay longer, and that he had agreed to do so. MP II 11 288 23
I could no longer bear to stay the end of, and knowing in MP II 13 299 5
Mrs. Norris called out, "stay, stay, Fanny! what are you MP III 1 325 60
Norris called out, "stay, stay, Fanny! what are you about?- MP III 1 325 60
him to stay dinner; it was really a necessary compliment. MP III 3 335 7
being persuaded to stay at Lessingby till that very day! MP III 4 354 48
Her mother, however, could not stay long enough to suspect MP III 7 378 10
in the parlour, and why should we stay in the passage?-- MP III 7 378 12
Perhaps I may be to stay longer. MP III 11 410 15
My dear little creature, do not stay at Portsmouth to lose MP III 12 416 3
His stay must be on Edmund alone. MP III 16 452 14
But he was pressed to stay for Mrs. Fraser's party; his MP III 17 467 20
She would be very glad to stay." E I 2 19 13
"It is unfortunate that they cannot stay longer--but it E I 9 79 63
I think, Emma, I shall try and persuade her to stay longer E I 9 80 66
She and the children might stay very well." E I 9 80 66
Isabella cannot bear to stay behind her husband." E I 9 80 67
the ten days of their stay at Hartfield it was not to be E I 11 91 1
Better not move at all, better stay in London altogether E I 12 106 58
to stay at home and take care of yourself to-night." E I 13 110 9
view or his feelings, to stay at home himself, and keep E I 13 113 26
If he could stay only a couple of days, he ought to come; E I 14 122 22
him that it was safe to stay; and while the others were E I 15 128 17
18
why do not you stay at home like poor Mr. Elton?" E I 16 138 18
19
never failed him during the rest of his stay at Hartfield. E I 16 139 20
persuade his daughter to stay behind with all her children, E I 17 140 1
without any doubt, to stay considerably longer with them E I 18 144 2
though she did not seem to stay half a moment there, soon E II 3 177 52
During his present short stay, Emma had barely seen him; E II 4 182 7
Cole, you would stay a little longer than you might wish. E II 7 210 20
for Jane, could hardly stay even to be grateful, before E II 8 229 98
upon some business, and he asked him to stay dinner." E II 9 232 17
if I thought I should go and stay there again next summer." E II 9 232 19
I could not stay two minutes. E II 10 244 45
about you and me in return; but I cannot stay to hear it." E II 10 245 49
term of Frank Churchill's stay in Surry; for, in spite of E II 12 257 1
to stay at home than engage in schemes of pleasure." E II 14 274 29
promised their daughter to stay at least till midsummer, E II 15 285 14
would not be displeased, she would rather stay at home." E II 16 291 5
up being in company and stay at home; and she could now E II 16 291 5
They will stay a good while when they do come, and he will E II 17 304 27
he wished to stay longer at Hartfield, he must hurry off." E III 1 316 4
He dared not stay longer than to see her well; these E III 3 334 8
a few hardships for yourself, and be contented to stay?" E III 6 365 63
You will stay, and go with us?" E III 6 365 67
"Then pray stay at Richmond." E III 6 365 71
you wish me to stay, and join the party, I will." E III 6 366 74
75
It was before tea--stay--no, it could not be before tea, E III 8 382 29
Let it stay, however,' said she; 'give it house-room till E III 8 384 33
Mr. Weston, who "could not stay five minutes, and wanted E III 10 392 1
even of the time he could stay--but that there had been E III 10 397 47
tell you, he could stay with us but a quarter of an hour.-- E III 10 398 57
had said that he could not stay five minutes--and his E III 11 410 35
"Emma, that I fear is a word--no, I have no wish--stay, E III 13 429 33
so much keen anxiety for her, that he could stay no longer. E III 13 433 41
stay longer; her fortnight was likely to be month at least. E III 17 463 16
it possible for her to stay behind, till she might convey P III 5 33 6
Anne had better stay, for nobody will want her in Bath." P III 5 33 7
country, and her own dear country, readily agreed to stay. P III 5 33 9
He said he should not stay out long; but he has never come P III 5 37 25
to hear papa invite him to stay dinner--how sorry when he P III 7 54 4
Anne will stay; Anne undertakes to stay at home and take P III 7 57 18
Kellynch as to a home, to stay as long as he liked, being P III 9 73 1
She could not stay. P III 9 80 34
were not all together, but she could stay for none of it. P III 9 80 34
strength apace, and she had nothing else to stay for. P III 11 93 4
They were consequently to stay the night there, and not to P III 11 94 8
they might wish to stay; though, with regard to any P III 12 113 56
"that you stay, and that I take care of your sister home. P III 12 114 61
if Anne will stay, no one so proper, so capable as Anne!" P III 12 114 61
"You will stay, I am sure; you will stay and nurse her;" P III 12 114 63
and had the best right to stay in Henrietta's stead! P III 12 115 65
gone who deserved not to stay, and that Kellynch-Hall had P IV 1 125 17
The Harvilles had promised to come with her and stay at P IV 2 134 31
You must stay to be acquainted with Mrs. Wallis, the P IV 4 145 1
but yield to such joint entreaties, and promise to stay. P IV 4 145 2
of her, apologised for his stay, was grieved to have kept P IV 7 177 16
goodness to ring for Mary--stay, I am sure you will have P IV 9 202 68
of the fact;--stay--can I be mistaken in the place?-- S 1 365 1
always attend a short stay there--one is never able to S 1 367 1
a home for the rest of her stay as their humbler house in S 3 378 1
They'll stay their six weeks.-- S 6 393 1
very neighbourly, I beleive Miss Clara & I must stay."---- S 6 394 1
& stay at Sanditon house, she will find herself mistaken.-- S 7 401 1
D. being too much tired of them all, to stay any longer.-- S 8 404 1
come, & meant to get into lodgings & make some stay."-- S 9 407 1
intending to make some stay, & without appearing to have S 10 412 1

STAY-AT-HOME (1)
to an indolent, stay-at-home man; and Mr. Crawford's being MP I 5 47 26

STAYED (3)
"She had better have stayed at home," cried Elizabeth; " PP III 5 293 67
I should certainly have stayed; but I knew nothing that MP III 4 354 50
"To be sure, I had much rather she had stayed in harbour, MP III 7 378 12

STAYING (82)
my brother's departure jealous, it may be, of his staying. LS 24 291 16
each other; and after staying long enough in the Pump-Room NA I 5 35 2
without any excuse for staying at home; and, in the second, NA I 12 92 4
have no hope here, and it is only staying to be miserable." NA II 4 150 4
a chamber, and scarcely staying to hope she would find it NA II 5 162 28
Edward had been staying several weeks in the house before SS I 3 16 7
They were scarcely ever without some friends staying with SS I 7 32 1
particular friend who was staying at the park, but who was SS I 7 33 4
that he had been staying with some friends near Plymouth. SS I 16 87 26
whenever any one is staying either with them, or with us." SS I 19 109 41
Somehow or other I never happened to be staying at Barton SS I 20 114 44
sister and me was often staying with my uncle, and it was SS I 22 130 28
"Oh! yes; he had been staying a fortnight with us. SS I 22 134 48
been staying a fortnight with some friends near Plymouth." SS I 22 134 49
After staying with them half an hour, he asked Elinor to SS II 11 223 15
whom her sisters were staying, by no means unworthy her SS II 12 229 1
concluded them to be staying in Harley-Street; and this SS II 14 248 6
be no occasion for their staying above a week at Cleveland, SS III 3 280 6
"Yes; once, while she was staying in this house, I SS III 5 299 37
be speedy; and therefore staying only till she could leave SS III 7 316 30
and said, "there is no use in staying here; I must be off." SS III 8 331 70
71
where she thinks of staying three or four weeks with Mrs. SS III 13 370 37
and from thence, after staying there a couple of nights, SS III 13 372 46
have them now frequently staying with you, for as Colonel SS III 14 375 9
And without staying for an answer, she turned again to W 330 11
no entreaties for his staying longer cd now avail,--for he W 359 28
Against staying longer, however, Elizabeth was positively PP I 12 59 1
manner how long Mr. Darcy had been staying there. PP I 16 77 8
find comfort in staying at home at any period of her life. PP I 18 99 63
I insist upon your staying and hearing Mr. Collins." PP I 19 104 6
They had frequently been staying with her in town. PP II 2 139 2
of travelling and staying at home, of new books and music, PP II 8 172 3
came into Kent again she would be staying there too. PP II 10 182 1
Catherine's being rather displeased by her staying at home. PP II 10 187 41
and who was actually staying in his Colonel's family, that PP III 5 282 1
friends, who were still staying at Pemberley; but it was PP III 10 324 2
that the little girl's staying with them, at least as MP I 1 9 10
to Lady Bertram's staying at home, could only be sorry. MP I 8 76 4
"that you should be staying at home instead of Fanny." MP I 8 79 24
they are inventing excuses themselves for staying away." MP I 9 86 13
Mr. Crawford's going or staying--but his good wishes for MP II 2 194 21
But at any rate his staying away at a time, when, MP II 11 287 17
you like your cousin Edmund's staying away so long?-- MP II 11 287 18
Does his staying longer surprize you?" MP II 11 287 18
Is it Christmas gaieties that he is staying for?" MP II 11 288 22
"You were near staying there?" MP III 4 354 49
for a day or two, was staying at the crown, had MP III 10 400 7
after morning service and staying till dinner-time. MP III 11 408 4
He had already ate, and declined staying for their meal. MP III 15 445 29
Mrs. Fraser's party; his staying was made of flattering MP III 17 467 20
Harriet's staying away so long was beginning to make her E I 8 67 56
people's not staying comfortably at home when they can! E I 13 113 26
She wanted me to nurse my cold by staying at home to-day, E I 15 125 5
I had no intention, I thought I had no power of staying E II 1 162 32
She is staying here on a visit to her grandmamma and aunt, E II 5 194 45
You will not like staying late. you will get very tired E II 7 210 14
of staying as late as Mrs. Weston, but on your account. E II 7 211 21
"Perhaps Miss Fairfax has never been staying here so long E II 8 216 23
to Enscombe to propose staying a few days beyond his E II 11 256 59
His wish of staying longer evidently did not please; but E II 12 257 2
"Ah! there is nothing like staying at home, for real E II 14 274 30
bringing them, and staying one whole day at Hartfield-- E II 16 292 7
on the subject, was his staying only a quarter of an hour, E III 1 316 4
I dare say there was a difference when I was staying with E III 17 465 27
as to have been already staying there more than once, in P III 2 15 15
I really think poor Mrs. Clay may be staying here in P III 5 35 14
Here Anne had often been staying. P III 5 36 21
She had never been staying there before, without being P III 6 42 1
Wentworth's visit;--staying five minutes behind their P III 7 54 4
Harville, and a Captain Benwick, who was staying with them. P III 11 96 11
The usefulness of her staying!-- P III 12 114 59
as was evident by her staying so long, she had found more P IV 2 129 3
the same time honoured for staying away in such a cause.-- P IV 5 158 21
"What an immense time Mrs. Clay has been staying with " P IV 6 163 7
Instead of staying at Lyme, he went off to Plymouth, and P IV 6 171 33
"Is not this song worth staying for?" said Anne, suddenly P IV 8 190 49
is nothing worth my staying for;" and he was gone directly. P IV 8 190 50
friend, the lady now staying with you, whom I have heard P IV 9 206 88
themselves) and has been staying there ever since; that P IV 9 206 88
It's amount was such as determined her on staying not S 3 378 1
I think they are great fools for not staying at home. S 7 401 1
Miss Capper happened to be staying with Mrs D. when Mrs G. S 9 408 1

STAYS (8)
The longer he stays, the worse it will be for him at last. NA II 4 150 4
No Emma, whoever stays at home this winter, it shan't be W 320 2
As long as she stays there, it is all very well. PP I 7 32 32
but with Mrs. Grant, and Fanny stays at home with her." MP I 5 51 42
She stays with her aunt. MP I 8 78 17
He stays till to-morrow, and Miss Fairfax has been E III 18 476 45
But as to the rest;--as to the others;--if one stays to P III 12 114 61
go to bed too, for if he stays up by himself, he will S 12 424 1

STEAD (1)
and had the best right to stay in Henrietta's stead! P III 12 115 65

STEADFAST (2)
It was an earnest, steadfast gaze, but she often doubted PP II 9 181 29
to her room, and grew steadfast and fearless in the P IV 11 245 77

STEADFASTLY (1)
regret, on finding how steadfastly both she and her uncle PP III 10 327 3

STEADIER (3)
eldest daughter, whose steadier judgment rejected several SS I 3 14 1
She spoke of it, Fanny, with a steadier voice than I can." MP III 16 456 29
And in a louder, steadier tone, he concluded with, "he E III 13 426 13

STEADIEST (2)
certain ideas to the coldest heart and the steadiest brain. E III 3 334 9
If Jemima were not the trustiest, steadiest creature in P III 6 45 9

STEADILY (19)
He steadily refused to accompany his father into NA II 15 248 16
steadily declared his intention of offering her his hand. NA II 15 248 16
Marianne looked at her steadily, and said, "you know SS II 13 244 46
his visit were most steadily resisted, the coach conveyed PP I 16 75 1
body went on; but Elizabeth steadily opposed the scheme. PP II 16 223 25
gallantry; and while she steadily repressed it, could not PP II 18 233 25
Her feelings have been steadily against it from first to MP II 2 187 1
Will not you engage to attend with your eyes steadily MP II 5 227 65
He remained steadily inclined to gratify so amiable a MP II 8 252 1
Fanny protested her ignorance as steadily as her MP II 10 277 18
set herself very steadily against admitting any such thing. MP III 6 371 14
was not capable of being steadily attached to any one MP III 15 438 5
for them, he was very steadily earnest in the pursuit of MP III 17 471 28
to: but he had gone steadily on, with these objects in E I 2 16 6
her instrument stand steadily, it was not quite firm; an E II 10 240 5
but he said, and very steadily, that he was sorry for the E II 12 262 40
41
Frank was standing by her, but not steadily; there was a E III 2 320 7
It was all read, however, steadily, attentively, and E III 15 447 21
use of Friction alone steadily persevered in, (& I rubbed S 5 386 1

STEADINESS (15)
it requires uncommon steadiness of reason to resist the NA I 7 50 44

at the park, with his steadiness in concealing its cause, SS I 14 70 1
The shortness of his visit, the steadiness of his purpose SS I 19 102 2
The steadiness of his manner, and the intelligence of his SS III 8 318 21
22
disposition, greater steadiness than first attachments PP II 17 227 26
in his sincerity, his steadiness, his integrity, which MP I 7 65 13
of the consistence, the steadiness, the solicitude, and MP I 12 115 4
of her having such a steadiness and regularity of conduct, MP II 12 294 16
Mr. Crawford's steadiness was honoured, and Fanny was MP III 2 329 12
almost every style; but steadiness had always been wanting; E I 6 44 19
do not altogether build upon his steadiness or constancy.-- E II 13 265 4
to a girl of such steadiness of character and good E III 10 400 65
the steadiness and delicacy of principle that it wants. E III 15 448 30
could not, with such steadiness of opinion, and such P III 4 27 5
There, he had learnt to distinguish between the steadiness P IV 11 242 63

STEADY (57)
at another irritated; always distressed, but always steady. NA I 13 99 9
appearance, acting on a steady affection, would naturally NA II 14 237 21
happiness of having such steady well-wishers as Mr. and NA II 14 239 28
opposition of his son, steady as the sanction of reason NA II 15 247 15
Their tempers were mild, but their principles were steady, NA II 16 249 2
The son, a steady respectable young man, was amply SS I 1 3 2
and again; with the same steady conviction and SS II 9 201 2
to it all with the most steady and submissive attention, SS II 10 212 1
sink into a quiet, steady, and to all appearance SS III 7 315 25
just so violent and so steady as to preserve her from that SS III 14 373 1
Between him and Darcy there was a very steady friendship, PP I 4 16 14
or crushing it. steady to his purpose, he scarcely spoke PP I 12 60 4
from indignant contempt to a composed and steady gravity. PP I 18 100 67
Elizabeth preserved as steady a silence as either Mrs. PP I 18 103 75
The steady countenance which Miss Lucas had commanded in PP I 22 124 14
15
It needed all Jane's steady mildness to bear these attacks PP I 23 129 14
respectability, and Charlotte's prudent, steady character. PP II 1 135 12
her mild and steady candour always pleaded for allowances, PP II 1 138 31
done in education without steady and regular instruction, PP II 6 165 32
was to the last so steady, that in his will he PP II 12 200 5
favourite, and whose steady sense and sweetness of temper PP II 19 239 10
Their mutual affection will steady them; and I flatter PP III 7 305 37
Mrs. Norris could not help thinking that some steady old MP I 4 36 7
either Fanny or the steady old coachman, who always MP I 7 66 15
steady young man, so I hope Miss Julia will be very happy." MP I 12 118 20
There should always be one steady head to superintend so MP I 15 141 22
though she could not give them in a very steady voice. MP I 18 168 18
but as a well-judging steady young man, with better MP II 1 186 35
very safe; you know how steady Stephen is, and Charles has MP II 2 189 5
weather--but only by a steady contrary wind, or a calm. MP II 5 225 57
to the steady sobriety and orderly silence of the other. MP II 7 240 9
not but imagine that steady, unceasing discouragement from MP III 2 331 18
it is not by telling you that my affections are steady. MP III 3 343 41
you by his steady affection, will give him his reward. MP III 4 348 21
young woman of five-and-twenty, to be as steady as himself. MP III 5 361 16
steady and quiet, and not living merely for himself. MP III 17 462 4
But I have done with expecting any course of steady E I 5 37 7
of youthful expression to the steady eyes of the artist. E I 6 46 24
into as strong and steady an attachment as her youth and E I 9 69 2
But Emma still shook her head in steady scepticism. E II 10 244 36
steady friend, when she might not bear to see herself. E III 8 379 9
by, the boy going a good pace, and driving very steady. E III 8 383 31
hems with a commiseration and good sense, true and steady. E III 9 388 13
believe; but Emma's countenance was as steady as her words. E III 10 396 40
seriously, and, after steady reflection, thus-- "very bad-- E III 15 445 14
15
in a conscious, low, yet steady voice, "how you can bear E III 18 480 78
79
world, to have created so steady and persevering an E III 19 482 4
That Lady Russell, of steady age and character, and P III 1 5 8
"Mrs. Musgrove thinks all her servants so steady, that it P III 6 45 9
"he was grown so steady, and such an excellent P III 8 67 27
one style by a couple of steady, sensible women, whose P IV 1 126 21
conjecture, steady and matter of fact as I may call myself. P IV 2 132 20
He was steady, observant, moderate, candid; never run away P IV 4 146 6
half filled: a party of steady old friends were seated P IV 10 221 32
company, those regular, steady, private families of S 1 368 1
She was a general favourite;--the influence of her steady S 3 379 1
And Sir Edw: is a very steady man in the main, & has got S 7 400 1

STEAK (1)
is time to dress a steak, and we have no butcher at hand. MP III 7 379 14

STEAKS (1)
of their making it into steaks, nicely fried, as our's are E II 3 171 16
17

STEAL (1)
quite appalled by darkness, steal out and look once more. NA II 8 189 19

STEALING (3)
she quitted it again, stealing away through the winding SS III 6 302 8
returns; & Robert watson stealing a veiw of his own head W 357 28
see Mrs. Clay stealing, a glance at Elizabeth and herself. P IV 4 145 2

STEALTH (1)
take him by stealth; neither of them very like therefore. E I 6 45 21

STEDFAST (1)
"Marianne is as stedfast as ever, you see," said Elinor, " SS I 17 93 31

STEDFASTLY (2)
which his cousin had stedfastly given him would naturally PP I 20 110 1
to be in his power; and stedfastly was she persuaded that PP II 13 204 1

STEELES (27)
attractions to the Miss Steeles, as he had been already SS I 21 119 5
he had been already boasting of the Miss Steeles to them. SS I 21 119 5
and endurance of the Miss Steeles towards her offspring, SS I 21 120 6
the alarm of the Miss Steeles, and every thing was SS I 21 121 10
by one of the Miss Steeles, who was on her knees to attend SS I 21 121 10
This speciman of the Miss Steeles was enough. SS I 21 124 32
Not so, the Miss Steeles.-- SS I 21 124 33
on the side of the Miss Steeles, their party would be too SS I 21 124 33
by making the Miss Steeles acquainted with whatever he SS I 21 125 34
The Miss Steeles, as she expected, had now all the benefit SS I 21 125 37
be pleased with the Miss Steeles, or to encourage their SS I 22 127 1
After sitting with them a few minutes, the Miss Steeles SS I 22 135 56
knowledge of the Miss Steeles as to Norland and their SS II 1 139 1
be quite alone, except her mother and the two Miss Steeles. SS II 1 143 9
The visit of the Miss Steeles at Barton Park was SS II 2 151 43
way; and as for the Miss Steeles, especially Lucy, they SS II 3 157 19
The Miss Steeles kept their station at the park, and were SS II 3 158 22
About this time, the two Miss Steeles, lately arrived at SS II 10 217 19
by her hearing that the Miss Steeles were also to be at it. SS II 12 230 7
convenient to the Miss Steeles, as soon as the Dashwoods' SS II 12 230 8
with which the Miss Steeles courted its continuance, SS II 12 233 16
and the two Miss Steeles, by whom their company was in SS II 14 246 2
myself to ask the Miss Steeles to spend a few days with us. SS II 14 253 24
you know; but the Miss Steeles may not be in town any more. SS II 14 253 24
He saw the necessity of inviting the Miss Steeles SS II 14 253 25
The Miss Steeles removed to Harley-Street, and all that SS II 14 254 28
To the Middletons, the Palmers, the Steeles, to every SS III 10 346 28

STEEP (10)
plantations, and the steep woody hills rising behind to NA II 7 177 19
possible speed down the steep side of the hill which led SS I 9 41 6
I shall call hills steep, which ought to be bold; surfaces SS I 18 97 4
I call it a very fine country--the hills are steep, the SS I 18 97 4
is a pretty steep flight of steps up to the room we dine W 344 20
to follow her, ran up a steep bank, cleared a slight hedge E III 3 333 5
and carefully down the steep flight, excepting Louisa; she P III 12 109 32
yards from the brow of a steep, but not very lofty cliff-- S 4 384 1
"Not, as to mere distance, but the hill is so steep!-- S 10 416 1
field open before them--a steep bank & pales never crossed S 12 427 1

STEEPER (2)
gradually acquired a steeper form beyond its grounds; and E III 6 360 38
entering upon the still steeper street of the town itself, P III 11 95 8

STEEPEST (1)
it branched out again between two of the steepest of them. SS I 6 29 3

STEEPISH (1)
I was suddenly, upon turning the corner of a steepish MP II 7 241 13

STEM (1)
But we must stem the tide of malice, and pour into the PP III 5 289 42

STEP (53)
Now here one can step out of doors and get a thing in five NA I 3 29 46
and from politics, it was an easy step to silence. NA I 14 111 29
Isabella now entered the room with so eager a step, and a NA I 15 117 4
of air, a dignified step, which caught the eye, but could NA II 8 182 2
it was some minutes before she could advance another step. NA II 9 193 6
At that moment Catherine thought she heard her step in the NA II 13 222 9
Marianne had at first the advantage, but a false step SS I 9 41 7
They saw him step into his carriage, and in a minute it SS I 15 76 17
To be fond of dancing was a certain step towards falling PP I 3 9 1
He began to wish to know more of her, and as a step PP I 6 24 13
the door and with quick step pass her towards the PP I 20 110 1
so material a step without her ladyship's concurrence." PP I 22 123 8
and detestable as such a step must make her were it known, PP II 18 230 14
of the water, and every step was bringing forward a nobler PP III 1 253 55
when Bingley's quick step was heard on the stairs, and in PP III 2 261 5
believe him, but this step (and let us rejoice over it) PP III 4 273 3
Could he expect that her friends would not step forward? PP III 5 282 1
know nothing of the effects that such a step might produce. PP III 5 283 8
Lydia has no brothers to step forward; and he might PP III 5 283 8
one false step involves her in endless ruin--that her PP III 5 289 43
Lydia's last letter, she had prepared her for such a step. PP III 5 290 50
They agree with me in apprehending that this false step in PP III 6 297 11
He called it, therefore, his duty to step forward, and PP III 10 322 2
them, Mr. Darcy's next step was to make your uncle PP III 10 323 2
without a gravel walk to step on, or a bench fit for use. MP I 6 57 31
Starting, the lady instinctively moved a step or two, but MP I 9 88 21
own, that were he now to step forth the owner of Mansfield MP I 12 114 2
It was necessary for him to step forward too and assist MP II 1 183 23
never respected when they step out of their proper sphere. MP II 5 220 30
instructions about the living he is to step into so soon. MP II 5 226 61
suddenly the sound of a step in regular approach was heard- MP III 1 312 4
was heard--a heavy step, an unusual step in that part of MP III 1 312 4
heavy step, an unusual step in that part of the house; it MP III 1 312 4
The next step was to communicate with Portsmouth. MP III 6 371 17
to give himself the next step as soon as possible, or MP III 7 375 2
her; came with no indolent step; and, falling on her neck, MP III 15 447 37
could not but regard the step she had taken, as opening MP III 16 452 13
They arrived, the carriage turned, the step was let down, E I 13 114 28
she thought she would just step in and see how it went on; E II 3 177 52
he may get there from the crown in a hop, step, and jump." E II 5 195 48
I will step to Mrs. Goddard in a moment, if you wish it." E II 7 209 11
at the conviction, that she must proceed another step. E II 8 228 90
Pray take care, Mrs. Weston, there is a step at the E II 9 239 53
Miss Smith, the step at the turning." E II 9 239 53
person will sometimes step behind a window-curtain, and E II 11 252 31
step upon--I shall never forget his extreme politeness.-- E III 2 323 19
She would not stir a step, nor drop a hint. E III 3 335 11
very promising step of the mind on its way to resignation. E III 19 483 9
and early gained the other step in rank--and must now, by P III 4 29 8
seat for herself, on the step of a stile, was very well P III 10 86 21
They were in Union-Street, when a quicker step behind, a P IV 11 239 55
the world, shall you stir a step on any business of mine.-- S 9 411 1
nothing to do but to step back again, & say not a word.-- S 12 426 1

STEPD (1)
She stepd again to the window--but instead of the W 338 17

STEPHEN (1)
safe; you know how steady Stephen is, and Charles has been MP II 2 189 5

STEPPED (10)
and, twice before she stepped into bed, she stole gently NA II 8 188 19
she stepped quietly forward, and opened the door. NA II 13 223 9
embrace of each, as she stepped from the carriage, she NA II 14 233 9
Her mother stepped forwards, embraced her, and welcomed PP III 9 315 3
Grant's saying, as she stepped from the carriage, "as MP I 8 80 29
Yates; and Mr. Rushworth stepped forward with great MP I 15 138 2
stepped forward, feeling the necessity of doing something. MP II 1 176 3
He stepped back again to the door to say, "take care of MP III 8 388 2
stepped to Lady Dalrymple, to request her assistance. P IV 7 174 2
Sir Walter and his two ladies stepped forward to meet her. P IV 8 184 17

STEPPING (18)
beginning to think of stepping into bed, when, on giving a NA II 6 168 10
General's disapprobation, be kept from stepping forward. NA II 7 179 29
at the door, and stepping across the turf, obliged her to SS I 19 105 13
"For me?" cried Marianne, stepping hastily forward. SS II 5 169 17
away, and they were just stepping in as he came off; poor SS III 1 259 7
at his mother and stepping forwards with an honest & W 331 11
and stepping forward with eagerness, pronounced her name. PP II 12 195 2
And as for Fanny's just stepping down to my house for me, MP I 7 73 53
Mr. Crawford smiled his acquiescence, and stepping forward MP I 9 88 20
its just importance, and stepping out of his place to MP I 9 92 45
"The nonsense and folly of people's stepping out of their MP II 5 221 32
and Henry Crawford's stepping forward with a most earnest MP II 7 239 8
of stepping aside to say something agreeable of Fanny. MP II 10 276 14
Did you speak?" stepping eagerly to Fanny, and addressing MP III 3 340 25
His kindness in stepping forward to her relief--the manner- P III 9 80 34
little subdued, when, on stepping back from the group, to P IV 8 184 18
The moment of her stepping forward in the Octagon-Room to P IV 11 244 71
Miss B. into her head--& stepping to the pales, she saw S 12 426 1

STEPS (43)
found that her ladyship's steps would be bent thither; and LS 27 297 4
passing in and out, up the steps and down; people whom NA I 4 31 1
hastened away with eager steps and a beating heart to pay NA I 12 91 3
some one seemed with swift steps to ascend the stairs, by NA II 9 194 6
morning direct their steps, attracted by the partial SS I 9 40 3
the door, advanced a few steps towards the stairs, and SS II 4 161 7
chain, the door approached by a flight of stone steps.-- W 322 2
a pretty steep flight of steps up to the room we dine in-- W 344 20
Steps were distinguished, first along the paved Footway W 355 28
They were the steps of a man. W 355 28
something to say to him before he had advanced many steps. PP I 11 54 2
When they ascended the steps to the hall, Maria's alarm PP II 6 161 9
"And this," cried Darcy, as he walked with quick steps PP II 11 192 22
remained, they bent their steps, after having seen all the PP II 19 240 12
were standing on the steps of the house, as they entered PP III 5 286 21
to the spacious stone steps before the principal entrance. MP I 8 83 37
open on a flight of steps which led immediately to turf MP I 9 89 32
A considerable flight of steps landed them in the MP I 9 91 38
A few steps farther brought them out at the bottom of the MP I 9 95 67
desire of hearing their steps and their voices again. MP I 10 97 1
She followed their steps along the bottom walk, and had MP I 10 103 49
On reaching the bottom of the steps to the terrace, Mrs. MP I 10 103 50
actually practising her steps about the drawing-room as MP II 10 272 4
I jumped up, and made but two steps to the platform. MP III 7 380 20
I had gone a few steps, Fanny, when I heard the door open MP III 16 459 30
was so glorious--the steps so quick, from the accidental E II 4 181 4
walking briskly with long steps through the passage, was E II 11 254 47
48
He moved a few steps nearer, and those few steps were E III 2 326 32
Two steps, Jane, take care of the two steps. E III 2 329 45
And, after proceeding a few steps, she added--"I stopped E III 13 429 32
whenever my uncle dies, he steps into very pretty property. P III 9 76 15
When they came to the steps, leading upwards from the P III 12 104 6

agreed to get down the steps to the lower, and all were P III 12 109 32
her enjoyment, ran up the steps to be jumped down again. P III 12 109 32
would have fallen on the steps, but for Captain Benwick P III 12 109 34
able to trace the exact steps of, had staid a few hours P IV 1 126 20
man who had stood on the steps at Lyme, admiring Anne as P IV 7 177 16
as she could, the few steps of unnecessary intimacy she P IV 10 214 11
be to measure back our steps into the turnpike road & S 1 367 1
to tread in Richardson's steps, so far as man's determined S 8 404 1
was on the steps & had rung, but the door was not opened, S 9 406 1
to be attributed the giddiness & false steps of many.-- S 11 421 1
round about, & added two steps to the ascent of the hill. S 11 422 1

STEPT (7)
of the shutters; and she stept boldly forward, carelessly NA II 6 167 10
chance, if Henry stept in before the articles were signed." MP I 17 162 17
He stept to the door, rejoicing at that moment in having MP II 1 182 22
for them at the door, stept forward, and more intent on MP III 7 377 7
Isabella stept in after her father; John Knightley, E I 15 128 23
not belong to their party, stept in after his wife very E I 15 128 23
she stept forward and put an end to all further singing. E II 8 229 98

STERLING (2)
face, of strong natural, sterling insignificance, though SS II 11 220 3
more and more the sterling good of principle and temper, MP III 17 471 29

STERN (1)
all breathed the same stern resolution of not engaging in P IV 9 209 97

STERNE (1)
and a chapter from Sterne, are eulogized by a thousand NA I 5 37 4

STERNNESS (2)
with a good deal of cold sternness, said, "it is of no use, MP III 1 318 39
aware how much it concealed the sternness of her purpose. MP III 2 327 6

STEWARD (10)
A letter form my steward tells me that my presence is NA II 2 139 7
about writing a letter to his steward in the country. SS III 1 259 7
was the son of old Wickham, the late Mr. Darcy's steward. PP I 18 94 45
the son of Mr. Darcy's steward, and of that, I can assure PP I 18 95 46
son of her late master's steward, who had been brought up PP III 1 247 9
that business with his steward had occasioned his coming PP III 1 256 61
the son of his late father's steward, to be his brother? PP III 14 357 62
carving, talking to the steward, writing to the attorney, MP I 4 34 1
might be borrowed of the steward, or that perhaps Dr. MP I 4 36 7
life, to see his steward and his bailiff--to examine and MP II 2 190 9

STEWARD'S (1)
To the right is the steward's house; he is a very MP I 8 82 34

STEWPONDS (1)
Then, there is a dove-cote, some delightful stewponds, and SS II 8 197 22

STICK (2)
But when you men have a point to carry, you never stick at NA I 8 57 23
I was surprised to see Sir Henry such a stick. MP I 13 122 2

STIFF (2)
A very stiff meeting between these near neighbours ensued-- W 327 8
That stiff old Mrs E. has never done tea."-- W 333 13

STIFFEST (1)
mrs edwards put on her very stiffest look at the sound.-- W 338 17

STIFFLY (2)
drawing herself up more stiffly than ever, pronounced in SS II 12 235 37
stiffly to Elizabeth, "I hope you are well, Miss Bennet. PP III 14 351 4
5

STIFFNESS (3)
been no formality, no stiffness, he had soon felt PP I 4 16 15
avoid her but by stiffness of manner and resentful silence. PP I 21 115 1
The stiffness of the meeting soon gave way before their MP II 10 273 8

STIFLING (2)
His mother, stifling her own mortification, tried to sooth W 330 11
Here, its power was only a glare, a stifling, sickly glare, MP III 15 439 9

STILE (19)
the elegant & expensive stile of living there, as from her LS 3 246 1
soon perceived by the stile of Frederica's letters, that LS 42 311 1
great; Miss Osborne perhaps, or something in that stile.--" W 319 2
have a noble house you see, & they live quite in stile. W 322 2
of the stile of the mother who had brought her up.-- W 322 3
The stile of her last partner had probably led him to W 334 13
with the very humble stile in which they were obliged to W 345 21
half-awkward, half-fearless stile of his former remarks.-- W 346 21
(I suppose) in a superior stile, you are returned upon W 352 26
Ld Osborne's stile of overdrawing himself on both cards.-- W 359 28
The change in her home society, & stile of life in W 361 31
she had no conversation, no stile, no taste, no beauty. PP I 8 35 3
"My stile of writing is very different from yours." PP I 10 48 21
There is something very pompous in his stile.-- PP I 13 64 17
herself, on the step of a stile, was very well satisfied P III 10 86 21
former station, by the stile, felt some comfort in their P III 10 89 35
surmounting an opposite stile; and the Admiral was putting P III 10 91 39
with his extraordinary stile of compliment, she gravely S 7 398 1
they could dress in a stile much beyond what they ought to S 11 421 1

STILED (1)
elegance than precision, stiled Willoughby, called at the SS I 10 46 1

STILES (2)
quick pace, jumping over stiles and springing over puddles PP I 7 32 41
In all their walks, he had had to jump her from the stiles; P III 12 109 32

STILISH (1)
Did you ever see her? a smart, stilish girl they say, but SS II 8 194 10

STILISHNESS (1)
stilishness of Miss Thorpe's, had more real elegance. NA I 8 55 11

STILL (570)
But as for myself, I am still unconvinced; & plausibly as LS 3 247 1
self-important De Courcies still lower, to convince Mrs LS 7 254 3
but is still greatly inferior to our friend at Langford. LS 10 258 3
Yet Reginald still thinks Lady Susan the best of mothers-- LS 17 271 7
of mothers--still condemns Frederica as a worthless girl! LS 17 271 7
had it's effect, he is still hurt I am sure at her LS 20 278 9
ever, while mine will be found still fresh & implacable. LS 22 282 7
& with still greater energy, I must warn you of one thing. LS 23 283 4
him again, in seeing him still worthy your esteem, still LS 23 285 7
your esteem, still capable of forming your happiness! LS 23 285 7
In spite of this release, Frederica still looks unhappy, LS 24 291 16
still looks unhappy, still fearful perhaps of her mother's LS 24 291 16
I have not, for tho' he is still in my power, I have given LS 25 294 6
I have still another motive for your coming. LS 26 295 4
I am still doubtful at times, as to marriage. LS 29 299 3
be still more insupportable, the displeasure of Mr Vernon. LS 30 300 3
is still here, & they have been all closeted together. LS 32 303 2
for some time existed, & still continues to exist between LS 36 305 1
But she is still so fond of her husband & frets so much LS 38 307 2
any body might expect, she still lived on--lived to have NA I 1 13 1
Still they moved on--something better was yet in view; and NA I 2 21 9
But I think we had better sit still, for one gets so NA I 2 22 19
The wish of a numerous acquaintance in Bath was still NA I 3 25 1
enjoyments, they were still resolute in meeting in NA I 5 37 4
still sitting down all the discredit of wanting a partner. NA I 8 53 2
She returned it with pleasure, and then advancing still NA I 8 54 4
This was accordingly done, Mr. Tilney still continuing NA I 8 54 10
in the hope of finding him still with them--a hope which, NA I 8 58 25
The others walked away, John Thorpe was still in view, and NA I 10 75 24
sounds very well; but still they are so very different.-- NA I 10 77 34
of life; and with his eye still directed towards her, she NA I 10 80 59
on each return that, if it still kept on raining another NA I 11 83 14
The clock struck twelve, and it still rained.-- NA I 11 83 14
But whether Catherine might still expect her friends, NA I 11 83 16
cannot go indeed, for you know Miss Tilney may still call." NA I 11 84 18
Still, however, and during the length of another street, NA I 11 87 53
towards that, she still looked at intervals with pleasure; NA I 11 88 54
shall think you quite unkind, if you still refuse." NA I 13 99 3
The three others still continued together, walking in a NA I 13 99 9
and her arm was still linked within Isabella's, though NA I 13 99 9
of them; and the servant still remaining at the open door, NA I 13 102 25
But whether her brother had still exceeded her in NA I 13 102 26
Catherine was still unconvinced; but glad that Anne should NA I 14 115 55
disengaged; but I would have given the world to sit still." NA II 1 134 37
of the ancient building still making a part of the present NA II 2 141 13
And, you know, we shall still be sisters." NA II 3 145 13
"Never more so; for the edge of a blooming check is still NA II 3 147 27
leaving Isabella still sitting with Captain Tilney. NA II 3 147 28
Perceiving her still to look doubtful and grave, he added, NA II 4 152 29
unpleasant feelings; but still she was far from being at NA II 5 154 2
thoughts and her eyes were still bent on the object so NA II 6 164 3
how strangely mysterious!--the door was still immoveable. NA II 6 168 10
The storm still raged, and various were the noises, more NA II 6 170 12
to open however, was still something remarkable, for she NA II 7 173 4
of his meditations, he could still smile with them. NA II 8 182 1
noises convinced her that the servants must still be up. NA II 8 189 19
Upon this trust she dared still to remain in his presence, NA II 9 192 4
head)--or it may be of something still less pardonable." NA II 9 196 25
Her thoughts being still chiefly fixed on what she had NA II 10 199 2
There were still some subjects indeed, under which she NA II 10 201 4
and grieved, that I cannot still love her, that I am never NA II 10 207 39
and her heart was still bounding with joy, when Henry, NA II 11 210 7
satisfaction; or, if he still harbours any doubt, a line NA II 12 217 2
to enter the room, and a still greater to speak when there. NA II 13 223 9
with firmness, but with eyes still cast down, soon went on. NA II 13 223 13
Were your friends, the Allens, still in Bath, you might go NA II 13 225 23
though Sarah indeed still indulged in the sweets of NA II 14 234 10
to their hopes, they were still perfectly unsuspicious of NA II 14 235 13
She could neither sit still, nor employ herself for ten NA II 15 240 1
he might have been made still more respectable than he was: SS I 1 5 7
Elinor, too, was deeply afflicted; but still she could SS I 1 7 13
occurred to give still greater eligibility, according to SS I 3 14 3
which her mother and sister still considered as certain. SS I 4 22 18
time, (which was still more common,) to make her uncivil. SS I 4 23 19
and to Edward she gave one with still greater affection. SS I 5 25 3
still more interesting, in the midst of an heavy rain. SS I 9 42 10
Marianne was still handsomer. SS I 10 46 2
the horse is still yours, though you cannot use it now. SS I 12 59 6
day, which placed this matter in a still clearer light. SS I 12 60 8
was still more unfortunate, for they did not go at all. SS I 13 63 1
Secrecy may be advisable; but still I cannot help SS I 15 79 29
and silent meditations, still produced occasional SS I 16 83 4
where the country, though still rich, was less wild and SS I 16 85 15
was attentive, and kind; but still he was not in spirits. SS I 17 90 1
"are you still to be a great orator in spite of yourself?" SS I 17 90 2
"But you would still be reserved," said Marianne, "and SS I 17 94 45
equally evident that he still distinguished her by the SS I 18 96 1
and it ended in an absence of mind still more settled. SS I 18 99 14
two or three days, though still very unequal, were greatly SS I 19 101 1
he should go when he left them--but still, go he must. SS I 19 101 1
I always preferred the church, as I still do. SS I 19 102 4
a very striking proof, by still loving and respecting that SS I 19 104 11
She still screamed and sobbed lustily, kicked her two SS I 21 121 10
still, for there is not the smallest alteration in him." SS I 21 124 29
Elinor, though greatly shocked, still felt unable to SS I 22 130 22
her; and there is so much still to be done to the basket, SS II 1 145 19
this speech, and Lucy was still the first to end it. SS II 2 150 35
occurred to you, there is still one objection which, in my SS II 3 156 9
and over the mantlepiece still hung a landscape in SS II 4 160 3
Her spirits still continued very high, but there was a SS II 4 161 6
weather, and still happier in her expectation of a frost. SS II 5 168 7
her sister to go, for still she had seen nothing of SS II 5 170 28
long delayed; and she was still more eagerly bent on this SS II 5 171 38
But still I might not have believed it, for where the mind SS II 5 173 44
for however Marianne might still feed her own wishes, she SS II 6 178 17
Her indignation would have been still stronger than it was, SS II 6 178 17
given her, and on those still more severe which might SS II 6 179 18
bursts of grief which still obliged her, at intervals, to SS II 7 180 4
sooth and tranquillize her still more, had not Marianne SS II 7 180 5
she might wound Marianne still deeper by treating their SS II 7 184 15
I have been expecting to hear from you, and still more to SS II 7 187 40
she could, while Marianne still remained on the bed, was SS II 8 193 5
served to identify the man still more:--as soon as the SS II 8 199 37
how eagerly she would still justify him if she could." SS II 8 200 42
the heart of Mrs. Jennings still lower in her estimation; SS II 9 202 4
withdrew, still referring her to the letter for comfort. SS II 9 202 8
Her mother, still confident of their engagement, and SS II 9 202 8
grieving still more fondly over its effect on her mother. SS II 9 203 10
Elinor, affected by his relation, and still more by his SS II 9 206 25
for him as strong, still as strong as her own, and with a SS II 9 210 32
On the contrary, every friend must be made still more her SS II 9 210 32
"Is she still in town?" SS II 9 211 41
delight of Lucy in finding her still in town. SS II 10 217 20
I had not found you here still," said she repeatedly, with SS II 10 217 21
"but however there is still a great deal to be done. SS II 11 226 37
because she believed them still so very much attached to SS II 12 229 4
Elinor was pleased that he had called; and still more SS II 12 230 5
to be carrying the pain still farther by persuading her, SS II 12 231 11
that was worth hearing, and his wife had still less. SS II 12 233 18
Mrs. Ferrars and Fanny still more, did not see the SS II 12 234 25
Elinor wished to talk of something else, but Lucy still SS II 13 239 7
and the appearance of secrecy must still be kept up. SS II 13 241 19
and another struggle, another effort still improved them. SS II 13 241 20
but his embarrassment still exceeded that of the ladies in SS II 13 241 21
as the consequences of her still continuing in an error SS II 13 244 47
Dashwoods; but, what was still worse, must be subject to SS II 14 248 6
was anxious to hear; and still more anxious to know how SS III 1 260 9
opposition to this, if he still persisted in this low SS III 1 266 38
is gone, or whether he is still in town, I do not know; SS III 1 268 48
Elinor avoided it upon principle, as tending to fix still SS III 2 270 1
Her mind was so much weakened that she still fancied SS III 2 270 2
Still farther in confirmation of her hopes, in the SS III 3 281 9
own sake, and as a friend of yours, I wish it still more. SS III 3 282 19
declining it likewise, still seemed so desirous of its SS III 3 283 20
Edward, she believed, was still in town, and fortunately SS III 3 283 20
His marriage must still be a distant good;--at least, I am SS III 3 284 23
I know he has, still greater pleasure in bestowing it; but, SS III 4 289 35
and still without forfeiting her expectation of the first. SS III 4 292 54
perhaps, had not Elinor still, as from the first, believed SS III 6 305 16
had-- assisted by the still greater imprudence of sitting SS III 6 305 17
Mr. Harris, who attended her every day, still talked SS III 7 309 7
Her sister, however, still sanguine, was willing to SS III 7 310 9
It was lower and quicker than ever! and Marianne, still SS III 7 311 14
Marianne's ideas were still, at intervals, fixed SS III 7 312 18
She had been for three months her companion, was still SS III 7 313 20
But he judged it unnecessary; he had still something more SS III 7 313 21
At seven o'clock, leaving Marianne still sweetly asleep, SS III 7 315 27
"Marianne's note, by assuring me that I was still as dear SS III 8 325 53
short note from Marianne-- still affectionate, open, SS III 8 327 55
to possess; and by that still ardent love for Marianne, SS III 9 333 2
tears of joy, though still unable to speak, embraced SS III 9 334 4
was unsubdued, and she still tried to appear cheerful and SS III 11 352 19
but conclude him to be still at Oxford;" which was all the SS III 11 353 21
to Elinor, who, though still much disordered, had so far SS III 11 353 25
for since Edward would still be unable to marry Miss SS III 13 369 33
He had nothing to urge against it, but still resisted the SS III 13 372 45
none, still remained some weeks longer unpardoned. SS III 14 376 11
done to succeed to it, might have puzzled them still more. SS III 14 377 12
to be married,--and who still sought the constitutional SS III 14 378 15
he is married to another woman, while I am still single.-- W 316 2
"But still she may like our brother." W 321 2

Context	Reference
& there seemed something still more suspicious in the	W 324 3
Still she hesitated.	W 339 18
can be, but I still profess my preference of a white skin.	W 357 28
She still suffered from them in the contemplation of their	W 361 31
which perhaps will be still better, for as you are as	PP I 1 4 19
They found Mr. Bennet still up.	PP I 3 12 15
character and make it still better, and say nothing of the	PP I 4 14 9
Mrs. Hurst and her sister allowed it to be so--but still	PP I 4 17 16
pleasure; but Elizabeth still saw superciliousness in	PP I 6 21 1
well--and indeed so I do still at my heart; and if a smart	PP I 7 29 12
She was still very poorly, and Elizabeth would not quit	PP I 8 37 21
at her because he disliked her, was still more strange.	PP I 10 51 46
at whom it was all aimed, was still inflexibly studious.	PP I 11 56 10
her education, and who still resides with them.	PP I 11 67 7
and the whole party were still standing and talking	PP I 15 72 8
was nothing; but he had still at intervals a kind listener	PP I 16 76 5
venture still to think of both gentlemen as I did before."	PP I 18 96 55
gone on Saturday, and to Saturday he still meant to stay.	PP I 21 115 2
heightened into something still more interesting, from the	PP I 21 117 14
But still he would be her husband.--	PP I 22 122 3
There are few people whom I really love, and still fewer	PP II 1 135 11
Mrs. Bennet still continued to wonder and repine at his	PP II 1 137 26
this point, as well as the still more interesting one of	PP II 2 142 16
think me obstinate if I still assert, that, considering	PP II 3 148 26
She had already learnt that Lady Catherine was still in	PP II 5 157 6
said Elizabeth, still addressing Colonel Fitzwilliam.	PP II 8 175 22
of course recommended him still more; and Elizabeth was	PP II 9 180 28
all that Jane had suffered, and still continued to suffer.	PP II 10 186 38
day after the next, and a still greater, that in less than	PP II 11 188 1
The park paling was still the boundary on one side, and	PP II 12 195 1
the letter, and to her still increasing wonder, perceived	PP II 12 196 3
which, though still existing, and existing to an equal	PP II 12 198 5
and constant intimacy, and still more as one of the	PP II 12 202 5
Many of his expressions were still fresh in her memory.	PP II 13 206 5
of his address, she was still full of indignation; but	PP II 14 212 17
to recommend them; but still more was she grieved for the	PP II 17 224 2
But there was still something lurking behind, of which	PP II 17 227 25
She still cherished a very tender affection for Bingley.	PP II 17 227 26
The elder Miss Bennets alone were still able to eat, drink,	PP II 18 229 1
with her sister, there was still less to be learnt--for	PP II 19 238 5
lakes; and still thought there might have been time enough.	PP II 19 239 8
that some acquaintance still remained, they bent their	PP II 19 240 12
in defiance of every thing, she was still dear to him.	PP III 1 253 55
It is impossible that he should still love me."	PP III 1 255 60
done away; but, had she still felt any, it could hardly	PP III 2 261 5
Elizabeth again, having still a great deal to say to her,	PP III 2 264 12
her, but for loving her still well enough, to forgive all	PP III 2 265 16
her fancy told her she still possessed, of bringing on the	PP III 2 266 16
though I have still something more to ask of the former.	PP III 4 275 5
not yet deserted her; she still expected that it would all	PP III 5 287 33
of her sister's ruin still more certain; and even Jane,	PP III 6 295 4
even Jane, who believed still less of it, became almost	PP III 6 295 4
town, but his debts of honour were still more formidable.	PP III 6 298 12
His debts to be discharged, and something still to remain!	PP III 7 304 30
former friends, there are still some who are able and	PP III 8 312 19
Lydia was Lydia still; untamed, unabashed, wild, noisy,	PP III 9 315 4
question, that Wickham still cherished the hope of more	PP III 10 323 2
was still with him, but would quit town the next morning.	PP III 10 323 2
to his friends, who were still staying at Pemberley; but	PP III 10 324 2
was acknowledged; but she still thought him partial to	PP III 11 332 18
time, that his affection and wishes must still be unshaken.	PP III 11 334 37
"He could be still amiable, still pleasing, to my uncle	PP III 12 339 4
of saying, "is your sister at Pemberley still?"	PP III 12 341 20
	21
She then sat still five minutes longer; but unable to	PP III 13 345 12
	13
awkward enough; but her's she thought was still worse.	PP III 13 346 22
To all the objections I have already urged, I have still	PP III 14 357 62
If your feelings are still what they were last April, tell	PP III 16 366 7
twenty; and such I might still have been but for you,	PP III 16 369 24
He still loves me, and we are engaged."	PP III 17 372 5
Miss Bennet still looked all amazement.	PP III 17 373 8
Elizabeth, still more affected, was earnest and solemn in	PP III 17 376 36
Bennet sat quite still, and unable to utter a syllable.	PP III 17 378 42
consent, there was still something to be wished for.	PP III 17 378 46
whether your sister were still partial to Bingley, and if	PP III 18 382 16
in a different style; and still different from either, was	PP III 18 383 22
she still was occasionally nervous and invariably silly.	PP III 19 385 1
A large and still increasing family, an husband disabled	MP I 1 4 2
towards their relation; but still they cannot be equals.	MP I 1 11 17
thank you;" but he still persevered, and no sooner had he	MP I 2 15 10
nursing him, my spirits still worse, all my peace in this	MP I 3 29 46
came, Sir Thomas was still abroad, and without any near	MP I 4 37 9
but still he was the gentleman, with a pleasing address.	MP I 5 44 2
beauty; but as she still continued to think Mr. Crawford	MP I 5 48 30
had still more to say on the subject next his heart.	MP I 6 55 17
The subject of improving grounds meanwhile was still under	MP I 6 60 53
gone, and still no horse was announced, no Edmund appeared.	MP I 7 67 15
and Miss Crawford still on horseback, but attended by	MP I 7 68 17
Vexed as Edmund was with his mother and aunt, he was still	MP I 7 74 58
made Mrs. Rushworth still think she wished to come, till	MP I 8 76 2
gates; but we have nearly a mile through the park still.	MP I 8 82 34
Norris, and Julia, were still far behind; for Julia, whose	MP I 9 90 36
He still reasoned with her, but in vain.	MP I 9 96 76
passed away, and Fanny was still thinking of Edmund, Miss	MP I 10 97 1
key again; but still this did not remove the present evil.	MP I 10 98 4
as fast as you could; but still it is some distance, you	MP I 10 102 46
It was a beautiful evening, mild and still, and the drive	MP I 10 106 58
After a short pause, however, the subject still continued,	MP I 13 124 13
Edmund had little to hope but he was still urging the	MP I 13 129 38
was already at work, while a play was still to seek.	MP I 14 130 1
by the housemaids, and still the play was wanting; and as	MP I 14 130 1
leaves with the hope of still discovering such a scene,	MP I 15 138 1
well, I am sure--but I still think you see things too	MP I 15 140 14
an hour or two; there was still a great deal to be settled;	MP I 15 142 25
The consultation upon the play still went on, and Miss	MP I 15 148 58
exceedingly"--Edmund still held his peace, and shewed his	MP I 15 148 60
bed full of it, her nerves still agitated by the shock of	MP I 16 150 1
the books, which she was still glad to keep there, from	MP I 16 151 1
"But still it has not your approbation.	MP I 16 155 18
Edmund might still look grave, and say he did not like the	MP I 17 158 1
She had loved, she did love still, and she had all the	MP I 17 162 19
the attentions which were still carrying on there, some	MP I 17 162 19
ourselves--and so am I still;-- and as soon as I am a	MP I 18 167 7
	8
But Fanny still hung back.	MP I 18 171 29
the shock of her words, he still kept his station and	MP II 1 175 2
twice as long on his passage, or were still in Antigua.	MP II 1 176 4
for a few minutes, and still remained so sensibly animated	MP II 1 179 9
Still Mrs. Norris was at intervals urging something	MP II 1 180 10
"Still the same anxiety for every body's comfort, my dear	MP II 1 180 11
"It is time to think of our visitors," said Maria, still	MP II 1 182 19
from the billiard room to astonish him still further.	MP II 1 182 22
Mr. Yates was still talking.	MP II 1 185 28
morning--and all the evening too was still expecting him.	MP II 2 192 11
country; and November is a still more serious month, and I	MP II 3 199 15
and only to three people, still it was dining out, and all	MP II 5 219 27
and as of course he will still live at home, it will be	MP II 5 226 61
had been suspended, and still hoped uncertain and at a	MP II 5 227 69
immediately, for he was still only a midshipman; and as	MP II 6 233 14
But with William and Fanny Price, it was still a sentiment	MP II 6 235 18
do with it, but much was still owing to Sir Thomas's more	MP II 7 238 1
I am not born to sit still and do nothing.	MP II 7 243 25
Thomas, in a more every day tone, but still with feeling.	MP II 7 247 37
Wednesday morning, Fanny, still unable to satisfy herself,	MP II 8 256 14
Fanny still resisted, and from her heart.	MP II 8 258 17
consciousness of looking well, made her look still better.	MP II 10 272 4
and she was soon made still happier; for in following her	MP II 10 272 4
other circumstances, but Fanny's happiness still prevailed.	MP II 10 273 5
Fanny's blushes, still thought she must be doing so--when	MP II 10 277 17
But still his attentions made no part of her satisfaction.	MP II 10 278 20
the two dances with Edmund still to look forward to,	MP II 10 278 20
he found himself still impelled to seek her again, she had	MP II 10 279 21
couple, who were still hard at work--and then, creeping	MP II 10 280 33
still more might be imputed to difference of circumstances.	MP II 11 285 15
All this was bad, but she had still more to feel when	MP II 11 286 16
Saturday came and still no Edmund--and when, through the	MP II 11 286 16
His still refusing to tell her what he had gone for, was	MP II 12 291 1
in the midst of all this, still speaking at intervals to	MP II 12 296 31
much trouble in vain, she still went on, after a civil	MP II 13 298 1
was so full and her senses still so that she could listen	MP II 13 300 7
While her heart was still bounding with joy and gratitude	MP II 13 301 7
But he was still talking on, describing his affection,	MP II 13 301 7
Her astonishment and confusion increased; and though still	MP II 13 301 7
But she still tried to believe it no more than what he	MP II 13 306 26
and as Mrs. Norris was still in the house, there seemed	MP III 1 311 2
to your finding one still better worth listening to.--	MP III 1 314 16
and I should have said still more,--if I had been quite	MP III 1 315 19
attentions, and who was still overpowered by the	MP III 2 326 3
declared, that he would still love, and still hope!	MP III 2 327 5
the connection was still the most desirable in the world.	MP III 2 329 12
a measure which he would still have avoided, if possible,	MP III 2 331 19
And still pursuing the same cheerful thoughts, she soon	MP III 2 333 28
with judgment, Edmund was still more and more pleased.	MP III 3 340 24
Edmund's advertisements were still of the first utility.	MP III 3 343 40
But still I am not frightened.	MP III 3 344 41
there is something in him which I object to still more.	MP III 4 349 25
warm-hearted friend was still run away with a little, by	MP III 4 353 46
Still, however, Fanny, was oppressed and wearied; he saw	MP III 4 355 55
Her secret was still her own; and while that was the case,	MP III 5 365 34
there were bad feelings still remaining which made the	MP III 6 367 4
personal kindness, had still been Miss Crawford, still	MP III 6 367 5
still been Miss Crawford, still shewn a mind led astray	MP III 6 367 5
and his own observations, still feeling a right, by all	MP III 6 368 7
of what she felt; but still there were emotions of	MP III 6 369 11
her there still when he came in, from his first cruise!	MP III 6 372 18
last evening at Mansfield Park must still be wretchedness.	MP III 6 374 28
to her kissing him, though still entirely engaged in	MP III 7 377 8
but, as there was still no appearance of tea, nor, from	MP III 7 381 24
as they were still kicking each other's shins, and	MP III 7 383 31
of home, there were still to her own perfect consciousness,	MP III 8 388 1
still, and nobody could command attention when they spoke.	MP III 8 392 11
and after chapel he still continued with them, and made	MP III 11 408 3
"I wish you were not so tired,"--said he, still detaining	MP III 11 411 20
I am sure he still means to impose on me if possible, and	MP III 11 411 20
The wonderful improvement which she still fancied in Mr.	MP III 11 413 32
last Saturday, and one still more to be dwelt on the next	MP III 12 415 1
	2
me till you were tired still more; but it is impossible to	MP III 12 415 2
and so it still was, but it must be applied to Mansfield.	MP III 14 431 8
Still, however, it was her private regale.--	MP III 14 431 8
evil of solitude, or the still greater evil of a restless,	MP III 14 432 10
she could not comprehend how both could still keep away.	MP III 14 432 11
either, however, I should still prefer you, because it	MP III 14 434 13
To have him still the acquaintance, the flirt, perhaps, of	MP III 14 436 15
of a week, she had still the same feeling when it did come.	MP III 15 437 1
his sister still said that he cared for nobody else.	MP III 15 438 6
She could still think of little else all the morning; but	MP III 15 438 8
of cheering, made her still more melancholy; for sun-shine	MP III 15 439 9
He is still able to think and act; and I write, by his	MP III 15 442 23
again, though his voice still faltered, his manner showed	MP III 15 444 29
him up, the case would still have been hopeless, for Mrs.	MP III 16 450 11
the woman he adored; but still more the folly of--poor	MP III 16 454 18
the impulse of the moment to resist, and still walked on.	MP III 16 459 30
of his sufferings, but still it was a sort of thing which	MP III 16 460 31
must make her, she would still have been happy without any	MP III 17 461 2
dinners in one week, they still lived together; for Mary,	MP III 17 469 24
Timid, anxious, doubting as she was, it was still	MP III 17 471 28
They lived beyond their income, but still it was nothing	E I 2 15 3
He had still a small house in Highbury, where most of his	E I 2 16 5
by surprize at his being still able to pity "poor Miss	E I 2 18 12
the new-married pair; but still the cake was eaten; and	E I 2 19 14
I say that if you should still be in this country when Mr.	E I 4 31 24
to be out, and that you must still fight your own battle."	E I 5 36 5
thrown over my senses, must still see, hear, and remember.	E I 5 37 9
But still I cannot imagine she would not be persuaded."	E I 6 44 18
or four years old stand still you know; nor can it be very	E I 6 45 21
She must allow him to be still frequently coming to look;	E I 6 47 26
"Well," said the still waiting Harriet;--"well--and--and	E I 7 51 6
and though the letter was still in her hand, it was not	E I 7 53 22
The idea of Mr. Elton was certainly cheering; but still,	E I 7 56 42
"A very serious sort, I assure you;" still smiling.	E I 8 59 22
She did not repent what she had done; she still thought	E I 8 65 50
"But still, you will be an old maid! and that's so	E I 10 85 18
of the place, and recal the still greater within.	E I 10 87 27
this means the others were still able to keep ahead,	E I 10 88 33
Mr. Elton was still talking, still engaged in some	E I 10 88 34
It was not closed however, it still remained ajar; but by	E I 10 89 38
Still, however, though every thing had not been	E I 10 90 41
"But still, not near enough to give me a chance of being	E I 12 99 9
"I have still the advantage of you by sixteen years'	E I 12 99 10
care; but as there must still remain a degree of	E I 13 110 8
in love with Harriet; but still, he cannot refuse an	E I 13 111 13
are put off, I am still afraid that some excuse may be	E I 14 122 21
with snow, and of its still snowing fast, with a strong	E I 15 125 7
to get away; and they were still discussing the point,	E I 15 127 16
of delay, there was still such an evil hanging over her in	E I 16 139 20
and regret; but still he looked forward with the hope of	E I 18 144 1
and out of temptation; but still, as it was desirable that	E I 18 144 4
"Yes; all the advantages of sitting still when he ought to	E I 18 148 24
well still, thank God! with the help of spectacles.	E II 1 157 10
It was easy to decide that she was still too young; and	E II 2 164 6
Still, however, affection was glad to catch at any	E II 2 165 9
like any other pork--but still it is pork--and, my dear	E II 3 171 16
	17
not think about it;" but still she talked of it--still she	E II 3 180 56
still she talked of it--still she could talk of nothing	E II 3 180 56
There was instant pleasure in the sight of them, and still	E II 5 188 6
	7
Highbury itself, Hartfield still more, and professed	E II 5 191 26
through Emma's brain; but still if it were a falsehood, it	E II 5 191 26
Mr. Frank Churchill still declined it, looking as serious	E II 5 195 48
who had nursed him was still living, walked in quest of	E II 6 197 3
families described, he was still unwilling to admit that	E II 6 198 5
her own indifference--(for still her resolution held of	E II 7 206 2
still more lucky, she wanted exactly the advice they gave.	E II 7 206 5
still I have no doubt that James will take you very safely.	E II 7 210 14
of their own claims; but still they must feel that any	E II 7 210 19
Emma to think her own way, and still listen to Mrs. Cole.	E II 8 215 15
old petticoat either--for still it would last a great	E II 8 225 78
by somebody else, and he was still talking to Mrs. Cole.	E II 8 230 99
and while she was still hanging over muslins and changing	E II 9 233 24
was amused enough; quite enough still to stand at the door.	E II 9 233 24
so beautiful, would still never match her yellow pattern.	E II 9 235 35

who was still sitting at it, to play something more. E II 10 242 16
She was in the adjoining chamber while she still spoke, E II 10 243 32
But Emma still shook her head in steady scepticism. E II 10 244 36
And (raising his voice still more) I do not see why Miss E II 10 245 49
But still she had inclination enough for shewing people E II 11 247 2
But still he went on measuring, and still he ended with, " E II 11 249 15
16

Still, however, having proceeded so far, one is unwilling E II 11 250 18
still was not it too small for any comfortable supper? E II 11 254 44
She is still nearer.-- E II 11 254 50
"If I can come again, we are still to have our ball. E II 12 260 19
than usual; she was still busy and cheerful; and, pleasing E II 13 264 1
was to mark their parting; but still they were to part. E II 13 264 1
Still, however, I must be on my guard. E II 13 265 4
warmth, that she could still do without the writer, and E II 13 266 6
grief was comforted away, still remained powerful enough E II 13 268 13
allowed to exist; but still she had declined it!" E II 15 285 14
and might now have been still, who had been long talking, E II 17 303 23
may, a fire in the evening was still very pleasant. E III 2 320 5
and Henry and John were still asking every day for the E III 3 336 13
and the gipsies, and still tenaciously setting her right E III 3 336 13
again, "here is something still more valuable, I mean that E III 4 339 16
The Eltons were still talking of a visit from the E III 5 343 1
and Jane Fairfax was still at her grandmother's; and as E III 5 343 1
wait, and every projected party be still only talked of. E III 6 352 2
well; and he could sit still with Mrs. Weston, while the E III 6 356 30
Still Mrs. Elton insisted on being authorized to write an E III 6 359 37
seated and busy, and still Frank Churchill did not come. E III 6 361 41
"You will soon be cooler, if you sit still." said Emma. E III 6 364 54
"But if I do, I shall be crosser still. E III 6 366 72
She still intended him for her friend. E III 7 368 3
endured than allowed, perhaps, but I must still use it. E III 7 374 55
56

thing of that sort, but still he cannot keep his father E III 8 383 29
She was warmly gratified--and in another moment still more E III 9 385 7
"Break it to me," cried Emma, standing still with terror.-- E III 10 393 10
"You may well be amazed," returned Mrs. Weston, still E III 10 395 35
given her credit for--and still am disposed to give her E III 10 400 65
Emma had promised; but still Harriet must be excepted. E III 11 403 2
"What did Mr. Weston tell you?"--said Emma, still E III 11 404 7
head and heart!--she sat still, she walked about, she E III 11 411 43
estimate of her own--but still, from family attachment and E III 12 415 1
that misconduct can bring, it is still not less misconduct. E III 12 419 8
was most probable--still, in knowing her as she ought, and E III 12 421 17
case to be obliged still to lower herself in his opinion. E III 13 427 18
which he still spoke--"I should like to take another turn. E III 13 429 32
still be greater when the flutter should have passed away. E III 14 434 1
She could only resolve at last, that she would still avoid E III 14 435 4
But I have been forgiven by one who had still more to E III 14 436 8
better yet; still insane either from happiness or misery. E III 14 439 8
I must still add to this long letter. E III 14 440 8
ceased, the subject could still maintain itself, by the E III 15 444 1
not been in the case--I should still have distrusted him." E III 15 445 13
his letter as I am; but still you must, at least I hope E III 15 448 29
than he deserves: but still as he is, beyond, a doubt, E III 15 448 30
The fear of being still unwelcome, determined her, though E III 16 452 8
acquainted with what was still a secret to other people. E III 16 453 12
She was still looking in him with the most speaking E III 18 471 15
If Emma had still, at intervals, an anxious feeling for E III 19 481 1
John and Isabella were still at Hartfield, to allow them E III 19 483 8
Still, however, he was not happy. E III 19 483 9
his youth; and, at fifty-four, was still a very fine man. P III 1 4 5
death, and they were still near neighbours and intimate P III 1 5 7
It was so with Elizabeth; still the same handsome Miss P III 1 6 11
She was fully satisfied of being still quite as handsome P III 1 7 12
This very awkward history of Mr. Elliot, was still, after P III 1 8 17
the man for himself, and still more for being her father's P III 1 8 17
there is still more due to the character of an honest man." P III 2 12 4
where they might still have Lady Russell's society, still P III 2 14 9
Lady Russell's society, still be near Mary, and still have P III 2 14 9
still be near Mary, and still have the pleasure of P III 2 14 9
wait on Admiral Croft, who still remained at Taunton, and P III 3 24 35
Sir Walter was not very wise; but still he had experience P III 3 24 36
He had always been lucky; he knew he should be so still.-- P III 4 27 3
which, with Lady Russell, still resident in Kellynch, and P III 4 31 12
deserted grounds, and still worse to anticipate the new P III 5 36 19
of her acquaintance; but still, saved as we all are by P III 5 41 45
she could, that the same brother must still be in question. P III 6 49 25
the father and the aunt, still they were all to hope the P III 7 54 4
to dine alone, though he still wanted her to join them in P III 7 58 20
I wished for him again the next summer, when I had still P III 8 67 23
bad thing for her, and still worse for me; and therefore P III 9 76 16
had no doubt of their still being--in some spot or other. P III 10 87 21
trodden under foot, is still in possession of all the P III 10 88 26
Her own emotions still kept her fixed. P III 10 89 34
Anne was still in the lane; and though instinctively P III 10 91 41
attached to another, still he could not see her suffer, P III 10 91 42
and entering upon the still steeper street of the town P III 11 95 8
sweeps of country, and still more its sweet retired bay, P III 11 95 9
looking rooms, and still descending, soon found themselves P III 11 96 10
Scott and Lord Byron, and still as unable, as before, and P III 12 107 23
at their door, and still accompanied by Captain Benwick, P III 12 108 30
supplied, to Henrietta, still tried, at intervals, to P III 12 111 44
could do no good; yet was still unwilling to be away, till P III 12 114 59
to go to Lyme, and his account was still encouraging. P IV 1 122 4
that Mrs. Clay should still be with them, Anne would have P IV 1 124 11
had burst on her; but still it must be talked of, she must P IV 1 124 12
still remain to suffer from the concussion hereafter!-- P IV 1 126 21
doing very well, it was still impossible to say when she P IV 2 129 1
They had drawn back from many introductions, and still P IV 3 138 4
Still, however, she had the sensation of there being P IV 3 140 11
But still, there certainly were a dreadful multitude of P IV 3 142 13
Anne presumed, however, still to smile about it; and at P IV 4 147 7
had not been very happy, still it had existed so many P IV 4 147 8
very agreeable, she would still have been ashamed of the P IV 4 149 14
Miss Carteret, with still less to say, was so plain and so P IV 4 150 14
nothing in themselves, but still maintained that as a P IV 4 150 15
older than herself, but still from the want of near P IV 5 152 2
relative to Anne, but still there were questions enough P IV 5 157 14
distinguish her arms; but still, it is a handsome carriage, P IV 5 158 19
And it was not only that her feelings were still adverse P IV 5 160 26
Warmth and enthusiasm did captivate her still. P IV 5 161 28
to be recovering fast, was still at Lyme; and she was P IV 6 162 1
gratified; but she was still obliged to wait, for the P IV 6 170 30
she found the others still waiting for the carriage, and P IV 7 175 5
Still, however, she had enough to feel! P IV 7 175 6
as if the remembrance were still too painful; but in a P IV 8 182 6
His choice of subjects, his expressions, and still more P IV 8 185 21
Miss Larolles,--but still she did it, and not with much P IV 8 189 46
She was still in the astonishment and confusion excited by P IV 9 194 19
am sure you will have the still greater goodness of going P IV 9 202 68
I found it with others still more trivial from different P IV 9 203 70
hastened him away from the concert room, still governed. P IV 10 221 32
"Anne," cried Mary, still at her window, "there is Mrs. P IV 10 222 34
features, and protesting still more positively that it was P IV 10 222 37
Charles and Mary still talked on in the same style; he, P IV 10 224 50
reserving the advantage of still teasing his wife, by P IV 10 225 55
a calmer hour; for while still hearing the sounds he had P IV 10 225 61
still to defer her explanatory visit in Rivers-Street. P IV 11 229 1
heaven had given them wings, by many hours sooner still! P 1 6 235 31
afforded much to be said, but the concert still more. P IV 11 244 71
and I felt that I had still a motive for remaining here." P IV 11 245 76

But, though discomfited and disappointed, he could still P IV 12 250 7
dark, his conversation was still giving information, to S 2 371 1
from the family, still she had given nothing for it."-- S 3 375 1
had no doubt been long, & still continued to be, well S 3 376 1
But you know, (still looking back) one loves to look at an S 4 381 1
pleasanter still--Morgan, with his "dinner on table."-- S 5 389 1
& which their groom was leading about still in her sight.-- S 7 394 1
conscious that Lady D. was still talking on in the same S 7 402 1
There was a great deal of surprise but still more pleasure S 9 406 1
Here Mr P. drew his chair still nearer to his sister, & S 9 408 1
or their own, & was still the most alert of the three.-- S 10 414 1

STILL-BORN (1)
a still-born son, nov. 5, 1789; mary, born nov. 20, 1791." P III 1 3 1

STILLNESS (1)
left to the silence and stillness which reigned in it with MP I 9 89 30

STILTON (1)
come in herself for the Stilton cheese, the north E I 10 88 34

STIMULANT (1)
preventing such an examination was an additional stimulant. NA II 8 186 6

STIMULATE (1)
Where Miss Taylor failed to stimulate, I may safely affirm E I 5 37 7

STIMULATED (1)
Oh! if he should be so far stimulated by your genius as to SS I 4 22 17

STIMULATIVE (2)
grew so potent and stimulative, that Fanny found it MP III 9 398 9
Gratifying, however, and stimulative as was the letter in E II 13 266 6

STING (3)
There's the sting. NA II 1 136 48
entirely insensible of the sting; for she calmly replied, " SS II 13 243 39
40

sting of the last word given to you and Miss Fairfax? E III 5 349 27

STINGS (1)
suffering wife, and left him to the stings of conscience. NA II 8 186 6

STIPULATE (2)
"He did not stipulate for any particular sum, my dear SS I 2 9 6
even without the harp, stipulate for what you chose;--and E II 17 301 18

STIPULATED (2)
Mrs. Norris having stipulated for there never being a fire MP I 16 151 1
Almost must be stipulated--for there were vacant spaces--& S 12 426 1

STIPULATION (3)
to make any parading stipulation; but the decent NA II 16 249 2
did not forget that stipulation, and though Mrs. Norris MP I 8 75 1
and only made the usual stipulation of not sitting at the E II 16 291 4

STIR (20)
said I--but all in vain--he would not stir an inch. NA I 8 56 14
And you are never to stir out of doors, till you can prove, PP III 6 300 30
every thing, who will not stir a finger for the MP I 11 111 28
left to sit down and stir the fire in thoughtful vexation. MP I 13 128 33
She would not stir farther from the east-room than the MP II 13 302 12
If they are not put off, he cannot stir. E I 14 120 11
his own house, too wise to stir out; and to hear him say E I 16 138 18
19

I am afraid--they did not stir last spring--I am afraid it E II 12 259 15
own good will, would never stir beyond the park paling.' E II 14 274 30
She would not stir a step, nor drop a hint. E III 3 335 11
"No--I shall not stir. E III 6 365 66
You knew I should not stir till my Lord and master E III 16 457 36
I am not to be allowed to stir;--and yet, I am sure, I am P III 7 56 10
But not a bit did Walter stir. P III 9 80 32
But there was nobody to stir in it. P IV 9 210 98
did not mean to stir, and tried to be cool and unconcerned. P IV 10 222 37
concerned--and would not stir without her for the world. P IV 11 238 45
A thing of this kind soon makes a stir in a lonely place S 1 370 1
about & who I have to deal with, before I stir a finger.-- S 7 399 1
the world, shall you stir a step on any business of mine.-- S 9 411 1

STIRRED (3)
infirm to mix with the world, and never stirred from home. SS I 9 40 2
Mrs. Price, it appeared, scarcely ever stirred out of MP III 10 401 10
imagined even by him, stirred no more; and his daughter E III 6 361 42

STIRRING (6)
her gone before he was stirring in the morning, that he NA II 13 226 25
arrival, without once stirring from her seat, or altering SS II 6 175 1
her resolution of not stirring from Cleveland as long as SS III 7 308 3
till noon, scarcely stirring from her sister's bed, her SS III 7 313 21
soon done--done while Mrs. Bennet was stirring the fire. PP I 15 71 4
of her stirring out of her house in the fogs of December. E I 6 48 40

STIRRUPS (1)
so regularly in their stirrups, and numerous out-riders NA II 5 156 4

STIRS (1)
and depend upon it, Mr. Bingley never stirs without him." PP II 2 141 13

STOCK (5)
have been a very pleasant addition to our own stock here." SS I 2 13 27
all employed in his stock, and so forth; and though, with E I 4 30 20
what she ought to the stock of their scanty comforts. E II 1 155 2
he asked whether we were not got to the end of our stock. E II 9 238 51
at Exeter all the usual stock of accomplishments, and were P III 5 40 45

STOCKED (3)
which I built and stocked myself about ten years ago, for NA II 7 175 15
find your woods by any means worse stocked than they were. MP II 1 181 16
"We are always well stocked, said he, with all the common S 1 367 1

STOCKINGS (6)
Shirts, stockings, cravats and waistcoats faced her in NA II 7 172 2
pair of silk stockings, and came off with the Richardsons." SS III 2 274 16
in her wet shoes and stockings--given Marianne a cold so SS III 6 305 17
stockings, and a face glowing with the warmth of exercise. PP I 7 32 41
My dear, did you change your stockings?" E II 16 294 25
deserted nursery to mend stockings, and dress all the P IV 1 121 3

STOCKS (2)
indeed; for the stocks were at the time so low, that if I SS II 11 225 33
a vessel in the stocks which they all went to look at. MP III 10 403 15

STOKE (3)
it, or the great house at Stoke, if the drawing-room were PP III 8 310 8
and ride over to Stoke, and settle with one of them." MP I 15 148 58
into the rough lanes about Stoke, where what with frost MP II 2 189 5

STOLE (3)
she stepped into bed, she stole gently from her room to NA II 8 188 19
on the downs, she directly stole away towards the lanes; SS I 16 85 15
to herself, she stole a sly look at him, to see how he PP III 1 255 59

STOLEN (6)
their knives and scissars stolen away, and felt no doubt SS I 21 120 6
their nests, or being stolen by a fox, or in the rapid SS III 6 303 10
"How the pleasing plague had stolen on him" he could not MP II 12 292 8
soon; and half an hour stolen afterwards to go over the E III 14 435 5
torn down--apples stolen--caught in the fact; and P III 3 23 28
in finding a proper spot for their stolen Interveiws.-- S 12 426 1

STOMACH (8)
head, a weakened stomach, and a general nervous faintness. SS II 7 185 16
His own stomach could bear nothing rich, and he could E I 2 19 14
and not roast it, for no stomach can bear roast port--I E II 3 171 16
17

every disorder, of the stomach, the lungs or the blood; S 2 373 1
wholesome, I think it a very bad thing for the stomach. S 10 417 1
butter to soften it, it hurts the coats of the stomach. S 10 417 1
Very bad indeed for the coats of the stomach--but there is S 10 417 1
secure the coats of his stomach;--& besides, he only S 10 417 1

STOMACHER (1)
aunt the pattern of a stomacher, or knit a pair of garters E I 10 86 23

STONE (12)
of its massy walls of grey stone, rising amidst a grove of NA II 5 161 24
In the high-arched passage, paved with stone, which NA II 8 188 17
a new-built substantial stone house, with its semi- NA II 11 212 17
Not a stone must be added to its walls, not an inch to its SS I 14 72 7

There is not a stone laid of Fanny's greenhouse, and SS II 11 226 37
chain, the door approached by a flight of stone steps.-- W 322 2
It was a large, handsome, stone building, standing well on PP III 1 245 3
was called away upon business to that horrid man Mr. Stone. PP III 9 319 25
to the spacious stone steps before the principal entrance. MP I 8 83 37
But I left no stone unturned. MP II 2 189 3
a stone to people in general; and the devil of a temper." E I 14 121 13
view at the end over a low stone wall with high pillars, E III 6 360 38

STONE'S (2)
village, and the parsonage-house within a stone's throw. SS II 8 197 22
within a stone's throw of the said knoll and church. MP II 7 241 13

STONE-WORK (1)
and the heaviest stone-work, for painted glass, dirt and NA II 5 162 26

STONES (1)
and snow upon beds of stones, it was worse than any thing MP II 2 189 5

STOOD (84)
Every thing being then arranged, the servant who stood at NA I 9 62 10
attention was claimed by John Thorpe, who stood behind her. NA I 10 75 25
stood among the lookers-on, immediately behind her partner. NA I 10 80 59
said Catherine, as she stood watching at a window. NA I 11 82 8
every thing else, she stood gazing on it in motionless NA II 6 163 1
2
A could sweat stood on her forehead, the manuscript fell NA II 6 170 12
rich in Gothic ornaments, stood forward for admiration. NA II 7 177 19
at the further end of the gallery, stood before her! NA II 9 191 4
from the rest of it, stood the parsonage, a new-built NA II 11 212 17
Eleanor, and only Eleanor, stood there. NA II 13 223 9
She felt that Edward Stood very high in her opinion. SS I 4 21 11
her complexion varied, she stood firm in incredulity and SS I 22 129 15
first engaged, and it has stood the trial so well, that I SS II 2 147 10
of the terms on which they stood with each other, of their SS II 5 174 45
The parties stood thus: the two mothers, though each SS II 12 234 21
22
I could not have stood it. SS II 13 240 17
I only stood at the door, and heard what I could. SS III 2 274 20
and Elinor, while they stood at the window, the gratitude SS III 3 284 24
In what state the affair stood at present between them, SS III 13 366 20
by my mother, and stood to all appearance without a friend SS III 13 367 22
parish in which the castle stood, Mrs Blake, a widow- W 329 9
this sudden reverse;--he stood the picture of W 330 11
of talking to Charles, stood to look at his partner.-- W 331 11
"I thought you were to have stood up with Mr James, the W 336 14
He stood for a few seconds, in silent amazement.-- W 355 28
"What's your game?"--cried he, as they stood round the W 358 28
Mr. Darcy stood near them in silent indignation at such a PP I 6 25 25
we stood--the sort of preference which was often given me." PP I 16 80 32
They stood for some time without speaking a word; and she PP I 18 91 8
Kitty followed, but Lydia stood her ground, determined to PP I 20 114 31
She stood several minutes before the picture in earnest PP III 1 250 47
his character, and as she stood before the canvas, on PP III 1 251 48
They stood a little aloof while he was talking to their PP III 1 251 52
herself not tired, and they stood together on the lawn. PP III 1 257 66
any, it could hardly have stood its ground against the PP III 2 261 5
He stood by her, however, for some minutes, in silence; PP III 12 342 25
"Good gracious!" cried Mrs. Bennet, as she stood at a PP III 17 374 20
the work of a day, but had stood the test of many months PP III 17 376 36
for Mrs. Bennet luckily stood in such awe of her intended PP III 17 378 46
as well as her sister, stood in too much awe of him to PP III 18 384 27
into the park, and make towards the spot where she stood. MP I 7 68 17
and running to where he stood with Miss Crawford and Fanny; MP I 9 89 25
gate and stood there, without seeming to know what to do. MP I 10 101 33
I stood out as long as I could, till the tears almost came MP I 10 105 55
gave her away--her mother stood with salts in her hand, MP II 3 203 29
round from the lane I stood in to the north-east, that is, MP II 7 242 23
diffused, and they all stood about and talked and laughed, MP II 10 273 6
Thomas's thoughts as he stood, and having, in spite of all MP II 10 276 14
Edmund to tell him how she stood affected on the present MP III 6 366 1
something better, and she stood for a moment expecting to MP III 7 377 10
the gentlemen, as they stood at the door, could do more MP III 10 403 13
Fanny stood aghast. MP III 15 438 4
by her brothers, where stood the tea-board never MP III 15 439 9
evils, that she could have stood against a great deal more MP III 16 448 3
in which affairs then stood with the young people. MP III 16 450 9
Miss Bates stood in the very worst predicament in the E I 3 21 4
which I heard to be wholly unmodulated as I stood here." E I 4 33 32
She paused over it, while Harriet stood anxiously watching E I 7 51 4
turned away confused, and stood thoughtfully by the fire; E I 7 53 22
and displeasure, as he stood up, in tall indignation, and E I 8 60 31
32
and we shook hands, and stood talking some time; but I E II 3 178 52
and I answered--and I stood for a minute, feeling E II 3 179 52
Highbury, with Mrs. Weston, stood for Hartfield; and she E II 6 196 1
A very few to-morrows stood between the young people of E III 1 318 12
foot of which the Abbey stood, gradually acquired a E III 6 360 38
It is not every body that would have stood out in such a E III 8 381 15
chaise, and the ostler had stood out and seen it pass by, E III 8 383 31
While he stood, as if meaning to go, but not going--her E III 9 385 5
them, as they had always stood in her estimation, from the E III 11 412 45
with Mr. Elton as he stood before them, could impair.-- E III 19 482 6
Precisely such had the paragraph originally stood from the P III 1 3 2
with Frederick Wentworth, as he stood in her memory. P III 4 28 7
so long as the others all stood about her; but when Louisa P III 10 86 21
He stood his chance for the rest--wrote up for leave of P III 12 108 28
The horror of that moment to all who stood around! P III 12 109 33
It stood the record of many sensations of pain, once P IV 1 123 8
and once, as he had stood in a shop in Bond-Street, he had P IV 3 141 13
He endured too well,--stood too well with everybody. P IV 5 161 29
him and the man who had stood on the steps at Lyme, P IV 7 177 16
He stood, as opposed to Captain Wentworth, in all his own P IV 10 212 1
that he was inviting her to join him where he stood. P IV 11 231 12
The window at which he stood, was at the other end of the P IV 11 231 12
His wife fervently hoped it was--but stood, terrified & S 1 364 1
village of Sanditon, which stood at the foot of the hill S 4 382 1

STOOLS (1)
with their books & camp stools--and in turning the corner S 4 383 1

STOOP (4)
to which I should hardly stoop under any circumstances. LS 12 261 4
in a situation which he must know she would never stoop to. MP II 5 228 69
She had seemed more sensible of Mr. Elton's being to stoop E III 11 414 50
the creation to stoop in charity to a secret engagement.-- E III 14 437 8

STOOPING (5)
so likely to give it as standing and stooping in a hot sun. MP I 7 72 45
do her good after being stooping among the roses; for MP I 7 73 55
of her half-boot, and stooping down in complete occupation E I 10 88 33
the bulky forms and stooping shoulders of the elderly men, E III 2 326 32
strawberries the stooping-- glaring sun--tired to death-- E III 6 358 35

STOOPS (2)
Goldsmith tells us, that when lovely woman stoops to folly, E III 9 387 12
but to die; and when she stoops to be disagreeable, it is E III 9 387 12

STOP (47)
I would not try to stop him, for I knew what his feelings LS 23 284 5
Do let us turn back, Mr. Thorpe; stop and speak to my NA I 9 65 29
"Stop, stop, Mr. Thorpe, she impatiently cried, it is Miss NA I 11 87 53
Stop, stop, I will get out this moment and go to them." NA I 11 87 53
the length of another street, she intreated him to stop. NA I 11 87 53
"Pray, pray stop, Mr. Thorpe.-- NA I 11 87 53
Mr. Thorpe so earnestly to stop; I called out to him as NA I 12 94 8
The entrance of her father put a stop to the civility, NA II 2 139 5
the window; and to have it stop at the sweep-gate was a NA II 14 233 8
and Margaret, unable to stop herself to assist her, was SS I 9 41 7
them in begging her to stop, and she turned round with SS I 16 86 20
and by changing the subject, put a stop to her entreaties. SS I 20 114 43
Marianne's feelings did not stop here. SS II 12 236 39
Her exertions did not stop her; for she soon afterwards SS II 13 241 23
when another lucky stop in Marianne's performance brought SS III 3 281 9
10
I will not reason here--now will I stop for you to SS III 8 321 34
to stop the ruin which had begun before your marriage?-- SS III 11 350 9
blunder, in proposing to stop at the milleners, before she W 322 2
allowed in any attempt to stop him farther, and he PP I 19 105 9
10
and endeavoured to put a stop to the exclamations of her PP I 23 126 4
Stop me whilst you can." PP II 1 136 19
the morning, to stop at the gates and look into the park. PP II 12 195 2
my aunt has got a fancy in her head, nothing can stop her." MP I 12 120 26
Thomas, stop a moment--I have something to say to you." MP II 5 217 11
then called out, "Oh! cousin, stop a moment, pray stop." MP II 9 261 3
passed along, and made no stop any where, till they MP III 7 376 5
Holla--you there--Sam--stop your confounded pipe, or I MP III 7 383 30
He came--not to stop--but to join them; he was asked to MP III 11 408 1
on the side of prudence to stop him or make his progress MP III 17 471 28
obliged to entreat them to stop, and acknowledge her E I 10 89 36
Mr. Elton, I must beg leave to stop at your house, and ask E I 10 89 37
Emma's attempts to stop her father had been vain; and when E I 12 106 59
She tried to stop him; but vainly; he would go on, and say E I 15 129 24
in common honesty to stop and admit that her own behaviour E I 16 136 9
All this spoken extremely fast obliged Miss Bates to stop E II 1 158 11
I shall just go round by Mrs. Cole's; but I shall not stop E II 3 176 50
that nothing should stop me from getting away-- and then-- E II 3 179 52
She was obliged to stop and think. E II 3 179 53
Mr. Knightley cannot stop. E II 10 245 52
not stopped, he would not stop for more than a word--but E III 1 316 4
Stop, stop, let us stand a little back, Mrs. Elton is E III 2 329 45
he had been obliged to stop at her door, and go in for a E III 3 334 7
Stop; Mr. Knightley was standing just here, was not he?-- E III 4 340 19
It was possible that he might stop in his way home, to ask P IV 3 142 17
his knowing where to stop,--it was all the operation of a P IV 3 143 19
I shall not stop. P IV 6 169 29
which you know to be either false or improbable, stop me. P IV 9 206 88

STOPPED (55)
I could not have stopped myself, had I begun. LS 24 291 14
humiliations to which I have stopped within these few days. LS 25 293 4
opposite Union-Passage; but here they were stopped. NA I 7 44 1
as belonging to her, stopped likewise, and Catherine, NA I 8 54 4
to increase till they stopped in Pulteney-Street again, NA I 9 66 32
happiness of being stopped in their way along narrow, NA I 11 88 54
have stopped, I would have jumped out and run after you." NA I 12 94 8
easily forget its having stopped two hours at Petty-France. NA II 5 156 5
taking out his watch, he stopped short to pronounce it NA II 5 162 27
She stopped for a moment, and then added, with great NA II 7 180 34
Wherever they went, some pattened girl stopped to curtsey, NA II 8 184 4
reaching that point, they stopped to look around them, and SS I 16 85 15
least I think"--he stopped a moment; then added in a voice SS II 8 199 39
He stopped. SS II 9 204 18
Again he stopped to recover himself; and Elinor spoke her SS II 9 208 27
When they stopped at the door, Mrs. Jennings recollected SS II 11 220 2
five minutes after it stopped at the door, a punctuality SS II 14 249 9
from Harley-Street, so he stopped over directly, and as SS III 1 257 5
Here he stopped to be thanked; which being done he went on. SS III 1 266 37
with the most contempt, stopped him, by saying, "it is SS III 8 320 30
31
Elinor stopped him with a reproof. SS III 8 332 78
stopped beyond a doubt at the garden gate of the parsonage. W 354 28
well manage before the carriage stopped at Longbourn house. PP I 16 84 59
door, and the carriage stopped at the small gate, which PP II 5 155 3
sometimes coming there stopped her, and instead of PP II 12 195 1
again; her uncle and aunt stopped also, and while the PP III 1 251 50
She stopped--Henry Crawford looked rather foolish, and as MP I 14 136 18
depend on, when she was stopped by Sir Thomas's saying MP II 7 245 34
This would not do; she immediately stopped, under pretence E I 10 88 33
Vicarage-Lane, or when it stopped, they found themselves, E I 15 132 37
That was well done of me; but there I should have stopped, E I 16 137 11
while warm from her heart, for he stopped to hand her out. E II 8 213 7
He stopped.-- E II 15 287 29
also at Mrs. Weston; but stopped, on perceiving that Mrs. E II 16 297 48
In this style she ran on; never thoroughly stopped by any E II 17 302 21
22
She was stopped by a slight fit of coughing, and Mr. E II 18 308 29
as he passed--he had not stopped, he would not stop for E III 1 316 4
They had stopped at Mrs. Bates's door to offer the use of E III 2 320 6
She was stopped by a cough. E III 7 373 42
have judged better, she thought, if he had not stopped.-- E III 9 386 7
She stopped to breathe. E III 10 395 31
He stopped at Highbury, at the bates's, I fancy, some time- E III 10 398 57
And, after proceeding a few steps, she added--"I stopped E III 13 429 32
He stopped in his earnestness to look the question, and E III 13 430 34
He stopped.-- E III 18 472 21
Mr. Musgrove, who just stopped and spoke through the P III 5 38 29
found him, when they were stopped by the eldest boy's P III 7 53 2
the little grounds, and stopped for no other purpose than P III 10 83 4
down, politely drew back, and stopped to give them way. P III 12 104 6
This decision checked Mary's eagerness, and stopped her P IV 2 133 24
He stopped. P IV 8 182 9
She stopped, regretting with a deep blush that she had P IV 9 197 34
"I am not yet so much changed," cried Anne, and stopped, P IV 10 225 60
Their preparations, however, were stopped short. P IV 10 226 63
opposite to them, & they all stopped for a few minutes. S 12 425 1

STOPPING (21)
Thorpe; and this lady stopping to speak to her, they, as NA I 8 54 4
delay, beyond that of stopping five minutes to order NA II 8 182 1
doors, and without stopping to look or breathe, rushed NA II 9 193 6
could require; and stopping only to change horses, she NA II 14 232 6
They was stopping in a chaise at the door of the new SS III 11 354 27
of the day, without stopping, or I shall not be satisfied. W 341 19
two ladies stopping in a low phaeton at the garden gate. PP II 5 158 13
But perhaps," added he, stopping in his walk, and turning PP II 11 192 22
She had instinctively turned away; but, stopping on his PP III 1 251 52
with either, and just stopping short of the consistence, MP I 12 115 4
But, Fanny,"--stopping her by taking her hand, and MP II 9 268 31
pass quietly away; stopping at the entrance door, like the MP II 10 280 33
"My dearest Henry," cried Mary, stopping short, and MP II 12 297 32
her apartment, till he, stopping short as he entered, said, MP III 1 312 5
before!"--and after stopping to look about her, and MP III 5 358 7
"I do not think it will," stopping to look once more at E I 10 87 27
They were stopping, however, in the first place at Mrs. E II 9 233 25
an arch look, but soon stopping--it was better, however, E II 15 287 26
himself the pleasure of stopping at Hartfield, as he was E III 3 332 2
He began--stopping, however, almost directly to say, "had E III 15 444 6
I can never get by this shop without stopping. P IV 6 169 25

STOPS (1)
to stops, and a very frequent ignorance of grammar." NA I 3 27 32

STOPT (28)
pleasing her; but she was stopt by Miss Tilney's saying, NA II 7 177 17
circumstances"----here he stopt suddenly; appeared to SS I 11 57 17
He stopt. SS I 15 76 16
Mrs. Palmer's barouche stopt at the door, and in a few SS II 4 164 21
He stopt a moment for recollection, and then, with another SS II 9 205 21
be feeling as the carriage stopt at the door,--of her SS III 7 316 30
He stopt. SS III 8 325 46
She stopt.-- SS III 10 344 18
He stopt at their gate. SS III 12 358 8
on perceiving Mr. Darcy he stopt with a bow of superior PP I 18 92 22
After a few minutes, they stopt entirely, Edmund was close MP I 7 67 16
Her conscience stopt her in the middle, but Edmund was MP I 16 156 26

Dr. Grant was in the vestibule, and as they stopt to speak MP II 4 215 47
She stopt, felt herself getting into a puzzle, and could MP III 3 341 27
The moment they stopt, a trollopy-looking maid-servant, MP III 7 377 7
usual up stairs, they were stopt by the knock of a visitor, MP III 10 399 2
He stopt; and, ungentlemanlike as he looked, Fanny was MP III 10 401 11
They often stopt with the same sentiment and taste, MP III 11 409 7
He stopt.-- MP III 16 455 20
leaving the room, and only stopt to say, with a very E I 6 43 10
11
He was afraid not even Miss Woodhouse"--he stopt a moment-- E I 9 71 9
She stopt to blush and laugh at her own relapse, and then E I 16 137 12
Presently the carriage stopt; she looked up; it was stopt E II 5 188 6
instead of passing on, he stopt for several minutes at the E II 6 197 5
He stopt again, rose again, and seemed quite embarrassed.-- E II 12 261 34
She never stopt till she had gone through the whole; and E III 15 444 1
He did so, but very soon stopt again to say, "the piano- E III 15 446 18
even the clergyman--" she stopt a moment to consider what P III 3 20 17

STORE (4)
And from Shakespeare she gained a great store of NA I 1 16 7
a rich reward in store, for every present inconvenience. SS III 7 316 28
"To think of your sending us all your store apples. E II 10 245 52
It was well to have a comfort in store on Harriet's behalf, E II 13 267 8

STORE-HOUSE (1)
she could from this store-house of knowledge, by running NA II 8 182 2

STORE-ROOM (2)
Her store-room she thought might have been good enough for MP I 3 31 59
from the Hartfield store-room must have been poison. E III 11 403 2

STORES (2)
could enrich their intellectual stores at present. E III 6 352 1
to an examination of her stores; and some arrow-root of E III 9 391 20

STORIES (4)
ridiculous stories of an old Irish groom of my uncle's. MP I 10 99 12
and recur to old stories: and he was not without agitation. E III 1 316 4
I hear strange stories of her; she is always upon the gad: P III 6 45 9
histories are against you, all stories, prose and verse. P IV 11 234 27

STORING (1)
He was storing his memory with anecdotes and noble names. PP II 6 166 41

STORM (15)
Manwaring will storm of course, but you may easily pacify LS 9 256 1
She may whimper, & the Vernons may storm; I regard them LS 39 308 1
after your arrival, you will probably have a violent storm. NA II 5 159 19
The storm too abroad so dreadful!-- NA II 6 170 12
The storm still raged, and various were the noises, more NA II 6 170 12
I will hope that the storm may be weathered without our SS III 1 265 36
I shall offer to pay him to-morrow; he will rant and storm PP III 17 377 39
was anxious to get away till the storm was blown over. PP III 18 383 26
as if I could rant and storm, or sigh, or cut capers in MP I 13 123 6
To storm through Baron Wildenhaim was the height of his MP I 14 132 8
and horses to be making their way through a storm of snow." E I 15 126 8
and brilliant after a storm, been more attractive to her. E III 13 424 1
I felt for your dear father very much in the storm of E III 14 436 7
We have all the grandeur of the storm, with less real S 4 381 1
The terrific grandeur of the ocean in a storm, its glassy S 7 396 1

STORMING (1)
Yates is storming away in the dining room. MP I 18 169 21

STORMS (5)
had witnessed, and such storms ushered in; and most NA II 6 166 9
storms and sleeplessness are nothing when they are over. NA II 7 174 5
original strength, has outlived all the storms of autumn. P III 10 88 26
windows and doors against the winter storms to be expected. P III 11 98 17
The Hilliers did not seem to feel the storms last winter S 4 381 1

STORMY (4)
The night was stormy; the wind had been rising at NA II 6 166 9
The night was cold and stormy. SS III 7 316 28
have hoped for after so stormy a morning; but she trusted, MP III 1 324 58
A cold stormy rain set in, and nothing of July appeared E III 12 421 18

STORY (69)
Your friend Mr Smith's story however cannot be quite true, LS 6 252 2
I trust I shall be able to make my story as good as her's. LS 16 268 2
of it however, & told my story with great success to Mrs. LS 22 280 1
I, deeply sighing at the recital of so lame a story. LS 24 287 10
Depend upon it, I can make my own story with Reginald. LS 33 303 1
I cannot suppose that the old story of Mrs Manwaring's LS 35 304 1
provided they were all story and no reflection, she had NA I 1 15 3
marrying her, than at any other part of the story." NA II 10 204 20
He must tell his own story." NA II 11 209 2
the hero of a favourite story; and in his carrying her SS I 9 43 11
The whole story would have been speedily formed under her SS I 11 57 17
till the door was opened before she told her story. SS I 19 106 20
her, in the middle of her story, to receive the rest of SS I 19 106 21
Jennings continued her story as she walked through the SS I 19 106 21
have probably heard the whole story long ago." SS III 8 321 34
fancied him, since the story of that unfortunate girl"----- SS III 10 344 17
of beginning her story directly, or postponing it till SS III 10 345 23
heard Willoughby's story from himself--had she witnessed SS III 11 349 2
from the whole of the story--that all Willoughby's SS III 11 352 16
17
She told the story however with great spirit among her PP I 3 12 14
he soon found that he had a very different story to hear. PP I 3 12 15
with several parts of the story, and has learnt the rest PP I 18 96 55
commanded in telling her story, gave way to a momentary PP I 22 124 14
15
Sir William, how can you tell such a story?-- PP I 23 126 2
at the time, she had the same story to repeat every day. PP II 1 137 26
But, alas! the story which followed of his designs on PP II 13 206 4
country, he had told his story to no one but herself; but PP II 13 207 5
did not know the whole story before the end of the day?" PP III 5 292 63
time--and Miss Crawford, it is plain, has heard the story." MP I 5 50 35
"And a very pretty story it is, and with more truth in it, MP I 5 50 36
a single entertaining story about "my friend such a one." MP I 6 52 1
Fanny would rather have had Edmund tell the story, but his MP I 6 60 47
She told her story. MP I 10 97 2
she made the best of the story, he was evidently mortified MP I 10 101 33
to the end of the story; and when it was over, could give MP II 1 184 25
Her story began; and Fanny immediately slipped out of the MP II 5 218 12
to speak and fill up the blanks in his mother's story. MP II 5 218 16
Fanny, anxious to get the story over, hastened to give the MP II 10 274 9
of the second story, for his mother and for Rebecca. MP III 7 381 26
She had so much to do, that not even the horrible story of MP III 15 443 25
as she wished of the circumstances attending the story. MP III 16 449 7
But as he proceeded in his story, these fears were over. MP III 16 454 18
own story a great deal better than I can tell it for her." E II 1 162 31
as some convenience: the story told well; he had not E II 4 181 4
and thought it a very good story; but that Mrs. Weston did E II 7 205 1
and the substance of the story, the end of all the E II 8 214 13
you know--there is a sad story against them, in general. E II 14 277 38
and her own share in the story, under a colouring the E II 15 282 3
This was the amount of the whole story,--of his E III 3 334 8
asking every day for the story of Harriet and the gipsies, E III 3 336 13
conduct, discretion, and indiscretion, told the same story. E III 5 343 2
It was too old a story.-- E III 6 361 40
story of Jane Fairfax, that was quite sunk and lost.-- E III 11 408 33
yet dread making the story known to Colonel Campbell.'" E III 12 419 8
And old story, probably--a common case--and no more than E III 13 427 19
"It is a very simple story. E III 18 471 20
The same story and the same raptures were repeated, when P III 7 54 5
To finish the interest of the story, the friendship P III 11 97 12
with his wife, had perfectly understood the whole story. P IV 3 139 9
I will tell you the whole story another time. P IV 6 170 29
He told me the whole story. P IV 9 201 59
If there is any thing in my story which you know to be P IV 9 206 88
least the comfort of telling the whole story her own way. P IV 9 210 99
have had every advantage of us in telling their own story. P IV 11 234 28
Those who tell their own story you know must be listened S 3 376 1
& the interest of his story increased very much with the S 3 378 1
pervading hero of the story, it leaves us full of generous S 8 403 1
of the villain of the story outweighed all his absurdities S 8 404 1
But I seem to be spinning out my story to an endless S 9 408 1

STOUT (15)
He was a stout young man of middling height, who, with a NA I 7 45 5
for his health last winter, and came away quite stout." NA I 8 54 7
upon my soul!--stout, active,--looks as young as his son. NA I 12 95 18
Have you a stout heart?-- NA II 5 158 13
her room with a tolerably stout heart; and her spirits NA II 6 167 9
them; and she is very stout and healthy, and hardly forty. SS I 2 10 20
No, no, they must get a stout girl of all works.-- SS III 2 277 28
"Yes--but unless they are so stout as to injure their W 345 21
"Of a fine, stout, healthy love it may. PP I 9 44 34
Lydia was a stout, well-grown girl of fifteen, with a fine PP I 9 45 36
But Baddeley was stout. MP III 1 325 61
"And I, Mr. Knightley, am equally stout in my confidence E I 5 39 22
children, headed by a stout woman and a great boy, all E III 3 333 6
The younger boy, a remarkable stout, forward child, of two P III 9 79 28
Lady D. was of middle height, stout, upright & alert in S 6 391 1

STOUTER (1)
brother & a great deal Stouter--broad made & Lusty--and S 10 413 1

STOUTEST (1)
intent, just then the stoutest of the three; for the very MP II 1 176 3

STOUTLY (7)
Thorpe defended himself very stoutly, declared he had NA I 11 87 53
You talked so stoutly beforehand, that I was sadly afraid W 343 19
"Oh!" said Lydia stoutly, "I am not afraid; for though I PP I 2 8 27
He believed this very stoutly while he was in Mansfield MP II 2 191 10
"No," said Fanny stoutly, "I do not expect it at all." MP II 11 289 35
But this he stoutly denied. MP II 12 292 9
"I am delighted to hear you speak so stoutly on the E III 11 405 13

STOVE (1)
care, a bright Bath stove, mahogany wardrobes and neatly- NA II 9 193 6

STOVES (1)
days, and in the stoves and hot closets of the present. NA II 8 183 3

STRAFFORD (1)
quite unconnected; nothing to do with the Strafford family. P III 3 23 33

STRAGGLER (1)
& then a fresh gentleman straggler, who if not enough in W 328 8

STRAIGHT (9)
I admire them much more if they are tall, straight and SS I 18 98 8
"They come straight from town, as Miss Lucy--Mrs. Ferrars SS III 11 354 36
be half a mile long in a straight line, for we have never MP I 9 94 62
then in (for there was a straight green walk along the MP I 9 96 76
He always speaks to the purpose; open, straight forward, E I 8 59 27
among them, and went straight to the sofa to see what was P III 9 79 28
She could not speak the name, and look straight forward to P IV 1 124 12
brought him out of the straight line to stand near her, P IV 8 181 1
her attention to the orchestra, and look straight forward. P IV 8 188 41

STRAIGHT-FORWARD (2)
"A straight-forward, open-hearted man, like weston, and a E I 1 13 44
but their straight-forward emotions left no room for the E I 15 132 37

STRAIGHTENED (1)
where the passage was straightened by tables, Mrs E. & her W 332 11

STRAIN (5)
From such a moralizing strain as this, she was suddenly NA I 8 55 10
in a very moralizing strain, to observe that our pleasures NA II 11 210 7
Such a strain of shallow artifice could not impose even NA II 12 218 3
I am very apt to get into this sort of wondering strain. MP II 4 209 16
Certainly, there was no strain of doubtful sentiment, nor S 7 399 1

STRAINING (3)
With a cheek flushed by hope, and an eye straining with NA II 6 169 11
one room to another--straining one's eyes and one's MP I 9 95 71
To see them straining away! MP II 2 189 5

STRAINS (2)
strains of the trash with which the press now groans. NA I 5 37 4
Mr. Dashwood's strains were more solemn. SS III 13 371 38

STRAITENED (1)
means will be rather straitened, if the Antigua estate is MP I 3 30 54

STRANGE (85)
What a strange, unaccountable character!--for with all NA I 1 14 1
This was strange indeed! NA I 1 16 10
But strange things may be generally accounted for if their NA I 1 16 10
laughing, "be so-----" she had almost said, strange. NA I 3 28 43
They must think it so strange; so rude of me! to go by NA I 11 87 53
It was a strange, wild scheme." NA I 11 89 62
Catherine thought this reproach equally strange and unkind. NA I 13 98 3
How strange that she should not perceive his admiration! NA II 3 148 28
"This is strange indeed! NA II 6 163 2
prematurely by some strange violence; and, on the centre NA II 6 163 2
If not originally their's, by what strange events could it NA II 6 164 2
The key was in the door, and she had a strange fancy to to NA II 6 168 10
strange that it should fall to her lot to discover it! NA II 6 170 12
was of a piece with the strange unseasonableness of his NA II 8 187 14
it, was not perhaps very strange, and yet that he could NA II 9 190 2
in performing it! this made it so particularly strange! NA II 10 201 5
And how strange an infatuation on Frederick's side! NA II 10 205 30
high, and often produced strange and sudden noises NA II 13 227 26
If, indeed, by any strange mischance his father should NA II 14 231 3
that, "it was a strange business, and that he must be a NA II 14 234 10
that he must be a very strange man," grew enough for all NA II 14 234 10
"This has been a strange acquaintance," observed Mrs. NA II 14 236 15
it would be very strange and unreasonable if he did. SS I 2 12 24
"How strange this is! what can be the meaning of it! SS I 8 39 18
strange and more incompatible with the disposition of both. SS I 14 71 3
But for this strange kind of secrecy maintained by them SS I 14 71 4
"It is all very strange. SS I 15 77 23
that at first seemed strange to me as well as to you." SS I 15 78 24
This is strange indeed, when your eyes have been SS I 15 79 32
"How strange this is! SS I 15 80 38
"But with a strange kind of tenderness, if he can leave SS I 15 80 40
"How strange!" said Marianne to herself as she walked on. SS I 16 88 37
"Strange if it would!" cried Marianne. SS I 17 91 8
to be bold; surfaces strange and uncouth, which ought to SS I 18 97 4
excuse for every thing strange on the part of her son. SS I 19 101 2
abilities, and at the strange unsuitableness which often SS I 21 118 1
"I am sure you think me very strange, for inquiring about SS I 22 128 7
"It is strange," replied Elinor in a most painful SS I 22 131 31
"No; considering our situation, it was not strange. SS I 22 131 32
at the time have appeared strange to every body, and which SS II 9 209 30
My behaviour must have seemed strange to you then; but now SS II 9 210 32
"Something so strange! SS III 1 257 5
That is strange!-- SS III 1 258 7
"This is very strange!--sure he need not wait to be older." SS III 3 281 12
a question, it might be strange that he should feel so SS III 13 361 2
"You are a very strange creature by way of a friend!-- PP I 6 24 22
at her because he disliked her, was still more strange. PP I 10 51 46
"How strange!" cried Elizabeth. PP I 16 81 38
It was very strange that he should come to Longbourn PP I 23 128 11
"That is very strange. PP II 6 164 24
It would have been strange if they had. PP II 17 228 35
How strange must it appear to him! PP III 1 252 54
"How strange this is! PP III 7 304 34
"La! you are so strange! but I must tell you how it went PP III 9 318 24
But it is so strange!" PP III 15 364 23
The place became less strange, and the people less MP I 2 17 21
How strange!-- MP I 2 18 23
What strange creatures brothers are! MP I 6 59 43
not go, and the very strange appearance there would MP I 8 78 23

"A strange business this in America, Dr. Grant!-- MP I 12 119 22
He told the whole, and she had only to add, "so strange! MP II 5 218 16
"This is very strange!" said Sir Thomas, in a voice of MP III 1 315 27
Here was another strange revolution of mind!-- MP III 9 393 1
And the consequence was, that Fanny, strange as it was-- MP III 10 401 10
Fanny, strange as it was--strange, awkward, and MP III 10 401 10
for her to understand much of this strange letter. MP III 15 438 4
It was very strange! MP III 15 438 6
There was a strange rumour in Highbury of all the little E I 2 19 15
indeed--and really it is strange; it is out of the common E I 9 74 25
"Well," said she to herself, "this is most strange!-- E I 13 111 13
ill behind!-- most strange indeed!-- but there is, I E I 13 111 13
What a strange thing love is! he can see ready wit in E I 13 111 13
The difficulty was great of driving his strange E I 13 111 13
bear to think of--and in strange hands--a mere common E I 14 118 4
which must make it very strange to be in different E I 15 132 38
But I believe I am nice; I do not like strange voices; and E II 1 159 20
It was through a series of strange blunders!" E II 14 279 54
Did you ever hear any thing so strange? E III 2 331 54
that supposing--that if--strange as it may appear--. E III 11 404 6
What ever strange things I said or did during that E III 11 407 28
him first for something strange, and then, in few words, E III 14 439 8
It would have been strange if I had not gone." E III 17 465 28
nursery-maid: I hear strange stories of her; she is always P III 5 39 37
eye will seek; and a very strange stranger it must be, who P III 6 45 9
"It was very strange!--very remarkable!--very P III 11 95 9
S 10 419 1

STRANGE-LOOKING (1)
There goes a strange-looking woman! NA I 2 23 21

STRANGELY (4)
much advantage; but was strangely harassed by a queer, NA I 3 26 22
how strangely mysterious!--the door was still immoveable. NA II 6 168 10
that, you know, things are strangely misrepresented." PP III 10 327 14
long watching for, and long thinking strangely delayed. MP III 3 344 42

STRANGENESS (2)
must be in liquor;--the strangeness of such a visit, and SS III 8 318 16
17
The strangeness of Mr. Collins's making two offers of PP I 22 125 18

STRANGER (34)
This question answered, as it readily was, the stranger NA I 4 31 2
Though we have not known him long, he is no stranger in SS I 15 81 44
I am a stranger here, & know nobody but the Edwardses; my W 320 2
least, a nobleman & a stranger, was really distressing.-- W 344 21
"So Emma, said he, you are quite the stranger at home. W 351 26
his wife's views on the stranger would be disappointed; PP I 3 12 15
"The person of whom I speak, is a gentleman and a stranger. PP I 13 61 3
"A gentleman and a stranger! PP I 13 61 3
by the sight of the stranger, and Elizabeth happening to PP I 15 73 8
her contemplation of one stranger was soon put an end to PP I 15 73 11
the stranger, were become "stupid, disagreeable fellows." PP I 15 74 11
From this day you must be a stranger to one of your PP I 20 112 19
to a stranger, and wondered it had escaped her before. PP II 13 207 5
Instead of viewing them as a stranger, I might have PP III 1 246 6
they could have little to fix the attention of a stranger. PP III 1 250 47
speaking) a stranger to our family, should have been PP III 9 320 33
I am no stranger to the particulars of your youngest PP III 14 357 62
be less unpleasant to me than to have a perfect stranger." MP I 15 148 59
Consider what it would be to act Amelia with a stranger. MP I 16 154 14
to be acting with a stranger; and as she probably engaged MP I 16 154 14
A stranger among them would have been the destruction of MP I 17 158 2
the presence of a stranger superior to Mr. Yates must have MP II 2 194 21
Stranger things have happened. MP II 11 289 34
stranger, from what he was in his own family at home. MP III 10 402 12
"My dear sir, do not make a stranger of me." E I 8 57 4
"One would rather have a stranger preferred than one's E II 6 202 33
friend--with a stranger it might not recur again--but the E II 6 202 33
But stranger things have happened; and when we cease to E II 13 267 7
She was almost sure that for a young woman, a stranger, a E II 14 270 4
to be snatched off by a stranger without alliance or P III 4 27 3
seek; and a very strange stranger it must be, who does not P III 11 95 9
She had before conjectured him to be a stranger like P III 12 104 7
to have been only a stranger on each side as to which P IV 2 129 2
Mrs G.-- being a stranger at Sanditon, was anxious for a S 10 419 1

STRANGER'S (3)
All were struck with the stranger's air, all wondered who PP I 15 72 8
the town, are what the stranger's eye will seek; and a P III 11 95 9
But the stranger's pace did not allow this to be S 9 406 1

STRANGERS (22)
slighted for strangers, I, who love you so excessively! NA I 13 98 2
friendship by strangers, does cut me to the quick, I own. NA I 13 98 2
two entire strangers of the party, and wished for no more. SS I 7 34 4
no affection for strangers, no profession, and no SS I 17 90 4
I am so little at my ease among strangers of gentility!" SS I 17 94 42
"Well," said he, "we have brought you some strangers. SS I 19 105 14
introduced the two strangers; Mrs. Dashwood and Margaret SS I 19 106 21
Poor fellow!--to see him in a circle of strangers!--to be SS III 5 299 35
if I can--but you know they will be all strangers to me." W 320 2
were therefore all but strangers to her, & tho' her W 322 3
her brothers & sisters strangers to Emma, but in her W 348 23
"I should like to know how he behaves among strangers." PP II 8 174 17
but I am ill qualified to recommend myself to strangers." PP II 8 175 21
world, is ill-qualified to recommend himself to strangers. PP II 8 175 22
We neither of us perform to strangers." PP II 8 176 26
the sight of so many strangers threw her back into herself; MP II 10 273 7
to marry--and to marry strangers too--and the other half E II 3 177 51
Now they were as strangers; nay, worse than strangers, for P III 8 64 3
of being oppressed by the presence of so many strangers. P III 11 99 22
Strangers filling their place!" P IV 1 126 18
and all this among strangers--with the absolute necessity P IV 5 154 9
calculated to make the strangers easy--and as Mrs P--was S 1 370 1

STRANGEST (4)
"That is the most unpromising circumstance, the strangest NA II 10 206 31
It must have the strangest appearance! MP I 8 78 23
The strangest things do take place!" E I 9 74 24
But now, the matter has taken the strangest turn of all; P IV 6 171 33

STRAPPERS (1)
No want of under strappers----- MP I 13 129 38

STRATAGEMS (1)
be reduced to tricks and stratagems to find it out." PP III 9 320 34

STRAW (2)
on the welfare of her new straw bonnet:--and she was NA II 5 161 25
The shops were deserted--the straw hats & pendant lace S 6 389 1

STRAWBERRIES (8)
Come, and eat my strawberries. E III 6 354 8
and gather the strawberries ourselves, and sit under trees; E III 6 355 20
When you are tired of eating strawberries in the garden, E III 6 355 21
accepting, or talking--strawberries, and only strawberries, E III 6 358 35
and only strawberries, could now be thought or spoken of.-- E III 6 358 35
of all--price of strawberries in London--abundance about E III 6 358 35
objection to gathering strawberries the stooping-- glaring E III 6 358 35
except that you were too late for the best strawberries. E III 7 368 5

STRAWBERRY (1)
as the others did, and collect round the strawberry beds.-- E III 6 358 35

STRAWBERRY-BEDS (1)
Donwell was famous for its strawberry-beds, which seemed a E III 6 354 9

STRAWS (2)
I will answer for it he never cared three straws about her. PP II 16 220 14
"But Miss Bertram does not care three straws for him; that MP I 5 45 14

STRAY (2)
from exercise, or a stray letter-boy on an obstinate mule, E II 9 233 24
stray letter near him, how beautifully Emma had written it. E III 5 347 20

STRAYING (1)
She played till Fanny's eyes, straying to the window on MP II 4 207 6

STREAKS (1)
cups and saucers wiped in streaks, the milk a mixture of MP III 15 439 9

STREAM (11)
hill;-- and in front, a stream of some natural importance PP III 1 245 3
overspreading many, and occasionally part of the stream. PP III 1 253 57
allowed room only for the stream, and a narrow walk amidst PP III 1 253 57
parts of the stream where there was usually most sport. PP III 1 255 60
But the woods are fine, and there is a stream, which, I MP I 6 56 26
rising hills; a small stream before me to be forded, a MP II 7 241 13
Then the stream--something must be done with the stream; MP II 7 242 23
to meadows washed by a stream, of which the Abbey, with E III 6 358 35
The stream is as good as at first; the little rubbish it P IV 9 204 82
to an inconsiderable stream, & formed at its mouth, a 3d S 4 383 1
very fine dark coloured stream--and at the same moment, S 10 417 1

STREAMED (1)
only by the tears which streamed from her eyes with SS II 9 202 8

STREET (70)
Wigmore Street, till she becomes a little more reasonable. LS 2 246 1
days last week, & called several times in Edward Street. LS 9 256 1
running away from Wigmore Street, she resolved on getting LS 19 273 1
progress down the street from the drawing-room window; NA I 4 34 7
point; it is indeed a street of so impertinent a nature, NA I 7 44 1
heard a carriage in the street, or saw a speck upon her NA I 9 60 1
one, but they break down before we are out of the street. NA I 9 61 1
street, and there I can only go and call on Mrs. Allen." NA I 10 79 54
watched him down the street, when her notice was claimed NA I 11 84 17
on her brother's arm, walking slowly down the street. NA I 11 87 53
Still, however, and during the length of another street, NA I 11 87 53
as she retired down the street, could not withhold one NA I 12 91 3
At the bottom of the street, however, she looked back NA I 12 91 3
new writing-desk from being thrown out into the street.-- NA II 5 155 4
Sir John met him somewhere in the street this morning." SS II 5 171 38
Bond street, January. my dear SS II 7 183 13
Berkeley Street, January. how surprised you will be, SS II 7 186 38
day, when she saw him crossing the street to the house. SS II 10 218 26
at the other end of the street, on whom she ought to call; SS II 11 220 2
Mr E. lived in the best house in the street, & the best in W 322 2
street, & he came ready to tell what ever might interest.-- W 323 3
the window to examine the street, & was on the point of W 338 17
Their eyes were immediately wandering up in the street in PP I 15 72 7
led the way across the street, under pretence of wanting PP I 15 72 8
and Darcy and Bingley were seen riding down the street. PP I 15 72 8
Jones's shop boy in the street, who had told her that they PP I 15 73 11
he walked up and down the street, and had Mr. Wickham PP I 15 74 11
that day in Grosvenor street, where Mr. Hurst had a house. PP I 21 116 8
a place as Gracechurch street, but he would hardly think a PP II 2 141 13
a gentleman and lady in a curricle, driving up the street. PP III 1 260 1
with me to Gracechurch street, and then we may consult PP III 5 288 37
brother, and persuaded him to come to Gracechurch street. PP III 6 295 5
They were in ---- street. PP III 10 322 2
have been in a bad school for matrimony, in hill street." MP I 5 46 21
The Andersons of Baker Street. MP I 5 49 35
of a street, and you are only a fly in the comparison." MP I 9 94 59
time, did not we? when the hand-organ was in the street? MP II 7 250 59
rattled into a narrow street, leading from the high street, MP III 7 376 6
leading from the high street, and drawn up before the door MP III 7 376 6
She was gone again to the street door, to welcome William. MP III 7 378 10
It is very inconvenient to have no butcher in the street. MP III 7 379 14
for she will open one of the best houses in Wimpole Street. MP III 9 394 1
walking towards the high street, with Mr. Crawford. MP III 10 401 10
were hardly in the high street, before they met her father, MP III 10 401 11
for his daughters' errands in the high street. MP III 10 402 13
I dined twice in Wimpole Street, and might have been there MP III 13 423 2
near Bedford Square; but I forgot their name and street. MP III 14 434 13
it must relate to Wimpole Street and Mr. Crawford, and MP III 15 438 4
"And don't they live in Wimpole Street?" MP III 15 439 11
of Mr. R. of Wimpole Street; the beautiful Mrs. R. whose MP III 15 440 14
had removed from Wimpole Street two or three weeks before, MP III 16 450 8
Very soon after the Rushworths' return to Wimpole Street, MP III 16 450 8
counteracted in Wimpole Street by the influence of Mr. MP III 16 450 9
event in Wimpole Street, to which he felt himself MP III 17 462 4
though irregular, main street of the place; and, as may be E I 10 83 2
She regained the street--happy in this, that though much E II 1 162 33
on the other side of the street, and there are a great E II 5 195 47
coachman can tell you where you had best cross the street." E II 5 195 47
from one end of the street to the other; and though in E II 6 197 3
of asking Mr. Perry; I happened to meet him in the street. E II 9 237 46
said she, beginning again when they were all in the street. E II 9 237 49
"He had seen a group of old acquaintance in the street as E III 1 316 4
upon the still steeper street of the town itself, that it P III 11 95 8
the town, the principal street almost hurrying into the P III 11 95 9
near her, as soon as they were all fairly in the street. P III 12 107 23
in the lowest part of the street; but his evident surprise P III 12 115 68
If you look across the street, you will see Admiral Brand P IV 6 170 29
and distinctly, Captain Wentworth walking down the street. P IV 7 175 4
as to have him in view the greater part of the street. P IV 7 178 28
the way, and this part of street, as being the handsomest P IV 7 179 30

STREET-DOOR (1)
The General attended her himself to the street-door, NA I 13 103 28

STREETS (13)
far as the length of two streets in her journey, when she LS 19 273 1
through those streets which conducted them to the hotel. NA I 2 19 5
If it keeps raining, the streets will be very wet." NA I 11 82 9
the tower threatened, the streets of London flowing with NA I 14 113 39
in a house in one of the streets near Portman-Square. SS II 3 153 1
She saw with the creative eye of fancy, the streets of PP II 18 232 22
and variety, by the streets, the shops, and the children.-- E III 14 435 4
the long course of streets from the old bridge to Camden- P IV 2 135 33
progress through the streets to be, however disagreeable, P IV 2 135 34
very plain faces he was continually passing in the streets. P IV 3 141 13
Such scare-crows as the streets were full of! P IV 3 142 13
old friend or other; the streets full of them every P IV 6 170 29
have passed along the streets of Bath, than Anne was P IV 9 192 3

STREIGHTENED (1)
This was a cruel aggravation of actually streightened P IV 9 210 98

STREIGHTENS (1)
operation, and it streightens him as to many things. P IV 10 218 22

STREIGHTS (1)
But I never went beyond the Streights--and never was in P III 8 70 52

STRENGTH (66)
on which their strength was founded. R. De Courcy. LS 36 306 2
a continued exertion of strength and ingenuity they found NA I 2 21 9
The strength of her feelings she could not express; the NA I 15 118 8
be the exertion of her strength, that, unless secured by NA II 6 164 3
and tried to turn it; but it resisted her utmost strength. NA II 6 168 10
The strength of these feelings, however, was far from NA II 14 235 14
On the strength of this, the General, soon after Eleanor's NA II 16 252 7
each other, and adding strength to their attachment, I NA II 16 252 7
with all the strength and urgency which illness could SS I 1 5 5
effectual, possessed a strength of understanding, and SS I 1 6 11
"and so much on the strength of your own imagination, that SS I 10 51 27
it; and of the strength of her own, she gave a very SS I 19 104 11
If the strength of your reciprocal attachment had failed, SS II 2 147 8
and with youth, natural strength, and her mother's SS III 10 340 1
and I have recovered my strength," said she, "we will take SS III 10 343 9
did not continue to gain strength as she had done; but SS III 11 352 19
Jane united with great strength of feeling, a composure of PP I 6 21 1
too much, she feared, for the strength of his attachment. PP I 23 129 13
He concluded with representing to her the strength of that PP II 11 189 6
been brought on by the strength of her love, rather than PP III 9 318 19
I know my own strength, and I shall never be embarrassed PP III 12 339 6
Though unworthy, from inferiority of age and strength, to MP I 2 17 21

or walked beyond her strength at the instigation of the MP I 4 36 7
Her merit in being gifted by nature with strength and MP I 7 69 23
"I wish Fanny had half your strength, ma'am." MP I 7 73 54
Luckily the strength of the piece did not depend upon him. MP I 13 122 2
evening afforded him an opportunity of trying his strength. MP I 13 124 14
she might inhale a breeze of mental strength herself. MP I 16 152 3
But her chief strength lay in Sotherton. MP II 2 188 3
indulging on the strength of her brother's description, no MP II 7 248 47
fatigue, to have strength and partners for about half the MP II 9 267 22
Her inclination and strength for more were pretty well at MP II 10 279 22
truth, or at least the strength of her indifference, might MP III 2 328 7
over her with renewed strength, and it seemed as if to be MP III 6 370 11
it, for she wanted strength for a two hours' saunter of MP III 11 409 6
temper, and genuine strength of feeling, made her think it MP III 15 442 21
vanity was not of a strength to fight long against reason. MP III 16 459 31
enough to warrant any strength of language in which he MP III 17 471 28
though strength of understanding must not be expected. E I 4 26 2
I am much mistaken if Emma's doctrines give any strength E I 5 39 15
recovered her usual strength, they must forbid her E II 2 165 9
Her regard was receiving strength by invariable praise of E II 4 184 10
The strength of the song falls on the second." E II 11 229 95
What strength, or what constancy of affection he might be E II 12 262 38
sensations, and think she had undervalued their strength. E II 13 265 5
had been willing to hope, had been lately gaining strength. E II 13 267 8
"It is too small--wants strength. E II 16 297 50
"No, it by no means wanted strength--it was not a large E II 16 297 51
able to speak, had just strength enough to reach Hartfield, E III 3 334 7
scruple of mine with multiplied strength and refinement.-- E III 14 440 8
The strength, resolution, and presence of mind of the Mr. E III 19 484 10
and consequently full of strength and courage, till for a P III 6 49 18
19
for ever, and all the strength of his faults forgotten, P III 6 51 32
as to the fashion and strength of any old pelisse, which P III 8 65 16
Their time and strength, and spirits, were, therefore, P III 10 83 6
the lady shewed her strength, and when he recommended the P III 10 86 17
requiring fortitude and strength of mind, if she have not P III 10 87 26
original strength, has outlived all the storms of autumn. P III 10 88 26
strength apace, and she had nothing else to stay for. P III 11 93 4
tone of despair, and as if all his own strength were gone. P III 12 110 35
Anne, attending with all the strength and zeal, and P III 12 111 44
its weakness and not its strength that appears in a sick P IV 5 156 11
stronger because her strength was not tried, was quite P IV 7 180 32
years; and that, on the strength of this present income, P IV 10 217 20
the sea, nobody wanted spirits, nobody wanted strength.-- S 2 373 1
& where some degree of strength of mind is given, it is S 9 410 1

STRENGTHEN (3)
her fortitude under it, must strengthen every attachment. SS II 9 210 32
served to strengthen them in believing they had no faults. MP I 4 35 4
try to compose her spirits, and strengthen her mind. MP III 1 322 50

STRENGTHENED (13)
ended, with rather a strengthened belief of there being a NA I 9 64 26
"No," said he, "my father's hands need not be strengthened, NA II 11 209 2
and strengthened her distaste for every thing before her. NA II 13 228 27
influence there, strengthened her expectation of the event. SS II 14 254 28
acknowledged, and now strengthened by the hollow eye, the SS III 10 340 2
On the contrary, with a mind and body alike strengthened SS III 10 343 8
to being obliged, were strengthened by the sight of MP I 16 153 3
them; and the hope strengthened when it was understood E I 2 18 9
the conviction was strengthened by what followed. E II 5 191 26
argumentative mind might have strengthened yours." E II 12 260 26
such a proof in her of strengthened character, and E III 9 388 14
was certainly much strengthened by one part, and a very P III 2 15 13
him; her nerves were strengthened by these circumstances; P IV 7 180 32

STRENGTHENER (1)
An advantage this, a strengthener of love, in which even MP II 6 234 18

STRENGTHENING (2)
She feared it was a strengthening regard. SS II 5 169 12
of strengthening his views in favour of Northamptonshire. MP II 7 247 37

STRENUOUS (1)
strenuous opposer of Sir Walter's making a second match. P IV 9 208 92

STRENUOUSLY (3)
I should have advised her most strenuously to engage one. PP II 6 165 32
of Longbourn, I should very strenuously have opposed it. PP III 15 364 22
"Mr. Wingfield most strenuously recommended it, sir--or we E I 12 101 21

STRESS (2)
and having a particular stress on those words, "that your SS II 2 150 34
"Do you consider the forms of introduction, and the stress PP I 2 7 18

STRETCH (9)
It was the greatest stretch of forbearance I could LS 24 291 14
and more open, a long stretch of the road which they had SS I 16 85 15
Mr. Hurst had therefore nothing to do, but to stretch PP I 11 54 3
which asked no extraordinary stretch of belief. PP III 10 326 3
when there was any stretch of road behind them, or when he MP I 8 81 31
I admit to be sometimes too hard a stretch upon the mind. MP I 9 88 18
I assure you the utmost stretch of public fame would not E II 6 200 16
became for a considerable stretch very retired; and when E III 3 333 5
The horror and distress you were involved in--the stretch P IV 8 183 15

STRETCHED (6)
have stretched much farther than your candour. SS I 10 51 24
newspaper, stretched himself, and looked at them all round. SS I 19 108 37
door, she saw Marianne stretched on the bed, almost choked SS II 7 182 12
She saw all the glories of the camp; its tents stretched PP II 18 232 22
to say, with his hand stretched towards Fanny's head, "do MP II 6 235 19
and without dignity, was stretched before them; an P III 10 85 14

STRETCHING (4)
through a beautiful wood, stretching over a wide extent. PP III 1 245 2
ample gardens stretching down to meadows washed by a E III 6 358 35
avenue of limes, which stretching beyond the garden at an E III 6 360 38
line of cliffs stretching out to the east of the town, are P III 11 95 9

STREWED (2)
to a pillow strewed with thorns and wet with tears. NA I 11 90 65
strewed with his litter of books, guns, and great coats. NA II 8 183 2

STRICT (18)
state are not so strict as your partner might wish? NA I 10 77 37
a minute to receive a strict charge against taking her NA II 7 181 41
who was then abroad, had left strict orders on that head. SS I 12 62 28
far from him as she could, and maintained a strict silence. SS III 12 359 13
The division of gratifying sensations ought not, in strict MP I 1 8 9
the first, fancied a very strict line of economy necessary; MP I 1 8 9
But dear Maria has such a strict sense of propriety, so MP I 12 117 14
His sense of decorum is strict." MP I 13 127 26
two, and shall give her a strict charge to be on the look- E II 17 300 10
None of that upright integrity, that strict adherence to E III 10 397 48
of this one great deviation from the strict rule of right. E III 10 400 65
She was of strict integrity herself, with a delicate sense P III 2 11 2
correct in her conduct, strict in her notions of decorum, P III 2 11 2
He is so very strict and scrupulous in his notions; over- P III 12 103 2
too strict to suit the unfeudal tone of the present day! P IV 3 139 7
thoughtless, gay set, without any strict rules of conduct. P IV 9 201 64
some Aberration from the strict line of Primitive S 8 403 1
Mrs G. did never deviate from the strict Medecinal page.-- S 11 422 1

STRICTER (1)
of income by the evident necessity of stricter economy. MP I 3 23 1

STRICTEST (7)
convinced her that the strictest punctuality to the family NA II 5 162 27
the strictest legal covenant had bound us to each other." SS II 7 188 44
discharged it in the strictest sense, by watching over her SS II 9 208 28
and established all his strictest notions of what was due PP I 15 70 3
of the day might stand the strictest investigation. MP II 3 203 29
He pressed for the strictest forbearance and silence MP III 2 332 20
again soon, and that the strictest injunctions had been P IV 11 229 2

STRICTLY (7)
increasing them, if not strictly reasonable, is too common LS 30 300 2
I clearly understand it now, and I will strictly fulfil my SS I 2 12 25
strictly attending to her views for his aggrandizement. SS I 4 22 18
were strictly honourable, and my feelings blameless. SS III 8 321 34
"The conduct of neither, if strictly examined, will be PP III 16 367 13
Mr. Dixon, you say, is not, strictly speaking, handsome." E II 3 176 46
speak more openly than might have been strictly correct.-- E III 16 459 46

STRICTURES (1)
What would I give to hear your strictures on them!" PP I 6 27 47

STRIKE (25)
must be childish indeed, if such things do not strike her. LS 17 271 7
myself to dwell on them; they will strike you sufficiently. LS 24 291 14
The name seemed to strike them all; and, after speaking to NA I 4 32 4
of her power; she could strike out nothing new in NA I 9 64 27
will so incomprehensibly strike you, that you will not be NA II 5 158 17
did not strike her less than the number of their offices. NA II 8 184 4
in the gallery before the clocks had ceased to strike. NA II 9 193 6
Come, Miss Marianne, let us strike hands upon the bargain, SS II 3 154 4
fond of you, but so it happened to strike her. SS II 11 227 50
to his friend seemed to strike him forcibly, and his eyes PP I 18 92 24
In what a disgraceful light might it not strike so vain a PP III 1 252 54
felt that he would probably strike into some other path. PP III 1 254 57
either side; and it might strike them that they could be PP III 5 282 7
strike into another path, she was overtaken by Wickham. PP III 10 327 4
Does not it strike you so, Fanny? MP II 16 155 14
occurrence too common to strike her, and she thought MP III 1 324 60
woman, before it began to strike him whether a very MP III 17 470 25
of the man may very likely strike us with equal force. E I 11 95 18
noise of numbers, was a circumstance to strike him deeply. E II 17 302 23
I wonder the arms did not strike me! P III 12 106 16
and whether it might not strike him, that, like all other P III 12 116 72
marrying for money is too common to strike one as it ought. P IV 9 201 64
those very cases which strike us the most) may be P IV 11 234 30
he must naturally wish to strike out something new, to S 8 405 2
It could not but strike her rather unfavourably with S 12 426 1

STRIKES (7)
It always strikes me as the most comfortable apartment in NA II 9 196 21
"To be sure it is: and, indeed, it strikes me that they SS I 2 10 15
It strikes me as if it would do exactly. MP I 14 132 7
prefer you, because it strikes me, that they have all MP III 14 434 13
softness, but it strikes me that his manners are softer E I 4 34 42
"Exactly so; that is what principally strikes me. E I 6 42 6
than heretofore, it strikes me as a possible thing, Emma, E II 18 312 48

STRIKING (39)
approached its fine and striking environs, and afterwards NA I 2 19 5
striking; but I think I could place them in such a view.-- NA I 10 77 33
it so striking an object from almost every opening in Bath. NA I 14 106 1
awful sensations this striking exemplification of what NA II 6 169 11
which she was treated striking at that instant on her mind NA II 13 228 27
figure is not striking; it has none of that grace which I SS I 3 17 18
At first sight, his address is certainly not striking; and SS I 4 20 9
her figure tall and striking, and her address graceful. SS I 6 31 8
of height, was more striking; and her face was so lovely, SS I 10 46 2
Willoughby, an equally striking opposition of character SS I 10 49 12
sufficiently striking to those of his brother elect. SS I 16 87 23
"I wish," said Margaret, striking out a novel thought, " SS I 17 92 18
her own, she gave a very striking proof, by still loving SS I 19 104 11
times, the most striking resemblance between this baby and SS II 14 248 5
the favour they were in, as must be universally striking. SS II 14 254 28
was not less striking than it had been on him. SS III 5 298 33
by the Orchestra's striking up a favourite air, which W 328 9
and the imprudence of another had indeed been striking.-- W 361 31
"This is no very striking resemblance of your own PP I 18 91 16
At last it arrested her--and she beheld a striking PP III 1 250 47
and niece, that such a striking civility as Miss Darcy's, PP III 2 266 17
nor any other striking beauty; exceedingly timid and shy, MP I 2 12 2
age, which produced as striking a difference between the MP I 2 13 4
nothing more striking or more solemn than the profusion of MP I 9 85 6
for half an hour together without striking it out." MP I 9 94 56
There is nothing very striking in Mr. Rushworth's manners, MP II 2 190 6
Sir Thomas's return made a striking change in the ways of MP II 3 196 1
clock at Mansfield Park, striking three, made her feel MP II 4 214 46
striking out a better)--you may give it a higher character. MP II 7 243 27
can say any thing new or striking, any thing that rouses MP III 3 341 28
There could be nothing very striking, because it is clear MP III 4 350 30
and admire all the striking parts of his dress--listening MP III 7 384 35
His perception of the striking improvement of Harriet's E I 6 42 1
Her name was not mentioned;--and there was so striking a E I 17 140 3
We are rather out of distance of the very striking E II 14 274 29
only in those striking inferiorities, which always brought E III 13 432 41
in company with two men, striking instances of what I am P III 3 19 16
eagerness, was very striking--and very amusing--or very S 7 396 1
& circumstances, however striking at first, involved S 10 419 1

STRIKINGLY (7)
The resemblance between her and her mother was strikingly SS I 1 6 12
Their taste was strikingly alike. SS I 10 47 3
And his behaviour, so strikingly altered,--what could it PP III 1 252 54
I have always thought her pretty--not strikingly pretty-- MP II 6 230 6
right--which church was strikingly large and handsome for MP II 7 241 13
assure you, as far as I could observe, are strikingly like. E II 14 273 21
it had been in the Octagon Room was strikingly great.-- P IV 8 190 47

STRING (5)
the resistless pressure of a long string of passing ladies. NA I 10 76 29
and as soon as the string of carriages before them would SS II 6 175 2
can you give me a bit of string?' and once Henry asked me E I 9 80 72
ribband or string, or any thing just to keep my boot on." E I 10 89 37
over a dirty bone, and a string of dawdling children round E II 9 233 24

STRINGER (1)
that old Stringer & his son have a higher claim. S 4 381 1

STRINGERS (1)
to buy the cheif of our consumption of the Stringers.--" S 4 382 1

STRINGS (2)
of portly chaperons, & strings of smartly-dressed girls W 328 8
Bertram, who might be said to have two strings to her bow. MP I 8 81 33

STRIP (2)
In a long strip of meadow-land, where there was ample P III 10 90 37
little cottage Ornee, on a strip of waste ground Lady D. S 3 377 1

STRIVE (2)
attention; and could strive to rouse her mother to similar SS I 1 7 13
natural, so inevitable to strive against an inclination of E I 17 142 12

STRIVING (8)
in conversation or of striving to improve their SS I 22 127 1
All Meryton seemed striving to blacken the man, who, but PP III 6 294 4
She sat intently at work, striving to be composed, and PP III 11 335 39
If I lose the game, it shall not be from not striving for MP II 7 243 25
knowing his heart, and striving to avoid his confidence, MP III 6 370 12
most unvarying kindness, striving to occupy and amuse her, E I 17 142 10
You are not striving to look taller than any body else. E II 8 214 10
been occupied by them, striving to catch sounds, which yet P IV 11 233 24

STROKE (6)
I counted every stroke. NA I 7 46 9
have given the finishing stroke to what the ill-humour of SS II 14 250 12
What a stroke was this for poor Jane! who would willingly PP II 17 224 9
This was a stroke of civility for which she was quite PP III 1 254 58
each was feeling it a stroke the most unwelcome, most ill- MP II 1 175 1
have been quite without resentment under such a stroke. E III 16 451 2

STROKES (1)
made one of the cleanest strokes that perhaps ever was NA I 12 96 20

STROLL (7)
invited them to take a stroll in the garden, which was PP II 5 156 4
that when the evening stroll was over, and the two MP I 7 65 14
former pain; and many a stroll and many a sigh were P III 4 30 10

agreed to stroll down to the sea before breakfast.-- P III 12 102 1
They came also for a stroll till breakfast was likely to P III 12 103 5
Anne return from any stroll of solitary indulgence in her P IV 2 133 26
stroll on the cliff gave way to an immediate return home.-- S 6 390 1

STROLLING (3)

Her ladyship is comforting herself meanwhile by strolling LS 15 267 4
to be met with, strolling about near home, was their P III 10 85 13
groom, who was strolling about near the two inns as they P III 12 104 7

STRONG (189)

His admiration was at first very strong, but no more than LS 8 255 2
dark lank hair, and strong features;--so much for her NA I 1 13 1
confirmation strong, "as proofs of Holy Writ." NA I 1 16 7
with a strong inclination for continuing the acquaintance. NA I 3 29 52
My attachments are always excessively strong. NA I 6 40 14
With real interest and strong admiration did her eye now NA I 10 80 60
and John is just the same; he has amazing strong feelings. NA I 11 90 64
I am sure they are too strong for my own peace; and to see NA I 13 98 2
of delight were so strong, that without waiting for any NA II 7 177 19
Open, candid, artless, guileless, with affections strong NA II 10 206 31
this little excursion, so strong was her desire to be NA II 11 210 7
material passages of her letter with strong indignation. NA II 12 218 4
Mr. John Dashwood had not the strong feelings of the rest SS I 1 5 6
But Mrs. John Dashwood was a strong caricature of himself;- SS I 1 5 7
and her feelings were strong; but she knew how to govern SS I 1 6 11
in that respect as earnest, as his abilities were strong. SS I 10 49 10
To her it was but the natural consequence of a strong SS I 11 54 4
"Months!" cried Marianne, with strong surprise. SS I 16 85 13
very easily;--with strong affections it was impossible, SS I 19 104 11
their party would be too strong for opposition, and that SS I 21 124 33
been as painful as it was strong, had not an immediate SS I 22 129 15
was such a proof, so strong, so full, of the importance of SS II 3 155 6
a strong sensibility, and the graces of a polished manner. SS II 9 201 4
strong resemblance between them, as well in mind as person. SS II 9 205 23
24
an affection for him as strong, still as strong as her own, SS II 9 210 32
him as strong, still as strong as her own, and with a mind SS II 9 210 32
said she repeatedly, with a strong emphasis on the word. SS II 10 217 21
of a person and face, of strong natural, sterling SS II 11 220 3
mother without that strong anxiety which had once promised SS II 12 230 6
by giving it the strong characters of pride and ill nature. SS II 12 232 15
horror; and urged by a strong impulse of affectionate SS II 12 236 39
40
of her feelings, strong in itself, and strongly spoken. SS II 13 242 23
seem strong, feel all her own disappointment over again. SS III 1 261 11
late discovery, nor her strong desire to affront her by SS III 5 294 3
have represented it to Edward in a very strong light. SS III 5 300 37
With strong concern, and with many reproaches for not SS III 7 313 20
within Elinor's breast was satisfaction, silent and strong. SS III 7 315 24
up to the house; and so strong was the persuasion that she SS III 7 316 29
no sentiment superior to strong esteem and lively SS III 14 378 15
communication which strong family affection would SS III 14 380 21
"She had not thought a strong likeness at all incompatible W 324 3
Every thing nourishes what is strong already. PP I 9 44 34
which often expose a strong understanding to ridicule." PP I 11 57 22
herself, and making a strong effort for it, was able to PP I 22 125 16
"I must think your language too strong in speaking of both, PP II 1 136 14
half-hour's acquaintance, as to a real strong attachment. PP II 2 140 8
to say, that there is a strong appearance of duplicity in PP II 3 148 26
cannot have a right to such very strong local attachment. PP II 9 179 23
"I understood that there were some very strong objections PP II 10 185 30
"There were some very strong objections against the lady," PP II 10 186 39
words, and these strong objections probably were, her PP II 10 186 39
to have inspired unconsciously so strong an affection. PP II 11 193 31
heart retained a strong impression of his kindness to her PP II 12 201 5
hope of revenging himself on me, was a strong inducement. PP II 12 202 5
With a strong prejudice against every thing he might say, PP II 13 204 1
"But I hope there is no strong attachment on either side," PP II 16 220 13
Miss Bennet's astonishment was soon lessened by the strong PP II 17 224 2
have used such very strong expressions in speaking of PP II 17 226 20
and to Mrs. Gardiner it had a peculiarly strong attraction. PP II 19 239 7
far from expecting them to make so strong an impression. PP III 16 368 15
affectionate heart, and a strong desire of doing right; MP I 2 16 20
character of Edmund, his strong good sense and uprightness MP I 2 20 33
from her, as no feelings could be strong enough to pay. MP I 4 37 8
He wrote in April, and had strong hopes of settling every MP I 4 40 14
and, indeed, his being the eldest was another strong claim. MP I 5 47 27
"Ungrateful is a strong word. MP I 7 63 7
she, as she sprang down with his help; "I am very strong. MP I 7 68 20
You know I am strong enough now to walk very well." MP I 7 70 29
and though the sun was strong, it was not so very hot. MP I 7 73 55
proof as she has given, that her feelings are not strong." MP I 12 116 10
an itch for acting so strong among young people, that he MP I 13 121 2
It gave her a very strong claim on my good will." MP I 16 156 24
though irrational hope, with a strong sense of ill-usage. MP I 17 162 19
Yet, how strong the impression that only a few weeks will MP II 3 197 4
him was sometimes very strong; he could look back on a MP II 8 255 10
forward to with a more equal degree of strong interest. MP II 8 256 13
had not words strong enough to satisfy her own humility. MP II 9 264 18
and the impression was so strong, that though her uncle MP II 10 275 11
She was afraid she had used some strong--some contemptuous MP II 11 286 15
said, and feared its too strong effect on him, she now MP II 11 286 17
Her affections were evidently strong. MP II 12 294 16
had been, and used such strong expressions, was so MP II 13 300 7
You are not strong. MP III 1 312 10
said she with another strong effort, "but I am so MP III 1 320 43
he had given her another strong motive for exertion, in MP III 1 322 50
her brother, she must have a strong feeling of gratitude. MP III 2 328 7
But taste was too strong in her. MP III 3 337 10
The dissimilarity is not so strong. MP III 4 348 23
Crawford's ideas; by the strong effect on her mind which MP III 5 357 6
as might warrant strong suspicion in a predisposed mind. MP III 5 362 17
she must have had a strong attack of them, when she first MP III 6 369 11
suddenly seized with a strong inclination to go with them-- MP III 6 372 21
no motive for writing, strong enough to overcome the MP III 7 376 4
in which he had a strong right of interest, being to MP III 7 377 8
feel yourself at all less strong, or comfortable than MP III 11 411 16
books, which had been so strong in Fanny, with a MP III 12 418 7
sake, she had so strong a desire of not appearing ignorant, MP III 12 418 7
Her prejudices, I trust, are not so strong as they were. MP III 13 422 2
with respect to some strong hectic symptoms, which seemed MP III 14 429 1
there must have been some strong indiscretion, since her MP III 15 438 6
with happiness, so strong in that best of blessings, an MP III 16 448 3
undoubted attachment, and strong probability of success; MP III 16 452 15
The high spirit and strong passions of Mrs. Rushworth MP III 17 464 10
pleasure was too strong for a mind unused to make any MP III 17 467 20
feelings on her side, more strong than he had supposed.-- MP III 17 468 21
each other, their mutual attachment became very strong. MP III 17 472 30
by sweetness of temper, and strong feelings of gratitude. MP III 17 472 31
that any caprice could be strong enough to affect one so E I 2 17 7
strong a likeness of his cockade as you would wish to see. E I 6 45 21
though plain, was strong and unaffected, and the E I 7 50 4
is too strong and concise; not diffuse enough for a woman. E I 7 51 5
the result with impatience, but not without strong hopes. E I 7 53 22
of a strong passion at war with all interested motives. E I 8 67 57
themselves into as strong and steady an attachment as her E I 9 69 2
She was not a woman of strong understanding or any E I 11 92 4
and a strong habit of regard for every old acquaintance. E I 11 92 4
and generally a strong sense of what was due to him; but E I 11 93 5
"There was a strong expectation of his coming soon after E I 11 95 21
man, than a man of strong feelings; he takes things as he E I 11 96 26
and valuable in the strong domestic habits, the all- E I 11 97 27
part of his life, and whose attachments were strong. E I 12 100 16
Will not the old prejudice be too strong?" E I 12 104 44
"Mr. Perry," said he, in a voice of very strong E I 12 106 60
snowing fast, with a strong drifting wind; concluding with E I 15 125 7
and it needed a very strong effort to appear attentive and E I 15 133 38
He may have as strong a sense of what would be right, as E I 18 148 19
"Then, it would not be so strong a sense. E I 18 148 20
you must have had very strong eyes to see as you do--and E II 1 158 10
what had appeared to him strong encouragement; and not E II 4 181 3
other, which had taken strong possession of her mind, had E II 5 192 33
were the persons; and I thought it a very strong proof." E II 6 202 30
"Certainly--very strong it was; to own the truth, a great E II 6 202 31
say that their petticoats were all very strong.'" E II 8 225 78
I have a very strong notion that it comes from him. E II 8 226 83
It was hardly right; but it had been so strong an idea, E II 9 231 2
Emma is not strong. E II 11 249 11
father, never to marry, a strong attachment certainly must E II 13 264 1
Her sensibilities, I suspect, are strong--and her temper E II 15 289 40
was not a large hand, but very clear and certainly strong. E II 16 297 51
That is, I always had a strong persuasion he would be here E II 18 308 27
were merely imaginary, or that she was as strong as ever. E III 1 317 6
before they quitted the ball-room, she had strong hopes. E III 3 332 1
I feel a strong persuasion, this morning, that I shall E III 6 365 62
the other parties, too strong for any fine prospects, or E III 7 367 1
The impression of it is strong on my memory." E III 11 406 23
her own appearance, and a strong sense of justice by E III 11 408 33
but her judgment was as strong as her feelings, and as E III 13 431 38
as her feelings, and as strong as it had ever been before, E III 13 431 38
the writer, and the very strong attraction which any E III 15 444 1
was, at this moment, so strong to Emma's feelings, and so E III 18 473 27
Emma's feelings, and so strong was the recollection of all E III 18 473 27
who had been brought, by strong attachment to herself, to P III 1 5 6
father's heir, and whose strong family pride could see P III 1 8 17
woman, and capable of strong attachments; most correct in P III 2 11 2
to me; I have two strong grounds of objection to it. P III 3 19 16
conference, expressed as strong an inclination for the P III 3 21 18
was growing so strong for a removal, that she was happy to P III 3 24 37
want of more money, and a strong inclination for a P III 6 43 5
and mentioning him in strong, though not perfectly well P III 6 52 33
mother were in much too strong and recent alarm to bear P III 7 55 5
"A strong mind, with sweetness of manner," made the first P III 7 62 40
She had a strong impression of his having said, in a vext P III 9 80 34
heavily, uniting very strong feelings with quiet, serious, P III 11 97 12
a little lame; and from strong features, and want of P III 11 97 14
completely; and that the strong feelings which alone could P III 11 100 23
left a very strong impression in his disfavour with me." P IV 2 133 23
the room presented as strong a contrast as could be wished, P IV 2 134 28
was a strong proof of his opinions on the subject. P IV 3 139 7
He had strong feelings of family-attachment and family- P IV 4 146 6
which fancied itself strong feeling; and yet, with a P IV 4 146 6
in Bath, who had the two strong claims on her attention, P IV 5 152 2
as a girl of fourteen, of strong sensibility and not high P IV 5 152 2
A submissive spirit might be patient, a strong P IV 5 154 8
first effects of strong surprise were over with her. P IV 7 175 6
last impressions of Lyme must have been strong disgust." P IV 8 183 15
feelings as to a first, strong attachment,--sentences P IV 8 185 21
careless habits, and not strong understanding, much more P IV 9 209 95
"Ah!" cried Captain Harville, in a tone of strong feeling, P IV 11 234 31
strong sense of duty is no bad part of a woman's portion." P IV 11 246 80
of, under circumstances of otherwise strong felicity. P IV 12 251 10
He had strong reason to beleive that one family had been S 2 372 1
in the world for a man of strong understanding, but not of S 2 372 1
appearance secured a very strong hold in Lady D.'s regard. S 3 379 1
exhibit the progress of strong passion from the first Germ S 8 403 1
we see the strong spark of woman's Captivations elicit S 8 403 1
having by nature a very strong head, the graces, the S 8 404 1
before him--and he felt a strong curiosity to ascertain S 8 405 2
the weak of mind & the strong--between those who can act & S 9 410 1
"What! said he--do you venture upon two dishes of strong S 10 418 1

STRONGER (48)

What stronger proof of her dangerous abilities can be LS 8 255 1
But I believe my feelings are stronger than any body's; I NA I 13 98 2
partial though stronger illumination of a treacherous lamp. NA II 9 190 1
a yet stronger interest, would have left it unwillingly. NA II 9 191 3
having a stronger head, they have not yet injured himself. NA II 12 218 7
Believe them to be stronger than I have declared; believe SS I 4 21 15
"On the contrary, nothing can be a stronger proof of it, SS I 13 68 72
She was stronger alone, and her own good sense so well SS II 1 141 6
Her indignation would have been still stronger than it was, SS II 6 178 17
which now raised a much stronger curiosity than before, SS II 7 186 37
Her pulse was much stronger, and every symptom more SS III 7 310 8
Marianne growing visibly stronger every twelve hours, Mrs. SS III 10 340 4
it till Marianne were in stronger health;--and they crept SS III 10 345 23
to me, there were stronger impulses even than pride." PP I 16 81 39
With a stronger voice she soon added, "I have this comfort PP II 1 134 8
But Bingley has great natural modesty, with a stronger PP II 12 199 5
have made a stronger impression on his mind than on hers. PP II 13 209 10
stronger than their virtue, she could easily conjecture. PP III 8 312 17
stronger desire of generally pleasing than any other man." PP III 12 343 32
care, but with great regret that she was not stronger. MP I 9 96 76
only a softened air and stronger expressions of regret. MP II 2 193 18
it was a love which his stronger spirits, and bolder MP II 6 234 17
to interfere with the stronger claims, the truer kindness MP II 9 271 40
endeavour to reason yourself into a stronger frame of mind. MP III 1 321 48
honouring her in rather stronger terms than Sir Thomas MP III 3 335 6
On his side, the inclination was stronger, on hers less MP III 6 367 4
were in the house; "I wish I left you in stronger health.-- MP III 11 411 20
room in a juster and stronger light than all Lady MP III 14 429 2
at last the longing grew stronger, it overthrew caution, MP III 14 431 8
withdraw with infinitely stronger feelings to a retirement MP III 17 464 12
Harriet smiled again, and her smiles grew stronger. E I 7 56 47
never had his smile been stronger, nor his eyes more E I 13 111 12
higher, fix his interest stronger with the people he E I 18 147 18
the truth, a great deal stronger than, if I had been Miss E II 6 202 31
I saw," brought him yet stronger suspicion of there being E III 5 344 2
She had scarcely a stronger regret than for her past E III 9 389 16
by its apparently stronger effect on Harriet's mind, E III 11 403 2
one, at times much stronger,) that Harriet might have E III 12 416 1
stronger heads than Sir Walter's have found too much.-- P III 2 15 13
of sense and consciousness were believed to be stronger. P IV 1 122 4
away for a week or ten days, till her head were stronger. P IV 2 133 25
and fancying herself stronger because her strength was not P IV 7 180 32
Can any thing be stronger?" P IV 9 204 75
& he cd almost feel his ancle getting stronger already.-- S 4 384 1
They have only weaker constitutions & stronger minds than S 5 385 1
you get your cocoa stronger & stronger every eveng"--, S 10 417 1
your cocoa stronger & stronger every eveng"--, with S 10 417 1
reply of "tis rather stronger than it should be tonight"-- S 10 417 1

STRONGEST (20)

that nothing but the strongest conviction of duty, could LS 30 301 4
shutter, felt the strongest conviction of the wind's force. NA II 6 167 10
would represent in the strongest manner to her mother the SS II 4 165 30
do, and on your prudence I have the strongest dependence. SS II 5 173 44
back the past in the strongest and most afflicting manner, SS II 10 213 3
With no expectation of pleasure, but with the strongest PP II 12 196 3
It is he who sees and worships your merit the strongest, MP III 3 344 41
being previously in the strongest state, her heart was MP III 5 365 35
at times, hold out the strongest hope of success, though MP III 17 471 28
anxious to bind by the strongest securities all that MP III 17 471 29
looks of love, the strongest of admiration were for her, E II 8 214 12
Harriet, is the strongest reproach you can make me. E II 13 268 10
I know what you mean--but Emma's hand is the strongest." E II 16 297 46
be mentioned, the two of strongest promise to Harriet, E III 11 410 35

give, by letters of the strongest approbation; and Mrs. E III 17 467 30
him to all that was strongest and best in his cellars. P III 7 53 1
the strongest examples of moral and religious endurances. P III 11 101 24
Surprise was the strongest emotion raised by their P IV 10 216 18
as our bodies are the strongest, so are our feelings; P IV 11 233 22
"Your feelings may be the strongest," replied Anne, "but P IV 11 233 23
STRONGLY (40)
more strongly they operate on Mr Vernon's generous temper. LS 6 251 2
afforded me, nor how strongly I felt the contract between LS 29 299 2
felt my loss perhaps as strongly as one so young could NA II 7 180 34
merit; she felt it too strongly for expression; and should NA II 14 232 5
outward behaviour, they strongly resembled each other in SS I 7 32 1
propensity, in which he strongly resembled and peculiarly SS I 10 48 9
strongly partook of the emotion which overpowered Marianne. SS I 15 75 2
Mrs. Palmer, on the contrary, who was strongly endowed by SS I 19 106 23
Mrs. Ferrars were both strongly prepossessed that neither SS II 11 228 53
of her feelings, strong in itself, and strongly spoken. SS II 13 242 23
to this act, were strongly felt, and warmly expressed. SS III 3 283 20
&c. she urged him so strongly to remain, that he, who was SS III 7 309 5
E.--, very strongly--but I am not sensible of the others.-- W 324 3
The distinction had perhaps been felt too strongly. PP I 5 18 1
Strongly anywhere else.-- PP I 16 77 14
"Take care, Lizzy; that speech savours strongly of PP II 4 154 20
But she had never felt so strongly as now, the PP II 19 236 2
In no countenance was attentive curiosity so strongly PP III 3 269 8
family, that I am strongly inclined to hope the best. PP III 5 282 1
Mrs Bennet had been strongly inclined to ask them to stay PP III 11 338 60
Active and fearless, and, though rather small, strongly MP I 7 66 15
and in no one more strongly than in him who was now master MP I 13 123 6
think you see things too strongly; and I really cannot MP I 15 140 14
was so warmly asked, so strongly wished for? what might be MP I 16 153 3
Edmund was so strongly calculated to inspire; but with MP I 18 169 22
and at such a time, as strongly as his son had ever MP II 2 187 2
He had vanity, which strongly inclined him, in the first MP III 2 326 1
Lady Bertram's admiration was expressed, and strongly too. MP III 3 338 17
always more inclined to silence when feeling most strongly. MP III 6 369 11
his confidential treatment touched her strongly. MP III 13 425 5
the sun's rays falling strongly into the parlour, instead MP III 15 439 9
talent for--thinks strongly and clearly--and when he takes E I 7 51 5
of it, she was very strongly persuaded; and though not E I 14 119 5
should not be strongly recommending each to the other. E III 3 335 10
How directly, how strongly had he expressed himself to her E III 12 415 1
Not too strongly for the offence--but far, far too E III 12 415 1
far, far too strongly to issue from any feeling softer E III 12 415 1
Mr. Knightley felt as strongly as herself; but the E III 15 448 31
of condition and rank more strongly than most people. P III 5 35 14
than he really was, strongly enforced the invitation. P IV 11 231 12
STRUCK (113)
not wonder at his being struck by the gentleness & LS 8 255 2
notion that has recently struck me, your kind impression LS 18 272 1
This idea struck me at the moment, & I instantly LS 24 288 11
Mrs. Allen was quite struck by his genius. NA I 3 28 39
Tetbury as the town-clock struck eleven; and I defy any NA I 7 45 7
When the orchestra struck up a fresh dance, James would NA I 8 57 21
employment till the clock struck one; and from habitude NA I 9 60 1
of duties which struck you, as rendering the conditions NA I 10 77 35
The clock struck twelve, and it still rained.-- NA I 11 83 14
boys and girls, always struck me as a hard fate; and NA I 14 109 24
The clock struck ten while the trunks were carrying down, NA II 5 155 4
Dorothy meanwhile, no less struck by your appearance, NA II 5 158 17
solemnity of any kind, struck her as odd and inconsistent. NA II 5 161 25
round the room, she was struck by the appearance of a high, NA II 6 168 10
the closing of a distant door struck on her affrighted ear. NA II 6 170 12
the wind, which struck at intervals on her startled ear. NA II 6 170 12
She was struck however, beyond her expectation, by the NA II 7 177 19
firs; and Catherine, struck by its gloomy aspect, and NA II 7 179 29
so much wished for, struck Catherine as very remarkable. NA II 7 181 41
undressed, it suddenly struck her as not unlikely, that NA II 8 188 17
just opposite her own, it struck her that, if judiciously NA II 8 188 19
then, when the clock had struck twelve, and all was quiet, NA II 8 189 19
The clock struck twelve--and Catherine had been half an NA II 8 189 19
went down when the clock struck five, with a broken heart, NA II 10 199 1
Its inconsistencies, contradictions, and falsehood, struck NA II 12 218 3
that had particularly struck him, when Edward interrupted SS I 18 96 4
her curiosity; for it struck her as being rather ill- SS I 21 126 41
Elinor said no more; it immediately struck her that she SS II 4 160 5
Mrs. Jennings was not struck by the same thought; for, SS II 8 198 30
You saw it all; and was not you quite struck with it?" SS II 13 239 4
thing else; and a thought struck him during the evening, SS II 14 252 20
Marianne seemed much struck.-- SS III 1 262 24
must have struck a less interested person with concern. SS III 7 313 20
The clock struck eight. SS III 7 316 29
& she was immediately struck with the fine countenance & W 330 11
Emma's calm curtsey in reply must have struck him as very W 335 13
But you must have liked him, you must have been struck W 342 19
It struck me as very becoming in so young a man, but I am W 344 20
The clock struck nine, while he was thus agreably occupied; W 359 28
quite struck with Jane as she was going down the dance. PP I 3 13 16
towards them, he was struck with the notion of doing a PP I 6 26 37
38
When the clock struck three, Elizabeth felt that she must PP I 7 33 45
Elizabeth was chiefly struck with his extraordinary PP I 13 64 16
All were struck with the stranger's air, all wondered who PP I 15 72 8
and he was so much struck with the size and furniture of PP I 16 75 2
It now first struck her, that she was selected from among PP I 17 88 14
reflections which often struck her, and though by no means PP I 22 124 11
"I like her appearance," said Elizabeth, struck with other PP II 5 158 18
of listening much; but it struck her in the course of PP II 10 182 1
She was now struck with the impropriety of such PP II 13 207 5
The justice of the charge struck her too forcibly for PP II 13 209 10
change was so great, and struck so forcibly on her mind, PP III 2 263 10
It suddenly struck her that it might be from Lady PP III 15 361 8
her to be little struck with the duet they were so good as MP I 2 14 7
Mr. Rushworth was from the first struck with the beauty of MP I 4 38 10
But was there nothing in her conversation that struck you MP I 7 63 3
"I thought you would be struck. MP I 7 63 5
arrangements till, as if struck by a sudden recollection, MP I 15 143 27
in their own noise, to be struck by unusual noise in the MP I 18 172 33
the billiard room door struck him especially, but he had MP II 1 182 22
before, and often been struck with the inconveniences they MP II 2 191 10
this shrubbery I am more struck with its growth and beauty. MP II 4 208 12
Henry Crawford was as much struck with it as any. MP II 6 235 19
over, for Edmund was so struck with the circumstance, so MP II 9 262 11
but she was so much more struck with her own kindness in MP II 10 277 15
She was struck, quite struck, when on returning from her MP III 1 322 51
for others which had formerly so struck and disgusted her. MP III 2 328 9
exists, you cannot be struck as I am with all that is MP III 2 330 14
for the purpose, she was struck with the idea of there MP III 6 372 21
passage and staircase, struck her beyond her imagination. MP III 7 387 47
a doubt of the manner in which Mr. Crawford must be struck. MP III 10 402 11
are very much struck with his gentleman-like appearance. MP III 12 416 2
and Edmund, particularly struck by the alteration in MP III 15 446 34
Lady Bertram had been struck by the difference, and all MP III 16 451 13
She was not struck by any thing remarkably clever in Miss E I 3 23 10
must yourself be struck with the difference in Mr. Martin. E I 4 32 32
Were not you struck? E I 4 33 32
I am sure you must have been struck by his awkward look E I 4 33 32
Mr. Elton seemed very properly struck and delighted by the E I 6 46 22
her own danger, but the idea of it struck her forcibly. E I 7 53 25
especially struck with the complimentary conclusion. E I 9 78 51
she was particularly struck with the very appearance and E II 2 167 12
The clock struck twelve as she passed through the hall. E II 5 189 20
"If you were never particularly struck by her manners E II 5 194 44
She was particularly struck by his manner of considering E II 6 203 42
entered the room had been struck by the sight of a E II 8 214 13
to more advantage, it struck me that she was heated, and E II 8 223 63
thought, but for Mrs. Weston, it would not have struck her. E II 8 228 88
When she became sensible of this, it struck her that she E II 13 264 1
but he had been very much struck with the loveliness of E II 13 266 6
She was quite struck by the likeness!-- E II 14 272 18
Every body who sees it is struck by its beauty; but to me, E II 14 273 19
momentary glance; and she was herself struck by his warmth. E II 15 286 19
of mind of each at this period, it struck her the more. E III 3 335 10
She was most forcibly struck. E III 7 376 62
and Jane Fairfax's, struck her; one was every thing, the E III 8 384 32
33
It struck her with dreadful force, and she was ready to E III 11 408 33
Donwell Abbey, was never struck with any sense of injury E III 15 449 35
that something should be struck out by one or the other to P III 1 10 21
before, without being struck by it, or without wishing P III 6 42 1
should have been suddenly struck, this very day, with a P III 6 51 31
and there was one speech of Louisa's which struck her. P III 10 84 7
She roused herself to say, as they struck by order into P III 10 85 12
to say, "that man is struck with you,--and even I, at this P III 12 104 6
The elegant little clock on the mantle-piece had struck " P IV 3 144 23
Such personal praise might have struck her, especially as P IV 4 146 4
He was more obviously struck and confused by the sight of P IV 7 175 6
every word, was struck, gratified, confused, and beginning P IV 8 183 11
said Anne, suddenly struck by an idea which made her yet P IV 8 190 49
"Perhaps," cried Anne, struck by a sudden idea, "you P IV 9 201 60
Presently, struck by a sudden thought, Charles said, P IV 11 240 55
56
well, he was very much struck by his personal claims, and P IV 12 248 2
It struck her however, as he poured out this rather weak S 10 417 1
STRUGGLE (24)
I spoke, to see the struggle between returning tenderness LS 25 293 3
Isabella, in a low voice, "there is no great struggle." NA I 13 100 12
but still she could struggle, she could exert herself. SS I 1 7 13
small income, and could struggle with any poverty for him; SS II 2 147 7
It should not, must not be a struggle." SS II 3 154 5
and another struggle, another effort still improved them. SS II 13 241 20
The struggle was great--but it ended too soon. SS III 8 323 40
Every lingering struggle in his favour grew fainter and PP II 13 207 6
I must struggle through my sorrows and difficulties as I MP I 3 29 46
"The mind which does not struggle against itself under one MP I 9 88 18
of education and decorum to struggle through." MP I 13 124 12
Maria had a moment's struggle as she listened, and only a MP II 3 200 21
Fanny felt that there must be a struggle in Edmund's MP II 10 273 6
great, though short struggle--half a wish of yielding to MP III 16 458 30
and the consciousness of being born to struggle and endure. MP III 17 473 31
of a struggle than she could foresee in her own feelings. E II 13 264 1
general state, had carried her off after a short struggle. E III 9 387 11
After a short struggle, however, Charles Hayter seemed to P III 10 82 2
she had to struggle against a great tendency to lowness. P III 11 98 16
It was a struggle between propriety and vanity; but vanity P IV 10 219 29
at once, and have to struggle with a few difficulties P IV 11 230 7
and privations, and dangers enough to struggle with. P IV 11 233 23
immediate struggle; but after a while she could do no more. P IV 11 238 45
however, without a struggle; his sisters accusing him of S 10 417 1
STRUGGLED (9)
necessary, and she struggled so resolutely against the SS I 22 134 53
that though Jane always struggled to support her spirits, PP II 4 152 6
agitated manner, and thus began, "in vain have I struggled. PP II 11 189 3
4
she might not have struggled through so much to obtain MP II 3 204 32
Fanny struggled for speech, and said, "I am very sorry MP II 9 268 30
her for having so struggled as to make the purchase MP III 9 397 7
November evening must be struggled through at Hartfield, E I 1 7 9
a mind to take it up; but she struggled, and let it pass. E I 11 96 27
Anxious to omit no possible precaution, Anne struggled, P IV 11 239 48
49
STRUGGLES (5)
that it cost him a few struggles to relinquish her, she PP II 5 150 26
I with greater policy concealed my struggles, and flattered PP II 11 192 22
other struggles than what such a purpose must comprehend. PP III 16 370 33
and with fewer struggles for politeness, replied, "it is E I 15 130 29
30
and be making some struggles to become truly acquainted P IV 12 249 3
STRUGGLING (8)
torn asunder by any common effort of a struggling assembly. NA I 2 21 9
During all this time he was evidently struggling for SS II 6 177 8
"You know, replied Emma struggling with her tears, my W 352 26
He was struggling for the appearance of composure, and PP II 11 190 8
struggling against discontent and envy for some days past. MP I 7 74 59
hand of her uncle with struggling sobs, because she had MP III 6 374 28
which she had been struggling for at least two years, she MP III 9 397 7
the duty and benefit of struggling against affliction, P III 11 100 23
STUBBORN (6)
entirely; since he will be stubborn, he must be tricked. LS 5 249 1
a bad temper; was seldom stubborn, scarcely ever NA I 1 14 1
But Catherine could be stubborn too; and Mrs. Allen just NA II 3 147 28
You shall find me as stubborn as you can be artful. I have SS I 10 52 28
I never thought Edward so stubborn, so unfeeling before. SS III 1 266 38
getting her to Delaford!--but her spirit was stubborn. SS III 9 339 25
STUBBORNNESS (1)
There is a stubbornness about me that never can bear to be PP II 8 174 13
STUCCO (1)
towards the ceiling and stucco of the room; and that when MP II 1 183 24
STUCK (2)
though I hate being stuck up in the barouche-landau E II 14 274 30
And yet, here are two gentlemen stuck up in it mightily at P IV 6 169 25
STUDIED (12)
all the great variety that you have known and studied." NA II 10 206 36
representation, no studied appeal to their passions. NA II 14 237 21
I have seen a great deal of him, have studied his SS I 4 20 9
sprung, nor observe the studied attentions with which the SS II 12 233 16
She studied every sentence: and her feelings towards its PP II 14 212 17
Presuming, however, that this studied avoidance spoke PP III 2 264 11
When you have studied the character, I am sure you will MP I 14 135 17
art of reading has been studied! how little a clear manner, MP III 3 339 23
If I had studied a twelvemonth, I could never have made E I 9 76 28
he was affected by the studied elegance of her dress, and E III 2 320 13
rising, said, with studied politeness, "I beg your pardon, P III 8 72 58
59
world, by those who have studied right sides & green tea S 10 418 1
STUDIER (1)
Bingley immediately, "that you were a studier of character. PP I 9 42 15
STUDIES (4)
I had entered on my studies at Oxford, while you were a NA I 14 107 11
not pursuing their usual studies with quite so much vigour SS III 11 352 20
He studies too much for words of four syllables.-- PP I 10 48 20
Kitty is slight and delicate, and Mary studies so much, PP III 5 292 66
STUDIOUS (2)
at whom it was all aimed, was still inflexibly studious. PP I 11 56 10
give pain to one who has been so studious of your comfort. MP II 9 263 16
STUDIOUSLY (4)
other subjects being studiously brought forward and NA II 11 213 20
which had appeared so studiously to avoid him throughout MP III 3 337 11
her by the noise he was studiously making with the child, P III 9 80 34
In general, his voice and manner were studiously calm. P III 12 116 70
STUDY (20)
But here she was obliged to look and consider and study NA II 9 191 3
anxiously recommending the study of her comfort and NA II 13 220 1
this less abstruse study of it, which my family approved. SS I 19 103 4

and am determined to enter on a course of serious study. SS III 10 343 9
in retirement and study, as afterwards in her more calm SS III 14 378 16
It must be an amusing study." PP I 9 42 15
"can in general supply but few subjects for such a study. PP I 9 42 17
But it has been the study of my life to avoid those PP I 11 57 22
They found Mary, as usual, deep in the study of thorough PP I 12 60 7
of the moment, or are the result of previous study?" PP I 14 68 10
by education and habitual study to decide on what is right PP I 18 97 61
He had found the law a most unprofitable study, and was PP II 12 201 5
and trick of composition are oftener an object of study. MP III 3 341 28
"I had only my own family to study from. E I 6 45 21
sigh and languish, and study for compliments rather more E I 6 49 44
It was much easier to chat than to study; much pleasanter E I 9 69 3
His manner had no air of study or exaggeration. E II 5 191 26
degree of sedate civility entreated her to study it. E III 5 348 23
man, just engaged in the study of the law; and Elizabeth P III 1 8 15
of prose in his daily study; and on being requested to P III 11 101 24
STUDYING (7)
she were to be studying his character for a twelve-month. PP I 6 23 10
He had some intention, he added, of studying the law, and PP II 12 200 5
In town I believe he chiefly lived, but his studying the PP II 12 201 5
little opportunity of studying her spirits, amidst the PP II 15 217 16
Without studying the business, however, or knowing what he MP I 7 65 13
to studying it, without seeming to recollect her existence. MP III 7 382 28
talked, with grave faces, of his studying himself to death. P III 10 82 2
STUFF (8)
so full of nonsense and stuff; there had not been a NA I 7 48 34
"Yes, that's the book; such unnatural stuff!-- NA I 7 49 40
I guessed what sort of stuff it must be before I saw it: NA I 7 49 40
Mine is famous good stuff to be sure. NA I 9 64 24
and the bed, of dark green stuff or purple velvet, NA II 5 158 15
basket full of garden stuff and fruit arrived from the SS I 6 30 6
Lord! how Charlotte and I did stuff the only time we were SS II 8 197 22
"Phoo! phoo!" cried the Admiral, "what stuff these young P III 8 65 12
STUFF'D (1)
There is a monstrous curious stuff'd fox there, & a Badger- W 333 12
STUFFED (1)
her, and her mouth stuffed with sugar plums by the other. SS I 21 121 10
STUFFY (1)
to the broad-faced stuffy uncle Philips, breathing port PP I 16 76 3
STUMBLING (2)
a man without now and then stumbling on something witty." PP II 17 226 17
a tongue that has been stumbling at Miss Price for at MP II 13 303 15
STUNNED (2)
Fanny was almost stunned. MP III 7 382 28
I was like a man stunned. MP III 16 455 21
STUPEFACTION (1)
At first, it was a sort of stupefaction; but every moment MP III 15 440 19
STUPID (39)
We shall be as stupid as possible. LS 5 250 2
She is a stupid girl, & has nothing to recommend her. LS 7 252 1
for she was often inattentive, and occasionally stupid. NA I 1 14 1
Not that Catherine was always stupid,--by no means; she NA I 1 14 1
thinking of that other stupid book, written by that woman NA I 7 49 38
not pleasure in a good novel, must be intolerably stupid. NA I 14 106 7
if you had ever seen how stupid they can be for a whole NA I 14 109 26
And you, Miss Morland--my stupid sister has mistaken all NA I 14 113 39
were in bed, by stupid pamphlets, was not very likely. NA II 8 187 16
or grave, or ingenious or stupid than they really are, and SS I 17 93 37
Sir John is as stupid as the weather." SS I 20 111 8
The stupid indifference, insolence, and discontent of her SS I 20 112 26
having escaped the company of a stupid old woman so long. SS II 14 247 5
I owe such a grudge to myself for the stupid, rascally SS III 8 324 45
Now, however, his good-natured, honest, stupid soul, full SS III 8 330 69
to dress, said he--I am waiting for my stupid fellow.-- W 327 7
pulpit--I do not like the stupid air & artificial W 343 20
see you standing about by yourself in this stupid manner. PP I 3 11 8
the stranger, were become "stupid, disagreeable fellows." PP I 15 74 11
Stupid men are the only ones worth knowing, after all." PP II 4 154 19
Their table was superlatively stupid. PP II 6 166 41
thought her prodigiously stupid, and for the first two or MP I 2 18 23
Did you ever hear any thing so stupid?" MP I 2 18 23
tell you another thing of Fanny, so odd and so stupid." MP I 2 19 28
"To be sure, my dear, that is very stupid indeed, and MP I 2 19 29
As for Fanny's being stupid at learning, "she could only MP I 2 20 31
but some people were stupid, and Fanny must take more MP I 2 20 31
twelve thousand a year, he would be a very stupid fellow." MP I 4 40 13
is a stupid old fellow, and does not know how to drive. MP I 8 77 13
Anhalt a very stupid fellow, he soon decided for the count. MP I 15 138 1
"I feel quite stupid. MP II 11 283 5
Fetch the cards,--I feel so very stupid." MP II 11 283 5
in writing for that stupid woman's service, and all this MP II 12 296 31
to be the drudge of some attorney, and too stupid to rise. E II 4 183 9
She had never seen Frank Churchill so silent and stupid. E III 7 367 2
then whispering--"our companions are excessively stupid. E III 7 369 16
equally; some looked very stupid about it, and Mr. E III 7 371 35
36
to sea, because he was stupid and unmanageable on shore; P III 6 50 28
as you say, & I have made an abominably stupid blunder.-- S 1 367 1
STUPIDER (1)
You have liked many a stupider person." PP I 4 14 5
STUPIDEST (3)
all the others, they are the stupidest things in creation." NA I 7 48 34
The stupidest fellow! E I 9 71 9
she had herself been the stupidest of beings in not having E III 17 467 31
STUPIDITY (14)
Where pride & stupidity unite, there can be no LS 4 248 2
Forgive her stupidity. NA I 14 113 39
the latter she could only attribute to her own stupidity. NA II 1 129 1
The stupidity with which he was favoured by nature, must PP I 22 122 2
laughing at his stupidity, proved that he was generally PP II 9 180 29
we may laugh at their stupidity in not knowing it before. PP II 17 226 23
Mrs. Gardiner abused her stupidity. PP II 19 240 15
My stupidity was abominable, for here we have all the MP I 15 139 6
I should dread the stupidity of the day, if there were not MP II 3 199 18
demands of her aunt's stupidity, working with her, and for MP II 12 296 31
The indignities of stupidity, and the disappointments of MP III 17 464 12
But, be it sweetness or be it stupidity in her --quickness E II 6 202 35
"This sensation of listlessness, weariness, stupidity, E II 12 262 39
solely in the elegant stupidity of private parties, in P IV 7 180 32
STUPIFIED (3)
time, he believed, half stupified between the wonder, the SS III 13 364 13
Did Admiral Crawford apply?--how was it?--I am stupified." MP II 13 300 6
She was an altered creature, quieted, stupified, MP III 16 448 2
STUPOR (1)
more quiet--not more herself--remained in an heavy stupor. SS III 7 313 21
STURDY (5)
you talking of; cried the husband with sturdy pleasantry--. W 325 4
first by the sturdy independence of your country customs. MP I 6 58 39
"Not half a mile," was his sturdy answer; for he was not MP I 9 94 61
His sturdy spirit to bend as it did! MP III 5 358 9
so much, that his little sturdy hands were unfastened from P III 9 80 33
STYLE (107)
to form the easy style of writing for which ladies are so NA I 3 27 28
to me that the usual style of letter-writing among women NA I 3 27 30
her air, and dressing in the same style, did very well. NA I 4 34 8
You really have done your hair in a more heavenly style NA I 10 70 1
that by their method and style, they are perfectly well NA I 14 109 25
him in general; but he is not at all in my style of beauty. NA II 1 135 41
her admiration of the style in which they travelled, of NA II 5 156 4
use, and fitted up in a style of luxury and expense which NA II 6 165 6
in a complimentary style, which so well concealed his NA II 9 192 4
discovering; aiming at a style of life which their fortune NA II 15 246 12
would only enlarge their style of living if they felt sure SS I 2 11 23
written in so friendly a style as could not fail of giving SS I 4 23 20
for though her former style of life rendered many SS I 6 29 4
his manners were as friendly as the style of his letter. SS I 6 30 6
lived in a style of equal hospitality and elegance. SS I 7 32 1
thing were conducted in style and her two eldest children SS I 11 55 6
in the usual style of a complete party of pleasure. SS I 12 62 28
with Mrs. Jennings's style of living, and set of SS II 5 168 11
though adorned in the first style of fashion. SS II 11 220 3
Her house, her style of living, all bespeak an exceeding SS II 11 226 42
There was something in her style of beauty, to please them SS II 11 227 50
are something in Miss Morton's style of painting, ma'am?-- SS II 12 235 31
32
style of life would venture to settle on--and he said so. SS III 3 284 22
from his style of education it was always to be expected. SS III 5 299 35
The merest awkward country girl, without style, or SS III 5 299 37
And in short--what do you think of my wife's style of SS III 8 328 61
substance made me any amends for the defect of the style." SS III 13 365 17
ever appeared in Robert's style of living or of talking, SS III 14 377 12
Their other engagements were few; as the style of living PP II 7 169 5
He answered her in the same style, and the subject dropped. PP II 10 184 16
used to characterize her style, and which, proceeding from PP II 11 188 1
satisfied her; his style was not penitent, but haughty. PP II 13 204 1
When she remembered the style of his address, she was PP II 14 212 17
civility to his ordinary style? for I dare not hope," he PP II 18 234 33
was in a different style; and still different from either, PP III 18 383 22
lady's horse of her own in the style of her cousins. MP I 4 36 7
doubts of her sister's style of living and tone of society; MP I 4 41 16
I would have every thing done in the best style, and made MP I 6 53 9
In any particular style of building?" MP I 6 56 25
You have but one style among you. MP I 6 59 43
That is the true manly style; that is a complete brother's MP I 6 59 43
I find it better, grander, more complete in its style, MP I 10 98 7
in its style, though that style may not be the best. MP I 10 98 7
understand the different style of the characters, and MP I 15 138 1
be resolved into a better style of dress and your having MP II 6 230 6
according to the usual style of the Grants, and too much MP II 7 238 3
so perfectly gratifying in the occasion and the style. MP II 9 265 19
in a very handsome style, with all the heightenings of MP II 11 283 7
the subject of William's appointment in their own style. MP II 13 304 18
scruples and fears as to style, she would have felt them MP II 13 307 30
31
even a careless, slovenly style of reading can destroy; MP III 3 340 25
Miss Crawford's style of writing, lively and affectionate, MP III 7 376 4
as it ought to be, in a style that any of her connections MP III 12 416 2
of preferring her style to that of any printed author. MP III 12 419 7
common-place, amplifying style, so that a very little MP III 13 425 6
more warm and genuine than her aunt's style of writing. MP III 13 427 12
Fanny, in the same diffuse style, and the same medley of MP III 13 427 12
finished in a different style, in the language of real MP III 13 427 12
thing in so superior a style to what she had been used to, E I 3 23 10
a much more satisfactory style; and on the present evening E I 3 25 15
She played and sang;--and drew in almost every style; but E I 6 44 19
perhaps the most; her style was spirited; but had there E I 6 44 20
The style of the letter was much above her expectation. E I 7 50 4
and yet it is not the style of a woman; no, certainly, it E I 7 51 5
in the true English style, burying under a calmness that E I 12 99 14
And in this style he talked on for some time very properly, E I 15 124 3
It was a style of beauty, of which elegance was the E II 2 167 12
shew off in higher style her own very superior performance. E II 2 168 15
By his style, I should imagine it just settled." E II 3 174 32
her, written in the very style to touch; a small mixture E II 4 184 11
The style of the visit, and the shortness of it, were then E II 5 187 4
style of living, second only to the family at Hartfield. E II 7 207 6
one set of people, and one style of living; that if not E II 14 272 16
are always pleased with any thing in the same style." E II 14 273 21
home, and we live in a style which could not make the E II 15 283 9
was in the first style of guileless simplicity and warmth. E II 15 284 12
packs in the true style--and more waiters engaged for the E II 16 290 3
In this style she ran on; never thoroughly stopped by any E II 17 302 21
22
I never saw any thing equal to the comfort and style-- E III 2 329 45
the respectable size and style of the building, its E III 6 358 35
A style of living almost equal to Maple Grove--and as to E III 8 382 23
One man's style must not be the rule of another's. E III 15 445 7
bordering on it in her style, which increased the E III 16 451 2
him to go on in the same style; but his mind was the next E III 18 478 60
61
could materially alter his style of living in a house P III 2 13 7
To be claimed as a good, though in an improper style, is P III 5 33 9
in the old English style; containing only two houses P III 5 36 20
Anne had always thought such a style of intercourse highly P III 5 40 44
The father and mother were in the old English style, and P III 5 40 45
some amusement at their style of driving, which she P III 10 92 48
so unlike the usual style of give-and-take invitations, P III 11 98 16
be canvassed only in one style by a couple of steady, P IV 1 126 21
the style of the fitting-up, or the taste of the furniture. P IV 3 137 4
was living in very good style in Marlborough buildings, P IV 3 139 8
three months, in laura-place, and would be living in style. P IV 4 149 12
In London, perhaps, in your present quiet style of living, P IV 4 151 19
lessons are not often in the elevated style you describe. P IV 5 156 11
there is nothing in the style of Captain Wentworth's P IV 6 172 42
We were principally in town, living in very good style. P IV 9 199 55
never been equal to their style of living, and that from P IV 9 209 95
to have the difference of style, the reduction of servants, P IV 10 219 29
Charles and Mary still talked on in the same style; he, P IV 10 224 50
a great deal in the same style of open-hearted P IV 11 230 5
I am astonished at the chearful style of the letters, S 5 388 1
sentences from the style of our most approved writers.-- S 8 404 1
measures in that masterly style was ill-suited to his S 8 405 2
in the order and the importance of her style of living.-- S 12 427 1
STYLES (3)
"Mr Norton, & Mr Styles." W 337 15
"And who is Mr Styles?" W 337 15
We shall see if our styles suit.-- E III 2 324 21
STYLISH (1)
of meaning to be the most stylish girls in the place.-- S 11 421 1
SUAVITY (1)
general politeness and suavity, she had been too quick in P IV 12 249 3
SUBDUE (10)
coquetry to subdue his judgement to her own purposes. LS 11 259 1
she could not entirely subdue the hope of some traditional NA II 2 141 11
especially, which required some trouble and time to subdue. SS I 19 104 9
But as it was her determination to subdue it, and to SS I 19 104 9
gravity as nothing could subdue, no curiosity touch, no MP I 17 160 8
Fanny could not subdue her agitation; and the dejection MP II 9 264 17
in order to subdue me; at least, it appeared so to me. MP III 16 459 30
he must exert himself to subdue so proud a display of MP III 17 467 20
try to subdue the feelings this picture excited. P IV 5 160 26
a smile, "I must endeavour to subdue my mind to my fortune. P IV 11 247 84
SUBDUED (16)
I have subdued him entirely by sentiment & serious LS 10 258 2
every feature when we last parted, were partially subdued. LS 25 292 2
the artifices which had subdued me, than to despise myself LS 36 306 2
Catherine was distressed, but not subdued. NA I 13 97 1
for a short time was subdued, and the pleasure of seeing NA II 14 233 9
Marianne was shortly subdued; and she promised not to SS I 12 59 5
Her flattery had already subdued the pride of Lady SS II 14 254 27
Marianne was quite subdued.-- SS III 1 264 30
gaiety of heart was much subdued; the sight of so many MP II 10 273 7
The fever was subdued; the fever had been his complaint, MP III 14 429 1

a voice a little subdued, but very audible to every body. E II 17 303 26
in a more broken and subdued accent, "the feelings of the E III 13 426 13
little tranquillized and subdued--and in the course of the E III 14 434 4
If I had followed her judgment, and subdued my spirits to E III 14 440 8
The delightful emotions were a little subdued, when, on P IV 8 184 18
& Medecine, more relaxed in air, & more subdued in voice. S 10 413 1

SUBDUING (5)
There is exquisite pleasure in subduing an insolent spirit, LS 7 254 3
of her conscience in subduing her first inclination, and MP III 17 467 19
the acquaintance, of subduing feelings, concealing E I 16 137 12
Rousing from reflection, therefore, and subduing her E III 11 408 33
Can you conceive any thing more subduing, more melting, S 7 397 1

SUBJECT (444)
about Reginald would subject him to an alarm which might LS 8 254 1
between them, implied by the discussion of such a subject. LS 15 266 1
amusing; & let the subject be ever so serious that he may LS 18 272 1
his discourse than the subject required; said many things LS 20 276 3
my uncle or aunt on the subject; & this being the case, I LS 21 279 1
conversed with her on the subject of it, in order to LS 22 281 5
not to have prevented your speaking to me on the subject. LS 24 286 7
speaking to you on the subject, from a fear of your LS 24 289 12
Why should I subject you to entreaties, which I refused to LS 24 289 12
a second marriage, must subject me to the censure of the LS 30 300 3
Her anxiety on the subject made her press for an early LS 42 311 2
Persecution on the subject of Sir James was entirely at an LS 42 312 3
"A general deficiency of subject, a total inattention to NA I 3 27 32
him on the subject of muslins till the dancing recommenced. NA I 3 29 47
to tease you on this subject whenever we meet, and nothing NA I 3 29 51
It was a subject, however, in which she often indulged NA I 5 36 2
often any resemblance of subject, for Mrs. Thorpe talked NA I 5 36 3
Let us drop the subject." NA I 6 42 32
at length to vary the subject by a question which had been NA I 7 48 32
some time, the original subject seemed entirely forgotten; NA I 8 57 21
His knowledge and her ignorance of the subject, his NA I 9 64 27
on the subject, "that James's gig will break down?" NA I 9 65 27
his real opinion on the subject; but she checked herself, NA I 9 66 31
to give any, from not having heard a word of the subject. NA I 10 72 8
read her a lecture on the subject only the Christmas NA I 10 73 22
Their drive, even when this subject was over, was not NA I 11 88 54
But now every commendation on every subject is comprised NA I 14 108 16
from her on that lady's merits, closed the subject.-- NA I 14 110 28
to her treatment of the subject I will only add in justice NA I 14 111 29
once, Henry suffered the subject to decline, and by an NA I 14 111 29
met, they had a far more interesting subject to discuss. NA II 1 135 42
John desired me to speak to you on the subject, and NA II 3 145 16
She spoke to Henry Tilney on the subject, regretting his NA II 4 150 1
"I can have no opinion on that subject." NA II 4 151 18
resolved never to think so seriously on the subject again. NA II 4 153 30
solemnity either of subject or voice, and was obliged to NA II 5 160 23
to get rid of the subject; "and storms and sleeplessness NA II 7 174 5
house, soon revived the subject; and her father being, NA II 8 182 1
She believed she must wave the subject altogether. NA II 10 203 9
From this time, the subject was frequently canvassed by NA II 11 208 1
sentiments on the subject of money, which she had more NA II 11 208 1
like an opinion on the subject could be drawn from her. NA II 11 214 25
was her mind on the subject of his expectations, that, NA II 11 215 28
forward so unpleasant a subject, she took the first NA II 13 220 2
Catherine had never thought on the subject till that NA II 13 229 31
stairs upon much such a subject, about young girls that NA II 15 241 6
before he mentioned the subject; and as he proceeded to NA II 15 244 11
She begged him to think again on the subject. SS I 2 8 3
and said no more on the subject; but the kind of SS I 4 19 3
it was impossible for Elinor to feel easy on the subject. SS I 4 22 18
which means there was one subject always to be recurred to SS I 6 31 9
concern which the same subject had drawn from him the day SS I 7 33 4
many witty things on the subject of lovers and husbands; SS I 7 34 5
on the subject of illness, which I cannot conceal from you. SS I 8 38 14
any anxiety at all on the subject, it has been in SS I 8 39 15
to question him on the subject of books; her favourite SS I 10 47 3
extraordinary dispatch of every subject for discourse? SS I 10 47 4
Opposition on so tender a subject would only attach her SS I 12 59 5
and much was said on the subject of rain by both of them. SS I 12 62 27
and Willoughby on the subject, which they must know to be SS I 14 71 3
"Yet not a syllable has been said to you on the subject, SS I 15 79 35
the subject, and with me it almost outweighs every other." SS I 15 80 37
of every subject which her feelings connected with him. SS I 15 82 47
trying to laugh off the subject, she said to him, "do not SS I 17 95 49
This was a subject which ensured Marianne's attention, and SS I 18 96 4
The subject was continued no farther; and Marianne SS I 18 98 10
I was too old when the subject was first started to enter SS I 19 103 4
past and the future, on a subject so interesting, must be SS I 19 105 12
and by changing the subject, put a stop to her entreaties. SS I 20 114 43
husband and mother on that subject went for nothing at all. SS I 21 118 2
reprimand on the subject five or six times every day. SS I 21 118 2
She wished very much to have the subject continued, though SS I 21 126 41
It was broken by Lucy, who renewed the subject again by SS I 22 128 8
9
with Lucy on the subject, she soon felt an earnest wish of SS II 1 141 7
painful to hear on the subject than had already been told, SS II 1 142 7
subject, without any risk of being heard at the card-table. SS II 1 145 23
its continuance, or no farther curiosity on its subject. SS II 2 146 2
agitated feelings, "on such a subject I certainly will not. SS II 2 150 31
me from giving any opinion on the subject had I formed one. SS II 2 150 33
even partly determined never to mention the subject again. SS II 2 150 35
From this time that subject was never revived by Elinor, SS II 2 151 42
said no more on the subject, and began directly to speak SS II 4 162 11
much more curiosity on the subject than she had ever felt. SS II 4 162 13
be said to myself on the subject, the more my feelings SS II 8 195 17
Elinor, for her sister's sake, could not press the subject SS II 8 196 21
of the card parties, the subject was necessarily dropped. SS II 8 200 43
they had gone through the subject again and again; with SS II 9 201 2
On such a subject," sighing heavily, "I can have little SS II 9 205 20
Ah! Miss Dashwood--a subject such as this--untouched for SS II 9 208 28
day, or twice, if the subject occurred very often, by SS II 10 215 14
it was all over; and one subject only engaged the ladies SS II 12 233 19
to say any thing that might introduce another subject. SS II 13 242 28
any other raillery on the subject, than what she was kind SS II 14 247 4
was still worse, must be subject to all the unpleasantness SS II 14 248 6
as the subject might naturally be supposed to produce. SS III 1 260 8
As Mrs. Jennings could talk on no other subject, Elinor SS III 1 260 10
had to say upon the subject, with an unchanging complexion, SS III 1 265 33
state, its was not a subject on which either of them were SS III 2 270 1
She had wandered away to a subject on which Elinor had SS III 2 272 13
Miss Steele was going to reply on the same subject, but SS III 2 275 24
anxious to be alone, than to be mistress of the subject. SS III 4 287 23
becoming so important a subject, "knows nothing about it SS III 5 295 18
of the living, and was very inquisitive on the subject. SS III 5 298 33
entrance of Mrs. John Dashwood put an end to the subject. SS III 5 300 38
let me be pained by hearing any thing more on the subject." SS III 8 320 31
the discussion of such a subject may well be--your SS III 8 322 37
on any interesting subject, and therefore instead of an SS III 9 336 11
on that subject, Elinor?"--hesitatingly it was said.-- SS III 10 344 14
15
of reviving the subject again, should Marianne fail to do SS III 10 348 34
pursuing the first subject, immediately continued, "one SS III 11 352 16
17
on so prohibited a subject, but conclude him to be still SS III 11 353 21
Between them no subject is finished, no communication is SS III 13 364 9
What he might say on the subject a twelvemonth after, must SS III 13 366 20
much attention, as to be entirely mistress of the subject. SS III 13 368 31
talk only of Robert,--a subject on which he had always SS III 14 376 11
in the manner in which Mr E. took up the subject.-- W 324 3
So far, the subject was very often carried;--but Mr & Mrs W 325 4
it, changed the subject to one of less anxiety to all.-- W 326 6
by way of changing the subject, he added--"I am just come W 352 26
ran away from a subject which was odious to her feelings.-- W 360 29
could ask on the subject was sufficient to draw from her PP I 3 9 1
another branch of the subject, and related, with much PP I 3 13 19
friend to mention such a subject to him, which immediately PP I 6 24 17
18
"With great energy;--but it is a subject which always PP I 6 24 19
by Miss Bingley, "I can guess the subject of your reverie." PP I 6 27 44
45
their effusions on this subject, Mr. Bennet coolly PP I 7 29 5
6
satisfied with this reply as to continue the subject. PP I 8 40 58
Mr. Bingley on the subject of the ball, and abruptly PP I 9 45 36
before we proceed on this subject, to arrange with rather PP I 10 50 38
And, if I may mention so delicate a subject, endeavour to PP I 10 52 55
of the whole party on the subject, seemed to justify her. PP I 11 54 3
if you please, by attempting to laugh without a subject. PP I 11 57 18
They had often attempted it before, but it was a subject PP I 13 62 8
My mind however is now made up on the subject, for having PP I 13 62 12
could say much on the subject, but that I am cautious of PP I 13 65 25
and therefore started a subject in which he expected him PP I 14 66 1
The subject elevated him to more than usual solemnity of PP I 14 66 1
Mr. Wickham began the subject himself. PP I 16 77 8
unwilling to let the subject drop, added, "he is a man of PP I 16 77 9
Elizabeth found the interest of the subject increase, and PP I 16 78 21
"I will not trust myself on the subject," replied Wickham, PP I 16 80 35
no answer, and seemed desirous of changing the subject. PP I 18 92 22
be the case, there can at least be no want of subject.-- PP I 18 93 29
had wandered far from the subject, as soon afterwards PP I 18 93 32
to make inquiries on the same subject of Bingley. PP I 18 95 48
which on every other subject shall be my constant guide, PP I 18 97 61
It was an animating subject, and Mrs. Bennet seemed PP I 18 99 63
by my feelings on this subject, perhaps it will be PP I 19 105 8
(unasked too!) on this subject; and it was but the very PP I 19 105 10
to you next on this subject I shall hope to receive a more PP I 19 108 16
17
she likewise began on the subject, calling on Miss Lucas PP I 20 113 26
felt an anxiety on the subject which drew off her PP I 21 116 6
you my feelings on this subject, but I will not leave the PP I 21 118 14
Can there be any other opinion on the subject?" PP I 21 118 15
what she felt on the subject, and had soon the pleasure of PP I 21 120 29
mutually silent on the subject; and Elizabeth felt PP I 23 127 9
Jane nor Elizabeth were comfortable on this subject. PP I 23 129 12
and Elizabeth, therefore, the subject was never alluded to. PP I 23 129 14
It was a subject, in short, on which reflection would be PP II 1 134 3
with Elizabeth afterwards, she spoke more on the subject. PP II 2 140 6
felt a solicitude on the subject which convinced her, on PP II 2 142 16
speak to Elizabeth on the subject before she left PP II 2 142 18
Here consequently was an inexhaustible subject of PP II 2 143 20
body had as much to say or to hear on the subject as usual. PP II 3 146 19
Their first subject was her sister; and she was more PP II 4 152 6
her opinion on every subject in so decisive a manner as PP II 6 163 15
The subject was pursued no farther, and the gentlemen soon PP II 7 171 12
what he would say on the subject of their hasty departure, PP II 9 177 3
4
to leave the trouble of finding a subject to him. PP II 9 178 11
A short dialogue on the subject of the country ensued, on PP II 9 179 26
it right to press the subject, from the danger of raising PP II 9 181 30
He answered her in the same style, and the subject dropped. PP II 10 184 16
The agitation and tears which the subject occasioned, PP II 10 187 41
more eloquent on the subject of tenderness than of pride. PP II 11 189 5
On this subject, what can you have to say? PP II 11 191 17
On this subject I have nothing more to say, no other PP II 12 199 5
But when this subject was succeeded by his account of Mr. PP II 13 204 2
Their first subject was the diminution of the Rosings PP II 14 210 3
defects of her family a subject of yet heavier chagrin. PP II 14 212 17
she once entered on the subject, of being hurried into PP II 15 217 17
"It was a subject which they could not mention before me." PP II 17 228 34
Mr. Bennet saw that her whole heart was in the subject; PP II 18 231 19
20
She saw that he wanted to engage her on the old subject of PP II 18 235 39
herself; and when the subject was revived the next morning, PP II 19 241 17
She related the subject of the pictures, the dimensions of PP III 1 249 37
soon led again to the subject; and she dwelt with energy PP III 1 249 37
to talk, but there seemed an embargo on every subject. PP III 1 257 66
been highly gratified by her niece's beginning the subject. PP III 3 272 20
and talking on the subject, to give greater--what shall I PP III 5 284 10
on this interesting subject, by its repeated discussion, PP III 5 285 19
comprehend all her fears and solicitude on the subject. PP III 5 288 40
Impossible; the former continued the subject, by saying, " PP III 5 290 45
46
ventured to introduce the subject; and then, on her PP III 6 299 19
that the subject might never be mentioned to him again. PP III 8 312 18
"I think there cannot be too little said on the subject." PP III 9 318 23
secret," said Jane, "say not another word on the subject. PP III 9 319 28
by introducing the subject of it; and she was pleased to PP III 11 330 1
The subject which had been so warmly canvassed between PP III 11 332 21
therefore, to be importuned no farther on the subject." PP III 14 357 61
and Elizabeth was spared from much teazing on the subject. PP III 15 361 5
add a short hint on the subject of another; of which we PP III 15 362 14
word from you will silence me on this subject for ever." PP III 16 366 7
was too painful a subject to each, to be dwelt on farther. PP III 16 370 34
of promise, for I ought not to have mentioned the subject? PP III 18 381 13
possible flight which the subject will afford, and unless PP III 18 382 21
wrote to her family on the subject till actually married. MP I 1 4 1
When the subject was brought forward again, her views were MP I 1 9 10
On pursuing the subject, he found that dear as all these MP I 2 15 12
"to what any young person says on the subject of marriage. MP I 4 43 25
Maria's notions on the subject were more confused and MP I 5 44 2
with his head full of the subject, and very eager to be MP I 6 52 1
The subject had been already handled in the drawing-room; MP I 6 52 1
had still more to say on the subject next his heart. MP I 6 55 17
"You could not be expected to have thought on the subject MP I 6 58 38
The subject of improving grounds meanwhile was still under MP I 6 60 53
next day, after thinking some time on the subject himself. MP I 7 63 1
this period, and on this subject, there began now to be MP I 7 64 12
requires," was Edmund's only reply, and the subject dropt. MP I 8 79 26
of the cloth with more respect," and turned the subject. MP I 9 89 29
many courtesies on the subject of pheasants, had taken her MP I 10 103 50
his daughters felt on the subject of his return, and would MP I 11 107 4
of the letters, and the subject was dropt; but after tea, MP I 11 108 4
"You taught me to think and feel on the subject, cousin." MP I 11 113 37
her aunt Norris on this subject, as well as to her MP I 12 116 11
change of expression and subject necessary, as Fanny, in MP I 12 119 22
subject, and to boast of the past his only consolation. MP I 13 121 1
After a short pause, however, the subject still continued, MP I 13 124 13
returning to the former subject, posture, and voice, as MP I 13 126 23
he was still urging the subject, when Henry Crawford MP I 13 129 38
to harangue all the rest upon a subject of this kind.-- MP I 15 140 14
animating support, thought the subject better avoided. MP I 15 142 24
just getting deep in the subject when a most welcome MP I 15 142 25
the morrow might produce in continuation of the subject. MP I 16 150 1
without considering the subject enough to know what was MP I 16 154 14
The whole subject of it was love--a marriage of love was MP I 18 167 12
The Crawfords were more warm on the subject than Mr. Yates, MP II 1 177 5
And then he would have changed the subject, and sipped his MP II 1 184 25
Mr. Yates took the subject from his friend as soon as MP II 1 184 27
to find our sentiments on this subject so much the same. MP II 1 186 34
Her only resource was to get out of the subject as fast as MP II 2 188 3
his opinion on one subject--his decided preference of a MP II 2 190 6

while this branch of the subject was under discussion, MP II 2 193 17
he had done with the subject, and only added more MP II 3 198 9
at all interested in the subject, I did not like--I MP II 3 198 12
wish on the subject, was concerned at her own neglect;-- MP II 4 206 5
subject, he grew thoughtful and indisposed for any other. MP II 4 216 50
were present; but the subject involving, as it did, her MP II 5 217 11
for to hear herself the subject of any discussion with her MP II 5 218 12
engaged her on some other subject, but her answers were so MP II 5 226 59
thoroughly master of the subject, or had in fact become at MP II 6 232 13
hide her interest in the subject by an eager attention to MP II 7 244 28
voice, not meant to reach far, and the subject dropped. MP II 7 246 35
himself on the same subject to Sir Thomas, in a more every MP II 7 247 37
should not have thought much on the subject, Mr. Crawford. MP II 7 247 42
you can make on the subject, to your entire satisfaction. MP II 7 250 61
passing around him on the subject, from morning till night. MP II 8 256 13
upstairs, and were soon deep in the interesting subject. MP II 8 257 15
It is a subject on which I should never ask advice. MP II 9 269 35
It is the sort of subject on which it had better never be MP II 9 269 35
men assured him, that the subject might be gently touched MP II 10 272 4
beginning to speak on the subject, when Fanny, anxious to MP II 10 274 9
greater advantage on the subject, than his Lady Did, soon MP II 10 276 14
said, "he is best off as he is," and turned the subject. MP II 11 290 38
wild I have been on the subject, I will not attempt to MP II 13 299 5
She would hardly join even when William was the subject, MP II 13 304 17
the subject of William's appointment in their own style. MP II 13 304 18
a great favour of you never to mention the subject again. MP II 13 307 31
coming up to speak to her whatever might be the subject.-- MP III 1 312 4
spoke to me on this subject yesterday--and I told him MP III 1 314 17
spirit of reproach, exerted on a more momentous subject. MP III 1 323 53
flatter herself that the subject would be finally MP III 1 324 59
thing would soon be as if no such subject had existed. MP III 1 324 59
had never thought on the subject enough to be in danger; MP III 2 326 3
impossible, that the subject was most painful to her, that MP III 2 327 5
opinion, one wish on the subject; the influence of all who MP III 2 329 12
From this hour, the subject is never to be revived between MP III 2 330 16
And now, my dear Fanny, this subject is closed between us." MP III 2 331 16
obliged to mention the subject to his niece, to prepare MP III 2 331 19
The subject of reading aloud was farther discussed. MP III 3 339 22
The subject is more justly considered. MP III 3 339 23
shewing it to be a subject on which he had thought before, MP III 3 340 24
improperly?--lightly, irreverently on the subject?-- MP III 3 342 33
I should not have mentioned the subject, though very MP III 4 351 36
a moment, and on such a subject, was a bitter aggravation. MP III 4 354 47
The subject of it so very--very--what shall I say? MP III 5 358 9
thoughts on the subject, some surmises as to what might be. MP III 5 362 18
of long talking on the subject, explaining and dwelling on MP III 6 370 14
good deal of alarm on the subject of their journey, for MP III 6 372 21
That a letter from Edmund should be a subject of terror! MP III 6 374 27
knowing her wish on the subject, he would not distress her MP III 7 375 3
as he was, in that subject, more than once tried to make MP III 7 380 23
But here, one subject swallowed up all the rest. MP III 7 382 29
seasons, a regulation of subject, a propriety, an attempt MP III 7 382 29
herself cheerfully on the subject of home, there were MP III 8 388 1
for ever on the sore subject of the silver knife, MP III 9 396 7
Her greatest wonder on the subject soon became--not that MP III 9 397 8
They talked of William, a subject on which Mrs. Price MP III 10 400 7
After talking a little more about Mansfield, a subject in MP III 10 401 10
It was a subject which she must learn to speak of, and the MP III 10 406 20
As for the main subject of the letter--there was nothing MP III 13 424 4
subject in the world for a little medical imposition. MP III 14 429 1
"On the subject of my last, I had actually begun a letter MP III 14 430 4
I really am quite agitated on the subject. MP III 14 434 13
channel, that the subject was for a moment out of her head. MP III 15 438 8
keenly felt to be a subject of the slightest communication. MP III 16 453 16
evening that Edmund began to talk to her on the subject. MP III 16 453 17
repetition--it would be a subject prohibited entirely--he MP III 16 453 17
the subject in a manner which he owned had shocked him. MP III 16 454 18
made it natural to her to treat the subject as she did. MP III 16 456 25
almost sorry that the subject had been entered on at all. MP III 16 457 30
Where she could be placed, became a subject of most MP III 17 464 13
his early opinion on the subject when the poor little MP III 17 471 29
All manner of solemn nonsense was talked on the subject, E I 1 12 41
from Farmer Mitchell's, I made up my mind on the subject. E I 1 12 41
There was not a dissentient voice on the subject, either E I 2 17 9
Her situation was altogether the subject of hours of E I 2 18 12
of consulting Mr. Perry, the apothecary, on the subject. E I 2 19 14
in her power, but on this subject questions were vain. E I 4 27 3
he were here, for he thinks exactly as I do on the subject. E I 5 36 6
own and Mr. Weston's on the subject, as much as possible. E I 5 41 31
chose rather to take up her own line of the subject again. E I 8 63 43
more philosophic on the subject of beauty than they are E I 8 63 44
he had spoken to on the subject, did not at present E I 9 70 6
my wishes on the subject have been ever since I knew you. E I 9 73 20
Mr. Woodhouse came in, and very soon led to the subject E I 9 78 49
led to such a branch of the subject as must raise them. E I 9 80 68
poor family, however, were the first subject on meeting. E I 10 87 31
for him to chuse his own subject in the adjoining room. E I 10 89 38
an unsafe subject, "I must beg you not to talk of the sea. E I 12 101 23
she added soon afterwards--as if quite another subject. E I 13 110 8
Emma thought with pleasure of some change of subject. E I 13 114 28
quiet Mr. Elton, the subject was so completely past that E I 14 118 4
Emma liked the subject so well, that she began upon it, to E I 14 121 14
subject, was ready to listen with most friendly smiles. E I 15 124 2
it off and bring the subject back into its proper course, E I 15 125 4
so rapidly did another subject succeed; for Mr. John E I 15 125 7
as much at ease on the subject as his nervous constitution E I 15 128 17
than she found her subject cut up--her hand seized--her E I 15 129 24
at all,--he resumed the subject of his own passion, and E I 15 130 28
on the subject, for the first start of its possibility. E I 16 135 6
in all her ideas on one subject, all her observations, all E I 17 141 5
There will be but one subject throughout the parishes of E I 18 149 29
getting rid of the subject as they returned;-- but it E II 1 155 1
on the subject of Weymouth and the Dixons than any thing. E II 2 169 16
other half she could give to her own view of the subject. E II 3 177 51
brought on a more interesting subject, and a warmer manner. E II 5 186 4
were too numerous for any subject of conversation to be E II 8 214 13
body who spoke on the subject was equally convinced that E II 8 215 15
your <u>thoughts</u> on this subject are very much like mine." E II 8 216 26
but by the others, the subject was almost immediately E II 8 220 45
in dwelling on the subject; and having so much to ask and E II 8 220 46
"No," said he, smiling, "that is no subject of regret at E II 8 222 53
train of thinking on the subject of Mrs. Weston's E II 8 227 87
"That you do not give another half-second to the subject. E II 9 235 41
passed by the two young people in schemes on the subject. E II 11 247 2
I bring a new proposal on the subject:--a thought of my E II 11 250 21
of affection he might be subject to, was another point; E II 12 262 38
Every consideration of the subject, in short, makes me E II 13 265 4
longer"--but no change of subject could avail, and the E II 13 267 9
The very first subject after being seated was Maple Grove, E II 14 272 18
indignation, changed the subject directly: "I do not ask E II 14 276 34
35
after a moment's pause, Mrs. Elton chose another subject. E II 14 278 43
heard all Mrs. Elton's knight-errantry on the subject.-- E II 15 282 4
aloud on that part of the subject, before the few who knew E II 15 285 16
It was natural to have some civil hopes on the subject, E II 16 293 10
11
you did not mention the subject to her; till the time E II 17 300 11
disengaged, he necessarily began on the subject with her. E II 17 304 30
decided her belief on the subject, was his staying only a E III 1 316 4
continued, "to have no reserves with you on this subject. E III 4 337 4
because I shall never speak to you again on the subject. E III 4 342 39
"if I must speak on this subject, there is no denying that E III 5 345 16

body to go, concluded the subject; and with a short final E III 6 366 74
What Mr. Elton had learnt from the ostler on the subject, E III 8 383 31
it united with the subject which already engaged her mind. E III 8 384 32
On that subject poor Miss Bates was very unhappy, and very E III 9 391 19
He came to speak to his father on a subject,--to announce E III 10 395 30
hand, and entered on the subject in a manner to prove, E III 10 400 69
given her a hint on the subject; but she felt completely E III 11 402 1
speak so stoutly on the subject," replied Emma, smiling; " E III 11 405 13
for as to the subject which had first introduced it, the E III 11 408 33
join them, he changed the subject, and began talking about E III 11 410 35
On the subject of the first of the two circumstances, she E III 11 410 36
had he expressed himself to her on the subject!-- E III 12 415 1
It would do neither of them good, it would do the subject E III 12 416 2
a little from the one subject which had engrossed them, E III 12 417 3
as to bring her to converse on the important subject. E III 12 418 5
much pleased with all that she had said on the subject. E III 12 418 5
feared had been made a subject of material distress to the E III 12 421 17
could not, feel equal to lead the way to any such subject. E III 13 425 2
immediate feeling was to avert the subject, if possible. E III 13 429 26
You will find, whenever the subject becomes freed from its E III 14 438 8
this charm ceased, the subject could still maintain itself, E III 15 444 1
or merely of love, as the subject required; concluding, E III 15 445 14
15
Emma, my mind has been hard at work on one subject." E III 15 448 30
The subject followed; it was in plain, unaffected, E III 15 448 31
could alter his wishes or his opinion on the subject. E III 15 449 32
I do not know, for I never heard the subject talked of." E III 16 456 31
tempted to introduce a subject, to ask questions, to speak E III 16 459 46
with Harriet Smith; but it was too tender a subject.-- E III 17 463 15
we could enter without ceremony or reserve on the subject." E III 17 464 22
She must not make it a more decided subject of misery to E III 17 465 28
praise of her gave the subject even a kind of welcome; and E III 17 466 30
meeting, to consider the subject in the most serviceable E III 17 467 30
been able to finish the subject better than by saying--" E III 17 467 31
"There is one subject," he replied, "I hope but one, on E III 18 470 8
in the meanwhile, we need not talk much on the subject." E III 18 471 16
materially changed since we talked on this subject before." E III 18 474 32
was no longer a want of subject or animation--or of E III 18 476 46
47
When first sounded on the subject, he was so miserable, E III 19 483 9
Lady Russell was most anxiously zealous on the subject, P III 2 11 2
Mr. Shepherd was eloquent on the subject; pointing out all P III 3 22 24
Anne's conduct, for the subject was never alluded to,--but P III 4 29 8
assure you, that upon the subject of marriage they are P III 5 35 14
with a heart full of the subject which had been completely P III 6 42 1
Her own spirits improved by change of place and subject, P III 6 46 12
had been said on the subject at the other house, where the P III 6 49 25
listened to anew on this subject, and afterwards, of all P III 6 51 32
for I have thought on the subject more than most men." P III 7 62 41
Anne had a moment's astonishment on the subject herself; P III 11 98 17
and entered into the subject, as ready to do good by P III 12 103 3
affected to renew the subject--and when he spoke again, it P III 12 108 29
awkwardness at first in their discourse on another subject. P IV 1 124 12
She could have said more on the subject; for she had in P IV 1 125 17
civil enough, took up the subject again, to say, "the next P IV 1 128 29
the many anxious feelings she had wasted on the subject. P IV 1 128 32
was a strong proof of his opinions on the subject. P IV 3 139 7
His tone, his expressions, his choice of subject, his P IV 3 143 19
on a subject which she thought unworthy to excite them. P IV 4 148 10
certainty she felt on the subject, she would venture on P IV 5 159 22
She could not distinguish, but she must guess the subject; P IV 8 181 2
It was impossible for her to enter on such a subject; and P IV 8 183 11
12
impossible to pursue the subject farther; and Anne felt P IV 9 198 52
to repeat half that I used to hear him say on that subject. P IV 9 202 66
at all hours--but I need not be particular on this subject. P IV 9 207 90
He little surmised that it was a subject acting now P IV 10 214 12
I had not thought seriously on this subject before. P IV 11 242 65
the subject of Sanditon, a complete enthusiast.-- S 2 371 1
& are subject to a variety of very serious disorders.-- S 5 385 1
But while we are on the subject of poetry, what think you S 7 397 1
Already had he had many musings on the subject. S 8 405 2
to Mrs D. more doubtingly on the subject of Sanditon.-- S 9 409 1
I am very subject to Perspiration, and there cannot be a S 10 416 1
like herself, & the subject had supplied letters & S 11 420 1
And while you are on the subject of subscriptions Mary, I S 12 424 1

SUBJECT'S (1)

the first time of the subject's occurring to her again, MP I 3 24 7

SUBJECTION (5)

subjection of reason to common-place and mistaken notions. SS I 11 53 2
My doctrine has never aimed at the subjection of the SS I 17 94 39
The subjection in which his father had brought him up, had PP I 15 70 1
and a subjection of the fancy to the understanding. E I 5 37 7
talents, and must have been under subjection to her." E I 5 37 9

SUBJECTS (57)

chatting on indifferent subjects for a short time, said to LS 23 284 6
Their conversation turned upon those subjects, of which NA I 4 33 7
by his conversation on subjects very different--returned NA II 5 161 24
as careless on such subjects as most people, he did look NA II 6 166 6
There were still some subjects indeed, under which she NA II 10 201 4
pained by it; and other subjects being studiously brought NA II 11 213 20
a short trial of other subjects, Mrs. Allen again returned NA II 14 238 27
and heard his opinion on subjects of literature and taste; SS I 4 20 9
information on various subjects, and he has always SS I 10 51 20
subjects of raillery as delighted her husband and mother. SS I 12 62 27
will dispatch more subjects than can really be in common SS III 13 363 9
"can in general supply but few subjects for such a study. PP I 9 42 17
After many pauses and many trials of other subjects, PP I 16 82 44
45
We have tried two or three subjects already without PP I 18 93 26
It is of all subjects my delight. PP II 8 173 6
and various were the subjects which occupied them; Lady PP II 16 222 21
in crayons, whose subjects were usually more interesting, PP III 1 250 46
to think on serious subjects; and for the last half year, PP III 5 283 10
Lydia led voluntarily to subjects, which her sisters would PP III 9 316 6
interruption on those subjects that must deaden them more. PP III 12 339 1
other subjects took place of the improvements of Sotherton. MP I 6 55 14
to leave people to their own devices on such subjects. MP I 9 87 15
lively mind can hardly be serious even on serious subjects. MP I 9 87 16
zeal after poachers,--subjects which will not find their MP I 12 115 4
on people or subjects which she wished to be respected. MP II 4 208 11
Bertram one of the worst subjects to work on, in any MP II 4 212 30
sentiment and feeling, and seriousness on serious subjects. MP III 3 340 24
mass of hearers, on subjects limited, and long worn thread- MP III 3 341 28
that he does not think as he ought, on serious subjects." MP III 4 350 31
subjects, which I believe to be a good deal the case. MP III 4 350 32
of their higher-toned subjects, all of which ended, if MP III 7 375 2
to recover itself, were subjects for endless conjecture, MP III 12 417 4
Their conversations, however, were not always on subjects MP III 12 419 8
talk on indifferent subjects could never be long supported. MP III 15 445 33
word from him on the subjects that were weighing him down. MP III 15 445 34
her thoughts to other subjects, and revive some interest MP III 16 449 6
I quit such odious subjects as soon as I can, impatient to MP III 17 461 1
Mr. Knightleys; their subjects totally distinct, or very E I 12 100 15
information on all subjects which will enable him to E I 18 150 31
so much of late on these subjects who must have been so E II 3 175 42
Their subjects in general were such as belong to an E II 5 191 27
"You get upon delicate subjects, Emma," said Mrs. Weston E II 6 201 23
She said no more, other subjects took their turn; and the E II 8 219 43
of their principal subjects:--the post-office--catching E II 17 299 1
modes, till other subjects were started, that, though <u>may</u>, E III 2 320 5
I have a right to talk on such subjects, without being E III 6 361 40

On these subjects, her perplexity and distress were very E III 14 435 4
you, in the confusion of so many subjects, mistake him?-- E III 18 473 26
on each side continual subjects of offence, neither family P III 5 40 44
in all the other common subjects of house-keeping, P III 6 42 3
in the discussion of subjects, which his usual companions P III 11 100 23
Uppercross, before all subjects suddenly ceased, on seeing P III 12 103 5
The subjects of which her heart had been full on leaving P IV 1 124 11
Mutual enquiries on common subjects passed; neither of P IV 7 176 8
and care, and though his subjects were principally such as P IV 7 178 24
His choice of subjects, his expressions, and still more P IV 8 185 21
was startled to other subjects by Henrietta, eager to make P IV 10 225 61

SUBJOIN (1)
whom I shall subjoin a list, according to his information. PP III 8 313 19

SUBLIME (2)
the tender and the sublime of pleasure to Harriet's share. E I 9 82 84
more fraught with the deep sublime than that line?-- S 7 397 1

SUBLIMITIES (1)
as shew her in the Sublimities of intense feeling--such as S 8 403 1

SUBLIMITY (3)
be less of both if the sublimity of nature were more MP I 11 113 35
even the more simple sublimity of resolving to refuse him E III 13 431 38
in praise of their sublimity, & descriptive of the S 7 396 1

SUBMISSION (16)
at once into the utmost submission, & rendered more LS 25 293 3
a letter of proper submission from him, addressed perhaps SS III 13 371 39
"A letter of proper submission!" repeated he; "would they SS III 13 372 41
I can make no submission--I am grown neither humble nor SS III 13 372 41
I know of no submission that *is* proper for me to make." SS III 13 372 41
of a letter of proper submission; and therefore, to make SS III 13 372 45
but between his submission to *her* taste, and his having MP I 6 55 17
Miss Crawford listened with submission, and said to MP I 6 56 27
but with all that submission to Edmund could do, and all MP I 12 116 11
Her habits of ready submission, on the contrary, made her MP III 5 357 5
it rather from submission, however, than conviction, for MP III 6 370 14
and expediency of submission and forbearance, saw also MP III 9 397 8
into submission, as to be very tolerably cheerful again. MP III 17 462 5
escape her, and his submission to all that she told, was a E II 9 231 2
of her outward submission left a heavy arrear due of E III 6 353 3
He made no answer; merely looked, and bowed in submission; E III 7 373 45
46

SUBMISSIVE (5)
the most steady and submissive attention, made neither SS II 10 212 1
not be able to appear properly submissive and indifferent. MP II 5 218 12
could only give a submissive sigh; and as Emma saw his E I 9 80 68
Harriet kissed her hand in silent and submissive gratitude. E III 4 342 40
A submissive spirit might be patient, a strong P IV 5 154 8

SUBMISSIVELY (1)
Harriet listened submissively, and said "it was very true-- E II 13 267 9

SUBMIT (35)
to which she must now submit, I can only suppose that the LS 6 252 2
painful necessity, but I will endeavour to submit to it. LS 15 267 6
is too old ever to submit to school confinement, and have LS 20 277 5
in restoring peace than I ever intended to submit too. LS 25 292 1
Tell me that you submit to my arguments, & do not reproach LS 30 301 5
is an humiliation to which I know not how to submit. LS 35 305 1
know it is impossible to submit to such an extremity while LS 38 306 1
getting away, was obliged to give up the point and submit. NA I 11 87 53
"This will not do," said Catherine; "I cannot submit to NA I 13 100 18
might bring herself to submit to the offices of a nurse, SS I 8 38 10
Who would submit to the indignity of being approved by SS I 10 50 17
affair; and for some time she refused to submit to them. SS I 12 58 3
happy, and determined to submit to the greatest SS I 13 63 2
Is her son determined to submit to this, and to all the SS II 2 148 14
my love and esteem, must submit to my open commendation." SS II 13 244 40
in an error might be, she was obliged to submit to it. SS II 13 244 47
Dashwood was obliged to submit not only to the exceedingly SS II 14 248 6
which it was given, obliged him to submit to her authority. SS III 5 295 13
of the past, to submit--and therefore, after such an SS III 14 373 3
firm, & the gentleman found himself obliged to submit. W 340 18
Her niece was, therefore, obliged to submit, and they took PP III 1 254 57
Mrs. Bennet was forced to submit to a separation, which, PP III 11 330 2
I have not been used to submit to any person's whims. PP III 14 356 48
was too much vexed to submit with a very good grace, and MP I 8 79 23
after being obliged to submit to all this attention, and MP II 4 206 3
for though she must submit, as her own propriety of mind MP II 5 223 48
companion myself, I must submit to your finding one still MP III 1 314 16
There was nothing to be done, however, but to submit MP III 5 356 3
Gladly would I submit to all the increased pain of losing MP III 16 456 25
She will never submit to any thing requiring industry and E I 5 37 7
done with so little labour as she would ever submit to. E I 6 44 19
Emma must submit to stand second to Mrs. Elton, though she E III 2 325 31
she believed she must now submit to feel that another P III 6 42 1
Anne, after a little observation, felt she must submit to. P IV 4 147 8
She had only to submit, sit down, be outwardly composed, P IV 11 229 2

SUBMITTED (26)
she cheerfully submitted to the wish of Mr. Allen, which NA I 10 81 61
Catherine submitted; and though sorry to think that NA I 13 105 41
and mischievous tricks to which her cousins submitted. SS I 21 120 6
kind of intimacy must be submitted to, which consists of SS I 21 124 33
to which both of them submitted without any reluctance, SS II 2 151 41
Elinor submitted to the arrangement which counteracted her SS II 3 158 20
opinion, and she submitted to it therefore without SS II 10 214 6
weak for conversation, submitted readily to the silence SS III 9 334 5
that she submitted to the change without much reluctance. PP III 19 386 5
Mrs. Rushworth submitted, and the question of surveying MP I 9 89 32
been forced on her, she submitted to it without any alarm MP I 17 160 8
Suspense must be submitted to, and must not be allowed to MP III 12 418 6
That his judgment submitted to all his own peculiar and MP III 16 453 16
He submitted to believe, that Tom's illness had influenced MP III 16 459 31
She had submitted the best to the disappointment in Henry MP III 17 466 18
Harriet submitted, though her mind could hardly separate E I 9 77 43
she would gladly have submitted to feel yet more mistaken-- E I 16 134 1
This was not submitted to by either lady. E II 16 297 51
preference herself--she submitted, therefore, and only E III 9 390 19
Harriet submitted, and approved, and was grateful. E III 12 417 2
She checked herself, however, and submitted quietly to a E III 18 475 36
of retrenchment, which was at last submitted to Sir Walter. P III 2 12 3
to my judgment, submitted to an amicable compromise. P III 3 23 28
"Altered beyond his knowledge!" Anne fully submitted, in P III 7 60 34
Anne had never submitted more reluctantly to the jealous P III 12 115 66
As it was, she instantly submitted, and with all the P IV 9 197 34

SUBMITTING (5)
I am tired of submitting my will to the caprices of others- LS 39 308 1
herself at nineteen, submitting to new attachments, SS III 14 378 16
matrimonial point of submitting your own will, and doing E I 5 38 11
thinking the better of him for submitting to their whims. E I 18 147 18
But I mean, that I was right in submitting to her, and P IV 11 246 80

SUBORDINATE (2)
obtain them, and could better bear a subordinate situation. MP II 3 204 32
to both to have every subordinate arrangement concluded as E III 14 442 8

SUBORDINATION (1)
place the Martins under proper subordination in her fancy. E II 3 180 57

SUBSCRIBE (2)
I do not subscribe to it. MP I 5 45 14
That of being able to subscribe myself, your obliged E III 14 443 8

SUBSCRIBER (1)
She became a subscriber--amazed at being any thing *in* MP III 9 398 9

SUBSCRIBERS (1)
The list of Subscribers was but commonplace. S 6 389 1

SUBSCRIPTION (4)
library, & the library Subscription book, & Charlotte was S 6 389 1
& sound her ladyship as to a Subscription for them. S 12 423 1
beleive we must set a Subscription on foot--& therefore S 12 423 1
to promote a little Subscription for their releif, S 12 423 1

SUBSCRIPTIONS (2)
I am not fond of charitable subscriptions in a place of S 12 423 1
And while you are on the subject of subscriptions Mary, I S 12 424 1

SUBSEQUENT (12)
wealth, than by his subsequent malicious overthrow of it; NA II 16 251 6
In the whole of her subsequent manner, she traced the SS III 10 342 7
his subsequent language, she lost all compassion in anger. PP II 11 189 6
her subsequent absence from home, had since lain dormant. MP I 8 75 1
their power, which no subsequent connections can supply; MP II 6 235 18
by a divorce which no subsequent connection can justify, MP II 6 235 18
of a scheme for his subsequent consolation and happiness. E II 13 266 6
Emma was not required, by any subsequent discovery, to E II 15 281 1
or of deriving it, except in subsequent ridicule. E III 8 378 3
must be paid; but his subsequent object was to lament over E III 16 457 37
away, and one or two subsequent moments, marked by P IV 11 244 71
to admit from subsequent observation, that they appeared S 6 391 1

SUBSERVIENT (1)
us merely to be subservient to those of our neighbours. SS I 17 94 38

SUBSIDE (3)
I may therefore expect it will sooner subside; & perhaps LS 22 282 7
to Mr. Knightley's marrying did not in the least subside. E II 8 227 87
Their affection was always to subside into friendship. E II 13 264 1

SUBSIDED (5)
subsided) to doubt whether she had been perfectly right. NA I 13 103 29
the tempest subsided, or she unknowingly fell fast asleep. NA II 6 171 12
His apparent partiality had subsided, his attentions were PP II 3 149 28
Fanny's sick feelings subsided; but when tea was soon MP II 1 181 17
Her own attachment had really subsided into a mere nothing; E III 1 315 1

SUBSIST (2)
them by letter, could subsist only under a positive SS I 22 134 53
no real confidence could ever subsist between them again. PP I 23 127 9

SUBSISTANCE (1)
supplying the means of respectable subsistance hereafter. E II 2 164 5

SUBSISTED (5)
That some kind of engagement had subsisted between SS II 6 178 17
we are to call it--has subsisted through all the knowledge SS III 9 336 14
especially, there subsisted a very particular regard. PP II 2 139 2
and confidence subsisted between Mr. Darcy and herself. PP III 10 327 3
such a friendship as has subsisted between him and Captain P IV 6 173 46

SUBSISTING (4)
the degree of intimacy subsisting between them, implied by LS 15 266 1
ill-will continually subsisting between Fanny and Lucy, in SS III 14 377 11
as the degree of intimacy subsisting between the parties?" PP I 10 50 38
Dear sir, the disagreement subsisting between PP I 13 62 12

SUBSTANCE (19)
person of taste; the substance of its papers so often NA I 5 38 4
then--how mournfully superior in reality and substance! NA II 13 227 26
his father a man of substance and credit, whereas the NA II 15 246 12
substance made me any amends for the defect of the style." SS III 13 365 17
Had Lydia and her mother known the substance of her PP II 18 232 22
the substance of their conversation was impossible. PP III 14 359 77
its motive, and the substance of her conversation with PP III 16 367 9
It made the substance of one other confidential discourse MP III 6 373 26
This, as well as I understand, is to be the substance of MP III 12 415 2
after giving the substance of it, "has agitated us MP III 13 426 11
Their substance was great anger at the *folly* of each. MP III 16 454 18
I have told you the substance of all that she said. MP III 16 457 30
or the substance of it, from the open-hearted Mr. Weston.-- E I 14 119 6
in fact heard the whole substance of Jane Fairfax's letter, E II 1 162 33
He had caught both substance and shadow--both fortune and E II 4 182 5
pianoforte; and the substance of the story, the end of all E II 8 214 13
The substance of this letter was forwarded to Emma, in a E II 12 258 8
"My dear Harriet, I perfectly remember the substance of E III 11 406 23
of the narration, a substance to sink her spirit-- E III 11 409 34

SUBSTANTIAL (6)
if not accompanied by something more substantial. LS 3 247 1
parsonage, a new-built substantial stone house, with its NA II 11 212 17
yet add something more substantial, in the improvement of PP I 8 39 51
could remember no more substantial good than the general PP II 13 206 4
gates, and old trees, substantial and unmodernized--and P III 5 36 20
Mrs. Musgrove was of a comfortable substantial size, P III 8 68 29

SUBSTITUTE (3)
give up the lakes, and substitute a more contracted tour; PP II 19 238 7
and last as her substitute, she was established at MP III 17 472 31
"I leave an excellent substitute in my daughter. E I 8 57 5

SUBSTITUTED (2)
being accordingly substituted, every thing was considered MP I 1 8 9
bad air, bad smells, substituted for liberty, freshness, MP III 14 432 9

SUBSTITUTION (1)
and vexation, at the substitution of one sister for the P III 12 115 68

SUBTERRANEOUS (1)
that there is a secret subterraneous communication between NA II 5 159 21

SUBTLETIES (1)
of Mr. Elliot's subtleties, in endeavouring to prevent it. P IV 10 215 13

SUCCEED (26)
with her, & if he cannot succeed, to bring her to LS 15 266 4
a bright afternoon would succeed, and justified the NA I 11 83 16
after a few efforts, succeed in opening,--and, with your NA II 5 159 19
The anxieties of common life began soon to succeed to the NA II 10 201 5
pass away and repentance succeed it? and she only wanted NA II 13 227 27
means however they might succeed by establishing his SS I 20 112 28
done to succeed to it, might have puzzled them still more. SS III 14 377 12
it would succeed, if Miss de Bourgh were out of the way. PP I 21 119 20
because he was not so happy as to succeed with you?" PP I 22 125 15
not try to part us; if he were so, they could not succeed. PP II 1 137 24
in my life--trying to entertain her--and succeed so ill! MP II 6 230 7
before he could succeed; for Mrs. Norris had not MP III 1 323 57
was understood, he should succeed?--he believed it fully. MP III 2 327 4
But (with an affectionate smile), let him succeed at last, MP III 4 347 18
let him succeed at last, Fanny, let him succeed at last. MP III 4 347 18
"Oh! never, never, never; he never will succeed with me." MP III 4 347 19
I do not think that even *he* could now hope to succeed with MP III 16 457 29
affections for an object worthy to succeed her in them. MP III 17 470 25
did another subject succeed; for Mr. John Knightley now E I 15 125 7
She had not been prepared to have Jane Fairfax succeed Mr. E II 1 156 6
trying to be useful; tell me if you think I shall succeed." E II 10 240 3
(returning into the room,) I have not been able to succeed. E II 10 245 52
She would not allow any other anxiety to succeed directly E III 16 452 6
But alas! there were very different thoughts to succeed. P IV 8 191 51
and if such parties succeed, how should a Captain P IV 12 248 1
Domains, but he cd not succeed in the veiws of permanently S 3 375 1

SUCCEEDED (54)
me six years ago, & which never succeeded at last. LS 5 249 1
mortification succeeded another, and from the whole she NA I 8 55 10
A silence of several minutes succeeded their first short NA I 9 63 10
The general pause which succeeded his short disquisition NA I 14 111 29
A reverie succeeded this conviction--and when Isabella NA I 15 120 23
In the pause which succeeded, a sound like receding NA II 6 170 12
a bright morning had succeeded the tempest of the night. NA II 7 172 1
Tilney, which have not succeeded; but I do not understand NA II 12 218 6
how frequently are they succeeded by such opinions as are SS I 11 56 17
too much astonished to speak, and another pause succeeded. SS I 15 76 16
After a short silence which succeeded the first surprise SS I 16 87 24
A short pause succeeded this speech, which was first SS I 21 123 21
many minutes' duration, succeeded this speech, and Lucy SS II 2 150 35
letter how ill she had succeeded in laying any foundation SS II 9 203 10
A short pause of mutual thoughtfulness succeeded. SS III 8 327 56
suppose his plan to have succeeded, & imagine him W 336 14
To this discovery succeeded some others equally mortifying. PP I 6 23 12
again, she was eagerly succeeded at the instrument by her PP I 6 25 23

to their father, and succeeded him in the business, and a PP I 7 28 2
Miss Bingley succeeded no less in the real object of her PP I 11 56 12
next to Jane in birth and beauty, succeeded her of course. PP I 15 71 4
But when this subject was succeeded by his account of Mr. PP II 13 204 2
as such pauses must always be, succeeded for a few moments. PP III 3 267 4
man who had recently succeeded to one of the largest MP I 4 38 9
Mr. Rushworth has made it since he succeeded to the estate. MP I 8 82 34
A general silence succeeded. MP I 9 94 57
A short silence succeeded her leaving them; but her MP I 14 136 21
A fine blush having succeeded the previous paleness of her MP II 1 178 7
few words, of his having succeeded in the object he had MP II 13 298 3
She succeeded. MP III 5 357 5
he had succeeded in getting your brother's commission." MP III 5 363 26
At length, a something like composure succeeded. MP III 12 418 6
it is probable that Mr. Yates would never have succeeded. MP III 17 466 18
ceased to form hopes, succeeded to a stall in Westminster, MP III 17 469 23
after Fanny's removal, succeeded so naturally to her MP III 17 472 31
"John, how are you?" succeeded in the true English style, E I 12 99 14
very happily, and others succeeded of similar moment, and E I 12 104 50
when she thought she had succeeded, and after speaking E II 1 155 1
And not all that could be urged to detain her succeeded. E II 1 162 33
passed away; the dessert succeeded, the children came in, E II 8 219 43
As Frank Churchill's arrival had succeeded Mr. Elton's E II 13 267 8
discussion; and to them succeeded one, which must be at E II 17 299 1
trying not to smile; and succeeded without difficulty, E II 18 312 51
When had he succeeded to that place in her affection, E III 11 412 45
it; but no such bustle succeeded as poor Miss Bates had E III 16 452 8
To Emma's entreaties and assurances succeeded Mr. E III 17 466 30
Elizabeth had succeeded, at sixteen, to all that was P III 1 5 8
complaisance; had never succeeded in any point which she P III 2 16 16
It succeeded, however; and though Sir Walter must ever P III 3 24 35
more; and that they were succeeded, not merely by P IV 8 185 21
and a short pause succeeded, which seemed to ensure that P IV 10 222 37
a keener interest had succeeded, and she was not so little P IV 11 229 1
these good people have succeeded in setting the Carge to S 1 367 1
of Sanditon had succeeded in removing her & her large S 3 375 1

SUCCEEDING (25)
The succeeding morning promised something better. NA II 9 191 3
them; and a shortly succeeding ray of common sense added NA II 9 193 6
nature; but the four succeeding years--years, which if SS II 1 140 2
I have no right, and I could have no chance of succeeding. SS II 5 173 44
she and Elinor luckily succeeding to chairs, placed SS II 6 175 2
Long letters from her, quickly succeeding each other, SS II 10 213 2
The third day succeeding their knowledge of the SS III 2 271 4
was not even mentioned in any of the succeeding letters. SS III 11 353 21
on which succeeding events have built so immoveable a PP II 11 193 28
had never yet despaired of succeeding at last. PP II 16 223 26
"His being so sure of succeeding, was wrong," said she; " PP II 17 224 3
communicated, and every succeeding day was expected to PP III 6 296 9
enjoyment, and every succeeding morrow renewed a tete-a- MP II 6 234 17
He had received a good education, but on succeeding early E I 2 15 1
to come with me, that I might be sure of succeeding." E II 9 236 44
But, said I, I shall be more sure of succeeding if one of E II 9 236 46
her the idea of Harriet's succeeding her in his affections. E II 13 266 6
Tell me, then, have I no chance of ever succeeding?" E III 13 430 33
dear mother's place, succeeding to all her rights, and all P IV 5 159 25
Towards the close of it, in the interval succeeding an P IV 8 186 24
the new-formed hope of succeeding in the object of her P IV 9 210 99
which he had occupied, succeeding to the very spot where P IV 11 237 41
42
profession--succeeding as eldest son to the property which S 2 371 1
the fairest chance of succeeding to the greater part of S 3 377 1
commission with pleasure, & have no doubt of succeeding.-- S 5 387 1

SUCCEEDS (1)
their own; and with many men, I dare say, it succeeds. PP I 8 40 56

SUCCESS (63)
told my story with great success to Mrs. Vernon who, LS 22 280 1
tho' with little hope of success, was resolved to leave LS 42 311 2
than this assurance of success; and every particular was NA I 15 122 28
disappointed at her ill success thus far, it would be NA II 6 169 11
that her success was speedy, and for the time complete. SS I 22 134 53
who had traded with success in a less elegant part of the SS II 3 153 1
though almost hopeless of success, she forced herself to SS II 3 157 17
hope of Colonel Brandon's success, whatever the event of SS II 5 174 45
I had no hope of interfering with success; and sometimes I SS II 9 210 32
to make a civil answer, though doubting her own success. SS II 13 240 14
application, of whose success he was almost as confident SS III 7 313 21
over in private, to wish success to her friend, and yet in SS III 9 339 27
"Well," said Charlotte, "I wish Jane success with all my PP I 6 23 10
The usual inquiries as to his success were made by the PP I 16 83 49
success, and what we are to talk of next I cannot imagine." PP I 18 93 26
"And what is your success?" PP I 18 93 39
more spirit, or finer success; and happy did she think it PP I 18 101 72
have felt almost sure of success if he had not been to PP I 22 121 1
attempt known till its success could be known likewise; PP I 22 121 1
and whenever he came to Hunsford; but without much success. PP II 9 181 29
friend from your sister, or that I rejoice in my success. PP II 11 191 15
on you; but his success is not perhaps to be wondered at. PP II 12 202 5
the probability of each statement--but with little success. PP II 13 205 3
she was most sure of success, for those to whom she PP III 2 262 7
could result from the success of his endeavours, and when PP III 2 263 10
somewhat nettled, she had all the success she expected. PP III 3 271 16
any success, no such people had been seen to pass through. PP III 4 275 5
Mr. Gardiner himself did not expect any success from this PP III 6 295 5
wished to converse with her, he might have better success. PP III 12 342 25
in witnessing their success and enjoyment at the expense MP I 4 35 5
all the good-humour of success, she said, "thank you, my MP I 10 100 22
with such talent and such success, went off with her to MP II 2 195 22
into the enjoyment and success of his lady, but in vain; MP II 7 240 10
touched again when the ladies withdrew, with more success. MP II 10 272 4
seeing such confidence of success in the principal, Sir MP III 2 329 11
have enlightened witnesses of the progress of his success. MP III 2 331 19
as to his feelings and success; questions which being made MP III 3 340 24
with this idea--but he could hardly tell with what success. MP III 6 366 1
and strong probability of success; and who in every thing MP III 16 452 15
been every probability of success and felicity for him. MP III 17 467 19
out the strongest hope of success, though it remained for MP III 17 471 28
general well-doing and success of the other members of the MP III 17 473 31
And after such success you know!-- E I 1 12 41
I planned the match from that hour; and when such success E I 1 12 41
"I do not understand what you mean by 'success;'" said Mr. E I 1 12 42
"Success supposes endeavour. E I 1 12 42
do you talk of success? where is your merit?--what are you E I 1 12 42
lines about the mouth--I have not a doubt of your success. E I 6 44 16
The same civilities and courtesies, the same success and E I 6 47 30
earnestly wishing you success: but had I supposed that she E I 15 131 34
Miss Bates was obliged to return without success; Jane was E III 9 390 18
I have already met with such success in two applications E III 14 437 8
Lady Russell's had no success at all--could not be put up P III 2 13 6
improper, hardly capable of success, and not deserving it. P III 4 27 5
She had little hope of success; but Elizabeth, who in the P III 5 34 12
more of the general success and produce of the evening P IV 9 192 5
desire it, as what could alone crown all my other success. P IV 11 247 84
Sanditon,--the success of Sanditon as a small, fashionable S 2 371 1
Not that he had any personal concern in the success of the S 4 383 1
But success more than repays.-- S 5 387 1
the first offering to the success of the season, was busy S 6 390 1
more anxious for its success & mourned over its S 8 404 1
of a few broken sentences of self-approbation & success.-- S 10 416 1

SUCCESSFUL (15)
being successful in your application to your fair friend?" NA II 2 139 5
she believed herself successful; but how strangely NA II 6 168 10
wish him successful, she heartily wished him indifferent. SS I 10 50 12
contemplation of his successful love; for Mrs. Bennet, PP I 20 110 1
that his sisters would be successful in keeping him away. PP I 23 129 13
delight, can never be successful; and general PP II 19 237 4
A successful scheme of this sort generally brings on MP I 7 70 30
Mr. Rushworth came back from the parsonage successful; and MP I 8 77 7
She found herself more successful in sending away, than in MP I 10 103 48
and the ball, and herself, as to be finally successful. MP II 8 258 17
A very successful visit:--I saw all the three ladies; and E II 6 198 7
their advice for her going was most prompt and successful. E II 7 208 8
Every invitation was successful. E II 16 291 7
He soon joined them again, successful, of course; Lady P IV 7 174 2
She had been too successful however for much fatigue; for S 10 414 1

SUCCESSFULLY (6)
while Mrs. Morland was successfully confirming her own NA II 14 239 28
marmalade had been successfully applied for a bruised SS I 21 121 10
of his friends successfully combated by the more natural PP II 2 142 16
it was delightful to see the effort so successfully made. MP II 10 273 6
minute, Emma felt the glory of having schemed successfully. E I 10 90 39
And she talked in this way so long and successfully that, E I 12 104 45

SUCCESSION (8)
explanations, became in succession her's, with the NA II 14 237 22
To him therefore the succession to the Norland estate was SS I 1 3 2
succession, she wept for him, more than for herself. SS II 1 140 4
to promise the quickest succession; one gentleman only was SS II 11 220 3
the ball with all this succession of company--& Emma was W 338 17
ball, there was such a succession of rain as prevented PP I 17 88 15
table, it was a quick succession of busy nothings till the MP I 10 104 52
After a little succession of these sort of debates and P III 10 86 18

SUCCESSION-HOUSES (1)
"How were Mr. Allen's succession-houses worked?" NA II 7 178 24

SUCCESSIVE (4)
to recollect how many successive springs her ladyship LS 6 251 1
For nine successive mornings, Catherine wondered over the NA II 10 201 6
a borough in three successive parliaments, exertions of P III 1 3 3
4
now, by successive captures, have made a handsome fortune. P III 4 29 8

SUCCESSIVELY (7)
finding herself successively in a billiard-room, and in NA II 8 183 2
She was here shewn successively into three large bed- NA II 8 185 5
and for many days successively, and he did not repent. SS I 1 5 8
Five daughters successively entered the world, but yet the PP III 8 308 3
Four fine mornings successively were spent in this manner, MP I 7 70 30
were successively dismissed with yet warmer objections. MP I 14 130 3
many, many months successively, without being at any ball E II 11 247 1

SUCCESSLESS (1)
If it were love, it might be simple, single, successless E II 2 168 13

SUCCESSOR (1)
As her successor in that house, she regarded her with PP I 23 130 16

SUCCOUR (1)
succour, and watching almost every look and every breath. SS III 7 315 25

SUCH-LIKE (1)
Such and such-like were the reasonings of Sir Thomas-- MP II 3 201 22

SUCKING (1)
She might have been unconsciously sucking in the sad E II 2 168 13

SUCKLINGS (5)
of a visit from the Sucklings, and of the use to be made E III 5 343 1
explore to box hill though the Sucklings did not come? E III 6 352 2
and pic-nic parade of the Eltons and the Sucklings. E III 6 352 2
Except the Sucklings and Bragges, there is not such E III 8 382 23
except the little Sucklings and little Bragges, there are E III 8 382 23

SUCKLINGS' (1)
which for a while the Sucklings' coming had been united, E III 6 352 1

SUDDEN (89)
beleive; for in fact, the sudden disclosure of so LS 20 277 6
I always disliked him from the first, it is not a sudden LS 21 279 1
Guess then what I must feel at the sudden disturbance of LS 22 281 4
not more sudden in forming, than unsteady in keeping them. LS 23 284 6
to do in perfecting a sudden intimacy between two young NA I 4 33 7
and the blush, which his sudden reappearance raised in NA I 8 53 3
a sudden gust of wind, and of being left in total darkness. NA I 11 88 54
On the beginning of the fifth, however, the sudden view of NA I 12 92 4
difficulty arising, no sudden recollection, no unexpected NA I 14 106 1
A sudden scud of rain driving full in her face, made it NA II 5 161 25
but at that moment a sudden knocking at the door of the NA II 6 164 3
building and close with sudden fury a distant door, felt NA II 6 166 9
was no danger of its sudden extinction, it had yet some NA II 6 169 12
A violent gust of wind, rising with sudden fury, added NA II 6 170 12
Her illness was sudden and short; and, before I arrived it NA II 8 186 12
"the seizure which which ended in her death was sudden. NA II 9 196 25
Catherine had not read three lines before her sudden NA II 10 202 8
ease as to the necessity of any sudden removal of her own. NA II 11 208 2
arrival was often as sudden, if not quite so unseasonable, NA II 13 222 7
produced strange and sudden noises throughout the house, NA II 13 227 26
the cause, or collect the particulars of her sudden return. NA II 14 233 10
fancy or other, all of a sudden grew tired of having her NA II 14 237 21
entrance, asked her, with sudden alacrity, if Mr. and Mrs. NA II 15 242 9
or expense of so sudden a removal, her beloved Elinor SS I 4 23 19
The sudden termination of Colonel Brandon's visit at the SS I 14 70 1
concern and alarm which this sudden departure occasioned. SS I 15 77 18
It was quite a sudden thing our coming at all, and I knew SS I 20 110 2
caught those words by a sudden pause in Marianne's music.-- SS II 2 148 20
countenance glowing with sudden delight, she would have SS II 6 176 3
bear any sudden noise, was startled by a rap at the door. SS II 9 203 11
and confusion were very great on his so sudden appearance. SS III 4 288 26
"No," replied he, with sudden consciousness, "not to find SS III 4 289 34
and of dinner by their sudden reverse, from eating much;-- SS III 7 315 27
so wonderful and so sudden;--a perplexity which they had SS III 12 360 26
he feared, might give a sudden turn to his constitution, SS III 14 373 3
more so under this sudden reverse;--he stood the picture W 330 11
well had taken the sudden resolution of attending the W 338 18
He loved to take people by surprise, with sudden visits at W 355 28
His answer to this sudden attack was delightful to their PP I 9 45 36
her surprise at their sudden return home, which, as their PP I 15 73 11
The sudden acquisition of ten thousand pounds was the most PP II 3 149 28
ready for a walk, a sudden noise below seemed to speak the PP II 5 158 11
she could, to a change so sudden and so important, fatigue, PP II 13 209 12
in Lambton, with false excuses for their sudden departure. PP III 4 281 29
her disappointment at its sudden interruption; which PP III 16 370 33
The reason of this sudden removal was soon evident. PP III 18 383 26
on being introduced into company is frequently too sudden. MP I 5 49 32
that in her head; and the sudden change which Edmund's MP I 7 74 59
She was again roused from disagreeable musings by sudden MP I 10 100 24
in consequence of the sudden breaking-up of a large party MP I 13 121 1
representation, when the sudden death of one of the MP I 13 121 1
till, as if struck by a sudden recollection, she exclaimed, MP I 15 143 27
were so warmed by his sudden arrival, as to place her MP II 1 179 9
form of hurried walks and sudden removals from her own MP II 2 188 3
they were forced by the sudden swell of a cold gust MP II 4 208 11
when Mrs. Grant, with sudden recollection, turned to her MP II 4 215 47
how welcome was his sudden resolution of coming to them MP II 5 223 48
the shrubbery, in her caution to avoid any sudden attack. MP III 5 357 4
at least delayed by the sudden change in Miss Crawford's MP III 5 357 6
half an hour, was from a sudden burst of her father's, not MP III 7 383 30
out at sudden starts immediately under their father's eye. MP III 7 383 31
seconded a sudden wish of her's, to have Harriet's picture. E I 6 43 8
a very sudden trial of our stability in good thoughts. E I 10 87 29
30
vicarage pales, when a sudden resolution, of at least E I 10 89 36
with the surprize of so sudden a journey, and his fears E I 17 141 4
But now she made the sudden resolution of not passing E II 1 155 3
water, and she, by the sudden whirling round of something E II 1 160 23

So sudden!-- E II 1 161 31
perhaps--when, all of a sudden, who should come in--to be E II 3 178 52
Martin's saying, all of a sudden, that she thought Miss E II 5 186 4
A sudden freak seemed to have seized him at breakfast, and E II 7 205 1
About half a mile beyond Highbury, making a sudden turn, E III 3 333 5
her, was liable to such sudden variation as might E III 6 361 41
But is not this a sudden scheme?" E III 9 385 3
now he seemed more sudden than usual in his disappearance. E III 9 386 7
A sudden seizure of a different nature from any thing E III 9 387 11
confusion of sudden and perplexing emotions, must create.-- E III 11 409 34
The change had perhaps been somewhat sudden;--her proposal E III 13 431 38
slow effects, sudden bursts, perseverance and weariness, E III 14 437 8
Emma spoke her pity so very kindly, that, with a sudden E III 18 477 58
59
befriended, not by any sudden illumination of Mr. E III 19 483 10
Suppose I were to be seized of a sudden in some dreadful P III 5 37 24
that there may not be a sudden change half an hour hence? P III 7 56 10
She had seen too much of the world, to expect sudden or P IV 5 154 9
from laura-place, with a sudden invitation from Lady P IV 5 156 14
A sudden recollection seemed to occur, and to give him P IV 8 182 9
"Perhaps," cried Anne, struck by a sudden idea, "you P IV 9 201 60
Presently, struck by a sudden thought, Charles said, P IV 11 240 55
56
& overwhelmed by the sudden tempest, all were eagerly & S 7 396 1

SUDDENLY (64)
objects around them, he suddenly addressed her with--"I NA I 3 25 2
From such a moralizing strain as this, she was suddenly NA I 8 55 10
her mind, when she suddenly found herself addressed and NA I 10 75 24
an idea of the truth suddenly darted into her mind; and, NA I 15 117 7
fall'--when your lamp suddenly expires in the socket, and NA II 5 160 21
when her eye suddenly fell on a large high chest, standing NA II 6 163 1
last effort, the door suddenly yielded to her hand: her NA II 6 168 10
while she undressed, it suddenly struck her as not NA II 8 188 17
Her dying so suddenly," (slowly, and with hesitation it NA II 9 196 24
opportunity of being suddenly alone with Eleanor, and of NA II 13 220 2
so suddenly too; but I am not offended, indeed I am not. NA II 13 224 14
of hospitality, and so suddenly turned all his partial NA II 14 234 10
minutes longer, when suddenly the clouds united over their SS I 9 41 6
a false step brought her suddenly to the ground, and SS I 9 41 7
he stopt suddenly; appeared to think that he had said too SS I 11 57 17
make Colonel Brandon leave my breakfast table so suddenly." SS I 13 63 6
wonder on his going so suddenly away, which Mrs. Jennings SS I 14 71 3
So suddenly to be gone! SS I 15 77 23
silent, till a new object suddenly engaged her attention. SS I 18 98 10
Only think of their coming so suddenly! SS I 19 106 20
when a loud one was suddenly heard which could not be SS II 4 161 7
But last February, almost a twelvemonth back, she suddenly SS II 9 208 28
of my leaving Barton so suddenly, which I am sure must at SS II 9 209 30
slumber, when Marianne, suddenly awakened by some SS III 7 310 10
11
the knife-case, she was suddenly called to the front door, W 344 21
in trimming a hat, he suddenly addressed her with, "I hope PP I 2 6 1
2
Miss Bennet, she turned suddenly towards him and said, "by PP I 11 55 5
6
when they were suddenly arrested by the sight of the PP I 15 73 8
when she found herself suddenly addressed by Mr. Darcy, PP I 18 90 5
not to break it; till suddenly fancying that it would be PP I 18 91 8
appeared by her suddenly exclaiming, "I remember hearing PP I 18 93 32
she observed, "how very suddenly you all quitted PP II 9 177 3
4
While settling this point, she was suddenly roused by the PP II 11 188 3
of being closed, when he suddenly reminded them, with some PP II 15 217 8
the owner of it himself suddenly came forward from the PP III 1 251 50
a word, he suddenly recollected himself, and took leave. PP III 1 252 53
their niece was taken suddenly ill;--but satisfying them PP III 4 280 26
a precious occasion, she suddenly got up, and saying to PP III 13 345 12
13
the other had sat down, suddenly rose, and whispering a PP III 13 346 22
their attention was suddenly drawn to the window, by the PP III 14 351 1
It suddenly struck her that it might be from Lady PP III 15 361 8
Unfavourable circumstances had suddenly arisen at a moment MP I 4 38 9
at the pianoforte, she suddenly revived it by turning MP I 11 108 4
and turning it over, suddenly exclaimed, "Lovers' Vows! MP I 14 132 7
suddenly on a footing which must do away all restraints. MP I 16 154 14
thoughtfulness, till suddenly looking up at the end of a MP II 4 210 22
I was suddenly, upon turning the corner of a steepish MP II 7 241 13
very comfortable, when suddenly the sound of a step in MP III 1 312 4
of ignorance men, when suddenly called to the necessity of MP III 3 339 22
on something else, suddenly called her attention, by MP III 5 364 30
visions of enjoyment so suddenly opened, she could speak MP III 6 369 11
in the carriage, and suddenly seized with a strong MP III 6 372 21
It seemed as if her eyes were suddenly opened, and she E III 3 332 1
way into it, they had suddenly perceived at a small E III 3 333 5
from some fancy or other, he suddenly let it go.-- E III 9 386 7
to London; and going so suddenly; and going on horseback, E III 9 386 9
You cannot imagine how suddenly it has come on me! how E III 18 473 24
by Mrs. Croft's suddenly saying,-- "it was you, and not P III 6 49 18
19
should have been suddenly struck, this very day, with a P III 6 51 31
Musgroves were gone too, suddenly resolving to walk to the P III 7 59 25
were silent; till Henrietta suddenly began again, with, P III 12 102 1
2
before all subjects suddenly ceased, on seeing Louisa and P III 12 103 5
"Now, this must be very bad for you," said he, suddenly P IV 1 127 24
"Is not this song worth staying for?" said Anne, suddenly P IV 8 190 49

SUDDENNESS (8)
James's arrival, & the suddenness of it requires some LS 20 276 5
The suddenness of her reputed illness; the absence of her NA II 8 188 16
with astonishment the suddenness, continuance and extent NA II 15 245 12
and though the suddenness of their removal surprised her, PP I 21 116 8
overpowered by the suddenness of addresses so wholly MP III 2 326 3
but the rarity and the suddenness of it made it very E II 8 230 100
yesterday; but the suddenness, and, in one light, the E III 14 440 8
"But that was only the effect of the suddenness of your P III 7 56 11

SUE (2)
had certainly too much wit to let them Sue for detection. NA II 9 194 6
girls--come, fan--come, Sue--take care of yourselves--keep MP III 10 403 14

SUFFER (69)
she must not be even left to suffer from the dread of it. LS 20 278 11
But at the same time, it is not for me to suffer such a LS 25 292 3
that he would not really suffer his sister and his friend NA I 9 66 31
I would not have you suffer half what I have done! NA I 15 118 13
nothing to explore or to suffer; and might go to her NA II 6 167 9
Oh! happy house, could you know what I suffer in now SS I 5 27 8
herself from appearing to suffer more than what all her SS I 19 104 9
detecting falsehood might suffer to linger in her mind, SS I 22 132 26
you suffer; for her sake you must exert yourself." SS II 7 185 21
Elinor, you cannot have an idea of what I suffer." SS II 7 185 22
Much as you suffer now, think of what you would have SS II 7 186 29
certainty on either side will be ease to what I now suffer. SS II 7 188 42
Elinor, Elinor, they who suffer little may be proud and SS II 7 189 52
To suffer you all to be so deceived; to see your sister-- SS II 9 210 32
Now, though at first she will suffer much, I am sure she SS II 9 211 34
I would not have you suffer on my account; for I assure SS III 1 263 27
for I assure you I no longer suffer materially myself. SS III 1 263 27
His heart was softened in seeing mine suffer; and so much SS III 8 330 69
He will suffer enough in them." SS III 10 345 24
of nature that she should suffer from it many years." W 326 6
We can never suffer this--it is against the rules of the W 334 13
"I cannot suffer it indeed. W 339 18
suffer more from it herself, than I can possibly do." W 352 26
"Ah! you do not know what I suffer." PP I 1 5 30
the fire, lest she should suffer from the change of room; PP I 11 54 2
would have much to suffer when the affair became public. PP I 17 86 8
a manner which he is likely to suffer from all his life." PP I 18 92 21
People who suffer as I do from nervous complaints can have PP I 20 113 28
Nobody can tell what I suffer!-- PP I 20 113 28
and Elizabeth had only to suffer from the uncomfortable PP I 21 115 1
We do not suffer by accident. PP II 2 140 7
more suffer him to call on Jane in such a part of London! PP II 2 141 13
But in matters of greater weight, I may suffer from the PP II 10 183 12
all that Jane had suffered, and still continued to suffer. PP II 10 186 38
Who should suffer but myself? PP III 6 299 19
know, no one can know how much I suffer from what she says. PP III 11 333 28
will not suffer from the heat as she would have done then. MP I 7 68 19
and we must not suffer her good nature to be imposed on. MP I 14 134 15
Julia did suffer, however, though Mrs. Grant discerned it MP I 17 162 19
home, she had nothing to suffer on that score; for as her MP II 4 206 4
a something to do and to suffer for it, which she could MP II 5 226 64
would arise, from the very conviction, that he did suffer. MP II 10 279 21
to suffer in seeing him on the stage with Miss Bertram. MP III 3 337 10
tone, "no wonder--you must feel it--you must suffer. MP III 15 446 34
that the heart which knew no guile, should not suffer. MP III 16 455 23
could occur to make me suffer more, but that she had been MP III 16 457 30
in his own conduct as a parent, was the longest to suffer. MP III 17 461 4
husband was to suffer, suffered a great deal more herself. E I 18 144 3
of what the poor must suffer in winter, and receiving no E II 1 155 1
for attendance, we could not suffer it to be so, you know. E II 1 162 31
they might resent, how naturally Harriet must suffer. E II 5 187 4
Mrs. Weston (poor Miss Taylor that was) would suffer it." E II 11 252 30
only be the greater; I should suffer more from comparison. E II 17 301 17
of chance,) who will suffer an unfortunate acquaintance to E III 7 373 44
And how suffer him to leave her without saying one word of E III 7 376 62
To suffer her to engage herself--to suffer her even to E III 10 397 50
and wanted to walk with her, but she would not suffer it. E III 14 440 8
Mr. Woodhouse would not suffer him to deceive himself long; E III 15 448 31
had to suffer from the recurrence of any such uncertainty. E III 19 481 1
"Nobody knew how much she should suffer. P III 6 48 17
see her suffer, without the desire of giving her relief. P III 10 91 42
as of the sort which must suffer heavily, uniting very P III 11 97 12
you are very likely to suffer the most of the two; your P IV 1 125 15
16
which Lady Russell would suffer in entering the house P IV 1 125 17
still remain to suffer from the concussion hereafter!-- P IV 1 126 21
so long, she had found more to enjoy than to suffer.-- P IV 2 129 3
not high spirits, must suffer at such a time; and Miss P IV 5 152 2
Whoever suffered inconvenience, she must suffer none, but P IV 7 174 3
She had something to suffer perhaps when they came into P IV 12 250 5

SUFFERABLE (1)
were to set about copying him, he would not be sufferable. E I 4 34 42

SUFFERANCE (1)
upon, "in corporal sufferance feels a pang as great NA I 1 16 8

SUFFERED (81)
dearly purchased by all that you have previously suffered. LS 23 283 1
on her fancy was not suffered therefore to weaken. NA I 5 36 2
Catherine had fortitude too; she suffered, but no murmur NA I 8 53 2
wisdom at once, Henry suffered the subject to decline, and NA I 14 111 29
seeing and wondering, he suffered the girls at last to NA II 7 179 27
She could not contradict it, and therefore suffered NA II 9 195 19
The malady itself, one from which she had often suffered, NA II 9 196 25
present time, that she suffered her mind to be at ease as NA II 11 208 2
never have voluntarily suffered; and that, in forcing her NA II 14 234 10
and before it was suffered to close, she was enabled to NA II 15 243 10
than what all her family suffered on his going away, she SS I 19 104 9
had been saying; but Lucy's countenance suffered no change. SS I 22 132 41
I only wonder that I am alive after what I have suffered SS I 22 133 42
after she had first suffered the extinction of all her SS II 1 141 4
Much as she had suffered from her first conversation with SS II 1 141 7
such language could be suffered to announce it; nor could SS II 7 183 14
of what you would have suffered if the discovery of his SS II 7 186 29
she felt as if, till that instant, she had never suffered. SS II 9 202 7
gloom,--even now the recollection of what I suffered----" SS II 9 206 24
what I feared, may be imagined; and what I suffered too." SS II 9 209 28
I would not have suffered myself to trouble you with this SS II 9 210 32
to tell all that she suffered and thought; to express her SS II 10 213 2
of his mother; and have suffered the punishment of an SS III 1 264 29
you may suppose that I have suffered now. SS III 1 264 29
"Your sister," he continued, "has suffered dreadfully. SS III 1 265 36
"What poor Mrs. Ferrars suffered, when first Fanny broke SS III 1 266 38
certainly would not have suffered you to give me SS III 2 274 19
God! though we have suffered dreadfully, we are both quite SS III 2 277 29
30
friend Mr. Ferrars has suffered from his family; for if I SS III 3 282 17
though no question was suffered to speak it, talked of SS III 10 348 34
of what the latter had suffered through his means, now SS III 11 349 1
you might have been suffered to practise it, but beyond SS III 11 350 9
He would then have suffered under the pecuniary distresses SS III 11 351 13
how much she really suffered, and in a moment afterwards, SS III 11 353 24
suffering as she then had suffered for Marianne. SS III 11 355 46
of women--poor Fanny had suffered agonies of sensibility-- SS III 13 371 38
other, a man who had suffered no less than herself under SS III 14 378 15
She still suffered from them in the contemplation of their W 361 31
on in the wild manner that you are suffered to do at home." PP I 9 42 14
his pride was hurt, he suffered in no other way. his PP I 20 112 24
and all that he had suffered from him, was now openly PP II 1 138 30
all that Jane had suffered, and still continued to suffer. PP II 10 186 38
dear Lizzy, only consider what he must have suffered. PP II 17 225 12
deter him from such foul misconduct as I have suffered by. PP II 18 234 38
caused their confusion, suffered no variation of colour. PP III 9 316 5
As for Wickham and Lydia, their characters suffered no PP III 19 386 6
The very idea of her having been suffered to grow up at a MP I 1 7 6
Do you think the minds which are suffered, which are MP I 9 87 16
and would have moved too, but this was not suffered. MP I 9 96 76
originally plain, had suffered all the ill-usage of MP I 16 152 2
of being suffered to sit silent and unattended to. MP II 5 223 48
have been at sea, and seen and done and suffered as much. MP II 6 236 22
But this could not be suffered. MP II 13 300 7
His hopes from both gentleman and lady suffered a small MP III 1 320 45
It was with reluctance that he suffered her to go, but MP III 2 328 8
a great deal more suffered than a stander-by can judge of." MP III 5 363 23
But as such were Fanny's persuasions, she suffered very MP III 6 367 6
and of what she had suffered in being torn from them, came MP III 6 370 11
suffered the less because reminded by it of the east-room. MP III 9 398 9
He had suffered, and he had learnt to think, two MP III 17 462 4
husband was to suffer, suffered a great deal more herself. E I 18 144 3
Mr. Elton could not have suffered long; but she was sorry E II 3 177 51
was arranged, he never suffered beforehand from the E II 5 193 35
Such talents as her's must not be suffered to remain E II 15 282 5
She had suffered very much from cramp after dancing, and E III 3 333 5
The heat was excessive; he had never suffered any thing E III 6 363 53
They must both have suffered a great deal under such a E III 10 398 53
"On the misery of what she had suffered, during the E III 12 418 6
Are you disposed to pity me for what I must have suffered E III 14 443 8
had supposed--and he had suffered, and was very sorry--and E III 15 444 1
He does seem to have suffered in finding her ill.-- E III 15 447 28
Other poultry-yards in the neighbourhood also suffered.-- E III 19 483 10
The only time that I ever really suffered in body or mind, P III 8 71 54
of what she had suffered herself, by observing, with a P IV 2 134 30
concern for what she must have suffered in witnessing it. P IV 3 144 22
Whoever suffered inconvenience, she must suffer none, but P IV 7 174 3
I am afraid you must have suffered from the shock, and the P IV 8 181 4
One does not love a place the less for having suffered in P IV 8 184 16
I was right, much as I suffered from it, that I was P IV 11 246 79

80
otherwise, I should have suffered more in continuing the P IV 11 246 80
it up, because I should have suffered in my conscience. P IV 11 246 80

SUFFERER (8)
James was the sufferer. NA II 4 149 1
as likely to assuage the agonies of the little sufferer. SS I 21 121 10
a sufferer is denied me, because you have always so much." PP III 11 333 29
Julia was a sufferer too, though not quite so blamelessly. MP I 17 160 7
at home, I consider you as the greatest sufferer.-- MP II 11 287 18
flatter myself, the poor sufferer will soon be able to MP III 13 426 11
most attached to Maria, was really the greatest sufferer. MP III 16 448 1
to her merits, because he had been a sufferer from them. P IV 11 241 61

SUFFERERS (2)
They were two solitary sufferers, or connected only by MP I 17 163 20
to the sufferers, it has done all that is truly important. E I 10 87 30

SUFFERING (77)
myself for suffering you to form a connection so imprudent. LS 30 300 2
suffering wife, and left him to the stings of conscience. NA II 8 186 6
Without suffering any romantic alarm, in the consideration NA II 14 234 10
by habitual suffering, to receive and enjoy felicity. NA II 16 251 5
at a moment when she was suffering under the cold and SS I 4 23 20
was not suffering under the insatiable appetite of fifteen. SS I 7 32 2
I am now suffering under a very heavy disappointment!" SS I 15 75 4
her till this excess of suffering had somewhat spent SS II 7 182 12
13
of impatient suffering, she at first refused to do. SS II 8 197 25
So altered--so faded--worn down by acute suffering of SS II 9 207 26
preserved her from suffering under any other of Mrs. SS II 13 238 1
to represent herself as suffering much, any otherwise than SS III 1 261 12
my misery, who have seemed to be only suffering for me!-- SS III 1 264 31
It was a night of almost equal suffering to both. SS III 7 312 17
pictured to herself her suffering mother arriving too late SS III 7 312 18
one image of grief, one suffering friend to another, and SS III 7 313 21
after week so constantly suffering, oppressed by anguish SS III 10 341 6
suffering as she then had suffered for Marianne. SS III 11 355 46
might have a daughter suffering almost as much, certainly SS III 11 356 46
before;--& Emma, tho' suffering a good deal from curiosity, W 359 28
occurrences, or any communication of present suffering. PP II 11 188 1
affliction you are now suffering under, of which we were PP III 6 296 11
and to see your sister suffering from it, must be MP I 11 111 29
been sometimes much of suffering to her--though her MP I 16 152 2
and she had all the suffering which a warm temper and a MP I 17 162 19
credit, and make it a very suffering exhibition to herself. MP I 18 170 24
away his plate--and has been suffering ever since." MP I 18 171 27
which not even innocence could keep from suffering. MP II 1 176 4
enjoyment was followed by hours of acute suffering. MP II 2 192 11
You do not know how much we have been suffering, nor what MP II 4 212 30
of all this, and suffering the more from that involuntary MP II 7 248 47
It was barbarous to be happy when Edmund was suffering. MP II 10 279 21
Upon my representation of what you were suffering, he MP III 1 321 47
all her time between suffering from that of to-day, and MP III 13 427 13
the sight of him in his suffering, helpless state, and MP III 14 429 1
the attendant, supporter, cheerer of a suffering brother. MP III 14 429 2
must be suffering, brought back all her own first feelings. MP III 15 444 28
He looked very ill; evidently suffering under violent MP III 15 445 30
By one of the suffering party within, they were expected MP III 15 447 37
He was aware of what Edmund must be suffering on his own MP III 16 452 15
He was suffering from disappointment and regret, grieving MP III 17 461 3
in great danger of suffering from intellectual solitude. E I 1 6 7
a single pleasure, or suffering an hour's ennui, from the E I 2 18 11
not suffering any disappointment that need be cared for. E I 16 135 7
poor Harriet would be suffering, with the awkwardness of E I 16 137 12
she had been in a very suffering state (so said her E II 12 258 7
She had been particularly unwell, however, suffering from E II 12 263 42
Her nerves were under continual irritation and suffering; E III 1 317 7
"Poor Mrs. Churchill! no doubt she had been suffering a E III 9 387 13
and that she was suffering under severe headachs, and a E III 9 389 16
She listened with much inward suffering, but with great E III 11 409 34
had shown how deeply she was suffering from consciousness. E III 12 418 5
been a state of perpetual suffering to me; and so it ought. E III 12 419 8
for a little respite of suffering;--she was now in an E III 14 434 1
first object to prevent her from suffering unnecessarily.-- E III 15 446 20
heat he was suffering, and the walk he had had for nothing. E III 16 457 37
She could not bear to see him suffering, to know him E III 19 483 9
part of our suffering, as it always does of our conduct. P III 2 12 4
not be in danger of suffering as much where there was no P III 3 22 24
with a few months ended Anne's share of suffering from it. P III 4 28 6
must involve least suffering, to go with the others. P III 5 33 6
to banish, and the poor suffering one to attend and soothe; P III 7 53 3
characters of worth and suffering, as occurred to her at P III 11 101 24
completely rational, was suffering most, Captain Wentworth, P III 12 110 43
on her attention, of past kindness and present suffering. P IV 5 152 2
from home, and suffering as a girl of fourteen, of strong P IV 5 152 2
confined to her bed, and suffering under severe and P IV 5 154 9
He looked very well, not as if he had been suffering in P IV 7 176 8
whether he were really suffering much from disappointment P IV 7 178 24
unless it has been all suffering, nothing but suffering-- P IV 8 184 16
but suffering--which was by no means the case at Lyme. P IV 8 184 16
she sacrificed to politeness with a more suffering spirit. P IV 8 190 47
Elizabeth was, for a short time, suffering a good deal. P IV 10 219 29
Six years of separation and suffering might have been P IV 11 247 84
Anne knew that Lady Russell must be suffering some pain in P IV 12 249 3
though it found me suffering under a more severe attack S 5 386 1
She has been suffering much from the headache and six S 5 387 1

SUFFERINGS (26)
her past adventures and sufferings, which might otherwise NA I 4 34 9
he might have thought her sufferings rather too acute. NA I 8 54 10
not, in our concern for his sufferings, undervalue your's. NA II 10 206 38
Woodston, added to her sufferings, and when within the NA II 14 230 1
"Her sufferings have been very severe. SS II 8 199 40
She will feel her own sufferings to be nothing. SS II 9 210 32
her sympathy in her sufferings was very sincere. SS III 7 313 20
heart, that all my past sufferings under it are only SS III 8 324 45
commiseration for the sufferings produced by them, which SS III 9 333 2
felt that to his sufferings and his constancy far more SS III 9 335 5
I saw that my own feelings had prepared my sufferings, and SS III 10 345 28
gave her a keener sense of her sister's sufferings. PP II 11 188 1
complaints of her own sufferings and ill usage; blaming PP III 5 287 34
The sufferings which Lady Bertram did not see, had little MP III 13 427 12
The mother's sufferings, the father's--there, she paused. MP III 15 442 21
Time would undoubtedly abate somewhat of his sufferings, MP III 16 460 31
The wants and sufferings of the poor family, however, were E I 10 87 31
picture of her present sufferings acted as a cure of every E III 8 379 9
"His sufferings," replied Emma drily, "do not appear to E III 10 398 54
involve and advance the sufferings of her friend, who must E III 15 450 37
all the worst of her sufferings had been unsuspected.-- E III 16 452 8
in any of the sufferings it occasioned; but if Henrietta P III 9 77 18
without sufferings which made her worse than helpless! P III 12 114 59
to the inevitable sufferings of her situation, had been P IV 9 209 96
With all their sufferings, you perceive how much they are S 5 388 1
rest of their sufferings was from fancy, the love of S 10 412 1

SUFFERS (4)
His circumstances are now unembarrassed--he suffers from SS III 11 351 13
is very ill indeed, and suffers a vast deal, though with PP I 9 42 7
You will find how very much he suffers." E III 15 447 23
you comprehend what a man suffers when he takes a last P IV 11 234 31

SUFFICE (8)
Another meeting will suffice to explain his sentiments on SS I 10 47 4
of Elinor's company, or suffice to say half that was to be SS III 13 363 9
Any room in this house might suffice." MP I 13 123 6
suffice me; and I hope may suffice all who care about me." MP II 7 242 24
Suffice it, that he has behaved in the most gentleman-like MP III 1 321 47
now it is too long ago; suffice it, that every thing was MP III 12 416 2
and tempers, by that sense of duty which can alone suffice. MP III 17 463 8
a silent rumination might suffice to restore him to the E I 12 105 51

SUFFICED (3)
for half a glance sufficed to ascertain written characters; NA II 6 169 11
divisions of the grounds sufficed him for his long walk, E I 4 26 1
A moment sufficed to convince her that something E III 3 333 3

SUFFICIENCY (1)
its sufficiency, began to take the matter in another point. MP II 13 305 23

SUFFICIENT (49)
of prudence were sufficient to soften his heart, & make LS 3 247 1
I allude; Langford--Langford--that word will be sufficient. LS 34 304 1
So far her improvement was sufficient--and in many other NA I 1 16 10
scullery were deemed sufficient at Fullerton, were here NA II 8 184 4
equal openness,) seemed sufficient vouchers for his truth; NA II 15 245 12
would have been a sufficient objection to outweigh every SS I 4 23 20
park; as to a stable, the merest shed would be sufficient. SS I 12 58 3
Brandon," Marianne eagerly, "will it not be sufficient?" SS I 13 64 23
Willoughby may undoubtedly have very sufficient reasons SS I 15 79 29
tried to find in it a motive sufficient for their silence. SS I 16 84 7
to her fortune, nor sufficient for her comfortable SS II 9 207 26
This would not, in itself, have been sufficient for the SS III 3 279 1
probably have been sufficient to unite them in friendship, SS III 13 370 36
With an income sufficient to their wants thus secured to SS III 14 374 6
ask on the subject was sufficient to draw from her husband PP I 3 9 1
Having now a good house and very sufficient income, he PP I 15 70 2
This he considered sufficient encouragement, and the PP II 11 189 5
For such an attachment as this, she might have sufficient PP III 4 279 24
judgment, he had sufficient confidence to make him go MP I 3 32 62
received a very sufficient invitation for his cousin, Mrs. MP I 8 79 23
but this was not quite sufficient to do away the pain of MP I 10 103 49
and a fortnight of sufficient leisure in the intervals of MP I 12 114 3
A very few words between them were sufficient. MP II 1 176 3
thing, the sweep of every preparation would be sufficient. MP II 2 187 2
very few weeks would be sufficient for such arrangements MP II 3 202 27
there would remain sufficient for a round game, and every MP II 7 239 4
But compliments may be sufficient here.-- MP II 11 288 22
sufficient recommendation to you, had there been no other. MP III 1 316 27
every young man, with a sufficient income, settled as soon MP III 1 317 34
dislike on her side, would have been sufficient. MP III 1 318 38
attachment, and no sufficient principle on either side, MP III 15 441 20
could he have found sufficient exultation in overcoming MP III 17 467 19
There was always sufficient reason for such an attention; E II 1 155 2
sufficient; but nothing else, she feared, would cure her. E II 4 183 10
they know you do not dine out," was not quite sufficient. E II 7 207 7
had been deemed barely sufficient for five couple, was now E II 11 249 12
could; but it was fully sufficient for Mrs. Elton, who E II 14 273 20
came to a sufficient explanation, and quite undesignedly. E III 4 340 28
A few minutes were sufficient for making her acquainted E III 11 407 32
of concealing the truth she did not think sufficient.-- E III 14 440 8
fortunate in having a sufficient reason for asking it, E III 16 451 3
as if no other reception of her were felt sufficient.-- E III 16 452 8
natural, happy, and sufficient cure, at her time of life, P III 4 28 7
and there being no sufficient reason against it, he ought P III 7 55 7
her manner being soon sufficient to convince him, where P III 7 58 20
A bed on the floor in Louisa's room would be sufficient P III 12 114 63
no enquiries, there was voluntary communication sufficient. P IV 2 133 25
lately occupying, a sufficient explanation of what he P IV 4 151 22
so much; but less would hardly have been sufficient. P IV 9 197 34

SUFFICIENTLY (29)
be overcome; & I hope I was afterwards sufficiently keen. LS 22 282 7
I never can sufficiently regret that I wrote to you at all. LS 24 285 1
myself to dwell on them; they will strike you sufficiently. LS 24 291 14
a year ago, she was sufficiently recovered to think it NA II 11 214 25
sufficiently striking to those of his brother elect. SS I 16 87 23
or any other game that was sufficiently noisy. SS II 1 143 8
of the Meryton assembly was sufficiently characteristic. PP I 4 16 15
They always continue to grow sufficiently unlike PP I 6 23 10
Elizabeth took up some needlework, and was sufficiently PP I 10 47 2
happy expression, as sufficiently marked how well she was PP I 18 95 48
Kenelworth, Birmingham, &c. are sufficiently known. PP II 19 240 12
for her appearance spoke sufficiently on that point. MP II 1 178 7
Mr. Yates's family and connections were sufficiently known MP II 1 183 23
and were at least sufficiently friends to make each of MP II 3 203 32
by, his absence may sufficiently account for any MP III 9 393 1
but allow that he was sufficiently open to the charms of MP III 11 409 7
sentiments had been sufficiently known to him to render MP III 17 461 4
or put Edmund Bertram sufficiently out of her head. MP III 17 469 24
He was looked on as sufficiently belonging to the place to E I 2 17 7
quick eye sufficiently acquainted with Mr. Robert Martin. E I 4 31 27
conversation, it was sufficiently clear to her friend that E I 9 74 21
answer, but altogether sufficiently awake to the terror of E I 15 124 3
admired Hartfield sufficiently for Mr. Woodhouse's ear; E II 6 196 2
seated by him; and was sufficiently employed in looking E II 10 240 6
am that you cannot feel them sufficiently to act upon them. E II 13 268 12
time, the Randalls' party just sufficiently before them. E III 2 319 2
As soon as Mrs. Weston was sufficiently recovered to admit E III 17 465 28
harden her nerves sufficiently to feel the continual P III 4 30 10
No, she was a very sober-minded young lady, sufficiently S 6 391 1

SUFFISE (1)
another day or two would suffise to wipe away every MP II 2 190 9

SUFFRAGE (1)
off without being able to receive his uncle's suffrage.-- W 332 11

SUGAR (1)
her, and her mouth stuffed with sugar plums by the other. SS I 21 121 10

SUGGEST (23)
"It is amazingly; it may well suggest amazement if they do- NA I 14 107 11
If able to suggest a hint, Isabella could never understand NA II 4 150 1
Oh! that I could suggest any thing in extenuation! NA II 13 225 19
to suggest the propriety of some self-command to Marianne. SS I 11 53 2
thing was affection could suggest as likely to assuage the SS I 21 121 10
Dashwood, "is my dear prudent Elinor going to suggest? SS II 3 156 11
might suggest a hint of what was practicable to Marianne. SS III 1 261 12
had even vouchsafed to suggest some herself,--some shelves PP I 14 66 1
might suggest to be advisable for continuing their pursuit. PP III 6 298 13
to say, in her anxiety to suggest some comfort, "perhaps MP I 13 128 34
proving incompetent to suggest any reply, she had recourse, MP I 16 150 1
evening, and could even suggest the possibility of the MP II 1 177 5
his imagination could suggest; and Fanny, from a different MP II 9 266 21
his consciousness might suggest, a suspicion of his having MP II 12 291 5
and reason, which might suggest the expediency of making MP III 8 390 8
prudence might originally suggest; and more than a E I 8 67 57
about any body, is apt to suggest suspicions of there E II 6 203 41
Therefore, Sir Walter, what I would take leave to suggest P III 3 17 4
tried, at intervals, to suggest comfort to the others, P III 12 111 44
Anne was considering whether she should venture to suggest P IV 3 142 17
did; but now she could safely suggest the name of "Louisa." P IV 6 170 32
When you had the presence of mind to suggest that benwick P IV 8 182 6
neither able to do or suggest anything--& receiving her S 1 364 1

SUGGESTED (30)
soothing; it sometimes suggested the dread of his calm NA II 14 231 4
the very person who had suggested them, from Thorpe NA II 15 246 12
It suggested no other surprise than that Elinor and SS I 21 121 6
rather ill-natured, and suggested the suspicion of that SS I 21 126 41
their guests, had suggested the propriety of their being SS II 14 252 20
when a plan was suggested, which, though detaining them SS III 3 279 1
if such an idea had been suggested, his behaviour during PP I 12 60 4
gallantry, from the idea it suggested of something more.-- PP I 17 87 14
She had once or twice suggested to Elizabeth the PP II 9 181 30
Nothing had ever suggested it before, but they now felt PP III 2 260 1
benevolence of her heart suggested, had not yet deserted PP III 5 287 33
which his own children suggested, Sir Thomas did not MP I 2 21 34

but a more tender nature suggested that her feelings were MP I 3 32 64
Mr. Crawford suggested the greater desirableness of some MP I 9 84 1
harm, and it was suggested, I know; but Lord Ravenshaw, MP I 13 122 4
his measurements, had suggested and removed at least two MP I 14 130 1
or diversion in the playful conceits they suggested. MP I 17 159 6
measures and such amusements should have been suggested. MP II 2 188 3
from Norfolk, which, suggested by Dr. Grant, advised by MP II 5 223 48
By some such improvements as I have suggested, (I do not MP II 7 243 27
mischievous which her imagination had suggested at first. E II 2 168 13
the room, he would acknowledge none which they suggested. E II 6 198 5
little friend," suggested to her the idea of Harriet's E II 13 266 6
His companions suggested only what could palliate E III 10 401 69
mischief; with having suggested such feelings as might E III 11 402 1
possible cause for it, suggested by her fears, was, that E III 13 424 1
away, when Anne eagerly suggested, "Captain Benwick, would P III 12 110 40 41
suggested suspicions not favourable of what he had been. P IV 5 161 27
past, and a question has suggested itself, whether there P IV 11 247 82
circumstances having suggested to himself, & the other S 2 371 1

SUGGESTING (8)
her journey, and, upon suggesting it to her with most NA II 13 229 31
that she could not help suggesting it to her mother. SS I 16 84 7
Elinor could have given her immediate relief by suggesting SS II 12 232 14
amuse myself with suggesting and arranging such little PP I 14 68 11
alterations as I was suggesting just now, such as moving a MP I 13 127 29
every other heart was suggesting "what will become of us? MP II 1 175 1
different rooms, some suggesting, some attending, and all E II 11 256 60
could hardly fail of suggesting certain ideas to the E III 3 334 9

SUGGESTION (10)
in the flattering suggestion for half a minute, till the NA II 7 173 4
by Mrs. Jennings's suggestion; and she could not help SS III 6 305 16
It appeared to her merely the suggestion of Caroline's PP I 21 120 28
the match, by every suggestion and contrivance, likely to MP I 4 39 10
at her apparent suggestion, they rose into a canter; and MP I 7 67 16
The suggestion was generally welcome. MP I 14 132 8
who at his suggestion now seated themselves round the fire. MP II 1 178 8
her horror at the first suggestion, that she could MP II 10 275 11
not avoid the internal suggestion of "can it really be as E I 14 118 4
little room; but that was scouted as a wretched suggestion. E II 11 254 45

SUGGESTIONS (8)
Catherine's blood ran cold with the horrid suggestions NA II 8 186 13
her comfortable suggestions to have had no good effect, NA II 14 236 18
Mrs. Norris was ready with her suggestions as to the rooms MP II 8 253 7
every thing easy by her suggestions, and tried to make MP II 8 257 15
future, the sobering suggestions of her own good E II 2 164 6
When the suggestions of hope, however, which must follow E III 12 415 1
real use to him in some suggestions as to the duty and P III 11 100 23
to defy the suggestions of very opposite feelings. P IV 10 227 69

SUIT (59)
manner of living did not suit her situation or feelings, I LS 6 252 2
between us, it would ill suit the feelings of either to LS 25 292 3
you can get lodgings to suit me within a short distance of LS 25 294 7
of Sir Reginald, will not suit the freedom of my spirit; & LS 29 299 3
Sam Fletcher, has got one to sell that would suit any body. NA I 10 76 28
said that Tuesday would suit her as well, it was quite NA I 13 100 19
The word 'nicest,' as you used it, did not suit him; and NA I 14 108 14
urge his suit, and say all manner of pretty things to you. NA II 3 144 10
of Lady Middleton, did not suit the fancy of Mrs. Jennings, SS II 12 229 3
that would suit us quite as well as our present situation." SS III 9 338 24
It did not suit them, it did not suit Capt. O'brien that I W 326 5
her vanity, but did not suit her pride, & she wd rather W 347 22
Elizabeth assured him that she could suit herself PP I 8 38 28
How can they suit each other?-- PP I 16 82 45
as much to encourage my suit as would be consistent with PP I 19 108 16 17
If therefore she actually persists in rejecting my suit, PP I 20 110 4
"Your cousin's conduct does not suit my feelings. PP II 10 185 34
was wounding, but was very unlikely to recommend his suit. PP II 11 189 5
man, who, in disposition and talents, would most suit her. PP III 8 312 15
that any thing could ever suit her like the old grey poney; MP I 4 37 8
you were about of course--but that would not suit me. MP I 6 57 29
It did not suit his sense of propriety, and he was MP I 6 57 32
and inquire whether Wednesday would suit him or not. MP I 8 75 1
they may not be able to find any play to suit them. MP I 13 128 34
The business of finding a play that would suit every body, MP I 14 130 1
had been proposed before so likely to suit them all. MP I 14 132 8
studied the character, I am sure you will feel it suit you. MP I 14 135 17
have another fine fancy suit by way of a shooting dress.-- MP I 15 138 3
there is nothing that will suit us altogether so well, MP I 15 139 6
Will twenty minutes after four suit you?" MP II 5 221 37
attended them; but they would not altogether suit us now. MP II 8 252 1
It was just the plan to suit Fanny; and with a great deal MP II 8 257 15
It will exactly suit my cross. MP II 9 262 8
and--and love--to suit the sort of friendly acquaintance MP II 11 287 22
not much longer persevere in a suit so distressing to her? MP III 11 414 32
morals and discretion to suit--for to their house Mr. MP III 16 450 8
He is an excellent young man, and will suit Harriet E I 6 49 44
of his near approach afraid, so fatal to my suit before. E I 9 78 54
natured and too silly to suit me; but, in general, she is E I 10 85 19
very person to suit her in age, character and condition. E I 14 119 5
which she hoped would best suit his half and half state, E I 15 129 24 25
than would suit your notions of man's perfection. E I 18 148 23
that the place might suit her better than her father." E II 14 276 34
little doubt of hearing of something to suit her shortly.-- E II 15 284 9
of any situation likely to suit her, and professions of E II 17 299 1
"Aye, that may suit your humble ideas of yourself;--I know E II 17 301 16
We shall see if our styles suit.-- E III 2 324 21
were out of hearing:--"how well they suit one another!-- E III 7 372 40
that a daughter would suit both father and mother best. E III 17 461 1
disposed to think it must suit them all; and as to her P III 2 14 12
It did not happen to suit the Miss Musgroves, I suppose, P III 5 38 29
found, slightly, as might suit a former slight P III 7 59 23
Admiral Croft's manners were not quite of the tone to suit P IV 1 127 23
too strict to suit the unfeudal tone of the present day! P IV 3 139 7
for some time which will at once suit her and myself.-- P IV 5 157 16
think highly of him," said Anne; "but we should not suit." P IV 5 159 24
a part of Bath as it might suit Miss Elliot and himself to P IV 6 165 9
each of them every thing that would not suit the other. P IV 6 166 19
tea with him them, would suit her best,--& therefore the S 6 390 1

SUITABLE (19)
It was performed with suitable quietness and uneventful NA I 2 19 4
what, if you had had a suitable fortune, he would have NA II 1 136 46
The dining-parlour was a noble room, suitable in its NA II 6 165 6
in her inquiries for a suitable dwelling in the SS I 3 14 1
on as the most suitable period for its accomplishment. SS I 5 27 6
reached an age highly suitable for dancing, and not very SS III 14 380 20
his five cousins at a suitable hour to Meryton; and the PP I 16 75 1
and their furniture suitable to the fortune of their PP III 1 246 5
"The party seemed so well selected, so suitable one with PP III 12 343 30
She had not waited her arrival to look out for a suitable MP I 4 42 17
character, easy fortune, suitable age and pleasant manners; E I 1 6 6
Mr. Elton's situation was most suitable, quite the E I 4 35 44
of the building, its suitable, becoming, characteristic E III 6 358 35
every respect so proper, suitable, and unexceptionable a E III 17 467 31
bring a choice of more suitable intimates within Miss P III 2 16 17
A most suitable connection every body must consider it-- P IV 5 159 23
Where can you look for a more suitable match? P IV 9 196 30
visiting young lady a suitable knowledge of the person S 3 375 1
& every thing had a suitable air of property & order.-- S 12 427 1

SUITABLENESS (4)
of eligibility and suitableness, and excessively generous PP I 15 70 2
One enjoyment was certain--that of suitableness as PP II 19 239 11
as companions; a suitableness which comprehended health PP II 19 239 11
his company, or opinion of the suitableness of the match. E II 2 169 16

SUITABLY (2)
make her incapable of suitably sharing the distress even MP III 15 443 24
none: Elizabeth would, one day or other, marry suitably. P III 1 6 10

SUITE (2)
we go up every staircase, and into every suite of rooms?" NA I 11 86 43
a progress through a long suite of lofty rooms, exhibiting NA I 11 88 54

SUITED (26)
her of former delight, was exactly what suited her mind. SS I 2 8 2
of comfort and ease, and suited the prudence of her eldest SS I 3 14 1
objects, and equally suited to the advancement of each. SS I 19 104 9
pianoforte, whenever it suited her, and unrestrained even SS II 14 250 11
air in Mr H. which suited her--& in a few minutes W 333 13
to consider his house as her home when it suited her. PP I 4 15 13
in a manner so little suited to recommend them; but still PP II 17 224 2
It would have suited me in every respect." PP III 10 328 26
so properly happy, so well suited, and so much the thing! MP I 12 118 16
would have been much more suited to her capacity, than the MP III 8 390 5
matters, which exactly suited Mr. Woodhouse, full of E I 3 21 4
in the plaintive tone which just suited her father. E I 11 94 12
it suited neither; it was a jumble without taste or truth. E I 16 134 4
as such seclusion exactly suited her brother, whose E I 16 139 20
as, in every respect, it suited Emma best to lead, she E II 8 227 85
all the rapidity which suited his feelings, he was apt to E II 18 308 28
for a fuller view of her face than it suited her to give. E III 13 425 2
goodhumoured playfulness, which exactly suited me. E III 14 438 8
which, however, had not suited him; that accidentally P III 3 21 18
It suited Mary best to think Henrietta the one preferred, P III 9 75 12
suited, and there remain till dear Louisa could be moved. P IV 1 122 5
Charles Hayter had been at Lyme oftener than suited her, P IV 2 129 3
the Crofts' arrival, it suited her best to leave her P IV 6 168 25
manners had not suited her own ideas, she had been too P IV 12 249 3
Every body's taste & every body's finances may be suited-- S 1 369 1
And accordingly, long before they had suited themselves S 11 422 1

SUITES (1)
But suites of apartments did not spring up with her wishes. NA II 8 183 2

SUITING (1)
does not lose much by not suiting his fancy; for he is a PP I 3 13 20

SUITOR (1)
her old friend could have made so indifferent a suitor. SS III 3 282 15

SUITS (7)
He has a fine dignified manner, which suits the head of MP I 17 162 16
sort of manner--though it suits him very well; his figure E I 4 34 42
equal that of a parent, it suits my ideas of comfort E I 10 86 21
Then I will speak the truth, and nothing suits me so well. E II 6 200 20
"Well, whenever it suits you.-- P IV 1 127 26
It suits us very well. P IV 6 170 29
I know how little it suits you to be pressing matters upon S 12 425 1

SULKINESS (1)
I wish there may not be a little sulkiness of temper--her MP I 2 13 5

SULLEN (2)
The lock yielded to her hand, and, luckily, with no sullen NA II 9 193 6
him; she could only be sullen to her mother, aunt, and MP I 7 70 30

SULLENLY (1)
go any further," said he sullenly; "I see nothing of them. MP I 10 101 35

SULLENNESS (1)
parting in apparent sullenness, she looked out with voice E III 7 376 62

SULLYING (1)
passed away without sullying her heroic importance. NA I 8 53 3

SULTANESS SCHEHERAZADE'S (1)
the Sultaness Scheherazade's head, must live another day. P IV 11 229 1

SUM (20)
lay by a considerable sum from the produce of an estate SS I 1 4 4
spare so considerable a sum with little inconvenience."-- SS I 1 5 8
rob his child, and his only child too, of so large a sum? SS I 2 8 3
"He did not stipulate for any particular sum, my dear SS I 2 9 6
when Harry will regret that so large a sum was parted with. SS I 2 9 8
for all parties if the sum were diminished one half.-- SS I 2 9 10
To be tied down to the regular payment of such a sum, on SS I 2 11 21
for, except a trifling sum, the whole of his fortune SS I 3 15 5
Depend upon it that whatever unemployed sum may remain, SS I 14 72 10
to have the necessary sum in my banker's hands, I must SS II 11 225 33
in lieu, so considerable a sum as three thousand pounds, PP II 13 205 3
A small sum could not do all this." PP III 7 304 30
How is half such a sum to be repaid?" PP III 7 304 32
he had laid by an annual sum, for the better provision of PP III 8 308 1
Lydia's expences had been very little within that sum. PP III 8 309 4
and Easter, I suppose, will be the sum total of sacrifice." MP II 5 226 61
nobody would believe what a sum they cost Sir Thomas every MP II 13 305 24
It had very early occurred to her, that a small sum of MP III 9 396 7
Half the sum of attraction, on either side, might have P III 4 26 1
really have raised the sum we wanted for putting them all S 12 424 1

SUMMARILY (1)
The Admiral wound it all up summarily by exclaiming, "ay, P IV 1 126 21 22

SUMMARY (1)
This was just such a summary view of the affair as NA II 14 237 20

SUMMER (69)
in the course of the summer--an accession of dignity that NA II 16 250 4
the neighbourhood, for in summer he was for ever forming SS I 7 32 2
them, at least, twice every summer for the last ten years. SS I 12 62 28
I know the summer will pass happily away. SS III 10 343 9
himself in the small summer breakfast parlour at Rosings; PP I 16 75 2
was, that Mr. Bingley must be down again in the summer. PP II 1 137 26
tour of pleasure which they proposed taking in the summer. PP II 4 154 21
that it was much better worth looking at in the summer. PP II 6 162 13
them to have been together the whole of last summer." PP II 10 185 28
But last summer he was again most painfully obtruded on my PP II 12 201 5
her in London; and last summer she went with the lady who PP II 12 201 5
When my niece Georgiana went to ramsgate last summer, I PP II 14 211 13
what one wears this summer, after the ----shire have left PP II 16 219 4
I do so want papa to take us all there for the summer! PP II 16 219 6
Only think what a miserable summer else we shall have!" PP II 16 220 6
Netherfield again in the summer; and I have enquired of PP II 17 228 27
back again, and summer finery and summer engagements arose. PP II 19 238 6
little alarm, whether the family were down for the summer. PP II 19 241 17
here; and Miss Darcy is always down for the summer months." PP III 1 248 25
whose northern aspect rendered it delightful for summer. PP III 3 267 2
miraculous consequence of travelling in the summer. PP III 3 271 14
for the evening, in summer; the windows are full west." PP III 14 352 11
and leaving Antigua before the end of the summer. MP I 4 40 14
foliage of summer, was enough to catch any man's heart. MP I 7 65 13
Another summer will hardly improve it to me." MP I 10 98 7
and Brighton is almost as gay in winter as in summer. MP II 3 203 31
it all and all, I never spent so happy a summer.-- MP II 4 210 19
him and some part of this family in the summer and autumn. MP III 5 363 21
He particularly built upon a very happy summer and autumn MP III 10 405 18
it; a summer and autumn infinitely superior to the last. MP III 10 405 18
her quitting it; and the change was from winter to summer. MP III 15 446 35
trees with Fanny all the summer evenings, he had so well MP III 17 462 5
about a great deal in the summer, and in winter dressed E I 3 22 5
"But, my dear papa, it is supposed to be summer; a warm E I 6 48 37
papa, it is supposed to be summer; a warm day in summer. E I 6 48 37
Her visit to abbey-mill, this summer, seems to have done E I 8 59 25
was as happy as possible with the Martins in the summer. E I 8 63 42
They had not intended to go over till the summer, but she E II 1 159 20
in one afternoon next summer, and take their tea with us -- E II 7 209 10
The dews of a summer evening are what I would not expose E II 7 209 10
In the summer it might have passed; but what can any E II 8 217 32
if I thought I should go and stay there again next summer." E II 9 232 19

a visit in the spring, or summer at farthest," continued E II 14 274 28
We explored to King's-Weston twice last summer, in that E II 14 274 28
that kind here, I suppose, Miss Woodhouse, every summer?" E II 14 274 28
said that I hoped I should in the course of the summer. E II 14 280 54
month--merely looked forward to the summer in general." E II 17 299 3
serious in wishing nothing to be done till the summer. E II 17 301 19
with her, how very happy a summer must be before her! E III 3 332 1
that ought to be treated rather as winter than summer. E III 5 347 19
summer there is dust, and in winter there is dirt." E III 6 356 26
opinion, when one is exploring about the country in summer. E III 7 372 37
were carried off; the sun appeared; it was summer again. E III 13 424 1
this present time, (the summer of 1814,) wearing black P III 1 8 17
Somersetshire, in the summer of 1806; and having no parent P III 4 26 1
think she has been in this house three times this summer." P III 5 37 24
I wished for him again the next summer, when I had still P III 8 67 23
for putting it off till summer; and to Lyme they were to P III 11 94 7
She had died the preceding summer, while he was at sea. P III 11 96 12
be called a young mourner--only last summer, I understand." P III 12 108 25
He is only a commander, it is true, made last summer, and P IV 6 171 37
swear "to visit them this summer, but my first visit to " P IV 9 203 72
Did he see you last summer or autumn, 'somewhere down in P IV 9 205 86
to get to Sanditon this summer, could hardly be expected S 2 372 1
So shady in summer!" S 4 381 1
any during the whole summer, excepting one family of S 4 383 1
me at Sanditon house, as I did last summer--but I shan't.-- S 7 399 1
I had them with me last summer about this time, for a week; S 7 399 1
Matters are altered with me since last summer you know--. S 7 401 1

SUMMER-DAY (1)
a very fair English Summer-day,--not only was there no S 10 413 1

SUMMER-HOUSE (2)
having a very handsome summer-house in their garden, where E I 4 27 4
summer-house, large enough to hold a dozen people." E I 4 27 4

SUMMER-ROOMS (1)
make it one of the pleasantest summer-rooms in England." SS I 13 69 76

SUMMERS (11)
under the care of Miss Summers in Wigmore Street, till she LS 2 246 1
to be attended to, while she remains with Miss Summers. LS 7 252 1
He is if possible to prevail on Miss Summers to let LS 15 266 4
in my life as by a letter this morning from Miss Summers. LS 16 268 1
If Miss Summers will not keep her, you must find me out LS 16 268 1
informing her that Miss Summers had absolutely refused to LS 17 269 1
had, but while Miss Summers declares that Miss Vernon LS 17 271 7
which prevented Miss Summers from keeping the girl; & it LS 19 274 2
for us all to spend our summers in; and my aunt and I went MP I 6 57 31
There will be work for five summers at least before the MP II 7 241 21
the influence of four summers and two children; and, on P III 5 37 21
22

SUMMIT (3)
he had placed near its summit, to oaks in general, to NA I 14 111 29
as they gained the summit of a long hill, and was not more MP I 8 81 32
again, they gained the summit of the most considerable P III 10 85 13

SUMMITS (2)
enjoyment of air on their summits, were an happy SS I 9 40 3
fancy that from their summits Combe Magna might be seen. SS III 6 302 8

SUMMON (5)
one of the children to summon him; but Mr. Morland was NA II 15 242 9
I can summon more than one witness of undoubted veracity. PP II 12 199 5
Mr. Rushworth, shall we summon a council on this lawn?" MP I 9 90 34
one whom she could summon at any time to a walk, would be E I 4 26 1
difficulty that she could summon enough of her usual self E III 14 434 2

SUMMONED (11)
to dine with them, and summoned by the latter to guess the NA I 7 51 54
into the dining room as soon as they were summoned to it. SS II 8 193 5
till Mrs. Jennings was summoned to her chaise to take SS III 10 341 5
and at half past six Elizabeth was summoned to dinner. PP I 8 35 1
dining-parlour, and sat with her till summoned to coffee. PP I 8 37 21
The two young ladies were summoned from the shrubbery PP I 17 86 9
Mrs. Bennet rang the bell, and Miss Elizabeth was summoned PP I 20 111 14
From these instructions they were summoned by the arrival PP II 6 166 42
This was a hard duty, and she was never summoned to it, MP II 10 273 7
summoned to town and must be absent on the very day. E II 16 292 9
& three or four of them summoned to attend their master-- S 1 364 1

SUMMONS (12)
He seemed astonished at the summons, and looked as if half LS 25 292 2
no unexpected summons, no impertinent intrusion to NA I 14 106 1
friend, and expecting a summons herself from the angry NA II 9 192 4
No summons however arrived; and at last, on seeing a NA II 9 192 4
as the shock of such a summons could be lessened to her, SS III 7 311 16
He was interrupted by a summons to dinner; and the girls PP I 13 65 26
the cause of their summons, reading the two letters aloud, PP III 4 280 26
instead of the expected summons, when they approached her, PP III 7 301 1
Miss Crawford before this summons came, but no sentiment MP III 13 427 12
pressing, joyful cares attending this summons to herself. MP III 15 443 24
Miss Smith receiving her summons, was with her without E II 5 186 3
She smiled her acceptance; and nothing less than a summons E III 6 366 76

SUMS (2)
and sold for incredible sums; of racing matches, in which NA I 9 66 31
Even you, used as you are to great sums, would hardly E III 8 382 23

SUN (22)
The morrow brought a very sober looking morning; the sun NA I 11 82 1
if the clouds would only go off, and the sun keep out." NA I 11 82 1
with the last beams of the sun playing in beautiful NA II 5 161 24
them:--"the rays of the sun were not too cheerful for him, NA II 7 179 29
high; at four o'clock, the sun was now two hours above the NA II 9 193 5
of a western sun gaily poured through two sash windows! NA II 9 193 6
dispersing across the sky, and the sun frequently appeared. SS I 13 63 2
The clouds seem parting too, the sun will be out in a SS II 5 168 9
fire the next day, or the sun gained any power over a cold, SS II 7 180 1
so likely to give it as standing and stooping in a hot sun. MP I 7 72 45
and though the sun was strong, it was not so very hot. MP I 7 73 55
Yes, certainly, the sun shines and the park looks very MP I 10 99 17
the same soil and the same sun should nurture plants MP II 4 209 16
brisk soft wind, and bright sun, occasionally clouded for MP III 11 409 6
The sun was yet an hour and half above the horizon. MP III 15 439 9
As the sun is out, I believe I had better take my three E I 8 57 3
Under a bright mid-day sun, at almost midsummer, Mr. E III 6 357 33
the stooping-- glaring sun--tired to death--could bear it E III 6 358 35
comfort, seen under a sun bright, without being oppressive. E III 6 360 39
were carried off; the sun appeared; it was summer again. E III 13 424 1
observed the same beautiful effect of the western sun!-- E III 14 434 2
who neglect the reigning power to bow to the rising sun. P IV 10 224 48

SUN'S (2)
with the sun's first rays she was determined to peruse it. NA II 6 170 12
months there; and the sun's rays falling strongly into the MP III 15 439 9

SUN-SHINE (2)
more melancholy; for sun-shine appeared to her a totally MP III 15 439 9
There was neither health nor gaiety in sun-shine in a town. MP III 15 439 9

SUNDAY (34)
a doubt of it; for a fine Sunday in Bath empties every NA I 5 35 1
body discovers every Sunday throughout the season, they NA I 5 35 2
Sunday only now remain to be described, and close the week. NA I 13 97 1
It was Sunday, an the whole time between morning and NA II 9 190 1
As to-morrow is Sunday, Eleanor, I shall not return." NA II 11 211 14
of Sunday groups, and speedy shall be her descent from it. NA II 14 232 7
so fine, so beautiful a Sunday as to draw many to SS III 2 271 4
and of a Sunday evening when he has nothing to do." PP I 10 50 39
On Sunday, after morning service, the separation, so PP I 12 60 5
occasional absence on a Sunday, provided that some other PP I 13 63 12
Saturday, Sunday and Monday, endurable to Kitty and Lydia. PP I 17 88 15
de Bourgh on the ensuing Sunday at church, and I need not PP II 5 157 6
7
us on Sunday to drink tea and spend the evening at Rosings. PP II 6 160 2
They left Brighton together on Sunday night, and were PP III 4 277 14
Mr. Gardiner left Longbourn on Sunday; on Tuesday, his PP III 6 295 5
They met again on Sunday and then I saw him too. PP III 10 324 2
go to church twice every Sunday and preach such very good MP I 11 112 30
into a good humour every Sunday, it will be bad enough to MP I 11 112 31
not to be dressed till Sunday, because I know how much MP II 4 212 31
Grant would enjoy it on Sunday after the fatigues of the MP II 4 212 31
he might ride over, every Sunday, to a house nominally MP II 7 247 42
the other family which Sunday produced, she learnt that he MP II 11 286 16
therefore of seeing your friend either to-morrow or Sunday. MP III 4 354 48
out of doors, except of a Sunday; she owned she could MP III 10 401 10
of beauty, and every Sunday dressed them in their cleanest MP III 11 408 2
Sunday always brought this comfort to Fanny, and on this MP III 11 408 2
to Fanny, and on this Sunday she felt it more than ever. MP III 11 408 2
But Sunday made her a very creditable and tolerably MP III 11 408 2
the ramparts every fine Sunday throughout the year, always MP III 11 408 4
and it was not till Sunday evening that Edmund began to MP III 16 453 17
Sitting with her on Sunday evening--a wet Sunday evening-- MP III 16 453 17
Mrs. Goddard had dressed it on a Sunday, and asked all the E I 4 28 8
no church for her on Sunday any more than on Christmas-Day; E I 16 138 17
She came away from Marlborough-Buildings only on Sunday; P IV 9 197 40

SUNDAY-TRAVELLING (1)
bad habits; that Sunday-travelling had been a common thing; P IV 5 161 27

SUNDAYS (2)
expected for half a dozen Sundays together; but not for a MP III 3 341 30
He had been absent only two Sundays; and when they parted, P III 9 78 19

SUNG (3)
They had sung together once or twice, it appeared, at E II 8 227 87
"You have sung quite enough for one evening--now, be quiet. E II 8 229 94
anxious to have a general idea of what was next to be sung. P IV 8 190 47

SUNK (38)
serious enough--for to be sunk, tho' but an hour, in your LS 35 305 1
Her companion's discourse now sunk from its hitherto NA I 7 48 32
mounted, sunk a little under this consequent inconvenience. NA II 5 156 4
It was not only with herself that she was sunk--but with NA II 10 199 1
but, after a few minutes, sunk again, without knowing it NA II 15 241 7
be supported for ever; it sunk within a few days into a SS I 16 83 4
were all sunk in Mrs. Dashwood's romantic delicacy. SS I 16 85 10
Marianne looked again; her heart sunk within her; and SS I 16 86 20
As she said this, she sunk into a reverie for a few SS I 16 88 33
Elinor's security sunk; but her self-command did not sink SS I 22 131 33
almost overcome--her heart sunk within her, and she could SS I 22 134 53
Marianne's countenance sunk. SS II 3 156 10
and unable to stand, sunk into her chair, and Elinor, SS II 6 177 12
after breakfast, which sunk the heart of Mrs. Jennings SS II 9 202 4
Her voice sunk with the word, but presently reviving she SS III 10 344 14
15
And to the pang of a friend disgracing herself and sunk in PP I 22 125 18
person to blame, and saying your opinion of him is sunk. PP II 1 136 14
His character sunk on every review of it; and as a PP II 3 149 27
His affection for her soon sunk into indifference; her's PP III 19 387 8
the despondence that sunk her little heart was severe. MP I 2 14 8
Lady Bertram, sunk back in one corner of the sofa, the MP I 13 126 19
Fanny's heart sunk, but there was no leisure for thinking MP II 10 275 10
I have;" but her heart sunk under the appalling prospect MP III 1 317 38
It would be sunk into a badge of disgrace; for what can be MP III 6 368 8
She looked at him, but he was leaning back, sunk in a MP III 15 447 35
to pay his addresses to her had sunk him in her opinion. E I 16 135 7
The worn-out past was sunk in the freshness of what was E II 5 188 8
The dignity of Miss Woodhouse, of Hartfield, was sunk E II 14 276 33
could prompt such behaviour sunk them both very much.-- E II 15 281 3
She is poor; she has sunk from the comfort's she was born E III 7 375 61
on entering the carriage, sunk back for a moment overcome-- E III 7 376 62
natural key of his voice, sunk it immediately, to say, E III 10 392 1
2
It has sunk him, I cannot say how it has sunk him in my E III 10 397 48
story of Jane Fairfax, that was quite sunk and lost.--- E III 11 408 33
or fortune; or rather sunk by him into a state of most P III 4 27 3
but any indisposition sunk her completely; she had no P III 5 37 21
Their concerns had been sunk under those of Uppercross, P IV 1 124 11
to raise even the unfounded hopes which sunk with him. P IV 12 250 6

SUNNY (1)
Anne found a nice seat for her, on a dry sunny bank, under P III 10 87 21

SUNRISE (1)
do you stay in this heavenly place?--till sunrise?"-- W 335 13

SUNSHINE (9)
him, declined giving any absolute promise of sunshine. NA I 11 82 1
A gleam of sunshine took her quite by surprize; she looked NA I 11 83 16
attracted by the partial sunshine of a showery sky, and SS I 9 40 3
there was a gleam of sunshine, she hoped not to be driven MP I 16 151 2
is no more like her's, than a lamp is like sunshine." E II 9 231 6
the dread of a future war all that could dim her sunshine. P IV 12 252 12
I wd rather them run about in the sunshine than not. S 4 381 1
to the sea, dancing & sparkling in sunshine & freshness.-- S 4 384 1
Mariners tempting it in sunshine & overwhelmed by the S 7 396 1

SUP (1)
and Miss Prince, and Miss Richardson, to sup with her." E I 4 28 8

SUPER-ADDED (2)
same himself, with the super-added objects of professing MP I 6 55 17
an evil which no super-added elegance or harmony could MP III 8 391 11

SUPER-EXCELLENT (1)
understanding, and super-excellent disposition of Jane, PP III 13 347 33

SUPERADDED (2)
with the superadded dread of what the morrow might produce MP I 16 150 1
So much superadded decision of character! E I 6 42 6

SUPERANNUATED (1)
of three to old superannuated servants by my father's will, SS I 2 10 20

SUPERCILIOUS (1)
it did not render him supercilious; on the contrary, he PP I 5 18 1

SUPERCILIOUSNESS (3)
To behave to her guest with such superciliousness!-- NA II 1 130 1
there was no superciliousness; she was very civil." NA II 1 130 2
Elizabeth still saw superciliousness in their treatment of PP I 6 21 1

SUPERFICIAL (2)
should be more than superficial, & I flatter myself that LS 7 253 1
so fully supporting the superficial, that she was at first, P IV 4 146 6

SUPERFINE (1)
Where was this superfine, extraordinary sort of gallantry P III 8 69 39

SUPERFLUITY (3)
and despondence, such a superfluity of children, and such MP I 1 4 2
understanding for him out of the superfluity of your own! MP II 5 224 53
found vent for his superfluity of sensation as a Projector, S 10 412 1

SUPERINTEND (3)
from whence they could superintend the progress of the SS III 14 374 7
There should always be one steady head to superintend so MP I 15 141 22
It was no longer in Emma's power to superintend his E I 11 91 1

SUPERINTENDANCE (2)
taking the office of superintendance intirely from her W 360 30
to my father's active superintendance, and when PP I 16 81 37

SUPERINTENDED (2)
by the lady who superintended her education, and who still PP I 11 67 7
Susan had only superintended their final removal from the S 10 414 1

SUPERINTENDING (2)
occupied in superintending the fortunes of her eldest MP I 4 38 9
of the company, superintending their various dresses with MP I 17 163 21

SUPERINTENDS (1)
a lady lives with her, and superintends her education." PP I 16 82 43

SUPERIOR (124)
that you will be superior to such as allow nothing for a LS 12 260 1
her, for losing by the superior attractions of another LS 14 264 4
Manwaring is indeed beyond compare superior to Reginald-- LS 16 269 3
in everything but the power of being with me. LS 16 269 3

She is an amiable girl, & has a very superior mind to what LS 23 284 4
sense of superior integrity which is peculiarly insolent. LS 25 292 1
Her taste for drawing was not superior; though whenever NA I 1 14 1
She is a most amiable girl; such a superior understanding! NA I 7 50 49
me of your being superior in good-nature yourself to all NA II 1 133 28
one on the same plan, but superior in length and breadth. NA II 8 184 5
then--how mournfully superior in reality and substance! NA II 13 227 26
while, till one of these superior blessings could be SS I 3 16 6
beneath shut up their superior beauties; and towards one SS I 9 40 3
in the world," said Marianne, "superior to this?-- SS I 9 41 5
It was the desire of appearing superior to other people. SS I 20 112 28
informed by it of Lucy's superior claims on Edward, and be SS II 1 142 7
Edward will marry Lucy; he will marry a woman superior in SS III 1 263 27
forget that he ever thought another superior to her."-- SS III 1 263 27
men, I do not know that one is superior to the other." SS III 5 297 29
to fancy himself as much superior to people in general, as SS III 6 304 15
her's; and whose mind--Oh! how infinitely superior!"-- SS III 8 322 36
her, and Elinor, though superior to her in fortune and SS III 14 377 11
and with no sentiment superior to strong esteem and lively SS III 14 378 15
you up (I suppose) in a superior stile, you are returned W 352 26
In understanding Darcy was the superior. PP I 4 16 14
myself--for I am fond of superior society; but I did not PP I 6 26 36
distinguishing the much superior solicitude of Mr. PP I 8 35 1
and I think it infinitely superior to Miss Grantley's." PP I 10 48 15
Miss de Bourgh is far superior to the handsomest of her PP I 14 67 7
walk, as they were superior to the broad-faced stuffy PP I 16 76 3
he stopt with a bow of superior courtesy to compliment him PP I 18 92 22
Such very superior dancing is not often seen. PP I 18 92 23
the superior in consequence, to begin the acquaintance.-- PP I 18 97 60
superior to his sister as well by nature as education. PP II 2 139 2
of your clothes is superior to the rest, there is no PP II 6 160 6
Our instrument is a capital one, probably superior to---- PP II 6 164 18
as capable as any other woman's of superior execution." PP II 8 175 25
Your superior knowledge of your sister must make the PP II 12 197 5
to introduce you to very superior society, and from our PP II 15 215 4
to be infinitely superior to any thing they had expected. PP III 1 257 67
your husband; unless you looked up to him as a superior. PP III 17 376 35
In society so superior to what she had generally known, PP III 19 385 4
other, and Julia was not superior to the hope of some MP I 17 162 19
presence of a stranger superior to Mr. Yates must have MP II 2 194 21
it appeared to her, with superior tone and expression; and MP II 4 207 10
Believe me, I have no pleasure in the world superior to MP II 9 262 9
could not but admit the superior power of one pleasure MP II 9 262 11
the way of a rich, superior, longworded, arbitrary uncle. MP II 12 297 35
given it to him with superior and more heartfelt MP III 1 319 39
You are infinitely my superior in merit; all that I know.-- MP III 3 343 41
for an action with some superior force, which (supposing MP III 7 375 2
at intervals by the superior noise of Sam, Tom, and MP III 7 382 27
it; a summer and autumn infinitely superior to the last. MP III 10 405 18
of every thing in so superior a style to what she had been E I 3 23 10
his sisters, from a superior education, are not to be E I 4 30 22
manners are superior to Mr. Knightley's or Mr. Weston's. E I 4 34 41
42
She is not the superior young woman which Emma's friend E I 5 36 6
are infinitely superior to what she received from nature." E I 6 42 2
As to anything superior for you, I suppose she is quite in E I 7 56 41
for he is as much her superior in sense as in situation. E I 8 61 38
She is superior to Mr. Robert Martin." E I 8 62 41
I can imagine, that before she had seen anybody superior, E I 8 65 48
He is so very superior. E I 9 74 22
"I must see somebody very superior to any one I have seen E I 10 84 13
doubt you were much my superior in judgment at that period E I 12 99 7
Our part of London is so very superior to most others!-- E I 12 103 37
very accomplished and superior!--and exactly Emma's age." E I 12 104 49
in fortune and consequence she was greatly his superior. E I 16 136 9
should not be of that superior sort in which the feelings E I 16 138 15
that Harriet was the superior creature of the two--and E I 17 142 9
rather than to what is superior, engaged the affections of E II 2 165 7
shew off in higher style her own very superior performance. E II 2 168 15
it certainly is, so very superior to all other pork, that E II 3 173 30
31
to another as superior, of course, to the first, as under E II 4 181 3
it did not appear that she was at all Harriet's superior. E II 4 183 9
minutes at the two superior sashed windows which were open E II 6 197 5
the terms on which the superior families would visit them. E II 7 207 6
Jane Fairfax did look and move superior; but Emma E II 8 219 44
conceal from herself, was infinitely superior to her own. E II 8 227 86
Harriet is my superior in all the charm and all the E II 13 269 16
He is just as superior as ever;--but being married, you E II 14 271 15
to shine and be very superior, but with manners which had E II 14 272 16
Highbury had long known that you are a superior performer." E II 14 276 35
A superior performer!--very far from it, I assure you. E II 14 276 36
herself coming with superior knowledge of the world, to E II 15 281 1
than return to the superior companions who have always E II 15 285 13
civilities by one very superior party--in which her card E II 16 290 3
on my side; with your superior talents, you have a right E II 17 301 18
Mr. Weston might be his son's superior.-- E III 2 325 32
Elton was not the superior creature she had believed him. E III 3 332 1
Emma was quite eager to see this superior treasure. E III 4 339 17
could just catch the words, "so superior to Mr. Elton!" E III 4 341 33
be too greatly your superior in situation to think of you. E III 4 341 35
He is your superior, no doubt, and there do seem E III 4 342 39
superior intelligence, of those five letters so arranged. E III 5 348 23
elegant way, infinitely superior to the bustle and E III 6 352 2
infinitely superior--no comparison--the others hardly E III 6 358 35
Delightful, charming, superior, first circles, spheres, E III 6 359 37
"To a Mrs. Smallridge--charming woman--most superior--to E III 8 380 13
some arrow-root of very superior quality was speedily E III 9 391 20
Considering the very superior claims of the object, it E III 11 403 2
It was her superior duty. E III 11 403 2
how infinitely superior he is to every body else, I should E III 11 405 18
feel how superior he was to every other being upon earth." E III 11 406 24
that occasion, found her much superior to his expectation. E III 11 409 35
The superior degree of confidence towards Harriet, which E III 11 410 35
as infinitely the superior, or when his regard for her had E III 11 412 45
wife for him, they could not have found her superior.-- E III 13 428 23
The superior hopes which gradually opened were so much the E III 13 432 40
and judgment had been ever so superior to her own. E III 18 475 39
us with two characters so much superior to our own." E III 18 478 69
You can have no superior, but most true on mine.-- E III 18 479 70
very superior character to any thing deserved by his own. P III 1 4 6
only two houses superior in appearance to those of the P III 5 36 20
he was undoubtedly superior to his wife; but not of powers, P III 6 43 5
since there was neither superior affection, confidence, P III 6 46 12
nothing superior to the accommodations of a man of war. P III 8 69 37
very superior in cultivation and manners to all the rest. P III 9 74 5
make her infinitely superior to thousands of those who P IV 5 155 9
and only superior to her in being more highly valued! P IV 5 160 25
Fanny Harville was a very superior creature; and his P IV 8 183 10
There is someone in most families privileged by superior S 4 382 1
Sir Edwd was much her superior in air & manner;--certainly S 7 394 1
divided again--the two superior ladies being at one end of S 7 395 1

SUPERIORITIES (1)
superiorities of the house, as they were detailed to her. P IV 10 219 28

SUPERIORITY (34)
pre-determined to dislike, acknowledge one's superiority. LS 7 254 3
That is--I should not think the superiority was always on NA I 3 27 29
Their superiority of abode was no more to them than their NA II 2 141 12
abode was no more to them than their superiority of person. NA II 2 141 12
by establishing his superiority in ill-breeding, were not SS I 20 112 28
any material superiority by nature, merely from the SS II 14 250 12
But pride--where there is a real superiority of mind, PP I 11 57 24
showed rather conscious superiority than any solicitude to MP I 6 52 1
Bertrams, with every superiority in their own apartments, MP I 16 151 1
their own sense of superiority could demand, were entirely MP I 16 151 1
, on farther observation, admit no right of superiority. MP III 9 395 3
with circumstances of superiority undescribable. MP III 10 405 18
others only established her superiority in wretchedness. MP III 16 448 2
he had acknowledged Fanny's mental superiority. MP III 17 471 28
she had no intellectual superiority to make atonement to E I 3 21 4
She had no sense of superiority then. E I 8 63 42
Mr. Elton's superiority had very ample acknowledgment. E I 9 74 21
he will have the advantage over negligent superiority. E I 13 111 17
the display of his own superiority; to be dispensing his E I 18 150 32
Jane's decided superiority both in beauty and acquirements. E II 2 164 7
awes Mrs. Elton by her superiority both of mind and manner; E II 15 286 23
think of his infinite superiority to all the rest of the E III 4 341 36
repetition, and all the insolence of imaginary superiority. E III 14 442 8
sensible of Mr. Knightley's high superiority of character. E III 18 480 80
She could do justice to the superiority of Lady Russell's P III 4 30 10
comfortable feeling of superiority from wishing for the P III 5 41 45
most topics, he had the superiority, for while Mary P III 6 43 5
such a consciousness of superiority in the Miss Musgroves, P III 9 74 6
or heard of; and the superiority was not less in the style P IV 3 137 4
There was no superiority of manner, accomplishment, or P IV 4 150 14
and confidence of superiority, into a poor, infirm, P IV 5 153 6
Cobb, and at Captain Harville's, had fixed her superiority. P IV 11 242 62
and felt that his superiority of appearance might be not P IV 12 248 2
balanced against her superiority of rank; and all this, P IV 12 248 2

SUPERIORS (2)
so many, infinitely her superiors--who seemed so little MP II 13 305 26
among his equals or superiors, may be of use in diverting P IV 4 151 21

SUPERLATIVELY (1)
Their table was superlatively stupid. PP II 6 166 41

SUPERNATURAL (1)
unless secured by supernatural means, the lid in one NA II 6 164 3

SUPERNUMERARY (3)
Mrs. Rushworth in a supernumerary glass or two, was all MP II 3 203 30
gone home with all the supernumerary jellies to nurse a MP II 11 283 4
little disposed for supernumerary exertion, always quitted S 11 422 1

SUPERSEDE (2)
potent intelligence, as to supersede the necessity of more. LS 35 305 1
This brief account of the family is intended to supersede NA I 4 34 9

SUPERSEDED (4)
Allen were not to be superseded; but on some other day he NA I 13 103 28
mind every idea was superseded by Lydia's situation, PP III 4 276 6
the cottage, and all idle topics were superseded. E I 10 86 24
He might be superseded by another; he certainly would E II 4 183 10

SUPINE (1)
but which her more supine and yielding temper would have MP III 9 395 4

SUPINENESS (1)
could be urged by the supineness of his mother, or the MP I 4 36 7

SUPPER (30)
now, I am resolved to finish the basket after supper." SS II 1 144 12
Let her name her own supper, and go to bed. SS II 8 195 16
that will hold ten couple, and where can the supper be?' SS II 14 252 18
and let the supper be set out in the saloon.' SS II 14 252 18
him at supper, while he went home to dinner himself.-- W 359 28
staid he must sit down to supper in less than ten minutes-- W 359 28
however, by duets after supper, while he could find no PP I 8 40 59
lottery tickets, and a little bit of hot supper afterwards. PP I 15 74 11
mutual satisfaction till supper put an end to cards; and PP I 16 84 59
noise of Mrs. Philips's supper party, but his manners PP I 16 84 59
all the dishes at supper, and repeatedly fearing that he PP I 16 84 59
When they sat down to supper, therefore, she considered it PP I 18 98 63
of tranquillity; for when supper was over, singing was PP I 18 100 68
Netherfield gentlemen to supper; but their carriage was PP III 12 342 27
He scarcely needed an invitation to stay supper; and PP III 13 345 19
Mr. Bennet joined them at supper, his voice and manner PP III 13 348 34
remaining till after supper; unless when some barbarous PP III 13 349 43
table, on which the supper tray yet remained, brought a MP I 7 74 57
have her own way with the supper, and whom she could not MP II 9 267 22
body's dress, or any body's place at supper, but her own. MP II 11 282 4
supper, wound up the enjoyments and fatigues of the day. MP III 7 376 5
was in distress about the supper; and Mr. Woodhouse E II 11 248 10
still was not it too small for any comfortable supper? E II 11 254 44
tolerate the prospect of being miserably crowded at supper. E II 11 254 44
Mrs. Weston proposed having no regular supper; merely E II 11 254 45
A private dance, without sitting down to supper, was E II 11 254 45
lights and music, tea and supper, made themselves; or were E II 11 255 59
The two last dances before supper were begun, and Harriet E III 2 326 33
Supper was announced. E III 2 328 44
Mr. Knightley till after supper; but, when they were all E III 2 330 46

SUPPER-HOUR (1)
Mrs. Norris, about the supper-hour, were all for the sake MP II 10 278 20

SUPPER-ROOM (2)
quitted the supper-room on the day of Henry's departure. NA II 13 222 7
It regarded a supper-room. E II 11 254 44

SUPPER-TABLE (1)
unusual rate; and the supper-table, which always closed E I 3 24 11

SUPPERS (3)
Remember we never eat suppers."-- W 351 25
but his conviction of suppers being very unwholesome made E I 3 24 12
At the time of the ball-room's being built, suppers had E II 11 254 44

SUPPLANTED (8)
and to see myself supplanted in your friendship by NA I 13 98 2
to both, that he had entirely supplanted his brother. SS III 14 376 11
All are supplanted sooner or later. MP II 10 277 17
I could not bear to have Henry supplanted.-- E II 8 224 68
in the dread of being supplanted, found how inexpressibly E III 12 415 1
be forgotten, that is, supplanted; but this could not be E III 15 450 38
Martin had thoroughly supplanted Mr. Knightley, and was E III 19 481 1
She had never been supplanted. P IV 11 241 61

SUPPLEMENT (1)
or in the anxious supplement from Mary, of "upon my word, P III 6 42 1

SUPPLEMENTARY (1)
was the great supplementary comfort of Sir Thomas's life. MP III 17 465 15

SUPPLICATED (1)
it, and entreated and supplicated never to do so again?" MP II 4 211 26

SUPPLICATION (7)
supplication, could not allow it to influence her. NA I 13 98 2
up, was begged of me with the most earnest supplication. SS II 7 189 46
rather of command than supplication, "Miss Dashwood, for SS III 8 317 1
2
a research; in which supplication had been necessary to a PP III 10 326 3
to this, Henry Crawford continued his supplication. MP I 14 135 17
not by dint of several minutes of supplication and waiting. MP III 3 341 27
too decided to invite supplication; and in this state of E I 15 132 37

SUPPLICATIONS (2)
again attacked with supplications or reproaches, and her NA I 13 99 9
She was immediately surrounded by supplications, every MP I 18 171 28

SUPPLIED (27)
had much meaning, was supplied by the General: the NA II 8 182 2
and affectionate embrace supplied the place of language in NA II 13 229 31
and abroad, however, supplied all the deficiencies of SS I 7 32 1
for it supplied her with endless jokes against them both. SS I 8 36 2
the gentlemen had supplied the discourse with some variety- SS II 12 233 19
his morning's lounge had supplied him with, & they chatted W 323 3
At present, indeed, they were well supplied both with news PP I 7 28 3
most abundantly supplied with coffee and muffin. PP I 16 76 5
or the imagination supplied what the eye could not reach. MP I 7 67 16
of no door had ever supplied her, she turned the lock in MP II 1 177 7
with himself for having supplied every thing else;-- MP II 10 276 13
Every thing supplied an amusement to the high glee of MP III 7 375 2

sense and good breeding supplied its place; and as to the MP III 8 392 11
all the uneasiness it supplied, it connected her with the MP III 9 394 2
and her place had been supplied by an excellent woman as E I 1 5 2
Emma allowed her father to talk--but supplied her visitors E I 3 25 15
The gruel came and supplied a great deal to be said--much E I 12 104 50
It was a very useful note, for it supplied them with fresh E I 17 141 4
effect was justified; it supplied a very useful check,-- E III 9 386 9
So far went his understanding; and his vanity supplied a P III 3 24 36
to former days, supplied anecdotes in abundance to occupy P III 11 100 23
thought, which instinct supplied, to Henrietta, still P III 12 111 44
were supplied by her husband to all who needed them. P III 12 111 50
(smiling at Anne) "well supplied, and want for nothing.-- P IV 11 234 27
accidental omission is supplied in a moment by Ly D.'s S 4 381 1
they may be supplied at a fair rate--(poor Mr Hollis's S 6 393 1
& the subject had supplied letters & extracts & messages S 11 420 1
SUPPLIES (2)
and while these prime supplies of good remained, she might P IV 12 252 12
It supplies us, as before, with all the fruit & vegetables S 4 380 1
SUPPLY (53)
as heroines must read to supply their memories with those NA I 1 15 3
appear to her that life could supply any greater felicity. NA I 10 75 24
which its walls could supply--the happiness of a progress NA I 11 88 54
of her husband a nightly supply of coarse food, was the NA II 8 187 16
in his home; for to supply her loss, he invited and SS I 1 3 1
ready money enough to supply all that was wanted of SS I 6 29 4
Neither Lady Middleton nor Mrs. Jennings could supply to SS I 11 54 6
is gossip, and she only likes me now because I supply it." SS II 9 201 3
china, &c. to supply the place of what was taken away. SS II 11 225 35
Delaford living could supply such an income, as any body SS III 3 284 22
own attentive care, to supply to her the place of the SS III 7 308 3
pounds a-year would supply them with the comforts of life. SS III 13 369 32
in life, could but ill supply the deficiency of his. PP I 7 28 1
family with her stay, and bring back a supply of clothes. PP I 7 34 45
"The country," said Darcy, "can in general supply but few PP I 9 42 17
The party did not supply much conversation. PP II 6 163 14
intelligence, which might supply it among themselves if PP II 19 239 11
at the same time to supply him with fishing tackle, and PP III 1 255 60
made every body eager for another, to supply the idea. PP III 15 360 1
a very small income to supply their wants, made her eager MP I 1 4 2
needful solicitude, which there were no children to supply. MP I 1 8 9
He could not think Lady Bertram quite equal to supply his MP I 3 32 62
how well Edmund could supply his place in carving, talking MP I 4 34 1
If you have no work of your own, I can supply you from the MP I 7 71 34
No piece could be proposed that did not supply somebody MP I 14 131 3
the forbearance it would supply, to save Sir Thomas from MP II 1 183 23
supply of the most amiable and innocent enjoyments. MP II 3 201 22
connections can supply; and it must be by a long and MP II 6 235 18
terrific scenes, which such a period, at sea, must supply. MP II 6 235 19
to supply as a duty what the heart was deficient in. MP III 2 329 9
You will supply the rest; and a most fortunate man he is MP III 4 351 32
be read deliberately, to supply matter for much reflection, MP III 12 417 4
with her, because Susan remained to supply her place.-- MP III 17 472 31
They ready wit the word will soon supply, may its approval E I 9 71 14
Thy ready wit the word will soon supply E I 9 72 15
in all probability, to supply every sort of sensation that E I 10 86 21
it is incumbent on me to supply her place, if I can; and I E II 7 209 11
dear part of Emma, her fancy, received an amusing supply. E II 8 214 13
from Donwell--some of Mr. Knightley's most liberal supply. E II 9 238 51
supply; for I have a great many more than I can ever use. E II 9 238 51
I had, you desired me to supply him; and so I took mine E III 4 338 12
seemed every day to supply a different report, and the E III 6 352 1
state could no longer supply his aunt with a pretence for P III 8 63 1
she could, every possible supply from Uppercross had been P IV 2 129 2
understanding would supply resolution, but here was P IV 5 154 8
so busy about, and which supply me with the means of doing P IV 5 155 9
all that such an evening could supply, from Lady Russell. P IV 5 158 21
but not of capacity to supply the cooler reflection which S 2 372 1
Sanditon could be made to supply by the gratitude of those S 2 374 1
The Gardiner there, is glad enough to supply us--. S 4 380 1
to have a nominal supply you know, that poor old Andrew S 4 382 1
well-read in novels to supply her imagination with S 6 391 1
drink Asses milk I could supply her)--and as soon as she S 7 401 1
SUPPLYING (9)
a thought occurred, and supplying the place of many ideas NA I 8 52 1
Good-will supplying the place of experience, his character NA II 16 249 1
her enfeebled spirits, supplying every succour, and SS III 7 315 25
families I have been the means of supplying in that way. PP II 6 165 32
venison cut up without supplying one pleasant anecdote of MP I 6 52 1
the heat only supplying inconvenience enough to be talked MP I 7 70 30
Emma must do Harriet good: and by supplying her with a new E I 5 36 4
supplying the means of respectable subsistence hereafter. E II 2 164 5
of the Eltons for supplying all the discipline of pointed E III 3 332 1
SUPPORT (74)
You must support & encourage me--you must urge the LS 15 267 6
I am not sorry for, as I know no better support of love. LS 16 269 3
injured you with your family, how am I to support myself. LS 30 300 3
My sweet Catherine, do support me, persuade your brother NA I 8 57 23
to provide for the support of the woman; the woman to make NA I 10 77 35
With Mr. Allen to support her, she felt no dread of the NA I 14 106 1
next day, endeavouring to support her spirits, and while NA I 15 121 26
is not a trifle that will support a family now-a-days; and NA II 3 146 16
Human nature could support no more. NA II 6 170 12
In support of the plausibility of this conjecture, it NA II 8 188 17
being thus without any support, at the end of a quarter of NA II 15 242 9
incapable of giving the young people even a decent support. NA II 15 246 12
provision than 7000l. would support her in affluence. SS I 3 14 2
spite of all that he and Marianne could say in its support. SS I 10 49 9
visitor, endeavoured to support something like discourse SS I 16 89 42
herself, and which was more than she felt equal to support. SS II 1 141 5
of all your mutual affection to support you under them. SS II 2 146 6
expected to receive any support in her endeavour to SS II 3 154 6
always find something to support its doubts, if I had not, SS II 5 173 44
I had hoped that her regard for me would support her under SS II 9 205 24
to shew, and the master's ability to support it. SS II 12 233 18
were equally earnest in support of their own descendant. SS II 12 234 23
I have many things to support me. SS III 1 263 27
with a view of better support, she would do all in her SS III 1 267 38
just in time to receive and support her as she entered it. SS III 9 333 3
instantly that praise and support which her frankness and SS III 10 346 29
Mrs Robert offered not another word in support of the game. W 358 28
of domestic comfort, & as little hope of future support.-- W 361 31
to support her spirits, there were periods of dejection. PP II 4 152 6
She knew not how to support herself, and from actual PP II 11 193 31
pounds would be a very insufficient support therein. PP II 12 200 5
then Georgiana, unable to support the idea of grieving and PP II 12 202 5
to her support, and consequently preferred her husband's. PP III 1 256 61
On his quitting the room, she sat down, unable to support PP III 4 276 9
insufficient to their support; and whenever they changed PP III 19 387 8
body else, his single support could not bring her forward, MP I 2 22 35
of her support, and the obligation of her future provision. MP I 3 24 7
with barely enough to support me in the rank of a MP I 3 29 46
and gave it her full support, declaring that in her MP I 6 61 58
occasioned, made her hardly know how to support herself. MP I 7 74 59
Maria, wanting Henry Crawford's animating support, thought MP I 15 142 24
had driven Julia away, was to her the sweetest support. MP II 1 176 3
Her greatest support and glory was in having formed the MP II 2 188 3
it at the park to support her sister's spirits, and MP II 3 203 30
who had done most for his support and advancement; and MP II 6 233 14
She was one of his two dearest--that must support her. MP II 9 264 17
but so much the better; his spirits will support yours. MP III 4 348 23
pleasantness and gaiety will be a constant support to you. MP III 4 348 23
met, was Fanny's only support in looking forward to it. MP III 5 356 4
be quite enough to support the spirits he was watching.-- MP III 6 368 7
known there only as William's friend, was some support. MP III 10 399 4
To be deriving support from the commendations of Mrs. MP III 12 417 4
the support of their own bad sense to her too lively mind. MP III 13 421 2
possible for them to support life and reason under such MP III 15 442 21
May God support you under *your* share. MP III 15 442 23
of Susan herself, was all serving to support her spirits. MP III 15 444 25
from her the smallest support or attempt at support. MP III 16 448 2
His spirits required support. E I 1 7 10
daughter, and you must support your claim to that station E I 4 30 22
"Mr. Weston would undoubtedly support me, if he were here, E I 5 36 6
not she give him her support?--would not she add her E I 15 125 4
I am sure of your kind support and aid." E I 15 125 5
father gave his hearty support by calling out, "my good E II 5 195 48
I shall be no support to Mrs. Weston. E II 9 234 32
to what was right and support her in it very tolerably. E II 13 268 13
character of hospitality and ancient dignity to support.-- P III 2 13 7
informed--the mother to support and keep from hysterics-- P III 7 53 3
The Admiral's kind urgency came in support of his wife's; P III 10 91 41
I can support her myself. P III 12 110 36
against the wall for his support, exclaimed in the P III 12 110 37
38
Their being in the back ground was a support to Anne; she P IV 8 181 1
as he could do to support the appearance of a gentleman. P IV 9 199 55
library, which Mr P. was anxiously wishing to support.-- S 2 374 1
could say no more in support of hers, which was his object, S 12 425 1
SUPPORTABLE (1)
affairs, no health to make all the rest supportable. P IV 5 154 8
SUPPORTED (35)
who had reared and supported a boy accidentally found at NA I 1 16 10
meant, nor consistently supported; and its unkindness she NA I 15 121 25
Her resolution was supported by Isabella's behaviour in NA II 4 153 31
too far; but they were supported by such appearances as NA II 8 188 18
brought forward and supported by Henry, at the same time NA II 11 213 20
of nature and education; supported the good spirits of Sir SS I 7 32 1
But how is your acquaintance to be long supported, under SS I 10 47 4
Such violence of affliction indeed could not be supported SS I 16 83 4
perhaps two, and hunters, cannot be supported on less." SS I 17 91 14
dared not longer doubt; supported as it was too on every SS II 1 139 1
Supported by the conviction of having done nothing to SS II 1 140 4
own good sense so well supported her, that her firmness SS II 1 141 6
he is undoubtedly supported by the same trust in your's. SS II 2 147 8
be divided in future, her mind might be always supported. SS II 6 179 18
her mind was no longer supported by the fever of suspense, SS II 7 185 16
matter; and having thus supported the dignity of her own SS II 10 215 14
"So calm!--so cheerful!--how have you been supported?"-- SS III 1 262 22
She was supported into the drawing-room between her SS III 9 334 4
supported by an affection, on his side, much less certain. SS III 11 350 9
Dashwood's assistance, supported her into the other room. SS III 11 353 25
My father supported him at school, and afterwards at PP II 12 200 5
but while they were supported by their mother's indulgence, PP II 14 213 17
How Wickham and Lydia were to be supported in tolerable PP III 8 312 17
with which you have supported this extraordinary PP III 14 357 61
part of Amelia if well supported--that is, if every thing MP I 15 144 38
and her friend;--he had supported her cause, or explained MP I 16 152 2
Her spirit supported her, but the agony of her mind was MP II 2 193 18
talk on indifferent subjects could never be long supported. MP III 15 445 33
and, supported by her mistress, was not to be silenced. MP III 16 450 10
married, and properly supported by her own family, people MP III 16 457 29
in every comfort, and supported by every encouragement to MP III 17 465 13
generously supported by her father, had disappointed her. P III 1 7 13
and Anne, who caught and supported her between them. P III 12 109 34
Louisa was raised up and supported more firmly between P III 12 110 37
38
kind of woman, who supported herself by receiving such S 11 420 1
SUPPORTER (2)
and is the determined supporter of every thing mercenary MP III 13 421 2
the attendant, supporter, cheerer of a suffering brother. MP III 14 429 2
SUPPORTING (4)
that though Catherine's supporting opinion was not NA I 10 72 8
and were it only in supporting the spirits of her aunt MP III 14 432 10
the view of supporting her hopes and raising her spirits. P III 12 116 70
the solid so fully supporting the superficial, that she P IV 4 146 6
SUPPORTS (3)
own innocence and good intentions supports your spirits. SS II 7 189 51
With these supports, she hoped that the acquaintance P III 4 31 12
to consider what powerful supports would be his! P IV 11 244 72
SUPPOSE (358)
not quite weak enough to suppose a woman who has behaved LS 3 247 1
appearance one would not suppose her more than five & LS 6 251 1
now submit, I can only suppose that the wish of LS 6 252 2
hardly suppose that Lady Susan's veiws extend to marriage. LS 11 259 1
I do not suppose that you would deliberately form an LS 12 260 1
I am to thank my sister I suppose, for having represented LS 14 263 1
his tender feelings I suppose on this distressing occasion. LS 15 267 4
She meant I suppose to go to the Clarkes in Staffordshire, LS 16 268 1
that I can only suppose the lady to be governed by the LS 19 274 2
Can you possibly suppose that I was aware of her LS 24 289 12
I cannot suppose that the old story of Mrs Manwaring's LS 35 304 1
in town--not as you may suppose with any doubt of the fact- LS 41 310 1
before; but I suppose Mrs. Morland objects to novels." NA I 6 41 20
look at that creature, and suppose it possible if you can." NA I 7 46 9
"I suppose you mean Camilla?" NA I 7 49 39
"well, Miss Morland, I suppose you and I are to stand up NA I 8 59 35
Why you do not suppose a man is overset by a bottle? NA I 9 63 20
"He never comes to the Pump-Room, I suppose?" NA I 10 73 17
That, I suppose, was the difference of duties which struck NA I 10 77 35
the rest of them here, I suppose I should be too happy! NA I 10 79 56
"It is very odd! but I suppose they thought it would be NA I 11 85 40
to it:--"well, my dear," said she, "suppose you go."-- NA I 11 86 49
miles; and, I suppose, we have at least eight more to go. NA I 11 88 54
intentions, and could suppose it to be only a mistake, why NA I 12 94 11
"The nicest;--by which I suppose you mean the neatest. NA I 14 107 13
I do not suppose he ever thinks of me." NA II 1 130 7
I suppose he saw Isabella sitting down, and fancied she NA II 1 132 17
Yes, I suppose he may. NA II 1 135 41
my dear, we are not to suppose but what, if you had had a NA II 1 136 46
I cannot suppose your brother cares so very much about me. NA II 3 145 13
she gives you reason to suppose that the part of the Abbey NA II 5 158 17
as she could then suppose, by the negligence of a servant NA II 7 172 2
To suppose that a manuscript of many generations back NA II 7 173 2
"Her picture, I suppose," blushing at the consummate art NA II 7 180 38
And did she not suppose her friend might be glad of some NA II 8 185 5
"It remains as it was, I suppose?" said she, in a tone of NA II 8 186 7
"You were with her, I suppose, to the last?" NA II 8 186 10
of policy she should be allowed to suppose herself so. NA II 9 192 4
She sent you to look at it, I suppose? NA II 9 196 21
Eleanor, I suppose, has talked of her a great deal?" NA II 9 196 23
"It contained something worse than any body could suppose!- NA II 10 204 13
Thorpe's prudence, to suppose that she would part with one NA II 10 206 31
for poor James, I suppose he will hardly ever recover it." NA II 10 206 37
You feel, I suppose, that, in losing Isabella, you lose NA II 10 207 38
carry us to Woodston, I suppose; we shall be in the NA II 11 210 6
"Then you do not suppose he ever really cared about her?" NA II 12 219 8
But, suppose he had made her very much in love with him?" NA II 12 219 12
"But we must first suppose Isabella to have had a heart to NA II 12 219 13
by her wishes) to suppose that a much longer visit had NA II 13 221 2
but which I can hardly suppose you to have any concern in, NA II 13 225 21
I do not suppose, Mrs. Morland, you ever saw a better-bred NA II 14 238 26
it was not their way to suppose any evil could be told. NA II 16 249 1
He could hardly suppose I should neglect them. SS I 2 9 6
But one must not expect every thing; though I suppose it SS I 6 29 4

SUPPOSE/SUPPOSE

I can easily suppose that his age may appear much greater SS I 8 37 5
her fortune small, I can suppose that she might bring SS I 8 38 10
I suppose it is something he is ashamed of." SS I 13 65 39
stairs, and a kitchen that smokes, I suppose," said Elinor. SS I 14 72 12
Do you suppose him really indifferent to her?" SS I 15 80 38
If you were to see them at the altar, you would suppose SS I 15 80 42
"We are all unanimous in that wish, I suppose," said SS I 17 92 20
What can you suppose?" SS I 17 95 48
"The consequence of which, I suppose, will be," said Mrs. SS I 19 103 5
it must be some other place that is so pretty I suppose." SS I 20 111 17
I suppose you were very sorry to leave Sussex." SS I 21 123 21
I suppose you have not so many in this part of the world; SS I 21 123 26
I suppose your brother was quite a beau, Miss Dashwood, SS I 21 124 28
Elinor could not suppose that Sir John would be more nice SS I 21 125 36
How could you suppose so? SS II 2 146 4
for she could not suppose it to be to any other person. SS II 5 171 38
But I will not suppose this possible, and I hope very soon SS II 7 187 40
is gone to her own room I suppose to moan by herself. SS II 8 195 14
I suppose has been hanging over her head as long as that. SS II 8 195 16
Little did Mr. Willoughby imagine, I suppose, when his SS II 9 209 30
"I suppose you will go and stay with your brother and SS II 10 218 30
"Not so large, I dare say, as many people suppose. SS II 11 225 31
"Nothing at all, I should rather suppose; for she has only SS II 11 226 43
In a week or two, I suppose, we shall be going; and, I SS II 13 243 31
contradicted, as I must suppose to be the case, you ought SS II 13 244 46
You do not suppose that I have ever felt much.-- SS III 1 263 29
you may suppose that I have suffered now. SS III 1 264 29
"You have heard, I suppose," said he with great solemnity, SS III 1 265 34
too as you may well suppose by my arguments, and Fanny's SS III 1 266 38
And then lowering her voice, "I suppose Mrs. Jennings has SS III 2 271 8
"I cannot suppose it possible that she should." SS III 2 272 11
I suppose Lady Middleton won't ask us any more this bout. SS III 2 276 25
for he did not suppose it possible that Delaford living SS III 3 284 22
"You mean to go to Delaford after them I suppose," said SS III 4 285 6
And I suppose you had no great difficulty--you did not SS III 4 291 47
suppose two or three months will complete his ordination." SS III 4 291 50
"Fanny is in her own room, I suppose," said he;--"I will SS III 5 294 6
I suppose, however--on recollection--that the case may SS III 5 295 12
"the lady, I suppose, has no choice in the affair." SS III 5 296 25
26

"I only mean, that I suppose from your manner of speaking, SS III 5 296 28
Just the kind of girl I should suppose likely to captivate SS III 5 299 37
The servants, I suppose, forgot to tell you that Mr. SS III 8 317 3
time cannot leave you to suppose that I have nothing to SS III 8 322 36
can I suppose it a relief to your own conscience." SS III 8 329 64
not thinking at all, I suppose-- giving way to SS III 9 336 12
"I would suppose him,--Oh! how gladly would I suppose him, SS III 10 345 22
"I suppose you know, ma'am, that Mr. Ferrars is married." SS III 11 353 22
23

She will hardly be less hurt, I suppose, by Robert's SS III 13 366 18
creature, how could I suppose, when she so earnestly, so SS III 13 367 22
"No, but she might suppose that something would occur in SS III 13 367 23
After that, I suppose, I was wrong in remaining so much in SS III 13 368 28
be married, on purpose we suppose to make a shew with, and SS III 13 370 37
Yes I can suppose so. W 317 2
I suppose you did not know what her particular business W 317 2
I suppose my aunt brought you up to be rather refined." W 318 2
I suppose I shall know him as soon as I enter the ball- W 319 2
"Do you suppose Miss Edwardes inclined to like him?" W 321 2
I suppose she is grown somewhat older since that time.-- W 325 4
I suppose so."--tho' she felt that she had no better W 332 12
As Tom Musgrave was seen no more, we may suppose his plan W 336 14
I suppose your set was not a very full one."-- W 340 19
I suppose you know among yourselves."-- W 344 20
she was willing to suppose that he had either known W 347 22
"I suppose, said Margt rather quickly to Emma, you & I are W 351 25
us & breeding you up (I suppose) in a superior stile, you W 352 26
a great while, were not you? a fortnight I suppose?"-- W 356 28
kindness & situation, to suppose to offer could appear in W 362 32
"Oh!--you mean Jane, I suppose--because he danced with her PP I 5 18 6
I entreat you not to suppose that I moved this way in PP I 6 26 39
this morning, which, I I suppose, is to be imputed to my PP I 7 31 29
30

She hardly knew how to suppose that she could be an object PP I 10 51 46
But these, I suppose, are precisely what you are without." PP I 11 57 21
We cannot suppose he would help it, if he could.-- PP I 13 64 17
You are very cautious, I suppose, as to its being created." PP I 18 93 32
could not for a moment suppose that those wishes, however PP I 21 120 28
Miss Bennet was the only creature who could suppose there PP II 1 138 31
"Oh, yes!--of that kind of love which I suppose him to PP II 2 141 10
and while able to suppose that it cost him a few struggles PP II 5 150 26
But I suppose you had no opportunity. PP II 6 164 24
There are few people in England, I suppose, who have more PP II 8 173 6
neighbourhood of Longbourn, I suppose, would appear far." PP II 9 179 20
they could at last only suppose his visit to proceed from PP II 9 180 28
would vanish, if she could suppose him to be in her power. PP II 9 181 30
Unless the elder brother is very sickly, I suppose you PP II 10 184 15
have no right to suppose that Bingley was the person meant. PP II 10 185 24
Mr. Darcy, if you suppose that the mode of your PP II 11 192 23
24

delayed his determination, I do not suppose that it would PP II 12 198 5
young man--and I do not suppose there is the least chance PP II 17 228 27
And so, I suppose, they often talk of having Longbourn PP II 17 228 33
Oh! my dear father, can you suppose it possible that they PP II 18 231 18
But he is a liberal master, I suppose, and that in the eye PP III 1 258 74
can I suppose her so lost to every thing?--impossible. PP III 4 275 5
and though she did not suppose Lydia to be deliberately PP III 4 279 24
no reason, I suppose, to believe them fond of each other." PP III 5 285 17
a doubt, I suppose, of their being really married?" PP III 5 290 49
there is reason to suppose, as my dear Charlotte informs PP III 6 297 11
"Do you suppose them to be in London?" PP III 6 299 22
"but the terms, I suppose, must be complied with." PP III 7 303 24
for I was thinking, you may suppose, of my dear Wickham. PP III 9 319 24
She would not betray her trust, I suppose, without bribery PP III 10 322 2
You know pretty well, I suppose, what has been done for PP III 10 324 2
And you saw the old housekeeper, I suppose? PP III 10 327 11
"Some acquaintance or other, my dear, I suppose; I am sure PP III 11 334 33
I suppose you have heard of it; indeed, you must have seen PP III 11 336 49
His regiment is there; for I suppose you have heard of his PP III 11 337 51
and I suppose he has two or three French cooks at least. PP III 12 342 28
That lady I suppose is your mother." PP III 14 351 5
"And that I suppose is one of your sisters." PP III 14 352 7
injure him so much as to suppose the truth of it possible, PP III 14 353 26
can have no reason to suppose he will make an offer to me." PP III 14 354 41
only came, I suppose, to tell us the Collinses were well. PP III 14 359 76
I suppose she had nothing particular to say to you, Lizzy?" PP III 14 359 76
but it was natural to suppose the he thought much higher PP III 15 360 2
"And your assurance of it, I suppose, carried immediate PP III 16 371 44
But now suppose as much as you chuse; give a loose to your PP III 18 382 21
Suppose her a pretty girl, and seen by Tom or Edmund for MP I 1 7 6
But breed her up with them from this time, and suppose her MP I 1 7 6
I suppose, sister, you will put the child in the little MP I 1 9 12
of her clothes, for I suppose you would not think it fair MP I 1 9 12
I suppose you have had as little to vex you, since you MP I 3 25 12
white house, I suppose, as soon as she is removed there." MP I 3 25 20
If I could suppose my aunt really to care for me, it would MP I 3 27 34
misled Sir Thomas to suppose it really intended for Fanny. MP I 3 28 38
I suppose he thought it best." MP I 3 29 43
"So I should suppose. MP I 5 45 8
I think too well of Miss Bertram to suppose she would ever MP I 5 45 14
she says so little, that I can hardly suppose she is." MP I 5 48 30
it is now, in its old state; but I do not suppose I shall." MP I 6 56 22
not be so easy as you suppose; our farmers are not in the MP I 6 58 38
Yes, we must suppose the faults of the niece to have been MP I 7 64 9
And what right had she to suppose, that you would not MP I 7 64 10
Suppose you let her have your aromatic vinegar; I always MP I 7 72 45
"There is no hardship, I suppose, nothing unpleasant," MP I 8 78 14
They have been buried, I suppose, in the parish church. MP I 9 86 7
"Suppose we turn down here for the present," said Mrs. MP I 9 90 33
You must suppose me designed for some profession, and MP I 9 91 39
not misunderstand me, or suppose I mean to call them the MP I 9 93 49
"Which you suppose has biassed me." MP I 11 109 15
"that I can hardly suppose;--and since you push me so hard, MP I 11 111 28
Besides, I cannot but suppose that whatever there may be MP I 11 111 30
but Lord Ravenshaw, who I suppose is one of the most MP I 13 122 4
you might just as well suppose he would object to our MP I 13 127 29
that she could hardly suppose her cousins could be aware MP I 14 137 23
I cannot but suppose you will when you have read it MP I 15 140 11
"If any part could tempt you to act, I suppose it would be MP I 15 144 40
the meanwhile will be taking a trip into china, I suppose. MP I 16 156 27
"None of it, I suppose. MP I 18 169 21
"Well then, Lady Bertram, suppose you speak for tea MP II 1 180 12
speak for tea directly, suppose you hurry Baddeley a MP II 1 180 12
No young people's are, I suppose, when those they look up MP II 3 197 3
"I suppose I am graver than other people," said Fanny. MP II 3 197 5
I hope she does not suppose there is any dislike on his MP II 3 199 13
I can even suppose it pleasant to spend half the year in MP II 4 210 21
and her--"but she did not suppose it would be in her power, MP II 4 215 47
"Suppose you take my father's opinion, ma'am." MP II 5 217 7
and Easter, I suppose, will be the sum total of sacrifice." MP II 5 226 61
They belong to the living, I suppose. MP II 7 242 23
house, such as one might suppose a respectable old country MP II 7 243 27
And as for this necklace, I do not suppose I have worn it MP II 8 260 22
is not it fair to suppose that she would rather not part MP II 9 263 13
"She must not suppose it not wanted, not acceptable at MP II 9 263 14
had too much reason to suppose, was at the parsonage; and MP II 9 267 22
"Suppose I were to find him there again to-day!" said she MP II 9 267 23
till she could suppose herself no longer looked at. MP II 10 276 13
laughing, "I must suppose it to be purely for the pleasure MP II 10 277 19
"And there is no reason to suppose," added Sir Thomas, " MP II 11 284 9
"The Miss Owens," said she soon afterwards--"suppose you MP II 11 289 34
by ambition, I can suppose it her; but ask her to love you, MP II 12 293 15
Price, that if I could suppose the next Mrs. Crawford MP II 12 296 29
not such a coxcomb as to suppose her feelings more lasting MP II 12 297 33
knowing how to suppose him serious, she could hardly stand. MP II 13 301 7
I chuse to suppose that the assurance of my consent will MP II 13 303 15
suppose you will ever harbour resentment on that account.-- MP III 1 313 12
brother, which I should suppose would have been almost MP III 1 316 27
If, as I am willing to suppose, you wish to shew me any MP III 1 321 48
It would have made no difference to you, I suppose, MP III 1 323 54
You cannot suppose me capable of trying to persuade you to MP III 2 330 16
She could not, though only eighteen, suppose Mr. MP III 2 331 18
Do you suppose you are ever present to my imagination MP III 3 344 41
You cannot suppose me uninformed. MP III 4 346 8
"Do you suppose that we think differently? MP III 4 346 12
But how could you possibly suppose me against you? MP III 4 346 14
I cannot suppose that you have not the wish to love him-- MP III 4 348 21
I suppose no time can ever wear out the impression I have MP III 5 358 9
suppose to have been her own fault, or her own fancy. MP III 6 371 17
She had reason to suppose herself not yet forgotten by Mr. MP III 7 375 4
that Fanny could not but suppose it meant for him to hear; MP III 7 376 4
was not unreasonable to suppose, that Fanny might be MP III 10 400 8
have more good qualities than she had been wont to suppose. MP III 10 405 16
I suppose it will not be less." MP III 11 410 13
good as to say that--I suppose I shall soon hear from him." MP III 11 412 27
"This distressing intelligence, as you may suppose," MP III 13 426 11
not suppose any school-boy's bosom to feel more keenly. MP III 14 431 7
and she was beginning to suppose that she might never know MP III 14 433 12
I suppose, Mrs. R.'s Easter holidays will not last much MP III 14 434 13
all necessary, she must suppose her return would be MP III 14 436 15
of being never able to suppose that other people could E I 1 7 10
You do not think I could mean you, or suppose Mr. E I 1 10 32
not like her so well as we do, sir, if we could suppose it. E I 1 11 38
"I suppose you have heard of the handsome letter Mr. Frank E I 2 18 9
"Mr. Martin, I suppose, is not a man of information beyond E I 4 29 9
"Yes, to be sure--I suppose there are. E I 4 31 23
that she could not suppose any thing wanting which a E I 6 42 1
How could you suppose me ignorant? E I 6 43 14
"I should say so, but that I suppose there may be a E I 6 49 44
No doubt he is a sensible man, and I suppose may have a E I 7 51 5
As to anything superior for you, I suppose she is quite in E I 7 56 41
Now, as we may fairly suppose, he would not allow much E I 8 60 27
it is fair to suppose that views, and plans, and projects E I 8 66 51
Harriet, "and therefore I suppose, and believe, and hope E I 9 74 22
this morning-- (dropt, we suppose, by a fairy)--containing E I 9 78 50
as you may suppose, Isabella, most frequently here. E I 11 94 14
My dear Emma, suppose we all have a little gruel." E I 12 100 18
Emma could not suppose any such thing, knowing, as she did, E I 12 101 19
I suppose there is not a man in such practice any where. E I 12 101 25
daughter is married, I suppose Colonel and Mrs. Campbell E I 12 104 46
is entirely a mistake to suppose the place unhealthy; and E I 12 105 55
She could not but suppose it to be a match that every body E I 14 119 5
to marry him!--should suppose himself her equal in E I 16 135 8
done; and she could suppose herself but an indifferent E I 17 142 11
What has Mr. Frank Churchill done, to make you suppose him E I 18 145 9
Standing up in the middle of the room, I suppose, and E I 18 147 17
Do you suppose she does not often say all this to herself? E I 18 149 26
"Well! that is quite----- I suppose there never was a E II 3 173 29
people; and the Perrys--I suppose there never was a E II 3 175 39
with her," said Emma, "nothing I suppose can be known. E II 3 175 39
40

understanding as to suppose they meant to marry till it E II 5 193 35
I shall have no difficulty, I suppose, in finding the E II 5 193 37
and it is natural to suppose that we should be intimate,-- E II 6 203 39
The regular and best families Emma could hardly suppose E II 7 207 6
accounting for it with "I suppose they will not take the E II 7 207 7
"One can suppose nothing else," added Mrs. Cole, "and I E II 8 215 14
"Me!--I suppose I smile for pleasure at Col. Campbell's E II 8 216 20
"Indeed you injure me if you suppose me unconvinced. E II 8 218 42
At first, while I suppose you satisfied that Col. Campbell E II 8 219 42
oftener than I should suppose such a circumstance would, E II 8 226 81
is no reason to suppose the instrument is indifferent. E II 9 234 33
William Larkins and said every thing, as you may suppose. E II 9 239 51
real workmen, I suppose, hold their tongues; but we E II 10 242 15
say nothing less, for I suppose Miss Woodhouse and Mr. E II 10 245 49
if you suppose Mr. Perry to be that sort of character. E II 11 251 28
Suppose I go and invite Miss Bates to join us?" E II 11 255 50
there whom he could suppose to feel any interest in him; E II 12 258 9
You have many parties of that kind here, I suppose, Miss E II 14 274 28
"We cannot suppose," said Emma, smiling, "that Mr. Elton E II 14 277 37
There was no reason to suppose Mr. Elton thought at all E II 15 281 2
no idea that you will suppose her talents can be unknown." E II 15 283 6
Let me not suppose that she dares go about, Emma Woodhouse- E II 15 284 10
"We cannot suppose that she has any great enjoyment at the E II 15 285 17
said she, "and you soon silenced Mr. Cole, I suppose?" E II 15 288 37
not one in a million, I suppose, actually lost! E II 16 296 42
that would be the way, I suppose, if I were very bad.-- E II 16 297 48
Mrs. Elton, very willing to suppose a particular E II 18 305 2
That fact is, I suppose, that she is tired of Enscombe. E II 18 307 20
very great, and, as you may suppose, most gratifying to me. E II 18 309 30
"Very well--and as Randalls, I suppose, it not likely to E II 18 312 48
easy--but Miss Fairfax does not disapprove it, I suppose." E III 2 324 24
not the presumption to suppose--indeed I am not so mad.-- E III 4 341 36
"--Mrs. Weston, I suppose," interrupted Mrs. Elton, rather E III 6 354 16

He did not suppose they could be damp now, in the middle E III 6 356 30
You will all be going soon I suppose; the whole party E III 6 364 55
I suppose you have heard--and are come to give us joy. E III 8 378 8
a situation, I suppose, as no young woman before ever met E III 8 379 8
"Mrs. Elton, I suppose, has been the person to whom Miss E III 8 380 14
"Miss Fairfax, I suppose, though you were not aware of it, E III 8 381 20
While poor Mrs. Churchill lived, I suppose there could not E III 10 398 55
"Well," said Emma, "I suppose we shall gradually grow E III 10 399 61
This was a device, I suppose, to sport with my curiosity, E III 10 400 68
Am I to suppose then?-----" E III 11 405 15
"She loves him then excessively, I suppose. E III 12 419 9
to suppose, would soon cease to belong to Highbury. E III 12 422 20
I can suppose, however, that I may have under-rated him. E III 13 427 21
"You are going in, I suppose," said he. E III 13 429 31
Had you witnessed my behaviour there, I can hardly suppose E III 14 441 8
"And the next news, I suppose, will be, that we are to E III 16 460 52
But it was so, I suppose. E III 17 465 27
I could suppose she might in time--but can she already?-- E III 18 473 26
"Do you dare to suppose me so great a blockhead, as not to E III 18 474 28
as there was no reason to suppose it perpetuated by P III 1 8 17
I shall forget my own name soon, I suppose. P III 3 23 28
moment-- "you mean Mr. Wentworth, I suppose," said Anne. P III 3 23 29
30
Suppose I were to be seized of a sudden in some dreadful P III 5 37 24
It did not happen to suit the Miss Musgroves, I suppose, P III 5 38 29
"I suppose you will not like to call at the great house P III 5 39 41
yourself, suppose you were to go, as well as your husband. P III 7 57 15
she had no reason to suppose his eye wandering towards her P III 8 63 2
"And so then, I suppose," said Mrs. Musgrove, in a low P III 8 66 18
"I cannot imagine why they should suppose I should not P III 10 83 5
I suppose you know he wanted to marry Anne?" P III 10 88 28
long be so unjust as to suppose she would shrink P III 12 116 69
I suppose he was afraid of finding it dull; but upon my P IV 2 130 5
was come, she could not suppose herself at all wanted;" P IV 4 145 1
I suppose (smiling) I have more pride than any of you; but P IV 4 151 18
different tone, "I do not suppose the situation my friend P IV 5 156 12
13
"I do not know; but I can hardly suppose that, at Admiral P IV 6 166 14
of writing to make you suppose he thinks himself ill-used P IV 6 172 46
But I have no reason to suppose it so. P IV 8 182 10
If in that light, if there is any thing which you suppose P IV 9 195 25
"Not before he married, I suppose?" P IV 9 198 47
He has changed his hour of going, I suppose, that is all-- P IV 10 223 39
was saying, we shall never agree I suppose upon this point. P IV 11 234 27
I should deserve utter contempt if I dared to suppose that P IV 11 235 32
(as Mr H. had been apt to suppose) from any design of S 2 371 1
You are not rheumatic I suppose?--". S 10 415 1

SUPPOSED (160)

her infancy, would have supposed her born to be an heroine. NA I 1 13 1
Mrs. Morland will be naturally supposed to be most severe. NA I 2 18 2
In marriage, the man is supposed to provide for the NA I 10 77 35
would have supposed she had any wretchedness about her. NA I 12 92 4
be offended at being supposed to have no higher aim; and NA I 14 109 25
She looked at him with great admiration, and even supposed NA II 1 131 15
necessaries of life; he supposed, however, "that she must NA II 6 166 6
size, and much less than she supposed it to be at first. NA II 7 172 1
Mr. Allen, he supposed, must feel these inconveniences as NA II 7 178 21
The side of the quadrangle, in which she supposed the NA II 8 188 19
Till midnight, she supposed it would be in vain to watch; NA II 8 189 19
where her ashes were supposed to slumber, were she to NA II 9 190 2
than she could have supposed it possible in the beginning NA II 10 201 4
But as it was not to be supposed that Captain Tilney, NA II 11 208 2
she hardly supposed there were any thing worse to be told. NA II 13 223 13
or, at least, not supposed to be connected with it. NA II 13 226 25
only of being less rich than he had supposed her to be. NA II 15 244 11
It was very well known that no affection was ever supposed SS I 2 8 3
How is it to be supposed that Willoughby, persuaded as he SS I 15 80 36
by such a situation of his affairs as you have supposed. SS I 15 81 43
supposed that any one can estimate its beauties as we do." SS I 21 123 25
with whatever he knew or supposed of his cousins' SS I 21 125 34
hopes, no one would have supposed from the appearance of SS II 1 141 4
could not be supposed to meet for the sake of conversation. SS II 1 142 8
If you could be supposed to be biassed in any respect by SS II 2 150 34
but I had not supposed any secrecy intended, as they SS II 5 173 42
it; nor could she have supposed Willoughby capable of SS II 7 183 14
of the room, as if she supposed her young friend's SS II 8 192 4
is not to be supposed that it could make any impression on SS II 9 205 22
It is not to be supposed that any prior attachment on your SS II 11 224 24
as the subject might naturally be supposed to produce. SS III 1 260 8
for him, was it to be supposed that he could be all the SS III 1 266 38
to do so;--but supposed it to be the proper etiquette. SS III 3 281 9
as Mrs. Jennings had supposed her to do, made very light SS III 3 283 20
Though it is not to be supposed that Mrs. Ferrars can have SS III 5 296 19
late behaviour, is she supposed to feel at all?--she has SS III 5 296 19
They would soon, she supposed, be settled at Delaford.-- SS III 12 357 3
constant as she had ever supposed it to be,--she was SS III 13 363 8
fate, it is to be supposed, in spite of the jealousy with SS III 13 366 20
his spirits, he might be supposed no less contented with SS III 14 377 12
and not very ineligible for being supposed to have a lover. SS III 14 380 20
Emma could not help entering into what she supposed her W 357 28
said, as might be supposed, that she had caught a violent PP I 7 33 44
"That is exactly what I should have supposed of you," said PP I 9 42 9
that the friend who is supposed to desire his return to PP I 10 50 34
of such a case as you have supposed about Mr. Bingley. PP I 10 50 37
by talking of their supposed marriage, and planning his PP I 10 52 54
Something he supposed might be attributed to his PP I 15 74 13
he might almost have supposed himself in the small summer PP I 16 75 2
very ill of him-- I had supposed him to be despising his PP I 16 80 33
which he supposed a regular part of the business. PP I 19 104 1
lament; it was not to be supposed that their absence from PP I 21 116 8
but she could not have supposed it possible that when PP I 22 125 18
of it, Elizabeth supposed he must be often forgotten. PP II 5 157 5
But then I have always supposed it to be my own fault-- PP II 8 175 25
She supposed, if he meant any thing, he must mean an PP II 10 182 1
asked her why she supposed Miss Darcy likely to give them PP II 10 184 20
It is not to be supposed that there was much affection in PP II 10 186 36
It was not to be supposed that any other people could be PP II 10 186 38
But such as they were, it may be well supposed how eagerly PP II 13 204 1
time than she could have supposed, seated in the carriage, PP III 4 281 29
He had never before supposed that, could Wickham be PP III 8 309 4
terms, it was not to be supposed that Mr. Darcy would PP III 8 311 12
It was not to be supposed that time would give Lydia that PP III 9 317 10
she might have supposed him capable of coming there, with PP III 11 332 18
of breaking off her supposed engagement with Mr. Darcy. PP III 15 360 1
as warmly as a man violently in love can be supposed to do. PP III 16 366 8
You supposed more than really existed. PP III 18 382 21
supposed the girls so nearly of an age as they really were. MP I 2 13 4
she would probably have supposed it unnecessary, for they MP I 2 20 31
She had not supposed before, that any thing could ever MP I 4 37 8
Till now, I could not have supposed it possible to be MP I 5 49 32
Having visited many more rooms than could be supposed to MP I 9 85 5
Fanny supposed she must have been mistaken, and meant to MP I 12 116 11
Fanny seemed nearer being right than Edmund had supposed. MP I 14 130 1
one might have supposed--but it is only as Agatha that I MP I 14 136 18
exertion and confidence than you can be supposed to have.-- MP I 15 140 15
as his son had ever supposed he must; he felt it too much MP II 2 187 2
Mr. Yates felt it as acutely as might be supposed. MP II 2 191 10
not acute; he had never supposed them to be so; but her MP II 3 201 22
no one would have supposed, from her confident triumph, MP II 3 203 30
though it was not to be supposed so--and Miss Crawford MP II 5 227 68
she supposed all the other young ladies would appear in? MP II 8 254 8
cousins: he wanted, she supposed, to cheat her of her MP II 8 260 24
had, or must have been supposed to have, by the many young MP II 9 266 22
saw her only as the supposed inmate of Mansfield parsonage, MP II 12 295 22
She could not have supposed it in the power of any MP II 13 303 13
And further, how could it be supposed that his sister, MP II 13 306 26
of a character the very reverse of what I had supposed. MP III 1 318 39
"Of course," continued her uncle, "it cannot be supposed MP III 1 321 48
You have qualities which I had not before supposed to MP III 3 343 41
believe to be just, he supposed she had all those feelings, MP III 5 356 3
into a woman, and he supposed would be wanting a husband MP III 7 380 22
If tenderness could be ever supposed wanting, good sense MP III 8 392 11
A week was gone since Edmund might be supposed in town, MP III 10 399 1
and did not like to be supposed otherwise; but take it all MP III 11 410 7
might not it be fairly supposed, that he would not much MP III 11 414 32
should resent any former supposed slight to Miss Bertram. MP III 13 423 2
She supposed he could not yet leave his son, but it was a MP III 14 430 6
of it, and such as she supposed would convey to the MP III 14 436 16
I replied that I had not supposed it possible, coming in MP III 16 457 30
supposed to have in her wish for a complete reconciliation. MP III 16 459 31
found greater than he had supposed, in his other children. MP III 17 461 4
supposed that their tempers became their mutual punishment. MP III 17 465 14
feelings on her side, more strong than he had supposed.-- MP III 17 468 21
widower-father may be supposed to have felt; but as they E I 2 16 4
"But, my dear papa, it is supposed to be summer; a warm E I 6 48 37
than they are generally supposed; till they do fall in E I 8 63 44
of character, indeed, which I had not supposed possible! E I 15 130 30
you success: but had I supposed that she were not your E I 15 131 34
She had taken up the idea, she supposed, and made every E I 16 134 3
supposed it could make him unjust to the merit of another. E I 18 150 37
body had supposed they must be so fond of each other." E II 2 166 11
it was to be rather supposed that Miss Taylor had formed E II 5 192 29
and interest much oftener than Emma could have supposed. E II 6 196 2
it could not be fairly supposed that he had been ever E II 6 197 4
You are not afraid of being supposed ashamed. E II 8 214 10
all that she might be supposed to have lost on the side of E II 9 231 1
me! I never could have supposed it. but I live out of the E II 11 252 32
much less than she had supposed before--indeed very E II 11 255 59
He was more in love with her than Emma had supposed; and E II 12 261 34
could be supposed attractive, with spirit and precision. E II 13 265 5
and it was not to be supposed that poor Harriet should not E II 14 270 3
it might be fairly supposed from her easy conceit, had E II 14 272 17
"Worse than I had supposed. E II 14 279 52
one young lady might be supposed to recommend the other, E II 15 282 4
No--till Cole alluded to my supposed attachment, it had E II 15 289 40
And how could it be supposed that his uncle and aunt would E II 18 308 27
and why I am to be supposed in danger of wanting leisure E II 18 312 50
I am all amazement! could not have supposed any thing!-- E III 2 330 45
had ever supposed--and continual pain would try the temper. E III 9 387 13
and voice; so, she supposed, had poor Mrs. Weston felt E III 11 404 3
possible that I could be supposed to mean any other person. E III 11 405 18
She supposed she must say more before she were entitled to E III 13 427 18
less wrong than she had supposed--and he had suffered, and E III 15 444 1
Harriet expressed herself very much as might be supposed, E III 16 451 2
herself, resulting, she supposed, from doubt of what might E III 16 455 19
to whom you might be supposed to owe them, is so perfectly E III 16 459 48
now be contented;" and supposed "she had always meant to E III 17 469 36
could they have been supposed in the secret of Sir P III 3 23 34
and found it all as she supposed; and the reperusal of P III 6 51 32
reckoning, and then, she supposed, they must meet; and P III 7 53 1
jealousy, at not being supposed a good walker, "Oh, yes, I P III 10 83 4
the happiness that a hazel-nut can be supposed capable of." P III 10 88 26
"Upon my word," said she, "I should not have supposed that P IV 2 132 20
Anne could not have supposed it possible that her first P IV 3 144 24
"Merely Gowland," he supposed. P IV 4 145 3
Benwick's being "supposed to be an admirer of yours. P IV 6 165 8
No, it was not to be supposed that Lady Russell would P IV 7 179 28
I should not have supposed that you could have found any P IV 8 183 15
He ought not to be supposed to be paying his addresses to P IV 9 196 31
you see, I was not romancing so much as you supposed." P IV 9 205 82
Nobody supposed that you were his first inducement. P IV 9 205 86
Anne's refutation of the supposed engagement changed the P IV 9 210 99
Mary, resenting that she should be supposed not to know P IV 10 222 37
hours after his being supposed to be out of Bath; for P IV 10 228 70
him nearer than she had supposed, and half inclined to P IV 11 233 24
While supposed to be writing only to Captain Benwick, he P IV 11 237 41
if her sentiments for him were what the Harvilles supposed. P IV 11 243 66
For the title, it was to be supposed that she had married-- S 3 376 1

SUPPOSES (1)

"Success supposes endeavour. E I 1 12 42

SUPPOSING (64)

You were mistaken my dear Alicia, in supposing me fixed at LS 2 244 1
injured that lady, by supposing the worst, where the LS 14 264 2
while they dined, & supposing I should be wanted left the LS 20 275 1
for her folly, in supposing that among such a crowd they NA I 10 75 24
supposing them to be now admitted as synonimous." NA I 14 109 25
what were you to live upon, supposing you came together? NA II 3 145 16
or Miss Thorpe's, for supposing that her affection, or at NA II 4 152 28
You have erred in supposing him not attached to her. NA II 9 197 27
Catherine, supposing some uneasiness on Captain Tilney's NA II 13 223 9
A doubt of her regard, supposing him to feel it, need not SS I 4 22 18
"You are mistaken, Elinor," said she warmly, "in supposing SS I 12 58 4
Supposing it possible that they are not engaged, what SS I 16 84 9
You are very right in supposing how my money would be SS I 17 92 26
The consideration of Mrs. Dennison's mistake, in supposing SS II 14 252 20
a living of that value--supposing the late incumbent to SS III 5 295 12
length of time, and even supposing her heart again free, SS III 9 338 20
Edward could only attempt an explanation by supposing, SS III 13 364 11
"But, my dear sister, can I be happy, even supposing the PP I 21 119 23
"You persist, then, in supposing his sisters influence him. PP II 1 136 20
this may be from better feelings than you are supposing. PP II 1 137 24
By supposing such an affection, you make every body acting PP II 1 137 24
Without supposing them, from what she saw, to be very PP II 2 142 18
She accounted for it, however, by supposing that her last PP II 3 147 21
understood; he must be supposing her to be thinking of PP II 9 179 21
"And remember that I have not much reason for supposing it PP II 10 185 28
but I cannot help supposing that the hope of revenging PP II 12 202 5
for it herself, by supposing that she did not like to go PP II 14 211 5
6
a quarter, than by supposing a partiality for their niece. PP III 2 260 1
Mr. and Mrs. Gardiner had hurried back in alarm, supposing, PP III 4 280 26
"Well, then--supposing them to be in London. PP III 5 282 7
Supposing him to be attached to me, would my refusing to PP III 14 357 61
myself mistaken in supposing, as I had done, that your PP III 16 371 40
wish; but if you are supposing it a frequent thing, that MP I 9 87 16
How can two sermons a week, even supposing them worth MP I 9 92 46
them worth hearing, supposing the preacher to have the MP I 9 92 46
he was mistaken in supposing she would wish to make any. MP I 13 129 40
for the pattern, and supposing Fanny was now preparing for MP I 15 147 57
he was quite mistaken in supposing she had the smallest MP II 3 200 21
Were you even less pleasing--supposing her not to love you MP II 12 293 15
because, so far from supposing her to consider him with MP III 3 335 6
you know your duty too well for me to--even supposing-----" MP III 3 341 26
But even supposing it is so, allowing Mr. Crawford to have MP III 4 353 45
must have thought it so, supposing he had meant nothing. MP III 4 353 45
way, and was as far from supposing as from wishing him to MP III 5 362 21
supposing the first three or four days could produce any. MP III 6 366 2
superior force, which (supposing the first lieutenant out MP III 7 375 2
but she was not right in supposing that such an interval MP III 9 393 1
She was mistaken, however, in supposing that Edmund gave MP III 16 452 15
Pray excuse me; but supposing any little inconvenience may E I 5 40 24
Waving that point, however, and supposing her to be, as E I 8 63 44
you have been entirely mistaken in supposing it. E I 15 132 35
36

and attention, as (supposing her real motive unperceived) E I 16 136 9
"I am not supposing him at all an unnatural creature, in E I 18 145 10
solitary grandeur, even supposing the omission to be E II 7 208 7
to her; but as without supposing it possible that she E III 8 383 30
But I hope, Miss Woodhouse, that supposing--that if-- E III 11 407 28
Supposing even that they had never become intimate friends; E III 12 421 17
"As to all that," rejoined Sir Walter coolly, "supposing I P III 3 18 8
too had been accused of supposing sailors to be living on P III 8 64 4
"Every body is always supposing that I am not a good P III 10 83 5
two or three besides, supposing they might wish to stay; P III 12 113 56
supposing such attachment to be real, and returned. P IV 5 159 22
which you have been supposing, in whatever pleasure the P IV 9 197 33
hand alone, supposing it could be applied instantly.-- S 5 386 1
SUPPOSITION (10)
time--all favoured the supposition of her imprisonment.-- NA II 8 188 16
If in the supposition of his seeking to marry herself, his SS II 1 140 3
The supposition did not pain her. PP I 10 51 46
but for the mortifying supposition of his viewing it all PP I 13 65 26
with the same kind of supposition, which had appeased Mrs. PP III 15 361 5
was heightened by the supposition of its being in some PP III 15 361 8
This is in the supposition of his attachment continuing E II 13 265 4
and it was only on the supposition of his being P III 2 15 14
get abroad--in the supposition of which, as I was going to P III 3 17 4
And under such a supposition, which would have been most P IV 9 211 102
SUPPOSITIONS (2)
questions, ingenious suppositions, and distant surmises; PP I 3 9 1
in answer to her suppositions, "yes, here I am, Sophia, P III 7 61 38 39
SUPPOSITITIOUS (1)
be introduced, and a supposititious funeral carried on. NA II 9 191 2
SUPPRESS (7)
at length resolving to suppress every particular in which PP II 17 224 1
and she could hardly suppress a smile, at his being now PP III 1 254 58
Maria was trying to suppress shewed how well it was MP I 14 133 12
After a moment's pause, Sir Thomas, trying to suppress a MP III 1 313 13
violent emotions, which he was determined to suppress. MP III 15 445 30
creature who would so designedly suppress her own merit.-- E III 14 439 8
this morning on poor Arthur's trying to suppress a cough. S 5 387 1
SUPPRESSED (8)
died away, or were suppressed by his friends' interference; PP II 1 134 3
These bitter accusations might have been suppressed, had I PP II 11 192 22
have been suppressed for just the three days we wanted. MP I 13 122 4
her own perfect consciousness, many drawbacks suppressed. MP III 8 388 1
he saw confusion suppressed or laughed away, he had E III 5 346 17
Anne suppressed a smile, and listened kindly, while Mrs. P III 8 64 7
to be communicated, but as what ought to be suppressed. P III 12 107 21
expressions begun and suppressed, with which Charles was P III 12 115 68
SUPPRESSING (1)
"My dear Eleanor," cried Catherine, suppressing her NA II 13 224 14
SURE (793)
To be sure, when we consider that I did take some pains to LS 5 249 1
Charles is very rich I am sure; when a man has once got LS 5 250 2
I am sure of Sir James at any time, & could make him renew LS 7 253 1
His opinion of her I am sure, was as low as of any woman LS 8 255 1
with her as I am sure he is, does really astonish me. LS 8 255 2
that I am sure he would marry either of you with pleasure. LS 9 257 1
On my side, you may be sure of it's never being more, for LS 10 258 2
read your letter, and I am sure has not had the business LS 13 262 1
You will, I am sure my dear sir, feel the truth of this LS 14 265 4
Her kindhearted uncle you may be sure, was too fearful of LS 17 271 6
I am sure I cannot say that it had, but while Miss Summers LS 17 271 7
Sometimes he is sure that she is deficient in LS 17 271 8
kind impression in her favour will I am sure be heightened. LS 18 272 1
must be highly prepossessing, & I am sure she feels it so. LS 18 272 1
She is extremely young to be sure, has had a wretched LS 18 273 2
The poor girl however I am sure dislikes him; and tho' his LS 20 276 2
I am sure my dear sister, you will excuse my remaining LS 20 277 5
he is still hurt I am sure at her allowing of such a man's LS 20 278 9
be confusion, for it is impossible to be sure of servants. LS 31 302 1
I thought myself sure of you at 7. LS 33 303 1
Her manner, to be sure, was very kind & proper--& Mr LS 41 310 3
music; and Catherine was sure she should like it, for she NA I 1 14 1
But, dear Mrs. Allen, are you sure there is nobody you NA I 2 23 20
Nature may have done something, but I am sure it must be NA I 3 27 28
measured nine; but I am sure it cannot be more than eight; NA I 3 29 46
"That is artful and deep, to be sure; but I had rather be NA I 3 29 49
Isabella was very sure that he must be a charming young NA I 5 36 2
young man; and was equally sure that he must have been NA I 5 36 2
novel, is sure to turn over its insipid pages with disgust. NA I 5 37 4
I am sure I have been here this half hour. NA I 6 39 4
I know it must be a skeleton, I am sure it is Laurentina's NA I 6 39 7
"Yes, pretty well; but are they all horrid, are you sure NA I 6 40 11
"Yes, quite sure; for a particular friend of mine, a Miss NA I 6 40 12
at you so earnestly--I am sure he is in love with you." NA I 6 41 16
I am sure you would be miserable if you thought so." NA I 6 41 18
My dear Isabella, I am sure there must be Laurentina's NA I 6 41 19
"He does look very hot to be sure." NA I 7 46 10
"I am sure I cannot guess at all." NA I 7 46 12
"And I am sure," said Catherine, "I know so little of such NA I 7 46 14
"No sure; was it? NA I 7 49 38
I was sure I should never be able to get through it." NA I 7 49 40
otherwise; and the Allens I am sure are very kind to you?" NA I 7 51 51
sick of it, that I am sure he should not complain, for it NA I 8 54 5
Mrs. Thorpe said she was sure you would not have the least NA I 8 55 10
I am sure of this--that if every half was to drink their NA I 9 63 20
Mine is famous good stuff to be sure. NA I 9 64 24
However, I am sure James does not drink so much." NA I 9 64 25
the mother is; yes, I am sure Mrs. Tilney is dead, because NA I 9 68 48
are such a sly thing, I am sure you would have made some NA I 10 71 3
besides, I am sure it would never have entered my head." NA I 10 71 6
I felt so sure of his being quite gone away." NA I 10 73 11
"To be sure not. NA I 10 77 32
"Yes, to be sure, as you state it, all this sounds very NA I 10 77 34
"Nay, I am sure you cannot have a better; for if I do not NA I 10 78 40
it did not rain, which Catherine was sure it would not. NA I 10 80 61
"No, he is not," said Catherine warmly, "for I am sure he NA I 11 89 57
I am sure I pity every body that is. NA I 11 90 63
I am sure you do. NA I 11 90 63
It was amazingly shocking to be sure; but the Tilneys were NA I 11 90 64
I am sure John and I should not have minded it. NA I 11 90 64
"Nay, I am sure by your look, when you came into the box, NA I 12 95 13
She was sure her dearest, sweetest Catherine would not NA I 13 98 2
than any body's; I am sure they are too strong for my own NA I 13 98 2
"Oh, no; Catherine was sure they would not have the least NA I 13 103 28
I am glad you do not think of going; I am sure Mrs. NA I 13 104 31
I am sure if I had known it to be improper, I would not NA I 13 104 35
"I am sure," cried Catherine, "I did not mean to say any NA I 14 108 15
Miss Anne, "and I am sure I do not envy them their drive. NA I 14 115 50
"She will never forgive me, I am sure; but, you know, how NA I 15 116 3
But my secret I was always sure would be safe with you." NA I 15 118 13
As for myself, I am sure I only wish our situations were NA I 15 119 18
"I am sure they will consent," was her frequent NA I 15 119 19
declaration; "I am sure they will be delighted with you." NA I 15 119 19
"I am sure I shall be miserable if we do not. NA I 15 120 22
"I am sure I think it a very good one." NA I 15 122 31
I am sure of a good income of my own; and if she had not a NA I 15 124 46
her friend; she was sure there had been no insolence in NA II 1 131 14
she was very sure Miss Thorpe did not mean to dance at all. NA II 1 132 16
your dear brother, I am sure he would have been miserable NA II 1 134 39
Amazingly conceited, I am sure. NA II 1 135 41
for I am sure he must be an excellent good hearted man. NA II 1 135 44
more, for I am sure he must be a most liberal-minded man." NA II 1 136 46
can think better of Mr. Morland than I do, I am sure. NA II 1 136 47
"I am very sure," said she, "that my father has promised NA II 1 136 47
to be sure that a much smaller income would satisfy me. NA II 1 136 48
came--and I am pretty sure that you and John were alone in NA II 3 145 12
of your's, Isabella, I am sure; but you know very well NA II 3 145 13
"Since that is the case, I am sure I shall not tease you NA II 3 145 16
You have both of you something to be sure, but it is not a NA II 3 146 16
here he comes; never mind, he will not see us, I am sure." NA II 3 147 20
Henry smiled and said, "I am sure my brother would not NA II 4 150 4
Not that James has ever told me so, but I am sure he is NA II 4 150 7
"And are you sure it is my brother's doing?" NA II 4 151 8
"Yes, very sure." NA II 4 151 9
But I am sure she cannot mean to torment, for she is very NA II 4 151 13
brother's intentions from all this; but I am sure I cannot. NA II 4 152 27
Sure, if your father were to speak to him, he would go." NA II 4 152 27
He cannot think this--and you may be sure that he would NA II 4 152 28
with some grandeur, to be sure, but it was a heavy and NA II 5 156 5
"To be sure I have. NA II 5 157 12
"Oh! but this will not happen to me, I am sure." NA II 5 158 16
I am sure your housekeeper is not really Dorothy.-- NA II 5 159 18
"Miss Tilney, she was sure, would never put her into such NA II 5 160 23
To be sure, the pointed arch was preserved--the form of NA II 5 162 26
Mr. Allen's house, he was sure, must be exactly of the NA II 6 166 7
now, to be sure, there is nothing to alarm one." NA II 6 167 9
of you young ladies, I am sure your father, Miss Morland, NA II 7 176 15
"To be sure you must miss him very much." NA II 7 180 35
"Yes; I am sure I should be very sorry to leave you so NA II 10 204 17
I must go and prepare a dinner for you to be sure." NA II 11 211 9
"I am sure it is quite unnecessary upon your sister's NA II 11 211 13
his absence; and Wednesday she was very sure would be wet. NA II 11 211 16
"You are too good, I am sure, to think the worse of me for NA II 13 223 13
"I am sure," said she, "I am very sorry if I have offended NA II 13 225 22
receive a letter from me, I am sure I had better not write. NA II 13 228 29
I have a notion you danced with him, but am not quite sure. NA II 14 238 26
"I am sure I do not care about the bread. NA II 15 241 5
some day or other, because I am sure it will do you good." NA II 15 241 6
young house-keeper to be sure," was her mother's NA II 16 249 1
"Why, to be sure," said her husband, very gravely, "that SS I 2 9 8
"To be sure it would." SS I 2 9 9
"To be sure it is: and, indeed, it strikes me that they SS I 2 10 15
If they marry, they will be sure of doing well, and if SS I 2 10 15
"To be sure," said she, "it is better than parting with SS I 2 10 18
of annuities, that I am sure I would not pin myself down SS I 2 11 20
of living if they felt sure of a larger income, and would SS I 2 11 23
"To be sure it will. SS I 2 12 24
I am sure I cannot imagine how they will spend half of it; SS I 2 12 24
your opinion, I am sure you could never be civil to him." SS I 4 19 4
"I am sure," replied Elinor with a smile, "that his SS I 4 20 7
see me, I am sure I will find none in accommodating them." SS I 5 25 2
"As for the house itself, to be sure," said she, "it is SS I 6 29 4
I am sure Edward Ferrars is not well. SS I 8 38 14
"Know him! to be sure I do. SS I 9 43 15
be a trifle; mama she was sure would never object to it; SS I 12 58 3
I am sure she will be married to Mr. Willoughby very soon." SS I 12 60 9
I am sure they will be married very soon, for he has got a SS I 12 60 11
I am almost sure it is, for I saw him cut it off. SS I 12 60 13
guess where he is; at his own house at Norland to be sure. SS I 12 61 23
"Well then he is lately dead, Marianne, for I am sure SS I 12 62 26
"Yes; it is about Miss Williams, I am sure." SS I 13 66 55
I am sure you must have heard of her before. SS I 13 66 57
be the reason of it; was sure there must be some bad news, SS I 14 70 1
"Something very melancholy must be the matter, I am sure," SS I 14 70 2
and to be sure must have cleared the estate by this time. SS I 14 70 2
He must and does love her I am sure." SS I 15 80 39
"He has, he has," cried Marianne, "I am sure he has. SS I 16 86 19
I am sure I am not extravagant in my demands. SS I 17 91 14
This has always been your doctrine, I am sure." SS I 17 94 38
why yourselves, and the Careys, and Whitakers to be sure.-- SS I 18 99 20
But the time will come I hope . . . . I am sure you will SS I 18 100 29
I am sure I shall be very happy to chaperon you at any SS I 20 110 4
I am sure you will like it of all things. SS I 20 113 33
am sure, though we could not get him to own it last night." SS I 20 116 58
Nothing can be like it to be sure! SS I 20 116 60
You will be delighted with them I am sure. SS I 21 119 4
"Nay, my dear, I'm sure I don't pretend to say that there SS I 21 123 28
I'm sure there's a vast many smart beaux in Exeter; but SS I 21 123 28
her married so young to be sure," said she, "and I hear he SS I 21 125 35
very agreeable young man to be sure; I know him very well." SS I 21 126 39
"I am sure you think me very strange, for inquiring about SS I 22 128 7
I am sure I would rather do any thing in the world than be SS I 22 128 9
And I am sure I should not have the smallest fear of SS I 22 128 9
"I dare say you are, and I am sure I do not at all wonder SS I 22 129 11
continued Lucy; "for to be sure you could have had no idea SS I 22 129 16
I am sure has been faithfully kept so by me to this hour. SS I 22 129 16
It does not do him justice to be sure, but yet I think you SS I 22 131 35
"I am sure," said she, "I have no doubt in the world of SS I 22 132 39
I have not known you long to be sure, personally at least, SS I 22 132 42
must perceive, and I am sure I was in the greatest fright SS I 22 133 42
I am sure I wonder my heart is not quite broke." SS I 22 133 42
"To be sure," continued Lucy, after a few minutes silence SS I 22 133 46
this evening; for I am sure it must hurt your eyes to work SS II 1 144 11
would not, I am sure she depends upon having it done." SS II 1 144 13
I felt sure that you was angry with me; and have been SS II 2 146 5
would make you overlook every thing else I am sure." SS II 2 146 5
but in such a case I am sure I could not be deceived." SS II 2 148 12
your interest, which I am sure you would be kind enough to SS II 2 149 25
To be sure, your brother and sister will ask you to come SS II 2 151 38
Lord, I am sure your mother can spare you very well, and I SS II 3 153 2
I am sure your mother will not object to it; for I have SS II 3 153 2
"Nay," cried Mrs. Jennings. "I am sure I shall be SS II 3 154 4
I have no such scruples, and I am sure, I could put up SS II 3 156 14
"Aye, to be sure, I thought as much. SS II 4 163 18
"Are you quite sure of it?" she replied. SS II 4 165 26
"Here is some mistake I am sure--some dreadful mistake. SS II 6 177 10
Grey herself, else I am sure I should not have believed it; SS II 8 192 3
I am sure if I knew of any thing she would like, I would SS II 8 194 8
if I can to go early to bed, for I am sure she wants rest." SS II 8 195 15
I am sure if I had had a notion of it, I would not have SS II 8 195 16
I made sure of its being nothing but a common love letter, SS II 8 195 16
"It would be unnecessary I am sure, for you to caution Mrs. SS II 8 195 17
as for your sister, I am sure I would not mention a word SS II 8 196 18
I bring you something that I am sure will do you good." SS II 9 202 5 6
so suddenly, which I am sure must at the time have SS II 9 209 30
Now, though at first she will suffer much, I am sure she SS II 9 211 34
It was a great comfort to her, to be sure of exciting no SS II 10 215 12
I was almost sure you would not leave London yet awhile; SS II 10 217 21
And now to be sure you will be in no hurry to be gone. SS II 10 217 21
My cousins say they are sure I have made a conquest; but SS II 10 218 26
I think she might see us; and I am sure we would not speak SS II 10 219 39
Elinor; "but I am very sure that Colonel Brandon has not SS II 11 223 23
good-natured woman, I am sure it would give her great SS II 11 224 24
"Why to be sure," said he, seeming to recollect himself, " SS II 11 227 48
Such a woman as I am sure Fanny will be glad to know. SS II 11 228 53
I am sure it will all end well, and there will be no SS II 13 239 9
seem low--you don't speak;--sure you an't well." SS II 13 239 11
I am sure if ever you tell your sister what I think of her, SS II 13 240 15
"I am sure I should have seen it in a moment, if Mrs. SS II 13 240 17
sure that conscience only kept Edward from Harley-Street. SS II 13 243 39 40
her hair, she was almost sure of being told that upon "her SS II 14 249 8
I am sure you will like them; indeed, you do like them, SS II 14 253 24

She was sure it was very ill--it cried, and fretted, and   SS III 1 257 5
it came into my head, I am sure I do not know how I   SS III 1 257 5
I never happened to see them together, or I am sure I   SS III 1 258 7
all so fond of Lucy, to be sure they will make no   SS III 1 258 7
house, for your sister was sure she would be in hysterics   SS III 1 259 7
should not marry; for I am sure Mrs. Ferrars may afford to   SS III 1 259 7
I wish him very happy; and I am so sure of his always   SS III 1 263 27
'There, to be sure,' said she, 'I might have thought   SS III 1 266 38
"Poor young man!" cried Mrs. Jennings, "I am sure he   SS III 1 268 51
I am sure, for my part, I should never have known he did   SS III 2 272 12
But, to be sure, Lucy would not give ear to such kind of   SS III 2 273 16
To be sure you must know better than that.   SS III 2 274 18
And I am sure Lucy would have done just the same by me;   SS III 2 274 20
them to you; and to be sure they did send us home in their   SS III 2 275 22
I know they will; but I am sure I would not do such a   SS III 2 275 22
should want company, I am sure we should be very glad to   SS III 2 275 25
I am sure you will be glad to hear, as likewise dear Mrs.   SS III 2 277 30
are not very bright, to be sure, but we must wait, and   SS III 2 277 30
living to bestow, am very sure you will not forget us, and   SS III 2 277 30
Yes, yes, I will go and see her, sure enough.   SS III 2 278 32
"This is very strange!--sure he need not wait to be older."   SS III 3 281 12
Aye, to be sure, he must be ordained in readiness; and I   SS III 4 286 17
Should not the Colonel write himself?--sure, he is the   SS III 4 286 17
But whether she would do for a lady's maid, I am sure I   SS III 4 287 22
you--a concern which I am sure Marianne, myself, and all   SS III 4 289 31
I am sure it would put me quite out of patience!--   SS III 4 291 51
Sure, somebody else might be found that would do as well;   SS III 4 291 51
Sure you do not mean to persuade me that the Colonel only   SS III 4 291 53
Michaelmas; and I am sure I sha'nt go if Lucy an't there."   SS III 4 292 57
to her presently, for I am sure she will not have the   SS III 5 294 6
of strangers!--to be sure it was pitiable enough!--but,   SS III 5 299 35
known to me than my own,--and I am sure they are dearer."   SS III 8 325 50
One person I was sure would represent me as capable of   SS III 8 331 69
Marianne to be sure is lost to me for ever.   SS III 8 332 77
I am very sure myself, that had Willoughby turned out as   SS III 9 338 22
know, what it really is, I am sure it must be a good one."   SS III 9 339 26
when they come back, they'd make sure to come and see you."   SS III 11 354 27
They will soon be back again, and then they'd be sure and   SS III 11 354 38
Pratt, I think-- nay, I am sure, it would never have   SS III 13 362 5
at home, and was always sure of a welcome; and accordingly   SS III 13 362 5
"Dear sir, being very sure I have long   SS III 13 365 14
I can safely say I owe you no ill-will, and am sure you   SS III 13 365 14
Mr. Edward, who, she was sure, had quite doted upon the   SS III 13 370 37
confidently run over as sure of attending, & sanguine   W 314 1
home perhaps--but you are sure of some comfortable soup.--   W 315 1
"That will not be for my happiness I am sure.--   W 318 2
by her absence--but I am sure she is mistaken, & that he   W 319 2
"To be sure I would.--   W 319 2
I am sure I shd never have forgiven the person who kept me   W 320 2
"Unless Sam feels on sure grounds with the lady herself,   W 321 2
"Mine is all to come I am sure--said eliz: giving another   W 321 2
am very sure there is no resemblance between her & Sam."--   W 324 3
30 years ago; I am pretty sure I danced with her in the   W 325 4
of the assembly--& I am sure it will never be patronised   W 334 13
so young a man, but I am sure I had no claim to expect it;   W 344 20
"I am sure we shall be great friends"--she observed, with   W 349 24
"Oh! single, my dear, to be sure!   PP I 1 3 14
Lizzy is not a bit better than the others; and I am sure   PP I 1 4 26
I was sure you loved your girls too well to neglect such   PP I 2 7 24
Bingley was sure of being liked wherever he appeared,   PP I 4 16 14
To be sure that did seem as if he admired her--indeed I   PP I 5 18 6
"Are you quite sure, ma'am?--is not there a little mistake?   PP I 5 19 11
You cannot refuse to dance, I am sure, when so much beauty   PP I 6 26 38
no objection, I am sure, to oblige us for one half hour."   PP I 6 26 41
you were sure that they would not offer to send her home."   PP I 7 30 22
my dear, your father cannot spare the horses, I am sure.   PP I 7 30 25
it, Mr. Darcy, I am sure," said Miss Bingley; "and I am   PP I 8 36 7
"In nursing your sister I am sure you have pleasure," said   PP I 8 37 25
"Neglect! I am sure you neglect nothing that can add to   PP I 8 38 33
do all this, and I am sure I never heard a young lady   PP I 8 39 45
"Nor I, I am sure," said Bingley.   PP I 8 39 47
My sister, I am sure, will not hear of her removal."   PP I 9 41 4
"I am sure," she added, "if it was not for such good   PP I 9 42 7
I do not like to boast of my own child, but to be sure,   PP I 9 44 31
was sure he would make her an offer before we came away.   PP I 9 44 31
trouble, and was sure Jane would have caught cold again.--   PP I 12 60 6
I know of nobody that is coming I am sure, unless   PP I 13 61 2
It is Mr. Bingley I am sure.   PP I 13 61 3
Well, I am sure I shall be extremely glad to see Mr.   PP I 13 61 3
own children; and I am sure if I had been you, I should   PP I 13 61 7
"No, that I am sure I shall not; and I think it was very   PP I 13 62 10
are very kind, sir, I am sure; and I wish with all my   PP I 13 65 21
22
"That is all very proper and civil, I am sure," said Mrs.   PP I 14 66 2
In his library he had been always sure of leisure and   PP I 15 71 6
resemblance of your own character, I am sure," said he.   PP I 18 91 16
I am sure we never read the same, or not with the same   PP I 18 93 28
third person; in which case you may be sure of my pardon."   PP I 18 95 49
I am sure we owe him no such particular civility as to be   PP I 18 99 65
have great pleasure, I am sure, in obliging the company   PP I 18 101 71
I am sure Lizzy will be very happy--I am sure she can have   PP I 19 104 4
and we shall very soon settle it with her, I am sure."   PP I 20 111 5
a husband at all--and I am sure I do not know who is to   PP I 20 113 28
Miss Bingley I am sure cannot.   PP I 21 119 20
she would have felt almost sure of success if he had not   PP I 22 121 1
Mr. Collins to be sure was neither sensible nor agreeable;   PP I 22 122 3
secondly, she was very sure that Mr. Collins had been   PP I 23 127 5
and delicacy she was sure her opinion could never be   PP I 23 128 9
and wherever she went she was sure of hearing it talked of.   PP I 23 129 16
officers Mr. Wickham was sure to be one; and on these   PP II 2 142 18
depend on your resolution and good conduct, I am sure.   PP II 3 144 2
"My dearest Lizzy will, I am sure, be incapable of   PP II 3 148 26
were to happen again, I am sure I should be deceived again.   PP II 3 148 26
very sure that anxiety for her brother is the cause of it.   PP II 3 148 26
I am sure you will be very comfortable there. "your's, &c.   PP II 3 149 26
"You cannot be more that twenty, I am sure,--therefore you   PP II 6 166 39
"I believe she did--and I am sure she could not have   PP II 9 178 13
Mrs. Collins will be very glad of your company, I am sure."   PP II 14 211 6
"I am sure there is not on his.   PP II 16 220 14
"His being so sure of succeeding, was wrong," said she; "   PP II 17 224 3
I am sure you must feel it so."   PP II 17 225 12
"Lizzy, when you first read that letter, I am sure you   PP II 17 226 18
Well, my comfort is, I am sure Jane will die of a broken   PP II 17 228 29
"I am sure," said she, "I cried for two days together when   PP II 18 229 4
"I am sure I shall break mine," said Lydia.   PP II 18 229 5
"And my aunt Philips is sure it would do me a great deal   PP II 18 229 9
it, I am sure you would judge differently in the affair."   PP II 18 231 16
"I am sure I know none so handsome; but in the gallery up   PP III 1 247 18
much to his credit, I am sure, that you should think so."   PP III 1 248 29
Some people call him proud; but I am sure I never saw any   PP III 1 249 38
"Whatever can give his sister any pleasure, is sure to be   PP III 1 250 45
"There is something a little stately in him to be sure,"   PP III 1 257 68
"To be sure.   PP III 1 257 70
But to be sure, the good lady who shewed us the house, did   PP III 1 258 74
most to fail, she was most sure of success, for those to   PP III 2 262 7
What he means to do, I am sure I know not; but his   PP III 4 276 5
I am sure there was some great neglect or other on their   PP III 5 287 35
I am sure, but I did not think it right for either of them.   PP III 5 292 66
"Sure he will not leave London before he has found them.   PP III 6 298 14
My dear Jane, I am in such a flutter, that I am sure I   PP III 7 306 47
An airing would do me a great deal of good, I am sure.   PP III 7 307 49
To be sure it would have been more for the advantage of   PP III 8 309 6
Good gracious! when I went away, I am sure I had no more   PP III 9 316 7
I am sure my sisters must all envy me.   PP III 9 317 11
He did every thing best in the world; and she was sure he   PP III 9 318 20
To be sure London was rather thin, but however the little   PP III 9 319 25
If he had another motive, I am sure it would never   PP III 10 322 2
She was sure they should be married some time or other,   PP III 10 323 2
do himself; though I am sure (and I do not speak it to be   PP III 10 324 2
If she heard me, it was by good luck, for I am sure she   PP III 10 325 2
revolt from the connection. he had to be sure done much.   PP III 10 326 3
One ought not repine;--but, to be sure, it would have been   PP III 10 328 28
He is nothing to us, you know, and I am sure I never want   PP III 11 331 14
"Some acquaintance or other, my dear, I suppose; I am sure   PP III 11 334 33
be welcome here to be sure; but else I must say that I   PP III 11 334 35
"It is a delightful thing, to be sure, to have a daughter   PP III 11 336 51
I am sure he will be vastly happy to oblige you, and will   PP III 11 337 53
I am sure I sha'nt get a wink of sleep all night.   PP III 13 348 40
I was sure you could not be so beautiful for nothing!   PP III 13 348 40
"He made a little mistake to be sure; but it is to the   PP III 13 350 50
It was a rational scheme to be sure! but from what the   PP III 15 360 1
me then devoid of every proper feeling, I am sure you did.   PP III 16 368 16
My sole dependence was on you; and I am sure nobody else   PP III 17 372 5
Are you quite sure that you feel what you ought to do?"   PP III 17 373 11
Mr. Bingley; "but I am sure it will be too much for Kitty.   PP III 17 374 24
He is rich, to be sure, and you may have more fine clothes   PP III 17 376 31
To be sure, you know no actual good of me--but nobody   PP III 18 380 5
I am sure Wickham would like a place at court very much,   PP III 19 386 7
Jane or herself were sure of being applied to, for some   PP III 19 387 8
one's own hands; and I am sure I should be the last person   MP I 1 6 6
of my sisters?--and I am sure Mr. Norris is too just--but   MP I 1 6 6
It is, in fact, the only sure way of providing against the   MP I 1 6 6
and I am sure we shall never disagree on this point.   MP I 1 7 8
mention of such a thing she was sure would distract him.   MP I 1 9 10
thing there, and be sure of having the room to ourselves."   MP I 2 16 15
I am sure I should have been ashamed of myself, if I had   MP I 2 18 25
"To be sure, my dear, that is very stupid indeed, and   MP I 2 19 29
"Never, my dear; but you are sure of a comfortable home.   MP I 3 25 16
You have good sense, and a sweet temper, and I am sure you   MP I 3 26 29
Sure Sir Thomas could not seriously expect such a thing!   MP I 3 28 42
Nobody that wishes me well, I am sure, would propose it.   MP I 3 28 42
I am sure in his heart he could not wish me to do it."   MP I 3 29 44
She is in good hands, and sure of doing well.   MP I 3 29 46
They are sure of being well provided for.   MP I 3 30 53
She was sure Sir Thomas had never intended it; and she   MP I 4 36 7
"No, I am sure you are too good.   MP I 4 43 23
plain; he was plain, to be sure, but then he had so much   MP I 5 44 2
I am sure Miss Bertram is very much attached to Mr.   MP I 5 45 14
It would be a very flat business, she was sure.   MP I 6 52 1
cried Mrs. Norris, "I am sure you need not regard it.   MP I 6 53 9
Its natural beauties, I am sure, are great.   MP I 6 61 53
I am sure William would never have used me so, under any   MP I 7 64 10
"I was sure she would ride well," said Julia; "she has the   MP I 7 69 24
I am sure I almost broke my back by cutting it out.   MP I 7 71 34
at her attentively; "I am sure you have the headach?"   MP I 7 71 36
"Go out! to be sure she did," said Mrs. Norris; "would you   MP I 7 72 41
"I am sure I do not know how it was to have been done   MP I 7 73 53
"To be sure not, but I cannot do without her."   MP I 8 78 19
of the kind, and I am sure ma'am you would be glad to give   MP I 8 78 21
settle it your own way, I am sure I do not care about it."   MP I 8 79 23
"I am sure she ought to be very much obliged to you,"   MP I 8 79 25
"Oh! I know nothing of your furlongs, but I am sure it is   MP I 9 95 64
than your manner, I am sure, and I dare say you walked as   MP I 10 102 46
I am sure you ought to be very much obliged to your aunt   MP I 10 105 53
living creatures of that sort; and so to be sure it will.   MP I 10 106 57
"But that I am sure it has not," cried Fanny.   MP I 11 109 16
am sure my father was too conscientious to have allowed it.   MP I 11 109 17
"We cannot prove the contrary, to be sure--but I wish you   MP I 11 112 31
"There goes good humour I am sure," said he presently.   MP I 11 112 34
respect, had she been sure that she was seeing clearly,   MP I 12 115 5
"It is not worth complaining about, but to be sure the   MP I 13 122 4
Not these countenances I am sure," looking towards the   MP I 13 123 6
think our time very well spent, and so I am sure will he.--   MP I 13 126 18
"To be sure, my dear mother, your anxiety--I was unlucky   MP I 13 126 21
I am sure he encouraged it in us as boys.   MP I 13 126 25
And I am sure, my name was Norval, every evening of my   MP I 13 126 25
be thought of; he was very sure his sister had no wish of   MP I 14 133 10
Cottager's wife; and I am sure I set her the example of   MP I 14 134 14
through; he is solemn and pathetic enough I am sure.   MP I 14 134 14
When you have studied the character, I am sure you will   MP I 14 135 17
to be Agatha, and I am sure I will do nothing else; and as   MP I 14 136 20
which she began of, "I am sure I would give up the part to   MP I 14 136 21
mean very well, I am sure--but I still think you see   MP I 15 140 14
To be sure Julia is dressed by this time."   MP I 15 141 16
I am sure she would argue so.   MP I 15 141 21
I am sure that would be a discredit to us all.   MP I 15 141 22
them to father, you may be sure; mother had chanced to   MP I 15 141 22
am sure you must be sick of all our noise and difficulties.   MP I 15 143 26
"You chose very wisely, I am sure," replied Miss Crawford,   MP I 15 144 30
breakfast," said he, "and am sure of giving pleasure there.   MP I 16 156 27
I am sure Julia does not, or she would not have flirted as   MP I 17 162 16
Fanny, I am sure you know the part."   MP I 18 172 31
"Sure, my dear Sir Thomas, a basin of soup would be a much   MP II 1 180 10
on that stage; but he was sure there could not be a finer.   MP II 1 182 22
a young man whom he felt sure of disapproving, and whose   MP II 1 183 23
leaders so often now, that I am sure there is no fear.'   MP II 2 189 5
I am sure I do.   MP II 3 198 10
Could they be much together I feel sure of their liking   MP II 3 199 13
We are to be sure a miracle every way--but our powers of   MP II 4 209 12
"To be sure.   MP II 4 213 38
I cannot spare her, and I am sure she does not want to go.-   MP II 5 217 1
say, no; but I am sure, my dear mother, she would like to   MP II 5 217 2
"To be sure, so I shall."   MP II 5 217 6
"To walk and ride with me, to be sure."   MP II 6 229 2
of improvement, I am sure it may all be resolved into a   MP II 6 230 6
the view is really very pretty; I am sure it may be done.   MP II 7 242 23
sure I can answer for your being kindly received by both.   MP II 7 245 32
My uncle says nothing, but I am sure he will do every   MP II 7 250 55
be a sacrifice--I am sure you will, upon consideration,   MP II 9 263 16
have the meaning, is not in your nature I am sure.   MP II 9 263 16
I think, I hope, I am sure she is not serious--but I would   MP II 9 268 29
in Fanny; she was not sure whether Colonel Harrison had   MP II 11 283 4
to live there--and I am sure she is better off here--and   MP II 11 285 14
it was very short; indeed I am sure it was but a few lines.   MP II 11 288 23
or some days longer, I am not quite sure which."   MP II 11 288 23
every woman who plays herself is sure to ask about another.   MP II 11 288 28
I am sure of an excellent tenant at half a word.   MP II 12 295 20
to buy, though to be sure his father and mother would be   MP II 13 305 19
I am sure you will not disappoint my opinion of you, by   MP III 1 313 12
my exact words--but I am sure I told him that I would not   MP III 1 315 19
I am sure I said as much as that and more; and I should   MP III 1 315 19
had been before; she was sure he did not mean there should   MP III 1 323 53
You mean me, Baddeley, I am sure; Sir Thomas wants me, not   MP III 1 325 60
could not love him, was sure she never could love him: MP III 2 327 5
wish me to do differently from what I have done, I am sure.   MP III 2 333 24
25
Yes, I am sure you would miss me too much for that."   MP III 2 333 25
"I am sure he fell in love with you at the ball, I am sure   MP III 2 333 28
"I am sure he fell in love with you at the ball, I am sure   MP III 2 333 28
I shall tell Sir Thomas that I am sure it was done that   MP III 2 333 28
parlour, that she was sure they must be talking of her;   MP III 3 334 5
And sure enough there was a book on the table which had   MP III 3 336 9
"You have a great turn for acting, I am sure, Mr. Crawford,   MP III 3 338 19
saying, "no," he added, "are you sure you did not speak?   MP III 3 340 25

I am sure his sisters, rating him as they do, must have MP III 4 353 45
You are sure therefore of seeing your friend either to- MP III 4 354 48
To be sure, your uncle's returning that very evening! MP III 5 360 14
the air of a gentleman, and now, I am sure, she was wrong. MP III 5 361 16
Oh, I am sure it is not in woman's nature to refuse such a MP III 5 363 22
She had made a sure push at Fanny's feelings here. MP III 5 364 27
I am sure of meeting again and again, and all but you. MP III 5 364 32
are very right, but I am sure I shall miss her very much." MP III 6 371 16
You will set things going in a better way, I am sure. MP III 6 372 20
"To be sure, I had much rather she had stayed in harbour, MP III 7 378 12
I am sure I told her to bring some coals half an hour ago. MP III 7 379 17
was sure her sister must want something after her journey." MP III 7 383 32
"Her year!" cried Mrs. Price; "I am sure I hope I shall be MP III 7 385 39
to please--and I am sure the place is easy enough, for MP III 7 385 39
sure of her, and been delighted with his own sagacity. MP III 8 388 1
been glad to have been sure of such a letter every week. MP III 9 394 2
When you know her as well as I do, I am sure you will MP III 11 410 16
I am sure he still means to impose on me if possible, and MP III 11 411 20
They are very fond of her; but I am sure she does not love MP III 13 421 2
I am sure he has been very ill. MP III 13 427 12
If it be so, I am sure you must be included in that part, MP III 14 433 13
at Twickenham (as to be sure you know), and is not yet MP III 14 434 13
I am sure it will be all hushed up, and nothing proved by MP III 15 437 3
about that carpet, I am sure I have spoke at least a dozen MP III 15 440 18
Settle it as you like; say what is proper; I am sure you MP III 15 443 23
We must go in the carriage to be sure." E I 1 8 16
And as for James, you may be very sure he will always like E I 1 8 18
upon any account; and I am sure she will make a very good E I 1 9 19
I am sure she will be an excellent servant; and it will be E I 1 9 19
half a mile apart, and were sure of meeting every day." E I 1 11 35
I am sure she will miss her more than she thinks for." E I 1 11 36
"Mr. Elton is a very pretty young man to be sure, and a E I 1 14 47
was sure whenever he married he would make a good husband. E I 4 28 6
He is in Highbury every now and then, and he is sure to E I 4 29 13
"To be sure. E I 4 29 15
"To be sure, so it is. E I 4 30 21
"Yes, to be sure--I suppose there are. E I 4 31 23
"To be sure. E I 4 31 25
am sure I shall not wish for the acquaintance of his wife. E I 4 31 25
"To be sure," said Harriet, in a mortified voice, "he is E I 4 32 31
I am sure you must have been struck by his awkward look E I 4 33 32
I am sure you always thought me unfit for the office I E I 5 38 10
I am sure of having their opinions with me." E I 5 40 23
"Great has been the pleasure, I am sure. E I 6 43 7
a little like-- but to be sure it did not do him justice." E I 6 45 21
You will express yourself very properly, I am sure. E I 7 51 11
"Oh! no, I am sure you are a great deal too kind to---- E I 7 52 20
"No, to be sure you could not; but I never thought of that E I 7 54 26
"And I am sure I should never want to go there; for I am E I 7 55 39
I am sure Miss Nash would--for Miss Nash thinks her own E I 7 55 40
"He is very obliging," said Emma; "but is he sure that E I 8 59 26
"Oh! to be sure," cried Emma, "it is always E I 8 60 33
Even your satisfaction I made sure of. E I 8 61 38
"To be sure!" cried she playfully. E I 8 64 46
of prudence, she was very sure did not belong to Mr. Elton. E I 8 67 57
him, but he was very sure there must be a lady in the case, E I 8 68 58
I am sure, a month ago, I had no more idea myself!-- E I 9 74 24
I am sure I have not got one half so good." E I 9 77 39
parts, so as to feel quite sure that her friend were not E I 9 77 43
I am sure I was very much surprized when I first heard she E I 9 79 60
I am sure she will be pleased with the children. E I 9 80 69
I am sure I do not know who is not." E I 9 80 71
friend on their account; her father was sure of his rubber. E I 9 81 79
He may be sure of every woman's approbation while he E I 9 82 82
And, without love, I am sure I should be a fool to change E I 10 84 15
of the poor were as sure of relief from her personal E I 10 86 24
"Why to be sure," said Mr. Woodhouse--"yes, certainly--I E I 11 94 16
I am sure nobody ought to be, or can be, a greater E I 11 95 19
"To be sure--our discordancies must always arise from my E I 12 99 5
I am sure it almost killed me once." E I 12 101 22
place unhealthy; and I am sure he may be depended on, for E I 12 105 55
"We are sure of excellent fires," continued he, "and every E I 13 115 43
that we are by no means so sure of seeing Mr. Frank E I 14 121 16
Isabella: "and I am sure I never think of that poor young E I 14 121 17
on his side; but I am sure there is a great wish on the E I 14 122 21
I am sure of your kind support and aid." E I 15 125 5
the utmost good-will was sure that accommodation might be E I 15 126 11
and felt sure that he would want to be talking nonsense. E I 15 129 23
No!--(in an accent meant to be insinuating)--I am sure you E I 15 131 31
To be sure, the charade, with its "ready wit"--but then, E I 16 134 4
so very much, I am sure I have not an idea of any body E I 16 137 11
unclosed, they will be sure to open to sensations of E I 16 137 13
of his being a weak young man: I feel sure that he is not. E I 18 148 23
The mention of the Coles was sure to be followed by that E II 1 156 5
I was sure it could not be far off; but I had put my E II 1 157 10
very lately that I was almost sure it must be on the table. E II 1 157 10
--And then I tell her, I am sure she would contrive to E II 1 157 10
--every word of it--I am sure she would pore over it till E II 1 157 10
Jane often says, when she is here, 'I am sure, grandmama, E II 1 158 10
I am sure there is nobody's praise that could give us so E II 1 158 12
she is sure to hear; but then she is used to my voice. E II 1 158 14
same obliging things. I am sure she will be as happy to E II 1 159 18
to her letter, and I am sure she tells her own story a E II 1 162 31
I am sure Miss Fairfax must have found the evening E II 3 170 2
said her father instantly; "that I am sure you are not. E II 3 170 4
Emma, unless one could be sure of their making it into E II 3 171 16
17

had every thing they could wish for, I am sure it is us. E II 3 174 31
Well, that is so very!--I am sure if Jane is tired, you E II 3 177 50
who should come in--to be sure it was so very odd!--but E II 3 178 52
I am sure she saw me, but she looked away directly, and E II 3 178 52
I am sure I must have been as white as my gown. I could E II 3 178 52
I am sure they were talking of me; and I could not help E II 3 178 52
either marries or dies, is sure of being kindly spoken of. E II 4 181 1
every day Harriet was sure just to meet with him, or just E II 4 184 10
and again into his room, to be sure that all is right." E II 5 189 20
I am sure they will bring him soon." E II 5 190 20
Emma was directly sure that he knew how to make himself E II 5 191 26
He understood what would be welcome; he could be sure of E II 5 192 28
"To be sure we do," cried his father; "Mrs. Bates-- we E II 5 194 38
They will be extremely glad to see you, I am sure, and one E II 5 195 45
mortify the Coles, I am sure, sir; friendly, good sort of E II 7 210 19
I am sure, rather than run the risk of hurting Mr. and Mrs. E II 7 210 20
home cold, she would be sure to warm herself thoroughly; E II 7 211 22
No, I am perfectly sure that he is not trifling or silly." E II 8 212 3
"Yes I should, I am sure I should. E II 8 213 10
This is like giving ourselves a slap, to be sure! and it E II 8 215 16
bought--or else I am sure we ought to be ashamed of it.-- E II 8 216 16
the right; but I am sure there must be a particular cause E II 8 217 32
"No, I am sure it is not form the Campbells. Miss Fairfax E II 8 218 41
And she,--"only to be sure it was paying him too great a E II 8 220 47
soul! she was as grateful as possible, you may be sure. E II 8 223 63
I was quite surprized;--very glad, I am sure; but really E II 8 223 63
marrying; and I am sure it is not at all likely. E II 8 224 66
I am sure he has not the least idea of it. E II 8 225 74
In the way of love, I am sure he does not. E II 8 225 76
"If it would be good to her, I am sure it would be evil to E II 8 225 78
I am sure he was particularly silent when Mrs. Cole told E II 8 226 83
he replied;--"but you must often wish it, I am sure." E II 8 228 90
I am sure I had much rather hear you. E II 9 231 7
"Are you sure? E II 9 232 11
to come with me, that I might be sure of succeeding." E II 9 236 44

Oh! then, said I, I must run across, I am sure Miss E II 9 236 46
But, said I, I shall be more sure of succeeding if one of E II 9 236 46
And I am sure, by his manner, it was no compliment. E II 9 238 51
'I am sure you must be,' said he, 'and I will send you E II 9 238 51
He told Patty this, but bid her not mind it, and be sure E II 9 239 51
Miss Woodhouse, I am quite concerned, I am sure you hit E II 9 239 53
of the upper notes I am sure is exactly what he and all E II 10 241 8
You must have heard every thing to be sure. E II 10 245 54
I am sure, neither your father nor Mrs. Weston (poor Miss E II 11 252 30
If I could be sure of the rooms being thoroughly aired-- E II 11 252 35
She will enjoy the scheme, I am sure; and I do not know a E II 11 255 55
No, the young lady, to be sure. E II 11 255 57
I am sure we do. E II 12 260 22
I am sure you did not much expect to like us. E II 12 260 22
I am sure it will. E II 13 269 16
She was almost sure that for a young woman, a stranger, a E II 14 270 4
I am sure she does. E II 15 283 7
I am a great advocate for timidity--and I am sure one does E II 15 283 7
I am sure they will like her extremely; and when she gets E II 15 284 9
principle, you may be sure that Miss Fairfax awes Mrs. E II 15 286 23
were to ask her--and I am very sure I shall never ask her." E II 15 287 30
this morning, or I am sure you must have been wet.-- E II 16 293 10
11

I know Mr. John Knightley too well--I am very sure he E II 16 293 22
"My dear Miss Fairfax, young ladies are very sure to be E II 16 294 27
You do us a great deal of honour to-day, I am sure. E II 16 294 27
Yes, I am sure you are much too reasonable. E II 16 295 33
had my writing-desk, I am sure I could produce a specimen. E II 16 298 52
"I must spend some time with them; I am sure they will E II 17 300 9
little more nice, and I am sure the good Campbells will be E II 17 301 18
do all that, I am very sure; but you sing as well as play;- E II 17 301 18
Jane, "they are pretty sure to be equal; however, I am E II 17 301 19
I am sure Mr. Elton will lose no time in calling on him; E II 18 305 4
Frank will be extremely happy, I am sure.-- E II 18 305 5
be here again soon, I was sure something favourable would E II 18 308 27
untowardly one month, they are sure to mend the next." E II 18 308 27
and exclaim that he was sure at this rate it would be may E II 18 308 28
at least--I am almost sure that old Mr. Suckling had E II 18 310 34
every thing is down at full length there we may be sure. E II 18 311 37
38

You may be very sure I shall always take care of them." E III 2 321 17
Oh! and I am sure our thanks are due to you, Mrs. Weston, E III 2 322 19
My dear Jane, are you sure you did not wet your feet?-- E III 2 323 19
to be avoided: she was sure he would not--and she was E III 2 326 33
have great pleasure, I am sure--for, though beginning to E III 2 327 36
Well, I am sure, Mr. Churchill--only it seems too good-- E III 2 330 45
If one leads you wrong, I am sure the other tells you of E III 2 330 53
"It is my duty, and I am sure it is my wish," she E III 4 337 4
I am sure I never suspected it, you did it so naturally." E III 4 339 14
he did not dream it--I am sure I have sometimes the oddest E III 5 345 16
"That I am sure you would. E III 6 356 28
have been absent--but I am sure we shall be wanted, and I E III 6 362 44
"Is Miss Woodhouse sure that she would like to hear what E III 7 369 18
I shall be sure to say three dull things as soon as ever I E III 7 370 24
"Ah!--well--to be sure. E III 7 371 28
I am sure I do not know." E III 7 371 33
I am sure I should like any body fixed on by you. E III 7 373 46
laid down upon the bed, and I am sure you are ill enough." E III 8 378 4
I am sure she will be here presently." E III 8 378 6
'Oh!' said I, 'it is Miss Woodhouse: I am sure you will E III 8 379 8
and over again--and I am sure I had no more idea that she E III 8 380 15
her; she would wait--and, sure enough, yesterday evening E III 8 381 15
"Yes; Jane says she is sure they will; but yet, this is E III 8 382 29
and so will Jane, I am sure, if she gets out at all. E III 8 383 29
Emma was sure he had not forgiven her; he looked unlike E III 9 385 5
It ought to be a first object, as I am sure poor Miss E III 9 387 10
"I am very sure that I never said any thing of either to E III 10 399 62
You may be very sure that if I had, I should have E III 11 405 11
I am sure, but for believing that you entirely approved E III 11 405 18
"To be sure I am. E III 11 406 20
I am sure the service Mr. Frank Churchill had rendered you, E III 11 406 21
But you are too good for that, I am sure." E III 11 407 28
circumstances, would, I am sure, have been as constantly E III 12 419 12
I am sure she is very good--I hope she will be very happy. E III 12 420 13
Be sure to give me intelligence of the letter as soon as E III 12 420 16
"After waiting a moment, as if to be sure she intended to E III 13 425 6
7

him; and no one, I am sure, could be more effectually E III 13 427 19
any thing he wrote, she was sure she was incapable of it.-- E III 14 436 6
of thinking myself too sure of your's, and of those among E III 14 437 8
object--but I am sure you will believe the declaration, E III 14 438 8
She was sure of Mrs. Weston's wishing it to be E III 15 444 2
"And I have not forgotten," said Emma, "how sure you were E III 15 445 12
"I am sure William Larkins will not like it. E III 15 449 33
he must have left a message for you, I am sure he must.-- E III 16 458 42
I am sure I would not have such a creature as his Harry E III 16 458 42
And I will own to you, (I am sure it will be safe), that E III 16 460 56
"I am sure you were of use to me," cried Emma. E III 17 462 8
I am very sure you did me good. E III 17 462 8
Isabella, to be sure, was no very quick observer; yet if E III 17 463 16
better; and she was very sure that he would be a great E III 17 466 29
He would not deny that he did, she was sure.-- E III 17 466 29
"Oh! good I am sure.-- E III 18 470 5
Time, you may be very sure, will make one or the other of E III 18 471 16
To speak, she was sure would be to betray a most E III 18 472 21
But, Mr. Knightley, are you perfectly sure that she has E III 18 473 26
Are you quite sure that you understand the terms on which E III 18 474 29
"I am quite sure," he replied, speaking very distinctly, " E III 18 474 30
I am sure you had.-- E III 18 478 65
I am sure it was a consolation to you." E III 18 478 65
I am sure it was a source of high entertainment to you, to E III 18 478 67
weather-beaten, to be sure, but not much; and quite the P III 3 22 23
You remember him, I am sure." P III 3 23 32
reply was, "then I am sure Anne had better stay, for P III 5 33 7
thing in the world, I am sure, would induce my father to P III 5 35 14
all this morning--very unfit to be left alone, I am sure. P III 5 37 24
I am sure, Anne, if you would, you might persuade him that P III 6 44 7
things, that they are sure to come back sick and cross for P III 6 44 8
But to be sure, in general they are so spoilt! P III 6 44 8
it in question; but I am sure, without exaggeration, that P III 6 45 9
was so; and is perfectly sure that this must be the very P III 6 50 27
going on, men are always sure to get out of it, and P III 7 56 10
to stir;--and yet, I am sure, I am more unfit than any P III 7 56 10
told him to keep quiet, he was sure to begin kicking about. P III 7 56 12
To be sure I may just as well go as not, for I am of no P III 7 57 16
Oh! I will certainly go; I am sure I ought if I can, quite P III 7 57 16
I should not go, you may be sure, if I did not feel quite P III 7 57 16
"To be sure you did.-- P III 8 65 14
"And I am sure, sir," said Mrs. Musgrove, "it was a lucky P III 8 67 24
"Ay, to be sure.-- P III 8 71 55
answer; but then she was sure of his having asked his P III 8 72 58
himself say, was very sure that he had not made less than P III 9 75 10
any future war; and he was sure Captain Wentworth was as P III 9 75 10
between us; and I am sure you would have thought as I did, P III 9 77 16
thought you would have it; I always thought you sure. P III 9 78 20
Mr. and Mrs. Musgrove were sure all could not be right, P III 10 82 2
with her own seat,--was sure Louisa had got a much better P III 10 86 21
it would not do; she was sure Louisa had found a better P III 10 87 21
You are never sure of a good impression being durable. P III 10 88 26
"Miss Elliot, I am sure you are tired," cried Mrs. Croft. P III 10 91 40
for her,--and I am sure she would be glad to get to a P III 12 102 2
I was sure that would come out, if it was so. P III 12 106 16

so it did, otherwise, I am sure, I should have observed P III 12 106 16
Yes, I am sure, carry her gently to the inn." P III 12 111 47
Wentworth, Anne was sure could never be forgotten by her; P III 12 112 54
"You will stay, I am sure; you will stay and nurse her;" P III 12 114 63
felt the parish to be so sure of a good example, and the P IV 1 125 17
A very good man, and very much the gentleman I am sure-- P IV 1 127 28
"And I am sure," cried Mary warmly, "it was very little to P IV 2 131 10
is it, Lady Russell? I am sure you will agree with me." P IV 2 131 10
and soul; and I am sure from his manner that you will have P IV 2 131 12
I am sure you will not like him." P IV 2 132 16
"I am sure Lady Russell would like him. P IV 2 132 18
It had been a frosty morning, to be sure, a sharp frost, P IV 3 142 13
him; every woman's eye was sure to be upon Colonel Wallis." P IV 3 142 13
She was sure that he had not been happy in marriage. P IV 4 147 6
be very sure is a matter of perfect indifference to them." P IV 4 151 18
In one point, I am sure, my dear cousin, (he continued, P IV 4 151 21
in the room) in one point, I am sure, we must feel alike. P IV 4 151 21
to bestow on me, she is sure to have something that makes P IV 5 155 9
They were only asked, she was sure, because Lady Dalrymple P IV 5 157 14
"I am sure I had not. P IV 6 163 7
of them every morning; sure to have plenty of chat; and P IV 6 170 29
Here are pretty girls enough, I am sure. P IV 6 173 49
He will be here in a moment, I am sure." P IV 7 177 15
She was sure of a pleasant reception; and her friend P IV 9 192 4
I am sure you have, somehow or other, imbibed such a P IV 9 195 25
To be sure by next week I may be allowed to think it all P IV 9 195 27
I am sure you hear nothing but good of him from Colonel P IV 9 196 30
"To be sure I did, very often. P IV 9 201 61
How sure to be mistaken! P IV 9 201 63
ring for Mary--stay, I am sure you will have the still P IV 9 202 68
"Why, to be sure, ma'am," said she, "it would not prevent P IV 9 208 92
sure he has always been a very kind, liberal father to me. P IV 10 218 22
They do every thing to confer happiness, I am sure. P IV 10 218 23
"To be sure he is. P IV 10 218 26
I am sure she would rather not come--she cannot feel easy P IV 10 220 29
"there is Mrs. Clay, I am sure, standing under the P IV 10 222 34
Anne will not be sorry to join us, I am sure. P IV 10 223 41
at her father's; and I am sure neither Henrietta nor I P IV 10 224 51
where she might be sure of being as silent as she chose. P IV 10 227 68
"To be sure I will, if you wish it. P IV 11 239 52
to marry, they are pretty sure by perseverance to carry P IV 12 248 1
They had their great cousins, to be sure, to resort to for P IV 12 251 9
good people can be with him in three minutes I am sure. S 1 365 1
much business--to be sure, if gentlemen were to be often S 1 366 1
"Not down in the Weald I am sure sir, replied the S 1 366 1
Bad things for a country;--sure to raise the price of S 1 368 1
for every thing, & the sure resort of the very best S 1 368 1
to your leg--& I am sure by your lady's countenance that S 1 368 1
I am sure we agree my dear, in wishing our boys to be as S 1 370 1
"Yes indeed, I am sure we do--& I will get Mary a little S 4 381 1
"And I am sure they must be very extraordinary ones.--said S 4 381 1
We wanted just to see you & make sure of your being really S 5 388 1
sure of getting a woman of fortune, if he chuses it."-- S 6 391 1
You understand me I am sure?" S 7 400 1
venture,--for I am sure there is Lumbago hanging about him- S 8 403 1
I am very sure that the largest house at Sanditon cannot S 9 407 1
to doubt it as long as you possibly can, I am sure.--" S 9 409 1
I am sure it does.-- S 10 415 1
"It sounds rather odd to be sure--answered Charlotte S 10 417 1
S 10 418 1

SURELY (29)
Surely it is not to Lady Susan's credit that he should be LS 15 267 7
Consideration & esteem as surely follow command of LS 16 268 2
Lady Susan is surely too severe, because Frederica does LS 17 270 4
The probability of their marrying is surely heightened. LS 24 291 17
Her idle love for Reginald too; it is surely my duty to LS 25 294 5
It would surely be much more to the purpose to get LS 26 295 1
It will surely therefore be advisable to delay our union, LS 30 301 4
One moment surely might be spared; and, so desperate NA II 6 164 3
In this there was surely something mysterious, and she NA II 7 173 4
But in the central part of England there was surely some NA II 10 200 3
Surely you must be mistaken. SS I 20 115 49
but surely there must be some mistake of person or name. SS I 22 131 29
If you know it already, as surely you must, I may be SS II 8 199 35
Surely this comparison must have its use with her. SS II 9 210 32
If you can think me capable of ever feeling--surely you SS III 1 264 29
Surely, after doing so, she cannot be imagined liable to SS III 5 296 19
"You are over scrupulous surely. PP I 1 4 25
It would surely be much more rational if conversation PP I 11 55 8
Miss Bennet paused a little and then replied, "surely PP II 17 226 22
"But surely," said she, "I may enter his county with PP II 19 239 9
for those who have surely some right to guide you--without MP III 1 318 39
had any meaning; and surely I was not to be teaching MP III 4 353 45
'Open the windows!--but surely, Mr. Churchill, nobody E II 11 251 30
so extremely fond of it--there can be no danger, surely." E II 14 277 39
She opened the packet; it was too surely so;--a note from E III 14 436 6
estate would as surely be his hereafter as the title. P IV 3 140 11
But surely, you may put off this old lady till to-morrow. P IV 5 157 15
Surely, this must be calm enough. P IV 9 196 33
of rational dependance--"surely, if there be constant P IV 10 221 33

SURER (2)
disregarded them all; he had a surer test of distance. NA I 7 45 7
and there cannot be a surer sign of nervousness.--" S 10 416 1

SUREST (2)
be severe on us, and our surest way of disappointing him, PP I 11 56 13
their wishes, might be their surest means of forwarding it. MP III 2 330 14

SURFACE (2)
Even the smooth surface of family-union seems worth P IV 9 198 53
in a storm, its glassy surface in a calm, it's Gulls & its S 7 396 1

SURFACES (1)
I shall call hills steep, which ought to be bold; surfaces SS I 18 97 4

SURGEON (18)
Sam is only a surgeon you know.-- W 321 2
I dare say a very clever surgeon, but his complexion has W 324 3
The next bustle brought in Mr. Campbell, the surgeon of MP III 7 384 36
"A surgeon!" said Anne. P III 12 110 39
only "true, true, a surgeon this instant," was darting P III 12 110 40
41
He knows where a surgeon is to be found." P III 12 110 41
The surgeon was with them almost before it had seemed P III 12 112 52
person to fetch a surgeon, you could have little idea of P IV 8 182 6
you to send off one of these good people for the surgeon." S 1 365 1
"The surgeon sir!--replied Mr Heywood--I am afraid you S 1 365 1
afraid you will find no surgeon at hand here, but I dare S 1 365 1
are you expecting to find a surgeon in that cottage?-- S 1 365 1
We have neither surgeon nor partner in the parish I assure S 1 365 1
"Then sir, I can bring proof of your having a surgeon in S 1 366 1
me of there being a surgeon in Willingden,--for having S 1 366 1
for a surgeon to get a house at the top of the hill.-- S 1 366 1
hunt for an advertising surgeon, was also plainly stated;-- S 2 371 1
for the good of such surgeon--nor (as Mr H. had been apt S 2 371 1

SURGEON'S (2)
go to their house--and wait the surgeon's arrival there. P III 12 111 50
in these cases to have a surgeon's opinion without loss of S 1 365 1

SURMISE (11)
It was a bold surmise, for he was Isabella's brother; and NA I 9 66 32
This bold surmise, however, she soon learnt comprehended NA I 15 117 8
"If I understand you rightly, you had formed a surmise of NA II 9 197 29
absence than if her first surmise had been just, every PP I 18 89 3
"That is not an unnatural surmise," said Fitzwilliam, "but PP II 10 186 37
their pity, more than she hoped they would ever surmise. MP I 18 170 24
Say not a word of it--hear nothing, surmise nothing, MP III 15 437 3
that he had nothing more to say or surmise about Hartfield. E I 5 41 31
of a single unpleasant surmise, without a glance forward E II 5 193 35
that Mrs. Weston was quite mistaken in that surmise. E II 12 258 6
To that surmise, you say nothing, of course; but confess, E III 2 330 48

SURMISED (3)
Harriet had not surmised her own danger, but the idea of E I 7 53 25
She may not have surmised the whole, but her quickness E III 14 438 8
He little surmised that it was a subject acting now P IV 10 214 12

SURMISES (4)
the boldness of her own surmises, and sometimes hoped or NA II 8 188 18
and distant surmises; but he eluded the skill of them all; PP I 3 9 1
thoughts on the subject, some surmises as to what might be. MP III 5 362 18
Emma saw its artifice, and returned to her first surmises. E II 2 169 16

SURMISING (1)
quite unequal to surmising or soliciting any thing more. MP II 4 210 20

SURMOUNT (1)
she could not wholly surmount even in speaking to Mr. PP I 18 89 3

SURMOUNTING (2)
After surmounting your unconquerable horror of the bed, NA II 5 159 19
the lane, and were surmounting an opposite stile; and the P III 10 91 39

SURPASS (4)
but it could not surpass the alarm of the Miss Steeles, SS I 21 121 10
who does not greatly surpass what is usually met with. PP I 8 39 50
Do not we rather surpass your expectations? E II 12 260 22
in society as Mrs. Elton's consequence only could surpass. E II 15 281 1

SURPASSED (2)
that Isabella far surpassed her in tender anticipations.-- NA I 15 118 9
at her want of thought could not be surpassed by his. SS I 18 98 12

SURPASSING (4)
in her sister even surpassing his expectation, gave her SS III 7 314 22
"His regard for her, infinitely surpassing anything that SS III 9 336 14
of Mrs. Bennet perhaps surpassing the rest; though when PP I 2 7 23
conviction of very much surpassing her sex in general by MP I 7 66 15

SURPLICE (1)
prayers in a white surplice, and publishing the banns of SS III 5 298 33

SURPRISE (147)
examining the terrified face of Frederica with surprise. LS 20 275 2
reasonable, is too common to excite surprise or resentment. LS 30 300 2
My surprise is the greater, because on Wednesday, the very LS 41 309 1
no other emotion than surprise at there being any men in NA I 2 20 8
said Marianne, "I may consider it with some surprise. SS I 3 17 18
They heard her with surprise. SS I 5 25 1
this, and, in a voice of surprise and concern, which SS I 5 25 1
his head, to the great surprise of her ladyship, who SS I 6 31 9
of it created no other surprise, than that she, or any of SS I 12 60 7
it; and great was her surprise when she found that every SS I 13 68 67
Mrs. Dashwood looked at Elinor with surprise. SS I 15 76 13
"Months!" cried Marianne, with strong surprise. SS I 16 85 13
round with surprise to see and welcome Edward Ferrars. SS I 16 86 20
Marianne saw and listened with increasing surprise. SS I 16 87 23
After a short silence which succeeded the first surprise SS I 16 87 24
one, and could not help looking with surprise at them both. SS I 19 107 27
her account of their surprise, the evening before, on SS I 19 107 28
times over, that it had been quite an agreeable surprise. SS I 19 107 28
"You surprise me very much. SS I 20 115 49
Lady Middleton without the smallest surprise or distrust. SS I 21 120 6
It suggested no other surprise than that Elinor and SS I 21 121 6
In some surprise at the familiarity of this question, or SS I 21 123 22
Elinor heard all this with attention and surprise. SS I 21 126 41
well concealed her surprise and solicitude--"may I ask if SS I 22 130 17
18
I express some surprise at so unnecessary a communication. SS I 22 132 40
She remembered too, her own surprise at the time, at his SS I 22 134 49
Dashwoods to express his surprise on seeing them in town, SS II 5 171 30
I do assure you that nothing would surprise me more than SS II 7 182 9
more than surprise, when you know that I am in town. SS II 7 186 38
Marianne, to the surprise of her sister, determined on SS II 8 192 5
leave them exposed to a surprise; and chance had less in SS II 10 213 4
face, and found him with some surprise to be her brother. SS II 11 221 6
civilities with some surprise, but much more pleasure. SS II 12 230 6
But at last she found herself with some surprise, accosted SS III 2 271 5
first ebullition of surprise and satisfaction was over, " SS III 4 292 55
or future, would ever surprise her, for she believed her SS III 5 293 2
"You surprise me; I should think it must nearly have SS III 5 296 21
With great surprise therefore, did she find herself SS III 6 303 11
taken their mother by surprise on the following forenoon. SS III 7 308 4
It gave her no surprise that she saw nothing of Mrs. SS III 7 309 6
my marriage, I had seen without surprise or resentment. SS III 8 330 69
"At Longstaple!" he replied, with an air of surprise-- "no, SS III 12 359 18
name, which does not surprise us; but to our great SS III 13 371 38
39
was a partnership which cd not be noticed without surprise. W 331 11
The surprise of the young ladies may be imagined. W 344 21
He loved to take people by surprise, with sudden visits at W 355 28
As it happened however, he did not give more surprise than W 355 28
Compliments always take you by surprise, and me never. PP I 4 14 5
where her appearance created a great deal of surprise.-- PP I 7 32 42
He repeated the question, with some surprise at her PP I 10 52 49
eagerly expressing her surprise at their sudden return PP I 15 73 11
took their brother by surprise, and hurrying off as if PP I 17 86 9
who took her so much by surprise in his application for PP I 18 90 5
of surprise, Mrs. Bennet instantly answered, "Oh dear!-- PP I 19 104 3
4
in the business, was the surprise it must occasion to PP I 22 123 3
---- and to the great surprise of all the party, when Mr. PP II 7 170 7
surprise, Mr. Darcy, and Mr. Darcy only, entered the room. PP II 9 177 1
It must have been a most agreeable surprise to Mr. Bingley PP II 9 177 4
to catch her words with no less resentment than surprise. PP II 11 190 8
She could not yet recover from the surprise of what had PP II 12 195 1
"is not this nice? is not this an agreeable surprise?" PP II 16 219 2
and all surprise was shortly lost in other feelings. PP II 17 224 2
seemed immoveable from surprise; but shortly recovering PP III 1 251 51
gardener's expression of surprise, on beholding his master, PP III 1 251 52
"What will be his surprise," thought she, "when he knows PP III 1 255 58
The surprise of such an application was great indeed; it PP III 1 256 64
no small degree of surprise to her relations, by PP III 2 260 1
surprise in her uncle and aunt, as made every thing worse. PP III 2 260 2
to own the truth, with Wickham!--imagine our surprise. PP III 4 273 3
Surprise was the least of her feelings on this PP III 4 279 24
her mind, she was all surprise--all astonishment that PP III 4 279 24
first exclamations of surprise and horror, Mr. Gardiner PP III 4 280 26
to the door, the joyful surprise that lighted up their PP III 5 286 21
at your surprise tomorrow morning, as soon as I am missed. PP III 5 291 60
it, for it will make the surprise the greater, when I PP III 5 291 60
was another very welcome surprise; for his chief wish at PP III 8 309 5
me is to give you great surprise; I hope at least it will PP III 10 325 2
Jane looked at Elizabeth with surprise and concern. PP III 11 334 36
she saw, to her infinite surprise, there was reason to PP III 13 346 22
The surprise of the rest of the family, on hearing who PP III 15 361 5
Darcy, in a tone of surprise and emotion, "that you have PP III 16 365 4
"No indeed; I felt nothing but surprise." PP III 16 370 30
"Your surprise could not be greater than mine in being PP III 16 370 31
His surprise was great. PP III 16 371 40
Sir Thomas heard, with some surprise, that it would be MP I 1 9 10
Edmund expressed his pleasure and surprise. MP I 6 57 33
Guess my surprise, when I found that I had been asking the MP I 6 58 37
This is rather a surprise to me." MP I 9 91 38
"Why should it surprise you? MP I 9 91 39
however, gives me no surprise; for there is nothing in the MP I 9 95 71
expressed his extreme surprise and vexation, and he walked MP I 10 101 33
What is there to surprise you in it?" MP I 13 125 16
Surprise, consciousness, and pleasure, appeared in each of MP I 18 169 23
said, with much surprise, "why have you no fire to-day?" MP III 1 312 5

SURPRISE/SURPRIZED

This cannot have taken-you by surprise. MP III 1 316 29
Sir Thomas looked at her with deeper surprise. MP III 1 316 31
Fanny, I have had a very agreeable surprise this morning. MP III 2 332 23
His surprise was not so great as his father's, at her MP III 3 335 6
The surprise of your refusal, Fanny, seems to have been MP III 4 352 44
He took me wholly by surprise. MP III 4 353 45
Fanny, to her great surprise, that she had previously seen MP III 7 383 32
If the talking aunt had taken me quite by surprise, it E II 6 198 7
not hear the sound of at first, without great surprise. E III 2 319 3
Frank Churchill, with a look of surprise and displeasure.-- E III 2 324 24
could imagine with what surprise and mortification she E III 2 327 38
could not but feel some surprise, and a little displeasure, E III 6 353 3
Quite a surprise to me! E III 8 381 15
It is impossible to express our surprise. E III 10 395 30
Emma even jumped with surprise;--and, horror-struck, E III 10 395 33
34
Every moment had brought a fresh surprise; and every E III 11 411 43
and every surprise must be matter of humiliation to her.-- E III 11 411 43
comparison, exciting no surprise, presenting no disparity, E III 11 413 48
now you are come back, that will rather surprise you." E III 13 425 2
3
restraints, that it did not take her wholly by surprise. E III 14 438 8
stating her extreme surprise at not having had the E III 14 442 8
not take him wholly by surprise, that he was rather in E III 17 465 25
The news was universally a surprise wherever it spread; E III 17 468 33
There, the surprise was not softened by any satisfaction. E III 17 469 36
I have been silent from surprise merely, excessive E III 18 473 24
have been silent from surprise merely, excessive surprise. E III 18 473 24
"I was just going to tell you of our agreeable surprise in E III 18 476 45
that I will not greatly surprise me if, with all our P III 3 17 4
"Indeed!" was the reply, and with a look of surprise. P III 3 19 15
that it was rather a surprise to her to find Mary alone; P III 5 36 21
hours, &c.; and their surprise at his accounts, at P III 8 64 4
The surprise of finding himself almost alone with Anne P III 9 78 22
street; but his evident surprise and vexation, at the P III 12 115 68
surprise, that he had not been at all aware of who she was. P IV 3 143 18
and it did not surprise her, therefore, that Lady Russell P IV 4 147 7
and surprise, with Admiral and Mrs. Croft's compliments. P IV 6 162 1
"well, now you shall hear something that will surprise you. P IV 6 170 30
31
first effects of strong surprise were over with her. P IV 7 175 6
It did not surprise, but it grieved Anne to observe that P IV 7 176 9
encounter Lady Russell's surprise; and now, if she were by P IV 7 178 27
consider his attaching himself to her, with some surprise. P IV 8 182 10
Elliot, and as general a surprise that Miss Elliot should P IV 9 206 88
not but express some surprise at Mrs. Smith's having P IV 9 211 100
Surprise was the strongest emotion raised by their P IV 10 216 18
Anne's only surprise was, that affairs should be in P IV 10 217 20
latter could not be more than the surprise of the moment. P IV 10 221 32
other; and checking the surprise which she could not but P IV 10 222 39
of doubtful meaning, of surprise rather than gratification, P IV 10 226 65
Only think, Miss Elliot, to my great surprise I met with P IV 10 228 71
All the surprise and suspense, and every other painful P IV 11 245 77
for the accident--some surprise at any body's attempting S 1 365 1
There was a great deal of surprise but still more pleasure S 9 406 1
at surprise, by the grandeur of her own conceptions.-- S 10 418 1

SURPRISED (111)

temper I should not be surprised at her appealing to her LS 2 245 1
that he could not be surprised at any effect produced on LS 8 255 2
said, "I was never more surprised in my life than by Sir LS 20 276 5
I should not be surprised if he were to change his mind at LS 23 284 6
My dear madam Your letter has surprised me beyond LS 41 309 1
Mrs Vernon surprised & incredulous, knew not what to LS 42 312 4
Chagrined and surprised, they were obliged, though SS I 9 41 6
Elinor could not be surprised at their attachment. SS I 11 53 2
surprised her by its extravagant testimony of both. SS I 12 58 1
Surprised and alarmed they proceeded directly into the SS I 15 75 2
Her mother was surprised, and Elinor again became uneasy. SS I 16 84 5
"A fortnight!" she repeated, surprised at his being so SS I 16 87 25
Mrs. Dashwood was surprised only for a moment at seeing SS I 17 90 1
Elinor looked surprised at his emotion, but trying to SS I 17 95 49
Marianne was surprised and confused, yet she could not SS I 18 100 28
29
She surprised Elinor very much as they returned into the SS I 20 113 40
therefore I am a little surprised, I confess, at so SS I 22 128 10
I dared tell you all, you would not be so much surprised. SS I 22 129 11
"You may well be surprised," continued Lucy; "for to be SS I 22 129 16
I confess myself so totally surprised at what you tell me, SS I 22 131 29
which had often surprised her, the picture, the letter, SS II 1 139 1
So surprised at their coming to town, though it was what SS II 4 164 21
He looked surprised and said, "I beg your pardon, I am SS II 5 173 42
Berkeley Street, January. how surprised you will be, SS II 7 186 38
By which the Colonel was surprised to find that she was SS III 3 284 22
I am not in the least surprised at it; from his style of SS III 5 299 35
You would be surprised to hear how often I watched you, SS III 8 326 55
pained, surprised and not surprised, was silent attention. SS III 9 336 9
possession of the living, surprised her a little at first. SS III 12 357 2
to us, and should not be surprised to see him walk in to- SS III 12 358 6
seemed the only person surprised at her not giving more. SS III 14 374 5
I should not be surprised if you were to be thought one of W 315 1
"You will not be surprised at Charles's impatience, said W 330 11
He was evidently surprised & discomposed.-- W 334 13
old friends were quite surprised to see me amongst them--& W 344 20
who, though extremely surprised, was not unwilling to PP I 6 26 38
"I am no longer surprised at your knowing only six PP I 8 39 52
Every body was surprised; and Darcy, after looking at her PP I 9 43 20
Elizabeth was surprised, but agreed to it immediately. PP I 11 56 12
Elizabeth could not but look surprised. PP I 16 77 11
"You may well be surprised, Miss Bennet, at such an PP I 16 77 12
and she was rather surprised to find that he entertained PP I 17 87 12
Bingley; what it contains, had surprised me a good deal. PP I 21 116 6
7
of their removal surprised her, she saw nothing in it PP I 21 116 8
equally surprised to find that he meditated a quick return. PP I 22 124 11
replied, "why should you be surprised, my dear Eliza?-- PP I 22 124 14
15
Charlotte,--"you must be surprised, very much surprised,-- PP I 22 125 17
be surprised, very much surprised,--so lately as Mr. PP I 22 125 17
Jane confessed herself a little surprised at the match; PP I 23 127 7
not have been at all surprised by her ladyship's asking us PP II 6 160 2
"I am the less surprised at what has happened," replied PP II 6 160 3
"I should not be surprised," said Darcy, "if he were to PP II 9 178 10
Elizabeth looked surprised. PP II 9 179 24
The tete a tete surprised them. PP II 9 179 26
instead of being again surprised by Mr. Darcy, she saw on PP II 10 182 2
Elizabeth was surprised, but said not a word. PP II 11 189 3
and preparing her to be surprised, she related to her the PP II 17 224 1
He looked surprised, displeased, alarmed; but with a PP II 18 233 27
manner, they were again surprised, and Elizabeth's PP III 1 254 57
That he was surprised by the connexion was evident; he PP III 1 255 59
"I was never more surprised than by his behaviour to us. PP III 1 257 69
Mrs. Gardiner was surprised and concerned; but as they PP III 1 258 76
Elizabeth was not surprised at it, as Jane had written the PP III 4 273 1
Elizabeth was surprised, however, that Wickham should PP III 8 314 22
I must confess myself surprised by your application; I did PP III 10 321 2
Your uncle is as much surprised as I am--and nothing but PP III 10 321 2
said, "I was surprised to see Darcy in town last month. PP III 10 328 15
16
They were of course all intending to be surprised; but PP III 14 351 2
Now, Lizzy, I think I have surprised you. PP III 15 363 18
"I must ask whether you were surprised?" said Elizabeth. PP III 16 370 37
Mrs. Price seemed rather surprised that a girl should be MP I 1 11 19
in being so surprised, and persuade her to speak openly. MP I 2 15 10
Fanny was too much surprised to do more than repeat her MP I 3 25 8
In extent it is a mere nothing--you would be surprised at MP I 6 61 54
She was a little surprised that he could spend so many MP I 7 66 14
"I am just as much surprised now as I was at first that MP I 9 93 53
She began to be surprised at being left so long, and to MP I 10 97 1
"I am rather surprised," said she, "that Mr. Crawford MP I 12 115 5
I was surprised to see Sir Henry such a stick. MP I 13 122 2
"I am not at all surprised," said Miss Crawford, after a MP I 15 144 32
Fanny, quite surprised, endeavoured to show herself MP I 18 168 16
If they are not perfect, I shall be surprised. MP I 18 169 21
Sir Thomas had been a good deal surprised to find candles MP II 1 182 22
have been very much surprised had either of my daughters, MP III 1 319 39
I should have been much surprised, and much hurt, by such MP III 1 319 39
I may be sorry, I may be surprised--though hardly that, MP III 4 347 16
undertake the part, we must not be surprised at the rest." MP III 4 350 28
What chiefly surprised Edmund was, that Crawford's sister, MP III 6 366 3
I saw him draw back surprised, and I was sorry that Mr. MP III 13 423 2
Never had she been more surprised, seldom more delighted, E III 2 328 40
Emma was a good deal surprised; but begged her to speak. E III 4 337 3
"I am not at all surprised at you, Harriet. E III 4 347 37
Mrs. Weston looked surprised, and said, "I did not know E III 5 344 6
probably have been less surprised than any of us, for you E III 13 425 10
11
She had been extremely surprised, never more so, than when E III 17 467 31
I never was more surprised--but it does not make me E III 18 471 19
who would not be surprised to find themselves in a house P III 3 18 5
6
not have been surprised if Sir Walter had asked more;--had P III 3 22 23
and she was not at all surprised, at the end of it, to P III 5 41 46
It would have surprised Anne, if Louisa could have readily P III 10 88 27
that Anne was not surprised to see Mrs. Clay stealing, a P IV 4 145 2
"Ha! he was surprised at that;" and added, "certainly you P IV 4 146 3
"Westgate-Buildings must have been rather surprised by the P IV 5 157 19
will be surprised to hear that they "have never gone home. P IV 6 163 7
when we were "rather surprised not to find Captain Benwick P IV 6 164 8
"I shall be surprised at least if you ever received a " P IV 6 164 8
"Mr. Elliot!" repeated Anne, looking up surprised. P IV 9 194 21
"I hardly know," replied Captain Wentworth, surprised. P IV 11 240 57
He surprised her by quitting clara immediately on their S 7 396 1
"I dare say I do look surprised, said she--because these S 9 410 1
She was already helped to tea--which surprised him--so S 10 416 1

SURPRISES (5)

Many surprises were awaiting him. MP III 3 334 1
the full value of the other joyful surprises at hand. MP III 3 334 2
questions must be answered, and surprises be explained. E III 3 333 4
untaught feeling on his side, and this surprises me. P IV 8 183 10
but I have heard nothing which really surprises me. P IV 9 207 91

SURPRISING (5)

cordiality is not very surprising--& yet it shews an LS 5 249 1
and it seemed rather surprising to him that anybody could SS II 14 251 16
You see the house in the most surprising manner. MP I 6 53 2
more surprising that the place can have been so improved. MP I 6 55 17
Woodhouse, for such surprising good fortune--(again E III 8 379 8

SURPRIZE (58)

by your reply, and surprize is more easily assumed, and NA I 3 26 8
"Do you indeed!--you surprize me; I thought it had not NA I 6 42 24
aloud with grateful surprize; and her companion NA I 9 62 10
A gleam of sunshine took her quite by surprize; she looked NA I 11 83 16
had observed with some surprize, that John Thorpe, who was NA I 12 95 17
felt something more than surprize, when she thought she NA I 12 95 17
His manner might sometimes surprize, but his meaning must NA I 14 114 49
"I cannot take surprize to myself on that head. NA II 1 133 34
wonder at your surprize; and I am really fatigued to death. NA II 1 134 37
pronounce it with surprize within twenty minutes of five! NA II 5 162 27
She was gazing on it with the first blush of surprize. NA II 6 165 4
The General was flattered by her looks of surprize, which NA II 7 178 21
He was prevented, however, from even looking his surprize NA II 10 203 8
be unhappy; but my surprize would be greater at NA II 10 204 20
also her concern and surprize, began to inquire into Miss NA II 10 205 25
found, with some surprize, that her two young friends were NA II 11 208 1
they would take him by surprize there some day or other, NA II 11 209 5
first perturbation of surprize had passed away, in a "good NA II 13 222 7
and great was their surprize, and warm their displeasure, NA II 14 237 21
"Catherine took us quite by surprize yesterday evening," NA II 14 237 21
Mr. and Mrs. Morland's surprize on being applied to by Mr. NA II 16 249 1
Mrs. Jennings received the refusal with some surprize, and SS II 3 153 1
indeed it took me by surprize, as I had not the smallest MP II 1 184 25
this, and looked with some surprize at the speaker. MP II 1 186 32
and with greater surprize therefore he must regard her MP II 2 188 3
(at least Robert) by surprize, and I shall lose every one; MP II 4 212 31
life, that she was all surprize and embarrassment; and MP II 4 215 47
with, "I have something to tell you that will surprize you. MP II 5 218 12
Sir Thomas, as if waiting more to accomplish the surprize. MP II 5 218 13
The only surprize I can feel is that this should be the MP II 5 218 18
This is quite a surprize, Fanny. MP II 5 223 46
She saw decision in his looks, and her surprize and MP II 8 253 4
the door, what was her surprize to find her cousin Edmund MP II 9 261 1
help an exclamation of surprize, a hint of her unfitness, MP II 10 275 11
Does his staying longer surprize you?" MP II 11 287 18
something planned as a pleasant surprize to herself. MP II 12 291 1
And the next day did bring a surprize to her. MP II 12 291 1
But this was only the beginning of her surprize. MP II 12 291 3
The surprize was now complete; for in spite of whatever MP II 12 291 5
There was even pleasure with the surprize. MP II 12 292 5
was sometimes taken by surprize at his being still able to E I 2 18 12
"You surprize me! E I 5 36 4
actually looked red with surprize and displeasure, as he E I 8 60 31
32
and found to his great surprize that Mr. Elton was E I 8 68 58
Emma saw Mrs. Weston's surprize, and felt that it must be E I 15 125 6
Her father was quite taken up with the surprize of so E I 17 141 4
in all the favouring warmth of surprize and conjecture. E II 4 184 10
to have her share of surprize, introduction, and pleasure. E II 5 190 21
and it was an agreeable surprize to her, therefore, to E II 6 196 2
dialogue which ensued of surprize, and inquiry, and E II 8 214 13
They might chuse to surprize her." E II 8 215 14
of it, the mystery, the surprize, is more like a young E II 8 217 29
took her agreeably by surprize--a second, slightly but E II 8 227 86
"Oh! no--there is nothing to surprize one at all.-- E II 14 271 12
Emma's only surprize was that Jane Fairfax should accept E II 15 285 12
The extent of your admiration may take you by surprize E II 15 287 26
of my admiration for her will ever take me by surprize.-- E II 15 288 36
by the best judges, for surprize--but there was great joy. E II 17 302 23

SURPRIZED (44)

"Why should you be surprized, sir?" NA I 3 26 7
For a moment Catherine was surprized; but Mrs. Thorpe and NA I 4 33 5
which at once surprized and amused her companion. NA I 10 72 9
a moment's silence, "how surprized I was to see him again. NA I 10 72 11
people that had surprized her so much a few mornings back. NA I 11 84 17
had no scruple in owning herself greatly surprized by it. NA I 13 102 26
was then most agreeably surprized by General Tilney's NA I 13 103 28
have been abroad then?" said Henry, a little surprized. NA I 14 106 3
You bid me be surprized on your friend's account, and NA II 1 133 34
much was Catherine then surprized by the General's NA II 5 156 4
She knew not that she had any right to be surprized, but NA II 5 161 25
came I up that staircase!" he replied, greatly surprized. NA II 9 194 7
"No, and I am very much surprized. NA II 9 195 20
Upon this conviction, she would not be surprized if even NA II 10 200 3
and they pretended to be quite surprized to see me out. NA II 12 217 2
The young people could not be surprized at a decision like NA II 16 250 3
But he will be very much surprized that Mrs. Grant should MP II 5 217 10

and I cannot but be surprized that such an elegant lady as MP II 5 220 30
He was surprized; but after a few moments silent MP II 5 226 59
with him, nobody was surprized except her brother and his E I 2 15 2
I should be surprized if, after seeing them, you could be E I 4 32 32
that you cannot be surprized, Mr. Knightley, at this E I 5 40 24
She was so surprized she did not know what to do. E I 7 50 1
She read, and was surprized. E I 7 50 4
would be very much surprized if she knew what had happened. E I 7 55 40
"Certainly," replied he, surprized, "I do not absolutely E I 8 60 29
equal; and am rather surprized indeed that he should have E I 8 61 37
"She will not be surprized, papa, at least." E I 9 79 59
I am sure I was very much surprized when I first heard she E I 9 79 60
Some people are surprized, I believe, that the eldest was E I 9 80 72
Perry was surprized to hear you had fixed upon south end." E I 12 105 54
every body was either surprized or not surprized, and had E I 15 126 9
either surprized or not surprized, and had some question E I 15 126 9
Emma was most agreeably surprized.-- E I 17 140 3
For half an hour Mr. Weston was surprized and sorry; but E I 18 144 2
I do not know that I ever saw anybody more surprized. E II 1 157 7
Every body is so surprized; and every body says the same E II 1 159 18
she was so completely surprized that she could not avoid a E II 3 173 25
and Emma was rather surprized to see the constitution of E II 6 198 5
was only surprized that there could ever have been a doubt. E II 8 215 14
I was quite surprized;--very glad, I am sure; but really E II 8 223 63
glad, I am sure; but really quite surprized. E II 8 223 63
"I am not at all surprized that he should have fallen in E II 14 271 11
And so I am not to be surprized that Jane Fairfax accepts E II 15 288 39

SURPRIZES (1)
Surprizes are foolish things. E II 8 228 92

SURPRIZING (3)
It was to Catherine the most surprizing insensibility. NA I 15 125 48
of a ball was no longer surprizing to her; she felt it to MP II 10 272 4
"Well! that is quite surprizing, for we have had a vast E I 1 10 26

SURRENDER (2)
over, Emma could fairly surrender all her attention to the E II 8 214 13
Elton in vain--by the surrender of all the dangerous E II 8 219 44

SURROUND (1)
If two moments, however, can surround with difficulties, a MP III 15 437 2

SURROUNDED (23)
living in the world & surrounded with temptation, should LS 14 264 3
When she saw her indeed surrounded only by their immediate NA II 4 149 1
rooms she had now seen surrounded three sides of the court, NA II 8 183 2
where every man is surrounded by a neighbourhood of NA II 9 197 29
So surrounded, so caressed, she was even happy! NA II 14 233 9
The hills which surrounded the cottage terminated the SS I 6 29 3
you seem to me to be surrounded with difficulties, and you SS II 2 146 6
Mary was surrounded by red coats the whole eveng. W 337 15
already overstocked, surrounded by inferior minds with W 361 31
She wrote cheerfully, seemed surrounded with comforts, and PP II 3 146 19
and of course, so surrounded by admirers, must be MP I 4 39 10
I made my bow in form, and as Mrs. Sneyd was surrounded by MP I 5 51 40
on a little lawn, surrounded by shrubs in the rich foliage MP I 7 65 13
She was immediately surrounded by supplications, every MP I 18 171 28
the equal of those who surrounded her, to be at peace from MP III 6 370 11
She was in high spirits, and surrounded by those who were MP III 13 421 2
fortunate creature, and surrounded with blessings in such E I 3 21 4
or rather surrounded, by the whole gang, demanding more. E III 3 334 6
and sorrowful regret that had ever surrounded it.-- E III 14 435 4
Had you not been surrounded by other friends, I might have E III 16 459 46
Miss Elliot, surrounded by her cousins, and the principal P IV 8 186 23
if he would; she was so surrounded and shut in: but she P IV 8 188 42
in the kingdom, surrounded by three great proprietors, P IV 10 217 20

SURROUNDING (12)
of forty surrounding families cannot prevent her. NA I 1 16 11
its buildings an surrounding country, whether she drew, or NA I 8 56 11
same aspect; the walls surrounding which I built and NA II 7 175 15
pleasure from the surrounding objects, she soon began to NA II 7 181 41
the general good opinion of their surrounding acquaintance. SS I 1 3 1
affliction as rendered her careless of surrounding objects. SS I 3 16 7
The house and the garden, with all the objects surrounding SS I 9 40 1
fresh admiration of the surrounding country; in his walk SS I 18 96 4
in the minds of the surrounding families, that he is PP I 1 3 2
awed, by the grandeur surrounding him, that he had but PP II 6 162 11
Of all the sources of evil surrounding the former, since E III 12 421 17
Immediately surrounding Mrs. Musgrove were the little P IV 2 134 29

SURRY (14)
The first winter assembly in the Town of D. in Surry was W 314 1
in Shropshire, what is passing of that nature in Surry?-- W 320 2
than usual absent from Surry, were exciting of course E I 11 91 2
in a regular way by their Surry connections, or seen at E I 11 91 2
their confined society in Surry; the pleasure of looking E I 18 145 5
There was one person among his new acquaintance in Surry, E II 7 206 4
Frank Churchill's stay in Surry; for, in spite of Mr. E II 12 257 1
Surry is full of beauties." E II 14 273 23
Surry is the garden of England." E II 14 273 24
are called the garden of England, as well as Surry." E II 14 273 25
"I never heard any county but Surry called so." E II 14 274 26
a rich West Indian from Surry, the other, a most S 5 387 1
from Surry & Camberwell, were an ever-ready consolation.-- S 6 389 1
Surry & the family from Camberwell were one & the same.-- S 11 420 1

SURVEY (8)
They took a slight survey of all; and Catherine was NA II 8 184 4
at the cottage, came to take a survey of the guest. SS I 18 99 15
wished to avoid any survey of the past that might weaken SS III 11 352 16 17
a short survey, to be decent looking rooms, walked on. PP III 14 352 19
full survey of her face and her frock in easy indifference. MP I 2 12 3
manner would he choose, to take a survey of the grounds?-- MP I 9 84 1
come to take his daily survey of how things went on, and MP III 10 403 15
Emma was not sorry to have such an opportunity of survey; E I 4 31 27

SURVEYING (4)
As they were surveying the last, the General, after NA II 8 185 5
word, and, after briefly surveying them and their SS I 19 106 22
Elizabeth, after slightly surveying it, went to a window PP III 1 246 5
Mrs. Rushworth submitted, and the question of surveying MP I 9 89 32

SURVEYOR (3)
I expect my surveyor from Brockham with his report in the NA II 11 210 6
Who is surveyor now?"-- W 349 24
"Kellynch will be with a surveyor, to tell me how to bring P IV 9 203 72

SURVIVE (3)
His own father did not long survive mine, and within half PP II 12 200 5
not in rational expectation survive such a blow as this. PP III 8 311 13
it is, when undue influence does not survive the grave!-- E III 10 398 55

SURVIVED (2)
He survived his uncle no longer; and ten thousand pounds, SS I 1 4 4
of his children, and of his wife, if she survived him. PP III 8 308 1

SURVIVING (3)
of surviving my share in this disappointment. S. V. LS 37 306 1
of his incivility in surviving her loss--he always SS III 14 379 19
solicitude for the surviving friends; and, in a reasonable E III 9 387 12

SURVIVOR (1)
Let us flatter ourselves that I may be the survivor." PP I 23 130 18

SUSAN (158)
Lady Susan Vernon to Mr Vernon. Langford, Decr. LS 1 243 1
Lady Susan to Mrs Johnson. Langford. LS 2 244 1
Lady Susan in a letter to her brother, has declared her LS 3 246 1
Susan, & we shall depend on his joining our party soon. LS 3 247 1
that I can gather, Lady Susan possesses a degree of LS 4 248 2
Lady Susan to Mrs Johnson. Churchill. LS 5 249 1
that I have seldom seen so lovely a woman as Lady Susan. LS 6 251 1
of confidence in Lady Susan; but her countenance is LS 6 251 1
Lady Susan to Mrs Johnson. Churchill. LS 7 252 1
Lady Susan has certainly contrived in the space of a LS 8 255 1
Mrs Johnson to Lady Susan. Edward St. LS 9 256 1
you my dearest Susan, Mr De Courcy may be worth having. LS 9 256 1
Lady Susan to Mrs Johnson. Churchill. LS 10 257 1
life, to know that you were married to Lady Susan Vernon. LS 12 261 4
your partiality for Lady Susan is no secret to your LS 12 261 5
Lady Susan, to a young man of his age & high expectations. LS 13 262 1
from Lady Susan to contradict the late shocking reports. LS 13 262 1
to think well of Lady Susan, that his assurances as to LS 13 262 1
To impute such a design to Lady Susan would be taking from LS 14 263 1
I can have no veiw in remaining with Lady Susan than to LS 14 263 1
beyond the hope of conviction against Lady Susan. LS 14 264 2
which have been attributed to selfishness in Lady Susan. LS 14 264 2
Lady Susan had heard something so materially to the LS 14 264 3
to the prejudice of Lady Susan, as I am now convinced how LS 14 264 4
Lady Susan was far from intending such a conquest, & on LS 14 265 4
I know that Lady Susan in coming to Churchill was governed LS 14 265 5
my real sentiments of Lady Susan; you will know from this LS 14 265 6
of marrying Lady Susan--not that he is in no danger of LS 15 266 1
is a sad thing & of course highly afflicting to Lady Susan. LS 15 266 2
Lady Susan to Mrs Johnson. Churchill. LS 16 268 1
Lady Susan had received a line from him by that day's post LS 17 269 1
Lady Susan who had been shedding tears before & shewing LS 17 269 2
Lady Susan is surely too severe, because Frederica does LS 17 270 4
severity of Lady Susan, & the silent dejection of LS 17 270 5
Yet Reginald still thinks Lady Susan the best of mothers-- LS 17 271 7
readily credit what Lady Susan has made him & wants to LS 17 271 7
Lady Susan finds it necessary for her own justification LS 17 272 8
Susan she would always appear to much greater advantage. LS 18 273 3
Lady Susan to Mrs Johnson. Churchill. LS 19 273 1
In the breakfast room we found Lady Susan & a young man of LS 20 275 2
Lady Susan behaved with great attention to her visitor, & LS 20 276 3
over again, & told Lady Susan three times that he had seen LS 20 276 3
At length Lady Susan, weary I believe of her situation, LS 20 276 4
As we went upstairs Lady Susan begged permission to attend LS 20 276 5
discourse with Lady Susan has since had it's effect, he is LS 20 278 9
Even Lady Susan seemed a little disconcerted by this LS 20 278 10
Lady Susan to Mrs Johnson. Churchill. LS 22 280 1
my return to the parlour, Lady Susan entered the room. LS 23 284 6
James is gone, Lady Susan vanquished, & Frederica at peace. LS 23 285 8
The quarrel between Lady Susan & Reginald is made up, & we LS 24 285 1
I have entirely misunderstood Lady Susan, & was on the LS 24 287 9
Frederica does not know her mother--Lady Susan means LS 24 287 9
Lady Susan therefore does not always know what will make LS 24 287 9
Lady Susan I beleive wishes to speak to you about it, if LS 24 287 9
Reginald was glad to get away, & I went to Lady Susan; LS 24 287 10
I see how closely she observes him & Lady Susan. LS 24 291 16
Lady Susan to Mrs Johnson. Churchill. LS 25 291 1
Mrs Johnson to Lady Susan. Edward St. LS 26 295 1
How long Lady Susan will be in town, or whether she LS 27 297 3
Mrs Johnson to Lady Susan. Edward St. LS 28 297 1
Lady Susan to Mrs Johnson. Upper Seymour St. LS 29 298 1
Lady Susan to Mr De Courcy. Upper Seymour St. LS 30 299 1
Lady Susan to Mrs Johnson. Upper Seymour St. LS 31 301 1
Mrs Johnson to Lady Susan. Edward St. LS 32 302 1
Lady Susan to Mrs Johnson. Upper Seymour St. LS 33 303 1
Mr De Courcy to Lady Susan. hotel. LS 34 304 1
Lady Susan to Mr De Courcy. Upper Seymour St. I LS 35 304 1
Mr De Courcy to Lady Susan. hotel. LS 36 305 1
Lady Susan to Mr De Courcy. Upper Seymour St. LS 37 306 1
Mrs Johnson to Lady Susan. Edward St. LS 38 306 1
Adeiu, my dearest Susan. LS 38 307 3
Lady Susan to Mrs Johnson. Upper Seymour St. LS 39 307 1
Lady Susan, but to tell us that they are parted forever! LS 40 308 1
unwelcome visit from Lady Susan, looking all chearfulness LS 41 309 1
But Lady Susan declared that as she was now about to fix LS 41 310 3
passed between him & Lady Susan to sink the latter lower LS 42 311 2
Mrs Vernon waited on Lady Susan, shortly after her arrival LS 42 311 2
Frederica was no more altered than Lady Susan; the same LS 42 311 3
No unkindness however on the part of Lady Susan appeared. LS 42 312 3
Lady Susan was unable to express her sense of such LS 42 312 5
offer of it, & tho' Lady Susan continued to resist, her LS 42 312 5
Lady Susan announced her being married to Sir James Martin. LS 42 312 6
which Lady Susan had doubtless resolved on from the first. LS 42 313 7
Whether Lady Susan was, or was not happy in her second LS 42 313 9
you will be so useful to Susan, and you will teach Betsey, MP III 6 372 20
were her two sisters, Susan, a well-grown fine girl of MP III 7 377 9
Susan, you should have taken care of the fire." MP III 7 379 17
"I was up stairs, mamma, moving my things;" said Susan, in MP III 7 379 18
between herself and Susan, one of whom was clerk in a MP III 7 381 26
Within the room all was tranquil enough, for Susan having MP III 7 382 28
Susan and an attendant girl, whose inferior appearance MP III 7 383 32
necessary for the meal; Susan looking as she put the MP III 7 383 32
glad of a little tea, and Susan immediately set about MP III 7 383 33
Susan had an open, sensible countenance; she was like MP III 7 384 33
of Rebecca, against whom Susan had also much to depose, MP III 7 385 38
Fanny, in those early days, had preferred her to Susan; MP III 7 386 40
Up jumped Susan, claiming it as her own, and trying to get MP III 7 386 42
mother's protection, and Susan could only reproach, which MP III 7 386 42
"Now, Susan," cried Mrs. Price in a complaining voice, " MP III 7 386 44
Poor little Betsey; how cross Susan is to you! MP III 7 386 44
You know I told you not to touch it, because Susan is so MP III 7 386 44
Susan have my knife, mamma, when I am dead and buried.'-- MP III 7 386 44
chamber that she was to share with Susan. MP III 7 387 47
the remonstrances of Susan, given as they were--though MP III 8 390 8
knowledge of Susan, and a hope of being of service to her. MP III 9 395 4
Susan had always behaved pleasantly to herself, but the MP III 9 395 4
Susan saw that much was wrong at home, and wanted to set MP III 9 395 4
Susan was only acting on the same truths, and pursuing the MP III 9 395 4
Susan tried to be useful, where she could only have gone MP III 9 395 4
away and cried; and that Susan was useful she could MP III 9 395 4
In every argument with her mother, Susan had in point of MP III 9 396 5
and gradually placed Susan before her sister as an object MP III 9 396 6
Susan, she found, looked up to her and wished for her good MP III 9 396 6
give occasional hints to Susan, and endeavour to exercise MP III 9 396 6
in an act of kindness by Susan, which after many MP III 9 396 7
possession of her desired; Susan was established in the MP III 9 396 7
Susan shewed that she had delicacy; pleased as she was to MP III 9 397 7
all that must be hourly grating to a girl like Susan. MP III 9 397 8
soon became--not that Susan should have been provoked into MP III 9 397 8
Fanny had peace, and Susan learnt to think it no MP III 9 398 9
Susan had read nothing, and Fanny longed to give her a MP III 9 398 9
every day--as she and Susan were preparing to remove as MP III 10 399 2
herself and Susan, within ten minutes, walking towards the MP III 10 401 10
agreeable, and letting Susan have her share of MP III 10 404 15
use, and Susan was entertained in a way quite new to her. MP III 10 404 15
kind and proper in the notice he took of Susan. MP III 10 406 21
he, addressing himself to Susan, "which I think the MP III 11 410 16
readings and conversation with Susan were much suspended. MP III 12 418 5
to Susan, and again awakened the same interest in them. MP III 12 418 6
Susan was growing very fond of her, and though without any MP III 12 418 7
Susan, who had an innate taste for the genteel and well- MP III 12 419 8
Poor Susan was very little better fitted for home than her MP III 12 419 9
would have a material drawback in leaving Susan behind. MP III 12 419 9
Susan was her only companion and listener on this, as on MP III 13 428 14
Susan was always ready to hear and to sympathize. MP III 13 428 14
My father wishes you to invite Susan to go with you, for a MP III 15 443 23
and with leave to take Susan, was altogether such a MP III 15 443 24
must be spoken to, Susan prepared, every thing got ready. MP III 15 443 25
of Susan herself, was all serving to support her spirits. MP III 15 443 25
her thoughts, and as for Susan, now unexpectedly gratified MP III 15 444 26
Does Susan go?"--were questions following each other MP III 15 445 29

Just before their setting out from Oxford, while Susan was MP III 15 446 34
a humiliation; and Susan to feel with some anxiety, that MP III 15 446 35
Susan, too, was a grievance. MP III 16 448 3
By her other aunt, Susan was received with quiet kindness. MP III 16 448 3
to kiss and like her; and Susan was more than satisfied, MP III 16 448 3
But it was possible to part with her, because Susan MP III 17 472 31
Susan became the stationary niece--delighted to be so!-- MP III 17 472 31
Susan could never be spared. MP III 17 472 31
offering odds that either Susan Diana or Arthur wd appear S 5 385 1
Susan & Arthur!-- S 9 407 1
Susan able to come too!-- S 9 407 1
"And how has Susan born the journey?--& how is Arthur?--& S 9 407 1
"Susan has born it wonderfully. S 9 407 1
I sounded Susan--the same thought had occurred to her.-- S 9 409 1
Susan never eats I grant you--& just at present I shall S 9 411 1
Susan had only superintended their final removal from the S 10 414 1
I must hurry home, for Susan is to have Leaches at one S 12 424 1
SUSAN'S (24)
Lady Susan's intentions are of course those of absolute LS 8 256 4
the very rapid increase of Lady Susan's influence. LS 11 259 1
hardly suppose that Lady Susan's veiws extend to marriage. LS 11 259 1
Lady Susan's age is itself a material objection, but her LS 12 260 2
the true motive of Lady Susan's conduct, & removes all the LS 14 264 3
while he is so very eager in Lady Susan's justification. LS 15 266 2
Surely it is not to Lady Susan's credit that he should be LS 15 267 7
nor so blooming as Lady Susan's--& she has quite the LS 17 270 5
these few days at Lady Susan's request, into her dressing LS 17 271 7
who came by Lady Susan's direction to call Frederica down. LS 20 275 1
at seeing Reginald come out of Lady Susan's dressing room. LS 24 287 8
was derived from Lady Susan's asking her whether she LS 42 312 4
Lady Susan's maternal fears were then too much awakened LS 42 312 6
eyes, meaning to screen it at the same time from Susan's. MP III 7 386 40
love or assist; and of Susan's temper, she had many doubts. MP III 8 391 9
was the means of opening Susan's heart to her, and giving MP III 9 397 7
A quick looking girl of Susan's age was the very worst MP III 10 403 15
She hoped it was not wrong; though after a time, Susan's MP III 12 419 8
her father and mother to Susan's going with her--the MP III 15 444 25
to find any thing to hold Susan's clothes, because Rebecca MP III 15 444 26
of Portsmouth, and how Susan's face wore its broadest MP III 15 445 32
of every resolution; but Susan's presence drove him quite MP III 15 445 33
But in truth, I doubt whether Susan's nerves wd be equal S 5 387 1
sister Susan's, are more distressing than all the rest.--" S 5 388 1
SUSCEPTIBILITIES (2)
with the refined susceptibilities, the tender emotions NA I 2 19 3
His genius & his susceptibilities might lead him into some S 7 398 1
SUSCEPTIBILITY (2)
shall I call it? susceptibility to her feelings; which are PP III 5 284 10
Germ of incipient susceptibility to the utmost Energies of S 8 403 1
SUSCEPTIBLE (1)
weak, and her nerves susceptible to the highest extreme of P IV 2 129 1
SUSPECT (60)
& of insensibility to yours, you will hardly suspect me. LS 30 301 4
knew not what to suspect, & without any change in her own LS 42 312 4
"I suspect," said Isabella, in a low voice, "there is no NA I 13 100 12
"Oh! I know no harm of him; I do not suspect him of pride. NA II 1 130 9
to suspect her friend, could not help watching her closely. NA II 4 149 1
but Henry began to suspect the truth, and something, in NA II 10 204 18
entered their heads to suspect an attachment on either NA II 16 249 1
as she had reason to suspect that the misery of SS I 11 55 8
And, after all, what is it you suspect him of?" SS I 15 79 28
It must be Willoughby therefore whom you suspect. SS I 15 81 42
"I suspect," said Elinor, "that to avoid one kind of SS I 18 97 6
"I begged him to exert himself for fear you should suspect SS I 22 134 52
on serious reflection to suspect it in the present case, SS II 1 139001
"Then I rather suspect that my interest would do very SS II 2 149 28
whom I would not rather suspect of evil than Willoughby, SS II 7 189 50
brought so forward between them, and nobody suspect it! SS III 1 258 7
his real favourite, to make her suspect it herself. SS III 6 305 16
of the neighbourhood, to suspect any part of what had SS III 8 324 42
only is it horrible to suspect a person, who has been what SS III 10 345 20
"I suspect the Dr to have an attack of the asthma,--& that W 318 2
in general, but did not suspect him of descending to such PP I 16 80 33
of her ladyship, I suspect his gratitude misleads him, and PP I 16 83 57
And that made the men suspect something, and then they PP II 16 221 17
You must not suspect me. PP III 12 343 32
I suspect that in this comprehensive and (may I say) MP I 11 110 24
that she was inclined to suspect the truth and purity of MP I 16 153 3
archly--you suspect a confederacy between us, and that MP II 8 259 20
"to convince me that you suspect no trick, and are as MP II 8 259 22
had not been obliged to suspect that his previous MP II 10 278 20
Her mother, however, could not stay long enough to suspect MP III 7 378 10
would not have him really suspect a circumstance as her E I 1 11 33
wife in the case; she did suspect danger to her poor E I 4 27 5
or other, depending, I suspect, much more upon what is E I 11 96 26
"I suspect they do not satisfy Mrs. Weston. E I 18 149 26
(Harriet, as Emma must suspect, as ready as the best of E II 5 187 4
I smile because you smile, and shall probably suspect E II 8 216 27
whatever I find you suspect; but at present I do not see E II 8 216 27
I do suspect he would not have had a pair of horses for E II 8 223 63
That she was not immediately ready, Emma did suspect to E II 10 240 6
I do suspect that he is not really necessary to my E II 13 264 2
Her sensibilities, I suspect, are strong--and her temper E II 15 289 40
as you may suspect--but this is quite between ourselves. E II 18 307 18
not to be angry with you, I suspect, whatever he may be.-- E III 2 330 48
she let it pass, and seem to suspect nothing?-- E III 4 341 34
He began to suspect him of some double dealing in his E III 5 343 2
Mr. Knightley began to suspect him of some inclination to E III 5 343 2
She did not suspect him. E III 6 361 40
full of intrigue, that he should suspect it in others.-- E III 15 446 15
not help saying, "I do suspect that in the midst of your E III 18 478 64
65
"Oh! no, no, no--how can you suspect me of such a thing?-- E III 18 478 66
Perhaps I am the readier to suspect, because, to tell you E III 18 478 67
praise, such as made Anne suspect that her keener powers P III 10 92 47
to suspect) to prevent his thinking of a second choice. P IV 4 147 6
"I suspect," said Sir Walter coolly, "that Admiral Croft P IV 6 166 15
Why was she to suspect herself of another motive? P IV 7 175 6
replied Anne; "but I suspect that you are considering me P IV 9 195 25
and half inclined to suspect that the pen had only fallen, P IV 11 233 24
It was impossible for Charlotte not to suspect a good deal S 10 412 1
you than I suspect you are in the habit of taking."-- S 10 416 1
Charlotte could not but suspect him of adopting that line S 10 418 1
SUSPECTED (56)
assured that Mr Johnson suspected nothing of your LS 5 249 1
I am suspected of matrimonial veiws in my behaviour to her. LS 14 263 1
Mr Johnson has for some time suspected de courcy of LS 32 303 1
of what she had only suspected before, that she might have LS 42 313 7
No longer could he be suspected of indifference for a play; NA I 12 92 4
She had long suspected the family to be very high, and NA II 1 129 1
never suspected him of liking me till this moment?" NA II 3 146 17
For the world would she not have her weakness suspected; NA II 7 174 5
her, exactly over this suspected range of cells, and the NA II 8 188 17
just opened; "if I had suspected the letter of containing NA II 10 204 12
natural result of the suspected engagement, and at others NA II 11 209 5
She rather suspected it to be so, on the very first SS I 8 36 1
Willoughby certainly does not deserve to be suspected. SS I 15 81 44
been suspected of a much nearer connection with her. SS II 9 208 28
your brother or sister suspected a word of the matter;-- SS III 1 258 7
Happy to find that she was not suspected of any SS III 1 260 8
If she suspected any prepossession elsewhere, it could not SS III 1 266 38
and ashamed to be suspected of half her economical SS III 12 357 3
Not a soul suspected anything of the matter, not even SS III 13 370 37
I have suspected it some time, but I am now convinced." PP I 7 29 6
Miss Bingley saw, or suspected enough to be jealous; and PP I 10 52 53
answer; and Elizabeth suspected herself to be the first PP II 6 166 38
particulars, and I only suspected it to be Bingley from PP II 10 185 28
suspected that every power of pleasing would fail her. PP III 2 260 1
"Colonel Forster did own that he had often suspected some PP III 5 290 46
which could not be suspected by Jane, to whom she had PP III 11 334 36
"I suspected as much," replied Elizabeth. PP III 13 349 46
and her own, it was suspected by her father that she PP III 19 386 5
save her from being suspected of something better; or, MP I 3 28 38
may be fairly suspected, you think?" said Edmund. MP I 11 109 20
"Oh! dear, ma'am--nobody suspected you----- MP I 13 126 23
it was a pleasant joke--suspected only of concealing MP II 12 291 1
before she had suspected for what she was detained. MP II 13 301 7
Fanny suspected what was going on. MP III 3 334 5
herself, and grieved lest they should have been suspected. MP III 7 377 10
He had suspected his agent of some underhand dealing--of MP III 10 404 15
and could he have suspected how many privations, besides MP III 11 412 30
of wealth; and this, she suspected, was all the conquest MP III 14 436 16
desirable to have them suspected; and the quiet transition E I 5 41 31
half-syllables very much suspected that he was announcing E I 14 118 4
never, for an instant, suspected it to mean any thing but E I 16 134 5
move superior; but Emma suspected she might have been glad E II 8 219 44
and throw up a sash, without its being suspected. E II 11 252 31
to find fault, but she suspected that there was no E II 14 270 4
She suspected that it had; that it would not have been so E II 16 298 58
things I assure you are suspected; and yet by their E II 18 310 34
I am sure I never suspected it, you did it so naturally." E III 4 339 14
Mr. Knightley suspected in Frank Churchill the E III 5 346 17
without being suspected of introducing Robert Martin."-- E III 6 361 40
than to care for Mr. Martin, or to be suspected of it." E III 11 411 37
Poor Mr. Woodhouse little suspected what was plotting E III 14 434 3
Donwell and Highbury, the truth must have been suspected.-- E III 14 441 8
single so long for our sakes, need be suspected now. P III 5 35 14
of being vague;--they suspected great injury, but knew not P III 7 54 4
share in it she suspected; and that Mr. Elliot's idea P III 12 107 21
"You should not have suspected me now; the case so P IV 11 244 73
SUSPECTING (19)
I cannot help suspecting the truth of everything she said. LS 20 278 8
enough to feel, that in suspecting General Tilney of NA II 15 247 14
afraid of his sister's suspecting any thing, that was SS I 22 131 32
on the other hand, suspecting that it would not be in her SS II 10 214 7
time, however, slyly suspecting that another year would SS II 14 253 25
her carpet-work, little suspecting what was to come--for SS III 1 258 7
Elizabeth was far from suspecting that she was herself PP I 6 23 12
to join them; but suspecting them to be playing high she PP I 8 37 21
Now, do not be suspecting me of a pun, I entreat." MP I 6 60 49
future, that her father might not be again suspecting her. MP II 3 201 23
in the least suspecting that she was addressing a lover.-- E I 6 47 31
unnatural creature, in suspecting that he may have learnt E I 18 145 10
but I cannot help suspecting either that, after making his E II 8 217 32
I cannot help suspecting him. E II 8 226 79
Sometimes, indeed, I have thought you were half suspecting E III 18 474 34
not been able to avoid suspecting before; and instead of P IV 6 167 19
or always suspecting the other of being worse than it was. P IV 7 175 6
little suspecting that to my eye you could never alter." P IV 11 243 67
had been too quick in suspecting them to indicate a P IV 12 249 3
SUSPECTS (4)
I am persuaded that Mrs. Smith suspects his regard for SS I 15 78 26
and that if she suspects the nature of my feelings for him, PP I 21 118 15
can serve them best, or suspects them to be less in MP I 11 109 18
Mrs. Grant, I believe, suspects him of a preference for MP I 12 116 8
SUSPENCE (1)
As for Jane, her anxiety under this suspence was, of PP I 23 129 14
SUSPEND (2)
"I would by no means suspend any pleasure of yours," he PP I 18 94 43
and not a word to suspend decision was uttered by her. P III 3 24 37
SUSPENDED (17)
the comedy so well suspended her care, that no one, NA I 12 92 4
the Abbey--for some time suspended by his conversation on NA II 5 161 24
Eleanor's work was suspended while she gazed with NA II 10 204 18
Every hope, every expectation from him suspended, at least, NA II 13 226 25
and crying; her voice often totally suspended by her tears. SS I 16 83 3
me--ought he not to have suspended his belief? ought he SS II 7 190 56
when its action was suspended by his hastily advancing, SS III 8 317 1
2
weather, which totally suspended the improvement of her PP I 17 88 15
likeness of Mr. Wickham suspended, amongst several other PP III 1 247 9
Listening and wondering were all suspended for a time, for MP I 12 118 22
an eagerness which was suspended only by intervals of MP I 14 137 23
But the concerns of the theatre were suspended only for an MP I 15 142 25
the entrance of Edmund the next moment, suspended it all. MP I 18 169 22
Jealousy and bitterness had been suspended: selfishness MP II 1 175 2
a blow that had been suspended, and still hoped uncertain MP II 5 227 69
readings and conversation with Susan were much suspended. MP III 12 418 5
misuse, when a knock at the door suspended every thing. P IV 3 142 17
SUSPENSE (39)
any cause in suspense, cannot be too cautiously concealed. LS 20 277 5
and keeping her in suspense at a most interesting part, by NA I 14 107 9
Her suspense was of full five minutes' duration; and she NA II 1 132 16
while the affair was in suspense, and every thing secured NA II 2 138 1
The past suspense of the morning had been ease and quiet NA II 2 138 1
through the varieties of suspense, security, and NA II 2 140 11
Every thing in such suspense and uncertainty; and seeing SS I 22 133 42
of the many years of suspense in which it may involve you, SS II 2 148 14
by the fever of suspense, the consequence of all this was SS II 7 185 16
suspense in which she must now be travelling towards them. SS III 7 315 26
moment's horrible suspense, she ran immediately into the SS III 9 333 3
He was brought, not from doubt or suspense, but from SS III 13 361 3
A pause of suspense ensued.-- W 355 28
cooking, & anxious suspense however they were obliged to W 360 30
of increasing my love by suspense, according to the usual PP I 19 108 19
Darcy, in wretched suspense, could only say something PP III 4 277 11
She could not bear such suspense; and hastily seizing a PP III 9 320 32
them so many previous months of suspense and vexation. PP III 13 347 28
the test of many months suspense, and enumerating with PP III 17 376 36
Their suspense lasted an hour or two. MP III 6 373 23
and to leave every thing in greater suspense than ever. MP III 12 417 4
Suspense must be submitted to, and must not be allowed to MP III 12 418 6
Let there be an end of this suspense. MP III 13 424 4
While you were at all in suspense I kept my feelings to E I 7 53 24
Such events are very interesting, but the suspense of them E III 3 333 4
I have been walking all this way in complete suspense. E III 10 394 27
We both abhor suspense. E III 10 394 27
cause to him, for my suspense while all was at stake?-- E III 14 443 8
In this state of suspense they were befriended, not by any E III 19 483 10
all such solicitudes and suspense been theirs, without P III 4 29 8
she was soon spared all suspense; for after the Miss P III 7 60 31
32
looked rather in suspense, and as if waiting for more. P III 8 67 25
a dreadful extension of suspense; and Captain Wentworth P III 12 114 64
standing in a moment's suspense, was obliged, and not P IV 7 180 36
suspense good or bad, her affection would be his for ever. P IV 9 192 2
After the usual period of suspense, the usual sounds of P IV 10 216 17
or two, every thing seemed to be in suspense, or at an end. P IV 10 216 19
possible, any thing might be defied rather than suspense. P IV 11 237 41
All the surprise and suspense, and every other painful P IV 11 245 77
SUSPENSION (5)
suspicion at the total suspension of all Isabella's NA I 8 57 21
suspension of agony by creeping far underneath the clothes. NA II 6 170 12
awhile, till another suspension brought Mrs. Elton's tones E III 2 324 22
there having been a suspension of all intercourse by P IV 4 148 12

returned, after a short suspension, to ruin the concert; P IV 11 241 60
SUSPICION (73)
& no longer harbour a suspicion which cannot be more LS 14 263 1
could not avoid a little suspicion at the total suspension NA I 8 57 21
herself, or one moment's suspicion of any past scenes of NA II 5 161 25
the suspicion of there being many chambers secreted. NA II 8 183 2
as his merit, and the suspicion--the hope of his affection SS I 4 21 15
This suspicion was given by some words which accidentally SS I 11 55 8
The lady would probably have passed without suspicion, had SS I 11 57 17
But suspicion of something unpleasant is the inevitable SS I 15 79 29
"I love Willoughby, sincerely love him; and suspicion of SS I 15 81 43
and suggested the suspicion of that lady's knowing, or SS I 21 126 41
every suspicion of the truth from her mother and sisters. SS II 1 140 4
was enough inclined for suspicion, to have found out the SS II 2 147 12
a suspicion could never have entered her head! SS III 1 266 38
that suspicion in his mind which had recently entered it. SS III 4 290 36
hand-writing altogether, immediately gave her a suspicion. SS III 8 328 61
Not the smallest suspicion, therefore, had ever occurred SS III 13 364 13
crime, because, had any suspicion of it occurred to the SS III 13 371 38
served to prevent every suspicion of good-will, she issued SS III 14 373 3
or of talking, to give a suspicion of his regretting the SS III 14 377 12
"No indeed, I had not the smallest suspicion of it. W 317 2
But in an instant arose the dreadful suspicion of his PP I 18 89 1
2
was, my confidence was as natural as your suspicion. PP II 3 148 26
Wickham has created, a suspicion of their nature shall not PP II 12 200 5
power, and suspicion certainly not in your inclination. PP II 12 202 5
and had this led to no suspicion, the faces of both as PP III 13 346 22
suspicion, she was not distressed by his repeating it. PP III 15 364 25
He had never had the slightest suspicion. PP III 16 371 40
nor any thing else, awakened a suspicion of the truth. PP III 17 372 1
Though suspicion was very far from Miss Bennet's general PP III 17 372 3
A week had passed in this way, and no suspicion of it MP I 2 15 9
she may exert all her powers of pleasing without suspicion. MP I 5 45 12
I had not a suspicion that I could be doing any thing MP I 5 51 40
to meet them with a great anxiety to avoid the suspicion. MP I 7 68 17
Sir Thomas would have been deeply mortified by a suspicion MP I 11 107 4
to be less liable to the suspicion of wanting sincerity or MP I 11 110 22
"If you have such a suspicion, something must be done, and MP I 17 162 18
I had not the smallest suspicion of your acting having MP II 1 184 25
to them than she had any suspicion of, and each found it MP II 7 250 56
might suggest, a suspicion of his having any such views MP II 12 291 5
Then, her understanding was beyond every suspicion, quick MP II 12 294 16
Not to excite suspicion by her look or manner was now an MP III 1 322 50
might be going on; a suspicion rushed over her mind which MP III 1 325 60
Of that, he had no suspicion. MP III 2 326 3
as might warrant strong suspicion in a predisposed mind. MP III 5 362 17
suspicion of being so; darkened, yet fancying itself light. MP III 6 367 5
protested against her suspicion as most injurious, and E I 15 130 28
thought, at first, could not escape her father's suspicion. E I 17 140 3
At this moment, an ingenious and animating suspicion E II 1 160 21
22
Emma wondered whether the same suspicion of what might be E II 5 192 33
or suspicion, was a most comfortable circumstance. E II 5 193 35
Bates was speaking, a suspicion darted into my head, and I E II 8 224 65
think you can hardly be quite without suspicion"----- E II 12 260 29
She was not present when the suspicion first arose. E III 5 343 2
brought him yet stronger suspicion of there being a E III 5 344 2
every former ungenerous suspicion, and left her nothing E III 8 379 9
he had had no previous suspicion of--and there was every E III 10 399 57
I never had the slightest suspicion, till within the last E III 11 405 11
A mind like her's, once opening to suspicion, made rapid E III 11 407 32
But Harriet rejected the suspicion with spirit. E III 11 410 36
not conceive that any suspicion could be excited by it; or E III 12 417 5
she was not without suspicion; but I have no doubt of her E III 14 438 8
thither as often as might be, and with the least suspicion. E III 14 439 8
it to delicacy, and a suspicion, from some appearances, E III 17 463 15
I wonder whether Jane has any suspicion." E III 17 468 34
But is it possible that you had no suspicion?-- E III 18 477 53
Elizabeth could not conceive that such an absurd suspicion P III 5 34 13
Elizabeth, though resenting the suspicion, might yet be P III 5 35 17
suspicion of Mrs. Croft's side, to give a bias of any sort. P III 6 48 18
without the smallest suspicion of his possessing the P IV 3 144 19
have been open to the suspicion of overturning them on S 1 364 1
did not quarrel with the suspicion of his finding her S 7 395 1
was laying her open to suspicion by Lady D's giving a S 7 400 1
This glorious sentiment seemed quite to remove suspicion. S 7 400 1
SUSPICIONS (30)
You see, Miss Morland, the injustice of your suspicions. NA I 14 107 9
the examples to justify even the blackest suspicions!-- NA II 8 186 13
explain to Eleanor the suspicions, from which the other NA II 9 193 5
the dreadful nature of the suspicions you have entertained. NA II 9 197 29
the grossly injurious suspicions which she must ever blush NA II 10 200 3
privy to the shocking suspicions which she had so idly NA II 14 230 3
This, and Marianne's blushing, gave new suspicions to SS I 18 100 22
nice in proclaiming his suspicions of her regard for SS I 21 125 36
with the uneasiness and suspicions they had caused to Mrs. SS II 4 162 13
that had passed, her suspicions of Willoughby's SS II 5 172 39
This person's suspicions, therefore, I have had to oppose, SS III 1 263 29
would guard her from the suspicions of the impertinent. PP I 6 21 1
The suspicions which had just arisen of Mr. Darcy and PP III 2 261 6
She saw that the suspicions of the whole party were PP III 3 268 8
The vague and unsettled suspicions which uncertainty had PP III 10 326 3
convinced him that the suspicions whence, he must confess MP II 10 280 32
previous to the suspicions of this very day; she could E I 15 129 23
suspicions of there there being something to conceal." E II 6 203 41
I told you that your suspicions would guide mine." E II 8 217 29
"If so, you must extend your suspicions and comprehend Mr. E II 8 217 30
I do not require you to adopt all my suspicions, though E II 8 217 32
of Mrs. Weston's suspicions, to which the sweet sounds of E II 8 227 87
suspicions of Jane Fairfax's feelings to Frank Churchill. E II 9 231 2
endeavour to avoid the suspicions of others, to save your E II 13 268 11
12
suspicions, and imagined capable of pitiful resentment. E II 16 290 4
for though her suspicions were by no means removed, she E III 5 350 28
the particulars of his suspicions, every look described, E III 5 351 38
from the abominable suspicions of an improper attachment E III 12 421 17
than any of us, for you have had your suspicions.-- E III 13 425 10
11
suggested suspicions not favourable of what he had been. P IV 5 161 27
SUSPICIOUS (11)
to act an ungenerous, a suspicious part by our family, he SS I 15 81 43
expression that could give her words a suspicious tendency. SS II 2 147 9
something still more suspicious in the manner in which Mr W 324 3
Mrs. Gardiner, rendered suspicious by Elizabeth's warm PP II 2 142 18
Miss Crawford, a little suspicious and resentful of a MP II 7 242 25
If I avoided his name entirely, it would look suspicious. MP III 12 416 2
How cheerful, how animated, how suspicious, how busy their E I 7 56 46
No suspicious flourishes now of apology or concern; it was E II 13 265 5
Admiral Croft?" was Sir Walter's cold suspicious inquiry. P III 3 21 19
of Monkford, however suspicious appearances may be, but a P III 4 26 1
should see nothing suspicious or inconsistent, nothing to P IV 4 147 7
SUSPICIOUSLY (3)
She looked suspiciously at her sister; Maria's countenance MP I 14 135 18
She was disgustingly, was suspiciously reserved. E II 2 169 15
feeling before, passed suspiciously through Emma's brain; E II 5 191 26
SUSSEX (13)
stay in Sussex that they may have some hunting together. LS 8 254 1
The family of Dashwood had been long settled in Sussex. SS I 1 3 1
so far distant from Sussex as Devonshire, which, but a few SS I 4 23 20
hearts behind them in Sussex, and pretended to see them SS I 7 34 5
she brought with her from Sussex, was more likely to be SS I 11 54 5
"Have you been lately in Sussex?" said Elinor. SS I 16 87 27
I suppose you were very sorry to leave Sussex." SS I 21 123 21
not as many genteel young men in Devonshire as Sussex?" SS I 21 123 27
in remaining so much in Sussex, and the arguments with SS III 13 368 28
at the expense of a journey from Sussex to do them honour. SS III 14 375 8
towards that part of the Sussex coast which lies between S 1 363 1
found along the coast of Sussex;--the most favoured by S 1 368 1
fixed on the coast of Sussex, but was undecided as to the S 9 408 1
SUSTAIN (1)
might have as much hope to sustain them as possible. MP III 4 345 2
SUSTAINED (3)
sustained in his purpose by a conviction of its justice. NA II 15 247 15
was evident; he sustained it however with fortitude, and PP III 1 255 59
The young people were all at home, and sustained their MP I 2 12 3
SWALLOW (6)
These Tilneys seem to swallow up every thing else." NA I 13 98 2
but she had appetite, and could not swallow many mouthfuls. NA II 13 228 27
exorbitant; but she will swallow any thing; and the SS I 21 120 6
she could scarcely swallow two mouthfuls before tears MP I 2 13 4
feelings created, made it easier to swallow than to speak. MP I 7 74 57
Now, if I were to swallow only one such dish--what do you S 10 418 1
SWALLOWED (9)
I arrived last night about five, & had scarcely swallowed LS 29 299 2
back to the hotel, swallowed their dinner in haste, to NA I 15 116 1
all her thinking powers swallowed up in the reflection of NA II 14 237 20
and Elinor, as she swallowed the chief of it, reflected SS II 8 198 29
on them all, soon swallowed up every private care; and PP III 4 278 20
This deeper anxiety swallowed them up. MP I 16 157 28
ill-flavour, and then be swallowed and forgotten; for I am MP II 12 297 33
But here, one subject swallowed up all the rest. MP III 7 382 29
of my right side, before I had swallowed it 5 minutes.-- S 10 418 1
SWAY (1)
Every body may sway it; let those who would be happy be P III 10 88 26
SWAYED (2)
You think me unsteady--easily swayed by the whim of the MP III 3 343 41
Harriet, tempted by every thing and swayed by half a word, E II 9 233 24
SWEAR (1)
"They are gone back to Kellynch, and almost made me swear " P IV 9 203 72
SWEARING (1)
parading to her, or swearing at them; so different from NA II 5 157 5
SWEARS (1)
Mrs. Charles quite swears by her, I know; but I just give P III 6 45 9
SWEAT (1)
A could sweat stood on her forehead, the manuscript fell NA II 6 170 12
SWEEP (8)
with its semi-circular sweep and green gates, and, as they NA II 11 212 17
chuse papers, project shrubberies, and invent a sweep. SS III 14 374 7
end of the town with a shrubbery & sweep in the country.-- W 322 2
thing, the sweep of every preparation would be sufficient. MP II 2 187 2
him at last most impatiently in the sweep, and cried out. MP II 12 291 1
his, and walking along the sweep as if not knowing where MP II 12 291 4
He had gone beyond the sweep--some way along the Highbury E I 15 127 16
"Now,"--said Emma, when they were fairly beyond the sweep E III 10 392 8
SWEEP-GATE (3)
to have it stop at the sweep-gate was a pleasure to NA II 14 233 8
they passed through the sweep-gate, "will be to find E I 13 116 46
had they passed the sweep-gate and joined the other E I 15 129 24
SWEEPGATE (1)
when the great iron sweepgate opened, and two persons E III 3 332 3
SWEEPING (2)
well as what now is, sweeping round from the lane I stood MP II 7 242 23
to say she thought the kitchen chimney wanted sweeping. E II 9 236 46
SWEEPS (1)
grounds and extensive sweeps of country, and still more P III 11 95 9
SWEET (81)
is absolutely sweet, & her voice & manner winningly mild. LS 6 251 1
When you have the happiness of bestowing your sweet little LS 20 277 5
She is a sweet girl, & deserves a better fate. LS 23 284 4
of mine, a Miss Andrews, a sweet girl, one of the sweetest NA I 6 40 12
My sweet Catherine, do support me, persuade your brother NA I 8 57 23
friend exclaim aloud to James, "what a sweet girl she is! NA I 9 62 8
so feeling a heart, so sweet a temper, to be so easily NA I 13 98 2
Now, my sweet Catherine, all our distresses are over; you NA I 13 100 17
"Oh! my sweet Catherine, in your generous heart I know it NA I 15 119 18
"As to that, my sweet Catherine, there cannot be a doubt, NA II 1 136 48
"My sweet love, do not be so abominably affected. NA II 3 144 8
Oh! what a sweet little cottage there is among the trees-- NA II 11 214 23
was determined, were such sweet proofs of her importance NA II 13 221 6
no sweet elation of spirits can lead me into minuteness. NA II 14 232 7
all good; her smile was sweet and attractive, and in her SS I 10 46 2
I always thought it such a sweet place, ma'am! (turning to SS I 19 107 24
Do but look, mama, how sweet! SS I 19 108 36
I never was at his house; but they say it is a sweet SS I 20 111 14
You cannot think what a sweet place Cleveland is; and we SS I 20 113 33
It is a sweet place by all accounts." SS I 20 116 60
"And here is my sweet little Annamaria," she added, SS I 21 121 9
"What a sweet woman Lady Middleton is!" said Lucy Steele. SS I 21 122 13
same; and had the natural sweet disposition of the one SS II 9 208 28
(with a great deal about sweet and love, you know, and all SS III 2 273 16
sweet figure I cut!--what an evening of agony it was!-- SS III 8 327 55
I had seen Marianne's sweet face as white as death.-- SS III 8 327 55
by so long and sweet a sleep to the extent of her hopes. SS III 9 333 3
You must have a sweet temper indeed;--I never met with any W 320 2
which with a lively eye, a sweet smile, & an open W 328 9
"Sweet little darling!--cried Margt--it quite broke my W 350 24
and pronounced her to be a sweet girl, and one whom they PP I 4 17 16
Miss Bennet was therefore established as a sweet girl, and PP I 4 17 16
she is really a very sweet girl, and I wish with all my PP I 8 36 14
You have a sweet room here, Mr. Bingley, and a charming PP I 9 42 7
"He is a sweet tempered, amiable, charming man. PP I 16 82 47
Jane met her with a smile of such sweet complacency, a PP I 18 95 48
mind gave a glow of such sweet animation to her face, as PP III 13 348 34
was sweet, and when she spoke her countenance was pretty. MP I 2 12 2
You have good sense, and a sweet temper, and I am sure you MP I 3 26 29
she was most allowably a sweet pretty girl, while they MP I 5 44 1
with only walking in this sweet wood; but the next time we MP I 9 94 57
And the morning wore away in satisfactions very sweet, if MP I 17 159 6
man;--his sister a sweet, pretty, elegant, lively girl." MP II 1 186 30
Her eyes should be darker, but she has a sweet smile; but MP II 6 230 6
I know her disposition to be as sweet and faultless as MP II 9 269 31
The gentlemen joined them; and soon after began the sweet MP II 10 273 6
You will have a sweet little wife; all gratitude and MP II 12 292 7
openness of heart, and sweet peculiarity of manner, that MP III 4 351 36
She was in a reverie of sweet remembrances. MP III 5 358 8
Oh! it was sweet beyond expression. MP III 5 358 9
Poor little sweet creature! MP III 7 387 44
Adieu, my dear sweet Fanny, this is a long letter from MP III 9 394 1
and her aunt as having the sweetest of all sweet tempers. MP III 10 405 17
sparkling sea, and your sweet looks and conversation were MP III 12 415 1
2
whose warm heart and sweet temper made him think every E I 2 15 3
Harriet certainly was not clever, but she had a sweet, E I 4 26 2
presented a very sweet mixture of youthful expression to E I 6 46 24
"Thank you, thank you, my own sweet little friend. E I 7 54 31
Only think of those sweet verses--'to Miss ----.' E I 9 74 22
"Such sweet lines!" continued Harriet--"these two last!-- E I 9 76 37
Harriet's was-- "Oh! what a sweet house!-- E I 10 83 3
4
"That sweet, amiable Jane Fairfax!" said Mrs. John E I 12 104 46
comfortable, in the sweet dependence of his having a most E I 13 109 6
"My dearest Emma, do not pretend, with your sweet temper, E I 14 123 25
suspicions, to which the sweet sounds of the united voices E II 8 227 87

I hope we shall have many sweet little concerts together. E II 14 277 38
A sweet, interesting creature. E II 15 282 5
We must not allow them to be verified in sweet Jane E II 15 283 5
It was a sweet view--sweet to the eye and the mind. E III 6 360 39
Harriet's sweet easy temper will not mind it." E III 6 364 58
there are not such elegant sweet children any where. E III 8 382 23
And is he to be rewarded with that sweet young woman?-- E III 13 426 16
Oh! she is a sweet creature! E III 16 454 13
You need not be afraid, Miss Elliot, of your own sweet P III 3 18 7
all the influence so sweet and so sad of the autumnal P III 5 33 6
them so much trash and sweet things, that they are sure to P III 6 44 8
The sweet scenes of autumn were for a while put by--unless P III 10 85 12
and still more its sweet retired bay, backed by dark P III 11 95 9
Dear, sweet Louisa!" P III 12 116 71
married 7 years--& had 4 sweet children at home;--that he S 2 371 1
And Mrs P. was as evidently a gentle, amiable, sweet S 2 372 1
SWEET-CAKE (1)
about her mother's, and sweet-cake from the beaufet--"Mrs. E II 1 155 4
SWEET-TEMPERED (3)
either of the dear sweet-tempered boys in love with her. MP I 1 7 6
Weston, like a sweet-tempered woman and a good wife, had E II 11 255 59
I regard Louisa Musgrove as a very amiable, sweet-tempered P IV 8 182 10
SWEETBREAD (2)
a delicate fricassee O sweetbread and some asparagus E III 2 329 45
loves better than sweetbread and asparagus--so she was E III 2 329 45
SWEETER (2)
With a yet sweeter smile, he said every thing that need be NA I 12 94 9
nor did she ever enjoy a sweeter feeling than the hope of P IV 5 161 30
SWEETEST (20)
a sweet girl, one of the sweetest creatures in the world, NA I 6 40 12
She is netting herself the sweetest cloak you can conceive. NA I 6 40 12
My sweetest Catherine, how have you been this long age? NA I 10 70 1
"My sweetest Catherine, is not this delightful? NA I 11 84 19
She was sure her dearest, sweetest Catherine would not NA I 13 98 2
between two of the sweetest girls in the world, who had NA I 14 114 50
"Nay, my beloved, sweetest friend," continued the other, " NA I 15 117 6
"Nay, my sweetest Catherine, this is being quite absurd! NA II 3 144 10
Lose no time, my dearest, sweetest Catherine, in writing NA II 12 218 2
by the sweetest confidence in his regret and resentment. NA II 14 231 4
assure them of their being the sweetest girls in the world. SS I 21 119 3
well knew that the sweetest girls in the world were to be SS I 21 119 3
without exception, the sweetest temper I ever met with. PP I 9 42 7
Oh! my sweetest Lizzy! how rich and how great you will be! PP III 17 378 43
had driven Julia away, was to her the sweetest support. MP III 1 176 3
smile upon him with your sweetest smiles this afternoon, MP III 13 303 15
hopes--yes, dearest, sweetest Fanny--nay--(seeing her draw MP III 3 344 41
and her aunt as having the sweetest of all sweet tempers. MP III 10 405 17
she was giving up the sweetest hours of the twenty-four to E III 8 377 1
dinner, to see how this sweetest and best of all creatures, E III 13 433 41
SWEETEST-TEMPERED (1)
Was always the sweetest-tempered, most generous-hearted, PP III 1 249 33
SWEETLY (4)
At seven o'clock, leaving Marianne still sweetly asleep, SS III 7 315 27
so easily impressed--so sweetly disposed--had in short, to E II 4 181 4
touches the instrument--though she played sweetly. E II 14 277 40
& soft blue eyes, a sweetly modest & yet naturally S 6 391 1
SWEETMEATS (1)
by a variety of sweetmeats and olives, and a good fire. SS II 8 193 7
SWEETNESS (28)
& there is peculiar sweetness in her look when she speaks LS 17 270 5
good, and the g sweetness of his countenance, is perceived. SS I 4 20 9
She thanked him again and again; and with a sweetness of SS I 9 42 10
it did not give much sweetness to the manners of one SS II 10 219 42
your sister just the same--all sweetness and affability!" SS II 13 239 6
says into a compliment on the sweetness of my temper. PP I 10 49 31
there was a mixture of sweetness and archness in her PP I 10 52 52
Your sweetness and disinterestedness are really angelic; I PP II 1 134 9
whose steady sense and sweetness of temper exactly adapted PP II 19 239 10
It is only that he is blessed with greater sweetness of PP III 12 343 32
The gentleness, modesty, and sweetness of her character MP II 12 294 16
expatiated on, that sweetness which makes so essential a MP II 12 294 16
with such ineffable sweetness and patience, to all the MP II 12 296 31
You have given the name such reality of sweetness, that MP III 3 344 41
yet higher value on the sweetness of her temper, the MP III 17 468 21
by sweetness of temper, and strong feelings of gratitude. MP III 17 472 31
and a look of great sweetness; and before the end of the E I 3 23 9
She had all the natural grace of sweetness of temper and E I 6 42 3
it does, real, thorough sweetness of temper and manner, a E I 8 63 44
The extreme sweetness of her temper must hurt his. E I 11 93 5
But, be it sweetness or be it stupidity in her --quickness E II 6 202 35
only love the blooming sweetness and the artless manner, E II 8 219 44
manner towards her; a manner of kindness and sweetness!-- E III 11 409 35
an elegance of mind and sweetness of character, which must P III 1 5 8
"A strong mind, with sweetness of manner," made the first P III 7 62 40
would always give some sweetness to the memory of her two P III 11 93 4
"Elegance, sweetness, beauty," Oh! there was no end of P IV 2 131 9
Beauty, sweetness, poverty & dependance, do not want the S 3 378 1
SWEETS (7)
in arm, again tasted the sweets of friendship in an NA I 5 35 2
still indulged in the sweets of incomprehensibility, NA II 14 234 10
and shrubs, and all the sweets of pleasure-grounds, as by MP I 9 89 32
of Fanny's, on the sweets of so protracted an autumn, they MP II 4 208 11
"The sweets of housekeeping in a country village!" said MP II 4 212 32
farmer, counteracting the sweets of poetical despondence, P III 10 85 13
The toils of the business were over, the sweets began. P IV 4 149 13
SWELL (6)
of accepted love to swell his heart, and raise his spirits. SS III 13 361 3
your porridge,"--and I shall keep mine to swell my song. PP I 6 24 22
were forced by the sudden swell of a cold gust shaking MP II 4 208 11
Let my accents swell to Mickleham on one side, and Dorking E III 7 369 16
Circumstances that might swell to half an hour's relation, E III 11 410 35
for (with a sigh) let me swell out the causes ever so E III 13 427 19
SWELLED (6)
Catherine's heart swelled; she drew away her arm, and NA I 13 100 13
natural importance was swelled into greater, but without PP III 1 245 3
hand, her wounded heart swelled again with injury, and MP II 1 175 2
She knelt in spirit to her uncle, and her bosom swelled to MP II 1 185 27
How her heart swelled with joy and gratitude, as she MP III 15 445 32
Miss Bates said a great deal; Mrs. Elton swelled at the E III 7 369 17
SWELLING (7)
me in the first angry swelling of his proud heart, without LS 25 293 3
Catherine's swelling heart needed relief. NA II 13 226 25
Marianne entered the house with an heart swelling with SS III 6 302 8
answer, and walked on, her heart swelling with indignation. PP II 10 185 33
the other, and her heart swelling with emotion, Crawford MP II 13 299 4
and in this state of swelling resentment, and mutually E I 15 132 37
they have a knack of swelling out, till they are quite as E I 18 147 19
SWEPT (7)
Catherine could have raved at the hand which had swept NA II 8 184 4
They are seen only as a nuisance, swept hastily off, and SS I 16 88 31
The party passed on--Mrs E's Sattin gown swept along the W 327 8
Three or four prices might have been swept away, any or MP III 13 428 15
and the papers swept away;-- "particularly pleasant. E II 3 170 2
towards her, and resolutely swept away by her unexamined. E III 5 349 25
no. --, Camden-Place, was swept away for many days; for P IV 4 148 10
SWERVED (1)
on such a footing as cannot be afterwards swerved from.-- MP III 11 412 20
SWIFT (1)
some one seemed with swift steps to ascend the stairs, by NA II 9 194 6
SWIFTLY (4)
of men by the door, as swiftly as the necessary caution NA I 2 21 9
half had ever gone off so swiftly before, as Catherine was NA I 9 67 33
Swiftly therefore shall her post-boy drive through the NA II 14 232 7
wish otherwise, but that the days did not pass so swiftly. E I 13 108 1
SWIFTNESS (1)
of her extraordinary swiftness in entering the house, he NA I 13 102 27
SWIMMING (1)
consideration of Fanny's swimming eyes, nothing more was MP II 11 284 9
SWINGING (1)
in the maids' room, or swinging a cot somewhere," they P III 12 113 56
SWISSERLAND (4)
They were looking over views in Swisserland. E III 6 364 59
"That may be--but not by sketches in Swisserland. E III 6 365 61
You will never go to Swisserland. E III 6 365 61
It is not Swisserland, but it will be something for a E III 6 365 67
SWITCH (1)
in the hedge with his switch; and when Mary began to P III 10 90 37
SWITZERLAND (1)
delineation; and Italy, Switzerland, and the south of NA II 10 200 3
SWOLLEN (1)
Her eyes were red and swollen; and it seemed as if her SS I 15 82 46
SWOON (1)
and felt in no danger of an hysterical fit, or a swoon. SS I 22 129 15
SWORD-CASE (1)
"Curricle-hung you see; seat, trunk, sword-case, splashing- NA I 7 46 13
SWORE (2)
in the world, but swore off many sentences in his praise. NA I 15 121 27
Motherbank; he swore and he drank, he was dirty and gross. MP III 8 389 3
SWORN (1)
woman, she & I are sworn friends; & Howard's a very W 358 28
SYLLABLE (34)
am much mistaken if a syllable of his uttering, escape her. LS 18 272 1
tho' I did not know a syllable of it till afterwards, for LS 32 302 1
as ever, & not a syllable, not a hint was dropped of any LS 41 309 1
by the exchange of a syllable with any of her fellow NA I 2 21 10
that no syllable of such a nature ever passed between us. NA II 3 144 11
meaning, which one short syllable would have given, NA II 15 242 9
"Yet not a syllable has been said to you on the subject, SS I 15 79 35
maintained; but not a syllable escaped her lips, and the SS II 8 193 6
And not a creature knowing a syllable of the matter except SS III 1 258 7
I will take my oath he never dropt a syllable of being SS III 2 273 16
without her catching a syllable, when another lucky stop SS III 3 281 9
10
She caught every syllable with panting eagerness; her hand, SS III 10 348 33
Not a syllable passed aloud. SS III 12 359 10
Scarcely a syllable was uttered that did not relate to the PP II 6 166 41
Not a syllable had ever reached her of Miss Darcy's PP III 3 270 10
without there being a syllable said of her father, or the PP III 11 336 49
Not a syllable was uttered by either; and Elizabeth was on PP III 13 346 22
Bennet sat quite still, and unable to utter a syllable. PP III 17 378 42
I never spoke a syllable about it to Sir Thomas, nor he to MP I 3 28 42
he had not breathed a syllable of it even to Mary; while MP II 13 300 7
of help had Fanny given; not a syllable for or against. MP III 3 337 10
herself capable of uttering a syllable at such a moment. MP III 10 399 4
Oh, no! shark is only one syllable. E I 9 73 17
I did not mention a syllable of it in the other room. E I 14 120 11
his house; and he was out before another syllable passed.-- E I 15 132 37
acquainted; but not a syllable of real information could E II 2 169 17
not another syllable of communication could rest with him. E II 3 172 23
attention, and every syllable of their conversation was as E II 10 243 32
that she heard every syllable of a dialogue which just E III 2 327 34
syllable of it before, of course it must have been a dream. E III 5 345 13
of deep mortification, and not another syllable followed. E III 13 429 29
indeed, and that she had not a syllable to say for him. E III 16 458 41
connexions, by whom no syllable, she believed, would ever P III 4 30 10
The six months had long been over--& not a syllable was S 3 379 1
SYLLABLES (3)
"I have not wanted syllables where actions have spoken so SS I 15 79 36
ideas; and of the few syllables that did escape her, not SS II 12 232 15
He studies too much for words of four syllables.-- PP I 10 48 20
SYMMETRY (2)
an uncommon union of symmetry, brilliancy and grace. LS 6 251 1
one failure of perfect symmetry in her form, he was forced PP I 6 23 12
SYMPATHETIC (6)
of sympathetic early rising did not advance her composure. NA II 7 175 11
to the other by the sympathetic alacrity with which they MP II 6 233 15
'When two sympathetic hearts meet in the marriage state, MP III 5 358 9
saw also with sympathetic acuteness of feeling, all that MP III 9 397 8
and the Admiral, with sympathetic cordiality, observed to P III 5 32 4
and she had this sympathetic touch in the evening, from P III 6 48 16
SYMPATHISE (1)
and myself sincerely sympathise with you, and all your PP III 6 296 11
SYMPATHISED (1)
them; and they sympathised with each other in an insipid SS II 12 229 2
SYMPATHISING (1)
having one such truly sympathising friend as Lady Russell. P III 6 42 2
SYMPATHIZE (5)
which alone could sympathize with her own, was estimable SS I 7 35 9
though she could not sympathize in his wish that the count MP I 15 138 1
Susan was always ready to hear and to sympathize. MP III 13 428 14
and very inadequate to sympathize in an attachment to Mr. E I 17 142 11
woman, and a heart to sympathize in any of the sufferings P III 9 77 18
SYMPATHIZED (1)
They praised the morning; gloried in the sea; sympathized P III 12 102 1
2
SYMPATHIZER (1)
or persuaded out, his patient listener and sympathizer. E III 6 357 33
SYMPATHIZING (1)
sympathizing in praise of Fanny's kind offices. MP I 18 170 23
SYMPATHY (20)
affectionate sympathy as Isabella chose to consider her. NA I 15 119 14
Her kindness is not sympathy; her good nature in not SS II 9 201 3
the personal sympathy of her mother, and doomed her to SS II 10 214 6
The rest of Mrs. Palmer's sympathy was shewn in procuring SS II 10 215 11
her sympathy in *her* sufferings was very sincere. SS III 7 313 20
not justify so warm a sympathy--or rather not thinking at SS III 9 336 12
be pitied;" were the kind responses of listening sympathy. MP I 13 122 3
assurance of sympathy than what a slight bow conveyed. MP II 1 184 25
She had neither sympathy nor assistance from those who MP II 5 219 27
kindness and sympathy without the sincerest gratitude." MP II 9 270 38
voice of kindness and sympathy in return, was every thing MP III 16 449 5
one of whose affectionate sympathy he was quite convinced. MP III 16 453 17
troubles with ready sympathy, and always gave her E I 10 86 24
the rest is empty sympathy, only distressing to ourselves." E I 10 87 30
"Oh! yes, sir," cried she with ready sympathy, "how you E I 11 93 7
have lavished every distinction of regard or sympathy. E III 9 389 16
There was little sympathy to be spared for any body else. E III 11 403 2
more curiosity and sympathy than she found in the separate, P III 6 42 1
doing it with so much sympathy and natural grace, as P III 8 67 28
The sympathy and good-will excited towards Captain Benwick P III 11 97 12
SYMPTOM (15)
for Bath, nothing could induce him to have a gouty symptom. LS 28 298 1
No sooner did she perceive any symptom of love in his SS I 3 17 14
a loss, nothing gave any symptom of that indigence which SS II 12 233 18
Her pulse was much stronger, and every symptom more SS III 7 310 8
Half an hour passed away, and the favourable symptom yet SS III 7 314 22
examination, that every symptom of recovery continued, and SS III 7 315 25
The gentlemen, who had hitherto disregarded every symptom, W 346 21
could she discern any symptom of love; and from the whole PP II 8 176 29
as ever, but without any symptom of peculiar regard, and I PP II 12 197 5
I can remember no symptom of affection on either side; and PP III 5 285 18
any symptom of resentment, or any unnecessary complaisance. PP III 11 335 39
never seen much symptom of it, but I wish it may be so. MP I 12 116 8
no letter, no message--no symptom of a softened heart--no MP II 3 201 24

Context	Work	Vol.	Ch.	Page	Line
was not the smallest symptom of any knowledge or suspicion	P	III	6	48	18
L. to have the smallest symptom of a decline, or any	S		11	422	1
SYMPTOMS (23)					
with all these symptoms of profligacy at ten years old,	NA	I	1	14	1
numerous openings, and symptoms of a winding stair-case,	NA	II	8	185	5
the atmosphere, the certain symptoms of approaching frost.	SS	II	5	168	10
next morning produced no abatement in these happy symptoms.	SS	III	10	342	8
The advice was followed readily, for the feverish symptoms	PP	I	7	33	44
Could there be finer symptoms?	PP	II	2	141	9
Do you see no symptoms there?"	MP	I	12	118	17
round it, to see other symptoms of recent habitation, and	MP	II	1	182	22
Edmund did not discern any symptoms of regret, and thought	MP	III	6	366	2
of Dr. Grant's gouty symptoms and Mrs. Grant's morning	MP	III	13	425	6
to some strong hectic symptoms, which seemed to seize the	MP	III	14	429	1
in a decline, that the symptoms are most alarming, and	MP	III	14	433	13
of this speech, and saw no alarming symptoms of love.	E	I	4	31	26
The symptoms were favourable.--	E	I	7	53	22
He could not understand it; but there were symptoms of	E	III	5	343	2
thought so at least--symptoms of admiration on his side,	E	III	5	343	2
"I have lately imagined that I saw symptoms of attachment	E	III	5	350	36
no absolutely alarming symptoms, nothing touching the	E	III	9	389	16
Emma saw symptoms of it immediately in the expression of	E	III	16	453	12
					13
No symptoms worse than before had appeared.	P	IV	1	121	2
and, wherever she looked, saw symptoms of the same.	P	IV	10	226	63
at Tunbridge Wells, & symptoms of the gout and a winter at	S		2	373	1
could perceive no symptoms of illness which she, in the	S		10	413	1

T (1)
the last letter to be a T; and yet that it should be any NA II 6 164 2
T'IS (1)
eagerly called out, "T'is uncle Sidney mama, it is indeed." S 12 425 1
T'OTHER (5)
"Neither one nor t'other; I might have got it for less I NA I 7 46 15
The Monk; I read that t'other day; but as for all the NA I 7 48 34
fright in the world t'other day, when Edward's name was SS I 22 133 42
Nancy,' my cousin said t'other day, when she saw him SS II 10 218 26
Two maids and two men indeed!--as I talked of t'other day.- SS III 2 277 28
T'WERE (1)
T'were Pseudo-philosophy to assert that we do not feel S 8 404 1
T. MUSGRAVE (3)
It is some foolery of that idle fellow T. Musgrave. W 348 22
And when T. Musgrave was met with again, he was W 348 22
T. Musgrave never came, & Margt was at no pains to conceal W 360 30
TABLE (163)
sit down at the end of a table, at which a large party NA I 2 22 10
The gentlemen and ladies at this table look as if they NA I 2 22 14
understand it without a table;--however I did beat him. NA I 12 96 20
violence, ordered "dinner to be on table directly!" NA II 6 165 5
at table; and, luckily, it had been the General's choice. NA II 7 175 12
As soon as she dared leave the table she hurried away to NA II 10 203 8
Catherine took her place at the table, and, after a short NA II 10 203 9
the young ladies making allowance for a bachelor's table. NA II 11 210 6
They had seldom seen him eat so heartily at any table but NA II 11 215 27
upon the elegance of her table, and of all her domestic SS I 7 32 2
make Colonel Brandon leave my breakfast table so suddenly." SS I 13 63 6
to table, which Sir John observed with great contentment. SS I 13 67 61
room and took her place at the table without saying a word. SS I 15 82 46
sat down to table indignant against all selfish parents. SS I 17 90 1
the table and continued to read it as long as he staid. SS I 19 106 22
Lucy directly drew her work table near her and reseated SS II 1 144 14
side by side at the same table, and with the utmost SS II 1 145 23
sat down to the card table with the melancholy persuasion SS II 2 151 41
found her turning from the table with a sorrowful SS II 4 165 25
sat down to the breakfast table with a happy countenance. SS II 5 167 3
His card was on the table, when they came in from the SS II 5 169 13
A note was just then brought in, and laid on the table. SS II 5 169 16
placed themselves at no great distance from the table. SS II 6 175 2
round the common working table, when a letter was SS II 7 181 7
remained fixed at the table where Elinor wrote, watching SS II 9 203 10
Twice was his card found on the table, when they returned SS II 12 230 5
them seats at her table; but as Lady Middleton's guests SS II 12 231 9
it, she walked silently towards the table, and sat down. SS III 8 317 7
and when, as he waited at table, he had satisfied the SS III 11 353 22
23
"I meant," said Elinor, taking up some work from the table, SS III 12 359 19
when they all sat down to table at four o'clock, about SS III 13 361 3
It happened close by Lady Osborne's Cassino Table; Mr W 332 11
was lounging on a vacant table near her, call Tom Musgrave W 333 13
the whole time at the same table in the same room, with W 336 14
to the other end of the table, that they might not offend W 344 20
for the profusion on the table, & absolutely protesting W 353 27
best Pembroke table, with the best tea things before her. W 355 28
carriage--but the old card table being set out, & the fish W 357 28
your game?"--cried he, as they stood round the table.-- W 358 28
He proved a very useful addition to their table; without W 359 28
a mere nothing, that had great effect at a card table. W 359 28
to preside at his table, nor was Mrs. Hurst, who had PP I 4 15 13
then walked towards a table where a few books were lying. PP I 8 37 26
The loo table, however, did not appear. PP I 10 47 1
little design for a table, and I think it infinitely PP I 10 48 15
another table with Mr. Bennet, and prepared for backgammon. PP I 14 69 17
he received at the other table between Elizabeth and Lydia. PP I 16 76 8
gathered round the other table, and Mr. Collins took his PP I 16 82 49
persons sit down to a card table, they must take their PP I 16 83 50
table at Rosings, in the absence of more eligible visitors. PP I 17 88 14
amongst the thanks of the table, the hint of a hope that PP I 18 100 68
seat at the bottom of the table, by her ladyship's desire, PP II 6 162 14
when any dish on the table proved a novelty to them. PP II 6 163 14
Their table was superlatively stupid. PP II 6 166 41
A great deal more passed at the other table. PP II 6 166 41
there being only one card table in the evening, every such PP II 7 169 5
took a newspaper from the table, and, glancing over it, PP II 9 179 24
25
books, and a billiard table, but gentlemen cannot be PP II 9 180 28
triumphantly displayed a table set out with such cold meat PP II 16 219 2
some news for you," said Lydia, as they sat down to table. PP II 16 220 8
of Maria across the table, after the welfare and poultry PP II 16 222 21
And what sort of table do they keep? PP II 17 228 31
and peaches, soon collected them round the table. PP III 3 268 6
manner till dinner was on table, they left her to vent all PP III 5 288 39
while they waited at table, and judged it better that one PP III 5 288 40
of grave reflection, soon after they were seated at table, PP III 5 289 41
42
Elizabeth took the letter from his writing table, and they PP III 7 305 43
at the head of her table, and in spirits oppressively high. PP III 8 310 7
ourselves, so there will be just room at table for him." PP III 11 333 26
Jane resolutely kept her place at the table; but Elizabeth, PP III 11 333 31
always kept a very good table, she did not think any thing PP III 11 338 60
Mr. Darcy was almost as far from her, as the table could PP III 12 340 13
had crowded round the table, where Miss Bennet was making PP III 12 341 16
room, and from all the others when they sat down to table. PP III 17 372 1
In a few minutes he approached the table where she was PP III 17 375 28
near the bottom of the table, fully expecting to feel a MP I 6 52 1
at the upper end of the table, and in observing Mr. MP I 6 52 1
to whisper across the table to Mrs. Norris, "that Dr. MP I 6 54 13
to her seat at the table, and had taken up her work again; MP I 7 71 35
going quietly to another table, on which the supper tray MP I 7 74 57
of their sitting down to table, it was a quick succession MP I 10 104 52
was allowed at the second table, and she has turned away MP I 10 105 55
are speaking what you have been told at your uncle's table. MP I 11 110 24
he took a newspaper from table, and looking over it said MP I 12 118 22
want to make a table for Mrs. Rushworth, you know.-- MP I 12 119 23
"To want to nail me to a card table for the next two hours MP I 12 119 26
passed at table, did not evince the least disapprobation. MP I 13 124 13
of plays that lay on the table, and turning it over, MP I 14 132 7
which had been left on the table, and begin to acquaint MP I 14 137 23
in committee at a separate table, with the play open MP I 15 142 25
the other three at the table, while his sister made her MP I 15 143 26
to the party round the table; and standing by them, seemed MP I 15 143 27
table--(looking round)--it certainly will not be taken." MP I 15 144 38
"Fanny," cried Tom Bertram, from the other table, where MP I 15 145 43
the opposite side of the table close to Fanny, saying to MP I 15 147 56
The table between the windows was covered with work-boxes MP I 16 153 3
a volume on the table and then taking up some others.) MP I 16 156 27
nonsense of acting, and sit comfortably down to your table. MP I 16 156 27
the fate of the billiard table, he was not proceeding MP II 1 183 24
they sat round the same table, which made Mr. Yates think MP II 2 191 10
numbers to sit down to table; and I cannot but be MP II 5 220 30
And round their enormous great wide table too, which fills MP II 5 220 30
Had the doctor been contented to take my dining table when MP II 5 220 30
wider than the dinner table here--how infinitely better it MP II 5 220 30
Five, only five to be sitting around that table! MP II 5 221 30
found, while they were at table, such a happy flow of MP II 5 223 48
and as a whist table was formed after tea--formed really MP II 5 227 68
behold either the wide table or the number of dishes on it MP II 7 238 3
after making up the whist table there would remain MP II 7 239 4
Grant, being seated at the table of prime intellectual MP II 7 239 8
to the game; and the round table was altogether a very MP II 7 240 9
but when the whist table broke up at the end of the second MP II 7 246 36
to find her cousin Edmund there writing at the table! MP II 9 261 1
Sir Thomas said no more; but when they sat down to table MP II 10 272 4
She went accordingly to the table, where she was in the MP II 13 307 30
Sir Thomas came towards the table where she sat in MP III 1 318 39
And sure enough there was a book on the table which had MP III 3 336 9
Lady Bertram's being just on the other side of the table MP III 3 343 40
you here, sitting at this table at work; and then your MP III 5 360 14
and Betsey's eating at table without restraint, and MP III 10 407 23
hashes, brought to table as they all were, with such MP III 11 413 30
her father's head, to the table cut and knotched by her MP III 15 439 9
down to the breakfast table, which by dint of much unusual MP III 15 445 31
a piece of paper on the table containing, as he said, a E I 9 71 10
A piece of paper was found on the table this morning-- (E I 9 78 50
taking the paper from the table, she returned it----- "Oh! E I 9 81 79
80
on the table, took it up, and examined it very attentively. E I 9 82 81
and replacing it on the table,) he would consider it as E I 9 82 83
the upper end of the table) has so few vagaries herself, E I 14 120 11
very lately that I was almost sure it must be on the table. E II 1 157 10
the others; but when the table was again safely covered, E II 8 218 38
39
Frank Churchill, at a table near her, most deedily E II 10 240 1
All the minor arrangements of table and chair, lights and E II 11 255 59
at the bottom of the table himself, with the usual regular E II 16 291 4
Dinner was on table.-- E II 16 298 56
till her being seated at table and taking up her spoon. E III 2 328 44
and this was left upon the table as good for nothing. E III 4 339 18
the large modern circular table which Emma had introduced E III 5 347 18
after examining a table behind him, which he could reach E III 5 347 19
and producing the box, the table was quickly scattered E III 5 347 20
She gave a slight glance round the table, and applied E III 5 347 21
should have looked on the table instead of looking just E III 5 348 21
She was immediately up, and wanting to quit the table; but E III 5 349 25
be all out of doors--a table spread in the shade, you know. E III 6 355 20
will be to have the table spread in the dining-room. E III 6 355 21
Mr. Knightley had another reason for avoiding a table in E III 6 356 29
They sat down to tea--the same party round the same table-- E III 14 434 2
had left it open on the table near her, had she closed it, P III 1 7 12
Journeys, London, servants, horses, table,--contradictions P III 2 13 6
seating himself near the table, and taking up the P III 9 79 27
sitting down to the same table with him now, and the P III 11 99 21
as he sat near a table, leaning over it with folded arms, P III 12 112 54
On one side was a table, occupied by some chattering girls, P IV 2 134 29
rise, to walk to a distant table, and, leaning there in P IV 5 160 26
at home," were laid on the table, with a courteous, P IV 10 226 64
Materials were all at hand, on a separate table; he went P IV 11 229 4
towards the distant table, Captain Wentworth's pen ceased P IV 11 231 10
though nearer to Captain Wentworth's table, not very near. P IV 11 231 12
She had only time, however, to move closer to the table P IV 11 236 40
the room to the writing table, and standing with his back P IV 11 236 40
of her own at her own table; to their protection she must P IV 11 237 41
42
pleasanter still--Morgan, with his "dinner on table."-- S 5 389 1
but the sopha & the table, & the establishment in general S 10 413 1
TABLE-CLOTH (1)
and Thomas and the table-cloth, now alike needless, were SS III 11 355 45
TABLES (13)
Not tables, toilettes, wardrobes, or drawers, but on one NA II 5 158 17
was straightened by tables, Mrs E. & her party were for a W 332 11
On entering the Tearoom, in which two long tables were W 332 11
dining room, where the tables were prepared, & the neat W 336 14
I had seven tables last week in my drawingroom. W 350 24
They all paint tables, cover skreens and net purses. PP I 8 39 45
When the card tables were placed, he had an opportunity of PP I 16 76 6
joined them, and tea was over, the card tables were placed. PP II 6 166 41
long as they chose, the tables were broke up, the carriage PP II 6 166 42
When the tea-things were removed, and the card tables PP III 12 342 26
They were confined for the evening at different tables, PP III 12 342 26
party--in which her card tables should be set out with E II 16 290 3
flower-stands and little tables placed in every direction. P III 5 40 44
TABLETS (1)
We will provide ourselves with tablets and a pencil. MP II 5 227 65
TACIT (2)
unworthy retraction of a tacit consent, no reversing NA II 15 247 15
To his tacit engagement with Miss de Bourgh? PP III 14 355 43
TACITLY (2)
it was more than being tacitly brought up as his uncle's E I 2 17 7
the very time that I was--tacitly, if not openly-- E III 11 404 11
TACITURN (1)
We are each of an unsocial, taciturn disposition, PP I 18 91 15
TACK (1)
But you must come up and tack on my patterns all the same." MP I 3 25 9
TACKLE (1)
supply him with fishing tackle, and pointing out those PP III 1 255 60
TAINTED (1)
than manner; it appears as if the mind itself was tainted." MP II 9 269 33
TAKE (513)
I take town in my way to that insupportable spot, a LS 2 245 1
To be sure, when we consider that I did take some pains to LS 5 249 1
I take on my lap & sigh over for his dear uncle's sake. LS 5 250 2
take all possible pains to prevent his marrying Catherine. LS 12 260 2
But it was impossible to take her any where else, & she is LS 15 267 5
but if you do not take my part, & persuade her to break it LS 21 279 1
if you have any letter therefore he can take it. LS 23 283 4
He was so good as to take it immediately; I dared not look LS 24 286 5
My removal therefore, which must at any rate take place LS 25 293 3
to take her to town, & marry her immediately to Sir James. LS 25 294 5
Besides, if you take my advice, & resolve to marry de LS 26 295 3
it will at least be handsome to take your personal leave. LS 35 305 1
long be in her power to take Frederica into the country LS 42 312 5
take her assurance of it, on either side of the question? LS 42 313 9
always preferring those which she was forbidden to take.-- NA I 1 13 1
entree into life could not take place till after three or NA I 2 20 8
Catherine," said she, "do take this pin out of my sleeve; NA I 3 28 35
"Men commonly take so little notice of those things," said NA I 3 28 39
Miss Thorpe, and take a turn with her about the room. NA I 4 33 6
who, if she accidentally take up a novel, is sure to turn NA I 5 37 4
The men take notice of that sometimes you know." NA I 6 42 25
Morland must take care of you." NA I 7 48 31
Did not we agree together to take a drive this morning? NA I 9 61 3
plunge or two, and perhaps take the rest for a minute; but NA I 9 62 9
"Yes; we agreed to take a turn in the Crescent, and there NA I 9 68 40
I would not take eight hundred guineas for them. NA I 10 76 28
Take care, or you will forget to be tired of it at the NA I 10 78 43
I would much rather take a chair at any time." NA I 11 83 11
and her brother to call on me to take a country walk. NA I 11 85 32
mistake, why should you be so ready to take offence?" NA I 12 94 11
"Me!--I take offence!" NA I 12 94 12
fair, the party should take place on the following morning; NA I 13 97 1
She had that moment settled with Miss Tilney to take their NA I 13 97 1
of an hour, she rose to take leave, and was then most NA I 13 103 28
I am fond of history--and am very well contented to take NA I 14 109 23
and with whom I like, and the devil take the rest, say I.-- NA I 15 123 44
sensibility did not take immediate alarm, and lay it down NA II 1 132 16
"I cannot take surprize to myself on that head. NA II 1 133 34
as long as I possibly could, but he would take no denial. NA II 1 134 39
long as I possibly could, but he would take no denial. NA II 1 134 39
who introduced him, might take it ill if I did not: and NA II 1 134 39
he should be old enough to take it; no trifling deduction NA II 1 135 42
and if our union could take place now upon only fifty NA II 1 136 48
Take my word for it, that if you are in too great a hurry, NA II 3 146 20
Gloucestershire was to take place within a few days, and NA II 4 150 1

rays of a single lamp to take in its size--its walls hung NA II 5 158 15
"She should take her time; she should not hurry herself; NA II 6 167 10
Mrs. Allen used to take pains, year after year, to make me NA II 7 174 7
to more frequent exercise than you would otherwise take. NA II 7 174 8
you may believe I take care that it shall not be a bad one. NA II 7 176 15
it will be wisest to take the morning while it is so fine; NA II 7 177 17
And was not it odd that he should always take his walk so NA II 7 177 18
out:--"I was going to take you into what was my mother's NA II 8 186 6
rather wonder that Eleanor should not take it for her own. NA II 9 196 21
The liberty which her imagination had dared to take with NA II 10 199 1
"Will you take the trouble of reading to us the passages NA II 10 205 22
to Woodston, they would take him by surprize there some NA II 11 209 5
"Well, well, we will take our chance some one of those NA II 11 210 6
upon me; but he is the last man whose word I would take. NA II 12 217 2
Well, I am certain of-----I shall be able to take leave NA II 13 224 17
ease; a few hours would take you there; but a journey of NA II 13 225 23
impossible, might speedily take place, to unite them again NA II 16 250 3
To take three thousand pounds from the fortune of their SS I 2 8 3
Brandon will be jealous, if she does not take care." SS I 9 44 23
"Take care, Margaret. SS I 12 60 12
of exhilaration I am now come to take my farewel of you." SS I 15 76 6
You had rather take evil upon credit than good. SS I 15 78 28
to talk, and unwilling to take any nourishment; giving SS I 16 83 1
affront, and affecting to take no notice of what passed, SS I 18 98 13
at the cottage, came to take a survey of the guest. SS I 18 99 15
not been able to take your usual walk to Allenham to-day." SS I 20 111 10
When is it to take place?" SS I 20 115 52
disposed as herself to take advantage of any that occurred; SS II 1 142 8
in till another rubber, or will you take your chance now?" SS II 1 145 22
my plan is that he should take orders as soon as he can, SS II 2 149 25
I always pity them when they do; they seem to take it so SS II 5 167 1
mingle in the croud, and take their share of the heat and SS II 6 175 2
entreat Lady Middleton to take them home, as she was too SS II 6 178 15
was at length persuaded to take, were of use; and from SS II 7 191 65
Do take it to your sister." SS II 8 198 27
to be a secret--it would take place even within a few SS II 8 199 37
for we were obliged to take Harry to see the wild beasts SS II 11 221 9
employ Edward to take care of us in our return to Barton. SS II 13 243 31
"Perhaps, Miss Marianne," cried Lucy, eager to take some SS II 13 243 38
knowing till the last moment, where it was to take her. SS II 14 249 7
The carriage was at the door ready to take my poor cousins SS III 1 259 7
I will take my oath he never dropt a syllable of being SS III 2 273 16
and they agreed he should take orders directly, and they SS III 2 274 16
in her coach, and would take one of us to Kensington SS III 2 274 16
any thing should happen to take you and your sister away, SS III 2 275 25
will excuse the liberty I take of writing to her; but I SS III 2 277 29
30
moving to the window to take more expeditiously the SS III 3 280 9
calm voice, "I am afraid it cannot take place very soon." SS III 3 281 9
10
Colonel should be able to take leave of them, as he SS III 3 282 15
I understand that he intends to take orders. SS III 3 282 19
least, I am afraid it cannot take place very soon.--" SS III 3 284 23
understanding you mean to take orders, he has great SS III 4 288 28
Take my word for it, that, if I am alive, I shall be SS III 4 292 57
really sold the presentation, is old enough to take it.-- SS III 5 295 12
had rung up the maid to take her place by her sister, she SS III 7 311 14
her at its conclusion to take some rest before her SS III 7 315 27
and allow her to take her place by Marianne; but Elinor SS III 7 315 27
was unwilling to take her where there might be infection. SS III 9 335 6
summoned to her chaise to take comfort in the gossip of SS III 10 341 5
said she, "we will take long walks together every day. SS III 10 343 9
give her five guineas to take her down to Exeter, where SS III 13 370 37
And I must say that Lucy's crossness not to take her along SS III 13 371 37
Perhaps Tom Musgrave may take notice of you--but I would W 315 1
ask why it did not take place, & why he is married to W 316 2
Do not trust her with any secrets of your own, take W 317 2
at the object that could take her away, from Stanton just W 317 2
"You will take notice who Mary Edwards dances with."-- W 320 2
direction of the reins to take the right turning, & making W 322 2
"But you may come to Wickstead & see mama, & she can take W 332 12
by them, that we do not know how to take this neglect."-- W 334 13
from the bottom to the top, & would make me take his arm.-- W 344 20
Tho' Emma could not but take the compliment of the visit W 345 21
briskly after Nanny "to tell Betty to take up the fowls."-- W 346 21
I am one of those who always take things as they find them. W 351 25
He loved to take people by surprise, with sudden visits at W 355 28
imported that she meant to take the visit to herself.-- W 355 28
immediately; that he is to take possession before PP I 1 3 10
You take delight in vexing me. PP I 1 5 28
if you decline the office, I will take it on myself." PP I 2 7 16
Compliments always take you by surprise, and me never. PP I 4 14 5
But to be candid without ostentation or design--to take PP I 4 14 9
to see you at it I should take away your bottle directly." PP I 5 20 22
that neighbourhood, and take Pemberley for a kind of model. PP I 8 38 35
"I wish I might take this for a compliment; but to be so PP I 9 42 12
you to follow my example, and take a turn about the room.-- PP I 11 56 11
and Mr. Bennet was glad to take his guest into the drawing- PP I 14 68 13
"As to her younger daughters she could not take upon her PP I 15 71 3
"I should take him, even on my slight acquaintance, to be PP I 16 78 17
to a card table, they must take their chance of these PP I 16 83 50
of the evening, and I take this opportunity of soliciting PP I 17 87 13
Elizabeth however did not chuse to take the hint, being PP I 17 88 14
(glancing at her sister and Bingley,) shall take place. PP I 18 92 23
"But if I do not take your likeness now, I may never have PP I 18 94 42
When at length they arose to take leave, Mrs. Bennet was PP I 18 103 76
to my family, and may take possession of Longbourn estate PP I 19 107 16
my favour; and you should take it into farther PP I 19 108 19
But I tell you what, Miss Lizzy, if you take it into your PP I 20 113 28
a more happy idea, since you will not take comfort in mine. PP I 21 119 22
dinner, she would take care to have two full courses. PP I 21 120 30
home, and be satisfied that we shall take no offence." PP I 22 124 9
it necessary, I shall now take the liberty of wishing them PP I 22 124 10
that she wished it to take place as soon as possible, PP I 23 128 10
for her, and live to see her take my place in it!" PP I 23 130 17
"And men take care that they should." PP II 1 136 15
Let me take it in the best light, in the light in which it PP II 1 137 24
I will take care of myself, and of Mr. Wickham too. PP II 3 144 5
and when she rose to take leave, Elizabeth, ashamed of her PP II 3 145 11
shall take the opportunity of calling in Grosvenor-Street." PP II 3 147 22
Kitty and Lydia take his defection much more to heart than PP II 3 150 29
March was to take Elizabeth to Hunsford. PP II 4 151 1
"Take care, Lizzy; that speech savours strongly of PP II 4 154 20
Collins invited them to take a stroll in the garden, which PP II 5 156 4
make a very low bow, and take his seat without saying a PP II 6 162 11
obliged to take her ladyship's praise into his own hands. PP II 6 167 42
fault-- because I would not take the trouble of practising. PP II 8 175 25
her ladyship's carriage was ready to take them all home. PP II 8 176 30
But perhaps Mr. Bingley did not take the house so much for PP II 9 178 9
"Care of him!--yes, I really believe Darcy does take care PP II 10 184 24
"You take an eager interest in that gentleman's concerns," PP II 11 191 18
only for a few minutes to take leave, but that Colonel PP II 13 209 13
it will be in my power to take one of you as far as London, PP II 14 211 10
I do so want papa to take us all there for the summer! PP II 16 219 6
Take your choice, but you must be satisfied with only one. PP II 17 225 10
event should ever take place, I shall merely be able to PP II 17 227 25
They will take care not to outrun their income. PP II 17 228 33
If you, my dear father, will not take the trouble of PP II 18 231 18
to go into the house and take some refreshment; but this PP III 1 257 66
"Your great men often are; and therefore I shall not take PP III 1 258 72
season; but this did not take place till after many a PP III 3 268 6
Adieu. I take up my pen again to do, what I have just told PP III 4 275 5
Is there nothing you could take, to give you present PP III 4 276 9
but poor dear Lydia had nobody to take care of her. PP III 5 287 35
If you are a good girl for the next ten years, I will take PP III 6 300 32
"May we take my uncle's letter to read to her?" PP III 7 305 41
"Take whatever you like, and get away." PP III 7 305 42
"Mrs. Bennet, before you take any, or all of these houses, PP III 8 310 9
sister, "Ah! Jane, I take your place now, and you must go PP III 9 317 9
and I will take care to get good partners for them all." PP III 9 317 13
Will you be very angry with me, my dear Lizzy, if I take PP III 10 325 2
for me, or else I could take it in my way to Newcastle. PP III 10 327 11
"It must be something particular, to take him there at PP III 10 328 17
to take a family dinner with us, as soon as you returned. PP III 11 338 58
"Oh, Jane, take care." PP III 12 339 7
see whether Bingley would take the place, which, in all PP III 12 340 11
leave, would take an early opportunity of waiting on them. PP III 13 344 3
and then added, "may I take the liberty of asking your PP III 14 352 12
13
begged her ladyship to take some refreshment; but Lady PP III 14 352 16
17
I should be glad to take a turn in it, if you will favour PP III 14 352 17
you have the presumption to aspire, can never take place. PP III 14 354 40
round, she added, "I take no leave of you, Miss Bennet. PP III 14 358 72
73
and how he might take a similar representation of the PP III 15 360 2
you will be inclined to take immediate advantage of." PP III 15 362 15
which induced you to take so much trouble, and bear so PP III 16 366 5
first, but my anger soon began to take a proper direction." PP III 16 369 28
She could not determine how her mother would take it; PP III 17 375 27
that a woman may take liberties with her husband, which a PP III 19 388 11
power to take any share in the personal charge of her. MP I 1 9 10
she should then be glad to take her turn, and think MP I 1 9 10
dress her you know, and take care of her clothes, for I MP I 1 9 12
it, they were soon able to take a full survey of her face MP I 2 12 3
"Yes, when you have written the letter I will take it to MP I 2 16 19
stupid, and Fanny must take more pains; she did not know MP I 2 20 31
my sister always meant to take you when Mr. Norris died. MP I 3 25 9
Even your constant little heart need not take fright at MP I 3 27 35
He could not say he wished me to take Fanny. MP I 3 29 44
Sir Thomas will take care of that." MP I 3 30 53
be obliged to take daily refuge in the dining of the park. MP I 4 38 9
He only conditioned that the marriage should not take MP I 4 40 14
her situation--Mr. Crawford must take care of himself." MP I 5 44 3
What is this, but a take in?" MP I 5 46 22
the same airs and take the same liberties as if they were, MP I 5 50 39
But if I had more room, I should take a prodigious delight MP I 6 54 9
world; and when obliged to take up the pen to say that MP I 6 59 43
to take Mr. Crawford away, interposed with an amendment. MP I 6 61 58
I dare say Mr. Crawford would take my two nieces and me in MP I 6 62 58
You should learn to think of other people; and take my MP I 7 71 34
Mrs. Grant to alight and the others to take their places. MP I 8 80 29
this will be a good opportunity for you to take a lesson." MP I 8 80 29
I wish you had my seat, but I dare say you will not take MP I 8 81 32
manner would he choose, to take a survey of the grounds?-- MP I 9 84 1
I will take you in this way, if you will excuse me." MP I 9 85 5
"Upon my word, it is really a pity that it should not take MP I 9 88 24
"Yes, I shall take orders soon after my father's return-- MP I 9 89 28
as I was at first that you should intend to take orders. MP I 9 93 53
old gardener would make me take; but if it is in your way, MP I 10 105 55
There Fanny, you shall carry that parcel for me--take MP I 10 105 55
Take care of the cheese, Fanny. MP I 10 106 55
would quite force upon me; she would not take a denial. MP I 10 106 57
him in proposing to take his passage in the September MP I 11 107 2
"What! take orders without a living! MP I 11 109 21
man is neither to take orders with a living, nor without? MP I 11 109 22
or of inclination to take the trouble of being agreeable, MP I 11 110 23
"I have been so little addicted to take my opinions from MP I 11 111 28
occur when he was once gone, to take him elsewhere. MP I 12 115 5
Yates's being invited to take Mansfield in his way, MP I 13 121 1
resign his to me, it was impossible to take it, you know. MP I 13 122 2
"You take up a thing so seriously! as if we were going to MP I 13 125 18
"I know my father as well as you do, and I'll take care MP I 13 127 27
Manage your own concerns, Edmund, and I'll take care of MP I 13 127 27
take their course, without attempting it through her. MP I 13 128 37
and will be happy to take the part of any old Duenna or MP I 13 129 38
month at her own cost, and take up her abode in their's, MP I 13 129 40
One could not expect any body to take such a part----- MP I 14 131 3
I take any part you choose to give me, so as it be comic. MP I 14 131 5
before, I am determined to take any thing and do my best. MP I 14 132 7
Henry Crawford was ready to take either. MP I 14 132 8
thing humorous, let her take Cottager's speeches instead MP I 14 134 14
The first use she made of her solitude was to take up the MP I 14 137 23
Maria blushed in spite of herself as she answered, "I take MP I 15 139 8
Maria with renewed zeal, "Julia would certainly take it." MP I 15 141 19
of himself,) I'll take the boards to your father, dick; so MP I 15 142 22
"Your brother should take the part," said Mr. Yates, in a MP I 15 144 34
Take the part with a good grace, and let us hear no more MP I 15 146 53
see any where, so I will take my horse early to-morrow MP I 15 148 58
I must take Anhalt myself. MP I 16 154 10
Things should take their course; she cared not how it MP I 16 157 28
there, and then gladly take her share in any thing that MP I 17 161 9
acts was certainly to take place in the evening; Mrs. MP I 18 171 25
all dinner; he would take nothing, nothing till tea came-- MP II 1 180 10
I hope you will take a day's sport there yourself, sir, MP II 1 181 16
days to Brighton, and take a house there for some weeks. MP II 3 203 31
horses out to take her home, with which she was threatened. MP II 4 206 4
asked to call again, to take them in her walk whenever she MP II 4 207 10
it all and all, I never spent so happy a summer.-- MP II 4 210 19
We may sometimes take greater liberties in November than MP II 4 212 29
of whether she should take leave of not just then, and how, MP II 4 214 46
Mr. Edmund Bertram, I dare say, would take their chance. MP II 4 215 49
"Suppose you take my father's opinion, ma'am." MP II 5 217 7
Mrs. Grant thinks it a civility due to us to take a little MP II 5 220 28
Had the doctor been contented to take my dining table when MP II 5 220 30
mind to what may happen, and take your things accordingly." MP II 5 221 34
she was not required to take any part--there was so much MP II 5 223 48
The assurance of Edmund's being so soon to take orders, MP II 5 227 69
exercise only to my body, and I must take care of my mind. MP II 6 229 3
be all animation when I take it and talk to her; to think MP II 6 231 9
to drive about the grounds, and see his genius take fire. MP II 7 244 30
To take what had been the gift of another person--of a MP II 8 259 20
and seemed resolved either to take another or none at all. MP II 8 259 20
found you, take the necklace, and say no more about it. MP II 8 259 22
Excuse the liberty--but take care how you talk to me. MP II 9 269 36
they were not at home to take their own place in the room, MP II 10 275 12
She was happy even when they did take place; but not from MP II 10 278 20
or to have any thing take place at all in the way she MP II 10 280 32
view the happy scene, and take a last look at the five or MP II 10 280 33
I will not take her from Northamptonshire. MP II 12 295 20
chusing by any means to take so much trouble in vain, she MP II 13 298 1
its sufficiency, began to take the matter in another point. MP II 13 305 23
Now, here are my Sister Price's children;--take them all MP II 13 305 24
you will excuse my begging you to take no further notice. MP II 13 307 31
That was what she most earnestly desired;--go and take his MP III 1 311 1
spoken of their journey as what would take place ere long. MP III 1 311 1
You will take in the whole of the past, you will consider MP III 1 313 12
She had no one to take her part, to counsel, or speak for MP III 1 321 46
and more than half a mind to take orders and preach myself. MP III 3 341 28
"I will speak to her, sir; I will take the first MP III 4 345 5
whom she is wild to get married, and wants Henry to take. MP III 5 360 16
Every thing shall take its course. MP III 5 362 18
in the breakfast parlour, I must take leave of you here. MP III 5 364 30
And I do take leave, longing for a happy re-union, and MP III 5 364 30

TAKE / TAKEN

When it came to the moment of parting, he would take her MP III 5 365 36
carriage, she was able to take leave of the old coachman, MP III 7 375 1
They entered Oxford, but she could take only a hasty MP III 7 376 5
anybody in England would take her for an eight-and-twenty. MP III 7 380 20
the passage, he exclaimed, "devil take those young dogs! MP III 7 383 30
He stepped back again to the door to say, "take care of MP III 8 388 2
I charge you, take care of Fanny." MP III 8 388 2
for, take away his rants, and the poor Baron has nothing. MP III 9 394 1
and her daughters, to take their walk without loss of time. MP III 10 401 10
"Would she not then persuade her daughters to take MP III 10 401 10
an offer of Mr. Price's to take Mr. Crawford into the dock- MP III 10 402 13
fan--come, Sue--take care of yourselves--keep a sharp look MP III 10 403 14
Price's, who was come to take his daily survey of how MP III 10 403 15
which he could sometimes take advantage of, to look in her MP III 11 409 7
be supposed otherwise; but take it all in all, he was MP III 11 410 7
will immediately come down, and take you back to Mansfield. MP III 11 411 16
of; so you must take it upon my word, to be inestimable. MP III 12 417 3
dear Fanny, "I take up my pen to communicate some MP III 13 425 7
8

This was a great deal better than to have to take up the MP III 13 426 9
such guilt, and began to take in some part of the misery MP III 15 440 19
comfort, and with leave to take Susan, was altogether such MP III 15 443 24
Persuade him to let things take their course. MP III 16 457 29
I only doubt whether he will ever take us anywhere else. E I 1 9 18
years ago; and to have it take place, and be proved in the E I 1 11 39
Depend upon it, a man of six or seven-and-twenty can take E I 1 14 48
to care for, offered to take the whole charge of the E I 2 16 4
a most proper attention, that the visit should take place. E I 2 17 9
take any pains to marry him, she would probably repent it. E I 4 30 18
plenty of people who would take pleasure in degrading you." E I 4 30 22
be very safely recommended to take Mr. Elton as a model. E I 4 34 42
me, Mr. Knightley, if I take the liberty (I consider E I 5 40 24
take him by stealth; neither of them very like therefore. E I 6 45 21
nor can it be very easy to take any likeness of them, E I 6 45 21
in a pet, and vowed I would never take another likeness. E I 6 45 21
Mr. Elton was to take the drawing to London, chuse the E I 6 49 42
take Emma's advice and go out for a quarter of an hour. E I 8 57 3
As the sun is out, I believe I had better take my three E I 8 57 3
And therefore I think I will beg your excuse and take my E I 8 57 5
chose rather to take up her own line of the subject again. E I 8 63 43
another moment's pause, "take it," said Emma, smiling, and E I 9 71 12
13

Take your own." E I 9 71 13
The strangest things do take place!" E I 9 74 24
But take it away, and all appropriation ceases, and a very E I 9 77 42
"Ah! it is no difficulty to see who you take after! E I 9 78 53
54

Your friend will not take it amiss I hope. E I 9 82 80
read more; if I give up music, I shall take to carpet-work. E I 10 85 21
You and I, Emma, will venture to take the part of the poor E I 11 95 18
a mind to take it up; but she struggled, and let it pass. E I 11 96 27
in the usual way, and to take the child out of her arms E I 12 98 2
Poor Perry is bilious, and he has not time to take care of E I 12 101 25
me he has not time to take care of himself--which is very E I 12 101 25
will call upon her to-morrow, and take my children.-- E I 12 102 31
Mr. Weston would take no denial; they must all dine at E I 13 108 2
Indeed you should take care of yourself as well as of your E I 13 109 7
to stay at home and take care of yourself to-night." E I 13 110 9
before, you may as well take it into consideration now." E I 13 112 20
This to me! you forget yourself--you take me for my friend- E I 15 130 25
state of mind, he tried to take her hand again, as he E I 15 131 32
33

It was foolish, it was wrong, to take so active part in E I 16 136 10
him to follow the lead, or take the lead, just as E I 18 150 31
To take a dislike to a young man, only because he appeared E I 18 150 37
the meeting in Dublin, and take them back to their country- E II 1 159 20
I hope you mean to take an interest in this news. E II 3 175 41
42

my dear Miss Woodhouse; but we really must take leave. E II 3 176 50
She meant to take her in the carriage, leave her at the E II 4 185 13
on business, sir, I will take the opportunity of paying a E II 5 193 36
37

to whom and to Highbury he seemed to take very cordially. E II 6 196 1
my side which was prone to take disgust towards a girl so E II 6 203 39
than I have yet been, to take the trouble of conquering E II 6 203 41
"I suppose they will not take the liberty with you; they E II 7 207 7
afternoon next summer, and take their tea with us --take E II 7 209 10
take their tea with us --take us in their afternoon walk; E II 7 209 10
and Mr. Knightley too, to take care of her, I cannot wish E II 7 209 10
James could take the note. E II 7 209 13
still I have no doubt that James will take you very safely. E II 7 210 14
if hungry, that she would take something to eat; that her E II 7 211 22
and would therefore be particularly liable to take cold. E II 8 223 63
carriage had brought, and was to take them home again.' E II 8 223 63
My dear Mrs. Weston, do not take to match-making. E II 8 225 72
"You take up an idea, Mrs. Weston, and run away with it; E II 8 226 84
And I could take the pattern gown home any day. E II 9 235 36
it sent to Hartfield, and take it home with me at night. E II 9 235 40
I meant to take them over to John Saunders the first thing E II 9 236 46
be so very obliging as to take some, 'Oh!' said he E II 9 238 51
Pray take care, Mrs. Weston, there is a step at the E II 9 239 53
Pray take care, Miss Woodhouse, ours is rather a dark E II 9 239 53
Miss Smith, pray take care. E II 9 239 53
The preparations must take their time, nothing could be E II 12 257 1
after breakfast, and take leave of the few friends there E II 12 258 9
and did sigh, could not but agree, and rise to take leave. E II 12 261 35
I fancy I need not take much pains to dwell on them. E II 14 275 32
The extent of your admiration may take you by surprize E II 15 287 26
for me to presume to take such a liberty with you. E II 15 288 35
of my admiration for her will ever take me by surprize.-- E II 15 288 36
parties which are to take place in the barouche-landau." E II 15 288 39
Young ladies should take care of themselves.-- E II 16 294 25
They should take care of their health and their complexion. E II 16 294 25
It is a sign I was not there to take care of you." E II 16 295 30
sad girl, and do not know how to take care of yourself.-- E II 16 295 32
But I would not wish you to take the trouble of making any E II 17 300 9
"I know you, I know you; you would take up with any thing; E II 17 301 18
only a few lines--will not take you long; read it to Emma." E II 17 303 25
You must take care of yourself, Mrs. Elton.-- E II 18 305 7
I always take the part of my own sex. E II 18 306 12
my numerous engagements take place without your being of E II 18 312 50
You may be very sure I shall always take care of them." E III 2 321 17
I made her take her shawl--for the evenings are not warm-- E III 2 322 19
No coffee, I thank you, for me--never take coffee.-- E III 2 323 19
he must have danced, would he but take the trouble.-- E III 2 326 32
Two steps, Jane, take care of the two steps. E III 2 329 45
Every thing was to take its natural course, however, E III 3 335 11
But take care of yourself. E III 4 342 39
judged it wisest to take their exercise early, as the E III 5 344 3
The dream must be borne with, and Mr. Knightley must take E III 5 347 18
she positively refused to take her friend's negative, E III 6 359 37
a chair close to them, take an interest in their E III 6 364 59
Richmond was to take him back before the following evening. E III 6 366 76
Come, Jane, take my other arm." E III 7 372 39
harmless absurdity to take its chance, I would not quarrel E III 7 375 61
She would not take a denial. E III 8 380 15
as she did, and refuse to take Jane's answer; but she E III 8 381 15
sent to Randall's to take Mr. Frank Churchill to Richmond. E III 8 383 29
To take her--be it only an hour or two--from her aunt, to E III 9 390 16
was a thing she could not take--and, moreover, she E III 9 391 20
her father, that she would take her walk now, she and Mr. E III 10 392 7
"Nay, dear Emma, now I must take his part; for though he E III 10 397 49
Well, and how did Mr. Churchill take it?" E III 10 398 54
They must take the consequence, if they have heard each E III 10 399 61
Were this most unequal of all connexions to take place, on E III 11 413 47
If all took place that might take place among the circle E III 12 422 19
"Take a little time, consider, do not commit yourself." E III 13 429 28
which he still spoke--"I should like to take another turn. E III 13 429 32
What totally different feelings did Emma take back into E III 14 434 1
say;--when I called to take leave of her, I remember that E III 14 438 8
restraints, that it did not take her wholly by surprise. E III 14 438 8
I will take it home with me at night." E III 15 444 3
my information did not take him wholly by surprise, that E III 17 465 25
might not be so very bad if the marriage did take place. E III 17 467 30
matters will take care of themselves; the young people E III 17 467 31
days ago, and I got him to take charge of some papers E III 18 471 20
They were going to take the two eldest boys to Astley's. E III 18 471 20
Then might she again take up the book of books with as P III 1 7 12
"I must take leave to observe, Sir Walter," said Mr. P III 3 17 1
Therefore, Sir Walter, what I would take leave to suggest P III 3 17 4
What do you take his age to be?' P III 3 20 16
"Then I take it for granted," observed Sir Walter, "that P III 3 22 22
Came there about the year --5, I take it. P III 3 23 32
found it most natural to take her almost daily walk to P III 5 32 1
of her own, which must take her from Kellynch for several P III 5 33 6
They are both so very large, and take up so much room! P III 5 39 39
me, they are always tempting her to take a walk with them." P III 6 45 9
be always putting herself forward to take place of mamma. P III 6 46 10
Her brother's return was the first comfort; he could take P III 7 54 4
Anne will stay; Anne undertakes to stay at home and take P III 7 57 18
Anne was now at hand to take up her own cause, and the P III 7 58 20
Doubtless it was so; and she could take no revenge, for he P III 7 61 34
When she could let her attention take its natural course P III 8 64 7
remain where he was, and take all the charms and P III 9 73 1
near them, seemed to leave every thing to take its chance. P III 9 74 9
She would take place of me then, and Henrietta would not P III 9 75 11
that they were going to take a long walk, and, therefore, P III 10 83 4
They meant to take a long drive this morning; perhaps we P III 10 84 8
My dear Admiral, that post!--we shall certainly take that P III 10 92 47
which his servants take care to publish where he goes. P III 12 106 16
whom they had appointed to take their last walk about Lyme. P III 12 107 22
Rub her hands, rub her temples; here are salts,--take them, P III 12 110 36
rub her temples; here are salts,--take them, take them." P III 12 110 36
Musgrove, take care of the others." P III 12 111 48
"that you stay, and that I take care of your sister home. P III 12 114 61
the Uppercross horses to take them back, would be a P III 12 114 64
be much better for him to take a chaise from the inn, and P III 12 114 64
And take it altogether, now that we have been into most of P IV 1 128 30
But every thing must take its chance. P IV 4 146 4
to give me any notice, or offer to take "any thing. P IV 6 164 7
"How Charles could take such a thing into his head was " P IV 6 165 8
There, take my arm; that's right; I do not feel P IV 6 169 27
take them home, and would call for them in a few minutes. P IV 7 174 2
Shall I take any message?" P IV 9 198 43
My father was certainly disposed to take very kind and P IV 9 200 58
Mrs. Smith did not want to take blame to herself, and was P IV 9 209 95
Oh! you may as well take back that tiresome book she would P IV 10 215 15
to take place in a few months, quite as soon as Louisa's. P IV 10 217 20
She tried to be calm, and leave things to take their P IV 10 221 33
Take a box for to-morrow night! P IV 10 223 43
of some sort or other, to take you back into the world P IV 11 232 19
take care of yourself, that you may be fit for the evening. P IV 11 238 46
take my place, and give Anne your arm to her father's door. P IV 11 240 58
When any two young people take it into their heads to P IV 12 248 1
wrong, and to take up a new set of opinions and of hopes. P IV 12 249 3
on being first required to take that direction, had S 1 364 1
are extremely obliging sir, & I take you at your word.-- S 1 365 1
Two hours take us home, from Hailsham--and when once at S 1 367 1
"I do not mean to take exceptions to any place in S 1 368 1
of another being then to take her place;--but in selecting S 3 379 1
For her particular gratification, they were then to take a S 6 390 1
their house, & obliged to take her tea with him them, S 6 390 1
Ten fees, one after another, did the man take who sent him S 6 394 1
My young folks, as I call them sometimes, for I take them S 7 399 1
I always take care to know what I am about & who I have to S 7 399 1
just as they take our empty houses--and (between ourselves) S 7 401 1
If people want to be by the sea, why dont they take S 7 402 1
to come & take one of these lodgings for a fortnight.-- S 7 402 1
coat & sent him off to the terrace, to take us lodgings.-- S 9 407 1
I shall take only one however, & that, but for a week S 9 410 1
merit to his civility in wishing her to take his chair.-- S 10 414 1
I shall be out every morning before breakfast--& take S 10 416 1
his earnest invitation to her to take both cocoa & toast.-- S 10 416 1
No--it acts on me like poison and wd entirely take away S 10 418 1
I will take an opportunity of seeing Lady D. myself.-- S 12 425 1

TAKE-LEAVE (1)

almost every house in the parish, as a sort of take-leave. P III 5 39 34

TAKEN (246)

some pains are taken to prevent her being much with me. LS 17 270 6
& have taken great pains to overcome her timidity. LS 18 273 3
me for the liberty he had taken in coming to Churchill, LS 20 276 3
& since matters have now taken so favourable a turn, I am LS 23 283 1
Where my own resolution was taken, I could not wish for LS 24 289 12
"I beg your pardon sir, for the liberty I have taken in LS 25 292 3
distress; the most unfortunate event has just taken place. LS 28 297 1
promising, till affairs have taken a more favourable turn. LS 30 301 4
had early in the evening taken pains to know who her NA I 3 30 52
Taken in that light certainly, their resemblance is not NA I 10 77 33
She had never taken a country walk since her arrival in NA I 10 80 61
projected walk should be taken as soon as possible; and, NA I 12 95 16
It seemed as if a good view were no longer to be taken NA I 14 110 28
be taken by government to prevent its coming to effect." NA I 14 112 34
she soon learned that the party to Clifton had taken place. NA I 14 115 50
I told him he had taken a very unlikely way to prevail NA II 1 134 39
that the lodgings should be taken for another fortnight. NA II 2 138 1
the place whence she had taken them," which had filled her NA II 7 172 2
Having taken her into every division, and led her under NA II 7 179 27
A face once taken was taken for generations. NA II 9 191 3
the country, it would be taken exceedingly amiss; and it NA II 11 210 6
at six o'clock, the General having taken his coffee, the NA II 11 215 28
Many girls might have been taken in, for never was such NA II 12 217 2
but I am not such a fool as to be taken in by them. NA II 12 217 2
conduct by the manner in which her proposal might be taken. NA II 13 220 1
to be taken post by you, at your age, alone, unattended!" NA II 13 225 23
and should a dislike be taken against them, should they be NA II 14 232 5
His lodgings were taken the very day after he left them, NA II 14 238 27
live fifteen years, we shall be completely taken in." SS I 2 10 18
sorry he was that she had taken an house at such a SS I 5 25 4
and Lady Middleton had taken the wise precaution of SS I 6 31 9
cold provisions were to be taken, open carriages only to SS I 12 62 28
declared to have taken place, Elinor could not imagine. SS I 14 71 3
be that Barton cottage was taken; and I felt an immediate SS I 14 73 17
I have just received my dispatches, and taken my farewel SS I 15 76 6
unfortunate quarrel had taken place between him and her SS I 15 77 19
old lady, "you have taken Charlotte off my hands, and SS I 20 112 25
for no farther notice was taken of Mr. Ferrars's name by SS I 21 126 41
One or two meetings of this kind had taken place, without SS II 1 143 9
and what he meant, before many meetings had taken place. SS II 4 159 1
She had taken care to have the intelligence conveyed to SS II 10 217 16
china, &c. to supply the place of what was taken away. SS II 11 225 35
where they had taken a very good house for three months. SS II 12 230 6
She met him with a hand that would be taken, and a voice SS II 13 242 23
the means that were to be taken for promoting its end, was SS III 2 276 27
time no notice had been taken by them of his wife's SS III 5 293 3

till after the breach had taken place, when it was not for SS III 5 299 37
of the mother she had taken her from; and Elinor found her SS III 7 308 3
taken their mother by surprise on the following forenoon. SS III 7 308 4
At last, however, my resolution was taken, and I had SS III 8 321 34
affection which I had already taken such pains to display. SS III 8 321 34
inquiry, had intuitively taken the same direction, was SS III 11 353 24
The servant, who saw only that Miss Marianne was taken ill, SS III 11 353 25
But so little interest had he taken in the matter, that he SS III 13 368 31
measures would have been taken to prevent the marriage; SS III 13 371 38
her mother, might not be taken amiss; for we all know the SS III 13 371 39
when Marianne was taken from them, Margaret had reached an SS III 14 380 20
goes to see;--& she has taken a vast deal of trouble about W 317 2
feelings & more natural smiles than they had taken away.-- W 323 3
being unusually well had taken the sudden resolution of W 338 18
No notice was taken. W 340 18
why Mr Howard had not taken the same privilege of coming, W 347 22
"Do not you want to know who has taken it?" cried his wife PP I 1 3 7
says that Netherfield is taken by a young man of large PP I 1 3 10
If my vanity had taken a musical turn, you would have been PP I 6 24 22
She will be taken good care of. PP I 7 31 32
Elizabeth was glad to be taken to her immediately; and PP I 7 33 43
not attempt to have it taken, for what painter could do PP I 10 53 57
When this information was given, and they had all taken PP I 16 75 2
Elizabeth felt herself completely taken in. PP I 17 87 14
glad to find that he had taken himself out of the way. PP I 18 94 45
had he and his companion taken leave, than a glance from PP I 21 116 6
that Mr. Collins had been taken in; thirdly, she trusted PP I 23 127 5
neatness of the entrance, taken into the house; and as PP II 5 155 3
Your mother should have taken you to town every spring for PP II 6 164 24
That he had been concerned in the measures taken to PP II 10 186 38
Long before it had taken place, my opinion of you was PP II 11 191 17
Forgive me for having taken up so much of your time, and PP II 11 193 29
About a year ago, she was taken from school, and an PP II 12 201 5
She says Lizzy had better have taken Mr. Collins; but I do PP II 16 221 17
who had taken a liking to the room, when last at Pemberley. PP III 1 249 43
Mrs. Reynolds informed them, that it had been taken in his PP III 1 250 47
to be assured it has taken place, for there is but too PP III 4 274 3
that their niece was taken suddenly ill;--but satisfying PP III 4 280 26
And since this sad affair has taken place, it is said, PP III 5 291 54
My mother was taken ill immediately, and the whole house PP III 5 292 62
of the business that had taken him away, and it was some PP III 6 299 18
pity that Lydia should be taken from a regiment where she PP III 8 313 20
her house, they would have taken up their abode with her. PP III 10 322 2
He had followed them purposely to town, he had taken on PP III 10 326 3
it is very hard to have her taken such a way from me. PP III 11 336 51
must have taken place with that gentleman's concurrence. PP III 13 346 20
Lady Catherine it appeared, had actually taken the trouble PP III 15 360 1
an absolute breach between the sisters had taken place. MP I 1 3 1
child one had in a manner taken into one's own hands; and MP I 1 6 6
friend, she was taken to finish her sorrows in bed. MP I 2 13 4
no measures were taken for mounting her again, "because," MP I 4 35 7
dear aunt and myself, have taken to reason, coax, or trick MP I 4 42 21
He will be taken in at last." MP I 5 46 16
"But I would not have him taken in, I would not have him MP I 5 46 17
"Oh! dear--let him stand his chance and be taken in. MP I 5 46 18
Every body is taken in at some period or other." MP I 5 46 18
hundred of either sex, who is not taken in when they marry. MP I 5 46 20
more taken in and deceived than the parties themselves." MP I 5 46 23
The mare was only to be taken down to the parsonage half MP I 7 66 14
Edmund, who had taken down the mare and presided at the MP I 7 66 15
seat at the table, and had taken up her work again; and MP I 7 71 35
to have them, and then you know they must be taken home." MP I 7 72 49
Having been out some time, and taken a different route to MP I 8 75 2
account, because he had taken the opportunity as he walked MP I 8 79 23
Mrs. Rushworth proposed that the chaise should be taken MP I 9 84 2
principal stair-case, and taken them through all the rooms MP I 9 89 31
Crawford when they had taken one turn on the terrace, and MP I 9 91 37
We have taken such a very serpentine course; and the wood MP I 9 94 62
subject of pheasants, had taken her to the dairy, told her MP I 10 103 50
and the junction which had taken place at last seemed, to MP I 10 104 51
had chose, he would have taken a ---- not a good temper MP I 11 111 30
received his orders and taken his measurements, had MP I 14 130 1
Henry Crawford, who meanwhile had taken up the play, and MP I 14 133 11
table--(looking round)--it certainly will not be taken." MP I 15 144 38
I have hardly taken out a gun since the 3d. MP II 1 181 16
worth any trouble that might be taken to establish it. MP II 2 190 6
the morning, and Tom had taken the opportunity of MP II 2 191 10
had taken place, which gave Sotherton another mistress. MP II 3 202 28
has taken place in her looks within the last six weeks. MP II 6 229 5
in having for many years taken in the paper esteemed to MP II 6 232 13
again--had been often taken on shore by the favour of his MP II 6 236 21
the matter over and taken his resolution in quiet MP II 8 252 1
What would she have been if we had not taken her by the MP II 10 272 3
Norris, who was entirely taken up at first in fresh MP II 10 272 4
which would otherwise have taken place about this time. MP II 11 284 10
is taken away; that is, there is a great difference felt. MP II 11 289 32
observed, that joy had taken away her appetite, she was MP II 13 304 16
even where pains had been taken to please him--who thought MP II 13 305 26
The note was held out and must be taken; and as she MP II 13 307 35
This cannot have taken you by surprise. MP III 1 316 29
a situation which her fancy had never taken into account. MP III 2 326 3
a purport fulfilled as had taken him away, he would have MP III 3 334 2
could imagine her to be taken perfectly unprepared, but MP III 3 335 6
Poor Janet has been sadly taken in; and yet there was MP III 5 361 16
It had, in fact, occurred to her, that, though taken to MP III 6 373 24
She was then taken into a parlour, so small that her first MP III 7 377 10
Susan, you should have taken care of the fire." MP III 7 379 17
But you should not have taken it out, my dear, when I sent MP III 7 386 44
Maxwell, only six weeks before she was taken for death. MP III 7 387 44
Well, she was taken away from evil to come. MP III 7 387 44
Mrs. Norris, however, had gone home and taken down two old MP III 7 387 45
from it was, that nothing decisive had yet taken place. MP III 12 417 4
"He is just come, my dear Fanny, and is taken up stairs; MP III 13 427 12
regard the step she had taken, as opening the worst MP III 16 452 13
with Miss Crawford had taken place, from which Edmund MP III 16 452 15
He would have taken no pains to be on terms with Mrs. MP III 16 456 23
when that marriage had taken place, which would have given MP III 17 467 19
her father, was sometimes taken by surprize at his being E I 2 18 12
many--perhaps with most people, unless taken moderately. E I 2 19 14
Had it taken place only once a year, it would have been a E I 3 20 3
She had taken up a wrong idea, fancying it was a mother E I 4 27 5
that if she were not taken care of, she might be required E I 4 27 5
"Did you ever have your likeness taken, Harriet?" said she: E I 6 43 9
had taken in the affair, was provoking him exceedingly. E I 8 66 55
and Harriet, who had taken the first hint of it from her, E I 9 69 4
Poor Isabella!--she is sadly taken away from us all!-- and E I 9 79 58
two or three days are not to be taken out for the Abbey. E I 9 79 63
The room they were taken into was the one he chiefly E I 10 89 38
There is something so shocking in a child's being taken E I 11 96 25
This had just taken place and with great cordiality, when E I 12 99 14
wondering at its not being taken every evening by every E I 12 101 19
20
horses and four servants taken out for nothing but to E I 13 113 26
they had all taken their places, that he was close to her. E I 14 118 4
She had taken up the idea, she supposed, and made every E I 16 134 3
Her father was quite taken up with the surprize of so E I 17 141 4
with them, and she had taken a piece of cake and been so E II 1 155 4
drawings of the place, views that he had taken himself. E II 1 160 20
This event had very lately taken place; too lately for any E II 2 165 8
each other, which had taken strong possession of her mind, E II 5 192 33
If the talking aunt had taken me quite by surprise, it E II 6 198 7
have taken to each other whenever she visited her friends. E II 6 203 39
chiefly among the single men, had already taken place. E II 7 207 6
and that Highbury, taken in its best, might reasonably E II 8 221 49
Before he could return to his chair, it was taken by Mrs. E II 8 222 58
second, slightly but correctly taken by Frank Churchill. E II 8 227 86
From that moment, Emma could have taken her oath that Mr. E II 8 228 93
"But really, I am half ashamed, and wish I had never taken E II 10 243 26
declare, that had the ball taken place, she did not think E II 12 263 42
However, my resolution is taken as to noticing Jane E II 15 284 9
"another thing must be taken into consideration too-- Mrs. E II 15 286 22
23
Could he by a touch of his finger have instantly taken E II 17 303 23
it in his way, and had taken the liberty of opening it. E II 17 303 24
"She has taken it into her head that Enscombe is too cold E II 18 307 20
which he had taken away, it would be very distressing. E III 1 315 1
dear friends--for the house was taken for may and June. E III 1 317 8
very quietly and properly taken, Mrs. Elton was evidently E III 2 324 20
"Knightley has taken pity on poor little Miss Smith!-- E III 2 328 42
43
walked out together, and taken a road, the Richmond road, E III 3 333 5
taken place, there have been matches of greater disparity. E III 4 342 39
to himself, had certainly taken an early dislike to Frank E III 5 343 2
nephews taken away their alphabets--their box of letters? E III 5 347 19
Mr. Woodhouse, who had already taken his little round in E III 6 361 42
herself for having taken no leave, making no E III 7 376 62
situation, and that her health will be taken good care of. E III 9 387 10
greater disparity had taken place than between Mr. Frank E III 11 407 28
Emma came, and he had taken pains (as she was convinced) E III 11 410 35
turn that every thing has taken, and the kindness I am now E III 12 419 8
a little relieved, she had taken a few turns, when she saw E III 13 424 1
to Harriet had been all taken as the language of her own E III 13 430 38
It was his jealousy of Frank Churchill that had taken him E III 13 432 41
anxiously hoping might not have taken cold from his ride.-- E III 14 434 3
Emma, it would not have been taken with such indifference." E III 15 444 6
Mr. Woodhouse taken from Hartfield!-- E III 15 449 31
How could he be so taken in?-- E III 17 469 36
I have taken some pains for your sake, and for Robert E III 18 474 34
How Anne's more rigid requisitions might have been taken, P III 2 13 6
The hint was immediately taken up by Mr. Shepherd, whose P III 2 13 7
let him have taken ever so many before--hey, Shepherd?" P III 3 17 2
Every thing in and about the house would be taken such P III 3 18 7
A house was never taken good care of, Mr. Shepherd P III 3 22 24
and all that he had told her would follow, had taken place. P III 4 29 8
world, but I know it is taken notice of by many persons." P III 6 46 10
They had taken out a young dog, who had spoilt their sport, P III 10 83 6
He and his wife had taken their intended drive, and were P III 10 90 38
Captain Harville had taken his present house for half a P III 11 97 12
pavement on the lower Cobb, and was taken up lifeless! P III 12 109 32
She must be taken to their house--all must go to their P III 12 111 50
which had been taken, and her regret that Mrs. Clay should P IV 1 124 11
She had been taken to Charmouth too, and she had bathed, P IV 2 130 3
connection, as he had formerly taken pains to shew neglect. P IV 2 135 35
Sir Walter had taken a very good house in Camden-Place, a P IV 3 137 1
she nor her friend had taken cold the day before, &c. &c." P IV 3 143 18
politely taken as possible, but her part must follow then. P IV 3 143 18
Lady Dalrymple had taken a house, for three months, in P IV 4 149 12
by far too much trouble taken to procure the acquaintance. P IV 4 150 18
lodgings in Westgate-Buildings, as Anne chose to be taken. P IV 5 153 5
journey, and had hardly taken possession of her lodgings, P IV 5 154 9
has generally taken me, when I have called on Mrs. Smith." P IV 5 157 18
"the care that will be taken of her; and it would be much " P IV 6 163 7
But now, the matter has taken the strangest turn of all; P IV 6 171 33
There were many things to be taken into the account. P IV 9 198 53
But then, it had been taken up by his father and mother. P IV 10 216 19
& some refreshment taken, & very cordially pressing them S 1 367 1
person's claims to be taken into account, those of the S 3 377 1
the inhabitants may be taken totally unawares, by one of S 4 381 1
not taken place, or we should have seen him in his way.-- S 5 387 1
sisters, for the object which had taken him to Willingden. S 6 393 1
I should not chuse to have my 2 housemaids time taken up S 7 401 1
The use of my right side is entirely taken away for S 10 418 1
A long journey from Hampshire taken for nothing--a brother S 11 420 1

TAKEN-IN (1)
I am not very easily taken-in my dear." S 7 399 1

TAKES (39)
When that wretched event takes place, Frederica must LS 24 291 17
fear the separation takes place too late to do us any good. LS 27 296 1
wind takes your hair and your bonnet in every direction. NA I 13 104 32
My father has recollected an engagement that takes our NA II 13 224 13
by no means desirable: it takes away one's independence." SS I 2 11 21
be almost completely fitted up as soon as she takes it." SS I 2 13 26
as every one must be who takes a very lively interest in SS I 14 70 1
settle on him a thousand a-year, if the match takes place. SS II 11 224 28
When the marriage takes place, I fear she must hear of it SS III 5 296 18
When Edward's unhappy match takes place, depend upon it SS III 5 296 20
I defy you not to be delighted with him if he takes notice W 319 2
in some of the measures he takes for becoming so.-- W 342 19
Elizth always takes care to have a room to herself."-- W 351 25
when this desirable event takes place, as to the advantage PP I 10 52 55
when the melancholy event takes place--which, however, as PP I 19 106 10
is on my side, nobody takes part with me, I am cruelly PP II 3 113 26
Mr. Bingley, and takes a prodigious deal of care of him." PP II 10 184 23
He takes them now for people of fashion." PP III 1 255 58
"No," said her father, "Wickham's a fool, if he takes her PP III 7 304 31
"But the motives of a man who takes orders with the MP I 11 109 20
I find he takes orders in a few weeks. MP II 5 226 61
to be dictated to; she takes her own independent walk MP III 1 323 56
It takes me quite unawares. MP III 7 378 10
and clearly--and when he takes a pen in hand, his thoughts E I 7 51 5
man of strong feelings; he takes things as he finds them, E I 11 96 26
The introduction must be unpleasant, whenever it takes E I 14 122 20
One takes up a notion, and runs away with it. Mr. Dixon, E II 3 176 46
you shall see how she takes it;--whether she colours." E II 8 222 56
The interest he takes in her--his anxiety about her health E II 8 226 79
home than the one he takes her from; and he who can do it, E III 13 428 23
the building in which N. takes M. for better, for worse." E III 17 463 14
She always takes the right time for applying. P IV 5 155 9
Look, he sees us; he kisses his hand to you; he takes you P IV 6 170 29
that; it takes a bend or two, but nothing of consequence. P IV 9 204 82
what a man suffers when he takes a last look at his wife P IV 11 234 31
She cannot look forward quite as I would have her--& takes S 3 376 1
which always takes, will give us the command of lodgers--. S 4 380 1
time, said he, but cocoa takes a great deal of boiling."-- S 10 416 1
"If Arthur takes my advice, he will go to bed too, for if S 12 424 1

TAKING (163)
My dear Alicia You are very good taking notice of LS 7 252 1
To impute such a design to Lady Susan would be taking from LS 14 263 1
the likelihood of it's taking place to any one, because I LS 20 277 5
great kindness of taking my part with her, & persuading LS 21 279 1
this letter, I know it is taking so great a liberty, I am LS 21 279 1
point--continued she, taking me affectionately by the hand. LS 24 289 12
The poor girl's heart was almost broke at taking leave of LS 41 310 4
taking her hand with affection, "may be proud of." NA I 7 50 47
language, and now he is taking the same liberty with you. NA I 14 107 14
very nice day, and we are taking a very nice walk, and you NA I 14 108 16
General's proposal of her taking his place in his son's NA II 5 156 4
one in particular, when taking out his watch, he stopped NA II 5 162 27
that he should be taking them out of doors against his own NA II 7 177 17
against taking her friend round the Abbey till his return. NA II 7 181 41
for his character, taking an early occasion of saying to NA II 9 192 4
see him myself without taking pains to converse with him." SS I 10 50 16
Willoughby's behaviour in taking leave of them, his SS I 15 77 19
Dashwood, accidentally taking up a volume of Shakespeare, SS I 16 85 11

12
She was sitting by Edward, and in taking his tea from Mrs. SS I 18 98 10
without taking that liberty, she begged to be excused. SS I 19 105 17
be doing any thing, or in taking patterns of some elegant SS I 21 120 6
said she, on his taking Miss Steele's pocket handkerchief, SS I 21 121 7
Then taking a small miniature from her pocket, she added, " SS I 22 131 35
"I was afraid you would think I was taking a great liberty SS I 22 132 42
I heard from him just before I left Exeter;" taking a SS I 22 134 52
No positive engagement indeed! after taking her all over SS II 8 196 20
sides, and I have not a doubt of its taking place in time. SS II 11 224 28
Whereas, in my opinion, by her taking so much notice of SS II 11 227 46
in my power, as my taking them out this evening shews. SS II 14 253 21
Lord! what a taking poor Mr. Edward will be in when he SS III 1 259 7
"I am so glad to meet you;" said Miss Steele, taking her SS III 2 271 8
on, and the time of its taking place remained as SS III 2 276 26
as soon as he could say any thing, after taking a chair. SS III 4 288 26
desire to affront her by taking Edward's part, could SS III 5 294 3
"Of one thing, my dear sister," kindly taking her hand, SS III 5 297 31
and Marianne, after taking so particular and lengthened a SS III 10 341 5
your restraints, by taking any part in those offices of SS III 10 346 28
"I meant," said Elinor, taking up some work from the table, SS III 12 359 19
was made against Edward's taking orders for the sake of SS III 14 374 4
Musgrave?--" said Emma, as they were taking their seats.-- W 358 28
the day before; and taking the office of superintendance W 360 30
And taking her hand, he would have given it to Mr. Darcy, PP I 6 26 38
Then taking the disengaged arm of Mr. Darcy, she left PP I 10 53 62
he readily engaged for taking the earliest opportunity of PP I 18 103 76
When they had gained their own room, Jane taking out the PP I 21 116 6
7
may depend upon my not taking so material a step without PP I 22 123 8
tour of pleasure which they proposed taking in the summer. PP II 4 154 21
finally resolved against taking orders, he hoped I should PP II 12 200 5
to taking you both, as you are neither of you large." PP II 14 211 10
"And yet I meant to be uncommonly clever in taking so PP II 17 225 17
and affectionately taking her hand, said in reply, "do not PP II 18 231 19
20
desire, did not in taking place, bring all the PP II 19 237 3
As they passed into other rooms, these objects were taking PP III 1 246 5
returned down stairs, and taking leave of the housekeeper, PP III 1 251 49
Colonel F. who instantly taking the alarm, set off from B. PP III 4 274 5
"What is there of good to be expected?" said he, taking PP III 7 302 11
Their taking her home, and affording her their personal PP III 7 305 36
your resolution of never taking orders, and that the PP III 10 329 31
Elizabeth had the satisfaction of seeing her father taking PP III 17 379 47
cruelty instead of kindness in taking her from her family. MP I 1 6 5
Lady Bertram, without taking half so much trouble, or MP I 2 12 2
Mrs. Norris had not the smallest intention of taking her. MP I 3 28 38
could I have in taking such a charge upon me as Fanny! MP I 3 29 46
ever speak again about my taking Fanny, you will be able MP I 3 30 56
Mansfield shall cure you both--and without any taking in. MP I 5 47 25
over to Sotherton, and taking a bed there; when Mrs. MP I 6 61 58
Maria, "I know that Mr. Crawford depends upon taking us. MP I 8 77 11
"And my dear Edmund," added Mrs. Norris, "taking out two MP I 8 77 12
would consequently be in taking her, which seemed to her a MP I 8 78 23
Her eye was eagerly taking in every thing within her reach; MP I 8 82 35
Mrs. Rushworth, civilly taking the hint and following them. MP I 9 90 33
"my dear companion may do me the honour of taking an arm." MP I 9 94 58
of an hour here," said Edmund, taking out his watch. MP I 9 95 65
By taking a circuitous, and as it appeared to her, very MP I 10 100 23
not last, and therefore taking no notice, only asked her MP I 10 101 29
she thought that he was taking particular pains, during MP I 10 104 51
good old Mrs. Whitaker, but my taking one of the cheeses. MP I 10 105 55
events; your sister's marriage, and your taking orders." MP I 11 108 8
"My taking orders I assure you is quite as voluntary as MP I 11 108 13
Come, Fanny,"--taking her hand--"do not be dawdling any MP I 12 119 24
It would be taking liberties with my father's house in his MP I 13 127 28
by the same speaker, who taking up one of the many volumes MP I 14 132 7
"I should be but too happy in taking the part if it were MP I 15 144 33
kindness; and when from taking notice of her work and MP I 15 147 57
You in the meanwhile will be taking a trip into china, I MP I 16 156 27
a volume on the table and then taking up some others.) MP I 16 156 27
setting in all at once, taking every body (at least Robert) MP II 4 212 31
He too was taking leave.-- MP II 4 215 47
"She will be late," said Sir Thomas, taking out his watch, MP II 5 218 15
at the parsonage, you are not to be taking place of her. MP II 5 221 32
"Bertram," said Crawford some time afterwards, taking the MP II 7 240 13
which Edmund was quietly taking from the servant to bring MP II 7 251 66
she now urged Fanny's taking one for the cross and to keep MP II 8 258 15
offering, nor you from taking it on that account, it ought MP II 9 263 14
But, Fanny,"--stopping her by taking her hand, and MP II 9 268 31
The very gown you have been taking notice of, is your own MP II 10 272 3
and taking an arm of each, they followed with the rest. MP II 10 275 9
instantly to Fanny, and taking out some letters said, with MP II 13 298 2
because he was taking, what seemed, very idle notice of me. MP III 4 353 45
reproach, and taking her hand, seemed hardly able to help MP III 5 357 6
herself remaining; and he taking out a newspaper--the MP III 7 382 28
with any idea of taking him for a model in dress; but (as MP III 10 402 12
Her father asked him to do them the honour of taking his MP III 10 406 22
the ramparts, taking her first lesson, I presume, in love. MP III 12 415 2
I mean about our taking you back into Northamptonshire. MP III 12 416 3
Her awe of her uncle, and her dread of taking a liberty MP III 14 436 15
and had engaged him in taking Fanny home to her aunt, with MP III 16 452 15
thing; and Mrs. Martin talks of taking a boy another year." E I 4 30 21
I had a great passion for taking likenesses, and attempted E I 6 43 13
Emma--but what has all that to do with taking likenesses? E I 6 43 15
down the rule of their taking turns, which ever began E I 9 81 75
to make his bow, when taking the paper from the table, she E I 9 81 79
80
"My poor dear Isabella," said he, fondly taking her hand, E I 12 100 18
my taking my family to one part of the coast or another?-- E I 12 106 60
believed him to be really taking comfort in some society E I 16 138 18
19
weather and business, of taking a personal leave of Mr. E I 17 140 2
perceived that she was taking the other side of the E I 18 145 5
It will be taking out my freedom.-- E II 6 200 14
too large about the wrist; but Jane is taking them in." E II 9 237 48
Weston and her companion taking leave also, could allow E II 10 246 55
made to hold--and then in taking the dimensions of the E II 11 247 2
Miss Bates's good-will or taking it for granted that the E II 15 281 2
your friends to have you taking up with any thing that may E II 17 301 16
for the purpose of taking her opinion as to the propriety E III 2 319 2
till her being seated at table and taking up her spoon. E III 2 328 44
promised them money, and taking out her purse, gave them a E III 3 334 6
Mrs. Elton, they were all taking the scheme as a E III 6 357 31
she recommended his taking some refreshment; he would find E III 6 364 56
sudden;--her proposal of taking another turn, her renewing E III 13 431 38
She was pleased, on taking leave, to find Miss Fairfax E III 16 459 45
46
indeed you are," cried Emma, warmly, and taking her hand. E III 16 459 48
Weston, whose marriages taking them from Hartfield, had, E III 17 466 29
to you, to feel that you were taking us all in.-- E III 18 478 67
especially after taking the young man so publicly by the P III 1 8 16
happy thought of their taking no present down to Anne, as P III 1 9 19
Depend upon me for taking care that no tenant has more P III 3 19 10
of Admiral Croft's really taking Kellynch-Hall, she P III 4 30 10
at sea in her; and after taking privateers enough to be P III 8 65 16
himself the pleasure of taking the precious volume into P III 8 66 22
The Admiral, after taking two or three refreshing turns P III 8 68 31
32
"My feelings, you see, did not prevent my taking Mrs. P III 8 69 44
near the table, and taking up the newspaper; and Captain P III 9 79 27
from him; some one was taking him from her, though he had P III 9 80 33
Louisa more eagerly, and taking her sister aside, seemed P III 10 85 16
"Do let us have the pleasure of taking you home. P III 10 91 40
His lameness prevented him from taking much exercise; but P III 11 99 18
of the household, and taking his seat, to drive off. P III 12 105 9
off for the town, Charles taking care of his sister, and P III 12 115 66
They must be taking off some trouble from the good people P IV 1 122 5
themselves, had been taking as much pains to seek the P IV 2 135 35
the pains he had been taking on this, the first P IV 3 139 7
Lord! what a boat it is!" taking a last look at the P IV 6 169 27
While Admiral Croft was taking this walk with Anne, and P IV 7 174 1
and taking a station, with less bare-faced design, by Anne. P IV 10 225 56
Mrs. Croft was taking leave. P IV 11 236 35
Here sir--(taking out his pocket book--) if you will do me S 1 366 1
Taking hold of Charlotte's arm with the ease of one who S 7 399 1
the quantity of Luggage taking off, bringing it might be S 9 406 1
offered his assistance in taking the house for Mrs G.-- S 9 410 1
I have been taking some Bitters of my own decocting, which S 9 411 1
you than I suspect you are in the habit of taking."-- S 10 416 1
Mrs G.-- to encourage Miss Lambe in taking her first Dip. S 12 424 1
law, who was most kindly taking it for granted that he was S 12 425 1

TALE (3)
She shall find that she has poured forth her tender tale LS 22 282 8
Mrs. Jennings wrote to tell the wonderful tale, to vent SS III 13 370 37
distance telling the same tale, before Mr. Elliot or any P IV 3 144 23

TALENT (24)
talent, as the cheif of my time is spent in conversation. LS 16 268 2
never had the convenient talent of affecting sensations LS 20 277 6
7
a Chit, a child, without talent or education, whom he had LS 22 282 6
Every body allows that the talent of writing agreeable NA I 3 27 28
in that total want of talent and taste which confined SS I 7 32 1
that you possess the talent of flattering with delicacy. PP I 14 68 10
"I certainly have not the talent which some people possess, PP II 8 175 24
feelings without some talent on one side, or some MP I 12 115 4
Nobody is fonder of the exercise of talent in young people, MP I 13 126 25
judgment than Tom, more talent and taste than Mr. Yates.-- MP I 18 165 3
The curtain over which she had presided with such talent MP II 2 195 22
judgment by all that talent, manner, attention, and MP II 6 231 11
and spirit of a man of talent too, that he sought her for MP III 2 328 6
but to read him well aloud, is no every-day talent." MP III 3 338 14
to end, and who had no talent, no conversation, no MP III 8 390 6
There is always some talent in it. E I 1 13 43
to exercise so charming a talent in favour of your friend. E I 6 43 14
may have a natural talent for--thinks strongly and clearly- E I 7 51 5
was her inferior in talent, and all the elegancies of mind. E I 16 136 9
in London, every lighter talent had been done full justice E II 2 164 6
That I thought, in a man of known musical talent, was some E II 6 201 28
with my curiosity, and exercise my talent of guessing. E III 10 400 68
said Emma, "I begin to doubt my having any such talent. E III 11 404 11
The Coruscations of talent, elicited by impassioned S 7 398 1

TALENTS (28)
she expatiated on the talents of her sons, and the beauty NA I 4 32 2
What his pursuits, his talents and genius?" SS I 9 44 18
together; his musical talents were considerable; and he SS I 10 48 8
have no more talents than inclination for a public life!" SS I 17 90 3
advantage of person and talents, united a disposition SS III 8 331 70
from any extraordinary talents or miraculous virtue, and PP II 6 161 9
ill-judged a direction of talents; talents which rightly PP II 19 236 2
a direction of talents; talents which rightly used, might PP II 19 236 2
man, who, in disposition and talents, would most suit her. PP III 8 312 15
Your lively talents would place you in the greatest danger PP III 17 376 35
with all their promising talents and early information, MP I 2 19 30
for men and women, her talents for the light and lively. MP I 8 81 31
such a degree of lively talents and comic taste, as were MP I 13 123 6
appreciate the talents of your company a little better." MP I 14 134 13
Her talents will be wanted in Amelia. MP I 14 135 15
He would enjoy her liveliness--and she has talents to MP II 3 199 13
his talents could not have recommended him at any time. E I 1 7 8
She inherits her mother's talents, and must have been E I 5 37 9
and make every body's talents conduce to the display of E I 18 150 32
So mild and ladylike--and with such talents!-- E II 15 282 5
I assure you I think she has very extraordinary talents. E II 15 282 5
Such talents as her's must not be suffered to remain E II 15 282 5
no idea that you will suppose her talents can be unknown." E II 15 283 6
parties to draw out her talents, and shall be constantly E II 15 284 9
talents, you have a right to move in the first circle. E II 17 301 18
abroad, no talents, or accomplishments for home, to occupy. P III 1 9 18
tempted, by some man of talents and independence, to enter P III 4 29 7
to possess, & such talents as he did also give himself S 8 405 2

TALES (4)
beleived the scandalous tales invented by Charles Smith to LS 14 264 4
much in awe of me, to tell tales; but if the mildness of LS 16 268 2
And here are Crabbe's Tales, and the Idler, at hand to MP I 16 156 27
tales, but--but--but. your's, affectionately." MP III 12 416 2

TALK (250)
& talk to him about Frederica that he may not forget her. LS 7 253 1
law's reserve, & listening to her husband's insipid talk. LS 10 258 3
over every new novel to talk in threadbare strains of the NA I 5 37 4
My dearest creature, do not talk of it. NA I 6 41 18
Talk of the curiosity of women, indeed!--'tis nothing. NA I 8 57 18
It would make us the talk of the place, if we were not to NA I 8 57 21
talk, began and ended with himself and his own concerns. NA I 9 66 31
there I met her, and we had a great deal of talk together. NA I 9 68 38
joined some gentlemen to talk over the politics of the day NA I 10 71 8
if he talks to me, I must talk to him again; but there are NA I 10 78 38
it is impossible for me to talk to them; and, besides, I NA I 10 78 40
them; and, besides, I do not want to talk to any body." NA I 10 78 40
You will be able to talk of Bath, and of all that you did NA I 10 79 55
I shall never be in want of something to talk of again to NA I 10 79 56
Let us sit down and talk in comfort. NA I 15 117 6
He made no reply, and was beginning to talk of something NA II 4 150 4
having heard the general talk of his preserving them in NA II 5 162 26
eye was employed, began to talk of the smallness of the NA II 5 162 27
injury; and she began to talk with easy gaiety of the NA II 7 179 29
can feel I myself-----but I must not talk of what I felt. NA II 13 225 19
I did not quite like, at breakfast, to hear you talk so NA II 15 241 4
to mention any favourite amusement to engage her to talk. SS I 10 47 3
all are delighted to see, and nobody remembers to talk to." SS I 10 50 14
know; but you shall not talk me out of my trust in it. SS I 15 78 26
She got up with an headache, was unable to talk, and SS I 16 83 1
one reserved who does not talk as fast, and admire what SS I 17 95 49
"Lord! Anne," cried her sister, "you can talk of nothing SS I 21 124 31
Did you never hear him talk of Mr. Pratt?" SS I 22 130 26
tired of me, they might talk to one another, and laugh at SS II 3 154 4
side, they continued to talk, both of them out of spirits, SS II 4 162 12
to look at Marianne and talk to Elinor, who often derived SS II 5 168 12
and calmly continuing her talk, as soon as Marianne SS II 7 181 7
8
"For shame, for shame, Miss Dashwood! how can you talk so! SS II 7 182 10
who have no sorrow of their own to talk of exertion! SS II 7 185 22
"You must not talk so, Marianne. SS II 7 186 29
But I cannot talk." SS II 7 186 36
Whom did I ever hear him talk of as young and attractive SS II 7 190 58
Elinor encouraged her as much as possible to talk of what SS II 9 201 2
be, when her mother could talk of fortitude! mortifying SS II 10 213 2
were by themselves, "I come to talk to you of my happiness. SS II 13 238 4
Elinor wished to talk of something else, but Lucy still SS II 13 239 7
You shan't talk me out of my satisfaction. SS II 13 239 9
He and I had a great deal of talk about it; and the best SS III 1 259 7
As Mrs. Jennings could talk on no other subject, Elinor SS III 1 260 10
a most serious aspect to talk over the dreadful affair, SS III 1 265 33
Elinor tried to talk of something else; but Miss Steele SS III 2 275 21

After this had been settled, Colonel Brandon began to talk SS III 3 283 20
my dear, I must be gone before I have had half my talk out. SS III 4 286 10
11
talk of it; and can the Colonel wait two or three months! SS III 4 291 51
the affair to me, to talk to him myself, and dissuade him SS III 5 299 37
a much greater exertion, began to talk of going likewise.-- SS III 7 308 5
"Do not talk to me of my wife," said he with an heavy sigh. SS III 8 329 65
I, you may well believe, could talk of nothing but my SS III 9 336 12
"Oh! my love, I could not then talk of hope to him or to SS III 9 337 18
her daughter's wishes began to talk of removing to Barton. SS III 10 340 4
left by themselves, to talk of the travellers, and feel SS III 10 341 5
the spot!--shall we ever talk on that subject, Elinor?"-- SS III 10 344 14
15
I can talk of it now, I hope, as I ought to do."-- SS III 10 344 15
I do not mean to talk to you of what my feelings have been SS III 10 344 17
Long before I was enough recovered to talk, I was SS III 10 345 28
Instead of talking of Edward, they came gradually to talk SS III 14 376 11
they were alone, you must talk to me all the rest of the W 341 19
he had done, & glad to talk of it, over his own fireside.-- W 343 19
wd not have had to talk to such a great man for the world. W 347 22
When the tea-things were removed, Tom began to talk of his W 357 28
risks, as she had rather talk of Croydon to Jane, with W 361 30
"Design! nonsense, how can you talk so! PP I 1 4 18
Bennets should meet to talk over a ball was absolutely PP I 5 18 3
They could talk of nothing but officers; and Mr. Bingley's PP I 7 29 4
Pray do not talk of that odious man. PP I 13 61 7
were ready enough to talk, and Mr. Collins seemed neither PP I 13 64 21
therefore at leisure to talk to Elizabeth, and she was PP I 16 77 8
ball to prepare for and talk of, the younger Miss Bennets PP I 17 88 15
him to talk, she made some slight observation on the dance. PP I 18 91 8
"Do you talk by rule then, while you are dancing?" PP I 18 91 12
success, and what we are to talk of next I cannot imagine." PP I 18 93 26
"No--I cannot talk of books in a ball-room; my head is PP I 18 93 30
Her mother would talk of her views in the same PP I 18 100 67
"How can you talk so?"--said Jane faintly smiling,-- "you PP I 21 119 25
in which she did not talk of Bingley, express her PP I 23 129 14
but to hear Lady Catherine talk, which she did without any PP II 6 163 15
"He did not talk to me of his own arts," said Fitzwilliam PP II 10 185 32
Well, now let us be quite comfortable and snug, and talk PP II 16 221 17
in Jane, whenever she might wish to talk again of either. PP II 17 227 25
There is no talk of his coming to Netherfield again in the PP II 17 228 27
And so, I suppose, they often talk of having Longbourn PP II 17 228 33
But I make no doubt, they often talk of it between PP II 17 228 35
She wanted to talk, but there seemed an embargo on every PP III 1 257 66
her from trying to talk to the latter, had they not been PP III 3 268 5
though they could not all talk, they could all eat; and PP III 3 268 6
herself much more to talk; and Elizabeth saw that he was PP III 3 269 8
It is useless to talk of it." PP III 7 305 38
Her husband allowed her to talk on without interruption, PP III 8 310 9
The bride and her mother could neither of them talk fast PP III 9 316 6
as I said before, they had a great deal of talk together. PP III 10 323 2
too much afraid of him to talk; Elizabeth was secretly PP III 16 365 1
I want to talk very seriously. PP III 17 373 15
so far as to talk of giving them a hint to be gone. PP III 19 387 9
"I shall not talk to you, Henry, but I know you will like MP I 5 45 9
easy in her manners, and as ready to talk as to listen. MP I 5 51 40
not saying much to the purpose, could talk of nothing else. MP I 6 52 1
doing several things that Sir Thomas and I used to talk of. MP I 6 54 9
confides in me, and will talk to me by the hour together, MP I 6 59 43
I like to hear her talk. MP I 7 63 2
gaieties of small talk, he began to be agreeable to her. MP I 7 65 13
be keenly felt, and Mr. Yates could talk of nothing else. MP I 13 121 1
it will be too absurd to talk of expense;--and as long as MP I 13 127 31
attention continued to talk to her and endeavour to raise MP I 15 147 56
It was not in Miss Crawford's power to talk Fanny into any MP I 16 150 1
play is all over, we will talk to him seriously, and make MP I 17 162 18
not one of those who can talk and work at the same time.-- MP I 18 167 9
him again, and hear him talk, to have her ear amused and MP II 1 179 9
He might talk of necessity, but she knew his independence.- MP II 2 193 18
I love to hear my uncle talk of the West Indies. MP II 3 197 5
"Oh! don't talk so, don't talk so," cried Fanny, MP II 3 198 9
respect; and I only wish you would talk to him more.-- MP II 3 198 9
"But I do talk to him more than I used. MP II 3 198 10
forbearance, and she began to talk of something else. MP II 3 199 16
when I take it and talk to her; to think as I think, be MP II 6 231 9
William as before, and talk to him, as her heart had been MP II 6 233 17
of those who would talk and those who would listen; and MP II 7 238 3
You talk of giving it the air of a gentleman's residence. MP II 7 243 27
"Oh! my dear William, do not talk so, do not be so MP II 7 250 55
of, and each found it necessary to talk of something else. MP II 7 250 56
Let me talk to you a little. MP II 9 268 31
I only want to talk to you." MP II 9 269 35
Excuse the liberty--but take care how you talk to me. MP II 9 269 36
had he been able to talk another five minutes, there is no MP II 9 270 40
She talked to her aunt Bertram--she must talk to somebody MP II 11 282 4
Talk to me for ever. MP II 12 292 7
"I will not talk of my own happiness," said he, "great as MP II 13 299 5
she had so comfortable a talk with him about William as to MP II 13 303 12
late,--he began to talk of going away; but the comfort of MP II 13 306 28
I begged him never to talk to me in that manner again.-- MP III 1 315 19
said, "it is of no use, I perceive, to talk to you. MP III 1 318 39
It was all known at the parsonage, where he loved to talk MP III 2 331 19
books we open, and we all talk Shakespeare, use his MP III 3 338 14
You must talk to me. MP III 4 346 8
to talk or to be silent, to be grave or to be gay. MP III 4 349 23
We had a long talk about it. MP III 4 351 36
of going, he loved to talk of it; and when once with her MP III 6 367 4
Of pleasant talk between the brother and sister, there was MP III 7 375 2
loved, and talk to him of his infant preference of herself. MP III 7 381 25
of an hour of earnest talk between the gentlemen, noise MP III 7 384 36
Norfolk was what he had mostly to talk of; there had been MP III 10 404 15
as well to talk of something else, and turned to Mansfield. MP III 10 405 17
My dear, dear Fanny, if I had you here, how I would talk MP III 12 415 2
at him; but, when able to talk or be talked to, or read to, MP III 14 429 2
talk on indifferent subjects could never be long supported. MP III 15 445 33
To talk over the dreadful business with Fanny, talk and MP III 16 449 5
evening that Edmund began to talk to her on the subject. MP III 16 453 17
Let us talk over this sad business. MP III 16 454 18
She went on, began to talk of you;--yes, then she began to MP III 16 455 21
then she began to talk of you, regretting, as well she MP III 16 455 21
Till that happened, they continued to talk of Miss MP III 16 459 31
afterwards,--why do you talk of success? where is your E I 1 12 42
shy, not unwilling to talk--and yet so far from pushing, E I 3 23 10
Emma allowed her father to talk--but supplied her visitors E I 3 25 15
them, and now loved to talk of the pleasures of her visit, E I 4 27 4
led Harriet to talk more of Mr. Martin,--and there was E I 4 28 6
"Oh! you would rather talk of her person than her mind, E I 5 39 17
Emma's side to talk of the weather, but he made no answer. E I 8 65 50
Elton may talk sentimentally, but he will act rationally. E I 8 66 53
back, not to think of Mr. Martin, but to talk of Mr. Elton. E I 8 68 58
How nicely you talk; I love to hear you. E I 9 76 28
"Dear me!--it is so odd to hear a woman talk so!"-- E I 10 84 14
To walk by the side of this child, and talk to and E I 10 88 33
he was soon led on to talk of them all in the usual way, E I 12 98 2
the sake of comfortable talk with his dear Isabella, and E I 12 100 15
an unsafe subject, "I must beg you not to talk of the sea. E I 12 101 23
And for a little while she hoped he would not talk of it, E I 12 105 51
She allowed him to talk, and arranged the glasses, and E I 13 114 27
But--that he should talk of encouragement, should consider E I 16 135 8
To you, he will talk of farming; to me, of drawing or E I 18 150 31
made Emma immediately talk of something else, though she E I 18 150 36
Oh! Miss Woodhouse, do talk to me and make me comfortable E II 3 179 52

of it--still she could talk of nothing else; and Emma, at E II 3 180 56
manner, and a readiness to talk, which convinced her that E II 5 190 22
My dear Emma, I am longing to talk to you. E II 8 222 59
She might talk on; and if he wanted to say any thing E II 8 226 79
himself, he would only talk louder, and drown her voice. E II 8 226 79
quite laid up; do not let them talk of such a wild thing. E II 11 249 11
Pray do not let them talk of it. E II 11 249 11
perhaps, when we come to talk it over--but these sort of E II 11 252 32
morning, we may talk it over, and see what can be done." E II 11 252 32
talk a great deal of the length of this passage, my dear. E II 11 254 47
48
I am very fond of hearing Miss Bates talk. E II 11 255 53
There was hardly time to talk over the first letter from E II 13 267 8
for my sake; think less, talk less of Mr. Elton for my E II 13 268 11
12
You will laugh at my warmth--but upon my word, I talk of E II 15 282 5
does not talk to Miss Fairfax as she speaks of her. E II 15 286 22
23
acquaintance and a quiet girl, and he could talk to her. E II 16 292 10
Put it up, put it up; we will have a good talk about it E II 17 304 27
to want others to talk, was very well satisfied with what E II 17 304 29
difficulty, upon Mrs. Elton's beginning to talk to him. E II 18 312 51
He was in high spirits; as ready to talk and laugh as ever, E III 1 316 4
Do not we often talk of Mr. Frank Churchill?-- E III 2 323 19
It was the very event to engage those who talk most, the E III 3 336 12
If you wish me to talk to Mrs. Hodges, or to inspect E III 6 355 22
I really must talk to him about purchasing a donkey. E III 6 356 26
at his ease, ready to talk with pleasure of what had been E III 6 357 33
I have a right to talk on such subjects, without being E III 6 361 40
and, at last, made himself talk nonsense very agreeably. E III 6 364 59
They shall talk. E III 7 369 16
And poor John's son came to talk to Mr. Elton about relief E III 8 383 29
I shall talk about it to him; he will settle for me; he E III 8 384 33
to talk over Jane Fairfax's situation with Mr. Knightley.-- E III 9 386 8
as governess, and could talk of it cheerfully, but Mr. E III 9 387 9
To talk would be only to irritate.-- E III 12 416 2
proved even too joyous to talk as usual, had been a E III 12 418 5
"If I loved you less, I might be able to talk about it E III 13 430 37
And now, let me talk to you of something else. E III 15 448 30
visits; now she could talk, and she could listen with true E III 16 451 4
in the meanwhile, we need not talk much on the subject." E III 18 471 16
When we first began to talk of her.-- E III 18 478 62
They talk and laugh a great deal too much for me. P III 5 38 31
disposition led him, to talk; and "that was in the year P III 8 63 2
cried the Admiral, "what stuff these young fellows talk! P III 8 65 12
"We had better not talk about it, my dear," replied Mrs. P III 10 92 45
While Captain Wentworth and Harville led the talk on one P III 11 100 23
done a good deed in making that poor fellow talk so much. P III 12 107 24
overcome-- "don't talk of it, don't talk of it," he cried. P III 12 116 70
71
and he wants to talk to you about them; he has found out P IV 2 131 9
enquiries to make, before the talk must be all their own. P IV 3 137 3
As soon as he could, he began to talk to her of Lyme, P IV 3 143 19
indulgence now and then to talk to him about Lyme, which P IV 4 148 9
You talk of being proud, I am called proud I know, and I P IV 4 151 21
did, in fact, think and talk a great deal more about the P IV 6 168 23
me the name of the young lady I am going to talk about. P IV 6 170 31
She had no longer any inclination to talk to him. P IV 8 188 43
animate her features, and make her rejoice to talk of it. P IV 9 192 5
I want you to talk about me to Mr. Elliot. P IV 9 195 24
She must talk to Lady Russell, tell her, consult with her, P IV 10 212 1
she began to talk of spending the morning in Rivers-Street. P IV 10 215 14
He had begun to talk of it a week ago; and by way of doing P IV 10 216 19
and when one can but get him to talk, he has plenty to say. P IV 10 218 26
They seem deep in talk. P IV 10 222 34
"Don't talk to me about heirs and representatives," cried P IV 10 224 48
silence, or insipid talk, to meet the heartless elegance P IV 10 226 63
and not disposed to talk, she could not avoid hearing many P IV 11 230 5
had met again and again to talk it over; what my brother P IV 11 230 5
The two ladies continued to talk, to re-urge the same P IV 11 231 11
Songs and proverbs, all talk of woman's fickleness. P IV 11 234 27
He could talk of it for ever.-- S 2 372 1
But let us talk of pleasanter things.-- S 5 389 1
He began, in a tone of great taste & feeling, to talk of S 7 396 1
his side--but why he shd talk so much nonsense, unless he S 7 398 1
He & I often talk that matter over.-- S 7 400 1
But--after a short pause--if Miss Esther thinks to talk me S 7 401 1
by no means indisposed to talk;--and while the other 4 S 10 415 1

TALKATIVE (5)
Lady Bertram became talkative, and what were the MP II 1 180 13
Lady Bertram was quite talkative. MP III 2 333 27
and with that sort of lock--and not very talkative." E II 3 176 44
Mr. John Knightley proved more talkative than his brother. E II 18 311 37
grew talkative and gay, making her his first object. E III 7 367 3

TALKATIVENESS (1)
Emma encouraged her talkativeness--amused by such a E I 4 27 4

TALKED (253)
I talked to him about you & your daughter, & he is so from LS 9 257 1
Sir James talked a good deal, & made many civil excuses to LS 20 276 3
de courcy could be talked, flattered & finessed into an LS 42 313 8
talked of once, she might have danced with George Parry. NA I 2 23 25
He talked with fluency and spirit--and there was an NA I 3 25 2
almost forgot Mr. Tilney while she talked to Miss Thorpe. NA I 4 33 6
conversation;--they talked much, and with much enjoyment; NA I 5 35 2
subject, for Mrs. Thorpe talked chiefly of her children, NA I 5 36 3
not behaved, he had not talked, like the married men to NA I 8 53 3
with her, and readily talked therefore whenever she could NA I 8 56 11
such, that as she never talked a great deal, so she could NA I 9 60 1
Mrs. Hughes talked to me a great deal about the family." NA I 9 68 42
"Oh! a vast deal indeed; she hardly talked of any thing NA I 9 68 44
Isabella smiled incredulously, and talked the rest of the NA I 10 71 7
This was of course vehemently talked down as no reason at NA I 11 84 19
Thorpe talked to his horse, and she meditated, by turns, NA I 11 87 51
talked in phrases which conveyed scarcely any idea to her. NA I 14 110 28
He talked of fore-grounds, distances, and second distances- NA I 14 111 29
You talked of expected horrors in London--and instead of NA I 14 113 39
She wished Isabella had talked more like her usual self, NA II 3 148 28
Isabella talked of his attentions; she had never been NA II 3 148 29
Eleanor, I suppose, has talked of her a great deal?" NA II 9 196 23
And yet, when we talked about it in Bath, you little NA II 10 204 19
had been in the country, talked every now and then of NA II 11 209 5
A very short visit to Mrs. Allen, in which Henry talked at NA II 15 243 10
He so frequently talked of the increasing expenses of SS I 5 27 6
talked a great deal, seemed very happy, and rather vulgar. SS I 7 34 5
"But he talked of flannel waistcoats," said Marianne; "and SS I 8 38 12
my invitation, when I talked of his coming to Barton. SS I 8 39 15
and deceitful:--had I talked only of the weather and the SS I 10 48 5
They read, they talked, they sang together; his musical SS I 10 48 8
So wondered, so talked Mrs. Jennings, her opinion varying SS I 14 70 3
the lanes; if they talked of the valley, she was as speedy SS I 16 85 15
Mrs. Jennings, in the mean time, talked on as loud as she SS I 19 107 28
account for, or if he had talked more of one lady than SS II 2 147 12
to Mrs. Jennings, talked with her, laughed with her, and SS II 4 160 2
that she was, and then talked of head-aches, low spirits, SS II 4 162 10
correspond, and their marriage is universally talked of." SS II 5 173 42
have you really, ma'am, talked yourself into a persuasion SS II 7 181 9
Oh! no one, no one--he talked to me only of myself." SS II 7 190 58
It must be terrible for you to hear it talked of; and as SS II 8 196 18
beg you will contradict it, if you ever hear it talked of." SS II 10 218 28
satisfied, and soon talked of something else. "we spent SS II 13 243 32
to bring her to hear it talked of by others, without SS III 1 260 10
and when Mrs. Jennings talked of Edward's affection, it SS III 1 265 33

Harley-Street, and been talked to by his mother and all of SS III 2 273 16
So then he was monstrous happy, and talked on some time SS III 2 274 16
Two maids and two men indeed!--as I talked of t'other day.- SS III 2 277 28
They then talked on for a few minutes longer without her SS III 3 281 9
10
vastly well,--she will not like to hear it much talked of." SS III 5 295 16
her carpet-work; they talked of the friends they had left SS III 6 303 12
confidante of himself, talked to her a great deal of the SS III 6 305 16
Mr. Harris, who attended her every day, still talked SS III 7 309 7
to be material, and talked of the relief which a fresh SS III 7 312 19
was suffered to speak it, talked of nothing but Willoughby, SS III 10 348 34
to be open, she sat down again and talked of the weather. SS III 12 359 12
politeness with which he talked of his doubts, he did not, SS III 13 366 20
You talked so stoutly beforehand, that I was sadly afraid W 343 19
so early, and talked of giving one himself at Netherfield. PP I 3 10 6
If he had been so very agreeable he would have talked to PP I 5 19 14
He then sat down by her, and talked scarcely to any one PP I 11 54 2
Lydia talked incessantly of lottery tickets, of the fish PP I 16 84 59
I talked about the dance, and you ought to make some kind PP I 18 91 9
was over, singing was talked of, and she had the PP I 18 100 68
detached from the rest, and talked only to each other. PP I 18 103 75
She talked to Elizabeth again and again; coaxed and PP I 20 112 23
She talked on, therefore, without interruption from any of PP I 20 113 29
30
and the concern of every body was well talked over.-- PP I 21 115 3
and wherever she went she was sure of hearing it talked of. PP I 23 129 16
with which Charlotte talked of the healthfulness of the PP II 5 156 4
Scarcely any thing was talked of the whole day or next PP II 6 160 4
by Lady Catherine; who talked of his coming with the PP II 7 170 6
of a well-bred man, and talked very pleasantly; but his PP II 7 171 10
He now seated himself by her, and talked so agreeably of PP II 8 172 3
Lady Catherine listened to half a song, and then talked, PP II 8 174 12
the conversation, talked on indifferent matters till they PP II 10 186 38
And then we were so merry all the way home! we talked and PP II 16 222 22
talked of Matlock and Dove Dale with great perseverance. PP III 1 257 66
Sometimes she could fancy, that he talked less than on PP III 2 262 8
Mrs. Gardiner and Elizabeth talked of all that had PP III 3 271 20
They talked of his sister, his friends, his house, his PP III 3 272 20
unfortunate affair; and will probably be much talked of. PP III 5 289 42
But there was much to be talked of, in marrying her; and PP III 8 309 6
and talked with them both, Wickham repeatedly, Lydia once. PP III 10 321 2
I talked to her repeatedly in the most serious manner, PP III 10 325 2
what I told you on that point, when first we talked of it." PP III 10 329 32
I can hardly bear to hear it thus perpetually talked of. PP III 11 333 28
and their mother talked on, of her dislike of Mr. Darcy, PP III 11 334 36
There he had talked to her friends, when he could not to PP III 11 335 43
and was really persuaded that she talked as much as ever. PP III 11 337 56
her feelings, though she talked to Bingley of nothing else, PP III 13 348 34
In this manner Lady Catherine talked on, till they were at PP III 14 358 72
73
The acknowledged lovers talked and laughed, the PP III 17 372 2
But we considered it, we talked of it as impossible. PP III 17 373 11
"You might have talked to me more when you came to dinner." PP III 18 381 11
Mrs. Bingley and talked of Mrs. Darcy may be guessed. PP III 19 385 1
It was William whom she talked of most and wanted most to MP I 2 15 12
He talked to her more, and from all that she said, was MP I 2 16 20
it gave me to hear it talked of as likely to do me good;--(MP I 3 27 36
his lips if horses were talked of) and then think of the MP I 3 27 36
She talked to her, listened to her, read to her; and the MP I 4 35 6
it every where as a matter not to be talked of at present. MP I 4 39 12
of inclination, but it would only do to be talked of. MP I 5 48 29
talked and laughed till I did not know which way to look. MP I 5 50 35
by any common rule, he talked no nonsense, he paid no MP I 7 65 13
enough to be talked of with pleasure--till the fourth day, MP I 7 70 30
any thing else should be talked of, for Mrs. Norris was in MP I 8 75 2
Mr. Rushworth talked of the west front." MP I 8 82 35
And she talked and laughed about it with so little caution, MP I 9 88 24
more engaging, and they talked with mutual satisfaction. MP I 9 96 76
a whole hour, when he had talked of only a few minutes, MP I 10 103 49
She started no difficulties that were not talked down in MP I 13 129 40
were otherwise much talked of, for Edmund's disapprobation MP I 15 142 24
had soon talked away all that could be said of either. MP I 15 142 24
Miss Crawford talked of something else, and soon MP I 15 144 36
had read and written, and talked and laughed, till within MP I 15 150 1
the privacy and propriety which was talked about at first. MP I 16 153 8
was insufficient, that she might have talked in vain. MP II 2 188 3
down for but to be talked to about it, and entreated and MP II 4 211 26
When we talked of her last night, you none of you seemed MP II 6 229 5
might be all talked over as well without doors as within. MP II 8 257 15
How many a time have we talked over her little errors! MP II 9 270 38
that he might not have talked away all Miss Crawford's MP II 9 270 40
they all stood about and talked and laughed, and every MP II 10 273 6
sometimes, when he talked of William, he was really not un- MP II 10 278 20
You will not want to be talked to. MP II 10 278 20
They had talked--and they had been silent--he had reasoned- MP II 10 279 21
She talked to her aunt Bertram--she must talk to somebody MP II 11 282 4
Had Henry returned, as he talked of doing, at the end of MP II 11 287 17
proper name; but when he talked of her having such a MP II 12 294 16
different from what they were when he talked to the others. MP II 13 304 16
He talked therefore for several minutes without Fanny's MP III 1 314 16
standing by the fire, talked over the too common neglect MP III 3 339 22
It is anger to be talked of, rather than felt. MP III 4 352 42
looks, it could not be talked away, and attempting it no MP III 4 355 55
within a fortnight, he talked of going, he loved to talk MP III 6 367 4
the mode of it came to be talked of, and Mrs. Norris found MP III 6 372 21
and Fanny were talked of as already advanced one stage. MP III 6 374 29
smell of spirits; and he talked on only to his son, and MP III 7 380 23
home, not to stand and be talked to, but to run about and MP III 7 381 25
and the navy-list; he talked only of the dock-yard, the MP III 8 389 3
They talked of William, a subject on which Mrs. Price MP III 10 400 7
heard a little news, talked over the badness of the MP III 11 408 4
My uncle talked of two months. MP III 11 410 13
when able to talk or be talked to, or read to, Edmund was MP III 14 429 2
aunt, how she could have talked to her, and tried at once MP III 14 432 10
Mrs. Price talked of her poor sister for a few minutes-- MP III 15 444 26
evenings, he had so well talked his mind into submission, MP III 17 462 5
We talked it all over with Mr. Weston last night. E I 1 8 18
Some people even talked of a promise to his wife on her E I 1 12 41
All manner of solemn nonsense was talked on the subject, E I 1 12 41
His coming to visit his father had been often talked of E I 2 17 8
yards forward, while they talked together, soon made her E I 4 31 27
Mrs. Weston, I am not to be talked out of my dislike of E I 5 39 21
He talked of Harriet, and praised her so warmly, that she E I 6 42 1
and sooner than had been talked of, and with an agitated, E I 7 50 1
"Nonsense, errant nonsense, as ever was talked!" cried Mr. E I 8 65 49
Miss Nash had told her all this, and had talked a great E I 8 68 58
arrival, the many to be talked to, welcomed, encouraged, E I 11 92 3
The brothers talked of their own concerns and pursuits, E I 12 100 16
And she talked in this way so long and successfully that, E I 12 104 45
affection, Mr. Perry was talked of, and Harriet herself E I 13 109 5
the time talked of: "for I cannot depend upon his coming. E I 14 121 14
While he talked to Isabella, however, Emma found an E I 14 122 19
And in this style he talked on for some time very properly, E I 15 124 3
could;" and James was talked to, and given a charge to go E I 15 128 22
very day; she could have talked to him of Harriet, and the E I 15 129 23
"Here have I," said she, "actually talked poor Harriet E I 16 137 11
Mr. Woodhouse talked over his alarms, and Emma was in E I 17 141 4
but meant, having once talked him handsomely over, to be E II 1 156 6
as Mr. Woodhouse had been talked into what was necessary, E II 3 170 2
about it;" but still she talked of it--still she could E II 3 180 56
was over, she had talked herself into all the sensations E II 3 180 57
about it all! she had talked her into love; but alas! she E II 4 183 10
but alas! she was not so easily to be talked out of it. E II 4 183 10
many vacancies of Harriet's mind was not to be talked away. E II 4 183 10
common-place had been talked almost all the time --till E II 5 186 4
she hoped Mr. Elton would now be talked of no more. E II 5 188 8
The Frank Churchill so long talked of, so high in interest E II 5 190 22
Woodhouse was to be talked into an acquiescence of his E II 7 208 9
and Mr. Elton were talked over, Emma could fairly E II 8 214 13
came in, and were talked to and admired amid the usual E II 8 219 43
They talked at first only of the performance. E II 8 228 88
and Mr. Frank Churchill talked a great deal about your E II 9 232 9
Nobody talked about it. E II 9 232 11
"They talked a great deal about him, especially Anne Cox. E II 9 232 19
these apples, and we talked about them and said how much E II 9 238 51
She had great pleasure in hearing Frank Churchill talked E II 13 264 1
first contribution and talked with a good grace of her E II 15 281 2
After Emma had talked about it for ten minutes, Mr. E II 16 291 4
"When I talked of your being altered by time, by the E II 16 294 23
The varieties of hand-writing were farther talked of, and E II 16 297 44
Dining once with the Coles--and having a ball talked of, E II 18 312 50
Somebody talked of rain.-- E III 2 321 14
While she talked of his son, Mr. Weston's attention was E III 2 321 16
wait, and every projected party be still only talked of. E III 6 352 2
She has talked of it since. E III 7 375 59
I wish you could have heard how she talked of it--with E III 7 375 59
While they talked, they were advancing towards the E III 7 375 62
and by the time they had talked it all over together, and E III 10 401 69
over together, and he had talked it all over again with E III 10 401 69
When we talked about him, it was clear as possible." E III 11 406 20
and walked by her, and talked so very delightfully!-- E III 11 409 35
at first, he had talked to her in a more particular way E III 11 410 35
were put by, they had talked a good deal of the present E III 12 418 5
She talked with a great deal of reason, and at least equal E III 12 420 14
from Mr. Perry, and talked on with much self-contentment, E III 14 434 3
Of the pianoforte so much talked of, I feel it only E III 14 439 8
When they had all talked a little while in harmony of the E III 16 454 16
17
I do not know, for I never heard the subject talked of." E III 16 456 31
used to be talked to by each, on every fair occasion.-- E III 17 466 30
"You are materially changed since we talked on this E III 18 474 32
I have often talked to her a good deal. E III 18 474 34
she had moved about, and talked to herself, and laughed E III 18 475 37
He was invited to Kellynch Hall; he was talked of and P III 1 8 15
the highest terms, he was talked into allowing Mr. P III 3 24 35
But was not easy till she had talked Charles into driving P III 6 48 17
she heard his voice--he talked to Mary, said all that was P III 7 59 25
Mary talked, but she could not attend. P III 7 60 27
When he talked, she heard the same voice, and discerned P III 8 64 4
a pleasure to hear him talked of, by such a good friend." P III 8 66 20
talked, with grave faces, of his studying himself to death. P III 10 82 2
They talked of coming into this side of the country. P III 10 84 8
Captain Wentworth talked of going there again himself; it P III 11 94 7
restraints; and having talked of poetry, the richness of P III 11 100 23
but no, he reasoned and talked in vain; she smiled and P III 12 109 32
her; but still it must be talked of, she must make P IV 1 124 12
He had talked of going down to Plymouth for a week, and P IV 2 133 25
them, while Mr. Elliot's frequent visits were talked of. P IV 3 140 11
in Marlborough buildings, were talked of the whole evening. P IV 3 141 13
Sir Walter talked of his youngest daughter; "Mr. Elliot P IV 3 143 18
Dalrymple and Miss Carteret," were talked of to every body. P IV 4 149 13
In the course of a second visit she talked with great P IV 5 153 8
in having been very much talked of between her friend and P IV 5 158 21
agreeable man,--that he talked well, professed good P IV 5 160 27
Admiral, than the Admiral ever thought or talked about him. P IV 6 168 23
health or spirits, and he talked of Uppercross, of the P IV 7 176 8
love-song must not be talked of,--but it is as nearly the P IV 8 186 25
They talked for a few minutes more; the improvement held; P IV 8 190 47
the tall Irish officer, who is talked of for one of them." P IV 9 193 8
When I talked of a whole history therefore, you see, I was P IV 9 205 82
My heart bled for you, as I talked of happiness. P IV 9 211 101
wedding-clothes to be talked of: she had imagined such P IV 10 217 20
Charles and Mary still talked on in the same style; he, P IV 10 224 50
Anne talked of being perfectly ready, and tried to look it; P IV 10 225 62
had reached him while she talked with Captain Harville; P IV 11 241 60
itself could not be talked of long, without the S 3 375 1
thing requiring rest, & talked of going home again S 6 390 1
He came into the room remarkably well, talked much--& very S 7 394 1
clear brain she presumed, & talked a good deal by rote.-- S 7 398 1
like a true great lady, talked & talked only of her own S 7 399 1
true great lady, talked & talked only of her own concerns, S 7 399 1
She talked however, the whole evening as incessantly as S 10 413 1

TALKER (12)

Mrs. Thorpe, however, had one great advantage as a talker, NA I 4 32 2
latter was an everlasting talker, and from the first had SS I 11 54 6
she was a most determined talker; but being likewise PP I 16 76 8
Mr. Rushworth, however, though not usually a great talker, MP I 6 55 17
He had the best right to be the talker; and the delight of MP II 1 178 8
William was often called on by his uncle to be the talker. MP II 6 236 21
and though never a great talker, she was always more MP III 6 369 11
She was a great talker upon little matters, which exactly E I 3 21 4
most communicative, and who was always the greater talker. E I 12 100 16
aunt was such an eternal talker! --and she was made such a E II 2 166 11
right of being principal talker, which a day spent any E II 17 303 24
I am a talker, you know; I am rather a talker; and now and E III 5 346 16

TALKERS (2)

The party being now all united, and the chief talkers MP II 5 227 68
The two young men were the only talkers, but they, MP III 3 339 22

TALKING (211)

She has been talking a great deal about it to me, she LS 15 267 4
& sat with him in his room, talking over the whole matter. LS 24 285 2
sisters, and cousins, talking both together, far more NA I 4 32 2
Isabella, who had been talking to James on the other side NA I 8 52 2
lively as ever, and was talking with interest to a NA I 8 53 3
We are not talking about you." NA I 8 57 16
What can it signify to you, what we are talking of? NA I 8 57 20
Perhaps we are talking about you, therefore I would advise NA I 8 57 20
will, and they continued talking together as long as both NA I 10 72 8
I really believe I shall always be talking of Bath, when I NA I 10 79 56
You are talking of the man you danced with last night, are NA I 11 85 35
He replied by asking her to make room for him, and talking NA I 12 95 15
While talking to each other, she had observed with some NA I 12 95 17
whether she had seen him talking with General Tilney:--"he NA I 12 95 18
But what do you think we have been talking of?-- NA I 12 96 20
It does not signify talking. NA I 13 101 22
Miss Morland has been talking of nothing more dreadful NA I 14 113 39
But this is idle talking! NA I 15 120 22
us distress our dear Catherine by talking of such things. NA II 1 136 46
"He did not know what he was talking of, I dare say; ten SS I 2 9 5
on the occasion, talking to her so expressively of her SS I 4 23 19
"I rather think you are mistaken, for when I was talking SS I 8 39 17
one day, when they were talking of him together, "whom SS I 10 50 14
they were whispering and talking together as fast as could SS I 12 60 13
discourse with him by talking of their present residence, SS I 16 89 42
you will never offend me by talking of former times. SS I 17 92 26
what passed, by instantly talking of something else, she SS I 18 98 13
with us; and so we began talking of my brother and sister, SS I 20 115 50
"Oh! they are talking of their favourite beaux, I dare say. SS II 2 148 20
he had been previously talking, he felt the necessity of SS II 6 177 11
Well, it don't signify talking, but when a young man, be SS II 8 194 10
And what good does talking ever do you know?" SS II 8 196 18
pleasure while they were talking, and who expected to see SS II 8 200 43
"Aye, aye; that is very pretty talking--but it won't do-- SS II 10 218 27
Elinor, that this is a kind of talking which I cannot bear. SS II 13 244 46

hour's conversation; for, talking of his brother, and SS II 14 250 12
I left her this morning with her lawyer, talking over the SS III 1 269 53
give ear to such kind of talking; so she told him directly SS III 2 273 16
and Marianne, still talking wildly of mama, her alarm SS III 7 311 14
become indifferent to me; talking to myself of our past SS III 8 326 53
But I am talking like a fool. SS III 8 328 63
of Margaret's return, and talking of the dear family party SS III 10 343 8
not look up;--he never was a gentleman much for talking." SS III 11 354 31
hard labour of incessant talking will dispatch more SS III 13 363 9
Instead of talking of Edward, they came gradually to talk SS III 14 376 11
style of living or of talking, to give a suspicion of his SS III 14 377 12
"So late, my dear, what are you talking of; cried the W 325 4
of talking to Charles, stood to look at his partner.-- W 331 11
"Aye do--& if you find she does not want much talking to, W 333 13
"That's odd sort of talking!-- W 352 26
frequently cd not endure talking at all, the affair was so W 361 30
"I do not mind his not talking to Mrs. Long," said Miss PP I 5 20 15
collect by your manner of talking, you must be two of the PP I 7 29 5
6
"I am talking of possibilities, Charles." PP I 8 38 37
expostulation with her brother for talking such nonsense. PP I 10 51 40
disliking her guest, by talking of their supposed marriage, PP I 10 52 54
collection, but really talking to Mr. Bennet, with little PP I 15 71 6
were still standing and talking together very agreeably, PP I 15 72 8
of it, and they continued talking together with mutual PP I 16 84 59
had the refreshment of talking of Wickham, and of hearing PP I 18 90 5
interruption has made me forget what we were talking of." PP I 18 93 24
25
Your sister has been talking to me about him, and asking PP I 18 94 45
find that her mother was talking to that one person (Lady PP I 18 98 63
bore it; but Jane was very composedly talking to Bingley. PP I 18 100 68
"Of what are you talking?" PP I 20 111 9
"What do you mean, Mr. Bennet, by talking in this way? PP I 20 112 21
I have no pleasure in talking to undutiful children.-- PP I 20 113 28
Not that I have much pleasure indeed in talking to any PP I 20 113 28
complaints can have no great inclination for talking. PP I 20 113 28
convinced that they were talking of the Longbourn estate, PP I 23 130 16
seem by her manner of talking, as if she wanted to PP II 3 148 26
The evening was spent chiefly in talking over PP II 5 157 10
What is it you are talking of? PP II 8 173 4
who called out to know what they were talking of. PP II 8 176 27
She was afraid of talking longer of his friend; and, PP II 9 178 11
herself the trouble of talking or of listening much; but PP II 10 182 1
and laughing and talking with more violence than ever; PP II 18 230 12
In talking over their route the evening before, Mrs. PP II 19 240 12
great pleasure in talking of her master and his sister. PP III 1 248 23
They stood a little aloof while he was talking to their PP III 1 251 52
talking to the man about them, that he advanced but little. PP III 1 254 57
when the others were talking together, and in a tone which PP III 2 262 8
her power by thinking and talking on the subject, to give PP III 5 284 10
as her fears; and, after talking with her in this manner PP III 5 288 39
and talking away just as if she was reading a sermon. PP III 9 319 24
But in spite of all this fine talking, my dear Lizzy, you PP III 10 324 2
My dear Mr. Bennet," cried his wife, "what are you talking PP III 13 348 40
for the pleasure of talking of her; and when Bingley was PP III 13 349 44
no occasion for talking to him, except just now and then. PP III 17 375 26
at her lively, sportive manner of talking to her brother. PP III 19 387 11
As far as walking, talking, and contriving reached, she MP I 1 8 9
Mrs. Norris had been talking to her the whole way from MP I 2 13 4
he made reading useful by talking to her of what she read, MP I 2 22 35
his place in carving, talking to the steward, writing to MP I 4 34 1
than Mrs. Norris's talking of it every where as a matter MP I 4 39 12
Talking does no good. MP I 5 46 16
to have it so; a talking pretty young woman like Miss MP I 5 47 26
Mrs. Norris was talking to Julia, and did not hear. MP I 7 72 48
places at once; and I was talking to Mr. Green at that MP I 7 73 53
very walk they had been talking of; and standing back, MP I 9 95 67
"What are you talking of? MP I 14 134 13
of Mr. Yates, was talking with forced gaiety to him alone, MP I 17 160 8
Some one was talking there in a very loud accent--he did MP II 1 182 22
know the voice--more than talking--almost hallooing. MP II 1 182 22
Mr. Yates was still talking. MP II 1 185 28
We were talking of you at the parsonage, and those were MP II 3 198 13
yourself forward, and talking and giving your opinion as MP II 5 221 32
the tea-table, he began talking of them with more MP II 5 224 49
deserted card-table, talking very comfortably and not MP II 7 249 49
of conveying your brother and talking of you by the way." MP II 10 277 19
"I have been talking incessantly all night, and with MP II 10 278 20
Colonel Harrison had been talking of Mr. Crawford or of MP II 11 283 4
her an opportunity of talking over Thursday night with Mrs. MP II 11 283 7
This is a sort of talking which is very unpleasant to me. MP II 13 301 7
But he was still talking on, describing his affection, MP II 13 301 7
She was talking at Fanny, and resenting this private walk MP III 1 324 57
she was sure they must be talking of her; and when tea at MP III 3 334 5
for me to find any relief in talking of what I feel." MP III 4 346 11
"My uncle thought me wrong, and I knew he had been talking MP III 4 347 15
"I should like to sit talking with you here all day, but MP III 5 364 30
and now by dint of long talking on the subject, explaining MP III 6 370 14
to defend themselves, all talking together, but Rebecca MP III 7 382 27
first only in working and talking; but after a few days, MP III 9 398 9
After talking a little more about Mansfield, a subject in MP III 10 401 10
the pleasure of talking of Mansfield was so very great! MP III 10 406 21
And my poor aunt talking of me every hour!" MP III 13 424 3
and she found herself talking of what she should do when MP III 14 431 8
And being always with her, and always talking MP III 17 470 27
those soft blue eyes, in talking and listening, and E I 3 24 11
I can hardly imagine the young man whom I saw talking with E I 7 51 5
from his general way of talking in unreserved moments, E I 8 66 53
Mr. Elton was still talking, still engaged in some E I 10 88 34
"Are you talking about me?-- E I 11 95 19
It does not bear talking of." E I 12 105 51
her five children, and talking over what she had done E I 13 108 1
and felt sure that he would want to be talking nonsense. E I 15 129 23
opinion, been talking enough of Mr. Elton for that day. E II 1 155 1
and her more active, talking daughter, almost ready to E II 1 155 4
to sit some time with us, talking of Jane; for as soon as E II 1 156 7
I am sure they were talking of me; and I could not help E II 3 178 52
we shook hands, and stood talking some time; but I know no E II 3 178 52
happy man he ought to be; talking only of himself and his E II 4 182 5
If the talking aunt had taken me quite by surprise, it E II 6 198 7
and said he did not know what he was talking about. E II 6 204 43
did know what he was talking about, and that he shewed a E II 6 204 43
warm regard, was fond of talking of him--said he would be E II 7 205 2
Woodhouse was soon composed enough for talking as usual. E II 7 209 13
There will be a great many people talking at once. E II 7 210 16
before Miss Fairfax, and talking to her; but as to its E II 8 222 57
No; he was talking to Mrs. Cole--he was looking on E II 8 230 99
by somebody else, and he was still talking to Mrs. Cole. E II 8 230 99
"What was I talking of?" said she, beginning again when E II 9 237 49
"I declare I cannot recollect what I was talking of.-- E II 9 237 51
"there will be plenty of time for talking every thing over. E II 11 252 34
for Mrs. Elton, who only wanted to be talking herself. E II 14 273 20
they waited for dinner, he was talking to Miss Fairfax. E II 16 292 10
almost always either talking together or silent together. E II 17 299 1
still, who had been long talking, and might have been E II 17 303 23
and he sat smiling and talking to them the whole time, in E II 17 303 26
Miss Bates, who came in talking, and had not finished her E III 2 322 18
Much better employed talking to the young ladies. E III 2 323 19
At this moment Frank began talking so vigorously, that E III 2 324 22
Talking about spruce beer.-- E III 4 339 19
The Eltons were still talking of a visit from the E III 5 343 1
and his feelings were too much irritated for talking. E III 5 351 38
gathering, accepting, or talking--strawberries, and only E III 6 358 35
what Mrs. Elton and Jane Fairfax were talking of.-- E III 6 359 37
found them more engaged in talking than in looking around. E III 6 360 40
is rather too much to be talking nonsense for the E III 7 369 15
bustle on her approach; a good deal of moving and talking. E III 8 378 4
Poor dear Jane was talking of it just now.-- E III 8 384 33
"I was wrong," he continued, "in talking of its being E III 10 393 17
averting her eyes, and talking on with eagerness, that E III 10 395 35
to be sensible of his talking to her much more than he had E III 11 409 35
the subject, and began talking about farming:--the second, E III 11 410 35
was his having sat talking with her nearly half an hour E III 11 410 35
do the subject no good, to be talking of it farther.-- E III 12 416 2
"I would rather be talking to you," he replied; "but as it E III 15 444 5
You were both talking of other things; of business, shows E III 18 473 26
to know what a man is talking of?-- what do you deserve?" E III 18 474 28
The others had been talking of the child, Mrs. Weston E III 18 479 73
instances of what I am talking of, Lord St. Ives, whose P III 3 19 16
almost all the time they were talking the matter over. P III 3 22 24
But Mrs. Clay was talking so eagerly with Miss Elliot, P III 3 23 26
one of them, after talking of rank, people of rank, and P III 6 46 10
the talking, laughing, and singing of their daughters. P III 6 46 12
To hear them talking so much of Captain Wentworth, P III 6 52 33
There had been music, singing, talking, laughing, all that P III 7 58 22
"My dear Frederick, you are talking quite idly. P III 8 69 43
"But I hate to hear you talking so, like a fine gentleman, P III 8 70 45
"Now you are talking nonsense, Mary," was therefore his P III 9 76 15
She then found them talking of "Frederick." P III 10 92 43
together some time, talking as before of Mr. Scott and P III 12 107 23
Lady Russell began talking of something else. P IV 2 132 22
to her for ten minutes, talking with a very raised voice, P IV 2 134 29
remembering former partialities and talking over old times. P IV 5 153 6
The high-spirited, joyous, talking Louisa Musgrove, and P IV 6 166 19
what they might be talking of, as they walked along in P IV 6 168 24
and a bustle, and a talking, which must make all the P IV 7 176 10
ladies of Captain Wentworth's party began talking of them. P IV 7 177 17
After talking however of the weather and Bath and the P IV 8 181 3
4
Had I known it, I would have had the pleasure of talking P IV 9 194 23
her own cousin, began talking very warmly about the family P IV 10 222 37
The party before her were Mrs. Musgrove, talking to Mrs. P IV 11 229 2
talking of, Harville, now, if you will give me materials." P IV 11 229 2
3
D.'s elbow, listening & talking with smiling attention or S 7 396 1
or a natural love of talking, she immediately said in a S 7 399 1
time Miss Esther begins talking about the dampness of S 7 402 1
that Lady D. was still talking on in the same way, allowed S 7 402 1
only had she by walking & talking down a thousand S 10 414 1
All said & done, in less time than you have been talking S 12 423 1

TALKS (22)
makes conversation easy, & talks very well, with a happy LS 6 251 1
deal about it to me, she talks vastly well, I am afraid of LS 15 267 4
I should say she talks too well to feel so very deeply. LS 15 267 4
before her mother, she talks enough when alone with me, to LS 18 273 3
I tell Mr. Allen, when he talks of being sick of it, that NA I 8 54 5
my brother's, that if he talks to me, I must talk to him NA I 10 78 38
in all she does--sometimes talks a great deal and always SS I 17 93 35
deny it, because you know it is what every body talks of. SS I 20 115 46
"Edward talks of going to Oxford soon," said she, "but now SS III 2 275 22
that my uncle Philips talks of turning away Richard, and PP I 14 68 13
14
"Perhaps he will always stay longer than he talks of. MP II 11 287 20
Mrs. Norris often talks of her luck; what will she say now? MP II 12 292 7
"I shall see your cousin in town soon; he talks of being MP III 5 364 32
She talks of you almost every hour, and I am sorry to find MP III 13 423 2
thing; and Mrs. Martin talks of taking a boy another year." E I 4 30 21
What nonsense one talks, Miss Woodhouse, when hard at work, E II 10 242 15
when hard at work, if one talks at all;--your real workmen, E II 10 242 15
My mother often talks of your goodnature. E III 2 323 19
from his poor little boy; talks of his being on so well! P III 7 56 10
"Oh! he talks of you," cried Charles, "in such terms,"-- P IV 2 131 8
I declare, Anne, he never talks of you at all." P IV 2 131 8
Mr. Elliot talks unreservedly to Colonel Wallis of his P IV 9 205 82

TALL (37)
and twenty, was rather tall, had a pleasing countenance, a NA I 3 25 2
a doubt, for he was tall and handsome, and Henry's father. NA II 1 129 1
her figure tall and striking, and her address graceful. SS I 6 31 8
The person is not tall enough for him, and has not his air. SS I 16 86 18
I admire them much more if they are tall, straight and SS I 18 98 8
boys were both remarkably tall for their age, and could SS II 12 234 24
with tall Lombardy poplars, shut out the offices. SS III 6 302 7
of the room by his fine, tall person, handsome features, PP I 3 10 5
said Miss Bingley; "will she be as tall as I am?" PP I 8 38 40
I assure you that if Darcy were not such a great tall PP I 10 50 39
He was a tall, heavy looking young man of five and twenty. PP I 13 64 21
Lady Catherine was a tall, large women, with strongly- PP II 6 162 11
Miss Darcy was tall, and on a larger scale than Elizabeth; PP III 2 261 4
That tall, proud man." PP III 11 334 34
Such a charming man!--so handsome! so tall!-- PP III 17 378 43
seventeen and sixteen, and tall of their age, had all the MP I 2 12 3
their duets, and grow tall and womanly; and their father MP I 2 20 33
Had she been tall, full formed, and fair, it might have MP I 5 44 1
avenue immediately beyond tall iron palisades and gates. MP I 9 85 4
She is too tall and robust. MP I 14 135 16
Antwerp at the bottom, in letters as tall as the main-mast. MP I 16 152 2
This is only because there were no tall women to compare MP II 6 230 6
She was interrupted by a fine tall boy of eleven years old, MP III 7 377 7
"You have made her too tall, Emma," said Mr. Knightley. E I 6 48 33
no! certainly not too tall; not in the least too tall. E I 6 48 34
35
as he stood up, in tall indignation, and said, "then she E I 8 60 31
32
Mr. John Knightley was a tall, gentleman-like, and very E I 11 92 5
everybody would think tall, and nobody could think very E II 2 167 12
nobody could think very tall; her figure particularly E II 2 167 12
starting on this appeal; "is he--is he a tall man?" E II 3 174 37
I mean in person--tall, and with that sort of look--and E II 3 176 44
His tall, firm, upright figure, among the bulky forms and E III 2 326 32
Mrs. Croft, though neither tall nor fat, had a squareness, P III 6 48 18
Captain Harville was a tall, dark man, with a sensible, P III 11 97 14
the tall Irish officer, who is talked of for one of them." P IV 9 193 8
Elegantly tall, regularly handsome, with great delicacy of S 6 391 1
to find him quite as tall as his brother & a great deal S 10 413 1

TALLER (4)
about Miss Elizabeth Bennet's height, or rather taller." PP I 8 38 41
so much taller, and produces all these charms and graces! MP II 6 230 8
and moving all the taller, firmer, and more graceful for MP III 7 384 34
You are not striving to look taller than any body else. E II 8 214 10

TALLEST (5)
delighted to see you: the tallest is Isabella, my eldest; NA I 4 32 3
was the tallest, politely decided in favour of the other. SS II 12 234 21
22
afraid; for though I am the youngest, I'm the tallest." PP I 2 8 27
the tallest, seemed to fit him peculiarly for the Baron. MP I 14 132 8
not been considerably the tallest of the two, Miss B.'s S 12 426 1

TAMBOUR (1)
Mrs. Grant and her tambour frame were not without their MP I 7 65 13

TAMBOURED (1)
her spotted and her tamboured muslin, and nothing but the NA I 10 73 22

TAME (5)
Oh! mama, how spiritless, how tame was Edward's manner in SS I 3 17 18
spirits; I cannot bear them if they are tame and quiet." SS I 21 122 19
think of tame and quiet children with any abhorrence." SS I 21 123 20

tame confidante, that you may not like to do yourselves." MP I 13 129 38
Tender, elegant, descriptive--but tame.-- S 7 397 1
TAMENESS (1)
Mr. Yates, indeed, exclaimed against his tameness and MP I 18 165 3
TAN (1)
"men's beavers" and "York tan" were bringing down and E II 6 200 16
TANDEM (1)
concluding in favour of a Tandem, little Mary's young eyes S 12 425 1
TANNED (1)
than her being rather tanned,--no miraculous consequence PP III 3 271 14
TAP (3)
A tap at the door roused her in the midst of this attempt MP I 16 153 3
of an hour, when a gentle tap at the door was followed by MP I 18 168 14
half the scene, when a tap at the door brought a pause, MP I 18 169 22
TAPESTRY (4)
Nerves fit for sliding pannels and tapestry?" NA II 5 158 13
walls hung with tapestry exhibiting figures as large as NA II 5 158 15
a division in the tapestry so artfully constructed as to NA II 5 159 19
large, and contained neither tapestry nor velvet.-- NA II 6 163 1
TAPPING (1)
The next moment she was tapping at her husband's dressing- P III 7 57 17 18
TARDINESS (1)
lecture; and that his tardiness was chiefly resented from NA II 5 154 2
TARDY (1)
But the fortune, which had been so tardy in coming, was SS I 1 4 4
TARNISHED (1)
The lock was silver, though tarnished from age; at each NA II 6 163 2
TART (2)
the sight of a gooseberry tart towards giving her comfort; MP I 2 13 4
Miss Bates, let Emma help you to a little bit of tart--a E I 3 24 14
TARTS (2)
tarts and preserves, my cook contrives to get them all." MP I 6 54 13
Ours are all apple tarts. E I 3 25 14
TASK (4)
From Thompson, that -----"it is a delightful task NA I 1 15 6
Elinor therefore the whole task of telling lies when SS I 21 122 14
for the hardship of such a task, and grieving still more SS II 9 203 10
But unwelcome as such a task must be, it was necessary to SS III 1 261 11
TASTE (161)
I want her to play & sing with some portion of taste, & a LS 7 253 1
Indeed she had no taste for a garden; and if she gathered NA I 1 13 1
Her taste for drawing was not superior; though whenever NA I 1 14 1
In every power, of which taste is the foundation, NA I 3 28 34
which have only genius, wit, and taste to recommend them. NA I 5 37 4
disgust a young person of taste; the substance of its NA I 5 38 4
taste which marked the reasonableness of that attachment. NA I 6 39 1
Well, my taste is different. NA I 6 42 30
formed into pictures, with all the eagerness of real taste. NA I 14 110 28
She knew nothing of drawing--nothing of taste:--and she NA I 14 110 28
satisfied of her having a great deal of natural taste. NA I 14 111 29
I cannot say I admire her taste; and for my part I was NA I 14 115 52
His taste and manners were beyond a doubt decidedly NA II 1 131 15
her seeing nothing to her taste--though never in her life NA II 5 154 2
was in all the profusion and elegance of modern taste. NA II 5 162 26
Besides, a taste for flowers is always desirable in your NA II 7 174 8
He was enchanted by her approbation of his taste, NA II 7 175 12
the taste of ladies in regard to places as well as men. NA II 7 175 15
every thing that money and taste could do, to give comfort NA II 8 185 5
speedily be furnished: it waits only for a lady's taste!" NA II 11 214 22
Davis: I pitied his taste, but took no notice of him. NA II 12 217 2
besides all this, I am afraid, mama, he has no real taste. SS I 3 17 18
I could not be happy with a man whose taste did not in SS I 3 17 18
by Cowper!--but we must allow for difference of taste. SS I 3 18 20
Marianne, "that Edward should have no taste for drawing." SS I 4 19 1
"No taste for drawing," replied Elinor; "why should you SS I 4 19 2
taste, though he has not had opportunities of improving it. SS I 4 19 2
of taste, which in general direct him perfectly right." SS I 4 19 2
which, in her opinion, could alone be called taste. SS I 4 19 3
"you do not consider him as deficient in general taste. SS I 4 19 4
subjects of literature and taste; and, upon the whole, I SS I 4 20 9
just and correct, and his taste delicate and pure. SS I 4 20 9
of improving that natural taste for your favourite pursuit SS I 4 22 17
total want of talent and taste which confined their SS I 7 32 1
of encouraging their taste by admitting them to a SS I 7 33 3
had reasonably forfeited by their shameless want of taste. SS I 7 35 9
Their taste was strikingly alike. SS I 10 47 3
Marianne, "that he has neither genius, taste, nor spirit. SS I 10 51 26
my ignorance and want of taste if we come to particulars. SS I 18 96 4
tries to describe with the taste and elegance of him who SS I 18 97 7
your taste very much, for I think he is extremely handsome. SS I 20 111 12
or even difference of taste from herself, was at this time SS I 22 127 1
to infer that she could taste no greater delight than in SS II 1 144 14
delicacy of his taste, proved to be beyond his politeness. SS II 11 220 3
as a man of taste, will, I dare say, be pleased with them. SS II 12 234 27
many people who had real taste for the performance, and a SS II 14 250 10
generous temper, simple taste, and diffident feelings. SS III 6 305 15
she have given me!--her taste, her opinions--I believe SS III 8 325 50
you are at all at a loss for she has a very good taste.-- W 315 1
to inspire devotion, & shews a much better taste.-- W 344 20
Mary had neither genius nor taste; and though vanity had PP I 6 25 24
she had no conversation, no stile, no taste, no beauty. PP I 8 35 3
I never saw such capacity, and taste, and application, and PP I 8 40 54
pleasure of despising my taste; but I always delight in PP I 10 52 50
This gallantry was not much to the taste of some of his PP I 13 65 21 22
and roads, were all to her taste, and Lady Catherine's PP II 3 146 19
enjoyment of music than myself, or a better natural taste. PP II 8 173 6
She has a very good notion of fingering, though her taste PP II 8 176 28
mixing with them many instructions on execution and taste. PP II 8 176 30
beauty had been so little counteracted by an awkward taste. PP III 1 245 3
with admiration of his taste, that it was neither gaudy PP III 1 246 5
seldom able to indulge the taste, was very fond of fishing, PP III 1 254 57
marked his intelligence, his taste, or his good manners. PP III 1 255 59
similarity of feeling and taste between her and himself. PP III 13 347 33
hours, he encouraged her taste, and corrected her judgment; MP I 2 22 35
Court deserves every thing that taste and money can do. MP I 6 53 9
knows what the natural taste of our apricot is; he is MP I 6 54 13
his submission to her taste, and his having always MP I 6 55 17
and where the natural taste is equal, the player must MP I 6 59 41
with an expression and taste which were peculiarly MP I 7 64 12
She had none of Fanny's delicacy of taste, of mind, of MP I 8 81 31
and amply furnished in the taste of fifty years back, with MP I 9 84 3
all laudable ambition, of taste for good company, or of MP I 11 110 23
not at least been given a taste for nature in early life. MP I 11 113 36
"A trifling part," said he, "and not at all to my taste, MP I 13 122 2
taste, as were exactly adapted to the novelty of acting. MP I 13 123 6
reciting kind, I think he has always a decided taste. MP I 13 126 25
Your brother's taste, and your sisters', seem very MP I 13 128 34
honourable mention--her taste and her time were considered- MP I 17 160 6
judgment than Tom, more talent and taste than Mr. Yates.-- MP I 18 165 3
and spring, when her own taste could have fairer play. MP II 3 202 26
performance, and who shewed herself not wanting in taste. MP II 4 207 6
I must admire the taste Mrs. Grant has shewn in all this. MP II 4 209 14
feelings and directed her taste; for Lady Bertram never MP II 5 219 27
disposition, and so much taste as belonged to her, she MP II 6 231 11
It was a picture which Henry Crawford had moral taste MP II 6 235 20
man of education, taste, modern manners, good connections. MP II 7 244 27
no confidence in her own taste--the "how she should be MP II 8 254 8
sister, whose acknowledged taste would certainly bear her MP II 8 256 14
all her best judgment and taste, made every thing easy by MP II 8 257 15
I endeavoured to consult the simplicity of your taste, but MP II 9 261 2
But taste was too strong in her. MP III 3 337 10
general observation and taste, a more critical knowledge MP III 3 340 23
interest and quick taste--without any touch of that spirit MP III 3 340 24
without offending the taste, or wearing out the feelings MP III 3 341 28
We have not one taste in common. MP III 4 348 22
pleasures, and inspire a taste for the biography and MP III 9 398 9
They often stopt with the same sentiment and taste, MP III 11 409 7
Susan, who had an innate taste for the genteel and well- MP III 12 419 8
could satisfy the better taste she had acquired at MP III 17 469 24
fears from opposition of taste, no need of drawing new MP III 17 471 28
that there was no want of taste, though strength of E I 4 26 2
intelligent person whose taste could be depended on; and E I 6 48 40
Emma felt the bad taste of her friend, but let it pass E I 7 54 33
Emma assisted with her invention, memory and taste; and as E I 9 70 4
to the taste of everybody, though single and though poor. E I 10 85 19
it suited neither; it was a jumble without taste or truth. E I 16 134 4
judgment, of knowledge of taste, as one proof among others E I 16 134 5
his conversation to the taste of every body, and has the E I 18 150 31
and spared her from a taste of such enjoyments of ease and E II 2 165 9
"Well," said Emma, "there is no disputing about taste.-- E II 6 199 11
taste, but I know nothing of the matter myself.-- E II 6 201 28
credit; she wanted neither taste nor spirit in the little E II 8 227 86
taste, to look about, and see what became of Mr. Knightley. E II 8 229 99
Mr. Cole said how much taste you had; and Mr. Frank E II 9 232 9
taste, and that he valued taste much more than execution." E II 9 232 9
she had execution, but I did not know she had any taste. E II 9 232 11
I heard a good deal of Col. Campbell's taste at Weymouth; E II 10 241 8
either a compliment to her taste, or a remembrance of what E II 13 266 5
am not entirely devoid of taste; but as to any thing else, E II 14 276 36
She could not have believed it possible that the taste or E II 15 285 12
quits, before we condemn her taste for what she goes to." E II 15 286 17
to her, and Maple Grove had given her a taste for dinners. E II 16 290 3
my taste than modern ease; modern ease often disgusts me. E II 17 302 22
a bride, but my natural taste is all for simplicity; a E II 17 302 22
Emma perceived that her taste was not the only taste on E III 2 319 4
any man of sense and taste to such a woman as Mrs. Elton. E III 2 331 55
mark of good taste which I shall always know how to value." E III 4 342 39
I would wish every thing to be as much to your taste as E III 6 356 27
Disputable, however, as might be the taste of such a E III 6 360 38
than in a total want of taste for what he saw, for he was E III 6 362 43
When they all sat down it was better; to her taste a great E III 7 367 3
I hope I have a better taste than to think of Mr. Frank E III 11 405 18
where the parties have no taste for finery or parade; and E III 19 484 12
involving the loss of any indulgence of taste or pride. P III 1 10 21
Elliot: an extraordinary taste, certainly, could they have P III 3 23 34
girl, with gentleness, modesty, taste, and feeling.-- P III 4 26 1
Lady Russell had little taste for wit; and of any thing P III 4 27 4
her taste, in the small limits of the society around them. P III 4 28 7
to, or encouraged by any just appreciation or real taste. P III 6 47 13
the speed which a clear head and quick taste could allow. P III 7 61 38
taste cannot tolerate,--which ridicule will seize. P III 8 68 30
influence on the mind of taste and tenderness, that season P III 10 84 7
and a decided taste for reading, and sedentary pursuits. P III 11 97 12
house for half a year, his taste, and his health, and his P III 11 97 12
He was evidently a young man of considerable taste in P III 11 100 23
the very feelings which ought to taste it but sparingly. P III 11 100 23
seeing, for as he has a taste for those sort of things, I P IV 2 131 12
Every body has their taste in noises as well as in other P IV 2 135 33
the style of the fitting-up, or the taste of the furniture. P IV 3 137 4
Miss Anne Elliot, you have the most extraordinary taste! P IV 5 157 15
into a person of literary taste, and sentimental P IV 6 167 20
There is something about Frederick more to our taste." P IV 6 172 39
and to give him some taste of that emotion which was P IV 8 182 9
or the gapes, as real or affected taste for it prevailed. P IV 8 189 45
I used to think she had some taste in dress, but I was P IV 10 215 15
"That cannot be much to your taste, I know," said she; " P IV 10 218 25
with every advantage of taste and delicacy which good Mrs. P IV 11 230 5
Every body's taste & every body's finances may be suited-- S 1 369 1
He began, in a tone of great taste & feeling, to talk of S 7 396 1
"If I understand you aright--said Charlotte--our taste in S 8 404 1
TASTED (4)
Here Catherine and Isabella, arm in arm, again tasted the NA I 5 35 2
down to the Pump-Room, tasted the water, and laid out some NA I 15 116 1
tasted, so I have brought a glass of it for your sister. SS II 8 197 27
She had tasted of consequence in its most flattering form; MP III 6 366 1
TASTEFUL (2)
in many articles of tasteful attire; could discover a NA I 4 33 7
As it is, he does what he can--& is running up a tasteful S 3 377 1
TASTES (6)
We soon found out that our tastes were exactly alike in NA I 10 71 3
his inclinations and tastes as you have; but I have the SS I 4 19 6
and from these tastes had arisen his principal enjoyments. PP II 19 236 1
You have tastes in common. MP III 4 348 23
You have moral and literary tastes in common. MP III 4 348 23
no two hearts so open, no tastes so similar, no feelings P III 8 63 3
TASTING (1)
her account of tasting a little before the morning closed. P IV 11 229 2
TATTERED (1)
I do not like ruined, tattered cottages. SS I 18 98 8
TATTERSAL'S (1)
he observed, "once at Tattersal's, and twice in the lobby P III 1 8 16
TAUGHT (42)
As a very distinguished flirt, I have been always taught LS 4 248 1
or education, whom he had been always taught to despise? LS 22 282 6
any thing before she was taught; and sometimes not even NA I 1 14 1
Writing and accounts she was taught by her father; French NA I 1 14 1
Consider--if reading had not been taught, Mrs. Radcliffe NA I 14 110 27
Once or twice indeed, since James's engagement had taught NA II 2 138 1
Could not the adventure of the chest have taught her NA II 7 173 2
"Your sister taught me; I cannot tell how. NA II 7 174 7
It taught him that he had been scarcely more misled by by NA II 16 251 6
which one of her sisters had resolved never to be taught. SS I 1 6 11
she beheld what no foresight had taught her to expect. SS I 15 75 2
claims on Edward, and be taught to avoid him in future? SS II 1 142 7
as her own wounded heart taught her to think of with SS II 12 236 39 40
Wickstead, that his uncle taught him Latin, that he was W 331 11
I do assure you that my intimacy has not yet taught me PP I 11 57 18
"Then, who taught you? who attended to you? PP II 6 165 30
But she is very young; she has never been taught to think PP III 5 283 10
"It taught me to hope," said he, "as I had scarcely ever PP III 16 367 10
As a child I was taught what was right, but I was not PP III 16 369 24
was right, but I was not taught to correct my temper. PP III 16 369 24
encouraged, almost taught me to be selfish and overbearing, PP III 16 369 24
You taught me a lesson, hard indeed at first, but most PP III 16 369 24
her cousins; if Miss Lee taught her nothing, she would MP I 1 10 15
Fanny could read, work, and write, but she had been taught MP I 2 18 23
In every thing but disposition, they were admirably taught. MP I 2 19 30
Miss Lee taught her French, and heard her read the daily MP I 2 22 35
pitied who have not been taught to feel in some degree as MP I 11 113 36
"You taught me to think and feel on the subject, cousin." MP I 11 113 37
would sing if they were taught--or sing all the better for MP II 11 288 28
all the better for not being taught--or something like it." MP II 11 288 28
His acting had first taught Fanny what pleasure a play MP III 3 337 10
a slattern, who neither taught nor restrained her children, MP III 8 390 6
had never been properly taught to govern their MP III 17 463 8
and a very few months had taught him, by the force of MP III 17 468 21
years--how she had taught and how she had played with her E I 1 6 6
of character, have taught her to think on points which had E I 6 42 5
She has been taught nothing useful, and is too young and E I 8 61 38
fixed there; of her being taught only what very limited E II 2 163 3
way, but they ought to be taught that it was not for them E II 7 207 6

Who but herself had taught her, that she was to elevate — E III 11 414 50
madam,' she continued, 'that I was taught wrong. — E III 12 419 8
As soon as I could use my hands, she taught me to knit, — P IV 5 155 9
TAUNTINGLY (1)
"Yes, that he will!" exclaimed Mary, tauntingly. — P IV 2 132 19
TAUNTON (6)
the quarter sessions at Taunton; and indeed, he had — P III 3 21 18
and had come down to Taunton in order to look at some — P III 3 21 18
He had seen Mrs. Croft, too; she was at Taunton with the — P III 3 22 24
at Taunton, and fix a day for the house being seen. — P III 3 24 35
a deal, my dear, in spite of what they told us at Taunton. — P III 5 32 4
Taunton, which is some of the best land in the country. — P III 9 76 15
TAUTOLOGY (1)
all the feebleness and tautology of the narration, a — E III 11 409 34
TAVERNS (1)
about at his own charge now, at lodgings and taverns." — SS III 1 268 51
TAWNY (1)
of the year upon the tawny leaves and withered hedges, and — P III 10 84 7
TAX (8)
that the youngest should tax Mr. Bingley with having — PP I 9 45 35
and perhaps a greater tax on his forbearance; and though — PP III 18 384 27
to contribute to the window tax, and find employment for — MP I 9 85 5
brief, and certainly never tax her kindness in the same — MP III 16 453 17
night, which was the tax for such an evening, she found — E III 14 434 4
has its tax--I, John Shepherd, might conceal any family- — P III 3 17 4
wife, but she must pay the tax of quick alarm for — P IV 12 252 12
this kind--it is a sort of tax upon all that come--yet as — S 12 423 1
TAXED (2)
"She taxed me with the offence at once, and my confusion — SS III 8 323 40
good manners were severely taxed to conceal her vexation — MP I 7 70 30
TAXES (1)
the house, and terms, and taxes, than the Admiral himself, — P III 3 22 25
TEA (105)
They came while we were at tea, & I never saw any creature — LS 17 269 1
Every body was shortly in motion for tea, and they must — NA I 2 21 10
Here are no tea things for us, you see." — NA I 2 22 18
After some time they received an offer of tea from one of — NA I 2 23 22
when they were seated at tea, she found him as agreeable — NA I 3 25 2
away from their party at tea, to attend that of his — NA I 8 59 38
"I remember too, Miss Andrews drank tea with us that — NA I 15 118 13
his uncritical palate, the tea was as well flavoured from — NA II 7 175 12
Mr. Tilney drank tea with us, and I always thought him a — NA II 14 238 26
Last night after tea, when you and mama went out of the — SS I 12 60 13
She was sitting by Edward, and in taking his tea from Mrs. — SS I 18 98 10
park the next day, or to drink tea with them that evening. — SS I 18 99 16
"You must drink tea with us to night," said he, "for we — SS I 18 99 17
tea, but it never entered my head that it could be them. — SS I 19 106 20
The tea things were brought in, and already had Marianne — SS II 4 161 7
Elinor now began to make the tea, and Marianne was obliged — SS II 4 163 19
The former left them soon after tea to fulfil her evening — SS II 4 166 31
She sat by the drawing room fire after tea, till the — SS II 6 175 1
Colonel Brandon came in while the party were at tea, and — SS II 8 198 30
the library may be open for tea and other refreshments; — SS II 14 252 18
she joined Mrs. Jennings in the drawing-room to tea. — SS III 7 315 27
over, as soon as I had made tea for him; & I should be — W 319 2
The entrance of the tea things at 7 o'clock was some — W 326 7
excuse me, & I will certainly dance with you after tea." — W 330 11
found they were to drink tea;--Miss E. gave her a caution — W 331 11
Osborne will keep her word with me, when tea is over?" — W 332 12
On rising from tea, there was again a scramble for the — W 333 13
I shall find her in the tea room. — W 333 13
That stiff old Mrs E. has never done tea."-- — W 333 13
but was prevailed on to come down & drink tea with them.-- — W 354 28
after tea, that he was going home to an 8 o'clock dinner.-- — W 355 28
best Pembroke table, with the best tea things before her. — W 355 28
to throw off his greatcoat, & drink tea with them. — W 355 28
When tea was over, Mr. Hurst reminded his sister-in-law of — PP I 11 54 3
again, and when tea was over, glad to invite him to read — PP I 14 68 13
us on Sunday to drink tea and spend the evening at Rosings. — PP II 6 160 2
When the gentlemen had joined them, and tea was over, the — PP II 6 166 41
cousins to Rosings, where they were engaged to drink tea. — PP II 10 187 41
"We have dined nine times at Rosings, besides drinking tea — PP II 15 217 13
It was not till the afternoon, when he joined them at tea, — PP III 6 299 19
by Miss Bennet, who came to fetch her mother's tea. — PP III 6 299 27
Miss Bennet was making tea, and Elizabeth pouring out the — PP III 12 341 16
After tea, Mr. Bennet retired to the library, as was his — PP III 13 344 11
for that purpose soon after tea; for as the others were — PP III 13 346 21
Dinner was soon followed by tea and coffee, a ten miles' — MP I 10 104 52
was dropt; but after tea, as Miss Crawford was standing at — MP I 11 108 4
being renewed after tea, when the bustle of receiving Sir — MP II 1 177 5
nothing till tea came--he would rather wait for tea. — MP II 1 180 10
of soup would be a much better thing for you than tea. — MP II 1 180 10
"But indeed I would rather have nothing but tea." — MP II 1 180 11
"Well then, Lady Bertram, suppose you speak for tea — MP II 1 180 12
feelings subsided; but when tea was soon afterwards — MP II 1 181 17
"She always makes tea, you know, when my sister is not — MP II 5 219 21
table was formed after tea--formed really for the — MP II 5 227 68
her uncle was soon after tea called out of the room; an — MP III 1 324 60
be talking of her; and when tea at last brought them away, — MP III 3 334 5
and the scene which the tea things afforded, she must have — MP III 3 335 5
meat, or only a dish of tea after your journey, or else I — MP III 7 378 14
Perhaps you would like some tea, as soon as it can be got." — MP III 7 379 14
was still no appearance of tea, nor, from Betsey's reports — MP III 7 381 24
directly, that he might have his tea in comfort afterwards. — MP III 7 381 24
when they should have got tea--and she was sure her sister — MP III 7 383 32
be very glad of a little tea, and Susan immediately set — MP III 7 383 33
carpet as usual, while the tea was in preparation--and — MP III 15 439 9
such thoughts; but when tea came, it was impossible for — E I 1 8 10, 11
when Mrs. Perry drank tea with Mrs. and Miss Bates, or — E I 2 17 9
old lady, almost past every thing but tea and quadrille. — E I 3 21 4
year they were all to drink tea:--a very handsome summer- — E I 4 27 4
Mr. Woodhouse was soon ready for his tea; and when he had — E I 15 124 1
and when he had drank his tea he was quite ready to go — E I 15 124 1
next summer, and take their tea with us --take us in their — E II 7 209 10
staying late. you will get very tired when tea is over." — E II 7 210 14
Emma's going away directly after tea might be giving — E II 7 210 19
the room shewed them that tea was over, and the instrument — E II 8 226 85
chair, lights and music, tea and supper, made themselves; — E II 11 255 59
Tea was carrying round, and Mr. Weston, having said all — E II 18 310 35
After tea, Mr. and Mrs. Weston, and Mr. Elton sat down — E II 18 311 36
A little tea if you please, sir, by and bye,--no hurry--Oh! — E III 2 323 19
Tea was made down stairs, biscuits and baked apples and — E III 2 329 45
father, pressed them all to go in and drink tea with him. — E III 5 344 3
Tea passed pleasantly, and nobody seemed in a hurry to — E III 5 347 18
It was before tea--stay--no, it could not be before tea, — E III 8 382 29
yet it was before tea, because I remember thinking--Oh! no, — E III 8 382 29
now I have it; something happened before tea, but not that. — E III 8 382 29
Mr. Elton was called out of the room before tea, old John — E III 8 383 29
That was what happened before tea. — E III 8 383 29
It was after tea that Jane spoke to Mrs. Elton." — E III 8 383 29
soon after tea, and dissipated every melancholy fancy. — E III 12 422 19
They sat down to tea--the same party round the same table-- — E III 14 434 2
party, some of them did decide on going in quest of tea. — P IV 8 188 44
to get a good dish of tea within 3 miles of the place--& — S 1 369 1
& obliged to take her tea with him them, would suit her — S 6 390 1
will not have you hurry your tea on my account.-- — S 6 390 1
I know you like your tea late.-- — S 6 390 1
No, no, Miss Clara & I will get back to our own tea.-- — S 6 390 1
being really come--, but we get back to our own tea."-- — S 6 391 1
to the servant as they entered, to bring tea directly. — S 6 391 1
The tea things were brought in.-- — S 6 394 1
& sister & herself were entreated to drink tea with them.-- — S 10 413 1
with the tea things, as a very fortunate interruption.-- — S 10 416 1
She was already helped to tea--which surprised him--so — S 10 416 1
obliged to you, replied Charlotte--but I prefer tea." — S 10 417 1
upon two dishes of strong green tea in one eveng?-- — S 10 418 1
studied right sides & green tea scientifically & — S 10 418 1
Soon after tea, a letter was brought to Miss D. P-- from — S 10 418 1
TEA-BOARD (2)
The solemn procession, headed by Baddely, of tea-board, — MP III 3 344 43
where stood the tea-board never thoroughly cleaned, the — MP III 15 439 9
TEA-HOUSE (1)
alterations about the tea-house, proposed it as no — NA II 7 179 27
TEA-MAKER'S (1)
washing of the young tea-maker's, a cup and saucer; and — MP III 7 384 36
TEA-ROOM (1)
at last arrived in the tea-room, she felt yet more the — NA I 2 21 10
TEA-TABLE (4)
all seated round the tea-table, which Mrs. Morland had — NA II 14 233 9
across the room to the tea-table where Elinor presided, — SS II 8 198 30
considerably nearer the tea-table, and gave all her — MP I 15 145 42
Grant occupied at the tea-table, he began talking of them — MP II 5 224 49
TEA-THINGS (8)
They quitted it only with the removal of the tea-things. — SS II 1 144 10
by the removal of the tea-things, and the arrangement of — SS II 8 200 43
When the tea-things were removed, Tom began to talk of his — W 357 28
When the tea-things were removed, and the card tables — PP III 12 342 26
me!" said Lady Bertram, when the tea-things were removed. — MP II 11 283 5
and tell her to bring in the tea-things as soon as she can. — MP III 7 379 15
welcome; it was for the tea-things, which she had begun — MP III 7 383 32
on to carry away the tea-things, and Mrs. Price had walked — MP III 7 385 37
TEA-TIME (1)
By tea-time however the dose had been enough, and Mr. — PP I 14 68 13
TEA-VISIT (1)
occasional holiday of a tea-visit; and having formerly — E I 3 22 5
TEACH (24)
of familiarity which I shall teach him to correct. — LS 7 254 3
task "to teach the young idea how to shoot." — NA I 1 15 6
teach her to think of Norland with less regret than ever. — SS I 11 54 6
and time and habit will teach him to forget that he ever — SS III 1 263 27
notion of me, and teach you not to believe a word I say. — PP II 8 174 15
Let us hope, therefore, that her being there may teach her — PP II 18 232 20
But no such happy marriage could now teach the admiring — PP III 8 312 16
if he marry prudently, his wife may teach him. — PP III 10 325 2
We all love to instruct, though we can teach only what is — PP III 12 343 37
girls to teach, or only two--there can be no difference. — MP I 1 9 12
that the housekeeper could teach, and was now almost — MP I 9 84 3
which it is their duty to teach and recommend; and it will, — MP I 9 93 49
Learn part, and we will teach you all the rest. — MP I 15 146 50
was at great pains to teach him how to learn, giving him — MP I 18 166 4
I know nothing about it, but Fanny must teach me." — MP II 7 239 7
and Miss Price, and teach them, it was settled; and Sir — MP II 7 239 8
Her father's house would, in all probability, teach her — MP III 6 369 10
you will teach Betsey, and make the boys love and mind you. — MP III 6 372 20
out of her head, and teach her to think of her cousin — MP III 8 391 10
to marry greatly, and teach her to be satisfied with — E I 8 64 47
than she is obliged to do, because she will have to teach. — E II 9 232 11
to teach, should not have their powers in exercise again. — E III 17 461 1
might teach her humility and circumspection in future. — E III 18 475 39
she must teach herself to be insensible on such points. — P III 6 52 33
TEACHABLENESS (1)
is the thing; and a teachableness of disposition in a — NA II 7 174 10
TEACHER (3)
I would rather be teacher at a school (and I can think of — W 318 2
"I would rather do any thing than be teacher at a school-- — W 318 2
pride or refinement in the teacher of a school, Harriet. — E I 7 56 41
TEACHERS (3)
Mrs. Goddard, and the teachers, and the girls, and the — E I 4 27 4
and asked all the three teachers, Miss Nash, and Miss — E I 4 28 8
the adoration of all the teachers and great girls in the — E I 17 143 15
TEACHES (2)
My understanding is at length restored, & teaches me no — LS 36 306 2
and where the same master teaches, it is natural enough. — E II 16 297 45
TEACHING (8)
Her mother was three months in teaching her only to repeat — NA I 1 14 1
occupied in lying-in and teaching the little ones, that — NA I 1 15 3
spirits, and of teaching her that her present pursuits are — PP II 18 231 18
way--teaching them, playing with them, and loving them. — PP II 19 239 10
be in the habit of teaching others their duty every week, — MP I 11 112 30
surely I was not to be teaching myself to like him only — MP III 4 353 45
increased the evil, by teaching them to repress their — MP III 17 463 7
boys have very little teaching after an early age, and — E II 16 297 45
TEAPOTS (1)
with almost as many Teapots &c as there were persons in — S 10 416 1
TEAR (8)
You tear them to pieces." — PP I 2 6 8
Had she known that her sister sought to tear her from such — PP II 18 232 23
him go without a tear!--it was a shameful insensibility." — MP I 3 33 64
those spikes--you will tear your gown--you will be in — MP I 10 99 21
Not a tear, and hardly a long face to be seen. — E I 1 11 35
a tear in the eye, shewed that it was felt beyond a laugh. — E II 16 294 24
in me--(twinkling away a tear or two)--but it will be very — E III 8 378 8
when a visitor arrived to tear Emma's thoughts a little — E III 12 417 3
TEARING (2)
Elliot's appearing and tearing her away, and one or two — P IV 11 244 71
very gallant despair in tearing himself away, & they — S 7 399 1
TEAROOM (3)
when she moved into the Tearoom; & Emma was accordingly on — W 331 11
for refreshment;--the Tearoom was a small room within the — W 332 11
On entering the Tearoom, in which two long tables were — W 332 11
TEARS (77)
Lady Susan who had been shedding tears before & shewing — LS 17 269 2
Frederica's bursting into tears as soon <as> we were — LS 17 270 2
sadness, and drown her in tears for the last day or two of — NA I 2 18 2
to a pillow strewed with thorns and wet with tears. — NA I 11 90 65
and the fair ladies mingled in embraces and tears of joy. — NA I 15 118 8
Mrs. Thorpe, with tears of joy, embraced her daughter, her — NA I 15 121 27
The embraces, tears, and promises of the parting fair ones — NA II 4 153 31
way or other her destroyer, affected her even to tears. — NA II 9 190 1
They had reached the end of the gallery; and with tears of — NA II 9 198 30
Tears filled her eyes, and even ran down her cheeks as she — NA II 10 203 8
then speaking through her tears, she added, "I do not — NA II 10 204 11
had equally restrained her tears, but no sooner was she — NA II 13 226 25
in a violent burst of tears, she was conveyed some miles — NA II 14 230 1
Her eyes filled with tears as she pictured her — NA II 14 236 18
Many were the tears shed by them in their last adieus to a — SS I 5 27 8
small indeed!-- but the tears which recollection called — SS I 6 28 2
as if her tears were even then restrained with difficulty. — SS I 15 82 46
was quite overcome, she burst into tears and left the room. — SS I 15 82 46
and crying; her voice often totally suspended by her tears. — SS I 16 83 3
her; but she dispersed her tears to smile on him, and in — SS I 16 86 21
With such a reward for her tears, the child was too wise — SS I 21 121 10
much oppressed even for tears; but as Mrs. Jennings was — SS II 6 178 16
as fast as a continual flow of tears would permit her. — SS II 7 180 1
gave way to a burst of tears, which at first was scarcely — SS II 7 182 12
reproach her only by the tears which streamed from her — SS II 9 202 8
to shew by her tears that she felt it to be impossible. — SS II 10 212 1
it, and at first shed no tears; but after a short time — SS II 10 217 17
her face on Elinor's shoulder, she burst into tears.-- — SS II 12 236 41
with tears as she spoke, "don't think of my health. — SS II 13 242 26
she could have no share, without shedding many tears. — SS III 6 302 4
misery, she rejoiced in tears of agony to be at Cleveland; — SS III 6 303 9
gave her confidence, comfort, and tears of joy. — SS III 7 314 22

there, shedding tears of joy, though still unable to speak, SS III 9 334 4
closely pressed her sister's, and tears covered her cheeks. SS III 10 348 33
articulate through her tears, "tell mama," withdrew from SS III 10 348 34
tears of joy, which at first she thought would never cease. SS III 12 360 26
Marianne could speak her happiness only by tears. SS III 13 363 7
"You know, replied Emma struggling with her tears, my W 352 26
The agitation and tears which the subject occasioned, PP II 10 187 41
Kitty was the only one who shed tears; but she did weep PP II 18 235 40
to enter Meryton without tears; an event of such happy PP II 19 238 6
She burst into tears as she alluded to it, and for a few PP III 4 277 11
no less, thanked him with tears of gratitude; and all PP III 4 280 26
replied Elizabeth, with tears in her eyes, "that a PP III 5 283 10
embraced her, whilst tears filled the eyes of both, lost PP III 5 286 23
and thanked them both, with alternate smile and tears. PP III 5 287 32
as might be expected; with tears and lamentations of PP III 5 287 34
"I do, I do like him," she replied, with tears in her eyes, PP III 17 376 34
two mouthfuls before tears interrupted her, and sleep MP I 2 13 4
of years that he had been absent without tears in her eyes. MP I 6 60 47
She wished to be able to decline it; but the tears which a MP I 7 74 57
I stood out as long as I could, till the tears almost came MP I 10 105 55
and then at Fanny, whose tears were beginning to show MP I 15 147 56
affection which made her tears delightful--and the whole MP I 16 152 2
aunt, cost her some tears of gratitude when she was alone. MP II 5 222 40
Till she had shed many tears over this deception, Fanny MP II 9 264 17
Fanny was too urgent, however, and had too many tears in MP II 10 280 30
inarticulately through her tears, "I am very sorry indeed." MP III 1 319 41
Another burst of tears; but in spite of that burst, and in MP III 1 320 44
but of less anger, "well, child, dry up your tears. MP III 1 320 44
There is no use in these tears; they can do no good. MP III 1 320 44
Check these tears; they do but exhaust you. MP III 1 321 48
she could; did check her tears, did earnestly try to MP III 1 322 50
I feel that we are born to be connected; and those tears MP III 5 359 10
She had tears for every room in the house, much more for MP III 6 374 28
and wiping away her tears, was able to notice and admire MP III 7 384 35
Not even Fanny had tears for aunt Norris--not even when MP III 17 466 16
Emma turned away her head, divided between tears and E I 1 11 37
though she could not speak of her loss without many tears. E I 13 109 5
and the sight of Harriet's tears made her think that she E I 17 141 6
Her tears fell abundantly--but her grief was so truly E I 17 142 9
There she sat--and who would have guessed how many tears E II 8 219 44
silent; and Emma felt the tears running down her cheeks E III 7 376 63
blind yourself'--for tears were in her eyes perpetually. E III 8 379 8
dispersing her tears)--but, poor dear soul! if you were to E III 8 379 8
Mrs. Weston kissed her with tears of joy; and when she E III 10 396 42
would sometimes fill with tears as she sat at the P III 8 71 56

TEASE (8)
as I am authorized to tease you on this subject whenever NA I 3 29 51
winter, that if he was to tease me all night, I would not NA I 6 40 14
"Since that is the case, I am sure I shall not tease you NA II 3 145 16
never tease the other beyond what is known to be pleasant." NA II 4 152 28
disposed to follow and tease me, before you went away. NA II 12 216 2
"I hope she will not tease my poor pug," said Lady Bertram; MP I 1 10 16
Her cousins might attack, but could hardly tease her. MP I 16 157 28
and as I have no desire to tease her, I shall never force MP III 9 394 1

TEASED (2)
at half-price: they teased me into it; and I was NA II 12 217 2
over; he was no longer teased by being wished joy of so E I 2 19 14

TEASING (3)
How can you be so teasing; only conceive, my dear NA I 8 57 21
is cross and teasing--but do not let us mind them;" and MP I 15 147 56
the advantage of still teasing his wife, by persisting P IV 10 225 55

TEAZE (7)
Teaze him--laugh at him.-- PP I 11 57 17
Teaze calmness of temper and presence of mind! PP I 11 57 18
I will not teaze you. MP III 5 362 18
She would hesitate, she would teaze, she would condition, MP III 12 417 4
on going, and that it would be of no use to teaze him. P III 7 55 9
his aunt would not let him teaze his sick brother, he P III 9 79 29
Walter; I told you not to teaze your aunt;" and could P III 9 80 34

TEAZED (4)
only to be teazed about Dr. Davies to be perfectly happy. SS II 12 233 17
"It will be her turn soon to be teazed," said Miss Lucas. PP I 6 24 21
She was teazed by Mr. Collins, who continued most PP I 18 102 73
into bad hands, may be teazed, and kept at a distance from E I 14 122 22

TEAZING (9)
"Could she not see that we wanted her gone!--how teazing SS II 13 244 44
acquainted with him myself; how can you be so teazing?" PP I 2 7 15
was teazing Colonel Forster to give us a ball at Meryton?" PP I 6 24 17
18
uncivil to her, and more teazing than usual to himself. PP I 12 59 4
Teazing, teazing, man! PP III 12 339 4
and Elizabeth was spared from much teazing on the subject. PP III 15 361 5
me to find occasions for teazing and quarrelling with you PP III 18 381 7
But this is teazing you. MP III 4 353 44
be always scolding and teazing a poor child when it is ill; P III 7 56 12

TEDIOUS (7)
and while away the many tedious hours before the delivery NA I 15 121 26
But many were the tedious hours which must yet intervene. NA II 6 170 12
a moment's attention, she found no stage of it tedious. NA II 14 231 5
a disposition to be otherwise than tedious and unpleasant. SS I 6 28 1
not in them, if their parties are grown tedious and dull. SS I 19 109 42
tedious in the usual process of such a meeting. PP I 11 55 8
and my pace would be tedious to you; and besides, you have E I 8 58 7

TEDIOUSLY (1)
and therefore so tediously--no creature to speak to--my SS III 8 325 45

TEDIOUSNESS (5)
The tediousness of a two hours' bait at Petty-France, in NA II 5 156 4
to this, and to all the tediousness of the many years of SS II 2 148 14
her vexation at the tediousness of Mrs. Palmer, whose eye SS II 4 165 24
What was tranquillity and comfort to Fanny was tediousness MP II 11 285 15
served to lighten the tediousness of a long hill, or a S 3 375 1

TEETH (8)
Her teeth are tolerable, but not out of the common way; PP III 3 271 15
much countenance, and his teeth were so good, and he was MP I 5 44 2
teeth, and how you do your hair, and who makes your shoes. MP III 5 360 16
She had bright dark eyes, good teeth, and altogether an P III 6 48 18
She has accordingly had 3 teeth drawn, & is decidedly S 5 387 1
Three teeth drawn at once!--frightful!-- S 5 388 1
as possible, but those 3 teeth of your sister Susan's, are S 5 388 1
Miss P-- whom, remembering the three teeth drawn in one S 10 413 1

TEIZING (2)
He has been teizing me to allow of his coming into this LS 16 269 3
our reconciliation, or by marrying & teizing him for ever. LS 25 293 4

TELESCOPE (1)
at nothing through a Telescope, attracted many an eye S 11 422 1

TELL (421)
My dear mother I am very sorry to tell you that it LS 3 246 1
I need not tell you how much I miss him--how perpetually LS 5 250 3
He desires me to tell you that the present open weather LS 8 254 1
I honestly tell you my sentiments & intentions. LS 12 261 4
but I felt it my duty to tell you that your partiality for LS 12 261 5
Tell him so, with my congratulations; but between LS 15 266 1
too much in awe of me, to tell tales; but if the mildness LS 16 268 2
This was no explanation; I begged her to tell me what she LS 20 275 1
But remember what I tell you of Frederica; you must make LS 23 284 4
When I next write, I shall be able I hope to tell you that LS 23 285 8
"Did not I tell you, said she with a smile, that your LS 24 287 11
"But what, said I, was your ladyship going to tell me LS 24 289 12
& I can hardly tell which would have been worse for her. LS 27 296 1
& in particular tell me what you mean to do with Manwaring. LS 28 298 2
Tell me that you submit to my arguments, & do not reproach LS 30 301 5
Lady Susan, but to tell us that they are parted forever! LS 40 308 1
"Shall I tell you what you ought to say?" NA I 3 26 24
I had rather be told at once that you will not tell me." NA I 3 29 49
and tell their acquaintance what a charming day it is. NA I 5 35 1
Oh! I would not tell you what is behind the black veil for NA I 6 39 6
But do not tell me--I would not be told upon any account. NA I 6 39 7
Oh! I must tell you, that just after we parted yesterday, NA I 6 41 16
I tell Mr. Allen, when he talks of being sick of it, that NA I 8 54 5
I tell him he is quite in luck to be sent here for his NA I 8 54 5
so I tell Mr. Allen he must not be in a hurry to get away." NA I 8 54 9
"I tell you, Mr. Morland," she cried, "I would not do such NA I 8 57 21
He wants me to dance with him again, though I tell him NA I 8 57 21
Tell him, that it would quite shock you to see me do such NA I 8 58 23
speak to my brother, and tell him how very unsafe it is." NA I 9 65 29
Catherine could not tell a falsehood even to please NA I 9 67 33
"And what did she tell you of them?" NA I 9 68 43
"Did she tell you what part of Gloucestershire they come NA I 9 68 45
I tell him he ought to be ashamed of himself, but you and NA I 10 75 23
How could you tell me they were gone?-- NA I 11 87 53
Did not they tell me that Mr. Tilney and his sister were NA I 12 93 5
"It would be so easy to tell Miss Tilney that you had just NA I 13 98 1
"Dear madam," said Catherine, "they why did not you tell NA I 13 104 35
hoped you would tell me, if you thought I was doing wrong." NA I 13 104 35
Tell her that you think very highly of the understanding NA I 14 113 44
"But pray tell me what you mean." NA II 1 133 25
Isabella, you had something in particular to tell me?" NA II 3 144 5
Pray undeceive him as soon as you can, and tell him I beg NA II 3 145 13
"But do you only ask what I can be expected to tell?" NA II 4 151 22
"Your sister taught me; I cannot tell how. NA II 7 174 7
rather domestic, who can tell, the sentiment once raised, NA II 7 174 8
for ladies can best tell the taste of ladies in regard to NA II 7 175 15
as he soon forced her to tell him in words, that she had NA II 7 178 21
remain to tell what nothing else was allowed to whisper? NA II 9 194 6
she could hardly tell where, made her pause and tremble. NA II 9 194 6
I think it my duty to tell you, that every thing is at an NA II 10 202 6
7
He must tell his own story." NA II 11 209 2
"But he will tell only half of it." NA II 11 209 3
"How shall I tell you!-- NA II 13 223 11
Oh! how shall I tell you!" NA II 13 223 11
weeks longer, how can I tell you that your kindness is not NA II 13 223 13
But--how can I tell you?-- NA II 13 224 18
When you tell me to love him as a brother, I shall no more SS I 4 21 10
well worth catching, I can tell you, Miss Dashwood; he has SS I 9 44 23
setting your cap at, I can tell you, in spite of all this SS I 9 45 32
the offer, and to tell Willoughby when she saw him next, SS I 12 59 5
"Oh! Elinor," she cried, "I have such a secret to tell you SS I 12 60 9
her sister, and saying, "I must not tell, may I, Elinor?" SS I 12 61 15
"I must not tell, ma'am. SS I 12 61 22
Nobody could tell. SS I 13 63 5
"Perhaps it is to tell you that your cousin Fanny is SS I 13 64 14
Tell me that not only your house will remain the same, but SS I 14 74 19
You will tell me, I know, that this may, or may not have SS I 15 78 26
"I can hardly tell you myself.-- SS I 15 79 29
I can hardly tell why, or in what the deception originated. SS I 17 93 37
What am I to tell you? SS I 17 95 48
Shall I tell you my guess?" SS I 18 100 23
"Shall I tell you?" SS I 18 100 25
Charlotte is very pretty, I can tell you. SS I 19 105 16
"Did not I tell you, Sir John, when you spoke to me about SS I 20 111 20
you and your sisters I can tell you, and you can't think SS I 20 114 42
Colonel Brandon tell you of it! SS I 20 115 49
was so, for all that, and I will tell you how it happened. SS I 20 115 50
wherever he goes, and so you may tell your sister. SS I 20 116 58
for the cottage to tell the Miss Dashwoods of the Miss SS I 21 119 3
but you know, how could I tell what smart beaux there SS I 21 123 28
"Upon my word," replied Elinor, "I cannot tell you, for I SS I 21 124 29
"but pray do not tell it, for it's a great secret." SS I 21 125 38
Then perhaps you cannot tell me what sort of a woman she SS I 22 128 5
But if I dared tell you all, you would not be so much SS I 22 129 11
I confess myself so totally surprised at what you tell me, SS I 22 131 29
"I will honestly tell you of one scheme which has lately SS II 2 149 25
to tell you, that you will certainly see her to-morrow." SS II 4 163 17
come confusion; "indeed, Marianne, I have nothing to tell." SS II 5 170 25
We have neither of us any thing to tell; you, because you SS II 5 170 26
to tell her, sat for some time without saying a word. SS II 5 172 40
Tell me that it is all absolutely resolved on, that any SS II 5 173 44
Tell me, Willoughby; for heaven's sake tell me, what is SS II 6 177 10
Tell him I must see him again--must speak to him instantly. SS II 6 177 13
it is no such thing, I can tell you, for it has been known SS II 7 182 10
I tell every body of it and so does Charlotte." SS II 7 182 10
Tell me what it is, explain the grounds on which you acted, SS II 7 188 42
Delaford is a nice place, I can tell you; exactly what I SS II 8 196 22
He knows nothing of it; do tell him, my dear." SS II 8 198 30
whom I knew to be engaged--but how shall I tell you? SS II 8 199 35
"You have something to tell me of Mr. Willoughby, that SS II 9 204 19
secrecy, she would tell nothing, would give no clue, SS II 9 209 28
But now, after such dishonourable usage, who can tell what SS II 9 210 32
each other, arrived to tell all that she suffered and SS II 10 213 2
tell everybody she saw, how good-for-nothing he was." SS II 10 215 10
She could soon tell at what coachmaker's the new carriage SS II 10 215 11
to tell her that his mistress waited for them at the door. SS II 11 222 12
before her, till able to tell her that his marriage with SS II 12 229 4
of seeing Elinor alone, to tell her how happy she was. SS II 13 238 2
I am sure if ever you tell your sister what I think of her, SS II 13 240 15
encouragement to hope that she should tell her sister. SS II 13 240 16
attention: and who could tell that they might not expect SS II 14 248 6
so I often tell my mother, when she is grieving about it. SS II 14 251 13
'my dear ferrars, do tell me how it is to be managed. SS II 14 252 18
at my house; and so I would tell him if I could see him. SS III 1 268 51
She will tell you any thing if you ask. SS III 2 271 6
too, that she would tell any thing without being asked, SS III 2 271 7
it's no such a thing I can tell you; and it's quite a SS III 2 272 14
three days, I could not tell what to think myself; and I SS III 2 272 16
called from below to tell me Mrs. Richardson was come in SS III 2 274 16
They will tell me I should write to the doctor, to get SS III 2 275 22
about it myself, but pray tell her I am quite happy to SS III 2 275 25
Will you be so good as to tell him that the living of SS III 3 282 19
besides, you must long to tell your sister all about it." SS III 4 286 11
"Certainly, ma'am, I shall tell Marianne of it; but I SS III 4 286 13
"Then you would not have me tell it Lucy, for I think of SS III 4 286 14
she would do for a lady's maid, I am sure I can't tell. SS III 4 287 22
of, and what she had to tell him, made her feel SS III 4 288 26
But I thought I would just tell you of this, because I SS III 5 297 31
tell!-- with such knowledge it was impossible to be calm. SS III 7 316 30
The servants, I suppose, forgot to tell you that Mr. SS III 8 317 3
"For God's sake tell me, is she out of danger, or is she SS III 8 318 12
Tell me honestly"--a deeper glow overspreading his cheeks-- SS III 8 318 15
"Did you tell her that you should soon return?" SS III 8 324 44
Well, at last, as I need not tell you, you were forced on SS III 8 327 55
You tell me that she has forgiven me already. SS III 8 330 67
Tell her of my misery and my penitence--tell her that my SS III 8 330 67
"I will tell her all that is necessary to what may SS III 8 330 68
I tell what horrid projects might not have been imputed? SS III 8 330 69
Time, a very little time, I tell him, will do everything;-- SS III 9 337 18
through her tears, "tell mama," withdrew from her sister SS III 10 348 34
"But did she tell you she was married, thomas?" SS III 11 354 28
Mrs. Jennings wrote to tell the wonderful tale, to vent SS III 13 370 37
in hopes, as I tell her, to fall in with the doctor again. SS III 13 370 37
deal at home, nobody can tell what may happen--for, when SS III 14 375 9
to get married--she would as good as tell you so herself.-- W 316 2
at Chichester; she wont tell us with whom, but I beleive W 317 2
My conduct must tell you how I have been brought up. W 318 2

Context	Work	Vol.	Ch.	Page	Para.
"You will not find him in the ballroom I can tell you, you	W			319	2
I have had no leisure to tell you anything--but indeed I	W			321	2
by a man in livery with a powder'd head, I can tell you."	W			322	2
street, & he came ready to tell what ever might interest.--	W			323	3
And now tell me how you like them all, & what I am to say	W			341	19
Nobody can tell how much I hate quarrelling.	W			343	19
briskly after Nanny "to tell Betty to take up the fowls."--	W			346	21
motive of being able to tell the Miss Watsons, whom he	W			355	28
Ly. Osborne would tell me that I were growing as careless	W			357	28
I will tell you how it was.--	W			358	28
"You want to tell me, and I have no objection to hearing	PP	I	1	3	8
"I am sorry to hear that; but why did not you tell me so	PP	I	2	7	22
At our time of life, it is not so pleasant I can tell you,	PP	I	2	8	26
face, and desired he would tell her what lady had the	PP	I	6	27	49
					50
Well, Jane, make haste and tell us; make haste, my love."	PP	I	7	30	15
"I wonder my aunt did not tell us of that."	PP	I	7	30	18
I often tell my other girls they are nothing to her.	PP	I	9	42	7
I shall tell Colonel Forster it will be quite a shame if	PP	I	9	46	38
"Pray tell your sister that I long to see her."	PP	I	10	47	9
"Tell your sister I am delighted to hear of her	PP	I	10	48	15
I have therefore made up my mind to tell you, that I do	PP	I	10	52	50
however, she could only tell her nieces what they already	PP	I	15	73	11
the young man forgot to tell you, among his other	PP	I	18	94	45
forgotten him; but I have nothing satisfactory to tell you.	PP	I	18	95	50
Tell her that you insist upon her marrying him."	PP	I	20	111	12
by Kitty, who came to tell the same news, and no sooner	PP	I	20	113	26
But I tell you what, Miss Lizzy, if you take it into your	PP	I	20	113	28
Nobody can tell what I suffer!--	PP	I	20	113	28
Sir William, how can you tell such a story?--	PP	I	23	126	2
I am very glad to hear what you tell us, of long sleeves."	PP	II	2	140	4
He could tell her nothing new of the wonders of his	PP	II	4	152	4
"If you will only tell me what sort of girl Miss King is,	PP	II	4	153	10
tell how many trees there were in the most distant clump.	PP	II	5	156	4
such a sight to be seen! I will not tell you what it is.	PP	II	5	158	11
					12
Elizabeth asked questions in vain; Maria would tell her	PP	II	5	158	13
Mrs. Collins, did I tell you of Lady Metcalfe's calling	PP	II	6	165	32
Lady Catherine; "and pray tell her from me, that she	PP	II	8	173	8
I often tell young ladies, that no excellence in music is	PP	II	8	173	10
You must allow me to tell you how ardently I admire and	PP	II	11	189	4
The feelings which, you tell me, have long prevented the	PP	II	11	190	7
insulting me, you chose to tell me that you liked me	PP	II	11	190	10
I shall give you pain--to what degree you only can tell.	PP	II	12	200	5
How much I shall have to tell!"	PP	II	15	217	13
I shall merely be able to tell what Bingley may tell in a	PP	II	17	227	25
Bingley may tell in a much more agreeable manner himself.	PP	II	17	227	25
But, Lizzy, you can tell us whether it is like or not."	PP	III	1	247	12
not tell, but he certainly had not seen her with composure.	PP	III	1	253	55
But how came you to tell us that he was so disagreeable?"	PP	III	1	257	70
them wait for that, but tell Lydia she shall have as much	PP	III	5	288	38
Tell him what a dreadful state I am in,--that I am	PP	III	5	288	38
And tell my dear Lydia, not to give any directions about	PP	III	5	288	38
subject, by saying, "but tell me all and every thing about	PP	III	5	290	45
					46
Tell him I hope he will excuse me when he knows all, and	PP	III	5	291	60
me when he knows all, and tell him I will dance with him	PP	III	5	291	60
but I wish you would tell sally to mend a great slit in my	PP	III	5	292	60
But, on second thoughts, perhaps Lizzy could tell us, what	PP	III	6	295	6
and tell the good, good news to my sister Phillips.	PP	III	7	307	49
"La! you are so strange! but I must tell you how it went	PP	III	9	318	24
certainly tell you all, and then Wickham would be angry."	PP	III	9	320	30
dear aunt, if you do not tell me in an honourable manner,	PP	III	9	320	34
writing will not comprise what I have to tell you.	PP	III	10	321	2
He came to tell Mr. Gardiner that he had found out where	PP	III	10	321	2
It is a relation which you tell me is to give you great	PP	III	10	325	2
but I would not tell you how little I was satisfied with	PP	III	10	325	2
therefore what I now tell you, can give you no fresh pain.	PP	III	10	325	2
How Mr. Darcy looked, therefore, she could not tell.	PP	III	11	336	50
thing to be privileged to tell him, that his kindness was	PP	III	12	340	13
Your own heart, your own conscience, must tell you why I	PP	III	14	353	23
"Tell me once for all, are you engaged to him?"	PP	III	14	356	54
his affairs, I cannot tell; but you have certainly no	PP	III	14	357	61
only came, I suppose, to tell us the Collinses were well.	PP	III	14	359	76
to know what he had to tell her, was heightened by the	PP	III	15	361	8
Mrs. Bennet had time to tell him of their having seen his	PP	III	16	365	1
If your feelings are still what they were last April, tell	PP	III	16	366	7
themselves I can hardly tell, but I believe in about half	PP	III	16	370	32
I feel more than I ought to do, when I tell you all."	PP	III	17	373	12
Will you tell me how long you have loved him?"	PP	III	17	373	15
How little did you tell me of what passed at Pemberley and	PP	III	17	374	18
But my dearest love, tell me what dish Mr. Darcy is	PP	III	17	378	45
But tell me, what did you come down to Netherfield for?	PP	III	18	381	15
have it in her power to tell them, as she now and then did	MP	I	1	4	2
Let us walk out in the park, and you shall tell me all	MP	I	2	15	11
my cousin cannot tell the principal rivers in Russia--or	MP	I	2	18	23
But I must tell you another thing of Fanny, so odd and so	MP	I	2	19	28
"Do not I tell you, that I like her best at first?"	MP	I	5	45	10
a great deal of pleasure, if you will tell me what about."	MP	I	5	49	34
nothing was ever juster,) tell one what is expected; but I	MP	I	5	51	40
But if dear Sir Thomas were here, he could tell you what	MP	I	6	54	9
Whenever I do see it, you will tell me how it has been	MP	I	6	56	24
brother, I entreat you to tell him that my harp is come,	MP	I	6	59	41
Fanny would rather have had Edmund tell the story, but his	MP	I	6	60	47
Of various admirals, I could tell you a great deal; of	MP	I	6	60	49
She could not tell Miss Crawford that "those woods	MP	I	8	81	33
And to tell you the truth," speaking rather lower, "I do	MP	I	10	98	7
"Or if we are, Miss Price will be so good as to tell him,	MP	I	10	99	20
spare time to tell us his errand, and where you all were."	MP	I	10	101	30
Miss Crawford demanded, to tell of races and Weymouth, and	MP	I	12	114	1
forward with great alacrity to tell him the agreeable news.	MP	I	15	138	2
I must now, my dear Maria, tell you, that I think it	MP	I	15	139	11
I forgot to tell Tom of something that happened to me this	MP	I	15	141	22
many spoke together to tell the same melancholy truth--	MP	I	15	143	28
consideration; "and I can tell Mr. Maddox, that I shall	MP	I	15	149	61
"You had better tell Miss Bertram to think of Mr.	MP	I	17	161	13
You are best off, I can tell you; but if nobody did more	MP	I	18	166	6
desired to exercise it and tell them all their faults; but	MP	I	18	170	24
They'll tell you all about it."	MP	II	1	181	15
but you should tell your father he is not above five feet	MP	II	1	186	31
Little observation there was necessary to tell him that	MP	II	3	200	20
with, "I have something to tell you that will surprize you.	MP	II	5	218	12
affectionate brother, "and tell you how I like you; and as	MP	II	5	222	42
I could not tell what she would be at yesterday.	MP	II	6	230	7
feelings; he had heard her tell Mrs. Grant that she should	MP	II	8	256	12
You see how it is; and could tell me, perhaps better than	MP	II	9	268	31
better than I could tell you, how and why I am vexed.	MP	II	9	268	31
Do not tell me any thing now, which hereafter you may be	MP	II	9	269	36
Tell me whatever you like."	MP	II	9	270	39
And she looked around as if longing to tell him so.	MP	II	10	275	9
you can tell me why my brother goes to town to-morrow.	MP	II	10	277	17
He says, he has business there, but will not tell me what.	MP	II	10	277	17
His still refusing to tell her what he had gone for, was	MP	II	12	291	1
But tell me all about it.	MP	II	12	292	7
Tell me more.	MP	II	12	293	11
he was as happy to tell as she could be to listen, and a	MP	II	12	293	16
tell her uncle that he was wrong--"you are quite mistaken.	MP	III	1	315	19
way; and let me tell you, Fanny, that you may live	MP	III	1	319	39
what has passed; I shall not even tell your aunt Bertram.	MP	III	1	322	48
"I will tell you what, Fanny," said she.--	MP	III	2	333	28
I shall tell Sir Thomas that I am sure it was done that	MP	III	2	333	28
added,--"and I will tell you what, Fanny--which is more	MP	III	2	333	28
interested her, and to tell her that he had been hearing	MP	III	3	335	6
afterwards--"and I will tell you what, I think you will	MP	III	3	338	19
I fancied you might be going to tell me I ought to be more	MP	III	3	340	25
Are not you going to tell me so?"	MP	III	3	340	25
Only tell me if I was.	MP	III	3	342	33
Only tell me if I was wrong.	MP	III	3	342	33
every body, cousin, there can be nothing for me to tell."	MP	III	4	346	9
No one but you can tell me them.	MP	III	4	346	10
I wish he had not been obliged to tell you what he was	MP	III	4	348	21
Had I received any letter from Mansfield, to tell me how	MP	III	4	354	50
with all that Fanny could tell, or could leave to be	MP	III	5	356	1
But were I to attempt to tell you of all the women whom I	MP	III	5	362	16
He watched her with this idea--but he could hardly tell	MP	III	6	366	1
applied to Edmund to tell him how she stood affected on	MP	III	6	366	1
done away--nobody could tell how; and the doubts and	MP	III	6	367	4
You will tell my mother how it all ought to be, and you	MP	III	6	372	20
I could not tell whether you would be for some meat, or	MP	III	7	378	14
and tell her to bring in the tea-things as soon as she can.	MP	III	7	379	15
to see their sister, and tell that the thrush was gone out	MP	III	7	381	25
Shall I tell you how Mrs. Rushworth looked when your name	MP	III	9	393	1
of dress now-a-days to tell tales, but--but--but.	MP	III	12	416	2
natural that she should tell you enough of her own	MP	III	13	420	2
It will be a comfort to me to tell you how things now are,	MP	III	13	420	2
Having once begun, it is a pleasure to me to tell you all	MP	III	13	422	2
Tell me the real truth, as you have it form the fountain	MP	III	14	434	13
Dear Fanny, write directly, and tell us to come.	MP	III	14	435	14
will tell you every thing, and then have done for ever.	MP	III	16	455	19
to tell him the whole delightful and astonishing truth.	MP	III	17	471	28
He will be able to tell her how we all are."	E	I	1	9	19
shall be happy to tell you, for we all behaved charmingly.	E	I	1	11	35
find out who were the parents; but Harriet could not tell.	E	I	4	27	3
She was ready to tell every thing in her power, but on	E	I	4	27	3
what Mrs. Goddard chose to tell her; and looked no farther.	E	I	4	27	3
Did not I tell you what he said of you the other day?"	E	I	4	34	42
to have happened which she was longing to tell.	E	I	7	50	1
Pray, dear Miss Woodhouse, tell me what I ought to do?"	E	I	7	52	16
compliment, so I will tell you that you have improved her.	E	I	8	58	12
or places, but I must tell you that I have good reason to	E	I	8	58	19
					20
"I will tell you something, in return for what have told	E	I	8	60	30
and good-natured, let me tell you, that in the degree she	E	I	8	63	44
(she must be allowed to tell herself, in spite of Mr.	E	I	8	67	57
I could never tell whether an attachment between you and	E	I	9	74	20
so apt to tell every thing relative to every body about me,	E	I	10	84	16
"But you should tell them of the letter, my dear," said	E	I	11	95	22
Whether it was his own idea you know, one cannot tell.	E	I	11	96	22
Tell your aunt, little Emma, that she ought to set you a	E	I	12	99	10
at Donwell, he had to tell what every field was to bear	E	I	12	100	16
dryness, "if Mr. Perry can tell me how to convey a wife	E	I	12	106	60
She could tell nothing of Hartfield, in which Mrs. Weston	E	I	14	117	1
--And then I tell her, I am sure she would contrive to	E	II	1	157	10
I must tell you what an unlucky thing happened to me, as	E	II	1	162	31
own story a great deal better than I can tell it for her."	E	II	1	162	31
to tell me, I hope, that you had not a pleasant evening."	E	II	3	171	9
unchecked, ran eagerly through what she had to tell.	E	II	3	177	52
you know, one can't tell how; and then I took courage, and	E	II	3	179	52
for him to do, than to tell her christian name, and say	E	II	4	181	2
coachman can tell you where you had best cross the street."	E	II	5	195	47
I need not tell you what is to be done.	E	II	7	210	14
And when you get there, you must tell him at what time you	E	II	7	210	14
of doing it, but I honestly tell you what they are."	E	II	8	217	32
yourself, and I must tell them while the idea is fresh.	E	II	8	222	59
His good-nature, his humanity, as I tell you, would be	E	II	8	224	72
You find me trying to be useful; tell me if you think I	E	II	10	240	3
Tell me how Miss Fairfax is."	E	II	10	244	35
Do not tell his father, but that young man is not quite	E	II	11	249	11
be our object--if one could but tell what that would be."	E	II	11	254	49
"She will be all delight and gratitude, but she will tell	E	II	11	255	52
interested in the absent!--she will tell me every thing.	E	II	12	261	36
"Oh! do not tell me.	E	II	16	295	32
Anne, my dear, did not I always tell you so, and you would	E	II	17	304	27
Oh! Mr. Frank Churchill, I must tell you my mother's	E	III	2	323	19
Then changing from a frown to a smile--"no, do not tell me-	E	III	2	325	28
Otway; she will love to tell you all about it herself to-	E	III	2	329	45
Does my vain spirit ever tell me I am wrong?"	E	III	2	330	52
that I should like to tell you--a sort of confession to	E	III	4	337	1
					2
and how they parted, Mr. Knightley could not tell.	E	III	5	349	25
As I tell Mr. E., you are a thorough humourist.--	E	III	6	356	28
I will tell you.--	E	III	7	371	34
I must, I will,--I will tell you truths while I can,	E	III	7	375	61
be considered by the rest of the party, she could not tell.	E	III	8	377	1
I must, I will tell you truths while I can."	E	III	8	377	1
said she, "but I do not know; they tell me she is well.	E	III	8	378	6
Time, however, she thought, would tell him that they ought	E	III	9	385	5
"Good God!--Mr. Weston, tell me at once.--	E	III	10	393	10
Tell me, I charge you tell me this moment what it is."	E	III	10	393	10
It does relate to him, and I will tell you directly;" (	E	III	10	394	30
continued, "I will farther tell you, that there was a	E	III	10	396	41
How could he tell what mischief he might be doing?--	E	III	10	396	44
How could he tell that he might not be making me in love	E	III	10	396	44
tell you, he could stay with us but a quarter of an hour.--	E	III	10	398	57
Common sense would have directed her to tell Harriet, that	E	III	11	402	1
"What did Mr. Weston tell you?"--said Emma, still	E	III	11	404	7
Emma, I must tell what you will not ask, though I may wish	E	III	13	429	27
I will tell you exactly what I think."	E	III	13	429	32
Tell me, then, have I no chance of ever succeeding?"	E	III	13	430	33
my dearest, most beloved Emma--tell me at once.	E	III	13	430	35
Bear with the truths I would tell you now, dearest Emma,	E	III	13	430	37
She must tell you herself what she is--yet not by word,	E	III	14	439	8
the next day to tell me that we never were to meet again.--	E	III	14	442	8
eldest daughter?--he must tell her; and Miss Bates being	E	III	17	468	35
with, "I have something to tell you, Emma; some news."	E	III	18	470	1
					2
"No, I have not; I know nothing; pray tell me."	E	III	18	470	11
now tell me every thing; make this intelligible to me.	E	III	18	471	19
"I was just going to tell you of our agreeable surprise in	E	III	18	476	45
Perhaps I am the readier to suspect, because, to tell you	E	III	18	478	67
More than I can recollect in a moment: but I can tell you	P	III	5	38	34
would not do; but I shall tell you, Miss Anne, because you	P	III	6	45	9
"And I will tell you our reason," she added, "and all	P	III	6	50	27
I will tell you why she is out of spirits.	P	III	6	50	27
I will go and tell Charles, and get ready directly.	P	III	7	57	16
"Oh!--but, Charles, tell Captain Wentworth, he need not be	P	III	8	66	20
"Pray," said Captain Wentworth, immediately, "can you tell	P	III	12	105	11
There the news must follow him, but who was to tell it?	P	III	12	108	28
tell how, and brought a rather improving account of Louisa.	P	IV	1	125	14
You will tell Sir Walter what we have done, and that Mr.	P	IV	1	127	28
"And that you are very likely to do very soon, I can tell	P	IV	2	131	12
together; and I have something to tell you as we go along.	P	IV	6	169	27
"Did you say that you had something to tell me, sir?"	P	IV	6	169	28
I will tell you the whole story another time.	P	IV	6	170	29
"We do not like our lodgings here the worse, I can tell	P	IV	6	170	29
But first of all, you must tell me the name of the young	P	IV	6	170	31
She had already been obliged to tell Lady Russell that	P	IV	7	178	27
"By all means," said she; "only tell me all about it, when	P	IV	7	180	34
He delighted in being asked, but he would not tell.	P	IV	8	187	33
All that she could tell, she told most gladly; but the all	P	IV	9	192	5
You need not tell me that you had a pleasant evening.	P	IV	9	194	14
"Do tell me how it first came into your head."	P	IV	9	197	35
Then do tell me what he was at that time of life.	P	IV	9	198	51
doubting and considering as to what I ought to tell you.	P	IV	9	198	53

I will only tell you what I have found him. P IV 9 199 55
be with a surveyor, to tell me how to bring "it with best P IV 9 203 72
"Yes," said Anne, "you tell me nothing which does not P IV 9 207 91
Mrs. Smith had been able to tell her what no one else P IV 10 212 1
She must talk to Lady Russell, tell her, consult with her, P IV 10 212 1
You need not tell her so, but I thought her dress hideous P IV 10 215 15
Come, and tell me. P IV 10 222 34
"Tell me not that I am too late, that such precious " P IV 11 237 42
Tell me if, when I returned to England in the year eight, P IV 11 247 82
My sensations tell me so already."-- S 1 367 1
may have given rise to--allow me to tell you who we are. S 1 367 1
Those who tell their own story you know must be listened S 3 376 1
it, but my feelings tell me too plainly that in my present S 5 387 1
I will not tell you how many people I have employed in the S 5 387 1
to be respectable I cannot tell,--but they are obliged to S 7 402 1
I will tell you how I got at her. S 9 412 1

TELL-TALE (1)
who will see in the tell-tale compression of the pages NA II 16 250 4

TELLING (58)
in the habit therefore of telling lies to increase their NA I 9 65 31
And here have I been telling all my acquaintance that I NA I 10 75 26
And it all ended, at last, in his telling Henry one NA II 11 209 5
for months, without telling her of his affection;--that SS I 15 80 36
of telling lies when politeness required it, always fell. SS I 21 122 14
in telling the name, as Miss Steele had in hearing it. SS I 21 125 37
liberty with you," said she, "in telling you all this. SS I 22 132 42
the staircase, and telling Marianne that he was gone, SS II 6 178 15
Your telling it will be the greatest act of friendship SS II 9 204 19
comfort; and therefore telling him at once that his stay SS III 7 309 5
when she is recovered, what I have been telling you?-- SS III 8 330 67
resist the temptation of telling me what he knew ought to-- SS III 8 330 69
running away without telling us that you were coming out." PP I 10 53 61
Lucas had commanded in telling her story, gave way to a PP I 22 124 14
15
honestly telling her what she thought, she thus went on: PP II 3 144 1
2
Hertfordshire news, and telling again what had been PP II 5 157 10
What are you telling Miss Bennet? PP II 8 173 4
"I am thinking of what you have been telling me," said she. PP II 10 185 34
she, one evening, "by telling me, that he was totally PP III 13 349 45
Mrs. Grant has been telling her of its fine views, and I MP I 7 69 28
Fanny by Tom Bertram's telling her, with infinite regret, MP I 15 148 58
worse, cook has just been telling me that the turkey, MP II 4 212 31
all his heart to her, telling her all his hopes and fears, MP II 6 234 18
season, (as he was then telling her,) though that MP II 7 246 37
Thomas, as you have perhaps heard me telling Miss Price. MP II 7 247 38
it is not by telling you that my affections are steady. MP III 3 343 41
Lady Bertram had been telling her niece in the evening to MP III 6 373 26
and more intent on telling the news, than giving them any MP III 7 377 7
Her son answered cheerfully, telling her that every thing MP III 7 378 11
a minute's privacy for telling Fanny that his only MP III 10 406 21
encouraging, and telling her to come very often; and as E I 4 26 1
his mother and sisters, telling how much more beautiful is E I 7 56 44
Miss Nash had been telling her something, which she E I 8 68 58
I have been always telling you, my love, that I had no E I 11 94 15
"I did not thoroughly understand what you were telling E I 12 104 44
But John, as to what I was telling you of my idea of E I 12 106 61
was on the point of telling you that when I called at Mrs. E I 13 114 31
I believe you did not hear me telling the others in the E I 14 119 7
Mr. Weston, I dare say, has been telling you exactly how E I 14 121 14
to dancing--Mrs. Cole was telling me that dancing at the E II 1 156 7
her before, and as I was telling Mrs. Cole, we shall E II 1 158 14
be telling Miss Campbell about his own home in Ireland. E II 1 159 20
Mrs. Cole was telling that she had been calling on Miss E II 8 214 13
was but yesterday I was telling Mr. Cole, I really was E II 8 215 16
I was this moment telling Jane, I thought you would begin E III 2 324 23
every where.-- I was telling you of your grandmamma, Jane,- E III 2 329 45
Mr. Knightley had been telling him something about brewing E III 4 339 18
Jane, don't you remember grandmamma's telling us of it E III 5 346 16
had no objection to her telling us, of course, but it was E III 5 346 16
"How much I am obliged to you," said he, "for telling me E III 7 368 4
what John ostler had been telling him, and then it came E III 8 383 29
I remember her telling me at the ball, that I owed Mrs. E III 14 439 8
adopted the expedient of telling her briefly what she P IV 1 124 12
fine--I overheard him telling Henrietta all about it--and P IV 2 131 9
to be heard at a distance telling the same tale, before Mr. P IV 3 144 23
Alicia and Mrs. Frankland were telling me of last night. P IV 7 179 30
least the comfort of telling the whole story her own way. P IV 9 210 99
Men have had every advantage of us in telling their own P IV 11 234 28

TELLS (21)
I read it a little as a duty, but it tells me nothing that NA I 14 108 22
A letter form my steward tells me that my presence is NA II 2 139 7
book that tells her how to admire an old twisted tree. SS I 17 92 25
He never tells me any thing! SS I 20 110 2
At least I believe so--but she tells me nothing. W 318 2
that because Miss Bingley tells you her brother greatly PP I 21 119 20
take care of himself--he tells me he has not time to take E I 12 101 25
the voice of nature, which tells man, in every thing given E I 13 113 26
letter, and I am sure she tells her own story a great deal E II 1 162 31
Perry tells me that Mr. Cole never touches malt liquor. E II 7 210 20
to know a little more, and this tells me quite enough. E II 8 218 38
39
"For my companion tells me," said she, "that I absolutely E II 9 234 26
This letter tells us--it is a short letter--written in a E II 18 305 7
to give us notice--it tells us that they are all coming up E II 18 305 7
If one leads you wrong, I am sure the other tells you of E III 2 330 53
Goldsmith tells us, that when lovely woman stoops to folly, E III 9 387 12
receiving, is what my conscience tells me ought not to be. E III 12 419 8
to spoil her; for she tells me, they are always tempting P III 6 45 9
him yesterday, in which he tells us of it, and he had just P IV 6 172 41
silly wife, to whom he tells things which he had better P IV 9 205 82
Mrs. Wallis has an amusing idea, as nurse tells me, that P IV 9 208 92

TEMPER (157)
that in the fury of her temper I should not be surprised LS 2 245 1
more strongly they operate on Mr Vernon's generous temper. LS 6 251 2
poor Frederica's temper could never bear opposition well. LS 15 267 6
seem to have the sort of temper to make severity necessary. LS 17 270 4
Her mother has insinuated that her temper is untractable, LS 17 270 5
& at others that her temper only is in fault. LS 17 271 8
plain sense, with a good temper, and, what is more NA I 1 13 1
a bad heart nor a bad temper; was seldom stubborn, NA I 1 14 1
of quiet, inactive good temper, and a trifling turn of NA I 2 20 8
a temper, to be so easily persuaded by those she loved. NA I 13 98 2
it is not a little matter that puts me out of temper." NA I 15 117 3
but though his temper injured her, his judgment never did. NA II 9 197 27
His temper is not happy, and something has now occurred to NA II 13 225 21
circumstance could work upon a temper like the General's? NA II 16 250 4
at first, severe; but his temper was cheerful and sanguine, SS I 1 4 4
In seasons of cheerfulness, no temper could be more SS I 2 8 2
she knew his heart to be warm and his temper affectionate. SS I 3 16 13
for however dissimilar in temper and outward behaviour, SS I 7 32 1
of spirits, than of any natural gloominess of temper. SS I 10 50 12
I once knew a lady who in temper and mind greatly SS I 11 57 17
She knew her sister's temper. SS I 12 59 5
His temper might perhaps be a little soured by finding, SS I 20 112 28
variation of form, face, temper, and understanding. SS I 21 119 3
"I am rather of a jealous temper too by nature, and from SS II 2 147 12
too much for her temper; but she was saved the trouble of SS II 10 219 42
of elegance--want of spirits--or want of temper. SS II 12 233 18
generous temper, simple taste, and diffident feelings. SS III 6 305 15
open and honest, and a feeling, affectionate temper. SS III 8 331 70
merits, and a temper irritated by their very attention.-- SS III 10 346 28
it--my feelings shall be governed and my temper improved. SS III 10 347 30
has married a woman of a less amiable temper than yourself. SS III 11 351 13
He would have had a wife of whose temper he could make no SS III 11 351 13
to domestic happiness, than the mere temper of a wife." SS III 11 351 13
him to Barton in a temper of mind which needed all the SS III 13 369 35
an habitual gloom of temper, or died of a broken heart, SS III 14 379 18
She must have too masculine & bold a temper.-- W 318 2
You must have a sweet temper indeed;--I never met with any W 320 2
social temper more than half seconded, gave the invitation. W 359 28
disappointment, or repress the peevishness of her temper--. W 360 30
to an aunt whose amiable temper had delighted to give her W 361 31
understanding, little information, and uncertain temper. PP I 1 5 34
and less pliancy of temper than her sister, and with a PP I 4 15 11
knew the easiness of his temper, whether he might not PP I 4 15 12
ductility of his temper, though no disposition could offer PP I 4 16 14
feeling, a composure of temper and a uniform cheerfulness PP I 6 21 1
without exception, the sweetest temper I ever met with. PP I 9 42 7
says into a compliment on the sweetness of my temper. PP I 10 49 31
Teaze calmness of temper and presence of mind! PP I 11 57 18
My temper I dare not vouch for.-- PP I 11 58 28
My temper would perhaps be called resentful.-- PP I 11 58 28
I have a warm, unguarded temper, and I may perhaps have PP I 16 80 27
He had not a temper to bear the sort of competition in PP I 16 80 32
of his resentments, of his having an unforgiving temper. PP I 16 80 34
of temper, she could not contribute much to my felicity." PP I 20 110 4
Jane's temper was not desponding, and she was gradually PP I 21 120 29
on that easiness of temper, that want of proper resolution PP II 1 133 3
allowance enough for difference of situation and temper. PP II 1 135 12
temper, her heart was not likely to be easily touched.-- PP II 12 197 5
her temper to be happy; and all was soon right again. PP II 19 239 8
sense and sweetness of temper exactly adapted her for PP II 19 239 10
comprehended health and temper to bear inconveniences-- PP II 19 239 11
His understanding and temper, though unlike her own, would PP III 8 312 15
was right, but I was not taught to correct my temper. PP III 16 369 24
even to his easy temper, or her affectionate heart. PP III 19 385 3
She was not of so ungovernable a temper as Lydia, and, PP III 19 385 4
tranquil feelings, and a temper remarkably easy and MP I 1 4 1
I wish there may not be a little sulkiness of temper--her MP I 2 13 5
of an obliging, yielding temper; and they could not but MP I 2 17 21
You have good sense, and a sweet temper, and I am sure you MP I 3 26 29
She is of a temper to do a great deal for any body she MP I 3 27 33
Mrs. Norris could not speak with any temper of such MP I 3 31 59
I am of a cautious temper, and unwilling to risk my MP I 4 43 23
love; but with sense and temper which ought to have made MP I 5 45 3
Julia was vexed, and her temper was hasty, but she felt it MP I 10 101 29
It is a great defect of temper, made worse by a very MP I 11 111 29
taken a ---- not a good temper into it; and as he must MP I 11 111 30
"There goes a temper which would never give pain! MP I 11 112 34
suffering which a warm temper and a high spirit were MP I 17 162 19
With no material fault of temper, or difference of opinion, MP I 17 162 19
already; be plagued very often and never lose your temper." MP II 4 213 34
temper, made it as natural for him to express as to feel. MP II 6 234 17
Her temper he had good reason to depend on and to praise. MP II 12 294 16
any reason, child, to think ill of Mr. Crawford's temper?" MP III 1 317 36
free from wilfulness of temper, self-conceit, and every MP III 1 318 39
Here is a young man of sense, of character, of temper, of MP III 1 319 39
favourable opinion of his understanding, heart, and temper. MP III 1 321 47
and concern, that to a temper of vanity and hope like MP III 2 328 7
"it is not merely in temper that I consider him as totally MP III 4 349 25
fretfulness of a fearful temper, or been unreasonable in MP III 6 371 17
love or assist; and of Susan's temper, she had many doubts. MP III 8 391 9
The living in incessant noise was to a frame and temper, MP III 8 391 11
and yielding temper would have shrunk from asserting. MP III 9 395 4
Her temper was open. MP III 9 397 8
to irritate an imperfect temper; and she had the happiness MP III 9 397 8
to faults of judgment or temper, or disproportion of age, MP III 13 421 2
of Miss Crawford's temper, of being urged again; and MP III 15 437 1
principles, unsuspicious temper, and genuine strength of MP III 15 442 21
Her's are not faults of temper. MP III 16 456 25
or his being acquainted with their character and temper. MP III 17 463 9
conviction, rendered her temper so bad, and her feelings MP III 17 464 10
elopement, her temper had been in a state of such MP III 17 466 16
Her temper was naturally the easiest of the two, her MP III 17 466 17
on the sweetness of her temper, the purity of her mind, MP III 17 468 21
Mrs. Grant, with a temper to love and be loved, must have MP III 17 469 24
new hopes of happiness from dissimilarity of temper. MP III 17 471 28
good of principle and temper, and chiefly anxious to bind MP III 17 471 29
by sweetness of temper, and strong feelings of gratitude. MP III 17 472 31
the mildness of her temper had hardly allowed her to E I 1 5 3
his heart and his amiable temper, his talents could not E I 1 7 8
cheerful mind and social temper by entering into the E I 2 15 1
warm heart and sweet temper made him think every thing due E I 2 15 3
He had never been an unhappy man; his own temper had E I 2 17 6
It was her own universal good-will and contented temper E I 3 21 4
She had all the natural grace of sweetness of temper and E I 6 42 3
thorough sweetness of temper and manner, a very humble E I 8 63 44
and such temper, the highest claims a woman could possess." E I 8 63 44
has a tendency to contract the mind, and sour the temper. E I 10 85 19
They were alike too, in a general benevolence of temper, E I 11 92 4
such a reproach; but his temper was not his great E I 11 92 5
The extreme sweetness of her temper must hurt his. E I 11 93 5
and your brother, I do not know his equal for temper. E I 11 95 19
those of the elder, whose temper was by much the most E I 12 100 16
There is such perfect good temper and good will in Mr. E I 13 112 17
a stone to people in general; and the devil of a temper." E I 14 121 13
his aunt's spirits and pleasure; in short, upon her temper. E I 14 121 16
"My dearest Emma, do not pretend, with your sweet temper, E I 14 123 25
and she had difficulty in behaving with temper. E I 15 125 4
temper and happiness when this visit of hardship were over. E I 15 128 21
sober: but a sanguine temper, though for ever expecting E I 18 144 2
and with Mrs. Churchill's temper, before we pretend to E I 18 146 15
change, restlessness of temper, which must be doing E II 7 205 1
He appeared to have a very open temper--certainly a very E II 7 205 2
and the character of his temper; but for all the purposes E II 11 250 19
She has not the open temper which a man would wish for in E II 15 288 36
Her sensibilities, I suspect, are strong--and her temper E II 15 289 40
I think, than she used to be--and I love an open temper. E II 15 289 40
on the unmanageable good-will of Mr. Weston's temper. E III 6 353 3
Some faults of temper John Knightley had; but Isabella had E III 6 358 35
Harriet's sweet easy temper will not mind it." E III 6 364 58
your temper under your own command rather than mine." E III 7 369 11
had ever supposed--and continual pain would try the temper. E III 9 387 13
to have done, for his temper and spirits--his delightful E III 12 419 12
Mr. Weston's sanguine temper was a blessing on all his E III 15 445 11
His sanguine temper, and fearlessness of mind, operated P III 4 27 4
elder sister, Mary had not Anne's understanding or temper. P III 5 37 21
agreeable; in sense and temper he was undoubtedly superior P III 6 43 5
which his own decided, confident temper could not endure. P III 7 61 36
very good humour with her, was out of temper with his wife. P III 10 90 37
feel, that a persuadable temper might sometimes be as much P III 12 116 72
How her temper and understanding might bear the P IV 3 140 11
in her temper, manners, mind, a model of female excellence. P IV 5 159 21
There are on both sides good principles and good temper." P IV 8 182 7
He seems to have a calm, decided temper, not at all open P IV 9 196 33
of warm feelings, easy temper, careless habits, and not P IV 9 209 95
that she was exactly in a temper to admire every thing as P IV 10 219 28
steady conduct & mild, gentle temper was felt by everybody. S 3 379 1
of an indolent temper--& to be determined on having no S 10 418 1

TEMPERAMENT (1)
Anne, judging from her own temperament, would have deemed P IV 2 134 30

TEMPERATE (3)
He is a very temperate man, and you could not fancy him in NA I 9 63 19

But Mrs. Dashwood, trusting to the temperate account of SS III 9 335 7
a great deal while I am here, if the weather is temperate. S 10 416 1

TEMPERED (9)
"He is a sweet tempered, amiable, charming man. PP I 16 82 47
to her, especially when tempered with the silence and PP I 19 106 10
change on a gentle tempered girl like Fanny; but there was MP III 2 329 11
She is pretty, and she is good tempered, and that is all. E I 8 61 38
I believe he is one of the very best tempered men that E I 11 95 19
Mr. Weston is rather an easy, cheerful tempered man, than E I 11 96 26
happiness with any good tempered man; but with him, and in E III 19 482 4
though with more tempered and pardonable pride, received P III 4 26 2
a gentle, amiable, sweet tempered woman, the properest S 2 372 1

TEMPERS (12)
Their tempers were mild, but their principles were steady, NA II 16 249 2
be left by tempers so frank, to discover it by accident. SS I 12 60 7
Your tempers are by no means unlike. PP III 13 348 38
there is a decided difference in your tempers, I allow. MP III 4 348 23
I am perfectly persuaded that the tempers had better be MP III 4 349 23
and her aunt as having the sweetest of all sweet tempers. MP III 10 405 17
An attachment, originally as tranquil as their tempers, MP III 13 428 15
and tempers, by that sense of duty which can alone suffice. MP III 17 463 8
supposed that their tempers became their mutual punishment. MP III 17 465 14
With quickness in understanding the tempers of those she MP III 17 472 31
You do not know what it is to have tempers to manage." E I 18 146 11
Various as were the tempers in her father's house, he P IV 5 161 29

TEMPEST (5)
the hall, listened to the tempest with sensations of awe; NA II 6 166 9
the tempest subsided, or she unknowingly fell fast asleep. NA II 6 171 12
a bright morning had succeeded the tempest of the night. NA II 7 172 1
been undisturbed by the tempest, with an arch reference to NA II 7 174 5
overwhelmed by the sudden tempest, all were eagerly & S 7 396 1

TEMPESTS (1)
Neither robbers nor tempests befriended them, nor one NA I 2 19 4

TEMPLARS (1)
gales dispense to Templars modesty, to parsons sense.' MP I 17 161 15

TEMPLE (5)
who had chambers in the temple, made a very good SS I 19 102 4
applied for a bruised temple, the same remedy was eagerly SS I 21 121 10
where, from its Grecian temple, her eye, wandering over a SS III 6 302 8
She had depended on a twilight walk to the Grecian temple, SS III 6 303 11
he had chambers in the temple, and it was as much as he P IV 9 199 55

TEMPLES (4)
to be seated, rubbed her temples with lavender-water, and NA II 13 223 9
her, and slammed the parlour door till her temples ached. MP III 7 381 25
Lady Russell's temples had long been a distress to him. P III 1 6 11
Rub her hands, rub her temples; here are salts,--take them, P III 12 110 36

TEMPORALLY (1)
considered, temporally and eternally--which has the MP I 9 92 45

TEMPORARY (7)
happiness, produced a temporary alteration in the disposal SS II 14 246 2
might be more than a temporary accommodation to yourself-- SS III 4 289 28
to acknowledge a temporary revival, tried to keep her SS III 7 314 22
witnessed, however temporary its existence might prove, PP III 2 263 10
considered it only as a temporary interruption, a disaster MP II 1 177 5
Emma's, though under temporary gloom at night, the return E I 16 137 13
He had been detained by a temporary increase of illness in E III 6 363 53

TEMPORISING (1)
same inevitable necessity of temporising with his mother. SS I 19 102 2

TEMPT (20)
this lively place; we can tempt you neither by amusement NA II 2 139 7
and she promised not to tempt her mother to such imprudent SS I 12 59 5
"And that will tempt you, Miss Marianne." SS I 18 99 18
How much could it not tempt her to forgive! SS II 1 140 1
absence--Oh! no, nothing should tempt me to leave her. SS II 3 154 5
They only knew how little he had had to tempt him to be SS III 2 270 1
appeared; such as might tempt the daughter's wishes and SS III 10 344 11
there seemed nothing to tempt the avarice or the vanity of SS III 13 367 22
but not handsome enough to tempt me; and I am in no humour PP I 3 11 13
any consideration would tempt me to accept the man, who PP II 11 190 10
We know how little there is to tempt any one to our humble PP II 15 215 2
She has no money, no connections, nothing that can tempt PP III 4 277 11
I may say, that nothing shall ever tempt me to it again. MP I 13 125 14
"If any part could tempt you to act, I suppose it would be MP I 15 144 40
"That circumstance would by no means tempt me," he replied, MP I 15 145 41
"There does, indeed, seem as little to tempt her to break E I 5 41 30
Nothing should tempt her to go, if they did; and she E II 7 207 6
to tempt the lady, who only wanted to be going somewhere. E III 6 354 9
However, I think it answered so far as to tempt one to go E III 16 454 18
"If I thought it would not tempt her to go out in sharp P IV 3 142 16

TEMPTATION (25)
world & surrounded with temptation, should be accused of LS 14 264 3
Smith, to resist the temptation of returning here soon, SS I 15 81 43
present case, where no temptation could be answerable to SS II 1 139001
with Mrs. Jennings, was a temptation we could not resist. SS II 7 187 38
heavily, "I can have little temptation to be diffuse." SS II 9 205 20
could not resist the temptation of telling me what he knew SS III 8 330 69
unable to resist the temptation, added, "when you met us PP I 18 92 18
the two cousins found a temptation from this period of PP II 9 180 28
reason away, was such a temptation to openness as nothing PP II 15 217 17
His temptation is not adequate to the risk." PP III 5 282 1
Lydia on so slight a temptation as one hundred a-year PP III 7 304 29
he had apparently least to do, and least temptation to go. PP III 9 320 32
to be proof against the temptation of immediate relief. PP III 10 323 2
you rank highly as temptation and reward to the soldier MP I 11 110 22
hold out the greatest temptation, and would, in all MP II 3 201 22
Curiosity and vanity were both engaged, and the temptation MP III 17 467 20
She wanted, rather, to be quiet, and out of temptation; E I 18 144 4
his while; whenever there is any temptation of pleasure." E I 18 146 14
to have resisted the temptation of any delay, and spared E II 2 165 9
I can much more readily enter into the temptation of E II 15 288 39
Many circumstances assisted the temptation. E III 13 427 19
For my temptation to think it a right, I refer every E III 14 437 8
"He trifles here," said he, "as to the temptation. E III 15 445 11
She would be never led into temptation, nor left for it to E III 19 482 4
never had the smallest temptation to say, "very true." P III 6 44 6

TEMPTATIONS (4)
where the temptations must be greater than at home. PP II 18 230 14
Yet in spite of all these temptations, let me warn my PP III 15 362 15
ignorance and their temptations, had no romantic E I 10 86 24
& among so many pretty temptations, & with so much good S 6 390 1

TEMPTED (33)
of that kind, might have been tempted to order a new set. NA II 7 175 12
him utter, and which tempted her to think his disposition NA II 11 208 1
by the fire, was to be tempted to eat by every delicacy in SS II 8 193 7
Perhaps Emma may be tempted to go back with us, & stay W 350 24
tempted to eat a bit, for it is rather a favourite dish." W 354 27
make a round game he may be tempted to sit down with us."-- W 354 28
two years, when he was tempted by an accidental PP I 4 16 13
ladies, who were usually tempted thither three or four PP I 7 28 3
and my friend Denny tempted me farther by his account of PP I 16 79 23
fellow creatures if I am tempted, or how am I even to know PP II 3 145 7
I should be almost tempted to say, that there is a strong PP II 3 148 26
any possible way that would have tempted me to accept it." PP II 11 192 25 26
part of the lane, she was tempted, by the pleasantness of PP II 12 195 2
gate, not fastened, had tempted them very soon after their MP I 10 103 49
be tempted to give the young people a dance at Mansfield. MP II 8 252 2
though nothing could have tempted her to turn her eyes to MP II 13 304 16
the whim of the moment--easily tempted--easily put aside. MP III 3 343 41
end of a week, Fanny was tempted to apply to them Dr. MP III 8 392 12
from me at such a time, I should not like to be tempted. MP III 12 416 3
I have seen yet, to be tempted; Mr. Elton, you know, (E I 10 84 13
I would rather not be tempted.
environs could be tempted to attend, were mentioned; but E I 10 84 13
not know that she might not have been tempted to accept. E II 6 198 5
Harriet, tempted by every thing and swayed by half a word, E II 7 208 7
and persuasively, "I certainly do feel tempted to give. E II 9 233 24
or two spent at Donwell, be tempted away to his misery. E II 16 295 33
and I was very foolishly tempted to say and do many things E III 6 356 29
I was tempted by his attentions, and allowed myself to E III 13 426 15
I might have been tempted to introduce a subject, to ask E III 13 427 19
any thing, which he had not been very much tempted to do. E III 16 459 46
for Anne's being tempted, by some man of talents and P III 1 5 8
as he could be properly tempted; actually looking round, P III 4 29 7
all her money would have tempted Elliot, and Sir Walter P III 7 61 38
P IV 3 139 9

TEMPTING (6)
you out of doors, and tempting you to more frequent NA II 7 174 8
The weather was not tempting enough to draw the two others SS I 9 41 3
To herself, individually, it was most tempting. MP III 14 435 15
and her purse were too tempting, and she was followed, or E III 3 334 6
me, they are always tempting her to take a walk with them." P III 6 45 9
it's Mariners tempting it in sunshine & overwhelmed by the S 7 396 1

TEMPTINGLY (1)
with an outward door, temptingly open on a flight of steps MP I 9 89 32

TEN (182)
five & twenty, tho' she must in fact be ten years older. LS 6 251 1
In about ten minutes after my return to the parlour, Lady LS 23 284 6
a little dissipation for a ten weeks' penance at Churchill. LS 25 294 4
to present, in having been scarcely ten months a widow. LS 29 299 3
of her due by a woman ten years older than herself. LS 42 313 10
A family of ten children will be always called a fine NA I 1 13 1
symptoms of profligacy at ten years old, she had neither a NA I 1 14 1
Such was Catherine Morland at ten. NA I 1 14 2
only ten guineas, and promised her more when she wanted it. NA I 2 19 3
hardly had she been seated ten minutes before a lady of NA I 4 31 2
"Oh! these ten ages at least. NA I 6 39 4
out a list of ten or twelve more of the same kind for you." NA I 6 40 8
make my horse go less than ten miles an hour in harness; NA I 7 45 7
"You have lost an hour," said Morland; "it was only ten NA I 7 45 8
"Ten o'clock! it was eleven, upon my soul! NA I 7 46 9
than ten miles an hour: tie his legs and he will get on. NA I 7 46 11
I might have sold it for ten guineas more the next day; NA I 7 47 19
was roused, at the end of ten minutes, to a pleasanter NA I 8 53 3
be got into, and now it is ten thousand to one, but they NA I 9 61 1
its inevitable pace was ten miles an hour) by no means NA I 9 62 10
The wheels have been fairly worn out these ten years at NA I 9 65 28
and yet she lay awake ten minutes on Wednesday night NA I 10 73 22
their six weeks into ten or twelve, and go away at last NA I 10 78 45
Ten minutes more made it certain that a bright afternoon NA I 11 83 16
cried Thorpe, "we shall be able to do ten times more. NA I 11 84 21
I had rather, ten thousand times rather get out now, and NA I 11 87 53
But I had ten thousand times rather have been with you; NA I 12 93 5
same part of the house for ten minutes together, was NA I 12 95 17
Thus passed a long ten minutes, till they were again NA I 13 100 13
Ten to one but he guesses the reason, and that is exactly NA II 1 131 13
income, no niggardly assignment to one of ten children. NA II 1 135 42
The clock struck ten while the trunks were carrying down, NA II 5 155 4
myself about ten years ago, for the benefit of my son. NA II 7 175 15
shall be in the carriage by ten; so, about a quarter NA II 11 210 6
By ten o'clock, the chaise-and-four conveyed the trio from NA II 11 212 17
was the same which only ten days ago she had so happily NA II 14 230 1
Yes, only ten days ago had he elated her by his pointed NA II 14 230 2
It is ten to one but you are thrown together again in the NA II 14 236 17
backwards and forwards some ten times a-day, with an heart NA II 14 237 20
She could neither sit still, nor employ herself for ten NA II 15 240 1
of you; for ten to one whether you ever see him again. NA II 15 240 4
more in reserve, and the ten or fifteen thousand pounds NA II 15 245 12
But her death, which happened ten years before his own, SS I 1 3 1
He survived his uncle no longer; and ten thousand pounds, SS I 1 4 4
"He did not know what he was talking of, I dare say; ten SS I 2 9 5
They will have ten thousand pounds divided amongst them. SS I 2 10 15
together on the interest of ten thousand pounds." SS I 2 10 15
In the present case it took up ten minutes to determine SS I 6 31 9
once in ten minutes, this reproach would have been spared." SS I 10 48 5
them, at least, twice every summer for the last ten years. SS I 12 62 28
By ten o'clock the whole party were assembled at the park, SS I 13 63 2
to her; and after a ten minutes' interval of earnest SS I 13 69 76
And now after only ten minutes notice--gone too without SS I 15 77 23
Not above ten miles, I dare say." SS I 20 111 12
and paid ten or twelve shillings more than we did." SS II 10 218 24
There is not a room in this cottage that will hold ten SS II 14 252 18
When the note was shewn to Elinor, as it was within ten SS II 14 254 27
Colonel Brandon, who was here only ten minutes ago, has SS III 4 288 28
you for the sake of giving ten guineas to Mr. Ferrars!" SS III 4 291 53
to drop in for ten minutes; and I saw quite enough of her. SS III 5 299 37
after an absence of only ten days, his readiness to SS III 6 305 16
At ten o'clock, she trusted, or at least not much later, SS III 7 315 26
Had it been ten, Elinor would have been convinced that at SS III 7 316 29
for half an hour--for ten minutes--I entreat you to stay." SS III 8 317 1 2
eight o'clock, and the only ten minutes I have spent out SS III 8 318 20
the ten thousand pounds, which had been given with Fanny. SS III 14 374 4
ball was not lessened by a ten years enjoyment, had some W 315 1
an only child, & will have at least ten thousand pounds."-- W 321 2
Mama said I should be asleep before ten.-- W 332 12
half so handsome as eliz: watson had been ten years ago.-- W 337 17
hands of Miss Watson only ten minutes ago, said he--I met W 338 18
A week or ten days rolled quietly away after this visit, W 348 23
out of his road merely to call for ten minutes at Stanton. W 355 28
down to supper in less than ten minutes--which to a man W 359 28
visit, and sat about ten minutes with him in his library. PP I 3 9 3
after his entrance, of his having ten thousand a year. PP I 3 10 5
In nine cases out of ten, a woman had better show more PP I 6 22 2
purpose, he scarcely spoke ten words to her, through the PP I 12 60 4
A clear ten thousand per annum. PP I 16 77 10
in the eyes of a man of ten times his consequence. PP I 18 90 8
About ten or a dozen years ago, before her marriage, she PP II 2 142 19
The sudden acquisition of ten thousand pounds was the most PP II 3 149 28
to get a girl with only ten thousand pounds, you want to PP II 4 153 9
as he frequently sat there ten minutes together without PP II 9 180 29
My sister, who is more than ten years my junior, was left PP II 12 201 5
loud, that any body might have heard us ten miles off!" PP II 16 222 22
Had they been only ten minutes sooner, they should have PP III 1 252 54
With a triumphant smile, they were told, that it was ten PP III 1 253 57
My dear Lizzy, they must have passed within ten miles of PP III 4 274 3
He could not speak a word for full ten minutes. PP III 5 292 62
have spent ten minutes of every day in a rational manner." PP III 6 300 30
If you are a good girl for the next ten years, I will take PP III 6 300 32
he takes her with a farthing less than ten thousand pounds. PP III 7 304 31
"Ten thousand pounds! PP III 7 304 32
him, I cannot believe that ten thousand pounds, or any PP III 7 304 35
How could he spare half ten thousand pounds?" PP III 7 304 35
He would scarcely be ten pounds a-year the loser, by the PP III 8 309 4
I could not bear to have her ten miles from me; and as for PP III 8 310 8
Their visitors were not to remain above ten days with them. PP III 9 318 17
However, I did not hear above one word in ten, for I was PP III 9 319 24
"Well, and so we breakfasted at ten as usual; I thought it PP III 9 319 25
But luckily, he came back again in ten minutes time, and PP III 9 319 25
the appetite and pride of one who had ten thousand a-year. PP III 11 338 60
for London, but was to return home in ten days time. PP III 13 344 1
Ten thousand a year! PP III 17 378 43
Ten thousand a year, and very likely more! PP III 17 378 45
allow in a sister more than ten years younger than himself. PP III 19 388 11
Her eldest was a boy of ten years old, a fine spirited MP I 1 5 2

into the world, and ten to one but she has the means of MP I 1 6 6
Fanny Price was at this time just ten years old, and MP I 2 12 2
one word where he spoke ten, by the mere aid of a good- MP I 2 12 2
of seventeen will always think fair with a child of ten. MP I 2 17 22
You have robbed Edmund for ten, twenty, thirty years, MP I 3 23 3
sixteen in some respects too much like his sister at ten." MP I 3 33 64
ten miles of indifferent road, to pay a morning visit. MP I 4 39 10
"Well, and if they were ten," cried Mrs. Norris, "I am MP I 6 53 9
it has probably been these ten days, in spite of the MP I 6 57 33
Between ten and eleven, Edmund and Julia walked into the MP I 7 71 31
Ten miles there, and ten back, you know. MP I 8 76 3
and women might lie another ten minutes in bed, when they MP I 9 87 15
you with Irish anecdotes during a ten miles' drive." MP I 10 99 14
Dinner was soon followed by tea and coffee, a ten miles' MP I 10 104 52
where they had spent ten days together in the same society, MP I 13 121 1
a weak voice, always hoarse after the first ten minutes! MP I 13 122 2
great lubberly fellow of ten years old you know, who ought MP I 15 142 22
or you should have gone into the army ten years ago." MP II 4 214 44
However, you will have dinner enough on it for ten I dare MP II 5 221 30
as possible; and scarcely ten days had passed since Fanny MP II 6 233 14
they did, and be back in ten minutes--but he was gone MP II 12 291 1
till the butler re-appeared ten minutes afterwards, and MP III 1 324 60
received at the end of about ten years' happy marriage." MP III 4 354 46
William had obtained a ten days' leave of absence to be MP III 6 368 7
With such thoughts as these among ten hundred others, MP III 7 376 5
called him to Everingham ten days ago, or perhaps he only MP III 9 393 1
herself and Susan, within ten minutes, walking towards the MP III 10 401 10
My poor aunt always felt affected, if within ten miles of MP III 12 416 3
And it would not be ten minutes work." MP III 15 440 18
doing ever since her being ten years old, her mind in so MP III 17 470 27
At ten years old, she had the misfortune of being able to E I 5 37 9
less, or had there been ten times more, the delight and E I 6 44 20
For ten minutes she could hear nothing but herself. E I 10 89 38
of interest; and during the ten days of their stay at E I 11 91 1
not accommodate more than ten comfortably; and for my part, E I 13 116 43
soon try for miss somebody else with twenty, or with ten. E I 16 135 7
there, just called in for ten minutes, and had been so E II 1 155 4
than five--or at least ten--for I had got my bonnet and E II 3 173 27
thing in the world, full ten minutes, perhaps--when, all E II 3 178 52
as would always be called ten; a point of some dignity, as E II 4 181 4
did not forget either at ten, or eleven, or twelve o'clock, E II 5 189 19
Ten minutes would have been all that was necessary, E II 6 199 7
and who have been your neighbours these ten years." E II 7 210 19
"coming at least ten minutes earlier than I had calculated. E II 10 240 3
couple would be at least ten, and a very interesting E II 11 248 9
was now endeavoured to be made out quite enough for ten. E II 11 249 12
Ten couple may stand here very well." E II 11 249 13
"I think there will be very tolerable room for ten couple." E II 11 249 15
16

Ten couple, in either of the Randalls rooms, would have E II 11 250 23
After Emma had talked about it for ten minutes, Mr. E II 16 291 4
but it is not your being ten years older than myself which E II 16 294 22
to hope, Miss Fairfax, that ten years hence you may have E II 16 294 23
only visit from Frank Churchill in the course of ten days. E III 1 316 6
and suffering; and by the ten days' end, her nephew's E III 1 317 7
she wished she had left her ten minutes earlier;--it would E III 9 386 8
Churchill had been promising a visit the last ten years. E III 9 388 15
One morning, about ten days after Mrs. Churchill's decease, E III 10 392 1
you have ever shown me, and ten thousand for the E III 14 443 8
might be growing older ten years hence--to have his E III 17 461 1
in one of my amiable fits, about ten years ago. E III 17 462 12
In ten minutes, however, the child had been perfectly well E III 18 479 73
at twenty-nine than she was ten years before; and, P III 1 6 11
away for a week or ten days, till her head were stronger. P IV 2 133 25
sat down close to her for ten minutes, talking with a very P IV 2 134 29
he pretend to say that ten years had not altered almost P IV 3 141 12
It was ten o'clock. P IV 3 142 17
Ten minutes were enough to certify that. P IV 3 143 19
The first ten minutes had its awkwardness and its emotion. P IV 5 153 6
morning, about a week or ten days after the Crofts' P IV 6 168 25
She had learnt, in the last ten minutes, more of his P IV 8 184 17
"I had not waited even these ten days, could I have read " P IV 11 237 42
tranquillized her; but the ten minutes only, which now P IV 11 238 44
share of ten thousand pounds which must be hers hereafter. P IV 12 248 1
Ten fees, one after another, did the man take who sent him S 6 394 1

TENACIOUS (2)
Her affections were not acute, nor was her mind tenacious. MP III 16 449 6
if she were not so very tenacious; especially, if she P III 6 46 10

TENACIOUSLY (2)
the gipsies, and still tenaciously setting her right if E III 3 336 13
heir expectant had formerly been so tenaciously regarded. E III 15 449 35

TENANT (18)
now established only as a tenant, Miss Bingley was by no PP I 4 15 13
for your not influencing your son against such a tenant?" MP II 7 247 38
But, Crawford, though I refuse you as a tenant, come to me MP II 7 247 41
I am sure of an excellent tenant at half a word. MP II 12 295 20
griping fellow for a tenant, instead of an honest man, to MP III 11 412 20
in thinking a sailor might be a very desirable tenant. P III 3 18 7
I am not particularly disposed to favour a tenant. P III 3 18 8
I am very little disposed to grant a tenant of Kellynch P III 3 18 8
every thing plain and easy between landlord and tenant. P III 3 18 9
10

Depend upon me for taking care that no tenant has more P III 3 19 10
a naval officer as tenant, had been gifted with foresight; P III 3 21 18
proof of his being a most responsible, eligible tenant. P III 3 21 18
family, which made him peculiarly desirable as a tenant. P III 3 22 24
secret of Sir Walter's estimate of the dues of a tenant. P III 3 23 34
a more unobjectionable tenant, in all essentials, than P III 3 24 36
fixed and expedited by a tenant at hand; and not a word to P III 3 24 37
I know what is due to my tenant." P IV 6 162 5
His sister married my tenant in Somersetshire,--the Croft, P IV 8 188 40

TENANTRY (1)
for all the afflicted tenantry and cottagers who might P III 5 35 18

TENANTS (8)
earliest tenants might be "our friends from Fullerton." NA II 8 185 5
hospitality, to assist his tenants, and relieve the poor. PP I 16 81 41
There is not one of his tenants or servants but what will PP III 1 249 38
He had introduced himself to some tenants, whom he had MP III 10 404 15
for having a choice of tenants, very responsible tenants. P III 3 17 1
tenants as any set of people one should meet with. P III 3 17 4
happiness of being the tenants of Sir Walter Elliot: an P III 3 23 34
so very fortunate in his tenants, felt the parish to be so P IV 1 125 17

TEND (6)
her actions will hereafter tend to promote the general NA I 2 19 7
She had found in her every thing that could tend to make a SS II 13 238 1
"May I ask to what these questions tend?" PP I 18 93 37
of the licence which every rehearsal must tend to create. MP I 16 154 14
any strength of mind, or tend at all to make a girl adapt E I 5 39 15
of the place--wd in fact tend to bring a prodigious influx; S 2 372 1

TENDED (2)
effect on her in that point to which it principally tended. SS I 5 25 3
passed during the visit, tended to assure him of the sense, SS I 10 46 1

TENDENCY (24)
This tendency to excuse her conduct, or to forget it in LS 8 256 3
may concern, whether the tendency of this work be NA II 16 252 7
Their tendency is gross and illiberal; and if their SS I 9 45 30
Her systems have all the unfortunate tendency of setting SS I 11 56 13
expression that could give her words a suspicious tendency. SS II 2 147 9
to have a putrid tendency, and allowing the word " SS III 7 307 3
"There is, I believe, in every disposition a tendency to PP I 11 58 30
can have any evil tendency; and I am so far from objecting PP I 17 87 13
An union of a different tendency, and precluding the PP III 8 312 16
than such an absence has a tendency to produce at first. MP II 3 197 3
arose which had a tendency rather to forward his views of MP II 6 232 12
absence was really in its cause and its tendency a relief. MP II 11 285 15
self-conceit, and every tendency to that independence of MP III 1 318 39
the world, Mary on something of less philosophic tendency. MP III 5 360 13
a wife's happiness, as a tendency to fall in love himself, MP III 5 363 24
And I hope you will not be cruelly concealing any tendency MP III 11 411 18
Fanny checked the tendency of these thoughts as well as MP III 13 424 4
it, had such a softening tendency, that it was E I 7 55 35
has a tendency to contract the mind, and sour the temper. E I 10 85 19
It's tendency would be to raise and refine her mind--and E III 4 342 40
perfectly free from any tendency to being attached to me, E III 14 438 8
They were of sobering tendency; they allayed agitation; P III 7 61 35
she had to struggle against a great tendency to lowness. P III 11 98 16
had given them an early tendency at various times, to S 10 412 1

TENDER (62)
worthy than she has yet done, of her mother's tender care. LS 14 265 5
his tender feelings I suppose on this distressing occasion. LS 15 267 4
I infinitely prefer the tender & liberal spirit of LS 16 269 3
watched her with so much tender solicitude that I, who LS 17 270 3
it was achieved at the tender age of sixteen we shall LS 19 274 2
She shall find that she has poured forth her tender tale LS 22 282 8
susceptibilities, the tender emotions which the first NA I 2 19 3
feeling of awe, and left nothing but tender affection. NA I 4 33 7
and though pained by such tender, such flattering NA I 13 98 2
Maria's intelligence concluded with a tender effusion of NA I 15 116 2
that Isabella far surpassed her in tender anticipations.-- NA I 15 118 9
interest excited by this tender remembrance, shewed itself NA II 7 179 31
of going, and her own tender love for all her three SS I 1 6 10
his emotion with the tender recollection of past regard. SS I 11 57 17
Opposition on so tender a subject would only attach her SS I 12 59 5
pressing her hand with tender compassion, her small degree SS I 15 82 46
in her declaration of tender regard for him, and she SS II 1 141 7
the partiality of tender recollection, there is a very SS II 9 205 23
24

of tender concern, at the fate of his unfortunate friend. SS II 9 208 27
feminine--was it not?" SS III 8 328 61
with his earnest, tender, constant, affection for Marianne. SS III 9 336 12
to raise anything less tender than pity, and in its SS III 10 342 7
declare an affection as tender, as constant as she had SS III 13 363 8
to me by such a proof of tender respect for my aunt."-- W 352 26
"Musgrave!"--ejaculated Margaret in a tender voice.-- W 355 28
grieved to the soul by a thousand tender recollections. PP I 16 78 20
to interest all her tender feelings; and nothing therefore PP I 17 85 1
She still cherished a very tender affection for Bingley. PP II 17 227 26
interest, if not quite so tender, at least as reasonable PP III 11 334 36
her cousins', but a more tender nature suggested that her MP I 3 32 64
all that was respectful, grateful, confiding, and tender. MP I 4 37 8
of the Antwerp," was a tender apostrophe of Fanny's, very MP I 11 111 27
and a hot climate, every tender feeling was increased, and MP II 1 178 7
till in the midst of some tender ejaculation of Fanny's, MP II 4 208 11
most unfeigned and truly tender regret, that they were not MP II 10 275 12
expressions of tender gallantry as had blessed the morning. MP II 10 278 20
man might exercise her tender enthusiasm, and that the MP II 11 282 2
remembrances, and tender associations, when her own fair MP III 3 334 1
went on as if there had been no such tender interruption. MP III 3 341 27
She is tender, and not used to rough it like the rest of MP III 8 388 2
She had a few tender reveries now and then, which he could MP III 11 409 7
him with silent, but most tender concern, was almost sorry MP III 16 457 30
"What a precious deposit!" said he with a tender sigh, as E I 6 49 43
that Harriet, with many tender embraces could articulate E I 9 74 21
After a little thinking, and a very tender sigh, he added, E I 9 78 53
54

the tender and the sublime of pleasure to Harriet's share. E I 9 82 84
his head and fixing his eyes on her with tender concern.-- E I 12 105 51
to give with so much tender caution; hardly knowing E II 3 180 56
something like a look of spring, a tender smile even there. E II 5 189 16
Every thing tender and charming was to mark their parting; E II 13 264 1
in lamenting, with tender melancholy, over the departure E III 5 347 20
which Mr. Woodhouse's tender habits required almost every E III 5 351 38
pleasure, excited by such tender consideration, replied, " E III 13 426 14
15

with Harriet Smith; but it was too tender a subject.-- E III 17 463 15
His tender compassion towards oppressed worth can go no E III 17 465 24
while put by--unless some tender sonnet, fraught with he P III 10 85 12
she had feelings for the tender, spirits for the gay, P IV 8 186 24
to herself, and was most tender of throwing any on her P IV 9 209 95
will authorise me to assert that our are the most tender. P IV 11 233 23
first projected; more tender, more tried, more fixed in a P IV 11 240 59
Tender, elegant, descriptive--but tame.-- S 7 397 1
She was about 17, half Mulatto, chilly & tender, had a S 11 421 1

TENDER-HEARTED (3)
how much more their tender-hearted cousin, who wandered MP II 3 204 33
yourself grateful and tender-hearted; and then you will be MP III 4 347 18
was tender-hearted again towards the rejected Mr. Martin. E I 7 56 42

TENDER-HEARTEDNESS (1)
that romantic tender-heartedness which will always ensure LS 26 295 1

TENDERED (1)
animal was one minute tendered to his use again; and the MP II 6 237 23

TENDERER (1)
to each other, was yet a dearer, tenderer recollection. E I 1 6 6

TENDEREST (6)
and she thought with the tenderest compassion of that SS I 15 77 20
The tenderest caresses followed this confession. SS III 1 264 32
and reading with the tenderest emotion these words, "my MP II 9 265 19
He has the tenderest spirit of gallantry towards us all!-- E I 9 77 45
by making you an object of the tenderest affection to me. E III 17 462 7
acquainted with all the tenderest songs of the one poet, P III 11 100 23

TENDERLY (8)
Edward is very amiable, and I love him tenderly. SS I 3 17 18
Annamaria," she added, tenderly caressing a little girl of SS I 21 121 9
tenderly attached is too much for an indifferent person." SS II 2 150 33
Elinor tenderly invited her to be open. SS III 10 344 16
and embracing her most tenderly, she even shook hands with PP I 12 60 5
tent, tenderly flirting with at least six officers at once. PP II 18 232 22
Both were kissed very tenderly, but Tom she wanted to keep MP III 7 381 25
a doating mother, and so tenderly attached to her father E I 11 92 4

TENDERNESS (69)
She speaks of her with so much tenderness & anxiety, LS 6 251 1
it as a very happy mixture of circumspection & tenderness. LS 7 253 2
mothers, she is accused of wanting maternal tenderness. LS 14 265 5
& without betraying the least tenderness of spirit. LS 17 269 2
illtimed expressions of tenderness to which I listened LS 22 281 4
between returning tenderness & the remains of displeasure. LS 25 293 3
gradation of increasing tenderness, that there was shortly NA I 5 36 4
of his fraternal tenderness, for he asked each of them how NA I 7 49 43
of peculiar tenderness towards the spotted, the sprigged, NA I 10 74 22
of being wanting in tenderness towards herself and her NA I 11 90 64
speaking peace and tenderness in every line, and NA I 15 116 1
Her heart was overflowing with tenderness. NA I 15 121 27
Her tenderness for her friend seemed rather the first NA II 4 153 31
tenderness which would prompt a visit like yours. NA II 9 196 23
all, you know, the same tenderness of disposition--and I NA II 9 197 27
think of him with less tenderness than she did at that NA II 14 236 18
To Marianne it had all the distinguishing tenderness which SS I 14 71 5
"But with a strange kind of tenderness, if he can leave SS I 15 80 40
tenderness, pity, approbation, censure, and doubt. SS I 19 104 12
but she saw, with less tenderness of feeling, the thorough SS I 22 127 2
seemed to feel all the tenderness of this behaviour, and SS II 7 182 12
unsolicited proofs of tenderness, not warranted by SS II 7 188 43
is not sympathy; her good nature in not tenderness. SS II 9 201 3
Willoughby, full of tenderness and contrition, explanatory SS II 9 202 7

and this, with such tenderness towards her, such affection SS II 9 202 8
She could therefore only look her tenderness, and after SS II 13 241 19
with the most speaking tenderness, sometimes at Edward and SS II 13 242 25
such attractions, to have withstood such tenderness!-- SS III 8 321 34
recal the tenderness which, for a very short time, had the SS III 8 322 36
from her family with a tenderness, a regret, rather in SS III 9 333 2
any embellishment of tenderness to lead the fancy astray. SS III 11 349 2
instantly with soothing tenderness, had not Elinor, who SS III 11 349 5
too much engrossed her tenderness, and led her away to SS III 11 356 46
for we all know the tenderness of Mrs. Ferrars's heart, SS III 13 371 39
care of a parent, & of tenderness to an aunt whose amiable W 361 31
With a renewal of tenderness, however, they repaired to PP I 8 37 21
more eloquent on the subject of tenderness than of pride. PP II 11 189 5
not untinctured by tenderness, and a wish of saying more PP III 2 262 8
the air, were all favourable to tenderness and sentiment. MP I 7 65 13
had been awful in his dignity seemed lost in tenderness. MP II 1 178 7
think that with so much tenderness of disposition, and so MP II 6 231 11
dignity or pride, or tenderness or remorse, or whatever MP III 3 337 10
And having said so, with a degree of tenderness and MP III 5 358 9
emotions of tenderness that could not be clothed in words-- MP III 6 369 11
Every feeling of duty, honour, and tenderness was wounded MP III 7 386 43
to tenderness in his former treatment of herself. MP III 8 389 3
If tenderness could be ever supposed wanting, good sense MP III 8 392 11
and never was there any maternal tenderness to buy her off. MP III 9 396 5
her eldest cousin, her tenderness of heart made her feel MP III 13 428 13
of carrying with me the right of tenderness and esteem. MP III 16 458 30
into the esteem and tenderness of Fanny Price, there would MP III 17 467 19
impossible that such tenderness as hers should not, at MP III 17 471 28
"There is no charm equal to tenderness of heart," said she E II 13 269 16
Warmth and tenderness of heart, with an affectionate, open E II 13 269 16
It is tenderness of heart which makes my dear father so E II 13 269 16
of his feeling the same tenderness in the same degree. E III 1 316 3
Every body had a degree of gravity and sorrow; tenderness E III 9 387 12
intelligible tenderness as was tolerably convincing.-- E III 13 430 37
tenderness of manner, be continually advising her in vain. P III 4 27 5
and good humour, than tenderness and sentiment; and while P III 8 68 29
the mind of taste and tenderness, that season which has P III 10 84 7
the highest extreme of tenderness; and though she might be P IV 2 129 1
his having felt some dawning of tenderness toward herself. P IV 6 167 19
and regard, but by the tenderness of the past; yes, some P IV 8 185 21
of the past; yes, some share of the tenderness of the past. P IV 8 185 21
There was no longer any thing of tenderness due to him. P IV 10 212 1
Anne was tenderness itself, and she had the full worth of P IV 12 252 12
her friends wish that tenderness less; the dread of a P IV 12 252 12
Discomfitures with more tenderness than cd ever have been S 8 404 1

TENDING (6)
by any information tending to that end, and her's must be SS II 9 204 19
Elinor avoided it upon principle, as tending to fix still SS III 2 270 1
of his idle vanity was tending; but, thoughtless and MP I 12 114 3
day thus unemployed, was tending to increase his sense of MP I 18 164 1
side, tending to reconcile his wife to the arrangement. MP II 11 284 10
on satisfaction, so tending to ease, and so much in MP III 17 461 3

TENEMENT (1)
as indifferent a double tenement as any in the parish, and S 1 366 1

TENEMENTS (1)
tenements of the village, without a saddened heart.-- P IV 1 123 8

TENFOLD (1)
effect on him, she now felt and feared it all tenfold more. MP II 11 286 17

TENOR (2)
so gratifying had been the tenor of his conduct throughout NA II 11 215 28
would pass, the quiet tenor of their usual employments, PP II 5 157 10

TENOUR (1)
How are your absent cousins to understand the tenour of NA I 3 27 28

TENS (2)
She saw herself the object of attention, to tens and to PP II 18 232 22
He is a very liberal thanker, with his thousands and tens E III 15 447 28

TENT (1)
tent, tenderly flirting with at least six officers at once. PP II 18 232 22

TENTH (2)
more severe: but, on the tenth, when she entered the NA II 10 201 6
half Mr. Crawford's estate, or a tenth part of his merits. MP III 1 319 39

TENTS (1)
She saw all the glories of the camp; its tents stretched PP II 18 232 22

TERM (7)
driving into Oxford, last term: 'Ah! Thorpe,' said he, 'do NA I 7 46 11
"My brother's heart, as you term it, on the present NA II 4 151 24
increase with the shortness of the term for indulgence.-- W 347 21
And though he exclaimed at the term, she found that it had PP III 16 370 39
a day within the granted term of Frank Churchill's stay in E II 12 257 1
You misled me by the term gentleman. P III 3 23 33
permanent long before the term in question, the two P IV 10 217 20

TERMED (3)
end of half an hour, be termed by the courtesy of her NA II 14 233 10
give her consent to what she termed so disgraceful a match. PP III 15 363 22
offended by what they termed "airs"--for as she neither MP III 9 395 3

TERMINATED (2)
The gallery was terminated by folding doors, which Miss NA II 8 185 6
The hills which surrounded the cottage terminated the SS I 6 29 3

TERMINATION (4)
The sudden termination of Colonel Brandon's visit at the SS I 14 70 1
and would formerly have rejoiced in its termination. PP III 4 279 23
shortly give the proper termination to the elopement, they PP III 8 311 11
be the taste of such a termination, it was in itself a E III 6 360 38

TERMS (82)
of late, it has been in terms of more extraordinary praise, LS 8 255 2
They are now on terms of the most particular friendship, LS 11 259 1
intentions, could see the terms on which we now are LS 20 278 7
credit in being on good terms with Reginald, which at LS 25 294 6
daughter, acknowledging in terms of grateful delight that LS 42 312 3
familiar, spoke of them in terms which made her all NA I 10 80 61
while we praise Udolpho in whatever terms we like best. NA I 14 108 17
"Then we are on very unequal terms, for I understand you NA II 1 132 22
spoke her astonishment in very plain terms to her partner. NA II 1 133 30
intent; and of her continuing on the best terms with James. NA II 10 201 5
hastily informed in angry terms of Miss Morland's NA II 15 244 10
Thorpe, most happy to be on speaking terms with a man of NA II 15 244 12
on such terms as destroyed half the value of the bequest. SS I 1 4 3
requested me, in general terms, to assist them, and make SS I 2 9 6
It was the offer of a small house, on very easy terms, SS I 4 23 20
in the most sociable terms with his family, and pressed SS I 6 30 6
but said only in general terms that they had kept in the SS I 13 67 60
doubt the nature of the terms on which they are together. SS I 15 80 38
we have it on very hard terms, if we are to dine at the SS I 19 109 41
meeting in conversation on terms of equality, and whose SS I 22 127 2
by themselves of the terms on which they stood with each SS II 5 174 45
must understand the terms on which it was given, obliged SS III 5 295 13
nothing so much as to be on good terms with her children." SS III 13 371 39
Ferrars, were on the best terms imaginable with the SS III 14 377 11
did not wish to be on terms of intimacy with the proposer-- W 339 18
for me to be on good terms with any one, with whom it had PP I 13 62 12
terms, without forming at it any useful acquaintance. PP I 15 70 1
We are not on friendly terms, and it always gives me pain PP I 16 78 20
"There was just such an informality in the terms of the PP I 16 79 27
shall speak in the highest terms of your modesty, economy, PP I 19 107 15
terms on the happy prospect of their nearer connection. PP I 20 110 1
spoke of him in terms of the highest admiration, and PP II 7 170 6
family were mentioned, in terms of such mortifying, yet PP II 13 208 10
fate in terms as unreasonable as her accent was peevish. PP II 18 230 12
terms of perfect composure, at least of perfect civility. PP III 1 251 51
and he had spoken in such terms of Elizabeth, as to leave PP III 3 270 12
each other again on such terms of cordiality as had marked PP III 4 279 23
"And are they upon such terms as for her to disclose the PP III 4 281 28
to live with him on any other terms than marriage?" PP III 5 283 9
he was on terms of particular friendship with any of them. PP III 6 297 12
"And may I ask?" said Elizabeth, "but the terms, I suppose, PP III 7 303 24
In terms of grateful acknowledgment for the kindness of PP III 8 309 4
on the most honourable terms, it was not to be supposed PP III 8 311 12
speak her approbation in terms warm enough to satisfy her PP III 13 348 34
and we shall be on good terms again; though we can never PP III 13 349 47
then pray do not pain me by speaking of him in such terms." PP III 17 376 34
the Gardiners, they were always on the most intimate terms. PP III 19 388 13
His terms are five guineas a day." MP I 6 53 8
else wanted, though the terms in which she sometimes spoke MP I 16 151 1
The sister with whom she was used to be on easy terms, was MP I 17 162 19
people now, who would give me my own terms and thank me." MP II 12 295 20
her in rather stronger terms than Sir Thomas could quite MP III 3 335 6
He would have taken no pains to be on terms with Mrs. MP III 16 456 23
acquaintance, but such as would visit him on his own terms. E I 3 20 1
in most respectful terms, to be allowed to bring Miss E I 3 22 7
any danger of being thought extravagant in my terms." E II 5 192 32
the terms on which the superior families would visit them. E II 7 207 6
terms of being "elegantly dressed, and very pleasing." E II 14 270 3
you to name your own terms, have as many rooms as you like, E II 17 301 18
abominable folly of Miss Bickerton in the warmest terms. E III 3 335 11
Are you quite sure that you understand the terms on which E III 18 474 29
family, in the usual terms: how it had been first settled P III 1 3 3
4
at once, than remain in it on such disgraceful terms." P III 2 13 6
terms, and as a great favor, that he would let it at all. P III 2 15 14
smallest difficulty about terms;--only wanted a P III 3 22 23
about the house, and terms, and taxes, than the Admiral P III 3 22 25
to rent it on the highest terms, he was talked into P III 3 24 35
the Crofts were approved, terms, time, every thing, and P III 5 32 3
She was always on friendly terms with her brother-in-law; P III 6 43 4
The two families had always been on excellent terms, there P III 9 74 6
many years, been on such terms as to make the power of P III 12 106 18
"Oh! he talks of you," cried Charles, "in such terms,"-- P IV 2 131 8
then "Miss Elliot" was spoken of in the highest terms!-- P IV 2 131 9
His declining to be on cordial terms with the head of his P IV 2 133 23
whole happiness in being on intimate terms in Camden-Place. P IV 3 139 10
to gain by being on terms with Sir Walter, nothing to risk P IV 3 140 11
people, to be on good terms with the head of his family; P IV 4 147 7
Though I have forgot the exact terms, I have a perfect P IV 9 204 75
I found them on the most friendly terms when I arrived." P IV 9 205 83
that they appeared to be on very comfortable terms.-- S 6 391 1
a Mrs Darling, who is on terms of constant correspondence S 9 408 1
has been represented to me in the most affecting terms.-- S 12 424 1

TERRACE (21)
the bowling-green a long terrace walk, backed by iron MP I 9 90 36
busy consultation on the terrace by Edmund, Miss Crawford MP I 9 90 36
had taken one turn on the terrace, and were drawing a MP I 9 91 37
beauty, compared with the bowling-green and the terrace. MP I 9 91 38
On reaching the bottom of the steps to the terrace, Mrs. MP I 10 103 50
the sands & the terrace always attracted some--.and the S 4 384 1
houses, called the terrace, with a broad walk in front, S 4 384 1
distance behind the terrace, the travellers were safely S 4 384 1
the end house of the terrace,--& extra beds at the hotel.-- S 5 388 1
& tranquillity on the terrace, the cliffs, & the sands.-- S 6 389 1
on together to the terrace--which altogether gave an hasty S 7 395 1
get out themselves;--the terrace was the attraction to all; S 7 395 1
must begin with the terrace, & there, seated on one of the S 7 395 1
D.'s invitation of remaining on the terrace with her.-- S 7 398 1
Here are a great many empty houses--3 on this very terrace; S 7 402 1
from the sands to the terrace, a gentleman's carriage with S 9 406 1
coat & sent him off to the terrace, to take us lodgings.-- S 9 407 1
They were in one of the terrace houses--& she found them S 10 413 1
the terrace, & you will often see me at Trafalgar house."-- S 10 416 1
The corner house of the terrace was the one in which Miss S 11 422 1
always quitted the terrace, in his way to his brothers by S 11 422 1

TERRIBLE (14)
"Oh! that would be terrible indeed," said Miss Steele-- " SS II 1 145 21
It must be terrible for you to hear it talked of; and as SS II 8 196 18
So up he flew directly, and a terrible scene took place, SS III 1 259 7
to each other, is terrible-- Mrs. Ferrars does not know SS III 3 282 19
having had a most terrible, cold, dark dreadful journey.-- W 356 28
The annoyance of the bells must be terrible. MP I 8 82 34
It was a terrible pause; and terrible to every ear were MP II 1 175 1
for independent of that terrible nuisance, I never saw a MP II 7 243 27
which would have been terrible; but at the same time there MP II 10 274 8
The past, present, future, every thing was terrible. MP III 1 321 46
leave his son, but it was a cruel, a terrible delay to her. MP III 14 430 6
and acknowledge it to be terrible and grievous, or it was MP III 15 443 24
She knew it must be so, but it was terrible to her. MP III 15 445 30
Her uncle's displeasure was terrible to her; but what MP III 16 452 14

TERRIBLY (3)
autumn came on, was so terribly haunted by these ideas, in MP I 4 38 9
long it is, how terribly long since you were here! E I 12 100 18
knowledge as seemed terribly like a would-be lover, and E I 14 118 4

TERRIERS (2)
a proposed exchange of terriers between them, interest her NA I 8 55 10
three terriers, was ready to receive and make much of them. NA II 11 212 17

TERRIFIC (5)
Catherine from this terrific separation must oppress her NA I 2 18 2
were the noises, more terrific even than the wind, which NA II 6 170 12
They all exclaimed against such terrific ideas; and Mr. PP III 5 287 36
terrific scenes, which such a period, at sea, must supply. MP II 6 235 19
The terrific grandeur of the ocean in a storm, its glassy S 7 396 1

TERRIFIED (4)
examining the terrified face of Frederica with surprise. LS 20 275 2
The terrified General pronounced the name of Allen with an NA II 15 246 13
and exceedingly terrified, she had been obliged to remain. E III 3 333 5
His wife fervently hoped it was--but stood, terrified & S 1 364 1

TERROR (20)
been terror and dislike before, was now absolute aversion. NA II 7 181 40
of his presence, and to Catherine terror upon terror. NA II 9 191 4
With a feeling of terror not very definable, she fixed her NA II 9 194 6
had with such causeless terror felt and done, nothing NA II 10 199 2
lay awake, hour after hour, without curiosity or terror. NA II 13 227 26
you must be in continual terror of my decay; and it must SS I 8 37 7
"Not yet," replied the other, concealing her terror, and SS III 7 311 12
Mrs. Dashwood, whose terror as they drew near the house SS III 9 334 4
crept about in constant terror of something or other; MP I 2 14 9
had soon all the terror of other complaints from him.-- MP I 18 164 2
The terror of his former occasional visits to that room MP III 1 312 4
threat to Fanny, and she lived in continual terror of it. MP III 5 356 4
That a letter from Edmund should be a subject of terror! MP III 6 374 27
sufficiently awake to the terror of a bad sore throat; and E I 15 124 3
was moving away--but her terror and her purse were too E III 3 334 6
The terror which the woman and boy had been creating in E III 3 334 7
he had spoken of her terror, her naivete, her fervor as E III 3 335 11
"Break it to me," cried Emma, standing still with terror.-- E III 10 393 10
down, waiting in great terror till Harriet should answer. E III 11 405 16
while it was only an interchange of perplexity and terror. P III 12 113 57

TERRORS (8)
The journey in itself had not terrors for her; and she NA II 14 230 1
The affrighted Catherine, amidst all the terrors of NA II 15 244 11
to dread riding, what terrors it gave me to hear it talked MP I 3 27 36
to bring its daily terrors--and if reading could banish MP III 9 398 10
being all re-seated, the terrors that occurred of what MP III 10 399 4
Lady Bertram wrote her daily terrors to her niece, who MP III 13 427 13
happened the next day, or the next, to weaken her terrors. MP III 15 442 22
away, I hope, by the terrors of my father's little rooms. E II 11 250 21

TERSENESS (1)
I will not promise even to equal the elegant terseness of E III 17 463 14

TEST (5)
disregarded them all; he had a surer test of distance. NA I 7 45 7
pretty well put to the test, by our long, very long SS II 2 147 10
a day, but had stood the test of many months suspense, and PP III 17 376 36
and care, and put the cheerfullest spirits too the test. MP I 3 28 42
hardly one woman in a thousand could stand the test of. P IV 3 142 13
TESTIFIED (2)
to accept it, when Jane testified such concern in parting PP I 7 33 45
the inclination he soon testified of renewing those PP II 18 233 25
TESTIFIES (1)
your countenance testifies that your thoughts on this E II 8 216 26
TESTIFY (2)
for her society, and testify respect and consideration. E III 9 389 16
and rather sought to testify that her conversation was the P III 9 80 34
TESTIFYING (3)
business, but that of testifying by the coldness of her W 334 13
omit an occasion of testifying his respect towards any PP I 18 101 71
in every thing testifying such an ingenuousness of E I 17 141 7
TESTIMONIES (1)
or to be known by such testimonies, that no private P IV 9 204 76
77
TESTIMONY (8)
"Thank you, Eleanor;--a most honourable testimony. NA I 14 107 9
surprised her by its extravagant testimony of both. SS I 12 58 1
very material; but any testimony in his favour, however SS I 20 116 59
received the gratifying testimony of Lady Middleton's SS II 12 235 28
Brandon means it as a testimony of his concern for what SS III 4 289 31
more particularly to the testimony of Colonel Fitzwilliam, PP II 12 202 5
nature, by the testimony so highly in his favour, and PP III 2 265 16
give as authentic oral testimony as you can desire, of P IV 9 204 80
TESTS (1)
Miss Nash has put down all the tests he has ever preached E I 9 75 26
TETBURY (3)
think we have been running it from Tetbury, Miss Morland?" NA I 7 45 5
out of the inn-yard at Tetbury as the town-clock struck NA I 7 45 7
"it was only ten o'clock when we came from Tetbury." NA I 7 45 8
TETE A TETE (3)
The tete a tete surprised them. PP II 9 179 26
a tete so much less painful than her fears had predicted. MP III 5 365 33
the sight of this tete a tete produced, Charlotte cd not S 12 426 1
TETE-A-TETE (13)
the extasies of another tete-a-tete; and before it was NA II 15 243 10
to run the risk of a tete-a-tete with a woman, whom SS III 5 294 3
interrupt the lovers' first tete-a-tete before breakfast. SS III 13 369 34
for a whole day's tete-a-tete between two women can never PP I 7 30 17
a quarter of an hour's tete-a-tete with Mrs. Bennet before PP I 15 70 3
ideas were nearly worn out before the tete-a-tete was over. PP III 1 257 66
security in such a tete-a-tete from any sound of MP I 4 35 6
to nothing worse than a tete-a-tete with the person one MP II 4 210 21
morrow renewed a tete-a-tete, which Sir Thomas could not MP II 6 234 17
on them, and that they were to have a tete-a-tete drive. E I 15 128 23
It was an odd tete-a-tete; but she was glad to see it.-- E III 6 360 40
objected only to a tete-a-tete--they might be able to act E III 12 416 2
It reminded her of their first forlorn tete-a-tete, on the E III 12 422 19
TEXEL (1)
now, that he thought you would be sent first to the Texel. MP III 7 380 20
TEXTURE (1)
it is biassed by the texture of their muslin, and how NA I 10 74 22
THAMES (1)
The baronet will never set the Thames on fire, but there P III 5 32 4
THANK (114)
I am to thank my sister I suppose, for having represented LS 14 263 1
know what I feel now; tho' thank heaven! you cannot have LS 20 277 5
Catherine grew tired at last, and would thank her no more. NA I 2 21 9
"Thank you; for now we shall soon be acquainted, as I am NA I 3 29 51
"Thank you," said Catherine, in some distress, from a NA I 7 47 24
"Thank you; but will not your horse want rest?" NA I 7 47 26
"Thank you, sir. NA I 8 54 7
Thank God! we have got a better. NA I 9 65 28
"Yes, ma'am, I thank you; we could not have had a nicer NA I 9 68 35
You are to thank your brother and me for the scheme; it NA I 11 84 19
"Thank ye," cried Thorpe, "but I did not come to Bath to NA I 13 99 7
"Thank you, Eleanor;--a most honourable testimony. NA I 14 107 9
"Thank you; but it is quite a matter of indifference to me. NA I 14 115 54
Would he thank you, either on his own account or Miss NA II 4 152 28
Thank God! NA II 10 202 7
"No, I thank you," (sighing as she spoke,) "they are all NA II 10 203 10
Thank God! we leave this vile place to-morrow. NA II 12 216 2
"None at all, ma'am, I thank you." SS I 13 63 9
"Thank you, Willoughby. SS I 14 72 10
Thank heaven! SS I 17 91 5
"Thank you," cried Lucy warmly, "for breaking the ice; you SS II 2 146 3
"I thank you, ma'am, sincerely thank you," said Marianne, SS II 3 154 5
and thank heaven! you are what you always were!" SS II 13 242 29
but proceed to say that, thank God! though we have SS III 2 277 29
30
Thank you, my dear, for shewing it me. SS III 2 278 32
"Thank you, ma'am," said Elinor. SS III 4 285 2
Thank heaven! it did torture me. SS III 8 324 45
with an honest & simple thank you Maam was instantly ready W 331 11
"Thank you--but I always mend my own." PP I 10 47 12
You will not thank me for detaining you from the PP I 18 92 23
I thank you again and again for the honour you have done PP I 19 109 20
Thank God! PP II 1 134 7
"Thank you, sir, but a less agreeable man would satisfy me. PP II 1 138 28
Thank heaven! PP II 4 154 19
tell you of Lady Metcalfe's calling yesterday to thank me? PP II 6 165 32
"I may thank you, Eliza, for this piece of civility. PP II 7 170 7
8
"Perfectly so--I thank you." PP II 9 177 5
and if I could feel gratitude, I would now thank you. PP II 11 190 7
I thank you for explaining it so fully. PP II 11 192 22
"No, I thank you;" she replied, endeavouring to recover PP III 4 276 10
Mary and Kitty, thank heaven! are quite well." PP III 5 286 30
"I thank you for my share of the favour," said Elizabeth; " PP III 9 317 16
"Thank you," said Lydia, "for if you did, I should PP III 9 320 30
Thank heaven! he has some friends, though perhaps not so PP III 11 337 51
Let me thank your again and again, in the name of all my PP III 16 366 5
"If you will thank me," he replied, "let it be for PP III 16 366 6
I thank you, again and again, for not going to the lakes. PP III 18 382 21
a "no, no--not at all--no, thank you;" but he still MP I 2 15 10
I ever thank you as I ought, for thinking so well of me? MP I 3 26 30
"Thank you, but I am not at all tired." MP I 9 94 59
of success, she said, "thank you, my dear Fanny, but I and MP I 10 100 22
"Thank you for your good word, Fanny, but it is more than MP I 11 109 17
"Thank you--I am quite warm, very warm. MP I 18 168 17
"Thank you--but there is no escaping these little MP II 4 213 35
"Thank you, I am so glad," was Fanny's instinctive reply; MP II 5 219 26
Thank your uncle, William, thank your uncle." MP II 8 252 2
"I cannot attempt to thank you," she continued in a very MP II 9 261 5
His niece, meanwhile, did not thank him for what he had MP II 10 280 32
people now, who would give me my own terms and thank me." MP II 12 295 20
"Oh! I thank you, I have quite done, just done--it will be MP II 13 307 34
At the moment she could only thank and accept. MP III 6 369 11
Before they parted, she had to thank him for another MP III 10 406 22
"Thank God!" said he. MP III 16 455 23
I thank you for your patience, Fanny. MP III 16 459 30
"Thank you. E I 5 38 12
"Thank you, thank you, my own sweet little friend. E I 7 54 31
"Thank you, sir, thank you; I am going this moment myself; E I 8 58 8
"Thank you. E I 8 58 13
as to leave with us; thank you for the sight of it. E I 9 81 79
80
"I thank you; but I assure you you are quite mistaken. E I 13 112 23
"Thank you. E II 1 157 10
well still, thank God! with the help of spectacles. E II 1 157 10
"Thank you. E II 1 159 18
Thank you, we do indeed. E II 3 177 50
"Thank you for rousing me," he replied. E II 8 222 56
to thank Mrs. Weston, look sorrowful, and have done. E II 8 230 101
Very well I thank you.-- E II 9 236 44
Thank ye, the gloves do very well--only a little too large E II 9 237 48
I must speak to him if possible, just to thank him. E II 10 243 31
Very well, I thank you. E II 10 243 33
"No, I thank you. E II 10 244 42
"No, not now, I thank you. E II 10 244 45
A pleasant "thank you" seemed meant to laugh it off, but a E II 16 294 24
"Thank you, but I would rather you did not mention the E II 17 300 11
"Very well, I thank you, ma'am. E III 2 322 19
Thank you, my mother is remarkably well. E III 2 322 19
Very well I thank you, quite well. E III 2 323 19
Very well, I thank you. E III 2 323 19
No coffee, I thank you, for me--never take coffee.-- E III 2 323 19
There it goes, and there is an end, thank heaven! of Mr. E III 4 340 26
"I have not the least wish for it, I thank you." E III 6 355 23
"Thank you, thank you--but on no account.-- E III 6 362 48
"Thank you, dear Miss Woodhouse. yes, indeed, there is E III 8 382 23
I had an opportunity, to thank you--I could not thank you E III 12 419 12
to thank you--I could not thank you too much--for every E III 12 419 12
"Thank you," said he, in an accent of deep mortification, E III 13 429 29
"Thank you, dear Miss Woodhouse, you are all kindness.-- E III 16 455 20
"Thank you, thank you.-- E III 16 460 57
Much of this, I have no doubt, she may thank you for." E III 18 474 34
her and say, "I have to thank you, Miss Woodhouse, for a E III 18 476 46
47
Thank God! P III 8 71 54
She could not even thank him. P III 9 80 34
The tone, the look, with which "thank God!" was uttered by P III 12 112 54
"Another time, sir, I thank you, not now." P IV 1 127 25
near her on purpose to thank her most cordially, again and P IV 2 134 30
Thank you, thank you. P IV 6 169 25
"None, I thank you, unless you will give me the pleasure P IV 6 169 26
"No, I thank you: no, certainly not. P IV 9 198 44
But not now: no, I thank you, I have nothing to trouble P IV 9 198 44
"The name of Walter I can drop, thank God! and I desire " P IV 9 203 73
which she had been meditating over, and say, "thank you. P IV 9 204 76
77
his house myself, I will thank you to send off one of S 1 365 1
of life, we shall not much thank them Mr Parker."-- S 6 392 1
subscriptions Mary, I will thank you to mention a very S 12 424 1
THANKED (34)
She thanked me however most affectionately for my kind LS 20 277 6
7
He thanked her for her fears, and said that he had quitted NA I 8 54 4
her own praise; of being thanked at least, on his sister's NA II 5 157 5
She thanked him as heartily as if he had written it NA II 10 201 6
She thanked him again and again; and with a sweetness of SS I 9 42 10
They thanked her; but were obliged to resist all her SS I 20 110 5
Lady Middleton looked as if she thanked heaven that she SS II 1 145 16
Here he stopped to be thanked; which being done he went on. SS III 1 266 37
Elinor's heart thanked her for such kindness towards SS III 1 268 52
She thanked him for it with all her heart, spoke of SS III 3 283 20
She thanked him with brief, though fervent gratitude, and SS III 7 311 15
Emma thanked him--but professed herself very unwilling to W 339 18
Elizabeth thanked him from her heart, and then walked PP I 8 37 26
was; and Elizabeth having thanked her for the kindness of PP II 3 145 10
Elizabeth, though expecting no less, thanked him with PP III 4 280 26
Jane ran to her uncle and aunt, and welcomed and thanked PP III 5 287 32
I do not speak it to be thanked, therefore say nothing PP III 10 324 2
Jane went to him instantly, kissed him, and thanked him PP III 13 348 37
"I would have thanked you before, my dear aunt, as I ought PP III 18 382 21
Henry bowed and thanked her. MP I 4 42 20
for which nobody thanked her, and saying, with delighted MP I 17 163 21
weariness, and she was thanked and pitied; but she MP I 18 170 24
She thanked him for his great attention, his paternal MP II 3 200 21
and as he cordially thanked him, he hoped to be expressing MP III 3 337 11
Fanny thanked him, but tried to laugh it off. MP III 11 411 17
Fanny thanked him again, but was affected and distressed MP III 11 411 19
She thanked Miss Crawford, but gave a decided negative.-- MP III 14 436 15
Emma thanked him, but could not allow of his disappointing E I 9 81 79
He thanked her, observing, "how lucky that we should E II 8 213 9
He was very warmly thanked both by mother and daughter; to E II 10 242 16
He never can bear to be thanked. E II 10 245 52
have given, and only thanked Mrs. Elton coolly; "but their E II 14 276 34
invited him irresistibly to come to her and be thanked. E III 2 330 46
He thanked her with all his heart, and continued some time E III 18 476 49
THANKER (1)
He is a very liberal thanker, with his thousands and tens E III 15 447 28
THANKFUL (37)
I am thankful that my last letter will precede this by so LS 24 291 18
here, which I am most thankful for, it is impossible for NA II 7 180 34
of his son; and thankful for Mr. Thorpe's communication, NA II 15 245 12
and she was very thankful that she had never been SS II 10 215 10
to herself; and was very thankful that Marianne was not SS II 11 226 40
had seen enough to be thankful for her own sake, that one SS II 13 238 1
she added, "I am thankful to find that I can look with so SS III 10 344 14
15
enough, how to be enough thankful for his release without SS III 13 363 6
thankful; and then you may say whatever you like of me." PP I 10 51 42
Mrs. Philips was very thankful for his compliance, but PP I 16 76 7
I am most thankful that the discovery is made in time for PP I 18 97 57
"Let us be thankful that you are preserved from a state of PP I 23 130 23
"I never can be thankful, Mr. Bennet, for any thing about PP I 23 130 24
and Elizabeth was thankful to find that they did not see PP II 7 168 1
How thankful am I, that we never let them know what has PP III 4 274 3
And for this we are to be thankful. PP III 7 304 34
but that it was no worse, she had need to be thankful. PP III 7 307 51
I should be most thankful to any Mr. Repton who would MP I 6 57 29
Even Edmund was very thankful for an arrangement which MP I 8 80 28
must be infinitely more thankful for a decision; and I do MP I 15 143 26
sake, and he might be thankful to his fair daughter Julia MP II 2 191 10
She could not but be thankful.-- MP II 4 215 47
He would soon be always gone; and she was thankful that MP II 11 284 8
his infatuation, and be thankful for the right reason in MP III 1 324 59
Fanny was very thankful. MP III 7 383 33
Fanny fatigued and fatigued again, was thankful to accept MP III 7 387 46
made her a most attentive, profitable, thankful pupil. MP III 12 418 7
28th, and we ought to be thankful, papa, that we are to E I 9 79 63
have been thankful to be assured of never seeing him again. E II 4 182 7
thankful that my happiness is not more deeply involved.-- E II 13 265 4
I feel very thankful that I have so many myself as to be E II 18 307 21
And from her great, her more than commonly thankful E III 16 455 20
We shall have him very thankful to any body that will P III 8 70 46
would have been more thankful to ascertain, even than Mr. P IV 4 145 1
She was most thankful for her own knowledge of him. P IV 10 212 1
to Monday; and very delighted & thankful they were.-- S 7 399 1
as a screen, & was very thankful for every inch of back & S 10 415 1
THANKFULLY (12)
neighbours; it was thankfully accepted, and this NA I 2 23 22
and most thankfully feel their present release from it. NA II 13 220 1
us--how joyfully, how thankfully on my side!--as to your NA II 13 223 13
kindness I shall always thankfully remember, as well SS III 2 277 30
accepted the offer most thankfully; acknowledging that as W 339 18
could produce, made her thankfully turn to a book.-- W 361 31

Elizabeth most thankfully consented, and a servant was PP I 7 34 45
accepted the offer most thankfully, assuring them of her MP I 1 11 19
of his intention, was thankfully acknowledged--quite MP II 6 232 13
acknowledged--quite thankfully and warmly, for she was MP II 6 232 13
she had thankfully passed six weeks not six months ago?-- E II 5 187 4
indeed, she must thankfully say that their petticoats were E II 8 225 78

THANKFULNESS (4)
The thankfulness of Mrs Blake was more diffuse;--with a W 331 11
with many speeches of thankfulness on Mr. Collins's side, PP II 6 166 42
Serious she was, very serious in her thankfulness, and in E III 18 475 40
and fearless in the thankfulness of her enjoyment. P IV 11 245 77

THANKING (10)
unaffected benevolence; thanking him for such an attention NA II 15 242 7
Elizabeth took an opportunity of thanking her. PP I 22 121 1
thing her ladyship said, thanking her for every fish he PP II 6 166 41
I can no longer help thanking you for your unexampled PP III 16 365 3
My resolution of thanking you for your kindness to Lydia PP III 18 381 13
and therefore, thanking them, said, "he preferred MP II 1 177 5
He got as near as he could to thanking her for Miss E II 5 192 29
To have her haunting the Abbey, and thanking him all day E II 8 225 78
and longed to be thanking him; and though too distant for E III 2 328 40
Thanking them for their invitation, but "that was quite S 9 407 1

THANKLESS (1)
fall to the share of her thankless son, and treated as MP III 13 425 6

THANKS (41)
to her--in spite of his thanks, invitations, and NA II 1 129 1
little more than grateful thanks, and the thousand good NA II 14 236 14
"Undoubtedly; and after all you have no thanks for it. SS I 2 11 22
Elinor's thanks followed this speech with grateful SS II 9 211 33
"I must hurry away then, to give him those thanks which SS III 4 290 42
Edward, having carried his thanks to Colonel Brandon, SS III 5 293 1
to pour forth her thanks to him for fetching her mother, SS III 10 340 1
present," said he, "after thanks so ungraciously delivered SS III 13 368 30
No thanks to his gallantry for that. PP I 4 14 5
began repeating her thanks to Mr. Bingley for his kindness PP I 9 45 35
not say the same, but thanks to Lady Catherine de Bourgh, PP I 16 83 50
on receiving amongst the thanks of the table, the hint of PP I 18 100 68
Accept my thanks for the compliment you are paying me. PP I 19 106 12
from me a letter of thanks for this, as well as for every PP I 22 124 10
The promised letter of thanks from Mr. Collins arrived on PP I 23 128 10
again, and promised their father another letter of thanks. PP II 2 139 1
apologies and thanks which he would have thought necessary. PP II 6 161 10
not leave the house without receiving her thanks for it. PP II 15 215 2
Elizabeth was eager with her thanks and assurances of PP II 15 215 3
not forgetting his thanks for the kindness he had received PP II 15 217 8
thanks for their kindness to you while you have been here." PP II 15 217 9
wishes, which may seem purposely to ask for your thanks. PP III 4 278 20
Mr. Crawford bowed his thanks. MP II 7 248 45
before their happiness and thanks were all expressed. MP II 8 253 4
renewed but, less happy thanks accepted the necklace again, MP II 8 260 23
in a very agitated manner, "thanks are out of the question. MP II 9 261 5
for to-morrow: but your thanks are far beyond the occasion. MP II 9 262 9
With thanks for the honour of your note, I remain, MP II 13 307 31
with care and kindness, thanks for their visit, solicitude E II 1 155 4
They had music; Emma was obliged to play; and the thanks E II 2 168 15
Full of thanks, and full of news, Miss Bates knew not E II 3 172 23
a thousand thanks, and says you really quite oppress her." E II 3 173 29
many, many thanks,--'there was no occasion to trouble us, E II 8 223 63
Oh! and I am sure our thanks are due to you, Mrs. Weston, E III 2 322 19
and thanks, but is quite unequal to any exercise." E III 9 390 16
17
returned, with a thousand thanks from Miss Bates, but " E III 9 391 20
I could not bear these thanks;--for, Oh! Mrs. Weston, if E III 12 420 13
A thousand and a thousand thanks for all the kindness you E III 14 443 8
Woodhouse received the thanks for coming, which he asked E III 18 476 44
to avoid hearing her thanks, and rather sought to testify P III 9 80 34
Many thanks my dear Tom for the kindness with respect to S 5 386 1

THAT'S (45)
"Yes, that's the book; such unnatural stuff!-- NA I 7 49 40
"Not expect me! that's a good one! NA I 9 61 5
"Do you?--that's honest, by heavens! NA I 15 122 32
"Oh, if that's all," cried Miss Steele, "we can just as SS II 10 219 41
There, I said you were very refined;--& that's an instance W 319 2
"That's odd sort of talking!-- W 352 26
That's the long & the short of the business. W 352 26
Only do not oblige me to chuse the game, that's all. W 354 28
"Yes, I dare say you will; that's natural enough. MP I 3 25 12
If I can but make both ends meet, that's all I ask for." MP I 3 29 48
carpenter's work--and that's all; and as the carpenter's MP I 13 127 31
That's something, is not it?-- MP I 15 139 10
It just stands for a gentleman, and that's all. MP II 4 211 23
"That's well thought of. MP II 5 217 8
"That's right; and in London, of course, a house of your MP II 12 295 27
"Ha!" cried William, "that's just where I should have put MP III 7 380 21
"Then, there's the devil to pay among them, that's all. MP III 15 439 13
That's very like. E I 6 45 21
"Aye, that's very just, indeed, that's very properly said. E I 9 78 52
"But still, you will be an old maid! and that's so E I 10 85 18
"That's true," she cried--"very true. E I 12 99 11
That's a consideration indeed.-- E I 12 106 61
"That's easily said, and easily felt by you, who have E I 18 145 11
"That's right, my dear, very right. E II 3 172 19
A Miss Hawkins--that's all I know. E II 3 173 27
That's right. E II 11 256 60
"Ah! that's a great pity; for I assure you, Miss Woodhouse, E II 14 275 32
"Oh! that's all. E III 4 340 22
"That's quite unnecessary; I see Jane every day:--but as E III 6 355 20
There she is--no, that's somebody else. E III 7 374 53
That's one of the ladies in the Irish car party, not at E III 7 374 53
"Very soon, very soon indeed; that's the worst of it. E III 8 382 27
"Ah! you clever creature, that's very true. E III 16 456 33
"No, no, that's to-morrow; and I particularly wanted to E III 16 457 40
replied Sir Walter, "that's all I have to remark. P III 3 17 2
"Dear me! that's a very good thought, very good indeed. P III 7 57 16
poor fellow for a week; that's what he did, and nobody P III 12 108 28
There, take my arm; that's right; I do not feel P IV 6 169 27
Do not forget me when you are married, that's all. P IV 9 196 32
That's the worst of him." P IV 10 217 20
"Yes, yes--that's likely enough. S 4 381 1
things--and I have heard that's very much the case with S 6 392 1
"Aye my dear--that's very sensibly said cried Lady D--and S 7 401 1
That's right; all right & clean. S 9 408 1
"That's a great blessing.-- S 10 415 1

THAW (1)
state between frost and thaw, which is of all others the E I 16 138 17

THE BRIDE OF ABYDOS (1)
and The Bride of Abydos; and moreover, how the Giaour was P III 11 100 23

THE LADY OF THE LAKE (1)
or The Lady of the Lake were to be preferred, and how P III 11 100 23

THE MONK (1)
Tom Jones, except The Monk; I read that t'other day; but NA I 7 48 34

THE REV. PHILIP ELTON (1)
to The Rev. Philip Elton, White-Hart, Bath, was to be seen E II 5 186 1

THEATRE (44)
at the upper rooms, the theatre, and the concert; and how NA I 3 25 2
"Have you been to the theatre?" NA I 3 26 12
see each other across the theatre at night, and say their NA I 4 34 7
Catherine was not so much engaged at the theatre that NA I 5 35 1
met in the evening at the theatre; and, as Catherine and NA I 10 70 1
with the others to the theatre that night; but it must be NA I 12 92 4
To the theatre accordingly they all went; no Tilneys NA I 12 92 4
this, their spacious theatre; and, when the genius of NA II 8 183 3
No theatre, no rooms to prepare for. NA II 9 195 18
The General, perceiving his son one night at the theatre NA II 15 244 12
was rather thin, but however the little theatre was open. PP III 9 319 25
Ecclesford and its theatre, with its arrangements and MP I 13 121 1
Happily for him, a love of the theatre is so general, an MP I 13 121 2
theatre at Mansfield, and ask you to be our manager." MP I 13 123 5
"Oh! for the Ecclesford theatre and scenery to try MP I 13 123 6
Bertrams, "and for a theatre, what signifies a theatre? MP I 13 123 6
make the performance, not the theatre, our object. MP I 13 124 9
If we are to act, let it be in a theatre completely fitted MP I 13 124 10
It is the very room for a theatre, precisely the shape and MP I 13 125 14
way; and I think a theatre ought not to be attempted.-- MP I 13 127 28
Something of a theatre we must have undoubtedly, but it MP I 13 127 31
out, "no want of hands in our theatre, Miss Bertram. MP I 13 129 38
to be called the theatre, and Miss Bertram's resolving to MP I 14 136 22
it could be proposed and accepted in a private theatre! MP I 14 137 23
But the concerns of the theatre were suspended only for an MP I 15 142 25
Tom was engrossed by the concerns of his theatre, and saw MP I 17 163 21
Every thing was now in a regular train; theatre, actors, MP I 18 164 1
her to creep into the theatre, and attend the rehearsal of MP I 18 165 3
chairs, not made for a theatre, I dare say; much more MP I 18 169 21
I heard him as I came up stairs, and the theatre is MP I 18 169 21
every body was in the theatre at an early hour, and having MP I 18 171 25
To the theatre he went, and reached it just in time to MP II 1 182 22
himself on the stage of a theatre, and opposed to a MP II 1 182 22
"I come from your theatre," said he composedly, as he sat MP II 1 184 25
him on the topic of the theatre, would torment him with MP II 1 184 25
and very little will remain of the theatre to-morrow.-- MP II 2 193 13
of Sotherton, or the theatre at Mansfield Park; but he MP III 2 328 7
a theatre, some time or other, at your house in Norfolk. MP III 3 338 19
I think you will fit up a theatre at your house in Norfolk. MP III 3 339 19
No theatre at Everingham! MP III 3 339 20
"that lady will never allow a theatre at Everingham." MP III 3 339 20
of his unjustifiable theatre, made an impression on his MP III 17 462 4
The theatre or the rooms, where he was most likely to be, P IV 7 180 32
I have been to the theatre, and secured a box for to- P IV 10 223 41

THEATRES (1)
and shopping, and the evening at one of the theatres. PP II 4 152 5

THEATRICAL (7)
the same time without any theatrical grimace or violence.-- W 343 20
for it had been a theatrical party; and the play, in which MP I 13 121 1
was the height of his theatrical ambition, and with the MP I 14 132 8
entreaty from the theatrical board, and the really good MP I 15 147 56
Edmund, between his theatrical and his real part, between MP I 17 163 21
in the midst of theatrical nonsense, and forced in so MP II 1 183 23
destruction of every theatrical preparation at Mansfield, MP II 2 194 21

THEATRICALS (4)
praise of the private theatricals at Ecclesford, the seat MP I 13 121 1
In a general light, private theatricals are open to some MP I 13 125 17
that "the Mansfield theatricals would enliven the whole MP I 15 148 60
"I shall always look back on our theatricals with MP II 5 225 55

THEFT (1)
procured by some theft or contrivance unknown to herself. SS I 18 98 13

THEIR'S (8)
If not originally their's, by what strange events could it NA II 6 164 2
and garden in which their's might at present be deficient. SS I 6 30 6
their's, she should pay her visit and return for them. SS II 11 220 2
left her own party for a short time, to join their's. SS III 2 271 5
to censure in a plan like their's, comprehending only MP I 13 128 38
and take up her abode in their's, that every hour might be MP I 13 129 40
that 'the world is not their's, nor the world's law.'" E III 10 400 66
as if ever willing to change his own home for their's!-- E III 12 422 20

THEME (3)
were instantly the theme of general admiration, and the SS I 9 43 11
of manner and goodness of heart were the exhaustless theme. MP II 12 294 16
not but indulge herself in dwelling on so beloved a theme. MP III 12 419 8

THENCE (10)
and may I not thence infer, that your notions of the NA I 10 77 37
in purses and spars; thence adjourned to eat ice at a NA I 15 116 1
return to Northanger, and thence made him the bearer of NA II 16 252 7
I have business there; from thence to town in a day or two. SS III 8 331 73
But does it thence follow that had he married you, he SS III 11 351 13
needed to it; and from thence, after staying there a SS III 13 372 46
cottages;--and from thence returning to town, procured the SS III 14 376 11
the breakfast room; from thence to the library;--their PP III 7 301 4
5
that in removing thence she might be considered rather as P III 11 93 2
They had been to Trafalgar house, & been directed thence S 6 390 1

THEORETICAL (1)
My theoretical and his practical knowledge together, could MP III 4 348 21

THEORETICALLY (2)
"I should have thought so theoretically myself, but"--and MP II 4 210 19
They had been instructed theoretically in their religion, MP III 17 463 8

THEORY (1)
As to the management of their children, his theory was P III 6 44 6

THERE'S (8)
There's the sting. NA II 1 136 48
I'm sure there's a vast many smart beaux in Exeter; but SS I 21 123 28
Now there's Mr. Rose at Exeter, a prodigious smart young SS I 21 123 28
There's for you, my dear!-- SS III 1 258 7
Charles instantly pointed him out to Emma--"there's Lord W 332 11
There's for you! PP II 16 220 10
There's Arcturus looking very bright." MP I 11 113 38
"Then, there's the devil to pay among them, that's all. MP III 15 439 13

THEREABOUTS (2)
that you would find them at that knoll, or thereabouts." MP I 10 101 34
a woman of 10,000l. or thereabouts; and he had gained her E II 4 181 4

THEREBY (4)
which she must have been thereby involved filling the NA II 13 229 31
His character is thereby complete." PP I 4 14 3
As all conversation was thereby at an end, Elizabeth soon PP I 8 40 55
of Northampton, and to be thereby raised to the rank of a MP I 1 3 1

THEREIN (1)
pounds would be a very insufficient support therein. PP II 12 200 5

THEREON (1)
distinctions consequent thereon, she found, while they MP II 5 223 48

THEREUPON (2)
we discuss the discretion of his behaviour thereupon. PP I 10 50 37
to express her concern thereupon, he assured her with much PP I 16 83 49

THEY'D (2)
when they come back, they'd make sure to come and see you." SS III 11 354 27
They will soon be back again, and then they'd be sure and SS III 11 354 38

THEY'LL (2)
They'll tell you all about it." MP II 1 181 15
They'll stay their six weeks.-- S 6 393 1

THICK (10)
he would not drive her, because she had such thick ancles. NA I 15 117 3
nothing worse than a thick mizzling rain; and having given NA II 5 161 25
It was a narrow winding path through a thick grove of old NA II 7 179 29
and the acacia, and a thick screen of them altogether, SS III 6 302 7
the end of Jane's second song, her voice grew thick. E II 8 229 93
the lower buttons of his thick leather gaiters, and either E II 15 287 27
28
Quite thick shoes. E III 2 322 19
her from Randall's--a very thick letter;--she guessed what E III 14 436 6
dark November day, a small thick rain almost blotting out P IV 1 123 8
all, and her boots were so thick! much thicker than Miss P IV 7 174 3

THICK-HEADED (2)
Who could have seen through such thick-headed nonsense? E I 16 134 4
nothing better than a thick-headed, unfeeling, P III 6 51 29

THICKER (2)
one evening, when a thicker letter than usual from Mary P IV 6 162 1

were so thick! much thicker than Miss Anne's; and, in P IV 7 174 3
THICKEST (1)
that his cousin Anne's boots were rather the thickest. P IV 7 174 3
THICKLY (1)
The woods and walks thickly covered with dead leaves." SS I 16 87 30
THICKNESS (3)
and point out a quiz through the thickness of a crowd. NA I 4 33 7
it seemed, as far as the thickness of the walls would NA II 13 222 7
man at their back--and a great thickness of air, in aid--. S 12 427 1
THIN (17)
She had a thin awkward figure, a sallow skin without NA I 1 13 1
I am grown wretchedly thin I know; but I will not pain you NA I 15 118 13
very unwell, has lost her colour, and is grown quite thin. SS II 11 227 48
Mrs. Ferrars was a little, thin woman, upright, even to SS II 12 232 14
But if it be only a slight, thin sort of inclination, I am PP I 9 44 34
Who would have thought she could be so thin and small!" PP II 5 158 15
Maria's astonishment, at her being so thin, and so small. PP II 6 162 12
Her face is too thin; her complexion has no brilliancy; PP III 3 271 15
To be sure London was rather thin, but however the little PP III 9 319 25
of motes floating in thin blue, and the bread and butter MP III 15 439 9
could meet with, into a thin quarto of hot-pressed paper, E I 9 69 3
by a basin of nice smooth gruel, thin, but not too thin. E I 12 104 50
must expect to see her grown thin, and looking very poorly. E II 1 162 31
medium, between fat and thin, though a slight appearance E II 2 167 12
them now that she was faded and thin, to excite his esteem. P III 1 6 10
he thought her "less thin in her person, in her checks; P IV 4 145 3
or manner--tho' more thin & worn by illness & Medecine, S 10 413 1
THING (1413)
If you can get him away, it will be a good thing. Yrs LS 11 259 2
is a sad thing & of course highly afflicting to Lady Susan. LS 15 266 2
& with still greater energy, I must warn you of one thing. LS 23 283 4
for hers, nor for my own, could such a thing be desirable. LS 24 289 12
She never could learn or understand any thing before she NA I 1 14 1
to see her children every thing they ought to be; but her NA I 1 15 3
Every thing indeed relative to this important journey was NA I 2 19 3
and seeing every thing herself as any young lady could be. NA I 2 20 8
placed, without having any thing to do there, or any body NA I 2 22 10
For my part I have not seen any thing I like so well in NA I 2 22 11
"Indeed I shall say no such thing." NA I 3 26 23
Now here one can step out of doors and get a thing in five NA I 3 29 46
coloured, and said, "I was not thinking of any thing." NA I 3 29 48
day wished for the same thing was at length to have its NA I 4 31 2
Every thing is so insipid, so uninteresting, that does not NA I 6 41 16
time rather more than any thing else in the world, NA I 6 42 33
looking out for some light thing of the kind, though I had NA I 7 46 11
to want such a little thing as this? it is a capital one NA I 7 46 11
of doing a kind thing by a friend, I hate to be pitiful." NA I 7 47 17
would be reckoned a cheap thing by some people, for I NA I 7 47 19
You hardly mentioned any thing of her, when you wrote to NA I 7 50 48
thing to say, and had courage and leisure for saying it. NA I 8 56 11
I never saw any thing half so beautiful! NA I 8 57 16
But be satisfied, for you are not to know any thing at all NA I 8 57 18
"Well, I declare I never knew any thing like you. NA I 8 57 20
she cried, "I would not do such a thing for all the world. NA I 8 57 21
is a most improper thing, and entirely against the rules. NA I 8 57 21
men have a point to carry, you never stick at any thing. NA I 8 57 23
shock you to see me do such a thing; now would not it?" NA I 8 58 23
an eternity finding out a thing fit to be got into, and NA I 9 61 1
Every thing being then arranged, the servant who stood at NA I 9 62 10
without a plunge or a caper, or any thing like one. NA I 9 62 10
"A famous thing for his next heirs. NA I 9 63 14
Why should you think of such a thing? NA I 9 63 19
It would be a famous good thing for us all." NA I 9 63 20
Now, for instance, it was reckoned a remarkable thing at NA I 9 64 24
You would not often meet with any thing like it in Oxford-- NA I 9 64 24
Did you ever see such a little tittuppy thing in your life? NA I 9 65 28
knows how to drive it; a thing of that sort in good hands NA I 9 65 30
accounts of the same thing; for she had not been brought NA I 9 65 31
"Oh! a vast deal indeed; she hardly talked of any thing NA I 9 68 44
that is a settled thing--even your modesty cannot doubt NA I 10 70 1
world; you are such a sly thing, I am sure you would have NA I 10 71 3
One thing, however, I must observe. NA I 10 77 37
"Oh!" expressing every thing needful; attention to his NA I 10 80 60
"I shall like it," she cried, "beyond any thing in the NA I 10 80 61
experience, she scarcely saw any thing during the evening. NA I 10 81 61
augured from it, every thing most favourable to her wishes. NA I 11 82 1
for he had rather do any thing in the world than walk out NA I 11 83 13
Kingsweston! aye, and Blaize Castle too, and any thing NA I 11 84 21
of good, as might console her for almost any thing. NA I 11 86 50
I shall have no pleasure at Clifton, nor in any thing else. NA I 11 87 53
about its being a d---- thing to be miserly; and that if NA I 11 89 61
I never mind going through any thing, where a friend is NA I 11 90 64
I shall not be easy till I have explained every thing." NA I 12 91 1
rendered every thing else of the kind "quite horrid." NA I 12 92 4
I never thought of such a thing; but I begged Mr. Thorpe NA I 12 94 8
With a yet sweeter smile, he said every thing that need be NA I 12 94 9
placed, it is not in the power of any thing to change them. NA I 13 98 2
These Tilneys seem to swallow up every thing else." NA I 13 98 2
regardless of every thing but her own gratification. NA I 13 98 3
upon any account in the world, do so improper a thing." NA I 13 99 4
When every thing was settled, when Miss Tilney herself NA I 13 100 19
street-door, saying every thing gallant as they went down NA I 13 103 28
She reached home without seeing any thing more of the NA I 13 103 29
These schemes are not at all the thing. NA I 13 104 31
Allen however discouraged her from doing any such thing. NA I 13 105 40
therefore at neither seeing nor hearing any thing of them. NA I 14 106 1
"I did not mean to say any thing wrong; but it is a nice NA I 14 108 15
it is a very nice word indeed!--it does for every thing. NA I 14 108 16
on, I conclude, as any thing that does not actually pass NA I 14 109 23
of knowing any thing, should conceal it as well as she can. NA I 14 111 28
to desire any thing more in woman than ignorance. NA I 14 111 29
that she would give any thing in the world to be able to NA I 14 111 29
to see beauty in every thing admired by him, and her NA I 14 111 29
to be more horrible than any thing we have met with yet." NA I 14 112 31
Where could you hear of such a thing?" NA I 14 112 32
I shall expect murder and every thing of the kind." NA I 14 112 33
unjust thing of any woman at all, or an unkind one of me." NA I 14 114 48
It must be the dullest thing in the world, for there is NA I 14 115 50
It sees through every thing." NA I 15 117 4
Never had Catherine listened to any thing so full of NA I 15 117 8
it always is with me; the first moment settles every thing. NA I 15 118 11
were acquainted with every thing, and who seemed only to NA I 15 120 25
and am promised that every thing in their power shall be NA I 15 121 26
was pledged to make every thing easy; and by what means NA I 15 122 28
"a famous good thing this marrying scheme, upon my soul! NA I 15 122 30
so much, so much of every thing; and then you have such-- NA I 15 123 38
And to marry for money I think the wickedest thing in NA I 15 124 47
not to be delayed by any thing in his nature to urge; and NA I 15 124 47
sparkling eyes to every thing he said; and, in finding him NA II 1 131 15
Isabella on having every thing so pleasantly settled. NA II 1 135 43
was in suspense, and every thing secured when it was NA II 2 138 1
Every thing honourable and soothing, every present NA II 2 140 8
Every thing seemed to co-operate for her advantage. NA II 2 140 11
Allen's side, without any thing to say or to hear; and NA II 3 143 1
Well, the thing is this, I have just had a letter from NA II 3 144 6
And as to making me an offer, or any thing like it, there NA II 3 144 11
I could not have misunderstood a thing of that kind, you NA II 3 144 11
expected, nor wished for any thing of the kind from him. NA II 3 145 13
"You do acquit me then of any thing wrong?-- NA II 3 146 17
I do not think any thing would justify me in wishing you NA II 3 146 20
I am sorry for it; I am sorry they find any thing so NA II 3 147 26
"Is not it the same thing?" NA II 4 151 11
loiter about without any thing to see, next followed--and NA II 5 156 4
spirits, and scarcely any thing was said but by himself; NA II 5 156 4
he could not propose any thing improper for her; and, in NA II 5 156 5
I should be too much frightened to do any such thing." NA II 5 159 20
without perceiving any thing very remarkable in either. NA II 5 160 21
without discovering any thing of importance--perhaps NA II 5 160 21
for her to observe any thing farther, and fixed all her NA II 5 161 25
the room, whether any thing within her observation, would NA II 5 161 26
the furniture, where every thing being for daily use, NA II 5 162 27
examination of any thing, as she greatly dreaded NA II 6 163 1
and, forgetting every thing else, she stood gazing on it NA II 6 163 1
2
without being able to distinguish any thing with certainty. NA II 6 164 2
yet that it should be any thing else in that house was a NA II 6 164 2
thing, but it was so very odd, after what Henry had said. NA II 6 168 10
every thing seemed to speak the awfulness of her situation. NA II 6 168 10
eye could not discern any thing unusual, a double range of NA II 6 168 10
Not one was left unsearched, and in not one was any thing NA II 6 169 11
idea of finding any thing in any part of the cabinet, and NA II 6 169 11
The mere habit of learning to love is the thing; and a NA II 7 174 10
nothing, it is not an object, but employment is the thing. NA II 7 176 15
fitted up; every thing that money and taste could do, to NA II 8 185 5
The day was unmarked therefore by any thing to interest NA II 9 190 1
grossly mistaken in every thing else!--in Miss Tilney's NA II 9 193 6
Is there any thing extraordinary to be seen there?" NA II 9 195 10
and where roads and newspapers lay every thing open? NA II 9 197 29
on alarm, and every thing forced to bend to one purpose by NA II 10 199 2
heretofore, of continual improvement by any thing he said. NA II 10 201 4
and when she promised a thing, she was so scrupulous in NA II 10 201 5
that every thing is at an end between Miss Thorpe and me.-- NA II 10 202 6
7
your brother of every thing but the folly of too easily NA II 10 202 7
directly; but Catherine could hardly eat any thing. NA II 10 203 8
letter of containing any thing unwelcome, I should have NA II 10 204 12
and fickleness, and every thing that is bad in the world?" NA II 10 204 19
"But how can you think of such a thing, after what the NA II 11 211 12
give yourself any trouble, because any thing would do." NA II 11 211 12
but why he should say one thing so positively, and mean NA II 11 211 15
Far be it from me to say otherwise; and any thing in NA II 11 213 19
ourselves, if there is one thing more than another my NA II 11 213 19
is beyond any thing; and every body one cares for is gone. NA II 12 216 2
Pray explain every thing to his satisfaction; or, if he NA II 12 217 2
"There is but one thing that I cannot understand. NA II 12 218 6
she hardly supposed there were any thing worse to be told. NA II 13 223 13
Oh! that I could suggest any thing in extenuation! NA II 13 225 19
It was the last thing I would willingly have done. NA II 13 225 22
be of none; but to every thing else it is of the greatest NA II 13 225 23
When every thing was done they left the room, Catherine NA II 13 227 27
and strengthened her distaste for every thing before her. NA II 13 228 27
around her, enjoying every thing present, and fearing NA II 13 228 27
thing to startle and recall them to the present moment. NA II 13 228 27
her from noticing any thing before her, when once beyond NA II 14 231 5
soothed beyond any thing that she had believed possible. NA II 14 233 9
In the joyfulness of family love every thing for a short NA II 14 233 9
time of it; but as for any thing else, it is no matter now; NA II 14 234 12
have not left any thing behind you in any of the pockets." NA II 14 234 12
could not be a desirable thing to have him engaged to a NA II 14 236 19
thing--a time for balls and plays, and a time for work. NA II 15 240 2
that moment in his power to say any thing to the purpose. NA II 15 242 8
to his son of doing every thing in his power to attach her, NA II 15 245 12
to do every thing in his power to make them comfortable. SS I 1 5 6
She was sensible and clever; but eager in every thing; her SS I 1 6 12
amiable, interesting: she was every thing but prudent. SS I 1 6 12
A continuance in a place where every thing reminded her of SS I 2 8 2
not have thought of such a thing as begging you to give SS I 2 9 5
"Oh! beyond any thing great! SS I 2 9 11
"I would not wish to do any thing mean," he replied. SS I 2 9 12
died, and afterwards it turned out to be no such thing. SS I 2 11 20
"It is certainly an unpleasant thing," replied Mr. SS I 2 11 21
I would not bind myself to allow them any thing yearly. SS I 2 11 22
"But, however, one thing must be considered. SS I 2 12 26
have left almost every thing in the world to them." SS I 2 13 28
It implies every thing amiable. SS I 3 16 8
is not in every thing equal to your sense of his merits. SS I 4 19 5
6
I think him every thing that is worthy and amiable." SS I 4 20 6
he assured her that every thing should be done to it which SS I 4 23 20
than till every thing were ready for her inhabiting it. SS I 5 25 1
of every thing that interested her, was soon done.-- SS I 5 26 5
letter to Norland, every thing was so far settled in their SS I 5 27 7
But one must not expect every thing; though I suppose it SS I 6 29 4
better not have any thing to do with matrimony together. SS I 8 37 9
a man of thirty-five any thing near enough to love, to SS I 8 38 11
prompted; and every thing that passed during the visit, SS I 10 46 1
recommended him to her affection beyond every thing else. SS I 10 48 7
Every thing he did, was right. SS I 11 54 3
Every thing he said, was clever. SS I 11 54 3
husband, provided every thing were conducted in style and SS I 11 55 6
imagination; and every thing established in the most SS I 11 57 17
"But indeed this is quite another thing. SS I 12 60 11
to be employed, and every thing conducted in the usual SS I 12 62 28
said Sir John, "when once you are determined on any thing. SS I 13 65 32
I am not sensible of having done any thing wrong in SS I 13 68 74
a year, and his brother left every thing sadly involved. SS I 14 70 2
I would give any thing to know the truth of it. SS I 14 70 2
tone, "with all and every thing belonging to it;--in no SS I 14 73 13
which has made every thing belonging to you so dear to me." SS I 14 74 19
"Is any thing the matter with her?" cried Mrs. Dashwood as SS I 15 75 3
account for every thing that at first seemed strange to me SS I 15 78 24
every thing to me at once: but this is not the case. SS I 15 81 44
The slightest mention of any thing relative to Willoughby SS I 15 82 47
He valued their kindness beyond any thing, and his SS I 19 101 1
excuse for every thing strange on the part of her son. SS I 19 101 2
me employment, or afford me any thing like independence. SS I 19 102 4
In feeling, in action, in condition, in every thing." SS I 19 103 6
of the parlour and every thing in it burst forth. SS I 19 106 23
Only look, sister, how delightful every thing is! SS I 19 107 24
their friends, without ceasing till every thing was told. SS I 19 107 28
would be a shocking thing, as we go away again to-morrow. SS I 20 110 2
It was quite a sudden thing our coming at all, and I knew SS I 20 110 2
He never tells me any thing! SS I 20 110 2
"Such weather makes every thing and every body disgusting. SS I 20 110 8
body, and his general abuse of every thing before him. SS I 20 112 28
"No;" said he, "I never said any thing so irrational. SS I 20 113 38
with something so droll--all about any thing in the world." SS I 20 113 39
and sister, and one thing and another, and I said to him, ' SS I 20 115 50
happened to be doing any thing, or in taking patterns of SS I 21 120 6
but she will swallow any thing; and the excessive SS I 21 120 6
and quiet--never was there such a quiet little thing!" SS I 21 121 9
Miss Steeles, and every thing was affection could suggest SS I 21 121 10
To do him justice, he did every thing in his power to SS I 21 125 34
" twill be a fine thing to have her married so young to be SS I 21 125 35
Marianne, who had never much toleration for any thing like SS I 22 127 1
I am sure I would rather do any thing in the world than be SS I 22 128 9
sister's suspecting any thing, that was reason enough for SS I 22 131 32
Every thing in such suspense and uncertainty; and seeing SS I 22 133 42
as I know the very mention of such a thing would do. SS I 22 133 44
and distress beyond any thing she had ever felt before. SS I 22 135 55
blind him to every thing but her beauty and good nature; SS II 1 140 2
a shocking thing to disappoint dear Annamaria after all." SS II 1 145 20
would make you overlook every thing else I am sure." SS II 2 146 5
"That conviction must be every thing to you; and he is SS II 2 147 8

very likely secure every thing to Robert, and the idea of SS II 2 148 15
to almost every thing else, she was carried by her SS II 3 154 6
you will scarcely have any thing at all, and you will SS II 3 156 13
to consider the separation as any thing short of eternal. SS II 3 158 21
Every thing was silent; this could not be borne many SS II 4 161 7
fatigues; and of every thing to which she could decently SS II 4 162 10
Aye, it is a fine thing to be young and handsome. SS II 4 163 18
abstracted from every thing actually before them, from all SS II 4 164 24
no pleasure from any thing; was only impatient to be at SS II 4 165 24
eye was caught by every thing pretty, expensive, or new; SS II 4 165 24
'tis a said thing for sportsmen to lose a day's pleasure. SS II 5 167 1
Every thing in her household arrangements was conducted on SS II 5 168 11
We have neither of us any thing to tell; you, because you SS II 5 170 26
Is every thing finally settled? SS II 5 173 44
nor attempted to eat any thing; and Elinor's attention was SS II 7 181 6
for her rug, to see any thing at all; and calmly SS II 7 181 7
8
senses; but it is no such thing, I can tell you, for it SS II 7 182 10
Indeed, you are doing a very unkind thing in spreading the SS II 7 182 11
I am much concerned to find there was any thing in my SS II 7 183 13
heart gave him with every thing that passed, Elinor forgot SS II 7 184 16
"I only wish," replied her sister, "there were any thing I SS II 7 185 18
This, as every thing else would have been, was too much SS II 7 185 19
Poor thing! she looks very bad.-- SS II 8 192 3
Well, poor thing! SS II 8 192 3
in ignorance of every thing that was passing before her. SS II 8 193 6
thing was due to her which might make her at all less so. SS II 8 193 7
I am sure if I knew of any thing she would like, I would SS II 8 194 8
Well, it is the oddest thing to me, that a man should use SS II 8 194 8
But then you know, how should I guess such a thing? SS II 8 195 16
of appearing to know any thing about it when she is SS II 8 195 17
pretty canal; and every thing, in short, that one could SS II 8 197 22
said it did him more good than any thing else in the world. SS II 8 198 27
assertion that every thing was now finally settled SS II 8 199 37
One thing, especially, I remember, because it served to SS II 8 199 37
In that, if in any thing, we may find an explanation." SS II 8 199 38
In one thing, however, she was uniform, when it came to SS II 9 201 2
"This is beyond every thing!" exclaimed Elinor. SS II 9 209 31
at Barton, where every thing within her view would be SS II 10 213 3
"What a charming thing it is that Mrs. Dashwood can spare SS II 10 218 34
place; the most complete thing of its kind, he said, that SS II 11 222 11
ever was, and you all seemed to enjoy it beyond any thing. SS II 11 222 11
In short, it is a kind of thing that"--lowering his voice SS II 11 224 24
"It is not actually settled, but there is such a thing in SS II 11 224 28
Her inviting you to town is certainly a vast thing in your SS II 11 226 42
At her time of life, any thing of an illness destroys the SS II 11 227 50
almost without having any thing to say to them; for of the SS II 12 229 3
in the habit of giving any thing, they determined to give SS II 12 230 6
were numerous, and every thing bespoke the mistress's SS II 12 233 18
as he would have done any thing painted by Miss Dashwood; SS II 12 234 28
But she does every thing well." SS II 12 235 33
She had found in her every thing that could tend to make a SS II 13 238 1
Could any thing be so flattering as Mrs. Ferrars's way of SS II 13 239 4
like me, if she did not, and her liking me is every thing. SS II 13 239 9
But now, there is one good thing, we shall be able to meet, SS II 13 240 15
a word; and almost every thing that was said, proceeded SS II 13 241 22
This would almost make amends for every thing!" SS II 13 242 24
to say any thing that might introduce another subject. SS II 13 242 28
not a thing to be urged against the wishes of everybody. SS II 14 246 2
thought it a delightful thing for the girls to be together; SS II 14 247 5
One thing did disturb her; and of that she made her daily SS II 14 247 5
injured by the expectation of any thing better from them. SS II 14 248 6
curiosity; she saw every thing, and asked every thing; was SS II 14 249 8
thing, and asked every thing; was never easy till she knew SS II 14 249 8
at liberty to fix on any thing else; and a thought struck SS II 14 252 20
by time and address, to do every thing that Lucy wished. SS II 14 254 27
glad there never was any thing in it), Mr. Edward Ferrars, SS III 1 258 7
Could you have believed such a thing possible?-- SS III 1 258 7
is the foundation on which every thing good may be built.-- SS III 1 263 27
Nothing has proved him unworthy; nor has any thing SS III 1 264 29
in her sister, made Elinor feel equal to any thing herself. SS III 1 265 33
is a good one, and her resolution equal to any thing. SS III 1 265 36
Duty, affection, every thing was disregarded. SS III 1 266 38
And there is one thing more preparing against him, which SS III 1 269 53
"Can any thing be more galling to the spirit of a man," SS III 1 269 56
She will tell you any thing if you ask. SS III 2 271 6
that she would tell any thing without being asked, for SS III 2 271 7
"That is a good thing. SS III 2 272 10
a new bonnet, nor do any thing else for me again, so long SS III 2 272 12
Lucy, for it's no such a thing I can tell you; and it's SS III 2 272 14
pounds, and no hope of any thing else; and if he was to go SS III 2 273 16
I am sure I would not do such a thing for all the world.-- SS III 2 275 22
directly, 'I wonder how you could think of such a thing. SS III 2 275 22
the same; and if any thing should happen to take you and SS III 2 275 25
it would be;--every thing depended, exactly after her SS III 2 276 26
readily gained, every thing relative to their return was SS III 3 280 7
a thing, somehow or other he will soon find an opportunity. SS III 4 285 5
I have not heard of any thing to please me so well since SS III 4 287 20
have been the easiest thing in the world; but she equally SS III 4 287 24
as soon as he could say any thing, after taking a chair. SS III 4 288 26
to the probability of their not waiting for any thing more SS III 4 292 58
cannot be interested in any thing that befalls him.-- SS III 5 296 19
eldest son;--and as to any thing else, they are both very SS III 5 297 29
"Of one thing, my dear sister," kindly taking her hand, SS III 5 297 31
be very wrong to say any thing about it--but I have it SS III 5 297 31
the danger of hearing any thing more from her brother, by SS III 5 297 32
I found, to do any thing, for unluckily, I was not in the SS III 5 299 37
every thing that was most affectionate and graceful. SS III 5 300 38
and Elinor could have forgiven every thing but her laugh. SS III 6 304 13
be in vain, that every thing had been delayed too long, SS III 7 312 18
is worth the trial however, and you shall hear every thing. SS III 8 319 29
Such a beginning as this cannot be followed by any thing.-- SS III 8 320 31
Do not let me be pained by hearing any thing more on the SS III 8 320 31
therefore, was not a thing to be thought of;--and with a SS III 8 320 32
But one thing may be said for me, even in that horrid SS III 8 320 32
affluence, lost every thing that could make it a blessing." SS III 8 321 32
her ignorance of the world--every thing was against me. SS III 8 323 40
have felt it too certain a thing, to trust myself near him. SS III 8 327 55
But what could I do?--we were engaged, every thing in SS III 8 328 63
like mine, any thing was to be done to prevent a rupture. SS III 8 328 63
and wished any thing rather than Mrs. Willoughby's death. SS III 9 335 5
which fashioned every thing delightful to her, as it chose. SS III 9 336 13
Every thing that the most zealous affection, the most SS III 10 341 6
she, "that I see every thing--as you can desire me to do." SS III 11 349 4
concluded that every thing had been expressly softened at SS III 11 355 46
him, should overlook every thing but the risk of delay. SS III 12 357 2
it might be, that any thing but the most disinterested SS III 13 367 22
Every thing was explained to him by Mrs. Dashwood, and he SS III 13 370 35
The secrecy with which every thing had been carried on SS III 13 371 38
of not marrying till every thing was ready, and the SS III 14 374 6
and direct every thing as they liked on the spot;--could SS III 14 374 7
His property here, his place, his house, every thing in SS III 14 375 9
she was in every thing considered, and always openly SS III 14 377 11
Could a sister do such a thing?-- W 316 2
a sort of thing that shocks me; I cannot understand it. W 318 2
"I would rather do any thing than be teacher at a school-- W 318 2
eliz: warmly--do you think I would do such a thing?-- W 320 2
temper indeed;--I never met with any thing like it!-- W 320 2
day after a ball, it is a thing quite out of rule I assure W 340 18
& what do you thing of Ld Osborne Miss Watson?" W 340 19
Poor thing!-- W 341 19
attention; it is a hard thing for a woman to stand against W 343 19
It was a new thing with him to wish to please a woman; it W 346 21
to assert a very unlikely thing, & describe a very odd W 347 22
without leaving every thing that he had to dispose of, or W 352 26
wait, said she, so I put on the first thing I met with.-- W 353 26
What a fine thing for our girls!" PP I 1 4 14
but I do not pretend to be any thing extraordinary now. PP I 1 4 20
"I desire you will do no such thing. PP I 1 4 26
"I do not believe Mrs. Long will do any such thing. PP I 2 6 5
every day; but for your sakes, we would do any thing. PP I 2 8 26
disposition, which delighted in any thing ridiculous. PP I 3 12 14
I never in my life saw any thing more elegant than their PP I 3 13 18
every thing in his favour, should think highly of himself. PP I 5 20 18
of doing a very gallant thing, and called out to her, "my PP I 6 26 37
38
mother, "as to think of such a thing, in all this dirt! PP I 7 32 34
She is a great reader and has no pleasure in any thing PP I 8 37 23
Every thing nourishes what is strong already. PP I 9 44 34
the most shameful thing in the world if he did not keep it. PP I 9 45 36
The power of doing any thing with quickness is always much PP I 10 49 27
"Have you any thing else to propose for my domestic PP I 10 52 56
How much sooner one tires of any thing than of a book!-- PP I 11 55 4
it is quite a settled thing; and as soon as Nicholls has PP I 11 55 7
Mr. Darcy in any thing, and persevered therefore in PP I 11 56 14
"I never heard any thing so abominable. PP I 11 57 16
Why Jane--you never dropt a word of this; you sly thing! PP I 13 61 3
I do think it is the hardest thing in the world, that your PP I 13 61 7
his commendation of every thing would have touched Mrs. PP I 13 65 26
but he had never seen any thing but affability in her. PP I 14 66 1
beholding it, (for every thing announced it to be from a PP I 14 68 13
I could forgive him any thing and everything, rather than PP I 16 78 20
by extravagance, imprudence, in short any thing or nothing. PP I 16 79 27
of having really done any thing to deserve to lose it. PP I 16 79 27
to--but he gave up every thing to be of use to the late Mr. PP I 16 81 37
names, facts, every thing mentioned without ceremony.-- PP I 17 85 5
of every thing in Mr. Darcy's looks and behaviour. PP I 17 86 10
thing indeed, and I wonder how he could presume to do it. PP I 18 94 45
his enemies, and every thing else gave way before the hope PP I 18 95 48
It was, moreover, such a promising thing for her younger PP I 18 99 63
Before Elizabeth had time for any thing but a blush of PP I 19 104 3
4
that I think it a right thing for every clergyman in easy PP I 19 105 9
10
You will find her manners beyond any thing I can describe; PP I 19 106 10
In every thing else she is as good natured a girl as ever PP I 20 111 5
"I do not pretend to regret any thing I shall leave in PP I 21 116 8
would allow, every thing was settled between them to the PP I 22 121 2
Risk any thing rather than her displeasure; and if you PP I 22 124 9
The very mention of any thing concerning the match threw PP I 23 129 16
"I should not mind any thing at all." PP I 23 130 21
"I never can be thankful, Mr. Bennet, for any thing about PP I 23 130 24
"To oblige you, I would try to believe almost any thing, PP II 1 135 13
Mr. Darcy before they had known any thing of the matter. PP II 1 138 30
Every thing, however, went on smoothly, and was finally PP II 4 151 1
the laurel hedge, every thing declared they were arriving. PP II 5 155 3
But though every thing seemed neat and comfortable, she PP II 5 156 4
When Mr. Collins said any thing of which his wife might PP II 5 156 4
and convenient; and every thing was fitted up and arranged PP II 5 157 5
Scarcely any thing was talked of the whole day or next PP II 6 160 4
to the rest, there is no occasion for any thing more. PP II 6 160 6
all; told her how every thing ought to be regulated in so PP II 6 163 15
I never heard of such a thing. PP II 6 164 28
Mr. Collins was employed in agreeing to every thing her PP II 6 166 41
glad to see them; any thing was a welcome relief to him at PP II 8 172 3
the privilege of hearing you, can think any thing wanting. PP II 8 176 26
her marrying Mr. Collins as the wisest thing she ever did. PP II 9 178 15
Any thing beyond the very neighbourhood of Longbourn, I PP II 9 179 20
difficulty of finding any thing to do, which was the more PP II 9 180 28
She supposed, if he meant any thing, he must mean an PP II 10 182 1
you chose, or procuring any thing you had a fancy for?" PP II 10 183 11
to the lady's family, it would be an unpleasant thing." PP II 10 185 26
Neither could any thing be urged against my father, who, PP II 10 187 40
denying that I did every thing in my power to separate my PP II 11 191 15
inclination; by reason, by reflection, by every thing. PP II 11 192 22
impossible to think of any thing else, and totally PP II 12 195 1
Ignorant as you previously were of every thing concerning PP II 12 202 5
For the truth of every thing here related, I can appeal PP II 12 202 5
With a strong prejudice against every thing he might say, PP II 13 204 1
scarcely knowing any thing of the last page or two, put it PP II 13 204 2
She perfectly remembered every thing that had passed in PP II 13 206 5
How differently did every thing now appear in which he was PP II 13 207 6
of his wishes, but his eagerness to grasp at any thing. PP II 13 207 6
with his ways, seen any thing that betrayed him to be PP II 13 207 6
thing that spoke him of irreligious or immoral habits. PP II 13 207 6
gross a violation of every thing right could hardly have PP II 13 208 6
felt depressed beyond any thing she had every known before. PP II 13 209 11
the greatest dislike in the world to that sort of thing.-- PP II 13 211 13
that we have done every thing in our power to prevent your PP II 15 215 2
There is in every thing a most remarkable resemblance of PP II 15 216 6
scheme, and I dare say would hardly cost any thing at all. PP II 16 219 6
Who could about such a nasty little freckled thing?" PP II 16 220 14
never will be able to make both of them good for any thing. PP II 17 225 10
too! and having to relate such a thing to his sister! PP II 17 225 12
One may be continually abusive without saying any thing PP II 17 226 17
But I cannot find out that Jane saw any thing of him in PP II 17 227 27
at the dulness of every thing around them, threw a real PP II 19 237 3
call him proud; but I am sure I never saw any thing of it. PP III 1 249 38
most unfortunate, the most ill-judged thing in the world! PP III 1 252 54
in defiance of every thing, she was still dear to him. PP III 1 253 55
to be infinitely superior to any thing they had expected. PP III 1 257 67
spots in its environs, to think of any thing else. PP III 1 258 76
surprise in her uncle and aunt, as made every thing worse. PP III 2 260 2
Neither had any thing occurred in the intelligence of PP III 2 264 14
I never could perceive any thing extraordinary in them. PP III 3 271 15
house, his fruit, of every thing but himself; yet PP III 3 272 20
can I suppose her so lost to every thing?--impossible. PP III 4 275 5
assistance would be every thing in the world; he will PP III 4 276 5
Her power was sinking; every thing must sink under such a PP III 4 278 19
was soon lost to every thing else; and, after a pause of PP III 4 278 20
my absence, nor have I any thing to plead in excuse of my PP III 4 278 20
Would to heaven that any thing could be either said or PP III 4 278 20
every thing relating to their journey was speedily settled. PP III 4 280 26
"But can you think that Lydia is so lost to every thing PP III 5 283 9
She has been doing every thing in her power by thinking PP III 5 284 10
either side; and had any thing of the kind been PP III 5 285 18
asking whether any thing had been heard of the fugitives. PP III 5 286 23
"But now that my dear uncle is come, I hope every thing PP III 5 286 24
girl to do such a thing, if she had been well looked after. PP III 5 287 35
and every thing about it, which I have not already heard. PP III 5 290 45
46
Had they no apprehension of any thing before the elopement PP III 5 290 45
Denny denied knowing any thing of their plan, and would PP III 5 290 48
and try if any thing could be made out from them. PP III 5 293 69
Colonel Forster will, I dare say, do every thing in his PP III 6 295 6
These are conditions, which, considering every thing, I PP III 7 302 14
I shall write again as soon as any thing more is PP III 7 303 14
thousand pounds, or any thing like it, has been advanced. PP III 7 304 35
I knew how it would be--I knew he would manage every thing. PP III 7 306 44
we have ever had any thing from him, except a few presents. PP III 7 306 47
Girls, can I do any thing for you in Meryton? PP III 7 307 49
never heard nor saw any thing of which she chose to be PP III 9 316 8
see the ring, and then I bowed and smiled like any thing." PP III 9 316 8
"I should like it beyond any thing!" said her mother. PP III 9 317 14

He did every thing best in the world; and she was sure he PP III 9 318 20
Not one party, or scheme, or any thing. PP III 9 319 25
Every thing being settled between them, Mr. Darcy's next PP III 10 323 2
I believe I have now told you every thing. PP III 10 325 2
with a nice little pair of ponies, would be the very thing. PP III 10 325 2
restoration of Lydia, her character, every thing to him. PP III 10 326 3
to be sure, it would have been such a thing for me! PP III 10 328 28
"It is no such thing. PP III 11 331 12
I am glad of one thing, that he comes alone; because we PP III 11 332 17
"I wish I could say any thing to comfort you," replied PP III 11 333 29
not answer without confusion, said scarcely any thing. PP III 11 335 43
of her father, or the place where she lived, or any thing. PP III 11 336 49
"It is a delightful thing, to be sure, to have a daughter PP III 11 336 51
them a year ago, every thing, she was persuaded, would be PP III 11 337 54
she did not think any thing less than two courses, could PP III 11 338 60
at times, have given any thing to be privileged to tell PP III 12 340 13
I think every thing has passed off uncommonly well, I PP III 12 342 28
Bingley was every thing that was charming, except the PP III 13 345 18
declined eating any thing; and then rising up, said to PP III 14 352 16
17

"I have said no such thing. PP III 14 358 68
a peculiar way, with every thing the heart of mortal can PP III 15 362 15
Busy to know any thing about it, they found at last, on PP III 16 370 35
a case, but his reliance on mine, made every thing easy. PP III 16 371 45
I was obliged to confess one thing, which for a time, and PP III 16 371 45
She coloured as she spoke; but neither that, nor any thing PP III 17 372 1
The evening passed quietly, unmarked by any thing PP III 17 372 2
Oh, Lizzy! do any thing rather than marry without PP III 17 373 11
Let me know every thing that I am to know, without delay. PP III 17 373 15
never dare refuse any thing, which he condescended to ask. PP III 17 376 35
And so, Darcy did every thing; made up the match, gave the PP III 17 377 39
these violent young lovers carry every thing their own way. PP III 17 377 39
Every thing was too recent for gaiety, but the evening PP III 17 377 41
there was no longer any thing material to be dreaded, and PP III 17 377 41
Every thing that is charming! PP III 17 378 43
me hope, and I was determined at once to know every thing." PP III 18 381 14
drew him oftener from home than any thing else could do. PP III 19 385 2
her; and in spite of every thing, was not wholly without PP III 19 386 6
a want of almost every thing else, as could not but MP I 1 4 2
propriety of doing every thing one could by way of MP I 1 6 6
Norris; "you are every thing that is generous and MP I 1 7 8
the necessaries of life, than do an ungenerous thing. MP I 1 7 8
substituted, every thing was considered as settled, and MP I 1 8 9
mention of such a thing she was sure would distract him. MP I 1 9 10
and every thing to hope for her, from the association." MP I 1 10 14
its being a most difficult thing, encouraged him to hope MP I 1 11 18
and praise, to have any thing like natural shyness, and MP I 2 12 3
idea of its being a wicked thing for her not to be happy. MP I 2 13 4
about any thing in her lesson that he could explain? MP I 2 15 10
Did she, in short, want any thing he could possibly get MP I 2 15 10
thing there, and be sure of having the room to ourselves." MP I 2 16 15
Did you ever hear any thing so stupid?" MP I 2 18 23
as well as in every thing else, and therefore you must MP I 2 19 27
But I must tell you another thing of Fanny, so odd and so MP I 2 19 28
In every thing but disposition, they were admirably taught. MP I 2 19 30
guided in every thing important by Sir Thomas, and in MP I 2 19 31
harm in the poor little thing--and always found her very MP I 2 20 31
every thing that could satisfy his anxiety. MP I 2 20 33
any thing at all promising in their situation or conduct. MP I 2 21 34
effect than any thing he had yet been able to say or do. MP I 3 23 2
In the fulness of his belief that such a thing must be, he MP I 3 24 7
of living with her aunt with any thing like satisfaction. MP I 3 25 17
"It has every thing else in its favour. MP I 3 26 23
I love this house and every thing in it. MP I 3 26 24
"Every thing--my situation--my foolishness and awkwardness. MP I 3 26 28
present occasion, but as a thing to be carefully avoided. MP I 3 28 38
Fanny live with me! the last thing in the world for me MP I 3 28 42
Me! a poor helpless, forlorn widow, unfit for any thing, MP I 3 28 42
Sure Sir Thomas could not seriously expect such a thing! MP I 3 28 42
He could not but wonder at her refusing to do any thing MP I 3 30 57
every thing at Mansfield went on for some time as usual. MP I 3 31 58
she naturally became every thing to Lady Bertram during MP I 4 35 6
seemed with him but one thing to be done, and that "Fanny MP I 4 36 7
that some steady old thing might be found among the MP I 4 36 7
She had not supposed before, that any thing could ever MP I 4 37 8
She regarded her cousin as an example of every thing good MP I 4 37 8
uncertainty in which every thing was then involved, MP I 4 38 9
hopes of settling every thing to his entire satisfaction, MP I 4 40 14
To any thing like a permanence of abode, or limitation of MP I 4 41 16
Grant immediately gave them credit for every thing else. MP I 4 41 17
can persuade him into any thing of the sort, it will be a MP I 4 42 21
thing which Miss Crawford's habits made her likely to feel. MP I 5 47 27
and found almost every thing in his favour, a park, a real MP I 5 48 28
immediately up to every thing--and perhaps when one has MP I 5 49 32
That is worse than any thing--quite disgusting!" MP I 5 50 39
I had not a suspicion that I could be doing any thing MP I 5 51 40
see Compton," said he, "it is the most complete thing! MP I 6 53 2
"It wants improvement, ma'am, beyond any thing. MP I 6 53 4
I would have every thing done in the best style, and made MP I 6 53 9
Such a place as Sotherton Court deserves every thing that MP I 6 53 9
For my own part, if I had any thing within the fiftieth MP I 6 53 9
It would be too ridiculous for me to attempt any thing MP I 6 53 9
He could hardly ever get out, poor man, to enjoy any thing, MP I 6 54 9
I would have every thing as complete as possible in the MP I 6 57 31
most impossible thing in the world, had offended all the MP I 6 58 37
London maxim, that every thing is to be got with money, I MP I 6 58 39
Bath seems full, and every thing as usual. MP I 6 59 43
"Do you know any thing of my cousin's captain?" said MP I 6 60 48
"You are fond of the sort of thing?" said Julia. MP I 6 61 55
the trouble of writing any thing worth reading, to his MP I 7 64 10
have a listener, and every thing was soon in a fair train. MP I 7 64 12
in harmony; and as every thing will turn to account when MP I 7 65 13
Every thing answered; it was all gaiety and good-humour, MP I 7 70 30
Poor thing! MP I 7 72 44
any occasion, but really I cannot do every thing at once. MP I 7 73 53
His own forgetfulness of her was worse than any thing MP I 7 74 58
that the properest thing to be done, was for him to walk MP I 8 75 1
It was hardly possible indeed that any thing else should MP I 8 75 2
because it was her own, than from any thing else. MP I 8 79 23
She felt that she had arranged every thing extremely well, MP I 8 79 23
who sat by her; in every thing but a value for Edmund, MP I 8 80 31
Her eye was eagerly taking in every thing within her reach; MP I 8 82 35
portraits, no longer any thing to any body but Mrs. MP I 9 84 3
while Fanny, to whom every thing was almost as interesting MP I 9 85 3
delighted to connect any thing with history already known, MP I 9 85 3
it is a formidable thing, and what nobody likes: and if MP I 9 87 15
supposing it a frequent thing, that is to say, a weakness MP I 9 87 16
It was the very thing of all others to be wished, it was MP I 10 97 4
"It is undoubtedly the best thing we can do now, as we are MP I 10 98 5
whether she had seen any thing of Miss Crawford and Edmund. MP I 10 101 33
At first he scarcely said any thing; his looks only MP I 10 101 33
of any thing useful with regard to the object of the day. MP I 10 104 51
"It is the same sort of thing," said Fanny, after a short MP I 11 109 18
to be in the army, and nobody sees any thing wrong in that. MP I 11 109 18
It has every thing in its favour; heroism, danger, bustle, MP I 11 109 19
palate consulted in every thing, who will not stir a MP I 11 111 28
than he would if he had been any thing but a clergyman." MP I 11 112 30
Mansfield, without any thing but pleasure in view, and his MP I 12 114 2
Every thing returned into the same channel as before his MP I 12 115 4
Fanny was the only one of the party who found any thing to MP I 12 115 5
so properly happy, so well suited, and so much the thing! MP I 12 118 16
"It is not a settled thing, ma'am, yet.-- MP I 12 118 21
in spite of every thing, could hardly help laughing at.-- MP I 12 119 22
It raises my spleen more than any thing, to have the MP I 12 120 26
as to oblige one to do the very thing--whatever it be! MP I 12 120 26
I feel as if I could be any thing or every thing, as if I MP I 13 123 6
But one good thing I have just ascertained. MP I 13 125 14
father's room, is the very thing we could have desired, if MP I 13 125 14
more than injudicious, to attempt any thing of the kind. MP I 13 125 17
delicate one, considering every thing, extremely delicate." MP I 13 125 17
"You take up a thing so seriously! as if we were going to MP I 13 125 18
my father; and for any thing of the acting, spouting, MP I 13 126 25
"It was a very different thing.-- MP I 13 127 26
"For every thing of that nature, I will be answerable,"-- MP I 13 127 29
is employed, every thing will be right with Sir Thomas.-- MP I 13 127 31
we had better do any thing than be altogether by the ears." MP I 13 128 37
mad, that could see any thing to censure in a plan like MP I 13 128 38
purport of the message than on any thing else. MP I 13 129 39
as any thing pursued by youth and zeal could hold out. MP I 14 130 2
gamester, presented any thing that could satisfy even MP I 14 130 3
Any thing but that, my dear Tom. MP I 14 131 3
play, but every thing of higher consequence was against it. MP I 14 131 4
the greater our credit in making any thing of it. MP I 14 131 5
part, but the sort of thing I should not dislike, and as I MP I 14 132 7
before, I am determined to take any thing and do my best. MP I 14 132 7
Maria as willing to do any thing; when Julia, meaning like MP I 14 133 8
bent against every thing humorous, let her take Cottager's MP I 14 134 14
be impossible to make any thing of it fit for your sister, MP I 14 134 15
all the morning, knew any thing of the matter; but when he MP I 15 138 2
and it is so useful to have any thing of a model!-- MP I 15 139 6
"Do not act any thing improper, my dear," said Lady MP I 15 140 16
and if we are so very nice, we shall never act any thing." MP I 15 141 21
"I was just going to say the very same thing," said Mrs. MP I 15 141 22
says, if there is any thing a little too warm (and it is MP I 15 141 22
is, if every thing went well--I shall be sorry to be an MP I 15 144 38
I could not act any thing if you were to give me the world. MP I 15 145 46
have no objection to any thing that you all think eligible. MP I 15 148 59
She could go there after any thing unpleasant below, and MP I 16 151 2
Every thing was a friend, or bore her thoughts to a friend; MP I 16 152 2
"There is but one thing to be done, Fanny. MP I 16 154 10
"No, I cannot think of any thing else." MP I 16 155 19
There was no longer any thing to disturb them in their MP I 17 158 1
in the complaisance of the moment, to promise any thing. MP I 17 158 2
she had no share in any thing; she might go or stay, she MP I 17 159 6
She could almost think any thing would have been MP I 17 160 6
take her share in any thing that brought cheerfulness to MP I 17 161 9
been nobody to put him in the way of doing any thing yet." MP I 17 161 14
Every thing seems to depend upon Sir Thomas's return." MP I 17 162 15
Every thing was now in a regular train; theatre, actors, MP I 18 164 1
Mrs. Grant spoilt every thing by laughing, that Edmund was MP I 18 164 2
it was misery to have any thing to do with Mr. Rushworth, MP I 18 164 2
you think there is any thing so very fine in all this? MP I 18 165 3
As to his ever making any thing tolerable of them, nobody MP I 18 166 4
not perceive that any thing of the kind was necessary, and MP II 1 177 5
his death were to be the thing unfolded; and was now MP II 1 180 10
bustle without having any thing to bustle about, and MP II 1 180 10
of soup would be a much better thing for you than tea. MP II 1 180 10
days, but there has been no attempting any thing since. MP II 1 181 16
He was gone before any thing had been said to prepare him MP II 1 181 17
Crawford's heart, and caring little for any thing else.-- MP II 1 182 19
so often encouraged the sort of thing in us formerly. MP II 1 184 26
of affairs; relating every thing with so blind an interest MP II 1 184 27
It is having too much of a good thing. MP II 1 186 33
and saying scarcely any thing, he did his best towards MP II 1 186 35
You will find Fanny every thing you could wish." MP II 2 187 1
The reproof of an immediate conclusion of every thing, the MP II 2 187 2
thing you can imagine, I was quite in an agony about him. MP II 2 189 5
the removal of every thing appertaining to the play; he MP II 2 194 21
could he regret any thing but the exclusion of the Grants. MP II 3 196 2
there would certainly be every thing else in her favour. MP II 3 201 22
very happy to think any thing of his daughter's MP II 3 201 22
In every thing else the etiquette of the day might stand MP II 3 203 29
match--she had done every thing--and no one would have MP II 3 203 30
she was doing the kindest thing by Fanny, and giving her MP II 4 205 2
never thought of as any thing, or capable of becoming any MP II 4 208 12
or capable of becoming any thing; and now it is converted MP II 4 208 12
ever aspired to a shrubbery or any thing of the kind." MP II 4 209 15
quite unequal to surmising or soliciting any thing more. MP II 4 210 20
"I mean to be too rich to lament or to feel any thing of MP II 4 213 36
"I cannot intend any thing which it must be so completely MP II 4 213 39
in no situation to do any thing for you, or to mortify you MP II 4 213 40
I must look down upon any thing contented with obscurity MP II 4 214 42
I am glad to hear you have any thing so good in the house. MP II 4 215 49
will consider it a right thing by Mrs. Grant, as well as MP II 5 217 9
in the case, could any thing in my opinion be more natural. MP II 5 218 18
"Yes, ma'am, I should not think of any thing else." MP II 5 221 33
Dr. Grant, and of every thing, and all together between Mr. MP II 5 223 48
that in my opinion, every thing had gone quite far enough." MP II 5 225 58
Seven hundred a year is a fine thing for a younger brother; MP II 5 226 61
what had passed to be in a humour for any thing but music. MP II 5 227 68
of expression enough when she has any thing to express. MP II 6 229 5
proceeds from any thing but your own idleness and folly." MP II 6 230 6
Fraternal love, sometimes almost every thing, is at others MP II 6 235 18
the opinion of all who had hearts to value any thing good. MP II 6 235 19
can reconcile me to any thing"--and saw, with lively MP II 6 235 19
thing that could deserve or promise well. MP II 6 236 21
With spirits, courage, and curiosity up to any thing, MP II 6 237 23
He was in high spirits, doing every thing with happy ease, MP II 7 240 9
moved, I grant you; but I am not aware of any thing else. MP II 7 241 22
therefore, you cannot but give it, if you do any thing. MP II 7 243 27
possibly engage in any thing of the sort at Thornton Lacey, MP II 7 244 30
to the first Lord than any thing else," was William's only MP II 7 246 35
sure he will do every thing in his power to get you made. MP II 7 250 55
she had been present than remembered any thing about her. MP II 7 251 62
an occasion for such a thing, you would be tempted to give MP II 8 252 2
She must be the doer of every thing; Lady Bertram would of MP II 8 253 4
The ball was now a settled thing, and before the evening a MP II 8 254 8
the evening a proclaimed thing to all whom it concerned. MP II 8 254 8
perfect in disinterested attachment as in every thing else. MP II 8 255 10
and taste, made every thing easy by her suggestions, and MP II 8 257 15
tried to make every thing agreeable by her encouragement. MP II 8 257 15
for her sake, saying every thing she could think of to MP II 8 258 15
"Oh! this is beautiful indeed! this is the very thing, MP II 9 262 8
than the having any thing returned on our hands, which we MP II 9 263 12
It was the only thing approaching to a letter which she MP II 9 265 19
To her, the hand-writing itself, independent of any thing MP II 9 265 19
was saying at once every thing in favour of its happiness MP II 9 266 21
the fatigue of such a journey, to think of any thing else. MP II 9 266 21
at last to think every thing an evil belonging to the ball, MP II 9 267 22
am very sorry that any thing has occurred to distress you. MP II 9 268 30
"One thing more. MP II 9 269 36
Do not tell me any thing now, which hereafter you may be MP II 9 269 36
incapable of any thing else, though perhaps some might not. MP II 9 270 39
I cannot be afraid of hearing any thing you wish to say. MP II 9 270 39
Now, every thing was smiling. MP II 9 270 40
for each other by every thing real and imaginary--and put MP II 9 271 40
she felt only one thing; and her eyes, bright as they had MP II 10 274 9
in a flutter that forbad its fixing on any thing serious. MP II 10 275 10
the general arrangements and see how every thing was done. MP II 10 275 10
every thing else;--education and manners she owed to him. MP II 10 276 13
odd, or thought her any thing rather than insensible of MP II 10 277 20
consulted, or to have any thing take place at all in the MP II 10 280 32
in spite of every thing, that a ball was indeed delightful. MP II 10 280 33
and said and thought every thing by William, that was due MP II 11 282 3

Context	Work	Vol	Ch	Page	Line
Every thing that a considerate parent ought to feel was	MP	II	11	285	10
for her use; and every thing that an affectionate mother	MP	II	11	285	10
want of it to derive any thing but irritation from	MP	II	11	285	15
He could not have devised any thing more likely to raise	MP	II	11	286	15
He would have sent you a description of every thing and	MP	II	11	288	24
It is a regular thing.	MP	II	11	288	28
The impossibility of not doing every thing in the world to	MP	II	12	296	30
before, and that every thing he had done for William, was	MP	II	13	301	7
severely resentful of any thing that injured only herself;	MP	II	13	301	7
himself, hand, fortune, every thing to her acceptance.	MP	II	13	301	7
She was feeling, thinking, trembling, about every thing;--	MP	II	13	302	10
She opened her note immediately, glad to have any thing to	MP	II	13	303	14
she could hardly eat any thing; and when Sir Thomas good	MP	II	13	304	16
the way of getting every thing very cheap--but she was	MP	II	13	305	19
him a commission for any thing else that is worth having.	MP	II	13	305	25
There was every thing in the world against their being	MP	II	13	305	26
Every thing natural, probable, reasonable was against it;	MP	II	13	305	26
such points--who was every thing to every body, and seemed	MP	II	13	305	26
any thing of a serious nature in such a quarter?	MP	II	13	306	26
Every thing might be possible rather than serious	MP	II	13	306	26
any thing so imperfectly understood was most distressing.	MP	II	13	307	30
not to appear to think any thing really intended, she	MP	II	13	307	30
					31
but I am so unequal to any thing of the sort, that I hope	MP	II	13	307	31
without her being obliged to know any thing of the matter.	MP	III	1	311	3
but there should be moderation in every thing.--	MP	III	1	312	12
and shewn you every thing placed on a basis the most	MP	III	1	314	16
How could Mr. Crawford say such a thing?	MP	III	1	315	19
certain of his meaning any thing seriously, but I did not	MP	III	1	315	19
to you, with every thing to recommend him; not merely	MP	III	1	315	27
very, very different from any thing that I had imagined.	MP	III	1	318	39
The past, present, future, every thing was terrible.	MP	III	1	321	46
I do not want to add to any thing you may now be feeling,	MP	III	1	321	47
Any thing might be bearable rather than such reproaches.	MP	III	1	322	49
almost any thing that might save her from her aunt Norris.	MP	III	1	322	50
thing which caught her eye was a fire lighted and burning.	MP	III	1	322	51
thing would soon be as if no such subject had existed.	MP	III	1	324	59
Every thing was said that could encourage, every	MP	III	2	329	13
can, dismissing the recollection of every thing unpleasant.	MP	III	2	331	16
he would have expected any thing rather than a look of	MP	III	3	334	2
trusted that every thing would work out a happy conclusion.	MP	III	3	335	6
A sermon, good in itself, is no rare thing.	MP	III	3	341	28
hands; who can say any thing new or striking, any thing	MP	III	3	341	28
thing new or striking, any thing that rouses the attention,	MP	III	3	341	28
was trying, by every thing in the power of her modest	MP	III	3	342	32
Is there any thing in my present intreaty that you do not	MP	III	3	342	36
any thing like it--but beyond what one fancies might be.	MP	III	3	344	41
It proves him, in short, every thing that I had been used	MP	III	4	350	30
he will make you happy; but you will make him every thing."	MP	III	4	351	32
to anything!--fancying every thing too much for you!	MP	III	4	351	34
depended upon her seeing every thing in so just a light.	MP	III	4	351	35
					36
right to every thing he may wish for, at the first moment.	MP	III	4	352	40
persuade; but that every thing should be left to	MP	III	5	356	2
feel it quite impossible to do any thing but love you."	MP	III	5	359	9
who can think of him with any thing like indifference.	MP	III	5	362	16
Every thing shall take its course.	MP	III	5	362	18
she thought she could resign herself to almost every thing.	MP	III	5	365	34
Quite unlike his usual self, he scarcely said any thing.	MP	III	5	365	35
she convinced that every thing was now in a fairer train	MP	III	6	366	4
The thing was good in itself, and could not be done at a	MP	III	6	368	9
and arranging every thing there, without wretchedness.--	MP	III	6	370	12
set herself very steadily against admitting any such thing.	MP	III	6	371	14
She knew so much already, that she must know every thing.	MP	III	6	373	26
Fanny, when I have any thing worth writing about; any	MP	III	6	373	26
worth writing about; any thing to say, that I think you	MP	III	6	373	26
Every thing supplied an amusement to the high glee of	MP	III	7	375	2
however, could not stay long enough to suspect any thing.	MP	III	7	378	10
with you, and here every thing comes upon me at once."	MP	III	7	378	10
Her son answered cheerfully, telling her that every thing	MP	III	7	378	11
the walls, brought every thing so close to her, that ,	MP	III	7	382	28
it as a proof of any thing more than their being for the	MP	III	7	383	31
servant, brought in every thing necessary for the meal;	MP	III	7	383	32
for setting off; every thing was ready, William took leave,	MP	III	7	384	36
Every thing in that quarter failed her, except William's	MP	III	8	388	2
Every thing where she now was was in full contrast to it.	MP	III	8	391	10
by the prevalence of every thing opposite to them here.	MP	III	8	391	10
and distance from every thing that had been wont to	MP	III	9	393	1
opinion; and new as any thing like an office of authority	MP	III	9	396	6
She became a subscriber--amazed at being any thing in	MP	III	9	398	9
been some time, and every thing there was rising in	MP	III	10	404	15
in the vicinity of every thing so dear--for as to any	MP	III	10	405	19
and pulling every thing about as she chose, were what	MP	III	10	407	23
for a minute; and every thing looked so beautiful under	MP	III	11	409	6
Thomas cannot settle every thing for coming himself, or	MP	III	11	410	16
Is there any thing I can do for you in town?	MP	III	11	411	20
directly, and put every thing at once on such a footing as	MP	III	11	412	20
suffice it, that every thing was just as it ought to be,	MP	III	12	416	2
good), one very material thing I had to say from Henry and	MP	III	12	416	3
and to leave every thing in greater suspense than ever.	MP	III	12	417	4
of her's, though, every thing considered, she thought he	MP	III	12	418	4
great admiration of every thing said or done in her	MP	III	12	419	8
That a girl so capable of being made, every thing good,	MP	III	12	419	9
supporter of every thing mercenary and ambitious, provided	MP	III	13	421	2
creature, capable of every thing noble, and I am ready to	MP	III	13	421	2
Were it a decided thing, an actual refusal, I hope I	MP	III	13	422	2
Considering every thing, I think a letter will be	MP	III	13	422	2
and where the mind is any thing short of perfect decision,	MP	III	13	423	2
of its being a very happy thing, and a great blessing to	MP	III	13	428	15
It was weeks since she had heard any thing of Miss	MP	III	14	433	12
She had a rule to apply to, which settled every thing.	MP	III	14	436	15
which hardly any thing would have seemed to justify.	MP	III	14	436	15
correspondent, the hope of every thing she was wishing for.	MP	III	14	436	16
it was not likely that any thing unpleasant should have	MP	III	15	438	4
her a totally different thing in a town and in the country.	MP	III	15	439	9
must be spoken to, Susan prepared, every thing got ready.	MP	III	15	443	25
how to find any thing to hold Susan's clothes, because	MP	III	15	444	26
offices of Rebecca, every thing was rationally and duly	MP	III	15	444	27
quieted, stupified, indifferent to every thing that passed.	MP	III	16	448	2
and an indigent niece, and every thing most odious.	MP	III	16	448	3
at this time, for every thing like comfort; Edmund trying	MP	III	16	449	4
in return, was every thing that could be done for her.	MP	III	16	449	5
He was doing all in his power to quiet every thing, with	MP	III	16	450	9
Every thing was by that time public beyond a hope.	MP	III	16	450	10
He called it a bad thing, done in the worst manner, and at	MP	III	16	452	13
success; and who in every thing but this despicable	MP	III	16	452	15
must be opened, and every thing told--no one else in the	MP	III	16	453	17
will tell you every thing, and then have done for ever.	MP	III	16	455	19
as I had done, that any thing could occur to make me	MP	III	16	457	30
but still it was a sort of thing which he never could get	MP	III	16	460	31
of knowing, must have been happy in spite of every thing.	MP	III	17	461	2
time will do almost every thing, and though little comfort	MP	III	17	461	4
It had appeared to her the only thing to be done.	MP	III	17	467	18
and happier nerves made every thing easy to her there.--	MP	III	17	472	31
in her eyes, as every thing else, within the view and	MP	III	17	473	33
Taylor had done as sad a thing for herself as for them,	E	I	1	7	10
"Dear Emma bears every thing so well," said her father.	E	I	1	11	36
would never marry again, may comfort me for any thing."	E	I	1	11	39
it would be a very good thing for Miss Taylor if Mr.	E	I	1	12	42
matters, it might not have come to any thing after all.	E	I	1	13	43
That will be a much better thing.	E	I	1	14	47
with you entirely that it will be a much better thing.	E	I	1	14	48
made him think every thing due to her in return for the	E	I	2	15	3
old lady, almost past every thing but tea and quadrille.	E	I	3	21	4
an establishment, or any thing which professed, in long	E	I	3	21	5
She was not struck by any thing remarkably clever in Miss	E	I	3	23	10
by the appearance of every thing in so superior a style to	E	I	3	23	10
the credit of doing every thing well and attentively, with	E	I	3	24	11
rather sorry to see any thing put on it; and while his	E	I	3	24	12
his visitors to every thing, his care for their health	E	I	3	24	12
Smith's intimacy at Hartfield was soon a settled thing.	E	I	4	26	1
It was quite a different sort of thing--a sentiment	E	I	4	26	2
there was nothing to be done; for Harriet every thing.	E	I	4	27	2
She was ready to tell every thing in her power, but on	E	I	4	27	3
of them--and in every thing else he was so very obliging!	E	I	4	28	6
believed he was very clever, and understood every thing.	E	I	4	28	6
a good deal--but not what you would think any thing of.	E	I	4	29	10
to impossible that he should have realised any thing yet."	E	I	4	30	20
thing; and Mrs. Martin talks of taking a boy another year."	E	I	4	30	21
to that station by every thing within your own power, or	E	I	4	30	22
the market to think of any thing else--which is just as it	E	I	4	34	40
Emma and Harriet Smith, but I think it a bad thing."	E	I	5	36	1
"A bad thing!	E	I	5	36	2
Do you really think it a bad thing?--why so?"	E	I	5	36	2
She will never submit to any thing requiring industry and	E	I	5	37	7
never remember Emma's omitting to do any thing I wished."	E	I	5	37	8
herself, and looks upon Emma as knowing every thing.	E	I	5	38	15
How can Emma imagine she has any thing to learn herself,	E	I	5	38	15
Can you imagine any thing nearer perfect beauty than Emma	E	I	5	39	18
It would not be a bad thing for her to be very much in	E	I	5	41	29
any thing wanting which a little time would not add.	E	I	6	42	1
The only thing I do not thoroughly like is, that she seems	E	I	6	48	36
"You, sir, may say any thing," cried Mr. Elton; "but I	E	I	6	48	39
The next thing wanted was to get the picture framed; and	E	I	6	48	40
man is determined not to lose any thing for want of asking.	E	I	7	50	2
Harriet, that every thing considered, I think one of his	E	I	7	51	5
of your not being intelligible, which is the first thing.	E	I	7	51	11
should not be hesitating--it is a very serious thing.--	E	I	7	52	20
of being intimate with you for any thing in the world."	E	I	7	54	26
that is quite a different thing from--and you know, though	E	I	7	54	30
Nobody cares for a letter; the thing is, to be always	E	I	7	55	34
me as doing a very rude thing, I shall take Emma's advice	E	I	8	57	3
I can think of but one thing--who is in love with her?	E	I	8	59	23
He told me every thing; his circumstances and plans, and	E	I	8	59	27
"Nonsense! a man does not imagine any such thing.	E	I	8	60	34
young and too simple to have acquired any thing herself.	E	I	8	61	38
at your knowing so little of Emma as to say any such thing.	E	I	8	62	39
at present recollect any thing of the riddle kind; but he	E	I	9	70	6
"Oh no! he had never written, hardly ever, any thing of	E	I	9	71	9
I never saw any thing so hard.	E	I	9	72	17
It will give you every thing that you want--consideration,	E	I	9	74	20
It is so much beyond any thing I deserve.	E	I	9	74	22
"It is a sort of thing which nobody could have expected.	E	I	9	74	24
You understand every thing.	E	I	9	76	28
a twelvemonth, I could never have made any thing like it."	E	I	9	76	28
"It is one thing," said she, presently--her cheeks in a	E	I	9	76	35
else, and if there is any thing to say, to sit down and	E	I	9	76	35
He loves any thing of the sort, and especially any thing	E	I	9	77	45
Have you got any thing fresh?"	E	I	9	78	49
She read it to him, just as he liked to have any thing	E	I	9	78	51
There will not be time for any thing."	E	I	9	79	62
If he were, every thing else must give way; but otherwise	E	I	9	81	78
it would be a different thing! but I never have been in	E	I	10	84	15
so apt to tell every thing relative to every body about me,	E	I	10	84	16
How trifling they make every thing else appear!-- I feel	E	I	10	87	25
her, was the most natural thing in the world, or would	E	I	10	88	33
consoling reflection; "any thing interests between those	E	I	10	89	35
thing will serve as introduction to what is near the heart.	E	I	10	89	35
ribband or string, or any thing just to keep my boot on."	E	I	10	89	37
and endeavouring to make every thing appear to advantage.	E	I	10	89	38
Still, however, though every thing had not been	E	I	10	90	41
herself expect--that any thing beyond occasional,	E	I	11	91	1
could sometimes act an ungracious, or say a severe thing.	E	I	11	93	5
of any body who proposed such a thing to any body else."	E	I	11	96	25
upon family affection, or any thing that home affords."	E	I	11	96	26
if requisite, to do every thing for the good of the other.	E	I	12	99	14
brother ever left him any thing to inquire about, his	E	I	12	100	16
Emma could not suppose any such thing, knowing, as she did,	E	I	12	101	19
It is a dreadful thing to have you forced to live there!--	E	I	12	103	36
it, she had never been able to get any thing tolerable.	E	I	12	105	50
a possible thing in preference to a division of the party.	E	I	13	108	2
habits and inclination being consulted in every thing.	E	I	13	108	4
It was a done thing; Mr. Elton was to go, and never had	E	I	13	111	12
their duties, that any thing gives way to it--and this	E	I	13	111	13
What a strange thing love is! he can see ready wit in	E	I	13	111	13
her fair friend, the last thing before he prepared for the	E	I	13	111	14
a most agreeable fellow; I could not do such a thing.	E	I	13	113	26
which tells man, in every thing given to his view or his	E	I	13	113	26
which I did the very last thing before I returned to dress,	E	I	13	114	31
continued he, "and every thing in the greatest comfort.	E	I	13	115	43
oddities, or of any thing else unpleasant, and enjoy all	E	I	14	117	2
"I am sorry there should be any thing like doubt in the	E	I	14	120	12
which I imagine to be the most certain thing in the world."	E	I	14	121	15
It is what we happily have never known any thing of; but	E	I	14	121	17
try to conceal any thing relative to the Churchills from	E	I	14	122	18
Neither wine nor conversation was any thing to him; and	E	I	14	122	18
is so very unreasonable; and every thing gives way to her."	E	I	14	123	23
to whom she owes every thing, while she exercises	E	I	14	123	24
have the power of directly saying any thing to the purpose.	E	I	15	125	6
we do come to any thing very bad, I can get out and walk.	E	I	15	127	14
home; and it is not the sort of thing that gives me cold."	E	I	15	127	14
most extraordinary sort of thing in the world, for in	E	I	15	127	15
the world, for in general every thing does give you cold.	E	I	15	127	15
Mr. Elton, my astonishment is much beyond any thing I can	E	I	15	130	30
Every thing that I have said or done, for many weeks past,	E	I	15	131	31
"No, sir," cried Emma, "it confesses no such thing.	E	I	15	131	34
were wanted to make every thing go well: for Mr. John	E	I	15	132	38
Such an overthrow of every thing she had been wishing for!-	E	I	16	134	1
Such a development of every thing most unwelcome!---	E	I	16	134	1
Harriet into liking the man, I could have born any thing.	E	I	16	134	2
up the idea, she supposed, and made every thing bend to it.	E	I	16	134	3
any thing but grateful respect to her as Harriet's friend.	E	I	16	134	5
but in trade, or any thing to recommend him to notice but	E	I	16	136	9
further service, for any thing was welcome that might	E	I	16	138	16
Mr. Elton's absence just at this time was the very thing	E	I	17	140	3
nobody--and in every thing testifying such an	E	I	17	141	7
Harriet did not consider herself as having any thing to	E	I	17	141	8
care very little for any thing but his own pleasure, from	E	I	18	145	10
"There is one thing, Emma, which a man can always do, if	E	I	18	146	16
that if he turn out any thing like it, he will be the most	E	I	18	150	32
Emma, "you turn every thing to evil. we are both	E	I	18	150	33
apartment, which was every thing to them, the visitors	E	II	1	155	4
chance of my hearing any thing of Miss Fairfax to-day."	E	II	1	159	19
The very thing that we have always been rather afraid of;	E	II	1	160	23
But you see, every thing turns out for the best.	E	II	1	160	23
"Jane caught a bad cold, poor thing! so long ago as the	E	II	1	161	29
I must tell you what an unlucky thing happened to me, as	E	II	1	162	31
for fear of there being any thing in them to distress her.	E	II	1	162	31
his own return to England put any thing in his power.	E	II	2	163	4
place; too lately for any thing to be yet attempted by her	E	II	2	165	8
for the recovery of her health, than on any thing else.	E	II	2	166	10
impossible to feel any thing but compassion and respect;	E	II	2	167	13
from his wife, or of any thing mischievous which her	E	II	2	168	13
and every thing was relapsing much into its usual state.	E	II	2	168	15

If any thing could be more, where all was most, she was E II 2 169 16
on the subject of Weymouth and the Dixons than any thing. E II 2 169 16
If any thing, you are too attentive. E II 3 170 4
trifling presents, of any thing uncommon--now we have E II 3 171 16
17
had every thing they could wish for, I am sure it is us. E II 3 174 31
My dear sir, if there is one thing my mother loves better E II 3 175 39
40
really do not think she cares for any thing but boiled E II 3 177 50
Pork: when we dress the leg it will be another thing. E II 3 177 50
"And so, there she had set, without an idea of any thing E II 3 178 52
did--but I hardly knew where I was, or any thing about it. E II 3 179 52
Oh! Miss Woodhouse, I would rather done any thing than E II 3 179 52
coaches past; and every thing in this world, excepting E II 5 186 1
door, the sight of every thing which had given her so much E II 5 186 2
We shall enjoy him completely; every thing has turned out E II 5 188 7
up to happiness; every thing wore a different air; James E II 5 189 16
far; but in coming home I felt I might do any thing." E II 5 190 25
that, considering every thing, I had not expected more E II 5 192 30
He was delighted with every thing; admired Hartfield E II 6 196 2
She who could do any thing in Highbury! E II 6 198 5
a mixture would be any thing, or that there would be the E II 6 198 5
"Oh! yes, gloves and every thing. E II 6 200 15
But her account of every thing leaves so much to be E II 6 200 19
ever been any thing but my friend and my dearest friend." E II 6 201 24
hand, to do every thing better than one does oneself!-- E II 6 202 33
She owned that, considering every thing, she was not E II 7 208 9
But the idea of any thing to be done in a moment, was E II 7 209 12
Mr. Weston must be quiet, and every thing deliberately E II 7 209 12
But you will do every thing right. E II 7 210 14
see that every thing were safe in the house, as usual. E II 7 211 22
perhaps may never make any thing of it; and there is poor E II 8 215 16
of music, has not any thing of the nature of an instrument, E II 8 215 16
for any thing of peculiar anxiety to be observable. E II 8 218 37
and thought it the most natural thing in the world. E II 8 219 42
points) he could with time persuade her to any thing. E II 8 221 49
I never saw any thing so outree!-- E II 8 222 56
she:--"one can get near every body, and say every thing. E II 8 222 59
sort of thing that so few men would think of. E II 8 223 63
to do the sort of thing--to do any thing really good- E II 8 223 64
sort of thing--to do any thing really good-natured, useful, E II 8 223 64
"Dear Mrs. Weston, how could you think of such a thing?-- E II 8 224 66
I am amazed that you should think of such a thing." E II 8 224 66
For his own sake, I would not have him do so mad a thing." E II 8 225 72
She might talk on; and if he wanted to say any thing E II 8 226 79
But I do not think it is at all a likely thing for him to E II 8 226 80
at the close of the song, and every thing usual followed. E II 8 227 86
thing was rapidly clearing away, to give proper space. E II 8 229 98
"Those who knew any thing about it, must have felt the E II 9 232 8
Harriet, tempted by every thing and swayed by half a word, E II 9 233 24
"I do not believe any such thing," replied Emma.-- E II 9 234 33
I meant to take them over to John Saunders the first thing E II 9 236 46
one thing, then another, there is no saying what, you know. E II 9 236 46
never known any thing but the greatest attention from them. E II 9 236 46
I say one thing and then I say another, and it passes off. E II 9 237 46
He seems every thing the fondest parent could. . . . E II 9 238 51
William Larkins and said every thing, as you may suppose. E II 9 239 51
master's profit than any thing; but Mrs. Hodges, he said, E II 9 239 51
and be sure not to say any thing to us about it, for Mrs. E II 9 239 51
I would not have Mr. Knightley know any thing about it for E II 9 239 51
a direct answer before he would hear her in any thing else. E II 10 244 36
Can I do any thing for you?" E II 10 244 39
Can I do any thing for you?" E II 10 244 41
Mr. Frank Churchill; I never saw any thing equal to it." E II 10 245 48
Mr. Frank Churchill are hearing every thing that passes. E II 10 245 49
He asked me if he could do any thing" . . . . E II 10 245 52
Jane, "we heard his kind offers, we heard every thing." E II 10 245 53
You must have heard every thing to be sure. E II 10 245 54
'Can I do any thing for you at Kingston?' said he; so I E II 10 245 54
quite laid up; do not let them talk of such a wild thing. E II 11 249 11
tell his father, but that young man is not quite the thing. E II 11 249 11
you against him, but indeed he is not quite the thing!" E II 11 249 11
She knew the importance of it, and said every thing in her E II 11 249 12
too anxious for securing any thing to like to yield. E II 11 250 23
I never heard of such a thing. E II 11 252 30
"there will be plenty of time for talking every thing over. E II 11 252 34
That is a great thing. E II 11 252 35
"I can answer for every thing of that nature, sir, because E II 11 252 36
some little distress; and he, finding every thing perfect. E II 11 253 40
yellow and forlorn than any thing I could have imagined." E II 11 253 41
We never see any thing of it on our club-nights." E II 11 253 42
One thing was wanting to make the prospect of the ball E II 12 257 1
were immediately followed by the overthrow of every thing. E II 12 258 7
When once it had been read, there was no doing any thing, E II 12 259 10
"Ah! that ball!--why did we wait for any thing?--why not E II 12 259 17
I was a right thing to do. E II 12 260 27
I shall hear of every thing that is going on among you. E II 12 261 36
interested in the absent!--she will tell me every thing. E II 12 261 36
Every thing tender and charming was to mark their parting; E II 13 264 1
"He is undoubtedly very much in love--every thing denotes E II 13 265 3
then, it will be a good thing over; for they say every E II 13 265 4
and describing every thing exterior and local that could E II 13 265 5
Such expressions, assisted as they were by every thing E II 13 269 15
being married, you know, it is quite a different thing. E II 14 271 15
meet with any thing at all like what one has left behind. E II 14 273 19
are always pleased with any thing in the same style." E II 14 273 21
without saying any thing of our carriage, we should be E II 14 274 28
society, it is a very bad thing; and that it is much more E II 14 275 30
of taste; but as to any thing else, upon my honour my E II 14 276 36
To those who had no resources it was a different thing; E II 14 276 36
"But every thing of that kind," said Emma, "will soon be E II 14 278 41
I have no idea of that sort of thing. E II 15 283 9
Mrs. Elton's invitations I should have imagined any thing E II 15 286 20
silence, he said, "another thing must be taken into E II 15 286 22
23
would soon shew them how every thing ought to be arranged. E II 16 290 3
You sad girl, how could you do such a thing?-- E II 16 295 30
You look as if you would not do such a thing again." E II 16 295 33
"Oh! she shall not do such a thing again," eagerly E II 16 295 34
"We will not allow her to do such a thing again:"--and E II 16 295 34
The thing is determined, that is (laughing affectedly) as E II 16 296 36
any thing without the concurrence of my Lord and master. E II 16 296 36
the difficulty of procuring exactly the desirable thing." E II 17 299 6
charge to be on the look-out for any thing eligible." E II 17 300 10
you taking up with any thing that may offer, any inferior, E II 17 301 16
"I know you, I know you; you would take up with any thing; E II 17 301 18
in not wishing any thing to be attempted at present for me. E II 17 301 19
thoroughly stopped by any thing till Mr. Woodhouse came E II 17 302 21
22
simplicity of dress,--shew and finery are every thing. E II 17 302 22
black gentleman when any thing is to be done; most likely E II 17 304 27
But it is an excellent thing to have Frank among us again, E II 17 304 27
"Depend on it, Mrs. Churchill does every thing that any E II 18 306 13
You seem shut out from every thing--in the most complete E II 18 307 21
Nobody but yourself could imagine such a thing possible. E II 18 308 25
do not believe I have any thing more to say about the boys; E II 18 311 37
38
every thing is down at full length there we may be sure. E II 18 311 37
38
When did it happen before, or any thing like it? E II 18 311 46
strikes me as a possible thing, Emma, that Henry and John E II 18 312 48
He did not believe it to proceed from any thing that care E III 1 317 6
One good thing was immediately brought to a certainty by E III 1 318 11
Mr. Weston's ball was to be a real thing. E III 1 318 12
May was better for every thing than February. E III 1 318 13
any thing the matter with them, while dear Emma were gone. E III 1 318 13
reached Randall's before dinner, and every thing was safe. E III 2 319 1
They all walked about together, to see that every thing E III 2 319 3
Jane, Jane, look--did you ever see any thing? E III 2 322 19
by Mr. Knightley's not dancing, than by any thing else.-- E III 2 325 32
Any thing else I should be most happy to do, at your E III 2 327 37
the passage, though every thing has been done--one door E III 2 328 45
I never saw any thing equal to the comfort and style-- E III 2 329 45
I am all amazement! could not have supposed any thing!-- E III 2 330 45
It was a very extraordinary thing! E III 3 335 10
It seemed as if every thing united to promise the most E III 3 335 10
Every thing was to take its natural course, however, E III 3 335 11
Did he ever give you any thing?" E III 4 338 7
I must get rid of every thing.-- E III 4 340 26
too much; and against any thing like such an unreserve as E III 4 341 34
in thinking such an attachment no bad thing for her friend. E III 4 342 40
Every thing declared it; his own attentions, his father's E III 5 343 2
I know I do sometimes pop out a thing before I am aware. E III 5 346 16
and then I have let a thing escape me which I should not. E III 5 346 16
for it she never betrayed the least thing in the world. E III 5 346 16
not spoken a word--"I was just going to say the same thing. E III 5 349 24
She would rather busy herself about any thing than speak. E III 5 350 31
He owed it to her, to risk any thing that might be E III 5 350 31
welfare; to encounter any thing, rather than the E III 5 350 31
convinced her that every thing need not be put off. E III 6 352 2
lame carriage-horse threw every thing into sad uncertainty. E III 6 353 6
morning scheme, you know, Knightley; quite a simple thing. E III 6 355 20
Every thing as natural and simple as possible. E III 6 355 20
The thing would be for us all to come on donkies, Jane, E III 6 356 26
I would wish every thing to be as much to your taste as E III 6 356 27
You have hit upon the very thing to please me." E III 6 356 28
lines, ranks, every thing--and Mrs. Elton was wild to have E III 6 359 37
at present engage in any thing, repeating the same motives E III 6 359 37
The heat was excessive; he had never suffered any thing E III 6 363 53
find abundance of every thing in the dining-room--and she E III 6 364 56
I am thwarted in every thing material. E III 6 365 64
"It comes to the same thing. E III 7 369 12
It is the very last thing I would stand the brunt of just E III 7 369 19
Let me hear any thing rather than what you are all E III 7 370 19
"It is a sort of thing," cried Mrs. Elton emphatically, " E III 7 370 20
indeed--quite unheard of--but some ladies say any thing. E III 7 370 22
each of you either one thing very clever, be it prose or E III 7 370 23
or she would not have said such a thing to an old friend." E III 7 371 28
the sort of clever thing that is wanted, and Mr. Weston E III 7 371 35
36
cannot attempt--I am not at all fond of the sort of thing. E III 7 371 37
half way down the hill, and every thing left far behind. E III 7 376 62
She heard Miss Bates's voice, some thing was to be done in E III 8 378 4
is every thing in the world that can make her happy in it. E III 8 382 23
crown, ostler, and every thing of that sort, but still he E III 8 383 29
struck her; one was every thing, the other nothing--and E III 8 384 32
33
with a repetition of every thing that she could venture to E III 8 384 34
Have you any thing to send or say, besides the 'love,' E III 9 385 2
Richmond to throw every thing else into the back-ground. E III 9 387 11
A sudden seizure of a different nature from any thing E III 9 387 11
guidable man, to be persuaded into any thing by his nephew. E III 9 388 13
thing that message could do was tried--but all in vain. E III 9 390 18
Jane would hardly eat any thing:--Mr. Perry recommended E III 9 391 19
nourishing food; but every thing they could command (and E III 9 391 19
being sent back; it was a thing she could not take--and, E III 9 391 20
her saying, that she was not at all in want of any thing." E III 9 391 20
no doubt--putting every thing together--that Jane was E III 9 391 21
not, on this occasion, have found any thing to reprove. E III 9 391 21
her more good than any thing else in the world could do. E III 10 396 42
creature from any thing I had ever seen him before.-- E III 10 399 57
"I am very sure that I never said any thing of either to E III 10 399 62
you to say and look every thing that may set his heart at E III 10 400 65
almost every thing may be fairly said in her favour. E III 10 400 65
and persuasion to think the engagement no very bad thing. E III 10 400 69
it the very best thing that Frank could possibly have done. E III 10 401 69
thing she could offer of assistance or regard be repulsed. E III 11 403 2
Did you ever hear any thing so strange? E III 11 404 6
not immediately say any thing; and when she did speak, it E III 11 405 17
it seems as if such a thing even as this, may have E III 11 407 28
choose me, it will not be any thing so very wonderful." E III 11 411 39
Was it new for any thing in this world to be unequal, E III 11 413 48
as, considering every thing, she thought such a visit E III 12 417 5
her own mind as every thing had so long been, and was very E III 12 418 5
fortunate turn that every thing has taken, and the E III 12 419 8
the only source whence any thing like consolation or E III 12 423 21
indeed--I have had no idea of their meaning any thing.-- E III 13 427 19
disinterestedness; every thing in his favour,--equality of E III 13 428 23
Every thing turns out for his good.-- E III 13 428 23
to ask my opinion of any thing that you may have in E III 13 429 32
that she was every thing herself; that what she had been E III 13 430 38
herself, from whom every thing was due; a separation for E III 14 435 4
any thing he wrote, she was sure she was incapable of it.-- E III 14 436 6
To any thing, every thing--to time, chance, circumstance, E III 14 437 8
I should myself have shrunk from any thing so hasty, and E III 14 440 8
One thing only.-- E III 14 443 8
My Emma, does not every thing serve to prove more and more E III 15 446 15
the first thing to call for more than a word in passing. E III 15 446 19
that she had done a wrong thing in consenting to the E III 15 446 20
Mrs. John Knightley was delighted to be of use; any thing E III 16 451 3
she should attend to any thing Jane might communicate. E III 16 452 7
warmth; there was every thing which her countenance or E III 16 453 8
of what might be said, and impatience to say every thing. E III 16 455 19
They seem not able to do any thing without him.-- E III 16 455 23
I fancy Mr. E. and Knightley have every thing their own E III 16 456 27
could do such a thing by you, of all people in the world! E III 16 458 42
Oh! if you knew how much I love every thing that is E III 16 460 57
I never can call you any thing but 'Mr. Knightley.' E III 17 463 14
Had he said any thing to bear a different construction, I E III 17 464 20
"My Emma, he means no such thing. E III 17 464 21
If any thing could increase her delight, it was perceiving E III 17 468 32
be a Mrs. Knightley to throw cold water on every thing.-- E III 17 469 36
I can hardly imagine that any thing which pleases or E III 18 470 7
now tell me every thing; make this intelligible to me. E III 18 471 19
Could I mention any thing more fit to be done, than to go E III 18 474 30
Every thing would be a pleasure. E III 18 475 41
had I broken the bond of secrecy and told you every thing." E III 18 477 55
"Oh! no, no, no--how can you suspect me of such a thing?-- E III 18 478 66
very superior character to any thing deserved by his own. P III 1 4 6
any thing, which he had not been very much tempted to do. P III 1 5 8
of indifference for every thing but justice and equity. P III 2 12 3
could secure, and saw no dignity in any thing short of it. P III 2 12 5
contemplated as a possible thing, because we know how P III 3 17 4
Every thing in and about the house would be taken such P III 3 18 7
I might impose on the pleasure-grounds, is another thing. P III 3 18 8
every thing plain and easy between landlord and tenant. P III 3 18 9
10
be on a station that would lead to every thing he wanted. P III 4 27 4
Lady Russell had little taste for wit; and of any thing P III 4 27 4
She was persuaded to believe the engagement a wrong thing-- P III 4 27 5
terms, time, every thing, and every body, was right; and P III 5 32 3
think that, every thing considered, she wished to remain. P III 5 33 6
of claiming Anne when any thing was the matter, was P III 5 33 7
some use, glad to have any thing marked out as a duty, and P III 5 33 9

much with me; not that any thing in the world, I am sure, P III 5 35 14
And one thing I have had to do, Mary, of a more trying P III 5 39 34
neither was there any thing among the other component P III 6 43 4
away, without benefit from books, or any thing else. P III 6 43 5
he would not think there was any thing the matter with me. P III 6 44 7
any thing amiss, you need not be afraid of mentioning it." P III 6 45 9
time, and help play at any thing, or dance any where; and P III 6 47 15
Musgrove more than any thing else, and often drew this P III 6 47 15
to hear whether any thing had been said on the subject at P III 6 49 25
who had never done any thing to entitle himself to more P III 6 51 29
It was an afternoon of distress, and Anne had every thing P III 7 53 3
And, in short, he had looked and said every thing with P III 7 54 4
Only think, if any thing should happen!" P III 7 55 6
Anne will send for me if any thing is the matter." P III 7 55 8
If there is any thing disagreeable going on, men are P III 7 56 10
I have not nerves for the sort of thing." P III 7 56 12
You can make little Charles do any thing; he always minds P III 7 57 16
a moment's notice, if any thing is the matter; but I dare P III 7 57 16
be able to persuade him to do any thing he did not like. P III 7 57 18
on board without any thing to eat, or any cook to dress it P III 8 64 4
Lucky fellow to get any thing so soon, with no more P III 8 65 12
to the Asp, to see what an old thing they had given you." P III 8 65 16
Ah! it would have been a happy thing, if he had never left P III 8 67 27
thing of Harville's from the world's end, if he wanted it. P III 8 69 40
ever called them any thing in the whole course of her life. P III 8 70 53
She felt that he had every thing to elevate him, which P III 8 71 57
his ceremonious grace, were worse than any thing. P III 8 72 60
of flattery, and of every thing most bewitching in his P III 9 73 1
near them, seemed to leave every thing to take its chance. P III 9 74 9
That would be a noble thing, indeed, for Henrietta! P III 9 75 11
Charles Hayter; a very bad thing for her, and still worse P III 9 76 16
to Louisa, but had been almost every thing to Henrietta. P III 9 78 19
in his claim to any thing good that might be giving away. P III 9 79 28
to produce, of every thing being to be communicated, and P III 10 83 4
be communicated, and every thing being to be done together, P III 10 83 4
What!--would I be turned back from doing a thing that I P III 10 87 23
Every thing now marked out Louisa for Captain Wentworth; P III 10 90 37
one of the inns, the next thing to be done was P III 11 95 9
it as a thing of course that they should dine with them. P III 11 98 15
improvements; and if every thing else was done, sat down P III 11 99 18
Do not you agree with me, that it is the best thing he P III 12 102 2
My doubt is, whether any thing could persuade him to leave P III 12 102 2
if people thought there was any thing to complain of." P III 12 103 2
look upon her as able to persuade a person to any thing! P III 12 103 4
between them, and every thing was done that Anne had P III 12 110 37
38
They had looked forward and arranged every thing, before P III 12 113 56
One thing more, and all seemed arranged. P III 12 114 64
Captain Wentworth now hurried off to get every thing ready P III 12 115 65
A speedy cure must not be hoped, but every thing was going P IV 1 121 2
meet Lady Russell with any thing like the appearance of P IV 1 124 11
more pleasure than almost any thing else would have done. P IV 1 126 20
one corner, and another great thing that I never go near." P IV 1 128 28
Every thing was safe enough, and she smiled over the many P IV 1 128 32
it is a very clear thing that he admires you exceedingly.-- P IV 2 131 9
"You will not find any thing very agreeable in him, I P IV 2 132 16
when one drops one's scissors, or any thing that happens. P IV 2 132 19
used to the sight of any thing tolerable, by the effect P IV 3 142 13
misuse, when a knock at the door suspended every thing. P IV 3 142 17
to make him quite the thing, are more absurd, I believe, P IV 3 144 20
Had she been using any thing in particular?" P IV 4 145 3
But every thing must take its chance. P IV 4 146 4
Every thing united in him; good understanding, correct P IV 4 146 6
for himself in every thing essential, without defying P IV 4 146 6
is by no means a dangerous thing in good company, on the P IV 4 150 17
They were not much interested in any thing relative to P IV 5 157 14
Every thing that revolts other people, low company, paltry P IV 5 157 15
had been a common thing; that there had been a period of P IV 5 161 27
said a careless or a hasty thing, than of those whose P IV 5 161 28
out of the way when any thing "desirable is going on; P IV 6 163 7
to give me any notice, or offer to take "any thing. P IV 6 164 7
"Charles joins me in love, and every thing proper. P IV 6 164 7
offering to convey any thing to you; a very "kind, P IV 6 164 8
him attached to "Louisa; I never could see any thing of it. P IV 6 165 8
"How Charles could take such a thing into his head was " P IV 6 165 8
each of them every thing that would not suit the other. P IV 6 166 19
in every thing, and to walk for her life, to do him good. P IV 6 168 24
But what a thing here is, by way of a boat. P IV 6 169 25
interrupted her with, "and the thing is certainly true. P IV 6 172 40
41
cold or friendly, or any thing so certainly as embarrassed. P IV 7 175 7
A day or two passed without producing any thing.-- P IV 7 179 32
her to be preferring him, it would have been another thing. P IV 8 182 10
have found any thing in Lyme to inspire such a feeling. P IV 8 183 15
behind her, which rendered every thing else trivial. P IV 8 188 37
to interest her, by every thing in situation, by his own P IV 9 192 2
If in that light, if there is any thing which you suppose P IV 9 195 25
It is a thing of course among us, that every man is P IV 9 195 30
I have no reason, from any thing that has fallen within my P IV 9 196 33
it to be the most probable thing in the world to be wished P IV 9 197 36
Can any thing be stronger?" P IV 9 204 75
This is full proof undoubtedly, proof of every thing you P IV 9 204 77
If there is any thing in my story which you know to be P IV 9 206 88
two friends, as the only thing to be done; and Colonel P IV 9 207 90
changed the face of every thing, and while it took from P IV 9 210 99
to her friend every thing relative to Mrs. Smith, in which P IV 9 211 103
There was no longer any thing of tenderness due to him. P IV 10 212 1
quite sincere, but now she saw insincerity in every thing. P IV 10 214 11
the destruction of every thing like peace and comfort. P IV 10 215 13
or two, every thing seemed to be in suspense, or at an end. P IV 10 216 19
mother's party, that every thing might be comfortable and P IV 10 217 19
They do every thing to confer happiness, I am sure. P IV 10 218 23
a temper to admire every thing as she ought, and enter P IV 10 219 28
heavens, Charles! how can you think of such a thing? P IV 10 223 42
43
I will not allow books to prove any thing." P IV 11 234 28
"But how shall we prove any thing?" P IV 11 234 29
We never can expect to prove any thing upon such a point. P IV 11 234 30
No, I believe you capable of every thing great and good in P IV 11 235 32
Any thing was possible, any thing might be defied rather P IV 11 237 41
seemed to secure every thing, but which had been followed P IV 11 240 59
influenced him in every thing he had said and done, or P IV 11 241 60
There, he had seen every thing to exalt in his estimation P IV 11 242 63
best corrective of every thing dangerous in such high- P IV 11 245 77
and Mrs. Croft, every thing of peculiar cordiality and P IV 11 246 78
ready to say almost every thing else in her favour; and as P IV 12 251 10
The very thing perhaps to be wished for. S 1 364 1
the horses round, the best thing we can do will be to S 1 367 1
Saline air & immersion will be the very thing.-- S 1 367 1
the demand for every thing, & the sure resort of the very S 1 368 1
A thing of this kind soon makes a stir in a lonely place S 1 370 1
The young ladies approached & said every thing that was S 1 370 1
not named Trafalgar--for Waterloo is more the thing now. S 4 380 1
Sidney says any thing you know. S 4 382 1
And it would be a fine thing for the place!-- S 4 382 1
The library of course, afforded every thing; all the S 6 390 1
the walk of a mile as any thing requiring rest, & talked S 6 390 1
dear sir, she cried, how could you think of such a thing? S 6 393 1
Can you conceive any thing more subduing, more melting, S 7 397 1
"Yes, my dear--& it is not the only kind thing I have done S 7 400 1
I had not expected any thing so bad.-- S 7 402 1
And that she was to belong to them, was a thing of course." S 9 407 1
There was but one thing for me to do.-- S 9 408 1
"But you have not told me any thing of the other family S 9 411 1
recollection of having written or felt any such thing.-- S 10 412 1
I am not afraid of any thing so much as damp.--" S 10 415 1
every evening, agrees with me better than any thing."-- S 10 417 1
wholesome, I think it a very bad thing for the stomach. S 10 417 1
proved to be the simplest thing in the world, by those who S 10 418 1
she added--"the oddest thing that ever was!--a Miss Lambe S 10 419 1
naturally preferring any thing to smallness & retirement, S 11 421 1
"The easiest thing in the world--cried Miss Diana Parker S 12 423 1
She is so frightened, poor thing, that I promised to come S 12 424 1
& every thing had a suitable air of property & order.-- S 12 427 1

THINGS (249)

saying those delightful things which put one in good LS 10 258 3
must be childish indeed, if such things do not strike her. LS 17 271 7
required; said many things over and over again, & told LS 20 276 3
perfectly justified, all things considered, in desiring LS 22 281 3
alteration of his present plan; things have gone too far. LS 23 284 7
I have many things to compass. LS 25 293 4
All things considered therefore, it seems encumbent on me LS 25 294 5
Facts are such horrid things! LS 32 303 1
But strange things may be generally accounted for if their NA I 1 16 10
Here are no tea things for us, you see." NA I 2 22 18
"Men commonly take so little notice of those things," said NA I 3 28 39
The whole being explained, many obliging things were said NA I 4 33 6
I have an hundred things to say to you. NA I 6 39 4
things that I cannot judge whether it was cheap or dear." NA I 7 46 14
all the others, they are the stupidest things in creation." NA I 7 48 34
She said the highest things in your praise that could NA I 7 50 47
I have a thousand things to say to you; but make haste and NA I 9 62 7
insights, in making those things plain which he had before NA I 9 66 31
she had such thousands of things to say to her, it NA I 9 67 33
few of the many thousand things which had been collecting NA I 10 70 1
"But they are such very different things!--" NA I 10 76 30
amusements, a variety of things to be seen and done all NA I 10 78 46
"They are disagreeable things to carry. NA I 11 83 11
in money could not afford things, he did not know who NA I 11 89 61
Open carriages are nasty things. NA I 13 104 32
"That is, I can read poetry and plays, and things of that NA I 14 108 20
I will not allow myself to think of such things, till we NA I 15 120 22
My notion of things is simple enough. NA I 15 124 46
Of all things in the world inconstancy is my aversion. NA II 1 130 5
upon me; for, of all things in the world, I hated fine NA II 1 134 39
us distress our dear Catherine by talking of such things. NA II 1 136 46
urge his suit, and say all manner of pretty things to you. NA II 3 144 10
All those things should be allowed for in youth and high NA II 3 146 18
But above all things, my dear Catherine, do not be in a NA II 3 146 20
"Why do you put such things into my head? NA II 3 147 22
natural course of things, she must ere long be released. NA II 8 188 16
And, upon my word, there are some things that seem very NA II 10 206 35
Henry, in having such things to relate of his father, was NA II 15 247 15
them to move their things, and sending them presents of SS I 2 12 24
over had said many witty things on the subject of lovers SS I 7 34 5
Barton was, in her opinion, of all things the most natural. SS I 17 90 1
He said so repeatedly; other things he said too, which SS I 19 101 1
soon forgot that there were any such things in the room. SS I 19 108 36
I am sure you will like it of all things. SS I 20 113 33
your praises, he did nothing but say fine things of you." SS I 20 115 54
to it, I dare say he would have liked it of all things. SS I 20 117 64
And they both long to see you of all things, for they have SS I 21 119 4
The tea things were brought in, and already had Marianne SS II 4 161 7
a world of little odd things to do after one has been away SS II 4 163 14
The real state of things between Willoughby and her sister SS II 5 173 45
Lord bless you! they care no more about such things!--" SS II 8 194 8
things, the better, the sooner 'tis blown over and forgot. SS II 8 196 18
his family was, above all things, the most material to her SS II 14 254 26
I have many things to support me. SS III 1 263 27
arm--"for I wanted to see you of all things in the world." SS III 2 271 8
can't repeat such kind of things you know)--she told him SS III 2 273 16
I am very glad to find things are so forward between you. SS III 4 286 17
as well, or better, perhaps, all things considered. SS III 5 297 31
their way, which of all things was the most unlikely to SS III 6 301 1
But I can see in a great many things that you are very W 318 2
The entrance of the tea things at 7 o'clock was some W 326 7
"It is so delightful to me, said she, to have things going W 343 19
alienation; she had heard things which made her dread her W 348 23
"I hope you will find things tolerably comfortable Jane"-- W 351 25
I am one of those who always take things as they find them. W 351 25
best Pembroke table, with the best tea things before her. W 355 28
Vanity and pride are different things, though the words PP I 5 20 20
a great reader, and I have pleasure in many things." PP I 8 37 24
night all the foolish things that were said in the morning. PP I 10 49 28
Things are settled so oddly." PP I 13 65 22
for such things I know are all chance in this world. PP I 13 65 24
These are the kind of little things which please her PP I 14 67 9
their chance of these things,--and happily I am not in PP I 16 83 50
How wonderfully these sort of things occur! PP I 18 96 57
for there are certainly other things to be attended to. PP I 18 101 71
A thousand things may arise in six months!" PP I 21 120 27
Let us hope for better things. PP I 23 130 18
They may wish many things besides his happiness; they may PP II 1 136 23
But these things happen so often! PP II 2 140 6
things may come out, as will shock your relations to hear." PP II 8 174 15
I am excessively attentive to all those things. PP II 14 212 13
am very glad you have somebody who thinks of those things. PP II 14 212 15
we first came!--and yet how many things have happened!" PP II 15 217 11
Mamma would like to go too of all things! PP II 16 220 6
I dare say he often hears worse things said than I am PP II 16 220 10
And, above all things, keep Mr. Bennet from fighting. PP III 5 288 38
But there are two things that I want very much to know;-- PP III 7 304 27
I will put on my things in a moment. PP III 7 306 44
afterwards; but the things should be ordered immediately." PP III 7 306 47
and yet there have been things enough happened in the time. PP III 9 316 7
I shall like it of all things. PP III 9 317 13
from the reason of things, that their elopement had been PP III 9 318 19
At such a distance as that, you know, things are strangely PP III 10 327 14
He smiled, looked handsome, and said many pretty things. PP III 11 330 7
for it; and really, all things considered, I begin to PP III 18 380 5
not you know that of all things upon earth that is the MP I 1 6 6
least as things then were, was quite out of the question. MP I 1 9 10
the better; but then there is moderation in all things." MP I 2 13 5
her ignorant of many things with which they had been long MP I 2 18 23
But all things considered, I do not know whether it is not MP I 2 19 29
he told her such charming things of what William was to do, MP I 2 21 34
and, plied well with good things, would soon pop off." MP I 3 24 5
me to be reconciled to things that I disliked at first, MP I 3 25 18
Fanny sighed, and said, "I cannot see things as you do; MP I 3 27 34
"I hope, sister, things are not so very bad with you MP I 3 29 49
A great many things were due from poor Mr. Norris as MP I 3 30 50
The approach now is one of the finest things in the MP I 6 53 2
doing several things that Sir Thomas and I used to talk of. MP I 6 54 9
walked about and settled things, and then we could all MP I 6 62 58
Your lap seems full of good things, and here is a basket MP I 10 105 54
Mr. Rushworth has set a good example, and such things are MP I 12 118 16
them myself, I shall let things take their course, without MP I 13 128 37
There were, in fact, so many things to be attended to, so MP I 14 130 2
"We see things very differently," cried Maria--"I am MP I 15 140 12
I still think you see things too strongly; and I really MP I 15 140 14
I hope in preventing waste and making the most of things. MP I 15 141 22
Things should take their course; she cared not how it MP I 16 157 28
"Sir Thomas is to achieve mighty things when he comes home, MP I 17 161 15
How am I ever to look him in the face and say such things? MP I 18 168 19

and it spread as those things always spread you know, sir--	MP	II	1	184	26
It entertains me more than many other things have done--	MP	II	3	197	5
mind to what may happen, and take your things accordingly."	MP	II	5	221	34
I first heard of such things being done in England I could	MP	II	6	235	19
Only think what grand things were produced there by our	MP	II	7	244	30
I see things very differently now.	MP	II	7	245	31
"My dear Fanny, you feel these things a great deal too	MP	II	9	262	9
back to the state of things in the autumn, to what they	MP	II	10	276	12
Stranger things have happened.	MP	II	11	289	34
that he would have many things to buy, though to be sure	MP	II	13	305	19
But, poor things! they cannot help it; and you know it	MP	II	13	305	25
things only in part, and judging partially by the event.--	MP	III	1	313	12
he had hoped better things; he had thought that an hour's	MP	III	2	329	11
who are always doing mistaken and very disagreeable things.	MP	III	2	332	19
Edmund had great things to hear on his return.	MP	III	3	334	1
the scene which the tea things afforded, she must have	MP	III	3	335	5
was an unnatural state of things; a state which he must	MP	III	4	345	4
"I must hope better things.	MP	III	4	347	21
from all the holds upon things animate and inanimate,	MP	III	4	347	21
Oh! why will such things ever pass away?"	MP	III	5	358	7
You will set things going in a better way, I am sure.	MP	III	6	372	20
I am to do about Sam's things, they will never be ready in	MP	III	7	378	10
"I was up stairs, mamma, moving my things;" said Susan, in	MP	III	7	379	18
In this more placid state of things William re-entered,	MP	III	7	384	34
it told her of people and things about whom she had never	MP	III	9	394	2
she could perceive; that things, bad as they were, would	MP	III	9	395	4
his daily survey of how things went on, and who must prove	MP	III	10	403	15
She turned away, and wished he would not say such things.	MP	III	10	405	16
the two or three other things which she wished he had not	MP	III	10	406	21
And if in little things, must it not be so in great?	MP	III	11	414	32
It will be a comfort to me to tell you how things now are,	MP	III	13	420	2
I want to know the state of things at Mansfield Park, and	MP	III	14	433	13
too, would be the best way of preventing such things."	MP	III	15	440	13
It was the imprudence which had brought things to	MP	III	16	455	19
Persuade him to let things take their course.	MP	III	16	457	29
and wish for impossible things, till her father awoke, and	E	I	1	7	10
foretel things, for whatever you say always comes to pass.	E	I	1	12	40
silly things, and break up one's family circle grievously."	E	I	1	13	45
herself for contriving things so well; but the quiet	E	I	3	22	6
clearing the nicer things, to say: "Mrs. Bates, let me	E	I	3	24	13
					14
Things must come to a crisis soon now."	E	I	9	72	15
The strangest things do take place!"	E	I	9	74	24
Such things in general cannot be too short."	E	I	9	76	33
Your dear mother was so clever at all those things!	E	I	9	78	54
strong feelings; he takes things as he finds them, and	E	I	11	96	26
began to speak of other things, and in a voice of the	E	I	13	115	36
Contrary to the usual course of things, Mr. Elton's	E	I	16	135	7
and ashamed, and resolved to do such things no more.	E	I	16	137	10
quite longing to go to Ireland, from his account of things"	E	II	1	160	20
You are very obliging to say such things-- but certainly	E	II	1	161	27
in the common course of things it was to be rather	E	II	5	192	29
so, but certainly silly things do cease to be silly if	E	II	8	212	2
					3
One might guess twenty things without guessing exactly the	E	II	8	217	32
a few clever things said, a few downright silly, but by	E	II	8	219	43
Little things do not irritate him.	E	II	8	226	79
would, in the common course of things, occur to him."	E	II	8	226	81
nor spirit in the little things which are generally	E	II	8	227	86
Surprizes are foolish things.	E	II	8	228	92
these sort of things require a good deal of consideration.	E	II	11	252	32
"men never know when things are dirty or not;" and the	E	II	11	253	43
to say, "of all horrid things, leave-taking is the worst."	E	II	12	259	12
					13
But stranger things have happened; and when we cease to	E	II	13	267	7
of insensibility to other things; but it was now too	E	II	13	267	8
that a married woman has many things to call her attention.	E	II	14	277	40
We feel things differently.	E	II	15	286	23
One says those sort of things, of course, without any idea	E	II	15	288	35
of my life, that if things are going untowardly one month,	E	II	18	308	27
courtship, when, because things did not go quite right,	E	II	18	308	28
though a good many things I assure you are suspected; and	E	II	18	310	34
them; and we used sometimes to say very cutting things!	E	III	2	321	15
for the cruel state of things before, and for the very	E	III	2	328	41
"No--I cannot call them gifts: but they are things that I	E	III	4	338	8
actually found happiness in treasuring up these things?"	E	III	4	340	23
Harriet, more wonderful things have taken place, there	E	III	4	342	39
it of all things," was not plainer in words than manner.	E	III	6	354	9
or repeated--or two things moderately clever--or three	E	III	7	370	23
clever--or three things very dull indeed, and she engages	E	III	7	370	23
'Three things very dull indeed.'	E	III	7	370	24
I shall be sure to say three dull things as soon as ever I	E	III	7	370	24
These kind of things are very well at Christmas, when one	E	III	7	372	37
I am not one of those who have witty things at every	E	III	7	372	37
"Such things do occur, undoubtedly."--	E	III	7	373	42
It was felt as such things must be felt.	E	III	9	387	12
a disagreeable business--but things might be much worse.--	E	III	10	393	17
It may make many things intelligible and excusable which	E	III	10	398	53
me that more wonderful things had happened; that there had	E	III	11	406	18
that more wonderful things had happened, matches of	E	III	11	407	28
for "such things," he observed, "always got about."	E	III	12	417	5
to say and do many things which may well lay me open to	E	III	13	426	15
What ever strange things I said or did during that	E	III	14	439	8
lady's in the case, "you know all other things give place."	E	III	16	454	13
Things did not seem--that is, there seemed a little cloud	E	III	16	454	18
We never heard of such things at Maple Grove."	E	III	16	456	29
You were both talking of other things; of business, shows	E	III	18	473	26
But though I was always doing wrong things, they were very	E	III	18	477	55
very bad wrong things, and such as did me no service.--	E	III	18	477	55
"A great many things, I assure you.	P	III	5	38	34
But all these things took up a great deal of time."	P	III	5	39	34
so much trash and sweet things, that they are sure to come	P	III	6	44	8
you may be able to set things to rights, that I have no	P	III	6	45	9
And upon looking over his letters and things, she found it	P	III	6	50	27
can, that she may not be dwelling upon such gloomy things."	P	III	6	50	27
an eldest son, and he saw things as an eldest son himself.	P	III	9	76	14
occasion, when all these things should have been seen by	P	III	9	77	17
her too, when it comes to things of consequence, when they	P	III	10	87	26
towards her which all these things made apparent.	P	III	10	91	42
I do not like having such things so long in hand.	P	III	10	92	46
her; all but the recollection that such things had been.	P	IV	1	123	8
a taste for those sort of things, I thought that would be	P	IV	2	131	12
had mentioned one or two things relative to the marriage,	P	IV	3	139	8
She had hoped better things from their high ideas of their	P	IV	4	148	11
shall buy all the high-priced things I have in hand now."	P	IV	5	156	13
breathe very quick, and feel a hundred things in a moment.	P	IV	8	183	11
There were many things to be taken into the account.	P	IV	9	198	53
"Oh! those things are too common.	P	IV	9	201	64
other men, about those things; and when I came to examine	P	IV	9	203	70
wife, to whom he tells things which he had better not, and	P	IV	9	205	82
of things, and the reports beginning to prevail.--	P	IV	9	206	90
operation, and it streightens him as to many things.	P	IV	10	218	22
She tried to be calm, and leave things to take their	P	IV	10	221	33
"And so, ma'am, all these things considered," said Mrs.	P	IV	11	230	6
Bad things for a country;--sure to raise the price of	S		1	368	1
we now & then, see things differently, Miss H.--	S		3	376	1
But let us talk of pleasanter things.--	S		5	389	1
thing; all the useless things in the world that cd not be	S		6	390	1
by raising the price of things--and I have heard that's	S		6	392	1
The tea things were brought in.--	S		6	394	1
& he is the heir, things do not stand between us in the	S		7	400	1
with the tea things, as a very fortunate interruption.--	S		10	416	1
I could no more mention these things to Lady D.-- than I	S		12	424	1
THINK (1541)					
Mr Vernon I think was a great deal too kind to her, when	LS		3	246	1
Disposed however as he always is to think the best of	LS		3	247	1
you my dear madam, tho@ I think you had better not	LS		8	254	1
the justice of her opinion of me, I think I may defy her.	LS		10	257	1
Let her think & act as she chuses however; I have never	LS		10	258	2
affection on a man who had dared to think so meanly of me.	LS		10	258	2
for a father's anxiety, & think themselves privileged to	LS		12	260	1
I should blush to see him, to hear of him, to think of him.	LS		12	261	4
shall enclose to you, as I think you will like to see it;	LS		13	262	1
such a determination to think well of Lady Susan, that his	LS		13	262	1
Frederica is too shy I think, & too much in awe of me, to	LS		16	268	2
my neice; she is shy, & I think I can see that some pains	LS		17	270	6
her instead of him; I think I should have discovered the	LS		17	271	6
I think my dear madam, you would not disapprove of her as	LS		18	272	2
& perhaps may think me negligent for not writing before.	LS		19	273	1
days; hoped we would not think it odd, was aware of it's	LS		20	278	10
How unpleasant, one would think, must his reflections be!	LS		22	282	8
"My love, replied I, do not think it necessary to	LS		24	286	4
Do you think that your uncle & I should not have espoused	LS		24	286	6
Do you think me destitute of every honest, every natural	LS		24	289	12
If you think your daughter at all attached to Reginald,	LS		24	290	12
at the same time began to think that we had perhaps been	LS		24	290	13
You should think more of yourself, & less of your daughter.	LS		26	295	1
Do not think me unkind for such an exercise of my power,	LS		30	299	1
he is full as handsome I think as Manwaring, & with such	LS		38	307	3
I wish I could think so too!	LS		41	310	3
much awakened for her to think of anything but Frederica's	LS		42	312	6
Who would not think so?	NA	I	2	18	2
But I think we had better sit still, for one gets so	NA	I	2	22	19
I think you must know somebody."	NA	I	2	23	20
"I see what you think of me," said he gravely--"I shall	NA	I	3	26	20
That is--I should not think the superiority was always on	NA	I	3	27	29
You do not think too highly of us in that way."	NA	I	3	27	33
"And pray, sir, what do you think of Miss Morland's gown?"	NA	I	3	28	41
do not think it will wash well; I am afraid it will fray."	NA	I	3	28	42
in these words:--"I think, madam, I cannot be mistaken; it	NA	I	4	31	2
to continue to think of him; and his impression on her	NA	I	5	36	2
I think her as beautiful as an angel, and I am so vexed	NA	I	6	40	12
The men think us incapable of real friendship you know,	NA	I	6	40	14
"But you should not persuade me that I think so very much	NA	I	6	41	17
"It is not like Udolpho at all; but yet I think it is very	NA	I	6	42	23
the world, and think themselves of so much importance!--	NA	I	6	42	28
Something between both, I think.	NA	I	6	42	29
He took out his watch: "how long do you think we have been	NA	I	7	45	5
What do you think of my gig, Miss Morland? a neat one, is	NA	I	7	46	11
And how much do you think he did, Miss Morland?"	NA	I	7	46	11
"I think you must like Udolpho, if you were to read it; it	NA	I	7	48	35
whenever she could think of any thing to say, and had	NA	I	8	56	11
"And is that likely to satisfy me, do you think?"	NA	I	8	57	19
"No, not at all; but if you think it wrong, you had much	NA	I	8	58	24
Catherine did not think the portrait a very inviting one,	NA	I	9	62	10
of his horse, he should think it necessary to alarm her	NA	I	9	62	10
Why should you think of such a thing?	NA	I	9	63	19
"You do not really think, Mr. Thorpe," said Catherine,	NA	I	9	65	27
lament her ill-luck, and think over what she had lost,	NA	I	9	69	51
I think it does not look amiss; the sleeves were entirely	NA	I	10	70	3
"You cannot think," added Catherine after a moment's	NA	I	10	72	11
Do you think her pretty?"	NA	I	10	73	15
"Perhaps we----- yes, I think we certainly shall."	NA	I	10	73	20
"I wonder you should think so, for you never asked me."	NA	I	10	75	26
"Oh, no; they will never think of me, after such a	NA	I	10	76	27
"--That you think they cannot be compared together."	NA	I	10	77	31
striking; but I think I could place them in such a view.--	NA	I	10	77	33
the same light, nor think the same duties belong to them."	NA	I	10	77	35
"I do not think I should be tired, if I were to stay here	NA	I	10	78	44
and those who go to London may think nothing of Bath.	NA	I	10	78	46
it to clear up, and I do think it looks a little lighter.	NA	I	11	83	15
She could not think the Tilneys had acted quite well by	NA	I	11	86	50
They must think it so strange; so rude of me! to go by	NA	I	11	87	53
you; but you men think yourselves of such consequence."	NA	I	11	90	63
And lucky may she think herself, if she get another good	NA	I	11	90	65
But what do you think we have been talking of?--	NA	I	12	96	20
"And what do you think I said?" (lowering his voice)	NA	I	12	96	22
I think you cannot stand out any longer now.	NA	I	13	99	3
shall think you quite unkind, if you still refuse."	NA	I	13	99	3
"I did not think you had been so obstinate, Catherine,"	NA	I	13	99	10
think with pleasure that he might be sometimes depended on.	NA	I	13	102	27
"Well," said he, "and do you think of going too?"	NA	I	13	104	29
"No, certainly not; and I am glad you do not think of it.	NA	I	13	104	31
I am glad you do not think of going; I am sure Mrs.	NA	I	13	104	31
Do not you think these kind of projects objectionable?"	NA	I	13	104	31
Do not you think it has an odd appearance, if young ladies	NA	I	13	104	33
I do not think you would have found me hard to persuade."	NA	I	13	105	37
Catherine submitted; and though sorry to think that	NA	I	13	105	41
I am proud when I reflect on it, and I think it must	NA	I	14	107	9
But now really, do not you think Udolpho the nicest book	NA	I	14	107	12
tiresome: and yet I often think it odd that it should be	NA	I	14	108	22
"Historians, you think," said Miss Tilney, "are not happy	NA	I	14	109	23
which, as I used to think, nobody would willingly ever	NA	I	14	109	24
"You think me foolish to call instruction a torment, but	NA	I	14	109	26
you mean to have her think you intolerably rude to your	NA	I	14	113	40
Tell her that you think very highly of the understanding	NA	I	14	113	44
"Miss Morland, I think very highly of the understanding of	NA	I	14	113	45
"Miss Morland, no one can think more highly of the	NA	I	14	114	47
I think you and I are very well off to be out of the	NA	I	14	115	50
Oh! heavens! when I think of them I am so agitated!"	NA	I	15	117	6
I will not allow myself to think of such things, till we	NA	I	15	120	22
What do you think of it, Miss Morland?	NA	I	15	122	30
"I am sure I think it a very good one."	NA	I	15	122	31
But I have a notion, Miss Morland, you and I think pretty	NA	I	15	124	44
I think like you there.	NA	I	15	124	47
And to marry for money I think the wickedest thing in	NA	I	15	124	47
Let me entreat you never to think of him again, my dear	NA	II	1	130	5
that some people might think him handsomer than his	NA	II	1	131	15
and she was beginning to think it a very long quarter of	NA	II	1	132	16
but it was very good-natured in him to think of it.	NA	II	1	132	17
"I cannot think how it could happen!	NA	II	1	133	31
After what you told him from me, how could he think of	NA	II	1	133	33
to my brother, I really think Miss Thorpe has by no means	NA	II	1	134	36
the room he could bear to think of; and it was not that he	NA	II	1	134	39
For myself, it is nothing; I never think of myself."	NA	II	1	136	45
"Nobody can think better of Mr. Morland than I do, I am	NA	II	1	136	47
prevailed on to give the waters what I think a fair trial.	NA	II	2	138	2
"Psha! my dear creature," she replied, "do not think me	NA	II	3	143	2
very well that if I could think of one man more than	NA	II	3	145	13
I only wonder John could think of it; he could not have	NA	II	3	146	16
I do not think any thing would justify me in wishing you	NA	II	3	146	20
That he should think it worth his while to fancy himself	NA	II	3	148	29
"I think Mr. Morland would acknowledge a difference.	NA	II	4	151	12
"Yes, I think so; for you must know your brother's heart."	NA	II	4	151	23
He cannot think this--and you may be sure that he would	NA	II	4	152	28
you may be sure that he would not have you think it.	NA	II	4	152	28
resolved never to think so seriously on the subject again.	NA	II	4	153	30
"Oh! yes--I do not think I should be easily frightened,	NA	II	5	158	14
it, you will probably think you discern (for your lamp is	NA	II	5	159	19
and she could think of her friends in Bath without one	NA	II	6	166	8
was beginning to think of stepping into bed, when, on	NA	II	6	168	10
I think it would be acknowledged by the most impartial eye	NA	II	7	175	15
younger children, I should think any profession necessary	NA	II	7	176	15
Which did his daughter think would most accord her fair	NA	II	7	177	17

Tilney, "that I always think it the best and nearest way.	NA	II	7	179	28
inclination for writing, I think it my duty to tell you,	NA	II	10	202	6
					7
I am ashamed to think how long I bore with it; but if ever	NA	II	10	202	7
"I do not think I shall ever wish for a letter again!"	NA	II	10	204	11
I think you must be deceived so far.	NA	II	10	204	20
When I think of his past declarations, I give him up.--	NA	II	10	206	31
"You think it is all for ambition then?--	NA	II	10	206	35
and which tempted her to think his disposition in such	NA	II	11	208	1
His brother and sister knew not what to think.	NA	II	11	209	5
"And when do you think, sir, I may look forward to this	NA	II	11	209	5
I think I can answer for the young ladies making allowance	NA	II	11	209	5
But on Wednesday, I think, Henry, you may expect us; and	NA	II	11	210	6
"But how can you think of such a thing, after what the	NA	II	11	210	6
as the General seemed to think an apology necessary for	NA	II	11	211	12
sufficiently recovered to think it prettier than any	NA	II	11	212	17
your time pleasantly, but am afraid you never think of me.	NA	II	11	214	25
She must think me an idiot, or she could not have written	NA	II	12	216	2
because I do not think Isabella has any heart to lose.	NA	II	12	218	4
Isabella's letter; and tried to think no more of it.	NA	II	12	219	12
could not but think that if Mr. and Mrs. Morland were	NA	II	12	219	16
If you think it long-----"	NA	II	13	221	2
"You are too good, I am sure, to think the worse of me for	NA	II	13	221	5
Do not think about that.	NA	II	13	223	13
of what she had dared to think and look for, of her	NA	II	13	226	24
How Henry would think, and feel, and look, when he	NA	II	14	231	3
She could never forget Henry Tilney, or think of him with	NA	II	14	231	4
after such behaviour, we cannot think at all well of her.	NA	II	14	236	18
immediately added, "only think, my dear, of my having got	NA	II	14	236	19
My dear, do not you think these silk gloves were very well?	NA	II	14	238	22
for home by great acquaintance--'the mirror' I think.	NA	II	14	238	24
did not think it could ever be repeated too often.	NA	II	15	241	6
Morland's departure, and ordered to think of her no more.	NA	II	15	243	9
doubling what he chose to think the amount of Mr.	NA	II	15	244	10
She begged him to think again on the subject.	NA	II	15	245	12
No one, at least, can think I have not done enough for	SS	I	2	8	3
lady, "but we are not to think of their expectations: the	SS	I	2	10	12
"Certainly--and I think I may afford to give them five	SS	I	2	10	13
They think themselves secure, you do no more than what is	SS	I	2	10	14
I think, be amply discharging my promise to my father."	SS	I	2	11	22
your giving them more, it is quite absurd to think of it.	SS	I	2	11	23
"I think you will like him," said Elinor, "when you know	SS	I	2	12	24
for drawing," replied Elinor; "why should you think so?	SS	I	3	16	9
Had he ever been in the way of learning, I think he would	SS	I	4	19	2
Indeed, I think I may say that you cannot, for your	SS	I	4	19	2
I think him every thing that is worthy and amiable."	SS	I	4	19	4
Elinor, "no one can, I think, be in doubt, who has seen	SS	I	4	20	6
At present, I know him so well, that I think him really	SS	I	4	20	9
"I shall very soon think him handsome, Elinor, if I do not	SS	I	4	20	9
"I do not attempt to deny," said she, "that I think very	SS	I	4	20	10
never been disposed to think her amiable; and I am very	SS	I	4	21	12
she might think necessary, if the situation pleased her.	SS	I	4	21	15
money, as I dare say I shall, we may think about building.	SS	I	4	23	20
Mrs. Dashwood, who could not think a man five years	SS	I	6	29	4
though you may not think it intentionally ill-natured.	SS	I	8	37	3
and twenty, I should not think Colonel Brandon's being	SS	I	8	37	4
"I rather think you are mistaken, for when I was talking	SS	I	8	38	9
You will be setting your cap at him now, and never think	SS	I	8	39	17
"for one morning I think you have done pretty well.	SS	I	9	45	29
"That is exactly what I think of him," cried Marianne.	SS	I	10	47	4
teach her to think of Norland with less regret than ever.	SS	I	10	50	15
no such encouragement to think only of Marianne, and in	SS	I	11	54	6
suddenly; appeared to think that he had said too much, and	SS	I	11	55	7
But, however, I hope you will think better of it.	SS	I	11	57	17
I do think he must have been sent for about money matters,	SS	I	13	65	32
How little did I then think that the very first news I	SS	I	14	70	2
You are resolved to think him blameable, because he took	SS	I	14	73	17
to love, and no reason in the world to think ill of?	SS	I	15	78	28
You must think wretchedly indeed of Willoughby, if after	SS	I	15	79	28
"No, I cannot think that.	SS	I	15	80	38
been more to his honour I think, as well as more	SS	I	15	80	39
or a deviation from what I may think right and consistent."	SS	I	15	81	43
was then at liberty to think over the representations of	SS	I	15	81	43
cried out, "indeed, Marianne, I think you are mistaken.	SS	I	15	82	45
	SS	I	16	86	17
					18
"How can you think of dirt, with such objects before you?"	SS	I	16	88	35
"Why should you think so!" replied he, with a sigh.	SS	I	17	93	34
"Nor do I think it a part of Marianne's," said Elinor; "I	SS	I	17	93	35
"I think, Edward," said Mrs. Dashwood, as they were at	SS	I	19	102	3
"that I have long thought on this point, as you think now.	SS	I	19	102	4
"I think," replied Edward, "that I may defy many months to	SS	I	19	103	8
her leisure enough to think of Edward, and of Edward's	SS	I	19	104	12
Only think of their coming so suddenly!	SS	I	19	106	20
I said to Sir John, I do think I hear a carriage; perhaps	SS	I	19	106	20
					21
Only think, mama, how it is improved since I was here last!	SS	I	19	107	24
your taste very much, for I think he is extremely handsome.	SS	I	20	111	12
Charlotte laughed heartily to think that her husband could	SS	I	20	112	26
You cannot think how happy I shall be!	SS	I	20	113	29
You cannot think what a sweet place Cleveland is; and we	SS	I	20	113	33
tell you, and you can't think how disappointed he will be	SS	I	20	114	42
so much there, I do not think Mr. Palmer would visit him,	SS	I	20	114	44
He seems an excellent man; and I think him uncommonly	SS	I	20	115	55
but they all think him extremely agreeable I assure you.	SS	I	20	116	58
However I don't think her hardly at all handsomer than you,	SS	I	20	116	58
you, I assure you; for I think you both excessively pretty,	SS	I	20	116	58
You can't think how much I longed to see you!	SS	I	20	116	60
But mama did not think the match good enough for me,	SS	I	20	116	62
you shall come--you can't think how you will like them.	SS	I	21	119	4
"I have a notion," said Lucy, "you think the little	SS	I	21	122	19
think of tame and quiet children with any abhorrence."	SS	I	21	123	20
think some apology necessary for the freedom of her sister.	SS	I	21	123	24
"I think every one must admire it," replied Elinor, "who	SS	I	21	123	25
for my part, I think they are a vast addition always."	SS	I	21	123	26
"But why should you think," said Lucy, looking ashamed of	SS	I	21	123	27
For my part, I think they are vastly agreeable, provided	SS	I	21	123	28
will make Miss Dashwood believe you think of nothing else."	SS	I	21	124	31
"You will think my question an odd one, I dare say," said	SS	I	22	128	3
Elinor did think the question a very odd one, and her	SS	I	22	128	4
"I am sure you think me very strange, for inquiring about	SS	I	22	128	7
"I cannot bear to have you think me impertinently curious.	SS	I	22	128	8
					9
And I do not think Mr. Ferrars can be displeased, when he	SS	I	22	130	16
"I think I have," replied Elinor, with an exertion of	SS	I	22	130	27
It does not do him justice to be sure, but yet I think you	SS	I	22	131	35
"I was afraid you would think I was taking a great liberty	SS	I	22	132	42
You can't think how much I go through in my mind from it	SS	I	22	133	42
after wiping her eyes, "I think whether it would not be	SS	I	22	133	44
dear as he is to me--I don't think I could be equal to it.	SS	I	22	133	44
Did not you think him dreadful low-spirited when he was at	SS	I	22	133	46
to you, that I was afraid you would think him quite ill."	SS	I	22	133	46
Did you think he came directly from town?"	SS	I	22	134	48
"Did not you think him sadly out of spirits?" repeated	SS	I	22	134	50
and Elinor was then as liberty to think and be wretched.	SS	I	22	135	56
I think for her labour singly, to finish it this evening.	SS	II	1	145	19
nobody of whose judgment I think so highly as I do of	SS	II	2	150	32
my hands, that she will think me a very fit person to have	SS	II	3	153	2
Lord bless me! how do you think I can live poking by	SS	II	3	154	4
"My objection is this; though I think very well of Mrs.	SS	II	3	156	12
likewise, as she did not think it proper that Marianne	SS	II	3	156	15
you think he said when he heard of your coming with mama?	SS	II	4	164	22
It was not so yesterday, I think.	SS	II	5	168	9
Because you are so sly about it yourself, you think nobody	SS	II	7	182	10
Think of your mother; think of her misery while you suffer;	SS	II	7	185	21
Much as you suffer now, think of what you would have	SS	II	7	186	29
on receiving this; and I think you will feel something	SS	II	7	186	38
It would grieve me indeed to be obliged to think ill of	SS	II	7	188	42
"The lady then--Miss Grey I think you called her--is very	SS	II	8	194	9
For my part, I think the less that is said about such	SS	II	8	196	18
almost asleep; and as I think nothing will be of so much	SS	II	8	198	28
"That a gentleman, whom I had reason to think--in short,	SS	II	8	199	35
"It may be so; but Willoughby is capable--at least I think"	SS	II	8	199	39
But your sister does not--I think you said so--she does	SS	II	8	200	41
of being useful-----I think I am justified-- though where	SS	II	9	204	18
gravity, you might think me incapable of having ever felt.	SS	II	9	205	24
"A man of whom he had always had such reason to think well!	SS	II	10	214	9
at the end of two days, to think that, instead of	SS	II	10	216	15
had for some time ceased to think at all of Mr. Ferrars.	SS	II	10	216	15
laughs at me so about the doctor, and I cannot think why.	SS	II	10	218	26
I never think about him from one hour's end to another.	SS	II	10	218	26
My beau, indeed! said I--I cannot think who you mean.	SS	II	10	218	26
"No, I do not think we shall."	SS	II	10	218	31
I think she might see us; and I am sure we would not speak	SS	II	10	219	39
But to-morrow I think I shall certainly be able to call in	SS	II	11	222	9
He seems a most gentlemanlike man; and I think, Elinor, I	SS	II	11	223	18
"More than you think it really and intrinsically worth."	SS	II	11	225	32
"And do you not think it more likely that she should leave	SS	II	11	227	45
to know more of it; and I think I can answer for your	SS	II	11	227	50
in his appearance, to think his acquaintance worth having;	SS	II	11	228	52
added, "do you not think they are something in Miss	SS	II	12	235	31
					32
for her?-- it is Elinor of whom we think and speak."	SS	II	12	235	34
					35
heart taught her to think of with horror; and urged by a	SS	II	12	236	39
					40
You would not think it perhaps, but Marianne was	SS	II	12	237	43
will be no difficulties at all, to what I used to think.	SS	II	13	239	9
I am sure if ever you tell your sister what I think of her,	SS	II	13	240	15
"Oh! don't think of me!" she replied, with spirited	SS	II	13	242	26
with tears as she spoke, "don't think of my health.	SS	II	13	242	26
"I think, Elinor," she presently added, "we must employ	SS	II	13	243	31
some revenge on her, "you think young men never stand upon	SS	II	13	243	38
which Lucy was proud to think of and administer at other	SS	II	14	247	4
school, she could not think of Edward's abode in Mr.	SS	II	14	251	14
"You reside in Devonshire, I think"--was his next	SS	II	14	251	15
Elinor agreed to it all, for she did not think he deserved	SS	II	14	252	19
good kind of girls; and I think the attention is due to	SS	II	14	253	24
not know how I happened to think of it, but it came into	SS	III	1	257	5
sister's indisposition, I think it advisable to say, that	SS	III	1	258	5
So you may think what a blow it was to all her vanity and	SS	III	1	258	7
And I must say, I think she was used very hardly; for your	SS	III	1	259	7
Now, I can think and speak of it with little emotion.	SS	III	1	263	27
If you can think me capable of ever feeling--surely you	SS	III	1	264	29
She says she never shall think well of anybody again; and	SS	III	1	265	36
But I don't think mine would be, to make one son	SS	III	1	269	54
Whatever Lucy might think about it herself, you know, it	SS	III	2	272	14
I could not tell what to think myself; and I believe in my	SS	III	2	272	16
He could not bear to think of her doing no better, and so	SS	III	2	273	16
Miss Dashwood, do you think people make love when any body	SS	III	2	274	18
directly, 'I wonder how you could think of such a thing.	SS	III	2	275	22
hope Mrs. Jennings won't think it too much trouble to give	SS	III	2	277	30
How attentive she is, to think of every body!--	SS	III	2	278	32
afterwards good reason to think her object gained; for, on	SS	III	3	280	9
her lips that she did not think that any material	SS	III	3	281	9
"I shall always think myself very much obliged to you."	SS	III	3	281	13
					14
day's post, is his, if he think it worth his acceptance--	SS	III	3	282	19
serve him farther, I must think very differently of him	SS	III	3	284	23
in the world, I think I shall know where to look for them."	SS	III	4	285	5
"Then you would not have me tell it Lucy, for I think of	SS	III	4	286	14
I think it ought not to be mentioned to any body else.	SS	III	4	286	15
speech; neither did she think it worth inquiring into; and	SS	III	4	286	18
However, you will think of all that at your leisure."	SS	III	4	287	22
"Colonel Brandon, I think, lodges in St. James's-Street,"	SS	III	4	290	40
					41
by poor Mr. Ferrars, I do think it is not worth while to	SS	III	4	291	51
on the ground-floor, and I think the housekeeper told me,	SS	III	4	292	55
"You surprise me; I should think it must nearly have	SS	III	5	296	21
"We think now"--said Mr. Dashwood, after a short pause, "	SS	III	5	296	24
I have good reason to think--indeed I have it from the	SS	III	5	297	31
But had I been informed of it a few hours earlier--I think	SS	III	5	299	37
inclined from the first to think Marianne's complaint more	SS	III	7	307	3
his cheeks--"do you think me most a knave or a fool?"	SS	III	8	318	15
She began to think that he must be in liquor;--the	SS	III	8	318	16
					17
and in spite of herself made her think him sincere.	SS	III	8	319	25
Perhaps you will hardly think the better of me,--it is	SS	III	8	319	29
Do not think yourself excused by any weakness, any natural	SS	III	8	322	37
and I persuaded myself to think that nothing else in	SS	III	8	323	40
I cannot think of it.--	SS	III	8	324	45
Relate only what in your conscience you think necessary	SS	III	8	325	52
And in short--what do you think of my wife's style of	SS	III	8	328	61
society, they already think me an unprincipled fellow,	SS	III	8	328	63
letter will only make them think me a blackguard one.'	SS	III	8	328	63
probably he did not think it would --vex me horridly.--	SS	III	8	330	69
"And you do think something better of me than you did?"--	SS16			331	75
If, however, I am allowed to think that you and yours feel	SS	III	8	332	77
was the general result, to think even of her sister.	SS	III	9	333	1
by them, which made her think of him as now separated for	SS	III	9	333	2
of her joy to think only of what would increase it.	SS	III	9	335	7
be as ready as yourself to think our connection the	SS	III	9	337	17
and Elinor withdrew to think it all over in private, to	SS	III	9	339	27
to think that something more than gratitude already dawned.	SS	III	10	340	3
if I could be allowed to think that he was not always	SS	III	10	344	17
could be assured of that, you think you should be easy."	SS	III	10	344	18
					19
My illness has made me think-----	SS	III	10	345	28
in a tone that implied--"do you really think him selfish?"	SS	III	11	351	10
observation may, I think, be fairly drawn from the whole	SS	III	11	352	16
					17
Mrs. Dashwood could think of no other question, and Thomas	SS	III	11	355	45
lost, and Margaret might think herself very well off, that	SS	III	11	355	45
of her daughter, to think the attachment, which one she	SS	III	11	355	46
the care of Mr. Pratt, I think-- nay, I am sure, it would	SS	III	13	362	5
And Lucy perhaps at first might think only of procuring	SS	III	13	364	12
with him as I once used to think I might be with you; but	SS	III	13	365	14
"I was simple enough to think, that because my faith was	SS	III	13	368	28
he must think I have never forgiven him for offering."	SS	III	13	368	30
quite enough in love to think that three hundred and fifty	SS	III	13	369	32
"I do think," she continued, "nothing was ever carried on	SS	III	13	370	37
that his sister and I both think a letter of proper	SS	III	13	371	39
offended;--and I should think you might now venture so far	SS	III	13	372	42
a reconciliation, I shall think that even John and Fanny	SS	III	13	372	45
to attract him--yet I think it would altogether be	SS	III	14	375	9
"I think I have heard you speak of him before, said Emma.	W			315	1
Penelope makes light of her conduct, but I think such	W			316	2
I do not think Tom Musgrave should be named with him in	W			316	2
I would rather be teacher at a school (and I can think of	W			318	2
yourself,--but I do not think there are many very	W			318	2
very disagreable men;--I think I could like any good	W			318	2
"My dearest Emma cried eliz: warmly--do you think I would	W			320	2
Sometimes I think she does like him.	W			321	2
me that he should be encouraged to think of her at all."--	W			321	2
"A young man must think of somebody. said eliz:--& why	W			321	2

I shall long to know what you think of Tom Musgrave." W 321 2
coming.--which I think is doing pretty well, tho' it would W 322 2
"You are paying Miss Emma no great compliment I think Mary, W 324 3
I do not much think she is like any of the family but Miss W 324 3
him, he began with, "I think Miss Emma, I remember your W 325 4
"Mr Turner had not been dead a great while I think? W 325 5
& mother think it has given him rather an unsettled turn.-- W 328 8
which made her think her brother Sam's a hopeless case.-- W 328 8
Emma did not think, or reflect;--she felt & acted--. W 330 11
Do you think Miss Osborne will keep her word with me, when W 332 12
fox there, & a Badger--anybody would think they were alive. W 333 12
"I think there is no occasion for their engaging W 337 15
"It is making it too much of a fatigue I think, to stay so W 340 19
"I do not think her handsome." replied Emma, to whom all W 340 19
& I do not think I could have done it myself.-- W 341 19
me, you will not encourage him to think of Miss Edwards.-- W 341 19
She danced twice with Capt. Hunter, & I think shews him in W 341 19
as you well know, Emma;--but you must think him agreable. W 342 19
"I should like to know the man you do think agreable." W 343 19
I cannot think of him, but as playing cards with ly W 343 19
which made his Lordship think;--and when he addressed her W 346 21
you, but you know every body must think her an old fool.-- W 352 26
I think there is powder enough in my hair for my wife & W 353 26
It has been excessively admired;--but sometimes I think W 353 26
I shall wear one tomorrow that I think you will prefer to W 353 26
I think a snug chat infinitely better. W 354 28
Mrs Robert Smartly--but we think a month very little. W 356 28
I think even you must be a convert to a brown complexion."- W 357 28
Croydon now, said Mrs Robert--we never think of any other. W 358 28
I think it is a much better game than speculation. W 358 28
not engage--you will not think of me unless you see me."-- W 360 28
she seemed no longer to think about, found the continuance W 360 30
She was at leisure, she could read & think,--tho' her W 361 31
vex you more than you think for, if you stay at home.--" W 362 32
"In such cases, a woman has not often much beauty to think PP I 1 4 21
Only think what an establishment it would be for one of PP I 1 4 24
and therefore, as she will think it an act of kindness, if PP I 2 7 16
Only think of that my dear; he actually danced with her PP I 3 12 16
in censuring any one; but I always speak what I think." PP I 4 14 8
entitled to think well of themselves, and meanly of others. PP I 4 15 11
by such commendation to think of her as he chose. PP I 4 17 16
Lodge, where he could think with pleasure of his own PP I 5 18 1
and whether he did not think there were a great many PP I 5 19 7
every thing in his favour, should think highly of himself. PP I 5 20 18
vanity to what we would have others think of us." PP I 5 20 20
to him to-morrow, I should think she had as good a chance PP I 6 23 10
him and said, "did not you think, Mr. Darcy, that I PP I 6 24 17
18

"Do you not think it would be a proper compliment to the PP I 6 26 32
you should be so ready to think your own children silly. PP I 7 29 8
If I wished to think slightingly of any body's children, PP I 7 29 8
as to think our two youngest daughters uncommonly foolish." PP I 7 29 11
When they get to our age I dare say they will not think PP I 7 29 12
"How can you be so silly," cried her mother, "as to think PP I 7 32 34
"and I am inclined to think that you would not wish to see PP I 8 36 7
"I think I have heard you say, that their uncle is an PP I 8 36 15
"Upon my word, Caroline, I should think it more possible PP I 8 38 38
"I think she will. PP I 8 38 41
"Yes, all of them, I think. PP I 8 39 45
who arrived about the same time, think it at all advisable. PP I 9 41 2
Mr. Jones says we must not think of moving her. PP I 9 41 3
You will not think of quitting it in a hurry I hope, PP I 9 42 7
But that gentleman," looking at Darcy, "seemed to think PP I 9 43 23
Not that I think Charlotte so very plain--but then she is PP I 9 44 29
She longed to speak, but could think of nothing to say; PP I 9 45 35
How odious I should think them!" PP I 10 47 7
and I think it infinitely superior to Miss Grantley's." PP I 10 48 15
if not estimable, you think at least highly interesting. PP I 10 48 27
for he would certainly think the better of me, if under PP I 10 49 31
great moment, should you think ill of that person for PP I 10 50 37
I do think it is the hardest thing in the world, that your PP I 13 61 7
"No, that I am sure I shall not; and I think it was very PP I 13 62 10
"He must be an oddity, I think," said she. PP I 13 64 17
"No, my dear; I think not. PP I 13 64 18
is not wholly new, yet I think it is well expressed." PP I 13 64 19
"I think you said she was a widow, sir? has she any family? PP I 14 67 4
same house with him, and I think him very disagreeable." PP I 16 77 13
together, as I think you said, in the closest manner!" PP I 16 80 36
She could think of nothing but of Mr. Wickham, and of what PP I 16 84 59
to be done, but to think well of them both, to defend the PP I 17 85 1
Do clear them too, or we shall be obliged to think ill of PP I 17 85 3
One does not know what to think." PP I 17 86 6
"I beg your pardon;--one knows exactly what to think." PP I 17 86 7
But Jane could think with certainty on only one point,-- PP I 17 86 8
I think it no sacrifice to join occasionally in evening PP I 17 87 11
he did, whether he would think it proper to join in the PP I 17 87 12
You think it a faithful portrait undoubtedly." PP I 18 91 16
"I do not think we were speaking at all. PP I 18 93 26
"What think you of books?" said he, smiling. PP I 18 93 27
"I am sorry you think so; but if that be the case, there PP I 18 93 29
But perhaps you have been too pleasantly engaged to think PP I 18 95 49
venture still to think of both gentlemen as I did before." PP I 18 96 55
it was such a comfort to think how fond the two sisters PP I 18 99 63
And I do not think it of light importance that he should PP I 18 101 71
I cannot acquit him of that duty; nor could I think well PP I 18 101 71
success; and happy did she think it for Bingley and her PP I 18 101 72
are, first, that I think it a right thing for every PP I 19 105 9
10

your wit and vivacity I think must be acceptable to her, PP I 19 106 10
"Were it certain that Lady Catherine would think so," said PP I 19 107 15
What do you think has happened this morning?-- PP I 20 112 25
"Why will you think so? PP I 21 117 14
her again. I really do not think Georgiana Darcy has her PP I 21 117 14
is not misleading me, I think, when I call Charles most PP I 21 118 14
"What think you of this sentence, my dear Lizzy?-- said PP I 21 118 15
"I did not think you would;--and that being the case, I PP I 21 120 26
us again, which I should think exceedingly probable, stay PP I 22 124 9
Do you think it incredible that Mr. Collins should be able PP I 22 125 15
But when you have had time to think it all over, I hope PP I 22 125 17
whom he had been used to think tolerably sensible, was as PP I 23 127 6
did not come back, she should think herself very ill used. PP I 23 129 14
"Indeed, Mr. Bennet," said she, "it is very hard to think PP I 23 130 17
"I cannot bear to think that they should have all this PP I 23 130 20
to like him, she could not think without anger, hardly PP II 1 133 3
She could think of nothing else, and yet whether Bingley's PP II 1 134 3
You wish to think all the world respectable, and are hurt PP II 1 135 11
I only want to think you perfect, and you set yourself PP II 1 135 11
whom I really love, and still fewer of whom I think well. PP II 1 135 11
for him, I should only think worse of her understanding, PP II 1 135 13
"I must think your language too strong in speaking of both, PP II 1 136 14
displease you by saying what I think of persons you esteem. PP II 1 136 19
What sister would think herself at liberty to do it, PP II 1 137 24
It is something to think of, and gives her a sort of PP II 1 137 27
"True," said Mr. Bennet, "but it is a comfort to think PP II 1 138 29
every body was pleased to think how much they had always PP II 1 138 30
But, Lizzy! Oh, sister! it is very hard to think that she PP II 2 140 4
neighbours who think of themselves before anybody else. PP II 2 140 4
of independent fortune to think no more of a girl, whom he PP II 2 140 7
But do you think she would be prevailed on to go back with PP II 2 141 10
My dear aunt, how could you think of it? PP II 2 141 13
but he would hardly think a month's ablution enough to PP II 2 141 13
he ought to have, I should think you could not do better. PP II 3 144 2
I think to be wisest; and now, I hope you are satisfied." PP II 3 145 9
so far resigned as to think it inevitable, and even PP II 3 145 11
"I did not think Caroline in spirits," were her words, " PP II 3 147 23
proved you right, do not think me obstinate if I still PP II 3 148 26
every painful thought, and think only of what will make me PP II 3 148 26
the least unwilling to think her a very good sort of girl. PP II 3 150 29
were not of a kind to make her think him less agreeable. PP II 4 152 4
I should be sorry to think our friend mercenary." PP II 4 153 8
sort of girl Miss King is, I shall know what to think." PP II 4 153 10
I should be sorry, you know, to think ill of a young man PP II 4 153 18
Lady Catherine will not think the worse of you for being PP II 6 161 6
"your father's estate is entailed on Mr. Collins, I think. PP II 6 164 15
16

But really, ma'am, I think it would be very hard upon PP II 6 165 35
I think it would not be very likely to promote sisterly PP II 6 165 35
in which his wife did not think it necessary to go PP II 7 168 3
was at a ball--and at this ball, what do you think he did? PP II 8 175 18
No one admitted to the privilege of hearing you, can think PP II 8 176 26
It was absolutely necessary, therefore, to think of PP II 9 177 3
4

a short pause, added, "I think I have understood that Mr. PP II 9 177 6
7

and Mrs. Collins did not think it right to press the PP II 9 181 30
"Unless where they like women of fortune, which I think PP II 10 183 13
I think I have heard you say that you know them." PP II 10 184 21
I have reason to think Bingley very much indebted to him. PP II 10 185 24
she could think without interruption of all that she heard. PP II 10 186 38
It was some consolation to think that his visit to Rosings PP II 11 188 1
She could not think of Darcy's leaving Kent, without PP II 11 188 2
been favourable, do you think that any consideration would PP II 11 190 10
"I have every reason in the world to think ill of you. PP II 11 191 12
it was impossible to think of any thing else, and totally PP II 12 195 1
I first began to think of him in a very different manner. PP II 12 200 5
he hoped I should not think it unreasonable for him to PP II 12 200 5
Of neither Darcy nor Wickham could she think, without PP II 13 208 7
She could think only of her letter. PP II 13 209 13
niece; nor could she think, without a smile, of what her PP II 14 210 2
to feel it most acutely, more I think than last year. PP II 14 210 3
the humble home scene, I think we may flatter ourselves PP II 15 215 4
parsonage, I should not think any one abiding in it an PP II 15 216 4
I do not think it is very pretty; but I thought I might as PP II 16 219 3
to trim it with fresh, I think it will be very tolerable. PP II 16 219 4
Only think what a miserable summer else we shall have!" PP II 16 220 6
"What do you think? PP II 16 220 8
Elizabeth was shocked to think that, however incapable of PP II 16 220 15
aunt Philips wants you so to get husbands, you can't think. PP II 16 221 17
but I do not think there would have been any fun in it. PP II 16 221 17
and then, what do you think we did? we dressed up PP II 16 221 17
on purpose to pass for a lady,--only think what fun! PP II 16 221 17
we got to the George, I do think we behaved very PP II 16 222 22
But I think Mr. Darcy improves on acquaintance." PP II 18 234 32
"And do not you think him a very handsome gentleman, ma'am? PP III 1 247 16
much to his credit, I am sure, that you should think so." PP III 1 248 29
Not like the wild young men now-a-days, who think of PP III 1 249 38
She knew not what to think, nor how to account for it. PP III 1 252 54
his resentment had not made him think really ill of her. PP III 1 256 64
spots in its environs, to think of any thing else. PP III 1 258 76
she could do nothing but think, and think with wonder, of PP III 1 259 77
do nothing but think, and think with wonder, of Mr. PP III 1 259 77
Of Mr. Darcy it was now a matter of anxiety to think well; PP III 2 264 14
I know not what to think. PP III 4 275 5
My father and mother believe the worst, but I cannot think PP III 4 275 5
"Do you really think so?" cried Elizabeth, brightening up PP III 5 282 2
I cannot think so very ill of Wickham. PP III 5 282 3
would do as little, and think as little about it, as any PP III 5 283 8
"But can you think that Lydia is so lost to every thing PP III 5 283 9
But she is very young; she has never been taught to think PP III 5 283 10
"But you see that Jane," said her aunt, "does not think so PP III 5 284 11
"Of whom does Jane ever think ill? PP III 5 284 12
"And did Colonel Forster appear to think ill of Wickham PP III 5 291 53
guess with who, I shall think you a simpleton, for there PP III 5 291 60
I should never be happy without him, so think it no harm PP III 5 291 60
I am sure, but I did not think it right for either of them. PP III 5 292 66
Bennet, I am inclined to think that her own disposition PP III 6 297 11
I should be sorry to think so ill of him, in the very PP III 7 304 31
refuge in her own room, that she might think with freedom. PP III 7 307 50
And I think you will agree with me, in considering a PP III 8 312 19
on to think as they thought, and act as they wished. PP III 8 314 22
"Only think of its being three months," she cried, "since PP III 9 316 7
the breakfast room, "and what do you think of my husband? PP III 9 317 11
more desirable to such as did think, than such as did not. PP III 9 318 18
"No really," replied Elizabeth; "I think there cannot be PP III 9 318 23
which Lydia seems to think necessary; and then I must PP III 9 320 33
Don't think me angry, however, for I only mean to let you PP III 10 321 2
She was ashamed to think how much. PP III 10 326 3
"I often think," said she, "that there is nothing so bad PP III 11 330 10
good table, she did not think any thing less than two PP III 11 338 60
I will think no more about him." PP III 12 339 4
"My dear Lizzy, you cannot think me so weak, as to be in PP III 12 339 8
"I think you are in very great danger of making him as PP III 12 339 9
She could think of nothing more to say; but if he wished PP III 12 342 25
I think every thing has passed off uncommonly well, I PP III 12 342 28
And what do you think she said besides? PP III 12 342 28
I do think Mrs. Long is as good a creature as ever lived-- PP III 12 342 28
I think she will be pleased with the hermitage." PP III 14 352 18
"How could I ever think her like her nephew?" said she, as PP III 14 353 21
You have widely mistaken my character, if you think I can PP III 14 357 61
for many hours, learn to think of it less than incessantly. PP III 15 360 1
matters as these; but I think I may defy even your PP III 15 362 12
Now, Lizzy, I think I have surprised you. PP III 15 363 18
I did not think Mrs. Gardiner was so little to be trusted. PP III 16 366 4
I cannot think of it without abhorrence." PP III 16 367 12
"Did it," said he, "did it soon make you think better of PP III 16 368 18
we have both reason to think my opinions not entirely PP III 16 368 21
But think no more of the letter. PP III 16 368 23
Think only of the past as its remembrance gives you PP III 16 369 23
my own family circle, to think meanly of all the rest of PP III 16 369 24
think meanly of their sense and worth compared with my own. PP III 16 369 24
What will you think of my vanity.? PP III 16 369 26
You will only think I feel more than I ought to do, when I PP III 17 373 12
But let me advise you to think better of it. PP III 17 376 35
Lord bless me! only think! dear me! Mr. Darcy! PP III 17 378 43
"My dearest child," she cried, "I can think of nothing PP III 17 378 45
"Wickham, perhaps, is my favourite; but I think I shall PP III 17 379 48
considered, I begin to think it perfectly reasonable. PP III 18 380 5
she must sometimes think the pleasure dearly bought, when PP III 18 384 26
you have nothing else to do, I hope you will think of us. PP III 19 386 7
very much, and I do not think we shall have quite money PP III 19 386 7
what did Sir Thomas think of Woolwich? or how could a boy MP I 1 5 2
"I think we cannot do better," said she, "let us send for MP I 1 5 4
glad to take her turn, and think nothing of the MP I 1 9 10
I suppose you would not think it fair to expect Ellis to MP I 1 9 12
"That is exactly what I think," cried Mrs. Norris, "and MP I 1 10 15
are, without making them think too lowly of their cousin; MP I 1 10 17
of seventeen will always think fair with a child of ten. MP I 2 17 22
"Dear mamma, only think, my cousin cannot put the map of MP I 2 18 23
Of the rest she saw nothing; nobody seemed to think of her MP I 2 21 34
be so small, she could not think of living with her aunt MP I 3 25 17
But you are now of an age to be treated better; I think MP I 3 26 25
were talked of) and then think of the kind pains you took MP I 3 27 36
to Mrs. Norris,-- "I think, sister, we need not keep Miss MP I 3 28 38
39

thing in the world for me think of, or for any body to MP I 3 28 42
sake, I would not do so unjust a think by the poor girl. MP I 3 29 46
I should be very glad to think I could have a little MP I 3 30 52
He could not think Lady Bertram quite equal to supply his MP I 3 32 62
one of those persons who think nothing can be dangerous or MP I 3 32 63
Bertram was beginning to think matrimony a duty; and as a MP I 4 38 10
therefore, she did not forget to think of it seriously. MP I 4 42 18
Nobody can think more highly of the matrimonial state than MP I 4 43 23
I think too well of Miss Bertram to suppose she would ever MP I 5 45 14
as she still continued to think Mr. Crawford very plain, MP I 5 48 30
"No," replied Edmund, "I do not think she has ever been to MP I 5 51 42
"No wonder that Mr. Rushworth should think so at present," MP I 6 53 5
As he has done so well by Smith, I think I had better have MP I 6 53 8
If I were you, I should not think of the expense. MP I 6 53 9
I think I shall have repton." MP I 6 55 15
water meadows; so that I think, if so much could be done MP I 6 55 17
amazingly which makes me think that repton, or any body of MP I 6 55 17
Does not it make you think of Cowper? MP I 6 56 20
Mr. Rushworth is quite right, I think, in meaning to give MP I 6 56 26
"I am to have it to-morrow; but how do you think it is to MP I 6 58 35
but when you do think of it, you must see the importance MP I 6 58 38
a correspondent, makes her think you too severe upon us." MP I 6 59 45
"And very ungrateful I think." MP I 7 63 60
"Do not you think," said Fanny, after a little MP I 7 63 8
But I think her present home must do her good. MP I 7 64 9
She did not think very much about it, however; he pleased MP I 7 65 13
parted again, he should think it right to attend Mrs. MP I 7 65 14
Crawford, but he seemed to think it enough that the MP I 7 66 14
She could not but think indeed that Mr. Crawford might as MP I 7 67 16
She began to think it rather hard upon the mare to have MP I 7 68 16
I cannot but think that good horsemanship has a great deal MP I 7 69 25
to stay at home, I think Miss Crawford would be glad to MP I 7 69 28
remarks on the stars, to think beyond themselves; but when MP I 7 71 31
You should learn to think of other people; and take my MP I 7 71 34
I think nobody can justly accuse me of sparing myself upon MP I 7 73 53
of a mile, I cannot think I was unreasonable to ask it. MP I 7 73 53
He was ashamed to think that for four days together she MP I 7 74 58
made Mrs. Rushworth still think she wished to come, till MP I 8 76 2
you could drive, Julia, I think this will be a good MP I 8 80 29
"It was foolish of me not to think of all that, but I am MP I 9 86 8
there is some reason to think that the linings and MP I 9 86 9
Do you think the minds which are suffered, which are MP I 9 87 16
"Do you think the church itself never chosen then?" MP I 9 92 43
conversation which means not very often, I do think it. MP I 9 92 44
"I do not think you ever will," said she with an arch MP I 9 93 53
Do not you think we have?" MP I 9 94 60
"Do you think we are walking four miles an hour?" MP I 9 95 65
was left on the bench to think with pleasure of her MP I 9 96 76
rather lower, "I do not think that I shall ever see MP I 10 98 7
If other people think Sotherton improved, I have no doubt MP I 10 98 8
"You think her more light-hearted than I am." MP I 10 99 13
I am as lively as Julia, but I have more to think of now." MP I 10 99 15
and protection, or I think you might with little MP I 10 99 18
with my assistance; I think it might be done, if you MP I 10 99 18
and could allow yourself to think it not prohibited." MP I 10 99 18
"But they cannot be very far off, and I think I am equal MP I 10 100 26
After an interval of silence, "I think they might as well MP I 10 102 38
"I do not think him at all handsome." MP I 10 102 42
I think he is an ill-looking fellow. MP I 10 102 43
"Well," said he, "if you really think I had better go; it MP I 10 103 48
"I think you have done pretty well yourself, ma'am. MP I 10 105 54
It was much pleasanter to think of Henry Crawford than of MP I 11 107 1
of their father; and to think of their father in England MP I 11 107 1
Nor can I think it wrong that it should. MP I 11 109 17
I have no doubt that I was biassed, but I think it was MP I 11 109 17
may be fairly suspected, you think?" said Edmund. MP I 11 109 20
"There are such clergymen, no doubt, but I think they are MP I 11 110 24
command than he has now, I think more would have been made MP I 11 111 30
It must make him think, and I have no doubt that he MP I 11 112 30
"I think the man who could often quarrel with Fanny," said MP I 11 112 32
"You taught me to think and feel on the subject, cousin." MP I 11 113 37
almost think that he admired her more than Julia." MP I 12 116 9
mistaken, and meant to think differently in future; but MP I 12 116 11
Mr. Crawford's choice, she knew not always what to think. MP I 12 116 11
"I think, ma'am," said Mrs. Norris--her eyes directed MP I 12 117 12
looking on now, and I think it was rather a pity they MP I 12 117 13
I cannot but think of dear Sir Thomas's delight. MP I 12 118 16
I always come to you to know what I am to think of public MP I 12 119 22
"It was a hard case, upon my word;" and, "I do think you MP I 13 122 3
two hundred miles off, I think there would have been no MP I 13 122 4
you amends, Yates, I think we must raise a little theatre MP I 13 123 5
I can stand it no longer, and I think, I may say, that MP I 13 125 14
"I think it would be very wrong. MP I 13 125 17
are circumstanced, I must think it would be highly MP I 13 125 17
it would be imprudent, I think, with regard to Maria, MP I 13 125 17
We may be trusted, I think, in choosing some play most MP I 13 125 18
think our time very well spent, and so I am sure will he.-- MP I 13 126 18
reciting kind, I think he has always a decided taste. MP I 13 126 25
way; and I think a theatre ought not to be attempted.-- MP I 13 127 28
"I should think my aunt Norris would be on your side." MP I 13 128 36
to be of any use, but I think we could not choose worse." MP I 14 131 3
in prison? I think I see you coming in with your basket." MP I 14 135 17
whole, and who could not think of her as under the MP I 14 136 20
appearance would be, to think of the others, or draw any MP I 15 138 1
tell you, that I think it exceedingly unfit for private MP I 15 139 11
I am sure--but I still think you see things too strongly; MP I 15.140 14
There would be the greatest indecorum I think." MP I 15 140 14
"Oh! she might think the difference between us--the MP I 15 141 21
The maids do their work very well, and I think we shall be MP I 15 141 22
"Do not you think he would?" MP I 15 144 34
sharply, "but I shall think her a very obstinate, MP I 15 147 55
have no objection to any thing that you all think eligible. MP I 15 148 59
I cannot think of it with any patience--and it does appear MP I 16 154 8
in every respect; but I can think of no other alternative. MP I 16 154 12
Think it a little over. MP I 16 154 14
To think only of the licence which every rehearsal must MP I 16 154 14
you are known to think will be disagreeable to my uncle. MP I 16 155 15
"No, I cannot think of any thing else." MP I 16 155 19
most unwelcome news; and she could think of nothing else. MP I 16 156 28
the mouth, and seemed to think it as great an escape to be MP I 17 158 2
She could almost think any thing would have been MP I 17 160 6
Think of Mr. Rushworth." MP I 17 161 12
"You had better tell Miss Bertram to think of Mr. MP I 17 161 13
I often think of Mr. Rushworth's property and independence, MP I 17 161 13
and wish them in other hands--but I never think of him. MP I 17 161 13
I do not think we do so well without him. MP I 17 162 16
I think she likes Sotherton too well to be inconstant." MP I 17 162 16
you think there is any thing so very fine in all this? MP I 18 165 3
I think you may give me your help in putting it together.-- MP I 18 166 6
if he were, I do not think I could go through it with him, MP I 18 168 17
I did not think much of it at first--but, upon my word--. MP I 18 168 19
and besides, he did not think it would be fair by the MP II 1 177 5
her say, "how do you think the young people have been MP II 1 180 13
I do not think you will find your woods by any means worse MP II 1 181 16
"It is time to think of our visitors," said Maria, still MP II 1 182 19
"If I must say what I think," continued Mr. Rushworth, "in MP II 1 186 33
I think we are a great deal better employed, sitting MP II 1 186 33
She never ceased to think of what was due to you. MP II 2 187 1
to the bottom of Sandcroft Hill, what do you think I did? MP II 2 189 5
"I hope we shall always think the acquaintance worth any MP II 2 190 6
which made Mr. Yates think it wiser to let him pursue his MP II 2 191 10
"When do you think of going?" MP II 2 193 15
"Do you think so?" said Fanny. MP II 3 196 3
I think he values the very quietness you speak of, and MP II 3 196 3
it is not more I think than such an absence has a tendency MP II 3 197 3
"To-morrow, I think, my uncle dines at Sotherton, and you MP II 3 199 17
and very happy to think any thing of his daughter's MP II 3 201 22
He should not have to think of her as pining in the MP II 3 202 25
something fresh to see and think of was thus extended to MP II 4 206 3
more wonderful than the rest, I do think it is memory. MP II 4 208 12
One does not think of extent here--and between ourselves, MP II 4 209 15
You will think me rhapsodizing; but when I am out of doors, MP II 4 209 16
What do you think we have been sitting down for but to be MP II 4 211 26
own sister, I think I had a right to alarm you a little." MP II 4 212 30
These are something like grievances, and make me think the MP II 4 212 31
not envy you; I do not much think I shall even respect you. MP II 4 213 40
"How came she to think of asking Fanny?-- MP II 5 217 1
"I cannot imagine why Mrs. Grant should think of asking MP II 5 217 3
accepted or not; and I think he will consider it a right MP II 5 217 9
"Indeed I think you may." MP II 5 219 20
above themselves, makes me think it right to give you a MP II 5 221 32
"Yes, ma'am, I should not think of any thing else." MP II 5 221 33
"And if it should rain, which I think exceedingly likely, MP II 5 221 34
I hope you do not think me too fine." MP II 5 222 43
I think my friend Julia knows better than to entertain her MP II 5 224 52
I think if we had had the disposal of events--if Mansfield MP II 5 225 57
I think, Miss Price, we would have indulged ourselves with MP II 5 225 57
it, which she could not think lightly of; but she checked MP II 5 226 64
She had begun to think of him--she felt that she had--with MP II 5 227 69
a smile, "and how do you think I mean to amuse myself, MP II 6 229 1
for the intermediate days, and what do you think it is?" MP II 6 229 1
I used to think she had neither complexion nor countenance; MP II 6 229 5
it and talk to her; to think as I think, be interested in MP II 6 231 9
talk to her; to think as I think, be interested in all my MP II 6 231 9
Fanny one of them, or to think that with so much MP II 6 231 11
at Mansfield--ready to think of every member of that home MP II 6 234 18
that he first began to think, that any one in the habit of MP II 7 238 2
I think the house and premises may be made comfortable, MP II 7 242 24
You think with me, I hope--(turning with a softened voice MP II 7 244 27
Only think how useful he was at Sotherton! MP II 7 244 30
Only think what grand things were produced there by our MP II 7 244 30
Do not think of me as I appeared then." MP II 7 245 31
of the rest, till some of the rest began to think of them. MP II 7 249 49
You must think of that; you must try to make up your mind MP II 7 249 53
When you are a lieutenant!--only think, William, when you MP II 7 249 53
"I begin to think I shall never be a lieutenant, Fanny. MP II 7 250 54
but I trust we shall both think she acquits herself like a MP II 7 250 60
I believe, we must not think of a Northampton ball. MP II 8 252 1
I think of giving at Mansfield, will be for their cousins. MP II 8 252 3
as to the rooms he would think fittest to be used, but MP II 8 253 7
not, on his own account, think very much of the evening, MP II 8 256 13
and she had reason to think Mr. Crawford likewise out, she MP II 8 256 14
every thing she could think of to obviate the scruples MP II 8 258 15
have," said she, "more by half than I ever use or think of. MP II 8 258 16
"When I wear this necklace I shall always think of you," MP II 8 258 18
"You must think of somebody else too when you wear that MP II 8 259 19
"You must think of Henry, for it was his choice in the MP II 8 259 19
Do you think Henry will claim the necklace as mine, and MP II 8 259 20
very pretty--but I never think of it; and though you would MP II 8 260 22
am the last person to think that could be--but they have MP II 9 263 16
To think of him as Miss Crawford might be justified in MP II 9 264 18
the fatigue of such a journey, to think of any thing else. MP II 9 266 21
was worn down at last to think every thing an evil MP II 9 267 22
believed he had soon ceased to think of her countenance. MP II 9 268 27
And he looked so conscious, that Fanny could think but of MP II 9 268 28
I think, I hope, I am sure she is not serious--but I would MP II 9 268 29
She does not think evil, but she speaks it--speaks it in MP II 9 269 31
I begin to think it most improbable; the chances grow less MP II 9 269 38
befell me, I could think of your kindness and sympathy MP II 9 270 38
Only think, my dear Sir Thomas, what extraordinary MP II 10 272 3
It was but to think of her conversation with Edmund; and MP II 10 273 5
her own claims as to think, that if Mr. Crawford had not MP II 10 274 8
Miss Crawford knew Mrs. Norris too well to think of MP II 10 277 16
Did she think of being up before you set off?" MP II 10 279 27
Mr. Crawford, I think you call for him at half past nine?" MP II 10 280 29
that she could never even think of her aunt Norris in the MP II 11 282 3
The evening was heavy like the day--"I cannot think what MP II 11 283 5
She could think of William the next day more cheerfully, MP II 11 283 7
They are all going away I think. MP II 11 284 9
We shew Fanny what a good girl we think her by praising MP II 11 285 11
is a comfort to think that we shall always have her." MP II 11 285 12
then, but she would not think of asking her to live there-- MP II 11 285 14
Yes--I think it must be compliments. MP II 11 287 22
not think him likely to marry at all--or not at present." MP II 11 289 36
When did you begin to think seriously about her?" MP II 12 292 7
Mary, she is not like her cousins; but I think I shall not MP II 12 293 14
From my soul I do not think she would marry you without MP II 12 293 15
"The more I think of it," she cried, "the more am I MP II 12 294 19
"Well, well, we do not think quite alike here. MP II 12 296 28
"Henry, I think so highly of Fanny Price, that if I could MP II 12 296 29
said he, "great as it is, for I think only of yours. MP II 13 299 5
No, no, don't think of me. MP II 13 302 8
for though he might think nothing of what had passed, it MP II 13 303 12
She did not know what to do, or what to think. MP II 13 304 16
and she was able to think as she would, while her aunts MP II 13 304 18
They little think how much it comes to, or what their MP II 13 305 24
I think I will have two shawls, Fanny." MP II 13 305 25
wishing not to appear to think any thing really intended, MP II 13 307 30
31
"You cannot think I mean to hurry you," said he, in an MP II 13 307 33
made up the note; "you cannot think I have any such object. MP II 13 307 33
distinction; but I think too well of you, Fanny, to MP III 1 313 12
I am half inclined to think, Fanny, that you do not quite MP III 1 316 29
This is so much my opinion, that I am sorry to think how MP III 1 317 34
any reason, child, to think ill of Mr. Crawford's temper?" MP III 1 317 36
For I had, Fanny, as I think my behaviour must have shewn, MP III 1 318 39
You think only of yourself; and because you do not feel MP III 1 318 39
it, Sir Thomas began to think a little relenting, a little MP III 1 320 44
all, perhaps all, would think her selfish and ungrateful. MP III 1 321 46
She wondered that Sir Thomas could have leisure to think MP III 1 322 51
"I do not think you would answer the purpose at all." MP III 1 325 61
in the first place, to think she did love him, though she MP III 2 326 1
the felicity of having a fire to sit over and think of it. MP III 2 329 10
The promised departure was all that Fanny could think of MP III 2 331 17
"No, my dear, I should not think of missing you, when such MP III 2 333 26
of mind--but he did not think he could have gone on MP III 3 336 7
Crawford;--but I do not think I have had a volume of MP III 3 338 13
I will tell you what, I think you will have a theatre, MP III 3 338 19
I think you will fit up a theatre at your house in Norfolk. MP III 3 339 19
Did you think me speaking improperly?--lightly, MP III 3 342 33
Did you think I ought?" MP III 3 343 38
You think me unsteady--easily swayed by the whim of the MP III 3 343 41
No, it is 'Fanny' that I think of all day, and dream of MP III 3 344 41
easily learn to think she was wanting him to break through. MP III 4 345 4
"I am afraid we think too differently, for me to find any MP III 4 346 11
"Do you suppose that we think differently? MP III 4 346 12
"As far as you have gone, Fanny, I think you perfectly MP III 4 347 16
time to attach yourself; but I think you perfectly right. MP III 4 347 16
herself, "that I think, I never shall, as far as the MP III 4 347 20
be answered for--I think I never shall return his regard." MP III 4 347 20
Between us, I think we should have won you. MP III 4 348 21
the other night, will think you unfitted as companions? MP III 4 348 23
in that respect, I think the difference between us too MP III 4 349 25
I do think that Mr. Rushworth was sometimes very jealous." MP III 4 350 27

I am shocked whenever I think that Maria could be capable	MP	III	4	350	28
if Julia did not think he was paying her attentions."	MP	III	4	350	29
sisters' good qualities, I think it very possible that	MP	III	4	350	30
"I am persuaded that he does not think as he ought, on	MP	III	4	350	31
Let him have all the perfections in the world, I think it	MP	III	4	353	45
claims which his sisters think he has, how was I to be	MP	III	4	353	45
And, and--we think very differently of the nature of women,	MP	III	4	353	45
I think I see him now, trying to be as demure and composed	MP	III	5	358	9
gentle Fanny! when I think of this being the last time of	MP	III	5	359	9
I can think only of the friends I am leaving; my excellent	MP	III	5	359	12
It is you only, you, insensible Fanny, who can think of	MP	III	5	362	16
"I cannot think well of a man who sports with any woman's	MP	III	5	363	23
If any man ever loved a woman for ever, I think Henry will	MP	III	5	363	24
she was much inclined to think his, she would have been	MP	III	6	366	4
she should be able to think of him as in London, and	MP	III	6	370	12
that she did not like to think of; and that part of the	MP	III	6	370	13
any thing to say, that I think you will like to hear, and	MP	III	6	373	26
speak, nor look, nor think, when the last moment came with	MP	III	6	374	28
And they think she will have her orders in a day or two.	MP	III	7	377	7
I began to think you would never come.	MP	III	7	378	14
I cannot think what Rebecca has been about.	MP	III	7	379	17
think of Fanny, and her long absence and long journey.	MP	III	7	380	23
in time, was at leisure to think of her eldest daughter	MP	III	7	385	37
And yet, I do not think I am a very difficult mistress to	MP	III	7	385	39
As she now sat looking at Betsey, she could not but think	MP	III	7	385	40
Aunt Norris lives too far off, to think of such little	MP	III	7	387	44
She soon learnt to think with respect of her own little	MP	III	7	387	47
Betsey too, a spoilt child, trained up to think the	MP	III	8	391	9
her to think of her cousin Edmund with moderated feelings.	MP	III	8	391	10
On the contrary, she could think of nothing but Mansfield,	MP	III	8	391	10
see each other, and I do really think we were a little.--	MP	III	9	393	1
I did not use to think her wanting in self possession, but	MP	III	9	393	1
learnt to think it no misfortune to be quietly employed.	MP	III	9	398	9
which she never failed to think over and calculate every	MP	III	10	399	2
Nothing of all that she had been used to think of as the	MP	III	10	400	7
completely unsuited to her, and ought not to think of her.	MP	III	10	405	16
It often grieved her to the heart--to think of the	MP	III	11	408	2
contrast between them--to think that where nature had made	MP	III	11	408	2
"You have been here a month, I think?" said he.	MP	III	11	410	8
Two months is an ample allowance, I should think six weeks	MP	III	11	410	16
I think the confinement of Portsmouth unfavourable to.	MP	III	11	410	16
and she could not think of his returning to town, and	MP	III	11	413	31
own family, and I do not think him so very ill-looking as	MP	III	12	416	2
so I think has he, though he will not acknowledge it."	MP	III	12	417	3
When I think of her great attachment to you, indeed, and	MP	III	13	421	2
She is the only woman in the world whom I could ever think	MP	III	13	421	2
I am refused, that, I think, will be the honest motive.	MP	III	13	422	2
Considering every thing, I think a letter will be	MP	III	13	422	2
than of an immediate hasty impulse; I think I am.	MP	III	13	422	2
I must think this matter over a little.	MP	III	13	423	2
I think I shall certainly write.	MP	III	13	423	2
'The only woman in the world, whom he could ever think of	MP	III	13	424	4
again; Lady Bertram could think nothing less, and Fanny	MP	III	14	429	1
say when there might be leisure to think of, or fetch her?	MP	III	14	430	6
Fanny was disposed to think the influence of London very	MP	III	14	433	12
she had some reason to think lightly of the friendship	MP	III	14	433	12
Do not you think Edmund would have been in town again long	MP	III	14	435	13
She had only learnt to think nothing of consequence but	MP	III	14	436	16
She had begun to think he really loved her, and to fancy	MP	III	15	438	6
She could still think of little else all the morning: but	MP	III	15	438	8
I don't know what Sir Thomas may think of such matters; he	MP	III	15	439	13
of feeling, made her think it scarcely possible for them	MP	III	15	442	21
He is still able to think and act; and I write, by his	MP	III	15	442	23
She was obliged to call herself to think of it, and	MP	III	15	443	24
Fanny, think of me!"	MP	III	15	446	34
Lady Bertram did not think deeply, but, guided by Sir	MP	III	16	449	5
Fanny to advise her, to think little of guilt and infamy.	MP	III	16	449	5
His present state, Fanny could hardly bear to think of.	MP	III	16	451	13
they were in reason to think that one interview with Miss	MP	III	16	452	15
but think that for me, for my feelings, she would-----	MP	III	16	456	25
of losing her, rather than have to think of her as I do.	MP	III	16	456	25
I do not think that even he could now hope to succeed with	MP	III	16	457	29
she might soon learn to think more justly, and not owe the	MP	III	16	458	30
He had suffered, and he had learnt to think, two	MP	III	17	462	4
She had been always used to think herself a little	MP	III	17	466	17
way, and a disposition to think a little too well of	E	I	1	5	4
she had then only to sit and think of what she had lost.	E	I	1	6	5
was very much disposed to think Miss Taylor had done as	E	I	1	7	10
"I am very glad I did think of her.	E	I	1	9	19
not have had poor James think himself slighted upon any	E	I	1	9	19
You do not think I could mean you, or suppose Mr.	E	I	1	10	32
you cannot think that I shall leave off match-making."	E	I	1	12	41
one idle day, 'I think it would be a very good thing for	E	I	1	12	42
You have drawn two pretty pictures--but I think there may	E	I	1	13	43
I think you must know Hartfield enough to comprehend that."	E	I	1	13	43
I think very well of Mr. Elton, and this is the only way I	E	I	1	13	46
and sweet temper made him think every thing due to her in	E	I	2	15	3
be missed; and could not think, without pain, of Emma's	E	I	2	18	11
I do not think it could disagree with you."	E	I	3	25	14
a good deal--but not what you would think any thing of.	E	I	4	29	10
I thought him very plain at first, but I do not think him	E	I	4	29	13
Not that I think Mr. Martin would ever marry any body but	E	I	4	31	25
"Only think of our happening to meet him!--	E	I	4	32	29
He did not think we ever walked this road.	E	I	4	32	29
What do you think of him?	E	I	4	32	29
Do you think him so very plain?"	E	I	4	32	29
"I think, Harriet, since your acquaintance with us, you	E	I	4	32	32
He was a great deal too full of the market to think of any	E	I	4	34	40
On the contrary, I think a young man might be very safely	E	I	4	34	42
She feared it was what every body else must think of and	E	I	4	35	44
Emma and Harriet Smith, but I think it a bad thing."	E	I	5	36	1
Do you really think it a bad thing?--why so?"	E	I	5	36	2
"I think they will neither of them do the other any good."	E	I	5	36	3
Not think they will do each other any good!	E	I	5	36	4
"Perhaps you think I am come on purpose to quarrel with	E	I	5	36	5
think you would have spoken a good word for me to any body.	E	I	5	37	10
I think her the very worst sort of companion that Emma	E	I	5	38	15
"I think her all you describe.	E	I	5	39	21
add this praise, that I do not think her personally vain.	E	I	5	39	21
of hinting that I do not think any possible good can arise	E	I	5	40	24
made to "what does weston think of the weather; shall we	E	I	5	41	31
"I am glad you think I have been useful to her; but	E	I	6	42	3
to think on points which had not fallen in her way before."	E	I	6	42	5
"Do you think so?" replied he.	E	I	6	48	32
her shoulders--and it makes one think she must catch cold."	E	I	6	48	36
I think one of his sisters must have helped him.	E	I	7	51	5
"You think I ought to refuse him then," said Harriet,	E	I	7	52	12
Do you think I had better say 'no?'"	E	I	7	53	20
every other person; if you think him the most agreeable	E	I	7	53	21
Do you think I am right?"	E	I	7	53	23
"I do not think he is conceited either, in general," said	E	I	7	54	30
However, I do really think Mr. Martin a very amiable young	E	I	7	54	30
mother and sisters would think and say, and was so anxious	E	I	7	55	35
Some time afterwards it was, "I think Mrs. Goddard would	E	I	7	55	40
"Let us think of those among our absent friends who are	E	I	7	56	44
We invalids think we are privileged people."	E	I	8	57	3
And therefore I think I will beg your excuse and take my	E	I	8	57	5
myself; and I think the sooner you go the better.	E	I	8	58	8
and I am inclined to think very well of her disposition.	E	I	8	58	10
"I am glad you think so; and the good hands, I hope, may	E	I	8	58	11
I can think of but one thing--who is in love with her?	E	I	8	59	23
"I have reason to think," he replied, "that Harriet Smith	E	I	8	59	25
her partiality for Harriet, will think this a good match."	E	I	8	62	38
What! think a farmer, (and with all his sense and all his	E	I	8	62	39
I wonder you should think it possible for me to have such	E	I	8	62	39
I much think your statement by no means fair.	E	I	8	62	39
sex in general would not think such beauty, and such	E	I	8	63	44
reason you have, is almost enough to make me think so too.	E	I	8	64	45
"We think so very differently on this point, Mr. Knightley,	E	I	8	65	48
decidedly, I think, as must prevent any second application.	E	I	8	65	48
"Robert Martin has no great loss--if he can but think so;	E	I	8	66	51
elton is the man, I think it will be all labour in vain."	E	I	8	66	51
that let Mr. Knightley think or say what he would, she had	E	I	8	67	56
back, not to think of Mr. Martin, but to talk of Mr. Elton.	E	I	8	68	58
could prefer, she should think the luckiest woman in the	E	I	8	68	58
had the benefit of this; I think this would convince you.	E	I	9	72	15
Do you think it is a good one?	E	I	9	72	17
Oh! Miss Woodhouse, do you think we shall ever find it out?	E	I	9	73	17
the application, which I think, my dear Harriet, you	E	I	9	73	18
Only think of those sweet verses--'to Miss ----.'	E	I	9	74	22
How little did I think!--	E	I	9	75	26
"I do think it is, without exception, the best charade I	E	I	9	76	30
But I think, my dear, you said you had got it."	E	I	9	79	54
The name makes me think of poor Isabella; for she was very	E	I	9	79	56
I think, Emma, I shall try and persuade her to stay longer	E	I	9	80	66
been able to accomplish, and I do not think you ever will.	E	I	9	80	67
I wonder which she will think the handsomest, Henry or	E	I	9	80	69
I think their father is too rough with them very often."	E	I	9	81	72
him with other papas, you would not think him rough.	E	I	9	81	73
Emma could not think it too soon; for with all his good	E	I	9	82	84
said she; "but I cannot think of any tolerable pretence	E	I	10	83	7
She pondered, but could think of nothing.	E	I	10	84	8
not my way, or my nature; and I do not think I ever shall.	E	I	10	84	15
I feel now as if I could think of nothing but these poor	E	I	10	87	25
"Poor creatures! one can think of nothing else."	E	I	10	87	26
"And really, I do not think the impression will soon be	E	I	10	87	27
"I do not think it will," stopping to look once more at	E	I	10	87	27
child on, was beginning to think how she might draw back a	E	I	10	88	33
"I think, indeed," said John Knightley pleasantly, "that	E	I	11	95	18
Mr. Weston, I think there is nothing he does not deserve.	E	I	11	95	19
I really never could think well of any body who proposed	E	I	11	96	25
"Nobody ever did think well of the Churchills, I fancy,"	E	I	11	96	26
it is, that we think alike about our nephews and nieces.	E	I	12	98	2
					3
these children are concerned, we might always think alike."	E	I	12	98	4
give me a chance of being right, if we think differently.	E	I	12	99	9
Now I cannot say, that I think you are any of you looking	E	I	12	103	38
I hope you will think better of their looks to-morrow; for	E	I	12	103	39
I trust, at least, that you do not think Mr. Knightley	E	I	12	103	39
I think Mr. John Knightley very far from looking well."	E	I	12	103	40
that my father does not think you looking well--but I hope	E	I	12	103	42
Woodhouse was persuaded to think it a possible thing in	E	I	13	108	2
to-morrow will bring, I think it would be no more than	E	I	13	110	9
I think your manners to him encouraging.	E	I	13	112	22
He must think himself a most agreeable fellow; I could not	E	I	13	113	26
indeed, that she began to think he must have received a	E	I	13	114	28
"Yes," said John Knightley, "and I think we shall have a	E	I	13	115	38
"Quite seasonable; and extremely fortunate we may think	E	I	13	115	39
them, and people think little of even the worst weather.	E	I	13	115	39
I think you will agree with me, (turning with a soft air	E	I	13	116	43
a soft air to Emma,) I think I shall certainly have your	E	I	13	116	43
and she determined to think as little as possible of Mr.	E	I	14	117	2
to be a match that every body who knew them must think of.	E	I	14	119	5
That Mr. and Mrs. Weston did think of it, she was very	E	I	14	119	5
If you think he will come, I shall think so too; for you	E	I	14	120	12
I used to think she was not capable of being fond of any	E	I	14	120	13
"and I am sure I never think of that poor young man	E	I	14	121	17
who can think of Miss Smith, when Miss Woodhouse is near!	E	I	15	130	31
I think seriously of Miss Smith?--Miss Smith is a very	E	I	15	131	35
as for myself, I am not, I think, quite so must at a loss.	E	I	15	132	35
he could never bear to think of--and in strange hands--a	E	I	15	132	38
away, and Emma sat sat down to think and be miserable.--	E	I	16	134	1
and blushed to think how much truer a knowledge of his	E	I	16	135	6
for she is as modest and humble as I used to think him.	E	I	16	137	11
Harriet's tears made her think that she should never be in	E	I	17	141	6
Harriet did think him all perfection, and maintain the non-	E	I	17	142	12
people in authority, I think they have a knack of swelling	E	I	18	147	19
Can you think your friend behind-hand in these sort of	E	I	18	149	26
"You seem determined to think ill of him."	E	I	18	149	27
"I do not want to think ill of him. I should be as ready	E	I	18	149	28
Frank Churchill; we shall think and speak of nobody else."	E	I	18	149	29
"He is a person I never think of from one month's end to	E	I	18	150	36
She could not think that Harriet's solace or her own sins	E	II	1	155	1
'well, Hetty, now I think you will be put to it to make	E	II	1	157	10
And I think she wrote us word that he had shewn them some	E	II	1	160	20
of her habit--(I can never think of it without trembling?)	E	II	1	160	23
Colonel and Mrs. Campbell think she does quite right, just	E	II	1	161	25
I think they judge wisely.	E	II	1	161	26
kind friends the Campbells think she had better come home,	E	II	1	161	29
of it now to her, that she does not think much about it.	E	II	1	162	31
as almost everybody would think tall, and nobody could	E	II	2	167	12
tall, and nobody could think very tall; her figure	E	II	2	167	12
He had been used to think her unjust to Jane, and had now	E	II	3	170	1
been handed round once, I think it would have been enough."	E	II	3	170	4
I think you understand me, therefore."	E	II	3	171	5
"You think her diffident.	E	II	3	171	8
and amused to think how little information I obtained."	E	II	3	171	10
can bear roast port--I think we had better send the leg--	E	II	3	171	16
					17
we had better send the leg--do not you think so, my dear?"	E	II	3	171	16
					17
article in my way hither that I think will interest you."	E	II	3	172	20
Emma had not had time even to think of Mr. Elton, and she	E	II	3	173	25
I go down instead? for I think you have a little cold, and	E	II	3	173	27
I say, sir," turning to Mr. Woodhouse, "I think there are	E	II	3	175	39
think I am particularly quick at those sort of discoveries.	E	II	3	176	44
Where I have a regard, I always think a person well-	E	II	3	176	49
We think she is the better for Highbury already.	E	II	3	177	50
really do not think she cares for any thing but boiled	E	II	3	177	50
Woodhouse, what do you think has happened!" which	E	II	3	177	52
Dear Miss Woodhouse! only think.	E	II	3	178	52
to speak to me --(do you think he was, Miss Woodhouse?)--	E	II	3	178	52
away-- and then--only think!--I found he was coming up	E	II	3	179	52
She was obliged to stop and think.	E	II	3	179	53
occur again, and therefore you need not think about it."	E	II	3	180	55
Harriet said, "very true;" and she "would not think about	E	II	3	180	56
She could think of nothing better: and though there was	E	II	4	185	14
"Think of me to-morrow, my dear Emma, about four o'clock,"	E	II	5	189	15
or twelve o'clock, that she was to think of her at four.	E	II	5	189	19
" tis twelve, I shall not forget to think of you four	E	II	5	190	20
to her, and she did not think too much had been said in	E	II	5	190	22
seemed as if he could not think so ill of any two persons'	E	II	5	193	35
before," said she, "I think you will to-day. you will see	E	II	5	194	44
and could now engage to think of them all at Randalls any	E	II	5	195	49
"And how did you think Miss Fairfax looking?"	E	II	6	199	8
any body, that I really think you may say what you like of	E	II	6	200	19
"I certainly do forget to think of her," said Emma, "as	E	II	6	201	24
"You think so, do you?--	E	II	6	201	28
I think, who must have felt it: Miss Fairfax herself.	E	II	6	202	35
I have no reason to think ill of her--not the least--	E	II	6	203	41
could not think any man to be pitied for having that house.	E	II	6	204	42
As for his going, Emma did not wish him to think it	E	II	7	208	9
I think it would be much better if they would come in one	E	II	7	209	10
They are good-natured people, and think little of their	E	II	7	210	19

You would not think it to look at him, but he is bilious--	E II 7 210 20
You think you carry it off very well, I dare say, but with	E II 8 213 10
loss, quite bewildered to think who could possibly have	E II 8 214 13
Emma to think her own way, and still listen to Mrs. Cole.	E II 8 215 15
"That is a grand pianoforte, and he might think it too	E II 8 216 25
If I had been there, I think I should have made some	E II 8 218 36
in the secret herself, to think the appearance of	E II 8 220 45
did think there were some looks a little like Mr. Elton."	E II 8 220 47
sort of thing that so few men would think of.	E II 8 223 63
I am very much inclined to think that it was for their	E II 8 223 63
The more I think of it, the more probable it appears.	E II 8 224 65
"Dear Mrs. Weston, how could you think of such a thing?--	E II 8 224 66
I am amazed that you should think of such a thing."	E II 8 224 66
"My dear Emma, I have told you what led me to think of it.	E II 8 224 67
And, upon my word, I do not think Mr. Knightley would be	E II 8 225 78
for him, but whether he wishes it; and I think he does.	E II 8 226 79
I think he is just the person to do it, even without being	E II 8 226 79
But I do not think it is at all a likely thing for him to	E II 8 226 80
And Frank Churchill was heard to say, "I think you could	E II 8 229 95
"Oh! dear--I think you play the best of the two.	E II 9 231 7
I think you play quite as well as she does.	E II 9 231 7
"Well, I always shall think that you play quite as well as	E II 9 232 9
How did you think the Coxes looked?"	E II 9 232 11
I think they are, without exception, the most vulgar girls	E II 9 233 22
--I do not know--no, I think, Miss Woodhouse, I may just	E II 9 235 40
'Oh!' said he, 'I do think I can fasten the rivet; I like	E II 9 237 51
he was so pleased to think his master had sold so many;	E II 9 239 51
You find me trying to be useful; tell me if you think I	E II 10 240 3
Do not you think so?"	E II 10 241 8
I dare say they often think of you, and wonder which will	E II 10 241 12
"She is not entirely without it, I think."	E II 10 243 28
Who do you think is here?--	E II 10 244 42
I think Miss Fairfax dances very well; and Mrs. Weston is	E II 10 245 49
"To think of your sending us all your store apples.	E II 10 245 52
I really do not think there will."	E II 11 248 6
He does not think of the draught.	E II 11 249 11
"I think there will be very tolerable room for ten couple."	E II 11 249 15
	16
I think it admirable; and, as far as I can answer for	E II 11 251 24
Papa, do you not think it an excellent improvement?"	E II 11 251 24
nobody would think of opening the windows at Randalls.	E II 11 251 30
her father, engaging to think it all over while she was	E II 11 253 40
room, observed, "I do not think it *is* so very small.	E II 11 254 45
	46
I think we do want a larger council.	E II 11 255 50
rather hesitating, "if you think she will be of any use."	E II 11 255 51
I shall think you a great blockhead, Frank, if you bring	E II 11 255 57
confidence, she could not think it so very impossible that	E II 12 257 1
If the Westons think it worth while to be at all this	E II 12 257 3
"In short," said he, "perhaps, Miss Woodhouse-----I think	E II 12 260 29
to all the rest, made her think that she *must* be a little	E II 12 262 38
taken place, she did not think Jane could *have* attended it;	E II 12 263 42
Not that I imagine he can think I have been encouraging	E II 13 265 4
sensations, and think she had undervalued their strength.	E II 13 265 5
"I must not think of it.	E II 13 267 7
was not worth while to think about them--and she would not	E II 13 267 9
them--and she would not think about them any longer"--but	E II 13 267 9
Harriet for my sake; think less, talk less of Mr. Elton	E II 13 268 11
	12
(with a gentle sigh,) what do you think of her?--	E II 14 271 6
"I think her beautiful, quite beautiful."	E II 14 271 9
And now, Miss Woodhouse, I do not think I shall mind	E II 14 271 15
I am afraid you will think you have over-rated Hartfield.	E II 14 273 22
	23
They would hardly come in their chaise, I think, at that	E II 14 274 28
for entire seclusion. I think, on the contrary, when	E II 14 275 30
'But,' said I, 'to be quite honest, I do not think I can	E II 14 277 36
I think, Miss Woodhouse, you and I must establish a	E II 14 277 38
If *we* exert ourselves, I think we shall not be long in	E II 14 277 38
She was your governess, I think?"	E II 14 278 44
"And who do you think came in while we were there?"	E II 14 278 48
Decidedly, I think, a very gentleman-like man."	E II 14 279 50
Though I think he had better not have married.	E II 14 279 54
I assure you I think she has very extraordinary talents.	E II 15 282 5
"I cannot think there is any danger of it," was Emma's	E II 15 283 6
And I think she feels it.	E II 15 283 7
"I know how highly you think of Jane Fairfax," said Emma.	E II 15 287 24
"Yes," he replied, "any body may know how highly I think	E II 15 287 25
by Mrs. Weston, and did not herself know what to think.	E II 15 287 29
The result of his reverie was, "no, Emma, I do not think	E II 15 288 36
She is reserved, more reserved, I think, than she used to	E II 15 289 40
When you have lived to my age, you will begin to think	E II 16 293 16
a post-office, I think, must always have power to draw me	E II 16 294 22
The spring I always think requires more than common care.	E II 16 295 33
and from *us* I really think, my dear Jane, you can have no	E II 16 295 34
Isabella and Emma, I think, do write very much alike.	E II 16 297 45
rich; my mortifications, I think, would only be the	E II 17 301 17
Only think of his gallantry in coming away before the	E II 17 302 22
Oh! I assure you I began to think my caro sposo would be	E II 17 302 22
Selina's choice--handsome, I think, but I do not know	E II 17 302 22
Do you think it will look well?"	E II 17 302 22
"Well, he is coming, you see; good news, I think.	E II 17 303 27
"Indeed!--from Yorkshire, I think.	E II 18 305 8
Mrs. Elton began to think she had been wrong in	E II 18 307 17
I think it is so.	E II 18 309 30
I think it is the state of mind which gives most spirit	E II 18 309 30
"Only think! well, that must be infinitely provoking!	E II 18 310 34
Your description of Mrs. Churchill made me think of them	E II 18 310 34
manners they evidently think themselves equal even to my	E II 18 310 34
You think so, do not you?"	E II 18 311 41
time for them, I do not think they would fare much better	E II 18 312 50
he had the vanity to think they would be disappointed if	E III 1 316 4
she was rather inclined to think it implied a dread of her	E III 1 316 5
"I think she must be here soon," said he.	E III 2 320 8
much of her. it cannot be long, I think, before she comes."	E III 2 320 8
I think him a very handsome young man, and his manners are	E III 2 321 15
think it as much her duty as Mrs. Weston's to receive them.	E III 2 322 18
So kind of her to think of my mother!	E III 2 322 19
No hairdresser from London I think could.--	E III 2 323 19
Mrs. Elton then said, "nobody can think less of dress in	E III 2 324 20
	21
"She will think Frank ought to ask her."	E III 2 325 30
It was almost enough to make her think of marrying.	E III 2 325 31
She did not think he was quite so hardened as his wife,	E III 2 328 42
	43
say, and all that, but I think her very ill-tempered and	E III 4 337 6
and Mrs. John Knightley came--I think the very evening.--	E III 4 338 12
Perhaps Harriet might think her cold or angry if she did;	E III 4 341 34
be too greatly your superior in situation to think of you.	E III 4 341 35
him at a distance--and to think of his infinite	E III 4 341 36
Yes, honourable, I think, to choose so well and so	E III 4 342 39
not persuade himself to think entirely void of meaning,	E III 5 343 2
Emma, you are a great dreamer, I think?"	E III 5 345 14
likely to Randall's; yes, I think it was to Randall's.	E III 5 346 16
earnest kindness, "do you think you perfectly understand	E III 5 350 32
"Have you never at any time had reason to think that he	E III 5 350 34
furniture, I think is best observed by meals within doors.	E III 6 355 21
Robert Martin had probably ceased to think of Harriet.--	E III 6 361 40
to think of him--but she was very glad to see him.	E III 6 363 53
I can never bear to think of you all there without me."	E III 6 366 72
Do not you all think I shall?"	E III 7 370 24
They only knew each other, I think, a few weeks in Bath!	E III 7 372 40
on first going out--do not think us ungrateful, Miss	E III 8 379 8
To look at her, nobody would think how delighted and happy	E III 8 379 8
However, *I* shall always think it a very pleasant party,	E III 8 381 19
have been myself, I should think five times the amount of	E III 8 382 24
say, come ma'am, do not let us think about it any more."	E III 8 382 27
Now Emma was obliged to think of the piano forte; and the	E III 8 384 34
circumstance which I must think of at least half a day,	E III 10 395 37
Weston; and I must say, that I think him greatly to blame.	E III 10 396 44
herself--to suffer her even to think of such a measure!"	E III 10 397 50
But I shall always think it a very abominable sort of	E III 10 399 61
and persuasion to think the engagement no very bad thing.	E III 10 400 69
must not allow herself to think of him, and that there	E III 11 402 1
therefore, I should not think of mentioning it to any body	E III 11 404 6
You do not think I care about Mr. Frank Churchill."	E III 11 405 12
I hope I have a better taste than to think of Mr. Frank	E III 11 405 18
too great a presumption almost, to dare to think of him.	E III 11 405 18
You must think one five hundred million times more above	E III 11 407 28
encouraging her to think of him, Harriet had begun to be	E III 11 409 35
"I never should have presumed to think of it at first,"	E III 11 411 39
It was horrible to Emma to think how it must sink him in	E III 11 413 48
Harriet Smith might think herself not unworthy of being	E III 12 415 1
on his side, for I think the merit will be all on her's."	E III 12 420 13
regard, must, I think, be the happiest of mortals.--	E III 13 428 23
I will tell you exactly what I think."	E III 13 429 32
She did not think it in Harriet's nature to escape being	E III 14 435 4
I think we shall never materially disagree about the	E III 14 436 7
by weather, I think every body feels a north-east wind.--	E III 14 436 7
For my temptation to *think* it a right, I refer every	E III 14 437 8
will think I ought to *add*, with the deepest humiliation.--	E III 14 438 8
When I think of the kindness and favour I have met with,	E III 14 439 8
My plea of concealing the truth she did not think	E III 14 440 8
Think, then, what I must have endured in hearing it	E III 14 442 8
If you think me in a way to be happier than I deserve, I	E III 14 443 8
emma:--but yet, I think--had *you* not been in the case--I	E III 15 445 13
at least I hope you must, think the better of him for it.	E III 15 448 29
that I cannot think any longer about Frank Churchill.	E III 15 448 30
She promised to think of it, and advised him to think of	E III 15 449 32
She promised, however, to think of it; and pretty nearly	E III 15 449 34
promised, moreover, to think of it, with the intention of	E III 15 449 34
Think she must of the possible difference to the poor	E III 15 449 35
but she could not think of her in London without objects	E III 16 452 5
with, "do not you think, Miss Woodhouse, our saucy little	E III 16 454 16
	17
Do not you think her cure does Perry the highest credit?--(	E III 16 454 17
But yet I think there was something wanting.	E III 16 454 18
However, I think it answered so far as to tempt one to go	E III 16 454 18
anywhere else I should think it necessary to apologize:	E III 16 455 20
	21
some people may not think *you* perfection already.--	E III 16 457 33
We must do whatever is to *be* done quickest, and I think	E III 16 459 50
I could not think about you so much without doating on you,	E III 17 462 7
young woman might think him rather cool in her praise.	E III 17 464 19
time, as worthy of your affection, as you think me already.	E III 17 464 20
He will think all the happiness, all the advantage, on	E III 17 464 24
She must not appear to think it a misfortune.--	E III 17 465 28
admitted it, he began to think that some time or other--in	E III 17 467 30
She had such a regard for Mr. Knightley, as to think he	E III 17 467 31
Some might think him, and others might think her, the most	E III 17 468 36
Did not think him at all in love--not in the least.--	E III 17 469 36
replied, "I hope but one, on which we do not think alike."	E III 18 470 8
one or the other of us think differently; and, in the	E III 18 471 16
She must wait a moment, or he would think her mad.	E III 18 472 21
I think Harriet is doing extremely well.	E III 18 473 24
hope I know better than to think of Robert Martin," that	E III 18 473 27
and I think I can give you a proof that it must be so.	E III 18 474 30
"I can never think of it," she cried, "without extreme	E III 18 477 52
"I know you saw my letter, and think you may remember my	E III 18 477 59
to tell you the truth, I think it might have been some	E III 18 478 67
I think there is a little likeness between us."	E III 18 478 67
"I can never think of it without laughing.--	E III 18 480 77
He began to think it was to be, and that he could not	E III 19 483 9
Few women could think more of their personal appearance	P III 1 4 5
alarm, set seriously to think what could be done, and had	P III 1 9 19
Elizabeth, inclined her to think that the sacrifice of one	P III 2 13 5
She disliked Bath, and did not think it agreed with her--	P III 2 14 9
in short, and disposed to think it must suit them all; and	P III 2 14 12
I chose, for nobody would think it worth their while to	P III 3 17 4
follow, I should think any from our wealthy naval	P III 3 17 4
Here Anne spoke,-- "the navy, I think, who have done much	P III 3 19 11
	12
to inhabit that house, and think them infinitely too well	P III 3 24 35
indeed, a throwing away, which she grieved to think of!	P III 4 26 3
from what she had been made to think at nineteen.--	P III 4 29 8
think that, every thing considered, she wished to remain.	P III 5 33 6
I really think poor Mrs. Clay may be staying here in	P III 5 35 14
"I think very differently," answered Elizabeth, shortly; "	P III 5 35 16
I think it rather unnecessary in you to be advising me."	P III 5 35 16
I began to think I should never see you.	P III 5 37 22
at the time; and I do not think I ever was so ill in my	P III 5 37 24
I do not think she has been in this house three times this	P III 5 37 24
And I think it very likely that my illness to-day may be	P III 5 39 39
Then, forgetting to think of it, she was at the other end	P III 5 39 40
"I should never think of standing on such ceremony with	P III 5 40 42
what part of Bath do you think they will settle in?" and	P III 6 42 1
in future, and think with heightened gratitude of the	P III 6 42 2
he would not think there was any thing the matter with me.	P III 6 44 7
She could not think of much else on the 29th of September;	P III 6 48 16
I am glad I did not think of it before.	P III 6 48 16
off, and only be sorry to think that the cottage party,	P III 7 54 5
Only think, if any thing should happen!"	P III 7 55 6
I did not think Charles would have been so unfeeling.	P III 7 56 10
I really think Charles might as well have told his father	P III 7 57 14
"Well--if you do not think it too late to give notice for	P III 7 57 15
Mr. and Mrs. Musgrove cannot think it wrong, while I	P III 7 57 15
not think differently, let him think of her as he would.	P III 7 61 34
you will think very differently, when you are married.'	P III 8 70 48
by it, and to think Captain Wentworth very much in the way.	P III 9 73 3
It would be but a new creation, however, and I never think	P III 9 75 11
It suited Mary best to think Henrietta the one preferred,	P III 9 75 12
"You know," said she, "I cannot think him at all a fit	P III 9 75 13
I do not think any young woman has a right to make a	P III 9 76 13
she could not but think, as far as she might dare to judge	P III 10 82 1
I think we had better turn back; I am excessively tired."	P III 10 85 15
and papa and mamma always think it was her great friend	P III 10 89 33
They think Charles might not be learned and bookish enough	P III 10 89 33
too, long enough, one would think, to make up his mind.	P III 10 92 44
think how her own comfort was likely to be affected by it.	P III 11 93 1
them together, she might think that he had too much self-	P III 11 93 3
the heart could think capable of accommodating so many.	P III 11 98 17
I do think he had better leave Uppercross entirely, and	P III 12 102 2
Indeed I think it quite melancholy to have such excellent	P III 12 102 2
I really think they ought.	P III 12 102 2
Do not you think, Anne, it is being over-scrupulous?	P III 12 103 2
Do not you think it is quite a mistaken point of	P III 12 103 2
Do you think he had the Elliot countenance?	P III 12 106 16
but I think he had something of the Elliot countenance.	P III 12 106 16
I think my father certainly ought to hear of it; do	P III 12 107 20
any other two readers, to think exactly alike of the	P III 12 107 23
You may think, Miss Elliot, whether he is dear to us!"	P III 12 108 28
Anne did think on the question with perfect decision, and	P III 12 108 29
they could hardly bear to think of not finding room for	P III 12 113 56
She, however, was soon persuaded to think differently.	P III 12 114 59

to assist Mrs. Harville, I think it need be only one.-- P III 12 114 61
sufficient for her, if Mrs. Harville would but think so." P III 12 114 63
Do you think this a good plan?" P III 12 117 74
she said, in observing, "I think you are very likely to P IV 1 125 15
16
that it was frightful to think, how long Miss Musgrove's P IV 1 126 21
But" (checking himself) "you will not think it a good P IV 1 127 26
I am sure--but I should think, Miss Elliot" (looking with P IV 1 127 28
reflection) "I should think he must be rather a dressy man P IV 1 127 28
said Mary, "I think he is rather my acquaintance, for I P IV 2 132 14
"I think Lady Russell would like him. P IV 2 132 17
I think she would be so much pleased with his mind, that P IV 2 132 17
Do you think Lady Russell would like that?" P IV 2 132 19
Her mother could even think of her being able to join P IV 2 134 31
Mr. Elliot appeared to think that he (Sir Walter) was P IV 3 141 12
They could think of no one else. P IV 3 142 17
friend could sometimes think differently; and it did not P IV 4 147 7
They did not always think alike. P IV 4 148 10
she added, "I certainly do think there has been by far too P IV 4 150 18
who forget to think seriously till it is almost too late." P IV 5 156 11
her think worse of the world, than she hoped it deserved. P IV 5 156 12
"No, sir, she is not one and thirty; but I do not think I P IV 5 157 16
"But what does Lady Russell think of this acquaintance?" P IV 5 157 17
disposed to accept him, I think there would be every P IV 5 159 23
consider it--but I think it might be a very happy one." P IV 5 159 23
think highly of him," said Anne; "but we should not suit." P IV 5 159 24
and, though he might now think very differently, who could P IV 5 161 27
"little people think of letters in such a place as Bath. P IV 6 162 7
"Between ourselves, I think it a great pity Henrietta did " P IV 6 163 7
"Let me know what you think of this. P IV 6 163 7
to Bath "almost immediately; they think the Admiral gouty. P IV 6 163 7
"I do not think they improve at all as neighbours. P IV 6 164 7
as the Harvilles; and "what do you think was the reason? P IV 6 164 8
"Oh! no, I think not. P IV 6 166 16
and did, in fact, think and talk a great deal more about P IV 6 168 23
failed to think of them, and never failed to see them. P IV 6 168 24
What queer fellows your fine painters must be, to think P IV 6 169 25
is more than you would think for, perhaps, for that soft P IV 6 171 37
and there is nothing very unforgiving in that, I think." P IV 6 173 47
I think we must get him to Bath. P IV 6 173 49
Do not you think, Miss Elliot, we had better try to get P IV 6 173 49
think, it would be more prudent to let me get you a chair." P IV 7 177 14
He came in with eagerness, appeared to see and think only P IV 7 177 16
"She is pretty, I think; Anne Elliot; very pretty, when P IV 7 177 21
But just now she could think only of Captain Wentworth. P IV 7 178 24
exactly forward--"but there I think ends the resemblance. P IV 8 182 8
thus, "I confess that I do think there is a disparity, too P IV 8 182 9
10
far as to say, "you were a good while at Lyme, I think?" P IV 8 183 11
12
than she dared to think of! and she gave herself up to the P IV 8 184 17
Anne could think of no one so likely to have spoken with P IV 8 187 35
It was misery to think of Mr. Elliot's attentions.-- P IV 8 191 51
I do not think they were." P IV 9 193 9
with the person, whom you think the most agreeable in the P IV 9 194 16
To be sure by next week I may be allowed to think it all P IV 9 195 27
of yours, and then he will think little of the trouble P IV 9 196 32
and he is not a man, I think, to be known intimately soon. P IV 9 196 33
"She could not make a very long history, I think, of one P IV 9 197 41
"I think you spoke of having known Mr. Elliot many years?" P IV 9 198 45
However, I have determined; I think I am right; I think P IV 9 199 53
At nineteen, you know, one does not think very seriously, P IV 9 199 55
I think differently now; time and sickness, and sorrow, P IV 9 201 64
And indeed, to own the truth, I do not think nurse in her P IV 9 208 92
Anne went home to think over all that she had heard. P IV 10 212 1
I used to think she had some taste in dress, but I was P IV 10 215 15
But she does not do him justice, nor think enough about P IV 10 218 22
I hope you think Louisa perfectly recovered now?" P IV 10 218 23
Nobody doubts it; and I hope you do not think I am so P IV 10 218 26
heavens, Charles! how can you think of such a thing? P IV 10 223 42
43
Your father might have asked us to dinner, I think, if he P IV 10 223 44
should think it scandalous to go for the sake of his heir. P IV 10 224 48
herself, she should not think herself very well used, if P IV 10 224 50
She could think only of the invitation she had with such P IV 10 226 65
"Only think of Elizabeth's including every body!" P IV 10 227 66
Only think, Miss Elliot, to my great surprise I met with P IV 10 228 71
afterwards persuaded to think might do very well," and a P IV 11 230 5
yet altogether we did not think it fair to stand out any P IV 11 230 6
I always think that no mutual-----" P IV 11 230 7
I think, all parents should prevent as far as they can." P IV 11 231 9
I do not think I shall grant) it does not apply to benwick. P IV 11 232 20
sounds, which yet she did not think he could have caught. P IV 11 233 24
the argument, and I do not think I ever opened a book in P IV 11 234 27
And when I think of benwick, my tongue is tied." P IV 11 236 34
"For you alone I think and plan.-- P IV 11 237 42
"your feelings, as I think you must have penetrated mine. P IV 11 237 42
"Do you think so? P IV 11 239 51
Was it unpardonable to think it worth my while to come? P IV 11 243 70
I could think of you only as one who had yielded, who had P IV 11 245 74
It is not that I did not think of it, or desire it, as P IV 11 247 84
morng in London--I think you will be convinced that I am S 1 366 1
man & boy 57 years, I think I must have known of such a S 1 366 1
entreating them not to think of proceeding till the ancle S 1 367 1
disposed the Travellor to think rather more as he had done S 1 367 1
I only think our coast is too full of them altogether--but S 1 368 1
Mr Parker could not think of very little besides.-- S 2 371 1
That is--we think differently, we now & then, see things S 3 376 1
You will not think I have made a bad exchange, when we S 4 380 1
Well, I think I have done something in my day.-- S 4 383 1
But if you think it advisable for the interest of the S 5 387 1
company worth having; & think we may safely reckon on S 5 387 1
"Why to own the truth, said Mrs P.--I do think the Miss S 5 388 1
You often think they wd better, if they wd leave S 5 388 1
I know you think it a great pity they shd give him such a S 5 388 1
money so freely, never think of whether they may not be S 6 392 1
"Lord! my dear sir, she cried, how could you think of such S 6 393 1
she was inclined to think not very favourably; for tho' S 7 395 1
she cd not but think him a man of feeling--till he began S 7 396 1
But while we are on the subject of poetry, what think you S 7 397 1
She began to think him downright silly.-- S 7 398 1
Charlotte cd think of nothing more harmless to be said, S 7 399 1
I wd not have you think that I only notice them, for poor S 7 399 1
I do not think I was ever over-reached in my life; & that S 7 399 1
will think so--for Sir Edwd must marry for money.-- S 7 400 1
I do not think we have had an heiress here, or even a Co-- S 7 401 1
I think they are great fools for not staying at home. S 7 401 1
Don't you think that will be very fair?-- S 7 402 1
much wind that I did not think he cd safely venture,--for S 9 407 1
"I think you are doing too much, said Mr P. S 9 411 1
My sisters think me bilious, but I doubt it.--" S 10 415 1
"No more do I--said he exceedingly pleased--we think quite S 10 417 1
So far from dry toast being wholesome, I think it a very S 10 417 1
dish--what do you think it's effect would be upon me?--" S 10 418 1
mean to go with them)--I think you had better mention the S 12 423 1
Charlotte cd not but think of the extreme difficulty which S 12 426 1

THINKING (200)

I cannot help thinking his pressing invitation to her to LS 3 247 1
"What are you thinking of so earnestly?" said he, as they NA I 3 29 47
Catherine coloured, and said, "I was not thinking of any NA I 3 29 48
Aye, I remember, so it was; I was thinking of that other NA I 7 49 38
mind and incapacity for thinking were such, that as she NA I 9 60 1
You women are always thinking of men's being in liquor. NA I 9 63 20
her own observation help thinking, that they might have NA I 11 86 50
Mrs. Allen, are not you of my way of thinking? NA I 13 104 31
of the river, "without thinking of the south of France." NA I 14 106 2
her; I could not sleep a wink all night for thinking of it. NA I 15 118 13
"That is just my way of thinking. NA I 15 123 44
would agree with me in thinking it expedient to give every NA II 7 176 15
the impossibility of thinking well of a man so kindly NA II 8 185 5
could win Catherine from thinking, that some very NA II 8 187 16
had been in the habit of thinking bearing always an equal NA II 9 191 3
the folly of too easily thinking his affection returned. NA II 10 202 7
"I do not know what I was thinking of," (blushing again NA II 10 205 23
interesting, she added, thinking aloud, "Monday--so soon NA II 13 224 17
for soon were all her thinking powers swallowed up in the NA II 14 237 20
for Mrs. Morland, thinking it probable, as a secondary NA II 15 243 9
world; has been abroad; has read, and has a thinking mind. SS I 10 51 20
you of what I am always thinking of every moment of my SS II 2 146 5
Jennings, had leisure enough for thinking over the past. SS II 6 178 16
comforted herself by thinking, that though their longer SS II 10 214 7
down stairs, thinking about writing a letter to his SS III 1 259 7
"If such is your way of thinking," said Marianne, "if the SS III 1 263 28
And after thinking it all over and over again, he said, it SS III 2 273 16
She wondered indeed at his thinking it necessary to do so;- SS III 3 281 9
But at the same time, she could not help thinking that no SS III 3 283 20
"I have just been thinking of Betty's sister, my dear. SS III 4 287 21
22
of what she had been thinking of, and what she had to tell SS III 4 288 26
"My dear ma'am," said Elinor, "what can you be thinking of? SS III 4 291 52
I cannot help thinking, in short, that means might have SS III 5 300 37
Careless of her happiness, thinking only of my own SS III 8 320 29
Elinor was half inclined to ask her reason for thinking so, SS III 9 336 11
my own, and he perhaps, thinking that mere friendship, as SS III 9 336 12
sympathy--or rather not thinking at all, I suppose-- SS III 9 336 12
and manner of thinking, would probably have been SS III 13 370 36
"I was thinking of it's being something to amuse my father, W 354 28
"Not absolutely--he answered--but I was thinking of you,-- W 357 28
You must know that I am thinking of his marrying one of PP I 1 4 16
she ought to give over thinking of her own beauty." PP I 1 4 20
gentleman, and he was thinking of her with some PP I 6 27 44
45
The latter was thinking only of his breakfast. PP I 7 33 42
seeing him before, nor thinking of him since, with the PP I 16 76 3
had the consolation of thinking that Mr. Bingley would be PP I 21 120 30
Without thinking highly either of men or of matrimony, PP I 22 122 3
who marries him, cannot have a proper way of thinking. PP II 1 135 13
Lizzy, not to pain me by thinking that person to blame, PP II 1 136 14
what I should feel in thinking ill of him or his sisters. PP II 1 137 24
be supposing her to be thinking of Jane and Netherfield, PP II 9 179 21
"I am thinking of what you have been telling me," said she. PP II 10 185 34
Charlotte and I have but one mind and one way of thinking. PP II 15 216 6
It was impossible for her to see the word without thinking PP II 19 239 9
"I have been thinking it over again, Elizabeth," said her PP III 5 282 1
She has been doing every thing in her power by thinking PP III 5 284 10
"I comfort myself with thinking," replied Jane, "that he PP III 7 304 35
I will believe, that he is come to a right way of thinking. PP III 7 305 37
for I was thinking, you may suppose, of my dear Wickham. PP III 9 319 24
great pleasure in thinking you will be so happily settled. PP III 13 348 38
Heaven and earth!--of what are you thinking? PP III 14 357 62
and looking, and thinking for your approbation alone. PP III 18 380 5
up her sister, and thinking no more of the matter: but Mrs. MP I 1 4 1
You are thinking of your sons--but do not you know that of MP I 1 6 6
use and no beauty, thinking more of her pug than her MP I 2 19 31
I ever thank you as I ought, for thinking so well of me? MP I 3 26 30
walking all day, thinking every body ought to walk as much. MP I 4 36 7
Mrs. Norris could not help thinking that some steady old MP I 4 36 7
the risk of his father's thinking he had done too much. MP I 4 37 8
And Fanny, what was she doing and thinking all this while? MP I 5 48 30
"That is what I was thinking of. MP I 6 53 8
next day, after thinking some time on the subject himself. MP I 7 63 1
had a good chance of her thinking like him; though at this MP I 7 64 12
and Fanny was still thinking of Edmund, Miss Crawford, and MP I 10 97 1
he had been very near thinking whether he should not bring MP I 10 98 4
Rushworth prevented her thinking so much of their MP I 10 101 33
of the park, and will be thinking how it may be improved; MP I 10 102 47
He is thinking of November." MP I 11 108 4
he is really thinking of, more than the woman herself. MP I 12 116 10
walking about in, and thinking, and of which she had now MP I 16 150 1
him so little, and thinking his return a misfortune; and MP II 1 178 7
of Mr. Yates's habits of thinking from the beginning to MP II 1 184 25
for that sentence to be thinking of Edmund, such a memento MP II 4 207 10
loving her, without ever thinking like her, without any MP II 4 208 11
to Mrs. Grant for thinking of you, and to your aunt for MP II 5 220 28
very comfortably and not thinking of the rest, till some MP II 7 249 49
Mrs. Norris was obliged to be satisfied with thinking just MP II 8 254 7
Your goodness in thinking of me in such a way is beyond"--- MP II 9 262 5
might be justified in thinking, would in her be insanity. MP II 9 264 18
Fanny's heart sunk, but there was no leisure for thinking MP II 10 275 10
Sir Thomas perhaps might not be thinking of her health. MP II 10 281 34
Thomas, I have been thinking--and I am very glad we took MP II 11 285 10
she could not help thinking of him continually when absent, MP II 11 286 15
But you are not thinking of me. MP II 13 302 8
She was feeling, thinking, trembling, about every thing;-- MP II 13 302 10
habits and ways of thinking, and all her own demerits.-- MP II 13 305 26
I will, therefore, only add, as thinking it my duty to MP III 1 318 39
honoured, and whether thinking of herself or her brother, MP III 2 328 7
before, he had been thinking of as seventy miles off, and MP III 3 334 1
times out of twenty I am thinking how such a prayer ought MP III 3 340 25
long watching for, and long thinking strangely delayed. MP III 3 344 42
I know what you are thinking of. MP III 4 346 8
How well I remember what I was thinking of as I came along; MP III 5 360 14
Thinking, I hope, of one who is always thinking of you. MP III 5 360 16
Crawford; and she sat thinking deeply of it till Mary, who MP III 5 364 30
as nearly desperate, for thinking that if Edmund's MP III 6 367 5
and she could not help thinking her poor dear Sister Price MP III 6 372 21
only the best, and never thinking beyond what she heard, MP III 14 429 1
than former zeal, and thinking she could never do enough MP III 16 449 4
of a marriage which, thinking as I now thought of her MP III 16 457 30
in a fair way of not thinking of him again; and when the MP III 17 466 18
For some time she was amused, without thinking beyond the E I 4 27 5
appearances, and thinking of nothing but profit and loss." E I 4 33 38
fourteen--I remember thinking it did her judgment so much E I 5 37 7
I were quite agreed in thinking it very like)--only too E I 6 45 21
At this moment whom are you thinking of?" E I 7 53 21
thinking me the best friend and counsellor man ever had. E I 8 59 27
a visitor, without thinking him at all a tiresome wretch." E I 8 60 27
He was thinking. E I 8 66 50
My dear Harriet, what are you thinking of? E I 9 73 18
After a little thinking, and a very tender sigh, he added, E I 9 78 53
54
very cross--and of thinking that the rest of the visit E I 14 119 6
thinking the better of him for submitting to their whims. E I 18 147 18
me; and I could not help thinking that he was persuading E II 3 178 52
After much thinking, she could determine on nothing better, E II 4 185 13
be thinking of the possibility of their all calling here. E II 5 190 20
his certainly thinking it worth while to try to please her. E II 5 191 28
She had no doubt of what Mr. Weston was often thinking E II 5 192 34
together so long, and thinking so much alike, Emma felt E II 6 203 42
and without ever thinking how many advantages and E II 6 204 43
Emma divined what every body present must be thinking. E II 8 220 47
she fell into a train of thinking on the subject of Mrs. E II 8 227 87
"That will do," said he, when it was finished, thinking E II 8 229 94
Those who are standing by are usually thinking of E II 12 258 3

constant habit of never thinking of herself, she had not E II 12 258 7
she was very often thinking of him, and quite impatient E II 13 264 1
and farther, though thinking of him so much, and, as she E II 13 264 1
with herself, and thinking much of her own importance; E II 14 272 16
Ah! there I am--thinking of him directly. E II 14 279 52
"I did not mean, I was not thinking of the slave-trade," E II 17 300 15
it was not worth thinking of;--but if he, who had E III 1 315 1
good Mr. Woodhouse, not thinking the asparagus quite E III 2 329 45
Emma was not thinking of it at the moment, which made the E III 4 340 28
Emma was very decided in thinking such an attachment no E III 4 342 40
was not very likely you should be thinking of at Enscombe. E III 5 345 14
to be renewed--gardeners thinking exactly different--no E III 6 358 35
Emma had not been thinking of him, she had forgotten to E III 6 363 53
that she desires to know what you are all thinking of." E III 7 369 16
that she would like to hear what we are all thinking of?" E III 7 369 18
me hear any thing rather than what you are all thinking of. E III 7 370 19
what you may all be thinking of, and only requires E III 7 370 23
her at once, that upon thinking over the advantages of Mrs. E III 8 381 15
tea, because I remember thinking--Oh! no, now I recollect, E III 8 382 29
"ay, I see what you are thinking of, the piano forte. E III 8 384 32
33
"Yes--rather--I have been thinking of it some little time." E III 9 385 4
her most earnestly in thinking an airing might be of the E III 9 390 18
"If a woman can ever be excused for thinking only of E III 10 400 66
and not far from thinking it the very best thing that E III 10 401 69
but I was thinking of something very different at the time. E III 11 406 24
No! (with some elevation) I was thinking of a much more E III 11 406 24
She had been thinking of him the moment before, as E III 13 424 1
inclination for thinking of anybody else, when a letter E III 14 436 6
I may be in danger of thinking myself too sure of your's, E III 14 437 8
much of his opinion in thinking him likely to be happier E III 15 448 30
He had been thinking it over most deeply, most intently; E III 15 448 31
What a thinking brain you have! E III 16 456 33
over Highbury; and were thinking of themselves, as the E III 17 468 35
It was an alarming change; and Emma was thinking of it one E III 18 470 1
thinking better and better of him as you know him more. E III 18 472 22
her very much for thinking of sending for Perry, and only E III 18 479 73
every day was giving her fresh reason for thinking so.-- E III 19 481 3
only half a fool, for thinking himself and Elizabeth as P III 1 6 11
she could not admit him to be worth thinking of again. P III 1 8 17
in thinking a sailor might be a very desirable tenant. P III 3 18 7
Mary, often a little unwell, and always thinking a great P III 5 33 7
Mrs. Croft should be thinking and speaking of Edward, and P III 6 49 22
mamma; she is thinking so much of poor Richard! P III 6 50 27
From thus listening and thinking, she was roused by a P III 8 64 5
6
in a low voice, as if thinking aloud, "so then he went P III 8 66 18
one of the girls; "mamma is thinking of poor Richard." P III 8 67 26
might be interrupting, thinking only of his thoughts, P III 8 68 31
32
Now, I cannot help thinking it a pity that he does not P III 12 102 2
Every one capable of thinking felt the advantage of the P III 12 110 42
"It was what she had been thinking of, and wishing to be P III 12 114 63
and a pleasure even in thinking that it might, perhaps, be P III 12 115 67
I have been thinking whether you had not better remain in P III 12 117 74
how much more she was thinking of Lyme, and Louisa P IV 1 124 11
either!" continued the Admiral, after thinking a moment. P IV 1 127 28
occasionally thinking of Captain Benwick, from this time. P IV 2 133 26
to suspect) to prevent his thinking of a second choice. P IV 4 147 6
at Lyme; and she was thinking of them all very intently P IV 6 162 1
and the dejected, thinking, feeling, reading Captain P IV 6 166 19
I cannot help thinking Frederick's manners better than his. P IV 6 172 39
She was thinking only of the last half hour, and as they P IV 8 185 21
She could not help thinking much of the extraordinary P IV 9 192 2
I assure you that nothing of the sort you are thinking of P IV 9 195 28
she said, "I have been thinking over the past, and trying P IV 11 246 79
80
But I too have been thinking over the past, and a question P IV 11 247 82
was very far from thinking it a bad match for her. P IV 12 248 2
Yes, yes, my dear, depend upon it, you will be thinking of S 6 393 1

THINKS (66)

never satisfied till he thinks he has ascertained the LS 16 268 2
Yet Reginald still thinks Lady Susan the best of mothers-- LS 17 271 7
He thinks very differently of her, from what he used to do, LS 24 291 16
"Yes, very much indeed, I fancy; Mr. Allen thinks her the NA I 7 51 50
late to go on to-day; your sister thinks so as well as I. NA I 11 88 54
Yes, by heavens!--and the General thinks you the finest NA I 12 96 20
I do not suppose he ever thinks of me." NA II 1 130 7
"That is exactly what I say; he never thinks of you.-- NA II 1 130 7
John thinks very well of him, and John's judgment-----" NA II 1 130 9
You know what he thinks of Cowper and Scott; you are SS I 10 47 4
"Oh! dear! one never thinks of married mens' being beaux-- SS I 21 124 30
'Lord!' thinks she to herself, 'they are all so fond of SS III 1 258 7
of a passion!--and Mr. Donavan thinks just the same. SS III 1 259 7
himself, he thinks that nobody else can marry on less. SS III 4 292 57
He thinks Marianne's affection too deeply rooted for any SS III 9 338 20
evil of that kind; and he thinks only that he has married SS III 11 351 13
down to Exeter, where she thinks of staying three or four SS III 13 370 37
She thinks everything fair for a husband; I trusted her, W 316 2
"Your Lordship thinks we always have our own way.-- W 346 21
he thinks our due, the wish is certainly to his credit." PP I 13 63 15
He can be a conversible companion if he thinks it worth PP I 16 82 48
I am very glad you have somebody who thinks of those PP II 14 212 15
me--but nobody thinks of _that_ when they fall in love." PP III 18 380 5
She thinks of nothing but the Isle of Wight, and she calls MP I 2 18 25
find, who thinks it very fit for private representation." MP I 15 140 12
Ask your uncle what he thinks, and you will hear MP II 3 197 6
"Your uncle thinks you very pretty, dear Fanny--and that MP II 3 197 8
I wonder what she thinks of my father! MP II 3 199 13
When one thinks of it, how astonishing a variety of nature! MP II 4 209 16
Mrs. Grant thinks it a civility due to _us_ to take a little MP II 5 220 28
such a woman as he thinks does not exist in the world. MP II 12 293 10
of a sister, who thinks her brother has a right to every MP III 4 352 40
should be done, and thinks best on every account, and I MP III 13 426 11
of a moment's _etourderie_ thinks of nobody but you. MP III 15 437 3
I am sure she _will_ miss her more than she thinks for." E I 1 11 36
"Emma never thinks of herself, if she can do good to E I 1 13 45
he were here, for he thinks exactly as I do on the subject. E I 5 36 6
and Isabella always thinks as he does; except when he is E I 5 40 23
She thinks so little of her own beauty. E I 6 44 17
a natural talent for--thinks strongly and clearly--and E I 7 51 5
I am sure Miss Nash would--for Miss Nash thinks her own E I 7 55 40
Mr. Wingfield thinks the vicinity of Brunswick Square E I 12 103 37
"Yes, she would be, but that she thinks there will be E I 14 120 11
Mr. Frank Churchill, in my opinion, as his father thinks. E I 14 121 16
"And those times are, whenever he thinks it worth his E I 18 146 14
killed a porker, and Emma thinks of sending them a loin or E II 3 171 16
17
"My dear Emma, as long as he thinks so, it is so; but if E II 8 225 75
"That fellow," said he, indignantly, thinks of nothing but E II 8 229 97
Miss Nash thinks either of the Coxes would be very glad to E II 9 233 21
I believe it is the only way that Mr. Woodhouse thinks the E II 9 237 46
for William, you know, thinks more of his master's profit E II 9 239 51
Five couple are nothing, when one thinks seriously about E II 11 248 8
If one thinks of all that it has to do, and all that it E II 16 296 40
the whole winter, and thinks Enscombe too cold for her--so E II 18 305 7
She thinks nobody equal to him." E II 18 309 30
"I will answer for it, that mine thinks herself full as E III 6 356 25
"She thinks herself wrong, then, for having consented to a E III 12 418 7
"Mrs. Musgrove thinks all her servants so steady, that it P III 6 45 9
thinks it the greatest improvement the house ever had. P IV 1 127 28
in one of them which he thinks--Oh! I cannot pretend to P IV 2 131 9
to make you suppose he thinks himself ill-used by his P IV 6 172 46
cold-blooded being, who thinks only of himself; who, for P IV 9 199 53
"He thinks Mrs. Clay afraid of him, aware that he sees P IV 9 208 92
is quite of my opinion & thinks it a pity to lose any more S 1 370 1
Aye--that young lady smiles I see;--I dare say she thinks S 6 393 1
But--after a short pause--if Miss Esther thinks to talk me S 7 401 1

THINNER (3)

has fretted herself thinner & uglier than ever, is still LS 32 303 2
she saw that he was grown thinner and had the burnt, MP II 1 178 7
we, probably with rather thinner clothing than usual, E I 13 113 26

THINNESS (1)

The smallness of the house, and thinness of the walls, MP III 7 382 28

THINNING (1)

his way through the then thinning rows, spoke with like NA I 12 93 5

THIRD (48)

I am afraid, brother, you will not have room for a third." NA I 7 48 30
"A third indeed! no, no; I did not come to Bath to drive NA I 7 48 31
Tilney should ask her a third time to dance, her wishes, NA I 10 74 23
But on the second, or at farthest the _third_ night after NA II 5 159 19
drops of blood, and in a third the remains of some NA II 5 160 21
seized a second, a third, a fourth; each was equally empty. NA II 6 169 11
a third, a fourth, and a fifth presented nothing new. NA II 7 172 2
On the third day, in short as soon as she could be NA II 9 196 25
A more considerable degree of wandering attended the third NA II 14 238 22
without a hint; but when a third night's rest had neither NA II 15 240 2
raised to detain her, a third, almost as well known as SS I 16 86 20
It was painful to him to keep a third cousin to himself. SS I 21 119 3
They reached town by three o'clock the third day, glad to SS II 4 160 2
it for ever, and at a third could resist it with energy. SS II 9 201 2
About the third or fourth morning after their being thus SS III 1 257 2
3
The third day succeeding their knowledge of the SS III 2 271 4
in the forenoon of the third they drove up to Cleveland. SS III 6 302 6
Two delightful twilight walks on the third and fourth SS III 6 305 17
On the morning of the third day however, the gloomy SS III 7 310 8
Here they were interrupted by the entrance of a third SS III 9 339 27
Then, the two third he danced with Miss King, and the two PP I 3 13 16
third person; in which case you may be sure of my pardon." PP I 18 95 49
the refusal is repeated a second or even a third time. PP I 19 107 13
Yet it did, and even a third. PP II 10 182 1
her in the course of their third rencontre that he was PP II 10 182 1
spent there; but on the third, her repining was over, and PP III 4 273 1
But on the third morning after his arrival in PP III 11 333 30
of a nature to make a third very useful, especially when MP I 2 17 21
especially when that third was of an obliging, yielding MP I 2 17 21
Two of them were hunters; the third, a useful road-horse: MP I 4 37 8
a useful road-horse: this third he resolved to exchange MP I 4 37 8
he was plain; and after a third interview, after dining in MP I 5 44 2
for the first time;--the third act would bring a scene MP I 18 167 12
while, and do have the goodness to hear me my third act. MP I 18 168 17
hitherto held so humble a third, it was impossible for her MP II 4 205 1
of there being room for a third in the carriage, and MP III 6 372 21
age was the very worst third in the world--totally MP III 10 403 15
with difficulties, a third can disperse them; and before MP III 15 437 2
have overlooked, when the third day did bring the MP III 15 442 22
with no prospect of a third to cheer a long evening. E I 1 6 5
a third--a something between the do-nothing and the do-all. E I 1 13 43
with the second rate and third rate of Highbury, who were E II 1 155 3
be properly ready till the third week were entered on, and E II 12 257 1
confidence, and about the third time of their meeting, she E II 15 282 4
It included nearly a third part of her own life. P III 7 60 28
a way not endurable to a third person, or driving out in a P III 9 73 2
could not endure to make a third in a one horse chaise. P III 10 90 38
called a second time, a third; had been pointedly P IV 2 135 35

THIRDLY (2)

to my happiness; and thirdly--which perhaps I ought to PP I 19 105 10
had been taken in; thirdly, she trusted that they would PP I 23 127 5

THIRDS (1)

to the feelings of two thirds of her auditors, and was so SS II 13 244 41

THIRTEEN (13)

"I was only thirteen when it happened; and though I felt NA II 7 180 34
sense, she did not, at thirteen, bid fair to equal her SS I 1 7 14
That will make thirteen with ourselves, so there will be PP III 11 333 26
Three months comprised thirteen weeks. MP I 11 107 3
Much might happen in thirteen weeks. MP I 11 107 3
in love with you ever since you were thirteen at least." E III 17 462 7
me, except falling in love with her when she is thirteen." E III 17 462 8
Thirteen years had passed away since Lady Elliot's death, P III 1 5 7
that she had begun to be thirteen years ago; and Sir P III 1 6 11
Thirteen years had seen her mistress of Kellynch Hall, P III 1 6 12
For thirteen years had she been doing the honours, and P III 1 6 12
Thirteen winters' revolving frosts had seen her opening P III 1 7 12
afforded; and thirteen springs shewn their blossoms, as P III 1 7 12

THIRTY (36)

the truth in the course of a thirty mile journey. LS 17 271 6
perform a journey of thirty miles: such was the distance NA II 5 155 4
wrong side of five and thirty; but though his face was not SS I 7 34 6
that a man of five and thirty might well have outlived all SS I 7 35 9
a silent man of five and thirty hope, when opposed by a SS I 10 50 12
Yes, Marianne, even in a man between thirty and forty. SS I 10 51 20
They were soon within thirty yards of the gentleman. SS I 16 86 20
"Much nearer thirty," said her husband. SS I 20 111 13
eldest, who was nearly thirty, with a very plain and not a SS I 21 120 6
of the late Lord Morton, with thirty thousand pounds. SS II 11 224 28
(for Miss Morton has thirty thousand pounds,) I cannot SS III 1 268 50
like Miss Morton, with thirty thousand pounds to her SS III 2 272 16
from Barton, and not thirty from Combe Magna; and before SS III 6 302 8
of a nobleman with thirty thousand pounds, while Miss SS III 14 373 3
we have been only five & thirty minutes coming.--which _I_ W 322 2
was an agreable-looking man, a little more than thirty.-- W 330 10
Colonel Fitzwilliam, who led the way, was about thirty, PP II 7 170 9
fortune, which is thirty thousand pounds; but I cannot PP II 12 202 5
of happiness, were within thirty miles of each other. PP III 19 385 3
About thirty years ago, Miss Maria Ward of Huntingdon, MP I 1 3 1
You have robbed Edmund for ten, twenty, thirty years, MP I 3 23 3
as was formed by the last thirty minutes of expectation MP II 6 233 17
who were ordained twenty, thirty, forty years ago, the MP III 3 339 23
dear Miss Woodhouse, he would be thirty years old!" E I 4 30 19
of an hundred and thirty miles with no greater expense or E I 12 106 60
Hartfield, the heiress of thirty thousand pounds, were not E I 16 135 7
years longer in the world than her real eight and thirty. P III 6 48 18
Any body between fifteen and thirty may have me for asking. P III 7 62 39
He seemed about thirty, and, though not handsome, had an P III 12 105 7
be proud of between two walls, perhaps thirty feet asunder. P IV 3 138 5
face would be followed by thirty, or five and thirty P IV 3 141 13
by thirty, or five and thirty frights; and once, as he had P IV 3 141 13
"No, sir, she is not one and thirty; but I do not think I P IV 5 157 16
A poor widow, barely able to live, between thirty and P IV 5 158 19
widow in Bath between thirty and forty, with little to P IV 5 158 20
wish for her original thirty thousand pounds among them, S 3 376 1

THIRTY-FIVE (4)

But thirty-five has nothing to do with matrimony." SS I 8 37 8
"Perhaps," said Elinor, "thirty-five and seventeen had SS I 8 37 9
being thirty-five any objection to his marrying _her_." SS I 8 38 9
could feel for a man of thirty-five any thing near enough SS I 8 38 11

THIRTY-ONE (1)

makes thirty-one;--four in hand and eight in crib.-- MP II 11 283 6

THIRTY-SIX (1)

disproportion between thirty-six and seventeen, brought SS III 13 369 35

THISTLES (1)

I am not fond of nettles, or thistles, or heath blossoms. SS I 18 98 8

THITHER (34)

I led her thither accordingly, & as soon as the door was LS 20 276 5
steps would be bent thither; and tho' he professed himself LS 27 297 4
soon found some accomodating business to call him thither. LS 42 311 2
from what had attended her thither the Monday before. NA I 10 74 23
had likewise retreated thither, and were at that moment NA II 10 203 8
to turn her thoughts, and thither she one day abruptly, SS II 3 153 1
for Marianne brought him thither, and who saw that SS II 9 204 17
with Charlotte, she went thither every morning as soon as SS II 14 246 2
who were usually tempted thither three or four times a PP I 7 28 3
library to himself; for thither Mr. Collins had followed PP I 15 71 6
on following him thither, that he may not be obliged to PP I 21 117 10
11
very seriously of going thither; but Charlotte, she soon PP II 4 151 1
received any invitation thither, for while there were PP II 8 172 1
from this period of walking thither almost every day. PP II 9 180 28
over it, to ramsgate; and thither also went Mr. Wickham, PP II 12 201 5
through which their route thither lay; Oxford, Blenheim, PP II 19 240 12
She followed him thither; and her curiosity to know what PP III 15 361 8
and was welcomed thither quite as gladly by those whom he MP I 12 115 3
of making his passage thither in a private vessel, instead MP II 1 178 8
that he might convey her thither; he had heard her speak MP II 8 256 12
have hoped her return thither, to be as distant as she was MP III 6 366 4
Price would have turned thither directly, without the MP III 10 402 13
what he had intended, and they all walked thither together. MP III 11 408 1
Thither they now went; Mr. Crawford most happy to consider MP III 11 409 5
his being conveyed thither too early, as a return of fever MP III 13 427 13
look which hurrying thither with a full heart was likely E II 3 177 52
They walked thither directly. E II 6 196 1
had agreed to choose some fine morning and drive thither. E III 6 352 2
thither as often as might be, and with the least suspicion. E III 14 439 8
and a project for going thither was the consequence. P III 11 94 6
Vague wishes of getting Sarah thither, had occurred before P IV 1 122 3
to Bath, Captain Wentworth was already on his way thither. P IV 7 174 1
friends at Willingden thither; and his endeavours in the S 2 372 1
the West-Indians were very much disposed to go thither.-- S 9 408 1

THO' (78)

so speedy a distinction, tho' I always imagined from her LS 3 246 1
overlooked it at all; & tho' as his brother's widow & in LS 3 247 1
some description of her, tho' I hope you will soon be able LS 6 250 1
five & twenty, tho' she must in fact be ten years older. LS 6 251 1
I was certainly not disposed to admire her, tho' always LS 6 251 1
tho' I have so long been convinced of the contrary. LS 6 251 1
reputation by following, tho' late, the path of propriety, LS 6 252 2
I hear the young man well spoken of, & tho' no one can LS 9 256 1
expediency, tho' I am not quite determined on following it. LS 10 257 1
tho' perhaps my desire of dominion was never more decided. LS 10 258 2
without some alarm, tho' I can hardly suppose that Lady LS 11 259 1
Poor woman! tho' I have reasons enough for my dislike, I LS 15 266 2
She is very pretty, tho' not so handsome as her mother, LS 17 270 5
Tho' totally without accomplishment, she is by no means so LS 18 273 3
We are very good friends, & tho' she never opens her lips LS 18 273 3
fixed on that point, tho' I have not yet quite resolved on LS 19 275 4
The poor girl however I am sure dislikes him; and tho' his LS 20 276 2
tho' to me as a mother, it is highly flattering. LS 20 276 5
will know what I feel now; tho' thank heaven! you cannot LS 20 277 5
entirely engrossed him; & tho' a little private discourse LS 20 278 9
torment him, as Sir James tho' extremely gallant to me, LS 22 280 2
Everything however was going on calmly & quietly; & tho' I LS 22 281 4
I reproach myself for having ever, tho' so innocently, LS 24 290 13
of her mother's anger, & tho' dreading my brother's LS 24 291 16
in fact I have not, for tho' he is still in my power, I LS 25 294 6
was so great, that tho' Mr Johnson was her guardian & I do LS 26 296 5
would be bent thither; and tho' he professed himself quite LS 27 297 4
of marrying him--& tho' this was too idle & nonsensical an LS 29 299 2
I have received your letter; & tho' I do not attempt to LS 30 299 1
her guardian's presence, tho' I did not know a syllable of LS 32 302 1
enough--for to be sunk, tho' but an hour, in your opinion, LS 35 305 1
I am greived, tho' I cannot be astonished at your rupture LS 38 306 1
under her own care; & tho' with little hope of success, LS 42 311 2
with her daughter; & as, tho' her own plans were not yet LS 42 312 5
Mrs Vernon however persevered in the offer of it, & tho' LS 42 312 5
six weeks; but her mother, tho' inviting her to return in LS 42 313 7
any girl so well since, tho' he is always behaving in a W 316 1
No, tho' I am nine years older than you are, I would not . W 320 2
doing pretty well, tho' it would be nothing for Penelope.-- W 322 2
but strangers to her, & tho' her spirits were by no means W 322 3
these ideas;--the mother tho' a very friendly woman, had a W 322 3
however sanctioned--& tho' complacently veiwing her W 323 3
to the two young ladies; & tho' Miss Edwards was rather W 326 7
much the finest person;--tho' nearly 50, she was very W 329 9
second promise;--but tho' he contrived to utter with an W 330 11
Tho' rather distressed by such observation, Emma could not W 331 11
Her little partner she found, tho' bent cheifly on dancing, W 331 11
I suppose so."--tho' she felt that she had no better W 332 12
unwilling to leave her, tho' his friend Ld Osborne was W 334 13
In himself, she thought him as agreable as he looked; tho' W 335 13
by whom she had been, tho' in some respects unpleasantly, W 336 14
& spirit of the meeting. tho' as he had been fixed the W 336 14
Tho' they are not written down, I bring your sister's W 339 18
Emma said this--tho' against her conscience.-- W 340 19
"That he would be handsome even, tho' he were not a Lord-- W 340 19
"You did very right; tho' I wonder at your forbearance, & W 341 19
that I could not say no, tho' it rather went against me to W 341 19
You do not offend me, tho' I hardly know how to beleive W 342 19
Now, tho' we have had nothing but fried beef, how good it W 343 19
a riding-whip cd give--& tho' charged by Miss W. to let W 344 21
Tho' Emma could not but take the compliment of the visit W 345 21
from such mortification--& tho' shrinking under a general W 345 21
when you are out visitting, tho' you do not at home." W 353 26
her sister in law, Emma (tho' in no spirits to make such W 353 26
justify eliz.'s opinions tho' Margaret's modest smiles W 355 28
saying before;--& Emma, tho' suffering a good deal from W 359 28
He played with spirit, & had a great deal to say & tho' W 359 28
She was at leisure, she could read & think,--tho' her W 361 31
Elizth gave them her interest, tho' evidently against her W 362 32
name perhaps--tho' I am by no means the first of my family, S 1 368 1
Sidney laughs at him--but it really is no joke--tho' S 5 385 1
He, I am happy to say is tolerably well--tho' more languid S 5 387 1
unagreable countenance--& tho' her manner was rather S 6 391 1
of butcher's meat in time--tho' you may not happen to have S 6 393 1
not very favourably; for tho' sitting thus apart with him (S 7 395 1
in person or manner--tho' more thin & worn by illness & S 10 413 1
hung last assizes at York, tho' we really have raised the S 12 424 1
& well-furnished;--tho' it was furniture rather originally S 12 427 1

THOMAS PALMER, ESQ. (1)

the lady of Thomas Palmer, Esq. was safely delivered of a SS II 14 246 1

THOMAS'S (42)

Thomas's intelligence seemed over. SS III 11 355 40
silence, awed by Sir Thomas's grave looks, and quite MP I 2 14 8
to a small house of Sir Thomas's in the village, and MP I 3 23 1
somewhat easier to Sir Thomas's conscience, he could not MP I 3 23 2
"Why, you know Sir Thomas's means will be rather MP I 3 30 54
all the others, when Sir Thomas's assurances of their both MP I 4 34 2
him to wait till Sir Thomas's return, and then Sir Thomas MP I 4 36 7
for not waiting till Sir Thomas's return in September, for MP I 4 37 9
Sir Thomas's sending away his son, seemed to her so like a MP I 4 38 9
It was some months before Sir Thomas's consent could be MP I 4 39 12
I cannot but think of dear Sir Thomas's delight. MP I 12 118 16
his persuasion of Sir Thomas's disapprobation of the whole, MP I 16 153 3
Every thing seems to depend upon Sir Thomas's return." MP I 17 162 15
of her claims on Sir Thomas's affection was much too MP II 1 176 4
by many fears of Sir Thomas's disapprobation when the MP II 1 179 10
She carried this point, and Sir Thomas's narrative MP II 1 180 12
discernment to catch Sir Thomas's meaning, or diffidence, MP II 1 184 25
fixed--from seeing Sir Thomas's dark brow contract as he MP II 1 184 27
Sir Thomas's look implied, "on your judgment, Edmund, I MP II 1 185 27
pleased with Sir Thomas's good opinion, and saying MP II 1 186 35
the current of Sir Thomas's ideas into a happier channel. MP II 2 188 3
Mr. Yates was beginning now to understand Sir Thomas's MP II 2 191 10
Sir Thomas's return made a striking change in the ways of MP II 3 196 1
And Sir Thomas's wishing just at first to be only with his MP II 3 199 14
was still owing to Sir Thomas's more than toleration of MP II 7 238 1
the odd trick by Sir Thomas's capital play and her own, MP II 7 245 32
she was stopped by Sir Thomas's saying with authority, "I MP II 7 245 34
Whatever effect Sir Thomas's little harangue might really MP II 7 248 47
To be urging her opinion against Sir Thomas's, was a proof MP II 10 275 11
She was attractive, she was modest, she was Sir Thomas's MP II 10 276 13
Miss Crawford saw much of Sir Thomas's thoughts as he MP II 10 276 14
"We miss our two young men," was Sir Thomas's observation MP II 11 284 9
A great deal of good sense followed on Sir Thomas's side, MP II 11 284 10
feelings, before Sir Thomas's politeness and apologies MP II 13 302 9
as these; and upon Sir Thomas's information of her being MP III 4 345 5
Mr. Crawford gone, Sir Thomas's next object was, that he MP III 6 366 1
they were to quit Sir Thomas's carriage, she was able to MP III 7 375 1
the circumstance of Sir Thomas's being in Parliament, got MP III 13 425 6
Sir Thomas's parental solicitude, and high sense of honour MP III 15 442 21
wrote to recommend Sir Thomas's coming to London himself, MP III 16 450 8
was the great supplementary comfort of Sir Thomas's life. MP III 17 465 15
It was a match which Sir Thomas's wishes had even MP III 17 471 29

THOMPSON (1)

From Thompson, that -----"it is a delightful task NA I 1 15 6

THOMSON (1)

Thomson, Cowper, Scott-- she would buy them all over and SS I 17 92 25

THORNBERRY (1)

He had been prevented setting off for Thornberry, but I P IV 10 228 71

THORNBERRY-PARK (1)

to his friends at Thornberry-Park for the whole day to- P IV 10 213 9

THORNS (3)

to a pillow strewed with thorns and wet with tears. NA I 11 90 65
We have cleared away all the old thorns that grew in SS II 11 226 39
rows of old thorns following its line almost every where.-- S 12 426 1

THORNTON LACEY (19)

I found myself in short in Thornton Lacey." MP II 7 241 13
it was not Thornton Lacey--for such it certainly was." MP II 7 241 15
a hedge that it was Thornton Lacey, and he agreed to it." MP II 7 241 17
Thornton Lacey was the name of his impending living, as MP II 7 241 19
your plan for Thornton Lacey will ever be put in practice. MP II 7 242 24
proceeded, and Crawford began again about Thornton Lacey. MP II 7 243 26
of the sort at Thornton Lacey, without accepting his help. MP II 7 244 30
scheme about Thornton Lacey, and not being able to catch MP II 7 246 37
that Edmund will occupy his own house at Thornton Lacey. MP II 7 247 39
the clergyman of Thornton Lacey every seventh day, for MP II 7 247 42
"I repeat again," added Sir Thomas, "that Thornton Lacey MP II 7 248 44
Owens settled at Thornton Lacey; how should you like it? MP II 11 289 34
relative to Thornton Lacey were completed--perhaps, within MP III 6 367 4
There may be some old woman at Thornton Lacey to be MP III 9 394 1
"Mansfield, Sotherton, Thornton Lacey," he continued, " MP III 10 405 19
any partnership in Thornton Lacey, as Edmund Bertram once MP III 10 405 19
at home, that I may have your opinion about Thornton Lacey. MP III 13 423 2
at Mansfield and Thornton Lacey; and when I hear of you MP III 16 458 30
After settling her at Thornton Lacey with every kind MP III 17 472 30

THOROUGH (29)

in which the most thorough knowledge of human nature, the NA I 5 38 4
of feeling, the thorough want of delicacy, of rectitude, SS I 22 127 2
Elinor was from feeling thorough contentment about it, yet SS II 5 167 7
Nothing but a thorough change of sentiment could account SS II 6 178 17
turn off his servants, and make a thorough reform at once? SS II 8 194 10
My affection for Marianne, my thorough conviction of her SS III 8 323 40
A woman must have a thorough knowledge of music, singing, PP I 8 39 50
They found Mary, as usual, deep in the study of thorough PP I 12 60 7
"A thorough, determined dislike of me--a dislike which I PP I 16 80 32
this last day a day of thorough enjoyment, was out snipe MP II 9 267 22
that it was to be a very thorough attack, that looks and MP III 3 341 31
Even Dr. Grant does shew a thorough confidence in my MP III 5 361 16
much longer; no doubt they are thorough holidays to her. MP III 14 434 13
all that he could, with thorough self-approbation, E I 3 24 13
14
He knows I have a thorough regard for him and all his E I 8 59 27
as it does, real, thorough sweetness of temper and manner, E I 8 63 44
And that excellent Miss Bates!--such thorough worthy E I 12 102 31
Mr. Weston entered into the idea with thorough enjoyment, E II 11 247 3
Then she is no rule for Mrs. Churchill, who is as thorough E II 18 306 16
Maple Grove has given me a thorough disgust of people of E II 18 310 34
As I tell Mr. E., you are a thorough humourist.-- E III 6 356 28
They parted thorough friends, however; she could not be E III 9 386 8
and habit, and thorough excellence of mind, he had loved E III 12 415 1
I know what thorough justice you will do it, and have E III 14 436 7
"Oh!" she cried with more thorough gaiety, "if you fancy E III 17 464 24
A morning of thorough confusion was to be expected. P IV 10 221 32
him, though it was from thorough absence of mind, became P IV 11 231 12
private families of thorough gentility & character, who S 1 368 1
in general, it was a thorough pause of company, it was S 6 389 1

THOROUGHLY (75)

long enough at school to understand anything thoroughly. LS 7 253 1
her thoroughly uncomfortable till she does accept him. LS 7 253 2
The purport of it frightened her so thoroughly that with a LS 19 273 1
I was thoroughly unwilling to let her go, & so was her LS 41 310 3
good sense, and is so thoroughly unaffected and amiable; I NA I 7 50 47
the following question, thoroughly artless in itself, NA I 12 94 11
not to examine it thoroughly while she was about it." NA II 6 169 11
Henry's address, short as it had been, had more thoroughly NA II 10 199 1
own command, made her thoroughly sensible of the restraint NA II 13 220 1
His countenance was thoroughly good-humoured; and his SS I 6 30 6
It was impossible for any one to be more thoroughly good- SS I 20 112 26
whole heart she felt thoroughly possessed, and whom she SS II 1 141 4
of which she seemed so thoroughly aware that he was weary. SS II 2 151 41
That Marianne, fastidious as she was, thoroughly SS II 3 155 6
she saw her mother so thoroughly pleased with the plan, SS II 3 158 20
Mrs. Jennings, with a thoroughly good-humoured concern for SS II 7 185 16
to convince me, as thoroughly as he was convinced himself, SS II 9 209 28
continuance, without thoroughly despising them all four. SS II 12 233 16
and Edward himself, now thoroughly enlightened on her SS III 13 366 21
good-hearted girl, and thoroughly attached to himself. SS III 13 366 21
made farther conversation most thoroughly undesirable.-- W 321 2
From what he said of Miss Darcy, I was thoroughly prepared PP III 5 284 14
and in your heart, you thoroughly despised the persons who PP III 18 380 5
education, fortune, or connections, did it very thoroughly. MP I 1 3 1
"I thoroughly understand you," cried Mrs. Norris; "you are MP I 1 7 8
reached, she was thoroughly benevolent, and nobody knew MP I 1 8 9
and very thoroughly relished the means it afforded her of MP I 4 35 5
beauty of her own, she thoroughly enjoyed the power of MP I 4 42 17
ladyship, who had been thoroughly awakened by Mrs. MP I 7 72 42
them as thoroughly perhaps in the animation of a card- MP II 3 202 28
had made himself thoroughly master of the subject, or had MP II 6 232 13
to know him pretty thoroughly, is, perhaps, not uncommon; MP III 3 338 14
A thoroughly good sermon, thoroughly well delivered, is a MP III 3 341 28
Some opposition here is, I am thoroughly convinced, MP III 4 349 23
being for the time thoroughly fagged, which their hot MP III 7 383 31
and who did seem so thoroughly without a single MP III 7 385 38
and some degree of elegance, was thoroughly acceptable.-- MP III 9 393 1
The deed thoroughly answered; a source of domestic MP III 9 397 7
himself, and thoroughly investigate the merits of the case. MP III 10 404 15
and as Fanny grew thoroughly to understand this, she began MP III 12 419 9
He thoroughly knows his own mind, and acts up to his MP III 13 423 2

well to hope they would thoroughly understand;--and who MP III 14 430 6
the tea-board never thoroughly cleaned, the cups and MP III 15 439 9
thoroughly up, could really close such a conversation. MP III 16 459 31
to her heart, and as thoroughly perfect in her eyes, as MP III 17 473 33
excellent man, that he thoroughly deserves a good wife;-- E I 1 8 12
The only thing I do not thoroughly like is, that she seems E I 6 48 36
"I did not thoroughly understand what you were telling E I 12 104 44
be depended on, for he thoroughly understands the nature E I 12 105 55
and he had besides, so thoroughly cleared off his ill- E I 16 139 20
Time, she knew, must be allowed for this being thoroughly E I 17 142 11
and if it is very thoroughly boiled, just as Serle boils E II 3 172 19
She was not thoroughly comfortable herself. E II 3 179 53
what she knew to be thoroughly deserved by Mrs. Weston; E II 5 191 28
be sure to warm herself thoroughly; if hungry, that she E II 7 211 22
that Mr. Woodhouse thinks the fruit thoroughly wholesome. E II 9 237 46
it shews it to have been so thoroughly from the heart. E II 10 242 21
If I could be sure of the rooms being thoroughly aired-- E II 11 252 35
In this style she ran on; never thoroughly stopped by any E II 17 302 21
22
But as I have always had a thoroughly good opinion of Miss E III 10 399 64
To understand, thoroughly understand her own heart, was E III 11 412 44
Within half an hour, he had passed from a thoroughly E III 13 432 40
You will soon, I earnestly hope, know her thoroughly E III 14 439 8
Robert Martin had thoroughly supplanted Mr. Knightley, and E III 19 481 1
No second attachment, the only thoroughly natural, happy, P III 4 28 7
as he liked, being as thoroughly the object of the P III 9 73 1
She only consulted Lady Russell, who entered thoroughly P IV 5 153 5
and nurse Rooke thoroughly understands when to speak. P IV 5 155 9
as thoroughly as it appeared to have influenced her fate. P IV 6 167 20
She could thoroughly comprehend the sort of fascination he P IV 7 179 28
The Heywoods were a thoroughly respectable family, & every S 2 370 1
She was as thoroughly amiable as she was lovely--& since S 3 379 1
thoroughly know them, have an extraordinary appearance.-- S 5 385 1
"She is thoroughly mean. S 7 402 1
tea scientifically & thoroughly understand all the S 10 418 1

THORPE (126)

pronounced her's to be Thorpe; and Mrs. Allen immediately NA I 4 31 2
Mrs. Thorpe, however, had one great advantage as a talker, NA I 4 32 2
"Here come my dear girls," cried Mrs. Thorpe, pointing at NA I 4 32 3
For a moment Catherine was surprized; but Mrs. Thorpe and NA I 4 33 5
college, of the name of Thorpe; and that he had spent the NA I 4 33 5
Miss Thorpe, and take a turn with her about the room. NA I 4 33 6
almost forgot Mr. Tilney while she talked to Miss Thorpe. NA I 4 33 6
Miss Thorpe, however, being four years older than Miss NA I 4 33 7
it together, that Miss Thorpe should accompany Miss NA I 4 34 7
Mrs. Thorpe was a widow, and not a very rich one; she was NA I 4 34 8
minute detail from Mrs. Thorpe herself, of her past NA I 4 34 9
nods and smiles of Miss Thorpe, though they certainly NA I 5 35 1
am we have met with Mrs. Thorpe!"--and she was as eager in NA I 5 36 3
of it by the side of Mrs. Thorpe, in what they called NA I 5 36 3
of subject, for Mrs. Thorpe talked chiefly of her children, NA I 5 36 3
the independence of Miss Thorpe, and her resolution of NA I 6 43 44
the bright eyes of Miss Thorpe were incessantly NA I 7 44 4
John Thorpe, who in the mean time had been giving orders NA I 7 45 5
"Three-and-twenty!" cried Thorpe; "five and twenty if it NA I 7 45 7
last term: 'Ah! Thorpe,' said he, 'do you happen to want NA I 7 46 11
Edgar's Buildings, and pay their respects to Mrs. Thorpe. NA I 7 47 18
John Thorpe kept of course with Catherine, and, after a NA I 7 47 19
it was, "have you ever read Udolpho, Mr. Thorpe?" NA I 7 48 32
Thorpe, who had descried them from above, in the passage. NA I 7 49 43
how do you like my friend Thorpe?" instead of answering, NA I 7 50 44
of such a girl as Miss Thorpe even you, Catherine," taking NA I 7 50 47
and friend as Isabella Thorpe, it would be impossible for NA I 7 51 51
part, in praise of Miss Thorpe, till they reached Pulteney- NA I 7 51 54
Mrs. Thorpe and Mrs. Allen, between whom she now remained. NA I 8 52 2
the non-appearance of Mr. Thorpe, for she not only longed NA I 8 53 2
by seeing, not Mr. Thorpe, but Mr. Tilney, within three NA I 8 53 3
an acquaintance of Mrs. Thorpe; and this lady stopping to NA I 8 54 4
Here they were interrupted by a request from Mrs. Thorpe NA I 8 54 10
really felt it, that had Thorpe, who joined her just NA I 8 54 10
any how get to Miss Thorpe, and Mrs. Thorpe said she was NA I 8 55 10
to Miss Thorpe, and Mrs. Thorpe said she was sure you NA I 8 55 10
John Thorpe, in the meanwhile, had walked away; and NA I 8 58 25
to Mrs. Allen and Mrs. Thorpe as fast as she could, in the NA I 8 58 25
"Well, my dear," said Mrs. Thorpe, impatient for praise of NA I 8 58 25
"Indeed he is, Mrs. Allen," said Mrs. Thorpe, smiling NA I 8 58 33
gracious reply, when John Thorpe came up to her soon NA I 8 59 35
her brother driving Miss Thorpe in the second, before John NA I 9 61 1
the second, before John Thorpe came running up stairs, NA I 9 61 1
in her going with Mr. Thorpe, as Isabella was going at the NA I 9 61 6
in her praise, after Thorpe had procured Mrs. Allen's NA I 9 62 7
"You will not be frightened, Miss Morland," said Thorpe, NA I 9 62 9
she sat peaceably down, and saw Thorpe sit down by her. NA I 9 62 10
"You do not really think, Mr. Thorpe," said Catherine, NA I 9 65 27
Do let us turn back, Mr. Thorpe; stop and speak to my NA I 9 65 29
of requesting from Mr. Thorpe a clearer insight into his NA I 9 66 31
"So Mrs. Thorpe said; she was vastly pleased at your all NA I 9 68 36
"You have seen Mrs. Thorpe then?" NA I 9 68 37
and that John Thorpe himself was quite disagreeable. NA I 9 69 51
The female part of the Thorpe family, attended by James NA I 10 71 8
But I really had been engaged the whole day to Mr. Thorpe." NA I 10 72 11
She had then been exulting in her engagement to Thorpe, NA I 10 74 23
fidgetted about if John Thorpe came towards her, hid NA I 10 74 23
The others walked away, John Thorpe was still in view, and NA I 10 75 24
so narrowly escape John Thorpe, and to be asked, so NA I 10 75 24
attention was claimed by John Thorpe, who stood behind her. NA I 10 75 25
"Mr. Thorpe is such a very particular friend of my NA I 10 78 38
"Isabella, my brother, and Mr. Thorpe, I declare! NA I 11 84 18
John Thorpe was soon with them, and his voice was with NA I 11 84 18
"You croaking fellow!" cried Thorpe, "we shall be able to NA I 11 84 21
"Not they indeed," cried Thorpe; "for, as we turned into NA I 11 85 33
Thorpe talked to his horse, and she meditated, by turns, NA I 11 87 51
"Stop, stop, Mr. Thorpe, she impatiently cried, it is Miss NA I 11 87 53
Thorpe only lashed his horse into a brisker trot; the NA I 11 87 53
"Pray, pray stop, Mr. Thorpe.-- NA I 11 87 53
But Mr. Thorpe only laughed, smacked his whip, encouraged NA I 11 87 53
"How could you deceive me so, Mr. Thorpe?-- NA I 11 87 53
Thorpe defended himself very stoutly, declared he had NA I 11 87 53
"we had better go back, Thorpe; it is too late to go on to- NA I 11 88 54
"It is all one to me," replied Thorpe rather angrily; and NA I 11 88 55
Thorpe then said something in the loud, incoherent way to NA I 11 89 61
she was gone out with Mr. Thorpe, the lady had asked NA I 11 89 62
a thing; but I begged Mr. Thorpe so earnestly to stop; I NA I 12 94 8
indeed I did; and, if Mr. Thorpe would only have stopped, NA I 12 94 8
some surprize, that John Thorpe, who was never in the same NA I 12 95 17
"How came Mr. Thorpe to know your father?" was her anxious NA I 12 95 17
When the entertainment was over, Thorpe came to assist NA I 12 95 18
Thorpe, however, would see her to her chair, and, till she NA I 12 96 23
"that could not be, for Thorpe did not know that he might NA I 13 99 4
"But why cannot Mr. Thorpe drive one of his other sisters? NA I 13 99 6
"Thank ye," cried Thorpe, "but I did not come to Bath to NA I 13 99 7
But her words were lost on Thorpe, who had turned abruptly NA I 13 99 8
they were again joined by Thorpe, who coming to them with NA I 13 100 13
Isabella, however, caught hold of one hand; Thorpe of the NA I 13 100 19
Mr. Thorpe had no business to invent any such message. NA I 13 100 20
how do I know that Mr. Thorpe has-----he may be mistaken NA I 13 101 20
Thorpe told her it would be in vain to go after the NA I 13 101 21
Let me go, Mr. Thorpe; Isabella, do not hold me." Tilneys; NA I 13 101 20
Thorpe would have darted after her, but Morland withheld NA I 13 101 22
Thorpe never finished the simile, for it could hardly have NA I 13 101 24
Catherine found that John Thorpe had given the message; NA I 13 102 26
It is not right; and I wonder Mrs. Thorpe should allow it. NA I 13 104 31
not have gone with Mr. Thorpe at all; but I always hoped NA I 13 104 35
you, my dear, not to go out with Mr. Thorpe any more." NA I 13 105 38
in her to write to Miss Thorpe, and explain the indecorum NA I 13 105 40
Mrs. Thorpe is too indulgent beyond a doubt; but however NA I 13 105 40
overtook the second Miss Thorpe, as she was loitering NA I 14 114 50
Mrs. Thorpe and her son, who were acquainted with every NA I 15 120 25
Mrs. Thorpe, with tears of joy, embraced her daughter, her NA I 15 121 27
were ascertained, John Thorpe, who had only waited its NA I 15 122 29
thought her friend, Miss Thorpe, would have any objection NA II 1 132 16
she was very sure Miss Thorpe did not mean to dance at all. NA II 1 132 16
wish of dancing with Miss Thorpe to good-nature alone, NA II 1 133 28
I really think Miss Thorpe has by no means chosen ill in NA II 1 134 36
the gentle Mrs. Thorpe, looking anxiously at her daughter. NA II 1 135 44
"Yes, yes, my darling Isabella," said Mrs. Thorpe, "we NA II 1 136 49
partiality for Miss Thorpe, and entreating him to make NA II 4 150 1
I have myself told him that Miss Thorpe is engaged. NA II 4 150 6
"Is it my brother's attentions to Miss Thorpe, or Miss NA II 4 151 10
The mess-room will drink Isabella Thorpe for a fortnight, NA II 4 153 29
that every thing is at an end between Miss Thorpe and me.-- NA II 10 202 6
7
Poor Thorpe is in town: I dread the sight of him; his NA II 10 202 7
His marrying Miss Thorpe is not probable. NA II 10 204 20
He has his vanities as well as Miss Thorpe, and the chief NA II 12 218 7
be much distressed by the disappointment of Miss Thorpe. NA II 12 219 15
She trusted he would never speak of Miss Thorpe; and NA II 13 222 8
"Very true: we soon met with Mrs. Thorpe, and then we NA II 14 238 24
John Thorpe had first misled him. NA II 15 244 12
inquired of Thorpe, if he knew more of her than her name. NA II 15 244 12
Thorpe, most happy to be on speaking terms with a man of NA II 15 244 12
had suggested them, from Thorpe himself, whom he had NA II 15 246 12
inquiring look; and here too Thorpe had learnt his error. NA II 15 246 13

THORPE'S (21)

that the lace on Mrs. Thorpe's pelisse was not half so NA I 4 32 2
the easy gaiety of Miss Thorpe's manners, and her frequent NA I 4 33 7
stairs, and watched Miss Thorpe's progress down the street NA I 4 34 7
them to the door of Mrs. Thorpe's lodgings, and the NA I 7 49 43
stilishness of Miss Thorpe's, had more real elegance. NA I 8 55 11
was broken by Thorpe's saying very abruptly, "old Allen is NA I 9 63 10
Thorpe's ideas then all reverted to the merits of his own NA I 9 64 27
They all spent the evening together at Thorpe's. NA I 11 89 63
The affair thus determined, and Thorpe's approbation NA I 13 97 1
politeness as recalled Thorpe's information to her mind, NA I 13 102 27
of every thought of Mr. Thorpe's being in love with her, NA II 3 144 11
The compliment of John Thorpe's affection did not make NA II 3 148 29
or Miss Thorpe's admission of them, that gives the pain?" NA II 4 151 10
his own account or Miss Thorpe's, for supposing that her NA II 4 152 28
in which Miss Thorpe's name was included, passed his lips. NA II 10 204 18
began to inquire into Miss Thorpe's connexions and fortune. NA II 10 205 25
Moreover, I have too good an opinion of Miss Thorpe's NA II 10 206 31
Mrs. Thorpe's being there was such a comfort to us, was NA II 14 238 22
Thorpe's interest in the family, by his sister's NA II 15 245 12
and thankful for Mr. Thorpe's communication, he almost NA II 15 245 12
more misled by by Thorpe's first boast of the family NA II 16 251 6

THORPES (13)

The Miss Thorpes were introduced; and Miss Morland, who NA I 4 32 4
were said by the Miss Thorpes of their wish of being NA I 4 33 6
As soon as divine service was over, the Thorpes and Allens NA I 5 35 2
From the Thorpes she could learn nothing, for they had NA I 5 36 2
sitting an hour with the Thorpes, set off to walk together NA I 7 50 44
The Thorpes and James Morland were there only two minutes NA I 8 52 1
The younger Miss Thorpes being also dancing, Catherine was NA I 8 52 2
The Allens, Thorpes, and Morlands, all met in the evening NA I 10 70 1
As soon as they were joined by the Thorpes, Catherine's NA I 10 74 23
the eager cry of both the Thorpes; they must go to Clifton NA I 13 97 1
of her brother and the Thorpes for the following day. NA I 13 103 29
The two youngest Miss Thorpes were by themselves in the NA I 15 116 1
The Thorpes spent the last evening of Catherine's stay in NA II 4 153 31

THOU (3)

able to decipher 'Oh! thou--whomsoever thou mayst be, into NA II 5 160 21
'Oh! thou--whomsoever thou mayst be, into whose hands NA II 5 160 21
the pronouns he or she and thou, the plainest-spoken E II 15 286 23

THOUGHT (880)

thought it better to lay aside the scheme for the present. LS 2 245 1
but herself I can affirm, would ever have thought possible. LS 14 263 1
to her visitor, & yet I thought I could perceive that she LS 20 276 3
to any one, because I thought that while Frederica LS 20 277 5
& that I shall not find out I have thought too well of her. LS 20 278 11
assure you sir, I always thought him silly & impertinent & LS 21 279 1
was done, I thought I never should have courage to give it. LS 24 286 5
colouring again, but I thought that Mr De Courcy could do LS 24 286 7
mortified to find it as I thought so ill bestowed. LS 24 290 13
I thought myself sure of you at 7. LS 33 303 1
before entertained a thought, has for some time existed, & LS 36 305 1
asking her whether she thought Frederica looked quite as LS 42 312 4
they would now have thought her exceedingly handsome. NA I 2 24 27
Such words had their due effect; she immediately thought NA I 2 24 28
"I have sometimes thought," said Catherine, doubtingly, " NA I 3 27 29
Whether she thought of him so much, while she drank her NA I 3 29 52
how little they had thought of meeting in Bath, and what a NA I 4 32 2
originality of thought, and literary taste which marked NA I 6 39 1
I am very sorry for it; but really I thought I was in very NA I 6 39 3
I am sure you would be miserable if you thought so." NA I 6 41 18
"Do you indeed!--you surprize me; I thought it had not NA I 6 42 24
By the bye, though I have thought of it a hundred times, I NA I 6 42 28
I never much thought about it. NA I 6 42 29
thought her friend quite as pretty as she could do herself. NA I 7 44 4
the new hat, that John thought her the most charming girl NA I 7 50 44
"Because I thought I should soon see you myself. NA I 7 50 49
to each other whenever a thought occurred, and supplying NA I 8 52 1
he might have thought her sufferings rather too acute. NA I 8 54 10
so I thought perhaps he would ask you, if he met with you." NA I 8 58 30
"I dare say she thought I was speaking of her son." NA I 8 59 34
of a drive, and who thought there could be no impropriety NA I 9 61 6
all drink a great deal more wine than I thought you did. NA I 9 64 25
not look amiss; the sleeves were entirely my own thought. NA I 10 70 3
"He must have thought it very odd to hear me say I was NA I 10 72 11
not seeing him any where, I thought he must be gone. NA I 10 73 13
I thought you and I were to dance together." NA I 10 75 25
"No, indeed, I never thought of that." NA I 10 77 36
"I thought how it would be," said Mrs. Allen. NA I 11 82 3
"Any body would have thought so indeed. NA I 11 83 13
of Mrs. Allen, who had "always thought it would clear up." NA I 11 83 16
"It is very odd! but I suppose they thought it would be NA I 11 85 40
especially rather than be thought ill of by the Tilneys, NA I 11 88 54
You must have thought me so rude; but indeed it was not my NA I 12 93 5
a pleasant walk; I never thought of such a thing; but I NA I 12 94 8
"Well, nobody would have thought you had no right who saw NA I 12 95 15
than surprize, when she thought she could perceive herself NA I 12 95 17
and she joyfully thought, that there was not one of the NA I 12 96 24
Catherine thought this reproach equally strange and unkind. NA I 13 98 3
A pretty good thought of mine--hey?" NA I 13 100 15
"A most heavenly thought indeed! NA I 13 100 17
If I had thought it right to put it off, I could have NA I 13 100 20
If I could not be persuaded into doing what I thought NA I 13 101 22
I did not care what you thought of me.-- NA I 13 102 25
elasticity, though she had never thought of it before. NA I 13 103 29
hoped you would tell me, if you thought I was doing wrong." NA I 13 104 35
and after a moment's thought, asked Mr. Allen whether it NA I 13 105 40
would the Tilneys have thought of her, if she had broken NA I 13 105 41
But I really thought before, young men despised novels NA I 14 107 10
natural affection; for no thought of Isabella or James had NA I 14 114 50
She thought it would be something very fine. NA I 14 115 52

It appeared that Blaize Castle had never been thought of; NA I 15 116 2
him, I thought I never saw any body so handsome before." NA I 15 118 11
endowments, she had never in her life thought him handsome. NA I 15 118 12
so heavenly, that I thought your brother must certainly NA I 15 118 13
her acquaintance; and she thought her friend never looked NA I 15 119 19
"Perhaps we may; but it is more than I ever thought of. NA I 15 124 45
I thought it was all settled." NA II 1 130 12
protested against every thought of dancing himself, but NA II 1 131 15
to know, if she thought her friend, Miss Thorpe, would NA II 1 132 16
Besides, I thought Mrs. Hughes, who introduced him, might NA II 1 134 39
to forget that she had for a minute thought otherwise. NA II 1 137 50
desired to be favourably thought of, outstripped even her NA II 2 141 11
accused of being arch, thought the present a fine NA II 3 143 2
"But I thought, Isabella, you had something in particular NA II 3 144 5
her innocence of every thought of Mr. Thorpe's being in NA II 3 144 11
of it, that I never thought, nor expected, nor wished for NA II 3 145 13
But I confess, as soon as I read this letter, I thought it NA II 3 145 16
to her good will, and she thought with sincere compassion NA II 4 149 1
a plan, and her first thought was to decline it; but her NA II 5 156 5
had it moved, because I thought it might sometimes be of NA II 6 165 4
Why, as he had such rooms, he thought it would be simple NA II 6 166 7
it to be neat and simple, thought it right to encourage NA II 7 175 12
But he thought he could discern.-- NA II 7 177 17
no uniformity of architecture had been thought necessary. NA II 8 184 4
and, as Catherine thought, rather angrily back, demanding NA II 8 185 6
"So much the worse!" thought Catherine; such ill-timed NA II 8 187 14
and, besides, she thought the examination itself would be NA II 9 192 5
It was no time for thought; she hurried on, slipped with NA II 9 193 6
I thought you did not mean to come back till to-morrow." NA II 9 195 11
father, I thought--perhaps had not been very fond of her." NA II 9 196 24
He had--she thought he had, once or twice before this NA II 10 199 1
about it in Bath, you little thought of its ending so. NA II 10 204 19
so very, very much afflicted as one would have thought." NA II 10 207 39
The very painful reflections to which this thought led, NA II 11 208 1
Catherine was ashamed to say how pretty she thought it, as NA II 11 212 17
o'clock, when Catherine scarcely thought it could be three. NA II 11 214 26
she had, her leaving them was not even to be thought of. NA II 13 221 6
avoided, she thought she could behave to him very civilly. NA II 13 222 8
At that moment Catherine thought she heard her step in the NA II 13 222 9
who sat as deep in thought as herself; and the appearance NA II 13 228 27
Catherine had never thought on the subject till that NA II 13 229 31
which led to it, and thought of Henry, so near, yet so NA II 14 230 1
There was a thought yet nearer, a more prevailing, more NA II 14 231 4
The pressing anxieties of thought, which prevented her NA II 14 231 5
them, should they be thought of unfavourably, on their NA II 14 232 5
They never once thought of her heart, which, for the NA II 14 235 13
and, after long thought and much perplexity, to be very NA II 14 235 14
I am sorry it happens so, for Mrs. Allen thought them very NA II 14 236 15
friend; and Mrs. Allen thought his expressions quite good NA II 14 237 22
relaxation of anger, or any material digression of thought. NA II 14 238 22
Mr. Tilney drank tea with us, and I always thought him a NA II 14 238 26
had been the only cause of giving her a serious thought. NA II 15 243 9
He then really thought himself equal to it. SS I 1 5 8
He thought of it all day long, and for many days SS I 1 5 8
Had he been in his right senses, he could not have thought SS I 2 9 5
do less than give it: at least I thought so at the time. SS I 2 9 6
The assistance he thought of, I dare say, was only such as SS I 2 12 24
Your father thought only of them. SS I 2 13 28
it himself, and she thought of it for her daughters' sake SS I 3 14 2
I thought so at the time; but you would give him Cowper." SS I 3 18 19
Elinor had always thought it would be more prudent for SS I 4 24 21
thought which particularly recommended the action to her. SS I 9 43 11
saying too much what he thought on every occasion, without SS I 10 48 9
Her mother too, in whose mind not one speculative thought SS I 10 49 11
Willoughby thought the same; and their behaviour, at all SS I 11 53 2
be softened than she had thought it possible before, by SS I 11 54 5
your sister, who thought and judged like her, but who from SS I 11 57 17
imprudence and want of thought, surprised her by its SS I 12 58 1
Elinor thought it wisest to touch that point no more. SS I 12 59 5
interval of earnest thought, she came to her sister again, SS I 13 69 76
be some bad news, and thought over every kind of distress SS I 14 70 1
She thought of what had just passed with anxiety and SS I 15 77 19
was indubitable; and she thought with the tenderest SS I 15 77 20
I have thought it all over I assure you, and I can SS I 15 78 24
How could such a thought occur to you? SS I 15 80 36
Marianne would have thought herself very inexcusable had SS I 16 83 1
Elinor thought this generosity overstrained, considering SS I 16 85 10
thought he ought to be treated from the family connection. SS I 16 89 42
"I wish," said Margaret, striking out a novel thought, " SS I 17 92 18
"But I thought it was right, Elinor," said Marianne, "to SS I 17 93 38
I thought our judgments were given us merely to be SS I 17 94 38
I have frequently thought that I must have been intended SS I 17 94 42
But I should have thought her hair had been darker." SS I 18 98 11
at her want of thought could not be surpassed by his. SS I 18 98 12
What! you thought nobody could dance because a certain SS I 18 100 20
"I do assure you," he replied, "that I have long thought SS I 19 102 4
I thought I heard a carriage last night, while we were SS I 19 106 20
I thought of nothing but whether it might not be Colonel SS I 19 106 20
21

I always thought it such a sweet place, ma'am! (turning to SS I 19 107 24
I thought you would, he is so pleasant; and Mr. Palmer is SS I 20 114 42
She thought it probable that as they lived in the same SS I 20 114 43
time in her life, she thought Mrs. Jennings deficient SS I 21 126 41
"Indeed!" replied Lucy; "I wonder at that, for I thought SS I 22 128 5
in the world than be thought so by a person whose good SS I 22 128 9
secrecy; and I really thought my behaviour in asking so SS I 22 129 16
Besides in the present case, I really thought some SS I 22 132 42
forfeit her esteem, she thought she could even now, under SS II 1 140 4
Such a thought would never enter either Sir John or Lady SS II 1 143 8
not one novelty of thought or expression, and nothing SS II 1 143 10
to be done to it than I thought there was; and it would be SS II 1 145 20
"All this," thought Elinor, "is very pretty; but it can SS II 2 148 13
Elinor thought it wisest to make no answer to this, lest SS II 2 150 35
the merrier say I, and I thought it would be more SS II 3 154 4
Elinor thought she could distinguish a large W. in the SS II 4 161 5
"Aye, to be sure, I thought as much. SS II 4 163 18
"I had not thought of that. SS II 5 167 2
"I thought you were both in Devonshire," said he. SS II 5 171 31
conduct from censure, she thought it most prudent and kind, SS II 5 174 45
I thought it had been only a joke, but so serious a SS II 7 182 9
Sometimes I thought it had been--but it never was." SS II 7 186 34
Mrs. Jennings was not struck by the same thought; for, SS II 8 198 30
I thought we had been safe." SS II 9 203 12
encouraged, because I thought it probable that I might SS II 9 204 18
I knew him to be a very good sort of man, and I thought SS II 9 209 28
What I thought, what I feared, may be imagined; and what I SS II 9 209 28
I thought your sister's influence might yet reclaim him. SS II 9 210 32
all that she suffered and thought; to express her anxious SS II 10 213 2
Sir John could not have thought it possible. SS II 10 214 9
wrong in the other, she thought herself at liberty to SS II 10 215 14
"But I always thought I should. SS II 10 217 21
But I thought, at the time, that you would most likely SS II 10 217 21
Dr. Davies was coming to town, and so we thought we'd join SS II 10 218 24
parent than the other, thought the boys were both SS II 12 234 24
had no opinion to give, as she had never thought about it. SS II 12 234 25
Perhaps Fanny thought for a moment that her mother had SS II 12 235 30
31

she would have thought herself amply rewarded for the SS II 14 247 4
Mrs. Jennings, that she thought it a delightful thing for SS II 14 247 5
Lady Elliott was delighted with the thought. SS II 14 252 18
on any thing else; and a thought struck him during the SS II 14 252 20
minutes before, that she thought to make a match between SS III 1 258 7
forget that he ever thought another superior to her."-- SS III 1 263 27
my prospects; and told me, as I thought, with triumph.-- SS III 1 263 29
house; merely because she thought they deserved some SS III 1 266 36
might have thought myself safe.' thought myself safe.' SS III 1 266 38
I never thought Edward so stubborn, so unfeeling before. SS III 1 266 38
he had done otherwise, I should have thought him a rascal. SS III 1 267 43
Once Lucy thought to write to him, but then her spirit SS III 2 273 16
earnestly did I, as I thought my duty required, urge him SS III 2 277 30
She had not thought her old friend could have made so SS III 3 282 15
thought of late, there was nothing more likely to happen." SS III 4 285 3
For a short time he sat deep in thought, after Elinor had SS III 4 290 36
37

a man apologising, as I thought, for a house that to my SS III 4 292 55
from observing, that she thought Fanny might have borne SS III 5 295 17
the question--not to be thought of or mentioned--as to any SS III 5 297 31
But I thought I would just tell you of this, because I SS III 5 297 31
eyes, while Mrs. Jennings thought only of his behaviour;-- SS III 6 305 16
to deprive them both, she thought, of every comfort; and SS III 7 309 5
the latter, was a thought which immediately followed the SS III 7 311 14
her more, by hints of what her mistress had always thought. SS III 7 312 17
She was calm, except when she thought of her mother, but SS III 7 313 21
friend from indulging a thought of its continuance;--and SS III 7 314 22
By their uncertain light she thought she could discern it SS III 7 316 29
was not a thing to be thought of;--and with a meanness, SS III 8 320 32
to engage her regard, without a thought of returning it.-- SS III 8 320 32
But I thought of her, I believe, every moment of the day. SS III 8 327 55
Yet when I thought of her to-day as really dying, it was a SS III 8 327 55
allowable, governed every thought; and the connection, for SS III 8 331 70
her own interest in every thought, courting the favour of SS III 12 357 3
the whole, of the case, thought it incumbent on her to be SS III 12 359 13
tears of joy, which at first she thought would never cease. SS III 12 360 26
which he must have thought of almost with despair, as soon SS III 13 361 3
Longstaple with what I thought, at the time, a most SS III 13 362 5
She was pretty too--at least I thought so then, and I had SS III 13 362 5
your affections, I have thought myself at liberty to SS III 13 365 14
curiosity to see, but thought I would first trouble you SS III 13 365 14
with which he had once thought of Colonel Brandon, in SS III 13 366 20
"I thought it my duty," said he, "independent of my SS III 13 367 22
that he long thought of Colonel Brandon with envy, and of SS III 14 379 18
I should not be surprised if you were to be thought one of W 315 1
Every body thought it would have been a match." W 316 2
in the thought of all that was to precede them. W 322 3
Emma thought she could perceive a faint blush accompany W 324 3
"She had not thought a strong likeness at all incompatible W 324 3
she might like to be thought a beautiful girl by Lord or W 334 13
In himself, she thought him as agreable as he looked; tho' W 335 13
"I thought you were to have stood up with Mr James, the W 336 14
I thought it had been for the 2 dances after, if we staid W 337 14
Nobody could have thought of the Edwards' letting you have W 341 19
not offend Mr Watson--which I thought very kind of him.-- W 344 20
We thought it too dirty." W 345 21
Who would have thought of Ld Osborne's coming to Stanton.-- W 347 22
"Very much"--replied Emma, who thought a comprehensive W 350 24
I thought turner had been reckoned an extraordinary W 352 26
pounds, there was a young man who wd have thought of her." W 353 26
Penelope was the only creature to be thought of. W 355 28
likely to lessen; & when thought had been freely indulged, W 361 31
refusal accepted; as they thought too highly of their own W 362 32
thought her quite beautiful, and danced with her twice. PP I 3 12 16
women in the room, and which he thought the prettiest? PP I 5 19 7
and who had not thought her handsome enough to dance with. PP I 6 23 12
not say nay to him; and I thought Colonel Forster looked PP I 7 29 12
ill themselves; and then thought no more of the matter: PP I 8 35 1
Mrs. Hurst thought the same, and added, "she has nothing, PP I 8 35 3
4

I thought Miss Elizabeth Bennet looked remarkably well, PP I 8 36 7
"It must not be thought of. PP I 9 41 4
Perhaps he thought her too young. PP I 9 44 31
from a rapidity of thought and carelessness of execution, PP I 10 48 27
Mr. Darcy smiled; but Elizabeth thought she could perceive PP I 10 51 40
Mrs. Bennet wondered at their coming, and thought them PP I 12 60 6
ago I answered it, for I thought it a case of some PP I 13 61 6
were withdrawn, he thought it time to have some PP I 14 66 1
father's estate; and he thought it an excellent one, full PP I 15 70 2
He meant to provide for me amply, and thought he had done PP I 16 79 25
Elizabeth honoured him for such feelings, and thought him PP I 16 80 30
"I had not thought Mr. Darcy so bad as this--though I have PP I 16 80 33
liked him, I had not thought so very ill of him-- I had PP I 16 80 33
Elizabeth was again deep in thought, and after a time PP I 16 80 36
This information made Elizabeth smile, as she thought of PP I 16 83 56
brother; and Elizabeth thought with pleasure of dancing a PP I 17 86 10
that though my brother thought he could not well avoid PP I 18 94 45
Who would have thought of my meeting with--perhaps--a PP I 18 96 57
It was really a very handsome thought. PP I 16 98 62
to Mr. Collins, she thought with equal certainty, and with PP I 18 103 77
He thought too well of himself to comprehend on what PP I 20 112 24
"If we thought alike of Miss Bingley," replied Jane, "your PP I 21 119 21
Mrs. Bennet wished to understand by it that he thought of PP I 22 124 11
so clever as herself, she thought that if encouraged to PP I 22 124 11
it in what ever manner he thought best; but her sister's PP II 1 133 3
involved in it, as she thought he must be sensible himself. PP II 1 133 3
It was possible, and sometimes she thought it probable, PP II 2 142 16
honestly telling her what she thought, she thus went on: PP II 3 144 1
2

to banish every painful thought, and think only of what PP II 3 148 26
She had not at first thought very seriously of going PP II 4 151 1
Who would have thought she could be so thin and small!" PP II 5 158 15
rank, she thought she could witness without trepidation. PP II 6 161 9
apologies and thanks which he would have thought necessary. PP II 6 161 10
Maria thought speaking out of the question, and the PP II 6 163 14
It was not thought necessary in Sir Lewis de Bourgh's PP II 6 164 16
fish he won, and apologising if he thought he won too many. PP II 6 166 41
and Jane; and she thought he looked a little confused as PP II 7 171 12
As she had heard no carriage, she thought it not unlikely PP II 9 177 1
thought it necessary to turn back and walk with her. PP II 10 182 1
"Is this," thought Elizabeth, "meant for me?" and she PP II 10 183 15
When she thought of her mother indeed, her confidence gave PP II 10 187 40
I thought too ill of him, to invite him to Pemberley, or PP II 12 201 5
way to every variety of thought; re-considering events, PP II 13 209 12
How grievous then was the thought that, of a situation so PP II 14 213 18
right way, that Maria thought herself obliged, on her PP II 14 213 20
I do not think it is very pretty; but I thought I might as PP II 16 219 3
"Yes," thought Elizabeth, "that would be a delightful PP II 16 220 7
You thought the waiter must not hear, as if he cared! PP II 16 220 10
I thought I should have died. PP II 16 221 17
I thought we never should have got into the coach. PP II 16 222 22
"I never thought Mr. Darcy so deficient in the appearance PP II 17 225 16
I thought I should have broke my heart." PP II 18 229 4
"But it is fortunate," thought she, "that I have something PP II 19 237 4
lakes; and still thought there might have been time enough. PP II 19 239 8
She blushed at the very idea; and thought it would be PP II 19 240 16
"And of this place," thought she, "I might have been PP III 1 246 6
"Except," thought Elizabeth, "when she goes to ramsgate." PP III 1 248 26
Elizabeth thought this was going pretty far; and she PP III 1 248 30
"Can this be Mr. Darcy!" thought she. PP III 1 249 34
"In what an amiable light does this place him!" thought PP III 1 249 39
eyes upon herself, she thought of his regard with a deeper PP III 1 251 48
mind; in what manner he thought of her, and whether, in PP III 1 253 55
could go no farther, and thought only of returning to the PP III 1 254 57
"What will be his surprise," thought she, "when he knows PP III 1 255 58
now walked on in silence; each of them deep in thought. PP III 1 256 65
"I really should not have thought that he could have PP III 1 258 74

Context	Work	Vol	Ch	Page	Line
and I believe you thought her rather pretty at one time."	PP	III	3	271	17
know what Mrs. Gardiner thought of him, and Mrs. Gardiner	PP	III	3	272	20
thought, could flatter herself with such an expectation.	PP	III	4	279	24
related the whole, nor I, thought it necessary to make our	PP	III	5	285	16
I always thought they were very unfit to have the charge	PP	III	5	287	35
It had come with a fare from London; and as he thought the	PP	III	5	293	69
thought her presence might be serviceable to her nieces.	PP	III	6	294	3
in town, as Mr. Bennet thought it possible they might have	PP	III	6	295	5
It would have spared her, she thought, one sleepless night	PP	III	6	299	17
with, as far as I thought myself privileged, for you.	PP	III	7	302	14
"Wickham is not so undeserving, then, as we have thought	PP	III	7	303	16
in thought, continued silent till they reached the house.	PP	III	7	304	33
What a triumph for him, as she often thought, could he	PP	III	8	311	14
on to think as they thought, and act as they wished.	PP	III	8	314	22
was wretched in the thought of what her sister must endure.	PP	III	9	315	1
though I thought it would be very good fun if I was."	PP	III	9	316	7
"Well, and so we breakfasted at ten as usual; I thought it	PP	III	9	319	25
that he had before thought it beneath him, to lay his	PP	III	10	322	2
Since such were her feelings, it only remained, he thought,	PP	III	10	323	2
I thought him very sly;--he hardly ever mentioned your	PP	III	10	325	2
I thought I understood from the Gardiners that you had."	PP	III	10	328	18
"I have heard from authority, which I thought as good,	PP	III	10	328	29
but she still thought him partial to Jane, and she wavered	PP	III	11	332	18
"Yet it is hard," she sometimes thought, "that this poor	PP	III	11	332	19
to her eyes, as she thought for that space of time, that	PP	III	11	334	37
He looked serious as usual; and she thought, more as he	PP	III	11	335	40
The gentlemen came; and she thought he looked as if he	PP	III	12	341	16
awkward enough; but her's she thought was still worse.	PP	III	13	346	22
I thought how likely it was that you should come together.	PP	III	13	348	40
to dinner, which he thought himself obliged to accept.	PP	III	13	349	43
through Meryton, thought she might as well call on you.	PP	III	14	359	76
natural to suppose the he thought much higher of her	PP	III	15	360	2
I thought it my duty to give the speediest intelligence of	PP	III	15	363	22
Much as I respect them, I believe, I thought only of you."	PP	III	16	366	6
There was too much to be thought, and felt, and said, for	PP	III	16	366	9
You thought me then devoid of every proper feeling, I am	PP	III	16	368	16
"I am almost afraid of asking what you thought of me; when	PP	III	16	369	29
Who would have thought it!	PP	III	17	378	43
marriage; but as she thought it advisable to retain the	PP	III	19	387	10
of their acquaintance as thought Miss Ward and Miss	MP	I	1	3	1
He thought of his own four children--of his two sons--of	MP	I	1	6	5
Poor woman! she probably thought change of air might agree	MP	I	1	11	19
"After all that I said to her as we came along, I thought	MP	I	2	13	5
Fanny thought it a bold measure, but offered no farther	MP	I	2	16	20
Thomas and Mrs. Norris thought with greater satisfaction	MP	I	2	18	23
been long familiar, they thought her prodigiously stupid,	MP	I	2	18	23
thought too lowly of her own claims to feel injured by it.	MP	I	2	20	32
I thought you had settled it with Sir Thomas?"	MP	I	3	28	41
I suppose he thought it best."	MP	I	3	29	43
"No, he only said he thought it very likely--and I thought	MP	I	3	29	45
"No, he only said he thought it very likely--and I thought	MP	I	3	29	45
We both thought it would be a comfort to you.	MP	I	3	29	45
Her store-room she thought might have been good enough for	MP	I	3	31	59
had danced with; but thought too lowly of her own	MP	I	4	35	6
and had Lady Bertram ever thought about her own objection	MP	I	4	37	9
married," she very often thought; always when they were in	MP	I	4	38	9
"And now," added Mrs. Grant, "I have thought of something	MP	I	4	42	19
for Miss Bertram is in general thought the handsomest."	MP	I	5	45	7
Tom Bertram must have been thought pleasant, indeed, at	MP	I	5	47	28
But Miss Bertram thought it most becoming to reply: "the	MP	I	6	55	17
					18
passing another, I thought it would be only ask and have,	MP	I	6	58	37
"You could not be expected to have thought on the subject	MP	I	6	58	38
"I thought you would be struck.	MP	I	7	63	5
of the park; but she thought it a very bad exchange, and	MP	I	7	65	14
She did not seem to have a thought of fear.	MP	I	7	69	22
But I thought it would rather do her good after being	MP	I	7	73	55
pompous woman, who thought nothing of consequence, but as	MP	I	8	75	2
I believe it would be generally thought the favourite seat.	MP	I	8	78	15
party; and Mrs. Norris thought it an excellent plan, and	MP	I	8	80	28
I thought that was always the lot of the youngest, where	MP	I	9	92	42
risked an original thought of his own beyond a wish that	MP	I	10	97	3
She could almost have thought, that Edmund and Miss	MP	I	10	100	23
I thought Maria and Mr. Crawford were with you."	MP	I	10	100	24
"Miss Bertram thought you would follow her."	MP	I	10	102	39
Fanny thought she discerned in his standing there, an	MP	I	10	102	47
much more gay, and she thought that he was taking	MP	I	10	104	51
and moving about, that I thought something would certainly	MP	I	12	115	5
first ball, being the thought only of the afternoon, built	MP	I	12	117	11
dancing with Edmund herself, and had not thought about her.	MP	I	12	117	15
honour to be asked by him, she thought it must happen.	MP	I	12	118	22
If I had not luckily thought of standing up with you, I	MP	I	12	120	26
would probably have thought his introduction at Mansfield	MP	I	13	121	1
Sir Henry thought the duke not equal to Frederick, but	MP	I	13	122	2
Our Agatha was inimitable, and the duke was thought very	MP	I	13	122	2
This, though the thought of the moment, did not end with	MP	I	13	123	6
The thought returned again and again.	MP	I	13	123	6
If I must give my opinion, I have always thought it the	MP	I	14	131	3
How came it never to be thought of before?	MP	I	14	132	7
Mr. Crawford desired that might not be thought of; he was	MP	I	14	133	10
play in London, and had thought Anhalt a very stupid	MP	I	15	138	1
The wonder is that it should not have been thought of	MP	I	15	139	6
"I should not have thought it the sort of play to be so	MP	I	15	139	9
Maria, wanting Henry Crawford's animating support, thought	MP	I	15	142	24
Mr. Rushworth; "but I thought I should like the count best-	MP	I	15	143	29
After a moment's thought, Miss Crawford calmly replied, "	MP	I	15	148	59
pursuit, or some train of thought at hand.-- her plants,	MP	I	16	151	2
of family profiles thought unworthy of being anywhere else,	MP	I	16	152	2
I thought you would have entered more into Miss Crawford's	MP	I	16	155	22
to the quarrel, or rather thought it a lucky occurrence,	MP	I	17	160	9
had ever had a serious thought of each other, she could	MP	I	17	161	9
She knew that Mr. Yates was in general thought to rant	MP	I	18	164	2
Maria she also thought acted well--too well;--and after	MP	I	18	165	3
and that Mrs. Norris thought her quite as well off as the	MP	I	18	166	6
Fanny did not share her aunt's composure; she thought of	MP	I	18	167	12
I thought he began to look a little queer, so I turned it	MP	I	18	169	21
But Mr. Yates, having never been with those who thought	MP	II	1	177	5
of our acting," said Tom after a moment's thought.	MP	II	1	184	26
I thought we should never have got through them, though we	MP	II	2	189	5
that you had not been thought very pretty before; but the	MP	II	3	197	8
I did not like--I thought it would appear as if I wanted	MP	II	3	198	12
about the house, and thought of them, and felt for them,	MP	II	3	204	33
be more looked at, more thought of and attended to, than	MP	II	4	205	1
side of the field, never thought of as any thing, or	MP	II	4	208	12
And following the latter train of thought, she soon	MP	II	4	208	12
back her own mind to what she thought must interest.	MP	II	4	209	13
"I should have thought so theoretically myself, but"--and	MP	II	4	210	19
down for a few minutes can be hardly thought imprudent.	MP	II	4	212	29
But I have long thought Mr. Bertram one of the worst	MP	II	4	212	30
should be miserable if I thought myself without any chance-	MP	II	4	214	45
"That's well thought of.	MP	II	5	217	8
for Lady Bertram never thought of being useful to any body,	MP	II	5	219	27
Her niece thought it perfectly reasonable.	MP	II	5	221	35
I hope it is not too fine; but I thought I ought to wear	MP	II	5	222	43
"Will he not feel this?" thought Fanny.	MP	II	5	227	67
She had thought her influence more.	MP	II	5	227	69
I have always thought her pretty--not strikingly pretty--	MP	II	6	230	6
She had by no means forgotten the past, and she thought as	MP	II	6	232	11
respecting that long thought of, dearly earned, and justly	MP	II	6	234	18
in the same trim, I thought they were mad; but Fanny can	MP	II	6	235	19
of the old intimacy had thought ever likely to be again.	MP	II	7	238	1
thought that Mr. Crawford was the admirer of Fanny Price.	MP	II	7	238	2
Sir Thomas, after a moment's thought, recommended	MP	II	7	239	6
It is perfectly natural that you should not have thought	MP	II	7	247	42
had then given, was not given to be thought of no more.	MP	II	8	252	1
in general; and having thought the matter over and taken	MP	II	8	252	1
thought and exertion, and it would all fall upon her.	MP	II	8	253	4
his hopes, and when he thought of her acknowledged	MP	II	8	255	10
and after a moment's thought, urged Fanny's returning with	MP	II	8	257	15
Miss Crawford thought she had never seen a prettier	MP	II	8	259	20
the deepest blushes Fanny protested against such a thought.	MP	II	8	259	21
Fanny, "I should not have thought of returning it; but	MP	II	9	263	13
As she walked slowly up stairs she thought of yesterday;	MP	II	9	267	23
been Miss Crawford's, "you are all considerate thought!--	MP	II	9	269	38
a smile--she thought there was a smile--which made her	MP	II	10	274	8
No other man would have thought of it.	MP	II	10	274	9
Whenever she had thought on the minutiae of the evening,	MP	II	10	275	11
Fanny's blushes, still thought she must be doing so--when	MP	II	10	277	17
she did not smile, and thought her over-anxious, or	MP	II	10	277	20
her over-anxious, or thought her odd, or thought her any	MP	II	10	277	20
or thought her odd, or thought her any thing rather than	MP	II	10	277	20
having done and said and thought every thing by William,	MP	II	11	282	3
Fanny thought and thought again of the difference which	MP	II	11	283	6
Maria; and as Sir Thomas thought it best for each daughter	MP	II	11	284	10
But I thought it might have been to Lady Bertram or you.	MP	II	11	288	24
she thought must know; and her spirits were clouded again.	MP	II	11	289	33
The Admiral hated marriage, and thought it never	MP	II	12	292	9
principles in a wife, thought he was too little accustomed	MP	II	12	294	16
clever thought indeed. you will both find your good in it."	MP	II	12	295	19
She thought Lady Bertram sat longer than ever, and began	MP	II	13	304	18
taken to please him--who thought so slightly, so	MP	II	13	305	26
She thought he was wishing to speak to her unheard by the	MP	II	13	306	27
to Fanny's nervousness, thought not remarkably late,--he	MP	II	13	306	28
Fanny thought she had never known a day of greater	MP	II	13	308	36
I thought it might all pass for nothing with him."	MP	III	1	315	19
He was deep in thought.	MP	III	1	316	33
His niece was deep in thought likewise, trying to harden	MP	III	1	316	33
can judge, matrimony makes no part of his plans or thought.	MP	III	1	317	34
He, indeed, I have lately thought has seen the woman he	MP	III	1	317	34
I had thought you peculiarly free from wilfulness of	MP	III	1	318	39
I should have thought it a gross violation of duty and	MP	III	1	319	39
He thought her all this.	MP	III	1	319	40
exceedingly nervous; and thought it not improbable that	MP	III	1	320	44
had brought her into, he thought there might be as much	MP	III	1	320	45
As a general reflection on Fanny, Sir Thomas thought	MP	III	1	323	57
time, to what degree he thought well of his niece, or how	MP	III	1	323	57
to strike her, and she thought nothing of it till the	MP	III	1	324	60
He considered her rather as one who had never thought on	MP	III	2	326	3
So thought Fanny in good truth and sober sadness, as she	MP	III	2	329	10
better things; he had thought that an hour's intreaty from	MP	III	2	329	11
and at that moment she thought that, but for the	MP	III	3	335	5
few circumstances occurred which he thought more promising.	MP	III	3	336	8
of a hint, he thought, was rather favourable than not.	MP	III	3	339	21
thought reading was reading, and preaching was preaching.	MP	III	3	339	23
a subject on which he had thought before, and thought with	MP	III	3	340	24
had thought before, and thought with judgment, Edmund was	MP	III	3	340	24
sir, I thought it was a pity you did not always know	MP	III	3	343	39
departure; and Sir Thomas thought it might be as well to	MP	III	4	345	2
be of service to her, he thought he must be of service to	MP	III	4	345	4
I had thought it might be a relief."	MP	III	4	346	10
But I thought you blamed me.	MP	III	4	346	13
I thought you were against me.	MP	III	4	346	13
"My uncle thought me wrong, and I knew he had been talking	MP	III	4	347	15
I have not thought well of him from the time of the play.	MP	III	4	349	25
"Say rather, that he has not thought at all upon serious	MP	III	4	350	32
"I should have thought," said Fanny, after a pause of	MP	III	4	353	45
must have thought it so, supposing he had meant nothing.	MP	III	4	353	45
the more improper for me ever to have thought of him.	MP	III	4	353	45
I thought I could understand you.	MP	III	4	353	46
in her before, and now thought only too becoming, she	MP	III	5	358	9
understand how your power over Henry is thought of there!	MP	III	5	360	16
of it! it was his own doing entirely, his own thought.	MP	III	5	362	20
she thought she could resign herself to almost every thing.	MP	III	5	365	34
Edmund did not discern any symptoms of regret, and thought	MP	III	6	366	2
thought Fanny ought to go, and therefore that she must.	MP	III	6	370	14
days before we had any thought of it; and I do not know	MP	III	7	378	10
I thought to have had such a comfortable evening with you,	MP	III	7	378	10
But old Scholey was saying just now, that he thought you	MP	III	7	380	20
Yet she thought it would not have been so at Mansfield.	MP	III	7	382	29
dread of being thought to demean herself by such an office.	MP	III	7	383	32
Poor Mary little thought it would be such a bone of	MP	III	7	386	44
of a week, he would have thought Mr. Crawford sure of her,	MP	III	8	388	1
His last thought on leaving home was for her.	MP	III	8	388	2
time for writing; that he thought himself lucky in seeing	MP	III	10	400	8
he had not said, she thought him altogether improved since	MP	III	10	406	21
he known all, might have thought his niece in the most	MP	III	11	413	30
conjecture, and to be thought of on that day and many days	MP	III	12	417	4
A house in town!--that she thought must be impossible.	MP	III	12	417	4
considered, she thought he would go without delay.	MP	III	12	418	4
to her cousin, she thought it very likely, most likely,	MP	III	12	418	5
She thought he was really good-tempered, and could fancy	MP	III	12	419	9
I have sometimes thought of going to London again after	MP	III	13	422	2
it was not long before he thought so ill of himself, as to	MP	III	13	426	10
and family which had been thought of in uninterrupted	MP	III	13	427	13
Lady Bertram would have thought little about it; or	MP	III	13	428	15
cousin--except when she thought of Miss Crawford--but Miss	MP	III	14	430	3
I thought little of his illness at first.	MP	III	14	433	13
She had thought better of him.	MP	III	14	436	15
weeks without her being thought at all necessary, she must	MP	III	14	436	15
from it as impossible--when she thought it could not be.	MP	III	15	441	20
distress even of those whose distress she thought of most.	MP	III	15	443	24
guided by Sir Thomas, she thought justly on all important	MP	III	16	449	5
She thought he did, but she wanted to be assured of it.	MP	III	16	453	16
which, thinking as I now thought of her brother, should	MP	III	16	457	30
words, that for five minutes she thought they had done.	MP	III	16	459	31
himself this consoling thought, that considering the many	MP	III	16	459	31
Fanny thought exactly the same; and they were also quite	MP	III	16	460	31
or thought she felt, for the distress of those around her.	MP	III	17	461	2
that Emma first sat in mournful thought of any continuance.	E	I	1	6	5
she could speak every thought as it arose, and who had	E	I	1	6	6
What a pity it is that Mr. Weston ever thought of her!"	E	I	1	8	11
"No, papa, nobody thought of your walking.	E	I	1	8	16
Nobody thought of Hannah till you mentioned her--James is	E	I	1	9	18
as her not being thought perfect by every body.	E	I	1	11	33
I thought you cleverer--for depend upon it, a lucky guess	E	I	1	13	43
single any longer--and I thought when he was joining their	E	I	1	13	46
she might well be thought, where the only regret was for a	E	I	2	18	10
thought it no hardship for either James or the horses.	E	I	3	20	3
to every body's merits; thought herself a most fortunate	E	I	3	21	4
in her youth, and now thought herself entitled to the	E	I	3	22	5
knew Mr. Knightley thought highly of them--but they must	E	I	3	23	10
"Well done, Mrs. Martin!" thought Emma.	E	I	4	28	7
I thought him very plain at first, but I do not think him	E	I	4	29	13
with gentlemen, she thought he must lose all the ground he	E	I	4	31	27
He thought we walked towards Randalls most days.	E	I	4	32	29
for having ever thought him at all agreeable before.	E	I	4	32	32
which Emma thought might be safely left to itself.	E	I	4	34	41
and said she had always thought Mr. Elton very agreeable.	E	I	4	34	43
She thought it would be an excellent match; and only too	E	I	4	34	44
property; and she thought very highly of him as a good-	E	I	4	35	44
She had already satisfied herself that he thought Harriet	E	I	4	35	45
Weston, smiling, "that I thought so then;--but since we	E	I	5	37	8
I am sure you always thought me unfit for the office I	E	I	5	38	10
and was thought to have a tolerable eye in general.	E	I	6	43	13

Yes, good man!--thought Emma--but what has all that to do E I 6 43 15
regard it as a most happy thought, the placing of Miss E I 6 48 39
"He was too good!--she could not endure the thought!-- she E I 6 49 41
the directions; and Emma thought she could so pack it as E I 6 49 42
"This man is almost too gallant to be in love," thought E I 6 49 44
"Who could have thought it! E I 7 50 1
marriage; and a very good letter, at least she thought so. E I 7 50 1
I thought--but I beg your pardon, perhaps I have been E I 7 52 13
be too powerful, she thought it best to say, "I lay it E I 7 52 18
19
I thought it my duty as a friend, and older than yourself, E I 7 52 19
"No, to be sure you could not; but I never thought of that E I 7 54 26
making him unhappy, and thought so much of what his mother E I 7 55 35
He came to ask me whether I thought it would be imprudent E I 8 59 27
so early; whether I thought her too young: in short, E I 8 59 27
before, he would have thought highly of me then; and, I E I 8 59 27
Her friends evidently thought this good enough for her; E I 8 62 42
girl, and must be thought so by ninety-nine people out of E I 8 63 44
"I have always thought it a very foolish intimacy," said E I 8 64 47
She did not repent what she had done; she still thought E I 8 65 50
Mr. Knightley saw no such passion, and of course thought E I 8 67 57
much, something, he thought, might come from that quarter. E I 9 70 6
I thought it must be so. E I 9 73 20
I thought I could not be so deceived; but now, it is clear; E I 9 73 20
And how beautiful we thought he looked! E I 9 75 26
"I thought he meant to try his skill, by his manner of E I 9 76 29
Have you thought, my dear, where you shall put her--and E I 9 79 56
have him called Henry, which I thought very pretty of her. E I 9 80 72
Harriet; and if I thought I should ever be like Miss Bates! E I 10 84 16
such an errand as this," thought Emma; "to meet in a E I 10 87 32
"Cautious, very cautious," thought Emma; "he advances inch E I 10 90 40
He thought much of the evils of the journey for her, and E I 11 91 3
I should never have thought of Miss Taylor but as the most E I 11 95 19
I thought it very well done of him indeed. E I 11 96 22
Well, I could not have thought it--and he was but two E I 11 96 24
She thought it was time to make up. E I 12 98 2
Emma thought with pleasure of some change of subject. E I 13 114 28
She had frequently thought--especially since his father's E I 14 119 5
to: and though it is thought necessary to invite them once E I 14 120 11
it was such a look as she thought must restore him to his E I 15 125 6
Angry as she was, the thought of the moment made her E I 15 129 24
As she thought less of his inebriety, she thought more of E I 15 130 29
30
I never thought of Miss Smith in the whole course of my E I 15 130 31
I have thought only of you. E I 15 131 31
thought you judged ill in making your visits so frequent. E I 15 131 34
Smith?--that you have never thought seriously of her?" E I 15 131 34
He protested that he had never thought seriously of E I 16 134 3
Certainly she had often, especially of late, thought his E I 16 134 5
She thought nothing of his attachment, and was insulted by E I 16 135 7
She might never have thought of him but for me; and E I 16 137 11
never would have thought of him with hope, if I had not E I 16 137 11
thought, at first, could not escape her father's suspicion. E I 17 140 3
with fresh matter for thought and conversation during the E I 17 141 4
a friend as Miss Woodhouse would have thought it possible. E I 17 141 8
burst out again when she thought she had succeeded, and E II 1 155 1
The expense shall not be thought of; and though he is E II 1 162 31
I had no intention, I thought I had no power of staying E II 1 162 32
which she wanted to be thought herself; and though the E II 2 166 11
"He was generally thought so." E II 2 169 17
I had not thought of it before, but that was the best way. E II 3 172 19
"There is my news:--I thought it would interest you," said E II 3 173 26
every moment--but she thought she might get to Hartfield E II 3 177 52
up a gown for her, she thought she would just step in and E II 3 177 52
I thought I should have fainted. E II 3 178 52
sorry we never met now; which I thought almost too kind! E II 3 178 52
going to Hartfield, he thought I had much better go round E II 3 179 52
Oh! dear, I thought it would have been the death of me! E II 3 179 52
wonder that she had ever thought him pleasing at all; and E II 4 182 7
Of the lady, individually, Emma thought very little. E II 4 183 9
all of a sudden, that she thought Miss Smith was grown, E II 5 186 4
To know that she thought his coming certain was enough to E II 5 188 8
of half a moment's thought, she hoped Mr. Elton would now E II 5 188 8
When she looked at the hedges, she thought the elder at E II 5 189 16
He was very much pleased with Randalls, thought it a most E II 5 191 26
any danger of being thought extravagant in my terms." E II 5 192 32
Her own father's perfect exemption from any thought of the E II 5 193 35
Fairfax could be thought only ordinarily gifted with it. E II 5 194 43
one proof of her being thought to play well:--a man, a E II 6 201 28
That I thought, in a man of known musical talent, was some E II 6 201 28
were the persons; and I thought it a very strong proof." E II 6 202 30
His father only called him a coxcomb, and thought it a E II 7 205 1
admired her extremely--thought her very beautiful and very E II 7 206 3
be more thought of than any other person's in the room. E II 7 210 19
I had not thought of Mrs. Dixon. E II 8 217 29
and thought it the most natural thing in the world. E II 8 219 42
moments afterwards, heard what each thought of the other. E II 8 220 47
of Highbury altogether-- thought it so abundant in E II 8 220 48
for I thought it would be making her comfortable at once. E II 8 223 63
Mr. Knightley has any thought of marrying Jane Fairfax." E II 8 226 84
His admiration was certainly very warm; yet she thought, E II 8 228 88
if I thought I should go and stay there again next summer." E II 9 232 19
Emma thought it most prudent to go with her. E II 9 233 23
"I thought you meant to go with me. E II 9 234 29
great an attention! and I always thought you meant it." E II 9 234 34
At one time Patty came to say she thought the kitchen E II 9 236 46
But I thought he would have staid now, and it would have E II 10 245 52
It can be allowable only as the thought of the moment." E II 11 248 8
I bring a new proposal on the subject:--a thought of my E II 11 250 21
"No; he thought it very far from an improvement--a very E II 11 251 26
and the gentlemen perhaps thought each to himself, "women E II 11 253 43
enjoyed the thought of it to an extraordinary degree. E II 12 258 4
He thought principally of Mrs. Churchill's illness, and E II 12 259 11
He sat really lost in thought for the first few minutes; E II 12 259 12
13
"Yes--I have called there; passing the door, I thought it E II 12 260 27
At first, she thought it was a good deal; and afterwards, E II 13 264 1
Could he have thought himself encouraged, his looks and E II 13 265 4
Emma thought at least it would turn out so. E II 14 270 4
Miss Hawkins perhaps wanted a home, and thought this the E II 14 271 14
I had been used to, I really could not give it a thought. E II 14 277 36
Always the first person to be thought of! E II 14 279 52
little judgment that she thought herself coming with E II 15 281 1
There was no reason to suppose Mr. Elton thought at all E II 15 281 2
"Poor Jane Fairfax!"--thought Emma.-- E II 15 284 10
I never had a thought of her in that way, I assure you." E II 15 288 36
herself the inferior in thought, word, or deed; or in her E II 15 288 39
and pleasure always--but with no thought beyond." E II 15 289 40
The persons to be invited, required little thought. E II 16 291 5
She thought it in reality a sad exchange for herself, to E II 16 292 8
"I have often thought them the worst of the two," replied E II 16 293 21
She thought there was an air of greater happiness than E II 16 298 58
Mrs. Elton, who can have thought of it as I have done?" E II 17 299 7
her agitation, which she rather thought was considerable. E II 17 304 28
or he might not have thought either Mr. Woodhouse or Mr. E II 17 304 30
He is generally thought a fine young man, but do not E II 18 309 30
"We thought you were to bring them." E III 2 320 12
I was this moment telling Jane, I thought you would begin E III 2 324 23
She must not flatter herself that he thought of her E III 2 326 32
That Frank Churchill thought less of her than he had done, E III 2 326 32
There was one, however, which Emma thought something of.-- E III 2 326 33
It was his idea to bring her to Hartfield: he had thought E III 3 334 7
So Emma thought, at least. E III 3 335 9
I should not have thought it possible you could forget E III 4 338 12
when should I ever have thought of putting by in cotton a E III 4 339 15
"And when," thought Emma, "will there be a beginning of Mr. E III 4 340 27
you to do and so"--and thought no more of it, till after a E III 4 340 28
between them--he thought so at least--symptoms of E III 5 343 2
It was owing to her persuasion, as she thought his being E III 5 344 9
known to nobody else, and only thought of about three days. E III 5 345 16
spirits one morning because she thought she had prevailed. E III 5 346 16
From Frank Churchill's face, where he thought he saw E III 5 346 17
Emma was pleased with the thought; and producing the box, E III 5 347 20
away; and Mr. Knightley thought he saw another collection E III 5 349 25
So she thought at first;--but a little consideration E III 6 352 2
"But I thought you would. E III 6 353 4
He thought it very well done of Mr. Knightley to invite E III 6 357 30
and only strawberries, could now be thought or spoken of.-- E III 6 358 35
had quite given up every thought of coming, till very late; E III 6 363 53
for his attentions, and thought them all, whether in E III 7 368 3
I thought I had seen you first in February." E III 7 369 14
should not have thought myself privileged to inquire into. E III 7 370 20
Emma, I had not thought it possible." E III 7 374 55
perhaps, more in thought than fact; scornful, ungracious. E III 8 377 1
It was not unlikely, she thought, that she might see Mr. E III 8 377 2
the first; and though I thought he would come, because Mrs. E III 8 381 19
Time, however, she thought, would tell him that they ought E III 9 385 5
He would have judged better, she thought, if he had not E III 9 386 7
it happened, but she thought nothing became him more.-- E III 9 386 7
woman, who would have thought it!" and resolved, that his E III 9 388 13
He thought she had undertaken more than she was equal to, E III 9 389 16
so plainly, and she thought only of how she might best E III 9 390 18
Emma thought first of herself, and then of Harriet. E III 10 395 31
I thought I knew him." E III 10 395 35
"Ah!" thought Emma, "he would have done as much for E III 10 398 56
I thought you had lost half your property, at least. E III 10 400 68
"I should not have thought it possible," she began, "that E III 11 405 18
else, I should not have thought it possible that I could E III 11 405 18
way to--I should not have thought it possible--but if you, E III 11 406 18
have an idea of anybody else--and so I thought you knew. E III 11 406 20
Neither of them thought but of Mr. Knightley and E III 11 408 33
Is not it possible, that when enquiring, as you thought, E III 11 410 36
no disparity, affording nothing to be said or thought.-- E III 11 413 48
every thing, she thought such a visit could not be paid E III 12 417 5
Mr. Weston had thought differently; he was extremely E III 12 417 5
in every sensation; thought so much of Jane; so much of E III 12 418 5
She thought well of Frank in almost every respect; and, E III 12 420 14
sake; if he were to be thought of hereafter, as finding in E III 12 422 20
She thought he neither looked nor spoke cheerfully; and E III 13 424 1
She thought he was often looking at her, and trying for a E III 13 425 2
I thought them a habit, a trick, nothing that called for E III 13 427 19
silent; and, as far as she could judge, deep in thought. E III 13 427 20
the wonderful velocity of thought, had been able--and yet E III 13 430 38
and if he could have thought of Frank Churchill then, he E III 13 433 42
She even wept over the idea of it, as a sin of thought. E III 14 435 4
She was displeased; I thought unreasonably so: I thought E III 14 440 8
scrupulous and cautious: I thought her even cold. E III 14 440 8
She absolutely refused to allow me, which I then thought E III 14 441 8
suppose you would ever have thought well of me again. E III 14 441 8
She thought so well of the letter, that when Mr. Knightley E III 15 444 2
an hesitation which Emma thought infinitely more becoming E III 16 459 47
"Oh! as to all that, of course nothing can be thought of E III 16 460 53
Emma, smiling--"but, excuse me, it must be thought of." E III 16 460 54
Jane answered, "you are very right; it has been thought of. E III 16 460 55
56
I did it because I thought it would offend you; but, as E III 17 462 12
from her not being thought of; but Emma was rather E III 17 463 15
her first arrival she had thought her out of spirits, E III 17 463 16
in not having thought of it, and wished it long ago.-- E III 17 467 31
Sometimes, indeed, I have thought you were half suspecting E III 18 474 34
a sudden accession of gay thought, he cried, "Ah! by the E III 18 477 58
59
detailed by her husband, thought it all extremely shabby, E III 19 484 12
for, should have no thought of a second marriage, needs no P III 1 5 8
added the happy thought of their taking no present down to P III 1 9 19
she did, what nobody else thought of doing, she consulted P III 2 12 3
Sir Walter had at first thought more of London, but Mr. P III 2 14 10
that Lady Russell, who thought it a friendship quite out P III 2 15 15
He thought it a very degrading alliance; and Lady Russell, P III 4 26 2
at seven and twenty, thought very differently from what P III 4 29 8
back through the park, "I thought we should soon come to a P III 5 32 4
all; and Anne, glad to be thought of some use, glad to P III 5 33 9
thought, have reason to reproach her for giving no warning. P III 5 34 12
And as to my father, I really should not have thought that P III 5 35 14
Anne had always thought such a style of intercourse highly P III 5 40 44
for while Mary thought it a great shame that such a P III 6 43 5
performance was little thought of, only out of civility, P III 6 46 13
more agreeable they thought him than any individual among P III 7 54 4
recent alarm to bear the thought; and Anne, in the joy of P III 7 55 5
just now that I would come, and he thought me quite right. P III 7 55 8
"Dear me! that's a very good thought, very good indeed. P III 7 57 16
An excellent thought of yours, indeed, Anne! P III 7 57 16
Henrietta asked him what he thought of you, when they went P III 7 60 32
He had thought her wretchedly altered, and, in the first P III 7 61 36
a woman since whom he thought her equal; but, except from P III 7 61 37
for I have thought on the subject more than most men." P III 7 62 41
There must be the same immediate association of thought, P III 8 63 2
lost in only a sloop, nobody would have thought about me." P III 8 66 16
Henrietta fully thought so herself, before Captain P III 9 74 7
upon the Hayters, and thought it would be quite a P III 9 75 12
I am sure you would have thought as I did, unless you had P III 9 77 16
She had thought only of avoiding Captain Wentworth; but an P III 9 77 17
"Well, I am very glad indeed, but I always thought you P III 9 78 20
thought you would have it; I always thought you sure. P III 9 78 20
and could only say, "I thought the Miss Musgroves had been P III 9 78 22
He had, probably, never heard, and never thought of any P III 10 82 1
and that being the case, thought it best to accept the P III 10 83 4
"These would have been all my friends," was her thought; P III 11 98 16
Anne thought she left great happiness behind her when they P III 11 99 19
and to say, that she thought it was the misfortune of P III 11 100 23
if people thought there was any thing to complain of." P III 12 103 2
looks, that he thought hers very lovely, and by the P III 12 104 7
He advised her against it, thought the jar too great; but P III 12 109 32
strength and zeal, and thought, which instinct supplied, P III 12 111 44
away, till touched by the thought of her father and mother, P III 12 114 59
that it ever had been thought of, he burst forth, as if P III 12 116 70
71
She thought it could scarcely escape him to feel, that a P III 12 116 72
And so much was said in this way, that Anne thought she P IV 1 122 5
what she thought of the attachment between him and Louisa. P IV 1 124 12
No, except when she thought of her mother, and remembered P IV 1 126 18
and for my part, I thought it was all settled; when behold! P IV 2 130 5
my word I should have thought we were lively enough at the P IV 2 130 5
those sort of things, I thought that would be a good P IV 2 131 12
Sir Walter thought much of Mrs. Wallis; she was said to be P IV 3 141 13
"If I thought it would not tempt her to go out in sharp P IV 3 142 16
Mrs. Clay decidedly thought it Mr. Elliot's knock." P IV 3 142 17
continually; thought they must be a most delightful set of P IV 3 144 19
fine mind did not appear to excite a thought in her sister. P IV 4 145 2
on her improved looks; he thought her "less thin in her P IV 4 145 3
on a subject which she thought unworthy to excite them. P IV 4 148 10
neither Lady Russell nor Mr. Elliot thought unimportant. P IV 4 149 12
all this passed, now thought it advisable to leave the P IV 5 158 20
He thought her a most extraordinary young woman; in her P IV 5 159 21

"if you remember, I never thought him attached to "Louisa; P IV 6 165 8
He is thought to be gouty." P IV 6 165 11
when she thought of Captain Wentworth unshackled and free. P IV 6 167 21
Admiral, than the Admiral ever thought or talked about him. P IV 6 168 23
Well, this Miss Louisa, we all thought, you know, was to P IV 6 171 33
"I thought Captain Benwick a very pleasing young man," P IV 6 171 36
I thought them particularly pleasing, and I will answer P IV 6 172 38
he had ever thought of this Miss (what's her name?) for P IV 6 173 47
I should have thought your last impressions of Lyme must P IV 8 183 15
Anne saw nothing, thought nothing of the brilliancy of the P IV 8 185 21
She thought of her father--of Lady Russell. P IV 8 190 47
he has any thought of doing), I shall not accept him. P IV 9 196 33
trusted and loved him, and thought him as good as himself. P IV 9 199 55
He described one Miss Elliot, and I thought very P IV 9 201 59
I thought it coming on, before our acquaintance ceased, P IV 9 207 90
was odious; and when she thought of his cruel conduct P IV 10 214 11
You need not tell her so, but I thought her dress hideous P IV 10 215 15
she wanted to see; it was thought a good opportunity for P IV 10 217 19
She generally thought he would come, because she generally P IV 10 227 69
because she generally thought he ought; but it was a case P IV 10 227 69
near as bad; and so we thought they had better marry at P IV 11 230 6
I little thought then--but no matter. P IV 11 232 15
and Mrs. Musgrove, who thought only of one sort of illness, P IV 11 238 47
Captain Harville has no thought but of going." P IV 11 239 50
Presently, struck by a sudden thought, Charles said, P IV 11 240 55
56
I had not thought seriously on this subject before. P IV 11 242 65
"I should have thought," said Anne, "that my manner to P IV 11 245 75
admired than she thought about or cared for, she had P IV 11 245 78
& thought he would have vouchsafed me an answer.-- S 5 385 1
her so little that we thought it right to change our S 5 387 1
We came out with no other thought.-- S 6 391 1
praise that Charlotte thought she had never beheld a more S 6 391 1
may sometimes be thought the better half, of the pair)-- S 7 394 1
Sober-minded as she was, she thought him agreable, & did S 7 395 1
Poor dear Sir Harry (between ourselves) thought at first S 7 399 1
The very name of Sir Edward he thought, carried some S 8 405 2
I sounded Susan--the same thought had occurred to her.-- S 9 409 1
dinner, you wd have thought me a very poor creature.--" S 10 415 1
"I thought I should have been in time, said he, but cocoa S 10 416 1
Here perhaps they had thought themselves so perfectly S 12 427 1

THOUGHTFUL (20)

Thoughtful & pensive in general her countenance always LS 18 272 1
After her entrance, Colonel Brandon became more thoughtful SS II 4 163 20
for they are all very thoughtful and considerate; SS II 8 196 18
the whole evening more serious and thoughtful than usual. SS II 8 200 43
she grew silent and thoughtful, and turning away her face SS III 10 342 7
a little, Fitzwilliam asked her why she was so thoughtful. PP II 10 185 33
"This was so thoughtful and kind!"--and would he only have MP I 3 33 64
Each was thoughtful. MP I 9 94 57
left to sit down and stir the fire in thoughtful vexation. MP I 13 128 33
But then"--with a more thoughtful air and lowered voice--" MP II 4 210 19
subject, he grew thoughtful and indisposed for any other. MP II 4 216 50
minutes silent, each thoughtful; Fanny meditating on the MP III 5 360 13
Such a very kind attention--and so thoughtful an attention! E II 8 223 63
Very thoughtful of Col. Campbell, was not it?-- E II 10 242 21
He seemed hardly to hear her; he was thoughtful--and in a E II 15 287 33
34
Mr. Knightley was thoughtful again. E II 15 288 36
He was thoughtful. E III 2 324 20
They were both silent--Mrs. Smith very thoughtful. P IV 9 198 52
Captain Harville seemed thoughtful and not disposed to P IV 11 230 5
thoughtful expression which seemed its natural character. P IV 11 232 12

THOUGHTFULLY (4)

and Marianne remained thoughtfully silent, till a new SS I 18 98 10
Elinor was employed in walking thoughtfully from the fire SS II 7 190 55
56
Edmund was standing thoughtfully by the fire, while Lady MP I 13 125 14
confused, and stood thoughtfully by the fire; and though E I 7 53 22

THOUGHTFULNESS (9)

together in silent thoughtfulness, with downcast eyes and NA II 8 187 13
His gravity and thoughtfulness returned on him in their SS I 17 95 50
on her side, and thoughtfulness on his own,--"how you may SS III 8 319 29
A short pause of mutual thoughtfulness succeeded. SS III 8 327 56
the restless, unquiet thoughtfulness in which she had been SS III 11 349 3
together in a similarity of thoughtfulness and silence. SS III 11 355 46
that his gravity and thoughtfulness there, had arisen from PP III 16 370 33
relapsed into thoughtfulness, till suddenly looking up at MP II 4 210 22
know all this," said Anne, after a little thoughtfulness. P IV 9 208 93

THOUGHTLESS (12)

and perhaps sometimes a thoughtless young man; he has had NA II 4 152 26
They were all thoughtless or indolent. SS III 12 358 5
Thoughtless and indiscreet I can easily believe him, but PP III 4 273 3
"Oh! thoughtless, thoughtless Lydia!" cried Elizabeth when PP III 5 292 61
drawing her arm within his, "how thoughtless I have been! MP I 9 94 58
was tending; but, thoughtless and selfish from prosperity MP I 12 114 3
cold-hearted ambition--his thoughtless vanity. MP III 14 435 15
That young man (speaking lower) is very thoughtless. E II 11 249 11
"Ah! sir--but a thoughtless young person will sometimes E II 11 252 31
Not that Emma was gay and thoughtless from any real E III 7 368 3
to have you now, in thoughtless spirits, and the pride of E III 7 375 61
thoughtless, gay set, without any strict rules of conduct. P IV 9 201 64

THOUGHTLESSNESS (8)

did not make amends for this thoughtlessness in his sister. NA II 3 148 29
thoughtlessness which Catherine could not but resent. NA II 4 149 1
Thoughtlessness, want of attention to other people's PP II 1 136 17
Imprudence or thoughtlessness in money matters, would be PP III 13 348 39
Lydia's thoughtlessness first betrayed to me that you had PP III 16 366 5
the thoughtlessness and selfishness of his previous habits. MP III 17 462 4
inconsideration and thoughtlessness; and I am very much of E III 15 448 30
consequence of much thoughtlessness and much imprudence; P IV 1 126 21

THOUGHTS (157)

how much I miss him--how perpetually he is in my thoughts. LS 5 250 3
At present my thoughts are fluctuating between various LS 25 293 4
Frederica runs much in my thoughts, & when Reginald has LS 40 309 1
long uppermost in her thoughts; it was, "have you ever NA I 7 48 32
Oh! I am in such extasies at the thoughts of a little NA I 11 84 19
Dejected and humbled, she had even some thoughts of not NA I 12 92 4
heroes' mouths, their thoughts and designs--the chief of NA I 14 108 22
but so active were her thoughts, that when these inquiries NA II 2 141 13
of fixing mine, when my thoughts are an hundred miles off. NA II 3 143 4
what your thoughts and designs in time past may have been. NA II 3 146 18
and fixed all her thoughts on the welfare of her new straw NA II 5 161 25
in motionless wonder, while these thoughts crossed her:-- NA II 6 163 1
2
Her progress was not quick, for her thoughts and her eyes NA II 6 164 3
Such were her thoughts, but she kept them to herself, and NA II 7 177 18
Her thoughts being still chiefly fixed on what she had NA II 10 199 2
cried Catherine, whose second thoughts were clearer. NA II 10 205 23
of the General's conduct dwelt much on her thoughts. NA II 11 211 15
Eleanor made no answer; and Catherine's thoughts recurring NA II 13 224 17
here; and I have some thoughts of throwing the passage SS I 6 29 4
by carrying back her thoughts to Willoughby, whose manners SS I 16 87 23
Her mind was inevitably at liberty; her thoughts could not SS I 19 105 12
I cannot bear the thoughts of making him so miserable, as SS I 22 133 44
own music and her own thoughts, had by this time forgotten SS II 1 145 23
of January to turn her thoughts, and thither she one day SS II 3 153 1
out of spirits, and the thoughts of both engaged elsewhere. SS II 4 162 12
from seeing her sister's thoughts as clearly as she did, " SS II 5 167 4
Elinor's thoughts were full of what might be passing in SS II 5 169 16
lost in her own thoughts and insensible of her sister's SS II 6 175 1
the abstraction of her thoughts preserved her in ignorance SS II 8 193 6
well able to collect her thoughts within herself, and be SS II 11 221 4
visit at Gray's, his thoughts took a cheerfuller turn, and SS II 11 226 41
You know how I dreaded the thoughts of seeing her;--but SS II 13 239 4
enough to collect her thoughts, she was able to give such SS III 1 260 8
fix still more upon her thoughts, by the too warm, too SS III 2 270 1
orders, as he had some thoughts, he could get nothing but SS III 2 273 16
She began, however, seriously to turn her thoughts towards SS III 3 279 1
She had no such object for her lingering thoughts to fix SS III 6 302 5
her sister's bed, her thoughts wandering from one image of SS III 7 313 21
to her charge and her thoughts, and retired to her own SS III 7 316 27
The original was all her own--her own happy thoughts and SS III 8 328 63
Her thoughts were silently fixed on the irreparable injury SS III 8 331 70
was constantly in her thoughts; she would not but have SS III 9 334 6
to enjoy his own thoughts, & gape without restraint.-- W 332 11
It was an expectation to fill the thoughts of the sisters W 348 23
engrossed by his own thoughts to perceive that Sir William PP I 6 25 25
"I had once some thoughts of fixing in town myself--for I PP I 6 26 36
might turn her mother's thoughts, now asked her if PP I 9 43 26
what she said, for her thoughts had wandered far from the PP I 18 93 32
Her mother's thoughts she plainly saw were bent the same PP I 18 98 63
"My dear, do not give way to such gloomy thoughts. PP I 23 130 18
were no otherwise in her thoughts at the time, than as she PP II 2 142 17
Could he have Colonel Fitzwilliam in his thoughts? PP II 10 182 1
Elizabeth awoke the next morning to the same thoughts and PP II 12 195 1
In this perturbed state of mind, with thoughts that could PP II 13 205 3
From herself to Jane--from Jane to Bingley, her thoughts PP II 13 208 9
and to banish from her thoughts that continual breach of PP II 19 236 2
object of her happiest thoughts; it was her best PP II 19 237 3
a way, as plainly spoke the distraction of his thoughts. PP III 1 252 52
Her thoughts were all fixed on that one spot of Pemberley PP III 1 253 55
Her thoughts were instantly driven back to the time when PP III 1 256 62
In seeing Bingley, her thoughts naturally flew to her PP III 2 262 8
As for Elizabeth, her thoughts were at Pemberley this PP III 2 265 16
Her own thoughts were employing her. PP III 3 268 5
he was uppermost in her thoughts; and the various PP III 3 269 10
designed to turn his thoughts from Elizabeth, seemed to PP III 3 270 11
you may easily believe was far enough from my thoughts." PP III 5 285 16
From Elizabeth's thoughts it was never absent. PP III 5 285 19
But, on second thoughts, perhaps Lizzy could tell us, what PP III 6 295 6
by leading her thoughts to the obligations which Mr. PP III 7 306 45
accomplishment, and her thoughts and her words ran wholly PP III 8 310 7
one among them who ran more in her thoughts than the rest. MP I 2 15 12
some place in the thoughts and conversation of the ladies. MP I 3 32 61
to turn all his thoughts towards England, and the very MP I 4 38 9
Her own thoughts and reflections were habitually her best MP I 8 80 31
difficulty of fixing our thoughts as we could wish; but if MP I 9 87 16
Fanny's thoughts were now all engrossed by the two who had MP I 10 103 49
Every thing was a friend, or bore her thoughts to a friend; MP I 16 152 2
all these fearful thoughts, while the other three, no MP II 1 176 4
Tom understood his father's thoughts, and heartily wishing MP II 1 183 24
Maria, were much in her thoughts on seeing him; but no MP II 5 224 48
Having regulated her thoughts and comforted her feelings MP II 9 265 20
before her, and her thoughts were put into another channel MP II 10 274 8
And her thoughts flew to those absent cousins with most MP II 10 275 12
Miss Crawford saw much of Sir Thomas's thoughts as he MP II 10 276 14
had a moment's share in your thoughts on this occasion. MP III 1 318 39
And still pursuing the same cheerful thoughts, she soon MP III 2 333 28
His thoughts and beauties are so sread abroad that one MP III 3 338 13
be more attentive, and not allow my thoughts to wander. MP III 3 340 25
was the result of such thoughts as these; and upon Sir MP III 4 345 5
Full well could Fanny guess where his thoughts were now. MP III 4 349 24
After leaving him to his happier thoughts for some minutes, MP III 4 349 25
thoughts on the subject, some surmises as to what might be. MP III 5 362 18
as from wishing him to have any serious thoughts of me. MP III 5 362 21
She proclaimed her thoughts. MP III 6 372 21
With such thoughts as these among ten hundred others, MP III 7 376 5
her, she called back her thoughts, reproved herself, and MP III 7 377 10
The only interruption which thoughts like these received MP III 7 383 30
cousin Edmund to direct her thoughts or fix her principles. MP III 9 397 8
useful in diverting her thoughts from pursuing Edmund to MP III 9 398 10
comfort of anything within the current of her thoughts. MP III 11 413 32
You have my thoughts exactly as they arise, my dear Fanny; MP III 13 422 2
Fanny checked the tendency of these thoughts as well as MP III 13 424 4
It was impossible to banish the letter from her thoughts, MP III 15 438 7
was much more in her thoughts, and as for Susan, now MP III 15 444 26
impossible to direct her thoughts to other subjects, and MP III 16 449 6
to keep him from such thoughts; but when tea came, it was E I 1 8 10
11
But the Martins occupied her thoughts a good deal; she had E I 4 27 4
Part of her meaning was to conceal some favourite thoughts E I 5 41 31
a pen in hand, his thoughts naturally find proper words. E I 7 51 5
"though I have kept my thoughts to myself; but I now E I 8 64 47
The result of his thoughts appeared at last in these words. E I 8 66 50
a very sudden trial of our stability in good thoughts. E I 10 87 29
30
I have no thoughts of matrimony at present." E I 15 132 36
These were very cheering thoughts; and the sight of a E I 16 138 16
and conversation, to drive Mr. Elton from her thoughts. E I 17 142 10
coxcomb, he will not occupy much of my time or thoughts." E I 18 150 30
Mr. Woodhouse, whose thoughts were on the bates's, said---- E II 3 171 16
17
your thoughts on this subject are very much like mine." E II 8 216 26
It will be the object of all my thoughts and cares!-- and E II 12 259 15
He looked at her, as if wanting to read her thoughts. E II 12 260 30
A thousand vexatious thoughts would recur. E II 14 270 3
All this ran so glibly through her thoughts, that by the E II 14 279 53
Little Henry was in her thoughts, and a mixture of alarm E II 15 287 24
that your raising your thoughts to him, is a mark of good E III 4 342 39
that Highbury is in your thoughts when you are absent. E III 5 345 14
He remained at Hartfield after all the rest, his thoughts E III 5 349 26
Harriet,) whose thoughts I might not be afraid of knowing." E III 7 370 19
He might even have Harriet in his thoughts at the moment; E III 7 373 51
scheme to box hill was in Emma's thoughts all the evening. E III 8 377 1
So then, I try to put it out of her thoughts, and say, E III 8 382 27
In the hope of diverting her father's thoughts from the E III 9 386 9
How it would affect Frank was among the earliest thoughts E III 9 388 13
the following night, were hardly enough for her thoughts.-- E III 11 411 43
the presumption to raise her thoughts to Mr. Knightley!-- E III 11 414 50
soon it appeared when her thoughts were in one course. E III 12 416 2
arrived to tear Emma's thoughts a little from the one E III 12 417 3
But she probably had something of that in her thoughts. E III 12 419 12
There, with spirits freshened, and thoughts a little E III 13 424 1
wanted only to have her thoughts to herself--and as for E III 14 436 6
to Donwell, Emma had already had her own passing thoughts. E III 15 449 32
Larkins the whole morning, to have his thoughts to himself. E III 15 449 32
penetrate Mrs. Elton's thoughts, and understand why she E III 16 453 12
only means so far as your having some thoughts of marrying. E III 17 465 26
Knightley came in, and distressing thoughts were put by. E III 18 470 1
hints of Mr. Shepherd, his agent, from his thoughts. P III 1 9 19
was not out of his thoughts, when he more seriously P III 7 62 40
Musgrove at all near his thoughts, looked rather in P III 8 67 25
thinking only of his thoughts, began with, "if you had P III 8 68 31
32
These were some of the thoughts which occupied Anne, while P III 8 72 58
in diverting his thoughts from those who are beneath him." P IV 4 151 21
These were thoughts, with their attendant visions, which P IV 8 186 22
But alas! there were very different thoughts to succeed. P IV 8 191 51
immediately into her thoughts all those parts of his P IV 10 214 12
They are never out of my thoughts when I walk here.-- S 7 396 1
"Happy, happy wind, to engage Miss Heywood's thoughts!--" S 7 398 1
same way, allowed her thoughts to form themselves into S 7 402 1
"Upon second thoughts Mary, said her husband, I will not S 12 425 1

THOUSAND (142)
A thousand alarming presentiments of evil to her beloved NA I 2 18 2
are eulogized by a thousand pens,--there seems almost a NA I 5 37 4
into, and now it is ten thousand to one, but they break NA I 9 61 1
I have a thousand things to say to you; but make haste and NA I 9 62 7
be bound to go two miles in it for fifty thousand pounds." NA I 9 65 28
thousand pounds, and five hundred to buy wedding-clothes. NA I 9 68 46
some few of the many thousand things which had been NA I 10 70 1
I had rather, ten thousand times rather get out now, and NA I 11 87 53
But I had ten thousand times rather have been with you; NA I 12 93 5
a thousand apologies to make for not answering them sooner. NA II 12 216 1
2
and the thousand good wishes of a most affectionate heart. NA II 14 236 14
and the ten or fifteen thousand pounds which her father NA II 15 245 12
poor, and that Catherine would have three thousand pounds. NA II 16 251 6
their father only seven thousand pounds in his own SS I 1 4 2
the three girls, he left them a thousand pounds a-piece. SS I 1 4 3
He survived his uncle no longer; and ten thousand pounds, SS I 1 4 4
of his sisters by the present of a thousand pounds a-piece. SS I 1 5 8
The prospect of four thousand a-year, in addition to his SS I 1 5 8
"Yes, he would give them three thousand pounds: it would SS I 1 5 8
Three thousand pounds! he could spare so considerable a SS I 1 5 8
To take three thousand pounds from the fortune of their SS I 2 8 3
but that something need not be three thousand pounds. SS I 2 9 7
each have above three thousand pounds on their mother's SS I 2 10 14
They will have ten thousand pounds divided amongst them. SS I 2 10 15
together on the interest of ten thousand pounds." SS I 2 10 15
on the interest of seven thousand pounds, besides the SS I 2 12 24
pounds, besides the thousand pounds belonging to each of SS I 2 12 24
reckoned more than two thousand a year, and his brother SS I 14 70 2
"About eighteen hundred or two thousand a-year; not more SS I 17 91 12
"Two thousand a-year! SS I 17 91 13
"And yet two thousand a-year is a very moderate income," SS I 17 91 14
"He has only two thousand pounds of his own; it would be SS II 2 147 7
"Fifty thousand pounds, my dear. SS II 8 194 10
Fifty thousand pounds! and by all accounts it wo'nt come SS II 8 194 10
Two thousand a-year without debt or drawback--except the SS II 8 196 22
To my fancy, a thousand times prettier than Barton Park, SS II 8 197 22
likewise heard that Miss Grey has fifty thousand pounds? SS II 8 199 38
"I believe about two thousand a-year." SS II 11 223 21
"Two thousand a-year;" and then working himself up to a SS II 11 223 22
settle on him a thousand a-year, if the match takes place. SS II 11 224 28
of the late Lord Morton, with thirty thousand pounds. SS II 11 224 28
A thousand a-year is a great deal for a mother to give SS II 11 224 28
once been within some thousand pounds of being obliged to SS II 12 233 18
brings in a good thousand a-year; offered even, when SS III 1 266 38
His own two thousand pounds she protested should be his SS III 1 267 38
The interest of two thousand pounds--how can a man live on SS III 1 268 50
in the receipt of two thousand, five hundred a-year, (for SS III 1 268 50
Miss Morton has thirty thousand pounds,) I cannot picture SS III 1 268 50
Miss Morton, with thirty thousand pounds to her fortune, SS III 2 272 16
he had nothing but two thousand pounds, and no hope of any SS III 2 273 16
the interest of his two thousand pounds, and what little SS III 2 276 28
dear; because he has two thousand a-year himself, he SS III 4 292 57
A thousand inquiries sprung up from her heart, but she SS III 10 347 33
bribing one son with a thousand a-year, to do the very SS III 13 366 18
regard, and who had only two thousand pounds in the world. SS III 13 367 22
Edward had two thousand pounds, and Elinor one, which, SS III 13 369 32
a nobleman with thirty thousand pounds, while Miss SS III 14 373 3
endowed with a thousand pounds a-year, not the smallest SS III 14 374 4
the ten thousand pounds, which had been given with Fanny. SS III 14 374 4
as usual, a thousand disappointments and delays, from the SS III 14 374 6
an only child, & will have at least ten thousand pounds."-- W 321 2
as Robert, who has got a good wife & six thousand pounds?" W 321 2
It is a thousand pities that he should be so deprived of W 325 4
he had been clerk, with a fortune of six thousand pounds.-- W 348 23
for having had that six thousand pounds, & for being now W 349 23
that the aunt could never have had six thousand pounds.-- W 350 24
I beleive if Margt had had a thousand or fifteen hundred W 353 26
A single man of large fortune; four or five thousand a PP I 1 3 14
men of four thousand a year come into the neighbourhood." PP I 1 5 31
after his entrance, of his having ten thousand a year. PP I 3 10 5
had a fortune of twenty thousand pounds, were in the habit PP I 4 15 11
of nearly an hundred thousand pounds from his father, who PP I 4 15 11
in an estate of two thousand a year, which, unfortunately PP I 7 28 1
attorney in Meryton, and had left her four thousand pounds. PP I 7 28 1
with five or six thousand a year, should want one of my PP I 7 29 12
A clear ten thousand per annum. PP I 16 77 10
grieved to the soul by a thousand tender recollections. PP I 16 78 20
him, and asking me a thousand questions; and I find that PP I 18 94 45
with; and that one thousand pounds in the 4 per cents. PP I 19 106 10
A thousand things may arise in six months!" PP I 21 120 27
The sudden acquisition of ten thousand pounds was the most PP II 3 149 28
get a girl with only ten thousand pounds, you want to find PP II 4 153 9
I suppose you would not ask above fifty thousand pounds." PP II 10 184 15
There was also a legacy of one thousand pounds. PP II 12 200 5
that the interest of one thousand pounds would be a very PP II 12 200 5
receive it, and accepted in return three thousand pounds. PP II 12 201 5
fortune, which is thirty thousand pounds; but I cannot PP II 12 202 5
as three thousand pounds, again was she forced to hesitate. PP II 13 205 3
Colonel Forster believed that more than a thousand pounds PP III 6 298 12
equal share of the five thousand pounds, secured among PP III 7 302 14
he takes her with a farthing less than ten thousand pounds. PP III 7 304 31
"Ten thousand pounds! PP III 7 304 32
thousand pounds, or any thing like it, has been advanced. PP III 7 304 35
How could he spare half ten thousand pounds?" PP III 7 304 35
Five thousand pounds was settled by marriage articles on PP III 8 308 4
considerably more than a thousand pounds, another thousand PP III 10 324 2
thousand pounds, another thousand in addition to her own PP III 10 324 2
the appetite and pride of one who had ten thousand a-year. PP III 11 338 60
Why, he has four or five thousand a-year, and very likely PP III 13 348 40
Ten thousand a year! PP III 17 378 43
Ten thousand a year, and very likely more! PP III 17 378 45
with only seven thousand pounds, had the good luck to MP I 1 3 1
three thousand pounds short of any equitable claim to it. MP I 1 3 1
felicity with very little less than a thousand a year. MP I 1 3 1
Mrs. Grant had ever had more than five thousand pounds." MP I 3 31 59
twelve thousand a year, he would be a very stupid fellow." MP I 4 40 13
estate in Norfolk, the daughter twenty thousand pounds. MP I 4 40 15
for a girl of twenty thousand pounds, with all the MP I 4 42 17
"Four thousand a year." MP I 12 118 19
Four thousand a year is a pretty estate, and he seems a MP I 12 118 20
He is not a shining character, but he has a thousand good MP II 2 190 7
were now spending from two to three thousand a year in." MP II 7 243 27
Fanny, overpowered by a thousand feelings of pain and MP II 9 261 3
I would not have been out of the way for a thousand pounds. MP III 7 380 20
to him, though her twenty thousand pounds had been forty. MP III 16 453 15
intimate with, who have all twenty thousand pounds apiece." E I 8 66 53
the heiress of thirty thousand pounds, were not quite so E I 16 135 7
for the sake of the future twelve thousand pounds. E II 2 169 16
a thousand thanks, and says you really quite oppress her." E II 3 173 29
or working, forming a thousand amusing schemes for the E II 13 264 1
A thousand vexatious thoughts would recur. E II 14 270 3
was returned, with a thousand thanks from Miss Bates, but " E III 9 391 20
of his brother, the thousand inconveniences to himself.-- E III 11 413 48
had exposed her to a thousand inquietudes, and made her E III 12 419 12
Fairfax's peace in a thousand instances; and on box hill, E III 12 421 17
without delay; I am impatient for a thousand particulars. E III 14 439 8
so: I thought her, on a thousand occasions, unnecessarily E III 14 440 8
A thousand and a thousand thanks for all the kindness you E III 14 443 8
ever shown me, and ten thousand for the attentions your E III 14 443 8
though very eccentric, he had a thousand good qualities.-- E III 17 469 36
to receive him; while a thousand feelings rushed on Anne, P III 7 59 25
had not made less than twenty thousand pounds by the war. P III 9 75 10
herself some few of the thousand poetical descriptions P III 10 84 7
hardly one woman in a thousand could stand the test of. P IV 3 142 13
One of the five thousand Mr. Smiths whose names are to be P IV 5 157 15
year eight, with a few thousand pounds, and was posted P IV 11 247 82
Captain Wentworth, with five-and-twenty thousand pounds, P IV 12 248 1
share of ten thousand pounds which must be hers hereafter. P IV 12 248 1
for her original thirty thousand pounds among them, the S 3 376 1
me, I have had a thousand fears for her--but she had kept S 9 407 1
She desired her best love, with a thousand regrets at S 9 407 1
walking & talking down a thousand difficulties at last S 10 414 1

THOUSANDS (14)
"Oh! Lord, it would be the saving of thousands. NA I 9 64 22
and, though she had such thousands of things to say to her, NA I 9 67 33
been made and used some thousands of times before, under NA I 10 72 8
She has only to fix on her number of thousands a year, and MP II 4 213 39
fortune, of so many thousands as would always be called E II 4 181 4
So seldom that a letter, among the thousands that are E II 16 296 42
He is a very liberal thanker, with his thousands and tens E III 15 447 28
thanker, with his thousands and tens of thousands.-- E III 15 447 28
The fate of thousands. E III 17 461 5
and were now, like thousands of other young ladies, living P III 5 40 45
for; and among the thousands that may just as well go to P III 8 65 11
infinitely superior to thousands of those who having only P IV 5 155 9
invalid--the very spot which thousands seemed in need of.-- S 1 369 1
she had many thousands a year to bequeath, & three S 3 376 1

THREAD (2)
her needle or broke her thread, if she heard a carriage in NA I 9 60 1
of two needlefulls of thread or a second hand shirt button MP II 6 236 21

THREAD-BARE (2)
some new observations of thread-bare morality to listen to. PP I 12 60 7
limited, and long worn thread-bare in all common hands; MP III 3 341 28

THREAD-CASES (1)
of making these little thread-cases, pin-cushions and card- P IV 5 155 9

THREADBARE (3)
new novel to talk in threadbare strains of the trash with NA I 5 37 4
dullest, most threadbare topic might be rendered PP I 16 76 4
became common-place, threadbare, stale in the comparison, E III 11 413 48

THREADING (1)
through the crowds, and threading the gutters of that NA I 7 44 1

THREAT (2)
threat to Fanny, and she lived in continual terror of it. MP III 5 356 4
This threat was so palpably disregarded, that though MP III 7 383 31

THREATEN (4)
to threaten her reason--how is she to be consoled? LS 36 306 1
and threaten her with all its possible ill consequences. MP I 1 4 1
For the world would not she have seemed to threaten me.-- E III 14 442 8
often of a nature, to threaten existence immediately--& as S 9 410 1

THREATENED (11)
attacked, the tower threatened, the streets of London NA I 14 113 39
Brandon: he has threatened me with rain when I wanted it SS I 10 52 28
from the frightful solitude which had threatened her. SS II 1 143 10
again and again; coaxed and threatened her by turns. PP I 20 112 23
horses out to take her home, with which she was threatened. MP II 4 206 4
When the meeting with which she was threatened for the MP III 1 324 59
The maid-servant of Mrs. Rushworth, senior, threatened MP III 16 450 9
which threatened alloy to her many enjoyments. E I 1 5 4
for a few minutes had threatened to ruin the rest of her E III 3 332 1
early, as the weather threatened rain; Mr. and Mrs. Weston E III 5 344 3
Till now that she was threatened with its loss, Emma had E III 12 415 1

THREATENING (6)
minutes to the clock, threatening on each return that, if NA I 11 83 14
fair, and that every threatening cloud would be drawn off SS I 9 41 3
and you must not set forward while it is so threatening. MP II 4 207 9
for I never saw it more threatening for a wet evening in MP II 5 221 34
self, such a burst of threatening evil, such a confusion E III 11 409 34
The prospect before her now, was threatening to a degree E III 12 422 19

THREATS (3)
his mother's threats, for a woman who could not reward him. SS III 1 268 46
Kitty, who took all these threats in a serious light, PP III 6 300 31
scolded away by Mrs. Norris's threats of catching cold. MP I 11 113 43

THREE (415)
for I have seldom spent three months more agreably than LS 2 244 1
& if she had not staid three months there before she LS 6 252 2
that he is in no danger of doing so three months hence. LS 15 266 1
We all three went down altogether, & I saw my brother LS 20 275 2
again, & told Lady Susan three times that he had seen Mrs LS 20 276 3
Hamiltons to the lakes; & three years ago when I had a LS 28 298 1
with her uncle & aunt, & three weeks afterwards Lady Susan LS 42 312 6
Three months might have done it in general, but Reginald's LS 42 313 8
She had three sons before Catherine was born; and instead NA I 1 13 1
Her mother was three months in teaching her only to repeat NA I 1 14 1
not take place till after three or four days had been NA I 2 20 8
the company only seen her three years before, they would NA I 2 24 27
among women is faultless, except in three particulars." NA I 3 27 30
stations than any other three beings ever were, Mrs. Allen NA I 4 32 2
Mrs. Thorpe, pointing at three smart looking females, who, NA I 4 32 3
was repeated by them all, two or three times over. NA I 4 32 5
be expected to occupy the three or four following chapters; NA I 4 34 9
This evil had been felt and lamented, at least three times NA I 7 44 1
"Three-and-twenty!" cried Thorpe; "five and twenty if it NA I 7 45 7
Three hours and a half indeed coming only three-and-twenty NA I 7 46 9
notice, that she looked back at them only three times. NA I 7 47 18
continued as they were for three minutes longer, when NA I 8 52 2
but Mr. Tilney, within three yards of the place where they NA I 8 53 3
"Yes, sir--and Dr. Skinner and his family were here three NA I 8 54 9
"you have been at least three hours getting ready. NA I 9 62 7
into the house:--"past three o'clock!" it was NA I 9 67 33
delay them, and they all three set off in good time for NA I 10 71 8
I have three now, the best that ever were back'd. NA I 10 76 28
but there are hardly three young men in the room besides NA I 10 78 38
containing the same three people that had surprized her so NA I 11 84 17
good night's rest in the course of the next three months. NA I 11 90 65
The three others still continued together, walking in a NA I 13 99 9
of the other; and remonstrances poured in from all three. NA I 13 100 19
to be tormented for two or three years of one's life, for NA I 14 110 27
is shortly to come out, in three duodecimo volumes, two NA I 14 113 39
to herself a mob of three hundred men assembling in St. NA I 14 113 39
three lines, and in one moment all was joyful security. NA I 15 121 26
He cannot be the instigator of the three villains in NA II 1 131 15
of waiting between two and three years before they could NA II 1 135 43
now comprised in another three weeks, and her happiness NA II 2 138 1
hardly aware that two or three days had passed away, NA II 3 143 1
out, though there were three people to go in it, and his NA II 5 155 4
At last, however, the door was closed upon the three NA II 5 155 4
Catherine had heard three proclaimed by all the clocks in NA II 6 171 12
business required and would keep him two or three days. NA II 7 175 13
poured forth;--the first three received a ready NA II 7 180 37
had now seen surrounded three sides of the court, she NA II 8 183 2
She was here shewn successively into three large bed- NA II 8 185 5
when I went away; but three hours ago I had the pleasure NA II 9 195 12
Catherine had not read three lines before her sudden NA II 10 202 8
canvassed by the three young people; and Catherine found, NA II 11 208 1
and shall probably be obliged to stay two or three days." NA II 11 209 5
Two hours and three quarters will carry us to Woodston, I NA II 11 210 6
three terriers, was ready to receive and make much of them. NA II 11 212 17
o'clock, when Catherine scarcely thought it could be three. NA II 11 214 26
several phaetons, and three waiting-maids in a travelling NA II 14 232 7
It was not three months ago since, wild with joyful NA II 14 237 20
Three months ago had seen her all this; and now, how NA II 14 237 20
transactions of the two or three last weeks proved him to NA II 15 246 12

poor, and that Catherine would have three thousand pounds. NA II 16 251 6
Dashwood had one son: by his present lady, three daughters. SS I 1 3 2
in children of two or three years old; an imperfect SS I 1 4 3
the three girls, he left them a thousand pounds a-piece. SS I 1 4 3
"Yes, he would give them three thousand pounds: it would SS I 1 5 8
Three thousand pounds! he could spare so considerable a SS I 1 5 8
tender love for all her three children determined her SS I 1 6 10
To take three thousand pounds from the fortune of their SS I 2 8 3
but that something need not be three thousand pounds. SS I 2 9 7
they will each have above three thousand pounds on their SS I 2 10 14
with the payment of three to old superannuated servants by SS I 2 10 20
of their servants to three; two maids and a man, with whom SS I 5 26 5
you can be artful. I have three unanswerable reasons for SS I 10 52 28
She had already repeated her own history to Elinor three SS I 11 54 6
come over from Newton, the three Miss Dashwoods walked up SS I 13 65 32
Mrs. Jennings for two or three days; she was a great SS I 14 70 1
His spirits, during the last two or three days, though SS I 19 101 1
every body agreed, two or three times over, that it had SS I 19 107 28
was not more than two or three and twenty, they SS I 21 120 6
caressing a little girl of three years old, who had not SS I 21 121 9
I have had it above these three years." SS I 22 131 35
We three shall be able to go very well in my chaise; and SS II 3 153 2
was the only one of the three, who seemed to consider the SS II 3 158 21
They were three days on their journey, and Marianne's SS II 4 160 2
They reached town by three o'clock the third day, glad to SS II 4 160 2
Nothing occurred during the next three or four days, to SS II 6 175 1
letter in her hand, and two or three others lying by her. SS II 7 182 12
forgot that she had three letters on her lap yet unread, SS II 7 184 16
Elinor said no more, and turning again to the three SS II 7 186 37
Beyond you three, is there a creature in the world whom I SS II 7 189 50
they are forced to send three miles for their meat, and SS II 8 197 22
"It was nearly three years after this unhappy period SS II 9 207 26
guilty connection, who was then about three years old. SS II 9 208 28
It is now three years ago, (she had just reached her SS II 9 208 28
than what was comprised in three or four very broad stares; SS II 11 220 3
where they had taken a very good house for three months. SS II 12 230 6
were not only all three together, but were together SS II 13 241 19
Miss Steele was the lest discomposed of the three, by SS II 14 247 4
and laid before me three different plans of Bonomi's. SS II 14 251 17
nothing, and was heard three times to say, "yes, ma'am."-- SS III 1 265 33
for his own folly, within three months have been in the SS III 1 268 50
he went away; leaving the three ladies unanimous in their SS III 1 269 57
did not come near us for three days, I could not tell what SS III 2 272 16
might now be at home in little more than three weeks' time. SS III 3 280 6
I have seen Mr. Ferrars two or three times in Harley- SS III 3 282 19
suppose two or three months will complete his ordination." SS III 4 291 50
"Two or three months!" cried Mrs. Jennings; "Lord! my dear, SS III 4 291 51
talk of it; and can the Colonel wait two or three months! SS III 4 291 51
it is not worth while to wait two or three months for him. SS III 4 291 51
He promised to call again in the course of three or four SS III 7 313 19
She had been for three months her companion, was still SS III 7 313 20
Those three or four weeks were worse than all. SS III 8 327 55
Her three notes--unluckily they were all in my pocket-book, SS III 8 329 63
Marianne had been two or three days at home, before the SS III 10 344 11
In the evening, when they were all three together, SS III 11 349 3
saw on the two or three following days, that Marianne did SS III 11 352 19
at four o'clock, about three hours after his arrival, he SS III 13 361 3
in love to think that three hundred and fifty pounds a- SS III 13 369 32
A three weeks' residence at Delaford, where, in his SS III 13 369 35
she thinks of staying three or four weeks with Mrs. SS III 13 370 37
After a visit on Colonel Brandon's side of only three or SS III 13 372 46
with no more than three; but when she found that, though SS III 14 373 3
For now we have a quiet little whist club that meets three W 325 4
formally seated, while three or four officers were W 327 8
before yesterday that I saw them all three in this town. W 334 13
at five minutes before three, was beginning to bustle into W 344 21
& a visit of two or three days from Mr & Mrs Robert Watson, W 348 23
for two or three nights, without making a peice of work. W 351 25
that the experience of three and twenty years had been PP I 1 5 34
of the lucases and two or three officers joined eagerly in PP I 6 25 24
usually tempted thither three or four times a week, to pay PP I 7 28 3
The distance is nothing, when one has a motive; only three PP I 7 32 37
Elizabeth accepted their company, and the three young PP I 7 32 39
That she should have walked three miles so early in the PP I 7 32 42
When the clock struck three, Elizabeth felt that she must PP I 7 33 45
The sisters, on hearing this, repeated three or four times PP I 8 35 1
"To walk three miles, or four miles, or five miles, or PP I 8 36 10
invitation, the mother and three daughters all attended PP I 9 41 2
The path just admitted three. PP I 10 53 62
monotonous solemnity, read three pages, she interrupted PP I 14 68 13
14

We have tried two or three subjects already without PP I 18 93 26
so rich, and living but three miles from them, were the PP I 18 99 63
at Netherfield, in the course of three or four months. PP I 18 103 77
might be concluded in three or four days, but as we are PP I 21 117 10
11

the loss of the three, of whom we shall deprive you." PP I 21 117 11
offers of marriage within three days, was nothing in PP I 22 125 18
At his own ball he offended two or three young ladies, by PP II 2 141 9
While they were dressing, he came two or three times to PP II 6 161 7
and could observe the three ladies before her composedly.-- PP II 6 162 11
"With three younger sisters grown up," replied Elizabeth PP II 6 166 37
of the three others, or relating some anecdote of herself. PP II 6 166 41
shortly afterwards the three gentlemen entered the room. PP II 7 170 9
"my eldest sister has been in town these three months. PP II 7 171 10
11

After walking two or three times along that part of the PP II 12 195 2
by herself, by your three younger sisters, and PP II 12 198 5
receive it, and accepted in return three thousand pounds. PP II 12 201 5
and dissipation. for about three years I heard little of PP II 12 201 5
as three thousand pounds, again was she forced to hesitate. PP II 13 205 3
It was the second week in may, in which the three young PP II 16 219 1
but there were two or three much much uglier in the shop; PP II 16 219 4
I will answer for it he never cared three straws about her. PP II 16 220 14
She is almost three and twenty! PP II 16 221 17
I should be of not being married before three and twenty! PP II 16 221 17
When Denny, and Wickham, and Pratt, and two or three more PP II 16 221 17
for we treated the other three with the nicest cold PP II 16 222 22
other, and out of their three months' acquaintance they PP II 18 230 11
having a couple of--or I may say, three very silly sisters. PP II 18 231 20
Darcy's having both spent three weeks at Rosings, and PP II 18 233 26
"Nearly three weeks." PP II 18 234 28
After the first fortnight or three weeks of her absence, PP II 19 238 6
occupy the chief of their three weeks; and to Mrs. PP II 19 239 7
The picture gallery, and two or three of the principal bed- PP III 1 250 46
On this point she was soon satisfied; and two or three PP III 2 262 8
Gardiner, who, with two or three other gentlemen from the PP III 3 268 8
of gratitude; and all three being actuated by one spirit, PP III 4 280 26
but three months before, had been almost an angel of light. PP III 6 294 4
"Only think of its being three months," she cried, "since PP III 9 316 7
But it was two or three days before he could get from her PP III 10 322 2
Not these two or three years perhaps." PP III 11 330 4
she has got three couple of ducks, just fit to be killed." PP III 11 331 15
The others have been gone on to Scarborough, these three PP III 12 342 24
and I suppose he has two or three French cooks at least. PP III 12 342 28
of the remaining three continued, though with little PP III 14 351 1
sister had been in town three months last winter, that I PP III 16 371 45
Three daughters married! PP III 17 378 43
But before she had been three minutes in her own room, her PP III 17 378 44
"I admire all my three sons-in-law highly," said he. PP III 17 379 48
three days of happiness, and immediately wrote as follows. PP III 18 382 20
Any place would do, of about three or four hundred a hear; PP III 19 386 7

three thousand pounds short of any equitable claim to it. MP I 1 3 1
Miss Lee, whether she has three girls to teach, or only MP I 1 9 12
to have my chief counsellor away for three days. MP I 1 9 12
and for the first two or three weeks were continually MP I 2 18 23
He had three horses of his own, but not one that would MP I 4 37 8
woman, Mary had not been three hours in the house before MP I 4 42 17
I have three very particular friends who have been all MP I 4 42 21
"But Miss Bertram does not care three straws for him; that MP I 5 45 14
There have been two or three fine old trees cut down that MP I 6 55 17
Three years ago, the Admiral, my honoured uncle, bought a MP I 6 57 31
to be improved; and for three months we were all dirt and MP I 6 57 31
age three months before Everingham was all that it is now. MP I 6 61 56
with two or three grooms, standing about and looking on. MP I 7 67 16
of what they found in the three ladies sitting there, for MP I 7 71 31
I sat three quarters of an hour in the flower garden, MP I 7 72 42
How often do I pace it three times a-day, early and late, MP I 7 73 53
"What!" cried Julia; "go box'd up three in a post-chaise MP I 8 77 10
form into parties, these three were found in busy MP I 9 90 36
The remaining three, Mrs. Rushworth, Mrs. Norris, and MP I 9 90 36
at least; the middle of November was three months off. MP I 11 107 3
Three months comprised thirteen weeks. MP I 11 107 3
have been suppressed for just the three days we wanted. MP I 13 122 4
It was but three days; and being only a grand-mother, and MP I 13 122 4
run up, doors in flat, and three or four scenes to be let MP I 13 123 8
as if we were going to act three times a week till my MP I 13 125 18
good management, of full three quarters of a yard), and MP I 14 130 1
was wanting; and as two or three days passed away in this MP I 14 130 1
but every character first-rate, and three principal women. MP I 14 130 3
Three of the characters were now cast, besides Mr. MP I 14 133 8
Mr. Rushworth followed him to say, "I come in three times, MP I 15 139 10
soon seated with the other three at the table, while his MP I 15 143 26
within the last three years, when she had quitted them.-- MP I 15 150 1
done for the drawing-room, three transparencies, made in a MP I 16 152 2
transparencies, for the three lower panes of one window, MP I 16 152 2
There are but three seams, you may do them in a trice.-- MP I 18 166 6
Bertram, "there will be three acts rehearsed to-morrow MP I 18 167 10
a great deal,--for if the three acts were rehearsed, MP I 18 167 12
appeared in each of the three on this unexpected meeting; MP I 18 169 23
The first regular rehearsal of the three first acts was MP I 18 171 25
then the stoutest of the three; for the very circumstance MP II 1 176 3
thoughts, while the other three, no longer under any MP II 1 176 4
Tolerable sport the first three days, but there has been MP II 1 181 16
of the arrangement, the three gentlemen returned to the MP II 1 183 24
We were going through the three first acts, and not MP II 1 185 28
daughter within the first three or four days after Henry MP II 3 201 24
but after another three or four days, when there was no MP II 3 201 24
Fanny went to her every two or three days; it seemed a MP II 4 208 11
Three years ago, this was nothing but a rough hedgerow MP II 4 208 12
and perhaps in another three years we may be forgetting-- MP II 4 208 12
Mansfield Park, striking three, made her feel that she had MP II 4 214 46
half a mile and only to three people, still it was dining MP II 5 219 27
and pleased looks of the three others standing round him, MP II 5 223 48
I am grown too old to go out more than three times a week; MP II 6 229 1
the rules of the game in three minutes, he had yet to MP II 7 240 8
I had two or three ideas." MP II 7 242 23
"And I have two or three ideas also," said Edmund, "and MP II 7 242 24
were now spending from two to three thousand a year in." MP II 7 243 27
day, for three or four hours, if that would content him. MP II 7 247 42
which his money purchased three years ago, before he knew MP II 8 259 20
necessary caution--"it is three o'clock, and your sister MP II 10 279 24
of doing, at the end of three or four days, she should now MP II 11 287 17
"Three grown up." MP II 11 288 25
young ladies--about any three sisters just grown up; for MP II 11 288 28
little variation of words three times over, his sister MP II 12 292 8
I could name three people now, who would give me my own MP II 12 295 20
but I have not cared much for her these three years." MP III 5 359 12
She took three days to consider of his proposals; and MP III 5 361 16
and during those three days asked the advice of every body MP III 5 361 16
time, perhaps two or three weeks; but then I considered it MP III 5 362 21
supposing the first three or four days could produce any. MP III 6 366 2
be allowed to make her absence three) must do her good. MP III 6 370 12
She had heard repeatedly from his sister within the three MP III 7 375 4
She is gone out of harbour already, three days before we MP III 7 378 10
minutes afterwards the three boys all burst into the room MP III 7 383 31
of them were gone--for the three boys, in spite of their MP III 7 384 36
found that the best of the three younger ones was gone in MP III 8 390 8
of love at the end, no three or four lines passionees from MP III 9 393 1
There were three different conclusions to be drawn from MP III 10 399 1
of this and the two or three other things which she wished MP III 10 406 21
He went to while away the next three hours as he could, MP III 11 412 29
I will say, then, that we have seen him two or three times, MP III 12 416 2
Mrs. Fraser (no bad judge), declares she knows but three MP III 12 416 2
appearing in the course of three or four days more, she MP III 12 418 5
I was three weeks in London, and saw her (for London) very MP III 13 420 2
Three or four prices might have been swept away, any or MP III 13 428 15
it would soon be almost three months instead of two that MP III 14 430 6
To be finding herself, perhaps, within three days, MP III 14 435 15
She felt that she had, indeed, been three months there; MP III 15 439 9
It was three months, full three months, since her quitting MP III 15 446 35
It had been a miserable party, each of the three believing MP III 16 448 1
from Wimpole Street two or three weeks before, on a visit MP III 16 450 8
on apoplexy and death, by three great institutionary MP III 17 469 24
This is three times as large.-- E I 1 8 13
which for the last two or three generations had been E I 2 15 1
when his wife died after a three years' marriage, he was E I 2 16 4
Bates and Mrs. Goddard, three ladies almost always at the E I 3 20 3
but the quiet prosings of three such women made her feel E I 3 22 6
"He had gone three miles round one day, in order to bring E I 4 28 6
Sunday, and asked all the three teachers, Miss Nash, and E I 4 28 8
You do not know it I dare say, but two or three years ago E I 6 43 13
Then, here come all my attempts at three of those four E I 6 45 21
is no making children of three or four years old stand E I 6 45 21
As the sun is out, I believe I had better take my three E I 8 57 3
beg your excuse and take my three turns--my winter walk." E I 8 57 5
had written out at least three hundred; and Harriet, who E I 9 69 4
They owed to him their two or three politest puzzles; and E I 9 70 7
and distinctly, and two or three times over, with E I 9 78 51
two or three days are not to be taken out for the Abbey. E I 9 79 63
invite them once in two or three years, they always are E I 14 120 11
and it was as much as his three companions could do, to E I 15 124 1
what had passed except the three principals, and E I 16 138 15
justify their all three being quite asunder at present. E I 16 138 16
fixed, in the same place, was bad for each, for all three. E I 17 143 14
that Frank's coming two or three months later would be a E I 18 144 2
A man at his age--what is he?--three or four-and-twenty-- E I 18 145 10
"It is not to be conceived that a man of three or four-and- E I 18 146 12
By only raising my voice, and saying anything two or three E II 1 158 14
she is to be three months with us at least. E II 1 159 20
Three months, she says so, positively, as I am going to E II 1 159 20
they have no doubt that three or four months at Highbury E II 1 161 29
By birth she belonged to Highbury: and when at three years E II 2 163 3
she did not like through three long months!--to be always E II 2 166 11
but I shall not stop three minutes: and, Jane, you had E II 3 176 50
I set; and I had not got three yards from the door, when E II 3 179 52
Emma saw him only once; but two or three times every day E II 4 184 10
If he had come at Christmas he could not have staid three E II 5 188 7
"Four o'clock!--depend upon it he will be here by three," E II 5 189 16
They were all three walking about together for an hour or E II 6 196 2
A very successful visit:--I saw all the three ladies; and E II 6 198 7
sitting with them very nearly three quarters of an hour. E II 6 199 7
Only three of us--besides dear Jane at present--and she E II 9 237 46
promise to have them done three times--but Miss Woodhouse E II 9 238 51

"You and Miss Smith, and Miss Fairfax, will be three, and E II 11 248 4
You and Miss Smith, and Miss Fairfax, will be three, and E II 11 248 4
I went in for three minutes, and was detained by Miss E II 12 260 27
She had had three weeks of happy exemption from Mr. Elton; E II 13 267 8
vain artifice retreated three months ago, to lace up her E II 14 270 3
Jane had come to Highbury professedly for three months; E II 15 285 14
were gone to Ireland for three months; but now the E II 15 285 14
For two or three months longer I shall remain where I am, E II 17 301 19
There were three others, Jane says, which they hesitated E III 2 323 19
asunder;--they were all three soon in the hall, and E III 3 333 3
You wrote me word of it three months ago." E III 5 344 7
known to nobody else, and only thought of about three days. E III 5 345 16
Two or three more of the chosen only were to be admitted E III 6 352 2
way, scarcely any three together, they insensibly followed E III 6 360 38
"Dating from three o'clock yesterday. E III 7 369 13
"Three o'clock yesterday! E III 7 369 14
moderately clever--or three things very dull indeed, and E III 7 370 23
'Three things very dull indeed.' E III 7 370 24
I shall be sure to say three dull things as soon as ever I E III 7 370 24
you will be limited as to number--only three at once." E III 7 370 26
the charge of her three little girls--delightful children. E III 8 380 13
I have really for some time past, for at least these three E III 10 396 41
They never could have been all three together, without her E III 12 421 17
"So early in life--at three and twenty--a period when, if E III 13 428 23
At three and twenty to have drawn such a prize!-- E III 13 428 23
could be in love with more than <u>three</u> men in one year. E III 15 450 38
There must be three months, at <u>least</u>, of deep mourning; E III 16 460 56
He went to town on business three days ago, and I got him E III 18 471 20
couple engaged of the three, were the first to be married. E III 19 483 6
representing a borough in three successive parliaments, P III 1 3 3
4
Three girls, the two eldest sixteen and fourteen, was an P III 1 4 6
There had been three alternatives, London, Bath, or P III 2 13 7
of her having been three years at school there, after her P III 2 14 11
know, Sir Walter, some time back, for two or three years. P III 3 23 32
among the only three of her own friends in the secret of P III 4 30 10
past being known to those three only among her connexions, P III 4 30 10
and Mary fixed only three miles off, must be anticipated, P III 4 31 12
I do not think she has been in this house three times this P III 5 37 24
at a distance of only three miles, will often include a P III 6 42 1
subject, by being removed three miles from Kellynch: P III 6 46 12
So passed the first three weeks. P III 6 47 16
The Admiral, after taking two or three refreshing turns P III 8 68 31
32
and the three children, round from Portsmouth to Plymouth. P III 8 69 39
Three days had passed without his coming once to P III 10 82 2
were thus divided--forming three distinct parties; and to P III 10 90 37
and to that party of the three which boasted least P III 10 90 37
Here is excellent room for three, I assure you. P III 10 91 40
coming after them, with three companions, all well known P III 11 96 11
Captain Benwick looked and was the youngest of the three, P III 11 97 14
be said which of the three, who were completely rational, P III 12 110 43
finding room for two or three besides, supposing they P III 12 113 56
Charles, Henrietta, and Captain Wentworth were the three P III 12 113 57
The first three or four days passed most quietly, with no P IV 1 125 14
and blows hard, which may not happen three times a winter. P IV 1 128 30
that Lady Russell lived three miles off, his heart failed P IV 2 130 6
three months, in laura-place, and would be living in style. P IV 4 149 12
three lines of scrawl from the Dowager Viscountess. P IV 4 149 13
a time; and Miss Hamilton, three years older than herself, P IV 5 152 2
It was three weeks since she had heard at all. P IV 6 162 1
She has a blister on one of her heels, as large as a three P IV 6 170 29
expect accommodation for all the three Camden-Place ladies. P IV 7 174 3
Could she have believed it a week ago--three hours ago! P IV 8 190 51
"I have not seen Mr. Elliot these three years," was Mrs. P IV 9 198 52
common, "but I have lived three and twenty years in the P IV 9 203 72
the kingdom, surrounded by three great proprietors, each P IV 10 217 20
other; and to two of the three, at least, Charles Hayter P IV 10 217 20
They all three called in Rivers-Street for a couple of P IV 10 220 30
pass between two or three of the lady visitors, as if they P IV 10 222 37
been seen with Mr. Elliot three hours after his being P IV 10 228 70
Haymakers at the time, & three or four of them summoned to S 1 364 1
One of these good people can be with him in three minutes S 1 365 1
Shepherd lives at one end, & three old women at the other." S 1 366 1
attempts of two or three speculating people about S 1 369 1
& their mother. (two or three genteel looking young women S 1 370 1
a year to bequeath, & three distinct sets of people to be S 3 376 1
attacked;--and of these three divisions, Mr P. did not S 3 376 1
a home, & at the end of three days calling for her bill, S 3 378 1
to Charlotte, & two or three of the best of them were S 4 383 1
hours without intermission)--he was well in three days.-- S 5 386 1
Three teeth drawn at once!--frightful!-- S 5 388 1
terrace; no fewer than three lodging papers staring me in S 7 402 1
for they were all three come, & meant to get into lodgings S 9 407 1
"All three come!-- S 9 407 1
I trust there are not three people in England who have so S 9 410 1
Charlotte had only two or three veiws of Miss Diana S 10 413 1
Miss P-- whom, remembering the three teeth drawn in one S 10 413 1
hand, took drops two or three times from one, out of the S 10 413 1
or their own, & was still the most alert of the three.-- S 10 414 1
from Camberwell, & the three young ladies under her care, S 10 419 1
She had several more under her care than the three who S 11 421 1
Of these three, & indeed of all, Miss Lambe was beyond S 11 421 1
at least one family out of three, throughout the kingdom; S 11 421 1
six new dresses each for a three days visit, were S 11 421 1
oclock--which will be a three hours business,--therefore I S 12 424 1
proposing to spend two or three days, as it might happen, S 12 425 1

THREE DECKERS (1)
the number of three deckers now in commission, their MP III 10 403 13

THREE-AND-TWENTY (5)
Three hours and a half indeed coming only three-and-twenty NA I 7 46 9
"Rest! he has only come three-and-twenty miles to-day; all NA I 7 47 27
"My dear papa, he is three-and-twenty.-- E I 11 96 23
"Three-and-twenty!--is he indeed?-- E I 11 96 24
What! at three-and-twenty to be the king of his company -- E I 18 150 32

THREE-QUARTERS (1)
and the three-quarters of a mile would have seemed but one. E I 15 129 23

THREW (27)
so becoming in a hero, threw a fresh grace in Catherine's NA I 5 35 2
a violence which almost threw him on his haunches, and the NA I 7 44 3
He asked fifty guineas; I closed with him directly, threw NA I 7 46 13
"Make haste! make haste!" as he threw open the door--" put NA I 11 84 18
Her resolute effort threw back the lid, and gave to her NA II 6 164 3
accession of dignity that threw him into a fit of good- NA II 16 250 4
It was <u>that</u> which threw this gloom,--even now the SS II 9 206 24
for though she often threw out expressions of pity for her SS II 14 247 4
mother's expected arrival, threw her altogether into an SS III 9 333 3
an old woman who threw herself away on an Irish captain.-- W 349 24
She then yawned again, threw aside her book, and cast her PP I 11 55 5
6
and by so doing, threw a languor over the whole party, PP I 18 102 75
The very mention of any thing concerning the match threw PP I 23 129 16
and threw back the praise on her sister's warm affection. PP II 1 135 10
every thing around them, threw a real gloom over their PP II 19 237 3
in Derbyshire; and as she threw a retrospective glance PP III 4 279 23
The contents of this letter threw Elizabeth into a flutter PP III 10 326 3
But the spiritless condition which this event threw her PP III 11 331 13
this extraordinary visit threw Elizabeth into, could not PP III 15 360 1
sister as he sealed and threw the letter from him, and MP II 6 229 1
sight of so many strangers threw her back into herself; MP II 10 273 7
admiration, and then threw her arms round his neck to sob MP III 7 384 34
Mr. and Mrs. Churchill, who threw her off with due decorum. E I 2 15 3
lame carriage-horse threw every thing into sad uncertainty. E III 6 353 6
wonder too, as Elizabeth threw open the folding-doors, and P IV 3 138 5
He omitted no opportunity of being with them, threw P IV 9 207 90
& a curve <u>there</u> threw them to a better distance. S 12 426 1

THRILL (3)
nerve in Elinor's body thrill with transport, now arrived SS III 13 370 37
had time for only one thrill of horror, before he declared MP III 10 406 22
felt it in a nervous thrill all over her, and at the same P IV 11 231 10

THRILLING (1)
These were thrilling words, and wound up Catherine's NA II 2 140 8

THRIVE (2)
"I am so glad to see the evergreens thrive!" said Fanny in MP II 4 209 16
And I have no doubt that he <u>will</u> thrive and be a very rich E I 4 34 40

THRIVES (1)
"The tree thrives well beyond a doubt, madam," replied Dr. MP I 6 54 10

THRIVING (1)
else--which is just as it should be, for a thriving man. E I 4 34 40

THROAT (17)
up very warm about the throat, when you come from the NA I 2 18 2
affection, it cost her only a spasm in her throat.-- SS III 1 265 33
feeling, in her head and throat, the beginning of an heavy SS III 6 305 16
a cough, and a sore throat, a good night's rest was to SS III 6 306 17
seeing round your lovely throat an ornament which his MP II 8 259 20
he knew there was such a throat in the world?--or perhaps-- MP II 8 259 20
in little Bella's throat,--both sea air and bathing." E I 12 101 21
you had better let him look at little Bella's throat." E I 12 102 27
"Oh! my dear sir, her throat is so much better that I have E I 12 102 28
friend's complaint;--"a throat very much inflamed, with a E I 13 109 6
charm away a sore throat; it is a most severe cold indeed. E I 13 114 32
a bad sore throat; and Emma was quite in charity with him. E I 15 124 3
of its being a bad sore throat on her account, than on E I 15 124 4
the danger of catching an ulcerated sore throat herself! E I 15 125 5
It was but a very few days before I had my sore throat-- E III 4 338 12
Observe the turn of her throat. E III 18 479 70
After clearing his throat, however, he proceeded thus, "I P IV 8 182 9
10

THROATS (1)
Charges' shoulders & throats, led the way up the wide W 327 7

THRONG (1)
made her way through the throng of men by the door, as NA I 2 21 9

THROUGHOUT (23)
discovers every Sunday throughout the season, they NA I 5 35 2
she had been triumphant throughout, had carried her point NA I 13 103 29
tenor of his conduct throughout the whole visit, so well NA II 11 215 28
and sudden noises throughout the house, she heard it all NA II 13 227 26
Mrs. Ferrars's conduct throughout the whole, has been such SS III 1 268 45
house, on every monthly return throughout the winter.-- W 314 1
a great air of comfort throughout, and by Charlotte's PP II 5 157 5
must make him entirely blameless throughout the whole. PP II 13 205 3
to act in your name, throughout the whole of this business, PP III 7 303 14
reigned in it with few interruptions throughout the year. MP I 9 89 30
of the proportion of virtue to vice throughout the kingdom. MP I 9 93 49
in every feeling throughout the whole, now ventured to say, MP I 13 128 34
Fanny is the only one who has judged rightly throughout, MP II 2 187 1
and followed his advice throughout, as far as she could; MP III 1 322 50
studiously to avoid him throughout the day, were turned MP III 3 337 11
every fine Sunday throughout the year, always going MP III 11 408 4
There will be but one subject throughout the parishes of E I 18 149 29
In general he was judged, throughout the parishes of E II 7 206 4
almost every evening throughout the year, he soon E III 5 351 38
The delicacy of her mind throughout the whole engagement, E III 14 439 8
of all naval matters throughout the party; and he was very P III 8 64 4
are printed in one week throughout the kingdom, you wd not S 1 366 1
family out of three, throughout the kingdom; they had S 11 421 1

THROW (38)
& indelicate feelings to throw herself into the protection LS 22 282 6
circumstance that might throw blame on the memory of one, LS 24 288 11
Something must and will happen to throw a hero in her way. NA I 1 17 11
and fortune as likely to throw great difficulties in the NA II 11 208 1
behind her friend to throw a parting glance on every well- NA II 13 227 27
the probability of wishing to throw ridicule on his age. SS I 8 37 3
throw herself into his arms, when Colonel Brandon appeared. SS II 4 161 7
village, and the parsonage-house within a stone's throw. SS II 8 197 22
She would not be so weak as to throw away the comfort of a SS III 5 296 19
will throw off at Stanton wood on Wednesday at 9 o'clock.-- W 347 21
He was persuaded without much difficulty to throw off his W 355 28
though I must throw in a good word for my little Lizzy." PP I 1 4 25
the conduct of each, and throw into the account of PP I 17 85 1
marrying so greatly must throw them in the way of other PP I 18 99 63
and hasten to Lucas Lodge to throw himself at her feet. PP I 22 121 1
Mr. Collins had a compliment, and an allusion to throw in PP II 14 210 4
for him and Mrs. F. but no one can throw any blame on them. PP III 4 275 5
in the corps might throw on a dishonourable elopement with PP III 5 283 8
as much as possible, to throw off your unworthy child from PP III 6 297 11
"and far be it from me to throw any fanciful impediment in MP I 1 7 7
and trusting they would never have cause to throw her off. MP I 1 11 19
do not like to have people throw themselves away; but MP I 4 43 27
than immediately to throw the business into the hands of a MP I 6 61 58
aunt, and cousin, and throw as great a gloom as possible MP I 7 70 30
that she could do was to throw a mist over it, and hope MP I 11 107 3
within a stone's throw of the said knoll and church. MP II 7 241 13
that very day, and to throw her into all the agitation of MP III 15 437 2
and as she meant to throw in a little improvement to the E I 6 47 27
I am convinced that he does not mean to throw himself away. E I 8 66 53
be necessary for her to throw coldness into her air; and E II 8 212 4
and throw up a sash, without its being suspected. E II 11 252 31
that I am now going to throw them both behind the fire, E III 4 340 22
The following day brought news from Richmond to throw E III 9 387 11
own it all to his uncle, throw himself on his kindness, E III 10 398 51
Oh! no; there would be a Mrs. Knightley to throw cold E III 17 469 36
beauty, and mind, to throw herself away at nineteen; P III 4 26 3
have made, she has no right to throw herself away. P III 9 75 13
of the day, would throw me into such a Perspiration!-- S 10 416 1

THROWING (21)
his life was his throwing her off forever on her marriage. LS 2 245 1
arts & sciences; it is throwing time away; to be mistress LS 7 253 1
seemed no chance of her throwing a whole party into NA I 1 16 10
thus unthinkingly throwing away a fair opportunity of NA I 8 53 3
instantly arise, and throwing your dressing-gown around NA II 5 159 19
I have some thoughts of throwing the passage into one of SS I 6 29 4
throwing it out of window--"he is full of monkey tricks." SS I 21 121 7
"Forgive me, forgive me," throwing her arms round her SS II 7 185 24
'My dear courtland,' said I, immediately throwing them all SS II 14 252 17
went against me to be throwing you together, so well as I W 341 19
spite of Mrs. Philips' throwing up the parlour window, and PP I 15 73 10
her in throwing off this last incumbrance of mystery. PP II 17 227 25
for Mrs. Crawford, without throwing a shade on the Admiral. MP I 7 63 7
a much brisker tone, and throwing down the newspaper again- MP I 12 118 22
"By Jove! this won't do"--cried Tom, throwing himself into MP I 13 126 21
by a single attempt at throwing ridicule on his cause. MP II 7 248 47
in a wild fit of folly, throwing away from you such an MP III 1 318 39
short, and dexterously throwing it into a ditch, was E I 10 89 36
indeed, a throwing away, which she grieved to think of! P III 4 26 3
He had never had an idea of throwing himself off; he had P IV 3 138 7
and was most tender of throwing any on her husband; but P IV 9 209 95

THROWN (66)
very showery, and that would have thrown me into agonies! NA I 6 39 4
But the hindrance thrown in the way of a very speedy NA I 8 56 11
meanwhile, was entirely thrown away, for Mrs. Allen, not NA I 9 61 6
sole as it did, was not thrown away; it brought a more NA I 12 93 7
new writing-desk from being thrown out into the street.-- NA II 5 155 4
Her habit therefore was thrown off with all possible haste, NA II 6 163 1

means, the lid in one moment should be thrown back. NA II 6 164 3
a victory, and having thrown open each folding door, the NA II 6 168 10
Tilney, advancing, had thrown open, and passed through, NA II 8 185 6
thing in reason--a bow thrown out, perhaps--though, NA II 11 213 19
It is ten to one but you are thrown together again in the NA II 14 236 17
He and I have been at times thrown a good deal together, SS I 4 20 9
Elinor recover from the alarm into which it had thrown her. SS I 12 62 27
and Lady Middleton was thrown into no little alarm on the SS I 21 118 2
the day before had thrown them into unceasing delight. SS I 21 120 6
but the book was soon thrown aside, and she returned to SS II 4 166 31
hearing Willoughby's name mentioned, was not thrown away. SS II 10 214 8
by the door's being thrown open, the servant's announcing SS II 13 240 18
How they could be thrown together, and by what attraction SS III 13 364 10
that brother had been thrown off by his family--it was SS III 13 364 10
when people are much thrown together, and see little of SS III 14 375 9
way than the other was thrown open, & he beheld a circle W 355 28
occurrences had thrown on many of the Longbourn family. PP II 1 138 30
would make him abundantly regret what he had thrown away. PP II 3 149 27
Wilfully and wantonly to have thrown off the companion of PP II 12 196 5
It might seem as if she had purposely thrown herself in PP III 1 252 54
has thrown herself into the power of--of Mr. Wickham. PP III 4 277 11
ours is not a family, on which it could be thrown away. PP III 5 285 18
the door was thrown open, and she ran into the room. PP III 9 315 3
till the door was thrown open, and their visitor entered. PP III 14 351 1
eat, and the doors were thrown open to admit them through MP I 9 84 1
will be all so much money thrown away--and I am sure that MP I 15 141 22
animation of being thus thrown together--of comparing MP I 18 170 23
the door of the room was thrown open, and Julia appearing MP I 18 172 33
Poor Fanny's mind was thrown into the most distressing of MP III 5 364 30
an advantage entirely thrown away; she had been unable to MP III 16 448 2
and his recovery so much thrown back by it, that even Lady MP III 16 451 13
Such was his opinion of the set into which she had thrown MP III 16 452 13
'He has thrown away,' said she, 'such a woman as he will MP III 16 455 21
he could not bear to be thrown off by the woman whose MP III 17 467 20
his lovely daughter, was in no danger of being thrown away. E I 3 20 2
"But I," he soon added, "who have had no such charm thrown E I 5 37 9
"Why, to own the truth, I am afraid you are rather thrown E I 5 38 13
You would have thrown yourself out of all good society. E I 7 54 27
made a push--of having thrown a die; and she imagined he E I 9 81 78
dear Miss Woodhouse, what a flurry it has thrown me in! E II 1 161 31
Her caution was thrown away. E II 2 169 16
when the door was thrown open, and Miss Bates and Miss E II 3 172 22
23
pass without their being thrown together again, with any E II 3 180 58
told well; he had not thrown himself away--he had gained a E II 4 181 4
are where fine instruments are absolutely thrown away. E II 8 215 16
To know that he has not thrown himself away, is such a E II 14 272 15
now in such retirement, such obscurity, so thrown away.-- E II 15 283 7
incessant attentions of Mrs. Weston, were not thrown away. E III 2 326 33
It was not thrown away on her, she bounded higher than E III 2 328 41
and a lovely young woman thrown together in such a way, E III 3 334 9
sort of intimacy into which we were immediately thrown.-- E III 14 438 8
No additional agitation should be thrown at this period E III 16 452 6
was so hot and tired, that all this wit seemed thrown away. E III 16 457 37
spirits exceedingly, and thrown her into greater grief for P III 6 51 32
he had feared that he was thrown off, but knew not why; P IV 3 138 7
They had been thrown together several weeks; they had been P IV 6 167 19
were by any chance to be thrown into company with Captain P IV 7 178 27
forward by some cousins, thrown by chance into Mr. P IV 9 202 66
and the door was thrown open for Sir Walter and Miss P IV 10 226 63
kept him from trying to regain her when thrown in his way. P IV 11 242 63

THROWS (1)
luck in some of her throws: and she inquired a great deal E III 2 329 45

THRUSH'S (2)
he has got one of the Thrush's boats, and is going off to MP III 7 377 7
particulars of the Thrush's going out of harbour, in which MP III 7 377 8

THUMPING (1)
At a more than ordinary pitch of thumping and hallooing in MP III 7 383 30

THUNDER (1)
Peals of thunder so loud as to seem to shake the edifice NA II 5 159 19

THUNDERBOLT (1)
was in town was--in the same language--a thunderbolt.-- SS III 8 325 50

THUNDERBOLTS (1)
Thunderbolts and daggers!--what a reproof would she have SS III 8 325 50

THURSDAY (21)
My dear mother Mr Vernon returned on Thursday night, LS 17 269 1
She arrived with her uncle last Thursday fortnight, when LS 19 273 1
I shall not be at home myself till Wednesday or Thursday, LS 23 283 4
& on Thursday next, we & our little ones will be with you. LS 41 310 2
She entered the rooms on Thursday evening with feelings NA I 10 74 23
Monday, Tuesday, Wednesday, Thursday, Friday and Saturday NA I 13 97 1
ride over to-morrow, and ask him to dinner on Thursday." SS I 9 43 13
nothing of him not all Thursday, Friday, and Saturday, and SS III 2 272 16
Thursday and Friday, on purpose to get the better of it. SS III 2 273 16
Thursday was to be the wedding day, and on Wednesday Miss PP II 3 145 11
away; and was so good as to stay till Thursday with me. PP III 5 292 66
day, and was to leave town again on Wednesday or Thursday. PP III 10 325 2
He comes down on Thursday at the latest, very likely on PP III 11 331 15
I observed he was hoarse on Thursday night." MP II 5 222 39
Thursday was the day of the ball: and on Wednesday morning, MP II 8 256 14
Thursday, predestined to hope and enjoyment, came; and MP II 9 265 21
of talking over Thursday night with Mrs. Grant and Miss MP II 11 283 7
They reached Mansfield on Thursday, and it was not till MP III 16 453 17
"You sent me such a good account of yourself on Thursday!" P III 5 37 23
It was quite unkind of you not to come on Thursday." P III 5 38 31
from Thursday to Saturday evening his absence was certain. P IV 10 214 13

THWARTED (3)
Young people do not like to be always thwarted." NA I 13 105 36
It makes me very nervous and poorly, to be thwarted so in PP II 2 140 4
I am thwarted in every thing material. E III 6 365 64

THY (1)
Thy ready wit the word will soon supply E I 9 72 15

TICKETS (4)
a new name on her tickets, and a brilliant exhibition of NA I 15 122 28
lottery tickets, and a little bit of hot supper afterwards. PP I 15 74 11
extremely fond of lottery tickets, she soon grew too much PP I 16 76 8
Lydia talked incessantly of lottery tickets, of the fish PP I 16 84 59

TIDE (5)
a disgust which turned the tide of his popularity; for he PP I 3 10 5
But we must stem the tide of malice, and pour into the PP III 5 289 42
watching the flow of the tide, for sitting in unwearied P III 11 95 9
They went to the sands, to watch the flowing of the tide, P III 12 102 1
some--.and the tide must be flowing--about half-tide now.-- S 4 384 1

TIDINGS (15)
Pondering over these heart-rendering tidings, Catherine NA I 11 89 62
A day or two passed away and brought no tidings of Captain NA II 11 209 5
Elinor grew impatient for some tidings of Edward. SS III 11 352 21
after day passed off, and brought no letter, no tidings. SS III 12 358 4
bringing any other tidings of him than the report which PP I 23 129 12
am able to send you some tidings of my niece, and such as, PP III 7 302 14
to have the earliest tidings of it, that the period of PP III 11 333 30
"Mr. Bertram," said she, "I have tidings of my harp at MP I 6 57 33
The approach of September brought tidings of Mr. Bertram MP I 12 114 1
and had heard no tidings beyond a friendly note of MP II 2 192 11
would bring the first tidings, he found her trembling with MP II 6 232 12
To Isabella, the relief of such tidings was very great, E I 15 128 17
Although in one instance the bearers of not good tidings, E II 7 206 5
thought you would begin to be impatient for tidings of us." E III 2 324 23
not come; and the next tidings were that he was married. P III 1 8 15

TIDY (4)
house, and made unusually tidy on the occasion; an NA II 11 213 21
a troop of tidy, happy villagers please me better than the SS I 18 98 8
There is the parsonage; a tidy looking house, and I MP I 8 82 34
butcher with his tray, a tidy old woman travelling E II 9 233 24

TIE (6)
than ten miles an hour: tie his legs and he will get on. NA I 7 46 11
could all wish him disengaged from every tie of business. NA II 7 176 15
in which even the conjugal tie is beneath the fraternal. MP II 6 234 18
connected as they were by tie upon tie, all friends, all MP III 15 441 20
as they were by tie upon tie, all friends, all intimate MP III 15 441 20
The child to be born at Randall's must be a tie there even E III 12 422 20

TIED (5)
The whole was tied up for the benefit of this child, who, SS I 1 4 3
To be tied down to the regular payment of such a sum, on SS I 2 11 21
the advantage of being tied up from much gaming at present, MP I 5 48 28
She, poor soul, is tied by the leg. P IV 6 170 29
And when I think of benwick, my tongue is tied." P IV 11 236 34

TIES (2)
So long divided, and so differently situated, the ties of MP III 13 428 15
higher ties, a warmer love might have seemed impossible. E I 11 92 4

TIGHT (1)
the compact, tight parsonage, enclosed in its own neat P III 5 36 20

TIGHTENED (1)
tightened for the moment by the very idea of separation. MP III 4 347 21

TILED (1)
was regular, the roof was tiled, the window shutters were SS I 6 28 2

TILNEY (196)
gentlemanlike young man as a partner;--his name was Tilney. NA I 3 25 2
guessed it, madam," said Mr. Tilney, looking at the muslin. NA I 3 28 36
Mr. Tilney was polite enough to seem interested in what NA I 3 29 47
How proper Mr. Tilney might be as a dreamer or a lover, NA I 3 30 52
herself of seeing Mr. Tilney there before the morning were NA I 4 31 1
no smile was demanded--Mr. Tilney did not appear. NA I 4 31 1
almost forgot Mr. Tilney while she talked to Miss Thorpe. NA I 4 33 6
an inquiring eye for Mr. Tilney in every box which her eye NA I 5 35 1
Mr. Tilney was no fonder of the play than the Pump-Room. NA I 5 35 1
about Mr. Tilney, for perhaps I may never see him again." NA I 6 41 17
I have not forgot your description of Mr. Tilney;--'a NA I 6 42 30
not Mr. Thorpe, but Mr. Tilney, within three yards of the NA I 8 53 3
entered her head that Mr. Tilney could be married; he had NA I 8 53 3
Mr. Tilney and his companion, who continued, though slowly, NA I 8 54 4
Tilney with seats, as they had agreed to join their party. NA I 8 54 10
This was accordingly done, Mr. Tilney still continuing NA I 8 54 10
that part of the room where she had left Mr. Tilney. NA I 8 55 10
behind her, attended by Miss Tilney and a gentleman. NA I 8 55 10
to each other, Miss Tilney expressing a proper sense of NA I 8 55 10
Miss Tilney had a good figure, a pretty face, and a very NA I 8 55 11
her relationship to Mr. Tilney, was desirous of being NA I 8 56 11
of all Isabella's impatient desire to see Mr. Tilney. NA I 8 57 21
ever willing to give Mr. Tilney an opportunity of NA I 8 58 25
"Did you meet Mr. Tilney, my dear?" said Mrs. Allen. NA I 8 58 28
The rest of the evening she found very dull; Mr. Tilney NA I 8 59 38
that of his partner; Miss Tilney, though belonging to it, NA I 8 59 38
acquaintance with Miss Tilney, and almost her first NA I 9 60 1
desire of seeing Miss Tilney again could at that moment NA I 9 61 6
met Mrs. Hughes, and Mr. and Miss Tilney walking with her." NA I 9 68 40
Miss Tilney was in a very pretty spotted muslin, and I NA I 9 68 42
Mrs. Tilney was a Miss Drummond, and she and Mrs. Hughes NA I 9 68 46
"And are Mr. and Mrs. Tilney in Bath?" NA I 9 68 47
is; yes, I am sure Mrs. Tilney is dead, because Mrs. NA I 9 68 48
wedding-day and that Miss Tilney had got now, for they NA I 9 68 48
"And is Mr. Tilney, my partner, the only son?" NA I 9 69 49
already; and as for Mr. Tilney--but that is a settled NA I 10 70 1
Catherine's resolution of endeavouring to meet Miss Tilney NA I 10 71 8
of speaking to Miss Tilney, whom she most joyfully saw NA I 10 72 8
Miss Tilney met her with great civility, returned her NA I 10 72 8
Miss Tilney could only bow. NA I 10 72 11
Mrs. Hughes now joined them, and asked Miss Tilney if she NA I 10 73 19
dared not expect that Mr. Tilney should ask her a third NA I 10 74 23
and again solicited to dance, by Mr. Tilney himself. NA I 10 75 24
joining her, asked by Mr. Tilney, as if he had sought her NA I 10 75 24
"Tilney," he repeated, "hum--I do not know him. NA I 10 76 28
Mr. Tilney was very much amused. NA I 10 79 55
saw him presently address Mr. Tilney in a familiar whisper. NA I 10 80 59
It is General Tilney, my father." NA I 10 80 59
In chatting with Miss Tilney before the evening concluded, NA I 10 80 61
Miss Tilney, to whom all the commonly-frequented environs NA I 10 80 61
rain for Miss Tilney to venture, must yet be a question. NA I 11 83 16
cannot go indeed, for you know Miss Tilney may still call." NA I 11 84 18
smile) "I expect Miss Tilney and her brother to call on me NA I 11 85 32
of that, for I heard Tilney hallooing to a man who was NA I 11 86 46
Catherine looked round and saw Miss Tilney leaning on her NA I 11 87 53
she impatiently cried, it is Miss Tilney; it is indeed.-- NA I 11 87 53
I must go back to Miss Tilney." NA I 11 87 53
hardly give up the point of its having been Tilney himself. NA I 11 87 53
there be any harm in my calling on Miss Tilney to-day? NA I 12 91 1
only put on a white gown; Miss Tilney always wears white." NA I 12 91 2
looked at the door, and inquired for Miss Tilney. NA I 12 91 3
The man believed Miss Tilney to be at home, but was not NA I 12 91 3
he had been mistaken, for that Miss Tilney was walked out. NA I 12 91 3
She felt almost persuaded that Miss Tilney was at home, NA I 12 91 3
but issuing from the door, she saw Miss Tilney herself. NA I 12 91 3
sudden view of Mr. Henry Tilney and his father, joining a NA I 12 92 4
Henry Tilney, without being once able to catch his eye. NA I 12 92 4
The play concluded--the curtain fell--Henry Tilney was no NA I 12 93 5
by the latter: "Oh! Mr. Tilney, I have been quite wild to NA I 12 93 5
Did not they tell me that Mr. Tilney and his sister were NA I 12 93 5
Henry Tilney at least was not. NA I 12 94 9
"Oh! do not say Miss Tilney was not angry," cried NA I 12 94 9
Tilney, why were you less generous than your sister? NA I 12 94 11
conversation with General Tilney; and she felt something NA I 12 95 17
She feared General Tilney did not like her appearance: she NA I 12 95 17
him talking with General Tilney:--"he is a fine old fellow, NA I 12 95 18
That General Tilney, instead of disliking, should admire NA I 12 96 24
had left them for a few minutes to speak to Miss Tilney. NA I 13 97 1
She had that moment settled with Miss Tilney to take their NA I 13 97 1
I am engaged to Miss Tilney. NA I 13 97 1
"It would be so easy to tell Miss Tilney that you had just NA I 13 98 1
more affection for Miss Tilney, though she had known her NA I 13 98 2
I have been to Miss Tilney, and made your excuses." NA I 13 100 13
I must run after Miss Tilney directly and set her right." NA I 13 100 18
When every thing was settled, when Miss Tilney herself NA I 13 100 19
to put it off, I could have spoken to Miss Tilney myself. NA I 13 100 20
in her engagement to Miss Tilney, to have retracted a NA I 13 101 25
she had spoken to Miss Tilney she could not be at ease; NA I 13 101 25
she must speak with Miss Tilney that moment, and hurrying NA I 13 102 25
the drawing-room with General Tilney, his son and daughter. NA I 13 102 25
the message; and Miss Tilney had no scruple in owning NA I 13 102 26
was introduced by Miss Tilney to her father, and received NA I 13 102 27
Miss Tilney added her own wishes. NA I 13 103 28
"No; I had just engaged myself to walk with Miss Tilney NA I 13 104 30
"Yes," added Miss Tilney, "and I remember that you NA I 14 107 8
"Henry," said Miss Tilney, "you are very impertinent. NA I 14 107 14
"Historians, you think," said Miss Tilney, "are not happy NA I 14 109 23
Miss Tilney, to whom this was chiefly addressed, was NA I 14 112 30
gallant Capt. Frederick Tilney, in the moment of charging NA I 14 113 39
"And now, Henry," said Miss Tilney, "that you have made us NA I 14 113 40
It was no effort to Catherine to believe that Henry Tilney NA I 14 114 49
into the house, and Miss Tilney, before they parted, NA I 14 114 49
I dine with Miss Tilney to-day, and must now be going home. NA I 15 123 35
received by General Tilney, and kindly welcomed by his NA II 1 129 1
in acquaintance with Miss Tilney, from the intercourse of NA II 1 129 1
instead of seeing Henry Tilney to greater advantage than NA II 1 129 1
"But as for General Tilney, I assure you it would be NA II 1 130 8

as heretofore: Miss Tilney took pains to be near her, and NA II 1 131 14
elder brother, Captain Tilney, was expected almost every NA II 1 131 15
happiness with Henry Tilney, listening with sparkling eyes NA II 1 131 15
At the end of the first dance, Captain Tilney came towards NA II 1 132 16
as fact, that Captain Tilney must have heard some NA II 1 132 16
with Captain Tilney preparing to give them hands across. NA II 1 133 29
Tilney, made but a small part of Catherine's speculation. NA II 2 138 1
visited Miss Tilney, and poured forth her joyful feelings. NA II 2 138 1
stay, than Miss Tilney told her of her father's having NA II 2 138 1
"Perhaps," said Miss Tilney in an embarrassed manner, "you NA II 2 139 4
General Tilney was not less sanguine, having already NA II 2 140 9
Miss Tilney was earnest, though gentle, in her secondary NA II 2 140 10
to her passion for Henry Tilney--and castles and abbies NA II 2 141 11
was eager to make of Miss Tilney; but so active were her NA II 2 141 13
Tilney says it is always the case with minds of a certain NA II 3 144 4
Tilney says, there is nothing people are so often deceived NA II 3 147 20
Catherine, looking up, perceived Captain Tilney; and NA II 3 147 21
leaving Isabella still sitting with Captain Tilney. NA II 3 147 28
It seemed to her that Captain Tilney was falling in love NA II 3 148 28
not looked so well pleased at the sight of Captain Tilney. NA II 3 148 28
For poor Captain Tilney too she was greatly concerned. NA II 4 149 1
In this distress, the intended departure of the Tilney NA II 4 150 1
But Captain Tilney had at present no intention of removing; NA II 4 150 1
She spoke to Henry Tilney on the subject, regretting his NA II 4 150 1
Does not he want Captain Tilney to go away?-- NA II 4 152 27
to be secured by her seeing nothing of Captain Tilney? NA II 4 152 28
Henry Tilney must know best. NA II 4 153 30
Her happiness in going with Miss Tilney, however, NA II 5 154 1
at his laziness when Captain Tilney at last came down. NA II 5 154 2
Tilney, without being able to hope for his good-will. NA II 5 155 2
the door; for with Miss Tilney she felt no restraint; and, NA II 5 155 4
been nothing; but General Tilney, though so charming a man, NA II 5 156 4
"Oh! Mr. Tilney, how frightful!-- NA II 5 159 18
"Miss Tilney, she was sure, would never put her into such NA II 5 160 23
hurried away by Miss Tilney in such a manner as convinced NA II 5 162 27
a quadrangle, before Miss Tilney led the way into a NA II 5 162 28
events could it have fallen into the Tilney family? NA II 6 164 2
of surprize, when Miss Tilney, anxious for her friend's NA II 6 165 4
is not it?" said Miss Tilney, as Catherine hastily closed NA II 6 165 4
Miss Tilney gently hinted her fear of being late; and in NA II 6 165 5
unfounded, for General Tilney was pacing the drawing-room, NA II 6 165 5
absence of General Tilney, with much positive cheerfulness. NA II 6 166 8
on perceiving that Miss Tilney slept only two doors from NA II 6 167 9
Heaven forbid that Henry Tilney should ever know her folly! NA II 7 173 3
been pointed out to her by Miss Tilney the evening before. NA II 7 173 5
Why was Miss Tilney embarrassed? NA II 7 177 18
"This is so favourite a walk of mine," said Miss Tilney, " NA II 7 179 28
Catherine had never heard Mrs. Tilney mentioned in the NA II 7 179 31
Miss Tilney continuing silent, she ventured to say, "her NA II 7 180 33
in the deceased Mrs. Tilney augmented with every question, NA II 7 180 37
Miss Tilney, understanding in part her friend's curiosity NA II 8 182 1
folding doors, which Miss Tilney, advancing, had thrown NA II 8 185 6
Miss Tilney drew back directly, and the heavy doors were NA II 8 185 5
"No," said Miss Tilney, sighing; "I was unfortunately from NA II 8 186 12
the probability that Mrs. Tilney yet lived, shut up for NA II 8 187 16
of the unfortunate Mrs. Tilney, must be, as certainly as NA II 8 188 17
of Mrs. Tilney, which immediately fronted the family pew. NA II 9 190 1
proposed to Miss Tilney the accomplishment of her promise. NA II 9 191 3
Would the veil in which Mrs. Tilney had last walked, or NA II 9 194 6
"Mr. Tilney!" she exclaimed in a voice of more than common NA II 9 194 6
even in Henry and Eleanor Tilney, some slight imperfection NA II 10 200 3
be over before Captain Tilney makes his engagement known, NA II 10 202 7
need of my being played off to make her secure of Tilney. NA II 10 202 7
for me to be in the same house with Captain Tilney." NA II 10 204 17
Miss Tilney, at Catherine's invitation, now read the NA II 10 205 25
and if the heir of the Tilney property had not grandeur NA II 11 208 1
But as it was not to be supposed that Captain Tilney, NA II 11 208 2
two passed away and brought no tidings of Captain Tilney. NA II 11 209 5
"Oh! why do not you fit up this room, Mr. Tilney? NA II 11 214 21
I must mean Captain Tilney, who, as you may remember, was NA II 12 216 2
should not say I shut myself up because Tilney was gone. NA II 12 217 2
face I believe, at least Tilney told me so at the time, NA II 12 217 2
I see that she has had designs on Captain Tilney, which NA II 12 218 6
what Captain Tilney has been about all this time. NA II 12 218 6
acquaintance with Captain Tilney, and comforting herself NA II 13 222 8
And all this by such a man as General Tilney, so polite, NA II 13 226 25
There was yet another point which Miss Tilney was anxious NA II 13 229 31
such a measure, General Tilney had acted neither NA II 14 234 10
home, and our comfort does not depend upon General Tilney." NA II 14 234 12
her promise to Miss Tilney, whose trust in the effect of NA II 14 235 14
harder for her to write than in addressing Eleanor Tilney. NA II 14 235 14
She could never forget Henry Tilney, or think of him with NA II 14 236 18
night; for General Tilney, from some odd fancy or other, NA II 14 237 21
Mr. Tilney drank tea with us, and I always thought him a NA II 14 238 26
"Then you are fretting about General Tilney, and that is NA II 15 240 4
daughter as "Mr. Henry Tilney," with the embarrassment of NA II 15 241 7
in suspecting General Tilney of either murdering or NA II 15 247 14
being applied to by Mr. Tilney, for their consent to his NA II 16 249 1
The marriage of Eleanor Tilney, her removal from all the NA II 16 250 5

TILNEYS (19)
beginning, and she saw nothing of the Tilneys. NA I 10 74 23
should even meet with the Tilneys in any reasonable time, NA I 10 75 24
She could not think the Tilneys had acted quite well by NA I 11 86 50
phaetons and false hangings, Tilneys and trap-doors. NA I 11 87 51
into a brisker trot; the Tilneys, who had soon ceased to NA I 11 87 53
be thought ill of by the Tilneys, she would willingly have NA I 11 88 54
It was amazingly shocking to be sure; but the Tilneys were NA I 11 90 64
To the theatre accordingly they all went; no Tilneys NA I 12 92 4
These Tilneys seem to swallow up every thing else." NA I 13 98 2
Let me go, Mr. Thorpe; Isabella, do not hold me." Tilneys; NA I 13 101 20
for what would the Tilneys have thought of her, if she had NA I 13 105 41
The Tilneys called for her at the appointed time; and no NA I 14 106 1
The Tilneys were soon engaged in another on which she had NA I 14 110 28
When the Tilneys were gone, she became amiable again, but NA I 14 114 50
Isabella's opinion of the Tilneys did not influence her NA II 1 131 14
To have her acquaintance with the Tilneys end so soon, was NA II 2 138 1
The Tilneys, they, by whom above all, she desired to be NA II 2 141 11
of an ancestor of the Tilneys on its dissolution, of a NA II 2 141 13
acquaintance like the Tilneys ought to have with her, NA II 14 239 28

TILNEYS' (1)
that in spite of the Tilneys' advantage in the outset, NA I 13 102 25

TIMBER (8)
woods seem full of fine timber, and the valley looks SS I 18 97 4
lawn was dotted over with timber, the house itself was SS III 6 302 7
have not seen such timber any where in Dorsetshire, as SS III 14 375 9
estimation; such a happy fall of ground, and such timber! MP I 6 61 53
fine timber, but the situation of the house is dreadful. MP I 8 82 34
very pretty meadows they are, finely sprinkled with timber. MP II 7 242 23
its abundance of timber in rows and avenues, which neither E III 6 358 35
which an abundance of very fine timber could give.-- S 12 426 1

TIMBERS (1)
people sat down upon some timbers in the yard, or found a MP III 10 403 15

TIME (1425)
It is time for me to be gone; I have therefore determined LS 2 245 1
much--engaging at the same time & in the same house the LS 4 248 2
took place exactly at the time of his marriage--& LS 5 249 1
might for a time make her wish for retirement. LS 6 252 2
moment of your precious time by sending her to Edward St, LS 7 252 1
& sciences; it is throwing time away; to be mistress of LS 7 253 1
I am sure of Sir James at any time, & could make him renew LS 7 253 1
You may well wonder how I contrive to pass my time here--& LS 7 254 3
You must not expect Reginald back again for some time. LS 8 254 1
continuing here beyond the time originally fixed for his LS 8 255 1
of them at the time, nor can now have forgotten them. LS 12 260 2
than to enjoy for a short time (as you have yourself LS 14 263 2
talent, as the cheif of my time is spent in conversation. LS 16 268 2
& did not return for some time; when she did, her eyes LS 17 270 2
fond of books & spending the cheif of her time in reading. LS 18 273 3
when of course I lost no time in demanding the reason of LS 19 273 1
The poor girl sat all this time without opening her lips; LS 20 276 3
I have for some time been more particularly resolved on LS 22 280 1
I was calm for some time, but the greatest degree of LS 22 282 7
subjects for a short time, said to me, "I find from Wilson LS 23 284 6
I was resolved to lose no time in clearing up these LS 24 288 11
however, & at the same time began to think that we had LS 24 290 13
thus trespassing on your time, but I owed it to my own LS 24 290 13
But at the same time, it is not for me to suffer such a LS 25 292 3
without loss of time, but that you leave Frederica behind. LS 26 295 1
Here we shall in time be at peace. LS 27 297 2
much impatience to the time when Reginald according to our LS 29 299 2
of delaying that hour beyond the time originally fixed. LS 30 299 1
I might perhaps harden myself in time against the LS 30 300 3
At the same time do not forget my real interest; say all LS 31 302 1
All is by this time known to de courcy, who is now alone LS 32 303 1
Mr Johnson has for some time suspected de courcy of LS 32 303 1
a thought, has for some time existed, & still continues to LS 36 305 1
Can you, dare you deny it? & all this at the time when I LS 36 305 1
Reginald may not be in town again by that time! LS 41 310 2
uncle & aunt, till such time as Reginald de courcy could LS 42 313 8
they ought to be; but her time was so much occupied in NA I 1 15 3
this time the intimate friend and confidante of her sister. NA I 2 19 3
It was a splendid sight, and she began, for the first time NA I 2 21 9
For some time her young friend felt obliged to her for NA I 2 21 9
After some time they received an offer of tea from one of NA I 2 23 22
it, which was the only time that any body spoke to them NA I 2 23 22
comfort; and now was the time for a heroine, who had not NA I 2 23 27
After chatting some time on such matters as naturally NA I 3 25 2
be mistaken; it is a long time since I had the pleasure of NA I 4 31 2
and, after observing how time had slipped away since they NA I 4 32 2
been for a short time forgotten, was introduced likewise. NA I 4 32 4
sorry for it; but really I thought I was in very good time. NA I 6 39 3
Those will last us some time." NA I 6 40 10
interested her at that time rather more than any thing NA I 6 42 33
John Thorpe, who in the mean time had been giving orders NA I 7 45 5
"I know it must be five-and-twenty," said he, "by the time NA I 7 45 7
bid me sixty at once; Morland was with me at the time." NA I 7 47 19
The time of the two parties uniting in the Octagon Room NA I 7 51 54
Pulteney-Street reached the Upper-Rooms in very good time. NA I 8 52 1
up, Isabella had only time to press her friend's hand and NA I 8 52 2
better to be here than at home at this dull time of year. NA I 8 54 5
"So I told your brother all the time--but he would not NA I 8 56 14
In this common-place chatter, which lasted some time, the NA I 8 57 21
and scarcely had she time to inform Catherine of there NA I 9 61 1
time with James, was therefore obliged to speak plainer. NA I 9 61 6
allowed the two others time enough to get through a few NA I 9 62 7
well in his time, I dare say; he is not gouty for nothing. NA I 9 63 18
venturing after some time to consider the matter as NA I 9 65 27
She reflected on the affair for some time in much NA I 9 66 31
the immeasurable length of time which had divided them.-- NA I 10 70 1
all three set off in good time for the Pump-Room, where NA I 10 71 8
in that manner for some time, till Catherine began to NA I 10 71 8
of the time prevented her buying a new one for the evening. NA I 10 73 22
should ask her a third time to dance, her wishes, hopes NA I 10 74 23
lady has at some time or other known the same agitation. NA I 10 74 23
Catherine had neither time nor inclination to answer. NA I 10 75 24
Tilneys in any reasonable time, had just passed through NA I 10 75 24
agreeableness belongs solely to each other for that time. NA I 10 76 29
or you will forget to be tired of it at the proper time.-- NA I 10 78 43
"But then you spend your time so much more rationally in NA I 10 79 49
I would much rather take a chair at any time." NA I 11 83 11
This is just the time of day for it to clear up, and I do NA I 11 83 15
is not time to be lost--we are going to Bristol.-- NA I 11 84 18
is over, if there is time for it, go on to Kingsweston." NA I 11 84 19
in England--worth going fifty miles at any time to see." NA I 11 85 23
It was now but an hour later than the time fixed on for NA I 11 86 50
"I was not within at the time; but I heard of it from NA I 12 94 10
and he being hurried for time, and not caring to have it NA I 12 94 10
He remained with them some time, and was only too NA I 12 95 16
to set off very early, in order to be at home in good time. NA I 13 97 1
This was the first time of her brother's openly siding NA I 13 99 4
when he had overtaken them, and were at home by this time. NA I 13 101 20
to have failed a second time in her engagement to Miss NA I 13 101 25
The Tilneys called for her at the appointed time; and no NA I 14 106 1
it in two days--my hair standing on end the whole time." NA I 14 106 7
of the most advanced reason and mature time of life. NA I 14 109 25
she was amiable for some time to little effect; Mrs. Allen NA I 14 114 50
for there is not a soul at Clifton at this time of year. NA I 14 115 50
For heaven's sake, waste no more time. NA I 15 120 24
exertion, for as the time of reasonable expectation drew NA I 15 121 26
she drew back for some time, forgetting to speak or to NA II 1 133 29
change which could at that time be given; but as it was NA II 1 133 30
be the last, was for some time a question, to which NA II 2 138 1
daughter time to speak, "has been forming a very bold wish. NA II 2 139 7
convent at the time of the Reformation, of its having NA II 2 141 13
alone in the parlour, some time before you left the house." NA II 3 145 12
what your thoughts and designs in time past may have been. NA II 3 146 18
Absence will in time make him comfortable again; but he NA II 4 150 4
but a very short time, perhaps only a few days behind us. NA II 4 152 29
It was the first time of her being decidedly in his NA II 5 155 3
Half the time would have been enough for the curricle, and NA II 5 156 5
father's, and some of my time is necessarily spent there." NA II 5 157 7
drawer;--but for some time without discovering any thing NA II 5 160 21
of the Abbey--for some time suspended by his conversation NA II 5 161 24
which Catherine had only time to discover looked into a NA II 5 162 28
she resolved to lose no time in particular examination of NA II 6 163 1
her, spent the rest of his time in scolding his daughter, NA II 6 165 6
the time the party broke up, it blew and rained violently. NA II 6 166 9
felt for the first time that she was really in an Abbey.-- NA II 6 166 9
"She should take her time; she should not hurry herself; NA II 6 167 10
It was some time however before she could unfasten the NA II 6 169 11
once raised, but you may in time come to love a rose?" NA II 7 174 8
me, and in fine weather I am out more than half my time.-- NA II 7 174 9
The manufacture was much improved since that time; he had NA II 7 175 12
The weather was at present favourable, and at this time of NA II 7 176 17
father's account, he always walks out at this time of day." NA II 7 177 17
the Abbey, as she saw it for the first time from the lawn. NA II 7 177 19
At that time indeed I used to wonder at her choice. NA II 7 180 32
with the painting, and for some time it had no place. NA II 7 180 39
His endowments of this spot alone might at any time have NA II 8 183 3
And nine years, Catherine knew was a trifle of time, NA II 8 186 10
time--all favoured the supposition of her imprisonment.-- NA II 8 188 16
It was Sunday, an the whole time between morning and NA II 9 190 1
was expected on the morrow, there was no time to be lost. NA II 9 193 5
It was no time for thought; she hurried on, slipped with NA II 9 193 6
the first time in their acquaintance, wish to leave him. NA II 9 195 19
"For a time, greatly so. NA II 9 197 27
and the lenient hand of time did much for her by NA II 10 201 4
I am undeceived in time! NA II 10 202 7
From this time, the subject was frequently canvassed by NA II 11 208 1
than at the present time, that she suffered her mind to be NA II 11 208 2
making Miss Morland's time at Northanger pass pleasantly. NA II 11 209 5
But then it was such a dead time of year, no wild-fowl, no NA II 11 209 5
if a small sacrifice of time and attention can prevent it. NA II 11 210 6
be with you early, that we may have time to look about us. NA II 11 210 6

Context	Work	Vol.	Ch.	Page	Para.
Because no time is to be lost in frightening my old	NA	II	11	211	9
He went; and, it being at any time a much simpler	NA	II	11	211	15
by Henry, at the same time that a tray full of	NA	II	11	213	20
but in this horrid place one can find time for nothing.	NA	II	12	216	2
I hope you spend your time pleasantly, but am afraid you	NA	II	12	216	2
The last time we met was in Bath-Street, and I turned	NA	II	12	217	2
I knew their spite:--at one time they could not be civil	NA	II	12	217	2
Tilney told me so at the time, and said every eye was upon	NA	II	12	217	2
Lose no time, my dearest, sweetest Catherine, in writing	NA	II	12	218	2
what Captain Tilney has been about all this time.	NA	II	12	218	6
The happiness with which their time now passed, every	NA	II	13	220	1
Aware that if she gave herself much time, she might feel	NA	II	13	220	2
company for a much longer time--had been misled (perhaps	NA	II	13	221	2
so well-sufficient for the time to themselves, that it was	NA	II	13	222	7
indeed, as he must by this time be ashamed of the part he	NA	II	13	222	8
In such considerations time passed away, and it was	NA	II	13	222	8
Let me be called in time."	NA	II	13	226	24
of choice as to the time or mode of her travelling; of two	NA	II	13	226	25
made her for a short time sensible only of resentment.	NA	II	13	228	27
said by either during the time of their remaining together.	NA	II	13	229	31
Short, however, was that time.	NA	II	13	229	31
saved her at the same time from watching her progress; and	NA	II	14	231	5
every thing for a short time was subdued, and the pleasure	NA	II	14	233	9
but scarcely, within the time, could they at all discover	NA	II	14	233	10
"they must have a sad time of it; but as for any thing	NA	II	14	234	12
of your journey at the time; but now it is all over	NA	II	14	234	12
trust in the effect of time and distance on her friend's	NA	II	14	235	14
"If so, my dear, I dare say you will meet again some time	NA	II	14	236	17
happen within that time to make a meeting dreadful to her.	NA	II	14	236	18
I put them on new the first time of our going to the Lower	NA	II	14	238	24
house rather than remain fixed for any time in the parlour.	NA	II	15	240	1
Your head runs too much upon Bath; but there is a time for	NA	II	15	240	2
thing--a time for balls and plays, and a time for work.	NA	II	15	240	2
home, because there you must spend the most of your time.	NA	II	15	241	4
anxious to lose no time in attacking so dreadful a malady.	NA	II	15	241	7
It was some time before she could find what she looked for;	NA	II	15	241	7
her heart at ease for a time, and gladly therefore did she	NA	II	15	242	8
to Catherine for the first time since her mother's	NA	II	15	242	9
being at that time not only in daily expectation of	NA	II	15	244	12
Catherine herself could not be more ignorant at the time	NA	II	15	245	12
to communicate at this time to Catherine, how much of it	NA	II	15	247	14
a letter, as, at that time, happened pretty often, they	NA	II	16	250	3
of such a nature at such a time, and he promised to do	SS	I	1	5	6
say; ten to to one but he was light-headed at the time.	SS	I	2	9	5
do less than give it: at least I thought so at the time.	SS	I	2	9	6
The time may come when Harry will regret that so large a	SS	I	2	9	8
to him, and, for a long time, she firmly relied on the	SS	I	3	14	2
who had since spent the greatest part of his time there.	SS	I	3	15	4
for she was, at that time, in such affliction as rendered	SS	I	3	16	7
I thought so at the time; but you would give him Cowper."	SS	I	3	18	19
time, (which was still more common,) to make her uncivil.	SS	I	4	23	19
She needed no time for deliberation or inquiry.	SS	I	4	23	20
Now was the time when her son-in-law's promise to his	SS	I	5	27	6
her; and she had at this time ready money enough to supply	SS	I	6	29	4
In the mean time, till all these alterations could be made	SS	I	6	29	5
employments were in existence only half the time.	SS	I	7	32	1
not likely that the room would be wanted for some time."	SS	I	8	39	17
time did he most unaccountably follow me out of the room.	SS	I	8	39	18
clever, time has long ago destroyed all its ingenuity."	SS	I	9	45	30
than he can spend, more time than he knows how to employ,	SS	I	10	51	25
arise to occupy their time as shortly presented themselves,	SS	I	11	53	1
were partners for half the time; and when obliged to	SS	I	11	54	3
affair; and for some time she refused to submit to them.	SS	I	12	58	3
It is not time or opportunity that is to determine	SS	I	12	59	4
The reasons for this alteration were at the same time	SS	I	12	59	6
by being left some time in the parlour with only him and	SS	I	12	60	8
considering the time of year, and that it had rained every	SS	I	12	62	29
"What can you have to do in town at this time of year?"	SS	I	13	64	20
hours before his usual time, on purpose to go to Whitwell."	SS	I	13	65	32
party; but at the same time declared it to be unavoidable.	SS	I	13	65	33
"Then I must bid you farewell for a longer time than I	SS	I	13	66	48
and spent a considerable time there in walking about the	SS	I	13	67	65
been sensible of it at the time, for we always know when	SS	I	13	68	72
and to be sure must have cleared the estate by this time.	SS	I	14	70	2
time twelvemonth, that Barton cottage were inhabited!	SS	I	14	73	17
a part in his behaviour to your sister all this time?"	SS	I	15	80	38
he was going away for some time, he should seem to act an	SS	I	15	81	43
They saw nothing of Marianne till dinner time, when she	SS	I	15	82	46
nor speak, and after some time, on her mother's silently	SS	I	15	82	46
happiness forgot for a time her own disappointment.	SS	I	16	86	21
looks much as it always does at this time of year.	SS	I	16	87	30
At my time of life opinions are tolerably fixed.	SS	I	17	93	30
them, without giving oneself time to deliberate and judge."	SS	I	17	93	37
fullest extent--and he sat for some time silent and dull.	SS	I	17	95	50
Edward's embarrassment lasted some time, and it ended in	SS	I	18	99	14
But the time will come I hope . . . . I am sure you will	SS	I	18	100	29
a sigh--declared his time to be wholly disengaged--even	SS	I	19	101	1
wishes and his own, and without any restraint on his time.	SS	I	19	101	1
your time and give an interest to your plans and actions.	SS	I	19	102	3
would not be able to give them so much of your time.	SS	I	19	102	3
Your mother will secure to you, in time, that independence	SS	I	19	103	7
especially, which required some trouble and time to subdue.	SS	I	19	104	9
down stairs at the same time, and they all sat down to	SS	I	19	106	21
She came in with a smile, smiled all the time of her visit,	SS	I	19	106	22
Mrs. Jennings, in the mean time, talked on as loud as she	SS	I	19	107	28
to chaperon you at any time till I am confined, if Mrs.	SS	I	20	110	4
Will you come and spend some time at Cleveland this	SS	I	20	112	29
whims; and such of their time as could be spared from the	SS	I	21	120	6
said, and for the first time in her life, she thought Mrs.	SS	I	21	126	41
from herself, was at this time particularly ill-disposed,	SS	I	22	127	1
to me at present,--but the time may come--how soon it will	SS	I	22	129	11
She remembered too, her own surprise at the time, at his	SS	I	22	134	49
that her success was speedy, and for the time complete.	SS	I	22	134	53
been its dupe, for a short time made her feel only for	SS	II	1	139	1
She might in time regain tranquillity; but he, what had he	SS	II	1	140	1
while the same period of time, spent on her side in	SS	II	1	140	2
a hope of finding time for conversation at the park.	SS	II	1	144	10
her own end, and pleased Lady Middleton at the same time.	SS	II	1	145	23
own thoughts, had by this time forgotten that any body was	SS	II	1	145	23
A mutual silence took place for some time.	SS	II	2	149	24
upon, and we might trust to time and chance for the rest."	SS	II	2	149	25
for a time, we should be happier perhaps in the end.	SS	II	2	149	30
From this time that subject was never revived by Elinor,	SS	II	2	151	42
of not leaving their mother at that time of year.	SS	II	3	153	1
A short, a very short time however must now decide what	SS	II	4	159	1
Elinor was disappointed too; but at the same time her	SS	II	4	162	8
one has been away for any time; and then I have had	SS	II	4	163	14
I warrant you she is a fine size by this time."	SS	II	4	163	16
own, though at the same time she would never have forgiven	SS	II	4	164	21
none, and dawdled away her time in rapture and indecision.	SS	II	4	165	24
the game, but though her time was therefore at her own	SS	II	4	166	31
At this time of year, and after such a series of rain, we	SS	II	5	167	3
and Marianne was all the time busy in observing the	SS	II	5	168	8
time with much concern his continued regard for her sister.	SS	II	5	168	12
to tell her, sat for some time without saying a word.	SS	II	5	172	40
It was not the first time of her feeling the same kind of	SS	II	5	172	40
short time, on the answer it would be most proper to give.	SS	II	5	173	45
might be, and at the same time wished to shield her	SS	II	5	174	45
They were engaged about the end of that time to attend	SS	II	6	175	1
They arrived in due time at the place of destination, and	SS	II	6	175	2
After some time spent in saying little and doing less,	SS	II	6	175	2
During all this time he was evidently struggling for	SS	II	6	177	8
In a short time Elinor saw Willoughby quit the room by the	SS	II	6	178	15
was that she was writing for the last time to Willoughby.	SS	II	7	180	4
till breakfast time, avoiding the sight of every body.	SS	II	7	180	5
it lasted a considerable time, and they were just setting	SS	II	7	181	7
behaviour, and after some time thus spent in joint	SS	II	7	182	12
She paused over it for some time with indignant	SS	II	7	184	15
whom she reached just in time to prevent her from falling	SS	II	7	185	16
I wish you may receive this in time to come here to-night,	SS	II	7	187	38
You had better come earlier another time, because we are	SS	II	7	187	40
bed at all, and for some time was fearful of being	SS	II	7	191	65
were of use; and from that time till Mrs. Jennings	SS	II	7	191	65
You saw I did not all dinner time.	SS	II	8	196	18
Lord! how Charlotte and I did stuff the only time we were	SS	II	8	197	22
"A man who has nothing to do with his own time has no	SS	II	9	204	16
to that end, and her's must be gained by it in time.	SS	II	9	204	19
I cannot remember the time when I did not love Eliza; and	SS	II	9	205	24
difficulty, and for some time it did; but at last the	SS	II	9	205	24
Life could do nothing for her, beyond giving time for a	SS	II	9	207	26
girls of about the same time of life; and for two years I	SS	II	9	208	28
I am sure must at the time have appeared strange to every	SS	II	9	209	30
to be anywhere, at that time, that at Barton, where every	SS	II	10	213	3
It was only the last time they met that he had offered him	SS	II	10	215	9
had for some time ceased to think at all of Mr. Ferrars.	SS	II	10	216	15
tears; but after a short time they would burst out, and	SS	II	10	217	17
About this time, the two Miss Steeles, lately arrived at	SS	II	10	217	19
But I thought, at the time, that you would most likely	SS	II	10	217	21
Dashwood can spare you both for so long a time together!"	SS	II	10	218	34
"Long a time, indeed!" interposed Mrs. Jennings.	SS	II	10	219	35
Elinor lost no time in bringing her business forward, and	SS	II	11	221	6
have a brother and I a sister settling at the same time.	SS	II	11	224	26
sides, and I have not a doubt of its taking place in time.	SS	II	11	224	28
a comfortable one, and I hope will in time be better.	SS	II	11	225	31
for the stocks were at the time so low, that if I had not	SS	II	11	225	33
At her time of life, any thing of an illness destroys the	SS	II	11	227	50
a very short time, by twice calling in Berkeley-Street.	SS	II	12	230	5
to see him for the first time after all that passed, in	SS	II	12	231	10
is nobody here but you, that can feel for me.--	SS	II	12	231	13
her at the same time, that they were done by Miss Dashwood.	SS	II	12	235	28
by Lucy's eyes at the time, but was declared over again	SS	II	13	238	2
and Edward spends half his time with his sister--besides,	SS	II	13	240	15
When that was once done, however, it was time for the	SS	II	13	242	23
in the disposal of her time, and influenced, in a like	SS	II	14	246	2
which about this time befell Mrs. John Dashwood.	SS	II	14	248	6
they might not expect to go out with her a second time?	SS	II	14	248	6
private tuition, at the most critical time of his life?	SS	II	14	251	13
any time, and collect a few friends about me, and be happy.	SS	II	14	251	17
another year; at the same time, however, slyly suspecting	SS	II	14	253	25
to have been always meant to end in two days time.	SS	II	14	254	26
it gave her, for the first time, some share in the	SS	II	14	254	27
by time and address, to do every thing that Lucy wished.	SS	II	14	254	27
give up the whole of her time to her; and contenting	SS	III	1	257	1
wonderful; and giving her time only to form that idea,	SS	III	1	257	2
					3
to them by that time, little dreaming what was going on.	SS	III	1	259	7
Here Mrs. Jennings ceased, and as Elinor had had time	SS	III	1	260	8
No time was to be lost in undeceiving her, in making her	SS	III	1	260	10
But Marianne for some time would give credit to neither.	SS	III	1	261	13
of the engagement, and the length of time it had existed.--	SS	III	1	262	14
of detail; and for some time all that could be done was to	SS	III	1	262	14
to half her sex; and time and habit will teach him to	SS	III	1	263	27
And all this has been going on at a time, when, as you too	SS	III	1	264	29
that he could be all the time secretly engaged to another	SS	III	1	266	38
usual, had prevented her going to them within that time.	SS	III	2	270	3
of Edward, and for some time nothing of anybody who could	SS	III	2	271	5
left her own party for a short time, to join their's.	SS	III	2	271	5
I have had such a time of it!	SS	III	2	272	12
So then he was monstrous happy, and talked on some time	SS	III	2	274	16
so he must go there for a time; and after that, as soon as	SS	III	2	275	22
I have not time to speak to Mrs. Jennings about it myself,	SS	III	2	275	25
to come and stay with her for as long a time as she likes.	SS	III	2	275	25
Such was her parting concern; for after this, she had time	SS	III	2	276	26
powers of reflection some time, though she had learnt very	SS	III	2	276	26
determined on, and the time of its taking place remained	SS	III	2	276	26
but however, at the same time, gratefully acknowledge many	SS	III	2	277	30
which would fix the time of her returning to that dear	SS	III	3	280	6
might now be at home in little more than three weeks' time.	SS	III	3	280	6
acquainted in a short time, but I have seen enough of him	SS	III	3	282	19
But at the same time, she could not help thinking that no	SS	III	3	283	20
It is of importance that no time should be lost with him,	SS	III	4	286	15
manner; though at the same time, I should have been	SS	III	4	288	27
will most likely be some time--it is not probable that I	SS	III	4	288	27
but she was at the same time so unwilling to appear as the	SS	III	4	290	36
For a short time he sat deep in thought, after Elinor had	SS	III	4	290	36
					37
even conjecture as to the time, or the preparation	SS	III	4	291	50
the excess of it by the time he reached Bartlett's	SS	III	5	293	1
So far was she, at the same time, from any backwardness to	SS	III	5	293	2
and as since that time no notice had been taken by them of	SS	III	5	293	3
it must nearly have escaped her memory by this time."	SS	III	5	296	21
Elinor said no more, and John was also for a short time	SS	III	5	297	30
which she had for the last time enjoyed those hopes, and	SS	III	6	301	4
She returned just in time to join the others as they	SS	III	6	303	10
with no traits at all unusual in his sex and time of life.	SS	III	6	304	15
Marianne got up the next morning at her usual time; to	SS	III	7	307	1
away, in about seven days from the time of their arrival.	SS	III	7	309	6
Two days passed away from the time of Mr. Palmer's	SS	III	7	309	7
fixing on the time when Marianne would be able to travel.	SS	III	7	310	8
it, lasted a considerable time; and anxious to observe the	SS	III	7	310	9
It was not time for hesitation.	SS	III	7	311	15
exactness the time in which she might look for his return.	SS	III	7	312	17
which for some time kept her silent, even to her friend--	SS	III	7	314	22
The time was now drawing on, when Colonel Brandon might be	SS	III	7	315	26
the progress of time which yet kept them in ignorance!	SS	III	7	315	26
sir"--said Elinor impatiently--"I have no time to spare."	SS	III	8	317	8
For once, Miss Dashwood--it will be the last time, perhaps-	SS	III	8	318	15
since that time, procured me a nuncheon at Marlborough."	SS	III	8	318	20
than to pass my time pleasantly while I was obliged to	SS	III	8	319	29
it had been for some time my intention to re-establish my	SS	III	8	320	32
softened, "believe yourself at one time attached to her."	SS	III	8	321	33
I do not mean to justify myself, but at the same time	SS	III	8	322	36
a very short time, had the power of creating any return.	SS	III	8	322	36
of my time that I had bestowed on her, in my present visit.	SS	III	8	323	40
I was in town the whole time,) what I felt is--in the	SS	III	8	325	50
I say awakened, because time and London, business and	SS	III	8	326	53
notice; and for some time I was even determined not to	SS	III	8	326	53
was--for the first time these two months--he spoke to me.--	SS	III	8	330	69
Elinor, for some time after he left her, for some time	SS	III	9	333	1
Short was the time, however, in which that fear could	SS	III	9	333	3
just in time to receive and support her as she entered it.	SS	III	9	333	3
Yet after a time I did say, for at first I was quite	SS	III	9	337	18
Time, a very little time, I tell him, will do everything;--	SS	III	9	337	18
it under a great length of time, and even supposing her	SS	III	9	338	20
at the same time, there is something much more pleasing in	SS	III	9	338	20
"His fortune too!--for at my time of life you know,	SS	III	9	339	26
than six, and from that time till dinner I shall divide	SS	III	10	343	9
least for a time this fair prospect of busy tranquillity.	SS	III	10	343	10
my own health, as I had felt even at the time to be wrong.	SS	III	10	345	28
my desire to live, to have time for atonement to my God,	SS	III	10	345	28
Elinor, who had now been for some time reflecting on the	SS	III	10	347	32
she had been for some time previously sitting--her rising	SS	III	11	349	3
could safely trust to the effect of time upon her health.	SS	III	11	352	19
By that time, Marianne was rather better, and her mother	SS	III	11	353	25

they was they had not time to come on and see you, but SS III 11 354 27
expressly softened at the time, to spare her from an SS III 11 355 46
what I thought, at the time, a most unconquerable SS III 13 362 5
any object to engage my time and keep me at a distance SS III 13 362 5
the greatest part of my time there from eighteen to SS III 13 362 5
the time an unnatural, or an inexcusable piece of folly." SS III 13 362 5
brother's affairs might have done, if applied to in time. SS III 13 364 11
he had been for some time, he believed, half stupified SS III 13 364 13
in your favour; that your own family might in time relent. SS III 13 367 23
for having spent so much time with them at Norland, when SS III 13 368 25
of having, for the first time since her living at Barton, SS III 13 369 34
otherwise have waited the effect of time and judgment. SS III 13 370 36
and after waiting some time for their completion, after SS III 14 374 6
with no other sacrifice than that of time and conscience. SS III 14 376 11
would convince her in time, another visit, another SS III 14 376 11
with, procured her in time the haughty notice which SS III 14 377 11
and sisters spent much more than half their time with her. SS III 14 378 13
her whole heart became, in time, as much devoted to her SS III 14 379 17
him & given up a great deal of time to no purpose as yet.-- W 317 2
away the other day she said it should be the last time.- W 317 2
I considered her engagement to Mrs Shaw just at that time W 317 2
This is the second time within this twelvemonth that she W 319 2
him; & I should be with you by the time the dancing began." W 319 2
spare him, & just now it is a sickly time at Guilford--" W 321 2
young ladies were carefully recommended to lose no time.-- W 323 3
I suppose she is grown somewhat older since that time.-- W 325 4
her own perturbation in time to see a blush on Miss E.'s W 326 5
are determined to be in good time I see, as usual.-- W 327 7
glances; & after a time Ld Osborne himself came & under W 331 11
turned away her eyes in time, to avoid seeming to hear her W 332 11
Away we went--Ld Osborne after him--& Emma lost no time in W 333 13
solicited without loss of time--& Emma, however she might W 334 13
be more fortunate another time--& seeming unwilling to W 334 13
it is a shameful length of time since I was at Stanton.-- W 335 13
had been fixed the whole time at the same table in the W 336 14
no time to be lost on Emma's side in preparing for it.-- W 340 19
ourselves, continued eliz: & then we shall lose no time.-- W 341 19
the same time without any theatrical grimace or violence.-- W 343 20
more to say for some time, & could only gratify his eye by W 345 21
a woman; it was the first time that he had ever felt what W 346 21
Ld Osborne's parting Compts took some time, his W 347 21
for such a length of time as must do away all natural W 352 26
It was an unusual sound in Stanton at any time of the day, W 354 28
really been gone a month! 'tis amazing how time flies.--" W 356 28
dreaded the meeting, & at the same time longed for it.-- W 356 28
We got here so late, that I had not time even to put a W 357 28
I have had some pleasant hours at speculation in my time-- W 358 28
can possibly get here in time--but I shoot with Ld Osborne,- W 360 28
were alone for a short time the next morng; & had W 360 29
At our time of life, it is not so pleasant I can tell you, PP I 2 8 26
and during part of that time, Mr. Darcy had been standing PP I 3 11 7
enjoy her smiles, for you are wasting your time with me." PP I 3 12 13
With a book he was regardless of time; and on the present PP I 3 12 15
the only creature in the room that he asked a second time. PP I 3 12 16
much flattered by his asking me to dance a second time. PP I 4 14 4
He was at the same time haughty, reserved, and fastidious, PP I 4 16 14
"Another time, Lizzy," said her mother, "I would not dance PP I 5 20 16
I have suspected it some time, but I am now convinced." PP I 7 29 6
I remember the time when I liked a red coat myself very PP I 7 29 12
their mirth for some time at the expense of their dear PP I 8 37 20
for the short time she could stay below with a book. PP I 8 37 21
spoken of for the first time, without being informed that PP I 8 39 45
by a housemaid, and some time afterwards from the two PP I 9 41 1
who arrived about the same time, think it at all advisable. PP I 9 41 2
time most likely Captain Carter would be at Meryton again. PP I 9 45 38
"My ideas flow so rapidly that I have not time to express PP I 10 48 23
though they were at one time left by themselves for half PP I 12 60 4
After amusing himself some time with their curiosity, he PP I 13 61 6
the breach; but for some time I was kept back by my own PP I 13 62 12
Mr. Collins was punctual to his time, and was received PP I 13 64 21
seeing them all in due time well disposed of in marriage. PP I 13 64 21
withdrawn, he thought it time to have some conversation PP I 14 66 1
"They arise chiefly from what is passing at the time, and PP I 14 68 11
maintaining at the same time the most resolute composure PP I 14 68 12
his cousins, their time passed till they entered Meryton. PP I 15 72 7
readiness at the same time perfectly correct and PP I 15 72 8
and I should at this time have been in possession of a PP I 16 79 23
"Some time or other he will be--but it shall not be by me. PP I 16 80 29
Elizabeth was again deep in thought, and after a time PP I 16 80 36
devoted all his time to the care of the Pemberley property. PP I 16 81 37
home; but there was not time for her even to mention his PP I 16 84 59
a pitiable state at this time, for from the day of the PP I 17 88 15
They stood for some time without speaking a word; and she PP I 18 91 8
she addressed him a second time with "it is your turn to PP I 18 91 8
9

I am most thankful that the discovery is made in time for PP I 18 97 57
humility of behaviour is at the same time maintained. PP I 18 97 60
61

him time to speak, replied with an air of distant civility. PP I 18 98 61
it was so pleasant at her time of life to be able to PP I 18 99 63
Let the other young ladies have time to exhibit." PP I 18 101 69
devoting too much of our time to music, for there are PP I 18 101 71
He must write his own sermons; and the time that remains PP I 18 101 71
was gone, which gave them time to see how heartily they PP I 18 102 75
at any time, without the ceremony of a formal invitation. PP I 18 103 76
whither he was obliged to go the next day for a short time. PP I 18 103 76
Having resolved to do it without loss of time, as his PP I 19 104 1
Before Elizabeth had time for any thing but a blush of PP I 19 104 3
4

Let me do it without farther loss of time. PP I 19 106 12
the refusal is repeated a second or even a third time. PP I 19 107 13
their happiness on the chance of being asked a second time. PP I 19 107 14
She would not give him time to reply, but hurrying PP I 20 111 6
Charlotte had hardly time to answer, before they were PP I 20 113 26
"I found," said he, "as the time drew near, that I had PP I 21 115 4
The whole party have left Netherfield by this time, and PP I 21 116 7
be so, and at the same time convinced that when Charles PP I 21 117 10
11

it amply repaid her for the little sacrifice of her time. PP I 22 121 1
In as short a time as Mr. Collins's long speeches would PP I 22 121 2
She had gained her point, and had time to consider of it. PP I 22 122 3
and he was at the same time exercising great self-denial, PP I 22 123 3
But when you have had time to think it all over, I hope PP I 22 125 17
It was a long time before she became at all reconciled to PP I 22 125 18
to Longbourn only in time to make an apology for his PP I 23 129 15
regret at not having had time to pay his respects to his PP II 1 133 1
A little time therefore.-- PP II 1 134 7
Elizabeth could not oppose such a wish; and from this time PP II 1 137 25
at the time, she had the same story to repeat every day. PP II 1 137 26
Now is your time. PP II 1 138 27
by this time, had not it been for her own perverseness. PP II 2 140 4
However, your coming just at this time is the greatest of PP II 2 140 4
Every time they met, it was more decided and remarkable. PP II 2 141 9
in her thoughts at the time, than as she hoped that, by PP II 2 142 17
time in that very part of Derbyshire, to which he belonged. PP II 2 142 19
"I am not likely to leave Kent for some time. PP II 3 146 16
and not a note, not a line, did I receive in the mean time. PP II 3 148 26
Mrs. Gardiner about this time reminded Elizabeth of her PP II 3 149 28
and, in short, as the time drew near, she would have been PP II 4 151 1
in time, and the plan became perfect as plan could be. PP II 4 151 1
"A man in distressed circumstances has not time for all PP II 4 153 15
he welcomed them a second time with ostentatious formality PP II 5 155 3
and the latter said not a word to her all dinner time. PP II 6 163 14
"Oh! then--some time or other we shall be happy to hear PP II 6 164 18
for the chief of the time between breakfast and dinner was PP II 7 168 1
the whole she spent her time comfortably enough; there PP II 7 169 5
was so fine for the time of year, that she had often great PP II 7 169 5
Elizabeth had scarcely time to disclaim all right to the PP II 7 170 9
Collins, sat for some time without speaking to any body. PP II 7 171 10
the time, but Mr. Darcy they had only seen at church. PP II 8 172 1
The first time of my ever seeing him in Hertfordshire, you PP II 8 175 18
"I had not at that time the honour of knowing any lady in PP II 8 175 19
You have employed your time much better. PP II 8 176 26
that he may spend very little of his time there in future. PP II 9 177 8
He has many friends, and he is at a time of life when PP II 9 178 8
to do, which was the more probable from the time of year. PP II 9 180 28
How it could occur a second time therefore was very odd!-- PP II 10 182 1
Forgive me for having taken up so much of your time, and PP II 11 193 29
He had by that time reached it also, and holding out a PP II 12 195 2
walking in the grove some time in the hope of meeting you. PP II 12 195 2
He spoke of it as a certain event, of which the time alone PP II 12 197 5
alike sensible that no time was to be lost in detaching PP II 12 198 5
At one time she had almost resolved on applying to him, PP II 13 206 4
it, she might by this time have been presented to her, as PP II 14 210 2
our power to prevent your spending your time unpleasantly." PP II 15 215 2
to hear that you have passed your time not disagreeably. PP II 15 215 3
4

and must, at the same time, so highly gratify whatever of PP II 15 217 17
answers were at the same time so vague and equivocal, that PP II 16 223 26
It was some time, however, before a smile could be PP II 17 225 11
Elizabeth was now to see Mr. Wickham for the last time. PP II 18 233 25
and her preference secured at any time by their renewal. PP II 18 233 25
to the manner in which her time had passed at Hunsford, PP II 18 233 26
and, though Kitty might in time regain her natural degree PP II 19 237 3
The time fixed for the beginning of their northern tour PP II 19 238 7
lakes; and still thought there might have been time enough. PP II 19 239 8
points, and drove for some time through a beautiful wood, PP III 1 245 2
It was drawn at the same time as the other--about eight PP III 1 247 11
say he may spend half his time here; and Miss Darcy is PP III 1 248 25
them, that it had been taken in his father's life time. PP III 1 250 47
his enquiries as to the time of her having left Longbourn, PP III 1 252 52
but is was some time before Elizabeth was sensible of any PP III 1 253 55
them again, after some time, in a descent among hanging PP III 1 253 57
offering at the same time to supply him with fishing PP III 1 255 60
After walking some time in this way, the two ladies in PP III 1 255 61
Her thoughts were instantly driven back to the time when PP III 1 256 62
At such a time, much might have been said, and silence was PP III 1 257 65
Yet time and her aunt moved slowly--and her patience and PP III 1 257 66
on her; and she had barely time to express her PP III 2 261 5
that it "was a very long time since he had had the PP III 2 262 8
admitted, had for some time ceased to be repugnant to her PP III 2 265 16
He had been some time with Mr. Gardiner, who, with two or PP III 3 268 8
in time, though not enough to be able to speak any more. PP III 3 270 11
and I believe you thought her rather pretty at one time." PP III 3 271 17
Without allowing herself time for consideration, and PP III 4 274 4
"By this time, my dearest sister, you have received my PP III 4 274 5
though not confined for time, my head is so bewildered PP III 4 274 5
losing a moment of the time so precious; but as she PP III 4 276 6
in a shorter space of time than she could have supposed, PP III 4 281 29
She has been allowed to dispose of her time in the most PP III 5 283 10
was to leave Meryton in a week or fortnight's time. PP III 5 285 16
But to be guarded at such a time, is very difficult. PP III 5 292 64
but at such a time, they had hoped for exertion. PP III 6 294 1
more especially as the time was now come, when if they had PP III 6 295 4
from a cause which no time can remove. no arguments shall PP III 6 296 11
though, at the same time, for the consolation of yourself PP III 6 297 11
to London, at the same time that Mr. Bennet came from it. PP III 6 298 15
Elizabeth, who was by this time tolerably well acquainted PP III 6 298 17
some time before his daughters had courage to speak of it. PP III 6 299 18
Away ran the girls, too eager to get in to have time for PP III 7 301 4
I shall send this by express, that no time may be lost in PP III 7 302 14
she then intreat him to lose no more time before he wrote. PP III 7 303 19
By this time she is actually with them! PP III 7 305 36
as may in time make their past imprudence forgotten." PP III 7 305 37
know, and it is the first time we have ever had any thing PP III 7 306 47
In a short time, I shall have a daughter married. PP III 7 306 47
depended; but at the same time, there was no one, whose PP III 8 311 12
and yet there have been things enough happened in the time. PP III 9 316 7
It was not to be supposed that time would give Lydia that PP III 9 317 10
of them; and in the mean time, she went after dinner to PP III 9 317 10
she made the most of the time, by visiting about with her PP III 9 318 18
And there was my aunt, all the time I was dressing, PP III 9 319 24
aunt were horrid unpleasant all the time I was with them. PP III 9 319 25
But luckily, he came back again in ten minutes time, and PP III 9 319 25
to our family, should have been amongst you at such a time. PP III 9 320 33
Mrs. Younge, who was some time ago governess to Miss Darcy, PP III 10 322 2
She was sure they should be married some time or other, PP III 10 323 2
They battled it together for a long time, which was more PP III 10 324 2
probable, and at the same time dreaded to be just, from PP III 10 326 3
particular, to take him there at this time of year." PP III 10 328 17
"I did hear, too, that there was a time, when sermon- PP III 10 329 31
But you know married women have never much time for PP III 11 330 6
neighbours every time they go away, and come back again." PP III 11 332 25
for the first time after receiving his explanatory letter. PP III 11 334 36
time, that his affection and wishes must still be unshaken. PP III 11 334 37
"It is a long time, Mr. Bingley, since you went away," PP III 11 336 47
mother, "but at the same time, Mr. Bingley, it is very PP III 11 336 51
and engaged to dine at Longbourn in a few days time. PP III 11 338 57
Her resolution was for a short time involuntarily kept by PP III 12 339 5
of their punctuality as sportsmen, were in very good time. PP III 12 340 11
His behaviour to her sister was such, during dinner time, PP III 12 340 13
for London, but was to return home in ten days time. PP III 13 344 1
"Next time you call," said she, "I hope we shall be more PP III 13 344 2
He should be particularly happy at any time, &c. &c.; and PP III 13 344 3
He came, and in such very good time, that the ladies were PP III 13 344 6
a considerable time, without making any impression on them. PP III 13 345 11
unless Mr. Darcy returned within the stated time. PP III 13 345 20
Bingley, from this time, was of course a daily visitor at PP III 13 349 43
Elizabeth had now but little time for conversation with PP III 13 349 44
good luck, I may meet with another Mr. Collins in time." PP III 13 350 54
of Jane, was enough, at a time when the expectation of one PP III 15 360 1
had looked forward to as possible, at some future time. PP III 15 360 1
before Mrs. Bennet had time to tell him of their having PP III 16 365 1
never spare time, but the remaining five set off together. PP III 16 365 1
to you at the time, had merited the severest reproof. PP III 16 367 12
me;--though it was some time, I confess, before I was PP III 16 367 14
on examining their watches, that it was time to be at home. PP III 16 370 35
I was obliged to confess one thing, which for a time, and PP III 16 371 45
This is the last time I shall ever remember it myself." PP III 17 373 7
after laughing at her some time, allowed her at last to go- PP III 17 377 40
and the comfort of ease and familiarity would come in time. PP III 17 377 41
"I am more likely to want time than courage, Elizabeth. PP III 18 382 18
with delight to the time when they should be removed from PP III 18 384 27
spent the chief of time with her two elder sisters. PP III 19 385 4
that for some time all intercourse was at an end. PP III 19 388 12
reach; and before he had time to devise any other method MP I 1 3 1
or Edmund for the first time seven years hence, and I dare MP I 1 7 6
But breed her up with them from this time, and suppose her MP I 1 7 6
up every moment of her time, and the very mention of such MP I 1 9 10
Fanny Price was at this time just ten years old, and MP I 2 12 2
It required a longer time, however, than Mrs. Norris was MP I 2 14 6
He continued with her the whole time of her writing, to MP I 2 16 20
I cannot remember the time when I did not know a great MP I 2 18 25
She had not time for such cares. MP I 2 19 31

Context	Work	Vol	Ch	Page	Para
From about the time of her entering the family, Lady	MP	I	2	20	33
The time was now come when Sir Thomas expected his sister-	MP	I	3	24	7
to his wife; and the first time of the subject's occurring	MP	I	3	24	7
I do with a girl at her time of life, a girl of fifteen!	MP	I	3	28	42
which at the same time that it was advantageous and	MP	I	3	30	57
every thing at Mansfield went on for some time as usual.	MP	I	3	31	58
a bad character in her time, but this was a way of going	MP	I	3	31	59
of others at their present most interesting time of life.	MP	I	3	32	62
Tome Bertram had of late spent so little of his time at	MP	I	4	34	1
grey poney, and for some time she was in danger of feeling	MP	I	4	35	7
her cousins' horses at any time when they did not want	MP	I	4	35	7
of any real pleasure, that time of course never came.	MP	I	4	35	7
Edmund was absent at this time, or the evil would have	MP	I	4	36	7
expense of his stable at a time when a large part of his	MP	I	4	36	7
too much, and at the same time procure for Fanny the	MP	I	4	37	8
Mrs. Grant having by this time run through the usual	MP	I	4	41	15
They sometimes pass in such very little time from reserve	MP	I	5	49	32
I felt that I must be the jest of the room at the time--	MP	I	5	50	35
To be neglected before one's time, must be very vexatious.	MP	I	5	51	41
Mansfield, for the first time since the Crawfords' arrival.	MP	I	6	52	1
every improvement in time which his heart can desire."	MP	I	6	53	5
"The house was built in Elizabeth's time, and is a large,	MP	I	6	56	26
The hire of a cart at any time, might not be so easy as	MP	I	6	58	38
"I shall understand all your ways in time; but coming down	MP	I	6	58	39
next day, after thinking some time on the subject himself.	MP	I	7	63	1
with it in excellent time, before either Fanny or the	MP	I	7	66	15
"For there is more than time enough for my cousin to ride	MP	I	7	68	19
have her for a longer time--for a whole morning in short.	MP	I	7	69	28
time, and doubly enjoyed again in the evening discussion.	MP	I	7	70	30
ever since she came back from your house the second time."	MP	I	7	72	46
to Mr. Green at that very time about your mother's	MP	I	7	73	53
Having been out some time, and taken a different route to	MP	I	8	75	2
She has time enough before her; and her going now is quite	MP	I	8	76	5
his appearance just in time to learn what had been settled	MP	I	8	77	7
her pleasure at any time, but her opposition to Edmund now	MP	I	8	79	23
was fitted up as you see it, in James the Second's time.	MP	I	9	86	9
own way--to choose their own time and manner of devotion.	MP	I	9	87	15
restraint, the length of time--altogether it is a	MP	I	9	87	15
have foreseen that the time would ever come when men and	MP	I	9	87	15
house of Rushworth did many a time repair to this chapel?	MP	I	9	87	15
had not interposed with a doubt of there being time enough.	MP	I	9	89	31
we shall not have time for what is to be done out of doors.	MP	I	9	89	31
No objection was made, but for some time there seemed no	MP	I	9	90	36
and when after a little time the others began to form into	MP	I	9	90	36
and were drawing a second time to the door in the middle	MP	I	9	91	37
They all felt the refreshment of it, and for some time	MP	I	9	91	38
sweet wood; but the next time we come to a seat, if it is	MP	I	9	94	57
for the first time, made him a little forgetful of Fanny.	MP	I	9	94	59
distance, or reckon time, with feminine lawlessness.	MP	I	9	94	61
spare time to tell us his errand, and where you all were."	MP	I	10	101	30
By the time I get to the knoll, they may be gone some	MP	I	10	101	35
judges of time, and every half a minute seems like five."	MP	I	10	102	46
and "wished he had had the key about him at the time."	MP	I	10	102	47
It was evident that they had been spending their time	MP	I	10	103	49
conversing about all that time; and the result of the	MP	I	10	103	49
there to lounge away the time as they could with sofas,	MP	I	10	104	51
of hours, and from the time of their sitting down to table,	MP	I	10	104	52
this present time the guest of my own brother, Dr. Grant.	MP	I	11	111	28
he would have had less time and obligation--where he might	MP	I	11	111	30
and Miss Crawford had only time to say in a pleasant	MP	I	11	112	33
to be in time, she did not believe she could accept him.	MP	I	12	114	2
returned to it at the time appointed, and was welcomed	MP	I	12	115	3
the second time--"we shall see some happy faces again now."	MP	I	12	117	12
Listening and wondering were all suspended for a time, for	MP	I	12	118	22
well spare time to sit down herself, because of her fringe.	MP	I	12	119	23
a choice, and at the same time addressed in such a way as	MP	I	12	120	26
not have died at a worse time; and it is impossible to	MP	I	13	122	4
"There would not be time, and other difficulties would	MP	I	13	124	9
think our time very well spent, and so I am sure will he.--	MP	I	13	126	18
How many a time have we mourned over the dead body of	MP	I	13	126	25
"We are wasting time most abominably.	MP	I	14	131	5
For about the fifth time he then proposed the heir at law,	MP	I	14	131	6
When this had lasted some time, the division of the party	MP	I	14	136	22
To be sure Julia is dressed by this time."	MP	I	15	141	16
too distressing at the time, to make the remembrance when	MP	I	16	150	1
Miss Crawford had protected her only for the time; and if	MP	I	16	150	1
she had now for some time been almost equally mistress.	MP	I	16	150	1
The room had then become useless, and for some time was	MP	I	16	151	1
and spent more of her time there; and having nothing to	MP	I	16	151	1
mention--her taste and her time were considered--her	MP	I	17	160	6
busy with his play to have time for more than one	MP	I	17	160	9
we will send him off, though he is Henry, for a time."	MP	I	17	162	18
and other claims on her time and attention, she was as far	MP	I	18	166	5
not one of those who can talk and work at the same time.--	MP	I	18	167	9
together for the first time;--the third act would bring a	MP	I	18	167	12
at once of having her time to herself, and of avoiding the	MP	I	18	168	14
glad to remain behind and gain a little breathing time.	MP	II	1	176	4
her pleasure; her own time had been irreproachably spent	MP	II	1	179	9
"It is time to think of our visitors," said Maria, still	MP	II	1	182	19
To the theatre he went, and reached it just in time to	MP	II	1	182	22
he had scarcely more than time to feel astonished at all	MP	II	1	182	22
There was little time, however, for the indulgence of any	MP	II	1	183	23
But at your time of life to feel all this, is a most	MP	II	1	186	34
a party, and at such a time, as strongly as his son had	MP	II	2	187	2
To be a second time disappointed in the same way was an	MP	II	2	191	10
should now lose no time in declaring himself, and she was	MP	II	2	191	11
to Mansfield, at any time required by the party; he was	MP	II	2	192	11
"It is about my uncle's usual time."	MP	II	2	193	14
He was gone--he had touched her hand for the last time, he	MP	II	2	193	18
at this time, for any engagements but in one quarter.	MP	II	3	196	1
and trust to his seeing as much beauty of mind in time."	MP	II	3	197	6
of way, allowing for the difference of the time of year."	MP	II	3	199	14
were over, it would be time for the wider range of London.	MP	II	3	203	31
them exceedingly glad to be with the other at such a time.	MP	II	3	203	32
at Mansfield, a chasm which required some time to fill up.	MP	II	3	204	33
unusually mild for the time of year; and venturing	MP	II	4	208	11
together one day: "every time I come into this shrubbery I	MP	II	4	208	12
How wonderful, how very wonderful the operations of time,	MP	II	4	208	12
at this time of year, by being up before they can begin?"	MP	II	4	211	24
It was the first time of his seeing them together since	MP	II	4	211	25
blowing on you the whole time--for here are some of my	MP	II	4	212	31
it is for a person at your time of life, with such limited	MP	II	4	213	40
You have not much time before you; and your relations are	MP	II	4	213	40
Edmund began at the same time to recollect, that his	MP	II	4	214	46
day; and Fanny had barely time for an unpleasant feeling	MP	II	4	215	47
that this should be the first time of its being paid.	MP	II	5	218	18
said, "Fanny, at what time would you have the carriage	MP	II	5	221	35
"My niece walk to a dinner engagement at this time of the	MP	II	5	221	37
as good time as his own correctly punctual habits required.	MP	II	5	222	41
There was no occasion, there was no time for Fanny to say	MP	II	5	223	47
By the time he is four or five-and-twenty he will have	MP	II	5	226	63
fixed on him the whole time--as I shall do--not to lose a	MP	II	5	227	65
of fruition; it was some time even before her happiness	MP	II	6	233	17
That time however, did gradually come, forwarded by an	MP	II	6	234	17
the influence of time and absence only in its increase.	MP	II	6	235	18
was long enough for the time his measured manner needed;	MP	II	7	240	10
"Bertram," said Crawford some time afterwards, taking the	MP	II	7	240	13
due time in the very place which I had a curiosity to see.	MP	II	7	241	13
William, you are quite out of luck; but the next time you	MP	II	7	245	32
he could come to at any time, a little homestall at his	MP	II	7	246	37
It was time to have done with cards if sermons prevailed,	MP	II	7	248	48
admirals have all experienced, more or less, in their time.	MP	II	7	249	53
a time when you will have nothing of that sort to endure.	MP	II	7	249	53
We used to jump about together many a time, did not we?	MP	II	7	250	59
Fanny look distressed) it must be at some other time.	MP	II	7	250	61
elegance, and in admirable time, but in fact he could not	MP	II	7	251	62
A ball at such a time!	MP	II	8	253	4
it be allowable at such a time, in the midst of all the	MP	II	8	254	8
Edmund was at this time particularly full of cares; his	MP	II	8	254	10
within a very short time, as soon as the variety of	MP	II	8	255	10
that it should be here in time for to-morrow: but your	MP	II	9	262	9
It was some time before she could get his attention to her	MP	II	9	262	11
she was able, in due time, to go down and resume her usual	MP	II	9	265	20
it is to be the last time that she ever will dance with me.	MP	II	9	268	29
The time may come-----"	MP	II	9	269	36
The time will never come.	MP	II	9	269	38
No such time as you allude to will ever come.	MP	II	9	269	38
How many a time have we talked over her little errors!	MP	II	9	270	38
terrible; but at the same time there was a pointedness in	MP	II	10	274	8
herself for the first time near Miss Crawford, whose eyes	MP	II	10	274	9
courteous words as she had time for, amid so much	MP	II	10	277	16
The first time he ever denied me his confidence!	MP	II	10	277	17
From that time, Mr. Crawford sat down likewise.	MP	II	10	279	22
It will be the last time you know, the last morning."	MP	II	10	280	28
Your brother will find my ideas of time and his own very	MP	II	10	280	31
which would otherwise have taken place about this time.	MP	II	11	284	10
as it did at the very time of her brother's going away, of	MP	II	11	286	15
But at any rate his staying away at a time, when,	MP	II	11	287	17
"He did not, the only time he went to see Mr. Owen before."	MP	II	11	287	21
I do not like the idea of leaving Mrs. Grant now the time	MP	II	11	289	30
have been all this time?" he had only to say that he had	MP	II	12	291	1
"You must give us more than half your time," said he; "I	MP	II	12	295	23
were less accordant; time would discover it to him; but	MP	II	12	296	29
object would have detained me half the time from Mansfield.	MP	II	13	299	5
It was no time for further assurances or entreaty, though	MP	II	13	302	9
inconvenience just at that time, to give him something	MP	II	13	304	19
had there been time for scruples and fears as to style,	MP	II	13	307	30 31
She sat some time in a good deal of agitation, listening,	MP	III	1	311	3
"I am not cold, sir--I never sit here long at this time of	MP	III	1	312	7
of you, by failing at any time to treat your aunt Norris	MP	III	1	313	12
acquaintance of to-day, you have now known him some time.	MP	III	1	316	27
"you must have been some time aware of a particularity in	MP	III	1	316	29
wishing even for a little time to consider of it--a little	MP	III	1	318	39
of it--a little more time for cool consideration, and for	MP	III	1	318	39
of marriage at any time, which might carry with it only	MP	III	1	319	39
Fanny was by this time crying so bitterly, that angry as	MP	III	1	319	40
such a state, as a little time, a little pressing, a	MP	III	1	320	44
But there is no time fixed, perhaps to-morrow, or whenever	MP	III	1	321	48
A fire! it seemed too much; just at that time to be giving	MP	III	1	322	51
I could very ill spare the time, and you might have saved	MP	III	1	323	54
now, or at any other time, to what degree he thought well	MP	III	1	323	57
be able in time to make those feelings what he wished.	MP	III	2	326	1
her conduct at this very time, by speaking the	MP	III	2	326	3
time, that her not loving him now was scarcely regretted.	MP	III	2	327	4
She must do her duty, and trust that time might make her	MP	III	2	331	17
discouragement from herself would put an end to it in time.	MP	III	2	331	18
How much time she might, in her own fancy, allot for its	MP	III	2	331	18
Sir Thomas, indeed, was, by this time, not very far from	MP	III	2	332	19
next time pug has a litter you shall have a puppy."	MP	III	2	333	28
He had not given her time to attach herself.	MP	III	3	335	6
it a second time, by any word, or look, or movement.	MP	III	3	335	6
"We have not been so silent all the time," replied his	MP	III	3	336	9
a theatre, some time or other, at your house in Norfolk.	MP	III	3	338	19
My conduct shall speak for me--absence, distance, time	MP	III	3	343	41
of her being at that very time walking alone in the	MP	III	4	345	5
time to attach yourself; but I think you perfectly right.	MP	III	4	347	16
This, we know, must be a work of time.	MP	III	4	347	18
quit Mansfield will for a time be arming you against him.	MP	III	4	348	21
I must hope, however, that time proving him (as I firmly	MP	III	4	348	21
I have not thought well of him from the time of the play.	MP	III	4	349	25
which--in short, at the time of the play, I received an	MP	III	4	349	25
The time of the play, is a time which I hate to recollect.	MP	III	4	349	26
did she say--did she speak--was she there all the time?"	MP	III	4	352	43
the hope of being loved in time, and of having his	MP	III	4	354	46
"You spent your time pleasantly there."	MP	III	4	355	51
on Crawford's side, and time must be given to make the	MP	III	5	356	1
very long allowances of time and habit were necessary for	MP	III	5	356	3
I suppose no time can ever wear out the impression I have	MP	III	5	358	9
of this being the last time of seeing you; for I do not	MP	III	5	359	9
better time for the visit--but now I cannot put her off.	MP	III	5	359	12
Oh! that I could transport you for a short time into our	MP	III	5	360	16
yet it was a most desirable match for Janet at the time.	MP	III	5	361	16
I had my doubts at the time about her being right, for he	MP	III	5	361	16
was not half afraid at the time, of its being so; for	MP	III	5	362	21
sensible of it some little time, perhaps two or three	MP	III	5	362	21
Henry Crawford came and sat some time with them; and her	MP	III	5	365	35
which at the time she had felt, or fancied an evil.	MP	III	6	366	1
to Portsmouth, and spend a little time with her own family.	MP	III	6	368	9
not be done at a better time; and he had no doubt of it	MP	III	6	368	9
to give up all her own time to her as requested) and in	MP	III	6	371	15
By the time Mrs. Price's answer arrived, there remained	MP	III	6	372	21
He had intended, about this time, to be going to London,	MP	III	6	373	25
feeling it to be the last time in which Miss Crawford's	MP	III	6	373	26
which the progress of time and variation of circumstances	MP	III	6	374	27
left behind, and by the time their first stage was ended,	MP	III	7	375	1
the chaise door himself, called out, "you are just in time.	MP	III	7	377	7
six, and hoped you would be here in time to go with him."	MP	III	7	377	7
commence his career of seamanship in her at this very time.	MP	III	7	377	8
in time; for she may have her orders to-morrow, perhaps.	MP	III	7	378	10
is time to dress a steak, and we have no butcher at hand.	MP	III	7	379	14
By g--, you are just in time.	MP	III	7	380	20
Old Scholey ran in at breakfast time, to say she had	MP	III	7	380	20
After sitting some time longer, a candle was obtained; but,	MP	III	7	381	24
than their being for the time thoroughly fagged, which	MP	III	7	383	31
at the same time to carry back his neighbour's newspaper.	MP	III	7	384	36
walked about the room some time looking for a shirt sleeve,	MP	III	7	385	37
of getting Sam ready in time, was at leisure to think of	MP	III	7	385	37
Mansfield, had for a short time been quite afflicted.--	MP	III	7	386	40
eyes, meaning to screen it at the same time from Susan's.	MP	III	7	386	40
I must hide it another time, Betsey.	MP	III	7	386	44
Her heart and her time were already quite full; she had	MP	III	8	389	4
These shared her heart; her time was given chiefly to her	MP	III	8	389	4
means of address which she had spirits or time to attempt.	MP	III	8	391	8
sake of being travelling at the same time that you were.	MP	III	9	393	1
not it time for you to write to Fanny?' to spur me on.	MP	III	9	393	1
at home, that it took some time to determine that it would	MP	III	9	396	7
and especially at this time, hoped it might be useful in	MP	III	9	398	10
One morning about this time, Fanny having now been nearly	MP	III	10	399	2
eyes away, and giving her time to recover, while he	MP	III	10	399	5
and propriety, at the same time with a degree of	MP	III	10	399	5
By the time he had given all this information, it was not	MP	III	10	400	8
love, but had had no time for writing; that he thought	MP	III	10	400	8
the words, "then by this time it is all settled," passed	MP	III	10	401	9
and her daughters, to take their walk without loss of time.	MP	III	10	401	10
seldom, with her large family, find time for a walk.--	MP	III	10	401	10
than himself; and after a time the two officers seemed	MP	III	10	403	15
of; there had been some time, and every thing there was	MP	III	10	404	15
Norfolk at all, at this unusual time of year, was given.	MP	III	10	404	15
of his time there--always there, or in the neighbourhood.	MP	III	10	405	18
that they wished, or had time for, the others were ready	MP	III	10	406	21
with them, and Fanny had time for only one thrill of	MP	III	10	406	22
It made her uncomfortable for a time--but yet there were	MP	III	11	409	5
I have not time for writing much, but it would be out of	MP	III	12	415	2

with the names of people and parties, that fill up my time. MP III 12 415 2
Only keep your cousin Edmund from me at such a time, I MP III 12 416 3
Time did something, her own exertions something more, and MP III 12 418 6
She hoped it was not wrong; though after a time, Susan's MP III 12 419 8
and shall be giving her time for reflection before she MP III 13 422 2
The last time I saw Crawford was at Mrs. Fraser's party. MP III 13 423 2
going to Bath, occur at a time when she could make no MP III 13 425 6
letters, and pass all her time between suffering from that MP III 13 427 13
at this distressing time, so very trying to my spirits.-- MP III 14 431 8
in London at such a time--through an illness, which had MP III 14 432 11
I have not time or patience to give half Henry's messages; MP III 14 435 14
Her representation of her cousin's state at this time, was MP III 14 436 16
it was now full time for her to hear again from her aunt. MP III 15 442 22
At any other time, this would have been felt dreadfully. MP III 15 442 23
heart in a glow, and for a time, seemed to distance every MP III 15 443 24
She had not time to be miserable. MP III 15 443 25
When Mansfield was considered, time was precious; and the MP III 15 445 29
the same moment, just in time to spend a few minutes with MP III 15 445 31
parted with, and just in time to prevent their sitting MP III 15 445 31
Lady Bertram could not give her much time, or many words, MP III 16 448 3
dependant on them, at this time, for every thing like MP III 16 449 4
After a time, Fanny found it not impossible to direct her MP III 16 449 6
Mr. Rushworth had been gone, at this time, to Bath, to MP III 16 450 8
Every thing was by that time public beyond a hope. MP III 16 450 10
The two ladies, even in the short time they had been MP III 16 450 10
There was but one of his children who was not at this time MP III 16 451 13
manner, and at the worst time; and though Julia was yet as MP III 16 452 13
Sunday evening--the very time of all others when if a MP III 16 453 17
to Richmond for the whole time of her being at Twickenham-- MP III 16 455 19
Time would undoubtedly abate somewhat of his sufferings, MP III 16 460 31
My Fanny indeed at this very time, I have the satisfaction MP III 17 461 2
These were reflections that required some time to soften; MP III 17 461 4
some time to soften; but time will do almost every thing, MP III 17 461 4
Something must have been wanting within, or time would MP III 17 463 8
convincing him that either time had done her much MP III 17 465 15
it, and of chusing that time to pay a visit to her other MP III 17 466 18
She had been allowing his attentions some time, but with MP III 17 466 18
must vary much as to time in different people.-- MP III 17 470 26
that exactly at the time when it was quite natural that it MP III 17 470 26
been first agitated, as time is for ever producing between MP III 17 471 29
his talents could not have recommended him at any time. E I 1 7 8
welcome, and at this time more welcome than usual, as E I 1 9 21
circumstance and animated Mr. Woodhouse for some time. E I 1 9 21
must be at Miss Taylor's time of life to be settled in a E I 1 11 38
Your time has been properly and delicately spent, if you E I 1 12 42
"With a great deal of pleasure, sir, at any time," said Mr. E I 1 14 48
He had, by that time, realized an easy competence--enough E I 2 16 5
It was now some time since Miss Taylor had begun to E I 2 16 6
Now was the time for Mr. Frank Churchill to come among E I 2 18 9
he fancied himself at any time unequal to company, there E I 3 20 1
to sit and watch the due time, was all set out and ready, E I 3 24 11
Quick and decided in her ways, Emma lost no time in E I 4 26 1
she could summon at any time to a walk, would be a E I 4 26 1
For some time she was amused, without thinking beyond the E I 4 27 5
One does not, you know, after a time. E I 4 29 13
luck, he may be rich in time, it is next to impossible E I 4 30 20
He was so busy the last time he was at Kingston that he E I 4 32 29
and abrupt; what will he be at Mr. Weston's time of life?" E I 4 33 36
and be a very rich man in time--and his being illiterate E I 4 34 40
She, therefore, said no more for some time. E I 4 34 41
connections; at the same time not of any family that could E I 4 35 44
that I preserved it some time; and I dare say she may have E I 5 37 7
to be an excellent wife all the time you were at Hartfield. E I 5 38 11
any thing wanting which a little time would not add. E I 6 42 1
in executing it! he could ride to London at any time. E I 6 49 40
breakfast; and after a time, had gone home to return again E I 7 50 1
Some time afterwards it was, "I think Mrs. Goddard would E I 7 55 40
but still, after a time, she was tender-hearted again E I 7 56 42
more than half her time there, and gradually getting to E I 8 57 1
called, and sat some time with Mr. Woodhouse and Emma, E I 8 57 2
he would not allow much time to pass before he spoke to E I 8 60 27
No--pray let her have time to look about her." E I 8 64 46
however, but that a little time and the return of Harriet E I 8 67 56
could not remember them! but he hoped he should in time." E I 9 70 5
and at the same time, as she could perceive, most E I 9 70 7
When I look back to the first time I saw him! E I 9 75 26
Your soft eyes shall chuse their own time for beaming. E I 9 76 38
"Yes, my dear, if there is time.-- E I 9 79 62
There will not be time for any thing." E I 9 79 62
to have the whole of the time they can give to the country, E I 9 79 63
so near as to give Emma time only to say farther, "Ah! E I 10 87 29
30

They did as they were desired; and by the time she judged E I 10 88 33
You forget how time passes." E I 11 96 23
Well, time does fly indeed!--and my memory is very bad. E I 11 96 24
She thought it was time to make up. E I 12 98 2
Concession must be out of the question; but it was time to E I 12 98 2
Poor Perry is bilious, and he has not time to take care of E I 12 101 25
tells me he has not time to take care of himself--which is E I 12 101 25
young woman hired for the time, who never had been able to E I 12 104 50
The cold, however, was severe; and by the time the second E I 13 112 24
air to produce a very white world in a very short time. E I 13 112 24
At another time Emma might have been amused, but she was E I 13 115 42
Well, sir, the time must come when you will be paid for E I 13 116 45
has been full of it; but he cannot command his own time. E I 14 119 9
the time talked of: "for I cannot depend upon his coming. E I 14 121 14
And in this style he talked on for some time very properly, E I 15 124 3
She had not time to know how Mr. Elton took the reproof, E I 15 125 7
it to be snowing some time, but had not said a word, lest E I 15 126 11
first exclamation, and all that he could say for some time. E I 15 126 12
should have stopped, and left the rest to time and chance. E I 16 137 11
But now, poor girl, her peace is cut up for some time. E I 16 137 11
reflections some time longer, and she went to bed at last E I 16 137 12
Mr. Elton's absence just at this time was the very thing E I 17 140 3
she should have as much time as possible for getting the E I 17 141 5
for the time convinced that Harriet was the superior E I 17 142 9
Time, she knew, must be allowed for this being thoroughly E I 17 142 11
state of composure by the time of Mr. Elton's return, as E I 17 142 11
When the time proposed drew near, Mrs. Weston's fears were E I 18 144 1
a much better plan; better time of year; better weather; E I 18 144 2
Emma was not at this time in a state of spirits to care E I 18 144 4
It ought to have been an habit with him by this time, of E I 18 148 22
coxcomb, he will not occupy much of my time or thoughts." E I 18 150 30
and after speaking some time of what the poor must suffer E II 1 155 1
disagreeable,--a waste of time--tiresome women--and all E II 1 155 3
was so kind as to sit some time with us, talking of Jane; E II 1 156 7
because it is not her time for writing;' and when I E II 1 157 7
great deal at my mother's time of life--and it really is E II 1 158 14
Fairfax should be allowed to come to you at such a time. E II 1 160 21
22

Fairfax prefers devoting the time to you and Mrs. Bates?" E II 1 161 24
A long time, is not it, for a cold to hang upon her? E II 1 161 29
family to maintain, and is not to be giving away his time. E II 1 162 31
entirely, only visiting her grandmother from time to time. E II 2 164 4
She had never been quite well since the time of their E II 2 165 9
It was her own choice to give the time of their absence to E II 2 166 10
eagerly refuted at the time, there were moments of self- E II 2 166 11
saw Jane Fairfax the first time after any considerable E II 2 167 12
Mr. Frank Churchill had been at Weymouth at the same time. E II 2 169 17
"No," said Mr. Knightley, nearly at the same time; "you E II 3 170 5
He had time only to say, "no, not at Randalls; I have not E II 3 172 22
23

Emma had not had time even to think of Mr. Elton, and she E II 3 173 25
At the same time, nobody could wonder if Mr. Elton should E II 3 176 44
It was now about the time that she was likely to call. E II 3 177 51
and stood talking some time; but I know no more what I E II 3 178 52
By that time, it was beginning to hold up, and I was E II 3 179 52
so soon, as to allow no time for insidious applications or E II 4 185 13
She went on herself, to give that portion of time to an E II 5 186 2
been talked almost all the time --till just at last, when E II 5 186 4
much to herself at this time, that she soon felt the E II 5 187 4
some time; the man believed they were gone to Hartfield. E II 5 187 5
him to-morrow by dinner time to a certainty--he is at E II 5 188 7
in a humour to resolve that they should both come in time. E II 5 189 18
hours hence; and by this time to-morrow, perhaps, or a E II 5 190 20
being a day before his time, and her father was yet in the E II 5 190 21
told you all that he would be here before the time named. E II 5 190 24
And there was time enough for Emma to form a reasonable E II 6 196 2
of every sort; and by this time were, in fortune and style E II 7 207 6
And when you get there, you must tell him at what time you E II 7 210 14
to bed at your usual time--and the idea of that would E II 7 211 21
again, and for a longer time than hitherto; of judging of E II 8 212 4
be, who were now seeing them together for the first time. E II 8 212 4
points) he could with time persuade her to any thing. E II 8 221 49
"I have been here a week to-morrow--half my time. E II 8 221 51
He has no occasion to marry, either to fill up his time or E II 8 225 74
with it; as you have many a time reproached me with doing. E II 8 226 84
They combated the point some time longer in the same way; E II 8 226 85
themselves off, Emma found time, in spite of the E II 8 229 99
At one time Patty came to say she thought the kitchen E II 9 236 46
the business to be going forward just at this time?-- E II 10 241 12
to time, to depend upon contingencies and conveniencies?" E II 10 241 12
not enjoy them as I did; you appeared tired the whole time. E II 10 242 17
We were just in time; my mother just ready for us. E II 10 243 33
Emma found it really time to be at home; the visit had E II 10 246 55
I felt how right you were the whole time, but was too E II 11 250 23
"But, unfortunately, sir, my time is so limited-----" E II 11 252 33
"Oh!" interrupted Emma, "there will be plenty of time for E II 11 252 34
At the time of the ball-room's being built, suppers had E II 11 254 44
And Mr. Weston at the same time, walking briskly with long E II 11 254 47
48

settled at any time between Mrs. Weston and Mrs. Stokes.-- E II 11 255 59
The preparations must take their time, nothing could be E II 12 257 1
Mrs. Weston added, "that he could only allow himself time E II 12 258 9
Emma was ready for her visitor some time before he E II 12 259 12
that all the rest of my time might be given to Hartfield. E II 12 261 32
33

doubtful, said, "it was time to go;" and the young man, E II 12 261 35
said; and in the very last time of its meeting her eye, E II 13 266 5
own imagination, fix a time for coming to Randalls again. E II 13 266 5
There was hardly time to talk over the first letter from E II 13 267 8
It was an awkward ceremony at any time to be receiving E II 14 271 5
Mrs. Elton; "and that will be our time for exploring. E II 14 274 28
Indeed, when the time draws on, I shall decidedly E II 14 274 28
Many a time has Selina said, when she has been going to E II 14 274 30
Many a time has she said so; and yet I am no advocate for E II 14 275 30
Happily it was now time to be gone. E II 14 279 51
her thoughts, that by the time her father had arranged E II 14 279 53
and about the third time of their meeting, she heard all E II 15 282 4
of Jane Fairfax, at any time, the least inconvenient.-- E II 15 283 9
We scarcely got home in time. E II 16 293 11
"When I talked of your being altered by time, by the E II 16 294 23
to imply the change of situation which time usually brings. E II 16 294 23
Time will generally lessen the interest of every E II 16 294 23
By this time, the walk in the rain had reached Mrs. Elton, E II 16 295 29
be particularly careful, especially at this time of year. E II 16 295 33
time to reflect, "now, how am I going to introduce him?-- E II 16 297 48
If Jane repressed her for a little time, she soon began E II 17 299 1
"I must spend some time with them; I am sure they will E II 17 300 9
subject to her; till the time draws nearer, I do not wish E II 17 300 11
"But, my dear child, the time is drawing near; here is E II 17 300 12
When I am quite determined as to the time, I am not at all E II 17 300 13
talking to them the whole time, in a voice a little E II 17 303 26
when they do come, and he will be half his time with us. E II 17 304 27
good talk about it some other time, but it will not do now. E II 17 304 27
I am sure Mr. Elton will lose no time in calling on him; E II 18 305 4
they are all to move southward without loss of time." E II 18 305 7
She has now been a longer time stationary there, than she E II 18 307 20
Now will be the time. E II 18 309 30
At the same time it is fair to observe, that I am one of E II 18 309 31
Witness this very time. E II 18 311 46
that if aunt Emma has not time for them, I do not think E II 18 312 50
time, induced them to name as early a day as possible. E III 1 318 11
The time of year lightened the evil to him. E III 1 318 13
time, the Randalls' party just sufficiently before them. E III 2 319 2
as to offer, but another time it will be quite unnecessary. E III 2 321 17
'Oh! Mrs. Stokes,' said I--but I had not time for more."-- E III 2 322 19
so obliged to you for the carriage!--excellent time.-- E III 2 322 19
others, Jane says, which they hesitated about some time. E III 2 323 19
Mrs. Elton had undoubtedly the advantage, at this time, in E III 2 325 32
any time to stand up with an old friend like Mrs. Gilbert." E III 2 327 36
"How I could so long a time be fancying myself!. . ." E III 4 337 6
some time with what was left, before he gave it back to me. E III 4 338 12
She then took a longer time for consideration. E III 4 341 34
all that I felt at the time--when I saw him coming--his E III 4 342 38
have no doubt, some time or other; only a little premature. E III 5 345 14
At the same time, I will not positively answer for my E III 5 346 16
There was no time for farther remark or explanation. E III 5 347 18
It is time for us to be going indeed. E III 5 349 24
"Have you never at any time had reason to think that he E III 5 350 34
Before this time last year I assure you we had had a E III 6 354 7
Weston engaged to lose no time in writing, and spare no E III 6 357 31
be tired, and sit all the time with him, remained, when E III 6 357 33
Morning decidedly the best time--never tired--every sort E III 6 358 35
It was hot; and after walking some time over the gardens E III 6 360 38
There had been a time when he would have scorned her as a E III 6 360 40
There had been a time also when Emma would have been sorry E III 6 360 40
You will have my sketches, some time or other, to look at-- E III 6 364 60
That it was time for every body to go, concluded the E III 6 366 74
and the vicarage, and every body was in good time. E III 7 367 1
there is generally time to recover from it afterwards. E III 7 373 44
time or other do me greater justice than you can do now." E III 7 375 61
Time did not compose her. E III 7 376 63
satisfaction at the time, and more to be abhorred in E III 8 377 1
'Well,' said she, 'it must be borne some time or other, E III 8 379 8
"Whenever the time may come, it must be unwelcome to her E III 8 381 22
Miss Bates would hardly give Emma time to say how E III 8 383 30
no time to spare, and therefore must now be gone directly. E III 9 385 1
2

"Yes--rather--I have been thinking of it some little time." E III 9 385 4
Time, however, she thought, would tell him that they ought E III 9 385 5
have happened at a better time--and to have had longer E III 9 386 8
time, curiosity to know where she would be buried. E III 9 387 12
of her going to Mrs. Smallridge's at the time proposed. E III 9 389 16
"can you come to Randall's at any time this morning?-- E III 10 392 1
2

You will know it all in time. E III 10 392 6
He is half way to Windsor by this time." E III 10 394 20
Emma might have time to recover--"you may well be amazed. E III 10 395 35
Harriet;--and for some time she could only exclaim, and E III 10 395 36
I have really for some time past, for at least these three E III 10 396 41
He had not time to enter into much explanation. E III 10 397 47
the full use even of the time he could stay--but that E III 10 397 47
bates's, I fancy, some time--and then came on hither; but E III 10 398 57

that he now only wanted time and persuasion to think the E III 10 400 69
objections; and by the time they had talked it all over E III 10 401 69
Poor Harriet! to be a second time the dupe of her E III 11 402 1
another woman at the very time that I was--tacitly, if not E III 11 404 11
to deny that there was a time--and not very distant either- E III 11 405 13
but I was thinking of something very different at the time. E III 11 406 24
From that evening, or at least from the time of Miss E III 11 409 35
they had been walking some time before Emma came,-and he E III 11 410 35
her estimation, from the time of latter's becoming known E III 11 412 45
as they must at any time have been compared by her, had it- E III 11 412 45
She saw that there never had been a time when she did not E III 11 412 45
call till a little time had passed, and Mr. Churchill E III 12 417 5
and Mrs. Weston's heart and time would be occupied by it. E III 12 422 20
father, she lost no time in hurrying into the shrubbery.-- E III 13 424 1
There was time only for the quickest arrangement of mind. E III 13 424 1
low, "time, my dearest Emma, time will heal the wound.-- E III 13 425 12
13

Latterly, however--for some time, indeed--I have had no E III 13 427 19
"Take a little time, consider, do not commit yourself." E III 13 429 28
And not only was there time for these convictions, with E III 13 431 38
happiness; there was time also to rejoice that Harriet's E III 13 431 38
and silence, as for the time crushed every hope;--she had E III 13 431 38
to the hope, that, in time, he might gain her affection E III 13 432 40
much to have been done, even had his time been longer.-- E III 13 432 41
her removed just now for a time from Highbury, and-- E III 14 435 4
To any thing, every thing--to time, chance, circumstance, E III 14 437 8
mean to be reconciled in time; but I was the injured E III 14 441 8
a few lines at the same time by the post, stating her E III 14 442 8
I reached Highbury at the time of the day when, from my E III 14 443 8
It will not be so great a loss a time: but if you dislike E III 15 445 8
body else, which at the time she had wholly imputed to the E III 15 449 35
Such a partner in all those duties and cares to which time E III 15 450 36
In time, of course, Mr. Knightley would be forgotten, that E III 15 450 38
Harriet really wished, and had wished some time, to E III 16 451 3
act on herself by anticipation before the appointed time.-- E III 16 452 6
"We can finish this some other time, you know. E III 16 453 13
word, Perry has restored her in a wonderful short time!-- E III 16 454 17
like morning visits, and Mr. Elton's time is so engaged." E III 16 455 22
In all probability she was at this very time waited for E III 16 458 44
as to--I have not time for half that I could wish to say. E III 16 459 47
quickest, and I think our feelings will lose no time there. E III 16 459 50
rightly by you--oftener than I would own at the time. E III 17 462 8
time, as worthy of your affection, as you think me already. E III 17 464 20
at this time for my marrying any more than at another.-- E III 17 465 27
The time was coming when the news must be spread farther, E III 17 465 28
such a time, and follow up the beginning she was to make.-- E III 17 465 28
given; time and continual repetition must do the rest.-- E III 17 466 30
began to think that some time or other--in another year or E III 17 467 30
had calculated from the time of its being known at E III 17 468 35
Time passed on. E III 18 470 1
But in time they will. E III 18 471 16
Time, you may be very sure, will make one or the other of E III 18 471 16
and Henry; and that at one time they were in such a crowd, E III 18 472 20
I could suppose she might in time--but can she already?-- E III 18 473 26
"I hope so--for at the time I was a fool." E III 18 474 33
again, there was for some time such a blank in the circle, E III 18 476 46
I hope time has not made you less willing to pardon. E III 18 476 47
He thanked her with all his heart, and continued some time E III 18 476 49
time when you found fault with her for being so pale?-- E III 18 478 62
time, you had very great amusement in tricking us all.-- E III 18 478 64
65

Perhaps, indeed, at that time she scarcely saw Mr. Elton, E III 19 482 6
it is a time of life at which scarcely any charm is lost. P III 1 6 11
He was at that time a very young man, just engaged in the P III 1 8 15
she was at this present time, (the summer of 1814,) P III 1 8 17
Could not be a better time, Sir Walter, for having a P III 3 17 1
me over at any time, to save you the trouble of replying." P III 3 17 4
seldom leaves a man's looks to the natural effect of time. P III 3 20 17
almost all the time they were talking the matter over. P III 3 22 24
resident at Monkford since the time of old Governor Trent." P III 3 23 27
know, Sir Walter, some time back, for two or three years. P III 3 23 32
and, at the same time, can never make a baronet look small. P III 3 24 36
He was, at that time, a remarkably fine young man, with a P III 4 26 1
Her attachment and regrets had, for a long time, clouded P III 4 28 6
had reached its close; and time had softened down much, P III 4 28 7
had been too dependant on time alone; no aid had been P III 4 28 7
sufficient cure, at her time of life, had been possible to P III 4 28 7
a single man at the time, she had a fond dependance on no P III 4 28 7
were approved, terms, time, every thing, and every body, P III 4 30 10
no time to be lost in making every dependant arrangement. P III 5 32 3
that all the intervening time should be divided between P III 5 33 5
Anne walked up at the same time, in a sort of desolate P III 5 34 10
very far from well at the time; and I do not think I ever P III 5 35 18
understood in time what was intended as to the waggons. P III 5 37 24
But all these things took up a great deal of time." P III 5 38 34
though, at the same time, Anne could believe, with Lady P III 5 39 34
zeal, but sport; and his time was otherwise trifled away, P III 6 43 5
they would come at any time, and help play at any thing, P III 6 43 5
Richard's captain, at one time, I do not know when or P III 6 47 15
little cared for at any time by his family, though quite P III 6 50 27
any impression at the time; and that Mrs. Musgrove should P III 6 50 28
It must be a work of time to ascertain that no injury had P III 6 51 31
her up stairs, she was in time for the whole conversation, P III 7 55 7
P III 7 57 17
18

not have waited till this time; he would have done what P III 7 58 21
From this time Captain Wentworth and Anne Elliot were P III 8 63 1
There _had_ been a time, when of all the large party now P III 8 63 3
say he would have been just such another by this time." P III 8 64 5
6

better men than himself applying for her at the same time. P III 8 65 12
It was a great object with me, at that time, to be at sea,- P III 8 65 13
of foul weather all the time I was at sea in her; and P III 8 65 16
poor old Asp, in half the time; our touch with the great P III 8 66 16
The only time that I ever really suffered in body or mind, P III 8 71 54
in body or mind, the only time that I ever fancied myself P III 8 71 54
I lived in perpetual fright at that time, and had all P III 8 71 54
from that time cousin Charles had been very much forgotten. P III 9 74 7
One morning, about this time, Charles Musgrove and Captain P III 10 83 3
Their time and strength, and spirits, were, therefore, P III 10 83 6
own observations, the last time I was in company with him, P III 10 87 26
time; but I believe about a year before he married Mary. P III 10 89 33
which had been some time heard, was just coming up, and P III 10 90 38
cannot afford to make long courtships in time of war. P III 10 92 44
How many days was it, my dear, between the first time of P III 10 92 44
The time now approached for Lady Russell's return; the day P III 11 93 1
he spent so much of his time at Uppercross, that in P III 11 93 2
would not leave much time for seeing a new place, after P III 11 94 8
would not have more than time for looking about them, P III 11 95 8
Captain Benwick had some time ago been first lieutenant of P III 11 96 12
Anne found herself by this time growing so much more P III 11 99 21
no difficulty at his time of life, and with his character. P III 12 102 2
family; she had only time, however, for a general answer, P III 12 103 5
collected to look, by the time the owner of the curricle P III 12 105 9
I wish we had been aware in time, who it was, that he P III 12 106 16
At the same time, however, it was a secret gratification P III 12 106 19
met with him the second time; luckily Mary did not much P III 12 106 19
our seeing Mr. Elliot, the next time you write to Bath. P III 12 107 20
they walked together some time, talking as before of Mr. P III 12 107 23
to be impossible; but in time, perhaps--we know what time P III 12 108 25
perhaps--we know what time does in every case of P III 12 108 25
walking enough by the time he reached home, determined the P III 12 108 30
By all their calculations there was just time for this; P III 12 108 30

By this time the report of the accident had spread among P III 12 111 49
been off,--the impossibility of being in tolerable time. P III 12 113 57
share of delay; yet the time required by the Uppercross P III 12 114 64
among them for some time, Henrietta leaning back in the P III 12 117 73
The remainder of Anne's time at Uppercross, comprehending P IV 1 121 1
yesterday--(the first time since the accident) had brought P IV 1 126 20
"Another time, sir, I thank you, not now." P IV 1 127 25
You can slip in from the shrubbery at any time. P IV 1 127 26
he must be rather a dressy man for his time of life.-- P IV 1 127 28
again, to say, "the next time you write to your good P IV 1 128 29
mother, who must return in time to receive their younger P IV 2 129 1
heard him mention Anne twice all the time I was there. P IV 2 131 8
occasionally thinking of Captain Benwick, from this time. P IV 2 133 26
He had called in Camden-Place; had called a second time, a P IV 2 135 35
time of life was another concern, and rather a fearful one. P IV 3 140 11
eye, but, at the same time, "must lament his being very P IV 3 141 12
under-hung, a defect which time seemed to have increased; P IV 3 141 12
"The last time I saw her, she had a red nose, but I hope P IV 3 142 14
the same inn at the same time, to give his own route, P IV 3 143 19
you;" and she was in full time to hear her father say, "my P IV 4 145 1
and has a very large acquaintance, has time to be vexed. P IV 4 146 5
Mr. Elliot, at a mature time of life, should feel it a P IV 4 147 7
process in the world of time upon a head naturally clear, P IV 4 147 7
Time will explain." P IV 4 147 7
same time, there had been an unlucky omission at Kellynch. P IV 4 148 12
must suffer at such a time; and Miss Hamilton, three years P IV 5 152 2
give Mrs. Smith, and Anne therefore lost no time in going. P IV 5 153 5
There had been a time, Mrs. Smith told her, when her P IV 5 154 9
chanced to be at liberty just in time to attend her.-- P IV 5 154 9
She always takes the right time for applying. P IV 5 155 9
for some time which will at once suit her and myself.-- P IV 5 157 16
the same time honoured for staying away in such a cause.-- P IV 5 158 21
meaning to gain Anne in time, as of his deserving her; and P IV 5 159 22
I only mean that if Mr. Elliot should some time hence pay P IV 5 159 23
me more delight than is often felt at my time of life!" P IV 5 160 25
"What an immense time Mrs. Clay has been staying with " P IV 6 163 7
that, at Admiral Croft's time of life, and in his P IV 6 166 14
I will tell you the whole story another time. P IV 6 170 29
and the very next time Anne walked out, she saw him. P IV 7 174 1
time to settle the point of civility between the other two. P IV 7 174 3
For the first time, since their renewed acquaintance, she P IV 7 175 6
Time had changed him, or Louisa had changed him. P IV 7 176 8
without further loss of time, and before the rain P IV 7 177 16
you," being all that she had time for, as she passed away. P IV 7 177 16
She hoped to be wise and reasonable in time; but alas! P IV 7 178 25
She looked at her however, from time to time, anxiously; P IV 7 179 28
and she was just in time by a side glance to see a slight P IV 8 181 2
and the more from its not overpowering you at the time." P IV 8 181 4
must be broken up for a time; but slight was the penance P IV 8 184 17
She was just in time to see him turn into the concert room. P IV 8 184 18
she must consent for a time to be happy in an humbler way. P IV 8 186 22
"No, no--some time or other perhaps, but not now. P IV 8 187 34
her from home at the time when Mr. Elliot would be most P IV 9 192 1
time, more than all the rest of the world put together." P IV 9 194 16
you must have so many pleasanter demands upon your time." P IV 9 194 18
Then do tell me what he was at that time of life. P IV 9 198 51
You might, some time or other, be differently affected P IV 9 199 53
It must have been about the same time that he became known P IV 9 200 56
and as to his marriage, I knew all about it at the time. P IV 9 200 57
But I should like to know why, at that time of his life, P IV 9 200 58
She checked herself just in time. P IV 9 201 62
I think differently now; time and sickness, and sorrow, P IV 9 201 64
Now you are to understand that time had worked a very P IV 9 206 90
fixing himself here for a time, with the view of renewing P IV 9 207 90
But since he must be absent some time or other, I do not P IV 9 208 92
The husband had died just in time to be spared the full P IV 9 209 96
most miserable, when time had disclosed all, too late? P IV 9 211 102
Morning visits are never fair by women at her time of life, P IV 10 215 16
of being seen; but last time I called, I observed the P IV 10 215 16
Elizabeth was, for a short time, suffering a good deal. P IV 10 219 29
She was intreated to give them as much of her time as P IV 10 220 31
She was just in time to ascertain that it really was Mr. P IV 10 222 39
You did not use to like cards; but time makes many changes. P IV 10 225 59
to lose no time, lest somebody else should come in. P IV 10 225 61
neither arriving quite in time, nor the first to arrive. P IV 11 229 2
There was no delay, no waste of time. P IV 11 229 2
To begin without knowing that at such a time there will be P IV 11 231 9
Neither time, nor health, nor life, to be called your own. P IV 11 233 23
She had only time, however, to move closer to the table P IV 11 236 40
that Anne had not, at any time lately, slipped down, and P IV 11 238 47
But there are hopes of her being forgiven in time. P IV 11 247 82
among his Haymakers at the time, & three or four of them S 1 364 1
opinion without loss of time; and as the road does not S 1 365 1
Where people can be found with money or time to go to them! S 1 368 1
a pity to lose any more time--and here come my girls to S 1 370 1
her husband by this time, not much less disposed for it--a S 1 370 1
resentment at the time of Mr. Hollis's death;--the latter, S 3 377 1
time, we can always buy what we want at Sanditon-House.-- S 4 380 1
for little Mary at any time, or a large bonnet at Jebb's-- S 4 381 1
very well--that is, there has not been time enough yet.-- S 4 382 1
At the same time last year, (late in July) there had not S 4 383 1
He had fancied it just the time of day for them to be all S 4 384 1
health is;--& at the same time, they are such excellent S 5 385 1
poor Arthur, that, at his time of life he shd be S 5 388 1
will come to care about such matters herself in time. S 6 393 1
of butcher's meat in time--tho' you may not happen to have S 6 393 1
milk--& I have two Milch Asses at this present time.-- S 6 393 1
Mrs P.-- in the drawing room in time to see them all.-- S 7 394 1
If there are young ladies in the world at her time of life, S 7 395 1
as soon as she had time to speak, but I am not poetic S 7 397 1
I had them with me last summer about this time, for a week; S 7 399 1
I should not chuse to have my 2 housemaids time taken up S 7 401 1
so, my dear, the next time Miss Esther begins talking S 7 402 1
had both gone home some time before, she proceeded for S 9 406 1
over by the time we reached the hotel--so that we got her S 9 407 1
Our dinner is not ordered till six--& by that time I hope S 9 411 1
to see you at any time, but as soon as I get back I shall S 9 411 1
to Mrs G. herself--time not allowing for the circuitous S 10 414 1
You would see me all in a Bath by the time I got there!-- S 10 416 1
"I thought I should have been in time, said he, but cocoa S 10 416 1
& very ignorant, their time being divided between such S 11 421 1
All said & done, in less time than you have been talking S 12 423 1
bed myself at this present time, for I am hardly able to S 12 424 1
they could not for some time make out what sort of S 12 425 1
This adventure afforded agreable discussion for some time. S 12 425 1

TIMED (2)

post, which contained a proposal particularly well timed. SS I 4 23 20
instead! her liveliness had been never worse timed. PP I 17 87 14

TIMES (137)

days last week, & called several times in Edward Street. LS 9 256 1
times that he had seen Mrs Johnson a few evenings before. LS 20 276 3
I am still doubtful at times, as to marriage. LS 29 299 3
by it; & in happier times, when your situation is as LS 39 307 1
I have heard my sister say so forty times, when she has NA I 3 28 45
was repeated by them all, two or three times over. NA I 4 32 5
By the bye, though I have thought of it a hundred times, I NA I 6 42 28
This evil had been felt and lamented, at least three times NA I 7 44 1
notice, that she looked back at them only three times. NA I 7 47 18
and used some thousands of times before, under that roof, NA I 10 72 8
Dress is at all times a frivolous distinction, and NA I 10 73 22
cried Thorpe, "we shall be able to do ten times more. NA I 11 84 21
I had rather, ten thousand times rather get out now, and NA I 11 87 53

Text	Work	Vol	Ch	Page	Line
I would fifty times rather you should have them than	NA	I	11	90	64
But I had ten thousand times rather have been with you;	NA	I	12	93	5
to poor Catherine; some times not a word was said,	NA	I	13	99	9
I took him down several times you know in my way."	NA	II	1	135	41
carving of former times, was contracted to a Rumford, with	NA	II	5	162	26
by whom they had at times been honoured, turned with a	NA	II	8	185	5
and forwards some ten times a-day, with an heart light,	NA	II	14	237	20
He and I have been at times thrown a good deal together,	SS	I	4	20	9
There was, at times, a want of spirits about him which, if	SS	I	4	22	18
at all times, was an illustration of their opinions.	SS	I	11	53	2
to Elinor three or four times; and had Elinor's memory	SS	I	11	54	6
you will never offend me by talking of former times.	SS	I	17	92	26
every body at times, whatever be their education or state.	SS	I	19	103	7
her spirits at different times could produce;--with	SS	I	19	104	12
times over, that it had been quite an agreeable surprise.	SS	I	19	107	28
reprimand on the subject five or six times every day.	SS	I	21	118	2
"But then at other times I have not resolution enough for	SS	I	22	133	44
her affectionately several times, and then gave way to a	SS	II	7	182	12
To my fancy, a thousand times prettier than Barton Park,	SS	II	8	197	22
hoped, cheat Marianne, at times, into some interest beyond	SS	II	10	213	3
Every qualification is raised at times, by the	SS	II	10	215	13
times, she feared they would despise her for offering.	SS	II	14	247	4
perceive at different times, the most striking resemblance	SS	II	14	248	5
nothing, and was heard three times to say, "yes, ma'am."--	SS	III	1	265	33
I have seen Mr. Ferrars two or three times in Harley-	SS	III	3	282	19
Willoughby's eyes at times, which I did not like."	SS	III	9	338	20
made, till it has been made at least twenty times over.	SS	III	13	364	9
club that meets three times a week at the White Hart, & if	W			325	4
by the hand & wished her "goodbye" at least a dozen times.	W			335	13
& as eliz: had at all times more good will than method in	W			348	23
in her coughs," said her father; "she times them ill."	PP	I	2	6	8
He could not help seeing that you were about five times as	PP	I	4	14	5
house, and has since dined in company with him four times.	PP	I	6	22	7
thither three or four times a week, to pay their duty to	PP	I	7	28	3
The sisters, on hearing this, repeated three or four times	PP	I	8	35	1
in the eyes of a man of ten times his consequence.	PP	I	18	90	8
occurring at different times between Jane and herself,	PP	II	4	152	6
While they were dressing, he came two or three times to	PP	II	6	161	7
She asked her at different times, how many sisters she had,	PP	II	6	163	15
I have told Miss Bennet several times, that she will never	PP	II	8	173	10
They called at various times of the morning, sometimes	PP	II	9	180	28
After walking two or three times along that part of the	PP	II	12	195	2
feelings towards its writer were at times widely different.	PP	II	14	212	17
"We have dined nine times at Rosings, besides drinking tea	PP	II	15	217	13
They met several times, for there was much to be discussed.	PP	III	10	323	2
He has been accused of many faults at different times; but	PP	III	10	324	2
We passed each other several times.	PP	III	10	328	16
It was in the times and the courier, I know; though it was	PP	III	11	336	49
mind; and she would, at times, have given any thing to be	PP	III	12	340	13
The soup was fifty times better than what we had at the	PP	III	12	342	28
How often do I pace it three times a-day, early and late,	MP	I	7	73	53
of the family in former times, its rise and grandeur,	MP	I	9	85	3
It was a valuable part of former times.	MP	I	9	86	12
We must all feel at times the difficulty of fixing our	MP	I	9	87	16
we were going to act three times a week till my father's	MP	I	13	125	18
Mr. Rushworth followed him to say, "I come in three times,	MP	I	15	139	10
given her at different times, principally by Tom; and she	MP	I	16	153	3
she cried, "these are fine times for you, but you must not	MP	I	18	166	6
be exactly at one of the times when they were trying not	MP	I	18	169	21
might each have killed six times as many; but we respect	MP	II	1	181	16
I am grown too old to go out more than three times a week;	MP	II	6	229	1
But at other times doubt and alarm intermingled with his	MP	II	8	255	10
suppose I have worn it six times; it is very pretty--but I	MP	II	8	260	22
variation of words three times over, his sister eagerly	MP	II	12	292	8
past, you will consider times, persons, and probabilities,	MP	III	1	313	12
at Fanny) that nineteen times out of twenty I am thinking	MP	III	3	340	25
been a consideration of times and seasons, a regulation of	MP	III	7	382	29
That her manner was wrong, however, at times very wrong--	MP	III	9	396	6
each of them at times being held the most probable.	MP	III	10	399	1
I will say, then, that we have seen him two or three times.	MP	III	12	416	2
What Fanny told her of former times, dwelt more on her	MP	III	12	419	7
perhaps they are some times contradictory, but it will not	MP	III	13	422	2
not one who was not more useful at times to her son.	MP	III	14	429	2
I have spoke at least a dozen times; have not I, Betsey?--	MP	III	15	440	18
house Mr. Crawford had constant access at all times.	MP	III	16	450	8
as hers should not, at times, hold out the strongest hope	MP	III	17	471	28
This is three times as large.--	E	I	1	8	13
She knew that at times she must be missed; and could not	E	I	2	18	11
"That may be--and I may have seen him fifty times, but	E	I	4	29	14
her drawing up at various times of books that she meant to	E	I	5	37	7
where Emma errs once, she is in the right a hundred times."	E	I	5	40	22
or had there been ten times more, the delight and	E	I	6	44	20
asked for it five or six times, allowing them to hear your	E	I	7	56	44
do not pretend to fix on times or places, but I must tell	E	I	8	58	19
					20
and two or three times over, with explanations of every	E	I	9	78	51
That is, I know you must have seen her a hundred times--	E	I	10	86	22
Every letter from her is read forty times over; her	E	I	10	86	23
with his neighbours five times a-week, than upon family	E	I	11	96	26
which we have been applying at times ever since August."	E	I	12	102	28
"my son," repeated several times over; and from a few	E	I	14	118	4
I have no doubt of his having, at times, considerable	E	I	14	123	25
"And those times are, whenever he thinks it worth his	E	I	18	146	14
He may, at times, be able to do a great deal more than he	E	I	18	146	15
anything two or three times over, she is sure to hear; but	E	II	1	158	14
Emma saw him only once; but two or three times every day	E	II	4	184	10
considerable address at times, that he could get away, or	E	II	8	221	48
to have them done three times--but Miss Woodhouse will be	E	II	9	238	51
two Miss Coxes five," had been repeated many times over.	E	II	11	248	4
He came four times a day for a week.	E	II	11	253	38
plaister, one of the very last times we ever met in it!--	E	III	4	338	12
Miss Woodhouse, we all know at times what it is to be	E	III	6	363	50
I should think five times the amount of what I have even	E	III	8	382	24
You must think one five hundred million times more above	E	III	11	407	28
but there was a hope (at times a slight one, at times much	E	III	12	416	1
(at times a slight one, at times much stronger,) that	E	III	12	416	1
sight; seen him a hundred times; came to consult me once,	P	III	3	23	28
personal misfortunes, though I know you must fifty times.	P	III	5	35	14
I do not think she has been in this house three times this	P	III	5	37	24
I have been several times in the garden with Mackenzie,	P	III	5	38	34
to the proof; former times must undoubtedly be brought to	P	III	8	63	2
I have crossed the Atlantic four times, and have been once	P	III	8	70	52
been above four or five times in the Miss Musgroves'	P	III	9	75	9
and blows hard, which may not happen three times a winter.	P	IV	1	128	30
the particulars of their first meeting a great many times.	P	IV	4	148	9
remembering former partialities and talking over old times.	P	IV	5	153	6
Here and there, human nature may be great in times of	P	IV	5	156	11
Anne had called several times on her friend, before the	P	IV	5	156	14
a "million times better than marrying among the Hayters."	P	IV	6	165	8
summer, and these are bad times for getting on, but he has	P	IV	6	171	37
which I never could quite reconcile with present times.	P	IV	9	200	56
It is a very fair match, as times go; and I have liked	P	IV	10	218	22
"There is at times said he--a little self-importance--but	S		3	376	1
early tendency at various times, to various disorders;--	S		10	412	1
took drops two or three times from one, out of the several	S		10	413	1
TIMID (7)					
She looks perfectly timid, dejected & penitent.	LS		17	270	4
manners, the same timid look in the presence of her mother	LS		42	311	3
beauty; exceedingly timid and shy, and shrinking from	MP	I	2	12	2
a canter; and to Fanny's timid nature it was most	MP	I	7	67	16
He knew her to be very timid, and exceedingly nervous; and	MP	III	1	320	44
Timid, anxious, doubting as she was, it was still	MP	III	17	471	28
She is very timid and silent.	E	II	15	283	7
TIMIDITY (7)					
& have taken great pains to overcome her timidity.	LS		18	273	3
by great sensibility of her situation, and great timidity.	MP	I	2	16	20
Fanny, with all her faults of ignorance and timidity, was	MP	I	2	20	32
timidity of her mind by the flow of her love for William.	MP	II	6	232	13
with, and no natural timidity to restrain any consequent	MP	III	17	472	31
I am a great advocate for timidity--and I am sure one does	E	II	15	283	7
It had been weakness and timidity.	P	III	7	61	36
TINGE (1)					
to her professed opinions, sometimes a tinge of wrong.	MP	II	9	269	31
TINGED (1)					
of her's, so frequently tinged with a blush as it was	MP	II	6	229	5
TINKLING (1)					
for she was very fond of tinkling the keys of the old	NA	I	1	14	1
TINTERN ABBEY (1)					
one window, where Tintern Abbey held its station between a	MP	I	16	152	2
TIP (1)					
her heart almost to the tip of her tongue, by asking, in a	NA	I	12	95	18
TIP-TOE (1)					
On tip-toe she entered; the room was before her; but it	NA	II	9	193	6
TIPPET (3)					
the price and weigh the merits of a new muff and tippet.	NA	I	7	51	54
Here is your tippet.	E	III	2	328	45
Mrs. Weston begs you to put on your tippet.	E	III	2	328	45
TIPTOE (1)					
She then went away, walking on tiptoe out of the room, as	SS	II	8	192	4
TIRE (3)					
at hand to relieve you, if you tire of the great book.	MP	I	16	156	27
Mrs. Price could never tire; and Mr. Crawford was as warm	MP	III	10	400	7
will be enough to tire even the friendship of a Fanny.	MP	III	13	423	2
TIRED (74)					
I am tired of submitting my will to the caprices of others-	LS		39	308	1
Catherine grew tired at last, and would thank her no more.	NA	I	2	21	9
of disappointment--she was tired of being continually	NA	I	2	21	10
eight; and it is such a fag--I come back tired to death.	NA	I	3	29	46
the room till they were tired; "and how pleasant it would	NA	I	4	31	1
a capital one of the kind, but I am cursed tired of it.'	NA	I	7	46	11
"He was with us just now, and said he was so tired of	NA	I	8	58	30
besides, I am tired, and do not mean to dance any more."	NA	I	8	59	36
Take care, or you will forget to be tired of it at the	NA	I	10	78	43
You ought to be tired at the end of six weeks."	NA	I	10	78	43
"I do not think I should be tired, if I were to stay here	NA	I	10	78	44
Oh! who can ever be tired of Bath?"	NA	I	10	79	56
morning together, and how tired my poor mother is at the	NA	I	14	109	26
Morland's horse was so tired he could hardly get it along.	NA	I	15	116	1
She was so amazingly tired, and it was so odious to parade	NA	II	3	147	28
extension of their walk, if Miss Morland were not tired.	NA	II	7	179	27
She was tired of the woods and the shrubberies--always so	NA	II	11	212	16
all of a sudden grew tired of having her there, and almost	NA	II	14	237	21
He was tired, I dare say, for he had just filled the sheet	SS	I	22	134	52
off for town, when you are tired of Barton, without saying	SS	II	3	154	3
because if they got tired of me, they might talk to one	SS	II	3	154	4
would not have been a bit tired: and to say the truth it	SS	II	5	171	36
dropt a syllable of being tired of her, or of wishing to	SS	III	2	273	16
Elinor, dreading her being tired, led her towards home;	SS	III	10	348	34
tired of a conversation in which she had no share.--	PP	I	11	58	33
of "Lord, how tired I am!" accompanied by a violent yawn.	PP	I	18	103	75
She must own that she was tired of great houses; after	PP	II	19	240	14
herself not tired, and they stood together on the lawn.	PP	III	1	257	66
"I wonder that I should be tired with only walking in this	MP	I	9	94	57
I hope you are not very tired.	MP	I	9	94	58
"Thank you, but I am not at all tired."	MP	I	9	94	59
"I am really not tired, which I almost wonder at; for we	MP	I	9	94	60
"I am afraid you are very tired, Fanny," said Edmund,	MP	I	9	95	68
"That she should be tired now, however, gives me no	MP	I	9	95	71
for her, had she not been tired already; but this was not	MP	I	10	103	49
down the newspaper again--"for I am tired to death.	MP	I	12	118	22
"Yes, very;--only I am soon tired."	MP	II	7	250	58
"You look tired and fagged, Fanny.	MP	II	9	267	24
How can you be tired so soon?"	MP	II	10	279	23
"Poor dears! how tired you must both be!--and now what	MP	III	7	378	14
"I wish you were not so tired,"--said he, still detaining	MP	III	11	411	20
You should listen to me till you were tired, and advise me	MP	III	12	415	2
advise me till you were tired still more; but it is	MP	III	12	415	2
And how tired you must be after your journey!	E	I	12	100	18
they were a little more tired than usual, from their	E	I	12	103	39
Well, that is so very!--I am sure if Jane is tired, you	E	II	3	177	50
You will not like staying late. you will get very tired	E	II	7	210	14
"But you would not wish me to come away before I am tired,	E	II	7	210	15
"Oh! no, my love; but you will soon be tired.	E	II	7	210	16
You will not regard being tired.	E	II	7	211	20
You did not enjoy them as I did; you appeared tired the	E	II	10	242	17
That fact is, I suppose, that she is tired of Enscombe.	E	II	18	307	20
persuaded--Miss Smith, you walk as if you were tired.	E	III	5	345	11
When you are tired of eating strawberries in the garden,	E	III	6	355	21
there on purpose to be tired, and sit all the time with	E	III	6	357	33
Morning decidedly the best time--never tired--every sort	E	III	6	358	35
stooping-- glaring sun--tired to death--could bear it no	E	III	6	358	35
I am tired of doing nothing.	E	III	6	365	62
I am really tired of exploring so long on one spot.	E	III	7	372	39
Even Emma grew tired at last of flattery and merriment,	E	III	7	374	54
Mr. Elton was so hot and tired, that all this wit seemed	E	III	16	457	37
the poor boys saying, 'uncle seems always tired now.'"	E	III	17	465	27
She is never tired of playing."	P	III	8	72	58
I think we had better turn back; I am excessively tired."	P	III	10	85	15
Winthrop, as she felt so tired, she resolutely answered, "	P	III	10	86	17
Anne, really tired herself, was glad to sit down; and she	P	III	10	87	22
She joined Charles and Mary, and was tired enough to be	P	III	10	90	37
who might be particularly tired; it would save her full a	P	III	10	90	38
The Miss Musgroves were not at all tired, and Mary was	P	III	10	90	38
"Miss Elliot, I am sure you are tired," cried Mrs. Croft.	P	III	10	91	40
And they were by no means tired of wondering and admiring;	P	III	11	96	11
D. being too much tired of them all, to stay any longer.--	S		8	404	1
the space of seven hours, confessed herself a little tired.	S		10	414	1
Tired as she was, she must instantly repair to the hotel,	S		10	419	1
TIRES (2)					
How much sooner one tires of any thing than of a book!--	PP	I	11	55	4
I wish Jane Fairfax very well; but she tires me to death."	E	I	10	86	23
TIRESOME (15)					
But enough of this tiresome girl.	LS		7	254	2
that, it is the most tiresome place in the world.'	NA	I	10	78	45
at all--it is very tiresome: and yet I often think it odd	NA	I	14	108	22
Bennet," replied his wife, "how can you be so tiresome!	PP	I	1	4	16
What can he mean by being so tiresome as to be always	PP	III	17	374	20
father had made a most tiresome piece of work of it; and	MP	I	3	24	4
The mother I could not avoid, as long as my tiresome aunt	MP	I	10	101	32
Tiresome wretches!"	E	I	8	58	17
"Harriet may not consider every body tiresome that you	E	I	8	58	18
a visitor, without thinking him at all a tiresome wretch."	E	I	8	60	27
waste of time--tiresome women--and all the horror of being	E	II	1	155	3
The aunt was as tiresome as ever; more tiresome, because	E	II	2	168	15
but, as a constant companion, must be very tiresome.	E	II	15	286	17
and tiresome; but her pride is arrogance and insolence!	E	II	18	309	33
Oh! you may as well take back that tiresome book she would	P	IV	10	215	15
TIROCINIUM (1)					
a line or two of Cowper's Tirocinium for ever before her.	MP	III	14	431	7
TIS (1)					
conscious reply of "tis rather stronger than it should be	S		10	417	1
TISSUES (1)					
or those vapid tissues of ordinary occurrences from which	S		8	403	1
TITLE (7)					

One title I know she might have had, besides baronets. LS 26 296 5
His unexpected accession to title and fortune had removed NA II 16 251 5
all honoured with the title of seduction, had been PP III 6 294 4
estate would as surely be his hereafter as the title. P IV 3 140 11
got nothing but her title from the family, still she had S 3 375 1
For the title, it was to be supposed that she had married-- S 3 376 1
deal in his air & address; and his title did him no harm." S 7 395 1

TITLES (1)
over the titles of half a shelf, and was ready to proceed. NA II 8 182 2

TITTLE-TATTLE (1)
can hardly be among the tittle-tattle of Highbury yet. E I 7 56 41

TITTUPPY (1)
Did you ever see such a little tittuppy thing in your life? NA I 9 65 28

TO---- (1)
"Oh! no, I am sure you are a great deal too kind to---- E I 7 52 20

TO-DAY (63)
of leaving this place to-day, I feel it my duty to entreat LS 25 292 3
He leaves London he says to-day. LS 38 306 1
"Rest! He has only come three-and-twenty miles to-day; all NA I 7 47 27
"No walk for me to-day," sighed Catherine;--"but perhaps NA I 11 82 4
But, however, I cannot go with you to-day, because I am NA I 11 84 19
late to go on to-day; your sister thinks so as well as I. NA I 11 88 54
there be any harm in my calling on Miss Tilney to-day? NA I 12 91 1
again to-day the moment he came into the billiard-room. NA I 12 96 20
I dine with Miss Tilney to-day, and must now be going home. NA I 15 123 35
"Woodston will make but a sombre appearance to-day." NA II 7 175 13
Was she out with him to-day?" SS I 9 44 20
not been able to take your usual walk to Allenham to-day." SS I 20 111 10
Why did not you ask the Gilberts to come to us to-day?" SS I 20 111 19
"John is in such spirits to-day!" said she, on his taking SS I 21 121 7
came you to conjure out that I should be in town to-day?" SS II 4 163 14
"your sister looks unwell to-day," or "your sister seems SS II 5 172 40
the servant let me in to-day, accidentally seen a letter SS II 5 173 44
And so the letter that came to-day finished it! SS II 8 195 16
it Lucy, for I think of going as far as Holborn to-day." SS III 4 286 14
Yet when I thought of her to-day as really dying, it was a SS III 8 327 55
to see him walk in to-day or to-morrow, or any day." SS III 12 358 6
compassionate as to dine to-day with Louisa and me, we PP I 7 30 17
ordered a good dinner to-day, because I have reason to PP I 13 61 1
unlucky! there is not a bit of fish to be got to-day. PP I 13 61 3
She comes to us to-day. PP III 7 303 14
mamma, do the people here abouts know I am married to-day? PP III 9 316 8
here-abouts in which Lizzy may lose her way again to-day?" PP III 17 374 22
Even your mother was out to-day for above an hour." MP I 7 72 41
I came here to-day intending to rehearse it with Edmund-- MP I 18 168 17
"I may perhaps get as far as Banbury to-day." MP II 2 193 16
"Suppose I were to find him there again to-day!" said she MP II 9 267 23
said, with much surprise, "why have you no fire to-day?" MP III 1 312 5
And he is not an acquaintance of to-day, you have now MP III 1 316 27
from that of to-day, and looking forward to to-morrow's. MP III 13 427 13
she returns to Wimpole-Street to-day, the old lady is come. MP III 14 435 14
was joining their hands to-day, he looked so very much as E I 1 13 46
should try not to go out to-day--and dissuade my father E I 13 110 9
Such a sad loss to our party to-day!" E I 13 114 34
She wanted me to nurse my cold by staying at home to-day, E I 15 125 5
chance of my hearing any thing of Miss Fairfax to-day." E II 1 159 19
always do: and so I began to-day with my usual caution; E II 1 162 31
is at Oxford to-day, and he comes for a whole fortnight; I E II 5 188 7
at Weymouth which"----- "Oh! go to-day, go to-day. E II 5 194 39
40
I know he had horses to-day--for we arrived together; and E II 8 223 64
How is she to-day? E II 10 244 35
have power to draw me out, in worse weather than to-day." E II 16 294 22
You do us a great deal of honour to-day, I am sure. E II 16 294 27
We have notice of it in a letter to-day. E II 18 305 5
will be on his coming in to-day or to-morrow, and at any E II 18 309 30
"It is hotter to-day." E III 7 368 7
I am perfectly comfortable to-day." E III 7 368 8
your own management; but to-day you are got back again-- E III 7 369 11
must go and see him to-day; and so will Jane, I am sure, E III 8 383 29
"Oh! no; the meeting is certainly to-day," was the abrupt E III 16 456 29
wanted to see Knightley to-day on that very account.-- E III 16 457 40
I have not seen one of them to-day, except Mr. Musgrove, P III 5 38 29
And I think it very likely that my illness to-day may be P III 5 39 39
alarmed yesterday, but the case is very different to-day." P III 7 57 14
I wonder whereabouts they will upset to-day. P III 10 84 8
hers to call at Winthrop to-day--and yet she was as near P III 10 87 23
"The carriage is gone to-day, to bring Louisa and the " P IV 6 163 7
"his consent, and Captain Benwick is expected to-day. P IV 6 165 8
and of yesterday and to-day there could scarcely be an end. P IV 11 241 59

TO-DO (1)
I have no notion of people's making such a to-do about SS III 1 259 7

TO-MORROW (122)
To-morrow I shall fetch her from Churchill, & let Maria LS 39 308 1
shall make but a poor figure in your journal to-morrow." NA I 3 26 20
"I will drive you up Lansdown hill to-morrow." NA I 7 47 25
Well, I will drive you up Lansdown hill to-morrow; mind, I am NA I 7 48 29
"Shall you be at the cotillion ball to-morrow?" NA I 10 73 19
world; and do not let us put it off--let us go to-morrow." NA I 10 80 61
take their promised walk to-morrow; it was quite NA I 13 97 1
they must go to Clifton to-morrow, they would not go NA I 13 97 1
and now we may all go to-morrow with a safe conscience. NA I 13 100 13
going to Clifton with us to-morrow, you could not have the NA I 13 100 15
it to-night to Salisbury, we may have it to-morrow.-- NA I 15 120 22
To-morrow?-- NA I 15 120 22
I thought you did not mean to come back till to-morrow." NA II 9 195 11
As to-morrow is Sunday, Eleanor, I shall not return." NA II 11 211 14
Thank God! we leave this vile place to-morrow. NA II 12 216 2
To-morrow morning is fixed for your leaving us, and not NA II 13 224 18
honour of calling to-morrow to inquire after Miss Dashwood. SS I 9 42 10
That is good news however; I will ride over to-morrow, and SS I 9 43 13
You cannot go to town till to-morrow, brandon, that is all. SS I 13 64 25
"Shall we see you to-morrow to dinner?" said Mrs. Dashwood SS I 14 74 21
be quite alone--and to-morrow you must absolutely dine SS I 18 99 17
would be a shocking thing, as we go away again to-morrow. SS I 20 110 2
to-morrow, and then I hope she will not much mind it." SS II 1 144 11
basket was not finished to-morrow, for though I told her SS II 1 144 13
to tell you, that you will certainly see her to-morrow." SS II 4 163 17
to say, "depend upon it he will call again to-morrow." SS II 5 169 14
Wait only till to-morrow." SS II 6 177 14
At any rate I shall expect you to-morrow. SS II 7 187 38
Cannot we be gone to-morrow?" SS II 7 190 60
"To-morrow, Marianne!" SS II 7 190 61
"It would be impossible to go to-morrow. SS II 7 191 63
But I shall see them to-morrow." SS II 8 195 16
But to-morrow I think I shall certainly be able to call in SS II 11 222 9
I go to Oxford to-morrow." SS III 4 288 27
no longer hope that to-morrow would find her recovered; SS III 7 308 4
and the idea of what to-morrow would have produced, but SS III 7 308 4
me, it will be better recollected and explained to-morrow." SS III 8 318 17
to see him walk in to-day or to-morrow, or any day." SS III 12 358 6
"To-morrow fortnight." PP I 2 6 12
she were married to him to-morrow, I should think she had PP I 6 23 10
I shall walk to Meryton to-morrow to hear more about it, PP I 14 68 14
"My aunt," she continued, "is going to-morrow into that PP II 3 147 22
I am going to-morrow where I shall find a man who has not PP II 4 154 19
present from my master; she comes here to-morrow with him." PP III 1 248 22
not be here till to-morrow; and indeed, before we left PP III 1 256 61
"They will join me early to-morrow," he continued, "and PP III 1 256 61
is obliged to be at Brighton again to-morrow evening. PP III 4 276 5
"Can you come to-morrow?" PP III 13 344 4
Yes, he had no engagement at all for to-morrow; and her PP III 13 344 5
I shall offer to pay him to-morrow; he will rant and storm PP III 17 377 39
is particularly fond of, that I may have it to-morrow." PP III 17 378 45
write to my poor sister to-morrow, and make the proposal; MP I 1 7 8
"I am to have it to-morrow; but how do you think it is to MP I 6 58 35
However, I am to have my harp fetched to-morrow. MP I 6 58 39
"I shall not ride to-morrow, certainly," said Fanny; "I MP I 7 70 29
But I dare say it will be well to-morrow. MP I 7 72 45
will take my horse early to-morrow morning, and ride over MP I 15 148 58
be three acts rehearsed to-morrow evening, and that will MP I 18 167 10
You will hear enough of it to-morrow, sir. MP II 1 181 16
to-morrow evening, I should not be afraid of the result. MP II 1 185 28
and very little will remain of the theatre to-morrow.-- MP II 2 193 13
"To-morrow, I think, my uncle dines at Sotherton, and you MP II 3 199 17
the fatigues of the day, will not keep beyond to-morrow. MP II 4 212 31
insists upon the turkey's being dressed to-morrow." MP II 4 215 48
for to-morrow: but your thanks are far beyond the occasion. MP II 9 262 9
Wear the necklace, as you are engaged to do to-morrow MP II 9 263 16
not this very week, this very day--to-morrow I leave home." MP II 9 268 29
you can tell me why my brother goes to town to-morrow. MP II 10 277 17
"Well then, Fanny, you shall not get up to-morrow before I MP II 10 279 25
my ideas of time and his own very different to-morrow." MP II 10 280 31
But there is no time fixed, perhaps to-morrow, or whenever MP III 1 321 48
therefore of seeing your friend either to-morrow or Sunday. MP III 4 354 48
in time; for she may have her orders to-morrow, perhaps. MP III 7 378 10
I should not wonder if you had your orders to-morrow; but MP III 7 380 20
Good bye; I wish you a pleasant journey to-morrow. MP III 11 412 23
But Sir Thomas hopes he will be better to-morrow, and says MP III 13 427 12
To-morrow! to leave Portsmouth to-morrow! MP III 15 443 24
that he quite forgot it, but he goes again to-morrow. E I 4 32 29
Bond-Street till just before he mounts his horse to-morrow. E I 7 56 46
first chapters, and the intention of going on to-morrow. E I 9 69 3
relative to every body about me, I would marry to-morrow. E I 10 84 16
"I hope he will be here to-morrow, for I have a question E I 12 101 27
Good old Mrs. Bates--I will call upon her to-morrow, and E I 12 102 31
I hope you will think better of their looks to-morrow; for E I 12 103 39
I shall see you at the Abbey to-morrow morning I hope, and E I 12 107 61
voice and what fatigues to-morrow will bring, I think it E I 13 110 9
yesterday, and may not be said and heard again to-morrow. E I 13 113 26
complaints, and I hope to-morrow morning will bring us E I 13 114 34
I shall, therefore, set off to-morrow.'-- E I 18 146 16
Frank comes to-morrow--I had a letter this morning--we see E II 5 188 7
this morning--we see him to-morrow by dinner time to a E II 5 188 7
"Think of me to-morrow, my dear Emma, about four o'clock," E II 5 189 15
hence; and by this time to-morrow, perhaps, or a little E II 5 190 20
"I have been here a week to-morrow--half my time. E II 8 221 51
A week to-morrow!-- E II 8 221 51
done; most likely they will be there to-morrow or Saturday. E II 17 304 27
his coming in to-day or to-morrow, and at any hour, may E II 18 309 30
all about it herself to-morrow: her first partner was Mr. E III 2 329 45
sick of England--and would leave it to-morrow, if I could." E III 6 365 62
"We are going to box hill to-morrow;--you will join us. E III 6 365 67
"But you may come again in the cool of to-morrow morning." E III 6 365 69
that the meeting at the crown is not till to-morrow.-- E III 16 456 28
"No, no, that's to-morrow; and I particularly wanted to E III 16 457 40
He stays till to-morrow, and Miss Fairfax has been E III 18 476 45
under the constant dependance of seeing him to-morrow. P III 10 82 2
that they would go, go to-morrow, fix themselves at the P IV 1 122 5
But surely, you may put off this old lady till to-morrow. P IV 5 157 15
She goes into the warm Bath to-morrow, and for the rest of P IV 5 157 16
gone to-day, to bring Louisa and the "Harvilles to-morrow. P IV 6 163 7
be much "more convenient to me to dine there to-morrow. P IV 6 163 7
me to-morrow if I may not have many more visits from you." P IV 7 180 35
and felt safe till to-morrow, when she heard that he was P IV 10 212 2
for the whole day to-morrow, I had compassion on him." P IV 10 213 9
They will be delighted to come to-morrow evening. P IV 10 220 29
nine this morning, and does not come back till to-morrow." P IV 10 222 35
been to the theatre, and secured a box for to-morrow night. P IV 10 223 41
Take a box for to-morrow night! P IV 10 223 43
engaged to Camden-Place to-morrow night? and that we were P IV 10 223 43
he would go to the play to-morrow, if nobody else would." P IV 10 225 55
"To-morrow evening, to meet a few friends, no formal party. P IV 10 226 64
He wanted to know how early he might be admitted to-morrow. P IV 10 228 71
He was full of "to-morrow;" and it is very evident that I P IV 10 228 71

TO-MORROW'S (2)
He must like him less after to-morrow's visit, for we MP II 3 199 18
from that of to-day, and looking forward to to-morrow's. MP III 13 427 13

TO-MORROWS (2)
A very few to-morrows stood between the young people of E III 1 318 12
A few more to-morrows, and the party from London would be E III 18 470 1

TO-NIGHT (11)
have you settled what to wear on your head to-night? NA I 6 42 24
Morland says that by sending it to-night to Salisbury, we NA I 15 120 22
hardly last longer--nay, perhaps it may freeze to-night!" SS II 5 167 3
I wish you may receive this in time to come here to-night, SS II 7 187 38
The Parrys and Sandersons luckily are coming to-night you SS II 8 192 3
I hope he will come to-night. SS II 8 196 22
hurry Baddeley a little, he seems behind hand to-night." MP II 1 180 12
nothing more can be done to-night; but if you will give us MP II 1 185 28
Mrs. Rushworth and Julia to-night!" and Mrs. Norris paid MP II 10 277 16
to stay at home and take care of yourself to-night." E I 13 110 9
To-night we may have the pleasure of all meeting again, at P IV 11 236 36

TOAST (8)
sally and help make the toast, and spread the bread and MP III 7 383 32
up ready-prepared in the toast rack--and till it was all S 10 416 1
his earnest invitation to her to take both cocoa & toast.-- S 10 416 1
conversation on dry toast, & hear no more of his sisters.-- S 10 417 1
"I hope you will eat some of this toast, said he, I reckon S 10 417 1
I hope you like dry toast."-- S 10 417 1
So far from dry toast being wholesome, I think it a very S 10 417 1
himself; but when her toast was done, & he took his own in S 10 417 1

TOASTED (1)
the boys begging for toasted cheese, her father calling MP III 7 387 46

TOASTER (1)
reckon myself a very good Toaster; I never burn my Toasts-- S 10 417 1

TOASTING (1)
his own satisfaction & toasting some slices of bread, S 10 416 1

TOASTS (1)
Toaster; I never burn my Toasts--I never put them too near S 10 417 1

TODAY (7)
"Catherine, said he, I am going home today. LS 23 283 4
should receive this letter today, for it is on business SS I 13 64 19
"I do beg & entreat that no turkey may be seen today. W 354 27
my dear Emma & returns today, is more interesting to me, W 360 29
left Chichester at the same hour today--& here we are.--" S 9 409 1
As to seeing me again today--I cannot answer for it; the S 9 411 1
If you had seen me today before dinner, you wd have S 10 415 1

TOGETHER (439)
stay in Sussex that they may have some hunting together. LS 8 254 1
in long conversations together, & she has contrived by the LS 11 259 1
is tolerable, we pace the shrubbery for hours together. LS 16 268 2
an hour together, in earnest conversation with Reginald. LS 17 271 7
we left the two gentlemen together to put on our pelisses. LS 20 276 4
on which we now are together, & understand the real LS 20 278 7
St, & we may be always together, there or here, for I LS 26 296 4
is still here, & they have been all closeted together. LS 32 303 2
or two of their being together; and advice of the most NA I 2 18 2
since they were last together, how little they had thought NA I 4 32 2
cousins, talking both together, far more ready to give NA I 4 32 2
when they all quitted it together, that Miss Thorpe should NA I 4 34 7
and dirt, and shut themselves up, to read novels together. NA I 5 37 4
we will read the Italian together; and I have made out a NA I 6 40 8
Thorpes, set off to walk together to Mr. Allen's, and NA I 7 50 44

I hope you will be a great deal together while you are in NA I 7 50 49
you and I are to stand up and jig it together again." NA I 8 59 35
engaged in conversing together, that the latter had no NA I 8 59 38
Did not we agree together to take a drive this morning? NA I 9 61 3
than all his companions together; and described to her NA I 9 66 31
if they were never to be together again; so, with smiles NA I 9 67 33
there I met her, and we had a great deal of talk together. NA I 9 68 38
"Yes, we walked along the Crescent together for half an NA I 9 68 42
and Isabella sat together, there was then an opportunity NA I 10 70 1
the ladies walked about together, noticing every new face, NA I 10 71 8
they continued talking together as long as both parties NA I 10 72 8
I thought you and I were to dance together." NA I 10 75 25
A good figure of a man; well put together.-- NA I 10 76 28
"--That you think they cannot be compared together." NA I 10 77 31
marry can never part, but must go and keep house together. NA I 10 77 32
They all spent the evening together at Thorpe's. NA I 11 89 63
gone out in a phaeton together? and then what could I do? NA I 12 93 5
house for ten minutes together, was engaged in NA I 12 95 17
we had a little touch together, though I was almost afraid NA I 12 96 20
The three others still continued together, walking in a NA I 13 99 9
very well; but going to inns and public places together! NA I 13 104 31
be for a whole morning together, and how tired my poor NA I 14 109 26
Who knows when we may be together again?-- NA I 15 123 36
They retired whispering together; and, though her delicate NA II 1 132 16
The friends were not able to get together for any NA II 1 134 37
her seeing Isabella for more than a few minutes together. NA II 3 143 1
It would be hideous to be always together; we should be NA II 3 143 2
what were you to live upon, supposing you came together? NA II 3 145 16
they ran down stairs together, in an alarm not wholly NA II 6 165 5
drawing-room for an hour together in silent thoughtfulness, NA II 8 187 13
and young men never know their minds two days together. NA II 12 216 2
said by either during the time of their remaining together. NA II 13 229 31
It is ten to one but you are thrown together again in the NA II 14 236 17
herself for ten minutes together, walking round the garden NA II 15 240 1
that we are all hastening together to perfect felicity. NA II 16 250 4
together on the interest of ten thousand pounds." SS I 2 10 15
impossible to have lived together so long, had not a SS I 3 14 3
He and I have been at times thrown a good deal together, SS I 4 20 9
Nay, the longer they were together the more doubtful SS I 4 22 18
evening of their being together, from his listening so SS I 8 36 1
better not have any thing to do with matrimony together. SS I 8 37 9
evening of their being together! in Edward's farewell SS I 8 39 18
Twice did I leave them purposely together in the course of SS I 8 39 18
off from their hills; and the two girls set off together. SS I 9 41 3
They read, they talked, they sang together; his musical SS I 10 48 8
they were talking of him together, "whom every body speaks SS I 10 50 14
stand together and scarcely spoke a word to any body else. SS I 11 54 3
together by mutual consent, while the others were dancing. SS I 11 55 8
As Elinor and Marianne were walking together the next SS I 12 58 1
Of John I know very little, though we have lived together SS I 12 59 4
whispering and talking together as fast as could be, and SS I 12 60 13
as they were all got together, they must do something by SS I 13 66 60
been since spent by us together, you would degrade to the SS I 14 73 17
doubt the nature of the terms on which they are together. SS I 15 80 38
read nothing but what they had been used to read together. SS I 16 83 3
care how cross he was to her, as they must live together. SS I 20 112 26
Sometimes he won't speak to me for half a day together. SS I 20 113 39
that we should never have been in the country together. SS I 20 114 44
an hour or two together in the same room almost every day. SS I 21 124 33
more was required; to be together was, in his opinion, to SS I 21 124 33
they had never dined together, without his drinking to her SS I 21 125 36
day as they were walking together from the park to the SS I 22 128 3
drinking, and laughing together, playing at cards, or SS II 1 143 8
her husband united them together in one noisy purpose, SS II 1 143 9
for them to be together; because if they got tired of me, SS II 3 154 4
and happily together with our books and our music! SS II 3 155 8
and especially in being together; and if Elinor would ever SS II 3 157 16
they should not be long together; and the restless state SS II 7 180 5
Did not I see them together in Devonshire every day, and SS II 7 182 10
Have you forgot the last evening of our being together at SS II 7 189 46
my acquaintance leagued together to ruin me in his opinion, SS II 7 189 50
But the family are all rich together. SS II 8 194 10
while the sisters were together in their own room after SS II 9 202 4
We were within a few hours of eloping together for SS II 9 206 24
covert, and they were kept waiting for two hours together. SS II 10 214 9
Dashwood can spare you both for so long a time together!" SS II 10 218 34
which he could not conceal when they were together. SS II 12 231 11
walked up the stairs together--for the Middletons arrived SS II 12 231 13
were not only all three together, but were together SS II 13 241 19
but were together without the relief of any other person. SS II 13 241 19
for the girls to be together; and generally congratulated SS II 14 247 5
five minutes of their being together, when it was finished. SS II 14 249 8
I never happened to see them together, or I am sure I SS III 1 258 7
together, without any diminution of her usual cordiality.-- SS III 1 264 32
We consulted together, however, as to what should be done, SS III 1 266 38
clapped her hands together, and cried, "gracious God! can SS III 1 267 39
"you were all in the same room together, were not you?" SS III 2 274 17
No, no; they were shut up in the drawing-room together, SS III 2 274 18
I had so many secrets together, she never made any bones SS III 2 274 20
friendship, which together prompted Colonel Brandon to SS III 3 283 26
He too was much distressed, and they sat down together in SS III 4 288 26
together in Delaford parsonage before Michaelmas. SS III 5 293 2
be the last time, perhaps-- let us be cheerful together.-- SS III 8 318 15
said she, "we will take long walks together every day. SS III 10 343 9
and their conversation together; and was carefully minute SS III 10 348 34
In the evening, when they were all three together, SS III 11 349 3
His demands and your inexperience together on a small, SS III 11 350 9
together in a similarity of thoughtfulness and silence. SS III 11 355 46
conversation together, and yet enjoy, as she wished, the SS III 13 363 6
How they could be thrown together, and by what attraction SS III 13 364 10
They were brought together by mutual affection, with the SS III 13 369 32
or four days, the two gentlemen quitted Barton together.-- SS III 13 372 46
Mrs. Jennings's prophecies, though rather jumbled together, SS III 14 374 7
as they were walking together one morning before the gates SS III 14 375 9
people are much thrown together, and see little of anybody SS III 14 375 9
could exceed the harmony in which they all lived together. SS III 14 377 11
and Colonel Brandon together was hardly earnest, though SS III 14 378 13
The girls, dressing in some measure together, grew W 323 3
together, passing in & out from the adjoining card-room.-- W 327 8
you should not be here, but we had better all be together." W 334 13
me to be throwing you together, so well as I knew his W 341 19
with much sentiment, as they were sitting together.-- W 349 24
us--if it be for months together.--& I am sorry, (with a W 350 24
Emma, you & I are to be together; Elizth always takes care W 351 25
is never for many hours together; and as they always see PP I 6 22 6
every moment should be employed in conversing together. PP I 6 22 6
spent together--and four evenings may do a great deal." PP I 6 22 8
their company, and the three young ladies set off together. PP I 7 32 39
Miss Bingley left them together, could attempt little PP I 7 33 43
"I hope," said she, as they were walking together in the PP I 10 52 55
up and down the room together, with either of which PP I 11 56 12
standing and talking together very agreeably, when the PP I 15 72 8
together, as I think you said, in the closest manner!" PP I 16 80 36
of our youth was passed together; inmates of the same PP I 16 81 37
they continued talking together with mutual satisfaction PP I 16 84 59
silent for half an hour together, and yet for the PP I 18 91 13
towards Bingley and Jane, who were dancing together. PP I 18 92 24
Mr. Bingley and Jane were standing together, a little PP I 18 103 75
one of the younger girls together, soon after breakfast, PP I 19 104 1
2

And gathering her work together, she was hastening away, PP I 19 104 4
5

Mr. Collins and me have a little conversation together." PP I 20 113 30
him for so many hours together, might be more than I could PP I 21 115 4
No one who has ever seen you together, can doubt his PP I 21 119 20
away, just as they were all getting so intimate together. PP I 21 120 30
together; and fourthly, that the match might be broken off. PP I 23 127 5
Bennet's leaving them together, after a longer irritation PP II 1 134 4
5

you will be convinced of it, by seeing them happy together. PP II 1 136 14
As they went down stairs together, Charlotte said, "I PP II 3 146 11
12

shall not be jumbled together in our imaginations; nor, PP II 4 154 23
together, and now and then accompanied by their aunt. PP II 9 180 28
sat there ten minutes together without opening his lips; PP II 9 180 29
did turn, and they walked towards the parsonage together. PP II 10 183 6
them to have been together the whole of last summer." PP II 10 185 28
we have been concerned together; and if you do not PP II 12 202 5
brought them much together, and given her a sort of PP II 13 207 6
young ladies set out together from Gracechurch-Street, for PP II 16 219 1
"I am sure," said she, "I cried for two days together when PP II 18 229 4
I know, when they were together; and a good deal is to be PP II 18 235 38
merits, as they proceeded together up the great staircase. PP III 1 249 37
together, were some of the most uncomfortable of her life. PP III 1 252 52
took her place by her niece, and they walked on together. PP III 1 256 61
herself not tired, and they stood together on the lawn. PP III 1 257 66
They had not been long together, before Darcy told her PP III 2 261 5
the others were talking together, and in a tone which had PP III 2 262 8
when we were all dancing together at Netherfield." PP III 2 262 8
They are gone off together from Brighton. PP III 4 277 11
They left Brighton together on Sunday night, and were PP III 4 277 14
few minutes conversation together, received them exactly PP III 5 287 34
and then we may consult together as to what is to be done." PP III 5 288 37
They must have seen them together for ever." PP III 5 290 45
Elizabeth were walking together in the shrubbery behind PP III 7 301 1
from his writing table, and they went up stairs together. PP III 7 305 43
How merry we shall be together when we meet!" PP III 7 306 44
who were only brought together because their passions were PP III 8 312 17
My uncle and aunt and I were to go together; and the PP III 9 319 24
And then, you know, when once they get together, there is PP III 9 319 25
as I said before, they had a great deal of talk together. PP III 10 323 2
They battled it together for a long time, which was more PP III 10 324 2
soon as they were alone together, she said, "I saw you PP III 11 331 16
17

of bringing them together; that the whole of the visit PP III 12 340 14
Bennet spent the morning together, as had been agreed on. PP III 13 346 21
and Bingley standing together over the hearth, as if PP III 13 346 22
I have not a doubt of your doing very well together. PP III 13 348 38
I thought how likely it was that you should come together. PP III 13 348 40
the family were sitting together in the dining room, their PP III 14 351 1
of her sister must bring them more frequently together. PP III 15 360 1
that their living together before the marriage took place, PP III 15 363 22
never spare time, but the remaining five set off together. PP III 16 365 1
was unabated, I felt no doubt of their happiness together." PP III 16 371 40
they would be, always together like brothers and sisters? MP I 1 6 6
and they went together into the breakfast room, where MP I 2 16 20
put the map of Europe together--or my cousin cannot tell MP I 2 18 23
delight in being together, their hours of happy mirth, and MP I 2 21 34
to their living together, but even to give it the most MP I 3 24 7
men were not often seen together even in London, and that MP I 5 47 27
and on their all dining together at the park soon after MP I 6 52 1
talk to me by the hour together, has never yet turned the MP I 6 59 43
walking down the hill together to the village; nor did her MP I 7 69 21
had been left four days together without any choice of MP I 7 74 58
He was ashamed to think that for four days together she MP I 7 74 58
Fanny, and Miss Crawford remained in a cluster together. MP I 9 86 11
for half an hour together without striking it out." MP I 9 94 56
On this rencontre they all returned to the house together, MP I 10 104 51
were close to her; they were all in a cluster together. MP I 12 117 15
they had spent ten days together in the same society, and MP I 13 121 1
The many laughs we have had together would infallibly come MP I 14 133 11
Henry Crawford conversed together in an under voice, and MP I 14 136 21
Mr. Yates walking off together to consult farther in the MP I 14 136 22
Agatha might be to act together, nor wait very patiently MP I 15 138 1
There is no occasion to put them so very close together. MP I 15 141 22
For a moment no one spoke; and then many spoke together to MP I 15 143 28
Tom, "but unluckily the butler and Anhalt are in together. MP I 15 144 33
a great many of my own, before we rehearse together.-- MP I 15 149 61
whole was now so blended together, so harmonized by MP I 16 152 2
prospect of acting the fool together with such unanimity. MP I 16 156 27
of all his parts together, and make him more ready to MP I 18 164 1
I think you may give me your help in putting it together.-- MP I 18 166 6
would then be acting together for the first time;--the MP I 18 167 12
of being thus thrown together--of comparing schemes--and MP I 18 170 23
They must now rehearse together. MP I 18 170 24
as he did--all collected together exactly as he could have MP II 1 178 8
have been nearly confined to the house for days together. MP II 1 181 16
to the drawing-room together, Sir Thomas with an increase MP II 1 183 24
began, without bringing them together in some way or other. MP II 2 192 11
I could listen to him for an hour together. MP II 3 197 5
Could they be much together I feel sure of their liking MP II 3 199 13
She went however, and they sauntered about together many MP II 4 208 11
they were thus sitting together one day: "every time I MP II 4 208 12
It was the first time of his seeing them together since MP II 4 211 25
while you do wrong together I can overlook a great deal." MP II 4 211 28
The two cousins walked home together; and except in the MP II 4 216 50
young people like to be together, I can see no reason why MP II 5 219 18
of every thing, and all together between Mr. Crawford and MP II 5 223 48
to recommend yourself, for we are a great deal together." MP II 6 231 10
On the morrow they were walking about together with true MP II 6 234 17
variety of danger, which sea and war together could offer. MP II 6 236 21
They had been hunting together, and were in the midst of a MP II 7 240 13
must be all laid together of course; very pretty meadows MP II 7 242 23
They remained together at the otherwise deserted card- MP II 7 249 49
We used to jump about together many a time, did not we? MP II 7 250 59
Dr. and Mrs. Grant, who were together in the drawing-room. MP II 8 257 15
They must and shall be worn together. MP II 9 262 8
They proceeded up stairs together, their rooms being on MP II 9 268 27
down their two dances together with such sober· MP II 10 278 20
when they first danced together, but it was not her gaiety MP II 10 279 21
when they had been last together; much less could her MP II 11 282 3
there for a whole day together, and he was gone on whom MP II 11 284 8
and Lady Bertram were together, and unless she had Fanny MP II 11 287 18
the sort of friendly acquaintance we have had together?-- MP II 11 287 22
is a clergyman, and they are all clergymen together. MP II 11 289 34
Then we shall be all together." MP II 12 295 21
What can Sir Thomas and Edmund together do, what do they MP II 12 297 35
The two ladies were together in the breakfast-room, and MP II 13 298 1
by my uncle, after the evening they passed together." MP II 13 300 5
children;--take them all together, I dare say nobody would MP II 13 305 24
and were unhappy too!--it was all wretchedness together. MP III 1 321 46
soon as they were alone together afterwards,--and she MP III 2 332 23
walking together through the village, as he rode into it.-- MP III 3 334 1
and wit, and good nature together, could do; or at least, MP III 3 340 24
for half a dozen Sundays together; but not for a constancy; MP III 3 341 30
long while since we have had a comfortable walk together." MP III 4 346 6
more is necessary than merely pacing this gravel together. MP III 4 346 8
My theoretical and his practical knowledge together, could MP III 4 348 21
be tolerably happy together, even if I could like him. MP III 4 348 22
probability of your happiness together: do not imagine it. MP III 4 348 23
we were all wrong together; but none so wrong as myself. MP III 4 349 26
say; and they walked on together some fifty yards in MP III 4 351 35
I found the two sisters together by themselves; and when MP III 4 352 38
were to pass all their middle and latter life together. MP III 7 375 2

themselves, all talking together, but Rebecca loudest, and MP III 7 382 27
all burst into the room together and sat down, Fanny could MP III 7 383 31
at last all in motion together, the moment came for MP III 7 384 36
By sitting together up stairs, they avoided a great deal MP III 9 398 9
while they walked on together at their own hasty pace. MP III 10 403 14
satisfied in going about together and discussing matters MP III 10 403 15
what he had intended, and they all walked thither together. MP III 11 408 1
I hope they get on pretty well together. MP III 13 423 2
it and her cousin Edmund together, would have made her (as MP III 14 435 15
friends, all intimate together!--it was too horrible a MP III 15 441 20
short time they had been together, had disagreed; and the MP III 16 450 10
"How long were you together?" MP III 16 456 28
than sought--all this together most grievously convinced MP III 16 457 30
She hoped to marry him, and they continued together till MP III 17 464 10
private, where, shut up together with little society, on MP III 17 465 14
in every transaction together from that period, in their MP III 17 465 15
first inclination, and brought them very often together. MP III 17 467 19
They lived together; and when Dr. Grant had brought on MP III 17 469 24
week, they still lived together; for Mary, though MP III 17 469 24
they had been living together as friend and friend very E I 1 5 3
were left to dine together, with no prospect of a third to E I 1 6 5
to their spending half the evenings in the week together. E I 2 18 11
wife, who all lived together; but when it appeared that E I 4 27 5
while they talked together, soon made her quick eye E I 4 31 27
They remained but a few minutes together, as Miss E I 4 32 28
They will read together. E I 5 36 6
they might decide together on the best size for Harriet. E I 6 44 19
whether she had not better leave them together at once. E I 6 46 22
You and Mr. Elton are by situation called together; you E I 9 75 25
the Knightleys together, as she does about Jane Fairfax. E I 10 86 23
was sickness and poverty together which she came to visit; E I 10 86 24
25
side of the lane, leaving them together in the main road. E I 10 88 33
They now walked on together quietly, till within view of E I 10 89 36
The lovers were standing together at one of the windows. E I 10 90 39
You and I will have a nice basin of gruel together. E I 12 100 18
as they walked on slowly together in conversation about E I 13 109 6
They joined company and proceeded together. E I 13 109 6
Mrs. Weston and Emma were sitting together on a sopha. E I 15 124 1
They must keep as much together as they could;" and James E I 15 128 22
they had to continue together a few minutes longer, for E I 15 132 37
to take so active part in bringing any two people together. E I 16 136 10
Emma and Harriet had been walking together one morning, E II 1 155 1
together--not able to come if anything was to happen. E II 1 160 23
They continued together with unabated regard however, till E II 2 165 7
more beauty in them all together than she had remembered; E II 2 167 12
It is such a happiness when good people get together--and E II 3 175 39
their being thrown together again, with any necessity, or E II 3 180 58
perceive them walking up to the house together, arm in arm. E II 6 196 2
But on seeing them together, she became perfectly E II 6 196 2
They were all three walking about together for an hour or E II 6 196 2
been children and women together; and it is natural to E II 6 203 39
He perfectly agreed with her: and after walking together E II 6 203 42
be, who were now seeing them together for the first time. E II 8 212 4
to them as they sat together after dinner; and while her E II 8 213 6
I know he had horses to-day--for we arrived together; and E II 8 223 64
They sang together once more; and Emma would then resign E II 8 227 86
They had sung together once or twice, it appeared, at E II 8 227 87
"Don't class us together, Harriet. E II 9 231 6
all the music to her, and they looked it over together.-- E II 10 243 23
young people set off together without delay for the crown. E II 11 253 40
we shall walk back together, and I must be off immediately. E II 12 260 25
I hope we shall have many sweet little concerts together. E II 14 277 38
exertion of getting them together, or some other cause, E II 15 287 27
28
happy wife together, without feeling uncomfortable. E II 16 291 5
Mr. Woodhouse considered eight persons at dinner together E II 16 292 7
almost always either talking together or silent together. E II 17 299 1
of such a situation together," said Jane, "they are pretty E II 17 301 19
The two ladies looked over it together; and he sat smiling E II 17 303 26
has not been able to leave the sopha for a week together. E II 18 306 11
They all walked about together, to see that every thing E III 2 319 3
together for the purpose of preparatory inspection. E III 2 319 3
less expected to see together--Frank Churchill, with E III 3 332 3
the ball, had walked out together, and taken a road, the E III 3 333 5
young woman thrown together in such a way, could hardly E III 3 334 9
their appearance together, and heard their history of it, E III 3 335 9
No, let them be ever so happy together, it will not give E III 4 337 6
should unite, and go together; and that as Mrs. Elton had E III 6 353 3
way, scarcely any three together, they insensibly followed E III 6 360 38
They took a few turns together along the walk.-- E III 6 361 40
Emma and Harriet went together; Miss Bates and her niece, E III 7 367 1
The Eltons walked together; Mr. Knightley took charge of E III 7 367 1
"Mr. Frank Churchill and Miss Woodhouse flirted together E III 7 368 3
Understanding and gratification came together. E III 7 371 35
every thing together--that Jane was resolved to receive no E III 9 391 21
together and on their way at a quick pace for Randall's. E III 10 392 7
I shall leave you together. E III 10 394 25
had talked it all over together, and he had talked it all E III 10 401 69
When they had been all walking together, he had so often E III 11 409 35
when able to see them together again, she might at least E III 12 416 2
They never could have been all three together, without her E III 12 421 17
In half a minute they were together. E III 13 424 1
They walked together. E III 13 425 2
"I have no doubt of their being happy together," said Emma; E III 13 428 22
of the evil day, when they must all be together again. E III 14 435 4
Had we been met walking together between Donwell and E III 14 441 8
Mrs. Bates and Mrs. Elton were together. E III 16 453 11
and Knightley are shut up together in deep consultation.-- E III 16 456 25
you and I should make, if we could be shaken together. E III 16 456 33
right that equal worth can give, to be happy together. E III 17 465 25
Shocking plan, living together. E III 17 469 36
been great, and they had gone on together most happily. P III 1 5 8
they must have been seen together," he observed, "once at P III 1 8 16
Accordingly their removal was made together, and Anne was P III 5 36 19
and agreement together, that good-humoured mutual P III 5 41 45
as they were connected together, at all a dangerous P III 6 43 5
to them by the hour together; a kindness which always P III 6 47 15
but the two sisters were together; and as it chanced that P III 6 48 17
pleasure of seeing them set off together in high spirits. P III 7 58 20
They were soon dining in company together at Mr. P III 8 63 1
evening they spent together: and though his voice did not P III 8 63 2
They had no conversation together, no intercourse but what P III 8 63 3
and sitting down together to pore over it, with the P III 8 64 7
fellow, like you, do ashore, for half a year together?-- P III 8 65 14
I knew that we should either go to the bottom together, or P III 8 65 16
A friend of mine, and I, had such a lovely cruise together P III 8 67 23
While we were together, you know, there was nothing to be P III 8 70 54
as long as we could be together, nothing ever ailed me, P III 8 71 54
together, equally without error, and without consciousness. P III 8 72 58
generally out of doors together, interesting themselves in P III 9 73 2
were not all together, but she could stay for none of it. P III 9 80 34
Anne had soon been in company with all the four together P III 10 82 1
being gone a shooting together, as the sisters in the P III 10 83 3
to be done together, however undesired and inconvenient. P III 10 83 4
the whole six set toward together in the direction chosen P III 10 83 6
hope, and spring, all gone together, blessed her memory. P III 10 85 12
afterwards collected, and once more in motion together. P III 10 89 35
now very glad to be together again, did not admit a doubt. P III 10 89 36
sitting down together in our lodgings at North Yarmouth?" P III 10 92 44
would never be persuaded that we could be happy together. P III 10 92 45
Lady Russell to see them together, she might think that he P III 11 93 3

circumstances together," said Captain Wentworth, "we must P III 12 106 17
to be all together, and out of doors as long as they could. P III 12 107 22
again; and they walked together some time, talking as P III 12 107 23
They had been all in lodgings together. P IV 2 129 2
chancing to be alone together, he began to compliment her P IV 4 145 3
would be every possibility of your being happy together. P IV 5 159 23
They had been thrown together several weeks; they had been P IV 6 167 19
them their country habit of being almost always together. P IV 6 168 24
of your company the little way our road lies together. P IV 6 169 26
Yes, yes, we will have a snug walk together; and I have P IV 6 169 27
He very handsomely hopes they will be happy together, and P IV 6 173 47
They had, by dint of being so very much together, got to P IV 7 176 8
moment they walked off together, her arm under his, a P IV 7 177 16
time, more than all the rest of the world put together." P IV 9 194 16
how much you were together, and feeling it to be the most P IV 9 197 36
than most others, and we were almost always together. P IV 9 199 55
been as before always together, and Mr. Elliot had led his P IV 9 208 95
They were wretched together. P IV 9 211 101
an opportunity of bringing him and Sir Walter together. P IV 10 213 5
Charles's leaving them together, was listening to Mrs. P IV 10 220 31
common friends must be soon bringing them together again. P IV 10 221 32
solicitude never appeased for five minutes together. P IV 10 227 69
together, than be involved in a long engagement. P IV 11 230 7
our walking together at Lyme, and grieving for him? P IV 11 232 15
the other two proceeding together; and soon words enough P IV 11 240 59
The sea air & sea bathing together were nearly infallible, S 2 373 1
than are often met with, either separate or together.-- S 5 385 1
a day for 10 days together releived her so little that we S 5 387 1
I have heard nothing of Sidney since your being together S 5 387 1
laugh for half an hour together I declare I by myself, can S 5 387 1
but for walking on together to the terrace--which S 7 395 1
Nobody could live happier together than us--& he was a S 7 400 1
The two ladies continued walking together till rejoined by S 8 403 1
I have dined, said he, & we will go about together."-- S 9 410 1
4 were cheifly engaged together, he evidently felt it no S 10 415 1

TOIL (3)
I see him now;--his toil and his despair. MP II 5 224 53
professions, there is a toil and a labour of the mind, if P III 3 20 17
Mary never wrote to Bath herself; all the toil of keeping P III 12 107 21

TOILETTE (5)
arm into her gown, her toilette seemed so nearly finished, NA II 6 164 3
during the whole of her toilette, which it received from SS II 14 249 8
When the ladies were separating for the toilette, he said PP II 6 160 5
6
One came from her books, and the other from her toilette. PP III 5 289 41
be hurried down from her toilette, with all her glossy S 6 390 1

TOILETTES (2)
Not tables, toilettes, wardrobes, or drawers, but on one NA II 5 158 17
nieces, assisting their toilettes, displaying their MP I 4 34 3

TOILING (2)
You are always labouring and toiling, exposed to every P IV 11 233 23
in toiling up it's long ascent half rock, half sand.-- S 1 363 1

TOILS (4)
Fanny felt the advantage; and, drawing back from the toils MP II 10 273 8
The toils of the business were over, the sweets began. P IV 4 149 13
I have valued myself on honourable toils and just rewards. P IV 11 247 84
When his toils were over however, he moved back his chair S 10 416 1

TOILSOME (1)
of the present, by a toilsome walk to Camden-Place, there P IV 10 227 69

TOKEN (4)
they quickly perceived, in token of the coachman's PP II 16 219 1
is, a token of the love of one of your oldest friends." MP II 9 261 2
better pleased that such a token of friendship had passed. MP III 5 365 36
Mr. Churchill had made a point of it, as a token of E III 11 403 2

TOKENS (1)
her heart. those dearest tokens so formed for each other MP II 9 271 40

TOLD (364)
I gave him hopes of Frederica's relenting, & told him a LS 9 257 1
He has told me so in a warmth of manner which spoke his LS 11 259 1
over and over again, & told Lady Susan three times that he LS 20 276 3
the best of it however, & told my story with great success LS 22 280 1
He then told me, mixing in his speech a few insolent LS 22 281 4
How dared he beleive what she told him in my disfavour! LS 22 282 6
"He told us nothing of all this last night, said she LS 23 284 6
"Frederica, said I, you ought to have told me all your LS 24 286 6
I have told him that I am not quite well, & must be alone-- LS 31 302 1
Mrs Manwaring can have told you, to occasion so LS 35 304 1
Allen; "and so I told Miss Morland when she bought it." NA I 3 28 44
I had rather be told at once that you will not tell me." NA I 3 29 49
advantage now; but we are told to "despair of nothing we NA I 4 31 2
produced the book, and told its name; though the chances NA I 5 38 4
But do not tell me--I would not be told upcn any account. NA I 6 39 7
I told Capt. Hunt at one of our assemblies this winter, NA I 6 40 14
Her brother told her that it was twenty-three miles." NA I 7 45 6
The very easy manner in which he then told her that he had NA I 8 55 10
"So I told your brother all the time--but he would not NA I 8 56 14
He told her of horses which he had bought for a trifle and NA I 9 66 31
dead, because Mrs. Hughes told me there was a very NA I 9 68 48
You would have told us that we seemed born for each other, NA I 10 71 5
You would be told so by people of all descriptions, who NA I 10 78 45
As she entered the house, the footman told her, that a NA I 11 89 62
setting off; that, when he told them she was gone out with NA I 11 89 62
Told her you had sent me to say, that having just NA I 13 100 15
Thorpe told her it would be in vain to go after the NA I 13 101 21
to go--I told them from the first I could not go.-- NA I 13 102 25
Miss Tilney before they told me of it; and therefore you NA I 13 104 30
may depend on it; for as I told Mrs. Morland at parting, I NA I 13 104 36
After what you told him from me, how could he think of NA II 1 133 33
I told him he had taken a very unlikely way to prevail NA II 1 134 39
stay, than Miss Tilney told her of her father's having NA II 2 138 1
We leave Bath, as she has perhaps told you, on Saturday NA II 2 139 7
I have myself told him that Miss Thorpe is engaged. NA II 4 150 6
Not that James has ever told me so, but I am sure he is NA II 4 150 7
I only ask what I want to be told." NA II 4 151 21
Henry had certainly been only in jest in what he had told NA II 6 167 6
looks of surprize, which told him almost as plainly, as he NA II 7 178 21
part; though, on being told that, with the addition of the NA II 8 183 2
in her progress, by being told, that she was treading what NA II 8 183 2
He told me the other day, that he only valued money as it NA II 10 205 30
I believe, at least Tilney told me so at the time, and NA II 12 217 2
gratified look on being told that her stay was determined, NA II 13 221 6
she hardly supposed there were any thing worse to be told. NA II 13 223 13
portion must yet remain to be told in a letter from James. NA II 15 247 14
it was not their way to suppose any evil could be told. NA II 16 249 1
Mr. John Dashwood told his mother again and again how SS I 5 25 4
intelligence; and he told them that Mr. Willoughby had no SS I 9 44 23
contemptuously, "he has told you that in the East Indies SS I 10 51 21
"He would have told me so, I doubt not, had I made any SS I 10 51 22
If it will be any satisfaction to you, however, to be told, SS I 10 52 28
Marianne told her, with the greatest delight, that SS I 12 58 1
without hesitation, and told her sister of it in raptures. SS I 12 58 1
replied Margaret; "it was you who told me of it yourself." SS I 12 61 19
"Then you would have told me, that it might or might not SS I 15 78 28
till the door was opened before she told her story. SS I 19 106 20
their friends, without ceasing till every thing was told. SS I 19 107 28
just before we left town, and he told me of it directly." SS I 20 115 48
have told them it is all very true, and a great deal more. SS I 21 119 4
veracity; "I remember he told us, that he had been staying SS I 22 134 49
than had already been told, she did not mistrust her own SS II 1 142 7
to-morrow, for though I told her it certainly would not, I SS II 1 144 13
afraid I had offended you by what I told you that Monday." SS II 2 146 3
"So my daughter Middleton told me, for it seems Sir John SS II 5 171 38

and when at last they were told that Lady Middleton waited	SS II 6 175 1
"But he told you that he loved you?"--	SS II 7 186 33
I have been told that you were asked to be of the party.	SS II 7 187 40
only to deceive, let it be told as soon as possible.	SS II 7 188 42
When he told me that it might be many weeks before we meet	SS II 7 189 46
ought he not to have told me of it, to have given me the	SS II 7 190 56
Mrs. Taylor told me of it half an hour ago, and she was	SS II 8 192 3
an hour ago, and she was told it by a particular friend of	SS II 8 192 3
in Conduit-Street in my way home, and told them of it.	SS II 8 195 16
I have never told you how this was brought on.	SS II 9 206 24
however, in communicating to her what I have told you.	SS II 9 210 32
from her son-in-law had told her that he and his wife were	SS II 10 213 5
yet awhile; though you told me, you know, at Barton, that	SS II 10 217 21
not to be told, they could do nothing at present but write.	SS II 11 230 4
disappointment when she told her that Edward certainly	SS II 12 231 11
was almost sure of being told that upon "her word she	SS II 14 249 8
call when Mrs. Ferrars is told of it, for she was sent for	SS III 1 259 7
November, she told me in confidence of her engagement."	SS III 1 262 16
It was told me,--it was in a manner forced on my by the	SS III 1 263 29
my prospects; and told me, as I thought, with triumph.--	SS III 1 263 29
his marrying Miss Morton; told him that she would settle	SS III 1 266 38
than one; for Miss Godby told Miss Sparks, that nobody in	SS III 2 272 16
kind of talking; so she told him directly (with a great	SS III 2 273 16
of things you know)--she told him directly, she had not	SS III 2 273 16
remember, as well Edward too, who I have told of it.	SS III 2 277 30
When she told Marianne what she had done, however, her	SS III 3 279 2
Elinor told him that it was.	SS III 3 282 18
"Mrs. Jennings told me," said he, "that you wished to	SS III 4 288 27
from his chair Elinor told him the number of the house.	SS III 4 290 40
	41
I think the housekeeper told me, could make up fifteen	SS III 4 292 55
He expressed great pleasure in meeting Elinor, told her	SS III 5 294 4
My mother was the first person who told me of it, and I,	SS III 5 299 35
its deficiencies, and told her what he meant to do himself	SS III 6 305 16
injunction of distrust, told herself likewise not to hope.	SS III 7 314 22
horses; and this, while it told the excess of her poor	SS III 7 316 29
"Had they told me," he cried with vehemence, "that Mr.	SS III 8 317 4
and common sense might have told her how to find it out."	SS III 8 322 38
her deep regret, when I told her that I was obliged to	SS III 8 324 42
"I do not know what I told her," he replied, impatiently; "	SS III 8 324 45
Had he not told me as an inducement that you and your	SS III 8 327 55
As bluntly as he could speak it, therefore, he told me	SS III 8 330 69
He has told me so himself."	SS III 9 336 8
its foundations as far as we are told they once reached.	SS III 10 343 9
relief to me--what Elinor told me this morning--I have now	SS III 11 350 5
	6
"Who told you that Mr. Ferrars was married, thomas?"	SS III 11 354 26
straight from town, as Miss Lucy--Mrs. Ferrars told me."	SS III 11 354 36
the mind may be told to consider it, and certainty itself.	SS III 12 357 1
and how he was received, need not be particularly told.	SS III 13 361 3
Elinor remembered what Robert had told her in Harley-	SS III 13 364 11
I felt that I admired you, but I told myself it was only	SS III 13 368 28
argument in her power;--told him, that in Miss Morton he	SS III 14 373 3
many people come yet was told by the waiter as she knew	W 327 7
two dances; Mrs Tomlinson told me he was gone to ask you--	W 336 14
He related the dishes & told what he had ate himself.	W 344 20
Long has just been here, and she told me all about it."	PP I 1 3 5
She told the story however with great spirit among her	PP I 3 12 14
Mrs. Long told me last night that he sat close to her for	PP I 5 19 10
"Miss Bingley told me," said Jane, "that he never speaks	PP I 5 19 13
"I have already told her so once, by your desire."	PP I 10 47 10
When you told Mrs. Bennet this morning that if you ever	PP I 10 49 27
and by that means, as I told Lady Catherine myself one day,	PP I 14 67 9
My aunt told me so herself on Saturday.	PP I 14 68 14
and though prepared, as he told Elizabeth, to meet with	PP I 15 71 6
boy in the street, who had told her that they were not to	PP I 15 73 11
to be told, the history of his acquaintance with Mr. Darcy.	PP I 16 77 8
and of what he had told her, all the way home; but there	PP I 16 84 59
eagerly applied, and who told them that Wickham had been	PP I 18 89 1
	2
on her spirits; and having told all her griefs to	PP I 18 90 4
came up to them and told her with great exultation that he	PP I 18 96 56
it remains to be told why my views were directed to	PP I 19 106 10
I told you in the library, you know, that I should never	PP I 20 113 28
liked her going, that he told her to write to him, and	PP II 4 151 2
management of them all; told her how every thing ought to	PP II 6 163 15
running into the other, told the girls what an honour they	PP II 7 170 7
	8
I have told Miss Bennet several times, that she will never	PP II 8 173 10
welcome, as I have often told her, to come to Rosings	PP II 8 173 10
But when Elizabeth told of his silence, it did not seem	PP II 9 180 28
of him could not have told her; and as she would have	PP II 9 180 29
From something that he told me in our journey hither, I	PP II 10 185 24
What he told me was merely this; that he congratulated	PP II 10 185 28
"He only told me, what I have now told you."	PP II 10 185 32
You may possibly wonder why all this was not told you last	PP II 12 202 5
had been known in Hertfordshire but what he told himself.	PP II 13 206 4
the country, he had told his story to no one but herself;	PP II 13 207 5
She was immediately told, that the two gentlemen from	PP II 13 209 13
I told Mrs. Collins so before you came.	PP II 14 211 8
before she told her sister of Mr. Darcy's proposals.	PP II 15 217 17
other, and the waiter was told that he need not stay.	PP II 16 220 9
"But you will know it, when I have told you what happened	PP II 17 224 8
I want to be told whether I ought, or ought not to make	PP II 17 226 21
I told my sister Philips so the other day.	PP II 17 227 27
The housekeeper came forward, and told them it was the	PP III 1 247 9
on beholding his master, must immediately have told it.	PP III 1 251 52
With a triumphant smile, they were told, that it was ten	PP III 1 253 57
They had not been long together, before Darcy told her	PP III 2 261 5
the power, which her fancy told her she still possessed,	PP III 2 266 16
Adieu. I take up my pen again to do, what I have just told	PP III 4 275 5
"John told us Mr. Darcy was here when you sent for us;--	PP III 4 280 26
"Yes; and I told him we should not be able to keep our	PP III 4 281 27
"I told you the other day, of his infamous behaviour to Mr.	PP III 5 284 14
her and all her family, told her that he meant to be in	PP III 5 287 36
"Oh, Jane had we been less secret, had we told what we	PP III 5 291 55
a letter from him; it told them, that on his arrival, he	PP III 6 295 5
Through letters, whatever of good or bad was to be told,	PP III 6 296 9
When Mrs. Bennet was told of this, she did not express so	PP III 6 298 13
You were not by, when I told mamma, and the others, all	PP III 9 318 22
I believe I have now told you every thing.	PP III 10 325 2
Yes, there was something in that; I told you so from the	PP III 10 329 30
You may remember what I told you on that point, when first	PP III 10 329 32
the truth of it; and she told me that it was certain true.	PP III 11 331 15
She was going to the butcher's, she told me, on purpose to	PP III 11 331 15
day, Lizzy, when my aunt told us of the present report;	PP III 11 331 16
	17
and moved away from each other, would have told it all.	PP III 13 346 22
I was told, that not only your sister was on the point of	PP III 14 353 26
been told, by some of the good-natured, gossiping lucases.	PP III 15 362 14
she could listen, and he told her of feelings, which, in	PP III 16 366 8
My conscience told me that I deserved no extraordinary	PP III 16 370 31
He then told her of Georgiana's delight in her	PP III 16 370 33
I told him of all that had occurred to make my former	PP III 16 371 40
I told him, moreover, that I believed myself mistaken in	PP III 16 371 40
said she, "when you told him that my sister loved him, or	PP III 16 371 42
Elizabeth told her the motives of her secrecy.	PP III 17 374 19
To complete the favourable impression, she then told him	PP III 17 377 38
have behaved better; I told her how much might depend upon	MP I 2 13 5
"William did not like she should come away--he had told	MP I 2 16 12
"Yes, he had promised he would, but he had told her to	MP I 2 16 12
her cousin Edmund; and he told her such charming things of	MP I 2 21 34
As soon as she met with Edmund, she told him her distress.	MP I 3 25 17
"Yes, my aunt Bertram has just told me so.	MP I 3 25 20
in the house before she told her what she had planned.	MP I 4 42 17
I told Smith I did not know where I was.	MP I 6 53 2
It was seen by some farmer, and he told the miller, and	MP I 6 57 33
the miller, and the miller told the butcher, and the	MP I 6 57 33
seemed impossible, so I told my maid to speak for one	MP I 6 58 37
was a very long one, told them that she was on the sofa.	MP I 7 71 33
I told Mrs. Rushworth so.	MP I 8 78 17
When Edmund, therefore, told her in reply, as he did when	MP I 8 79 23
"Go into the law! with as much ease as I was told to go	MP I 9 94 54
She told her story.	MP I 10 97 2
taken her to the dairy, told her all about their cows, and	MP I 10 103 50
You are speaking what you have been told at your uncle's	MP I 11 110 24
When he had told of his horse, he took a newspaper from	MP I 12 118 22
so infinitely worse, to be told that she must do what was	MP I 16 150 1
her meaning, he had told her not to cry, or had given her	MP I 16 152 2
He had told her the most extraordinary, the most	MP I 16 156 28
What is the play about, Fanny, you have never told me?"	MP I 18 167 8
"The all will be soon told," cried Tom hastily, and with	MP II 1 181 16
Fanny told of their departure, and delivered their message.	MP II 1 182 20
had done and were doing, told him of the gradual increase	MP II 1 184 27
Do you want to be told that you are only unlike other	MP II 3 197 6
With solemn kindness Sir Thomas addressed her; told her	MP II 3 200 21
If any body told me a year ago that this place would be my	MP II 4 210 17
He told the whole, and she had only to add, "so strange!	MP II 5 218 16
told you what happened to me yesterday in my ride home."	MP II 7 240 13
"I told you I lost my way after passing that old farm	MP II 7 241 13
to ask; but I have not told you that with my usual luck--	MP II 7 241 13
But I told a man mending a hedge that it was Thornton	MP II 7 241 17
I had forgotten having ever told you half so much of the	MP II 7 241 18
home again; and what was done there is not to be told!"	MP II 7 244 30
before, and though it told her no more than what she had	MP II 9 264 17
was a stab;--for it told of his own convictions and views.	MP II 9 264 17
one knows, without being told, exactly what they are--all	MP II 11 288 28
wishes more than could be told, that Fanny could not have	MP II 13 300 7
even to what he told her of William, and saying only when	MP II 13 300 7
"Sir Thomas told me 10l. would be enough."	MP II 13 305 22
Mr. Crawford ought to know--he must know that--I told him	MP III 1 314 17
subject yesterday--and I told him without disguise that it	MP III 1 314 17
the contrary, I told him--I cannot recollect my exact	MP III 1 315 19
words--but I am sure I told him that I would not listen to	MP III 1 315 19
She told him, that she did not love him, could not love	MP III 2 327 5
I have told him so, that it never will be in my power-----"	MP III 2 330 15
I must just speak of it once, I told Sir Thomas I must	MP III 2 333 23
I told them, that you were of all human creatures the one,	MP III 4 354 46
He told Fanny of it.	MP III 6 373 26
I am sure I told her to bring some coals half an hour ago.	MP III 7 379 17
You know I told you not to touch it, because Susan is so	MP III 7 386 44
her with the absent, it told her of people and things	MP III 9 394 2
What Fanny told her of former times, dwelt more on her	MP III 12 419 7
Crawford told me that you were wishing to hear from me,	MP III 13 420 2
recollecting what you once told me, and I acknowledge that	MP III 13 423 2
to be capable of!--yet her judgment told her it was so.	MP III 15 441 20
opened, and every thing told--no one else in the room,	MP III 16 453 17
I told her so."	MP III 16 456 25
"Yes, when I left her I told her so."	MP III 16 456 27
I have told you the substance of all that she said.	MP III 16 457 30
and the only one who ever told her of them: and though	E I 1 11 33
Mr. Woodhouse told me of it.	E I 2 18 9
Mrs. Martin had told her one day, (and there was a blush	E I 4 28 6
He told me every thing; his circumstances and plans, and	E I 8 59 27
"I will tell you something, in return for what have told	E I 8 60 30
had seen him, and he had told Miss Nash, that as he was	E I 8 68 58
with him about it, and told him how shabby it was in him,	E I 8 68 58
in the case, and he told him so; and Mr. Elton only looked	E I 8 68 58
Miss Nash had told her all this, and had talked a great	E I 8 68 58
a knife, but I told him knives were only for grandpapas.	E I 9 80 72
He had been most agreeable, most delightful; he had told	E I 10 90 39
though perhaps I never told you so before, that the sea is	E I 12 101 22
Mr. Wingfield told me that he had never known them more	E I 12 102 33
I assure you Mr. Wingfield told me, that he did not	E I 12 103 39
I returned to dress, I was told that Miss Smith was not	E I 13 114 31
snow, came back again, and told them that he had been out	E I 15 127 16
but truth, though there might be some truths not told.	E II 2 166 10
Mr. Knightley had once told her it was because she saw in	E II 2 166 11
into what was necessary, told that he understood, and the	E II 3 170 2
"I always told you she was--a little; but you will soon	E II 3 171 7
Cole told Mrs. Cole of it, she sat down and wrote to me.	E II 3 173 27
Jane, if you remember, I told you yesterday he was	E II 3 174 39
I told you he was plain."	E II 3 176 47
convenience: the story told well; he had not thrown	E II 4 181 4
"I told you yesterday," cried Mr. Weston with exultation, "	E II 5 190 24
told you all that he would be here before the time named.	E II 5 190 24
that was proper; and I had told my father I should	E II 6 199 7
The circumstance was told him at Hartfield; for the moment,	E II 7 206 4
I told you that your suspicions would guide mine."	E II 8 217 29
"Yes, and what you told me on the head, confirmed an idea	E II 8 217 32
He told her that he had	E II 8 220 48
"My dear Emma, I have told you what led me to think of it.	E II 8 224 67
had intended to give her one, he would have told her so."	E II 8 226 82
I am sure he was particularly silent when Mrs. Cole told	E II 8 226 83
submission to all that she told, was a compliment to her	E II 9 231 2
"They told me something," said Harriet rather hesitatingly,	E II 9 232 13
Emma was obliged to ask what they had told her, though	E II 9 232 14
"They told me--that Mr. Martin dined with them last	E II 9 232 15
Mrs. Weston told me you were here.--	E II 9 236 46
He told Patty this, but bid her not mind it, and be sure	E II 9 239 51
And so Patty told me, and I was excessively shocked indeed!	E II 9 239 51
You told us it would be so.--	E II 12 259 17
he had almost told her that he loved her.	E II 12 262 38
He gave me a quiet hint; I told him he was mistaken; he	E II 15 288 38
I always told you he would be here again soon, did not I?--	E II 17 304 27
She was told that now he wrote with the greatest	E III 1 317 8
You know I candidly told you I should form my own opinion;	E III 2 321 15
I set off without saying a word, just as I told you.	E III 2 329 45
He had told her that he could not allow himself the	E III 3 332 2
gipsy, though she had told no fortune, might be proved to	E III 4 340 28
conduct, discretion, and indiscretion, told the same story.	E III 5 343 2
Mrs. Perry had told somebody, and was extremely happy	E III 5 344 9
She had been often remiss, her conscience told her so;	E III 8 377 1
Emma's conscience told her that there was not the same	E III 8 378 7
at present--and so she told Mrs. Elton over and over again-	E III 8 380 15
Jane took Mrs. Elton aside, and told her at once, that	E III 8 381 15
I was so astonished when she first told me what she had	E III 8 382 29
Mr. Elton came back, he told us what John ostler had been	E III 8 383 29
Mrs. and Miss Bates, Mr. Knightley, as I told you before.	E III 9 385 6
"He told me at parting, that he should soon write; and he	E III 10 398 53
of owning it to me, for Mr. Weston has told me himself.	E III 11 404 6
He told me it was to be a great secret; and, therefore, I	E III 11 404 6
"Oh! he told me all about it; that Jane Fairfax and Mr.	E III 11 404 8
At first, if you had not told me that more wonderful	E III 11 406 18
I told you that I did not wonder at your attachment; that	E III 11 406 23
minutes--and his having told her, during their	E III 11 410 35
You told me to observe him carefully, and let his	E III 11 411 39
Had she left her where she ought, and where he had told	E III 11 413 49
told that she did not forbid his attempt to attach her.--	E III 13 432 40
unsuspicious of what they could have told him in return.	E III 14 434 3
all that need be told by letter; that it would be	E III 14 435 4
got near the house, and he told me I should not find his	E III 16 458 43
single; and told of poor Isabella, and poor Miss Taylor.--	E III 17 466 29
Only let me be told when I may speak out.--	E III 17 468 34

He told her the news. E III 17 468 35
against any young man who told her he loved her." E III 18 473 25
very distinctly, "that he told me she had accepted him; E III 18 474 30
hardly had they been told of the baby, and Mr. Woodhouse E III 18 476 44
had I broken the bond of secrecy and told you every thing." E III 18 477 55
live amongst us once; she told me so herself: sister to P III 3 22 25
and all that he had told her would follow, had taken place. P III 4 29 8
She often told herself it was folly, before she could P III 4 30 10
a deal, my dear, in spite of what they told us at Taunton. P III 5 32 4
He would go, though I told him how ill I was. P III 5 37 25
told him how ill I was, not one of them have been near me. P III 5 38 29
I was told that they wished it. P III 5 39 34
the child," said he, "so I told my father just now that I P III 7 55 8
told him to keep quiet, he was sure to begin kicking about. P III 7 56 12
I really think Charles might as well have told his father P III 7 57 14
been here--Mrs. Musgrove told me I should find them here," P III 9 78 22
minded me, Walter; I told you not to teaze your aunt;" and P III 9 80 34
I am afraid of her, as I have told you before, quite P III 12 103 4
When this was told, his name distressed her no longer. P IV 1 125 12
We told you about the laundry-door, at Uppercross. P IV 1 127 28
I told him the distance and the road, and I told him of P IV 2 131 12
The name of Musgrove would have told him enough. P IV 3 144 19
she was at first, as she told Anne, almost ready to P IV 4 146 6
There had been a time, Mrs. Smith told her, when her P IV 5 154 9
Anne could listen no longer; she could not even have told P IV 6 162 6
well; and "Jemima has just told me that the butcher says P IV 6 164 8
men walking about here, who, I am told, are sailors. P IV 6 166 16
All that she could tell, she told most gladly; but the all P IV 9 192 5
and she it was who told me you were to marry Mr. Elliot. P IV 9 197 40
He told me the whole story. P IV 9 201 59
All that he understood of himself, he readily told, for he S 2 371 1
I told you my sisters were excellent women, miss h----." S 5 388 1
& my Milch-Asses--& I have told Mrs Whitby that if any S 6 393 1
Charlotte's first glance told her that Sir Edw:'s air was S 7 395 1
He only told me, & that but once, that he shd wish his S 7 400 1
I told you in my letter, of the two considerable families, S 9 408 1
told me that this was an occasion which called for me. S 9 409 1
"But you have not told me any thing of the other family S 9 411 1
It was not a week, since Miss Diana Parker had been told S 10 412 1
to look about, & to be told by Mrs P. that the whole- S 12 427 1

TOLERABLE (56)
as she has my hand & arm, & a tolerable voice. LS 7 253 1
is tolerable, we pace the shrubbery for hours together. LS 16 268 2
its expressions within the language of tolerable calmness. NA II 2 140 8
doors, which commanded a tolerable view of every body NA II 3 143 1
The Dashwoods were now settled at Barton with tolerable SS I 9 40 1
might be allowed to be a tolerable judge, for he had SS I 12 62 28
a tolerable composure of mind by driving about the country. SS I 13 66 60
whose elegance,--whose tolerable gentility even, she could SS I 21 118 2
Marianne to behave with tolerable politeness: and resolved SS II 3 156 15
If the morning's tolerable, pray do us the honour of W 347 21
and coldly said, "she is tolerable; but not handsome PP I 3 11 13
where he had made a tolerable fortune and risen to the PP I 5 18 1
Poor Eliza!--to be only just tolerable." PP I 5 19 9
of being able to send a tolerable answer to the enquiries PP I 9 41 1
could hardly reply with tolerable civility to the polite PP I 18 89 3
breast there was a tolerable powerful feeling towards her, PP I 18 94 43
able to assure her with tolerable firmness that the PP I 22 125 16
mildness to bear these attacks with tolerable tranquillity. PP I 23 129 14
His behaviour to herself could now have had no tolerable PP II 13 207 6
good health, and in as tolerable spirits as could be PP II 14 210 1
to trim it with fresh, I think it will be very tolerable. PP II 16 219 4
beyond youth and a tolerable person; and from the PP II 18 231 18
Her teeth are tolerable, but not out of the common way; PP III 3 271 15
How Wickham and Lydia were to be supported in tolerable PP III 8 312 17
she received them with tolerable ease, and with a PP III 11 335 39
she was able to join the others with tolerable composure. PP III 17 377 41
son of a Lord with a tolerable independence; and Sir MP I 13 121 1
Not a tolerable woman's part in the play----- MP I 14 131 3
merest common-place--not a tolerable speech in the whole. MP I 14 134 13
As to his ever making any thing tolerable of them, nobody MP I 18 166 4
Tolerable sport the first three days, but there has been MP II 1 181 16
to encounter her share of it with tolerable calmness. MP II 2 193 17
is removed, there may be a very tolerable approach to it." MP II 7 242 22
how different would it be--how far more tolerable! MP II 9 264 17
Was she as much plagued as herself to get tolerable MP III 7 385 38
enough inured to, for her often to make a tolerable meal. MP III 10 407 23
her own feelings, to furnish a tolerable guess at mine.-- MP III 13 420 2
to tolerable comfort, and to have done with all the rest. MP III 17 461 1
and was thought to have a tolerable eye in general. E I 6 43 13
he is attached to her, and can write a tolerable letter." E I 7 54 31
I cannot think of any tolerable pretence for going in;--no E I 10 83 7
rights so as to be able to walk home in tolerable comfort. E I 10 89 36
it was never met with tolerable;--but, unfortunately, E I 12 104 50
it, she had never been able to get any thing tolerable. E I 12 105 50
of body and mind to be discharged with tolerable comfort. E II 2 165 9
"I think there will be very tolerable room for ten couple." E II 11 249 15
16
upon the whole, a tolerable account of Mrs. Churchill, and E III 8 383 31
in tolerable order by more cake than is good for them." P III 6 45 8
and eat their dinner in tolerable ease of mind; and then P III 7 54 4
pretty shelves, for a tolerable collection of well-bound P III 11 99 18
been off,--the impossibility of being in tolerable time. P III 12 113 57
another, without there being a tolerable face among them. P IV 3 141 13
the sight of any thing tolerable, by the effect which a P IV 3 142 13
She exclaimed, however, with a very tolerable imitation of P IV 10 228 70
71
any circumstance of tolerable similarity, give such advice. P IV 11 246 80
the kingdom; they had tolerable complexions, shewey S 11 421 1

TOLERABLY (62)
Her feelings are tolerably lively, & she is so charmingly LS 19 274 2
As soon as I was tolerably composed, I returned to the LS 24 291 15
than the commonest flirtation; & he is tolerably appeased. LS 29 299 4
there had not been a tolerably decent one come out since NA I 7 48 34
he did look upon a tolerably large eating-room as one of NA II 6 166 6
to enter her room with a tolerably stout heart; and her NA II 6 167 9
At the further end of the village, and tolerably NA II 11 212 17
we will make ourselves tolerably comfortable for the SS I 6 29 4
At my time of life opinions are tolerably fixed. SS I 17 93 30
of manner, which tolerably well concealed her surprise and SS I 22 130 17
18
Could he ever be tolerably happy with Lucy Steele; could SS II 1 140 1
even the chance of being tolerably happy in marriage, SS II 2 151 41
Very early in April, and tolerably early in the day, the SS III 6 301 3
It had no park, but the pleasure-grounds were tolerably SS III 6 302 7
"I hope you will find things tolerably comfortable Jane"-- W 351 25
fish & counters with a tolerably clean pack brought W 357 28
But though Bingley and Jane meet tolerably often, it is PP I 6 22 6
for Charlotte had been tolerably encouraging, he was PP I 22 121 1
Charlotte herself was tolerably composed. PP I 22 122 3
friend to be tolerably happy in the lot she had chosen. PP I 22 125 18
had been used to think tolerably sensible, was as foolish PP I 23 127 6
The dear Colonel rallied his spirits tolerably till just PP II 14 210 3
it almost impossible for her to appear tolerably cheerful. PP II 14 213 19
she might be so tolerably reasonable as not to mention an PP II 19 238 6
answered the question in a tolerably dis-engaged tone. PP III 3 269 10
"My mother is tolerably well, I trust; though her spirits PP III 5 286 30
The faces of both, however, were tolerably calm; and no PP III 5 289 41
who was by this time tolerably well acquainted with her PP III 6 298 17
Seriously, however, she felt tolerably persuaded that all PP III 13 346 20
of her eldest niece, as tolerably to quiet her nerves. MP I 4 38 9
Poor Julia, the only one out of the nine not tolerably MP I 9 91 36
on Fanny's account, was tolerably resigned to her having MP I 16 151 1
observing them, had seen enough to be tolerably satisfied. MP II 10 279 21
"but that his visits to us may now be tolerably frequent. MP II 11 284 9
be tolerably happy together, even if I could like him. MP III 4 348 22
therefore said to her tolerably soon, in a low voice, "I MP III 5 357 5
he talks of being there tolerably soon; and Sir Thomas, I MP III 5 364 32
spoken to; and she was tolerably able to bear his eye, and MP III 10 400 8
But Sunday made her a very creditable and tolerably MP III 11 408 2
Though tolerably secure of not seeing Mr. Crawford again, MP III 11 413 31
his being at least tolerably domestic and quiet; and, at MP III 17 462 4
into submission, as to be very tolerably cheerful again. MP III 17 462 5
was over, she had been tolerably soon in a fair way of not MP III 17 466 18
to get her father tolerably through the evening, and be E I 1 9 20
But I hope it all went off tolerably well. E I 1 10 27
the young ladies from tolerably regular exercise; and on E I 10 83 1
I do not know but that the place agrees with her tolerably. E I 11 94 8
"And do you see her, sir, tolerably often?" asked Isabella E I 11 94 12
and left her at last tolerably comfortable, in the sweet E I 13 109 6
before her, and to depend on getting tolerably out of it. E I 16 138 14
more than a very tolerably well-looking woman of a certain E II 5 192 30
to what was right and support her in it very tolerably. E II 13 268 13
to speak, she was very tolerably capable of attending. E II 14 279 53
Seats tolerably in the shade were found; and now Emma was E III 6 359 37
he could only be kept tolerably comfortable by almost E III 12 422 19
And now I can tolerably comprehend his behaviour. E III 13 427 19
At last, and tolerably in his usual tone, he said, "I have E III 13 427 20
21
intelligible tenderness as was tolerably convincing.-- E III 13 430 37
merits, can never have been reckoned tolerably pretty! P III 5 35 14
He was tolerably cheerful. P IV 1 121 2
She was persuaded that any tolerably pleasing young woman P IV 6 167 19
He, I am happy to say is tolerably well--tho' more languid S 5 387 1

TOLERATE (6)
Mrs. Norris could tolerate its being for Fanny's use; and MP I 4 37 9
that you could tolerate nothing that you were not used to; MP III 4 354 46
she had seen anybody superior, she might tolerate him. E I 8 65 48
tolerate the prospect of being miserably crowded at supper. E II 11 254 44
attentions and tolerate Mrs. Elton as she seemed to do. E II 15 285 12
taste cannot tolerate,--which ridicule will seize. P III 8 68 30

TOLERATED (3)
Murder was not tolerated, servants were not slaves, and NA II 10 200 3
They were never tolerated at Maple Grove. E III 2 321 15
have been tolerated in Camden-Place but for her birth. P IV 4 150 14

TOLERATION (2)
Marianne, who had never much toleration for any thing like SS I 22 127 1
toleration of the neighbourly attempts at the parsonage. MP II 7 238 1

TOM (78)
"We are off at last, said his Lordship to Tom--how much W 335 13
"If it were not a breach of confidence, replied Tom with W 340 19
"And so, you really did not dance with Tom M. at all?-- W 342 19
Tom had nothing to say for himself, he knew it very well, W 346 21
Tom was very agreable, was not he?-- W 347 22
Tom made no reply.-- W 357 28
When the tea-things were removed, Tom began to talk of his W 357 28
I know you do, Tom."-- W 358 28
"Oh! me! cried Tom. W 358 28
Suppose her a pretty girl, and seen by Tom or Edmund for MP I 1 7 6
to endure on the part of Tom, than that sort of merriment MP I 2 17 22
"I blush for you, Tom," said he, in his most dignified MP I 3 23 3
Tom listened with some shame and some sorrow; but escaping MP I 3 24 4
Tom arrived safely, bringing an excellent account of his MP I 4 38 9
"My dear Tom," cried his aunt soon afterwards, "as you are MP I 12 119 23
Tom returning from them into the drawing-room, where MP I 13 125 14
"You are not serious, Tom, in meaning to act?" said Edmund MP I 13 125 15
"By Jove! this won't do"--cried Tom, throwing himself into MP I 13 126 21
"I know all that," said Tom displeased. MP I 13 127 27
I will be answerable,"--said Tom, in a decided tone.-- MP I 13 127 29
Tom walked out of the room as he said it, and Edmund was MP I 13 128 33
no influence with either Tom or my sisters that could be MP I 13 128 37
quite as determined in the cause of pleasure, as Tom.-- MP I 13 128 38
Any thing but that, my dear Tom. MP I 14 131 3
discussion was high between Tom, Maria, and Mr. Yates; and MP I 15 138 2
Tom would be quite angry; and if we are so very nice, we MP I 15 141 21
I only wish Tom had known his own mind when the carpenters MP I 15 141 22
I forgot to tell Tom of something that happened to me this MP I 15 141 22
giving fresh courage, Tom, Maria, and Mr. Yates, soon MP I 15 142 25
Tom, "but unluckily the butler and Anhalt are in together. MP I 15 144 33
"I shall not ask him," replied Tom, in a cold determined MP I 15 144 35
Her entreaty had no effect on Tom; he only said again what MP I 15 146 53
and it was not merely Tom, for the requisition was now MP I 15 146 53
Tom repeated his resolution of going to him early on the MP I 15 148 60
an attack from her cousin Tom, so public and so persevered MP I 16 150 1
authoritative urgency that Tom and Maria were capable of; MP I 16 150 1
times, principally by Tom; and she grew bewildered as to MP I 16 153 3
I am well aware that nothing else will quiet Tom." MP I 16 154 10
But it is absolutely impossible to let Tom go on in this MP I 16 155 22
If Tom is up, I shall go to him directly and get it over; MP I 16 156 27
"Perhaps," said Tom, "Fanny may be more disposed to oblige MP I 17 158 3
Tom was engrossed by the concerns of his theatre, and saw MP I 17 163 21
Tom himself began to fret over the scene painter's slow MP I 18 164 1
judgment than Tom, more talent and taste than Mr. Yates.-- MP I 18 165 3
on the occasion; Tom was enjoying such an advance towards MP I 18 171 25
Tom, as Cottager, was in despair. MP I 18 171 28
"The all will be soon told," cried Tom hastily, and with MP II 1 181 16
"Then poor Yates is all alone," cried Tom. MP II 1 182 21
Tom understood his father's thoughts, and heartily wishing MP II 1 183 24
"This was in fact the origin of our acting," said Tom MP II 1 184 26
Tom was the only one at all ready with an answer, but he MP II 1 185 30
chief of the morning, and Tom had taken the opportunity of MP II 2 191 10
a chair between herself and Tom, ask the latter in an MP II 2 192 11
It was well at that moment that Tom had to speak and not MP II 2 193 13
In himself he was wearisome, but as the friend of Tom and MP II 2 194 21
seem out of spirits, and Tom is certainly not at his ease. MP II 3 196 2
was gone out of harbour; Tom and Charles: Charles had been MP III 7 381 25
Fanny's going away, but Tom she had often helped to nurse, MP III 7 381 25
Both were kissed very tenderly, but Tom she wanted to keep MP III 7 381 25
Tom, however, had no mind for such treatment: he came home, MP III 7 381 25
the superior noise of Sam, Tom, and Charles chasing each MP III 7 382 27
state of the house, from Tom and Charles being gone to MP III 8 388 1
and John, Richard, Sam, Tom, and Charles, occupied all the MP III 8 389 4
ones was gone in him; Tom and Charles being at least as MP III 8 390 8
her rash squabbles with Tom and Charles, and petulance MP III 8 391 9
Tom had gone from London with a party of young men to MP III 13 426 10
Tom dangerously ill, Edmund gone to attend him, and the MP III 13 427 12
and poor invalids, till Tom was actually conveyed to MP III 13 427 12
Poor Tom, I am quite grieved for him, and very much MP III 13 427 12
When Tom is better, I shall go." MP III 14 430 4
Fanny began to dread the meeting with her aunts and Tom, MP III 15 446 35
neither Lady Bertram nor Tom had received from her the MP III 16 448 2
There was comfort also in Tom, who gradually regained his MP III 17 462 4
seeming to have got a cold, Tom had been sent off E III 8 383 31
"My dear Tom, we were all much greived at your accident, & S 5 386 1
Many thanks my dear Tom for the kindness with respect to S 5 386 1
My dear Tom I am so glad to see you walk so well. S 9 408 1
"No, my dear Tom, upon no account in the world, shall you S 9 411 1

TOM BERTRAM (13)
she had fixed on Tom Bertram; the eldest son of a baronet MP I 4 42 17
Tom Bertram must have been thought pleasant, indeed, at MP I 5 47 28
"We must have a curtain," said Tom Bertram, "a few yards MP I 13 123 7
settled but that Tom Bertram would prefer a comedy, and MP I 13 124 13
on the comic, Tom Bertram, not quite alone, because it was MP I 14 130 3
"This will never do," said Tom Bertram at last. MP I 14 131 5

But this was immediately opposed by Tom Bertram, who MP I 14 133 10
Tom Bertram began again. MP I 14 136 18
was completed by Tom Bertram and Mr. Yates walking off MP I 14 136 22
"Fanny," cried Tom Bertram, from the other table, where MP I 15 145 43
from Fanny by Tom Bertram's telling her, with infinite MP I 15 148 58
Crawford, that Tom Bertram spoke so quick he would be MP I 18 164 2
of his rehearsals, Tom Bertram entered at the other end of MP II 1 182 22
TOM JONES (1)
one come out since Tom Jones, except The Monk; I read that NA I 7 48 34
TOM MUSGRAVE (21)
Perhaps Tom Musgrave may take notice of you--but I would W 315 1
"When first we knew Tom Musgrave, continued Miss W. W 316 2
I do not think Tom Musgrave should be named with him in W 316 2
disappointed in Tom Musgrave, who afterwards transferred W 317 2
"Your account of this Tom Musgrave, Elizabeth, gives me W 319 2
"Dislike & despise Tom Musgrave! W 319 2
Well, we shall see how irresistable Mr Tom Musgrave & I W 319 2
I shall long to know what you think of Tom Musgrave." W 321 2
10 years old, & Mr Tom Musgrave; who probably imprisoned W 329 9
who was certainly a genteel, good looking young man.-- W 329 9
Tom Musgrave who was dancing with Miss Carr, gave her many W 331 11
near her, call Tom Musgrave towards him & say, "why do not W 333 13
at the moment by Tom Musgrave, who requesting Mrs E. aloud W 334 13
disposed to favour Tom Musgrave himself, that she had W 334 13
As Tom Musgrave was seen no more, we may suppose his plan W 336 14
And so, you would not come home with Tom Musgrave?"-- W 341 19
as you do, of Tom Musgrave; my heart did misgive me that W 343 19
hold the parlour door open for Ld Osborne & Tom Musgrave.-- W 344 21
longer, while Tom Musgrave was chattering to Elizth, till W 346 21
He is very handsome--but Tom Musgrave looks all to nothing, W 347 22
The door opened, & displayed Tom Musgrave in the wrap of a W 355 28
TOM MUSGRAVE'S (4)
the notion of Tom Musgrave's being more seriously in love W 319 2
to stand up--& Tom Musgrave's curiosity was appeased, on W 335 13
obliged to listen to Tom Musgrave's farther account. W 338 18
me much more ease & confidence than Tom Musgrave's." W 342 19
TOM OLIVER (1)
Tom Oliver is a very clever fellow, and Charles Maddox is MP I 15 148 58
TOM'S (9)
But Tom's extravagance had, previous to that event, been MP I 3 23 2
Tom's extreme impatience to be removed to Mansfield, and MP III 13 427 13
his return to Mansfield, Tom's immediate danger was over, MP III 14 429 1
letter when called away by Tom's illness, but I have now MP III 14 430 4
Tom's amendment was alarmingly slow. MP III 14 430 5
It astonished her that Tom's sisters could be satisfied MP III 14 432 11
Julia's, Tom's, Edmund's--there, a yet longer pause. MP III 15 442 21
Tom's complaints had been greatly heightened by the shock MP III 16 451 13
He submitted to believe, that Tom's illness had influenced MP III 16 459 31
TOMBSTONES (1)
of two tombstones and a lantern--do you understand?-- NA I 14 113 39
TOMBUCTOO (1)
the neighbourhood of Tombuctoo might not afford some S 8 405 2
TOME (1)
Tome Bertram had of late spent so little of his time at MP I 4 34 1
TOMORROW (7)
of your company till tomorrow--but if you can not W 339 18
Stokes is to call for it tomorrow, for his uncle is going W 341 19
I shall wear one tomorrow that I think you will prefer to W 353 26
we expect him tomorrow, with a large party of friends." PP III 1 246 8
at your surprise tomorrow morning, as soon as I am missed. PP III 5 291 60
It is only four weeks tomorrow since I left Mansfield." MP III 11 410 9
lodgings or other & be settled after breakfast tomorrow.-- S 9 411 1
TOMORROW'S (1)
at first, but by tomorrow's dinner, everything will be LS 33 303 2
TON (1)
He must not head mobs, or set the ton in dress. MP I 9 92 45
TONE (109)
"Why, indeed!" said he, in his natural tone--"but some NA I 3 26 8
it will be wet," broke from her in a most desponding tone. NA I 11 82 2
and he replied in a tone which retained only a little NA I 12 93 7
who, in rather a solemn tone of voice, uttered these words, NA I 14 111 29
"It remains as it was, I suppose?" said she, in a tone of NA II 8 186 7
moment, in his loudest tone, resounded through the NA II 9 191 4
"Yes," cried he in the same eager tone, "with all and SS I 14 73 13
Then continuing his former tone, he said, "and yet this SS I 14 73 17
In a firm, though cautious tone, Elinor thus began. SS II 2 146 1
Lucy first put an end to it by saying in a lower tone, SS II 2 149 24
25
his name in a tone of affection, held out her hand to him. SS II 6 176 7
silent anxiety, said, in a tone of the most considerate SS II 7 180 1
2
she added, in a firmer tone, "Elinor, I have been cruelly SS II 7 189 47
48
"Mrs. Ferrars," added he, lowering his voice to the tone SS III 5 295 18
of her brother's tone, calmly replied, "the lady, I SS III 5 296 25
26
"Has she!"--he cried, in the same eager tone.-- SS III 8 319 27
on one side, calling me Willoughby in such a tone!-- SS III 8 327 55
in a tone that implied--"do you really think him selfish?" SS III 11 351 10
"Capt. Hunter." was repeated, in a very humble tone--"hum!- W 337 15
country I understand, said he in the tone of a gentlen. W 346 21
Margt to Mrs Robert in her most languishing tone.-- W 350 24
appearance were over; the tone of artificial sensibility W 351 25
and manner of walking, the tone of her voice, her address PP I 8 39 50
In a softened tone she declared herself not at all PP I 13 65 26
would talk of her views in the same intelligible tone. PP I 18 100 67
she added in a melancholy tone, "for nobody is on my side, PP II 3 113 26
ill-natured tone that she "wished they might be happy." PP II 3 145 11
in so authoritative a tone, as marked her self-importance, PP II 6 162 11
I cannot catch their tone of conversation, or appear PP II 8 175 24
herself, said in a lively tone, "and pray, what is the PP II 10 183 15
in a less tranquil tone, and with a heightened colour. PP II 11 191 18
added in a gayer tone, "is it in address that he improves? PP II 18 234 33
and more serious tone, "that he is improved in essentials." PP II 18 234 33
talking together, and in a tone which had something of PP III 2 262 8
answered the question in a tolerably dis-engaged tone. PP III 3 269 10
refrain from saying, in a tone of gentleness and PP III 4 276 9
"Miss Bennet," replied her ladyship, in any angry tone, " PP III 14 353 26
"I am sorry, exceedingly sorry," replied Darcy, in a tone PP III 16 365 4
style of living and tone of society; and it was not till MP I 4 41 16
numerous words and louder tone convinced her of the truth. MP I 8 76 2
in a tone not much louder, "if he would give her away?" MP I 9 88 21
"I am glad of it," said he in a much brisker tone, and MP I 12 118 22
in the heavy tone of one half roused,--"I was not asleep." MP I 13 126 22
I will be answerable,"--said Tom, in a decided tone.-- MP I 13 127 29
"Lovers' Vows!"--in a tone of the greatest amazement, was MP I 15 139 5
to her, with superior tone and expression; and though MP II 4 207 10
No, Miss Crawford," he added, in a more serious tone, " MP II 4 214 45
without me, ma'am," said Fanny in a self-denying tone----- MP II 5 217 4
Her tone of calm languor, for she never took the trouble MP II 5 218 12
"Walk!" repeated Sir Thomas, in a tone of most MP II 5 221 37
And then changing his tone again to one of gentle MP II 5 224 53
"We are unlucky, Miss Price," he continued in a lower tone, MP II 5 225 57
face, said with a firmer tone than usual, "as far as I am MP II 5 225 58
in a calmer, graver tone, and as if the candid result of MP II 5 226 59
and resentful of a certain tone of voice and a certain MP II 7 242 25
Thomas, in a more every day tone, but still with feeling. MP II 7 247 37
a journey with an animation which had "no" in every tone. MP II 8 256 12
And in a lower tone to Fanny, "I shall have only a MP II 10 280 31
Never did tone express indifference plainer. MP II 11 288 30
and in a cooler tone, "Mrs. Rushworth will be very angry. MP II 12 297 33
it, "well," said he, in a tone of becoming gravity, but of MP III 1 320 44
it, and in the language, tone, and spirit of a man of MP III 2 328 6
in a fearless, self-defending tone, which startled Fanny. MP III 7 379 18
tone, "no wonder--you must feel it--you must suffer. MP III 15 446 34
to abbey-mill again," was said in rather a sorrowful tone. E I 7 55 37
But--(in a very depressed tone)--she is coming for only E I 9 79 62
in the plaintive tone which just suited her father. E I 11 94 12
about, his inquiries even approached a tone of eagerness. E I 12 100 16
Harriet at parting; in the tone of his voice while E I 13 111 14
"Indeed! (in a tone of wonder and pity,) I had no idea E I 13 116 45
or fancy any tone of voice, less allied with real love. E I 16 135 7
Harriet was further unfortunate in the tone of her E I 17 143 15
If he would say so to her at once, in the tone of decision E I 18 146 16
to ask and to say as to tone, touch, and pedal, totally E II 8 220 46
prove to have an indifferent tone--what shall I say? E II 9 234 32
The tone implied some old acquaintance--and how could she E II 14 278 49
Harriet say in a very serious tone, "I shall never marry." E III 4 340 28
said, in a lively tone, "well, I have so little confidence E III 7 373 45
46
For a moment he was silent; and then added, in a tone much E III 10 394 23
24
And Emma distinctly heard him add, in a lower tone, before E III 10 394 25
him thus saying, in a tone of great sensibility, speaking E III 13 425 12
13
And in a louder, steadier tone, he concluded with, "he E III 13 426 13
At last, and tolerably in his usual tone, he said, "I have E III 13 427 20
21
soon resumed; and in a tone of such sincere, decided, E III 13 430 37
low, but very feeling tone, "this is most kind, indeed!-- E III 16 453 8
9
I went over the fields too--(speaking in a tone of great E III 16 457 40
subject of misery to him, by a melancholy tone herself. E III 17 465 28
and then, in a graver tone, began with, "I have something E III 18 470 1
2
from debt, a much higher tone of indifference for every P III 2 12 3
been possible to the nice tone of her mind, the P III 4 28 7
with Mary's saying, in a tone of great exultation, "I mean P III 7 57 17
18
his having said, in a vext tone of voice, after Captain P III 9 80 34
"Had you?" cried he, catching the same tone; "I honour you! P III 10 85 11
Then, returning to his former earnest tone: "my first wish P III 10 88 26
said Mrs. Croft, in a tone of calmer praise, such as made P III 10 92 47
tone of despair, and as if all his own strength were gone. P III 12 110 35
The tone, the look, with which "thank God!" was uttered by P III 12 112 54
past, became in a decided tone, "I must call on Mrs. Croft; P IV 1 125 14
Admiral Croft's manners were not quite of the tone to suit P IV 1 127 23
too strict to suit the unfeudal tone of the present day! P IV 3 139 7
His tone, his expressions, his choice of subject, his P IV 3 143 19
soon added in a different tone, "I do not suppose the P IV 5 156 12
13
she cried, in her natural tone of cordiality, "I beg your P IV 9 198 52
53
just in that inconvenient tone of voice which was P IV 11 230 5
But (in a deep tone) it was not done for her. Miss Elliot, P IV 11 232 15
"Ah!" cried Captain Harville, in a tone of strong feeling, P IV 11 234 31
He began, in a tone of great taste & feeling, to talk of S 7 396 1
she immediately said in a tone of great satisfaction--& S 7 399 1
though with more decision & less mildness in her tone. S 9 407 1
TONED (2)
for it is the very best toned piano-forte I ever heard." SS II 1 145 17
of high toned genius, the grovellings of a common mind.-- S 7 398 1
TONES (4)
a sensible man;--his loud tones did very well in the open MP III 10 402 12
brought Mrs. Elton's tones again distinctly forward.-- E III 2 324 22
"You sink your voice, but I can distinguish the tones of " P IV 11 237 42
those sentiments and those tones which had reached him P IV 11 241 60
TONGUE (17)
almost to the tip of her tongue, by asking, in a NA I 12 95 18
She does not know how to hold her tongue, as you must SS I 22 133 42
conjectured that she might as well have held her tongue. SS II 3 157 18
advantage of holding her tongue; and if you can compass it, PP I 10 52 55
Lydia was bid by her two eldest sisters to hold her tongue; PP I 14 69 15
16
enough to hold her tongue before the servants, while they PP III 5 288 40
the infinite relief of a tongue that has been stumbling at MP II 13 303 15
was continually on her tongue, as the truest description MP III 14 431 7
at all, for she has an aunt who never holds her tongue." E II 5 194 44
to be quite certain that she ought to have held her tongue. E II 9 231 2
no limits to the licentiousness of that woman's tongue!" E II 15 284 10
to Mr. Knightley,) and I will try to hold my tongue. E III 7 371 28
allowed to judge when to speak and when to hold my tongue. E III 7 372 37
which had kept her face averted, and her tongue motionless. E III 7 375 62
Had she not, with a folly which no tongue could express, E III 11 413 49
presence of mind never varied, whose tongue never slipped. P IV 5 161 28
And when I think of benwick, my tongue is tied." P IV 11 236 34
TONGUE'S (2)
plan, and had it at her tongue's end, and was on the point MP I 8 80 28
mails;--it was at her tongue's end--but she abstained. E II 16 298 59
TONGUES (2)
all of you, hold your tongues, and let Mr. Collins and me PP I 20 113 30
I suppose, hold their tongues; but we gentlemen labourers E II 10 242 15
TONIC (1)
except in favour of some Tonic pills, which a cousin of S 11 422 1
TONIGHT (3)
The Osbornes will certainly be at the ball tonight.-- W 323 3
"I wish we may be able to have a game of cards tonight," W 354 28
than it should be tonight"--convinced her that Arthur was S 10 417 1
TOO-COMMANDING (1)
could hazard among the too-commanding claims of the others. P IV 10 214 12
TOO-COMMON (1)
She had only meant to oppose the too-common idea of spirit P IV 6 172 40
41
TOO-SUFFICIENT (1)
castle, on the too-sufficient plea of Mr Watson's infirm W 348 22
TOOK (275)
especially as the sale took place exactly at the time of LS 5 249 1
soon <as> we were seated, took her out of the room & did LS 17 270 2
took from me the power of speaking with any clearness. LS 20 277 6
very impertinent, but he took the liberty of a relation, & LS 20 278 10
I have not a doubt but that the girl took this opportunity LS 22 282 6
door, & he, merry as usual, soon afterwards took his leave. LS 24 291 15
I took care to see her alone, that I might say all this, & LS 41 310 4
Under these unpromising auspices, the parting took place, NA I 2 19 4
The following conversation, which took place between the NA I 6 39 1
He took out his watch: "how long do you think we have been NA I 7 45 5
An inquiry now took place into the intended movements of NA I 7 47 18
I took up the first volume once, and looked it over, but I NA I 7 49 40
This, on arriving on Pulteney-Street, took the direction NA I 9 60 1
Catherine took the advice, and ran off to get ready. NA I 9 61 7
of events and conversation took place; Mr. Allen, after NA I 10 71 8
immediately took her usual place by the side of her friend. NA I 10 71 8
wish of Mr. Allen, which took them rather early away, and NA I 10 81 61
A gleam of sunshine took her quite by surprize; she looked NA I 11 83 16
with somebody else, she took to herself all the shame of NA I 12 93 4
made in this world-----I took his ball exactly-----but I NA I 12 96 20
had really been, she took occasion to mention before Mr. NA I 13 103 29
of waiting for me, you took the volume into the Hermitage- NA I 14 107 8
I was saying so to Emily and Sophia when you over took us." NA I 14 115 54
call her sister, Catherine took the opportunity of asking NA I 15 116 1
a matter in which her disinterested spirit took no concern. NA I 15 122 28
took a rapid flight over its attendant felicities. NA I 15 122 28
took pains to be near her, and Henry asked her to dance. NA II 1 131 14
I took him down several times you know in my way." NA II 1 135 41

He approached immediately, and took the seat to which her NA II 3 147 21
She could not, in whatever direction she took it, believe NA II 6 164 2
She took her candle and looked closely at the cabinet. NA II 6 168 10
They took a slight survey of all; and Catherine was NA II 8 184 4
Catherine took her place at the table, and, after a short NA II 10 203 9
Davis: I pitied his taste, but took no notice of him. NA II 12 217 2
above, am afraid he took something in my conduct amiss. NA II 12 217 2
unpleasant a subject, she took the first opportunity of NA II 13 220 2
"Catherine took us quite by surprize yesterday evening," NA II 14 237 21
Catherine took up her work directly, saying, in a dejected NA II 15 240 3
and consequence, which took place in the course of the NA II 16 250 4
body smiled; and, as this took place within a twelve-month NA II 16 252 7
Mrs. Dashwood now took pains to get acquainted with him. SS I 3 16 13
She took the first opportunity of affronting her mother-in- SS I 4 23 19
Mrs. Dashwood took the house for a twelvemonth; it was SS I 5 26 5
In the present case it took up ten minutes to determine SS I 6 31 9
rendered necessary, took her up in his arms without SS I 9 42 8
of her, and presently he took up her scissars and cut off SS I 12 60 13
Among the rest there was one for Colonel Brandon;--he took SS I 13 63 3
He then took leave of the whole party. SS I 13 66 45
Willoughby took his usual place between the two elder Miss SS I 13 67 61
Mrs. Dashwood's visit to Lady Middleton took place the SS I 15 75 1
He then hastily took leave of them all and left the room. SS I 15 76 17
You are resolved to think him blameable, because he took SS I 15 78 28
room and took her place at the table without saying a word. SS I 15 82 46
Elinor took no notice of this, and directing her attention SS I 16 89 42
the parting, which shortly took place, and left an SS I 19 104 9
them and their apartments, took up a newspaper from the SS I 19 106 22
She took them all most affectionately by the hand, and SS I 20 110 1
Mr. Palmer took no notice of her. SS I 20 113 36
to these young ladies took place, they found in the SS I 21 120 6
Here she took her handkerchief; but Elinor did not feel SS I 22 133 43
took such a liberty as to trouble you with my affairs. SS II 2 146 5
A mutual silence took place for some time. SS II 2 149 24
Even Lady Middleton took the trouble of being delighted, SS II 3 157 19
Their departure took place in the first week in January. SS II 3 158 22
To atone for this conduct therefore, Elinor took immediate SS II 4 160 2
But Marianne, not convinced, took it instantly up. SS II 5 169 19
may endeavour to deserve her,"--took leave, and went away. SS II 5 174 46
herself on the bed, took her hand, kissed her SS II 7 182 12
one of its post, again took up Willoughby's letter, and SS II 7 190 55
56

He saw her concern, and coming to her, took her hand, SS II 9 206 25
of being able to call on them the next day, took leave. SS II 11 222 13
at Gray's, his thoughts took a cheerfuller turn, and he SS II 11 226 41
visit should begin a few days before the party took place. SS II 12 230 8
And so saying, she took the screens out of her sister-in- SS II 12 235 36
should seem to say, she had quite took a fancy to me. SS II 13 239 4
it in a moment, if Mrs. Ferrars had took a dislike to me. SS II 13 240 17
word, and never after had took any notice of me, and never SS II 13 240 17
So up he flew directly, and a terrible scene took place, SS III 1 259 7
discovery that took place under our roof yesterday." SS III 1 265 34
said about them, and I took care to keep mine out of sight. SS III 2 275 22
an explanation immediately took place, by which both SS III 4 292 54
He took the opposite chair, and for half a minute not a SS III 8 317 7
A discovery took place,"--here he hesitated and looked SS III 8 321 34
of guilt that almost took from me the power of dissembling. SS III 8 324 42
immediately afterwards took his solitary way to Delaford. SS III 10 341 5
Mrs. Dashwood immediately took all that trouble on herself; SS III 11 353 25
youngest Miss Steele; so I took off my hat, and she knew SS III 11 354 27
dignified, and therefore took a seat as far from him as SS III 12 359 13
the dryness of the season, a very awful pause took place. SS III 12 359 14
not knowing what to do; took up a pair of scissars that SS III 12 360 22
23

ceremony took place in Barton church early in the autumn. SS III 14 374 6
their husbands of course took a part, as well as the SS III 14 377 11
in the manner in which Mr E. took up the subject.-- W 324 3
much concern they took their seats--Ld. Osborne near Emma, W 345 21
Ld Osborne's parting Compts took some time, his W 347 21
what the owner said in its praise, and took it immediately. PP I 4 16 13
Elizabeth took up some needlework, and was sufficiently PP I 10 47 2
"Mr. Darcy took her advice, and did finish his letter. PP I 10 51 44
Darcy took up a book; Miss Bingley did the same; and Mrs. PP I 11 54 3
the separation, so agreeable to almost all, took place. PP I 12 60 5
took leave of the whole party in the liveliest spirits. PP I 12 60 5
what passed, took leave and rode on with his friend. PP I 15 73 9
table, and Mr. Collins took his station between his cousin PP I 16 82 49
with an activity which took their brother by surprise, and PP I 17 86 9
by Mr. Darcy, who took her so much by surprise in his PP I 18 90 5
Elizabeth made no answer, and took her place in the set, PP I 18 90 8
He took the hint, and when Mary had finished her second PP I 18 100 68
69

that the business which took him to London, might be PP I 21 117 10
11

merit than when he took leave of you on Tuesday, or that PP I 21 119 20
Elizabeth took an opportunity of thanking her. PP I 22 121 1
He took leave of his relations at Longbourn with as much PP II 2 139 1
and Jane; but as he took up his abode with the lucases, PP II 3 145 11
The wedding took place; the bride and bridegroom set off PP II 3 146 19
accompanied him, Charlotte took her sister and friend over PP II 5 156 5
had likewise foretold, he took his seat at the bottom of PP II 6 162 14
He took the hint, and soon began with, "this seems a very PP II 9 178 12
he drew back his chair, took a newspaper from the table, PP II 9 179 24
25

its ever happening again, took care to inform him at first, PP II 10 182 1
which she instinctively took, said with a look of PP II 12 195 2
might allow, and if he took orders, desired that a PP II 12 200 5
others appeared; and he took the opportunity of paying the PP II 15 215 1
a word, he suddenly recollected himself, and took leave. PP III 1 252 53
Her niece was, therefore, obliged to submit, and they took PP III 1 254 57
Mr. Darcy took her place by her niece, and they walked on PP III 1 256 61
appeared, and this formidable introduction took place. PP III 2 261 3
exact; and he afterwards took occasion to ask her, when PP III 2 262 9
the imprudence of anger, took the first opportunity of PP III 3 269 8
9

apprehension of any thing before the elopement took place? PP III 5 290 45
Jane then took it from her pocket-book, and gave it to PP III 5 291 59
But the horror of what might possibly happen, almost took PP III 5 292 64
number of the hackney coach which took them from Clapham. PP III 5 293 69
The coach, therefore, took them the first stage of their PP III 6 298 15
Kitty, who took all these threats in a serious light, PP III 6 300 31
news from town, so I took the liberty of coming to ask." PP III 7 301 1
Elizabeth took the letter from his writing table, and they PP III 7 305 43
then, sick of this folly, took refuge in her own room, PP III 7 307 50
this happy day, she again took her seat at the head of her PP III 8 310 7
living with Wickham, a fortnight before they took place. PP III 8 310 10
eagerly round the room, took notice of some little PP III 9 315 4
glass next to him, and took off my glove, and let my hand PP III 9 316 8
She then took a large house in Edward-Street, and has PP III 10 322 2
once more when the wedding took place, and all money PP III 10 324 2
my love, I want to speak to you," took her out of the room. PP III 13 345 12
13

to it, till their visitor took his leave for the night; PP III 13 348 35
36

disdain, "I wonder you took the trouble of coming so far. PP III 14 353 27
the marriage took place, should be so generally known. PP III 15 363 22
in spite of the pains you took to disguise yourself, your PP III 18 380 5
arising from all this took from the season of courtship PP III 18 384 27
just now, poor Mr. Norris took up every moment of her time, MP I 1 9 10
of the kind pains you took to reason and persuade me out MP I 3 27 36
to adopt; but as she took early care to make him, as well MP I 3 30 57
Mrs. Norris took possession of the white house, the Grants MP I 3 31 58
of his affairs, and he took his eldest son with him in the MP I 3 32 61
They took their cheerful rides in the fine mornings of MP I 4 36 7
It was not long before a good understanding took place MP I 4 39 10
other subjects took place of the improvements of Sotherton. MP I 6 55 14
and it was a mere nothing before repton took it in hand. MP I 6 55 15
ride to Mansfield common took place the next morning;--the MP I 7 70 30
in a moment, the latter took her seat within, in gloom and MP I 8 80 30
its being a most happy event to her whenever it took place. MP I 9 88 24
She took it, however, as she spoke, and the gratification MP I 9 94 59
Bertram back to Mansfield, took Mr. Crawford into Norfolk. MP I 12 114 3
When he had told of his horse, he took a newspaper from MP I 12 118 22
an Agatha in the question, took on her to decide it, by MP I 14 132 8
a scene, she very kindly took his part in hand, and MP I 15 138 1
Edmund almost immediately took the opportunity of saying, " MP I 15 139 11
Julia made no communication, and Fanny took no liberties. MP I 17 163 20
He had learned his part--all his parts--for he took every MP I 18 164 1
Fanny took the work very quietly without attempting any MP I 18 167 7
8

The first day I went over Mansfield wood, and Edmund took MP II 1 181 16
in every respect indeed it took me by surprize, as I had MP II 1 184 25
Mr. Yates took the subject from his friend as soon as MP II 1 184 27
She took to herself all the credit of bringing Mr. MP II 2 188 3
Such was the origin of the sort of intimacy which took MP II 4 207 11
Her tone of calm languour, for she never took the trouble MP II 5 218 12
so--and Miss Crawford took her harp, she had nothing to do MP II 5 227 68
had been, and rather took it for granted that she had been MP II 7 251 62
herself to him, took an opportunity of stepping aside to MP II 10 276 14
I am very glad we took Fanny as we did, for now the others MP II 11 285 10
my dear Henry, and this is what took you to London! MP II 12 292 8
She took the letters as he gave them. MP II 13 298 3
minutes longer," and he took her hand and led her back to MP II 13 301 7
Accordingly, on this principle Sir Thomas took the first MP III 2 330 14
Lady Bertram took it differently. MP III 2 332 22
He came to her, sat down by her, took her hand, and MP III 3 335 5
Crawford took the volume. MP III 3 336 10
turned his back, and took up a newspaper, very sincerely MP III 3 341 31
He took me wholly by surprise. MP III 4 353 45
I took uneasiness with me, and there was no getting rid of MP III 4 355 52
form the east room, and took no solitary walk in the MP III 5 357 4
Fanny naturally turned up stairs, and took her guest to MP III 5 357 6
She took three days to consider of his proposals; and MP III 5 361 16
thing was ready, William took leave, and all of them were MP III 7 384 36
lady at home, that it took some time to determine that it MP III 9 396 7
He took care, however, that they should be allowed to go MP III 10 403 13
kind and proper in the notice he took of Susan. MP III 10 406 21
divide, but Mr. Crawford took care not to be divided from MP III 11 408 3
Mrs. Price took her weekly walk on the ramparts every fine MP III 11 408 4
clothes, because Rebecca took away all the boxes and MP III 15 444 26
to the recent event, took her hand, and said in a low, but MP III 15 446 34
from the marriage, and it took place to the infinite E I 2 15 3
I took him, as he was sleeping on the sofa, and it is as E I 6 45 21
success and satisfaction, took place on the morrow, and E I 6 47 30
He was the brother of her friends, and he took pains to E I 8 65 48
on the table, took it up, and examined it very attentively. E I 9 82 81
could, she soon afterwards took possession of a narrow E I 10 88 33
She had not time to know how Mr. Elton took the reproof, E I 15 125 7
like her usual self, she took care to express as much E I 18 144 4
When he did return, he sought out the child and took E II 2 163 4
When she took in her history, indeed, her situation, as E II 2 167 13
as fast as she could, and took shelter at Ford's."-- E II 3 177 52
looked away directly, and I took no notice; and they both E II 3 178 52
can't tell how; and then I took courage, and said it did E II 3 179 52
graceful bow from the other, the two gentlemen took leave. E II 5 195 49
"hum! just the trifling, silly fellow I took him for." E II 7 206 4
"Well, sir," cried Mr. Weston, "as I took Miss Taylor away, E II 7 209 11
She said no more, other subjects took their turn; and the E II 8 219 43
at her service before it took us home; for I thought it E II 8 223 63
One accompaniment to her song took her agreeably by E II 8 227 86
extremely wholesome, for I took the opportunity the other E II 9 237 46
He took some music from a chair near the pianoforte, and E II 10 242 20
21

Emma took the opportunity of whispering, "you speak too E II 10 243 23
24

her; but she took the compliment, and forgave the rest. E II 11 250 19
She then took another line of expediency, and looking into E II 11 254 45
46

Mrs. Elton took a great fancy to Jane Fairfax; and from E II 15 282 4
I fancy I am rather a favourite; he took notice of my gown. E II 17 302 22
It was well that he took every body's joy for granted, or E II 17 304 30
that he wanted, soon took the opportunity of walking away. E II 18 310 35
Coles--and having a ball talked of, which never took place. E II 18 312 50
a dialogue which just then took place between him and Mrs. E III 2 327 34
operations of justice; they took themselves off in a hurry. E III 3 336 13
me to supply him; and so I took mine out and cut him a E III 4 338 12
put it down; but when he took out his pencil, there was so E III 4 339 18
She then took a longer time for consideration. E III 4 341 34
fondly pointing out, as he took up any stray letter near E III 5 347 20
finding out none, directly took it up, and fell to work. E III 5 348 21
year, he soon afterwards took a hasty leave, and walked E III 5 351 38
They took a few turns together along the walk.-- E III 6 361 40
of Frank Churchill; others took it very composedly; but E III 6 366 74
The Eltons walked together; Mr. Knightley took charge of E III 7 367 1
Jane took Mrs. Elton aside, and told her at once, that E III 8 381 15
say of the good wishes which she really felt, took leave. E III 8 384 34
He took her hand;--whether she had not herself made the E III 9 386 7
rather offered it--but he took her hand, pressed it, and E III 9 386 7
daughter-in-law elect, and took Hartfield in her way home, E III 12 417 3
If all took place that might take place among the circle E III 12 422 19
at Astley's, my brother took charge of Mrs. John Knightley E III 18 472 20
his own amusement, never took up any book but the P III 1 3 1
She knew, that when he now took up the Baronetage, it was P III 1 9 19
took out a gun, but never killed;--quite the gentleman. P III 3 22 23
to Bath till Lady Russell took her, and that all the P III 5 34 10
But all these things took up a great deal of time." P III 5 39 34
Mr. and Mrs. Musgrove took me, and we were so crowded! P III 5 39 39
And Mrs. Musgrove took the first opportunity of being P III 6 44 8
The Crofts took possession with true naval alertness, and P III 6 48 17
Musgrove were sitting, took a place by the latter, and P III 8 67 28
She took hardly any notice of Charles Hayter yesterday. P III 9 77 16
than all the medicine he took; and, that being by the sea, P III 12 102 2
have been civil enough, took up the subject again, to say, P IV 1 128 29
She longed to see the Crofts, but when the meeting took P IV 6 168 22
Lady Russell took her out in her carriage almost every P IV 6 168 24
took their station by one of the fires in the Octagon Room. P IV 8 181 1
passed to their seats, her mind took a hasty range over it. P IV 8 185 21
every thing, and while it took from her the new-formed P IV 9 210 99
The visitors took their leave; and Charles, having civilly P IV 10 223 40
41

He took the peices of paper as he spoke--& having looked S 1 366 1
It took us half an hour to climb your hill.-- S 1 367 1
She took up a book; it happened to be a vol: of <u>Camilla</u>. S 6 390 1
She went on however towards Trafalgar house & took S 6 391 1
Here have I lived 70 good years in the world & never took S 6 394 1
nearer to his sister, & took her hand again most S 9 408 1
for <u>us</u>, instantly took up her pen & forwarded the S 9 408 1
with salts in her hand, took drops two or three times from S 10 413 1
He took his own cocoa from the tray,--which seemed S 10 416 1
her toast was done, & he took his own in hand, Charlotte S 10 417 1

TOOTH (3)

There was a tooth amiss. E III 16 451 3
Mrs. Clay had freckles, and a projecting tooth, and a P III 5 34 12
That tooth of her's! and those freckles! P III 5 35 14

TOOTHPICK-CASE (3)
He was giving orders for a toothpick-case for himself, and SS II 11 220 3
of an hour over every toothpick-case in the shop, were SS II 11 220 3
the possession of the toothpick-case, drew on his gloves SS II 11 221 5
TOOTHPICK-CASES (2)
of the different toothpick-cases presented to his SS II 11 221 4
who had given them a lecture on toothpick-cases at Gray's. SS II 14 250 11
TOP (17)
they gained even the top of the room, their situation was NA I 2 21 9
remaining ground till she gained the top of Milsom-Street. NA I 13 101 25
longer to be taken from the top of an high hill, and that NA I 14 110 28
that when they gained the top of Beechen Cliff, she NA I 14 111 29
out: having gained the top, they turned in an opposite NA II 8 184 5
from the bottom to the top, & would make me take his arm.-- W 344 20
found themselves at the top of a considerable eminence, PP III 1 245 3
from the west front to the top of the hill you know," MP I 6 55 17
presented themselves at the top, just ready for the MP I 10 103 50
by Mr. Crawford to the top of the dancers, couple after MP II 10 275 11
to Emma, had secured her hand, and led her up to the top. E II 8 229 98
a slight hedge at the top, and made the best of her way by E III 3 333 5
Emma read the words most precious treasures on the top. E III 4 338 9
hairs of a side, and nothing but a dab of powder at top.-- P III 3 19 16
rest of the party waited for them at the top of the hill. P III 10 86 18
for a surgeon to get a house at the top of the hill.-- S 1 366 1
house, & saw the top of the house itself among its groves. S 4 383 1
TOPIC (11)
You will soon have exhausted each favourite topic. SS I 10 47 4
different people to quit the topic, it fell to the ground. SS I 12 62 27
trying to converse upon a topic which always left her more SS III 2 270 1
dullest, most threadbare topic might be rendered PP I 16 76 4
less impenetrable on any topic than that of his regret at MP I 15 142 24
would keep him on the topic of the theatre, would torment MP II 1 184 25
He could not have chosen better; that was a topic to bring MP III 10 405 17
This topic was discussed very happily, and others E I 12 104 50
by any troublesome topic, and to wander at large amongst E II 1 156 6
discussion of one topic had better be avoided; and hoping, E III 12 416 2
The sad accident at Lyme was soon the prevailing topic; P IV 1 126 20
TOPICS (8)
unnatural characters, and topics of conversation, which no NA I 5 38 4
chatting on the commonest topics he had a sensible, W 335 13
Mr. Wickham began to speak on more general topics, Meryton, PP I 16 78 22
They were now approaching the cottage, and all idle topics E I 10 86 24
The like reserve prevailed on other topics. E II 2 169 17
restricted to the other topics with which for a while the E III 6 352 1
but here, as on most topics, he had the superiority, for P III 6 43 5
on topics which had by nature the first claim on her. P IV 1 124 11
TOPS (3)
tops of the trees of the wilderness immediately adjoining. MP I 9 90 36
of the air, below the tops of the trees--and the S 4 381 1
buildings, waving linen, & tops of houses, to the sea, S 4 384 1
TORE (1)
who pulled her about, tore her clothes, and put an end to SS I 7 34 7
TORMENT (17)
who was born to be the torment of my life, chose to set LS 2 245 1
for me really to torment him, as Sir James tho' extremely LS 22 280 2
I must torment my sister-in-law for the insolent triumph LS 25 293 4
Do not torment yourself with fears on my account. LS 33 303 1
be labouring only for the torment of little boys and girls, NA I 14 109 24
well qualified to torment readers of the most advanced NA I 14 109 25
I use the verb 'to torment,' as I observed to be your own NA I 14 109 25
"You think me foolish to call instruction a torment, but NA I 14 109 26
you would allow that to torment and to instruct might NA I 14 109 26
not hearts, we have eyes; and they give us torment enough." NA II 3 147 25
he loves; it is the woman only who can make it a torment." NA II 4 151 12
But I am sure she cannot mean to torment, for she is very NA II 4 151 13
I will not torment myself any longer by remaining among SS I 15 76 16
But I will not torment you with vain wishes, which may PP III 4 278 20
of the theatre, would torment him with questions and MP II 1 184 25
own property, without the torment of trying for more; it P III 3 20 17
had been the retarding weight, the doubt, the torment. P IV 11 241 60
TORMENTED (5)
"That little boys and girls should be tormented," said NA I 14 109 25
well worth while to be tormented for two or three years of NA I 14 110 27
her back on him,) I hope your eyes are not tormented now." NA II 3 147 26
imagination had tormented her on her first arrival, was NA II 13 227 26
her own, and with a mind tormented by self-reproach, which SS II 9 210 32
TORMENTING (5)
My dear friend, That tormenting creature Reginald is LS 31 301 1
of elegance which consists in tormenting a respectable man. PP I 19 108 20
of such irritation, as to make her every where tormenting. MP III 17 466 16
Those were the words; in them lay the tormenting ideas E III 11 402 1
writing, inviting & tormenting her, & whom she was S 3 378 1
TORMENTS (1)
Whether the torments of absence were softened by a NA II 16 250 3
TORN (9)
torn asunder by any common effort of a struggling assembly. NA I 2 21 9
"It would have been very shocking to have it torn," said NA I 2 22 11
sleeve; I am afraid it has torn a hole already; I shall be NA I 3 28 35
I wonder you was not afraid of its being torn." SS III 2 276 25
dear lock--all, every memento was torn from me." SS III 8 329 63
interest he had outwardly torn himself, now, when no SS III 8 331 70
she had suffered in being torn from them, came over her MP III 6 370 11
which must, at any rate, have been torn from me now. MP III 16 458 30
into his orchard--wall torn down--apples stolen--caught in P III 3 23 28
TORRENT (1)
Elinor could no longer witness this torrent of unresisted SS II 7 185 20
TORRENTS (2)
the rain beat in torrents against the windows, and every NA II 6 168 10
no sooner was she gone than they burst forth in torrents. NA II 13 226 25
TORTURE (7)
of some instrument of torture; but there being nothing in NA II 5 160 21
But a justification so full of torture to herself, she NA II 14 231 3
leave me, hate me, forget me! but do not torture me so. SS II 7 185 22
the torture of penitence, without the hope of amendment. SS III 2 270 2
Then came your dear mother to torture me farther, with all SS III 8 324 45
Thank heaven! it did torture me. SS III 8 324 45
They shall no longer worry others, nor torture myself. SS III 10 347 30
TORTURED (3)
to be called, only tortured her more, by hints of what her SS III 7 312 17
the moment, she ceased to be tortured by their effects.-- W 361 31
conceive, how they have tortured me;--though it was some PP III 16 367 14
TORTURING (1)
the sentiments and expressions which were torturing me. MP III 13 421 2
TOSSED (2)
She shuddered, tossed about in her bed, and envied every NA II 6 170 12
nothing of it--she would as lieve be tossed out as not." P III 10 84 8
TOSSES (1)
"And then their uncle comes in, and tosses them up to the E I 9 81 74
TOTAL (29)
So very great, so total a change from the intimacy of LS 25 292 3
or have been left in total solitude, & I can hardly tell LS 27 296 1
"A general deficiency of subject, a total inattention to NA I 3 27 32
a little suspicion at the total suspension of all NA I 8 57 21
a sudden gust of wind, and of being left in total darkness. NA I 11 88 54
expires in the socket, and leaves you in total darkness." NA II 5 160 21
each other in that total want of talent and taste which SS I 7 32 1
consolation for the total indifference of her sister. SS I 11 55 7
"This," said he, "cannot hold; but a change, a total SS I 11 56 17
but that one is the total silence of both on the subject, SS I 15 80 37
said Elinor, "in a total misapprehension of character in SS I 17 93 37
at his total silence with respect even to their names. SS I 22 134 49
In short, it ended in a total breach. SS III 8 323 40
My total ignorance of the connection must plead my apology. PP I 18 97 57
were made, seemed in danger of sinking into total silence. PP II 9 177 3
in comparison of that total want of propriety so PP II 12 198 5
from their cousin's total want of it, they were soon able MP I 2 12 3
a certainty, they felt the total destruction of the scheme MP II 1 177 5
and Easter, I suppose, will be the sum total of sacrifice." MP II 5 226 61
of the qualification, the total inattention to it, in the MP III 3 339 22
and because he could not endure a longer total separation. MP III 10 406 21
The evil lies yet deeper; in her total ignorance, MP III 16 456 25
total want of spirits when he did come might redeem him. E II 12 259 12
to a child, than in a total want of taste for what he saw, E III 6 362 43
The delightful assurance of her total indifference towards E III 13 432 40
include a total change of conversation, opinion, and idea. P III 6 42 1
performance, and total indifference to any other person's, P III 6 47 13
and there had been total silence among them for some time, P III 12 117 73
the smallest wish for a total change, she only deviated so P IV 8 183 11
12
TOTALLY (70)
As to Mrs Manwaring's jealousy, it was totally his own LS 14 264 4
Tho' totally without accomplishment, she is by no means so LS 18 273 3
so often, and proved so totally ineffectual, that NA I 2 21 9
You totally disallow any similarity in the obligations; NA I 10 77 37
himself to have been totally mistaken in his opinion of NA II 15 246 12
totally she disregarded her disapprobation of the match. SS I 5 25 3
and crying; her voice often totally suspended by her tears. SS I 16 83 3
Lady Middleton, and totally unlike her in every respect. SS I 19 106 22
"unless it had been under totally different circumstances. SS I 21 122 12
I confess myself so totally surprised at what you tell me, SS I 22 131 29
however, were so totally unsuspected by Mrs. Jennings, SS II 14 247 5
As for Lucy Steele, she considered her so totally SS III 1 261 13
so, because it is totally out of our power to assist him." SS III 1 268 50
of considerate propriety, totally unlike the half-awkward, W 346 21
in a sharp quick accent, totally unlike the first--"have W 351 24
& his attention was so totally engaged in the business & W 359 28
"Your conjecture is totally wrong, I assure you. PP I 6 27 48
in weather, which totally suspended the improvement of her PP I 17 88 15
"Yes, there can; for mine is totally different.-- PP I 21 118 16
influence a young man so totally independent of every one. PP I 21 120 28
of any thing else, and totally indisposed for employment, PP II 12 195 1
He declared himself to have been totally unsuspicious of PP II 13 208 9
he was totally ignorant of my being in town last spring! PP III 13 349 45
Your retrospections must be so totally void of reproach, PP III 16 369 24
That it would be totally out of Mrs. Norris's power to MP I 1 9 10
and Fanny, though almost totally separated from her family, MP I 2 21 34
appearance are, generally speaking, so totally different. MP I 5 49 32
in dilapidations, and their habits were totally dissimilar. MP I 6 55 14
am convinced that my father would totally disapprove it." MP I 13 126 24
their different ways so totally improper for home MP I 14 137 23
They were totally pre-occupied. MP I 17 163 21
as made him not only totally unconscious of the uneasy MP II 1 184 27
On the contrary, she was so totally unused to have her MP II 10 280 32
I am totally unequal to it." MP III 1 320 44
dispositions were so totally dissimilar, as to make mutual MP III 2 327 5
became necessary from the totally opposite feelings of Mr. MP III 2 331 19
seemed to occupy her totally; how it fell from her hand MP III 3 337 11
is totally distinct from giving his sense as you gave it. MP III 3 338 14
"We are so totally unlike," said Fanny, avoiding a direct MP III 4 348 22
that I consider him as totally unsuited to myself; though MP III 4 349 25
understand a disposition so totally different from her own. MP III 9 395 4
worst third in the world--totally different from Lady MP III 10 403 15
her a totally different thing in a town and in the country. MP III 15 439 9
without a pause of misery, the night was totally sleepless. MP III 15 441 20
young people, must be the totally opposite treatment which MP III 17 463 7
grateful disposition; was totally free from conceit; and E I 4 26 2
that he could be so very clownish, so totally without air. E I 4 32 30
He will be a completely gross, vulgar farmer--totally E I 4 33 38
their subjects totally distinct, or very rarely mixing-- E I 12 100 15
I need not so totally despair of an equal alliance, as to E I 15 132 35
tone, touch, and pedal, totally unsuspicious of that wish E II 8 220 46
first-rate qualities, which Mrs. Elton is totally without. E III 2 331 55
or perhaps if she were totally silent, it might only drive E III 4 341 34
rather of a totally different nature:--it is impossible E III 5 350 37
The house was larger than Hartfield, and totally unlike it, E III 6 358 35
completely misspent, more totally bare of rational E III 8 377 1
under a delusion, totally ignorant of her own heart--and, E III 11 412 45
She made her plan; she would speak of something totally E III 13 429 26
27
What totally different feelings did Emma take back into E III 14 434 1
much self-contentment, totally unsuspicious of what they E III 14 434 3
to admire in her, (so totally different were her delicate P III 1 6 10
of opinions, on his side, totally unconvinced and P III 4 28 5
when he spoke again, it was of something totally different. P III 12 108 29
He is totally beyond the reach of any sentiment of justice P IV 9 199 53
Your father and mother seem so totally free from all those P IV 10 218 23
between two persons of totally opposite interests, she P IV 10 222 39
On that point perhaps we may not totally disagree;--at S 1 369 1
inhabitants may be taken totally unawares, by one of those S 4 381 1
surprised him--so totally self-engrossed had he been.-- S 10 416 1
be two families; such a totally distinct set of people as S 10 419 1
TOTTERING (1)
the low hedge, and tottering footstep which ended the E I 10 87 27
TOUCH (32)
was suddenly roused by a touch on the shoulder, and NA I 8 55 10
soul, you might shake it to pieces yourself with a touch. NA I 9 65 28
bye; and we had a little touch together, though I was NA I 12 96 20
Elinor thought it wisest to touch that point no more. SS I 12 59 5
brothers for offering to touch her, and all their united SS I 21 121 10
He could not then avoid it, but her touch seemed painful SS II 6 177 8
Whenever he had a touch of his old cholicky gout, he said SS II 8 198 27
But, my dear, we must touch up the Colonel to do something SS III 4 292 55
her notice by a friendly touch, said "your goodness to W 333 13
have it in my dear, but I assure you I shan't touch it."-- W 354 27
"You scarcely touch me," said he. MP I 9 94 59
could subdue, no curiosity touch, no wit amuse; or MP I 17 160 8
quick taste--without any touch of that spirit of banter or MP III 3 340 24
The preacher who can touch and affect such an MP III 3 341 28
You know I told you not to touch it, because Susan is so MP III 7 386 44
Mr. Elton fidgetting behind her and watching every touch. E I 6 46 24
But Harriet was in a tremor, and could not touch it; and E I 9 71 14
Weston, her smile, her touch, her voice was grateful to E I 14 117 2
in the very style to touch; a small mixture of reproach, E II 4 184 11
Emma could imagine she saw a touch of the arm at this E II 5 188 11
ask and to say as to tone, touch, and pedal, totally E II 8 220 46
instrument long enough to touch it without emotion; she E II 10 240 6
touch it seldom; for evil in that quarter was at hand. E II 13 267 8
Could he Ly a touch of his finger have instantly taken E II 17 303 23
It did not seem to touch the rest of the party equally; E III 7 371 35
36
It was a commission to touch every favourite feeling. E III 7 373 51
The touch seemed immediate. E III 8 378 7
she had this sympathetic touch in the evening, from Mary, P III 6 48 16
Asp, in half the time; our touch with the great nation not P III 8 66 16
unseen, but was obliged to touch as well as address him P IV 6 169 25
a touch on her shoulder obliged Anne to turn round.-- P IV 8 190 47
I dare say, but their measures seem to touch on extremes.-- S 5 388 1
TOUCHED (23)
slightly and carelessly touched the hand of Isabella, on NA I 7 45 5
I shall go to the piano-forte; I have not touched it since SS II 1 144 15
of every thing would have touched Mrs. Bennet's heart, but PP I 13 65 26
Mr. Wickham, after a few moments, touched his hat--a PP I 15 73 8
Her heart had been but slightly touched, and her vanity PP II 3 149 28
temper, her heart was not likely to be easily touched.-- PP II 12 197 5

with ease; whatever she touched she expected to injure, MP I 2 14 9
the new calico that was bought last week, not touched yet. MP I 7 71 34
He was gone--he had touched her hand for the last time, he MP II 2 193 18
It ought not to have touched on the confines of her MP II 9 264 18
touched again when the ladies withdrew, with more success. MP II 10 272 4
way, it should never be touched on by him; but after a day MP III 4 345 1
Crawford and herself, touched her in comparison, slightly. MP III 12 418 4
his confidential treatment touched her strongly. MP III 13 425 5
When really touched by affliction, her active powers had MP III 16 448 2
and the tree is touched with such inimitable spirit! E I 6 48 39
injurious, and slightly touched upon his respect for Miss E I 15 130 28
life was just enough touched on to shew how keenly it was E II 13 265 5
She touched--she admitted--she acknowledged the whole E III 11 407 32
to be away, till touched by the thought of her father and P III 12 114 59
and she was not so little touched by Mr. Elliot's conduct, P IV 11 229 1
were eagerly & fluently touched;--rather commonplace S 7 396 1
his pleasures of hope has touched the extreme of our S 7 397 1

TOUCHES (4)

so sread abroad that one touches them every where, one is MP III 3 338 13
You have some touches of the angel in you, beyond what-- MP III 3 344 41
Perry tells me that Mr. Cole never touches malt liquor. E II 7 210 20
Selina has entirely given up music--never touches the E II 14 277 40

TOUCHING (4)

At last, however, by touching a secret spring, an inner NA II 5 160 21
as if some one was touching the very doorway--and in NA II 13 222 9
And touching Miss Bates, who at the moment passed near-- " E II 8 229 97
symptoms, nothing touching the pulmonary complaint, which E III 9 389 16

TOUCHSTONE (1)

As a sort of touchstone, however, she began to speak of E II 8 228 88

TOUGH (1)

He fancied it tough--sent away his plate--and has been MP I 18 171 27

TOUR (8)

tour of pleasure which they proposed taking in the summer. PP II 4 154 21
of her northern tour was a constant source of delight. PP II 5 155 1
"I have been making the tour of the park," he replied, "as PP II 10 183 4
Her tour to the lakes was now the object of her happiest PP II 19 237 3
The time fixed for the beginning of their northern tour PP II 19 238 7
a more contracted tour; and, according to the present plan, PP II 19 238 7
time or other, to look at--or my tour to read--or my poem. E III 6 364 60
absence in a tour to the sea-side, which was the plan.-- E III 19 483 8

TOURS (1)

He read all the Essays, letters, Tours & criticisms of the S 8 404 1

TOUT ENSEMBLE (1)

And then--her air, her manner, her tout ensemble is so MP II 6 230 5

TOWER (2)

the bank attacked, the tower threatened, the streets of NA I 14 113 39
You may see the church tower over the hedge, & the White W 321 2

TOWERS (1)

"But now really--are there towers and long galleries?" NA I 11 85 28

TOWN (283)

best private schools in town, where I shall have an LS 1 244 1
I hope a comfortable day with you in town within this week. LS 2 245 1
I take town in my way to that insupportable spot, a LS 2 245 1
My young lady accompanies me to town, where I shall LS 2 246 1
I will send you a line, as soon as I arrive in town.-- LS 2 246 2
Miss Vernon is to be placed at a school in town before her LS 3 247 1
Alicia, just before I left town, & rejoice to be assured LS 5 249 1
very little company, and never go to town but on business. LS 5 250 2
her ladyship spent in town, while her daughter was left in LS 6 251 1
when he comes to town; ask him to your house occasionally, LS 7 253 1
I have seen Sir James,--he came to town for a few days LS 9 256 1
Mr Vernon set off for town as soon as she had determined LS 15 266 4
I have sent Charles to town to make matters up if he can, LS 16 268 1
Mr & Mrs Vernon; & I cannot just now afford to go to town. LS 19 275 4
I have also an idea of being soon in town, & whatever may LS 25 294 4
to take her to town, & marry her immediately to Sir James. LS 25 294 5
advice; that you come to town yourself without loss of LS 26 295 1
misery enough; & come yourself to town, as soon as you can. LS 26 295 1
Manwaring came to town last week, & has contrived, in LS 26 295 3
She is going to town, to see her particular friend, Mrs LS 27 296 1
How long Lady Susan will be in town, or whether she LS 27 297 3
if he intended being in town this winter, as soon as I LS 27 297 4
when Reginald according to our agreement is to be in town. LS 29 299 2
many of my friends are in town--among them, the Manwarings. LS 30 301 5
keep him longer in the country, has hastened him to town. LS 31 301 1
in town, & had just watched him to your door herself! LS 32 302 1
Miss Manwaring is just come to town to be with her aunt, & LS 38 307 3
Reginald's being gone to town, for he is returned, LS 40 308 1
she got back to town, than as if parted from him for ever. LS 41 309 1
since his arrival in town--not as you may suppose with any LS 41 310 1
Reginald may not be in town again by that time! LS 41 310 2
about to fix herself in town for several months, she could LS 41 310 3
But I shall not be easy till I can go to town & judge of LS 41 310 4
it personally in town, ceased writing minutely or often. LS 42 311 1
after her arrival in town; & she was met with such an easy LS 42 311 2
Manwaring, who coming to town & putting herself to an LS 42 313 10
some new part of the town to be looked at; and the Pump- NA I 3 25 1
Well hung; town built; I have not had it a month. NA I 7 46 11
were within view of the town of Keynsham, when a halloo NA I 11 88 54
There are few people much about town that I do not know. NA I 12 96 20
did not know that he might not go to town on Tuesday." NA I 13 99 4
delay, walked out into the town, and in Bond-Street NA I 14 114 50
specimens when last in town, and had he not been perfectly NA II 7 175 12
Poor Thorpe is in town: I dread the sight of him; his NA II 10 202 7
call at Putney when next in town, might set all to rights. NA II 12 217 2
chanced to meet again in town, and who, under the NA II 15 246 12
It came from town, and is merely a letter of business." SS I 13 63 11
business which requires my immediate attendance in town." SS I 13 64 19
"In town!" cried Mrs. Jennings. SS I 13 64 20
"What can you have to do in town at this time of year?" SS I 13 64 20
You cannot go to town till to-morrow, brandon, that is all. SS I 13 64 25
you can conveniently leave town; and we must put off the SS I 13 65 35
"You do not go to town on horseback, do you?" added Sir SS I 13 65 41
you and your sisters in town this winter, Miss Dashwood?" SS I 13 66 46
May be she is ill in town; nothing in the world more SS I 14 70 2
He had no pleasure at Norland; he detested being in town; SS I 19 101 1
first circles, and drove about town in very knowing gigs. SS I 19 102 4
however we shall meet again in town very soon, I hope." SS I 20 110 2
"Not go to town!" cried Mrs. Palmer, with a laugh, "I SS I 20 110 4
me persuade the Miss Dashwoods to go to town this winter." SS I 20 110 9
spoke to him indeed; but I have seen him for ever in town. SS I 20 114 44
I assure you I heard of it in my way through town." SS I 20 115 46
just before we left town, and he told me of it directly." SS I 20 115 48
Did you think he came directly from town?" SS I 22 134 48
"Shall you be in town this winter, Miss Dashwood?" said SS II 2 150 36
a less elegant part of the town, she had resided every SS II 3 153 1
chaise; and when we are in town, if you do not like to go SS II 3 153 2
So I would advise you two, to set off for town, when you SS II 3 154 3
It is very right that you should go to town; I would have SS II 3 156 8
account, was not to be in town before February; and that SS II 3 157 15
whether she went to town or not, and when she saw her SS II 3 158 20
intentions were; in all probability he was already in town. SS II 4 159 1
They reached town by three o'clock the third day, glad to SS II 4 160 2
spent seven years at a great school in town to some effect. SS II 4 160 3
Willoughby were then in town, but she was afraid of giving SS II 4 162 12
came you to conjure out that I should be in town to-day?" SS II 4 163 14
So surprised at their coming to town, though it was what SS II 4 164 21
"If she had not known him to be in town she would not have SS II 4 165 29
in town, how odd that he should neither come nor write! SS II 4 165 29
John and Lady Middleton in town by the end of next week." SS II 5 167 4
them of her being in town; and Marianne was all the time SS II 5 168 8
scarcely settled in town, Sir John had contrived to SS II 5 170 29
since their arrival in town, as he was careful to avoid SS II 5 171 30
surprise on seeing them in town, though Colonel Brandon SS II 5 171 30
Mrs. Dashwood, and asked how long they had been in town. SS II 6 176 7
of your arrival in town, which you were so good as to send SS II 6 177 11
came to town with me on purpose to buy wedding clothes? SS II 7 182 10
you, for it has been known all over town this ever so long. SS II 7 182 10
had sent him on their arrival in town, was to this effect. SS II 7 186 37
more than surprise, when you know that I am in town. SS II 7 186 38
she would like, I would send all over the town for it. SS II 8 194 8
were ranging over the town and making what acquaintance SS II 9 209 28
and when he returned to town, which was within a fortnight SS II 9 211 38
"Is she still in town?" SS II 9 211 41
at least equally safe in town as in the country, since his SS II 10 213 4
and his wife were to be in town before the middle of SS II 10 213 5
The Willoughbys left town as soon as they were married; SS II 10 217 18
delight of Lucy in finding her still in town. SS II 10 217 20
Dr. Davies was coming to town, and so we thought we'd join SS II 10 218 24
when they come to town," said Lucy, returning, after a SS II 10 218 30
Elinor found that he and Fanny had been in town two days. SS II 11 221 8
but one has always so much to do on first coming to town. SS II 11 221 9
day, as soon as we came to town, aware that money could SS II 11 224 28
"your expenses both in town and country must certainly be SS II 11 225 29
30
Her inviting you to town is certainly a vast thing in your SS II 11 226 42
whether Edward was then in town; but nothing would have SS II 12 229 4
though he had arrived in town with Mr. and Mrs. Dashwood. SS II 11 230 4
Edward assured them himself of his being in town, within a SS II 12 230 5
health, their coming to town, &c. which Edward ought to SS II 13 241 22
you know; but the Miss Steeles may not be in town any more. SS II 14 253 24
by bringing Elinor to town as Colonel Brandon's wife, and SS II 14 253 25
or whether he is still in town, I do not know; for we of SS III 1 268 48
Willoughbys were again in town, and had a constant dread SS III 2 271 4
more than two months in town, and Marianne's impatience to SS III 3 279 1
Edward, she believed, was still in town, and fortunately SS III 3 283 20
were so soon to leave town, as she hoped to see more of SS III 5 300 38
the brother and sisters in town;--and a faint invitation SS III 6 301 1
My journey to town--travelling with my own horses, and SS III 8 325 45
"All!--no,--have you forgot what passed in town?-- that SS III 8 325 48
did, for I was in town the whole time,) what I felt is--in SS III 8 325 50
To know that Marianne was in town was--in the same SS III 8 325 50
Not aware of their being in town, however, I blundered on SS III 8 326 55
to be happy, and afterwards returned to town to be gay.-- SS III 8 329 65
"Are you going back to town?" SS III 8 331 72
I have business there; from thence to town in a day or two. SS III 8 331 73
"They come straight from town, as Miss Lucy--Mrs. Ferrars SS III 11 354 36
They were married, married in town, and now hastening down SS III 12 357 2
with an air of surprise-- "no, my mother is in town." SS III 12 359 18
The letters from town, which a few days before would have SS III 13 370 37
couple of nights, he was to proceed on his journey to town. SS III 13 372 46
from thence returning to town, procured the forgiveness of SS III 14 376 11
They settled in town, received very liberal assistance SS III 14 377 11
The Edward's were people of fortune who lived in the town W 314 1
on the pitching of the town--the jumbling & noise of which W 321 2
end of the town with a shrubbery & sweep in the country.-- W 322 2
Is not it a nice town?-- W 322 2
He had lived long enough in the idleness of a town to W 325 4
before yesterday that I saw them all three in this town. W 334 13
Mr. Bingley was obliged to be in town the following day, PP I 3 9 4
She could not imagine what business he could have in town PP I 3 10 4
private seminaries in town, had a fortune of twenty PP I 4 15 11
in a small market town; and quitting them both, he had PP I 5 18 1
"You have a house in town, I conclude?" PP I 6 26 34
"I had once some thoughts of fixing in town myself--for I PP I 6 26 36
independence, a most country town indifference to decorum." PP I 8 36 10
an express to town for one of the most eminent physicians. PP I 8 40 59
as much of that going on in the country as in town." PP I 9 43 19
leave it; and when I am in town it is pretty much the same. PP I 9 43 22
country as in town, which you must acknowledge to be true." PP I 9 43 24
my brother Gardiner's in town, so much in love with her, PP I 9 44 31
prevents her being in town; and by that means, as I told PP I 14 67 9
about it, and to ask when Mr. Denny comes back from town." PP I 14 68 14
him the day before from town, and he was happy to say had PP I 15 72 8
had been obliged to go to town on business the day before, PP I 18 89 1
2
He joined them on their entering the town and attended PP I 21 115 3
to town; and without any intention of coming back again. PP I 21 116 7
to follow their brother to town directly, and of their PP I 21 116 8
that when Charles gets to town, he will be in no hurry to PP I 21 117 10
11
She follows him to town in the hope of keeping him there, PP I 21 118 18
They had frequently been staying with her in town. PP II 2 139 2
We live in so different a part of town, all our PP II 2 141 12
Jane had been a week in town, without either seeing or PP II 3 147 21
into that part of the town, and I shall take the PP II 3 147 22
could discover to Mr. Bingley her sister's being in town. PP II 3 147 24
He knows of my being in town, I am certain, from something PP II 3 148 26
Your mother should have taken you to town every spring for PP II 6 164 24
"my eldest sister has been in town these three months. PP II 7 171 10
11
so far as to conceal from him your sister's being in town. PP II 12 199 5
to invite him to Pemberley, or admit his society in town. PP II 12 201 5
In town I believe he chiefly lived, but his studying the PP II 12 201 5
in town, had there renewed a slight acquaintance. PP II 13 205 4
I must be in town next Saturday." PP II 14 211 7
for the town of ---- in Hertfordshire; and, as they drew PP II 16 219 1
The families who had been in town for the winter came back PP II 19 238 6
The town where she had formerly passed some years of her PP II 19 239 7
To the little town of Lambton, the scene of Mrs. PP II 19 240 12
to be married privately in town than to pursue their first PP III 4 275 5
as they drove from the town; "and really, upon serious PP III 5 282 1
"Is my father in town?" PP III 5 286 25
As soon as I get to town, I shall go to my brother, and PP III 5 288 37
And now do, when you get to town, find them out, wherever PP III 5 288 38
to pursue, while in town, for the recovery of his daughter. PP III 5 293 68
the principal hotels in town, as Mr. Bennet thought it PP III 6 295 5
know in what part of the town he has now concealed himself. PP III 6 295 6
He owed a good deal in the town, but his debts of honour PP III 6 298 12
news from town, so I took the liberty of coming to ask." PP III 7 301 1
We have heard nothing from town." PP III 7 301 2
for your coming to town again; therefore, stay quietly at PP III 7 303 14
Lydia Bennet come upon the town; or, as the happiest PP III 8 309 6
and came to town with the resolution of hunting for them. PP III 10 321 2
He had been some days in town, before he was able to PP III 10 322 2
to her for intelligence of him, as soon as he got to town. PP III 10 322 2
was still with him, but would quit town the next morning. PP III 10 323 2
He dined with us the next day, and was to leave town again PP III 10 325 2
He had followed them purposely to town, he had taken on PP III 10 326 3
said, "I was surprised to see Darcy in town last month. PP III 10 328 15
16
"for when you went to town last winter, you promised to PP III 11 338 58
my uncle and aunt, when he was in town; and why not to me? PP III 12 339 4
he was totally ignorant of my being in town last spring! PP III 13 349 45
"Would you believe it, Lizzy, that when he went to town PP III 13 350 49
Lady Catherine might see him in her way through town; and PP III 15 361 3
your sister had been in town three months last winter, PP III 16 371 45
A house in town! PP III 17 378 43
They may easily get her from Portsmouth to town by the MP I 1 8 8
gave up the house in town, which she had been used to MP I 2 20 33
as ensure her the house in town, which was now a prime MP I 4 38 10
having seen Mr. Bertram in town, she knew that objection MP I 4 42 18
scene painter arrived from town, and was at work, much to MP I 18 164 1
formerly were ever merry, except when my uncle was in town. MP II 3 197 3

when you are settled in town and I come to see you, I dare MP II 4 213 35
him on his return to town to apply for information as to MP II 6 232 13
my brother's not being in town by several days so soon as MP II 9 261 2
Mr. Crawford meant to be in town by his uncle's MP II 9 266 21
you can tell me why my brother goes to town to-morrow. MP II 10 277 17
for permission to go to town with Maria; and as Sir Thomas MP II 11 284 10
time into our circle in town, that you might understand MP III 5 360 16
"I shall see your cousin in town soon; he talks of being MP III 5 364 32
He was to go to town, as soon as some business relative to MP III 6 367 4
They passed the Drawbridge, and entered the town; and the MP III 7 376 6
in any errand in the town; and though spurning the MP III 8 390 8
A week was gone since Edmund might be supposed in town, MP III 10 399 1
her cousin Edmund was in town, had been in town he MP III 10 400 8
was in town, had been in town he understood, a few days; MP III 10 400 8
in the town, which they would be very glad to do."-- MP III 10 401 10
Is there any thing I can do for you in town? MP III 11 411 20
"Is there nothing I can do for you in town?" MP III 11 412 24
think of his returning to town, and being frequently with MP III 11 413 31
she knows but three men in town who have so good a person, MP III 12 416 2
A house in town!--that she thought must be impossible. MP III 12 417 4
She was yet more impatient for another letter from town MP III 12 418 5
not be till after Easter, when he has business in town. MP III 13 423 2
she had to lose in passing March and April in a town. MP III 14 431 9
her other connections in town, except through Mansfield, MP III 14 433 12
Do not you think Edmund would have been in town again long MP III 14 435 13
her a totally different thing in a town and in the country. MP III 15 439 9
There was neither health nor gaiety in sun-shine in a town. MP III 15 439 9
the name of your great cousins in town, fan?" MP III 15 439 9
and bring her back to town, and Maria was with these MP III 16 450 8
Sir Thomas, however, remained yet a little longer in town, MP III 16 451 12
others, to get him out of town, and had engaged him in MP III 16 452 15
"I heard you were in town," said she--"I wanted to see you. MP III 16 454 18
was renewed in town, and Mr. Rushworth's house became MP III 17 466 18
almost amounting to a town, to which Hartfield, in spite E I 1 7 10
either in his business in town or among his friends here, E I 1 12 41
Mr. John Knightley must be in town again on the 28th, and E I 9 79 63
Mr. Wingfield in town as her father could be of Mr. Perry. E I 11 92 4
in any other part of the town;--there is hardly any other E I 12 103 37
except now and then for a moment accidentally in town! E I 12 104 46
and the Campbells leave town in their way to Holyhead the E II 1 161 31
I had known the Campbells a little in town; and at E II 6 200 20
of means--the house in town had yielded greater profits, E II 7 207 6
you have a charming collection of new ribbons from town. E II 9 237 48
if my uncle and aunt go to town this spring--but I am E II 12 259 15
summoned to town and must be absent on the very day. E II 16 292 9
"Col. and Mrs. Campbell are to be in town again by mid- E II 17 300 9
There are places in town, offices, where inquiry would E II 17 300 13
In town next week, you see--at the latest, I dare say; for E II 17 304 27
thing to have Frank among us again, so near as town. E II 17 304 27
He is to be in town next week, if not sooner. E II 18 305 5
they are all coming up to town directly, on Mrs. E II 18 305 7
is so impatient to be in town, that she means to sleep E II 18 306 11
The Enscombe family were not in town quite so soon as had E III 1 315 3
I saw you the other day as you rode through the town----- E III 2 323 19
He went to town on business three days ago, and I got him E III 18 471 20
The Mr. Churchills were also in town; and they were only E III 19 483 7
The following spring he was seen again in town, found P III 1 8 15
He had given her some hints of it the last spring in town; P III 1 9 19
in the neighbouring market town, and Lady Russell, were P III 1 10 21
One day last spring, in town, I was in company with two P III 3 19 16
steeper street of the town itself, that it was very P III 11 95 8
situation of the town, the principal street almost P III 11 95 9
out to the east of the town, are what the stranger's eye P III 11 95 9
a shop, invited them all to go back with her into the town. P III 12 103 5
care, and was off for the town with the utmost rapidity. P III 12 110 42
and they set off for the town, Charles taking care of his P III 12 115 66
in the littlenesses of a town; and she must sigh, and P IV 3 138 5
in the lower part of the town, and return alone to Camden- P IV 6 168 25
We were principally in town, living in very good style. P IV 9 199 55
solitary progress up the town (and she felt almost certain P IV 11 238 47
you going? only to Gay-Street, or farther up the town?" P IV 11 240 56
last half of our being in town;--when everything was in S 1 367 1
your being together in town, but conclude his scheme to S 5 387 1
Clergymen may be, or Lawyers from town, or half pay S 7 401 1
TOWN OF D. (1)
The first winter assembly in the Town of D. in Surry was W 314 1
TOWN-CLOCK (1)
at Tetbury as the town-clock struck eleven; and I defy any NA I 7 45 7
TOYS (2)
some of their least valued toys, and leave her to herself, MP I 2 14 7
he glued; he made toys for the children, he fashioned new P III 11 99 18
TRACE (10)
I could not trace her beyond her first seducer, and there SS II 9 207 26
and could easily trace it to whatever cause best pleased SS II 13 243 32
of the Priory, and try to trace its foundations as far as SS III 10 343 9
of the valley, as far as she could trace it, with delight. PP III 1 246 5
as he looked at her, he was trying to trace a resemblance. PP III 2 262 8
the alarm, set off from B. intending to trace their route. PP III 4 274 5
He did trace them easily to Clapham, but no farther; for PP III 4 274 5
to keep by her, to try to trace the features of the baby MP III 7 381 25
perhaps, trying to trace in them the ruins of the face P III 8 72 58
she had not been able to trace the exact steps of, had P IV 1 126 20
TRACED (6)
as if the whole might be traced to the influence of that NA II 10 200 2
In the whole of her subsequent manner, she traced the SS III 10 342 7
traced to pride;--and pride has often been his best friend. PP I 16 81 39
on Sunday night, and were traced almost to London, but not PP III 4 277 14
They cannot be traced. MP III 15 442 23
beginnings, hardly to be traced as to what came first, and MP III 16 453 17
TRACES (3)
been a cloister, having traces of cells pointed out, and NA II 8 183 2
than that which yet bore the traces of monastic division? NA II 8 188 17
And, besides, no traces of them were to be found on the PP III 5 282 6
TRACT (1)
eye, wandering over a wide tract of country to the south- SS III 6 302 8
TRACTABLE (3)
& rendered more tractable, more attached, more devoted LS 25 293 3
she is one of the most tractable creatures in the world. PP II 10 184 21
clever, she showed a tractable disposition, and seemed MP I 2 18 23
TRADE (11)
brother's fortune and their own had been acquired by trade. PP I 4 15 11
Sir William Lucas had been formerly in trade in Meryton, PP I 5 18 1
a brother settled in London in a respectable line of trade. PP I 7 28 2
that a man who lived by trade, and within view of his own PP II 2 139 2
have not been bred to the trade,--a set of gentlemen and MP I 13 124 12
Did not you hear me ask him about the slave trade last MP II 3 198 10
But Miss Price had not been brought up to the trade of MP II 9 267 22
He quitted the militia and engaged in trade, having E I 2 16 5
any alliances but in trade, or any thing to recommend him E I 16 136 9
dignity of his line of trade had been very moderate also. E II 4 183 9
were of low origin, in trade, and only moderately genteel. E II 7 207 6
TRADED (1)
Since the death of her husband, who had traded with SS II 3 153 1
TRADERS (1)
Our Butchers & Bakers & Traders in general cannot get rich S 6 392 1
TRADES (1)
employments, professions, and trades as Columella's." SS I 19 103 5
TRADESMAN (2)
He was declared to be in debt to every tradesman in the PP III 6 294 4
She proved to be the daughter of a tradesman, rich enough E III 19 481 3
TRADESMAN'S (2)
seduction, had been extended into every tradesman's family. PP III 6 294 4
I dare say there is always some reputable tradesman's wife MP I 1 8 8
TRADESPEOPLE (1)
the heavy bills of his tradespeople, and the unwelcome P III 1 9 19
TRADITIONAL (1)
subdue the hope of some traditional legends, some awful NA II 2 141 11
TRADUCED (1)
as I am now convinced how greatly they have traduced her. LS 14 264 4
TRAFALGAR (11)
He was in the Trafalgar action, and has been in the East P III 3 21 21
exchange, when we reach Trafalgar house--which by the bye, S 4 380 1
not named Trafalgar--for Waterloo is more the thing now. S 4 380 1
Trafalgar house, on the most elevated spot on the down was S 4 384 1
At Trafalgar house, rising at a little distance behind the S 4 384 1
They had been to Trafalgar house, & been directed thence S 6 390 1
She went on however towards Trafalgar house & took S 6 391 1
she proceeded for Trafalgar house with as much alacrity as S 9 406 1
the terrace, & you will often see me at Trafalgar house."-- S 10 416 1
an acquaintance with the Trafalgar House-Family, & with S 11 421 1
it for granted that he was on his way to Trafalgar house. S 12 425 1
TRAFFIC (1)
Much could not be hoped from the traffic of even the E II 9 233 24
TRAGEDIANS (1)
that could satisfy even tragedians; and the rivals, the MP I 14 130 3
TRAGEDIES (1)
Let us have no ranting tragedies. MP I 14 131 3
TRAGEDY (6)
capers in any tragedy or comedy in the English language. MP I 13 123 6
and Henry Crawford a tragedy, and that nothing in the MP I 13 124 13
should be at once both tragedy and comedy, that there did MP I 14 130 2
Though Julia fancies she prefers tragedy, I would not MP I 14 134 12
There is nothing of tragedy about her. MP I 14 134 12
Tragedy may be your choice, but it will certainly appear MP I 14 135 17
TRAGIC (4)
On the tragic side were the Miss Bertrams, Henry Crawford, MP I 14 130 3
fine tragic parts in the rest of the Dramatis Personae. MP I 14 131 6
Here are two capital tragic parts for Yates and Crawford, MP I 14 132 7
Her features are not tragic features, and she walks too MP I 14 134 12
TRAIN (14)
pinned up each other's train for the dance, and were not NA I 5 37 4
of a countess, with a long train of noble relations in NA II 14 232 7
At their conclusion the Osbornes & their train were all on W 335 13
and Mr. Bingley, and the train of agreeable reflections PP I 18 98 63
have a listener, and every thing was soon in a fair train. MP I 7 64 12
in some pursuit, or some train of thought at hand.-- her MP I 16 151 2
Every thing was now in a regular train; theatre, actors, MP I 18 164 1
And following the latter train of thought, she soon MP II 4 208 12
thing was now in a fairer train for Miss Crawford's MP III 6 366 4
It was no wonder that a train of twenty young couple now E I 3 22 5
mind; and she fell into a train of thinking on the subject E II 8 227 87
kind," said Emma, "will soon be in so regular a train-----" E II 14 278 41
Now we all follow in her train. E III 2 329 45
for the circuitous train of intelligence which had been S 10 414 1
TRAINED (2)
Betsey too, a spoilt child, trained up to think the MP III 8 391 9
a vine and a pear-tree trained round its casements; but P III 5 36 20
TRAINING (1)
But from fifteen to seventeen she was in training for a NA I 1 15 3
TRAIT (1)
some distinguished trait of integrity or benevolence, that PP II 13 206 4
TRAITS (2)
with no traits at all unusual in his sex and time of life. SS III 6 304 15
but there are some traits in her character which make it E II 18 309 33
TRAMPERS (1)
How the trampers might have behaved, had the young ladies E III 3 333 6
TRANQUIL (18)
Nay, I know not whether I ought to be quite tranquil now, LS 25 292 1
Look up it, and be tranquil if you can. SS I 16 88 33
themselves under the tranquil and well-bred direction of SS II 1 143 9
countenance and saw its expression becoming more tranquil. SS II 6 177 8
followed, she was everything by turns but tranquil. SS III 13 363 8
even for half a day, the tranquil & affectionate W 348 23
Mr. Bennet's emotions were much more tranquil on the PP I 23 127 6
in a less tranquil tone, and with a heightened colour. PP II 11 191 18
Lady Bertram, who was a woman of very tranquil feelings, MP I 1 4 1
were unbending, his attentions tranquil and simple. MP I 7 65 13
Within the room all was tranquil enough, for Susan having MP III 7 382 28
An attachment, originally as tranquil as their tempers, MP III 13 428 15
he saw nothing--of the tranquil manner in which the MP III 15 445 31
something to alter her present composed and tranquil state. E III 1 315 2
in tranquil observation of the beautiful views beneath her. E III 7 374 54
the blessing of one tranquil hour:'--and the quivering lip, E III 12 418 6
sensation of nature, tranquil, warm, and brilliant after a E III 13 424 1
by the tranquil & morbid virtues of any opposing character. S 8 404 1
TRANQUILITY (2)
to her spirits, or any degree of tranquility to her heart. SS III 13 363 8
save your health and credit, and restore your tranquility. E II 13 268 11 12
TRANQUILLISE (1)
and Fanny remained to tranquillise herself as she could. MP II 9 264 17
TRANQUILLITY (39)
grave reflections troubled the tranquillity of Catherine. NA I 10 74 22
Her tranquillity was not improved by the General's NA II 5 154 2
her spirits were gradually raised to a modest tranquillity. NA II 10 199 2
She might in time regain tranquillity; but he, what had he SS II 1 140 1
what a few months of tranquillity at Barton might do SS III 6 302 5
left her no moment of tranquillity till the arrival of Mr. SS III 7 314 22
least for a time this fair prospect of busy tranquillity. SS III 10 343 10
sure of leisure and tranquillity; and though prepared, as PP I 15 71 6
But not long was the interval of tranquillity; for when PP I 18 100 68
mildness to bear these attacks with tolerable tranquillity. PP I 23 129 14
With assumed tranquillity he then replied, "I have no wish PP II 11 191 15
been injurious to her own health and their tranquillity. PP II 17 227 26
inroads on the tranquillity of all, and not least of MP I 2 17 21
read to her; and the tranquillity of such evenings, her MP I 4 35 6
wealth, ease, and tranquillity, was just falling into a MP I 13 126 19
or any endeavour at rational tranquillity for herself.-- MP I 17 160 8
him not to risk his tranquillity by too much admiration MP I 17 161 9
where nothing was wanted but tranquillity and silence. MP II 1 180 10
value for domestic tranquillity, for a home which shuts MP II 1 186 34
home, restraint, and tranquillity; by the misery of MP II 3 202 26
other, she remained in tranquillity; and as a whist table MP II 5 227 68
but to listen, and her tranquillity remained undisturbed MP II 5 227 68
to cheat her of her tranquillity as he had cheated them; MP II 8 260 24
with such sober tranquillity as might satisfy any looker- MP II 10 278 20
conform to the tranquillity of the present quiet week. MP II 11 283 7
What was tranquillity and comfort to Fanny was tediousness MP II 11 285 15
could not help noticing their apparently deep tranquillity. MP III 3 336 8
Something like tranquillity might now be hoped for, and MP III 7 385 37
all, the peace and tranquillity of Mansfield, were brought MP III 8 391 10
the purchase necessary for the tranquillity of the house. MP III 9 397 7
heart, and the rational tranquillity of her ways.-- MP III 17 469 24
But neither geography nor tranquillity could come all at E II 5 189 18
as they entered, was tranquillity itself; Mrs. Bates, E II 10 240 1
Such a man, to quit the tranquillity and independence of E II 17 303 23
was out, which accounted for the previous tranquillity. E III 16 453 11
in a sort of desolate tranquillity, to the lodge, where P III 5 35 18
The rest was all tranquillity; till just as they were P III 6 49 23 24
of her situation, could do nothing towards tranquillity. P IV 11 238 44
& tranquillity on the terrace, the cliffs, & the sands.-- S 6 389 1
TRANQUILLIZE (4)
each other, we shall tranquillize the sisterly fears of LS 30 301 4

tried to sooth and tranquillize her still more, had not — SS II 7 180 5
Here's what may tranquillize every care, and lift the — MP I 11 113 35
For the present you have only to tranquillize yourself. — MP III 1 321 48

TRANQUILLIZED (7)
I have not yet tranquillized myself enough to see — LS 22 282 8
Catherine's spirits however were tranquillized but for an — NA II 13 223 9
were soon a little tranquillized, by seeing the party in — MP I 7 68 17
feelings were at all tranquillized, before she had given — MP II 3 201 24
frightened herself, tranquillized this excess of — E I 13 110 8
began to be a little tranquillized and subdued--and in the — E III 14 434 4
reflection might have tranquillized her; but the ten — P IV 11 238 44

TRANQUILLY (3)
yet it required some consideration to be tranquilly happy. — LS 23 284 5
but the evening passed tranquilly away; there was no — PP III 17 377 41
or all of the rest, he tranquilly said, "Mr. and Miss — MP II 1 185 29

TRANSACT (1)
off to transact, is invented as an excuse to dismiss him. — SS I 15 78 26

TRANSACTED (1)
while her young friends transacted their's, she should pay — SS II 11 220 2

TRANSACTION (2)
from Antigua: in every transaction together from that — MP III 17 465 15
a man should display in every transaction of his life." — E III 10 397 48

TRANSACTIONS (5)
credit, whereas the transactions of the two or three last — NA II 15 246 12
acquainted with every particular of these transactions. — PP II 12 202 5
of all the pecuniary transactions in which they had been — PP III 1 258 75
that it is, of all transactions, the one in which people — MP I 5 46 20
have reason to be long sorry for this day's transactions." — MP III 1 320 42

TRANSCRIBED (2)
that they had transcribed it some pages ago already. — E I 9 70 7
Of course I have not transcribed beyond the eight first — E I 9 82 80

TRANSCRIBING (1)
was the collecting and transcribing all the riddles of — E I 9 69 3

TRANSFER (4)
Park, and learning to transfer in its favour much of her — MP I 2 20 32
passions, and the transfer of unchanging attachments, must — MP III 17 470 26
beginning to transfer his affections from Harriet to me?-- — E I 14 118 4
her to entreat him to transfer his affection from herself — E III 13 431 38

TRANSFERRED (3)
or she has since transferred it to her daughter, for Sir — LS 20 276 2
who afterwards transferred his attentions from me to her, — W 317 2
of himself, were transferred for the rest of the day to — PP I 21 115 1

TRANSFORMATION (1)
Such a transformation!-- — E III 2 323 19

TRANSFORMED (1)
and twelve years had transformed the fine-looking, well- — P IV 5 153 6

TRANSGRESSED (3)
therefore could have transgressed none, still remained — SS III 14 376 11
She doubted whether she had not transgressed the duty of — E II 9 231 2
moral duty evidently transgressed; but yet she would have — P IV 5 160 27

TRANSGRESSION (1)
It would have been a much better transgression had I — E III 18 477 55

TRANSGRESSIONS (1)
Lady Russell, in spite of all her former transgressions, — P IV 12 251 10

TRANSIENT (6)
admiration but what was very moderate and very transient. — NA I 1 16 10
which she had caught a transient glimpse, communicating by — NA II 8 188 17
effect of a common and transient liking, which ceased when — PP II 1 137 26
acquainted with the transient, varying, unsteady nature of — MP III 2 330 14
of him; but it was too transient an indulgence of self- — P III 8 67 28
It was transient, cleared away in an instant, but Anne — P IV 10 228 70

TRANSITION (5)
decline, and by an easy transition from a piece of rocky — NA I 14 111 29
to make a voluntary transition to the oddities of her — PP I 18 90 4
and the quiet transition which Mr. Knightley soon — E I 5 41 31
Mrs. Weston; and the transition from Highbury to Enscombe, — E II 13 265 5
With all the eagerness which such a transition gives, Emma — E III 13 424 1

TRANSLATE (1)
of the language, to translate at sight these inverted, — P IV 8 186 26

TRANSMITTED (2)
were as regularly transmitted to Fanny, in the same — MP III 13 427 12
The Kellynch estate should be transmitted whole and entire, — P III 1 10 20

TRANSMITTING (1)
exacted her promise of transmitting the character of every — NA I 2 19 3

TRANSPARENCIES (2)
drawing-room, three transparencies, made in a rage for — MP I 16 152 2
made in a rage for transparencies, for the three lower — MP I 16 152 2

TRANSPARENCY (1)
Her skin was very brown, but from its transparency, her — SS I 10 46 2

TRANSPIRE (1)
hope that it would never transpire farther, and that it — NA II 10 199 2

TRANSPIRED (3)
for it had just transpired that he had left gaming debts — PP III 6 297 12
from her, all the particulars which had yet transpired. — MP III 16 449 7
as to names--which have but lately transpired.-- — S 9 408 1

TRANSPIRES (1)
Nothing satisfactory transpires as to her reason for — LS 17 270 6

TRANSPLANTATION (2)
seemed to do, to her transplantation to Mansfield, he was — MP II 10 276 13
that such a transplantation would be a risk of her — E III 15 448 31

TRANSPLANTED (2)
Whenever you are transplanted, like me, Miss Woodhouse, — E II 14 273 19
unworthy member of the one she was now transplanted into.-- — P III 6 43 3

TRANSPORT (3)
body thrill with transport, now arrived to be read with — SS III 13 370 37
Oh! what hours of transport we shall spend! — PP II 4 154 23
Oh! that I could transport you for a short time into our — MP III 5 360 16

TRANSPORTED (3)
minutes, the party were transported from the quiet warmth — W 327 7
within three days, transported to Mansfield, was an image — MP III 14 435 15
Knightley, were to be transported and placed all at once — E I 18 147 19

TRANSPORTING (1)
"Oh!" cried Marianne, "with what transporting sensations — SS I 16 87 31

TRANSPORTS (2)
the violence of these transports, by leading her thoughts — PP III 7 306 45
When the first transports of rage which had produced his — PP III 8 309 5

TRANSPOSED (1)
sight these inverted, transposed, curtailed Italian lines, — P IV 8 186 26

TRAP-DOORS (1)
phaetons and false hangings, Tilneys and trap-doors. — NA I 11 87 51

TRASH (3)
strains of the trash with which the press now groans. — NA I 5 37 4
and gives them so much trash and sweet things, that they — P III 6 44 8
The mere trash of the common circulating library, I hold — S 8 403 1

TRAVEL (12)
down to work, "and with how heavy a heart does he travel?" — SS I 15 77 22
"What magnificent orders would travel from this family to — SS I 17 92 25
my dear," said Mrs. Jennings, "and how did you travel?" — SS II 10 218 23
fixing on the time when Marianne would be able to travel. — SS III 7 310 8
of Fanny, they were to travel post, when she saw Sir — MP III 6 372 21
and if one is to travel, there is not much to chuse — E I 12 106 58
altogether than travel forty miles to get into a worse air. — E I 12 106 58
him alter his plan, and travel earlier, later, and quicker, — E II 5 190 23
to be allowed to travel--but she would not hear of it. — E II 8 221 49
I ought to travel. — E III 6 365 62
And how does he travel now?-- — E III 18 480 75
& independant as Mrs G.--can travel & chuse for herself.-- — S 9 411 1

TRAVELLED (20)
distressing her, to ask many questions as they travelled. — LS 17 271 6
the inquiry which had travelled from her heart almost to — NA I 12 95 18
travelled through, in the 'mysteries of uholpho.' — NA I 14 106 4
the style in which they travelled, of the fashionable — NA II 5 156 4
Unfortunately, the road she now travelled was the same — NA II 14 230 1
to change horses, she travelled on for about eleven hours — NA II 14 232 6
"She travelled all the way post by herself, and knew — NA II 14 237 21
the road which they had travelled on first coming to — SS I 16 85 15
wishing they had not travelled quite so fast, nor made — SS I 19 107 29
behaviour as they travelled was a happy speciman of what — SS II 4 160 2
She was before me, constantly before me, as I travelled, — SS III 8 327 55
"He opened his whole heart to me yesterday as we travelled. — SS III 9 336 12
They travelled as expeditiously as possible; and sleeping — PP III 5 285 20
Seven miles were travelled in expectation of enjoyment, — E III 7 367 1
their blossoms, as she travelled up to London with her — P III 1 7 12
They had travelled half their way along the rough lane, — P III 10 91 43
waiting the return, travelled night and day till he got to — P III 12 108 28
Sir Walter wanted to know whether the Crofts travelled — P IV 6 165 9
I have travelled so little, that every fresh place would — P IV 8 184 16
simple gig in which they travelled, & which their groom — S 7 394 1

TRAVELLER (5)
all the attention that a traveller like herself could — NA II 14 232 6
The chaise of a traveller being a rare sight in Fullerton, — NA II 14 233 8
the comfort of the poor traveller, whose pale and jaded — NA II 14 233 9
"What a great traveller you must have been, ma'am!" said — P III 8 70 51
the Weald I am sure sir, replied the traveller, pleasantly. — S 1 366 1

TRAVELLER'S (1)
as likely to catch the traveller's eye, as the more — P III 5 36 20

TRAVELLERS (8)
Marianne slept through every blast, and the travellers-- — SS III 7 316 28
to talk of the travellers, and feel their own dulness, — SS III 10 341 5
shall not be like other travellers, without being able to — PP II 4 154 23
than those those of the generality of travellers." — PP II 4 154 23
With respect to Wickham, the travellers soon found that he — PP III 2 265 15
of those days the young travellers were in a good deal of — MP III 6 372 21
to feel for their fatigues and wants as travellers. — MP III 7 378 13
behind the terrace, the travellers were safely set down, & — S 4 384 1

TRAVELLERS' (1)
The earliest intelligence of the travellers' safe arrival — MP I 4 34 2

TRAVELLING (28)
the time or mode of her travelling; of two days, the — NA II 13 226 25
waiting-maids in a travelling chaise-and-four, behind her, — NA II 14 232 7
find no difficulty in travelling so far to see me, I am — SS I 5 25 2
on their travelling so far towards Barton without any — SS III 6 301 1
and Mr. Palmer, travelling more expeditiously with Colonel — SS III 6 301 3
suspense in which she must now be travelling towards them. — SS III 7 315 26
My journey to town--travelling with my own horses, and — SS III 8 325 45
and Hertfordshire, of travelling and staying at home, of — PP II 8 172 3
Where there is fortune to make the expence of travelling — PP II 9 179 22
the idea of two young women travelling post by themselves. — PP II 14 211 13
the rest of the party with whom he had been travelling. — PP III 1 256 61
At last she recollected that she had been travelling, and — PP III 1 257 66
miraculous consequence of travelling in the summer. — PP III 3 271 14
by every creature travelling the road; especially as there — MP II 7 244 27
who enjoyed the idea of travelling post with four horses — MP II 9 266 21
The novelty of travelling, and the happiness of being with — MP III 7 375 1
sake of being travelling at the same time that you were. — MP III 9 393 1
It was presumed that Mr. Crawford was travelling back to — MP III 12 415 1 2
when they chose; travelling could be no difficulty to them, — MP III 14 432 11
The cousin who was travelling towards them, could hardly — MP III 15 444 27
administered by his travelling companion; but she had — E I 13 113 27
opinion completely for travelling round to its object, he — E II 5 192 29
There was certainly no harm in his travelling sixteen — E II 7 205 1
tray, a tidy old woman travelling homewards from shop with — E II 9 233 24
friends contrived--no travelling difficulty allowed to — E II 15 285 14
is up at all hours, and travelling in all weather; and — P III 3 20 17
A gentleman & lady travelling from Tunbridge towards that — S 1 363 1
While I have been travelling, with this object in veiw, I — S 9 410 1

TRAVELLING-CHAISE (1)
be forced into a travelling-chaise and four, which will — NA II 1 131 15

TRAVELLOR (3)
& displayed Tom Musgrave in the wrap of a Travellor.-- — W 355 28
upright again, the Travellor said--"you are extremely — S 1 365 1
his foot disposed the Travellor to think rather more as he — S 1 367 1

TRAVELLORS (1)
For a whole fortnight the travellors were fixed at — S 2 370 1

TRAVELS (2)
plays, and things of that sort, and do not dislike travels. — NA I 14 108 20
She always travels with her own sheets; and excellent — E II 18 306 12

TRAY (7)
at the same time that a tray full of refreshments was — NA II 11 213 20
into the parlour with the tray & the knife-case, she was — W 344 21
have looked so awkward;--just the tray did not signify.--" — W 347 22
going, even the sandwich tray, and Dr. Grant doing the — MP I 7 65 13
table, on which the supper tray yet remained, brought a — MP I 7 74 57
on the butcher with his tray, a tidy old woman travelling — E II 9 233 24
He took his own cocoa from the tray,--which seemed — S 10 416 1

TRAYS (1)
other were tressels and trays, bending under the weight of — P IV 2 134 29

TREACHEROUS (3)
partial though stronger illumination of a treacherous lamp. — NA II 9 190 1
He was, perhaps, but at treacherous play with her. — MP I 14 135 18
clandestine, insidious, treacherous admirer of Maria — MP III 2 327 6

TREACHERY (6)
The treachery, or the folly, of my cousin's maid betrayed — SS II 9 206 24
of her conduct, but I think such treachery very bad. — W 316 2
Rivalry, treachery between sisters!-- — W 316 2
forward at any possible treachery in his guest, give way — E II 5 193 35
of hypocrisy and deceit,--espionage, and treachery?-- — E III 10 399 61
of any cruelty, or any treachery, that could be — P IV 9 199 53

TREAD (5)
That "the poor beetle, which we tread upon, "in — NA I 1 16 8
her obliging manners down to her light and graceful tread. — MP I 11 112 33
no abrupt bursts, no tread of violence was ever heard; all — MP III 8 391 11
but it was dangerous, perhaps, to tread such ground. — MP III 15 441 21
as have since appeared to tread in Richardson's steps, so — S 8 404 1

TREADING (4)
being told, that she was treading what had once been a — NA II 8 183 2
It was like treading old ground again." — MP II 1 184 26
a diminution of cares since her treading that path before. — MP II 8 260 25
wife, they set forward, treading back with feelings — P III 12 111 49

TREASON (1)
that it would be high treason to call it in question; but — P III 6 45 9

TREASURE (10)
hasten with the precious treasure into your own chamber, — NA II 5 160 21
Well read in the art of concealing a treasure, the — NA II 6 169 11
she finds Miss Pope a treasure. — PP II 6 165 32
Catherine,' said she, 'you have given me a treasure.' — PP II 6 165 32
The new mare proved a treasure; with a very little trouble, — MP I 4 37 8
That Mrs. Whitaker is a treasure! — MP I 10 105 55
writing to her, as a treasure beyond all her hopes, and — MP II 9 265 19
him, he will be a treasure at Highbury, we do not often — E I 18 149 29
could not help making a treasure of it--so I put it by — E III 4 338 12
Emma was quite eager to see this superior treasure. — E III 4 339 17

TREASURED (2)
Elinor joyfully treasured her words as she answered, "if — SS III 10 344 18 19
Mrs. Bennet treasured up the hint, and trusted that she — PP I 15 71 5

TREASURES (3)
held all her smaller treasures; but on opening the door, — MP II 9 261 1
Emma read the words most precious treasures on the top. — E III 4 338 9
to do for the sake of these treasures of his existence! — P IV 11 235 31

TREASURING (1)
actually found happiness in treasuring up these things?" — E III 4 340 23

TREAT (19)

must be sensible, to treat my daughter with some severity LS 15 267 6
treat them with spirit, and make them keep their distance." NA I 6 42 26
on her arrival, and treat her with proper attention; and SS I 1 7 13
having often wished you to treat out acquaintance in SS I 17 94 39
of appearing to treat them with attention: and who could SS II 14 248 6
"We may treat it as a joke," said he at last, recovering SS III 5 298 35
To treat her with unkindness, to speak of her slightingly SS III 8 329 64
chose to doubt it--or to treat it as a merely conditional PP I 16 79 27
a time exclaimed, "to treat in such a manner, the godson, PP I 16 80 36
You have done all this! and yet you can treat the mention PP II 11 192 21
"And we mean to treat you all," added Lydia; "but you must PP II 16 219 3
I am sure you could not treat the matter as you do now." PP II 17 226 18
by failing at any time to treat your aunt Norris with the MP III 1 313 12
in existence, who could treat as a trifle this sin of the MP III 15 441 19
made it natural to her to treat the subject as she did. MP III 16 456 25
I treat you without ceremony Mr. Knightley. E I 8 57 3
be used, and looked at it now and then as a great treat." E III 4 338 12
so much alone, her conversation I assure you is a treat." P IV 5 155 9
will be much better--that will be a novelty and a treat. P IV 10 220 29

TREATED (46)
has never done her justice, or treated her affectionately. LS 17 270 5
it clear that if properly treated by Lady Susan she would LS 18 273 3
beleives that Frederica will now be treated with affection. LS 41 310 3
with which she was treated striking at that instant on her NA II 13 228 27
hearing how she had been treated,--though Mrs. Morland's NA II 14 237 21
how Catherine had been treated, on comprehending his NA II 15 247 15
As such, however, they were treated by her with quiet SS I 2 8 1
or displeasure, and treated him as she thought he ought to SS I 16 89 42
thought he ought to be treated from the family connection. SS I 16 89 42
from Edward, it was treated by the former with calmness SS II 2 151 42
Mrs. Jennings on her side treated them both with all SS II 4 160 2
good joke, and which she treated accordingly, by hoping, SS II 7 181 7
She treated her therefore, with all the indulgent fondness SS II 8 193 7
to have been, and from the first he treated her unkindly. SS II 9 206 24
I mean,--if I had been treated in that forbidding sort of SS II 13 240 17
anxious that he should be treated as one in all worldly SS III 5 293 2
treated with all the philosophic dignity of twenty-four. SS III 13 362 4
them, was rationally treated as enormously heightening the SS III 13 371 38
to see them, and always treated them with the make-believe SS III 14 375 10
the unkindness she was treated with, procured her in time SS III 14 377 11
Our assemblies have been used to be so well treated by W 334 13
I always wish to be treated quite "en famille" when I come W 351 25
for the extraordinary kindness she was treated with. PP I 7 33 43
Wickham has treated Mr. Darcy in a most infamous manner. PP I 18 94 45
The idea of his returning no more Elizabeth treated with PP I 21 120 28
Mr. Bennet treated the matter differently. PP II 1 137 27
very handsomely, for we treated the other three with the PP II 16 222 22
and if you would have gone, we would have treated you too. PP II 16 222 22
of the regiment, who treated her with more distinction, PP III 5 285 18
But you are now of an age to be treated better; I think MP I 3 26 25
While she treated it as a joke, therefore, she did not MP I 4 42 18
And they will now see their cousin treated as she ought to MP II 12 297 33
of her thankless son, and treated as concisely as possible MP III 13 425 6
that I depend upon being treated better than I deserve-- MP III 14 433 13
had herself been treated, as from sensibility for her son. MP III 16 450 10
That the manner in which she treated the dreadful crime MP III 16 457 30
and treated as the friend best worth attending to. MP III 17 462 4
which Miss Woodhouse had treated her all the evening, and E I 3 25 15
to know how she was treated; and as for the ball, it was E II 12 259 11
that ought to be treated rather as winter than summer. E III 5 347 19
Jane will be treated with such regard and kindness!-- E III 8 382 23
side; the young man was treated liberally; it was all as E III 19 482 4
at Kellynch-Hall were treated as of such general publicity P III 6 42 1
there, was her being treated with too much confidence by P III 6 44 7
Mrs. Charles knows no more how they should be treated!-- P III 6 45 8
But how were you treated?-- S 5 386 1

TREATIES (1)
had also opened so many Treaties with cooks, housemaids, S 10 414 1

TREATING (13)
I have no notion of treating men with such respect. NA I 6 43 43
Miss Morland, he is treating you exactly as he does his NA I 14 107 14
him to judge--of their treating her with parental kindness. NA II 15 245 12
Marianne still deeper by treating their disengagement, not SS II 7 184 15
much notice of you, and treating you in this kind of way, SS II 11 227 46
flattering as Mrs. Ferrars's way of treating me yesterday? SS II 13 239 4
lately; and who, treating her at once as the disinterested SS III 6 305 16
and Mr. Palmer, though treating their apprehensions as SS III 7 307 3
places Mr. Darcy, to be treating his father's favourite in PP I 17 85 4
of her brother, treating him, they say, quite like a son. MP I 7 63 4
It was treating her like her cousins! MP II 10 275 12
not but feel that it was treating her improperly and MP II 13 301 7
This is treating me like a friend. P IV 6 169 25

TREATMENT (25)
author;--and to her treatment of the subject I will only NA I 14 111 29
case, she would have met with very different treatment." NA II 12 219 13
his contemptuous treatment of every body, and his general SS I 20 112 28
their treatment of you;--but as that was not the case"----- SS II 13 239 8
which a fresh mode of treatment must procure, with a SS III 7 312 19
Her affection for me deserved better treatment, and I SS III 8 322 36
in their treatment of every body, hardly excepting even PP I 6 21 1
borne without anger such treatment; but Sir William's good PP I 23 126 3
the present Mr. Darcy's treatment of him, she tried to PP II 2 143 20
for his affectionate treatment of herself, she endeavoured PP II 19 236 2
often mortified by their treatment of her, she thought too MP I 2 20 32
her now with rights that demanded different treatment. MP III 2 328 7
to value a fond treatment, and from having hitherto known MP III 5 365 33
Tom, however, had no mind for such treatment: he came home, MP III 7 381 25
to tenderness in his former treatment of herself. MP III 8 389 3
his confidential treatment touched her strongly. MP III 13 425 5
be the totally opposite treatment which Maria and Julia MP III 17 463 7
Rushworth Maria Bertram again in her treatment of himself. MP III 17 467 20
With this treatment, Mr. Woodhouse was soon composed E II 7 209 13
found a broader vent in contemptuous treatment of Harriet. E II 15 282 3
the family, nor of the treatment I have met with; and, E II 18 309 33
would be entirely guided by your treatment of her.-- E III 7 375 61
weary her by negligent treatment--and had he and all his E III 13 428 23
whole system of whose treatment of her, by the bye, has E III 14 441 8
"Oh! I always deserve the best treatment, because I never E III 18 474 29

TREATS (1)
treats her with all the respect which she has a claim to. E II 15 286 23

TREATY (1)
to proceed in the treaty, and authorising him to wait on P III 3 24 35

TREBLE (1)
single, or double, or treble, gave the arrangement their E II 2 166 10

TREBLING (1)
Morland's preferment, trebling his private fortune, NA II 15 245 12

TREE (12)
book that tells her how to admire an old twisted tree. SS I 17 92 25
in the country: and such a mulberry tree in one corner! SS II 8 196 22
every field and every tree brought some peculiar, some SS III 10 342 7
is now grown such a noble tree, and getting to such MP I 6 54 9
"The tree thrives well beyond a doubt, madam," replied Dr. MP I 6 54 10
of a moor park apricot, as the fruit from that tree. MP I 6 54 12
In some countries we know the tree that sheds its leaf is MP II 4 209 16
Look at the tree." E I 6 48 37
and the tree is touched with such inimitable spirit! E I 6 48 39
a fence, the felling of a tree, and the destination of E I 12 100 16
a glimpse of a fine large tree, with a bench round it, E II 14 273 21
for having dismembered himself from the paternal tree. P IV 2 136 35

TREES (24)
trees, hens and chickens, all very much like one another.-- NA I 1 14 1
The remainder was shut off by knolls of old trees, or NA II 7 177 19
little cottage there is among the trees--apple trees too! NA II 11 214 23
And you, ye well-known trees!--but you will continue the SS I 5 27 8
I do not like crooked, twisted, blasted trees. SS I 18 98 8
The old walnut trees are all come down to make room for it. SS II 11 226 39
in the rest, where the trees were the oldest, and the SS III 6 305 17
tell how many trees there were in the most distant clump. PP II 5 156 4
by an opening in the trees that bordered the park nearly PP II 5 156 4
scene, the river, the trees scattered on its banks, and PP III 1 246 5
where the opening of the trees gave the eye power to PP III 1 253 57
There have been two or three fine old trees cut down that MP I 6 55 17
something of it here--something of the more distant trees. MP I 8 83 36
tops of the trees of the wilderness immediately adjoining. MP I 9 90 36
at last; and had been sitting down under one of the trees. MP I 10 103 49
farm house, with the yew trees, because I can never bear MP II 7 241 13
freshest green; and the trees, though not fully clothed, MP III 15 446 35
After wandering about and sitting under trees with Fanny MP III 17 462 5
where as one of his trees--I believe there is two of them. E II 9 238 51
ourselves, and sit under trees;--and whatever else you may E III 6 355 20
July appeared but in the trees and shrubs, which the wind E III 12 421 18
great gates, and old trees, substantial and unmodernized-- P III 5 36 20
where the scattered forest trees and orchards of luxuriant P III 11 95 9
below the tops of the trees--and the inhabitants may be S 4 381 1

TREMBLE (9)
& let Maria Manwaring tremble for the consequence. LS 39 308 1
she could hardly tell where, made her pause and tremble. NA II 9 194 6
believed they must always tremble;--the mention of a chest NA II 10 201 4
tremble lest her mother should be exposing herself again. PP I 9 45 35
Lord bless me! how you did tremble when Sir Thomas first MP I 7 69 22
friends, he began to tremble for his credit and his lungs MP I 13 123 5
it as often, and began to tremble again, at the idea of MP III 1 312 4
I know no more what I said-- I was in such a tremble!-- E II 3 178 52
really when I look round among my acquaintance, I tremble. E II 14 277 40

TREMBLED (12)
Catherine trembled at the emphasis with which he spoke, NA II 6 165 6
Her heart fluttered, her knees trembled, and her cheeks NA II 6 169 11
Catherine trembled from head to foot. NA II 6 170 12
She trembled a little at the idea of any one's approaching NA II 13 223 9
She trembled, her eyes were fixed on the ground, and her SS III 10 347 33
Now she should hear more; and she trembled in expectation SS III 12 358 8
Elizabeth hesitated, but her knees trembled under her, and PP III 4 276 8
good;--(Oh! how I have trembled at my uncle's opening his MP I 3 27 36
was over, she trembled and blushed at her own daring. MP II 5 225 59
as his voice; she had trembled at it as often, and began MP III 1 312 4
Poor Mr. Woodhouse trembled as he sat, and, as Emma had E III 3 336 12
She had spoken it; but she trembled when it was done, P IV 10 225 54

TREMBLING (16)
and seizing, with trembling hands, the hasp of the lock, NA II 6 164 3
on the postscript of the last, with trembling energy.-- PP III 4 280 26
She had found a seat, where in excessive trembling she was MP II 1 176 4
tidings, he found her trembling with joy over this letter, MP II 6 232 12
While her hand was trembling under these letters, her eye MP II 13 299 4
She was feeling, thinking, trembling, about every thing;-- MP II 13 302 10
wrote thus, in great trembling both of spirits and hand: MP II 13 307 30 31
of agitation, listening, trembling, and fearing to be sent MP III 1 311 3
table where she sat in trembling wretchedness, and with a MP III 1 318 39
is so prevalent, that I confess I cannot help trembling. MP III 14 433 13
to so low and wan and trembling a condition as no mother-- MP III 15 442 22
her father, who had been trembling for the dangers of a E I 15 132 38
of her habit--(I can never think of it without trembling?) E II 1 160 23
In this state Frank Churchill had found her, she trembling E III 3 334 7
indeed no idea?" said Mrs. Weston in a trembling voice. E III 10 394 28
of her hopes with great, though trembling delight.-- E III 11 408 34

TREMBLINGS (2)
my wits; and have such tremblings, such flutterings, all PP III 5 288 38
Emma's tremblings as she asked, and as she listened, were E III 11 409 34

TREMENDOUS (1)
his safety by any tremendous weather--but only by a steady MP II 5 225 57

TREMOR (1)
But Harriet was in a tremor, and could not touch it; and E I 9 71 14

TREMORS (1)
Every body was satisfied--and she was left to the tremors MP I 18 172 32

TREMOUR (1)
and sat in such a general tremour as made her fear it SS II 7 181 7

TREMULOUS (4)
the key with a very tremulous hand and tried to turn it; NA II 6 168 10
With hasty indignation therefore, and a tremulous voice, MP I 14 136 18
with words, whose tremulous inequality showed E III 9 390 18
he repeated, with such tremulous feeling, the various P III 11 100 23

TREMULOUSLY (1)
(speaking low and tremulously) "there are so many who P IV 5 156 11

TRENCHES (1)
of opening the first Trenches of an acquaintance with such S 10 414 1

TREPIDATION (3)
rank, she thought she could witness without trepidation. PP II 6 161 9
a great increase of the trepidation with which she MP II 5 223 47
perceiving the amazing trepidation with which she made up MP II 13 307 33

TRESPASS (3)
We must trespass a little longer on your kindness." PP I 9 41 3
and shall probably trespass on your hospitality till the PP I 13 63 12
I remember, about a trespass of one of his neighbours; P III 3 23 28

TRESPASSED (1)
fancy, though it had trespassed lately once or twice, NA II 8 186 6

TRESPASSING (1)
Escuse me, my dearest sister, for thus trespassing on your LS 24 290 13

TRESSELS (1)
and on the other were tressels and trays, bending under P IV 2 134 29

TRIAL (26)
When properly to relax is the trial of judgment; and, NA II 1 134 36
It was doomed to be a day of trial. NA II 2 138 1
prevailed on to give the waters what I think a fair trial. NA II 2 138 2
A very short trial convinced her that a curricle was the NA II 5 156 5
dignity was put to the trial--Eleanor brought no message. NA II 13 227 27
Catherine could not answer; and, after a short trial of NA II 14 238 27
and it has stood the trial so well, that I should be SS II 2 147 10
The next morning brought a farther trial of it, in a visit SS III 1 265 33
is worth the trial however, and you shall hear every thing. SS III 8 319 29
Even Elizabeth might have found some trial of her patience PP I 17 88 15
had given somewhat of a trial to the latter method, in her PP III 4 279 24
further trial at her uncle's house, to find another home. MP I 4 40 15
might have been more of a trial; but as it was, there MP I 5 44 1
The second day's trial was not so guiltless. MP I 7 66 15
the sisters, under such a trial as this, had not affection MP I 17 162 19
seemed complete, for upon trial the one given her by Miss MP II 9 270 40
be hoped, more prosperous trial of the state--if duped, to MP III 17 464 12
a very sudden trial of our stability in good thoughts. E I 10 87 29 30
This would be a trial. E II 8 229 99
few minutes more, however, completed the present trial. E II 12 261 35
"It must be a severe trial to them all. E III 8 380 9
in the hands of others; a trial of fortitude, which P III 2 15 13
eight years ago,--was a new sort of trial to Anne's nerves. P III 6 52 33
It will be some trial to us both." P IV 1 125 14
trial on this point, in her intercourse in Camden-Place. P IV 4 146 5
may be great in times of trial, but generally speaking it P IV 5 156 11

TRIALS (2)
We have had great trials, and great persecutions, but SS III 2 277 30
After many pauses and many trials of other subjects, PP I 16 82 44 45

TRIBE (2)
We have entirely done with the whole medical Tribe. S 5 386 1
Oh! Oh! pray, let us have none of the Tribe at Sanditon. S 6 393 1

TRIBUTE (10)
James accepted this tribute of gratitude, and qualified NA I 7 51 53
received from him the smiling tribute of recognition. NA I 8 54 4
When they had paid their tribute of politeness by SS II 6 175 2
and in bestowing her tribute of praise on the character of PP II 2 143 20
attended to, she paid her tribute of admiration to Miss MP I 5 48 30
I wish you could have overheard her tribute of praise; I MP III 4 352 42
and by his honourable tribute to its inhabitants allowed MP III 10 405 17
Do not be overpowered by such a little tribute of E I 9 77 47
that it should be the tribute of warm female friendship. E II 8 219 42
Mrs. Clay had paid her tribute of more decent attention, P IV 6 166 17
TRICE (1)
There are but three seams, you may do them in a trice.-- MP I 18 166 6
TRICK (19)
It is such an abominable trick, to be ill here, instead of LS 28 298 2
round, you were gone!--this is a cursed shabby trick! NA I 10 75 26
you know what a foolish trick I have of fixing mine, when NA II 3 143 4
I dare say, and invented this trick for getting out of it. SS I 13 65 30
coax, or trick him into marrying, is inconceivable! MP I 4 42 21
"That is a very foolish trick, Fanny, to be idling away MP I 7 71 34
trick for a young person to be always lolling upon a sofa; MP I 7 71 34
"A pretty trick, upon my word! MP I 10 100 26
it was a scheme--a trick; she was slighted, Maria was MP I 14 133 12
followed securing the odd trick by Sir Thomas's capital MP II 7 245 32
me that you suspect no trick, and are as unsuspicious of MP II 8 259 22
and trick of composition are oftener an object of study. MP III 3 341 28
ought to be serious, a trick of what ought to be simple. E I 16 137 10
These letters were but the vehicle for gallantry and trick. E III 5 348 21
principle, that disdain of trick and littleness, which a E III 10 397 48
very pretty trick you have been playing me, upon my word! E III 10 400 67
68
I thought them a habit, a trick, nothing that called for E III 13 427 19
They played me a pitiful trick once--got away some of my P IV 6 170 29
complication of mutual trick, or some overbearing P IV 10 228 70
TRICKED (4)
entirely; since he will be stubborn, he must be tricked. LS 5 249 1
what I thought wrong, I never will be tricked into it." NA I 13 101 22
I cannot descend to be tricked out of assurances, that are SS II 13 244 46
I must make him know that I will not be tricked on the MP III 11 411 20
TRICKING (3)
He was proud of his conquest, proud of tricking Edward, SS III 14 376 11
matter what, with a good tricking, shifting after-piece, MP I 13 124 10
time, you had very great amusement in tricking us all.-- E III 18 478 64
65
TRICKS (9)
with a relation of its tricks, congratulated herself NA I 9 62 10
She is a vain coquette, and her tricks have not answered. NA II 12 218 4
his own way, many cunning tricks, and a great deal of SS I 1 4 3
to hear, "I have found you out in spite of all your tricks. SS I 13 67 61
and mischievous tricks to which her cousins submitted. SS I 21 120 6
throwing it out of window--"he is full of monkey tricks." SS I 21 121 7
so well as I knew his tricks;--but I did long to see you, W 341 19
be reduced to tricks and stratagems to find it out." PP III 9 320 34
One of my senseless tricks!-- E III 4 339 13
TRIDENT (1)
Or a trident? or a mermaid? or a shark? E I 9 73 17
TRIED (112)
Isabella then tried another method. NA I 13 98 2
and tried to turn it; but it resisted her utmost strength. NA II 6 168 10
Alarmed, but not discouraged, she tried it another way; a NA II 6 168 10
Anne Mitchell had tried to put on a turban like mine, as I NA II 12 217 2
She resolved on not answering Isabella's letter; and tried NA II 12 219 16
She tried to eat, as well to save herself from the pain of NA II 13 228 27
Catherine hoped so too, and tried to feel an interest in NA II 14 235 13
She tried to explain the real state of the case to her SS I 4 21 11
This of course made every body laugh; and Elinor tried to SS I 12 61 16
Elinor could not deny the truth of this, and she tried to SS I 16 84 7
He tried to smile as he replied, "your sister's engagement SS II 5 173 40
moment to see her faint, tried to screen her from the SS II 6 177 12
power; and she would have tried to sooth and tranquillize SS II 7 180 5
Had she tried to speak, or had she been conscious of half SS II 8 193 6
might be as reasonably tried on herself as on her sister. SS II 8 198 29
they chose; and he tried to convince me, as thoroughly as SS II 9 209 28
Elinor tried very seriously to convince him that there was SS II 11 228 51
indigence which he had tried to infer from it;--no poverty SS II 12 233 18
Elinor tried to make a civil answer, though doubting her SS II 13 240 14
Edward tried to return her kindness as it deserved, but SS II 13 242 25
was; though she earnestly tried to drive away the notion SS III 1 260 9
Elinor tried to talk of something else; but Miss Steele SS III 2 275 21
upon my honour, I tried to keep out of hearing, I could SS III 4 285 1
that she was better, and tried to prove herself so, by SS III 7 307 1
delay; though Elinor tried to raise her spirits, and make SS III 7 308 4
He tried to reason himself out of fears, which the SS III 7 309 7
a temporary revival, tried to keep her young friend from SS III 7 314 22
I tried--but could not frame a sentence. SS III 8 327 55
unsubdued, and she still tried to appear cheerful and easy, SS III 11 352 19
His mother, stifling her own mortification, tried to sooth W 330 11
She often tried to provoke Darcy into disliking her guest, PP I 10 52 54
go so soon, and repeatedly tried to persuade Miss Bennet PP I 12 59 3
have tried long ago to do something or other about it." PP I 13 61 7
want of presence of mind; Charlotte tried to console her. PP I 18 90 5
We have tried two or three subjects already without PP I 18 93 26
Elizabeth tried hard to dissuade him from such a scheme; PP I 18 97 60
she sat down again, and tried to conceal by incessant PP I 19 104 7
putting the letter away, tried to join with her usual PP I 21 116 6
treatment of him, she tried to remember something of that PP II 2 143 20
She tried, however, to compose herself to answer him with PP II 11 189 6
every moment; yet she tried to the utmost to speak with PP II 11 192 23
24
She tried to recollect some instance of goodness, some PP II 13 206 4
tried to unite civility and truth in a few short sentences. PP II 15 216 5
Elizabeth tried to be diverted by them; but all sense of PP II 18 229 10
Elizabeth tried to join in her father's pleasantry, but PP III 15 363 19
she needed encouragement, tried to be all that was MP I 2 12 2
He tried to console her. MP I 2 15 10
and he earnestly tried to impress his eldest son with the MP I 3 23 2
was not till after she had tried in vain to persuade her MP I 4 41 16
All that English abilities can do, has been tried already. MP I 4 42 21
of his acquiescence, and tried to make out something MP I 6 55 17
attention from without, and it would not be tried so long." MP I 9 88 17
on Maria's account, tried to understand her feelings. MP II 3 200 20
to be agitated--her aunt tried to cry--and the service was MP II 3 203 29
His sister tried to laugh off her feelings by saying, " MP II 5 226 62
and let it pass; and tried to look calm and unconcerned MP II 5 226 64
Fanny gave a quick negative, and tried to hide her MP II 7 244 28
tried to make every thing agreeable by her encouragement. MP II 8 257 15
He evidently tried to please her--he was gallant--he was MP II 8 260 24
Thomas smiled, tried to encourage her, and then looked too MP II 10 275 11
in excellent spirits and tried to impart them to her, but MP II 10 276 13
He had often seen it tried. MP II 12 294 16
She tried to get the better of it, tried very hard as the MP II 13 303 13
But she still tried to believe it no more than what he MP II 13 306 26
sentiments himself, and he tried to turn the conversation; MP III 1 323 57
to turn the conversation; tried repeatedly before he could MP III 1 323 57
undertones were to be well tried, he sank as quietly as MP III 3 341 31
subject, more than once tried to make his father think of MP III 7 380 23
Susan tried to be useful, where she could only have gone MP III 9 395 4
Fanny thanked him, but tried to laugh it off. MP III 11 411 17
have talked to her, and tried at once to make her feel the MP III 14 432 10
She confined herself, or tried to confine herself to the MP III 15 441 21
She tried to speak carelessly; but she was not so careless MP III 16 458 30
had, therefore, earnestly tried to dissuade them from E I 2 19 14
vain, as earnestly tried to prevent any body's eating it. E I 2 19 14
crayon, and water-colours had been all tried in turn. E I 6 44 19
Emma made no answer, and tried to look cheerfully E I 8 65 50
to absent himself, and tried very much to persuade him to E I 8 68 58
business as the girls, and tried very often to recollect E I 9 70 5
opinion; and though she tried to laugh it off and bring E I 15 125 4
Mrs. Weston and Emma tried earnestly to cheer him and turn E I 15 126 9
She tried to stop him; but vainly; he would go on, and say E I 15 129 24
sanguine state of mind, he tried to take her hand again, E I 15 131 32
33
having, as usual, tried to persuade his daughter to stay E I 17 140 1
she listened to her and tried to console her with all her E I 17 142 9
"My father tried it more than once, formerly; but without E II 14 275 31
If he was quite sincere, if he really tried to come, it E III 1 316 6
And Mr. Weston tried, in vain, to make them harmonize E III 7 367 1
Emma recollected, blushed, was sorry, but tried to laugh E III 7 374 57
thing that message could do was tried--but all in vain. E III 9 390 18
Emma wished she could have seen her, and tried her own E III 9 390 18
she walked about, she tried her own room, she tried the E III 11 411 43
tried her own room, she tried the shrubbery--in every E III 11 411 43
every way her due; had she tried to know her better; had E III 12 421 17
I have not forgotten that you once tried to give me a E III 13 425 11
Like him, she had tried the scheme and rejected it; but E III 15 449 32
spread farther, and other persons' reception of it tried. E III 17 465 28
to him, and he tried earnestly to dissuade her from it. E III 17 466 29
She knew a family near Maple Grove who had tried it, and E III 17 469 36
is the very reason why my feelings should not be tried. P III 7 56 10
She tried to dissuade Mary from going, but in vain; and P III 10 83 4
attention, Anne quietly tried to convince her that their P III 12 106 18
to Henrietta, still tried, at intervals, to suggest P III 12 111 44
comfort to the others, tried to quiet Mary, to animate P III 12 111 44
In her own room she tried to comprehend it. P IV 6 166 18
was not tried, was quite impatient for the concert evening. P IV 7 180 32
Elliot's had better not be tried; but it was not till his P IV 9 209 96
She tried to be calm, and leave things to take their P IV 10 221 33
to take their course; and tried to dwell much on this P IV 10 221 33
did not mean to stir, and tried to be cool and unconcerned. P IV 10 222 37
Anne talked of being perfectly ready, and tried to look it; P IV 10 225 62
more tender, more tried, more fixed in a knowledge of each P IV 11 240 59
TRIES (2)
Every body pretends to feel and tries to describe with the SS I 18 97 7
and tries to persuade you that he does not care about you." PP I 21 118 18
TRIFLE (36)
He told her of horses which he had bought for a trifle and NA I 9 66 31
be sure, but it is not a trifle that will support a family NA II 3 146 16
And nine years, Catherine knew was a trifle of time, NA II 8 186 10
As to an additional servant, the expence would be a trifle; SS I 12 58 3
live with him upon a trifle, and how little so ever he SS III 2 273 16
mere trifle, and begged she would not make herself uneasy. PP I 16 83 49
the lady felt no inclination to trifle with his happiness. PP I 22 121 2
ever dared to trifle with so much dignified impertinence. PP II 6 166 38
"I would not on any account trifle with her affectionate PP III 13 347 26
companion added, "you are too generous to trifle with me. PP III 16 366 7
Do not let us be frightened from a good deed by a trifle. MP I 1 6 6
could have a little trifle among them, worth their having." MP I 3 30 52
as gladly by those whom he came to trifle with farther. MP I 12 115 3
body, proved to be no trifle; and the carpenter had MP I 14 130 1
speeches," returned Mr. Rushworth, "which is no trifle." MP I 15 144 31
in a trifle of this sort,--so kind as they are to you!-- MP I 15 146 53
the last week, to get up a few scenes, a mere trifle. MP II 1 181 16
Such a trifle is not worth half so many words." MP II 8 260 22
of this little trifle--a chain for William's cross. MP II 9 261 2
no want of delicacy on his part could make a trifle to her. MP II 13 301 7
use of such words and offers, if they meant but to trifle? MP II 13 302 10
to think of such a trifle again; but she soon found, from MP III 1 322 51
side of the table was a trifle, for she might always be MP III 3 343 40
They really go on Monday! and I was within a trifle of MP III 4 354 48
To be losing such pleasures was no trifle; to be losing MP III 14 432 9
of post, judge of my anxiety, and do not trifle with it. MP III 14 434 13
who could treat as a trifle this sin of the first MP III 15 441 19
as a mere trifle, and quite unworthy of being dwelt on. E II 3 180 54
now she was too ill to trifle, and must entreat him to set E II 12 258 7
him of some inclination to trifle with Jane Fairfax. E III 5 343 2
"Mr. Weston do not trifle with me.-- E III 10 393 12
so overcome by such a trifle; but so it was; and it P III 9 81 34
to resist idle interference in such a trifle as this. P III 10 87 26
The rain was a mere trifle, and Anne was most sincere in P IV 7 174 3
But the rain was also a mere trifle to Mrs. Clay; she P IV 7 174 3
might be a mere trifle of reproach remaining for herself.-- S 11 420 1
TRIFLED (6)
though for a day or two trifled with or denied, would SS III 6 305 17
herself for having trifled with so many days of illness, SS III 7 312 18
serious, & when he had trifled with her long enough, he W 317 2
tone, "you ought to know, that I am not to be trifled with. PP III 14 353 26
Henry Crawford had trifled with her feelings; but she had MP I 17 160 8
his time was otherwise trifled away, without benefit from P III 6 43 5
TRIFLER (1)
have always been prevented by some silly trifler or other. NA II 12 216 2
TRIFLES (4)
the rest, that -----"trifles light as air, "are, NA I 1 16 7
You should never fret about trifles." NA II 15 240 4
or were left as mere trifles to be settled at any time E II 11 255 59
"He trifles here," said he, "as to the temptation. E III 15 445 11
TRIFLING (43)
It would have been trifling with my reputation, to allow LS 25 292 1
good temper, and a trifling turn of mind, were all that NA I 2 20 8
inconceivable vexation on every little trifling occurrence. NA I 8 56 11
a trifling request to a friend who loved her so dearly. NA I 13 98 2
to the larger and more trifling part of the sex, NA I 14 111 29
enough to take it; no trifling deduction from the family NA II 1 135 42
change of manners was so trifling that, had it gone no NA II 4 149 1
was altogether but of trifling size, and much less than NA II 7 172 1
delusion, each trifling circumstance receiving importance NA II 10 199 2
prudence, for, except a trifling sum, the whole of his SS I 3 15 5
income would be so trifling in comparison with their own, SS I 5 26 4
of the party under some trifling pretext of employment; SS I 15 75 1
great agitation, "was of trifling weight--was nothing--to SS II 9 206 24
as a mere idle, trifling, business, shrugging up my SS III 8 326 53
her uncle, were neither trifling, nor likely to lessen; & W 361 31
People do not die of little trifling colds. PP I 7 31 32
in leaving the girls to their own trifling amusements. PP I 14 69 17
bestowed on him by Mrs. Reynolds was of no trifling nature. PP III 1 250 48
His acquaintance with Elizabeth was very trifling." PP III 1 257 69
That it would be done with such trifling exertion on his PP III 8 309 5
too, of so long a journey, became soon no trifling evil. MP I 2 13 4
any smiles, or agreeable trifling, and the venison cut up MP I 6 52 1
"A trifling part," said he, "and not at all to my taste, MP I 13 122 2
nobody else wants it--a trifling part, but the sort of MP I 14 132 7
If the part is trifling she will have more credit in MP I 14 134 14
parts--for he took every trifling one that could be united MP I 18 164 1
irksome; but of him, trifling and confident, idle and MP II 2 194 21
She considered it all as nonsense, as mere trifling and MP II 13 301 7
were short, they were trifling, they were as a drop of MP III 8 392 11
a fuss himself in any trifling disorder, and was chiefly MP III 14 433 13
of his becoming less trifling--of his being at least MP III 17 462 4
How trifling they make every thing else appear!-- I feel E I 10 87 25
"My mother's deafness is very trifling you see--just E II 1 158 14
venture to do--small, trifling presents, of any thing E II 3 171 16
17
"hum! just the trifling, silly fellow I took him for." E II 7 206 4
Mr. Knightley, he is not a trifling, silly young man. E II 8 212 3
No, I am perfectly sure that he is not trifling or silly." E II 8 212 3

this without effort; the first part is so very trifling. E II 8 229 95
very trifling; and here ended the difficulties of decision. E II 11 255 59
My acquaintance with him has been but trifling.-- E III 13 427 21
fait as to the newest modes of being trifling and silly. P IV 5 155 9
The injury to my leg is I dare say very trifling, but it S 1 365 1
her--& takes alarm at a trifling present expence, without S 3 376 1
TRIM (3)
She vowed at first she would never trim me up a new bonnet, SS III 2 272 12
to trim it with fresh, I think it will be very tolerable. PP II 16 219 4
appeared in the same trim, I thought they were mad; but MP II 6 235 19
TRIMMING (3)
Observing his second daughter employed in trimming a hat, PP I 2 6 1
2
I have some notion of putting such a trimming as this to E II 17 302 22
How do you like my trimming?-- E III 2 324 20
TRIMMINGS (1)
muslin robe with blue trimmings--plain black shoes-- NA I 3 26 22
TRINKET-BOX (2)
She was answered by having a small trinket-box placed MP II 8 257 15
to any other in my trinket-box, you have happened to fix MP II 8 260 22
TRINKETS (2)
keys, and assorting her trinkets, to trying to convince P IV 10 220 31
all her glossy curls & smart trinkets to wait on her.-- S 6 390 1
TRIO (2)
By ten o'clock, the chaise-and-four conveyed the trio from NA II 11 212 17
They were now a miserable trio, confined within doors by a MP II 11 286 15
TRIP (1)
You in the meanwhile will be taking a trip into china, I MP I 16 156 27
TRIPPED (1)
to join in a glee, she tripped off to the instrument, MP I 11 112 33
TRIPPING (1)
and be forgiven; tripping lightly through the church-yard, NA I 12 91 3
TRIUMPH (39)
I must torment my sister-in-law for the insolent triumph LS 25 293 4
quit this scene of public triumph and oblige your friend NA II 2 139 7
native village, in the triumph of recovered reputation, NA II 14 232 7
of their malignant triumph, my dear sister, by seeing how SS II 7 189 51
The triumph of seeing me so may be open to all the world. SS II 7 189 52
any reply to this civil triumph, by the door's being SS II 13 240 18
my prospects; and told me, as I thought, with triumph.-- SS III 1 263 29
was sincere, it must triumph, with little difficulty, over SS III 3 280 6
under it are only triumph and exultation to me now. SS III 8 324 45
Vanity, while seeking its own guilty triumph at the SS III 8 331 70
He had more than the ordinary triumph of accepted love to SS III 13 361 3
gained a complete victory over him, continued her triumph. PP I 9 43 20
Lady Lucas could not be insensible of triumph on being PP I 23 127 8
Mr. Collins's triumph in consequence of this invitation PP II 6 160 1
is lessening the honour of my cousin's triumph very sadly." PP II 10 186 37
Elizabeth could not but be pleased, could not but triumph. PP III 1 255 59
Kitty then owned, with a very natural triumph on knowing PP III 5 290 50
Let them triumph over us at a distance, and be satisfied." PP III 5 293 67
No sentiment of shame gave a damp to her triumph. PP III 8 310 7
What a triumph for him, as she often thought, could he PP III 8 311 14
But while he was mortal, there must be a triumph. PP III 8 312 14
preferred; the smile of triumph which Maria was trying to MP I 14 133 12
Mrs. Norris related again her triumph over Dick Jackson, MP I 15 142 24
It will be such a triumph to the others!" MP I 16 155 15
"They will not have much cause of triumph, when they see MP I 16 155 16
But, however, triumph there certainly will be, and I must MP I 16 155 16
Maria felt her triumph, and pursued her purpose careless MP I 17 163 19
of giving Crawford the triumph of governing her actions, MP II 3 201 23
from her confident triumph, that she had ever heard of MP II 3 203 30
might seem a state of triumph, she followed her uncle out MP II 5 221 38
39
sure it is not in woman's nature to refuse such a triumph." MP III 5 363 22
between the agreeable triumph of shewing her activity and MP III 7 383 32
"And have you never known the pleasure and triumph of a E I 1 13 43
who was pursuing his triumph rather unfeelingly. E I 15 126 9
Mr. Weston, with triumph of a different sort, was E I 15 126 11
Elton himself arrived to triumph in his happy prospects, E II 4 181 2
in the triumph of Miss Fairfax's mind over Mrs. Elton. E II 15 288 39
On her side, all was warmth, energy, and triumph--and she E III 6 359 37
There was no triumph, no pitiful triumph in his manner. P III 10 82 1
TRIUMPHANT (10)
I am again myself;--gay and triumphant. LS 25 291 1
now that she had been triumphant throughout, had carried NA I 13 103 29
With a triumphant smile of self-satisfaction, the general NA II 7 178 23
her feelings soon hardened into even a triumphant delight. NA II 15 244 11
familiar curiosity & triumphant compassion;--the loss of W 349 24
With a triumphant smile, they were told, that it was ten PP III 1 253 57
Elizabeth with a triumphant sensation, looked towards his PP III 12 340 12
It was, indeed, a triumphant day to Mr. Bertram and Maria. MP I 17 158 1
in another light, so triumphant and secure, she was in MP III 5 356 4
Mr. Knightley, however, shewed no triumphant happiness. E II 12 262 40
TRIUMPHANTLY (5)
"Well, but Miss Dashwood," speaking triumphantly, "people SS III 2 272 14
and triumphantly believing there was no chance of it. PP I 18 99 63
After welcoming their sisters, they triumphantly displayed PP II 16 219 2
"Well, Mrs. Weston," said Emma triumphantly when he left E II 15 289 41
"Well," continued Mrs. Smith triumphantly, "grant my P IV 9 206 88
TRIUMPHING (3)
enjoy the pleasure of triumphing over a mind prepared to LS 10 257 1
sure, be incapable of triumphing in her better judgment, PP II 3 148 26
his views, but in triumphing over the discretion, which, MP III 17 468 21
TRIUMPHS (1)
to give, no similar triumphs to press on the unwilling and NA I 4 32 2
TRIVIAL (10)
to be again overcome by trivial appearances of alarm, or NA II 13 223 9
in silence, and few and trivial were the sentences NA II 13 227 27
she did not feel, however trivial the occasion; and upon SS I 21 122 14
The most trivial, paltry, insignificant part; the merest MP I 14 134 13
thank him for another pleasure, and one of no trivial kind. MP III 10 406 22
full of trivial communications and harmless gossip. E I 3 21 4
them, they are not trivial recommendations to the world in E I 8 63 44
She merely said, in the course of some trivial chat, "well, E III 4 340 28
behind her, which rendered every thing else trivial. P IV 8 188 37
it with others still more trivial from different people P IV 9 203 70
TROD (2)
It came--it was fine--and Catherine trod on air. NA II 11 212 17
same path which she had trod herself, and were before her. MP I 10 97 1
TRODDEN (3)
which already she had trodden with peculiar awe, she well NA II 8 188 17
spirits since last she had trodden that well-known road. NA II 14 237 20
have fallen and been trodden under foot, is still in P III 10 88 26
TROLLOPY-LOOKING (1)
The moment they stopt, a trollopy-looking maid-servant, MP III 7 377 7
TROOP (3)
at the head of his troop, knocked off his horse by a NA I 14 113 39
than a watch-tower--and a troop of tidy, happy villagers SS I 18 98 8
On the stairs were a troop of little boys and girls, whose PP II 4 152 5
TROPHIES (1)
up by her friend, and ornamented with cyphers and trophies. E I 9 69 3
TROT (1)
Thorpe only lashed his horse into a brisker trot; the NA I 11 87 53
TROTTED (2)
My horse would have trotted to Clifton within the hour, if NA I 11 88 56
The old mare trotted heavily on, wanting no direction of W 322 2
TROUBLE (120)
I shall trouble you meanwhile to prevent his forming any LS 7 253 1
but be the occasion of so much vexation & trouble. LS 13 263 1
greatest distress, or I should be ashamed to trouble you. LS 21 279 1
now, for I have had more trouble in restoring peace than I LS 25 292 1
I am satisfied--& will trouble you no more when these few LS 37 306 1
spared herself all the trouble of urging a removal, which LS 42 313 7
"You need not give yourself that trouble, sir." NA I 3 25 3
"No trouble I assure you, madam." NA I 3 26 4
to leave to him all the trouble of seeking an explanation, NA I 12 93 4
but to be at so much trouble in filling great volumes, NA I 14 109 24
Henry smiled, and said, "how very little trouble it can NA II 1 132 18
"Will you take the trouble of reading to us the passages NA II 10 205 22
give yourself any trouble, because any thing would do." NA II 11 211 12
a great deal of needless trouble," said her mother at last; NA II 14 234 10
I have known a great deal of the trouble of annuities; for SS I 2 10 20
and then there was the trouble of getting it to them; and SS I 2 11 20
Well, I wish him out of all his trouble with all my heart, SS I 14 70 2
especially, which required some trouble and time to subdue. SS I 19 104 9
I am; but however there is no occasion to trouble you. SS I 22 128 9
took such a liberty as to trouble you with my affairs. SS II 2 146 5
Even Lady Middleton took the trouble of being delighted, SS II 3 157 19
have suffered myself to trouble you with this account of SS II 9 210 32
but she was saved the trouble of checking it, by Lucy's SS II 10 219 42
A very little trouble on your side secures him. SS II 11 223 24
won't think it too much trouble to give us a call, should SS III 2 277 30
Mrs. Dashwood immediately took all that trouble on herself; SS III 11 353 25
but thought I would first trouble you with these few lines, SS III 13 365 14
has taken a vast deal of trouble about him & given up a W 317 2
Emma was saved the trouble of apologizing, by their being W 334 13
herself very unwilling to give him so much trouble. W 339 18
"The trouble was of course, honour, pleasure, delight. W 339 18
Emma was not inclined to give herself much trouble for his W 345 21
trouble, and was sure Jane would have caught cold again.-- PP I 12 60 6
they may have the trouble of saying as little as possible." PP I 18 91 13
she may have less trouble in achieving a second; in which PP I 21 119 20
But her commendation, though costing her some trouble, PP II 6 167 42
It is because he will not give himself the trouble." PP II 8 175 23
fault-- because I would not take the trouble of practising. PP II 8 175 25
to leave the trouble of finding a subject to him. PP II 9 178 11
did she give herself the trouble of talking or of PP II 10 182 1
Does your charge give you much trouble? PP II 10 184 19
If you, my dear father, will not take the trouble of PP II 18 231 18
gown, and give as much trouble as I can,--or, perhaps, I PP III 6 300 28
for you," said Jane, "if you dislike the trouble yourself." PP III 7 303 21
was to have as little trouble in the business as possible. PP III 8 309 5
And will you give yourself the trouble of carrying similar PP III 8 313 19
taken on himself all the trouble and mortification PP III 10 326 3
disdain, "I wonder you took the trouble of coming so far. PP III 14 353 27
Lady Catherine it appeared, had actually taken the trouble PP III 15 360 1
you to take so much trouble, and bear so many PP III 16 366 5
It will save me a world of trouble and economy. PP III 17 377 39
There--I have saved you the trouble of accounting for it; PP III 18 380 5
"I must trouble you once more for congratulations. PP III 18 383 23
The trouble and expense of it to them, would be nothing MP I 1 5 4
child to Mansfield; you shall have no trouble about it. MP I 1 7 8
My own trouble, you know, I never regard. MP I 1 7 8
I am not one of those that spare their own trouble; and MP I 1 9 12
taking half so much trouble, or speaking one word where he MP I 2 12 2
disposition, and seemed likely to give them little trouble. MP I 2 18 23
"You are very good, but do not trouble yourself about them. MP I 3 30 53
expense of any personal trouble, and the charge was made MP I 4 35 5
The new mare proved a treasure; with a very little trouble, MP I 4 37 8
fruit should be so little worth the trouble of gathering." MP I 6 54 10
will not give himself the trouble of writing any thing MP I 7 64 10
well have saved him the trouble; that it would have been MP I 7 67 16
who had not been at the trouble of visiting Mrs. Rushworth MP I 8 76 7
one will do, would be trouble for nothing; and between MP I 8 77 12
"It is a pity that he should have so much trouble for MP I 10 101 31
income ready made, to the trouble of working for one; and MP I 11 110 23
the trouble of being agreeable, which make men clergymen. MP I 11 110 23
Nobody was at the trouble of an answer; the others soon MP I 15 142 23
worth any trouble that might be taken to establish it. MP II 2 190 6
as might save him the trouble of ever coming back again. MP II 2 192 11
Her tone of calm languor, for she never took the trouble MP II 5 218 12
ducks and drakes with, and earned without much trouble. MP II 5 226 61
Sir Thomas engaged for its giving her very little trouble, MP II 8 253 6
trouble, indeed she could not imagine there would be any." MP II 8 253 6
all this gave her no trouble, and as she had foreseen, " MP II 8 254 9
foreseen, "there was in fact no trouble in the business." MP II 8 254 9
any means to take so much trouble in vain, she still went MP II 13 298 1
might have saved me the trouble, if you would only have MP III 1 323 54
The Admiral hates trouble, and scorns asking favours; and MP III 5 364 29
enough to overcome the trouble, and that at Portsmouth MP III 7 376 4
poor sister Bertram must be in a great deal of trouble." MP III 13 428 14
To all, she must have saved some trouble of head or hand; MP III 14 432 10
And now, do not trouble yourself to be ashamed of either MP III 14 434 13
know, and be no trouble to our friends at Mansfield Park. MP III 14 435 14
We had had a great deal of trouble in persuading him to E I 6 46 21
She need not trouble herself to pity him. he only wanted E I 16 135 7
trouble of conquering any body's reserve to procure one. E II 6 203 41
was no occasion to trouble us, for Mr. Knightley's E II 8 223 63
Harriet, to give Mrs. Ford the trouble of two parcels." E II 9 235 37
"No trouble in the world, ma'am," said the obliging Mrs. E II 9 235 39
while to be at all this trouble for a few hours of noisy E II 12 257 3
It saves trouble, and is a something to get me out. E II 16 293 12
But I would not wish you to take the trouble of making any E II 17 300 9
"Trouble! aye, I know your scruples. E II 17 300 10
You are afraid of giving me trouble; but I assure you, my E II 17 300 10
draws nearer, I do not wish to be giving any body trouble." E II 17 300 11
by so often, and knowing how much trouble you must have. E III 2 322 19
he must have danced, would he but take the trouble.-- E III 2 326 32
I will not trouble you to give any other invitations." E III 6 354 13
It would only be giving trouble and distress. E III 6 362 44
at any trouble to check them, extraordinary as they were. E III 7 376 63
me over at any time, to save you the trouble of replying." P III 3 17 4
hands to save them the trouble, and once more read aloud P III 8 66 22
and Anne was well repaid the first trouble of exertion. P III 11 100 23
the Harvilles in such trouble, did not admit a doubt. P III 12 112 56
It would be going only to multiply trouble to the others, P IV 1 121 3
They must be taking off some trouble from the good people P IV 1 122 5
by far too much trouble taken to procure the acquaintance. P IV 4 150 18
and had been at the trouble of inviting both Lady Russell P IV 5 158 21
is safe, and I shall give myself no more trouble about him. P IV 9 196 32
will think little of the trouble required, which it is P IV 9 196 32
But not now: no, I thank you, I have nothing to trouble P IV 9 198 44
engaging in a fruitless trouble, and, under a cold P IV 9 209 97
that a little trouble in the right place might do it, and P IV 9 210 98
of saving her sister trouble, which determined her to wait P IV 10 215 14
No part of it however seemed to trouble her long. S 11 420 1
I will not trouble you to speak about the Mullins's.-- S 12 425 1
TROUBLED (3)
But not one of these grave reflections troubled the NA I 10 74 22
should certainly have troubled him with her best regards NA I 15 125 48
Had the Grants been at home, I would not have troubled you, MP III 14 434 1
3000
TROUBLES (6)
Edward, after all the troubles we have went through lately, SS III 2 277 29
30
you in many certain troubles and disappointments, in which SS III 11 350 9
"Penelope however has had her troubles--continued Miss W.-- W 317 2
entered into their troubles with ready sympathy, and E I 10 86 24
about Jane, whose troubles and whose ill health having, of E III 11 403 2
Troubles soon arose. P III 4 26 2
TROUBLESOME (20)
deal to say, but he is sometimes impertinent & troublesome. LS 16 268 2
but it was a heavy and troublesome business, and she could NA II 5 156 5

the climate is hot, and the mosquitoes are troublesome." SS I 10 51 21
amongst them by her solicitude about her troublesome boys. SS I 11 55 6
Marianne was spared from the troublesome feelings of SS II 11 221 4
was also very inconvenient and exceedingly troublesome.-- PP I 23 128 11
the house-keeper with troublesome directions, and insulted MP II 1 180 10
or keep her from being troublesome where she was; the MP III 7 382 27
a fanciful, troublesome creature!" said Emma playfully. E I 1 10 30
"I am afraid I am sometimes very fanciful and troublesome." E I 1 10 31
not give him such a troublesome office for the world"-- E I 6 49 41
I really am a most troublesome companion to you both, but E I 10 89 37
A few minutes more, and Emma hoped to see one troublesome E I 15 128 21
incommoded by any troublesome topic, and to wander at E II 1 156 6
an arrangement, so needlessly troublesome to your servant. E II 16 296 37
"And if you find them troublesome, you must send them home E II 18 311 40
"this is the most troublesome parish that ever was. E III 16 456 29
Bless me, how troublesome they are sometimes!-- P III 6 45 8
ill fortune of a very troublesome, hopeless son; and the P III 6 50 28
You are extremely troublesome. P III 9 80 30

TROUBLING (1)
to Jane, with an apology for troubling him also with Lizzy. PP I 9 45 35

TROUT (1)
appearance of some trout in the water, and talking to the PP III 1 254 57

TRUE (191)
Your friend Mr Smith's story however cannot be quite true, LS 6 252 2
perfectly well, which is true must raise abhorrence LS 8 255 1
It is true that I am vain enough to beleive it within my LS 10 257 1
And this circumstance while it explains the true motive of LS 14 264 3
Langford, I wish it may be true, but his intelligence must LS 15 266 1
that with a mixture of true girlish perverseness & folly, LS 19 273 1
It is true that Reginald had not in any degree grown cool LS 22 280 1
He can have no true regard for me, or he would not have LS 22 282 6
where the resentment which true love would have dictated LS 22 282 6
Is it true that he leaves Churchill this morning?" LS 23 284 6
I was mistaken, it is true, but I beleived myself to be LS 24 289 12
be able to chuse our own society, & have true enjoyment. LS 26 296 4
Can it be true that they are really separated--& for ever? LS 41 309 1
There she fell miserably short of the true heroic height. NA I 1 16 10
"Very true, my dear; and if we knew anybody we would join NA I 2 22 17
I gave but five shillings a yard for it, and a true Indian NA I 3 28 38
doze at most; for if it be true, as a celebrated writer NA I 3 29 52
"It is very true, upon my honour, but I see how it is; you NA I 6 41 16
"Such true blood! NA I 7 46 9
misconduct of another the true source of her debasement, NA I 8 53 2
couch, which is the true heroine's portion; to a pillow NA I 11 90 65
"Very true," said Henry, "and this is a very nice day, and NA I 14 108 16
am very well contented to take the false with the true. NA I 14 109 23
"Very true. NA I 15 124 47
'tis true, we can offer you nothing like the gaieties of NA II 2 139 7
must be exactly of the true size for rational happiness. NA II 6 166 7
"It is very true, however; you shall read James's letter NA II 10 205 21
"Very true: we soon met with Mrs. Thorpe, and then we NA II 14 238 24
"That is very true, and, therefore, I do not know whether, SS I 2 10 16
and written in the true spirit of friendly accommodation. SS I 4 23 20
Elinor could hardly believe this to be true, as it seemed SS I 13 68 66
circumstance related by Mrs. Jennings was perfectly true. SS I 13 68 67
"I am afraid it is but too true," said Marianne; "but why SS I 18 97 5
"It is very true," said Marianne, "that admiration of SS I 18 97 7
true, is not what I should expect Colonel Brandon to do." SS I 20 115 49
Is it true, pray? for of course you must know, as you have SS I 20 115 50
to be true, so from that moment I set it down as certain. SS I 20 115 52
have told them it is all very true, and a great deal more. SS I 21 119 4
What Lucy had asserted to be true, therefore, Elinor could SS II 1 139 1
"That is very true," replied her mother; "but of her SS II 3 156 13
"That is true," cried Marianne in a cheerful voice, and SS II 5 167 2
Aye, it is but too true. SS II 8 192 3
Well, said I, all I can say is, that if it is true, he has SS II 8 192 3
"Well, my dear, 'tis a true saying about an ill wind, for SS II 8 196 22
but only Elinor and Marianne understood its true merit. SS III 2 270 1
This living of Colonel Brandon's--can it be true?--has he SS III 5 294 8
"It is perfectly true.-- SS III 5 294 9
But is it true?--is it really true?" SS III 8 318 10
"It is very true. SS III 11 351 12
I have lost Purvis, it is true but very few people marry W 317 2
"That is very true," replied Elizabeth, "and I could PP I 5 20 19
country as in town, which you must acknowledge to be true." PP I 9 43 24
said of myself to be true, and I believe it at this moment. PP I 10 49 28
Lady Catherine herself says that in point of true beauty, PP I 14 67 7
"Very true, indeed;--and now, my dear Jane, what have you PP I 17 85 3
which a marriage of true affection could bestow; and she PP I 18 98 63
consistent with the true delicacy of the female character." PP I 19 108 16
17
Is it true?" PP I 20 111 15
"True," said Mr. Bennet, "but it is a comfort to think PP II 1 138 29
"very true, it will be wise in me to refrain from that. PP II 3 145 7
"Very true, my dear, that is exactly what I say. she is PP II 5 157 9
I suppose, who have more true enjoyment of music than PP II 8 173 6
"True; and nobody can ever be introduced in a ball room. PP II 8 175 20
the true Darcy spirit, she may like to have her own way." PP II 10 184 19
of events, which, if true, must overthrow every cherished PP II 13 204 2
are wanting, the true philosopher will derive benefit from PP II 19 236 1
"That is very true," said Elizabeth; "though it had not PP III 7 304 30
"Very true; and if I had my will, we should. PP III 9 317 12
faults at different times; but this is the true one. PP III 10 324 2
were proved beyond their greatest extent to be true! PP III 10 326 3
"True. PP III 10 327 8
the truth of it; and she told me that it was certain true. PP III 11 331 15
at Michaelmas; but, however, I hope it is not true. PP III 11 336 49
"If you believed it impossible to be true," said Elizabeth, PP III 14 353 27
"True. PP III 14 356 52
And is it really true? PP III 17 378 43
"Very true," cried Mrs. Norris, "which are both very MP I 1 9 12
"Very true, indeed, my dears, but you are blessed with MP I 2 19 27
too much, he was always true to her interests, and MP I 2 21 34
"Very true. MP I 3 27 36
but coming down with the true London maxim, that every MP I 6 58 39
That is the true manly style; that is a complete brother's MP I 6 59 43
"Very true; but, in short, it had not occurred to me. MP I 9 92 40
propriety, so much of that true delicacy which one seldom MP I 12 117 14
"True, to see real acting, good hardened real acting; but MP I 13 124 12
right, and shew them what true delicacy is.-- in all MP I 15 140 13
and their blindness to its true cause, must be imputed to MP I 17 163 21
of true acting as he would not have lost upon any account. MP II 1 182 22
and her chariot, with true dowager propriety, to Bath-- MP II 3 202 28
But Edmund goes;--true--it is upon Edmund's account. MP II 5 222 39
It was plain that he could have so serious views, no true MP II 5 228 69
On the morrow they were walking about together with true MP II 6 234 17
True enough, he had once seen Fanny dance; and it was MP II 7 251 62
dance; and it was equally true that he would now have MP II 7 251 62
general resemblance in true generosity and natural MP II 9 263 16
and the privilege of true solicitude for him by a sound MP II 9 265 18
immediately improved this compliment by adding, "very true. MP II 11 285 11
And she has some true friends in it. MP II 12 292 7
"Edmund--true, I believe he is (generally speaking) kind MP II 12 297 35
"Very true, sister, as you say. MP II 13 305 25
offensive to Fanny, he had true pleasure in satisfying; MP III 3 340 24
"Yes, very true. MP III 5 359 12
It is as true as that I sit here. MP III 5 362 21
her there with looks of true kindness, and with features MP III 7 377 9
cannot be true--it must mean some other people." MP III 15 440 15
"Indeed, I hope it is not true," said Mrs. Price MP III 15 440 18
It is true, that Edmund was very far from happy himself. MP III 17 461 3
year, to be in need of the true kindness of her sister's MP III 17 469 24
With so much true merit and true love, and no want of MP III 17 473 32
It was true that her friend was going only half a mile E I 1 6 7
"I believe it is very true, my dear, indeed," said Mr. E I 1 10 31
"Such an eye!--the true hazle eye--and so brilliant! E I 5 39 20
let it pass with a "very true; and it would be a small E I 7 54 33
Emma knew this was too true for contradiction, and E I 8 58 19
more true gentility than Harriet Smith could understand." E I 8 65 49
resentfully to be true, than what he knew anything about. E I 8 67 57
The course of true love never did run smooth-- E I 9 75 25
"Yes, very true. E I 9 76 28
Very true. E I 9 78 52
"Aye, very true.-- E I 9 79 56
This was too true for contradiction. E I 9 80 68
"Very true," said Harriet. E I 10 87 26
"That's true," she cried--"very true. E I 12 99 11
you?" succeeded in the true English style, burying under a E I 12 99 14
"True, true," cried Mr. Knightley, with most ready E I 12 106 61
Mr. Knightley, with most ready interposition--"very true. E I 12 106 61
to emulate the "very true, my love," which must have been E I 13 113 27
gentleness of his address, true elegance was sometimes E I 16 134 5
the way of cure, there could be no true peace for herself. E I 17 143 15
"Very true, very true, indeed. E II 1 160 23
"True, sir; and Emma, because she had Miss Fairfax." E II 3 171 13
"Very true, Miss Woodhouse, so she will. E II 3 174 39
Harriet said, "very true;" and she "would not think about E II 3 180 56
True, true, you are acquainted with Miss Fairfax; I E II 5 194 38
to belong to the place, to be a true citizen of Highbury. E II 6 200 14
"Mrs. Dixon! very true indeed. E II 8 217 29
"Very true.-- E II 8 223 63
True affection only could have prompted it." E II 10 242 21
"Very true," he gravely replied; "it was very bad." E II 11 249 15
"Aye, very true. E II 11 253 38
"Yes, very true," cried Frank, "very true. E II 11 254 50
us in that sort of true disinterested friendship which I E II 13 267 7
Harriet listened submissively, and said "it was very true-- E II 13 267 9
and unbroken packs in the true style--and more waiters E II 16 290 3
"This is very true," said she, "at least as far as relates E II 16 291 6
"Very true, Mr. Weston, perfectly true. E II 18 308 28
though not exactly true, for she was perfectly well, and E III 3 336 12
"Ay, very true, my dear," cried the latter, though Jane E III 5 349 24
She could not endure to give him the true explanation; for E III 5 350 28
true gentility, untainted in blood and understanding.-- E III 6 358 35
and he murmured, in reply, "very true, my love, very true. E III 7 370 21
In the warmth of true contrition, she would call upon her E III 8 377 1
The most indefatigable, true friend. E III 8 380 15
Very true. E III 8 384 33
hems with a commiseration and good sense, true and steady. E III 9 388 13
"True. E III 10 399 64
It was true that she had not to charge herself, in this E III 11 402 1
Very true; he did not come till Miss Fairfax was here." E III 15 445 11
and she could listen with true happiness, unchecked by E III 16 451 4
"Ah! you clever creature, that's very true. E III 16 456 33
young ladies a sample of true conjugal obedience--for who E III 16 457 36
That was all very true. E III 17 466 29
added, with a look of true sensibility, "there is a E III 18 478 69
"True, true," he answered, warmly. E III 18 479 70
"No, not true on your side. E III 18 479 70
You can have no superior, but most true on mine.-- E III 18 479 70
of the small band of true friends who witnessed the E III 19 484 12
reductions; and that the true dignity of Sir Walter Elliot P III 2 12 4
"Very true, very true. P III 3 19 13
What Miss Anne says, is very true," was Mr. Shepherd's P III 3 19 13
14
never had the smallest temptation to say, "very true." P III 6 44 6
The Crofts took possession with true naval alertness, and P III 6 48 17
"Ay, true enough," (with a deep sigh) "only June." P III 12 108 26
at once, and saying only "true, true, a surgeon this P III 12 110 40
41
and saying only "true, true, a surgeon this instant," was P III 12 110 40
41
This was very wonderful, if it were true; and Lady Russell P IV 2 135 35
who could answer for the true sentiments of a clever, P IV 5 161 27
"True, upon my honour. P IV 6 164 8
He is only a commander, it is true, made last summer, and P IV 6 171 37
interrupted her with, "and the thing is certainly true. P IV 6 172 40
41
true parental hearts to promote their daughter's comfort. P IV 8 182 8
Is this true? P IV 9 205 86
So far it is very true. P IV 9 205 87
"Oh dear! very true. P IV 10 228 71
"True," said Anne, "very true; I did not recollect; but P IV 11 233 21
I believe in a true analogy between our bodily frames and P IV 11 233 22
true attachment and constancy were known only by woman. P IV 11 235 32
"Yes," said he, "very true; here we separate, but Harville P IV 11 236 38
"You do believe that there is true attachment and P IV 11 237 42
poetry, Wordsworth has the true soul of it--Campbell in S 7 397 1
is, Lady Denham like a true great lady, talked & talked S 7 399 1

TRUER (4)
the stronger claims, the truer kindness of another, she MP II 9 271 40
a better daughter, or a kinder sister, or a truer friend? E I 5 39 22
blushed to think how much truer a knowledge of his E I 16 135 6
You never wrote a truer line." E III 15 446 20

TRUEST (5)
Believe me," and Elinor spoke it with the truest sincerity, SS II 2 146 4
While she with the truest affection had been planning a SS III 1 266 38
ever breathed, and the truest friend I ever had; and I can PP I 16 78 20
was sensible of the truest satisfaction in hearing of any MP I 2 21 34
on her tongue, as the truest description of a yearning MP III 14 431 7

TRULY (52)
you, for I do beleive her truly deserving of our regard, & LS 18 272 1
of her own conduct, and truly rejoiced to be preserved by NA I 13 105 41
if not permanently, he was truly afflicted by her death." NA II 9 197 27
of her character and truly loved her society, I must NA II 15 243 9
say--your friends are all truly anxious to see you well SS II 11 224 24
a saint, but was moreover truly anxious that he should be SS III 5 293 2
"It is truly astonishing!"--he cried, after hearing what SS III 5 295 14
feminine--was it not?" SS III 8 328 61
She professes to keep her own counsel; she says, & truly W 318 2
You have seen Miss Osborne?--she is my model for a truly W 357 28
believe, truly amiable, be in friendship with such a man? PP I 16 82 44
45
but in person and address most truly the gentleman. PP II 7 170 9
impartial conviction, as truly as I wished it in reason.-- PP II 12 197 5
proved her to be more truly well bred than either of the PP III 3 267 4
I am truly glad, dearest Lizzy, that you have been spared PP III 4 275 5
"Mr. Collins moreover adds," "I am truly rejoiced that my PP III 15 363 22
respectable, unless you truly esteemed your husband; PP III 17 376 35
wanting, because, though a truly anxious father, he was MP I 2 19 30
Sir Thomas, however, was truly happy in the prospect of an MP I 4 40 14
so truly feminine, as to be no very good picture of a man. MP I 18 169 22
with most unfeigned and truly tender regret, that they MP II 10 275 12
and she looked so truly the astonishment she felt, that he MP II 12 291 5
Fanny will be so truly your sister!" MP II 12 295 23
It was truly dramatic.-- MP III 3 337 10
And I do seriously and truly believe that he is attached MP III 5 363 24
She felt truly for them all. MP III 13 427 12
a well-judging and truly amiable woman could be, and must E I 2 17 6
I never met with a disposition more truly amiable." E I 6 43 7
could I expect to be so truly beloved and important; so E I 10 84 15
to the sufferers, it has done all that is truly important. E I 10 87 30
Her tears fell abundantly--but her grief was so truly E I 17 142 9
information could Emma procure as to what he truly was. E II 2 169 17

approver, (a much safer character,) she was truly welcome. E II 11 256 60
And she appears so truly good--there is something so E II 14 278 44
truly the gentleman, without the least conceit or puppyism. E III 2 321 15
the appearance of the penitence, so justly and truly hers. E III 8 377 2
They were both so truly respectable in their happiness, so E III 12 418 5
Mr. Knightley, always so kind, so feeling, so truly E III 15 450 38
having one such truly sympathising friend as Lady Russell. P III 6 42 2
alone could estimate it truly, were the very feelings P III 11 100 23
Anne did not shrink from it; on the contrary, she truly P IV 1 125 15
16
This is breaking a head and giving a plaister truly!" P IV 1 127 22
She had weathered it however, and could truly say that it P IV 5 154 9
How could it ever be ascertained that his mind was truly P IV 5 161 27
"I shall be truly glad to have them back again. P IV 6 164 8
rest of my life, to be only yours "truly, "Wm. Elliot." P IV 9 203 73
He truly wants to marry you. P IV 9 204 80
Anne felt truly obliged to her for such kindness; and P IV 10 224 52
53
"It would not be the nature of any woman who truly loved." P IV 11 232 18
truly acquainted with, and do justice to Captain Wentworth. P IV 12 249 3
of Sanditon with a spirit truly admirable--though now & S 3 376 1
truly breathed the Immortal Incence which is her due.--" S 7 397 1
TRUNK (6)
"Curricle-hung you see; seat, trunk, sword-case, splashing- NA I 7 46 13
good-will than experience intent upon filling the trunk. NA II 13 227 27
all the work of the morning, and pack her trunk afresh. PP III 14 213 20
carrying up his sister's trunk, which he would manage all MP III 7 379 19
where, at that moment, a trunk, directed to The Rev. E II 5 186 1
that trunk and the direction, was consequently a blank. E II 5 186 1
TRUNKS (4)
The clock struck ten while the trunks were carrying down, NA II 5 155 4
At length the chaise arrived, the trunks were fastened on, PP II 15 216 8
to divide, and all my trunks to repack, from not having P III 5 38 34
of the Luggage, & helping old Sam uncord the trunks.-- S 9 407 1
TRUST (83)
I trust I shall be able to make my story as good as her's. LS 16 268 2
to my heart; & therefore I trust you will beleive me when LS 20 277 6
7
I trust however my dear mother, that we have no reason to LS 23 284 7
I trust I am in no danger of sinking in your opinion." LS 24 290 13
will, I trust, gradually overcome this youthful attachment. LS 27 297 2
usual good spirits, (as I trust he soon will) we will try LS 40 309 1
Upon this trust she dared still to remain in his presence, NA II 9 192 4
"I trust," said the General, with a most satisfied smile, " NA II 11 214 22
did or could love, and I trust you will convince him of it. NA II 12 216 2
difficult to know whom to trust, and young men never know NA II 12 216 2
He went away to his regiment two days ago, and I trust I NA II 12 217 2
to be repaid by-----but I must not trust myself with words. NA II 13 223 13
of all its insult; yet, I trust you will acquit me, for NA II 13 225 19
I will trust to your own kindness of heart when I am at a NA II 13 229 30
to Miss Tilney, whose trust in the effect of time and NA II 14 235 14
eye made her mother trust that this good-natured visit NA II 15 242 8
their own hearts made them trust that it could not be very NA II 16 249 2
know; but you shall not talk me out of my trust in it. SS I 15 78 26
but from her venturing to trust her on so short a personal SS II 1 142 7
Could you have a motive for the trust, that was not SS II 2 146 4
he is undoubtedly supported by the same trust in your's. SS II 2 147 8
upon, and we might trust to time and chance for the rest." SS II 2 149 25
him, that she dared not trust herself to speak, lest she SS II 7 184 15
"I will not trust to that," retreating to her own room. SS II 9 204 16
It was a valued, a precious trust to me; and gladly would SS II 9 208 28
and so imperfectly have I discharged my trust!" SS II 9 211 40
we shall be going; and, I trust, Edward will not be very SS II 13 243 31
betraying my trust, I never could have convinced you." SS III 1 262 25
dear Mrs. Jennings too, trust she will speak a good word SS III 2 277 30
alarm, allowed herself to trust in his judgment, and SS III 7 314 23
have felt it too certain a thing, to trust myself near him. SS III 8 327 55
could safely trust to the effect of time upon her health. SS III 11 352 19
Do not trust her with any secrets of your own, take W 317 2
take warning by me, do not trust her; she has her good W 317 2
I do not trust my own partiality. PP I 9 44 31
"I will not trust myself on the subject," replied Wickham, PP I 16 80 35
preference which I trust my cousin Jane will attribute to PP I 17 87 13
do, and trust he will excuse my not having done it before. PP I 18 97 57
I have been in early preferment; and I trust I am resigned. PP I 20 114 32
them, and I trust you will not esteem them unreasonable. PP I 21 118 14
Darcy, that she would not trust herself with an answer; PP II 10 186 38
in the discharge of his trust, naturally inclined my PP II 12 199 5
of; and altogether I trust it does not appear that your PP II 15 216 6
"My mother is tolerably well, I trust; though her spirits PP III 5 286 30
one whom they could most trust, should comprehend all her PP III 5 288 40
I would not trust you so near it as East Bourne, for fifty PP III 6 300 30
side," said Jane: "I hope and trust they will yet be happy. PP III 7 305 37
She would not betray her trust, I suppose, without bribery PP III 10 322 2
But when they see, as I trust they will, that their PP III 13 349 47
I trust, can they be dangerous for her associates. MP I 1 10 14
I am driven on, and I trust I may pity your feelings as a MP I 3 23 3
fancies she prefers tragedy, I would not trust her in it. MP I 14 134 12
I should not be afraid to trust either of the Olivers or MP I 15 148 58
and trust to his seeing as much beauty of mind in time." MP II 3 197 6
to Brighton, William, as I trust you may soon have more MP II 7 245 34
was a little girl; but I trust we shall both think she MP II 7 250 60
She must do her duty, and trust that time might make her MP III 2 331 17
feelings, you will be persuaded into them I trust. MP III 4 351 34
willing than his son to trust to the future, he could not MP III 5 356 3
You all give me a feeling of being able to trust and MP III 5 359 12
Her prejudices, I trust, are not so strong as they were. MP III 13 422 2
in our small circle, but I trust and hope he will find the MP III 13 426 11
my mind, and fear to trust the influence of friends. MP III 14 430 4
I trust and hope, and sincerely wish you may never be MP III 14 431 8
Let Sir Thomas trust to his honour and compassion, and it MP III 16 457 29
love, and was willing to trust to there being no harm in E I 8 61 38
Trust to me." E I 9 76 38
I trust, at least, that you do not think Mr. Knightley E I 12 103 39
But, as it is, the disappointment is single, and, I trust, E I 15 132 36
They would feel that they could trust him; that the nephew, E I 18 147 18
see no objection, and I trust you cannot, my father hopes E II 11 250 23
"Can you trust me with such flatterers?-- E III 2 330 52
continue there, I trust, till we may carry her northward.-- E III 18 477 57
be whispered, and in the trust that among his, the brother P III 4 30 10
Well, my dear Miss Elliot, I hope and trust you will be P IV 9 196 32
their protection she must trust, and sinking into the P IV 11 237 41
42
I trust to being in charity with her soon. P IV 11 247 82
She was felt to be worthy of trust--to be the very S 3 379 1
to be ventured on--(as I trust we shall) then, we shall be S 4 380 1
I trust it may.-- S 5 385 1
for us & that we must trust to our own knowledge of our S 5 386 1
No, no; they are very deserving themselves, or trust me, S 7 399 1
I trust there are not three people in England who have so S 9 410 1
TRUSTED (45)
not yet wholly fixed, she trusted it would ere long be in LS 42 312 5
and my sister has often trusted me in the choice of a gown. NA I 3 28 38
but on some other day he trusted, when longer notice could NA I 13 103 28
If the evidence of sight might be trusted, she held a NA II 7 172 2
He trusted, however, that an opportunity might ere long NA II 7 175 12
She trusted he would never speak of Miss Thorpe; and NA II 13 222 8
torture to herself, she trusted would not be in his power. NA II 14 231 3
when he knows I have trusted you, because I know he has SS I 22 130 16
on her at night, trusted, like Marianne, to the certainty SS III 7 307 1
At ten o'clock, she trusted, or at least not much later, SS III 7 315 26
if she lived, as I trusted she might, my greatest SS III 9 337 18
being the result as she trusted of serious reflection, SS III 10 341 6
Mrs. Dashwood, however, conforming, as she trusted, to the SS III 12 359 11
She thinks everything fair for a husband; I trusted her, W 316 2
A woman should never be trusted with money. W 351 26
Mrs. Bennet treasured up the hint, and trusted that she PP I 15 71 5
the result of which he trusted he had every reason to be PP I 20 110 1
taken in; thirdly, she trusted that they would never be PP I 23 127 5
as possible, which he trusted would be an unanswerable PP I 23 128 10
in question--of which he trusted there could be little PP II 12 201 5
hopes, and said he feared W. was not a man to be trusted. PP III 4 275 5
I did not think Mrs. Gardiner was so little to be trusted. PP III 16 366 4
and in quitting it he trusted would extend its respectable MP I 2 20 33
had lately been, Edmund trusted that her losses both of MP I 8 75 1
We may be trusted, I think, in choosing some play most MP I 13 125 18
Her judgment may be quite as safely trusted.-- MP I 15 147 54
stormy a morning; but she trusted, in the first place, MP III 1 324 58
trusted that every thing would work out a happy conclusion. MP III 3 335 6
of a good income; and he trusted that she would be the MP III 6 369 10
roof with Edmund, she trusted that Miss Crawford would MP III 7 376 4
have trusted to her sense of what was due to her cousin. MP III 15 438 7
His displeasure against herself she trusted, reasoning MP III 16 452 14
The young man had been the first admirer, but she trusted E I 4 31 26
beautiful girl, which she trusted, with such frequent E I 4 35 45
No, no; she has qualities which may be trusted; she will E I 5 40 22
"Might he be trusted with the commission, what infinite E I 6 49 40
she trusted to its bearing the same construction with him. E II 6 196 1
being thoroughly aired--but is Mrs. Stokes to be trusted? E II 11 252 35
into the cardroom, looking (Emma trusted) very foolish. E III 2 328 42
the sacrifice of this, he trusted his dearest Emma would E III 15 449 31
be obtained--which, she trusted, would be attended with no E III 17 465 28
felt that he could not be trusted in London, and had been P III 2 14 10
He was the intimate friend of my dear husband, who trusted P IV 9 199 55
His judgement is evidently not to be trusted.-- S 7 402 1
he was not to be trusted;--and he maintaining that he only S 10 417 1
TRUSTIEST (1)
If Jemima were not the trustiest, steadiest creature in P III 6 45 9
TRUSTING (16)
herself to her fate, and trusting to the animal's boasted NA I 9 62 10
the smallest fear of trusting you; indeed I should be very SS I 22 128 9
But Mrs. Dashwood, trusting to the temperate account of SS III 9 335 7
in trusting themselves with me, even on a race course.-- W 339 18
"But that would have been trusting me with money, replied W 351 26
unsubdued of his heart, trusting that it was not more than PP I 18 89 1
Catherine de Bourgh, and trusting their opinion of her-- PP II 4 151 3
and trusting they would never have cause to throw her off. MP I 1 11 19
Henry Crawford, without trusting that it would create MP I 17 163 19
propitious, and though trusting altogether to her MP II 8 255 10
I came away on Monday, trusting that many posts would not MP II 13 299 5
a happy re-union, and trusting, that when we meet again, MP III 5 364 30
discreet resolution of not trusting himself with her long. E III 1 316 5
faithful counsel, and trusting that you will some time or E III 7 375 61
my writing-desk; and I, trusting that I had written enough, E III 14 442 8
humour, such an open, trusting liberality on the Admiral's P III 5 32 2
TRUSTS (1)
and the same medley of trusts, hopes, and fears, all MP III 13 427 12
TRUTH (164)
You will, I am sure my dear sir, feel the truth of this LS 14 265 4
the truth in the course of a thirty mile journey. LS 17 271 6
I cannot help suspecting the truth of everything she said. LS 20 278 8
discover the real truth, but she seems to wish to avoid me. LS 20 278 11
from the fullest conviction of the truth of what I say. LS 23 284 4
When I wrote to you the other day, I was in truth in high LS 25 291 1
But I have little heart to jest; in truth, I am serious LS 35 305 1
my dear, here you are;" a truth which she had no greater NA I 9 67 34
spoken with simplicity and truth, and without personal NA I 10 72 8
to his words, and perfect reliance on their truth. NA I 10 80 60
"To say the truth, I do not much like any other." NA I 14 108 18
to awake: an idea of the truth suddenly darted into her NA I 15 117 7
then you know, we may try the truth of this same old song." NA I 15 123 34
And as to most matters, to say the truth, there are not NA I 15 124 45
Catherine, with all the earnestness of truth, expressed NA II 3 144 11
To doubt her truth or good intentions was impossible; and NA II 3 148 28
Henry began to suspect the truth, and something, in which NA II 10 204 18
To say the truth, though I am hurt and grieved, that I NA II 10 207 39
vouchers for his truth; and to these were added the NA II 15 245 12
Indeed, to say the truth, I am convinced within myself SS I 2 12 24
of her mother and herself had outstripped the truth. SS I 4 22 16
truth was less violently outraged than usually happens. SS I 10 46 2
this wo'nt do, Colonel; so let us hear the truth of it." SS I 13 63 12
I would give any thing to know the truth of it. SS I 14 70 2
There is great truth, however, in what you have now urged SS I 15 79 29
Elinor could not deny the truth of this, and she tried to SS I 16 84 7
every suspicion of the truth from her mother and sisters. SS II 1 140 4
to have found out the truth in an instant, if there had SS II 2 147 12
risk of her displeasure for a while by owning the truth?" SS II 2 148 14
be the less when the whole truth were revealed, and now on SS II 3 157 17
Whatever the truth of it might be, and far as Elinor was SS II 5 167 7
bit tired: and to say the truth it was not very pretty of SS II 5 171 36
gain very little by the inforcement of the real truth. SS II 8 196 21
more truth in it than I could believe possible at first." SS II 8 198 33
truth; though irresolute what to do when it was known. SS II 9 210 32
Not that Marianne appeared to distrust the truth of any SS II 10 212 1
entirely on reason, and certainly not at all on truth. SS II 12 231 11
her fancy so far to outrun truth and probability, that on SS II 14 248 6
acquainted with the real truth, and in endeavouring to SS III 1 260 10
giving any hint of the truth; and I owed it to my family SS III 1 262 23
Truth obliged her to acknowledge some small share in the SS III 4 290 36
and opened a window-shutter, to be satisfied of the truth. SS III 7 316 29
to declare only the simple truth, and lay open such facts SS III 11 349 2
reality of reason and truth, one of the happiest of men. SS III 13 361 3
perfectly admitting the truth of her representation, he SS III 14 373 3
Emma with perfect truth could assure her that she could W 331 11
simplicity, such shameless truth rather bewildered him.-- W 346 21
It is a truth universally acknowledged, that a single man PP I 1 3 1
a neighbourhood, this truth is so well fixed in the minds PP I 1 3 2
of accomplishments," said Darcy, "has too much truth. PP I 8 39 46
had fallen short of the truth; and added, that he did not PP I 13 64 21
Besides, there was truth in his looks." PP I 17 86 5
as a rational creature speaking the truth from her heart." PP I 19 109 20
sister, and to confess the truth, we are scarcely less PP I 21 117 14
to be positive as to the truth of his information, he PP I 23 126 3
that she had somehow or other got pretty near the truth. PP II 10 184 20
I am ignorant; but of the truth of what I shall relate, I PP II 12 199 5
For the truth of every thing here related, I can appeal PP II 12 202 5
she was referred for the truth of every particular to PP II 13 206 4
In truth I must acknowledge, that with all the PP II 15 216 4
tried to unite civility and truth in a few short sentences. PP II 15 216 5
"I say no more than the truth, and what every body will PP III 1 248 30
He acknowledged the truth of it all; and said that PP III 1 256 61
to own the truth, with Wickham!--imagine our surprise. PP III 4 273 3
Conceal the unhappy truth as long as it is possible. PP III 4 278 21
upon such terms as for her to disclose the real truth! PP III 4 281 28
Colonel Fitzwilliam, I was ignorant of the truth myself. PP III 5 284 16
Perhaps there was some truth in this; though I doubt PP III 10 324 2
the truth of it; and she told me that it was certain true. PP III 11 331 15
so much as to suppose the truth of it possible, I PP III 14 353 26
nor any thing else, awakened a suspicion of the truth. PP III 17 372 1
I speak nothing but the truth. PP III 17 372 5
again, and more seriously assured her of its truth PP III 17 373 8
but to say the truth, I was too cross to write. PP III 18 382 21
"There is a great deal of truth in what you say," replied MP I 1 7 7
"And a very pretty story it is, and with more truth in it, MP I 5 50 36

"The truth is, ma'am," said Mrs. Grant, pretending to MP I 6 54 13
"The truth is, that our inquiries were too direct; we sent MP I 6 57 33
numerous words and louder tone convinced her of the truth. MP I 8 76 2
said Maria; "but the truth is, that Wilcox is a stupid old MP I 8 77 13
And to tell you the truth," speaking rather lower, "I do MP I 10 98 7
To own the truth, Henry and I were partly driven out this MP I 11 111 28
melancholy truth--that they had not yet got any Anhalt. MP I 15 143 28
inclined to suspect the truth and purity of her own . MP I 16 153 3
"To own the truth, Sir Thomas, we were in the middle of a MP II 1 185 28
But the truth is that my father hardly knows them. MP II 3 196 2
pretty before; but the truth is, that your uncle never did MP II 3 197 8
some part of the truth--that Mr. Rushworth was an inferior MP II 3 200 19
"To say the truth," replied Miss Crawford, "I am something MP II 4 209 17
The truth is, that she was the only girl in company for MP II 6 230 6
She would rather die than own the truth, and she hoped by MP III 1 317 33
hope like Crawford's, the truth, or at least the strength MP III 2 328 7
So thought Fanny in good truth and sober sadness, as she MP III 2 329 10
considered how much of the truth was unknown to him, she MP III 2 331 17
I said what I could for you; but in good truth, as they MP III 4 352 44
"My dear, dear Fanny, now I have the truth. MP III 4 353 46
I know this to be the truth; and most worthy of you are MP III 4 353 46
When she comes to know the truth, she will very likely MP III 5 360 16
This is the truth. MP III 13 422 2
there was no reason why Fanny should not know the truth. MP III 14 429 1
Tell me the real truth, as you have it form the fountain MP III 14 434 13
to for the truth, his sisters not being within my reach. MP III 14 434 1
3000
own amusements cut up, as to shut their eyes to the truth. MP III 14 434 13
The truth rushed on her; and how she could have spoken at MP III 15 440 16
to tell him the whole delightful and astonishing truth. MP III 17 471 28
situation she should not have discovered the truth. E I 4 27 3
"Why, to own the truth, I am afraid you are rather thrown E I 5 38 13
affections, which is in truth the great point of E I 10 85 21
extent we ourselves anticipated--which is the exact truth." E I 11 94 14
"Ah! my poor dear child, the truth is, that in London it E I 12 102 36
To you--to my two daughters, I may venture on the truth. E I 14 121 16
it suited neither; it was a jumble without taste or truth. E I 16 134 4
or goodness --and did, in truth, prove herself more E I 17 142 12
him spoken of with cooling moderation or repellant truth. E I 17 143 15
but truth, though there might be some truths not told. E II 2 166 10
On that article, truth seemed attainable. E II 4 183 9
Then I will speak the truth, and nothing suits me so well. E II 6 200 20
"Certainly--very strong it was; to own the truth, a great E II 6 202 31
The truth is, Harriet, that my playing is just good enough E II 9 232 8
A disagreeable truth would be palateable through her lips, E II 9 234 32
Emma doubted the truth of this sentiment. E II 14 273 22
find he has outstepped the truth more than may be pardoned, E II 14 277 37
Emma heard the sad truth with fortitude. E III 2 325 29
that I have been speaking truth, I am now going to destroy- E III 4 337 6
"Why, to own the truth," cried Miss Bates, who had been E III 5 345 16
The truth of his representation there was no denying. E III 7 376 62
if his eyes received the truth from her's, and all that E III 9 385 7
"Indeed, the truth was, that poor dear Jane could not bear E III 9 390 18
This is the simple truth." E III 10 396 41
that strict adherence to truth and principle, that disdain E III 10 397 48
all on an equal footing of truth and honour, with two E III 10 399 61
She must communicate the painful truth, however, and as E III 11 403 2
touched--she admitted--she acknowledged the whole truth. E III 11 407 32
You hear nothing but truth from me.-- E III 13 430 37
and comprehend the exact truth of the whole; to see that E III 13 430 38
Seldom, very seldom, does complete truth belong to any E III 13 431 39
a moment of confessing the truth, and I then fancied she E III 14 438 8
My plea of concealing the truth she did not think E III 14 440 8
Donwell and Highbury, the truth must have been suspected.-- E III 14 441 8
truth and sincerity in all our dealings with each other?" E III 15 446 15
but the truth is, that I am waiting for my Lord and master. E III 16 455 20
21
because, to tell you the truth, I think it might have been E III 18 478 67
some rumour of the truth should get abroad--in the P III 3 17 4
And all this was said with a truth and sincerity of P III 12 113 56
the day before; but the truth was, that Mrs. Harville left P IV 1 121 2
How was the truth to reach him? P IV 8 191 51
"To confess the truth," said Mrs. Smith, assuming her P IV 9 195 24
"though there is no truth in my having this claim on Mr. P IV 9 198 43
Hear the truth, therefore, now, while you are unprejudiced. P IV 9 199 53
and ignorance in another, can hardly have much truth left." P IV 9 205 85
And indeed, to own the truth, I do not think nurse in her P IV 9 208 92
speak the truth of him, than if he had been your husband. P IV 9 211 101
The truth was, that Elizabeth had been long enough in Bath, P IV 10 226 64
Captain Harville, who had in truth been hearing none of it, P IV 11 231 12
of each other's character, truth, and attachment; more P IV 11 240 59
but I believe it to be truth; and if such parties succeed, P IV 12 248 1
Why, in truth sir, I fancy we may apply to Brinshore, that S 1 370 1
But in truth, I doubt whether Susan's nerves wd be equal S 5 387 1
"Why to own the truth, said Mrs P.--I do think the Miss S 5 388 1
I have difficulty in depending on the truth of his S 7 398 1
He was all ardour & truth!-- S 7 398 1
The truth was the Sir Edw: whom circumstances had confined S 8 404 1
To say the truth nerves are the worst part of my S 10 415 1
the hotel, to investigate the truth & offer her services.-- S 10 419 1

TRUTHS (10)

all the unhappy truths which attended the affair; and for SS I 12 58 3
the most solid truths; and, besides, there is more general MP III 3 340 23
Susan was only acting on the same truths, and pursuing the MP III 9 395 4
can, after having had truths before him so long in vain.-- MP III 13 424 4
truths, half a sense of shame--but habit, habit carried it. MP III 16 458 30
but truth, though there might be some truths not told. E II 2 166 10
I will,--I will tell you truths while I can, satisfied E III 7 375 61
I must, I will tell you truths while I can." E III 8 377 1
Bear with the truths I would tell you now, dearest Emma, E III 13 430 37
re-urge the same admitted truths, and enforce them with P IV 11 231 11

TRY (81)

I would not try to stop him, for I knew what his feelings LS 23 284 5
trust he soon will) we will try to rob him of his heart LS 40 309 1
night; and I wish you would try to keep some account of NA I 2 18 2
then you know, we may try the truth of this same old song." NA I 15 123 34
You have had a long run of amusement, and now you must try NA II 15 240 2
When does she try to avoid society, or appear restless and SS I 8 39 18
And there can be no reason why you should not try for him. SS II 11 223 24
to bed, to try one or two of the simplest of the remedies. SS III 6 306 17
had still something more to try, some fresh application, SS III 7 313 21
After dinner she would try her piano-forte. SS III 10 342 7
ruins of the Priory, and try to trace its foundations as SS III 10 343 9
him to Barton, and Miss Marianne must try to comfort him." SS III 13 371 37
I shall certainly try to get the better." PP II 1 134 7
"To oblige you, I would try to believe almost any thing, PP II 1 135 13
Why should they try to influence him? PP II 1 136 22
If they believed him attached to me, they would not try to PP II 1 137 24
I will try again. PP II 3 144 7
But really, and upon my honour, I will try to do what I PP II 3 145 9
to try some other dish, and fearing she were indisposed. PP II 6 163 14
one, probably superior to----you shall try it some day.-- PP II 6 164 18
with Colonel Forster instantly, to try to discover her. PP III 4 275 5
and try if any thing could be made out from them. PP III 5 293 69
or at least it was impossible not to try for information. PP III 9 320 32
I came to try you. PP III 14 358 71
She must try to find amusement in what was passing at the MP I 6 52 1
"I must try to do something with it," said Mr. Rushworth, " MP I 6 53 6
concerned, or would have hesitated to try their skill. MP I 13 122 2
"Oh! for the Ecclesford theatre and scenery to try MP I 13 123 6
and try to dissuade them, and that is all I can do." MP I 13 128 35
I will not entirely give it up, however--I will try what MP I 15 144 33
To this nest of comforts Fanny now walked down to try its MP I 16 152 3
hands with Edmund, meant to try to lose the disagreeable MP II 2 187 2
You must try not to mind growing up into a pretty woman." MP II 3 198 8
I must try to get the better of this. MP II 6 230 7
possessions and pleasures, try to keep me longer at MP II 6 231 9
You must think of that; you must try to make up your mind MP II 7 249 53
felt it to be her duty, to try to overcome all that was MP II 9 264 18
for her to get to Fanny and try to learn something more. MP II 11 287 17
usual cheerfulness, she had nothing further to try her own. MP II 12 291 1
try to compose her spirits, and strengthen her mind. MP III 1 322 50
over; and in vain did she try to move away--in the same MP III 3 342 34
mind, and try what his influence might do for his friend. MP III 4 345 1
For this letter she must try to arm herself. MP III 6 374 27
wanted to keep by her, to try to trace the features of the MP III 7 381 25
that Fanny found it impossible not to try for books again. MP III 9 398 9
him--provided he does not try to displace me;--but it MP III 11 412 20
She would try to be more ambitious than her heart would MP III 12 417 4
bear it; and till I am, I can never cease to try for her. MP III 13 422 2
first magnitude, who could try to gloss it over, and MP III 15 441 19
Mr. Elton, I believe I shall try what I can do. E I 6 43 15
Do try to find it out, Miss Woodhouse. E I 9 72 17
"I thought he meant to try his skill, by his manner of E I 9 76 29
I think, Emma, I shall try and persuade her to stay longer E I 9 80 66
any other party, I should try not to go out to-day--and E I 13 110 9
believed, would scarcely try to conceal any thing relative E I 14 122 18
soon try for miss somebody else with twenty, or with ten. E I 16 135 7
I wish you would try to understand what an amiable young E I 18 148 21
wish her to try her native air, as she has not been quite E II 1 161 25
had better come home, and try an air that always agrees E II 1 161 29
however, she seemed to try to be very friendly, and we E II 3 178 52
She exerted herself; and did try to make her comfortable, E II 3 180 54
his certainly thinking it worth while to try to please her. E II 5 191 28
Now you have nothing to try for. E II 8 214 10
Woodhouse may be prevailed with to try it this evening." E II 8 216 16
to pause and consider, and try to understand the value of E II 11 250 19
I shall try for it with a zeal!-- E II 12 259 15
Why does not he try Bath?-- E II 14 275 30
to Mr. Knightley,) and I will try to hold my tongue. E III 7 371 28
So then, I try to put it out of her thoughts, and say, E III 8 382 27
had ever supposed--and continual pain would try the temper. E III 9 387 13
against it, and try to put difficulties in the way. E III 11 407 28
Soon, however, she began to reason with herself, and try P III 7 60 28
and he had sat down to try to make out an air which he P III 8 72 58
not try to hear it; yet she caught little very remarkable. P III 10 84 7
Captain Wentworth away, to try for a gleaning of nuts in P III 10 86 21
try to subdue the feelings this picture excited. P IV 5 160 26
Do not you think, Miss Elliot, we had better try to get P IV 6 173 49
But I will try to command myself. P IV 9 199 55
They had previously known embarrassments enough to try the P IV 9 209 96
to, and daring not even to try to observe their effect. P IV 10 225 54
them altogether--but had we not better try to get you"---- S 1 368 1

TRYING (109)

to sell it, but it was a trying circumstance, especially LS 5 249 1
That horrid girl of mine has been trying to run away.-- LS 16 268 1
"About a week, sir," replied Catherine, trying not to NA I 3 26 5
She drew back, trying to beg their pardon, but was, with NA II 10 203 8
"I hope not," he replied, trying to look cheerful; and SS I 15 75 4
Elinor looked surprised at his emotion, but trying to SS I 17 95 49
as this, and, therefore, trying to smile, replied, "and SS II 7 181 9
there is something very trying to a young woman who has SS II 12 236 43
cries out upon myself, I have been trying to do it away." SS III 1 264 31
soon failed her, in trying to converse upon a topic which SS III 2 270 1
of the event; and though trying to speak comfort to Elinor, SS III 7 313 20
acting in this manner, trying to engage her regard, SS III 8 320 32
And since then, she has been trying to make some match at W 317 2
"I am trying to make it out." PP I 18 93 38
or dejection, or by trying to avoid her but by stiffness PP I 21 115 1
and now, because he is trying to get a girl with only ten PP II 4 153 9
as he looked at her, he was trying to trace a resemblance. PP III 2 262 8
This observation would not have prevented her from trying PP III 3 268 5
"I dare say she will; she has got over the most trying age. PP III 10 328 23
of her feelings, trying to make her good qualities MP I 2 21 34
obliged to you for trying to reconcile me to what must be. MP I 3 27 34
very dreadful fears, and trying to make Edmund participate MP I 4 34 2
Sitting and calling to pug, and trying to keep him from MP I 7 74 56
he found Mrs. Norris trying to make up her mind as to MP I 8 77 8
The same evening afforded him an opportunity of trying his MP I 13 124 14
but very unsuccessfully, trying to persuade the others MP I 14 131 6
triumph which Maria was trying to suppress shewed how well MP I 14 133 12
Julia wavered: but was he only trying to soothe and pacify MP I 14 135 18
Mr. Yates, who was trying to make himself agreeable to MP I 15 142 24
had been most anxiously trying to make it out to be MP I 15 148 58
It must be a great relief to her," said Fanny, trying for MP I 16 155 23
directions in her power, trying to make an artificial MP I 18 166 4
trying not to embrace, and Mr. Rushworth was with me. MP I 18 169 21
unfolded; and was now trying to be in a bustle without MP II 1 180 10
We have just been trying, by way of doing something, and MP II 1 181 16
out of their rank and trying to appear above themselves, MP II 5 221 32
indefatigable patience in trying to make it possible for MP II 5 224 53
him to learn his part--in trying to give him a brain which MP II 5 224 53
sorry to see you trying at it, than almost any other man." MP II 5 227 66
I never was in company with a girl in my life--trying to MP II 6 230 7
days, he could not help trying to procure a companion; and MP II 9 265 21
hints to Sir Thomas, and trying to move all the chaperons MP II 10 277 16
said Miss Crawford, trying to appear gay and unconcerned, " MP II 11 288 28
I dare say they are trying for it. MP II 11 289 34
trying to understand what Mr. and Miss Crawford were at. MP II 13 305 26
She fancied he was trying for it the whole evening at MP II 13 306 27
a chair for him, and trying to appear honoured; and in her MP III 1 312 5
After a moment's pause, Sir Thomas, trying to suppress a MP III 1 313 13
His niece was deep in thought likewise, trying to harden MP III 1 316 33
You cannot suppose me capable of trying to persuade you to MP III 2 330 16
to one whom she had been always trying to depress. MP III 2 332 20
lover; and as earnestly trying to bury every sound of the MP III 3 341 31
arrangements, was trying, by every thing in the power of MP III 3 342 32
refrained from at least trying to get away in spite of all MP III 3 344 42
means of effecting it would be by not trying him too long. MP III 4 345 3
he had not been obliged to tell you what he was trying for. MP III 4 348 21
I think I see him now, trying to be as demure and composed MP III 5 358 9
Oh! she has been trying for him to such a degree! MP III 5 360 16
You must have seen that he was trying to please you, by MP III 5 362 18
in a great hurry; William trying in vain to send Betsey MP III 7 382 27
Up jumped Susan, claiming it as her own, and trying to get MP III 7 386 42
While trying to keep herself alive, their visitor, who had MP III 10 399 5
distressing occasion, as it would be too trying for me. MP III 13 426 11
at this distressing time, so very trying to my spirits.-- MP III 14 431 8
like comfort; Edmund trying to bury his own feelings in MP III 16 449 4
As to the pretence of trying her native air, I look upon E II 8 217 32
Miss Woodhouse would do them the honour of trying it. E II 8 226 85
the interesting counter,--trying, with all the force of E II 9 235 35
You find me trying to be useful; tell me if you think I E II 10 240 3
assisting Miss Fairfax in trying to make her instrument E II 10 240 5
baked apple for her, and trying to make her help or advise E II 10 240 6
on what she had said, and trying to understand the manner. E II 12 261 32
her own feelings, and trying to understand the degree of E II 17 304 28
Mr. Knightley seemed to be trying not to smile; and E II 18 312 51
Harriet looked white and frightened, and he was trying to E III 3 333 3
Miss Bates, who had been trying in vain to be heard the E III 5 345 16
a situation of such danger, without trying to preserve her. E III 5 349 26
He was not in his best spirits, but seemed trying to E III 6 364 59
two)--but it will be very trying for us to part with her, E III 8 378 8
"Well," said she at last, trying to recover herself; "this E III 10 395 37

Well, (checking herself, and trying to be more lively), E III 12 420 13
She thought he was often looking at her, and trying for a E III 13 425 2
She considered--resolved--and, trying to smile, began-- " E III 13 425 2
3
"Mr. Knightley," said Emma, trying to be lively, but E III 13 426 17
followed her into the shrubbery with no idea of trying it. E III 13 432 40
You are trying not to smile." E III 18 470 5
"Perry!" said he to Emma, and trying, as he spoke, to E III 18 479 75
she too was really hearing him, though trying to seem deaf. E III 18 480 76
She had been repeatedly very earnest in trying to get Anne P III 2 16 16
without the torment of trying for more; it is only their P III 3 20 17
herself from trying to make it perceptible to her sister. P III 5 34 12
garden with Mackenzie, trying to understand, and make him P III 5 38 34
And one thing I have had to do, Mary, of a more trying P III 5 39 34
features, perhaps, trying to trace in them the ruins of P III 8 72 58
though more fearfully, trying to induce his wife to go too. P III 10 86 17
to the first-rate poets, trying to ascertain whether P III 11 100 23
his soul, and trying by prayer and reflection to calm them. P III 12 112 54
number, and I have been trying to find out which it could P IV 7 179 30
a glimpse of him, without even trying to discern him. P IV 8 186 22
her trinkets, to trying to convince her that she was not P IV 10 220 31
kept him from trying to regain her when thrown in his way. P IV 11 242 63
that I had no right to be trying whether I could attach P IV 11 242 65
over the past, and trying inpartially to judge of the P IV 11 246 79
80
A twinge or two, in trying to move his foot disposed the S 1 367 1
those good people who are trying to add to the number, are S 1 369 1
deterred last year from trying Sanditon on that account--& S 2 372 1
this morning on poor Arthur's trying to suppress a cough. S 5 387 1
She has been trying to get round me every way, with her S 7 399 1
case, & had now been long trying with cautious assiduity S 8 405 2

TUESDAY (41)
Who should come on Tuesday but Sir James Martin? LS 22 280 1
Mr Johnson leaves London next Tuesday. LS 26 295 4
"Yes, sir, I was at the play on Tuesday." NA I 3 26 13
Monday, Tuesday, Wednesday, Thursday, Friday and Saturday NA I 13 97 1
and must only beg to put off the walk till Tuesday." NA I 13 98 1
If they would only put off their scheme till Tuesday, NA I 13 99 4
did not know that he might not go to town on Tuesday." NA I 13 99 4
not have the pleasure of walking with her till Tuesday. NA I 13 100 15
She said very well, Tuesday was just as convenient to her; NA I 13 100 15
Tilney herself said that Tuesday would suit her as well, NA I 13 100 19
not come on Monday; and Tuesday will be a busy one with me. NA II 11 210 6
Tuesday, therefore, we may say is out of the question. NA II 11 210 6
in Berkeley-Street last Tuesday, and very much regretted SS II 6 177 9
be in Harley-Street on Tuesday, and even hoped to be SS II 12 231 11
The important Tuesday came that was to introduce the two SS II 12 231 12
Surry was to be held on Tuesday Octr Ye 13th, & it was W 314 1
till the following Tuesday, which would exactly finish PP I 12 59 1
have the carriage before Tuesday; and in her postscript it PP I 12 59 1
at Netherfield, which was fixed for the following Tuesday. PP I 17 86 9
less than a dance on Tuesday, could have made such a PP I 17 88 15
he took leave of you on Tuesday, or that it will be in her PP I 21 119 20
Mr. Collins arrived on Tuesday, addressed to their father, PP I 23 128 10
"Yes he went on Tuesday as I wrote you word." PP III 5 286 26
My aunt Phillips came to Longbourn on Tuesday, after my PP III 5 292 66
Mr. Gardiner left Longbourn on Sunday; on Tuesday, his PP III 6 295 5
I am glad he dines here on Tuesday. PP III 12 339 6
They did not see the gentlemen again till Tuesday; and Mrs. PP III 12 339 10
On Tuesday there was a large party assembled at Longbourn; PP III 12 340 11
"I did not arrive here till Tuesday evening." MP III 11 410 11
not have heard from her before next Tuesday or Wednesday." E II 1 159 18
let James know that the carriage will be wanted on Tuesday. E II 7 210 14
With Tuesday came the agreeable prospect of seeing him E II 8 212 4
had not a spare moment on Tuesday, as you know, for Miss E II 13 266 5
perhaps it was the Tuesday or Wednesday before that E III 4 339 18
I did not quite like your looks on Tuesday, but it was an E III 14 436 7
very much in the storm of Tuesday afternoon and yesterday E III 14 436 7
for I have not dined at the other house since Tuesday." P III 7 57 18
when behold! on Tuesday night, he made a very awkward sort P IV 2 130 5
"She and the Harvilles came on Tuesday very safely, and in P IV 6 164 8
had much better go back, and change the box for Tuesday. P IV 10 224 51
It was soon generally agreed that Tuesday should be the P IV 10 225 55

TUITION (2)
of escaping from the tuition of masters which brought on LS 17 271 7
private tuition, at the most critical time of his life? SS II 14 251 13

TUMBLE (2)
They want to get their tumble over." NA I 9 61 1
"My dear, you tumble my gown," was Mrs. Allen's reply. NA I 12 93 6

TUMBLED (2)
sit still, for one gets so tumbled in such a crowd! NA I 2 22 19
her hair, for it was all tumbled down her back; and he SS I 12 60 13

TUMBLER (1)
A small half glass--put into a tumbler of water? E I 3 25 14

TUMBLING (4)
my younger sister in spite of all this tumbling down hills. SS I 9 44 23
spite of all this tumbling about and spraining of ancles." SS I 9 45 32
other up and down stairs, and tumbling about and hallooing. MP III 7 382 27
them be nearer the shore for fear of their tumbling in.-- S 4 383 1

TUMULT (5)
though when the first tumult of joy was over, she began to PP I 2 7 23
The tumult of her mind was now painfully great. PP II 11 193 31
The tumult of Elizabeth's mind was allayed by this PP II 17 227 25
or to bury the tumult of her feelings under the restraint MP II 2 193 18
compared with the ceaseless tumult of her present abode. MP III 8 392 11

TUNBRIDGE (3)
of Bath with those of Tunbridge; its fashions with the NA I 4 33 7
I do not call Tunbridge or Cheltenham the country; and MP II 3 199 15
A gentleman & lady travelling from Tunbridge towards that S 1 363 1

TUNBRIDGE WELLS (2)
Smith, Esq. of Tunbridge Wells," and dated from London, as P IV 9 203 71
month at Tunbridge Wells, & symptoms of the gout and a S 2 373 1

TUNBRIDGE-WARE (1)
was a pretty little Tunbridge-Ware box, which Harriet E III 4 338 9

TUNE (4)
about, hummed a tune, and seemed wholly self-occupied. NA I 15 122 29
carelessly humming a tune, to assure herself of its being NA II 6 167 10
"What felicity it is to hear a tune again which has made E II 10 242 19
when he has got a wife, he will sing a different tune. P III 8 70 46

TUNED (1)
the piano-forte; I have not touched it since it was tuned." SS II 1 144 15

TUPMAN (1)
People of the name of Tupman, very lately settled there, E II 18 310 34

TUPMANS (1)
positively known of the Tupmans, though a good many things E II 18 310 34

TURBAN (1)
Anne Mitchell had tried to put on a turban like mine, as I NA II 12 217 2

TURF (2)
and stepping across the turf, obliged her to open the SS I 19 105 13
which led immediately to turf and shrubs, and all the MP I 9 89 32

TURKEY (8)
entrance of the roast turkey--which formed the only W 353 27
"I do beg & entreat that no turkey may be seen today. W 354 27
Let us have no turkey I beseech you."-- W 354 27
"My dear, replied Eliz. the turkey is roasted, & it may W 354 27
been telling me that the turkey, which I particularly MP II 4 212 31
It certainly may secure all the myrtle and turkey part of MP II 4 213 36
Grant, smiling--"the turkey--and I assure you a very fine MP II 4 215 48
A turkey or a goose, or a leg of mutton, or whatever you MP II 4 215 49

TURKEY'S (1)
insists upon the turkey's being dressed to-morrow." MP II 4 215 48

TURKIES (1)
of all her turkies--evidently by the ingenuity of man. E III 19 483 10

TURN (137)
now taken so favourable a turn, I am quite sorry that I LS 23 283 1
promising, till affairs have taken a more favourable turn. LS 30 301 4
affection as made her almost turn from her with horror. LS 42 311 2
temper, and a trifling turn of mind, were all that could NA I 2 20 8
Miss Thorpe, and take a turn with her about the room. NA I 4 33 6
novel, is sure to turn over its insipid pages with disgust. NA I 5 37 4
"then pray let us turn back; they will certainly meet with NA I 9 65 29
Do let us turn back, Mr. Thorpe; stop and speak to my NA I 9 65 29
"Yes; we agreed to take a turn in the Crescent, and there NA I 9 68 40
allowed would generally turn to rain, but a cloudy one NA I 11 82 1
"Well, I saw him at that moment turn up the Lansdown road,- NA I 11 85 37
We had much better put it off till another day, and turn NA I 11 88 54
and tried to turn it; but it resisted her utmost strength. NA II 6 168 10
The dimness of the light her candle emitted made her turn NA II 6 169 12
was a something in the turn of his features which spoke NA II 7 180 37
or being able to turn aright when she left them; and NA II 8 183 2
"And may I not, in my turn," said he, as he pushed back NA II 9 194 8
On discovering his error, to turn her from the house NA II 15 244 11
But Edward had no turn for great men or barouches. SS I 3 16 6
turn back, for no shelter was nearer than their own house. SS I 9 41 6
the turn of his feelings and gave the lie to his actions. SS I 19 101 1
But from such vain wishes, she was forced to turn for SS I 19 102 2
This desponding turn of mind, though it could not be SS I 19 104 9
Elinor was obliged to turn from her, in the middle of her SS I 19 106 21
endowed by nature with a turn for being uniformly civil SS I 19 106 23
And then to turn the discourse, she began admiring the SS I 21 124 31
the approach of January to turn her thoughts, and thither SS II 3 153 1
turn off his servants, and make a thorough reform at once? SS II 8 194 10
doubtless will, turn with gratitude towards her own SS II 9 210 32
took a cheerfuller turn, and he began to congratulate SS II 11 226 41
She began, however, seriously to turn her thoughts towards SS III 3 279 1
turn from the house, her husband accidentally came out. SS III 5 294 4
you at ease, did I turn away from every exertion of duty SS III 10 346 28
might give a sudden turn to his constitution, and carry SS III 14 373 3
& mother think it has given him rather an unsettled turn.-- W 328 8
was now free enough to hazard a few questions in his turn. W 332 12
good stars prompted me to turn my horses heads--she was at W 338 18
but it cannot turn a small income into a large one."-- W 346 21
to seek, he did not turn away from the chair close to W 356 28
could produce, made her thankfully turn to a book.-- W 361 31
"It will be her turn soon to be teazed," said Miss Lucas. PP I 6 24 21
If my vanity had taken a musical turn, you would have been PP I 6 24 22
something that might turn her mother's thoughts, now asked PP I 9 43 26
But I am afraid you are giving it a turn which that PP I 10 49 31
you to follow my example, and take a turn about the room.-- PP I 11 56 11
may turn you all out of this house as soon as he pleases." PP I 13 61 6
The dinner too in its turn was highly admired; and he PP I 13 65 26
"it is your turn to say something now, Mr. Darcy.-- PP I 18 91 8
9
always seen a great similarity in the turn of our minds.-- PP I 18 91 15
Her disappointment in Charlotte made her turn with fonder PP I 23 128 9
estate, and resolving to turn herself and her daughters PP I 23 130 16
When is your turn to come? PP II 1 138 27
It became her turn to listen. PP II 2 139 3
thought it necessary to turn back and walk with her. PP II 10 182 1
And accordingly she did turn, and they walked towards the PP II 10 183 6
infamous, was capable of a turn which must make him PP II 13 205 3
It was often that she could turn her eyes on Mr. Darcy PP III 2 263 10
which had been designed to turn his thoughts from PP III 3 270 11
The Collinses will turn us out, before he is cold in his PP III 5 287 35
Mrs. Bennet had no turn for economy, and her husband's PP III 8 308 3
I hope she will turn out well." PP III 10 328 22
The venison was roasted to a turn--and everybody said, PP III 12 342 28
Kitty simpered and smiled, and hoped her turn was coming PP III 13 348 34
I should be glad to take a turn in it, if you will favour PP III 14 352 17
sport for our neighbours, and laugh at them in our turn?" PP III 15 364 22
The turn of your countenance I shall never forget, as you PP III 16 368 16
Mrs. Price in her turn was injured and angry; and an MP I 1 4 1
then be glad to take her turn, and think nothing of the MP I 1 9 10
when he was beginning to turn all his thoughts towards MP I 4 38 9
all dying for him in their turn; and the pains which they, MP I 4 42 21
and as every thing will turn to account when love is once MP I 7 65 13
She could not turn her eyes from the meadow, she could not MP I 7 67 16
"Suppose we turn down here for the present," said Mrs. MP I 9 90 33
when they had taken one turn on the terrace, and were MP I 9 91 37
of the ha-ha,) and perhaps turn a little way in some other MP I 9 96 76
as fast as possible, and turn the current of Sir Thomas's MP II 2 188 3
Nay, Fanny, do not turn away about it--it is but an uncle. MP II 3 198 8
to make money--how to turn a good income into a better. MP II 5 226 61
"but which way did you turn after passing Sewell's farm?" MP II 7 241 14
The Portsmouth girls turn up their noses at any body who MP II 7 249 52
twice attempted in vain to turn away from him, she got up MP II 13 301 7
could have tempted her to turn her eyes to the right hand MP II 13 304 16
himself, and he tried to turn the conversation; tried MP III 1 323 57
all were given in turn; for with the happiest knack, the MP III 3 337 10
"You have a great turn for acting, I am sure, Mr. Crawford, MP III 3 338 19
Do not turn away from me." MP III 4 353 44
under any other distress, I should turn to for consolation. MP III 13 422 2
crayon, and water-colours had been all tried in turn. E I 6 44 19
but in good hands she will turn out a valuable woman." E I 8 58 10
his, might be easily led aright and turn out very well. E I 8 61 38
Till you chose to turn her into a friend, her mind had no E I 8 63 42
and she imagined he was come to see how it might turn up. E I 9 81 78
The only way of proving it, however, will be to turn to E I 12 107 61
to him, was able to turn away and welcome her dear Emma. E I 14 117 3
hope that all would yet turn out right, she was even E I 14 118 4
But at last there seemed a perverse turn; it seemed all at E I 15 124 4
Mrs. Weston and Emma tried earnestly to cheer him and turn E I 15 126 9
"Never, madam," cried he, affronted, in his turn: never, I E I 15 131 35
warmly, "is, that if he turn out any thing like it, he E I 18 150 32
"I will say no more about him," cried Emma, "you turn E I 18 150 33
Jane writes about, we will turn to her letter, and I am E II 1 162 31
She said no more, other subjects took their turn; and the E II 8 219 43
to be heard in his turn, for most resolutely and E II 10 244 34
35
could be worse than dancing without space to turn in?" E II 11 249 14
Emma thought at least it would turn out so. E II 14 270 4
with, she drew back in her turn and gradually became much E II 15 281 3
something favourable would turn up--but nobody believed me. E II 18 308 27
About half a mile beyond Highbury, making a sudden turn, E III 3 333 5
and double-dealing seemed to meet him at every turn. E III 5 348 21
right; and the fortunate turn that every thing has taken, E III 12 419 8
not under-rated him hitherto, he may yet turn out well.-- E III 13 427 21
which he still spoke--"I should like to take another turn. E III 13 429 32
proposal of taking another turn, her renewing the E III 13 431 38
Observe the turn of her throat. E III 18 479 70
and honourable in its turn, it is only the lot of those P III 3 20 17
in; but when listening in turn to Mary's reproach of " P III 6 44 6
it in the voice, or the turn of sentiment and expression. P III 6 48 17
it probably would, turn out to be the very same Captain P III 6 52 33
I think we had better turn back; I am excessively tired." P III 10 85 15
of Captain Harville, to turn the deficiencies of lodging- P III 11 98 17
of grief, and could only turn his eyes from one sister, to P III 12 110 43
Anne was obliged to turn away, to rise, to walk to a P IV 5 160 26
But now, the matter has taken the strangest turn of all; P IV 6 171 33
of seeing her sister turn away with unalterable coldness. P IV 7 176 9
She was just in time to see him turn into the concert room. P IV 8 184 18
a touch on her shoulder obliged Anne to turn round.-- P IV 8 190 47
again, when able to turn and look as she had done before, P IV 8 190 48
Clay, not daring, however, to turn her eyes towards Anne. P IV 10 213 6

Context	Reference	Line
I saw them turn the corner from Bath-Street just now.	P IV 10 222	34
see it; and if I do not turn back now, I have no chance.	P IV 11 240	58
and followed in turn, is but a state of half enjoyment.	P IV 12 251	9
turn of mind, with more imagination than judgement.	S 2 372	1
pity they shd give him such a turn for being ill.--"	S 5 388	1
they were then to take a turn on the cliff--but as they	S 6 390	1
altogether gave an hasty turn to Charlotte's fancy, cured	S 7 395	1
fact, with an unfortunate turn for Medecine, especially	S 10 412	1
He was certainly very happy to turn the conversation on	S 10 417	1
TURNED (196)		
Catherine turned away her head, not knowing whether she	NA I 3 26	19
Their conversation turned upon those subjects, of which	NA I 4 33	7
"Hot! he had not turned a hair till we came to Walcot	NA I 7 46	11
on the other side of her, turned again to his sister and	NA I 8 52	2
Catherine followed her orders and turned away, but not too	NA I 9 62	8
ask you again, but when I turned round, you were gone!--	NA I 10 75	26
wrong in her appearance, she turned away her head.	NA I 10 80	59
"Not they indeed," cried Thorpe; "for, as we turned into	NA I 11 85	33
her father, and they turned up towards Edgar's-Buildings.	NA I 12 92	3
But her words were lost on Thorpe, who had turned abruptly	NA I 13 99	8
After addressing her with his usual politeness, he turned	NA II 2 139	5
turned up an Abbey, and she was to be its inhabitant.	NA II 2 141	11
Catherine hastily closed it and turned away to the glass.	NA II 6 165	4
A glance at the old chest, as she turned away from this	NA II 6 167	10
He turned away; and Catherine was shocked to find how much	NA II 7 179	29
gained the top, they turned in an opposite direction from	NA II 8 184	5
at times been honoured, turned with a smiling countenance	NA II 8 185	5
She turned into the drawing-room for privacy, but Henry	NA II 10 203	8
oppose the connexion, turned her feelings moreover with	NA II 11 208	1
The last time we met was in Bath-Street, and I turned	NA II 12 217	2
Though it has turned out so well for us, I do not like him	NA II 12 219	12
the fourth week would be turned, and perhaps it might seem	NA II 13 220	1
Her voice faltered, and her eyes were turned to the ground	NA II 13 223	13
Turned from the house, and in such a way!--	NA II 13 226	25
she might have been turned from the house without even the	NA II 13 229	31
and so suddenly turned all his partial regard for their	NA II 14 234	10
having her there, and almost turned her out of the house.	NA II 14 237	21
died, and afterwards it turned out to be no such thing.	SS I 2 11	20
Edward turned hastily towards her, on hearing this, and,	SS I 5 25	1
Marianne was vexed at it for her sister's sake, and turned	SS I 7 34	5
it turned out to be only the miniature of our great uncle."	SS I 12 60	10
Their intended excursion to Whitwell turned out very	SS I 13 63	1
Marianne turned away in great confusion.	SS I 13 67	65
He turned round on their coming in, and his countenance	SS I 15 75	2
her to stop, and she turned round with surprise to see and	SS I 16 86	20
When we met him, he turned back and walked with us; and so	SS I 20 115	50
She turned towards Lucy in silent amazement, unable to	SS I 22 129	15
And without farther ceremony, she turned away and walked	SS II 1 144	15
and disappointed voice, as she turned away to the window.	SS II 4 165	28
Elinor turned involuntarily to Marianne, to see whether it	SS II 6 176	3
At last he turned round again, and regarded them both; she	SS II 6 176	7
so good as to send me," turned hastily away with a slight	SS II 6 177	11
who turned away her face without attempting to answer.	SS II 8 192	2
I had allowed her, (imprudently, as it has since turned	SS II 9 208	28
She turned her eyes towards his face, and found him with	SS II 11 221	6
That sentence is very prettily turned.	SS III 2 278	32
Edward made no answer; but when she had turned away her	SS III 4 290	39
at the devil, it would not have turned me from the door.	SS III 8 317	4
I am very sure myself, that had Willoughby turned out as	SS III 9 338	22
than Marianne turned her eyes around it with a look of	SS III 10 342	7
pausing with her eyes turned towards it, Marianne calmly	SS III 10 344	12
		13
turned into the parlour to fulfil her parting injunction.	SS III 10 348	34
her; she turned away her head from every sketch of him.	SS III 12 357	4
her mother and Marianne both turned their eyes on him.	SS III 12 360	20
After a cordial reception of Emma, he turned to his	W 323	3
that point; & Mr Edwards now turned to something else.--	W 325	4
And without staying for an answer, she turned again to	W 330	11
& lively gratitude, she turned to her neighbour with	W 331	11
(said the former as she turned him) you have got a better	W 331	11
to Ly. O. & him, had just turned away her eyes in time, to	W 332	11
gave a disgust which turned the tide of his popularity;	PP I 3 10	5
Elizabeth to do it, she turned to him and said, "did not	PP I 6 24	17
		18
Elizabeth looked archly, and turned away.	PP I 6 26	44
after looking at her for a moment, turned silently away.	PP I 9 43	20
not help observing as she turned over some music books	PP I 10 51	46
Miss Bingley's eyes were instantly turned towards Darcy,	PP I 11 54	2
ball to Miss Bennet, she turned suddenly towards him and	PP I 11 55	5
		6
Elizabeth turned away to hide a smile.	PP I 11 57	25
every female eye was turned, and Elizabeth was the happy	PP I 16 76	4
with him, and turned away with a degree of ill humour,	PP I 18 89	3
Recovering himself, however, shortly, he turned to his	PP I 18 93	24
		25
of her own to pursue, she turned her attention almost	PP I 18 98	63
and in compassion to her nieces turned the conversation.	PP II 2 140	5
unseldom, she involuntarily turned her eye on Charlotte.	PP II 5 156	4
remains of a white frost, turned back; and while Sir	PP II 5 156	5
of Mr. Darcy, she turned her eyes on the daughter, she	PP II 6 162	12
his bow as the carriage turned into the park, hurried home	PP II 7 170	7
His eyes had been soon and repeatedly turned towards them	PP II 8 172	3
		4
first convenient pause, turned to him with an arch smile,	PP II 8 174	12
		13
"No, I should have turned in a moment."	PP II 10 183	5
of entering the park, she turned up the lane, which led	PP II 12 195	1
She had turned away, but on hearing herself called, though	PP II 12 195	2
And then, with a slight bow, turned again into the	PP II 12 195	2
him, her anger was turned against herself; and his	PP II 14 212	17
off his embarrassment, he turned to her again, and said in	PP II 18 234	37
		38
turned in at the lodge, her spirits were in a high flutter.	PP III 1 245	1
by her uncle; and she turned away with alarm, while Mrs.	PP III 1 246	8
she added, "but I am afraid he has turned out very wild."	PP III 1 247	9
below, she had willingly turned to look at some drawings	PP III 1 250	46
the river, Elizabeth turned back to look again; her uncle	PP III 1 251	50
She had instinctively turned away; but, stopping on his	PP III 1 251	52
so far from going away, turned back with them, and entered	PP III 1 255	59
The conversation soon turned upon fishing, and she heard	PP III 1 255	60
to its acceptance, but Elizabeth had turned away her head.	PP III 2 263	11
And so saying, he turned back with them, and walked	PP III 7 303	23
Their reception from Mr. Bennet, to whom they then turned,	PP III 9 315	4
She turned from sister to sister, demanding their	PP III 9 315	4
the army, and she was afraid had-- not turned out well.	PP III 10 327	14
seen his eyes likewise turned towards Mr. Darcy, with an	PP III 12 340	12
his eyes were so often turned towards her side of the room,	PP III 12 342	26
of both as they hastily turned round, and moved away from	PP III 13 346	22
turned to his daughter and said, "Jane, I congratulate you.	PP III 13 348	35
		36
Lady Catherine rose also, and they turned back.	PP III 14 357	64
up her mouth, and turned from me with such an air!	MP I 5 50	35
together, has never yet turned the page in a letter; and	MP I 6 59	43
expressive profile as he turned with a smile to Julia, or	MP I 8 81	32
of the cloth with more respect," and turned the subject.	MP I 9 89	29
She watched them till they had turned the corner, and	MP I 9 96	76
bottom walk, and had just turned up into another, when the	MP I 10 103	49
she has turned away two housemaids for wearing white gowns.	MP I 10 105	55
Fanny turned farther into the window; and Miss Crawford	MP I 11 112	33
of having his eyes soon turned like her's towards the	MP I 11 112	35
to Mr. Rushworth; and he turned towards his brother and	MP I 15 139	5
The boy looked very silly and turned away without offering	MP I 15 142	22
last, when Mr. Rushworth turned to her with a black look,	MP I 18 165	3
I thought he began to look a little queer, so I turned it	MP I 18 169	21
closed the page and turned away exactly as he wanted help.	MP I 18 170	24
After a pause of perplexity, some eyes began to be turned	MP I 18 171	28
been white before, she turned out of the room, saying "I	MP II 1 175	2
ever supplied her, she turned the lock in desperation, and	MP II 1 177	7
To her he soon turned, repeating much of what he had	MP II 2 193	18
with sudden recollection, turned to her and asked for the	MP II 4 215	47
though when she had turned from him and shut the door, she	MP II 5 219	26
The house must be turned to front the east instead of the	MP II 7 242	23
Fanny's eyes were turned on Crawford for a moment with an	MP II 7 244	31
He turned back.	MP II 9 261	4
but of one errand, which turned her too sick for speech.--	MP II 9 268	28
and had no composure till he turned away to some one else.	MP II 10 274	8
her on a sofa very near, turned round before she began to	MP II 10 276	14
Miss Crawford turned her eye on her, as if wanting to hear	MP II 11 289	32
said, "he is best off as he is," and turned the subject.	MP II 11 290	38
losing another moment, turned instantly to Fanny, and	MP II 13 298	2
up quite impossible, turned away his own eyes, and without	MP III 1 313	15
throughout the day, were turned and fixed on Crawford,	MP III 3 337	11
possible into a corner, turned his back, and took up a	MP III 3 341	31
Fanny naturally turned up stairs, and took her guest to	MP III 5 357	6
becoming, she turned away for a moment to recover herself.	MP III 5 358	9
a fine morning so often turned off, that it was wisest for	MP III 10 401	10
Mr. Price would have turned thither directly, without the	MP III 10 402	13
She turned away, and wished he would not say such things.	MP III 10 405	16
as well to talk of something else, and turned to Mansfield.	MP III 10 405	17
and she turned in to her more simple one immediately.	MP III 11 412	29
He turned away to recover himself, and when he spoke again,	MP III 15 444	29
She turned extremely red.	MP III 16 458	30
Emma turned away her head, divided between tears and	E I 1 11	37
Instead of answering, Harriet turned away confused, and	E I 7 53	22
Harriet turned away; but Emma could receive him with the	E I 9 81	78
Mr. Elton then turned back to accompany them.	E I 10 87	31
They arrived, the carriage turned, the step was let down,	E I 13 114	28
He turned to Mrs. Weston to implore her assistance, "would	E I 15 125	4
Isabella turned to Mrs. Weston for her approbation of the	E I 15 127	16
Without knowing when the carriage turned into Vicarage-	E I 15 132	37
Miss Bates turned to her again and seized her attention.	E II 1 158	13
"This is too bad," cried Emma, as they turned away.	E II 5 187	6
We shall enjoy him completely; every thing has turned out	E II 5 188	7
coming out; and when she turned round to Harriet, she saw	E II 5 189	16
communication of Mrs. Cole's, turned to Frank Churchill.	E II 8 216	17
Emma restrained her indignation, and only turned from her	E II 8 220	47
I hope you turned directly."	E II 16 293	11
but ever since her being turned into a Churchill she has	E II 18 310	33
Mrs. Elton turned to Mrs. Weston.	E III 2 321	17
Frank turned instantly to Emma, to claim her former	E III 2 325	31
he had involuntarily turned to her's; but she was indeed	E III 5 346	17
those who had made the attack, and turned towards her aunt.	E III 5 349	23
as a companion, and turned from her with little ceremony.	E III 6 360	40
aunt!" said Emma, as she turned back into the hall again.	E III 6 363	52
Frank Churchill turned towards her to listen.	E III 7 373	42
He had turned away, and the horses were in motion.	E III 7 376	62
distance, and with face turned from her, did not	E III 11 405	17
Emma turned round to look at her in consternation, and	E III 11 407	29
		30
subduing her emotion, she turned to Harriet again, and, in	E III 11 408	33
partly remained as she turned towards him, and said in a	E III 18 480	78
		79
pity and contempt, as he turned over the almost endless	P III 1 3	1
assure them all, their heads were both turned by him!--	P III 7 54	4
He was rich, and being turned on shore, fully intended to	P III 7 61	38
glance, as he turned away, which Anne knew the meaning of.	P III 10 86	20
She turned through the same gate,--but could not see them.-	P III 10 87	21
What!--would I be turned back from doing a thing that I	P III 10 87	23
"She would have turned back then, but for you?"	P III 10 87	24
without saying a word, turned to her, and quietly obliged	P III 10 91	41
Captain Wentworth turned in to call on his friend; the	P III 11 96	10
Captain Wentworth's eyes were also turned towards her.	P III 12 111	46
They were people whom her heart turned to very naturally.	P IV 6 162	2
The idea of Louisa Musgrove turned into a person of	P IV 6 167	20
and Mrs. Clay, therefore, turned into Molland's, while Mr.	P IV 7 174	2
He spoke to her, and then turned away.	P IV 7 175	7
Wentworth, watching them, turned again to Anne, and by	P IV 7 176	10
Lady Russell's eyes being turned exactly in the direction	P IV 7 179	28
Elizabeth had turned from him, Lady Russell overlooked him;	P IV 7 180	32
of contempt, and turned away, that she might neither see	P IV 10 227	67
He turned back and walked with me to the Pump-Yard.	P IV 10 228	71
listening, and he turned round the next instant to give a	P IV 11 231	10
The peace turned him on shore at the very moment, and he	P IV 11 233	20
will be better for us."--turned again to Mr H--& said--"	S 1 367	1
her distress,--so, she turned from the drawers of rings &	S 6 390	1
The conversation turned entirely upon Sanditon, its	S 6 392	1
TURNER'S (1)		
I have been to Turner's about your mess; it is all in a to	MP III 7 380	20
TURNING (117)		
ruining her character, or turning her out of doors.	NA I 2 19	7
"And which way are they gone?" said Isabella, turning	NA I 6 43	37
"How delightful that will be!" cried Isabella, turning	NA I 7 48	30
and therefore, instead of turning of a deathlike paleness,	NA I 8 53	3
on the shoulder, and turning round, perceived Mrs. Hughes	NA I 8 55	10
turning his horse, they were on their way back to Bath.	NA I 11 88	55
and resolutely turning away her eyes, that she might not	NA I 12 91	3
me." Tilneys; they were turning the corner into Brock-	NA I 13 101	20
they were but just turning into their lodgings as she came	NA I 13 102	25
I hope this pleases you, (turning her back on him,) I hope	NA II 3 147	26
able to breathe, was turning to close the former with	NA II 9 191	4
A new idea now darted into Catherine's mind, and turning	NA II 13 223	12
view before she was capable of turning her eyes towards it.	NA II 14 230	1
of five, she passed the turning which led to it, and	NA II 14 230	1
could not wonder at his even turning her from his house.	NA II 14 231	3
That would be turning your visit into an evil indeed.	NA II 15 241	4
After a couple of minutes unbroken silence, Henry, turning	NA II 15 242	9
good to the cause, by turning very red, and saying in an	SS I 12 61	17
		18
within her; and abruptly turning round, she was hurrying	SS I 16 86	20
parlour door open, and, turning round, was astonished to	SS I 18 96	2
I always thought it such a sweet place, ma'am! (turning to	SS I 19 107	24
followed, she found her turning from the table with a	SS II 4 165	25
from the servant, and, turning of a death-like paleness,	SS II 7 181	7
turning eagerly to Willoughby's letter, read as follows:	SS II 7 182	12
		13
Elinor said no more, and turning again to the three	SS II 7 186	37
she made no scruple of turning away her eyes from the	SS II 14 250	11
interval of Marianne's turning from one lesson to another,	SS III 3 281	9
impulse of her heart in turning instantly to quit the room,	SS III 8 317	1
		2
Miss Dashwood at this point, turning her eyes on him with	SS III 8 320	30
		31
Elinor again and again, turning from her at intervals to	SS III 9 334	4
and thoughtful, and turning away her face from their	SS III 10 342	7
her turning pale, and fell back in her chair in hysterics.	SS III 11 353	24
The next turning will bring us to the turnpike.	W 321	2
reins to take the right turning, & making only one blunder,	W 322	2
"I am sorry it happens so--she added, turning good-	W 346	21
"Which do you mean?" and turning round, he looked for a	PP I 3 11	13
"You begin to comprehend me, do you?" cried he, turning	PP I 9 42	10
on one effort more; and, turning to Elizabeth, said,	PP I 11 56	10
		11
my uncle Philips talks of turning away Richard, and if he	PP I 14 68	13
		14

Then turning to Mr. Bennet, he offered himself as his PP I 14 69 17
the two gentlemen turning back had reached the same spot. PP I 15 72 8
"I beg your pardon," replied Miss Bingley, turning away PP I 18 95 47
parsonage, and every turning expected to bring it in view. PP II 5 155 2
For your sake," turning to Charlotte, "I am glad of it; PP II 6 164 16
But perhaps," added he, stopping in his walk, and turning PP II 11 192 22
This idea lasted while a turning in the walk concealed him PP III 1 254 57
view; the turning past, he was immediately before them. PP III 1 254 57
of the carriage, when turning hastily round, she added, "I PP III 14 358 72
73

know," turning to Miss Bertram particularly as he spoke. MP I 6 55 17
they were all agreed in turning joyfully through it, and MP I 9 91 38
Perhaps," turning to Miss Crawford, "my dear companion may MP I 9 94 58
suddenly revived it by turning round towards the group and MP I 11 108 4
Fanny," said he, turning his back on the window; and as it MP I 11 113 42
and turning it over, suddenly exclaimed, "Lovers' Vows! MP I 14 132 7
was turning over the first act, soon settled the business. MP I 14 133 11
You must not, indeed you must not--(turning to her.) MP I 14 133 11
You will undertake it I hope?" turning to her with a look MP I 14 135 15
while he was slowly turning over the leaves with the hope MP I 15 138 1
us," replied Edmund, turning away to the fire where sat MP I 15 139 9
Then turning away towards any or all of the rest, he MP II 1 185 29
of larger fortune, and turning from the cheerful round of MP II 4 210 21
fine one; for, my dear"--turning to her husband--"cook MP II 4 215 48
And then turning the conversation, he would have engaged MP II 5 226 59
I was suddenly, upon turning the corner of a steepish MP II 7 241 13
You think with me, I hope--(turning with a softened voice MP II 7 244 27
The game will be yours, turning to her again--it will MP II 7 244 28
And turning to his uncle, who was now close to them--"is MP II 7 250 59
obliged to insist on turning back, was unwilling to lose MP II 8 257 15
have to say, Fanny," smiling and turning away again----- MP II 9 262 6
sound was impaired by his turning to her the next moment, MP II 13 306 28
And, Fanny, (turning back again for a moment) I shall make MP III 1 322 48
But here is my sister, sir, here is Fanny;" turning and MP III 7 380 21
turning pale about, when Mr. Crawford walked into the room. MP III 10 399 3
She began to feel the possibility of his turning out well MP III 10 405 16
If, therefore, (turning again to Fanny) you find yourself MP III 11 411 16
Knightley looking ill,"--turning her eyes with E I 12 103 39
the path to Langham, of turning it more to the right that E I 12 106 61
I think you will agree with me, (turning with a soft air E I 13 116 43
Then turning to Isabella, who had not been attending E I 14 121 16
drive from Vicarage-Lane--turning a corner which he could E I 15 132 38
I say, sir," turning to Mr. Woodhouse, "I think there are E II 3 175 39
"Well, well, I am ready;"--and turning again to Emma, "but E II 5 189 13
a neighbour of yours, (turning to Emma,) a lady residing E II 5 193 37
The turning to Mrs. Weston, with a look of gentle reproach- E II 7 209 10
take care, Mrs. Weston, there is a step at the turning. E II 9 239 53
Miss Smith, the step at the turning." E II 9 239 53
turning to Emma, said, "here is something quite new to me. E II 10 242 20
21

But you, (turning to Mr. Knightley,) who know how very, E II 18 312 50
and by only turning her head a little she saw it all. E III 2 327 34
to rights, she was just turning to the house with spirits E III 3 332 3
"Here," resumed Harriet, turning to her box again, "here E III 4 339 16
As they were turning into the grounds, Mr. Perry passed by E III 5 344 4
Yes, I see what she means, (turning to Mr. Knightley,) and E III 7 371 28
Will you? (turning to Emma.) E III 7 373 46
its all turning out well, and ready to hope that it may. E III 10 398 53
how could you so mistake me?" turning away distressed. E III 11 405 14
"How is it possible?" cried Emma, turning her flowing E III 13 425 8
And again, on Emma's merely turning her head to look at E III 16 454 14
15

"Is not she looking well?" said he, turning his eyes E III 18 477 50
selection of Mrs. Clay; turning from the society of so P III 2 16 16
This peace will be turning all our rich navy officers P III 3 17 1
She hoped, on turning her head, to see the master of the P III 9 79 25
as she might be useful in turning back with her sister, P III 10 83 4
Pray sir," (turning to the waiter), "did not you hear,-- P III 12 106 14
and nurse her;" cried he, turning to her and speaking with P III 12 114 63
He was devoted to Henrietta; always turning towards her; P III 12 116 70
It was all your doing," (turning to Anne.) P IV 2 130 6
comforted, that power of turning readily from evil to good, P IV 5 154 8
"Well," (turning away) "now, where are you bound? P IV 6 169 25
I forget what we are to have next," turning to the bill. P IV 8 187 29
He is turning away. P IV 10 222 38
turning his back on them all, was engrossed by writing. P IV 11 229 4
of all meeting again, at your party," (turning to Anne.) P IV 11 236 36
the Carge to rights & turning the horses round, the best S 1 367 1
There my dear--(turning with exultation to his wife)--you S 1 370 1
& camp stools--and in turning the corner of the baker's S 4 383 1
& Miss Diana another, & turning completely to the fire, S 10 416 1

TURNINGS (1)

rubbish it collects in the turnings, is easily moved away. P IV 9 204 82

TURNIP (1)

of, with a boiled turnip, and a little carrot or parsnip, E II 3 172 19

TURNIPS (1)

of every acre for wheat, turnips, or spring corn, was E I 12 100 16

TURNPIKE (4)

The next turning will bring us to the turnpike. W 321 2
they passed thro' the turnpike gate & entered on the W 321 2
up the lane, which led her farther from the turnpike road. PP II 12 195 1
back our steps into the turnpike road & proceed to S 1 367 1

TURNPIKE-ROAD (1)

of a mile from the turnpike-road, so 'tis never dull, for SS II 8 197 22

TURNPIKES (1)

renewing them at all the turnpikes, and at the inns in PP III 4 275 5

TURNS (26)

"But then you know, madam, muslin always turns to some NA I 3 28 45
with half a dozen turns in the Pump-Room, but required, NA I 4 34 7
especially as it turns out, that the very family we are NA I 10 79 56
Thorpe talked to his horse, and she meditated, by turns, NA I 11 87 51
about (but however, as it turns out, I am monstrous glad SS III 1 258 7
as such was it dwelt on by turns in Marianne's imagination; SS III 6 302 6
Her daughter, feeling by turns both pleased and pained, SS III 9 336 9
followed, she was everything by turns but tranquil. SS III 13 363 8
again and again; coaxed and threatened her by turns. PP I 20 112 23
looked at Jane, and smiled, and shook her head by turns. PP III 11 331 13
fails, human nature turns to another; if the first MP I 5 46 23
in all the lively turns, quick resources, and playful MP II 7 240 9
Your wicked project upon her peace turns out a clever MP II 12 295 19
she had nothing; but he turns out ill-tempered, and MP III 5 361 16
I observe she always turns the lock of the door the right E I 1 9 19
I believe I had better take my three turns while I can. E I 8 57 3
beg your excuse and take my three turns--my winter walk." E I 8 57 5
turns, which ever began would never give way to the other." E I 9 81 75
But you see, every thing turns out for the best. E II 1 160 23
They took a few turns together along the walk.-- E III 6 361 40
of condolence, it turns out to be one of congratulation.-- E III 10 400 68
she had taken a few turns, when she saw Mr. Knightley E III 13 424 1
Every thing turns out for his good.-- E III 13 428 23
The Admiral, after taking two or three refreshing turns P III 8 68 31
32

it is in sight, and then turns away and says, "God knows P IV 11 234 31
breakfast--& take several turns upon the terrace, & you S 10 416 1

TUSCANY (1)

Udolpho, or at least in Tuscany and the south of France!-- NA I 11 83 15

TUTOR (1)

friend, Mr Howard formerly Tutor to Ld Osborne, now W 329 9

TWELVE (38)

even twelve years becomes in comparison of small account. LS 12 260 2
out a list of ten or twelve more of the same kind for you." NA I 6 40 8
At about half past twelve, a remarkably loud rap drew her NA I 9 61 1
six weeks into ten or twelve, and go away at last because NA I 10 78 45
At twelve o'clock, they were to call for her in Pulteney- NA I 10 80 61
o'clock," was her parting speech to her new friend. NA I 10 80 61
it may come to nothing, or it may hold up before twelve." NA I 11 82 4
The clock struck twelve, and it still rained.-- NA I 11 83 14
I shall not give it up till a quarter after twelve. NA I 11 83 15
There, it is twenty minutes after twelve, and now I shall NA I 11 83 15
At half past twelve, when Catherine's anxious attention to NA I 11 83 16
They promised to come at twelve, only it rained; but now, NA I 11 85 32
when the clock had struck twelve, and all was quiet, she NA II 8 189 19
The clock struck twelve--and Catherine had been half an NA II 8 189 19
a very fine place about twelve miles from Barton, SS I 12 62 28
and paid ten or twelve shillings more than we did." SS II 10 218 24
desperate, to make it twelve hundred; and in opposition to SS III 1 266 38
It was then about twelve o'clock, and she returned to her SS III 7 312 17
visibly stronger every twelve hours, Mrs. Dashwood, urged SS III 10 340 4
twelve ladies and seven gentlemen with him to the assembly. PP I 3 10 4
hearing, that instead of twelve, he had brought only six PP I 3 10 4
An express came at twelve last night, just as we were all PP III 4 273 3
They were off Saturday night about twelve, as is PP III 4 274 3
Julia Bertram was only twelve, and Maria but a year older. MP I 2 13 4
twelve thousand a year, he would be a very stupid fellow." MP I 4 40 13
people enough to form twelve or fourteen couple; and could MP II 8 253 7
meaning to read more ever since she was twelve years old. E I 5 37 7
And ever since she was twelve, Emma has been mistress of E I 5 37 9
in writing that note, at twelve o'clock at night, on E I 11 95 19
for the sake of the future twelve thousand pounds. E II 2 169 16
or twelve o'clock, that she was to think of her at four. E II 5 189 19
The clock struck twelve as she passed through the hall. E II 5 189 20
" tis twelve, I shall not forget to think of you four E II 5 190 20
Twelve years were gone since they had parted, and each P IV 5 153 6
Twelve years had changed Anne from the blooming, silent, P IV 5 153 6
invariably gentle; and twelve years had transformed the P IV 5 153 6
in six months, or even in twelve, but a long engagement!" P IV 11 231 8
the while hoping for them twelve hours sooner, and seeing P 1 6 235 31

TWELVE-MONTH (3)

took place within a twelve-month from the first day of NA II 16 252 7
she were to be studying his character for a twelve-month. PP I 6 23 10
Such were its immediate effects, and within a twelve-month MP I 1 5 4

TWELVEMONTH (31)

hope to see her the wife of Sir James within a twelvemonth. LS 7 253 1
be reasonably looked for in the course of a twelvemonth. LS 42 313 8
had been so tardy in coming, was his only one twelvemonth. SS I 1 4 4
Mrs. Dashwood took the house for a twelvemonth; it was SS I 5 26 5
time twelvemonth, that Barton cottage were inhabited! SS I 14 73 17
to Mrs. Smith are never repeated within the twelvemonth." SS I 15 76 10
But last February, almost a twelvemonth back, she suddenly SS II 9 208 28
been engaged above this twelvemonth to my cousin Lucy!-- SS III 1 258 7
end;--they will wait a twelvemonth, and finding no good SS III 2 276 28
gain in the course of a twelvemonth a great deal of SS III 10 343 9
idle; and for the first twelvemonth afterwards, I had not SS III 13 362 5
What he might say on the subject a twelvemonth after, must SS III 13 366 20
This is the second time within this twelvemonth that she W 319 2
seen her for a twelvemonth, prevented their coming lower. PP II 4 152 5
half year, nay, for a twelvemonth, she has been given up PP III 5 283 10
Newcastle, was likely to continue at least a twelvemonth. PP III 11 330 2
about a twelvemonth ago, was now brought forward again. PP III 11 332 21
and Jane remained at Netherfield only a twelvemonth. PP III 19 385 3
with the probability of being nearly a twelvemonth absent. MP I 3 32 61
I did not see her again for a twelvemonth. MP I 5 50 35
It was only the spring twelvemonth before Mr. Norris's MP I 6 54 9
"No, I dare say, nor if he were to be gone a twelvemonth, MP I 6 59 43
party for at least a twelvemonth! and being so near, to MP I 13 121 1
They had not been here a twelvemonth when he left England. MP II 3 196 2
which Mr. Rushworth had used for a twelvemonth before. MP II 3 203 29
If I had studied a twelvemonth, I could never have made E I 9 76 28
kindness last September twelvemonth in writing that note, E I 11 95 19
Mrs. Goddard's; and a twelvemonth might pass without their E II 3 180 58
by baronet-blood within the next twelvemonth or two. P III 1 7 12
to Dr. Shirley, after his illness, last spring twelvemonth. P III 12 102 2
Till within the last twelvemonth, Mr P. had considered Sir S 3 377 1

TWELVEMONTH'S (2)

a twelvemonth's abode in the family might have prompted. PP I 23 128 10
coming back after a twelvemonth's absence perhaps, and P 1 6 235 31

TWENTIETH (2)

twentieth part of a moment, did such an idea occur to me. E III 5 350 35
before he reached his twentieth year; that he had been P III 6 50 28

TWENTY (79)

five & twenty, tho' she must in fact be ten years older. LS 6 251 1
He seemed to be about four or five and twenty, was rather NA I 3 25 2
which had passed twenty years before, be minutely repeated. NA I 4 34 9
"Three-and-twenty!" cried Thorpe; "five and twenty if it NA I 7 45 7
will last about twenty years after it is fairly worn out. NA I 9 65 30
her father gave her twenty thousand pounds, and five NA I 9 68 46
There, it is twenty minutes after twelve, and now I shall NA I 11 83 15
to Pulteney-Street without her speaking twenty words. NA I 11 89 61
Woodston, which is nearly twenty miles from my father's, NA II 5 157 7
some cousin or kin died in it about twenty years before. NA II 5 158 15
pronounce it with surprize within twenty minutes of five! NA II 5 162 27
which bad weather, or twenty other causes may prevent, I NA II 11 210 7
agreeable drive of almost twenty miles, they entered NA II 11 212 17
spire which would announce her within twenty miles of home. NA II 14 232 6
Lady Middleton was not more than six or seven and twenty; SS I 6 31 8
He may live twenty years longer. SS I 8 37 8
is single at seven and twenty, I should not think Colonel SS I 8 38 9
"A woman of seven and twenty," said Marianne, after SS I 8 38 10
that a woman of seven and twenty could feel for a man of SS I 8 38 11
delight for about twenty minutes longer, when suddenly the SS I 9 41 6
any young man of five and twenty must have been insensible SS I 10 47 3
lively one of five and twenty? and as she could not even SS I 10 50 12
of sitting down nearly twenty to table, which Sir John SS I 13 67 61
man of five or six and twenty, with an air of more fashion SS I 19 106 22
than two or three and twenty, they acknowledged SS I 21 120 6
nearly twenty young people, and to amuse them with a ball. SS II 5 170 29
made, till it has been made at least twenty times over. SS III 13 364 9
He had quitted Oxford within four and twenty hours after SS III 13 366 20
them with consideration these twenty years at least." PP I 1 5 29
"It will be no use to us, if twenty such should come since PP I 1 5 32
"Depend upon it, my dear, that when there are twenty, I PP I 1 5 33
experience of three and twenty years had been insufficient PP I 1 5 34
in town, had a fortune of twenty thousand pounds, were in PP I 4 15 11
I know we dine with four and twenty families." PP I 9 43 25
He was a tall, heavy looking young man of five and twenty. PP I 13 64 21
"You cannot be more that twenty, I am sure,--therefore you PP II 6 166 39
"I am not one and twenty." PP II 6 166 40
She is almost three and twenty! PP II 16 221 17
I should be of not being married before three and twenty! PP II 16 221 17
endured on a similar occasion, five and twenty years ago. PP II 18 229 3
They were within twenty yards of each other, and so abrupt PP III 1 251 51
Such I was, from eight to eight and twenty; and such I PP III 16 369 24
You have robbed Edmund for ten, twenty, thirty years, MP I 3 23 3
The son had a good estate in Norfolk, the daughter twenty MP I 4 40 15
too good for a girl of twenty thousand pounds, with all MP I 4 42 17
perhaps at Cambridge, and at one and twenty executed. MP I 6 61 56
A quarter of an hour, twenty minutes, passed away, and MP I 10 97 1
Perhaps it might cost a whole twenty pounds.-- MP I 13 127 31
could put Mrs. Grant right the other day in twenty places. MP I 18 172 31
agitation than she had been for the last twenty years. MP II 1 179 9
Will twenty minutes after four suit you?" MP II 5 221 37
a lad who, before he was twenty, had gone through such MP II 6 236 22
income, settled as soon after four and twenty as he can. MP III 1 317 34
those who were ordained twenty, thirty, forty years ago, MP III 3 339 23

nineteen times out of twenty I am thinking how such a MP III 3 340 25
Price for more than twenty years; and it would be a help MP III 6 372 21
and another twenty years' absence, perhaps, begun. MP III 6 373 24
to him, though her twenty thousand pounds had been forty. MP III 16 453 15
"Five and twenty minutes. MP III 16 456 29
or twenty years of his life passed cheerfully away. E I 2 16 5
It was no wonder that a train of twenty young couple now E I 3 22 5
intimate with, who have all twenty thousand pounds apiece." E I 8 66 53
soon try for miss somebody else with twenty, or with ten. E I 16 135 7
twenty miles off would administer most satisfaction. E II 4 182 7
One might guess twenty things without guessing exactly the E II 8 217 32
The iron gates and the front door were not twenty yards E III 3 333 3
I shall be at home in twenty minutes." E III 6 362 46
"So early in life--at three and twenty--a period when, if E III 13 428 23
At three and twenty to have drawn such a prize!-- E III 13 428 23
Anne, at seven and twenty, thought very differently from P III 4 29 8
ladies of nineteen and twenty, who had brought from a P III 5 40 45
He knows there must have been twenty better men than P III 8 65 12
had not made less than twenty thousand pounds by the war. P III 9 75 10
quite unknowingly, within twenty miles of each other. P III 11 94 6
"The notions of a young man of one or two and twenty," P IV 3 144 20
little woman of seven and twenty, with every beauty P IV 5 153 6
and twenty years in the world, "and have seen none like it. P IV 9 203 72
young woman of two and twenty, the eldest of the daughters S 2 374 1
reflected that at two & twenty there cd be no excuse for S 6 390 1

TWENTY-FIRST (1)

Being now in her twenty-first year, Maria Bertram was MP I 4 38 10

TWENTY-FIVE (2)

an hour in harness; that makes it exactly twenty-five." NA I 7 45 7
Mrs. Churchill, after being disliked at least twenty-five E III 9 387 12

TWENTY-FOUR (12)

treated with all the philosophic dignity of twenty-four. SS III 13 362 4
It was a journey of only twenty-four miles, and they began PP II 4 152 5
themselves for the next twenty-four hours; the sound of a MP II 4 205 3
of the difference which twenty-four hours had made in that MP II 11 283 6
having spent scarcely twenty-four hours in London after MP III 10 400 8
Within twenty-four hours she was hoping to be gone; her MP III 15 443 25
able to join them for twenty-four hours at any given time, E III 1 318 11
sweetest hours of the twenty-four to his comfort; and E III 8 377 1
or waking, the last twenty-four hours--Mrs. Weston, who E III 12 417 3
A little disordered always the first twenty-four hours of P III 8 71 54
it was so essential to obtain every twenty-four hours. P IV 1 122 4
him, though only twenty-four hours in the place, but he P IV 3 138 6

TWENTY-NINE (1)

a woman is handsomer at twenty-nine than she was ten years P III 1 6 11

TWENTY-ONE (1)

and had lived nearly twenty-one years in the world with E I 1 5 1

TWENTY-SEVEN (3)

woman, about twenty-seven, was Elizabeth's intimate friend. PP I 5 18 2
and at the age of twenty-seven, without having ever been PP I 22 123 3
to my poor father twenty-seven years; and now, poor old E III 8 383 29

TWENTY-SIX (1)

the respective ages of twenty-six and eighteen, is to do NA II 16 252 7

TWENTY-THREE (2)

Her brother told her that it was twenty-three miles." NA I 7 45 6
that the man who at twenty-three had seemed to understand P IV 1 125 13

TWENTY-TWO (1)

rejoiced to see her at twenty-two, so respectably removed P III 4 28 7

TWICE (71)

Twice was he called almost from the door by her eagerness NA I 15 120 24
Once or twice indeed, since James's engagement had taught NA II 2 138 1
trespassed lately once or twice, could not mislead her NA II 8 186 6
prison of his wife; and, twice before she stepped into bed, NA II 8 188 19
He had--she thought he had, once or twice before this NA II 10 199 1
to dinner, and once or twice began even to calculate the NA II 11 209 5
They have half a buck from Northanger twice a year; and I NA II 11 210 6
the general," was uttered twice after Mr. Allen left the NA II 14 238 22
and by merely adding twice as much for the grandeur of the NA II 15 245 12
Twice every year these annuities were to be paid; and then SS I 2 11 20
"Yes; and the set of breakfast china is twice as handsome SS I 2 13 28
Twice did I leave them purposely together in the course of SS I 8 39 18
openly shewn; and once or twice did venture to suggest the SS I 11 53 2
them, at least, twice every summer for the last ten years. SS I 12 62 28
He had not seen me then above twice, for it was before I SS I 20 117 64
not seen them more than twice, before the eldest of them SS I 21 125 34
"Though we have seen him once or twice at my uncle's, it SS I 21 126 40
him so seldom--we can hardly meet above twice a-year. SS I 22 133 42
since; I have been once or twice to Delaford for a few SS II 4 162 12
about once every day, or twice, if the subject occurred SS II 10 215 14
all my heart, it were twice as much, for your sake." SS II 11 223 22
a very short time, by twice calling in Berkeley-Street. SS II 12 230 5
Twice was his card found on the table, when they returned SS II 12 230 5
with visiting her once or twice a day, returned from that SS III 1 257 1
added Elinor; "and once or twice I have attempted it;--but SS III 1 262 25
Miss Penelope--& once or twice there has been a glance of W 324 3
After this discovery she had walked twice to the window to W 338 17
She danced twice with Capt. Hunter, & I think shews him in W 341 19
Mr. Bingley had danced with her twice, and she had been PP I 3 12 15
thought her quite beautiful, and danced with her twice. PP I 3 12 16
actually danced with her twice; and she was the only PP I 3 12 16
mean Jane, I suppose--because he danced with her twice. PP I 5 18 6
She had also asked him twice to dine at Rosings, and had PP I 14 66 1
of calling patroness. twice has she condescended to give PP I 19 105 10
I spoke to him twice myself, without receiving an answer. PP II 2 141 9
Once or twice she could discern a faint blush; but in PP II 5 156 4
We dine at Rosings twice every week, and are never allowed PP II 5 157 7
Rosings was repeated about twice a week; and, allowing for PP II 7 169 5
She had once or twice suggested to Elizabeth the PP II 9 181 30
times at Rosings, besides drinking tea there twice!-- PP II 15 217 13
occasions, and once or twice pleased herself with the PP III 2 262 8
for my cousin to ride twice as far as she ever goes," said MP I 7 68 19
the hot park to your house, and doing it twice, ma'am?-- MP I 7 72 47
"But were there roses enough to oblige her to go twice?" MP I 7 73 50
and say their prayers here twice a day, while they are MP I 9 86 13
week, cannot go to church twice every Sunday and preach MP I 11 112 30
twice as long on his passage, or were still in Antigua. MP II 1 176 4
In that house which she had hardly entered twice a year MP II 4 205 2
Twice had Sir Thomas inquired into the enjoyment and MP II 7 240 10
herself; and after having twice drawn back her hand, and MP II 13 301 7
drawn back her hand, and twice attempted in vain to turn MP II 13 301 7
in the room; for once or twice a look seemed forced on her MP II 13 306 26
and then, perhaps, once or twice in the spring, after MP III 3 341 30
Mr. Crawford," repeated twice over; and in vain did she MP III 3 342 34
she had seen him only twice, in a short and hurried way, MP III 8 388 2
I dined twice in Wimpole Street, and might have been there MP III 13 423 2
twice over before the good old lady could comprehend it. E II 1 158 13
travelling sixteen miles twice over on such an errand; but E II 7 205 1
They had sung together once or twice, it appeared, at E II 8 227 87
have them baked more than twice, and Mr. Woodhouse made us E II 9 238 51
We explored to King's-Weston twice last summer, in that E II 14 274 28
You will hardly believe me--but twice in one week he and E II 18 306 10
and twice in the lobby of the House of Commons." P III 1 8 16
I meet them wherever I go; and I declare, I never go twice P III 6 45 9
meeting, once or twice, after their coming back from P III 6 52 33
I have never been in the house above twice in my life." P III 10 86 19
ladies, for it proved twice as fine as the first report. P III 12 111 49
"I declare, Charles, I never heard him mention Anne twice P IV 2 131 8
She can only speak in a whisper--and fainted away twice S 5 387 1
& never took physic above twice--and never saw the face of S 6 394 1
good deal for a woman to say that has been married twice.-- S 7 399 1

TWICKENHAM (4)

bought a cottage at Twickenham for us all to spend our MP I 6 57 31
with the Aylmers at Twickenham (as to be sure you know), MP III 14 434 13
the Easter holidays, to Twickenham, with a family whom she MP III 16 450 8
time of her being at Twickenham--her putting herself in MP III 16 455 19

TWILIGHT (4)

She had depended on a twilight walk to the Grecian temple, SS III 6 303 11
Two delightful twilight walks on the third and fourth SS III 6 305 17
Fanny looking out on a twilight scene, while the Miss MP I 11 108 4
Cowper and his fire at twilight, "myself creating what I E III 5 344 2

TWINGE (1)

A twinge or two, in trying to move his foot disposed the S 1 367 1

TWINKLING (1)

joy, indeed, in me--(twinkling away a tear or two)--but it E III 8 378 8

TWISTED (5)

twisted in the fall, and she was scarcely able to stand. SS I 9 42 8
book that tells her how to admire an old twisted tree. SS I 17 92 25
I do not like crooked, twisted, blasted trees. SS I 18 98 8
He addressed her with easy civility, and twisted his head SS II 14 250 12
hand, it was not mechanically twisted about without regard. E I 7 53 22

TWISTING (1)

"And then you know"--twisting himself about and forcing a NA I 15 123 34

TWO (966)

house the affections of two men who were neither of them LS 4 248 2
is scarcely possible that two men should be so grossly LS 6 252 2
got as far as the length of two streets in her journey, LS 19 273 1
we left the two gentlemen together to put on our pelisses. LS 20 276 4
perhaps, but a year or two will rectify that, & he is in LS 20 276 5
with whom she had scarcely ever exchanged two words before. LS 22 282 6
For a minute or two I remained in the same spot, LS 23 284 5
My dear mother, every hope which but two hours ago made me LS 24 285 1
I got up this morning before it was light--I was two hours LS 24 286 5
For an hour or two, I was even stagger'd in my resolution LS 29 299 2
She staid nearly two hours, was as affectionate & agreable LS 41 309 1
her to return in one or two affectionate letters, was very LS 42 313 7
stay, & in the course of two months ceased to write of her LS 42 313 7
& in the course of two more, to write to her at all. LS 42 313 7
which impoverished her for two years, on purpose to secure LS 42 313 10
He had a considerable independence, besides two good NA I 1 13 1
tears for the last day or two of their being together; and NA I 2 18 2
The season was full, the room crowded, and the two ladies NA I 2 20 9
hearing, two gentlemen pronounced her to be a pretty girl. NA I 2 24 28
felt more obliged to the two young men for this simple NA I 2 24 28
was repeated by them all, two or three times over. NA I 4 32 5
a sudden intimacy between two young ladies; such as dress, NA I 4 33 7
been only two days in Bath before they met with Mrs. Allen. NA I 5 36 2
the intercourse of the two families, as her young charge NA I 5 36 3
took place between the two friends in the Pump-Room one NA I 6 39 1
Do you know, there are two odious young men who have been NA I 6 43 33
"Only," she added, "perhaps we may overtake the two young NA I 6 43 40
fast as they could walk, in pursuit of the two young men. NA I 6 43 44
and within view of the two gentlemen who were proceeding NA I 7 44 1
overtook and passed the two offending young men in Milsom- NA I 7 47 18
between the other two; but Catherine heard neither the NA I 7 48 32
On his two younger sisters he then bestowed an equal NA I 7 49 43
was, that, when the two Morlands, after sitting an hour NA I 7 50 44
The time of the two parties uniting in the Octagon Room NA I 7 51 54
The Thorpes and James Morland were there only two minutes NA I 8 52 1
The two dances were scarcely concluded before Catherine NA I 8 56 12
"Oh, no; I am much obliged to you, our two dances are over; NA I 8 59 36
in the room; my two younger sisters and their partners. NA I 8 59 37
Catherine of there being two open carriages at the door, NA I 9 61 1
Can you spare me for an hour or two? shall I go?" NA I 9 61 6
having scarcely allowed the two others time enough to get NA I 9 62 7
He will, most likely, give a plunge or two, and perhaps NA I 9 62 9
I would not be bound to go two miles in it for fifty NA I 9 65 28
knew not how to reconcile two such very different accounts NA I 9 65 31
and over again, that no two hours and a half had ever gone NA I 9 67 33
by the approach of the same two open carriages, containing NA I 11 84 17
and the two others walked in, to give their assistance. NA I 11 84 19
two hours ago if it had not been for this detestable rain. NA I 11 84 19
And in two minutes they were off. NA I 11 86 49
declared he had never seen two men so much alike in his NA I 11 87 53
box; and, for the space of two entire scenes, did she thus NA I 12 92 4
was never withdrawn from the stage during two whole scenes. NA I 12 92 4
it in two days--my hair standing on end the whole time." NA I 14 106 7
a very nice walk, and you are two very nice young ladies. NA I 14 108 16
my father; and I have two brothers who do not dislike it. NA I 14 109 24
while to be tormented for two or three years of one's life, NA I 14 110 27
in three duodecimo volumes, two hundred and seventy-six NA I 14 113 39
of two tombstones and a lantern--do you understand?-- NA I 14 113 39
Edgar's Buildings between two of the sweetest girls in the NA I 14 114 50
The two youngest Miss Thorpes were by themselves in the NA I 15 116 1
The two friends, with hearts now more united than ever, NA I 15 120 25
in their felicity; and two "dears" at once before the name NA I 15 121 27
of waiting between two and three years before they could NA II 1 135 43
The long, long, endless two years and half that are to NA II 1 136 48
was hardly aware that two or three days had passed away, NA II 3 143 1
from Bath, to be now divided into two equal stages. NA II 5 155 4
The tediousness of a two hours' bait at Petty-France, in NA II 5 156 4
of him, and appeared to lengthen the two hours into four.-- NA II 5 156 4
easily forget its having stopped two hours at Petty-France. NA II 5 156 5
of St. Anthony, scarcely two miles off--could you shrink NA II 5 159 21
that Miss Tilney slept only two doors from her, to enter NA II 6 167 9
Two others, penned by the same hand, marked an expenditure NA II 7 172 2
But this was quite an old set, purchased two years ago. NA II 7 175 12
business required and would keep him two or three days. NA II 7 175 13
Perhaps it may seem odd, that with only two younger NA II 7 176 15
The whole building enclosed a large court; and two sides NA II 7 177 19
a ready affirmative, the two others were passed by; and NA II 7 180 37
was to be done by two pair of female hands at the utmost. NA II 8 184 4
o'clock, the sun was now two hours above the horizon, and NA II 9 193 5
of a western sun gaily poured through two sash windows! NA II 9 193 6
There were two other doors in the chamber, leading NA II 9 194 6
Upon his opinion of her danger, two others were called in NA II 9 197 25
her; but to the other two her distress was equally visible. NA II 10 203 8
some surprize, that her two young friends were perfectly NA II 11 208 1
A day or two passed away and brought no tidings of Captain NA II 11 209 5
and shall probably be obliged to stay two or three days." NA II 11 209 5
Two hours and three quarters will carry us to Woodston, I NA II 11 210 6
I must go away directly, two days before I intended it." NA II 11 210 7
Newfoundland puppy and two or three terriers, was ready to NA II 11 212 17
consisting of a walk round two sides of a meadow, on which NA II 11 214 25
Catherine, I received your two kind letters with the NA II 12 216 1
2
and young men never know their minds two days together. NA II 12 216 2
He went away to his regiment two days ago, and I trust I NA II 12 217 2
The last two days he was always by the side of Charlotte NA II 12 217 2
ruin their comfort; and the two girls agreeing in NA II 13 222 7
mode of her travelling; of two days, the earliest fixed on, NA II 13 226 25
unlooked for by all but the two youngest children, a boy NA II 14 233 8
The two houses were only a quarter of a mile apart; and, NA II 14 236 19
For two days Mrs. Morland allowed it to pass even without NA II 15 240 2
On his return from Woodston, two days before, he had been NA II 15 244 10
the transactions of the two or three last weeks proved him NA II 15 246 12
unusual in children of two or three years old; an SS I 1 4 3
the side of the former, the two ladies might have found it SS I 3 14 3
But two advantages will proceed from this delay. SS I 4 22 17
A room or two can easily be added; and if my friends find SS I 5 25 2
of their servants to three; two maids and a man, with whom SS I 5 26 5
Four bed-rooms and two garrets formed the rest of the SS I 6 28 2
it branched out again between two of the steepest of them. SS I 6 29 3
two entire strangers of the party, and wished for no more. SS I 7 34 4
She had only two daughters, both of whom she had lived to SS I 8 36 1

the settled rain of the two preceding days had occasioned.	SS	I	9	40	3
The weather was not tempting enough to draw the two others	SS	I	9	41	3
off from their hills; and the two girls set off together.	SS	I	9	41	3
Margaret, we will walk here at least two hours."	SS	I	9	41	5
A gentleman carrying a gun, with two pointers playing	SS	I	9	42	8
gained two such sons-in-law as Edward and Willoughby.	SS	I	10	49	11
than he knows how to employ, and two new coats every year."	SS	I	10	51	25
conducted in style and her two eldest children attended	SS	I	11	55	6
of her own father, who had himself two wives, I know not.	SS	I	11	56	11
Consider, here are the two Miss Careys come over from	SS	I	13	65	32
and Mr. Willoughby got up two hours before his usual time,	SS	I	13	65	32
Willoughby took his usual place between the two elder Miss	SS	I	13	67	61
It is a corner room, and has windows on two sides.	SS	I	13	69	76
wonder of Mrs. Jennings for two or three days; she was a	SS	I	14	70	1
The estate at Delaford was never reckoned more than two	SS	I	14	70	2
place the next day, and two of her daughters went with her;	SS	I	15	75	1
"About eighteen hundred or two thousand a-year; not more	SS	I	17	91	12
"Two thousand a-year!	SS	I	17	91	13
"And yet two thousand a-year is a very moderate income,"	SS	I	17	91	14
perhaps two, and hunters, cannot be supported on less."	SS	I	17	91	14
His spirits, during the last two or three days, though	SS	I	19	101	1
Jennings, but there were two others, a gentleman and lady,	SS	I	19	105	13
Middleton introduced the two strangers; Mrs. Dashwood and	SS	I	19	106	21
and every body agreed, two or three times over, that it	SS	I	19	107	28
the next day, and the two families at Barton were again	SS	I	21	118	1
In a morning's excursion to Exeter, they had met with two	SS	I	21	118	2
to receive a visit from two girls whom she had never seen	SS	I	21	118	2
at the park within a day or two, and then left them in	SS	I	21	119	5
who was not more than two or three and twenty, they	SS	I	21	120	6
made a noise for the last two minutes; "and she is always	SS	I	21	121	9
She still screamed and sobbed lustily, kicked her two	SS	I	21	121	10
this medicine, and as the two boys chose to follow, though	SS	I	21	122	10
an hour or two together in the same room almost every day.	SS	I	21	124	33
his favourite joke of the two, as being somewhat newer and	SS	I	21	125	36
joined them at dinner only two hours after she had first	SS	II	1	141	4
One or two meetings of this kind had taken place, without	SS	II	1	143	9
be quite alone, except her mother and the two Miss Steeles.	SS	II	1	143	9
Lucy made room for her with ready attention, and the two	SS	II	1	145	23
"He has only two thousand pounds of his own; it would be	SS	II	2	147	7
high; the power of dividing two people so tenderly	SS	II	2	150	33
discourse of the two ladies was therefore at an end, to	SS	II	2	151	41
prevailed on to stay nearly two months at the park, and to	SS	II	2	151	43
So I would advise you two, to set off for town, when you	SS	II	3	154	3
two, to the number of inhabitants in London, was something.	SS	II	3	157	19
As dinner was not to be ready in less than two hours from	SS	II	4	160	4
"had not you better defer your letter for a day or two?"	SS	II	4	160	4
Well, Colonel, I have brought two young ladies with me,	SS	II	4	163	18
After an hour or two spent in what her mother called	SS	II	4	164	23
Mrs. Palmer and two elderly ladies of Mrs. Jennings's	SS	II	4	166	31
In another day or two perhaps; this extreme mildness can	SS	II	5	167	3
couple, with two violins, and a mere side-board collation.	SS	II	5	170	29
letter in her hand, and two or three others lying by her.	SS	II	7	182	12
For a moment or two she could say no more; but when this	SS	II	7	189	47
					48
"Well, then, another day or two, perhaps; but I cannot	SS	II	7	191	64
cast down this last week or two, for this matter I suppose	SS	II	8	195	16
Two thousand a year without debt or drawback--except the	SS	II	8	196	22
Two ladies were waiting for their carriage, and one of	SS	II	8	199	37
when I heard, about two years afterwards, of her divorce.	SS	II	9	206	24
same time of life; and for two years I had every reason to	SS	II	9	208	28
covert, and they were kept waiting for two hours together.	SS	II	10	214	9
him, began, at the end of two days, to think that, instead	SS	II	10	216	15
About this time, the two Miss Steeles, lately arrived at	SS	II	10	217	19
any other attention on the two ladies, than what was	SS	II	11	220	3
Elinor found that he and Fanny had been in town two days.	SS	II	11	221	8
"I believe about two thousand a-year."	SS	II	11	223	21
"Two thousand a-year;" and then working himself up to a	SS	II	11	223	22
into Fanny's hands to the amount of two hundred pounds.	SS	II	11	224	28
"Another year or two may do much towards it," he gravely	SS	II	11	226	37
ask them to spend a week or two in Conduit-Street: and it	SS	II	12	230	8
The important Tuesday came that was to introduce the two	SS	II	12	231	12
The parties stood thus: the two mothers, though each	SS	II	12	234	21
					22
The two grandmothers, with not less partiality, but more	SS	II	12	234	23
Again they all sat down, and for a moment or two all were	SS	II	13	242	25
In a week or two, I suppose, we shall be going; and, I	SS	II	13	243	31
to the feelings of two thirds of her auditors, and was so	SS	II	13	244	41
had his visit lasted two hours, soon afterwards went away.	SS	II	13	244	43
to Lady Middleton and the two Miss Steeles, by whom their	SS	II	14	246	2
It so happened that while her two sisters with Mrs.	SS	II	14	248	6
produced within a day or two afterwards, cards of	SS	II	14	248	6
But while she wondered at the difference of the two young	SS	II	14	250	12
to have been always meant to end in two days time.	SS	II	14	254	26
a little bigger--with two maids and two men; and I believe	SS	III	1	260	7
bigger--with two maids and two men; and I believe I could	SS	III	1	260	7
His own two thousand pounds she protested should be his	SS	III	1	267	38
The interest of two thousand pounds--how can a man live on	SS	III	1	268	50
have been in the receipt of two thousand, five hundred a-	SS	III	1	268	50
Nothing new was heard by them, for a day or two afterwards,	SS	III	2	270	3
for he had nothing but two thousand pounds, and no hope of	SS	III	2	273	16
same by me; for a year or two back, when Martha Sharpe and	SS	III	2	274	20
she had gave us a day or two before; but however, nothing	SS	III	2	275	22
with the interest of his two thousand pounds, and what	SS	III	2	276	28
Two maids and two men indeed!--as I talked of t'other day.-	SS	III	2	277	28
dear Mrs. Jennings, I spent two happy hours with him	SS	III	2	277	30
The Miss Dashwoods had now been rather more than two	SS	III	3	279	1
we shall sit and gape at one another as dull as two cats."	SS	III	3	280	8
or attempting to divide, two young people long attached to	SS	III	3	282	19
I have seen Mr. Ferrars two or three times in Harley-	SS	III	3	282	19
The preferment, which only two days before she had	SS	III	3	283	20
the living--it is about two hundred a-year--were much more	SS	III	4	289	28
but he said only these two words, "Colonel Brandon!"	SS	III	4	289	29
					30
suppose two or three months will complete his ordination."	SS	III	4	291	50
"Two or three months!" cried Mrs. Jennings; "Lord! my dear,	SS	III	4	291	51
talk of it; and can the Colonel wait two or three months!	SS	III	4	291	51
it is not worth while to wait two or three months for him.	SS	III	4	291	51
"The Colonel is a ninny, my dear; because he has two	SS	III	4	292	57
"About two hundred a-year."	SS	III	5	295	11
'the least evil of the two, and she would be glad to	SS	III	5	297	31
They had scarcely been two minutes by themselves, before	SS	III	5	298	33
to Cleveland in a day or two, completed the intercourse of	SS	III	6	301	1
early in the day, the two parties from Hanover-Square and	SS	III	6	301	3
they were to be more than two days on their journey, and	SS	III	6	301	3
The two gentlemen arrived the next day to a very late	SS	III	6	304	14
the nicest observer of the two;-- she watched his eyes,	SS	III	6	305	16
Two delightful twilight walks on the third and fourth	SS	III	6	305	17
as, though for a day or two trifled with or denied, would	SS	III	6	305	17
to bed, to try one or two of the simplest of the remedies.	SS	III	6	306	17
to join her in a day or two; and whither she was almost	SS	III	7	308	3
Two days passed away from the time of Mr. Palmer's	SS	III	7	309	7
was--for the first time these two months--he spoke to me.--	SS	III	8	330	69
I have business there; from thence to town in a day or two.	SS	III	8	331	73
her first desire; and in two minutes she was with her	SS	III	9	334	5
Marianne will be the most happy with him of the two."	SS	III	9	336	10
At the end of another day or two, Marianne growing visibly	SS	III	10	340	4
On her measures depended those of her two friends; Mrs.	SS	III	10	341	4
maid for the loss of her two young companions; and Colonel	SS	III	10	341	5
The Dashwoods were two days on the road, and Marianne bore	SS	III	10	341	6
Marianne had been two or three days at home, before the	SS	III	10	344	11
kiss of gratitude and these two words just articulate	SS	III	10	348	34
Elinor, according to her expectation, saw on the two or	SS	III	11	352	19
"No, ma'am, only they two."	SS	III	11	354	34
two rational creatures, yet with lovers it is different.	SS	III	13	363	9
regard, and who had only two thousand pounds in the world.	SS	III	13	367	22
Edward had two thousand pounds, and Elinor one, which,	SS	III	13	369	32
their being in love with two sisters, and two sisters fond	SS	III	13	370	36
love with two sisters, and two sisters fond of each other,	SS	III	13	370	36
on so sly; for it was but two days before Lucy called and	SS	III	13	370	37
or four days, the two gentlemen quitted Barton together.--	SS	III	13	372	46
For many years of her life she had had two sons; but the	SS	III	14	373	2
orders for the sake of two hundred and fifty at the utmost;	SS	III	14	374	4
that one or two interviews would settle the matter.	SS	III	14	376	11
a former attachment, whom, two years before, she had	SS	III	14	378	15
On the present occasion, as only two of Mr W.'s children	W			315	1
He has been very much in love with her these two years, &	W			321	2
most of its neighbours with two windows on each side the	W			322	2
Horses for two carriages are ordered from the White Hart,	W			323	3
attired in one of the two Sattin gowns which went thro'	W			323	3
You had better meet every night, & break up two hours	W			325	4
afternoon was long to the two young ladies; & tho' Miss	W			326	7
engagement formed for the two first dances, which made her	W			328	8
The two first dances were not quite over, when the	W			329	9
At the conclusion of the two dances, Emma found herself,	W			330	11
kind as to promise to dance the two 1st dances with him."--	W			330	11
I am going to dance these two dances with Coln Beresford.	W			330	11
enquiry that he had two brothers & a sister, that they &	W			331	11
On entering the Tearoom, in which two long tables were	W			332	11
to be increased by one or two of the card parties having	W			333	13
of her hand in the next two dances, to which as hasty an	W			333	13
was continually at Howard's elbow during the two dances.--	W			335	13
The two dances seemed very short, & she had her partner's	W			335	13
distinguished, & the two dances which followed & concluded	W			336	14
up with Mr James, the last two dances; Mrs Tomlinson told	W			336	14
say two minutes before that you were not engaged."--	W			336	14
Capt. Hunter assured me it was for those very two.--"	W			337	14
astonished by finding it two o'clock, & considering that	W			338	17
"We had two dances more."--	W			340	19
declared it seemed only two days since he had seen her.--"	W			342	19
to nothing, the smartest & most fashionable man of the two.	W			347	22
intercourse of the two sisters, whose mutual regard was	W			348	23
of Margaret, & a visit of two or three days from Mr & Mrs	W			348	23
I hope I can put up with a small apartment for two or	W			351	25
When there is only one or two of you at home, you must be	W			354	28
The wheels rapidly approached;--in two minutes the general	W			354	28
She has two neices of her own.	PP	I	2	6	5
Mr. Bingley, his two sisters, the husband of the eldest,	PP	I	3	10	4
gentlemen, to sit down for two dances; and during part of	PP	I	3	11	7
was, and got introduced, and asked her for the two next.	PP	I	3	13	16
Then, the two third he danced with Miss King, and the two	PP	I	3	13	16
with Maria Lucas, and the two fifth with Jane again, and	PP	I	3	13	16
and the two sixth with Lizzy, and the boulanger-----"	PP	I	3	13	16
Mr. Bingley had not been of age two years, when he was	PP	I	4	16	13
a doubt, there cannot be two opinions on that point."	PP	I	5	19	7
with them, was expressed towards the two eldest.	PP	I	6	21	1
After a song or two, and before she could reply to the	PP	I	6	25	23
some of the lucases and two or three officers joined	PP	I	6	25	24
entirely in an estate of two thousand a year, which,	PP	I	7	28	1
The two youngest of the family, Catherine and Lydia, were	PP	I	7	28	3
you must be two of the silliest girls in the country.	PP	I	7	29	5
					6
as to think our two youngest daughters uncommonly foolish."	PP	I	7	29	11
between two women can never end without a quarrel.	PP	I	7	30	17
In Meryton they parted; the two youngest repaired to the	PP	I	7	32	41
At five o'clock the two ladies retired to dress, and at	PP	I	8	35	1
from the two elegant ladies who waited on his sisters.	PP	I	9	41	1
Mrs. Bennet, accompanied by her two youngest girls,	PP	I	9	41	1
The two girls had been whispering to each other during the	PP	I	9	45	35
to the remarks of the two ladies and Mr. Darcy; the latter	PP	I	9	46	39
"And which of the two do you call my little recent piece	PP	I	10	48	26
about, in the hope of being at home again in a day or two.	PP	I	10	53	66
she was welcomed by her two friends with many professions	PP	I	11	54	1
that he could imagine but two motives for their chusing to	PP	I	11	56	12
therefore in requiring an explanation of his two motives.	PP	I	11	56	14
occasionally for a week or two, to visit his relations.	PP	I	14	66	1
Lydia was bid by her two eldest sisters to hold her tongue;	PP	I	14	69	15
					16
that she might soon have two daughters married; and the	PP	I	15	71	5
the two gentlemen turning back had reached the same spot.	PP	I	15	72	8
On distinguishing the ladies of the group, the two	PP	I	15	72	8
to see her nieces, and the two eldest, from their recent	PP	I	15	73	11
had seen pass between the two gentlemen; but though Jane	PP	I	15	74	12
Certain it is, that the living became vacant two years ago,	PP	I	16	79	27
that she and her cousin will unite the two estates."	PP	I	16	83	55
The two young ladies were summoned from the shrubbery	PP	I	17	86	9
The two ladies were delighted to see their dear friend	PP	I	17	86	9
in the society of her two friends, and the attentions of	PP	I	17	86	10
Miss Elizabeth, for the two first dances especially,--a	PP	I	17	87	13
The two first dances, however, brought a return of	PP	I	18	90	4
was to last through the two dances, and at first was	PP	I	18	91	8
Sir William could not have interrupted any two people in	PP	I	18	93	26
We have tried two or three subjects already without	PP	I	18	93	26
of endeavouring even to like Bingley's two sisters.	PP	I	18	98	63
to think how fond the two sisters were of Jane, and to be	PP	I	18	99	63
She looked at his two sisters, and saw them making signs	PP	I	18	100	68
That his two sisters and Mr. Darcy, however, should have	PP	I	18	102	72
"My dear," replied her husband, "I have two small favours	PP	I	20	112	22
misery of disobliging his two sisters is more than	PP	I	21	119	24
dinner, she would take care to have two full courses.	PP	I	21	120	30
of coming out a year or two sooner than they might	PP	I	22	122	3
within the last day or two; but that Charlotte could	PP	I	22	124	12
					13
The strangeness of Mr. Collins's making two offers of	PP	I	22	125	18
Two inferences, however, were plainly deduced from the	PP	I	21	127	5
by them all; and on these two points she principally dwelt	PP	I	21	127	5
The united efforts of his two unfeeling sisters and of his	PP	I	23	129	13
A day or two passed before Jane had courage to speak of	PP	II	1	134	4
					5
I have met with two instances lately; one I will not	PP	II	1	135	11
You mentioned two instances.	PP	II	1	136	14
Between the two eldest and herself especially, there	PP	II	2	139	2
Two of her girls had been on the point of marriage, and	PP	II	2	139	3
At his own ball he offended two or three young ladies, by	PP	II	2	141	9
have led them round his two meadows, but the ladies not	PP	II	5	156	5
two ladies stopping in a low phaeton at the garden gate.	PP	II	5	158	13
Mr. Collins no sooner saw the two girls than he began to	PP	II	5	159	20
While they were dressing, he came two or three times to	PP	II	6	161	7
to play at cassino, the two girls had the honour of	PP	II	6	166	41
There were two nephews of Lady Catherine to require them,	PP	II	7	170	7
people who lived in it, the two cousins found a temptation	PP	II	9	180	28
There could not exist in the world two men, over whom Mr.	PP	II	10	186	38
After walking two or three times along that part of the	PP	II	12	195	2
an envelope containing two sheets of letter paper, written	PP	II	12	196	3
"Two offences of a very different nature, and by no means	PP	II	12	196	5
to which the separation of two young persons, whose	PP	II	12	196	5
I joined them unexpectedly a day or two before the	PP	II	12	202	5
thing of the last page or two, put it hastily away,	PP	II	13	204	2
After wandering along the lane for two hours, giving way	PP	II	13	209	12
She was immediately told, that the two gentlemen from	PP	II	13	209	13
The two gentlemen left Rosings the next morning; and Mr.	PP	II	14	210	1
I expected you to stay two months.	PP	II	14	211	8
the idea of two young women travelling post by themselves.	PP	II	14	211	13
made a point of her having two men servants go with her.--	PP	II	14	211	13
"it seems but a day or two since we first came!--and yet	PP	II	15	217	11

These two girls had been above an hour in the place, PP II 16 219 1
"Oh! but there were two or three much more ugly in the PP II 16 219 4
and so she asked the two Harringtons to come, but Harriet PP II 16 221 17
When Denny, and Wickham, and Pratt, and two or three more PP II 16 221 17
mismanagement in the education of those two young men. PP II 17 225 15
She had got rid of two of the secrets which had weighed on PP II 17 227 25
"I am sure," said she, "I cried for two days together when PP II 18 229 4
months' acquaintance they had been intimate two. PP II 18 230 11
asked as she has, and more too, for I am two years older." PP II 18 230 13
The children, two girls of six and eight years old, and PP II 19 239 10
and eight years old, and two younger boys, were to be left PP II 19 239 10
their direct road, nor more than a mile or two out of it. PP II 19 240 12
The picture gallery, and two or three of the principal bed- PP III 1 250 46
to assure the other two that they now saw Mr. Darcy, the PP III 1 251 52
After walking some time in this way, the two ladies in PP III 1 255 61
two ladies in front, the two gentlemen behind, on resuming PP III 1 255 61
On this point she was soon satisfied; and two or three PP III 2 262 8
lay awake two whole hours, endeavouring to make them out. PP III 2 265 16
of manner, where their two selves only were concerned, was PP III 2 265 16
He had been some time with Mr. Gardiner, who, with two or PP III 3 268 8
justified by the receipt of two letters from her at once, PP III 4 273 1
its object, and even before two words have been exchanged, PP III 4 279 24
their summons, reading the two letters aloud, and dwelling PP III 4 280 26
about him for the first two months; but he never PP III 5 285 18
In the afternoon, the two elder Miss Bennets were able to PP III 5 289 45
spared her, she thought, one sleepless night out of two. PP III 6 299 17
Two days after Mr. Bennet's return, as Jane and Elizabeth PP III 7 301 1
But there are two things that I want very much to know;-- PP III 7 304 27
what they had feared, only two hours ago, she felt all the PP III 7 307 51
but the cheeks of the two who caused their confusion, PP III 9 316 5
of being married, to Mrs. Hill and the two housemaids. PP III 9 317 10
"And then when you go away, you may leave one or two of my PP III 9 317 15
as she was sitting with her two elder sisters, she said to PP III 9 318 21
22
But it was two or three days before he could get from her PP III 10 322 2
that she is uncommonly improved within this year or two. PP III 10 328 22
Not these two or three years perhaps." PP III 11 330 4
down in a day or two, to shoot there for several weeks. PP III 11 331 13
of civility, which made her two daughters ashamed, PP III 11 335 41
think any thing less than two courses, could be good PP III 11 338 60
at Longbourn; and the two, who were most anxiously PP III 12 340 11
Mrs. Bennet had designed to keep the two Netherfield PP III 12 342 27
and I suppose he has two or three French cooks at least. PP III 12 342 28
Two obstacles of the five being thus removed, Mrs. Bennet PP III 13 345 11
A report of a most alarming nature, reached me two days PP III 14 353 26
I did not know before, that I had two daughters on the PP III 15 362 10
I had narrowly observed her during the two visits which I PP III 16 371 43
Mrs. Bennet got rid of her two most deserving daughters. PP III 19 385 1
spent the chief of time with her two elder sisters. PP III 19 385 4
under the direction of two persons so extravagant in their PP III 19 387 8
She had two sisters to be benefited by her elevation; and MP I 1 3 1
He thought of his own four children--of his two sons--of MP I 1 6 5
girls to teach, or only two--there can be no difference. MP I 1 9 12
became immediately the less awful character of the two. MP I 2 12 2
The two girls were more at a loss from being younger and MP I 2 12 3
There was in fact but two years between the youngest and MP I 2 13 4
she could scarcely swallow two mouthfuls before tears MP I 2 13 4
on finding that she had but two sashes, and had never MP I 2 14 7
stupid, and for the first two or three weeks were MP I 2 18 23
except William; her heart was divided between the two. MP I 2 22 35
You speak as if you were going two hundred miles off, MP I 3 26 31
The two families will be meeting every day in the year. MP I 3 27 31
Two of them were hunters; the third, a useful road-horse: MP I 4 37 8
the intercourse of the two families was carried on without MP I 4 39 12
to whom they showed the greatest fondness of the two. MP I 4 40 15
very fine young men, that two such young men were not MP I 5 47 27
very plain, in spite of her two cousins having repeatedly MP I 5 48 30
When anderson first introduced me to his family, about two MP I 5 50 35
her and a little girl or two in the room--the governess MP I 5 50 35
Mrs. and the two Miss Sneyds, with others of their MP I 5 51 40
There have been two or three fine old trees cut down that MP I 6 55 17
"Yes, the profession is well enough under two MP I 6 60 51
as if reading in her two nieces' minds their little MP I 6 61 58
I dare say Mr. Crawford would take my two nieces and me in MP I 6 62 58
stroll was over, and the two families parted again, he MP I 7 65 14
with two or three grooms, standing about and looking on. MP I 7 67 16
and having asked one or two questions about the dinner, MP I 7 71 31
indeed; but I cannot be in two places at once; and I was MP I 7 73 53
and accept of our two dear girls and myself without her. MP I 8 76 3
and walk half way down the park with the two other ladies. MP I 8 77 7
"And my dear Edmund," added Mrs. Norris, "taking out two MP I 8 77 12
The next meeting of the two Mansfield families produced MP I 8 79 28
amid the good wishes of the two remaining ladies, and the MP I 8 80 30
Bertram, who might be said to have two strings to her bow. MP I 8 81 33
admit them through one or two intermediate rooms into the MP I 9 84 1
of some carriage which might convey more than two. MP I 9 84 1
They would have two chances at least in their favour. MP I 9 88 17
Starting, the lady instinctively moved a step or two, but MP I 9 88 21
It is past two, and we are to dine at five." MP I 9 89 31
was a planted wood of about two acres, and though chiefly MP I 9 91 38
How can two sermons a week, even supposing them worth MP I 9 92 46
two, but I forestall you; remember I have forestalled you." MP I 9 94 55
Fanny's thoughts were now all engrossed by the two who had MP I 10 103 49
It was late before the Miss Bertrams and the two gentlemen MP I 10 104 51
of the other two, and restore general good humour. MP I 10 104 51
she has turned away two housemaids for wearing white gowns. MP I 10 105 55
between the two above-mentioned ladies was forced on her. MP I 12 117 11
different from what it was the two last dances!" MP I 12 117 14
"To want to nail me to a card table for the next two hours MP I 12 119 26
borne a part, was within two days of representation, when MP I 13 121 1
Lord Ravenshaw and the duke had appropriated the only two MP I 13 122 2
whereas it was certainly in the best hands of the two. MP I 13 122 2
and all happening two hundred miles off, I think there MP I 13 122 4
only just a side wing or two run up, doors in flat, and MP I 13 123 8
and removed at least two sets of difficulties, and having MP I 14 130 1
play was wanting; and as two or three days passed away in MP I 14 130 1
Here are two capital tragic parts for Yates and Crawford, MP I 14 132 7
She was acknowledged to be quite right, and the two parts MP I 14 132 8
We cannot have two Agathas, and we must have one MP I 14 134 14
"I come in three times, and have two and forty speeches. MP I 15 139 10
servants' hall door with two bits of deal board in his MP I 15 141 22
two bits of board for he could not no how do without them. MP I 15 141 22
only for an hour or two; there was still a great deal to MP I 15 142 25
"The count has two and forty speeches," returned Mr. MP I 15 144 31
You have only two scenes, and as I shall be Cottager, I'll MP I 15 146 50
and there are one or two that would not disgrace us.-- MP I 15 148 58
For a day or two after the affront was given, Henry MP I 17 160 9
promote the pleasure of the two so dear to her. MP I 17 161 9
They were two solitary sufferers, or connected only by MP I 17 163 20
The inattention of the two brothers and the aunt to MP I 17 163 21
the first rehearsal or two, Fanny began to be their only MP I 18 165 3
knowledge of his two and forty speeches became much less. MP I 18 165 4
will be hung in a day or two,--there is very little in a MP I 18 167 11
A glimpse, as she passed through the hall, of the two MP I 18 168 14
a little, for really there is a speech or two----- MP I 18 168 17
We must have two chairs at hand for you to bring forward MP I 18 169 21
Fanny, and a voice or two, to say, "if Miss Price would be MP I 18 171 28
Her going roused the rest; and at the same moment, the two MP II 1 176 3
every question of his two sons almost before it was put. MP II 1 178 8
minutes seemed to mark him the most at home of the two. MP II 1 183 23
hopes that another day or two would suffice to wipe away MP II 2 190 9
from the house, and within two hours afterwards from the MP II 2 193 18

Another day or two, and Mr. Yates was gone likewise. MP II 2 194 21
The bride was elegantly dressed--the two bridemaids were MP II 3 203 29
in a supernumerary glass or two, was all joyous delight-- MP II 3 203 30
The two sisters were so kind to her and so pleasant, that MP II 4 206 4
out was known only to her two aunts, she was perfectly MP II 4 206 4
Fanny went to her every two or three days; it seemed a MP II 4 208 11
A friendship between two so very dear to him was exactly MP II 4 211 25
"Upon my word," cried Miss Crawford, "you are two of the MP II 4 212 30
The two cousins walked home together; and except in the MP II 4 216 50
There are his own two men pushing it back into its old MP II 5 222 46
Bath, so much between the two young men about hunting, so MP II 5 223 48
and warmly urged by the two sisters, was soon in MP II 5 223 48
Her two absent cousins, especially Maria, were much in her MP II 5 224 48
two about the equinox, there would have been a difference. MP II 5 225 57
when the two gentlemen shortly afterwards joined them. MP II 5 226 64
You ought to be satisfied with her two cousins." MP II 6 229 4
She must be grown two inches, at least, since October." MP II 6 230 5
every body in quest of two needlefulls of thread or a MP II 6 236 21
The intercourse of the two families was at this period MP II 7 238 1
full of business, having two persons' cards to manage as MP II 7 240 8
I had two or three ideas." MP II 7 242 23
"And I have two or three ideas also," said Edmund, "and MP II 7 242 24
to generation, through two centuries at least, and were MP II 7 243 27
were now spending from two to three thousand a year in." MP II 7 243 27
some awkward sensations in two of the others, two of his MP II 7 248 47
in two of the others, two of his most attentive listeners, MP II 7 248 47
Edmund's feelings were for the other two. MP II 8 253 5
in the consideration of two important events now at hand, MP II 8 254 10
Independent of his two cousins' enjoyment in it, the MP II 8 256 13
any other appointed meeting of the two families might be. MP II 8 256 13
To engage her early for the two first dances, was all the MP II 8 256 13
I would not have the shadow of a coolness between the two MP II 9 263 16
little, "between the two dearest objects I have on earth." MP II 9 264 16
She was one of his two dearest--that must support her. MP II 9 264 17
his two dearest, before the words gave her any sensation. MP II 9 264 17
Two lines more prized had never fallen from the pen of the MP II 9 265 19
spent principally with her two aunts, she was often under MP II 9 267 22
"I wished to engage Miss Crawford for the two first dances, MP II 9 268 28
those memorials of the two most beloved of her heart, MP II 9 271 40
to table the eyes of the two young men assured him, that MP II 10 272 4
me, Fanny; you must keep two dances for me; any two that MP II 10 272 4
dances for me; any two that you like, except the first." MP II 10 272 4
his engaging her almost instantly for the two first dances. MP II 10 274 8
Mrs. Grant coming up to the two girls and taking an arm of MP II 10 275 9
she went to her after the two first dances and said, with MP II 10 277 17
she was happy in having the two dances with Edmund still MP II 10 278 20
and they went down their two dances together with such MP II 10 278 20
When her two dances with him were over, her inclination MP II 10 279 22
I hope we shall keep it up these two hours. MP II 10 279 23
in the room for the next two hours beyond the reckonings MP II 11 283 6
"We miss our two young men," was Sir Thomas's observation MP II 11 284 9
Two play on the piano-forte, and one on the harp--and all MP II 11 288 28
that there could not be two persons in existence, whose MP II 12 296 29
bitter pills, it will have two moments ill-flavour, and MP II 12 297 33
The two ladies were together in the breakfast-room, and MP II 13 298 1
young price, and inclosing two more, one from the MP II 13 298 3
I think I will have two shawls, Fanny." MP II 13 305 25
from the woman whom, two moments before, he had been MP III 3 334 1
it, or within a page or two, quite near enough to satisfy MP III 3 336 10
The two young men were the only talkers, but they, MP III 3 339 22
by him; but after a day or two of mutual reserve, he was MP III 4 345 1
There never were two people more dissimilar. MP III 4 348 22
"Yes, when I reached the house I found the two sisters MP III 4 352 38
They are two distinct orders of being. MP III 4 355 54
composed as Anhalt ought, through the two long speeches. MP III 5 358 9
'When two sympathetic hearts meet in the marriage state, MP III 5 358 9
particular friend of the two; but I have not cared much MP III 5 359 12
After this speech, the two girls sat many minutes silent, MP III 5 360 13
some little time, perhaps two or three weeks; but then I MP III 5 362 21
I have two favours to ask, Fanny; one is your MP III 5 364 32
a year or two, and sees others made commanders before him? MP III 6 368 8
Edmund too--to be two months from him, (and perhaps, she MP III 6 370 12
Their suspense lasted an hour or two. MP III 6 373 23
he delayed for a week or two longer a journey which he was MP III 6 373 25
And they think she will have her orders in a day or two. MP III 7 377 7
A stare or two at Fanny, as William helped her out of the MP III 7 377 8
her; and there were her two sisters, Susan, a well-grown MP III 7 377 9
I jumped up, and made but two steps to the platform. MP III 7 380 20
I was upon the platform two hours this afternoon, looking MP III 7 380 20
As he left the room, two rosy-faced boys, ragged and dirty, MP III 7 381 25
home; there remained only two brothers between herself and MP III 7 381 26
A day or two might shew the difference. MP III 7 382 29
her own two were the very worst, engrossed her completely. MP III 7 385 38
she gave it me to keep, only two hours before she died. MP III 7 386 44
Mrs. Norris, however, had gone home and taken down two old MP III 7 387 45
Of her two sisters, Mrs. Price very much more resembled MP III 8 390 5
In a review of the two houses, as they appeared to her MP III 8 392 12
Upon the whole Julia was in the best looks of the two, at MP III 9 394 1
I was in it two years ago, when it was Lady Lascelles's, MP III 9 394 1
struggling for at least two years, she yet feared that her MP III 9 397 7
was nothing alike in the two apartments; and she often MP III 9 398 9
was come for a day or two, was staying at the crown, had MP III 10 400 7
met with a navy officer or two of his acquaintance, since MP III 10 400 7
The conclusion of the two gentlemen's civilities was an MP III 10 402 13
regulation of it, as the two girls, he found, would have MP III 10 403 14
and after a time the two officers seemed very well MP III 10 403 15
proposed, I hope I foresee two objections, two fair, MP III 10 405 19
two fair, excellent, irresistible objections to that plan." MP III 10 405 19
in spite of this and the two or three other things which MP III 10 406 21
she wanted strength for a two hours' saunter of this kind, MP III 11 409 6
"And it is to be a two months' visit, is not it?" MP III 11 410 12
My uncle talked of two months. MP III 11 410 13
for me to be fetched exactly at the two months' end." MP III 11 410 15
Two months is an ample allowance, I should think six weeks MP III 11 410 16
waiting for the two months to be ended--that must not be MP III 11 411 16
around her; a friend or two of her father's, as always MP III 11 413 32
of him at Mr. Price's; and two days afterwards, it was a MP III 12 415 1
2
to Portsmouth, and these two said walks, and his MP III 12 415 2
I will say, then, that we have seen him two or three times, MP III 12 416 2
Seven weeks of the two months were very nearly gone, when MP III 13 420 1
I look upon her intimacy with those two sisters, as the MP III 13 421 2
beyond a brief question or two if she saw her daughter MP III 13 428 14
three months instead of two that she had been absent from MP III 14 430 6
a line or two of Cowper's Tirocinium for ever before her. MP III 14 431 7
If he is to die, there will be two poor young men less in MP III 14 434 13
Its object was unquestionable; and two moments were enough MP III 15 437 2
If two moments, however, can surround with difficulties, a MP III 15 437 2
mistake, and that a day or two will clear it up--at any MP III 15 437 3
They were the two on whom it would fall most horribly. MP III 15 442 21
Two posts came in, and brought no refutation, public or MP III 15 442 22
We have been here two days, but there is nothing to be MP III 15 442 23
from the inn, the other two were standing by the fire; and MP III 15 446 34
removed from Wimpole Street two or three weeks before, on MP III 16 450 8
The two ladies, even in the short time they had been MP III 16 450 10
What can equal the folly of our two relations?"-- MP III 16 454 18
He had suffered, and he had learnt to think, two MP III 17 462 4
Her temper was naturally the easiest of the two, her MP III 17 466 17
After what had passed to wound and alienate the two MP III 17 469 23
than possibility of the two young friends finding their MP III 17 471 29
to become, perhaps, the most beloved of the two.-- MP III 17 472 31
which under each of its two former owners, Fanny had never MP III 17 473 33

She was the youngest of the two daughters of a most E I 1 5 2
it must be better to have only one to please, than two." E I 1 10 29
"Especially when one of those two is such a fanciful, E I 1 10 30
Miss Taylor has been used to have two persons to please; E I 1 11 34
gallantry, and borrowed two umbrellas for us from Farmer E I 1 12 41
You have drawn two pretty pictures--but I think there may E I 1 13 43
family, which for the last two or three generations had E I 2 15 1
Her father never went beyond the shrubbery, where two E I 4 26 1
Two such could never be granted. E I 4 26 2
Two such she did not want. E I 4 26 2
a good deal; she had spent two very happy months with them, E I 4 27 4
of Mrs. Martin's having "two parlours, two very good E I 4 27 4
having "two parlours, two very good parlours indeed; one E I 4 27 4
of their having eight cows, two of them Alderneys, and one E I 4 27 4
A degree or two lower, and a creditable appearance might E I 4 29 14
I had imagined him, I confess, a degree or two nearer E I 4 32 30
Knightley, feelingly; and for a moment or two he had done. E I 5 37 9
You do not know it I dare say, but two or three years ago E I 6 43 13
admiration of her two companions would have been the same. E I 6 44 20
actually found, besides the two songs which she had lent E I 7 50 1
She was obliged to go the next morning for an hour or two E I 8 57 1
He came to the Abbey two evenings ago, on purpose to E I 8 59 27
may be the richest of the two, but he is undoubtedly her E I 8 62 39
They owed to him their two or three politest puzzles; and E I 9 70 7
There cannot be two opinions about him. E I 9 74 22
The two Abbotts and I ran into the front room and peeped E I 9 75 26
"Such sweet lines!" continued Harriet--"these two last!-- E I 9 76 37
"Leave out the two last lines, and there is no reason why E I 9 77 40
"Oh! but those two lines are"----- E I 9 77 41
slowly and distinctly, and two or three times over, with E I 9 78 51
two or three days are not to be taken out for the Abbey. E I 9 79 63
but so good a charade must not be confined to one or two. E I 9 82 81
82

be no possibility of the two friends passing it without a E I 10 83 2
But she had not been there two minutes when she found that E I 10 88 33
Well, I could not have thought it--and he was but two E I 11 96 24
Now, Mr. Knightley, a word or two more, and I have done. E I 12 99 11
and the little party made two natural divisions; on one E I 12 100 15
daughter; on the other the two Mr. Knightleys; their E I 12 100 15
that article as herself;--and two basins only were ordered. E I 12 101 19
or two to ask him about myself of some consequence. E I 12 101 27
visit to Donwell, with his two eldest boys, whose healthy, E I 13 109 6
such circumstances, fall short by two than exceed by two. E I 13 116 43
to her, "we want only two more to be just the right number. E I 14 119 6
7

I should like to see two more here,--your pretty little E I 14 119 7
to invite them once in two or three years, they always are E I 14 120 11
To you--to my two daughters, I may venture on the truth. E I 14 121 16
road impassable; and we are two carriages; if one is blown E I 15 126 10
of there being but two spare rooms in the house. E I 15 126 11
able to reply: and two moments of silence being ample E I 15 131 32
33

Elton had first entered not two years ago, to make his way E I 16 136 9
to take so active part in bringing any two people together. E I 16 136 10
superior creature of the two--and that to resemble her E I 17 142 9
that Frank's coming two or three months later would be a E I 18 144 2
so short a letter--only two pages you see--hardly two--and E II 1 157 10
two pages you see--hardly two--and in general she fills E II 1 157 10
By only raising my voice, and saying anything two or three E II 1 158 14
at all deafer than she was two years ago; which is saying E II 1 158 14
it really is full two years, you know, since she was here. E II 1 158 14
who could bring only the freshness of a two years absence. E II 2 166 10
on her arrival, after a two years' interval, she was E II 2 167 12
which for those two whole years she had been depreciating. E II 2 167 12
seemed to point out the likeliest evil of the two. E II 2 167 12
a whole evening by two such young women; sometimes with E II 3 170 2
Miss Hawkins was the youngest of the two daughters of a E II 4 183 9
in a great way, near Bristol, who kept two carriages! E II 4 183 9
Emma saw him only once; but two or three times every day E II 4 184 10
She had seen only Mrs. Martin and the two girls. E II 5 186 4
she had been measured last September, with her two friends. E II 5 187 4
She opened the parlour door, and saw two gentlemen sitting E II 5 190 21
an opportunity, while their two fathers were engaged with E II 5 191 28
not think so ill of any two persons' understanding as to E II 5 193 35
the sad evils of sleeping two nights on the road, and E II 5 193 35
graceful bow from the other, the two gentlemen took leave. E II 5 195 49
together for an hour or two--first round the shrubberies E II 6 196 2
for several minutes at the two superior sashed windows E II 6 197 5
but the last year or two had brought them a considerable E II 7 207 6
of her dress, to make the two ladies all the amends in her E II 8 213 6
believed (excepting one of two points) he could with time E II 8 221 49
was the most used of the two to yield; till a little E II 8 226 85
Two dances, unfortunately, were all that could be allowed. E II 8 230 101
and there were two points on which she was not quite easy. E II 9 231 2
"Oh! dear--I think you play the best of the two. E II 9 231 7
shop with her full basket, two curs quarrelling over a E II 9 233 24
The scene enlarged; two persons appeared; Mrs. Weston and E II 9 233 25
You could make it into two parcels, Mrs. Ford, could not E II 9 235 36
Harriet, to give Mrs. Ford the trouble of two parcels." E II 9 235 37
Voices approached the shop--or rather one voice and two E II 9 235 43
And, by the bye, every body ought to have two pair of E II 9 236 46
where as one of his trees--I believe there is two of them. E II 9 238 51
I could not stay two minutes. E II 10 244 45
only to walk with the two young ladies to Hartfield gates, E II 10 246 55
passed by the two young people in schemes on the subject. E II 11 247 2
two Miss Coxes five," had been repeated many times over. E II 11 248 4
"And there will be the two Gilberts, young Cox, my father, E II 11 248 4
will be three, and the two Miss Coxes five; and for five E II 11 248 4
The doors of the two rooms were just opposite each other. E II 11 248 10
May I hope for the honour of your hand for the two first E II 11 250 21
while she was gone, the two young people set off together E II 11 253 40
positively secured for the two first dances by the hero of E II 11 256 60
Two days of joyful security were immediately followed by E II 12 258 7
when writing to her nephew two days before, though from E II 12 258 7
great spirit to the last two weeks--indescribable spirit; E II 12 262 38
but I did assure him that two carriages were not necessary E II 14 277 36
that was--and of the two Milmans, now Mrs. Bird and Mrs. E II 14 277 40
She was a little shocked at the want of two drawing rooms, E II 16 290 3
The two eldest little Knightleys were engaged to pay their E II 16 292 7
"I have often thought them the worst of the two," replied E II 16 293 21
Better wait an hour or two, or even half a day for your E II 16 295 33
She could have made an inquiry or two, as to the E II 16 298 59
to prevent their making two distinct parties;--with so E II 17 299 1
I shall write Mrs. Partridge in a day or two, and shall E II 17 300 10
For two or three months longer I shall remain where I am, E II 17 301 19
The two ladies looked over it together; and he sat smiling E II 17 303 26
that she means to sleep only two nights on the road.-- E II 18 306 11
very, very seldom I am ever two hours from Hartfield, why E II 18 312 50
the most in love of the two, were to be returning with the E III 1 315 1
If a separation of two months should not have cooled him, E III 1 315 1
the blessing of having two months before him of such near E III 1 317 8
Two months must bring it to the proof. E III 1 317 9
Miss Bates and Miss Fairfax, escorted by the two gentlemen, E III 2 322 18
But two such offers in one day!-- E III 2 322 19
It was but a drop or two, but I am so afraid:--but Mr. E III 2 323 19
The two last dances before supper were begun, and Harriet E III 2 326 33
Two steps, Jane, take care of the two steps. E III 2 329 45
Well, I was persuaded there were two. E III 2 329 45
I was convinced there were two, and there is but one. E III 2 329 45
up for the demands of the two little boys, as well as of E III 3 332 3
iron sweepgate opened, and two persons entered whom she E III 3 332 3
by another road, a mile or two beyond Highbury--and E III 3 334 7
or not--except that of the two I had rather not see him-- E III 4 337 6
likely to remain there full two months longer, provided at E III 5 343 1
vain to be heard the last two minutes, "if I must speak on E III 5 345 16
The two other gentlemen waited at the door to let her pass. E III 5 346 17
two of his daily meals had, for forty years, been crowded. E III 5 347 18
one seemed so much disposed to employ as their two selves. E III 5 347 20
and distrust, to observe also his two blinded companions. E III 5 348 22
for one another, as any two beings in the world can be. E III 5 350 37
Two or three more of the chosen only were to be admitted E III 6 352 2
had failed her, that the two parties should unite, and go E III 6 353 3
or two spent at Donwell, be tempted away to his misery. E III 6 356 29
He had not been at Donwell for two years. E III 6 356 30
with many comfortable and one or two handsome rooms.-- E III 6 358 35
In two minutes, however, he relented in his own favour; E III 6 364 57
they could: but during the two whole hours that were spent E III 7 367 1
There are one or two, perhaps, (glancing at Mr. Weston and E III 7 370 19
original or repeated--or two things moderately clever--or E III 7 370 23
What two letters of the alphabet are there, that express E III 7 371 32
Hazel eyes excepted, two years more might make her all E III 7 373 51
away a tear or two)--but it will be very trying for us to E III 8 378 8
To take her--be it only an hour or two--from her aunt, to E III 9 390 16
even for an hour or two, might do her good; and the E III 9 390 16
Her mind was divided between two ideas--her own former E III 10 395 36
been known to no being in the world but their two selves." E III 10 399 60
of truth and honour, with two people in the midst of us E III 10 399 61
A glance or two between him and his wife, convinced him E III 10 400 69
difference between the two, as to me or as to anybody. E III 11 407 28
in his behaviour ever since those two decisive dances.-- E III 11 409 35
who now heard them; but the two latest occurrences to be E III 11 410 35
to be mentioned, the two of strongest promise to Harriet, E III 11 410 35
On the subject of the first of the two circumstances, she E III 11 410 36
She looked back; she compared the two--compared them, as E III 11 412 45
For a moment or two nothing was said, and she was E III 13 425 12
13

the most worthy of the two--or even the more simple E III 13 431 38
evening, she found one or two such very serious points to E III 14 434 4
I have already met with such success in two applications E III 14 437 8
We removed to Windsor; and two days afterwards I received E III 14 442 8
of the head; a word or two of assent, or disapprobation; E III 15 445 14
15

In such cases my interference was giving you two bad E III 17 462 9
in our estimation of the two,"--interrupted she, with a E III 17 464 22
of the two recommendations to Mr. Woodhouse's mind.-- E III 17 467 30
other--in another year or two, perhaps--it might not be so E III 17 467 30
They were going to take the two eldest boys to Astley's. E III 18 471 20
through the blind, of two figures passing near the window. E III 18 476 44
us with two characters so much superior to our own." E III 18 478 69
into a comparison of the two men, she felt, that pleased E III 18 480 80
married; forming altogether two handsome duodecimo pages, P III 1 3 3
4

Three girls, the two eldest sixteen and fourteen, was an P III 1 4 6
(having met with one or two private disappointments in P III 1 5 8
His two other children were of very inferior value. P III 1 5 8
by baronet-blood within the next twelvemonth or two. P III 1 7 12
had finally proposed these two branches of economy: to cut P III 1 9 19
Their two confidential friends, Mr. Shepherd, who lived in P III 1 10 21
were great, from the opposition of two leading principles. P III 2 11 2
Two material advantages of Bath over London had of course P III 2 14 10
house, with the additional burthen of two children. P III 2 15 15
beg leave to add, that two hours will bring me over at any P III 3 17 4
"Yes; it is in two points offensive to me; I have two P III 3 19 16
One day last spring, in town, I was in company with two P III 3 19 16
know, Sir Walter, some time back, for two or three years. P III 3 23 32
This meeting of the two parties proved highly satisfactory, P III 5 32 2
style; containing only two houses superior in appearance P III 5 36 20
The two families were so continually meeting, so much in P III 5 36 21
of four summers and two children; and, on Anne's appearing, P III 5 37 21
22

There was a numerous family; but the only two grown up, P III 5 40 45
With the prospect of spending at least two months at P III 6 43 3
She had no dread of these two months. P III 6 43 4
was not at home, but the two sisters were together; and as P III 6 48 17
abroad had worked its way to Uppercross, two years before. P III 6 50 28
captain, written the only two letters which his father and P III 6 51 30
that is to say, the only two disinterested letters; all P III 6 51 30
fine dashing fellow, only two perticular about the school- P III 6 52 33
they parted, that the two young aunts were able so far to P III 7 54 4
were repeated, when the two girls came with their father, P III 7 54 5
In two minutes after Charles's preparation, the others P III 7 59 25
there could have been no two hearts so open, no tastes so P III 8 63 3
and especially by the two Miss Musgroves, who seemed P III 8 64 4
Reported fit for home service for a year or two,--and so I P III 8 64 9
of me; and I never had two days of foul weather all the P III 8 65 16
The Admiral, after taking two or three refreshing turns P III 8 68 31
32

at his father's house, only two miles from Uppercross. P III 9 73 4
The two families had always been on excellent terms, there P III 9 74 6
Which of the two sisters was preferred by Captain P III 9 74 8
in the course of a year or two; and you will please to P III 9 76 15
The estate at Winthrop is not less than two hundred and P III 9 76 15
estranged, as might in two meetings extinguish every past P III 9 77 19
He had been absent only two Sundays; and when they parted, P III 9 78 19
The younger boy, a remarkable stout, forward child, of two P III 9 79 28
accepting must be the word) of two young women at once. P III 10 82 1
by the looks of the two girls, that it was precisely what P III 10 83 4
between Charles and his two sisters, that he, and P III 10 86 18
they walked side by side, nearly as much as the other two. P III 10 90 37
"He certainly means to have one or other of those two P III 10 92 44
and there must be intercourse between the two families. P III 11 93 2
to the memory of her two months visit there, but he was P III 11 93 4
of at Uppercross for two whole days, appeared again among P III 11 94 5
wound which he received two years before, and Captain P III 11 94 6
much past noon before the two carriages, Mr. Musgrove's P III 11 95 8
They had been a year or two waiting for fortune and P III 11 96 12
near the two inns as they came back, should be his servant. P III 12 104 7
and as unable as any other two readers, to think exactly P III 12 107 23
of a dead young lady, nay, two dead young ladies, for it P III 12 111 49
of not finding room for two or three besides, supposing P III 12 113 56
Between those two, she could want no possible attendance P III 12 113 56
The other two warmly agreed to what he said, and she then P III 12 114 62
to be soon followed by the two ladies. when the plan was P III 12 115 65
comprehending only two days, was spent entirely at the P IV 1 121 1
the receipt of a note or two from Lyme, which found their P IV 1 125 14
to suffer the most of the two; your feelings are less P IV 1 125 15
16

We asked him to come home with us for a day or two; P IV 2 130 5
from the tyranny of the two children from the cottage, P IV 2 134 29
be proud of between two walls, perhaps thirty feet asunder. P IV 3 138 5
had mentioned one or two things relative to the marriage, P IV 3 139 8
In all probability he was already the richer of the two, P IV 3 140 11
apparent by a glance or two between them, while Mr. P IV 3 140 11
"The notions of a young man of one or two and twenty," P IV 3 144 20
in Bath, who had the two strong claims on her attention, P IV 5 152 2
two years before, had left his affairs dreadfully involved. P IV 5 152 4
to one or two very poor families in this neighbourhood. P IV 5 155 9
And yet, here are two gentlemen stuck up in it mightily at P IV 6 169 25
into any comparison of the two friends," but the Admiral P IV 6 172 40
41

Mr. Elliot was attending his two cousins and Mrs. Clay. P IV 7 174 2
time to settle the point of civility between the other two. P IV 7 174 3
that she was betraying the least sensibility of the two. P IV 7 175 6
A day or two passed without producing any thing.-- P IV 7 179 32

Context	Work	Vol.	Ch.	Page	Para.
Sir Walter, his two daughters, and Mrs. Clay, were the	P	IV	8	181	1
We were only in anxiety and distress during the last two	P	IV	8	184	16
Sir Walter and his two ladies stepped forward to meet her.	P	IV	8	184	17
The party was divided, and disposed of on two contiguous	P	IV	8	186	23
"The Ibbotsons--were they there? and the two new beauties,	P	IV	9	193	8
But I never heard it spoken of till two days ago."	P	IV	9	197	36
least, till within the last two years of her life, and can	P	IV	9	200	57
that; it takes a bend or two, but nothing of consequence.	P	IV	9	204	82
came to Bath for a day or two, as he happened to do a	P	IV	9	206	90
This was agreed upon between the two friends, as the only	P	IV	9	207	90
and that he would be gone the greater part of two days.	P	IV	10	214	13
Henrietta, and Captain Harville, beside their two selves.	P	IV	10	216	19
or two, every thing seemed to be in suspense, or at an end.	P	IV	10	216	19
the term in question, the two families had consented to	P	IV	10	217	20
than the other; and to two of the three, at least, Charles	P	IV	10	217	20
should happen: and that of two sisters, who both deserve	P	IV	10	217	21
Money, you know, coming down with money--two daughters at	P	IV	10	218	22
They have not seen two such drawing rooms before.	P	IV	10	220	29
invitation was given to the two present, and promised for	P	IV	10	220	29
glances pass between two or three of the lady visitors, as	P	IV	10	222	37
friendly conference between two persons of totally	P	IV	10	222	39
Two minutes after her entering the room, Captain Wentworth	P	IV	11	229	2
					3
The two ladies continued to talk, to re-urge the same	P	IV	11	231	11
of the room from where the two ladies were sitting, and	P	IV	11	231	12
To lose the possibility of speaking two words to Captain	P	IV	11	238	47
two moments preparation for the sight of Captain Wentworth.	P	IV	11	239	55
again, and the other two proceeding together; and soon	P	IV	11	240	59
her away, and one or two subsequent moments, marked by	P	IV	11	244	71
When any two young people take it into their heads to	P	IV	12	248	1
She had but two friends in the world to add to his list,	P	IV	12	251	10
instead of depriving her of one friend, secured her two.	P	IV	12	251	11
& gratitude & while one or two of the men lent their help	S		1	365	1
length sir"--offering him the two little oblong extracts.--	S		1	366	1
There are two Willingdens in this country--& your	S		1	366	1
mile or two of a Willingden, I sought no farther . . .	S		1	367	1
Two hours take us home, from Hailsham--and when once at	S		1	367	1
A twinge or two, in trying to move his foot disposed the	S		1	367	1
your eye--the attempts of two or three speculating people	S		1	369	1
themselves & their mother. (two or three genteel looking	S		1	370	1
eldest of the two former indeed, by collateral inheritance,	S		2	371	1
Excepting two journeys to London in the year, to receive	S		2	373	1
pleasing young woman of two and twenty, the eldest of the	S		2	374	1
old lady, who had buried two husbands, who knew the value	S		3	375	1
what returns it will make her in a year or two.	S		3	376	1
delight to Charlotte, & two or three of the best of them	S		4	383	1
court of an old farm house, two females in elegant white	S		4	383	1
deal of imagination in my two sisters' complaints--but it	S		5	385	1
Two years ago I happened to be calling on Mrs Sheldon when	S		5	386	1
reckon on securing you two large families, one a rich West	S		5	387	1
Two large families--one, for prospect house probably, the	S		5	388	1
These two large families are just what we wanted--but--	S		5	389	1
she reflected that at two & twenty there cd be no excuse	S		6	390	1
library they were met by two ladies whose arrival made an	S		6	390	1
Miss Diana Parker's two large families were not forgotten.	S		6	392	1
milk--& I have two Milch Asses at this present time.--	S		6	393	1
there, seated on one of the two green benches by the	S		7	395	1
divided again--the two superior ladies being at one end of	S		7	395	1
She had read it, in an anxious glance or two on his side--	S		7	398	1
in considering the contrast between her two companions.--	S		7	399	1
us in the way they commonly do between those two parties.--	S		7	400	1
for them, but either of the two others are nice little	S		7	402	1
The two ladies continued walking together till rejoined by	S		8	403	1
I told you in my letter, of the two considerable families,	S		9	408	1
most desirable of the two--as the best of the good--prove	S		9	408	1
when I wrote to you;--but two days ago;--yes, the day	S		9	409	1
but Charlotte had only two or three veiws of Miss Diana	S		10	413	1
in her hand, took drops two or three times from one, out	S		10	413	1
from the hotel, bringing two heavy boxes herself, & Arthur	S		10	414	1
Mr & Mrs P.-- & Charlotte had seen two post chaises	S		10	414	1
Their visitors answered for two Hack-chaises.--	S		10	414	1
that two hack chaises could never contain a seminary.--	S		10	414	1
"What! said he--do you venture upon two dishes of strong	S		10	418	1
The two Mrs Griffiths!--	S		10	419	1
that there should not be two families; such a totally	S		10	419	1
There must be two families.--	S		10	419	1
had all entered Sanditon in those two hack chaises.	S		11	420	1
in the reports of the two, might very fairly be placed to	S		11	420	1
The other girls, two Miss Beauforts were just such young	S		11	421	1
round about, & added two steps to the ascent of the hill.	S		11	422	1
"He was just come from Eastbourne, proposing to spend two	S		12	425	1
was expecting to be joined there by a friend or two."--	S		12	425	1
the tallest of the two, Miss B.'s white ribbons might not	S		12	426	1
The house was large & handsome; two servants appeared, to	S		12	427	1
TWO'S (1)					
Another hour or two's snow can hardly make the road	E	I	15	126	10
TWO-AND-FORTY (2)					
"Poor Rushworth and his two-and-forty speeches!" continued	MP	II	5	224	53
ever want him to make two-and-forty speeches to her"--	MP	II	5	224	53
TWO-AND-TWENTY (1)					
She had been solicited, when about two-and-twenty, to	P	III	4	28	7
TWO-FOLD (1)					
Fanny's attractions increased--increased two-fold--for the	MP	II	6	235	20
TWO-PENNY (2)					
to get that letter conveyed for her to the two-penny post.	SS	II	4	161	5
The next morning brought Elinor a letter by the two-penny	SS	III	2	277	29
TWOFOLD (2)					
interest, in twofold motives, in views and wishes more	MP	II	13	300	7
at Jane Fairfax with twofold complacency; the sense of	E	II	2	167	13
TYING (1)					
being at once blushing, tying her gown, and forming wise	NA	II	6	165	5
TYRANNIC (2)					
at others again, so tyrannic, so beyond controul!--	MP	II	4	209	12
but as it was not the tyrannic influence of youth on youth,	E	I	2	16	6
TYRANNICAL (1)					
moral, so infamously tyrannical as Sir Thomas.	MP	II	2	191	10
TYRANNY (4)					
with few interruptions of tyranny; she was moreover noisy	NA	I	1	14	1
recommend parental tyranny, or reward filial disobedience.	NA	II	16	252	7
had known the pains of tyranny, of ridicule, and neglect,	MP	I	16	152	2
guarding from the tyranny of the two children from the	P	IV	2	134	29
TYTHES (3)					
anxious that his tythes should be raised to the utmost;	SS	III	5	293	2
the land, and rate of the tythes, to Elinor herself, who	SS	III	13	368	31
such an agreement for tythes as may be beneficial to	PP	I	18	101	71

UDOLPHO (17)
Have you gone on with Udolpho?" NA I 6 39 4
when you have finished Udolpho, we will read the Italian NA I 6 40 8
him; but while I have Udolpho to read, I feel as if nobody NA I 6 41 19
should never have read Udolpho before; but I suppose Mrs. NA I 6 41 20
"It is not like Udolpho at all; but yet I think it is very NA I 6 42 23
it was, "have you ever read Udolpho, Mr. Thorpe?" NA I 7 48 32
"Udolpho! NA I 7 48 33
"I think you must like Udolpho, if you were to read it; it NA I 7 48 35
"Udolpho was written by Mrs. Radcliff," said Catherine, NA I 7 49 37
over the pages of Udolpho, lost from all worldly concerns NA I 7 51 54
In spite of Udolpho and the dress-maker, however, the NA I 8 52 1
Oh! that we had such weather here as they had at Udolpho, NA I 11 83 15
exploring an edifice like Udolpho, as her fancy NA I 11 86 50
The Mysteries of Udolpho, when I had once begun it, I NA I 14 106 7
and now I shall never be ashamed of liking Udolpho myself. NA I 14 107 10
But now really, do not you think Udolpho the nicest book NA I 14 107 12
while we praise Udolpho in whatever terms we like best. NA I 14 108 17
UGLIER (2)
fretted herself thinner & uglier than ever, is still here, LS 32 303 2
two or three much much uglier in the shop; and when I have PP II 16 219 4
UGLY (7)
them how they did, and observed they both looked very ugly. NA I 7 49 43
Had he been even old, ugly, and vulgar, the gratitude and SS I 9 42 9
"Is it very ugly?" continued Mrs. Palmer--"then it must be SS I 20 111 17
And when her sisters abused it as ugly, she added, with PP II 16 219 4
But he is an ugly fellow! PP II 16 220 10
It is not ugly, you see, at this end; there is some fine MP I 8 82 34
a dreadful multitude of ugly women in Bath; and as for the P IV 3 142 13
ULCERATED (1)
the danger of catching an ulcerated sore throat herself! E I 15 125 5
ULTIMATE (3)
your health--and as much for your ultimate happiness, too." MP I 3 27 37
poor Mr. Bertram has a bad chance of ultimate recovery. MP III 14 433 13
likely to be necessary to each other's ultimate comfort. P IV 12 248 1
ULTIMATELY (1)
Ultimately have prevented the marriage, had it not been PP II 12 199 5
UMBRELLA (4)
How I hate the sight of an umbrella!" NA I 11 82 10
himself went out with an umbrella, there was nothing to be MP II 4 205 3
me directly; but he did not; he was busy with the umbrella. E II 3 178 52
see," (pointing to a new umbrella) "I wish you would make P IV 7 177 14
UMBRELLAS (4)
"There are four umbrellas up already. NA I 11 82 10
and borrowed two umbrellas for us from Farmer Mitchell's, E I 1 12 41
"I will see that there are umbrellas, sir," said Frank to E III 2 321 14
And there you will find we keep our umbrellas, hanging up P IV 1 127 26
UMPIRE (1)
umpire, was now added to the advantages of a quiet evening. P III 9 77 17
UN-AGREEABLE (1)
he was really not un-agreeable, and shewed even a warmth MP II 10 278 20
UN-ARMED (1)
Heaven defend me from meeting such a man un-armed."-- S 7 397 1
UN-INFLUENCED (1)
Emma was of course un-influenced, except to greater esteem W 362 32
UN-OSTENTATIOUS (1)
for an act of un-ostentatious kindness, there is nobody E II 8 223 64
UN-SMART (1)
very un-smart family equipage perceived a neat curricle.-- W 338 17
UNABASHED (1)
Lydia was Lydia still; untamed, unabashed, wild, noisy, PP III 9 315 4
UNABATED (4)
His medicines had failed;--the fever was unabated; and SS III 7 313 21
was unabated, I felt no doubt of their happiness together." PP III 16 371 40
and was discussed with unabated eagerness, every one's MP I 13 124 13
They continued together with unabated regard however, till E II 2 165 7
UNABLE (54)
Lady Susan was unable to express her sense of such LS 42 312 5
Unable of course to repress your curiosity in so NA II 5 159 19
they entered the hall, unable to leave the house without NA II 13 229 31
at being unable to get any smart young men to meet them. SS I 7 33 4
of a showery sky, and unable longer to bear the SS I 9 40 3
the ground, and Margaret, unable to stop herself to assist SS I 9 41 7
"Yes, for I am unable to keep my engagement with you. SS I 15 75 6
She got up with an headache, was unable to talk, and SS I 16 83 1
She turned towards Lucy in silent amazement, unable to SS I 22 129 15
Elinor, though greatly shocked, still felt unable to SS I 22 130 22
"You are expecting a letter then?" said Elinor, unable to SS II 5 169 21
of mind by such an address, and was unable to say a word. SS II 6 176 7
Marianne, now looking dreadfully white, and unable to SS II 6 177 12
The latter, though unable to speak, seemed to feel all the SS II 7 182 12
Elinor, unable herself to determine whether it were better SS II 9 203 9
compassion on being unable to see Edward, though he had SS II 11 230 4
to you, yet unable to prepare you for it in the least.-- SS III 1 263 29
her hand, which she was unable to read, or in lying, weary SS III 7 307 1
rising, confessed herself unable to sit up, and returned SS III 7 307 2
of joy, though still unable to speak, embraced Elinor SS III 9 334 4
Edward would still be unable to marry Miss Morton, and his SS III 13 369 33
Mrs. Bennet deigned not to make any reply; but unable to PP I 2 6 7
unable to accept the honour of their invitation, &c. PP I 3 9 4
She answered in the affirmative, and, unable to resist the PP I 18 92 18
would have been unable to give him a gentleman's education. PP II 12 200 5
and then Georgiana, unable to support the idea of grieving PP II 12 202 5
of her mind, wholly unable to ward off any portion of that PP II 18 231 18
overcome with confusion, and unable to lift up her eyes. PP III 3 269 10
On his quitting the room, she sat down, unable to support PP III 4 276 9
ease, which she felt very unable to equal in her replies. PP III 9 316 6
and when occasionally, unable to resist the impulse of PP III 11 335 43
She then sat still five minutes longer; but unable to PP III 13 345 12
13
of seeing *you* unable to respect your partner in life. PP III 17 376 35
Bennet sat quite still, and unable to utter a syllable. PP III 17 378 42
by Mrs. Bennet's being quite unable to sit alone. PP III 19 386 5
cried Mrs. Norris, unable to be longer deaf; "unless I had MP I 7 73 53
and finding herself quite unable to attend as she ought to MP II 4 214 46
am sorry to say that I am unable to answer your question. MP II 7 250 60
morning, Fanny, still unable to satisfy herself, as to MP II 8 256 14
distressed, and for some moments unable to speak. MP II 13 301 7
for love, and therefore unable to blame; and knowing her MP III 7 375 3
Fraser, and I at a distance, unable to help my own cause. MP III 13 422 2
the party broke up, being unable to move, had been left by MP III 13 426 10
unable to direct or dictate, or even fancy herself useful. MP III 16 448 2
"What news do you mean?" replied Emma, unable to guess, by E III 11 404 5
Emma looked at her, quite unable to speak. E III 11 404 9
several weeks, she was unable to give the full invitation P III 5 33 6
Lord Byron, and still as unable, as before, and as unable P III 12 107 23
unable, as before, and as unable as any other two readers, P III 12 107 23
In speaking of the Harvilles, he seemed unable to satisfy P IV 1 121 2
in a very humble way, unable even to afford herself the P IV 5 152 4
her friend's penetration, unable to imagine how any report P IV 9 194 19
"Oh! dear Mrs. Croft," cried Mrs. Musgrove, unable to let P IV 11 230 8
sit down on the bank, unable to stand--"there is something S 1 364 1
UNABSURD (1)
all that was real and unabsurd in the parent's feelings. P III 8 67 28
UNACCEPTABLE (1)
on having been no unacceptable companion myself, I must MP III 1 314 16
UNACCOUNTABLE (17)
What a strange, unaccountable character!--for with all NA I 1 14 1
thing like it, there must be some unaccountable mistake. NA II 3 144 11
and mean another all the while, was most unaccountable! NA II 11 211 15
of their behaviour to each other has been unaccountable! SS I 8 39 18
a continuation of that unaccountable coldness which she SS I 16 87 23
sex, that through some unaccountable bias in favour of SS I 20 112 28
It was an unaccountable business. SS II 10 214 9
Unaccountable, however, as the circumstances of his SS III 13 361 1
and unaccountable circumstances she had ever heard. SS III 13 364 10
and delays, from the unaccountable dilatoriness of the SS III 14 374 6
"Here's an unaccountable honour! cried eliz: at last. W 347 22
It is unaccountable! in every view it is unaccountable!" PP II 1 135 11
The most unaccountable business! E III 10 392 6
Very odd! very unaccountable! after the note I sent him E III 16 457 38
perfectly satisfied--unaccountable as it was!--that Robert E III 19 481 1
in the world, the most unaccountable and absurd! P IV 7 175 5
The words "unaccountable officiousness!-- S 9 410 1
UNACCOUNTABLENESS (1)
no service; as her unaccountableness was confirmed, his MP III 1 317 36
UNACCOUNTABLY (2)
led on, though so unaccountably, to mention the NA II 10 207 41
time did he most unaccountably follow me out of the room. SS I 8 39 18
UNACKNOWLEDGED (3)
what is meant at present to be unacknowledged to any one. SS I 16 84 9
lovers talked and laughed, the unacknowledged were silent. PP III 17 372 2
of pure, though unacknowledged friendship; it was a proof P III 10 91 42
UNACQUAINTED (2)
whom she was so wholly unacquainted, that she could not NA I 2 21 10
say, but since he is unacquainted with several parts of PP I 18 96 55
UNADMIRED (1)
Emma in the meanwhile was not unobserved, or unadmired W 328 9
UNADORNED (1)
of its meeting her eye, unadorned as it was by any such E II 13 266 5
UNADVISABLE (1)
that it would be highly unadvisable for them to meet at LS 26 295 3
UNAFFECTED (25)
more extensive and unaffected pleasure than those of any NA I 5 37 4
In a few moments Catherine, with unaffected pleasure, NA I 6 43 36
and is so thoroughly unaffected and amiable; I always NA I 7 50 47
simple professions of unaffected benevolence; thanking him NA II 15 242 7
The Miss Dashwoods were young, pretty, and unaffected. SS I 7 33 3
good opinion; for to be unaffected was all that a pretty SS I 7 33 3
to Barton Park with unaffected sincerity; and as he SS I 7 33 4
out her hand with the most unaffected good humour.-- W 330 11
he had a sensible, unaffected, way of expressing himself, W 335 13
had a pleasant countenance, and easy, unaffected manners. PP I 3 10 5
Elizabeth, easy and unaffected, had been listened to with PP I 6 25 24
its ground against the unaffected cordiality with which he PP III 2 261 5
natured, and as unaffected, though not quite so chatty. PP III 11 337 56
Elizabeth looked with unaffected astonishment. PP III 14 353 24
was new, attended with unaffected earnestness to all that MP I 9 85 3
Pleasant, good-humoured, unaffected girls. MP III 4 355 54
Good-humoured, unaffected girls, will not do for a man who MP III 4 355 54
weston, and a rational unaffected woman, like Miss Taylor, E I 1 13 44
plain, was strong and unaffected, and the sentiments it E I 7 50 4
With men he can be rational and unaffected, but when he E I 13 111 16
The subject followed; it was in plain, unaffected, E III 15 448 31
"Very good humoured, unaffected girls, indeed," said Mrs. P III 10 92 47
was a perfect gentleman, unaffected, warm, and obliging. P III 11 97 15
to say;" and the unaffected, easy kindness of manner which P IV 11 231 12
offers; & in an unaffected manner calculated to make the S 1 370 1
UNAFFECTEDLY (3)
being so genuinely and unaffectedly ill-natured or ill- SS I 20 112 28
Mr. Bingley was unaffectedly civil in his answer, and PP I 9 45 35
Bingley is most unaffectedly modest. PP III 16 371 45
UNAGREEABLE (1)
air--but not an unagreeable countenance--& tho' her manner S 6 391 1
UNALLIED (1)
in the world, and wholly unallied to the family! PP III 14 355 43
UNALLOYED (5)
pleasures untasted and unalloyed, and free from the NA II 14 237 20
was by no means unalloyed; his coming was a sort of notice W 347 22
impelled by unqualified, unalloyed inclination; by reason, PP II 11 192 22
to with such unbroken unalloyed enjoyment as by his wife, MP II 1 179 9
safely say, I have no pleasure so complete, so unalloyed. MP II 9 262 9
UNALTERABLE (3)
opinions not entirely unalterable, they are not, I hope, PP III 16 368 21
the spirit of each and every one is unalterable affection." MP III 14 435 14
of seeing her sister turn away with unalterable coldness. P IV 7 176 9
UNALTERABLY (2)
her marriage; no, I am unalterably fixed on that point, LS 19 275 4
And may you always regard me as unalterably yours S. LS 39 308 2
UNAMIABLE (1)
her so totally unamiable, so absolutely incapable of SS III 1 261 13
UNAMUSED (1)
Fanny looked on and listened, not unamused to observe the MP I 14 131 4
UNANIMITY (2)
prospect of acting the fool together with such unanimity. MP I 16 156 27
the continuance of such unanimity and delight, as had been MP I 18 164 1
UNANIMOUS (4)
"We are all unanimous in that wish, I suppose," said SS I 17 92 20
the ladies were unanimous in agreeing to go early to bed. SS II 4 164 20
leaving the three ladies unanimous in their sentiments on SS III 1 269 57
such a one as your family are unanimous in disapproving.' SS III 5 300 37
UNANSWERABLE (7)
I must have unanswerable motives for all that I had done! LS 22 282 6
The silence of the lady proved it to be unanswerable. NA II 7 176 16
artful. I have three unanswerable reasons for disliking SS I 10 52 28
To the possibility of motives unanswerable in themselves, SS I 15 79 28
he trusted would be an unanswerable argument with his PP I 23 128 10
unanswerable dignity, and coming farther into the room.-- MP II 5 221 37
"Your gallantry is really unanswerable. E III 7 369 15
UNANSWERABLY (1)
resolve to disallow, have been unanswerably proved to me. LS 36 305 1
UNANSWERED (3)
For a few moments she was unanswered. MP I 9 87 16
Such a conclusion could not pass unanswered by Mrs. Weston. E III 12 420 14
He had done,--and was unanswered. P III 10 88 27
UNAPPEASABLE (1)
that your resentment once created was unappeasable. PP I 18 93 32
UNAPPROACHABLE (1)
be in any doubtful, or distant, or unapproachable region." MP II 11 289 32
UNAPPROPRIATED (1)
the envied seat, the post of honour, was unappropriated. MP I 8 80 29
UNASKED (2)
to give me her opinion (unasked too!) on this subject; and PP I 19 105 10
from it; and Mr. Weston, unasked, promised to get Frank E III 6 357 31
UNASSAILED (2)
and with a judgment too unassailed by any attention to PP I 4 15 11
At a distance unassailed by his looks or his kindness, and MP III 6 370 12
UNASSISTED (2)
she had, by her own unassisted observation, already NA II 11 211 15
That a girl of fourteen, acting only on her own unassisted MP III 9 395 4
UNASSUMING (4)
perfectly correct and unassuming; and the whole party were PP I 15 72 8
"He is perfectly well behaved, polite, and unassuming," PP III 1 257 67
face, and her manners were perfectly unassuming and gentle. PP III 2 261 4
amiable, gentle, unassuming, conducting herself uniformly S 3 378 1
UNATTAINABLE (1)
animate, and reward those duties might yet be unattainable. MP II 8 255 10
UNATTEMPTED (1)
to leave nothing unattempted that might offer a chance of LS 42 311 2
UNATTENDED (6)
to be taken post by you, at your age, alone, unattended!" NA II 13 225 23
to ask her, when unattended to by any of the rest, whether PP III 2 262 9
of being suffered to sit silent and unattended to. MP II 5 223 48
without delay, and unattended by any alarming young man. E II 5 186 3

almost alone, and quite unattended to, in tranquil E III 7 374 54
At last Miss Elliot and her friend, unattended but by the P IV 7 176 10
UNAVAILING (3)
But her curiosity was unavailing, for no farther notice SS I 21 126 41
reflection would be long indulged, and must be unavailing. PP II 1 134 3
in excuse of my stay, but real, though unavailing, concern. PP III 4 278 20
UNAVOIDABLE (6)
no longer than was unavoidable, it had not produced the SS I 5 25 3
party; but at the same time declared it to be unavoidable. SS I 13 65 33
One meeting was unavoidable. SS II 9 211 35
duty, and to fret over unavoidable evils, or augment them PP II 18 232 21
her in Mrs. Goddard's unavoidable absences, and raise her E I 13 109 6
Quite unavoidable.-- S 9 407 1
UNAVOIDABLY (3)
in themselves, though unavoidably secret for a while? SS I 15 79 28
measure together, grew unavoidably better acquainted; Emma W 323 3
father's will, has been unavoidably acquainted with every PP II 12 202 5
UNAWARE (1)
Of this she was perfectly unaware;--to her he was only the PP I 6 23 12
UNAWARES (4)
unawares, without giving any notice, as generally happens." NA II 5 158 14
It came out quite unawares, quite undesignedly. SS III 9 336 12
It takes me quite unawares. MP III 7 378 10
may be taken totally unawares, by one of those dreadful S 4 381 1
UNBECOMING (6)
of the ladies with no unbecoming ease, & continuing to W 338 17
"but it is confined to his air, and is not unbecoming. PP III 1 257 68
for what can be more unbecoming, or more worthless, than MP III 6 368 8
it would not be unbecoming in her to make such a present. MP III 9 396 7
her unbecoming indifference to the languor of ill-health. E II 12 263 42
But, fair or not fair, there are unbecoming conjunctions, P III 8 68 30
UNBELIEVING (1)
on the unwilling and unbelieving ear of her friend, and NA I 4 32 2
UNBENDING (3)
self-consequence, or unbending reserve as now, when no PP III 2 263 10
were unbending, his attentions tranquil and simple. MP I 7 65 13
totally unconvinced and unbending, and of his feeling P III 4 28 5
UNBIASSED (3)
unbiassed opinion, by an eager sign, engaged her silence. SS III 11 349 5
of her own meditations, unbiassed by his bewildering MP III 6 370 14
accept another man from unbiassed inclination, it was not E III 19 481 1
UNBIDDEN (1)
themselves unbidden to your mind, I am persuaded. E I 7 51 11
UNBLEACHED (1)
The stain of illegitimacy, unbleached by nobility or E III 19 482 3
UNBLEMISHED (2)
a faith unbroken--a character unblemished, to Marianne. SS III 11 349 1
once to be as happy, as dignity unblemished could make him. PP III 15 361 3
UNBOUND (1)
the destruction of every unbound copy of "Lovers' Vows" in MP II 2 190 9
UNBOUNDED (3)
an unbounded affection, to be miserable for my sake." SS III 10 346 28
of your refusal, Fanny, seems to have been unbounded. MP III 4 352 44
of high conceptions, unbounded veiws, illimitable ardour, S 8 403 1
UNBROKEN (4)
After a couple of minutes unbroken silence, Henry, turning NA II 15 242 9
Nothing could restore him with a faith unbroken--a SS III 11 349 1
he listened to with such unbroken unalloyed enjoyment as MP II 1 179 9
separate candles and unbroken packs in the true style--and E II 16 290 3
UNCANDID (1)
He did not address himself to an uncandid judge or a NA II 15 242 7
UNCEASING (9)
In this unceasing recurrence of doubts and inquiries, on NA II 14 231 5
the day before had thrown them into unceasing delight. SS I 21 120 6
though it obliged her to unceasing exertion, was no SS II 1 141 5
on her side of her unceasing good wishes for his happiness SS III 4 290 43
The kindness, the unceasing kindness of Mrs. Jennings, I SS III 10 346 28
Lucy's marriage, the unceasing and reasonable wonder among SS III 13 364 10
of what an earnest, an unceasing attention to self- SS III 14 376 11
was very evident by the unceasing agitation of his W 330 11
but imagine that steady, unceasing discouragement from MP III 2 331 18
UNCEASINGLY (1)
and which continued unceasingly to increase till they NA I 9 66 32
UNCENSURED (1)
hoped at least to pass uncensured through the crowd. NA I 2 20 8
UNCEREMONIOUS (1)
It would be something so very unceremonious, so bordering MP I 8 78 23
UNCEREMONIOUSNESS (1)
her arms with all the unceremoniousness of perfect amity. E I 12 98 2
UNCERTAIN (25)
was uncertain, she fretted herself almost into a fever. NA II 4 151 13
But it is so uncertain, when I may have it in my power to SS I 13 65 36
must be at a very uncertain distance; and even secrecy, as SS I 15 81 44
preference seemed very uncertain; and the reservedness of SS I 18 96 1
displeased with his uncertain behaviour to herself, she SS I 19 101 2
the weather was uncertain and not likely to be good. SS I 19 109 40
his own prospects, his uncertain behaviour towards herself, SS II 1 139 1
remained as absolutely uncertain, as she had concluded it SS III 2 276 26
He was nice in his eating, uncertain in his hours; fond of SS III 6 304 15
By their uncertain light she thought she could discern it SS III 7 316 29
yet the event being uncertain, and possibly far distant, SS III 8 320 32
Though uncertain that any one were to blame, she found SS III 12 358 4
understanding, little information, and uncertain temper. PP I 1 5 34
fortune, and however uncertain of giving happiness, must PP I 22 122 3
and still hoped uncertain and at a distance, was felt with MP II 5 227 69
it even to Mary; while uncertain of the issue, he could MP II 13 300 7
It is very uncertain when my interest might have got MP III 1 316 28
The future must be very uncertain. MP III 2 331 16
What she was, must be uncertain; but who she was, might be E II 4 183 9
he, "it was quite uncertain when we might see him again, E II 18 308 27
in the chances of a most uncertain profession, and no P III 4 26 3
immediate wretchedness, such uncertain future good.-- P III 4 29 8
giving you, but I have been uncertain what I ought to do. P IV 9 198 52
53
"Yes, dear ma'am," said Mrs. Croft, "or an uncertain P IV 11 231 9
"I must go, uncertain of my fate; but I shall return " P IV 11 237 43
UNCERTAINTY (13)
year the uncertainty was very great of its continuing so.-- NA II 7 176 17
Every thing in such suspense and uncertainty; and seeing SS I 22 133 42
am not deceived by the uncertainty, the partiality of SS II 9 205 23
24
And so, he departed, delighted with the uncertainty in W 360 28
The vague and unsettled suspicions which uncertainty had PP III 10 326 3
and the very great uncertainty in which every thing was MP I 4 38 9
do it in the most complete uncertainty of any provision." MP I 11 109 20
and hoping in uncertainty--at the risk--in her opinion, E II 12 257 1
"Ah!--(shaking his head)--the uncertainty of when I may be E II 12 259 15
Mrs. Elton, whether the uncertainty of our meetings, the E II 18 309 30
lame carriage-horse threw every thing into sad uncertainty. E III 6 353 6
had to suffer from the recurrence of any such uncertainty. E III 19 481 1
of the uncertainty of all human events and calculations. P IV 5 159 23
UNCHANGED (4)
find you and yours as unchanged as your dwelling; and that SS I 14 74 19
your opinion on that point is unchanged, I presume?" SS I 17 93 29
My affections and wishes are unchanged, but one word from PP III 16 366 7
Her intentions were unchanged. E II 13 266 6
UNCHANGING (2)
the subject, with an unchanging complexion, dissented from SS III 1 265 33
and the transfer of unchanging attachments, must vary much MP III 17 470 26
UNCHECKED (3)
in her life, as in this unchecked, equal, fearless MP II 6 234 18
unchecked, ran eagerly through what she had to tell. E II 3 177 52
with true happiness, unchecked by that sense of injustice, E III 16 451 4
UNCHEERFUL (3)
and the air of the room altogether far from uncheerful. NA II 6 163 1
her eyes were red, her countenance was not uncheerful. SS I 15 77 21
serious, so earnest, so uncheerful, as seemed to say, that SS III 4 290 39
UNCIVIL (8)
The manner in which it was done so grossly uncivil; NA II 13 226 25
time, (which was still more common,) to make her uncivil. SS I 4 23 19
uncivil to her, and more teazing than usual to himself. PP I 12 59 4
and often uncivil, boisterously exclaimed, "good Lord! PP I 23 126 1
2
not this some excuse for incivility, if I was uncivil? PP II 11 190 10
and dull to a degree, that almost made her uncivil. PP III 12 341 14
always bordering on the uncivil, and I never spoke to you PP III 18 380 3
that Mrs. Wallis can be uncivil and give a very rude E II 9 236 46
UNCLE (206)
uncle should get anything from her, I am not afraid. LS 16 268 2
she speaks either to her uncle or me, for as we behave LS 17 270 5
Her kindhearted uncle you may be sure, was too fearful of LS 17 271 6
She arrived with her uncle last Thursday fortnight, when LS 19 273 1
feelings are much as both her uncle & I beleive them to be. LS 20 278 11
ever speaking to my uncle or aunt on the subject; & this LS 21 279 1
me never to speak to you or my uncle about it,--&--" LS 24 286 5
Do you think that your uncle & I should not have espoused LS 24 286 6
was her uncle; & all that could be urged, we did urge. LS 41 310 3
Frederica returned to Churchill with her uncle & aunt, & LS 42 312 6
Frederica was therefore fixed in the family of her uncle & LS 42 313 8
on the affections of his uncle, by such attractions as are SS I 1 4 3
He survived his uncle no longer; and ten thousand pounds, SS I 1 4 4
it turned out to be only the miniature of our great uncle." SS I 12 60 10
It may be only the hair of some great uncle of his." SS I 12 60 12
Mama saw him here once before;--but I was with my uncle at SS I 20 114 44
"And who was this uncle? SS I 21 126 41
"Your uncle!" SS I 22 130 25
"He was four years with my uncle, who lives at Longstaple, SS I 22 130 28
was often staying with my uncle, and it was there our SS I 22 130 28
the conduct of one, who was at once her uncle and guardian. SS II 9 205 24
Why would you be persuaded by my uncle, sir Robert, SS II 14 251 13
is due to them, as their uncle did so very well by Edward. SS II 14 253 24
is a rich old Dr Harding, uncle to the friend she goes to W 317 2
mama all lived with his uncle at Wickstead, that his uncle W 331 11
at Wickstead, that his uncle taught him Latin, that he was W 331 11
whisper aloud "Oh! uncle, do look at my partner. W 332 11
uncle is going within a mile of Guilford the next day.--" W 341 19
The evils arising from the loss of her uncle, were neither W 361 31
of hope & solicitude of an uncle who had formed her mind W 361 31
"I think I have heard you say, that their uncle is an PP I 8 36 15
Do let the portraits of your uncle and aunt Philips be PP I 10 52 57
Put them next to your great uncle the judge. PP I 10 53 57
dined lately with their uncle, a private had been flogged, PP I 12 60 7
you know, mama, that my uncle Philips talks of turning PP I 14 68 13
14
to the broad-faced stuffy uncle Philips, breathing port PP I 16 76 3
the profession which your uncle, Mr. Philips, appears to PP I 16 81 37
and the invariable kindness of my dear uncle and aunt. PP II 3 148 26
to accompany her uncle and aunt in a tour of pleasure PP II 4 154 21
the younger son of his uncle, Lord ---- and to the great PP II 7 170 7
were, her having one uncle who was a country attorney, and PP II 10 186 39
"My uncle is to send a servant for us." PP II 14 212 14
Your uncle!-- PP II 14 212 15
She is gone down to her uncle at Liverpool; gone to stay. PP II 16 220 10
Four weeks were to pass away before her uncle and aunt's PP II 19 239 10
own, and welcomed to them as visitors my uncle and aunt.-- PP III 1 246 6
could never be: my uncle and aunt would have been lost to PP III 1 246 6
At length, however, the question was asked by her uncle; PP III 1 246 8
and was grateful to her uncle for saying, "there are very PP III 1 248 31
32
back to look again; her uncle and aunt stopped also, and PP III 1 251 50
repeated appeals of her uncle and aunt, and seemed to PP III 1 253 55
every sentence of her uncle, which marked his intelligence, PP III 1 255 59
The observations of her uncle and aunt now began; and each PP III 1 257 67
well behaved, polite, and unassuming," said her uncle. PP III 1 257 67
a little whimsical in his civilities," replied her uncle. PP III 1 258 72
Her uncle and aunt were all amazement; and the PP III 2 260 1
surprise in her uncle and aunt, as made every thing worse. PP III 2 260 2
or hints from her uncle and aunt, she staid with them only PP III 2 264 12
letters came in; and her uncle and aunt, leaving her to PP III 4 273 2
I know my dear uncle and aunt so well, that I am not PP III 4 275 5
"Oh ! where, where is my uncle?" cried Elizabeth, darting PP III 4 276 6
Elizabeth," said her uncle, as they drove from the town; " PP III 5 282 1
"But now that my dear uncle is come, I hope every thing PP III 5 286 24
Jane ran to her uncle and aunt, and welcomed and thanked PP III 5 287 32
was going on, and their uncle promised, at parting, to PP III 6 294 2
what news? what news? have you heard from my uncle?" PP III 7 301 7
8
is, how much money your uncle has laid down, to bring it PP III 7 304 27
"Money! my uncle!" cried Jane, "what do you mean, sir?" PP III 7 304 28
Though our kind uncle has done something towards clearing PP III 7 304 35
The kindness of my uncle and aunt can never be requited. PP III 7 305 36
"it is all very right; who should do it but her own uncle? PP III 7 306 47
have been indebted to her uncle, for whatever of honour or PP III 8 308 1
My uncle and aunt and I were to go together; and the PP III 9 319 24
are to understand, that my uncle and aunt were horrid PP III 9 319 25
came to the door, my uncle was called away upon business PP III 9 319 25
know what to do, for my uncle was to give me away; and if PP III 9 319 25
Your uncle is as much surprised as I am--and nothing but PP III 10 321 2
from Longbourn, your uncle had a most unexpected visitor. PP III 10 321 2
next step was to make your uncle acquainted with it, and PP III 10 323 2
properly consult as your uncle, and therefore readily PP III 10 323 2
Your father was gone, your uncle at home, and, as I said PP III 10 323 2
it,) your uncle would most readily have settled the whole. PP III 10 324 2
But at last your uncle was forced to yield, and instead of PP III 10 324 2
assured, that your uncle would never have yielded, if we PP III 10 324 2
both she and her uncle had been persuaded that affection PP III 10 327 3
And so, my dear sister, I find from our uncle and aunt, PP III 10 327 9
mother's presence be what he was before her uncle and aunt. PP III 11 335 40
"He could be still amiable, still pleasing, to my uncle PP III 12 339 4
ashamed to find, that her uncle and aunt had already lost PP III 18 382 20
but the visits of her uncle and aunt from the city. PP III 19 388 12
of the match, and her uncle, the lawyer, himself, allowed MP I 1 3 1
as your uncle will frank it, it will cost William nothing." MP I 2 16 17
"My uncle!" repeated Fanny with a frightened look. MP I 2 16 18
to appear before her uncle, nor did her aunt Norris's MP I 2 17 21
The living was hereafter for Edmund, and had his uncle MP I 3 23 2
She cried bitterly over this reflection when her uncle was MP I 3 33 64
Three years ago, the Admiral, my honoured uncle, bought a MP I 6 57 31
was much disposed to admire, speak so freely of her uncle. MP I 6 57 32
"Oh! yes, she ought not to have spoken of her uncle as she MP I 7 63 4
An uncle with whom she has been living so many years, and MP I 7 63 4
I do not know that her uncle has any claim to her MP I 7 63 7
And you know there is generally an uncle or a grandfather MP I 9 92 40
Your uncle, and his brother admirals, perhaps, knew little MP I 11 110 26
take my opinions from my uncle," said Miss Crawford, "that MP I 11 111 28
you are known to think will be disagreeable to my uncle. MP I 16 155 15
considering only her uncle, she must condemn altogether. MP I 17 160 6
What would your governess and your uncle say to see them MP I 18 169 21
habitual dread of her uncle was returning, and with it MP II 1 176 4
to perform the dreadful duty of appearing before her uncle. MP II 1 177 6
She knelt in spirit to her uncle, and her bosom swelled to MP II 1 185 27
being to meet his uncle at Bath without delay, but if MP II 2 192 11
his uncle for attending them whenever he might be wanted. MP II 2 192 11
due to his uncle, his engagements were all self-imposed.-- MP II 2 193 18

"In my opinion, my uncle would not like any addition. MP II 3 196 3
than we used to be; I mean before my uncle went abroad. MP II 3 196 3
formerly were ever merry, except when my uncle was in town. MP II 3 197 3
I love to hear my uncle talk of the West Indies. MP II 3 197 5
Ask your uncle what he thinks, and you will hear MP II 3 197 6
"Your uncle thinks you very pretty, dear Fanny--and that MP II 3 197 8
your uncle never did admire you till now--and now he does. MP II 3 197 8
Nay, Fanny, do not turn away about it--it is but an uncle. MP II 3 198 8
more seriously, "your uncle is disposed to be pleased with MP II 3 198 9
It would have pleased your uncle to be inquired of farther. MP II 3 198 11
"To-morrow, I think, my uncle dines at Sotherton, and you MP II 3 199 17
I hope my uncle may continue to like Mr. Rushworth." MP II 3 199 17
with her uncle, was more than her nerves could bear. MP II 5 218 12
or staid?--but if her uncle were to be a great while MP II 5 218 12
the compliment is intended to your uncle and aunt, and me. MP II 5 220 28
triumph, she followed her uncle out of the room, having MP II 5 221 38
39
"The new dress that my uncle was so good as to give me on MP II 5 222 43
My uncle disapproved it all so entirely when he did arrive, MP II 5 225 58
which her uncle was most collectedly dictating in reply. MP II 6 232 12
of seven years, and the uncle who had done most for his MP II 6 233 14
William was often called on by his uncle to be the talker. MP II 6 236 21
My uncle says nothing, but I am sure he will do every MP II 7 250 55
"She was checked by the sight of her uncle much nearer to MP II 7 250 56
And turning to his uncle, who was now close to them--"is MP II 7 250 59
dance, made more than a momentary impression on his uncle. MP II 8 252 1
Thank your uncle, William, thank your uncle." MP II 8 252 2
My uncle meant it so." MP II 9 268 30
"Yes, that uncle and aunt! MP II 9 269 33
Her uncle and both her aunts were in the drawing-room when MP II 10 272 1
She was introduced here and there by her uncle, and forced MP II 10 273 7
strong, that though her uncle spoke the contrary, she MP II 10 275 11
be nearer her uncle, "I must get up and breakfast with him. MP II 10 279 28
change; and there her uncle kindly left her to cry in MP II 11 282 2
She sat and cried con amore as her uncle intended, but it MP II 11 282 2
in the same room with her uncle, hear his voice, receive MP II 11 284 8
"I only heard a part of the letter; it was to my uncle-- MP II 11 288 23
He knew his uncle too well to consult him on any MP II 12 292 9
the way of a rich, superior, longworded, arbitrary uncle. MP II 12 297 35
But though my uncle entered into my wishes with all the MP II 13 299 5
My uncle, who is the very best man in the world, has MP II 13 299 5
by my uncle, after the evening they passed together." MP II 13 300 5
haste towards the door, crying out, "I will go to my uncle. MP II 13 300 7
My uncle ought to know it as soon as possible." MP II 13 300 7
She rushed out at an opposite door from the one her uncle MP II 13 302 9
to go down and be with her uncle, and have all the MP II 13 302 12
a vast difference to his uncle, for it was unknown how MP II 13 304 19
how much he had cost his uncle; and indeed it would make MP II 13 304 19
"I understand," cried her uncle recollecting himself, and MP III 1 312 12
Fanny's colour grew deeper and deeper; and her uncle MP III 1 313 15
the sanction of the uncle, who seemed to stand in the MP III 1 314 16
to her uncle, in the utmost perturbation and dismay.-- MP III 1 314 16
tell her uncle that he was wrong--"you are quite mistaken. MP III 1 315 19
After such a picture as her uncle had drawn, for not MP III 1 316 28
She had hoped that to a man like her uncle, so discerning, MP III 1 318 38
In about a quarter of an hour her uncle returned; she was MP III 1 321 47
"Of course," continued her uncle, "it cannot be supposed MP III 1 321 48
She walked out directly as her uncle recommended, and MP III 1 322 50
She saw nothing more of her uncle, nor of her aunt Norris, MP III 1 323 53
these sort of hopes, her uncle was soon after tea called MP III 1 324 60
had been long used; her uncle read well--her cousins all-- MP III 3 337 10
"My uncle thought me wrong, and I knew he had been talking MP III 4 347 15
It proves him unspoilt by his uncle. MP III 4 350 30
She desires the connection as warmly as your uncle or MP III 4 351 36
That very evening brought your most unwelcome uncle. MP III 5 358 9
was intended, when her uncle first made her the offer of MP III 6 369 11
she kissed the hand of her uncle with struggling sobs, MP III 6 374 28
possession of herself, her uncle having given her 10l. at MP III 9 396 7
in speaking of her uncle as all that was clever and good, MP III 10 405 17
My uncle talked of two months. MP III 11 410 13
no notice, no message from the uncle on whom all depended. MP III 14 430 6
Her awe of her uncle, and her dread of taking a liberty MP III 14 436 15
"Her uncle, she understood, meant to fetch her; and as her MP III 14 436 15
her uncle and obtained his permission, was giving her ease. MP III 15 437 2
and others of the son and the uncle not letting him. E I 1 12 41
"And then their uncle comes in, and tosses them up to the E I 9 81 74
It is such enjoyment to them, that if their uncle did not E I 9 81 75
He is but young, and his uncle perhaps-----" E I 11 96 22
to come; but his uncle and aunt will not spare him." E I 18 145 7
a speech as that to the uncle and aunt, who have brought E I 18 147 17
died some years ago, an uncle remained--in the law line-- E II 4 183 9
right; he spoke of his uncle with warm regard, was fond of E II 7 205 2
his aunt where his uncle could do nothing, and on her E II 8 221 49
and cares!-- and if my uncle and aunt go to town this E II 12 259 15
And how could it be supposed that his uncle and aunt would E II 18 308 27
Your uncle and aunt will never allow you to leave England." E III 6 365 61
at once, own it all to his uncle, throw himself on his E III 10 398 51
a hurry to get back to his uncle, to whom he is just now E III 10 398 57
My uncle has been too good for me to encroach.-- E III 14 440 8
I must speak to my uncle. E III 14 443 8
I remember one evening the poor boys saying, 'uncle seems E III 17 465 27
that my uncle means to give her all my aunt's jewels. E III 18 479 70
whenever my uncle dies, he steps into very pretty property. P III 9 76 15
eagerly called out, "T'is uncle Sidney mama, it is indeed." S 12 425 1

UNCLE KNIGHTLEY (1)
much better with Uncle Knightley, who is absent from home E II 18 312 50

UNCLE'S (50)
I take on my lap & sigh over for his dear uncle's sake. LS 5 250 2
"Though we have seen him once or twice at my uncle's, it SS I 21 126 40
He was under my uncle's care, you know, a considerable SS I 22 130 24
"Did he come from your uncle's then, when he visited us?" SS I 22 134 47
a young man under her uncle's care, the son of a woman SS III 1 267 45
married in town, and now hastening down to her uncle's. SS III 12 357 2
off without being able to receive his uncle's suffrage.-- W 332 11
"My uncle's sense is not at all impeached in my opinion, W 352 26
The event has been unfortunate, but my uncle's memory is W 352 26
has erred--but my uncle's conduct was faultless. W 352 26
with her tears, my uncle's melancholy state of health.-- W 352 26
the officers, to whom her uncle's good dinners and her own PP I 9 45 36
their uncle's invitation, and was then in the house. PP I 16 75 1
In such an exigence my uncle's advice and assistance would PP III 4 276 5
has written to beg my uncle's immediate assistance, and we PP III 4 277 15
be done for Lydia, her uncle's interference seemed of the PP III 4 280 26
said Mrs. Gardiner, "I begin to be of your uncle's opinion. PP III 5 282 3
Oh! it must be my uncle's doings! PP III 7 304 30
"May we take my uncle's letter to read to her?" PP III 7 305 41
Had it been your uncle's doing, I must and would have paid PP III 17 377 39
how I have trembled at my uncle's opening his lips if MP I 3 27 36
In their uncle's house they had found a kind home. MP I 4 40 15
further trial at her uncle's house, to find another home. MP I 4 40 15
Certainly, my home at my uncle's brought me acquainted MP I 6 60 49
ridiculous stories of an old Irish groom of my uncle's. MP I 10 99 12
You are speaking what you have been told at your uncle's MP I 11 110 24
"It is about my uncle's usual time." MP II 2 193 14
If you cannot bear an uncle's admiration what is to become MP II 3 198 8
"My uncle's gardener always says the soil here is better MP II 4 209 16
and without the smallest hesitation on your uncle's side. MP II 5 219 25
herself alone; and her uncle's consideration of her, MP II 5 222 40
Mr. Crawford meant to be in town by his uncle's MP II 9 266 21
of the house; it was her uncle's; she knew it as well as MP III 1 312 4
But her uncle's anger gave her the severest pain of all. MP III 1 321 46
Her uncle's behaviour to her was then as nearly as MP III 1 323 53
hope, secondly, that her uncle's displeasure was abating, MP III 1 324 58
Her uncle's kind expressions, however, and forbearing MP III 2 331 17
None such had occurred since his seeing her in her uncle's MP III 3 343 40
To be sure, your uncle's returning that very evening! MP III 5 360 14
No, in her uncle's house there would have been a MP III 7 382 29
thing said or done in her uncle's house, and earnest MP III 12 419 8
such a preference of her uncle's house: it was always, " MP III 14 431 8
of her uncle's plantations, and the glory of his woods.-- MP III 14 432 9
who had quitted his uncle's house, as for a journey, on MP III 16 450 11
Her uncle's displeasure was terrible to her; but what MP III 16 452 14
Fanny was not in the secret of her uncle's feelings, Sir MP III 16 453 15
tacitly brought up as his uncle's heir, it had become so E I 2 17 7
conservatory without having both his arm and his uncle's! E II 18 306 11
and patience, and my uncle's generosity, I am mad with joy: E III 14 439 8
"I have some hope," resumed he, "of my uncle's being E III 18 477 57

UNCLES (4)
"If they had uncles enough to fill all Cheapside," cried PP I 8 37 18
Who are your uncles and aunts? PP III 14 356 52
up business, at the expence of your father and uncles. PP III 14 357 62
uncles and aunts pay for them in the course of the year. MP II 13 305 24

UNCLOSED (1)
enough to keep the eyes unclosed, they will be sure to E I 16 137 13

UNCLOSING (1)
Then here is my last"--unclosing a pretty sketch of a E I 6 45 21

UNCLOUDED (1)
in the brilliancy of an unclouded night, and the contrast MP I 11 112 35

UNCOMFORTABLE (43)
her thoroughly uncomfortable till she does accept him. LS 7 253 2
uncomfortable, & confirmed her in the plan of altering it. LS 42 311 3
"How uncomfortable it is," whispered Catherine, "not to NA I 2 22 12
with perfect serenity, "it is very uncomfortable indeed." NA I 2 22 13
It is so d---- uncomfortable, living at an inn." NA I 10 76 28
walking in a most uncomfortable manner to poor Catherine; NA I 13 99 9
Catherine's uncomfortable feelings began to lessen. NA II 1 136 50
ever told me so, but I am sure he is very uncomfortable." NA II 4 150 7
But is not your father uncomfortable about it?-- NA II 4 152 27
This was placing her in a very uncomfortable situation, NA II 5 155 2
him, he seemed so uncomfortable when he went away, with a NA II 12 217 2
and if her home be uncomfortable, or her fortune small, I SS I 8 38 10
place, and left an uncomfortable impression on Elinor's SS I 19 104 9
to manage in such an uncomfortable situation as I am; but SS I 22 128 9
in your manner, that made me quite uncomfortable. SS II 2 146 5
in spirits, she could not be very uncomfortable herself. SS II 5 167 7
who, though really uncomfortable herself, hoped at least SS II 12 232 14
made her feel particularly uncomfortable for some minutes. SS III 4 288 26
more heavy, restless, and uncomfortable than before. SS III 7 310 9
that he should feel so uncomfortable in the present case SS III 13 361 2
nor his home always uncomfortable; and his breed of horses SS III 14 379 18
she felt a little uncomfortable in the thought of all that W 322 3
Bingley was quite uncomfortable; his sisters declared that PP I 8 40 59
to suffer from the uncomfortable feelings necessarily PP I 21 115 1
I was uncomfortable enough. PP II 17 226 19
I was very uncomfortable, I may say unhappy. PP II 17 226 19
for all the uncomfortable hours, which the PP II 19 237 3
together, were some of the most uncomfortable of her life. PP III 1 252 52
Both sisters were uncomfortable enough. PP III 11 334 36
and though the uncomfortable feelings arising from all PP III 18 384 27
You know how uncomfortable I feel with her." MP I 3 26 24
seemed so decided, as to make Edmund quite uncomfortable. MP I 13 124 13
Many uncomfortable, anxious, apprehensive feelings she MP I 18 166 5
shy and uncomfortable when their visitor entered the room. MP II 13 303 13
It made her uncomfortable for a time--but yet there were MP III 11 409 5
Very uncomfortable she was and must continue till she MP III 15 438 7
She will grow just refined enough to be uncomfortable with E I 5 38 15
feeling uncomfortable and wanting him very much to be gone. E I 8 65 50
uncomfortable, and be an excuse for for his hurrying away. E I 15 126 11
happy wife together, without feeling uncomfortable. E II 16 291 5
now getting to the Box-Hill party, and grew uncomfortable. E III 15 447 21
And it is so very uncomfortable, not having a carriage of P III 5 39 39
but all that was uncomfortable in the meeting had soon P IV 5 153 6

UNCOMFORTABLY (2)
His sister, he said, was uncomfortably circumstanced--she NA II 5 157 5
known, or you will be uncomfortably circumstanced.-- NA II 10 202 7

UNCOMMON (20)
an uncommon union of symmetry, brilliancy and grace. LS 6 251 1
are united, it requires uncommon steadiness of reason to NA I 7 50 44
without personal conceit, might be something uncommon.-- NA I 10 72 8
great though not uncommon, from which one of the other sex NA I 10 73 22
to ruffle it in an uncommon degree; some disappointment, NA II 13 225 21
Lucy; for such a mark of uncommon kindness, vouchsafed on SS II 14 254 27
by that person of uncommon attraction, that open, SS III 9 333 2
You are charmingly group'd, and appear to uncommon PP I 10 53 65
"That is an uncommon advantage, and uncommon I hope it PP I 11 57 19
better; but his father's uncommon attachment to me, PP I 16 80 32
such instances of elegant breeding are not uncommon." PP II 6 160 3
of her uncommon good fortune in having such friends." MP I 1 10 13
is Fanny?" became no uncommon question, even without her MP II 4 205 1
is, perhaps, not uncommon; but to read him well aloud, is MP III 3 338 14
"A sermon, well delivered, is more uncommon even than MP III 3 341 28
Her daughter enjoyed a most uncommon degree of popularity E I 3 21 4
such collections on a very grand scale are not uncommon. E I 9 69 4
presents, of any thing uncommon--now we have killed a E I 3 171 16
17
It is a most uncommon complexion, with her dark eye-lashes E III 18 478 61
degree of hospitality so uncommon, so unlike the usual P III 11 98 16

UNCOMMONLY (20)
and Manwaring is so uncommonly pleasing that I was not LS 2 244 1
be got at market this morning, it is so uncommonly scarce." NA I 9 68 38
It is to be uncommonly dreadful. NA I 14 112 33
of his eyes, which are uncommonly good, and the g SS I 4 20 9
scale, and the rent so uncommonly moderate, as to leave SS I 4 24 21
his person, which was uncommonly handsome, received SS I 9 42 9
her complexion was uncommonly brilliant; her features were SS I 10 46 2
He seems an excellent man; and I think him uncommonly SS I 20 115 55
That was what I said immediately,--I was most uncommonly SS III 5 299 35
Blake's little boy, who was uncommonly fond of dancing.-- W 329 9
and there are several of them you see uncommonly pretty." PP I 3 11 10
to find it was rendered uncommonly intelligent by the PP I 6 23 12
that I expressed myself uncommonly well just now, when I PP I 6 24 17
18
as to think our two youngest daughters uncommonly foolish." PP I 7 29 11
"You write uncommonly fast." PP I 10 47 5
drily--"Mr. Darcy is uncommonly kind to Mr. Bingley, and PP II 10 184 23
"And yet I meant to be uncommonly clever in taking so PP II 17 225 17
"I have heard, indeed, that she is uncommonly improved PP III 10 328 22
I think every thing has passed off uncommonly well, I PP III 12 342 28
The day was uncommonly lovely. MP III 11 409 6

UNCOMPANIONABLE (1)
a mother and such uncompanionable sisters, home could not PP II 4 151 1

UNCONCERN (9)
With regard to herself, it was now a matter of unconcern SS II 3 158 20
The calm and polite unconcern of Lady Middleton on the SS II 10 215 12
Robert, who, by the gay unconcern, the happy self- SS III 5 298 32
letter, with the perfect unconcern with which her praises PP I 10 47 2
on her face with a calm unconcern which was not in the PP I 20 111 8
she added, with perfect unconcern, "Oh! but there were PP II 16 219 4
and with affected unconcern; "but it is not worth while to MP II 1 181 16
to the unconcern of his mother speaking entirely by rote. MP II 2 194 20
an air of affected unconcern; I always observe it whenever E II 8 213 10

UNCONCERNED (10)
she appeared perfectly unconcerned, & after chatting on LS 23 284 6
his daughter's being entirely unconcerned in the business. SS II 9 209 28

Bennet, "looking as unconcerned as may be, and caring no PP I 20 113 28
I am growing every moment more unconcerned and indifferent. PP II 17 225 13
tried to look calm and unconcerned when the two gentlemen MP II 5 226 64
to appear gay and unconcerned, "which every woman who MP II 11 288 28
to look cheerfully unconcerned, but was really feeling E I 8 65 50
Cole--he was looking on unconcerned; Jane was asked by E II 8 230 99
did not mean to stir, and tried to be cool and unconcerned. P IV 10 222 37
Elizabeth did nothing worse than look cold and unconcerned. P IV 12 248 1

UNCONGENIAL (1)
there being anything uncongenial in their characters, or MP III 2 327 5

UNCONNECTED (11)
their employments, unconnected with such as society SS I 7 32 1
of affording pleasure, unconnected with his general powers. PP II 2 142 19
he was asking some odd unconnected questions--about her PP II 10 182 1
be to know how a person unconnected with any of us, and (PP III 9 320 33
you, or to any person so wholly unconnected with me." PP III 14 358 68
She was safe; but peace and safety were unconnected here. MP I 17 159 6
He did not appear in spirits; something unconnected with MP II 9 268 27
in idle cares and selfish solicitudes unconnected with him. MP II 11 282 2
Mary's future fate as unconnected with Mansfield, as she MP III 6 366 4
found she was not quite unconnected in this country, any P III 3 22 25
Mr. Wentworth was nobody, I remember; quite unconnected; P III 3 23 33

UNCONQUERABLE (5)
After surmounting your unconquerable horror of the bed, NA II 5 159 19
at the time, a most unconquerable preference for his niece, SS III 13 362 5
doubtless are such unconquerable young ladies of eighteen (MP II 6 231 11
which she had deemed unconquerable a week before, for the MP II 11 287 17
aware that the cure of unconquerable passions, and the MP III 17 470 26

UNCONSCIOUS (9)
yet so unconscious, her grief and agitation were excessive. NA II 14 230 1
being the involuntary, unconscious object of a deception NA II 15 244 11
pretend to be unconscious, nor endeavour to be calm. SS I 4 23 19
No; you will continue the same; unconscious of the SS I 5 27 8
by remaining unconscious of it all; for she was as well SS II 11 221 4
When at last she returned to the unconscious Marianne, she SS III 9 333 3
him not only totally unconscious of the uneasy movements MP II 1 184 27
Emma could look perfectly unconscious and innocent, and E II 5 189 14
destiny, and quite unconscious on what her eyes were fixed, E III 8 384 32
33

UNCONSCIOUSLY (11)
Isabella, and Isabella unconsciously encouraging him; NA II 3 148 28
encouraging him; unconsciously it must be, for Isabella's NA II 3 148 28
herself could be, and unconsciously closed his book. PP I 11 56 12
It has been most unconsciously done, however, and I hope PP II 11 190 7
to have inspired unconsciously so strong an affection. PP II 11 193 31
refrain (though unconsciously) from giving a more willing MP II 7 238 1
Almost unconsciously she had now undone the parcel he had MP II 9 262 8
had, in fact, though unconsciously, been attributing many E I 12 107 62
She might have been unconsciously sucking in the sad E II 2 168 13
of her companions were at first unconsciously given. P III 10 91 43
he had been constant unconsciously, nay unintentionally; P IV 11 241 61

UNCONSCIOUSNESS (1)
and apparent unconsciousness, among the only three of her P III 4 30 10

UNCONSIDERED (1)
seeing how unknown, or unconsidered there, were the P III 6 42 1

UNCONTROULED (1)
Vain, ignorant, idle, and absolutely uncontrouled! PP II 18 231 18

UNCONVINCED (4)
But as for myself, I am still unconvinced; & plausibly as LS 3 247 1
Catherine was still unconvinced; but glad that Anne should NA I 14 115 55
"Indeed you injure me if you suppose me unconvinced. E II 8 218 42
on his side, totally unconvinced and unbending, and of his P III 4 28 5

UNCOQUETTISH (1)
brother, so pure and uncoquettish were her feelings, that, NA I 7 47 18

UNCORD (1)
of the Luggage, & helping old Sam uncord the trunks.-- S 9 407 1

UNCORDIAL (1)
proud-looking woman of uncordial address, who met her SS II 12 229 3

UNCOUTH (1)
surfaces strange and uncouth, which ought to be irregular SS I 18 97 4

UNCOUTHNESS (1)
abrupt manner--and the uncouthness of a voice, which I E I 4 33 32

UNCRITICAL (1)
for his part, to his uncritical palate, the tea was as NA II 7 175 12

UNCULTIVATED (1)
She has good natural sense, but quite uncultivated.-- S 3 376 1

UNDAUNTED (1)
He was quite as undaunted and as lively as ever; and after E II 8 212 2
3

UNDECEIVE (3)
Pray undeceive him as soon as you can, and tell him I beg NA II 3 145 13
"I have very often wished to undeceive yourself and my SS III 1 262 25
and if I endeavour to undeceive people as to the rest of PP II 17 226 23

UNDECEIVED (1)
I am undeceived in time! NA II 10 202 7

UNDECEIVING (1)
No time was to be lost in undeceiving her, in making her SS III 1 260 10

UNDECIDED (6)
Perhaps just at present he may be undecided; the smallness SS II 11 223 24
One question after this only remained undecided, between SS III 13 369 32
certain event, of which the time alone could be undecided. PP II 12 197 5
she had begun to feel undecided as to what she ought to do; MP I 16 152 3
which could neither be undecided nor dilatory, but now he E III 9 386 7
coast of Sussex, but was undecided as to the where, wanted S 9 408 1

UNDEFINED (2)
on the other of undefined discovery, all equally acute. NA I 15 121 25
of self-condemnation or undefined alarm, every other heart MP II 1 175 1

UNDENIABLE (1)
business--undeniable character--respectable references-- S 1 366 1

UNDENIABLY (1)
healthy as they all undeniably were--foresaw that every S 2 373 1

UNDER (323)
where I shall deposit her under the care of Miss Summers LS 2 246 1
to him, it must be under cover to you. yours ever, s. a. LS 5 250 3
I wish you could get Reginald home again, under any LS 11 259 1
to which I should hardly stoop under any circumstances. LS 12 261 4
I shall feel myself under an obligation to anyone who is LS 24 286 4
leaving the house under a false impression of her conduct. LS 24 287 9
Sir James is certainly under par--(his boyish manners make LS 24 288 11
I shall probably put off his arrival, under some pretence LS 29 299 2
meeting, I yet feel myself under the necessity of delaying LS 30 299 1
the imposition I have been under, & the absolute necessity LS 34 304 1
Under such circumstances you could not act otherwise. LS 39 307 1
that they were written under her mother's inspection, & LS 42 311 1
such a mother, & placed under her own care; & tho' with LS 42 311 2
Under these unpromising auspices, the parting took place, NA I 2 19 4
under it what particularly dignifies her character. NA I 8 53 2
herself sincerely on being under the care of so excellent NA I 9 62 10
thousands of times before, under that roof, in every Bath NA I 10 72 8
does not actually pass under one's own observation; and as NA I 14 109 23
which had been formed under their eye, and sent therefore NA II 2 140 11
she was to be for weeks under the same roof with the NA II 2 141 11
mounted, sunk a little under this consequent inconvenience. NA II 5 156 4
she was actually under the Abbey walls, was springing, NA II 5 161 25
his own inclination, under a mistaken idea of pleasing her; NA II 7 177 17
Having taken her into every division, and led her under NA II 7 179 27
to descend and meet him under the protection of visitors. NA II 9 192 4
There were still some subjects indeed, under which she NA II 10 201 4
warmly, "must be a comfort to him under any distress." NA II 10 204 14
and comforting herself under the unpleasant impression his NA II 13 222 8
least they should not meet under such circumstances as NA II 13 222 8
Direct to me at Lord Longtown's, and, I must ask it, under NA II 13 228 28
which she had first looked under impressions so different. NA II 14 230 1
Under a mistaken persuasion of her possessions and claims, NA II 15 244 11
of Miss Morland's being under their care, and--as soon as NA II 15 245 12
again in town, and who, under the influence of exactly NA II 15 246 12
and comfort, and under every pecuniary view, it was a NA II 16 249 2
when she was suffering under the cold and unfeeling SS I 4 23 20
under a cold invitation to her to defer her departure. SS I 5 27 6
of any change in those who walk under your shade!-- SS I 5 27 8
first seeing the place under the advantage of good weather, SS I 6 28 2
valley in that direction; under another name, and in SS I 6 29 3
was not suffering under the insatiable appetite of fifteen. SS I 7 32 2
But how is your acquaintance to be long supported, under SS I 10 47 4
The whole story would have been speedily formed under her SS I 11 57 17
Then, and then only, under such a roof, I might perhaps be SS I 14 73 13
"I flatter myself," replied Elinor, "that even under the SS I 14 73 14
from being of the party under some trifling pretext of SS I 15 75 1
I am now suffering under a very heavy disappointment!" SS I 15 75 4
in every part of England, under every possible variation SS I 21 119 3
"unless it had been under totally different circumstances. SS I 21 122 12
He was under my uncle's care, you know, a considerable SS I 22 130 24
"but I can give you no advice under such circumstances. SS I 22 133 45
letter, could subsist only under a positive engagement, SS I 22 134 53
"I did;" said Elinor, with a composure of voice, under SS I 22 135 55
she could even now, under the first smart of the heavy SS II 1 140 4
liberty among themselves under the tranquil and well-bred SS II 1 143 9
judged, she might safely, under the shelter of its noise, SS II 1 145 23
of all your mutual affection to support you under them. SS II 2 146 6
as between many people and under many circumstances it SS II 2 147 8
You will be under the care of a motherly good sort of SS II 3 156 8
a journey to London under her protection, and as her guest, SS II 4 159 1
to do away, knew not how, under such circumstances, to SS II 5 170 27
from her infancy, and under the guardianship of my father. SS II 9 205 24
I had hoped that her regard for me would support her under SS II 9 205 24
under a similar confinement, was my unfortunate sister. SS II 9 207 26
I saw her placed in comfortable lodgings, and under proper SS II 9 207 26
from school, to place her under the care of a very SS II 9 208 28
her fortitude under it, must strengthen every attachment. SS II 9 210 32
she would bear up with fortitude under this misfortune. SS II 10 213 2
who almost all laboured under one or other of these SS II 12 233 18
her from suffering under any other of Mrs. Ferrars's SS II 13 238 1
disposed as to determine, under pretence of fetching SS II 13 241 23
judgment, to place Edward under private tuition, at the SS II 14 251 13
reach the young ladies under your care as to their SS III 1 258 5
discovery that took place under our roof yesterday." SS III 1 265 34
with a young man under her uncle's care, the son of a SS III 1 267 45
the house itself was under the guardianship of the fir, SS III 6 302 7
her companion, was still under her care, and she was known SS III 7 313 20
more difficult to bury under exterior calmness, than all SS III 7 314 22
under it are only triumph and exultation to me now. SS III 8 324 45
for any changes in it under a great length of time, and SS III 9 338 20
of fortitude under them had almost led me to the grave. SS III 10 345 28
his distress, and been under the influence of his SS III 11 349 2
He would then have suffered under the pecuniary distresses SS III 11 351 13
She feared that under this persuasion she had been unjust, SS III 11 356 46
existence of each, under such a blow, with grateful wonder. SS III 13 371 38
no less than herself under the event of a former SS III 14 378 15
it was infinitely more so under this sudden reverse;--he W 330 11
Ld Osborne himself came & under pretence of talking to W 331 11
tho' shrinking under a general sense of inferiority, she W 345 21
passed;--a little peevish under immediate pain, & ill W 348 22
paved Footway which led under the windows of the house to W 355 28
Margt in the joy of her heart under circumstances, which W 360 29
to conceal her vexation under the disappointment, or W 360 30
was all in pursuit of Mr. Bingley, and under your orders." PP I 7 31 31
think the better of me, if under such a circumstance I PP I 10 49 31
of mind, pride will be always under good regulation." PP I 11 57 24
his life having been spent under the guidance of an PP I 15 70 1
the way across the street, under pretence of wanting PP I 15 72 8
Mr. Darcy often acknowledged himself to be under the PP I 16 81 37
and she felt capable under such circumstances, of PP I 18 98 63
and quitted the house under the delightful persuasion that, PP I 18 103 77
As for Jane, her anxiety under this suspence was, of PP I 23 129 14
"Well, then, you need not be under any alarm. PP II 3 144 5
to be Lady Catherine, and under the apprehension was PP II 9 177 1
her family under less than half the present distance." PP II 9 179 22
is under his sole care, he may do what he likes with her." PP II 10 184 17
Or under what misrepresentation, can you here impose upon PP II 11 191 17
is due to myself, I am under the necessity of relating PP II 12 197 5
I know not in what manner, under what form of falsehood he PP II 12 202 5
for those casual errors, under which she would endeavour PP II 13 206 4
Catherine, weak-spirited, irritable, and completely under PP II 14 213 17
the inn, was under frequent discussion between her parents. PP II 16 223 26
to her family as under the present circumstances." PP II 18 230 14
15
much too full of lines under the words to be made public. PP II 19 238 5
boys, were to be left under the particular care of their PP II 19 239 10
Elizabeth hesitated, but her knees trembled under her, and PP III 4 276 8
Her power was sinking; every thing must sink under such a PP III 4 278 19
she meant well, but , under such a misfortune as this, one PP III 5 293 67
you are now suffering under, of which we were yesterday PP III 6 296 11
or that may comfort you, under a circumstance that must be PP III 6 296 11
which Mr. Gardiner's behaviour laid them all under. PP III 7 306 45
Under such circumstances, however, he was not likely to be PP III 10 323 2
to know that they were under obligations to a person who PP III 10 326 3
Nor was it under many, many minutes, that she could PP III 17 378 42
My good qualities are under your protection, and you are PP III 18 381 7
such an income as theirs, under the direction of two PP III 19 387 8
society of this country under such very favourable MP I 1 6 6
to town by the coach, under the care of any creditable MP I 1 8 8
Under this infatuating principle, counteracted by no real MP I 1 8 9
cousin William, and sent him half a guinea under the seal. MP I 2 16 20
unnecessary, for they were under the care of a governess, MP I 2 20 31
so like a parent's care, under the influence of a MP I 4 38 9
to bring his mistress under his own roof; and to this Mrs. MP I 4 41 15
"Yes, the profession is well enough under two MP I 6 60 51
The subject of improving grounds meanwhile was still under MP I 6 60 53
one more sensible of the disadvantages she has been under. MP I 7 64 9
I am sure William would never have used me so, under any MP I 7 64 10
Mrs. Rushworth proceeded next, under the conviction that MP I 8 76 7
The whole party rose accordingly, and under Mrs. MP I 9 84 3
"The mind which does not struggle against itself under one MP I 9 88 18
She looked almost aghast under the new idea she was MP I 9 89 26
part of her education, made her miserable under it. MP I 9 91 36
nor my memory of they past under such easy dominion as one MP I 10 98 10
at last; and had been sitting down under one of the trees. MP I 10 103 49
preferred, comforted her under it, and enabled her to MP I 10 105 52
I shall get the dairy maid to set them under the first MP I 10 106 57
a great many more people under his command than he has now, MP I 11 111 30
No want of under strappers----- MP I 13 129 38
under the agitations of jealousy, without great pity. MP I 14 136 20
conversed together in an under voice, and the declaration MP I 14 136 21
Miss Crawford in an under voice, to Fanny, after some MP I 15 149 61
sinking under her aunt's unkind reflection and reproach. MP I 16 150 1
unsteadiness; and his happiness under it made her wretched. MP I 17 159 6
were likely to endure under the disappointment of a dear, MP I 17 162 19
the same, the sisters, under such a trial as this, had not MP I 17 162 19
She worked very diligently under her aunt's directions, MP I 18 168 14
Her spirits sank under the glow of theirs, and she felt MP I 18 170 24
other heart was sinking under some degree of self- MP II 1 175 1
the other three, no longer under any restraint, were MP II 1 176 4
did yet mean to stay a few days longer under his roof. MP II 2 191 10
Tom, ask the latter in an under voice, whether there were MP II 2 192 11

branch of the subject was under discussion, Maria, who MP II 2 193 17
the tumult of her feelings under the restraint of society; MP II 2 193 18
Under his government, Mansfield was an altered place. MP II 3 196 1
Nothing could be objected to when it came under the MP II 3 203 29
of the niece who had been brought up under her eye. MP II 3 203 30
to find shelter under the branches and lingering leaves of MP II 4 205 3
in the country, under certain circumstances--very pleasant. MP II 4 210 21
delightfully; but sink it under the chill, the MP II 4 211 24
the remaining six, under Miss Crawford's direction, were MP II 7 239 8
only answer, in an under voice, not meant to reach far, MP II 7 246 35
to sober her spirits even under the prospect of a ball MP II 8 254 8
To her, he could be nothing under any circumstances-- MP II 9 264 18
more at ease, but under circumstances of less novelty, MP II 9 266 22
was often under the influence of much less sanguine views. MP II 9 267 22
have been at least languid under any other circumstances, MP II 10 273 5
While her hand was trembling under these letters, her eye MP II 13 299 4
found that Mr. Crawford, under pretence of receiving the MP II 13 307 32
hurry you," said he, in an under voice, perceiving the MP II 13 307 33
have;" but her heart sunk under the appalling prospect of MP III 1 317 38
of her being never under any circumstances able to love Mr. MP III 2 329 10
her for what she had done under the influence of her MP III 3 335 6
you are ever present to my imagination under any other? MP III 3 344 41
Under the disadvantages, indeed, which both have had, is MP III 4 350 32
we meet again, it will be under circumstances which may MP III 5 364 30
And as to the not missing her, which under Mrs. Norris's MP III 6 371 14
When no longer under the same roof with Edmund, she MP III 7 376 4
kitchen, much hope of any under a considerable period, MP III 7 381 24
out at sudden starts immediately under their father's eye. MP III 7 383 31
a girl under her, and I often do half the work myself." MP III 7 385 39
them with an arm of each under his, and she did not know MP III 11 409 5
thing looked so beautiful under the influence of such a MP III 11 409 6
careless of the circumstances under which she felt them. MP III 11 409 6
his experiment farther, lest she might die under the cure. MP III 11 413 30
under any other distress, I should turn to for consolation. MP III 13 422 2
for us, my dear Fanny, under these distressing MP III 13 426 11
under different degrees of danger, lasted several weeks. MP III 14 432 11
a clergyman, it seemed, under certain conditions of wealth; MP III 14 436 16
to support life and reason under such disgrace; and it MP III 15 442 21
May God support you under <u>your</u> share. MP III 15 442 23
He looked very ill; evidently suffering under violent MP III 15 445 30
with her aunts and Tom, under so dreadful a humiliation; MP III 15 446 35
nephew, and all the house under her care, had been an MP III 16 448 2
Under any circumstances it would have been an unwelcome MP III 16 452 13
into such difficulties, under the idea of being really MP III 16 454 18
After wandering about and sitting under trees with Fanny MP III 17 462 5
a marriage contracted under such circumstances as to make MP III 17 464 12
the parsonage there, which under each of its two former MP III 17 473 33
old lady, under such untoward circumstances, can excite. E I 3 21 4
talents, and must have been under subjection to her." E I 5 37 9
I beg your pardon, perhaps I have been under a mistake. E I 7 52 13
Does any body else occur to you at this moment under such E I 7 53 21
of Highbury in general should be put under requisition. E I 9 70 7
This would not do; she immediately stopped, under pretence E I 10 88 33
nerves could not have born under any other cause, nor have E I 11 92 3
and women, and as little under the power of fancy and whim E I 12 98 4
English style, burying under a calmness that seemed all E I 12 99 14
home himself, and keep all under shelter that he can;-- E I 13 113 26
my part, I would rather, under such circumstances, fall E I 13 116 43
<u>man's</u> being being under such restraint, as not to be able E I 14 122 22
<u>coldly</u> and proudly; and, under indescribable irritation of E I 15 132 37
like Emma's, though under temporary gloom at night, the E I 16 137 13
the impossibility he was under, from various circumstances E I 17 140 2
so equal under particular circumstances to act up to it." E I 18 148 19
and here it is, only just under my huswife--and since you E II 1 157 10
on hurrying away directly under some slight excuse, when E II 1 158 13
under consumption and grief soon afterwards--and this girl. E II 2 163 2
varying spirits, seemed, under the most favourable E II 2 165 9
Manners were all that could be safely judged of, under a E II 2 169 17
place the Martins under proper subordination in her fancy. E II 3 180 57
course, to the first, as under such circumstances what is E II 4 181 3
Bath, was to be seen under the operation of being lifted E II 5 186 1
observe it whenever I meet you under those circumstances. E II 8 213 10
nature, sir, because it will be under Mrs. Weston's care. E II 11 252 36
her going into public under the auspices of a friend of E II 14 275 33
own share in the story, under a colouring the least E II 15 282 3
friend of Mrs. Elton, nor, under Mrs. Elton's guidance, E II 15 284 11
"To chuse to remain here month after month, under E II 15 285 13
"She must be under some sort of penance, inflicted either E II 15 285 15
or deed; or in her being under any restraint beyond her E II 15 288 39
friendship, were long under discussion; and to them E II 17 299 1
Her nerves were under continual irritation and suffering; E III 1 317 7
words, were soon lost under the incessant flow of Miss E III 2 322 18
not finished her speech under many minutes after her being E III 2 322 18
I deserve to be under a continual blush all the rest of my E III 4 339 13
ourselves, and sit under trees;--and whatever else you may E III 6 355 20
Under that peculiar sort of dry, blunt manner, I know you E III 6 356 28
Mr. Woodhouse must not, under the specious pretence of a E III 6 356 29
to box hill was again under happy consideration; and at E III 6 357 32
Under a bright mid-day sun, at almost midsummer, Mr. E III 6 357 33
comfort, seen under a sun bright, without being oppressive. E III 6 360 39
Emma looked at Harriet while the point was under E III 6 361 41
"You are comfortable because you are under command." E III 7 368 9
your temper under your own command rather than mine." E III 7 369 11
and that she was suffering under severe headachs, and a E III 9 389 16
very day on which she had, under the plea of being unequal E III 9 391 21
They must both have suffered a great deal under such a E III 10 398 53
Fairfax, I never could, under any blunder, have spoken ill E III 10 399 64
of course, the same origin, must be equally under cure.-- E III 11 403 2
had been thus practising on herself, and living under!-- E III 11 411 43
she had been entirely under a delusion, totally ignorant E III 11 412 45
of disposition, which, under any other circumstances, E III 12 419 12
Emma was almost ready to sink under the agitation of this E III 13 430 36
See me, then, under these circumstances, arriving on my E III 14 437 8
have been quite without resentment under such a stroke. E III 16 451 2
she was quite eager to have Harriet under her care.-- E III 16 451 3
heard you speak of, as under the patronage of your sister E III 16 456 32
She was aware herself, that, parting under any other E III 17 463 15
little alarm she had been under, the evening before, from E III 18 479 73
me the report, is passing under her eye--that the whole E III 18 480 77
have been under wretched alarm every night of his life. E III 19 483 10
and consideration under his present difficulties. P III 2 11 2
But it was not a merely selfish caution, under which she P III 4 27 5
was her chief consolation, under the misery of a parting-- P III 4 28 5
She was persuaded that under every disadvantage of P III 4 29 8
gradually growing shabby, under the influence of four P III 5 37 21
22

from the Laconia he had, under the influence of his P III 6 51 30
having been six months under his care, and mentioning him P III 6 52 33
seeing Captain Wentworth under his own roof, and welcoming P III 7 53 1
Mr. Musgrove, no longer under the first uneasiness about P III 7 54 5
Perhaps indifferent, if indifference could exist under P III 7 58 21
an excellent correspondent, while he was under your care! P III 8 67 27
on board; and no ship, under my command, shall ever convey P III 8 69 35
but she had staid at home, under the mixed plea of a head- P III 9 77 17
under the constant dependance of seeing him to-morrow. P III 10 82 2
who evidently considered the walk as under their guidance. P III 10 83 6
Anne found a nice seat for her, on a dry sunny bank, under P III 10 87 21
fallen and been trodden under foot, is still in possession P III 10 88 26
or to be more deeply afflicted under the dreadful change. P III 11 96 12
letters, but the Grappler was under orders for Portsmouth. P III 12 108 28
moment, Henrietta, sinking under the conviction, lost her P III 12 109 34
roof; and while Louisa, under Mrs. Harville's direction, P III 12 111 50
them; and in this manner, under these circumstances full P III 12 116 70
Their concerns had been sunk under those of Uppercross, P IV 1 124 11
and trays, bending under the weight of brawn and cold pies, P IV 2 134 29
her spirits rose under their influence; and, like Mrs. P IV 2 135 33
She heard it all under embellishment. P IV 3 140 11
to her bed, and suffering under severe and constant pain; P IV 5 154 9
they see it occasionally under every circumstance that can P IV 5 156 10
off together, her arm under his, a gentle and embarrassed P IV 7 177 16
reflection shewed her the mistake she had been under. P IV 9 194 21
In the warmth of the moment, and under a mistaken P IV 9 198 44
a fruitless trouble, and, under a cold civility, the same P IV 9 209 97
had been for many years under a sort of sequestration for P IV 9 210 98
And under such a supposition, which would have been most P IV 9 211 102
not possibly claim it under many years; and that, on the P IV 10 217 20
company with each other, under their present circumstances, P IV 10 221 33
standing under the colonnade, and a gentleman with her. P IV 10 222 34
he drew out a letter from under the scattered paper, P IV 11 236 40
with Captain Harville; and under the irresistible P IV 11 241 60
feelings which I had been smarting under year after year. P IV 11 245 74
Like other great men under reverses," he added with a P IV 11 247 84
heard of as established under his protection in London, it P IV 12 250 7
of, under circumstances of otherwise strong felicity. P IV 12 251 10
at home, & the one, who under her mother's directions had S 2 374 1
it found me suffering under a more severe attack than S 5 386 1
running off with 5 vols. under his arm to Sir Edward's gig- S 8 403 1
under her care, than on her own account or her daughters.-- S 9 409 1
young ladies under her care, to Miss D. P.'s notice.-- S 10 419 1
of one of the young ladies under her care, a Miss Lambe, a S 10 419 1
were at the same period (under another representation) S 11 420 1
She had several more under her care than the three who S 11 421 1
"Miss L. was under the constant care of an experienced S 11 422 1

UNDER-BRED (2)
all pert, every body under-bred; and she gave as little MP III 9 395 3
and all her airs of pert pretension and under-bred finery. E II 14 279 52

UNDER-HUNG (1)
his being very much under-hung, a defect which time seemed P IV 3 141 12

UNDER-RATED (2)
I can suppose, however, that I may have under-rated him. E III 13 427 21
And even if I have not under-rated him hitherto, he may E III 13 427 21

UNDER-SERVANTS (1)
and made five of the under-servants idle and dissatisfied; MP II 2 190 9

UNDER-SIZED (1)
Nobody can call such an under-sized man handsome. MP I 10 102 43

UNDER-VALUED (1)
and her comprehension under-valued; though she had known MP I 16 152 2

UNDERGO (2)
in, would undergo so speedy, so melancholy a reverse! LS 24 285 1
the very next day, to undergo the necessary penance of E I 17 141 5

UNDERGOING (2)
of all; for after undergoing an examination into the value SS II 14 249 8
glad to be secure of undergoing the anxiety of a first E I 14 121 14

UNDERGONE (3)
Elinor's heart, which had undergone many changes in the SS III 8 325 51
that her sentiments had undergone so material a change, PP III 16 366 8
estimation of him had undergone, relating her absolute PP III 17 376 36

UNDERHAND (1)
He had suspected his agent of some underhand dealing--of MP III 10 404 15

UNDERLET (1)
of the lodgings being in some instances underlet.-- S 6 392 1

UNDERMINE (1)
impression on her heart, and to undermine her principles.-- S 8 405 2

UNDERNEATH (2)
suspension of agony by creeping far underneath the clothes. NA II 6 170 12
At that instant a door underneath was hastily opened; some NA II 9 194 6

UNDERSIZED (1)
to see such an undersized, little, mean-looking man, set MP I 18 165 3

UNDERSTAND (246)
till I better understand her real meaning in coming to us. LS 3 247 1
long enough at school to understand anything thoroughly. LS 7 253 1
be one of contempt were he to understand her emotions. LS 19 274 3
& understand the real affection we feel for each other! LS 20 278 7
James, & gave her to understand that I was absolutely LS 22 280 1
party understand that his heart was devoted to my daughter. LS 22 280 2
of it, in order to understand the particulars & assure LS 22 281 5
She never could learn or understand any thing before she NA I 1 14 1
How are your absent cousins to understand the tenour of NA I 3 27 28
"Do you understand muslins, sir?" NA I 3 28 37
Catherine did not understand him--and he repeated his NA I 9 63 10
not been brought up to understand the propensities of a NA I 9 65 31
could they be made to understand how little the heart of NA I 10 74 22
which Catherine did not even endeavour to understand. NA I 11 89 61
understand it without a table;--however I <u>did</u> beat him. NA I 12 96 20
The little which she could understand however appeared to NA I 14 110 28
He laughed, and added, "come, shall I make you understand NA I 14 112 36
of two tombstones and a lantern--do you understand?-- NA I 14 113 39
"that you have made us understand each other, you may as NA I 14 113 40
well make Miss Morland understand yourself--unless you NA I 14 113 40
what she did not understand, she was almost as ready to NA I 14 114 49
you to understand the motive of other people's actions." NA II 1 132 18
"I do not understand you." NA II 1 132 21
"Then we are on very unequal terms, for I understand you NA II 1 132 22
We perfectly understand the present vexation; and every NA II 1 136 49
is one of the finest old places in England, I understand. NA II 3 143 2
make him understand what I mean, in the properest way. NA II 3 145 13
If able to suggest a hint, Isabella could never understand NA II 4 150 1
"I understand: she is in love with James, and flirts with NA II 4 151 14
"What! not when Dorothy has given you to understand that NA II 5 159 21
the only one of the party who did not understand him. NA II 7 175 12
"If I understand you rightly, you had formed a surmise of NA II 9 197 29
I cannot understand even now what she would be at, for NA II 10 202 7
as she was given to understand by his words as well as his NA II 11 208 1
Catherine did not hear enough of this speech to understand NA II 11 213 20
"There is but one thing that I cannot understand. NA II 12 218 6
succeeded; but I do not understand what Captain Tilney has NA II 12 218 6
I clearly understand it now, and I will strictly fulfil my SS I 2 12 25
the admiration of a person who can understand their worth. SS I 3 17 18
Sir John did not much understand this reproof; but he SS I 9 45 31
32

I understand, does not approve of second attachments." SS I 11 55 8
"I do not understand you," replied he, colouring. SS I 17 94 48
know my sister well enough to understand what she means? SS I 17 95 49
wanted more clearly to understand what Lucy really felt SS II 1 141 7
Norland living; which I understand is a very good one, and SS II 2 149 25
be impossible, when you understand that my affections have SS II 7 183 13
"I understand you," said Elinor. SS II 9 204 19
I understand she is a woman of very good fortune. SS II 11 222 9
excellent neighbours to you in the country, I understand." SS II 11 222 9
"I understand you.-- SS III 1 263 29
"I do not understand what you mean by interrupting them," SS III 2 274 17
his family; for if I understand the matter right, he has SS III 3 282 17
I understand that he intends to take orders. SS III 3 282 19
could not help catching enough to understand his business. SS III 4 285 1
idea, and she exclaimed;--"Oh ho!--I understand you. SS III 4 286 16
17

Elinor did not quite understand the beginning of Mrs. SS III 4 286 18
near neighbours, (for I understand the parsonage is almost SS III 4 290 38
and therefore must understand the terms on which it was SS III 5 295 13
certain connection--you understand me--it would have been SS III 5 297 31
"I understand you," he replied, with an expressive smile, SS III 8 318 18
more and more at a loss to understand what he would be at. SS III 8 318 19
speak--and to make them understand that she hoped no SS III 12 358 9
you may as well give her a chance--you understand me."-- SS III 14 375 9

a sort of thing that shocks me; I cannot understand it. W 318 2
He is reckoned remarkably agreable I understand.--" W 328 8
"You have not been long in this country I understand, said W 346 21
but Emma pretending to understand nothing extraordinary in W 360 29
insufficient to make his wife understand his character. PP I 1 5 34
This is not quite enough to make her understand his PP I 6 22 7
"Oh? yes--I understand you perfectly." PP I 9 42 11
asked Elizabeth whether she could at all understand him? PP I 11 56 12
a man of very large property in Derbyshire, I understand." PP I 16 77 9
fifteen or sixteen, and I understand highly accomplished. PP I 16 82 43
her mother gave her to understand that the probability of PP I 17 88 14
in vain; Mary would not understand them; such an PP I 18 100 68
I understand that Mr. Collins has made you an offer of PP I 20 111 15
Mrs. Bennet wished to understand by it that he thought of PP I 22 124 11
understand; and all for the sake of Mr. Collins too!-- PP I 23 130 24
I cannot understand it. PP II 3 148 26
of contentment, to understand her address in guiding, and PP II 5 157 10
she could not understand that sacrifice of so many hours. PP II 7 168 3
to the parsonage, it was more difficult to understand. PP II 9 180 29
With amazement did she first understand that he believed PP II 13 204 1
acquaintance in general understand Wickham's character." PP II 17 226 21
therefore gave them to understand, in as guarded a manner PP III 1 258 75
to Mrs. F. gave them to understand that they were going to PP III 4 274 5
calculated to make her understand her own wishes; and PP III 4 278 19
ignorant of what you and Jane seem so well to understand?" PP III 5 284 15
Elizabeth was at no loss to understand from whence this PP III 6 295 7
to Longbourn; and I understand from Mrs. Gardiner, that my PP III 8 313 19
by the bye, you are to understand, that my uncle and aunt PP III 9 319 25
Pray write instantly, and let me understand it--unless it PP III 9 320 33
If you do not choose to understand me, forgive my PP III 10 321 2
Miss Bennet, to understand the reason of my journey hither. PP III 14 353 22
23

You are to understand, Miss Bennet, that I came here with PP III 14 355 48
a few days," she added, "I shall know how to understand it. PP III 15 361 4
fluently, gave him to understand, that her sentiments had PP III 16 366 8
"I thoroughly understand you," cried Mrs. Norris; "you are MP I 1 7 8
and she cannot as yet understand how much she has changed MP I 2 13 5
well as Lady Bertram, understand that whatever she MP I 3 30 57
this was a way of going on that she could not understand. MP I 3 31 59
When he returned to understand how Fanny was situated, and MP I 4 36 7
She did not want to see or understand. MP I 5 44 3
"I begin now to understand you all, except Miss Price," MP I 5 48 30
"I shall understand all your ways in time; but coming down MP I 6 58 39
and could hardly understand it; for he was not pleasant by MP I 7 65 13
the other day, understand why a visit from the family were MP I 8 77 9
looking house, and I understand the clergyman and his wife MP I 8 82 34
Before that period, as I understand, the pews were only MP I 9 86 9
does not understand--admiring what one does not care for.-- MP I 9 95 71
My other sacrifice of course you do not understand." MP I 11 108 12
There is a very good living kept for you, I understand, MP I 11 109 14
but upon being made to understand the different style of MP I 15 138 1
All who can distinguish, will understand your motive.-- MP I 15 140 15
to you last night, to understand her unwillingness to be MP I 16 154 14
We bespeak your indulgence, you understand, as young MP II 1 185 28
Sir Thomas did not quite understand this, and looked with MP II 1 186 32
Mr. Yates was beginning now to understand Sir Thomas's MP II 2 191 10
on Maria's account, tried to understand her feelings. MP II 3 200 20
I understand you--and a very proper plan it is for a MP II 4 213 40
his fair bride are at Brighton, I understand--happy man!" MP II 5 224 49
I do not understand her. MP II 6 230 7
in seeking them, was to understand the recitor, to know MP II 6 236 21
when he did awake and understand, he was very decided in MP II 9 262 11
was almost more than she could understand herself. MP II 10 276 12
When she did understand it, however, and found herself MP II 13 301 7
trying to understand what Mr. and Miss Crawford were at. MP II 13 305 26
I have seen too much of Mr. Crawford not to understand his MP II 13 307 31
"I understand," cried her uncle recollecting himself, and MP III 1 312 12
himself, and not wanting to hear more-- "I understand. MP III 1 312 12
and (as far as I understand), received as much MP III 1 315 18
"Am I to understand," said Sir Thomas, after a few MP III 1 315 21
thing in my present intreaty that you do not understand? MP III 3 342 36
because I now understand more clearly your opinion of me. MP III 3 343 41
man as Henry Crawford, seems more than they can understand. MP III 4 352 44
I thought I could understand you. MP III 4 353 46
understand how your power over Henry is thought of there! MP III 5 360 16
He did not understand her; he felt that he did not; and MP III 6 366 1
understand a disposition so totally different from her own. MP III 9 395 4
This, as well as I understand, is to be the substance of MP III 12 415 2
grew thoroughly to understand this, she began to feel that MP III 12 419 9
persuaded myself that you would understand my silence.-- MP III 13 420 2
they would thoroughly understand;--and who could yet say MP III 14 430 6
for her to understand much of this strange letter. MP III 15 438 4
she was soon able to understand quite as much as she MP III 16 449 7
"I do not understand what you mean by 'success;'" said Mr. E I 1 12 42
I understand it was a very handsome letter, indeed. E I 2 18 9
came to understand the family better, other feelings arose. E I 4 27 5
"You understand the force of influence pretty well, E I 4 31 24
Yes, I understand the sort of mind. E I 7 51 5
more true gentility than Harriet Smith could understand." E I 8 65 49
Mr. Perry could not quite understand him, but he was very E I 8 68 58
she did not pretend to understand what his business might E I 8 68 58
more to Emma than to Harriet, which Emma could understand. E I 9 71 12
You understand every thing. E I 9 76 28
"Well, I cannot understand it." E I 9 81 76
One half of the world cannot understand the pleasures of E I 9 81 77
"I did not thoroughly understand what you were telling E I 12 104 44
never had been able to understand what she meant by a E I 12 104 50
And, by what I understand, you might have had lodgings E I 12 106 56
your sweet temper, to understand a bad one, or to lay down E I 14 123 25
I wish you would try to understand what an amiable young E I 18 148 21
Mrs. Dixon, I understand, has no remarkable degree of E II 1 161 26
I think you understand me, therefore." E II 3 171 5
An arch look expressed--"I understand you well enough;" E II 3 171 6
Miss Fairfax, you will understand that Mr. Elton is the E II 3 174 38
from her enough to understand the sort of meeting, and the E II 5 186 4
Mrs. Weston I should understand whom I might praise E II 5 192 32
She must see more of him to understand his ways; at E II 5 192 33
"And now that I understand your question, I must pronounce E II 6 200 18
He gave her to understand that Frank admired her extremely- E II 7 206 3
She must understand you." E II 10 243 24
I would have her understand me. E II 10 243 25
consider, and try to understand the value of his E II 11 250 19
But I do not understand how the room at the crown can be E II 11 251 28
is not as likely to understand the inclinations of the E II 11 254 50
on what she had said, and trying to understand the manner. E II 12 261 32
Woodhouse, you will understand how very delightful it is E II 14 273 19
I perfectly understand your situation, however, Miss E II 14 275 30
spirits, which, I understand, are sometimes much depressed. E II 14 275 32
"My dear, you do not understand me. E II 14 280 60
Her father was growing nervous, and could not understand E II 14 280 61
Fairfax's situation and understand what her home has been, E II 15 283 6
feelings, and trying to understand the degree of her E II 17 304 28
Mrs. Churchill, as we understand, has not been able to E II 18 306 11
I can understand you--(nodding at Mr. John Knightley)-- E II 18 312 50
I understand you were so kind as to offer, but another E III 2 321 17
So Frank Churchill is a capital dancer, I understand.-- E III 2 324 21
Emma could hardly understand him; he seemed in an odd E III 2 325 29
way as I have done, and I dare say you understand me." E III 4 337 4
He could not understand it; but there were symptoms of E III 5 343 2
you think you perfectly understand the degree of E III 5 350 32
Do you understand?" E III 7 371 34
I dare say she did not understand me." E III 7 374 58
as if she did not quite understand what was going on. E III 8 378 5
not pretend not to understand you; and to give you all the E III 10 396 39
extremely odd, that Emma did not know how to understand it. E III 11 404 9
gave me reason to understand that you did care about him?" E III 11 405 13
resolutely--"let us understand each other now, without the E III 11 406 19
How to understand it all! E III 11 411 43
How to understand the deceptions she had been thus E III 11 411 43
To understand, thoroughly understand her own heart, was E III 11 412 44
himself--"no, no, I understand you--forgive me--I am E III 13 426 16
But you understand me.-- E III 13 430 37
Yes, you see, you understand my feelings--and will return E III 13 430 37
We seemed to understand each other. E III 14 438 8
Whether Miss Woodhouse began really to understand me E III 14 438 8
Elton's thoughts, and understand why she was, like herself, E III 16 453 12
Yes, indeed, I quite understand--dearest Jane's prospects-- E III 16 455 20
"If I understand your brother, he only means so far as E III 17 465 26
of that visit (as I understand) he found an opportunity of E III 18 472 20
Are you quite sure that you understand the terms on which E III 18 474 29
Mackenzie, trying to understand, and make him understand, P III 5 38 34
and make him understand, which of Elizabeth's plants are P III 5 38 34
Husbands and wives generally understand when opposition P III 7 55 9
I perfectly understand Mr. Robinson's directions, and have P III 7 56 11
could not attempt to understand; even Captain Wentworth P III 10 89 36
be called a young mourner--only last summer, I understand." P III 12 108 25
had seemed to understand somewhat of the value of an Anne P IV 1 125 13
to give his own route, understand something of hers, and P IV 3 143 19
He gave her to understand that he had looked at her with P IV 4 148 9
could not be given to understand so much by her friend, P IV 5 159 21
"I do not understand it. P IV 6 163 7
Even Sophy could not understand it. P IV 6 171 33
"and I understand that he bears an excellent character." P IV 6 171 36
"Yes, yes, I understand you. P IV 6 173 47
crowd in the shop understand that Lady Dalrymple was P IV 7 176 10
She could not understand his present feelings, whether he P IV 7 178 24
can give; for I do not pretend to understand the language. P IV 8 186 25
I can understand. P IV 9 193 12
Mr. Elliot has sense to understand the value of such a P IV 9 196 32
Now you are to understand that time had worked a very P IV 9 206 90
"Lessening, I understand," replied Mrs. Smith. P IV 9 208 92
had heard enough to understand the present state of P IV 10 219 27
each side, our hearts must understand each other ere long. P IV 10 221 33
long enough in Bath, to understand the importance of a man P IV 10 226 64
Anne knew not how to understand it. P IV 11 236 39
She began not to understand a word they said, and was P IV 11 238 45
and only at Lyme had he begun to understand himself. P IV 11 241 61
I did not understand you. P IV 11 247 84
I shut my eyes, and would not understand you, or do you P IV 11 247 84
His chusing to walk with her, she had learnt to understand. S 7 398 1
You understand me I am sure?" S 8 403 1
"If I understand you aright--said Charlotte--our taste in S 8 404 1
said--"as far as I can understand what nervous complaints S 10 416 1
& thoroughly understand all the possibilities of their S 10 418 1

UNDERSTANDING (125)

to that excellent understanding which her bitterest LS 14 263 1
she is deficient in understanding, & at others that her LS 17 271 8
from our not rightly understanding each other's meaning. LS 24 287 11
Frederica has an excellent understanding, and Sir James LS 24 288 11
My understanding is at length restored, & teaches me no LS 36 306 2
She is a most amiable girl; such a superior understanding! NA I 7 50 49
Tell her that you think very highly of the understanding NA I 14 113 44
"Miss Morland, I think very highly of the understanding of NA I 14 113 45
think more highly of the understanding of women than I do. NA I 14 114 47
Catherine's understanding began to awake: an idea of the NA I 15 117 7
Miss Tilney, understanding in part her friend's curiosity NA II 8 182 1
Consult your own understanding, your own sense of the NA II 9 197 29
He is a deceased man--defunct in understanding. NA II 10 206 31
upon it, it is something not at all worth understanding." NA II 14 234 10
assisted by that right understanding of Mr. Morland's NA II 16 251 6
a strength of understanding, and coolness of judgment, SS I 1 6 11
His understanding was good, and his education had given it SS I 3 15 6
The excellence of his understanding and his principles can SS I 4 20 9
That his understanding has no brilliancy, his feelings no SS I 10 51 26
method of understanding the affair as satisfactory as this. SS I 15 78 26
has never aimed at the subjection of the understanding. SS I 17 94 39
variation of form, face, temper, and understanding. SS I 21 119 3
improvement to the understanding, must have opened his SS II 1 140 2
She had little difficulty in understanding thus much of SS II 1 142 7
The good understanding between the Colonel and Miss SS II 10 216 15
of demeanour, and a general want of understanding. SS II 12 229 2
Miss Dashwoods, and understanding them to be Mr. SS II 14 248 6
superior in person and understanding to half her sex; and SS III 1 263 27
me to say that, understanding you mean to take orders, he SS III 4 288 28
understanding--I do not mean, however, to defend myself. SS III 8 322 36
any natural defect of understanding on her side, in the SS III 8 322 37
good mind and a sound understanding must consider it; and SS III 11 350 9
and Margaret, understanding some part, but not the whole, SS III 12 359 13
silent, either not understanding the case, or waiting to W 339 18
She was a woman of mean understanding, little information, PP I 1 5 34
In understanding Darcy was the superior. PP I 4 16 14
is no compliment to the understanding of either." PP I 10 50 36
which often expose a strong understanding to ridicule." PP I 11 57 22
faults enough, but they are not, I hope, of understanding. PP I 11 58 28
with him should have an understanding of the first class." PP I 16 84 58
the scope of your understanding, but permit me to say that PP I 18 97 60
61

"I have not the pleasure of understanding you," said he, PP I 20 111 9
me the free use of my understanding on the present PP I 20 112 22
worse of her understanding, than I now do of her heart. PP II 1 135 13
My friend has an excellent understanding--though I am not PP II 9 178 15
and her not perfectly understanding the house, he seemed PP II 10 182 1
Her understanding excellent, her mind improved, and her PP II 10 186 40
less than a perfect understanding between the parties PP II 17 227 25
a woman whose weak understanding and illiberal mind, had PP II 19 236 1
understanding would preserve her from falling an easy prey. PP III 4 279 24
son and daughter, let us come to a right understanding. PP III 8 310 9
His understanding and temper, though unlike her own, would PP III 8 312 15
His understanding and opinions all please me; he wants PP III 10 325 2
basis the excellent understanding, and super-excellent PP III 13 347 33
for their present good understanding to the efforts of his PP III 16 367 9
It was not long before a good understanding took place MP I 4 39 10
Mr. Yates, from better understanding the family and MP II 1 177 5
though as far as ever from understanding their source. MP II 2 191 10
of their former good understanding; and were at least MP II 3 203 32
credit of the lover's understanding be it stated, that he MP II 4 211 25
understanding for him out of the superfluity of your own! MP II 5 224 53
understanding the question, was at no loss for an answer. MP II 7 247 40
Then, her understanding was beyond every suspicion, quick MP II 12 294 16
You have an understanding, which will prevent you from MP III 1 313 12
favourable opinion of his understanding, heart, and temper. MP III 1 321 47
had prevented her from understanding his attentions, and MP III 2 326 3
nothing could be hoped from attacking her understanding. MP III 2 333 27
It was a medicinal project upon his niece's understanding, MP III 6 369 10
from that hour Fanny understanding the worth of her MP III 9 397 8
be resisted by a good understanding, and given so mildly MP III 9 397 8
Now they came to an understanding. MP III 10 401 10
I must come to an understanding with him. MP III 11 411 20
as with a good clear understanding, made her a most MP III 12 418 7
been directed to the understanding and manners, not the MP III 17 463 8
without their understanding their first duties, or his MP III 17 463 9
With quickness in understanding the tempers of those she MP III 17 472 31
others;" rejoined Mr. Woodhouse, understanding but in part. E I 1 13 45
though strength of understanding must not be expected. E I 4 26 2

of useful understanding or knowledge of the world. E I 4 35 44
and a subjection of the fancy to the understanding. E I 5 37 7
deserve to have her understanding spoken of so slightingly. E I 8 63 44
She was not a woman of strong understanding or any E I 11 92 4
"Me, my love," cried his wife, hearing and understanding E I 11 95 19
her friend, so well understanding the gradations of rank E I 16 135 8
all her heart and understanding--really for the time E I 17 142 9
understanding, and warm-hearted, well meaning relations. E II 2 163 3
people, her heart and understanding had received every E II 2 164 6
of her own good understanding to remind her that all this E II 2 164 6
way that, if they had understanding, should convince them E II 4 185 13
to the same good understanding; and they were just growing E II 5 187 4
of any two persons' understanding as to suppose they meant E II 5 193 35
"There appeared such a perfectly good understanding among E II 6 202 38
There is no understanding a word of it. E II 9 232 11
his inferior in understanding; but he had been very much E II 13 266 6
had come to so good an understanding respecting the Eltons, E III 3 332 1
understanding even, between Frank Churchill and Jane. E III 5 344 2
more exact understanding of a house and grounds which must E III 6 357 34
true gentility, untainted in blood and understanding.-- E III 6 358 35
Understanding and gratification came together. E III 7 371 35
excusable in one who sets up as I do for understanding. E III 13 427 19
to herself--and as for understanding any thing he wrote, E III 14 436 6
Mystery; finesse--how they pervert the understanding! E III 15 446 15
Nature gave you understanding:--Miss Taylor gave you E III 17 462 7
and though her understanding almost acquiesced in the E III 19 483 9
any people of real understanding, was nobody with either P III 1 5 8
Hall being to let, and understanding his (Mr. Shepherd's) P III 3 21 18
So far went his understanding; and his vanity supplied a P III 3 24 36
elder sister, Mary had not Anne's understanding or temper. P III 5 37 21
seemingly perfect good understanding and agreement P III 5 41 45
that a woman of real understanding might have given more P III 6 43 5
how soon we came to an understanding, she would never be P III 10 92 45
listened with all his understanding and soul; and I am P IV 2 131 12
former good understanding was completely reestablished. P IV 3 138 6
Anne listened, but without quite understanding it. P IV 3 140 11
How her temper and understanding might bear the P IV 3 140 11
Every thing united in him; good understanding, correct P IV 4 146 6
no superiority of manner, accomplishment, or understanding. P IV 4 150 14
be patient, a strong understanding would supply resolution, P IV 5 154 8
deficient in understanding; but benwick is something more. P IV 8 182 10
A scheme, worthy of Mrs. Wallis's understanding, by all P IV 9 208 92
habits, and not strong understanding, much more amiable P IV 9 209 95
The Wallises; she had amusement in understanding them. P IV 11 246 78
suffering some pain in understanding and relinquishing Mr. P IV 12 249 3
gifted in this part of understanding than her young friend. P IV 12 249 4
for a man of strong understanding, but not of capacity to S 2 372 1

UNDERSTANDINGS (3)
injurious to your own peace than to our understandings. LS 14 263 1
understandings while they reason, feels the comfort of. MP I 11 107 3
years bring our understandings a good deal nearer?" E I 12 99 7

UNDERSTANDS (6)
She certainly understands _you_ better than you are MP II 3 198 13
"Sir Thomas," said Edmund, "undoubtedly understands the MP II 7 248 46
Serle understands boiling an egg better than any body. E I 3 24 14
on, for he thoroughly understands the nature of the air, E I 12 105 55
he understands the value of friendship as well as any body. E II 16 293 22
and nurse Rooke thoroughly understands when to speak. P IV 5 155 9

UNDERSTOOD (105)
eagerness; when I understood his intention however, & at LS 24 290 13
which interested, though it was hardly understood by her. NA I 3 25 2
more seriously)--your feelings are easily understood. NA I 6 41 16
firmness, you know, could only be understood by yourself." NA II 1 133 34
did not exactly know how this was to be understood. NA II 7 177 18
Catherine understood her:--the General must be watched NA II 8 186 7
How were people, at that rate, to be understood? NA II 11 211 15
of George or Harriet could never be exactly understood. NA II 14 233 8
He understood that she was in need of a dwelling, and SS I 4 23 20
and when its object was understood, she hardly knew SS I 8 36 2
Willoughby, as plainly denoted how well she understood him. SS I 14 73 16
Have we not perfectly understood each other? SS I 15 80 36
my feelings are not often shared, not often understood. SS I 16 88 33
so heartily at the question, as to shew she understood it. SS I 19 108 35
But really, I never understood that you were at all SS I 22 128 10
and Elinor, who now understood her sister, and saw to what SS II 3 154 6
Elinor perfectly understood her, and was forced to use all SS II 10 217 22
but only Elinor and Marianne understood its true merit. SS III 2 270 1
with me, at least I understood her so--or I certainly SS III 4 288 27
I did not even know, till I understood his design, that SS III 4 289 35
that self-denial is a word hardly understood by him. SS III 11 350 9
one she had so well understood, much slighter in reality, SS III 11 355 46
of the day must be understood, before Robert could let his W 356 28
but when Mrs. Philips understood from him what Rosings was, PP I 16 75 2
best light, in the light in which it may be understood." PP II 1 137 24
know that he had understood all the ladies to be within. PP II 9 177 2
added, "I think I have understood that Mr. Bingley has not PP II 9 177 6 7
Elizabeth fancied she understood; he must be supposing her PP II 9 179 21
"I understood that there were some very strong objections PP II 10 185 30
They could have been understood only by her mother, who PP II 18 232 23
knowing him better, his disposition was better understood." PP II 18 234 35 36
we left Bakewell, we understood that you were not PP III 1 256 61
were imperfectly understood, it was yet a well known fact PP III 2 265 15
Elizabeth soon observed, and instantly understood it. PP III 4 278 19
I thought I understood from the Gardiners that you had." PP III 10 328 18
"Let me be rightly understood. PP III 14 354 40
Her feelings were very acute, and too little understood to MP I 2 14 6
make her good qualities understood, and to conquer the MP I 2 21 34
amusement to me, as she understood I lived quite alone, to MP I 10 106 57
seven weeks; for I had understood he was so very fond of MP I 12 115 5
shewed how well it was understood, and before Julia could MP I 14 133 12
Tom understood his father's thoughts, and heartily wishing MP II 1 183 24
better than you are understood by the greater part of MP II 3 198 13
One of whom, having never before understood that thornton MP II 7 248 47
near, and she so little understood her own claims as to MP II 10 274 8
any thing so imperfectly understood was most distressing. MP II 13 307 30
his manners; if he understood me as well, he would, I dare MP II 13 307 31
I understood that you had the use of this room by way of MP III 1 312 10
Must it not follow of course, that when he was understood, MP III 2 327 4
she felt herself obliged to use, was not to be understood. MP III 2 327 5
When Sir Thomas understood this, he felt the necessity of MP III 2 332 19
and upon this being understood, he had a variety of MP III 3 340 24
of them, when she first understood what was intended, when MP III 6 369 11
had been in town he understood, a few days; that he had MP III 10 400 8
"Her uncle, she understood, meant to fetch her; and as her MP III 14 436 15
"Nothing, nothing to be understood. MP III 16 455 21
me that I had never understood her before, and that, as MP III 16 457 30
when it was understood that he had written to his new E I 2 18 9
She believed he was very clever, and understood every E I 4 28 6
She understood their ways, could allow for their ignorance E I 10 86 24
being listened to and understood, of being always E I 14 117 1
insinuating)--I am sure you have seen and understood me." E I 15 131 31
It confesses that you have long understood me." E I 15 131 33
So far from having long understood you, I have been in a E I 15 131 34
"Oh! yes--Mr. Elton, I understood--certainly as to dancing- E II 1 156 7
necessary, told that he understood, and the papers swept E II 3 170 2
He understood what would be welcome; he could be sure of E II 5 192 28
He looked as if he fully understood and honoured such a E II 6 201 25
Quite otherwise indeed, if I understood Miss Fairfax's E II 9 234 33
of Bath to the young are pretty generally understood. E II 14 275 32
"Having understood as much, I was rather astonished to E II 14 278 46

Emma saw how Mr. Weston understood these joyous prospects. E III 1 317 9
Her gestures and movements might be understood by any one E III 2 322 18
This was so very well understood between them, that Emma E III 6 353 3
I would be understood to mean, that it can be only weak, E III 7 373 44
She had understood it was to be delayed till Colonel E III 8 380 9
and excusable which now are not to be understood. E III 10 398 53
She understood it all; and as far as her mind could E III 11 403 2
not have encouraged me, then, if you had understood me. E III 11 407 26
Emma understood him; and as soon as she could recover from E III 13 426 14 15
Emma soon recollected, and understood him; and while she E III 18 480 76
She was a clever young woman, who understood the art of P III 2 15 15
understood in time what was intended as to the waggons. P III 5 38 34
Anne understood it. P III 7 59 23
be detected by any who understood him less than herself; P III 8 67 28
feelings, the alteration could not be understood too soon. P III 9 77 18
She understood him. P III 10 91 42
and visited again, to make the worth of Lyme understood. P III 11 95 9
as if he meant to be understood, that she ventured to hope P III 11 100 23
with his wife, had perfectly understood the whole story. P IV 3 139 9
asked, to make it understood what this old schoolfellow P IV 5 157 14
delighted to fancy she understood what they might be P IV 6 168 24
but I hope it may be understood to have worn out on each P IV 6 172 42
and exclaimed, "now, how I do wish I understood you! P IV 9 195 29 30
I have always understood they were not a happy couple. P IV 9 200 58
So much was pretty soon understood; but till Sir Walter P IV 10 216 18
"We had your sister's card yesterday, and I understood P IV 11 236 36
"Can you fail to have understood my wishes?-- P IV 11 237 42
"I am afraid, ma'am, that it is not perfectly understood. P IV 11 239 48 49
"Oh! my dear, it is quite understood, I give you my word. P IV 11 239 50
followed it, he had not understood the perfect excellence P IV 11 242 63
All that he understood of himself, he readily told, for he S 2 371 1
Her motives for such a match could be little understood at S 3 375 1
This was very fine;--but if Charlotte understood it at all, S 7 398 1
letter from Mrs Darling understood that Mrs G.--has S 9 409 1

UNDERTAKE (17)
I would undertake for five pounds to drive it to York and NA I 9 65 30
deserve; and promised to undertake the commission with SS III 3 283 20
She could undertake therefore to inform him of it, in the SS III 3 283 20
Your Cloathes I would undertake to find means of sending W 320 2
"What if they were among them to undertake the care of her MP I 1 5 4
you mean--but I will not undertake to answer the question. MP I 5 49 31
any Mr. Repton who would undertake it, and give me as much MP I 6 57 29
enough at this moment to undertake any character that ever MP I 13 123 6
speeches, _I_ would undertake him with all my heart." MP I 14 134 14
You _will_ undertake it I hope?" turning to her with a look MP I 14 135 15
and _I_ really cannot undertake to harangue all the rest MP I 15 140 14
If I were to undertake it, I should only disappoint you." MP I 15 146 51
impossible for him to undertake the part of Anhalt in MP I 15 148 58
good humour agreed to undertake the part for which Fanny MP I 17 159 6
undertake the part, we must not be surprised at the rest." MP III 4 350 28
I undertake the commission. E III 7 373 49
man there, I will undertake the commission with pleasure, S 5 387 1

UNDERTAKEN (8)
She then sought her eldest sister, who had undertaken to PP I 18 95 48
to be Count Cassel, but no one had yet undertaken Anhalt." MP I 15 143 28
in the object he had undertaken, the promotion of young MP II 13 298 3
His last journey to London had been undertaken with no MP II 13 300 7
He thought she had undertaken more than she was equal to, E III 9 389 16
health, wd not have undertaken to cure, by putting out the S 10 413 1
But now it was to be more resolutely undertaken, at a more S 12 423 1
& I have undertaken to collect whatever I can for her. S 12 424 1

UNDERTAKES (4)
Mrs. Weston undertakes to direct the whole." E II 11 252 36
'If _Miss Taylor_ undertakes to wrap Miss Emma up, you need E II 11 252 37
Anne will stay; Anne undertakes to stay at home and take P III 7 57 18
He undertakes it--(looking towards Captain Wentworth) he P IV 11 232 15

UNDERTAKING (8)
chance to see, was an undertaking to frighten away all her NA II 14 235 14
appeared rather a bold undertaking, considering the time SS I 12 62 29
merit in chearfully undertaking to drive her & all her W 315 1
in undertaking business, he was quick in its execution. PP III 8 309 5
"Yes, the expense of such an undertaking would be MP I 13 127 31
a possible, an hopeful undertaking to persuade her that MP III 17 470 25
certainly a very kind undertaking; highly becoming her own E I 3 24 10
Campbell of undertaking the whole charge of her education. E II 2 163 4

UNDERTONES (1)
attack, that looks and undertones were to be well tried, MP III 3 341 31

UNDERTOOK (6)
"and I remember that you undertook to read it aloud to me, NA I 14 107 8
& Mrs Robert Watson, who undertook to bring her home & W 348 23
and Mr. Rushworth undertook to count his speeches. MP I 17 158 2
door than Henry Crawford undertook to answer the anxious MP II 1 176 3
Weston most willingly undertook to play as long as they E II 11 247 3
a day or two; Charles undertook to give him some shooting, P IV 2 130 5

UNDERVALUE (3)
not, in our concern for his sufferings, undervalue your's. NA II 10 206 38
lively nor young, seemed resolved to undervalue his merits. SS I 10 50 13
God forbid that I should undervalue the warm and faithful P IV 11 235 32

UNDERVALUED (3)
In that point, however, I undervalued my own magnanimity, SS III 8 323 40
and whose merit she had undervalued; but to her own more PP III 11 334 36
sensations, and think she had undervalued their strength. E II 13 265 5

UNDERVALUING (2)
the capacity and undervaluing the labour of the novelist, NA I 5 37 4
to the other sex, by undervaluing their own; and with many PP I 8 40 56

UNDESCRIBABLE (2)
with circumstances of superiority undescribable. MP III 10 405 18
& descriptive of the _undescribable_ emotions they excite in S 7 396 1

UNDESERVED (1)
Mr. Darcy, for now they _do_ appear wholly undeserved." PP II 17 226 20

UNDESERVEDLY (1)
and I feel most undeservedly honoured, but I am so MP III 2 330 15

UNDESERVING (4)
"I should be undeserving of the confidence you have SS II 2 146 2
Well, he is a very undeserving young man--and I do not PP II 17 228 27
in her behaviour towards the undeserving of the other sex." PP III 5 289 43
"Wickham is not so undeserving, then, as we have thought PP III 7 303 16

UNDESIGNED (2)
Once it had, by an opening undesigned and unmerited, led MP III 17 467 19
in all her ways; and so much the worse, because undesigned. E I 5 38 15

UNDESIGNEDLY (2)
It came out quite unawares, quite undesignedly. SS III 9 336 12
came to a sufficient explanation, and quite undesignedly. E III 4 340 28

UNDESIRABLE (5)
a farther connection between the families, undesirable.-- SS II 13 238 1
made farther conversation most thoroughly undesirable.-- W 321 2
it became not undesirable to himself to be relieved from MP I 3 24 7
This, though very undesirable, would be no matter of agony E III 10 393 18
not avoid hearing many undesirable particulars, such as " P IV 11 230 5

UNDETERMINED (2)
himself quite undetermined, there there was a something in LS 27 297 4
the aunt; and she was undetermined whether most to be PP II 15 362 11 12

UNDEVIATING (1)
"Believe it to be most fervent, most undeviating in "F. W. P IV 11 237 42

UNDIMINISHED (1)
Mrs. Bennet rejoiced to see Jane in undiminished beauty; PP II 16 222 19 20

UNDISCERNED (1)

seen them, had passed undiscerned by her who now heard E III 11 410 35
UNDISCERNING (2)
not more undiscerning, than you are prejudiced and unjust." SS I 10 50 18
myself off as insensible even to the undiscerning Sir John. SS III 8 330 69
UNDISCOVERED (1)
could have remained undiscovered in a room such as that, NA II 7 173 2
UNDISMAYED (1)
I am undismayed however. LS 33 303 1
UNDISPUTED (1)
at one end of the chest in undisputed possession! NA II 6 164 3
UNDISTINGUISHED (1)
herself undistinguished in the dusk, and unthought of. MP III 7 379 20
UNDISTINGUISHING (2)
the innocent with the guilty in undistinguishing ill-will? NA II 14 231 5
prosing --so undistinguishing and unfastidious--and so apt E I 10 84 16
UNDISTURBED (5)
Catherine, meanwhile, undisturbed by presentiments of such NA II 1 131 15
hope of her having been undisturbed by the tempest, with NA II 7 174 5
These reflections were long indulged undisturbed by any NA II 13 228 27
in the east room, undisturbed, for a quarter of an hour, MP I 18 168 14
tranquillity remained undisturbed the rest of the evening, MP II 5 227 68
UNDIVIDED (2)
away, leaving him to the undivided consciousness of his NA I 15 124 47
to the enjoyment of undivided attention where his heart SS I 10 49 9
UNDO (2)
it will in all likelihood undo the effects of your PP I 19 108 19
obliged, on her return, to undo all the work of the PP II 14 213 20
UNDOING (1)
And as she spoke she was undoing a small parcel, which MP II 8 257 15
UNDONE (4)
very necessary business undone, and can be of no real PP I 10 49 27
Almost unconsciously she had now undone the parcel he had MP II 9 262 8
You left nothing undone. E II 3 170 2
never wished the past undone, she began now to have the P III 4 29 7
UNDOUBTED (4)
undoubted right to dispose of his own property as he chose. SS II 11 225 35
I can summon more than one witness of undoubted veracity. PP II 12 199 5
had been pursuing with undoubted attachment, and strong MP III 16 452 15
In one respect, my good fortune is undoubted, that of E III 14 443 8
UNDOUBTEDLY (51)
evening before; it is undoubtedly better to deceive him LS 5 249 1
quitting Churchill is undoubtedly in unison with our LS 25 292 3
proper measures will undoubtedly be taken by government to NA I 14 112 34
Abbey you inhabit is undoubtedly haunted, and informs you NA II 5 158 17
"Undoubtedly; and after all you have no thanks for it. SS I 2 11 22
"That is a material consideration undoubtedly. SS I 2 13 27
Willoughby may undoubtedly have very sufficient reasons SS I 15 79 29
"Undoubtedly. SS I 17 93 30
of his engagement was undoubtedly inferior in connections, SS II 1 140 3
he is undoubtedly supported by the same trust in your's. SS II 2 147 8
I do not mean to complain, however; it is undoubtedly a SS II 11 225 31
"Undoubtedly, if they had known your engagement," said she, SS II 13 239 8
He is undoubtedly a sensible man, and in his manners SS III 4 290 37
Bingley likes your sister undoubtedly; but he may never do PP I 6 22 2
"Undoubtedly," replied Darcy, to whom this remark was PP I 8 40 57
There are undoubtedly many who could not say the same, but PP I 16 83 50
You think it a faithful portrait undoubtedly." PP I 18 91 16
clothes, she should undoubtedly see her daughter settled PP I 18 103 77
Elizabeth quietly answered "undoubtedly;"--and after an PP I 22 125 18
for Mr. Collins would undoubtedly have been much less in PP II 7 168 1
also went Mr. Wickham, undoubtedly by design; for there PP II 12 201 5
her beloved friend, she undoubtedly would have refrained PP III 3 269 10
"Undoubtedly. PP III 10 328 18
"It is undoubtedly the best thing we can do now, as we are MP I 10 98 5
"You have undoubtedly--and there are situations in which MP I 10 99 16
Something of a theatre we must have undoubtedly, but it MP I 13 127 31
"Sir Thomas," said Edmund, "undoubtedly understands the MP II 7 248 46
our satisfaction would undoubtedly be more complete, but MP II 8 252 3
I go to London, as will now undoubtedly be the case.-- MP II 11 287 22
The Bertrams are undoubtedly some of the first people in MP II 12 293 11
and there is, undoubtedly, more liberality and candour on MP III 16 457 29
Time would undoubtedly abate somewhat of his sufferings, MP III 16 460 31
"He is very plain, undoubtedly--remarkably plain:--but E I 4 32 30
"Mr. Weston would undoubtedly support me, if he were here, E I 5 36 6
but he is undoubtedly her inferior as to rank in society.-- E I 8 62 39
pleasing young man undoubtedly, and very much in love with E I 13 111 13
would undoubtedly rush upon her without preparation. E II 3 177 51
but undoubtedly he could know very little of the matter. E II 5 191 28
"I have known her from a child, undoubtedly; we have been E II 6 203 39
Undoubtedly, if you wish it, I will endeavour to persuade E II 11 255 58
"He is undoubtedly very much in love--every thing denotes E II 13 265 3
Harriet undoubtedly was greatly his inferior in E II 13 266 6
A charming place, undoubtedly. E II 14 273 19
of;--but if he, who had undoubtedly been always so much E III 1 315 1
Mrs. Elton had undoubtedly the advantage, at this time, in E III 2 325 32
"Such things do occur, undoubtedly."-- E III 7 373 42
sense and temper he was undoubtedly superior to his wife; P III 6 43 5
former times must undoubtedly be brought to the P III 8 63 2
was undoubtedly a gentleman, and had an air of good sense. P III 12 106 19
Their house was undoubtedly the best in Camden-Place; P IV 3 137 4
This is full proof undoubtedly, proof of every thing you P IV 9 204 77
UNDOUBTING (2)
With undoubting decision she directly began her adieus; MP II 4 214 46
and many comments--undoubting decision of its E I 12 104 50
UNDOUBTINGLY (1)
and she relied so undoubtingly on Sir John's description SS I 5 26 6
UNDRAW (1)
on to undraw her purse, would as readily give 10Gs as 5.-- S 12 424 1
UNDRESSED (3)
Rooms, at dressed or undressed balls, was he perceivable; NA I 5 35 2
In revolving these matters, while she undressed, it NA II 8 188 17
She was soon undressed and in bed, and as she seemed SS II 6 178 16
UNDUE (3)
house, attributing an undue share of the change, MP III 15 446 34
What a blessing it is, when undue influence does not E III 10 398 55
of obscure birth into undue distinction, and raising men P III 3 19 16
UNDUTIFUL (1)
I have no pleasure in talking to undutiful children.-- PP I 20 113 28
UNEASINESS (43)
I always looked forward to her coming with uneasiness--but LS 11 259 2
herself, Sir James, & me, which gave him great uneasiness. LS 22 281 4
her adieu without much uneasiness, and returned home, NA I 14 115 55
With much uneasiness did she thus leave them. NA II 3 148 28
her uneasiness, or make her quit them in apprehension. NA II 4 153 31
He often expressed his uneasiness on this head, feared the NA II 11 209 5
In having this cause of uneasiness so pleasantly removed, NA II 13 221 6
Catherine, supposing some uneasiness on Captain Tilney's NA II 13 223 9
Elinor's uneasiness was at least equal to her mother's. SS I 15 77 19
Elinor saw, with great uneasiness, the low spirits of her SS I 18 96 1
that place, with the uneasiness and suspicions they had SS II 4 162 13
within herself, regarding her sister with uneasiness. SS II 4 165 29
to lessen the uneasiness of her mind on other points; she SS II 5 174 47
that she felt any uneasiness for her sister, or any SS III 1 260 10
his love was in so much uneasiness on her sister's account, SS III 7 309 5
for so great was her uneasiness about Marianne, that she SS III 9 335 6
off, that with so much uneasiness as both her sisters had SS III 11 355 45
always gave me much uneasiness, and since I have had the PP I 13 62 12
likely to give them any uneasiness, convinced her that she PP II 10 184 20
conveying the idea of uneasiness, with an attention which PP II 11 188 1
His sisters' uneasiness had been equally excited with my PP II 12 198 5
But Elizabeth had sources of uneasiness which could not be PP III 11 334 36
not help feeling some uneasiness as to the possible PP III 15 360 2
what may, in a mistaken light, have given you uneasiness. PP III 16 365 4
already given him much uneasiness; but his other children MP I 2 20 33
without a companion in uneasiness; quite as far from MP I 18 166 5
There is no giving you a moment's uneasiness. MP II 4 212 30
Miss Crawford's uneasiness was much lightened by this MP II 12 291 1
I took uneasiness with me, and there was no getting rid of MP III 4 355 52
and yet, with all the uneasiness it supplied, it connected MP III 9 394 2
many other sources of uneasiness was added the severe one MP III 10 400 6
became the prominent uneasiness; and when Harriet appeared, E I 8 67 56
so much better that I have hardly any uneasiness about it. E I 12 102 28
remain a degree of uneasiness which she could not wish to E I 13 110 8
But it is impossible not to feel uneasiness. E I 13 114 34
her father's being given a moment's uneasiness about it. E I 16 138 15
that Emma's uneasiness increased; and the moment they were E III 10 394 26
27
I recollect all the uneasiness I occasioned her, and how E III 14 439 8
lines, to satisfy her, remained without any uneasiness.-- E III 14 442 8
and no moment's uneasiness can ever occur between us again. E III 14 443 8
extreme difficulty and uneasiness, and it should have been E III 15 446 20
longer under the first uneasiness about his heir, could P III 7 54 5
uneasiness in leaving her to Mrs. Harville's care entirely. P III 12 113 56
UNEASY (43)
I see plainly that she is uneasy at my progress in the LS 10 257 1
I really grow quite uneasy my dearest mother about LS 11 259 1
of a matter which we foresaw would make him so uneasy. LS 13 262 1
& he is certainly less uneasy since Reginald's letter. LS 13 263 1
make herself & her family uneasy by apprehending an event, LS 14 263 1
uneasy, as the gentlemen had just left the Pump-Room. NA I 6 43 36
Catherine, relieved for herself, felt uneasy for Isabella; NA I 13 105 40
conveyed from her sight without very uneasy sensations. NA II 1 132 16
so; and therefore gaily said, "do not be uneasy, Isabella. NA II 3 143 2
She saw him grave and uneasy; and however careless of his NA II 4 149 1
I will not say, 'do not be uneasy,' because I know that NA II 4 152 28
are so, at this moment; but be as little uneasy as you can. NA II 4 152 28
is so fine; and do not be uneasy on my father's account, NA II 7 177 17
I am quite uneasy about your dear brother, not having NA II 12 216 2
you will meet again some time or other; do not be uneasy. NA II 14 236 17
his sister, to make her uneasy; and at the same time, (SS I 4 23 19
Her mother was surprised, and Elinor again became uneasy. SS I 16 84 5
it, so I said, 'My dear Lady Elliott, do not be uneasy. SS II 14 252 18
not therefore be very uneasy about it, he went away; SS III 1 269 57
Her sisters were uneasy for her, but her mother was PP I 7 31 28
mere trifle, and begged she would not make herself uneasy. PP I 16 83 49
to make her a little uneasy; and she resolved to speak to PP II 2 142 18
make yourself uneasy, my dear cousin, about your apparel. PP II 6 160 5
6
hand, said in reply, "do not make yourself uneasy, my love. PP II 18 231 19
20
I felt a little uneasy--a little fearful of my sister's PP III 5 290 50
grave; her daughters, alarmed, anxious, uneasy. PP III 9 315 2
Anxious and uneasy, the period which passed in the drawing- PP III 12 341 14
unconscious of the uneasy movements of many of his friends MP II 1 184 27
She need not have been uneasy. MP III 14 431 8
Now do not make yourself uneasy with any queer fancies, MP III 14 435 14
remarks, and evidently making Mr. Rushworth uneasy. MP III 16 450 8
staying away so long was beginning to make her uneasy. E I 8 67 56
to inquire if he were come--and she was a little uneasy.-- E III 6 359 36
His father would not own himself uneasy, and laughed at E III 6 361 41
well," exclaimed Miss Bates, "then I need not be uneasy. E III 7 370 24
apprehension of the family, Mr. Perry was uneasy about her. E III 9 389 16
she endeavoured not to be uneasy, and settling it with her E III 10 392 7
dear Emma, there is no occasion to be so uneasy about it. E III 10 393 17
were in such a crowd, as to make Miss Smith rather uneasy." E III 18 472 20
but Mr. Weston had been almost as uneasy as herself.-- E III 18 479 73
He was very uneasy; and but for the sense of his son-in- E III 19 483 10
letter to make you and Mrs. Croft particularly uneasy. P IV 6 172 42
But indeed, my dear, you need not be uneasy. P IV 11 239 52
UNEMBARRASSED (4)
His circumstances are now unembarrassed--he suffers from SS III 11 351 13
in her as acute and unembarrassed an observer as ever Mr. PP III 2 261 4
be perfectly easy and unembarrassed;--a resolution the PP III 3 268 8
good, their manners unembarrassed and pleasant; they were P III 5 40 45
UNEMPLOYED (5)
Depend upon it that whatever unemployed sum may remain, SS I 14 72 10
unemployed, felt all the right of missing him much more. MP I 12 115 4
and every day thus unemployed, was tending to increase his MP I 18 164 1
the time, I am not at all afraid of being long unemployed. E II 17 300 13
home in that house when unemployed, chanced to be at P IV 5 154 9
UNENGAGED (1)
grievously; and Julia, unengaged and unemployed, felt all MP I 12 115 4
UNEQUAL (25)
to whose care I consigned her, was unequal to the charge. LS 1 244 1
"Then we are on very unequal terms, for I understand you NA II 1 132 22
suspected; and yet, unequal to an absolute falsehood, was NA II 7 174 5
there was a general though unequal mixture of good and bad. NA II 10 200 3
days, though still very unequal, were greatly improved--he SS I 19 101 1
mortifications of unequal society, & family discord--from W 361 31
made her feel how unequal she was to encounter Charlotte's PP II 11 194 32
They were more disturbed, more unequal, than she had often PP III 11 332 20
connections were so unequal to his own, his aunt would PP III 15 360 2
place you in the greatest danger in an unequal marriage. PP III 17 376 35
Say that, on examining the part, you feel yourself unequal MP I 15 140 15
Fanny's heart beat quick, and she felt quite unequal to MP II 4 210 20
nothing; but I am so unequal to any thing of the sort, MP II 13 307 31
I am totally unequal to it." MP III 1 320 44
"As usual, believing yourself unequal to anything!-- MP III 4 351 34
himself at any time unequal to company, there was scarcely E I 3 20 1
Am I unequal to speaking his name at once before all these E II 16 297 48
and thanks, but is quite unequal to any exercise." E III 9 390 16
17
under the plea of being unequal to any exercise, so E III 9 391 21
Were this most unequal of all connexions to take place, on E III 11 413 47
Was it new for any thing in this world to be unequal, E III 11 413 48
any such alliance for him, as most unequal and degrading. E III 13 431 38
estimate, a very unequal, and in her character she P III 2 16 17
that at present she felt unequal to more, and fit only for P IV 10 227 68
as to coming & been unequal to the journey, was the very S 11 420 1
UNEQUAL'D (1)
Diana, you are unequal'd in serving your friends & doing S 9 409 1
UNEQUALLED (3)
of his excessive and unequalled attachment to her, she was MP II 13 301 7
ardent attachment and unequalled love and unexampled E I 15 129 24
And then again, that unequalled, unrivalled address to S 7 397 1
UNEQUALLY (1)
sentiments avowed, however unequally they may be returned. PP II 11 189 6
7
UNEQUIVOCAL (2)
joy, and soon with unequivocal cheerfulness, the SS III 7 314 23
Your meaning must be unequivocal; no doubts or demurs: and E I 7 51 11
UNEQUIVOCALLY (2)
immediately and more unequivocally directed as her MP II 10 274 9
She did unfeignedly and unequivocally regret the E II 9 231 3
UNEVENNESS (1)
was not quite firm; an unevenness in the floor, I believe. E II 10 240 5
UNEVENTFUL (2)
It was performed with suitable quietness and uneventful NA I 2 19 4
interest to a long, uneventful residence in one country P III 1 9 18
UNEXAMINED (1)
towards her, and resolutely swept away by her unexamined. E III 5 349 25
UNEXAMPLED (3)
declining entirely to profit by such unexampled attention. LS 42 312 5
I can no longer help thanking you for your unexampled PP III 16 365 3

and unequalled love and unexampled passion could not fail E I 15 129 24
UNEXCEPTIONABLE (19)
was far from unexceptionable, might for a time make her LS 6 252 2
but her family & character must be equally unexceptionable. LS 12 261 3
As a mother she is unexceptionable. LS 14 265 5
seems to have been unexceptionable, it is a sad thing & of LS 15 266 2
To disobey her mother by refusing an unexceptionable offer LS 19 274 2
& character is alike unexceptionable, you will know what I LS 20 277 5
make his pupil's manners as unexceptionable as his own.-- W 335 13
play most perfectly unexceptionable, and I can conceive no MP I 13 125 18
so well, nothing so unexceptionable, as Lovers' Vows. MP I 15 139 6
Had his choice been less unexceptionable, I should have MP III 2 330 14
duty to accept such a very unexceptionable offer as this." MP III 2 333 26
Mr. Weston was a man of unexceptionable character, easy E I 1 6 6
but his love and his complaisance were unexceptionable. E I 6 47 26
a most unexceptionable quarter:--Robert Martin is the man. E I 8 59 25
address, all were unexceptionable, and his countenance had E II 5 190 22
also, that nothing really unexceptionable may pass us." E II 17 302 20
her marrying the unexceptionable young man who would have E III 11 413 49
proper, suitable, and unexceptionable a connexion, and in E III 17 467 31
by some most unexceptionable applicant, on his own terms, P III 2 15 14
UNEXCEPTIONABLY (1)
had; but Isabella had connected herself unexceptionably. E III 6 358 35
UNEXHILARATING (1)
and was so very unexhilarating to Edward, that he very SS II 13 244 41
UNEXPECTED (32)
We have a very unexpected guest with us at present, my LS 20 275 1
we had a most unexpected & unwelcome visit from Lady Susan, LS 41 309 1
Catherine, by whom this meeting was wholly unexpected, NA I 7 44 4
sudden recollection, no unexpected summons, no impertinent NA I 14 106 1
She felt the unexpected compliment, and deeply regretted NA II 8 185 5
The next morning brought the following very unexpected NA II 12 216 1
2
His unexpected accession to title and fortune had removed NA II 16 251 5
He looked all the astonishment which such unexpected, such SS III 4 289 29
30
acknowledging a very unexpected and unpleasant alteration SS III 7 312 19
alarm, gave some explanation to such unexpected rapidity. SS III 7 316 29
revealed, and he was listened to with unexpected calmness. SS III 14 373 3
most expressive of unexpected pleasure, & lively gratitude, W 331 11
She might perhaps have met with some unexpected W 355 28
consequential feelings of early and unexpected prosperity. PP I 15 70 1
the play, she had the unexpected happiness of an PP II 4 154 21
spoken with such gentleness as on this unexpected meeting. PP III 1 252 54
arrival had been very unexpected-- "for your housekeeper," PP III 1 256 61
has occurred of a most unexpected and serious nature; but PP III 4 273 3
To Kitty, however, it does not seem so wholly unexpected. PP III 4 273 3
"This is wholly unexpected. PP III 6 298 12
from Longbourn, your uncle had a most unexpected visitor. PP III 10 321 2
was as disagreeable to Fanny as it had been unexpected. MP I 3 25 10
of the three on this unexpected meeting; and as Edmund was MP I 18 169 23
stairs to deposit this unexpected acquisition, this MP II 9 261 1
of addresses so wholly unexpected, and the novelty of a MP III 2 326 3
honour!' said she; 'well, that is quite unexpected. E II 1 157 7
and niece--entirely unexpected; that at first, by Miss E II 8 214 13
It was completely unexpected. E II 18 308 27
Knightley's going to London had been an unexpected blow. E III 9 387 9
A degree of unexpected cordiality, however, in the welcome P IV 3 137 2
Anne found an unexpected interest here. P IV 11 231 10
with such a powerful discharge of unexpected obligation. S 10 414 1
UNEXPECTEDLY (10)
day abruptly, and very unexpectedly by them, asked the SS II 3 153 1
Her curiosity however was unexpectedly relieved. PP I 16 77 8
her ramble within the park, unexpectedly meet Mr. Darcy.-- PP II 10 182 1
I joined them unexpectedly a day or two before the PP II 12 202 5
all at home--coming unexpectedly as he did--all collected MP II 1 178 8
as he sat down; "I found myself in it rather unexpectedly. MP II 1 184 25
enjoyment, for it came unexpectedly, and with no such MP III 3 337 10
and as for Susan, now unexpectedly gratified in the first MP III 15 444 26
John Knightley came; but Mr. Weston was unexpectedly E II 16 292 9
Anne's engagement burst on Mr. Elliot most unexpectedly. P IV 12 250 7
UNEXPENSIVE (1)
him to a residence unexpensive, and by the sea; and the P III 11 97 12
UNEXPENSIVELY (1)
and that little unexpensively; but the last year or two E II 7 207 6
UNEXPLORED (1)
The place in the middle alone remained now unexplored; and NA II 6 169 11
UNEXPRESSED (1)
an heavy cold, because unexpressed by words, entirely SS III 6 305 16
UNFAIR (5)
manner while enjoying so unfair a division of his mother's SS III 5 298 32
"It is very unfair to judge of any body's conduct, without E I 18 146 15
very moderate, it was not unfair to guess the dignity of E II 4 183 9
your question, I must pronounce it to be a very unfair one. E II 6 200 18
her former fanciful and unfair conjectures was so little E III 8 384 34
UNFAIRLY (7)
better than a death unfairly hastened, as, in the natural NA II 8 188 16
fear of condemning him unfairly, and established as a fact, SS II 1 139 1
How could you behave so unfairly by your sister?" SS III 2 274 19
the first place been so unfairly obtained, she confined SS III 2 276 27
such a friendship as theirs should be severed unfairly. P IV 6 166 18
appearance might be not unfairly balanced against her P IV 12 248 2
both; that she had been unfairly influenced by appearances P IV 12 249 3
UNFASHIONABLE (1)
appearance was by no means ungenteel or unfashionable. SS I 21 119 3
UNFASTEN (2)
It was some time however before she could unfasten the NA II 6 169 11
his own use, he has to unfasten it from all the holds upon MP III 4 347 21
UNFASTENED (1)
sturdy hands were unfastened from around her neck, and he P III 9 80 33
UNFASTIDIOUS (1)
undistinguishing and unfastidious--and so apt to tell E I 10 84 16
UNFATHERLY (1)
Mr. Palmer maintained the common, but unfatherly opinion SS II 14 248 5
UNFATHOMABLE (1)
Mr. Willoughby is unfathomable! SS II 8 199 36
UNFAVOURABLE (14)
have given his wife an unfavourable impression--but where LS 5 250 1
Should the result of her observations be unfavourable, she SS II 4 159 1
her most unfavourable opinion of his head and heart. SS III 5 298 32
that would not give one an unfavourable idea of his heart. PP III 1 258 74
hope to conceal its unfavourable beginning, from all those PP III 8 311 11
Unfavourable circumstances had suddenly arisen at a moment MP I 4 38 9
of the park; in that respect, unfavourable for improvement. MP I 6 56 26
I think the confinement of Portsmouth unfavourable to. MP III 11 410 16
feelings in a most unfavourable light, and severely MP III 16 452 13
Too late he became aware how unfavourable to the character MP III 17 463 7
apologized over as an unfavourable likeness, to every E I 6 46 21
not but observe, was unfavourable to a nervous disorder:-- E III 9 389 16
the weather was unfavourable, and she had grieved over the P IV 11 229 2
to do away with any unfavourable impression which the sort S 1 367 1
UNFAVOURABLY (3)
they be thought of unfavourably, on their father's account, NA II 14 232 5
to the absence of the family, were unfavourably answered. PP II 19 241 16
It could not but strike her rather unfavourably with S 12 426 1
UNFEELING (16)
the cold and unfeeling behaviour of her nearer connections. SS I 4 23 20
she considered it as an unfeeling reflection on the SS I 8 36 2
I never thought Edward so stubborn, so unfeeling before. SS III 1 266 38
The united efforts of his two unfeeling sisters and of his PP I 23 129 13
not justify it, and the unfeeling manner in which he had PP II 11 193 31
Unfeeling, selfish girl! PP III 14 357 65
disappointing and unfeeling kind friends I ever met with! MP II 4 212 30
How could you be so unfeeling to Miss Bates? E III 7 374 56
to her, "how could you be so unfeeling to your father?-- E III 8 377 1
how irrational, how unfeeling had been her conduct! E III 11 408 33
than a thick-headed, unfeeling, unprofitable Dick Musgrove, P III 6 51 29
Very unfeeling! P III 7 56 10
I must say it is very unfeeling of him, to be running away P III 7 56 10
I did not think Charles would have been so unfeeling. P III 7 56 10
He could not forgive her,--but he could not be unfeeling. P III 10 91 42
him to have been very unfeeling in his conduct towards her, P IV 9 208 94
UNFEELINGLY (4)
than when behaving so dishonourably and unfeelingly!-- MP II 5 225 56
so carelessly, so unfeelingly on all such points--who was MP II 13 305 26
so very improperly and unfeelingly, I may speak of it now MP III 4 349 25
who was pursuing his triumph rather unfeelingly. E I 15 126 9
UNFEIGNED (4)
and admitted with unfeigned joy, and soon with unequivocal SS III 7 314 23
absent cousins with most unfeigned and truly tender regret, MP II 10 275 12
unfeigned eagerness, to express his interest in the event. MP II 13 299 4
looked with most unfeigned satisfaction at her companion. E I 4 31 27
UNFEIGNEDLY (1)
She did unfeignedly and unequivocally regret the E II 9 231 3
UNFELT (4)
The compliment to herself and her sister, was not unfelt. PP II 13 209 11
was neither unknown nor unfelt by the whole of the family. PP III 12 340 13
could her higher powers of mind be unfelt by the parents. E II 2 165 7
difference in their manner of doing it could not be unfelt. P IV 3 144 22
UNFEUDAL (1)
too strict to suit the unfeudal tone of the present day! P IV 3 139 7
UNFINISHED (3)
it up as well as its unfinished state admitted, were MP I 18 171 25
countenance, and his unfinished gallantry;--it was all E III 9 386 8
foreground of unfinished buildings, waving linen, & tops S 4 384 1
UNFIT (19)
him every hour of the day, made her unfit for anything. SS II 5 169 15
in it, make it unfit to become the public conversation. SS II 8 196 19
which make her unfit for company or conversation." SS II 10 219 38
I really did not consider how unfit I was to be here or I W 357 28
such reflections as must make her unfit for conversation. PP II 13 209 12
I always thought they were very unfit to have the charge PP III 5 287 35
Me! a poor helpless, forlorn widow, unfit for any thing, MP I 3 28 42
language of the other, so unfit to be expressed by any MP I 14 137 23
I think it exceedingly unfit for private representation, MP I 15 139 11
It is highly unfit for you to sit--be it only half an hour MP III 1 312 10
What was unwholesome to him, he regarded as unfit for any E I 2 19 14
dinner-parties made him unfit for any acquaintance, but E I 3 20 1
and unpolished, and very unfit to be the intimates of a E I 3 23 10
I am sure you always thought me unfit for the office I E I 5 38 10
all this morning--very unfit to be left alone, I am sure. P III 5 37 24
I am more unfit than any body else to be about the child. P III 7 56 10
particularly unfit to meet any extraordinary expense. P IV 5 154 9
countenance she knew was unfit to be seen), she was yet P IV 7 179 28
injury on the fallen side as to be unfit for present use.-- S 1 370 1
UNFITNESS (1)
a hint of her unfitness, an entreaty even to be excused. MP II 10 275 11
UNFITTED (2)
unfitted for each other by nature, education, and habit. MP III 2 327 5
the other night, will think you unfitted as companions? MP III 4 348 23
UNFIXED (4)
judging for herself, and unfixed as were her general NA I 9 66 32
Catherine, whose expectations had been as unfixed as her NA II 1 135 43
estimation of Northanger had waited unfixed till that hour. NA II 7 178 19
unfixed, and without seeming much aware of it himself. MP II 3 200 19
UNFLEDGED (1)
catch the music; like unfledged sparrows ready to be fed. P IV 9 193 6
UNFOLD (1)
the present should induce me to unfold to any human being. PP II 12 201 5
UNFOLDED (11)
five minutes; the second unfolded thus much in detail,-- NA I 15 116 1
here, when the whole was unfolded, was an insult not to be NA II 14 233 10
elucidation, for this very morning first unfolded it to us. SS II 8 199 36
I do not imagine that much has been unfolded." PP I 6 22 9
between the houses, he unfolded the matter,--to an PP I 23 126 1
2
of the wishes which had been unfolded in her former letter. PP II 1 133 2
Your character was unfolded in the recital which I PP II 11 191 17
a minute the letter was unfolded again, and collecting PP II 13 205 3
were to be the thing unfolded; and was now trying to be in MP II 1 180 10
Harriet unfolded the parcel, and she looked on with E III 4 338 9
Mr Parker's character & history were soon unfolded. S 2 371 1
UNFOLDING (2)
shall not prevent me from unfolding his real character. PP II 12 200 5
"Look here," said he, unfolding a parcel in his hand, and P IV 11 232 13
UNFORESEEN (1)
If, however, by any unforeseen chance it should be in my SS III 3 284 23
UNFORGIVING (3)
of his resentments, of his having an unforgiving temper. PP I 16 80 34
"That is the most unforgiving speech," said Elizabeth, " PP III 13 350 48
and there is nothing very unforgiving in that, I think." P IV 6 173 47
UNFORGIVINGNESS (1)
to what a degree of unforgivingness it might with NA I 12 92 3
UNFORMED (1)
the blooming, silent, unformed girl of fifteen, to the P IV 5 153 6
UNFORTUNATE (52)
"Say rather that she has been unfortunate in her education. LS 24 288 11
and the unfortunate dread of me I have been mentioning. LS 24 289 12
distress; the most unfortunate event has just taken place. LS 28 297 1
But the unfortunate Mrs Manwaring, whose agonies while she LS 36 306 1
was most particularly unfortunate herself in having missed NA I 9 69 51
the very spot of this unfortunate woman's confinement-- NA II 8 188 17
the apartments of the unfortunate Mrs. Tilney, must be, as NA II 8 188 17
be considered, in comparison with the past, as unfortunate. SS I 7 33 3
belief of his being an unfortunate man, and she regarded SS I 10 50 12
Her systems have all the unfortunate tendency of setting SS I 11 56 13
a series of unfortunate circumstances"-----here he stopt SS I 11 57 17
was still more unfortunate, for they did not go at all. SS I 13 63 1
general regret on so unfortunate an event; concluding SS I 13 66 60
"This is very unfortunate. SS I 15 76 9
and the next that some unfortunate quarrel had taken place SS I 15 77 19
proposed for this unfortunate scratch, and a slight SS I 21 121 10
mother; and I am so unfortunate, that I have not a SS I 22 132 42
Your case is a very unfortunate one; you seem to me to be SS II 2 146 6
point I could be so unfortunate as to offend you, I SS II 7 183 13
but if I have been so unfortunate as to give rise to a SS II 7 183 13
Willoughby to be as unfortunate and as innocent as herself, SS II 9 201 2
it was, though from a different cause, no less unfortunate. SS II 9 205 24
under a similar confinement, was my unfortunate sister. SS II 9 207 26
of tender concern, at the fate of his unfortunate friend. SS II 9 208 27
I might have been very unfortunate indeed; for the stocks SS II 11 225 33
"Your indifference, however, towards that unfortunate girl- SS III 8 322 37
in encouraging the unfortunate attachment to Willoughby, SS III 9 335 7
fancied him, since the story of that unfortunate girl"----- SS III 10 344 17
know nothing of our unfortunate Edward, and can make no SS III 11 353 21
Mrs. Ferrars was the most unfortunate of women--poor Fanny SS III 13 371 38
to Mrs Shaw just at that time as very unfortunate for me. W 317 2
The event has been unfortunate, but my uncle's memory is W 352 26
friend has drawn an unfortunate--but on this point it will PP II 15 216 6
"How unfortunate that you should have used such very PP II 17 226 20
console the unfortunate for their folly or their vice. PP II 19 236 1
Her coming there was the most unfortunate, the most ill- PP III 1 252 54
This unfortunate affair will, I fear, prevent my sister's PP III 4 278 20
"This is a most unfortunate affair; and will probably be PP III 5 289 42

consider it as very unfortunate that she had; for, less MP III 5 356 3
devote herself to her unfortunate Maria, and in an MP III 17 465 14
that it will be a very unfortunate one for Harriet. E I 8 64 47
"It is unfortunate that they cannot stay longer--but it E I 9 79 63
Harriet was further unfortunate in the tone of her E I 17 143 15
and, but for such an unfortunate fancy for having his hair E II 7 206 2
"I was only going to observe, that though such unfortunate E III 7 373 44
who will suffer an unfortunate acquaintance to be an E III 7 373 44
has been a most unfortunate--most deplorable mistake!-- E III 11 407 25
She felt herself ill-used and unfortunate, as did her P III 1 10 19
pardonable pride, received it as a most unfortunate one. P III 4 26 2
looks, that the same unfortunate persuasion, which had P IV 10 221 32
grant you, it is unfortunate for poor Arthur, that, at his S 5 388 1
in fact, with an unfortunate turn for Medecine, especially S 10 412 1

UNFORTUNATELY (26)

Unfortunately one knows her too well. LS 6 251 1
a nature, so unfortunately connected with the great London NA I 7 44 1
This critique, the justness of which was unfortunately NA I 7 49 43
"No," said Miss Tilney, sighing; "I was unfortunately from NA II 8 186 12
Unfortunately, the road she now travelled was the same NA II 14 230 1
good character, was unfortunately too infirm to mix with SS I 9 40 2
and spirit which Edward had unfortunately wanted. SS I 10 48 8
Colonel Brandon, unfortunately for himself, had no such SS I 11 55 7
Marianne, "we could not be more unfortunately situated." SS I 16 88 39
But unfortunately my own nicety, and the nicety of my SS I 19 102 4
were therefore unfortunately founded, when she advised her SS I 21 118 2
But unfortunately in bestowing these embraces, a pin in SS I 21 121 10
"I can believe it," said Elinor; "but unfortunately he did SS II 7 188 45
that, perhaps, so unfortunately circumstanced as he is now, SS III 3 282 19
a year, which, unfortunately for his daughters, was PP I 7 28 1
She is unfortunately of a sickly constitution, which has PP I 11 67 7
Unfortunately an only son, (for many years an only child) PP III 16 369 24
which, unfortunately for himself, he certainly has imbibed. MP III 1 320 44
with tolerable;--but, unfortunately, among the failures E I 12 104 50
Two dances, unfortunately, were all that could be allowed. E II 8 230 101
"But, unfortunately, sir, my time is so limited-----" E II 11 252 33
what is ridiculous are most unfortunately blended in her." E III 7 375 60
But of that, unfortunately, there could be no chance. E III 11 404 3
But, unfortunately--in short, if your compassion does not E III 16 459 47
Anne's opinion, most unfortunately) were cousins of the P IV 4 148 10
in the world!--and unfortunately" (speaking low and P IV 5 156 11

UNFOUNDED (5)

in an alarm not wholly unfounded, for General Tilney was NA II 6 165 5
her first anticipations was proved to have been unfounded. MP I 18 166 5
to be hoped, would prove unfounded; but there was no MP III 14 429 1
I think, of one such little article of unfounded news." P IV 9 197 41
to raise even the unfounded hopes which sunk with him. P IV 12 250 6

UNFREQUENCY (1)

It was her manner, however, rather than any unfrequency of MP III 13 421 2

UNFREQUENTLY (2)

its good effects not unfrequently; more was not expected MP III 9 397 8
Not unfrequently, through Emma's persuasion, he had some E I 3 20 1

UNFRIENDLY (4)

Very unfriendly, certainly; and he must be a very odd man;- NA II 14 237 21
them at Northanger had been of the most unfriendly kind. NA II 15 247 15
characters, or anything unfriendly in their situations; MP III 2 327 5
of all others the most unfriendly for exercise, every E I 16 138 17

UNFULFILLED (1)

to Willoughby was yet unfulfilled, and feared she had that SS III 10 343 10

UNFURNISHED (1)

of which, though unfurnished, Catherine was delighted NA II 11 213 21

UNGALLANT (1)

careful that nothing ungallant, nothing that did not E I 9 70 7

UNGENEROUS (15)

inexcusably artful and ungenerous since our marriage was LS 3 247 1
how little the ungenerous representations of any one to LS 10 257 1
I am afraid of being ungenerous or I should say she talks LS 15 267 4
Yes, novels;--for I will not adopt that ungenerous and NA I 5 37 4
Isabella appeared to her ungenerous and selfish, NA I 13 98 3
because I would not be ungenerous, or set you against NA II 12 216 2
should seem to act an ungenerous, a suspicious part by our SS I 15 81 43
At any rate it would be most ungenerous. SS I 16 84 9
assure yourself that no ungenerous reproach shall ever PP I 19 106 10
Indeed, Mr. Darcy, it is very ungenerous in you to mention PP II 8 174 15
No motive can excuse the unjust and ungenerous part you PP II 11 191 12
the necessaries of life, than do an ungenerous thing. MP I 1 7 8
ungenerous, it would be really wrong to expose her to it. MP I 16 154 14
did arise at a perseverance so selfish and ungenerous. MP III 2 328 9
a cure of every former ungenerous suspicion, and left her E III 8 379 9

UNGENIAL (1)

Tuesday, but it was an ungenial morning; and though you E III 14 436 7

UNGENTEEL (2)

appearance was by no means ungenteel or unfashionable. SS I 21 119 3
on the principle of its being very ungenteel to be curious. P IV 3 144 19

UNGENTLEMANLIKE (1)

He stopt; and, ungentlemanlike as he looked, Fanny was MP III 10 401 11

UNGOVERNABLE (2)

enough to be formal, ungovernable & to have the gout--too LS 29 298 1
She was not of so ungovernable a temper as Lydia, and, PP III 19 385 4

UNGRACEFUL (1)

with a plain face and ungraceful form, seemed fearful of NA I 7 45 5

UNGRACIOUS (12)

So acutely did Mrs. Dashwood feel this ungracious SS I 1 6 10
Ungracious girl! SS I 15 80 42
after such an ungracious delay as she owed to her own SS III 14 373 3
ashamed of her mother's ungracious and reluctant good PP II 3 145 11
Oh! how heartily did she grieve over every ungracious PP III 10 327 3
air more than usually ungracious, made no other reply to PP III 14 351 3
which prevented her from being very ungracious. MP I 6 52 1
could sometimes act an ungracious, or say a severe thing. E I 11 93 5
appear in the ungracious character of the one preferred-- E I 17 141 5
perhaps, more in thought than fact; scornful, ungracious. E III 8 377 1
Apologies for her seemingly ungracious silence in their E III 12 418 5
This, though late and reluctant and ungracious, was yet P IV 8 181 2

UNGRACIOUSLY (2)

he, "after thanks so ungraciously delivered as mine were SS III 13 368 30
added--"I stopped you ungraciously, just now, Mr. E III 13 429 32

UNGRACIOUSNESS (1)

Her mother's ungraciousness, made the sense of what they PP III 12 340 13

UNGRATEFUL (21)

He was neither so unjust, nor so ungrateful, as to leave SS I 1 4 3
of Mrs. Jennings, I had repaid with ungrateful contempt. SS III 10 346 28
"I was not so ungrateful sir, said Emma warmly, as to wish W 326 5
"I hope I am not ungrateful, aunt," said Fanny, modestly. MP I 3 25 13
that her feelings were ungrateful, and she really grieved MP I 3 32 64
"And very ungrateful I think." MP I 7 63 60
"Ungrateful is a strong word. MP I 7 63 7
her a very obstinate, ungrateful girl, if she does not do MP I 15 147 55
ungrateful indeed, considering who and what she is." MP I 15 147 55
Self-willed, obstinate, selfish, and ungrateful. MP III 1 319 40
Selfish and ungrateful! to have appeared so to him! MP III 1 321 46
all, perhaps all, would think her selfish and ungrateful. MP III 1 321 46
"I must be a brute indeed, if I can be really ungrateful!" MP III 1 322 52
in soliloquy; "heaven defend me from being ungrateful!" MP III 1 322 52
should not fancy her ungrateful, that Emma believed if the E I 7 55 35
Oh! Miss Woodhouse, how ungrateful I have been!" E II 13 268 14
"You are ungrateful." E III 2 324 27
"Ungrateful!-- E III 2 325 28
out--do not think us ungrateful, Miss Woodhouse, for such E III 8 379 8
But she could not be long ungrateful; he was sacrificing P IV 11 239 54
ungrateful that it can hardly be made to yeild a Cabbage.-- S 1 369 1

UNGUARDED (10)

We have been unguarded in forming this hasty engagement; LS 30 300 1
unguarded in speaking of my partiality for the church!-- NA I 15 118 13
shamefully unguarded affection could expose me to"----- SS III 10 345 20
I have a warm, unguarded temper, and I may perhaps have PP I 16 80 27
and Lydia, always unguarded and often uncivil, PP I 23 126 1
2
him in unguarded moments, which Mr. Darcy could not have. PP II 12 200 5
public notice of Lydia's unguarded and imprudent manner; PP II 18 231 16
lively hints, the unguarded expressions of the moment, MP II 3 198 13
A short absence from home had left his fair one unguarded P III 9 74 4
I had been unguarded. P IV 11 242 65

UNGUARDEDLY (1)

desire rather more unguardedly than was perfectly prudent. MP III 4 350 30

UNHANDSOME (2)

betray her into any observations seemingly unhandsome. MP II 3 199 16
"Come, come, it would be very unhandsome in us to be MP II 4 210 21

UNHAPPILY (6)

us all; but my sister is unhappily prejudiced beyond the LS 14 264 2
"Her indifferent state of health unhappily prevents her PP I 14 67 9
Your portion is unhappily so small that it will in all PP I 19 108 19
character we were most unhappily deceived; and by her PP II 12 201 5
former home, grew up there not unhappily among her cousins. MP I 2 20 32
pleasures, and his absence was unhappily most welcome. MP I 3 32 64

UNHAPPINESS (15)

that I was aware of her unhappiness? that it was my LS 24 289 12
The progress of Catherine's unhappiness from the events of NA I 9 60 1
Of her unhappiness in marriage, she felt persuaded. NA II 7 180 37
to merit her present unhappiness, and consoled by the SS II 1 140 4
of Colonel Brandon's unhappiness, and was prevented even SS II 5 174 47
Concern for her unhappiness, and respect for her fortitude SS II 9 210 32
you too well know, it has not been my only unhappiness.-- SS III 1 264 29
of unhappiness to himself of a far more incurable nature. SS III 8 331 70
to her than ever by absence, unhappiness, and danger. SS III 9 334 5
her from an increase of unhappiness, suffering as she then SS III 11 355 46
unhappiness which her sister's refusal must have given him. PP II 17 224 2
and all the unhappiness she had brought on her family. PP III 10 325 2
There is no appearance of unhappiness. MP III 13 423 2
The unhappiness produced by the knowledge of that E II 4 184 11
have escaped the greatest unhappiness I have ever known.-- E III 14 440 8

UNHAPPY (82)

The poor girl looks so unhappy that my heart aches for her. LS 17 270 4
Do not let Frederica vernon be made unhappy by that Martin. LS 23 284 4
She blushed deeply as she answered, "I was so unhappy LS 24 286 5
She has no right to make you unhappy, & she shall not do LS 24 287 7
Depend upon it that you shall not be made unhappy any LS 24 287 7
Frederica makes me very unhappy. LS 24 289 12
ever, tho' so innocently, made her unhappy on that score. LS 24 290 13
In spite of this release, Frederica still looks unhappy, LS 24 291 16
Unhappy man!-- NA II 8 187 13
Poor James is so unhappy!-- NA II 10 204 13
one you love should be unhappy; but my surprize would be NA II 10 204 20
Her brother so unhappy, and her loss in Isabella so great; NA II 11 212 16
of the latter--I am quite unhappy about him, he seemed so NA II 12 217 2
But do not be unhappy, Eleanor. NA II 13 225 22
had delineated in that unhappy hour and in every brighter SS I 10 49 10
to comprehend all the unhappy truths which attended the SS I 12 58 3
It was evident that he was unhappy; she wished it were SS I 18 96 1
As for Marianne, on the pangs which so unhappy a meeting SS II 6 179 18
by saying, "poor Elinor! how unhappy I make you!" SS II 7 185 16
17
Every additional day of unhappy confidence, on your side, SS II 7 186 29
Their good friend saw that Marianne was unhappy, and felt SS II 8 193 7
"It was nearly three years after this unhappy period SS II 9 207 26
a pause, "has been the unhappy resemblance between the SS II 9 211 40
Elinor could not now be made unhappy by this behaviour.- SS II 12 232 16
Don't let them make you unhappy." SS II 12 236 40
you and my mother most unhappy whenever it were explained SS III 1 263 29
openly shewing that I was very unhappy."-- SS III 1 264 29
"I am sorry to say, ma'am, in a most unhappy rupture:-- SS III 1 268 48
to be unhappy, induced her to accept it with pleasure. SS III 3 279 1
When Edward's unhappy match takes place, depend upon it SS III 5 296 20
was known to have been greatly injured, and long unhappy. SS III 7 313 20
of dear Marianne's unhappy prepossession for that SS III 9 336 14
No;--not less when I knew you to be unhappy, than when I SS III 10 346 28
wished to see;--happy or unhappy,--nothing pleased her; SS III 12 357 4
"An unhappy alternative is before you, Elizabeth. PP I 20 112 19
unhappy, there may be error, and there may be misery. PP II 1 136 17
body acting unnaturally and wrong, and me most unhappy. PP II 1 137 24
of making any of you unhappy; but since we see every day PP II 3 145 7
as he was, she did not mean to be unhappy about him. PP II 11 188 2
my friend from what I esteemed a most unhappy connection.-- PP II 12 198 5
and regret; and in the unhappy defects of her family a PP II 14 212 17
I was very uncomfortable, I may say unhappy. PP II 17 226 19
Conceal the unhappy truth as long as it is possible. PP III 4 278 21
of replying, she added, "unhappy as the event must be for PP III 5 289 43
The present unhappy state of the family, rendered any PP III 6 298 17
"Well, well," said he, "do not make yourself unhappy. PP III 6 300 32
he was going to be made unhappy, and that it should be PP III 17 375 28
The little visitor meanwhile was as unhappy as possible. MP I 2 13 4
If you consider my unhappy state, how can she be any MP I 3 29 46
Unhappy Maria! MP I 8 80 30
was quite unhappy in having to communicate what had passed. MP I 10 101 33
unhappy by him as a sailor or soldier than as a clergyman. MP I 11 111 30
up, if she felt herself unhappy in the prospect of it. MP II 3 200 21
I do desire that you will not be making her really unhappy; MP II 6 230 8
and were unhappy too!--it was all wretchedness together. MP III 1 321 46
to be about as unhappy as most other married people. MP III 5 361 16
Anxious not to appear unhappy, she soon recovered herself: MP III 7 384 35
friend, and that whatever unhappy differences of opinion MP III 13 420 2
and though evidently unhappy in her marriage, places her MP III 13 421 2
to be mortified and unhappy, till some other pretty girl MP III 17 464 12
He had never been an unhappy man; his own temper had E I 2 17 6
alarmed, and might be made unhappy about her sister." E I 5 40 26
at the idea of making him unhappy, and thought so much of E I 7 55 35
sisters know--if he is unhappy, they will be unhappy too. E I 7 56 43
Poor little creatures, how unhappy she would have made E I 14 122 17
It made him so very unhappy, indeed, that it could not be E II 11 248 10
not admit herself to be unhappy, nor, after the first E II 13 264 1
"Your allowing yourself to be so occupied and so unhappy E II 13 268 10
She had an unhappy state of health in general for the E III 3 336 12
On that subject poor Miss Bates was very unhappy, and very E III 9 391 19
she need no longer be unhappy about Jane, whose troubles E III 11 403 2
She should not be made unhappy by any coldness now,) gave E III 11 408 33
Harriet, who had been standing in no unhappy reverie, was E III 11 408 34
"that I must often have contributed to make her unhappy." E III 12 419 11
little inferior to the pain of having made Harriet unhappy. E III 17 463 15
would now make me unhappy, but I cannot believe it. E III 18 471 17
surprised--but it does not make me unhappy, I assure you.-- E III 18 471 19
would not now make you unhappy; but I am afraid it gives E III 18 472 21
22
make a degrading match; but he might be rendered unhappy. P III 5 35 14
language; and, in an unhappy mood, thus spoke Mary:--"I do P III 6 44 7
Anne had gone unhappy to school, grieving for the loss of P IV 5 152 2
and had made herself so unhappy about it that, for a day P IV 10 216 19

UNHEALTHY (2)

South end is an unhealthy place. E I 12 105 54
to suppose the place unhealthy; and I am sure he may be E I 12 105 55

UNHEARD (5)

This part of his intelligence, though unheard by Lydia, PP I 18 89 3
She thought he was wishing to speak to her unheard by the MP II 13 306 27
Exactly so, indeed--quite unheard of--but some ladies say E III 7 370 22
it immediately, to say, unheard by her father, "can you E III 10 392 1

	2
Captain Wentworth, after being unseen and unheard of at	P III 11 94 5
UNIFORM (8)	
In one thing, however, she was uniform, when it came to	SS II 9 201 2
composure of temper and a uniform cheerfulness of manner,	PP I 6 21 1
made, to shew his happiness and describe his uniform.	MP III 6 368 7
delighted to shew his uniform there too, had not cruel	MP III 6 368 8
So the uniform remained at Portsmouth, and Edmund	MP III 6 368 8
more worthless, than the uniform of a lieutenant, who has	MP III 6 368 8
alteration of his uniform waist-coat, which he had been	MP III 7 381 26
He, complete in his lieutenant's uniform, looking and	MP III 7 384 34
UNIFORMITY (2)	
no uniformity of architecture had been thought necessary.	NA II 8 184 4
forth in beauteous uniformity of lines, crowded with the	PP II 18 232 22
UNIFORMLY (7)	
been attempted; all has been uniformly open and unreserved.	SS I 15 80 42
with a turn for being uniformly civil and happy, was	SS I 19 106 23
On that head, therefore, I shall be uniformly silent; and	PP I 19 106 10
"You are uniformly charming!" cried he, with an air of	PP I 19 109 21
so frequently, so almost uniformly betrayed by herself, by	PP II 12 198 5
Edmund was uniformly kind himself, and she had nothing	MP I 2 17 22
conducting herself uniformly with great good sense, &	S 3 378 1
UNIMPAIRED (1)	
between them continuing unimpaired by Mr. Elliot's	P IV 9 208 95
UNIMPEDED (1)	
as it ought to do, unimpeded by Miss Woodhouse, who	E II 15 281 2
UNIMPORTANT (5)	
of travelling unimportant, distance becomes no evil.	PP II 9 179 22
or the economy of his aunt, to make it appear unimportant.	MP I 4 36 7
of it, or that its purpose was unimportant--and staid.	MP III 17 467 20
neither Lady Russell nor Mr. Elliot thought unimportant.	P IV 4 149 12
thus oddly begun, was neither short nor unimportant.	S 2 370 1
UNINFLUENCED (2)	
But Mrs. Dashwood was alike uninfluenced by either	SS I 3 15 5
world capable of being uninfluenced by ambition, I can	MP II 12 293 15
UNINFORMED (3)	
and uninformed as the female mind at seventeen usually is.	NA I 2 18 1
that Fanny was yet uninformed of his sister's being there,	SS III 5 298 32
You cannot suppose me uninformed.	MP III 4 346 8
UNINHABITED (1)	
it has never been uninhabited and left deserted for years,	NA II 5 158 14
UNINTELLIGIBLE (8)	
I cannot speak well enough to be unintelligible."	NA II 1 133 23
in great agitation, and drops a few unintelligible hints.	NA II 5 158 17
He coloured, and stammered out an unintelligible reply.	SS III 12 359 12
as made her almost unintelligible, to fetch his master and	PP III 4 276 8
so quick he would be unintelligible, that Mrs. Grant	MP I 18 164 2
life, to find any charm in it, all this was unintelligible.	MP III 2 327 5
Beyond this, it must ever be unintelligible to Emma.	E III 19 481 2
unless he could do no better, was unintelligible.--	S 7 398 1
UNINTELLIGIBLY (1)	
one of that class, so unintelligibly moral, so infamously	MP II 2 191 10
UNINTENTIONAL (2)	
it has been quite unintentional on my side, I never had	NA II 3 145 13
what I can assure you to have been perfectly unintentional.	SS II 7 183 13
UNINTENTIONALLY (2)	
Unintentionally she returned to that part of the room; he	P III 8 72 58
	59
unconsciously, nay unintentionally; that he had meant to	P IV 11 241 61
UNINTERESTING (2)	
Every thing is so insipid, so uninteresting, that does not	NA I 6 41 16
to be, was no longer uninteresting when she knew his heart	SS I 3 16 13
UNINTERRUPTED (3)	
that it was not all uninterrupted enjoyment to the party	MP I 18 164 1
had been thought of in uninterrupted health, had probably	MP III 13 427 13
and half an hour's uninterrupted communication of all	E I 14 117 1
UNINTERRUPTEDLY (1)	
"I have not been working uninterruptedly," he replied, "I	E II 10 240 5
UNINTRICATE (1)	
passages, not wholly unintricate, connected the different	NA II 8 183 2
UNINVITED (1)	
might she have gone in uninvited and unnoticed to hear the	MP I 7 65 14
UNINVITING (1)	
calm and uninviting, that he had nothing to censure in her.	MP II 7 246 37
UNION (16)	
an uncommon union of symmetry, brilliancy and grace.	LS 6 251 1
at preventing their union, which have been attributed to	LS 14 264 2
begun to consider her union with Sir James as not very	LS 20 277 5
derived from him during an union of some years, I cannot	LS 30 300 3
It will surely therefore be advisable to delay our union,	LS 30 301 4
I hate money; and if our union could take place now upon	NA II 1 136 48
It was an union that must have been to the advantage of	PP III 8 312 15
An union of a different tendency, and precluding the	PP III 8 312 16
While in their cradles, we planned the union: and now, at	PP III 14 355 43
and entertaining their young cousin, produced little union.	MP I 2 14 7
There was a languor, a want of spirits, a want of union,	E III 7 367 1
It was an union to distance every wonder of the kind.--	E III 11 413 48
It was a union of the highest promise of felicity in	E III 17 468 31
were fully answered in the perfect happiness of the union.	E III 19 484 12
Their union, she believed, could not divide her more from	P IV 9 192 2
mixture of character, that union of littleness with	S 3 378 1
UNION-PASSAGE (2)	
opposite Union-Passage; but here they were stopped.	NA I 7 44 1
of coming opposite to Union-Passage, and within view of	NA I 7 44 1
UNION-STREET (3)	
off for Union-Street on a commission of Mrs. Clay's.	P IV 7 175 5
They were in Union-Street, when a quicker step behind, a	P IV 11 239 55
was at the bottom of Union-Street again, and the other two	P IV 11 240 59
UNISON (5)	
is undoubtedly in unison with our situation & with those	LS 25 292 3
in perfect unison with what she had heard and seen herself.	SS I 12 61 14
and was exactly in unison with her opinion of each.	PP I 10 47 2
silence; it was all in unison; words, conduct, discretion,	E III 5 343 2
no feelings so in unison, no countenances so beloved.	P III 8 63 3
UNITE (12)	
Where pride & stupidity unite, there can be no	LS 4 248 2
mine, it will unite us again in the same intimacy as ever.	LS 39 307 1
unite them again in the fullness of privileged affection.	NA II 16 250 3
have been sufficient to unite them in friendship, without	SS III 13 370 36
that she and her cousin will unite the two estates."	PP I 16 83 55
tried to unite civility and truth in a few short sentences.	PP II 15 216 5
who seemed as naturally to unite, and who after a short	MP I 9 90 36
for her happiness, would unite her to the lover, on whom	MP I 11 107 3
feelings yielded to love, and such love must unite them.	MP III 6 367 4
disposition, seemed to unite some of the best blessings of	E I 1 5 1
And to propose that she and I should unite to form a	E II 14 279 52
the two parties should unite, and go together; and that as	E III 6 353 3
UNITED (47)	
The females of the family are united against me.	LS 2 244 1
youth and diffidence are united, it requires uncommon	NA I 7 50 44
The two friends, with hearts now more united than ever,	NA I 15 120 25
I have united for their ease what they must divide for	NA II 15 247 14
To satisfy me, those characters must be united.	SS I 3 17 18
when suddenly the clouds united over their heads, and a	SS I 9 41 6
of the gentleman, he united frankness and vivacity, and	SS I 10 46 2
touch her, and all their united soothings were ineffectual	SS I 21 121 10
than when her husband united them together in one noisy	SS II 1 143 9
believed herself to be speaking their united inclinations.	SS II 3 153 1
too with such reliance, such confidence in me!--	SS III 8 324 42
of person and talents, united a disposition naturally open	SS III 8 331 70
soon brought, by their united request, to consider his own	SS III 10 341 4
At his and Mrs. Jennings's united request in return, Mrs.	SS III 10 341 4
in general, since Jane united with great strength of	PP I 6 21 1
and application, and elegance, as you describe, united."	PP I 8 40 54
The united efforts of his two unfeeling sisters and of his	PP I 23 129 13
air and manner, not often united with great sensibility.	PP II 13 208 9
Elizabeth had frequently united with Jane in an endeavour	PP II 14 213 17
hardly have found expression in their united volubility.	PP II 18 232 22
afterwards united to my nephew, my own nephew, Mr. Darcy.	PP III 14 353 26
in nothing else, were united in affection for these	MP I 4 40 15
hill, they were united, and a "there he is" broke at the	MP I 8 81 31
one that could be united with the butler, and began to be	MP I 18 164 1
The party being now all united, and the chief talkers	MP II 5 227 68
again, and every former united pain and pleasure retraced	MP II 6 234 18
match at last, and that, united by mutual affection, it	MP III 3 335 6
a young lady in the united kingdoms, who would not rather	MP III 10 402 11
may exist between us, we are united in our love of you.--	MP III 13 420 2
they are beyond what our incomes united could authorise.	MP III 13 421 2
see him; and from various united causes, from his long	E I 3 20 1
But, Ah! united, what reverse we have!	E I 9 71 14
But Ah! united (courtship, you know,) what reverse we have!	E I 9 73 18
of being a real friend, united to produce an offer from	E II 2 163 4
united; the shop first in size and fashion in the place.--	E II 3 178 52
of the united voices gave only momentary interruptions.	E II 8 227 87
It seemed as if every thing united to promise the most	E III 3 335 10
They all united; and, on reaching Hartfield gates, Emma,	E III 5 344 3
coming had been united, such as the last accounts of Mrs.	E III 6 352 1
it united with the subject which already engaged her mind.	E III 8 384 32
Sir Walter Elliot, who united these gifts, was the	P III 1 4 5
to her; her; and, united as they all seemed by the	P III 12 115 67
His daughter and Mrs. Clay united in hinting that Colonel	P IV 3 142 13
Every thing united in him; good understanding, correct	P IV 4 146 6
walk, they found the united denham party;--but though	S 7 395 1
denham party;--but though united in the gross, very	S 7 395 1
himself away, & they united their agreeableness--that is,	S 7 399 1
UNITEDLY (1)	
warm as friendship and design could unitedly dictate.	SS III 11 352 18
UNITES (1)	
fine country, because it unites beauty with utility--and I	SS I 18 97 4
UNITING (7)	
The time of the two parties uniting in the Octagon Room	NA I 7 51 54
such an evil seemed uniting to heighten the misery of	SS II 6 179 18
contriving manager, uniting at once a desire of smart	SS III 12 357 3
her into Derbyshire, had been the means of uniting them.	PP III 19 388 13
where a comfortable meal, uniting dinner and supper, wound	MP III 7 376 5
by uniting himself to a rich woman of inferior birth.	P III 1 8 15
must suffer heavily, uniting very strong feelings with	P III 11 97 12
UNIVERSAL (11)	
of absolute coquetry, or a desire of universal admiration.	LS 8 256 4
and to distrust his powers of giving universal pleasure.	NA I 9 66 32
It is a match that must give universal satisfaction.	SS II 11 224 24
agreable, an universal favourite wherever he goes.	W 315 1
of my encroaching on your privilege of universal good will.	PP II 1 135 11
The dejection was almost universal.	PP II 18 229 1
off any portion of that universal contempt which her rage	PP II 18 231 18
practice," said Edmund, "but not quite universal.	MP I 9 92 41
It was her own universal good-will and contented temper	E I 3 21 4
If he were a little spoilt by such universal, such eager	P III 8 71 57
opinion as to the universal felicity and advantage of	P III 12 116 72
UNIVERSALLY (11)	
now burst forth universally; and they all agreed again and	SS I 13 66 52
correspond, and their marriage is universally talked of."	SS II 5 173 42
the favour they were in, as must be universally striking.	SS II 14 254 28
and feeling herself universally ill, could no longer hope	SS III 7 308 4
It is a truth universally acknowledged, that a single man	PP I 1 3 1
of Wickham, and of hearing that he was universally liked.	PP I 18 90 5
"At once to insist upon having such a report universally	PP III 14 354 28
for her father was universally civil, but not one among	E I 1 7 10
power as well as the wish of being universally agreeable.	E I 18 150 31
She was proved to have been universally mistaken; and she	E III 11 413 47
The news was universally a surprise wherever it spread;	E III 17 468 33
UNIVERSE (2)	
I detest: I would not settle in London for the universe.	NA I 15 119 20
Not for the universe--but I shall never forget your	W 320 2
UNIVERSITIES (1)	
belonged to one of the universities, he had merely kept	PP I 15 70 1
UNIVERSITY (1)	
which belonging to the university would have given me, for	SS III 13 362 5
UNJUST (27)	
unjust thing of any woman at all, or an unkind one of me."	NA I 14 114 48
that the General's unjust interference, so far from being	NA II 16 252 7
He was neither so unjust, nor so ungrateful, as to leave	SS I 1 4 3
herself for being unjust to his merit before, in believing	SS I 3 14 2
not more undiscerning, than you are prejudiced and unjust."	SS I 10 50 18
How can you be so unjust?	SS I 16 88 40
I had been insolent and unjust; with an heart hardened	SS III 10 346 28
She feared that under this persuasion she had been unjust,	SS III 11 356 46
But I know the foundation is unjust.	PP I 21 119 21
No motive can excuse the unjust and ungenerous part you	PP II 11 191 12
to be unprincipled or unjust--any thing that spoke him of	PP II 13 207 6
and all the unjust accusations accompanying her rejection.	PP III 2 265 16
sake, I would not do so unjust a think by the poor girl.	MP I 3 29 46
This was a most unjust reflection, but Fanny could allow	MP I 10 101 29
nothing could be more unjust, though he had been so lately	MP III 1 323 57
"I know that you all love her really too well to be unjust	E I 5 40 24
Mr. Martin; but, as I said before, are unjust to Harriet.	E I 8 63 44
supposed it could make him unjust to the merit of another.	E I 18 150 37
He had been used to think her unjust to Jane, and had now	E II 3 170 1
Emma's colour was heightened by this unjust praise; and	E III 9 385 7
'His father's disposition:'--he is unjust, however, to his	E III 15 445 11
it with high and unjust resentment, though perfectly	P III 10 91 42
he would not long be so unjust as to suppose she would	P III 12 116 69
"Pardon me, my dear cousin, you are unjust to your own	P IV 4 151 19
"Unjust I may have been, weak and resentful I have been, "	P IV 11 237 42
angry; and he had been unjust to her merits, because he	P IV 11 241 61
sort of reading, it were unjust to say that he read	S 8 404 1
UNJUSTIFIABLE (8)	
no reversing decree of unjustifiable anger, could shake	NA II 15 247 15
her ideas of perfection, had been rash and unjustifiable.	SS I 10 49 10
situation in which the unjustifiable conduct of your	SS III 4 289 31
what their present feelings were, seemed unjustifiable.	PP III 5 291 56
Lady Catherine's unjustifiable endeavours to separate us,	PP III 18 381 14
his income was unsettled, seemed to her very unjustifiable.	MP I 4 36 7
intimacy of his unjustifiable theatre, made an impression	MP III 17 462 4
of very unwise & unjustifiable resentment at the time of	S 3 377 1
UNJUSTLY (2)	
when she considered how unjustly she had condemned and	PP II 14 212 17
thing, which for a time, and not unjustly, offended him.	PP III 16 371 45
UNKIND (23)	
I have been called an unkind mother, but it was the sacred	LS 2 245 1
Do not think me unkind for such an exercise of my power,	LS 30 299 1
Catherine thought this reproach equally strange and unkind.	NA I 13 98 3
shall think you quite unkind, if you still refuse."	NA I 13 99 3
unjust thing of any woman at all, or an unkind one of me."	NA I 14 114 48
The General certainly had been an unkind husband.	NA II 7 180 37
He meant not to be unkind however, and, as a mark of his	SS I 1 4 3
it; and it was the more unkind in my father, because,	SS I 2 11 20
Indeed, you are doing a very unkind thing in spreading the	SS II 7 182 11
at all, it would be quite unkind to keep her on to the	SS III 2 273 16
inattentive, nay, almost unkind, to her Elinor;--that	SS III 11 356 46
Nobody meant to be unkind, but nobody put themselves out	MP I 2 14 6
sinking under her aunt's unkind reflection and reproach.	MP I 16 150 1
himself, to say nothing unkind of the others; but there	MP II 2 187 1
it very unkind of her not to come by such an opportunity.	MP III 6 372 21

Mrs. Price was not unkind--but, instead of gaining on her MP III 8 389 4
of conduct, and grossly unkind and ill-judged; but she MP III 12 418 4
Thomas was quite unkind, both to her aunt and to herself.-- MP III 13 424 4
as no mother--not unkind, except Mrs. Price, could have MP III 15 442 22
too well to be unjust or unkind; but excuse me, Mr. E I 5 40 24
It was quite unkind of you not to come on Thursday." P III 5 38 31
No, it was too unkind! P III 12 115 65
He was very unkind to his first wife. P IV 9 211 101

UNKINDLY (2)
cried Willoughby, "you are now using me unkindly. SS I 10 51 28
to have been, and from the first he treated her unkindly. SS II 9 206 24

UNKINDNESS (15)
with inattention if not unkindness to her own child, LS 3 247 1
me on the impropriety & unkindness of allowing Sir James LS 22 281 4
No unkindness however on the part of Lady Susan appeared. LS 42 312 3
supported; and its unkindness she would hardly have NA I 15 121 25
aware of this double unkindness; but for remonstrance, NA II 4 150 1
which the neglect or unkindness of slight acquaintance NA II 14 239 28
opposition and unkindness, could be felt as a relief! SS II 1 140 3
she experienced great unkindness, overcame all her SS II 9 205 24
I have had to contend against the unkindness of his sister, SS III 1 264 29
"The unkindness of your own relations has made you SS III 4 289 33
To treat her with unkindness, to speak of her slightingly SS III 8 329 64
and gratitude for the unkindness she was treated with, SS III 14 377 11
really endured such unkindness, was enough to interest all PP I 17 85 1
from any sound of unkindness, was unspeakably welcome to a MP I 4 35 6
ashamed of their own abominable neglect and unkindness. MP II 12 297 33

UNKNOWINGLY (4)
the tempest subsided, or she unknowingly fell fast asleep. NA II 6 171 12
eagerness; her hand, unknowingly to herself, closely SS III 10 348 33
feelings, it was unknowingly done; and though the motives PP II 12 199 5
quite unknowingly, within twenty miles of each other. P III 11 94 6

UNKNOWN (27)
at their door--not one young man whose origin was unknown. NA I 1 16 10
lived, shut up for causes unknown, and receiving from the NA II 8 187 16
Middleton was entirely unknown to Mrs. Dashwood, she SS I 5 26 6
procured by some theft or contrivance unknown to herself. SS I 18 98 13
a gentleman and lady, who were quite unknown to her. SS I 19 105 13
only given her, because her real situation was unknown. SS II 13 238 2
from having been entirely unknown and unthought of before. SS III 11 350 9
opened to his nieces a source of felicity unknown before. PP I 7 28 4
the next evening, although utterly unknown to her before. PP I 15 74 13
in the case, unknown to the society of Hertfordshire; her PP II 1 138 31
his compliments to Mr. and Mrs. Gardiner, though unknown. PP II 15 217 8
to tens and to scores of them at present unknown. PP II 18 232 22
was neither unknown nor unfelt by the whole of the family. PP III 12 340 13
unknown to them, even inferior to what Elizabeth felt. PP III 14 351 2
falsehood had before been unknown to her; and in spite of PP III 19 386 6
It is unknown how much was consumed in our kitchen by odd MP I 3 30 50
to his uncle, for it was unknown how much he had cost his MP II 13 304 19
how much of the truth was unknown to him, she believed she MP III 2 331 17
though on his own estate, had been hitherto unknown to him. MP III 10 404 15
their real disposition unknown to him, and sending them MP III 17 463 7
name, I dare say, is not unknown to you, does not conceive E II 14 275 31
talents as her's must not be suffered to remain unknown.-- E II 15 282 5
no idea that you will suppose her talents can be unknown." E II 15 283 6
ordered was absolutely unknown to Miss F--, who would E III 14 439 8
advantage in seeing how unknown, or unconsidered there, P III 6 42 1
of an old pier of unknown date, were the Harvilles settled. P III 11 96 10
of Sanditon, may be unknown at this distance from the S 1 368 1

UNLESS (61)
another school, unless we can get her married immediately. LS 16 268 1
Reginald is never easy unless we are by ourselves, & when LS 16 268 2
ought to be, unless noted down every evening in a journal? NA I 3 27 28
satisfied with the day unless she spent the chief of it by NA I 5 36 3
would not dance with him, unless he would allow Miss NA I 6 40 14
of being too handsome unless he wore the dress of a groom, NA I 7 45 5
too much like a gentleman unless he were easy where he NA I 7 45 5
young man, unless circumstances are particularly untoward. NA I 14 111 29
understand yourself--unless you mean to have her think you NA I 14 113 40
of her strength, that, unless secured by supernatural NA II 6 164 3
will be very constant, unless a baronet should come in her NA II 10 206 34
He was not an ill-disposed young man, unless to be rather SS I 1 5 7
will listen to no cavil, unless you can point out any SS I 15 78 26
"Yet I hardly know how," cried Marianne, "unless it had SS I 21 122 12
with you, unless it were on the side of your wishes." SS II 2 150 31
He will never marry unless he can marry somebody very W 319 2
"Unless Sam feels on sure grounds with the lady herself, W 321 2
till the following morng, unless the Edwardses wd send her W 338 18
"Yes--but unless they are so stout as to injure their W 345 21
not engage--you will not think of me unless you see me."-- W 360 28
You know how I detest it, unless I am particularly PP I 3 11 9
never speaks much unless among his intimate acquaintance. PP I 5 19 13
I know of nobody that is coming I am sure, unless PP I 13 61 2
unwilling to speak, unless we expect to say something that PP I 18 91 15
to do it, unless there were something very objectionable? PP II 1 137 24
should meet at all, unless he really comes to see her." PP II 2 141 12
never play really well, unless she practises more; and PP II 8 173 10
"Unless where they like women of fortune, which I think PP II 10 183 13
Unless the elder brother is very sickly, I suppose you PP II 10 184 15
cleared of all blame, unless any could attach to the PP II 14 213 18
officer above once a day, unless by some cruel and PP II 19 238 6
Balls will be absolutely prohibited, unless you stand up PP III 6 300 30
They will then join his regiment, unless they are first PP III 8 313 19
Pray write instantly, and let me understand it--unless it PP III 9 320 33
unless Mr. Darcy returned within the stated time. PP III 13 345 20
till after supper; unless when some barbarous neighbour, PP III 13 349 43
happy nor respectable, unless you truly esteemed your PP III 17 376 35
your husband; unless you looked up to him as a superior. PP III 17 376 35
not to speak to him, unless it was in her power to offer PP III 17 378 46
subject will afford, and unless you believe me actually PP III 18 382 21
to be longer deaf; "unless I had gone myself indeed; but I MP I 7 73 53
not to lose my companion, unless she is afraid of the MP I 10 105 52
and no witnesses, unless the servants chiefly intent upon MP II 6 233 15
a determined rejection? unless it were an acceptance even MP II 8 255 10
unless she had Fanny to herself she could hope for nothing. MP II 11 287 18
the whole of his visit, unless actually sent for; and as MP III 1 311 2
many--perhaps with most people, unless taken moderately. E I 2 19 14
what he preferred, and, unless he fancied himself at any E I 3 20 1
the air and complexion, unless they are coarser featured E I 6 45 21
coolly said, "I shall not be satisfied, unless he comes." E I 14 123 26
pork--and, my dear Emma, unless one could be sure of their E II 3 171 16 17
it is a very dirty walk, unless you keep on the foot-path; E II 5 195 47
I have no pleasure in seeing my friends, unless I can E II 8 222 53
"I see no probability in it, unless you have any better E II 8 224 72
carry you far, unless you are persuaded of his liking you. E III 4 342 39
avoid observations which, unless it were like Cowper and E III 5 344 2
did, unless you had been determined to give it against me." P III 9 77 16
The sweet scenes of autumn were for a while put by--unless P III 10 85 12
"None, I thank you, unless you will give me the pleasure P IV 6 169 26
having suffered in it, unless it has been all suffering, P IV 8 184 16
unless he could do no better, was unintelligible.-- S 7 398 1

UNLIKE (35)
almost its equal in degree, however unlike in kind. NA I 11 86 50
her apartment was very unlike the one which Henry had NA II 6 163 1
"It is enough," said she; "to say that he is unlike Fanny SS I 3 16 8
unlike a lover, so unlike himself, greatly disturbed her. SS I 15 77 19
a serious accent, "to be as unlike myself as is possible. SS I 19 103 6
and fancy that any one unlike yourself must be happy. SS I 19 103 7
Lady Middleton, and totally unlike her in every respect. SS I 19 106 22
he is very unlike his brother--silly and a great coxcomb." SS II 2 148 19
woman of many words: for, unlike people in general, she SS II 12 232 15
& the complexion, & even the features be very unlike."-- W 324 3
have struck him as very unlike the encouraging warmth he W 335 13
propriety, totally unlike the half-awkward, half-fearless W 346 21
quick accent, totally unlike the first--"have you heard W 351 24
They always continue to grow sufficiently unlike PP I 6 23 10
His understanding and temper, though unlike her own, would PP III 8 312 15
Your tempers are by no means unlike. PP III 13 348 38
I roused, and interested you, because I was so unlike them. PP III 18 380 5
but a value for Edmund, Miss Crawford was very unlike her. MP I 8 80 31
have done--but then I am unlike other people I dare say." MP II 3 197 5
Do you want to be told that you are only unlike other MP II 3 197 6
"We are so totally unlike," said Fanny, avoiding a direct MP III 4 348 22
Your being so far unlike, Fanny, does not in the smallest MP III 4 348 23
the tempers had better be unlike; I mean unlike in the MP III 4 349 23
better be unlike; I mean unlike in the flow of the spirits, MP III 4 349 23
Quite unlike his usual self, he scarcely said any thing. MP III 5 365 35
my first reception was so unlike what I had hoped, that I MP III 13 421 2
her own little elegant figure!--and the face not unlike. E I 6 45 21
"In that respect how unlike dear Mrs. Elton, who wants to E II 15 288 39
The house was larger than Hartfield, and totally unlike it, E III 6 358 35
Emma was sure he had not forgiven her; he looked unlike E III 9 385 5
So unlike what a man should be!-- E III 10 397 48
so uncommon, so unlike the usual style of give-and-take P III 11 98 16
in prosperous love, all that was most unlike Anne Elliot! P IV 1 123 7
very unlike him--led by him, and probably despised by him. P IV 9 209 95
compassion, was not very unlike her sister in person or S 10 413 1

UNLIKELY (15)
I told him he had taken a very unlikely way to prevail NA II 1 134 39
struck her as not unlikely, that she might that morning NA II 8 188 17
true, as it seemed very unlikely that Willoughby should SS I 13 68 66
And yet it is not very unlikely." SS II 11 224 26
all things was the most unlikely to occur, with a more SS III 6 301 1
be to assert a very unlikely thing, & describe a very odd W 347 22
But, whatever may be their own wishes, it is very unlikely PP II 1 137 24
As she had heard no carriage, she thought it not unlikely PP II 9 177 1
was wounding, but was very unlikely to recommend his suit. PP II 11 189 5
It appears to me so very unlikely, that any young man PP III 5 282 1
It was most unlikely, therefore, that he should ever want E I 2 17 7
yesterday, it is not unlikely that he should be at Mrs. E I 8 60 27
It is too unlikely, for me to believe it without proof." E I 18 145 8
It was not unlikely, she thought, that she might see Mr. E III 8 377 2
is not unlikely to marry "again; he is quite fool enough. P IV 9 203 72

UNLIMITED (2)
Her father, instead of giving her an unlimited order on NA I 2 19 3
secret discourses and unlimited confidence, that she was NA I 9 60 1

UNLOCK (1)
eagerly advance to it, unlock its folding doors, and NA II 5 160 21

UNLOCKED (3)
having been at first unlocked, and of being herself its NA II 7 173 4
The instrument was unlocked, every body prepared to be SS I 7 35 8
sighing over it as she unlocked it, said, "this is full of P IV 9 202 69 70

UNLOCKING (2)
of unlocking a cabinet, the key of which was open to all! NA II 7 173 2
moving a book-case, or unlocking a door, or even as using MP I 13 127 29

UNLOOKED (2)
fancy--a pleasure quite unlooked for by all but the two NA II 14 233 8
but the complaisance of the others was unlooked for. P IV 3 137 3

UNLOOKED-FOR (6)
His unlooked-for return was enough in itself to make NA II 13 223 13
the kindness which her unlooked-for appearance, acting on NA II 14 237 21
relieved by such unlooked-for mildness, it was not just at NA II 15 242 8
his good fortune for the unlooked-for indulgence.-- W 355 28
lamenting over such an unlooked-for premature arrival as a MP II 1 176 4
which any marked or unlooked-for instance of Edmund's MP II 6 234 18

UNLOVELY (1)
its capriciousness, be unlovely, and seeing its increasing MP III 14 432 9

UNLOVER-LIKE (1)
Astonished and shocked at so unlover-like a speech, she SS III 3 281 11

UNLUCKILY (18)
My dear Catherine, Unluckily I was confined to my room LS 13 262 1
with jealousy; but unluckily it was impossible for me LS 22 280 2
was known to him; & unluckily she had wormed out of LS 32 302 1
it had not happened very unluckily that we should never SS I 20 114 44
to do any thing, for unluckily, I was not in the way at SS III 5 299 37
Her three notes--unluckily they were all in my pocket-book, SS III 8 329 63
"But unluckily she has left the pleasure of providing for W 352 26
the occupation, but unluckily no one passed the windows PP I 15 74 11
but their carriage was unluckily ordered before any of the PP III 12 342 27
But, unluckily for her ladyship, its effect had been PP III 16 367 9
Henry Crawford had, unluckily, a great dislike; he could MP I 4 41 16
No, you never can; and unluckily it is out of distance for MP I 6 56 23
spare room to day; and, unluckily, Fanny forgot to lock MP I 7 73 51
But unluckily that iron gate, that ha-ha, give me a MP I 10 99 17
Tom, "but unluckily the butler and Anhalt are in together. MP I 15 144 33
but unluckily, I had mentioned it before I was aware." E II 9 239 51
directly; and most unluckily it came into mamma's head, P III 6 50 27
no wind--but unluckily a damp air does not like me.-- S 10 415 1

UNLUCKY (28)
How unlucky that you should have been from home! LS 33 303 1
That unlucky visit to Langford! LS 38 307 3
"How unlucky that is! SS II 2 151 40
produced, but for this unlucky illness, made every ailment SS III 7 308 4
circumstance occurred--an unlucky circumstance, to ruin SS III 8 321 34
I have been unlucky enough, & I cannot say much for you, W 321 2
It is very unlucky; but as I have actually paid the visit, PP I 2 7 22
"Dining out," said Mrs. Bennet, "that is very unlucky." PP I 7 30 19
But--good Lord! how unlucky! there is not a bit of fish PP I 13 61 3
"He has been so unlucky as to lose your friendship," PP I 18 92 21
she considered it a most unlucky perverseness which placed PP I 18 98 63
"It is unlucky," said she, after a short pause, "that you PP I 21 117 9
it as exceedingly unlucky that the ladies should happen to PP I 21 120 30
I am particularly unlucky in meeting with a person so well PP II 8 174 15
and "charming," when some unlucky recollections obtruded, PP III 1 254 57
"How unlucky that you should have a reasonable answer to PP III 18 381 13
only say it was very unlucky, but some people were stupid, MP I 2 20 31
How unlucky that you are not ordained, Mr. Rushworth and MP I 9 89 25
"I am very sorry," said she; "it is very unlucky." MP I 10 102 37
"To be sure, my dear mother, your anxiety--I was unlucky MP I 13 126 21
"We are unlucky, Miss Price," he continued in a lower tone, MP II 5 225 57
all aware of her feelings, "we certainly were very unlucky. MP II 5 225 57
an adviser may, in an unlucky moment, lead it to do what MP III 13 423 2
I must tell you what an unlucky thing happened to me, as E II 1 162 31
How unlucky! E II 12 260 26
considered how peculiarly unlucky poor Mr. Elton was in E II 14 271 5
A circumstance rather unlucky occurred. E II 16 292 7
same time, there had been an unlucky omission at Kellynch. P IV 4 148 12

UNMANAGEABLE (6)
than such self-willed, unmanageable days often volunteer, MP II 9 265 21
However that might be, she was unmanageable. MP III 16 450 11
out, till they are quite as unmanageable as great ones. E I 18 147 19
on the unmanageable good-will of Mr. Weston's temper. E III 6 353 3
are so unmanageable that they do me more harm than good. P III 5 38 27
he was stupid and unmanageable on shore; that he had been P III 6 50 28

UNMARKED (3)
The day was unmarked therefore by any thing to interest NA II 9 190 1
The evening passed quietly, unmarked by any thing PP III 17 372 2
His manners, however, must have been unmarked, wavering, E I 16 134 3

UNMARRIED (1)
never can be any likeness, except in being unmarried." E I 10 85 17

UNMENTIONED (1)

at all checked by hearing that her friend was unmentioned. E III 17 464 18
UNMERCIFULLY (1)
between us, which has been knocking my elbow unmercifully." MP I 10 105 54
UNMERITED (4)
fallen avenues, once more I mourn your fate unmerited.'" MP I 6 56 20
Once it had, by an opening undesigned and unmerited, led MP III 17 467 19
and feeling that, unmerited as might be the degree of his E III 8 377 1
to be placing her in such a state of unmerited punishment. E III 15 450 37
UNMIRTHFUL (1)
to occupy her in most unmirthful reflections some time E I 16 137 12
UNMITIGATED (1)
it, and leaving the unmitigated glare of day behind. MP I 9 91 38
UNMIXED (2)
I was pleased to see not unmixed with jealousy; but LS 22 280 2
and express very genuine unmixed anxiety to know that he E II 5 193 35
UNMODERNIZED (1)
substantial and unmodernized--and the compact, tight P III 5 36 20
UNMODULATED (1)
which I heard to be wholly unmodulated as I stood here." E I 4 33 32
UNMOVED (4)
Mrs. Dashwood did not hear unmoved the vindication of her SS III 11 349 1
which proved him wholly unmoved by any feeling of remorse. PP II 11 191 13
not hear of such horrors unmoved, or without sometimes MP II 6 236 21
That man who can read them unmoved must have the nerves of S 7 396 1
UNNATURAL (16)
circumstances, unnatural characters, and topics of NA I 5 38 4
"Yes, that's the book; such unnatural stuff!-- NA I 7 49 40
had been used to call unnatural and overdrawn; but here NA II 7 181 40
acquaintance, it was not unnatural for me to be very often SS III 13 362 5
the time an unnatural, or an inexcusable piece of folly." SS III 13 362 5
"That is not an unnatural surmise," said Fitzwilliam, "but PP II 10 186 37
is unreasonable or unnatural, in comparison of what is so PP III 4 279 24
An odious, little, pert, unnatural, impudent girl. MP I 14 136 20
it must be by a long and unnatural estrangement, by a MP II 6 235 18
Nothing could be more unnatural in either. MP II 13 306 26
in some instances almost unnatural degree of ignorance men, MP III 3 339 22
and reserved, was an unnatural state of things; a state MP III 4 345 4
done, to make you suppose him such an unnatural creature?" E I 18 145 9
"I am not supposing him at all an unnatural creature, in E I 18 145 10
With him it was most unnatural. E III 13 425 2
grew older--the natural sequel of an unnatural beginning. P III 4 30 9
UNNATURALLY (2)
my heroine was most unnaturally able to fulfil her NA I 14 106 1
body acting unnaturally and wrong, and me most unhappy. PP II 1 137 24
UNNECESSARILY (7)
spontaneously & unnecessarily, & once had said something LS 22 280 1
did not often speak unnecessarily to Mr. Collins, she PP I 17 87 12
His absence was unnecessarily long. MP II 11 286 15
his manners to herself unnecessarily gallant; but it had E I 16 134 5
a thousand occasions, unnecessarily scrupulous and E III 14 440 8
first object to prevent her from suffering unnecessarily.-- E III 15 446 20
she would shrink unnecessarily from the office of a friend. P III 12 116 69
UNNECESSARY (43)
to her to visit us at Churchill perfectly unnecessary. LS 3 247 1
"I am sure it is quite unnecessary upon your sister's NA II 11 211 13
Any further definition of his merits must be unnecessary; NA II 16 251 5
it would be absolutely unnecessary, if not highly SS I 2 13 29
made such an excuse unnecessary before it had ceased to be SS I 10 48 7
to her not merely an unnecessary effort, but a disgraceful SS I 11 53 2
at least prevented from unnecessary increase, and her SS I 19 104 10
I express some surprise at so unnecessary a communication. SS I 22 132 40
on such an occasion would be perfectly unnecessary? SS II 2 149 26
"Dear ma'am, this kindness is quite unnecessary, Marianne SS II 8 195 15
"It would be unnecessary I am sure, for you to caution Mrs. SS II 8 195 17
in Elinor, and unnecessary in Mrs. Jennings, they all SS III 1 269 58
But he judged it unnecessary; he had still something more SS III 7 313 21
not to be kept away from her sister an unnecessary instant. SS III 7 315 27
Eager to save her mother from every unnecessary moment's SS III 9 333 3
"Indeed, Mr. Collins, all praise of me will be unnecessary. PP I 19 107 16
lowness of her spirits unnecessary; nothing, therefore, PP III 6 298 17
any symptom of resentment, or any unnecessary complaisance. PP III 11 335 39
Elizabeth's misery increased, at such unnecessary, such PP III 11 337 54
have supposed it unnecessary, for they were under the care MP I 2 20 31
Fanny soon learnt how unnecessary had been her fears of a MP I 3 31 58
exercise to be as unnecessary for every body as it was MP I 4 36 7
She could not but consider it as absolutely unnecessary, MP I 4 36 7
seemed to make allies unnecessary; and independent of this MP I 14 130 3
as she deemed it, most unnecessary rehearsal of the first MP I 18 168 14
agitation: "quite unnecessary!--a great deal too kind! MP II 5 221 38
39
But it is unnecessary here. MP II 9 269 38
brought up without unnecessary indulgences; but there MP III 1 312 12
Though their caution may prove eventually unnecessary, it MP III 1 313 12
and with only a little unnecessary bustle, and some few MP III 7 383 33
She would not voluntarily give unnecessary pain to any one, MP III 16 456 25
immediately afterwards walked in and made it unnecessary. E I 1 9 20
friend, this is quite unnecessary; Frank knows a puddle of E II 5 195 48
"We allowed unnecessary room. E II 11 249 13
were conveniently voted unnecessary by their four selves, E II 11 254 44
as to offer, but another time it will be quite unnecessary. E III 2 321 17
"That's quite unnecessary; I see Jane every day:--but as E III 6 355 20
to spare her from any unnecessary pain; how to make her E III 14 435 4
It seemed an unnecessary caution; Jane was wanting to give E III 16 457 34
to cut off some unnecessary charities, and to refrain from P III 1 9 19
I think it rather unnecessary in you to be advising me." P III 5 35 16
as not merely unnecessary to be communicated, but as what P III 12 107 21
of unnecessary intimacy she had been gradually led along. P IV 10 214 11
UNNOTICED (7)
had it gone no farther, it might have passed unnoticed. NA II 4 149 1
examining the furniture before, you had passed unnoticed. NA II 5 160 21
She instantly saw that it was not unnoticed by him, that SS II 4 162 8
gone in uninvited and unnoticed to hear the harp; neither MP I 7 65 14
at once here, delights you too much to pass unnoticed. E II 18 312 50
it should pass unnoticed or not, replied, "never marry!-- E III 4 341 29
30
inferred, had been unnoticed, because unsuspected by Emma. E III 11 409 35
UNOBJECTIONABLE (2)
family, a proper unobjectionable country family, whom the E II 8 214 13
to feel, that a more unobjectionable tenant, in all P III 3 24 36
UNOBSERVANT (2)
was equally unobservant; and Mrs. Norris was too busy in MP I 17 163 21
to such matters, so unobservant and incurious were they as P III 6 51 31
UNOBSERVED (3)
to Marianne, to see whether it could be unobserved by her. SS II 6 176 3
Emma in the meanwhile was not unobserved, or unadmired W 328 9
and desired nothing in return but to be unobserved. P III 8 71 56
UNOBTRUSIVE (3)
She saw only that he was quiet and unobtrusive, and she SS I 3 16 7
Elinor paid her every quiet and unobtrusive attention in SS II 7 180 5
Colonel Brandon's delicate unobtrusive inquiries were SS II 10 216 15
UNOBTRUSIVENESS (1)
than pity, and in its unobtrusiveness entitled to praise. SS III 10 342 7
UNOCCUPIED (1)
dimity bed, arranged as unoccupied with an housemaid's NA II 9 193 6
UNPACKED (2)
Marianne's pianoforte was unpacked and properly disposed SS I 6 30 5
said he would keep it unpacked to the last possible moment, P IV 11 240 58
UNPARDONABLE (16)
so well, that I should be unpardonable to doubt it now. SS II 2 147 10
you so obligingly bestowed on me'--that is unpardonable. SS II 7 190 56
that whatever other unpardonable folly might bring him to SS III 8 318 21
22
Robert's offence was unpardonable, but Lucy's was SS III 13 371 38
respect to Jane, his unpardonable assurance in PP II 11 193 31
in money matters, would be unpardonable in me." PP III 13 348 39
It was unpardonable. PP III 16 367 12
But in such cases as these, a good memory is unpardonable. PP III 17 373 7
how wretched, and how unpardonable, how hopeless and how MP III 1 324 58
must have betrayed her emotion in some unpardonable excess. MP III 3 335 5
that shrunk from it would soon be quite unpardonable. MP III 10 406 20
conduct; it had been unpardonable rudeness; and Mrs. E III 2 330 46
feelings; with unpardonable arrogance proposed to arrange E III 11 412 47
them both to an unpardonable degree.-- I believe I have E III 16 456 23
It would be unpardonable to fail. P IV 10 224 47
Was it unpardonable to think it worth my while to come? P IV 11 243 70
UNPARDONABLY (2)
Frederick could not be unpardonably guilty, while Henry NA II 12 219 16
herself, but had so unpardonably imparted; an idea which E III 12 421 17
UNPARDONED (1)
none, still remained some weeks longer unpardoned. SS III 14 376 11
UNPERCEIVED (2)
The danger, however, was at present so unperceived, that E I 1 5 4
her real motive unperceived) might warrant a man of E I 16 136 9
UNPERMITTED (1)
that not a breath of air can find its way unpermitted. E I 13 115 37
UNPERPLEXED (1)
was considered with sensations unqualified, unperplexed.-- P IV 10 212 1
UNPERSUADABLE (4)
Mr. Knightleys were as unpersuadable on that article as E I 12 101 19
The unpersuadable point, which he did not mention, Emma E II 8 221 50
Jane was quite unpersuadable; the mere proposal of going E III 9 390 18
her; but she was quite unpersuadable; and this being the P III 7 58 20
UNPIN (1)
and she was preparing to unpin the linen package, which NA II 6 163 1
UNPLEASANT (64)
I wish her to find her situation as unpleasant as possible. LS 7 253 1
How unpleasant, one would think, must his reflections be! LS 22 282 8
propensity towards any unpleasant vivacity, and (NA I 9 62 10
did away some of her unpleasant feelings; but still she NA II 5 154 2
conduct produced such unpleasant reflections, and found NA II 7 173 5
proposed it as no unpleasant extension of their walk, if NA II 7 179 27
To be found there, even by a servant, would be unpleasant; NA II 9 194 6
her to be receiving unpleasant news; and Henry, earnestly NA II 10 202 8
large and populous village, in a situation not unpleasant. NA II 11 212 17
to bring forward so unpleasant a subject, she took the NA II 13 220 2
herself under the unpleasant impression his conduct had NA II 13 222 8
"It is certainly an unpleasant thing," replied Mr. SS I 2 11 21
a disposition to be otherwise than tedious and unpleasant. SS I 6 28 1
But suspicion of something unpleasant is the inevitable SS I 15 79 29
many days longer, as unpleasant as they now were, she SS II 4 165 30
'for fear any unpleasant report should reach the young SS III 1 258 5
a very unexpected and unpleasant alteration in his patient, SS III 7 312 19
girl--I must say it, unpleasant to me as the discussion of SS III 8 322 37
secret reflections may be no more unpleasant than my own. SS III 10 345 24
the expectation of an unpleasant event, however certain SS III 12 357 1
giving her some very unpleasant feelings, with respect to W 322 3
there, was the only unpleasant part of her engagement, the W 335 13
the dissipation of unpleasant ideas which only reading W 361 31
to make her appear unpleasant in the eyes of a man of ten PP I 18 90 8
that scenes might arise unpleasant to more than myself." PP I 21 115 4
to relieve him from so unpleasant a situation, now put PP I 23 126 4
to the lady's family, it would be an unpleasant thing." PP II 10 185 26
indulge in all the delight of unpleasant recollections. PP II 14 212 16
aunt were horrid unpleasant all the time I was with them. PP III 9 319 25
were then, that every unpleasant circumstance attending it, PP III 16 368 23
We all know him to be a proud, unpleasant sort of man; but PP III 17 376 33
"Well, Fanny, and if the plan were not unpleasant to you, MP I 3 25 21
every body as it was unpleasant to herself; and Mrs. MP I 4 36 7
"There is no hardship, I suppose, nothing unpleasant," MP I 8 78 14
"Unpleasant!" cried Maria; "Oh! dear, I believe it would MP I 8 78 15
be less unpleasant to me than to have a perfect stranger." MP I 15 148 59
She could go there after any thing unpleasant below, and MP I 16 151 2
had barely time for an unpleasant feeling on the occasion, MP II 4 215 47
There can hardly be a more unpleasant sensation than the MP II 9 263 12
This is a sort of talking which is very unpleasant to me. MP II 13 301 7
him, that it was very unpleasant to me in every respect, MP III 1 315 19
that head,) I never perceived them to be unpleasant to you. MP III 1 316 29
can, dismissing the recollection of every thing unpleasant. MP III 2 331 16
which Fanny found quite as unpleasant as she had feared. MP III 7 376 4
letter, and chiefly for unpleasant meditation; and yet, MP III 9 394 2
likely that any thing unpleasant should have preceded them, MP III 15 438 4
already exposing her to unpleasant remarks, and evidently MP III 16 450 8
Some minutes passed in this unpleasant silence, with only E I 8 65 50
unpleasant, and enjoy all that was enjoyable to the utmost. E I 14 117 2
The introduction must be unpleasant, whenever it takes E I 14 122 20
this--which of all her unpleasant sensations was uppermost. E I 15 131 32
exciting or receiving unpleasant and most unsuitable ideas. E I 16 138 17
He could now, without the drawback of a single unpleasant E II 5 193 35
Her manners too--and Mr. Elton's, were unpleasant towards E II 15 281 3
be at least equally unpleasant to Jane--inquiries whether E II 17 299 1
young man's spirits now rose to a pitch almost unpleasant. E III 7 374 54
Something of a very unpleasant nature, I find, has E III 10 394 27
Emma with more food for unpleasant reflection, by E III 12 420 17
may well lay me open to unpleasant conjectures, but I have E III 13 426 15
W., in being unpleasant to Miss F., were highly blamable. E III 14 440 8
"It is very unpleasant, having such connexions! P III 10 86 19
Could there have been any unpleasant glances? P IV 8 190 47
It would have been very unpleasant to me in every respect. P IV 9 193 11
even an unpleasant report, were there no other ill effects. P IV 11 242 65
UNPLEASANTEST (1)
The very circumstance, in its unpleasantest form, which SS II 13 241 19
UNPLEASANTLY (4)
tho' in some respects unpleasantly, distinguished, & the W 336 14
our power to prevent your spending your time unpleasantly." PP II 15 215 2
not say that it was unpleasantly done, that there was MP II 10 278 20
found how much and how unpleasantly her having only walked MP III 1 323 53
UNPLEASANTNESS (3)
productive of much unpleasantness to her; that it was what NA II 14 234 10
every unpleasantness of that kind with very little effort." SS II 3 156 14
be subject to all the unpleasantness of appearing to treat SS II 14 248 6
UNPLEASANTNESSES (1)
that may, of the unpleasantnesses that must, arise from a MP I 16 154 14
UNPLEASING (4)
must have been highly unpleasing;--but in her mind there SS I 1 6 9
His appearance however was not unpleasing, in spite of his SS I 7 34 6
means unpleasing, though it could not be exactly defined. PP III 2 266 16
artless, maternal gratitude, which could not be unpleasing. MP III 10 400 6
UNPOLISHED (2)
they must be coarse and unpolished, and very unfit to be E I 3 23 10
inferior, retired, and unpolished way of living, and their P III 9 74 5
UNPRACTISED (3)
was almost lost on the unpractised eye of Catherine, who NA II 6 165 6
Quite unpractised in such sort of note-writing, had there MP II 13 307 30
31
on the very poor, so unpractised in removing evils, or MP III 9 396 7
UNPRECEDENTED (1)
Fanny, in dismay at such an unprecedented question, did MP II 7 250 60
UNPREJUDICED (3)
of the discerning and unprejudiced reader of Camilla gave NA I 7 49 43
by the opinion of an unprejudiced person what her own NA I 13 103 29
Hear the truth, therefore, now, while you are unprejudiced. P IV 9 199 53
UNPREMEDITATED (2)
In the country, an unpremeditated dance was very allowable; SS II 5 170 29
ended, occasionally, in an unpremeditated little ball. P III 6 47 15

UNPREPARED (5)
for which she was quite unprepared; and she could hardly PP III 1 254 58
to be taken perfectly unprepared, but Sir Thomas could not MP III 3 335 6
were not so absolutely unprepared to have the question MP III 5 362 18
He seems perfectly unprepared for that." E III 17 465 26
on me! how peculiarly unprepared I was!--for I had reason E III 18 473 24
UNPRETENDING (12)
by any design in behaviour so gentle and unpretending. LS 10 258 2
you see, is plain and unpretending; yet no endeavours NA II 2 139 7
The domestic, unpretending merits of a person never known, NA II 9 196 23
her imagination as the unpretending comfort of a well- NA II 11 212 16
I know no one more entitled, by unpretending merit, or NA II 16 251 5
good sense, a modest unpretending mind, & a great wish of W 323 3
He must know that she was as amiable and unpretending as PP III 5 284 14
and all this with such unpretending gentleness, so much as MP III 12 296 31
liberal, and unpretending; but, on the other hand, they E II 7 207 6
An unpretending, single-minded, artless girl--infinitely E III 2 331 55
to be done in a quiet, unpretending, elegant way, E III 6 352 2
kindest & most unpretending manner, to both husband & wife. S 2 370 1
UNPRETTY (1)
Her person was rather good; her face not unpretty; but E II 14 270 4
UNPRINCIPLED (6)
I am indeed provoked at the artifice of this unprincipled LS 8 255 1
She must be an unprincipled one, or she could not have NA II 10 205 30
from believing him so unprincipled as to have been SS II 6 178 17
for life, with an unprincipled man, as a deliverance the SS II 7 184 15
already think me an unprincipled fellow, this letter will SS III 8 328 63
betrayed him to be unprincipled or unjust--any thing that PP II 13 207 6
UNPRIVILEGED (1)
curiosity to be raised in the unprivileged younger sisters. NA I 15 120 25
UNPRODUCTIVE (1)
The letter was not unproductive. MP I 1 5 3
UNPRODUCTIVELY (1)
The anxious interval wore away unproductively. P IV 8 189 45
UNPROFITABLE (3)
He had found the law a most unprofitable study, and was PP II 12 201 5
She felt how unprofitable contention would be. MP III 2 333 27
unfeeling, unprofitable Dick Musgrove, who had never done P III 6 51 29
UNPROMISING (3)
Under these unpromising auspices, the parting took place, NA I 2 19 4
"That is the most unpromising circumstance, the strangest NA II 10 206 31
indifference, spoke a something almost as unpromising. SS I 4 22 18
UNPROMPTED (1)
It had really occurred to her, unprompted, that Fanny, MP II 9 271 41
UNPROPITIOUS (1)
not less unpropitious for heroism seemed her mind. NA I 1 13 1
UNPROSPEROUS (1)
had returned, after an unprosperous marriage, to her P III 2 15 15
UNPROTECTED (1)
girl who is by no means unprotected or friendless, and who PP III 5 282 1
UNPROVIDED (2)
expectations, unprovided with any pretence for further NA II 8 182 1
"Ah! there is one difficulty unprovided for," cried Emma. E III 15 449 33
UNPUNCTUALITY (1)
Their remoteness and unpunctuality, or their exorbitant MP II 4 213 35
UNPUNISHED (1)
and desire to have it unpunished, she could believe Miss MP III 15 441 19
UNQUALIFIED (6)
You into the belief of my being impelled by unqualified, PP II 11 192 22
Sir Thomas could not give so instantaneous and unqualified MP I 1 6 5
conveying to her that unqualified approbation and MP III 3 335 6
by meeting her with the most unqualified congratulations.-- E III 19 481 2
perfectly justify the unqualified bitterness of Mrs. Smith, P IV 9 208 94
was considered with sensations unqualified, unperplexed.-- P IV 10 212 1
UNQUESTIONABLE (1)
Its object was unquestionable; and two moments were enough MP III 15 437 2
UNQUESTIONABLY (7)
Mr. Wickham's chief object was unquestionably my sister's PP II 12 202 5
of an alliance so unquestionably advantageous, and of MP I 4 40 14
receiving a welcome, unquestionably friendly, from the MP III 3 334 1
moment before, as unquestionably sixteen miles distant.-- E III 13 424 1
applications will unquestionably follow, I should think P III 3 17 4
done was unquestionably to walk directly down to the sea. P III 11 95 9
These convictions must unquestionably have their own pain, P IV 1 125 17
UNQUIET (3)
will retire to rest, and get a few hours' unquiet slumber. NA II 5 159 19
again the scene of agitated spirits and unquiet slumbers. NA II 13 227 26
an effort, the restless, unquiet thoughtfulness in which SS III 11 349 3
UNQUIETNESS (1)
fidget, the hem! of unquietness, but prevented him even MP II 1 184 27
UNRAVELLED (1)
perhaps, or wanton cruelty--was yet to be unravelled. NA II 8 188 16
UNREAD (1)
letters on her lap yet unread, and so entirely forgot how SS II 7 184 16
UNREASONABLE (31)
to be fruitless, she felt to have been highly unreasonable. NA I 8 58 25
it would be very strange and unreasonable if he did. SS I 2 12 24
any unreasonable abridgment, might be previously finished. SS II 3 157 15
since, with the smallest degree of unreasonable admiration. PP I 16 76 3
them, and I trust you will not esteem them unreasonable. PP I 21 118 14
pain on her, your resentment has not been unreasonable. PP II 12 197 5
I should not think it unreasonable for him to expect some PP II 12 200 5
fate in terms as unreasonable as her accent was peevish. PP II 18 230 12
from such sources is unreasonable or unnatural, in PP III 4 279 24
not to be intimidated into anything so wholly unreasonable. PP III 14 357 61
been asking the most unreasonable, most impossible thing MP I 6 58 37
of a mile, I cannot think I was unreasonable to ask it. MP I 7 73 53
for avoiding whatever her unreasonable aunts might require. MP I 7 74 58
appeared to her, very unreasonable direction to the knoll, MP I 10 100 23
felt that she had been unreasonable in expecting it. MP I 12 118 22
of his being less unreasonable than he professed himself. MP III 2 328 8
his father a little unreasonable in supposing the first MP III 6 366 2
temper, or been unreasonable in wanting a larger share MP III 6 371 17
as ----- she checked herself; she was unreasonable. MP III 7 382 29
it was not unreasonable to suppose, that Fanny might be MP III 10 400 8
enough to refrain from unreasonable regrets at that E I 2 15 3
at that brother's unreasonable anger, nor from missing the E I 2 15 3
is so very unreasonable; and every thing gives way to her." E I 14 123 23
I was only betrayed into paying a most unreasonable visit. E II 6 199 7
"No, no," said she, "you are quite unreasonable. E II 11 249 17
in," she said, "was that of making her unreasonable. E III 12 419 12
to allow me, which I then thought most unreasonable. E III 14 441 8
He should have respected even unreasonable scruples, had E III 15 446 20
made perhaps an unreasonable difference in Emma's E III 16 452 5
would be to betray a most unreasonable degree of happiness. E III 18 472 21
in very unreasonable applications) prided himself on P III 1 5 8
UNREASONABLENESS (2)
in one light, the unreasonableness, with which the affair E III 14 440 8
bore with her unreasonableness sometimes to Anne's P III 6 43 5
UNREASONABLY (8)
It was by no means unreasonably large, and contained NA II 6 163 1
who could be coming so unreasonably early, she was all SS II 7 184 16
recollections that might not unreasonably have alarmed her. PP I 18 89 1
He was not an ill-tempered man, not so often unreasonably E I 11 92 5
"So unreasonably early!" she was going to exclaim; but she E III 2 319 3
She was displeased; I thought unreasonably so: I thought E III 14 440 8
is rather apt to be unreasonably discontented when a woman P III 1 5 8
but not at all unreasonably influenced by them; & while S 6 391 1
UNRELENTING (1)
shall be consigned to unrelenting contempt; but by all LS 4 248 2
UNREMITTING (2)
who watched with unremitting attention her continual SS III 7 310 10
11
& comforted with unremitting kindness--and as every office S 2 371 1
UNREPULSABLE (1)
and enquiries; and he unrepulsable was persisting in both. MP III 3 342 32
UNREQUITED (1)
of that sort unrequited, that she could not comprehend its E I 17 142 12
UNRESERVE (13)
whom you can speak with unreserve; on whose regard you can NA II 10 207 38
disgrace could attend unreserve; and to aim at the SS I 11 53 2
She used to be all unreserve, and to you more especially." SS I 16 84 8
power to promote their unreserve, by making the Miss SS I 21 125 34
increase of ease and unreserve; and was even partly SS II 2 150 35
recommendations was now added that of general unreserve. PP II 1 138 30
If he would now speak to her with the unreserve which had MP III 16 453 16
footing and perfect unreserve which had soon followed E I 1 6 6
Elton speak with more unreserve than she had ever done, E I 8 67 57
whom she spoke with such unreserve, as to his wife; not E I 14 117 1
to her, with a degree of unreserve which she would not E I 14 122 18
an offering to conjugal unreserve, and her own share in E II 15 282 3
any thing like such an unreserve as had been, such an open E III 4 341 34
UNRESERVED (8)
of friendship in an unreserved conversation;--they talked NA I 5 35 2
him often enough to engage him in unreserved conversation. SS I 4 20 9
been attempted; all has been uniformly open and unreserved. SS I 15 80 42
room; he was lively and unreserved, danced every dance, PP I 3 10 6
by a very frequent and most unreserved correspondence. PP I 21 116 8
been; that it should be equally unreserved was impossible. PP II 3 146 19
being a warm-hearted, unreserved woman, Mary had not been MP I 4 42 17
way of talking in unreserved moments, when there are only E I 8 66 53
UNRESERVEDLY (1)
Mr. Elliot talks unreservedly to Colonel Wallis of his P IV 9 205 82
UNRESISTED (1)
Elinor could no longer witness this torrent of unresisted SS II 7 185 20
UNRESTRAINED (3)
it suited her, and unrestrained even by the presence of a SS II 14 250 11
give them leisure for unrestrained conversation together, SS III 13 363 6
Mr. Darcy was eyeing him with unrestrained wonder, and PP I 18 98 61
UNRIVALLED (3)
it,--he did believe them to be unrivalled in the kingdom. NA II 7 178 21
or the perfect, unrivalled hold it possessed over his own. P IV 11 242 63
And then again, that unequalled, unrivalled address to S 7 397 1
UNSAFE (5)
speak to my brother, and tell him how very unsafe it is." NA I 9 65 29
"Unsafe! NA I 9 65 30
her countenance of their unsafe amusements, than that such MP II 2 188 3
"Come, come," cried Emma, feeling this to be an unsafe E I 12 101 23
I hold to be very unsafe and unwise, and what, I think, P IV 11 231 9
UNSAID (3)
She wished such words unsaid with all her heart. MP II 11 286 15
herself, and wished it unsaid; but there was no need of MP II 12 295 22
will not ask, though I may wish it unsaid the next moment." E III 13 429 27
UNSATISFACTORY (4)
Among other unsatisfactory feelings it once occurred to W 347 22
A few minutes were enough for such unsatisfactory MP II 1 183 24
unsatisfactory correspondence with Elizabeth fell on Anne. P III 12 107 21
had been there, and unsatisfactory for such an enquirer as P IV 9 192 5
UNSATISFIED (2)
fifty pounds a year, I should not have a wish unsatisfied. NA II 1 136 48
To retire to bed, however, unsatisfied on such a point, NA II 6 168 10
UNSEARCHED (1)
Not one was left unsearched, and in not one was any thing NA II 6 169 11
UNSEASONABLE (1)
if not quite so unseasonable, and accordingly she hurried NA II 13 222 7
UNSEASONABLENESS (1)
with the strange unseasonableness of his morning walks, NA II 8 187 14
UNSEASONABLY (1)
and make me think the weather most unseasonably close." MP II 4 212 31
UNSEEN (9)
unseen, "and waste its fragrance on the desert air." NA I 1 15 5
that she had either been unseen by the General, or that NA II 9 192 4
bringing her sister away unseen by Willoughby since his SS III 6 302 5
and screened by her bonnet, those smiles were unseen. MP III 15 445 32
That nature had given it in feature could not be unseen by E II 2 165 7
unseen, 'and waste its fragrance on the desert air.' E II 15 282 5
was unseen by the whole party till almost close to them. E III 3 334 7
Captain Wentworth, after being unseen and unheard of at P III 11 94 5
might have passed him unseen, but was obliged to touch as P IV 6 169 25
UNSELDOM (1)
unseldom, she involuntarily turned her eye on Charlotte. PP II 5 156 4
UNSELFISH (1)
in expense, or even the unselfish warmth of heart which E II 7 205 1
UNSENTIMENTAL (1)
that light, cheerful, unsentimental disposition which E II 8 219 44
UNSETTLE (1)
which might again unsettle the mind of Marianne, and ruin SS III 10 343 10
UNSETTLED (11)
carriage, were in a very unsettled state; divided between NA I 11 86 50
& mother think it has given him rather an unsettled turn.-- W 328 8
The vague and unsettled suspicions which uncertainty had PP III 10 326 3
mention Bingley; and the unsettled state of her own PP III 17 374 19
dismissed them to a home, was unsettled in the extreme. PP III 19 387 8
his income was unsettled, seemed to her very unjustifiable. MP I 4 36 7
She does not like his unsettled habits." MP I 12 116 6
for a few days, was so unsettled by it altogether, by what MP III 12 418 5
His unsettled affections, wavering with his vanity, MP III 15 441 20
the atmosphere in that unsettled state between frost and E I 16 138 17
in an hotel ensured a quick-changing, unsettled scene. P IV 10 221 32
UNSHACKLED (2)
his own importance, and unshackled by business, occupy PP I 5 18 1
when she thought of Captain Wentworth unshackled and free. P IV 6 167 21
UNSHAKEN (3)
that her firmness was as unshaken, her appearance of SS II 1 141 6
time, that his affection and wishes must still be unshaken. PP III 11 334 37
professions and vows of unshaken attachment might have as MP III 4 345 2
UNSHELTERED (1)
now comparatively unsheltered, remaining perhaps till in MP II 4 208 11
UNSISTERLY (1)
Mary was not so repulsive and unsisterly as Elizabeth, nor P III 6 43 4
UNSOCIAL (1)
We are each of an unsocial, taciturn disposition, PP I 18 91 15
UNSOFTENED (1)
ill-will, though unsoftened by one kind word or look on P III 4 27 5
UNSOLICITED (2)
constant to him only when unsolicited by any one else?-- NA II 4 152 28
which had hazarded such unsolicited proofs of tenderness, SS II 7 188 43
UNSOLICITOUS (1)
and shewn himself as unsolicitous of being longer noticed P III 1 8 16
UNSOPHISTICATED (1)
the first ardours of her young, unsophisticated mind! MP II 6 235 20
UNSPEAKABLE (3)
If you will therefore have the unspeakable great kindness LS 21 279 1
His words were echoed with unspeakable astonishment by all SS III 12 360 24
It would have been an unspeakable indulgence. MP II 10 280 32
UNSPEAKABLY (2)
of it appeared unspeakably great, and she contemplated it NA I 15 117 8
of unkindness, was unspeakably welcome to a mind which had MP I 4 35 6
UNSPENT (1)
reason to wish the money unspent, to improve his spirits. E II 8 212 2
UNSPOILT (1)
It proves him unspoilt by his uncle. MP III 4 350 30
UNSTEADINESS (3)
unsteadiness; and his happiness under it made her wretched. MP I 17 159 6

manner--this is an unsteadiness of character, indeed, E I 15 130 30
No, upon my honour, there is no unsteadiness of character. E I 15 131 31
UNSTEADY (8)
not more sudden in forming, than unsteady in keeping them. LS 23 284 6
What would be meant by such unsteady conduct, what her NA II 4 149 1
She seized, with an unsteady hand, the precious manuscript, NA II 6 169 11
as she spoke--and her unsteady voice, plainly shewed. SS III 11 349 3
Edmund, he believed of unsteady characters; and with MP II 2 188 3
the transient, varying, unsteady nature of love, as it MP III 2 330 14
You think me unsteady--easily swayed by the whim of the MP III 3 343 41
Her voice was not unsteady; but her mind was in all the E III 11 409 34
UNSTUDIED (3)
people, and their manly unstudied simplicity is much more SS III 9 338 22
always wish to give them as unstudied an air as possible." PP I 14 68 11
countenance, and frank, unstudied, but feeling and MP II 6 233 16
UNSUBDUED (2)
while her resolution was unsubdued, and she still tried to SS III 11 352 19
of all that remained unsubdued of his heart, trusting that PP I 18 89 1
UNSUCCESSFUL (1)
for him was equally unsuccessful, in morning lounges or NA I 5 35 2
UNSUCCESSFULLY (4)
the room, as to make him play as unsuccessfully as herself. PP III 12 342 26
earnestly, but very unsuccessfully, trying to persuade the MP I 14 131 6
three first acts, and not unsuccessfully upon the whole. MP II 1 185 28
She went--she had driven once unsuccessfully to the door, E III 16 452 8
UNSUITABLE (7)
such a woman therefore there would be nothing unsuitable. SS I 8 38 10
each other to an unsuitable increase of ease and unreserve; SS II 2 150 35
at all reconciled to the idea of so unsuitable a match. PP I 22 125 18
the children of so unsuitable a marriage, nor ever been so PP II 19 236 2
It was an unsuitable connection, and did not produce much E I 2 15 3
exciting or receiving unpleasant and most unsuitable ideas. E I 16 138 17
a little disparity of age, I can see nothing unsuitable." E II 8 225 73
UNSUITABLENESS (1)
and at the strange unsuitableness which often existed SS I 21 118 1
UNSUITED (3)
lady been, so wholly unsuited were they in age and SS II 4 159 1
consider him as totally unsuited to myself; though in that MP III 4 349 25
completely unsuited to her, and ought not to think of her. MP III 10 405 16
UNSULLIED (1)
short might be hoped to pass away in unsullied cordiality. E I 11 93 5
UNSUSCEPTIBLE (1)
their muslin, and how unsusceptible of peculiar tenderness NA I 10 74 22
UNSUSPECTED (5)
were so totally unsuspected by Mrs. Jennings, that she SS II 14 247 5
unsuspected vexation was probably ready to burst on him. MP II 1 178 7
been guarded in a way unsuspected by Miss Crawford, might MP II 6 231 11
inferred, had been unnoticed, because unsuspected by Emma. E III 11 409 35
all the worst of her sufferings had been unsuspected.-- E III 16 452 8
UNSUSPICIOUS (14)
and was wholly unsuspicious of danger to her daughter from NA I 2 18 2
perfectly unsuspicious of there being any deeper evil. NA II 14 235 13
He declared himself to have been totally unsuspicious of PP II 13 208 9
sensibility which he, unsuspicious of her fond attachment, MP I 8 79 27
no trick, and are as unsuspicious of compliment as I have MP II 8 259 22
unsuspicious calmness--"for I gave him only 10l." MP II 13 305 20
as unsuspicious of it at first!--indeed, indeed I was. MP III 5 362 21
upright principles, unsuspicious temper, and genuine MP III 15 442 21
and pedal, totally unsuspicious of that wish of saying as E II 8 220 46
Mr. Weston meanwhile, perfectly unsuspicious of the E II 17 303 24
was said, and she was unsuspicious of having excited any E III 13 425 12
13
He had, in fact, been wholly unsuspicious of his own E III 13 432 40
unsuspicious of what they could have told him in return. E III 14 434 3
unsuspicious of being inflicting any peculiar wound. P III 7 60 32
UNSUSPICIOUSNESS (1)
her total ignorance, unsuspiciousness of there being such MP III 16 456 25
UNTAINTED (2)
true gentility, untainted in blood and understanding.-- E III 6 358 35
It was likely to be as untainted, perhaps, as the blood of E III 19 482 3
UNTAMEABLE (1)
they were quite untameable by any means of address which MP III 8 391 8
UNTAMED (1)
Lydia was Lydia still; untamed, unabashed, wild, noisy, PP III 9 315 4
UNTASTED (2)
forward to pleasures untasted and unalloyed, and free from NA II 14 237 20
was yet an untasted pleasure, was quite alive at the idea. MP I 13 123 6
UNTAUGHT (2)
and her spontaneous, untaught felicity on the discovery, MP I 3 31 58
untaught feeling on his side, and this surprises me. P IV 8 183 10
UNTHINKING (1)
and it may be a little unthinking, might be led on to----- MP III 4 350 30
UNTHINKINGLY (2)
to be his sister; thus unthinkingly throwing away a fair NA I 8 53 3
"Dear sister, I beg your pardon, if I have unthinkingly W 316 2
UNTHOUGHT (3)
she had yet another source of joy unthought of by Elinor. SS III 9 335 7
from having been entirely unknown and unthought of before. SS III 11 350 9
herself undistinguished in the dusk, and unthought of. MP III 7 379 20
UNTHOUGHT-OF (1)
such unexpected, such unthought-of information could not SS III 4 289 29
30
UNTIDY (1)
Her hair so untidy, so blowsy!" PP I 8 36 5
UNTIED (1)
She saw their sashes untied, their hair pulled about their SS I 21 120 6
UNTIL (1)
he was happily employed until the gentlemen joined them; PP I 16 75 3
UNTINCTURED (2)
of Jane, not untinctured by tenderness, and a wish of PP III 2 262 8
allowable, when untinctured by ill humour of roughness; MP I 7 64 11
UNTITLED (1)
honourable, and ancient, though untitled families. PP III 14 356 50
UNTOUCHED (5)
Ah! Miss Dashwood--a subject such as this--untouched for SS II 9 208 28
They could not be untouched by his politeness, and had PP III 2 264 14
say nothing, and leave untouched all Miss Crawford's MP II 3 199 16
Miss Crawford, untouched and inattentive, had nothing to MP II 4 209 13
must now be shut up in London, untouched by any body." E II 8 216 24
UNTOWARD (8)
young man, unless circumstances are particularly untoward. NA I 14 111 29
very hearty wish that no untoward accident might ever NA II 7 173 3
wrong-headed folly, engrafted on an untoward disposition.-- W 361 31
She could hardly have made a more untoward choice. MP I 1 3 1
to work against a most untoward gravity of deportment--and MP I 2 12 2
arrival as a most untoward event, and without mercy MP II 1 176 4
and forced in so untoward a moment to admit the MP II 1 183 23
old lady, under such untoward circumstances, can excite. E I 3 21 4
UNTOWARDLY (1)
untowardly one month, they are sure to mend the next." E II 18 308 27
UNTRACTABLE (1)
Her mother has insinuated that her temper is untractable, LS 17 270 5
UNTRIED (1)
in an exercise hitherto untried since her illness required; SS III 10 344 12
13
UNTURNED (1)
But I left no stone unturned. MP II 2 189 3
UNUSED (5)
Unused to exert himself, & happy in contemplating her, he W 346 21
On the contrary, she was so totally unused to have her MP II 10 280 32
satisfied, the other so unused to endure; but still more MP II 11 285 15
But she was so wholly unused to confer favours, except on MP III 9 396 7
was too strong for a mind unused to make any sacrifice to MP III 17 467 20
UNUSUAL (20)
room, with a very unusual solemnity of countenance, & LS 22 281 4
not discern any thing unusual, a double range of small NA II 6 168 10
walks about the room in this way; it is nothing unusual." NA II 8 187 13
feelings, and of the unusual exertion and fatigue of such NA II 14 235 13
as are by no means unusual in children of two or three SS I 1 4 3
with no traits at all unusual in his sex and time of life. SS III 6 304 15
It was an unusual sound in Stanton at any time of the day, W 354 28
domestic felicity in so unusual a form, that she still was PP III 19 385 1
noise, to be struck by unusual noise in the other part of MP I 18 172 33
and chatty in a very unusual degree; and he was ready to MP II 1 178 8
on this occasion, with an unusual degree of wakefulness. MP II 9 271 41
heard--a heavy step, an unusual step in that part of the MP III 1 312 4
Norfolk at all, at this unusual time of year, was given. MP III 10 404 15
which by dint of much unusual activity, was quite and MP III 15 445 31
flew away at a very unusual rate; and the supper-table, E I 3 24 11
she had so many hours of unusual festivity before her.-- E III 2 325 32
a decision of action unusual to her, proposed a removal.-- E III 6 359 37
soon, with what appeared unusual speed, they were half way E III 7 376 62
Mrs. Elton met her with unusual graciousness, she hoped E III 16 453 11
for calling at so unusual an hour, but "he could not be so P IV 3 143 18
UNUSUALLY (4)
of the house, and made unusually tidy on the occasion; an NA II 11 213 21
in the patient, went unusually early to bed; her maid, who SS III 7 310 9
in consequence of being unusually well had taken the W 338 18
the weather being unusually mild for the time of year; and MP II 4 208 11
UNUTTERABLE (2)
of her own unutterable happiness, scarcely opened her lips, NA II 15 243 10
back with feelings unutterable, the ground which so lately, P III 12 111 49
UNVARYING (4)
you move in a very confined and unvarying society." PP I 9 43 17
sensation, and unvarying cheerfulness all dinner-time. MP III 3 334 3
and shewed her the most unvarying kindness, striving to E I 17 142 10
It was unvarying, warm admiration every where. P III 9 73 3
UNVISITED (1)
he could be unvisited by remembrance any more than herself. P III 8 63 2
UNWARILY (1)
of her favourite plants, unwarily exposed, and nipped by SS III 6 303 10
UNWEARIED (4)
the case, and though by unwearied diligence they gained NA I 2 21 9
we would attain," as "unwearied diligence out point would NA I 4 31 2
would gain;" and the unwearied diligence with which she NA I 4 31 2
the tide, for sitting in unwearied contemplation;--the P III 11 95 9
UNWEARYING (1)
with unwearying civility that they were perfectly needless. PP I 15 74 11
UNWELCOME (31)
How provoking it is my dear Catherine, that this unwelcome LS 13 263 1
had a most unexpected & unwelcome visit from Lady Susan, LS 41 309 1
marry, being, however unwelcome, no more than he had NA II 1 135 43
of containing any thing unwelcome, I should have given it NA II 10 204 12
The hand writing of her mother, never till then unwelcome, SS II 9 202 7
inquiries were never unwelcome to Miss Dashwood. SS II 10 216 15
each other should be checked by Lucy's unwelcome presence. SS II 13 242 25
But unwelcome as such a task must be, it was necessary to SS III 1 261 11
a little change was not unwelcome for its own sake. PP II 4 151 1
and parcels, and the unwelcome addition of Kitty's and PP II 16 220 16
help feeling how very unwelcome her appearance at PP III 3 267 1
does not follow that the interruption must be unwelcome." PP III 10 327 6
letters obliged them to do, was a most unwelcome exercise. MP I 11 107 1
most unwelcome news; and she could think of nothing else. MP I 16 156 28
the most unwelcome, most ill-timed, most appalling! MP II 1 175 1
of his son, exceedingly unwelcome; and it needed all the MP II 1 183 23
"His going, though only eight miles, will be an unwelcome MP II 7 247 42
of his determination once admitted, it was not unwelcome. MP II 12 292 5
he must have seen how unwelcome it was to her; and in that MP II 13 302 11
This was a most unwelcome hearing, for though he might MP II 13 303 12
That very evening brought your most unwelcome uncle. MP III 5 358 9
her return would be unwelcome at present, and that she MP III 14 436 15
Under any circumstances it would have been an unwelcome MP III 16 452 13
Unwelcome as it was, Mr. Woodhouse could only give a E I 9 80 68
Such a development of every thing most unwelcome!--- E I 16 134 1
might be involved in an unwelcome interference, rather E III 5 350 31
"Whenever the time may come, it must be unwelcome to her E III 8 381 22
The fear of being still unwelcome, determined her, though E III 16 452 8
patent; there any unwelcome sensations, arising from P III 1 3 1
tradespeople, and the unwelcome hints of Mr. Shepherd, his P III 1 9 19
in all his own unwelcome obtrusiveness; and the evil of P IV 10 212 1
UNWELL (17)
of "your sister looks unwell to-day," or "your sister SS II 5 172 40
that Marianne was unwell, was too polite to object for a SS II 6 178 16
very unwell, has lost her colour, and is grown quite thin. SS II 11 227 48
"I find myself very unwell this morning, which, I I PP I 7 31 29
30
Mrs. Collins, seeing that she was really unwell, did not PP II 10 187 41
you find yourself growing unwell, and any difficulties MP III 11 411 16
she should come here, than go to Ireland, if she is unwell. E II 1 161 29
the mention of her being unwell, than I burst out quite E II 1 162 31
Mrs. Churchill was unwell--far too unwell to do without E II 12 258 7
She had been particularly unwell, however, suffering from E II 12 263 42
"Is she unwell?" E III 10 392 3
of finding her so very unwell, which he had had no E III 10 399 57
Mary, often a little unwell, and always thinking a great P III 5 33 7
unwell and out of spirits, was almost a matter of course. P III 5 36 21
"I am sorry to find you unwell," replied Anne. P III 5 37 23
Oh! Anne, I am so very unwell! P III 5 38 31
I ever fancied myself unwell, or had any ideas of danger, P III 8 71 54
UNWHOLESOME (5)
What was unwholesome to him, he regarded as unfit for any E I 2 19 14
of suppers being very unwholesome made him rather sorry to E I 3 24 12
An egg boiled very soft is not unwholesome. E I 3 24 14
You need not be afraid of unwholesome preserves here. E I 3 25 14
carrot or parsnip, I do not consider it unwholesome." E II 3 172 19
UNWILLING (56)
She was very unwilling that Frederica should be allowed to LS 15 267 5
I was thoroughly unwilling to let her go, & so was her LS 41 310 3
triumphs to press on the unwilling and unbelieving ear of NA I 4 32 2
I am indeed a most unwilling messenger. NA II 13 223 13
much, that he is always unwilling to give his opinion on SS I 4 19 2
Most unwilling was she to awaken from such a dream of SS I 12 58 3
was unable to talk, and unwilling to take any nourishment; SS I 16 83 1
I was very unwilling to enter into it, as you may imagine, SS I 22 130 28
Marianne, though always unwilling to join any of their SS II 1 143 9
amusement abroad, than unwilling to run the risk of his SS II 5 170 28
Never had Marianne been so unwilling to dance in her life, SS II 5 171 35
mind is perhaps rather unwilling to be convinced, it will SS II 5 173 44
Willoughby's sake, would have been unwilling to believe. SS II 7 188 43
Edward will not be very unwilling to accept the charge." SS II 13 243 31
It was an office in short, from which, unwilling to give SS III 3 283 20
was at the same time so unwilling to appear as the SS III 4 290 36
did not find him very unwilling to accept your proposal?" SS III 4 291 47
Mr. Palmer, though very unwilling to go, as well from real SS III 7 308 5
was unwilling to take her where there might be infection. SS III 9 335 6
on dancing, was not unwilling to speak, when her questions W 331 11
another time--& seeming unwilling to leave her, tho' his W 334 13
Emma thanked him--but professed herself very unwilling to W 339 18
Bingley was by no means unwilling to preside at his table, PP I 4 15 13
surprised, was not unwilling to receive it, when she PP I 6 26 38
This, she would not hear of; but she was not so unwilling PP I 8 40 59
"About a month," said Elizabeth; and then, unwilling to PP I 16 77 9
taciturn disposition, unwilling to speak, unless we expect PP I 18 91 15
Unwilling as she was to admit an idea so destructive of PP I 23 129 13

the least unwilling to think her a very good sort of girl. PP II 3 150 29
to get rid of him; and unwilling for her sister's sake, to PP III 10 329 33
34
She had been unwilling to mention Bingley; and the PP III 17 374 19
what made you so unwilling to come to the point at last. PP III 18 381 7
I am of a cautious temper, and unwilling to risk my MP I 4 43 23
the lady could not be unwilling to have a listener, and MP I 7 64 12
by her early progress, to make her unwilling to dismount. MP I 7 66 15
resolved, however unwilling he must be to check a pleasure MP I 7 74 58
Cannot you imagine with what unwilling feelings the former MP I 9 87 15
observing her, but unwilling to exasperate his brother by MP I 15 146 53
the lady, not very unwilling at first, could refuse no MP I 18 170 24
on turning back, was unwilling to lose her walk, she MP II 8 257 15
Edmund was not unwilling to be persuaded to engage in the MP III 4 345 4
I am unwilling to fancy myself neglected for a young one. MP III 9 394 1
have all along been so unwilling to have their own MP III 14 434 13
inconveniently shy, not unwilling to talk--and yet so far E I 3 23 10
but she was not unwilling to have others deceived, or E I 6 44 19
I should be unwilling, I own, to live in any other part of E I 12 103 37
described, he was still unwilling to admit that the E II 6 198 5
very reserved, so very unwilling to give the least E II 6 200 19
of wine, for whatever unwilling self-denial his care of E II 8 213 6
Still, however, having proceeded so far, one is unwilling E II 11 250 18
to secure, was very unwilling to have her hurried away so P III 5 33 6
He must be either indifferent or unwilling. P III 7 58 21
no good; yet was still unwilling to be away, till touched P III 12 114 59
with most unwilling looks been constrained to pass by--. S 1 364 1
And as for poor Arthur, he wd not have been unwilling S 9 407 1
you to be pressing matters upon a mind at all unwilling."-- S 12 425 1

UNWILLINGLY (11)
and felt, as she unwillingly paced back the gallery, that NA II 8 185 5
a yet stronger interest, would have left it unwillingly. NA II 9 191 3
were obliged, though unwillingly, to turn back, for no SS I 9 41 6
Elinor was obliged, though unwillingly, to believe that SS I 10 49 12
by the coldness of her manner that she did it unwillingly. W 334 13
felt that she must go; and very unwillingly said so. PP I 7 33 45
and you have certainly bestowed it most unwillingly. PP II 11 190 7
bestow it unwillingly, but I demand it of your justice. PP II 12 196 4
though at first unwillingly admitted, had for some time PP III 2 265 16
and she sitting, most unwillingly, among the chaperons at MP I 12 116 11
was at last, though unwillingly, accepted as an excuse; P III 11 98 15

UNWILLINGNESS (15)
began to speak of her unwillingness that he should be NA II 7 177 17
Could there be any unwillingness on the General's side to NA II 7 177 18
and, above all, his unwillingness to accept her mother's SS I 15 77 19
Why else should he have shewn such unwillingness to accept SS I 15 78 23
Her unwillingness to quit her mother was her only SS II 3 158 21
overcome her unwillingness to be in her company again. SS III 5 294 3
of doing it, from an unwillingness to enter into an SS III 8 321 34
been this little unwillingness; but allow me to assure you PP I 19 105 8
that, added to her unwillingness to see Mr. Darcy, it PP II 10 187 41
From an unwillingness to confess how much her intimacy PP III 18 382 20
to understand her unwillingness to be acting with a MP I 16 154 14
though from her usual unwillingness to give pain, and E I 12 258 7
Mr. Woodhouse felt no unwillingness, and only made the E II 16 291 4
Mr. and Mrs. Elton, indeed, showed no unwillingness to mix, E III 7 367 1
best counteract this unwillingness to be seen or assisted. E III 9 390 18

UNWISE (3)
days were so few it would be unwise to fix on any earlier. MP II 8 253 7
to be very unsafe and unwise, and what, I think, all P IV 11 231 9
by expressions of very unwise & unjustifiable resentment S 3 377 1

UNWORTHILY (3)
to be certain she could never bestow a favour unworthily. PP I 18 98 62
her improperly and unworthily, and in such a way as she MP II 13 301 7
How unworthily occupied! P IV 1 126 18

UNWORTHINESS (1)
the most perfect conviction of his unworthiness can do. SS II 9 211 34

UNWORTHY (31)
Reginald has a good figure, & is not unworthy the praise LS 10 258 3
city of Bath, as unworthy to make part of a landscape. NA I 14 111 29
again, my dear Catherine; indeed he is unworthy of you." NA II 1 130 5
"Unworthy! NA II 1 130 7
She felt utterly unworthy of such respect, and knew not NA II 5 154 2
in the Abbey not unworthy her notice--and was proceeding NA II 5 162 27
directed to gain, no unworthy retraction of a tacit NA II 15 247 15
their falling into unworthy hands; and she would have SS I 17 92 25
"No, he is not so unworthy as you believe him. SS II 7 186 32
staying, by no means unworthy her notice; and as for Lady SS II 12 229 1
Nothing has proved him unworthy; nor has any thing SS III 1 264 29
and being unworthy to be compared with his friend. PP I 3 10 5
Mr. Darcy could be so unworthy of Mr. Bingley's regard; PP I 17 85 1
to me that my hand is unworthy your acceptance, or that PP I 19 108 19
to throw off your unworthy child from your affection for PP III 6 297 11
Though unworthy, from inferiority of age and strength, to MP I 2 17 21
family profiles thought unworthy of being anywhere else, MP I 16 152 2
But this was an unworthy feeling. MP II 8 258 18
Her poor mother now did not look so very unworthy of being MP III 11 408 2
What an unworthy attachment! MP III 12 417 4
The acquaintance she had already formed were unworthy of E I 3 23 10
and shaken off all that was unworthy in their authority. E I 18 148 22
from himself, was unworthy the real liberality of mind E I 18 150 37
as a mere trifle, and quite unworthy of being dwelt on. E II 3 180 54
nothing to denote him unworthy of the distinguished honour E II 7 206 2
Harriet Smith might think herself not unworthy of being E III 12 415 1
unworthy of it: all acquaintance between them had ceased. P III 1 8 16
unworthy member of the one she was now transplanted into.-- P III 6 43 3
determined him to be unworthy of the interest which he had P IV 2 133 26
on a subject which she thought unworthy to excite them. P IV 4 148 10
the better half, of the pair)--not unworthy notice.-- S 7 394 1

UNWOUNDED (2)
endeavouring to convince Lucy that her heart was unwounded. SS II 1 142 7
We returned unwounded, and the meeting, therefore, never SS II 9 211 38

UNYIELDING (1)
of his advice, quite as unyielding to his representation, MP I 13 128 38

UP-HILL (1)
must have very up-hill work, for there are all your early MP III 4 347 21

UPBRAID (1)
No lurking horrors were to upbraid him for his easy E III 6 356 30

UPBRAIDED (1)
she had condemned and upbraided him, her anger was turned PP II 14 212 17

UPBRAIDING (1)
that young lady, whose bright eyes are also upbraiding me." PP I 18 92 23

UPHELD (1)
well, no person, (however upheld for the present by S 2 373 1

UPHILL (1)
doubt--but at first it is Uphill work; and therefore we S 4 382 1

UPPER (20)
evening came which was to usher her into the upper rooms. NA I 2 20 8
you have been at the upper rooms, the theatre, and the NA I 3 25 2
Have you yet honoured the upper rooms?" NA I 3 26 10
assemblies; neither at the upper nor Lower Rooms, at NA I 5 35 2
knocked off his horse by a brickbat from an upper window. NA I 14 113 39
to the fireplace at the upper end, where one party only W 327 8
were prepared, & the neat upper maid was lighting the W 336 14
of ascertaining from an upper window, that he wore a blue PP I 3 9 3
Miss Lucas perceived him from an upper window as he walked PP I 22 121 1
in what was passing at the upper end of the table, and in MP I 6 52 1
a rough hedgerow along the upper side of the field, never MP II 4 208 12
of better help than the upper housemaid's, and when MP II 9 271 41
had previously seen the upper servant, brought in every MP III 7 383 32
and of her having an upper maid who had lived five-and- E I 4 27 4
there (nodding towards the upper end of the table) has so E I 14 120 11
and the softness of the upper notes I am sure is exactly E II 10 241 8
exaggeration, that her upper house-maid and laundry-maid, P III 6 45 9
Here is a nut," said he, catching one down from an upper P III 10 88 26
box which you will find on the upper shelf of the closet." P IV 9 202 68
of a harp might be heard through the upper casement.-- S 4 383 1

UPPER SEYMOUR ST (8)
in Upper Seymour St, & we may be always together, there or LS 26 296 4
Lady Susan to Mrs Johnson. Upper Seymour St. LS 29 298 1
Susan to Mr De Courcy. Upper Seymour St. LS 30 299 1
Susan to Mrs Johnson. Upper Seymour St. LS 31 301 1
Susan to Mrs Johnson. Upper Seymour St. LS 33 303 1
Upper Seymour St. I will not attempt to LS 35 304 1
Susan to Mr De Courcy. Upper Seymour St. LS 37 306 1
Upper Seymour St. my dear Alicia I yeild LS 39 307 1

UPPER-ROOMS (1)
Pulteney-Street reached the Upper-Rooms in very good time. NA I 8 52 1

UPPERCROSS (71)
Musgrove, Esq. of Uppercross, in the county of Somerset,"-- P III 1 3 2
Uppercross was a moderate-sized village, which a few years P III 5 36 20
She knew the ways of Uppercross as well as those of P III 5 36 21
Anne had not wanted this visit to Uppercross, to learn P III 6 42 1
at least two months at Uppercross, it was highly incumbent P III 6 43 3
and all her ideas in as much of Uppercross as possible. P III 6 43 3
There was a family of cousins within a walk of Uppercross, P III 6 47 15
abroad had worked its way to Uppercross, two years before. P III 6 50 28
Crofts to dine at Uppercross, by the end of another week. P III 7 53 1
the drawing-room at Uppercross, they would have found it P III 8 63 3
that had ever been at Uppercross); and sitting down P III 8 64 7
the attractions of Uppercross induced him to put this off. P III 9 73 1
It was soon Uppercross with him almost every day. P III 9 73 2
at his father's house, only two miles from Uppercross. P III 9 73 4
their connexion with Uppercross; this eldest son of course P III 9 74 5
A most improper match for Miss Musgrove, of Uppercross." P III 9 76 13
but to keep away from Uppercross; but there was such a P III 9 77 19
present curacy, and obtaining that of Uppercross instead. P III 9 78 19
The advantage of his having to come only to Uppercross, P III 9 78 19
his coming once to Uppercross; a most decided change. P III 10 82 2
hill, which parted Uppercross and Winthrop, and soon P III 10 85 13
first instant of their all setting forward for Uppercross. P III 10 89 36
her full a mile, and they were going through Uppercross. P III 10 90 38
so much of his time at Uppercross, that in removing thence P III 11 93 2
her removal from Uppercross, where she felt she had been P III 11 93 4
and unheard of at Uppercross for two whole days, appeared P III 11 94 5
seventeen miles from Uppercross; though November, the P III 11 94 7
The party from Uppercross passing down by the now deserted P III 11 96 10
I do think he had better leave Uppercross entirely, and P III 12 102 2
days in a place like Uppercross, where, excepting our P III 12 102 2
lived at Uppercross, and were intimate with Dr. Shirley. P III 12 103 4
amazingly, and wish we had such a neighbour at Uppercross." P III 12 103 4
another woman were at Uppercross, before all subjects P III 12 103 5
They ought to be setting off for Uppercross by one, and in P III 12 107 22
"Uppercross,--the necessity of some one's going to P III 12 113 57
of some one's going to Uppercross,--the news to be P III 12 113 57
Some must resolve on being off for Uppercross instantly. P III 12 113 58
time required by the Uppercross horses to take them back, P III 12 114 64
Dr. Shirley's leaving Uppercross; farther on, she had P III 12 115 66
in the neighbourhood of Uppercross, and there had been P III 12 117 73
When the distressing communication at Uppercross was over, P III 12 117 76
The remainder of Anne's time at Uppercross, comprehending P IV 1 121 1
her last morning at Uppercross better than in assisting P IV 1 122 5
of all that had given Uppercross its cheerful character. P IV 1 123 6
Scenes had passed in Uppercross, which made it precious. P IV 1 123 8
She knew who had been frequenting Uppercross. P IV 1 124 10
Their concerns had been sunk under those of Uppercross, P IV 1 124 11
We told you about the laundry-door, at Uppercross. P IV 1 127 28
their return to Uppercross, they drove over to the lodge.-- P IV 2 129 1
possible supply from Uppercross had been furnished, to P IV 2 129 2
church at Lyme than at Uppercross,--and all this, joined P IV 2 130 3
body to be living in Uppercross; and when he discovered P IV 2 130 6
to Uppercross than herself, must be left to be guessed. P IV 2 130 7
improve the noise of Uppercross, and lessen that of Lyme. P IV 2 133 27
not but feel that Uppercross was already quite alive again. P IV 2 134 28
with her and stay at Uppercross, whenever she returned. P IV 2 134 31
"not to call at Uppercross in the Christmas holidays." P IV 2 135 32
to the bustles of Uppercross and the seclusion of Kellynch. P IV 2 135 34
Uppercross excited no interest, Kellynch very little, it P IV 3 137 3
was growing very eager for news from Uppercross and Lyme. P IV 6 162 1
"You must be a great deal too happy to care for Uppercross, P IV 6 162 7
choosing to venture to Uppercross till he had an "answer P IV 6 164 8
from Harville, written upon the spot, from Uppercross. P IV 6 172 41
I fancy they are all at Uppercross." P IV 6 172 41
It would be of no use to go to Uppercross again, for that P IV 6 173 49
and he talked of Uppercross, of the Musgroves, nay, even P IV 7 176 8
Captain Wentworth of Uppercross; owned himself P IV 8 190 47
remained with Mr. Musgrove and Louisa at Uppercross. P IV 10 217 19
miles from Uppercross, and in a very fine country--fine P IV 10 217 20
the present state of Uppercross, and rejoice in its P IV 10 219 27
that only at Uppercross had he learnt to do his justice, P IV 11 241 61

UPPERCROSS COTTAGE (5)
to come to Uppercross Cottage, and bear her company as P III 5 33 7
be divided between Uppercross Cottage and Kellynch-Lodge. P III 5 34 10
Cottage, in the first stage of Lady Russell's journey. P III 5 36 19
residence; and Uppercross Cottage, with its viranda, P III 5 36 20
"A letter from Uppercross Cottage, sir." P IV 6 162 4

UPPERCROSS-HALL (1)
Anne had no Uppercross-Hall before her, no landed estate, P IV 12 250 5

UPPERMOST (8)
in Bath was still uppermost with Mrs. Allen, and she NA I 3 25 1
which had been long uppermost in her thoughts; it was, " NA I 7 48 32
a couple of minutes, from what was uppermost in her mind. SS III 2 275 21
the aunt's fortune was uppermost in her mind, at the W 349 24
comprehended that he was uppermost in her thoughts; and PP III 3 269 10
the morrow, was so much uppermost in Lady Bertram's mind, MP II 5 217 11
this--which of all her unpleasant sensations was uppermost. E I 15 131 32
He don't stand uppermost, beleive me.-- S 7 400 1

UPRIGHT (18)
however upright, can escape the malevolence of slander. LS 14 264 3
was a little, thin woman, upright, even to formality, in SS II 12 232 14
that was honourable and upright, whose views of happiness MP III 2 328 6
You have proved yourself upright and disinterested, prove MP III 4 347 18
whole of her judicious, upright conduct as a sister, she MP III 13 421 2
and decorum, Edmund's upright principles, unsuspicious MP III 15 442 21
a pretty height and size; such a firm and upright figure. E I 5 39 20
This amiable, upright, perfect Jane Fairfax was apparently E II 10 243 22
His tall, firm, upright figure, among the bulky forms and E III 2 326 32
None of that upright integrity, that strict adherence to E III 10 397 48
softer than upright justice and clear-sighted good will.-- E III 12 415 1
and to induce the most upright female mind in the creation E III 14 437 8
was a blessing on all his upright and honourable exertions; E III 15 445 11
She could soon sit upright on the sofa, and began to hope P III 5 39 40
and arrange in her air! and she sits so upright! P IV 10 215 15
in getting the carriage upright again, the Travellor said-- S 1 365 1
Lady D. was of middle height, stout, upright & alert in S 6 391 1
shewey figures, an upright decided carriage & an assured S 11 421 1

UPRIGHTLY (1)
Would he have persevered, and uprightly, Fanny must have MP III 17 467 19

UPRIGHTNESS (3)
strong good sense and uprightness of mind, bid most fairly MP I 2 20 33
fat, had a squareness, uprightness, and vigour of form, P III 6 48 18
their openness, their uprightness; protesting that she was P III 11 99 19

UPROAR (2)
and Mr. Donavan found the house in all this uproar. SS III 1 259 7

you are wanted immediately; we are all in an uproar. PP I 20 111 7
UPSET (2)
I wonder whereabouts they will upset to-day. P III 10 84 8
to be upset the next moment, which they certainly must be. P IV 6 169 25
UPSTAIRS (6)
As we went upstairs Lady Susan begged permission to attend LS 20 276 5
He then left me & ran upstairs. LS 23 284 5
The ladies were invited upstairs to prepare for dinner. W 351 25
upstairs, and were soon deep in the interesting subject. MP II 8 257 15
and luxury of a fire upstairs--wondering at the past and MP III 2 329 10
at the low windows upstairs, in order to close the blinds, S 11 422 1
UPSTART (3)
The upstart pretensions of a young woman without family, PP III 14 356 50
A little upstart, vulgar being, with her Mr. E., and her E II 14 279 52
claims: but in herself, I assure you, she is an upstart." E II 18 310 33
UPSTARTS (1)
I have quite a horror of upstarts. E II 18 310 34
UPWARDS (2)
When they came to the steps, leading upwards from the P III 12 104 6
many an eye upwards, & made many a Gazer gaze again.-- S 11 422 1
URBANITY (1)
and with all his mildest urbanity, said, "I am very sorry E II 16 294 24 25

URGE (26)
You must support & encourage me--you must urge the LS 15 267 6
I would urge them more myself, but that I am impatient to LS 31 302 1
was her uncle; & all that could be urged, we did urge. LS 41 310 3
"Do not urge me, Isabella. NA I 13 97 1
any thing in his nature to urge; and she hurried away, NA I 15 124 47
urge his suit, and say all manner of pretty things to you. NA II 3 144 10
"Nay, if you can use such a word, I can urge you no NA II 13 221 5
her sister had hoped, to urge her to exertion now; she SS III 2 270 2
thought my duty required, urge him to it for prudence sake, SS III 2 277 30
that I have nothing to urge-- that because she was injured SS III 8 322 36
sprung up from her heart, but she dared not urge one. SS III 10 347 33
He had nothing to urge against it, but still resisted the SS III 13 372 45
"Do not urge her, madam," said Edmund. MP I 15 146 54
"It is not fair to urge her in this manner.-- MP I 15 146 54
Do not urge her any more." MP I 15 147 54
"I am not going to urge her,"--replied Mrs. Norris sharply, MP I 15 147 55
to be satisfied perhaps to urge the matter quite so far as MP II 3 201 22
delicacy, ceased to urge to see you for the present." MP III 1 321 47
I will explain to you instantly all that makes me urge you MP III 3 342 36
She meant to urge him to persevere in the hope of being MP III 4 354 46
A letter arrived from Mr. Churchill to urge his nephew's E II 12 258 7
the same motives which she had been heard to urge before.-- E III 6 359 37
A note was written to urge it. E III 9 389 16
she had too much to urge for Emma's attention; it was soon E III 12 420 14
He knows he is wrong, and has nothing rational to urge.-- E III 15 445 11
I long to make apologies, excuses, to urge something for E III 16 459 47
URGED (32)
not in his nature to refuse, when urged in such a manner?" LS 24 290 12
was her uncle; & all that could be urged, we did urge. LS 41 310 3
she not been urged by the disappointment of the day before. NA I 10 72 8
He perceived her inclination, and having again urged the NA II 7 179 29
from the pain of being urged, as to make her friend NA II 13 228 27
There is great truth, however, in what you have now urged SS I 15 79 29
her sister's youth, and urged the matter farther, but in SS I 16 85 10
justice of what Elinor has urged, and if she were to be SS II 3 154 5
Marianne that he was gone, urged the impossibility of SS II 6 178 15
think of with horror; and urged by a strong impulse of SS II 12 236 39 40

not a thing to be urged against the wishes of everybody. SS II 14 246 2
"All this, however," he continued, "was urged in vain. SS III 1 267 42
fears and caution, urged the necessity of her immediate SS III 7 307 3
with her sister, &c. she urged him so strongly to remain, SS III 7 309 5
hours, Mrs. Dashwood, urged equally by her own and her SS III 10 340 4
Bingley urged Mr. Jones's being sent for immediately; PP I 8 40 59
needlessly long, she urged Jane to borrow Mr. Bingley's PP I 12 59 1
for allowances, and urged the possibility of mistakes--but PP II 1 138 31
Neither could any thing be urged against my father, who, PP II 10 187 40
marriage by her parents, urged him so earnestly, yet so PP III 8 314 22
To all the objections I have already urged, I have still PP III 14 357 62
or their brother Edmund urged her claims to their kindness, MP I 2 17 21
opposed whatever could be urged by the supineness of his MP I 4 36 7
Edmund urged her remaining where she was with an MP I 9 96 76
Edmund proposed, urged, entreated it--till the lady, not MP I 18 170 24
by Edmund, and warmly urged by the two sisters, was soon MP II 5 223 48
after a moment's thought, urged Fanny's returning with her MP II 8 257 15
the kindest manner she now urged Fanny's taking one for MP II 8 258 15
temper, of being urged again; and though no second letter MP III 15 437 1
Miss Crawford need not have urged secrecy with so much MP III 15 438 7
And not all that could be urged to detain her succeeded. E II 1 162 33
for the night, and kindly urged her to let him come and P III 7 58 20
URGENCY (7)
with all the strength and urgency which illness could SS I 1 5 5
now obliged to forego through the urgency of your debts." MP I 3 23 3
and Mr. Yates, with an urgency which differed from his, MP I 15 146 53
all the authoritative urgency that Tom and Maria were MP I 16 150 1
scalloped oysters with an urgency which she knew would be E I 3 24 11
"But, in spite of all her friend's urgency, and her own E II 1 161 24
The Admiral's kind urgency came in support of his wife's; P III 10 91 41
URGENT (19)
My kind friends here are most affectionately urgent with LS 1 243 1
But Isabella became only more and more urgent; calling on NA I 13 98 2
by the urgent entreaties of his fair one that he would go. NA I 15 120 24
most urgent for returning with his daughter to the house. NA II 7 181 41
in spite of Sir John's urgent entreaties that they would SS I 9 40 2
Sir John had been very urgent with them all to spend the SS I 19 108 40
in Willoughby, and she was wildly urgent to be gone. SS II 9 203 9
to go herself, was very urgent to prevent her sister's SS III 5 294 3
was almost equally urgent with her mother to accompany her. SS III 7 308 3
the general voice was so urgent with him to join the party, W 357 28
of packing, and was so urgent on the necessity of placing PP II 14 213 20
In the afternoon Lydia was urgent with the rest of the PP II 16 223 25
Say that urgent business calls us home immediately. PP III 4 278 21
You would not write to each other but upon the most urgent MP I 6 59 43
among the most urgent in requesting to hear the glee again. MP I 11 113 42
Fanny was too urgent, however, and had too many tears in MP II 10 280 30
own passion, and was very urgent for a favourable answer. E I 15 130 28
and so she wrote a very urgent letter to her mother--or E II 1 159 20
the occasion, answers to urgent applications from Mrs. P IV 9 209 97
URGING (13)
I have another reason for urging this. LS 26 295 2
wound my own feelings by urging a lengthened separation; & LS 30 301 4
all the trouble of urging a removal, which Lady Susan had LS 42 313 7
Willoughby's inconstancy, urging her by every plea of duty SS II 5 172 39
then all employed, not in urging her, not in pitying her, SS II 7 181 6
her own, in privately urging Emma to go--"you do not know W 362 32
civility especially, in urging the execution of the plan MP I 8 75 1
Edmund had little to hope but he was still urging the MP I 13 129 38
Still Mrs. Norris was at intervals urging something MP II 1 180 10
To be urging her opinion against Sir Thomas's, was a proof MP II 10 275 11
the others were variously urging and recommending, Mr. E I 15 128 17 18

to all, and had no scruple in urging him to the utmost.-- E III 17 467 31
her father to be proceeding, his friends to be urging him. P III 2 12 5
URN (1)
by Baddely, of tea-board, urn, and cake-bearers, made its MP III 3 344 43
USAGE (7)
But now, after such dishonourable usage, who can tell what SS II 9 210 32
usage, and most painful regrets at his being what he is. PP I 16 78 20
her own sufferings and ill usage; blaming every body but PP III 5 287 34
or apparent sense of ill usage; and yet Emma fancied there E III 16 451 2
tone of great ill usage,) which made it so much the worse. E III 16 457 40
most rough usage, and riding out the heaviest weather." P IV 11 233 22
of where to go for better usage, to leave the hotel at all S 3 378 1
USAGES (1)
there are established usages which make every thing plain P III 3 18 9 10

USE (186)
"Of what use my dear sister, could be any application to LS 24 289 12
sat erect, in the perfect use of her senses, and with NA I 8 53 3
I use the verb 'to torment,' as I observed to be your own NA I 14 109 25
that they never find it necessary to use more than half." NA I 14 114 47
her to use her own fancy in the perusal of Matilda's woes. NA II 5 160 23
every thing being for daily use, pretended only to comfort, NA II 5 162 27
by her mistress to be of use to Miss Morland; and though NA II 6 164 3
it might sometimes be of use in holding hats and bonnets. NA II 6 165 4
than the one in common use, and fitted up in a style of NA II 6 165 6
would be simple not to make use of them; but, upon his NA II 6 166 7
was not without its use; she scorned the causeless fears NA II 6 167 10
desire of making use of the present smiling weather.-- NA II 7 177 17
which Mrs. Allen had the use of for her plants in winter, NA II 7 178 25
to the rooms in common use, by passing through a few of NA II 8 183 2
aware of their leading from the offices in common use?" NA II 9 195 12
of past folly, however painful, might not be without use. NA II 10 201 4
expressed a wish of being of use or comfort to her. NA II 10 203 8
air, however, was of great use in dissipating these NA II 11 214 25
"Nay, if you can use such a word, I can urge you no NA II 13 221 5
that the General had made use of such expressions with NA II 14 230 2
good enough to be immediately made use of again by herself. NA II 14 237 22
Use those words again and I will leave the room this SS I 4 21 14
deceive yourself as to his having the use of his limbs!" SS I 8 37 5
You shall share its use with me. SS I 12 58 2
the horse is still yours, though you cannot use it now. SS I 12 59 6
use, and with modern furniture it would be delightful. SS I 13 69 76
with admiration for the use of Sir John Middleton, his SS I 21 124 33
could be of any use to you to know my opinion of her. SS I 22 128 10
cut out, I may be of some use to Miss Lucy Steele, in SS II 1 145 19
you would be kind enough to use out of friendship for him, SS II 2 149 25
Marianne was of no use on these occasions, as she would SS II 4 166 31
persuaded to take, were of use; and from that time till SS II 7 191 65
Well, it is the oddest thing to me, that a man should use SS II 8 194 8
Surely this comparison must have its use with her. SS II 9 210 32
Use your own discretion, however, in communicating to her SS II 9 210 32
Elinor perfectly understood her, and was forced to use all SS II 10 217 22
has not only been of great use to you hitherto, but in the SS II 11 226 42
It was censure in common use, and easily given. SS II 14 246 3
nor too speedily made use of; and the visit to Lady SS II 14 254 26
Why, Colonel Brandon's only object is to be of use to Mr. SS III 4 291 52
"A very simple one--to be of use to Mr. Ferrars." SS III 5 295 15
often by her better experience in nursing, of material use. SS III 7 308 3
Brandon, who was chiefly of use in listening to Mrs. SS III 7 309 7
and said, "there is no use in staying her; I must be off." SS III 8 331 70 71

prevailed on to accept the use of his carriage on her SS III 10 341 4
had so far recovered the use of her reason and voice as to SS III 11 353 25
had entreated her to use no ceremony contained a few lines W 338 18
intimacy which the use of his carriage must have created--. W 341 19
"My good creatures, replied Jane, use no ceremony with me, W 351 25
"It might have been secured to your future use, without W 352 26
And what was the use of my putting up your last new coat, W 353 26
himself, cd sometimes make use of the wit of an absent W 359 28
"It will be no use to us, if twenty such should come since PP I 1 5 32
up every thing to be of use to the late Mr. Darcy, and PP I 16 81 37
laughing that she could not use the short pause he allowed PP I 19 105 9 10

First, that you will allow me the free use of my PP I 20 112 22
You have sense, and we all expect you to use it. PP II 3 144 2
dining parlour for common use; it was a better sized room, PP II 7 168 1
"And what arts did he use to separate them?" PP II 10 185 31
public; for of what use could it apparently be to any one, PP III 5 285 16
She was of great use and comfort to us all, and Lady Lucas PP III 5 292 66
or any of her daughters, if they could be of use to us." PP III 5 292 66
of being allowed to be of use to his niece, was forced to PP III 10 324 2
Mary petitioned for the use of the library at Netherfield; PP III 13 349 42
so; it must be so, while he retains the use of his reason. PP III 14 354 36
"Lady Catherine has been of infinite use, which ought to PP III 18 381 15
which ought to make her happy, for she loves to be of use. PP III 18 381 15
of needlework, of little use and no beauty, thinking more MP I 2 19 31
gradually admit that the separation might have some use. MP I 2 21 34
"My object, Lady Bertram, is to be of use to those that MP I 3 30 52
my sole desire is to be of use to your family--and so if MP I 3 30 56
its being for Fanny's use; and had Lady Bertram ever MP I 4 37 9
without a gravel walk to step on, or a bench fit for use. MP I 6 57 31
that might be of some small use to you with their opinions; MP I 6 62 58
were not without their use; it was all in harmony; and as MP I 7 65 13
Why is not use to be made of my mother's chaise? MP I 8 77 9
supposed to be of any other use than to contribute to the MP I 9 85 5
It was only for the private use of the family. MP I 9 86 7
It is a handsome chapel, and was formerly in constant use MP I 9 86 9
"You do not make me of any use. MP I 9 94 59
that could be of any use; and if I cannot convince them MP I 13 128 37
to be of any use, but I think we could not choose worse." MP I 14 131 3
The first use she made of her solitude was to take up the MP I 14 137 23
I am of some use I hope in preventing waste and making the MP I 15 141 22
of the one making the use of the other so evidently MP I 16 151 1
resigned to her having the use of what nobody else wanted, MP I 16 151 1
"Whose stables do you use at Bath?" was the next question; MP II 2 193 17
one minute tendered to his use again; and the next, with MP II 6 237 23
use entirely so long as he remained in Northamptonshire. MP II 6 237 23
it was not merely for the use of it in the hunting season, MP II 7 246 37
have," said she, "more by half than I ever use or think of. MP II 8 258 16
in, was making use of your inkstand to explain my errand. MP II 9 261 2
maid to assist her; too late of course to be of any use. MP II 9 271 41
feel was advanced for her use; and every thing that an MP II 11 285 10
use of such words and offers, if they meant but to trifle? MP II 13 302 10
I understood that you had the use of this room by way of MP III 1 312 10
said, "it is of no use, I perceive, to talk to you. MP III 1 318 39
There is no use in these tears; they can do no good. MP III 1 320 44
of some use, and obliging her aunt: it is all her fault. MP III 1 323 56
she felt herself obliged to use, was not to be understood. MP III 2 327 5
we all talk Shakespeare, use his similies, and describe MP III 3 338 14
get your heart for his own use, he has to unfasten it from MP III 4 347 21
always fit for comfortable use; opening the door, however, MP III 5 357 6
She was of use to no one else; but there she might be MP III 6 370 13
She might scruple to make use of the words, but she must MP III 8 390 6
I did not use to think her wanting in self possession, but MP III 9 393 1
she will then feel--to use a vulgar phrase--that she has MP III 9 394 1
Her influence, or at least the consciousness and use of it, MP III 9 396 7
use, and Susan was entertained in a way quite new to her. MP III 10 404 15
She felt that she must have been of use to all. MP III 14 432 10
might be of infinite use to them; and, as to yourself, you MP III 14 435 14
As you will do it, it will indeed, to use your own words, E I 6 44 16
believe I had been of some use; but it is not every body E I 8 58 13
Mr. Knightley, that there can be no use in canvassing it. E I 8 65 48
Where would be the use of his bringing us a charade made E I 9 73 18
so before, that the sea is very rarely of use to any body. E I 12 101 22
bathing should have been of use to her--and if I had known E I 12 102 29
I may be allowed, I hope, the use of my judgment as well E I 12 106 60
Emma smiled and answered--"my visit was of use to the E I 13 114 32
"What as excellent device;" said he, "the use of a sheep- E I 13 115 36
Weston, at dinner, he made use of the very first interval E I 14 119 6

7
"One ought to use the same caution, perhaps, in judging of E I 14 123 23
and making use of Mrs. Weston's arguments against herself. E I 18 145 5
Such language for a young man entirely dependent, to use!-- E I 18 147 17
disposed--had in short, to use a most intelligible phrase, E II 4 181 4
about as he could, and not use his carriage so often as E II 8 213 7
to put it to a better use than we can; and that really is E II 8 216 16
"Or that he did not give her the use of their own E II 8 216 24
plain muslin it was of no use to look at figured; and that E II 9 235 35
For my mother had no use of her spectacles--could not put E II 9 236 46
supply; for I have a great many more than I can ever use. E II 9 238 51
"Might not they use both rooms, and dance across the E II 11 248 10
rather hesitating, "if you think she will be of any use." E II 11 255 51
"I do not find myself making any use of the word sacrifice, E II 13 264 2
could not fail of being of use to Mr. Woodhouse's spirits, E II 14 275 32
I use to be quite angry with Selina; but really I begin E II 14 277 40
Is it necessary for me to use any roundabout phrase?-- E II 16 297 48
They had stopped at Mrs. Bates's door to offer the use of E III 2 320 6
and begged them not to want more, or to use her ill.-- E III 3 334 6
the Sucklings, and of the use to be made of their barouche- E III 5 343 1
and persuade her father to use, instead of the small-sized E III 5 347 18
And, by the bye, can I or my housekeeper be of any use to E III 6 355 22
endured than allowed, perhaps, but I must still use it. E III 7 374 55
56
She wanted to be of use to her; wanted to show a value for E III 9 389 16
There is no use in delay. E III 10 394 25
did not allow the full use even of the time he could stay-- E III 10 397 47
make more than an allowable use of the sort of intimacy E III 14 438 8
Mrs. John Knightley was delighted to be of use; any thing E III 16 451 3
which she immediately made use of, to say, "it is well, E III 16 459 45
46
"I am sure you were of use to me," cried Emma. E III 17 462 8
nothing being of so much use to Mrs. Clay's health as a P III 3 18 7
not be allowed to be of any use, or any importance, in the P III 5 33 6
glad to be thought of some use, glad to have any thing P III 5 33 9
Clay's being of so much use, while Anne could be of none, P III 5 34 11
in him, who could be of no use at home, to shut himself up. P III 7 55 7
like to leave him yourself, but you see I can be of no use. P III 7 55 8
on going, and that it would be of no use to teaze him. P III 7 55 9
know that I am of any more use in the sick-room than P III 7 56 12
for I am of no use at home--am I? and it only harasses me. P III 7 57 16
you, Charles, for I am of no more use at home than you are. P III 7 57 17
18
or any servants to wait, or any knife and fork to use. P III 8 64 4
the hope of being of real use to him in some suggestions P III 11 100 23
the constant use of Gowland, during the spring months. P IV 4 146 3
to them will have its use in fixing your family (our P IV 4 150 17
or superiors, may be of use in diverting his thoughts from P IV 4 151 21
to preserve, and would not use her ill; and she had been P IV 5 154 9
As soon as I could use my hands, she taught me to knit, P IV 5 155 9
bad cold, was glad to make use of the relationship which P IV 5 157 14
Can I be of any use?" P IV 6 169 25
It would be of no use to go to Uppercross again, for that P IV 6 173 49
"I wish you would make use of it, if you are determined to P IV 7 177 14
to be of even the slightest use to you," replied Anne; " P IV 9 195 25
happy to be of use to you, in any way that I could. P IV 9 198 43
to use her own words, without knowing it to be you?" P IV 9 205 86
You did not use to like cards; but time makes many changes. P IV 10 225 59
by Henrietta, eager to make use of the present leisure for P IV 10 225 61
at a gunsmith's to be of use to her; and she set off with P IV 11 239 54
pressing them to make use of his house for both purposes.-- S 1 367 1
injury on the fallen side as to be unfit for present use.-- S 1 370 1
house--but by the immediate use of Friction alone steadily S 5 386 1
any occupation that may be of use to himself or others.-- S 5 388 1
exert ourselves to be of use of others, I am convinced S 9 410 1
and how can we be of use to you?"--and Mr P. warmly S 9 410 1
wd entirely take away the use of my right side, before I S 10 418 1
The use of my right side is entirely taken away for S 10 418 1
they moved in Sanditon" to use a proper phrase, for every S 11 421 1

USEABLE (1)

before the horse were useable, but no preparations could E III 6 353 6

USED (192)

is too often used I believe to make black appear white. LS 6 251 1
He thinks very differently of her, from what he used to do, LS 24 291 16
men to whom she had been used; he had never mentioned a NA I 8 53 3
made, nor an expression used by either which had not been NA I 10 72 8
had not been made and used some thousands of times before, NA I 10 72 8
said James; "you were not used to be so hard to persuade; NA I 13 99 10
at the open door, she used only the ceremony of saying NA I 13 102 25
The word 'nicest,' as you used it, did not suit him; and NA I 14 108 14
great volumes, which, as I used to think, nobody would NA I 14 109 24
if you had been as much used as myself to hear poor little NA I 14 109 26
instruct might sometimes be used as synonimous words." NA I 14 109 26
Miss Morland is not used to your odd ways." NA I 14 113 40
After being used to such a home as the Abbey, an ordinary NA II 5 157 10
into an apartment never used since some cousin or kin died NA II 5 158 15
been used to much better sized apartments at Mr. Allen's?" NA II 6 166 6
She had not been used to feel alarm from wind, but now NA II 6 170 12
Mrs. Allen used to take pains, year after year, to make me NA II 7 174 7
"I used to walk here so often with her!" added Eleanor; " NA II 7 179 32
At that time indeed I used to wonder at her choice. NA II 7 180 32
which Mr. Allen had been used to call unnatural and NA II 7 181 40
real drawing-room, used only with company of consequence.-- NA II 8 182 2
one, or she could not have used your brother so.-- NA II 10 205 30
song that she had been used to play to Willoughby, every SS I 16 83 3
She read nothing but what they had been used to read SS I 16 83 3
She used to be all unreserve, and to you more especially." SS I 16 84 8
she had never been used to find wit in the inattention of SS I 19 107 27
at Barton, if they had not so many as they used to have. SS I 21 123 28
I have been always used to a very small income, and could SS II 2 147 7
in any respect less happy at Longstaple than he used to be. SS II 2 147 12
always used till this winter to have Charlotte with me. SS II 3 154 4
My girls were nothing to her, and yet they used to be SS II 7 181 8
"Elinor, I have been cruelly used; but not by Willoughby." SS II 7 189 47
48
that if it is true, he has used a young lady of my SS II 8 192 3
you must remember the place, where old Gibson used to live. SS II 11 225 31
I remember Fanny used to say that she would marry sooner SS II 11 227 50
will be no difficulties at all, to what I used to think. SS II 13 239 9
Mr. Edward Ferrars, the very young man I used to joke with SS III 1 258 7
And I must say, I think she was used very hardly; for your SS III 1 259 7
To have his love used so scornfully! for they say he is SS III 1 259 7
you too, that had been used to live in Barton cottage!-- SS III 4 292 55
"But why should such precaution be used?-- SS III 5 296 19
happy with him as I once used to think I might be with you; SS III 13 365 14
I have not been very well used Emma among them, I hope you W 316 2
friend of Robert's, who used to be with us a great deal. W 316 2
Our assemblies have been used to be so well treated by W 334 13
warmth he had been used to receive from her sisters, & W 335 13
"And as to Mrs Edwardes' carriage being used the day after W 340 18
in her aunt's family been used to many of the elegancies W 345 21
Emma cd possibly have been used to in Shropshire, & W 350 24
to find she was not ill used) "I am sorry I am not to have W 351 25
you, than I have been used to be; but poor Margt's W 362 32
things, though the words are often used synonimously. PP I 5 20 20
"I have been used to consider poetry as the food of love," PP I 9 44 33
"You used us abominably ill," answered Mrs. Hurst, "in PP I 10 53 61
room in the house, he was used to be free from them there; PP I 15 71 6
me, I am cruelly used, nobody feels for my poor nerves." PP II 3 113 26
had been barbarously used by them all; and on these two PP I 21 127 5
Lucas, whom he had been used to think tolerably sensible, PP I 23 127 6
did not come back, she should think herself very ill used. PP I 23 129 14
Lucas, who had been little used to company, and she looked PP II 6 161 7
that she was not used to have her judgment controverted. PP II 6 163 15
Mr. Darcy looked just as he had been used to look in PP II 7 171 9
which had been used to characterize her style, and which, PP II 11 188 1
deficient in the appearance of it as you used to do." PP II 17 225 16
"How unfortunate that you should have used such very PP II 17 226 20
Though I shall always say that he used my daughter PP II 17 228 29
talents which rightly used, might at least have preserved PP II 19 236 2
and these miniatures are just as they used to be then. PP III 1 247 18
"And Lydia used to want to go to London," added Kitty. PP III 6 299 24
looks just like that man that used to be with him before. PP III 11 334 34
more as he had been used to look in Hertfordshire, than as PP III 11 335 40
I have not been used to submit to any person's whims. PP III 14 356 48
Having married on a narrower income than she had been used MP I 1 8 9
But they were too much used to company and praise, to have MP I 2 12 3
and the separation from every body she had been used to. MP I 2 14 6
How long ago it is, aunt, since we used to repeat the MP I 2 18 25
town, which she had been used to occupy every spring, and MP I 2 20 33
Ah! cousin, when I remember how much I used to dread MP I 3 27 36
habits of a young woman who had been mostly used to London. MP I 4 41 15
doing several things that Sir Thomas and I used to talk of. MP I 6 54 9
you that they are all passed over, and all very ill used. MP I 6 60 49
Everingham as it used to be was perfect in my estimation; MP I 6 61 53
I am sure William would never have used me so, under any MP I 7 64 10
and if the good people who used to kneel and gape in that MP I 9 87 15
been used to hear given, or than I can quite comprehend. MP I 9 92 46
At Oxford I have been a good deal used to have a man lean MP I 9 94 59
cried her cousin, "how ill you have been used by them! MP I 10 97 2
Miss Price has been more used to deserve praise than to MP I 11 112 33
He is used to much gayer places than Mansfield." MP I 12 116 5
The sister with whom she was used to be on easy terms, was MP I 17 162 19
her, you know,--you and I used to be very fond of a play MP I 18 167 7
8
and your uncle say to see them used for such a purpose? MP I 18 169 21
than we used to be; I mean before my uncle went abroad. MP II 3 196 3
"But I do talk to him more than I used. MP II 3 198 10
which Mr. Rushworth had used for a twelvemonth before. MP II 3 203 29
She used to ask your sisters now and then, but she never MP II 5 217 3
add, "so strange! for Mrs. Grant never used to ask her." MP II 5 218 16
I used to think she had neither complexion nor countenance; MP II 6 229 5
We used to jump about together many a time, did not we? MP II 7 250 59
would think fittest to be used, but found it all MP II 8 253 7
Did she love him well enough to forego what had used to be MP II 8 255 11
and your sister is not used to these sort of hours." MP II 10 279 24
She was afraid she had used some strong--some contemptuous MP II 11 286 15
solicitude had been, and used such strong expressions, was MP II 13 300 7
To good reading, however, she had been long used; her MP III 3 337 10
drawback as she had been used to suffer in seeing him on MP III 3 337 10
She had been used to consult him in every difficulty, and MP III 4 345 4
alike as they have been used to be: to the point--I MP III 4 346 12
It proves him, in short, every thing that I had been used MP III 4 350 30
worldly maxims, which she was been too much used to hear. MP III 4 351 36
which she was never used to do; and it had a sound of most MP III 4 352 42
nothing that you were not used to; and a great deal more MP III 4 354 46
will not do for a man who has been used to sensible women. MP III 4 355 54
She must be used to the consideration of his being in love MP III 5 356 1
She is tender, and not used to rough it like the rest of MP III 8 388 2
Nothing of all that she had been used to think of as the MP III 10 400 7
easy; for being now used to the sight of him in his MP III 14 429 1
She was speaking only, as she had been used to hear others MP III 16 456 25
She had been always used to think herself a little MP III 17 466 17
and people she had been used to; but the same happiness of MP III 17 469 24
of every body that he was used to, and hating to part with E I 1 7 10
Taylor to have somebody about her that she is used to see. E I 1 9 19
Miss Taylor has been used to have two persons to please; E I 1 11 34
style to what she had been used to, that she must have E I 3 23 10
and for which she had been used to sit and watch the due E I 3 24 11
But he is not the only gentleman you have been lately used E I 4 33 34
me that his manners are softer than they used to be. E I 4 34 42
You are so much used to live alone, that you do not know E I 5 36 6
of one of her own sex, after being used to it all her life. E I 5 36 6
"So many clever riddles as there used to be when he was E I 9 70 5
"He has been used to her in these complaints, and I hope E I 13 114 34
perhaps, from being used to the large parties of London, E I 13 116 43
and has been so little used to them at Hartfield, that she E I 14 120 11
I used to think she was not capable of being fond of any E I 14 120 13
for she is as modest and humble as I used to think him. E I 16 137 11
mind which she was always used to acknowledge in him; for E I 18 150 37
she is sure to hear; but then she is used to my voice. E II 1 158 14
his addresses--and as Jane used to be very often walking E II 1 159 20
skin, which she had been used to cavil at, as wanting E II 2 167 12
He had been used to think her unjust to Jane, and had now E II 3 170 1
She did not do any of it in the same way that she used; I E II 3 178 52
Part of every winter she had been used to spend in Bath; E II 4 183 9
I remembered what I used to do myself. E II 5 190 24
had been occasionally used as such;--but such brilliant E II 6 197 5
I have been used to hear her's admired; and I remember one E II 6 201 28
Used only to a large house himself, and without ever E II 6 204 43
she had been used to despise the place rather too much. E II 8 220 48
was for their accommodation the carriage was used at all. E II 8 223 63
Mrs. Weston was the most used of the two to yield; till a E II 8 226 85
me; and having always been used to a very musical society, E II 14 276 36
And as to smaller-sized rooms than I had been used to, I E II 14 277 36
that I should, considering what I have been used to. E II 15 283 9
She is reserved, more reserved, I think, than she used to E II 15 289 40
It is just what I used to say to a certain gentleman in E II 18 308 28
being much more engaged with company than you used to be. E II 18 311 46
them; and we used sometimes to say very cutting things! E III 2 321 15
be used, and looked at it now and then as a great treat." E III 4 338 12
It used to stand here. E III 5 347 19
to you as I have been used to do: a privilege rather E III 7 374 55
56
Even you, used as you are to great sums, would hardly E III 8 382 23
I should not have used the expression. E III 10 393 17
much more than he had been used to do, and of his having E III 11 409 35
He has used every body ill--and they are all delighted to E III 13 428 23
such as Mr. Knightley used even to the woman he was in E III 15 448 31
always at hand, when he were once got used to the idea.-- E III 17 466 29
used to be talked to by each, on every fair occasion.-- E III 17 466 30
every body by whom he was used to be guided assuring him E III 17 467 30
doubtful, in the words he used; and I think I can give you E III 18 474 30
"Better than she ever used to do?-- E III 18 477 50
In music she had been always used to feel alone in the P III 6 47 13
Frederick Wentworth had used such words, or something like P III 7 61 36
She had used him ill; deserted and disappointed him; and P III 7 61 36
bad connections to those who have not been used to them. P III 9 76 13
where she had been used to sit and preside, she had no P IV 1 126 18
It was evident how little the women were used to the sight P IV 3 142 13
She had been used to affluence,--it was gone. P IV 5 154 8
ay, or as we used to be even at North Yarmouth and deal. P IV 6 170 29
I used to boast of my own Anne Elliot, and vouch for your P IV 9 201 61
I found he had been used to hear of me. P IV 9 201 63
to repeat half that I used to hear him say on that subject. P IV 9 202 66
This is all in confirmation, rather, of what we used to P IV 9 202 67
"Oh!" cried Elizabeth, "I have been rather too much used P IV 10 213 5
She had been used before to feel that he could not be P IV 10 214 11
I used to think she had some taste in dress, but I was P IV 10 215 15
her that she was not ill used by any body; which Mary, P IV 10 220 31
very well used, if they went to the play without her. P IV 10 224 50
It is all very well, I used to say, for young people to be P IV 11 231 8
I have been used to the gratification of believing myself P IV 11 247 84
"Oh!--they are so used to the operation--to every S 5 388 1

looks, that you are nmot used to such quick measures."-- S 9 410 1
I see by the position of your foot, that you have used it S 9 411 1
It was impossible not to feel him hardly used; to be S 12 427 1

USEFUL (93)

it has not with-held him from being very useful to me. LS 5 250 1
Her mother was a woman of useful plain sense, with a good NA I 1 13 1
that nothing like useful knowledge could be gained from NA I 1 15 3
whole she deduced this useful lesson, that to go NA I 8 55 10
improved her in useful activity, nor given her a greater NA II 15 240 2
long run of amusement, and now you must try to be useful." NA II 15 240 2
desire of being useful-----I think I am justified-- though SS II 9 204 18
I am not as ready to be useful to him then, as I sincerely SS III 3 284 23
He proved a very useful addition to their table; without W 359 28
terms, without forming at it any useful acquaintance. PP I 15 70 1
let her be an active, useful sort of person, not brought PP I 19 105 10
her satisfaction in being useful, and that it amply repaid PP I 22 121 1
a little relief from home, may be as useful as anything." PP II 2 141 10
we may draw from it this useful lesson; that loss of PP III 5 289 43
herself considerably useful to both of them, in those PP III 13 349 44
Was there any chance of his being hereafter useful to Sir MP I 1 5 2
I only wish I could be more useful; but you see I do all MP I 1 9 12
to make a third very useful, especially when that third MP I 2 17 21
judgment; he made reading useful by talking to her of what MP I 2 22 35
enjoyed being avowedly useful as her aunt's companion, MP I 4 35 6
Two of them were hunters; the third, a useful road-horse: MP I 4 37 8
was quite at his service in any way that could be useful. MP I 6 61 58
himself useful, and proving his good-nature by any one? MP I 7 67 16
a good clergyman will be useful in his parish and his MP I 9 93 49
of any thing useful with regard to the object of the day. MP I 10 104 51
but as she might be useful, and that she would not allow MP I 14 133 10
and it is so useful to have any thing of a model!-- MP I 15 139 6
prompter, sometimes as spectator--was often very useful.-- MP I 18 165 3
She was occasionally useful to all; she was perhaps as MP I 18 166 5
and useful pursuits of all the young people as for her own. MP II 1 179 9
the most active in being useful to Fanny, in detecting her MP II 4 206 3
never thought of being useful to any body, and Mrs. Norris, MP II 5 219 27
Only think how useful he was at Sotherton! MP II 7 244 30
as useful as I can; but I am not qualified for an adviser. MP II 9 269 34
now it would all be useful in helping to fit up his cabin. MP II 13 304 19
without her so long, while she was so useful to herself.-- MP III 6 370 14
Now, when she knew better how to be useful and how to MP III 6 371 17
to be, and you will be so useful to Susan, and you will MP III 6 372 20
every other pleasure to that of being useful to them. MP III 6 373 23
Fanny was very anxious to be useful, and not to appear MP III 8 390 7
Susan tried to be useful, where she could only have gone MP III 9 395 4
cried; and that Susan was useful she could perceive; that MP III 9 395 4
the hope of being useful to a mind so much in need of help, MP III 9 397 8
time, hoped it might be useful in diverting her thoughts MP III 9 398 10
he had foreseen, had been useful to more than his first MP III 10 404 15
she considered how little useful, how little self-denying MP III 13 428 13
not one who was not more useful at times to her son. MP III 14 429 2
the longing to be useful to those who were wanting her! MP III 14 432 9
unable to direct or dictate, or even fancy herself useful. MP III 16 448 2
She was returned to Mansfield Park, she was useful, she MP III 17 461 2
He became what he ought to be, useful to his father, MP III 17 462 4
no useful influence that way, no moral effect on the mind. MP III 17 463 8
she was soon welcome, and useful to all; and after Fanny's MP III 17 472 31
well-informed, useful, gentle, knowing all the ways of the E I 1 6 6
were spent; and between useful occupation and the E I 2 16 5
Emma had very early foreseen how useful she might find her. E I 4 26 1
Harriet would be loved as one to whom she could be useful. E I 4 26 2
hope to be useful to their families in some way or other. E I 4 29 14
of useful understanding or knowledge of the world. E I 4 35 44
"I am glad you think I have been useful to her; but E I 6 42 3
She has been taught nothing useful, and is too young and E I 8 61 38
companion or useful helpmate, he could not do worse. E I 8 61 38
mind, by a great deal of useful reading and conversation, E I 9 69 3
It was a very useful note, for it supplied them with fresh E I 17 141 4
and each was occasionally useful as a check to the other. E II 4 184 11
really good-natured, useful, considerate, or benevolent. E II 8 223 64
not make our carriage more useful on such occasions. E II 8 228 89
You find me trying to be useful; tell me if you think I E II 10 240 3
conceive it would be at all more likely to be useful now." E II 14 275 31
bit of old pencil, but the court plaister might be useful." E III 4 340 25
He found he could not be useful, and his feelings were too E III 5 351 38
a very useful check,--interested, without disturbing him. E III 9 386 9
looked around eager to discover some way of being useful. E III 9 389 16
Who was so useful to him, who so ready to write his E III 17 466 29
enquiring companions, than of very useful assistants. P III 7 53 3
likewise, as she might be useful in turning back with her P III 10 83 4
near them, to be useful if wanted, at any rate, to enjoy P III 12 111 49
that could be instantly useful; and a look between him and P III 12 111 50
Why was not she to be useful as Anne? P III 12 115 65
that she was valued only as she could be useful to Louisa. P III 12 115 68
knowing herself extremely useful there, both as an P IV 1 121 1
conveyed back a far more useful person in the old nursery- P IV 1 121 3
so very useful, had made really an agreeable fortnight. P IV 2 130 3
You have been here only to be useful. P IV 4 145 1
year at school, had been useful and good to her in a way P IV 5 152 2
from it which could give useful connections or respectable S 2 374 1
had been particularly useful & obliging to them; who had S 2 374 1
they are such excellent useful women & have so much energy S 5 385 1
occurrences from which no useful Deductions can be drawn.-- S 8 403 1
to be as extensively useful as possible, & where some S 9 410 1
to let no opportunity of being useful escape them.-- S 9 410 1
employed; part was laid out in a zeal for being useful.-- S 10 412 1
kindness than by giving her the means of being useful.-- S 10 419 1

USEFULNESS (11)

The glory of heroism, of usefulness, of exertion, of MP II 6 236 22
her activity and usefulness, and the dread of being MP III 7 383 32
She had great pleasure in feeling her usefulness, but MP III 8 390 7
and an inclination for usefulness, as Fanny had been by MP III 17 472 31
In her usefulness, in Fanny's excellence, in William's MP III 17 473 31
Her first attempts at usefulness were in an endeavour to E I 4 27 3
his character, and more usefulness, rationality, and P III 6 43 5
Her usefulness to little Charles would always give some P III 11 93 4
exercise; but a mind of usefulness and ingenuity seemed to P III 11 99 18
The usefulness of her staying!-- P III 12 114 59
had been won by her usefulness when they were in distress. P IV 10 220 31

USELESS (18)

drawing-room and one useless anti-chamber, into a room NA II 8 182 2
But the knowledge would have been useless here, it was not NA II 13 227 27
of it, extend an useless resentment, and perhaps involve NA II 14 231 5
after a due course of useless conjecture, that, "it was a NA II 14 234 10
at Barton entirely useless, for her mother and sisters SS III 14 378 13
Vain indeed must be all her attentions, vain and useless PP I 16 83 56
and till he did, it was useless to quarrel about him. PP I 17 88 14
gratified my vanity, in useless or blameable distrust.-- PP II 13 208 8
"Do not give way to useless alarm," added he, "though it PP III 5 288 37
It is useless to talk of it." PP III 7 305 38
perfectly useless; for, of course, they were to have a son. PP III 8 308 3
To save herself from useless remonstrance, Mrs. Price MP I 1 4 1
The room had then become useless, and for some time was MP I 16 151 1
must not be allowed to wear her out, and make her useless. MP III 12 418 6
which might have made every previous caution useless?-- E III 14 441 8
it would have been useless to press the enquiry farther. P IV 6 173 48
or spraining his ancle, she remained equally useless.-- S 2 372 1
every thing; all the useless things in the world that cd S 6 390 1

USELESSLY (2)

would even rather lay it uselessly by than dispose of it SS I 14 72 10
it was neither gaudy nor uselessly fine; with less of PP III 1 246 5

USES (2)

of one of the last epistolary uses she could put them to. MP III 13 425 6
uses for his money, and a right to spend it as he liked. P III 6 43 5

USHER (2)

evening came which was to usher her into the upper rooms. NA I 2 20 8
abruptly to the Coles, to usher in a letter from her niece. E II 1 156 6

USHERED (8)

many words of preparation ushered in, had been foreseen by NA I 15 124 48
and such storms ushered in; and most heartily did she NA II 6 166 9
passage, opened the front door, and ushered her in himself. SS I 19 108 35
an early hour they were ushered into the breakfast room, MP II 2 192 11
pleased to wait a moment, and then ushered her in too soon. E III 8 378 4
herself, ushered in the letter from Frank to Mrs. Weston. E III 14 436 6
foot-boy could give, Mr. Elliot was ushered into the room. P IV 3 142 17
"Mr. and Mrs. Charles Musgrove" were ushered into the room. P IV 10 216 17

USING (12)

to my arguments, & do not reproach me for using such. LS 30 301 5
"Miss Dashwood," cried Willoughby, "you are now using me SS I 10 51 28
woman in the world, and that I was using her infamously. SS III 8 326 53
for as to Mr. Darcy's using him ill, it is perfectly false; PP I 18 94 45
a shadow of either, but in using the words so improperly. MP I 3 26 29
"That would not be a very handsome reason for using Mr. MP I 8 77 13
a door, or even as using the billiard-room for the space MP I 13 127 29
to her than to find her aunt using the same language.-- MP III 14 431 8
to London himself, and using his influence with his MP III 16 450 8
would be ready to quarrel with you for using such words. E II 5 192 31
Had she been using any thing in particular?" P IV 4 145 3
Mrs. Clay has been using it at my recommendation, and you P IV 4 146 3

USUAL (193)

that I have been acting with my usual foolish impetuosity. LS 24 287 9
Sir James's carriage was at the door, & he, merry as usual, LS 24 291 15
Reginald has recovered his usual good spirits, (as I trust LS 40 309 1
it appears to me that the usual style of letter-writing NA I 3 27 30
With more than usual eagerness did Catherine hasten to the NA I 4 31 1
having gone through the usual ceremonial of meeting her NA I 8 52 1
senses, and with cheeks only a little redder than usual. NA I 8 53 3
the next morning; and till usual moment of going to the NA I 10 71 8
immediately took her usual place by the side of her friend. NA I 10 71 8
to dance down enjoyed her usual happiness with Henry NA II 1 131 15
After addressing her with his usual politeness, he turned NA II 2 139 5
She wished Isabella had talked more like her usual self, NA II 3 148 28
only her retiring to dress half an hour earlier than usual. NA II 9 193 5
her, was that he paid her rather more attention than usual. NA II 10 199 1
and Catherine to all her usual ease of spirits. NA II 11 213 20
the moment gave more than usual propriety; it was that of SS I 9 41 6
in the usual style of a complete party of pleasure. SS I 12 62 28
hours before his usual time, on purpose to go to Whitwell." SS I 13 65 32
Willoughby took his usual place between the two elder Miss SS I 13 67 61
us with less affection than his usual behaviour has shewn. SS I 15 78 28
in their usual walk, instead of wandering away by herself. SS I 16 85 15
not been able to take your usual walk to Allenham to-day." SS I 20 111 10
every body,"--said his wife with her usual laugh. SS I 20 111 23
But this is the usual way of heightening alarm, where SS I 21 122 12
one it is; but that is not written so well as usual.-- SS I 22 134 52
Marianne, who, with her usual inattention to the forms of SS II 1 144 15
began to foresee with her usual cheerfulness, a variety of SS II 3 155 7
"Though with your usual anxiety for our happiness," said SS II 3 156 9
restored to all her usual animation, and elevated to more SS II 3 158 20
elevated to more than her usual gaiety, she could not be SS II 3 158 20
them in London, making the usual inquiries about their SS II 4 162 11
"Oh! Colonel," said she, with her usual noisy cheerfulness, SS II 4 163 14
the whole evening more serious and thoughtful than usual. SS II 8 200 43
Mrs. Jennings left them earlier than usual; for she could SS II 9 203 10
themselves were, as usual, in their own estimation, and SS II 14 250 10
together, without any diminution of her usual cordiality.-- SS III 1 264 32
usual, had prevented her going to them within that time. SS III 2 270 3
office, (breathing rather faster than usual as she spoke.) SS III 4 288 28
Prescriptions poured in from all quarters, and as usual, SS III 6 306 17
Marianne got up the next morning at her usual time; to SS III 7 307 1
catching it with all her usual warmth, was in a moment as SS III 9 334 4
and if not pursuing their usual studies with quite so much SS III 11 352 20
neither less frequent, nor less affectionate than usual. SS III 13 364 13
after experiencing, as usual, a thousand disappointments SS III 14 374 6
of the workmen, Elinor, as usual, broke through the first SS III 14 374 6
are determined to be in good time I see, as usual.-- W 327 7
of being shewn into the usual little sitting room, the W 355 28
Eliz. was the usual object of both. W 360 30
tedious in the usual process of such a meeting. PP I 11 55 8
uncivil to her, and more teazing than usual to himself. PP I 12 59 4
They found Mary, as usual, deep in the study of thorough PP I 12 60 7
The subject elevated him to more than usual solemnity of PP I 14 66 1
came directly towards them, and began the usual civilities. PP I 15 72 8
The usual inquiries as to his success were made by the PP I 16 83 49
She had dressed with more than usual care, and prepared in PP I 18 89 1
of the hand, "that it is usual with young ladies to reject PP I 19 107 13
according to the usual practice of elegant females." PP I 19 108 19
than usual, and on perceiving whom, she said to the girls, PP I 20 113 29
30

tried to join with her usual cheerfulness in the general PP I 21 116 6
rather oftener than usual to say how happy she was, though PP I 23 127 8
a longer irritation than usual about Netherfield and its PP II 1 134 4
5

who came as usual to spend the Christmas at Longbourn. PP II 2 139 2
body had as much to say or to hear on the subject as usual. PP II 3 146 19
the quiet tenor of their usual employments, the vexatious PP II 5 157 10
family returned to their usual employments, and Elizabeth PP II 7 168 1
his compliments, with his usual reserve, to Mrs. Collins; PP II 7 171 9
She answered him in the usual way, and after a moment's PP II 7 171 10
11

her, and moving with his usual deliberation towards the PP II 8 174 12
pray, what is the usual price of an earl's younger son? PP II 10 183 15
of appearing cheerful as usual, and the resolution of PP II 13 209 12
sleep, and pursue the usual course of their employments. PP II 18 229 1
on his side, of usual cheerfulness, but with no farther PP II 18 235 39
Mrs. Bennet was restored to her usual querulous serenity, PP II 19 238 6
his accent had none of its usual sedateness; and he PP III 1 252 52
more of fretfulness than usual, to the accents of Kitty. PP III 5 289 41
had all the appearance of his usual philosophic composure. PP III 6 299 18
mother was too happy, to be quite so obstinate as usual. PP III 7 307 48
"Well, and so we breakfasted at ten as usual; I thought it PP III 9 319 25
You must feel it; and the usual satisfaction of preaching PP III 11 333 29
Jane looked a little paler than usual, but more sedate PP III 11 335 39
He looked serious as usual; and she thought, more as he PP III 11 335 40
she immediately, with her usual condescension, expressed PP III 15 363 22
the neighbourhood with the usual fair report of being very MP I 3 24 6
every thing at Mansfield went on for some time as usual. MP I 3 31 58
this time run through the usual resources of ladies MP I 4 41 15
family did not, from his usual goings on, expect him back MP I 5 48 29
Bath seems full, and every thing as usual. MP I 6 59 43
made some important communications to her usual confidant. MP I 12 115 5
Mrs. Grant had with her usual good humour agreed to MP I 17 159 6
to do it away by the usual attack of gallantry and MP I 17 160 9
"It is about my uncle's usual time." MP II 2 193 14
much longer absent than usual, and brought the previous MP II 4 214 46
with a firmer tone than usual, "as far as I am concerned, MP II 5 225 58
according to the usual style of the Grants, and too much MP II 7 238 3
too much according to the usual habits of all to raise any MP II 7 238 3
not told you that with my usual luck--for I never do wrong MP II 7 241 13
to go down and resume her usual employments near her aunt MP II 9 265 20
the usual observances without any apparent want of spirits. MP II 9 265 20
he looked at her with his usual kindness, she believed he MP II 9 268 27
usual cheerfulness, she had nothing further to try her own. MP II 12 291 1
to feel and appear as usual; but it was quite impossible MP II 13 303 13

all on the lover's side, might work their usual effect on. MP III 1 320 44
They sat so much longer than usual in the dining parlour, MP III 3 334 5
"As usual, believing yourself unequal to anything!-- MP III 4 351 34
Quite unlike his usual self, he scarcely said any thing. MP III 5 365 35
own, and her father on his usual lounges, enabled her to MP III 8 388 1
The usual plea of increasing engagements was made in MP III 9 393 1
preparing to remove as usual up stairs, they were stopt by MP III 10 399 2
of being debarred from her usual, regular exercise; she MP III 11 409 6
or comfortable than usual, and will only let my sister MP III 11 411 16
what might come, that her usual readings and conversation MP III 12 418 5
most consistent with his usual kindness, and till she got MP III 12 418 5
the daily newspaper as usual, she was so far from MP III 15 438 8
over the ragged carpet as usual, while the tea was in MP III 15 439 9
Mansfield long before the usual dinner-time, and as they MP III 15 446 35
some interest in the usual occupations; but whenever Lady MP III 16 449 6
to speak; and so, with the usual beginnings, hardly to be MP III 16 453 17
what came first, and the usual declaration that if she MP III 16 453 17
to sleep after dinner, as usual, and she had then only to E I 1 6 5
time more welcome than usual, as coming directly from E I 1 9 21
by him would have all the usual weight and efficacy. E I 4 35 45
on; and Isabella, the usual doer of all commissions, must E I 6 48 40
Harriet had been at Hartfield, as usual, soon after E I 7 50 1
He was so much displeased, that it was longer than usual E I 9 69 1
the nursery for the children,--just as usual, you know.-- E I 9 79 57
could receive him with the usual smile, and her quick eye E I 9 81 78
"I have none of the usual inducements of women to marry. E I 10 84 15
Woman's usual occupations of eye and hand and mind will be E I 10 85 21
having been longer than usual absent from Surry, were E I 11 91 2
exciting of course rather more than the usual interest. E I 11 91 2
to talk of them all in the usual way, and to take the E I 12 98 2
than usual, from their journey and the happiness of coming. E I 12 103 39
thinner clothing than usual, setting forward voluntarily, E I 13 113 26
and cheerful till the usual hour of separating allowed her E I 15 133 38
Contrary to the usual course of things, Mr. Elton's E I 16 135 7
Mr. Woodhouse having, as usual, tried to persuade his E I 17 140 1
to persuade them away with all her usual promptitude. E I 17 141 4
in general, like her usual self, she took care to express E I 18 144 4
air, as she has not been quite so well as usual lately." E II 1 161 25
so I began to-day with my usual caution; but no sooner did E II 1 162 31
completely recovered her usual strength, they must forbid E II 2 165 9
and every thing was relapsing much into its usual state. E II 2 168 15
The charming Augusta Hawkins, in addition to all the usual E II 4 181 4
at home, till her usual hour of exercise; and on being E II 6 196 1
Woodhouse was soon composed enough for talking as usual. E II 7 209 13
of going to bed at your usual time--and the idea of that E II 7 211 21
see that every thing were safe in the house, as usual. E II 7 211 22
have discerned me to be more of a gentleman than usual.-- E II 8 213 9
to and admired amid the usual rate of conversation; a few E II 8 219 43
And, in short, from knowing his usual ways, I am very much E II 8 223 63
at the close of the song, and every thing usual followed. E II 8 227 86
William Larkins let me keep a larger quantity than usual E II 9 238 51
Bates, deprived of her usual employment, slumbering on one E II 10 240 1
before, though from her usual unwillingness to give pain, E II 12 258 7
for employment than usual; she was still busy and cheerful; E II 13 264 1
and only made the usual stipulation of not sitting at the E II 16 291 4
table himself, with the usual regular difficulty of E II 16 291 4
were farther talked of, and the usual observations made. E II 16 297 44
than usual--a glow both of complexion and spirits. E II 16 298 58
happy and cheerful as usual, and with all the right of E II 17 303 24
Poor old Mrs. Bates, civil and humble as usual, looked as E III 8 378 5
decidedly graver than usual, said, "I would not go away E III 9 385 1
2

now he seemed more sudden than usual in his disappearance. E III 9 386 7
His air and voice recovered their usual briskness: he E III 10 400 69
even too joyous to talk as usual, had been a gratifying, E III 12 418 5
At last, and tolerably in his usual tone, he said, "I have E III 13 427 20
21

could summon enough of her usual self to be the attentive E III 14 434 2
all her usual composure--"there would have been no danger. E III 16 459 47
I did not play with the children quite so much as usual. E III 17 465 27
respectable family, in the usual terms: how it had been P III 1 3 3
4

present down to Anne, as had been the usual yearly custom. P III 1 9 19
But the usual fate of Anne attended her, in having P III 2 14 9
fully believed, had the usual share, had even more than a P III 4 29 8
had even more than a usual share of all such solicitudes P III 4 29 8
a school at Exeter all the usual stock of accomplishments, P III 5 40 45
respectable forms in the usual places, or without the P III 6 46 12
On its being proposed, Anne offered her services, as usual, P III 8 71 56
his manners of their usual composure: he started, and P III 9 78 22
so uncommon, so unlike the usual style of give-and-take P III 11 98 16
of subjects, which his usual companions had probably no P III 11 100 23
glad to burst their usual restraints; and having talked of P III 11 100 23
the rest of the family were again in their usual quarters. P IV 2 133 27
when a thicker letter than usual from Mary was delivered P IV 6 162 1
him too; but I have my usual "luck, I am always out of the P IV 6 163 7
it was done with all his usual frankness and good humour. P IV 6 169 25
Mrs. Smith, assuming her usual air of cheerfulness, "that P IV 9 195 24
Was not it Mrs. Speed, as usual, or the maid? P IV 9 197 39
at the composure of her friend's usual state of mind. P IV 9 210 97
After the usual period of suspense, the usual sounds of P IV 10 216 17
The usual character of them has nothing for me. P IV 10 225 58
a more severe attack than usual of my old greivance, S 5 386 1
energy through all the usual phrases employed in praise of S 7 396 1
They were shewn into the usual sitting room, well- S 12 427 1

USUALLY (22)
and uninformed as the female mind at seventeen usually is. NA I 2 18 1
castles and abbies made usually the charm of those NA II 2 141 11
horses of a gentleman usually perform a journey of thirty NA II 5 155 4
truth was less violently outraged than usually happens. SS I 10 46 2
heart seemed more than usually open to every feeling of SS I 14 72 6
of consistency, were most usually attributed to his want SS I 19 102 2
He looked more than usually grave, and though expressing SS II 5 172 40
the park; from whence he usually returned in the morning, SS III 13 369 34
young ladies, who were usually tempted thither three or PP I 7 28 3
who does not greatly surpass what is usually met with. PP I 8 39 50
decisions are not usually influenced by my hopes or fears. PP II 12 197 5
meat as an inn larder usually affords, exclaiming, "is not PP II 16 219 2
were usually more interesting, and also more intelligible. PP III 1 250 46
parts of the stream where there was usually most sport. PP III 1 255 60
She entered the room with an air more than usually PP III 14 351 3
who was now more than usually insolent and disagreeable. PP III 14 353 20
Mr. Rushworth, however, though not usually a great talker, MP I 6 55 17
and where an opinion is general, it is usually correct. MP I 11 110 25
which must have been usually administered by his E I 13 113 27
Those who are standing by are usually thinking of E II 12 258 3
to imply the change of situation which time usually brings. E II 16 294 23
it was not more productive than such meetings usually are. E III 2 326 33

UTILITY (11)
hours of companionship, utility, and patient endurance, as NA II 16 251 5
it unites beauty with utility--and I dare say it is a SS I 18 97 4
mind, bid most fairly for utility, honour, and happiness MP I 2 20 33
and the hope of its utility to his son, reconciled Sir MP I 3 32 62
without employment or utility amongst them, as without a MP I 18 166 5
Edmund's advertisements were still of the first utility. MP III 3 343 40
a guide in every plan of utility or charity for Everingham, MP III 10 404 15
happiness in the affections and utility of domestic life.-- E III 18 474 34
there were no habits of utility abroad, no talents, or P III 1 9 18
"the profession has its utility, but I should be sorry to P III 3 19 13
14

She knew herself to be of the first utility to the child; P III 7 58 20

UTMOST (62)
of knowing that we have done our utmost to save him. LS 15 267 8
softened at once into the utmost submission, & rendered LS 25 293 3
Nothing but my being in the utmost distress for money, LS 26 296 4
with a man who goes beyond his four pints at the utmost. NA I 9 64 24
kind; her father, at the utmost, being contented with a NA I 9 65 31
over our faults in the utmost propriety of diction, while NA I 14 108 17
friend on a matter of the utmost importance, hastened NA I 15 116 1
and tried to turn it; but it resisted her utmost strength. NA II 6 168 10
The utmost care could not always secure the most valuable NA II 7 178 21
was to be done by two pair of female hands at the utmost. NA II 8 184 4
The General's utmost anger could not be to herself what it NA II 9 192 5
the utmost harmony engaged in forwarding the same work. SS II 1 145 23
was governed in it by an impulse of the utmost good-will. SS II 9 202 4
in a situation of the utmost distress, with no creditable SS II 9 209 30
Mrs. Ferrars, with the utmost liberality, will come SS II 11 224 28
hundred a-year, at the utmost, and I am very much deceived SS II 11 227 50
immediately did, with the utmost sang-froid, and go away SS III 3 282 15
should be raised to the utmost; and secretly resolved to SS III 5 293 2
arrangement with the utmost dispatch, and calculated with SS III 7 312 17
spirits oppressed to the utmost by the conversation of Mrs. SS III 7 313 21
"With me!"--in the utmost amazement--"well, sir--be quick-- SS III 8 317 5
how little could the utmost of your single management do SS III 11 350 9
appearance, with the utmost frugality, and ashamed to be SS III 12 357 3
in an accent of the utmost amazement;--and though Elinor SS III 12 360 22
her capable of the utmost meanness of wanton ill-nature. SS III 13 366 21
hundred and fifty at the utmost; nor was anything promised SS III 14 374 4
received him with the utmost civility, but had even PP I 15 74 13
he answered me with the utmost civility, and even paid me PP I 18 98 62
no more Elizabeth treated with the utmost contempt. PP I 21 120 28
yet she tried to the utmost to speak with composure when PP II 11 192 23
24

to have required the utmost force of passion to put aside, PP II 12 198 5
and they parted on each side with the utmost politeness. PP III 1 257 66
and opening it with the utmost impatience, read as follows: PP III 4 274 4
seemed of the utmost importance, and till he entered the PP III 4 280 26
His behaviour was attentive and kind to the utmost. PP III 5 290 46
high importance, received her with the utmost politeness. PP III 14 351 4
come to us," said Lady Bertram with the utmost composure. MP I 1 9 11
he escorted her, with the utmost kindness, into MP I 4 41 16
a point of honour to promote her enjoyment to the utmost. MP I 8 82 35
It was of the utmost consequence to her that Crawford MP II 2 191 11
down the east room in the utmost confusion of contrary MP II 13 302 9
to her uncle, in the utmost perturbation and dismay.-- MP III 1 314 16
attending to her with the utmost politeness and propriety, MP III 10 399 5
with Mr. Elton, of the utmost advantage to the latter. E I 9 69 2
unpleasant, and enjoy all that was enjoyable to the utmost. E I 14 117 2
at Randalls; and with the utmost good-will was sure that E I 15 126 11
There she was welcomed, with the utmost delight, by her E I 15 132 38
and modesty to the utmost; and all that was amiable, all E I 17 141 8
I assure you the utmost stretch of public fame would not E II 6 200 16
at dinner together as the utmost that his nerves could E II 16 292 7
A year and a half is the very utmost that they can have E II 18 310 34
They met with the utmost friendliness. E III 1 316 3
For her own advantage indeed, it was fit that the utmost E III 11 408 33
bitter feelings, made the utmost exertion necessary on E III 11 411 40
41

guard the comfort of both to the utmost, was the question. E III 14 434 4
to all, and had no scruple in urging him to the utmost.-- E III 17 467 31
day; she could dwell on it all with the utmost delight. E III 19 481 2
a good appearance to the utmost: I know no other set of P III 3 20 17
On one other question, which perhaps her utmost wisdom P III 7 60 31
32

care, and was off for the town with the utmost rapidity. P III 12 110 42
person, we are doing our utmost to send you company worth S 5 387 1
susceptibility to the utmost Energies of reason half- S 8 403 1

UTTER (23)
But to her utter amazement she found that to proceed along NA I 2 21 9
utter despondency, she bade her friend adieu and went on. NA I 9 67 33
for the latter to utter some few of the many thousand NA I 10 70 1
more than once heard him utter, and which tempted her to NA II 11 208 1
she did pity her,--to the utter amazement of Lucy, who, SS II 12 232 14
expressed the astonishment, which her lips could not utter. SS III 1 262 17
tho' he contrived to utter with an effort of boyish W 330 11
was too much fatigued to utter more than the occasional PP I 18 103 75
them an interval to utter the praises he asked for, every PP II 5 156 4
her utter amazement, she saw Mr. Darcy walk into the room. PP II 11 188 3
"Mr. Darcy!" repeated Elizabeth, in utter amazement. PP III 9 319 26
speech," said Elizabeth, "that I ever heard you utter. PP III 13 350 48
Bennet sat quite still, and unable to utter a syllable. PP III 17 378 42
part of my future days will be spent in utter seclusion. MP I 3 29 48
and her bosom swelled to utter, "Oh! not to him. MP II 1 185 27
speak, to utter something like an inquiry as to the result. MP II 9 268 28
nature, not in a state of utter barbarism, to be capable MP III 15 441 20
away, no pause; and, to my utter astonishment, I found, E II 6 199 7
Harriet felt this too much to utter more than a few words E II 13 268 11
She was quite determined not to utter a word that should E II 16 298 59
blessings that she could utter for her friend and herself. E III 3 334 8
he spoke, Anne felt the utter impossibility, from her P III 8 63 2
I should deserve utter contempt if I dared to suppose that P IV 11 235 32

UTTERANCE (2)
to him;--but she had no utterance, and was obliged to SS III 12 358 9
and when she could find utterance, assured her, that this E III 10 396 42

UTTERED (15)
This sentiment had been uttered so often in vain, that Mrs. NA I 4 31 2
"Good heaven! 'tis James!" was uttered at the same moment NA I 7 44 3
a solemn tone of voice, uttered these words, "I have heard NA I 14 111 29
with the general," was uttered twice after Mr. Allen left NA II 14 238 22
whose negative might be uttered in such a manner as must PP I 19 109 22
Scarcely a syllable was uttered that did not relate to the PP II 6 166 41
adieus of her sisters were uttered without being heard. PP II 18 235 40
every sentence that he uttered was increasing her PP III 1 252 52
Not a syllable was uttered by either; and Elizabeth was on PP III 13 346 22
uttered it, was an attestation that I felt at my heart." E III 12 418 6
and not a word to suspend decision was uttered by her. P III 3 24 37
The tone, the look, with which "thank God!" was uttered by P III 12 112 54
the latter part had been uttered, and in spite of all the P IV 8 183 11
hearing the sounds he had uttered, she was startled to P IV 10 225 61
She could not immediately have uttered another sentence; P IV 11 235 33

UTTERING (4)
am much mistaken if a syllable of his uttering, escape her. LS 18 272 1
never looked more lovely than in uttering the grand idea.-- NA I 15 119 19
of fond reflection, uttering only now and then a few half MP II 9 262 11
herself capable of uttering a syllable at such a moment. MP III 10 399 4

UTTERLY (3)
She felt utterly unworthy of such respect, and knew not NA II 5 154 2
the next evening, although utterly unknown to her before. PP I 15 74 13
They walked off, utterly heedless of Mr. Rushworth's MP II 1 176 3

VACANCIES (2)
The charm of an object to occupy the many vacancies of — E II 4 183 10
circle, to fill the vacancies which there were no habits — P III 1 9 18
VACANCY (3)
of Mrs. Allen, whose vacancy of mind and incapacity for — NA I 9 60 1
There seemed no vacancy anywhere--& everybody danced with — W 340 19
a single vacancy near her, which would admit of a chair. — PP III 12 341 16
VACANT (16)
of Delaford, now just vacant, as I am informed by this — SS III 3 282 19
now just vacant, and only wishes it were more valuable. — SS III 4 288 28
that the living was vacant; nor had it ever occurred to me — SS III 4 289 35
who was lounging on a vacant table near her, call Tom — W 333 13
their minds were more vacant than their sisters', and when — PP I 7 28 3
living of Hunsford was vacant; and the respect which he — PP I 15 70 1
Certain it is, that the living became vacant two years ago, — PP I 16 79 27
obliged to spend his vacant hours in a comfortless hotel. — PP I 21 117 10 11
family living might be his as soon as it became vacant. — PP II 12 200 5
He had not to wait and wish with vacant affections for an — MP III 17 470 25
of exchanging any vacant evening of his own blank solitude — E I 3 20 2
Compressed into the very lowest vacant corner were these — E II 13 266 5
"But perhaps if she were to leave the room vacant we " — P IV 6 163 7
Such was her situation, with a vacant space at hand, when — P IV 8 189 47
the house, and his carriage wheeled off to a vacant barn.-- — S 1 370 1
Almost must be stipulated--for there were vacant spaces--& — S 12 426 1
VACATE (1)
and sickly, and likely to vacate it soon--he might have — SS III 5 295 12
VACATION (2)
of the Christmas vacation with his family, near London. — NA I 4 33 5
Till this year, every long vacation since their marriage — E I 11 91 2
VAGARIES (1)
of the table) has so few vagaries herself, and has been so — E I 14 120 11
VAGUE (5)
Some vague report had reached her before of my attachment — SS III 8 328 61
were at the same time so vague and equivocal, that her — PP II 16 223 26
The vague and unsettled suspicions which uncertainty had — PP III 10 326 3
were the worse of being vague;--they suspected great — P III 7 54 4
Vague wishes of getting Sarah thither, had occurred before — P IV 1 122 3
VAIN (114)
on the occasion--but all in vain--she does not like me. — LS 5 249 1
have been bestowed in vain, & to persuade Reginald that — LS 7 254 3
It is true that I am vain enough to beleive it within my — LS 10 257 1
If I am vain of anything, it is of my eloquence. — LS 16 268 2
her tender tale of love in vain, & exposed herself forever — LS 22 282 8
made no remarks however, for words would have been in vain. — LS 24 287 10
prudent advice of your parents has not been given in vain. — LS 37 306 1
looking about them in vain for a more eligible situation, — NA I 2 22 10
This sentiment had been uttered so often in vain, that Mrs. — NA I 4 31 2
box which her eye could reach; but she looked in vain. — NA I 5 35 1
said I--but all in vain--he would not stir an inch. — NA I 8 56 14
But all in vain; Catherine felt herself to be in the right, — NA I 13 98 2
Thorpe told her it would be in vain to go after the — NA I 13 101 21
written in vain--or perhaps might not have written at all." — NA I 14 110 27
So it is in vain to affect ignorance." — NA II 3 144 10
on such a point, would be vain, since sleep must be — NA II 6 168 10
and she felt round each with anxious acuteness in vain. — NA II 6 169 11
it did open; and not vain, as hitherto, was her search; — NA II 6 169 11
health in vain, was too polite to make further opposition. — NA II 7 179 29
Till midnight, she supposed it would be in vain to watch; — NA II 8 189 19
She is a vain coquette, and her tricks have not answered. — NA II 12 218 4
the matter farther, but in vain; common sense, common care, — SS I 16 85 10
But from such vain wishes, she was forced to turn for — SS I 19 102 2
and explain the reason of my having expected this in vain. — SS II 7 187 40
"All this, however," he continued, "was urged in vain. — SS III 1 267 42
relief might soon be in vain, that every thing had been — SS III 7 312 18
The matter itself I could not deny, and vain was every — SS III 8 323 40
The world had made him extravagant and vain----- — SS III 8 331 70
On the contrary, he seems very vain, very conceited, — W 342 19
A person may be proud without being vain. — PP I 5 20 20
to be allowed the honour of her hand; but in vain. — PP I 6 26 40
reminded his sister-in-law of the card-table--but in vain. — PP I 11 54 3
Vain indeed must be all her attentions, vain and useless — PP I 16 83 56
Netherfield and looked in vain for Mr. Wickham among the — PP I 18 89 1
In vain did Elizabeth endeavour to check the rapidity of — PP I 18 99 64
of complaisance,--but in vain; Mary would not understand — PP I 18 100 68
In vain did she entreat him to stand up with somebody else, — PP I 18 102 73
Elizabeth asked questions in vain; Maria would tell her — PP II 5 158 13
agitated manner, and thus began, "in vain have I struggled. — PP II 11 189 3 4
They were ignorant, idle, and vain. — PP II 14 213 17
so very weak and vain and nonsensical as I knew I had! — PP II 17 226 19
In vain did Elizabeth attempt to make her reasonable, and — PP II 18 230 14
Vain, ignorant, idle, and absolutely uncontrouled! — PP II 18 231 18
of the rooms, and the price of the furniture, in vain. — PP III 1 249 37
In what a disgraceful light might it not strike so vain a — PP III 1 252 54
could have loved him, as now, when all love must be vain. — PP III 4 278 19
But I will not torment you with vain wishes, which may — PP III 4 278 20
But wishes were vain; or at best could serve only to amuse — PP III 4 281 29
that Mrs. Norris did not write to her sister in vain. — MP I 1 11 19
In vain were the well-meant condescensions of Sir Thomas, — MP I 2 13 4
would be a good girl; in vain did Lady Bertram smile and — MP I 2 13 4
with herself and pug, and vain was even the sight of a — MP I 2 13 4
after she had tried in vain to persuade her brother to — MP I 4 41 16
He still reasoned with her, but in vain. — MP I 9 96 76
Opposition was vain; and as to Mrs. Norris, he was — MP I 13 129 40
All the best plays were run over in vain. — MP I 14 130 3
was insufficient, that she might have talked in vain. — MP II 2 188 3
of his lady, but in vain; no pause was long enough for the — MP II 7 240 10
be settled otherwise; in vain however;--Sir Thomas smiled, — MP II 10 275 11
not like her cousins; but I think I shall not ask in vain." — MP II 12 293 14
to take so much trouble in vain, she still went on, after — MP II 13 298 1
and twice attempted in vain to turn away from him, she got — MP II 13 301 7
In vain was her "pray, sir, don't--pray, Mr. Crawford," — MP III 3 342 34
twice over; and in vain did she try to move away--in the — MP III 3 342 34
brother-in-law's money was vain, and that in spite of her — MP III 6 372 21
hurry; William trying in vain to send Betsey down again, — MP III 7 382 27
She is a cold-hearted, vain woman, who has married — MP III 13 421 2
can, after having had truths before him so long in vain.-- — MP III 13 424 4
that such hope was vain, and till the disappointment and — MP III 17 464 10
and he would not by a vain attempt to restore what never — MP III 17 465 13
vain, as earnestly tried to prevent any body's eating it. — E I 2 19 14
in her power, but on this subject questions were vain. — E I 4 27 3
add this praise, that I do not think her personally vain. — E I 5 39 21
elton is the man, I think it will be all labour in vain." — E I 8 66 51
Emma's attempts to stop her father had been vain; and when — E I 12 106 59
Many vain solicitudes would be prevented--many — E II 4 182 8
loved even Mr. Elton in vain--by the surrender of all the — E II 8 219 44
her opinion, the great risk, of its being all in vain. — E II 12 257 1
to which she had with such vain artifice retreated three — E II 14 270 3
and after waiting in vain for her friend to begin; "well, — E II 14 271 6
her that Mrs. Elton was a vain woman, extremely well — E II 14 272 16
enough to exclaim, "you are not vain, Mr. Knightley. — E II 15 287 31
from some one very dear, and that it had not been in vain. — E II 16 298 58
it had been soon acknowledged vain to attempt to fix a day. — E III 1 318 11
Does my vain spirit ever tell me I am wrong?" — E III 2 330 52
"Not your vain spirit, but your serious spirit.-- — E III 2 330 53
who had been trying in vain to be heard the last two — E III 5 345 16
watching her intently--in vain, however, if it were so-- — E III 5 346 17
Mrs. Weston looked, and looked in vain. — E III 6 361 41
And Mr. Weston tried, in vain, to make them harmonize — E III 7 367 1
She continued to look back, but in vain; and soon, with — E III 7 376 62
thing that message could do was tried--but all in vain. — E III 9 390 18
If Harriet, from being humble, were grown vain, it was her — E III 11 414 50
speaking to Harriet; and certainly did not speak in vain.-- — E III 18 472 20
I see it in her cheek, her smile, her vain attempt to — E III 18 480 77
so often, that it became vain to attempt concealing it — P III 1 9 19
experience--but always in vain; Elizabeth would go her own — P III 2 16 16
tenderness of manner, be continually advising her in vain. — P III 4 27 5
wives generally understand when opposition will be vain. — P III 7 55 9
reason will patronize in vain,--which taste cannot — P III 8 68 30
She spoke to him--ordered, intreated, and insisted in vain. — P III 9 80 29
She tried to dissuade Mary from going, but in vain; and — P III 10 83 4
he reasoned and talked in vain; she smiled and said, "I am — P III 12 109 32
Anne had prompted, but in vain; while Captain Wentworth, — P III 12 110 37 38
clamour of the children on his knees, generally in vain. — P IV 2 134 29
should find so much to be vain of in the littlenesses of a — P IV 3 138 5
sort of watch for him in vain; but at last, in returning — P IV 7 178 28
She wondered, and questioned him eagerly--but in vain. — P IV 8 187 33
now asked in vain for several particulars of the company. — P IV 9 192 5
But this was a vain idea. — P IV 10 212 1
for having watched in vain for some intimation of the — P IV 10 228 70
We have consulted physician after Phyn in vain, till we — S 5 386 1
In vain may we put them into a literary Alembic;--we — S 8 403 1
soon found that all her calculations of profit wd be vain. — S 11 422 1
VAINER (1)
Had she been older or vainer, such attacks might have done — NA I 7 50 44
VAINLY (2)
"Very agreeable indeed," she replied, vainly endeavouring — NA I 2 23 24
She tried to stop him; but vainly; he would go on, and say — E I 15 129 24
VALANCOURT (1)
poor Valancourt when she went with her aunt into Italy. — NA I 14 107 11
VALET (1)
than he did; now could the valet of any new made Lord be — P III 1 4 5
VALETUDINARIAN (1)
for having been a valetudinarian all his life, without — E I 1 7 8
VALID (1)
seem valid, exceeded all that she could believe possible. — PP III 8 310 10
VALLEY (18)
of its standing low in a valley, sheltered from the north — NA II 2 141 13
of Barton valley as they entered it gave them cheerfulness. — SS I 6 28 1
whole of the valley, and reached into the country beyond. — SS I 6 29 3
cottage terminated the valley in that direction; under — SS I 6 29 3
it in their way along the valley, but it was screened from — SS I 7 32 1
along the narrow winding valley of Allenham, which issued — SS I 9 40 2
if they talked of the valley, she was as speedy in — SS I 16 85 15
They walked along the road through the valley, and chiefly — SS I 16 85 15
Beyond the entrance of the valley, where the country, — SS I 16 85 15
his attention to the prospect, "here is Barton valley. — SS I 16 88 33
seen many parts of the valley to advantage; and the — SS I 18 96 4
of fine timber, and the valley looks comfortable and snug-- — SS I 18 97 4
the valley, into which the road with some abruptness wound. — PP III 1 245 3
of the valley, as far as she could trace it, with delight. — PP III 1 246 5
charming views of the valley, the opposite hills, with the — PP III 1 253 57
had yet visited; and the valley, here contracted into a — PP III 1 253 57
do more mischief in a valley, when they do arise than an — S 4 381 1
A branch only, of the valley, winding more obliquely — S 4 383 1
VALLEYS (1)
when the dirt of the valleys beneath shut up their — SS I 9 40 3
VALUABLE (41)
had made her a valuable companion, and in the promotion of — NA II 5 154 1
The utmost care could not always secure the most valuable — NA II 7 178 21
charge on the estate, or by any sale of its valuable woods. — SS I 1 4 3
A valuable legacy indeed! — SS I 2 13 27
at Norland (and very valuable they were) to your mother. — SS II 11 225 35
"She seems a most valuable woman indeed.-- — SS II 11 226 42
to appear to doubt; I only wish it were more valuable.-- — SS III 3 282 19
now just vacant, and only wishes it were more valuable. — SS III 4 288 28
not too clever to be a valuable neighbour to Mrs. Bennet.-- — PP I 5 18 2
has preferred me to the valuable rectory of this parish, — PP I 13 62 12
I doubt not will prove a valuable acquaintance, especially — PP I 13 63 13
in possession of a most valuable living, had it pleased — PP I 16 79 23
orders, desired that a valuable family living might be his — PP II 12 200 5
What praise is more valuable than the praise of an — PP III 1 250 48
The respect created by the conviction of his valuable — PP III 2 265 16
Lucas himself, to produce a more valuable son-in-law." — PP III 11 330 8
was to him, made his affection every moment more valuable. — PP III 16 366 8
with one, for it is so valuable a fruit, with a little — MP I 6 54 13
It was a valuable part of former times. — MP I 9 86 12
made her always valuable amongst them--but now she was — MP I 18 171 28
to say whether most valuable as a convenience or an — MP II 4 208 12
The gift was too valuable. — MP II 8 258 17
which might be least valuable; and was determined in her — MP II 8 258 17
her to her face--she is now a very valuable companion. — MP II 11 285 11
and not owe the most valuable knowledge we could any of us — MP III 16 458 30
to a walk, would be a valuable addition to her privileges. — E I 4 26 1
"Which makes his good manners the more valuable. — E I 4 33 36
Even this conquest would appear valuable in her eyes. — E I 7 56 41
but in good hands she will turn out a valuable woman." — E I 8 58 10
something honourable and valuable in the strong domestic — E I 11 97 27
with Mr. Elton; a most valuable, amiable, pleasing young — E I 13 111 13
is something still more valuable, I mean that has been — E III 4 339 16
that has been more valuable, because this is what did — E III 4 339 16
which made the information she received more valuable. — E III 4 340 28
These valuable pictures of yours, Sir Walter, if you chose — P III 3 18 7
as a most important and valuable assistant to the latter — P III 5 34 11
something curious and valuable from all the distant — P III 11 98 17
Every minute is valuable. — P III 12 113 58
those periods of her life when it had been most valuable. — P IV 5 152 2
a cheerful, independant, valuable character.--and her — S 3 376 1
there--but it was a most valuable proof of the increasing — S 4 383 1
VALUE (85)
Every person of sense however will know how to value & — LS 14 265 5
my power to make; if she value her own happiness as much — LS 24 290 13
four hundred pounds yearly value, was to be resigned to — NA II 1 135 42
An estate of at least equal value, moreover, was assured — NA II 1 135 42
must have been beyond the value of all the rest, for the — NA II 8 184 4
His value of her was sincere; and, if not permanently, he — NA II 9 197 27
on such terms as destroyed half the value of the bequest. — SS I 1 4 3
as to outweigh all the value of all the attention which, — SS I 1 4 3
I value not her censure any more than I should do her — SS I 13 68 74
to more than its real value; and she was sometimes worried — SS II 10 215 13
an examination into the value and make of her gown, the — SS II 14 249 8
fetch such a price!--what was the value of this?" — SS III 5 294 10
to a living of that value--supposing the late incumbent to — SS III 5 295 12
and so highly do I value and esteem him, that if Marianne — SS III 9 337 17
minutes afterwards, the value of her engagement increased, — W 333 13
such as it was, had a value as arising in all probability — PP I 6 21 1
No man of common humanity, no man who had any value for — PP I 17 85 4
begins to lose somewhat on its value in our estimation. — PP I 20 114 32
which no one seemed to value but herself, and where she — PP II 7 169 5
cannot be mine till it has lost all its value!" — PP II 17 227 25
and so fervently did she value his remembrance, and prefer — PP II 17 227 26
and the little value he put on his own good qualities. — PP III 13 350 51
as I value the impudence and hypocrisy of my son-in-law. — PP III 15 364 24
I always had a value for him. — PP III 17 374 18
but a value for Edmund, Miss Crawford was very unlike her. — MP I 8 80 31
gradually, as her value for the comforts of it increased, — MP I 16 151 1
and equally so that my value for domestic tranquillity, — MP II 1 186 34
would do justice to, he intended to value him very highly. — MP II 1 186 35
If he knew them better, he would value their society as it — MP II 3 196 2
her liveliness--and she has talents to value his powers. — MP II 3 199 13
Not only at home did her value increase, but at the — MP II 4 205 2
The value of an event on a wet day in the country, was — MP II 4 206 3

the opinion of all who had hearts to value any thing good. MP II 6 235 19
which Henry Crawford had moral taste enough to value. MP II 6 235 20
better than his nephew the value of such a loan, and some MP II 6 237 23
ourselves to enhance the value of such a situation in MP II 7 244 27
too dearly, and your brother does not offer half her value. MP II 7 244 28
Park family which was increasing in value to him every day. MP II 7 246 37
was to him of no higher value than any other appointed MP II 8 256 13
impossible for me to value, or for him to remember half. MP II 8 259 22
upon her mind, and seemed of greater value than at first. MP II 9 270 40
the full value of the other joyful surprises at hand. MP III 3 334 2
Her disposition was peculiarly calculated to value a fond MP III 5 365 33
a juster estimate of the value of that home of greater MP III 6 369 9
probability, teach her the value of a good income; and he MP III 6 369 10
body, into a much juster value for Mr. Crawford's good MP III 11 413 30
The value of a man like Henry on such an occasion, is what MP III 12 417 3
to place a yet higher value on the sweetness of her temper, MP III 17 468 21
that you do not know the value of a companion; and perhaps E I 5 36 6
He knows the value of a good income as well as anybody. E I 8 66 53
temper and good will in Mr. Elton as one cannot but value." E I 13 112 17
Emma was in the humour to value simplicity and modesty to E I 17 141 8
and she had herself the highest value for elegance. E II 2 167 12
character, or her own value for his company, or opinion of E II 2 169 16
and besides, what was the value of Harriet's description?-- E II 3 179 53
And it cannot be for the value of our custom now, for what E II 9 235 46
and try to understand the value of his preference, and the E II 11 250 19
he understands the value of friendship as well as any body. E II 16 293 22
few people seem to value simplicity of dress,--shew and E II 17 302 22
mark of good taste which I shall always know how to value." E III 4 342 39
She wanted to be of use to her; wanted to show a value for E III 9 389 16
of houses or lands can ever equal the value of.-- E III 14 437 8
I hope he may long continue to feel all the value of such E III 15 447 28
His two other children were of very inferior value. P III 1 5 8
of ancestry; she had a value for rank and consequence, P III 2 11 2
If you value her conduct or happiness, infuse as much of P III 10 88 26
became a sort of parting proof, its value did not lessen. P III 12 117 75
understand somewhat of the value of an Anne Elliot, should, P IV 1 125 13
and proclaim the value of the connection, as he had P IV 2 135 35
amiable and lovely, and a value for all the felicities of P IV 4 146 6
His value for rank and connexion she perceived to be P IV 4 148 10
collect good company around them, they had their value. P IV 4 150 15
how to value your kindness in coming to me this morning. P IV 9 194 18
Mr. Elliot has sense to understand the value of such a P IV 9 196 32
now, as a young man he had not the smallest value for it. P IV 9 202 66
in Mr. Elliot's opinions as to the value of a baronetcy. P IV 9 206 90
Not that he will value it as he ought," he observed, " P IV 10 217 20
I cannot make her attend to the value of the property. P IV 10 218 22
I have a great value for benwick; and when one can but get P IV 10 218 26
of earlier youth: but the value of such homage was P IV 11 243 68
to bestow on him which a man of sense could value. P IV 12 251 10
former transgressions, he could now value from his heart. P IV 12 251 10
two husbands, who knew the value of money, was very much S 3 375 1
just such a degree of value for it apparent now, as to S 3 376 1
be ours eventually in the increased value of our houses." S 6 393 1

VALUED (34)

but the loss of <u>his</u> valued esteem, I am as you well know, LS 30 300 3
the envy of every valued old friend in Putney, with a NA I 15 122 28
A portrait--very like--of a departed wife, not valued by NA II 7 181 39
He told me the other day, that he only valued money as it NA II 10 205 30
with having never enough valued her merits or kindness; NA II 14 235 14
but by Mrs. Dashwood it was valued and cherished. SS I 1 7 13
He valued their kindness beyond any thing, and his SS I 19 101 1
It was a valued, a precious trust to me; and gladly would SS II 9 208 28
was in fact as little valued, as it was professedly sought. SS II 14 246 2
the loss of what is most valued is so easily to be made up SS III 1 263 28
of doing anything in the world for those she really valued. SS III 5 293 2
constant enjoyment to her valued friend; and to see SS III 14 378 13
whose friendship she valued beyond that of any other PP I 22 123 3
person. ship she valued beyond that of any other person. PP I 22 123 3
That among his own connections he was esteemed and valued-- PP II 13 207 6
I, who have valued myself on my abilities! who have often PP II 13 208 8
her sister how sincerely she had been valued by his friend. PP II 17 227 25
you must be respected and valued; and you will not appear PP II 18 231 20
of some of their least valued toys, and leave her to MP I 2 14 7
The ensuing spring deprived her of her valued friend the MP I 4 35 7
dearly earned, and justly valued blessing of promotion-- MP II 6 234 18
had for the world, and which could never be valued enough. MP III 13 425 5
taste, and that he valued taste much more than execution." E II 9 232 9
Harriet so well, nor valued her affection so highly before. E II 13 269 15
gifts: but they are things that I have valued very much." E III 4 338 8
herself to such ill opinion in any one she valued! E III 7 376 62
dear and highly valued god-daughter, favourite and friend. P III 1 6 9
whom he had always valued highly, which must have stamped P III 11 96 12
that she was valued only as she could be useful to Louisa. P III 12 115 68
and only superior to her in being more highly valued! P IV 5 160 25
I have valued myself on honourable toils and just rewards. P IV 11 247 84
which she certainly valued, joined those of having been S 3 377 1
as of a person who valued herself on being free-spoken, S 6 391 1
Lady D. valued herself upon her liberal establishment, & S 12 427 1

VALUELESS (2)

and deference towards herself perfectly valueless. SS I 22 127 2
make <u>my</u> assertions valueless, you cannot be prevented by PP II 12 203 5

VALUES (2)

I think he values the very quietness you speak of, and MP II 3 196 3
he is exactly what one values, so hospitable, and so fond E I 13 116 43

VANISH (3)

observed Elinor, "and your difficulties will soon vanish." SS I 17 92 24
would vanish, if she could suppose him to be in her power. PP II 9 181 30
yet, who can say how soon it may all vanish from my mind?" E I 10 87 25

VANISHED (6)

& perhaps his may be vanished for ever, while mine will be LS 22 282 7
hope which but two hours ago made me so happy, is vanished. LS 24 285 1
Respect, esteem, and confidence, had vanished for ever; PP II 19 236 1
She certainly did not hate him. no; hatred had vanished PP III 2 265 16
alteration of person had vanished, and she could see in MP II 6 233 17
girl, but her bloom had vanished early; and as even in its P III 1 6 10

VANITIES (2)

He has his vanities as well as Miss Thorpe, and the chief NA II 12 218 7
evasions of a mind too weak to defend its own vanities.-- E II 8 212 3

VANITY (86)

in it,--nothing of vanity, of pretension, of levity--& she LS 8 255 2
may arise only from vanity, or a wish of gaining the LS 12 261 4
It's effect on Reginald justifies some portion of vanity, LS 25 293 3
it before--her humble vanity was contented--she felt more NA I 2 24 28
and impudent falsehoods the excess of vanity will lead. NA I 9 65 31
of administering to the vanity of others, which a sensible NA I 14 110 28
In vanity therefore she gained but little, her chief NA II 3 148 29
been perfectly without vanity of that kind, might have NA II 7 175 12
it; but if he had a vanity, it was in the arrangement of NA II 8 184 4
Catherine himself, his vanity induced him to represent the NA II 15 244 12
than his vanity and avarice had made him believe them. NA II 15 244 12
vanity was her greatest enjoyment in any of their parties. SS I 7 32 2
the blushes and the vanity of many a young lady by SS I 8 36 1
her at Norland; it was not an illusion of her own vanity. SS II 1 139 1
her interest and her vanity should so very much blind her, SS II 13 238 2
So you may think what a blow it was to all her vanity and SS III 1 258 7
Elinor had heard enough, if not to gratify her vanity, and SS III 5 297 32
But at first I must confess, my vanity only was elevated SS III 8 320 29
horrid state of selfish vanity, I did not know the extent SS III 8 320 32
sacrificed my feelings to vanity, to avarice?--or, what is SS III 8 320 32
Extravagance and vanity had made him cold-hearted and SS III 8 331 70
Vanity, while seeking its own guilty triumph at the SS III 8 331 70
accidentally meeting, the vanity of the one had been so SS III 13 364 11
tempt the avarice or the vanity of any living creature, SS III 13 367 22
which might please her vanity, but did not suit her pride, W 347 22
Vanity and pride are different things, though the words PP I 5 20 20
Pride relates more to our opinion of ourselves, vanity to PP I 5 20 20
There is so much of gratitude or vanity in almost every PP I 6 21 2
If my vanity had taken a musical turn, you would have been PP I 6 24 22
Mary had neither genius nor taste; and though vanity had PP I 6 25 24
"Such as vanity and pride." PP I 11 57 23
"Yes, vanity is a weakness indeed. PP I 11 57 24
It is very often nothing but our own vanity that deceives PP II 1 136 14
Her heart had been but slightly touched, and her vanity PP II 3 149 28
If his own vanity, however, did not mislead him, <u>he</u> was PP II 10 186 38
had been gratifying his vanity by encouraging the PP II 13 207 6
gratified my vanity, in useless or blameable distrust.-- PP II 13 208 8
But vanity, not love, has been my folly.-- PP II 13 208 8
whatever of her own vanity she had not yet been able to PP II 15 217 17
had been withdrawn, her vanity would be gratified and her PP II 18 233 25
she has been given up to nothing but amusement and vanity. PP III 5 283 10
soon felt that even her vanity was insufficient, when PP III 10 326 3
What will you think of my vanity.? PP III 16 369 26
Their vanity was in such good order, that they seemed to MP I 4 35 4
They are always acting upon motives of vanity--and there MP I 5 50 38
in as happy a flutter as vanity and pride could furnish, MP I 8 83 37
indulgence of his idle vanity was tending; but, MP I 12 114 3
his selfish vanity had raised in Maria and Julia Bertram. MP II 2 193 18
He had vanity, which strongly inclined him, in the first MP III 2 326 1
that to a temper of vanity and hope like Crawford's, the MP III 2 328 7
In my situation, it would have been the extreme of vanity MP III 4 353 45
vanity it would be good luck to have Edmund the only son. MP III 14 430 3
cold-hearted ambition--<u>his</u> thoughtless vanity. MP III 14 435 15
<u>His</u> unsettled affections, wavering with his vanity, MP III 15 441 20
vanity was not of a strength to fight long against reason. MP III 16 459 31
in the freaks of a cold-blooded vanity a little too long. MP III 17 467 19
Curiosity and vanity were both engaged, and the temptation MP III 17 467 20
He was entangled by his own vanity, with as little excuse MP III 17 468 21
own friends, enough of vanity, ambition, love, and MP III 17 469 24
out of health and into vanity--but a real, honest, old- E I 3 21 5
to be little occupied with it; her vanity lies another way. E I 5 39 21
gratitude of her young vanity to a very good purpose, for E I 6 42 1
Vanity working on a weak head, produces every sort of E I 8 64 47
have him, that vanity and prudence were equally contented. E II 4 181 4
Vanity, extravagance, love of change, restlessness of E II 7 205 1
of the wicked aids of vanity--to assist him first in E II 11 247 2
before--and no degree of vanity can prevent her E II 15 287 23
came into the room; her vanity had then a change of object, E II 17 302 21 22
a word--but he had the vanity to think they would be E III 1 316 4
was not the very first distinction in the scale of vanity. E III 2 319 4
at this time, in vanity completely gratified; for though E III 2 325 32
With insufferable vanity had she believed herself in the E III 11 412 47
last--my vanity was flattered, and I allowed his attention. E III 13 427 19
Vanity was the beginning and the end of Sir Walter P III 1 4 5
Elliot's character; vanity of person and of situation. P III 1 4 5
So far went his understanding; and his vanity supplied a P III 3 24 36
it to gratify her vanity, than Mary might have allowed. P IV 6 167 19
all selfish vanity, of the other all generous attachment. P IV 8 185 20
of pleasure and vanity which could be commanded without P IV 9 209 95
his modest cousin's vanity; he found, at least, that it P IV 10 214 12
It was a struggle between propriety and vanity; but vanity P IV 10 219 29
It was a struggle between propriety and vanity; but vanity P IV 10 219 29
for Anne, and no vanity flattered, to make him really P IV 12 248 2
I make no apologies for my heroine's vanity.-- S 7 395 1
vanity in all they did, as well as in all they endured.-- S 10 412 1
to the account of the vanity, the ignorance, or the S 11 420 1

VANITY-BAITS (1)

your sanction to such vanity-baits for poor young ladies." E II 14 280 59

VANQUISHED (3)

James is gone, Lady Susan vanquished, & Frederica at peace. LS 23 285 8
She was quite vanquished, & the fashions of Osborne-Castle W 358 28
encouraged; it had been vanquished at last by those P IV 11 241 60

VAPID (1)

of Amalgamation, or those vapid tissues of ordinary S 8 403 1

VARIANCE (2)

with whom it had always pleased him to be at variance.-- PP I 13 62 12
with Sir Walter, nothing to risk by a state of variance. P IV 3 140 11

VARIATION (11)

and to offer some little variation on the subject, "that NA I 9 65 27
articles with little variation; a third, a fourth, and a NA II 7 172 2
about it, should the least variation be perceptible. SS I 14 73 13
variation of form, face, temper, and understanding. SS I 21 119 3
her situation continued, with little variation, the same. SS III 7 309 7
The next variation which their visit afforded was produced PP III 3 268 6
caused their confusion, suffered no variation of colour. PP III 9 316 5
sentiment with a little variation of words three times MP II 12 292 8
the progress of time and variation of circumstances MP III 6 374 27
me then, as they are now; or with no important variation. E I 10 85 21
liable to such sudden variation as might disappoint her E III 6 361 41

VARIATIONS (4)

Oh! how delightful it was, to watch the variations of his LS 25 293 3
the wind, watching the variations of the sky and imagining SS II 5 168 8
mind, Emma would have been amused by its variations. E II 4 184 11
All the little variations of the last week were gone P IV 11 241 59

VARIED (10)

and though her complexion varied, she stood firm in SS I 22 129 15
After playing some Italian songs, Miss Bingley varied the PP I 10 51 47 48
Though her manner varied however, her determination never PP I 20 112 23
Their parties abroad were less varied than before; and at PP II 19 237 3
Her mind was quite determined and varied not. MP II 3 202 25
or his short, as the year varied; and since Mrs. Weston's E I 4 26 1
Her ideas only varied as to the how much. E II 13 264 1
setting her right if she varied in the slightest E III 3 336 13
an accidental division, but it never materially varied. E III 7 367 1
presence of mind never varied, whose tongue never slipped. P IV 5 161 28

VARIETIES (9)

delineation of its varieties, the liveliest effusions of NA I 5 38 4
feelings through the varieties of suspense, security, and NA II 2 140 11
of contradictions and varieties, sighed at the PP III 4 279 23
was thrown into the most distressing of all its varieties. MP III 5 364 30
rationally to the varieties of her situation in life.-- E I 5 39 15
The varieties of hand-writing were farther talked of, and E II 16 297 44
woody varieties of the cheerful village of up Lyme, and, P III 11 95 9
The varieties in the fitting-up of the rooms, where the P III 11 98 17
Such varieties of human nature as they are in the habit of P IV 5 156 10

VARIETY (46)

yet knew not from a variety of reasons how to part with LS 42 312 5
"Bath, compared with London, has little variety, and so NA I 10 78 45
own home; for here are a variety of amusements, a variety NA I 10 78 46
variety of amusements, a variety of things to be seen and NA I 10 78 46
there;--but here I see a variety of people in every street, NA I 10 79 54
had she beheld half such variety on a breakfast-table-- NA II 5 154 2
recollection a countless variety of dreadful situations NA II 6 166 9
After an evening, the little variety and seeming length of NA II 8 187 15
"Among all the great variety that you have known and NA II 10 206 36
such lasting amazement or variety of speculation, her SS I 14 71 3
in every possible variety which the different state of her SS I 19 104 12
her usual cheerfulness, a variety of advantages that would SS II 3 155 7
foresee it there from a variety of sources; she would SS II 3 157 16
in other words, in every variety of inquiry concerning all SS II 4 164 23
by a variety of sweetmeats and olives, and a good fire. SS II 8 193 7
A variety of occupations, of objects, and of company, SS II 10 213 3
the discourse with some variety--the variety of politics, SS II 12 233 19

with some variety--the variety of politics, inclosing land, SS II 12 233 19
party, and a very welcome variety to their conversations, SS III 6 304 14
little had seen so much variety in his address to her SS III 6 304 15
but his presence gave variety & secured good manners.-- W 359 28
He only meant that there were not such a variety of people PP I 9 43 24
by Jane, and by making a variety of remarks on the PP I 23 126 4
Collins, she addressed a variety of questions to Maria and PP II 6 163 15
giving way to every variety of thought; re-considering PP II 13 209 12
The park was very large, and contained great variety of PP III 1 245 2
cold meat, cake, and a variety of all the finest fruits in PP III 3 268 6
their whole bodies, in a variety of capers and frisks, was PP III 5 286 21
and poultry, was very much in want of some variety at home. MP I 4 41 15
it; but the tears which a variety of feelings created, MP I 7 74 57
When one thinks of it, how astonishing a variety of nature! MP II 4 209 16
sheds its leaf is the variety, but that does not make it MP II 4 209 16
variety of danger, which sea and war together could offer. MP II 6 236 21
time, as soon as the variety of business before him were MP II 8 255 10
From a variety of causes she was happy, and she was soon MP II 10 272 4
and snow, with nothing to do and no variety to hope for. MP II 11 286 15
a variety of excellence beyond what she had ever met with. MP III 3 337 10
understood, he had a variety of questions from Crawford as MP III 3 340 24
"No great variety of faces for you," said Emma. E I 6 45 21
And when one considers the variety of hands, and of bad E II 16 296 42
A variety of evils crossed his mind. E III 5 350 31
the exercise and variety which her spirits seemed to need. E III 6 361 42
and variety, by the streets, the shops, and the children.-- E III 14 435 4
year for any amusement or variety which Lyme, as a public P III 11 95 9
for variety; but Anne had never found an evening shorter. P IV 11 245 78
& are subject to a variety of very serious disorders.-- S 5 385 1

VARIOUS (40)
At present my thoughts are fluctuating between various LS 25 293 4
To effect all this I have various plans. LS 25 294 4
How are your various dresses to be remembered, and the NA I 3 27 28
The storm still raged, and various were the noises, more NA II 6 170 12
The various ascending noises convinced her that the NA II 8 189 19
me much information on various subjects, and he has always SS I 10 51 20
it; and thus amidst the various endeavours of different SS I 12 62 27
Many were the eyes, & various the degrees of approbation W 337 17
They attacked him in various ways; with barefaced PP I 3 9 1
to be the case; and after various conjectures, they could PP II 9 180 28
They called at various times of the morning, sometimes PP II 9 180 28
I had, in defiance of various claims, in defiance of PP II 12 196 5
her spirits, amidst the various engagements which the PP II 15 217 16
and hear the news: and various were the subjects which PP II 16 222 21
was enumerating the various pleasures of the morning to PP II 16 222 21
in her thoughts; and the various recollections connected PP III 3 269 10
that he will satisfy the various creditors of Mr. Wickham PP III 8 313 19
Of various admirals, I could tell you a great deal; of MP I 6 60 49
superintending their various dresses with economical MP I 17 163 21
his own horsemanship in various countries, of the MP II 6 237 23
of his own, over the various advertisements of "a most MP III 3 341 31
Farther discussion was prevented by various bustles; first, MP III 7 379 19
neck to sob out her various emotions of pain and pleasure. MP III 7 384 34
At last, after various attempts at meeting, I have seen MP III 9 393 1
of all her books and boxes, and various comforts there. MP III 9 398 9
how nursed her through the various illnesses of childhood. E I 1 6 6
and see him; and from various united causes, from his long E I 3 20 1
of her drawing up at various times of books that she meant E I 5 37 7
portfolio containing her various attempts at portraits, E I 6 44 19
he was under, from various circumstances of weather and E I 17 140 2
fire, to observe in their various modes, till other E III 2 320 5
tremulous feeling, the various lines which imaged a broken P III 11 100 23
as if overpowered by the various feelings of his soul, and P III 12 112 54
Various as were the tempers in her father's house, he P IV 5 161 29
and in spite of all the various noises of the room, the P IV 8 183 11
the various sources of mortification preparing for them! P IV 10 215 13
of various kinds to recommend her quickly and permanently. P IV 12 251 10
fully occupied in their various civilities & S 6 390 1
them an early tendency at various times, to various S 10 412 1
at various times, to various disorders;--the rest of their S 10 412 1

VARIOUSLY (2)
encouraged, and variously dispersed and disposed of, E I 11 92 3
while the others were variously urging and recommending, E I 15 128 17 18

VARNISH (2)
when he comes home find all the varnish scratched off." MP I 8 77 12
Varnish and gilding hide many stains. MP III 14 434 13

VARNISHED (1)
He drew, he varnished, he carpentered, he glued; he made P III 11 99 18

VARY (7)
ventured at length to vary the subject by a question which NA I 7 48 32
His plan did not vary on seeing them.-- PP I 15 70 3
may vary greatly with respect to me; and I could wish, PP I 18 94 41
her intentions did not vary for an instant, she was at PP II 11 189 6
vary the scene, and exercise our powers in something new. MP I 13 125 18
must vary much as to time in different people.-- MP III 17 470 26
alloy, the agitations to vary, the sameness and the P III 1 9 18

VARYING (11)
cast down, & her colour varying every instant, while LS 20 276 3
So wondered, so talked Mrs. Jennings, her opinion varying SS I 14 70 3
Elinor, without observing the varying complexion of her SS II 3 153 1
feelings and varying opinions on Marianne's, as before. SS II 9 201 2
in his melancholy eye and varying complexion as he looked SS III 10 340 2
must be relative, and depend on many varying circumstances. PP II 9 179 22
the frequent means of varying the humble home scene, I PP II 15 215 4
with the transient, varying, unsteady nature of love, as MP III 2 330 14
the other all varying and indescribable perturbation. MP III 15 444 27
with a weakened frame and varying spirits, seemed, under E II 2 165 9
such a confusion of varying, but very painful agitation, P III 9 80 34

VAST (22)
"Oh! a vast deal indeed; she hardly talked of any thing NA I 9 68 44
for my part, I think they are a vast addition always." SS I 21 123 26
I'm sure there's a vast many smart beaux in Exeter; but SS I 21 123 28
convenience; and it has cost me a vast deal of money." SS II 11 225 31
Her inviting you to town is certainly a vast thing in your SS II 11 226 42
I saw a vast deal more. SS II 13 239 6
I had a vast deal more to say to you, but I must not stay SS III 2 275 25
Well, I am convinced that there is a vast deal of SS III 5 295 12
to see;--& she has taken a vast deal of trouble about him W 317 2
ill indeed, and suffers a vast deal, though with the PP I 9 42 7
The country is a vast deal pleasanter, is not it, Mr. PP I 9 43 21
There is a vast deal of difference in memories, as well as MP I 2 19 27
We did a vast deal in that way at the parsonage; we made MP I 6 54 9
which would make a vast difference to his uncle, for it MP II 13 304 19
We had a vast deal to say.-- MP III 9 393 1
It would have been a vast deal pleasanter to have had her MP III 16 459 31
"Well! that is quite surprizing, for we have had a vast E I 1 10 26
of sighing animation, which had a vast deal of the lover. E I 6 43 8
"My dear Miss Woodhouse, a vast deal may be done by those E II 15 283 9
I saw a vast deal of that in the neighbourhood round Maple E II 17 299 8
You must know I have a vast dislike to puppies--quite a E III 2 321 15
with Mr. Woodhouse, a vast deal of chat, and backgammon.-- E III 2 329 45

VASTLY (11)
about it to me, she talks vastly well, I am afraid of LS 15 267 4
"So Mrs. Thorpe said; she was vastly pleased at your all NA I 9 68 36
that, though it is vastly well to be here for a few weeks, NA I 10 70 3
"Mr. Morland has behaved vastly handsome indeed," said the NA II 1 135 44
For my part, I think they are vastly agreeable, provided SS I 21 123 28
Harry was vastly pleased. SS II 11 221 9
upon "her word she looked vastly smart, and she dared to SS II 14 249 8
vastly well,--she will not like to hear it much talked of." SS III 5 295 16
very handsome young lady--and she seemed vastly contented." SS III 11 355 44
I am sure he will be vastly happy to oblige you, and will PP III 11 337 53
the park, that would do vastly well, or that one might be MP I 4 36 7

VAULT (2)
Were she even to descend into the family vault where her NA II 9 190 2
at rest in the family vault, than her husband is persuaded E III 10 398 55

VAULTED (3)
your hand, will pass through it into a small vaulted room." NA II 5 159 19
No, no, you will proceed into this small vaulted room, and NA II 5 160 21
In repassing through the small vaulted room, however, your NA II 5 160 21

VAULTS (1)
way along narrow, winding vaults, by a low, grated door; NA I 11 88 54

VAUNTED (1)
vaunted claims and disdain of Harriet, he had done nothing. E II 4 183 9

VEAL (2)
She says there was hardly any veal to be got at market NA I 9 68 38
preferring salmon to cod, or boiled fowls to veal cutlets. SS II 4 160 2

VEGETABLES (2)
with all the fruit & vegetables we want; & we have in fact S 4 380 1
help we can--& when any vegetables or fruit happen to be S 4 382 1

VEGETATION (2)
beginnings and progress of vegetation had delighted her.-- MP III 14 431 9
or the yearly nuisance of its decaying vegetation.-- S 4 380 1

VEHEMENCE (4)
coachman with all the vehemence that could most fitly NA I 7 44 1
the room; and as her vehemence made reserve impossible in SS III 1 269 58
"Had they told me," he cried with vehemence, "that Mr. SS III 8 317 4
of her joy, than the first vehemence of her disapprobation. PP III 17 375 27

VEHEMENT (1)
She was so wretched, and so vehement, complained so much P III 12 115 65

VEHEMENTLY (1)
This was of course vehemently talked down as no reason at NA I 11 84 19

VEHICLE (1)
These letters were but the vehicle for gallantry and trick. E III 5 348 21

VEIL (4)
it ever since I woke; and I am got to the black veil." NA I 6 39 5
Oh! I would not tell you what is behind the black veil for NA I 6 39 6
Oh! the dreadful black veil! NA I 6 41 19
Would the veil in which Mrs. Tilney had last walked, or NA II 9 194 6

VEILS (2)
They looked just the same; both well dressed, with veils MP I 5 51 40
"Very little white satin, very few lace veils; a most E III 19 484 12

VEIW (10)
however I must remain till I have something better in veiw. LS 2 246 1
anything more serious in veiw, but it mortifies me to see LS 8 256 4
I can have no veiw in remaining with Lady Susan than to LS 14 263 2
set him against me, with a veiw of gaining him herself, & W 316 2
liberal full veiw of her face than she had yet bestowed. W 346 21
& Robert watson stealing a veiw of his own head in an W 357 28
so low in every worldly veiw, as with all her natural S 3 379 1
Nook, without air or veiw, only one mile & 3 qrs from the S 4 380 1
While I have been travelling, with this object in veiw, I S 9 410 1
room, with a beautiful veiw of the sea if they had chosen S 10 413 1

VEIWED (1)
Physics, that Charlotte veiwed the entrance of the servant S 10 416 1

VEIWING (1)
tho' complacently veiwing her daughter's good looks, wd W 323 3

VEIWS (11)
hardly suppose that Lady Susan's veiws extend to marriage. LS 11 259 1
I am suspected of matrimonial veiws in my behaviour to her. LS 14 263 1
it was easy to see that her veiws extended to marriage. LS 14 264 4
of action, however my veiws may be directed, & at any rate, LS 25 294 4
compatible with your veiws, & I rejoice to find that the LS 37 306 1
any change in her own veiws, only feared greater LS 42 312 4
and bounded their veiws to carrying back one daughter with S 2 374 1
he cd not succeed in the veiws of permanently enriching S 3 375 1
conceptions, unbounded veiws, illimitable ardour, S 8 403 1
(according to his own veiws of society) to approach with S 8 405 2
had only two or three veiws of Miss Diana posting over the S 10 413 1

VELOCITY (1)
with all the wonderful velocity of thought, had been able-- E III 13 430 38

VELVET (4)
or purple velvet, presenting even a funereal appearance. NA II 5 158 15
large, and contained neither tapestry nor velvet.-- NA II 6 163 1
mahogany, and the crimson velvet cushions appearing over MP I 9 85 6
the gentlemen in brown velvet and the ladies in the blue P III 5 40 44

VENERABLE (1)
All that was venerable ceased here. NA II 8 184 4

VENERATING (1)
that kind of fervent, venerating tenderness which would NA II 9 196 23

VENERATION (2)
her high rank, and his veneration for her as his patroness, PP I 15 70 1
and veneration, which are so proper, in me especially." E III 4 341 36

VENETIAN (1)
in standing at her ample Venetian window, & looking over S 4 384 1

VENICE (1)
Place, Venice, when Frank Churchill entered the room. E III 6 363 53

VENISON (2)
The venison was roasted to a turn--and everybody said, PP III 12 342 28
trifling, and the venison cut up without supplying one MP I 6 52 1

VENT (7)
continual though gentle vent, was able not only to see the SS II 10 215 14
Mrs. Jennings wrote to tell the wonderful tale, to vent SS III 13 370 37
had he left them than her feelings found a rapid vent. PP I 23 126 5
on table, they left her to vent all her feelings on the PP III 5 288 39
any restraint, were giving vent to their feelings of MP II 1 176 4
found a broader vent in contemptuous treatment of Harriet. E II 15 282 3
the eldest brother found vent for his superfluity of S 10 412 1

VENTED (1)
politeness, and to have vented all her feelings in a quiet MP I 11 108 4

VENTING (1)
Miss Bingley was venting her feelings in criticisms on PP III 3 270 12

VENTURE (43)
& made him I may venture to say at least half in love with LS 10 258 2
her head, not knowing whether she might venture to laugh. NA I 3 26 19
rain for Miss Tilney to venture, must yet be a question. NA I 11 83 16
and, upon the whole, I venture to pronounce that his mind SS I 4 20 9
"I may venture to say that his observations have stretched SS I 10 51 24
and once or twice did venture to suggest the propriety of SS I 11 53 2
reasons--I wish I might venture; but however I hope you SS I 22 128 7
to stay at home, than venture into so public a place. SS III 2 271 4
style of life would venture to settle on--and he said so. SS III 3 284 22
was fine enough for an invalid like herself to venture out. SS III 10 344 11
think you might now venture so far as to profess some SS III 13 372 42
But if we do not venture, somebody else will; and after PP I 2 7 16
venture still to think of both gentlemen as I did before." PP I 18 96 55
not to venture near her, lest she might hear too much. PP I 18 98 63
is certain,--but I will venture to say that my PP II 12 197 5
in it; and sometimes did venture a short sentence, when PP III 3 267 4
off to advise him not to venture: he was putting on his MP II 2 189 5
though Fanny would not venture, even on his encouragement, MP II 4 215 47
your kindness, but I may venture to say that it had honour MP II 5 225 53
And as for Harriet, I will venture to say that she cannot E I 5 38 15
But really, I could almost venture, if Harriet would sit E I 6 43 13
You and I, Emma, will venture to take the part of the poor E I 11 95 18
To you--to my two daughters, I may venture on the truth. E I 14 121 16
to promise him not to venture into such hazard till he had E I 15 125 4
it is so little one can venture to do--small, trifling E II 3 171 16 17
Emma, laughing, "I will venture to ask, whether you did E II 12 260 22
said, "I hope you did not venture far, Miss Fairfax, this E II 16 293 10 11
I really cannot venture to name her salary to you, Miss E III 8 382 23

thing that she could venture to say of the good wishes E III 8 384 34
after a little reflection, venture the following question. E III 11 410 36
"Harriet, I will only venture to declare, that Mr. E III 11 411 40
41
therefore, thus much I venture upon, that I will not P III 3 17 4
I venture to hint, that Sir Walter Elliot cannot be half P III 3 19 10
Anne was considering whether she should venture to suggest P IV 3 142 17
on the subject, she would venture on little more than P IV 5 159 22
"and not choosing to venture to Uppercross till he had an " P IV 6 164 8
Elizabeth, may we venture to present him and his wife in P IV 6 166 15
think that any body would venture their lives in such a P IV 6 169 25
"I would not venture over a horsepond in it. P IV 6 169 25
in his eye, and could not venture to believe that he had P IV 10 226 65
a person, at least I may venture to say that he has not S 1 366 1
not think he cd safely venture,--for I am sure there is S 9 407 1
"What! said he--do you venture upon two dishes of strong S 10 418 1

VENTURED (32)

own sex is concerned, ventured at length to vary the NA I 7 48 32
Miss Tilney continuing silent, she ventured to say, "her NA II 7 180 33
to Catherine, and ventured to hope, that henceforward some NA II 8 185 5
She ventured, when next alone with Eleanor, to express her NA II 8 186 7
fancy of her daughter, ventured to clear Mrs. Jennings SS I 8 37 3
Elinor then ventured to doubt the propriety of her SS I 12 58 3
and herself, he would not have ventured to mention it. SS I 18 100 30
his being in London, now ventured to say, "depend upon it SS II 5 169 14
her foregoing distress, ventured to communicate her hopes. SS III 7 314 22
Mrs. Dashwood feared to hazard any remark, and ventured SS III 11 355 46
increasing intimacy, and ventured to predict the PP II 1 133 2
to accept it, she ventured to engage for her attendance, PP III 2 264 11
at tea, that Elizabeth ventured to introduce the subject; PP III 6 299 19
engagements which I have ventured to make on your side, I PP III 7 302 14
She had ventured only one glance at Darcy. PP III 11 335 40
Philips, and she ventured, without any permission, to do PP III 13 350 55
son-in-law, that she ventured not to speak to him, unless PP III 17 378 46
the whole, now ventured to say, in her anxiety to suggest MP I 13 128 34
the explanation which I ventured to make for you to your MP III 4 353 46
She had ventured once alone to Randalls, but it was not E I 4 26 1
indeed that he should have ventured to address her. E I 8 61 37
We admired it so much, that I have ventured to write it E I 9 82 80
would hardly have ventured had there been much snow on the E I 13 115 39
of Mrs. Elton, Mrs. Weston ventured this apology for Jane. E II 15 285 16
could be ventured on, and it was all melancholy stagnation. E III 6 353 6
He ventured among them again, however, though his spirits P III 11 100 22
be understood, that she ventured to hope he did not always P III 11 100 23
seniority of mind, she ventured to recommend a larger P III 11 101 24
having," and when Anne ventured to speak her opinion of P IV 4 150 15
which she had almost ventured to depend on, and a P IV 5 153 7
When they were got a little farther, Anne ventured to P IV 6 170 30
a little Crescent to be ventured on--(as I trust we shall) S 4 380 1

VENTURESOME (1)

little venturesome for myself, or any body I loved!-- S 5 388 1

VENTURING (8)

Thorpe," said Catherine, venturing after some time to NA I 9 65 27
assertion, but from her venturing to trust her on so short SS II 1 142 7
or Lady Catherine de Bourgh, by venturing to dance. PP I 17 87 12
must have restrained her from venturing at disapprobation. MP I 18 170 24
the time of year; and venturing sometimes even to sit down MP II 4 208 11
Bates, let me propose your venturing on one of these eggs. E I 3 24 13
14
dissuade my father from venturing; but as he has made up E I 13 110 9
much, sir," said he, "in venturing out in such weather, E I 15 126 10

VERACITY (4)

in favour of Lucy's veracity; "I remember he told us, that SS I 22 134 49
dependance on Lucy's veracity might be, it was impossible SS II 1 139001
nature to question the veracity of a young man of such PP I 17 85 1
I can summon more than one witness of undoubted veracity. PP II 12 199 5

VERANDA (1)

dripping, and comfortless veranda, or even notice through P IV 1 123 8

VERB (1)

I use the verb 'to torment,' as I observed to be your own NA I 14 109 25

VERBAL (3)

indisposition, beyond one verbal inquiry, Elinor began to SS III 5 293 3
that a verbal postscript from himself wd be requisite.--" W 338 17
The invitation was refused, and by a verbal message. E III 9 389 16

VERDURE (5)

hill, whose beautiful verdure and hanging coppice render NA I 14 106 1
day was adding to the verdure of the early trees. she was PP II 12 195 2
and look upon verdure, is the most perfect refreshment." MP I 9 96 72
freshness, fragrance, and verdure, was infinitely worse;-- MP III 14 432 9
English verdure, English culture, English comfort, seen E III 6 360 39

VERIFIED (2)

disclaimed, and the gentleman's predictions were verified. NA II 1 133 29
We must not allow them to be verified in sweet Jane E II 15 283 5

VERILY (3)

at breakfast-time, I verily believe at the same instant; NA I 11 84 19
His behaviour to myself has been scandalous; but I verily PP I 16 78 20
And I verily beleive if my poor dear Sir Harry had never S 6 394 1

VERNONS (4)

I passed off the letter as his wife's, to the Vernons, & LS 5 250 3
Her beauty is much admired by the Vernons, but it has no LS 19 274 3
at Churchill with the Vernons; but you are fitted for LS 26 295 1
She may whimper, & the Vernons may storm; I regard them LS 39 308 1

VERSE (2)

clever, be it prose or verse, original or repeated--or two E III 7 370 23
histories are against you, all stories, prose and verse. P IV 11 234 27

VERSES (5)

However, he wrote some verses on her, and very pretty they PP I 9 44 31
Only think of those sweet verses--'to Miss ----.' E I 9 74 22
way; and another, to write verses and charades like this." E I 9 76 35
elbow, reading verses, or whispering to her, all day long." P IV 10 218 24
"With all my heart sir--apply any verses you like to it-- S 1 370 1

VESSEL (3)

thither in a private vessel, instead of waiting for the MP II 1 178 8
a vessel in the stocks which they all went to look at. MP III 10 403 15
dashed from the vessel and that Mr. Dixon caught her.-- E II 8 218 37

VESTIBULE (9)

The bustle in the vestibule, as she passed along an inner SS III 7 316 31
dawdled about in the vestibule to watch for the end of PP I 20 110 1
She was met in the vestibule by Lydia, who, flying to her, PP I 20 112 25
kiss, hurried into the vestibule, where Jane, who came PP III 5 286 22
They ran through the vestibule into the breakfast room; PP III 7 301 4
5
Lydia's voice was heard in the vestibule; the door was PP III 9 315 3
Price dripping with wet in the vestibule, was delightful. MP II 4 205 3
Dr. Grant was in the vestibule, and as they stopt to speak MP II 4 215 47
she heard some other person crossing the little vestibule. P III 9 79 25

VEX (9)

it tells me nothing that does not either vex or weary me. NA I 14 108 22
probably he did not think it would --vex me horridly.-- SS III 8 330 69
vex you more than you think for, if you stay at home.--" W 362 32
It would vex me, indeed, to see you again the dupe of Miss PP III 13 350 48
I suppose you have had as little to vex you, since you MP I 3 25 12
if nothing had occurred to vex her, till she found towards MP II 13 303 12
years in the world with very little to distress or vex her. E I 1 5 1
you; but I confess it does vex me, that we should be so P IV 4 151 18
away, that she might neither see nor hear more to vex her. P IV 10 227 67

VEXATION (44)

my great vexation with all your fears about your brother. LS 13 262 1
but be the occasion of so much vexation & trouble. LS 13 263 1
Guess my astonishment & vexation--for as you well know, I LS 22 280 1
have been spared the vexation of knowing of Reginald's LS 40 308 1
inconceivable vexation on every little trifling occurrence. NA I 8 56 11
We perfectly understand the present vexation; and every NA II 1 136 49
disappointment, some vexation, which just at this moment NA II 13 225 21
pained Edward, her own vexation at her want of thought SS I 18 98 12
difficulty govern her vexation at the tediousness of Mrs. SS II 4 165 24
"it is Colonel Brandon!" said she, with vexation. SS II 9 203 13
14
not have given her half the vexation that this does. SS III 5 297 31
& soften the evident vexation of her sister in law, Emma (W 353 26
no pains to conceal her vexation under the disappointment, W 360 30
to have their share of vexation; and it is better to know PP I 6 23 10
for to her inexpressible vexation, she could perceive that PP I 18 99 64
blushed and blushed again with shame and vexation. PP I 18 100 67
where his regret and vexation, and the concern of every PP I 21 115 3
was a constant source of vexation and regret; and in the PP II 14 212 17
who shed tears; but she did weep from vexation and envy. PP II 18 235 40
off by the defence of some little peculiar vexation." PP II 19 237 4
She was overpowered by shame and vexation. PP III 1 252 54
as she had ever been fidgetty from alarm and vexation. PP III 7 306 43
them so many previous months of suspense and vexation. PP III 13 347 28
to conceal her vexation and anger, till she reached home. MP I 7 70 30
his extreme surprise and vexation, and he walked to the MP I 10 101 33
left to sit down and stir the fire in thoughtful vexation. MP I 13 128 33
Fanny, and seating himself with a look of great vexation. MP I 15 139 9
Every body began to have their vexation. MP I 18 164 1
to their feelings of vexation, lamenting over such an MP II 1 176 4
unsuspected vexation was probably ready to burst on him. MP II 1 178 7
and her surprize and vexation required some minutes MP II 8 253 4
they had parted at last with mutual vexation. MP II 10 279 21
and comfort to Fanny was tediousness and vexation to Mary. MP II 11 285 15
Her vexation did not end with the week. MP II 11 286 16
he saw rather a flush of vexation, he inclined to hope MP III 3 344 44
no small portion of vexation and regret--vexation that MP III 17 468 22
of vexation and regret--vexation that must rise sometimes MP III 17 468 22
Emma remained in a state of vexation too; but there was E I 8 67 56
with a degree of vexation, which made Emma immediately E I 18 150 36
vexation Mr. Knightley's provoking indifference about it. E II 12 257 2
his fate, removed the chief of even Emma's vexation. E II 16 292 9
In spite of her vexation, she could not help feeling it E III 11 403 3
his evident surprise and vexation, at the substitution of P III 12 115 68
Another momentary vexation occurred. P IV 11 239 54

VEXATIONS (4)

There were great vexations however attending such a garden NA II 7 178 21
however, to increase her vexations, by dwelling on them. PP II 18 232 21
and little vexations seemed every where smoothed away. MP I 18 171 25
no escaping these little vexations, Mary, live where we MP II 4 213 35

VEXATIOUS (8)

usual employments, the vexatious interruptions of Mr. PP II 5 157 10
would be hastening to the same vexatious conclusion. PP III 11 337 54
To be neglected before one's time, must be very vexatious. MP I 5 51 41
It was very vexatious, and she was heartily sorry for it; MP I 12 114 2
Mr. Yates might consider it only as a vexatious MP II 1 175 1
confident, idle and expensive, it was every way vexatious. MP II 2 194 21
A thousand vexatious thoughts would recur. E II 14 270 3
"Is not this most vexatious, Knightley?" she cried.-- E III 6 353 7

VEXED (39)

now; but I am excessively vexed that Sir Reginald should LS 13 262 1
I think her as beautiful as an angel, and I am so vexed NA I 6 40 12
She could not help being vexed at the non-appearance of Mr. NA I 8 53 2
Catherine was disappointed and vexed. NA I 8 59 35
and Catherine, angry and vexed as she was, having no power NA I 11 87 53
You do not know how vexed I am.-- NA I 11 87 53
She was very much vexed, and meant to make her apology as NA I 12 94 10
entered his, without being vexed in some way or other, by NA II 7 178 23
He really felt conscientiously vexed on the occasion; for SS I 5 26 4
Marianne was vexed at it for her sister's sake, and turned SS I 7 34 5
her severely; she was vexed and half angry; but resolving SS I 16 89 42
Disappointed, however, and vexed as she was, and sometimes SS I 19 101 2
vexed at, for he has been always so anxious to get it! SS I 22 132 37
I was so vexed to see him stand up with her; but, however, PP I 3 13 16
"I beg you would not put it into Lizzy's head to be vexed PP I 5 19 10
It vexed her to see him expose himself to such a man. PP I 18 98 61
other; and deeply was she vexed to find that her mother PP I 18 98 63
And upon Elizabeth's seeming really, with vexed and PP I 19 104 6
and as Miss Bingley, vexed and disappointed, dared not PP III 3 270 11
Mr. Darcy's behaviour astonished and vexed her. PP III 12 339 1
a proposal; yet was really vexed that her mother should be PP III 17 374 21
Vexed as Edmund was with his mother and aunt, he was still MP I 7 74 58
Mrs. Norris was too much vexed to submit with a very good MP I 8 79 23
and let it pass; Julia was vexed, and her temper was hasty, MP I 10 101 29
to decide it; if she were vexed and alarmed--but Maria MP I 14 135 18
alarm; but she was vexed by the manner of his return. MP II 1 179 10
Miss Crawford was too much vexed by what had passed to be MP II 5 227 68
I am only vexed for a moment. MP II 9 268 31
better than I could tell you, how and why I am vexed. MP II 9 268 31
Fanny, meanwhile, vexed with herself for not having been MP III 3 342 32
She was almost vexed into displeasure, and anger, against MP III 13 424 4
He was very much vexed. E I 8 66 55
She was vexed. E I 15 125 4
She did look vexed, she did speak pointedly--and at last, E III 6 359 37
She was vexed beyond what could have been expressed-- E III 7 376 62
"But, Captain Wentworth," cried Louisa, "how vexed you P III 8 65 16
to her there; and vexed her as much when she was away, as P IV 4 146 5
and has a very large acquaintance, has time to be vexed. P IV 4 146 5
the consciousness of which vexed and embarrassed her, and P IV 10 222 36

VEXES (1)

the warmth of admiration vexes me; & if I did not know LS 8 256 3

VEXING (1)

You take delight in vexing me. PP I 1 5 28

VEXT (1)

She had a strong impression of his having said, in a vext P III 9 80 34

VICAR (2)

Mrs. Bates, the widow of a former vicar of Highbury, was a E I 3 21 4
and a very respectable vicar of Highbury, but not at all E I 8 66 53

VICAR OF WAKEFIELD (1)

And I know he has read the Vicar of Wakefield. E I 4 29 10

VICARAGE (12)

He had a comfortable income; for though the vicarage of E I 4 35 44
down the lane rose the vicarage; an old and not very good E I 10 83 2
been within side the vicarage, and her curiosity to see it E I 10 83 6
till within view of the vicarage pales, when a sudden E I 10 89 36
the vicarage was spent by him in expressing his discontent. E I 13 113 25
bear to have the poor old vicarage without a mistress. E II 3 174 35
such society and friendship as the vicarage had to offer. E II 15 285 12
great enjoyment at the vicarage, my dear Emma--but it is E II 15 285 17
both have great pleasure in seeing him at the vicarage." E II 18 305 4
and the vicarage, and every body was in good time. E III 7 367 1
the vicarage quarter, which was now graciously overcome.-- E III 16 455 20
objection raised, except in one habitation, the vicarage.-- E III 17 468 36

VICARAGE-LANE (4)

Their road to this detached cottage was down Vicarage-Lane, E I 10 83 2
carriage turned into Vicarage-Lane, or when it stopped, E I 15 132 37
a solitary drive from Vicarage-Lane--turning a corner E I 15 132 38
But I do not like the corner into Vicarage-Lane." E II 14 280 54

VICARAGE-PEW (1)

her to sit in in the vicarage-pew, that she might hear the E II 3 175 39

VICE (10)

spirits, playful as can be, but there is no vice in him." NA I 9 62 9
in every possible vice, going on from crime to crime, NA II 9 190 2
as the idleness and vice of many years continuance. PP II 13 206 4
console the unfortunate for their folly or their vice. PP II 19 236 1
It was an encouragement of vice; and had I been the rector PP III 15 364 22
"Not, I should hope, of the proportion of virtue to vice MP I 9 93 49

farther vice, though all was lost on the side of character. MP III 16 451 12
than Maria as folly than vice, he could not but regard the MP III 16 452 13
affording his sanction to vice, or in seeking to lessen MP III 17 465 13
morality, & incentives to vice from the history of it's S 8 404 1

VICES (3)
pine forests and their vices, they might give a faithful NA II 10 200 3
I cannot forget the follies and vices of others so soon as PP I 11 58 28
Of Rears, and vices, I saw enough. MP I 6 60 49

VICINITY (7)
a cabinet so mysteriously closed in her immediate vicinity. NA II 6 168 10
was a removal from the vicinity of Norland beyond her SS I 4 24 21
So near a vicinity to her mother and Meryton relations was PP III 19 385 3
vicinity of Sotherton, the former had considerable effect. MP I 8 81 33
Its vicinity to my own room--but in every respect indeed MP II 1 184 25
small hunting-box in the vicinity of every thing so dear-- MP III 10 405 19
Mr. Wingfield thinks the vicinity of Brunswick Square E I 12 103 37

VICIOUS (2)
The vicious propensities--the want of principle which he PP II 12 200 5
Admiral Crawford was a man of vicious conduct, who chose, MP I 4 41 15

VICISSITUDES (3)
so soothing in the vicissitudes of their eventful lives. NA I 1 15 3
The vicissitudes of the human mind had not yet been MP III 6 374 27
Abysses, it's quick vicissitudes, it's direful deceptions, S 7 396 1

VICTIM (1)
by seeing him fall a victim to her mother's rapacity for PP III 12 342 26

VICTIMS (1)
greater misery of the victims, I do not know where it lies. E II 17 300 15

VICTORY (5)
was produced, & at best, the honour of victory is doubtful. LS 25 294 6
spared a contest, where victory itself was painful; and NA I 14 106 1
with exultation at such a victory, and having thrown open NA II 6 168 10
Mrs. Bennet, who fancied she had gained a complete victory PP I 9 43 20
Such a victory over Edmund's discretion had been beyond MP I 17 158 1

VIE (2)
I hear of Everingham, it may vie with any place in England. MP I 6 60 53
bid fair by her merits to vie in favour with Sir Edward, S 3 377 1

VIEW (130)
Still they moved on--something better was yet in view; and NA I 2 21 9
had a comprehensive view of all the company beneath her, NA I 2 21 9
Union-Passage, and within view of the two gentlemen who NA I 7 44 1
very object she had had in view; and this persuasion did NA I 8 59 35
view, and when he spoke to her pretended not to hear him. NA I 10 74 23
The others walked away, John Thorpe was still in view, and NA I 10 75 24
striking; but I think I could place them in such a view.-- NA I 10 77 33
mischance; and were within view of the town of Keynsham, NA I 11 88 54
On the beginning of the fifth, however, the sudden view of NA I 12 92 4
as she came within view of them; and the servant still NA I 13 102 25
It seemed as if a good view were no longer to be taken NA I 14 110 28
commanded a tolerable view of every body entering at NA II 3 143 1
check is still in view--at once too much and too little." NA II 3 147 27
she caught the last view of Bath without any regret, and NA II 5 155 4
to her astonished eyes the view of a white cotton NA II 6 164 3
small drawers appeared in view, with some larger drawers NA II 6 168 10
like Miss Morland's, a view of the accommodations and NA II 8 184 4
collected within its view, maintain so elevated an air, NA II 9 190 2
as it was in every other view, was favourable here; and NA II 9 191 3
staircase, and in a few moments it gave Henry to her view. NA II 9 194 6
to the ground, and the view from them pleasant, though NA II 11 213 21
view before she was capable of turning her eyes towards it. NA II 14 230 1
than sought for the first view of that well-known spire NA II 14 232 6
This was just such a summary view of the affair as NA II 14 237 20
view, it was a match beyond the claims of their daughter. NA II 16 249 2
this spot, from whence perhaps I may view you no more!-- SS I 5 27 8
their dejection, and a view of Barton valley as they SS I 6 28 1
hills, and formed a pleasant view from the cottage windows. SS I 6 29 3
from their view at home by the projection of an hill. SS I 7 32 1
him, and in every point of view he was charmed with the SS I 7 33 3
on the other you have a view of the church and village, SS I 13 69 76
I never passed within view of it without admiring its SS I 14 73 17
the distance of their view from the cottage, from a spot SS I 16 85 15
view of the whole, which had exceedingly pleased him. SS I 18 96 4
with a sneer--"I came into Devonshire with no other view." SS I 20 113 30
for the point she had in view, in such a party as this was SS II 1 143 9
animating object in view, the same possibility of hope. SS II 4 159 1
beauty within their view drew from her an exclamation of SS II 4 160 2
every thing within her view would be bringing back the SS II 10 213 3
family, to have a nearer view of their characters and her SS II 12 231 9
into any profession with a view of better support, she SS III 1 267 38
The flaring lamps of a carriage were immediately in view. SS III 7 316 29
other intention, no other view in the acquaintance than to SS III 8 319 29
house as to admit a full view of the hill, the important SS III 10 344 12
13

it appear to her in every view, as one of the most SS III 13 364 10
it was only with the view imputed to him by his brother. SS III 14 376 11
herself at last within view of the house, with weary PP I 7 32 41
family he had a wife in view, as he meant to chuse one of PP I 15 70 2
it was merely with the view of enjoying her society that PP I 23 128 10
It is unaccountable! in every view it is unaccountable!" PP II 1 135 11
lived by trade, and within view of his own warehouses, PP II 2 139 2
parsonage, and every turning expected to bring it in view. PP II 5 155 2
he asked for, every view was pointed out with a minuteness PP II 5 156 4
the windows, to admire the view, Mr. Collins attending PP II 6 162 13
the whole morning within view of the lodges opening into PP II 7 170 7
to command a full view of the fair performer's countenance. PP II 8 174 12
and to complete the view, she saw herself seated beneath a PP II 18 232 22
saw and admired every remarkable spot and point of view. PP III 1 245 3
view; the turning past, he was immediately before them. PP III 1 254 57
admitted a most refreshing view of the high woody hills PP III 3 267 2
there, with no other view than what was acknowledged; but PP III 11 332 18
a nice long walk, and Mr. Darcy has never seen the view." PP III 17 374 23
Darcy professed a great curiosity to see the view from the PP III 17 375 25
kindness, and with that view endeavoured, in the first MP I 2 17 20
the park, and command a view of the parsonage and all its MP I 7 67 16
There can be no comparison as to one's view of the country. MP I 8 78 15
the highest spirits; "her view of the country was charming, MP I 8 81 32
at some pains to get a view of the house, and observing MP I 8 82 35
and commanding a view over them into the tops of the trees MP I 9 90 36
I must go and look through that iron gate at the same view, MP I 9 96 73
They expected to have a better view of the house from that MP I 10 102 47
any thing but pleasure in view, and his own will to MP I 12 114 2
meeting, and not a fine dinner, is all we have in view. MP II 4 215 49
the view is really very pretty; I am sure it may be done. MP II 7 242 23
moment and no more," to view the happy scene, and take a MP II 10 280 33
be more encouraging to a man who had her love in view? MP II 12 294 16
undertaken with no other view than that of introducing her MP II 13 300 7
was also to dine there, screened her a little from view. MP II 13 303 14
Your happiness and advantage are all that I have in view. MP III 2 331 16
And to be having any one's improvement in view in her MP III 9 398 9
enjoyments in the day and in the view which would be felt. MP III 11 409 5
The loveliness of the day, and of the view, he felt like MP III 11 409 7
with eyes closed as if the view of cheerfulness oppressed MP III 15 447 35
to some view of convenience on Mr. Yates's account. MP III 16 450 8
with a view to his relief and benefit, no less than theirs. MP III 16 452 15
the view and patronage of Mansfield Park, had long been. MP III 17 473 33
with these objects in view, till they were accomplished. E I 2 16 6
Another view of man, my second brings, behold him there, E I 9 71 14
Another view of man, my second brings; behold him there, E I 9 73 18
With the view of passing off an awkward moment, Emma E I 9 82 81
82

They now walked on together quietly, till within view of E I 10 89 36
every thing given to his view or his feelings, to stay at E I 13 113 26
with the sole view of marking my adoration of yourself. E I 15 131 31
other half she could give to her own view of the subject. E II 3 177 51
more important view that appeared than having his hair cut. E II 7 205 1
Upon the whole, she was equally contented with her view of E II 13 265 3
With Mr. Weston's ball in view at least, there had been a E II 13 267 8
circle--but that is not the change I had in view for you. E II 16 294 23
you, was all that I had in view; widely different E II 17 300 15
It led to nothing; nothing but a view at the end over a E III 6 360 38
walk, and the view which closed it extremely pretty.-- . E III 6 360 38
It was a sweet view--sweet to the eye and the mind. E III 6 360 39
and towards this view she immediately perceived Mr. E III 6 360 40
with pleasure; but in her view it was a morning more E III 8 377 1
Mr. Weston in keeping his secret, than with any other view. E III 10 394 19
Martin--he might have Mr. Martin's interest in view?"-- E III 11 410 36
for a fuller view of her face than it suited her to give. E III 13 425 2
with no selfish view, no view at all, but of endeavouring, E III 13 432 40
with no selfish view, no view at all, but of endeavouring, E III 13 432 40
What a view this gives of her sense of his behaviour!-- E III 15 447 22
many, very many, points of view in which she was now E III 15 449 35
She would not acknowledge that it was with any view of E III 17 461 1
visits, Emma having it in view that her gentle reasonings E III 17 465 28
same view of escaping introduction when they were to meet. P III 7 59 23
it, with the professed view of finding out the ships which P III 8 64 7
and the day, from the view of the last smiles of the year P III 10 84 7
and soon commanded a full view of the latter, at the foot P III 10 85 13
She was very much affected by the view of his disposition P III 10 91 42
forward by their present view, and she gladly gave him all P III 12 109 31
the view of supporting her hopes and raising her spirits. P III 12 116 70
Bath; caught the first dim view of the extensive buildings, P IV 2 135 34
In a worldly view, he had nothing to gain by being on P IV 3 140 11
to be equalled by the folly of what they have in view." P IV 3 144 20
In Lady Russell's view, it was perfectly natural that Mr. P IV 4 147 7
was more than excusable in the view of defeating her. P IV 4 151 22
as to have him in view the greater part of the street. P IV 7 178 28
life, had one object in view--to make his fortune, and by P IV 9 200 59
here for a time, with the view of renewing his former P IV 9 207 90
explains my view of the nature of their attachments. P IV 11 233 23
compliance for public view; and smiles reined in and P IV 11 240 59

VIEWED (5)
If aware of her having viewed him as a murderer, she could NA II 14 231 3
her offspring, were viewed therefore by Lady Middleton SS I 21 120 6
fairly warrant, as she viewed the respectable size and E III 6 358 35
It might be safely viewed with all its appendages of E III 6 360 40
It was the choicest gift of heaven; and Anne viewed her P IV 5 154 8

VIEWING (6)
They were viewing the country with the eyes of persons NA I 14 110 28
know what I suffer in now viewing you from this spot, from SS I 5 27 8
discrimination in viewing them himself than he possesses. SS I 18 97 6
of his viewing it all as his own future property. PP I 13 65 26
The possibility of meeting Mr. Darcy, while viewing the PP II 19 240 16
Instead of viewing them as a stranger, I might have PP III 1 246 6

VIEWS (68)
different situations and views,--that John was at Oxford, NA I 4 32 2
the present bounded her views: the present was now NA II 2 138 1
its members, and his own views on another, (circumstances NA II 15 245 12
comprehending his father's views, and being ordered to NA II 15 247 15
strictly attending to her views for his aggrandizement. SS I 4 22 18
because she has other views for him,) and on that account SS I 15 78 26
"What are Mrs. Ferrars's views for you at present, Edward?" SS I 17 90 2
what," said she after a short silence, "are your views? SS II 2 148 14
cherishing all her hopes, and promoting all her views! SS II 14 254 26
in short, as might establish all your views of happiness." SS III 4 289 28
However little known the feelings or views of such a man PP I 1 3 2
He had rather hoped that all his wife's views on the PP I 3 12 15
Miss Bennet's lovely face confirmed his views, and PP I 15 70 3
Her mother would talk of her views in the same PP I 18 100 67
remains to be told why my views were directed to Longbourn PP I 19 106 10
But of all the views which his garden, or which the PP II 5 156 4
now the consequence of views solely and hatefully PP II 13 207 6
to pardon his interference in the views of his friend. PP II 18 229 10
and all his views of domestic happiness were overthrown. PP II 19 236 1
wander, were many charming views of the valley, the PP III 1 253 57
by him, when all her views were overthrown, by seeing him PP III 12 342 26
When the subject was brought forward again, her views were MP I 1 9 10
as well as the sanguine views and spirits of the boy even MP I 2 21 34
his sister-in-law's views; and she was from that moment MP I 3 30 57
telling her of its fine views, and I have no doubt of her MP I 7 69 28
There were many other views to the shewn, and though the MP I 7 70 30
their views and their plans might be more comprehensive. MP I 10 97 4
We must rather adopt Mr. Crawford's views, and make the MP I 13 124 9
gradual increase of their views, the happy conclusion of MP II 1 184 27
It was plain that he could have so serious views, no true MP II 5 228 69
rather to forward his views of pleasing her, inasmuch as MP II 6 232 12
of strengthening his views in favour of Northamptonshire. MP II 7 247 37
was a stab;--for it told of his own convictions and views. MP II 9 264 17
was often under the influence of much less sanguine views. MP II 9 267 22
of his having any such views never entered his sister's MP II 12 291 5
twofold motives, in views and wishes more than could be MP II 13 300 7
and upright, whose views of happiness were all fixed on a MP III 2 328 6
comfort in the determined views and sanguine perseverance MP III 2 329 11
of satisfaction, and views of good over and above what he MP III 6 368 9
confirm all the daughter's views of happiness in being MP III 6 371 17
Whose views might it not affect? MP III 15 441 21
which bounded his views, but in triumphing over the MP III 17 468 21
Your views for Harriet are best known to yourself; but as E I 8 66 51
it is fair to suppose that views, and plans, and projects E I 8 66 51
Her views of improving her little friend's mind, by a E I 9 69 3
previous conceptions and views to hear him impartially, or E I 13 110 10
from her, excepting those views on the young man, of which E I 14 122 18
error with respect to your views, till this moment. E I 15 131 34
a misconception of your views; not being aware, probably, E I 15 132 36
her as aware of his views, accepting his attentions, E I 16 135 8
drawings of the place, views that he had taken himself. E II 1 160 20
With their wealth, their views increased; their want of a E II 7 207 6
dispel those gloomy ideas and give him cheerfuller views! E II 18 308 28
had only accomplished some views of St. Mark's Place, E III 6 363 53
They were looking over views in Swisserland. E III 6 364 59
in tranquil observation of the beautiful views beneath her. E III 7 374 54
not have been induced by any selfish views to go on.-- E III 14 438 8
I add?--too cheerful in my views to be captious.-- E III 14 442 8
Knightley, and was now forming all her views of happiness. E III 19 481 1
might be his hold or his views on Sir Walter, would rather P III 2 11 1
Lady Russell, whose first views on the projected change P III 2 14 10
As to Captain Wentworth's views, she deemed it of more P III 9 77 18
which closed all their views of alliance, and Captain P III 11 97 12
interests of Henrietta's views had better have placed her P III 12 103 5
to Colonel Wallis of his views on you--which said Colonel P IV 9 205 82
Mr. Elliot's having any views on me will not in the least P IV 9 205 83
were not arrived with any views of accommodation in that P IV 10 216 18
state of recently-improved views, of fresh-formed P IV 10 220 31

VIGILANCE (1)
in the cause by the vigilance & caution of Miss Diana P--. S 11 420 1

VIGOROUS (5)
are neither sound nor acute--neither vigorous nor keen. NA I 14 112 36
Perhaps Mrs. Jennings was in hopes, by this vigorous SS III 3 280 9
at least planning a vigorous prosecution of them in future. SS III 11 352 20
Vigorous, decided, with sentiments to a certain point, not E I 7 51 5
She wanted more vigorous measures, a more complete P III 2 12 3

VIGOROUSLY (4)
but, exerting herself vigorously to repel the ill-natured PP III 3 269 10
sat down and practised vigorously an hour and a half. E II 9 231 3
At this moment Frank began talking so vigorously, that E III 2 324 22
He had staid on, however, vigorously, day after day--till E III 13 433 41

VIGOUR (9)
genius, or vigour of mind which will force itself forward." LS 24 288 11
bloom, but not past the vigour of life; and with his eye NA I 10 80 59
Fanny paused a moment, and then, with fresh vigour, said, " SS II 14 253 23 24
with quite so much vigour as when they first came to SS III 11 352 20
height--well made & plump, with an air of healthy vigour.-- W 328 9
You give me fresh life and vigour. PP II 4 154 23
by manoeuvring and finessing, but by vigour and resolution. E I 18 146 16
cuts up a man's youth and vigour most horribly; a sailor P III 3 19 16
and vigour of form, which gave importance to her person. P III 6 48 18
VILE (4)
Thank God! we leave this vile place to-morrow. NA II 12 216 2
"As vile a spot as I ever saw in my life," said Mr. Palmer. SS I 20 111 15
"Such a horribly vile billiard-table as ours, is not to be MP I 13 125 14
Those vile sea-breezes are the ruin of beauty and health. MP III 12 416 3
VILLAGE (62)
a country village, for I am really going to Churchill. LS 2 245 1
about Fullerton, the village in Wiltshire where the NA I 1 17 12
a young lady in her own village, she must seek them abroad, NA I 1 17 12
But I, who live in a small retired village in the country, NA I 10 78 46
A cottage in some retired village would be extasy. NA I 15 120 20
endless in length; a village of hot-houses seemed to arise NA II 7 178 21
large and populous village, in a situation not unpleasant. NA II 11 212 17
and the size of the village; but in her heart she NA II 11 212 17
At the further end of the village, and tolerably NA II 11 212 17
and through part of the village, with a visit to the NA II 11 214 26
her career, to her native village, in the triumph of NA II 14 232 7
drive through the village, amid the gaze of Sunday groups, NA II 14 232 7
The village of Barton was chiefly on one of these hills, SS I 6 29 3
was in their favourite village, and she soon found out SS I 9 43 11
a view of the church and village, and, beyond them, of SS I 13 69 76
and wandered about the village of Allenham, indulging the SS I 16 83 2
"I am going into the village to see my horses," said he, " SS I 18 96 3
in his walk to the village, he had seen many parts of the SS I 18 96 4
to advantage; and the village itself, in a much higher SS I 18 96 4
A butcher hard by in the village, and the parsonage-house SS II 8 197 22
I hear it is a large village,--indeed there certainly must SS III 9 338 24
walked out towards the village--leaving the others in the SS III 12 360 26
the mistress of a family, and the patroness of a village. SS III 14 378 16
the Watsons inhabited a village about 3 miles distant, W 314 1
said he--I met her in the village of Stanton, whither my W 338 18
"Your road through the village is infamous, eliz:; said he, W 349 24
time of the day, for the village was on no very public W 354 28
spirits to Longbourn, the village where they lived, and of PP I 3 12 15
The village of Longbourn was only one mile from Meryton; a PP I 7 28 3
sallied forth into the village to settle their differences, PP II 7 169 4
gone on business into the village, when she was startled PP II 9 177 1
enter my house again, nor even to pass through the village. PP III 6 300 30
"Did you go by the village of Kympton?" PP III 10 328 24
of Sir Thomas's in the village, and consoled herself for MP I 3 23 1
when the society of the village received an addition in MP I 4 40 15
no, nothing of that kind could be hired in the village. MP I 6 58 35
gently rising beyond the village road; and in Dr. Grant's MP I 7 67 16
the hill together to the village; nor did her attendant do MP I 7 69 21
Here begins the village. MP I 8 82 34
Fanny, having been sent into the village on some errand by MP II 4 205 3
"The sweets of housekeeping in a country village!" said MP II 4 212 32
midst of a retired little village between gently rising MP II 7 241 13
road through the village, must be all laid together of MP II 7 242 23
walking together through the village, as he rode into it.-- MP III 3 334 1
Highbury, the large and populous village almost amounting E I 1 7 10
acquainted with the whole village, and found matter of E II 6 196 2
close by her, in the village of Kellynch; and on her P III 1 5 6
of so altered a village, and be out of the way when P III 5 36 19
Uppercross was a moderate-sized village, which a few years P III 5 36 20
business, are gadding about the village, all day long. P III 6 45 9
to walk to the end of the village with the sportsmen: the P III 7 59 25
It would place her in the same village with Captain P III 11 93 2
varieties of the cheerful village of up Lyme, and, above P III 11 95 9
tenements of the village, without a saddened heart.-- P IV 1 123 8
visit of charity in the village, without wondering whether P IV 2 133 26
not to a small village like Sanditon, precluded by its S 1 368 1
A very few years ago, & it had been a quiet village of no S 2 371 1
They were now approaching the church & neat village of S 4 382 1
The village contained little more than cottages, but the S 4 383 1
in the success of the village itself; for considering it S 4 383 1
If the village could attract, the hill might be nearly S 4 383 1
a single Lodger in the village!--nor did he remember any S 4 383 1
VILLAGERS (1)
a troop of tidy, happy villagers please me better than the SS I 18 98 8
VILLAIN (4)
growing a fine hardened villain, fancying myself SS III 8 326 53
believing me the greatest villain upon earth, scorning, SS III 8 330 69
Frank Churchill was a villain.-- E III 13 433 42
the perseverance, of the villain of the story outweighed S 8 404 1
VILLAINS (1)
He cannot be the instigator of the three villains in NA II 1 131 15
VILLANOUS (1)
invectives against the villanous conduct of Wickham, and PP III 5 287 34
VILLANY (1)
which proclaimed its writer to be deep in hardened villany. SS II 7 183 14
VILLAS (1)
There are some charming little villas about Richmond." NA I 15 120 20
VINDICATED (1)
They vindicated him against the base aspersion. E II 16 297 51
VINDICATING (1)
He was anxious, while vindicating himself, to say nothing MP II 2 187 1
VINDICATION (7)
to the other in her vindication, had no means of knowing. NA I 13 102 26
remark, attempted no vindication of Willoughby, and seemed SS II 10 212 1
and a very earnest vindication of Edward from every charge SS III 1 261 12
not but have heard his vindication for the world, and now SS III 9 334 6
Mrs. Dashwood did not hear unmoved the vindication of her SS III 11 349 1
Nor was Darcy's vindication, though grateful to her PP II 17 225 9
on to say something in vindication of his behaviour to PP III 1 258 75
VINDICTIVE (1)
it shews an illiberal & vindictive spirit to resent a LS 5 249 1
VINE (1)
own neat garden, with a vine and a pear-tree trained round P III 5 36 20
VINEGAR (1)
Suppose you let her have your aromatic vinegar; I always MP I 7 72 45
VINGT-UN (4)
Vingt-un is the game at osborne castle; I have played W 358 28
osborne castle; I have played nothing but vingt-un of late. W 358 28
me!--cried Margt why should not we play at vingt-un?-- W 358 28
that they both like vingt-un better than commerce; but PP I 6 22 9
VIOLATED (2)
"No principle of either, would be violated by my marriage PP III 14 358 70
to me, all risk would incurred, and all duty violated." P IV 11 244 73
VIOLATING (1)
A girl who, before his eyes, is violating an engagement NA II 10 205 30
VIOLATION (4)
them, so gross a violation of every thing right could PP II 13 208 6
It is really too great a violation of decency, honour, and PP III 5 282 3
I should have thought it a gross violation of duty and MP III 1 319 39
seeing the letter was a violation of the laws of honour, P IV 9 204 76 77
VIOLENCE (19)
The violence of her feelings, which must wear her out, may LS 39 308 1
Cautions against the violence of such noblemen and NA I 2 18 2
checked with a violence which almost threw him on his NA I 7 44 3
by some strange violence; and, on the centre of the lid, NA II 6 163 2
quit her hold, and the lid closed with alarming violence. NA II 6 164 3
violence, ordered "dinner to be on table directly!" NA II 6 165 5
It could be nothing but the violence of the wind NA II 6 167 10
but was, with gentle violence, forced to return; and the NA II 10 203 8
They encouraged each other now in the violence of their SS I 1 7 13
Such violence of affliction indeed could not be supported SS I 16 83 4
eyes with passionate violence--a reproach, however, so SS II 9 202 8
If the violence of her passions, the weakness of her SS III 8 322 36
the same time without any theatrical grimace or violence.-- W 343 20
the most animated language of the violence of my affection. PP I 19 106 10
and talking with more violence than ever; whilst the PP II 18 230 12
give some relief to the violence of these transports, by PP III 7 306 45
bursts, no tread of violence was ever heard; all proceeded MP III 8 391 11
a while, and when the violence of grief was comforted away, E II 13 268 13
have worn out on each side equally, and without violence. P IV 6 172 42
VIOLENT (40)
I was quite cool, but he gave way to the most violent LS 22 282 7
of a man whose passions were so violent and resentful. LS 25 292 1
But these measures are each too violent to be adopted LS 25 293 4
on considerable weariness and a violent desire to go home. NA I 9 60 1
after your arrival, you will probably have a violent storm. NA II 5 159 19
forming wise resolutions with the most violent dispatch. NA II 6 165 5
A violent gust of wind, rising with sudden fury, added NA II 6 170 12
or remorse; till a violent death or a religious retirement NA II 9 190 2
Leaning back in one corner of the carriage, in a violent NA II 14 230 1
spot ceased to raise the violent emotion which it produced SS I 3 14 1
"Had he been only in a violent fever, you would not have SS I 8 38 13
the parlour apparently in violent affliction, with her SS I 15 75 2
compassion of that violent sorrow which Marianne was in SS I 15 77 20
This violent oppression of spirits continued the whole SS I 15 82 47
of gentleness, such violent screams, as could hardly be SS I 21 121 10
Business on Sir John's part, and a violent cold on her own, SS II 5 170 28
which at first was scarcely less violent than Marianne's. SS II 7 182 12
For where she does dislike, I know it is most violent." SS II 13 240 17
She fell into violent hysterics immediately, with such SS III 1 259 7
accompanied by violent agitation, nor impetuous grief.-- SS III 1 261 12
Marianne a cold so violent, as, though for a day or two SS III 6 305 17
sir--be quick--and if you can--less violent." SS III 8 317 5
Marianne gave a violent start, fixed her eyes upon Elinor, SS III 11 353 24
of Mrs. Ferrars, just so violent and so steady as to SS III 14 373 1
Amongst the most violent against him was Mrs. Bennet, PP I 3 11 6
that she had caught a violent cold, and that they must PP I 7 33 44
of "Lord, how tired I am!" accompanied by a violent yawn. PP I 18 103 75
Pray, how violent was Mr. Bingley's love?" PP II 2 141 8
up stairs in a violent hurry, and calling loudly after her. PP II 5 158 11
he was doubtless as violent in his abuse of me to others, PP II 12 201 5
The general prejudice against Mr. Darcy is so violent, PP II 17 226 23
obliged to leave off in a violent hurry, as Mrs. Forster PP II 19 238 5
She was now in an irritation as violent from delight, as PP III 7 306 43
these violent young lovers carry every thing their own way. PP III 17 377 39
He looked very ill; evidently suffering under violent MP III 15 445 30
Mr. Elton actually making violent love to her: availing E I 15 129 24
the real cause of that violent dislike of Mr. Knightley's E III 15 449 35
enthusiasm and violent agitation seldom really possess. P IV 4 146 6
Anne heard her, and made no violent exclamations. P IV 5 159 22
the attack was not very violent--nearly over by the time S 9 407 1
VIOLENTLY (14)
chose to set herself so violently against the match, that LS 2 245 1
"It is Mr. De Courcy, said she, colouring violently, Mama LS 20 275 1
Frederica had set herself violently against marrying Sir LS 24 288 11
part of the hanging more violently agitated than the rest. NA II 5 159 19
the time the party broke up, it blew and rained violently. NA II 6 166 9
truth was less violently outraged than usually happens. SS I 10 46 2
And soon afterwards, on the second boy's violently SS I 21 121 8
she saw her spirits less violently irritated than before, SS II 10 212 1
whom he was violently in love with only a few days before." PP II 2 140 7
"But that expression of 'violently in love' is so PP II 2 140 8
wondered why, without violently caring for her, he chose PP III 9 318 19
as warmly as a man violently in love can be supposed to do. PP III 16 366 8
But whether she were violently set against the match, or PP III 17 375 27
against the match, or violently delighted with it, it was PP III 17 375 27
VIOLIN (2)
the first scrape of one violin, blessed the ears of her W 327 7
the late acquisition of a violin player in the servants' MP I 12 117 11
VIOLINS (2)
couple, with two violins, and a mere side-board collation. SS II 5 170 29
They were in the ball-room, the violins were playing, and MP II 10 275 10
VIOLONCELLO (1)
of a harp, and a violoncello, would fix them at pleasure SS II 14 250 11
VIRANDA (1)
Cottage, with its viranda, French windows, and other P III 5 36 20
VIRTUE (21)
epitaph, in which every virtue was ascribed to her by the NA II 9 190 1
But it is not often that virtue can boast an interest such NA II 9 196 23
that fire, which at once announce virtue and intelligence. SS I 3 17 18
offence against virtue, in his behaviour to Eliza Williams. SS III 11 352 16 17
It has connected him nearer with virtue than any other PP I 16 81 39
talents or miraculous virtue, and the mere stateliness of PP II 6 161 9
established him at once in the possession of every virtue. PP II 13 206 4
by the predominance of virtue, atone for those casual PP II 13 206 4
that in the eye of a servant comprehends every virtue." PP III 1 258 74
that neither her virtue nor her understanding would PP III 4 279 24
decency and virtue in such a point should admit of doubt. PP III 5 283 10
lesson; that loss of virtue in a female is irretrievable-- PP III 5 289 43
stronger than their virtue, she could easily conjecture. PP III 8 312 17
But make a virtue of it by all means. PP III 18 381 7
"Not, I should hope, of the proportion of virtue to vice MP I 9 93 49
all the dignity of angry virtue, in the grounds of MP III 2 328 7
much as ought to be expected from human virtue at fourteen. MP III 15 444 26
not one of the barriers, which society gives to virtue. MP III 17 468 22
of extraordinary virtue from those, for whom education had E I 10 86 24
Mr. Weston, on his side, added a virtue to the account E II 7 206 3
Fine dancing, I believe, like virtue, must be its own E II 12 258 3
VIRTUES (8)
He must have all Edward's virtues, and his person and SS I 3 18 20
"I do not dispute his virtues--but I do not like his W 340 19
of all her many virtues, from her obliging manners down to MP I 11 112 33
We must not be nice and ask for all the virtues into the E I 18 149 29
and your popularity will stand upon your own virtues." E II 6 200 15
as well as to all her virtues, would be the highest P IV 5 159 25
in its domestic virtues than in its national importance. P IV 12 252 12
by the tranquil & morbid virtues of any opposing character. S 8 404 1
VIRTUOUS (3)
and in spite of all her virtuous indignation, she found NA II 7 181 41
of such rational employment and virtuous self-controul. SS III 10 343 10
are not only natural, they are philanthropic and virtuous. MP III 14 434 13
VIRULENCE (1)
the most ingratiating virulence,--the dear lock--all, SS III 8 329 63
VISCOUNT (3)
The influence of the viscount and viscountess in their NA II 16 251 6
Sir Walter had once been in company with the late viscount, P IV 4 148 12
death of that said late viscount, when, in consequence of P IV 4 148 12
VISCOUNTESS (5)
The influence of the viscount and viscountess in their NA II 16 251 6
arrival of the Dowager Viscountess Dalrymple, and her P IV 4 148 10
three lines of scrawl from the Dowager Viscountess. P IV 4 149 13
the cards of Dowager Viscountess Dalrymple, and the hon. P IV 4 149 13
back of the Dowager Viscountess Dalrymple before her, had P IV 8 185 20
VISIBLE (10)
her; but to the other two her distress was equally visible. NA II 10 203 8

the disturbance of his mind was visible in every feature. PP II 11 190 8
such as had been already visible below, she had willingly PP III 1 250 46
could hardly restrain her astonishment from being visible. PP III 2 263 10
calm; and no change was visible in either, except that the PP III 5 289 41
The same anxiety to get them by themselves, was visible PP III 13 344 11
She had no visible friends but what had been acquired at E I 3 23 8
day, which only made such cruel sights the longer visible. E III 12 421 18
There was no wound, no blood, no visible bruise; but her P III 12 109 33
they might be most visible; and "our cousins in laura- P IV 4 149 13
VISIBLY (6)
She blushed at this hint; but it was even visibly SS I 13 69 76
At the end of another day or two, Marianne growing visibly SS III 10 340 4
for the gloves which were visibly compressed in his hand.-- W 336 13
been so much to her, should not be more visibly regretted. MP III 6 366 3
feelings, they were visibly forming themselves into as E I 9 69 2
history of the large room visibly added; it had been built E II 6 197 5
VISION (1)
or see him with clear vision, was very well satisfied with E I 13 110 10
VISIONS (5)
The visions of romance were over. NA II 10 199 1
Afterwards, when familiarized with the visions of MP III 6 369 11
Visions of good and ill breeding, of old vulgarisms and MP III 15 446 35
These were thoughts, with their attendant visions, which P IV 8 186 22
may not have some flying visions of attending the next P IV 9 208 92
VISIT (319)
immediately--& as such a visit is in all probability LS 3 246 1
to her to visit us at Churchill perfectly unnecessary. LS 3 247 1
But I cannot forget the length of her visit to the LS 6 252 2
St, especially as every visit is so many hours deducted LS 7 252 1
visit which my brother's company would otherwise give me. LS 8 255 1
his visit, I should regret Mr Vernon's giving him any. LS 8 256 3
in the length of my visit, she would do more justice to us LS 14 264 2
not on my account shorten your visit here, even an hour. LS 25 292 3
society must; & my visit has already perhaps been too long. LS 25 293 3
His long visit is about to be concluded at last, but I LS 27 296 1
That unlucky visit to Langford! LS 38 307 3
You have owed us a visit many long weeks. LS 40 309 1
unexpected & unwelcome visit from Lady Susan, looking all LS 41 309 1
her press for an early visit to London; & Mr Vernon who, LS 42 311 2
Frederica's visit was nominally for six weeks; but her LS 42 313 7
thing of her, when you wrote to me after your visit there." NA I 7 50 48
a beating heart to pay her visit, explain her conduct, and NA I 12 91 3
With such news to communicate, and such a visit to prepare NA I 15 124 47
Catherine's expectations of pleasure from her visit in NA II 1 129 1
Isabella, on hearing the particulars of the visit, gave a NA II 1 129 1
If you can be induced to honour us with a visit, you will NA II 2 139 7
post their ready consent to her visit to Gloucestershire. NA II 2 140 11
promise, their first visit in consequence was to the NA II 9 191 3
tenderness which would prompt a visit like yours. NA II 9 196 23
I wish your visit at Northanger may be over before Captain NA II 10 202 7
of the village, with a visit to the stables to examine NA II 11 214 26
throughout the whole visit, so well assured was her mind NA II 11 215 28
in the fourth week of her visit; before the General came NA II 13 220 1
suppose that a much longer visit had been promised--and NA II 13 221 2
That would be turning your visit into an evil indeed. NA II 15 241 4
that this good-natured visit would at least set her heart NA II 15 242 8
A very short visit to Mrs. Allen, in which Henry talked at NA II 15 243 10
resulting from a long visit at Northanger, by which my NA II 16 251 5
to inhabit or visit it while such a woman was its mistress. SS I 4 24 20
and Mrs. John Dashwood to visit her at Barton; and to SS I 5 25 3
could be assured that her visit would be no inconvenience; SS I 6 30 7
and warmth; and her visit was long enough to detract SS I 6 31 8
On every formal visit a child ought to be of the party, by SS I 6 31 9
sang to them; and when the visit was returned by the SS I 8 36 1
to visit any family beyond the distance of a walk. SS I 9 40 2
that passed during the visit, tended to assure him of the SS I 10 46 1
and long before his visit concluded, they conversed with SS I 10 47 3
he had formed parties to visit them, at least, twice every SS I 12 62 28
The sudden termination of Colonel Brandon's visit at the SS I 14 70 1
Mrs. Dashwood's visit to Lady Middleton took place the SS I 15 75 1
to Barton, whither he was purposely coming to visit them. SS I 16 86 22
His visit afforded her but a very partial satisfaction, SS I 18 96 1
The shortness of his visit, the steadiness of his purpose SS I 19 102 2
She came in with a smile, smiled all the time of her visit, SS I 19 106 22
not think Mr. Palmer would visit him, for he is in the SS I 20 114 44
was very soon to receive a visit from two girls whom she SS I 21 118 2
When their promised visit to the park and consequent SS I 21 120 6
and since Edward's visit, they had never dined together, SS I 21 125 36
and alarming; and Edward's visit near Plymouth, his SS II 1 139 1
have been wanting us to visit them these several years! SS II 2 151 40
The visit of the Miss Steeles at Barton Park was SS II 2 151 43
her endeavour to prevent a visit, which she could not SS II 3 154 6
February; and that their visit, without any unreasonable SS II 3 157 15
inform her, that Willoughby had paid no second visit there. SS II 5 169 16
both attend her on such a visit, Elinor had some SS II 5 170 28
misfortune, carried me to visit him in a spunging-house, SS II 9 207 26
he put an end to his visit, receiving from her again the SS II 9 211 43
means not to shorten their visit to Mrs. Jennings; the SS II 10 213 3
her while paying that visit at Allenham on his marriage, SS II 10 213 4
great deal too far off to visit; she hated him so much SS II 10 215 10
"Why, their visit is but just begun!" SS II 10 219 35
their's, she should pay her visit and return for them. SS II 11 220 2
His visit was duly paid. SS II 11 222 14
his sisters, in his next visit at Gray's, his thoughts SS II 11 226 41
at home, and Sir John came in before their visit ended. SS II 11 228 52
visit should begin a few days before the party took place. SS II 12 230 8
and Mrs. Ferrars will visit now;--and Mrs. Ferrars and SS II 13 240 15
had his visit lasted two hours, soon afterwards went away. SS II 13 244 43
made use of; and the visit to Lady Middleton, which had SS II 14 254 26
from her ordinary visit to Mrs. Palmer, entered the SS III 1 257 2
3

The next morning brought a farther trial of it, in a visit SS III 1 265 33
of effusion, concluded his visit; and with repeated SS III 1 269 57
from the first to pay a visit of comfort and inquiry to SS III 2 270 3
alive, I shall be paying a visit at Delaford parsonage SS III 4 292 57
Elinor began to feel it necessary to pay her a visit.-- SS III 5 293 3
out by herself to pay a visit, for which no one could SS III 5 294 3
would now least chuse to visit, or wish to reside; for not SS III 6 301 2
parted, gave her a pressing invitation to visit her there. SS III 6 301 2
every symptom more favourable than on the preceding visit. SS III 7 310 8
Mr. Harris was punctual in his second visit;--but he came SS III 7 313 21
as the last, and his visit concluded with encouraging SS III 7 313 21
strangeness of such a visit, and of such manners, seemed SS III 8 318 16
17

of my time that I had bestowed on her, in my present visit. SS III 8 323 40
The past, the present, the future, Willoughby's visit, SS III 9 333 3
her mother, Colonel Brandon was invited to visit her. SS III 10 340 1
it by a visit at the cottage, in the course of a few weeks. SS III 10 341 4
visit were consequently spent in hearing and in wondering. SS III 13 370 35
After a visit on Colonel Brandon's side of only three or SS III 13 372 46
for she was able to visit Edward and his wife in their SS III 14 374 7
her in time, another visit, another conversation, was SS III 14 376 11
He was also obliged to put an end to his visit--for Mrs W 340 19
Tho' Emma could not but take the compliment of the visit W 345 21
To say that Emma was not flattered by Ld Osborne's visit, W 347 22
known that he wished the visit without presuming to make W 347 22
I cannot return the visit.-- W 348 22
A week or ten days rolled quietly away after this visit, W 348 23
return of Margaret, & a visit of two or three days from Mr W 348 23
Such a visit as this, I never heard of!-- W 350 24
imported that she meant to take the visit to herself.-- W 355 28
length of Robert & Jane's visit, was continually invaded W 360 30

and therefore you must visit him as soon as he comes." PP I 1 4 18
account, for in general you know they visit no new comers. PP I 1 4 24
will be impossible for us to visit him, if you do not." PP I 1 4 24
if twenty such should come since you will not visit them." PP I 1 5 32
dear, that when there are twenty, I will visit them all." PP I 1 5 33
He had always intended to visit him, though to the last PP I 2 6 1
after the visit was paid, she had no knowledge of it. PP I 2 6 1
said her mother resentfully, "since we are not to visit." PP I 2 6 3
It is very unlucky; but as I have actually paid the visit, PP I 2 7 22
visit, and determining when they should ask him to dinner. PP I 2 8 28
In a few days Mr. Bingley returned Mr. Bennet's visit, and PP I 3 9 3
that she would, and the argument ended only with the visit. PP I 5 20 23
The visit was returned in due form. PP I 6 21 1
she longed for such a visit, was delighted at her entrance. PP I 7 33 43
to visit Jane, and form her own judgment of her situation. PP I 9 41 1
other during the whole visit, and the result of it was, PP I 9 45 35
occasionally for a week or two, to visit his relations. PP I 14 66 1
and had once paid him a visit in his humble parsonage; PP I 14 66 1
single evening during his visit were most steadily PP I 16 75 1
as you can, bring her to Hunsford, and I will visit her.' PP I 19 106 10
might shorten his visit, but his plan did not appear in PP I 21 115 2
his other engagements might allow him to visit them. PP I 22 123 4
Lucas paid her farewell visit; and when she rose to take PP II 3 145 11
refuse, though she foresaw little pleasure in the visit. PP II 3 146 17
she must wait for her own visit there, to know the rest. PP II 3 147 19
She wrote again when the visit was paid, and she had seen PP II 3 147 23
My visit was not long, as Caroline and Mrs. Hurst were PP II 3 147 23
Caroline did not return my visit till yesterday; and not a PP II 3 148 26
also of Miss Bingley's visit in Gracechurch-Street, and PP II 4 152 6
She had also to anticipate how her visit would pass, the PP II 5 157 10
the whole day or next morning, but their visit to Rosings. PP II 6 160 4
Sir William staid only a week at Hunsford; but his visit PP II 7 168 1
In this quiet way, the first fortnight of her visit soon PP II 7 169 6
at last only suppose his visit to proceed from the PP II 9 180 28
It was some consolation to think that his visit to Rosings PP II 11 188 1
his visit to a wish of hearing that she were better. PP II 11 189 3
that your Hunsford visit cannot have been entirely irksome. PP II 15 215 4
In Lydia's imagination, a visit to Brighton comprised PP II 18 232 22
would bring his sister to visit her, the very day after PP III 2 260 1
of a small market-town, where the family did not visit. PP III 2 265 14
The next variation which their visit afforded was produced PP III 3 268 6
of the family intended a visit to Georgiana that morning. PP III 3 268 8
Their visit did not continue long after the question and PP III 3 270 12
had occurred, during their visit, as they returned, except PP III 3 271 20
"You are quite a visit in my debt, Mr. Bingley," she added, PP III 11 338 58
of Bingley, in half an hour's visit, had revived. PP III 12 339 10
that the whole of the visit would not pass away without PP III 12 340 14
A few days after this visit, Mr. Bingley called again, and PP III 13 344 1
which this extraordinary visit threw Elizabeth into, could PP III 15 360 1
before many days had passed after Lady Catherine's visit. PP III 16 365 1
over every morning visit; and as she was no longer PP III 19 386 5
them again, even for a visit, nobody at home seemed to MP I 2 21 34
Luckily the visit happened in the Christmas holidays, when MP I 2 21 34
ten miles of indifferent road, to pay a morning visit. MP I 4 39 10
dinner visit; "they are very elegant, agreeable girls." MP I 5 45 4
home, and Henry equally ready to lengthen his visit. MP I 5 47 26
day, understand why a visit from the family were not to be MP I 8 77 9
intimate friend of Mr. Bertram's just arrived on a visit. MP I 12 117 11
You will be to visit me in prison with a basket of MP I 14 135 17
you will not refuse to visit me in prison? I think I see MP I 14 135 17
my sister to pay the first visit, I am as certain as I sit MP II 2 188 3
My object was accomplished in the visit." MP II 2 190 5
from her, and the farewell visit, as it then became openly MP II 2 193 18
He must like him less after to-morrow's visit, for we MP II 3 199 18
might have enjoyed her visit could she have believed MP II 4 206 4
of her first dinner visit, when she found herself in an MP II 6 233 14
in the course of that very visit, that he first began to MP II 7 238 2
Fanny's last feeling in the visit was disappointment--for MP II 7 251 66
be the last day of his visit; but where the days were so MP II 8 253 7
which claimed a long visit from her in London, and of the MP II 8 256 12
nothing but the friends she was to visit, was before her. MP II 8 256 12
the object of her intended visit; and in the kindest MP II 8 258 15
She gave the history of her recent visit, and now her MP II 9 262 11
coming for a moment to visit her and working away his MP II 10 279 23
if she had wasted half his visit in idle cares and selfish MP II 11 282 2
Fanny had hoped, in the course of his yesterday's visit, MP III 1 311 1
during the whole of his visit, unless actually sent for; MP III 1 311 2
pause, proceeded in his account of Mr. Crawford's visit. MP III 1 313 15
The promised visit from her "friend," as Edmund called MP III 5 356 4
better time for the visit--but now I cannot put her off. MP III 5 359 12
sick of home before her visit ended; and that a little MP III 6 369 9
walk on the ramparts, no visit to the dock-yard, no MP III 8 388 2
that occurred of what this visit might lead to, were MP III 10 399 4
to Portsmouth neither on a visit to the port-admiral, nor MP III 10 400 7
they came out expressly to visit; and it did not delay MP III 10 403 13
"And it is to be a two months' visit, is not it?" MP III 11 410 12
except this said visit to Portsmouth, and these two said MP III 12 415 2
in Portsmouth, I hope, but this must not be a yearly visit. MP III 13 423 2
three weeks before, on a visit to some relations of Sir MP III 16 450 8
chusing that time to pay a visit to her other friends, in MP III 17 466 18
Christmas brought the next visit from Isabella and her E I 1 7 9
are the poor horses to be while we are paying our visit?" E I 1 8 17
His coming to visit his father had been often talked of E I 2 17 8
a most proper attention, that the visit should take place. E I 2 17 9
Miss Bates, or when Mrs. and Miss Bates returned the visit. E I 2 17 9
For a few days every morning visit in Highbury included E I 2 18 9
acquaintance, but such as would visit him on his own terms. E I 3 20 1
just returned from a long visit in the country to some E I 3 23 8
of the pleasures of her visit, and describe the many E I 4 27 4
But while I visit at Hartfield, and you are so kind to me, E I 4 31 23
certainly I had better not visit her, if I can help it." E I 4 31 25
return to Hartfield, to make a regular visit of some days. E I 8 57 1
Her visit to abbey-mill, this summer, seems to have done E I 8 59 25
Emma had a charitable visit to pay to a poor sick family, E I 10 83 1
together which she came to visit; and after remaining E I 10 86 24
25

His visit he would now defer; but they had a very E I 10 87 31
apprehensively happy in forestalling this too short visit. E I 11 91 2
The beginning, however, of every visit displayed none but E I 11 93 5
was now making her first visit to Hartfield, and very E I 12 98 2
and excellent aunt, when she comes to visit them! E I 12 104 46
Knightley, in this short visit to Hartfield, going about E I 13 108 1
It was a delightful visit;--perfect, in being much too E I 13 108 1
comfortless visit, and of their all missing her very much. E I 13 109 6
returning from the daily visit to Donwell, with his two E I 13 109 6
inclination to give up the visit;--but Emma, too eager and E I 13 110 10
made up his mind to the visit, that in spite of the E I 13 112 24
anticipated nothing in the visit that could be at all E I 13 113 25
Emma smiled and answered--"my visit was of use to the E I 13 114 32
This was a pleasure which perhaps the whole day's visit E I 14 117 2
he was announcing an early visit from his son; but before E I 14 118 4
that the rest of the visit could not possibly pass without E I 14 119 6
are invited to pay a visit at Enscombe in January; and E I 14 120 11
"And so you do not consider this visit from your son as by E I 14 122 20
19

circumstance of his coming away from them to visit us." E I 14 123 27
temper and happiness when this visit of hardship were over. E I 15 128 21
that he ought to pay this visit to his father; and while E I 18 147 18
kindness, thanks for their visit, solicitude for their E II 1 155 4
her; and now, when the due visit was paid, on her arrival, E II 2 167 12
In short, when she sat, during the first visit, looking at Jane E II 2 167 13
be denying herself this visit to Ireland, and resolving to E II 2 168 13

judged it best for her to return Elizabeth Martin's visit. E II 4 185 11
How that visit was to be acknowledged--what would be E II 4 185 12
Harriet's returning the visit; but in a way that, if they E II 4 185 13
allow the visit to exceed the proposed quarter of an hour. E II 5 186 2
The style of the visit, and the shortness of it, were then E II 5 187 4
country gives, and the greatest curiosity to visit it. E II 5 191 26
A reasonable visit paid, Mr. Weston began to move.-- E II 5 193 36
opportunity of paying a visit, which must be paid some day E II 5 193 36
37
She is staying here on a visit to her grandmamma and aunt, E II 5 194 45
as their visit included all the rest of the morning. E II 6 196 2
visit the day before, and asked him if he had paid it. E II 6 198 6
A very successful visit:--I saw all the three ladies; and E II 6 198 7
I was only betrayed into paying a most unreasonable visit. E II 6 199 7
visit hitherto had given her friend only good ideas of him. E II 7 205 2
Mr. and Mrs. Weston's visit this morning was in another E II 7 206 5
the terms on which the superior families would visit them. E II 7 207 6
The visit afforded her many pleasant recollections the E II 9 231 1
"And while Mrs. Weston pays her visit, I may be allowed, I E II 9 234 27
Emma found it really time to be at home; the visit had E II 10 246 55
hopes his friends will be so kind as to visit him there. E II 11 250 23
"This will not be your only visit to Randalls." E II 12 259 14
It was better to pay my visit, then"----- E II 12 260 27
right; it was most natural to pay your visit, then"----- E II 12 261 30
31
The visit was of course short; and there was so much E II 14 270 3
When the visit was returned, Emma made up her mind. E II 14 272 16
"My brother and sister have promised us a visit in the E II 14 274 28
their grandpapa and aunt a visit of some weeks in the E II 16 292 7
to speak of his former visit, and recur to old stories: E III 1 316 4
This was the only visit from Frank Churchill in the course E III 1 316 6
The Eltons were still talking of a visit from the E III 5 343 1
After being long fed with hopes of a speedy visit form Mr. E III 6 352 1
perhaps, he might come in while she were paying her visit. E III 8 377 2
herself to believe her visit had been long enough; and, E III 8 384 34
for she knew how much his visit would be enjoyed--but it E III 9 386 8
Churchill had been promising a visit the last ten years. E III 9 388 15
Emma came back from her visit, the very last morning of E III 11 410 35
Mrs. Weston had set off to pay the visit in a good deal of E III 12 417 5
thing, she thought such a visit could not be paid without E III 12 417 5
arriving on my first visit to Randall's;--and here I am E III 14 437 8
of wrong, for that visit might have been sooner paid. E III 14 437 8
will soon call on her; she is living in dread of the visit. E III 14 439 8
her words from Emma--"a congratulatory visit, you know.-- E III 16 456 23
in the course of that visit (as I understand) he found an E III 18 472 20
pay a visit at Randall's; he wants to be introduced to her. E III 18 477 57
get Anne included in the visit to London, sensibly open to P III 2 16 16
of place, (except in one visit to Bath soon after the P III 4 28 7
Anne had not wanted this visit to Uppercross, to learn P III 6 42 1
In all other respects, her visit began and proceeded very P III 6 46 12
and was glad to be within when the visit was returned. P III 6 48 17
The child's situation put the visit entirely aside, but P III 7 53 2
of Captain Wentworth's visit;--staying five minutes behind P III 7 54 4
with their new acquaintance, and their visit in general. P III 7 58 22
his sisters meaning to visit Mary and the child, and P III 7 59 24
and finished their visit at the cottage, she had this P III 7 60 31
32
for a ball, or a visit, which a few hours might comprehend. P III 8 68 34
soon into Shropshire, and visit the brother settled in P III 9 73 1
she should be frightened from the visit by such nonsense. P III 10 87 23
memory of her two months visit there, but he was gaining P III 11 93 4
The conclusion of her visit, however, was diversified in a P III 11 93 5
had promised them a visit in the evening; and he came, P III 11 99 22
Anne, have you courage to go with me, and pay a visit in P IV 1 125 14
acquaintance which this visit began, was fated not to P IV 1 128 31
away for a few weeks, to visit the connexions in the north P IV 1 128 31
afterwards to pay a formal visit here, he will make his P IV 2 131 12
father's grounds, or any visit of charity in the village, P IV 2 133 26
of course, during their visit; and Mr. Musgrove made a P IV 2 134 29
Every body was wanting to visit them. P IV 3 137 4
the satisfaction which a visit from Miss Elliot would give P IV 5 153 5
The visit was paid, their acquaintance re-established, P IV 5 153 6
widow, receiving the visit of her former protegee as a P IV 5 153 6
In the course of a second visit she talked with great P IV 5 153 8
and himself to visit in; but had little curiosity beyond. P IV 6 165 9
The visit of ceremony was paid and returned, and Louisa P IV 6 168 22
the more decided promise of a longer visit on the morrow. P IV 7 180 33
almost made me swear "to visit them this summer, but my P IV 9 203 72
this summer, but my first visit to "Kellynch will be with P IV 9 203 72
it, though he did not then visit in Camden-Place; but his P IV 9 206 90
paid them a long morning visit; but hardly had she P IV 10 212 2
The visit passed off altogether in high good humour. P IV 10 219 28
still to defer her explanatory visit in Rivers-Street. P IV 11 229 1
He wanted to secure the promise of a visit--to get as many S 2 373 1
were only now & then to visit her neighbours, in the old S 2 373 1
Mr P. could not be satisfied without an early visit to the S 6 389 1
each for a three days visit, were constrained to be S 11 421 1

VISITANTS (1)
present number of Visitants & the chances of a good season. S 6 392 1

VISITATION (2)
of attending the visitation that day, & that as his road W 338 18
the occurrences of a visitation--but when she heard Mr W 343 20

VISITED (33)
servant that he had visited you every day since your being LS 32 302 1
duties;--shops were to be visited; some new part of the NA I 3 25 1
visited Miss Tilney, and poured forth her joyful feelings. NA II 2 138 1
Large as was the building, she had already visited the NA II 8-183 2
He had formerly visited at Stanhill, but it was too long SS I 6 30 6
Before the middle of the day, they were visited by Sir SS I 18 99 15
"Did he come from your uncle's then, when he visited us?" SS I 22 134 47
had never dropped, she visited no one, to whom an SS II 5 168 11
proper attendants; I visited her every day during the rest SS II 9 207 26
family property,) she frequently visited me at Delaford. SS II 9 208 28
They were visited on their first settling by almost all SS III 14 375 8
and privately visited her in Bartlett's Buildings, it was SS III 14 376 11
Mr. Philips visited them all, and this opened to his PP I 7 28 4
than any they had yet visited; and the valley, here PP III 1 253 57
Their other aunt also visited them frequently, and always, PP III 6 294 3
With what delighted pride she afterwards visited Mrs. PP III 19 385 1
Having visited many more rooms than could be supposed to MP I 9 85 5
except by Fanny, when she visited her plants, or wanted MP I 16 151 1
hardly have less than visited their agitated spirits, one MP III 15 444 27
I could not have visited Mrs. Robert Martin, of Abbey-Mill E I 7 53 24
"You could not have visited me!" she cried, looking aghast. E I 7 54 26
have taken to each other whenever she visited her friends. E II 6 203 39
Every body in and about Highbury who had ever visited Mr. E II 16 290 1
as to have been visited, though against her own consent, E III 9 389 16
but the Musgroves were visited by every body, and had more P III 6 47 14
with true naval alertness, and were to be visited. P III 6 48 17
at work, they were visited at the window by the sisters P III 10 83 3
these places must be visited, and visited again, to make P III 11 95 9
and visited again, to make the worth of Lyme understood. P III 11 95 9
Captain Harville had visited, were more than amusing to P III 11 98 17
The neglect had been visited on the head of the sinner, P IV 4 149 12
They visited in laura-place, they had the cards of Dowager P IV 4 149 13
I should have visited Admiral Croft, however, at any rate. P IV 6 162 5

VISITING (26)
her intention of visiting us almost immediately--& as such LS 3 246 1
there only while he was visiting the old lady at Allenham SS I 9 44 23
Your sister need not have any scruple even of visiting her, SS II 11 228 53
contenting herself with visiting her once or twice a day, SS III 1 257 1
of Charlotte,--and in visiting her poultry-yard, where, in SS III 6 303 10
with all the honours of visiting round the fire, & Miss W 355 28
her daughters married; its solace was visiting and news. PP I 1 5 34
happily employed in visiting an opposite milliner, PP II 16 219 1
the most of the time, by visiting about with her daughter, PP III 9 318 18
You forced me into visiting him last year, and promised if PP III 11 332 23
to retain the right of visiting at Pemberley, she dropt PP III 19 387 10
He had been visiting a friend in a neighbouring county, MP I 6 52 1
of the plan for visiting Sotherton, which had been started MP I 8 75 1
been at the trouble of visiting Mrs. Rushworth on her MP I 8 76 7
inmates really worth visiting; and though infinitely above MP II 7 238 1
and at an earlier hour than common visiting warrants. MP II 13 298 1
made her the offer of visiting the parents and brothers, MP III 6 369 11
confess that since my visiting here I have seen people-- E I 7 54 30
her to refrain from visiting the sick chamber again, for E I 15 125 4
entirely, only visiting her grandmother from time to time. E II 2 164 4
Small heart had Harriet for visiting. E II 5 186 1
they made a point of visiting no fresh person; and that, E II 8 221 48
was exactly the sort of visiting that would be welcome to E III 5 344 3
Miss Anne Elliot to be visiting in Westgate-Buildings?-- P IV 5 157 15
"I have not had the pleasure of visiting in Camden-Place P IV 8 187 28
of road, and to give the visiting young lady a suitable S 3 375 1

VISITING-ENGAGEMENTS (1)
to you, if your visiting-engagements continue to increase E II 18 311 42

VISITINGS (1)
going on; that their visitings were among a range of great E II 8 221 48

VISITOR (48)
Lady Susan behaved with great attention to her visitor, & LS 20 276 3
at the appearance of my visitor; and at first observed Sir LS 22 280 2
daughter, her son, her visitor, and could have embraced NA I 15 121 27
She was to be their chosen visitor, she was to be for NA II 2 141 11
to be more than the visitor of an hour, had seemed too NA II 2 141 11
for her to forget for a moment that she was a visitor. NA II 5 154 2
in thus becoming her visitor; of hearing it ranked as real NA II 5 157 5
she knew not that a visitor had arrived within the last NA II 15 241 7
to the cottage to being a visitor at Barton Park; and she SS I 5 26 6
her attention to their visitor, endeavoured to support SS I 16 89 42
entertainment of their visitor, towards whose amusement he SS I 18 99 16
No other visitor appeared that evening, and the ladies SS II 4 164 20
rap foretold a visitor, and Colonel Brandon was announced. SS II 5 172 40
Colonel Brandon's wife, and Marianne as their visitor. SS II 14 253 25
word of mouth, when her visitor entered, to force her upon SS III 4 287 26
all waited in silence for the appearance of their visitor. SS III 12 359 10
The plan was warmly opposed by their visitor. W 339 18
You know what a sad visitor I make.-- W 356 28
fresh excuse for her, the visitor did at last appear; but PP II 3 147 25
by a ring at the door, the certain signal of a visitor. PP II 9 177 1
There, shut into her own room, as soon as their visitor PP II 10 186 38
and prepare for such a visitor, when Bingley's quick step PP III 2 261 5
from Longbourn, your uncle had a most unexpected visitor. PP III 10 321 2
But our visitor was very obstinate. PP III 10 324 2
to it, till their visitor took his leave for the night; PP III 13 348 35
36
Bingley, from this time, was of course a daily visitor at PP III 13 349 43
till the door was thrown open, and their visitor entered. PP III 14 351 1
on hearing who their visitor had been, was very great; but PP III 15 361 5
Lydia was occasionally a visitor there, when her husband PP III 19 387 9
The little visitor meanwhile was as unhappy as possible. MP I 2 13 4
wish to procure so agreeable a visitor for her sister?" MP II 5 218 17
joyful intelligence, which his visitor came to communicate. MP II 13 302 9
shy and uncomfortable when their visitor entered the room. MP II 13 303 13
"You are not aware, perhaps, that I have had a visitor MP III 1 313 14
the prospect of another visitor, whose approach he could MP III 6 368 7
stopt by the knock of a visitor, whom they felt they could MP III 10 399 2
While trying to keep herself alive, their visitor, who had MP III 10 399 5
The backgammon-table was placed; but a visitor immediately E I 1 9 20
Highbury, was a frequent visitor and always welcome, and E I 1 9 21
hoped to influence every visitor of the new-married pair; E I 2 19 14
to every morning visitor in Brunswick-Square;--and, as I E I 6 46 21
a visitor, without thinking him at all a tiresome wretch." E I 8 60 27
Emma was ready for her visitor some time before he E II 12 259 12
continually insulting her visitor with praise, E II 15 288 39
This point was just arranged, when a visitor arrived to E III 12 417 3
Isabella sent quite as good an account of her visitor as E III 17 463 16
all was ready, their visitor had bowed and was gone; the P III. 7 59 25
She was their earliest visitor in their settled life; and P IV 12 251 11

VISITORS (45)
But nothing of that kind occurred, no visitors appeared to NA I 10 71 8
to descend and meet him under the protection of visitors. NA II 9 192 4
sisters-in-law were degraded to the condition of visitors. SS I 2 8 1
Their visitors, except those from Barton Park, were not SS I 9 40 2
and such constant visitors as to leave them little leisure SS I 11 53 1
before; and when their visitors left them, he went SS I 18 100 23
hardly got their last visitors out of her head, had hardly SS I 21 118 1
among the earliest and best pleased of your visitors." SS II 11 227 50
with the chief of their visitors, who almost all laboured SS II 12 233 18
But they are Lady Middleton's visitors. SS II 14 253 21
the hindrance of more visitors than usual, had prevented SS III 2 270 3
his behaviour to all his visitors, and only occasionally SS III 6 304 15
The next morng brought a great many visitors. W 337 16
No visitors would have been welcome at such a moment; but W 344 21
such a moment; but such visitors as these--such a one as W 344 21
other with astonishment, when their visitors had withdrawn. W 347 22
representations--& the visitors departed without her.-- W 362 32
table at Rosings, in the absence of more eligible visitors. PP I 17 88 14
She hated having visitors in the house while her health PP I 23 128 11
to his wondering visitors, and of letting them see her PP II 6 160 1
such as to make her visitors forget their inferior rank. PP II 6 162 11
for while there were visitors in the house, they could not PP II 8 172 1
regretting that her visitors were to go, she did not seem PP II 15 216 7
own, and welcomed to them as visitors my uncle and aunt.-- PP III 1 246 6
after their own arrival at Lambton, these visitors came. PP III 2 260 1
feelings of each of her visitors, she wanted to compose PP III 2 262 7
Their visitors staid with them above half an hour, and PP III 2 263 11
herself, when their visitors left them, capable of PP III 2 264 12
Their visitors were not to remain above ten days with them. PP III 9 318 17
her better satisfied with their visitors, than Elizabeth. PP III 12 339 5
It was too early in the morning for visitors, and besides, PP III 14 351 1
"It is time to think of our visitors," said Maria, still MP II 1 182 19
would have welcomed his visitors to every thing, his care E I 3 24 12
Emma allowed her father to talk--but supplied her visitors E I 3 25 15
"Something has happened to delay her; some visitors E I 8 58 16
every thing to them, the visitors were most cordially and E II 1 155 4
opened the door; and her visitors walked up stairs without E II 9 239 52
and more callers, more visitors by invitation and by P III 6 47 14
two or three of the lady visitors, as if they believed P IV 10 222 37
The visitors took their leave; and Charles, having civilly P IV 10 223 40
41
Alarming sounds were heard; other visitors approached, and P IV 10 226 63
The popularity of the parkers brought them some visitors S 7 394 1
was cleared of morng visitors was to get out themselves;-- S 7 395 1
Their visitors answered for two Hack-chaises.-- S 10 414 1
lounge of all the visitors at Sanditon, & on one side, S 11 422 1

VISITS (39)
wife--but with him--and that he now visits you every day. LS 36 305 1
child, who, in occasional visits with his father and SS I 1 4 3
My visits to Mrs. Smith are never repeated within the SS I 15 76 10
She expressly conditioned, however, for paying no visits, SS II 11 220 1
in the frequency of her visits at Delaford; for her wish SS III 14 378 13
his visits & soon after marrying somebody else.-- W 316 2
He loved to take people by surprise, with sudden visits at W 355 28
Their visits to Mrs. Philips were now productive of the PP I 7 28 4
that was passing in the room during these visits. PP II 7 169 3

is merely adopted on his visits to his aunt, of whose good PP II 18 234 38
I had narrowly observed her during the two visits which I PP III 16 371 43
but the visits of her uncle and aunt from the city. PP III 19 388 12
rise and grandeur, regal visits and loyal efforts, MP I 9 85 3
Her visits there, beginning by chance, were continued by MP II 4 205 2
She had some extra visits from the housekeeper, and her MP II 8 254 9
"but that his visits to us may now be tolerably frequent. MP II 11 284 9
The terror of his former occasional visits to that room MP III 1 312 4
as to the frequency of his visits, at present or in future. MP III 2 329 12
If I had not promoted Mr. Weston's visits here and given E I 1 13 43
man, whose frequent visits were one of the comforts of Mr. E I 2 19 14
he could command visits of his own little circle, in a E I 3 20 1
They are very, very kind in their visits. E I 11 94 14
thought you judged ill in making your visits so frequent. E I 15 131 34
No, madam, my visits to Hartfield have been for yourself E I 15 132 35
36

guest, paying them long visits and growing a favourite E II 2 163 4
it must be left for the visits in form which were then to E II 14 270 1
prospect of frequent visits from Frank the whole spring-- E II 18 308 30
as those sort of visits conveyed, might shortly be over. E III 12 422 19
Now Emma could, indeed, enjoy Mr. Knightley's visits; now E III 16 451 4
like morning visits, and Mr. Elton's time is so engaged." E III 16 455 22
to admit Mr. Woodhouse's visits, Emma having it in view E III 17 465 28
late in the year for such visits to be made on foot, the P III 6 50 26
them, while Mr. Elliot's frequent visits were talked of. P IV 3 140 11
Her kind, compassionate visits to this old schoolfellow, P IV 5 158 21
me to-morrow if I may not have many more visits from you." P IV 7 180 35
I have no doubt, had a double motive in his visits there. P IV 9 206 88
Morning visits are never fair by women at her time of life, P IV 10 215 16
Anne, remembering the preconcerted visits, at all hours, P IV 10 216 17
our sensations--"like Angel's visits, few & far between." S 7 397 1

VISITTING (1)
when you are out visitting, tho' you do not at home." W 353 26

VISTA (1)
We looked down the whole vista, and saw it closed by iron MP I 9 94 63

VITIATED (1)
Fanny, of blunted delicacy and a corrupted, vitiated mind. MP III 16 456 25

VIVACITY (10)
towards any unpleasant vivacity, and (considering its NA I 9 62 10
voices, and their vivacity attended with so much laughter, NA I 10 72 8
he united frankness and vivacity, and above all, when she SS I 10 46 2
with a forced vivacity as he returned to his seat--"what SS III 8 318 15
on her wit and vivacity; and though more astonished than PP I 17 88 14
and your wit and vivacity I think must be acceptable to PP I 19 106 10
made--though with the vivacity of friendly interest and MP III 3 340 24
I have a great deal of vivacity in my own way, but I E III 7 372 37
His lady greeted him with some of her sparkling vivacity. E III 16 457 35
The whole of their mental vivacity was evidently not so S 10 412 1

VOCAL (1)
whose performance, both vocal and instrumental, she never E II 8 227 86

VOGUE (1)
vogue amongst the less polished societies of the world.-- PP I 6 25 27

VOICE (239)
is absolutely sweet, & her voice & manner winningly mild. LS 6 251 1
as she has my hand & arm, & a tolerable voice. LS 7 253 1
speaking in a lower voice & with still greater energy, I LS 23 283 4
look and voice as he spoke, which contradicted his words. LS 27 297 4
affectedly softening his voice, he added, with a simpering NA I 3 26 4
was bid in an important voice "to let him go," and off NA I 9 62 10
friend's dissenting voice, by not waiting for her answer. NA I 9 67 33
John Thorpe was soon with them, and his voice was with NA I 11 84 18
"And what do you think I said?" (lowering his voice) NA I 12 96 22
by Isabella; who in a voice of cold resentment said, "very NA I 13 99 4
"I suspect," said Isabella, in a low voice, "there is no NA I 13 100 12
in rather a solemn tone of voice, uttered these words, "I NA I 14 111 29
was; till, roused by the voice of Isabella, she looked up NA II 1 133 29
Catherine's countenance fell, and in a voice of most NA II 2 138 1
but she scarcely heard his voice while his father remained NA II 5 155 3
either of subject or voice, and was obliged to entreat her NA II 5 160 23
and increasing one," replied the other, in a low voice. NA II 7 180 34
"Mr. Tilney!" she exclaimed in a voice of more than common NA II 9 194 6
only--(dropping her voice)--your father was with us." NA II 9 195 15
Her voice faltered, and her eyes were turned to the ground NA II 13 223 13
the General?" said Catherine in a faltering voice. NA II 13 225 20
Happy the voice that proclaimed the discovery!-- NA II 14 233 8
voice, that "her head did not run upon Bath-----much." NA II 15 240 3
on hearing this, and, in a voice of surprise and concern, SS I 5 25 1
received additional charms from his voice and expression. SS I 9 42 9
his feelings no ardour, and his voice no expression." SS I 10 51 26
to him in a low voice, on being obliged to forego the SS I 12 59 6
he added in the same low voice--"but, Marianne, the horse SS I 12 59 6
Elinor then heard Willoughby say in a low voice to SS I 13 64 30
Then lowering her voice a little, she said to Elinor, "she SS I 13 66 57
been so, Marianne?" speaking to her in a lowered voice. SS I 14 73 17
and crying; her voice often totally suspended by her tears. SS I 16 83 3
"No," said Marianne in a low voice, "nor how many painful SS I 16 88 41
"And who is Willoughby?" said he, in a low voice, to miss SS I 18 100 22
and speaking in a low voice as if she meant to be heard by SS I 19 107 29
I believe," she added in a low voice, "he would have been SS I 20 116 62
years you have been engaged," said she with a firm voice. SS I 22 131 34
"I did;" said Elinor, with a composure of voice, under SS I 22 135 55
exhilarated by it in look, voice, and manner, restored to SS II 3 158 20
"How very odd!" said she in a low and disappointed voice, SS II 4 165 28
"That is true," cried Marianne in a cheerful voice, and SS II 5 167 2
by his asking her in a voice of some agitation, when he SS II 5 172 40
and after saying in a voice of emotion, "to your sister I SS II 5 174 46
to another in an audible voice, and entered a room SS II 6 175 2
Her face was crimsoned over, and she exclaimed in a voice SS II 6 176 7
to give way in a low voice to the misery of her feelings, SS II 6 177 15
indeed," before her voice was entirely lost in sobs. SS II 7 185 19
Had you seen his look, his manner, had you heard his voice SS II 7 189 46
"How do you do my dear?"--said she in a voice of great SS II 8 192 2
the intended match, in a voice so little attempting SS II 8 199 37
a moment; then added in a voice which seemed to distrust SS II 8 199 39
me," he continued, in a voice of great agitation, "was of SS II 9 206 24
and the gentleness of her voice whenever (though it did SS II 10 216 15
In short, it is a kind of thing that"--lowering his voice SS II 11 224 24
low, but eager, voice, "dear, dear Elinor, don't mind them. SS II 12 236 39
40

Colonel Brandon in a low voice, as soon as he could secure SS II 12 236 43
She met him with a hand that would be taken, and a voice SS II 13 242 23
And then lowering her voice, "I suppose Mrs. Jennings has SS III 2 271 8
calm voice, "I am afraid it cannot take place very soon." SS III 3 281 9
10

Elinor say, and with a voice which shewed her to feel what SS III 3 281 13
14

"Mrs. Ferrars," added he, lowering his voice to the tone SS III 5 295 18
and saying, in a voice rather of command than supplication, SS III 8 317 1
2

smile, and a voice perfectly calm, "yes, I am very drunk.-- SS III 8 318 18
said Elinor, while her voice, in spite of herself, SS III 8 329 64
being no more, had no voice to inquire after her, no voice SS III 9 334 4
to inquire after her, no voice even for Elinor; but she, SS III 9 334 4
Her voice sunk with the word, but presently reviving she SS III 10 344 14
15

She paused--and added in a lower voice, "if I could but SS III 10 347 31
as she spoke--and her unsteady voice, plainly shewed. SS III 11 349 3
For some moments her voice was lost; but recovering SS III 11 350 6
the use of her reason and voice as to be just beginning an SS III 11 353 25
She observed, in a low voice, to her mother, that they SS III 11 355 39
her own voice, now said, "is Mrs. Ferrars at Longstaple?" SS III 12 359 16
17

spoke, said, in an hurried voice, "perhaps you do not know- SS III 12 360 22
23

Such were the last audible sounds of Miss Watson's voice, W 321 2
Beleive me--added he lowering his voice--you are quite W 339 18
& artificial inflexions of voice, which your very popular W 343 20
was all affection & her voice all gentleness; continual W 349 23
Such, she feared would be Margaret's common voice, when W 351 25
"Oh!--(in a soften'd voice, & rather mortified to find she W 351 25
"Musgrave!"--ejaculated Margaret in a tender voice.-- W 355 28
Miss Watson, the general voice was so urgent with him to W 357 28
of the gentle voice beyond her calculation short. W 360 30
walking, the tone of her voice, her address and PP I 8 39 50
asked Elizabeth in a low voice whether her relation were PP I 16 83 51
"I am," said he, with a firm voice. PP I 18 93 33
a display; her voice was weak, and her manner affected.-- PP I 18 100 68
In a doleful voice Mrs. Bennet thus began the projected PP I 20 114 31
Far be it from me," he presently continued in a voice that PP I 20 114 32
she spoke in a low voice to Mr. Collins, was convinced PP I 23 130 16
With a stronger voice she soon added, "I have this comfort PP II 1 134 8
little, except in a low voice, to Mrs. Jenkinson, in whose PP II 6 162 12
it, said, in a colder voice, "are you pleased with Kent?" PP II 9 179 24
25

At length, in a voice of forced calmness, he said, "and PP II 11 190 8
9

called, though in a voice which proved it to be Mr. Darcy, PP II 12 195 2
His countenance, voice, and manner, had established him at PP II 13 206 4
Lucases; and Lydia, in a voice rather louder than any PP II 16 222 21
had been that in his voice, which was not like ease. PP III 1 253 55
hearing Miss Bingley's voice, Elizabeth was roused by PP III 3 268 5
"When I consider," she added, in a yet more agitated voice, PP III 4 277 12
of her situation by the voice of her companion, who, in a PP III 4 278 20
Lydia's voice was heard in the vestibule; the door was PP III 9 315 3
bringing the sound of his voice; and when occasionally, PP III 11 335 43
voice and manner plainly shewed how really happy he was. PP III 13 348 34
They are destined for each other by the voice of every PP III 14 356 50
did in an angry voice, that Fanny had got another child. MP I 1 4 2
was not vulgar, her voice was sweet, and when she spoke MP I 2 12 2
nor did her aunt Norris's voice make her start very much. MP I 2 17 21
very sorry to go away," said she, with a faltering voice. MP I 3 25 11
at him, and said in a low voice, "cut down an avenue! MP I 6 56 19
20

brother's situation; her voice was animated in speaking of MP I 6 60 47
Her own gentle voice speaking from the other end of the MP I 7 71 33
in a rather softened voice; "but I question whether her MP I 7 72 45
"I am disappointed," said she, in a low voice, to Edmund. MP I 9 85 6
to Maria, said, in a voice which she only could her, "I do MP I 9 88 20
up into another, when the voice and the laugh of Miss MP I 10 103 49
A little man, with a weak voice, always hoarse after the MP I 13 122 2
Edmund in a low voice, as his brother approached the fire. MP I 13 125 15
subject, posture, and voice, as soon as Lady Bertram began MP I 13 126 23
The influence of his voice was felt. MP I 14 135 18
With hasty indignation therefore, and a tremulous voice, MP I 14 136 18
together in an under voice, and the declaration with which MP I 14 136 21
should take the part," said Mr. Yates, in a low voice. MP I 15 144 34
Miss Crawford in an under voice, to Fanny, after some MP I 15 149 61
though she could not give them in a very steady voice. MP I 18 168 18
so completely maternal in her voice and countenance.' MP I 18 169 21
but with looks and voice so truly feminine, as to be no MP I 18 169 22
towards Fanny, and a voice or two, to say, "if Miss Price MP I 18 171 28
His manner seemed changed; his voice was quick from the MP II 1 178 7
know the voice--more than talking--almost hallooing. MP II 1 182 22
ask the latter in an under voice, whether there were any MP II 2 192 11
But then"--with a more thoughtful air and lowered voice--" MP II 4 210 19
the trouble of raising her voice, was always heard and MP II 5 218 12
of a certain tone of voice and a certain half-look MP II 7 242 25
me, I hope--(turning with a softened voice to Fanny).-- MP II 7 244 27
he added, in a low voice directed solely at Fanny, "I MP II 7 245 31
voice, not meant to reach far, and the subject dropped. MP II 7 246 35
arise," he repeated, his voice sinking a little, "between MP II 9 264 16
"Fanny," said a voice at that moment near her. MP II 9 267 24
with her uncle, hear his voice, receive his questions, and MP II 11 284 8
thus began, with a voice as well regulated as she could--" MP II 11 287 18
but there was no consciousness of past folly in his voice. MP II 13 303 14
was a something in his voice and manner in addressing her, MP II 13 304 16
you," said he, in an under voice, perceiving the amazing MP II 13 307 33
she knew it as well as his voice; she had trembled at it MP III 1 312 4
"This is very strange!" said Sir Thomas, in a voice of MP III 1 315 27
"Yes," said Fanny, in a faint voice, and looking down with MP III 1 316 28
afterwards, and in a voice of authority, said, "have you MP III 1 317 36
to make it clear that the voice was enough to convey the MP III 3 339 21
want of management of the voice, of proper modulation and MP III 3 339 22
her in a softened voice; and upon her saying, "no," he MP III 3 340 25
the same low eager voice, and the same close neighbourhood, MP III 3 342 34
tolerably soon, in a low voice, "I must speak to you for a MP III 5 357 5
I have of his looks and voice, as he said those words. MP III 5 358 9
by William's powerful voice, they were rattled into a MP III 7 376 6
himself, his own loud voice preceding him, as with MP III 7 379 19
voice, he instantly began--"ha! welcome back, my boy. MP III 7 379 20
Ay, Sam's voice louder than all the rest! MP III 7 383 30
"Now, Susan," cried Mrs. Price in a complaining voice, " MP III 7 386 44
At Mansfield, no sounds of contention, no raised voice, no MP III 8 391 11
Here, every body was noisy, every voice was loud, (MP III 8 392 11
It was a gentleman's voice; it was a voice that Fanny was MP III 10 399 3
she felt it quite the voice of a friend when he mentioned MP III 10 405 17
or his voice to the level of irritation and feebleness. MP III 14 429 2
a fearless face and bold voice would I say to any one, MP III 14 434 13
he spoke again, though his voice still faltered, his MP III 15 444 29
To be listened to and borne with, and hear the voice of MP III 16 449 5
how the agitation of his voice was watched, and how MP III 16 454 18
With a graver look and voice she then added--'I do not MP III 16 454 18
She spoke of it, Fanny, with a steadier voice than I can." MP III 16 456 29
There was not a dissentient voice on the subject, either E I 2 17 9
"To be sure," said Harriet, in a mortified voice, "he is E I 4 32 31
the uncouthness of a voice, which I heard to be wholly E I 4 33 32
"Mr. Perry," said he, in a voice of very strong E I 12 106 60
consider what demand of voice and what fatigues to-morrow E I 13 110 9
in the tone of his voice while assuring her that he should E I 13 111 14
excuse, in defiance of the voice of nature, which tells E I 13 113 26
His face lengthened immediately; and his voice was the E I 13 114 30
and his voice was the voice of sentiment as he answered. E I 13 114 30
and in a voice of the greatest alacrity and enjoyment. E I 13 115 36
her smile, her touch, her voice was grateful to Emma, and E I 14 117 2
or fancy any tone of voice, less allied with real love. E I 16 135 7
By only raising my voice, and saying anything two or three E II 1 158 14
she is sure to hear; but then she is used to my voice. E II 1 158 14
him, just to hear his voice, or see his shoulder, just to E II 4 184 10
himself, he would only talk louder, and drown her voice. E II 8 226 79
of her performance on the pianoforte, and of her voice! E II 8 226 79
acceptable, and could accompany her own voice well. E II 8 227 86
He was accused of having a delightful voice, and a perfect E II 8 227 86
of the matter, and had no voice at all, roundly asserted. E II 8 227 86
Towards the end of Jane's second song, her voice grew E II 8 229 93
thinks of nothing but shewing off his own voice. E II 8 229 97
she was receiving on her voice and her taste, to look E II 8 229 99
Voices approached the shop--or rather one voice and two E II 9 235 43
"This is a pleasure," said he, in rather a low voice, " E II 10 240 3
Campbell," said she, in a voice of forced calmness, "I can E II 10 241 14
And (raising his voice still more) I do not see why Miss E II 10 245 49
feature, nor air, nor voice, nor manner, were elegant. E II 14 270 4
A little quickness of voice there is which rather hurts E II 14 279 54
a voice a little subdued, but very audible to every body. E II 17 303 26
But (lowering her voice)--nobody speaks except ourselves, E III 7 369 15

She recovered her voice. E III 7 373 43
she looked out with voice and hand eager to show a E III 7 376 62
She heard Miss Bates's voice, some thing was to be done in E III 8 378 4
in the natural key of his voice, sunk it immediately, to E III 10 392 1
2
indeed no idea?" said Mrs. Weston in a trembling voice. E III 10 394 28
His air and voice recovered their usual briskness: he E III 10 400 69
Harriet's footstep and voice; so, she supposed, had poor E III 11 404 3
voice, whether Harriet could indeed have received any hint. E III 11 404 5
Her voice was lost; and she sat down, waiting in great E III 11 405 16
did speak, it was in a voice nearly as agitated as Emma's. E III 11 405 17
Her voice was not unsteady; but her mind was in all the E III 11 409 34
I wish I had attended to it--but--(with a sinking voice E III 13 425 11
At present, I ask only to hear, once to hear your voice." E III 13 430 37
the sound of Mrs. Elton's voice from the sitting-room had E III 16 453 10
bye,"--then sinking his voice, and looking demure for the E III 18 477 58
59
conscious, low, yet steady voice, "how you can bear such E III 18 480 78
79
Musgroves; but having no voice, no knowledge of the harp, P III 6 46 13
it in the voice, or the turn of sentiment and expression. P III 6 48 17
passed; she heard his voice--he talked to Mary, said all P III 7 59 25
together: and though his voice did not falter, and though P III 8 63 2
When he talked, she heard the same voice, and discerned P III 8 64 4
Mrs. Musgrove, in a low voice, as if thinking aloud, "so P III 8 66 18
with her, in a low voice, about her son, doing it with so P III 8 67 28
said, in a vext tone of voice, after Captain Wentworth's P III 9 80 34
Louisa's voice was the first distinguished. P III 10 87 22
In general, his voice and manner were studiously calm. P III 12 116 70
In a low, cautious voice, he said, "I have been P III 12 117 73
74
talking with a very raised voice, but, from the clamour of P IV 2 134 29
in spite of the agitated voice in which the latter part P IV 8 183 11
that inconvenient tone of voice which was perfectly P IV 11 230 5
"No," replied Anne, in a low feeling voice. P IV 11 232 16
It would be too hard indeed" (with a faltering voice) "if P IV 11 233 23
Well, Miss Elliot," (lowering his voice) "as I was saying, P IV 11 234 27
"You sink your voice, but I can distinguish the tones of " P IV 11 237 42
tones of "that voice, when they would be lost on others.-- P IV 11 237 42
gentleness of voice, & a great deal of conversation. S 7 394 1
& Medecine, more relaxed in air, & more subdued in voice. S 10 413 1
she heard nothing of his voice but the murmuring of a few S 10 416 1
VOICES (11)
in such whispering voices, and their vivacity attended NA I 10 72 8
every air in which their voices had been oftenest joined, SS I 16 83 3
hurrying back, when the voices of both her sisters were SS I 16 86 20
desire of hearing their steps and their voices again. MP I 10 97 1
She listened, and at length she heard; she heard voices MP I 10 97 1
of the united voices gave only momentary interruptions. E II 8 227 87
Voices approached the shop--or rather one voice and two E II 9 235 43
But I believe I am nice; I do not like strange voices; and E II 14 279 54
to hear more;--and the voices of the ladies were drowned E III 2 324 22
of persons and voices--but a few minutes ended it. P III 7 59 25
theirs; had heard voices--mirth continually; thought they P IV 3 144 19
VOID (4)
speak a mind at ease, or a conscience void of reproach."-- NA II 8 182 1
feel a void in your heart which nothing else can occupy. NA II 10 207 38
Your retrospections must be so totally void of reproach, PP III 16 369 24
himself to think entirely void of meaning, however he E III 5 343 2
VOLATILITY (1)
be affected by the wild volatility, the assurance and PP II 18 231 18
VOLS. (1)
whitby running off with 5 vols. under his arm to Sir S 8 403 1
VOLTAIRE (1)
never heard of half a mile from home."-- S 1 370 1
VOLUBILITY (4)
hardly have found expression in their united volubility. PP II 18 232 22
Mrs. Norris was all delight and volubility; and even Fanny MP I 8 82 35
easy indifference and volubility in the course of the MP II 1 183 23
volubility as before--less ease of look and manner. E III 8 378 7
VOLUBLE (1)
introduced by his easy, voluble friend, he muttered W 344 21
VOLUME (21)
of which a last volume is capable--whether by her NA I 2 19 7
and publishes in a volume some dozen lines of Milton, Pope, NA I 5 37 4
Now, had the same young lady been engaged with a volume of NA I 5 38 4
Miss Andrews could not get through the first volume." NA I 6 42 22
I took up the first volume once, and looked it over, but I NA I 7 49 40
for me, you took the volume into the Hermitage-walk, and I NA I 14 107 8
by running away with the volume, which, you are to observe, NA I 14 107 9
had last walked, or the volume in which she had last read, NA II 9 194 6
down stairs with the volume from which so much was hoped. NA II 15 241 7
lay aside the first volume of the mirror for a future hour. NA II 15 242 8
accidentally taking up a volume of Shakespeare, exclaimed, SS I 16 85 11
12
because it was the second volume of his, she gave a great PP I 11 55 4
Lydia gaped as he opened the volume, and before he had, PP I 14 68 13
14
was to take up the volume which had been left on the table, MP I 14 137 23
How does Lord Macartney go on?--(opening a volume on the MP I 16 156 27
of being very recently closed, a volume of Shakespeare.-- MP III 3 336 9
Crawford took the volume. MP III 3 336 10
do not think I have had a volume of Shakespeare in my hand MP III 3 338 13
at which the favourite volume always opened: "Elliot P III 1 3 1
of taking the precious volume into his own hands to save P III 8 66 22
for the insertion of the marriage in the volume of honour. P IV 12 248 2
VOLUMES (5)
trouble in filling great volumes, which, as I used to NA I 14 109 24
out, in three duodecimo volumes, two hundred and seventy- NA I 14 113 39
taking up one of the many volumes of plays that lay on the MP I 14 132 7
of well-bound volumes, the property of Captain Benwick. P III 11 99 18
A sick chamber may often furnish the worth of volumes." P IV 5 156 10
VOLUMINOUS (1)
by any part of that voluminous publication, of which NA I 5 38 4
VOLUNTARILY (29)
from its amendment, the sky began voluntarily to clear. NA I 11 83 16
retracted a promise voluntarily made only five minutes NA I 13 101 25
of Beechen Cliff, she voluntarily rejected the whole city NA I 14 111 29
an engagement voluntarily entered into with another man! NA II 10 205 30
they could never have voluntarily suffered; and that, in NA II 14 234 10
them at first, was voluntarily renewed, was sought for, SS I 1 7 13
and scarcely ever voluntarily speaking, except when any SS II 4 160 2
speaking to him, even voluntarily speaking, with a kind of SS II 10 212 1
have induced Fanny voluntarily to mention his name before SS II 12 229 4
to sit up, and returned voluntarily to her bed, Elinor was SS III 7 307 2
Marianne began voluntarily to speak of him again;--but SS III 11 349 3
and lively friendship, voluntarily to give her hand to SS III 14 378 15
To Elizabeth, however, he voluntarily acknowledged that PP I 21 115 3
did Mr. Bennet say voluntarily to Elizabeth, "I am glad PP II 16 222 19
20
His name had never been voluntarily mentioned before them PP III 6 298 16
pain: and Lydia led voluntarily to subjects, which her PP III 9 316 6
to Longbourn, and voluntarily seeking her was almost equal PP III 11 334 36
told him what Mr. Darcy had voluntarily done for Lydia. PP III 17 377 38
He was going--and if not voluntarily going, voluntarily MP II 2 193 18
than were most voluntarily bestowed by my uncle, after the MP II 13 300 5
voluntarily to say of her concern at this separation. MP III 6 366 3
So voluntarily, so freely, so coolly to canvass it!-- MP III 16 454 18
She would not voluntarily give unnecessary pain to any one, MP III 16 456 25
a reward very voluntarily bestowed--within a reasonable MP III 17 467 19
Harriet was not insensible of manner; she had voluntarily E I 4 32 27
usual, setting forward voluntarily, without excuse, in E I 13 113 26

that he had been ever voluntarily absenting himself; that E II 6 197 4
It made her animated--open hearted--she voluntarily said;-- E II 12 258 4
5
which had been so voluntarily formed and maintained--or to E III 11 408 33
VOLUNTARY (18)
by a neighbourhood of voluntary spies, and where roads and NA II 9 197 29
that it had been all a voluntary, self-created delusion, NA II 10 199 2
passed, every employment voluntary, every laugh indulged, NA II 13 220 1
nothing but motion was voluntary; and it seemed as if she NA II 15 240 1
his errand, this was his voluntary communication-- "I SS III 11 353 22
23
complete in the voluntary forgiveness of Mrs. Smith, who, SS III 14 379 18
Mr. Darcy gave him a voluntary promise of providing for me, PP I 16 81 37
was soon able to make a voluntary transition to the PP I 18 90 4
It seemed like wilful ill-nature, or a voluntary penance, PP II 10 182 1
"My taking orders I assure you is quite as voluntary as MP I 11 108 13
a voluntary partner secured against the dancing began. MP II 10 274 8
she soon found, from the voluntary information of the MP III 1 322 51
carriage, was all the voluntary notice which this brother MP III 7 377 8
other's punishment, and then induce a voluntary separation. MP III 17 464 10
with more voluntary praise than Emma had ever heard before. E I 8 58 9
To her voluntary communications Emma could get no more E II 12 257 2
3
that, with a much more voluntary, cheerful consent than E III 19 484 11
no enquiries, there was voluntary communication sufficient. P IV 2 133 25
VOLUNTEER (2)
who was obliged to volunteer all the information about her SS II 13 241 22
unmanageable days often volunteer, for soon after MP II 9 265 21
VOTED (1)
if cards were conveniently voted unnecessary by their four E II 11 254 44
VOUCH (5)
My temper I dare not vouch for.-- PP I 11 58 28
whose very countenance may vouch for your being amiable"-- PP I 16 80 36
Mr. Darcy; but he will vouch for the good conduct, the PP I 18 95 50
which Emma had formerly been so ready to vouch for!-- E III 19 482 3
I used to boast of my own Anne Elliot, and vouch for your P IV 9 201 61
VOUCHERS (1)
seemed sufficient vouchers for his truth; and to these NA II 15 245 12
VOUCHES (1)
Jane Fairfax's character vouches for her disinterestedness; E III 13 428 23
VOUCHSAFE (3)
Elinor would not vouchsafe any answer. SS II 11 224 25
I am delighted to find that you can vouchsafe to let your E III 5 350 37
to my friends, so long before you vouchsafe to come!-- E III 16 457 36
VOUCHSAFED (4)
of uncommon kindness, vouchsafed on so short an SS II 14 254 27
making, and had even vouchsafed to suggest some herself,-- PP I 14 66 1
than Miss Fairfax would have vouchsafed in half a year." E II 6 202 29
& thought he would have vouchsafed me an answer.-- S 5 385 1
VOUCHSAFING (1)
and for ever, without vouchsafing any motive, because he E III 13 431 38
VOW (2)
Kings, I vow! NA I 11 90 64
"Good gracious! Mr. Darcy!--and so it does I vow. PP III 11 334 35
VOWED (3)
John would have me go, for he vowed he would not drive her, NA I 15 117 3
She vowed at first she would never trim me up a new bonnet, SS III 2 272 12
in a pet, and vowed I would never take another likeness. E I 6 45 21
VOWEL (1)
What a difference a vowel makes!--if his rents were but MP III 9 394 1
VOWS (15)
It makes me miserable--but Mr Johnson vows that if I LS 38 306 1
marry Mr. Collins, for she vows she will not have him, and PP I 20 111 7
The play had been Lovers' Vows, and Mr. Yates was to have MP I 13 122 2
"Lovers' Vows were at an end, and Lord and Lady Ravenshaw MP I 13 123 5
and turning it over, suddenly exclaimed, "Lovers' Vows! MP I 14 132 7
And why should not Lovers' Vows do for us as well as for MP I 14 132 7
to business and Lovers' Vows, and was eagerly looking over MP I 14 136 21
"It is to be Lovers' Vows; and I am to be Count Cassel, MP I 15 138 3
"Lovers' Vows!"--in a tone of the greatest amazement, was MP I 15 139 5
so well, nothing so unexceptionable, as Lovers' Vows. MP I 15 139 6
It is about Lovers' Vows." MP I 18 167 9
unbound copy of "Lovers' Vows" in the house, for he was MP II 2 190 9
of a renewal of "Lovers' Vows", he should hold himself MP II 2 192 11
in the ways of the family, independent of Lovers' Vows. MP II 3 196 1
all his professions and vows of unshaken attachment might MP III 4 345 2
VOYAGE (2)
after a favourable voyage, was received; though not before MP I 4 34 2
information as to his voyage, and answer every question of MP II 1 178 8
VULGAR (16)
talked a great deal, seemed very happy, and rather vulgar. SS I 7 34 5
Had he been even old, ugly, and vulgar, the gratitude and SS I 9 42 9
The vulgar freedom and folly of the eldest left her no SS I 21 124 32
at the expense of their dear friend's vulgar relations. PP I 8 37 20
yet, whenever she did speak, she must be vulgar. PP III 18 384 27
though awkward, was not vulgar, her voice was sweet, and MP I 2 12 2
is not cramped into the vulgar compactness of a square MP II 7 243 27
will then feel--to use a vulgar phrase--that she has got MP III 9 394 1
But if he marries a very ignorant, vulgar woman, certainly E I 4 31 25
He will be a completely gross, vulgar farmer--totally E I 4 33 38
of the illiterate and vulgar all your life! I wonder how E I 7 54 29
there, not to be vulgar, was distinction, and merit. E II 2 167 12
"Just as they always do--very vulgar." E II 9 232 12
I think they are, without exception, the most vulgar girls E II 9 233 22
Elton's, probably some vulgar, dashing widow, who, with E II 14 275 33
A little upstart, vulgar being, with her Mr. E., and her E II 14 279 52
VULGARISMS (1)
Visions of good and ill breeding, of old vulgarisms and MP III 15 446 35
VULGARITY (8)
by her imprudence, vulgarity, or jealousy--whether by NA I 2 19 7
thing like impertinence, vulgarity, inferiority of parts, SS I 22 127 1
Mrs. Philips's vulgarity was another, and perhaps a PP III 18 384 27
and very distressing vulgarity of manner; but these are MP I 1 10 14
some excesses of very offensive indulgence and vulgarity. MP III 9 395 4
him driven away by the vulgarity of her nearest relations. MP III 10 402 11
appellation for them, deep enough in familiar vulgarity? E II 15 288 39
the Eltons with all the vulgarity of needless repetition, E III 14 442 8
VULNERABLE (1)
to assail her on her vulnerable side, she presently MP III 2 333 24
25

W. (13)
Elinor thought she could distinguish a large W. in the SS II 4 161 5
"There was a reason for that--replied Miss W. changing W 316 2
"When first we knew Tom Musgrave, continued Miss W. W 316 2
more to my mind--continued Mr W. or one better delivered.-- W 343 20
tho' charged by Miss W. to let nobody in, returned in half W 344 21
Mrs R. W. eyed her with much familiar curiosity & W 349 24
Mrs R. W. was indeed wondering what sort of a home Emma cd W 350 24
expressing his belief that W. never intended to go there, PP III 4 274 5
hopes, and said he feared W. was not a man to be trusted. PP III 4 275 5
had not made him ill. "your's ever, "A. W. " E III 14 436 7
Miss W. calls me the child of good fortune. E III 14 443 8
insult me with my second W. again, "meaning, for the rest P IV 9 203 73
a young W. Indian of large fortune, in delicate health."-- S 10 419 1
W. INDIANS (1)
"No people spend more freely, I beleive, than W. Indians." S 6 392 1
WADED (1)
It must be waded through, however. E III 14 436 6
WAFT (1)
The breeze had not seemed to waft the sighs of the NA II 5 161 25
WAFTED (1)
murdered to her; it had wafted nothing worse than a thick NA II 5 161 25
WAGER (1)
I would lay any wager it is about Miss Williams. SS I 14 70 2
WAGES (2)
gave her cook as high wages as they did at Mansfield Park, MP I 3 31 59
If they had hard places, they would want higher wages.--" S 7 401 1
WAGGON (1)
Not by a waggon or cart;--Oh! no, nothing of that kind MP I 6 58 35
WAGGONS (1)
understood in time what was intended as to the waggons. P III 5 38 34
WAINSCOT (4)
the pews were only wainscot; and there is some reason to MP I 9 86 9
marks and memorandums on the wainscot by the window. E II 5 187 4
dirty; and the wainscot is more yellow and forlorn than E II 11 253 41
portraits against the wainscot, could the gentlemen in P III 5 40 44
WAIST-COAT (1)
of his uniform waist-coat, which he had been promised to MP III 7 381 26
WAISTCOAT (2)
"and with me a flannel waistcoat is invariably connected SS I 8 38 12
the constitutional safe-guard of a flannel waistcoat! SS III 14 378 15
WAISTCOATS (2)
Shirts, stockings, cravats and waistcoats faced her in NA II 7 172 2
"But he talked of flannel waistcoats," said Marianne; "and SS I 8 38 12
WAIT (99)
could not require you to wait for his emancipation. LS 9 256 1
Miss Frederica therefore must wait a little. yours LS 19 275 4
spirit; & if I resolve to wait for that event, I shall LS 29 299 3
For this I shall impatiently wait; & meanwhile can safely LS 39 307 1
"But if we only wait a few minutes, there will be no NA I 6 43 42
Here was I, in my eagerness to get on, refusing to wait NA I 14 107 9
But for particulars Isabella could well afford to wait. NA I 15 122 28
ready lit, than to have to wait shivering in the cold till NA II 6 167 9
Can you wait for an invitation here?" SS I 15 76 11
had not patience enough to wait till the door was opened SS I 19 106 20
"Yes; and heaven knows how much longer we may have to wait. SS I 22 131 35
We must wait, it may be for many years. SS II 2 147 7
No, my dearest Marianne, you must wait. SS II 6 177 14
Wait only till to-morrow." SS II 6 177 14
to check her agitation, to wait, at least, with the SS II 6 177 15
I warrant you, Miss Marianne would have been ready to wait SS II 8 194 10
obtained her sister's consent to wait for that knowledge. SS II 9 203 9
to attend to their orders; and they were obliged to wait. SS II 11 220 3
and she should certainly wait on Mrs. John Dashwood very SS II 11 223 14
and they must wait to be married till he got a living. SS III 2 274 16
"Wait for his having a living!--aye, we all know how that SS III 2 276 28
will end;--they will wait a twelvemonth, and finding no SS III 2 276 28
to be sure, but we must wait, and hope for the best; he SS III 2 277 30
"This is very strange!--sure he need not wait to be older." SS III 3 281 12
talk of it; and can the Colonel wait two or three months! SS III 4 291 51
it is not worth while to wait two or three months for him. SS III 4 291 51
her sister's apartment to wait for the arrival of the SS III 7 312 17
evil hour, she resolved to wait till her sister's health SS III 10 343 10
them, they had nothing to wait for after Edward was in SS III 14 374 6
coming, he will wait in the passage, & come in with them.-- W 319 2
Nanny brought in the dinner;--"we will wait upon ourselves, W 341 19
wait, said she, so I put on the first thing I met with.-- W 353 26
"Oh! yes--it would be much better to wait till Jane was PP I 9 45 38
We may as well wait, perhaps, till the circumstance occurs, PP I 10 50 37
for his compliance, but could not wait for his reason. PP I 16 76 7
of Mrs. Bennet had to wait for their carriages a quarter PP I 18 102 75
she must wait for her own visit there, to know the rest. PP II 3 147 19
would not allow them to wait in the drawing-room, and PP II 4 152 5
Mr. Darcy would never have come so soon to wait upon me." PP II 7 170 8
My fingers wait your orders." PP II 8 175 20
It was not without an effort meanwhile that she could wait PP II 15 217 17
Bingley was also coming to wait on her; and she had barely PP III 2 261 5
to wait on her at Pemberley the following morning. PP III 2 266 17
And as for wedding clothes, do not let them wait for that, PP III 5 288 38
to wait, till her father was at leisure to be consulted. PP III 7 307 48
dear," said Mrs. Bennet, "you will wait on him of course." PP III 11 332 22
that it will be abominably rude if you do not wait on him. PP III 11 332 26
I was not in a humour to wait for any opening of your's. PP III 18 381 14
and she condescended to wait on them at Pemberley, in PP III 19 388 12
fair to expect Ellis to wait on her as well as the others. MP I 1 9 12
she only wanted him to wait till Sir Thomas's return, and MP I 4 36 7
have been long wishing to wait upon your good mother again; MP I 6 62 58
but they were so full blown, that one could not wait." MP I 7 72 44
Do wait for Mr. Rushworth." MP I 10 100 27
be to act together, nor wait very patiently while he was MP I 15 138 1
They did not wait long for the Crawfords, but there was no MP I 18 171 26
nothing till tea came--he would rather wait for tea. MP II 1 180 10
The rest might wait. MP II 3 202 26
The preparations of new carriages and furniture might wait MP II 3 202 26
I believe I must wait till there is an especial assembly MP II 4 214 45
not be happy to wait on Mr. Crawford as occupier." MP II 7 248 44
Sir Thomas was obliged or obliged himself to wait till the MP III 2 329 11
He had not to wait and wish with vacant affections for an MP III 17 470 25
But as she wanted to be drawing, the declaration must wait E I 6 46 22
a charge to go very slow and wait for the other carriage. E I 15 128 22
necessary preparations to wait for; and when he set out E II 4 182 6
and wait for her at Hartfield--if you are going home." E II 9 234 27
'Oh!' said he, 'wait half-a-minute till I have finished my E II 9 236 46
Emma would be "very happy to wait on Mrs. Bates, &c." and E II 9 237 47
48
"Ah! that ball!--why did we wait for any thing?--why not E II 12 259 17
She was out; and I felt it impossible not to wait till she E II 12 260 27
not having been able to wait on him and Mrs. Elton on this E II 14 280 54
Not to wait upon a bride is very remiss. E II 14 280 54
Better wait an hour or two, or even half a day for your E II 16 295 33
The gipsies did not wait for the operations of justice; E III 3 336 13
Her introductions and recommendations must all wait, and E III 6 352 2
pleased to wait a moment, and then ushered her in too soon. E III 8 378 4
wished her; she would wait--and, sure enough, yesterday E III 8 381 15
Emma found that she must wait; and now it required little E III 10 393 18
Let us wait, therefore, for this letter. E III 10 398 53
at home, to wait in the passage, and send up her name.-- E III 16 452 8
I assure you: yes, indeed, on purpose to wait on you all." E III 16 456 23
over, I imagine there will be nothing more to wait for." E III 16 460 56
not do me justice, only wait till my dear father is in the E III 17 464 24
She must wait a moment, or he would think her mad. E III 18 472 21
and authorising him to wait on Admiral Croft, who still P III 3 24 35
proposing also to wait on her for a few minutes, if not P III 7 59 24
or any servants to wait, or any knife and fork to use. P III 8 64 4
very pretty girl; and what were we to wait for besides?-- P III 10 92 46
go to their house--and wait the surgeon's arrival there. P III 12 111 50
only a maid-servant to wait, and at first, Mrs. Harville P IV 2 129 3
all her evening engagements in order to wait on her. P IV 5 158 21
she was still obliged to wait, for the Admiral had made up P IV 6 170 30
enough that they must wait till her brain was set to right. P IV 6 171 33
already, for I do not know what they should wait for." P IV 6 171 35
and having done her best, wait the event with as much P IV 10 212 1
her to wait till she might be safe from such a companion. P IV 10 215 14
too impatient to wait, had gone out the moment it had P IV 11 229 2
all her glossy curls & smart trinkets to wait on her.-- S 6 390 1
WAITED (44)
Mr Johnson, while he waited in the drawing room for me. LS 32 302 1
With a heart full of the matter, Mrs Vernon waited on Lady LS 42 311 2
and, while they waited in the lobby for a chair, he NA I 12 95 18
John Thorpe, who had only waited its arrival to begin his NA I 15 122 29
replied Catherine--finding that he waited for an answer. NA I 15 123 37
sanguine, having already waited on her excellent friends NA II 2 140 9
estimation of Northanger had waited unfixed till that hour. NA II 7 178 19
attentive pause with which she waited for something more. NA II 7 179 31
in the agreement; and she waited only for the disposal of SS I 5 26 5
told that Lady Middleton waited for them at the door, she SS II 6 175 1
left her, and while she waited the return of Mrs. Jennings, SS II 6 178 16
to tell her that his mistress waited for them at the door. SS II 11 222 12
judgment that she waited the very next day both on Mrs. SS II 12 229 1
Elinor, while she waited in silence, and immovable gravity, SS III 5 298 34
her sister's pulse;--she waited, watched, and examined it SS III 7 314 22
business; and when, as he waited at table, he had SS III 11 353 22
23
They all waited in silence for the appearance of their SS III 12 359 10
otherwise have waited the effect of time and judgment. SS III 13 370 36
Mr. Bennet was among the earliest of those who waited on PP I 2 6 1
The ladies of Longbourn soon waited on those of PP I 6 21 1
from Netherfield, and the servant waited for an answer. PP I 7 30 14
from the two elegant ladies who waited on his sisters. PP I 9 41 1
and Elizabeth, as they waited for the housekeeper, had PP III 1 245 4
the servants, while they waited at table, and judged it PP III 5 288 40
Mr. Gardiner had waited only for the letters before he set PP III 6 294 1
She had not waited her arrival to look out for a suitable MP I 4 42 17
and to being assisted and waited on by mistresses and MP II 4 206 3
Fanny felt that she must; and though she had not waited MP II 4 207 10
immediately, and only waited for courage to say so, when MP II 4 214 46
waited for, and a "let Sir Thomas know," to the servant. MP II 13 298 1
excite impatience, or be waited for, that before the MP III 10 403 13
dinner, and therefore pretended to be waited for elsewhere. MP III 11 411 19
Emma waited the result with impatience, but not without E I 7 53 22
Elton hardly waited for the affirmative before she went on. E II 14 278 45
they waited for dinner, he was talking to Miss Fairfax. E II 16 292 10
The two other gentlemen waited at the door to let her pass. E III 5 346 17
Square; and she only waited for breath to begin, when Mr. E III 13 429 26
27
In all probability she was at this very time waited for E III 16 458 44
again, he need not have waited till this time; he would P III 7 58 21
rest of the party waited for them at the top of the hill. P III 10 86 18
as Lady Dalrymple must be waited for, they took their P IV 8 181 1
I ought to have waited for official information. P IV 9 195 27
"I had not waited even these ten days, could I have read " P IV 11 237 42
He was waited on & nursed, & she cheered & comforted with S 2 371 1
WAITER (8)
come yet was told by the waiter as she knew she should, W 327 7
Jane and Elizabeth looked at each other, and the waiter PP II 16 220 9
You thought the waiter must not hear, as if he cared! PP II 16 220 10
is about dear Wickham; too good for the waiter, is not it? PP II 16 220 10
The waiter came into the room soon afterwards. P III 12 105 10
been got through, even by the smart rapidity of a waiter. P III 12 105 13
Pray sir," (turning to the waiter), "did not you hear,-- P III 12 106 14
cut of a laundress and a waiter, rather more of the P IV 9 192 5
WAITERS (2)
angry impatience at the waiters, made Catherine grow every NA II 5 156 4
the true style--and more waiters engaged for the evening E II 16 290 3
WAITING (98)
I have been waiting for you at least this age!" NA I 6 39 2
her that he had kept her waiting, did not by any means NA I 8 55 10
Have you been waiting long? NA I 9 61 1
friend's dissenting voice, by not waiting for her answer. NA I 9 67 33
Yes; I remember, I asked you while you were waiting in the NA I 10 75 26
answer a note, instead of waiting for me, you took the NA I 14 107 8
and the necessity of waiting between two and three years NA II 1 135 43
and the General were waiting to welcome her, without NA II 5 161 25
so strong, that without waiting for any better authority, NA II 7 177 19
in his wish of waiting on their worthy neighbours, that he NA II 15 243 9
denoting her intention of waiting on Mrs. Dashwood as soon SS I 6 30 7
curricle and servant in waiting at the cottage, and Mrs. SS I 15 75 2
Lady Middleton; I am only waiting to know whether you can SS II 1 144 12
Or have you none but that of waiting for Mrs. Ferrars' SS II 2 148 14
heart, he wo'nt keep her waiting much longer, for it is SS II 7 181 8
her return, and without waiting to have her request of SS II 8 192 1
Two ladies were waiting for their carriage, and one of SS II 8 199 37
covert, and they were kept waiting for two hours together. SS II 10 214 9
to the probability of their not waiting for any thing more. SS III 4 292 58
for Elinor; but she, waiting neither for salutation nor SS III 9 334 4
on that very day, without waiting for any farther SS III 9 335 6
her mother, without waiting for her assent, continued, " SS III 9 338 21
22
improvements; and after waiting some time for their SS III 14 374 6
"I am this moment going to dress, said he--I am waiting W 327 7
his friend Ld Osborne was waiting in the doorway for the W 334 13
or waiting to see how the young lady's inclination lay. W 339 18
of doing himself the honour of waiting on Mr Watson.-- W 344 21
without waiting for arguments to reason one into it. PP I 10 50 37
with the desire, without waiting to be argued into it?" PP I 10 50 37
the satisfaction of waiting on you and your family, Monday, PP I 13 63 12
mantlepiece, the interval of waiting appeared very long. PP I 16 75 3
earliest opportunity of waiting on her, after his return PP I 18 103 76
After waiting at home every morning for a fortnight, and PP II 3 147 25
very much objected to be kept waiting for her dinner.-- PP II 6 161 7
Collins having been in waiting near the lodges, to make PP II 14 210 1
leave, would take an early opportunity of waiting on them. PP III 13 344 3
where would be the harm of only waiting till September? MP I 4 37 7
in her eyes, for not waiting till Sir Thomas's return in MP I 4 37 9
home his son, and waiting the final arrangement by himself. MP I 4 38 9
I sat there an hour one morning waiting for anderson, with MP I 5 50 35
Fanny was ready and waiting, and Mrs. Norris was beginning MP I 7 67 15
for keeping you waiting--but I have nothing in the world MP I 7 68 18
The old coachman, who had been waiting about with his own MP I 7 69 21
son, and the poor fellow was waiting for me half an hour. MP I 7 73 53
and when people are waiting, they are bad judges of time, MP I 10 102 46
While waiting and wishing, looking now at the dancers and MP I 12 117 11
slow progress, and to feel the miseries of waiting. MP I 18 164 1
Lady Bertram seemed quite resigned to waiting.-- MP I 18 167 12
state admitted, were waiting only the arrival of Mrs. MP I 18 171 25
vessel, instead of waiting for the packet; and all the MP II 1 178 8
"Well," said Sir Thomas, as if waiting more to accomplish MP II 5 218 13
It came happily while she was thus waiting; and there MP II 6 233 15
irregularly round the fire, and waiting the final break up. MP II 7 249 49
I cannot bear to keep good old Wilcox waiting. MP II 7 251 64
I came to look for you, and after waiting a little while MP II 9 261 2
word; but Edmund, after waiting a moment, obliged her to MP II 9 262 10
his sister, who had been waiting for him to walk with her MP II 12 291 1
"What are you waiting for?" MP II 12 293 13

Mr. Crawford must not be kept longer waiting. MP III 1 318 39
Mr. Crawford has been kept waiting too long already. MP III 1 320 44
not by dint of several minutes of supplication and waiting. MP III 3 341 27
seemingly in waiting for them at the door, stept forward, MP III 7 377 7
the honour, however, of waiting on them again on the MP III 10 406 22
Rebecca's cookery and Rebecca's waiting, and Betsey's MP III 10 407 23
to Mansfield--without waiting for the two months to be MP III 11 411 16
must not be kept waiting; and Harriet then came running to E I 4 32 28
"Well," said the still waiting Harriet;--"well--and--and E I 7 51 6
to keep ahead, without any obligation of waiting for her. E I 10 88 33
earlier, but had been waiting the arrival of a folding- E II 7 208 9
kept his father's dinner waiting, it was not known at E II 8 212 1
While waiting till the other young people could pair E II 8 229 99
of my own," said Emma, "I am only waiting for my friend. E II 9 234 31
the house, and after waiting in vain for her friend to E II 14 271 6
While waiting for the carriage, she found Mr. Knightley by E III 7 374 55
You were kept waiting at the door--I was quite ashamed-- E III 8 379 8
keep you waiting--and extremely sorry and ashamed we were. E III 8 379 8
go home directly, without waiting at all, and his horse E III 8 383 31
Her voice was lost; and she sat down, waiting in great E III 11 405 16
"After waiting a moment, as if to be sure she intended to E III 13 425 6
7
but the truth is, that I am waiting for my Lord and master. E III 16 455 20
21
were also in town; and they were only waiting for November. E III 19 483 7
After waiting another moment-- "you mean Mr. Wentworth, I P III 3 23 29
30
and this, without much waiting for an answer;--or in the P III 6 42 1
looked rather in suspense, and as if waiting for more. P III 8 67 25
They had been a year or two waiting for fortune and P III 11 96 12
of absence, but without waiting the return, travelled P III 12 108 28
and a chaise and four in waiting, stationed for their P III 12 115 68
"How is Mary?" said Elizabeth; and without waiting for an P IV 6 165 10
The only wonder was, what they could be waiting for, till P IV 6 171 33
carriage, which was seen waiting at a little distance; she, P IV 7 174 2
found the others still waiting for the carriage, and Mr. P IV 7 175 5
at present, and adding, "I am only waiting for Mr. Elliot. P IV 7 177 15
grieved to have kept her waiting, and anxious to get her P IV 7 177 16
and the very party appeared for whom they were waiting. P IV 8 184 17
After waiting a few moments he said--and as if it were the P IV 10 225 60
have them all standing or waiting around her was P IV 11 238 45
But to be waiting so long in inaction, and waiting only P IV 11 243 70
needed, & so entirely waiting to be guided on every S 2 372 1

WAITING-MAIDS (1)

phaetons, and three waiting-maids in a travelling chaise- NA II 14 232 7

WAITING-WOMAN (1)

door, and Elizabeth saw that her waiting-woman was in it. PP III 14 353 20

WAITS (3)

follow command of language, as admiration waits on beauty. LS 16 268 2
speedily be furnished: it waits only for a lady's taste!" NA II 11 214 22
which waits only your approbation to be acted upon. E II 11 250 21

WAKEFULNESS (1)

on this occasion, with an unusual degree of wakefulness. MP II 9 271 41

WAKING (3)

"Louisa, you will not mind my waking Mr. Hurst." PP I 11 58 33
Sleeping or waking, my head has been full of this matter MP I 16 156 27
them, sleeping or waking, the last twenty-four hours--Mrs. E III 12 417 3

WALCOT (1)

"Hot! He had not turned a hair till we came to Walcot NA I 7 46 11

WALK (272)

space for the remainder to walk about in some comfort; and NA I 2 23 27
the graceful spirit of her walk, the fashionable air of NA I 4 34 7
on such an occasion to walk about and tell their NA I 5 35 1
fast as they could walk, in pursuit of the two young men. NA I 6 43 44
to ensure a pleasant walk to him who brought the double NA I 7 47 18
the Thorpes, set off to walk together to Mr. Allen's, and NA I 7 50 44
"Do not you?--then let us walk about and quiz people. NA I 8 59 37
I walk about here, and so I do there;--but here I see a NA I 10 79 54
She had never taken a country walk since her arrival in NA I 10 80 61
they they should join in a walk, some morning or other. NA I 10 80 61
"No walk for me to-day," sighed Catherine;--"but perhaps NA I 11 82 4
thing in the world than walk out in a great coat; I wonder NA I 11 83 13
and her brother to call on me to take a country walk. NA I 11 85 32
I suppose they thought it would be too dirty for a walk." NA I 11 85 40
Walk! you could no more walk than you could fly! it has NA I 11 85 41
for the beginning of their walk; and, in spite of what she NA I 11 86 50
thousand times rather get out now, and walk back to them. NA I 11 87 53
of the promised walk, and especially rather than be NA I 11 88 54
for wishing us a pleasant walk after our passing you in NA I 12 93 7
"But indeed I did not wish you a pleasant walk; I never NA I 12 94 8
when I called; I saw her walk out of the house the next NA I 12 94 9
were just preparing to walk out, and he being hurried for NA I 12 94 10
agreed that the projected walk should be taken as soon as NA I 12 95 16
daughter, rather than postpone his own walk a few minutes. NA I 12 95 17
to take their promised walk to-morrow; it was quite NA I 13 97 1
nothing to put off a mere walk for one day longer, and NA I 13 97 1
and must only beg to put off the walk till Tuesday." NA I 13 98 1
the elasticity of her walk, which corresponded exactly NA I 13 103 28
and was secure of her walk, she began (as the flutter of NA I 13 103 29
"No; I had just engaged myself to walk with Miss Tilney NA I 13 104 30
a very nice walk, and you are two very nice young ladies. NA I 14 108 16
The whole walk was delightful, and though it ended too NA I 14 114 49
of Isabella or James had crossed her during their walk. NA I 14 114 50
And was not it odd that he should always take his walk so NA II 7 177 18
extension of their walk, if Miss Morland were not tired. NA II 7 179 27
"This is so favourite a walk of mine," said Miss Tilney, " NA II 7 179 28
"It was my mother's favourite walk." NA II 7 179 30
"I used to walk here so often with her!" added Eleanor; " NA II 7 179 32
He did not love her walk:--could he therefore have loved NA II 7 180 37
herself again obliged to walk with him, listen to him, and NA II 7 181 41
objects, she soon began to walk with lassitude; the NA II 7 181 41
the mortification of a walk through scenes so fallen, had NA II 8 184 4
The General's early walk, ill-timed as it was in every NA II 9 191 3
on their quitting it to walk round the grounds, she was NA II 11 213 21
premises, consisting of a walk round two sides of a meadow, NA II 11 214 25
as if she could even walk about the house rather than NA II 15 240 1
They began their walk, and Mrs. Morland was not entirely NA II 15 243 9
of any change in those who walk under your shade!-- SS I 5 27 8
to visit any family beyond the distance of a walk. SS I 9 40 2
Margaret, we will walk here at least two hours." SS I 9 41 5
"I do not ask you to come in the morning, for we must walk SS I 14 74 21
in their usual walk, instead of wandering away by herself. SS I 16 85 15
If her sisters intended to walk on the downs, she directly SS I 16 85 15
country; in his walk to the village, he had seen many SS I 18 96 4
not been able to take your usual walk to Allenham to-day." SS I 20 111 10
Sir John wanted the whole family to walk to the park SS I 21 119 3
at their indifference, to walk home and boast anew of SS I 21 119 5
of their joining in a walk, where they might most easily SS II 1 142 8
hour, he asked Elinor to walk with him to Conduit-Street, SS II 11 223 15
walk out of the room again, as to advance farther into it. SS II 13 240 19
she could hardly walk; and Nancy, she was almost as bad. SS III 1 259 7
shrubbery, and closer wood walk, a road of Smith gravel SS III 6 302 7
She had depended on a twilight walk to the Grecian temple, SS III 6 303 11
We will walk to the farm at the edge of the down, and see SS III 10 343 9
children go on; we will walk to Sir John's new plantations SS III 10 343 9
arm, was authorised to walk as long as she could without SS III 10 344 11
to see him walk in to-day or to-morrow, or any day." SS III 12 358 6
The distance was not beyond a walk.--" W 339 18
Within a short walk of Longbourn lived a family with whom PP I 5 18 1
nothing better offered, a walk to Meryton was necessary to PP I 7 28 3
I do not wish to avoid the walk. PP I 7 32 37
Elizabeth continued her walk alone, crossing field after PP I 7 32 41
"To walk three miles, or four miles, or five miles, or PP I 8 36 10
Mr. Bingley, and a charming prospect over that gravel walk. PP I 9 42 7
At that moment they were met from another walk, by Mrs. PP I 10 53 59
I did not know that you intended to walk," said Miss PP I 10 53 60
arm of Mr. Darcy, she left Elizabeth to walk by herself. PP I 10 53 62
said,-- "this walk is not wide enough for our party. PP I 10 53 62
63
for their chusing to walk up and down the room together, PP I 11 56 12
I shall walk to Meryton to-morrow to hear more about it, PP I 14 68 14
his daughters in their walk; and Mr. Collins, being in PP I 15 71 6
countenance, air, and walk, as they were superior to the PP I 16 76 3
if she and her sisters did not very often walk to Meryton. PP I 18 93 18
and during the walk, he particularly attended to her. PP I 21 115 5
led by a short gravel walk to the house, amidst the nods PP II 5 155 3
Here, leading the way through every walk and cross walk, PP II 5 156 4
twice every week, and are never allowed to walk home. PP II 5 157 7
room getting ready for a walk, a sudden noise below seemed PP II 5 158 11
As the weather was fine, they has a pleasant walk of about PP II 6 161 8
Very few days passed in which Mr. Collins did not walk to PP II 7 168 3
Her favourite walk, and where she frequently went while PP II 7 169 5
of Charlotte and her sister, just returned from their walk. PP II 9 179 26
or the pleasantness of the walk to it, or of the people PP II 9 180 28
thought it necessary to turn back and walk with her. PP II 10 182 1
her utter amazement, she saw Mr. Darcy walk into the room. PP II 11 188 3
But perhaps," added he, stopping in his walk, and turning PP II 11 192 22
She was proceeding directly to her favourite walk, when PP II 12 195 1
point of continuing her walk, when she caught a glimpse of PP II 12 195 2
and almost resolving to walk after her till she could be PP II 13 209 13
went by without a solitary walk, in which she might PP II 14 212 16
a walk of Longbourn, they would be going there for ever. PP II 14 213 17
and he was obliged to walk about the room, while Elizabeth PP II 15 216 5
the rest of the girls to walk to Meryton and see how every PP II 16 223 25
They had now entered a beautiful walk by the side of the PP III 1 253 55
round the whole park, but feared it might be beyond a walk. PP III 1 253 57
walk amidst the rough coppice-wood which bordered it. PP III 1 253 57
The walk being here less sheltered than on the other side, PP III 1 254 57
This idea lasted while a turning in the walk concealed him PP III 1 254 57
He then asked her to walk into the house--but she declared PP III 1 257 66
Fatigued as she had been by the morning's walk, they had PP III 1 259 76
They had just been preparing to walk as the letters came PP III 4 273 2
with anxious parade, walk up to her mother's right hand, PP III 9 317 9
an intrusion, and walk away with him into the shrubbery. PP III 14 351 1
They proceeded in silence along the gravel walk that led PP III 14 353 20
Lizzy, you must walk out with him again, that he may not PP III 17 374 20
said Mrs. Bennet, "to walk to oakham mount this morning. PP III 17 374 23
It is a nice long walk, and Mr. Darcy has never seen the PP III 17 374 23
During their walk, it was resolved that Mr. Bennet's PP III 17 375 27
little know herself, as to walk home to the parsonage MP I 1 8 9
Let us walk out in the park, and you shall tell me all MP I 2 15 11
walking all day, thinking every body ought to walk as much. MP I 4 36 7
without a gravel walk to step on, or a bench fit for use. MP I 6 57 31
seeing one farm yard, nor walk in the shrubbery without MP I 6 58 37
I wish you had saved yourself this walk home." MP I 7 68 19
You know I am strong enough now to walk very well." MP I 7 70 29
persuaded, that when she does not ride, she ought to walk. MP I 7 73 55
nothing so refreshing as a walk after a fatigue of that MP I 7 73 55
to be done, was for him to walk down to the parsonage MP I 8 75 1
and walk half way down the park with the two other ladies. MP I 8 77 7
a long terrace walk, backed by iron palissades, and MP I 9 90 36
of it, and for some time could only walk and admire. MP I 9 91 38
at the bottom of the very walk they had been talking of; MP I 9 95 67
"Now, Miss Crawford, if you will look up the walk, you MP I 9 96 74
there was a straight green walk along the bottom by the MP I 9 96 76
was coming at a quick pace down the principal walk. MP I 10 100 24
She followed their steps along the bottom walk, and had MP I 10 103 49
acting; but I would hardly walk from this room to the next MP I 13 124 12
"I shall walk down immediately after breakfast," said he, " MP I 16 156 27
intervals of business, to walk into his stables and his MP II 2 190 9
again, to take them in her walk whenever she could, to MP II 4 207 10
yellow leaves about them, to jump up and walk for warmth. MP II 4 208 11
now it is converted into a walk, and it would be difficult MP II 4 208 12
There is such a quiet simplicity in the plan of the walk!-- MP II 4 209 14
it was a silent walk--for having finished that subject, he MP II 4 216 50
cried Mrs. Norris, red with anger, "Fanny can walk." MP II 5 221 36
"Walk!" repeated Sir Thomas, in a tone of most MP II 5 221 37
"My niece walk to a dinner engagement at this time of the MP II 5 221 37
"To walk and ride with me, to be sure." MP II 6 229 2
was unwilling to lose her walk, she explained her business MP II 8 257 15
minutes that she could walk about with him and hear his MP II 10 278 20
having seen her rather walk than dance down the shortening MP II 10 279 22
been waiting for him to walk with her in the garden, met MP II 12 291 1
when on returning from her walk, and going into the east MP III 1 322 51
Fanny would have had quite as good a walk there, I assure MP III 1 323 56
takes her own independent walk whenever she can; she MP III 1 323 56
and resenting this private walk half through the dinner. MP III 1 324 57
"I am come to walk with you, Fanny," said he. MP III 4 346 6
long while since we have had a comfortable walk together." MP III 4 346 6
to have a comfortable walk, something more is necessary MP III 4 346 8
room, and took no solitary walk in the shrubbery, in her MP III 5 357 4
There had been no free conversation, no walk on the MP III 8 388 2
the expediency of an early walk;--"it was a lovely morning, MP III 10 401 10
and her daughters, to take their walk without loss of time. MP III 10 401 10
seldom, with her large family, find time for a walk.-- MP III 10 401 10
dock-yard at once, and the walk would have been conducted (MP III 10 403 14
he absolutely would not walk away from them; and, at any MP III 10 403 14
and in the course of their walk back, Mr. Crawford MP III 10 406 21
Mrs. Price took her weekly walk on the ramparts every fine MP III 11 408 4
This was towards the close of their walk. MP III 11 411 19
that he had a delightful walk with you to the dock-yard MP III 12 415 1
2
He would walk round the ramparts, and join them with the MP III 15 445 29
I could not walk half so far." E I 1 8 15
I am afraid you must have had a shocking walk." E I 1 10 22
sufficed him for his long walk, or his short, as the year E I 4 26 1
to a walk, would be a valuable addition to her privileges. E I 4 26 1
made up his mind to walk out, was persuaded by his E I 8 57 2
beg your excuse and take my three turns--my winter walk." E I 8 57 5
you have another long walk before you, to Donwell Abbey." E I 8 58 7
"I do not often walk this way now," said Emma, as they E I 10 83 5
goodness to walk on, and she would follow in half a minute. E I 10 88 33
To walk by the side of this child, and talk to and E I 10 88 33
rights so as to be able to walk home in tolerable comfort. E I 10 89 36
in very good spirits, was one of the first to walk in. E I 15 124 1
we do come to any thing very bad, I can get out and walk. E I 15 127 14
Walk home!--you are prettily shod for walking home, I dare E I 15 127 15
She came solitarily down the gravel walk-- a Miss Martin E II 5 186 3
admired the situation, the walk to Highbury, Highbury E II 5 191 26
and it is a very dirty walk, unless you keep on the foot- E II 5 195 47
to chuse their walk, immediately fixed on Highbury.-- E II 6 196 1
us in their afternoon walk; which they might do, as our E II 7 209 10
Now I shall really be very happy to walk into the same E II 8 214 10
allow themselves only to walk with the two young ladies to E II 10 246 55
"Yes; my father is to join me here: we shall walk back E II 12 260 25
as he was returning from a walk with his little boys, when E II 16 293 10
A walk before breakfast does me good." E II 16 293 12
"Not a walk in the rain, I should imagine." E II 16 293 13
you chose to have your walk, for you were not six yards E II 16 293 15
16
By this time, the walk in the rain had reached Mrs. Elton, E II 16 295 29
kind," said Jane; "but I cannot give up my early walk. E II 16 296 35
as much as I can, I must walk somewhere, and the post- E II 16 296 35
know whether the wet walk of this morning had produced any. E II 16 298 58

should set off again, and walk half-a-mile to another	E II 17 302 23
She was then able to walk, though but slowly, and was	E III 3 334 6
The pleasantness of the morning had induced him to walk	E III 3 334 7
Emma and Harriet were going to walk; he joined them; and,	E III 5 344 3
persuaded--Miss Smith, you walk as if you were tired.	E III 5 345 11
We are to walk about your gardens, and gather the	E III 6 355 20
"Should not they walk?--	E III 6 359 37
walk, and the view which closed it extremely pretty.--	E III 6 360 38
In this walk Emma and Mr. Weston found all the others	E III 6 360 40
They took a few turns together along the walk.--	E III 6 361 40
Some are gone to the ponds, and some to the lime walk.	E III 6 362 44
"Certainly, if you wish it;--but you are not going to walk	E III 6 362 45
I walk fast.	E III 6 362 46
I would rather walk.--	E III 6 362 48
Shall we walk, Augusta?"	E III 7 372 38
that she would take her walk now, she and Mr. Weston were	E III 10 392 7
If we walk fast, we shall soon be at Randall's."	E III 10 393 17
again with Emma, in their walk to Hartfield, he was become	E III 10 401 69
He meant to walk with her, she found.	E III 13 424 1
and wanted to walk with her, but she would not suffer it.	E III 14 440 8
reply of, "beg her to walk up;"--and a moment afterwards	E III 16 452 8
He will have a hot walk."	E III 16 456 26
heat he was suffering, and the walk he had had for nothing.	E III 16 457 37
that I should have had this hot walk to no purpose."	E III 16 458 43
to take her almost daily walk to Lady Russell's, and keep	P III 5 32 1
and then she was well enough to propose a little walk.	P III 5 39 40
and when we have got that over, we can enjoy our walk."	P III 5 40 43
me, they are always tempting her to take a walk with them."	P III 6 45 9
There was a family of cousins within a walk of Uppercross,	P III 6 47 15
not dine from home, but he might walk in for half an hour."	P III 7 55 6
too, suddenly resolving to walk to the end of the village	P III 7 59 25
going to take a long walk, and, therefore, concluded Mary	P III 10 83 4
I am very fond of a long walk," Anne felt persuaded, by	P III 10 83 4
not like a long walk!" said Mary, as she went up stairs.	P III 10 83 5
for this walk, and they entered into it with pleasure.	P III 10 83 6
who evidently considered the walk as under their guidance.	P III 10 83 6
Her pleasure in the walk must arise from the exercise and	P III 10 84 7
Upon hearing how long a walk the young people had engaged	P III 10 90 38
done was unquestionably to walk directly down to the sea.	P III 11 95 9
into the water, the walk to the Cobb, skirting round the	P III 11 95 9
by him in their early walk, but she would have felt quite	P III 12 106 19
whom they had appointed to take their last walk about Lyme.	P III 12 107 22
what was to be their last walk; they would accompany them	P III 12 108 30
was such a general wish to walk along it once more, all	P III 12 108 30
last ill-judged, ill-fated walk to the Cobb, bitterly	P III 12 116 70
	71
When he came away, she was going to walk out with Captain	P IV 1 121 2
Anne was obliged to turn away, to rise, to walk to a	P IV 5 160 26
He was ordered to walk, to keep off the gout, and Mrs.	P IV 6 168 24
in every thing, and to walk for her life, to do him good.	P IV 6 168 24
Yes, yes, we will have a snug walk together; and I have	P IV 6 169 27
While Admiral Croft was taking this walk with Anne, and	P IV 7 174 1
Anne was most sincere in preferring a walk with Mr. Elliot.	P IV 7 174 3
as anxious to be left to walk with Mr. Elliot, as Anne	P IV 7 174 3
I walk.	P IV 7 176 11
if you are determined to walk; though, I think, it would	P IV 7 177 14
the present, by a toilsome walk to Camden-Place, there to	P IV 10 227 69
much on her own, before she was able to attempt the walk.	P IV 11 229 2
She must not walk."	P IV 11 238 46
How grave she will walk about with it, and fancy herself	S 4 381 1
broad walk in front, aspiring to be the Mall of the place.	S 4 384 1
was forced to move early & walk for health--but in general,	S 6 389 1
too active to regard the walk of a mile as any thing	S 6 390 1
Charlotte was fully consoled for the loss of her walk, by	S 6 391 1
benches by the gravel walk, they found the united denham	S 7 395 1
walk, & by addressing his attentions entirely to herself.--	S 7 396 1
They are never out of my thoughts when I walk here.--	S 7 396 1
His chusing to walk with her, she had learnt to understand.	S 7 398 1
My dear Tom I am so glad to see you walk so well.	S 9 408 1
replied--& mean to walk a great deal while I am here, if	S 10 416 1
"But you do not call a walk to traf: h. much exercise?--"	S 10 416 1
friend & her little girl, on this walk to Sanditon house.--	S 12 425 1

WALKED (241)

said he, as they walked back to the ball-room;--"not of	NA I 3 29 47
arm in arm when they walked, pinned up each other's train	NA I 5 37 4
Away they walked to the book; and while Isabella examined	NA I 6 43 34
John Thorpe, in the meanwhile, had walked away; and	NA I 8 58 25
Again Catherine excused herself; and at last he walked off	NA I 8 59 38
"Yes, we walked along the Crescent together for half an	NA I 9 68 42
and the ladies walked about together, noticing every new	NA I 10 71 8
rest of their party, they walked in that manner for some	NA I 10 71 8
John is just walked off, but he will be back in a moment."	NA I 10 75 23
The others walked away, John Thorpe was still in view, and	NA I 10 75 24
and the two others walked in, to give their assistance.	NA I 11 84 19
heart-rendering tidings, Catherine walked slowly up stairs.	NA I 11 89 62
he had been mistaken, for that Miss Tilney was walked out.	NA I 12 91 3
Away walked Catherine in great agitation, as fast as the	NA I 13 101 25
As she walked, she reflected on what had passed.	NA I 13 101 25
"I never look at it," said Catherine, as they walked along	NA I 14 106 2
without a moment's delay, walked out into the town, and in	NA I 14 114 50
bespoke an early dinner, walked down to the Pump-Room,	NA I 15 116 1
Without appearing to hear her, he walked to the window,	NA I 15 122 29
was passed on to the other, and he immediately walked away.	NA II 1 132 16
over; but then, as they walked about the room arm in arm,	NA II 1 134 37
her conversation, as she walked along the Pump-Room one	NA II 3 143 1
home, she joined her and walked out of the Pump-Room,	NA II 3 147 28
"How much better is this," said she, as she walked to the	NA II 6 167 9
breakfast room, Catherine walked to a window in the hope	NA II 7 175 13
Would the veil in which Mrs. Tilney had last walked, or	NA II 9 194 6
They walked slowly up the gallery.	NA II 9 195 19
Catherine walked on to her chamber, making up her mind as	NA II 13 222 8
mile apart; and, as they walked, Mrs. Morland quickly	NA II 14 236 19
As they walked home again, Mrs. Morland endeavoured to	NA II 14 239 28
the three Miss Dashwoods walked up from the cottage, and	SS I 13 65 32
When breakfast was over she walked out by herself, and •	SS I 16 83 2
They walked along the road through the valley, and chiefly	SS I 16 85 15
She walked eagerly on as she spoke; and Elinor, to screen	SS I 16 86 20
He dismounted, and giving his horse to his servant, walked	SS I 16 86 22
How have I delighted, as I walked, to see them driven in	SS I 16 87 31
"How strange!" said Marianne to herself as she walked on.	SS I 16 88 37
her story as she walked through the passage into the	SS I 19 106 21
When we met him, he turned back and walked with us; and so	SS I 20 115 50
Elinor made her a civil reply, and they walked on for a	SS I 21 128 8
And without farther ceremony, she turned away and walked	SS II 1 144 15
anxious for conversation, walked from one window to the	SS II 5 172 39
opened the door and walked in with a look of real concern.	SS II 8 192 1
after his entrance, she walked across the room to the tea-	SS II 8 198 30
He could say no more, and rising hastily walked for a few	SS II 9 206 25
than express admiration, walked off with an happy air of	SS II 11 221 5
to Fanny," said he, as he walked back with his sister.	SS II 11 228 53
"Pity me, dear Miss Dashwood!" said Lucy, as they walked	SS II 12 231 13
walked about the room, and said he did not know what to do.	SS III 1 259 7
Marianne got up, and walked about the room.	SS III 1 269 55
They walked up stairs into the drawing-room,--	SS III 5 294 4
it, she walked silently towards the table, and sat down.	SS III 8 317 7
He rose up, and walked across the room.	SS III 8 318 14
gay were my spirits, as I walked from the cottage to	SS III 8 324 42
withdrew from her sister and walked slowly up stairs.	SS III 10 348 34
He rose from his seat and walked to the window, apparently	SS III 12 360 22
	23
quitted the room, and walked out towards the village--	SS III 12 360 26
How soon he had walked himself into the proper resolution,	SS III 13 361 3
Colonel Brandon therefore walked every night to his old	SS III 13 369 34
Emma sorrowfully, as she walked into the dining room,	W 336 14
After this discovery she had walked twice to the window to	W 338 17
gouty foot--& Mr Howard walked by me from the bottom to	W 344 20
Mr. Darcy walked off; and Elizabeth remained with no very	PP I 3 12 14
He walked here, and he walked there, fancying himself so	PP I 3 13 20
"If we make haste," said Lydia, as they walked along, "	PP I 7 32 40
That she should have walked three miles so early in the	PP I 7 32 42
Elizabeth thanked him from her heart, and then walked	PP I 8 37 26
and soon afterwards got up and walked about the room.	PP I 11 56 10
Her figure was elegant, and she walked well;--but Darcy,	PP I 11 56 10
Mr. Denny and Mr. Wickham walked with the young ladies to	PP I 15 73 10
hour, she said, as he walked up and down the street, and	PP I 15 74 11
As they walked home, Elizabeth related to Jane what she	PP I 15 74 12
The gentlemen did approach; and when Mr. Wickham walked	PP I 16 76 3
He walked away again immediately, and she was left to fret	PP I 18 90 5
Mrs. Bennet and Kitty walked off, and as soon as they were	PP I 19 105 7
After breakfast, the girls walked to Meryton to inquire if	PP I 21 115 3
and another officer walked back with them to Longbourn,	PP I 21 115 5
Miss Lucas perceived him from an upper window as he walked	PP I 22 121 1
nephew; till the latter walked away from her, and moving	PP II 8 174 12
She was engaged one day as she walked, in re-perusing	PP II 10 182 2
"I did not know before that you ever walked this way."	PP II 10 182 2
	3
And accordingly she did turn, and they walked towards the	PP II 10 183 6
Elizabeth made no answer, and walked on, her heart	PP II 10 185 33
He sat down for a few moments, and then getting up walked	PP II 11 189 3
"And this," cried Darcy, as he walked with quick steps	PP II 11 192 22
rest on nothing, she walked on; but it would not do; in	PP II 13 205 3
Mr. Collins, and as they walked down the garden, he was	PP II 15 217 8
"This fine account," whispered her aunt, as they walked, "	PP III 1 249 40
said Elizabeth, as she walked towards one of the windows.	PP III 1 250 44
Elizabeth walked on in quest of the only face whose	PP III 1 250 47
As they walked across the lawn towards the river,	PP III 1 251 50
Mr. Darcy took her place by her niece, and they walked on	PP III 1 256 61
They now walked on in silence; each of them deep in	PP III 1 256 65
of being seen; and as she walked up and down the room,	PP III 2 260 2
has been very kind; she walked here on Wednesday morning	PP III 5 292 66
And so saying, he turned back with them, and walked	PP III 7 303 23
to write, and the girls walked into the breakfast-room.	PP III 7 304 33
of the house, for she had walked fast to get rid of him;	PP III 10 329 33
	34
As soon as they were gone, Elizabeth walked out to recover	PP III 12 339 1
Darcy had walked away to another part of the room.	PP III 12 341 18
young lady's whispering to Elizabeth again, he walked away.	PP III 12 342 25
a short survey, to be decent looking rooms, walked on.	PP III 14 352 19
to return into the house, walked quietly into it herself.	PP III 14 358 74
They walked towards the Lucases, because Kitty wished to	PP III 16 365 2
They walked on, without knowing in what direction.	PP III 16 366 9
day with one aunt, or walked beyond her strength at the	MP I 4 36 7
to one of her daughters, walked by her side all the way	MP I 5 51 40
while the rest of you walked about and settled things, and	MP I 6 62 58
rude and impatient; and walked to meet them with a great	MP I 7 68 17
Between ten and eleven, Edmund and Julia walked into the	MP I 7 71 31
Edmund got up and walked about the room, saying, "and	MP I 7 73 52
the opportunity as he walked with her through the hall, of	MP I 8 79 23
one impulse, one wish for air and liberty, all walked out.	MP I 9 89 32
of their regrets and difficulties, left them and walked on.	MP I 9 90 36
at; for we must have walked at least a mile in this wood.	MP I 9 94 60
we have walked a mile in it, I must speak within compass."	MP I 9 95 64
As she spoke, and it was with expression, she walked to	MP I 10 99 17
And she immediately scrambled across the fence, and walked	MP I 10 101 33
and vexation, and he walked to the gate and stood there,	MP I 10 101 33
sure, and I dare say you walked as fast as you could; but	MP I 10 102 46
He got up and walked to the gate again, and "wished he had	MP I 10 102 47
And letting himself out, he walked off without further	MP I 10 103 48
my word!" he indignantly exclaimed as they walked away.	MP I 12 119 26
Tom walked out of the room as he said it, and Edmund was	MP I 13 128 33
And so saying, she walked hastily out of the room, leaving	MP I 14 136 20
To this nest of comforts Fanny now walked down to try its	MP I 16 152 3
as she walked round the room her doubts were increasing.	MP I 16 152 3
They walked off, utterly heedless of Mr. Rushworth's	MP II 1 176 3
You will laugh at me--but I got out and walked up.	MP II 2 189 5
Henry Crawford was again in the house; he walked up with	MP II 2 192 11
a pleasant journey, as he walked with him to the hall door,	MP II 2 194 21
walked down to the parsonage on purpose to bring her back.	MP II 4 214 46
The two cousins walked home together; and except in the	MP II 4 216 50
and when Crawford walked up with the newspaper in his hand,	MP II 6 232 12
likewise out, she walked down to the parsonage without	MP II 8 256 14
satisfaction, she now walked home again--with a change	MP II 8 260 25
As she walked slowly up stairs she thought of yesterday;	MP II 9 267 23
looking at William, as he walked about at his ease in the	MP II 10 273 7
After seeing William to the last moment, Fanny walked back	MP II 11 282 2
conversation, and she walked home again in spirits which	MP II 12 291 1
and with averted eyes walked towards the fireplace, where	MP II 13 307 35
no particular meaning, he walked off by himself, leaving	MP III 1 320 45
She walked out directly as her uncle recommended, and	MP III 1 322 50
her having only walked out without her aunt's knowledge	MP III 1 323 53
you had walked in the shrubbery, or gone to my house."	MP III 1 323 54
When he and Crawford walked into the drawing-room, his	MP III 3 336 8
anything to say; and they walked on together some fifty	MP III 4 351 35
own way; and lastly in walked Mr. Price himself, his own	MP III 7 379 19
candle was brought, however, and he walked into the room.	MP III 7 379 19
smile over his face, walked up directly to Fanny--who,	MP III 7 384 34
sally-port; and Mr. Price walked off at the same time to	MP III 7 384 36
and Mrs. Price had walked about the room some time looking	MP III 7 385 37
turning pale about, when Mr. Crawford walked into the room.	MP III 10 399 3
while they walked on together at their own hasty pace.	MP III 10 403 14
what he had intended, and they all walked thither together.	MP III 11 408 1
"I had actually began folding my letter, when Henry walked	MP III 14 435 14
the impulse of the moment to resist, and still walked on.	MP III 16 459 30
immediately afterwards walked in and made it unnecessary.	E I 1 9 20
days absence, and now walked up to Hartfield to say that	E I 1 9 21
of twenty young couple now walked after her to church.	E I 3 22 5
He did not think we ever walked this road.	E I 4 32 29
He thought we walked towards Randalls most days.	E I 4 32 29
He walked off in more complete self-approbation than he	E I 8 67 56
the hero of this inimitable charade walked in again.	E I 9 81 78
say to Harriet, as they walked away, "these are the sights,	E I 10 86 24
	25
They walked on.	E I 10 87 29
They now walked on together quietly, till within view of	E I 10 89 36
towards it, and as they walked on slowly together in	E I 13 109 6
certainly very cold," and walked on, rejoicing in having	E I 13 110 10
nothing more;" and she walked on, amusing herself in the	E I 13 112 23
each gentleman as they walked into Mrs. Weston's drawing-	E I 14 117 1
open, and Miss Bates and Miss Fairfax walked into the room.	E II 3 172 22
	23
attached?--his air as he walked by the house--the very	E II 4 184 10
They walked thither directly.	E II 6 196 1
him was still living, walked in quest of her cottage from	E II 6 197 3
They had been speaking of it as they walked about Highbury	E II 7 208 7
Frank Churchill. in he walked, the first and the	E II 8 220 47
"They walked, I conclude.	E II 8 223 62
door; and her visitors walked up stairs without having any	E II 9 239 52
He hesitated, got up, walked to a window.	E II 12 260 28
He had returned to a late dinner, and walked to Hartfield	E II 17 302 23
They all walked about together, to see that every thing	E III 2 319 3
The whole party walked about, and looked, and praised	E III 2 320 5
by the two gentlemen, walked into the room; and Mrs. Elton	E III 2 322 18
He walked off to find his father, but was quickly back	E III 2 325 29
spoke to some, and walked about in front of them, as if to	E III 2 327 34

she walked about the lawn the next morning to enjoy.-- E III 3 332 1
also at the ball, had walked out together, and taken a E III 3 333 5
The young ladies of Highbury might have walked again in E III 3 336 13
He had walked up one day after dinner, as he very often E III 5 344 3
Mr. Weston had walked in. E III 5 346 17
walked home to the coolness and solitude of Donwell Abbey. E III 5 351 38
Mrs. Weston, while the dear girls walked about the gardens. E III 6 356 30
Mrs. Weston, who seemed to have walked there on purpose to E III 6 357 33
These were pleasant feelings, and she walked about and E III 6 358 35
was begun, however, Emma walked into the hall for the sake E III 6 362 43
and muttering something about spruce beer, walked off. E III 6 364 57
The Eltons walked together; Mr. Knightley took charge of E III 7 367 1
Jane declined it, however, and the husband and wife walked E III 7 372 40
They walked off, followed in half a minute by Mr. E III 7 374 54
Her eyes were towards Donwell as she walked, but she saw E III 8 378 2
entered the passage, nor walked up the stairs, with any E III 8 378 3
Emma's pensive meditations, as she walked home, were not E III 9 385 1
Emma's courage returned, and she walked on. E III 10 393 16
and walked by her, and talked so very delightfully!-- E III 11 409 35
sat still, she walked about, she tried her own room, she E III 11 411 43
but Mr. Knightley had walked in then, soon after tea, and E III 12 422 19
They walked together. E III 13 425 2
He had ridden home through the rain; and had walked up E III 13 433 41
cheeks; and as she walked along a favourite grove, said, P III 3 24 38
shew themselves: and Anne walked up at the same time, in a P III 5 35 18
be listened for, when the youngest Miss Musgrove walked in. P III 6 50 26
of the case, only nodded in reply, and walked away. P III 8 66 21
Captain Wentworth walked into the drawing-room at the P III 9 78 21
them here," before he walked to the window to recollect P III 9 78 22
and having found, and walked back with her to their former P III 10 89 35
they walked side by side, nearly as much as the other two. P III 10 90 37
the others walked on, and he was to join them on the Cobb. P III 11 96 10
seek her again; and they walked together some time, P III 12 107 23
He has walked with me, sometimes, from one end of the P IV 2 132 16
the folding-doors, and walked with exultation from one P IV 3 138 5
He had frequently observed, as he walked, that one P IV 3 141 13
He had never walked any where arm in arm with Colonel P IV 3 142 13
be talking of, as they walked along in happy independence, P IV 6 168 24
and the very next time Anne walked out, she saw him. P IV 7 174 1
She had hardly spoken the words, when Mr. Elliot walked in. P IV 7 177 16
in another moment they walked off together, her arm under P IV 7 177 16
cousin, if he would have walked by her side all the way to P IV 7 178 24
door opened again, and Captain Wentworth walked in alone. P IV 8 181 1
I walked and rode a great deal; and the more I saw, the P IV 8 183 13
were both Elizabeth and Anne Elliot as they walked in. P IV 8 185 20
of the morning, and Anne walked off with Charles and Mary, P IV 10 220 29
on one side, as Mrs. Clay walked quickly off on the other; P IV 10 222 39
I might not attend;" and walked back to her chair, P IV 10 223 39
Captain Wentworth left his seat, and walked to the fire- P IV 10 225 56
He turned back and walked with me to the Pump-Yard. P IV 10 228 71
He walked by her side. P IV 11 240 55
to all;--every body who walked, must begin with the S 7 395 1
said Mr P. as he walked with her to the door of the house-- S 9 411 1
cold that he had merely walked from one house to the other S 10 414 1
& celebrity from all who walked within the sound of her S 11 421 1

WALKER (7)
that one day Miss Walker hinted to her, that she believed SS II 8 194 12
in short, to recommend her, but being an excellent walker. PP I 8 35 3 4
much better fitted for a walker than a reader, was PP I 15 71 6
who was not a great walker, could go no farther, and PP III 1 254 57
but I am a very slow walker, and my pace would be tedious E I 8 58 7
not being supposed a good walker, "Oh, yes, I should like P III 10 83 4
body is always supposing that I am not a good walker! P III 10 83 5

WALKERS (2)
nor among the walkers, the horseman, or the curricle- NA I 5 35 2
of company on the hill--fewer carriages, fewer walkers. S 4 384 1

WALKING (160)
she may see her mother walking for an hour together, in LS 17 271 7
her situation, proposed walking, & we left the two LS 20 276 4
met Mrs. Hughes, and Mr. and Miss Tilney walking with her." NA I 9 68 40
on her brother's arm, walking slowly down the street. NA I 11 87 53
The three others still continued together, walking in a NA I 13 99 9
not have the pleasure of walking with her till Tuesday. NA I 13 100 15
gaily to Pulteney-Street; walking, as she concluded, with NA I 13 103 29
They determined on walking round Beechen Cliff, that noble NA I 14 106 1
saying she should join Mrs. Allen, proposed their walking. NA II 3 147 28
The pleasure of walking and breathing fresh air is enough NA II 7 174 9
of ease and good-humour, walking where they liked and when NA II 13 220 1
for ten minutes together, walking round the garden and NA II 15 240 1
As Elinor and Marianne were walking together the next SS I 12 58 1
in walking about the garden and going all over the house. SS I 13 67 65
walking over Mrs. Smith's grounds, or in seeing her house. SS I 13 68 74
window, and she saw a large party walking up to the door. SS I 19 105 13
"She is walking, I believe." SS I 19 105 19
her one day as they were walking together from the park to SS I 22 128 3
interesting employment of walking backwards and forwards SS II 4 166 31
and walking to the window as she spoke, to examine the day. SS II 5 167 2
Elinor was employed in walking thoughtfully from the fire SS II 7 190 55 56
She then went away, walking on tiptoe out of the room, as SS II 8 192 4
Mr. Ferrars, and Edward's immediately walking in. SS II 13 240 18
could not fancy dry or pleasant weather for walking. SS III 6 303 11
said John, as they were walking together one morning SS III 14 375 9
officer of the sett, walking off to the orchestra to order W 330 11
any chance conveyance, or did not mind walking so far.-- W 338 18
the question of, "have you been walking this morning?" W 345 21
their beauty, they are not fit for country walking."-- W 345 21
rest of the evening in walking about the room, speaking PP I 3 11 6
she was no horse-woman, walking was her only alternative. PP I 7 32 33
in her air and manner of walking, the tone of her voice, PP I 8 39 50
"I hope," said she, as they were walking together in the PP I 10 52 55
the greatest advantage in walking;--if the first, I should PP I 11 56 15
Lydia's intention of walking to Meryton was not forgotten; PP I 15 71 6
walking with an officer on the other side of the way. PP I 15 72 8
of rain as prevented their walking to Meryton once. PP I 17 88 15
with walking to the window and pretending not to hear. PP I 20 114 31
for Mr. Collins was walking the whole morning within view PP II 7 170 7
from this period of walking thither almost every day. PP II 9 180 28
After walking two or three times along that part of the PP II 12 195 2
walking in the grove some time in the hope of meeting you. PP II 12 195 2
Mrs. Gardiner, who was walking arm in arm with Elizabeth, PP III 1 255 60
After walking some time in this way, the two ladies in PP III 1 255 61
off, Elizabeth saw him walking slowly towards the house. PP III 1 257 66
They had been walking about the place with some of their PP III 2 260 1
He seemed scarcely to hear her, and was walking up and PP III 4 278 19
Jane and Elizabeth were walking together in the shrubbery PP III 7 301 1
my master, ma'am, he is walking towards the little copse." PP III 7 301 4 5
Some-where about the grounds, walking with a young man, PP III 14 352 8
to be alone with Jane, proposed their all walking out. PP III 16 365 1
was not in the habit of walking, Mary could never spare PP III 16 365 1
After walking several miles in a leisurely manner, and too PP III 16 370 35
"My dear Lizzy, where can you have been walking to?" was a PP III 17 372 1
Her father was walking about the room, looking grave and PP III 17 376 29
As far as walking, talking, and contriving reached, she MP I 1 8 9
walking all day, thinking every body ought to walk as much. MP I 4 36 7
Miss Crawford, as she was walking with the Mr. Bertrams. MP I 5 48 30
of each other; but by walking fifty yards from the hall MP I 7 67 16
that the others were walking down the hill together to the MP I 7 69 21
"What!" cried Edmund; "has she been walking as well as MP I 7 72 47
as well as cutting roses; walking across the hot park to MP I 7 72 47
should be tired with only walking in this sweet wood; but MP I 9 94 57
"Do you think we are walking four miles an hour?" MP I 9 95 65
dimensions of the wood by walking a little more about it. MP I 9 96 76
I have had walking enough." MP I 10 101 35
By their own accounts they had been all walking after each MP I 10 104 51
Miss Crawford, on walking up with her brother to spend the MP I 11 108 4
Tom Bertram and Mr. Yates walking off together to consult MP I 14 136 22
and more meet for walking about in, and thinking, and of MP I 16 150 1
you must not be always walking from one room to the other MP I 18 166 6
hall, of the two ladies walking up from the parsonage, MP I 18 168 14
on the propriety of their walking quietly home and leaving MP II 1 177 5
who then appeared walking towards them with Mrs. Grant. MP II 4 211 22
from the staircase window, and then they were walking." MP II 4 211 28
the very aweful ceremony of walking into the drawing-room. MP II 5 223 47
On the morrow they were walking about together with true MP II 6 234 17
and we were all walking after each other and bewildered." MP II 7 245 31
You have been walking too far." MP II 9 267 24
through difficulties of walking which she had deemed MP II 11 287 17
her arm within his, and walking along the sweep as if not MP II 12 291 4
was approaching, and was walking up and down the east room MP II 13 302 9
and getting up and walking about the room, with a frown, MP III 1 317 36
to work again; and Fanny, walking off in agitating MP III 1 325 62
walking together through the village, as he rode into it.-- MP III 3 334 1
walking alone in the shrubbery, he instantly joined her. MP III 4 345 5
walking towards the high street, with Mr. Crawford. MP III 10 401 10
believed it--but he was walking between them with an arm MP III 11 409 5
"No, papa, nobody thought of your walking. E I 1 8 16
for even solitary female walking, and in Mr. Weston's E I 2 18 11
As a walking companion, Emma had very early foreseen how E I 4 26 1
very next day, as they were walking on the Donwell road. E I 4 31 27
of survey; and walking a few yards forward, while they E I 4 31 27
He has not such a fine air and way of walking as Mr. E I 4 33 33
Compare their manner of carrying themselves; of walking; E I 4 33 34
"Good morning to you,"--said he, rising and walking off E I 8 66 55
I should not mind walking half the way. I could change my E I 15 127 14
Walk home!--you are prettily shod for walking home, I dare E I 15 127 15
Emma and Harriet had been walking together one morning, E II 1 155 1
used to be very often walking out with them--for Colonel E II 1 159 20
their daughter's not walking out often with only Mr. Dixon, E II 1 159 20
made her look around in walking home, and lament that E II 2 168 14
mental soliloquy, while walking down stairs from her own E II 5 189 20
perceive them walking up to the house together, arm in arm. E II 6 196 2
They were all three walking about together for an hour or E II 6 196 2
He perfectly agreed with her: and after walking together E II 6 203 42
be to have Jane Fairfax walking home again, late at night, E II 8 223 63
of Highbury;--Mr. Perry walking hastily by, Mr. William E II 9 233 24
they were walking into Highbury;--to Hartfield of course. E II 9 233 25
And Mr. Weston at the same time, walking briskly with long E II 11 254 47 48
half-hour they were all walking to and fro, between the E II 11 256 60
She heard of her walking with the Eltons, sitting with the E II 15 285 12
that he wanted, soon took the opportunity of walking away. E II 18 310 35
I forgot where we had been walking to--very likely to E III 5 346 16
Jane, Miss Bates, and me--and my caro sposo walking by. E III 6 356 26
It was hot; and after walking some time over the gardens E III 6 360 38
"But it is too far, indeed it is, to be walking quite E III 6 362 47
And for *me* to be afraid of walking alone!--I, who may so E III 6 362 48
not the *sort* of fatigue--quick walking will refresh me.-- E III 6 363 50
and wished herself rather walking quietly about with any E III 7 374 54
but, however, she is not; she is walking about the room. E III 8 379 8
It was settled so, upon the hill, while we were walking E III 8 381 17
I have been walking all this way in complete suspense. E III 10 394 27
When they had been all walking together, he had so often E III 11 409 35
The first, was his walking with her apart from the others, E III 11 410 35
where they had been walking some time before Emma came, E III 11 410 35
No longer walking in at all hours, as if ever willing to E III 12 422 20
heavy sigh, or even from walking about the room for a few E III 12 423 21
that Mr. Knightley, in walking up to Hartfield to E III 14 435 5
I have been walking over the country, and am now, I hope, E III 14 440 8
I was late; I met her walking home by herself, and wanted E III 14 440 8
Had we been met walking together between Donwell and E III 14 441 8
he had been walking away from William Larkins the whole E III 15 449 32
the chaise and four, and walking immediately after Lady P III 1 6 12
few months more, and *he*, perhaps, may be walking here." P III 3 24 38
end of it, to have their walking party joined by both the P III 5 41 46
And one day, when Anne was walking with only the Miss P III 6 46 10
seeing no cousin Charles walking along any path, or P III 10 85 16
"Oh! no, indeed!--walking up that hill again would do her P III 10 86 17
by whom she found herself walking, burst forth into P III 11 99 19
husband would have quite walking enough by the time he P III 12 108 30
and in this manner, Anne walking by her side, and Charles P III 12 111 49
There are several odd-looking men walking about here, who, P IV 6 166 16
Lady Russell to be often walking herself, but it so P IV 6 168 25
to Camden-Place; and in walking up Milsom-Street, she had P IV 6 168 25
and distinctly, Captain Wentworth walking down the street. P IV 7 175 4
no cousin returned) were walking off; and Captain P IV 7 176 10
I prefer walking." P IV 7 176 11
There were many other men about him, many groups walking P IV 7 179 28
ceaseless buzz of persons walking through, had P IV 8 183 11
Walter and Elizabeth were walking Mary into the other P IV 10 216 18
probably for the sake of walking away from it soon P IV 10 225 56
our walking together at Lyme, and grieving for him? P IV 11 232 15
observe Lady D. & Miss B. walking by--& there was S 7 395 1
for moving, but for walking on together to the terrace-- S 7 395 1
The two ladies continued walking together till rejoined by S 8 403 1
lawn, when she saw a lady walking nimbly behind her at no S 9 406 1
for not only had she by walking & talking down a thousand S 10 414 1
Walking up that hill, in the middle of the day, would S 10 416 1
At any rate, she was seen all the following morng walking S 11 420 1

WALKING-PARTY (1)
The walking-party had crossed the lane, and were P III 10 91 39

WALKS (25)
father's account, he always walks out at this time of day." NA II 7 177 17
"My father," she whispered, "often walks about the room in NA II 8 187 13
of his morning walks, and boded nothing good. NA II 8 187 14
in one of their earliest walks, discovered an ancient SS I 9 40 2
The whole country about them abounded in beautiful walks. SS I 9 40 3
recurred, her solitary walks and silent meditations, still SS I 16 83 4
had never happened to reach in any of their walks before. SS I 16 85 15
The woods and walks thickly covered with dead leaves." SS I 16 87 30
Two delightful twilight walks on the third and fourth SS III 6 305 17
said she, "we will take long walks together every day. SS III 10 343 9
by little beyond the walks to Meryton, sometimes dirty and PP II 4 151 1
her love of solitary walks, and her opinion of Mr. and Mrs. PP II 10 182 1
mother, "and shew her ladyship about the different walks. PP III 14 352 18
You will have the same walks to frequent, the same library MP I 3 27 35
How well she walks! and how readily she falls in with the MP I 11 112 34
Her features are not tragic features, and she walks too MP I 14 134 12
at in the form of hurried walks and sudden removals from MP II 2 188 3
and these two said walks, and his introduction to your MP III 12 415 2
might be; and how many walks up and down stairs she might MP III 14 432 10
had had in their moonlight walks and merry evening games; E I 4 28 6
Pleasant walks?-- E II 5 191 27
"He did not doubt there being very pleasant walks in every E II 6 196 1
up at home;--and very long walks, you know-----in summer E III 6 356 26
In all their walks, he had had to jump her from the stiles; P III 12 109 32
there had been so many walks between their lodgings and P IV 2 129 3

WALL (10)
and led her under every wall, till she was heartily weary NA II 7 179 27
have carried on the garden wall, and made the plantation MP I 6 54 9
apricot against the stable wall, which is now grown such a MP I 6 54 9
The lawn, bounded on each side by a high wall, contained MP I 9 90 36

and pinned against the wall, a small sketch of a ship sent MP I 16 152 2
taste, leaning against the wall, some minutes, to look and MP III 11 409 7
the end over a low stone wall with high pillars, which E III 6 360 38
She joined them at the wall, and found them more engaged E III 6 360 40
breaking into his orchard--wall torn down--apples stolen-- P III 3 23 28
staggering against the wall for his support, exclaimed in P III 12 110 37
38

WALLED (1)
farm-house--it is a solid walled, roomy, mansion-like MP II 7 243 27
WALLISES (3)
and obliging to us, the Wallises, always--I have heard E II 9 236 46
with him once at the Wallises, says he is the most P IV 7 177 20
The Wallises; she had amusement in understanding them. P IV 11 246 78
WALLS (25)
encouraged to expect another friend from within its walls. NA I 9 60 1
the happiness which its walls could supply--the happiness NA I 11 88 54
to take in its size--its walls hung with tapestry NA II 5 158 15
a glimpse of its massy walls of grey stone, rising amidst NA II 5 161 24
actually under the Abbey walls, was springing, with NA II 5 161 25
The walls were papered, the floor was carpeted; the NA II 6 163 1
attending her entrance within walls so solemn!-- NA II 6 166 9
in the same aspect; the walls surrounding which I built NA II 7 175 15
The walls seemed countless in number, endless in length; a NA II 7 178 21
convent, rich in the massy walls and smoke of former days, NA II 8 183 3
With the walls of the kitchen ended all the antiquity of NA II 8 184 4
as the thickness of the walls would allow them to judge, NA II 13 222 7
some miles beyond the walls of the Abbey before she raised NA II 14 230 1
green, nor were the walls covered with honeysuckles. SS I 6 28 2
drawings were affixed to the walls of their sitting room. SS I 6 30 5
Not a stone must be added to its walls, not an inch to its SS I 14 72 7
shut in with great garden walls that are covered with the SS II 8 196 22
five minutes within its walls, while the others were SS III 6 302 8
the bloom upon its walls, and listening to the gardener's SS III 6 303 10
I see walls of great pleasure. MP I 9 90 34
they might be secure of having four walls to themselves. MP III 5 357 6
The smallness of the house, and thinness of the walls, MP III 7 382 28
could only wander from the walls marked by her father's MP III 15 439 9
the 'squire, with its high walls, great gates, and old P III 5 36 20
be proud of between two walls, perhaps thirty feet asunder. P IV 3 138 5
WALNUT (1)
The old walnut trees are all come down to make room for it. SS II 11 226 39
WALNUTS (2)
order to bring her some walnuts, because she had said how E I 4 28 6
about the country to get walnuts for her, might very well E I 4 35 45
WALTER (107)
printer's hands; but Sir Walter had improved it by adding, P III 1 3 2
Elliot, Esq., great grandson of the second Sir Walter." P III 1 3 3
4
This friend, and Sir Walter, did not marry, whatever might P III 1 5 7
Be it known then, that Sir Walter, like a good father, (P III 1 5 8
years ago; and Sir Walter might be excused, therefore, in P III 1 6 11
Lady Elliot's death Sir Walter had sought the acquaintance, P III 1 7 14
Sir Walter had resented it. P III 1 8 16
by the family, as Sir Walter considered him unworthy of it: P III 1 8 16
the whole of which Sir Walter found himself obliged to P III 1 10 19
There was only a small part of his estate that Sir Walter P III 1 10 20
hold or his views on Sir Walter, would rather have the P III 2 11 1
all its due; and Sir Walter, independent of his claims as P III 2 11 2
was, as being Sir Walter, in her apprehension entitled to P III 2 11 2
of retrenchment, which was at last submitted to Sir Walter. P III 2 12 3
It did not appear to him that Sir Walter could materially P III 2 13 7
In any other place, Sir Walter might judge for himself; P III 2 13 7
Sir Walter would quit Kellynch-Hall;--and after a very few P III 2 13 8
Sir Walter had at first thought more of London, but Mr. P III 2 14 10
had been for Bath, Sir Walter and Elizabeth were induced P III 2 14 10
It would be too much to expect Sir Walter to descend into P III 2 14 11
neighbourhood for Sir Walter, was certainly much P III 2 15 13
Sir Walter could not have borne the degradation of being P III 2 15 14
approach it again; Sir Walter spurned the idea of its P III 2 15 14
Sir Walter and his family were to remove from the country. P III 2 15 15
"I must take leave to observe, Sir Walter," said Mr. P III 3 17 1
Could not be a better time, Sir Walter, for having a P III 3 17 1
If a rich Admiral were to come in our way, Sir Walter-----" P III 3 17 1
replied Sir Walter, "that's all I have to remark. P III 3 17 2
presume to observe, Sir Walter, that, in the way of P III 3 17 2
3
Therefore, Sir Walter, what I would take leave to suggest P III 3 17 4
Sir Walter only nodded. P III 3 18 5
These valuable pictures of yours, Sir Walter, if you chose P III 3 18 7
"As to all that," rejoined Sir Walter coolly, "supposing I P III 3 18 8
Your interest, Sir Walter, is in pretty safe hands. P III 3 19 10
"Nay, Sir Walter," cried Mrs. Clay, "this is being severe P III 3 20 17
"Then I take it for granted," observed Sir Walter, "that P III 3 22 22
been surprised if Sir Walter had asked more;--had inquired P III 3 22 23
And moreover, Sir Walter, I found she was not quite P III 3 22 25
He had the curacy of Monkford, you know, Sir Walter, some P III 3 23 32
them no service with Sir Walter, he mentioned it no more; P III 3 23 34
It succeeded, however; and though Sir Walter must ever P III 3 24 35
Sir Walter was not very wise; but still he had experience P III 3 24 36
Sir Walter, on being applied to, without actually P III 4 26 2
not but influence Sir Walter, who had besides been P III 5 32 2
Sir Walter, without hesitation, declared the Admiral to be P III 5 32 4
at Michaelmas, and as Sir Walter proposed removing to Bath P III 5 33 5
to go to Bath with Sir Walter and Elizabeth, as a most P III 5 34 11
was to draw Sir Walter, Miss Elliot, and Mrs. Clay to Bath. P III 5 35 18
The party drove off in very good spirits; Sir Walter P III 5 35 18
Little Charles does not mind a word I say, and Walter is P III 5 38 27
Miss Anne, Sir Walter and your sister are gone; and what P III 6 42 1
"Walter," said she, "get down this moment. P III 9 80 30
"Walter," cried Charles Hayter, "why do you not do as you P III 9 80 31
Come to me, Walter, come to cousin Charles." P III 9 80 31
But not a bit did Walter stir. P III 9 80 32
to have minded me, Walter; I told you not to teaze your P III 9 80 34
You will tell Sir Walter what we have done, and that Mr. P IV 1 127 28
Sir Walter had taken a very good house in Camden-Place, a P IV 3 137 1
He could refer Sir Walter to all who knew him; and, P IV 3 139 7
an ill-looking man, Sir Walter added) who was living in P IV 3 139 8
tempted Elliot, and Sir Walter was, moreover, assured of P IV 3 139 9
Sir Walter seemed to admit it as complete apology, and P IV 3 139 9
with Sir Walter, nothing to risk by a state of variance. P IV 3 140 11
They were describing him themselves; Sir Walter especially. P IV 3 141 12
Mr. Elliot appeared to think that he (Sir Walter) was P IV 3 141 12
last parted;" but Sir Walter had "not been able to return P IV 3 141 12
Sir Walter thought much of Mrs. Wallis; she was said to be P IV 3 141 13
Modest Sir Walter! P IV 3 142 13
"How is Mary looking?" said Sir Walter, in the height of P IV 3 142 14
Sir Walter talked of his youngest daughter; "Mr. Elliot P IV 3 143 18
When he questioned, Sir Walter and Elizabeth began to P IV 3 144 22
Sir Walter had once been in company with the late viscount, P IV 4 148 12
Sir Walter, however, would choose his own means, and at P IV 4 149 13
While Sir Walter and Elizabeth were assiduously pushing P IV 5 152 1
Sir Walter, Elizabeth and Mrs. Clay returned one morning P IV 5 156 14
was; and Elizabeth was disdainful, and Sir Walter severe. P IV 5 157 14
drawn up near its pavement!" observed Sir Walter.-- P IV 5 157 19
the set absent; for Sir Walter and Elizabeth had not only P IV 5 158 21
"What is this?" cried Sir Walter. P IV 6 162 3
Sir Walter wanted to know whether the Crofts travelled P IV 6 165 9
"Gout and decrepitude!" said Sir Walter. P IV 6 166 12
"I suspect," said Sir Walter coolly, "that Admiral Croft P IV 6 166 15
This was Sir Walter and Elizabeth's share of interest in P IV 6 166 17
Sir Walter, his two daughters, and Mrs. Clay, were the P IV 8 181 1
Sir Walter and his two ladies stepped forward to meet her. P IV 8 184 17
"A well-looking man," said Sir Walter, "a very well- P IV 8 188 38
Before Sir Walter had reached this point, Anne's eyes had P IV 8 188 41
"He had been introduced to Sir Walter and your sister P IV 9 200 57
"Give me joy: I have got rid of Sir Walter and Miss. P IV 9 203 72
"The name of walter I can drop, thank God! and I desire " P IV 9 203 73
with Miss Elliot and Sir Walter as long ago as September, (P IV 9 206 88
added another motive) to watch Sir Walter and Mrs. Clay. P IV 9 207 90
an opportunity of bringing him and Sir Walter together. P IV 10 213 5
as much to Sir Walter as she would have done otherwise. P IV 10 213 10
"And mine," added Sir Walter. P IV 10 215 16
in that house, Sir Walter and Elizabeth were able to rise P IV 10 216 18
So much was pretty soon understood; but till Sir Walter P IV 10 216 18
was thrown open for Sir Walter and Miss Elliot, whose P IV 10 226 63
The card was pointedly given, and Sir Walter and Elizabeth P IV 10 226 64
his lectures and restrictions on her designs on Sir Walter. P IV 10 228 70
Sir Walter made no objection, and Elizabeth did nothing P IV 12 248 1
Sir Walter indeed, though he had no affection for Anne, P IV 12 248 2
name, enabled Sir Walter at last to prepare his pen with a P IV 12 248 2
best hope of keeping Sir Walter single by the watchfulness P IV 12 250 7
sake, the possibility of scheming longer for Sir Walter. P IV 12 250 8
being the wife of Sir Walter, he may not be wheedled and P IV 12 250 8
It cannot be doubted that Sir Walter and Elizabeth were P IV 12 251 9
WALTER ELLIOT (13)
Sir Walter Elliot, of Kellynch-Hall, in Somersetshire, was P III 1 3 1
Vanity was the beginning and the end of Sir Walter P III 1 4 5
and the Sir Walter Elliot, who united these gifts, was the P III 1 4 5
a proper match for Sir Walter Elliot's eldest daughter. P III 1 8 17
but what Sir Walter Elliot was imperiously called on to do; P III 1 9 19
dignity of Sir Walter Elliot will be very far from P III 2 12 4
me, but Sir Walter Elliot has eyes upon him which it may P III 3 17 4
I venture to hint, that Sir Walter Elliot cannot be half P III 3 19 10
the tenants of Sir Walter Elliot: an extraordinary taste, P III 3 23 34
In all their dealings and intercourse, Sir Walter Elliot P III 3 24 36
Heir to Sir Walter Elliot!-- P III 12 106 16
but in Bath, Sir Walter Elliot and his family will always P IV 4 151 19
and dignity which ought to belong to Sir Walter Elliot. P IV 4 151 21
WALTZ (1)
beginning an irresistible waltz; and Frank Churchill, E II 8 229 98
WALTZES (1)
waltzes we danced last night;--let me live them over again. E II 10 242 17
WAN (2)
was reduced to so low and wan and trembling a condition as MP III 15 442 22
Do not pity me till I saw her wan, sick looks.-- E III 14 443 8
WANDER (6)
change of place, made her wander about the house till SS II 7 180 5
gave the eye power to wander, were many charming views of PP III 1 253 57
be more attentive, and not allow my thoughts to wander. MP III 3 340 25
and her eyes could only wander from the walls marked by MP III 15 439 9
troublesome topic, and to wander at large amongst all the E II 1 156 6
to let your imagination wander--but it will not do--very E III 5 350 37
WANDERED (6)
"Dear, dear Norland!" said Marianne, as she wandered alone SS I 5 27 8
out by herself, and wandered about the village of Allenham, SS I 16 83 2
She had wandered away to a subject on which Elinor had SS III 2 272 13
for her thoughts had wandered far from the subject, as PP I 18 93 32
She had only to say in reply, that they had wandered about, PP III 17 372 1
cousin, who wandered about the house, and thought of them, MP II 3 204 33
WANDERING (14)
own imaginations from wandering towards the perfections of NA I 10 77 33
But where am I wandering to?-- NA II 3 145 14
A more considerable degree of wandering attended the third NA II 14 238 22
in their usual walk, instead of wandering away by herself. SS I 16 85 15
Grecian temple, her eye, wandering over a wide tract of SS III 6 302 8
of country liberty, of wandering from place to place in SS III 6 303 9
bed, her thoughts wandering from one image of grief, one SS III 7 313 21
Their eyes were immediately wandering up in the street in PP I 15 72 7
After wandering along the lane for two hours, giving way PP II 13 209 12
Whilst wandering on in this slow manner, they were again PP III 1 254 57
her eyes from wandering between Edmund and Mary Crawford. MP II 10 273 8
After wandering about and sitting under trees with Fanny MP III 17 462 5
Fairfax had been seen wandering about the meadows, at some E III 9 391 21
to suppose his eye wandering towards her while he spoke, P III 8 63 2
WANDERINGS (1)
which are indulged in wanderings in a chapel, would be MP I 9 87 16
WANT (355)
marrying her, this want of cordiality is not very LS 5 249 1
I want her to play & sing with some portion of taste, & a LS 7 253 1
as I am not at present in want of money, & might perhaps LS 10 257 1
objection, but her want of character is one so much more LS 12 260 2
up if he can, for I do not by any means want her here. LS 16 268 1
her of ill-nature & sometimes to lament her want of sense. LS 17 272 8
I want to make him sensible of all this, for we know power LS 18 272 2
which equally marks her want of judgement, and the LS 24 289 12
come, no want of cordiality on my part will keep her away. LS 27 297 3
he, 'do you happen to want such a little thing as this? it NA I 7 46 11
"Thank you; but will not your horse want rest?" NA I 7 47 26
intimacy, by the frequent want of one or more of these NA I 8 56 11
They want to get their tumble over." NA I 9 61 1
mischievous creature, do you want to attract every body? NA I 10 70 1
Does he want a horse?-- NA I 10 76 28
them; and, besides, I do not want to talk to any body." NA I 10 78 40
I shall never be in want of something to talk of again to NA I 10 79 56
I want an appropriate simile;--as far as your friend Emily NA I 14 107 11
confessed and lamented her want of knowledge; declared NA I 14 111 29
Perhaps they may want observation, discernment, judgment, NA I 14 112 36
and who seemed only to want Mr. Morland's consent, to NA I 15 120 25
He could not be accountable for his children's want of NA II 1 129 1
of spirits, or for her want of enjoyment in his company. NA II 1 129 1
and that is exactly what I want to avoid, so I shall NA II 1 131 13
you do not consider how little you ever want, my dear." NA II 1 135 44
It is not the want of more money that makes me just at NA II 1 136 48
I only ask what I want to be told." NA II 4 151 21
Does not he want Captain Tilney to go away?-- NA II 4 152 27
"But I do not want any such pursuit to get me out of doors. NA II 7 174 9
in considering Isabella's want of consequence and fortune NA II 11 208 1
now begun to attribute her want of cheerfulness, hastily NA II 15 241 7
it strikes me that they can want no addition at all. SS I 2 10 15
what on earth can four women want for more than that?-- SS I 2 12 24
His eyes want all that spirit, that fire, which at once SS I 3 17 18
There was, at times, a want of spirits about him which, if SS I 4 22 18
each other in that total want of talent and taste which SS I 7 32 1
could want to make her mind as captivating as her person. SS I 7 33 3
had reasonably forfeited by their shameless want of taste. SS I 7 35 9
that he sometimes shewed a want of pleasure and readiness SS I 8 39 15
propriety, he displayed a want of caution which Elinor SS I 10 49 9
Marianne's imprudence and want of thought, surprised her SS I 12 58 1
"I do not want to pry into other men's concerns. SS I 13 65 39
"I want no proof of their affection," said Elinor; "but of SS I 15 79 33
attributing it to some want of liberality in his mother, SS I 17 90 1
my ignorance and want of taste if we come to particulars. SS I 18 96 4
at her want of thought could not be surpassed by his. SS I 18 98 12
His want of spirits, of openness, and of consistency, were SS I 19 102 2
usually attributed to his want of independence, and his SS I 19 102 2
"Come, come; this is all an effusion of immediate want of SS I 19 103 7
You want nothing but patience--or give it a more SS I 19 103 7
of the youngest, to her want of real elegance and SS I 21 124 32
mental improvement, her want of information in the most SS I 22 127 2
of feeling, the thorough want of delicacy, of rectitude, SS I 22 127 2
with ignorance; whose want of instruction prevented their SS I 22 127 2
all the world, and if you want me at the card-table now, I SS II 1 144 12
to compound for the want of much real enjoyment from any SS II 5 168 11
and giddy from a long want of proper rest and food; for it SS II 7 185 16

Context	Work	Vol.	Ch.	Page	Line
and with your pretty face you will never want admirers.	SS	II	8	192	3
settled in your little cottage and want for nothing!	SS	II	11	222	11
of demeanour, and a general want of understanding.	SS	II	12	229	2
for being agreeable--want of sense, either natural or	SS	II	12	233	18
of elegance--want of spirits--or want of temper.	SS	II	12	233	18
Lucy does not want sense, and that is the foundation on	SS	III	1	263	27
and Mrs. Jennings should want company, I am sure we should	SS	III	2	275	25
more than atoned for that want of recollection and	SS	III	6	304	13
herself, that she should want him to play at piquet of an	SS	III	7	309	5
great deal of instruction which I now feel myself to want."	SS	III	10	343	9
imprudence towards myself, and want of kindness to others.	SS	III	10	345	28
my sufferings, and that my want of fortitude under them	SS	III	10	345	28
of ignorance of the world--and want of employment.	SS	III	13	362	5
to her ignorance and a want of liberality in some of her	SS	III	13	366	21
imputed, by him, to her want of education; and till her	SS	III	13	366	21
& among so many officers, you will hardly want partners.	W			315	1
I want to dance with her--& I will come & stand by you."--	W			333	13
"Aye do--& if you find she does not want much talking to,	W			333	13
If she is like her sisters, she will only want to be	W			333	13
& he did not particularly want to compliment her; but Miss	W			357	28
in possession of a good fortune, must be in want of a wife.	PP	I	1	3	1
"Do not you want to know who has taken it?" cried his wife	PP	I	1	3	7
"You want to tell me, and I have no objection to hearing	PP	I	1	3	8
thousand a year, should want one of my girls, I shall not	PP	I	7	29	12
"I shall be very fit to see Jane--which is all I want."	PP	I	7	32	35
"You dislike an argument, and want to silence this."	PP	I	10	51	41
to tell you, that I do not want to dance a reel at all--	PP	I	10	52	50
He does not want abilities.	PP	I	16	82	48
want of presence of mind; Charlotte tried to console her.	PP	I	18	90	5
be the case, there can at least be no want of subject.--	PP	I	18	93	29
"I want to know," said she, with a countenance no less	PP	I	18	95	49
Come, Kitty, I want you up stairs."	PP	I	19	104	4
must be their pleasantest preservative from want.	PP	I	22	122	3
easiness of temper, that want of proper resolution which	PP	II	1	133	3
I only want to think you perfect, and you set yourself	PP	II	1	135	11
Thoughtlessness, want of attention to other people's	PP	II	1	136	17
feelings, and want of resolution, will do the business."	PP	II	1	136	17
which the want of fortune would make so very imprudent.	PP	II	3	144	2
withheld by immediate want of fortune, from entering into	PP	II	3	145	7
pounds, you want to find out that he is mercenary."	PP	II	4	153	9
than one young lady was sitting down in want of a partner.	PP	II	8	175	18
When have you been prevented by want of money from going	PP	II	10	183	11
of greater weight, I may suffer from the want of money.	PP	II	10	183	12
a deeper wound from the want of importance in his friend's	PP	II	10	187	40
than from their want of sense; and she was quite decided	PP	II	10	187	40
line of each, there was a want of that cheerfulness which	PP	II	11	188	1
aside, in my own case; the want of connection could not be	PP	II	12	198	5
comparison of that total want of propriety so frequently,	PP	II	12	198	5
The vicious propensities--the want of principle which he	PP	II	12	200	5
I do so want papa to take us all there for the summer!	PP	II	16	219	6
There is one point, on which I want your advice.	PP	II	17	226	21
I want to be told whether I ought, or ought not to make	PP	II	17	226	21
"And Lydia used to want to go to London," added Kitty.	PP	III	6	299	24
But there are two things that I want very much to know;--	PP	III	7	304	27
She was more alive to the disgrace, which the want of new	PP	III	8	310	10
There was no want of discourse.	PP	III	9	316	6
It was owing to him, to his reserve, and want of proper	PP	III	10	324	2
you know, and I am sure I never want to see him again.	PP	III	11	331	14
We want none of them; do we?"	PP	III	12	341	17
my love, I want to speak to you," took her out of the room.	PP	III	13	345	12, 13
and called out, "Lizzy, my dear, I want to speak with you."	PP	III	13	345	13, 14
but wonder at such a want of penetration, or fear that	PP	III	15	364	25
I want to talk very seriously.	PP	III	17	373	15
"I am more likely to want time than courage, Elizabeth.	PP	III	18	382	18
of children, and such a want of almost every thing else,	MP	I	1	4	2
to see her want, while I had a bit of bread to give her?	MP	I	1	7	8
from their cousin's total want of it, they were soon able	MP	I	2	12	3
Did she, in short, want any thing he could possibly get	MP	I	2	15	10
Do you know, she says she does not want to learn either	MP	I	2	19	28
indeed, and shows a great want of genius and emulation.	MP	I	2	19	29
with proper masters, and could want nothing more.	MP	I	2	20	31
nobody at home seemed to want her; but William determining,	MP	I	2	21	34
occasion; not for their sorrow, but for their want of it.	MP	I	3	32	64
any time when they did not want them;" and as the Miss	MP	I	4	35	7
and poultry, was very much in want of some variety at home.	MP	I	4	41	15
She did not want to see or understand.	MP	I	5	44	3
He did not want them to die of love; but with sense and	MP	I	5	45	3
got into a dreadful scrape last year from the want of them.	MP	I	5	51	40
To want a horse and cart in the country seemed impossible,	MP	I	6	58	37
"You can never want employment.	MP	I	6	61	57
"No, I do not know, not if you want the mare," was her	MP	I	7	69	27
"I do not want her at all for myself," said he; "but	MP	I	7	69	28
her to escape; while the want of that higher species of	MP	I	9	91	36
Your prospects, however, are too fair to justify want of	MP	I	10	99	16
Indolence and love of ease--a want of all laudable	MP	I	11	110	23
elder, she did not even want to attract him beyond what	MP	I	12	114	2
"if you want to dance, Fanny, I will stand up with you."--	MP	I	12	118	22
poor woman! must want a lover as much as any one of them.	MP	I	12	119	22
want to make a table for Mrs. Rushworth, you know.--	MP	I	12	119	23
"To want to nail me to a card table for the next two hours	MP	I	12	119	26
For mere amusement among ourselves, we should want nothing	MP	I	13	124	8
It would show great want of feeling on my father's account,	MP	I	13	125	17
We want no audience, no publicity.	MP	I	13	125	18
out, "no want of hands in our theatre, Miss Bertram.	MP	I	13	129	38
No want of under strappers-----	MP	I	13	129	38
Crawford, after a short pause, "at this want of an Anhalt.	MP	I	15	144	32
"They do not want me at all," said she, seating herself.	MP	I	15	144	36
and the conversation incessant, "we want your services."	MP	I	15	145	43
"Oh! we do not want to disturb you from your seat.	MP	I	15	145	45
We do not want your present services.	MP	I	15	145	45
We shall only want you in our play.	MP	I	15	145	45
"I want to consult.	MP	I	16	153	6
I want your opinion."	MP	I	16	153	6
You want to be reading.	MP	I	16	156	27
lookings on, at your ease, in this way,--I want you here.--	MP	I	18	166	6
his daughters helped to conceal the want of real harmony.	MP	II	2	191	11
She did not want exposure to be added to desertion.--	MP	II	2	194	19
she happened to be particularly in want of green baize.	MP	II	2	195	22
We are sometimes a little in want of animation among	MP	II	3	196	2
Do you want to be told that you are only unlike other	MP	II	3	197	6
Go to my father if you want to be complimented.	MP	II	3	197	6
Independence was more needful than ever; the want of it at	MP	II	3	202	25
And besides, I want to play something more to you--a very	MP	II	4	207	9
What can you want but a decent maintenance?	MP	II	4	213	40
We none of us want to hear the bill of fare.	MP	II	4	215	49
I cannot spare her, and I am sure she does not want to go.-	MP	II	5	217	1
Fanny, you do not want to go, do you?"	MP	II	5	217	1
to Lady Bertram's niece, could never want explanation.	MP	II	5	218	18
seemed to want to be encouraged even by her to resolve on.	MP	II	5	223	48
his lovely Maria will ever want him to make two-and-forty	MP	II	5	224	53
I only want her to look kindly on me, to give me smiles as	MP	II	6	231	9
I want nothing more."	MP	II	6	231	9
parcel by you that I want to get conveyed to your cousins."	MP	II	7	245	32
There was no want of respect in the young man's address;	MP	II	7	246	37
"I want to be your neighbour, Sir Thomas, as you have	MP	II	7	247	38
I want to consult you."	MP	II	9	262	7
"but what it is that you want to consult me about?"	MP	II	9	262	10
the usual observances without any apparent want of spirits.	MP	II	9	265	20
said, "if you only want me as a listener, cousin, I will	MP	II	9	269	34
when they want to be influenced against their conscience.	MP	II	9	269	35
I only want to talk to you."	MP	II	9	269	35
ma'am, how much we want dear Mrs. Rushworth and Julia to-	MP	II	10	277	16
You will not want to be talked to.	MP	II	10	278	20
herself for some little want of attention to her when they	MP	II	11	282	3
She felt the want of his society every day, almost every	MP	II	11	285	15
hour; and was too much in want of it to derive any thing	MP	II	11	285	15
I may be discovered by those who want to see me.	MP	II	11	289	32
the world, and you do not want for fortune; and as to her	MP	II	12	293	11
confide in her," said he; "and that is what I want."	MP	II	12	294	17
Fanny could not speak, but he did not want her to speak.	MP	II	13	298	3
no want of delicacy on his part could make a trifle to her.	MP	II	13	301	7
do not want, I cannot bear, I must not listen to such-----	MP	II	13	302	8
I do not want to add to any thing you may now be feeling,	MP	III	1	321	47
What should Sir Thomas want you for?	MP	III	1	325	60
Here was again a want of delicacy and regard for others	MP	III	2	328	9
How evidently was there a gross want of feeling and	MP	III	2	329	9
secondary causes, the want of management of the voice, of	MP	III	3	339	22
from the first cause, want of early attention and habit;	MP	III	3	339	22
I want to be set right.	MP	III	3	342	33
the match inconsiderately, there was no want of foresight.	MP	III	5	361	16
"I do not know how it is," said he, "but we seem to want	MP	III	6	372	20
But manner Fanny did not want.	MP	III	7	377	9
was sure her sister must want something after her journey."	MP	III	7	383	32
He did not want abilities; but he had no curiosity, and no	MP	III	8	389	3
herself, she should never want that again--and no reproach	MP	III	9	396	7
Fanny was most conveniently in want of rest.	MP	III	10	403	15
I want you at home, that I may have your opinion about	MP	III	13	423	2
in her marriage, from the want of other employment, and	MP	III	13	425	6
I want to know the state of things at Mansfield Park, and	MP	III	14	433	13
never do enough for one who seemed so much to want her.	MP	III	16	449	4
The want of common discretion, of caution--his going down	MP	III	16	455	19
have been too happy and too busy to want any other object.	MP	III	16	455	23
of six-and-twenty, with no want of sense, or good	MP	III	17	462	4
With so much true merit and true love, and no want of	MP	III	17	473	32
long enough to begin to want an increase of income, and	MP	III	17	473	32
The want of Miss Taylor would be felt every hour of every	E	I	1	6	6
"Well," said Emma, willing to let it pass--"you want to	E	I	1	11	35
But if you want to shew him any attention, my dear, ask	E	I	1	14	47
It was most unlikely, therefore, that he should ever want	E	I	2	17	7
an hour's ennui, from the want of her companionableness:	E	I	2	18	11
shewed that there was no want of taste, though strength of	E	I	4	26	2
Two such she did not want.	E	I	4	26	2
They have no in-doors man--else they do not want for any	E	I	4	30	21
I want to see you permanently well connected--and to that	E	I	4	31	24
is nothing, compared with his entire want of gentility.	E	I	4	32	30
not by her, there being a want of elegance of feature	E	I	4	35	45
This did not want much of being finished, when I put it	E	I	6	45	21
There was no want of likeness, she had been fortunate in	E	I	6	47	27
man is determined not to lose any thing for want of asking.	E	I	7	50	2
But do not imagine that I want to influence you."	E	I	7	52	19
"And I am sure I should never want to go there; for I am	E	I	7	55	39
Men of sense, whatever you may chuse to say, do not want	E	I	8	64	47
eyes; but at present I only want to keep Harriet to myself.	E	I	8	66	54
It will give you every thing that you want--consideration,	E	I	9	74	20
in;--no servant that I want to inquire about of his	E	I	10	83	7
Fortune I do not want; employment I do not want;	E	I	10	84	15
consequence I do not want: I believe few married women are	E	I	10	84	15
want of employment at forty or fifty than one-and-twenty.	E	I	10	85	21
point of inferiority, the want of which is really the	E	I	10	85	21
the want of respectful forbearance towards her father.	E	I	11	93	5
I only want to know that Mr. Martin is not very, very	E	I	12	99	11
I want his directions no more than his drugs."	E	I	12	106	60
imagining her blind and ignorant, and in want of counsel.	E	I	13	112	23
being so overcharged as to want only a milder air to	E	I	13	112	24
to her, "we want only two more to be just the right number.	E	I	14	119	6, 7
and felt sure that he would want to be just talking nonsense.	E	I	15	129	23
The very want of such equality might prevent his	E	I	16	136	9
He cannot want money--he cannot want leisure.	E	I	18	146	12
displeased; "I do not want to think ill of him. I should	E	I	18	149	28
They want her (Mr. and Mrs. Dixon) excessively to come	E	II	1	160	23
And besides, I must give you a hint, Frank; any want of	E	II	5	194	40
The want of proper families in the place, and the	E	II	6	198	5
A most deplorable want of complexion."	E	II	6	199	9
could make amends for the want of the fine glow of health.	E	II	6	199	10
But I must be more in want of a friend, or an agreeable	E	II	6	203	41
at Hartfield, to make Emma want their advice; and, which	E	II	7	206	5
With their wealth, their views increased; their want of a	E	II	7	207	6
I do not want the match--I do not want to injure dear	E	II	8	224	67
"But Mr. Knightley does not want to marry.	E	II	8	225	74
Miss Woodhouse looks as if she did not want me.	E	II	9	234	30
But then, Mrs. Goddard will want to see it.--	E	II	9	235	36
But I shall want the ribbon directly--so it had better go	E	II	9	235	36
I want to inquire after you all, but particularly your	E	II	10	244	35
You want your neighbours' opinions.	E	II	11	254	50
I think we do want a larger council.	E	II	11	255	50
total want of spirits when he did come might redeem him.	E	II	12	259	12
I want you to save yourself from greater pain.	E	II	13	268	12
Want gratitude to you!--	E	II	13	268	14
ourselves, I think we shall not be long in want of allies.	E	II	14	277	38
Cole does not want to be wiser or wittier than his	E	II	15	288	38
Mr. Knightley--"I do not accuse her of want of feeling.	E	II	15	289	40
She was a little shocked at the want of two drawing rooms,	E	II	16	290	3
If you want any further explanation," continued he,	E	II	16	296	43
them; I am sure they will want it;--afterwards I may	E	II	17	300	9
too communicative to want others to talk, was very well	E	II	17	304	29
lady; perhaps there was want of spirit in the pretence of	E	II	18	307	17
there, than she was before, and she begins to want change.	E	II	18	307	20
own praises, and did not want to hear more;--and the	E	III	2	324	22
do not tell me-- I do not want to know what you mean.--	E	III	2	325	28
but confess, Emma, that you did want him to marry Harriet."	E	III	2	330	48
and begged them not to want more, or to use her ill.--	E	III	3	334	6
I do not want to say more than is necessary--I am too much	E	III	4	337	4
I want to puzzle you again."	E	III	5	347	19
a child, than in a total want of taste for what he saw,	E	III	6	362	43
I want a change.	E	III	6	365	62
be something for a young man so much in want of a change.	E	III	6	365	67
There was a languor, a want of spirits, a want of union,	E	III	7	367	1
into her own room--I want her to lie down upon the bed.	E	III	8	379	8
Emma did not want to be classed with the Mrs. Eltons, the	E	III	9	390	19
her saying, that she was not at all in want of any thing."	E	III	9	391	20
I shall not be far off, if you want me."--	E	III	10	394	25
He seemed to want to be acquainted with her.	E	III	11	409	35
I am not in want of that sort of compassion.	E	III	13	426	15
I want to have your opinion of her looks.	E	III	14	439	8
Emma was gratified, and would soon have shown no want of	E	III	16	453	10
You and I shall not want opportunities.	E	III	16	453	13
But I want to set your heart at ease as to Mrs. S.--	E	III	16	454	13
I want you to call me something else, but I do not know	E	III	17	462	11
Whom did he ever want to consult on business but Mr.	E	III	17	466	29
there was no longer a want of subject or animation--or of	E	III	18	476	46, 47
as long as she should want her, instead of going to Bath.	P	III	5	33	7
Anne had better stay, for nobody will want her in Bath."	P	III	5	33	7
"I never want them, I assure you.	P	III	5	38	31
They were always perfectly agreed in the want of more	P	III	6	43	5
to courseness, however, or any want of good humour.	P	III	6	48	18
they were evidently in want, first, of being listened to	P	III	6	51	32
much as Charles, for they want me excessively to be	P	III	7	57	16
"This is the woman I want, said he.	P	III	7	62	41
The Admiral abused him for his want of gallantry.	P	III	8	68	34
"But, if I know myself," said he, "this is from no want of	P	III	8	68	35

There can be no want of gallantry, Admiral, in rating the P III 8 69 35
sailors' wives, who often want to be conveyed to one port P III 8 69 43
want of health, looking much older than Captain Wentworth. P III 11 97 14
Between those two, she could want no possible attendance P III 12 113 56
but still from the want of near relations and a settled P IV 5 152 2
seems designed to counterbalance almost every other want. P IV 5 154 8
I should never augur want of spirit from Captain Benwick's P IV 6 171 38
there had in fact been no want of looking about; that the P IV 9 193 13
"that is exactly the pleasure I want you to have. P IV 9 195 24
I want you to talk about me to Mr. Elliot. P IV 9 195 24
I want your interest with him. P IV 9 195 24
"Indeed, my dear Mrs. Smith, I want none," cried Anne. P IV 9 202 67
Mrs. Smith did not want to take blame to herself, and was P IV 9 209 95
weakness; and from employing others by her want of money. P IV 9 210 98
after all, her greatest want of composure would be in that P IV 10 212 1
I am so illiberal as to want every man to have the same P IV 10 218 26
if she could, but she did not want to lessen theirs. P IV 10 219 27
in the more, from the sad want of such blessings at home. P IV 10 220 31
He did not seem to want to be near enough for conversation. P IV 10 221 32
(smiling at Anne) "well supplied, and want for nothing.-- P IV 11 234 27
distress them beyond the want of graciousness and warmth.-- P IV 12 248 1
you like to it--but I want to see something applied to S 1 370 1
faults may be entirely imputed to her want of education. S 3 376 1
Beauty, sweetness, poverty & dependance, do not want the S 3 378 1
the fruit & vegetables we want; & we have in fact all the S 4 380 1
time, we can always buy what we want at Sanditon-House.-- S 4 380 1
If we any of us want to bathe, we have not a qr of a mile S 4 381 1
reading one of her own novels, for want of employment.-- S 6 389 1
some may be consumptive & want Asses milk--& I have two S 6 393 1
as good as new)--and what can people want for more?-- S 6 393 1
immediately gnawed by the want of an handsomer equipage S 7 394 1
If Scott has a fault, it is the want of passion.-- S 7 397 1
If they had hard places, they would want higher wages.--" S 7 401 1
If people want to be by the sea, why dont they take S 7 402 1
They are more likely to want a second.-- S 9 410 1
at present I shall want nothing; I never eat for about a S 9 411 1
in want of employment than of actual afflictions & releif. S 10 412 1
Br, who felt the decided want of some motive for action, S 10 415 1

WANTED (255)

I wanted her to be delighted at seeing me--I was as LS 5 249 1
& supposing I should be wanted left the nursery soon LS 20 275 1
sister I beleive wanted only opportunity for doing so. LS 22 281 3
it was the same, when I wanted to join the Hamiltons to LS 28 298 1
only ten guineas, and promised her more when she wanted it. NA I 2 19 3
more than she wanted, or careless in cutting it to pieces." NA I 3 28 45
about, and nobody wanted to see; and he only was absent. NA I 4 31 1
this morning, just as I wanted to set off; it looked very NA I 6 39 4
say; but I hate haggling, and poor Freeman wanted cash." NA I 7 46 15
wanted you to know her; and she seems very fond of you. NA I 7 50 47
the second, that it was a play she wanted very much to see. NA I 12 92 4
You know I wanted you, when we first came, not to buy that NA I 13 105 36
he wanted merely to dance, he wanted to be with me. NA II 1 134 39
me that my presence is wanted at home; and being NA II 2 139 7
failed, his own had often produced the perfection wanted. NA II 8 183 3
to her, "my father only wanted me to answer a note," she NA II 9 192 4
seemed always at hand when least wanted,) much worse!-- NA II 9 194 6
"No, I only wanted to see----- NA II 9 195 17
Catherine had never wanted comfort more, and he looked as NA II 10 199 1
succeed it? and she only wanted to know how far, after NA II 13 227 27
soon met with Mrs. Thorpe, and then we wanted for nothing. NA II 14 238 24
They wanted him to make a fine figure in the world in some SS I 3 15 6
all that was wanted of greater elegance to the apartments. SS I 6 29 4
manners had all the elegance which her husband's wanted. SS I 6 31 8
Conversation however was not wanted, for Sir John was very SS I 6 31 9
not likely that the room would be wanted for some time." SS I 8 39 17
and spirit which Edward had unfortunately wanted. SS I 10 48 8
me with rain when I wanted it to be fine; he has found SS I 10 52 28
it wanted it very much, when I was there six years ago." SS I 13 67 64
but Mr. Willoughby wanted particularly to shew me the SS I 13 69 76
"It was not inclination that he wanted, Elinor; I could SS I 15 78 24
"I have not wanted syllables where actions have spoken so SS I 15 79 36
whenever she wanted them, which at least satisfied herself. SS I 16 84 5
I wanted her to stay at home and rest this morning, but SS I 19 107 29
Sir John wanted the whole family to walk to the park SS I 21 119 3
She wanted to hear many particulars of their engagement SS II 1 141 7
repeated again, she wanted more clearly to understand what SS II 1 141 7
him, and she particularly wanted to convince Lucy, by her SS II 1 141 7
come before it's wanted; for they say he is all to pieces. SS II 8 194 10
to say, that he only wanted to know him to be rich, to be SS II 11 223 14
Elinor wanted very much to know, though she did not chuse SS II 12 229 4
and Lucy, who had long wanted to be personally known to SS II 12 231 9
and Miss Steele wanted only to be teazed about Dr. Davies SS II 12 233 17
"Could she not see that we wanted her gone!--how teazing SS II 13 244 44
be tricked out of assurances, that are not really wanted." SS II 13 244 46
and sharing the kindness which they wanted to monopolize. SS II 14 246 3
in his proper situation, and would have wanted for nothing. SS III 1 269 53
arm--"for I wanted to see you of all things in the world." SS III 2 271 8
and wanted to speak with him on very particular business. SS III 4 287 25
certain--and they only wanted something to live upon. SS III 13 369 32
conversation, was always wanted to produce this conviction. SS III 14 376 11
account, as everybody wanted to look again at the girl who W 337 16
But as he wanted neither sense nor a good disposition, he W 346 21
pretty figure, & rather wanted countenance than good W 349 23
They are wanted in the farm, Mr. Bennet, are not they?" PP I 7 31 25
"They are wanted in the farm much oftener than I can get PP I 7 31 26
Miss Bingley offered her the carriage, and she only wanted PP I 7 33 45
I fancy she was wanted about the mince pies. PP I 9 44 29
what to say in reply. you wanted me, I know, to say 'yes,' PP I 10 52 50
wanted only regimentals to make him completely charming. PP I 15 72 8
"Oh! Mr. Bennet, you are wanted immediately; we are all in PP I 20 111 7
of talking, as if she wanted to persuade herself that he PP II 3 148 26
but such of us as wished to learn, never wanted the means. PP II 6 165 31
Oh! how I wanted you!" PP II 17 226 19
She saw that he wanted to engage her on the old subject of PP II 18 235 39
She wanted to talk, but there seemed an embargo on every PP III 1 257 66
She wanted to ascertain the feelings of each of her PP III 2 262 7
each of her visitors, she wanted to compose her own, and PP III 2 262 7
his welfare; and she only wanted to know how far she PP III 2 266 16
wanted only encouragement to attach herself to any body. PP III 4 280 25
She wanted to hear of him, when there seemed the least PP III 8 311 13
or three days before he could get from her what he wanted. PP III 10 322 2
none of her friends, she wanted no help of his, she would PP III 10 322 2
Wickham of course wanted more than he could get; but at PP III 10 323 2
she could not be wanted to counteract her mother's schemes. PP III 13 346 21
dread, Bingley, who wanted to be alone with Jane, proposed PP III 16 365 1
to playfulness again, she wanted Mr. Darcy to account for PP III 18 380 1
It was William whom she talked of most and wanted most to MP I 2 15 12
as either were wanted; and added to these attentions, MP I 2 16 20
quick in carrying messages, and fetching what she wanted." MP I 2 20 31
parsonage had never been wanted, but the absolute MP I 3 28 38
Miss Bertrams regularly wanted their horses every fine day, MP I 4 35 7
being any hurry, she only wanted him to wait till Sir MP I 4 36 7
I never saw a place that wanted so much improvement in my MP I 6 53 4
was hot, there were shady lanes wherever they wanted to go. MP I 7 70 30
that it was not those she wanted, when Miss Bertram, Mr. MP I 10 97 1
excuse, but I went the very moment she said she wanted it." MP I 10 102 45
was because Sir Henry wanted the part himself; whereas it MP I 13 122 2
have been suppressed for just the three days we wanted. MP I 13 122 4
difference, they wanted a piece containing very few MP I 14 130 3
Her talents will be wanted in Amelia. MP I 14 135 15
know which to choose, and wanted Miss Bertram to direct MP I 15 138 1
visited her plants, or wanted one of the books, which she MP I 16 151 1
use of what nobody else wanted, though the terms in which MP I 16 151 1
for which Fanny had been wanted--and this was all that MP I 17 159 6
presence was wanted--she was sought for and attended, and MP I 17 160 6
in which her help was wanted; and that Mrs. Norris thought MP I 18 166 6
Fanny was wanted only to prompt and observe them. MP I 18 170 24
closed the page and turned away exactly as he wanted help. MP I 18 170 24
where nothing was wanted but tranquillity and silence. MP II 1 180 10
his uncle for attending them whenever he might be wanted. MP II 2 192 11
discussion, Maria, who wanted neither pride nor resolution, MP II 2 193 17
it would appear as if I wanted to set myself off at their MP II 3 198 12
even without her being wanted for any one's convenience. MP II 4 205 1
William had wanted to buy her a gold chain too, but the MP II 8 254 8
been to her cousins: he wanted, she supposed, to cheat her MP II 8 260 24
she would rather not part with it, when it is not wanted?" MP II 9 263 13
"She must not suppose it not wanted, not acceptable at MP II 9 263 14
Is not there a something wanted, Miss Price, in our MP II 11 287 22
not devise, for Miss Crawford certainly wanted no delay.-- MP III 1 311 1
the house, there seemed little danger of her being wanted. MP III 1 311 2
Depend upon it, it is not you that are wanted; depend upon MP III 1 325 60
engage in the business; he wanted to know Fanny's feelings. MP III 4 345 4
Happily for her companion, she wanted no answer. MP III 5 358 8
But Mrs. Norris wanted to persuade her that Fanny could be MP III 6 371 15
and in short could not really be wanted or missed. MP III 6 371 15
And besides, he wanted her so very much to see the thrush MP III 6 372 18
Both were kissed very tenderly, but Tom she wanted to keep MP III 7 381 25
Whatever was wanted, was halloo'd for, and the servants MP III 8 392 11
Susan saw that much was wrong at home, and wanted to set MP III 9 395 4
she needed it, for she wanted strength for a two hours' MP III 11 409 6
You are very much wanted. MP III 13 423 2
Julia had offered to return if wanted--but this was all.-- MP III 14 432 11
feel yourself to be so wanted there, that you cannot in MP III 14 435 14
If he wanted, he would send for her; and even to offer an MP III 14 436 15
No candle was now wanted. MP III 15 439 9
Never had Fanny more wanted a cordial. MP III 15 443 24
She thought he did, but she wanted to be assured of it. MP III 16 453 16
"I heard you were in town," said she--"I wanted to see you. MP III 16 454 18
but she was not so careless as she wanted to appear. MP III 16 458 30
Her mind, disposition, opinions, and habits wanted no half MP III 17 471 28
Fanny was indeed the daughter that he wanted. MP III 17 472 30
I wanted them to put off the wedding." E I 1 10 26
love her husband, but she wanted at once to be the wife of E I 2 15 3
neighbours and friends, and a home that wanted for nothing. E I 3 21 4
intimates of a girl who wanted only a little more E I 3 23 10
she wanted--exactly the something which her home required. E I 4 26 2
Not that she wanted him to marry. E I 4 28 6
Woodhouse's family and wanted another situation; I do not E I 5 37 10
wanted drawing out, and receiving a few, very few hints. E I 6 42 3
She had always wanted to do everything, and had made more E I 6 44 19
But as she wanted to be drawing, the declaration must wait E I 6 46 22
the only beauty she wanted,"--observed Mrs. Weston to him-- E I 6 47 31
The next thing wanted was to get the picture framed; and E I 6 48 40
any assistance being wanted, it was in fact given in the E I 7 55 35
But she was not wanted to speak. E I 9 73 19
of mind which she wanted, and he could sometimes act an E I 11 93 5
is very sad--but he is always wanted all round the country. E I 12 101 25
She wanted me to nurse my cold by staying at home to-day, E I 15 125 5
if her return only were wanted to make every thing go well: E I 15 132 38
He wanted to marry well, and having the arrogance to raise E I 16 135 7
She need not trouble herself to pity him. he only wanted E I 16 135 7
She wanted, rather, to be quiet, and out of temptation; E I 18 144 4
If Frank Churchill had wanted to see his father, he would E I 18 145 10
young woman, which she wanted to be thought herself; and E II 2 166 11
Emma, alone with her father, had half her attention wanted E II 3 177 51
where hitherto they had wanted either the courage or the E II 3 180 58
for which it was ever wanted was to accommodate a whist E II 6 197 5
I wanted the opinion of some one who could really judge. E II 6 201 28
The man must be a blockhead who wanted more. E II 6 204 42
still more lucky, she wanted exactly the advice they gave. E II 7 206 5
let James know that the carriage will be wanted on Tuesday. E II 7 210 14
is decisive with me. I wanted to know a little more, and E II 8 218 38
39

He had wanted very much to go abroad--had been very eager E II 8 221 49
She might talk on; and if he wanted to say any thing E II 8 226 79
perform with credit; she wanted neither taste nor spirit E II 8 227 86
convince her that if she wanted plain muslin it was of no E II 9 235 35
to say she thought the kitchen chimney wanted sweeping. E II 9 236 46
He would be so very . . . I wanted to keep it from Jane's E II 9 239 51
Mrs. Cole was saying the other day she wanted something E II 10 244 40
it was not so good but that many of them wanted a better. E II 11 248 10
This card-room would be wanted as a card-room now; or, if E II 11 254 44
As a counsellor she was not wanted; but as an approver, (a E II 11 256 60
Churchill's illness, and wanted to know how she was E II 12 259 11
married, the woman he had wanted to marry, and the woman E II 14 271 5
Miss Hawkins perhaps wanted a home, and thought this the E II 14 271 14
for Mrs. Elton, who only wanted to be talking herself. E II 14 273 20
whom she really wanted to make the eighth, Jane Fairfax.-- E II 16 291 5
"No, it by no means wanted strength--it was not a large E II 16 297 51
This is precisely what I wanted. E II 17 304 27
that he wanted, soon took the opportunity of walking away. E II 18 310 35
"I am ready," said Emma, "whenever I am wanted." E III 2 331 58
that evening, he wanted to make a memorandum in his pocket- E III 4 339 18
spruce beer, and he wanted to put it down; but when he E III 4 339 18
to tempt the lady, who only wanted to be going somewhere. E III 6 354 9
we shall be wanted, and I am determined to go directly.-- E III 6 362 44
of clever thing that is wanted, and Mr. Weston has done E III 7 371 35
36

before tea, old John Abdy's son wanted to speak with him. E III 8 383 29
She wanted to be of use to her; wanted to show a value for E III 9 389 16
five minutes, and wanted particularly to speak with her."-- E III 10 392 1
prove, that he now only wanted time and persuasion to E III 10 400 69
Miss Woodhouse, and only wanted invitation, to give the E III 11 408 34
society all that he wanted; if Harriet were to be the E III 12 422 20
he was not wanted there, preferred being out of doors."-- E III 13 424 1
Perhaps he wanted to speak to her, of his attachment to E III 13 425 2
with Frank Churchill; she wanted no explanations, she E III 14 436 6
no explanations, she wanted only to have her thoughts to E III 14 436 6
I was late; I met her walking home by herself, and wanted E III 14 440 8
her to Donwell; he had wanted to believe it feasible, but E III 15 448 31
which her countenance or manner could ever have wanted.-- E III 16 453 8
I only wanted to prove to you that Mrs. S. admits our E III 16 453 13
who can say, you know, how soon it may be wanted?" E III 16 457 36
"No, no, that's to-morrow; and I particularly wanted to E III 16 457 40
This is just what I wanted to be assured of.-- E III 16 460 57
He wanted her to look up and smile; and having now brought E III 18 473 23
24

She wanted to be alone. E III 18 475 37
Emma was delighted, and only wanted him to go on in the E III 18 478 60
61

She wanted more vigorous measures, a more complete P III 2 12 3
This was the principle on which Anne wanted her father to P III 2 12 5
She wanted it to be prescribed, and felt as a duty. P III 2 13 5
She wanted her to be more known. P III 2 15 12
which she wanted to carry, against previous inclination. P III 2 16 16
about terms;--only wanted a comfortable home, and to get P III 3 22 23
be on a station that would lead to every thing he wanted. P III 4 27 4
hurried away so soon, and wanted to make it possible for P III 5 33 6
Anne had not wanted this visit to Uppercross, to learn P III 6 42 1
alone, though he still wanted her to join them in the P III 7 58 20
I wanted to be doing something." P III 8 65 13
She did all that I wanted. P III 8 65 16
autumn, to fall in with the very French frigate I wanted.-- P III 8 65 16
You know how much he wanted money--worse than myself. P III 8 67 23

thing of Harville's from the world's end, if he wanted it. P III 8 69 40
I suppose you know he wanted to marry Anne?" P III 10 88 28
Her spirits wanted the solitude and silence which only P III 10 89 35
them, to be useful if wanted, at any rate, to enjoy the P III 12 111 49
could have been at all wanted, they were yet the first of P IV 2 129 1
Plymouth for a week, and wanted to persuade Captain P IV 2 133 25
suppose herself at all wanted;" for Elizabeth was replying, P IV 4 145 1
but it did all that was wanted, in bringing three lines of P IV 4 149 13
She wanted to hear much more than Mary communicated. P IV 6 162 1
Sir Walter wanted to know whether the Crofts travelled P IV 6 165 9
to go to the outer door; she wanted to see if it rained. P IV 7 175 6
You were a large party in yourselves, and you wanted P IV 9 193 12
Money, money, was all that he wanted. P IV 9 202 66
I have always wanted some other motive for his conduct as P IV 9 207 91
He wanted to animate her curiosity again as to how and P IV 10 214 12
her formerly praised; wanted very much to be gratified by P IV 10 214 12
His mother had some old friends in Bath, whom she wanted P IV 10 217 19
asked us to dinner, I think, if he had wanted to see us. P IV 10 223 44
He wanted to know how early he might be admitted to-morrow. P IV 10 228 71
Such a place as Sanditon sir, I may say was wanted, was S 1 369 1
He wanted to secure the promise of a visit--to get as many S 2 373 1
Nobody could catch cold by the sea, nobody wanted appetite S 2 373 1
the sea, nobody wanted spirits, nobody wanted strength.-- S 2 373 1
just as was wanted--sometimes one, sometimes the other.-- S 2 373 1
or fruit happen to be wanted--& it will not be amiss to S 4 382 1
amiss to have them often wanted, to have something or S 4 382 1
These two large families are just what we wanted--but-- S 5 389 1
We wanted just to see you & make sure of your being really S 6 391 1
She wanted to have the place fill faster, & seemed to have S 6 392 1
My sister wanted my counsel in the selection of some books. S 8 403 1
as to the where, wanted something private, & wrote to ask S 9 408 1
besides, he only wanted it now for Miss Heywood.-- S 10 417 1
girls & young ladies, as wanted either masters for S 11 420 1
raised the sum we wanted for putting them all out, yet if S 12 424 1

WANTING (99)

a motive will never be wanting; & as to money-matters, it LS 5 250 1
that nothing will be wanting on her part to counteract me; LS 10 257 1
mothers, she is accused of wanting maternal tenderness. LS 14 265 5
Nothing is wanting but to have you here, & it is our LS 40 309 1
still sitting down all the discredit of wanting a partner. NA I 8 53 2
and at a ball, without wanting to fix the attention of NA I 8 56 11
accused Isabella of being wanting in tenderness towards NA I 11 90 64
no endeavours shall be wanting on our side to make NA II 2 139 7
as to be always wanting to confine him to my elbow. NA II 3 143 2
and wanting in all that could give pleasure to Catherine. NA II 8 185 5
It gave to his intentions whatever of decision was wanting SS I 2 13 29
is a something wanting--his figure is not striking; it has SS I 3 17 18
agree that every kind of external comfort must be wanting. SS I 17 91 11
have been wanting us to visit them these several years! SS II 2 151 40
and no civility shall be wanting on my part, to make him SS II 11 224 24
Nothing was wanting on Mrs. Palmer's side that constant SS III 6 304 13
The old mare trotted heavily on, wanting no direction of W 322 2
The ladies were not wanting in civil returns; & Robert W 357 28
of a friend!-- always wanting me to play and sing before PP I 6 24 22
street, under pretence of wanting something in an opposite PP I 15 72 8
the privilege of hearing you, can think any thing wanting. PP II 8 176 26
of entertainment are wanting, the true philosopher will PP II 19 236 1
and a fortnight only was wanting of it, when a letter PP II 19 238 7
no arguments shall be wanting on my part, that can PP III 6 296 11
The children have been wanting me this half hour. PP III 10 325 2
for her, she seemed to be wanting to do more: and at MP I 1 5 4
Sir Thomas did not know what was wanting, because, though MP I 2 19 30
believed had never been wanting in comforts of any sort, MP I 3 31 59
The Crawfords, without wanting to be cured, were very MP I 5 47 26
seats in the kingdom, and wanting only to be completely MP I 5 48 28
that every body must be wanting to see Sotherton, to MP I 8 76 7
wanting sincerity or good intentions in the choice of his." MP I 11 110 22
and still the play was wanting; and as two or three days MP I 14 130 1
"Do not be afraid of my wanting the character," cried MP I 14 136 20
Maria, wanting Henry Crawford's animating support, thought MP I 15 142 24
Rushworth, who was wanting a prompter through every speech. MP I 18 164 2
felt the chief interest; wanting to be alone with his MP II 2 194 21
performance, and who shewed herself not wanting in taste. MP II 4 207 6
without much fear of wanting an opportunity for private MP II 8 256 14
Miss Crawford turned her eye on her, as if wanting to hear MP II 11 289 32
and of wanting to get away--"I will write directly." MP II 13 306 29
himself, and not wanting to hear more-- "I understand. MP III 1 312 12
easily learn to think she was wanting him to break through. MP III 4 345 4
or been unreasonable in wanting a larger share than any MP III 6 371 17
and he supposed would be wanting a husband soon, seemed MP III 7 380 22
If tenderness could be ever supposed wanting, good sense MP III 8 392 11
I did not use to think her wanting in self possession, but MP III 9 393 1
she had been so much wanting his affection to be cured, MP III 10 402 11
The early habit of reading was wanting. MP III 12 419 7
wanting, but nothing of that nature was ever in my power.-- MP III 13 420 2
the longing to be useful to those who were wanting her! MP III 14 432 9
Something must have been wanting within, or time would MP III 17 463 8
principle, had been wanting, that they had never been MP III 17 463 8
that encouragement from her should be long wanting. MP III 17 471 28
any thing wanting which a little time would not add. E I 6 42 1
had always been wanting; and in nothing had she approached E I 6 44 19
think so; and the good hands, I hope, may not be wanting." E I 8 58 11
feeling uncomfortable and wanting him very much to be gone. E I 8 65 50
Yes, Harriet, just so long have I been wanting the very E I 9 73 20
were wanting an embrocation, I would have spoken to-----" E I 12 102 29
"He has been wanting to come to us," continued Mr. Weston, E I 14 119 9
elegance was sometimes wanting; but, till this very day, E I 16 134 5
of things, Mr. Elton's wanting to pay his addresses to her E I 16 135 7
in the warmest corner, wanting even to give up her place E II 1 155 4
will be wanting the carriage himself one of those days. E II 1 159 18
been used to cavil at, as wanting colour, had a clearness E II 2 167 12
His extreme attention to my mother--wanting her to sit in E II 3 175 39
She was wanting to see him again, and especially to see E II 6 196 2
One thing was wanting to make the prospect of the ball E II 12 257 1
He looked at her, as if wanting to read her thoughts. E II 12 260 30
The charm of her own name was not wanting. E II 13 266 5
The idea of wanting gratitude and consideration for Miss E II 13 268 13
she must be wanting to assist and befriend her.-- E II 15 282 4
he looked at in silence--wanting only to observe enough E II 16 292 10
Mrs. Elton was wanting notice, which nobody had E II 18 311 36
in danger of wanting leisure to attend to the little boys. E II 18 312 50
Nothing wanting. E III 2 322 19
Mrs. Elton was evidently wanting to be complimented E III 2 324 20
that Mrs. Weston was wanting him to dance with Mrs. Elton E III 2 325 31
and Mr. Knightley not wanting to quarrel with her, how E III 3 332 1
She was immediately up, and wanting to quit the table; but E III 5 349 25
the conversation, wanting to hear the particulars of his E III 5 351 38
Nothing was wanting but to be happy when they got there. E III 7 367 1
But yet I think there was something wanting. E III 16 454 18
and churchwardens, are always wanting his opinion. E III 16 455 23
It seemed an unnecessary caution; Jane was wanting to give E III 16 457 34
of some papers which I was wanting to send to John.-- E III 18 471 20
They will be all wanting a home. P III 3 17 1
grandmamma is always wanting to see them, for she humours P III 6 44 8
giving him the independence which alone had been wanting. P III 7 58 21
the Harvilles had been wanting them to come to dinner P IV 2 129 2
an Elliot, or from not wanting to believe Anne a greater P IV 2 130 7
Every body was wanting to visit them. P IV 3 137 4
to talk to her of Lyme, wanting to compare opinions P IV 3 143 19
the place, but especially wanting to speak of the P IV 3 143 19
of what he is now wanting, and what he is now doing. P IV 9 204 80
by Captain Harville's wanting to come to Bath on business. P IV 10 216 19
to bring a prodigious influx;--nothing else was wanting. S 2 372 1
short chain, you see, between us, & not a link wanting. S 9 408 1

WANTON (3)

Its origin--jealousy perhaps, or wanton cruelty--was yet NA II 8 188 16
on her side, in the wanton cruelty so evident on yours. SS III 8 322 37
her capable of the utmost meanness of wanton ill-nature. SS III 13 366 21

WANTONLY (2)

Wilfully and wantonly to have thrown off the companion of PP II 12 196 5
inadvertence, and wantonly playing with our own happiness." P IV 10 221 33

WANTONNESS (1)

Weston may grow cross from the wantonness of comfort, or E I 5 38 13

WANTS (59)

Lady Susan has made him & wants to make me beleive, that LS 17 271 7
He wants to marry her--her mother promotes the match--but LS 23 284 4
myself) I know my father wants very much to see him. LS 24 286 4
exactly what Miss Andrews wants, for I must confess there NA I 6 41 16
my dear Catherine, what your brother wants me to do. NA I 8 57 21
He wants me to dance with him again, though I tell him NA I 8 57 21
Our foggy climate wants help." NA I 9 64 22
kindest way; and now he wants me to urge his suit, and say NA II 3 144 10
if I can to go early to bed, for I am sure she wants rest." SS II 8 195 15
All that she wants is gossip, and she only likes me now SS II 9 201 3
With an income sufficient to their wants thus secured to SS III 14 374 6
master wants to know why he be'nt to have his dinner."-- W 346 21
a formal circle, but one never wants them among friends." W 354 28
is in love with you, and wants him to marry Miss Darcy. PP I 21 118 18
Do not you know that Mr. Collins wants to marry Lizzy?" PP I 23 126 2
take care of him in those points where he most wants care. PP II 10 184 24
My aunt Philips wants you so to get husbands, you can't PP II 16 221 17
Nobody wants him to come. PP II 17 228 29
Her nose wants character; there is nothing marked in its PP III 3 271 15
His understanding and opinions all please me; he wants PP III 10 325 2
"If he wants our society, let him seek it. PP III 11 332 25
Your ladyship wants Mr. Darcy to marry your daughter; but PP III 14 357 61
whisper, "go to your father, he wants you in the library." PP III 17 375 28
so extravagant in their wants, and heedless of the future, PP III 19 387 8
income to supply their wants, made her eager to regain the MP I 1 4 2
"It wants improvement, ma'am, beyond any thing. MP I 6 53 4
for me--if nobody else wants it--a trifling part, but the MP I 14 132 7
modest young man who wants a great deal of encouragement, MP II 2 188 3
that the repose of his own family-circle is all he wants. MP II 3 196 3
"By moderation and economy, and bringing down your wants MP II 4 213 40
"Edmund wants her to go. but how can I spare her?" MP II 5 218 14
But a parish has wants and claims which can be known only MP II 7 247 42
Miss Crawford had anticipated her wants with a kindness MP II 8 258 18
will influence her in her opinion of the wants of others. MP III 1 313 12
You mean me, Baddeley, I am sure; Sir Thomas wants me, not MP III 1 325 60
whom she is wild to get married, and wants Henry to take. MP III 5 360 16
and exigeant; and wants a young woman, a beautiful young MP III 5 361 16
to feel for their fatigues and wants as travellers. MP III 7 378 13
"With what intense desire she wants her home," was MP III 14 431 7
But on the other hand, as Emma wants to see her better E I 5 36 6
The wants and sufferings of the poor family, however, were E I 10 87 31
a distance from those she wants to be with; but one cannot E I 14 122 22
"In that respect how unlike dear Mrs. Elton, who wants to E II 15 288 39
patience, self-controul; but it wants openness. E II 15 289 40
"It is too small--wants strength. E II 16 297 50
Mrs. Weston wants to see you. E III 10 392 2
it will be his to bestow the only advantages she wants.-- E III 13 428 23
the steadiness and delicacy of principle that it wants. E III 15 448 30
I have nothing to do with William's wants, but it really E III 16 458 43
pay a visit at Randall's; he wants to be introduced to her. E III 18 477 57
If a man has not a wife, he soon wants to be afloat again." P III 8 65 14
was the last of his wants, produced such a confusion of P III 9 80 34
recommendation, and he wants to talk to you about them; he P IV 2 131 9
I sincerely hope "Bath will do him all the good he wants. P IV 6 164 8
He truly wants to marry you. P IV 9 204 80
Lady D. was indeed a great lady beyond the common wants of S 3 376 1
Andrew now, & says he never brings her what she wants.-- S 4 381 2
sagacity--"Miss Esther wants me to invite her & her S 7 399 1
Your ancle wants rest. S 9 411 1

WAR (15)

family are at war, & Manwaring scarcely dares speak to me. LS 2 245 1
linked within Isabella's, though their hearts were at war. NA I 13 99 9
was spent in a sort of war of wit, a display of family NA I 15 121 25
variety of danger, which sea and war together could offer. MP II 6 236 21
London very much at war with all respectable attachments. MP III 14 433 12
of a strong passion at war with all interested motives. E I 8 67 57
Many a noble fortune has been made during the war. P III 3 17 1
nothing superior to the accommodations of a man of war. P III 8 69 37
luck to live to another war, we shall see him do as you P III 8 70 46
a man you of war; I speak, you know, of the higher rates. P III 8 70 54
had not made less than twenty thousand pounds by the war. P III 9 75 10
might be done in any future war; and he was sure Captain P III 9 75 10
If it were war, now, he would have settled it long ago.-- P III 10 92 44
cannot afford to make long courtships in time of war. P III 10 92 44
the dread of a future war all that could dim her sunshine. P IV 12 252 12

WAR-OFFICE (1)

arrangement at the war-office, another regiment should be PP II 19 238 6

WARD (5)

Her father had no ward, and the squire of the parish no NA I 1 16 10
her mind, wholly unable to ward off any portion of that PP II 18 231 18
About thirty years ago, Miss Maria Ward of Huntingdon, MP I 1 3 1
as thought Miss Ward and Miss Frances quite as handsome as MP I 1 3 1
Miss Ward, at the end of half a dozen years, found herself MP I 1 3 1

WARDED (1)

disappointment is only warded off by the defence of some PP II 19 237 4

WARDROBES (2)

Not tables, toilettes, wardrobes, or drawers, but on one NA II 5 158 17
Bath stove, mahogany wardrobes and neatly-painted chairs, NA II 9 193 6

WAREHOUSE (2)

saw all the clothes after they came from the warehouse." NA I 9 68 46
and at what warehouse Miss Grey's clothes might be seen. SS II 10 215 11

WAREHOUSES (2)

own warehouses, could have been so well bred and agreeable. PP II 2 139 2
me, for she does not know which are the best warehouses. PP III 5 288 38

WARFARE (2)

poor Mr. Woodhouse's feelings were in sad warfare. E I 3 24 12
Not merely when a state of warfare with one young lady E II 15 282 4

WARM (98)

"His disposition you know is warm, & he came to LS 24 290 13
We were both warm, & of course both to blame. LS 24 290 13
wrap yourself up very warm about the throat, when you come NA I 2 18 2
much, while she drank her warm wine and water, and NA I 3 29 52
as its beginning had been warm, and they passed so rapidly NA I 5 36 4
a specimen of their very warm attachment, and of the NA I 6 39 1
Catherine assented--and a very warm panegyric from her on NA I 14 110 28
chairs, on which the warm beams of a western sun gaily NA II 9 193 6
was their surprize, and warm their displeasure, on hearing NA II 14 237 21
she knew his heart to be warm and his temper affectionate. SS I 3 16 13
John, who was particularly warm in their praise, might be SS I 12 62 28
I can hardly keep my hands warm even in my muff. SS II 5 168 9
Mrs. Jennings was very warm in her praise of Edward's SS III 2 270 1
her thoughts, by the too warm, too positive assurances of SS III 2 270 1
a very warm invitation from Charlotte to go with them. SS III 3 279 1
to occur, with a more warm, though less public, assurance, SS III 6 301 1
it?) was scarcely less warm than her's; and whose mind--Oh! SS III 8 322 36
goes, would not justify so warm a sympathy--or rather not SS III 9 336 12
or feigned, as much more warm, as more sincere or constant- SS III 9 336 14
and the warm acknowledgment of peculiar obligation. SS III 10 340 2
warm as friendship and design could unitedly dictate. SS III 11 352 18
much--& Mr Edwards was as warm as herself, in praise of W 336 14

Were you not rather warm last Saturday about 9 or 10 W 358 28
I have a warm, unguarded temper, and I may perhaps have PP I 16 80 27
both him and herself in warm terms on the happy prospect PP I 20 110 1
and threw back the praise on her sister's warm affection. PP II 1 135 10
warm commendation of him, narrowly observed them both. PP II 2 142 18
They were all of them warm in their admiration; and at PP III 1 245 3
her approbation in terms warm enough to satisfy her PP III 13 348 34
My dear Sir Thomas, with all my faults I have a warm heart: MP I 1 7 8
With such warm feelings and lively spirits it must be MP I 7 63 7
known, or warm her imagination with scenes of the past. MP I 9 85 3
is any thing a little too warm (and it is so with most of MP I 15 141 22
all the suffering which a warm temper and a high spirit MP I 17 162 19
"Thank you--I am quite warm, very warm. MP I 18 168 17
The Crawfords were more warm on the subject than Mr. Yates, MP II 1 177 5
to breathe the spirit of chivalry and warm affections. MP II 4 211 23
affection on his side as warm as her own, and much less MP II 6 234 17
He honoured the warm hearted, blunt fondness of the young MP II 6 235 19
Her praise was warm, and he received it as she could wish, MP II 10 276 14
to warm his courage than his eyes could discern in hers. MP III 3 336 7
You have both warm hearts and benevolent feelings; and MP III 4 348 23
that she should now find a warm and affectionate friend in MP III 6 371 17
lines from himself, warm and determined like his speeches. MP III 7 375 4
as warm in his commendation, as even her heart could wish. MP III 10 400 7
His warm regard, his kind expressions, his confidential MP III 13 425 5
more warm and genuine than her aunt's style of writing. MP III 13 427 12
She spoke of you with high praise and warm affection; yet, MP III 16 455 23
to persuade her that her warm and sisterly regard for him MP III 17 470 25
she had a husband whose warm heart and sweet temper made E I 2 15 3
She then repeated some warm personal praise which she had E I 4 34 43
"But, my dear papa, it is supposed to be summer; a warm E I 6 48 37
It was short, but expressed good sense, warm attachment, E I 7 51 4
of our nature, eager curiosity and warm prepossession. E I 7 56 46
"You are a very warm friend to Mr. Martin; but, as I said E I 8 63 44
Yet he would be so anxious for her being perfectly warm, E I 14 118 4
The affection of the whole family, the warm attachment of E II 2 164 7
He fancied bathing might be good for it--the warm Bath-- E II 3 175 39
handsome praise, so much warm admiration, so much E II 5 191 28
Emma would not agree to this, and began a warm defence of E II 6 199 10
he spoke of his uncle with warm regard, was fond of E II 7 205 2
cold, she would be sure to warm herself thoroughly; if E II 7 211 22
while warm from her heart, for he stopped to hand her out. E II 8 213 7
know, of his being so warm an admirer of her performance." E II 8 217 31
that it should be the tribute of warm female friendship. E II 8 219 42
His admiration was certainly very warm; yet she thought, E II 8 228 88
Her approbation, at once general and minute, warm and E II 11 256 60
My regard for Hartfield is most warm"----- E II 12 261 33
his having a decidedly warm admiration, a conscious E II 12 262 38
His feelings are warm, but I can imagine them rather E II 13 265 4
of her face and the warm simplicity of her manner; and all E II 13 266 6
Her congratulations were warm and open; but Emma could not E II 17 304 28
I made her take her shawl--for the evenings are not warm-- E III 2 322 19
He was warm in his reprobation of Mr. Elton's conduct; it E III 2 330 46
The service he rendered you was enough to warm your heart." E III 4 342 37
A warm climate may be prescribed for her. E III 6 365 62
of nature, tranquil, warm, and brilliant after a storm, E III 13 424 1
health, by passing all the warm months with her at P III 2 14 12
fitted by her warm affections and domestic habits. P III 4 29 7
on the side of early warm attachment, and a cheerful P III 4 30 9
the Musgroves, in their warm gratitude for the kindness he P III 6 52 33
on him, and come back warm in his praise, and he was P III 7 53 1
could not help adding her warm protestations to theirs. P III 7 55 5
It was unvarying, warm admiration every where. P III 9 73 3
it was a proof of his own warm and amiable heart, which P III 10 91 42
from Lyme before; his warm praise of him as an excellent P III 11 96 12
was a perfect gentleman, unaffected, warm, and obliging. P III 11 97 15
correct opinions, knowledge of the world, and a warm heart. P IV 4 146 6
quitted the house but to be conveyed into the warm Bath.-- P IV 5 154 8
She goes into the warm Bath to-morrow, and for the rest of P IV 5 157 16
interesting--praise, warm, just, and discriminating, of P IV 7 178 24
to have been a man of warm feelings, easy temper, careless P IV 9 209 95
God forbid that I should undervalue the warm and faithful P IV 11 235 32
result, not the cause of a revival of his warm attachment. P IV 11 243 68
were as grateful & disinterested, as they were warm.-- S 2 372 1
"He is a warm friend to Sanditon--said Mr Parker--& his S 3 377 1
the most active, friendly, warm hearted being in existence, S 5 386 1
but such as called for warm rooms & good nourishment.-- S 10 418 1

WARM-HEARTED (4)

in her; and being a warm-hearted, unreserved woman, Mary MP I 4 42 17
satisfied, though your warm-hearted friend was still run MP III 4 353 46
understanding, and warm-hearted, well meaning relations. E II 2 163 3
man, and Mrs. Campbell a friendly, warm-hearted woman. E II 6 201 20

WARMED (4)

warmed his heart and made him feel capable of generosity.-- SS I 1 5 8
whose feelings were so warmed by his sudden arrival, as to MP II 1 179 9
His heart was warmed, his fancy fired, and he felt the MP II 6 236 22
Warmed by the sight of such a friend to her son, and MP III 10 400 6

WARMER (9)

have spread a new grace and inspired a warmer interest. NA II 4 149 1
were successively dismissed with yet warmer objections. MP I 14 130 3
or be followed by warmer wishes and higher commendation, MP II 13 300 5
my ideas of comfort better than what is warmer and blinder. E I 10 86 21
higher ties, a warmer love might have seemed impossible. E I 11 92 4
brought on a more interesting subject, and a warmer manner. E II 5 186 4
His ideas seemed more moderate--his feelings warmer. E II 6 203 42
herself, to spend in some warmer place than Enscombe--in E II 18 308 30
every warmer, but more agitating, delight, should be her's. E III 16 452 6

WARMEST (21)

I finish as I began, with the warmest congratulations. Yrs LS 23 285 8
affection, with the warmest approbation of their real SS III 13 369 32
of addressing her with the warmest civility.-- W 331 11
I have found her more than answer my warmest hopes.-- W 357 28
certain possession of his warmest affection, and secure of PP III 17 378 46
both ever sensible of the warmest gratitude towards the PP III 19 388 13
Edmund spoke of with the warmest satisfaction, as so MP II 4 216 50
that could justify the warmest hopes of lasting happiness MP III 2 326 3
well not to entertain the warmest hopes--yes, dearest, MP III 3 344 41
her own heart in the warmest eulogium, in speaking of her MP III 10 405 17
earliest flowers, in the warmest divisions of her aunt's MP III 14 432 9
was seated in the warmest corner, wanting even to give up E II 1 155 4
abominable folly of Miss Bickerton in the warmest terms. E III 3 335 11
of dry, blunt manner, I know you have the warmest heart. E III 6 356 28
Emma listened with the warmest concern; grieved for her E III 9 389 16
first reception, and the warmest expressions of the E III 12 418 5
warmest friendship--indignation--abominable scoundrel!"-- E III 13 426 13
With the greatest respect, and the warmest friendship, do E III 14 438 8
I assure you that I have heard the news with the warmest E III 18 477 59
the constant object of his warmest respect and devotion. P III 1 4 5
her merit, and excited the warmest curiosity to know her." P IV 8 187 34

WARMLY (73)

She has already almost persuaded me of her being warmly LS 6 251 1
& on finding how warmly Miss Manwaring resented her LS 14 265 4
He is so warmly attached to my daughter that he could LS 20 276 5
not have espoused your cause as warmly as my brother?" LS 24 286 6
"Yes, it does give a notion," said Catherine, warmly, "and NA I 9 64 25
"No, he is not," said Catherine warmly, "for I am sure he NA I 11 89 57
And if Catherine had not most warmly asserted his NA I 13 103 27
To have her company so warmly solicited! NA II 2 140 8
warmly, "must be a comfort to him under any distress." NA II 10 204 14
Catherine coloured as she warmly answered, "no friend can NA II 14 236 16
not perceive how you could express yourself more warmly." SS I 4 20 7
"That is an expression, Sir John," said Marianne, warmly, " SS I 9 45 30
"You are mistaken, Elinor," said she warmly, "in supposing SS I 12 58 4
cottage in the spring, he warmly opposed every alteration SS I 14 72 6
"You are a good woman," he warmly replied. SS I 14 74 19
"Thank you," cried Lucy warmly, "for breaking the ice; you SS II 2 146 3
and relying as warmly as ever on his constancy, had only SS II 9 202 8
to connoisseurship, warmly admired the screens, as he SS II 12 234 28
to this act, were strongly felt, and warmly expressed. SS III 3 283 20
Jennings's entreaty was warmly seconded by Mr. Palmer, who SS III 7 309 5
"But, upon my soul, I did not know it," he warmly replied; SS III 8 322 38
when she so earnestly, so warmly insisted on sharing my SS III 13 367 22
"My dearest Emma cried eliz: warmly--do you think I would W 320 2
"I was not so ungrateful sir, said Emma warmly, as to wish W 326 5
The plan was warmly opposed by their visitor. W 339 18
"My aunt may have erred--said Emma warmly--she has erred-- W 352 26
above, with her father, & warmly entreated to be his W 361 30
Miss Bingley warmly resented the indignity he had received, PP I 10 51 40
"As much as I ever wish to be," cried Elizabeth warmly,-- " PP I 16 77 13
said Elizabeth warmly; "but you must excuse my not being PP I 18 96 55
"Believe me, my dear sir, my gratitude is warmly excited PP I 22 124 10
"But you blame me for having spoken so warmly of Wickham." PP II 17 224 6
Her answer was warmly in his favour. PP II 18 233 27
The subject which had been so warmly canvassed between PP III 11 332 21
as warmly as a man violently in love can be supposed to do. PP III 16 366 8
this speech, enforced it warmly, persuaded that no MP I 6 61 58
Was she right in refusing what was so warmly asked, so MP I 16 153 3
advised by Edmund, and warmly urged by the two sisters, MP II 5 223 48
thankfully and warmly, for she was elevated beyond the MP II 6 232 13
She wished she had not spoken so warmly in their last MP II 11 286 15
of her character were warmly expatiated on, that sweetness MP II 12 294 16
She desires the connection as warmly as your uncle or MP III 4 351 36
thrush, though William, warmly interested, as he was, in MP III 7 380 23
warmly, and evidently hoping to interest Fanny on her side. MP III 7 386 42
for having contended so warmly, and from that hour Fanny MP III 9 397 8
He talked of Harriet, and praised her so warmly, that she E I 6 42 1
not own it, and Mr. Elton warmly added, "Oh, no! certainly E I 6 48 34 35
Mr. Knightley loudly and warmly; and with calmer asperity, E I 8 61 38
He perfectly knew his own meaning; and having warmly E I 15 130 28
and enter as warmly into Mr. and Mrs. Weston's E I 18 144 4
"And mine," said Mr. Knightley warmly, "is, that if he E I 18 150 32
I have heard him express himself so warmly on those points! E II 8 226 79
I do congratulate you, Mrs. Weston, most warmly. E II 9 238 51
He was very warmly thanked both by mother and daughter; to E II 10 242 16
"Sir," said Mr. Woodhouse, rather warmly, "you are very E II 11 251 28
"You are right, Mrs. Weston," said Mr. Knightley warmly, " E II 15 286 18
began to think she had been wrong in disclaiming so warmly. E II 18 307 17
a time be fancying myself!. . ." cried Harriet, warmly. E III 4 337 6
She was warmly gratified--and in another moment still more E III 9 385 7
expressing yourself very warmly as to your sense of that E III 11 406 23
indeed you are," cried Emma, warmly, and taking her hand. E III 16 459 48
"True, true," he answered, warmly. E III 18 479 70
"Mrs. Clay," said she warmly, "never forgets who she is; P III 5 35 14
He had been most warmly attached to her, and had never P III 7 61 37
her sister aside, seemed to be arguing the matter warmly. P III 10 85 16
His acquittal was complete, his friendship warmly honoured, P III 11 94 6
The other two warmly agreed to what he said, and she then P III 12 114 62
"And I am sure," cried Mary warmly, "it was very little to P IV 2 131 10
which made him enter warmly into her father and sister's P IV 4 148 10
began talking very warmly about the family features, and P IV 10 222 37
invariably serious, most warmly opposing it, and not P IV 10 224 50
Mr Parker spoke warmly of Clara Brereton, & the interest S 3 378 1
use to you?"--and Mr P. warmly offered his assistance in S 9 410 1

WARMTH (70)

have a doubt of the warmth of that friendship, I am far LS 7 252 1
or to forget it in the warmth of admiration vexes me; & if LS 8 256 3
He has told me so in a warmth of manner which spoke his LS 11 259 1
ladyship wonder that she should? cried I with some warmth. LS 24 288 11
the warmth she had been betrayed into, in speaking of him. SS I 4 21 11
of his frankness and warmth; and her visit was long enough SS I 6 31 8
all their feelings with a warmth which left her no SS I 11 54 4
"Margaret," said Marianne with great warmth, "you know SS I 12 61 25
Marianne, who shewed more warmth of regard in her SS I 16 87 23
at her earnestness and warmth; for had he not imagined it SS I 18 100 30
warmth than she felt, though with far less than Miss Lucy. SS I 21 122 14
you," said Marianne, with warmth; "your invitation has SS II 3 154 5
knowing that she received warmth from one, or discerning SS II 7 190 55 56
The same warmth of heart, the same eagerness of fancy and SS II 9 205 24
immediately to say with warmth, "this is admiration of a SS II 12 235 34 35
Elinor was much more hurt by Marianne's warmth, than she SS II 12 236 38
Marianne's mistaken warmth, nor to the repetition of any SS II 13 245 47
with the most grateful warmth, was ready to own all their SS III 5 293 2
"Upon my soul it is,"--was his answer, with a warmth which SS III 8 319 25
it with all her usual warmth, was in a moment as much SS III 9 334 4
she then meant in the warmth of her heart to be guided in SS III 12 359 11
from the quiet warmth of a snug parlour, to the bustle, W 327 7
unlike the encouraging warmth he had been used to receive W 335 13
stockings, and a face glowing with the warmth of exercise. PP I 7 32 41
diffuseness and warmth remained for Bingley's salutation. PP I 11 54 2
"Really, Mr. Collins," cried Elizabeth with some warmth, " PP I 19 108 18
were dwelt on with a warmth which seemed due to the PP II 11 189 5
her regard had all the warmth of first attachment, and PP II 17 227 26
its warmth, and softened its impropriety of expression. PP III 1 251 48
a warmth, a delight, which words could but poorly express. PP III 13 347 25
and shook hands with such warmth, as left no doubt of his PP III 17 374 22
had; and it is the warmth of her respect for her aunt's MP I 7 63 7
and the warmth which might excite general notice. MP I 12 115 4
to her," said Fanny, trying for greater warmth of manner. MP I 16 155 23
She could not equal them in their warmth. MP I 18 170 24
friendly reception and warmth of hand-shaking had already MP II 1 179 8
yellow leaves about them, to jump up and walk for warmth. MP II 4 208 11
entirely without warmth or character!-- MP II 4 211 23
lips, with almost as much warmth as if it had been Miss MP II 9 269 38
and shewed even a warmth of heart which did him credit. MP II 10 278 20
What could more delightfully prove that the warmth of her MP II 12 294 16
my wishes with all the warmth I could desire, and exerted MP II 13 299 5
sanguine spirit, of more warmth than delicacy, made her MP III 2 326 2
And she spoke with a warmth which quite astonished Edmund, MP III 4 347 19
of her language, and the warmth of her attachments.-- MP III 7 376 4
ill-timed and powerless warmth, was beginning to be MP III 8 390 8
secrecy with so much warmth, she might have trusted to her MP III 15 438 7
in all the favouring warmth of surprize and conjecture. E II 4 184 10
or even the unselfish warmth of heart which she had E II 7 205 1
had not added any lasting warmth, that she could still do E II 13 266 6
Warmth and tenderness of heart, with an affectionate, open E II 13 269 16
You will laugh at my warmth--but upon my word, I talk of E II 15 282 5
was in the first style of guileless simplicity and warmth. E II 15 284 12
momentary glance; and she was herself struck by his warmth. E II 15 286 19
returning with the same warmth of sentiment which he had E III 1 315 1
clearly heard Emma opposing it with eager laughing warmth. PP II 11 348 22
On her side, all was warmth, energy, and triumph--and she E III 6 359 37
In the warmth of true contrition, she would call upon her E III 8 377 1
There was consciousness, animation, and warmth; there was E III 16 453 8
had not been met with any warmth, he had persevered in P III 1 7 14
Such confidence, powerful in its own warmth, and P III 4 27 3
warmth!--she could imagine what Louisa was feeling. P III 10 88 27
them, before the light and warmth of the day were gone. P III 11 95 8
having more worth and warmth than any other set of men in P III 11 99 19
There was never any burst of feeling, any warmth of P IV 5 161 28
Warmth and enthusiasm did captivate her still. P IV 5 161 28
In the warmth of the moment, and under a mistaken P IV 9 198 44
It was a heartiness, and a warmth, and a sincerity which P IV 10 220 31

distress them beyond the want of graciousness and warmth.-- P IV 12 248 1
as her friend Anne's was in the warmth of her heart. P IV 12 252 12
WARN (7)
is no secret to your friends, & to warn you against her. LS 12 261 5
& with still greater energy, I must warn you of one thing. LS 23 283 4
I shall not be able to keep you--and so I warn you.-- PP I 20 113 28
change his mind another day, and warn me off his grounds." PP III 1 258 72
"You may well warn me against such an evil. PP III 6 299 21
Yet in spite of all these temptations, let me warn my PP III 15 362 15
I write, dear Fanny, to warn you against giving the least MP III 15 437 3
WARNED (2)
a great aunt might have warned her, for man only can be NA I 10 73 22
merely because you are warned against it; and, therefore, PP II 3 144 2
WARNING (3)
"or after such a warning, I should be the last to SS III 9 337 16
secrets of your own, take warning by me, do not trust her; W 317 2
thought, have reason to reproach her for giving no warning. P III 5 34 12
WARPED (1)
But your mind is warped by an innate principle of general NA II 12 219 15
WARRANT (13)
their fortune could not warrant; seeking to better NA II 15 246 12
affection for me may warrant, without imprudence or folly. SS I 4 21 15
I warrant you she is a fine size by this time." SS II 4 163 16
"Aye, my dear, I'll warrant you we do. SS II 5 167 5
I warrant you, Miss Marianne would have been ready to wait SS II 8 194 10
indeed! and the doctor is a single man, I warrant you." SS II 10 218 25
as early an intimacy as good manners would warrant. MP I 5 44 1
of decorum as might warrant any man in the fullest MP II 12 294 16
as might warrant strong suspicion in a predisposed mind. MP III 5 362 17
Her ideas are not higher than her own fortune may warrant, MP III 13 421 2
have been great enough to warrant any strength of language MP III 17 471 28
motive unperceived) might warrant a man of ordinary E I 16 136 9
proprietor could fairly warrant, as she viewed the E III 6 358 35
WARRANTED (1)
of tenderness, not warranted by anything preceding, and SS II 7 188 43
WARRANTS (1)
and at an earlier hour than common visiting warrants. MP II 13 298 1
WARRIOR (1)
portrait of some handsome warrior, whose features will so NA II 5 158 17
WARS (1)
The quarrels of popes and kings, with wars or pestilences, NA I 14 108 22
WARWICK (1)
lay; Oxford, Blenheim, Warwick, Kenelworth, Birmingham, &c. PP II 19 240 12
WARY (2)
conscience; a designing, wary, cold-blooded being, who P IV 9 199 53
She had been too wary to put anything out of her own power- S 3 375 1
WASH (2)
do not think it will wash well; I am afraid it will fray." NA I 3 28 42
poor father and our great wash that I have had no leisure W 321 2
WASHED (1)
down to meadows washed by a stream, of which the Abbey, E III 6 358 35
WASHER-WOMEN (1)
cooks, housemaids, Washer-women & bathing women, that Mrs S 10 414 1
WASHING (3)
they parted, how much her washing cost per week, and how SS II 14 249 8
and with some hasty washing of the young tea-maker's, a MP III 7 384 36
a little cold, and Patty has been washing the kitchen.' E II 3 173 27
WASHING-BILL (1)
might be trusted, she held a washing-bill in her hand. NA II 7 172 2
WASHING-BILLS (1)
him that collection of washing-bills, resulting from a NA II 16 251 5
WASTE (13)
unseen, "and waste its fragrance on the desert air." NA I 1 15 5
the inclosure of them, waste lands, crown lands and NA I 14 111 29
For heaven's sake, waste no more time. NA I 15 120 24
and though she dared not waste a moment upon a second NA II 6 164 3
longer; but unable to waste such a precious occasion, she PP III 13 345 12
13
drive home allowed no waste of hours, and from the time of MP I 10 104 52
I am of some use I hope in preventing waste and making the MP I 15 141 22
very disagreeable,--a waste of time--tiresome women--and E II 1 155 3
unseen, 'and waste its fragrance on the desert air.' E II 15 282 5
most, was that in all this waste of foresight and caution, P IV 7 179 31
After the waste of a few minutes in saying the proper P IV 10 226 64
There was no delay, no waste of time. P IV 11 229 2
Ornee, on a strip of waste ground Lady D. had granted him, S 3 377 1
WASTED (7)
Muslin can never be said to be wasted. NA I 3 28 45
prevent your whole youth from being wasted in discontent. SS I 19 103 7
is not to be wasted for ever on such a man as Willoughby.-- SS III 9 337 18
William was gone, and she now felt as if she had wasted MP II 11 282 2
would be finally wasted on her even in years of matrimony. MP III 6 367 5
graces should not be wasted on the inferior society of E I 3 23 10
the many anxious feelings she had wasted on the subject. P IV 1 128 32
WASTEFUL (1)
sister, and Mrs. Grant's wasteful doings to overlook, left MP I 4 34 3
WASTING (3)
enjoy her smiles, for you are wasting your time with me." PP I 3 12 13
moment, making artificial flowers or wasting gold paper. MP I 2 14 7
"We are wasting time most abominably. MP I 14 131 5
WATCH (47)
It has been delightful to me to watch his advances towards LS 10 257 2
Oh! how delightful it was, to watch the variations of his LS 25 293 3
and be able to watch the dances with perfect convenience. NA I 2 21 9
to watch the proceedings of these alarming young men. NA I 6 43 34
He took out his watch: "how long do you think we have been NA I 7 45 5
neither believe her own watch, nor her brother's, nor the NA I 9 67 33
till Morland produced his watch, and ascertained the fact; NA I 9 67 33
window to watch over and encourage the happy appearance. NA I 11 83 16
scenes, did she thus watch Henry Tilney, without being NA I 12 92 4
when taking out his watch, he stopped short to pronounce NA II 5 162 27
the drawing-room, his watch in his hand, and having, on NA II 6 165 5
Till midnight, she supposed it would be in vain to watch; NA II 8 189 19
"It is only a quarter past four, (shewing his watch) and NA II 9 195 18
Henry returned to what was now his only home, to watch NA II 16 250 3
Wherever they went, she was evidently always on the watch. SS II 4 164 24
the apothecary, and to watch by her the rest of the night. SS III 7 312 17
bent over her sister to watch--she hardly knew for what. SS III 7 314 22
Emma, who could not but watch her at such a moment, saw W 328 8
about in the vestibule to watch for the end of conference, PP I 20 110 1
not watch his behaviour when he first came into the room. PP III 3 268 8
of an hour here," said Edmund, taking out his watch. MP I 9 95 65
"Oh! do not attack me with your watch. MP I 9 95 66
A watch is always too fast or too slow. MP I 9 95 66
I cannot be dictated to by a watch." MP I 9 95 66
newspaper, watch the weather, and quarrel with his wife. MP I 11 110 23
"She will be late," said Sir Thomas, taking out his watch, MP II 5 218 15
She must watch the general arrangements and see how every MP II 10 275 10
Sir Thomas, producing his watch with all necessary caution- MP II 10 279 24
had been used to sit and watch the due time, was all set E I 3 24 11
Perry to be upon the watch, and as he went about so much, E I 9 70 6
on the watch, heard distinctly, and was sadly alarmed at. E II 1 162 31
shall be constantly on the watch for an eligible situation. E II 15 284 9
to be always on the watch, and employing my friends to E II 17 302 20
employing my friends to watch also, that nothing really E II 17 302 20
Frank Churchill seemed to have been on the watch; and E III 2 319 3
longer allow her eyes to watch; but Mr. Elton was so near, E III 2 327 34
\ child on the watch, came towards them to beg; and Miss E III 3 333 5
little distance from the window, evidently on the watch. E III 10 400 65
that you may be upon the watch; because, if you see any P III 6 45 9
boys, she was well able to watch for a likeness, and if it P III 6 48 17
They went to the sands, to watch the flowing of the tide, P III 12 102 1
Captain Wentworth was on the watch for them, and a chaise P III 12 115 68
and fearful sort of watch for him in vain; but at last, in P IV 7 178 28
added another motive) to watch Sir Walter and Mrs. Clay. P IV 9 207 90
and Anne seeming to watch him, though it was from thorough P IV 11 231 12
And when he died, I gave Sir Edwd his gold watch.--" S 7 400 1
his nephew to have his watch; but it need not have been S 7 400 1
WATCH-TOWER (1)
snug farm-house than a watch-tower--and a troop of tidy, SS I 18 98 8
WATCHED (45)
in such distress, & watched her with so much tender LS 17 270 3
in town, & had just watched him to your door herself! LS 32 302 1
Catherine then ran directly up stairs, and watched Miss NA I 4 34 7
and Catherine had barely watched him down the street, when NA I 11 84 17
of having continually watched in Isabella's every look and NA I 15 117 8
"what! always to be watched, in person or by proxy!" NA II 3 147 21
Catherine understood her:--the General must be watched NA II 8 186 7
her that, if judiciously watched, some rays of light form NA II 8 188 19
Mrs. Morland watched the progress of this relapse; and NA II 15 241 7
with which he often watched Marianne, and his spirits were SS II 5 169 12
Elinor watched his countenance and saw its expression SS II 6 177 8
it, must have its course, watched by her till this excess SS II 7 182 12
13
Mrs. Jennings, who had watched them with pleasure while SS II 8 200 43
of the two;-- she watched his eyes, while Mrs. Jennings SS III 6 305 16
and her sister, who watched with unremitting attention her SS III 7 310 10
11
pulse;--she waited, watched, and examined it again and SS III 7 314 22
than anything else, I watched you all safely out of the SS III 8 326 53
"Watched us out of the house!" SS III 8 326 54
You would be surprised to hear how often I watched you, SS III 8 326 55
early hour itself was watched for with some eagerness.-- W 326 7
his advances she eagerly watched, and whose astonishment PP I 18 97 61
sensations; and she watched her progress through the PP I 18 100 68
She watched him whenever they were at Rosings, and PP II 9 181 29
Your sister I also watched.-- PP II 12 197 5
Elizabeth, as they drove along, watched for the first PP III 1 245 1
Elizabeth soon saw that she was herself closely watched by PP III 3 268 5
Elizabeth eagerly watched to see whether Bingley would PP III 12 340 11
She watched them till they had turned the corner, and MP I 9 96 76
Henry, overjoyed to have her go, bowed and watched her off, MP II 13 298 2
Edmund watched the progress of her attention, and was MP III 3 337 11
He watched her with this idea--but he could hardly tell MP III 6 366 1
Fanny watched him with never-failing solicitude, and MP III 15 445 34
of his voice was watched, and how carefully her own eyes MP III 16 454 18
Emma watched her through the fluctuations of this speech, E I 4 31 26
Emma watched and decided, that with such feelings as were E II 6 197 4
Emma watched the entree of her own particular little E II 8 219 44
Emma watched them in, and then joined Harriet at the E II 9 235 35
She watched him well. E III 1 316 3
up, and seeing herself watched, blushed more deeply than E III 5 349 23
and watched her safely off with the zeal of a friend. E III 6 363 51
he had loved her, and watched over her from a girl, with E III 12 415 1
it; and having all kindly watched him as far up the hill P III 12 105 10
She watched--observed--reflected--and finally determined P IV 5 154 8
She always watched them as long as she could; delighted to P IV 6 168 24
out of Bath; for having watched in vain for some P IV 10 228 70
WATCHES (3)
on examining their watches, that it was time to be at home. PP III 16 370 35
long; and on examining watches, so much of the morning was E II 10 246 55
wife and children, and watches the boat that he has sent P IV 11 234 31
WATCHFUL (6)
caught Catherine's watchful eye, and "Oh! dear, I do NA I 11 82 2
Mrs. Dashwood, not less watchful of what passed than her SS III 10 340 3
was the office of each watchful companion, and each found SS III 10 341 6
bustle without, & watchful curiosity within, the important W 329 9
Elizabeth was watchful enough to see it all, but she could PP II 3 149 28
but in Mrs. Norris's watchful attention, and in Edmund's MP I 3 32 62
WATCHFULNESS (5)
which eluded all her watchfulness to ascertain the fact. SS II 5 167 7
and was, by her watchfulness, most abundantly supplied PP I 16 76 5
My watchfulness has been effectual; and though I should PP II 3 150 29
Her countenance, perhaps, might express some watchfulness; P IV 4 145 2
watchfulness which a son-in-law's rights would have given. P IV 12 250 7
WATCHING (45)
said Catherine, as she stood watching at a window. NA I 11 82 8
to suspect her friend, could not help watching her closely. NA II 4 149 1
and Henry, earnestly watching her through the whole letter, NA II 10 202 8
at the same time from watching her progress; and though no NA II 14 231 5
her, but likewise upon watching his behaviour to her SS II 4 159 1
direction of the wind, watching the variations of the sky SS II 5 168 8
where Elinor wrote, watching the advancement of her pen, SS II 9 203 10
the strictest sense, by watching over her education myself, SS II 9 208 28
though she soon perceived them to be narrowly watching her. SS II 13 241 20
succour, and watching almost every look and every breath. SS III 7 315 25
and therefore watching to very different effect, saw SS III 10 340 3
seated near him, was watching the progress of his letter, PP I 10 47 1
quite as much engaged in watching Mr. Darcy's progress PP I 11 54 4
She had been watching him the last hour, she said, as he PP I 15 74 11
at a drawing-room window watching their arrival; when they PP II 4 152 5
Mrs. Jenkinson was chiefly employed in watching how little PP II 6 163 14
After watching her a little, Fitzwilliam asked her why she PP II 10 185 33
an opposite milliner, watching the sentinel on guard, and PP II 16 219 1
was so much engaged in watching the occasional appearance PP III 1 254 57
the meadow, she could not help watching all that passed. MP I 7 67 16
had been watching with an interest almost equal to her own. MP I 7 69 21
to have leisure for watching the behaviour, or guarding MP I 17 163 21
In watching them she forgot herself; and agitated by the MP I 18 170 24
"I have been watching them.-- MP II 4 207 8
of a higher nature--watching in the hall, in the lobby, on MP II 6 233 14
Sir Thomas himself was watching her progress down the MP II 10 276 13
long watching for, and long thinking strangely delayed. MP III 3 344 42
Mary, who had been first watching her complacently, and MP III 5 364 30
be quite enough to support the spirits he was watching.-- MP III 6 368 7
Betsey and I have been watching for you this half hour. MP III 7 378 14
she had derived from watching the advance of that season MP III 14 432 9
affected, that Fanny, watching him with silent, but most MP III 16 457 30
Mr. Elton fidgetting behind her and watching every touch. E I 6 46 24
She paused over it, while Harriet stood anxiously watching E I 7 51 4
I am always watching her to admire; and I do pity her from E II 3 171 15
morning of some anxious watching, Frank Churchill, in all E III 2 319 1
to the door, he was watching for the sound of other E III 2 320 7
her eye--he seemed watching her intently--in vain, however, E III 5 346 17
even those she was watching, she did not know how to admit E III 12 416 2
Harriet; he might be watching for encouragement to begin.-- E III 13 425 2
It might have been an opportunity of watching the loves P III 9 80 34
it the happiest spot for watching the flow of the tide, P III 11 95 9
and Captain Wentworth, watching them, turned again to Anne, P IV 7 176 10
gave him an interest in watching all that was going on P IV 9 206 90
herself as she saw him watching his sisters, while he S 10 417 1
WATCHMAN (1)
silver sounds," and the watchman was beginning to be heard P IV 3 144 23
WATER (28)
drank her warm wine and water, and prepared herself for NA I 3 29 52
drinking his glass of water, joined some gentlemen to talk NA I 10 71 8
him, while she furnishes the fan and the lavender water. NA I 10 77 35
the Pump-Room, tasted the water, and laid out some NA I 15 116 1
The furniture was all sent round by water. SS I 5 26 4
began; and parties on the water were made and accomplished SS I 11 53 1
They contained a noble piece of water; a sail on which was SS I 12 62 28
of others, while reviving her with lavender water. SS II 6 177 12
walk by the side of the water, and every step was bringing PP III 1 253 55
to the edge of the water, in one of its narrowest parts. PP III 1 253 57

of some trout in the water, and talking to the man about PP III 1 254 57
without reckoning the water meadows; so that I think, if MP I 6 55 17
and water for her, would rather go without it than not. MP I 7 65 14
see if Rebecca has put the water on; and tell her to bring MP III 7 379 15
his rum and water, and Rebecca never where she ought to be. MP III 7 387 46
they were as a drop of water to the ocean, compared with MP III 8 392 11
of the sea now at high water, dancing in its glee and MP III 11 409 6
A small half glass--put into a tumbler of water? E I 3 25 14
out in that party on the water, and she, by the sudden E II 1 160 23
Frank knows a puddle of water when he sees it, and as to E II 5 195 48
water, will make you nearly on a par with the rest of us." E III 6 365 65
be a Mrs. Knightley to throw cold water on every thing.-- E III 17 469 36
We none of us expect to be in smooth water all our days." P III 8 70 45
almost hurrying into the water, the walk to the Cobb, P III 11 95 9
in Bath who drinks the water, gets all the new P IV 4 146 5
a young dab chick in the water; and benwick sits at her P IV 10 218 24
hard sand--deep water 10 yards from the shore--no mud--no S 1 369 1
proverbially detestable--water brackish beyond example, S 1 369 1
WATER-COLOURS (3)
know the difference between water-colours and crayons!-- MP I 2 18 23
crayon, and water-colours had been all tried in turn. E I 6 44 19
It was to be a whole-length in water-colours, like Mr. E I 6 46 23
WATER-PARTY (1)
A water-party; and by some accident she was falling E II 8 218 34
WATER-PLANT (1)
water-plant, there chanced to be a little alteration. PP III 1 255 61
WATERING (2)
a dormouse, feeding a canary-bird, or watering a rosebush. NA I 1 13 1
of such double danger as a watering place and a camp. PP II 19 237 3
WATERING-PLACE (4)
We hear of him for ever at some watering-place or other. E I 18 146 12
"At a watering-place, or in a common London acquaintance, E II 2 169 17
He meets with a young woman at a watering-place, gains her E III 13 428 23
quietest part of a watering-place day, when the important S 6 389 1
WATERLOO (3)
not named Trafalgar--for Waterloo is more the thing now. S 4 380 1
However, Waterloo is in reserve--& if we have S 4 380 1
shall be able to call it Waterloo Crescent--& the name S 4 380 1
WATERS (3)
He is going for his health to Bath, where if the waters LS 26 295 4
prevailed on to give the waters what I think a fair trial. NA II 2 138 2
Miss Woodhouse, where the waters do agree, it is quite E II 14 275 32
WATSONS (3)
The Edwardes' invitation to the Watsons followed of course. W 314 1
& kept their coach; the Watsons inhabited a village about W 314 1
able to tell the Miss Watsons, whom he depended on finding W 355 28
WAVE (3)
She believed she must wave the subject altogether. NA II 10 203 9
Collins, with a a formal wave of the hand, "that it is PP I 19 107 13
to wave her hand & collect them around her for choice.-- S 10 414 1
WAVED (1)
a solicitation must be waved for the present, the lady PP I 22 121 2
WAVER (1)
to wonder & waver between his influence & her brother's.-- W 326 5
WAVERED (3)
partial to Jane, and she wavered as to the greater PP III 11 332 18
Julia wavered; but was he only trying to soothe and pacify MP I 14 135 18
Mrs Darling's hands, had wavered as to coming & been S 11 420 1
WAVERING (6)
Allen's wavering convictions only made it more doubtful. NA I 12 91 3
If he had been wavering before, as to what he should do, PP III 15 361 3
There is not a shadow of wavering. MP III 13 423 2
His unsettled affections, wavering with his vanity, MP III 15 441 20
While you were in the smallest degree wavering, I said E I 7 53 24
His manners, however, must have been unmarked, wavering, E I 16 134 3
WAVERINGS (1)
to herself, in the waverings of Harriet's mind, Emma would E II 4 184 11
WAVES (1)
Woodhouse to say, that she waves her right of knowing E III 7 370 23
WAVING (2)
Waving that point, however, and supposing her to be, as E I 8 63 44
of unfinished buildings, waving linen, & tops of houses, S 4 384 1
WAX-CANDLES (1)
Wax-candles in the school-room! E II 17 300 8
WAXEN (1)
of the ease with which a waxen figure might be introduced, NA II 9 191 2
WAY (668)
an opportunity of leaving her myself, in my way to you. LS 1 244 1
I take town in my way to that insupportable spot, a LS 2 245 1
it has lately fallen in my way to hear some particulars of LS 4 248 1
is very infirm, & not likely to stand in your way long. LS 9 256 1
called, but I seldom hear any noise when I pass that way. LS 17 271 7
soon afterwards & was half way down stairs, when Frederica LS 20 275 1
Martin, & have no other way in the world of helping myself LS 21 279 1
I was quite cool, but he gave way to the most violent LS 22 282 7
that I may not in any way be instrumental in separating a LS 25 293 3
to get Manwaring out of the way, & you only can have LS 26 295 3
did what she could in that way, by drawing houses and NA I 1 14 1
Her love of dirt gave way to an inclination for finery, NA I 1 15 2
Something must and will happen to throw a hero in her way. NA I 1 17 11
Mrs. Allen made her way through the throng of men by the NA I 2 21 9
room was by no means the way to disengage themselves from NA I 2 21 9
You do not think too highly of us in that way." NA I 3 27 33
go;--eight miles is a long way; Mr. Allen says it is nine, NA I 3 29 46
Grandison herself; but new books do not fall in our way." NA I 6 41 21
"They are not coming this way, are they? NA I 6 43 35
"And which way are they gone?" said Isabella, turning NA I 6 43 37
That is the way to spoil them." NA I 6 43 43
James and Isabella led the way; and so well satisfied was NA I 7 47 18
reader of Camilla gave way to the feelings of the dutiful NA I 7 49 43
he seemed to be moving that way, but he did not see her, NA I 8 53 3
But the hindrance thrown in the way of a very speedy NA I 8 56 11
her once, made her way to Mrs. Allen and Mrs. Thorpe as NA I 8 58 25
It was looked upon as something out of the common way. NA I 9 64 24
within her, as she danced in her chair all the way home. NA I 10 81 61
Is not that a great way off?-- NA I 11 84 19
of being stopped in their way along narrow, winding vaults, NA I 11 88 54
turning his horse, they were on their way back to Bath. NA I 11 88 55
Thorpe then said something in the loud, incoherent way to NA I 11 89 61
Catherine, in deep mortification, proceeded on her way. NA I 12 92 3
appeared, and, making his way through the then thinning NA I 12 93 5
This is only doing it in a ruder way; and how do I know NA I 13 101 20
A sacrifice was always noble; and if she had given way to NA I 13 103 29
Mrs. Allen, are not you of my way of thinking? NA I 13 104 31
with Johnson and Blair all the rest of the way." NA I 14 108 14
"That is just my way of thinking. NA I 15 123 44
It is not my way to bother my brains with what does not NA I 15 124 46
I told him he had taken a very unlikely way to prevail NA II 1 134 39
I took him down several times you know in my way." NA II 1 135 41
inviting her to a secret conference, led the way to a seat. NA II 3 143 1
every body entering at either, "it is so out of the way." NA II 3 143 1
Modesty, and all that, is very well in its way, but really NA II 3 144 10
his advances in the kindest way; and now he wants me to NA II 3 144 10
make him understand what I mean, in the properest way. NA II 3 145 13
I will look another way. NA II 3 147 26
way, they could have passed it with ease in half a minute. NA II 5 156 5
We shall not have to explore our way into a hall dimly NA II 5 158 15
all this out of the common way, and your lamp being nearly NA II 5 160 21
before Miss Tilney led the way into a chamber, and NA II 5 162 28
In that corner, however, it is at least out of the way." NA II 6 165 4
Alarmed, but not discouraged, she tried it another way; a NA II 6 168 10
moving it in every possible way for some instants with the NA II 6 168 10
her hand, and groping her way to the bed, she jumped NA II 6 170 12
way so agitated, repose must be absolutely impossible. NA II 6 170 12
reflections, and found her way with all speed to the NA II 7 173 5
he led the way to it across a small portion of the park. NA II 7 178 20
in some way or other, by its falling short of his plan. NA II 7 178 23
Our best way is across the park." NA II 7 179 27
Tilney, "that I always think it the best and nearest way. NA II 7 179 28
Catherine, he led the way across the hall, through the NA II 8 182 2
an apartment, in its way, of equal magnificence, NA II 8 182 2
walks about the room in this way; it is nothing unusual." NA II 8 187 13
way or other her destroyer, affected her even to tears. NA II 9 190 1
Of the way to the apartment she was now perfectly mistress; NA II 9 193 5
"Because it is my nearest way from the stable-yard to my NA II 9 194 7
"Very;--and does Eleanor leave you to find your way into NA II 9 195 14
alluding in the slightest way to what had passed, was of NA II 10 201 4
should come in her way; that is Frederick's only chance.-- NA II 10 206 34
difficulties in the way of her marrying their brother. NA II 11 208 1
You are not to put yourself at all out of your way. NA II 11 210 6
A second engagement must give way to a first. NA II 13 224 14
me, I dare say, half the way--and then I shall soon be at NA II 13 224 17
Turned from the house, and in such a way!-- NA II 13 226 25
"She travelled all the way post by herself, and knew NA II 14 237 21
her if she would have the goodness to shew him the way. NA II 15 242 9
it was not their way to suppose any evil could be told. NA II 16 249 1
happened pretty often, they always looked another way. NA II 16 250 3
it was secured, in such a way, as to leave to himself no SS I 1 4 3
desire of having his own way, many cunning tricks, and a SS I 1 4 3
It will certainly be much the best way. SS I 2 11 23
Had he ever been in the way of learning, I think he would SS I 4 19 2
to you, by speaking, in so quiet a way, of my own feelings. SS I 4 21 15
be many difficulties in his way, if he were to wish to SS I 4 21 15
to be of the party, by way of provision for discourse. SS I 6 31 9
The ladies had passed near it in their way along the SS I 7 32 1
Margaret agreed, and they pursued their way against the SS I 9 41 6
will make conquests enough, I day say, one way or other. SS I 9 45 31
32
them give way to the reception of more general opinions." SS I 11 56 12
mind are obliged to give way, how frequently are they SS I 11 56 17
Margaret's sagacity was not always displayed in a way so SS I 12 61 15
they must do something by way of being happy; and after SS I 13 66 60
farewel of Allenham; and by way of exhilaration I am now SS I 15 76 6
quitted the parlour to give way in solitude to the concern SS I 15 77 18
way to as a relief, but feeding and encouraging as a duty. SS I 15 77 20
I have explained it to myself in the most satisfactory way; SS I 15 78 26
happy; but like every body else it must be in my own way. SS I 17 91 7
the effect of a sense of inferiority in some way or other. SS I 17 94 44
But before she was half way up stairs she heard the SS I 18 96 2
Elinor placed all that was astonishing in this way of SS I 19 101 2
You may see her if you look this way." SS I 19 105 16
and no expectation of pleasure from them in any other way. SS I 19 108 40
We do not live a great way from him in the country, you SS I 20 111 12
This is always the way with him! SS I 20 113 39
the opposition you know, and besides it is such a way off. SS I 20 114 44
I assure you I heard of it in my way through town." SS I 20 115 46
Their engagements at Exeter instantly gave way before such SS I 21 118 2
But this is the usual way of heightening alarm, where SS I 21 122 12
about her in such a way;" said Lucy, eyeing Elinor SS I 22 128 7
it would be the wisest way to put an end to the business SS II 2 149 29
30
me, for I shan't put myself at all out of my way for you. SS II 3 153 2
herself rather out of her way; and as for the Miss Steeles, SS II 3 157 19
She sat in silence almost all the way, wrapt in her own SS II 4 160 2
In this calm kind of way, with very little interest on SS II 4 162 12
his rival; and at length by way of saying something, she SS II 4 162 12
Mary always has her own way." SS II 5 167 5
incessantly to give way in a low voice to the misery of SS II 6 177 15
times, and then gave way to a burst of tears, which at SS II 7 182 12
"No, Marianne, in no possible way." SS II 7 190 57
I have no notion of men's going on in this way: and if SS II 8 192 3
But that won't do, now-a-days; nothing in the way of SS II 8 194 10
in Conduit-Street in my way home, and told them of it. SS II 8 195 16
hoped, in a way to get some quiet rest before she left her. SS II 8 197 25
"I could meet him in no other way. SS II 9 211 38
Design could never bring them in each other's way: SS II 10 213 4
Mrs. Palmer, in her way, was equally angry. SS II 10 215 10
came post all the way, and had a smart beau to attend us. SS II 10 218 24
you in this kind of way, she has given you a sort of claim SS II 11 227 46
got all his money in a low way; and Fanny and Mrs. Ferrars SS II 11 228 53
Could any thing be so flattering as Mrs. Ferrars's way of SS II 13 239 4
looked at me in a pleasant way-- you know what I mean,--if SS II 13 240 17
sort of way, I should have gave it all up in despair. SS II 13 240 17
This is the way in which I always consider the matter, and SS II 14 251 13
"If such is your way of thinking," said Marianne, "if the SS III 1 263 28
way, 'that we had asked your sisters instead of them.'" SS III 1 266 36
Everybody has a way of their own. SS III 1 269 54
I declare sometimes I do not know which way to look before SS III 2 272 12
it expedient to find her way back again to the first. SS III 2 272 13
call, should she come this way any morning, 'twould be a SS III 2 277 30
He had met Mrs. Jennings at the door in her way to the SS III 4 287 25
unluckily, I was not in the way at first, and knew nothing SS III 5 299 37
happen to be in their way, which of all things was the SS III 6 301 1
the knack of finding her way in every house to the library, SS III 6 304 12
and, attended the whole way by a servant of Mrs. Jennings, SS III 7 308 4
It is a great way, you know, from hence to Barton." SS III 7 311 12
of my own amusement, giving way to feelings which I had SS III 8 320 29
therefore on calling at the cottage, in my way to Honiton. SS III 8 324 42
speak in this way, either of Mrs. Willoughby or my sister. SS III 8 329 64
at all, I suppose-- giving way to irresistible feelings, SS III 9 336 12
immediately afterwards took his solitary way to Delaford. SS III 10 341 5
as it has since in every way been proved, it was not at SS III 13 362 5
altar, and are now on our way to Dawlish for a few weeks, SS III 13 365 14
always behaving in a particular way to one or another."-- W 316 1
I know nobody who likes a game of cards in a social way, W 325 4
& throats, led the way up the wide staircase, while no W 327 7
of it began soon to give way; the inspiriting sound of W 328 8
men, one now made his way to Miss Edwards, with an air of W 328 8
players being disposed to move exactly the different way. W 333 13
corner, exactly the other way, forgetting in her haste W 333 13
had a sensible, unaffected, way of expressing himself, W 335 13
It was the way of the place always to call on Mrs E. on W 337 16
see you, & it was a clever way of getting you home; W 341 19
"Your Lordship thinks we always have our own way.-- W 346 21
Robert watson was an attorney at Croydon, in a good way of W 348 23
I have been quarrelling with you all the way we came, have W 350 24
after a short silence, by way of changing the subject, he W 352 26
He had been in London & was now on his way home, & he had W 355 28
parlour a foot larger each way than the other was thrown W 355 28
I have not been in the way of it now for a long while.-- W 358 28
friend; & had a lively way of retailing a common-place, or W 359 28
Bennet, how can you abuse your own children in such a way? PP I 1 5 28
"We are not in a way to know what Mr. Bingley likes," said PP I 2 6 3
by this, as her mother could be, though in a quieter way. PP I 3 12 15
the first, and was in a way to be very much in love; but PP I 6 21 1
sound, and that you would never act in this way yourself." PP I 6 23 11
"You are a very strange creature by way of a friend!-- PP I 6 24 22
I entreat you not to suppose that I moved this way in PP I 6 26 39
to their aunt and to a milliner's shop just over the way. PP I 7 28 3
world, which is always the way with her, for she has, PP I 9 42 7
has been many a one, I fancy, overcome in the same way. PP I 9 44 32
"Charles writes in the most careless way imaginable. PP I 10 48 22
Elizabeth would lead the way, which the other as politely PP I 10 51 45
"how pleasant it is to spend an evening in this way! PP I 11 55 4

way of disappointing him, will be to ask nothing about it." PP I 11 56 13
be completely in your way;--and if the second, I can PP I 11 56 15
"Though it is difficult," said Jane, "to guess in what way PP I 13 63 15
walking with an officer on the other side of the way. PP I 15 72 8
to find out, led the way across the street, under pretence PP I 15 72 8
He was then, he said, on his way to Longbourn on purpose PP I 15 72 8
he had told her, all the way home; but there was not time PP I 16 84 59
say, in some way or other, of which we can form no idea. PP I 17 85 2
glad to find that he had taken himself out of the way, PP I 18 94 45
and every thing else gave way before the hope of Jane's PP I 18 95 48
the hope of Jane's being in the fairest way for happiness. PP I 18 95 48
of it he only made him a slight bow, and moved another way. PP I 18 98 61
saw were bent the same way, and she determined not to PP I 18 98 63
must throw them in the way of other rich men; and lastly, PP I 18 99 63
up high, but able to make a small income go a good way. PP I 19 105 10
Allow me, by the way, to observe, my fair cousin, that I PP I 19 106 10
in such a way as may convince you of its being one." PP I 19 108 18
"What do you mean, Mr. Bennet, by talking in this way? PP I 20 112 21
if we were at York, provided she can have her own way.-- PP I 20 113 28
offer of marriage in this way, you will never get a PP I 20 113 28
this time, and are on their way to town; and without any PP I 21 116 7
it would succeed, if Miss de Bourgh were out of the way. PP I 21 119 20
in telling her story, gave way to a momentary confusion PP I 22 124 14
15
no other way than as a piece of news to spread at Meryton. PP I 23 127 7
Mrs. Bennet, and they gave way only to the greater PP I 23 128 11
should be forced to make way for her, and live to see her PP I 23 130 17
"My dear, do not give way to such gloomy thoughts. PP I 23 130 18
"My dear Lizzy, do not give way to such feelings as these. PP II 1 135 12
who marries him, cannot have a proper way of thinking. PP II 1 135 13
"An excellent consolation in its way," said Elizabeth, " PP II 2 140 7
former friends, than she had been in the way of procuring. PP II 2 142 19
Here, leading the way through every walk and cross walk, PP II 5 156 4
constantly bowing whenever Miss de Bourgh looked that way. PP II 5 158 19
on the edge of her chair, not knowing which way to look. PP II 6 162 11
families I have been the means of supplying in that way. PP II 6 165 32
In this quiet way, the first fortnight of her visit soon PP II 7 169 6
Colonel Fitzwilliam, who led the way, was about thirty, PP II 7 170 9
She answered him in the usual way, and after a moment's PP II 7 171 10
11
She would be in nobody's way, you know, in that part of PP II 8 173 10
or he would never have called on us in this familiar way." PP II 9 180 27
"I did not know before that you ever walked this way." PP II 10 182 2
3
"He likes to have his own way very well," replied Colonel PP II 10 183 10
the true Darcy spirit, she may like to have her own way." PP II 10 184 19
indeed, her confidence gave way a little, but she would PP II 10 187 40
affected me in any other way, than as it spared me the PP II 11 192 23
24
any possible way that would have tempted me to accept it." PP II 11 192 25
26
park; he was moving that way; and fearful of its being Mr. PP II 12 195 2
Pursuing her way along the lane, she then began it. PP II 12 196 3
Of his former way of life, nothing had been known in PP II 13 206 4
After wandering along the lane for two hours, giving way PP II 13 209 12
she was alone, she gave way to it as the greatest relief; PP II 14 212 16
Mr. Darcy's letter, she was in a fair way of soon knowing PP II 14 212 17
gowns in the only right way, that Maria thought herself PP II 14 213 20
My dear Charlotte and I have but one mind and one way of PP II 15 216 6
comfortable and snug, and talk and laugh all the way home. PP II 16 221 17
endeavour to amuse her companions all the way to Longbourn. PP II 16 222 18
from Jane, who sat some way below her, and on the other, PP II 16 222 21
should have gone so all the way, if Kitty had not been PP II 16 222 22
And then we were so merry all the way home! we talked and PP II 16 222 22
way--teaching them, playing with them, and loving them. PP II 19 239 10
"And this is always the way with him," she added.-- PP III 1 250 45
a way, as plainly spoke the distraction of his thoughts. PP III 1 252 52
as if she had purposely thrown herself in his way again! PP III 1 252 54
submit, and they took their way towards the house on the PP III 1 254 57
After walking some time in this way, the two ladies in PP III 1 255 61
so cruel a way by any body, as he has done by poor Wickham. PP III 1 258 74
pleasures, every idea gave way to the charm of PP III 1 258 76
that there was no other way of accounting for such PP III 2 260 1
He enquired in a friendly, though general way, after her PP III 2 261 5
Her teeth are tolerable, but not out of the common way; PP III 3 271 15
in the best and safest way, and Colonel Forster is obliged PP III 4 276 5
It is every way horrible!" PP III 4 277 16
manner, and to adopt any opinions that came in her way. PP III 5 283 10
her fancy for him gave way, and others of the regiment, PP III 5 285 18
"Do not give way to useless alarm," added he, "though it PP III 5 288 37
his way towards a small wood on one side of the paddock. PP III 7 301 6
I will believe, that he is come to a right way of thinking. PP III 7 305 37
dear Lydia, I don't at all like your going such a way off. PP III 9 317 12
I do not particularly like your way of getting husbands." PP III 9 317 16
for me, or else I could take it in my way to Newcastle. PP III 10 327 11
it is very hard to have him taken such a way from me. PP III 11 336 51
She could settle it in no way that gave her pleasure. PP III 12 339 3
the meanwhile, was giving way to all the happy schemes. PP III 12 339 10
Lady Catherine might see him in her way through town; and PP III 15 361 3
to Bingley of coming again to Netherfield must give way. PP III 15 361 3
"This young gentleman is blessed in a peculiar way, with PP III 15 362 15
the smallest idea of their being ever felt in such a way." PP III 16 368 15
in any possible way, that would induce you to accept me." PP III 16 368 16
out with him again, that he may not be in Bingley's way." PP III 17 374 20
here-abouts in which Lizzy may lose her way again to-day?" PP III 17 374 22
these violent young lovers carry every thing their own way. PP III 17 377 39
knowledge which had never before fallen in her way. PP III 19 388 11
her nephew; and as she gave way to all the genuine PP III 19 388 12
aunt, her resentment gave way, either to her affection of PP III 19 388 12
every thing one could by way of providing for a child one MP I 1 6 6
It is, in fact, the only sure way of providing against the MP I 1 6 6
fanciful impediment in the way of a plan which would be so MP I 1 7 7
"There will be some difficulty in our way, Mrs. Norris," MP I 1 10 17
Mrs. Norris had been talking to her the whole way from MP I 2 13 4
put themselves out of their way to secure her comfort. MP I 2 14 6
A week had passed in this way, and no suspicion of it MP I 2 15 9
Do you know, we asked her last night, which way she would MP I 2 18 25
this was a way of going on that she could not understand. MP I 3 31 59
But he had ended his speech in a way to sink her in sad MP I 3 33 64
She knew it was her way. MP I 5 47 27
In a quiet way, very little attended to, she paid her MP I 5 48 30
talked and laughed till I did not know which way to look. MP I 5 50 35
Mothers certainly have not yet got quite the right way of MP I 5 50 36
walked by her side all the way home, and made myself as MP I 5 51 40
his own place in the same way; and though not saying much MP I 6 52 1
We did a vast deal in that way at the parsonage; we made MP I 6 54 9
London--but this morning we heard of it in the right way. MP I 6 57 33
better keep out of his way; and my brother-in-law himself, MP I 6 58 37
was quite at his service in any way that could be useful. MP I 6 61 58
Miss Price, I give way to you with a very bad grace; but I MP I 7 68 20
and walk half way down the park with the two other ladies. MP I 8 77 7
settle it your own way, I am sure I do not care about it." MP I 8 79 23
The rest of the way is such as it ought to be. MP I 8 82 34
marble, gilding and carving, each handsome in its way. MP I 9 84 3
I will take you in this way, if you will excuse me." MP I 9 85 5
Every body likes to go their own way--to choose their own MP I 9 87 15
Miss Bertram, displeased with her sister, led the way, and MP I 9 89 30
and perhaps turn a little way in some other direction, if MP I 9 96 76
After some minutes spent in this way, Miss Bertram MP I 10 97 4
the best, it was the only way of proceeding with any MP I 10 97 4
You and Julia were laughing the whole way." MP I 10 98 11
nonsense! I certainly can get out that way, and I will. MP I 10 99 19
speeches to Mrs. Rushworth, was ready to lead the way. MP I 10 104 52
if it is in your way, I will have it in my lap directly. MP I 10 105 55
myself in a wrong way, and I am sure my father was too MP I 11 109 17
which will not find their way to female feelings without MP I 12 115 4
over it said in a languid way, "if you want to dance, MP I 12 118 22
And to ask me in such a way too! without ceremony, before MP I 12 119 26
time addressed in such a way as to oblige one to do the MP I 12 120 26
to take Mansfield in his way, whenever he could, and by MP I 13 121 1
way; and I think a theatre ought not to be attempted.-- MP I 13 127 28
back, inclined the same way; but his determinateness and MP I 14 130 3
have another fine fancy suit by way of a shooting dress.-- MP I 15 138 3
while his sister made her way to Lady Bertram, and with MP I 15 143 26
of employing her in that way was not yet overcome, in MP I 15 145 44
of this attempt to find her way to her duty, and her MP I 16 153 3
to let Tom go on in this way, riding about the country in MP I 16 155 22
with all the glee of feelings gratified in every way. MP I 17 158 1
wrong herself, but she was disquieted in every other way. MP I 17 159 6
been nobody to put him in the way of doing any thing yet." MP I 17 161 14
giving an invitation to every family who came in his way. MP I 18 164 1
lookings on, at your ease, in this way,--I want you here.-- MP I 18 166 6
I have made my way to you on purpose to entreat your help." MP I 18 168 15
but he is not in the way; and if he were, I do not think I MP I 18 168 17
house, had proceeded some way, when the door of the room MP I 18 172 33
We have just been trying, by way of doing something, and MP II 1 181 16
To be a second time disappointed in the same way was an MP II 2 191 10
Mansfield wood, and all the way home; but there was a MP II 2 191 10
his own way, and feel the folly of it without opposition. MP II 2 191 10
began, without bringing them together in some way or other. MP II 2 192 11
confident, idle and expensive, it was every way vexatious. MP II 2 194 21
of way, allowing for the difference of the time of year." MP II 3 199 14
Mrs. Rushworth was quite ready to retire, and make way for MP II 3 202 28
believed herself not in the way, and could she have MP II 4 206 4
We are to be sure a miracle every way--but our powers of MP II 4 209 12
Fanny never dines there, you know, in this sort of way. MP II 5 217 1
in for a minute in his way from his plantation to his MP II 5 217 11
Edmund knocked at her door in his way to his own. MP II 5 219 24
company in this sort of way, or ever dining out at all; MP II 5 220 28
She heard them spoken of by him only in a general way, MP II 5 224 49
heart been guarded in a way unsuspected by Miss Crawford, MP II 6 231 11
himself and working his way to fortune and consequence MP II 6 236 22
in a grand and careless way that Mr. Crawford was somewhat MP II 7 238 1
been obliged to give up, and make the best of his way back. MP II 7 240 13
"I told you I lost my way after passing that old farm MP II 7 241 13
"It sounds like it," said Edmund; "but which way did you MP II 7 241 14
Sir Thomas, politely bowing, replied--"it is the only way, MP II 7 247 39
I am a pretty good dancer in my way, but I dare say you MP II 7 250 59
which way to look, or how to be prepared for the answer. MP II 7 250 60
shall you have by way of necklace?" said Miss Crawford. MP II 8 257 15
Your goodness in thinking of me in such a way is beyond"--- MP II 9 262 5
"No, it is not handsomer, not at all handsomer in its way, MP II 9 263 15
would have her own way with the supper, and whom she could MP II 9 267 22
The stiffness of the meeting soon gave way before their MP II 10 273 8
she was to lead the way and open the ball; an idea that MP II 10 275 11
of conveying your brother and talking of you by the way." MP II 10 277 19
take place at all in the way she could desire, that she MP II 10 280 32
To Mary it was every way painful. MP II 11 285 15
and she made her way to the park, through difficulties of MP II 11 287 17
It is the general way; all young men do." MP II 11 287 20
Edmund, who had not in some way or other continually MP II 12 294 16
Few fathers would have let me have my own way half so much. MP II 12 296 28
and so is Sir Thomas in his way, but it is the way of a MP II 12 297 35
the way of a rich, superior, longworded, arbitrary uncle. MP II 12 297 35
unworthily, and in such a way as she had not deserved; but MP II 13 301 7
to a servant in his way towards the room they were in. MP II 13 302 9
way of the happiness he sought, was a cruel necessity.-- MP II 13 302 9
be able to put him in the way of getting every thing very MP II 13 305 19
and being then in her way up stairs, she resolved there to MP III 1 311 2
I understood that you had the use of this room by way of MP III 1 312 10
handsome and disinterested way; and let me tell you, Fanny, MP III 1 319 39
you will not give way to these emotions, but endeavour to MP III 1 321 48
likes to go her own way to work; she does not like to be MP III 1 323 56
the influence of all who loved her must incline one way. MP III 2 329 12
he believed kindness might be the best way of working. MP III 2 330 14
missing you, when such an offer as this comes in your way. MP III 2 333 26
And by carefully giving way to the inclination of the MP III 3 336 10
This would be the way to Fanny's heart. MP III 3 340 24
if she did not lead the way, it should never be touched on MP III 4 345 1
points would be the likeliest way to produce an extreme. MP III 4 349 23
secure, she was in every way an object of painful alarm. MP III 5 356 4
her almost instantly rise and lead the way out of the room. MP III 5 357 5
and setting off to find my way to the east room, without MP III 5 360 14
it down as simply being his way, and was as far from MP III 5 362 21
he is attached to you in a way that he never was to any MP III 5 363 24
be attended to in the same way, that a friendship and MP III 5 364 29
Edmund considered it every way, and saw nothing but what MP III 6 368 9
Had she ever given way to bursts of delight, it must have MP III 6 369 11
You will set things going in a better way, I am sure. MP III 6 372 20
lieutenant out of the way--and William was not very MP III 7 375 2
way, though with no advantage of manner in receiving her. MP III 7 377 9
he would manage all his own way; and lastly in walked Mr. MP III 7 379 19
I would not have been out of the way for a thousand pounds. MP III 7 380 20
a short and hurried way, when he had come ashore on duty. MP III 8 388 2
above her home, or in any way disqualified or disinclined, MP III 8 390 7
some of hers found its way to a circulating library. MP III 9 398 9
doings in every way; to be a renter, a chuser of books! MP III 9 398 9
use, and Susan was entertained in a way quite new to her. MP III 10 404 15
mentioned it, and led the way to her fond exclamations in MP III 10 405 17
I know its way, I know its faults towards you. MP III 11 410 16
to have your comforts give way to the imaginary MP III 11 410 16
niece in the most promising way of being starved, both MP III 11 413 30
shew you Everingham in our way, and perhaps you would not MP III 12 416 3
in Parliament, got into the way of making and keeping MP III 13 425 6
too, would be the best way of preventing such things." MP III 15 440 13
that way, that there was no answering for anybody." MP III 15 440 17
her kindness in the same way again--she need not fear a MP III 16 453 17
At such a moment to give way to gaiety and to speak with MP III 16 456 24
My influence, which is not small, shall all go that way; MP III 16 457 29
She had sources of delight that must force their way. MP III 17 461 2
no useful influence that way, no moral effect on the mind. MP III 17 463 8
tolerably soon in a fair way of not thinking of him again; MP III 17 466 18
and unmerited, led him into the way of happiness. MP III 17 467 19
rather too much her own way, and a disposition to think a E I 1 5 4
horses to for such a little way;--and where are the poor E I 1 8 17
the lock of the door the right way and never bangs it. E I 1 9 19
I think very well of Mr. Elton, and this is the only way I E I 1 13 46
way in London, which afforded him a favourable opening. E I 2 16 5
Mr. Woodhouse was fond of society in his own way. E I 3 20 1
She lived with her single daughter in a very small way, E I 3 21 4
be sent to be out of the way and scramble themselves into E I 3 21 5
is sure to ride through every week in his way to Kingston. E I 4 29 13
hope to be useful to their families in some way or other. E I 4 29 14
He has not such a fine air and way of walking as Mr. E I 4 33 33
to be little occupied with it; her vanity lies another way. E I 5 39 21
the fairest way of falling in love, if not in love already. E I 6 42 1
to think on points which had not fallen in her way before." E I 6 42 5
of its being in every way a pretty drawing at last, and of E I 6 47 27
Emma, smiling graciously, "would I advise you either way. E I 7 53 21
way at that moment, he would have been accepted after all. E I 7 55 35
goes; and from his general way of talking in unreserved E I 8 66 53
in a very particular way indeed, that he was going on E I 8 68 58
This is feeling your way. E I 9 72 15
very good sense in a common way, like every body else, and E I 9 76 35

way; and another, to write verses and charades like this." E I 9 76 35
recollect of it--but it is very clever all the way through. E I 9 78 54
tosses them up to the ceiling in a very frightful way!" E I 9 81 74
turns, which ever began would never give way to the other." E I 9 81 75
If he were, every thing else must give way; but otherwise E I 9 81 78
a poor sick family, who lived a little way out of Highbury. E I 10 83 1
"I do not often walk this way now," said Emma, as they E I 10 83 5
not my way, or my nature; and I do not think I ever shall. E I 10 84 15
had been seen in a regular way by their Surry connections, E I 11 91 2
party the last half of the way; but his alarms were E I 11 91 3
Papa, if you speak in that melancholy way, you will be E I 11 94 14
of them all in the usual way, and to take the child out of E I 12 98 2
And she talked in this way so long and successfully that, E I 12 104 45
The only way of proving it, however, will be to turn to E I 12 107 61
that any thing gives way to it--and this must be the case E I 13 111 13
and smiled himself off in a way that left the balance of E I 13 111 14
of snow were finding their way down, and the sky had the E I 13 112 24
that not a breath of air can find its way unpermitted. E I 13 115 37
(in her way--allowing for little whims and caprices, and E I 14 120 13
is so very unreasonable; and every thing gives way to her." E I 14 123 23
to lay down rules for it: you must let it go its own way. E I 14 123 25
and horses to be making their way through a storm of snow." E I 15 126 8
He had gone beyond the sweep--some way along the Highbury E I 15 127 16
account for it only in one way; you are not yourself, or E I 15 130 26
27
you should have been giving way to any feelings----- E I 15 131 34
but it had passed as his way, as a mere error of judgment, E I 16 134 5
two years ago, to make his way as he could, without any E I 16 136 9
following morning in his way to Bath, where, in compliance E I 17 140 2
the way of cure, there could be no true peace for herself. E I 17 143 15
So very good of them to send her the whole way! E II 1 159 18
leave town in their way to Holyhead the Monday following-- E II 1 161 31
a pleasant evening," said Mr. Woodhouse, in his quiet way. E II 3 171 12
is very agreeable, and Mrs. Bates too, in a different way. E II 3 171 12
I had not thought of it before, but that was the best way. E II 3 172 19
You like news--and I heard an article in my way hither E II 3 172 20
If she were to meet Miss Bates in her way!--and upon its E II 3 177 51
She did not do any of it in the same way that she used; I E II 3 178 52
for I should find the near way quite floated by this rain. E II 3 179 52
in a great way, near Bristol, who kept two carriages! E II 4 183 9
the visit; but in a way that, if they had understanding, E II 4 185 13
and resolve on going home by way of Randalls to procure it. E II 5 187 4
in his guest, give way to all his natural kind-hearted E II 5 193 35
always the last to make his way in conversation; "then E II 5 194 45
one of my servants shall go with you to shew you the way." E II 5 195 45
The Coles were very respectable in their way, but they E II 7 207 6
if they are done by sensible people in an impudent way. E II 8 212 2
3
people come in a way which they know to be beneath them. E II 8 213 10
Emma to think her own way, and still listen to Mrs. Cole. E II 8 215 15
and her niece, made his way directly to the opposite side E II 8 220 47
done her hair in so odd a way--so very odd a way-- that I E II 8 222 56
very odd a way-- that I cannot keep my eyes from her. E II 8 222 56
his approbation, I made my way directly to Miss Bates, to E II 8 223 63
In the way of love, I am sure he does not. E II 8 225 76
They combated the point some time longer in the same way; E II 8 226 85
A Mrs. Knightley for them all to give way to!-- E II 8 228 87
I should be quite in the way. E II 9 234 30
But, perhaps--I may be equally in the way here. E II 9 234 30
I believe it is the only way that Mr. Woodhouse thinks the E II 9 237 46
'there is nothing in the way of fruit half so good, and E II 9 238 51
happy in their different way; she, in some little distress; E II 11 253 40
solicitude generally makes way for another. Emma, being E II 12 257 2
A pretty fortune; and she came in his way." E II 14 271 12
very much in the same way--just across the lawn; and I had E II 14 273 21
twice last summer, in that way, most delightfully, just E II 14 274 28
When he was speaking of it in that way, I honestly said E II 14 276 36
way, in doing too much, and being too careless of expense. E II 15 283 9
with others in a general way, in knowing what was felt, E II 15 284 11
never fell in Mrs. Elton's way before--and no degree of E II 15 287 23
sit with us in this comfortable way, if you were married." E II 15 288 35
I never had a thought of her in that way, I assure you." E II 15 288 36
that would be the way, I suppose, if I were very bad.-- E II 16 297 48
I really am ashamed of always leading the way." E II 16 298 57
it in his way, and had taken the liberty of opening it. E II 17 303 24
mention the circumstance to the others in a common way." E II 17 304 27
I met the letters in my way this morning, and seeing my E II 18 305 5
in what way she had best retract, when Mr. Weston went on. E II 18 307 17
half year has made a great difference in your way of life." E II 18 311 44
Emma, that Henry and John may be sometimes in the way. E II 18 312 48
Miss Fairfax, who were standing a little way behind her.-- E III 2 323 20
Mr. Weston and Mrs. Elton led the way, Mr. Frank Churchill E III 2 325 31
She was not yet dancing; she was working her way up from E III 2 327 34
When she was half way up the set, the whole group were E III 2 327 34
The baked apples and biscuits, excellent in their way, you E III 2 329 45
ladies had advanced some way into it, they had suddenly E III 3 333 5
made the best of her way by a short cut back to Highbury. E III 3 333 5
thrown together in such a way, could hardly fail of E III 3 334 9
way as I have done, and I dare say you understand me." E III 4 337 4
I do not advise you to give way to it, Harriet. E III 4 342 39
unpretending, elegant way, infinitely superior to the E III 6 352 2
prevail; and I shall call on Miss Bates in my way home." E III 6 355 19
was very ready to lead the way in gathering, accepting, or E III 6 358 35
Delightful to gather for one's self--the only way of E III 6 358 35
to be put out of their way--delicious fruit--only too rich E III 6 358 35
in a scattered, dispersed way, scarcely any three together, E III 6 360 38
Harriet distinct from the rest, quietly leading the way. E III 6 360 40
own way, and only say that I am gone when it is necessary." E III 6 363 50
and regret, in a reasonable way, that he should be so late. E III 6 364 59
very entertaining from each of you, in a general way. E III 7 370 23
be indulgent--especially to any one who leads the way." E III 7 371 30
I have a great deal of vivacity in my own way, but I E III 7 372 37
half way down the hill, and every thing left far behind. E III 7 376 62
her cheeks almost all the way home, without being at any E III 7 376 63
see Mr. Knightley in her way; or, perhaps, he might come E III 8 377 2
she hoped, might lead the way to a return of old feelings. E III 8 378 7
stood out in such a kind way as she did, and refuse to E III 8 381 15
looked around eager to discover some way of being useful. E III 9 389 16
It is impossible to refuse what you ask in such a way. E III 10 392 5
together and on their way at a quick pace for Randall's. E III 10 392 7
He is half way to Windsor by this time." E III 10 394 20
I have been walking all this way in complete suspense. E III 10 394 27
at least not communicated in a way to carry conviction.-- E III 10 397 51
each other spoken of in a way not perfectly agreeable!" E III 10 399 61
you to give way to your own feelings?-- E III 11 404 11
not have dared to give way to--I should not have thought E III 11 406 18
against it, and try to put difficulties in the way. E III 11 407 28
to her in a more particular way than he had ever done E III 11 410 35
in a very particular way indeed!--(Harriet could not E III 11 410 35
and took Hartfield in her way home, almost as much in duty E III 12 417 3
Fairfax, which was every way her due; had she tried to E III 12 421 17
She did not, could not, feel equal to lead the way to any E III 13 425 2
her that he might have called at Mrs. Goddard's in his way. E III 13 425 8
led me to act by them in a way that I must always be E III 13 426 15
His aunt is in the way.-- E III 13 428 23
Her way was clear, though not quite smooth.-- E III 13 431 38
If you think me in a way to be happier than I deserve, I E III 14 443 8
This letter must make its way to Emma's feelings. E III 15 444 1
fine complimentary opening:--but it is his way. E III 15 445 7
She would be a loser in every way. E III 15 450 37
fancy Mr. E. and Knightley have every thing their own way." E III 16 456 27
And nobody knew at all which way he was gone. E III 16 458 40

care of themselves; the young people will find a way."-- E III 17 467 31
They called for him in their way; were all extremely E III 18 472 20
very promising step of the mind on its way to resignation. E III 19 483 9
but by the operation of the same system in another way.-- E III 19 483 10
at home, and leading the way to the chaise and four, and P III 1 6 12
or relinquishing their comforts in a way not to be borne. P III 1 10 19
in whatever way he might choose to model his household." P III 2 13 7
Elizabeth would go her own way--and never had she pursued P III 2 16 16
If a rich Admiral were to come in our way, Sir Walter-----" P III 3 17 1
Sir Walter, that, in the way of business, gentlemen of the P III 3 17 2
3
who can live in a regular way, in the country, choosing P III 3 20 17
and keep out of the way till all was over; when she found P III 5 32 1
village, and be out of the way when Admiral and Mrs. Croft P III 5 36 19
in some dreadful way, and not able to ring the bell! P III 5 37 24
I suppose, and they never put themselves out of their way." P III 5 38 29
It is a pity you cannot put your sister in the way of P III 6 44 8
abroad had worked its way to Uppercross, two years before. P III 6 50 28
in Mrs. Charles musgrove's way, on account of the child; P III 7 58 22
her sister's in a common way; but she was perfectly P III 7 60 32
young woman who came in his way, excepting Anne Elliot. P III 7 61 38
and dawdling about in a way not endurable to a third P III 9 73 2
by it, and to think Captain Wentworth very much in the way. P III 9 73 3
retired, and unpolished way of living, and their own P III 9 74 5
in a very different sort of way; and with that property, P III 9 76 15
of going six miles another way; of his having, in every P III 9 78 19
as she knelt, in such a way that, busy as she was about P III 9 79 29
Anne's object was, not to be in the way of any body, and P III 10 84 7
her, as if making their way back, along the rough, wild P III 10 87 22
They had travelled half their way along the rough lane, P III 10 91 43
was diversified in a way which she had not at all imagined. P III 11 93 5
in maintaining her own way, bore down all the wishes of P III 11 94 7
down, politely drew back, and stopped to give them way. P III 12 104 6
Captain Wentworth looked round at her instantly in a way P III 12 104 6
on now for Crewkherne, in his way to Bath and London." P III 12 105 12
It was soon drawn per force another way. P III 12 109 31
could oppose when he gave way, there was no help for it: P III 12 115 65
"Oh God! that I had not given way to her at the fatal P III 12 116 71
And so much was said in this way, that Anne thought she P IV 1 122 5
Lyme, which found their way to Anne, she could not tell P IV 1 125 14
A new sort of way this, for a young fellow to be making P IV 1 126 22
he ever does, in a general way--but however, it is a very P IV 2 131 9
here, he will make his way over to Kellynch one day by P IV 2 131 12
Bath in November, in his way to London, when the P IV 3 138 6
had drawn him a different way, and now that he could P IV 3 140 11
It was possible that he might stop in his way home, to ask P IV 3 142 17
useful and good to her in a way which had considerably P IV 5 152 2
living in a very humble way, unable even to afford herself P IV 5 152 4
and she put me in the way of making these little thread- P IV 5 155 9
as Louisa; it would have "kept her a little out of his way. P IV 6 163 7
I am always out of the way when any thing "desirable is P IV 6 163 7
But what a thing here is, by way of a boat. P IV 6 169 25
of your company the little way our road lies together. P IV 6 169 26
I am glad they are not on this side of the way. P IV 6 170 29
blows through one of the cupboards just in the same way." P IV 6 170 29
not really Mrs. Croft, she must let him have his own way. P IV 6 170 30
But even then, there was something odd in their way of P IV 6 171 33
No, you would not guess, from his way of writing, that he P IV 6 173 47
or quiet attention, and the Admiral had it all his own way. P IV 6 173 48
to Bath, Captain Wentworth was already on his way thither. P IV 7 174 1
side all the way to Camden-Place, without saying a word. P IV 7 178 24
walking the same way, but there was no mistaking him. P IV 7 179 28
houses on this side of the way, and this part of street, P IV 7 179 30
she must consent for a time to be happy in an humbler way. P IV 8 186 22
enough to spread purification and perfume all the way. P IV 9 192 3
all your acquaintance have disposed of you in the same way. P IV 9 197 36
see you, and was delighted to be in the way to let you in. P IV 9 197 40
happy to be of use to you, in any way that I could. P IV 9 198 43
Colonel Wallis was to assist in every way that he could. P IV 9 207 90
threw himself in their way, called at all hours--but I P IV 9 207 90
least the comfort of telling the whole story her own way. P IV 9 210 99
father this morning, I gave way immediately, for I would P IV 10 213 5
He had begun to talk of it a week ago; and by way of doing P IV 10 216 19
Mary were included in it, by way of general convenience. P IV 10 217 19
to Mrs. Musgrove--put her quite out of her way. P IV 10 219 29
Her plan of sitting with Lady Russell must give way for P IV 10 220 30
When she reached the White Hart, and made her way to the P IV 11 229 2
"Captain Wentworth, which way are you going? only to Gay- P IV 11 240 56
kept him from trying to regain her when thrown in his way. P IV 11 242 63
at least put myself in the way of happiness, I could exert P IV 11 243 70
by putting her in the way of recovering her husband's P IV 12 251 11
"Nay sir, if he is not in the way, his partner will just S 1 365 1
to complete anything in the way of business you know till S 1 367 1
service to you & this lady in every way in their power."-- S 1 367 1
There was no blue shoe when we passed this way a month ago. S 4 383 1
not taken place, or we should have seen him in his way.-- S 5 387 1
of life he shd be encouraged to give way to indisposition. S 5 388 1
stroll on the cliff gave way to an immediate return home.-- S 6 390 1
She has been trying to get round me every way, with her S 7 399 1
us in the way they commonly do between those two parties.-- S 7 400 1
talking on in the same way, allowed her thoughts to form S 7 402 1
Her situation in every way called for it. S 8 405 2
Disorders & Recoveries so very much out of the common way, S 10 412 1
quitted the terrace, in his way to his brothers by this S 11 422 1
it for granted that he was on his way to Trafalgar house. S 12 425 1

WAYS (47)

My dear madam, I am not so ignorant of young ladies' ways NA I 3 27 28
Miss Morland is not used to your odd ways." NA I 14 113 40
"Yes, yes," (with a blush) "there are more ways than one NA II 3 145 14
to one another, and laugh at my odd ways behind my back. SS II 3 154 4
and moving different ways, Mrs. Jennings very plainly SS III 3 281 13
14
ways of a man, when he is bent upon pleasing her.--" W 343 19
The ways, & good jokes of osborne castle were now added to W 359 28
poor Margt's disagreable ways are new to you, & they would W 362 32
They attacked him in various ways; with barefaced PP I 3 9 1
They are young in the ways of the world, and not yet open PP II 3 150 29
sort of intimacy with his ways, seen any thing that PP II 13 207 6
ways, and to catch the best manner of conforming to them. MP I 2 17 21
"I shall understand all your ways in time; but coming down MP I 6 58 39
be best off, for she is gratified in more ways than one. MP I 6 59 41
Agatha and Amelia appeared to her in their different ways MP I 14 137 23
Sir Thomas's return made a striking change in the ways of MP II 3 196 1
Edmund, William, and Fanny, did, in their different ways, MP II 8 253 5
habits and ways of thinking, and all her own demerits.-- MP II 13 305 26
all our inclinations and ways, that I consider it as quite MP III 4 348 22
want some of your nice ways and orderliness at my father's. MP III 6 372 20
it, without altering her ways; wishing to be an economist, MP III 8 389 4
nothing but Mansfield, its beloved inmates, its happy ways. MP III 8 391 10
the manners, the amusements, the ways of Mansfield Park. MP III 12 419 8
heart, and the rational tranquillity of her ways.-- MP III 17 469 24
her smiles, and all her ways, as Mary Crawford had ever MP III 17 470 25
gentle, knowing all the ways of the family, interested in E I 1 6 6
he was a much older man in ways than in years; and though E I 1 7 8
Quick and decided in her ways, Emma lost no time in E I 4 26 1
She is a flatterer in all her ways; and so much the worse, E I 5 38 15
there may be a hundred different ways of being in love. E I 6 49 44
all remarkably clever; and they have so many pretty ways. E I 9 80 72
She understood their ways, could allow for their ignorance E I 10 86 24
even for this; but the ways of Hartfield and the feelings E I 11 92 3
"One ought to be at Enscombe, and know the ways of the E I 14 123 23
She must see more of him to understand his ways; at E II 5 192 33

She knows their ways best; but I should not consider their E II 8 215 14
And, in short, from knowing his usual ways, I am very much E II 8 223 63
I have now a key to all her odd looks and ways. E II 10 243 27
They, in their different homes, and their different ways, E III 8 377 1
herself--very ill in many ways,--but it was not so much E III 11 402 1
in the looks or ways of either, he repeated to them very E III 14 434 3
they are so neat and careful in all their ways! P III 3 18 7
She knew the ways of Uppercross as well as those of P III 5 36 21
another path, "is not this one of the ways to Winthrop?" P III 10 85 12
One man's ways may be as good as another's, but we all P IV 1 127 26
fell into all her wonted ways of attention and assistance, P IV 10 220 31
of ill consequence in many ways; and that I had no right P IV 11 242 65

WD (56)
There is nothing she wd not do to get married--she would W 316 2
If it was but a good day with my father, I wd wrap myself W 319 2
Yours among all your acquaintance wd be certain.-- W 320 2
And wd you really give up the ball, that I might be able W 320 2
Her father & mother wd never consent to it. W 320 2
prim & reserved; I do not always know what she wd be at."-- W 321 2
her daughter's good looks, wd give but a qualified W 321 2
& if he cd but have his health, how much he wd enjoy it." W 323 3
"Your club wd be better fitted for an invalid, said Mrs E. W 325 4
that a verbal postscript from himself wd be requisite.--" W 325 4
morng, unless the Edwardses wd send her which was hardly W 338 17
But Margt wd never forgive such words." W 338 18
once they had the inclination, the means wd soon follow."-- W 342 19
I am glad he did not say anything to me; I wd not have had W 345 21
I am glad Nanny had not laid the cloth however, it wd have W 347 22
not suit her pride, & she wd rather have known that he W 347 22
pounds, there was a young man who wd have thought of her." W 347 22
table; without him, it wd have been a party of such very W 353 26
I wd rather see his partner indeed--I would prefer the W 359 28
throughout the kingdom, you wd not persuade me of there S 1 365 1
of a medical man at hand wd very materially promote the S 1 366 1
& prosperity of the place--wd in fact tend to bring a S 2 372 1
the family as his own house wd contain, to follow him to S 2 372 1
that every one of them wd be benefited by the sea.-- S 2 373 1
lived with him, wd be principally remembered in her will. S 2 373 1
his hand wd be as liberal as his heart, had he the power.-- S 3 377 1
be the very companion who wd guide & soften Lady D--who wd S 3 377 1
& soften Lady D--who wd enlarge her mind & open her hand.-- S 3 379 1
I wd rather them run about in the sunshine than not. S 3 379 1
Who wd have expected such a sight at a Shoemaker's in old S 4 381 1
came from--or rather what wd Sidney say if he were here?-- S 4 383 1
Now, if he were here, I know he wd be offering odds that S 5 385 1
Susan Diana or Arthur wd appear by this letter to have S 5 385 1
you denominate it, nothing wd have been so judicious as S 5 385 1
line settled at Sanditon, it wd be no recommendation to us. S 5 386 1
state, the sea air wd probably be the death of me.-- S 5 386 1
And neither of my dear companions will leave me, or I wd S 5 387 1
But in truth, I doubt whether Susan's nerves wd be equal S 5 387 1
You often think they wd better, if they wd leave S 5 387 1
doing otherwise--& that it wd not do for her to be S 5 388 1
It wd be only encouraging our servants & the poor to fancy S 6 390 1
had never seen one neither, he wd have been alive now.-- S 6 393 1
Had he written nothing more, he wd have been Immortal. S 6 394 1
I wd not have you think that I only notice them, for poor S 7 397 1
or trust me, they wd not be so much in my company.-- S 7 399 1
And as for poor Arthur, he wd not have been unwilling S 7 399 1
feelings, that the sea air wd probably in her present S 9 407 1
of her own good health, wd not have undertaken to cure, by S 10 412 1
"If I were bilious, he continued, you know wine wd S 10 413 1
If you had seen me today before dinner, you wd have S 10 415 1
No--it acts on me like poison and wd entirely take away S 10 415 1
Mrs G.'s cheif solicitude wd be for the accomodation & S 10 418 1
soon found that all her calculations of profit wd be vain. S 10 419 1
the Miss Beauforts, who wd have been nothing at Brighton, S 11 422 1
If you wd mention the circumstance to Lady Denham!-- S 11 422 1
in the credit which Sidney's arrival wd give to the place. S 12 424 1
S 12 426 1

WE'D (1)
Dr. Davies was coming to town, and so we thought we'd join SS II 10 218 24

WEAK (30)
degree less contemptibly weak I certainly should, but I LS 2 245 1
but I am not quite weak enough to suppose a woman who has LS 3 247 1
she has not the blind & weak partiality of most mothers, LS 14 265 5
he appears both to Mr. Vernon & me a very weak young man. LS 20 276 2
feelings; but I am not so weak as to find indulgence in LS 34 304 2
She would not be so weak as to throw away the comfort of a SS III 5 296 19
and conscious of being too weak for conversation, SS III 9 334 5
such as might have plunged weak spirits in despondence.-- W 362 31
by the self-conceit of a weak head, living in retirement, PP I 15 70 1
a display; her voice was weak, and her manner affected.-- PP I 18 100 68
so very weak and vain and nonsensical as I knew I had! PP II 17 226 19
had married a woman whose weak understanding and illiberal PP II 19 236 1
"My dear Lizzy, you cannot think me so weak, as to be in PP III 12 339 8
to Elizabeth had appeared weak and ridiculous, contained PP III 15 361 2
A little man, with a weak voice, always hoarse after the MP I 13 122 2
so bewildered and so weak--and at others again, so MP II 4 209 12
You know the weak side of her character, and may imagine MP III 13 421 2
Vanity working on a weak head, produces every sort of E I 8 64 47
"Your amiable young man is a very weak young man, if this E I 18 148 22
I have not the least idea of his being a weak young man: I E I 18 148 23
evasions of a mind too weak to defend its own vanities.-- E II 8 212 3
he said, of being too weak to get into her conservatory E II 18 306 11
I would be understood to mean, that it can be only weak, E III 7 373 44
Not a puncture, not a weak spot any where.-- P III 10 88 26
clear, was exceedingly weak, and her nerves susceptible to P IV 2 129 1
She would not have been obstinate if I had not been weak. P IV 8 183 13
"Unjust I may have been, weak and resentful I have been," P IV 11 237 42
The world is pretty much divided between the weak of mind S 9 410 1
A large dish of rather weak cocoa every evening, agrees S 10 417 1
It struck her however, as he poured out this rather weak S 10 417 1

WEAK-SPIRITED (1)
Catherine, weak-spirited, irritable, and completely under PP II 14 213 17

WEAKEN (7)
on her fancy was not suffered therefore to weaken. NA I 5 36 2
of attempting to weaken her mother's dependence on the SS II 3 157 17
of the past that might weaken her sister's spirits; she SS III 11 352 16
17
and how to endeavour to weaken her hold on my heart--and MP III 13 422 2
Nothing happened the next day, or the next, to weaken her MP III 15 442 22
continual occupation and change soon weaken impressions." P IV 11 232 19
He would gladly weaken, by any fair means, whatever P IV 11 243 66

WEAKENED (6)
removed, the force of the other was likewise weakened. NA II 13 221 6
Absence might have weakened his regard, and convenience SS II 6 179 17
head, a weakened stomach, and a general nervous faintness. SS II 7 185 16
Her mind was so much weakened that she still fancied SS III 2 270 2
Charlotte again, and weakened her disgust of Mr. Collins. PP II 4 151 1
being compatible with a weakened frame and varying spirits, E II 2 165 9

WEAKENING (3)
to spare no pains in weakening his boasted interest and NA II 15 245 12
Marianne's illness, though weakening in its kind, had not SS III 10 340 1
might be even weakening her claims, was hard to bear! P IV 9 210 98

WEAKER (3)
My hopes are much weaker.-- MP III 13 420 2
a weaker state of health than she had been half a year ago. E III 1 317 6
They have only weaker constitutions & stronger minds than S 5 385 1

WEAKEST (1)
to his own, his aunt would address him on his weakest side. PP III 15 360 2

WEAKLY (1)
that she had acted most weakly; that she had been imposed E III 11 411 43

WEAKNESS (23)
despise myself for the weakness, on which their strength LS 36 306 2
The fears of the sister have added to the weakness of the NA I 14 113 39
For the world would she not have her weakness suspected; NA II 7 174 5
because, through her own weakness, it chanced to prove a SS II 9 202 4
If the violence of her passions, the weakness of her SS III 8 322 36
Do not think yourself excused by any weakness, any natural SS III 8 322 37
the posture of reclining weakness, and the warm SS III 10 340 2
"Yes, vanity is a weakness indeed. PP I 11 57 24
blaming herself for her own weakness, could not go on. PP I 18 92 19
from actual weakness sat down and cried for half an hour. PP II 11 193 31
family weakness, such an assurance of the deepest disgrace. PP III 4 278 19
such a weakness as a second proposal to the same woman? PP III 12 341 19
thing, that is to say, a weakness grown into a habit from MP I 9 87 16
private on the jealous weakness to which they attributed MP I 17 158 1
mixture of reason and weakness, she was able, in due time, MP II 9 265 20
She might scold herself for the weakness, but there was no MP III 10 400 6
to speak of, and the weakness that shrunk from it would MP III 10 406 20
but particularly for the weakness in little Bella's throat, E I 12 101 21
This, you know, speaks a great degree of weakness--but now E II 18 306 11
It had been weakness and timidity. P III 7 61 36
without pride or weakness; he lived with the liberality of P IV 4 146 6
speaking it is its weakness and not its strength that P IV 5 156 11
weakness, and from employing others by her want of money. P IV 9 210 98

WEAKNESSES (2)
His heart was now open to Elinor, all its weaknesses, all SS III 13 362 4
my life to avoid those weaknesses which often expose a PP I 11 57 22

WEALD (3)
off, on the other side of Battel--quite down in the Weald. S 1 366 1
sir--(speaking rather proudly) are not in the Weald."-- S 1 366 1
"Not down in the Weald I am sure sir, replied the S 1 366 1

WEALTH (34)
poverty itself is wealth: grandeur I detest: I would not NA I 15 119 20
had not grandeur and wealth enough in himself, at what NA II 11 208 1
of his peerage, his wealth, and his attachment, being to a NA II 16 251 5
first boast of the family wealth, than by his subsequent NA II 16 251 6
which happened soon afterwards, he added to his wealth. SS I 1 3 2
"What have wealth or grandeur to do with happiness?" SS I 17 91 8
"Grandeur has but little," said Elinor, "but wealth has SS I 17 91 9
Your competence and my wealth are very much alike, I dare SS I 17 91 11
One is my wealth! SS I 17 91 13
said Elinor, "in spite of the insufficiency of wealth." SS I 17 92 20
and acquisition of wealth to her brother, by which neither SS III 5 295 17
and his prospects of future wealth were exceedingly fair. PP I 22 122 3
may wish his increase of wealth and consequence; they may PP II 1 136 23
doubting whether all his wealth and grandeur would be PP III 17 375 27
the picture of health, wealth, ease, and tranquillity, was MP I 13 126 19
Miss Crawford may chuse her degree of wealth. MP II 4 213 39
you by the contrast of their own wealth and consequence. MP II 4 213 40
and beauty and wealth were all that excited her respect. MP III 2 332 22
A residence of eight or nine years in the abode of wealth MP III 6 369 10
There were none in her father's house; but wealth is MP III 9 398 9
or the employment of wealth, had brought him to Portsmouth. MP III 10 400 7
It is the habits of wealth that I fear. MP III 13 421 2
I say to any one, that wealth and consequence could fall MP III 14 434 13
certain conditions of wealth; and this, she suspected, was MP III 14 436 16
up to the care and the wealth of the Churchills, and he E I 2 16 4
My first displays the wealth and pomp of kings, lords of E I 9 71 14
My first displays the wealth and pomp of kings, lords of E I 9 73 18
If ever there were people who, without having great wealth E II 3 174 31
up much of wealth to be allowed an early establishment. E II 6 204 43
With their wealth, their views increased; their want of a E II 7 207 6
by nobility or wealth, would have been a stain indeed. E III 19 482 3
should have answered his ideas of wealth and independence. P IV 9 201 59
Lady D. had been a rich Miss Brereton, born to wealth but S 3 375 1
& indolent, as wealth & a hot climate are apt to make us. S 9 409 1

WEALTHY (8)
"Are they a wealthy family?" NA II 10 205 29
the family as yet more wealthy than his vanity and avarice NA II 15 244 12
facts of the Allens being wealthy and childless, of Miss NA II 15 245 12
by wealthy connexions; a forward, bragging, scheming race. NA II 15 246 12
very well, Biddy Henshawe; she married a very wealthy man. SS II 8 194 10
Brandon, of Mrs. Jennings, and of every wealthy friend. SS III 12 357 3
should think any from our wealthy naval commanders P III 3 17 4
her name) not being so wealthy & independant as Mrs G.-- S 9 411 1

WEAR (29)
The violence of her feelings, which must wear her out, may LS 39 308 1
But, my dearest Catherine, have you settled what to wear NA I 6 42 24
To be disgraced in the eye of the world, to wear the NA I 8 53 2
What gown and what head-dress she should wear on the NA I 10 73 22
A clean gown is not five minutes wear in them. NA I 13 104 32
I wear nothing but purple now: I know I look hideous in it, NA II 12 218 2
"I never saw you wear a ring before, Edward," she cried. SS I 18 98 11
But why should not I wear pink ribbons? SS III 2 272 12
"You should wear Half-boots."-- W 345 21
up your last new coat, if you are never to wear it."-- W 353 26
I shall wear one tomorrow that I think you will prefer to W 353 26
Nor did that day wear out her resentment. PP I 23 127 5
I hope it is not too fine; but I thought I ought to wear MP II 5 222 43
And yet not to wear it? MP II 8 254 8
therefore not to wear the cross might be mortifying him. MP II 8 254 8
as to what she ought to wear, determined to seek the MP II 8 256 14
"Shall not you wear your brother's cross?" MP II 8 257 15
either to wear the cross, or to refrain from wearing it. MP II 8 257 15
"When I wear this necklace I shall always think of you," MP II 8 258 18
"You must think of somebody else too when you wear that MP II 8 259 19
Wear the necklace, as you are engaged to do to-morrow MP II 9 263 16
She had, to oblige Edmund, resolved to wear it--but it was MP II 9 271 40
I suppose no time can ever wear out the impression I have MP III 5 358 9
must not be allowed to wear her out, and make her useless. MP III 12 418 6
her fears will completely wear off, for there really is E II 15 284 9
The year will wear away at this rate, and nothing done. E III 6 354 7
I shall wear a large bonnet, and bring one of my little E III 6 355 20
involved in--the stretch of mind, the wear of spirits!-- P IV 8 183 15
If she would only wear rouge, she would not be afraid of P IV 10 215 16

WEARER'S (1)
the freshness of its wearer's feelings, must be worn away. MP III 6 368 8

WEARIED (6)
Hour after hour passed away, and the wearied Catherine had NA II 6 171 12
that Jane could not have been wearied by long expectations. PP III 5 286 20
"Perhaps, sir," said Fanny, wearied at last into speaking-- MP III 3 343 39
Still, however, Fanny, was oppressed and wearied; he saw MP III 4 355 55
we all know at times what it is to be wearied in spirits. E III 6 363 50
more engaged; and Anne, wearied of such a state of P IV 7 180 32

WEARINESS (8)
on considerable weariness and a violent desire to go home. NA I 9 60 1
of this, the extreme weariness of his company, which crept NA I 9 66 32
of weariness, much oftener than she moved her needle.-- NA II 15 241 7
It was imputed to very reasonable weariness, and she was MP I 18 170 24
A weariness arising probably, in great measure, from the MP II 10 278 20
Edmund saw weariness and distress in her face, and MP III 4 354 48
"This sensation of listlessness, weariness, stupidity, E II 12 262 39
bursts, perseverance and weariness, health and sickness. E III 14 437 8

WEARING (8)
many hours of the most wearing anxiety seemed to make SS III 9 334 5
she has turned away two housemaids for wearing white gowns. MP I 10 105 55
either to wear the cross, or to refrain from wearing it. MP II 8 257 15
effort, to resolve on wearing Miss Crawford's necklace too. MP II 9 271 40
offending the taste, or wearing out the feelings of his MP III 3 341 28
(the summer of 1814,) wearing black ribbons for his wife, P III 1 8 17
state of most wearing, anxious, youth-killing dependance! P III 4 27 3
good all their lives, wearing out their last days in a P III 12 102 2

WEARISOME (3)
the gentlemen came, was wearisome and dull to a degree, PP III 12 341 14
In himself he was wearisome, but as the friend of Tom and MP II 2 194 21
and patience for the wearisome; and had never liked a P IV 8 186 24
WEARS (2)
only put on a white gown; Miss Tilney always wears white." NA I 12 91 2
Besides, it will not much signify what one wears this PP II 16 219 4
WEARY (15)
At length Lady Susan, weary I believe of her situation, LS 20 276 4
This was the last sentence by which he could weary NA I 10 76 29
it tells me nothing that does not either vex or weary me. NA I 14 108 22
till she was heartily weary of seeing and wondering, he NA II 7 179 27
of which she seemed so thoroughly aware that he was weary. SS II 2 151 41
and that Willoughby was weary of it, seemed equally clear; SS II 6 178 17
Mrs. Jennings was so far from being weary of her guests, SS III 3 280 7
to read, or in lying, weary and languid, on a sofa, did SS III 7 307 1
view of the house, with weary ancles, dirty stockings, and PP I 7 32 41
her, an affectation and a sameness to disgust and weary. PP II 18 233 25
half an hour's notice, whenever she was weary of the place. MP I 4 41 16
and Mrs. Rushworth, never weary in the cause, would have MP I 9 89 31
I have looked across the ha-ha till I am weary. MP I 9 96 73
Every body was growing weary of indecision, and the first MP I 14 132 8
her affection, cannot even weary her by negligent E III 13 428 23
WEARYING (2)
Delighted with her progress, and fearful of wearying her NA I 14 111 29
The danger would have been of my wearying you. E III 16 459 47
WEASEL (1)
of both to hunt after a weasel which he had a momentary P III 10 90 37
WEATHER (106)
He desires me to tell you that the present open weather LS 8 254 1
by ourselves, & when the weather is tolerable, we pace the LS 16 268 2
when her wishes for fine weather were answered by seeing a NA I 5 35 1
Oh! that we had such weather here as they had at Udolpho, NA I 11 83 15
that poor St. Aubin died!--such beautiful weather!" NA I 11 83 15
anxious attention to the weather was over, and she could NA I 11 83 16
agreed that, provided the weather were fair, the party NA I 13 97 1
me, and in fine weather I am out more than half my time.-- NA II 7 174 9
The weather was at present favourable, and at this time of NA II 7 176 17
desire of making use of the present smiling weather.-- NA II 7 177 17
on Wednesday, which bad weather, or twenty other causes NA II 11 210 7
Mrs. Morland's common remarks about the weather and roads. NA II 15 242 8
the advantage of good weather, they received an impression SS I 6 28 2
The weather was not tempting enough to draw the two others SS I 9 41 3
the next interval of fair weather that morning allowed him SS I 9 43 12
I talked only of the weather and the roads, and had I SS I 10 48 5
the weather was uncertain and not likely to be good. SS I 19 109 40
bowing to the ladies, began complaining of the weather. SS I 20 110 7
"Such weather makes every thing and every body disgusting. SS I 20 110 8
Sir John is as stupid as the weather." SS I 20 111 8
that occurred; for the weather was not often fine enough SS II 1 142 8
"If this open weather holds much longer," said Mrs. SS II 5 167 1
This weather will keep many sportsmen in the country." SS II 5 167 2
"It is charming weather for them indeed," she continued, SS II 5 167 3
weather, and still happier in her expectation of a frost. SS II 5 168 7
The weather was remarkably fine, and she readily consented. SS II 11 223 15
for any change of weather during their stay at Cleveland. SS III 6 303 11
could not fancy dry or pleasant weather for walking. SS III 6 303 11
"When the weather is settled, and I have recovered my SS III 10 343 9
days at home, before the weather was fine enough for an SS III 10 344 11
to be open, she sat down again and talked of the weather. SS III 12 359 12
"Ladies should ride in dirty weather.-- W 345 21
Fine open weather Miss Emma!-- W 357 28
in the day, in such dirty weather, and by herself, was PP I 7 32 42
trial of her patience in weather, which totally suspended PP I 17 88 15
As the weather was fine, they has a pleasant walk of about PP II 6 161 8
determine what weather they were to have on the morrow. PP II 6 166 42
with Charlotte, and the weather was so fine for the time PP II 7 169 5
you--and indeed, if the weather should happen to be cool, PP II 14 211 10
One likes to get out into a shrubbery in fine weather." MP I 6 55 16
the shewn, and though the weather was hot, there were MP I 7 70 30
less hot than the weather had lately been, Edmund trusted MP I 8 75 1
in this weather, when we may have seats in a barouche! MP I 8 77 10
newspaper, watch the weather, and quarrel with his wife. MP I 11 110 23
have foreseen that the weather would certainly clear at MP II 4 206 4
that her absence in such weather might occasion at home, MP II 4 206 4
This weather is all from the south." MP II 4 207 8
Grant's shrubbery, the weather being unusually mild for MP II 4 208 11
Our weather must not always be judged by the calendar. MP II 4 212 29
I could have altered the weather, you would have had a MP II 4 212 31
and make me think the weather most unseasonably close." MP II 4 212 31
continuance of the open weather, but her answers were as MP II 5 223 48
weather--but only by a steady contrary wind, or a calm. MP II 5 225 57
sailor's share--like bad weather and hard living--only MP II 7 249 53
party in the same bad weather, had they been put to the MP II 12 291 1
weather, and allow him the pleasure of attending them?"-- MP III 10 401 10
beauty of the weather, would soon have been knocked up now. MP III 11 409 6
does Weston think of the weather; shall we have rain!" E I 5 41 31
Emma's side to talk of the weather, but he made no answer. E I 8 65 50
there had yet been no weather to prevent the young ladies E I 10 83 1
in his carriage, if the weather were Mr. Elton's only E I 13 110 12
consciousness of the weather than either of the others; E I 13 112 24
The preparing and the going abroad in such weather, with E I 13 113 25
Going in dismal weather, to return probably in worse;-- E I 13 113 26
One is so fenced and guarded from the weather, that not a E I 13 115 37
Weather becomes absolutely of no consequence. E I 13 115 37
"Christmas weather," observed Mr. Elton. E I 13 115 39
them, and people think little of even the worst weather. E I 13 115 39
room from examining the weather, and opened on them all E I 15 125 7
"in venturing out in such weather, for of course you saw E I 15 126 10
and gravity of the weather and the night; but scarcely had E I 15 129 24
The weather was most favourable for her; though Christmas- E I 16 138 17
It was weather which might fairly confine every body at E I 16 138 18
19
to Mr. Knightley, whom no weather could keep entirely from E I 16 138 18
19
The weather soon improved enough for those to move who E I 17 140 1
various circumstances of weather and business, of taking a E I 17 140 2
time of year; better weather; and that he would be able, E I 18 144 2
The weather does not look well, and grandmamma will be E II 3 176 50
to expect that the weather would be detaining her at Mrs. E II 3 177 51
just the right weather for him, fine, dry, settled weather. E II 5 188 7
prevent it, provided the weather be what it ought, neither E II 7 209 10
have power to draw me out, in worse weather than to-day." E II 16 294 22
almost at the longest; weather genial and pleasant, always E II 18 308 30
of wet, damp, cheerless weather; there always is in E II 18 309 30
exercise early, as the weather threatened rain; Mr. and E III 5 344 3
his being out in bad weather did him a great deal of harm. E III 5 344 9
It was now the middle of June, and the weather fine; and E III 6 353 6
And such weather for exploring!-- E III 6 353 7
hill for the next,--the weather appearing exactly right. E III 6 357 32
I met one as I came--madness in such weather!--absolute E III 6 364 55
The weather added what it could of gloom. E III 12 421 18
The weather affected Mr. Woodhouse, and he could only be E III 12 422 19
The weather continued much the same all the following E III 13 424 1
by weather, I think every body feels a north-east wind.-- E III 14 436 7
while in harmony of the weather and Mrs. Weston, she found E III 16 454 16
17
to Box-Hill again, while the fine weather lasts?-- E III 16 455 18
and every weather, till they are not fit to be seen. P III 3 20 16
and travelling in all weather; and even the clergyman--" P III 3 20 17
had two days of foul weather all the time I was at sea in P III 8 65 16
"what glorious weather for the Admiral and my sister! P III 10 84 7
8
though November, the weather was by no means bad; and, in P III 11 94 7
"What dreadful weather we have had! P IV 6 163 7
After talking however of the weather and Bath and the P IV 8 181 3
4
punctually, however; the weather was unfavourable, and she P IV 11 229 2
most rough usage, and riding out the heaviest weather." P IV 11 233 22
a great deal while I am here, if the weather is temperate. S 10 416 1
WEATHER'S (1)
to the window on the weather's being evidently fair, spoke MP II 4 207 6
WEATHER-BEATEN (2)
man, a little weather-beaten, to be sure, but not much; P III 3 22 23
her reddened and weather-beaten complexion, the P III 6 48 18
WEATHERED (2)
be weathered without our being any of us quite overcome. SS III 1 265 36
She had weathered it however, and could truly say that it P IV 5 154 9
WEATHERS (2)
all weathers, to make a likeness to him very flattering." W 324 3
ay and in all weathers too, and say nothing about it." MP I 7 73 53
WEDDED (2)
Accepted or refused, his heart is wedded to her for ever.-- MP III 13 424 4
regard for him would be foundation enough for wedded love. MP III 17 470 25
WEDDING (26)
Did you ever hear the old song, 'going to one wedding NA I 15 122 32
I say, you will come to Belle's wedding, I hope." NA I 15 123 32
came to town with me on purpose to buy wedding clothes? SS II 7 182 10
new carriages and wedding clothes, she should undoubtedly PP I 18 103 77
for herself, she would have ordered her wedding clothes. PP I 21 119 20
Thursday was to be the wedding day, and on Wednesday Miss PP II 3 145 11
The wedding took place; the bride and bridegroom set off PP II 3 146 19
And as for wedding clothes, do not let them wait for that, PP III 5 288 38
But the clothes, the wedding clothes! PP III 7 306 44
all have a bowl of punch, to make merry at her wedding." PP III 7 307 49
Their sister's wedding day arrived; and Jane and Elizabeth PP III 9 315 1
I never gave you an account of my wedding, I believe. PP III 9 318 21
22
been prevented going, the wedding need not be put off, for PP III 9 319 25
Mr. Darcy had been at her sister's wedding. PP III 9 320 32
London once more when the wedding took place, and all PP III 10 324 2
return, and as Lydia informed you, attended the wedding. PP III 10 325 2
the expectation of one wedding, made every body eager for PP III 15 360 1
for such arrangements as must precede the wedding. MP II 3 202 27
It was a proper wedding. MP II 3 203 29
The wedding over and the bride-people gone, her father and E I 1 6 5
I wanted them to put off the wedding." E I 1 10 26
want to hear about the wedding, and I shall be happy to E I 1 11 35
The wedding was no distant event, as the parties had only E II 4 182 6
warm--her large new shawl--Mrs. Dixon's wedding present.-- E III 2 322 19
"Oh! the best nature in the world--a wedding." E III 13 425 5
The wedding was very much like other weddings, where the E III 19 484 12
WEDDING-CAKE (4)
an event; and the wedding-cake, which had been a great E I 2 19 14
them from having any wedding-cake at all, and when that E I 2 19 14
of inclination,) that wedding-cake might certainly E I 2 19 14
slice of Mrs. Weston's wedding-cake in their hands: but Mr. E I 2 19 15
WEDDING-CLOTHES (3)
thousand pounds, and five hundred to buy wedding-clothes. NA I 9 68 46
to come and buy wedding-clothes for herself and her sister; P IV 10 217 19
for Henrietta's wedding-clothes to be talked of: she had P IV 10 217 20
WEDDING-DAY (5)
his daughter on her wedding-day and that Miss Tilney had NA I 9 68 48
It was on the wedding-day of this beloved friend that Emma E I 1 6 5
His wedding-day was named. E II 13 267 8
of Mrs. Weston's wedding-day; but Mr. Knightley had walked E III 12 422 19
was able to fix her wedding-day--and Mr. Elton was called E III 19 484 11
WEDDING-GOWN (1)
it was to resolve on the quality of her wedding-gown. NA I 15 120 23
WEDDING-VISIT (1)
We must begin, we must go and pay our wedding-visit very E I 1 8 14
WEDDING-VISITS (1)
time to be receiving wedding-visits, and a man had need be E II 14 271 5
WEDDINGS (2)
weddings among all the young people of her acquaintance. SS I 8 36 1
The wedding was very much like other weddings, where the E III 19 484 12
WEDGING (1)
You see we have been wedging one leg with paper. E II 10 240 5
WEDNESDAY (31)
I shall not be at home myself till Wednesday or Thursday, LS 23 283 4
My surprise is the greater, because on Wednesday, the very LS 41 309 1
"Yes, sir, on Wednesday." NA I 3 26 15
lay awake ten minutes on Wednesday night debating between NA I 10 73 22
Monday, Tuesday, Wednesday, Thursday, Friday and Saturday NA I 13 97 1
But on Wednesday, I think, Henry, you may expect us; and NA II 11 210 6
a quarter before one on Wednesday, you may look for us." NA II 11 210 6
you at Woodston on Wednesday, which bad weather, or twenty NA II 11 210 7
From Saturday to Wednesday, however, they were now to be NA II 11 211 16
his absence; and Wednesday she was very sure would be wet. NA II 11 211 16
If Wednesday should ever come! NA II 11 212 16
from your brother's on Wednesday, and we saw nothing of SS III 2 272 16
how he had been sent for Wednesday to Harley-Street, and SS III 2 273 16
will throw off at Stanton wood on Wednesday at 9 o'clock.-- W 347 21
since the preceding Wednesday; several of the officers had PP I 12 60 7
comparatively diffident since the adventure of Wednesday. PP I 22 121 1
Thursday was to be the wedding day, and on Wednesday Miss PP II 3 145 11
He wrote me a few lines on Wednesday, to say that he had PP III 5 286 28
kind; she walked here on Wednesday morning to condole with PP III 5 292 66
by Jane's letter last Wednesday, that her conduct on PP III 10 325 2
day, and was to leave town again on Wednesday or Thursday. PP III 10 325 2
down on Thursday at the latest, very likely on Wednesday. PP III 11 331 15
to order in some meat on Wednesday, and she has got three PP III 11 331 15
and inquire whether Wednesday would suit him or not. MP I 8 75 1
had been settled for Wednesday, to attend Mrs. Rushworth MP I 8 77 7
find no inconvenience from narrow roads on Wednesday." MP I 8 77 13
Wednesday was fine, and soon after breakfast the barouche MP I 8 80 29
Thursday was the day of the ball: and on Wednesday morning, MP II 8 256 14
not have heard from her before next Tuesday or Wednesday." E II 1 159 18
it was the Tuesday or Wednesday before that evening, he E III 4 339 18
I said, 'I will be at Bath on Wednesday,' and I was. P IV 11 243 70
WEED (1)
sea weed, can end in nothing but their own disappointment. S 1 369 1
WEEDS (1)
the shore--no mud--no weeds--no slimey rocks--never was S 1 369 1
WEEK (183)
I hope a comfortable day with you in town within this week. LS 2 245 1
here--& for the first week, it was most insufferably dull. LS 7 254 3
days last week, & called several times in Edward Street. LS 9 256 1
Manwaring came to town last week, & has contrived, in LS 26 295 3
"About a week, sir," replied Catherine, trying not to NA I 3 26 5
that he had spent the last week of the Christmas vacation NA I 4 33 5
he had quitted it for a week, on the very morning after NA I 8 54 4
Sunday only now remain to be described, and close the week. NA I 13 97 1
The Allens had now entered on the sixth week of their stay NA II 2 138 1
determined upon quitting Bath by the end of another week. NA II 2 138 1
Tilney's concluding words, "by the end of another week!" NA II 2 138 1
to remain only one more week in Bath themselves, her NA II 5 154 1
mine, as I wore it the week before at the concert, but NA II 12 217 2
to go to London for a week; and he left Northanger NA II 13 220 1
she was now in the fourth week of her visit; before the NA II 13 220 1
came home, the fourth week would be turned, and perhaps it NA II 13 220 1
should not be exposed another week to such insinuations. SS I 4 23 19
led before the end of a week to hope and expect it; and SS I 10 49 11
had not known each other a week, I believe, before you SS I 12 60 10

Context	Work	Vol	Ch	Page	Line
"If he is not here by the end of the week, I shall go	SS	I	13	65	37
One evening in particular, about a week after Colonel	SS	I	14	72	6
One morning, about a week after his leaving the country,	SS	I	16	85	15
Edward remained a week at the cottage; he was earnestly	SS	I	19	101	1
Never had any week passed so quickly--he could hardly	SS	I	19	101	1
Yet he must leave them at the end of a week, in spite of	SS	I	19	101	1
We must go, for the Westons come to us next week you know.	SS	I	20	110	2
of similar distress last week, some apricot marmalade had	SS	I	21	121	10
force at the end of every week, they were prevailed on to	SS	II	2	151	43
Their departure took place in the first week in January.	SS	II	3	158	22
The Middletons were to follow in about a week.	SS	II	3	158	22
like leaving Barton next week; 'tis a said thing for	SS	II	5	167	1
John and Lady Middleton in town by the end of next week."	SS	II	5	167	4
About a week after their arrival it became certain that	SS	II	5	169	13
any answer to a note which I sent you above a week ago.	SS	II	7	187	39
					40
and so cast down this last week or two, for this matter I	SS	II	8	195	16
When I came to you last week and found you alone, I came	SS	II	9	210	32
by the end of a week that it would not be a match at all.	SS	II	10	216	15
to ask them to spend a week or two in Conduit-Street: and	SS	II	12	230	8
In a week or two, I suppose, we shall be going; and, I	SS	II	13	243	31
much her washing cost per week, and how much she had every	SS	II	14	249	8
"They had already spent a week in this manner in Conduit-	SS	II	14	253	22
Gardens, though it was only the second week in March.	SS	III	2	271	4
for their staying above a week at Cleveland, they might	SS	III	3	280	6
It was now above a week since John Dashwood had called in	SS	III	5	293	3
She, who had seen her week after week so constantly	SS	III	10	341	6
"I wrote to him, my love, last week, and rather expect to	SS	III	12	358	6
"Yes," said he, "they were married last week, and are now	SS	III	12	360	25
Edward was now fixed at the cottage at least for a week;--	SS	III	13	363	9
that less than a week should be given up to the enjoyment	SS	III	13	363	9
that meets three times a week at the White Hart, & if he	W			325	4
"Oh! yes--we have been engaged this week, cried the boy. &	W			330	11
hunting this country next week--I beleive they will throw	W			347	21
A week or ten days rolled quietly away after this visit,	W			348	23
I had seven tables last week in my drawingroom.	W			350	24
servants are to be in the house by the end of next week."	PP	I	1	3	10
three or four times a week, to pay their duty to their	PP	I	7	28	3
had better stay till next week,' you would probably do it,	PP	I	10	49	29
exactly finish Jane's week, could not bring herself to	PP	I	12	59	1
occasionally for a week or two, to visit his relations.	PP	I	14	66	1
she had not seen for a week, she was soon able to make a	PP	I	18	90	4
A week elapsed before she could see Elizabeth without	PP	I	23	127	5
now been gone a week, and nothing was heard of his return.	PP	I	23	128	9
After a week spent in professions of love and schemes of	PP	II	2	139	1
The Gardiners staid a week at Longbourn; and what with the	PP	II	2	142	18
Jane had been a week in town, without either seeing or	PP	II	3	147	21
We dine at Rosings twice every week, and are never allowed	PP	II	5	157	7
Sir William staid only a week at Hunsford; but his visit	PP	II	7	168	1
was repeated about twice a week; and, allowing for the	PP	II	7	169	5
Easter was approaching, and the week preceding it, was to	PP	II	7	170	6
till Easter-day, almost a week after the gentlemen's	PP	II	8	172	1
For the last week they had seen very little of either lady	PP	II	8	172	1
yet he had avoided the Netherfield ball the very next week.	PP	II	13	207	5
He wrote last week to hurry my return."	PP	II	14	211	9
there early in June, for a week; and as Dawson does not	PP	II	14	211	10
frequent during the last week of her stay, as they had	PP	II	14	213	20
It was the second week in may, in which the three young	PP	II	16	219	1
The first week of their return was soon gone.	PP	II	18	229	1
was to leave Meryton in a week or fortnight's time.	PP	III	5	285	16
It is not quite a week since they left Brighton.	PP	III	5	288	37
has our directions, and all will be completed in a week.	PP	III	8	313	19
we had at the Lucas's last week; and even Mr. Darcy	PP	III	12	342	28
One morning, about a week after Bingley's engagement with	PP	III	14	351	1
A week had passed in this way, and no suspicion of it	MP	I	2	15	9
was invited to spend a week with his sister in	MP	I	2	21	34
a week, she was quite ready to be fallen in love with.	MP	I	5	44	2
I went down to ramsgate for a week with a friend last	MP	I	5	51	40
beginning at the end of a week of such intercourse, to be	MP	I	7	65	13
There is all the new calico that was bought last week, not	MP	I	7	71	34
How can two sermons a week, even supposing them worth	MP	I	9	92	46
manners of a large congregation for the rest of the week?	MP	I	9	92	46
then, to let me engross her horse as I did all last week!	MP	I	9	95	69
others their duty every week, cannot go to church twice	MP	I	11	112	30
a week till my father's return, and invite all the country.	MP	I	13	125	18
for the space of a week without playing at billiards in it,	MP	I	13	127	29
the last week, to get up a few scenes, a mere trifle.	MP	II	1	181	16
Another week, only one other week, would have been enough	MP	II	5	225	57
of the winds just for a week or two about the equinox,	MP	II	5	225	57
I am grown too old to go out more than three times a week;	MP	II	6	229	1
to receive ordination in the course of the Christmas week.	MP	II	8	255	10
You ought to have had it a week ago, but there has been a	MP	II	9	261	2
not this very week, this very day--to-morrow I leave home."	MP	II	9	268	29
bad them good bye for a week, and mounted his horse for	MP	II	11	282	4
conform to the tranquillity of the present quiet week.	MP	II	11	283	7
The week which passed so quietly and peaceably at the	MP	II	11	285	15
a week, when her own departure from Mansfield was so near.	MP	II	11	286	15
Her vexation did not end with the week.	MP	II	11	286	16
had deemed unconquerable a week before, for the chance of	MP	II	11	287	17
have defied almost another week of the same small party in	MP	II	12	291	1
"It is above a week since I saw Miss Crawford."	MP	III	4	352	39
If I had the power of recalling any one week of my	MP	III	5	358	9
of my existence, it should be that week, that acting week.	MP	III	5	358	9
Thomas, though I certainly did hate him for many a week.	MP	III	5	358	9
to leave them even for a week, and therefore must	MP	III	6	373	23
of, he delayed for a week or two longer a journey which he	MP	III	6	373	25
felt before the end of a week, he would have thought Mr.	MP	III	8	388	1
Before the week ended, it was all disappointment.	MP	III	8	388	2
to her before the end of a week, Fanny was tempted to	MP	III	8	392	12
been glad to have been sure of such a letter every week.	MP	III	9	394	2
A week was gone since Edmund might be supposed in town,	MP	III	10	399	1
I am aware that you may be left here week after week, if	MP	III	11	410	16
before the middle of next week, that is, he cannot any how	MP	III	12	417	3
and for a week he was in a more alarming state than ever.	MP	III	13	427	13
of a week, she had still the same feeling when it did come.	MP	III	15	437	1
dinners in one week, they still lived together; for Mary,	MP	III	17	469	24
it should be so, and not a week earlier, Edmund did cease	MP	III	17	470	26
to their spending half the evenings in the week together.	E	I	2	18	11
week in which Emma could not make up a card-table for him.	E	I	3	20	1
is sure to ride through every week in his way to Kingston.	E	I	4	29	13
he has more invitations than there are days in the week.	E	I	9	75	26
I hope we shall have her here next week.	E	I	9	79	56
a very depressed tone)--she is coming for only one week.	E	I	9	79	62
You make the best of it--but after you have been a week at	E	I	12	103	38
Perry was a week at Cromer once, and he holds it to be the	E	I	12	105	56
I was snowed up at a friend's house once for a week.	E	I	13	115	39
coolly, "I cannot wish to be snowed up a week at Randalls."	E	I	13	115	40
					41
doubt of seeing him here about the second week in January."	E	I	14	120	9
be able to spend a week with his father, if he likes it."	E	I	14	122	22
"Oh, yes; next week."	E	II	1	159	16
Yes, next week.	E	II	1	159	18
from them so much as a week, which must make it very	E	II	1	159	20
A week had not passed since Miss Hawkins's name was first	E	II	4	181	2
"I have been here a week to-morrow--half my time.	E	II	8	221	51
A week to-morrow!--	E	II	8	221	51
He came four times a day for a week.	E	II	11	253	38
ready till the third week were entered on, and for a few	E	II	12	257	1
In town next week, you see--at the latest, I dare say; for	E	II	17	304	27
He is to be in town next week, if not sooner.	E	II	18	305	5
You will hardly believe me--but twice in one week he and	E	II	18	306	10
has not been able to leave the sopha for a week together.	E	II	18	306	11
Conceive what the events of a week have done in that	E	III	10	398	55
them to Highbury within a week, I would forward them after	E	III	14	442	8
in London again by the end of the first week in November.	E	III	19	484	10
to the lodge, where she was to spend the first week.	P	III	5	35	18
Crofts to dine at Uppercross, by the end of another week.	P	III	7	53	1
But a week must pass; only a week, in Anne's reckoning,	P	III	7	53	1
began to wish that she could feel secure even for a week.	P	III	7	53	1
with, "if you had been a week later at Lisbon, last spring,	P	III	8	68	31
					32
I am glad I was not a week later then."	P	III	8	68	33
"Not till the first week in August, when he came home from	P	III	12	108	28
The Laconia had come into Plymouth the week before; no	P	III	12	108	28
left the poor fellow for a week; that's what he did, and	P	III	12	108	28
a different creature from what he had been the first week.	P	IV	2	133	25
away for a week or ten days, till her head were stronger.	P	IV	2	133	25
He had talked of going down to Plymouth for a week, and	P	IV	2	133	25
and for the rest of the week you know we are engaged."	P	IV	5	157	16
on me since the second "week in January, except Charles	P	IV	6	163	7
that one morning, about a week or ten days after the	P	IV	6	168	25
He was courting her week after week.	P	IV	6	171	33
Could she have believed it a week ago--three hours ago!	P	IV	8	190	51
Next week?	P	IV	9	195	27
To be sure by next week I may be allowed to think it all	P	IV	9	195	27
"No," replied Anne, "nor next week, nor next, nor next.	P	IV	9	195	28
of the sort you are thinking of will be settled any week.	P	IV	9	195	28
He had begun to talk of it a week ago; and by way of doing	P	IV	10	216	19
All the little variations of the last week were gone	P	IV	11	241	59
that are printed in one week throughout the kingdom, you	S		1	366	1
& her brother to spend a week with me at Sanditon house,	S		7	399	1
I had them with me last summer about this time, for a week;	S		7	399	1
I shall take only one however, & that, but for a week	S		9	410	1
I never eat for about a week after a journey--but as for	S		9	411	1
It was not a week, since Miss Diana Parker had been told	S		10	412	1
a proper house at 8g pr week for Mrs G.--; she had also	S		10	414	1
house on her hands for a week, must have been some of her	S		11	420	1

WEEK'S (7)

Context	Work	Vol	Ch	Page	Line
man; he has had about a week's acquaintance with your	NA	II	4	152	26
with a week's calm in the Atlantic at that season."	MP	II	5	225	57
his consequence than this week's absence, occurring as it	MP	II	11	286	15
as it generally did upon a week's previous inactivity.	MP	III	11	409	6
At about the week's end from his return to Mansfield,	MP	III	14	429	1
William Larkins's week's account; much rather, I confess.--	E	II	12	257	3
and after giving him a week's indulgence, Lady Russell	P	IV	2	133	26

WEEKLY (4)

Context	Work	Vol	Ch	Page	Line
needs more lessons than a weekly sermon can convey, and	MP	II	7	248	42
a little respite of her weekly cares, and only discomposed	MP	III	11	408	2
Mrs. Price took her weekly walk on the ramparts every fine	MP	III	11	408	4
and have regular weekly meetings at your house, or ours.	E	II	14	277	38

WEEKS (116)

Context	Work	Vol	Ch	Page	Line
parted, of spending some weeks with you at Churchill, &	LS		1	243	1
& my wishes, he will be laid up with the gout many weeks.	LS		26	295	4
You have owed us a visit many long weeks.	LS		40	309	1
her uncle & aunt, & three weeks afterwards Lady Susan	LS		42	312	6
Frederica's visit was nominally for six weeks; but her	LS		42	313	7
of fellow; he ran it a few weeks, till, I believe, it was	NA	I	7	46	11
here for a few weeks, we would not live here for millions.	NA	I	10	70	3
You ought to be tired at the end of six weeks."	NA	I	10	78	43
'For six weeks, I allow Bath is pleasant enough; but	NA	I	10	78	45
winter, lengthen their six weeks into ten or twelve, and	NA	I	10	78	45
She saw herself at the end of a few weeks, the gaze and	NA	I	15	122	28
comprised in another three weeks, and her happiness being	NA	II	2	138	1
visitor, she was to be for weeks under the same roof with	NA	II	2	141	11
other, had been for many weeks a darling wish, though to	NA	II	2	141	11
as I hoped for many, many weeks longer, how can I tell you	NA	II	13	223	13
after an absence such as her's--an eleven weeks absence.	NA	II	14	231	5
of the two or three last weeks proved him to be neither;	NA	II	15	246	12
Edward had been staying several weeks in the house before	SS	I	3	16	7
In a very few weeks from the day which brought Sir John	SS	I	5	27	7
"No--nor many weeks."	SS	I	16	85	13
than by those which we received from them a few weeks ago.	SS	I	19	109	42
many weeks, I believe, before this engagement is fulfilled.	SS	II	7	183	13
"He *did* feel the same, Elinor--for weeks and weeks he felt	SS	II	7	188	46
When he told me that it might be many weeks before we meet	SS	II	7	189	46
place even within a few weeks, with many particulars of	SS	II	8	199	37
Knowing all this, as I have now known it many weeks, guess	SS	II	9	210	32
expected by all to comprise at least five or six weeks.	SS	II	10	213	3
she has had a nervous complaint on her for several weeks."	SS	II	11	227	49
them from home yet a few weeks longer, appeared to Elinor	SS	III	3	279	1
this attack, to the many weeks of previous indisposition	SS	III	7	313	21
in spite of the many, many weeks we had been separated,	SS	III	8	325	53
Those three or four weeks were worse than all.	SS	III	8	327	55
it by a visit at the cottage, in the course of a few weeks.	SS	III	10	341	4
way to Dawlish for a few weeks, which place your dear	SS	III	13	365	14
of staying three or four weeks with Mrs. Burgess, in hopes,	SS	III	13	370	37
of Edward a few weeks ago, had robbed her of one; the	SS	III	14	373	2
none, still remained some weeks longer unpardoned.	SS	III	14	376	11
coat, and it was now some weeks since they had received	PP	I	13	64	20
a pretty girl for a few weeks, and when accident separates	PP	II	2	140	6
Four weeks passed away, and Jane saw nothing of him.	PP	II	3	147	25
in the course of a few weeks, and though there were not	PP	II	7	170	6
The five weeks which she had now passed in Kent, had made	PP	II	12	195	2
the growth of only a few weeks, could bear no comparison.--	PP	II	12	196	5
"Why, at that rate, you will have been here only six weeks.	PP	II	14	211	8
She had spent six weeks with great enjoyment; and the	PP	II	15	215	3
having both spent three weeks at Rosings, and asked him if	PP	II	18	233	26
"Nearly three weeks."	PP	II	18	234	28
After the first fortnight or three weeks of her absence,	PP	II	19	238	6
the chief of their three weeks; and to Mrs. Gardiner it	PP	II	19	239	7
Four weeks were to pass away before her uncle and aunt's	PP	II	19	239	10
seems, of their being in love with each other, many weeks."	PP	III	5	290	50
down in a day or two, to shoot there for several weeks.	PP	III	11	331	13
A few weeks, he believed.	PP	III	11	337	52
have been gone on to Scarborough, these three weeks."	PP	III	12	342	24
world, though only a few weeks before, when Lydia had	PP	III	13	350	56
for the first two or three weeks were continually bringing	MP	I	2	18	23
who had, for many weeks past, felt the expediency of Mr.	MP	I	4	39	11
many weeks, it would bring his passion to an early proof.	MP	I	5	48	29
Three months comprised thirteen weeks.	MP	I	11	107	3
Much might happen in thirteen weeks.	MP	I	11	107	3
might have listened six weeks before with some interest,	MP	I	12	114	1
so long before, full seven weeks; for I had understood he	MP	I	12	115	5
spirits for the next few weeks, I shall think our time	MP	I	13	126	18
It was the first day for many, many weeks, in which the	MP	II	2	192	11
Yet, how strong the impression that only a few weeks will	MP	II	3	197	4
appeared that a very few weeks would be sufficient for	MP	II	3	202	27
days to Brighton, and take a house there for some weeks.	MP	II	3	203	31
I find he takes orders in a few weeks.	MP	II	5	226	61
has taken place in her looks within the last six weeks.	MP	II	6	229	5
for at least the last six weeks--I cannot let my brother	MP	II	13	303	15
time, perhaps two or three weeks; but then I considered it	MP	III	5	362	21
sister within the three weeks which had passed since their	MP	III	7	375	4
Maxwell, only six weeks before she was taken for death.	MP	III	7	387	44
now been nearly four weeks from Mansfield--a point which	MP	III	10	399	2
It is only four weeks tomorrow since I left Mansfield."	MP	III	11	410	9
Two months is an ample allowance, I should think six weeks	MP	III	11	410	16
Seven weeks of the two months were very nearly gone, when	MP	III	13	420	1
I was three weeks in London, and saw her (for London) very	MP	III	13	420	2
find how many weeks more she is likely to be without you.	MP	III	13	423	7
under different degrees of danger, lasted several weeks.	MP	III	14	432	11
It was weeks since she had heard any thing of Miss	MP	III	14	433	12
had continued so many weeks without her being thought at	MP	III	14	436	15
Street two or three weeks before, on a visit to some	MP	III	16	450	8

but a few weeks brought some alleviation to Mr. Woodhouse. E I 2 19 14
For some weeks past she had been spending more than half E I 8 57 1
Every thing that I have said or done, for many weeks past, E I 15 131 31
had engaged to spend a few weeks, and very much regretted E I 17 140 2
her convictions, all her prophesies for the last six weeks. E I 17 141 5
very long acquaintance. he has been gone only four weeks." E II 3 175 40
"Yes, he has been gone just four weeks, as you observe, E II 3 176 44
Miss Woodhouse," said Miss Bates, "four weeks yesterday.-- E II 3 176 44
few weeks ago, he would have been more cautiously gallant. E II 4 182 5
she had thankfully passed six weeks not six months ago?-- E II 5 187 4
this presumption so many weeks before it appeared, that E II 7 207 7
spirit to the last two weeks--indescribable spirit; the E II 12 262 38
in the world if I were not--for a few weeks at least. E II 12 262 39
She had had three weeks of happy exemption from Mr. Elton; E II 13 267 8
Mr. Cole gave me a hint of it six weeks ago." E II 15 287 28
and aunt a visit of some weeks in the spring, and their E II 16 292 7
letters to Enscombe, many weeks ago, with all these E III 5 345 13
It might be weeks, it might be only a few days, before the E III 6 353 6
They only knew each other, I think, a few weeks in Bath! E III 7 372 40
Isabella had been pleased with Harriet; and a few weeks E III 14 435 4
Such an end of the doleful disappointment of five weeks E III 18 475 40
for a few weeks annual enjoyment of the great world. P III 1 7 12
from Kellynch for several weeks, she was unable to give P III 5 33 6
in Kellynch for many weeks, she had expected rather more P III 6 42 1
So passed the first three weeks. P III 6 47 16
to be going away for a few weeks, to visit the connexions P IV 1 128 31
to calculate the number of weeks which would free him from P IV 5 159 22
It was three weeks since she had heard at all. P IV 6 162 1
at the great house very well, for a month "or six weeks. P IV 6 163 7
They had been thrown together several weeks; they had been P IV 6 167 19
"I was six weeks with Edward," said he, "and saw him happy. P IV 11 243 67
without spending at least 6 weeks by the sea every year.-- S 2 373 1
They'll stay their six weeks.-- S 6 393 1

WEEKS' (4)
a little dissipation for a ten weeks' penance at Churchill. LS 25 294 4
and dangers of a six weeks' residence in Bath, it may be NA I 2 18 1
might now be at home in little more than three weeks' time. SS III 3 280 6
A three weeks' residence at Delaford, where, in his SS III 13 369 35

WEEP (1)
Kitty was the only one who shed tears; but she did weep PP II 18 235 40

WEIGH (2)
the price and weigh the merits of a new muff and tippet. NA I 7 51 54
Happily, however, she was not left to weigh and decide MP III 14 436 15

WEIGHED (2)
She put down the letter, weighed every circumstance with PP II 13 205 3
She had got rid of two of the secrets which had weighed on PP II 17 227 25

WEIGHING (2)
word from him on the subjects that were weighing him down. MP III 15 445 34
She was a little occupied in weighing her own feelings, E II 17 304 28

WEIGHS (1)
Mrs. Weston, your argument weighs most with me. E II 15 288 39

WEIGHT (28)
The worst of it is that its weight makes it difficult to NA II 6 165 4
to get rid of such a weight on her mind, she very soon NA II 13 220 1
Sir John's joking intelligence must have had some weight. SS II 1 142 7
You know every well that my opinion would have no weight SS II 2 150 31
"that your judgment might justly have such weight with me. SS II 2 150 34
"was of trifling weight--was nothing--to what I felt when SS II 9 206 24
not in reason to have weight; by that person of uncommon SS III 9 333 2
sent back a weight upon your family, without a sixpence.-- W 352 26
for that will have more weight in the argument, Miss PP I 10 50 39
day must have material weight in confirming or crushing it. PP I 12 60 4
But in matters of greater weight, I may suffer from the PP II 10 183 12
there had material weight with Mr. Darcy, whose pride, she PP II 10 187 40
Lambton friends, that could materially lessen its weight. PP III 2 264 14
Elizabeth's mind was now relieved from a very heavy weight; PP III 17 377 41
What a difference in the weight of a woman's arm from that MP I 9 94 59
her brother gave his weight against her too, by saying, " MP I 14 133 12
of the importance of having an ally of such weight." MP II 1 186 34
had certainly some weight, feeling as he did, that in MP II 7 246 37
It is felt that distinctness and energy may have weight in MP III 3 340 23
But had she been less obstinate, or of less weight with MP III 16 450 11
by him would have all the usual weight and efficacy. E I 4 35 45
added a virtue to the account which must have some weight. E II 7 206 3
She could not be alone without feeling the full weight of E III 14 434 4
In such a party, Harriet would be rather a dead weight E III 15 450 37
sister: her word had no weight; her convenience was always P III 1 5 8
been given all their weight, its more convenient distance P III 2 14 10
trays, bending under the weight of brawn and cold pies, P IV 2 134 29
Jealousy of Mr. Elliot had been the retarding weight, the P IV 11 241 60

WEIGHTY (1)
to that other, more weighty accusation, of having injured PP II 12 199 5

WELCH (2)
and one a little Welch cow, a very pretty little Welch cow, E I 4 27 4
cow, a very pretty little Welch cow, indeed; and of Mrs. E I 4 27 4

WELCOME (92)
her ears now and then; and how welcome were the sounds! NA I 1 15 2
As for admiration, it was always very welcome when it came, NA I 2 20 8
seated with the kindest welcome among her new friends; but NA II 5 154 1
General were waiting to welcome her, without feeling one NA II 5 161 25
A ball itself could not have been more welcome to NA II 11 210 7
and accordingly she hurried down to welcome him. NA II 13 222 7
assembled at the door, to welcome her with affectionate NA II 14 233 9
little right to expect a welcome at Fullerton, and stating NA II 15 241 7
her children were always welcome there, and intreating him NA II 15 242 7
landlord, who called to welcome them to Barton, and to SS I 6 30 6
house in the neighbourhood to which you will be welcome? SS I 15 76 11
you will always be welcome; for I will not press you to SS I 15 76 14
round with surprise to see and welcome Edward Ferrars. SS I 16 86 20
He received the kindest welcome from her; and shyness, SS I 17 90 1
Brandon ensured his welcome with her, and she felt SS II 4 162 8
I must feel--I must be wretched--and they are welcome to SS II 7 190 52
whisper--"will be exceedingly welcome to all parties." SS II 11 224 24
guests they must be welcome; and Lucy, who had long wanted SS II 12 231 9
moment's recollection, to welcome him, with a look and SS II 13 241 20
am sure he should be very welcome to bed and board at my SS III 1 268 51
good-humour could do, to make them feel themselves welcome. SS III 6 304 13
of the party, and a very welcome variety to their SS III 6 304 14
of content as she brought to it, was particularly welcome. SS III 7 315 27
and was always sure of a welcome; and accordingly I spent SS III 13 362 5
the ring with my hair you are very welcome to keep." SS III 13 365 15
all the kindness of her welcome, and all the encouragement SS III 13 369 35
& retrospections which now ensued, over the welcome soup.-- W 336 14
No visitors would have been welcome at such a moment; but W 344 21
education, was if able to converse, a welcome companion.-- W 361 30
To Mr. Darcy it was welcome intelligence--Elizabeth had PP I 12 59 4
were particularly welcome, and she was eagerly expressing PP I 15 73 11
Indeed, Eliza, you will be as welcome to me as either of PP II 3 146 18
passage she was there to welcome them, and Elizabeth, PP II 4 152 5
see them; any thing was a welcome relief to him at Rosings; PP II 8 172 3
instrument, she is very welcome, as I have often told her, PP II 8 173 10
A most welcome negative followed the last question--and PP II 19 241 17
frisks, was the first pleasing earnest of their welcome. PP III 5 286 21
too, was another very welcome surprise; for his chief wish PP III 8 309 5
But, however, he is very welcome to come to Netherfield, PP III 11 331 14
Well, any friend of Mr. Bingley's will always be welcome PP III 11 334 35
she knew would be most welcome, she was almost ashamed to PP III 18 382 20
He had been considering her as a particularly welcome MP I 1 9 10
of being foremost to welcome her, and in the importance of MP I 2 12 1
pleasures, and his absence was unhappily most welcome. MP I 3 32 64
was unspeakably welcome to a mind which had seldom known a MP I 4 35 6
her, a measure quite as welcome on one side, as it could MP I 4 41 15
The suggestion was generally welcome. MP I 14 132 8
the subject when a most welcome interruption was given by MP I 15 142 25
death, she became a welcome, an invited guest; and in the MP II 4 205 2
How beautiful, how welcome, how wonderful the evergreen!-- MP II 4 209 16
round him, shewed how welcome was his sudden resolution of MP II 5 223 48
I could not expect to be welcome in such a smart place as MP II 7 245 33
would be most heartily welcome to any other in my trinket- MP II 8 260 22
occurred before, was almost as wonderful as it was welcome. MP II 9 261 1
At Mansfield Park Mr. Crawford would always be welcome; he MP III 2 329 12
found himself receiving a welcome, unquestionably friendly, MP III 3 334 1
How I am well aware, that I shall not be half so welcome MP III 5 360 16
She was gone again to the street door, to welcome William. MP III 7 378 10
voice, he instantly began--"ha! welcome back, my boy. MP III 7 379 20
home, she had not such a welcome, as ----- she checked MP III 7 382 29
brought something more welcome; it was for the tea-things, MP III 7 383 32
She was as welcome to wish herself there, as to be there. MP III 14 431 8
Edmund was almost as welcome to his brother, as Fanny to MP III 16 448 2
wishes, she was soon welcome, and useful to all; and after MP III 17 472 31
visitor and always welcome, and at this time more welcome E I 1 9 21
and at this time more welcome than usual, as coming E I 1 9 21
good sense, and a most welcome addition to every source E I 2 18 10
Smith with her; a most welcome request: for Miss Smith was E I 3 22 7
to him, was able to turn away and welcome her dear Emma. E I 14 117 3
for any thing was welcome that might justify their all E I 16 138 16
It was to herself an amusing and a very welcome piece of E II 3 177 51
midst of his very civil welcome and congratulations, when E II 5 190 21
He understood what would be welcome; he could be sure of E II 5 192 28
them, and not a less grateful welcome than at Randalls. E II 11 250 23
approver, (a much safer character,) she was truly welcome. E II 11 256 60
done his duty, and made every fair lady welcome and easy. E II 16 295 28
see him again, which makes this day's news doubly welcome. E II 18 308 27
of visiting that would be welcome to her father, pressed E III 5 344 3
subject even a kind of welcome; and he was soon used to be E III 17 466 30
which her disposition was most ready to welcome as a duty. E III 18 475 42
carriage exceedingly welcome; and yet, though desirous to P IV 1 123 8
"Any acquaintance of Anne's will always be welcome to me," P IV 2 132 13
A degree of unexpected cordiality, however, in the welcome P IV 3 137 2
to enjoy a welcome which depends so entirely upon place." P IV 4 151 20
who has been "calling much oftener than was welcome. P IV 6 163 7
he chose it; he was always welcome; he was like a brother. P IV 9 199 55
put on a decent air of welcome; and as soon as it became P IV 10 216 18
by themselves, and Anne had the kindest welcome from each. P IV 10 220 31
worth and all the prompt welcome which met her in his P IV 12 251 10
She went; was delighted with her welcome & the hospitality S 3 378 1
& a heartiness of welcome towards her old friends, which S 6 391 1
Mr P. into the hall to welcome the sister he had seen from S 9 406 1

WELCOMED (21)
where he was welcomed with great kindness by Mr. and Mrs. NA I 7 51 54
Tilney, and kindly welcomed by his daughter, though Henry NA II 1 129 1
house by Sir John, who welcomed them to Barton Park with SS I 7 33 4
He was welcomed by them all with great cordiality, but SS I 16 87 23
and were welcomed by them all with great cordiality. SS II 10 217 19
where she was welcomed by her two friends with many PP I 11 54 1
They were not welcomed home very cordially by their mother. PP I 12 60 6
Mrs. Collins welcomed her friend with the liveliest PP II 5 155 3
were in the parlour, he welcomed them a second time with PP II 5 155 3
own, and welcomed to them as visitors my uncle and aunt.-- PP III 1 246 6
Jane ran to her uncle and aunt, and welcomed and thanked PP III 5 287 32
Her mother stepped forwards, embraced her, and welcomed PP III 9 315 3
the whole party were welcomed by him with due attention. MP I 9 84 1
time appointed, and was welcomed thither quite as gladly MP I 12 115 3
dismissed from it as hospitably as she had been welcomed. MP III 15 445 31
hospitality would have welcomed his visitors to every E I 3 24 12
many to be talked to, welcomed, encouraged, and variously E I 11 92 3
There she was welcomed, with the utmost delight, by her E I 15 132 38
and even gratefully welcomed; the quiet neat old lady, who E II 1 155 4
most perfect alacrity he welcomed the relationship, P IV 3 143 18
extremely comfortable, welcomed every change from it which S 2 374 1

WELCOMING (5)
halfcrown, than on welcoming a sister, who was no longer W 349 24
After welcoming their sisters, they triumphantly displayed PP II 16 219 2
Highbury, instead of welcoming that perfect novelty which E II 2 166 10
whom he was so cordially welcoming, and so anxiously E III 14 434 3
under his own roof, and welcoming him to all that was P III 7 53 1

WELFARE (20)
my kind concern in the welfare of herself & her daughter, LS 20 277 6 7
whose welfare it is my first earthly duty to promote?" LS 24 289 12
solicitous only for the welfare & improvement of her LS 42 312 3
all her thoughts on the welfare of her new straw bonnet:-- NA II 5 161 25
convinced her that their welfare was dear to him, and, for SS I 3 14 2
Elinor, though she felt really interested in the welfare SS I 14 71 3
and his interest in their welfare again became perceptible. SS I 17 90 1
Indeed, brother, your anxiety for our welfare and SS II 11 227 47
the table, after the welfare and poultry of her eldest PP II 16 222 21
a real interest in his welfare; and she only wanted to PP III 2 266 16
how far she wished that welfare to depend upon herself, PP III 2 266 16
to his lively concern for the welfare of his friend. PP III 3 270 10
eagerness to promote the welfare of any of his family; and PP III 8 312 18
of a lease in which the welfare of a large and (he MP III 10 404 15
employer, and the welfare of the poor, is inconceivable. MP III 11 412 20
would be more for her own welfare and happiness than all E I 17 142 9
he gave her pain, and his welfare twenty miles off would E II 4 182 7
rather than her welfare; to encounter any thing, rather E III 5 350 31
the prospect of Harriet's welfare, she was really in E III 18 475 39
one but Louisa, or those who were wrapt up in her welfare. P III 12 115 66

WELL (1529)
her in every respect, as well from the elegant & expensive LS 3 246 1
I am glad to hear that my father continues so well, & am, LS 3 247 1
who is therefore well qualified to make the communication. LS 4 248 1
She is perfectly well bred indeed, & has the air of a LS 5 249 1
Well my dear Reginald, I have seen this dangerous creature, LS 6 250 1
Unfortunately one knows her too well. LS 6 251 1
easy, & talks very well, with a happy command of language, LS 6 251 1
I wish I could be as well satisfied as he is, that it was LS 6 252 2
You may well wonder how I contrive to pass my time here--& LS 7 254 3
who knew her perfectly well, which is true must raise LS 8 255 1
conviction, to be so well pleased with her as I am sure he LS 8 255 2
I hear the young man well spoken of, & tho' no one can LS 9 256 1
well acquainted, & whose character he so heartily despised. LS 11 259 2
let me, to point out as well as I could the danger of an LS 13 262 1
a determination to think well of Lady Susan, that his LS 13 262 1
But in this case, as well as in many others, the world has LS 14 264 2
It is well known that Miss Manwaring is absolutely on the LS 14 264 4
how to value & commend her well directed affection, & will LS 14 265 5
it to me, she talks vastly well, I am afraid of being LS 15 267 4
I should say she talks too well to feel so very deeply. LS 15 267 4
poor Frederica's temper could never bear opposition well. LS 15 267 6
Well, whatever may be his fate, we have the comfort of LS 15 267 8
I like him on the whole very well, he is clever & has a LS 16 268 2
person & address are very well, he appears both to Mr. LS 20 276 2
& that I shall not find out I have thought too well of her. LS 20 278 11
Guess my astonishment & vexation--for as you well know, I LS 22 280 1
purpose to get yourself well established by marrying Mr De LS 26 295 1
valued esteem, I am as you well know, ill fitted to endure; LS 30 300 3
You may be, you must be well assured that nothing but the LS 30 301 4
I have told him that I am not quite well, & must be alone-- LS 31 302 1
dinner, everything will be well again. adeiu. S. V. LS 33 303 2
Frederica looked quite as well as she had done at LS 42 312 4
and loved nothing so well in the world as rolling down the NA I 1 14 1
she came on exceedingly well; for though she could not NA I 1 16 10
in the world who could like them well enough to marry them. NA I 2 20 8

Context	Work	Vol	Ch	Page	Line
and the two ladies squeezed in as well as they could.	NA	I	2	20	9
For my part I have not seen any thing I like so well in	NA	I	2	22	11
"Well, Miss Morland," said he, directly, "I hope you have	NA	I	2	23	23
"Yes--I like it very well."	NA	I	3	26	17
"Particularly well; I always buy my own cravats, and am	NA	I	3	28	38
do not think it will wash well; I am afraid it will fray."	NA	I	3	28	42
"Well then, I will not."	NA	I	3	29	50
Their joy on this meeting was very great, as well it might,	NA	I	4	31	2
and felt grateful, as well she might, for the chance which	NA	I	4	34	7
her air, and dressing in the same style, did very well.	NA	I	4	34	8
I often read novels--it is really well for a novel."--	NA	I	5	37	4
"Yes, pretty well; but are they all horrid, are you sure	NA	I	6	40	11
"I know you very well; you have so much animation, which	NA	I	6	41	16
Where the heart is really attached, I know very well how	NA	I	6	41	16
Well, I never observed that.	NA	I	6	42	27
They always behave very well to me."	NA	I	6	42	27
"Very well, Catherine.	NA	I	6	42	30
Well, my taste is different.	NA	I	6	42	30
"Well, I am amazingly glad I have got rid of them!	NA	I	6	43	39
Well hung; town built; I have not had it a month.	NA	I	7	46	11
kind, though I had pretty well determined on a curricle	NA	I	7	46	11
James and Isabella led the way; and so well satisfied was	NA	I	7	47	18
Well, I will drive you up Lansdown to-morrow; mind, I am	NA	I	7	48	29
was closed on them, said, "well, Catherine, how do you	NA	I	7	50	44
"Well, sir, and I dare say you are not sorry to be back	NA	I	8	54	5
informing themselves how well the other liked Bath, how	NA	I	8	56	11
"Well, I declare I never knew any thing like you.	NA	I	8	57	20
though Catherine was very well pleased to have it dropped	NA	I	8	57	21
Well, remember that it is not my fault, if we set all the	NA	I	8	58	25
"Well, my dear," said Mrs. Thorpe, impatient for praise of	NA	I	8	58	25
afterwards, and said, "well, Miss Morland, I suppose you	NA	I	8	59	35
up stairs, calling out, "well, Miss Morland, here I am.	NA	I	9	61	1
"Well, ma'am, what do you say to it?	NA	I	9	61	6
well in his time, I dare say; he is not gouty for nothing.	NA	I	9	63	18
ease which his paces, as well as the excellence of the	NA	I	9	64	27
She followed him in all his admiration as well as she	NA	I	9	64	27
immediately greeted with, "well, my dear, here you are;" a	NA	I	9	67	34
young man Mrs. Hughes says, and likely to do very well."	NA	I	9	69	50
that, though it is vastly well to be here for a few weeks,	NA	I	10	70	3
"How well your brother dances!" was an artless exclamation	NA	I	10	72	9
"Yes, he does dance very well."	NA	I	10	72	10
Catherine knew all this very well; her great aunt had read	NA	I	10	73	22
A good figure of a man; well put together.--	NA	I	10	76	28
sounds very well; but still they are so very different.--	NA	I	10	77	34
"Well, other people must judge for themselves, and those	NA	I	10	78	46
"Well, I saw him at that moment turn up the Lansdown road,-	NA	I	11	85	37
"And well they might, for I never saw so much dirt in my	NA	I	11	85	41
Mrs. Allen was not inattentive to it:--"well, my dear,"	NA	I	11	86	49
She could not think the Tilneys had acted quite well by	NA	I	11	86	50
late to go on to-day; your sister thinks so as well as I.	NA	I	11	88	54
said he soon afterwards, "we might have done it very well.	NA	I	11	88	56
Well, pray do not let any body here be a restraint on you.	NA	I	11	90	63
I dare say we would do very well without you; but you men	NA	I	11	90	63
of pleasure; the comedy so well suspended her care, that	NA	I	12	92	4
reason of such incivility; but perhaps I can do it as well.	NA	I	12	94	10
"Well, nobody would have thought you had no right who saw	NA	I	12	95	15
"Well done, General, said I, I am quite of your mind."	NA	I	12	96	22
said, "very well, then there is an end of the party.	NA	I	13	99	4
with a gayer look, said, "well, I have settled the matter,	NA	I	13	100	13
She said very well, Tuesday was just as convenient to her;	NA	I	13	100	15
Tuesday would suit her as well, it was quite ridiculous,	NA	I	13	100	19
"Well," said he, "and do you think of going too?"	NA	I	13	104	29
Now and then it is very well; but going to inns and public	NA	I	13	104	31
"It is amazingly; it may well suggest amazement if they do-	NA	I	14	107	11
I am fond of history--and am very well contented to take	NA	I	14	109	23
If a speech be well drawn up, I read it with pleasure, by	NA	I	14	109	23
If people like to read their books, it is all very well,	NA	I	14	109	24
observe, that they might well be offended at being	NA	I	14	109	25
style, they are perfectly well qualified to torment	NA	I	14	109	25
that it is very well worth while to be tormented for two	NA	I	14	110	27
of knowing any thing, should conceal it as well as she can.	NA	I	14	111	28
too reasonable and too well informed themselves to desire	NA	I	14	111	29
each other, you may as well make Miss Morland understand	NA	I	14	113	40
I think you and I are very well off to be out of the	NA	I	14	115	50
Well, and so you guessed it the moment you had my note?--	NA	I	15	117	6
were not more than that beloved child now well earned.	NA	I	15	121	27
But for particulars Isabella could well afford to wait.	NA	I	15	122	28
"Well, Miss Morland," said he, on finding her alone in the	NA	I	15	122	29
Well, I wish you a good journey.	NA	I	15	123	35
Good heavens! well, some people's feelings are	NA	II	1	130	3
John thinks very well of him, and John's judgment-----"	NA	II	1	130	9
"Well, I shall see how they behave to me this evening; we	NA	II	1	130	10
very unequal terms, for I understand you perfectly well."	NA	II	1	132	22
"Me?--yes; I cannot speak well enough to be unintelligible.	NA	II	1	133	23
"Well then, I only meant that your attributing my	NA	II	1	133	28
However, he is very well.	NA	II	1	135	41
her brother, felt equally well satisfied, and heartily	NA	II	1	135	43
a doubt, and you know me well enough to be sure that a	NA	II	1	136	48
and as he is now pretty well, is in a hurry to get home."	NA	II	2	138	2
to his daughter and said, "well, Eleanor, may I	NA	II	2	139	5
"Well, proceed by all means.	NA	II	2	139	7
Well, the thing is this, I have just had a letter from	NA	II	3	144	6
Modesty, and all that, is very well in its way, but really	NA	II	3	144	10
Well, if you say it, it was so, I dare say--but for the	NA	II	3	145	13
you, and seeing him as well as the rest--but that we were	NA	II	3	145	13
am sure; but you know very well that if I could think of	NA	II	3	145	13
Well, my dear Catherine, the case seems to be, that you	NA	II	3	145	14
was as certain and well acknowledged as her engagement.	NA	II	3	148	28
not looked so well pleased at the sight of Captain Tilney.	NA	II	3	148	28
"It is probable that she will neither love so well, nor	NA	II	4	151	16
so well, nor flirt so well, as she might do either singly.	NA	II	4	151	16
"Well?"	NA	II	4	151	25
"Well!--	NA	II	4	151	26
"Well," said Catherine, after some moments' consideration,	NA	II	4	152	27
horses;--Henry drove so well,--so quietly--without making	NA	II	5	157	5
And then his hat sat so well, and the innumerable capes of	NA	II	5	157	5
Well, what then?"	NA	II	5	159	18
Well, go on."	NA	II	5	160	22
bent on the object so well calculated to interest and	NA	II	6	164	3
Well read in the art of concealing a treasure, the	NA	II	6	169	11
You have gained a new source of enjoyment, and it is well	NA	II	7	174	8
palate, the tea was as well flavoured from the clay of	NA	II	7	175	12
the taste of ladies in regard to places as well as men.	NA	II	7	175	15
as well as her father's, including church-yard and orchard.	NA	II	7	178	21
must feel these inconveniences as well as himself."	NA	II	7	178	21
features which spoke his not having behaved well to her.	NA	II	7	180	37
impossibility of thinking well of a man so kindly disposed	NA	II	8	185	5
permitted to see it, as well as all the rest of that side	NA	II	8	186	7
with peculiar awe, she well remembered the doors of which	NA	II	8	188	17
with those cells, might well have favoured the barbarous	NA	II	8	188	17
style, which so well concealed his resentful ire, as to	NA	II	9	192	4
and the dressing closets so well disposed!	NA	II	9	196	21
He loved her, I am persuaded, as well as it was possible	NA	II	9	197	27
intelligible answer to Eleanor's inquiry, if she was well.	NA	II	10	199	1
you," (sighing as she spoke,) "they are all very well.	NA	II	10	203	10
returned it saying, "well, if it is to be so, I can only	NA	II	10	205	24
understand by his words as well as his actions, she had	NA	II	11	208	1
"Well, well, we will take our chance some one of those	NA	II	11	210	6
"Well, if it was my house, I should never sit any where	NA	II	11	214	23
the whole visit, so well assured was her mind on the	NA	II	11	215	28
were such attentions; but I knew the fickle sex too well.	NA	II	12	217	2
He has his vanities as well as Miss Thorpe, and the chief	NA	II	12	218	7
"Well, then, I must say that I do not like him at all.	NA	II	12	219	12
Though it has turned out so well for us, I do not like him	NA	II	12	219	12
making up her mind as well as she could, to a further	NA	II	13	222	8
"I am quite well.	NA	II	13	223	9
feelings as well as she could, "do not be so distressed.	NA	II	13	224	14
Well, I am certain of-----I shall be able to take leave	NA	II	13	224	17
not be distressed, Eleanor, I can go on Monday very well.	NA	II	13	224	17
She tried to eat, as well to save herself from the pain of	NA	II	13	228	27
and have found your family well, and then, till I can ask	NA	II	13	228	28
and, hiding her face as well as she could with her	NA	II	13	229	31
pen of the contriver may well delight to dwell; it gives	NA	II	14	232	7
"Well," continued her philosophic mother, "I am glad I did	NA	II	14	234	12
Well, we must live and learn; and the next new friends you	NA	II	14	236	15
after such behaviour, we cannot think at all well of her.	NA	II	14	236	19
helpless creature, but can shift very well for herself."	NA	II	14	237	21
My dear, do not you think these silk gloves were very well?	NA	II	14	238	24
Desirous of Mr. Morland's assistance, as well in giving	NA	II	15	242	9
grounds he had done it so well, that Catherine did not	NA	II	15	243	9
but likewise pretty well resolved upon marrying Catherine	NA	II	15	244	12
loved his daughter so well in all her hours of	NA	II	16	251	5
eighteen, is to do pretty well; and professing myself	NA	II	16	252	7
but he was, in general, well respected; for he conducted	SS	I	1	5	7
It was very well known that no affection was ever supposed	SS	I	2	8	3
Perhaps it would have been as well if he had left it	SS	I	2	9	6
"Well, then, let something be done for them; but that	SS	I	2	9	7
If they marry, they will be sure of doing well, and if	SS	I	2	10	15
My sisters would feel the good effects of it as well as	SS	I	2	10	16
to his wishes, for we very well know that if he could, he	SS	I	2	13	28
when the sight of every well known spot ceased to raise	SS	I	3	14	1
the way of learning, I think he would have drawn very well.	SS	I	4	19	2
At present, I know him so well, that I think him really	SS	I	4	20	9
both her sons should marry well, and of the danger	SS	I	4	23	19
post, which contained a proposal particularly well timed.	SS	I	4	23	20
It was a pleasant fertile spot, well wooded., and rich in	SS	I	6	28	1
was upon the whole well satisfied; for though her former	SS	I	6	29	4
The young ladies, as well as their mother, were perfectly	SS	I	7	34	4
and Marianne, who say very well, at their request went	SS	I	7	35	8
played extremely well, and by her own was very fond of it.	SS	I	7	35	8
of five and thirty might well have outlived all acuteness	SS	I	7	35	9
Mrs. Jennings had been anxious to see Colonel Brandon well	SS	I	8	36	1
I know very well that Colonel Brandon is not old enough to	SS	I	8	37	8
I am sure Edward Ferrars is not well.	SS	I	8	38	14
"yes, yes, he is very well worth catching, I can tell you,	SS	I	9	44	23
already, and he is very well worth setting your cap at, I	SS	I	9	45	32
"Well, Marianne," said Elinor, as soon as he had left them,	SS	I	10	47	4
"for one morning I think you have done pretty well.	SS	I	10	47	4
"whom every body speaks well of, and nobody cares about;	SS	I	10	50	14
But I know very well what it is; and I know where he is	SS	I	12	61	22
"Well then he is lately dead, Marianne, for I am sure	SS	I	12	62	26
"Well, then, I know who it is from, Colonel.	SS	I	13	64	16
And I hope she is well."	SS	I	13	64	16
"Well then, when will you come back again?"	SS	I	13	65	34
"Well, as you are resolved to go, I wish you a good	SS	I	13	65	43
"Yes, yes, Mr. Impudence, I know that very well, and I was	SS	I	13	67	64
Well, I wish him out of all his trouble with all my heart,	SS	I	14	70	2
Willoughby, as plainly denoted how well she understood him.	SS	I	14	73	16
You must have seen the difference as well as I.	SS	I	15	77	23
that at first seemed strange to me as well as to you."	SS	I	15	78	24
by our family, he might well be embarrassed and disturbed.	SS	I	15	81	43
to his honour I think, as well as more consistent with his	SS	I	15	81	43
In books too, as well as in music, she courted the misery	SS	I	16	83	3
her, a third, almost as well known as Willoughby's, joined	SS	I	16	86	20
Indeed a man could not very well be in love with either of	SS	I	17	90	1
"You have no ambition, I well know.	SS	I	17	91	5
I wish as well as every body else to be perfectly happy;	SS	I	17	91	7
"A family cannot well be maintained on a smaller.	SS	I	17	91	14
"She knows her own worth too well for false shame,"	SS	I	17	94	44
know my sister well enough to understand what she means?	SS	I	17	95	49
instantaneously felt as well satisfied as Marianne; the	SS	I	18	98	13
"Well then, I guess that Mr. Willoughby hunts."	SS	I	18	100	27
to herself, she was very well disposed on the whole to	SS	I	19	101	2
The old, well established grievance of duty against will,	SS	I	19	102	2
"Well," said he, "we have brought you some strangers.	SS	I	19	105	14
"Well! what a delightful room this is!	SS	I	19	107	24
Well! how delightful!	SS	I	19	108	36
"Ah! well! there is not much difference.	SS	I	20	111	14
"Well--I am so glad you do.	SS	I	20	114	42
"Oh! dear; yes; I know him extremely well," replied Mrs.	SS	I	20	114	44
I know why you inquire about him, very well; your sister	SS	I	20	114	44
"Mr. Brandon was very well I hope."	SS	I	20	115	53
"Oh! yes, quite well; and so full of your praises, he did	SS	I	20	115	54
"Oh! yes, extremely well; that is, I do not believe many	SS	I	20	116	58
And I am so glad your sister is going to be well married!	SS	I	20	116	60
all the philosophy of a well bred woman, contenting	SS	I	21	118	2
much to be learned; Elinor well knew that the sweetest	SS	I	21	119	3
They came from Exeter, well provided with admiration for	SS	I	21	124	33
very agreeable young man to be sure; I know him very well."	SS	I	21	126	39
it is rather too much to pretend to know him very well."	SS	I	21	126	40
person whose good opinion is so well worth having as yours.	SS	I	22	128	9
"You may well be surprised," continued Lucy; "for to be	SS	I	22	129	16
of manner, which tolerably well concealed her surprise and	SS	I	22	130	17
					18
him too well to be so prudent as I ought to have been.--	SS	I	22	130	28
Though you do not know him so well as me, Miss Dashwood,	SS	I	22	130	28
one it is; but that is not written so well as usual.--	SS	I	22	134	52
And so well was she able to answer her own expectations,	SS	II	1	141	4
She was stronger alone, and her own good sense so well	SS	II	1	141	6
But indeed, while Elinor remained so well assured within	SS	II	1	142	7
though Lucy was as well disposed as herself to take	SS	II	1	142	8
there, she was too well convinced of the impossibility of	SS	II	1	143	10
perhaps you will be as well pleased not to cut in till	SS	II	1	145	22
him; but I love him too well to be the selfish means of	SS	II	2	147	7
"Edward's love for me," said Lucy, "has been pretty well	SS	II	2	147	10
so well, that I should be unpardonable to doubt it now.	SS	II	2	147	10
You know every well that my opinion would have no weight	SS	II	2	150	31
Lord, I am sure your mother can spare you very well, and I	SS	II	3	153	2
We three shall be able to go very well in my chaise; and	SS	II	3	153	2
well and good, you may always go with one of my daughters.	SS	II	3	153	2
get one of you at least well married before I have done	SS	II	3	153	2
could spare them perfectly well; and Elinor, who now	SS	II	3	154	6
"My objection is this; though I think very well of Mrs.	SS	II	3	156	12
conjectured that she might as well have held her tongue.	SS	II	3	157	18
"Oh! you did; well, and how do they all do at their house?	SS	II	4	163	16
"Mrs. Palmer appeared quite well, and I am commissioned to	SS	II	4	163	17
Well, Colonel, I have brought two young ladies with me,	SS	II	4	163	18
Well! I was young once, but I never was very handsome --	SS	II	4	163	18
reason of all that very well; if a certain person who	SS	II	5	171	36
of evil than Willoughby, whose heart I know so well?"	SS	II	7	189	50
"Well, then, another day or two, perhaps; but I cannot	SS	II	7	191	64
Well, said I, all I can say is, that if it is true, he has	SS	II	8	192	3
Well, poor thing!	SS	II	8	192	3
But "no, she would go down; she could bear it very well,	SS	II	8	193	5
her dress for her as well as she could, while Marianne	SS	II	8	193	5
Well, it is the oddest thing to me, that a man should use	SS	II	8	194	8
I remember her aunt very well, Biddy Henshawe; she married	SS	II	8	194	10
Well, it don't signify talking, but when a young man, be	SS	II	8	194	10
Well, by-and-by we shall have a few friends, and that will	SS	II	8	195	14
"Well, my dear, 'tis a true saying about an ill wind, for	SS	II	8	196	22
Well, I shall spirit up the Colonel as soon as I can.	SS	II	8	197	22
"we shall do very well with or without Colonel Brandon."	SS	II	8	197	23
"Marianne is not well," said she.	SS	II	8	198	32
strong resemblance between them, as well in mind as person.	SS	II	9	205	23

24
I called her a distant relation; but I am well aware that SS II 9 208 28
sort of man, and I thought well of his daughter--better SS II 9 209 28
"A man of whom he had always had such reason to think well! SS II 10 214 9
"Well, my dear," said Mrs. Jennings, "and how did you SS II 10 218 23
"I am sorry she is not well;" for Marianne had left the SS II 10 219 37
Miss Steele, "we can just as well go and see her." SS II 10 219 41
of it all; for she was as well able to collect her SS II 11 221 4
truly anxious to see you well settled; Fanny particularly, SS II 11 224 24
Our respected father, as you well know, bequeathed all the SS II 11 225 35
"Her daughters are both exceedingly well married, and SS II 11 227 46
"She is not well, she has had a nervous complaint on her SS II 11 227 49
So well had they recommended themselves to Lady Middleton, SS II 12 230 8
but she is in general reckoned to draw extremely well." SS II 12 234 27
But she does every thing well." SS II 12 235 33
I am sure it will all end well, and there will be no SS II 13 239 9
seem low--you don't speak;--sure you an't well." SS II 13 239 11
sake and her own, to do it well, that she forced herself, SS II 13 241 20
Elinor is well, you see. SS II 13 242 26
they have no mind to keep them, little as well as great." SS II 13 243 38
It is but natural that he should like to see her as well SS II 13 244 45
attributing Charlotte's well doing to her own care, and SS II 14 247 5
of invitation for them as well as for their brother and SS II 14 248 6
was as well fitted to mix in the world as any other man. SS II 14 250 12
If you had only sent him to Westminster as well as myself, SS II 14 251 13
every comfort may be as well enjoyed in a cottage as in SS II 14 252 18
They are very well behaved, good kind of girls; and I SS II 14 253 24
is due to them, as their uncle did so very well by Edward. SS II 14 253 24
Mrs. Palmer was so well at the end of a fortnight, that SS III 1 257 1
reason for alarm; I hope Mrs. Dashwood will do very well." SS III 1 258 5
Well, and so this was kept a great secret, for fear of Mrs. SS III 1 258 7
for they say he is monstrous fond of her, as well he may. SS III 1 259 7
may afford to do very well by her son, and though Lucy has SS III 1 259 7
of Marianne, she felt very well able to speak of the SS III 1 260 8
you too well know, it has not been my only unhappiness.-- SS III 1 264 29
She says she never shall think well of anybody again; and SS III 1 265 36
assisted too as you may well suppose by my arguments, and SS III 1 266 38
"Well may you wonder, Marianne," replied her brother, "at SS III 1 267 40
I have some little concern in the business, as well as SS III 1 267 43
"Well, sir," said Mrs. Jennings, "and how did it end?" SS III 1 268 47
"If he would only have done as well by himself," said John SS III 1 269 53
"Well!" said Mrs. Jennings, "that is her revenge. SS III 1 269 54
"Well, but Miss Dashwood," speaking triumphantly, "people SS III 2 272 14
But it was said, I know, very well, and by more than one; SS III 2 272 16
"Well," said Elinor, "it is a comfort to be prepared SS III 2 275 23
we are both quite well now, and as happy as we must always SS III 2 277 29
30
remember, as well Edward too, who I have told of it. SS III 2 277 30
"Very well indeed!--how prettily she writes!--aye, that SS III 2 278 32
Very well upon my word. SS III 2 278 32
enough of him to wish him well for his own sake, and as a SS III 3 282 19
thinking that no one could so well perform it as himself. SS III 3 283 20
"Well, Miss Dashwood," said Mrs. Jennings, sagaciously SS III 4 285 1
Well, my dear, I wish you joy of it again and again; and SS III 4 285 5
"Well, and whose fault is that? SS III 4 286 9
preparing to go, said--"well, my dear, I must be gone SS III 4 286 10
11
"Oh! very well," said Mrs. Jennings rather disappointed. SS III 4 286 14
Well, so much the better for him. SS III 4 286 17
Well, that is an odd kind of delicacy! SS III 4 287 20
I have not heard of any thing to please me so well since SS III 4 287 20
She is an excellent housemaid, and works very well at her SS III 4 287 22
I feel it--I would express it if I could--but as you well SS III 4 289 34
"Well, my dear," she cried, "I sent you up the young man. SS III 4 291 47
"Well, and how soon will he be ready?-- SS III 4 291 49
Sure, somebody else might be found that would do as well; SS III 4 291 51
Well, this is very astonishing!--no relationship!--no SS III 5 294 10
"Very well--and for the next presentation to a living of SS III 5 295 12
Well, I am convinced that there is a vast deal of SS III 5 295 12
"Well, well; whatever Colonel Brandon may be, Edward is a SS III 5 295 16
vastly well,--she will not like to hear it much talked of." SS III 5 295 16
There is no doubt of your doing exceedingly well--quite as SS III 5 297 31
as well, or better, perhaps, all things considered. SS III 5 297 31
It was a look, however, very well bestowed, for it SS III 5 298 34
His behaviour to her in this, as well as in every other SS III 6 305 16
her opinion, might very well justify Mrs. Jennings's SS III 6 305 16
very unwilling to go, as well from real humanity and good- SS III 7 308 5
behind him a person so well able to assist or advise Miss SS III 7 309 5
"With me!"--in the utmost amazement--"well, sir--be quick-- SS III 8 317 5
Well may it be doubted; for, had I really loved, could I SS III 8 320 32
of such a subject may well be--your indifference is no SS III 8 322 37
"Well, sir, and what said Mrs. Smith?" SS III 8 323 39
Well, I went, left all that I loved, and went to those to SS III 8 325 45
"Well, sir," said Elinor, who, though pitying him, grew SS III 8 325 47
shall be heartily glad to hear she is well married."-- SS III 8 326 53
I avoided the Middletons as much as possible, as well as SS III 8 326 55
Well, at last, as I need not tell you, you were forced on SS III 8 327 55
all that was--well, it does not signify; it is over now.-- SS III 8 327 55
Willoughby first rousing himself, broke it thus: "well, SS III 8 327 56
57
She was well paid for her impudence. SS III 8 328 61
Well, married we were, and came down to Combe Magna to be SS III 8 329 65
Let me be a little lightened too in her opinion as well as SS III 8 330 67
pitied, wished him well--was even interested in his SS III 8 332 76
said he, "I must rub through the world as well as I can. SS III 8 332 77
"Well"--he replied--"once more good bye. SS III 8 332 79
I, you may well believe, could talk of nothing but my SS III 9 336 12
said Elinor, "as an excellent man, is well established." SS III 9 337 15
his disposition, I am well convinced, is exactly the very SS III 9 338 20
kind I well know to be more solidly attaching to Marianne. SS III 9 338 21
22
that would suit us quite as well as our present situation." SS III 9 338 24
for other people as well as herself, engaged with pleasure SS III 10 341 4
Our own library is too well known to me, to be resorted to SS III 10 343 9
But there are many works well worth reading, at the park; SS III 10 343 9
My illness, I well knew, had been entirely brought on by SS III 10 345 28
which her frankness and her contrition so well deserved. SS III 10 346 29
dare say, you perceive, as well as myself, not only in SS III 11 350 9
"Did Mrs. Ferrars look well?" SS III 11 355 43
"Yes, ma'am, she said how she was very well; and to my SS III 11 355 44
might think herself very well off, that with so much SS III 11 355 45
which one she had so well understood, much slighter in SS III 11 355 46
obliged to hope that he had left Mrs. Ferrars very well. SS III 12 359 14
fear of Mrs. Ferrars, as well as not knowing how to get to SS III 13 370 37
you may as well give her a chance--you understand me."-- SS III 14 375 9
of course took a part, as well as the frequent domestic SS III 14 377 11
from her family as could well be contrived, without SS III 14 378 13
Mrs. Dashwood was acting on motives of policy as well as SS III 14 378 13
seemed to like any girl so well since, tho' he is always W 316 1
I have not been very well used Emma among them, I hope you W 316 2
I wish with all my heart she was well married. W 317 2
I could do very well single for my own part--a little W 317 2
Well, we shall see how irresistable Mr Tom Musgrave & I W 319 2
Well--you will have a good ball I dare say. W 321 2
doing pretty well, tho' it would be nothing for Penelope.-- W 322 2
to his daughter with "well Mary, I bring you good news.-- W 323 3
'Mr Watson!--cried Mr Edwardes, well, you astonish me.-- W 324 3
I remember your aunt very well about 30 years ago; I am W 325 4
Emma watson was not more than of the middle height--well W 328 9
Emma was very well pleased with the circumstance;--there W 333 13
"Very well my Lord--. W 333 13
Our assemblies have been used to be so well treated by W 334 13
hand--"that will do as well for me"--was Ld Osborne's W 335 13
But he had won 4 rubbers out of 5, & everything went well. W 336 14
of being unusually well had taken the sudden resolution of W 338 18
on the Edwardes', as well as wishing to go home herself, W 339 18
throwing you together, so well as I knew his tricks;--but W 341 19
He is out of luck as well as other people.-- W 342 19
Well--now begin, & give me an account of everything as it W 342 19
"Well--go on. W 342 19
It is well Margaret is not by.-- W 342 19
He is no favourite of mine, as you well know, Emma;--but W 342 19
my heart did misgive me that you would like him too well. W 343 19
He reads extremely well, with great propriety & in a very W 343 20
heard from Nanny, was not well enough to be down stairs;-- W 345 21
a half-boot; nankin galoshed with black looks very well.-- W 345 21
it's mild seriousness, as well as in the words themselves W 346 21
Tom had nothing to say for himself, he knew it very well, W 346 21
"Well, I only beg you will not set your neighbours against W 350 24
You must come to Croydon as well as the rest, & see what W 353 26
& it may just as well come in, as stay in the kitchen. W 354 27
Mr Watson had not been well enough to join the party at W 354 28
I always say cards are very well sometimes, to break a W 354 28
cd now avail,--for he well knew, that if he staid he must W 359 28
company of any kind too well, not to prefer being below, W 361 30
It was well for her that she was naturally chearful;--for W 362 31
this truth is so well fixed in the minds of the PP I 1 3 2
I was sure you loved your girls too well to neglect such PP I 2 7 24
Well, how pleased I am! and it is such a good joke, too, PP I 2 7 24
equally well married, I shall have nothing to wish for." PP I 3 9 2
Every body said how well she looked; and Mr. Bingley PP I 3 12 16
Well, he certainly is very agreeable, and I give you leave PP I 4 14 5
entitled to think well of themselves, and meanly of others. PP I 4 15 11
and his manners, though well bred, were not inviting. PP I 4 16 14
"You began the evening well, Charlotte," said Mrs. Bennet PP I 5 18 4
Well, that was very decided in deed--that does seem as if-- PP I 5 19 8
"Mr. Darcy is not so well worth listening to as his friend, PP I 5 19 9
but the desire of being well married; and if I were PP I 6 22 7
"Well," said Charlotte, "I wish Jane success with all my PP I 6 23 10
If the dispositions of the parties are ever so well known PP I 6 23 10
myself uncommonly well just now, when I was teazing PP I 6 24 17
18
however, she added, "very well; if it must be so, it must." PP I 6 24 22
though not playing half so well; and Mary, at the end of a PP I 6 25 24
At present, indeed, they were well supplied both with news PP I 7 28 3
a red coat myself very well--and indeed so I do still at PP I 7 29 12
eagerly calling out, while her daughter read, "well, Jane, PP I 7 30 14
15
Well, Jane, make haste and tell us; make haste, my love." PP I 7 30 15
"Well, my dear," said Mr. Bennet, when Elizabeth had read PP I 7 31 31
As long as she stays there, it is all very well. PP I 7 32 32
was very feverish and not well enough to leave her room. PP I 7 33 43
I thought Miss Elizabeth Bennet looked remarkably well, PP I 8 36 7
girl, and I wish with all my heart she were well settled. PP I 8 36 14
I hope it will soon be increased by seeing her quite well." PP I 8 37 25
to wait till Jane was well, and by that time most likely PP I 9 45 38
I mend pens remarkably well." PP I 10 47 11
We may as well wait, perhaps, till the circumstance occurs, PP I 10 50 37
to this request, as well as the degree of intimacy PP I 10 50 38
her sister, and seeing her well guarded from cold, PP I 11 54 1
Her figure was elegant, and she walked well;--but Darcy, PP I 11 56 10
But you have chosen your fault well.-- PP I 11 58 29
them to stay longer, she could spare them very well.-- PP I 12 59 1
at last very rapidly, as well as her affection for Jane; PP I 12 60 5
Well, I am sure I shall be extremely glad to see Mr. PP I 13 61 3
to apologise for it, as well as to assure you of my PP I 13 63 12
and self-importance in his letter, which promises well. PP I 13 64 18
is not wholly new, yet I think it is well expressed." PP I 13 64 19
seeing them all in due time well disposed of in marriage. PP I 13 64 21
that they were very well able to keep a good cook, and PP I 13 65 26
was extremely well pleased to close his large book, and go. PP I 15 71 6
"You may well be surprised, Miss Bennet, at such an PP I 16 77 12
I have known him too long and too well to be a fair judge. PP I 16 77 14
"I know very well, madam," said he, "that when persons sit PP I 16 83 50
for many years, but I very well remember that I never PP I 16 84 58
Whatever he said, was said well; and whatever he did, done PP I 16 84 59
well manage before the carriage stopped at Longbourn house. PP I 16 84 59
to be done, but to think well of them both, to defend the PP I 17 85 1
to take the hint, being well aware that a serious dispute PP I 17 88 14
"Very well.-- PP I 18 91 11
I do not know the particulars, but I know very well that PP I 18 94 45
thought he could not well avoid including him in his PP I 18 94 45
as sufficiently marked how well she was satisfied with the PP I 18 95 48
say that by his account as well as his sister's, Mr. PP I 18 95 50
him that her ladyship was quite well yesterday se'nnight." PP I 18 97 59
of saying, that he was so well convinced of Lady PP I 18 98 62
song, said aloud, "that will do extremely well, child. PP I 18 100 68
69
I cannot acquit him of that duty; nor could I think well PP I 18 101 71
on your father, since I am well aware that it could not be PP I 19 106 10
"Very well--and this offer of marriage you have refused?" PP I 20 111 15
"Very well. PP I 20 111 17
He thought too well of himself to comprehend on what PP I 20 112 24
I have certainly meant well through the whole affair. PP I 20 114 32
and the concern of every body was well talked over.-- PP I 21 115 3
little, hot pressed paper, well covered with a lady's fair, PP I 21 116 6
of thanks for this, as well as for every other mark of PP I 22 124 10
of having a daughter well married; and she called at PP I 23 127 8
whom I really love, and still fewer of whom I think well. PP II 1 135 11
man; you know he is, as well as I do; and you must feel, PP II 1 135 13
do; and you must feel, as well as I do, that the woman who PP II 1 135 13
superior to his sister as well by nature as education. PP II 2 139 2
own warehouses, could have been so well bred and agreeable. PP II 2 139 2
so different, and, as you well know, we go out so little, PP II 2 141 12
to place this point, as well as the still more interesting PP II 2 142 16
and known the late Mr. Darcy by character perfectly well. PP II 2 143 20
"Well, then, you need not be under any alarm. PP II 3 144 5
"Perhaps it will be as well, if you discourage his coming PP II 3 145 7
Her impatience for this second letter was as well rewarded PP II 3 147 21
He was well, but so much engaged with Mr. Darcy, that they PP II 3 147 23
a punishment for him, as well as a possible advantage to PP II 3 149 27
men must have something to live on, as well as the plain." PP II 3 150 29
something greater pleasure as well as greater certainty. PP II 3 148 26
desertion, and complimented her on bearing it so well. PP II 4 153 7
"Well," cried Elizabeth, "have it as you choose. PP II 4 153 17
seen her sister looking so well as to banish all fear for PP II 5 155 1
which was large and well laid out, and to the cultivation PP II 5 156 4
It was a handsome modern building, well situated on rising PP II 5 156 4
over the house, extremely well pleased, probably, to have PP II 5 156 5
It was rather small, but well built and convenient; and PP II 5 157 5
husband, and to acknowledge that it was all done very well. PP II 5 157 10
Yes, she will do for him very well. PP II 5 158 18
I am always glad to get a young person well placed out. PP II 6 165 32
had never been half so well entertained in that room PP II 8 172 3
of Lady Catherine herself, as well as of Mr. Darcy. PP II 8 172 3
she will never play really well, unless she practises more; PP II 8 173 10
not be alarmed though your sister does play so well. PP II 8 174 13
I am particularly unlucky in meeting with a person so well PP II 8 174 15
Well, Colonel Fitzwilliam, what do I play next? PP II 8 175 20
He and his sisters were well, I hope, when you left London. PP II 9 177 4
"Yes, indeed; his friends may well rejoice in his having PP II 9 178 15
in being with him, as well as by his evident admiration of PP II 9 180 28
"He likes to have his own way very well," replied Colonel PP II 10 183 10
But, perhaps his sister does as well for the present, and, PP II 10 184 17

Context	Work	Vol.	Ch.	Page	Line
He spoke well, but there were feelings besides those of	PP	II	11	189	5
"I might as well enquire," replied she, "why with so	PP	II	11	190	10
be little doubt, as he was well assured that I had no	PP	II	12	201	5
But such as they were, it may be well supposed how eagerly	PP	II	13	204	1
and collecting herself as well as she could, she again	PP	II	13	205	3
known its extent, agreed equally well with his own words.	PP	II	13	205	3
he had not been well assured of his cousin's corroboration.	PP	II	13	206	4
and reconciling herself as well as she could, to a change	PP	II	13	209	12
on this point it will be as well to be silent.	PP	II	15	216	6
Jane looked well, and Elizabeth had little opportunity of	PP	II	15	217	16
very pretty; but I thought I might as well buy it as not.	PP	II	16	219	3
Well, but now for my news: it is about dear Wickham; too	PP	II	16	220	10
Well, now let us be quite comfortable and snug, and talk	PP	II	16	221	17
of her gowns; and you cannot imagine how well he looked!	PP	II	16	221	17
"Well, Lizzy," said Mrs. Bennet one day, "what is your	PP	II	17	227	27
Well, he is a very undeserving young man--and I do not	PP	II	17	228	27
"Oh, well! it is just as he chooses.	PP	II	17	228	29
Well, my comfort is, I am sure Jane will die of a broken	PP	II	17	228	29
"Well, Lizzy," continued her mother soon afterwards, "and	PP	II	17	228	31
Well, well, I only hope it will last.	PP	II	17	228	31
Well, much good may it do them!	PP	II	17	228	33
Well, if they can be easy with an estate that is not	PP	II	17	228	35
should not ask me as well as Lydia," said she, "though I	PP	II	18	230	13
well over; the agitations of former partiality entirely so.	PP	II	18	233	25
of accents, "you, who so well know my feelings towards Mr.	PP	II	18	234	37
					38
It was a large, handsome, stone building, standing well on	PP	III	1	245	3
"He is perfectly well behaved, polite, and unassuming,"	PP	III	1	257	67
Elizabeth excused herself as well as she could; said that	PP	III	1	258	71
and on this account, as well as some others, found herself,	PP	III	2	264	12
Of Mr. Darcy it was now a matter of anxiety to think well;	PP	III	2	264	14
understood, it was yet a well known fact that, on his	PP	III	2	265	15
but for loving her still well enough, to forgive all the	PP	III	2	265	16
her to be more truly well bred than either of the others;	PP	III	3	267	4
am afraid of alarming you--be assured that we are all well.	PP	III	4	273	3
I know my dear uncle and aunt so well, that I am not	PP	III	4	275	5
You are not well enough;--you cannot go yourself."	PP	III	4	276	7
I am quite well.	PP	III	4	277	10
You know him too well to doubt the rest.	PP	III	4	277	11
But nothing can be done; I know very well that nothing can	PP	III	4	277	16
her share of business as well as her aunt, and amongst the	PP	III	4	281	29
"Well, then--supposing them to be in London.	PP	III	5	282	7
every chance of benefiting himself by marrying well?	PP	III	5	283	8
But Jane knows, as well as I do, what Wickham really is.	PP	III	5	284	12
Can she be ignorant of what you and Jane seem so well to	PP	III	5	284	15
my dear uncle is come, I hope every thing will be well."	PP	III	5	286	24
"My mother is tolerably well, I trust; though her spirits	PP	III	5	286	30
Mary and Kitty, thank heaven! are quite well."	PP	III	5	286	30
of her being perfectly well; and their conversation, which	PP	III	5	286	32
that it would all end well, and that every morning would	PP	III	5	287	33
girl to do such a thing, if she had been well looked after.	PP	III	5	287	35
moderation to her, as well in her hopes as her fears; and,	PP	III	5	288	39
"I must confess that he did not speak so well of Wickham	PP	III	5	291	54
You do not look well.	PP	III	5	292	65
"perhaps she meant well, but , under such a misfortune as	PP	III	5	293	67
was by this time tolerably well acquainted with her own	PP	III	6	298	17
"You may well warn me against such an evil.	PP	III	6	299	21
"Yes; where else can they be so well concealed?"	PP	III	6	299	23
"Well, well," said he, "do not make yourself unhappy.	PP	III	6	300	32
"Well, and what news does it bring? good or bad?"	PP	III	7	302	10
"Well," cried her mother, "it is all very right; who	PP	III	7	306	47
Well!	PP	III	7	306	47
How well it sounds.	PP	III	7	306	47
She is well, and begs to be dutifully remembered to you	PP	III	8	313	19
But Mrs. Bennet, was not so well pleased with it.	PP	III	8	313	20
"Well, mamma," said she, when they were all returned to	PP	III	9	317	11
Well, Monday morning came, and I was in such a fuss!	PP	III	9	319	24
"Well, and so we breakfasted at ten as usual; I thought it	PP	III	9	319	25
Well, and so just as the carriage came to the door, my	PP	III	9	319	25
Well, I was so frightened I did not know what to do, for	PP	III	9	319	25
not be put off, for Mr. Darcy might have done as well."	PP	III	9	319	25
had not been so well known, as to make it impossible for	PP	III	10	321	2
You know pretty well, I suppose, what has been done for	PP	III	10	324	2
the army, and she was afraid had-- not turned out well.	PP	III	10	327	14
I hope she will turn out well."	PP	III	10	328	22
"Exceedingly well.	PP	III	10	328	28
"Well, well, and so Mr. Bingley is coming down, sister," (	PP	III	11	331	14
"Well, so much the better.	PP	III	11	331	14
"Well, all I know is, that it will be abominably rude if	PP	III	11	332	26
My mother means well; but she does not know, no one can	PP	III	11	333	28
Well, any friend of Mr. Bingley's will always be welcome	PP	III	11	334	35
sure, to have a daughter well married," continued her	PP	III	11	336	51
"Well girls," said she, as soon as they were left to	PP	III	12	342	28
I think every thing has passed off uncommonly well, I	PP	III	12	342	28
The dinner was as well dressed as any I ever saw.	PP	III	12	342	28
partridges were remarkably well done; and I suppose he has	PP	III	12	342	28
"The party seemed so well selected, so suitable one with	PP	III	12	343	30
"We may as well leave them by themselves you know;" said	PP	III	13	345	16
when Bingley, who as well as the other had sat down,	PP	III	13	346	22
I have not a doubt of your doing very well together.	PP	III	13	348	38
stiffly to Elizabeth, "I hope you are well, Miss Bennet.	PP	III	14	351	4
					5
your ladyship whether you left Mr. and Mrs. Collins well."	PP	III	14	352	12
					13
"Yes, very well.	PP	III	14	352	14
It was the favourite wish of his mother, as well as of	PP	III	14	355	43
"It is well.	PP	III	14	358	69
Very well.	PP	III	14	358	71
only came, I suppose, to tell us the Collinses were well.	PP	III	14	359	76
through Meryton, thought she might as well call on you.	PP	III	14	359	76
sad business has been so well hushed up, and am only	PP	III	15	363	22
she might have seen how well the expression of heart-felt	PP	III	16	366	8
Your reproof, so well applied, I shall never forget 'had	PP	III	16	367	14
Perhaps I did not always love him so well as I do now.	PP	III	17	373	7
And do you really love him quite well enough?	PP	III	17	373	11
"It may do very well for the others," replied Mr. Bingley;	PP	III	17	374	24
"Well, my dear," said he, when she ceased speaking, "I	PP	III	17	377	37
I shall like your husband quite as well as Jane's."	PP	III	17	379	48
"You may as well call it impertinence at once.	PP	III	18	380	5
Console Lady Catherine as well as you can.	PP	III	18	383	23
though Mrs. Philips, as well as her sister, stood in too	PP	III	18	384	27
her a sensible, amiable, well informed woman for the rest	PP	III	19	385	1
If you love Mr. Darcy half as well as I do my dear Wickham,	PP	III	19	386	7
They were able to love each other, even as well as they	PP	III	19	387	11
Darcy, as well as Elizabeth, really loved them; and they	PP	III	19	388	13
which, from principle as well as pride, from a general	MP	I	1	3	1
of settling well, without farther expense to any body.	MP	I	1	6	6
Whatever I can do, as you well know, I am always ready	MP	I	1	7	8
well how to save her own as to spend that of her friends.	MP	I	1	8	9
indeed he should ever get well of his gouty complaints, it	MP	I	1	9	10
fair to expect Ellis to wait on her as well as the others.	MP	I	1	9	12
in the introduction very well, with much good humour, and	MP	I	2	12	3
might depend upon her acquitting herself well at first.	MP	I	2	13	5
There is a vast deal of difference in memories, as well as	MP	I	2	19	27
know whether it is not as well that it should be so, for,	MP	I	2	19	29
may be imagined; as well as the sanguine views and spirits	MP	I	2	21	34
a quick apprehension as well as good sense, and a fondness	MP	I	2	22	35
that she could do very well without him, and for her	MP	I	3	23	1
and, plied well with good things, would soon pop off."	MP	I	3	24	5
"Well, Fanny, and if the plan were not unpleasant to you,	MP	I	3	25	21
I ever thank you as I ought, for thinking so well of me?	MP	I	3	26	30
I know I am of none, and yet I love the place so well."	MP	I	3	27	34

Context	Work	Vol.	Ch.	Page	Line
be, I am inclined to hope you may always prophesy as well."	MP	I	3	27	36
render Fanny, might as well have been spared, for Mrs.	MP	I	3	28	38
Nobody that wishes me well, I am sure, would propose it.	MP	I	3	28	42
She is in good hands, and sure of doing well.	MP	I	3	29	46
They are sure of being well provided for.	MP	I	3	30	53
"Well, Lady Bertram," said Mrs. Norris, moving to go, "I	MP	I	3	30	56
early care to make him, as well as Lady Bertram,	MP	I	3	30	57
in Mrs. Grant's being so well settled in life without	MP	I	3	31	60
to find how very well they did even without his father,	MP	I	4	34	1
without his father, how well Edmund could supply his place	MP	I	4	34	1
their both being alive and well, made it necessary to lay	MP	I	4	34	2
they possessed its favour as well as its admiration.	MP	I	4	34	4
the loss in her health as well as in her affections, for	MP	I	4	35	7
park, that would do vastly well, or that one might be	MP	I	4	36	7
As the horse continued in name as well as fact, the	MP	I	4	37	9
to see their dear Maria well married," she very often	MP	I	4	38	9
address, the young lady was well pleased with her conquest.	MP	I	4	38	10
than her father's, as well as ensure her the house in town,	MP	I	4	38	10
of character which could so well distinguish merit.	MP	I	4	39	10
and a house commodious and well fitted up; and Mrs. Grant	MP	I	4	41	17
Matrimony was her object, provided she could marry well,	MP	I	4	42	18
(very clever women,) as well as my dear aunt and myself,	MP	I	4	42	21
so good, and he was so well made, that one soon forgot he	MP	I	5	44	2
I think too well of Miss Bertram to suppose she would ever	MP	I	5	45	14
It will do just as well.	MP	I	5	46	18
"Well done, sister!	MP	I	5	47	24
promised well, and there was nothing to call him elsewhere.	MP	I	5	47	26
Dr. Grant was exceedingly well contented to have it so; a	MP	I	5	47	26
modern-built house, so well placed and well screened as to	MP	I	5	48	28
house, so well placed and well screened as to deserve to	MP	I	5	48	28
It might do very well; she believed she should accept him;	MP	I	5	48	28
Manners as well as appearance are, generally speaking, so	MP	I	5	49	32
"Ah! you carry it off very well, but I cannot be quite so	MP	I	5	49	35
The close bonnet and demure air you describe so well, (and	MP	I	5	51	40
They looked just the same; both well dressed, with veils	MP	I	5	51	40
Does she dine out every where, as well as at my sister's?"	MP	I	5	51	41
As he has done so well by Smith, I think I had better have	MP	I	6	53	8
"Well, and if they were ten," cried Mrs. Norris, "I am	MP	I	6	53	9
to work upon these, and grounds that will well reward you.	MP	I	6	53	9
"The tree thrives well beyond a doubt, madam," replied Dr.	MP	I	6	54	10
I have no doubt that it will be all done extremely well."	MP	I	6	56	26
herself, "he is a well bred man; he makes the best of it."	MP	I	6	56	27
I might as well have asked for porters and a hand-barrow."	MP	I	6	58	35
"Yes, the profession is well enough under two	MP	I	6	60	51
"Well Fanny, and how do you like Miss Crawford now?" said	MP	I	7	63	1
"Very well--very much.	MP	I	7	63	2
nature it was most astonishing to see how well she sat.	MP	I	7	67	16
that Mr. Crawford might as well have saved him the trouble;	MP	I	7	67	16
"I was sure she would ride well," said Julia; "she has the	MP	I	7	69	24
You know I am strong enough now to walk very well."	MP	I	7	70	29
believe you," he replied; "I know your looks too well.	MP	I	7	72	38
But I dare say it will be well to-morrow.	MP	I	7	72	45
"What!" cried Edmund; "has she been walking as well as	MP	I	7	72	47
Mrs. Norris and her nieces were all well pleased with its	MP	I	8	75	1
so it will all do very well; and as for Edmund, as he is	MP	I	8	76	3
would hold four perfectly well, independent of the box, on	MP	I	8	77	8
She felt that she had arranged every thing extremely well,	MP	I	8	79	23
and would only say, "very well, very well, just as you	MP	I	8	79	23
only say, "very well, very well, just as you choose,	MP	I	8	79	23
Lady Bertram was very well pleased to have it so, and the	MP	I	8	80	28
Miss Crawford was not slow to admire; she pretty well	MP	I	8	82	35
Much was said, and much was ate, and all went well.	MP	I	9	84	1
was now almost equally well qualified to shew the house.	MP	I	9	84	3
the Julia of the barouche-box as could well be imagined.	MP	I	9	91	36
has its gradations, I hope, as well as the never.	MP	I	9	92	45
of; and standing back, well shaded and sheltered, and	MP	I	9	95	67
at the same view, without being able to see it so well."	MP	I	9	96	73
I was glad to see you so well entertained.	MP	I	10	98	11
but I and my gown are alive and well, and so good bye."	MP	I	10	100	22
It might have been as well, perhaps, if you had been in my	MP	I	10	100	28
After an interval of silence, "I think they might as well	MP	I	10	102	38
We did very well without them."	MP	I	10	102	43
"Well," said he, "if you really think I had better go; it	MP	I	10	103	48
Mrs. Norris had been too well employed to move faster.	MP	I	10	103	50
Julia's day was likely to end almost as well as it began.	MP	I	10	105	52
"Well, Fanny, this has been a fine day for you, upon my	MP	I	10	105	53
"I think you have done pretty well yourself, ma'am.	MP	I	10	105	54
Now I can manage the other parcel and the basket very well.	MP	I	10	106	55
and your father's convenience should accord so well.	MP	I	11	108	14
How well she walks! and how readily she falls in with the	MP	I	11	112	34
Norris on this subject, as well as to her feelings, and	MP	I	12	116	11
so properly happy, so well suited, and so much the thing!	MP	I	12	118	16
"Very well.--	MP	I	12	118	20
Your mother is quite anxious about it but cannot very well	MP	I	12	119	23
Well, the jointure may comfort him; and perhaps, between	MP	I	13	123	5
think our time very well spent, and so I am sure will he.--	MP	I	13	126	18
Well, Edmund," he continued, returning to the former	MP	I	13	126	23
My father wished us, as school-boys, to speak well, but he	MP	I	13	127	26
"I know my father as well as you do, and I'll take care	MP	I	13	127	27
in it, you might just as well suppose he would object to	MP	I	13	127	29
the charm of acting might well carry fascination to the	MP	I	13	129	39
And why should not Lovers' Vows do for us as well as for	MP	I	14	132	7
"This is not behaving well by the absent," said she.	MP	I	14	133	9
to suppress shewed how well it was understood, and before	MP	I	14	133	12
Amelia is a character more difficult to be well	MP	I	14	135	15
She would not do well.	MP	I	14	135	16
satisfaction, and Julia well knew that on this ground	MP	I	14	135	18
Mr. Rushworth liked the idea of his finery very well,	MP	I	15	138	1
so well, nothing so unexceptionable, as Lovers' Vows.	MP	I	15	139	6
Edmund;--you mean very well, I am sure--but I still think	MP	I	15	140	14
The maids do their work very well, and I think we shall be	MP	I	15	141	22
"Well, how do you go on?" and "what have you settled?" and	MP	I	15	143	26
give you joy, madam, as well as Mrs. Norris, and every	MP	I	15	143	26
Such a forward young lady may well frighten the men."	MP	I	15	144	32
the part of Amelia if well supported--that is, if every	MP	I	15	144	38
is, if every thing went well--I shall be sorry to be an	MP	I	15	144	38
"Yes, yes, you can act well enough for us.	MP	I	15	146	50
about; and you will do it very well I'll answer for it."	MP	I	15	146	50
You'll do it very well.	MP	I	15	146	52
Let her choose for herself as well as the rest of us.--	MP	I	15	147	54
she could work as well, and begging for the pattern, and	MP	I	15	147	57
I am well aware that nothing else will quiet Tom."	MP	I	16	154	10
of concentrating our folly, I shall be well repaid.	MP	I	16	155	16
They behaved very well, however, to him on the occasion,	MP	I	17	158	2
"Oh! very well."	MP	I	17	159	5
I do not think we do so well without him.	MP	I	17	162	16
I think she likes Sotherton too well to be inconstant."	MP	I	17	162	16
shameful towards herself, as well as towards Mr. Rushworth.	MP	I	17	162	19
came before her as well as the rest; and so decided to her	MP	I	18	164	2
Crawford acted well, and it was a pleasure to her to creep	MP	I	18	165	3
Maria she also thought acted well--too well;--and after	MP	I	18	165	3
thought her quite as well off as the rest, was evident by	MP	I	18	166	6
so I turned it off as well as I could, by whispering to	MP	I	18	169	21
Was not that well done of me?	MP	I	18	169	21
having lighted it up as well as its unfinished state	MP	I	18	171	25
Why was not Miss Crawford to be applied to as well?	MP	I	18	171	29
"Well then, Lady Bertram, suppose you speak for tea	MP	II	1	180	12
he might be always as well disposed to give them but	MP	II	1	183	24
It was well at that moment that Tom had to speak and not	MP	II	2	193	13
As well as I can recollect, it was always much the same.	MP	II	3	197	3
carelessly, "it does very well for a place of this sort.	MP	II	4	209	15
Well, shall we join and disappoint them of half their	MP	II	4	211	24

"Well," said Miss Crawford, "and do not you scold us for MP II 4 211 26
"Very well, very well," cried Dr. Grant, "all the better. MP II 4 215 49
"That's well thought of. MP II 5 217 8
thing by Mrs. Grant, as well as by Fanny, that being the MP II 5 217 9
Her cause meanwhile went on well. MP II 5 218 12
"Well," said Sir Thomas, as if waiting more to accomplish MP II 5 218 13
"Very well, then, Fanny may go, Edmund." MP II 5 219 23
"Well, Fanny, it is all happily settled, and without the MP II 5 219 25
"Oh! depend upon it, your aunt can do very well without MP II 5 220 30
life--you must manage as well as you can, and not be MP II 5 221 34
you how I like you; and as well as I can judge by this MP II 5 222 42
Well, I am much mistaken if his lovely Maria will ever MP II 5 224 53
I am glad to hear Bertram will be so well off. MP II 5 226 61
Bertram is certainly well off for a cadet of even a MP II 5 226 63
a new gown, and you never saw her so well dressed before. MP II 6 230 6
me, to give me smiles as well as blushes, to keep a chair MP II 6 231 9
Well, you will have opportunities enough of endeavouring MP II 6 231 10
method of pleasing her, as well as of his dutiful MP II 6 232 13
thing that could deserve or promise well. MP II 6 236 21
and he found it was as well to be a man of fortune at once MP II 6 236 23
till he returned safe and well, without accident or MP II 6 237 23
"Very well," was her ladyship's contented answer--"then MP II 7 239 7
cards to manage as well as his own--for though it was MP II 7 240 8
living, as Miss Crawford well knew; and her interest in a MP II 7 241 19
"Well" continued Edmund, "and how did you like what you MP II 7 241 20
The meadows beyond what will be the garden, as well as MP II 7 242 23
One might as well be nothing as a midshipman. MP II 7 249 52
He knows, as well as you do, of what consequence it is." MP II 7 250 55
in general, and was so well engaged in describing the MP II 7 251 63
night with her head full of happy cares as well as Fanny.-- MP II 8 254 8
Did she love him well enough to forego what had used to be MP II 8 255 11
she love him well enough to make them no longer essential? MP II 8 255 11
might be all talked over as well without doors as within. MP II 8 257 15
necklace round her and making her see how well it looked. MP II 8 258 17
"Well then," replied Miss Crawford more seriously but MP II 8 259 22
and now her raptures might well be over, for Edmund was so MP II 9 262 11
All went well--she did not dislike her own looks; and when MP II 9 270 40
The necklace really looked very well; and Fanny left her MP II 9 271 40
"Yes," said Lady Bertram, "she looks very well. MP II 10 272 2
"Look well! MP II 10 272 3
has good reason to look well with all her advantages: MP II 10 272 3
consciousness of looking well, made her look still better. MP II 10 272 4
"Yes, she does look very well," was Lady Bertram's placid MP II 10 277 15
Miss Crawford knew Mrs. Norris too well to think of MP II 10 277 16
"Well, then," replied Miss Crawford laughing, "I must MP II 10 277 19
for more were pretty well at an end; and Sir Thomas having MP II 10 279 22
"Well then, Fanny, you shall not get up to-morrow before I MP II 10 279 25
it ended in a gracious, "well, well," which was permission. MP II 10 280 30
very ball had in great measure sprung, were well founded. MP II 10 280 32
a languid "yes--yes--very well--did you? did he?--I did MP II 11 283 4
began, with a voice as well regulated as she could--"and MP II 11 287 18
Well, when your cousin comes back, he will find Mansfield MP II 11 288 30
It is every body's duty to do as well for themselves as MP II 11 289 34
He knew his uncle too well to consult him on any MP II 12 292 9
"Well, well, I am satisfied. MP II 12 293 11
the knowledge of her being well principled and religious. MP II 12 294 16
Well might his sister, believing as she really did that MP II 12 294 18
"Well, well, we do not think quite alike here. MP II 12 296 28
happiness of his joy as well as her own, and all the MP II 13 302 12
"Upon my word, he must have gone off with his pockets well MP II 13 305 21
me as well, he would, I dare say, behave differently. MP II 13 307 31
uncle's; she knew it as well as his voice; she had MP III 1 312 4
but I think too well of you, Fanny, to suppose you will MP III 1 313 12
and he had done it all so well, so openly, so liberally, MP III 1 314 16
"I--I cannot like him, sir, well enough to marry him." MP III 1 315 26
Well, there is nothing more to be said." MP III 1 316 32
his mind and cheered it, "well," said he, in a tone of MP III 1 320 44
but of less anger, "well, child, dry up your tears. MP III 1 320 44
There was comfort too in his words, as well as his manner, MP III 1 321 47
to what degree he thought well of his niece, or how very MP III 1 323 57
glory, as well as the felicity, of forcing her to love him. MP III 2 326 2
of her indifference, might well be questionable; and he MP III 2 328 7
to be overcoming, "well, Fanny, I have seen Mr. Crawford MP III 2 330 14
Yet, having chosen so well, his constancy has a MP III 2 330 14
Your feelings are as well known to me, as my wishes and MP III 2 330 16
"Well, Fanny," said she, as soon as they were alone MP III 2 332 23
extraordinary animation--"well, Fanny, I have had a very MP III 2 332 23
I could do very well without you, if you were married to a MP III 2 333 26
You did look remarkably well. MP III 2 333 28
long used; her uncle read well--her cousins all--Edmund MP III 3 337 10
cousins all--Edmund very well; but in Mr. Crawford's MP III 3 337 10
with you," said he; "you read as if you knew it well." MP III 3 338 12
but to read him well aloud, is no every-day talent." MP III 3 338 14
"No, indeed, you know your duty too well for me to--even MP III 3 341 26
"A sermon, well delivered, is more uncommon even than MP III 3 341 28
delivered, is more uncommon even than prayers well read. MP III 3 341 28
It is more difficult to speak well than to compose well; MP III 3 341 28
A thoroughly good sermon, thoroughly well delivered, is a MP III 3 341 28
and undertones were to be well tried, he sank as quietly MP III 3 341 31
know yourself as well as you seemed to do at that moment." MP III 3 343 39
"Well," said Crawford, after a course of rapid questions MP III 3 343 41
declare it, I know you too well not to entertain the MP III 3 344 41
thought it might be as well to make one more effort for MP III 4 345 2
and he loved her too well to bear to be denied her MP III 4 345 4
I wish he had known you as well as I do, Fanny. MP III 4 348 21
Full well could Fanny guess where his thoughts were now. MP III 4 349 24
I have not thought well of him from the time of the play. MP III 4 349 25
gentleness of character so well adapted to recommend them. MP III 4 351 32
Well, though I may not be able to persuade you into MP III 4 351 34
I have no common interest in Crawford's well doing. MP III 4 351 34
Fanny was too well aware of it, to have anything to say; MP III 4 351 35
His sisters should consider me as well as him. MP III 4 353 45
"Yes, very well. MP III 4 355 54
How well I remember what I was thinking of as I came along; MP III 5 360 14
How I am well aware, that I shall not be half so welcome MP III 5 360 16
And my friend does not manage him well; she does not seem MP III 5 361 16
"I cannot think well of a man who sports with any woman's MP III 5 363 23
that Fanny could be very well spared--(she being ready to MP III 6 371 15
He too had a sacrifice to make to Mansfield Park, as well MP III 6 373 25
Well, well, we are ready, whatever happens. MP III 7 380 20
the job was to be done, as well as it could, in a great MP III 7 382 27
better order than she could, acquitted herself very well. MP III 7 383 33
of the thrush, a very well behaved young man, who came to MP III 7 384 36
of females were pretty well composed, and the mother MP III 7 385 37
Well, she was taken away from evil to come. MP III 7 387 44
for there has been no 'well, Mary, when do you write to MP III 9 393 1
I hope she will recollect it, and be satisfied, as well MP III 9 394 1
himself, but that he was well, had left them all well at MP III 10 400 8
well, had left them all well at Mansfield, and was to dine, MP III 10 400 8
loud tones did very well in the open air, and there was MP III 10 402 12
two officers seemed very well satisfied in going about MP III 10 403 15
This was aimed, and well aimed, at Fanny. MP III 10 404 15
She began to feel the possibility of his turning out well MP III 10 405 16
as well to talk of something else, and turned to Mansfield. MP III 10 405 17
of nature, and very well able to express his admiration. MP III 11 409 7
She said she was very well, and did not like to be MP III 11 410 7
When you know her as well as I do, I am sure you will MP III 11 410 16
letter to Mary, 'I am well.'--and I know you cannot speak MP III 11 411 18
falsehood,--so long only shall you be considered as well." MP III 11 411 18
"I advise!--you know very well what is right." MP III 11 412 21
This, as well as I understand, is to be the substance of MP III 12 415 2
I hope they get on pretty well together. MP III 13 423 2
Fanny checked the tendency of these thoughts as well as MP III 13 424 4
Instead of being soon well enough to follow his friends, MP III 13 426 10
poor dear Sister Price to have them so well provided for. MP III 13 428 15
of course he would soon be well again; Lady Bertram could MP III 14 429 1
which she loved them too well to hope they would MP III 14 430 6
She saw the proof of it in Miss Crawford, as well as in MP III 14 433 12
roof in company with the well known and captivating Mr. C. MP III 15 440 14
and well situated as it was, with a melancholy aspect. MP III 15 447 36
you, regretting, as well she might, the loss of such a----. MP III 16 455 21
Well, she went on to say, that what remained now to be MP III 16 456 29
and it may all end well; but if he get his daughter away, MP III 16 457 29
I only said in reply, that from my heart I wished her well, MP III 16 458 30
summer evenings, he had so well talked his mind into MP III 17 462 5
whom he had rationally, as well as passionately loved. MP III 17 468 22
might not do just as well--or a great deal better; whether MP III 17 470 25
to be so!--and equally well adapted for it by a readiness MP III 17 472 31
to think a little too well of herself; these were the E I 1 5 4
to Hartfield to say that all were well in Brunswick-Square. E I 1 9 21
"Well! that is quite surprizing, for we have had a vast E I 1 10 26
Being pretty well aware of what sort of joy you must both E I 1 10 27
But I hope it all went off tolerably well. E I 1 10 27
"Well," said Emma, willing to let it pass--"you want to E I 1 11 35
"Dear Emma bears every thing so well," said her father. E I 1 11 36
"We should not like her so well as we do, sir, if we could E I 1 11 38
I think very well of Mr. Elton, and this is the only way I E I 1 13 46
how fortunate she might well be thought, where the only E I 2 18 10
be hoped would bear her well and happily through its E I 2 18 11
so apparent, that Emma, well as she knew her father, was E I 2 18 12
for contriving things so well; but the quiet prosings of E I 3 22 6
whom Emma knew very well by sight and had long felt an E I 3 22 7
They were a family of the name of Martin, whom Emma well E I 3 23 10
of doing every thing well and attentively, with the real E I 3 24 11
She believed every body spoke well of him. E I 4 28 6
"Well done, Mrs. Martin!" thought Emma. E I 4 28 7
him--but he knows you very well indeed--I mean by sight." E I 4 29 15
I know indeed that he is so; and as such wish him well. E I 4 30 16
"Well, and that is as early as most men can afford to E I 4 30 20
"You understand the force of influence pretty well, E I 4 31 24
I want to see you permanently well connected--and to that E I 4 31 24
what had had some education--and been very well brought up. E I 4 31 25
to give them up, for they are quite as well educated as me. E I 4 31 25
her father's gentleness with admiration as well as wonder. E I 4 32 27
Well, Miss Woodhouse, is he like what you expected? E I 4 32 29
At Hartfield you have had very good specimens of well E I 4 32 32
had very good specimens of well educated, well bred men. E I 4 32 32
it suits him very well; his figure and look, and situation E I 4 34 42
might very well be conquered by Mr. Elton's admiration. E I 4 35 45
good lists they were--very well chosen, and very neatly E I 5 37 7
How well she looked last night!" E I 5 39 16
Very well; I shall not attempt to deny Emma's being pretty. E I 5 39 17
"Very well; I will not plague you any more. E I 5 40 23
"I know that you all love her really too well to be unjust E I 5 40 24
said Mrs. Weston, "as can well be; and while she is so E I 5 41 30
"Well, if you give me such kind encouragement, Mr. Elton, E I 6 43 15
I do not know any body who draws so well as you do. E I 6 48 36
He will connect himself well if he can." E I 7 50 2
for her opinion, with a "well, well," and was at last E I 7 51 4
her opinion, with a "well, well," and was at last forced E I 7 51 4
would express himself so well, if left quite to his own E I 7 51 5
"Well," said the still waiting Harriet;--"well--and--and E I 7 51 6
your opinion, I must do as well as I can by myself; and I E I 7 53 22
23
sister very well married, and it is only a linen-draper." E I 7 55 40
"Well, I believe, if you will excuse me, Mr. Knightley, if E I 8 57 3
and I am inclined to think very well of her disposition. E I 8 58 10
"Well, well, means to make her an offer then. E I 8 59 27
the purpose; open, straight forward, and very well judging. E I 8 59 27
his, might be easily led aright and turn out very well. E I 8 61 38
Highbury, for the sake of her being settled so well. E I 8 61 38
They would be estimated very differently by others as well E I 8 62 39
I know him well. E I 8 63 42
Harriet's claims to marry well are not so contemptible as E I 8 63 44
He knows the value of a good income as well as anybody. E I 8 66 53
He is as well acquainted with his own claims, as you can E I 8 66 53
I shall leave off while I am well." E I 8 66 54
of the first order, in form as well as quantity. E I 9 70 4
hope and dulness, "very well, Mr. Elton, very well, indeed. E I 9 72 15
This is an attachment which a woman may well feel pride in E I 9 74 20
in the common phrase, be well married, here is the E I 9 75 27
"Very well," replied Emma, "a most natural feeling; and E I 9 77 45
inquiry of "well, me dears, how does your book go on?-- E I 9 78 49
She and the children might stay very well." E I 9 80 66
"Well, I cannot understand it." E I 9 81 76
Mr. Elton certainly did not very well know what to say. E I 9 82 81
very inferior, society, may well be illiberal and cross. E I 10 85 19
marrying, I shall be very well off, with all the children E I 10 85 21
I wish Jane Fairfax very well; but she tires me to death." E I 10 86 23
Well, (smiling,) I hope it may be allowed that if E I 10 87 30
But I hope she is pretty well, sir." E I 11 93 7
"Pretty well, my dear--I hope--pretty well.-- E I 11 94 8
saw Mrs. Weston better in my life--never looking so well. E I 11 94 10
I thought it very well done of him indeed. E I 11 96 22
Well, I could not have thought it--and he was but two E I 11 96 24
Well, time does fly indeed!--and my memory is very bad. E I 11 96 24
I really never could think well of any body who proposed E I 11 96 25
"Nobody ever did think well of the Churchills, I fancy," E I 11 96 26
"Why, pretty well; but not quite well. E I 12 101 25
I hope they are quite well. E I 12 102 31
"Why, pretty well, my dear, upon the whole. E I 12 102 32
that I think you are any of you looking well at present." E I 12 103 38
from any where, I am quite well myself; and if the E I 12 103 39
I think Mr. John Knightley very far from looking well." E I 12 103 40
well--but I hope it is only from being a little fatigued. E I 12 103 42
We all had our health perfectly well there, never found E I 12 105 55
"would do as well to keep his opinion till it is asked for. E I 12 106 60
I may be allowed, I hope, the use of my judgment as well E I 12 106 60
hours were to be early, as well as the numbers few; Mr. E I 13 108 4
Indeed you should take care of yourself as well as of your E I 13 109 7
Mr. Elton looked as if he did not very well know what E I 13 110 10
clear vision, was very well satisfied with his muttering E I 13 110 10
"Well," said she to herself, "this is most strange!-- E I 13 111 13
After I had got him off so well, to chuse to go into E I 13 111 13
before, you may as well take it into consideration now." E I 13 112 20
"I do not say it is so; but you will do well to consider E I 13 112 22
falling into; and not very well pleased with her brother E I 13 112 23
to see that it was cold, and too well wrapt up to feel it. E I 13 112 24
Well, sir, the time must come when you will be paid for E I 13 116 45
The misfortune of Harriet's cold had been pretty well gone E I 14 117 3
as I do: but she does not know the parties so well as I do. E I 14 120 11
Emma liked the subject so well, that she began upon it, to E I 14 121 14
improprieties, and be as well satisfied with him as before, E I 15 124 2
your spirit; and I dare say we shall get home very well. E I 15 126 10
which must be already well known, hoping--fearing--adoring- E I 15 129 24
I wish her extremely well: and, no doubt, there are men E I 15 132 35
I am exceedingly sorry: but it is well that the mistake E I 15 132 36
to make every thing go well: for Mr. John Knightley, E I 15 132 38
She looked back as well as she could; but it was all E I 16 134 3
He wanted to marry well, and having the arrogance to raise E I 16 135 7
down upon her friend, so well understanding the gradations E I 16 135 8
That was well done of me; but there I should have stopped, E I 16 137 11
to have her father so well satisfied with his being all E I 16 138 18
19

Harriet bore the intelligence very well--blaming nobody-- E I 17 141 7
by them; for they know, as well as he does, as well as all E I 18 147 18
as well as he does, as well as all the world must know, E I 18 147 18
personal; that he is well grown and good-looking, with E I 18 149 28
"Well, if he have nothing else to recommend him, he will E I 18 149 29
power as well as the wish of being universally agreeable. E I 18 150 31
to speak extremely well on each; that is my idea of him." E I 18 150 31
it to Harriet, that, as well as she could calculate, they E II 1 155 3
she went through it very well, with all the interest and E II 1 156 5
'Have you, upon your honour!' said she; 'well, that is E II 1 157 7
I hope she is well?" E II 1 157 9
My mother often wonders that I can make it out so well. E II 1 157 10
She often says, when the letter is first opened, 'well, E II 1 157 10
well still, thank God! with the help of spectacles. E II 1 157 10
I only wish my eyes may last me as well.'" E II 1 158 10
in Mr. Dixon's name as well as her own, to press their E II 1 159 20
air, as she has not been quite so well as usual lately." E II 1 161 25
I am going to read to you,) and has never been well since. E II 1 161 29
But however, she is so far from well, that her kind E II 1 161 29
If Jane does not get well soon, we will call in Mr. Perry. E II 1 162 31
Well, now I have just given you a hint of what Jane writes E II 1 162 31
understanding, and warm-hearted, well meaning relations. E II 2 163 3
She had never been quite well since the time of their E II 2 165 9
indeed, her situation, as well as her beauty; when she E II 2 167 13
of mutton for dinner, as well as to see exhibitions of new E II 2 168 15
An arch look expressed--"I understand you well enough;" E II 3 171 6
""Oh! my dear, said I--well, and just then came the note. E II 3 173 27
"Well! that is quite----- I suppose there never was a E II 3 173 29
We may well say that 'our lot is cast in a goodly heritage. E II 3 174 31
Well, Mr. Knightley, and so you actually saw the letter; E II 3 174 31
32

actually saw the letter; well"----- "it was short, merely E II 3 174 31
32

He seemed to me very well off as he was. E II 3 174 34
Well, I had always rather fancied it would be some young E II 3 176 44
"Well my dear Jane, I believe we must be running away. E II 3 176 50
The weather does not look well, and grandmamma will be E II 3 176 50
Well, that is so very!--I am sure if Jane is tired, you E II 3 177 50
Oh! dear, Miss Woodhouse--well, at last, I fancy, he E II 3 178 52
But she had believed them to be well meaning, worthy E II 3 179 53
Ambition, as well as love, had probably been mortified. E II 3 179 53
to have behaved extremely well; and it is over--and may E II 3 180 55
Human nature is so well disposed towards those who are in E II 4 181 1
point of some dignity, as well as some convenience: the E II 4 181 4
the story told well; he had not thrown himself away--he E II 4 181 4
She wished him very well; but he gave her pain, and his E II 4 182 7
sister, who was very well married, to a gentleman in a E II 4 183 9
been sitting with your father--glad to see him so well. E II 5 188 7
at his command, as well as the route and the method of his E II 5 188 9
"Well, well, I am ready;"--and turning again to Emma, "but E II 5 189 13
"Will Mr. Frank Churchill pass through Bath as well as E II 5 189 17
His son, too well bred to hear the hint, rose immediately E II 5 193 36
37

some day or other, and therefore may as well be paid now. E II 5 193 36
37

"another day would do as well; but there was that degree E II 5 194 39
40

Emma remained very well pleased with this beginning of the E II 5 195 49
"Well," said Emma, "there is no disputing about taste.-- E II 6 199 11
Then I will speak the truth, and nothing suits me so well. E II 6 200 20
She appeared to me to play well, that is, with E II 6 201 28
her being thought to play well:--a man, a very musical man, E II 6 201 28
Well, I am glad she is gone to settle in Ireland." E II 6 202 33
Emma felt herself so well acquainted with him, that she E II 6 203 42
Elton's house, which, as well as the church, he would go E II 6 203 42
so often and bowed so well; but there was one spirit among E II 7 206 4
He was soon pretty well resigned. E II 7 209 9
"Well, sir," cried Mr. Weston, "as I took Miss Taylor away, E II 7 209 11
Her father's comfort was amply secured, Mrs. Bates as well E II 8 213 6
You think you carry it off very well, I dare say, but with E II 8 213 10
She listened, and found it well worth listening to. E II 8 214 13
She must know as well as her father, how acceptable an E II 8 217 29
Very well. E II 8 217 31
Well!-- E II 8 218 36
Well, a little while ago it occurred to me how very sad it E II 8 223 63
"Well," said Mrs. Weston, smiling, "you give him credit E II 8 224 65
been a first favourite with him, as you very well know." E II 8 224 69
"Well," said Mrs. Weston, laughing, "perhaps the greatest E II 8 225 77
we have all been so well satisfied to consider it a E II 8 226 79
"Very well; and if he had intended to give her one, he E II 8 226 82
She knew the limitations of her own powers too well to E II 8 227 86
acceptable, and could accompany her own voice well. E II 8 227 86
and she found herself well matched in a partner. E II 8 230 100
"Perhaps it is as well," said Frank Churchill, as he E II 8 230 102
"Oh! if I could play as well as you and Miss Fairfax!" E II 9 231 5
I think you play quite as well as she does. E II 9 231 7
Every body last night said how well you played." E II 9 231 7
"Well, I always shall think that you play quite as well as E II 9 232 9
Besides, if she does play so very well, you know, it is no E II 9 232 11
"Well--if you advise it.-- E II 9 234 32
She might do very well by herself. E II 9 234 32
Woodhouse, I may just as well have it sent to Hartfield, E II 9 235 40
Very well I thank you.-- E II 9 236 44
"Very well, I am much obliged to you. E II 9 236 46
My mother is delightfully well; and Jane caught no cold E II 9 236 46
is nothing she likes so well as these baked apples, and E II 9 237 46
Well, Mrs. Weston, you have prevailed, I hope, and these E II 9 237 46
Thank ye, the gloves do very well--only a little too large E II 9 237 48
Very well, I thank you. E II 10 243 33
"Well," said he in a deliberating manner, "for five E II 10 244 43
"Well, I am so sorry!-- E II 10 245 48
I think Miss Fairfax dances very well; and Mrs. Weston is E II 10 245 49
Mrs. Hodges may well be angry. E II 10 245 52
Well, (returning into the room,) I have not been able to E II 10 245 52
Ten couple may stand here very well." E II 11 249 13
my father--and altogether--I might stand here very well." E II 11 250 18
"Well, Miss Woodhouse," he almost immediately began, "your E II 11 250 21
bodies, which (as you well know, sir) does the mischief." E II 11 251 29
"Well--if you please," said Mrs. Weston rather hesitating, E II 11 255 51
Emma could get no more approving reply, than, "very well. E II 12 257 2
3

Well! evil to some is always good to others. E II 12 262 39
I shall do very well again after a little while--and then, E II 13 265 4
It was well to have a comfort in store on Harriet's behalf, E II 13 267 8
Harriet so well, nor valued her affection so highly before. E II 13 269 15
she behaved very well, and was only rather pale and silent. E II 14 270 3
had need be all grace to acquit himself well through it. E II 14 271 5
"Well, Miss Woodhouse," said Harriet, when they had E II 14 271 6
for her friend to begin; "well, Miss Woodhouse, (with a E II 14 271 6
"Yes," said Harriet earnestly, "and well she might, nobody E II 14 271 15
Well, I wish them happy with all my heart. E II 14 271 15
a vain woman, extremely well satisfied with herself, and E II 14 272 16
are called the garden of England, as well as Surry." E II 14 273 25
be able to explore the different beauties extremely well. E II 14 274 28
You, Miss Woodhouse, I well know, play delightfully. E II 14 276 36
I could do very well without it. E II 14 276 36
"Well," said Mrs. Elton, laughing, "we shall see." E II 14 278 42
"Well, my dear," he deliberately began, "considering we E II 14 279 54
"Well, papa, if this is not encouragement to marry, I do E II 14 280 59
herself, were very well satisfied; so that Mrs. Elton's E II 15 281 2
I do not scruple to say that she plays extremely well. E II 15 282 5
"Well," said she, "and you soon silenced Mr. Cole, I E II 15 288 37

"Well, Mrs. Weston," said Emma triumphantly when he left E II 15 289 41
I know Mr. John Knightley too well--I am very sure he E II 16 293 22
he understands the value of friendship as well as any body. E II 16 293 22
I hope your good grandmamma and aunt are well. E II 16 294 27
and all that it does so well, it is really astonishing!" E II 16 296 40
"It is certainly very well regulated." E II 16 296 41
The public pays and must be served well." E II 16 297 43
"Well, well, I have that note; and can shew it after E II 16 298 54
very sure; but you sing as well as play;--yes, I really E II 17 301 18
"You may well class the delight, the honour, and the E II 17 301 19
Do you think it will look well?" E II 17 302 22
"Well, he is coming, you see; good news, I think. E II 17 303 27
Well, what do you say to it?-- E II 17 304 27
Well, pretty good news, is not it? E II 17 304 27
others to talk, was very well satisfied with what she did E II 17 304 29
It was well that he took every body's joy for granted, or E II 17 304 30
account--she has not been well the whole winter, and E II 18 305 7
"Only think! well, that must be infinitely provoking! E II 18 310 34
their getting on very well; for Mr. Knightley seemed E II 18 311 36
and he soon began with-- "well, Emma, I do not believe I E II 18 311 37
38

"Very well--and as Randalls, I suppose, it not likely to E II 18 312 48
She watched him well. E III 1 316 3
him in London; he might as well be at Enscombe; but E III 1 318 10
And Jane declares--well!--(as soon as she was within the E III 2 322 19
soon as she was within the door) well! E III 2 322 19
So well lighted up.-- E III 2 322 19
"Very well, I thank you, ma'am. E III 2 322 19
I hope you are quite well. E III 2 322 19
Thank you, my mother is remarkably well. E III 2 322 19
Very well I thank you, quite well. E III 2 323 19
Very well, I thank you. E III 2 323 19
Quite well, I am much obliged to you. E III 2 323 19
I like him very well." E III 2 324 21
How well you put it on!--so gratified! E III 2 329 45
Grandmamma was quite well, had a charming evening with Mr. E III 2 329 45
Well, here we are at the passage. E III 2 329 45
Well, I was persuaded there were two. E III 2 329 45
Well, this is brilliant! E III 2 330 45
I have seen nothing like it since--well, where shall we E III 2 330 45
Well, I am sure, Mr. Churchill--only it seems too good-- E III 2 330 45
of the two little boys, as well as of their grandpapa, E III 3 332 3
He dared not stay longer than to see her well; these E III 3 334 8
to be inquired after), as well as Miss Smith, were coming E III 3 336 12
for she was perfectly well, and Harriet not much otherwise, E III 3 336 12
have kept--I know that very well (blushing as she spoke).-- E III 4 337 6
Harriet opened: it was well lined with the softest cotton; E III 4 338 9
Well--(sitting down again) go on--what else?" E III 4 339 13
"Well, go on." E III 4 340 21
She merely said, in the course of some trivial chat, "well, E III 4 340 28
Yes, honourable, I think, to choose so well and so E III 4 342 39
Well, Frank, your dream certainly shows that Highbury is E III 5 345 14
the Coles knew of it as well as ourselves--but it was E III 5 345 16
what every body found so well worth seeing, and she and Mr. E III 6 352 2
This was so very well understood between them, that Emma E III 6 353 3
Well, I shall bring Jane with me--Jane and her aunt.-- E III 6 355 18
"Well--as you please; only don't have a great set out. E III 6 355 22
"Well--but if any difficulties should arise, my E III 6 355 24
He wished to persuade Mr. Woodhouse, as well as Emma, to E III 6 356 29
and Harriet, could go very well; and he could sit still E III 6 356 30
He thought it very well done of Mr. Knightley to invite E III 6 357 30
The invitation was every where so well received, that it E III 6 357 31
abruptness and grandeur, well clothed with wood;--and at E III 6 360 38
she behaved very well, and betrayed no emotion. E III 6 361 41
Mr. Woodhouse had been exceedingly well amused. E III 6 362 43
"As soon as my aunt gets well, I shall go abroad," said he. E III 6 364 60
and eat and drink a little more, and you will do very well. E III 6 365 65
last words to Emma were, "well;--if you wish me to stay, E III 6 366 74
75

as no English word but flirtation could very well describe. E III 7 368 3
"Oh! very well," exclaimed Miss Bates, "then I need not be E III 7 370 24
"Ah!--well--to be sure. E III 7 371 28
Mr. Weston has done very well for himself; but he must E III 7 371 35
36

These kind of things are very well at Christmas, when one E III 7 372 37
were out of hearing:--"how well they suit one another!-- E III 7 372 40
said, in a lively tone, "well, I have so little confidence E III 7 373 45
46

"Very well. E III 7 373 49
ready to have gone with her, but this will do just as well. E III 7 374 53
Well, I declare-----" E III 7 374 53
heard Miss Bates saying, "well, my dear, I shall say you E III 8 378 4
"I am afraid Jane is not very well," said she, "but I do E III 8 378 6
said she, "but I do not know; they tell me she is well. E III 8 378 6
has written her letters, she says she shall soon be well. E III 8 379 8
'Well,' said she, 'it must be borne some time or other, E III 8 379 8
be borne some time or other, and it may as well be now.' E III 8 379 8
the parish: he is very well to do himself, you know, being E III 8 383 29
"Well, my dear, and did you get there safely?-- E III 9 385 6
Harriet behaved extremely well on the occasion, with great E III 9 388 14
"Miss Fairfax was not well enough to write;" and when Mr. E III 9 389 16
but, as her friend was well, she endeavoured not to be E III 10 392 7
Well, well, never mind." E III 10 394 22
"Well, my dear," said he, as they entered the room--"I E III 10 394 25
"You may well be amazed," returned Mrs. Weston, still E III 10 395 35
Emma might have time to recover--"you may well be amazed. E III 10 395 35
"Well," said she at last, trying to recover herself; "this E III 10 395 37
its all turning out well, and ready to hope that it may. E III 10 398 53
Well, and how did Mr. Churchill take it?" E III 10 398 54
"Well," said Emma, "I suppose we shall gradually grow E III 10 399 61
She would soon be well, and happy, and prosperous.-- E III 11 403 2
In Jane's eyes she had been a rival; and well might any E III 11 403 2
"Well, Miss Woodhouse!" cried Harriet, coming eagerly into E III 11 404 4
Her own conduct, as well as her own heart, was before her E III 11 408 33
Methodical, or well arranged, or very well delivered, it E III 11 409 34
Well, (checking herself, and trying to be more lively), E III 12 420 13
She thought well of Frank in almost every respect; and, E III 12 420 14
"Are you well, my Emma?" was Mrs. Weston's parting E III 12 420 15
I am always well, you know. E III 12 420 16
She asked after their mutual friends; they were all well.-- E III 13 424 1
do many things which may well lay me open to unpleasant E III 13 426 15
not under-rated him hitherto, he may yet turn out well.-- E III 13 427 21
character and conduct, I shall certainly wish him well." E III 13 428 21
you now, dearest Emma, as well as you have borne with them. E III 13 430 37
We are quite well.-- E III 14 436 7
of Enscombe must be too well known to require definition; E III 14 437 8
suppose you would ever have thought well of me again. E III 14 441 8
She thought so well of the letter, that when Mr. Knightley E III 15 444 2
Well, he must be a most extraordinary-----" E III 15 447 22
"Well, there is feeling here.-- E III 15 447 28
"You do not appear so well satisfied with his letter as I E III 15 448 29
defer the disclosure till Mrs. Weston were safe and well. E III 16 452 6
Emma had never seen her look so well, so lovely, so E III 16 453 8
I managed it extremely well." E III 16 456 15
"it is well, perhaps, that I have not had the possibility. E III 16 459 45
46

a pity that any one who so well knew how to teach, should E III 17 461 1
You must have done well. E III 17 462 7
complimenter; and though I well know him to have, likewise, E III 17 464 19
secondly, as a good one--well aware of the nearly equal E III 17 468 30
In general, it was a very well approved match. E III 17 468 36
"Well!"-- E III 18 471 19

be expressing, she added, "well, now tell me every thing; E III 18 471 19
I think Harriet is doing extremely well. E III 18 473 24
my word, I believe you know her quite as well as I do.-- E III 18 473 26
"Is not she looking well?" said he, turning his eyes E III 18 477 50
demure for the moment--"I hope Mr. Knightley is well?" E III 18 477 58
59

evening before, from the infant's appearing not quite well. E III 18 479 73
In ten minutes, however, the child had been perfectly well E III 18 479 73
though the child seemed well now, very well considering, E III 18 479 73
seemed well now, very well considering, it would probably E III 18 479 73
character, and extremely well provided for, should have no P III 1 5 8
to them, as any body of sense and honesty could well be. P III 2 11 2
of business, gentlemen of the navy are well to deal with. P III 3 17 2
3

A name that I am so very well acquainted with; knew the P III 3 23 28
knew the gentleman so well by sight; seen him a hundred P III 3 23 28
think them infinitely too well off in being permitted to P III 3 24 35
would sound extremely well; very much better than to any P III 3 24 36
Each lady was previously well disposed for an agreement, P III 5 32 2
She knew the ways of Uppercross as well as those of P III 5 36 21
While well, and happy, and properly attended to, she had P III 5 37 21
but I was very far from well at the time; and I do not P III 5 37 24
"Well, you will soon be better now," replied Anne, P III 5 38 28
said you were perfectly well, and in no hurry for me; and P III 5 38 32
"Oh! well;"--and after a moment's pause, "but you have P III 5 39 35
I was very well yesterday; nothing at all the matter with P III 5 39 37
"I am very glad you were well enough, and I hope you had a P III 5 39 38
and then she was well enough to propose a little walk. P III 5 39 40
with people I know so well as Mrs. and the Miss Musgroves." P III 5 40 42
However, we may as well go and sit with them a little P III 5 40 43
was generally, as Anne very well knew, the least to blame. P III 5 41 46
my word, I shall be pretty well off, when you are all gone P III 6 42 1
who loved her nearly as well, and respected her a great P III 6 43 4
"I could manage them very well, if it were not for Mary's P III 6 44 6
other respects, her visit began and proceeded very well. P III 6 46 12
should not have done so well without the sight of Mr. and P III 6 46 12
civility, or to refresh the others, as she was well aware. P III 6 46 13
done, Miss Anne! very well done indeed! P III 6 47 15
her little boys, she was well able to watch for a likeness, P III 6 48 17
to persuade herself, as well as she could, that the same P III 6 49 25
In each letter he had spoken well of his captain; but yet, P III 6 51 31
though not perfectly well spelt praise, as "a fine dashing P III 6 52 33
child was going on so well--and he wished so much to be P III 7 55 6
The child had a good night, and was going on well the next P III 7 55 7
from his poor little boy; talks of his being on so well! P III 7 56 10
How does he know that he is going on well, or that there P III 7 56 10
I really think Charles might as well have told his father P III 7 57 14
"Well--if you do not think it too late to give notice for P III 7 57 15
yourself, suppose you were to go, as well as your husband. P III 7 57 15
To be sure I may just as well go as not, for I am of no P III 7 57 16
thousands that may just as well go to the bottom as not, P III 8 65 11
"I was as well satisfied with my appointment as you can P III 8 65 13
"I knew pretty well what she was, before that day;" said P III 8 65 16
"Pretty well, ma'am, in the fifteen years of my marriage; P III 8 70 52
'Lady Wentworth' sounds very well. P III 9 75 11
can get Captain Wentworth, I shall be very well satisfied." P III 9 76 15
And as to Captain Wentworth's liking Louisa as well as P III 9 77 16
"Well, I am very glad indeed, but I always thought you P III 9 78 20
moment, and released Captain Wentworth as well as herself. P III 9 79 23
It was evident that Charles Hayter was not well inclined P III 9 80 34
step of a stile, was very well satisfied so long as the P III 10 86 21
Henrietta looked a little ashamed, but very well pleased;-- P III 10 89 36
"Well, and I had heard of you as a very pretty girl; and P III 10 92 46
with three companions, all well known already by P III 11 96 11
must have stamped him well in the esteem of every listener, P III 11 96 12
and Anne was well repaid the first trouble of exertion. P III 11 100 23
which may be just as well performed by another person?-- P III 12 103 2
"I wish," said Henrietta, very well pleased with her P III 12 103 4
She was looking remarkably well; her very regular, very P III 12 104 6
was going on as well as the nature of the case admitted. P IV 1 121 2
If Louisa recovered, it would all be well again. P IV 1 123 7
Anne was conscious of not doing it so well as Lady Russell. P IV 1 124 12
"Well, whenever it suits you.-- P IV 1 127 26
Lady Russell and Mrs. Croft were very well pleased with P IV 1 128 31
be altogether doing very well, it was still impossible to P IV 2 129 1
"Oh! Captain Benwick is very well, I believe, but he is a P IV 2 130 5
said, "now Mary, you know very well how it really was.-- P IV 2 130 6
the church's being so very well worth seeing, for as he P IV 2 131 12
"Well, as your joint acquaintance, then, I shall be very P IV 2 132 15
Every body has their taste in noises as well as in other P IV 2 135 33
Colonel Wallis had known Mr. Elliot long, had been well P IV 3 139 9
She was certainly not a woman of family, but well educated, P IV 3 139 9
an interval of so many years, to be well received by them. P IV 3 140 11
"Well, it would serve to cure him of an absurd practice of P IV 3 144 19
first evening in Camden-Place could have passed so well! P IV 3 144 24
To your fine mind, I well know the sight of beauty is a P IV 4 145 1
you cannot be better than well; or I should recommend P IV 4 146 3
Very well. P IV 4 147 7
She knew it well; and she remembered another person's look P IV 4 148 9
in good company, on the contrary, it will do very well. P IV 4 150 17
"Well," said Anne, "I certainly am proud, too proud to P IV 4 151 20
and if they are intelligent may be well worth listening to. P IV 5 155 10
And it is not merely in its follies, that they are well P IV 5 156 10
and no doubt is well known to convey a Miss Elliot.-- P IV 5 158 19
"I am no match-maker, as you well know," said Lady Russell, P IV 5 159 23
Russell, "being much too well aware of the uncertainty of P IV 5 159 23
and all her popularity, as well as to all her virtues, P IV 5 159 25
man,--that he talked well, professed good opinions, seemed P IV 5 160 27
He endured too well,--stood too well with everybody. P IV 5 161 29
"which as you well know, affords little to write about. P IV 6 162 7
quite as well, if not "better, than her grand-children. P IV 6 163 7
"I can leave them at the great house very well, for a P IV 6 163 7
"I am sorry to say that I am very far from well; and " P IV 6 164 8
he had been invited as well as the Harvilles; and "what do P IV 6 164 8
"We are all very well pleased, however; for though it is P IV 6 165 8
Well might Charles wonder how Captain Wentworth would feel! P IV 6 166 18
as well as address him before she could catch his notice. P IV 6 169 25
"Well," (turning away) "now, where are you bound? P IV 6 169 25
It suits us very well. P IV 6 170 29
"well, now you shall hear something that will surprise you. P IV 6 170 30
31

Well, this Miss Louisa, we all thought, you know, was to P IV 6 171 33
"Well, she is to marry him. P IV 6 171 35
"Well, well, ladies are the best judges; but James benwick P IV 6 172 39
He looked very well, not as if he had been suffering in P IV 7 176 8
half serious, half arch, "Well, I heartily wish your P IV 7 180 35
her father had judged so well as to give him that simple P IV 8 181 2
I could not leave it till Louisa's doing well was quite P IV 8 183 13
at present, perhaps, it was as well to be asunder. P IV 8 185 18
Elliot had manoeuvred so well, with the assistance of his P IV 8 186 23
of the performance so well, and yet in allowance for his P IV 8 190 47
as if he saw a place on it well worth occupying; when, at P IV 8 190 47
or notoriety in Bath was well known by name to Mrs. Smith. P IV 9 193 5
and we were exceedingly well placed--that is for hearing; P IV 9 193 11
Well, my dear Miss Elliot, I hope and trust you will be P IV 9 196 32
"Well," continued Mrs. Smith triumphantly, "grant my P IV 9 206 88
He saw you then at Lyme, and liked you so well as to be P IV 9 206 88
"Well, my dear Penelope, you need not be so alarmed about P IV 10 213 9
"Very well," said Elizabeth, "I have nothing to send but P IV 10 215 15
Oh! you may as well take back that tiresome book she would P IV 10 215 15
to rise in cordiality, and do the honours of it very well. ? IV 10 216 18
dropped by Mary, as well as of some apparent confusion as P IV 10 216 18
who both deserve equally well, and who have always been P IV 10 217 21
My father would be as well pleased if the gentlemen were P IV 10 218 22
has done him no harm, for he has fought as well as read. P IV 10 219 26
part so well, that I have liked him the better ever since." P IV 10 219 26
and the change; and so well satisfied with the journey in P IV 10 219 28
by any body; which Mary, well amused as she generally was P IV 10 220 31
with the comfortable hope of having acquitted herself well. P IV 10 223 39
for coming, began with-- "well, mother, I have done P IV 10 223 40
41

Have not I done well, mother?" P IV 10 223 41
very well used, if they went to the play without her. P IV 10 224 50
Wentworth would move about well in her drawing-room. P IV 10 226 64
to think might do very well," and a great deal in the same P IV 11 230 5
It is all very well, I used to say, for young people to be P IV 11 231 8
I am in very good anchorage here," (smiling at Anne) "well P IV 11 234 27
Well, Miss Elliot," (lowering his voice) "as I was saying, P IV 11 234 27
disengaged, Frederick, are you not, as well as ourselves?" P IV 11 236 36
by daylight and eyed him well, he was very much struck by P IV 12 248 2
result of the most correct opinions and well regarded mind. P IV 12 249 3
It would be well for the eldest sister if she was equally P IV 12 250 6
She has abilities, however, as well as affections; and it P IV 12 250 8
pain as her mind could well be sensible of, under P IV 12 251 10
To those, however, he was very well disposed to attach P IV 12 251 10
here, but I dare say we shall do very well without him."-- S 1 365 1
the way, his partner will just as well--or rather better--. S 1 365 1
Well sir--I dare say it is as you say, & I have made an S 1 367 1
"We are always well stocked, said he, with all the common S 1 367 1
wife in the few words of "well my dear, I beleive it will S 1 367 1
other in the course of that fortnight, exceedingly well.-- S 2 371 1
inheritance, quite as well provided for as himself.-- S 2 371 1
no person cd be really well, no person, (however upheld S 2 373 1
her, were facts already well known, but some further S 3 375 1
40 years, but she had so well nursed & pleased Mr Hollis, S 3 375 1
She has a fine active mind, as well as a fine healthy S 3 376 1
& still continued to be, well attacked;--and of these S 3 376 1
by a moderate-sized house, well fenced & planted, & rich S 4 379 1
We are quite as well off for Gardenstuff as ever we were-- S 4 380 1
very well--that is, there has not been time enough yet.-- S 4 382 1
He will do very well beyond a doubt--but at first it is S 4 382 1
"Very well my love, that can be easily done--& cook will S 4 381 2
Well, I think I have done something in my day.-- S 4 383 1
hours without intermission)--he was well in three days.-- S 5 386 1
He, I am happy to say is tolerably well--tho' more languid S 5 387 1
"Well--said Mr P.--as he finished. S 5 387 1
"Well, well--my dear Mary--I grant you, it is unfortunate S 5 388 1
She observed them well.-- S 6 391 1
That sounds well. S 6 392 1
"Oh!--well.-- S 6 393 1
Well Mr Parker--and the other is a Boarding school, a S 6 393 1
We go on very well as we are. S 6 393 1
He came into the room remarkably well, talked much--& very S 7 394 1
Miss Denham's character was pretty well decided with S 7 396 1
perhaps--but doing very well from the lips of a handsome S 7 396 1
yes, he is very well to look at--& it is to be hoped that S 7 400 1
she got well, have her fall in love with Sir Edward!"-- S 7 401 1
They have Miss Clara's room to put to rights as well as my S 7 401 1
of the carriage extremely well, with only Mr Woodcock's S 9 407 1
My dear Tom I am so glad to see you walk so well. S 9 408 1
Well--now for the explanation of my being here.-- S 9 408 1
Well?"-- S 9 409 1
Well--and now, what house do you design to engage for them? S 9 409 1
with this object in veiw, I have been perfectly well."-- S 9 410 1
vanity in all they did, as well as in all they endured.-- S 10 412 1
the party continuing quite well, their brother & sister & S 10 413 1
Arthur was heavy in eye as well as figure, but by no means S 10 415 1
"I like the air too, as well as any body can; replied S 10 415 1
you see, there is not a corner but what is well browned.-- S 10 417 1
And having read a few lines, exclaimed aloud "well, this S 10 418 1
giving mood, you might as well speak in favour of another S 12 424 1
guinea from her on their behalf, it may as well be done.--" S 12 424 1
good & extremely well kept, than new or shewey--and as S 12 427 1

WELL-APPOINTED (1)
for the genteel and well-appointed, was eager to hear, and MP III 12 419 8

WELL-BEHAVED (4)
And Mrs. Jennings too, an exceeding well-behaved woman, SS II 11 228 53
were harmless, well-behaved girls, and would be pleasant SS III 1 266 36
a very pretty and a very well-behaved young lady indeed. E II 3 171 12
Mrs G. was a very well-behaved, genteel kind of woman, who S 11 420 1

WELL-BOUND (1)
of well-bound volumes, the property of Captain Benwick. P III 11 99 18

WELL-BRED (11)
so well-bred, and heretofore so particularly fond of her! NA II 13 226 25
that though perfectly well-bred, she was reserved, cold, SS I 6 31 8
I can only pronounce him to be a sensible man, well-bred, SS I 10 51 27
under the tranquil and well-bred direction of Lady SS II 1 143 9
readiness and ease of a well-bred man, and talked very PP II 7 171 10
Wildenhaim into the well-bred and easy Mr. Yates, making MP II 1 182 22
often look upon fine young men, well-bred and agreeable. E I 18 149 29
him; and there was a well-bred ease of manner, and a E II 5 190 22
He is not at all a well-bred young man. P IV 2 132 16
Elizabeth was certainly very handsome with well-bred, P IV 3 140 11
of little Mary, & a very well-bred bow & proper address to S 12 425 1

WELL-BUILT (1)
neat and pretty; and the house was modern and well-built. E II 14 272 18

WELL-CONNECTED (1)
comfort of a well-connected parsonage, something like NA II 11 212 16

WELL-DISPOSED (5)
was a good-humoured well-disposed girl; but as she had SS I 1 7 14
believed her to be a well-disposed, good-hearted girl, and SS III 13 366 21
"I hope she will prove a well-disposed girl," continued MP I 1 10 13
being a very well-disposed, good-humoured girl, and MP I 1 11 19
A well-disposed young woman, who did not marry for love, MP II 3 201 22

WELL-DOING (3)
wishes for her well-doing, which had proceeded before, PP III 8 309 6
and in the general well-doing and success of the other MP III 17 473 31
the satisfaction of her well-doing could be increased to E III 17 461 1

WELL-EDUCATED (1)
provision for well-educated young women of small fortune, PP I 22 122 3

WELL-FURNISHED (1)
well-proportioned & well-furnished;--tho' it was furniture S 12 427 1

WELL-GROUNDED (1)
He had every well-grounded reason for solid attachment; he MP III 2 326 3

WELL-GROWN (4)
Lydia was a stout, well-grown girl of fifteen, with a fine PP I 9 45 36
and all of them well-grown and forward of their age, which MP I 2 13 4
two sisters, Susan, a well-grown fine girl of fourteen, MP III 7 377 9
the fine-looking, well-grown Miss Hamilton, in all the P IV 5 153 6

WELL-INFORMED (8)
To come with a well-informed mind, is to come with an NA I 14 110 28
that his mind is well-informed, his enjoyment of books SS I 4 20 9
man, well-bred, well-informed, of gentle address, and I SS I 10 51 27
his delicacy, and well-informed mind, be satisfied with a SS II 1 140 1
intelligent, well-informed, useful, gentle, knowing all E I 1 6 6
do fall in love with well-informed minds instead of E I 8 63 44
Living constantly with right-minded and well-informed E II 2 164 6
the company of clever, well-informed people, who have a P IV 4 150 15
16

WELL-JUDGING (5)
so respectable and well-judging a friend, and to join in SS III 4 289 28
Rushworth; but as a well-judging steady young man, with MP II 1 186 35
as a well-judging your woman could permit herself to give. MP III 1 315 18
him how delightful a well-judging and truly amiable woman E I 2 17 6

sensible and well-judging, her first was to see Anne happy. P IV 12 249 4
WELL-KNOWN (8)
examination of every well-known ornament, they proceeded NA II 8 182 2
parting glance on every well-known cherished object, and NA II 13 227 27
the first view of that well-known spire which would NA II 14 232 6
spirits since last she had trodden that well-known road. NA II 14 237 20
And you, ye well-known trees!--but you will continue the SS I 5 27 8
recited, that well-known charade, my first doth affliction E I 9 70 7
especially, if to every well-known particular entitling E II 2 167 13
again, and returning through the well-known apartments. P IV 1 125 17
WELL-LOOKING (10)
family, the sons very well-looking, the daughters MP I 2 13 4
feet eight, or he will be expecting a well-looking man." MP II 1 186 31
I have a regard, I always think a person well-looking. E II 3 176 49
than a very tolerably well-looking woman of a certain age; E II 5 192 30
a very hale, hearty, well-looking man, a little weather- P III 3 22 23
certainly altogether well-looking, and possessed, in an P III 5 34 12
and determined that a well-looking groom, who was P III 12 104 7
"A well-looking man," said Sir Walter, "a very well- P IV 8 188 38
man," said Sir Walter, "a very well-looking man." P IV 8 188 38
who approached, were a well-looking hale, gentlemanlike S 1 364 1
WELL-MARRIED (1)
I declare I had rather have her well-married than myself."- W 317 2
WELL-MEANING (9)
well-meaning woman, and a very indulgent mother. NA I 4 34 8
He, her father, a well-meaning, but not a quick-sighted SS II 9 209 28
a well-meaning creature, but no conjurer, popt it all out. SS III 1 258 7
as well-meaning a fellow perhaps, as any in the world. SS III 5 298 35
and Mrs. Rushworth, a well-meaning, civil, prosing, MP I 8 75 2
He deprecated her mistaken, but well-meaning zeal. MP III 2 332 19
Norris as one of those well-meaning people, who are always MP III 2 332 19
as a good-humoured, well-meaning, respectable young man, E I 4 35 44
of conduct in a well-meaning young woman, and a heart to P III 9 77 18
WELL-MEANT (2)
of half Mrs. Jennings's well-meant but ill-judged SS II 8 193 6
In vain were the well-meant condescensions of Sir Thomas,. MP I 2 13 4
WELL-PREPARED (1)
been conveyed in a state of well-prepared insensibility! NA II 8 188 17
WELL-PROPORTIONED (4)
She saw a large, well-proportioned apartment, an handsome NA II 9 193 6
was of a commodious, well-proportioned size, and NA II 11 213 21
It was a large, well-proportioned room, handsomely fitted PP III 1 246 5
usual sitting room, well-proportioned & well-furnished;-- S 12 427 1
WELL-READ (2)
shake the doubts of the well-read Catherine, he led the NA II 8 182 2
young lady, sufficiently well-read in novels to supply her S 6 391 1
WELL-SOUNDING (1)
this, assisted by his well-sounding name, enabled Sir P IV 12 248 2
WELL-SPOKEN (1)
"And a very well-spoken, genteel, shrewd lady, she seemed P III 3 22 25
WELL-SUFFICIENT (1)
found themselves so well-sufficient for the time to NA II 13 222 7
WELL-TIED (1)
They went in; and while the sleek, well-tied parcels of " E II 6 200 16
WELL-TIMED (1)
heart were soon the better for such well-timed kindness. MP III 7 384 33
WELL-TRIED (1)
than his feet or his well-tried old horse could carry him, S 2 373 1
WELL-WISHER (3)
sincere well-wisher, friend, and sister, Lucy ferrars. SS III 13 365 14
and daughters, your well-wisher and friend, PP I 13 63 12
attention their well-wisher and friend, he does very MP II 7 248 42
WELL-WISHERS (2)
of having such steady well-wishers as Mr. and Mrs. Allen, NA II 14 239 28
who could not be my well-wishers, to see your cousin close P IV 11 244 72
WELL-WRITTEN (1)
It was a long, well-written letter, giving the particulars E II 13 265 5
WENTWORTH (189)
After waiting another moment-- "you mean Mr. Wentworth, I P III 3 23 29
30
"Wentworth was the very name! P III 3 23 32
Mr. Wentworth was the very man. P III 3 23 32
"Wentworth? P III 3 23 33
Oh! ay,--Mr. Wentworth, the curate of Monkford. P III 3 23 33
Mr. Wentworth was nobody, I remember; quite unconnected; P III 3 23 33
He was not Mr. Wentworth, the former curate of Monkford, P III 4 26 1
but a Captain Frederick Wentworth, his brother, who being P III 4 26 1
Captain Wentworth had no fortune. P III 4 27 4
with Frederick Wentworth, as he stood in her memory. P III 4 28 7
explained it to be Mr. Wentworth of whom she spoke, that P III 6 49 22
her brother, Captain Wentworth, is just returned to P III 6 50 27
they were gone, that Wentworth, or something very like it, P III 6 50 27
of the name of Wentworth, as connected with her son, P III 6 51 31
To hear them talking so much of Captain Wentworth, P III 6 52 33
be the very same Captain Wentworth whom they recollected P III 6 52 33
A very few days more, and Captain Wentworth was known to P III 7 53 1
by seeing Captain Wentworth under his own roof, and P III 7 53 1
Captain Wentworth made a very early return to Mr. P III 7 53 2
more full of Captain Wentworth than of little Charles. P III 7 54 4
for putting Captain Wentworth off, and only be sorry to P III 7 54 5
be introduced to Captain Wentworth, that, perhaps, he P III 7 55 6
His father very much wished him to meet Captain Wentworth, P III 7 55 7
Wentworth, and I know you do not mind being left alone. P III 7 57 16
it to her, if Frederick Wentworth were only half a mile P III 7 58 20
manners in Captain Wentworth, no shyness or reserve; they P III 7 58 22
following with captain Wentworth, his sisters meaning to P III 7 59 24
the child, and Captain Wentworth proposing also to wait on P III 7- 59 24
it inconvenient, Captain Wentworth would not be satisfied P III 7 59 24
from mary: "Captain Wentworth is not very gallant by you, P III 7 60 31
32
She had seen the same Frederick Wentworth. P III 7 61 34
Frederick Wentworth had used such words, or something like P III 7 61 36
From this time Captain Wentworth and Anne Elliot were P III 8 63 1
out the ships which Captain Wentworth had commanded. P III 8 64 7
I assure you;" replied Captain Wentworth, seriously.-- P III 8 65 13
"But, Captain Wentworth," cried Louisa, "how vexed you P III 8 65 16
been a gallant Captain Wentworth, in a small paragraph at P III 8 66 16
Wentworth where it was he first met with your poor brother. P III 8 66 18
from his former captain to Captain Wentworth." P III 8 66 19
"Oh!--but, Charles, tell Captain Wentworth, he need not be P III 8 66 20
the Laconia; and Captain Wentworth could not deny himself P III 8 66 22
Her feelings made her speak low; and Captain Wentworth, P III 8 67 25
I assure you, Captain Wentworth, we are very sorry he ever P III 8 67 27
screened, Captain Wentworth should be allowed some credit P III 8 68 29
now came up to Captain Wentworth, and without any P III 8 68 31
32
"Now I have done," cried Captain Wentworth--"when once P III 8 70 48
and no one seemed in higher spirits than Captain Wentworth. P III 8 71 57
Captain Wentworth was come to Kellynch as to a home, to P III 9 73 1
Wentworth, among the Musgroves and their dependencies. P III 9 73 3
by it, and to think Captain Wentworth very much in the way. P III 9 73 3
very altered manners, and of seeing Captain Wentworth. P III 9 74 4
herself, before Captain Wentworth came; but from that time P III 9 74 7
was preferred by Captain Wentworth was as yet quite P III 9 74 8
and wonder; and Captain Wentworth had not been above four P III 9 75 9
had once heard Captain Wentworth himself say, was very P III 9 75 10
and he was sure Captain Wentworth was as likely a man to P III 9 75 10
'Lady Wentworth' sounds very well. P III 9 75 11
Sir Frederick and Lady Wentworth! P III 9 75 11
can get Captain Wentworth, I shall be very well satisfied." P III 9 76 15
be wished that Captain Wentworth may soon put him quite P III 9 76 16
She had thought only of avoiding Captain Wentworth; but an P III 9 77 17
Captain Wentworth was to be regarded as the probable cause. P III 9 77 19
looking out for Captain Wentworth; and even Henrietta had P III 9 78 19
been present, Captain Wentworth walked into the drawing- P III 9 78 21
moment, and released Captain Wentworth as well as herself. P III 9 79 23
by the sight of Captain Wentworth, than Captain Wentworth P III 9 79 25
than Captain Wentworth had been by the sight of Anne. P III 9 79 25
Captain Wentworth, however, came from his window, P III 9 79 27
newspaper; and Captain Wentworth returned to his window. P III 9 79 27
away, before she knew that Captain Wentworth had done it. P III 9 80 33
Hayter was not well inclined towards Captain Wentworth. P III 9 80 34
Wentworth should do what he ought to have done himself. P III 9 80 34
that Captain Wentworth was not in love with either. P III 10 82 1
her, to believe Captain Wentworth not in the least aware P III 10 82 1
Musgrove and Captain Wentworth being gone a shooting P III 10 83 3
bursting forth, Captain Wentworth added, "what glorious P III 10 84 7
8
when Louisa drew Captain Wentworth away, to try for a P III 10 86 21
very soon heard Captain Wentworth and Louisa in the hedge- P III 10 87 22
After a moment's pause, Captain Wentworth said, "do you P III 10 89 29
30
considered by Captain Wentworth; and there had been just P III 10 89 34
understand; even Captain Wentworth did not seem admitted P III 10 89 36
Every thing now marked out Louisa for Captain Wentworth; P III 10 90 37
again, when Captain Wentworth cleared the hedge in a P III 10 91 39
a corner; and Captain Wentworth, without saying a word, P III 10 91 41
village with Captain Wentworth, within half a mile of him; P III 11 93 2
ever seeing Captain Wentworth at the hall;--those rooms P III 11 93 3
Lady Russell and Captain Wentworth never meeting any where. P III 11 93 3
Captain Wentworth, after being unseen and unheard of at P III 11 94 5
Captain Wentworth talked of going there again himself; it P III 11 94 7
Mary, Anne, Henrietta, Louisa, and Captain Wentworth. P III 11 94 7
which he drove Captain Wentworth, were descending the long P III 11 95 8
Captain Wentworth turned in to call on his friend; the P III 11 96 10
had parted with Captain Wentworth long, when they saw him P III 11 96 11
account which Captain Wentworth had given of him, on his P III 11 96 12
Captain Wentworth believed it impossible for man to be P III 11 96 12
want of health, looking much older than Captain Wentworth. P III 11 97 14
Captain Harville, though not equalling Captain Wentworth P III 11 97 15
the friends of Captain Wentworth, or more kindly P III 11 97 15
almost hurt that Captain Wentworth should have brought any P III 11 98 15
There was so much attachment to Captain Wentworth in all P III 11 98 16
While Captain Wentworth and Harville led the talk on one P III 11 100 23
on seeing Louisa and Captain Wentworth coming towards them. P III 12 103 5
Captain Wentworth looked round at her instantly in a way P III 12 104 6
"Ah!" cried Captain Wentworth, instantly, and with half a P III 12 105 10
"Pray," said Captain Wentworth, immediately, "can you tell P III 12 105 11
together," said Captain Wentworth, "we must consider it to P III 12 106 17
it, but that good fellow, (pointing to Captain Wentworth.) P III 12 108 28
Louisa; she must be jumped down them by Captain Wentworth. P III 12 109 32
Captain Wentworth, who had caught her up, knelt with her P III 12 109 34
which burst from Captain Wentworth, in a tone of despair, P III 12 110 35
in vain; while Captain Wentworth, staggering against the P III 12 110 37
38
suffering most, Captain Wentworth, Anne, or Charles, who, P III 12 110 43
Charles, to assuage the feelings of Captain Wentworth. P III 12 111 44
"Yes, yes, to the inn," repeated Captain Wentworth, P III 12 111 48
was uttered by Captain Wentworth, Anne was sure could P III 12 112 54
Charles, Henrietta, and Captain Wentworth were the three P III 12 113 57
after, a while, Captain Wentworth, exerting himself, said, P III 12 113 57
58
"Then it is settled, Musgrove," cried Captain Wentworth, " P III 12 114 61
of suspense; and Captain Wentworth proposed, and Charles P III 12 114 64
Captain Wentworth now hurried off to get every thing ready P III 12 115 65
Captain Wentworth was on the watch for them, and a chaise P III 12 115 68
found herself all at once addressed by Captain Wentworth. P III 12 117 73
morn, that captian Wentworth had been in Kellynch P IV 1 126 20
So ended all danger to Anne of meeting Captain Wentworth P IV 1 128 32
With regard to Captain Wentworth, though Anne hazarded no P IV 2 133 25
Hayter, nor Captain Wentworth were there, the room P IV 2 134 28
Captain Wentworth was gone, for the present, to see his P IV 2 134 31
to her marrying Captain Wentworth, it is infinitely " P IV 6 165 8
"Charles wonders what Captain Wentworth will say; but "if P IV 6 165 8
Well might Charles wonder how Captain Wentworth would feel! P IV 6 166 18
wonder; and if Captain Wentworth lost no friend by it, P IV 6 167 21
when she thought of Captain Wentworth unshackled and free. P IV 6 167 21
wish of getting Captain Wentworth to Bath, Captain P IV 7 174 1
to Bath, Captain Wentworth was already on his way thither. P IV 7 174 1
and distinctly, Captain Wentworth walking down the street. P IV 7 175 4
Captain Wentworth must be out of sight. P IV 7 175 6
the entrance of Captain Wentworth himself, among a party P IV 7 175 6
but yet it was Captain Wentworth not comfortable, not easy, P IV 7 176 8
walking off; and Captain Wentworth, watching them, turned P IV 7 176 10
Captain Wentworth recollected him perfectly. P IV 7 177 16
But just now she could think only of Captain Wentworth. P IV 7 178 24
company with Captain Wentworth, her imperfect knowledge of P IV 7 178 27
a good one, and Captain Wentworth was very fond of music. P IV 7 180 32
door opened again, and Captain Wentworth walked in alone. P IV 8 181 1
She was divided from Captain Wentworth. P IV 8 184 17
again by Captain Wentworth, she saw that he was gone. P IV 8 184 18
Mr. Wentworth, of Monkford, Captain Wentworth's brother. P IV 8 187 35
Wentworth--Captain Wentworth of the navy. P IV 8 188 40
distinguished Captain Wentworth, standing among a cluster P IV 8 188 41
with Captain Wentworth, if he gave her the opportunity. P IV 8 189 44
without seeing Captain Wentworth once more, without the P IV 8 189 45
space at hand, when Captain Wentworth was again in sight. P IV 8 189 47
more like the Captain Wentworth of Uppercross; owned P IV 8 190 47
Wentworth, in a reserved yet hurried sort of farewell. P IV 8 190 48
Captain Wentworth jealous of her affection! P IV 8 190 51
there been no Captain Wentworth in the case, was not worth P IV 9 192 2
for there was a Captain Wentworth: and be the conclusion P IV 9 192 2
how any report of Captain Wentworth could have reached her. P IV 9 194 19
He stood, as opposed to Captain Wentworth, in all his own P IV 10 212 1
and Charles came back with Captains Harville and Wentworth. P IV 10 221 32
"As she spoke, she felt that Captain Wentworth was looking P IV 10 222 36
I have engaged Captain Wentworth. P IV 10 223 41
who saw that Captain Wentworth was all attention, looking P IV 10 224 49
Captain Wentworth left his seat, and walked to the fire- P IV 10 225 56
Captain Wentworth was acknowledged again by each, by P IV 10 226 64
smile and one card more decidedly for Captain Wentworth. P IV 10 226 64
The present was that Captain Wentworth would move about P IV 10 226 64
"I do not wonder Captain Wentworth is delighted! P IV 10 227 66
question, of whether Captain Wentworth would come or not? P IV 10 227 69
Harville to Captain Wentworth, and she immediately heard P IV 11 229 2
Two minutes after her entering the room, Captain Wentworth P IV 11 229 2
3
He undertakes it--(looking towards Captain Wentworth) he P IV 11 232 15
Captain Wentworth was folding up a letter in great haste, P IV 11 236 37
Mrs. Croft left them, and Captain Wentworth having sealed P IV 11 236 39
two words to Captain Wentworth in the course of her quiet, P IV 11 238 47
and Captain Wentworth, that we hope to see them both." P IV 11 239 49
answer for it; and Captain Wentworth the same, I dare say." P IV 11 239 52
two moments preparation for the sight of Captain Wentworth. P IV 11 239 55
"Captain Wentworth, which way are you going? only to Gay- P IV 11 240 56
"I hardly know," replied Captain Wentworth, surprised. P IV 11 240 57
with Captain Wentworth, some moments of communication P IV 11 246 78
how should a Captain Wentworth and an Anne Elliot, with P IV 12 248 1
Captain Wentworth, with five-and-twenty thousand pounds, P IV 12 248 1
On the contrary, when he saw more of Captain Wentworth, P IV 12 248 2
truly acquainted with, and do justice to Captain Wentworth. P IV 12 249 3
agreeable that Captain Wentworth should be a richer man P IV 12 249 5
could but keep Captain Wentworth from being made a baronet, P IV 12 250 5
meaning to love Captain Wentworth as she ought, had no P IV 12 251 10

life; and Captain Wentworth, by putting her in the way of P IV 12 251 11
WEPT (4)
She was awake the whole night, and she wept the greatest SS I 16 83 1
succession, she wept for him, more than for herself. SS II 1 140 4
other, that she wept with agony through the whole of it. SS II 9 202 8
She even wept over the idea of it, as a sin of thought. E III 14 435 4
WEST (7)
before she set off for the west; and this, as she was SS I 5 26 5
for the evening, in summer; the windows are full west." PP III 14 352 11
avenue that leads from the west front to the top of the MP I 6 55 17
Mr. Rushworth talked of the west front." MP I 8 82 35
Every room on the west front looked across a lawn to the MP I 9 85 4
at west hall; and how they got their fortune nobody knows. E II 18 310 34
'somewhere down in the west,' to use her own words, P IV 9 205 86
WEST INDIA ESTATE (1)
losses on his West India Estate, in addition to his eldest MP I 3 24 7
WEST INDIAN (3)
to Sir Thomas in the concerns of his West Indian property? MP I 1 5 2
one a rich West Indian from Surry, the other, a most S 5 387 1
to secure for you--the West Indians, & the seminary.--" S 9 408 1
WEST INDIES (8)
my return from the West Indies--my friend Sneyd--you have MP I 5 51 40
I love to hear my uncle talk of the West Indies. MP II 3 197 5
He had been in the Mediterranean--in the West Indies--in MP II 6 236 21
a year or two,--and so I was sent off to the West Indies." P III 8 64 9
beyond the Streights--and never was in the West Indies. P III 8 70 52
do not call Bermuda or Bahama, you know, the West Indies." P III 8 70 52
her husband in the West Indies, which had been for many P IV 9 210 98
property in the West Indies; by writing for her, acting P IV 12 251 11
WEST INDY (1)
A West Indy family & a school. S 6 392 1
WEST-INDIANS (2)
"The West-Indians, she continued, whom I look upon as the S 9 408 1
the West-Indians were very much disposed to go thither.-- S 9 408 1
WEST-INJINES (1)
the case with your West-Injines--and if they come among us S 6 392 1
WESTERHAM (1)
Hunsford, near Westerham, Kent, 15th October. PP I 13 62 12
WESTERN (3)
of a western sun gaily poured through two sash windows! NA II 9 193 6
would have yielded the northern and western extremities. NA II 10 200 3
observed the same beautiful effect of the western sun!-- E III 14 434 2
WESTERN ISLANDS (1)
such a lovely cruise together off the Western Islands.-- P III 8 67 23
WESTGATE-BUILDINGS (7)
lodgings in Westgate-Buildings, as Anne chose to be taken. P IV 5 153 5
engaged, to spend that evening in Westgate-Buildings. P IV 5 156 14
"Westgate-Buildings!" said he; "and who is Miss Anne P IV 5 157 15
Miss Anne Elliot to be visiting in Westgate-Buildings?-- P IV 5 157 15
"Westgate-Buildings must have been rather surprised by the P IV 5 157 19
A widow Mrs. Smith, lodging in Westgate-Buildings!-- P IV 5 158 19
was sporting with from Camden-Place to Westgate-Buildings. P IV 9 192 3
WESTINDIAN (1)
Miss Lambe too!--a young Westindian of large fortune.-- S 10 419 1
WESTINDIANS (1)
The rich Westindians, & the young ladies seminary had all S 11 420 1
WESTMINSTER (4)
If you had only sent him to Westminster as well as myself, SS II 14 251 13
My plan was laid at Westminster--a little altered perhaps MP I 6 61 56
Grant to the deanery of Westminster or St. Paul's, and I MP II 4 212 33
succeeded to a stall in Westminster, which, as affording MP III 17 469 23
WESTONS (11)
We must go, for the Westons come to us next week you know. SS I 20 110 2
Now, pray do,--and come while the Westons are with us. SS I 20 113 29
The Westons will be with us, and it will be quite SS I 20 113 33
Real, long-standing regard brought the Westons and Mr. E I 3 20 2
of putting all the Mr. Westons aside as much as she can." E I 11 95 18
To her, it was real enjoyment to be with the Westons. E I 14 117 1
very invitation while the Westons were at Hartfield, which E II 7 208 8
When the Westons arrived, the kindest looks of love, the E II 8 214 12
If the Westons think it worth while to be at all this E II 12 257 3
Besides the Eltons, it must be the Westons and Mr. E II 16 291 5
and in compliment to the Westons--who I have no doubt are E III 2 324 20
21
WESTWARD (2)
"And are going farther westward?" SS III 11 354 37
if you are to cruize to the westward, with the Elephant. MP III 7 380 20
WET (22)
in meeting in defiance of wet and dirt, and shut NA I 5 37 4
it will be wet," broke from her in a most desponding tone. NA I 11 82 2
If it keeps raining, the streets will be very wet." NA I 11 82 9
to a pillow strewed with thorns and wet with tears. NA I 11 90 65
Miss Morland will get wet. NA II 7 179 27
his absence; and Wednesday she was very sure would be wet. NA II 11 211 16
But this he declined, as he was dirty and wet. SS I 9 42 10
She was prepared to be wet through, fatigued, and SS I 13 63 1
of sitting in her wet shoes and stockings--given Marianne SS III 6 305 17
is to be imputed to my getting wet through yesterday. PP I 7 31 29
30
it was only on its being a wet night, and on the PP I 16 76 4
Price dripping with wet in the vestibule, was delightful. MP II 4 205 3
The value of an event on a wet day in the country, was MP II 4 206 3
it more threatening for a wet evening in my life--you must MP II 5 221 34
Sitting with her on Sunday evening--a wet Sunday evening-- MP III 16 453 17
this morning, or I am sure you must have been wet.-- E II 16 293 10
11
know whether the wet walk of this morning had produced any. E II 16 298 58
there was a good deal of wet, damp, cheerless weather; E II 18 309 30
My dear Jane, are you sure you did not wet your feet?-- E III 2 323 19
He must have had a wet ride.-- E III 13 424 1
which at last, on some very wet day, is lent to yourself.-- P III 8 65 16
was entering Bath on a wet afternoon, and driving through P IV 2 135 33
WETTER (1)
in detecting her to be wetter than she would at first MP II 4 206 3
WETTEST (1)
grass was the longest and wettest, had-- assisted by the SS III 6 305 17
WEYMOUTH (21)
him here once before;--but I was with my uncle at Weymouth. SS I 20 114 44
to tell of races and Weymouth, and parties and friends, to MP I 12 114 1
Mr. Bertram's acquaintance with him had begun at Weymouth, MP I 13 121 1
of another friend, which he had left Weymouth to join. MP I 13 121 1
I remember it was written from Weymouth, and dated sept. E I 11 96 24
A little while ago, he was at Weymouth. E I 18 146 12
Ever since the service he rendered Jane at Weymouth, when E II 1 160 23
on the subject of Weymouth and the Dixons than any thing. E II 2 169 16
She and Mr. Frank Churchill had been at Weymouth at the E II 2 169 17
remember you knew her at Weymouth, and a fine girl she is. E II 5 194 38
at Weymouth which"----- "Oh! go to-day, go to-day. E II 5 194 39
40
"Did you see her often at Weymouth? E II 6 199 13
had known much of Miss Fairfax and her party at Weymouth." E II 6 200 17
I met her frequently at Weymouth. E II 6 200 20
in town; and at Weymouth we were very much in the same set. E II 6 200 20
had sung together once or twice, it appeared, at Weymouth. E II 8 227 87
I heard a good deal of Col. Campbell's taste at Weymouth; E II 10 241 8
If I mistake not that was danced at Weymouth." E II 10 242 19
Bought at Weymouth, you know--Mr. Dixon's choice. E III 2 322 19
at Weymouth, and kept a secret from everybody. E III 10 395 35
before we parted at Weymouth, and to induce the most E III 14 437 8
WHAT'S (7)
in hopes of Yr being drawn out to see what's going on.-- W 347 21
"What's your game?"--cried he, as they stood round the W 358 28
Mr. what's his name. PP III 11 334 34
his name, Fanny?--when we heard your footsteps." MP III 3 336 9
the name of your great cousins in town, fan?" MP III 15 439 9
he had ever thought of this Miss (what's her name?) for P IV 6 173 47
"Phoo? phoo!" replied Charles, "what's an evening party? P IV 10 223 44
WHEAT (1)
of every acre for wheat, turnips, or spring corn, was E I 12 100 16
WHEEDLED (1)
Walter, he may not be wheedled and caressed at last into P IV 12 250 8
WHEEL (2)
the school for scandal, wheel of fortune, heir at law, and MP I 14 130 3
I have employed in the business--wheel within wheel.-- S 5 387 1
WHEELED (2)
the chaise-and-four wheeled off with some grandeur, to be NA II 5 156 5
the house, and his carriage wheeled off to a vacant barn.-- S 1 370 1
WHEN (2018)
by your kind invitation when we last parted, of spending LS 1 243 1
when I shall be admitted into your delightful retirement. LS 1 243 1
You foretold how it would be, when I first came to LS 2 244 1
Mr Vernon I think was a great deal too kind to her, when LS 3 246 1
To be sure, when we consider that I did take some pains to LS 5 249 1
Charles buy vernon castle when we were obliged to sell it, LS 5 249 1
Charles is very rich I am sure; when a man has once got LS 5 250 2
wife's, to the Vernons, & when I write to him, it must be LS 5 250 3
visit to the Manwarings, & when I recollect on the LS 6 252 2
any other attachment when he comes to town; ask him to LS 7 253 1
He is lively & seems clever, & when I have inspired him LS 7 254 3
& it is impossible to say when you may see him in Kent. LS 8 254 1
when he entered the house was so decidedly against her? LS 8 255 1
of any woman in England, & when he first came it was LS 8 255 1
of her manners; but when he has mentioned her of late, it LS 8 255 2
& such abilities; & when I lamented in reply the badness LS 8 255 2
of another will avail, when opposed to the immediate LS 10 257 1
Reginald firmly beleived when he came to Churchill, is now LS 11 259 1
When your choice is so fixed as that no objection can be LS 12 261 3
I was confined to my room when your last letter came, by a LS 13 262 1
not refuse your father when he offered to read it to me, LS 13 262 1
Reginald is never easy unless we are by ourselves, & when LS 16 268 2
in my life as Frederica when she entered the room. LS 17 269 1
not return for some time; when she did, her eyes looked LS 17 270 2
sweetness in her look when she speaks either to her uncle LS 17 270 5
called, but I seldom hear any noise when I pass that way. LS 17 271 7
He scarcely dares even allow her to be handsome, & when I LS 17 271 7
In short when a person is always to deceive, it is LS 17 272 8
deserving of our regard, & when I have communicated a LS 18 272 1
brightens with a smile when Reginald says anything amusing; LS 18 272 1
mother, she talks enough when alone with me, to make it LS 18 273 3
or more obliging manners, when acting without restraint. LS 18 273 3
She arrived with her uncle last Thursday fortnight, when LS 19 273 1
when she was fortunately miss'd, pursued, & overtaken. LS 19 273 1
When she first came, I was at some pains to prevent her LS 19 274 3
was half way down stairs, when Frederica as pale as ashes LS 20 275 1
Frederica looked so shy, so confused, when we entered the LS 20 276 3
When you have the happiness of bestowing your sweet little LS 20 277 5
trust you will beleive me when I declare that much as I LS 20 277 6
7
When Sir James first came, he appeared all astonishment & LS 20 278 9
I had no great difficulty in convincing de courcy when we LS 22 281 3
When I found that he was not to be laughed out of his LS 22 281 4
parlour, when my brother called me out of the room. LS 23 283 3
You know his eager manner, my dear madam, when his mind is LS 23 283 3
with earnestness--I do not know when you will see me again. LS 23 284 4
When I next write, I shall be able I hope to tell you that LS 23 285 8
Little did I imagine my dear mother, when I sent off my LS 24 285 1
was two hours about it--& when my letter was done, I LS 24 286 5
What then was your intention when you insisted on her LS 24 289 12
not in his nature to refuse, when urged in such a manner?" LS 24 290 12
his general eagerness; when I understood his intention LS 24 290 13
When that wretched event takes place, Frederica must LS 24 291 17
When I wrote to you the other day, I was in truth in high LS 25 291 1
I had scarcely concluded my last, when Wilson brought me LS 25 292 1
The angry emotions which had marked every feature when we LS 25 292 2
when one wishes to influence the passions of another. LS 25 293 3
When my own will is effected, contrary to his, I shall LS 25 294 6
pleasure; it was the same, when I wanted to join the LS 28 298 1
lakes; & three years ago when I had a fancy for Bath, LS 28 298 1
It is impossible to say when I shall be able to see you. LS 28 298 2
swallowed my dinner when Manwaring made his appearance. LS 29 299 2
when Reginald according to our agreement is to be in town. LS 29 299 2
ill fitted to endure; & when to this, may be added the LS 30 300 3
will be evident to you when you have considered our LS 30 301 4
Mr De Courcy arrived, just when he should not. LS 32 302 1
afterwards, for I was out when both she & Reginald came, LS 32 302 1
Can you, dare you deny it? & all this at the time when I LS 36 305 1
I am satisfied--& will trouble you no more when these few LS 37 306 1
by it; & in happier times, when your situation is as LS 39 307 1
Frederica runs much in my thoughts, & when Reginald has LS 40 309 1
if she were to marry him when she got back to town, than LS 41 309 1
feels a pang as great "as when a giant dies." NA I 1 16 8
But when a young lady is to be a heroine, the perverseness NA I 1 16 11
and mental endowments, when about to be launched into all NA I 2 18 1
her person pleasing, and, when in good looks, pretty--and NA I 2 18 1
When the hour of departure drew near, the maternal anxiety NA I 2 18 2
warm about the throat, when you come from the rooms at NA I 2 18 2
only ten guineas, and promised her more when she wanted it. NA I 2 19 3
Catherine too made some purchases herself, and when all NA I 2 20 8
As for admiration, it was always very welcome when it came, NA I 2 20 8
she had imagined that when once fairly within the door, NA I 2 21 9
her fellow captives; and when at last arrived in the tea- NA I 2 21 10
discovered and joined by Mr. Allen when the dance was over. NA I 2 23 22
The company began to disperse when the dancing was over-- NA I 2 23 27
while they danced; but when they were seated at tea, she NA I 3 25 2
Allen; "and so I told Miss Morland when she bought it." NA I 3 28 44
I have heard my sister say so forty times, when she has NA I 3 28 45
They danced again; and, when the assembly closed, parted, NA I 3 29 52
bed, as to dream of him when there, cannot be ascertained; NA I 3 29 52
a family of children; and when she expatiated on the NA I 4 32 2
beauty of her daughters,--when she related their different NA I 4 32 2
Pump-Room, but required, when they all quitted it together, NA I 4 34 7
She hoped to be more fortunate the next day; and when her NA I 5 35 1
of friendship, to know when delicate raillery was properly NA I 5 36 2
properly called for, or when a confidence should be forced. NA I 5 36 2
were always arm in arm when they walked, pinned up each NA I 5 37 4
"Dear creature! how much I am obliged to you; and when you NA I 6 40 8
Laurentina's skelton; when her friend prevented her, by NA I 6 42 33
"it was only ten o'clock when we came from Tetbury." NA I 7 45 8
"Oh! d---- it, when one has the means of doing a kind NA I 7 47 17
Isabella's assuring her, when they withdrew to see the new NA I 7 50 44
the consequence was, that, when the two Morlands, after NA I 7 50 44
You hardly mentioned any thing of her, when you wrote to NA I 7 50 48
for three minutes longer, when Isabella, who had been NA I 8 52 2
I tell Mr. Allen, when he talks of being sick of it, that NA I 8 54 5
What could induce you to come into this set, when you knew NA I 8 56 12
When the orchestra struck up a fresh dance, James would NA I 8 57 21
But when you men have a point to carry, you never stick at NA I 8 57 23
with them--a hope which, when it proved to be fruitless, NA I 8 58 25
to a very gracious reply, when John Thorpe came up to her NA I 8 59 35
extraordinary hunger, and when that was appeased, changed NA I 9 60 1
point of her distress; for when there she immediately fell NA I 9 60 1
and Catherine was left, when it ended, with rather a NA I 9 64 26
When they arrived at Mrs. Allen's door, the astonishment NA I 9 67 33
a very large fortune; and, when she married, her father NA I 9 68 46

Context	Work	Vol	Ch	Page	Line
now, for they were put by for her when her mother died."	NA	I	9	68	48
was engaged the other evening, when he saw me sitting down.	NA	I	10	72	11
"When Henry had the pleasure of seeing you before, he was	NA	I	10	73	12
view, and when he spoke to her pretended not to hear him.	NA	I	10	74	23
passed through her mind, when she suddenly found herself	NA	I	10	75	24
of a place, however, when her attention was claimed by	NA	I	10	75	25
to ask you again, but when I turned round, you were gone!--	NA	I	10	75	26
girl in the room; and when they see you standing up with	NA	I	10	75	26
always to buy a good horse when I meet with one; but it	NA	I	10	76	28
of each; and that when once entered into, they belong	NA	I	10	77	33
Do you find Bath as agreeable as when I had the honour of	NA	I	10	78	41
However, when you sink into this abyss again, you will	NA	I	10	79	55
I really believe I shall always be talking of Bath, when I	NA	I	10	79	56
I hope Mr. Allen will put on his great coat when he goes,	NA	I	11	83	13
At half past twelve, when Catherine's anxious attention to	NA	I	11	83	16
him down the street, when her notice was claimed by the	NA	I	11	84	17
Their drive, even when this subject was over, was not	NA	I	11	88	54
of the town of Keynsham, when a halloo from Morland, who	NA	I	11	88	54
her setting off; that, when he told them she was gone out	NA	I	11	89	62
not see me this morning when I called; I saw her walk out	NA	I	12	94	9
"Nay, I am sure by your look, when you came into the box,	NA	I	12	95	13
agreeable for Catherine to be contented when he went away.	NA	I	12	95	16
more than surprize, when she thought she could perceive	NA	I	12	95	17
When the entertainment was over, Thorpe came to assist	NA	I	12	95	18
"I cannot help being jealous, Catherine, when I see myself	NA	I	13	98	2
When once my affections are placed, it is not in the power	NA	I	13	98	2
When every thing was settled, when Miss Tilney herself	NA	I	13	100	19
when he had overtaken them, and were at home by this time.	NA	I	13	101	20
and quickening her pace when she got clear of the Crescent,	NA	I	13	101	25
some other day he trusted, when longer notice could be	NA	I	13	103	28
most graceful bows she had ever beheld, when they parted.	NA	I	13	103	28
You know I wanted you, when we first came, not to buy that	NA	I	13	105	36
The Mysteries of Udolpho, when I had once begun it, I	NA	I	14	106	7
it aloud to me, and that when I was called away for only	NA	I	14	107	8
I am proud when I reflect on it, and I think it must	NA	I	14	107	9
poor Valancourt when she went with her aunt into Italy.	NA	I	14	107	11
so hopeful a scholar, that when they gained the top of	NA	I	14	111	29
When the Tilneys were gone, she became amiable again, but	NA	I	14	114	50
I was saying so to Emily and Sophia when you over took us."	NA	I	14	115	54
Oh! heavens! when I think of them I am so agitated!"	NA	I	15	117	6
done up in braids; and when I came into the drawing-room,	NA	I	15	118	11
A reverie succeeded this conviction--and when Isabella	NA	I	15	120	23
But when it did come, where could distress be found?	NA	I	15	121	26
When the contents of the letter were ascertained, John	NA	I	15	122	29
Who knows when we may be together again?--	NA	I	15	123	36
long quarter of an hour, when they both returned, and an	NA	II	1	132	16
When properly to relax is the trial of judgment; and,	NA	II	1	134	36
When the young ladies next met, they had a far more	NA	II	1	135	42
knows you; and I dare say when Mr. Morland sees you, my	NA	II	1	136	46
of Isabella's regret; and when she saw her at their next	NA	II	1	137	50
and every thing secured when it was determined that the	NA	II	2	138	1
were her thoughts, that when these inquiries were answered,	NA	II	2	141	13
of fixing mine, when my thoughts are an hundred miles off.	NA	II	3	143	4
When she saw her indeed surrounded only by their immediate	NA	II	4	149	1
But when Catherine saw her in public, admitting Captain	NA	II	4	149	1
When Catherine knew this, her resolution was directly made.	NA	II	4	150	1
constant to him only when unsolicited by any one else?--	NA	II	4	152	28
at his laziness when Captain Tilney at last came down.	NA	II	5	154	2
was her concern increased, when she found herself the	NA	II	5	154	2
to Eleanor, "how glad I shall be when you are all off."	NA	II	5	155	3
by this apprehension when he handed her in, that she had	NA	II	5	155	4
But you must be aware that when a young lady is (by	NA	II	5	158	15
Will not your mind misgive you, when you find yourself in	NA	II	5	158	15
echo can reach you--and when, with fainting spirits, you	NA	II	5	159	17
"What! not when Dorothy has given you to understand that	NA	II	5	159	21
Matilda may fall'--when your lamp suddenly expires in the	NA	II	5	160	21
of one in particular, when taking out his watch, he	NA	II	5	162	27
immediate accommodation, when her eye suddenly fell on a	NA	II	6	163	1
first blush of surprize, when Miss Tilney, anxious for her	NA	II	6	165	4
out of breath from haste, when there was not the least	NA	II	6	165	6
at the dinner-table, when the General's complacent smiles,	NA	II	6	165	6
sensations of awe; and, when she heard it rage round a	NA	II	6	166	9
of stepping into bed, when, on giving a parting glance	NA	II	6	168	10
storms and sleeplessness are nothing when they are over.	NA	II	7	174	5
on Catherine's notice when they were seated at table; and,	NA	II	7	175	12
some beautiful specimens when last in town, and had he not	NA	II	7	175	12
there are moments when we could all wish him disengaged	NA	II	7	176	15
"And when they had gone over the house, he promised	NA	II	7	176	17
But when did she judge amiss?--	NA	II	7	177	17
she should not know what was picturesque when she saw it.	NA	II	7	177	18
"I was only thirteen when it happened; and though I felt	NA	II	7	180	34
She had just settled this point, when the end of the path	NA	II	7	181	41
with him, listen to him, and even to smile when he smiled.	NA	II	7	181	41
When the General had satisfied his own curiosity, in a	NA	II	8	182	2
being able to turn aright when she left them; and lastly,	NA	II	8	183	2
spacious theatre; and, when the genius of others had	NA	II	8	183	3
amazed Mrs. Allen; and, when Catherine saw what was	NA	II	8	184	4
long reach of gallery, when the General, coming forwards,	NA	II	8	185	6
She ventured, when next alone with Eleanor, to express her	NA	II	8	186	7
And, when she saw him in the evening, while she worked	NA	II	8	187	13
When the butler would have lit his master's candle,	NA	II	8	187	15
vain to watch; but then, when the clock had struck twelve,	NA	II	8	189	19
was favourable here; and when she knew him to be out of	NA	II	9	191	3
with fearful caution, when the figure, the dreaded figure	NA	II	9	191	4
have escaped his eye; and when her friend, who with an	NA	II	9	192	4
softly as she had entered, when the sound of footsteps,	NA	II	9	194	6
seemed always at hand when least wanted,) much worse!--	NA	II	9	194	6
"I did not expect to be able to return sooner, when I went	NA	II	9	195	12
half an hour, went down when the clock struck five, with a	NA	II	10	199	1
But Isabella had promised and promised again; and when she	NA	II	10	201	5
severe: but, on the tenth, when she entered the breakfast-	NA	II	10	201	6
And yet, when we talked about it in Bath, you little	NA	II	10	204	19
When I think of his past declarations, I give him up.--	NA	II	10	206	31
I cannot forget, that, when she first knew what my father	NA	II	10	206	35
Henry one morning, that when he next went to Woodston,	NA	II	11	209	5
"And when do you think, sir, I may look forward to this	NA	II	11	209	5
still bounding with joy, when Henry, about an hour	NA	II	11	210	7
what the General said? when he so particularly desired you	NA	II	11	211	12
It did come, and exactly when it might be reasonably	NA	II	11	212	17
o'clock, when Catherine scarcely thought it could be three.	NA	II	11	214	26
anxiety as to the how or the when she might return to it.	NA	II	11	215	28
he seemed so uncomfortable when he went away, with a cold,	NA	II	12	217	2
call at Putney when next in town, might set all to rights.	NA	II	12	217	2
When she had finished it,--"so much for Isabella," she	NA	II	12	218	3
where they liked and when they liked, their hours,	NA	II	13	220	1
They had just reached the head of the stairs, when it	NA	II	13	222	7
her fancy of error, when the noise of something moving	NA	II	13	222	9
to enter the room, and a still greater to speak when there.	NA	II	13	223	9
Can you, when you return from this Lord's, come to	NA	II	13	224	14
"Come when you can, then."--	NA	II	13	224	16
"I could hardly believe my senses, when I heard it;--and	NA	II	13	225	19
Who could say when they might meet again?--	NA	II	13	226	25
When every thing was done they left the room, Catherine	NA	II	13	227	27
I will trust to your own kindness of heart when I am at a	NA	II	13	229	30
to her sufferings, and when within the distance of five,	NA	II	14	230	1
How Henry would think, and feel, and look, when he	NA	II	14	231	4
any thing before her, when once beyond the neighbourhood	NA	II	14	231	5
affronts:--but here, when the whole was unfolded, was an	NA	II	14	233	10
"I can allow for his wishing Catherine away, when he	NA	II	14	234	11
slept away; and though, when they all met the next morning,	NA	II	14	235	13
even without a hint; but when a third night's rest had	NA	II	15	240	2
I do not know when poor Richard's cravats would be done,	NA	II	15	240	2

Context	Work	Vol	Ch	Page	Line
endurance, as when he first hailed her, "your ladyship!"	NA	II	16	251	5
was very young when he married, and very fond of his wife.	SS	I	1	5	7
When he gave his promise to his father, he meditated	SS	I	1	5	8
of other people she could act when occasion required it.	SS	I	1	6	9
Consider," she added, "that when the money is once parted	SS	I	2	9	7
The time may come when Harry will regret that so large a	SS	I	2	9	8
always live for ever when there is any annuity to be paid	SS	I	2	10	20
When my mother removes into another house my services	SS	I	2	12	25
When your father and mother moved to Norland, though the	SS	I	2	12	26
any disinclination to move when the sight of every well	SS	I	3	14	1
produced for a while; for when her spirits began to revive,	SS	I	3	14	1
He was too diffident to do justice to himself; but when	SS	I	3	15	6
"I think you will like him," said Elinor, "when you know	SS	I	3	16	9
no longer uninteresting when she knew his heart to be warm	SS	I	3	16	13
When you tell me to love him as a brother, I shall no more	SS	I	4	21	10
There are moments when the extent of it seems doubtful;	SS	I	4	21	15
its limits, it was enough, when perceived by his sister,	SS	I	4	23	19
especially at a moment when she was suffering under the	SS	I	4	23	20
Now was the time when her son-in-law's promise to his	SS	I	5	27	6
of their being there; "when shall I cease to regret you!--	SS	I	5	27	8
to regret you!--when learn to feel a home elsewhere!--	SS	I	5	27	8
her own, was estimable when contrasted against the	SS	I	7	35	9
she sang to them; and when the visit was returned by the	SS	I	8	36	1
incomprehensible; and when its object was understood, she	SS	I	8	36	2
When is a man to be safe from such wit, if age and	SS	I	8	37	4
my invitation, when I talked of his coming to Barton.	SS	I	8	39	15
"I rather think you are mistaken, for when I was talking	SS	I	8	39	17
When is she dejected or melancholy?	SS	I	8	39	18
When does she try to avoid society, or appear restless and	SS	I	8	39	18
were an happy alternative when the dirt of the valleys	SS	I	9	40	3
glimpse of blue sky; and when they caught in their faces	SS	I	9	41	4
twenty minutes longer, when suddenly the clouds united	SS	I	9	41	6
within a few yards of Marianne, when her accident happened.	SS	I	9	42	8
face was so lovely, that when in the common cant of praise	SS	I	10	46	2
But when this passed away, when her spirits became	SS	I	10	46	2
spirits became collected, when she saw that to the perfect	SS	I	10	46	2
vivacity, and above all, when she heard him declare that	SS	I	10	46	2
She could not be silent when such points were introduced,	SS	I	10	47	3
to Elinor, when it ceased to be noticed by them.	SS	I	10	49	12
arose, was removed when his feelings began really to call	SS	I	10	49	12
of five and thirty hope, when opposed by a very lively one	SS	I	10	50	12
said Willoughby one day, when they were talking of him	SS	I	10	50	14
threatened me with rain when I wanted it to be fine; he	SS	I	10	52	28
Little had Mrs. Dashwood or her daughters imagined, when	SS	I	11	53	1
When Marianne was recovered, the schemes of amusement at	SS	I	11	53	1
When he was present she had no eyes for any one else.	SS	I	11	53	3
for half the time; and when obliged to separate for a	SS	I	11	54	3
one evening at the park, when they were sitting down	SS	I	11	55	8
no, do not desire it,--for when the romantic refinements	SS	I	11	56	17
she added, "and when it arrives, we will ride every day.	SS	I	12	58	2
Willoughby when she saw him next, that it must be declined.	SS	I	12	59	5
She was faithful to her word; and when Willoughby called	SS	I	12	59	6
When you leave Barton to form your own establishment in a	SS	I	12	59	6
to her eldest sister, when they were next by themselves.	SS	I	12	60	8
Last night after tea, when you and mama went out of the	SS	I	12	60	13
When Mrs. Jennings attacked her one evening at the park,	SS	I	12	61	15
"It shall not be put off when we are so near it.	SS	I	13	64	25
said Sir John, "when once you are determined on any thing.	SS	I	13	65	32
"Well then, when will you come back again?"	SS	I	13	65	34
But it is so uncertain, when I may have it in my power to	SS	I	13	65	36
When Sir John returned, he joined most heartily in the	SS	I	13	66	60
Marianne never looked happier than when she got into it.	SS	I	13	66	60
It is a very large one I know, and when I come to see you,	SS	I	13	67	64
it wanted it very much, when I was there six years ago."	SS	I	13	67	64
and great was her surprise when she found that every	SS	I	13	68	67
time, for we always know when we are acting wrong, and	SS	I	13	68	72
it is, because he looked so conscious when I mentioned her.	SS	I	14	70	2
unemployed sum may remain, when I make up my accounts in	SS	I	14	72	10
"How often did I wish," added he, "when I was at Allenham	SS	I	14	73	17
hear from Mrs. Smith, when I next came into the country,	SS	I	14	73	17
to dinner?" said Mrs. Dashwood when he was leaving them.	SS	I	14	74	21
account for, though when she considered what Marianne's	SS	I	15	77	19
This is strange indeed, when your eyes have been	SS	I	15	79	32
They saw nothing of Marianne till dinner time, when she	SS	I	15	82	46
bed in more need of repose than when she lay down in it.	SS	I	16	83	1
When breakfast was over she walked out by herself, and	SS	I	16	83	2
when circumstances make the revealment of it eligible.	SS	I	16	84	9
We will put it by, that when he comes again	SS	I	16	85	12
hills, and could never be found when the others set off.	SS	I	16	85	15
And was hastening to meet him, when Elinor cried out, "	SS	I	16	86	17 18
she was hurrying back, when the voices of both her sisters	SS	I	16	86	20
Edward?" said she, when dinner was over and they had drawn	SS	I	17	90	2
greater attention; but when have I advised you to adopt	SS	I	17	94	39
when I am only kept back by my natural awkwardness.	SS	I	17	94	42
particularly struck him, when Edward interrupted her by	SS	I	18	96	4
what she really felt--but when she saw how much she had	SS	I	18	98	12
puzzled him before; and when their visitors left them, he	SS	I	18	100	23
when his enjoyment among his friends was at the height.	SS	I	19	101	1
he should go when he left them--but still, go he must.	SS	I	19	101	1
She would have been glad to know when these difficulties	SS	I	19	102	2
opposition was to yield,--when Mrs. Ferrars would be	SS	I	19	102	2
at least--you would know where to go when you left them."	SS	I	19	102	3
side, but I was too old when the subject was first started	SS	I	19	103	4
There were moments in abundance, when, if not by the	SS	I	19	105	12
except when she laughed, and smiled when she went away.	SS	I	19	106	22
When Lady Middleton rose to go away, Mr. Palmer rose also,	SS	I	19	108	37
When they were seated in the dining room, Sir John	SS	I	20	111	18
"Did not I tell you, Sir John, when you spoke to me about	SS	I	20	111	20
and when he scolded or abused her, she was highly diverted.	SS	I	20	112	26
"How charming it will be," said Charlotte, "when he is in	SS	I	20	113	35
When we met him, he turned back and walked with us; and so	SS	I	20	115	50
When is it to take place?"	SS	I	20	115	52
unfortunately founded, when she advised her daughter not	SS	I	21	118	2
When their promised visit to the park and consequent	SS	I	21	120	6
for some kind of sense, when she saw with what constant	SS	I	21	120	6
of telling lies when politeness required it, always fell.	SS	I	21	122	14
She did her best when thus called on, by speaking of Lady	SS	I	21	122	14
when alluded to, or even openly mentioned by Sir John.	SS	I	21	126	41
upon herself--when we may be very intimately connected."	SS	I	22	129	11
And I do not think Mr. Ferrars can be displeased, when he	SS	I	22	130	16
She put it into her hands as she spoke, and when Elinor	SS	I	22	132	26
in the world t'other day, when Edward's name was mentioned	SS	I	22	133	42
Did not you think him dreadful low-spirited when he was at	SS	I	22	133	46
He was so miserable when he left us at Longstaple, to go	SS	I	22	133	46
"Did he come from your uncle's then, when he visited us?"	SS	I	22	134	47
"We did indeed, particularly so when he first arrived."	SS	I	22	134	51
I gave him a lock of my hair set in a ring when he was at	SS	I	22	135	54
Perhaps you might notice the ring when you saw him?"	SS	I	22	135	54
they now likely to be, when the object of his engagement	SS	II	1	140	3
her own expectations, that when she joined them at dinner	SS	II	1	141	4
engaging Lucy in private, when Sir John called at the	SS	II	1	143	9
of Lady Middleton than when her husband united them	SS	II	1	143	9
in his behaviour to me when we met, or any lowness of	SS	II	2	147	12
revived by Elinor, and when entered on by Lucy, who seldom	SS	II	2	151	42
well in my chaise; and when we are in town, if you do not	SS	II	3	153	2
So I would advise you two, to set off for town, when you	SS	II	3	154	3
When you and the Middletons are gone, we shall go on so	SS	II	3	155	8
You will find Margaret so improved when you come back	SS	II	3	155	8
or the faults of his wife, when I consider whose son he is,	SS	II	3	156	8
shock might be the less when the whole truth were revealed,	SS	II	3	157	17
went to town or not, and when she saw her mother so	SS	II	3	158	20

speaking, except when any object of picturesque beauty SS II 4 160 2
She could scarcely eat any dinner, and when they SS II 4 161 6
at a neighbouring door, when a loud one was suddenly heard SS II 4 161 7
throw herself into his arms, when Colonel Brandon appeared. SS II 4 161 7
you think he said when he heard of your coming with mama? SS II 4 164 22
eagerly up stairs, and when Elinor followed, she found her SS II 4 165 25
said Mrs. Jennings, when they met at breakfast the SS II 5 167 1
I always pity them when they do; they seem to take it so SS II 5 167 1
and his spirits were certainly worse than when at Barton. SS II 5 169 12
His card was on the table, when they came in from the SS II 5 169 13
She insisted on being left behind, the next morning, when SS II 5 169 15
glance at her sister when they returned was enough to SS II 5 169 16
The invitation was accepted: but when the hour of SS II 5 170 28
Elinor found, when the evening was over, that disposition SS II 5 170 29
"When do you go back again?" SS II 5 171 33
of him not to give you the meeting when he was invited." SS II 5 171 36
Her letter was scarcely finished, when a rap foretold a SS II 5 172 40
a voice of some agitation, when he was to congratulate her SS II 5 172 40
its doubts, if I had not, when the servant let me in to- SS II 5 173 44
to say anything, and even when her spirits were recovered, SS II 5 173 45
her sister's presence; and when at last they were told SS II 6 175 1
When they had paid their tribute of politeness by SS II 6 175 2
the common working table, when a letter was delivered to SS II 7 181 7
Pray, when are they to be married?" SS II 7 181 8
allow to be impossible, when you understand that my SS II 7 183 13
had been in the room, that when on hearing a carriage SS II 7 184 16
had really slept; and now, when her mind was no longer SS II 7 185 16
more than surprise, when you know that I am in town. SS II 7 186 38
condemned by the event, when Marianne, perceiving that she SS II 7 188 43
When he told me that it might be many weeks before we meet SS II 7 189 46
For a moment or two she could say no more; but when this SS II 7 189 47
48

But to appear happy when I am so miserable--Oh! who can SS II 7 190 54
Willoughby, where was your heart, when you wrote those SS II 7 190 56
When there, though looking most wretchedly, she ate more SS II 8 193 6
But when there is plenty of money on one side, and next to SS II 8 194 8
Well, it don't signify talking, but when a young man, be SS II 8 194 10
Sir John and my daughters will be when they hear it! SS II 8 195 16
to know any thing about it when she is present; and the SS II 8 195 17
In one thing, however, she was uniform, when it came to SS II 9 201 2
and in a determined silence when obliged to endure it. SS II 9 201 2
But the letter, when she was calm enough to read it, SS II 9 202 8
a quarter of an hour, when Marianne, whose nerves could SS II 9 203 11
"You shall; and, to be brief, when I quitted Barton last SS II 9 204 20
I cannot remember the time when I did not love Eliza; and SS II 9 205 24
when I heard, about two years afterwards, of her divorce. SS II 9 206 24
My first care, when I did arrive, was of course to seek SS II 9 207 26
Little did Mr. Willoughby imagine, I suppose, when his SS II 9 209 30
When I came to you last week and found you alone, I came SS II 9 210 32
truth; though irresolute what to do when it was known. SS II 9 210 32
towards her own condition, when she compares it with that SS II 9 210 32
that of my poor Eliza, when she considers the wretched and SS II 9 210 32
the name of her lover; and when he returned to town, which SS II 9 211 38
When the particulars of this conversation were repeated by SS II 10 212 1
avoiding Colonel Brandon when he called, in her speaking SS II 10 212 1
Marianne's affliction be, when her mother could talk of SS II 10 213 2
pitiable than when she first learnt to expect the event. SS II 10 217 17
most likely change your mind when it came to the point. SS II 10 217 21
day, when she saw him crossing the street to the house. SS II 10 218 26
and sister, Miss Dashwood, when they come to town," said SS II 10 218 30
When they stopped at the door, Mrs. Jennings recollected SS II 11 220 2
it, when another gentleman presented himself at her side. SS II 11 221 6
that in all probability when she dies you will not be SS II 11 226 42
Twice was his card found on the table, when they returned SS II 12 230 5
a severe disappointment when she told her that Edward SS II 12 231 11
which he could not conceal when they were together. SS II 12 231 11
When the ladies withdrew to the drawing-room after dinner, SS II 12 233 19
assertion; and Marianne, when called on for her's, SS II 12 234 25
being from home, when he called before in Berkeley-Street. SS II 13 241 20
When that was once done, however, it was time for the SS II 13 242 23
But what was that, when such friends were to be met?" SS II 13 243 37
But that was not enough; for when people are determined on SS II 14 248 6
five minutes of their being together, when it was finished. SS II 14 249 8
his name from the latter, when they both came towards her, SS II 14 250 11
so I often tell my mother, when she is grieving about it. SS II 14 251 13
to his wife, for her approbation, when they got home. SS II 14 252 20
When the note was shewn to Elinor, as it was within ten SS II 14 254 27
When I got to Mr. Palmer's, I found Charlotte quite in a SS III 1 257 5
Lord! what a taking poor Mr. Edward will be in when he SS III 1 259 7
that he may be within call when Mrs. Ferrars is told of it, SS III 1 259 7
When Lucy first came to Barton-Park last November, she SS III 1 262 16
And all this has been going on at a time, when, as you too SS III 1 264 29
one chair to another, and when Mrs. Jennings talked of SS III 1 265 33
"What poor Mrs. Ferrars suffered, when first Fanny broke SS III 1 266 38
a-year; offered even, when matters grew desperate, to make SS III 1 266 38
a man live on it!--and when to that is added the SS III 1 268 50
on which either of them were fond of dwelling when alone. SS III 2 270 1
Richard said himself, that when it came to the point, he SS III 2 272 16
Ferrars would be off; and when Edward did not come near us SS III 2 272 16
Miss Dashwood, do you think people make love when any body SS III 2 274 18
for a year or two back, when Martha Sharpe and I had so SS III 2 274 20
life I know what my cousins will say, when they hear of it. SS III 2 275 22
and the dear children, when you chance to see them, and SS III 2 278 30
of her good-will, when a plan was suggested, which, though SS III 3 279 1
When she told Marianne what she had done, however, her SS III 3 279 2
Jennings's address to him when he first called on her, SS III 3 280 8
how forlorn we shall be, when I come back!-- SS III 3 280 8
her catching a syllable, when another lucky stop in SS III 3 281 9
10

Such was the sentence which, when misunderstood, so justly SS III 3 284 24
as to that, when a man has once made up his mind to such a SS III 4 285 5
by word of mouth, when her visitor entered, to force her SS III 4 287 26
Edward made no answer; but when she had turned away her SS III 4 290 39
"When I see him again," said Elinor to herself, as the SS III 4 291 44
When Mrs. Jennings came home, though she returned from SS III 4 291 46
When the marriage takes place, I fear she must hear of it SS III 5 296 18
When Edward's unhappy match takes place, depend upon it SS III 5 296 20
him beyond measure;--and when to that was added the SS III 5 298 33
was so shocked in my life, as when it all burst forth. SS III 5 299 35
place, when it was not for me, you know, to interfere. SS III 5 299 37
He had just settled this point with great composure, when SS III 5 300 38
Jennings, but even Lucy, when they parted, gave her a SS III 6 301 2
to quit it, could not, when it came to the point, bid SS III 6 301 4
Elinor prevailed on her, when she went to bed, to try one SS III 6 306 17
of her amendment; and when, at last, she went early to bed, SS III 7 307 1
expectation of both; and when Marianne, after persisting SS III 7 307 2
were almost done away; for when Mr. Harris arrived, he SS III 7 310 8
fixing on the time when Marianne would be able to travel. SS III 7 310 8
from so painful a slumber, when Marianne, suddenly SS III 7 310 10
11

when the former--but not till after five o'clock--arrived. SS III 7 312 19
as for their mother, when Mrs. Jennings considered that SS III 7 313 20
She was calm, except when she thought of her mother, but SS III 7 313 21
Harris at four o'clock;--when his assurances, his SS III 7 314 22
of what anxiety was--but when she saw, on her frequent and SS III 7 315 25
The time was now drawing on, when Colonel Brandon might be SS III 7 315 26
was already on the lock, when its action was suspended by SS III 8 317 1
2

When I first became intimate in your family, I had no SS III 8 319 29
It is astonishing, when I reflect on what it was, and what SS III 8 320 29
what I spent with her, when I felt my intentions were SS III 8 321 34
Even then, however, when fully determined on paying my SS III 8 321 34

Her sorrow, her disappointment, her deep regret, when I SS III 8 324 42
reflections so cheerful--when I looked forward everything SS III 8 325 45
everything so inviting!--when I looked back at Barton, the SS III 8 325 45
"When the first of her's reached me, (as it immediately SS III 8 325 50
Yet when I thought of her to-day as really dying, it was a SS III 8 327 55
She knew I had no regard for her when we married.-- SS III 8 329 65
"Will you repeat to your sister when she is recovered, SS III 8 330 67
Sir John Middleton, and when he saw who I was--for the SS III 8 330 69
was done away, that when we parted, he almost shook me by SS III 8 330 69
torn himself, now, when no longer allowable, governed SS III 8 331 70
When at last she returned to the unconscious Marianne, she SS III 9 333 3
could be even prudent, when the life of a child was at SS III 9 334 5
When there, at her own particular request, for she was SS III 10 340 1
But here, Elinor could neither wonder nor blame; and when SS III 10 342 7
"When the weather is settled, and I have recovered my SS III 10 343 9
Her smile however changed to a sigh when she remembered SS III 10 343 10
the important hill behind, when pausing with her eyes SS III 10 344 12
13

at last with a sigh, "when I wish his secret reflections SS III 10 345 24
No;--not less when I knew you to be unhappy, than when I SS III 10 346 28
In the evening, when they were all three together, SS III 11 349 3
have led you, I know, when aware of your situation, to SS III 11 350 9
which afterwards, when his own were engaged, made him SS III 11 351 11
quite so much vigour as when they first came to Barton, at SS III 11 352 20
to Exeter on business; and when, as he waited at table, he SS III 11 353 22
23

when they come back, they'd make sure to come and see you." SS III 11 354 27
When the dessert and the wine were arranged, and Mrs. SS III 11 355 46
"When do you write to Colonel Brandon, ma'am?" was an SS III 12 358 5
Scarcely had she so determined it, when the figure of a SS III 12 358 8
Elinor's lips had moved with her mother's, and when the SS III 12 359 12
When Elinor had ceased to rejoice in the dryness of the SS III 12 359 14
This only need be said;--that when they all sat down to SS III 13 361 3
Had my mother given me some active profession when I was SS III 13 362 5
But when the second moment had passed, when she found SS III 13 363 8
head when the acquaintance between them first began. SS III 13 364 12
for what followed;--and when at last it burst on him in a SS III 13 364 13
the engagement or not, when I was renounced by my mother, SS III 13 367 22
how could I suppose, when she so earnestly, so warmly SS III 13 367 22
at Norland, when he must have felt his own inconstancy. SS III 13 368 25
"And when she has forgiven you, perhaps a little humility SS III 13 372 44
more than three; but when she found that, though perfectly SS III 14 373 3
tell what may happen--for, when people are much thrown SS III 14 375 9
When Robert first sought her acquaintance, and privately SS III 14 376 11
Some doubts always lingered in her mind when they parted, SS III 14 376 11
John and Mrs. Jennings, when Marianne was taken from them, SS III 14 380 20
he paid attention to, when he came into this country, six W 316 1
"When first we knew Tom Musgrave, continued Miss W. W 316 2
means anything serious, & when he had trifled with her W 317 2
When she went away the other day she said it should be the W 317 2
she is all gentleness & mildness when anybody is by.-- W 318 2
"I wonder I never mentioned it when I wrote. W 321 2
great wish of obliging--& when they returned to the W 323 3
as he helped her to wine, when they were drawn round the W 324 4
When an old lady plays the fool, it is not in the course W 326 6
& ate an additional muffin when they were going to sit up W 326 7
He came into possession of it, when he was very young, & W 328 8
The two first dances were not quite over, when the W 329 9
before his mother, wondering when they should begin.-- W 330 11
near her, when you know what a partner he is to have. W 330 11
not unwilling to speak, when her questions or remarks gave W 331 11
them both close to her when she moved into the Tearoom; & W 331 11
a little bustle & croud when they thus adjourned for W 332 11
Do you think Miss Osborne will keep her word with me, when W 332 12
"When shall you come to osborne castle?"-- W 332 12
her engagement increased, when as she was sitting in the W 333 13
Ld Osborne's remark, when his friend carried him the news-- W 335 13
I assure you--I shall not shew myself here again when I W 335 13
"I was always engaged when they asked me." W 336 14
"No--perhaps not--but I remember my dear when you & I did W 337 15
the bell & make enquiries, when the light sound of a W 338 17
ways of a man, when he is bent upon pleasing her.--" W 343 19
of a visitation--but when she heard Mr Howard spoken of as W 343 20
"I do not know when I have heard a discourse more to my W 343 20
He was at no loss for words;--but when Ld. Osborne had W 345 21
& I fancy Miss Watson--when once they had the inclination, W 345 21
his Lordship think;--and when he addressed her again, it W 346 21
The sisters looked on each other with astonishment, when W 347 22
Miss Penelope & Miss Margt were, when he first came in?-- W 347 22
Mr W was very far from being delighted, when he heard what W 348 22
And when T. Musgrave was met with again, he was W 348 22
being her constant resource when determined on pleasing.-- W 349 23
she did not like it better when she heard Margt 5 minutes W 351 24
Such, she feared would be Margaret's common voice, when W 351 25
I always wish to be treated quite "en famille" when I come W 351 25
It will be a sad break-up when he dies. W 353 26
Emma was glad when they were joined by the others; it was W 353 26
when you are out visitting, tho' you do not at home." W 353 26
Dinner came, & except when Mrs R. looked at her husband's W 353 27
When there is only one or two of you at home, you must be W 354 28
surprise than he received, when instead of being shewn W 355 28
When the tea-things were removed, Tom began to talk of his W 357 28
thus agreably occupied; & when Nanny came in with her W 359 28
made a confidante of Emma when they were alone for a short W 360 29
nor likely to lessen; & when thought had been freely W 361 31
When a woman has five grown up daughters, she ought to PP I 1 4 20
"But, my dear, you must indeed go and see Mr. Bingley when PP I 1 4 22
"Depend upon it, my dear, that when there are twenty, I PP I 1 5 33
When she was discontented she fancied herself nervous. PP I 1 5 34
"When is your next ball to be, Lizzy?" PP I 2 6 11
"Impossible, Mr. Bennet, impossible, when I am not PP I 2 7 15
the rest; though when the first tumult of joy was over, PP I 2 7 23
"What an excellent father you have, girls," said she, when PP I 2 8 26
visit, and determining when they should ask him to dinner. PP I 2 8 28
housekeeping, when an answer arrived which deferred it all. PP I 3 9 4
And when the party entered the assembly room, it PP I 3 10 4
When Jane and Elizabeth were alone, the former, who had PP I 4 14 1
But they are very pleasing women when you converse with PP I 4 15 10
deficient in good humour when they were pleased, nor in PP I 4 15 11
to consider his house as her home when it suited her. PP I 4 15 13
Mr. Bingley had not been of age two years, when he was PP I 4 16 13
When she is secure of him, there will be leisure for PP I 6 22 6
and when they next met, he looked at her only to criticise. PP I 6 23 12
uncommonly well just now, when I was teazing Colonel PP I 6 24 17
18

You cannot refuse to dance, I am sure, when so much beauty PP I 6 26 38
unwilling to receive it, when she instantly drew back, and PP I 6 26 38
her with some complacency, when thus accosted by Miss PP I 6 27 44
45

How long has she been such a favourite?--and pray when am PP I 6 27 51
than their sisters', and when nothing better offered, a PP I 7 28 3
in their eyes when opposed to the regimentals of an ensign. PP I 7 29 4
When they get to our age I dare say they will not think PP I 7 29 12
I remember the time when I liked a red coat myself very PP I 7 29 12
Miss Watson's as they did when they first came; she sees PP I 7 30 13
Breakfast was scarcely over when a servant from PP I 7 31 29
30

"Well, my dear," said Mr. Bennet, when Elizabeth had read PP I 7 31 31
You will not be fit to be seen when you get there." PP I 7 32 34
The distance is nothing, when one has a motive; only three PP I 7 32 37
She was not equal, however, to much conversation, and when PP I 7 33 43
When breakfast was over, they were joined by the sisters; PP I 7 33 44

Context					
to like them herself, when she saw how much affection and	PP	I	7	33	44
When the clock struck three, Elizabeth felt that she must	PP	I	7	33	45
pressing to accept it, when Jane testified such concern in	PP	I	7	33	45
indifference towards Jane when not immediately before them,	PP	I	8	35	1
and play at cards, who when he found her prefer a plain	PP	I	8	35	2
When dinner was over, she returned directly to Jane, and	PP	I	8	35	3
remarkably well, when she came into the room this morning.	PP	I	8	36	7
till late in the evening, when she had the comfort of	PP	I	8	37	21
of seeing her asleep, and when it appeared to her rather	PP	I	8	37	21
Charles, when you build your house, I wish it may be half	PP	I	8	38	33
answered this description, when Mr. Hurst called them to	PP	I	8	40	55
"Eliza Bennet," said Miss Bingley, when the door was	PP	I	8	40	56
"When I am in the country," he replied, "I never wish to	PP	I	9	43	22
leave it; and when I am in town it is pretty much the same.	PP	I	9	43	22
When she was only fifteen, there was a gentleman at my	PP	I	9	44	31
to keep my engagement; and when your sister is recovered,	PP	I	9	45	37
And when you have given your ball," she added, "I shall	PP	I	9	46	38
When you told Mrs. Bennet this morning that if you ever	PP	I	10	49	27
and of a Sunday evening when he has nothing to do."	PP	I	10	50	39
When that business was over, he applied to Miss Bingley	PP	I	10	51	45
mother-in-law a few hints, when this desirable event takes	PP	I	10	52	55
When the ladies removed after dinner, Elizabeth ran up to	PP	I	11	54	1
But when the gentlemen entered, Jane was no longer the	PP	I	11	54	2
When tea was over, Mr. Hurst reminded his sister-in-law of	PP	I	11	54	3
When I have a house of my own, I shall be miserable if I	PP	I	11	55	4
quest of some amusement; when hearing her brother	PP	I	11	55	5
					6
affection for Jane; and when they parted, after assuring	PP	I	12	60	5
The evening conversation, when they were all assembled,	PP	I	12	60	6
It is from my cousin, Mr. Collins, who, when I am dead,	PP	I	13	61	6
There is no knowing how estates will go when once they	PP	I	13	65	24
At present I will not say more, but perhaps when we are	PP	I	13	65	25
During dinner, Mr. Bennet scarcely spoke at all; but when	PP	I	14	66	1
drawing-room again, and when tea was over, glad to invite	PP	I	14	68	13
about it, and to ask when Mr. Denny comes back from town."	PP	I	14	68	14
Lady Catherine de Bourgh when the living of Hunsford was	PP	I	15	70	1
just gained the pavement when the two gentlemen turning	PP	I	15	72	8
together very agreeably, when the sound of horses drew	PP	I	15	72	8
fix his eyes on Elizabeth, when they were suddenly	PP	I	15	73	8
Bennets were come away, when her civility was claimed	PP	I	15	73	11
When this information was given, and they had all taken	PP	I	16	75	2
much gratification; but when Mrs. Philips understood from	PP	I	16	75	2
who was its proprietor, when she had listened to the	PP	I	16	75	2
The gentlemen did approach; and when Mr. Wickham walked	PP	I	16	76	3
When the card tables were placed, he had an opportunity of	PP	I	16	76	6
nothing of his going away when I was at Netherfield.	PP	I	16	78	19
done it; but when the living fell, it was given elsewhere."	PP	I	16	79	25
superintendance, and when immediately before my father's	PP	I	16	81	37
had lost every point; but when Mrs. Philips began to	PP	I	16	83	49
"I know very well, madam," said he, "that when persons sit	PP	I	16	83	50
would have much to suffer when the affair became public.	PP	I	17	86	8
When those dances were over she returned to Charlotte	PP	I	18	90	5
in conversation with her, when she found herself suddenly	PP	I	18	90	5
When the dancing recommenced, however, and Darcy	PP	I	18	90	8
had gone down the dance, when he asked her if she and her	PP	I	18	93	18
the temptation, added, "when you met us there the other	PP	I	18	92	18
often repeated, especially when a certain desirable event,	PP	I	18	92	23
They had not long separated when Miss Bingley came towards	PP	I	18	94	44
					45
his own inclination, and when she ceased speaking, replied	PP	I	18	97	60
					61
unrestrained wonder, and when at last Mr. Collins allowed	PP	I	18	98	61
When they sat down to supper, therefore, she considered it	PP	I	18	98	63
But not long was the interval of tranquillity; for when	PP	I	18	100	68
He took the hint, and when Mary had finished her second	PP	I	18	100	68
					69
When at length they arose to take leave, Mrs. Bennet was	PP	I	18	103	76
fair daughter Elizabeth, when I solicit for the honour of	PP	I	19	104	1
					2
away, when Elizabeth called out, "dear ma'am, do not go.--	PP	I	19	104	4
					5
to her, especially when tempered with the silence and	PP	I	19	106	10
be as little as possible, when the melancholy event takes	PP	I	19	106	10
reproach shall ever pass my lips when we are married."	PP	I	19	106	10
secretly mean to accept, when he first applies for their	PP	I	19	107	13
And you may be certain that when I have the honour of	PP	I	19	107	15
thus addressed her, "when I do myself the honour of	PP	I	19	108	16
					17
"and I am persuaded that when sanctioned by the express	PP	I	19	109	21
you," said he, when she had finished her speech.	PP	I	20	111	9
not know who is to maintain you when your father is dead.--	PP	I	20	113	28
is never so perfect as when the blessing dented begins to	PP	I	20	114	32
When they had gained their own room, Jane taking out the	PP	I	21	116	6
					7
I will read it to you--"when my brother left us yesterday,	PP	I	21	117	10
					11
same time convinced that when Charles gets to town, he	PP	I	21	117	10
					11
misleading me, I think, when I call Charles most capable	PP	I	21	118	14
from the notion that when there has been one intermarriage,	PP	I	21	119	20
of your merit than when he took leave of you on Tuesday,	PP	I	21	119	20
were so favourable that when they parted at night, she	PP	I	22	121	1
charged Mr. Collins when he returned to Longbourn to	PP	I	22	123	3
leave-taking was performed when the ladies moved for the	PP	I	22	123	4
But when you have had time to think it all over, I hope	PP	I	22	125	17
supposed it possible that when called into action, she	PP	I	22	125	18
authorised to mention it, when Sir William Lucas himself	PP	I	23	126	1
Hope was over, entirely over; and when Jane could attend	PP	II	1	133	2
liking, which ceased when he saw her no more; but though	PP	II	1	137	26
When is your turn to come?	PP	II	1	138	27
When this was done, she had a less active part to play.	PP	II	2	139	3
When alone with Elizabeth afterwards, she spoke more on	PP	II	2	140	6
girl for a few weeks, and when accident separates them, so	PP	II	2	140	6
When the engagement was for home, some of the officers	PP	II	2	142	18
reputed disposition when quite a lad, which might agree	PP	II	2	143	20
When I am in company with him, I will not be wishing.	PP	II	3	145	7
her farewell visit; and when she rose to take leave,	PP	II	3	145	11
herself to be; though, when the letters were read,	PP	II	3	146	19
arrival in London; and when she wrote again, Elizabeth	PP	II	3	147	20
She wrote again when the visit was paid, and she had seen	PP	II	3	147	23
judgment, at my expence, when I confess myself to have	PP	II	3	148	26
When she did come, it was very evident that she had no	PP	II	3	148	26
altered a creature, that when she went away, I was	PP	II	3	148	26
miss her, and who, when it came to the point, so little	PP	II	4	151	2
watching their arrival; when they entered the passage she	PP	II	4	152	5
And when we do return, it shall not be like other	PP	II	4	154	23
in our imaginations; nor, when we attempt to describe any	PP	II	4	154	23
When they left the high road for the lane to Hunsford,	PP	II	5	155	2
coming, when she found herself so affectionately received.	PP	II	5	155	3
When Mr. Collins said any thing of which his wife might	PP	II	5	156	4
When Mr. Collins could be forgotten, there was really a	PP	II	5	157	5
It was spoken of again while they were at dinner, when Mr.	PP	II	5	157	6
					7
with some portion of her notice when service is over.	PP	II	5	157	7
been already written; and when it closed, Elizabeth in the	PP	II	5	157	10
It is the greatest of favours when Miss de Bourgh comes in.	PP	II	5	158	17
When the ladies were separating for the toilette, he said	PP	II	6	160	5
					6
When they ascended the steps to the hall, Maria's alarm	PP	II	6	161	9
When, after examining the mother, in whose countenance and	PP	II	6	162	12
when any dish on the table proved a novelty to them.	PP	II	6	163	14
When the ladies returned to the drawing room, there was	PP	II	6	163	15
When the gentlemen had joined them, and tea was over, the	PP	II	6	166	41
relate to the game, except when Mrs. Jenkinson expressed	PP	II	6	166	41
When Lady Catherine and her daughter had played as long as	PP	II	6	166	42
him the country; but when he went away, the whole family	PP	II	7	168	1
when Mr. Collins returned the gentlemen accompanied him.	PP	II	7	170	7
no means so acceptable as when she could get nobody else;	PP	II	8	172	2
"We are speaking of music, madam," said he, when no longer	PP	II	8	173	5
It cannot be done too much; and when I next write to her,	PP	II	8	173	10
When coffee was over, Colonel Fitzwilliam reminded	PP	II	8	173	12
business into the village, when she was startled by a ring	PP	II	9	177	1
all impertinent questions, when the door opened, and to	PP	II	9	177	1
They then sat down, and when her enquiries after Rosings	PP	II	9	177	3
emergence recollecting when she had seen him last in	PP	II	9	177	3
					4
He and his sisters were well, I hope, when you left London.	PP	II	9	177	4
He has many friends, and he is at a time of life when	PP	II	9	178	8
Lady Catherine, I believe, did a great deal to it when mr.	PP	II	9	178	12
But when Elizabeth told of his silence, it did not seem	PP	II	9	180	28
opening his lips; and when he did speak, it seemed the	PP	II	9	180	29
not written in spirits, when, instead of being again	PP	II	10	182	2
When have you been prevented by want of money from going	PP	II	10	183	11
When she thought of her mother indeed, her confidence gave	PP	II	10	187	40
When they were gone, Elizabeth, as if intending to	PP	II	11	188	1
very differently affected, when, to her utter amazement,	PP	II	11	188	3
to answer him with patience, when he should have done.	PP	II	11	189	6
exasperate farther, and when he ceased, the colour rose	PP	II	11	189	6
					7
to speak with composure when she said, "you are mistaken,	PP	II	11	192	23
					24
She was proceeding directly to her favourite walk, when	PP	II	12	195	1
of continuing her walk, when she caught a glimpse of a	PP	II	12	195	2
to be in future secured, when the following account of my	PP	II	12	196	5
To persuade him against returning into Hertfordshire, when	PP	II	12	199	5
If Elizabeth, when Mr. Darcy gave her the letter, did not	PP	II	13	204	1
But when this subject was succeeded by his account of Mr.	PP	II	13	204	2
account of Mr. Wickham, when she read with somewhat	PP	II	13	204	2
This must be the grossest falsehood!"--and when she had	PP	II	13	204	2
So far each recital confirmed the other: but when she came	PP	II	13	205	3
But when she read, and re-read with the closest attention,	PP	II	13	205	3
allow that Mr. Bingley, when questioned by Jane, had long	PP	II	13	207	6
When she came to that part of the letter in which her	PP	II	13	208	10
When my niece Georgiana went to ramsgate last summer, I	PP	II	14	211	13
When she remembered the style of his address, she was	PP	II	14	212	17
full of indignation; but when she considered how unjustly	PP	II	14	212	17
When to these recollections was added the development of	PP	II	14	213	19
When they parted, Lady Catherine, with great condescension,	PP	II	14	214	21
the point of being closed, when he suddenly reminded them,	PP	II	15	217	8
And when her sisters abused it as ugly, she added, with	PP	II	16	219	4
uglier in the shop; and when I have bought some prettier-	PP	II	16	219	4
When Denny, and Wickham, and Pratt, and two or three more	PP	II	16	221	17
had not been sick; and when we got to the George, I do	PP	II	16	222	22
And then when we came away it was such fun!	PP	II	16	222	22
"But you will know it, when I have told you what happened	PP	II	17	224	8
"I do not know when I have been more shocked," said she.	PP	II	17	225	12
"Lizzy, when you first read that letter, I am sure you	PP	II	17	226	18
often talk of having Longbourn when your father is dead.	PP	II	17	228	33
"I am sure," said she, "I cried for two days together when	PP	II	18	229	4
while she added, "when I said that he improved on	PP	II	18	234	35
					36
His fear of her, has always operated, I know, when they	PP	II	18	235	38
When the party broke up, Lydia returned with Mrs. Forster	PP	II	18	235	40
When Elizabeth had rejoiced over Wickham's departure, she	PP	II	19	237	3
When Lydia went away, she promised to write very often and	PP	II	19	238	5
only was wanting of it, when a letter arrived from Mrs.	PP	II	19	238	7
Accordingly, when she retired at night, she asked the	PP	II	19	241	17
see the house herself; and when the subject was revived	PP	II	19	241	17
some perturbation; and when at length they turned in at	PP	III	1	245	1
one of miss Darcy, drawn when she was only eight years old.	PP	III	1	247	20
"Except," thought Elizabeth, "when she goes to ramsgate."	PP	III	1	248	26
"Yes, sir; but I do not know when that will be.	PP	III	1	248	28
When children, are good-natured when they grow up; and he	PP	III	1	249	33
who had taken a liking to the room, when last at Pemberley.	PP	III	1	249	43
Mrs. Reynolds anticipated Miss Darcy's delight, when she	PP	III	1	250	45
remembered to have sometimes seen, when he looked at her.	PP	III	1	250	47
When all of the house that was open to general inspection	PP	III	1	251	49
Nor did he seem much more at ease; when he spoke, his	PP	III	1	252	52
in rosing's park, when he put his letter into her hand!	PP	III	1	252	54
Elizabeth longed to explore its windings; but when they	PP	III	1	254	57
and "charming," when some unlucky recollections obtruded,	PP	III	1	254	57
"What will be his surprise," thought she, "when he knows	PP	III	1	255	58
Her thoughts were instantly driven back to the time when	PP	III	1	256	62
They soon outstripped the others, and when they had	PP	III	1	257	65
Mr. Darcy handed the ladies into the carriage, and when it	PP	III	1	257	66
she had liked him better when they met in Kent than before,	PP	III	1	258	71
there is something pleasing about his mouth when he speaks.	PP	III	1	258	74
with the same family, when the sound of a carriage drew	PP	III	2	260	1
for such a visitor, when Bingley's quick step was heard on	PP	III	2	261	5
He observed to her, at a moment when the others were	PP	III	2	262	8
We have not met since the 26th of November, when we were	PP	III	2	262	8
took occasion to ask her, when unattended to by any of the	PP	III	2	262	9
When she saw him thus seeking the acquaintance, and	PP	III	2	263	10
have been a disgrace; when she saw him thus civil, not	PP	III	2	263	10
unbending reserve as now, when no importance could result	PP	III	2	263	10
of his endeavours, and when even the acquaintance of those	PP	III	2	263	10
above half an hour, and when they arose to depart, Mr.	PP	III	2	263	11
others, found herself, when their visitors left them,	PP	III	2	264	12
Elizabeth was pleased, though, when she asked herself the	PP	III	2	266	17
sentence, when there was least danger of its being heard.	PP	III	3	267	4
not watch his behaviour when he first came into the room.	PP	III	3	268	8
When Darcy returned to the saloon, Miss Bingley could not	PP	III	3	270	12
continued, "I remember, when we first knew her in	PP	III	3	271	16
					17
"but that was only when I first knew her, for it is many	PP	III	3	271	18
he shook his head when I expressed my hopes, and said he	PP	III	4	275	5
"When I consider," she added, in a yet more agitated voice,	PP	III	4	277	12
"When my eyes were opened to his real character.--Oh! had	PP	III	4	277	18
could have loved him, as now, when all love must be vain.	PP	III	4	278	19
"John told us Mr. Darcy was here when you sent for us;--	PP	III	4	280	26
Darcy; and you, yourself, when last at Longbourn, heard in	PP	III	5	284	14
And when I returned home, the ----shire was to leave	PP	III	5	285	16
And even when it was settled that Lydia should go with Mrs.	PP	III	5	285	16
"When they all removed to Brighton, therefore, you had no	PP	III	5	285	17
When first he entered the corps, she was ready enough to	PP	III	5	285	18
entered the paddock; and when the carriage drove up to the	PP	III	5	286	21
When they were all in the drawing room, the questions	PP	III	5	287	33
And now do, when you get to town, find them out, wherever	PP	III	5	288	38
being gone to Scotland: when that apprehension first got	PP	III	5	290	46
"Yes; but when questioned by him Denny denied knowing any	PP	III	5	290	48
"My dear Harriet, "you will laugh when you know where I am	PP	III	5	291	60
when I write to them, and sign my name Lydia Wickham.	PP	III	5	291	60
Tell him I hope he will excuse me when he knows all, and	PP	III	5	291	60
I shall send for my clothes when I get to Longbourn; but I	PP	III	5	292	60
Lydia!" cried Elizabeth when she had finished it.	PP	III	5	292	61
When he was gone, they were certain at least of receiving	PP	III	6	294	2
as the time was now come, when if they had gone to	PP	III	6	295	4
most anxious part of each was when the post was expected.	PP	III	6	296	9
When Mrs. Bennet was told of this, she did not express so	PP	III	6	298	13
When Mr. Bennet arrived, he had all the appearance of his	PP	III	6	299	18
It was not till the afternoon, when he joined them at tea,	PP	III	6	299	19
of the expected summons, when they approached her, she	PP	III	7	301	1
stairs with their mother, when they were met by the butler,	PP	III	7	301	4
					5

be some little money, even when all his debts are PP III 7 302 14
"It is possible!" cried Elizabeth, when she had finished. PP III 7 303 15
What a meeting for her, when she first sees my aunt!" PP III 7 305 36
How merry we shall be together when we meet!" PP III 7 306 44
When first Mr. Bennet had married, economy was held to be PP III 8 308 3
When the first transports of rage which had produced his PP III 8 309 5
But when they had withdrawn, he said to her, "Mrs. Bennet, PP III 8 310 9
She became jealous of his esteem, when she could no longer PP III 8 311 13
She wanted to hear of him, when there seemed the least PP III 8 311 13
with him; when it was no longer likely they should meet. PP III 8 311 13
Lydia's being settled in the north, just when she had PP III 8 313 20
When Mr. Bennet wrote again to his brother, therefore, he PP III 8 314 22
their congratulations, and when at length they all sat PP III 9 315 4
Good gracious! when I went away, I am sure I had no more PP III 9 316 7
"Well, mamma," said she, when they were all returned to PP III 9 317 11
"And then when you go away, you may leave one or two of my PP III 9 317 15
You were not by, when I told mamma, and the others, all PP III 9 318 22
And then, you know, when once they get together, there is PP III 9 319 25
some time or other, and it did not much signify when. PP III 10 323 2
When all this was resolved on, he returned again to his PP III 10 324 2
be in London once more when the wedding took place, and PP III 10 324 2
He was exactly what he had been, when I knew him in PP III 10 325 2
respect, been as pleasing as when we were in Derbyshire. PP III 10 325 2
vanity was insufficient, when required to depend on his PP III 10 326 3
When I last saw her, she was not very promising. PP III 10 328 22
Did you ever hear Darcy mention the circumstance, when you PP III 10 328 28
"I did hear, too, that there was a time, when sermon- PP III 10 329 31
You may remember what I told you on that point, when first PP III 10 329 32
"Oh! my dear Lydia," she cried, "when shall we meet again?" PP III 11 330 3
look at me to day, Lizzy, when my aunt told us of the PP III 11 331 16
17
Happy shall I be, when his stay at Netherfield is over!" PP III 11 333 28
ashamed, especially when contrasted with the cold and PP III 11 335 41
There he had talked to her friends, when he could not to PP III 11 335 43
sound of his voice; and when occasionally, unable to PP III 11 335 43
More thoughfulness, and less anxiety to please than when PP III 11 336 43
"When you have killed all your own birds, Mr. Bingley," PP III 11 337 53
When first he came in, he had spoken to her but little; PP III 11 337 56
engaged, that she did not always know when she was silent. PP III 11 338 56
When the gentlemen rose to go away, Mrs. Bennet was PP III 11 338 57
Bingley," she added, "for when you went to town last PP III 11 338 58
my uncle and aunt, when he was in town; and why not to me? PP III 12 339 4
When they repaired to the dining-room, Elizabeth eagerly PP III 12 340 11
When the tea-things were removed, and the card tables PP III 12 342 26
to be soon joined by him, when all her views were PP III 12 342 26
advantage to her family, when in a happy humour, were so PP III 12 343 29
But when her mother was gone, Jane would not be prevailed PP III 13 344 10
Elizabeth would not observe her; and when at last Kitty PP III 13 345 11
But on returning to the drawing room, when her letter was PP III 13 346 22
point of going away again, when Bingley, who was as well as PP III 13 346 22
for half an hour; and when Mr. Bennet joined them at PP III 13 348 34
I remember, as soon as ever I saw him, when he first came PP III 13 348 40
till after supper; unless when some barbarous neighbour, PP III 13 349 43
of talking of her; and when Bingley was gone, Jane PP III 13 349 44
But when they see, as I trust they will, that their PP III 13 349 47
"Would you believe it, Lizzy, that when he went to town PP III 13 350 49
only a few weeks before, when Lydia had first run away, PP III 13 350 56
the door of the carriage, when turning hastily round, she PP III 14 358 72
73
was enough, at a time when the expectation of one wedding, PP III 15 360 1
If he is satisfied with only regretting me, when he might PP III 15 361 4
to herself; when her father continued, "you look conscious. PP III 15 362 11
12
she felt on the occasion; when it became apparent, that on PP III 15 363 22
Nay, when I read a letter of his, I cannot help giving him PP III 15 364 24
It was necessary to laugh, when she would rather have PP III 15 364 25
when Kitty left them, she went boldly on with him alone. PP III 16 365 2
"When I wrote that letter," replied Darcy, "I believed PP III 16 368 22
"I am almost afraid of asking what you thought of me; when PP III 16 369 29
When I went away, I felt that it would soon happen." PP III 16 370 38
"Did you speak from your own observation," said she, "when PP III 16 371 42
room, and from all the others when they sat down to table. PP III 17 372 1
She anticipated what would be felt in the family when her PP III 17 372 2
I feel more than I ought to do, when I tell you all." PP III 17 373 12
coming on so gradually, that I hardly know when it began. PP III 17 373 16
When convinced on that article, Miss Bennet had nothing PP III 17 373 17
Mr. Darcy appeared again, when, looking at him, she was a PP III 17 375 28
"Well, my dear," said he, when she ceased speaking, "I PP III 17 377 37
When her mother went up to her dressing-room at night, she PP III 17 377 42
"I can comprehend your going on charmingly, when you had PP III 18 380 1
me--but nobody thinks of that when they fall in love." PP III 18 380 5
What made you so shy of me, when you first called, and PP III 18 381 7
Why, especially, when you called, did you look as if you PP III 18 381 7
"You might have talked to me more when you came to dinner." PP III 18 381 11
I wonder when you would have spoken, if I had not asked PP III 18 381 13
pleasure dearly bought, when she saw Mr. Darcy exposed to PP III 18 384 26
He could even listen to Sir William Lucas, when he PP III 18 384 26
with delight to the time when they should be removed from PP III 18 384 27
He delighted in going to Pemberley, especially when he was PP III 19 385 2
It is a great comfort to have you so rich, and when you PP III 19 386 7
Their manner of living, even when the restoration of peace PP III 19 387 8
Lydia was occasionally a visitor there, when her husband PP III 19 387 9
Miss Ward's match, indeed, when it came to the point, was MP I 1 3 1
When the subject was brought forward again, her views were MP I 1 9 10
a girl should be fixed on, when she had so many fine boys, MP I 1 11 19
was sweet, and when she spoke her countenance was pretty. MP I 2 12 2
said Mrs. Norris when Fanny had left the room.-- MP I 2 13 5
never learnt French; and when they perceived her to be MP I 2 14 7
at her clothes; and when to these sorrows was added the MP I 2 14 8
of in the drawing-room when she left it at night, as MP I 2 14 9
her quiet passive manner, when she was found one morning MP I 2 15 9
"And when shall you do it?" MP I 2 16 12
"Yes, when you have written the letter I will take it to MP I 2 16 19
very useful, especially when that third was of an obliging, MP I 2 17 21
they could not but own, when their aunt inquired into her MP I 2 17 21
I cannot remember the time when I did not know a great MP I 2 18 25
indulgent to the latter, when it did not put herself to MP I 2 19 31
to the last, and the misery of the girl when he left her. MP I 2 21 34
Luckily the visit happened in the Christmas holidays, when MP I 2 21 34
Mr. Norris, which happened when Fanny was about fifteen, MP I 3 23 1
The time was now come when Sir Thomas expected his sister- MP I 3 24 7
her again, happening to be when Fanny was present, she MP I 3 24 7
my sister always meant to take you when Mr. Norris died. MP I 3 25 9
better already; and when you are her only companion, you MP I 3 26 25
Ah! cousin, when I remember how much I used to dread MP I 3 27 36
Miss Lee any longer, when Fanny goes to live with you?" MP I 3 28 38
39
She cried bitterly over this reflection when her uncle was MP I 3 33 64
it to all the others, when Sir Thomas's assurances of MP I 4 34 2
as her aunt's companion, when they called away the rest of MP I 4 35 6
horses at any time when they did not want them;" and as MP I 4 35 7
When he returned to understand how Fanny was situated, and MP I 4 36 7
of his stable at a time when a large part of his income MP I 4 36 7
return in September, for when September came, Sir Thomas MP I 4 37 9
arisen at a moment when he was beginning to turn all his MP I 4 38 9
very often thought; always when they were in the company MP I 4 38 9
her eighteenth year, when the society of the village MP I 4 40 15
Her brother was not handsome; no, when they first saw him, MP I 5 44 2
I could see it in her eyes, when he was mentioned. MP I 5 45 14
hundred of either sex, who is not taken in when they marry. MP I 5 46 20
that it must be so, when I consider that it is, of all MP I 5 46 20
When I am a wife, I mean to be just as staunch myself; and MP I 5 47 24
when one has seen her hardly able to speak the year before. MP I 5 49 32
When anderson first introduced me to his family, about two MP I 5 50 35
When we reached Albion Place they were out; we went after MP I 5 51 40
I declare when I got back to Sotherton yesterday, it MP I 6 53 2
a different place from what it was when we first had it. MP I 6 54 9
Guess my surprise, when I found that I had been asking the MP I 6 58 37
rather black upon me, when he found what I had been at." MP I 6 58 37
on the subject before, but when you do think of it, you MP I 6 58 38
in the world; and when obliged to take up the pen to say MP I 6 59 43
"When they are at a distance from all their family, said MP I 6 59 44
and taking a bed there; when Mrs. Norris, as if reading in MP I 6 61 58
worth reading, to his sisters, when they are separated. MP I 7 64 10
would not write long letters when you were absent?" MP I 7 64 10
perfectly allowable, when untinctured by ill humour of MP I 7 64 11
thing will turn to account when love is once set going, MP I 7 65 13
could she wonder, that when the evening stroll was over, MP I 7 65 14
at the park, and which, when Edmund's acquaintance with MP I 7 66 14
who always attended her when she rode without her cousins, MP I 7 66 15
Very different from you, miss, when you first began, six MP I 7 69 22
Lord bless me! how you did tremble when Sir Thomas first MP I 7 69 22
When they parted at night, Edmund asked Fanny whether she MP I 7 69 26
the fourth day, when the happiness of one of the party was MP I 7 70 30
beyond themselves; but when the first pause came, Edmund, MP I 7 71 31
said Lady Bertram; "but when the roses were gathered, your MP I 7 72 49
persuaded, that when she does not ride, she ought to walk. MP I 7 73 55
I could not, when the scheme was first mentioned the other MP I 8 77 9
in this weather, when we may have seats in a barouche! MP I 8 77 10
out two carriages when one will do, would be trouble for MP I 8 77 12
when he comes home find all the varnish scratched off." MP I 8 77 12
When Edmund, therefore, told her in reply, as he did when MP I 8 79 23
Fanny's gratitude when she heard the plan, was in fact MP I 8 79 27
and was on the point of proposing it when Mrs. Grant spoke. MP I 8 80 28
In looking back after Edmund, however, when there was any MP I 8 81 31
of road behind them, or when he gained on them in MP I 8 81 31
When Julia looked back, it was with a countenance of MP I 8 81 32
When they came within the influence of Sotherton MP I 8 81 33
had known nothing about, when Mr. Rushworth had asked her MP I 8 83 37
and pride could furnish, when they drove up to the MP I 8 83 37
the time would ever come when men and women might lie MP I 9 87 15
ten minutes in bed, when they woke with a headach, without MP I 9 87 15
horses most could be done, when the young people, meeting MP I 9 89 32
and Mr. Rushworth, and when after a little time the others MP I 9 90 36
"This is insufferably hot," said Miss Crawford when they MP I 9 91 37
"You need not hurry when the object is only to prevent my MP I 9 94 56
into it; and therefore when I say that we have walked a MP I 9 95 64
was not those she wanted, when Miss Bertram, Mr. Rushworth, MP I 10 97 1
the house already," said Mr. Crawford, when he was gone. MP I 10 98 5
quite into the house; and when people are waiting, they MP I 10 102 46
turned up into another, when the voice and the laugh of MP I 10 103 49
been left a whole hour, when he had talked of only a few MP I 10 103 49
She was quite shocked when I asked her whether wine was MP I 10 105 55
nature could make it; but when Mrs. Norris ceased speaking MP I 10 106 58
when the mist cleared away, she should see nothing else. MP I 11 107 3
praise than to hear it;" when being earnestly invited by MP I 11 112 33
When I look out on such a night as this, I feel as if MP I 11 113 35
the instrument, and when it ceased, he was close by the MP I 11 113 42
occur when he was once gone, to take him elsewhere. MP I 12 115 5
When he had told of his horse, he took a newspaper from MP I 12 118 22
But when my aunt has got a fancy in her head, nothing can MP I 12 120 26
days of representation, when the sudden death of one of MP I 13 121 1
still urging the subject, when Henry Crawford entered the MP I 13 129 38
willing to do any thing; when Julia, meaning like her MP I 14 133 8
as for Cottager himself, when he has got his wife's MP I 14 134 14
When you have studied the character, I am sure you will MP I 14 135 17
keeping your countenance when I come in with a basket of MP I 14 136 18
When this had lasted some time, the division of the party MP I 14 136 22
thing of the matter; but when he entered the drawing-room MP I 15 138 2
I cannot but suppose you will when you have read it MP I 15 140 11
I only wish Tom had known his own mind when the carpenters MP I 15 141 22
and was just coming out, when who should I see but Dick MP I 15 141 22
deep in the subject when a most welcome interruption was MP I 15 142 25
her present kindness; and when from taking notice of her MP I 15 147 57
course she would come out when her cousin was married. MP I 15 147 57
When the evening was over, she went to bed full of it, her MP I 16 150 1
to make the remembrance when she was alone much less so,-- MP I 16 150 1
found it quite as puzzling when she awoke the next morning. MP I 16 150 1
within the last three years, when she had quitted them.-- MP I 15 150 1
deserted, except by Fanny, when she visited her plants, or MP I 16 151 1
not to be driven from it entirely, even when winter came. MP I 16 151 2
my joining them now, when they are exceeding their first MP I 16 154 12
"They will not have much cause of triumph, when they see MP I 16 155 16
and get it over; and when we meet at breakfast we shall be MP I 16 156 27
of all their comfort," and when Edmund, pursuing that idea, MP I 17 158 2
the day; and even this, when imparted by Edmund brought a MP I 17 159 6
When Sir Thomas comes, I dare say he will be in for some MP I 17 161 14
"Sir Thomas is to achieve mighty things when he comes home, MP I 17 161 15
reasonable when you see him in his family, I assure you. MP I 17 162 16
Lady Bertram seems more of a cipher now than when he is at MP I 17 162 16
the day came at last, when Mr. Rushworth turned to her MP I 18 165 3
for a quarter of an hour, when a gentle tap at the door MP I 18 168 14
kick their feet against when they are learning a lesson. MP I 18 169 21
at one of the times when they were trying not to embrace, MP I 18 169 21
through half the scene, when a tap at the door brought a MP I 18 169 22
was giving the other; and when again alone and able to MP I 18 170 24
had proceeded some way, when the door of the room was MP I 18 172 33
being renewed after tea, when the bustle of receiving Sir MP II 1 177 5
might seem disrespectful, when this point was settled, and MP II 1 177 6
return a misfortune; and when, on having courage to lift MP II 1 178 7
Thomas's disapprobation when the present state of his MP II 1 179 10
of his passage to England, when the alarm of a French MP II 1 180 10
feelings subsided; but when tea was soon afterwards MP II 1 181 17
He will be no bad assistant when it all comes out." MP II 1 182 21
of the room; and that when he inquired with mild gravity MP II 1 183 24
the end of the story; and when it was over, could give him MP II 1 184 25
in the middle of a rehearsal when you arrived this evening. MP II 1 185 28
for him at every jolt, and when we got into the rough MP II 2 189 5
And when we got to the bottom of Sandcroft Hill, what do MP II 2 189 5
a something in Sir Thomas, when they sat round the same MP II 2 191 10
"When do you think of going?" MP II 2 193 15
They had not been here a twelvemonth when he left England. MP II 3 196 2
formerly were ever merry, except when my uncle was in town. MP II 3 197 3
No young people's are, I suppose, when those they look up MP II 3 197 3
But when did you or any body ever get a compliment from me, MP II 3 197 6
and only a moment's: when her father ceased, she was able MP II 3 200 21
three or four days, when there was no return, no letter, MP II 3 201 24
and spring, when her own taste could have fairer play. MP II 3 202 26
Nothing could be objected to when it came under the MP II 3 203 29
When the novelty of amusement there were over, it would be MP II 3 203 31
A civil servant she had withstood; but when Dr. Grant MP II 4 205 3
It was beginning to look brighter, when Fanny, observing a MP II 4 206 5
"South or north, I know a black cloud when I see it; and MP II 4 207 9
for being sought after now when nobody else was to be had; MP II 4 208 11
expense of her judgment, when it was raised by pleasantry MP II 4 208 11
When one thinks of it, how astonishing a variety of nature! MP II 4 209 16
You will think me rhapsodizing; but when I am out of doors, MP II 4 209 16
out of doors, especially when I am sitting out of doors, I MP II 4 209 16
cried Mrs. Grant, "for when I went up for my shawl I saw MP II 4 211 28
live where we may; and when you are settled in town and I MP II 4 213 35
with obscurity when it might rise to distinction." MP II 4 214 42
for courage to say so, when the sound of the great clock MP II 4 214 46
feeling on the occasion, when Mrs. Grant, with sudden MP II 4 215 47
she called him back again, when he had almost closed the MP II 5 217 11

"She always makes tea, you know, when my sister is not MP II 5 219 21
instinctive reply; though when she had turned from him and MP II 5 219 26
any body, and Mrs. Norris, when she came on the morrow, in MP II 5 219 27
Had the doctor been contented to take my dining table when MP II 5 220 30
never respected when they step out of their proper sphere. MP II 5 220 30
as Mrs. Norris could; and when Sir Thomas, soon afterwards, MP II 5 221 35
aunt, cost her some tears of gratitude when she was alone. MP II 5 222 40
in the drawing-room, when Edmund, being engaged apart in MP II 5 224 49
happier than when doing what you must know was no MP II 5 225 56
than when behaving so dishonourably and unfeelingly!-- MP II 5 225 56
My uncle disapproved it all so entirely when he did arrive, MP II 5 225 58
so angrily to any one; and when her speech was over, she MP II 5 225 59
when the two gentlemen shortly afterwards joined them. MP II 5 226 64
When is it to be? MP II 5 227 65
When will it be? MP II 5 227 65
of the evening, except when Mr. Crawford now and then MP II 5 227 68
When we talked of her last night, you none of you seemed MP II 6 229 5
of expression enough when she has any thing to express. MP II 6 229 5
are, and be all animation when I take it and talk to her; MP II 6 231 9
feel when I go away that she shall be never happy again. MP II 6 231 9
anchor, in Spithead; and when Crawford walked up with the MP II 6 232 12
of her first dinner visit, when she found herself in an MP II 6 233 14
fashion already, though when I first heard of such things MP II 6 235 19
could not believe it, and when Mrs. Brown, and the other MP II 6 235 19
When it was proved however to have done William no harm, MP II 6 237 23
the owner with a smile when the animal was one minute MP II 6 237 23
to dine at the parsonage, when the general invitation was MP II 7 238 2
from looking at her cards when the deal began, must direct MP II 7 240 8
distance from Mansfield, when his horse being found to MP II 7 240 13
The house is by no means bad, and when the yard is removed, MP II 7 242 22
I do not exactly know the distance, but when you get back MP II 7 245 32
he might depend on, when she was stopped by Sir Thomas's MP II 7 245 34
Crawford's behaviour; but when the whist table broke up at MP II 7 246 36
of Portsmouth, and of dancing too, when I cannot have you. MP II 7 249 52
a time when you will have nothing of that sort to endure. MP II 7 249 53
When you are a lieutenant!--only think, William, when you MP II 7 249 53
time, did not we? when the hand-organ was in the street? MP II 7 250 59
herself like a gentlewoman when we do see her, which MP II 7 250 60
next morning at breakfast, when, after recalling and MP II 8 252 1
it all prearranged; and when she would have conjectured MP II 8 253 7
with his hopes, and when he thought of her acknowledged MP II 8 255 10
burst of such enjoyment, when nothing but the friends she MP II 8 256 12
she should enjoy herself when once away, she was already MP II 8 256 12
parcel, which Fanny had observed in her hand when they met. MP II 8 257 15
"When I wear this necklace I shall always think of you," MP II 8 258 18
"You must think of somebody else too when you wear that MP II 8 259 19
sentences of praise; but when he did awake and understand, MP II 9 262 11
she would rather not part with it, when it is not wanted?" MP II 9 263 13
belonging to the ball, and when sent off with a parting MP II 9 267 22
when they want to be influenced against their conscience. MP II 9 269 35
All went well--she did not dislike her own looks; and when MP II 9 270 40
Miss Crawford had a claim; and when it was no longer to MP II 9 271 40
the upper housemaid's, and when dressed herself, she MP II 9 271 41
Mrs. Chapman had just reached the attic floor, when Miss MP II 9 271 41
Her uncle and both her aunts were in the drawing-room when MP II 10 272 1
generous present to her when dear Mrs. Rushworth married. MP II 10 272 3
Sir Thomas said no more; but when they sat down to table MP II 10 272 4
touched again when the ladies withdrew, with more success. MP II 10 272 4
expectation of a carriage, when a general spirit of ease MP II 10 273 6
When the carriages were really heard, when the guests MP II 10 273 7
When the company were moving into the ball-room she found MP II 10 274 9
to speak on the subject, when Fanny, anxious to get the MP II 10 274 9
And to have them away when it was given--and for her to be MP II 10 276 12
distinction now; but when she looked back to the state of MP II 10 276 12
had all been to each other when once dancing in that house MP II 10 276 12
Lady Did, soon afterwards, when Mary, perceiving her on a MP II 10 276 14
she must be doing so--when she went to her after the two MP II 10 277 17
his manner--and sometimes, when he talked of William, he MP II 10 278 20
She was happy even when they did take place; but not from MP II 10 278 20
Miss Crawford had been in gay spirits when they first MP II 10 279 21
It was barbarous to be happy when Edmund was suffering. MP II 10 279 21
When her two dances with him were over, her inclination MP II 10 279 22
want of attention to her when they had been last together; MP II 11 282 3
Crawford or of William, when he said he was the finest MP II 11 283 4
me!" said Lady Bertram, when the tea-things were removed. MP II 11 283 5
of him continually when absent, dwelling on his merit and MP II 11 286 15
a week, when her own departure from Mansfield was so near. MP II 11 286 15
All this was bad, but she had still more to feel when MP II 11 286 16
and brought no Edmund--when Saturday came and still no MP II 11 286 16
and still no Edmund--and when, through the slight MP II 11 286 16
But at any rate his staying away at a time, when, MP II 11 287 17
Well, when your cousin comes back, he will find Mansfield MP II 11 288 30
every noisy evil is missed when it is taken away; that is, MP II 11 289 32
gone above an hour; and when his sister, who had been MP II 12 291 1
When did you begin to think seriously about her?" MP II 12 292 7
"When Fanny is known to him," continued Henry, "he will MP II 12 293 10
by their proper name; but when he talked of her having MP II 12 294 16
When she had spoken it, she recollected herself, and MP II 12 295 22
of women, and that even when you ceased to love, she would MP II 12 296 29
saying only when he paused, "how kind! how very kind! MP II 13 300 7
When she did understand it, however, and found herself MP II 13 301 7
part with her at a moment when her modesty alone seemed to MP II 13 302 9
shy and uncomfortable when their visitor entered the room. MP II 13 303 13
different from what they were when he talked to the others. MP II 13 304 16
hardly eat any thing; and when Sir Thomas good humouredly MP II 13 304 16
She would hardly join even when William was the subject, MP II 13 304 17
Fanny, meanwhile, speaking only when she could not help it, MP II 13 305 26
Fanny had by no means forgotten Mr. Crawford, when she MP III 1 311 1
growing very comfortable, when suddenly the sound of a MP III 1 312 4
room, after breakfast, when Mr. Crawford was shewn in.-- MP III 1 313 14
become conscious of it, when, rising from his chair, he MP III 1 314 16
But now, when he has made his overtures so properly, and MP III 1 315 18
It is very uncertain when my interest might have got MP III 1 316 28
in consequence; but when he looked at his niece, and saw MP III 1 320 45
She was struck, quite struck, when on returning from her MP III 1 322 51
quarrelling with her: and when she found how much and how MP III 1 323 53
When the meeting with which she was threatened for the MP III 1 324 59
she was preparing to obey, when Mrs. Norris called out, " MP III 1 325 60
and which, secondly, when constrained at last to admit MP III 2 326 1
Must it not follow of course, that when he was understood, MP III 2 327 4
And when farther pressed, had added, that in her opinion MP III 2 327 5
of the lover; and when seeing such confidence of success MP III 2 329 11
were sensibly felt; and when she considered how much of MP III 2 331 17
When Sir Thomas understood this, he felt the necessity of MP III 2 332 19
Fanny coloured, and doubted at first what to say; when MP III 2 333 24
25
"No, my dear, I should not think of missing you, when such MP III 2 333 26
and tender associations, when her own fair self was before MP III 3 334 1
After dinner, when he and his father were alone, he had MP III 3 334 4
be talking of her; and when tea at last brought them away, MP III 3 334 5
When he and Crawford walked into the drawing-room, his MP III 3 336 8
his name, Fanny?--when we heard your footsteps." MP III 3 336 9
I mean when you are settled there. MP III 3 339 19
degree of ignorance men, when suddenly called to the MP III 3 339 22
in satisfying; and when Crawford proceeded to ask his MP III 3 340 24
There is something in the eloquence of the pulpit, when it MP III 3 341 28
By that right I do and will deserve you; and when once MP III 3 344 41
recollection of herself, when she saw his look, and heard MP III 4 347 19
"Yes, when I reached the house I found the two sisters MP III 4 352 38
by themselves; and when once we had begun, we had not done MP III 4 352 38
when she said that you should be Henry's wife. MP III 4 352 42
of having others present when they met, was Fanny's only MP III 5 356 4

She was safe in the breakfast-room, with her aunt, when MP III 5 357 5
I do not know when I shall have done scolding you," and MP III 5 357 6
'When two sympathetic hearts meet in the marriage state, MP III 5 358 9
I have not the heart for it when it comes to the point." MP III 5 359 9
gentle Fanny! when I think of this being the last time of MP III 5 359 9
And when I have done with her, I must go to her sister, MP III 5 359 12
astonishment when he opened the door at seeing me here! MP III 5 360 14
Another short fit of abstraction followed--when, shaking MP III 5 360 15
When she comes to know the truth, she will very likely MP III 5 360 16
I leave him entirely to your mercy; and when he has got MP III 5 363 24
Mary, presently, "than when he had succeeded in getting MP III 5 363 26
and trusting, that when we meet again, it will be under MP III 5 364 30
When it came to the moment of parting, he would take her MP III 5 365 36
that she heard, and when he had left the room, she was MP III 5 365 36
when once with her again, Fanny could not doubt the rest.-- MP III 6 367 4
a strong attack of them, when she first understood what MP III 6 369 11
what was intended, when her uncle first made her the offer MP III 6 369 11
always more inclined to silence when feeling most strongly. MP III 6 369 11
Afterwards, when familiarized with the visions of MP III 6 369 11
When he had really resolved on any measure, he could MP III 6 370 14
Now, when she knew better how to be useful and how to MP III 6 371 17
and how to forbear, and when her mother could be no longer MP III 6 371 17
her there still when he came in, from his first cruise! MP III 6 372 18
of their journey, for when the mode of it came to be MP III 6 372 21
they were to travel post, when she saw Sir Thomas actually MP III 6 372 21
his father and mother just when every body else of most MP III 6 373 25
shall write to you, Fanny, when I have any thing worth MP III 6 373 26
face, when she looked up at him, would have been decisive. MP III 6 374 26
nor look, nor think, when the last moment came with him, MP III 6 374 28
early in the morning; and when the small, diminished party MP III 6 374 29
effect on Fanny's spirits, when Mansfield Park was fairly MP III 7 375 1
When no longer under the same roof with Edmund, she MP III 7 376 4
to be invited on; but when she saw there was no other door, MP III 7 377 10
And when did you get anything to eat? MP III 7 378 14
in the parlour, except when drowned at intervals by the MP III 7 382 27
she did not know when they should have got tea--and she MP III 7 383 32
for, and accordingly, when Rebecca had been prevailed on MP III 7 385 37
her mother meant to part with her when her year was up. MP III 7 385 38
there not much younger when she went into Northamptonshire, MP III 7 385 40
her to Susan; and when the news of her death had at last MP III 7 386 40
But you should not have taken it out, my dear, when I sent MP III 7 386 44
such a bone of contention when she gave it me to keep, MP III 7 386 44
Susan have my knife, mamma, when I am dead and buried.'-- MP III 7 386 44
Could Sir Thomas have seen all his niece's feelings, when MP III 8 388 1
a short and hurried way, when he had come ashore on duty. MP III 8 388 2
was, she rather regretted when he went, for he was clever MP III 8 390 8
still, and nobody could command attention when they spoke. MP III 8 392 11
She was really glad to receive the letter when it did come. MP III 9 393 1
has been no 'well, Mary, when do you write to Fanny?--is MP III 9 393 1
Shall I tell you how Mrs. Rushworth looked when your name MP III 9 393 1
I was in it two years ago, when it was Lady Lascelles's, MP III 9 394 1
to gladden Henry's eyes, when he comes back--and send me MP III 9 394 1
turning pale about, when Mr. Crawford walked into the room. MP III 10 399 3
Good sense, like hers, will always act when really called MP III 10 399 4
crossings, or any crowd, when Mr. Price was only calling MP III 10 403 14
him an approving look when it was all frightened off, by MP III 10 404 15
the voice of a friend when he mentioned it, and led the MP III 10 405 17
Fanny was doubly silenced here; though when the moment was MP III 10 406 20
When Mr. Price and his friend had seen all that they MP III 10 406 21
for church the next day when Mr. Crawford appeared again. MP III 11 408 1
When you know her as well as I do, I am sure you will MP III 11 410 16
door of their own house, when he knew them to be going to MP III 11 411 19
When you give me your opinion, I always know what is right. MP III 11 412 22
"My love to your sister, if you please; and when you see MP III 11 412 27
next day, on the ramparts; when the balmy air, the MP III 12 415 1
2
air; and I must confess, when he dined here the other day, MP III 12 416 2
she began to feel that when her own release from MP III 12 419 9
Seven weeks of the two months were very nearly gone, when MP III 13 420 1
to Mansfield in a less assured state than when I left it. MP III 13 420 2
Had she been different when I did see her, I should have MP III 13 421 2
When I think of her great attachment to you, indeed, and MP III 13 421 2
not be till after Easter, when he has business in town. MP III 13 423 2
to Bath, occur at a time when she could make no advantage MP III 13 425 6
brought on a fever; and when the party broke up, being MP III 13 426 10
yet a keener solicitude, when she considered how little MP III 13 428 13
and look at him; but, when able to talk or be talked to, MP III 14 429 2
him was higher than ever when he appeared as the attendant, MP III 14 429 2
for her cousin--except when she thought of Miss Crawford-- MP III 14 430 3
actually begun a letter when called away by Tom's illness, MP III 14 430 4
When Tom is better, I shall go." MP III 14 430 4
say when there might be leisure to think of, or fetch her? MP III 14 430 6
When she had been coming to Portsmouth, she had loved to MP III 14 431 8
house: it was always, "when I go back into MP III 14 431 8
or when I return to Mansfield, I shall do so and so."-- MP III 14 431 8
she should do when she went home, before she was aware.-- MP III 14 431 8
They might return to Mansfield when they chose; travelling MP III 14 432 11
any more this spring, when the following letter was MP III 14 433 12
"I had actually began folding my letter, when Henry walked MP III 14 435 14
you are,) keep away, when you have the means of returning. MP III 14 435 14
of a week, she had still the same feeling when it did come. MP III 15 437 1
else all the morning; but when her father came back in the MP III 15 438 8
there were moments even when her heart revolted from it as MP III 15 441 20
from it as impossible--when she thought it could not be. MP III 15 441 20
could have overlooked, when the third day did bring the MP III 15 442 22
He turned away to recover himself, and when he spoke again, MP III 15 444 29
When shall you be ready?-- MP III 15 445 29
When Mansfield was considered, time was precious; and the MP III 15 445 29
since February; but, when they entered the park, her MP III 15 446 35
in that delightful state, when farther beauty is known to MP III 15 446 35
known to be at hand, and when, while much is actually MP III 15 446 35
solemn-looking servants, when Lady Bertram came from the MP III 15 447 37
When really touched by affliction, her active powers had MP III 16 448 2
any creature at Mansfield, when it was followed by another, MP III 16 450 9
addition to all the rest, when they were in reason to MP III 16 452 15
very time of all others when if a friend is at hand the MP III 16 453 17
"Yes, when I left her I told her so." MP III 16 456 27
all go that way; and, when once married, and properly MP III 16 457 29
and Thornton Lacey; and when I hear of you next, it may be MP III 16 458 30
I had gone a few steps, Fanny, when I heard the door open MP III 16 459 30
from Mr. Crawford, and when Sir Thomas came back she had MP III 17 461 2
Not even Fanny had tears for aunt Norris--not even when MP III 17 466 16
thinking of him again; and when the acquaintance was MP III 17 466 18
been obtained; especially when that marriage had taken MP III 17 467 19
When he returned from Richmond, he would have been glad to MP III 17 468 21
her infinitely more, when all the bustle of the intrigue MP III 17 468 21
They lived together; and when Dr. Grant had brought on MP III 17 469 24
that exactly at the time when it was quite natural that it MP III 17 470 26
opinion on the subject when the poor little girl's coming MP III 17 471 29
a match of affection, when he was now obliged to part with E I 1 7 10
from such thoughts; but when tea came, it was impossible E I 1 8 10
11
my odd humours, when she might have a house of her own?" E I 1 8 12
a very pretty manner; and when you have had her here to do E I 1 9 19
When this was over, Mr. Woodhouse gratefully observed, "it E I 1 10 21
22
I have a great regard for you and Emma; but when it comes E I 1 10 29
"Especially when one of those two is such a fanciful, E I 1 10 30
be proved in the right, when so many people said Mr. E I 1 11 39
with him in Broadway-Lane, when, because it began to E I 1 12 41
I planned the match from that hour; and when such success E I 1 12 41
any longer--and I thought when he was joining their hands E I 1 13 46

Captain Weston was a general favourite; and when the	E	I	2	15	2
worst of the bargain; for when his wife died after a three	E	I	2	16	4
on the subject, either when Mrs. Perry drank tea with Mrs.	E	I	2	17	9
Miss Bates, or when Mrs. and Miss Bates returned the visit.	E	I	2	17	9
and the hope strengthened when it was understood that he	E	I	2	18	9
pity "poor Miss Taylor," when they left her at Randalls in	E	I	2	18	12
wedding-cake at all, and when that proved vain, as	E	I	2	19	14
all lived together; but when it appeared that the Mr.	E	I	4	27	5
"And when she had come away, Mrs. Martin was so very kind	E	I	4	28	8
Whatever money he might come into when his father died,	E	I	4	30	20
still be in this country when Mr. Martin marries, I wish	E	I	4	31	24
no other advantage; and when he came to be contrasted with	E	I	4	31	27
The list she drew up when only fourteen--I remember	E	I	5	37	7
when he is not quite frightened enough about the children.	E	I	5	40	23
She was a beautiful creature when she came to you, but, in	E	I	6	42	2
This did not want much of being finished, when I put it	E	I	6	45	21
after all my pains, and when I had really made a very good	E	I	6	45	21
strongly and clearly--and when he takes a pen in hand, his	E	I	7	51	5
in, when the mystery of her parentage came to be revealed.	E	I	8	64	47
in unreserved moments, when there are only men present, I	E	I	8	66	53
prominent uneasiness; and when Harriet appeared, and in	E	I	8	67	56
He had frightened her a little about Mr. Elton; but when	E	I	8	67	57
to Hartfield again; and when they did meet, his grave	E	I	9	69	1
"So many clever riddles as there used to be when he was	E	I	9	70	5
articulate at first; but when they did arrive at something	E	I	9	74	21
"When Miss Smiths and Mr. Eltons get acquainted--they do	E	I	9	74	25
When I look back to the first time I saw him!	E	I	9	75	26
peeped through the blind when we heard he was going by,	E	I	9	75	26
she will be when she comes, not to see Miss Taylor here!"	E	I	9	79	58
I am sure I was very much surprized when I first heard she	E	I	9	79	60
about to make his bow, when taking the paper from the	E	I	9	81	79
					80
you do? how shall you employ yourself when you grow old?"	E	I	10	85	20
The lane made a slight bend; and when that bend was passed,	E	I	10	87	29
					30
But she had not been there two minutes when she found that	E	I	10	88	33
draw back a little more, when they both looked around, and	E	I	10	88	33
some disappointment when she found that he was only giving	E	I	10	88	34
of the vicarage pales, when a sudden resolution, of at	E	I	10	89	36
They had not been long seated and composed when Mr.	E	I	11	93	5
he was but two years old when he lost his poor mother!	E	I	11	96	24
of friendship, that when he came into the room she had one	E	I	12	98	2
I was sixteen years old when you were born."	E	I	12	99	6
This had just taken place and with great cordiality, when	E	I	12	99	14
or heavy--except when it has been quite an influenza."	E	I	12	102	33
and successfully that, when forced to give her attention	E	I	12	104	45
and excellent aunt, when she comes to visit them!	E	I	12	104	46
Emma's attempts to stop her father had been vain; and when	E	I	12	106	59
Elton's would be depressed when he knew her state; and	E	I	13	109	6
from Mrs. Goddard's door, when she was met by Mr. Elton	E	I	13	109	6
You appear to me a little hoarse already, and when you	E	I	13	110	9
But hardly had she so spoken, when she found her brother	E	I	13	110	12
nor his eyes more exulting than when he next looked at her.	E	I	13	111	12
of meeting her again, when he hoped to be able to give a	E	I	13	111	14
With men he can be rational and unaffected, but when he	E	I	13	111	16
good opinion of himself when he asks people to leave their	E	I	13	113	26
people's not staying comfortably at home when they can!	E	I	13	113	26
point of telling you that when I called at Mrs. Goddard's	E	I	13	114	31
Emma was rather in dismay when only half a minute	E	I	13	115	36
Well, sir, the time must come when you will be paid for	E	I	13	116	45
when you will have little labour and great enjoyment."	E	I	13	116	45
come and see his daughter, when the others appeared, and	E	I	14	117	3
her rather sorry to find, when they had all taken their	E	I	14	118	4
So it proved;--for when happily released from Mr. Elton,	E	I	14	119	6
					7
years, they always are put off when it comes to the point.	E	I	14	120	11
impossible for him to know beforehand when it will be."	E	I	14	123	25
Mr. Woodhouse was soon ready for his tea; and when he had	E	I	15	124	1
discussing the point, when Mr. Knightley, who had left the	E	I	15	127	16
temper and happiness when this visit of hardship were over.	E	I	15	128	21
made her resolve to restrain herself when she did speak.	E	I	15	129	24
who can think of Miss Smith, when Miss Woodhouse is near!	E	I	15	130	31
Without knowing when the carriage turned into Vicarage-	E	I	15	132	37
into Vicarage-Lane, or when it stopped, they found	E	I	15	132	37
When the time proposed drew near, Mrs. Weston's fears were	E	I	18	144	1
"Yes; all the advantages of sitting still when he ought to	E	I	18	148	24
could not endure such a puppy when it came to the point."	E	I	18	150	32
but it burst out again when she thought she had succeeded,	E	II	1	155	1
This she had been prepared for when she entered the house;	E	II	1	156	6
time for writing;' and when I immediately said, 'but	E	II	1	157	7
She often says, when the letter is first opened, 'well,	E	II	1	157	10
Jane often says, when she is here, 'I am sure, grandmama,	E	II	1	158	10
under some slight excuse, when Miss Bates turned to her	E	II	1	158	13
Ever since the service he rendered Jane at Weymouth, when	E	II	1	160	23
However, when I read on, I found it was not near so bad as	E	II	1	162	31
more than five minutes, when I first entered the house.	E	II	1	162	32
By birth she belonged to Highbury: and when at three years	E	II	2	163	3
When he did return, he sought out the child and took	E	II	2	163	4
had injured her; and now, when the due visit was paid, on	E	II	2	167	12
When she took in her history, indeed, her situation, as	E	II	2	167	13
as well as her beauty; when she considered what all this	E	II	2	167	13
not been near Randalls," when the door was thrown open,	E	II	3	172	22
					23
When you have been here a little longer, Miss Fairfax, you	E	II	3	174	38
It is such a happiness when good people get together--and	E	II	3	175	39
"When I have seen Mr. Elton," replied Jane, "I dare say I	E	II	3	175	43
But I gave what I believed the general opinion, when I	E	II	3	176	49
Pork: when we dress the leg it will be another thing.	E	II	3	177	50
been over five minutes, when in came Harriet, with just	E	II	3	177	52
full ten minutes, perhaps--when, all of a sudden, who	E	II	3	178	52
three yards from the door, when he came after me, only to	E	II	3	179	52
and perfectly amiable: and when Mr. Elton himself arrived	E	II	4	181	2
to wait for; and when he set out for Bath again, there was	E	II	4	182	6
when he next entered Highbury he would bring his bride.	E	II	4	182	6
about him; for, excepting when at Hartfield, she was	E	II	4	184	10
and sisters, when invited to come, would be ingratitude.	E	II	4	185	12
She went, however; and when they reached the farm, and she	E	II	5	186	2
local agitation; and when they parted, Emma observed her	E	II	5	186	2
time --till just at last, when Mrs. Martin's saying, all	E	II	5	186	4
happy,) when the carriage re-appeared, and all was over.	E	II	5	187	4
I do not know when I have been so disappointed."	E	II	5	187	6
When she looked at the hedges, she thought the elder at	E	II	5	189	16
soon be coming out; and when she turned round to Harriet,	E	II	5	189	16
and congratulations, when she appeared, to have her share	E	II	5	190	21
But when satisfied on all these points, and their	E	II	5	191	28
expression; and even, when he might have determined not to	E	II	5	193	34
You saw her with the Campbells when she was the equal of	E	II	5	194	40
knows a puddle of water when he sees it, and as to Mrs.	E	II	5	195	48
Mr. Woodhouse's ear; and when their going farther was	E	II	6	196	2
such a meeting; and even when particulars were given and	E	II	6	198	5
astonishment, I found, when he (finding me no where else)	E	II	6	199	7
Mr. Frank Churchill hardly knows what to say when you	E	II	6	201	23
When the gloves were bought and they had quitted the shop	E	II	6	201	26
before it appeared, that when the insult came at last, it	E	II	7	207	7
And when you get there, you must tell him at what time you	E	II	7	210	14
staying late. you will get very tired when tea is over."	E	II	7	210	14
She loves piquet, you know; but when she is gone home, I	E	II	7	211	21
There is always a look of consciousness or bustle when	E	II	8	213	10
When the Westons arrived, the kindest looks of love, the	E	II	8	214	12
"I declare, I do not know when I have heard anything that	E	II	8	215	16
orderly as the others; but when the table was again safely	E	II	8	218	38
					39
was again safely covered, when every corner dish was	E	II	8	218	38
					39
But when you mentioned Mrs. Dixon, I felt how much more	E	II	8	219	42
always the first to move when he could--that his father,	E	II	8	220	48
very near; and that even when days were fixed, and	E	II	8	221	48
When Mr. Cole had moved away, and her attention could be	E	II	8	222	54
I am sure he was particularly silent when Mrs. Cole told	E	II	8	226	83
"That will do," said he, when it was finished, thinking	E	II	8	229	94
presume to expect; and when her eyes fell only on the	E	II	9	233	24
and had all but knocked, when Emma caught their eye.--	E	II	9	233	25
My aunt always sends me off when she is shopping.	E	II	9	234	30
as your neighbours, when it is necessary; but there is no	E	II	9	234	33
"What was I talking of?" said she, beginning again when	E	II	9	237	49
And when I brought out the baked apples from the closet,	E	II	9	238	51
And when he was gone, she almost quarrelled with me--no, I	E	II	9	238	51
What nonsense one talks, Miss Woodhouse, when hard at work,	E	II	10	242	15
not help being amused; and when on glancing her eye	E	II	10	243	22
the remains of a smile, when she saw that with all the	E	II	10	243	22
I dare say he will come in when he knows who is here.	E	II	10	243	31
to body or mind;--but when a beginning is made--when the	E	II	11	247	1
when a beginning is made--when the felicities of rapid	E	II	11	247	1
Five couple are nothing, when one thinks seriously about	E	II	11	248	8
Mr. Perry is extremely concerned when any of us are ill.	E	II	11	251	28
However, this does make a difference; and, perhaps, when	E	II	11	252	32
complains; but it is right to spare our horses when we can.	E	II	11	252	35
Mr. Perry said, so many years ago, when I had the measles?	E	II	11	252	37
meant, "men never know when things are dirty or not;" and	E	II	11	253	43
Most cordially, when Miss Bates arrived, did she agree	E	II	11	256	60
(so said her husband) when writing to her nephew two days	E	II	12	258	7
When once it had been read, there was no doing any thing,	E	II	12	259	10
total want of spirits when he did come might redeem him.	E	II	12	259	12
the first few minutes; and when rousing himself, it was	E	II	12	259	12
					13
"Ah!--(shaking his head)--the uncertainty of when I may be	E	II	12	259	15
Mr. Weston, always alert when business was to be done, and	E	II	12	261	35
Oh! the blessing of a female correspondent, when one is	E	II	12	261	36
change; but when they did meet, her composure was odious.	E	II	12	263	42
When she became sensible of this, it struck her that she	E	II	13	264	1
in love indeed!--and when he comes again, if his affection	E	II	13	265	3
When his letter to Mrs. Weston arrived, Emma had the	E	II	13	265	5
sentiments, she yet found, when it was folded up and	E	II	13	266	6
But stranger things have happened; and when we cease to	E	II	13	267	7
wretched for a while, and when the violence of grief was	E	II	13	268	13
sense to depend on; and when she considered how peculiarly	E	II	14	271	5
"Well, Miss Woodhouse," said Harriet, when they had	E	II	14	271	6
When the visit was returned, Emma made up her mind.	E	II	14	272	16
only said in reply, "when you have seen more of this	E	II	14	273	22
					23
Indeed, when the time draws on, I shall decidedly	E	II	14	274	28
When people come into a beautiful country of this sort,	E	II	14	274	28
Many a time has Selina said, when she has been going to	E	II	14	274	30
I think, on the contrary, when people shut themselves up	E	II	14	275	30
I have always resided with when in Bath, would be most	E	II	14	275	32
I honestly said as much to Mr. E. when he was speaking of	E	II	14	276	36
When he was speaking of it in that way, I honestly said	E	II	14	276	36
"I should hope not; but really when I look round among my	E	II	14	277	40
Was not it lucky?--for, not being within when he called	E	II	14	278	50
When they had nothing else to say, it must be always easy	E	II	15	282	3
Not merely when a state of warfare with one young lady	E	II	15	282	4
Emma's calm answer--"and when you are better acquainted	E	II	15	283	6
particularly to my brother and sister when they come to us.	E	II	15	284	9
I am sure they will like her extremely; and when she gets	E	II	15	284	9
"Well, Mrs. Weston," said Emma triumphantly when he left	E	II	15	289	41
his little boys, when it had been just beginning to rain.	E	II	16	293	10
I always fetch the letters when I am here.	E	II	16	293	12
"No, but it did not absolutely rain when I set out."	E	II	16	293	14
yards from your own door when I had the pleasure of	E	II	16	293	15
					16
When you have lived to my age, you will begin to think	E	II	16	293	16
"When I talked of your being altered by time, by the	E	II	16	294	23
as it always is when I am not here, by my grandmamma's."	E	II	16	296	37
And when one considers the variety of hands, and of bad	E	II	16	296	42
"Oh! when a gallant young man, like Mr. Frank Churchill,"	E	II	16	298	55
When the ladies returned to the drawing-room after dinner,	E	II	17	299	1
When I am quite determined as to the time, I am not at all	E	II	17	300	13
when Mr. Weston made his appearance among them.	E	II	17	302	23
as the black gentleman when any thing is to be done; most	E	II	17	304	27
They will stay a good while when they do come, and he will	E	II	17	304	27
in what way she had best retract, when Mr. Weston went on.	E	II	18	307	17
to the society of Highbury when he comes again; that is,	E	II	18	307	23
"When Frank left us," continued he, "it was quite	E	II	18	308	27
"it was quite uncertain when we might see him again, which	E	II	18	308	27
in the days of courtship, when, because things did not go	E	II	18	308	28
When he was here before, we made the best of it; but there	E	II	18	309	30
She was nobody when he married her, barely the daughter of	E	II	18	310	33
When did it happen before, or any thing like it?	E	II	18	311	46
is absent one--and who, when he is at home, is either	E	II	18	312	50
Though much might be fancy, he could not doubt, when he	E	III	1	317	6
attention was chained; but when she got to Maple Grove, he	E	III	2	321	16
such an occasion as this, when everybody's eyes are so	E	III	2	324	20
					21
When are we to begin dancing?"	E	III	2	325	28
When she was half way up the set, the whole group were	E	III	2	327	34
till after supper; but, when they were all in the ball-	E	III	2	330	46
as of their grandpapa, when the great iron sweepgate	E	III	3	332	3
stretch very retired; and when the young ladies had	E	III	3	333	5
and at the very hour, when the other very person was	E	III	3	335	10
A very few days had passed after this adventure, when	E	III	4	337	1
					2
And secretly she added to herself, "Lord bless me! when	E	III	4	339	15
wanted to put it down; but when he took out his pencil,	E	III	4	339	18
"And when," thought Emma, "will there be a beginning of Mr.	E	III	4	340	27
that I felt at the time--when I saw him coming--his noble	E	III	4	342	38
She was not present when the suspicion first arose.	E	III	5	343	2
When he was again in their company, he could not help	E	III	5	344	2
I dream of every body at Highbury when I am away--and when	E	III	5	345	13
I dream of every body at Highbury when I am away--and when	E	III	5	345	13
that Highbury is in your thoughts when you are absent.	E	III	5	345	14
remember grandmamma's telling us of it when we got home?--	E	III	5	346	16
he had seen; so full, that when the candles came to assist	E	III	5	349	26
pigeon-pies and cold lamb, when a lame carriage-horse	E	III	6	353	6
When you are tired of eating strawberries in the garden,	E	III	6	355	21
time with him, remained, when all the others were invited	E	III	6	357	33
Grove--cultivation-- beds when to be renewed--gardeners	E	III	6	358	35
There had been a time when he would have scorned her as a	E	III	6	360	40
There had been a time also when Emma would have been sorry	E	III	6	360	40
was hardly there, when Jane Fairfax appeared, coming	E	III	6	362	43
"Will you be so kind," said she, "when I am missed, as to	E	III	6	362	44
Till they come in I shall not be missed; and when they do,	E	III	6	362	44
own way, and only say that I am gone when it is necessary."	E	III	6	363	50
Place, Venice, when Frank Churchill entered the room.	E	III	6	363	53
Some people were always cross when they were hot.	E	III	6	364	56
"You are not quite so miserable, though, as when you first	E	III	6	365	65
Nothing was wanting but to be happy when they got there.	E	III	7	367	1
When they all sat down it was better; to her taste a great	E	III	7	367	3
catch her meaning; but, when it burst on her, it could not	E	III	7	371	27
These kind of things are very well at Christmas, when one	E	III	7	372	37
opinion, when one is exploring about the country in summer.	E	III	7	372	37
allowed to judge when to speak and when to hold my tongue.	E	III	7	372	37
I shall go abroad for a couple of years--and when I return,	E	III	7	373	50
and your father, when her society must be so irksome."	E	III	7	375	59
seen grow up from a period when her notice was an honour,	E	III	7	375	61

She was just as determined when the morrow came, and went E III 8 377 2
When one is in great pain, you know one cannot feel any E III 8 379 8
steady friend, when she might not bear to see herself. E III 8 379 9
She would not let Jane say 'no;' for when Jane first heard E III 8 380 15
we were at Donwell,) when Jane first heard of it, she was E III 8 380 15
"And when is Miss Fairfax to leave you?" E III 8 382 26
I was so astonished when she first told me what she had E III 8 382 29
saying to Mrs. Elton, and when Mrs. Elton at the same E III 8 382 29
without some help; and so, when Mr. Elton came back, he E III 8 383 29
from some fancy or other, he suddenly let it go.-- E III 9 386 7
mind when it was all but done, she could not perceive.-- E III 9 386 7
Goldsmith tells us, that when lovely woman stoops to folly, E III 9 387 12
to do but to die; and when she stoops to be disagreeable, E III 9 387 12
"Miss Fairfax was not well enough to write;" and when Mr. E III 9 389 16
When Emma afterwards heard that Jane Fairfax had been seen E III 9 391 21
"Now,"--said Emma, when they were fairly beyond the sweep E III 10 392 8
What will you say, Emma--what will anybody say, when it is E III 10 395 32
part of our acquaintance, when I did like him, when I was E III 10 396 41
when I did like him, when I was very much disposed to be E III 10 396 41
Mrs. Weston kissed her with tears of joy; and when she E III 10 396 42
What a blessing it is, when undue influence does not E III 10 398 55
Your only blunder was confined to my ear, when you E III 10 399 63
Mr. Knightley had spoken prophetically, when he once said, E III 11 402 1
Mrs. Weston felt when she was approaching Randall's. E III 11 404 3
not very distant either--when you gave me reason to E III 11 405 13
say any thing; and when she did speak, it was in a voice E III 11 405 17
When we talked about him, it was clear as possible." E III 11 406 20
and asking me to dance, when Mr. Elton would not stand up E III 11 406 24
with me; and when there was no other partner in the room. E III 11 406 24
to be; but it contained, when separated from all the E III 11 409 34
When they had been all walking together, he had so often E III 11 409 35
at Hartfield--though, when he first came in, he had said E III 11 410 35
Is not it possible, that when enquiring, as you thought, E III 11 410 36
When Harriet had closed her evidence, she appealed to her E III 11 411 38
When had his influence, such influence begun?-- E III 11 412 45
When had he succeeded to that place in her affection, E III 11 412 45
She saw that there never had been a time when she did not E III 11 412 45
the superior, or when his regard for her had not been E III 11 412 45
When the suggestions of hope, however, which must follow E III 12 415 1
and she hoped, that when able to see them together again, E III 12 416 2
soon it appeared when her thoughts were in one course. E III 12 416 2
This point was just arranged, when a visitor arrived to E III 12 417 3
open the cause; but when these effusions were put by, they E III 12 418 5
of that in her thoughts, when alluding to the E III 12 419 12
to attempt to listen; and when Mrs. Weston ended with, "we E III 12 420 14
When it came to such a pitch as this, she was not able to E III 12 423 21
herself, and leave her less to regret when it were gone. E III 12 423 21
she had taken a few turns, when she saw Mr. Knightley E III 13 424 1
When had he left them?-- E III 13 424 1
"So early in life--at three and twenty--a period when, if E III 13 428 23
for breath to begin, when Mr. Knightley startled her, by E III 13 429 26
27

She was his own Emma, by hand and word, when they returned E III 13 433 42
still be greater when the flutter should have passed away. E III 14 434 1
fever continued; but when he was gone, she began to be a E III 14 434 4
of the evil day, when they must all be together again. E III 14 435 4
thinking of anybody else, when a letter was brought her E III 14 436 6
nature of my situation when I first arrived at Randall's; E III 14 437 8
fortnight, I cannot say;--when I called to take leave of E III 14 438 8
Acquit me here, and procure for me, when it is allowable, E III 14 439 8
When I think of the kindness and favour I have met with, E III 14 439 8
I am mad with joy: but when I recollect all the uneasiness E III 14 439 8
I doubted it more the next day on Box-Hill; when, provoked E III 14 441 8
I reached Highbury at the time of the day when, from my E III 14 443 8
every line agreeable; and when this charm ceased, the E III 15 444 1
She thought so well of the letter, that when Mr. Knightley E III 15 444 2
When he came to Miss Woodhouse, he was obliged to read the E III 15 445 14
15

When it was thus settled on her sister's side, Emma E III 16 451 3
which had haunted her when remembering how disappointed a E III 16 451 4
morning after Box-Hill, when poor Jane had been in such E III 16 452 8
poem at this moment: "for when a lady's in the case, "you E III 16 454 13
When they had all talked a little while in harmony of the E III 16 454 16
17

Oh! if you had seen her, as I did, when she was at the E III 16 454 17
And when Mrs. Bates was saying something to Emma, E III 16 454 17
"When I got to Donwell," said he, "Knightley could not be E III 16 457 38
of deep mourning; but when they are over, I imagine there E III 16 460 56
me, except falling in love with her when she is thirteen." E III 17 462 8
"How often, when you were a girl, have you said to me, E III 17 462 9
I do not say when, but perhaps you may guess where;--in E III 17 463 14
"He writes like a sensible man," replied Emma, when she E III 17 464 20
I dare say there was a difference when I was staying with E III 17 465 27
The time was coming when the news must be spread farther, E III 17 465 28
Knightley's absence, or when it came to the point her E III 17 465 28
always at hand, when he were once got used to the idea.-- E III 17 466 29
She had been extremely surprised, never more so, than when E III 17 467 31
Only let me be told when I may speak out.-- E III 17 468 34
to agitate and grieve her, when Mr. Knightley came in, and E III 18 470 1
my dear Emma, that you will not smile when you hear it." E III 18 470 6
How, where, when?-- E III 18 471 19
This is all that I can relate of the how, where, and when. E III 18 472 20
Your friend Harriet will make a much longer history when E III 18 472 20
which he asked for, when a glimpse was caught through the E III 18 476 44
When Mr. Weston joined the party, however, and when the E III 18 476 46
47

When the Campbells are returned, we shall meet them in E III 18 477 57
time when you found fault with her for being so pale?-- E III 18 478 62
When we first began to talk of her.-- E III 18 478 62
When first sounded on the subject, he was so miserable, E III 19 483 9
the Mr. Knightleys, that when once the event were over, E III 19 483 9
Selina would stare when she heard of it."-- E III 19 484 12
indifference to her when she was called on to quit them.-- P III 1 4 6
unreasonably discontented when a woman does marry again, P III 1 5 8
does marry again, than when she does not; but Sir Walter's P III 1 5 8
evil; and more than once, when her father had left it open P III 1 7 12
excursions to London, when Elizabeth was in her first P III 1 7 14
She knew, that when he now took up the Baronetage, it was P III 1 9 19
of their personableness when they cease to be quite young." P III 3 20 17
They were gradually acquainted, and when acquainted, P III 4 26 1
She had been solicited, when about two-and-twenty, to P III 4 28 7
the way till all was over; when she found it most natural P III 5 32 1
the habit of claiming Anne when any thing was the matter, P III 5 33 7
of the Kellynch-Hall plan, when it burst on her, which was P III 5 34 11
and be out of the way when Admiral and Mrs. Croft first P III 5 36 19
her own absence from home begin when she must give up Anne. P III 5 36 19
"You know I always cure you when I come. P III 5 38 28
"Where shall we go?" said she, when they were ready. P III 5 39 41
and when we have got that over, we can enjoy our walk." P III 5 40 43
off, when you are all gone away to be happy at Bath!" P III 6 42 1
good deal of faith in; but when listening in turn to P III 6 44 6
that was her due, when they dined at the great house with P III 6 45 10
And one day, when Anne was walking with only the Miss P III 6 46 10
She knew that when she played she was giving pleasure only P III 6 47 13
state of imaginary agitation, when she came back. P III 6 48 17
and was glad to be within when the visit was returned. P III 6 48 17
of being acquainted with, when he was in this country." P III 6 49 18
19

and was happy to feel, when Mrs. Croft's next words P III 6 49 22
be listened for, when the youngest Miss Musgrove walked in. P III 6 50 26
ready to be affronted, when Louisa made all right by P III 6 50 26
When the Crofts called this morning, (they called here P III 6 50 27
it came into mamma's head, when they were gone, that P III 6 50 27
at one time, I do not know when or where, but a great P III 6 50 27
scarcely at all regretted, when the intelligence of his P III 6 50 28
affected likewise; and when they reached the cottage, they P III 6 51 32
inevitably have found him, when they were stopped by the P III 7 53 2
to stay dinner--how sorry when he said it was quite out of P III 7 54 4
power--and how glad again, when he had promised in reply P III 7 54 4
The same story and the same raptures were repeated, when P III 7 54 5
a bold public declaration, when he came in from shooting, P III 7 55 7
Husbands and wives generally understand when opposition P III 7 55 9
and teazing a poor child when it is ill; and you saw, this P III 7 56 12
join them in the evening, when the child might be at rest P III 7 58 20
should have done long ago, when events had been early P III 7 58 21
same view of escaping introduction when they were to meet. P III 7 59 23
than beginning breakfast when Charles came in to say that P III 7 59 24
Henrietta asked him what he thought of you, when they went P III 7 60 32
This was his only secret exception, when he said to his P III 7 61 38
39

not out of his thoughts, when he more seriously described P III 7 62 40
There had been a time, when of all the large party now P III 8 63 3
When he talked, she heard the same voice, and discerned P III 8 64 4
Anne of the early days when she too had been ignorant, and P III 8 64 4
When she could let her attention take its natural course P III 8 64 7
vexed you must have been when you came to the Asp, to see P III 8 65 16
We had been six hours in the sound, when a gale came on, P III 8 66 16
"Ah! those were pleasant days when I had the Laconia! P III 8 67 23
I wished for him again the next summer, when I had still P III 8 67 23
day for us, when you were put captain into that ship. P III 8 67 24
"Ah! my dear," said the Admiral, when he has got a wife, P III 8 70 46
When he is married, if we have the good luck to live to P III 8 70 46
"Now I have done," cried Captain Wentworth--"when once P III 8 70 48
you will think very differently, when you are married.' P III 8 70 48
When you come to a frigate, of course, you are more P III 8 70 54
passed by myself at deal, when the Admiral (captain Croft P III 8 71 54
what to do with myself, or when I should hear from him P III 8 71 54
am so glad when they are over, and he is safe back again." P III 8 71 55
in the morning, when he had no companion at home, for the P III 9 73 2
not more than established, when a certain Charles Hayter P III 9 73 3
this critical period, and when he came back he had the P III 9 74 4
had but just reappeared, when Anne had to listen to the P III 9 75 9
A dinner at Mr. Musgrove's had been the occasion, when all P III 9 77 17
as became very alarming, when such a man as Captain P III 9 77 19
He had been absent only two Sundays; and when they parted, P III 9 78 19
When he came back, alas! the zeal of the business was gone P III 9 78 19
continued a few minutes, when, to her very great P III 9 79 25
like to go with them; and when Mary immediately replied, P III 10 83 4
When people come in this manner on purpose to ask us, how P III 10 83 5
it was not possible, that when within reach of Captain P III 10 84 7
shewed her strength, and when he recommended the advantage P III 10 86 17
all stood about her; but when Louisa drew Captain P III 10 86 21
When I have made up my mind, I have made it. P III 10 87 23
betide him, and her too, when it comes to things of P III 10 87 26
to things of consequence, when they are placed in P III 10 87 26
"When did that happen?" P III 10 89 32
hedge with his switch; and when Mary began to complain of P III 10 90 37
of it, was to cross; and when the party had all reached P III 10 90 38
horse into motion again, when Captain Wentworth cleared P III 10 91 39
would not consent; and when it came to be rationally P III 11 94 8
Captain Wentworth long, when they saw him coming after P III 11 96 11
Anne thought she left great happiness behind her when they P III 11 99 19
When the evening was over, Anne could not but be amused at P III 11 101 26
point of conscience, when a clergyman sacrifices his P III 12 103 2
When they came to the steps, leading upwards from the P III 12 104 6
They had nearly done breakfast, when the sound of a P III 12 105 8
When she could command Mary's attention, Anne quietly P III 12 106 18
Breakfast had not been long over, when they were joined by P III 12 107 22
"Not till the first week in August, when he came home from P III 12 108 28
when he spoke again, it was of something totally different. P III 12 108 29
was darting away, when Anne eagerly suggested, "Captain P III 12 110 40
41

The plan had reached this point, when Anne, coming quietly P III 12 114 60
the next morning early, when there would be the farther P III 12 114 64
by the two ladies. when the plan was made known to Mary, P III 12 115 65
of the others could oppose when he gave way, there was no P III 12 115 65
turning towards her; and when he spoke at all, always with P III 12 116 70
Once only, when she had been grieving over the last ill- P III 12 116 70
71

cried herself to sleep; when, as they were going up their P III 12 117 73
a great pleasure; and when it became a sort of parting P III 12 117 75
When the distressing communication at Uppercross was over, P III 12 117 76
to Lyme; and when the horses were baited, he was off. P III 12 117 76
When he came away, she was going to walk out with Captain P IV 1 121 2
When they came to converse, she was soon sensible of some P IV 1 124 11
those of Uppercross, and when Lady Russell reverted to P IV 1 124 11
minutes the day before, when a full account of the whole P IV 1 124 12
When this was told, his name distressed her no longer. P IV 1 125 12
No, except when she thought of her mother, and remembered P IV 1 126 18
grant you, but it is only when the wind is due north and P IV 1 128 30
far at present; for when it was returned, the Crofts P IV 1 128 31
still impossible to say when she might be able to bear the P IV 2 129 1
than suited her, and when they dined with the Harvilles P IV 2 129 3
it was all settled; when behold! on Tuesday night, he made P IV 2 130 5
living in Uppercross; and when he discovered that Lady P IV 2 130 6
"He will sit poring over his book, and not know when a P IV 2 132 19
when one drops one's scissors, or any thing that happens. P IV 2 132 19
And when he does, Mary, you may depend upon hearing my P IV 2 132 20
compliments to them once, when Anne could not but feel P IV 2 134 28
When Lady Russell, not long afterwards, was entering Bath P IV 2 135 33
rapid; for who would be glad to see her when she arrived? P IV 2 135 34
saying to herself, "Oh! when shall I leave you again?" P IV 3 137 2
Her making a fourth, when they sat down to dinner, was P IV 3 137 2
in his way to London, when the intelligence of Sir P IV 3 138 6
endeavours to meet, and, when they did meet, by such great P IV 3 138 6
knowing her but in public, and when very young himself. P IV 3 140 11
exactly as he had done when they last parted;" but Sir P IV 3 141 12
misuse, when a knock at the door suspended every thing. P IV 3 142 17
inn, which he had adopted, when quite a young man, on the P IV 3 144 19
When he questioned, Sir Walter and Elizabeth began to P IV 3 144 22
from easy about it, when she had been at home a few hours. P IV 4 145 1
and vexed her as much when she was away, as a person in P IV 4 146 5
that said late viscount, when, in consequence of a P IV 4 148 12
head of the sinner, for when poor Lady Elliot died herself, P IV 4 149 12
worth having," and when Anne ventured to speak her opinion P IV 4 150 15
those periods of her life when it had been most valuable. P IV 5 152 2
There had been a time, Mrs. Smith told her, when her P IV 5 154 9
a home in that house when unemployed, chanced to be at P IV 5 154 9
Every body's heart is open, you know, when they have P IV 5 155 9
and nurse Rooke thoroughly understands when to speak. P IV 5 155 9
Call it gossip if you will; but when nurse Rooke has half P IV 5 155 9
has generally taken me, when I have called on Mrs. Smith." P IV 5 157 18
probably not a short one) when he had been, at least, P IV 5 161 27
very intently one evening, when a thicker letter than P IV 6 162 1
I am always out of the way when any thing "desirable is P IV 6 163 7
to ask her how she did, when we were "rather surprised not P IV 6 164 8
of interest in the letter; when Mrs. Clay had paid her P IV 6 166 17
when she thought of Captain Wentworth unshackled and free. P IV 6 167 21
She longed to see the Crofts, but when the meeting took P IV 6 168 22
hearty shake of the hand when he encountered an old friend, P IV 6 168 24
eagerness of conversation when occasionally forming into a P IV 6 168 24
When he did perceive and acknowledge her, however, it was P IV 6 169 25
When they were got a little farther, Anne ventured to P IV 6 170 30
She had hoped, when clear of Milsom-Street, to have her P IV 6 170 30

When we came back from Minehead, he was gone down to P IV 6 171 33
just reached this point when Anne, as she sat near the P IV 7 175 4
She was lost; and when she had scolded back her senses, P IV 7 175 5
She had hardly spoken the words, when Mr. Elliot walked in. P IV 7 177 16
"She is pretty, I think; Anne Elliot; very pretty, when P IV 7 177 21
to time, anxiously; and when the moment approached which P IV 7 179 28
"By all means," said she; "only tell me all about it, when P IV 7 180 34
Mrs. Smith made no reply; but when she was leaving her, P IV 7 180 35
But hardly were they so settled, when the door opened P IV 8 181 1
When you had the presence of mind to suggest that benwick P IV 8 182 6
replied Anne: "but when pain is over, the remembrance of P IV 8 183 16
The delightful emotions were a little subdued, when, on P IV 8 184 18
When their places were determined on, and they were all P IV 8 186 22
When she could give another glance, he had moved away. P IV 8 188 42
Such was her situation, with a vacant space at hand, when P IV 8 189 47
must confess that he should not be sorry when it was over. P IV 8 190 47
it well worth occupying; when, at that moment, a touch on P IV 8 190 47
inevitably consumed; and when her own mistress again, when P IV 8 190 48
her own mistress again, when able to turn and look as she P IV 8 190 48
her from home at the time when Mr. Elliot would be most P IV 9 192 1
to come and sit with me, when you must have so many P IV 9 194 18
as an old friend, do give me a hint as to when I may speak. P IV 9 195 27
you do not design to be cruel, when the right moment comes. P IV 9 195 30
Do not forget me when you are married, that's all. P IV 9 196 32
who opened the door to you, when you called yesterday?" P IV 9 197 38
"Yes; he was not married when I knew him first." P IV 9 198 48
When one lives in the world, a man or woman's marrying for P IV 9 201 64
portion only of what I had to look over when I lost him. P IV 9 202 69
70

about those things; and when I came to examine his papers, P IV 9 203 70
When I talked of a whole history therefore, you see, I was P IV 9 205 82
I found them on the most friendly terms when I arrived." P IV 9 205 83
as September, (in short when they first came themselves) P IV 9 206 88
was going on there, and when Mr. Elliot came to Bath for a P IV 9 206 90
into the marriage articles when you and Mr. Elliot marry, P IV 9 208 92
character would allow, when Anne's refutation of the P IV 9 210 99
most miserable, when time had disclosed all, too late? P IV 9 211 102
when she heard that he was coming again in the evening. P IV 10 212 2
However, when I found how excessively he was regretting P IV 10 213 5
When I found he was really going to his friends at P IV 10 213 9
language, was odious; and when she thought of his cruel P IV 10 214 11
I have a great value for benwick; and when one can but get P IV 10 218 26
And this satisfied Elizabeth: and when the invitation was P IV 10 220 29
had been won by her usefulness when they were in distress. P IV 10 220 31
been there half an hour, when their dining-room, spacious P IV 10 221 32
all the others liked it, when Mary eagerly interrupted her P IV 10 223 42
43

be too abominable if you do! when you promised to go." P IV 10 223 45
She had spoken it; but she trembled when it was done, P IV 10 225 54
When she reached the White Hart, and made her way to the P IV 11 229 2
was beginning to say, when a slight noise called their P IV 11 233 24
what a man suffers when he takes a last look at his wife P IV 11 234 31
you the glow of his soul when he does see them again; when, P I 6 235 31
he does see them again; when, coming back after a P I 6 235 31
of loving longest, when existence or when hope is gone." P IV 11 235 32
And when I think of benwick, my tongue is tied." P IV 11 236 34
where he had been writing, when footsteps were heard P IV 11 236 40
"than when you almost broke it eight years and a half ago. P IV 11 237 42
tones of "that voice, when they would be lost on others.-- P IV 11 237 42
Will you promise me to mention it, when you see them again? P IV 11 239 51
They were in Union-Street, when a quicker step behind, a P IV 11 239 55
in their re-union, than when it had been first projected; P IV 11 240 59
He had imagined himself indifferent, when he had only been P IV 11 241 61
kept him from trying to regain her when thrown in his way. P IV 11 242 63
To a degree, I could contradict this instantly; but, when P IV 11 242 65
When I yielded, I though it was to duty; but no duty could P IV 11 244 73
Tell me if, when I returned to England in the year eight, P IV 11 247 82
When any two young people take it into their heads to P IV 12 248 1
On the contrary, when he saw more of Captain Wentworth, P IV 12 248 2
her own abilities; and when the awkwardness of the P IV 12 249 4
She had something to suffer perhaps when they came into P IV 12 250 5
of our being in town;--when everything was in the hurry & S 1 367 1
Two hours take us home, from Hailsham--and when once at S 1 367 1
coach which had been new when they married & fresh lined S 2 373 1
When Mr & Mrs Parker therefore ceased from soliciting a S 2 374 1
He had been an elderly man when she married him;--her own S 3 375 1
out of her own power--and when on Sir Harry's decease she S 3 375 1
points, when her love of money is carried greatly too far. S 3 376 1
When you see us in contact, you will judge for yourself."-- S 3 376 1
the hotel at all hazards, when the cousins, the politic & S 3 378 1
You will not think I have made a bad exchange, when we S 4 380 1
of those dreadful nights, when we had been literally S 4 381 1
more mischief in a valley, when they do arise than an open S 4 381 1
him what help we can--& when any vegetables or fruit S 4 382 1
There was no blue shoe when we passed this way a month ago. S 4 383 1
When they met before dinner, Mr P. was looking over S 5 385 1
Two years ago I happened to be calling on Mrs Sheldon when S 5 386 1
of a watering-place day, when the important business of S 6 389 1
capable state of judging, when Sir Edw: was gone, of how S 7 395 1
The first object of the parkers, when their house was S 7 395 1
They are never out of my thoughts when I walk here.-- S 7 396 1
The future might explain him further--but when there was a S 7 398 1
And when he died, I gave Sir Edwd his gold watch.--" S 7 400 1
Thus it is, when rich people are Sordid."-- S 7 402 1
decision--and even when the event is mainly anti- S 8 403 1
reached the little lawn, when she saw a lady walking S 9 406 1
the door was not opened, when the other crossed the lawn;-- S 9 406 1
crossed the lawn;--and when the servant appeared, they S 9 406 1
Woodcock's assistance--& when I left her she was directing S 9 407 1
Miss Capper happened to be staying with Mrs D. when Mrs G. S 9 408 1
This was the state of the case when I wrote to you;--but S 9 409 1
I hate to employ others, when I am equal to act myself-- S 9 409 1
negatived, it was "and when shall we see you again? and S 9 410 1
till the following day, when, being removed into lodgings S 10 413 1
When they were all finally seated, after some removals to S 10 414 1
standing at an open window when there is no wind--but S 10 415 1
When his toils were over however, he moved back his chair S 10 416 1
delighted himself; but when her toast was done, & he took S 10 417 1
& the blame, that probably when she had divided out their S 11 420 1
be the sort of person who, when once she is prevailed on S 12 424 1
hardly able to stand--and when the Leaches have done, I S 12 424 1
It was a close, misty morng, & when they reached the brow S 12 425 1

WHENCE (15)
from a quarter, whence I had least reason to apprehend it. LS 22 281 4
From whence arose so astonishing a misapprehension of your LS 24 289 12
The letter, whence sprang all this felicity, was short, NA I 15 122 28
of a servant in the place whence she had taken them," NA II 7 172 2
his own residence, from whence she might judge, herself, SS I 4 23 20
this spot, from whence perhaps I may view you no more!-- SS I 5 27 8
was at Allenham, from whence he hoped she would allow him SS I 9 42 10
at the park; from whence he usually returned in the SS III 13 369 34
the mansion-house, from whence they could superintend the SS III 14 374 7
from whence they were to set out early the next morning. PP II 18 235 40
of the higher grounds; whence, in spots where the opening PP III 1 253 57
Elizabeth was at no loss to understand from whence this PP III 6 295 7
him that the suspicions whence, he must confess to himself, MP II 10 280 32
of home to himself, whence resulted her brother's E I 11 97 27
the only source whence any thing like consolation or E III 12 423 21

WHERE'S (2)
Where's dear Mr. Richard?-- E III 2 323 19
"Where's the difficulty?-- S 12 424 1

WHERE-EVER (1)
Remember, where-ever you are, you must be the lowest and MP II 5 221 32

WHEREABOUTS (3)
the east room, without having an idea whereabouts it was! MP III 5 360 14
Whereabouts does the thrush lay at Spithead! MP III 7 378 12
I wonder whereabouts they will upset to-day. P III 10 84 8

WHEREAS (5)
increase as they went on, whereas she had imagined that NA I 2 21 9
of substance and credit, whereas the transactions of the NA II 15 246 12
Whereas, in my opinion, by her taking so much notice of SS II 11 227 46
whereas it was certainly in the best hands of the two. MP I 13 122 2
whereas the pain she hoped would return no more. MP II 13 308 36

WHEREBY (1)
and Edmund to detail, whereby a most considerable saving MP II 2 188 3

WHERES (1)
described, and all the wheres and hows of a circumstance E III 5 351 38

WHEREWITH (1)
the very security of his affection, wherewith to pity her. P IV 10 225 62

WHICHEVER (3)
escaped his observation; whichever were the case, though PP II 1 134 3
house, whichever it might be, where Mr. Darcy then was. PP III 1 253 55
Whichever Mr. Yates did not choose, would perfectly MP I 14 132 8

WHILE (590)
ladyship spent in town, while her daughter was left in LS 6 251 1
to be attended to, while she remains with Miss Summers. LS 7 252 1
And this circumstance while it explains the true motive of LS 14 264 3
while he is so very eager in Lady Susan's justification. LS 15 266 2
with some severity while she is here;--a most painful LS 15 267 6
They came while we were at tea, & I never saw any creature LS 17 269 1
I am sure I cannot say that it had, but while Miss Summers LS 17 271 7
sitting with my children while they dined, & supposing I LS 20 275 1
varying every instant, while Reginald observed all that LS 20 276 3
because I thought that while Frederica continued at school, LS 20 277 5
that such circumstances, while they continue from any LS 20 277 5
woman is a fool indeed who while insulted by accusation, LS 22 282 7
ever, while mine will be found still fresh & implacable. LS 22 282 7
It is a great while since I have seen my father & mother. LS 23 283 4
of his countenance while I spoke, to see the struggle LS 25 293 3
by ratifying it, while there is so much reason to fear the LS 30 300 1
Mr Johnson, while he waited in the drawing room for me. LS 32 302 1
But the unfortunate Mrs Manwaring, whose agonies while she LS 36 306 1
to such an extremity while any other alternative remains. LS 38 306 1
There was little leisure for speaking while they danced; NA I 3 25 2
Whether she thought of him so much, while she drank her NA I 3 29 52
almost forgot Mr. Tilney while she talked to Miss Thorpe. NA I 4 33 6
And while the abilities of the nine-hundredth abridger of NA I 5 37 4
Oh! it is only a novel!" replies the young lady; while she NA I 5 38 4
much pleased with him; but while I have Udolpho to read, I NA I 6 41 19
Away they walked to the book; and while Isabella examined NA I 6 43 34
could have leisure to do, while the bright eyes of Miss NA I 7 44 4
which were her due; for while he slightly and carelessly NA I 7 45 5
at the average of four hours every day while I am here." NA I 7 48 27
I hope you will be a great deal together while you are in NA I 7 50 49
the appearance of infamy while her heart is all purity, NA I 8 53 2
which he entered into while they were standing up, of the NA I 8 55 10
to have it dropped for a while, she could not avoid a NA I 8 57 21
with every body about her, while she remained in the rooms, NA I 9 60 1
silent; and, therefore, while she sat at her work, if she NA I 9 60 1
entirely repress a doubt, while she bore with the NA I 9 66 32
Yes; I remember, I asked you while you were waiting in the NA I 10 75 26
him, while she furnishes the fan and the lavender water. NA I 10 77 35
But while she did so, the gentleman retreated, and her NA I 10 80 59
While talking to each other, she had observed with some NA I 12 95 17
of his gallantry; and, while they waited in the lobby for NA I 12 95 18
had known her so little a while, than for her best and NA I 13 98 2
I had entered on my studies at Oxford, while you were a NA I 14 107 11
"While, in fact," cried his sister, "it ought only to be NA I 14 108 17
while we praise Udolpho in whatever terms we like best. NA I 14 108 17
that it is very well worth while to be tormented for two NA I 14 110 27
support her spirits, and while away the many tedious hours NA I 15 121 26
Her whole happiness seemed at stake, while the affair was NA II 2 138 1
That he should think it worth his while to fancy himself NA II 3 148 29
since they first met, and while my father's consent was NA II 4 151 13
scarcely heard his voice while his father remained in the NA II 5 155 3
The clock struck ten while the trunks were carrying down, NA II 5 155 4
While they snugly repair to their own end of the house, NA II 5 158 15
in motionless wonder, while these thoughts crossed her:-- NA II 6 163 1
2

not to examine it thoroughly while she was about it." NA II 6 169 11
written characters; and while she acknowledged with awful NA II 6 169 11
wisest to take the morning while it is so fine; and do not NA II 7 177 17
And, when she saw him in the evening, while she worked NA II 8 187 13
which could be done only while the household slept; and NA II 8 187 16
In revolving these matters, while she undressed, it NA II 8 188 17
not pretend to say that while she lived, she might not NA II 9 197 27
Eleanor's work was suspended while she gazed with NA II 10 204 18
and mean another all the while, was most unaccountable! NA II 11 211 15
Frederick could not be unpardonably guilty, while Henry NA II 12 219 16
His loss was not now what it had been while the general NA II 13 221 7
the sentences exchanged while they remained up stairs, NA II 13 227 27
ought to have with her, while she could preserve the good NA II 14 239 28
happiness depended; and while Mrs. Morland was NA II 14 239 28
were steady, and while his parent so expressly forbad the NA II 16 249 2
something for their mother while she lives rather than for SS I 2 10 16
which it produced for a while; for when her spirits began SS I 3 14 1
likewise; but in the mean while, till one of these SS I 3 16 6
frequent attention to her while she draws, that in fact he SS I 3 17 18
a good deal together, while you have been wholly engrossed SS I 4 20 9
to inhabit or visit it while such a woman was its mistress. SS I 4 24 20
mother answered for him, while he hung about her and held SS I 6 31 9
all the year round, while Sir John's independent SS I 7 32 1
his conversation with the others while every song lasted. SS I 7 35 9
listening so attentively while she sang to them; and when SS I 8 36 1
at their entrance, and while the eyes of both were fixed SS I 9 42 9
that he resided there only while he was visiting the old SS I 9 44 23
together by mutual consent, while the others were dancing. SS I 11 55 8
While they were at breakfast the letters were brought in. SS I 13 63 3
had kept in the lanes, while the others went on the downs. SS I 13 67 60
to enter the house while Mrs. Smith was in it, with whom SS I 13 68 66
"Yes, Marianne, but I would not go while Mrs. Smith was SS I 13 68 69
before of calling on her while they were absent, was SS I 15 75 1
schemes, and absent himself from Devonshire for a while. SS I 15 78 26
in themselves, though unavoidably secret for a while? SS I 15 79 28
while his own enjoyment in it appeared so imperfect. SS I 18 96 1
word which fell from him while at Barton, and above all to SS I 19 102 2
I thought I heard a carriage last night, while we were SS I 19 106 20
to look at one another, while Mrs. Jennings continued her SS I 19 106 21
Now, pray do,--and come while the Westons are with us. SS I 20 113 29
happened to be staying at Barton while he was at Allenham. SS I 20 114 44
"Yes, a great while; ever since my sister married.-- SS I 20 116 62
"I confess," replied Elinor, "that while I am at Barton SS I 21 123 20
to be intimate, and while his continual schemes for their SS I 21 124 33
was under my uncle's care, you know, a considerable while." SS I 22 130 24
by description a great while; and as soon as I saw you, I SS I 22 132 42
His imprudence had made her miserable for a while; but it SS II 1 140 1
her defects of education, while the same period of time, SS II 1 140 2
receive no assistance, while her self-command would SS II 1 141 6
But indeed, while Elinor remained so well assured within SS II 1 142 7
rival's intentions, and while she was firmly resolved to SS II 1 142 7
accompanied them, and while they remained there, she was SS II 1 143 10
risk of her displeasure for a while by owning the truth?" SS II 2 148 14
"If we could be certain that it would be only for a while! SS II 2 148 15
and the present incumbent not likely to live a great while. SS II 2 149 25

Context	Work	Vol	Ch	Page	Line
"I am sorry for that," returned the other, while her eyes	SS	II	2	150	38
matters; for it is a long while since I have been at home,	SS	II	4	163	14
contentment about it, yet while she saw Marianne in	SS	II	5	167	7
"Good God!" cried Marianne, "he has been here while we	SS	II	5	169	14
This event, while it raised the spirits of Elinor,	SS	II	5	169	15
began her letter directly, while Marianne, too restless	SS	II	5	172	39
of others, while reviving her with lavender water.	SS	II	6	177	12
sister then left her, and while she waited the return of	SS	II	6	178	16
Her own situation gained in the comparison; for while she	SS	II	6	179	18
lasted no longer than while she spoke, and was immediately	SS	II	7	180	4
Think of your mother; think of her misery while you suffer;	SS	II	7	185	21
And can you believe me to be so, while I see you so	SS	II	7	185	23
"I can have no pleasure while I see you in this state."	SS	II	7	186	27
her as well as she could, while Marianne still remained on	SS	II	8	193	5
Colonel Brandon came in while the party were at tea, and	SS	II	8	198	30
Mrs. Jennings, who had watched them with pleasure while	SS	II	8	200	43
Thus a circumstance occurred, while the sisters were	SS	II	9	202	4
directions for the future; while Marianne, who came into	SS	II	9	203	10
confined to the house, while the girls were ranging over	SS	II	9	209	28
might force him before her while paying that visit at	SS	II	10	213	4
it was resolved, that while her young friends transacted	SS	II	11	220	2
is, for we must live at a great expense while we are here."	SS	II	11	225	28
very good-natured fellow: while Lady Middleton saw enough	SS	II	11	228	52
most anxious to mortify; while she herself, who had	SS	II	12	232	16
But while she smiled at a graciousness so misapplied, she	SS	II	12	233	16
or two all were silent; while Marianne was looking with	SS	II	13	242	25
It so happened that while her two sisters with Mrs.	SS	II	14	248	6
But while the imaginations of other people will carry them	SS	II	14	248	6
But while she wondered at the difference of the two young	SS	II	14	250	12
of a private education; while he himself, though probably	SS	II	14	250	12
such, while Mrs. Jennings's engagements kept her from home.	SS	II	14	252	20
"What!--while attending me in all my misery, has this been	SS	III	1	262	20
But I did not love only him;--and while the comfort of	SS	III	1	263	27
while your kind friend there, was attending her daughter.	SS	III	1	266	36
While she with the truest affection had been planning a	SS	III	1	266	38
the feelings of Edward, while braving his mother's threats,	SS	III	1	268	46
regard his mother's anger, while he could have my	SS	III	2	277	30
Brandon and Elinor, while they stood at the window, the	SS	III	3	284	24
it is not worth while to wait two or three months for him.	SS	III	4	291	51
of his manner while enjoying so unfair a division of his	SS	III	5	298	32
Elinor, while she waited in silence, and immovable gravity,	SS	III	5	298	34
"Yes; once, while she was staying in this house, I	SS	III	5	299	37
minutes within its walls, while the others were busily	SS	III	6	302	8
every hour of every day while she remained with the	SS	III	6	303	9
she watched his eyes, while Mrs. Jennings thought only of	SS	III	6	305	16
of his behaviour;--and while his looks of anxious	SS	III	6	305	16
of following her; and while he was preparing to go,	SS	III	7	308	5
to send to Colonel away while his love was in so much	SS	III	7	309	5
at piquet of an evening, while Miss Dashwood was above	SS	III	7	309	5
and while attempting to sooth her, eagerly felt her pulse.	SS	III	7	311	14
fervent gratitude, and while he went to hurry off his	SS	III	7	311	15
by four horses; and this, while it told the excess of her	SS	III	7	316	29
to pass my time pleasantly while I was obliged to remain	SS	III	8	319	29
"it is hardly worth while, Mr. Willoughby, for you to	SS	III	8	320	30
					31
while my circumstances were so greatly embarrassed.	SS	III	8	321	34
You must have known, that while you were enjoying yourself	SS	III	8	322	37
blameable," said Elinor, while her voice, in spite of	SS	III	8	329	64
shook me by the hand while he reminded me of an old	SS	III	8	330	69
Vanity, while seeking its own guilty triumph at the	SS	III	8	331	70
self-evident sensations, while in the actions and words of	SS	III	10	340	3
as she had done; but while her resolution was unsubdued,	SS	III	11	352	19
further down for a little while, but however, when they	SS	III	11	354	27
always admitted a hope, while Edward remained single, that	SS	III	12	357	1
that lay there, and while spoiling both them and their	SS	III	12	360	22
					23
but I scorn to accept a hand while the heart was another's.	SS	III	13	365	14
humility may be convenient while acknowledging a second	SS	III	13	372	44
thirty thousand pounds, while Miss Dashwood was only the	SS	III	14	373	3
no means her eldest; for while Robert was inevitably	SS	III	14	374	4
Robert or Fanny; and while Edward was never cordially	SS	III	14	377	11
he is married to another woman, while I am still single.--	W			316	2
"Mr Turner had not been dead a great while I think?	W			325	5
Mrs Edwards carefully guarding her own dress, while she	W			327	7
way up the wide staircase, while no sound of a ball but	W			327	7
only were formally seated, while three or four officers	W			327	8
to order the dance, while Miss Osborne passing before her,	W			330	11
for some minutes longer, while Tom Musgrave was chattering	W			346	21
jumped up with apologies, while Elizth called briskly	W			346	21
"You were gone a great while, were not you? a fortnight I	W			356	28
"You may call a fortnight a great while Mr Musgrave, said	W			356	28
I have not been in the way of it now for a long while.--	W			358	28
The clock struck nine, while he was thus agreably occupied;	W			359	28
him at supper, while he went home to dinner himself.--	W			359	28
"While Mary is adjusting her ideas," he continued, "let us	PP	I	2	7	20
to declare that it was what she had expected all the while.	PP	I	2	7	23
He listened to her with perfect indifference, while she	PP	I	6	27	54
eagerly calling out, while her daughter read, "well, Jane,	PP	I	7	30	14
					15
sent for immediately; while his sisters, convinced that no	PP	I	8	40	59
by duets after supper, while he could find no better	PP	I	8	40	59
After sitting a little while with Jane, on Miss Bingley's	PP	I	9	41	2
every possible attention while she remains with us."	PP	I	9	41	5
But you would not wish to be dancing while she is ill."	PP	I	9	45	37
Mrs. Hurst sang with her sister, and while they were thus	PP	I	10	51	46
soon done--done while Mrs. Bennet was stirring the fire.	PP	I	15	71	4
be a conversible companion if he thinks it worth his while.	PP	I	16	82	48
"While I can have my mornings to myself," said she, "it is	PP	I	17	87	11
"Do you talk by rule then, while you are dancing?"	PP	I	18	91	12
of fatigue while enumerating the advantages of the match.	PP	I	18	99	63
than Mr. Bennet himself, while his wife seriously	PP	I	18	101	71
our pools at quadrille, while Mrs. Jenkinson was arranging	PP	I	19	105	10
While the family were in this confusion, Charlotte Lucas	PP	I	20	112	25
known, and in the mean while may lessen the pain of	PP	I	21	116	8
to say a great deal while Sir William remained; but no	PP	I	23	126	5
She hated having visitors in the house while her health	PP	I	23	128	11
Nothing, on the contrary, could be more natural; and while	PP	II	5	150	26
frost, turned back; and while Sir William accompanied him,	PP	II	5	156	5
It was spoken of again while they were at dinner, when Mr.	PP	II	5	157	6
					7
While they were dressing, he came two or three times to	PP	II	6	161	7
While Sir William was with them, Mr. Collins devoted his	PP	II	7	168	1
Her favourite walk, and where she frequently went while	PP	II	7	169	5
invitation thither, for while there were visitors in the	PP	II	8	172	1
that her ladyship after a while shared the feeling, was	PP	II	8	172	3
					4
and writing to Jane, while Mrs. Collins and Maria were	PP	II	9	177	1
He had ruined for a while every hope of happiness for the	PP	II	10	186	38
While settling this point, she was suddenly roused by the	PP	II	11	188	3
without attempting to interrupt her while she continued.	PP	II	11	191	11
At that ball, while I had the honour of dancing with you,	PP	II	12	197	5
After pausing on this point a considerable while, she once	PP	II	13	206	4
Catherine and Lydia; but while they were supported by	PP	II	14	213	17
While there was an officer in Meryton, they would flirt	PP	II	14	213	17
would flirt with him; and while Meryton was within a walk	PP	II	14	213	17
while they are sharers of our intimacy at Rosings."	PP	II	15	216	4
to walk about the room, while Elizabeth tried to unite	PP	II	15	216	5
thanks for their kindness to you while you have been here."	PP	II	15	217	9
frivolous gallantry; and while she steadily repressed it,	PP	II	18	233	25
While she spoke, Wickham looked as if scarcely knowing	PP	II	18	234	35
and anxious attention, while she added, "when I said that	PP	II	18	234	35
					36

Context	Work	Vol	Ch	Page	Line
The possibility of meeting Mr. Darcy, while viewing the	PP	II	19	240	16
drove to the door; and, while examining the nearer aspect	PP	III	1	245	4
turned away with alarm, while Mrs. Reynolds replied, that	PP	III	1	246	8
and aunt stopped also, and while the former was	PP	III	1	251	50
They stood a little aloof while he was talking to their	PP	III	1	251	52
adieu to the river for a while, ascended some of the	PP	III	1	253	57
This idea lasted while a turning in the walk concealed him	PP	III	1	254	57
as often as he chose, while he continued in the	PP	III	1	255	60
While these newly-born notions were passing in their heads,	PP	III	2	260	1
while it was passing, the enjoyment of it had been little.	PP	III	2	264	12
While thus engaged, Elizabeth had a fair opportunity of	PP	III	3	268	7
While she spoke, an involuntary glance shewed her Darcy	PP	III	3	269	10
above-mentioned; and while Mr. Darcy was attending them to	PP	III	3	270	12
While the contents of the first letter remained on her	PP	III	4	279	24
She had never perceived while the regiment was in	PP	III	4	280	25
it is not worth while to relate; but his lies about the	PP	III	5	284	14
which had been passing while Mr. and Mrs. Gardiner were	PP	III	5	286	32
before the servants, while they waited at table, and	PP	III	5	288	40
to pursue, while in town, for the recovery of his daughter.	PP	III	5	293	68
soon lagged behind, while her sister, panting for breath,	PP	III	7	301	7
					8
talk on without interruption, while the servants remained.	PP	III	8	310	9
But while he was mortal, there must be a triumph.	PP	III	8	312	14
laugh, that it was a great while since she had been there.	PP	III	9	315	4
and his easy address, while he claimed their relationship,	PP	III	9	316	5
with her behaviour while she staid with us, if I had not	PP	III	10	325	2
Did you see him while you were at Lambton?	PP	III	10	328	18
with her sister; for while he was present, Jane had no	PP	III	13	349	44
"It ought to be so; it must be so, while he retains the	PP	III	14	354	36
While in their cradles, we planned the union: and now, at	PP	III	14	355	43
They lagged behind, while Elizabeth, Kitty, and Darcy,	PP	III	16	365	1
to be executed, and, while her courage was high, she	PP	III	16	365	2
					3
sitting with Kitty; and, while pretending to admire her	PP	III	17	375	28
behaviour to Jane, while she was ill at Netherfield?"	PP	III	18	380	6
to see her want, while I had a bit of bread to give her?	MP	I	1	7	8
and leave her to herself, while they adjourned to whatever	MP	I	2	14	7
For a long while no answer could be obtained beyond a "no,	MP	I	2	15	10
His daughters he felt, while they retained the name of	MP	I	2	20	33
like it after a little while, and feel how right you	MP	I	3	27	36
her "my dear Fanny," while he said it, every former frown	MP	I	3	33	64
and affectionate preparatory speeches for a while.	MP	I	4	34	2
gave themselves no airs; while the praises attending such	MP	I	4	35	4
received; but in the mean while, as no one felt a doubt of	MP	I	4	39	12
While she treated it as a joke, therefore, she did not	MP	I	4	42	18
while they were the finest young women in the country.	MP	I	5	44	1
while? and what was her opinion of the new-comers?	MP	I	5	48	30
and, for a little while, other subjects took place of the	MP	I	6	55	14
hours with Mrs. Rushworth while the rest of you walked	MP	I	6	62	58
her sister to their home, while Mr. Crawford was devoted	MP	I	7	65	14
hour in the flower garden, while Fanny cut the roses, and	MP	I	7	72	42
She has not been out on horseback now this long while, and	MP	I	7	73	55
While she was gone, Mr. Rushworth arrived, escorting his	MP	I	8	75	1
While each of the Miss Bertrams was meditating how best,	MP	I	8	80	29
of civilly listening, while Fanny, to whom every thing was	MP	I	9	85	3
from any of the rooms, and while Fanny and some of the	MP	I	9	85	4
prayers here twice a day, while they are inventing excuses	MP	I	9	86	13
While this was passing, the rest of the party being	MP	I	9	88	19
gallantries of her lover, while Mrs. Rushworth spoke with	MP	I	9	88	24
to that lady's slow pace, while her aunt, having fallen in	MP	I	9	90	36
for her to escape; while the want of that higher species	MP	I	9	91	36
to you, I should be glad to sit down for a little while."	MP	I	9	94	57
After sitting a little while, Miss Crawford was up again.	MP	I	9	96	73
Her cousin was safe on the other side, while these words	MP	I	10	100	22
Such a penance as I have been enduring, while you were	MP	I	10	100	28
body who shuts their eyes while they look, or their	MP	I	11	107	3
understandings while they reason, feels the comfort of.	MP	I	11	107	3
out on a twilight scene, while the Miss Bertrams, Mr.	MP	I	11	108	4
It is a great while since we have had any star-gazing."	MP	I	11	113	41
to listen, for it was while all the other young people	MP	I	12	116	11
While waiting and wishing, looking now at the dancers and	MP	I	12	117	11
thoughtfully by the fire, while Lady Bertram was on the	MP	I	13	125	14
into a gentle doze, while Fanny was getting through the	MP	I	13	126	19
was already at work, while a play was still to seek.	MP	I	14	130	1
softened her a little; but while she hesited what to say,	MP	I	14	135	15
would be necessary--while Maria and Henry Crawford	MP	I	14	136	21
nor wait very patiently while he was slowly turning over	MP	I	15	138	1
about the house for one while,--I hate such greediness--so	MP	I	15	142	22
other three at the table, while his sister made her way to	MP	I	15	143	26
While he spoke, Maria was looking apprehensively round at	MP	I	15	148	59
mind as Fanny's, and while there was a gleam of sunshine,	MP	I	16	151	2
and which had all slept while she listened to him, were	MP	I	16	156	28
being very good friends while their interest were the same,	MP	I	17	162	19
Allow me to stay here a little while, and do have the	MP	I	18	168	17
most palpitating heart, while the others prepared to begin.	MP	I	18	172	32
these fearful thoughts, while the other three, no longer	MP	II	1	176	4
to be inevitably at hand; while Mr. Yates considered it	MP	II	1	177	5
"but it is not worth while to bore my father with it now.	MP	II	1	181	16
him to lead the discourse while he mingled among the	MP	II	1	184	25
He was anxious, while vindicating himself, to say nothing	MP	II	2	187	1
He believed this very stoutly while he was in Mansfield	MP	II	2	191	10
was the next question; and while this branch of the	MP	II	2	193	17
great attention to my mother and sisters while he was away.	MP	II	3	196	2
And while my cousins were sitting by without speaking a	MP	II	3	198	12
After a little while I dare say we shall be meeting again	MP	II	3	199	14
drawing-room for an hour while the rain continued, the	MP	II	4	206	3
and you must not set forward while it is so threatening.	MP	II	4	207	9
while you do wrong together I can overlook a great deal."	MP	II	4	211	28
and embarrassment; and while stammering out her great	MP	II	4	215	47
uncle were to be a great while considering and deciding,	MP	II	5	218	12
"A woman can never be too fine while she is all in white.	MP	II	5	222	44
thereon, she found, while they were at table, such a happy	MP	II	5	223	48
It came happily while she was thus waiting; and there	MP	II	6	233	15
the absorbed attention, while her brother was describing	MP	II	6	235	19
to whether it were worth while, "because Sir Thomas seemed	MP	II	7	238	2
I came to look for you, and after waiting a little while	MP	II	9	261	2
confusion of discontent; while Miss Crawford wondered she	MP	II	10	277	20
While her hand was trembling under these letters, her eye	MP	II	13	299	4
in not having it finished while I was in London!	MP	II	13	299	5
of it even to Mary; while uncertain of the issue, he could	MP	II	13	300	7
While her heart was still bounding with joy and gratitude	MP	II	13	301	7
to think as she would, while her aunts finished the	MP	II	13	304	18
While Fanny's mind was engaged in these sort of hopes, her	MP	III	1	324	60
It had every recommendation to him, and while honouring	MP	III	3	335	6
how it fell from her hand while she sat motionless over it-	MP	III	3	337	11
long while since we have had a comfortable walk together."	MP	III	4	346	6
Her secret was still her own; and while that was the case,	MP	III	5	365	34
a while towards him--because he really seemed to feel.--	MP	III	5	365	35
without her so long, while she was so useful to herself.--	MP	III	6	370	14
home for a while would be a great advantage to every body.	MP	III	6	372	19
Had she doubted his meaning while she listened, the glow	MP	III	6	374	26
the environs of Portsmouth while there was yet daylight	MP	III	7	376	6
pushed the maid aside, and while William was opening the	MP	III	7	377	7
While considering her with these ideas, Betsey, at a small	MP	III	7	386	40
not expected by one, who, while seeing all the obligation	MP	III	9	397	8
While trying to keep herself alive, their visitor, who had	MP	III	10	399	5
her time to recover, while he devoted himself entirely to	MP	III	10	399	5
while they walked on together at their own hasty pace.	MP	III	10	403	14
never-failing interest, while the young people sat down	MP	III	10	403	15
He went to while away the next three hours as he could,	MP	III	11	412	29
For a great while it was so; but at last the longing grew	MP	III	14	431	8
ragged carpet as usual, while the tea was in preparation--	MP	III	15	439	9

of being exquisitely happy, while so many were miserable. MP III 15 443 24
Just before their setting out from Oxford, while Susan was MP III 15 446 34
to be at hand, and when, while much is actually given to MP III 15 446 35
very happily in so doing, while those who might otherwise MP III 16 449 4
Nature resisted it for a while. MP III 16 459 31
as to make them for a while each other's punishment, and MP III 17 464 10
good humour and good luck; while she must withdraw with MP III 17 464 12
are the poor horses to be while we are paying our visit?" E I 1 8 17
It rained dreadfully hard for half an hour, while we were E I 1 10 26
any thing put on it; and while his hospitality would have E I 3 24 12
might constrain himself, while the ladies were comfortably E I 3 24 13
14

He had a very fine flock; and while she was with them, he E I 4 28 6
But while I visit at Hartfield, and you are so kind to me, E I 4 31 23
a few yards forward, while they talked together, soon made E I 4 31 27
while Harriet is presenting such a delightful inferiority? E I 5 38 15
"as can well be; and while she is so happy at Hartfield, I E I 5 41 30
much incommoding him, while he seemed mostly fearful of E I 6 49 42
She paused over it, while Harriet stood anxiously watching E I 7 51 4
For a little while Emma persevered in her silence; but E I 7 52 18
19

While you were at all in suspense I kept my feelings to E I 7 53 24
While you were in the smallest degree wavering, I said E I 7 53 24
While she was gone, Mr. Knightley called, and sat some E I 8 57 2
I believe I had better take my three turns while I can. E I 8 57 3
while, nobody within her reach will be good enough for her. E I 8 64 47
not, while she was at abbey-mill, find him disagreeable. E I 8 65 48
I shall leave off while I am well." E I 8 66 54
and saying to herself, while Harriet was puzzling over the E I 9 72 15
not have left the paper while I was by; but he rather E I 9 77 47
"We must ask Mr. and Mrs. Weston to dine with us, while E I 9 79 61
He sat musing a little while, and then said, "but I do not E I 9 80 65
66

company as she can while my brother and sister are here. E I 9 80 69
He may be sure of every woman's approbation while he E I 9 82 82
hesitating a good deal while he spoke, "I have no E I 9 82 83
While they were thus comfortably occupied Mr. Woodhouse E I 12 100 17
And for a little while she hoped he would not talk of it, E I 12 105 51
in the tone of his voice while assuring her that he should E I 13 111 14
She had sent while dressing, and the answer had been, " E I 13 114 28
Emma's project of forgetting Mr. Elton for a while, made E I 14 118 4
Harriet, from her mind, while he not only sat at her elbow, E I 14 118 4
of appearing very polite, while feeling very cross--and of E I 14 119 6
While he talked to Isabella, however, Emma found an E I 14 122 19
be most natural, that while she makes no sacrifice for the E I 14 123 24
whom she owes every thing, while she exercises incessant E I 14 123 24
blocked up at Randalls, while her children were at E I 15 127 13
should remain at Randalls, while she and her husband set E I 15 127 13
of any comfort for him while he continued at Randalls. E I 15 128 17
it was safe to stay; and while the others were variously E I 15 128 17
18

These feelings rapidly restored his comfort, while Mrs. E I 18 144 3
A little while ago, he was at Weymouth. E I 18 146 12
his while; whenever there is any temptation of pleasure." E I 18 146 14
visit to his father; and while meanly exerting their power E I 18 147 18
deceived aunt, while eagerly hunting for the letter.-- E II 1 157 10
She was pondering, in the mean while, upon the possibility, E II 1 158 13
to speak of his own place while he was paying his E II 1 159 20
settled, while Jane Fairfax had yet her bread to earn. E II 2 165 7
sucking in the sad poison, while a sharer of his E II 2 168 13
attention wanted by him, while he lamented that young E II 3 177 51
While he staid, the Martins were forgotten; and on the E II 4 185 11
her at the Abbey mill, while she drove a little farther, E II 4 185 13
she, in mental soliloquy, while walking down stairs from E II 5 189 20
to find an opportunity, while their two fathers were E II 5 191 28
his certainly thinking it worth while to try to please her. E II 5 191 28
ago for a ball-room, and while the neighbourhood had been E II 6 197 5
They went in; and while the sleek, well-tied parcels of " E II 6 200 16
Something occurred while they were at Hartfield, to make E II 7 206 5
It was the arrival of this very invitation while the E II 7 208 8
together after dinner; and while her father was fondly E II 8 213 6
while warm from her heart, for he stopped to hand her out. E II 8 213 7
to be general; and while politics and Mr. Elton were E II 8 214 13
in the drawing-room, while I do not know one note from E II 8 215 16
At first, while I suppose you satisfied that Col. Campbell E II 8 219 42
yourself, and I must tell them while the idea is fresh. E II 8 222 59
Well, a little while ago it occurred to me how very sad it E II 8 223 63
instance than I do; for while Miss Bates was speaking, a E II 8 224 65
it would last a great while--and, indeed, she must E II 8 225 78
While waiting till the other young people could pair E II 8 229 99
long at a purchase; and while she was still hanging over E II 9 233 24
"And while Mrs. Weston pays her visit, I may be allowed, I E II 9 234 27
"It is not worth while, Harriet, to give Mrs. Ford the E II 9 235 37
sit down with us a little while, and give us your opinion E II 9 235 44
She was in the adjoining chamber while she still spoke, E II 10 243 32
couple are not enough to make it worth while to stand up. E II 11 248 7
8

it might have been worth while to pause and consider, and E II 11 250 19
to think it all over while she was gone, the two young E II 11 253 40
If the Westons think it worth while to be at all this E II 12 257 3
I shall do very well again after a little while--and then, E II 13 265 4
was not worth while to think about them--and she would not E II 13 267 9
made her wretched for a while, and when the violence of E II 13 268 13
else; but it was not worth while to attack an error so E II 14 273 22
23

While they are with us, we shall explore a great deal, I E II 14 274 28
"And who do you think came in while we were there?" E II 14 278 48
I shall have her very often indeed while they are with me, E II 15 284 9
Instead of drawing his brother off to a window while they E II 16 292 10
They will stay a good while when they do come, and he will E II 17 304 27
A little while ago, every letter Isabella brought an E II 18 312 46
any thing the matter with them, while dear Emma were gone. E III 1 318 13
While she talked of his son, Mr. Weston's attention was E III 2 321 16
while smiles of high glee passed between him and his wife. E III 2 328 38
she had yet had with him, while Harriet had been partially E III 3 335 11
And I had plenty all the while in my pocket!-- E III 4 339 13
you to check your feelings while you can: at any rate do E III 4 342 39
But while so many were devoting him to Emma, and Emma E III 5 343 2
He sat a little while in doubt. E III 5 350 31
topics with which for a while the Sucklings' coming had E III 6 352 1
Mrs. Weston, while the dear girls walked about the gardens. E III 6 356 30
Emma looked at Harriet while the point was under E III 6 361 41
for his old friend, to while away the morning; and the E III 6 362 43
"No--it will not be worth while. E III 6 365 70
While he was so dull, it was no wonder that Harriet should E III 7 367 2
While waiting for the carriage, she found Mr. Knightley by E III 7 374 55
will tell you truths while I can, satisfied with proving E III 7 375 61
While they talked, they were advancing towards the E III 7 375 62
I must, I will tell you truths while I can." E III 8 377 1
perhaps, he might come in while she were paying her visit. E III 8 377 2
It was settled so, upon the hill, while we were walking E III 8 381 17
While he stood, as if meaning to go, but not going--her E III 9 385 5
prospects were closing, while Harriet's opened, and whose E III 9 389 16
he certainly did--while he really belonged to another?-- E III 10 396 44
Composure with a witness! to look on, while repeated E III 10 397 46
While poor Mrs. Churchill lived, I suppose there could not E III 10 398 55
His wife gave him a look which invited him in; and, while E III 10 400 65
have been privately engaged to one another this long while. E III 11 404 8
had; and she made the most of it while her friend related. E III 12 417 5
cheeks towards him; for while she spoke, it occurred to E III 13 425 8
While he spoke, Emma's mind was most busy, and, with all E III 13 430 38
While he lived, it must be only an engagement; but she E III 14 435 4

My courage rises while I write. E III 14 437 8
part of my conduct while belonging to you, which excites E III 14 438 8
While you considered me as having sinned against Emma E III 14 439 8
While I, to blind the world to our engagement, was E III 14 441 8
cause to him, for my suspense while all was at stake?-- E III 14 443 8
"Say nothing, my dear Emma, while you oblige me to read-- E III 15 447 26
"While her dear father lived, any change of condition must E III 15 448 31
of her face; and while paying her own compliments to Mrs. E III 16 453 12
13

When they had all talked a little while in harmony of the E III 16 454 16
17

to Box-Hill again, while the fine weather lasts?-- E III 16 455 18
observing her a little while, he added, "Emma, my love, E III 18 472 21
22

Emma soon recollected, and understood him; and while she E III 18 480 76
ought to be concluded while John and Isabella were still E III 19 483 8
While either of them protected him and his, Hartfield was E III 19 484 10
She had, while a very young girl, as soon as she had known P III 1 7 14
While Lady Elliot lived, there had been method, moderation, P III 1 9 19
would think it worth their while to observe me, but Sir P III 3 17 4
yet for something more, while Anne was nineteen, she would P III 4 28 7
Mary, had been at school while it all occurred--and never P III 4 31 11
while Anne could be of none, was a very sore aggravation. P III 5 34 11
While well, and happy, and properly attended to, she had P III 5 37 21
and sit with them a little while, and when we have got P III 5 40 43
had the superiority, for while Mary thought it a great P III 6 43 5
fell to the share of Anne, while the Admiral sat by Mary, P III 6 48 17
or where, but a great while before he died, poor fellow! P III 6 50 27
Mr. and Mrs. Musgrove cannot think it wrong, while I P III 7 57 15
delighted to receive him; while a thousand feelings rushed P III 7 59 25
eye wandering towards her while he spoke, Anne felt the P III 8 63 2
Anne suppressed a smile, and listened kindly, while Mrs. P III 8 64 7
an excellent correspondent, while he was under your care! P III 8 67 27
and sentiment; and while the agitations of Anne's slender P III 8 68 29
While we were together, you know, there was nothing to be P III 8 70 54
These were some of the thoughts which occupied Anne, while P III 8 72 58
with Mr. Musgrove's; and while the Musgroves were in the P III 9 74 5
husband nor wife; for while she considered Louisa to be P III 10 82 1
And there was silence between them for a little while. P III 10 85 11
The sweet scenes of autumn were for a while put by--unless P III 10 85 12
their aunt and cousins, while the rest of the party waited P III 10 86 18
This nut," he continued, with playful solemnity,--"while P III 10 88 26
While she remained, a bush or low rambling holly protected P III 10 88 27
being on the hedge side, while Anne was never incommoded P III 10 90 37
She had died the preceding summer, while he was at sea. P III 11 96 12
While Captain Wentworth and Harville led the talk on one P III 11 100 23
heard the carriage, sir, while you were at dinner; and P III 12 105 12
his very polite excuses, while she had never been near him P III 12 106 19
had prompted, but in vain; while Captain Wentworth, P III 12 110 37
38

all beneath his roof; and while Louisa, under Mrs. P III 12 111 50
They were sick with horror while he examined; but he was P III 12 112 52
while it was only an interchange of perplexity and terror. P III 12 113 57
but, after, a while, Captain Wentworth, exerting himself, P III 12 113 57
58

who was nothing to Louisa, while she was her sister, and P III 12 115 65
her, while I go in and break it to Mr. and Mrs. Musgrove. P III 12 117 74
to the Harvilles, while the Harvilles had been wanting P IV 2 129 2
them, while Mr. Elliot's frequent visits were talked of. P IV 3 140 11
Anne drew a little back, while the others received his P IV 3 143 18
While Sir Walter and Elizabeth were assiduously pushing P IV 5 152 1
Mrs. Clay, who had been present while all this passed, now P IV 5 158 20
While Admiral Croft was taking this walk with Anne, and P IV 7 174 1
turned into Molland's, while Mr. Elliot stepped to Lady P IV 7 174 2
While they were speaking, a whispering between her father P IV 8 181 2
far as to say, "you were a good while at Lyme, I think?" P IV 8 183 11
12

said Anne, conscious while she spoke, that there had in P IV 9 193 13
It is a great while since we met." P IV 9 194 22
Hear the truth, therefore, now, while you are unprejudiced. P IV 9 199 53
scattered here and there, while many letters and P IV 9 203 70
can ever be secure, while she holds her present influence. P IV 9 208 92
face of every thing, and while it took from her the new- P IV 9 210 99
While her father spoke, there was a knock at the door. P IV 10 216 17
over in a calmer hour; for while still hearing the sounds P IV 10 225 61
business, and they met no more while Anne belonged to them. P IV 10 227 68
of its kind in Bath, while harassing herself in secret P IV 10 227 69
was perfectly audible while it pretended to be a whisper. P IV 11 230 5
such a day,' but all the while hoping for them twelve P 1 6 235 31
I mean, while the woman you love lives, and lives for you. P IV 11 235 32
While supposed to be writing only to Captain Benwick, he P IV 11 237 41
immediate struggle; but after a while she could do no more. P IV 11 238 45
which had reached him while she talked with Captain P IV 11 241 60
brother's, meaning after a while to return to Kellynch, P IV 11 243 66
Was it unpardonable to think it worth my while to come? P IV 11 243 70
While he was not obliged to say that he believed her to P IV 12 251 10
did not fail her; and while these prime supplies of good P IV 12 252 12
& gratitude & while one or two of the men lent their help S 1 365 1
It gives me no pain while I am quiet,--and as soon as S 1 367 1
the evils of civilization, while the growth of the place, S 1 368 1
might get out;--and while making that home extremely S 2 374 1
In the mean while we have the canvas Awning, which gives S 4 381 1
simply rages & passes on--while down in this Gutter-- S 4 381 1
& mama & their children; while Charlotte having received S 4 384 1
& communications, while Charlotte having added her name to S 6 390 1
influenced by them; & while she pleased herself the first S 6 391 1
better half at least--(for while single, the gentleman may S 7 394 1
But while we are on the subject of poetry, what think you S 7 397 1
While I have been travelling, with this object in veiw, I S 9 410 1
& quick feelings--and while the eldest brother found vent S 10 412 1
indisposed to talk;--and while the other 4 were cheifly S 10 415 1
a great deal while I am here, if the weather is temperate. S 10 416 1
him watching his sisters, while he scrupulously scraped S 10 417 1
in all who came near her while she sketched--and to both, S 11 421 1
And while you are on the subject of subscriptions Mary, I S 12 424 1

WHILED (1)
of the morning was easily whiled away, in lounging round SS III 6 303 10

WHILST (4)
Stop me whilst you can." PP II 1 136 19
more violence than ever; whilst the luckless Kitty PP II 18 230 12
Whilst wandering on in this slow manner, they were again PP III 1 254 57
Elizabeth, as she affectionately embraced her, whilst PP III 5 286 23

WHIM (2)
You think me unsteady--easily swayed by the whim of the MP III 3 343 41
the power of fancy and whim in your dealings with them, as E I 12 98 4

WHIMPER (1)
She may whimper, & the Vernons may storm; I regard them LS 39 308 1

WHIMS (8)
of her whims, at the expense of her mother's inclination. LS 25 294 5
and humouring all their whims; and such of their time as SS I 21 120 6
Follies and nonsense, whims and inconsistencies do divert PP I 11 57 21
I have not been used to submit to any person's whims. PP III 14 356 48
(in her way--allowing for little whims and caprices, and E I 14 120 13
thinking the better of him for submitting to their whims. E I 18 147 18
than that "all young people would have their little whims." E II 7 205 1
observed, "all young people would have their little whims." E II 7 206 3

WHIMSICAL (2)
it, there was something whimsical, it was certainly a very NA II 6 168 10
"But perhaps he may be a little whimsical in his PP III 1 258 72

WHINE (1)
"No, no; Frederick is not a man to whine and complain; he P IV 6 172 45

WHIP (3)

and dexterity with which he had directed his whip. NA I 9 62 10
But Mr. Thorpe only laughed, smacked his whip, encouraged NA I 11 87 53
So there I have the whip hand of you." SS I 20 112 25
WHIRL (1)
attachment; but the whirl of a ball-room perhaps was not MP II 8 256 13
WHIRLING (1)
and she, by the sudden whirling round of something or E II 1 160 23
WHISKED (2)
moment she was herself whisked into the market-place. NA I 11 87 53
with which she had whisked away Mr. Rushworth's pink satin MP II 1 179 10
WHISPER (41)
on beholding her, no whisper of eager inquiry ran round NA I 2 23 27
she said, in a whisper to Catherine, "I dare say she NA I 8 59 34
saw him presently address Mr. Tilney in a familiar whisper. NA I 10 80 59
was Isabella's answer in the same half whisper. NA II 3 147 22
but these words, in a whisper to Eleanor, "how glad I NA II 5 155 3
remain to tell what nothing else was allowed to whisper? NA II 9 194 6
round to her and said, in a whisper, "I have been guessing. SS I 18 100 23
"Mr. Palmer is so droll!" said she, in a whisper, to SS I 20 112 27
"His name is Ferrars," said he, in a very audible whisper; SS I 21 125 38
whisper--"will be exceedingly welcome to all parties." SS II 11 224 24
in a whisper, a brief account of the whole shocking affair. SS II 12 236 41
and at last he said in a whisper, 'for fear any unpleasant SS III 1 258 5
and speaking in an awful whisper--"I may assure you;--and SS III 5 297 31
look at herself, and whisper a few sentences to each other. SS III 12 358 9
again, Emma in the low whisper which became the solemn W 327 8
whisper aloud "Oh! uncle, do look at my partner. W 332 11
"You may imagine, said Margt in a sort of whisper what are W 356 28
Miss Bingley, in a half whisper, "that this adventure has PP I 8 36 12
help cautioning her in a whisper not to be a simpleton and PP I 18 90 8
in a less audible whisper; for to her inexpressible PP I 18 99 64
to her, cried in a half whisper, "I am glad you are come, PP I 20 112 25
as for Mary, she was mistress enough of herself to whisper PP III 5 289 41
Her heart did whisper, that he had done it for her. PP III 10 326 3
whisper, "the men shan't come and part us, I am determined. PP III 12 341 16
17
Mrs. Bennet was privileged to whisper it to Mrs. Philips, PP III 13 350 55
whisper, "go to your father, he wants you in the library." PP III 17 375 28
Mrs. Grant, pretending to whisper across the table to Mrs. MP I 6 54 13
the proposal, added in a whisper--"we want to make a table MP I 12 119 23
thus addressing her in a whisper at once angry and audible: MP I 15 146 53
to her in a kind low whisper as she placed herself, "never MP I 15 147 56
moment, then added, in a whisper, "and I shall write to MP III 6 373 26
surmise nothing, whisper nothing, till I write again. MP III 15 437 3
"It is not fair," said Emma in a whisper, "mine was a E II 10 241 10
Mr. Weston whisper to his wife, "he has asked her, my dear. E II 11 256 60
"How do you like Mrs. Elton?" said Emma in a whisper. E III 2 324 25
whisper, "I mentioned no names, you will observe.-- E III 16 454 14
15
she was roused by a whisper of Mrs. Musgrove's, who, P III 8 64 5
6
in a sort of whisper, "that must not be any reason, indeed. P IV 4 145 1
was perfectly audible while it pretended to be a whisper. P IV 11 230 5
Musgrove in her powerful whisper, "though we could have P IV 11 230 6
She can only speak in a whisper--and fainted away twice S 5 387 1
WHISPERED (21)
"How uncomfortable it is," whispered Catherine, "not to NA I 2 22 12
again to his sister and whispered, "my dear creature, I am NA I 8 52 2
beads round her head," whispered Catherine, detaching her NA I 8 56 15
"Do not be frightened, my dear Catherine," whispered NA I 10 74 23
"Do not be so dull, my dearest creature," she whispered. NA I 11 90 64
"My father," she whispered, "often walks about the room in NA II 8 187 13
and whispered--"the Colonel looks as grave as ever you see. SS II 8 198 30
And drawing him a little aside, she whispered her SS II 13 244 43
Mrs. Jennings immediately whispered to Elinor, "get it all SS III 2 271 5
6
slighted--her name was whispered from one party to another, W 328 9
"How charming Emma is!--" whispered Margt to Mrs Robert in W 350 24
"Emma is delightful, is not she?--whispered Margt. W 357 28
"This fine account," whispered her aunt, as they walked, " PP III 1 249 40
expose her sister to the whispered gallantries of her MP I 9 88 24
the room; somebody had whispered something to her, she had MP II 11 283 4
ever-----Mrs. Cole once whispered to me--but I immediately E II 3 176 44
"It will not do," whispered Frank to Emma, "they are most E III 7 370 23
something to Emma, whispered farther, "we do not say a E III 16 454 17
believed, would ever be whispered, and in the trust that P III 4 30 10
"My brother," whispered one of the girls; "mamma is P III 8 67 26
including every body!" whispered Mary very audibly. P IV 10 227 66
WHISPERING (15)
into the ball-room, whispering to each other whenever a NA I 8 52 1
"But what is all this whispering about? NA I 8 57 17
was conveyed in such whispering voices, and their vivacity NA I 10 72 8
They retired whispering together; and, though her delicate NA II 1 132 16
of the room, they were whispering and talking together as SS I 12 60 13
The two girls had been whispering to each other during the PP I 9 45 35
young lady's whispering to Elizabeth again, he walked away. PP III 12 342 25
whispering a few words to her sister ran out of the room. PP III 13 346 22
as well as I could, by whispering to him, 'we shall have MP I 18 169 21
with their buyings, they began whispering to one another. E II 3 178 52
Emma took the opportunity of whispering, "you speak too E II 10 243 23
24
And then whispering--"our companions are excessively E III 7 369 16
his head, and whispering seriously) that my uncle means to E III 18 479 70
While they were speaking, a whispering between her father P IV 8 181 2
elbow, reading verses, or whispering to her, all day long." P IV 10 218 24
WHISPERS (2)
After a few whispers, indeed, which placed it beyond a E III 16 455 20
21
as many whispers, and disturb as many people as they could. P IV 8 185 19
WHIST (18)
She hates whist I know; but is there no round game she SS II 8 195 14
For now we have a quiet little whist club that meets three W 325 4
He says his head won't bear whist--but perhaps if we make W 354 28
of obliging her in return, by sitting down to whist. PP I 16 76 6
Mr. Wickham did not play at whist, and with ready delight PP I 16 76 8
The whist party soon afterwards breaking up, the players PP I 16 82 49
least regard his losses at whist, enumerating all the PP I 16 84 59
her mother's rapacity for whist players, and in a few PP III 12 342 26
old woman, who knows no more of whist than of algebra. MP I 12 119 26
in tranquillity; and as a whist table was formed after tea- MP II 5 227 68
that after making up the whist table there would remain MP II 7 239 4
on almost as soon as whist; and Lady Bertram soon found MP II 7 239 4
and being required either to draw a card for whist or not. MP II 7 239 4
Whist and speculation; which will amuse me most?" MP II 7 239 5
He was a whist player himself, and perhaps might feel that MP II 7 239 6
behaviour; but when the whist table broke up at the end of MP II 7 246 36
and drinking, and playing whist with his neighbours five E I 11 96 26
was to accommodate a whist club established among the E II 6 197 5
WHIST-CLUB (1)
though it was the whist-club night, which he had been E I 8 68 58
WHIST-PLAYERS (1)
and fathers, and whist-players, who were pretending to E III 2 325 32
WHIST-TABLE (1)
obliged to assist in making a whist-table for the others. SS II 4 166 31
WHITAKERS (1)
"Who! why yourselves, and the Careys, and Whitakers to be SS I 18 99 20
WHITBY'S (2)
you can get a parasol at Whitby's for little Mary at any S 4 381 1
vol:s they had left behind them on Mrs Whitby's shelves.-- S 6 391 1
WHITE (39)
is too often used I believe to make black appear white. LS 6 251 1
"Look at that young lady with the white beads round her NA I 8 56 15
"Go by all means, my dear; only put on a white gown; Miss NA I 12 91 2
only put on a white gown; Miss Tilney always wears white." NA I 12 91 2
eyes the view of a white cotton counterpane, properly NA II 6 164 3
a piece of white paper, and put it into his pocket-book." SS I 12 60 13
Marianne, now looking dreadfully white, and unable to SS II 6 177 12
reading prayers in a white surplice, and publishing the SS III 5 298 33
I had seen Marianne's sweet face as white as death.-- SS III 8 327 55
His complexion was white with agitation, and he looked as SS III 12 359 11
can be, but I still profess my preference of a white skin. W 357 28
has made white soup enough I shall send round my cards." PP I 11 55 7
Both changed colour, one looked white, the other red. PP I 15 73 8
encounter the remains of a white frost, turned back; and PP II 5 156 5
child in the little white attic, near the old nurseries. MP I 1 9 12
I am to leave Mansfield Park, and go to the white house, I MP I 3 25 20
to be remembered at such a distance as the white house. MP I 3 26 31
of Mansfield parish; the white house being only just large MP I 3 28 38
At the white house, matters must be better looked after. MP I 3 30 50
Mrs. Norris took possession of the white house, the Grants MP I 3 31 58
she has turned away two housemaids for wearing white gowns. MP I 10 105 55
You must get a brown gown, and a white apron, and a mob MP I 15 146 52
The little white attic, which had continued her sleeping MP I 16 150 1
almost as decidedly as the white attic;--the smallness of MP I 16 151 1
as red as she had been white before, she turned out of the MP II 1 175 2
"A woman can never be too fine while she is all in white. MP II 5 222 44
air to produce a very white world in a very short time. E I 13 112 24
I am sure I must have been as white as my gown. I could E II 3 178 52
The quarter of an hour brought her punctually to the white E II 5 186 3
such a trimming as this to my white and silver poplin. E II 17 302 22
Harriet looked white and frightened, and he was trying to E III 3 333 3
scarce--chili preferred--white wood finest flavour of all-- E III 6 358 35
"Very little white satin, very few lace veils; a most E III 19 484 12
which followed, added-- "he is rear Admiral of the white. P III 3 21 20
21
of September in all the white glare of Bath, and grieving P III 5 33 6
were smartened up with a white curtain & "lodgings to let"- S 4 383 1
two females in elegant white were actually to be seen with S 4 383 1
the pales of something white & Womanish in the field on S 12 426 1
of the two, Miss B.'s white ribbons might not have fallen S 12 426 1
WHITE HART (6)
tower over the hedge, & the White Hart is close by it.-- W 321 2
Horses for two carriages are ordered from the White Hart, W 323 3
times a week at the White Hart, & if he cd but have his W 325 4
a few days with Mrs. Musgrove, and were at the White Hart. P IV 10 216 18
forward to the White Hart, to see again the friends and P IV 10 220 30
When she reached the White Hart, and made her way to the P IV 11 229 2
WHITE-HART (1)
Rev. Philip Elton, White-Hart, Bath, was to be seen under E II 5 186 1
WHITEN (1)
places hardly enough to whiten the ground; a very few E I 15 127 16
WHITER (1)
her lips became whiter than even sickness had left them. SS III 10 347 33
WHITHER (15)
Why, or whither she intended to go, does not appear; but LS 15 266 2
He is now shut up in his apartment, whither I heard him go, LS 22 282 8
ladies; and, on finding whither they were going, it was NA I 7 47 18
rather angrily back, demanding whither she were going?-- NA II 8 185 6
directly into the house, whither Margaret was just arrived, SS I 9 42 8
to Barton, whither he was purposely coming to visit them. SS I 16 86 22
In the drawing-room, whither she then repaired, she was SS II 8 197 26
the other side of Bath; whither her husband promised, at SS III 7 308 3
her in a day or two; and whither she was almost equally SS III 7 308 3
the village of Stanton, whither my good stars prompted me W 338 18
whither he was obliged to go the next day for a short time. PP I 18 103 76
him again at Longbourn, whither he hoped to be able to PP I 23 128 10
Edmund to London, whither, on the authority of her aunt's MP III 9 398 10
to the editor of the newspaper, whither they were gone." MP III 15 440 14
the great question of whither he should go, was settled, P III 2 13 8
WHITWELL (6)
Their intended excursion to Whitwell turned out very SS I 13 63 1
presence is necessary to gain your admittance at Whitwell." SS I 13 64 21
hours before his usual time, on purpose to go to Whitwell." SS I 13 65 32
and we must put off the party to Whitwell till you return." SS I 13 65 35
could only be enjoyed at Whitwell, they might procure a SS I 13 66 60
of our intended party to Whitwell; and this was the reason SS II 9 209 30
WHOEVER (11)
I only wish that they--whoever they are--to whom I am LS 20 278 7
they may be--with whom I happen to be in company." NA I 14 113 45
This woman of whom he writes--whoever she be--or any one, SS II 7 189 50
Elinor would not contend, and only replied, "whoever may SS II 7 189 51
No Emma, whoever stays at home this winter, it shan't be W 320 2
the future incumbent, whoever he might be, would, in all MP I 3 24 4
"Whoever might be her parents," said Mr. Knightley, " E I 8 62 42
said Mr. Knightley, "whoever may have had the charge of E I 8 62 42
"This is an alliance which, whoever--whatever your friends E I 9 75 27
"Whoever Col. Campbell might employ," said Frank Churchill, E II 10 241 8
Whoever suffered inconvenience, she must suffer none, but P IV 7 174 3
WHOLE (391)
was ever more altered; the whole family are at war, & LS 2 245 1
delicious gratification of making a whole family miserable. LS 4 248 1
Upon the whole I commend my own conduct in this affair LS 7 253 2
like a coquette in the whole course of my life, tho' LS 10 258 2
whole of your family, far & near, must highly reprobate. LS 12 260 1
I like him on the whole very well, he is clever & has a LS 16 268 2
her arrival, & expected them impatiently the whole evening. LS 17 269 1
This pathetic representation lasted the whole evening, & LS 17 270 3
or perverseness during her whole stay in Wigmore St till LS 17 271 7
to acquaint yourself and Mr Vernon with the whole business. LS 20 277 5
to me, very soon made the whole party understand that his LS 22 280 2
& the whole business seemed most comfortably arranged. LS 22 281 3
to the contempt of the whole world, & the severest LS 22 282 8
& sat with him in his room, talking over the whole matter. LS 24 285 2
very ready to oblige the whole party by consenting to a LS 42 313 7
chance of her throwing a whole party into raptures by a NA I 1 16 10
any thing I like so well in the whole room, I assure you." NA I 2 22 11
The whole being explained, many obliging things were said NA I 4 33 6
I should like to spend my whole life in reading it. NA I 6 40 7
on her he bestowed a whole scrape and half a short bow. NA I 7 45 5
I did we should certainly be separated the whole evening." NA I 8 52 2
another, and from the whole she deduced this useful lesson, NA I 8 55 10
By him the whole matter seemed entirely forgotten; and all NA I 9 66 31
But I really had been engaged the whole day to Mr. Thorpe." NA I 10 72 11
so dirty the whole winter; it is ancle-deep every where." NA I 11 85 41
genuine merriment--no longer keep her whole attention. NA I 12 92 4
was never withdrawn from the stage during two whole scenes. NA I 12 92 4
the whole, left one of the happiest creatures in the world. NA I 12 95 16
it in two days--my hair standing on end the whole time." NA I 14 106 7
stupid they can be for a whole morning together, and how NA I 14 109 26
voluntarily rejected the whole city of Bath, as unworthy NA I 14 111 29
The whole walk was delightful, and though it ended too NA I 14 114 49
of the whole world, your brother would be my only choice." NA I 15 119 18
And so he hardly looked once at you the whole day?" NA II 1 130 3
have been miserable if I had sat down the whole evening. NA II 1 134 39
Her whole happiness seemed at stake, while the affair was NA II 2 138 1
a mistake--for I did not see him once that whole morning." NA II 3 145 11
"But that you certainly did, for you spent the whole NA II 3 145 12
the whole of their conversation her manner had been odd. NA II 3 148 28
She had resisted its approaches during the whole length of NA II 4 153 30
rising at intervals the whole afternoon; and by the time NA II 6 166 9
The whole building enclosed a large court; and two sides NA II 7 177 19
and a whole parish to be at work within the inclosure. NA II 7 178 21
It was Sunday, an the whole time between morning and NA II 9 190 1
and it seemed as if the whole might be traced to the NA II 10 200 2

Context	Work	Vol	Ch	Page	Para
watching her through the whole letter, saw plainly that it	NA	II	10	202	8
that Henry should lay the whole business before him as it	NA	II	11	208	2
his conduct throughout the whole visit, so well assured	NA	II	11	215	28
an engagement that takes our whole family away on Monday.	NA	II	13	224	13
sight in Fullerton, the whole family were immediately at	NA	II	14	233	8
here, when the whole was unfolded, was an insult not to be	NA	II	14	233	10
whole family to the General in a most respectable light.	NA	II	15	245	12
The whole was tied up for the benefit of this child, who,	SS	I	1	4	3
not know whether, upon the whole, it would not be more	SS	I	2	10	16
whole of his fortune depended on the will of his mother.	SS	I	3	15	5
and taste; and, upon the whole, I venture to pronounce	SS	I	4	20	9
accommodate them, and the whole of his letter was written	SS	I	4	23	20
A small green court was the whole of its demesne in front;	SS	I	6	28	1
whole of the valley, and reached into the country beyond.	SS	I	6	29	3
Mrs. Dashwood was upon the whole well satisfied; for	SS	I	6	29	4
But the whole of their behaviour to each other has been	SS	I	8	39	18
The whole country about them abounded in beautiful walks.	SS	I	9	40	3
The whole story would have been speedily formed under her	SS	I	11	57	17
This was all overheard by Miss Dashwood; and in the whole	SS	I	12	59	7
By ten o'clock the whole party was assembled at the park,	SS	I	13	63	2
He then took leave of the whole party.	SS	I	13	66	45
behaviour during the whole of the evening declared at once	SS	I	14	74	20
This violent oppression of spirits continued the whole	SS	I	15	82	47
She was awake the whole night, and she wept the greatest	SS	I	16	83	1
She spent whole hours at the pianoforte alternately	SS	I	16	83	3
The whole family perceived it, and Mrs. Dashwood,	SS	I	17	90	1
view of the whole, which had exceedingly pleased him.	SS	I	18	96	4
He was particularly grave the whole morning.	SS	I	18	99	14
very well disposed on the whole to regard his actions with	SS	I	19	101	2
was pronounced on the whole to be the most advantageous	SS	I	19	103	4
prevent your whole youth from being wasted in discontent.	SS	I	19	103	7
employed herself the whole day, neither sought nor avoided	SS	I	19	104	10
them, or lying awake the whole night to indulge meditation,	SS	I	19	104	12
Sir John wanted the whole family to walk to the park	SS	I	21	119	3
They have brought the whole coach full of playthings for	SS	I	21	119	4
upon Elinor therefore the whole task of telling lies when	SS	I	21	122	14
of a man, of whose whole heart she felt thoroughly	SS	II	1	141	4
less interesting than the whole of their discourse both in	SS	II	1	143	10
might be the less when the whole truth were revealed, and	SS	II	3	157	17
which filled the whole soul and beamed in the eyes of	SS	II	4	159	1
At that moment she first perceived him, and her whole	SS	II	6	176	3
My esteem for your whole family is very sincere; but if I	SS	II	7	183	13
the whole evening more serious and thoughtful than usual.	SS	II	8	200	43
other, that she wept with agony through the whole of it.	SS	II	9	202	8
in a whisper, a brief account of the whole shocking affair.	SS	II	12	236	41
the impression of what had passed, the whole evening.	SS	II	12	236	42
Middletons, spent the whole of every day in Conduit-Street.	SS	II	14	246	2
and minute account of the whole affair between Marianne	SS	II	14	247	4
home, she might spend a whole day without hearing any	SS	II	14	247	4
on it, during the whole of her toilette, which it received	SS	II	14	249	8
necessary to give up the whole of her time to her; and	SS	III	1	257	1
conduct throughout the whole, has been such as every	SS	III	1	268	45
She liked him, however, upon the whole much better than	SS	III	6	305	15
and nursing her the whole day, against Marianne's	SS	III	7	307	1
home; and, attended the whole way by a servant of Mrs.	SS	III	7	308	4
she resolved to sit with her during the whole of it.	SS	III	7	310	9
little intermission the whole afternoon, calming every	SS	III	7	315	25
for the past; to open my whole heart to you, and by	SS	III	8	319	23
"I insist on your hearing the whole of it," he replied.	SS	III	8	320	32
have probably heard the whole story long ago."	SS	III	8	321	34
did, for I was in town the whole time,) what I felt is--in	SS	III	8	325	50
You have proved yourself, on the whole, less faulty than I	SS	III	8	329	66
"He opened his whole heart to me yesterday as we travelled.	SS	III	9	336	12
In the whole of her subsequent manner, she traced the	SS	III	10	342	7
even by himself, and his whole conduct declares that self-	SS	III	11	350	9
"The whole of his behaviour," replied Elinor, "from the	SS	III	11	351	11
be fairly drawn from the whole of the story--that all	SS	III	11	352	16
					17
She recognised the whole of Lucy in the message, and was	SS	III	11	355	39
some part, but not the whole, of the case, thought it	SS	III	12	359	13
might appear to the whole family, it was certain that	SS	III	13	361	1
he did not, upon the whole, expect a very cruel reception.	SS	III	13	366	20
The whole of Lucy's behaviour in the affair, and the	SS	III	14	376	11
Marianne could never love by halves; and her whole heart	SS	III	14	379	17
that have escaped with a whole heart, and yet I was the	W			316	1
he cried, must not expect to engross you the whole evening.	W			334	13
as he had been fixed the whole time at the same table in	W			336	14
Mary was surrounded by red coats the whole eveng.	W			337	15
She had scarcely run her eye thro' the whole, before she	W			338	18
"Upon the whole, he added, I have had a very comfortable	W			344	20
of that day, & the whole of the next, which comprised the	W			360	30
and to crown the whole, he meant to be at the next	PP	I	3	9	1
The evening altogether passed off pleasantly to the whole	PP	I	3	12	15
remain the whole winter, and Meryton was the head quarters.	PP	I	7	28	3
rest of our lives, for a whole day's tete-a-tete between	PP	I	7	30	17
The rain continued the whole evening without intermission;	PP	I	7	31	28
On entering the drawing-room she found the whole party at	PP	I	8	37	21
than half a dozen, in the whole range of my acquaintance,	PP	I	8	39	46
to each other during the whole visit, and the result of it	PP	I	9	45	35
of the whole party on the subject, seemed to justify her.	PP	I	11	54	3
words to her, through the whole of Saturday, and though	PP	I	12	60	4
took leave of the whole party in the liveliest spirits.	PP	I	12	60	5
a person whom I never saw in the whole course of my life."	PP	I	13	61	4
and was received with great politeness by the whole family.	PP	I	13	64	21
and unassuming; and the whole party were still standing	PP	I	15	72	8
met with so much attention in the whole course of his life.	PP	I	15	74	13
that will amaze the whole room, and be handed down to	PP	I	18	91	15
Mr. Bingley does not know the whole of his history, and is	PP	I	18	95	50
Upon the whole, I am much pleased with him."	PP	I	18	98	62
make a point of remaining close to her the whole evening.	PP	I	18	102	73
threw a languor over the whole party, which was very	PP	I	18	102	75
in her hope of seeing the whole family soon at Longbourn;	PP	I	18	103	76
I have certainly meant well through the whole affair.	PP	I	20	114	32
The whole party have left Netherfield by this time, and	PP	I	21	116	7
The whole family in short were properly overjoyed on the	PP	I	22	122	3
in disbelieving the whole of the matter; secondly, she was	PP	I	23	127	5
plainly deduced from the whole; one, that Elizabeth was	PP	I	21	127	5
no more to Netherfield the whole winter; a report which	PP	I	23	129	12
The whole of what Elizabeth had already heard, his claims	PP	II	1	138	30
the house, amidst the nods and smiles of the whole party.	PP	II	5	155	3
below seemed to speak the whole house in confusion; and	PP	II	5	158	11
the whole party was asked to dine at Rosings the next day.	PP	II	5	159	20
the whole party) so immediately after your arrival!	PP	II	6	160	2
Scarcely any thing was talked of the whole day or next	PP	II	6	160	4
but when he went away, the whole family returned to their	PP	II	7	168	1
This however was no evil to Elizabeth, and upon the whole	PP	II	7	169	5
Collins was walking the whole morning within view of the	PP	II	7	170	7
of love; and from the whole of his behavior to Miss de	PP	II	8	176	29
them to have been together the whole of last summer."	PP	II	10	185	28
There is but one part of my conduct in the whole affair,	PP	II	12	199	5
before you the whole of his connection with my family.	PP	II	12	199	5
looked up to as a father, acknowledged the whole to me.	PP	II	12	202	5
she had gone through the whole letter, though scarcely	PP	II	13	204	2
must make him entirely blameless throughout the whole.	PP	II	13	205	3
she had never, in the whole course of their acquaintance,	PP	II	13	207	6
Brighton, and a whole campful of soldiers, to us, who have	PP	II	16	220	7
some contrivance, the whole party, with all their boxes,	PP	II	16	220	16
She then spoke of the letter, repeating the whole of its	PP	II	17	224	9
wickedness existed in the whole race of mankind, as was	PP	II	17	224	9
Mr. Bennet saw that her whole heart was in the subject;	PP	II	18	231	19
					20
Upon the whole, therefore, she found, what has been	PP	II	19	237	3

Context	Work	Vol	Ch	Page	Para
Were the whole arrangement complete, my disappointment	PP	II	19	237	4
and she looked on the whole scene, the river, the trees	PP	III	1	246	5
Mr. Gardiner expressed a wish of going round the whole	PP	III	1	253	57
to be out of sight of the inn the whole of that morning.	PP	III	2	260	1
The whole party before them, indeed, excited a lively	PP	III	2	261	6
lay awake two whole hours, endeavouring to make them out.	PP	III	2	265	16
was now employment for the whole party; for though they	PP	III	3	268	6
that the suspicions of the whole party were awakened	PP	III	3	268	8
glance over the whole of their acquaintance, so full of	PP	III	4	279	23
An hour, however, saw the whole completed; and Mr.	PP	III	4	281	29
but his lies about the whole Pemberley family are endless.	PP	III	5	284	14
to whom I related the whole, nor I, thought it necessary	PP	III	5	285	16
detain them from it long, during the whole of the journey.	PP	III	5	285	19
itself over their whole bodies, in a variety of capers and	PP	III	5	286	21
was now put an end to, by the approach of the whole party.	PP	III	5	286	32
My mother was taken ill immediately, and the whole house	PP	III	5	292	62
did not know the whole story before the end of the day?"	PP	III	5	292	63
The whole party were in hopes of a letter from Mr. Bennet	PP	III	6	294	1
such as, upon the whole, I hope will give you satisfaction.	PP	III	7	302	14
your name, throughout the whole of this business, I will	PP	III	7	303	14
instead of spending his whole income, he had laid by an	PP	III	8	308	1
and shall devote this whole morning to answering it, as I	PP	III	10	321	2
He generously imputed the whole to his mistaken pride, and	PP	III	10	322	2
it,) your uncle would most readily have settled the whole.	PP	III	10	324	2
the person, to whom the whole family were indebted for the	PP	III	11	334	36
was neither unknown nor unfelt by the whole of the family.	PP	III	12	340	13
them together; that the whole of the visit would not pass	PP	III	12	340	14
the she could, upon the whole, have no cause to repine."	PP	III	14	355	46
my expressions during the whole of it, is now, and has	PP	III	16	367	14
Mrs. Norris had been talking to her the whole way from	MP	I	2	13	4
He continued with her the whole time of her writing, to	MP	I	2	16	20
Upon the whole, it was a comfortable winter to her; for	MP	I	4	35	6
either sat at home the whole day with one aunt, or walked	MP	I	4	36	7
made up his mind, the whole business was soon completed.	MP	I	4	37	8
mare and presided at the whole, returned with it in	MP	I	7	66	15
have her for a longer time--for a whole morning in short.	MP	I	7	69	28
the whole party were welcomed by him with due attention.	MP	I	9	84	1
The whole party rose accordingly, and under Mrs.	MP	I	9	84	3
A whole family assembling regularly for the purpose of	MP	I	9	86	12
We looked down the whole vista, and saw it closed by iron	MP	I	9	94	63
You and Julia were laughing the whole way."	MP	I	10	98	11
Fanny had been hoping the whole morning to reach at last;	MP	I	10	103	49
pain of having been left a whole hour, when he had talked	MP	I	10	103	49
and the result of the whole was to her disappointment and	MP	I	10	103	49
have immortalized the whole party for at least a	MP	I	13	121	1
And upon the whole it would certainly have gone off	MP	I	13	122	2
Perhaps it might cost a whole twenty pounds.--	MP	I	13	127	31
feeling throughout the whole, now ventured to say, in her	MP	I	13	128	34
with her; and, as the whole arrangement was to bring very	MP	I	13	129	40
very few characters in the whole, but every character	MP	I	14	130	3
merest common-place--not a tolerable speech in the whole.	MP	I	14	134	13
Amelia as the most difficult character in the whole piece.	MP	I	14	135	15
a quiet auditor of the whole, and who could not think of	MP	I	14	136	20
Mrs. Norris completed the whole, by thus addressing her in	MP	I	15	146	53
would enliven the whole neighbourhood exceedingly"--Edmund	MP	I	15	148	60
tears delightful--and the whole was now so blended	MP	I	16	152	2
disapprobation of the whole, be enough to justify her in a	MP	I	16	153	3
into the whole affair, as could have but one effect on him.	MP	I	17	159	6
The whole subject of it was love--a marriage of love was	MP	I	18	167	12
and able to recall the whole, she was inclined to believe	MP	I	18	170	24
The comfort of the whole evening was destroyed.	MP	I	18	171	28
her ear amused and her whole comprehension filled by his	MP	II	1	179	9
he had ever given in the whole course of his rehearsals,	MP	II	1	182	22
hear the whole history of his disappointment at Ecclesford.	MP	II	1	184	25
three first acts, and not unsuccessfully upon the whole.	MP	II	1	185	28
a fair statement of the whole acting scheme, defending his	MP	II	2	187	1
but never in the whole course of his life, had he seen one	MP	II	2	191	10
She had been expecting to see him the whole morning--and	MP	II	2	192	11
wind blowing on you the whole time--for here are some of	MP	II	4	212	31
He told the whole, and she had only to add, "so strange!	MP	II	5	218	16
steadily fixed on him the whole time--as I shall do--not	MP	II	5	227	65
dearest indulgence of the whole) all the evil and good of	MP	II	6	234	18
and fortune through the whole evening; and if quick enough	MP	II	7	240	8
Upon the whole, it was a very joyous note.	MP	II	9	266	21
by William, that was due to him for a whole fortnight.	MP	II	11	282	3
had ever known there for a whole day together, and he was	MP	II	11	284	8
She fancied he was trying for it the whole evening at	MP	II	13	306	27
to remain, during the whole of his visit, unless actually	MP	III	1	311	2
You will take in the whole of the past, you will consider	MP	III	1	313	12
keeping the whole affair from the knowledge of her aunts.	MP	III	1	322	50
and to complete the whole, he was now the Mr. Crawford who	MP	III	2	328	6
The effect of the whole was a manner so pitying and	MP	III	2	328	7
Nothing could be more improper than the whole business.	MP	III	4	350	28
where she was; the whole of which, as almost every door in	MP	III	7	382	27
Upon the whole Julia was in the best looks of the two, at	MP	III	9	394	1
to you, indeed, and the whole of her judicious, upright	MP	III	13	421	2
It is an attachment to govern his whole life.	MP	III	13	424	4
her near relation--the whole family, both families	MP	III	15	441	20
down to Richmond for the whole time of her being at	MP	III	16	455	19
to tell him the whole delightful and astonishing truth.	MP	III	17	471	28
he has been here a whole year, and has fitted up his house	E	I	1	13	46
whole charge of the little Frank soon after her decease.	E	I	2	16	4
Martins of Abbey-Mill-Farm, it must have been the whole.	E	I	4	27	4
whole progress of the picture, which was rapid and happy.	E	I	6	47	30
Was not she the whole day with you?"	E	I	8	60	29
is destin'd to feel and my whole is the best antidote that	E	I	9	70	7
that we are to have the whole of the time they can give to	E	I	9	79	63
"Why, pretty well, my dear, upon the whole.	E	I	12	102	32
the purchase; and the whole of their drive to the vicarage	E	I	13	113	25
This was a pleasure which perhaps the whole day's visit	E	I	14	117	2
I never thought of Miss Smith in the whole course of my	E	I	15	130	31
was obliged to see the whole party set off, and return to	E	I	17	140	1
in general she fills the whole paper and crosses half.	E	II	1	157	10
So very good of them to send her the whole way!	E	II	1	159	18
she had in fact heard the whole substance of Jane	E	II	1	162	33
Campbell of undertaking the whole charge of her education.	E	II	2	163	4
The affection of the whole family, the warm attachment of	E	II	2	164	7
which for those two whole years she had been depreciating.	E	II	2	167	12
Upon the whole, Emma left her with such softened,	E	II	2	168	14
his approbation of the whole; not so openly as he might	E	II	3	170	1
ease to be entertained a whole evening by two such young	E	II	3	170	2
"My dear papa, I sent the whole hind-quarter.	E	II	3	172	18
be called; but, as the whole of the profits of his	E	II	4	183	9
and he comes for a whole fortnight; I knew it would be so.	E	II	5	188	7
or pleasing than his whole manner to her--nothing could	E	II	6	196	2
made acquainted with the whole village, and found matter	E	II	6	196	2
Upon the whole, she was very persuadable; and it being	E	II	7	208	9
near at hand, and spending the whole evening away from him.	E	II	7	208	9
one whole day, out of so few, in having your hair cut."	E	II	8	222	52
not enjoy them as I did; you appeared tired the whole time.	E	II	10	242	17
I felt how right you were the whole time, but was too	E	II	11	250	23
at all--not once the whole evening; and it is that	E	II	11	251	29
Mrs. Weston undertakes to direct the whole."	E	II	11	252	36
And I need not bring the whole family, you know."	E	II	11	255	53
Upon the whole, she was equally contented with her view of	E	II	13	265	3
them, and staying one whole day at Hartfield--which one	E	II	16	292	7
The whole party were but just reassembled in the drawing-	E	II	17	302	23
and talking to them the whole time, in a voice a little	E	II	17	303	26
of what the whole room must have overheard already.	E	II	17	304	29
has not been well the whole winter, and thinks Enscombe	E	II	18	305	7
visits from Frank the whole spring--precisely the season	E	II	18	308	30
ourselves, the whole blame of it is to be laid to her.	E	II	18	309	33

whole difference of seeing him always and seeing him never. E III 1 317 10
The whole party walked about, and looked, and praised E III 2 320 5
whole row of young men who could be compared with him.-- E III 2 326 32
When she was half way up the set, the whole group were E III 2 327 34
A few minutes made Emma acquainted with the whole. E III 3 333 4
or rather surrounded, by the whole gang, demanding more. E III 3 334 6
was unseen by the whole party till almost close to them. E III 3 334 7
This was the amount of the whole story,--of his E III 3 334 8
their panic began, and the whole history dwindled soon E III 3 336 13
of your attention to me in the whole of this scheme. E III 6 356 28
The whole party were assembled, excepting Frank Churchill, E III 6 358 35
She wished to see the whole extent."-- E III 6 359 37
You will all be going soon I suppose; the whole party E III 6 364 55
Mr. Weston directed the whole, officiating safely between E III 7 367 1
could: but during the two whole hours that were spent on E III 7 367 1
A whole evening of back-gammon with her father, was E III 8 377 1
aware of it, had been making up her mind the whole day." E III 8 381 20
containing, upon the whole, a tolerable account of Mrs. E III 8 383 31
Here have we been, the whole winter and spring, completely E III 10 399 61
"For the present, the whole affair was to be completely a E III 11 403 2
She touched--she admitted--she acknowledged the whole E III 11 407 32
the exact truth of the whole; to see that Harriet's hopes E III 13 430 38
She may not have surmised the whole, but her quickness E III 14 438 8
The delicacy of her mind throughout the whole engagement, E III 14 439 8
officious Mrs. Elton; the whole system of whose treatment E III 14 441 8
She never stopt till she had gone through the whole; and E III 15 444 1
he was obliged to read the whole of it aloud--all that E III 15 445 14
15

Larkins the whole morning, to have his thoughts to himself. E III 15 449 32
but yet, upon the whole, there was no serious objection E III 17 468 36
"You have, I believe, and know the whole." E III 18 470 10
under her eye--that the whole blunder is spread before her- E III 18 480 77
extent of the evil, the whole of which Sir Walter found P III 1 10 19
The Kellynch estate should be transmitted whole and entire, P III 1 10 20
the whole list of Lady Russell's too gentle reductions. P III 2 13 5
attentive listener to the whole, left the room, to seek P III 3 24 38
satisfactory, and decided the whole business at once. P III 5 32 2
I have not seen a creature the whole morning!" P III 5 37 22
I assure you, I have not seen a soul this whole long P III 5 37 25
admiration; and, upon the whole, though there was very P III 6 43 5
from him during the whole of his absence; that is to say, P III 6 51 30
to be spending the whole evening away from the poor boy?" P III 7 56 13
she was in time for the whole conversation, which began P III 7 57 17
18

ever called them any thing in the whole course of her life. P III 8 70 53
late to retract, and the whole six set toward together in P III 10 83 6
felt some comfort in their whole party being immediately P III 10 89 35
towards him; and, upon the whole, she believed she must, P III 11 93 2
of at Uppercross for two whole days, appeared again among P III 11 94 5
desire of considering the whole party as friends of their P III 11 97 15
Anne's curiosity, and the whole six were collected to look, P III 12 105 9
them, and get a bed elsewhere--and the whole was settled. P III 12 113 56
when a full account of the whole had burst on her; but P IV 1 124 12
Mary had had her evils; but upon the whole, as was evident P IV 2 129 3
holding high revel; the whole completed by a roaring P IV 2 134 29
with his wife, had perfectly understood the whole story. P IV 3 139 9
whole happiness in being on intimate terms in Camden-Place. P IV 3 139 10
in Marlborough buildings, were talked of the whole evening. P IV 3 141 13
He had spent his whole solitary evening in the room P IV 3 144 19
Having alluded to "an accident," he must hear the whole. P IV 3 144 22
Anne had the whole history of all that such an evening P IV 5 158 21
The conclusion of the whole was, that if the woman who had P IV 6 167 21
I will tell you the whole story another time. P IV 6 170 29
Upon Lady Russell's appearance soon afterwards, the whole P IV 8 185 19
with me on Monday evening, and gave me the whole history." P IV 9 197 40
"The whole history!" repeated Anne, laughing. P IV 9 197 41
He told me the whole story. P IV 9 201 59
When I talked of a whole history therefore, you see, I was P IV 9 205 82
least the comfort of telling the whole story her own way. P IV 9 210 99
for the whole day to-morrow, I had compassion on him." P IV 10 213 9
account of the whole; a narration in which she saw a great P IV 10 216 19
and listening with his whole soul; and that the last words P IV 10 224 49
Promising to be with them the whole of the following P IV 10 227 69
And with a quivering lip he wound up the whole by adding, " P IV 11 232 15
that we hope to see your whole party this evening. P IV 11 239 49
Only conceive sir, the advantage of saving a whole mile, S 1 369 1
For a whole fortnight the travellors were fixed at S 2 370 1
Upon the whole, Mr P. was evidently an aimable, family-man, S 2 372 1
he remember any during the whole summer, excepting one S 4 383 1
We have entirely done with the whole medical Tribe. S 5 386 1
of the party & to give her the whole of his conversation. S 7 396 1
The whole of their mental vivacity was evidently not so S 10 412 1
She talked however, the whole evening as incessantly as S 10 413 1
had been on her feet the whole morning, on Mrs G.'s S 10 414 1
Not all that the whole Parker race could say among S 11 420 1
from observation!--the whole field open before them--a S 12 427 1

WHOLE-LENGTH (3)
in small size, whole-length--"my last and my best--my E I 6 45 21
It was to be a whole-length in water-colours, like Mr. E I 6 46 23
by Mrs P. that the whole-length portrait of a stately S 12 427 1

WHOLE-LENGTHS (1)
Miniatures, half-lengths, whole-lengths, pencil, crayon, E I 6 44 19

WHOLESOME (10)
indulgence, without the wholesome alloy of labour, and I MP II 6 229 3
nothing, would awaken very wholesome regrets in her mind.-- MP III 6 366 1
the children plenty of wholesome food, let them run about E I 3 22 5
of its being exceedingly wholesome; and the day was E I 15 132 38
and they are extremely wholesome, for I took the E II 9 237 46
that Mr. Woodhouse thinks the fruit thoroughly wholesome. E II 9 237 46
in England--every body's favourite--always wholesome.-- E III 6 358 35
an object of interest, amusement, and wholesome exertion. P III 6 43 4
It has always some property that is wholesome & S 10 415 1
So far from dry toast being wholesome, I think it a very S 10 417 1

WHOLESOMENESS (1)
decision of its wholesomeness for every constitution, and E I 12 104 50

WHOLLY (71)
event takes place, Frederica must wholly belong to us. LS 24 291 17
least delay his journey to Bath, if not wholly prevent it. LS 28 298 1
own plans were not yet wholly fixed, she trusted it would LS 42 312 5
mischievousness, and was wholly unsuspicious of danger to NA I 2 18 2
all of whom she was so wholly unacquainted, that she could NA I 2 21 10
Catherine, by whom this meeting was wholly unexpected, NA I 7 44 4
about, hummed a tune, and seemed wholly self-occupied. NA I 15 122 29
our side to make Northanger Abbey not wholly disagreeable." NA II 2 139 7
together, in an alarm not wholly unfounded, for General NA II 6 165 5
occasional passages, not wholly unintricate, connected the NA II 8 183 2
workings of a mind not wholly dead to every sense of NA II 8 187 13
and at others that it was wholly incompatible with it. NA II 11 209 5
injunction of remaining wholly at Northanger in attendance NA II 13 221 7
They gave themselves up wholly to their sorrow, seeking SS I 1 7 13
would have been as well if he had left it wholly to myself. SS I 2 9 6
while you have been wholly engrossed on the most SS I 4 20 9
his attentions were wholly Marianne's, and a far less SS I 11 55 7
account; and it was so wholly contradictory to their SS I 14 71 4
"to be guided wholly by the opinion of other people. SS I 17 93 38
his time to be wholly disengaged--even doubted to what SS I 19 101 1
bear to have you so wholly estranged from each other." SS II 3 156 8
with that lady been, so wholly unsuited were they in age SS II 4 159 1
for this party, Marianne, wholly dispirited, careless of SS II 6 175 1
book; and soon laying it wholly aside, she drew near the PP I 8 38 39
The idea of the olive branch perhaps is not wholly new, PP I 13 64 19
which she could not wholly surmount even in speaking to Mr. PP I 18 89 3
inattentive to other people, and wholly engrossed by her. PP II 2 141 9
and so splendid a dinner might not wholly overpower them. PP II 6 160 4
which proved him wholly unmoved by any feeling of remorse. PP II 11 191 13
and at length wholly banished by the conviction that Mr. PP II 13 206 4
Mr. Darcy, for now they do appear wholly undeserved." PP II 17 226 20
Wholly inattentive to her sister's feelings, Lydia flew PP II 18 230 12
emptiness of her mind, wholly unable to ward off any PP II 18 231 18
heard not a word, and, wholly engrossed by her own PP III 1 252 54
To Kitty, however, it does not seem so wholly unexpected. PP III 4 273 3
cares that must now fall wholly upon her, in a family so PP III 4 280 26
Can you, yourself, Lizzy, so wholly give him up, as to PP III 5 282 3
but certain, and Miss Bennet could not assert to be wholly PP III 5 290 45
He added, that Mr. Bennet seemed wholly disinclined at PP III 6 295 5
"This is wholly unexpected. PP III 6 298 12
and her words ran wholly on those attendants of elegant PP III 8 310 7
from which she had been so wholly free at first. PP III 9 317 10
"You did! and it was not wholly without foundation. PP III 10 329 32
you," replied Elizabeth; "but it is wholly out of my power. PP III 11 333 29
Elizabeth, that if left wholly to himself, Jane's PP III 12 340 13
in the world, and wholly unallied to the family! PP III 14 355 43
I am not to be intimidated into anything so wholly PP III 14 357 61
you, or to any person so wholly unconnected with me." PP III 14 358 68
of every thing, was not wholly without hope that Darcy PP III 19 386 6
children of her own; but he found himself wholly mistaken. MP I 1 9 10
spring, and remained wholly in the country, leaving Sir MP I 2 20 33
many weeks, in which the families had been wholly divided. MP II 2 192 11
"I could so wholly and absolutely confide in her," said he; MP II 12 294 17
of addresses so wholly unexpected, and the novelty of a MP III 2 326 3
He took me wholly by surprise. MP III 4 353 45
But she was so wholly unused to confer favours, except on MP III 9 396 7
to her, were shut up, or wholly occupied each with the MP III 16 449 4
whose smiles had been so wholly at his command; he must MP III 17 467 20
which I heard to be wholly unmodulated as I stood here." E I 4 33 32
who had been almost wholly engrossed by her attentions to E I 14 117 3
would have retained her wholly; but this would be E II 2 165 9
appear of that absorbing nature as wholly to occupy her. E II 3 174 36
to--of course he was not wholly without apprehension. E II 14 276 36
He had, in fact, been wholly unsuspicious of his own E III 13 432 40
restraints, that it did not take her wholly by surprise. E III 14 438 8
I could have anticipated, wholly reconciled and complying; E III 14 443 8
which at the time she had wholly imputed to the amiable E III 15 449 35
rested, as it now almost wholly did, on Isabella's letters. E III 17 463 15
did not take him wholly by surprise, that he was rather in E III 17 465 25
She had too old a regard for him to be so wholly estranged, P III 9 77 19
of, he burst forth, as if wholly overcome-- "don't talk of P III 12 116 70
71

WHOMSOEVER (6)
it with pleasure, by whomsoever it may be made--and NA I 14 109 23
decipher 'Oh! thou--whomsoever thou mayst be, into whose NA II 5 160 21
to crime, murdering whomsoever they chose, without any NA II 9 190 2
With whomsoever he was, or was likely to be connected, his NA II 15 245 12
it to be settled by whomsoever it may concern, whether the NA II 16 252 7
offence of the kind, by whomsoever given or received, was SS I 1 6 9

WICK (2)
on horseback, that they were going as far as Wick Rocks." NA I 11 86 46
It was done completely; not a remnant of light in the Wick NA II 6 170 12

WICKED (6)
You have proved your heart less wicked, much less wicked. SS III 8 329 66
he never was so very wicked as my fears have sometimes SS III 10 344 17
idea of its being a wicked thing for her not to be happy. MP I 2 13 4
Your wicked project upon her peace turns out a clever MP II 12 295 19
hopeless and how wicked it was, to marry without affection. MP III 1 324 58
without any of the wicked aids of vanity--to assist him E II 11 247 2

WICKEDEST (2)
And to marry for money I think the wickedest thing in NA I 15 124 47
Every body declared that he was the wickedest young man in PP III 6 294 4

WICKEDNESS (5)
believing that so much wickedness existed in the whole PP II 17 224 9
to her all the wickedness of what she had done, and all PP III 10 325 2
there could be neither wickedness nor sorrow in the world; MP I 11 113 35
perhaps, from that wickedness on my side which was prone E II 6 203 39
Wickedness is always wickedness, but folly is not always E II 8 212 3

WICKET (1)
in front; and a neat wicket gate admitted them into it. SS I 6 28 1

WICKHAM (162)
introduce his friend, Mr. Wickham, who had returned with PP I 15 72 8
Mr. Wickham, after a few moments, touched his hat--a PP I 15 73 8
Mr. Denny and Mr. Wickham walked with the young ladies to PP I 15 73 10
the street, and had Mr. Wickham appeared Kitty and Lydia PP I 15 74 11
her husband call on Mr. Wickham, and give him an PP I 15 74 11
drawing-room, that Mr. Wickham had accepted their uncle's PP I 16 75 1
The gentlemen did approach; and when Mr. Wickham walked PP I 16 76 3
present party; but Mr. Wickham was as far beyond them all PP I 16 76 3
Mr. Wickham was the happy man towards whom almost every PP I 16 76 4
of the fair, as Mr. Wickham and the officers, Mr. Collins PP I 16 76 5
Mr. Wickham did not play at whist, and with ready delight PP I 16 76 8
Allowing for the common demands of the game, Mr. Wickham PP I 16 77 8
Mr. Wickham began the subject himself. PP I 16 77 8
"Yes," replied Wickham;--"his estate there is a noble one. PP I 16 77 10
"I have no right to give my opinion." said Wickham, "as to PP I 16 77 14
"I cannot pretend to be sorry," said Wickham, after a PP I 16 78 16
Wickham only shook his head. PP I 16 78 17
Mr. Wickham began to speak on more general topics, Meryton, PP I 16 78 22
"I will not trust myself on the subject," replied Wickham, PP I 16 80 35
"It is wonderful,"--replied Wickham,--"for almost all his PP I 16 81 39
a great degree," replied Wickham; "I have not seen her for PP I 16 84 58
She could think of nothing but of Mr. Wickham, and of what PP I 16 84 59
next day, what had passed between Mr. Wickham and herself. PP I 17 85 1
of a young man of such amiable appearance as Wickham.-- PP I 17 85 1
imposed on, than that Mr. Wickham should invent such a PP I 17 85 5
a great deal with Mr. Wickham, and of seeing a PP I 17 86 10
half the evening with Mr. Wickham, he was by no means the PP I 17 86 10
She had fully proposed being engaged by Wickham for those PP I 17 87 14
her acquaintance with Mr. Wickham; and nothing less than a PP I 17 88 15
looked in vain for Mr. Wickham among the cluster of red PP I 18 89 1
and who told them that Wickham had been obliged to go to PP I 18 89 1
2

forbearance, patience with Darcy, was injury to Wickham. PP I 18 89 3
of Wickham, and of hearing that he was universally liked. PP I 18 90 5
and allow her fancy for Wickham to make her appear PP I 18 90 8
"Mr. Wickham is blessed with such happy manners as may PP I 18 92 20
I hear you are quite delighted with George Wickham!-- PP I 18 94 44
45

was the son of old Wickham, the late Mr. Darcy's steward. PP I 18 94 45
Wickham has treated Mr. Darcy in a most infamous manner. PP I 18 94 45
bear to hear George Wickham mentioned, and that though my PP I 18 94 45
moment solicitude for Wickham, resentment against his PP I 18 95 48
than her sister's, "what you have learnt about Mr. Wickham. PP I 18 95 49
convinced that Mr. Wickham has deserved much less PP I 18 95 50
Mr. Wickham is by no means a respectable young man. PP I 18 95 50
"Mr. Bingley does not know Mr. Wickham himself?" PP I 18 96 51
of her allusions to Mr. Wickham, and rejoiced in it. PP I 18 102 74
Meryton to inquire if Mr. Wickham were returned, and to PP I 21 115 3
on each other, as Wickham and another officer walked back PP I 21 115 5
her attention even from Wickham; and no sooner had he and PP I 21 116 6
young ladies in the country. let Wickham be your man. PP II 1 138 27
it, of which officers Mr. Wickham was sure to be one; and PP II 2 142 18
To Mrs. Gardiner, Wickham had one means of affording PP II 2 142 19
in common; and, though Wickham had been little there since PP II 2 142 19
minute description which Wickham could give, and in PP II 2 143 20
I will take care of myself, and of Mr. Wickham too. PP II 3 144 5
At present I am not in love with Mr. Wickham; no, I PP II 3 144 7

My father, however, is partial to Mr. Wickham. PP II 3 144 7
The farewell between herself and Mr. Wickham was perfectly PP II 4 151 3
and brought Mr. Wickham immediately to Elizabeth's mind; PP II 6 162 11
former favourite George Wickham; and though, in comparing PP II 9 180 28
recital which I received many months ago from Mr. Wickham. PP II 11 191 17
he had mentioned Mr. Wickham, his cruelty towards whom he PP II 11 193 31
prosperity, and blasted the prospects of Mr. Wickham.-- PP II 12 196 5
of having injured Mr. Wickham, I can only refute it by PP II 12 199 5
Mr. Wickham is the son of a very respectable man, who had PP II 12 199 5
to him, and on George Wickham, who was his god-son, his PP II 12 199 5
But whatever may be the sentiments which Mr. Wickham has PP II 12 200 5
and his attachment to Mr. Wickham was to the last so PP II 12 200 5
from these events, Mr. Wickham wrote to inform me that, PP II 12 200 5
I knew that Mr. Wickham ought not to be a clergyman. PP II 12 201 5
and thither also went Mr. Wickham, undoubtedly by design; PP II 12 201 5
but I wrote to Mr. Wickham, who left the place immediately, PP II 12 202 5
hope, acquit me henceforth of cruelty towards Mr. Wickham. PP II 12 202 5
by his account of Mr. Wickham, when she read with somewhat PP II 13 204 2
of all that related to Wickham, and commanded herself so PP II 13 205 3
What Wickham had said of the living was fresh in her PP II 13 205 3
in conversation between Wickham and herself, in their PP II 13 206 5
and valued-- that even Wickham had allowed him merit as a PP II 13 207 6
That had his actions been what Wickham represented them, PP II 13 208 6
Of neither Darcy nor Wickham could she think, without PP II 13 208 7
Well, but now for my news: it is about dear Wickham; too PP II 16 220 10
Wickham is safe." PP II 16 220 10
When Denny, and Wickham, and Pratt, and two or three more PP II 16 221 17
She dreaded seeing Wickham again, and was resolved to PP II 16 223 25
"But you blame me for having spoken so warmly of Wickham." PP II 17 224 6
of its contents as far as they concerned George Wickham. PP II 17 224 9
"Wickham so very bad! PP II 17 225 12
"Poor Wickham; there is such an expression of goodness in PP II 17 225 14
in speaking of Wickham to Mr. Darcy, for now they do PP II 17 226 20
Wickham will soon be gone; and therefore it will not PP II 17 226 23
Elizabeth was now to see Mr. Wickham for the last time. PP II 18 233 25
"Indeed!" cried Wickham with a look which did not escape PP II 18 234 33
While she spoke, Wickham looked as if scarcely knowing PP II 18 234 35
Wickham passed all his youth there, you know." PP II 19 240 13
She approached, and saw the likeness of Mr. Wickham PP III 1 247 9
Lizzy," said her aunt, "he is not so handsome as Wickham; PP III 1 257 70
so cruel a way by any body, as he has done by poor Wickham. PP III 1 258 74
of his behaviour to Wickham; and therefore gave them to PP III 1 258 75
With respect to Wickham, the travellers soon found that he PP III 2 265 15
not approach nearer to Wickham, Georgiana also recovered PP III 3 270 11
to own the truth, with Wickham!--imagine our surprise. PP III 4 273 3
Imprudent as a marriage between Mr. Wickham and our poor PP III 4 274 3
has thrown herself into the power of--of Mr. Wickham. PP III 4 277 11
in her partiality for Wickham, and that its ill-success PP III 4 279 24
astonishment that Wickham should marry a girl, whom it was PP III 4 279 24
I cannot think so very ill of Wickham. PP III 5 282 3
Wickham will never marry a woman without some money. PP III 5 283 8
And we all know that Wickham has every charm of person and PP III 5 284 10
ill of Wickham, as to believe him capable of the attempt." PP III 5 284 11
But Jane knows, as well as I do, what Wickham really is. PP III 5 284 12
the villanous conduct of Wickham, and complaints of her PP III 5 287 34
and I know he will fight Wickham, wherever he meets him, PP III 5 287 35
"And was Denny convinced that Wickham would not marry? PP III 5 290 47
"And did Colonel Forster appear to think ill of Wickham PP III 5 291 53
"I must confess that he did not speak so well of Wickham PP III 5 291 54
when I write to them, and sign my name Lydia Wickham. PP III 5 291 60
in the regiment, whether Wickham has any relations or PP III 6 295 6
It was not known that Wickham had a single relation, with PP III 6 297 12
Who is to fight Wickham, and make him marry her, if he PP III 6 298 14
"Wickham is not so undeserving, then, as we have thought PP III 7 303 16
done for them, because Wickham has not sixpence of his own. PP III 7 305 36
How I long to see her! and to see dear Wickham too! PP III 7 306 44
he has pledged himself to assist Mr. Wickham with money." PP III 7 306 46
Mrs. Wickham! PP III 7 306 47
He had never before supposed that, could Wickham be PP III 8 309 4
living with Wickham, a fortnight before they took place. PP III 8 310 10
How Wickham and Lydia were to be supported in tolerable PP III 8 312 17
that Mr. Wickham had resolved on quitting the militia. PP III 8 312 18
various creditors of Mr. Wickham in and near Brighton, PP III 8 313 19
Elizabeth was surprised, however, that Wickham should PP III 8 314 22
an affectionate smile to Wickham, who followed his lady, PP III 9 315 3
Wickham was not at all more distressed than herself, but PP III 9 316 5
talk fast enough; and Wickham, who happened to sit near PP III 9 316 6
hear herself called "Mrs. Wickham," by each of them; and PP III 9 317 10
Mr. Wickham had received his commission before he left PP III 9 318 17
He was her dear Wickham on every occasion; no one was to PP III 9 318 20
for I was thinking, you may suppose, of my dear Wickham. PP III 9 319 24
"Oh, yes!--he was to come there with Wickham, you know. PP III 9 319 27
What will Wickham say? PP III 9 319 27
certainly tell you all, and then Wickham would be angry." PP III 9 320 30
where your sister and Mr. Wickham were, and that he had PP III 10 321 2
and talked with them both, Wickham repeatedly, Lydia once. PP III 10 321 2
acquainted with Wickham; and he went to her for PP III 10 322 2
Wickham indeed had gone to her, on their first arrival in PP III 10 322 2
He saw Wickham, and afterwards insisted on seeing Lydia. PP III 10 322 2
no help of his, she would not hear of leaving Wickham. PP III 10 322 2
Wickham, he easily learnt, had never been his design. PP III 10 323 2
But he found, in reply to this question, that Wickham PP III 10 323 2
Wickham of course wanted more than he could get; but at PP III 10 323 2
Lydia came to us; and Wickham had constant admission to PP III 10 325 2
so natural as abhorrence against relationship with Wickham. PP III 10 326 3
Brother-in-law of Wickham! PP III 10 326 3
strike into another path, she was overtaken by Wickham. PP III 10 327 4
"come, Mr. Wickham, we are brother and sister, you know. PP III 10 329 33
34

Mr. Wickham was so perfectly satisfied with this PP III 11 330 1
It was only said, 'lately, George Wickham, Esq. to Miss PP III 11 336 49
Wickham, Lydia, were all forgotten. PP III 13 349 41
the preference even over Wickham, much as I value the PP III 15 364 24
"Wickham, perhaps, is my favourite; but I think I shall PP III 17 379 48
kept, and though Mrs. Wickham frequently invited her to PP III 19 385 4
As for Wickham and Lydia, their characters suffered no PP III 19 386 6
If you love Mr. Darcy half as well as I do my dear Wickham, PP III 19 386 7
I am sure Wickham would like a place at court very much, PP III 19 386 7

WICKHAM'S (32)
Mr. Wickham's attention was caught; and after observing Mr. PP I 16 83 51
rest of the ladies their share of Mr. Wickham's attentions. PP I 16 84 59
Mr. Wickham's happiness and her own was per force delayed PP I 17 87 14
not less answerable for Wickham's absence than if her PP I 18 89 3
Mr. Wickham's society was of material service in PP II 1 138 30
Darcy's sister, as, by Wickham's account, she would make PP II 3 149 27
Mrs. Gardiner then rallied her niece on Wickham's PP II 4 153 7
Mr. Wickham's chief object was unquestionably my sister's PP II 12 202 5
immediately following of Wickham's resigning all PP II 13 205 3
not to lay to Mr. Wickham's charge, exceedingly shocked PP II 13 205 4
of Wickham's character, it may be easily believed that the PP II 14 213 19
There is no danger of Wickham's marrying Mary king. PP II 16 220 10
was no escaping the frequent mention of Wickham's name. PP II 16 222 18
acquaintance in general understand Wickham's character." PP II 17 226 21
Wickham's alarm now appeared in a heightened complexion PP II 18 234 37
38

When Elizabeth had rejoiced over Wickham's departure, she PP II 19 237 3
This accounted to Elizabeth for Mr. Wickham's being among PP III 1 247 19
Wickham's countenance, for his features are perfectly good. PP III 1 257 70
no means so faulty, nor Wickham's so amiable, as they had PP III 1 258 75
In Darcy's presence she dared not mention Wickham's name; PP III 3 269 10
entertained a hope of Wickham's meaning to marry her. no PP III 4 279 24
some fresh instance of Wickham's extravagance or PP III 6 294 3
particulars, that Mr. Wickham's circumstances are not so PP III 7 302 14
"No," said her father, "Wickham's a fool, if he takes her PP III 7 304 31
"If we are ever able to learn what Wickham's debts have PP III 7 305 36
It is Mr. Wickham's intention to go into the regulars; and, PP III 8 312 19
all the advantages of Wickham's removal from the ----shire, PP III 8 313 20
Wickham's affection for Lydia, was just what Elizabeth had PP III 9 318 19
Clement's, because Wickham's lodgings were in that parish. PP III 9 318 24
owing to himself that Wickham's worthlessness had not been PP III 10 321 2
consideration, that Wickham's character had been so PP III 10 324 2
Mr. Wickham's adieus were much more affectionate than his PP III 11 330 7

WICKSTEAD (2)
lived with his uncle at Wickstead, that his uncle taught W 331 11
"But you may come to Wickstead & see mama, & she can take W 332 12

WIDE (11)
many landing-places, brought them upon a long wide gallery. NA II 5 162 28
her eye, wandering over a wide tract of country to the SS III 6 302 8
He has a long face, & a wide mouth.-- W 324 3
led the way up the wide staircase, while no sound of a W 327 7
that as his road lay quite wide from r., it was impossible W 338 18
said,-- "this walk is not wide enough for our party. PP I 10 53 62
63
say that there must be a wide difference between the PP I 18 97 60
61
through a beautiful wood, stretching over a wide extent. PP III 1 245 2
And round their enormous great wide table too, which fills MP II 5 220 30
never behold either the wide table or the number of dishes MP II 7 238 3
general joy through a wide circle of great people. MP II 13 298 3

WIDELY (7)
But my affair is widely different; I bring back my heroine NA II 14 232 7
by a croud of ideas, widely differing in themselves, but SS III 9 333 1
Widely different was the effect of a second perusal.-- PP II 13 208 9
feelings towards its writer were at times widely different. PP II 14 212 17
You have widely mistaken my character, if you think I can PP III 14 357 61
received it, are now so widely different from what they PP III 16 368 23
all that I had in view; widely different certainly as to E II 17 300 15

WIDEN (1)
I suppose it would be no difficult matter to widen them. SS I 6 29 4

WIDER (3)
were over, it would be time for the wider range of London. MP II 3 203 31
one of his own, which is wider, literally wider than the MP II 5 220 30
which is wider, literally wider than the dinner table here- MP II 5 220 30

WIDEST (1)
"Indeed I can, both hands; & spread to their widest extent. W 343 19

WIDOW (28)
being only four months a widow, & to be as quiet as LS 2 244 1
& tho' as his brother's widow & in narrow circumstances it LS 3 247 1
to present, in having been scarcely ten months a widow. LS 29 299 3
I have now been but a few months a widow; & however little LS 30 300 3
Mrs. Thorpe was a widow, and not a very rich one; she was NA I 4 34 8
was all that remained for his widow and daughters. SS I 1 4 4
husband, "that I should assist his widow and daughters." SS I 2 9 4
to do more for the widow and children of his father, than SS I 2 13 29
Mrs. Jennings was a widow, with an ample jointure. SS I 8 36 1
that Mrs. Jennings was the widow of a man who had got all SS II 11 228 53
He might have provided decently for his widow, without W 352 26
Lady Catherine de Bourgh, widow of Sir Lewis de Bourgh, PP I 13 62 12
"I think you said she was a widow, sir? has she any family? PP I 14 67 4
should be of age, and the widow and younger children would PP III 8 308 3
Me! a poor helpless, forlorn widow, unfit for any thing, MP I 3 28 42
Here am I a poor desolate widow, deprived of the best of MP I 3 29 46
Mrs. Bates, the widow of a former vicar of Highbury, was a E I 3 21 4
in action abroad--of his widow sinking under consumption E II 2 163 2
some vulgar, dashing widow, who, with the help of a E II 14 275 33
friends; and one remained a widower, the other a widow. P III 1 5 7
Herself, the widow of only a Knight, she gave the dignity P III 2 11 2
She was a widow, and poor. P IV 5 152 4
a poor, infirm, helpless widow, receiving the visit of her P IV 5 153 6
A widow Mrs. Smith,--and who was her husband? P IV 5 157 15
"Sir Henry Russell's widow, indeed, has no honours to P IV 5 158 19
A widow Mrs. Smith, lodging in Westgate-Buildings!-- P IV 5 158 19
A poor widow, barely able to live, between thirty and P IV 5 158 19
Smith was not the only widow in Bath between thirty and P IV 5 158 20

WIDOW-SISTER (1)
stood, Mrs Blake, a widow-sister who lived with him, her W 329 9

WIDOWER (4)
with another; and for a moment wished Willoughby a widower. SS III 9 335 5
Mr. Weston, who had been a widower so long, and who seemed E I 1 12 41
friends; and one remained a widower, the other a widow. P III 1 5 7
it must be remembered, had not been a widower seven months. P IV 4 147 8

WIDOWER-FATHER (1)
Some scruples and some reluctance the widower-father may E I 2 16 4

WIDOWHOOD (2)
remaining restraints of widowhood, and leave him at P IV 5 159 22
After a widowhood of some years, she had been induced to S 3 375 1

WIDOWS (1)
town, or half pay officers, or Widows with only a jointure. S 7 401 1

WIDTH (1)
The fire-place, where she had expected the ample width and NA II 5 162 26

WIFE (280)
with his wife, his slighting me has an awkward look. LS 2 245 1
Charles vernon is my aversion, & I am afraid of his wife. LS 2 246 1
& wretchedness to his wife, & by her attentions to a young LS 4 248 1
My having prevented it, may perhaps have given his wife an LS 5 250 1
wife & sister, & lamentations on the cruelty of his fate. LS 5 250 3
I hope to see her the wife of Sir James within a LS 7 253 1
To the fortune of your wife, the goodness of my own, will LS 12 261 3
She may be Reginald's wife. LS 15 267 4
her, a better fate than to be Sir James Martin's wife. LS 20 278 11
to Charles vernon or his wife, & they had therefore no LS 22 281 3
can have influence enough to send him back to his wife. LS 26 295 3
You know how sincerely I regard both husband & wife. I LS 30 301 5
At any rate I hope he will plague his wife more than ever. LS 32 303 2
wife--but with him--and that he now visits you every day. LS 36 305 1
This event, if his wife live with you, it may be in your LS 39 308 1
Frederica shall be Sir James's wife before she quits my LS 39 308 1
"I wish she had been able to dance," said his wife, "I NA I 2 23 25
never mentioned a wife, and he had acknowledged a sister. NA I 8 53 3
"That is just what I was going to say," added his wife. NA I 13 105 39
A portrait--very like--of a departed wife, not valued by NA II 7 181 39
suffering wife, and left him to the stings of conscience. NA II 8 186 6
of an injured wife, before her room was put to rights. NA II 8 186 10
to the prison of his wife; and, twice before she stepped NA II 8 188 19
the existence even of a wife not beloved, in the laws of NA II 10 200 3
Frederick will not be the first man who has chosen a wife NA II 10 205 24
or shutting up his wife, she had scarcely sinned against NA II 15 247 14
more for the sake of his wife and daughters than for SS I 1 4 3
was very young when he married, and very fond of his wife. SS I 1 5 7
towards any body beyond himself, his wife, and their child. SS I 2 8 1
His wife hesitated a little, however, in giving her SS I 2 10 17
such kind of neighbourly acts as his own wife pointed out. SS I 2 13 29
to her son-in-law and his wife that she was provided with SS I 5 25 1
John, and gave exercise to the good-breeding of his wife. SS I 7 32 1
his wife, or Mrs. Jennings to be Lady Middleton's mother. SS I 7 34 6
for the sake of the provision and security of a wife. SS I 8 38 10
Colonel Brandon and his wife to the constant confinement SS I 8 38 11
and what he said to his wife a few minutes before he died. SS I 11 54 6
with all my heart, and a good wife into the bargain. SS I 14 70 2
her as his future wife, and that he felt for us the SS I 15 80 36
his wife, but of less willingness to please or be pleased. SS I 19 106 22
"My love, have you been asleep?" said his wife, laughing. SS I 19 108 38
"My love, you contradict every body,"--said his wife with SS I 20 111 23
were not likely to attach any one to him except his wife. SS I 20 112 28

between husband and wife, before Sir John's and Mrs. SS I 21 118 1
with a wife like her--illiterate, artful, and selfish? SS II 1 140 1
Elinor blushed for the insincerity of Edward's future wife, SS II 2 150 33
person who was to be his wife; but that he had not even SS II 2 151 41
or the faults of his wife, when I consider whose son he is, SS II 3 156 8
I wish with all my soul his wife may plague his heart out. SS II 8 192 3
told her that he and his wife were to be in town before SS II 10 213 5
that was worth hearing, and his wife had still less. SS II 12 233 18
to his wife, for her approbation, when they got home. SS II 14 252 20
Colonel Brandon's wife, and Marianne as their visitor. SS II 14 253 25
over the dreadful affair, and bring them news of his wife. SS III 1 265 33
occasionally rude to his wife and her mother; she found SS III 6 304 15
and importunity of his wife too great to be withstood. SS III 7 307 3
be frightened away by his wife, was persuaded at last by SS III 7 308 5
I had reason to believe myself secure of my present wife, SS III 8 323 40
"Your wife!-- SS III 8 328 62
Your wife has a claim to your politeness, to your respect, SS III 8 329 64
"Do not talk to me of my wife," said he with an heavy sigh. SS III 8 329 65
He would have had a wife of whose temper he could make no SS III 11 351 13
to domestic happiness, than the mere temper of a wife." SS III 11 351 13
In a sister it is bad enough, but in a wife!--how I have SS III 13 365 17
to forgive her son, his wife should never be acknowledged SS III 13 371 38
to visit Edward and his wife in their parsonage by SS III 14 374 7
and the cunning of his wife; and it was earned by them SS III 14 375 10
attachment to his wife and his home, and from the regular SS III 14 377 12
placed in a new home, a wife, the mistress of a family, SS III 14 378 16
His wife was not always out of humour, nor his home always SS III 14 379 18
was sickly & had lost his wife, one only could profit by W 315 1
as Robert, who has got a good wife & six thousand pounds?" W 321 2
to elderly ladies, or to a second choice added his wife. W 326 6
She had been an excellent wife to him. W 352 26
I think there is powder enough in my hair for my wife & W 353 26
in possession of a good fortune, must be in want of a wife. PP I 1 3 1
to know who has taken it?" cried his wife impatiently. PP I 1 3 7
"My dear Mr. Bennet," replied his wife, "how can you be so PP I 1 4 16
insufficient to make his wife understand his character. PP I 1 5 34
last always assuring his wife that he should not go; and PP I 2 6 1
"I am sick of Mr. Bingley," cried his wife. PP I 2 7 21
he left the room, fatigued with the raptures of his wife. PP I 2 8 25
"I hope, my dear," said Mr. Bennet to his wife, as they PP I 13 61 1
eagerly questioned by his wife and five daughters at once. PP I 13 61 5
"Oh! my dear," cried his wife, "I cannot bear to hear PP I 13 61 7
Longbourn family he had a wife in view, as he meant to PP I 15 70 2
Bennet himself, while his wife seriously commended Mr. PP I 18 101 71
with the design of selecting a wife, as I certainly did." PP I 19 105 8
resolving to chuse a wife from among his daughters, that PP I 19 106 10
be a very desirable wife to a man in my situation, who PP I 20 110 4
being his wife, I advise you by all means to refuse him." PP I 21 119 24
and his wife should make their appearance at St. James's. PP I 22 122 3
Charlotte the wife of Mr. Collins, was a most humiliating PP I 22 125 18
foolish as his wife, and more foolish than his daughter! PP I 23 127 6
her brother and his wife, who came as usual to spend the PP II 2 139 2
have been Mr. Collins's wife by this time, had not it been PP II 2 140 4
When Mr. Collins said any thing of which his wife might PP II 5 156 4
She will make him a very proper wife." PP II 5 158 18
towards himself and his wife, was exactly what he had PP II 6 160 1
and not many in which his wife did not think it necessary PP II 7 168 3
Collins appears very fortunate in his choice of a wife." PP II 9 178 14
the extravagance of his wife, would have been unable to PP II 12 200 5
from Mrs. Forster, the wife of the Colonel of the regiment, PP II 18 230 11
To his wife he was very little otherwise indebted, than as PP II 19 236 1
general wish to owe to his wife; but where other powers of PP II 19 236 1
which, in exposing his wife to the contempt of her own PP II 19 236 2
even if incapable of enlarging the mind of his wife. PP II 19 236 2
Lydia left a few lines for his wife, informing her of PP III 4 274 3
repeat the particulars of Lydia's note to his wife?" PP III 5 291 57
on Sunday; on Tuesday, his wife received a letter from him; PP III 6 295 5
of his children, and of his wife, if she survived him. PP III 8 308 1
if he marry prudently, his wife may teach him. PP III 10 325 2
His wife represented to him how absolutely necessary such PP III 11 332 24
My dear Mr. Bennet," cried his wife, "what are you talking PP III 13 348 40
"But the wife of Mr. Darcy must have such extraordinary PP III 14 355 46
Elizabeth will soon be the wife of Mr. Darcy. PP III 18 383 23
to Elizabeth, from his wife, the Longbourn family heard PP III 18 383 26
to her that, by his wife at least, if not by himself, such PP III 19 386 6
curiosity to see how his wife conducted herself; and she PP III 19 388 12
I dare say there is always some reputable tradesman's wife MP I 1 8 8
He had a wife about fifteen years his junior, but no MP I 3 24 6
its probability to his wife; and the first time of the MP I 3 24 7
I consider the blessing of a wife as most justly described MP I 4 43 23
When I am a wife, I mean to be just as staunch myself; and MP I 5 47 24
to her gratitude; his wife certainly had; and it is the MP I 7 63 7
one to the side of his wife: but it is natural and amiable MP I 7 63 7
the clergyman and his wife are very decent people. MP I 8 82 34
newspaper, watch the weather, and quarrel with his wife. MP I 11 110 23
makes a blunder, is out of humour with his excellent wife. MP I 11 111 28
Miss Price, than to be the wife of a man whose amiableness MP I 11 112 31
countrywoman; the Cottager's wife; you had, indeed, Julia. MP I 14 134 12
Cottager's wife is a very pretty part I assure you. MP I 14 134 12
You shall be Cottager's wife." MP I 14 134 12
"Cottager's wife!" cried Mr. Yates. MP I 14 134 13
must have one Cottager's wife; and I am sure I set her the MP I 14 134 14
"With all your partiality for Cottager's wife," said Henry MP I 14 134 15
You must be Cottager's wife." MP I 15 145 45
with his fair sister-in-law, could not spare his wife. MP I 18 171 26
enjoyment as by his wife, who was really extremely happy MP II 1 179 9
on the nerves of his wife and children, had sought no MP II 1 180 10
of the agitation which his wife had been apprehensive of MP II 3 203 30
of Mr. Rushworth's wife must be to fill her house, and MP II 4 210 21
Grant, by his attentive wife, though it was not to be MP II 5 227 68
communicated to his wife and sister; but that seemed MP II 7 251 65
His duties would be established, but the wife who was to MP II 8 255 10
Thomas had been bringing up no wife for his younger son. MP II 10 278 20
to recommend her as a wife by shewing her persuadableness. MP II 10 281 34
side, tending to reconcile his wife to the arrangement. MP II 11 284 10
You will have a sweet little wife; all gratitude and MP II 12 292 7
of good principles in a wife, thought he was too little MP II 12 294 16
I know you, I know that a wife you loved would be the MP II 12 296 29
of making his own wife and sister-in-law acquainted with MP III 2 332 19
when she said that you should be Henry's wife. MP III 4 352 42
of Mr. Fraser by a first wife, whom she is wild to get MP III 5 360 16
My own sister as a wife, Sir Thomas Bertram as a husband, MP III 5 361 16
family, he did induce his wife to let her go; obtaining it MP III 6 370 14
woman in the world whom I could ever think of as a wife. MP III 13 421 2
to hear my opinion of Maria's degree of comfort as a wife. MP III 13 423 2
in the world, whom he could ever think of as a wife.' MP III 13 424 4
as did a deeper punishment, the deeper guilt of his wife. MP III 17 464 12
thoroughly deserves a good wife;--and you would not have E I 1 8 12
comfortable without a wife, so constantly occupied either E I 1 12 41
Some people even talked of a promise to his wife on her E I 1 12 41
You like Mr. Elton, papa,--I must look about for a wife E I 1 13 46
fish and the chicken, but leave him to chuse his own wife. E I 1 14 48
except her brother and his wife, who had never seen him, E I 2 15 2
the wife of Captain Weston, and Miss Churchill of Enscombe. E I 2 15 3
the bargain; for when his wife died after a three years' E I 2 16 4
house, and obtained his wife; and was beginning a new E I 2 17 6
daughter, a son and son's wife, who all lived together; E I 4 27 5
no young Mrs. Martin, no wife in the case; she did suspect E I 4 27 5
being acquainted with his wife-- for though his sisters, E I 4 30 22
to be acquainted with the wife, who will probably be some E I 4 31 24
am sure I shall not wish for the acquaintance of his wife. E I 4 31 25
"You are better placed here; very fit for a wife, but not E I 5 38 11
But you were preparing yourself to be an excellent wife E I 5 38 11
him a wife, I should certainly have named Miss Taylor." E I 5 38 11
There will be very little merit in making a good wife to E I 5 38 12
in her family; a devoted wife, a doating mother, and so E I 11 92 4
with such a worshipping wife, it was hardly possible that E I 11 92 5
I, being a husband, and you not being a wife, the claims E I 11 95 18
"Me, my love," cried his wife, hearing and understanding E I 11 95 19
tell me how to convey a wife and five children a distance E I 12 106 60
such unreserve, as to his wife; not any one, to whom she E I 14 117 1
every body, calling on his wife to agree with him, that, E I 15 126 11
party, stept in after his wife very naturally; so that E I 15 128 23
He has a wife and family to maintain, and is not to be E II 1 162 31
affections from his wife, or of any thing mischievous E II 2 168 13
his wife, fewer and quieter, but not less to the purpose. E II 5 188 8
she saw a touch of the arm at this speech, from his wife. E II 5 188 11
her, from both husband and wife; the son approached her E II 8 214 12
woman and a good wife, had examined the passage again, and E II 11 255 59
Mr. Weston whisper to his wife, "he has asked her, my dear. E II 11 256 60
And for a wife--a sensible man's wife--it is invaluable. E II 13 269 16
young lady, and no doubt will make him a very good wife. E II 14 279 54
suppose Mr. Elton thought at all differently from his wife. E II 15 281 2
not the open temper which a man would wish for in a wife." E II 15 288 36
happy wife together, without feeling uncomfortable. E II 16 291 5
instantly taken back his wife, there would have been a E II 17 303 23
the inquiries of his wife as to his dinner, convincing her E II 17 303 24
Mr. Elton had just joined them, and his wife was E III 2 324 22 23
and she perceived that his wife, who was standing E III 2 327 34
while smiles of high glee passed between him and his wife. E III 2 328 38
She did not think he was quite so hardened as his wife, E III 2 328 42 43
of both husband and wife were so much alike; and his E III 3 332 1
him--but I do not envy his wife in the least; I neither E III 4 337 6
be giving pain to his wife; and she found herself E III 6 353 3
Jane declined it, however, and the husband and wife walked E III 7 372 40
I marry, I hope somebody will choose my wife for me. E III 7 373 45 46
Will you choose a wife for me?-- E III 7 373 46
You shall have a charming wife." E III 7 373 49
years--and when I return, I shall come to you for my wife. E III 7 373 50
as possible; and his wife sat sighing and moralizing over E III 9 388 13
Mr. Churchill, independent of his wife, was feared by E III 9 388 13
I promised my wife to leave it all to her. E III 10 392 9
His wife gave him a look which invited him in; and, while E III 10 400 65
A glance or two between him and his wife, convinced him E III 10 400 69
a token of respect to the wife he had so very recently E III 11 403 2
dearest, the friend, the wife to whom he looked for all E III 12 422 20
when, if a man chooses a wife, he generally chooses ill. E III 13 428 23
wife for him, they could not have found her superior.-- E III 13 428 23
"Donwell!" cried his wife?"my dear Mr. E., you have not E III 16 457 39
the indignity as a wife ought to do,) "I cannot imagine E III 16 458 42
all the constancy of his wife; but the wonder of it was E III 17 468 33
Mr. Elton cared little about it, compared with his wife; E III 17 469 36
the day of the month on which he had lost his wife. P III 1 3 2
them he must have owed a wife of very superior character P III 1 4 6
black ribbons for his wife, she could not admit him to be P III 1 8 17
observed to his wife as they drove back through the park, " P III 5 32 4
superior to his wife; but not of powers, or conversation, P III 6 43 5
take best care of his wife, and the second blessing was P III 7 54 4
But in this he was eagerly opposed by his wife, with "Oh, P III 7 55 6
If a man has not a wife, he soon wants to be afloat again." P III 8 65 14
He had a wife.-- P III 8 67 23
called to order by his wife, now came up to Captain P III 8 68 31 32
I would assist any brother officer's wife that I could, P III 8 69 40
"Ah! my dear," said the Admiral, when he has got a wife, P III 8 70 46
very thankful to any body that will bring him his wife." P III 8 70 46
perfections of Edward's wife upon credit a little longer. P III 9 73 1
probability, make him an affectionate, good-humoured wife. P III 9 77 18
neither husband nor wife; for while she considered Louisa P III 10 82 1
though more fearfully, trying to induce his wife to go too. P III 10 86 17
very good humour with her, was out of temper with his wife. P III 10 90 37
He and his wife had taken their intended drive, and were P III 10 90 38
himself from his wife, they were both with him; and Louisa P III 12 110 37 38
his wife, calling on him for help which he could not give. P III 12 110 43
Charles attending to his wife, they set forward, treading P III 12 111 49
look between him and his wife decided what was to be done. P III 12 111 50
My wife should have the credit of them, however. P IV 1 127 28
with his wife, had perfectly understood the whole story. P IV 3 139 9
The husband had not been what he ought, and the wife had P IV 5 156 12
Elizabeth, may we venture to present him and his wife in P IV 6 166 15
Brigden stares to see anybody with me but my wife. P IV 6 169 29
us; he kisses his hand to you; he takes you for my wife. P IV 6 170 29
"My dear Mrs. Smith, Mr. Elliot's wife has not been dead P IV 9 196 31
though I did not know his wife previously, (her inferior P IV 9 200 57
has a very pretty silly wife, to whom he tells things P IV 9 205 82
He was very unkind to his first wife. P IV 9 211 101
of still teasing his wife, by persisting that he would go P IV 10 225 55
takes a last look at his wife and children, and watches P IV 11 234 31
That neither Harville nor his wife entertained a doubt of P IV 11 242 65
her from being the wife of Sir Walter, he may not be P IV 12 250 8
caressed at last into making her the wife of Sir William. P IV 12 250 8
she had rendered, or ever meant to render, to his wife. P IV 12 251 11
She gloried in being a sailor's wife, but she must pay the P IV 12 252 12
his congratulations to his wife & himself--& sit down on S 1 364 1
His wife fervently hoped it was--but stood, terrified & S 1 364 1
My dear--(to his wife) I am very sorry to have brought you S 1 367 1
pleasure it will give my wife & daughters to be of service S 1 367 1
consulting his wife in the few words of "well my dear, I S 1 367 1
Mr Parker of Sanditon; this lady, my wife Mrs Parker.-- S 1 368 1
There my dear--(turning with exultation to his wife)--you S 1 370 1
kindest & most unpretending manner, to both husband & wife. S 2 370 1
family-man, fond of wife, Childn, brothers & sisters--& S 2 372 1
woman, the properest wife in the world for a man of strong S 2 372 1
Sanditon was a second wife & 4 children to him--hardly S 2 372 1
Now Mary, (smiling at his wife)--before I open it, what S 5 385 1
cd be kinder than her reception from both husband and wife. S 9 406 1
"No, indeed you should not, cried his wife, for dinner is S 9 411 1
"I will do whatever you wish me, replied his wife--but you S 12 423 1

WIFE'S (21)

I passed off the letter as his wife's, to the Vernons, & LS 5 250 3
Poor Manwaring gives me such histories of his wife's LS 26 296 5
is just gone; he brought me the news of his wife's arrival. LS 33 303 1
moiety of his first wife's fortune was also secured to her SS I 1 4 2
You are my cousins, and they are my wife's, so you must be SS I 21 119 4
been taken by them of his wife's indisposition, beyond one SS III 5 293 3
And in short--what do you think of my wife's style of SS III 8 328 61
wife's words, and parted with the last relics of Marianne. SS III 8 329 63
He had rather hoped that all his wife's views on the PP I 3 12 15
punctually repeated all his wife's offers of refreshment. PP II 5 155 3
adieus were much more affectionate than his wife's. PP III 11 330 7
instead of Cottager's wife's, and so change the parts all MP I 14 134 14
when he has got his wife's speeches, I would undertake him MP I 14 134 14
half so dangerous to a wife's happiness, as a tendency to MP III 5 363 24
pride is nothing to his wife's: his is a quiet, indolent, E II 18 309 33
Perry's setting up his carriage! and his wife's persuading E III 5 345 14
much affected by his wife's occasional lowness; bore with P III 6 43 5
much better than his wife's, and his practice not so bad.-- P III 6 44 6
of the Admiral's fraternal kindness as of his wife's. P III 9 73 1
The Admiral's kind urgency came in support of his wife's; P III 10 91 41
From his wife's account of him, she could discern Mr. P IV 9 209 95

WIG (1)
he was putting on his wig--so I said, 'coachman, you had MP II 2 189 5
WIGMORE ST (2)
come to me at No 10 Wigmore St--but I hope this may not be LS 2 245 1
her whole stay in Wigmore St till she was detected in this LS 17 271 7
WIGMORE STREET (2)
Wigmore Street, till she becomes a little more reasonable. LS 2 246 1
running away from Wigmore Street, she resolved on getting LS 19 273 1
WILCOX (2)
"but the truth is, that Wilcox is a stupid old fellow, and MP I 8 77 13
I cannot bear to keep good old Wilcox waiting. MP II 7 251 64
WILD (39)
girl who has been running wild the first fifteen years of LS 17 271 7
she was moreover noisy and wild, hated confinement and NA I 1 14 1
Are not you wild to know?" NA I 6 39 6
I really am quite wild with impatience. NA I 10 70 1
It was a strange, wild scheme." NA I 11 89 62
been quite wild to speak to you, and make my apologies. NA I 12 93 5
She was quite wild to go. NA I 14 115 52
It was not three months ago since, wild with joyful NA II 14 237 20
credit of a wild imagination will at least be all my own. NA II 15 243 9
almost driven me wild, pronounced with such impenetrable SS I 3 18 18
still rich, was less wild and more open, a long stretch of SS I 16 85 15
expensive, or new; who was wild to buy all, could SS II 4 165 24
to take Harry to see the wild beasts at Exeter Exchange: SS II 11 221 9
She really looked almost wild." PP I 8 35 4
on in the wild manner that you are suffered to do at home." PP I 9 42 14
himself to restrain the wild giddiness of his youngest PP II 14 213 17
must be affected by the wild volatility, the assurance and PP II 18 231 18
as made her quite wild; that she had a new gown, or a new PP II 19 238 5
she added, "but I am afraid he has turned out very wild." PP III 1 247 9
Not like the wild young men now-a-days, who think of PP III 1 249 38
She was wild to be at home--to hear, to see, to be upon PP III 4 280 26
period of extravagant and wild admiration, her fancy for PP III 5 285 18
Lydia was Lydia still; untamed, unabashed, wild, noisy, PP III 9 315 4
Conjectures as to the meaning of it, rapid and wild, PP III 9 320 32
six miles of us, who are wild to be admitted into our MP I 15 148 58
How impatient, how anxious, how wild I have been on the MP II 13 299 5
are, in a wild fit of folly, throwing away from you such MP III 1 318 39
whom she is wild to get married, and wants Henry to take. MP III 5 360 16
at this very moment, he is wild to see you, and occupied MP III 14 435 14
quite laid up; do not let them talk of such a wild thing. E II 11 249 11
Elton was wild to have the offer closed with immediately.-- E III 6 359 37
But here there was nothing to be shifted off in a wild E III 17 468 31
The girls were wild for dancing; and the evenings ended, P III 6 47 15
along the rough, wild sort of channel, down the centre. P III 10 87 22
The young people were all wild to see Lyme. P III 11 94 7
But the men are all wild after Miss Elliot. P IV 7 178 23
What wild imaginations one forms, where dear self is P IV 9 201 63
Charles Hayter was quite wild about it, and Henrietta was P IV 11 230 6
which the sort of wild goose-chace you find me in, may S 1 367 1
WILD-FOWL (1)
But then it was such a dead time of year, no wild-fowl, no NA II 11 209 5
WILDERNESS (10)
kind of a little wilderness on one side of your lawn. PP III 14 352 16 17
"I believe the wilderness will be new to all the party. MP I 9 90 35
"The Miss Bertrams have never seen the wilderness yet." MP I 9 90 35
tops of the trees of the wilderness immediately adjoining. MP I 9 90 36
to the door in the middle which opened to the wilderness. MP I 9 91 37
landed them in the wilderness, which was a planted wood of MP I 9 91 38
as much ease as I was told to go into this wilderness." MP I 9 94 54
law being the worst wilderness of the two, but I forestall MP I 9 94 55
They were just returned into the wilderness from the park, MP I 10 103 49
top, just ready for the wilderness, at the end of an hour MP I 10 103 50
WILDEST (1)
received my notes?" cried Marianne in the wildest anxiety. SS II 6 177 10
WILDLY (3)
"No, no, no," cried Marianne wildly, "he loves you, and SS II 7 186 26
in Willoughby, and she was wildly urgent to be gone. SS II 9 203 9
Marianne, still talking wildly of mama, her alarm SS III 7 311 14
WILDNESS (2)
was something more of wildness than in the rest, where the SS III 6 305 17
with feverish wildness, cried out-- "is mama coming?--" SS III 7 310 10 11
WILFUL (7)
but it was a degree of wilful thoughtlessness which NA II 4 149 1
I see nothing in it but your own wilful ignorance and the PP I 18 95 48
To such perseverance in wilful self-deception Elizabeth PP I 19 109 22
It seemed like wilful ill-nature, or a voluntary penance, PP II 10 182 1
But you have now shewn me that you can be wilful and MP III 1 318 39
no service to the wilful or nervous part of her disorder. E III 1 316 6
her womanly follies--her wilful intimacy with Harriet E III 17 463 15
WILFULLY (5)
"And yours, he replied with a smile, "is wilfully to PP I 11 58 32
Caroline is incapable of wilfully deceiving any one; and PP I 21 119 21
Wilfully and wantonly to have thrown off the companion of PP II 12 196 5
if you wilfully act against the inclinations of all. PP III 14 355 45
his advice, or even wilfully opposing him, insensible of E III 12 415 1
WILFULNESS (1)
I had thought you peculiarly free from wilfulness of MP III 1 318 39
WILLIAM (175)
at Merchant-Taylors', and William at sea,--and all of them NA I 4 32 2
"What did William mean by it? NA I 13 103 27
it seemed likely that William would lose the favour of his NA I 13 103 27
fingers, she fondly observed, "how playful William is!" SS I 21 121 8
second son William, who were nearly of the same age. SS II 12 233 19
Sir William and Lady Lucas are determined to go, merely on PP I 1 4 24
Sir William had been delighted with him. PP I 3 9 1
Sir William Lucas had been formerly in trade in Meryton, PP I 5 18 1
It was at Sir William Lucas's, where a large party were PP I 6 24 13
to perceive that Sir William Lucas was his neighbour, till PP I 6 25 25
Lucas was his neighbour, till Sir William thus began. PP I 6 25 25
Sir William only smiled. PP I 6 25 28
some discomposure to Sir William, "indeed, sir, I have not PP I 6 26 38
Elizabeth was determined; nor did Sir William at all shake PP I 6 26 40
What an agreeable man Sir William is, Mr. Bingley--is not PP I 9 44 27
At that moment Sir William Lucas appeared close to them, PP I 18 92 22
Sir William could not have interrupted any two people in PP I 18 93 26
Sir William and Lady Lucas were speedily applied to for PP I 22 122 3
likely to live; and Sir William gave it as his decided PP I 22 122 3
to mention it, when Sir William Lucas himself appeared, PP I 23 126 1
Sir William, how can you tell such a story?-- PP I 23 126 2
congratulations to Sir William, in which she was readily PP I 23 126 4
a great deal while Sir William remained; but no sooner had PP I 23 126 5
she could speak to Sir William or Lady Lucas without being PP I 23 127 5
Pray go to see them, with Sir William and Maria. PP II 3 149 26
She was to accompany Sir William and his second daughter. PP II 4 151 1
Sir William Lucas, and his daughter Maria, a good humoured PP II 4 152 4
back; and while Sir William accompanied him, Charlotte PP II 5 156 5
with the ladies; and Sir William, to Elizabeth's high PP II 5 158 19
happened," replied Sir William, "from that knowledge of PP II 6 160 3
and even Sir William did not look perfectly calm.-- PP II 6 161 9
In spite of having been at St. James's, Sir William was so PP II 6 162 11
by him, and then by sir William, who was now enough PP II 6 163 14
Lady Catherine, Sir William, and Mr. and Mrs. Collins sat PP II 6 166 41
Sir William did not say much. PP II 6 166 41
Sir William staid only a week at Hunsford; but his visit PP II 7 168 1
While Sir William was with them, Mr. Collins devoted his PP II 7 168 1
for the loss of Sir William, and there being only one card PP II 7 169 5
made acquainted, by Sir William Lucas's accidental PP II 12 197 5
I defy even Sir William Lucas himself, to produce a more PP III 11 330 8
I assure you it is much larger than Sir William Lucas's." PP III 14 352 10
He could even listen to Sir William Lucas, when he PP III 18 384 26
If he did shrug his shoulders, it was not till Sir William PP III 18 384 26
It was William whom she talked of most and wanted most to MP I 2 15 12
William, the eldest, a year older than herself, her MP I 2 15 12
"William did not like she should come away--he had told MP I 2 16 12
"But William will write to you, I dare say." MP I 2 16 12
Would it make you happy to write to William?" MP I 2 16 13
as your uncle will frank it, it will cost William nothing." MP I 2 16 17
He wrote with his own hand his love to his cousin William, MP I 2 16 20
of many years, had she the happiness of being with William. MP I 2 21 34
seemed to want her; but William determining, soon after MP I 2 21 34
charming things of what William was to do, and be MP I 2 21 34
except William; her heart was divided between the two. MP I 2 22 35
he hoped she might see William again in the course of the MP I 3 33 64
by adding, "if William does come to Mansfield, I hope you MP I 3 33 64
for though it brought no William to England, the never MP I 4 35 6
I am sure William would never have used me so, under any MP I 7 64 10
"Poor William! MP I 11 111 27
from the Mediterranean by William, with H. M. S. Antwerp MP I 16 152 2
He inquired next after her family, especially William; and MP II 1 178 7
William, her brother, the so long absent, and dearly loved MP II 6 232 12
timidity of her mind by the flow of her love for William. MP II 6 232 13
This dear William would soon be amongst them. MP II 6 233 14
William and Fanny soon shewed themselves; and Sir Thomas MP II 6 233 16
could see in him the same William as before, and talk to MP II 6 233 17
But with William and Fanny Price, it was still a sentiment MP II 6 235 18
William was often called on by his uncle to be the talker. MP II 6 236 21
Young as he was, William had already seen a great deal. MP II 6 236 21
he wished he had been a William price, distinguishing MP II 6 236 22
up to any thing, William expressed an inclination to hunt; MP II 6 237 23
She feared for William; by no means convinced by all that MP II 6 237 23
When it was proved however to have done William no harm, MP II 6 237 23
The return of Henry Crawford, and the arrival of William MP II 7 238 1
in any competition with William, was a work of some MP II 7 240 8
in a negociation for William price's knave increased. MP II 7 241 19
of her dealings with William price, and securing his knave MP II 7 242 25
William, you are quite out of luck; but the next time you MP II 7 245 32
your going to Brighton, William, as I trust you may soon MP II 7 245 34
William and Fanny were the most detached. MP II 7 249 49
"This is the assembly night," said William. MP II 7 249 50
"But you do not wish yourself at Portsmouth, William?" MP II 7 249 51
But never mind it, William. MP II 7 249 53
When you are a lieutenant!--only think, William, when you MP II 7 249 53
"Oh! my dear William, do not talk so, do not be so MP II 7 250 55
should come back for you, and Edmund, and William." MP II 7 251 64
he added, "I do not like, William, that you should leave MP II 8 252 1
Thank your uncle, William, thank your uncle." MP II 8 252 2
Edmund, William, and Fanny, did, in their different ways, MP II 8 253 5
William was required to be at Portsmouth on the 24th; the MP II 8 253 7
pretty amber cross which William had brought her from MP II 8 254 8
William had wanted to buy her a gold chain too, but the MP II 8 254 8
and as Edmund and William were gone to Northampton, and MP II 8 256 14
through all the heads of William and the cross, and the MP II 8 258 17
from Mr. Crawford to William stating, that as he found MP II 9 265 21
therefore hoped that if William could make up his mind to MP II 9 265 21
and William was invited to dine with him at the Admiral's. MP II 9 266 21
The proposal was a very pleasant one to William himself, MP II 9 266 21
original plan was that William should go up by the mail MP II 9 266 21
was too happy in having William spared from the fatigue of MP II 9 266 21
with Mr. Crawford, to see William enjoy himself, and be MP II 9 267 22
William, determined to make this last day a day of MP II 9 267 22
Since the first joy from Mr. Crawford's note to William MP II 9 270 40
seen and felt how full of William and Edmund they were, MP II 9 271 40
to it, without looking at William, as he walked about at MP II 10 273 7
when he talked of William, he was really not un-agreeable, MP II 10 278 20
She was happy whenever she looked at William, and saw how MP II 10 278 20
"Poor Fanny!" cried William, coming for a moment to visit MP II 10 279 23
"Oh! William." MP II 10 279 26
"Yes, half past nine," said Crawford to William, as the MP II 10 280 31
She had hoped to have William all to herself, the last MP II 10 280 32
over too; the last kiss was given, and William was gone. MP II 11 282 1
After seeing William to the last moment, Fanny walked back MP II 11 282 2
William was gone, and she now felt as if she had wasted MP II 11 282 2
by William, that was due to him for a whole fortnight. MP II 11 282 3
of Mr. Crawford or of William, when he said he was the MP II 11 283 4
She could think of William the next day more cheerfully, MP II 11 283 7
William was kindly commended and his promotion hoped for. MP II 11 284 9
brother's going away, of William price's going too, and MP II 11 286 15
the circumstance of Mr. William Price's commission as MP II 13 298 3
I could not require William price to excite a greater MP II 13 300 5
to what he told her of William, and saying only when he MP II 13 300 7
Dearest, dearest William!" she jumped up and moved in MP II 13 300 7
thing he had done for William, was to be placed to the MP II 13 301 7
Your kindness to William makes me more obliged to you than MP II 13 302 8
But William was a lieutenant.-- MP II 13 302 11
she could esteem him for his friendship to William! MP II 13 302 11
a talk with him about William as to make her feel as if MP II 13 303 12
She would hardly join even when William was the subject, MP II 13 304 17
"Now William would be able to keep himself, which would MP II 13 304 19
She was very glad that she had given William what she did MP II 13 304 19
Fanny, William must not forget my shawl, if he goes to the MP II 13 305 25
as far as they relate to my dearest William. MP II 13 307 31
very uncertain when my interest might have got William on. MP III 1 316 28
She is hurt, as you would be for William; but she loves MP III 4 352 40
What a happy creature William must be! MP III 5 364 29
The recollection of what had been done for William was MP III 5 364 30
William had obtained a ten days' leave of absence to be MP III 6 368 7
of her infancy, with William for the protector and MP III 6 369 11
to see William to the last hour of his remaining on land. MP III 6 369 11
speak more largely to William and Edmund of what she felt; MP III 6 369 11
William was almost as happy in the plan as his sister. MP III 6 371 18
Sir Thomas actually give William notes for the purpose, MP III 6 372 21
William and Fanny were horror-struck at the idea. MP III 6 373 22
party met at breakfast, William and Fanny were talked of MP III 6 374 29
happiness of being with William, soon produced their MP III 7 375 1
out of the way--and William was not very merciful to the MP III 7 375 2
William knew what had passed, and from his heart lamented MP III 7 375 3
the maid aside, and while William was opening the chaise MP III 7 377 7
A stare or two at Fanny, as William helped her out of the MP III 7 377 8
She was gone again to the street door, to welcome William. MP III 7 378 10
"Oh! my dear William, how glad I am to see you. MP III 7 378 10
"Ha!" cried William, "that's just where I should have put MP III 7 380 21
of the thrush, though William, warmly interested, as he MP III 7 380 23
a considerable period, William determined to go and change MP III 7 381 24
William was soon calling out from the landing-place of the MP III 7 381 26
could, in a great hurry; William trying in vain to send MP III 7 382 27
she was like William--and Fanny hoped to find her like him MP III 7 384 33
In this more placid state of things William re-entered, MP III 7 384 34
every thing was ready, William took leave, and all of them MP III 7 384 36
the hope of soon seeing William again, and the MP III 8 388 1
In the first place, William was gone. MP III 8 388 2
William was gone;--and the home he had left her in was-- MP III 8 388 3
She was fond of her sons, especially of William, but MP III 8 389 4
William was her pride; Betsey, her darling; and John, MP III 8 389 4
They talked of William, a subject on which Mrs. Price MP III 10 400 7
or all, except Fanny and William, and Lady Bertram would MP III 13 428 15
walking hastily by, Mr. William Cox letting himself in at E II 9 233 24
But, however, I found afterwards from Patty, that William E II 9 239 51
William did not seem to mind it himself, he was so pleased E II 9 239 51
had sold so many; for William, you know, thinks more of E II 9 239 51
not know who will ask her next, perhaps Mr. William Cox.' E III 2 329 45

William seemed rather out of humour. E III 16 458 43
He cannot bear the idea of not being Sir William. P IV 9 207 90
caressed at last into making her the wife of Sir William. P IV 12 250 8
WILLIAM COLLINS (1)
William Collins." PP I 13 63 12
WILLIAM COXE (2)
desirable for her;--William Coxe-- Oh! no, I could not E I 16 137 11
no, I could not endure William Coxe--a pert young lawyer." E I 16 137 11
WILLIAM GOULDING (1)
and we overtook William Goulding in his curricle, so I was PP III 9 316 8
WILLIAM HEELEY'S (1)
Look my dear Mary--look at William Heeley's windows.-- S 4 383 1
WILLIAM LARKINS (12)
William Larkins let me keep a larger quantity than usual E II 9 238 51
However, the very same evening William Larkins came over E II 9 239 51
William Larkins and said every thing, as you may suppose. E II 9 239 51
William Larkins is such an old acquaintance! E II 9 239 51
William Larkins mentioned it here. E II 10 245 52
he would have preferred the society of William Larkins. E II 12 258 6
He may spend the evening with his dear William Larkins now E II 12 262 39
Larkins the whole morning, to have his thoughts to himself. E III 15 449 32
"I am sure William Larkins will not like it. E III 15 449 33
"I met William Larkins," continued Mr. Elton, "as I got E III 16 458 43
towards Mr. Elton, if not towards William Larkins. E III 16 458 44
You laugh at me about William Larkins; but I could quite E III 18 473 22
WILLIAM LARKINS'S (1)
William Larkins's week's account; much rather, I confess.-- E II 12 257 3
WILLIAM WALTER ELLIOT, ESQ. (2)
Elliot, Esq., great grandson of the second Sir Walter." P III 1 3 3
4
The heir presumptive, the very William Walter Elliot, Esq. P III 1 7 13
WILLIAM'S (30)
Elinor, having once delivered her opinion on William's SS II 12 234 25
the other night at Sir William's in his regimentals." PP I 7 29 12
heard by Darcy; but Sir William's allusion to his friend PP I 18 92 24
partner, and said, "Sir William's interruption has made me PP I 18 93 24
25
such treatment; but Sir William's good breeding carried PP I 23 126 3
absurdities, but she had known Sir William's too long. PP II 4 152 4
side, and as many bows on Sir William's, they departed. PP II 6 166 42
for William's sake, "they can write long letters." MP I 6 59 44
"And Fanny had much rather it were William's," said Edmund, MP II 7 244 29
any thing else," was William's only answer, in an under MP II 7 246 35
William's desire of seeing Fanny dance, made more than a MP II 8 252 1
of this little trifle--a chain for William's cross. MP II 9 261 2
The chain will agree with William's cross beyond all MP II 9 263 15
William's good fortune returned again upon her mind, and MP II 9 270 40
bones and mustard in William's place, might but divide her MP II 11 282 2
joy and gratitude on William's behalf, she could not be MP II 13 301 7
conjectures as to what would now be William's destination. MP II 13 302 12
on the first day of hearing of William's promotion. MP II 13 303 13
the subject of William's appointment in their own style. MP II 13 304 18
restore the knowledge of William's advancement, whereas MP II 13 308 36
the Mr. Crawford who had procured William's promotion! MP III 2 328 6
William's promotion, with all its particulars, he was soon MP III 3 334 3
to the high glee of William's mind, and he was full of MP III 7 375 2
to fail, as, guided by William's powerful voice, they were MP III 7 376 6
William's concerns must be dearest--they always had been-- MP III 7 382 29
Every thing in that quarter failed her, except William's MP III 8 388 2
of the name, as that of "William's friend," though she MP III 10 399 4
known there only as William's friend, was some support. MP III 10 399 4
In her usefulness, in Fanny's excellence, in William's MP III 17 473 31
I have nothing to do with William's wants, but it really E III 16 458 43
WILLING (50)
away; and Catherine, ever willing to give Mr. Tilney an NA I 8 58 25
object was a letter, held out by Henry's willing hand. NA II 10 201 6
denied--their willing approbation was instantly to follow. NA II 16 249 2
But I was willing to shew you that I had not forgot our SS I 17 92 25
expected, Elinor was very willing to compound for the want SS II 5 168 11
"Do you like London?" said Edward, willing to say any SS II 13 242 28
that I have been willing to admit, have been the effect of SS III 1 264 29
on every occasion a most willing and active helpmate, SS III 7 308 3
Her sister, however, still sanguine, was willing to SS III 7 310 9
Willing therefore to delay the evil hour, she resolved to SS III 10 343 10
You will find Mrs Edwards' maid very willing to help you, W 315 1
not find a more willing or speedy messenger than myself--. W 338 18
his Lordship--but she was willing to suppose that he had W 347 22
and she was very willing to hear him, though what she PP I 16 77 8
design, and he was not willing to have the attempt known PP I 22 121 1
and was certain of a willing listener in Jane, whenever PP II 17 227 25
But I am willing to hope the best, and that his character PP III 4 273 3
being so; but if you are willing to perform the PP III 7 302 14
some who are able and willing to assist him in the army. PP III 8 312 19
without wanting to be cured, were very willing to stay. MP I 5 47 26
answered for by Maria as willing to do any thing; when MP I 14 133 8
autumn morning, to such a willing mind as Fanny's, and MP I 16 151 2
children: he was more willing to believe they felt their MP II 2 187 2
before, and apparently as willing to stay and be happy MP II 5 224 49
a more willing assent to invitations on that account. MP II 7 238 1
If, as I am willing to suppose, you wish to shew me any MP III 1 321 48
could answer; and she was willing to hope, secondly, that MP III 1 324 58
He was very willing to hope that Crawford saw clearer; and MP III 3 336 7
she had; for, less willing than his son to trust to the MP III 5 356 3
made her as able as she was willing to be generous. MP III 9 396 7
She was willing to allow he might have more good qualities MP III 10 405 16
"Well," said Emma, willing to let it pass--"you want to E I 1 11 35
to a man in love, and was willing to trust to there being E I 8 61 38
possible; and if his willing brother ever left him any E I 12 100 16
willing to prefer Cromer to south end as he could himself." E I 12 106 60
coming now, depends upon her being willing to spare him." E I 14 121 16
Mr. Frank Churchill, was willing to forget his late E I 15 124 2
Emma was very willing now to acquit her of having seduced E II 2 168 13
had been willing to hope, had been lately gaining strength. E II 13 267 8
Mrs. Elton, very willing to suppose a particular E II 18 305 2
herself, fagged, and very willing to be silent; and Emma E III 7 376 63
No longer walking in at all hours, as if ever willing to E III 12 422 20
"And I am changed also; for I am now very willing to grant E III 18 474 34
I hope time has not made you less willing to pardon. E III 18 476 47
afterwards found a more willing mind in her younger sister; P III 4 28 7
her feet, made him less willing upon the present occasion; P III 12 109 32
She expressed herself most willing, ready, happy to remain. P III 12 114 63
Lady Russell said not another word, willing to leave the P IV 5 160 26
I was willing to hope that you must fare better." P IV 9 211 101
to me, & my being willing to promote a little Subscription S 12 423 1
WILLINGDEN (15)
Am I not in Willingden?-- S 1 366 1
Is not this Willingden?" S 1 366 1
"Yes sir, this is certainly Willingden." S 1 366 1
being a surgeon in Willingden,--for having lived here ever S 1 366 1
other--which is Great Willingden, or Willingden Abbots, & S 1 366 1
mile or two of a Willingden, I sought no farther . . . S 1 367 1
were fixed at Willingden; Mr. P.'s sprain proving too S 2 370 1
induced him to expect to accomplish in Willingden.-- S 2 371 1
his good friends at Willingden thither; and his endeavours S 2 372 1
obliged them to be stationary and healthy at Willingden. S 2 373 1
& in their journey from Willingden to the coast, Mr Parker S 3 375 1
She had been necessarily often mentioned at Willingden,-- S 3 375 1
"It seems to have as many comforts about it as Willingden," S 4 379 1
I sent him an account of my accident from Willingden, & S 5 385 1
sisters, for the object which had taken him to Willingden. S 6 393 1
WILLINGDEN ABBOTS (1)
Willingden, or Willingden Abbots, & lies 7 miles off, on S 1 366 1
WILLINGDENS (1)
There are two Willingdens in this country--& your S 1 366 1
WILLINGLY (19)
the Tilneys, she would willingly have given up all the NA I 11 88 54
to think, nobody would willingly ever look into, to be NA I 14 109 24
economy; and would willingly have been spared the NA II 8 184 4
It was the last thing I would willingly have done. NA II 13 225 22
propitious, would willingly have made a confidante of Emma W 360 29
"Most willingly." PP I 21 118 17
poor Jane! who would willingly have gone through the world PP II 17 224 9
visible below, she had willingly turned to look at some PP III 1 250 46
though Mrs. Norris would willingly have answered for his MP I 8 75 1
Fanny was led off very willingly, though it was impossible MP I 12 119 25
the part to Julia most willingly, but that though I shall MP I 14 136 21
He certainly wished her to go willingly, but he as MP III 6 369 9
Poor Fanny! though going, as she did, willingly and MP III 6 374 28
Bertram, she could not be parted with willingly by her. MP III 17 472 31
were attached, he would willingly give up much of wealth E II 6 204 43
and Mrs. Weston most willingly undertook to play as long E II 11 247 3
feelings could have so willingly acknowledged as an equal. P III 1 8 17
that he would never willingly admit any ladies on board a P III 8 68 34
"Most willingly, fair questioner.-- S 8 403 1
WILLINGNESS (10)
his wife, but of less willingness to please or be pleased. SS I 19 106 22
declared a much greater willingness to make mean SS III 13 372 45
Mr. Gardiner declared his willingness, and Elizabeth was PP II 19 240 12
of society, a perfect willingness to accept it, she PP III 2 264 11
that was done, and his willingness to fulfil the PP III 8 309 4
"There can be no doubt of Mr. Crawford's willingness; but MP I 6 62 58
no comparison in the willingness of their attention, for MP I 9 85 3
in Frederick, he professed an equal willingness for that. MP I 14 132 8
assure you it makes none in my willingness to part with it. MP II 8 259 22
you cannot doubt my willingness to be of even the P IV 9 195 25
WILLOUGHBY (178)
His name, he replied, was Willoughby, and his present home SS I 9 42 10
knew any gentleman of the name of Willoughby at Allenham. SS I 9 43 12
"Willoughby!" cried Sir John; "what, is he in the country? SS I 9 43 13
he told them that Mr. Willoughby had no property of his SS I 9 44 23
smile, "that Mr. Willoughby will be incommoded by the SS I 9 44 24
than precision, stiled Willoughby, called at the cottage SS I 10 46 1
From Willoughby their expression was at first held back, SS I 10 46 2
Willoughby, on his side, gave every proof of his pleasure SS I 10 48 7
Willoughby was a young man of good abilities, quick SS I 10 48 7
Willoughby was all that her fancy had delineated in that SS I 10 49 10
gained two such sons-in-law as Edward and Willoughby. SS I 10 49 11
the affection of Mr. Willoughby, an equally striking SS I 10 49 12
he was slighted by Willoughby and Marianne, who, SS I 10 50 13
"Brandon is just the kind of man," said Willoughby one day, SS I 10 50 14
"That he is patronized by you," replied Willoughby, "is SS I 10 50 17
"Perhaps," said Willoughby, "his observations may have SS I 10 51 23
"Miss Dashwood," cried Willoughby, "you are now using me SS I 10 51 28
In every meeting of the kind Willoughby was included; and SS I 11 53 1
Willoughby thought the same; and their behaviour, at all SS I 11 53 2
Her heart was devoted to Willoughby, and the fond SS I 11 54 5
Willoughby was out of the question. SS I 11 55 7
greatest delight, that Willoughby had given her a horse, SS I 12 58 1
she warmly, "in supposing I know very little of Willoughby. SS I 12 58 4
in accepting a horse from my brother, than from Willoughby. SS I 12 59 4
years; but of Willoughby my judgment has long been formed." SS I 12 59 4
Willoughby when she saw him next, that it must be declined. SS I 12 59 5
She was faithful to her word; and when Willoughby called SS I 12 59 6
Willoughby had spent the preceding evening with them, and SS I 12 60 8
I am sure she will be married to Mr. Willoughby very soon." SS I 12 60 9
Willoughby opened the piano-forte, and asked Marianne to SS I 12 62 27
"You would not be six hours later," said Willoughby, "if SS I 13 64 28
Elinor then heard Willoughby say in a low voice to SS I 13 64 30
the cottage, and Mr. Willoughby got up two hours before SS I 13 65 32
Willoughby took his usual place between the two elder Miss SS I 13 67 61
leant behind her and Willoughby, and said to Marianne, SS I 13 67 61
"Did not you know," said Willoughby, "that we had been out SS I 13 67 63
very unlikely that Willoughby should propose, or Marianne SS I 13 68 66
there, and with no other companion than Mr. Willoughby." SS I 13 68 69
"Mr. Willoughby however is the only person who can have a SS I 13 68 70
go to Allenham; but Mr. Willoughby wanted particularly to SS I 13 69 76
of hundred pounds, Willoughby says, would make it one of SS I 13 69 76
of her sister and Willoughby on the subject, which they SS I 14 71 3
their power; for though Willoughby was independent, there SS I 14 71 4
"Thank you, Willoughby. SS I 14 72 10
"There certainly are circumstances," said Willoughby, " SS I 14 73 15
Willoughby, as plainly denoted how well she understood him. SS I 14 73 16
had been made by Willoughby the night before of calling on SS I 15 75 1
where they found only Willoughby, who was leaning against SS I 15 75 2
For shame, Willoughby. SS I 15 76 11
"I have only to add, my dear Willoughby, that at Barton SS I 15 76 14
"My engagements at present," replied Willoughby confusedly, SS I 15 76 15
This was broken by Willoughby, who said with a faint smile, SS I 15 76 16
"Our dear Willoughby is now some miles from Barton, Elinor, SS I 15 77 22
guilt for poor Willoughby, than an apology for the latter. SS I 15 78 28
Willoughby may undoubtedly have very sufficient reasons SS I 15 79 29
But it would have been more like Willoughby to acknowledge SS I 15 79 29
for Willoughby to be but little in Devonshire at present. SS I 15 79 31
do you accuse Willoughby and Marianne of concealment? SS I 15 79 32
How is it to be supposed that Willoughby, persuaded as he SS I 15 80 36
You must think wretchedly indeed of Willoughby, if after SS I 15 80 38
It must be Willoughby therefore whom you suspect. SS I 15 81 42
"I love Willoughby, sincerely love him; and suspicion of SS I 15 81 43
Willoughby certainly does not deserve to be suspected. SS I 15 81 44
The slightest mention of any thing relative to Willoughby SS I 15 82 47
sleep at all the first night after parting from Willoughby. SS I 16 83 1
been used to play to Willoughby, every air in which their SS I 16 83 3
No letter from Willoughby came; and none seemed expected SS I 16 84 5
said she, "whether she is or is not engaged to Willoughby? SS I 16 84 8
dear Willoughby went away before we could get through it. SS I 16 85 11
12
confidence in Willoughby and knowledge of his intentions. SS I 16 85 14
It is not Willoughby. SS I 16 86 18
being Willoughby, quickened her pace and kept up with her. SS I 16 86 20
forgiven for not being Willoughby; the only one who could SS I 16 86 21
back her thoughts to Willoughby, whose manners formed a SS I 16 87 23
cried Sir John, "that Willoughby were among us again." SS I 18 100 21
"And who is Willoughby?" said he, in a low voice, to miss SS I 18 100 22
"Well then, I guess that Mr. Willoughby hunts." SS I 18 100 27
a nothing between Mr. Willoughby and herself, he would not SS I 18 100 30
She began by inquiring if they saw much of Mr. Willoughby SS I 20 114 43
is going to be married to Mr. Willoughby of Combe Magna. SS I 20 115 50
"Is Mr. Willoughby much known in your part of SS I 20 116 57
Nobody is more liked than Mr. Willoughby wherever he goes, SS I 20 116 58
Mrs. Palmer's information respecting Willoughby was not SS I 20 116 59
eagerness to be with Willoughby again, made no further SS II 3 154 6
must then be writing to Willoughby, and the conclusion SS II 4 160 5
"Oh! Elinor, it is Willoughby, indeed it is!"" and seemed SS II 4 161 7
Elinor wished very much to ask whether Willoughby were SS II 4 162 12
I do not know what you and Mr. Willoughby will do between SS II 4 163 18
which declared that no Willoughby had been there. SS II 4 165 25
arrival it became certain that Willoughby was also arrived. SS II 5 169 13
inform her, that Willoughby had paid no second visit there. SS II 5 169 16
she had seen nothing of Willoughby; and therefore was not SS II 5 170 28
was again writing to Willoughby, for she could not suppose SS II 5 171 38
engagement to Mr. Willoughby is very generally known." SS II 5 173 40
hand, directed to Mr. Willoughby in your sister's writing. SS II 5 173 44
The real state of things between Willoughby and her sister SS II 5 173 45
affection for Willoughby, could leave no hope of Colonel SS II 5 174 45

happiness; to Willoughby that he may endeavour to deserve SS II 5 174 46
to her mother; for Willoughby neither came nor wrote. SS II 6 175 1
before Elinor perceived Willoughby, standing within a few SS II 6 176 3
Willoughby, what is the meaning of this? SS II 6 176 7
Tell me, Willoughby; for heaven's sake tell me, what is SS II 6 177 10
In a short time Elinor saw Willoughby quit the room by the SS II 6 178 15
had subsisted between Willoughby and Marianne she could SS II 6 178 17
not doubt; and that Willoughby was weary of it, seemed SS II 6 178 17
final separation from Willoughby--in an immediate and SS II 6 179 18
was that she was writing for the last time to Willoughby. SS II 7 180 4
that it must come from Willoughby, felt immediately such a SS II 7 181 7
received a letter from Willoughby, which appreared to her SS II 7 181 7
persuasion of my sister's being engaged to Mr. Willoughby? SS II 7 181 9
all events to know what Willoughby had written, hurried SS II 7 182 12
madam, your most obedient humble servant, John Willoughby. SS II 7 183 13
could she have supposed Willoughby capable of departing so SS II 7 183 14
surprised you will be, Willoughby, on receiving this; and SS II 7 186 38
am I to imagine, Willoughby, by your behaviour last night? SS II 7 187 41
42

"Elinor, I have been cruelly used; but not by Willoughby." SS II 7 189 47
48

of evil than Willoughby, whose heart I know so well?" SS II 7 189 50
Oh! Willoughby, Willoughby, could this be yours! SS II 7 190 56
Willoughby, where was your heart, when you wrote those SS II 7 190 56
against ever naming Mr. Willoughby, or making the SS II 8 195 17
I must do <u>this</u> justice to Mr. Willoughby--he has broken no SS II 8 196 19
If we <u>can</u> but put Willoughby out of her head!" SS II 8 197 22
Mr. Willoughby is unfathomable! SS II 8 199 36
The name of Willoughby, John Willoughby, frequently SS II 8 199 37
"It may be so; but Willoughby is capable--at least I think" SS II 8 199 39
Sometimes she could believe Willoughby to be as SS II 9 201 2
her a letter from Willoughby, full of tenderness and SS II 9 202 7
instantly followed by Willoughby himself, rushing eagerly SS II 9 202 7
Willoughby filled every page. SS II 9 202 8
her, such affection for Willoughby, and such a conviction SS II 9 202 8
in Willoughby, and she was wildly urgent to be gone. SS II 9 203 9
"You have something to tell me of Mr. Willoughby, that SS II 9 204 19
of your sister to Mr. Willoughby, and it was, though from SS II 9 205 24
cried Elinor, "could it be--could Willoughby!----- SS II 9 209 29
Little did Mr. Willoughby imagine, I suppose, when his SS II 9 209 30
"ever seen Mr. Willoughby since you left him at Barton?" SS II 9 211 34
no vindication of Willoughby, and seemed to shew by her SS II 10 212 1
by constantly placing Willoughby before her, such as she SS II 10 213 3
From all danger of seeing Willoughby again, her mother SS II 10 213 4
Sir John) that as Mrs. Willoughby would at once be a woman SS II 10 215 14
Marianne and Mr. Willoughby, she would have thought SS II 14 247 4
Edward seemed a second Willoughby; and acknowledging as SS III 1 261 13
and that confidence, in Willoughby, which were now SS III 6 301 4
Nor could she leave the place in which Willoughby remained, SS III 6 302 4
sister away unseen by Willoughby since his marriage, and SS III 6 302 5
drawing-room,--she entered it,--and saw only Willoughby. SS III 7 316 31
Willoughby, I advise you at present to return to Combe.-- SS III 8 318 16
17

recollection, "Mr. Willoughby, you <u>ought</u> to feel, and I SS III 8 318 21
22

brought all the former Willoughby to her remembrance, and SS III 8 319 25
hardly worth while, Mr. Willoughby, for you to relate, or SS III 8 320 30
31

"Remember," cried Willoughby, "from whom you received the SS III 8 322 36
"Why did you call, Mr. Willoughby?" said Elinor, SS III 8 324 41
"This is not right, Mr. Willoughby.-- SS III 8 325 52
on one side, calling me Willoughby in such a tone!-- SS III 8 327 55
Willoughby first rousing himself, broke it thus: "well, SS III 8 327 56
57

"But the letter, Mr. Willoughby, your own letter; have you SS III 8 328 60
"You are very wrong, Mr. Willoughby, very blameable," said SS III 8 329 64
speak in this way, either of Mrs. Willoughby or my sister. SS III 8 329 64
end of some minutes by Willoughby, who, rousing himself SS III 8 331 70
71

Willoughby, he, whom only half an hour ago she had SS III 9 333 2
most worthless of men, Willoughby, in spite of all his SS III 9 333 2
Willoughby, "poor Willoughby," as she now allowed herself SS III 9 334 6
with another; and for a moment wished Willoughby a widower. SS III 9 335 5
attachment to Willoughby, had contributed to place her;-- SS III 9 335 7
anything that Willoughby ever felt or feigned, as much SS III 9 336 14
is not to be wasted for ever on such a man as Willoughby.-- SS III 9 337 18
is not so handsome as Willoughby--but at the same time, SS III 9 338 20
I am very sure myself, that had Willoughby turned out as SS III 9 338 22
and yet in wishing it, to feel a pang for Willoughby. SS III 9 339 27
which the remembrance of Willoughby could be connected.-- SS III 10 342 7
procured for her by Willoughby, containing some of their SS III 10 342 7
that her promise to Willoughby was yet unfulfilled, and SS III 10 343 10
mound,--there I fell; and there I first saw Willoughby." SS III 10 344 12
13

As for Willoughby--to say that I shall soon or that I SS III 10 347 30
chief points on which Willoughby grounded his apology; did SS III 10 347 33
talked of nothing but Willoughby, and their conversation SS III 10 348 34
devoted to her husband, as it had once been to Willoughby. SS III 14 379 17
Willoughby could not hear of her marriage without a pang; SS III 14 379 18

WILLOUGHBY'S (35)
to the colour of Mr. Willoughby's pointer, than he could SS I 9 44 21
You have already ascertained Mr. Willoughby's opinion in SS I 10 47 4
The carriages were then ordered; Willoughby's was first, SS I 13 66 60
woman enquire of Mr. Willoughby's groom, and that she had SS I 13 67 65
They will one day be Mr. Willoughby's, and" . . . SS I 13 68 74
75

of attachment to them all, than Willoughby's behaviour. SS I 14 71 5
The promise was readily given, and Willoughby's behaviour SS I 14 74 20
On their return from the park they found Willoughby's SS I 15 75 2
Willoughby's behaviour in taking leave of them, his SS I 15 77 19
It was several days before Willoughby's name was mentioned SS I 16 85 11
12

as well known as Willoughby's, joined them in begging her SS I 16 86 20
extorted from her, for Willoughby's service, by her mother. SS I 19 101 2
particular account of Willoughby's general character, than SS I 20 114 43
occasional doubt of Willoughby's constancy, could not SS II 4 159 1
must now decide what Willoughby's intentions were; in all SS II 4 159 1
Elinor felt secure of its announcing Willoughby's approach, SS II 4 161 7
her suspicions of Willoughby's inconstancy, urging her by SS II 5 172 39
turning eagerly to Willoughby's letter, read as follows: SS II 7 182 12
13

Willoughby's sake, would have been unwilling to believe. SS II 7 188 43
post, again took up Willoughby's letter, and after SS II 7 190 55
56

I came only for Willoughby's sake--and now who cares for SS II 7 191 62
required of her for Willoughby's; since though Marianne SS II 8 196 21
forced calmness, "Mr. Willoughby's marriage with Miss Grey. SS II 8 199 36
She felt the loss of Willoughby's character yet more SS II 10 212 1
hearing Willoughby's name mentioned, was not thrown away. SS II 10 214 8
by what painter Mr. Willoughby's portrait was drawn, and SS II 10 215 11
from the receipt of Willoughby's letter, Elinor had the SS II 10 216 16
The past, the present, the future, Willoughby's visit, SS III 9 333 3
half an hour after Willoughby's leaving the house, she was SS III 9 333 3
and wished any thing rather than Mrs. Willoughby's death. SS III 9 335 5
Willoughby's eyes at times, which I did not like." SS III 9 338 20
pleasing to me than Willoughby's ever were, but they are SS III 9 338 21
22

Had Mrs. Dashwood, like her daughter, heard Willoughby's SS III 11 349 2
her own opinion of Willoughby's deserts;--she wished, SS III 11 349 2
of the story--that all Willoughby's difficulties have SS III 11 352 16
17

WILLOUGHBYS (3)
The Willoughbys left town as soon as they were married; SS II 10 217 18
who knew that the Willoughbys were again in town, and had SS III 2 271 4
She saw nothing of the Willoughbys, nothing of Edward, and SS III 2 271 5

WILSON (3)
"I find from Wilson that we are going to lose Mr De Courcy. LS 23 284 6
I had scarcely concluded my last, when Wilson brought me LS 25 292 1
I sent Wilson to say that I desired to speak with him LS 25 292 2

WILTSHIRE (3)
the village in Wiltshire where the Morlands lived, was NA I 1 17 12
breathe his parting sigh before he set off for Wiltshire. NA I 15 120 24
cheese, the north Wiltshire, the butter, the cellery, the E I 10 88 34

WIMPOLE STREET (9)
for she will open one of the best houses in Wimpole Street. MP III 9 394 1
I dined twice in Wimpole Street, and might have been there MP III 13 423 2
it must relate to Wimpole Street and Mr. Crawford, and MP III 15 438 4
"And don't they live in Wimpole Street?" MP III 15 439 11
of Mr. R. of Wimpole Street; the beautiful Mrs. R. whose MP III 15 440 14
had removed from Wimpole Street two or three weeks before, MP III 16 450 8
Very soon after the Rushworths' return to Wimpole Street, MP III 16 450 8
counteracted in Wimpole Street by the influence of Mr. MP III 16 450 9
event in Wimpole Street, to which he felt himself MP III 17 462 4

WIMPOLE-STREET (1)
she returns to Wimpole-Street to-day, the old lady is come. MP III 14 435 14

WIN (5)
I mean to win my sister in law's heart through her LS 5 250 2
compliment, could win Catherine from thinking, that some NA II 8 187 16
able to win a more favourable opinion of poor osborne.--" W 340 19
She could not win him, however, to any conversation; he PP I 11 55 4
she could, and win or lose a few sixpences by his fireside. E I 3 22 5

WIND (39)
a sudden gust of wind, and of being left in total darkness. NA I 11 88 54
You are splashed getting in and getting out; and the wind NA I 13 104 32
the frightful gusts of wind which accompany it, you will NA II 5 159 19
The night was stormy; the wind had been rising at NA II 6 166 9
It could be nothing but the violence of the wind NA II 6 167 10
The wind roared down the chimney, the rain beat in NA II 6 168 10
A violent gust of wind, rising with sudden fury, added NA II 6 170 12
She had not been used to feel alarm from wind, but now NA II 6 170 12
the wind, which struck at intervals on her startled ear. NA II 6 170 12
to acknowledge that the wind had kept her awake a little. NA II 7 174 5
emotion; and though the wind was high, and often produced NA II 13 227 26
of an high south-westerly wind, they pitied the fears SS I 9 41 4
their way against the wind, resisting it with laughing SS I 9 41 6
to see them driven in showers about me by the wind! SS I 16 87 31
the direction of the wind, watching the variations of the SS II 5 168 8
"Well, my dear, 'tis a true saying about an ill wind, for SS II 8 196 22
The wind roared round the house, and the rain beat against SS III 7 316 28
rude to keep Charlotte out of doors in all this wind. PP II 5 158 16
No banners, cousin, to be 'blown by the night wind of MP I 9 86 6
have had a good sharp east wind blowing on you the whole MP II 4 212 31
weather--but only by a steady contrary wind, or a calm. MP II 5 225 57
you cannot sail with this wind, if you are to cruize to MP III 7 380 20
The thrush had had her orders, the wind had changed, and MP III 8 388 2
its mild air, brisk soft wind, and bright sun, MP III 11 409 6
wind; concluding with these words to Mr. Woodhouse: E I 15 125 7
and shrubs, which the wind was despoiling, and the length E III 12 421 18
afternoon it cleared; the wind changed into a softer E III 13 424 1
by weather, I think every body feels a north-east wind.-- E III 14 436 7
youth restored by the fine wind which had been blowing on P III 12 104 6
There was too much wind to make the high part of the new P III 12 109 32
but it is only when the wind is due north and blows hard, P IV 1 128 30
The wind blows through one of the cupboards just in the P IV 6 170 29
at all aware of the wind being anything more than common." S 4 381 1
real danger, because the wind meeting with nothing to S 4 381 1
The wind I fancy must be Southerly." S 7 398 1
"Happy, happy wind, to engage Miss Heywood's thoughts!--" S 7 398 1
2 hours with a very fine wind blowing directly on shore; S 9 406 1
but there is so much wind that I did not think he cd S 9 407 1
no wind--but unluckily a damp air does not like <u>me</u>.-- S 10 415 1

WIND'S (1)
shutter, felt the strongest conviction of the wind's force. NA II 6 167 10

WIND-UP (1)
That was the wind-up of the history; that was the glory of E II 4 183 9

WINDING (10)
their way along narrow, winding vaults, by a low, grated NA I 11 88 54
It was a narrow winding path through a thick grove of old NA II 7 179 29
and symptoms of a winding stair-case, believed herself at NA II 8 185 5
After winding along it for more than a mile, they reached SS I 6 28 1
cottage, along the narrow winding valley of Allenham, SS I 9 40 2
a road of Smith gravel winding round a plantation, led to SS III 6 302 7
stealing away through the winding shrubberies, now just SS III 6 302 8
on its banks, and the winding of the valley, as far as she PP III 1 246 5
and that we have been winding in and out ever since we MP I 9 95 64
A branch only, of the valley, winding more obliquely S 4 383 1

WINDINGS (2)
Elizabeth longed to explore its windings; but when they PP III 1 254 57
and a few more windings brought them before her. MP I 10 103 49

WINDOW (100)
Poor creature! the prospect from her window is not very LS 17 271 7
from the drawing-room window; admired the graceful spirit NA I 4 34 7
can imagine, in a shop window in Milsom-Street just now-- NA I 6 39 4
drew her in haste to the window, and scarcely had she time NA I 9 61 1
said Catherine, as she stood watching at a window. NA I 11 82 8
window to watch over and encourage the happy appearance. NA I 11 83 16
again, and then, not at a window, but issuing from the NA I 12 91 3
knocked off his horse by a brickbat from an upper window. NA I 14 113 39
Without appearing to hear her, he walked to the window, NA I 15 122 29
The window curtains seemed in motion. NA II 6 167 10
saw nothing on either low window seat to scare her, and on NA II 6 167 10
Catherine walked to a window in the hope of catching NA II 7 175 13
room to the corresponding window in the gallery, to see if NA II 8 188 19
were immediately at the window; and to have it stop at the NA II 14 233 8
"You may see the house from this window, sir," was NA II 15 243 9
the roof was tiled, the window shutters were not painted SS I 6 28 2
The high downs which invited them from almost every window SS I 9 40 3
window, and she saw a large party walking up to the door. SS I 19 105 13
She was sitting near the window, and as soon as Sir John SS I 19 105 13
between the door and the window, as to make it hardly SS I 19 105 13
She came hallooing to the window, "how do you do , my dear? SS I 19 106 20
throwing it out of window--"he is full of monkey tricks." SS I 21 121 7
and disappointed voice, as she turned away to the window. SS II 4 165 28
window, in hopes of distinguishing the long-expected rap. SS II 4 166 31
and walking to the window as she spoke, to examine the day. SS II 5 167 2
walked from one window to the other, or sat down by the SS II 5 172 39
Marianne, who had seen him from the window, and who hated SS II 5 172 40
the door, she went to the window to see who could be SS II 7 184 16
from the fire to the window, from the window to the fire, SS II 7 190 55
56

to the window, from the window to the fire, without SS II 7 190 55
56

Marianne moved to the window----- "it is Colonel Brandon!" SS II 9 203 13
14

on Elinor's moving to the window to take more SS III 3 280 9
while they stood at the window, the gratitude expressed by SS III 3 284 24
from their notice, sat earnestly gazing through the window. SS III 10 342 7
figure of a man on horseback drew her eyes to the window. SS III 12 358 8
He rose from his seat and walked to the window, apparently SS III 12 360 22
23

pardon", & look in the window seat behind her for the W 336 13
After this discovery she had walked twice to the window to W 338 17
She stepd again to the window--but instead of the W 338 17
window, that he wore a blue coat and rode a black horse. PP I 3 9 3

or a really new muslin in a shop window, could recal them. PP I 15 72 7
up the parlour window, and loudly seconding the invitation. PP I 15 73 10
with walking to the window and pretending not to hear. PP I 20 114 31
Miss Lucas perceived him from an upper window as he walked PP I 22 121 1
was at a drawing-room window watching their arrival; when PP II 4 152 5
out of window in his own book room, which fronted the road. PP II 7 168 1
Elizabeth, after slightly surveying it, went to a window PP III 1 246 5
but from every window there were beauties to be seen. PP III 1 246 5
a carriage drew them to a window, and they saw a gentleman PP III 2 260 1
She retreated from the window, fearful of being seen; and PP III 2 260 2
hand just rest upon the window frame, so that he might see PP III 9 316 8
window, enter the paddock, and ride towards the house. PP III 11 333 30
her mother, went to the window--she looked,--she saw Mr. PP III 11 333 31
was suddenly drawn to the window, by the sound of a PP III 14 351 1
Bennet, as she stood at a window the next morning, "if PP III 17 374 20
and both placed near a window, cut down to the ground, and MP I 7 65 13
than to contribute to the window tax, and find employment MP I 9 85 5
was standing at an open window with Edmund and Fanny MP I 11 108 4
Fanny turned farther into the window; and Miss Crawford MP I 11 112 33
him continue at the window with her, in spite of the MP I 11 112 35
turning his back on the window; and as it advanced, she MP I 11 113 42
Fanny sighed alone at the window till scolded away by Mrs. MP I 11 113 43
three lower panes of one window, where Tintern Abbey held MP I 16 152 2
She played till Fanny's eyes, straying to the window on MP II 4 207 6
from the staircase window, and then they were walking." MP II 4 211 28
Susan was stationed at a window, in eager observation of MP III 15 446 34
of the window seats--but he reads all them to himself. E I 4 29 10
marks and memorandums on the wainscot by the window. E II 5 187 4
we passed her house--I saw Miss Bates at the window. E II 5 194 38
Shortly afterwards Miss Bates, passing near the window, E II 10 243 30
I will not open the window here; it would give you all E II 10 243 31
and the window was open, and Mr. Knightley spoke loud. E II 10 245 54
He hesitated, got up, walked to a window. E II 12 260 28
Instead of drawing his brother off to a window while they E II 16 292 10
in his carriage, with one window down, to partake of this E III 6 357 33
a little distance from the window, evidently on the watch. E III 10 400 65
through the blind, of two figures passing near the window. E III 18 476 44
and spoke through the window, but without getting off his P III 5 38 29
Charles shewed himself at the window, all was ready, their P III 7 59 25
Dr. Shirley: she was at window, looking out for Captain P III 9 78 19
before he walked to the window to recollect himself, and P III 9 78 22
He continued at the window; and after calmly and politely P III 9 79 24
Captain Wentworth, however, came from his window, P III 9 79 27
newspaper; and Captain Wentworth returned to his window. P III 9 79 27
at the window by the sisters from the mansion-house. P III 10 83 3
since entering Lyme) drew half the party to the window. P III 12 105 8
He was standing by himself, at a printshop window, with P IV 6 169 25
Anne, as she sat near the window, descried, most decidedly P IV 7 175 4
was in her station at a window overlooking the entrance to P IV 10 220 31
"Anne," cried Mary, still at her window, "there is Mrs. P IV 10 222 34
her own embarrassment, Anne did move quietly to the window. P IV 10 222 39
his seat, and moved to a window; and Anne seeming to watch P IV 11 231 12
The window at which he stood, was at the other end of the P IV 11 231 12
back window with something like the fondness of regret.-- S 4 380 1
More bills at the window than he had calculated on;--and a S 4 384 1
at her ample Venetian window, & looking over the S 4 384 1
only was there no open window, but the sopha & the table, S 10 413 1
out the fire, opening the window, & disposing of the drops S 10 413 1
distinguish from their window that there was an arrival at S 10 414 1
of standing at an open window when there is no wind--but S 10 415 1
WINDOW-CURTAIN (1)
step behind a window-curtain, and throw up a sash, without E II 11 252 31
WINDOW-CURTAINS (2)
looking after some window-curtains, which Lady Alicia and P IV 7 179 30
They described the drawing-room window-curtains of one of P IV 7 179 30
WINDOW-SEATS (1)
against one of the window-seats for the sake of all the SS II 7 180 1
WINDOW-SHUTTER (1)
and opened a window-shutter, to be satisfied of the truth. SS III 7 316 29
WINDOW-SHUTTERS (1)
The housemaid's folding back her window-shutters at eight NA II 7 172 1
WINDOWS (43)
of small rain upon the windows caught Catherine's watchful NA I 11 82 2
at the drawing-room windows, in expectation of seeing her NA I 12 91 3
the floor of a room without windows, doors, or furnitures. NA II 5 158 15
playing in beautiful splendour on its high Gothic windows. NA II 5 161 24
The windows, to which she looked with peculiar dependence, NA II 5 162 26
on the other side by windows which Catherine had only time NA II 5 162 28
floor was carpeted; the windows were neither less perfect, NA II 6 163 1
in torrents against the windows, and every thing seemed to NA II 6 168 10
glimmer through the lower windows, as he passed to the NA II 8 188 19
of a western sun gaily poured through two sash windows! NA II 9 193 6
It was a prettily-shaped room, the windows reaching to the NA II 11 213 21
hills, and formed a pleasant view from the cottage windows. SS I 6 29 3
It is a corner room, and has windows on two sides. SS I 13 69 76
windows; but Elinor, all happiness within, regarded it not. SS III 7 316 28
its neighbours with two windows on each side the door, the W 322 2
each side the door, the windows guarded by posts and chain, W 322 2
which led under the windows of the house to the front door, W 355 28
no one passed the windows now except a few of the officers, PP I 15 74 11
by his enumeration of the windows in front of the house, PP II 6 161 8
all sent to one of the windows, to admire the view, Mr. PP II 6 162 13
said Elizabeth, as she walked towards one of the windows. PP III 1 250 44
Its windows opening to the ground, admitted a most PP III 3 267 2
for the evening, in summer; the windows are full west." PP III 14 352 11
was looking grave and shaking his head at the windows. MP I 9 85 4
The table between the windows was covered with work-boxes MP I 16 153 3
descried from one of the windows endeavouring to find MP II 4 205 3
with as many roofs as windows--it is not cramped into the MP II 7 243 27
intently on one of the windows, was listening to her uncle, MP III 1 314 16
The lovers were standing together at one of the windows. E I 10 90 39
the two superior sashed windows which were open to look in E II 6 197 5
We shall have no occasion to open the windows at all--not E II 11 251 29
habit of opening the windows, letting in cold air upon E II 11 251 29
'Open the windows!--but surely, Mr. Churchill, nobody E II 11 251 30
nobody would think of opening the windows at Randalls. E II 11 251 30
Dancing with open windows!-- E II 11 252 30
Harriet was standing at one of the windows. E III 11 407 29
sashed windows below, and casements above, in Highbury. E III 14 437 8
with its viranda, French windows, and other prettinesses, P III 5 36 20
windows and doors against the winter storms to be expected. P III 11 98 17
to be discerned from the windows, was enough to make the P IV 1 123 8
Look my dear Mary--look at William Heeley's windows.-- S 4 383 1
At last, from the low French windows of the drawing room S 7 395 1
appearance at the low windows upstairs, in order to close S 11 422 1
WINDS (2)
had the government of the winds just for a week or two MP II 5 225 57
her to go out in sharp winds, and grow coarse, I would P IV 3 142 16
WINDSOR (5)
of a very old friend in Windsor, to whom Mr. Churchill had E III 9 388 15
He is half way to Windsor by this time." E III 10 394 20
We removed to Windsor; and two days afterwards I received E III 14 442 8
not a word of a certain young physician from Windsor.-- E III 16 454 17
I hope you have pleasant accounts from Windsor?" E III 16 459 50
WINDSOR-JULY (1)
To Mrs. Weston. Windsor-July. My dear Madam, "if I E III 14 436 8
WINDY (2)
kite for him that very windy day last Easter--and ever E I 11 95 19
be what it ought, neither damp, nor cold, nor windy." E II 7 209 10
WINE (26)
while she drank her warm wine and water, and prepared NA I 3 29 52
There is not the hundredth part of the wine consumed in NA I 9 64 22
"And yet I have heard that there is a great deal of wine NA I 9 64 23
all drink a great deal more wine than I thought you did. NA I 9 64 25
being a great deal of wine drank in Oxford, and the same NA I 9 64 26
A glass of wine, which Elinor procured for her directly, SS II 7 185 16 17
if she is not gone away without finishing her wine! SS II 8 194 8
the finest old Constantia wine in the house, that ever was SS II 8 197 27
if you will give me leave, I will drink the wine myself." SS II 8 198 28
When the dessert and the wine were arranged, and Mrs. SS III 11 355 46
as he helped her to wine, when they were drawn round the W 324 4
a pack of foxhounds, and drink a bottle of wine every day." PP I 5 20 21
breathing port wine, who followed them into the room. PP I 16 76 3
glass of wine;--shall I get you one?--you are very ill." PP III 4 276 9
a most spiritless manner, wine drank without any smiles, MP I 6 52 1
was glad to put an end to his speech by a proposal of wine. MP I 6 55 17
were not there to mix the wine and water for her, would MP I 7 65 14
She was quite shocked when I asked her whether wine was MP I 10 105 55
Mrs. Goddard, what say you to half a glass of wine? E I 3 25 14
Neither wine nor conversation was any thing to him; and E I 14 122 18
much of Mr. Weston's good wine, and felt sure that he E I 15 129 23
But Mr. Elton had only drunk wine enough to elevate his E I 15 130 28
cake and full glasses of wine, for whatever unwilling self- E II 8 213 6
and baked apples and wine before she came away: amazing E III 2 329 45
"If I were bilious, he continued, you know wine wd S 10 415 1
The more wine I drink (in moderation) the better I am.-- S 10 415 1
WINE-GLASS (1)
with a wine-glass, full of something, in her hand. SS II 8 197 26
WING (1)
"with only just a side wing or two run up, doors in flat, MP I 13 123 8
WINGS (2)
He came on the wings of disappointment, and with his head MP I 13 121 1
heaven had given them wings, by many hours sooner still! P I 6 235 31
WINK (5)
her; I could not sleep a wink all night for thinking of it. NA I 15 118 13
On finding him determined to go, Margt began to wink & nod W 359 28
I did not wink at you." PP III 13 345 12
I am sure I sha'nt get a wink of sleep all night. PP III 13 348 40
She had not a wink of sleep either the night before we set S 9 407 1
WINKING (2)
Bennet sat looking and winking at Elizabeth and Catherine PP III 13 345 11
What do you keep winking at me for? PP III 13 345 11
WINKS (1)
and so many nods and winks, as to excite general attention. SS I 21 125 36
WINNER (1)
infallibly foretold the winner; of shooting parties, in NA I 9 66 31
WINNING (1)
extremely judicious, they were not winning back her heart. E III 7 368 3
WINNINGLY (1)
is absolutely sweet, & her voice & manner winningly mild. LS 6 251 1
WINS (1)
and kind-hearted about her, that it wins upon one directly. E II 14 278 44
WINTER (76)
me fixed at this place for the rest of the winter. LS 2 244 1
of him to keep up our spirits these long winter evenings. LS 13 262 1
being in town this winter, as soon as I found that her LS 27 297 4
It has been a sad heavy winter hitherto, without Reginald, LS 40 309 1
Skinners were here this winter instead of last; or if the NA I 2 23 25
I told Capt. Hunt at one of our assemblies this winter, NA I 6 40 14
for his health last winter, and came away quite stout." NA I 8 54 7
who come regularly every winter, lengthen their six weeks NA I 10 78 45
so dirty the whole winter; it is ancle-deep every where." NA I 11 85 41
plants in winter, and there was a fire in it now and then." NA II 7 178 25
out of doors, and in winter his private balls were SS I 7 32 2
you and your sisters in town this winter, Miss Dashwood?" SS I 13 66 46
he replied; "but these bottoms must be dirty in winter." SS I 16 88 34
me persuade the Miss Dashwoods to go to town this winter." SS I 20 110 9
"Shall you be in town this winter, Miss Dashwood?" said SS II 2 150 36
she had resided every winter in a house in one of the SS II 3 153 1
always used till this winter to have Charlotte with me. SS II 3 154 4
The first winter assembly in the Town of D. in Surry was W 314 1
house, on every monthly return throughout the winter.-- W 314 1
No Emma, whoever stays at home this winter, it shan't be W 320 2
which went thro' the winter, & a new cap from the W 323 3
remain the whole winter, and Meryton was the head quarters. PP I 7 28 3
of the party will return into Hertfordshire this winter. PP I 21 117 10
Many of my acquaintance are already there for the winter; PP I 21 117 11
added Jane, "that he comes back no more this winter." PP I 21 117 12
"But if he returns no more this winter, my choice will PP I 21 120 27
to Netherfield the whole winter; a report which highly PP I 23 129 12
settled in London for the winter, and concluded with her PP II 1 133 1
at Longbourn in the winter, and his compliments to Mr. and PP II 15 217 8
The families who had been in town for the winter came back PP II 19 238 6
saw any one so much altered as she is since the winter. PP III 3 270 13
We shall be at Newcastle all the winter, and I dare say PP III 9 317 13
I shall get husbands for them before the winter is over." PP III 9 317 15
you went to town last winter, you promised to take a PP III 11 338 58
Kitty begged very hard for a few balls there every winter. PP III 13 349 42
in town three months last winter, that I had known it, and PP III 16 371 45
the course of the ensuing winter, and had charged her to MP I 3 33 64
The winter came and passed without their being called for; MP I 4 34 3
Upon the whole, it was a comfortable winter to her; for MP I 4 35 6
The return of winter engagements, however, was not without MP I 4 38 9
not to be driven from it entirely, even when winter came. MP I 16 151 2
it was in the middle of winter, and the roads almost MP II 2 189 3
I cured him at last; but he was very bad all the winter-- MP II 2 189 5
for her not finding Mansfield dull as winter comes on." MP II 3 199 15
and Brighton is almost as gay in winter as in summer. MP II 3 203 31
I might not have such another opportunity all the winter. MP II 5 222 43
himself the following winter, that he might have a home of MP II 7 246 37
Consider the house as half your own every winter, and we MP II 7 247 41
This will be the last winter of his belonging to us, as he MP II 11 284 9
Ross was dying for Henry the first winter she came out. MP III 5 362 16
her quitting it; and the change was from winter to summer. MP III 15 446 35
and in winter dressed their chilblains with her own hands. E I 3 22 5
beg your excuse and take my three turns--my winter walk." E I 8 57 5
"This will prove a spirited beginning of your winter E I 15 126 7 8
the poor must suffer in winter, and receiving no other E II 1 155 1
Part of every winter she had been used to spend in Bath; E II 4 183 9
not been well the whole winter, and thinks Enscombe too E II 18 305 7
that ought to be treated rather as winter than summer. E III 5 347 19
summer there is dust, and in winter there is dirt." E III 6 356 26
What!--engaged to her all the winter--before either of E III 10 395 37
Here have we been, the whole winter and spring, completely E III 10 399 61
of the approaching winter, had proved erroneous; no E III 12 422 19
and every future winter of her life to the past, it would E III 12 423 21
some part of every winter there; and to the very great P III 2 14 10
winter which she had afterwards spent there with herself. P III 2 14 11
shall be in Bath in the winter; but remember, papa, if we P III 6 42 1
ideas of danger, was the winter that I passed by myself at P III 8 71 54
family at Lyme for the winter; of their being, therefore, P III 11 94 6
retirement of Lyme in the winter, appeared exactly adapted P III 11 97 12
windows and doors against the winter storms to be expected. P III 11 98 17
and blows hard, which may not happen three times a winter. P IV 1 128 30
No, these were noises which belonged to the winter P IV 2 135 33
first set in Bath this winter, and as rank is rank, your P IV 4 150 17
of the gout and a winter at Bath;--but the maintenance, S 2 373 1
one of the girls of the family to pass the winter with her. S 3 378 1
The Hilliers did not seem to feel the storms last winter S 4 381 1
WINTERS' (1)
Thirteen winters' revolving frosts had seen her opening P III 1 7 12
WINTHROP (11)

The estate at Winthrop is not less than two hundred and P III 9 76 15
a fellow; and whenever Winthrop comes into his hands, he P III 9 76 15
another path, "is not this one of the ways to Winthrop?" P III 10 85 12
Winthrop, however, or its environs--for young men are, P III 10 85 13
parted Uppercross and Winthrop, and soon commanded a full P III 10 85 13
Winthrop, without beauty and without dignity, was P III 10 85 14
Mary exclaimed, "bless me! here is Winthrop--I declare I P III 10 85 15
a quarter of an hour at Winthrop, as she felt so tired, P III 10 86 17
made up hers to call at Winthrop to-day--and yet she was P III 10 87 23
does not do him justice, nor think enough about Winthrop. P IV 10 218 22
of mine, which you shot with one day, round Winthrop." P IV 11 240 58
WIPE (1)
or two would suffise to wipe away every outward memento of MP II 2 190 9
WIPED (2)
the cups and saucers wiped in streaks, the milk a mixture MP III 15 439 9
loss of a daughter, and a disgrace never to be wiped off. MP III 16 449 6
WIPING (2)
"Sometimes," continues Lucy, after wiping her eyes, "I SS I 22 133 44
recovered herself: and wiping away her tears, was able to MP III 7 384 35
WISDOM (7)
her with too much wisdom at once, Henry suffered the NA I 14 111 29
not the adventure of the chest have taught her wisdom? NA II 7 173 2
Her wisdom too limited the number of their servants to SS I 5 26 5
He was recalled from wit to wisdom, not by any reproof of SS III 5 298 34
how am I even to know that it would be wisdom to resist? PP II 3 145 7
been governed by motives of selfishness and worldly wisdom. MP III 17 461 4
On one other question, which perhaps her utmost wisdom P III 7 60 31
32
WISE (27)
here, & canvassed by the wise heads of Mr & Mrs Vernon; & LS 19 275 4
her wise lips in their parting conference in her closet. NA I 2 18 2
You are more nice than wise. NA I 14 108 17
forming wise resolutions with the most violent dispatch. NA II 6 165 5
in her life, they were wise enough to be contented with SS I 6 29 5
Middleton had taken the wise precaution of bringing with SS I 6 31 9
With such a reward for her tears, the child was too wise SS I 21 121 10
Mr & Mrs Edwards were so wise as never to pass that point; W 325 4
I hope I never ridicule what is wise or good. PP I 11 57 21
"very true, it will be wise in me to refrain from that. PP II 3 145 7
was ready to allow it a wise and desirable measure for PP II 5 150 26
I must rejoice that he is wise enough to assume even the PP II 18 234 37
38
people are not always wise; and in seeing him at last look PP III 3 271 16
only unlike other people in being more wise and discreet? MP II 3 197 6
in his own house, too wise to stir out; and to hear him E I 16 138 18
19
I would much rather have been merry than wise." E II 12 260 18
behalf, though it might be wise to let the fancy touch it E II 13 267 8
right to look as little wise, and to be as much affectedly, E II 14 271 5
If not wise or refined herself, she would have connected E II 14 272 17
You are wise--but I cannot be wise. E III 13 429 27
case, for lady, read ---- mum! a word to the wise.-- E III 16 454 13
Sir Walter was not very wise; but still he had experience P III 3 24 36
It would be most right, and most wise, and, therefore, P III 5 33 6
an opinion, though too wise to acknowledge as much at home, P III 10 82 1
Anne could only feel that Charles Hayter was wise. P III 10 83 2
She hoped to be wise and reasonable in time; but alas! P IV 7 178 25
she must confess to herself that she was not wise yet. P IV 7 178 25
WISELY (9)
wisely & command herself as she ought, she may now be easy. LS 24 290 13
Thus wisely fortifying her mind, as she proceeded up NA II 6 167 9
He wisely resolved to be particularly careful that no sign PP I 12 60 4
that he acted very wisely in leaving the girls to their PP I 14 69 17
faint blush; but in general Charlotte wisely did not hear. PP II 5 156 4
No sooner did he appear, than Elizabeth wisely resolved to PP III 3 268 8
"You chose very wisely, I am sure," replied Miss Crawford, MP I 15 144 30
countenance as ever, was wisely and kindly keeping his MP III 10 399 5
I think they judge wisely. E II 1 161 26
WISER (11)
at last, judging it wiser to affect the air of a cool, SS III 8 326 53
how can I promise to be wiser than so many of my fellow PP II 3 145 7
made Mr. Yates think it wiser to let him pursue his own MP II 2 191 10
that she would be the wiser and happier woman, all her MP III 6 369 10
might have been kinder and wiser to have resisted the E II 2 165 9
Cole does not want to be wiser or wittier than his E II 15 288 38
who wants to be wiser and wittier than all the world! E II 15 288 39
She believed it would be wiser for her to say and know at E III 4 341 34
Will it not be wiser to accept the society of these good P IV 4 150 17
not be always so much wiser than the other half, or always P IV 7 175 6
them, probably, much the wiser for what they heard, and P IV 7 176 8
WISEST (15)
"I believe it will be wisest to take the morning while it NA II 7 177 17
Elinor thought it wisest to touch that point no more. SS I 12 59 5
believe it would be the wisest way to put an end to the SS II 2 149 29
30
Elinor thought it wisest to make no answer to this, lest SS II 2 150 35
by it, she judged it wisest, from the experience of the SS III 14 373 3
The wisest and the best of men, nay, the wisest and best PP I 11 57 20
sensible that it would be wisest to get it over as soon PP I 19 104 7
I think to be wisest; and now, I hope you are satisfied." PP II 3 145 9
her marrying Mr. Collins as the wisest thing she ever did. PP II 9 178 15
the happiest, wisest, most reasonable end!" PP III 13 347 29
body, and what would be wisest for herself, which her own MP III 9 396 6
turned off, that it was wisest for everybody not to delay MP III 10 401 10
"His father's marriage," he said, "had been the wisest E II 5 192 28
Perhaps it will be wisest in you to check your feelings E III 4 342 39
themselves, judged it wisest to take their exercise early, E III 5 344 3
WISH (598)
I wish I could be as well satisfied as he is, that it was LS 6 252 2
might for a time make her wish for retirement. LS 6 252 2
can only suppose that the wish of establishing her LS 6 252 2
education, which I really wish to be attended to, while LS 7 252 1
I wish her to find her situation as unpleasant as possible. LS 7 253 1
towards her, as by the wish of hunting with Mr Vernon, & LS 8 255 1
I wish you could get Reginald home again, under any LS 11 259 1
only from vanity, or a wish of gaining the admiration of a LS 12 261 4
I do not wish to work on your fears, but on your sense & LS 12 261 4
you will like to see it; I wish it was more satisfactory, LS 13 262 1
to his deserts, & her wish of obtaining my sister's good LS 14 265 5
behaviour at Langford, I wish it may be true, but his LS 15 266 1
I wish it had been possible for me to fetch her instead of LS 17 271 6
I only wish that they--whoever they are--to whom I am LS 20 278 7
discover the real truth, but she seems to wish to avoid me. LS 20 278 11
of that; but I would wish to forget every circumstance LS 24 288 11
Where my own resolution was taken, I could not wish for LS 24 289 12
those of your family, the wish of increasing them, if not LS 30 300 2
Much as I wish him away however, I cannot help being LS 31 302 1
everything that you could wish to be concealed, was known LS 32 302 1
Yet, I wish she had staid quietly at Langford. LS 33 303 1
I wish matters did not go so perversely. LS 38 307 3
& it is our particular wish & entreaty that you would come LS 40 309 1
I wish we could bring dear Frederica too, but I am sorry LS 41 310 3
I wish I could think so too! LS 41 310 3
I wish there were a better prospect than now appears, of LS 41 310 5
the rooms at night; and I wish you would try to keep some NA I 2 18 2
every now and then, "I wish you could dance, my dear,--I NA I 2 21 9
you could dance, my dear,--I wish you could get a partner." NA I 2 21 9
I wish we had a large acquaintance here." NA I 2 22 15
"I wish we had any;--it would be somebody to go to." NA I 2 22 16
The Skinners were here last year--I wish they were here NA I 2 22 17
"I don't upon my word--I wish I did. NA I 2 23 21
I wish I had a large acquaintance here with all my heart, NA I 2 23 21
"I wish she had been able to dance," said his wife, "I NA I 2 23 25
his wife, "I wish we could have got a partner for her.-- NA I 2 23 25
The wish of a numerous acquaintance in Bath was still NA I 3 25 1
That, madam, is what I wish you to say." NA I 3 27 26
young ladies' ways as you wish to believe me; it is this NA I 3 27 28
the Miss Thorpes of their wish of being better acquainted NA I 4 33 6
Her daily expressions were no longer, "I wish we had some NA I 5 36 3
seems almost a general wish of decrying the capacity and NA I 5 37 4
I wish you knew Miss Andrews, you would be delighted with NA I 6 40 12
of young woman I could wish to see you attached to; she NA I 7 50 47
"Ah! he has got a partner, I wish he had asked you," said NA I 8 58 32
The first wish of her heart was to improve her NA I 9 60 1
state are not so strict as your partner might wish? NA I 10 77 37
submitted to the wish of Mr. Allen, which took them rather NA I 10 81 61
"But indeed I did not wish you a pleasant walk; I never NA I 12 94 8
"I wish I were too. NA I 14 108 22
Where people wish to attach, they should always be NA I 14 110 28
others, which a sensible person would always wish to avoid. NA I 14 110 28
could not help answering, "I wish you could have gone too. NA I 14 115 53
I only wish I were more worthy of him.-- NA I 15 117 6
As for myself, I am sure I only wish our situations were NA I 15 119 18
Well, I wish you a good journey. NA I 15 123 35
was comprehended in a wish for the young people's NA I 15 124 48
and fancied she might wish for a partner; but he is quite NA II 1 132 17
attributing my brother's wish of dancing with Miss Thorpe NA II 1 133 28
"I only wish I could do as much. NA II 1 135 44
"It is not on my own account I wish for more; but I cannot NA II 1 135 45
fifty pounds a year, I should not have a wish unsatisfied. NA II 1 136 48
daughter time to speak, "has been forming a very bold wish. NA II 2 139 7
for many weeks a darling wish, though to be more than the NA II 2 141 11
know!--and, as I ever wish to be believed, I solemnly NA II 3 144 11
"I wish your heart were independent. NA II 3 147 23
and said, "I am sure my brother would not wish to do that." NA II 4 150 4
of her friends in Bath without one wish of being with them. NA II 6 166 8
with a very hearty wish that no untoward accident might NA II 7 173 3
could all wish him disengaged from every tie of business. NA II 7 176 15
and then expressing his wish to examine the effect of some NA II 7 179 27
Eleanor, to express her wish of being permitted to see it, NA II 8 186 7
courage was not equal to a wish of exploring them after NA II 9 190 1
the first time in their acquaintance, wish to leave him. NA II 9 195 19
I wish your visit at Northanger may be over before Captain NA II 10 202 7
expressed a wish of being of use or comfort to her. NA II 10 203 8
"I do not think I shall ever wish for a letter again!" NA II 10 204 11
"I wish I could reason like you, for his sake and my own. NA II 11 211 14
for James or for me, and I wish I had never known her." NA II 12 218 4
becoming soon her only wish, she readily agreed to her NA II 14 235 13
consideration in his wish of waiting on their worthy NA II 15 243 9
"I would not wish to do any thing mean," he replied. SS I 2 9 12
with them, to wish was to hope, and to hope was to expect. SS I 4 21 11
in his way, if he were to wish to marry a woman who had SS I 4 21 15
I could wish the stairs were handsome. SS I 6 29 4
spirit overcame the wish of society for her children; and SS I 9 40 2
and made them wish to be better acquainted with it. SS I 9 40 2
which an evident wish of improving it could offer. SS I 10 48 7
wish him successful, she heartily wished him indifferent. SS I 10 50 12
"I wish it would be so easily settled. SS I 13 64 26
"Well, as you are resolved to go, I wish you a good SS I 13 65 43
you farewell for a longer time than I should wish to do." SS I 13 66 48
Well, I wish him out of all his trouble with all my heart, SS I 14 70 2
"How often did I wish," added he, "when I was at Allenham SS I 14 73 17
it is my wish to be candid in my judgment of every body. SS I 15 79 29
I have no wish to be distinguished; and I have every SS I 17 90 5
I wish as well as every body else to be perfectly happy; SS I 17 91 7
"I wish," said Margaret, striking out a novel thought, " SS I 17 92 18
"We are all unanimous in that wish, I suppose," said SS I 17 92 20
I never wish to offend, but I am so foolishly shy, that I SS I 17 94 42
"I wish with all my soul," cried Sir John, "that SS I 18 100 21
It was rather a wish of distinction she believed, which SS I 20 112 28
she left the house without any wish of knowing them better. SS I 21 124 32
there may be reasons--I wish I might venture; but however SS I 22 128 7
too hasty decision, or her wish of detecting falsehood SS I 22 132 26
wish of renewing it; and this for more reasons than one. SS II 1 141 7
a little pleasure, because Miss Dashwood does not wish it. SS II 3 154 3
the plan," she cried, "it is exactly what I could wish. SS II 3 155 8
might wish to conduct the affair, they must be engaged. SS II 4 160 5
emotion, "to your sister I wish all imaginable happiness; SS II 5 174 46
only beyond the reach of Marianne, it was beyond her wish. SS II 6 176 6
object for a moment to her wish of going away, and making SS II 6 178 16
"I only wish," replied her sister, "there were any thing I SS II 7 185 18
I wish you may receive this in time to come here to-night, SS II 7 187 38
of dreadful indecision; I wish to acquit you, but SS II 7 188 42
it,) I was once as dear to him as my own soul could wish. SS II 7 188 46
I wish with all my soul his wife may plague his heart out. SS II 8 192 3
in short, that one could wish for: and, moreover, it is SS II 8 197 22
My object--my wish--my sole wish in desiring it--I hope, I SS II 9 204 18
regrets, which she could wish her not to indulge! SS II 10 213 2
he added, "Elinor, I wish, with all my heart, it were SS II 11 223 22
Brandon has not the smallest wish of marrying me." SS II 11 223 23
I wish him very happy; and I am so sure of his always SS III 1 263 27
'I wish with all my heart,' says poor Fanny in her SS III 1 266 36
We all wish her extremely happy, and Mrs. Ferrars's SS III 1 268 45
I wish I could get him a living with all my heart.-- SS III 2 278 32
have seen enough of him to wish him well for his own sake, SS III 3 282 19
own sake, and as a friend of yours, I wish it still more. SS III 3 282 19
to appear to doubt; I only wish it were more valuable.-- SS III 3 282 19
his wish to put off so agreeable an office to another. SS III 3 283 20
to him then, as I sincerely wish I could be at present. SS III 3 284 23
in my life, and I wish you joy of it with all my heart." SS III 4 285 1
Well, my dear, I wish you joy of it again and again; and SS III 4 285 5
friend, and to join in his wish that the living--it is SS III 4 289 28
that he might hereafter wish the distance between the SS III 4 290 39
least chuse to visit, or wish to reside; for not only was SS III 6 301 2
was gratifying the first wish of his own heart by a SS III 7 309 5
I wish--I heartily wish it had never been. SS III 8 322 36
Had I sat down to wish for any possible good to my family, SS III 9 336 10
it all over in private, to wish success to her friend, and SS III 9 339 27
and cheerful society as the only happiness worth a wish. SS III 10 343 8
last with a sigh, "when I wish his secret reflections may SS III 10 345 24
But it was neither in Elinor's power, nor in her wish, to SS III 11 349 2
"I wish to assure you both," said she, "that I see every SS III 11 349 4
am now perfectly satisfied, I wish for no change. SS III 11 350 6
Marianne sighed, and repeated--"I wish for no change." SS III 11 350 8
So, I made free to wish her joy." SS III 11 354 29
Sincerely wish you happy in your choice, and it shall not SS III 13 365 14
They had in fact nothing to wish for, but the marriage of SS III 14 374 7
with his lot, no less free from every wish of an exchange. SS III 14 377 12
at Delaford; for her wish of bringing Marianne and Colonel SS III 14 378 13
mansion-house was equally the wish of Edward and Elinor. SS III 14 378 13
stay as late as you can wish for; if he does, he will W 315 1
I wish with all my heart she was well married. W 317 2
last she said--"I wish Elizabeth, you had not made a point W 319 2
my going to this ball, I wish you were going instead of me. W 319 2
mind, & a great wish of obliging--& when they returned to W 323 3
"I dare say he would sir--& I wish with all my heart he W 325 4
I do not wonder that you should not wish to go with her W 326 5
"I was not so ungrateful sir, said Emma warmly, as to wish W 326 5
I wish it could all come over again!--" W 336 14
the proposal--she did not wish to be on terms of intimacy W 339 18
entirely alone, it was her wish to return home to dinner.-- W 339 18
You had said so much against him that I could not wish W 341 19
"I wish Margt could have heard him profess his ignorance W 342 19
I wish everybody were as easily satisfied as you--but poor W 343 19

Context	Work	Vol	Ch	Page	Line
It was a new thing with him to wish to please a woman; it	W			346	21
I always wish to be treated quite "en famille" when I come	W			351	25
"I wish we may be able to have a game of cards tonight,"	W			354	28
dream over their cards--I wish you could see him overdraw	W			358	28
equally well married, I shall have nothing to wish for."	PP	I	3	9	2
I wish you had been there.	PP	I	3	12	16
I wish you had been there, my dear, to have given him one	PP	I	3	13	20
"I would wish not to be hasty in censuring any one; but I	PP	I	4	14	8
said Miss Lucas, "but I wish he had danced with Eliza."	PP	I	5	20	15
not worth speaking to, a wish of being better acquainted	PP	I	6	21	1
"Well," said Charlotte, "I wish Jane success with all my	PP	I	6	23	10
He began to wish to know more of her, and as a step	PP	I	6	24	13
such a favourite?--and pray when am I to wish you joy?"	PP	I	6	27	51
I do not wish to avoid the walk.	PP	I	7	32	37
not wish to see your sister make such an exhibition."	PP	I	8	36	7
girl, and I wish with all my heart she were well settled.	PP	I	8	36	14
"And I wish my collection were larger for your benefit and	PP	I	8	38	27
Charles, when you build your house, I wish it may be half	PP	I	8	38	33
"I wish it may."	PP	I	8	38	34
not alarming, she had no wish of her recovering	PP	I	9	41	2
"I wish I might take this for a compliment; but to be so	PP	I	9	42	12
"When I am in the country," he replied, "I never wish to	PP	I	9	43	22
But you would not wish to be dancing while she is ill."	PP	I	9	45	37
that Mr. Darcy did not wish for cards; and Mr. Hurst soon	PP	I	11	54	3
he thinks our due, the wish is certainly to his credit."	PP	I	13	63	15
sir, I am sure; and I wish with all my heart it may prove	PP	I	13	65	21
					22
always wish to give them as unstudied an air as possible."	PP	I	14	68	11
had nothing to do but to wish for an instrument, and	PP	I	16	75	3
"As much as I ever wish to be," cried Elizabeth warmly,-- "	PP	I	16	77	13
"I wish I could call her amiable.	PP	I	16	82	43
Do not wish me such an evil."	PP	I	18	90	7
may vary greatly with respect to me; and I could wish,	PP	I	18	94	41
I wish you very happy and very rich, and by refusing your	PP	I	19	107	16
to attribute it to your wish of increasing my love by	PP	I	19	108	19
there for the winter; I wish I could hear that you, my	PP	I	21	117	11
footing, her relations all wish the connection as much as	PP	I	21	118	14
return to Netherfield and answer every wish of her heart.	PP	I	21	120	29
that could make a woman wish for its continuance; and Miss	PP	I	22	122	2
who could by no means wish for so speedy a return,	PP	I	22	123	6
					7
to close with their kind wish of seeing him again at	PP	I	23	128	10
You wish to think all the world respectable, and are hurt	PP	II	1	135	11
They can only wish his happiness, and if he is attached to	PP	II	1	136	22
They may wish many things besides his happiness; they may	PP	II	1	136	23
his happiness; they may wish his increase of wealth and	PP	II	1	136	23
and consequence; they may wish him to marry a girl who has	PP	II	1	136	23
"Beyond a doubt, they do wish him to chuse Miss Darcy,"	PP	II	1	137	24
Elizabeth could not oppose such a wish; and from this time	PP	II	1	137	25
I wish I could see her.	PP	II	3	147	23
She would not even wish for any renewal of his attentions.	PP	II	3	149	27
did not quarrel with him for his wish of independence.	PP	II	3	149	28
measure for both, and could very sincerely wish him happy.	PP	II	5	150	26
detest his very name, and wish him all manner of evil.	PP	II	3	150	29
"It is a circumstance which Darcy of course would not wish	PP	II	10	185	26
partly by the wish of retaining Mr. Bingley for his sister.	PP	II	10	187	40
his visit to a wish of hearing that she were better.	PP	II	11	189	3
I might, perhaps, wish to be informed why, with so little	PP	II	11	190	9
With assumed tranquillity he then replied, "I have no wish	PP	II	11	191	15
so much in love as to wish to marry her in spite of all	PP	II	11	193	31
I must now mention a circumstance which I would wish to	PP	II	12	201	5
made her too angry to have any wish of doing him justice.	PP	II	13	204	1
been in her power, she had never felt a wish of enquiring.	PP	II	13	206	4
entered the house with the wish of appearing cheerful as	PP	II	13	209	12
heart most cordially wish you equal felicity in marriage.	PP	II	15	216	6
"But," he added, "you will of course wish to have your	PP	II	15	217	9
"Oh! Mary," said she, " I wish you had gone with us, for	PP	II	16	222	22
in Jane, whenever she might wish to talk again of either.	PP	II	17	227	25
is to be imputed to his wish of forwarding the match with	PP	II	18	235	38
a man would in general wish to owe to his wife; but where	PP	II	19	236	1
thought she, "that I have something to wish for.	PP	II	19	237	4
"Not so much as I could wish, sir; but I dare say he may	PP	III	1	248	25
Mr. Gardiner expressed a wish of going round the whole	PP	III	1	253	57
His wish of introducing his sister to her, was a .	PP	III	1	257	65
by tenderness, and a wish of saying more that might lead	PP	III	2	262	8
him in expressing their wish of seeing Mr. and Mrs.	PP	III	2	263	11
Elizabeth, construing all this into a wish of hearing her	PP	III	2	264	12
it was not their wish to force her communication.	PP	III	2	264	13
conceal it, from that very wish which Elizabeth had long	PP	III	3	270	10
my hurried letter; I wish this may be more intelligible,	PP	III	4	274	5
Mrs. Bennet, "that is exactly what I could most wish for.	PP	III	5	288	38
I get to Longbourn; but I wish you would tell sally to	PP	III	5	292	60
As Mrs. Gardiner began to wish to be at home, it was	PP	III	6	298	15
whether he would not wish them to make it known to her.	PP	III	7	305	39
surprise; for his chief wish at present, was to have as	PP	III	8	309	5
The wish of procuring her regard, which she had assured	PP	III	8	311	13
"It was greatly my wish that he should do so," he added, "	PP	III	8	312	19
"I wish I could say any thing to comfort you," replied	PP	III	11	333	29
"The first wish of my heart," said she to herself, "is	PP	III	11	337	55
and sensible young man, without having a wish beyond it.	PP	III	12	343	32
"But why should you wish to persuade me that I feel more	PP	III	12	343	36
It was the favourite wish of his mother, as well as of	PP	III	14	355	43
If you were sensible of your own good, you would not wish	PP	III	14	356	50
accept his hand, make him wish to bestow it on his cousin?	PP	III	14	357	61
I shall then give over every expectation, every wish of	PP	III	15	361	4
That the wish of giving happiness to you, might add force	PP	III	16	366	6
rest of the world, to wish at least to think meanly of	PP	III	16	369	24
on that article, Miss Bennet had nothing farther to wish.	PP	III	17	373	17
How earnestly did she then wish that her former opinions	PP	III	17	376	30
How could I be so silly as to wish it!	PP	III	18	382	21
I wish I could say, for the sake of her family, that the	PP	III	19	385	1
The darling wish of his sisters was then gratified; he	PP	III	19	385	3
"I wish you joy.	PP	III	19	386	7
as pride, from a general wish of doing right, and a desire	MP	I	1	3	1
not but own it to be her wish, that poor Mrs. Price should	MP	I	1	5	4
I only wish I could be more useful; but you see I do all	MP	I	1	9	12
We shall probably see much to wish altered in her, and	MP	I	1	10	14
I should wish to see them very good friends, and would, on	MP	I	1	11	17
I wish there may not be a little sulkiness of temper--her	MP	I	2	13	5
and friends, who all love you, and wish to make you happy.	MP	I	2	15	11
of, or for any body to wish that really knows us both.	MP	I	3	28	42
I am sure in his heart he could not wish me to do it."	MP	I	3	29	44
If I could wish it for my own sake, I would not do so	MP	I	3	29	46
It is for your children's good that I wish to be richer.	MP	I	3	30	52
myself; and I wish my friends in general would be so too.	MP	I	5	47	24
"I wish you could see Compton," said he, "it is the most	MP	I	6	53	2
I wish we could contrive it."	MP	I	6	56	23
"I do not wish to influence Mr. Rushworth," he continued, "	MP	I	6	56	28
"If I write, I will say whatever you wish me; but I do not	MP	I	6	59	42
led to his encouraging the wish, and the offer of his own	MP	I	7	66	14
I wish you may not be fatigued by so much exercise.	MP	I	7	68	19
I wish you had saved yourself this walk home."	MP	I	7	68	19
"I wish Fanny had half your strength, ma'am."	MP	I	7	73	54
Sotherton is the only place that could giver her a wish to	MP	I	8	76	3
If you could do without her, you would not wish to keep	MP	I	8	78	18
Mrs. Norris had no affection for Fanny, and no wish of	MP	I	8	79	23
I wish you had my seat, but I dare say you will not take	MP	I	8	81	32
had all the distinction with each that she could wish.	MP	I	9	84	1
our thoughts as we could wish; but if you are supposing it	MP	I	9	87	16
one impulse, one wish for air and liberty, all walked out.	MP	I	9	89	32
"I wish I could convince Miss Crawford too."	MP	I	9	93	52
beyond a wish that they had seen his friend Smith's place.	MP	I	10	97	3
the iron gate, expressed a wish of passing through it into	MP	I	10	97	4
whatever there may be to wish otherwise in Dr. Grant,	MP	I	11	111	30
"We cannot prove the contrary, to be sure--but I wish you	MP	I	11	112	31
I wish I could see Cassiopeia."	MP	I	11	113	39
never seen much symptom of it, but I wish it may be so.	MP	I	12	116	8
Mrs. Rushworth, that wish of avoiding particularity!--	MP	I	12	117	14
the offer was declined;--she did not wish to dance.--	MP	I	12	118	22
I wish my good aunt would be a little less busy!	MP	I	12	119	26
there were few who did not wish to have been a party	MP	I	13	122	2
Each sister could echo the wish; and Henry Crawford, to	MP	I	13	123	6
we could have desired, if we had set down to wish for it.	MP	I	13	125	14
would never wish his grown up daughters to be acting plays.	MP	I	13	127	26
he was mistaken in supposing she would wish to make any.	MP	I	13	129	40
I do not wish to make objections, I shall be happy to be	MP	I	14	131	3
sure his sister had no wish of acting, but as she might be	MP	I	14	133	10
not sympathize in his wish that the count and Agatha might	MP	I	15	138	1
I only wish Tom had known his own mind when the carpenters	MP	I	15	141	22
of the last who would wish to represent it on the stage."	MP	I	15	145	41
what her aunt and cousins wish her--very ungrateful indeed,	MP	I	15	147	55
and wish them in other hands--but I never think of him.	MP	I	17	161	13
made no change in her wish of retreat, and she worked and	MP	I	18	168	14
Edmund repeated his wish, and with a look of even fond	MP	I	18	172	32
You will find Fanny every thing you could wish."	MP	II	2	187	1
He seemed to feel exactly as one could wish."	MP	II	2	190	6
I could wish my father were more sensible of their very	MP	II	3	196	2
respect; and I only wish you would talk to him more.--	MP	II	3	198	9
information which he must wish his own daughters to feel."	MP	II	3	198	12
I wish they met more frequently!--	MP	II	3	199	13
to mind an early-expressed wish on the subject, was	MP	II	4	206	5
wish to procure so agreeable a visitor for her sister?"	MP	II	5	218	17
But as I conclude that she must wish to go, since all	MP	II	5	219	18
She could not wish him to stay, and would much rather not	MP	II	5	224	48
The wish was rather eager than lasting.	MP	II	6	236	23
in which I could not wish you established as a permanent	MP	II	7	247	39
"But you do not wish yourself at Portsmouth, William?"	MP	II	7	249	51
any body else who might wish to see Fanny dance, and to	MP	II	8	252	1
quickened by one sovereign wish she then called out, "Oh!	MP	II	9	261	3
For my own sake, I could wish there had been no ball just	MP	II	9	268	29
I cannot be afraid of hearing any thing you wish to say.	MP	II	9	270	39
She had nothing more to wish for.	MP	II	10	272	4
So often as she had heard them wish for a ball at home as	MP	II	10	276	12
Her praise was warm, and he received it as she could wish,	MP	II	10	276	14
"Yes," said Lady Bertram, "but I wish he was not going	MP	II	11	284	9
I wish they would stay at home."	MP	II	11	284	9
This wish was levelled principally at Julia, who had just	MP	II	11	284	10
foresee your happiness as heartily as I wish and desire it.	MP	II	12	292	7
I wish the discovery may do them any good.	MP	II	12	297	33
as she ought to be, and I wish they may be heartily	MP	II	12	297	33
I wish he may go to the East Indies, that I may have my	MP	II	13	305	25
She had hardly even attained the wish to do it.	MP	III	1	314	16
I wish he were more likely to fix."	MP	III	1	317	34
If, as I am willing to suppose, you wish to shew me any	MP	III	1	321	48
disposition to persevere that Sir Thomas could wish him.	MP	III	2	326	1
be but one opinion, one wish on the subject; the influence	MP	III	2	329	12
wish me to do differently from what I have done, I am sure.	MP	III	2	333	24
					25
You cannot wish me to marry; for you would miss me, me,	MP	III	2	333	25
"I wish Sir Thomas had been here."	MP	III	3	338	17
If it is not what you wish yourself, I have done.	MP	III	4	346	10
all your family should wish you could return it; but that	MP	III	4	346	12
I wish he had not been obliged to tell you what he was	MP	III	4	348	21
I wish he had known you as well as I do, Fanny.	MP	III	4	348	21
I cannot suppose that you have not the wish to love him--	MP	III	4	348	21
the wish to love him--the natural wish of gratitude.	MP	III	4	348	21
been used to wish to believe him, and feared he was not."	MP	III	4	350	30
right to every thing he may wish for, at the first moment.	MP	III	4	352	40
I wish you could have overheard her tribute of praise; I	MP	III	4	352	42
her tribute of praise; I wish you could have seen her	MP	III	4	352	42
I wish I had settled with Mrs. Fraser not to go to her	MP	III	5	359	12
she will very likely wish me in Northamptonshire again;	MP	III	5	360	16
I wish Margaret were married, for my poor friend's sake,	MP	III	5	361	16
I wish we could see him."	MP	III	5	364	29
to blame; and knowing her wish on the subject, he would	MP	III	7	375	3
I wish we could get the bell mended--but Betsey is a very	MP	III	7	379	15
By g--, I wish you may.	MP	III	7	380	20
I wish you would not be so quarrelsome.	MP	III	7	386	44
she could wish to overcome her own shyness and reserve.	MP	III	9	395	3
son, and regulated by the wish of appearing to advantage	MP	III	10	400	6
as warm in his commendation, as even her heart could wish.	MP	III	10	400	7
"I wish you were not so tired,"--said he, still detaining	MP	III	11	411	20
were in the house; "I wish I left you in stronger health.--	MP	III	11	411	20
Maddison is a clever fellow; I do not wish to displace him-	MP	III	11	412	20
Good bye; I wish you a pleasant journey to-morrow.	MP	III	11	412	23
cousin Edmund, I wish you would be so good as to say that--	MP	III	11	412	27
You will wish to hear my opinion of Maria's degree of	MP	III	13	423	2
"I never will--no, I certainly never will wish for a	MP	III	13	424	3
Her aunt often expressed a wish for her, but there was no	MP	III	14	430	6
I trust and hope, and sincerely wish you may never be	MP	III	14	431	8
She was as welcome to wish herself there, as to be there.	MP	III	14	431	8
I wish you may not repent it. "yours, &c."	MP	III	15	437	3
She spoke from the instinctive wish of delaying shame, she	MP	III	15	440	16
gratified in the first wish of her heart, and knowing	MP	III	15	444	26
his manner showed the wish of self-command, and the	MP	III	15	444	29
You do not wish me to be silent?--if you do, give me but a	MP	III	16	455	21
short struggle--half a wish of yielding to truths, half a	MP	III	16	458	30
supposed to have in her wish for a complete reconciliation.	MP	III	16	459	31
He had not to wait and wish with vacant affections for an	MP	III	17	470	25
No happiness of son or niece could make her wish the	MP	III	17	472	31
not but sigh over it and wish for impossible things, till	E	I	1	7	10
I wish she were here again.	E	I	1	8	11
I wish you may not catch cold."	E	I	1	10	24
Her father fondly replied, "Ah! my dear, I wish you would	E	I	1	12	40
I know indeed that he is so; and as such wish him well.	E	I	4	30	16
"I wish you may not get into a scrape, Harriet, whenever	E	I	4	30	22
when Mr. Martin marries, I wish you may not be drawn in,	E	I	4	31	24
am sure I shall not wish for the acquaintance of his wife.	E	I	4	31	25
at Hartfield, I cannot wish her to be forming any	E	I	5	41	30
seconded a sudden wish of her's, to have Harriet's picture.	E	I	6	43	8
strong a likeness of his cockade as you would wish to see.	E	I	6	45	21
pleased with the first day's sketch to wish to go on.	E	I	6	47	27
It was by no means his daughter's wish that the intellects	E	I	9	70	7
Ah! Mr. Knightley, I wish you had the benefit of this; I	E	I	9	72	15
assurance of it;--if they wish to have you settled in the	E	I	9	75	27
I wish I could recollect more of it.	E	I	9	79	56
"I wish we could contrive it," said she; "but I cannot	E	I	10	83	7
the question: and I do not wish to see any such person.	E	I	10	84	13
I wish Jane Fairfax very well; but she tires me to death."	E	I	10	86	23
I wish I were anywhere else."	E	I	10	88	32
which they could possibly wish for, without the smallest	E	I	11	92	3
"Not near so often, my dear, as I could wish."	E	I	11	94	13
Her wish of shewing you attention could not be doubted,	E	I	11	94	15
She had nothing to wish otherwise, but that the days did	E	I	13	108	1
but for her own earnest wish of being nursed by Mrs.	E	I	13	108	5
which she could not wish to reason away, which she would	E	I	13	110	8
"but where there is a wish to please, one ought to	E	I	13	111	17
coolly, "I cannot wish to be snowed up a week at Randalls."	E	I	13	115	40
					41
a great wish on the Churchills' to keep him to themselves.	E	I	14	122	21
on his coming, and I wish Mr. Weston were less sanguine."	E	I	14	122	21
I wish her extremely well: and, no doubt, there are men	E	I	15	132	35
Emma then felt it indispensable to wish him a good night.	E	I	15	132	37
It is a great deal more natural than one could wish, that	E	I	18	145	10

WISH/WISHED

I wish you would try to understand what an amiable young	E I 18 148 21
power as well as the wish of being universally agreeable.	E I 18 150 31
you are so kind as to wish to hear what she says;--but,	E II 1 157 10
I only wish my eyes may last me as well.'"	E II 1 158 10
urgency, and her own wish of seeing Ireland, Miss Fairfax	E II 1 161 24
indeed they particularly wish her to try her native air,	E II 1 161 25
Now, however, we must wish you and Mrs. Bates good morning.	E II 1 162 32
for her, and his own wish of being a real friend, united	E II 2 163 4
nobody that she could wish to scheme about for her.	E II 2 168 14
I knew you would wish it.	E II 3 172 18
had every thing they could wish for, I am sure it is us.	E II 3 174 31
I did so wish myself any where in the world but there.--	E II 3 178 52
Very sincerely did Emma wish to do so; but it was not	E II 3 179 53
every thing has turned out exactly as we could wish."	E II 5 188 7
more agreeably denote his wish of considering her as a	E II 6 196 2
resolved on, confessed his wish to be made acquainted with	E II 6 196 2
be giving her refusal less meaning than she could wish.	E II 7 207 6
As for his going, Emma did not wish him to think it	E II 7 208 9
take care of her, I cannot wish to prevent it, provided	E II 7 209 10
I will step to Mrs. Goddard in a moment, if you wish it."	E II 7 209 11
"But you would not wish me to come away before I am tired,	E II 7 210 15
You would not wish to disappoint and mortify the Coles, I	E II 7 210 19
Cole, you would stay a little longer than you might wish.	E II 7 210 20
He had no reason to wish his hair longer, to conceal any	E II 8 212 2
reason to wish the money unspent, to improve his spirits.	E II 8 212 2
please, and given all the consequence she could wish for.	E II 8 214 12
She did not wish to speak of the pianoforte, she felt too	E II 8 220 45
unsuspicious of that wish of saying as little about it as	E II 8 220 46
he said, he was beginning to have no longer the same wish.	E II 8 221 49
It is not that I am without the wish; but you know how	E II 8 228 89
he replied;--"but you must often wish it, I am sure."	E II 8 228 90
I really wish you to call with me.	E II 9 234 34
staircase--rather darker and narrower than one could wish.	E II 9 239 53
I wish I could conjecture how soon I shall make this rivet	E II 10 242 15
"But really, I am half ashamed, and wish I had never taken	E II 10 243 26
play as long as they could wish to dance; and the	E II 11 247 3
"I wish," said Mrs. Weston, "one could know which	E II 11 254 49
Undoubtedly, if you wish it, I will endeavour to persuade	E II 11 255 58
His wish of staying longer evidently did not please; but	E II 12 257 2
must laugh at; but that one would not wish to slight.	E II 12 260 27
of something absolutely serious, which she did not wish.	E II 12 260 30
own sake rather, I would wish it to be done, for the sake	E II 13 268 11 12
Well, I wish them happy with all my heart.	E II 14 271 15
marry, but I would always wish to pay every proper	E II 14 280 58
in spite of the very natural wish of a little change."	E II 15 286 21
Oh! no, upon my word I have not the smallest wish for your	E II 15 288 35
She has not the open temper which a man would wish for in	E II 15 288 36
I wish my health allowed me to be a better neighbour.	E II 16 294 27
"I have not even made any inquiry; I do not wish to make	E II 17 299 5
Mrs. Bragge's is the one I would most wish to see you in."	E II 17 300 8
But I would not wish you to take the trouble of making any	E II 17 300 9
draws nearer, I do not wish to be giving any body trouble."	E II 17 300 11
But this good old Mr. Woodhouse, I wish you had heard his	E II 17 302 22
for me to speak of her with the forbearance I could wish.	E II 18 309 33
often with them, almost as often as he could even wish.	E III 1 317 8
to do me honour--I would not wish to be inferior to others.	E III 2 324 20 21
It was no more than a wish.	E III 3 335 11
"It is my duty, and I am sure it is my wish," she	E III 4 337 4
However, I assure you, Miss Woodhouse, I wish her no evil.-	E III 4 337 6
it is my particular wish to do it in your presence, that	E III 4 338 6
them both behind the fire, and I wish you to see me do it."	E III 4 340 22
now, and wish I could forget as easily as I can burn them.	E III 4 340 24
might wish to escape any of Emma's errors of imagination.	E III 5 343 2
I am not like Jane; I wish I were.	E III 5 346 16
We really must wish you good night."	E III 5 349 24
have spoken to some others whom I would wish to meet you."	E III 6 354 11
If you wish me to talk to Mrs. Hodges, or to inspect	E III 6 355 22
"I have not the least wish for it, I thank you."	E III 6 355 23
"I wish we had a donkey.	E III 6 356 26
I would wish every thing to be as much to your taste as	E III 6 356 27
"Certainly, if you wish it;--but you are not going to walk	E III 6 362 45
you wish me to stay, and join the party, I will."	E III 6 366 74 75
I wish you could have heard how she talked of it--with	E III 7 375 59
candour and generosity. I wish you could have heard her	E III 7 375 59
up the stairs, with any wish of giving pleasure, but in	E III 8 378 3
I wish Hetty had not gone.	E III 8 378 6
her kindness--and with Emma it was grown into a first wish.	E III 9 389 16
before she could hint the wish, Miss Bates made it appear	E III 9 390 18
It was our darling wish that you might be attached to each	E III 10 396 43
grow reconciled to the idea, and I wish them very happy.	E III 10 399 61
Wish it she must, for his sake--be the consequence nothing	E III 12 416 1
It must be her ardent wish that Harriet might be	E III 12 416 2
much--for every wish and every endeavour to do her good.	E III 12 419 12
I wish I had attended to it--but--(with a sinking voice	E III 13 425 11
character and conduct, I shall certainly wish him well."	E III 13 428 21
A man would always wish to give a woman a better home than	E III 13 428 23
Emma, I must tell what you will not ask, though I may wish	E III 13 429 27
But if you have any wish to speak openly to me as a friend,	E III 13 429 32
"Emma, that I fear is a word--no, I have no wish--stay,	E III 13 429 33
attached to me, was as much my conviction as my wish.--	E III 14 438 8
I should wish it."	E III 15 445 9
"I wish you would read it with a kinder spirit towards him.	E III 15 447 27
The wish of distinguishing her, as far as civility	E III 16 457 34
as to--I have not time for half that I could wish to say.	E III 16 459 47
I wish I may not sink into 'poor Emma' with him at once.--	E III 17 464 24
"Ah!" he cried, "I wish your father might be half as	E III 17 465 25
I wish our opinions were the same.	E III 18 471 16
As far as the man is concerned, you could not wish your	E III 18 472 22
the brightest smiles, "and most sincerely wish them happy."	E III 18 474 31
What had she to wish for?	E III 18 475 39
began to doubt whether the wish now indulged, which she	E III 18 476 46
I was once very near--and I wish I had--it would have been	E III 18 477 55
letter, and think you may remember my wish in your favour.	E III 18 477 59
you must be aware that my wish would be to remain with	P III 5 38 32
"I wish you could persuade Mary not to be always fancying	P III 6 44 7
you are about it: but I wish any body could give Mary a	P III 6 46 10
began to wish that she could feel secure even for a week.	P III 7 53 1
seriously described the woman he should wish to meet with.	P III 7 62 40
Anne did not wish for more of such looks and speeches.	P III 8 72 60
I wish you had been there to see her behaviour.	P III 9 77 16
I wish you had been with us yesterday, for then you might	P III 9 77 16
what they did not wish, and admired again the sort of	P III 10 83 4
Then, returning to his former earnest tone: "my first wish	P III 10 88 26
We do so wish that Charles had married Anne instead.--	P III 10 88 28
I wish she had accepted him.	P III 10 89 33
I wish Frederick would spread a little more canvas, and	P III 10 92 46
environs of Lyme, to make him wish to know it better.	P III 11 95 9
I wish his friends would propose it to him.	P III 12 102 2
"I wish," said Henrietta, very well pleased with her	P III 12 103 4
with her companion, "I wish Lady Russell lived at	P III 12 103 4
amazingly, and wish we had such a neighbour at Uppercross."	P III 12 103 4
a general answer, and a wish that such another woman were	P III 12 103 5
I wish I had looked at him more.	P III 12 106 16
I wish we had been aware in time, who it was, that he	P III 12 106 16
I wish he could have such company oftener.	P III 12 107 24
there was such a general wish to walk along it once more,	P III 12 108 30
supposing they might wish to stay; though, with regard to	P III 12 113 56
Mrs. Charles Musgrove will, of course, wish to get back to	P III 12 114 61
Lady Russell had only to listen composedly, and wish them	P IV 1 125 13
I wish he may be induced to call here.	P IV 2 132 20
"He is a man," said Lady Russell, "whom I have no wish to	P IV 2 133 23
in rain, without any wish of seeing them better; felt	P IV 2 135 34
to Mary, of his being "a man whom she had no wish to see."	P IV 2 135 35
She had a great wish to see him.	P IV 2 135 35
Most earnestly did she wish that he might not be too nice,	P IV 3 140 11
to Lady Russell, in the wish of really comprehending what	P IV 3 144 22
lively a wish to see again, and to see more of, as herself.	P IV 4 148 9
and was reduced to form a wish which she had never	P IV 4 148 11
she had never foreseen--a wish that they had more pride;	P IV 4 148 11
that degree of consideration which we must all wish for."	P IV 4 150 17
I know, and I shall not wish to believe myself otherwise,	P IV 4 151 21
"I am glad you find Mr. Elliot so agreeable, and wish I "	P IV 6 163 7
I wish young ladies had not such a number of fine	P IV 6 171 33
Anne, and expressing his wish of getting Captain Wentworth	P IV 7 174 1
to a new umbrella) "I wish you would make use of it, if	P IV 7 177 14
arch, "well, I heartily wish your concert may answer; and	P IV 7 180 35
With all my soul I wish them happy, and rejoice over every	P IV 8 182 8
having not the smallest wish for a total change, she only	P IV 8 183 11 12
before her, had nothing to wish for which did not seem	P IV 8 185 20
"He must wish her good night.	P IV 8 190 48
and exclaimed, "now, how I do wish I understood you!	P IV 9 195 29 30
How I do wish I knew what you were at!	P IV 9 195 30
of her life, and can answer any question you wish to put."	P IV 9 200 57
I wish nature had made such hearts as yours more common, "	P IV 9 203 72
"I wish I had any name but Elliot.	P IV 9 203 73
he could spend, nothing to wish for on the side of avarice	P IV 9 206 90
I wish Sarah was here to doctor you, but I am no doctor	P IV 11 238 46
I am afraid there has been some mistake; and I wish you	P IV 11 239 49
"To be sure I will, if you wish it.	P IV 11 239 52
To consider it as the certain wish of every being who	P IV 11 244 72
ever make her friends wish that tenderness less; the dread	P IV 12 252 12
merely in consequence of a wish to establish some medical	S 2 371 1
who might very reasonably wish for her original thirty	S 3 376 1
by the bye, I almost wish I had not named Trafalgar--for	S 4 380 1
I wish we may get him to Sanditon.	S 4 382 1
Most sincerely do we wish you a good season at Sanditon, &	S 5 387 1
address & wish of paying attention & giving pleasure.--	S 7 394 1
of pleasing, I know them not, & never wish to know them.--	S 7 395 1
He only told me, & that but once, that he shd wish his	S 7 400 1
to act, he must naturally wish to strike out something new,	S 8 405 2
"I will do whatever you wish me, replied his wife--but you	S 12 423 1
I wish I could go with you myself--but in 5 minutes I must	S 12 424 1

WISHED (253)

Reginald has long wished I know to see this captivating	LS 3 247 1
you well know, I never wished him to be seen at Churchill.	LS 22 280 1
in so many words, that he wished to reason with me on the	LS 22 281 4
he never wished to inspire, nor solicited the avowal of.	LS 22 282 6
which I could have wished in my daughter, or had I even	LS 24 288 11
Her mother wished her to learn music; and Catherine was	NA I 1 14 1
Mrs. Morland was a very good woman, and wished to see her	NA I 1 15 3
which she had every day wished for the same thing was at	NA I 4 31 2
of some one whom they wished to avoid; and all have been	NA I 10 74 23
for the attentions of some one whom they wished to please.	NA I 10 74 23
Catherine wished to congratulate him, but knew not what to	NA I 15 120 24
Catherine wished him a good journey.	NA I 15 122 29
of its concealment, wished she could have known his	NA I 15 125 48
have known his intention, wished she could have seen him	NA I 15 125 48
expected, nor wished for any thing of the kind from him.	NA II 3 145 13
She wished Isabella had talked more like her usual self,	NA II 3 148 28
She wished by a gentle remonstrance, to remind Isabella of	NA II 4 150 1
almost have wished to return with him to Pulteney-Street.	NA II 5 154 1
wished for the protection of light after she were in bed."	NA II 6 167 10
the general wished he could do the same, for he never	NA II 7 178 23
so much wished for, struck Catherine as very remarkable.	NA II 7 181 41
mistress; and as she wished to get it over before Henry's	NA II 9 193 5
her with the place, wished the Lady Frasers had been in	NA II 11 209 5
and sister loved and even wished her to belong to them;	NA II 13 221 6
Eleanor saw that she wished to be alone; and believing it	NA II 13 226 24
Eleanor had wished to spare her form so painful a notion,	NA II 13 226 25
His consent was all that they wished for.	NA II 16 249 2
Mr. Dashwood had wished for it more for the sake of his	SS I 1 4 3
His mother wished to interest him in political concerns,	SS I 3 16 6
Mrs. John Dashwood wished it likewise; but in the mean	SS I 3 16 6
object as ever; and she wished to shew Mrs. John Dashwood	SS I 5 25 3
two entire strangers of the party, and wished for no more.	SS I 7 34 4
each wished to be benefited at the expense of the other."	SS I 8 38 10
wish him successful, she heartily wished him indifferent.	SS I 10 50 12
She only wished that it were less openly shewn; and once	SS I 11 53 2
He wished her a good morning, and attended by Sir John,	SS I 13 66 51
Is not it what you have often wished to do yourself?"	SS I 13 68 68
I am guilty, I confess, of having often wished you to	SS I 17 94 39
It was evident that he was unhappy; she wished it were	SS I 18 96 1
bound to contribute, he wished to engage them for both.	SS I 18 99 16
ill-natured or ill-bred as he wished to appear.	SS I 20 112 28
Sir John and Lady Middleton wished it very much.	SS I 20 116 62
before the eldest of them wished her joy on her sister's	SS I 21 125 34
She wished very much to have the subject continued, though	SS I 21 126 41
Elinor had often wished for an opportunity of attempting	SS II 3 157 17
Elinor wished very much to ask whether Willoughby were	SS II 4 162 12
be, and at the same time wished to shield her conduct from	SS II 5 174 45
he neither expected, nor wished to see her there, and, in	SS II 8 198 30
different from what she wished and expected, though she	SS II 10 214 6
Elinor wished that the same forbearance could have	SS II 10 214 8
She wished with all her heart Combe Magna was not so near	SS II 10 215 10
"I wished very much to call upon you yesterday," said he, "	SS II 11 221 9
Elinor wished to talk of something else, but Lucy still	SS II 13 239 7
young friends; for as she wished to be as much as possible	SS II 14 246 2
Lady Elliott wished to give a dance.	SS II 14 252 18
by time and address, to do every thing that Lucy wished.	SS II 14 254 27
"I have very often wished to undeceive yourself and my	SS III 1 262 25
for otherwise we both wished very much to have invited you	SS III 1 266 36
provocation, and he never wished to offend anybody,	SS III 1 267 44
herself which she rather wished to do away; and Marianne's	SS III 2 270 1
but as Elinor wished to spread as little as possible	SS III 2 276 27
mother, whom she so much wished to see, in a more eligible,	SS III 3 280 6
a man, that he rather wished any one to announce his	SS III 4 287 19
"Mrs. Jennings told me," said he, "that you wished to	SS III 4 288 27
Her sleep, though not so quiet as Elinor wished to see it,	SS III 7 310 9
she forgave, pitied, wished him well--was even interested	SS III 8 332 76
with another; and for a moment wished Willoughby a widower.	SS III 9 335 5
and wished any thing rather than Mrs. Willoughby's death.	SS III 9 335 5
guilt;--she was sorry for him;--she wished him happy.	SS III 11 349 1
deserts;--she wished, therefore, to declare only the	SS III 11 349 2
not Elinor, who really wished to hear her sister's	SS III 11 349 5
morning--I have now heard exactly what I wished to hear."--	SS III 11 350 5 6
felt their own error, wished to avoid any survey of the	SS III 11 352 16 17
Elinor looked as if she wished to hear more.	SS III 11 355 40
she wished to be acquainted with, and yet desired to avoid.	SS III 12 357 3
In Edward--she knew not what she saw, nor what she wished	SS III 12 357 4
forced complacency, gave him her hand, and wished him joy.	SS III 12 359 11
over, she wished that she had shaken hands with him too.	SS III 12 359 12
yet enjoy, as she wished, the sight and society of both.	SS III 13 363 6
the cottage, as he really wished not only to be better	SS III 13 368 30
lengthened the ceremony almost to the wished for moment.	W 326 7
by the hand & wished her "goodbye" at least a dozen times.	W 335 13
rather have known that he wished the visit without	W 347 22
to bring her home & wished to see their sister Emma.--	W 348 23

Mary wished to say something very sensible, but knew not	PP I 2 7 19
The astonishment of the ladies was just what he wished;	PP I 2 7 23
If I wished to think slightingly of any body's children,	PP I 7 29 8
him, I have frequently wished to heal the breach; but for	PP I 13 62 12
though what she chiefly wished to hear she could not hope	PP I 16 77 8
if he had not wished to avoid a certain gentleman here."	PP I 18 89 1
	2
He smiled, and assured her that whatever she wished him to	PP I 18 91 10
how heartily they were wished away by some of the family.	PP I 18 102 75
the affair as she wished, was excessively disappointed.	PP I 20 112 20
Mrs. Bennet wished to understand by it that he thought of	PP I 22 124 11
to her, and that she wished her all imaginable happiness.	PP I 22 125 16
his marriage, that she wished it to take place as soon as	PP I 23 128 10
much solemnity as before; wished his fair cousins health	PP II 2 139 1
ill-natured tone that she "wished they might be happy."	PP II 3 145 11
was exactly what he had wished for; and that an	PP II 6 160 1
but such of us as wished to learn, never wanted the means.	PP II 6 165 31
he never had; but she wished to see whether he would	PP II 7 171 12
--I did not believe her to be indifferent because I wished	PP II 12 197 5
impartial conviction, as truly as I wished it in reason.--	PP II 12 197 5
I rather wished, than believed him to be sincere; but at	PP II 12 200 5
She wished to discredit it entirely, repeatedly exclaiming,	PP II 13 204 2
with great condescension, wished them a good journey, and	PP II 14 214 21
She wished him to know that she had been assured of his	PP III 1 256 61
They had long wished to see him.	PP III 2 261 6
to know how far she wished that welfare to depend upon	PP III 2 266 16
Miss Darcy looked as if she wished for courage enough to	PP III 3 267 4
She wished, she feared that the master of the house might	PP III 3 268 5
she wished or feared it most, she could scarcely determine.	PP III 3 268 5
she most feared or wished for the appearance of Mr. Darcy,	PP III 3 268 7
sorrow for her distress, wished it a happier conclusion	PP III 4 278 22
Mr. Bennet had very often wished, before this period of	PP III 8 308 1
He now wished it more than ever.	PP III 8 308 1
on to think as they thought, and act as they wished.	PP III 8 314 22
followed his lady, and wished them both joy, with an	PP III 9 315 3
man whom he always most wished to avoid, and whose very	PP III 10 326 3
She could think of nothing more to say; but if he wished	PP III 12 342 25
his mother and aunt wished him to marry Miss de Bourgh.	PP III 14 355 44
They walked towards the Lucases, because Kitty wished to	PP III 16 365 2
consent, there was still something to be wished for.	PP III 17 378 46
He could not say he wished me to take Fanny.	MP I 3 29 44
Fanny had never heard the harp at all, and wished for it	MP I 6 59 40
Miss Crawford civilly wished him an early promotion.	MP I 6 60 47
were gathered, your aunt wished to have them, and then you	MP I 7 72 49
She wished to be able to decline it; but the tears which a	MP I 7 74 57
Rushworth still think she wished to come, till Mrs.	MP I 8 76 2
saying lately, that you wished you could drive, Julia, I	MP I 8 80 29
country was charming, she wished they could all see it, &c.	MP I 8 81 32
It was the very thing of all others to be wished, it was	MP I 10 97 4
Mr. Rushworth wished he had brought the key; he had been	MP I 10 98 4
be done; if you really wished to be more at large, and	MP I 10 99 18
He got up and walked to the gate again, and "wished he had	MP I 10 102 47
assured that Edmund had wished for her very much, and that	MP I 10 103 49
she wished, and Maria by the hints of Mr. Crawford himself.	MP I 12 115 4
My father wished us, as school-boys, to speak well, but he	MP I 13 127 26
For her own gratification she could have wished that	MP I 14 131 4
warmly asked, so strongly wished for? what might be so	MP I 16 153 3
own family circle was what they had particularly wished.	MP I 17 158 2
exactly as he could have wished, but dared not depend on.	MP II 1 178 8
on people or subjects which she wished to be respected.	MP II 4 208 11
what he could have wished; and to the credit of the	MP II 4 211 25
which I particularly wished not to be dressed till Sunday,	MP II 4 212 31
shameful contrast; and he wished he had been a William	MP II 6 236 22
means of conferring a kindness where he wished to oblige.	MP II 6 237 23
to be chusing what Miss Crawford least wished to keep.	MP II 8 258 17
what she had so much wished for, did not bring much	MP II 8 260 25
thing, precisely what I wished for! this is the only	MP II 9 262 8
"I wished to engage Miss Crawford for the two first dances,	MP II 9 268 28
so very soon, and she wished she had not been obliged to	MP II 10 278 20
She wished she had not spoken so warmly in their last	MP II 11 286 15
She wished such words unsaid with all her heart.	MP II 11 286 15
recollected herself, and wished it unsaid; but there was	MP II 12 295 22
She wished to prove to him that she did desire his comfort,	MP III 1 322 50
be able in time to make those feelings what he wished.	MP III 2 326 1
He wished him to be a model of constancy; and fancied the	MP III 4 345 3
they were quite mistaken who wished you to do otherwise.	MP III 4 347 18
He certainly wished her to go willingly, but he as	MP III 6 369 9
but he as certainly wished her to be heartily sick of home	MP III 6 369 9
respect, the very reverse of what she could have wished.	MP III 8 388 3
Susan, she found, looked up to her and wished for her good	MP III 9 396 6
no means to the extent he wished; he absolutely would not	MP III 10 403 14
Crawford could not have wished her more fatigued or more	MP III 10 403 15
to sit down; but he could have wished her sister away.	MP III 10 403 15
She turned away, and wished he would not say such things.	MP III 10 405 16
had seen all that they wished, or had time for, the others	MP III 10 406 21
other things which she wished he had not said, she thought	MP III 10 406 21
She wished the next day over, she wished he had come only	MP III 10 406 21
She could not command her attention as she wished.	MP III 12 418 5
was in preparation--and wished Rebecca would mend it; and	MP III 15 439 9
as she wished of the circumstances attending the story.	MP III 16 449 7
son, he would not have wished her to belong to him, though	MP III 16 453 15
I only said in reply, that from my heart I wished her well,	MP III 16 458 30
less equal than could be wished; but without presuming to	MP III 17 468 22
friendship she had always wished and promoted the match;	E I 1 6 6
"By the bye--I have not wished you joy.	E I 1 10 27
no longer teased by being wished joy of so sorrowful an	E I 2 19 14
could persuade her to read half so much as you wished.--	E I 5 37 7
never remember Emma's omitting to do any thing I wished."	E I 5 37 8
Emma wished to go to work directly, and therefore produced	E I 6 44 19
had rather said what he wished resentfully to be true,	E I 8 67 57
She hardly wished to have more leisure for them.	E I 11 91 1
he had not always the patience that could have been wished.	E I 11 93 5
I could have wished, however, as you know, that you had	E I 12 103 42
Often as she had wished for and ordered it, she had never	E I 12 105 50
nonsense, which she particularly wished to listen to.	E I 14 118 4
Emma wished she had been alone with Mrs. Weston.	E I 14 122 18
He wished the road might be impassable, that he might be	E I 15 126 11
and messages; but if he wished to do it, it might be done.	E I 18 146 16
doing more than she wished, and less than she ought!	E II 2 166 11
and I have often wished--but it is so little one can	E II 3 171 16
	17
She wished him very well; but he gave her pain, and his	E II 4 182 7
She had provided a plentiful dinner for them; she wished	E II 8 213 6
if Mr. Knightley really wished to marry, you would not	E II 8 224 67
she wished I had made him believe we had a great many left.	E II 9 238 51
Emma wished he would be less pointed, yet could not help	E II 10 243 22
It was precisely what Emma would have wished, had she	E II 16 291 5
She wished she might be able to keep him from an absolute	E III 1 315 2
he wished to stay longer at Hartfield, he must hurry off."	E III 1 316 4
It was the very circumstance he would have wished for.	E III 1 317 10
She wished he would love a ball-room better, and could	E III 2 326 32
Emma had never been to box hill; she wished to see what	E III 6 352 2
He wished to persuade Mr. Woodhouse, as well as Emma, to	E III 6 356 29
She wished to see the whole extent."--	E III 6 359 37
any thing like it--almost wished he had staid at home--	E III 6 363 53
excepted, two years more might make her all that he wished.	E III 7 373 51
and merriment, and wished herself rather walking quietly	E III 7 374 54
denial yesterday, as Jane wished her; she would wait--and,	E III 8 381 15
to Miss Bates, but she wished she had left her ten minutes	E III 9 386 8
All that remained to be wished was, that the nephew should	E III 9 388 13
any one at Highbury, who wished to show her kindness--and	E III 9 389 16
one room;--he could have wished it otherwise--and her good	E III 9 389 16

Emma wished she could have seen her, and tried her own	E III 9 390 18
in the first place had wished not to go at all at present,	E III 12 417 5
She wished him to speak, but he would not.	E III 13 427 18
He never wished to attach me.	E III 13 427 19
with a deep sigh, that he wished I might find as much	E III 14 443 8
Harriet really wished, and had wished some time, to	E III 16 451 3
Emma could have wished Mrs. Elton elsewhere; but she was	E III 16 453 11
in not having thought of it, and wished it long ago.--	E III 17 467 31
and decent enough to have always wished for concealment.--	E III 19 481 3
forming an intimacy, which she wished to see interrupted.	P III 2 15 15
man, and without children; the very state to be wished for.	P III 3 22 24
her own discretion, never wished the past undone, she	P III 4 29 7
the full invitation she wished; and Anne, though dreading	P III 5 33 6
think that, every thing considered, she wished to remain.	P III 5 33 6
which she often wished less, of her father's character,	P III 5 34 12
I was told that they wished it.	P III 5 39 34
more share than she wished, being appealed to by both	P III 6 43 5
She wished, however, to see the Crofts, and was glad to be	P III 6 48 17
going on so well--and he wished so much to be introduced	P III 7 55 6
His father very much wished him to meet Captain Wentworth,	P III 7 55 7
Had he wished ever to see her again, he need not have	P III 7 58 21
He wished to avoid seeing her.	P III 7 59 23
I wished for him again the next summer, when I had still	P III 8 67 23
air which he wished to give the Miss Musgroves an idea of.	P III 8 72 58
Hayter, whose pretensions she wished to see put an end to.	P III 9 75 12
it is very much to be wished that Captain Wentworth may	P III 9 76 16
was ready to do as Mary wished; but "no," said Charles	P III 10 85 16
She wished it might be possible for her to avoid ever	P III 11 93 3
He almost wished she had been prevailed on to come home	P IV 1 121 2
as could be wished, to the last state she had seen it in.	P IV 2 134 28
Elliot, in having been wished for, regretted, and at the	P IV 5 158 21
people in Bath as they wished for, and considered their	P IV 6 168 24
She wished him not so near her.	P IV 8 188 43
thing in the world to be wished for by everybody belonging	P IV 9 197 36
what the young people had wished, and what I said at first	P IV 11 230 5
"though we could have wished it different, yet altogether	P IV 11 230 6
I was hers in honour if she wished it.	P IV 11 242 65
The very thing perhaps to be wished for.	S 1 364 1
Machine with her if she wished it--and as soon as that is	S 12 424 1
WISHED-FOR (2)	
however, our kind friend procured the wished-for direction.	PP III 10 322 2
would my giving you the wished-for promise, make their	PP III 14 357 61
WISHES (142)	
her heart I am persuaded, she sincerely wishes him gone.	LS 20 278 10
the particulars & assure himself of her real wishes!	LS 22 281 5
Lady Susan I beleive wishes to speak to you about it, if	LS 24 287 9
when one wishes to influence the passions of another.	LS 25 293 3
& my wishes, he will be laid up with the gout many weeks.	LS 26 295 4
With anxious wishes, Yrs faithfully Alicia.	LS 32 303 2
obliged to her for these wishes; but they were repeated so	NA I 2 21 9
next day; and when her wishes for fine weather were	NA I 5 35 1
And this address seemed to satisfy all the fondest wishes	NA I 7 49 43
parting good wishes, they both hurried down stairs.	NA I 9 62 7
her wishes, hopes and plans all centered in nothing less.	NA I 10 74 23
augured from it, every thing most favourable to her wishes.	NA I 11 82 1
Miss Tilney added her own wishes.	NA I 13 103 28
father and mother would never oppose their son's wishes.--	NA I 15 119 14
"For my own part," said Isabella, "my wishes are so	NA I 15 119 20
begin on indeed, but your wishes, my dear Isabella, are so	NA II 1 135 44
Pulteney-Street, and obtained their sanction of his wishes.	NA II 2 140 9
of, outstripped even her wishes in the flattering measures	NA II 2 141 11
on to give more encouragement than one wishes to stand by.	NA II 3 146 18
effect of this last argument was equal to his wishes.	NA II 7 176 16
think would most accord her fair friend's wishes?--	NA II 7 177 17
But suites of apartments did not spring up with her wishes.	NA II 8 183 2
equally confident of the wishes of his son, Catherine	NA II 11 215 28
misled (perhaps by her wishes) to suppose that a much	NA II 13 221 2
and the thousand good wishes of a most affectionate heart.	NA II 14 236 14
Henry Dashwood to his wishes, which proceeded not merely	SS I 1 3 1
him, nor attention to his wishes, for we very well know	SS I 2 13 28
disposition to answer the wishes of his mother and sister,	SS I 3 15 6
All his wishes centered in domestic comfort and the quiet	SS I 3 16 6
of Norland beyond her wishes, she made no attempt to	SS I 4 24 21
consulted only her own wishes, she would have kept it; but	SS I 5 26 5
elegance of her appearance was favourable to their wishes.	SS I 6 31 8
it was the good wishes of an affectionate brother to both.	SS I 8 39 18
behaviour declared his wishes to be in that respect as	SS I 10 49 10
You cannot doubt your sister's wishes.	SS I 15 81 42
would prevent the denial which her wishes might direct."	SS I 16 84 9
Your wishes are all moderate."	SS I 17 91 5
wishes and his own, and without any restraint on his time.	SS I 19 101 1
But from such vain wishes, she was forced to turn for	SS I 19 102 2
and proofs, and contradicted by nothing but her own wishes.	SS II 1 139 1
with you, unless it were on the side of your wishes."	SS II 2 150 31
wishes, with less reluctance than she had expected to feel.	SS II 3 158 20
might still feed her own wishes, she could not attribute	SS II 6 178 17
till their mother's wishes could be known; and at length	SS II 9 203 9
not a thing to be urged against the wishes of everybody.	SS II 14 246 2
already mentioned their wishes to their kind hostess, who	SS III 3 279 1
receiving our good wishes, even if we had not been able to	SS III 4 288 28
now just vacant, and only wishes it were more valuable.	SS III 4 288 28
of her unceasing good wishes for his happiness in every	SS III 4 290 43
within herself--to his wishes than to his merits.	SS III 9 333 2
her daughter's wishes began to talk of removing to Barton.	SS III 10 340 4
full of respect and kind wishes as seemed due to her own	SS III 10 341 5
tempt the daughter's wishes and the mother's confidence;	SS III 10 344 11
as she trusted, to the wishes of that daughter, by whom	SS III 12 359 11
heart, and that she wishes for nothing so much as to be on	SS III 13 371 39
do us the honour of giving us your good wishes in person.--	W 347 21
on it, to consult the wishes of the present party; I am	PP I 11 55 6
to Elizabeth's wishes, for she was impatient to get home.	PP I 12 59 1
Lady Catherine de Bourgh's attention to his wishes, and	PP I 14 66 1
If he wishes to avoid seeing me, he must go.	PP I 16 78 20
She concluded with many good wishes that Lady Lucas might	PP I 18 99 63
friend Lizzy to comply with the wishes of all her family.	PP I 20 113 26
neither expects nor wishes me to be her sister; that she	PP I 21 118 15
of Caroline's interested wishes, and she could not for a	PP I 21 120 28
moment suppose that those wishes, however openly or	PP I 21 120 28
of the wishes which had been unfolded in her former letter.	PP II 1 133 2
But, whatever may be their own wishes, it is very unlikely	PP II 1 137 24
and reluctant good wishes, and sincerely affected herself,	PP II 3 145 11
even to Charlotte's wishes, to be the case; and after	PP II 9 180 28
and accept my best wishes for your health and happiness."	PP II 11 193 29
myself, by dwelling on wishes, which, for the happiness of	PP II 12 196 4
moments, she flattered herself that her wishes did not err.	PP II 13 205 3
of his wishes, but his eagerness to grasp at any thing.	PP II 13 207 6
Mrs. Bennet was diffuse in her good wishes for the	PP II 18 235 40
other point on which her wishes and hopes might be fixed,	PP II 19 237 3
"who more particularly wishes to be known to you,--will	PP III 1 256 63
wishes to predominate, she began to regret that he came.	PP III 3 268 7
her understand her own wishes; and never had she so	PP III 4 278 19
But I will not torment you with vain wishes, which may	PP III 4 278 20
But wishes were vain; or at best could serve only to amuse	PP III 4 281 29
her; and the good-natured wishes for her well-doing, which	PP III 8 309 6
the first object of her wishes, since Jane was sixteen,	PP III 8 310 7
though unlike her own, would have answered all her wishes.	PP III 8 312 15
with him would have been the last object of her wishes.	PP III 8 314 22
time, that his affection and wishes must still be unshaken.	PP III 11 334 37
to her, claimed the good wishes and affection of a sister.	PP III 13 347 33
Do you pay no regard to the wishes of his friends?	PP III 14 355 43
My affections and wishes are unchanged, but one word from	PP III 16 366 7
How soon any other wishes introduced themselves I can	PP III 16 370 32

Nobody that wishes me well, I am sure, would propose it. MP I 3 28 42
I know she wishes it very much. MP I 8 78 21
drove off amid the good wishes of the two remaining ladies, MP I 8 80 30
One wishes it were not so--but I have not yet left Oxford MP I 9 88 18
that Mary Crawford's wishes, though politely kept back, MP I 14 130 3
for even her activity to keep pace with her wishes? MP II 2 194 20
or staying--but his good wishes for Mr. Yates's having a MP II 2 194 21
fears, inquired into her wishes, entreated her to be open MP II 3 200 21
"Poor Fanny! not allowed to cheat herself as she wishes!" MP II 7 244 29
Fanny acknowledged her wishes and doubts on this point; MP II 8 257 15
But though her wishes were overthrown there was no spirit MP II 10 280 32
But though my uncle entered into my wishes with all the MP II 13 299 5
or be followed by warmer wishes and higher commendation, MP II 13 300 5
motives, in views and wishes more than could be told, that MP II 13 300 7
Thomas wishes to speak with you, ma'am, in his own room." MP III 1 324 60
heighten all his wishes, and confirm all his resolutions. MP III 2 326 3
their wishes, might be their surest means of forwarding it. MP III 2 330 14
Your feelings are as well known to me, as my wishes and MP III 2 330 16
and that in spite of her wishes and hints for a less MP III 6 372 21
My father wishes you to invite Susan to go with you, for a MP III 15 443 23
It was a match which Sir Thomas's wishes had even MP III 17 471 29
restrain any consequent wishes, she was soon welcome, and MP III 17 472 31
to the wishes of his own friendly and social disposition. E I 2 16 5
There were wishes at Randalls respecting Emma's destiny, E I 5 41 31
my wishes on the subject have been ever since I knew you. E I 9 73 20
He wishes his boys to be active and hardy; and if they E I 9 81 73
If she has fancied otherwise, her own wishes have misled E I 15 130 31
could be farther from my wishes--your attachment to my E I 15 131 34
"I do not know why you should say so. he wishes E I 18 145 7
"He will have everybody's wishes for his happiness." E II 3 174 33
You may guess how readily he came into my wishes; and E II 8 223 63
for him, but whether he wishes it; and I think he does. E II 8 226 79
Woodhouse, one naturally wishes them to see as much as E II 14 274 28
with all their wishes of giving Emma that distinction.-- E III 2 325 29
"If Mrs. Gilbert wishes to dance," said he, "I shall have E III 2 327 36
say of the good wishes which she really felt, took leave. E III 8 384 34
be done for Harriet; good wishes for the future were all E III 9 388 15
Had she followed Mr. Knightley's known wishes, in paying E III 12 421 17
the acquittal and good wishes of that said Emma Woodhouse, E III 14 439 8
Always deceived in fact by his own wishes, and regardless E III 15 445 15
could alter his wishes or his opinion on the subject. E III 15 449 32
But, in spite of these deficiencies, the wishes, the hopes, E III 19 484 12
All Anne's wishes had been for the latter. P III 2 14 9
felt obliged to oppose her dear Anne's known wishes. P III 2 14 11
at least, were her wishes on the side of early warm P III 4 30 9
as every captain wishes to get rid of, been six months on P III 6 51 30
in Mrs. Musgrove's kind wishes, as to her son, he had P III 8 67 28
even to the height of his wishes, in his prospect of soon P III 9 78 19
way, bore down all the wishes of her father and mother for P III 11 94 7
Vague wishes of getting Sarah thither, had occurred before P IV 1 122 3
would breathe my wishes that the name might never change." P IV 8 188 36
to the young people's wishes, and that their marriage was P IV 10 217 20
"Can you fail to have understood my wishes?-- P IV 11 237 42

WISHING (105)

& will join me in wishing that Frederica vernon may prove LS 14 265 5
by wishing with a laugh, that he might be really one soon. LS 20 278 10
interference;" said I, wishing to save her the explanation. LS 24 286 5
and looked as if half wishing and half fearing to be LS 25 292 2
the other no cause for wishing that he or she had bestowed NA I 10 77 33
to you at any rate for wishing us a pleasant walk after NA I 12 93 7
Eleanor, and she had been wishing ever since to see you, NA I 12 94 10
it, and very heartily wishing that it might be too NA I 14 115 55
I do not think any thing would justify me in wishing you NA II 3 146 20
She was almost as far from believing as from wishing it to NA II 3 148 29
however, prevented their wishing it otherwise; and, as NA II 5 154 1
positive conviction of his actually wishing their marriage. NA II 14 230 2
"I can allow for his wishing Catherine away, when he NA II 14 234 11
was not entirely mistaken in his object in wishing it. NA II 15 243 9
you cannot wonder at my wishing to avoid any encouragement SS I 4 21 15
the probability of wishing to throw ridicule on his age. SS I 8 37 3
I should scold her myself, if she were capable of wishing SS I 10 48 6
however, I can't help wishing they had not travelled quite SS I 19 107 29
hastily, and as if wishing to avoid any farther inquiry. SS II 4 160 5
"At any rate," said Elinor, wishing to prevent Mrs. SS II 5 167 4
was prevented even from wishing it removed, by her anxiety SS II 5 174 47
than Marianne, as if wishing to avoid her eye, and SS II 6 176 7
She had yet another reason for wishing her children to SS II 10 213 5
or of wishing to marry Miss Morton, or anything like it. SS III 2 273 16
her lips, was almost wishing to rouse her from so painful SS III 7 310 10
11
and yet in wishing it, to feel a pang for Willoughby. SS III 9 339 27
"I am not wishing him too much good," said Marianne at SS III 10 345 24
& of wishing for more attention than she bestowed. W 335 13
the Edwardes', as well as wishing to go home herself, she W 339 18
I knew you would be wishing me joy." PP I 6 27 52
and enough was said of wishing them to stay at least till PP I 12 59 2
and friends are all wishing him to marry elsewhere?" PP I 21 119 23
now take the liberty of wishing them health and happiness, PP I 22 124 10
lately as Mr. Collins was wishing to marry you. PP I 22 125 17
When I am in company with him, I will not be wishing. PP II 3 145 7
I do not at all comprehend her reason for wishing to be PP II 3 148 26
said not a word of wishing to see me again, and was in PP II 3 148 26
of bidding her adieu, wishing her every enjoyment, PP II 4 151 3
wishing to make her feel what she had lost in refusing him. PP II 5 155 4
all, of his wishing her to be acquainted with his sister. PP III 1 259 77
But Jane and Elizabeth, who agreed in wishing, for the PP III 8 314 22
I believed you to be wishing, expecting my addresses." PP III 16 369 26
to you without rather wishing to give you pain than not. PP III 18 380 3
My aunt is acting like a sensible woman in wishing for you. MP I 3 26 23
could never receive kindness without wishing to return it. MP I 3 26 29
own part I have been long wishing to wait upon your good MP I 6 62 58
his mother, "for wishing Fanny not to be of the party, but MP I 8 78 18
whom, good or bad, they were always wishing away." MP I 11 110 26
his attentions, and wishing him not to return; and a MP I 12 114 3
While waiting and wishing, looking now at the dancers and MP I 12 117 11
it is impossible to help wishing, that the news could have MP I 13 122 4
notice of her work and wishing she could work as well, and MP I 15 147 57
event, and without mercy wishing poor Sir Thomas had been MP II 1 176 4
Tom understood his father's thoughts, and heartily wishing MP II 1 183 24
And Sir Thomas's wishing just at first to be only with his MP II 3 199 14
an acknowledgment of her wishing very much to hear it, and MP II 4 206 5
I have been wishing it more than you can have any idea. MP II 13 298 2
She thought he was wishing to speak to her unheard by the MP II 13 306 27
decided feeling, that of wishing not to appear to think MP II 13 307 30
31
Here is a young man wishing to pay his addresses to you, MP III 1 315 27
wishing to marry at all so early is recommendatory to me. MP II 13 317 34
him at once, without wishing even for a little time to MP III 1 318 39
how very far he was from wishing to have his own MP III 1 323 57
newspaper, very sincerely wishing that dear little Fanny MP III 3 341 31
as from wishing him to have any serious thoughts of me. MP III 5 362 21
altering her ways; wishing to be an economist, without MP III 8 389 4
Crawford told me that you were wishing to hear from me, MP III 13 420 2
correspondent, the hope of every thing she was wishing for. MP III 14 436 16
over what was, and wishing for what could never be. MP III 17 461 3
She was humble and wishing to be forgiven, and Mr. Yates, MP III 17 462 4
into the drawing-room: wishing her joy--yet observing, E I 14 121 14
have been very earnestly wishing you success: but had I E I 15 131 34
Such an overthrow of every thing she had been wishing for!- E I 16 134 1
Emma saw his anxiety, and wishing to appease it, at least E II 3 171 14
15
return, and wishing to do more than she dared to confess. E II 4 184 11

have wished, had she deemed it possible enough for wishing. E II 16 291 5
in not wishing any thing to be attempted at present for me. E II 17 301 19
serious in wishing nothing to be done till the summer. E II 17 301 19
He was wishing to get the better of his attachment to E III 3 335 10
be cured of wishing that he would part with his black mare. E III 6 361 41
and solicitude--sincerely wishing that the circumstances E III 8 380 9
Mrs. Churchill, and only wishing him not to delay coming E III 8 383 31
I have no motive for wishing him ill--and for her sake, E III 13 428 21
He was wishing to confide in her--perhaps to consult her;-- E III 13 429 30
She was sure of Mrs. Weston's wishing it to be E III 15 444 2
I cannot comprehend a man's wishing to give a woman any E III 15 446 18
She had been decided in wishing for a Miss Weston. E III 17 461 1
handsome fortune, was wishing to settle in his own country, P III 3 21 18
of superiority from wishing for the possibility of P III 5 41 45
struck by it, or without wishing that other Elliots could P III 6 42 1
Miss Anne, I cannot help wishing Mrs. Charles had a little P III 6 44 8
I assure you, Miss Anne, it prevents my wishing to see P III 6 45 8
Was this like wishing to avoid her? P III 7 60 30
"It was what she had been thinking of, and wishing to be P III 12 114 63
appeared, in Mr. Elliot's wishing, after an interval of so P IV 3 140 11
not be so near without wishing to know that neither she P IV 3 143 18
herself, and not wishing to be answered, she added, "I P IV 4 150 18
admitted that his wishing to promote her father's getting P IV 4 151 22
Anne, far from wishing to cavil at the pleasure, replied, " P IV 5 155 10
references--wishing to form a separate establishment--you S 1 366 1
But very far from wishing their children to do the same, S 2 374 1
library, which Mr P. was anxiously wishing to support.-- S 2 374 1
I am sure we agree my dear, in wishing our boys to be as S 4 381 1
I was just upon the point of wishing you good evening. S 6 394 1
merit to his civility in wishing her to take his chair.-- S 10 414 1

WIT (40)

all the sense & all the wit of the conversation to herself; LS 19 274 3
which have only genius, wit, and taste to recommend them. NA I 5 37 4
the liveliest effusions of wit and humour are conveyed to NA I 5 38 4
people, who seldom aimed at wit of any kind; her father, NA I 9 65 31
observation, discernment, judgment, fire, genius, and wit." NA I 14 112 36
spent in a sort of war of wit, a display of family NA I 15 121 25
had certainly too much wit to let them Sue for detection. NA II 9 194 6
When is a man to be safe from such wit, if age and SS I 8 37 4
I abhor every common-place phrase by which wit is intended; SS I 9 45 30
Their attention and wit were drawn off to his more SS I 10 49 12
had never been used to find wit in the inattention of any SS I 19 107 27
Fanny, rejoicing in her escape, and proud of the ready wit SS II 14 253 26
He was recalled from wit to wisdom, not by any reproof of SS III 5 298 34
But I doubt whether ridicule,--has Penelope much wit?"-- W 318 2
deal to say & tho' with no wit himself, cd sometimes make W 359 28
sometimes make use of the wit of an absent friend; & had a W 359 28
convinced her that all was safe, her wit flowed long. PP I 6 27 54
at a compliment on her wit and vivacity; and though more PP I 17 88 14
I can describe; and your wit and vivacity I think must be PP I 19 106 10
It is such a spur to one's genius, such an opening for wit PP II 17 225 17
a beauty!--I should as soon call her mother a wit.' PP III 3 271 16
17
Never had his wit been directed in a manner so little PP III 15 363 19
The harp arrived, and rather added to her beauty, wit, and MP I 7 64 12
a bon-mot, for there is not the least wit in my nature. MP I 9 94 56
no curiosity touch, no wit amuse; or allowing the MP I 17 160 8
She was not to be won by all that gallantry and wit, and MP III 3 340 24
and with her little wit, is not very likely ever to have E I 8 61 38
They ready wit the word will soon supply, may its approval E I 9 71 14
Thy ready wit the word will soon supply E I 9 72 15
Humph--Harriet's ready wit! E I 9 72 15
a proof of love, with Mr. Elton's seeing ready wit in her. E I 10 83 6
What a strange thing love is! he can see ready wit in E I 13 111 13
To be sure, the charade, with its "ready wit"--but then, E I 16 134 4
It might be a very indifferent piece of wit; but Emma E III 7 371 35
I do not pretend to be a wit. E III 7 372 37
How could you be so insolent in your wit to a woman of her E III 7 374 56
Mr. Elton was so hot and tired, that all this wit seemed E III 16 457 37
Mr. Shepherd laughed, as he knew he must, at this wit, and P III 3 17 2
3
and bewitching in the wit which often expressed it, must P III 4 27 3
Lady Russell had little taste for wit; and of any thing P III 4 27 4

WITCH (1)

that quiz of a hat, it makes you look like an old witch? NA I 7 49 43

WITH-HELD (1)

it has not with-held him from being very useful to me. LS 5 250 1

WITHDRAW (6)

He has no business to withdraw the attention of my partner NA I 10 76 29
that you will not be able to withdraw your eyes from it. NA II 5 158 17
and was not sorry to withdraw; and to make you amends, MP I 13 123 5
luck; while she must withdraw with infinitely stronger MP III 17 464 12
it must be for her to withdraw her eyes, the astonishment P IV 7 179 28
of seeing Mr. Elliot withdraw; and no one of proper P IV 12 250 6

WITHDRAWING (4)

my dear madam, by thus withdrawing my pretensions to your PP I 20 114 32
had had the merit of withdrawing herself from it, and of MP III 17 466 18
She loved him; there was no withdrawing attentions, MP III 17 468 21
that there had been a withdrawing on the gentleman's side, P III 10 89 36

WITHDRAWN (12)

was never withdrawn from the stage during two whole scenes. NA I 12 92 4
as the gentleman had withdrawn, "I do not ask you what the SS III 4 285 1
other with astonishment, when their visitors had withdrawn. W 347 22
when the servants were withdrawn, he thought it time to PP I 14 66 1
his attentions had been withdrawn, her vanity would be PP II 18 233 25
But when they had withdrawn, he said to her, "Mrs. Bennet, PP III 8 310 9
reproachful; but on catching his were instantly withdrawn. MP II 7 244 31
Emma's eyes were instantly withdrawn; and she sat silently E III 11 407 32
All that were good would be withdrawn; and if to these E III 12 422 20
glance at her, instantly withdrawn, in the fear of giving E III 15 447 21
As her eyes fell on him, his seemed to be withdrawn from P IV 8 188 41
His application thus withdrawn, his sister could say no S 12 425 1

WITHDREW (12)

assuring her, when they withdrew to see the new hat, that NA I 7 50 44
return; and the others withdrew, after Eleanor had NA II 10 203 8
withdrew, still referring her to the letter for comfort. SS II 9 202 8
When the ladies withdrew to the drawing-room after dinner, SS II 12 233 19
third person, and Elinor withdrew to think it all over in SS III 9 339 27
withdrew from her sister and walked slowly up stairs. SS III 10 348 34
catching her eye, he withdrew his own and coldly said, " PP I 3 11 13
himself, Elizabeth withdrew to Miss Lucas; to whose PP I 18 96 56
and in silence withdrew; determined, if he persisted in PP I 19 109 22
With proper civilities the ladies then withdrew; all of PP I 22 124 11
In the evening soon after Mr. Bennet withdrew to the PP III 17 375 28
touched again when the ladies withdrew, with more success. MP II 10 272 4

WITHERED (2)

rocky fragment and the withered oak which he had placed NA I 14 111 29
the tawny leaves and withered hedges, and from repeating P III 10 84 7

WITHHELD (7)

Thorpe would have darted after her, but Morland withheld NA I 13 101 22
and he had been long withheld only by inferiority of NA II 16 251 5
Jane, who had only been withheld by the fear of giving PP I 7 33 43
one of Bingley's being withheld from seeing Jane, she felt PP II 2 142 16
young people are seldom withheld by immediate want of PP II 3 145 7
You have withheld the advantages, which you must know to PP II 11 192 21
because it was withheld, and determined him to have the MP III 2 326 2

WITHHOLD (4)

the street, could not withhold one glance at the drawing- NA I 12 91 3
Elinor could not withhold her credit; nor was she disposed SS I 12 61 14
her, at intervals, to withhold her pen, were proofs enough SS II 7 180 4
in the world to withhold my mite upon such an occasion. MP I 1 6 6

WITHHOLDING (1)

to, without actually withholding his consent, or saying it — P III 4 26 2

WITHSTAND (5)
as no attempt at grandeur or pathos can withstand. — NA II 14 232 7
withstand the melancholy influence of the word "last." — MP III 5 359 10
have been possible to withstand her father's ill-will, — P III 4 27 5
her husband could long withstand; and as none of the — P III 12 115 65
No one can withstand the charm of such a mystery. — P IV 8 187 33

WITHSTANDING (1)
She had not been withstanding them on selfish principles — NA I 13 101 25

WITHSTOOD (4)
and importunity of his wife too great to be withstood. — SS III 7 307 3
"To have resisted such attractions, to have withstood such — SS III 8 321 34
"My beauty you had early withstood, and as for my manners-- — PP III 18 380 3
A civil servant she had withstood; but when Dr. Grant — MP II 4 205 3

WITNESS (22)
deceit which must be pleasing to witness & detect. — LS 4 248 2
own observation can bear witness to her having received — NA II 9 197 25
Witness myself, at this present hour. — NA II 11 210 7
spite of all that had passed, was not prepared to witness. — SS II 3 155 6
constancy, could not witness the rapture of delightful — SS II 4 159 1
shocking as it was to witness it, must have its course, — SS II 7 182 12 13
Elinor could no longer witness this torrent of unresisted — SS II 7 185 20
Elinor could not hear the declaration, nor witness its — SS III 9 335 7
rank, she thought she could witness without trepidation. — PP II 6 161 9
I can summon more than one witness of undoubted veracity. — PP II 12 199 5
you have been a daily witness of; and altogether I trust — PP II 15 216 6
and that she had not to witness the continuance of such — MP I 18 164 1
to witness the first meeting of his father and his friend. — MP II 1 182 22
never have expected to witness; and to feel that it was in — MP II 1 185 27
can bear me witness, Fanny, that I have never been blinded. — MP II 9 270 38
have been gratified to witness, and that her own dress and — MP III 12 416 2
the family, and be a witness--but that he saw nothing--of — MP III 15 445 31
Witness this very time. — E II 18 311 46
The room at the crown was to witness it;--but it would be — E III 2 319 2
Composure with a witness! to look on, while repeated — E III 10 397 46
not without some degree of witness from Emma herself.-- — E III 11 410 35
as insensible, or to witness the hysterical agitations of — P III 12 110 43

WITNESSED (19)
which such buildings had witnessed, and such storms — NA II 6 166 9
of such an alteration as we have just witnessed in him. — SS I 15 79 29
with a smile, "from what I have witnessed this morning." — SS I 21 122 18
than it was, had she not witnessed that embarrassment — SS II 6 178 17
from himself--had she witnessed his distress, and been — SS III 11 349 2
as his friends had never witnessed in him before. — SS III 13 361 3
he had never in his life witnessed such behaviour in a — PP I 14 66 1
much distressed by the folly which he must have witnessed. — PP I 18 101 72
Miss Bennet was beyond what I had ever witnessed in him. — PP II 12 197 5
which she had yesterday witnessed, however temporary its — PP III 2 263 10
scene before her than ever that spot had yet witnessed. — MP III 5 357 6
After such behaviour, as I have witnessed during the last — E I 15 130 30
seen what\ she did, have witnessed their appearance — E III 3 335 9
Had you witnessed my behaviour there, I can hardly suppose — E III 14 441 8
band of true friends who witnessed the ceremony, were — E III 19 484 12
hall;--those rooms had witnessed former meetings which — P III 11 93 3
which the same spots had witnessed earlier in the morning. — P III 12 115 66
a dinner must betray, witnessed by those who had been — P IV 10 219 29
with such astonishment witnessed; and of the manner in — P IV 10 226 65

WITNESSES (3)
such witnesses he dared not say half what he really felt. — SS II 13 242 25
no interruption and no witnesses, unless the servants — MP II 6 233 15
have enlightened witnesses of the progress of his success. — MP III 2 331 19

WITNESSING (8)
about Reginald, from witnessing the very rapid increase of — LS 11 259 1
him opportunity of witnessing the excellencies of Marianne, — SS I 11 53 1
on first witnessing his altered behaviour in Derbyshire. — PP III 11 334 36
gratification in witnessing their success and enjoyment at — MP I 4 35 5
London, who hearing and witnessing a good deal to alarm — MP III 16 450 8
He would save himself from witnessing again such permitted, — E III 13 432 41
concern for what she must have suffered in witnessing it. — P IV 3 144 22
of human nature as they are in the habit of witnessing! — P IV 5 156 10

WITS (5)
old housekeeper out of her wits,--because I must go and — NA II 11 211 9
been forced to have your wits about you, with so much — NA II 14 234 12
I should have been frightened out of my wits, to have had — W 342 19
I am really frightened out of my wits with the number of — W 354 27
I am frightened out of my wits; and have such tremblings, — PP III 5 288 38

WITTICISMS (2)
were not so nice; their witticisms added pain to many a — SS I 16 85 11 12
in spite of all Miss Bingley's witticisms on fine eyes. — PP I 9 46 39

WITTIER (2)
Cole does not want to be wiser or wittier than his — E II 15 288 38
who wants to be wiser and wittier than all the world! — E II 15 288 39

WITTIEST (1)
its character as the wittiest letter in the alphabet had — SS I 21 125 36

WITTY (5)
was ever had said many witty things on the subject of — SS I 7 34 5
I am sorry, (with a witty smile) we have not been able to — W 350 24
a man without now and then stumbling on something witty." — PP II 17 226 17
a hasty or a witty word from herself about his manners. — E II 14 270 5
I am not one of those who have witty things at every — E III 7 372 37

WIVES (10)
business with the partners or wives of their neighbours." — NA I 10 76 29
of her own father, who had himself two wives, I know not. — SS I 11 56 11
must be referred to the imagination of husbands and wives. — SS III 13 366 20
of one of the officers' wives, and Elizabeth continued her — PP I 7 32 41
there are no husbands and wives in the case at present, I — E I 6 46 21
wives in the case at present indeed, as you observe. — E I 6 46 22
No husbands and wives," with so interesting a — E I 6 46 22
whatever you may chuse to say, do not want silly wives. — E I 8 64 47
Husbands and wives generally understand when opposition — P III 7 55 9
Pray, what would become of us poor sailors' wives, who — P III 8 69 43

WM. ELLIOT (1)
rest of my life, to be only yours "truly, "Wm. Elliot." — P IV 9 203 73

WO'NT (4)
Come, come, this wo'nt do, Colonel; so let us hear the — SS I 13 63 12
I hope, from the bottom of my heart, he wo'nt keep her — SS II 7 181 8
Come, come, this wo'nt do. — SS II 7 182 10
Fifty thousand pounds! and by all accounts it wo'nt come — SS II 8 194 10

WOE (4)
to censure those who "bear about the mockery of woe." — NA I 1 15 4
do!" would they often exclaim in the bitterness of woe. — PP II 18 229 2
I could not stand your countenance dressed up in woe and — MP I 14 133 11
aunt was in question;--and woe betide him, and her too, — P III 10 87 26

WOEFUL (2)
With woeful countenances they looked at each other. — MP III 6 373 23
her honest regret in this woeful change; but when they did — E II 12 263 42

WOES (1)
her to use her own fancy in the perusal of Matilda's woes. — NA II 5 160 23

WOKE (2)
"Yes, I have been reading it ever since I woke; and I am — NA I 6 39 5
minutes in bed, when they woke with a headach, without — MP I 9 87 15

WOMAN (477)
weak enough to suppose a woman who has behaved with — LS 3 247 1
What a woman she must be! — LS 4 248 2
indeed, & has the air of a woman of fashion, but her — LS 5 249 1
that I have seldom seen so lovely a woman as Lady Susan. — LS 6 251 1
which are now necessary to finish a pretty woman. — LS 7 253 1
drawing &c. will gain a woman some applause, but will not — LS 7 253 1
indeed provoked at the artifice of this unprincipled woman. — LS 8 255 1
His opinion of her I am sure, was as low as of any woman — LS 8 255 1
marriage, & that she was altogether a wonderful woman. — LS 8 255 2
of being captivated by a woman with whose principles he — LS 11 259 2
conversation of a clever woman for a short period, & of — LS 12 261 6
with so artful a woman as Lady Susan, to a young man of — LS 13 262 1
it) the conversation of a woman of high mental powers. — LS 14 263 2
attractions of another woman, the chance of being able to — LS 14 264 4
to do justice to the character of a very injured woman. — LS 14 265 4
Poor woman! tho' I have reasons enough for my dislike, I — LS 15 266 2
What can one say of such a woman, my dear mother?--such — LS 20 278 8
my resentment, but that woman is a fool indeed who while — LS 22 282 7
Silly woman, to expect constancy from so charming a man! — LS 26 296 5
for any other woman in the world, than her own mother. — LS 27 297 2
He has a right to require a woman of fortune in his — LS 30 300 2
Silly woman! what does she expect by such manoeuvres? — LS 33 303 1
in describing them to a woman who will glory in having — LS 34 304 2
of her due by a woman ten years older than herself. — LS 42 313 10
Her mother was a woman of useful plain sense, with a good — NA I 1 13 1
Mrs. Morland was a very good woman, and wished to see her — NA I 1 15 3
And that a young woman in love always looks -----" — NA I 1 16 9
his lady, a good-humoured woman, fond of Miss Morland, and — NA I 1 17 12
There goes a strange-looking woman! — NA I 2 23 21
is Isabella, my eldest; is not she a fine young woman? — NA I 4 32 3
well-meaning woman, and a very indulgent mother. — NA I 4 34 8
on the face of every woman they met; and Catherine, after — NA I 7 48 32
book, written by that woman they make such a fuss about, — NA I 7 49 38
is just the kind of young woman I could wish to see you — NA I 7 50 47
and pleasing-looking young woman, who leant on his arm, — NA I 8 53 3
Woman is fine for her own satisfaction alone. — NA I 10 74 22
No man will admire her the more, no woman will like her — NA I 10 74 22
the advantage of choice, woman only the power of refusal; — NA I 10 77 33
engagement between man and woman, formed for the advantage — NA I 10 77 33
for the support of the woman; the woman to make the home — NA I 10 77 35
support of the woman; the woman to make the home agreeable — NA I 10 77 35
I cannot be the only woman. — NA I 13 99 4
A woman especially, if she have the misfortune of knowing — NA I 14 111 28
to desire any thing more in woman than ignorance. — NA I 14 111 29
the woman; but she is by no means a simpleton in general." — NA I 14 113 39
unjust thing of any woman at all, or an unkind one of me." — NA I 14 114 48
There never was a young woman so beloved as you are by — NA II 1 136 46
of his present comfort the woman might be who had given — NA II 4 149 1
man's admiration of the woman he loves; it is the woman — NA II 4 151 12
he loves; it is the woman only who can make it a torment." — NA II 4 151 12
A woman in love with one man cannot flirt with another." — NA II 4 151 15
"Was she a very charming woman? — NA II 7 180 37
His cruelty to such a charming woman made him odious to — NA II 7 181 40
It represented a very lovely woman, with a mild and — NA II 9 191 3
The world, I believe, never saw a better woman. — NA II 9 196 23
I can never expect to know such another woman! — NA II 10 202 7
"Her mother is a very good sort of woman," was Catherine's — NA II 10 205 26
proudly! who found no woman good enough to be loved!" — NA II 10 206 30
Had he married a more amiable woman, he might have been — SS I 1 5 7
much the greater, and to a woman in Mrs. Dashwood's — SS I 1 6 9
death--a very comfortable fortune for any young woman." — SS I 2 10 14
a woman who had not either a great fortune or high rank." — SS I 4 21 15
danger attending any young woman who attempted to draw him — SS I 4 23 19
to inhabit or visit it while such a woman was its mistress. — SS I 4 24 20
five hundred a-year by a woman who never saved in her life, — SS I 6 29 5
a very cheerful agreeable woman, he hoped the young ladies — SS I 7 34 4
merry, fat, elderly woman, who talked a great deal, seemed — SS I 7 34 5
But if there should by any chance happen to be a woman who — SS I 8 38 9
"A woman of seven and twenty," said Marianne, after — SS I 8 38 10
In his marrying such a woman therefore there would be — SS I 8 38 10
"to convince you that a woman of seven and twenty could — SS I 8 38 11
and which was exactly calculated to carry a woman. — SS I 12 58 1
had actually made her own woman enquire of Mr. — SS I 13 67 65
"You are a good woman," he warmly replied. — SS I 14 74 19
husband of a very silly woman,--but she knew that this — SS I 20 112 28
philosophy of a well bred woman, contenting herself with — SS I 21 118 2
"What a sweet woman Lady Middleton is!" said Lucy Steele. — SS I 21 122 13
Then perhaps you cannot tell me what sort of a woman she — SS I 22 128 5
very capable of making a woman sincerely attached to him." — SS I 22 130 28
no fortune, and I fancy she is an exceeding proud woman." — SS I 22 132 39
But Mrs. Ferrars is a very headstrong proud woman, and in — SS II 2 148 15
alone could induce a woman to keep a man to an engagement, — SS II 2 151 41
I would have every young woman of your condition in life, — SS II 3 156 8
of woman, of whose kindness to you I can have no doubt. — SS II 3 156 8
heart, she is not a woman whose society can afford us — SS II 3 156 12
conversation with a very fashionable looking young woman. — SS II 6 176 3
saw a young woman so desperately in love in my life! — SS II 7 181 7 8
This woman of whom he writes--whoever she be--or any one, — SS II 7 189 50
"And yet this woman--who knows what her art may have been-- — SS II 7 190 58
The pity of such a woman as Lady Middleton! — SS II 7 191 64
care of a very respectable woman, residing in Dorsetshire, — SS II 9 208 28
would at once be a woman of elegance and fortune, to leave — SS II 10 215 14
I understand she is a woman of very good fortune. — SS II 11 222 9
a very good-natured woman, I am sure it would give her — SS II 11 224 24
"She seems a most valuable woman indeed.-- — SS II 11 226 42
which a conscientious woman would not disregard. — SS II 11 227 46
"Lady Middleton is really a most elegant woman! — SS II 11 228 53
Such a woman as I am sure Fanny will be glad to know. — SS II 11 228 53
And Mrs. Jennings too, an exceeding well-behaved woman, — SS II 11 228 53
even the former, even the woman with whom her sisters were — SS II 12 229 1
a little proud-looking woman of uncordial address, who met — SS II 12 229 3
Ferrars was a little, thin woman, upright, even to — SS II 12 232 14
ill nature. she was not a woman of many words: for, unlike — SS II 12 232 15
very trying to a young woman who has been a beauty, in the — SS II 12 236 43
Mrs. Ferrars is a charming woman, and so is your sister. — SS II 13 239 9
having escaped the company of a stupid old woman so long. — SS II 14 247 5
Edward will marry Lucy; he will marry a woman superior in — SS III 1 263 27
a very deserving young woman, but in the present case you — SS III 1 267 45
uncle's care, the son of a woman especially of such very — SS III 1 267 45
his mother's threats, for a woman who could not reward him. — SS III 1 268 46
Mr. Ferrars to give up a woman like Miss Morton, with — SS III 2 272 16
What an ill-natured woman his mother is, an't she? — SS III 2 275 22
deserving young woman--have I been rightly informed?-- — SS III 3 282 17
of a tete-a-tete with a woman, whom neither of the others — SS III 5 294 3
marry this young woman, I never will see him again.' — SS III 5 299 35
my circumstances by marrying a woman of fortune. — SS III 8 320 32
In the height of her morality, good woman! she offered to — SS III 8 323 40
woman in the world, and that I was using her infamously. — SS III 8 326 53
I was forced to play the happy lover to another woman!-- — SS III 8 327 55
which is delightful in a woman one loves, she opened the — SS III 8 328 61
has married a woman of a less amiable temper than yourself. — SS III 11 351 13
formed his misery, from a woman whom he had long ceased to — SS III 13 361 3
Morton he would have a woman of higher rank and larger — SS III 14 373 3
his marriage with a woman of character, as the source of — SS III 14 379 18
standard of perfection in woman;--and many a rising beauty — SS III 14 379 19
he is married to another woman, while I am still single.-- — W 316 2
Poverty is a great evil, but to a woman of education & — W 318 2
tho' a very friendly woman, had a reserved air, & a great — W 322 3
She was a very fine woman then--but like other people I — W 325 4
pleasant-looking little woman of 5 or 6 & 30, to a lady — W 330 11
it is a hard thing for a woman to stand against the — W 343 19
A woman never looks better than on horseback.--" — W 345 21
"But every woman may not have the inclination, or the — W 345 21
It was a new thing with him to wish to please a woman; it — W 346 21
ever felt what was due to a woman, in Emma's situation.-- — W 346 21
as Jane had been a woman of fortune, the preparations for — W 348 23
an old woman who threw herself away on an Irish captain.-- — W 349 24
A woman should never be trusted with money. — W 351 26
me with money, replied Emma, & I am a woman too.--" — W 351 26

I hope the old woman will smart for it." W 352 26
Mrs Blake is a nice little good-humoured woman, she & I W 358 28
When a woman has five grown up daughters, she ought to PP I 1 4 20
"In such cases, a woman has not often much beauty to think PP I 1 4 21
She was a woman of mean understanding, little information, PP I 1 5 34
She is a selfish, hypocritical woman, and I have no PP I 2 6 5
Your sisters are engaged, and there is not another woman PP I 3 11 9
five times as pretty as every other woman in the room. PP I 4 14 5
Lady Lucas was a very good kind of woman, not too clever PP I 5 18 2
The eldest of them, a sensible, intelligent young woman, PP I 5 18 2
If a woman conceals her affection with the same skill from PP I 6 21 2
In nine cases out of ten, a woman had better show more PP I 6 22 2
"But if a woman is partial to a man, and does not PP I 6 22 5
of fine eyes in the face of a pretty woman can bestow." PP I 6 27 48
The word is applied to many a woman who deserves it no PP I 8 39 46
a great deal in your idea of an accomplished woman." PP I 8 39 48
A woman must have a thorough knowledge of music, singing, PP I 8 39 50
"I never saw such a woman. PP I 8 40 54
"She seems a very pleasant young woman," said Bingley. PP I 9 44 30
had never been so bewitched by any woman as he was by her. PP I 10 52 52
Mrs. Bennet, "and I dare say she is a very agreeable woman. PP I 14 66 2
which marks the young woman of distinguished birth. PP I 14 67 7
never seen a more elegant woman; for she had not only PP I 15 74 13
Elizabeth was the happy woman by whom he finally seated PP I 16 76 4
being his patroness, she is an arrogant, conceited woman." PP I 16 83 57
Find such a woman as soon as you can, bring her to PP I 19 106 10
am the last woman in the world who would make you so.- PP I 19 107 14
charm that could make a woman wish for its continuance; PP I 22 122 2
as well as I do, that the woman who marries him, cannot PP II 1 135 13
and if he is attached to me, no other woman can secure it." PP II 1 136 22
woman, and a great favourite with all her Longbourn nieces. PP II 2 139 2
"Lady Catherine is a very respectable, sensible woman PP II 5 157 8
of woman whom one cannot regard with too much deference." PP II 5 157 9
"I do not mean to say that a woman may not be settled too PP II 9 179 22
eldest sister, to any other young woman in the country.-- PP II 12 197 5
This invaluable friend was a very young woman, and very PP II 18 230 11
the friendship of such a woman as Mrs. Forster, and the PP II 18 230 14
give, had married a woman whose weak understanding and PP II 19 236 1
The housekeeper came; a respectable-looking, elderly woman, PP III 1 246 5
genteel, agreeable-looking woman, whose endeavour to PP III 3 267 4
a design against a young woman of Lydia's connections, PP III 4 275 5
Wickham will never marry a woman without some money. PP III 5 283 8
charm of person and address that can captivate a woman." PP III 5 284 10
now, and you must go lower, because I am a married woman." PP III 9 317 9
any young woman of character, to love or confide in him. PP III 10 321 2
had been necessary to a woman whom he must abominate and PP III 10 326 3
affection for her, for a woman who had already refused him, PP III 10 326 3
such a weakness as a second proposal to the same woman? PP III 12 341 19
You will be a very happy woman." PP III 13 348 36
for conversation with a woman, who was now more than PP III 14 353 20
to be prevented by a young woman of inferior birth, of no PP III 14 355 43
The upstart pretensions of a young woman without family, PP III 14 356 50
I expected to find a more reasonable young woman. PP III 14 356 60
"She is a very fine-looking woman! and her calling here PP III 14 359 76
Mr. Darcy, who never looks at any woman but to see a PP III 15 363 18
my pretensions to please a woman worthy of being pleased." PP III 16 369 24
amiable, well informed woman for the rest of her life; PP III 19 385 1
began to comprehend that a woman may take liberties with PP III 19 388 11
Lady Bertram, who was a woman of very tranquil feelings, MP I 1 4 1
you know I am a woman of few words and professions. MP I 1 6 6
Poor woman! she probably thought change of air might agree MP I 1 11 19
She was a woman who spent her days in sitting nicely MP I 2 19 31
My aunt is acting like a sensible woman in wishing for you. MP I 3 26 23
horses of his own, but not one that would carry a woman. MP I 4 37 8
habits of a young woman who had been mostly used to London. MP I 4 41 15
a young man and woman of very prepossessing appearance. MP I 4 41 17
a warm-hearted, unreserved woman, Mary had not been three MP I 4 42 17
They were too handsome themselves to dislike any woman for MP I 5 44 1
An engaged woman is always more agreeable than a MP I 5 45 12
so; a talking pretty young woman like Miss Crawford, is MP I 5 47 26
She has the age and sense of a woman, but the outs and not MP I 5 49 31
A young woman, pretty, lively, with a harp as elegant as MP I 7 65 13
civil, prosing, pompous woman, who thought nothing of MP I 8 75 2
She has done no more than what every young woman would do; MP I 11 108 12
or intimate friend of the woman he is really thinking of, MP I 12 116 10
he is really thinking of, more than the woman herself. MP I 12 116 10
poor woman! must want a lover as much as any one of them. MP I 12 119 22
old woman, who knows no more of whist than of algebra. MP I 12 119 26
to be expressed by any woman of modesty, that she could MP I 14 137 23
am not the only young woman you find, who thinks it very MP I 15 140 12
eyes, and you will be a very proper, little old woman." MP I 15 146 52
You must try not to mind growing up into a pretty woman." MP II 3 198 8
For so young a woman it is remarkable! MP II 3 198 13
A well-disposed young woman, who did not marry for love, MP II 3 201 22
for the fortunate young woman whom her dear son had MP II 3 202 28
Becoming as she then did, the only young woman in the MP II 4 205 1
against common sense, that a woman could be plagued with. MP II 4 212 30
"A woman can never be too fine while she is all in white. MP II 5 222 44
"there, I will stake my last like a woman of spirit. MP II 7 242 25
as a sister, was careless as a woman and a friend. MP II 8 260 24
every woman who plays herself is sure to ask about another. MP II 11 288 28
She is exactly the woman to do away every prejudice of MP II 12 293 10
such a woman as he thinks does not exist in the world. MP II 12 293 10
They will now see what sort of woman it is that can attach MP II 12 297 33
as a well-judging your woman could permit herself to give. MP III 1 315 18
He, indeed, I have lately thought has seen the woman he MP III 1 317 34
friendly, from the woman whom, two moments before, he had MP III 3 334 1
gone on himself with any woman breathing, without MP III 3 336 7
of a woman, which I have always believed you born for." MP III 4 347 18
to such a creature--to a woman, who firm as a rock in her MP III 4 351 32
not rather fixed on some woman of distinction, or fortune. MP III 4 351 36
and exertion, "that every woman must have felt the MP III 4 353 45
be acceptable to every woman he may happen to like himself. MP III 4 353 45
if they can imagine a woman so very soon capable of MP III 4 353 45
and wants a young woman, a beautiful young woman of five- MP III 5 361 16
young woman of five-and-twenty, to be as steady as himself. MP III 5 361 16
that he never was to any woman before; that he loves you MP III 5 363 24
If any man ever loved a woman for ever, I think Henry will MP III 5 363 24
see him again till he were the husband of some other woman. MP III 5 365 35
woman, all her life, for the experiment he had devised. MP III 6 369 10
that she was grown into a woman, and he supposed would be MP III 7 380 22
She might have made just as good a woman of consequence as MP III 8 390 5
There may be some old woman at Thornton Lacey to be MP III 9 394 1
The woman who could speak of him, and speak only of his MP III 12 417 4
She is a cold-hearted, vain woman, who has married MP III 13 421 2
She is the only woman in the world whom I could ever think MP III 13 421 2
'The only woman in the world, whom he could ever think of MP III 13 424 4
attached to any one woman in the world, and shame him from MP III 15 438 5
A little flogging for man and woman too, would be the best MP III 15 440 13
bad; and if there was a woman of character in existence, MP III 15 441 19
she could believe Miss Crawford to be the woman! MP III 15 441 19
A woman married only six months ago, a man professing MP III 15 441 20
it as he must be from the woman, whom he had been pursuing MP III 16 452 15
in being drawn on by a woman whom he had never cared for, MP III 16 454 18
do what must lose him the woman he adored; but still more MP III 16 454 18
To hear the woman whom--no harsher name than folly given!-- MP III 16 454 18
For where, Fanny, shall we find a woman whom nature had so MP III 16 455 18
'He has thrown away,' said she, 'such a woman as he will MP III 16 455 21
meeting with any other woman who could--it was too MP III 16 460 31
had there been no young woman in question, had there been MP III 17 465 13
to be thrown off by the woman whose smiles had been so MP III 17 467 20
and so lost the woman whom he had rationally, as well as MP III 17 468 22

meet with such another woman, before it began to strike MP III 17 470 25
a very different kind of woman might not do just as well-- MP III 17 470 25
Let no one presume to give the feelings of a young woman MP III 17 471 28
supplied by an excellent woman as governess, who had E I 1 5 2
and a rational unaffected woman, like Miss Taylor, may be E I 1 13 44
for--enough to marry a woman as portionless even as Miss E I 2 16 5
and truly amiable woman could be, and must give him the E I 2 17 6
The aunt was a capricious woman, and governed her husband E I 2 17 7
She felt herself a most fortunate woman; and she had lived E I 2 18 10
for a woman neither young, handsome, rich, nor married. E I 3 21 4
And yet she was a happy woman, and a woman whom no one E I 3 21 4
She was a plain, motherly kind of woman, who had worked E I 3 22 5
with a good sort of young woman in the same rank as his E I 4 30 18
But if he marries a very ignorant, vulgar woman, certainly E I 4 31 25
man, a young man whom any woman not fastidious might like. E I 4 35 45
judge of the comfort a woman feels in the society of one E I 5 36 6
She is not the superior young woman which Emma's friend E I 5 36 6
it is not the style of a woman; no, certainly, it is too E I 7 51 5
is too strong and concise; not diffuse enough for a woman. E I 7 51 5
rule, Harriet, that if a woman doubts as to whether she E I 7 52 18 19

A woman is not to marry a man merely because she is asked, E I 7 54 31
but in good hands she will turn out a valuable woman." E I 8 58 10
a man that a woman should ever refuse an offer of marriage. E I 8 60 33
A man always imagines a woman to be ready for anybody who E I 8 60 33
He has too much real feeling to address any woman on the E I 8 63 42
and such temper, the highest claims a woman could possess." E I 8 63 44
Were you, yourself, ever to marry, she is the very woman E I 8 64 46
but she only knew that any woman whom Mr. Elton could E I 8 68 58
should think the luckiest woman in the world; for, beyond E I 8 68 58
he bends a slave, and woman, lovely woman, reigns, alone. E I 9 71 14
Can it be woman? E I 9 72 17
And woman, lovely woman, reigns alone. E I 9 72 17
Lord of the earth and sea, he bends a slave, and woman, E I 9 73 18
he bends a slave, and woman, lovely woman, reigns alone. E I 9 73 18
This is an attachment which a woman may well feel pride in E I 9 74 20
and especially any thing that pays woman a compliment. E I 9 77 45
'Woman, lovely woman.' E I 9 78 52
"Dear me!--it is so odd to hear a woman talk so!"-- E I 10 84 14
A single woman, with a very narrow income, must be a E I 10 85 19
and girls; but a single woman, of good fortune, is always E I 10 85 19
Mrs. John Knightley was a pretty, elegant little woman, of E I 11 92 4
She was not a woman of strong understanding or any E I 11 92 4
but as the most fortunate woman in the world; and as to E I 11 95 19
and by not being a pretty young woman and a spoiled child. E I 12 99 10
Little Emma, grow up a better woman than your aunt. E I 12 99 11
cook at south end, a young woman hired for the time, who E I 12 104 50
She is an odd woman!-- E I 14 120 13
and is a very odd-tempered woman; and his coming now, E I 14 121 16
A young woman, if she fall into bad hands, may be teazed, E I 14 122 22
They hardly can satisfy a woman of her good sense and E I 18 149 26
not be unseen by the young woman, nor could her higher E II 2 165 7
really accomplished young woman, which she wanted to be E II 2 166 11
Miss Hawkins,--I dare say, an excellent young woman. E II 3 175 39
by the house where a young woman was making up a gown for E II 3 177 52
away--he had gained a woman of 10,000l. or thereabouts; E II 4 181 4
tolerably well-looking woman of a certain age; I did not E II 5 192 30
that I was to find a pretty young woman in Mrs. Weston." E II 5 192 30
that you have spoken of her as a pretty young woman." E II 5 192 31
said Emma, "she is a very elegant young woman." E II 5 194 42
recollecting that an old woman who had nursed him was E II 6 197 3
man, and Mrs. Campbell a friendly, warm-hearted woman. E II 6 201 20
and in love with another woman--engaged to her--on the E II 6 201 28
yet never ask that other woman to sit down to the E II 6 201 28
If it were to be shared with the woman he loved, he could E II 6 204 42
transgressed the duty of woman by woman, in betraying her E II 9 231 2
the duty of woman by woman, in betraying her suspicions of E II 9 231 2
with his tray, a tidy old woman travelling homewards from E II 9 233 24
like a sweet-tempered woman and a good wife, had examined E II 11 255 59
She is a woman that one may, that one must laugh at; but E II 12 260 27
She was almost sure that for a young woman, a stranger, a E II 14 270 4
The woman was better off; she might have the assistance of E II 14 271 5
same room at once with the woman he had just married, the E II 14 271 5
he had just married, the woman he had wanted to marry, and E II 14 271 5
wanted to marry, and the woman whom he had been expected E II 14 271 5
"Oh! yes--very--a very pleasing young woman." E II 14 271 8
not every man's fate to marry the woman who loves him best. E II 14 271 14
She does seem a charming young woman, just what he E II 14 272 15
that Mrs. Elton was a vain woman, extremely well satisfied E II 14 272 16
that a married woman has many things to call her attention. E II 14 277 40
would make them the safest model for any young woman." E II 14 278 47
"Insufferable woman!" was her immediate exclamation. E II 14 279 52
on having brought such a woman to Highbury, as not even E II 15 281 2
affable, delightful woman--just as accomplished and E II 15 284 12
Such a woman as Jane Fairfax probably never fell in Mrs. E II 15 287 23
charming young woman--but not even Jane Fairfax is perfect. E II 15 288 36
A woman with fewer resources than I have, need not have E II 16 290 2
I always say a woman cannot have too many resources--and I E II 18 307 21
any man of sense and taste to such a woman as Mrs. Elton. E III 2 331 55
headed by a stout woman and a great boy, all clamorous, E III 3 333 6
The terror which the woman and boy had been creating in E III 3 334 7
man and a lovely young woman thrown together in such a way, E III 3 334 9
And she is a good-natured woman after all. E III 6 353 4
"No,"--he calmly replied,--"there is but one married woman E III 6 354 15
of necessary; for, let a woman have ever so many resources, E III 6 356 26
How could you be so insolent in your wit to a woman of her E III 7 374 56
Were she a woman of fortune, I would leave every harmless E III 7 375 61
I suppose, as no young woman before ever met with on first E III 8 379 8
"To a Mrs. Smallridge--charming woman--most superior--to E III 8 380 13
Mrs. Smallridge, a most delightful woman!-- E III 8 382 23
Goldsmith tells us, that when lovely woman stoops to folly, E III 9 387 12
and said, "Ah! poor woman, who would have thought it!" and E III 9 388 13
distinguish any one young woman with persevering attention, E III 10 396 44
to another woman, before her face, and not resent it.-- E III 10 397 46
"If a woman can ever be excused for thinking only of E III 10 400 66
him attached to another woman at the very time that I was-- E III 11 404 11
intentionally give any woman the idea of his feelings for E III 11 411 40 41

And is he to be rewarded with that sweet young woman?-- E III 13 426 16
for a woman to feel in confessing exactly the reverse.-- E III 13 426 17
With such a woman he has a chance.-- E III 13 428 21
of the love of such a woman--the disinterested love, for E III 13 428 23
A man would always wish to give a woman a better home than E III 13 428 23
He meets with a young woman at a watering-place, gains her E III 13 428 23
it as no other woman in England would have borne it.-- E III 13 430 37
in his brother's house; woman wore too amiable a form in E III 13 432 41
me the idea of a young woman likely to be attached; and E III 14 438 8
hasty engagement she had entered into with that woman----- E III 14 440 8
particularity to another woman, was she to be consenting E III 14 441 8
been impossible for any woman of sense to endure, she E III 14 441 8
against the share of it which that woman has known.-- E III 14 441 8
I cannot comprehend a man's wishing to give a woman any E III 15 446 18
Knightley used even to the woman he was in love with, how E III 15 448 31
young woman might think him rather cool in her praise. E III 17 464 19
Lady Elliot had been an excellent woman, sensible and P III 1 4 6
a sensible, deserving woman, who had been brought, by P III 1 5 6
discontented when a woman does marry again, than when she P III 1 5 8
It sometimes happens, that a woman is handsomer at twenty- P III 1 6 11
by uniting himself to a rich woman of inferior birth. P III 1 8 15
She was a woman rather of sound than of quick abilities, P III 2 11 2
She was a benevolent, charitable, good woman, and capable P III 2 11 2
She was a clever young woman, who understood the art of P III 2 15 15

yet have been a happier woman in maintaining the P III 4 29 8
If Mrs. Clay were a very beautiful woman, I grant you, it P III 5 35 14
improved him; and that a woman of real understanding might P III 6 43 5
her, and had never seen a woman since whom he thought her P III 7 61 37
young woman who came in his way, excepting Anne Elliot. P III 7 61 38
seriously described the woman he should wish to meet with. P III 7 62 40
"This is the woman I want, said he. P III 7 62 41
with your husband; and were the only woman on board." P III 8 69 38
any reasonable woman may be perfectly happy in one of them; P III 8 70 54
I do not think any young woman has a right to make a P III 9 76 13
in a well-meaning young woman, and a heart to sympathize P III 9 77 18
man to be more attached to woman than poor benwick had P III 11 96 12
I have always heard of Lady Russell, as a woman of the P III 12 103 4
a wish that such another woman were at Uppercross, before P III 12 103 5
at the possibility of that woman, who had been mistress of P IV 3 138 5
She was certainly not a woman of family, but well educated, P IV 3 139 9
moreover, assured of her having been a very fine woman. P IV 3 139 9
A very fine woman, with a large fortune, in love with him! P IV 3 139 9
of her as "a most charming woman, quite worthy of being P IV 3 141 13
she was said to be an excessively pretty woman, beautiful. P IV 3 141 13
hardly one woman in a thousand could stand the test of. P IV 3 142 13
Lady Russell had heard her spoken of as a charming woman. P IV 4 149 12
Lady Dalrymple had acquired the name of "a charming woman," P IV 4 150 14
than almost any other woman I know; but will it answer? P IV 4 150 17
to the elegant little woman of seven and twenty, with P IV 5 153 6
She is a shrewd, intelligent, sensible woman. P IV 5 155 9
expensive, fashionable woman, I believe--and of course P IV 5 156 13
He thought her a most extraordinary young woman; in her P IV 5 159 21
She was persuaded that any tolerably pleasing young woman P IV 6 167 19
The conclusion of the whole was, that if the woman who had P IV 6 167 21
I do not feel comfortable if I have not a woman there. P IV 6 169 27
from such a devotion of the heart to such a woman!-- P IV 8 183 10
accomplished for modesty to be natural in any other woman." P IV 8 187 28
Elliot has sense to understand the value of such a woman. P IV 9 196 32
"Did you observe the woman who opened the door to you, P IV 9 197 38
You must allow for an injured, angry woman. P IV 9 199 55
"But was not she a very low woman?" P IV 9 202 65
She was a fine woman, had had a decent education, was P IV 9 202 66
insinuating, handsome woman, poor and plausible, and P IV 9 206 88
by the influence of the woman he loved, and she had been P IV 9 210 99
with such a woman as you, it was not absolutely hopeless. P IV 9 211 101
"It would not be the nature of any woman who truly loved." P IV 11 232 18
Man is more robust than woman, but he is not longer-lived; P IV 11 233 23
No man and woman would, probably. P IV 11 234 27
true attachment and constancy were known only by woman. P IV 11 235 32
I mean, while the woman you love lives, and lives for you. P IV 11 235 32
"Dare not say that man forgets sooner than woman, that " P IV 11 237 42
in his estimation the woman he had lost, and there begun P IV 11 242 63
It is something for a woman to be assured, in her eight- P IV 11 243 68
But she was a very good woman, and if her second object P IV 12 249 4
himself from being cut out by one artful woman, at least. P IV 12 250 7
amiable, sweet tempered woman, the properest wife in the S 2 372 1
a very pleasing young woman of two and twenty, the eldest S 2 374 1
But she is a goodnatured woman, a very goodnatured woman,-- S 3 376 1
a fine healthy frame for a woman of 70, & enters into the S 3 376 1
With due exceptions--woman feels for woman very promptly & S 3 378 1
about with it, and fancy herself quite a little woman.-- S 4 381 1
beheld a more lovely, or more interesting young woman.-- S 6 391 1
I am not a woman of parade, as all the world knows, & if S 6 393 1
Miss D. was a fine young woman, but cold & reserved, S 7 394 1
of woman.-- "Oh! woman in our hours of ease--" S 7 397 1
The man who cannot do justice to the attributes of woman S 7 397 1
we were speaking of--"Oh! woman in our hours of ease"--. S 7 397 1
His soul was the altar in which lovely woman sat enshrined, S 7 397 1
sentiment)--nor can any woman be a fair judge of what a S 7 398 1
I am not the woman to help any body blindfold.-- S 7 399 1
good deal for a woman to say that has been married twice.-- S 7 399 1
sure of getting a woman of fortune, if he chuses it."-- S 7 400 1
determined pursuit of woman in defiance of every S 8 404 1
Miss Heywood, or any other young woman with any S 8 405 2
One sees clearly enough by all this, the sort of woman Mrs S 9 409 1
That good woman (I do not know her name) not being so S 9 411 1
to have a fine young woman next to him, requiring in S 10 415 1
Mrs G. was a very well-behaved, genteel kind of woman, who S 11 420 1
I almost promised the poor woman yesterday to get S 12 423 1
There is a poor woman in Worcestershire, whom some friends S 12 424 1

WOMAN'S (31)

spot of this unfortunate woman's confinement--might have NA II 8 188 17
I call Charles most capable of engaging any woman's heart. PP I 21 118 14
be able to procure any woman's opinion, because he was not PP I 22 125 15
as capable as any other woman's of superior execution." PP II 8 175 25
up Chamberlayne in woman's clothes, on purpose to pass for PP II 16 221 17
What a difference in the weight of a woman's arm from that MP I 9 94 59
Not a tolerable woman's part in the play----- MP I 14 131 3
The enthusiasm of a woman's love is even beyond the MP II 9 265 19
essential a part of every woman's worth in the judgment of MP II 12 294 16
writing for that stupid woman's service, and all this with MP II 12 296 31
that it is every young woman's duty to accept such a very MP III 2 333 26
Oh, I am sure it is not in woman's nature to refuse such a MP III 5 363 22
"I cannot think well of a man who sports with any woman's MP III 5 363 23
conquest of one amiable woman's affections, could he have MP III 17 467 19
woman's friendship and woman's feelings would not justify. E I 8 67 56
He may be sure of every woman's approbation while he E I 9 82 82
Woman's usual occupations of eye and hand and mind will be E I 10 85 21
is more like a young woman's scheme than an elderly man's. E II 8 217 29
no limits to the licentiousness of that woman's tongue!" E II 15 284 10
It is like a woman's writing." E II 16 297 50
on the difference of woman's destiny, and quite E III 8 384 32 33
which only woman's language can make interesting.-- E III 18 472 20
observing that every woman's eye was upon him; every P IV 3 142 13
him; every woman's eye was sure to be upon Colonel Wallis." P IV 3 142 13
When one lives in the world, a man or woman's marrying for P IV 9 201 64
I will not allow it to be more man's nature than woman's P IV 11 233 22
voice) "if woman's feelings were to be added to all this." P IV 11 233 23
which had not something to say upon woman's inconstancy. P IV 11 234 27
Songs and proverbs, all talk of woman's fickleness. P IV 11 234 27
strong sense of duty is no bad part of a woman's portion." P IV 11 246 80
see the strong spark of woman's Captivations elicit such S 8 403 1

WOMANISH (1)

of something white & Womanish in the field on the other S 12 426 1

WOMANLY (3)

figure was formed, and her appearance womanly and graceful. PP III 2 261 4
duets, and grow tall and womanly; and their father saw MP I 2 20 33
from the worst of all her womanly follies--her wilful E III 17 463 15

WOMEN (118)

Those women are inexcusable who forget what is due to LS 16 269 3
among women is faultless, except in three particulars." NA I 3 27 30
"I should no more lay it down as a general rule that women NA I 3 28 34
Talk of the curiosity of women, indeed!--'tis nothing. NA I 8 57 18
You women are always thinking of men's being in liquor. NA I 9 63 20
Young men and women driving about the country in open NA I 13 104 31
if they do--for they read nearly as many as women. NA I 14 107 11
nothing, and hardly any women at all--it is very tiresome: NA I 14 108 22
Perhaps the abilities of women are neither sound nor acute- NA I 14 112 36
and a great brute in your opinion of women in general. NA I 14 113 40
that you think very highly of the understanding of women." NA I 14 113 44
understanding of all the women in the world--especially of NA I 14 113 45
think more highly of the understanding of women than I do. NA I 14 114 47
what on earth can four women want for more than that?-- SS I 2 12 24
of being approved by such women as Lady Middleton and Mrs. SS I 10 50 17
such kind of women as Fanny would like to associate with. SS II 11 228 53
found her one of the most charming women in the world! SS II 12 229 1
They are both delightful women indeed---? SS II 13 239 9
They are such charming women!-- SS II 13 240 15
pleased with any young women in her life, as she was with SS II 14 254 28
she had asked these young women to her house; merely SS III 1 266 36
declared herself, one of the happiest women in the world. SS III 9 335 7
seen so little of other women, that I could make no SS III 13 362 5
Mrs. Ferrars was the most unfortunate of women--poor Fanny SS III 13 371 38
of the most fortunate young women in the world, as it is. SS III 14 375 9
some circumstances which even women cannot controul.-- W 346 21
to the less national, & important demands of the women.-- W 356 28
His sisters were fine women, with an air of decided PP I 3 10 5
handsome! and his sisters are charming women. PP I 3 13 18
But they are very pleasing women when you converse with PP I 4 15 10
women in the room, and which he thought the prettiest? PP I 5 19 7
between two women can never end without a quarrel. PP I 7 30 17
surprised at your knowing only six accomplished women. PP I 8 39 52
that they knew many women who answered this description, PP I 8 40 55
where I assure you there are many amiable young women. PP I 19 106 10
for well-educated young women of small fortune, and PP I 22 122 3
Women fancy admiration means more than it does." PP II 1 136 14
Lady Catherine was a tall, large women, with strongly- PP II 6 162 11
of the very few sensible women who would have accepted him, PP II 9 178 15
"Unless where they like women of fortune, which I think PP II 10 183 13
the idea of two young women travelling post by themselves. PP II 14 211 13
Young women should always be properly guarded and attended, PP II 14 211 13
The officers will find women better worth their notice. PP II 18 232 20
her as one of the handsomest women of my acquaintance." PP III 3 271 18
But you know married women have never much time for PP III 11 330 6
You were disgusted with the women who were always speaking PP III 18 380 5
in the world, as there are pretty women to deserve them. MP I 1 3 1
mothers, (very clever women,) as well as my dear aunt and MP I 4 42 21
while they were the finest young women in the country. MP I 5 44 1
for men and women, her talents for the light and lively. MP I 8 81 31
ever come when men and women might lie another ten minutes MP I 9 87 15
"Yes, his manners to women are such as must please. MP I 12 116 8
families, and by so many women of the first consideration; MP I 13 128 38
but every character first-rate, and three principal women. MP I 14 130 3
"Here are not women enough. MP I 14 133 9
"But what do you do for women?" said Edmund gravely, and MP I 15 139 7
of notice and praise as other women were of neglect. MP II 3 198 13
This is only because there were no tall women to compare MP II 6 230 6
Mrs. Brown, and the other women, at the Commissioner's, at MP II 6 235 19
To be placed above so many elegant young women! MP II 10 275 12
would be the happiest of women, and that even when you MP II 12 296 29
have expressed towards her cousins and fifty other women. MP II 13 306 26
modern days, even in young women, and which in young women MP III 1 318 39
women, and which in young women is offensive and MP III 1 318 39
And, and--we think very differently of the nature of women, MP III 4 353 45
will not do for a man who has been used to sensible women. MP III 4 355 54
But were I to attempt to tell you of all the women whom I MP III 5 362 16
of the general nature of women, which would lead her to MP III 6 367 6
The men appeared to her all coarse, the women all pert, MP III 9 395 3
prosings of three such women made her feel that every E I 3 22 6
"I have none of the usual inducements of women to marry. E I 10 84 15
I believe few married women are half as much mistress of E I 10 84 15
As to men and women, our opinions are sometimes very E I 12 98 3
your estimate of men and women, and as little under the E I 12 98 4
waste of time--tiresome women--and all the horror of being E II 1 155 3
evening by two such young women; sometimes with music and E II 3 170 2
we have been children and women together; and it is E II 6 203 39
And Jane Fairfax, too, of all women!" E II 8 224 68
will have their little nonsenses and needless cares." E II 11 253 43
men and women; and Mrs. Weston must not speak of it again. E II 11 254 45
in practice; for married women, you know--there is a sad E II 14 277 38
expect, we married women must begin to exert ourselves!-- E II 18 305 6
I always stand up for women--and I assure you, if you knew E II 18 306 12
Married women, you know, may be safely authorized. E III 6 354 14
parties--young ladies-- married women-----" E III 7 370 20
It is only by seeing women in their own homes, among their E III 7 372 40
men and women, I cannot imagine them to be very frequent. E III 7 373 44
and accomplished young women in England for your daughter." E III 10 400 68
as these, was one of the happiest women in the world. E III 17 468 32
Few women could think more of their personal appearance P III 1 4 5
who has had no society among women to make him nice?" P III 7 62 39
the accommodations on board, such as women ought to have. P III 8 68 35
in rating the claims of women to every personal comfort P III 8 69 35
I hate to hear of women on board, or to see them on board; P III 8 69 35
Women may be as comfortable on board, as in the best house P III 8 69 37
I believe I have lived as much on board as most women, and P III 8 69 37
Such a number of women and children have no right to be P III 8 69 42
women were all fine ladies, instead of rational creatures. P III 8 70 45
years of my marriage; though many women have done more. P III 8 70 52
especially the attention of all the young women could do. P III 8 71 57
accepting must be the word) of two young women at once. P III 10 82 1
couple of steady, sensible women, whose judgments had to P IV 1 126 21
The worst of Bath was, the number of its plain women. P IV 3 141 13
He did not mean to say that there were no pretty women, P IV 3 141 13
had counted eighty-seven women go by, one after another, P IV 3 141 13
dreadful multitude of ugly women in Bath; and as for the P IV 3 142 13
It was evident how little the women were used to the sight P IV 3 142 13
Women of that class have great opportunities, and if they P IV 5 155 10
make shelter desirable for women, and quite enough to make P IV 7 174 2
Till it does come, you know, we women never mean to have P IV 9 195 30
Morning visits are never fair by women at her time of life, P IV 10 215 16
field, men, women, women & children--not very far off.-- S 1 364 1
Shepherd lives at one end, & three old women at the other." S 1 366 1
genteel looking young women followed by as many maid S 1 370 1
Women are the only correspondents to be depended on.-- S 5 385 1
are such excellent useful women & have so much energy of S 5 385 1
I told you my sisters were excellent women, miss h----." S 5 388 1
Washer-women & bathing women, that Mrs G. would have S 10 414 1

WOMEN'S (3)

was not fond of women's company, & he never danced.-- W 329 10
in the masterly manner which I see so many women's do. PP II 8 175 25
than other women's, though I was the object of them. MP II 12 297 33

WON (10)

But he had won 4 rubbers out of 5, & everything went well. W 336 14
lost and the fish she had won, and Mr. Collins, in PP I 16 84 59
not more than might be won in the course of the evening. PP I 18 89 1
fish he won, and apologising if he thought he won too many. PP II 6 166 41
She was not to be won by all that gallantry and wit, and MP III 3 340 24
at least, she would not be won by them nearly so soon, MP III 3 340 24
It is not by equality of merit that you can be won. MP III 3 344 41
Between us, I think we should have won you. MP III 4 348 21
had been won by her usefulness when they were in distress. P IV 10 220 31
If she could not be won by affection, he must carry her S 8 405 2

WON'T (16)

said Charlotte, "when he is in Parliament!--won't it? SS I 20 113 35
He declares he won't. SS I 20 113 35
Sometimes he won't speak to me for half a day together, SS I 20 113 39
"You are very good, I hope it won't hurt your eyes--will SS II 1 144 13
I won't disturb her any longer, for she had better have SS II 8 192 3
But that won't do, now-a-days; nothing in the way of SS II 8 194 10
"Aye, aye; that is very pretty talking--but it won't do-- SS II 10 218 27
I suppose Lady Middleton won't ask us any more this bout. SS III 2 276 25
hope Mrs. Jennings won't think it too much trouble to give SS III 2 277 30
It won't do.-- SS III 8 324 45
our balls--but Mr Curtis won't often spare him, & just now W 321 2
Won't he Miss Edwards?"-- W 340 18
of getting you home; besides it won't do to be too nice.-- W 341 19
He says his head won't bear whist--but perhaps if we make W 354 28

"By Jove! this won't do"--cried Tom, throwing himself into MP I 13 126 21
You will be so good, won't you?" MP I 18 168 17

WONDER (220)

You may well wonder how I contrive to pass my time here--& LS 7 254 3
that I should not wonder at his being delighted with her, LS 8 255 2
was natural; & I did not wonder at his being struck by the LS 8 255 2
spot, overpowered by wonder--of a most agreable sort LS 23 284 5
"And can your ladyship wonder that she should? cried I LS 24 288 11
affect farther wonder at my meaning in bidding you adeiu. LS 36 306 2
Not one, however, started with rapturous wonder on NA I 2 23 27
"I wonder you should think so, for you never asked me." NA I 10 75 26
I wonder he should dislike it, it must be so comfortable." NA I 11 83 13
I wonder whether it will be a full ball or not! NA I 11 90 63
It is not right; and I wonder Mrs. Thorpe should allow it. NA I 13 104 31
listened to any thing so full of interest, wonder, and joy. NA I 15 117 8
wonder at your surprize; and I am really fatigued to death. NA II 1 134 37
I only wonder John could think of it; he could not have NA II 3 146 16
she gained but little, her chief profit was in wonder. NA II 3 148 29
in motionless wonder, while these thoughts crossed her:-- NA II 6 163 1
2
She paused a moment in breathless wonder. NA II 6 168 10
authority, she boldly burst forth in wonder and praise. NA II 7 177 19
At that time indeed I used to wonder at her choice. NA II 7 180 32
It was no wonder that the General should shrink from the NA II 8 186 6
rather wonder that Eleanor should not take it for her own. NA II 9 196 21
exclamations of sorrowing wonder, declared her to be NA II 10 202 8
Isabella--no wonder now I have not heard from her-- NA II 10 204 19
Eleanor only replied, "I cannot wonder at your feelings. NA II 13 228 30
she could not wonder at any degree of his indignation. NA II 14 231 3
could not wonder at his even turning her from his house. NA II 14 231 3
all their indignation and wonder; though Sarah indeed NA II 14 234 10
His wonder, his conjectures, and his explanations, became NA II 14 237 22
But no wonder; Milsom-Street you know."-- NA II 14 238 27
fully known, you cannot wonder at my wishing to avoid any SS I 4 21 15
on him with an evident wonder and a secret admiration SS I 9 42 9
the mind and raised the wonder of Mrs. Jennings for two or SS I 14 70 1
I wonder whether it is so. SS I 14 70 2
I wonder what it can be! SS I 14 70 2
could not bestow all the wonder on his going so suddenly SS I 14 71 3
of speculation, her wonder was otherwise disposed of. SS I 14 71 3
Her joy and expressions of regard long outlived her wonder. SS I 17 90 1
I wonder what I should do with it!" SS I 17 92 21
"Indeed!" replied Lucy; "I wonder at that, for I thought SS I 22 128 5
"I dare say you are, and I am sure I do not at all wonder SS I 22 129 11
I only wonder that I am alive after what I have suffered SS I 22 133 42
I am sure I wonder my heart is not quite broke." SS I 22 133 42
The card-table was then placed, and Elinor began to wonder SS II 1 144 10
"and I do not much wonder at it; for it is the very best SS II 1 145 17
No wonder. SS II 8 192 3
No wonder! dashing about with his curricle and hunters! SS II 8 194 10
Lord! no wonder she has been looking so bad and so cast SS II 8 195 16
But can we wonder that with such a husband to provoke SS II 9 206 24
I wonder I should never hear you say how agreeable Mrs. SS II 13 239 9
There is no great wonder in their liking one another; but SS III 1 258 7
I should not wonder, if he was to be in the greatest of a SS III 1 259 7
After a pause of wonder, she exclaimed, "four months!-- SS III 1 262 17
18
again; and one cannot wonder at it, after being so SS III 1 265 36
"Well may you wonder, Marianne," replied her brother, "at SS III 1 267 40
I wonder what curacy he will get!-- SS III 2 275 22
'La!' I shall say directly, 'I wonder how you could think SS III 2 275 22
I wonder you was not afraid of its being torn." SS III 2 276 25
I wonder he should be so improvident in a point of such SS III 5 295 12
"You are never like me, dear Elinor, or I should wonder at SS III 9 336 10
But here, Elinor could neither wonder nor blame; and when SS III 10 342 7
reflections gave me, I wonder at my recovery,-- wonder SS III 10 345 28
wonder at my recovery,-- wonder that the very eagerness of SS III 10 345 28
eyes were fixed on him with the same impatient wonder. SS III 12 360 22
Lucy's marriage, the unceasing and reasonable wonder among SS III 13 364 10
the wonder, the horror, and the joy of such a deliverance. SS III 13 364 13
existence of each, under such a blow, with grateful wonder. SS III 13 371 38
"You are afraid of him, I do not wonder at you."-- W 319 2
"I wonder I never mentioned it when I wrote. W 321 2
I do not wonder that you should not wish to go with her W 326 5
to wonder & waver between his influence & her brother's.-- W 326 5
"You did very right; tho' I wonder at your forbearance, & W 341 19
"I wonder every Lady Does not.-- W 345 21
once occurred to her to wonder why Mr Howard had not taken W 347 22
"I know you do; and it is that which makes the wonder. PP I 4 14 9
One cannot wonder that so very fine a young man, with PP I 5 20 18
Miss Eliza, we cannot wonder at his complaisance; for who PP I 6 26 43
"I wonder my aunt did not tell us of that." PP I 7 30 18
I rather wonder now at your knowing any." PP I 8 39 52
I wonder who first discovered the efficacy of poetry in PP I 9 44 32
"I wonder," said he, at the next opportunity of speaking, " PP I 16 78 18
I wonder that the very pride of this Mr. Darcy has not PP I 16 81 38
thing indeed, and I wonder how he could presume to do it. PP I 18 94 45
Mr. Darcy was eyeing him with unrestrained wonder, and PP I 18 98 61
Elizabeth would wonder, and probably would blame her; and PP I 22 123 3
than they have known me; no wonder if they love her better. PP II 1 137 24
Mrs. Bennet still continued to wonder and repine at his PP II 1 137 26
I cannot but wonder, however, at her having any such fears PP II 3 148 26
and rather looked with wonder at her friend that she could PP II 5 156 4
lane, in quest of this wonder; it was two ladies stopping PP II 5 158 13
I wonder he does not marry, to secure a lasting PP II 10 184 17
to her still increasing wonder, perceived an envelope PP II 12 196 3
You may possibly wonder why all this was not told you last PP II 12 202 5
had leisure to wonder at her being where she was. PP III 1 245 4
with Elizabeth, gave her a look expressive of her wonder. PP III 1 255 60
but think, and think with wonder, of Mr. Darcy's civility, PP III 1 259 77
but as it was a matter of confidence one cannot wonder. PP III 4 275 5
She could neither wonder nor condemn, but the belief of PP III 4 278 19
From such a connection she could not wonder that he should PP III 8 311 13
I wonder what he can be doing there." PP III 10 328 16
It was my brother Gardiner's drawing up too, and I wonder PP III 11 336 49
with me, which I cannot wonder at, since he might have PP III 13 349 47
disdain, "I wonder you took the trouble of coming so far. PP III 14 353 27
she could do nothing but wonder at such a want of PP III 15 364 25
and Jane!" was a wonder which introduced the discussion PP III 16 370 36
chair, get up, sit down again, wonder, and bless herself. PP III 17 378 42
But I wonder how long you would have gone on, if you had PP III 18 381 13
I wonder when you would have spoken, if I had not asked PP III 18 381 13
He could not but wonder at her refusing to do any thing MP I 3 30 57
"No wonder that Mr. Rushworth should think so at present," MP I 6 53 5
Fanny could not wonder that Edmund was at the parsonage MP I 7 65 14
harp; neither could she wonder, that when the evening MP I 7 65 14
She must not wonder at all this; what could be more MP I 7 67 16
No wonder her head aches." MP I 7 72 47
Fanny made the first interruption by saying, "I wonder MP I 9 94 57
"I am really not tired, which I almost wonder at; for we MP I 9 94 60
I should not wonder if he was not more than five foot MP I 10 102 43
Nobody can wonder that men are soldiers and sailors." MP I 11 109 19
"I do not wonder at your disapprobation, upon my word. MP I 11 111 29
and seldom without wonder or censure; and had her MP I 12 115 5
I wonder my son did not propose it." MP I 12 117 13
I only wonder how the good people can keep it up so long.-- MP I 12 118 22
The wonder is that it should not have been thought of MP I 15 139 6
"I rather wonder Julia is not in love with Henry," was her MP I 17 161 10
her behalf, "one cannot wonder, sister, that Fanny should MP I 18 167 7
8
Mrs. Norris began to look about her and wonder that his MP II 2 194 20
Edmund did not wonder that such should be his father's MP II 3 196 2
I wonder what she thinks of my father! MP II 3 199 13
evils of a rupture, the wonder, the reflections, the MP II 3 201 22
much obliged, so full of wonder at the performance, and MP II 4 207 6
no wonder in this shrubbery equal to seeing myself in it. MP II 4 209 17
I wonder any body can ever go to sea." MP II 6 236 21
she was more disposed to wonder and rejoice in having MP II 10 280 32
But if he wrote to his father, no wonder he was concise. MP II 11 288 24
I do not at all wonder or blame them.-- MP II 11 289 34
"I wonder at that. MP II 11 289 36
In London he would soon learn to wonder at his infatuation, MP III 1 324 59
had no right to wonder at the line of conduct he pursued. MP III 2 331 17
was almost ready to wonder at his friend's perseverance.-- MP III 3 336 7
You quite astonish me--I wonder how you can"----- MP III 3 342 35
"Do you wonder? MP III 3 342 36
I will not leave you to wonder long." MP III 3 342 36
With such an opinion, no wonder that----- MP III 3 343 41
No wonder. MP III 4 350 28
dozens and dozens! the wonder, the incredulity that will MP III 5 360 16
to look around her, and wonder at the new buildings.-- MP III 7 376 6
I should not wonder if you had your orders to-morrow; but MP III 7 380 20
Her greatest wonder on the subject soon became--not that MP III 9 397 8
She could just find selfishness enough to wonder whether MP III 13 427 12
have breathed--was afterwards matter of wonder to herself. MP III 15 440 16
tone, "no wonder--you must feel it--you must suffer. MP III 15 446 34
"We were all disposed to wonder--but it seems to have been MP III 16 455 23
It was no wonder that a train of twenty young couple now E I 3 22 5
her father's gentleness with admiration as well as wonder. E I 4 32 27
"I wonder he did not remember the book"--was all Harriet's E I 4 34 41
I wonder what will become of her!" E I 5 40 27
vulgar all your life! I wonder how the young man could E I 7 54 29
"I wonder what they are all doing--whether his sisters E I 7 56 43
I wonder you should think it possible for me to have such E I 8 62 39
I wonder who the friend was--and who could be the young E I 9 72 17
I wonder which she will think the handsomest, Henry or E I 9 80 69
"Aye, I wonder which she will. E I 9 80 70
began again-- "I do so wonder, Miss Woodhouse, that you E I 10 84 8
9
I should not wonder if it were to bring on the declaration. E I 10 87 32
she could not wonder at her brother-in-law's breaking out. E I 12 106 59
Why does he make it any business of his, to wonder at what E I 12 106 60
others; too full of the wonder of his own going, and the E I 13 112 24
"Indeed! (in a tone of wonder and pity,) I had no idea E I 13 116 45
acknowledging his wonder that Miss Smith should be E I 15 130 28
she had little right to wonder that he, with self-interest E I 16 136 9
Jane, you have never seen Mr. Elton!--no wonder that you E II 3 174 35
At the same time, nobody could wonder if Mr. Elton should E II 3 176 44
sensations of curiosity, wonder and regret, pain and E II 3 180 57
She was, in fact, beginning very much to wonder that she E II 4 182 7
"I rather wonder that it was never made before." E II 8 216 22
I dare say they often think of you, and wonder which will E II 10 241 12
I do not wonder at you. E II 11 254 50
Upon her speaking her wonder aloud on that part of the E II 15 285 16
"I should not wonder," said Mrs. Weston, "if Miss Fairfax E II 15 286 21
I wonder how she speaks of the Coles--what she calls them! E II 15 288 39
not wonder if it were to end in his being so at last. E II 15 289 42
too, that are to be deciphered, it increases the wonder!" E II 16 296 42
at an inn, you would not wonder at Mrs. Churchill's making E II 18 306 12
how there could be any one disengaged was the wonder!-- E III 2 326 33
But Emma's wonder lessened soon afterwards, on seeing Mr. E III 2 326 33
of shame and feeling divided between wonder and amusement. E III 4 339 15
with the gratitude, wonder, and veneration, which are so E III 4 341 36
While he was so dull, it was no wonder that Harriet should E III 7 367 2
One cannot wonder, one cannot wonder. E III 8 379 8
attached--and how it came to cease, is perhaps the wonder. E III 10 396 41
may be a matter of grateful wonder to you and myself. E III 10 396 44
I told you that I did not wonder at your attachment; that E III 11 406 23
"I do not wonder, Miss Woodhouse," she resumed, "that you E III 11 407 28
It was an union to distance every wonder of the kind.-- E III 11 413 48
the bye, I wonder how Mrs. Elton bears the disappointment." E III 15 447 25
No wonder you should hold my speeches in such affectionate E III 17 462 10
of his wife; but the wonder of it was very soon nothing; E III 17 468 33
I wonder whether Jane has any suspicion." E III 17 468 34
wonder in many a family circle, with great sagacity. E III 17 468 35
Her mind was in a state of flutter and wonder, which made E III 18 475 37
fears; and indeed, Mary, I cannot wonder at your husband. P III 7 56 11
such universal, such eager admiration, who could wonder? P III 8 71 57
disposed to speculate and wonder; and Captain Wentworth P III 9 75 9
I wonder whereabouts they will upset to-day. P III 10 84 8
I wonder the arms did not strike me! P III 12 106 16
The wonder was, how any family upon earth could bear with P IV 1 127 28
Could Anne wonder that her father and sister were happy? P IV 3 138 5
She might not wonder, but she must sigh that her father P IV 3 138 5
must sigh, and smile, and wonder too, as Elizabeth threw P IV 3 138 5
Well might Charles wonder how Captain Wentworth would feel! P IV 6 166 18
to excite lasting wonder; and if Captain Wentworth lost no P IV 6 167 21
I wonder where that boat was built!" (laughing heartily) P IV 6 169 25
The only wonder was, what they could be waiting for, till P IV 6 171 33
not so much as say, "I wonder at it, I have a reason of my P IV 6 173 47
"You will wonder," said she, "what has been fixing my eye P IV 7 179 30
solicitous to give, his wonder at Captain Benwick, his P IV 8 185 21
Anne's astonished air, and exclamation of wonder, made her P IV 9 199 54
55
only the more inclined to wonder at the composure of her P IV 9 210 97
"I do not wonder Captain Wentworth is delighted! P IV 10 227 66
How they can half of them be filled, is the wonder! S 1 368 1
I began to wonder the bustle should not have reached them.- S 1 370 1

WONDERED (37)

table look as if they wondered why we came here--we seem NA I 2 22 14
necessary, I have often wondered at the person's courage NA I 14 109 24
Catherine heard, admired, and wondered with more genuine NA II 8 182 2
For nine successive mornings, Catherine wondered over the NA II 10 201 6
of her ladyship, who wondered at his being so shy before SS I 6 31 9
Lady Middleton frequently called him to order, wondered SS I 7 35 9
She wondered with little intermission what could be the SS I 14 70 1
So wondered, so talked Mrs. Jennings, her opinion varying SS I 14 70 3
The motive was too common to be wondered at; but the means SS I 20 112 28
She wondered that Lucy's spirits could be so very much SS II 13 238 2
But while she wondered at the difference of the two young SS II 14 250 12
are, perhaps, a little less to be wondered at.-- SS III 1 263 28
She wondered indeed at his thinking it necessary to do so;- SS III 3 281 9
her gratitude, and only wondered, that after hearing such SS III 3 282 15
engagements, and wondered whether Mr. Palmer and Colonel SS III 6 303 12
Mrs. Bennet wondered at their coming, and thought them PP I 12 60 6
All were struck with the stranger's air, all wondered who PP I 15 72 8
manner which Elizabeth wondered lady Catherine could bear. PP II 6 163 14
Elizabeth at first had rather wondered that Charlotte PP II 7 168 1
on you; but his success is not perhaps to be wondered at. PP II 12 202 5
to a stranger, and wondered it had escaped her before. PP II 13 207 5
Elizabeth listened, wondered, doubted, and was impatient PP III 1 249 37
his; and she would have wondered why, without violently PP III 9 318 19
her shyness; Miss Lee wondered at her ignorance, and the MP I 2 14 8
wondered that Edmund should forget her, and felt a pang. MP I 7 67 16
let her not be much wondered at if, after making all these MP II 9 265 19
while Miss Crawford wondered she did not smile, and MP II 10 277 20
She wondered that Sir Thomas could have leisure to think MP III 1 322 51
He wondered that Fanny spoke so seldom of her, and had so MP III 6 366 3
house, he would have wondered that her looks were not much MP III 11 412 30
to be known, to be wondered at because she does not accept E I 8 64 46
be when he was young--he wondered he could not remember E I 9 70 5
Emma wondered whether the same suspicion of what might be E II 5 192 33
Emma wondered on what, of all the medley, she would fix. E II 9 237 50
been resorted to at all--wondered, grieved, and feared-- P III 5 34 11

Anne wondered whether it ever occurred to him now, to P III 12 116 72
She wondered, and questioned him eagerly--but in vain. P IV 8 187 33
WONDERER (1)
days; she was a great wonderer, as every one must be who SS I 14 70 1
WONDERFUL (46)
marriage, & that she was altogether a wonderful woman. LS 8 255 2
and it was not very wonderful that Catherine, who had by NA I 1 15 3
Mrs. Allen, by the communication of the wonderful event. NA I 15 124 48
It was wonderful that her friends should seem so little NA II 2 141 12
only by bolts of less wonderful construction than the lock, NA II 6 168 10
even enter the church, seemed wonderful to Catherine. NA II 9 190 2
her to hear something wonderful; and giving her time only SS III 1 257 2
3
in his situation, so wonderful and so sudden;--a SS III 12 360 26
Mrs. Jennings wrote to tell the wonderful tale, to vent SS III 13 370 37
"It is wonderful,"--replied Wickham,--"for almost all his PP I 16 81 39
hints, they parted; a wonderful instance of advice being PP II 3 145 10
It is wonderful how many families I have been the means of PP II 6 165 32
at least to make it very wonderful to Sir Thomas, that Mrs. MP I 1 4 2
from Northampton of her wonderful good fortune, and the MP I 2 13 4
but you are blessed with wonderful memories, and your poor MP I 2 19 27
and it is not very wonderful that with all their promising MP I 2 19 30
She has a wonderful play of feature! MP I 7 63 3
How wonderful, how very wonderful the operations of time, MP II 4 208 12
more wonderful than the rest, I do think it is memory. MP II 4 208 12
How beautiful, how welcome, how wonderful the evergreen!-- MP II 4 209 16
seemed sensible of the wonderful improvement that has MP II 6 229 5
smile; but as for this wonderful degree of improvement, I MP II 6 230 6
occurred before, was almost as wonderful as it was welcome. MP II 9 261 1
Fanny Price--wonderful--quite wonderful!-- MP II 12 293 11
as I am with all that is wonderful in a perseverance of MP III 2 330 14
is it not wonderful that they should be what they are? MP III 4 350 32
method of reform was not wonderful; and Fanny soon became MP III 9 395 4
The wonderful improvement which she still fancied in Mr. MP III 11 413 32
do agree, it is quite wonderful the relief they give. E II 14 275 32
"The post-office is a wonderful establishment!" said she.-- E II 16 296 40
Quite wonderful how she does her hair!-- E III 2 323 19
but yet, Harriet, more wonderful things have taken place, E III 4 342 39
It is so wonderful, that though perfectly convinced of the E III 10 395 35
At first, if you had not told me that more wonderful E III 11 406 18
own words, that more wonderful things had happened, E III 11 407 28
first introduced it, the wonderful story of Jane Fairfax, E III 11 408 33
choose me, it will not be any thing so very wonderful." E III 11 411 39
busy, and, with all the wonderful velocity of thought, had E III 13 430 38
Upon my word, Perry has restored her in a wonderful short E III 16 454 17
"That appears quite wonderful. E III 18 477 55
Woodhouse's mind, or any wonderful change of his nervous E III 19 483 10
state, where a scene so wonderful and so lovely is P III 11 95 9
This was very wonderful, if it were true; and Lady Russell P IV 2 135 35
It was almost too wonderful for belief; and it was with P IV 6 165 9
Mary, my love, is not she a wonderful creature?-- S 9 409 1
the love of distinction & the love of the wonderful.-- S 10 412 1
WONDERFULLY (7)
The manuscript so wonderfully found, so wonderfully NA II 6 170 12
He was quite young, wonderfully handsome, extremely PP I 3 9 1
How wonderfully these sort of things occur! PP I 18 96 57
the whole it would certainly have gone off wonderfully." MP I 13 122 2
her sense, and wonderfully borne with her manners before. MP III 17 465 15
"Susan has born it wonderfully. S 9 407 1
she had kept up wonderfully.--had no hysterics of S 9 407 1
WONDERING (29)
Catherine, though she could not help wondering that with NA I 9 62 10
Catherine replied only by a look of wondering ignorance. NA I 15 117 5
and she opened her eyes, wondering that they could ever NA II 7 172 1
weary of seeing and wondering, he suffered the girls at NA II 7 179 27
I cannot help wondering at its being practised by him." SS I 15 79 29
head, had hardly done wondering at Charlotte's being so SS I 21 118 1
as her guest, without wondering at her own situation, so SS II 4 159 1
wondering whether her mother ever recollected Edward. SS III 9 335 7
visit were consequently spent in hearing and in wondering. SS III 13 370 35
before his mother, wondering when they should begin.-- W 330 11
Mrs R. W. was indeed wondering what sort of a home Emma cd W 350 24
an audience not merely wondering, but incredulous; for Mrs. PP I 23 126 1
2
of his patroness to his wondering visitors, and of letting PP II 6 160 1
and could not help wondering as she listened; and glad MP I 12 116 11
Listening and wondering were all suspended for a time, for MP I 12 118 22
seemed to govern them all, and wondering how it would end. MP I 14 131 4
with many painful, many wondering emotions, and looked MP I 18 167 13
I am very apt to get into this sort of wondering strain. MP II 4 209 16
of a fire upstairs--wondering at the past and present, MP III 2 329 10
at the past and present, wondering at what was yet to come, MP III 2 329 10
creature--and rather wondering at yourself for having ever E I 4 32 32
about wondering that people should like her so much. E I 7 56 42
"I cannot help wondering at your knowing so little of Emma E I 8 62 39
length, by the eagerness of Harriet's wondering questions. E I 9 72 16
of gruel, with some wondering at its not being taken every E I 12 101 19
20
The Coxes were wondering last night whether she would get E II 9 232 11
And they were by no means tired of wondering and admiring; P III 11 96 11
without wondering whether she might see him or hear of him. P IV 2 133 26
at it, I have a reason of my own for wondering at it." P IV 6 173 47
WONDERINGS (1)
and, after a few more wonderings, Emma said, "you are E II 3 175 41
42
WONDERS (12)
He could tell her nothing new of the wonders of his PP II 4 152 4
seen all the principal wonders of the country; and within PP II 19 240 12
"This is an evening of wonders, indeed! PP III 17 377 39
Nobody wonders that they should prefer the line where MP I 11 109 18
to parade over the wonders of Sotherton in her evening- MP II 3 202 28
good-will and contented temper which worked such wonders. E I 3 21 4
and describe the many comforts and wonders of the place. E I 4 27 4
My mother often wonders that I can make it out so well. E II 1 157 10
One wonders how the names of many of our nobility become P III 3 23 33
the Cobb itself, its old wonders and new improvements, P III 11 95 9
"Charles wonders what Captain Wentworth will say; but "if P IV 6 165 8
some Bitters of my own decocting, which have done wonders. S 9 411 1
WONT (9)
in which you were wont to share at Bath, the very idea of NA II 10 207 38
had been wont to believe, or than it was now proved to be. SS III 11 355 46
match at Chichester; she wont tell us with whom, but I W 317 2
Wont it, Kitty?" PP III 17 375 24
of one, before whom all her doubts were wont to be laid. MP I 16 153 3
every thing that had been wont to interest her, a letter MP III 9 393 1
have more good qualities than she had been wont to suppose. MP III 10 405 16
as she had been wont with such pride of heart to feel and MP III 16 448 1
principally such as were wont to be always interesting-- P IV 7 178 24
WONTED (2)
He had to reinstate himself in all the wonted concerns of MP II 2 190 9
fell into all her wonted ways of attention and assistance, P IV 10 220 31
WOOD (27)
the expiring embers of a wood fire--nor be obliged to NA II 5 158 15
inlaid with some darker wood, and raised, about a foot NA II 6 163 2
immediately assisted by the cheerful blaze of a wood fire. NA II 6 167 9
and the beauty of its wood, and ornaments of rich carving NA II 8 184 5
to a beautiful hanging wood, and on the other you have a SS I 13 69 76
grey moss and brush wood, but these are all lost on me. SS I 18 97 4
open shrubbery, and closer wood walk, a road of Smith SS III 6 302 7
will throw off at Stanton wood on Wednesday at 9 o'clock.-- W 347 21
through a beautiful wood, stretching over a wide extent. PP III 1 245 2
eminence, where the wood ceased, and the eye was instantly PP III 1 245 3
The hill, crowned with wood, from which they had descended, PP III 1 246 5
his way towards a small wood on one side of the paddock. PP III 7 301 6
Here is a nice little wood, if one can but get into it. MP I 9 91 37
which was a planted wood of about two acres, and though MP I 9 91 38
only walking in this sweet wood; but the next time we come MP I 9 94 57
at; for we must have walked at least a mile in this wood. MP I 9 94 60
We have taken such a very serpentine course; and the wood MP I 9 94 62
am sure it is a very long wood; and that we have been MP I 9 95 64
dimensions of the wood by walking a little more about it. MP I 9 96 76
She seemed to have the little wood all to herself. MP I 10 100 23
The first day I went over Mansfield wood, and Edmund took MP II 1 181 16
I never saw Mansfield wood so full of pheasants in my life MP II 1 181 16
while he was in Mansfield wood, and all the way home; but MP II 2 191 10
preferred--white wood finest flavour of all--price of E III 6 358 35
well clothed with wood;--and at the bottom of this bank, E III 6 360 38
of a rare species of wood, excellently worked up, and with P III 11 98 17
situated among wood on a high eminence at some little S 1 364 1
WOODED (1)
It was a pleasant fertile spot, well wooded., and rich in SS I 6 28 1
WOODHOUSES (3)
The Woodhouses were first in consequence there. E I 1 7 10
He must know that the Woodhouses had been settled for E I 16 136 9
of consequence; and the Woodhouses had long held a high E I 16 136 9
WOODS (21)
sheltered from the north and east by rising woods of oak. NA II 2 141 13
She was tired of the woods and the shrubberies--always so NA II 11 212 16
charge on the estate, or by any sale of its valuable woods. SS I 1 4 3
The woods and walks thickly covered with dead leaves." SS I 16 87 30
To the left is Barton Park, amongst those woods and SS I 16 88 33
hills are steep, the woods seem full of fine timber, and SS I 18 97 4
condition!--and his woods!--I have not seen such timber SS III 14 375 9
They have some of the finest woods in the country." PP II 19 240 15
appearance of Pemberley woods with some perturbation; and PP III 1 245 1
or a finer reach of the woods to which they were PP III 1 253 55
They entered the woods, and bidding adieu to the river for PP III 1 253 57
with the long range of woods overspreading many, and PP III 1 253 57
in a descent among hanging woods, to the edge of the water, PP III 1 253 57
that pollution which its woods had received, not merely PP III 19 388 12
But the woods are fine, and there is a stream, which, I MP I 6 56 26
She could not tell Miss Crawford that "those woods MP I 8 81 33
night, and the contrast of the deep shade of the woods. MP I 11 112 35
I do not think you will find your woods by any means worse MP II 1 181 16
of her uncle's plantations, and the glory of his woods.-- MP III 14 432 9
perhaps to the Abbey mill, perhaps into his woods.-- E III 16 458 40
side was covered with the woods & enclosures of Sanditon S 4 382 1
WOODSTON (21)
at my own house in Woodston, which is nearly twenty miles NA II 5 157 7
Shortly after breakfast Henry left them for Woodston, NA II 7 175 13
"Woodston will make but a sombre appearance to-day." NA II 7 175 13
when he next went to Woodston, they would take him by NA II 11 209 5
I must be at Woodston on Monday to attend the parish NA II 11 209 5
Two hours and three quarters will carry us to Woodston, I NA II 11 210 6
to be acquainted with Woodston; and her heart was still NA II 11 210 7
of seeing you at Woodston on Wednesday, which bad weather, NA II 11 210 7
Fullerton had its faults, but Woodston probably had none.-- NA II 11 212 16
miles, they entered Woodston, a large and populous village, NA II 11 212 17
would have quitted Woodston with little anxiety as to the NA II 11 215 28
On Henry's arrival from Woodston, she made known to him NA II 12 218 4
of his curate at Woodston obliging him to leave them on NA II 13 221 7
friend, she exclaimed, "'tis a messenger from Woodston!" NA II 13 223 12
at her most compassionately--"it is no one from Woodston. NA II 13 223 13
in future, beyond Henry's going to Woodston for a day! NA II 13 228 27
in going to and from Woodston; and, for fourteen miles, NA II 14 230 1
Every mile, as it brought her nearer Woodston, added to NA II 14 230 1
the neighbourhood of Woodston, saved her at the same time NA II 14 231 5
On his return from Woodston, two days before, he had been NA II 15 244 10
almost instantly to Woodston; and, on the afternoon of the NA II 15 248 16
WOODY (5)
plantations, and the steep woody hills rising behind to NA II 7 177 19
of which were open downs, the others cultivated and woody. SS I 6 28 3
backed by a ridge of high woody hill;-- and in front, a PP III 1 245 3
view of the high woody hills behind the house, and of the PP III 3 267 2
contemplation;--the woody varieties of the cheerful P III 11 95 9
WOOED (1)
the other half might not be so very smoothly wooed. MP II 8 255 10
WOOL (1)
been bid more for his wool than any body in the country. E I 4 28 6
WOOLWICH (1)
of Woolwich? or how could a boy be sent out to the east? MP I 1 5 2
WORCESTERSHIRE (1)
There is a poor woman in Worcestershire, whom some friends S 12 424 1
WORD (316)
a man to whom that great word "respectable" is always LS 2 245 1
Miss S. writes word that she could not get the young lady LS 16 268 1
concluded my last, when Wilson brought me word of it. LS 25 292 1
I allude; Langford--Langford--that word will be sufficient. LS 34 304 1
Believe me, the single word of Langford is not of such LS 35 305 1
little other right to the word, for they were in general NA I 1 13 1
"I don't upon my word--I wish I did. NA I 2 23 21
"Upon my word! NA I 3 27 33
"I shall not speak another word to you all the rest of the NA I 10 70 1
to give any, from not having heard a word of the subject. NA I 10 72 8
rude of me! to go by them, too, without saying a word! NA I 11 87 53
some times not a word was said, sometimes she was again NA I 13 99 9
The word 'nicest,' as you used it, did not suit him; and NA I 14 108 14
Oh! it is a very nice word indeed!--it does for every NA I 14 108 16
on every subject is comprised in that one word." NA I 14 108 16
It was "dear John," and "dear Catherine" at every word;-- " NA I 15 121 27
Take my word for it, that if you are in too great a hurry, NA II 3 146 20
This seemed the word of separation, and Catherine found NA II 5 162 27
And, upon my word, there are some things that seem very NA II 10 206 35
upon me; but he is the last man whose word I would take. NA II 12 217 2
"Nay, if you can use such a word, I can urge you no NA II 13 221 5
of both, scarcely another word was said by either during NA II 13 229 31
and intreating him to say not another word of the past. NA II 15 242 7
Catherine,--said not a word; but her glowing cheek and NA II 15 242 8
that in no sense of the word were they necessitous or poor, NA II 16 251 6
"Upon my word," said Mr. Dashwood, "I believe you are SS I 2 12 25
who has every body's good word and nobody's notice; who SS I 10 51 25
stand together and scarcely spoke a word to any body else. SS I 11 54 3
"Upon my word, I am not acquainted with the minutia of her SS I 11 56 16
She was faithful to her word; and when Willoughby called SS I 12 59 6
room and took her place at the table without saying a word. SS I 15 82 46
mark of regard in look or word which fell from him while SS I 19 102 2
ladies, without speaking a word, and, after briefly SS I 19 106 22
"Upon my word," replied Elinor, "you know much more of the SS I 20 114 45
I hear, and mama sends me word they are very pretty, and SS I 20 115 50
"Upon my word," replied Elinor, "I cannot tell you, for I SS I 21 124 29
for I do not perfectly comprehend the meaning of the word. SS I 21 124 29
I shall speak a good word for you to all the young men, SS II 3 154 2
Barton, without saying a word to Miss Dashwood about it." SS II 3 154 3
Do not let me hear a word about the expense of it." SS II 3 156 11
to tell her, sat for some time without saying a word. SS II 5 172 40
of mind by such an address, and was unable to say a word. SS II 6 176 7
Scarcely a word was spoken during their return to Berkeley- SS II 6 178 16
she said, "upon my word I never saw a young woman so SS II 7 181 7
8
Elinor drew near, but without saying a word; and seating SS II 7 182 12
to fly off from his word only because he grows poor, and a SS II 8 194 10
I would not mention a word about it to her for the world. SS II 8 196 18
He would not speak another word to him, meet him where he SS II 10 214 9
without recollecting a word of the matter; and having thus SS II 10 215 14

said she repeatedly, with a strong emphasis on the word. SS II 10 217 21
I am amazingly glad you did not keep to your word." SS II 10 217 21
might see us; and I am sure we would not speak a word." SS II 10 219 39
"I am extremely glad to hear it, upon my word; extremely SS II 11 222 11
too sedulously divided in word and deed on every occasion. SS II 12 229 4
instance, without saying a word, and never after had took SS II 13 240 17
and would not say a word; and almost every thing that was SS II 13 241 22
being told that upon "her word she looked vastly smart, SS II 14 249 8
or sister suspected a word of the matter;--till this very SS III 1 258 7
that he said a word about being off, and not upon his own. SS III 2 273 16
she will speak a good word for us to Sir John, or Mr. SS III 2 277 30
Very well upon my word. SS III 2 278 32
giving the information by word of mouth, when her visitor SS III 4 287 26
it; but, upon my word, you owe nothing to my solicitation." SS III 4 289 35
Take my word for it, that, if I am alive, I shall be SS III 4 292 57
tendency, and allowing the word "infection" to pass his SS III 7 307 3
chair, and for half a minute not a word was said by either. SS III 8 317 7
Every line, every word, was--in the hackneyed metaphor SS III 8 325 50
Her voice sunk with the word, but presently reviving she SS III 10 344 14
15
Marianne said not a word.-- SS III 10 347 33
that self-denial is a word hardly understood by him. SS III 11 350 9
Marianne's lips quivered, and she repeated the word " SS III 11 351 10
at last, without saying a word, quitted the room, and SS III 12 360 26
make mean concessions by word of mouth than on paper, it SS III 13 372 45
And I have promised to write him word who she dances with." W 320 2
"Upon my word Charles you are in luck, (said the former as W 331 11
Do you think Miss Osborne will keep her word with me, when W 332 12
"Let us see you soon at the castle; & bring me word how W 335 13
"Upon my word, you are severe upon my friend!-- W 340 19
Emma" that she could hardly speak a word in a minute.-- W 349 24
& stay till Christmas, if you don't put in your word."-- W 350 24
Mrs Robert offered not another word in support of the game. W 358 28
though I must throw in a good word for my little Lizzy." PP I 1 4 25
this morning, and never said a word about it till now." PP I 2 7 24
"Upon my word!-- PP I 5 19 8
"I do not believe a word of it, my dear. PP I 5 19 14
"Upon my word, Caroline, I should think it more possible PP I 8 38 38
The word is applied to many a woman who deserves it no PP I 8 39 46
languages, to deserve the word; and besides all this, she PP I 8 39 50
and expressions, or the word will be but half deserved." PP I 8 39 50
probably not go--and, at another word, might stay a month." PP I 10 49 29
"Upon my word I cannot exactly explain the matter, Darcy PP I 10 50 33
Mrs. Bennet sent them word that they could not possibly PP I 12 59 1
Why Jane--you never dropt a word of this; you sly thing! PP I 13 61 3
polite young man, upon my word; and I doubt not will prove PP I 13 63 13
"Upon my word I say no more here than I might say in any PP I 16 77 15
They stood for some time without speaking a word; and she PP I 18 91 8
but he said not a word, and Elizabeth, though blaming PP I 18 92 19
she could not hear a word of it, she felt as if hearing it PP I 18 98 61
"Upon my word, sir," cried Elizabeth, "your hope is rather PP I 19 107 14
to you again, and you will find me as good as my word. PP I 20 113 28
calling before, said not a word of wishing to see me again, PP II 3 148 26
his seat without saying a word; and his daughter, PP II 6 162 11
and the latter said not a word to her all dinner time. PP II 6 163 14
"Upon my word," said her ladyship, "you give your opinion PP II 6 165 36
Elizabeth merely curtseyed to him, without saying a word. PP II 7 171 9
notion of me, and teach you not to believe a word I say. PP II 8 174 15
Elizabeth was surprised, but said not a word. PP II 11 189 3
But of this answer Lydia heard not a word. PP II 16 223 24
It was impossible for her to see the word without thinking PP II 19 239 9
"I have never had a cross word from him in my life, and I PP III 1 248 30
a word, he suddenly recollected himself, and took leave. PP III 1 252 53
but Elizabeth heard not a word, and, wholly engrossed by PP III 1 252 54
shall not take him at his word about fishing, as he might PP III 1 258 72
She found it difficult to obtain even a word from her PP III 2 261 3
that she could not speak a word, especially to Miss Darcy, PP III 3 268 5
to it, and for a few minutes could not speak another word. PP III 4 277 11
"Upon my word," said Mrs. Gardiner, "I begin to be of your PP III 5 282 3
that he has been profligate in every sense of the word. PP III 5 284 12
"Yes he went on Tuesday as I wrote you word." PP III 5 286 26
You need not send them word at Longbourn of my going, if PP III 5 291 60
He could not speak a word for full ten minutes. PP III 5 292 62
However, I did not hear above one word in ten, for I was PP III 9 319 24
I ought not to have said a word about it. PP III 9 319 27
"If it was to be secret," said Jane, "say not another word PP III 9 319 28
we agreed long ago never to mention a word about it. PP III 11 331 14
Not a word passed between the sisters concerning Bingley; PP III 13 345 20
Not a word, however, passed his lips in allusion to it, PP III 13 348 35
36
of the head, and sat down without saying a word. PP III 14 351 3
Elizabeth was too much embarrassed to say a word. PP III 16 366 7
My affections and wishes are unchanged, but one word from PP III 16 366 7
trouble, or speaking one word where he spoke ten, by the MP I 2 12 2
"There, Mrs. Grant, you see how he dwells on one word, and MP I 4 43 24
for instance, looks very demure, and never says a word. MP I 5 49 32
and I could hardly get a word or a look from the young MP I 5 50 35
and the butcher's son-in-law left word at the shop." MP I 6 57 33
"Ungrateful is a strong word. MP I 7 63 7
other people; and take my word for it, it is a shocking MP I 7 71 34
Upon my word, ma'am, it has been a very ill-managed MP I 7 73 52
"Upon my word, it is really a pity that it should not take MP I 9 88 24
"Never is a black word. MP I 9 92 44
"A pretty trick, upon my word! MP I 10 100 26
word!" said Mrs. Norris, as they drove through the park. MP I 10 105 53
"Thank you for your good word, Fanny, but it is more than MP I 11 109 17
"I do not wonder at your disapprobation, upon my word. MP I 11 111 29
"A pretty modest request upon my word!" he indignantly MP I 12 119 26
"It was a hard case, upon my word;" and, "I do think you MP I 13 122 3
away without offering a word, for I believe I might speak MP I 15 142 22
signify if nobody hears a word you say, so you may be as MP I 15 145 47
"We have but to speak the word; we may pick and choose.-- MP I 15 148 58
And not another word was said: but Fanny felt herself in MP I 17 159 5
him, and learning every word of his part herself, but MP I 18 166 4
I did not think much of it at first--but, upon my word--. MP I 18 168 19
"And I do believe she can say every word of it," added MP I 18 172 31
and exclamations, not a word was spoken for half a minute; MP II 1 175 1
'Upon my word, Mrs. Norris,' said Mrs. Grant, the other MP II 2 190 7
by without speaking a word, or seeming at all interested MP II 3 198 12
"Upon my word," cried Miss Crawford, "you are two of the MP II 4 212 30
"Upon my word, Fanny, you are in high luck to meet with MP II 5 220 28
I shall do--not to lose a word; or only looking off just MP II 5 227 65
Sotherton was a word to catch Mrs. Norris, and being just MP II 7 245 32
Mrs. Norris had not another word to say. MP II 8 253 4
Fanny had not a word to say against its becomingness, and MP II 8 258 18
without saying another word; but Edmund, after waiting a MP II 9 262 10
for her to hazard another word; and she found herself the MP II 10 275 11
"Advise" was his word, but it was the advice of absolute MP II 10 280 33
I am sure of an excellent tenant at half a word. MP II 12 295 20
To have seen you grow like the Admiral in word or deed, MP II 12 296 27
"Upon my word, he must have gone off with his pockets well MP II 13 305 21
spite of that great black word miserable, which served to MP III 1 320 44
it a second time, by any word, or look, or movement. MP III 3 335 6
Both gentlemen had a glance at Fanny, to see if a word of MP III 3 338 16
on to add another word, not by dint of several minutes of MP III 3 341 27
Yes, that was the word. MP III 3 343 38
Constancy, I am not afraid of the word. MP III 3 343 38
I see nothing alarming in the word. MP III 3 343 38
She assented to it all rather by look than word. MP III 4 346 7
withstand the melancholy influence of the word "last." MP III 5 359 10
Sharp is the word, you see. MP III 7 380 20
What a long letter!--one word more. MP III 12 417 3
of; so you must take it upon my word, to be inestimable. MP III 12 417 3
she was going home; the word had been very dear to her; MP III 14 431 8
Say not a word of it--hear nothing, surmise nothing, MP III 15 437 3
word from him on the subjects that were weighing him down. MP III 15 445 34
you do, give me but a look, a word, and I have done." MP III 16 455 21
No look or word was given. MP III 16 455 22
as she answered, 'a pretty good lecture upon my word. MP III 16 458 30
And as to my poor word 'success,' which you quarrel with, E I 1 13 43
think you would have spoken a good word for me to any body. E I 5 37 10
"Upon my word," she cried, "the young man is determined E I 7 50 2
"Upon my word, Emma, to hear you abusing the reason you E I 8 64 45
They ready wit the word will soon supply, may its approval E I 9 71 14
Soft, is the very word for her eye--of all epithets, the E I 9 72 15
Thy ready wit the word will soon supply E I 9 72 15
can give them a sharp word now and then; but he is an E I 9 81 73
Now, Mr. Knightley, a word or two more, and I have done. E I 12 99 11
But, upon my word, Mr. Elton, in your case, I should E I 13 110 9
time, but had not said a word, lest it should make Mr. E I 15 126 11
He was too angry to say another word; her manner too E I 15 132 37
The Churchills might not have a word to say in return; but E I 18 147 19
forward to prevent Harriet's being obliged to say a word. E II 1 156 5
to do it for her --every word of it--I am sure she would E II 1 157 10
she would pore over it till she had made out every word. E II 1 157 10
And I think she wrote us word that he had shewn them some E II 1 160 20
The word home made his father look on him with fresh E II 5 191 26
He did not advance a word of praise beyond what she knew E II 5 191 28
"Upon my word! you answer as discreetly as she could do E II 6 200 19
perpetual cautiousness of word and manner, such a dread of E II 6 203 41
from them very lately, and not a word was said about it. E II 8 215 14
"And upon my word, they have an air of great probability. E II 8 217 33
at him about it, but he said not a word that could betray." E II 8 223 64
And, upon my word, I do not think Mr. Knightley would be E II 8 225 78
There is no understanding a word of it. E II 9 232 11
Harriet, tempted by every thing and swayed by half a word, E II 9 233 24
of a word--Miss Fairfax said something about conjecturing. E II 10 242 15
A word was put in for a second young Cox; and at last, Mr. E II 11 248 9
however was gracious, gracious in fact, if not in word. E II 12 257 2
"I do not find myself making any use of the word sacrifice, E II 13 264 2
a hasty or a witty word from herself about his manners. E II 14 270 5
Upon my word it is enough to put one in a fright. E II 14 277 40
You will laugh at my warmth--but upon my word, I talk of E II 15 282 5
Oh! no, upon my word I have not the smallest wish for your E II 15 288 35
the inferior in thought, word, or deed; or in her being E II 15 288 39
Upon my word we shall be absolutely dissipated. E II 16 290 2
my word, I have scarcely ever had a bad morning before." E II 16 296 35
She was quite determined not to utter a word that should E II 16 298 59
Upon my word, if this is what I am to expect, we married E II 18 305 6
"Yes, upon my word, very considerable. E II 18 306 10
So Frank writes word. E II 18 306 11
"Upon my word," exclaimed Emma, "you amuse me! E II 18 312 50
not stop for more than a word--but he had the vanity to E III 1 316 4
Excellently contrived, upon my word. E III 2 322 19
I said to my mother, 'upon my word, ma'am-----.' E III 2 322 19
would be rude--but upon my word, Miss Woodhouse, you do E III 2 323 19
Upon my word, this is charming to be standing about among E III 2 323 19
I set off without saying a word, just as I told you. E III 2 329 45
Upon my word, Jane on one arm, and me on the other!-- E III 2 329 45
and impertinent in look, though not absolutely in word.-- E III 3 333 6
I have not a word to say for the bit of old pencil, but E III 4 340 25
You wrote me word of it three months ago." E III 5 344 7
"Upon my word I never heard of it till this moment." E III 5 345 10
Frank Churchill placed a word before Miss Fairfax. E III 5 347 21
The word was discovered, and with a faint smile pushed E III 5 347 21
eager after every fresh word, and finding out none, E III 5 348 21
The word was blunder; and as Harriet exultingly proclaimed E III 5 348 21
He saw a short word prepared for Emma, and given to her E III 5 348 22
directly handed over the word to Miss Fairfax, and with a E III 5 348 23
Mr. Knightley's excessive curiosity to know what this word E III 5 348 23
to be engaged by no other word that could be offered. E III 5 349 23
not spoken a word--"I was just going to say the same thing. E III 5 349 24
sting of the last word given to you and Miss Fairfax? E III 5 349 27
I saw the word, and am curious to know how it could be so E III 5 349 27
Emma had not another word to oppose. E III 6 363 51
as no English word but flirtation could very well describe. E III 7 368 3
And how suffer him to leave her without saying one word of E III 7 376 62
I did not know a word of it till it was all settled." E III 8 381 15
"Upon my word, Emma."-- E III 10 393 13
"Your word!--why not your honour!--why not say upon your E III 10 393 14
very pretty trick you have been playing me, upon my word! E III 10 400 67
68
"Upon my word," said Emma, "I begin to doubt my having any E III 11 404 11
She could not speak another word.-- E III 11 405 16
She had hardly been able to speak a word, and every look E III 12 418 5
"Emma, that I fear is a word--no, I have no wish--stay, E III 13 429 33
able--and yet losing a word--to catch and comprehend the E III 13 430 38
She was his own Emma, by hand and word, when they returned E III 13 433 42
She must tell you herself what she is--yet not by word, E III 14 439 8
a shake of the head; a word or two of assent, or E III 15 445 14
15
the first thing to call for more than a word in passing. E III 15 446 19
Emma's answer was ready at the first word. E III 15 448 31
Excuse me for being so entirely without word." E III 16 453 9
But not a word more. E III 16 454 13
case, for lady, read ---- mum! a word to the wise.-- E III 16 454 13
Upon my word, Perry has restored her in a wonderful short E III 16 454 17
farther, "we do not say a word of any assistance that E III 16 454 17
not a word of a certain young physician from Windsor.-- E III 16 454 17
"Upon my word it is, Miss Bates.-- E III 16 455 23
'Upon my word, Mr. E., I often say, rather you than I.-- E III 16 455 23
"Upon my word, my dear, I do not know, for I never heard E III 16 456 31
But hush!--not a word, if you please." E III 16 457 33
"Very pretty, sir, upon my word; to send me on here, to be E III 16 457 36
my word, I believe you know her quite as well as I do.-- E III 18 473 26
father or sister: her word had no weight; her convenience P III 1 5 8
Mr. Shepherd had once mentioned the word, "advertise;"-- P III 2 15 14
and not a word to suspend decision was uttered by her. P III 3 24 37
unsoftened by one kind word or look on the part of her P III 4 27 5
Little Charles does not mind a word I say, and walter is P III 5 38 27
me one word about our dinner at the Pooles yesterday." P III 5 39 35
from Mary, of "upon my word, I shall be pretty well off, P III 6 42 1
And she could send us word every hour how he was. P III 7 56 14
little Charles do any thing; he always minds you at a word. P III 7 57 16
Mrs. Musgrove had not a word to say in dissent; she could P III 8 70 53
"Upon my word it would," replied Mary. P III 9 75 11
accepting must be the word) of two young women at once. P III 10 82 1
without saying a word, turned to her, and quietly obliged P III 10 91 41
The word curricle made Charles Musgrove jump up, that he P III 12 105 9
He caught the word; it seemed to rouse him at once, and P III 12 110 40
41
it dull; but upon my word I should have thought we were P IV 2 130 5
one end of the sands to the other, without saying a word. P IV 2 132 16
"Upon my word," said she, "I should not have supposed that P IV 2 132 20
Upon my word, Miss Anne Elliot, you have the most P IV 5 157 15
Lady Russell said not another word, willing to leave the P IV 5 160 26
"I kept my letter open, that I might send you word how " P IV 6 164 8
"Oh! yes, yes, there is not a word to be said against P IV 6 171 37
side all the way to Camden-Place, without saying a word. P IV 7 178 24
had distinguished every word, was struck, gratified, P IV 8 183 11
And, upon my word, he is nothing to me. P IV 9 196 33
Here Mrs. Smith paused a moment; but Anne had not a word P IV 9 206 89
90
But, upon my word, I am scarcely sensible of his P IV 10 213 7

I only smirked and bowed, and said the word 'happy.' P IV 10 223 46
from Captain Harville, but from him not a word, nor a look. P IV 11 236 39
"A word, a look will be enough to decide whether I enter " P IV 11 238 43
She began not to understand a word they said, and was P IV 11 238 45
"Oh! my dear, it is quite understood, I give you my word. P IV 11 239 50
are extremely obliging sir, & I take you at your word.-- S 1 365 1
seeming to hear a word of Mrs P.'s orders to the servant S 6 391 1
met with your accident, but upon my word you deserved it.-- S 6 393 1
nothing to do but to step back again, & say not a word.-- S 12 426 1

WORDED (2)

worded in a page full of empty professions to Mr. Morland. NA II 16 252 7
worded than if it had arisen from an offer of marriage. SS III 3 284 24

WORDS (222)

informed me in so many words, that he wished to reason LS 22 281 4
with whom she had scarcely ever exchanged two words before. LS 22 282 6
I made no remarks however, for words would have been in LS 24 287 10
And yet this Reginald, whom a very few words from me LS 25 293 3
look and voice as he spoke, which contradicted his words. LS 27 297 4
pretty to day," were words which caught her ears now and NA I 1 15 2
Such words had their due effect; she immediately thought NA I 2 24 28
complaisance in these words:--"I think, madam, I cannot be NA I 4 31 2
to his words, and perfect reliance on their truth. NA I 10 80 60
through laura-place, without the exchange of many words. NA I 11 86 51
to Pulteney-Street without her speaking twenty words. NA I 11 89 61
did not quite confirm his words, said he had been mistaken, NA I 12 91 3
But her words were lost on Thorpe, who had turned abruptly NA I 13 99 8
And with these words she broke away and hurried off. NA I 13 101 22
words of Caractacus, Agricola, or Alfred the Great." NA I 14 109 23
instruct might sometimes be used as synonimous words." NA I 14 109 26
of voice, uttered these words, "I have heard that NA I 14 111 29
would have done, that such words could relate only to a NA I 14 113 39
The important affair, which many words of preparation NA I 15 124 48
There was a something, however, in his words which repaid NA II 1 133 29
Tilney's concluding words, "by the end of another week!" NA II 2 138 1
These were thrilling words, and wound up Catherine's NA II 2 140 8
nothing but these words, in a whisper to Eleanor, "how NA II 5 155 3
Henry's words, his descriptions of the ebony cabinet which NA II 6 168 10
forced her to tell him in words, that she had never seen NA II 7 178 21
died-----" were all her words; but few as they were, they NA II 8 186 6
horrid suggestions which naturally sprang from these words. NA II 8 186 13
a surmise of such horror as I have hardly words to----- NA II 9 197 29
given to understand by his words as well as his actions, NA II 11 208 1
generality;--or, in other words, I believe there are few NA II 11 213 19
must not indeed--"were Eleanor's first connected words. NA II 13 223 9
to be repaid by-----but I must not trust myself with words. NA II 13 223 13
all her perplexity of words in reply, the meaning, which NA II 15 242 9
gratitude, or, in other words, that a persuasion of her NA II 15 243 9
dare to clothe itself in words, could ill brook the NA II 15 247 15
Use those words again and I will leave the room this SS I 4 21 14
His kindness was not confined to words; for within an hour SS I 6 30 6
This suspicion was given by some words which accidentally SS I 11 55 8
was at first too great for words; but at length forcing SS I 22 130 17
18
expression that could give her words a suspicious tendency. SS II 2 147 9
caught those words by a sudden pause in Marianne's music.-- SS II 2 148 20
particular stress on those words, "that your judgment SS II 2 150 34
chat, or in other words, in every variety of inquiry SS II 4 164 23
These words, which conveyed to Elinor a direct avowal of SS II 5 173 45
Middletons', was in these words:-- "I cannot express my SS II 7 187 39
40
where was your heart, when you wrote those words? SS II 7 190 56
was not a woman of many words: for, unlike people in SS II 12 232 15
assured her as plainly as words could have done, that he SS II 14 250 12
At these words, Marianne's eyes expressed the astonishment, SS III 1 262 17
lesson to another, some words of the Colonel's inevitably SS III 3 281 9
brought her these words in the Colonel's calm voice, "I am SS III 3 281 9
10
but he said only these two words, "Colonel Brandon!" SS III 4 289 29
30
the past, recal the words and endeavour to comprehend all SS III 4 291 45
because unexpressed by words, entirely escaped the latter SS III 6 305 16
of solemnity, and a few words spoken too low to reach her SS III 7 312 17
to no outward demonstrations of joy, no words, no smiles. SS III 7 315 24
In honest words, her money was necessary to me, and in a SS III 8 328 63
wife's words, and parted with the last relics of Marianne. SS III 8 329 63
And with these words, he almost ran out of the room. SS III 8 332 84
while in the actions and words of Marianne she persuaded SS III 10 340 3
Elinor joyfully treasured her words as she answered, "if SS III 10 344 18
19
of gratitude and these two words just articulate through SS III 10 348 34
His words were echoed with unspeakable astonishment by all SS III 12 360 24
A sigh accompanied these words, which Emma respected in W 316 2
But Margt wd never forgive such words." W 342 19
He was at no loss for words;--but when Ld. Osborne had W 345 21
as well as in the words themselves which made his Lordship W 346 21
extraordinary in the words, made some very inapplicable W 360 29
Vanity and pride are different things, though the words PP I 5 20 20
He studies too much for words of four syllables.-- PP I 10 48 20
He leaves out half his words, and blots the rest." PP I 10 48 22
he scarcely spoke ten words to her, through the whole of PP I 12 60 4
the motion of his lips the words "apology," "Hunsford," PP I 18 98 61
rapidity of her mother's words, or persuade her to PP I 18 99 64
the mother in these words, "may I hope, madam, for your PP I 19 104 1
2
your refusal of my addresses is merely words of course. PP I 19 108 19
The next was in these words. PP I 21 116 8
"You shall have it in few words. PP I 21 118 18
"I did not think Caroline in spirits," were her words, " PP II 3 147 23
His words seemed to imply it. PP II 10 182 1
were Colonel Fitzwilliam's words, and these strong PP II 10 186 39
to catch her words with no less resentment than surprise. PP II 11 190 8
As she pronounced these words, Mr. Darcy changed colour; PP II 11 191 11
And with these words he hastily left the room, and PP II 11 193 30
known its extent, agreed equally well with his own words. PP II 13 205 3
as she recalled his very words, it was impossible not to PP II 13 205 3
Words were insufficient for the elevation of his feelings; PP II 15 216 5
to rejoice over her words, or to distrust their meaning. PP II 18 234 35
much too full of lines under the words to be made public. PP II 19 238 5
she had not got beyond the words "delightful," and " PP III 1 254 57
and even before two words have been exchanged, nothing can PP III 4 279 24
and her thoughts and her words ran wholly on those PP III 8 310 7
her spirits; or in other words, to dwell without PP III 12 339 1
whispering a few words to her sister ran out of the room. PP III 13 346 22
a warmth, a delight, which words could but poorly express. PP III 13 347 25
Those were your words. PP III 16 367 14
"Or in other words, you are determined to have him. PP III 17 376 31
spot, or the look, or the words, which laid the foundation. PP III 18 380 2
you know I am a woman of few words and professions. MP I 1 6 6
and a few artless words fully conveyed all their gratitude MP I 2 16 20
more than repeat her aunt's words, "going to leave you?" MP I 3 25 8
a shadow of either, but in using the words so improperly. MP I 3 26 29
her pleasure sprung, was beyond all her words to express. MP I 4 37 8
a relation dead, it is done in the fewest possible words. MP I 6 59 43
numerous words and louder tone convinced her of the truth. MP I 8 76 2
Her cousin was safe on the other side, while these words MP I 10 100 22
respectable author than in chattering in words of our own. MP I 13 125 18
spite of the shock of her words, he still kept his station MP II 1 175 2
A very few words between them were sufficient. MP II 1 176 3
so far as to speak a few words of calm approbation in MP II 1 183 24
opinion in better words than he could find himself. MP II 1 186 35
too much indeed for many words; and having shaken hands MP II 2 187 2
talking of you at the parsonage, and those were her words. MP II 3 198 13

long enough to hear these words spoken in angry agitation: MP II 5 221 38
39
Such a trifle is not worth half so many words." MP II 8 260 22
his two dearest, before the words gave her any sensation. MP II 9 264 17
had not words strong enough to satisfy her own humility. MP II 9 264 18
tenderest emotion these words, "my very dear Fanny, you MP II 9 265 19
the flow of the first four words, in the arrangement of " MP II 9 265 19
many smiles and courteous words as she had time for, amid MP II 10 277 16
She wished such words unsaid with all her heart. MP II 11 286 15
with a little variation of words three times over, his MP II 12 292 8
his nephew, in a few words, of his having succeeded in the MP II 13 298 3
a return, and, finally, in words so plain as to bear but MP II 13 301 7
more obliged to you than words can express; but I do not MP II 13 302 8
use of such words and offers, if they meant but to trifle? MP II 13 302 10
against their being serious, but his words and manner. MP II 13 305 26
in which the words "my aunt Norris" were distinguishable. MP III 1 312 11
cannot recollect my exact words--but I am sure I told him MP III 1 315 19
With a few words, therefore, of no particular meaning, he MP III 1 320 45
There was comfort too in his words, as well as his manner, MP III 1 321 47
And there was a half smile with the words which meant, "I MP III 1 325 61
proving, as far as words could prove it, and in the MP III 2 328 6
pitying and agitated, and words intermingled with her MP III 2 328 7
in parting to bely his words, or give her hopes of his MP III 2 328 8
of satisfaction, and words of simple, pleasant meaning. MP III 3 334 2
one object of curiosity and one set of words to another. MP III 3 343 40
a few minutes somewhere;" words that Fanny felt all over MP III 5 357 5
I have of his looks and voice, as he said those words. MP III 5 358 9
and some agitation of manner, accompanied these words. MP III 5 364 31
emotions of tenderness that could not be clothed in words-- MP III 6 369 11
She might scruple to make use of the words, but she must MP III 8 390 6
at any certainty; and the words, "then by this time it is MP III 10 401 9
his heart with only these words, just articulate, "my MP III 15 444 28
Lady Bertram could not give her much time, or many words, MP III 16 448 3
I cannot recall all her words. MP III 16 454 18
And such was Fanny's dependance on his words, that for MP III 16 459 31
As you will do it, it will indeed, to use your own words, E I 6 44 16
a pen in hand, his thoughts naturally find proper words. E I 7 51 5
The result of his thoughts appeared at last in these words. E I 8 66 50
his son; she heard the words "my son," and "Frank," and " E I 14 118 4
at an address which, in words and manner, was assuming to E I 15 125 6
wind; concluding with these words to Mr. Woodhouse: E I 15 125 7
And he repeated her words with such assurance of accent, E I 15 130 26
27
Sighs and fine words had been given in abundance; but she E I 16 135 7
the precise words--one has no business to remember them. E II 3 174 32
as it all was by the words and the countenance of his wife, E II 5 188 8
would be ready to quarrel with you for using such words. E II 5 192 31
It was not merely in fine words or hyperbolical compliment E II 6 196 2
you have the art of giving pictures in a few words. E II 11 249 18
vacant corner were these words--"I had not a spare moment E II 13 266 5
His recollection of Harriet, and the words which clothed E II 13 266 6
Harriet felt this too much to utter more than a few words E II 13 268 11
Mr. Knightley's words dwelt with her. E II 16 291 5
Her looks and words had nothing to restrain them. E II 17 304 28
on like Emma, but her words, every body's words, were soon E III 2 322 18
her words, every body's words, were soon lost under the E III 2 322 18
as much as her words, for something more than ordinary. E III 4 337 3
She held the parcel towards her, and Emma read the words E III 4 338 9
"Oh! no"--and Emma could just catch the words, "so E III 4 341 33
it was all in unison; words, conduct, discretion, and E III 5 343 2
They were rapidly forming words for each other, or for any E III 5 347 20
it of all things," was not plainer in words than manner. E III 6 354 9
Her parting look was grateful--and her parting words, "Oh! E III 6 363 51
so much, that his last words to Emma were, "well;--if you E III 6 366 74
75
impossible to quarrel with words, whose tremulous E III 9 390 18
believe; but Emma's countenance was as steady as her words. E III 10 396 40
and words that were never meant for both to hear.-- E III 10 399 61
Those were the words; in them lay the tormenting ideas E III 11 402 1
of secresy had been among Mr. Weston's parting words. E III 11 403 2
(those were your very words);--I should not have dared to E III 11 406 18
But you know they were your own words, that more wonderful E III 11 407 28
She had hoped for an answer here--for a few words to say E III 13 427 20
A few words which dropped from him yesterday spoke his E III 14 438 8
in a form of words perfectly intelligible to me.-- E III 14 441 8
Those were Miss Woodhouse's words, were they?-- E III 15 448 28
happiness--in other words his life--required Hartfield to E III 15 449 31
soon have shown no want of words, if the sound of Mrs. E III 16 453 10
And putting up her hand to screen her words from Emma--"a E III 16 456 23
was wanting to give her words, not to Mrs. Elton, but to E III 16 457 34
strange, and then, in few words, said, that if his consent E III 17 465 28
fresh the sound of those words, spoken with such emphasis, E III 18 473 27
nothing doubtful, in the words he used; and I think I can E III 18 474 30
his own Jane, and his next words were, "did you ever see E III 18 478 60
61
to die away with the words, and leave her without a care E III 19 481 2
and his family, these words, after the date of Mary's P III 1 3 2
when Mrs. Croft's next words explained it to be Mr. P III 6 49 22
grave, and spoke low words both to the father and the aunt, P III 7 54 4
These were words which could not but dwell with her. P III 7 61 35
Frederick Wentworth had used such words, or something like P III 7 61 36
answered such a speech--words of such interest, spoken P III 10 88 27
"Is there no one to help me?" were the first words which P III 12 110 35
rather than words, was offering his services to her. P IV 7 176 10
She had hardly spoken the words, when Mr. Elliot walked in. P IV 7 177 16
song, she explained the words of the song to Mr. Elliot.-- P IV 8 186 24
rather the meaning of the words, for certainly the sense P IV 8 186 25
Such she believed were his words; but scarcely had she P IV 8 188 37
mortification of finding such words applied to her father. P IV 9 204 76
to use her own words, without knowing it to be you?" P IV 9 205 86
"Oh! I lay no embargo on any body's words. P IV 10 213 7
words brought his enquiring eyes from Charles to herself. P IV 10 224 49
done, conscious that her words were listened to, and P IV 10 225 54
only a buzz of words in her ear, her mind was in confusion. P IV 11 231 11
the following words: "I can listen no longer in silence. P IV 11 237 41
42
To lose the possibility of speaking two words to Captain P IV 11 238 47
together; and soon words enough had passed between them to P IV 11 240 59
hopes which her looks, or words, or actions occasionally P IV 11 241 60
comparing it with former words, and feeling it to be the P IV 11 243 68
his wife in the few words of "well my dear, I beleive it S 1 367 1
the newest-fashioned hard words--had not a very clear S 7 398 1
he gathered only hard words & involved sentences from the S 8 404 1
The words "unaccountable officiousness!-- S 9 410 1

WORDSWORTH (1)

Montgomery has all the fire of poetry, Wordsworth has the S 7 397 1

WORE (21)

went to the Lower Rooms; wore my sprigged muslin robe with NA I 3 26 22
too handsome unless he wore the dress of a groom, and too NA I 7 45 5
I remember I wore my yellow gown, with my hair done up in NA I 15 118 11
with us that evening, and wore her puce-coloured sarsenet; NA I 15 118 13
The evening wore away with no abatement of this soothing NA II 10 199 2
Frederick too, who always wore his heart so proudly! who NA II 10 206 30
a turban like mine, as I wore it the week before at the NA II 12 217 2
were certain that Marianne wore his picture round her neck; SS I 12 60 10
proof of it which he constantly wore round his finger. SS I 19 102 2
where she gave genteel parties, & wore fine Cloathes.-- W 349 23
window, that he wore a blue coat and rode a black horse. PP I 3 9 3
Everything wore a happier aspect. PP II 19 238 6
of herself, necessarily wore away, and she was no longer MP I 2 17 21
And the morning wore away in satisfactions very sweet, if MP I 17 159 6
on the pianoforte nor wore fine pelisses, they could , on MP III 9 395 3

idea, till it gradually wore off, by no letters appearing MP III 12 418 5
face wore its broadest smiles, may be easily conceived. MP III 15 445 32
to happiness; every thing wore a different air; James and E II 5 189 16
his brother's house; woman wore too amiable a form in it; E III 13 432 41
The anxious interval wore away unproductively. P IV 8 189 45
To Anne, it chiefly wore the prospect of an hour of P IV 8 189 45

WORK (128)
I do not wish to work on your fears, but on your sense & LS 12 261 4
I would rather work for my bread than marry him. LS 21 279 1
general distress of the work, and how she will, probably, NA I 2 19 7
or, in short, only some work in which the greatest powers NA I 5 38 4
instead of such a work, how proudly would she have NA I 5 38 4
while she sat at her work, if she lost her needle or broke NA I 9 60 1
It is a most interesting work. NA I 14 108 17
and a whole parish to be at work within the inclosure. NA II 7 178 21
Northanger, all the dirty work of the house was to be done NA II 8 184 4
Eleanor's work was suspended while she gazed with NA II 10 204 18
concert, but made wretched work of it--it happened to NA II 12 217 2
thing--a time for balls and plays, and a time for work. NA II 15 240 2
Catherine took up her work directly, saying, in a dejected NA II 15 240 3
do right, applied to her work; but, after a few minutes, NA II 15 241 7
circumstance could work upon a temper like the General's? NA II 16 250 4
the tendency of this work be altogether to recommend NA II 16 252 7
down to work, "and with how heavy a heart does he travel?" SS I 15 77 22
It seems but the work of a moment. SS I 15 77 23
it must hurt your eyes to work fillagree by candlelight. SS II 1 144 11
Lucy directly drew her work table near her and reseated SS II 1 144 14
I should like the work exceedingly, if she would allow me SS II 1 145 19
as you really like the work, perhaps you will be as well SS II 1 145 22
the utmost harmony engaged in forwarding the same work. SS II 1 145 23
The work of one moment was destroyed by the next. SS II 9 202 7
Mrs. Ferrars, not aware of their being Elinor's work, SS II 12 235 28
selfish repining, now at work in introducing excess into a SS III 10 343 10
"I meant," said Elinor, taking up some work from the table, SS III 12 359 19
her head leaning over her work, in a state of such SS III 12 360 24
for two or three nights, without making a peice of work. W 351 25
A pretty peice of work your Aunt Turner has made of it!-- W 351 26
"It ought to be good," he replied. "it has been the work PP I 8 38 30
own work; my daughters are brought up differently. PP I 9 44 29
Elizabeth, at work in the opposite corner, saw it all with PP I 11 54 2
till the following day to work on Jane; and till the PP I 12 59 2
And gathering her work together, she was hastening away, PP I 19 104 4
5
To work in his garden was one of his most respectable PP II 5 156 4
passed by him either at work in the garden, or in reading PP II 7 168 1
She examined into their employments, looked at their work, PP II 7 169 3
Eliza, she sat herself seriously to work to find it out.-- PP II 9 180 29
had been given, was scarcely the work of a moment.-- PP II 12 199 5
had in fact been the work of her nearest relations, and PP II 13 209 11
all the work of the morning, and pack her trunk afresh. PP II 14 213 20
It is not the object of this work to give a description of PP II 19 240 12
My reproofs at Hunsford could not work such a change as PP III 1 255 60
with her, must be the work of her brother, and without PP III 1 256 64
She sat intently at work, striving to be composed, and PP III 11 335 39
her work, with an eagerness which it did not often command. PP III 11 335 40
at work to get every body away from him and her daughter. PP III 13 346 21
pretending to admire her work, said in a whisper, "go to PP III 17 375 28
his affection was not the work of a day, but had stood the PP III 17 376 36
but he had to work against a most untoward gravity of MP I 2 12 2
Fanny could read, work, and write, but she had been taught MP I 2 18 23
a most tiresome piece of work of it; and 3dly, that the MP I 3 24 4
You have space to work upon these, and grounds that will MP I 6 53 9
"I was astonished to find what a piece of work was made of MP I 6 58 37
If you have no work of your own, I can supply you from the MP I 7 71 34
and had taken up her work again; and Julia, who was in MP I 7 71 35
His curate does all the work, and the business of his own MP I 11 110 23
beside her arranging her work, thus began as he entered. MP I 13 125 14
getting through the few difficulties of her work for her. MP I 13 126 19
and a little carpenter's work--and that's all; and as the MP I 13 127 31
and as the carpenter's work may be all done at home by MP I 13 127 31
was already at work, while a play was still to seek. MP I 14 130 1
was the loss of half a day's work about those side-doors.-- MP I 15 141 22
The maids do their work very well, and I think we shall be MP I 15 141 22
you are most composedly at work upon these cottages and MP I 15 143 27
audible: "what a piece of work here is about nothing,--I MP I 15 146 53
from taking notice of her work and wishing she could work MP I 15 147 57
and wishing she could work as well, and begging for the MP I 15 147 57
faded footstool of Julia's work, too ill done for the MP I 16 152 2
from town, and was at work, much to the increase of the MP I 18 164 1
Fanny took the work very quietly without attempting any MP I 18 167 7
8
not one of those who can talk and work at the same time.-- MP I 18 167 9
made her escape with her work to the east room, that she MP I 18 168 14
as to put away her work, move pug from her side, and give MP II 1 179 9
a great deal of carpet work and made many yards of fringe; MP II 1 179 9
also set the carpenter to work in pulling down what had MP II 2 190 9
of the worst subjects to work on, in any little manoeuvre MP II 4 212 30
work in such a state as to prevent her being missed. MP II 5 220 29
eyes from her work to say, "dear me! how disagreeable.-- MP II 6 236 21
with William, was a work of some difficulty; and as for MP II 7 240 8
There will be work for five summers at least before the MP II 7 241 21
who were still hard at work--and then, creeping slowly up MP II 10 280 33
and had so little curiosity, that it was heavy work. MP II 11 282 4
I cannot work. MP II 11 283 5
as she leant over the work, then returning to her seat to MP II 12 296 31
the Admiral had set to work in the business, the other MP II 13 298 3
all on the lover's side, might work their usual effect on. MP III 1 320 44
likes to go her own way to work; she does not like to be MP III 1 323 56
to compose herself to work again; and Fanny, walking off MP III 1 325 62
trusted that every thing would work out a happy conclusion. MP III 3 335 6
silently at work as if there was nothing else to care for. MP III 3 336 8
All her attention was for her work. MP III 3 337 10
Nay, nay, I entreat you; for one moment put down your work. MP III 3 342 33
This, we know, must be a work of time. MP III 4 347 18
must have very up-hill work, for there are all your early MP III 4 347 21
sitting at this table at work; and then your cousin's MP III 5 360 14
a girl under her, and I often do half the work myself." MP III 7 385 39
And it would not be ten minutes work." MP III 15 440 18
the match; but it was a black morning's work for her. E I 1 6 6
Emma wished to go to work directly, and therefore produced E I 6 44 19
her imagination range and work at Harriet's fortune, than E I 9 69 3
him most intently at work with his recollections; and at E I 9 70 7
as you do--and so much fine work as you have done too!-- E II 1 158 10
It was the work of a moment. E II 8 218 37
help or advise him in his work, till Jane Fairfax was E II 10 240 6
What nonsense one talks, Miss Woodhouse, when hard at work, E II 10 242 15
patience; but it was heavy work to be for ever convincing E II 13 267 9
Emma hoped it must rapidly work Harriet's cure; but the E II 15 281 3
Mr. Knightley was hard at work upon the lower buttons of E II 15 287 27
28
work to make them peculiarly interesting to each other?-- E III 3 335 9
finding out none, directly took it up, and fell to work. E III 5 348 21
her work, and seeming resolved against looking up.) E III 10 394 30
themselves, that every kindly feeling was at work for them. E III 12 418 5
distant from her mind, that it had been all her own work? E III 12 422 20
The rest had been the work of the moment, the immediate E III 13 432 40
me instantly; but I must work on my father's compassion, E III 14 437 8
Emma, my mind has been hard at work on one subject." E III 15 448 30
reading her name in any other page of his favourite work. P III 1 6 10
Sailors work hard enough for their comforts, we must all P III 3 19 12
clerks were set to work, without there having been a P III 5 32 3
It must be a work of time to ascertain that no injury had P III 7 55 7
were mechanically at work, proceeding for half an hour P III 8 72 58
were sitting quietly at work, they were visited at the P III 10 83 3
where the ploughs at work, and the fresh-made path spoke P III 10 85 13
whose judgments had to work on ascertained events; and it P IV 1 126 21
was aware of his being in it--the work of an instant! P IV 11 236 40
at first it is Uphill work; and therefore we must give him S 4 382 1

WORK-BAGS (2)
about their ears, their work-bags searched, and their SS I 21 120 6
of new caps and new work-bags for her mother and herself; E II 2 168 15

WORK-BOXES (1)
The table between the windows was covered with work-boxes MP I 16 153 3

WORKBAGS (1)
with all their boxes, workbags, and parcels, and the the PP II 16 220 16

WORKBASKET (1)
Then having recourse to her workbasket, in excuse for E III 18 471 19

WORKED (27)
insulted by accusation, can be worked on by compliments. LS 22 282 7
There is something agreable in feelings so easily worked LS 25 293 3
I have given up too much--have been too easily worked on; LS 39 308 1
Scarcely had they worked themselves into the quiet NA I 10 75 25
arrived, had worked herself into a state of real distress. NA I 15 121 26
"How were Mr. Allen's succession-houses worked?" NA II 7 178 24
And, when she saw him in the evening, while she worked NA II 8 187 13
Catherine had expected to have her feelings worked, and NA II 9 193 6
expected to have her feelings worked, and worked they were. NA II 9 193 6
of the one had been so worked on by the flattery of the SS III 13 364 11
plain one in the family, worked hard for knowledge and PP I 6 25 23
How is such a man to be worked on? PP III 4 277 16
slit in my worked muslin gown, before they are packed up. PP III 5 292 60
you think I can be worked on by such persuasions as these. PP III 14 357 61
Mr. Rushworth was worked on. MP I 10 103 48
and so artlessly worked herself into it, that it was now MP I 16 151 1
She worked very diligently under her aunt's directions, MP I 18 168 14
wish of retreat, and she worked and meditated in the east MP I 18 168 14
It was of gold prettily worked; and though Fanny would MP II 8 258 17
Crawford could not have worked so little change on a MP III 2 329 11
He should have worked upon my plans. MP III 4 348 21
hesitations of delicacy, she at last worked herself up to. MP III 9 396 7
good-will and contented temper which worked such wonders. E I 3 21 4
She was a plain, motherly kind of woman, who had worked E I 3 22 5
abroad had worked its way to Uppercross, two years before. P III 6 50 28
of wood, excellently worked up, and with something curious P III 11 98 17
Now you are to understand that time had worked a very P IV 9 206 90

WORKING (21)
were a good little girl working your sampler at home!" NA I 14 107 11
eyes--will you ring the bell for some working candles? SS II 1 144 13
it, round the common working table, when a letter was SS II 7 181 7
"Two thousand a-year;" and then working himself up to a SS II 11 223 22
Mrs. Dashwood seemed actually working for her, herself; SS II 14 254 26
to counteract them by working on others;--and represented SS III 3 280 6
made, to the trouble of working for one; and has the best MP I 11 110 23
himself and working his way to fortune and consequence MP II 6 236 22
a moment to visit her and working away his partner's fan MP II 10 279 23
of her aunt's stupidity, working with her, and for her, MP II 12 296 31
he believed kindness might be the best way of working. MP III 2 330 14
herself, and blushing and working as hard as ever; but it MP III 3 337 11
and therefore set about working for Sam immediately, and MP III 8 390 7
Sam immediately, and by working early and late, with MP III 8 390 7
stairs, at first only in working and talking; but after a MP III 9 398 9
the reluctance, in working himself into the esteem and MP III 17 467 19
Vanity working on a weak head, produces every sort of E I 8 64 47
"I have not been working uninterruptedly," he replied, "I E II 10 240 5
as she sat drawing or working, forming a thousand amusing E II 13 264 1
She was not yet dancing; she was working her way up from E III 2 327 34
that he had not been working only for himself, by his S 10 416 1

WORKING-SILVERSMITH (1)
good livelihood as a working-silversmith at this rate." E II 10 240 4

WORKINGS (2)
What could more plainly speak the gloomy workings of a NA II 8 187 13
assiduities, and the natural workings of her own mind. MP III 5 356 2

WORKMEN (3)
dilatoriness of the workmen, Elinor, as usual, broke SS III 14 374 6
talks at all;--your real workmen, I suppose, hold their E II 10 242 15
had spread among the workmen and boatmen about the Cobb, P III 12 111 49

WORKS (13)
heroine; she read all such works as heroines must read to NA I 1 15 3
harshest epithets on such works, and scarcely ever NA I 5 37 4
I have read all Mrs. Radcliffe's works, and most of them NA I 14 106 7
Charming as were all Mrs. Radcliffe's works, and charming NA II 10 200 3
charming ever as were the works of all her imitators, it NA II 10 200 3
the excellence of such works, however disregarded before. SS I 10 47 3
No, no, they must get a stout girl of all works.-- SS III 2 277 28
She is an excellent housemaid, and works very well at her SS III 4 287 22
But there are many works well worth reading, at the park; SS III 10 343 9
writing desk, and her works of charity and ingenuity, were MP I 16 151 2
but when he has ladies to please every feature works." E I 13 111 16
mentioned such works of our best moralists, such P III 11 101 24
Such are the works which I peruse with delight, & I hope I S 8 403 1

WORLD (450)
But if the world could know my motive there, they they LS 2 245 1
all that knowledge of the world which makes conversation LS 6 251 1
which put one in good humour with oneself & all the world. LS 10 258 3
my dear Reginald, of seeing you settled in the world. LS 12 261 3
But in this case, as well as in many others, the world has LS 14 264 2
those who living in the world & surrounded with temptation, LS 14 264 3
to themselves & the opinion of the world. S. Vernon. LS 16 269 3
& have no other way in the world of helping myself but by LS 21 279 1
the contempt of the whole world, & the severest resentment LS 22 282 8
nor would for the world have such myself, but they are LS 25 293 3
She is not of a disposition to do you credit in the world, LS 26 295 1
for any other woman in the world, than her own mother. LS 27 297 2
the claims of our friends, or the opinion of the world. LS 30 300 1
me to the censure of the world, & incur what would be LS 30 300 3
ill-nature of the world had interpreted to my discredit? LS 35 304 1
me in common with the world in general, & gained my entire LS 36 305 1
Mr Johnson & he are the greatest friends in the world. LS 38 307 3
Above all disorders in the world, she most dreaded the LS 42 312 6
The world must judge from probability. LS 42 313 9
the latter into the world, as any body might expect, she NA I 1 13 1
nothing so well in the world as rolling down the green NA I 1 14 1
in the world who could like them well enough to marry them. NA I 2 20 8
meet, and nothing in the world advances intimacy so much." NA I 3 29 51
inhabitants, and all the world appears on such an occasion NA I 5 35 1
world, no species of composition has been so much decried. NA I 5 37 4
are conveyed to the world in the best chosen language. NA I 5 38 4
not tell you what is behind the black veil for the world! NA I 6 39 6
you, I would not have come away from it for all the world." NA I 6 40 7
creatures in the world, has read every one of them. NA I 6 40 12
They are the most conceited creatures in the world, and NA I 6 42 28
than any thing else in the world, Laurentina's skelton; NA I 6 42 33
there is nothing in the world in it but an old man's NA I 7 49 42
most charming girl in the world, and by John's engaging NA I 7 50 44
most charming girl in the world, and of being so very NA I 7 50 44
dear sister for all the world; for if I did we should NA I 8 52 2
To be disgraced in the eye of the world, to wear the NA I 8 53 2
she cried, "I would not do such a thing for all the world. NA I 8 57 21
that there is not a more agreeable young man in the world." NA I 8 58 33
would not be half the disorders in the world there are now. NA I 9 63 20
young man in the world; she saw him this morning you know: NA I 10 70 1
have had you by for the world; you are such a sly thing, I NA I 10 71 3
as your roses; I would not have had you by for the world." NA I 10 71 5
that, it is the most tiresome place in the world.' NA I 10 78 45

world; and do not let us put it off--let us go to-morrow." NA I 10 80 61
"She had no doubt in the world of its being a very fine NA I 11 82 1
rather do any thing in the world than walk out in a great NA I 11 83 13
I would not have had it happen so for the world.-- NA I 11 87 53
I would not be there for all the world. NA I 11 90 63
Is there a Henry in the world who could be insensible to NA I 12 94 9
the whole, left one of the happiest creatures in the world. NA I 12 95 16
ever was made in this world-----I took his ball exactly---- NA I 12 96 20
I would not, upon any account in the world, do so improper NA I 13 99 4
do not you think Udolpho the nicest book in the world?" NA I 14 107 12
give any thing in the world to be able to draw; and a NA I 14 111 29
of all the women in the world--especially of those-- NA I 14 113 45
the world, who had been her dear friends all the morning. NA I 14 114 50
It must be the dullest thing in the world, for there is NA I 14 115 50
delightful scheme in the world; that nobody could imagine NA I 15 116 1
of the whole world, your brother would be my only choice." NA I 15 119 18
in the world, but swore off many sentences in his praise. NA I 15 121 27
Of all things in the world inconstancy is my aversion. NA II 1 130 5
for she would not dance upon any account in the world." NA II 1 132 17
in good-nature yourself to all the rest of the world." NA II 1 133 28
disengaged; but I would have given the world to sit still." NA II 1 134 37
for, of all things in the world, I hated fine speeches and NA II 1 134 39
Modesty such as your's--but not for the world would I pain NA II 2 139 7
said he, "we may expect philosophy from all the world." NA II 2 140 9
I believe I am the most absent creature in the world. NA II 3 144 4
I am the last person in the world to judge you severely. NA II 3 146 18
"I would not for all the world be the means of hurrying NA II 3 146 20
prettiest equipage in the world; the chaise-and-four NA II 5 156 5
him, was certainly the greatest happiness in the world. NA II 5 157 5
occasion for hurry in the world: but Catherine could not NA II 6 165 6
For the world would she not have her weakness suspected; NA II 7 174 5
The world, I believe, never saw a better woman. NA II 9 196 23
She was quite impatient to know how the Bath world went on, NA II 10 201 5
and fickleness, and every thing that is bad in the world?" NA II 10 204 19
would not, for instance, now go to a ball for the world. NA II 10 207 38
that our pleasures in this world are always to be paid for, NA II 11 210 7
comfortable room in the world; but she was too guarded to NA II 11 213 18
room I ever saw;--it is the prettiest room in the world!" NA II 11 214 21
but I would not have followed him for all the world. NA II 12 217 2
appearance, propriety, to your family, to the world. NA II 13 225 23
Enraged with almost every body in the world but himself, NA II 15 247 13
to a precision the most charming young man in the world. NA II 16 251 5
in the world is instantly before the imagination of us all. NA II 16 251 5
pin myself down to the payment of one for all the world." SS I 2 11 20
have left almost every thing in the world to them." SS I 2 13 28
They wanted him to make a fine figure in the world in some SS I 3 15 6
I have the highest opinion in the world of Edward's heart. SS I 3 17 17
Mama, the more I know of the world, the more am I SS I 3 18 20
the highest opinion in the world of his goodness and sense. SS I 4 19 6
of any consequence in the world was beyond calculation SS I 5 27 6
I shall see how much I am before-hand with the world in SS I 6 29 4
nothing to do but to marry all the rest of the world. SS I 8 36 1
It would be a compact of convenience, and the world would SS I 8 38 10
infirm to mix with the world, and never stirred from home. SS I 9 40 2
"Is there a felicity in the world," said Marianne, " SS I 9 41 5
He has seen a great deal of the world; has been abroad; SS I 10 51 20
of enthusiasm and ignorance of the world cannot atone for. SS I 11 56 13
acquaintance with the world is what I look forward to as SS I 11 56 13
any other creature in the world, except yourself and mama. SS I 12 59 4
May be she is ill in town; nothing in the world more SS I 14 70 2
one whom I loved, for all the improvements in the world. SS I 14 72 10
handsomest dimensions in the world could possibly afford." SS I 14 73 17
to love, and no reason in the world to think ill of? SS I 15 79 28
of the world; and who has ever spoken to his disadvantage? SS I 15 81 44
"I would not ask such a question for the world. SS I 16 84 9
He was the only person in the world who could at that SS I 16 86 21
"As moderate as those of the rest of the world, I believe. SS I 17 91 7
and without them, as the world goes now, we shall both SS I 17 91 11
please me better than the finest banditti in the world." SS I 18 98 8
I could get the nicest house in the world for you, next SS I 20 110 4
with something so droll--all about any thing in the world." SS I 20 113 39
assure them of their being the sweetest girls in the world. SS I 21 119 3
the sweetest girls in the world were to be met with in SS I 21 119 3
beautiful creatures in the world; and I have told them it SS I 21 119 4
I suppose you have not so many in this part of the world; SS I 21 123 26
I am sure I would rather do any thing in the world than be SS I 22 128 9
greatest dependance in the world upon your secrecy; and I SS I 22 129 16
the highest opinion in the world of all your family, and SS I 22 130 16
"I am sure," said she, "I have no doubt in the world of SS I 22 132 39
the greatest fright in the world t'other day, when SS I 22 133 42
I would not disappoint the little angel for all the world, SS II 1 144 12
With almost every other man in the world, it would be an SS II 2 147 7
being so much more in the world than me, and our continual SS II 2 147 12
you know one has always a world of little odd things to do SS II 4 163 14
nervous irritability, not to speak to her for the world. SS II 7 180 5
"By all the world, rather than by his own heart. SS II 7 189 50
Beyond you three, is there a creature in the world whom I SS II 7 189 50
The triumph of seeing me so may be open to all the world. SS II 7 189 52
the only young man in the world worth having; and with SS II 8 192 3
I would not mention a word about it to her for the world. SS II 8 196 18
said it did him more good than any thing else in the world. SS II 8 198 27
the observation of all the world, at another she would SS II 9 201 2
Like half the rest of the world, if more than half there SS II 9 201 4
word to him, meet him where he might, for all the world! SS II 10 214 9
found her one of the most charming women in the world! SS II 12 229 1
smallest difference in the world between them; and Miss SS II 12 234 24
there was no reason in the world why Mrs. Ferrars should SS II 13 239 9
that have been the greatest comfort to me in the world!-- SS II 13 239 13
delicate conscience in the world; the most scrupulous in SS II 13 243 40
recollect that I am the last person in the world to do it. SS II 13 244 46
announced to the world, that the lady of Thomas Palmer, SS II 14 246 1
proposition of its being the finest child in the world. SS II 14 248 5
was as well fitted to mix in the world as any other man. SS II 14 250 12
the world but the red-gum;' and nurse said just the same. SS III 1 257 5
in the world but the red-gum, and then Charlotte was easy. SS III 1 257 5
in the world, nor one who more deserves a good husband." SS III 1 267 43
arm--"for I wanted to see you of all things in the world." SS III 2 271 8
not the least mind in the world to be off, for she could SS III 2 273 16
I am sure I would not do such a thing for all the world.-- SS III 2 275 22
of all people in the world, was fixed on to bestow it!-- SS III 3 283 20
I an't the least astonished at it in the world, for I have SS III 4 285 3
in the world, I think I shall know where to look for them." SS III 4 285 5
the easiest thing in the world; but she equally feared to SS III 4 287 24
of doing anything in the world for those she really valued. SS III 5 293 2
have the least objection in the world to seeing you.-- SS III 5 294 6
is one of the most affectionate mothers in the world." SS III 5 296 22
as well-meaning a fellow perhaps, as any in the world. SS III 5 298 35
her ignorance of the world--every thing was against me. SS III 8 323 40
woman in the world, and that I was using her infamously. SS III 8 326 53
she would appear to those, who saw her last in this world. SS III 8 327 55
The world had made him extravagant and vain----- SS III 8 331 70
"As to that," said he, "I must rub through the world as SS III 8 332 77
his vindication for the world, and now blamed, now SS III 9 334 6
declared herself, one of the happiest women in the world. SS III 9 335 7
mere friendship, as the world now goes, would not justify SS III 9 336 12
our connection the greatest blessing to us in the world. SS III 9 337 17
must henceforth be all the world to me; you will share my SS III 10 347 30
She would have given the world to be able to speak--and to SS III 12 358 9
of ignorance of the world--and want of employment. SS III 13 362 5
more with the world, as in such a case I must have done. SS III 13 362 5
I had therefore nothing in the world to do, but to fancy SS III 13 362 5
all appearance without a friend in the world to assist me. SS III 13 367 22
regard, and who had only two thousand pounds in the world. SS III 13 367 22
not seven shillings in the world;--so I was very glad to SS III 13 370 37
really believed, one of the happiest couple in the world. SS III 14 374 7
of the most fortunate young women in the world, as it is. SS III 14 375 9
There is not the least likeness in the world; Yr brother's W 324 3
You are like nobody else in the world.-- W 342 19
wd not have had to talk to such a great man for the world. W 347 22
both his own cards--it is worth anything in the world!"-- W 358 28
He was the proudest, most disagreeable man in the world, PP I 3 11 6
All the world are good and agreeable in your eyes. PP I 4 14 7
occupy himself solely in being civil to all the world. PP I 5 18 1
to be discovered by the world in general, since Jane PP I 6 21 1
poor consolation to believe the world equally in the dark. PP I 6 21 2
fashionable world, he was caught by their easy playfulness. PP I 6 23 12
vogue amongst the less polished societies of the world.-- PP I 6 25 27
men of any consideration in the world," replied Darcy. PP I 8 37 19
greatest patience in the world, which is always the way PP I 9 42 7
the most shameful thing in the world if he did not keep it. PP I 9 45 36
too little for the convenience of the world. PP I 11 58 28
I do think it is the hardest thing in the world, that your PP I 13 61 7
for such things I know are all chance in this world. PP I 13 65 24
The world is blinded by his fortune and consequence, or PP I 16 78 16
might proclaim to all the world; a sense of very great ill PP I 16 78 20
the highest opinion in the world of your excellent PP I 18 97 60
61
am the last woman in the world who would make you so.- PP I 19 107 14
You wish to think all the world respectable, and are hurt PP II 1 135 11
The more I see of the world, the more am I dissatisfied PP II 1 135 11
being so much design in the world as some persons imagine." PP II 1 136 16
They are young in the ways of the world, and not yet open PP II 3 150 29
in a part of the world, where I had hoped to pass myself PP II 8 174 15
world, is ill-qualified to recommend himself to strangers. PP II 8 175 22
she is one of the most tractable creatures in the world. PP II 10 184 21
There could not exist in the world two men, over whom Mr. PP II 10 186 38
generous heart in the world; and no one could say how PP II 10 186 38
"I have every reason in the world to think ill of you. PP II 11 191 12
one to the censure of the world for caprice and PP II 11 191 12
in the world whom I could ever be prevailed on to marry." PP II 11 193 28
been concealed from the world; and that friendship between PP II 13 208 6
I have the greatest dislike in the world to that sort of PP II 13 211 13
the little we see of the world, must make Hunsford PP II 15 215 2
cold luncheon in the world, and if you would have gone, we PP II 16 222 22
have gone through the world without believing that so much PP II 17 224 9
the least chance in the world of her ever getting him now. PP II 17 228 27
Our importance, our respectability in the world, must be PP II 18 231 18
If I was to go through the world, I could not meet with a PP III 1 249 33
most generous-hearted, boy in the world." PP III 1 249 33
most unfortunate, the most ill-judged thing in the world! PP III 1 252 54
be every thing in the world; he will immediately PP III 4 276 5
is but one man in the world I love, and he is an angel. PP III 5 291 60
wickedest young man in the world; and every body began to PP III 6 294 4
friend, that had attended her from that part of the world. PP III 6 298 16
The world has been deceived in that respect; and I am PP III 7 302 14
Five daughters successively entered the world, but yet the PP III 8 308 3
been secluded from the world, in some distant farm house. PP III 8 309 6
and knowledge of the world, she must have received benefit PP III 8 312 15
each of them to have the happiest memories in the world. PP III 9 316 6
which her sisters would not have alluded to for the world. PP III 9 316 6
He did every thing best in the world; and she was sure he PP III 9 318 20
beneath him, to lay his private actions open to the world. PP III 10 322 2
emotion, that she was the happiest creature in the world. PP III 13 346 23
and forgiving heart in the world, she knew it was a PP III 13 350 52
the luckiest family in the world, though only a few weeks PP III 13 350 56
I am almost the nearest relation he has in the world, and PP III 14 354 38
in the world, and wholly unallied to the family! PP III 14 355 43
all his friends, and make him the contempt of the world." PP III 14 358 69
or the indignation of the world, if the former were PP III 14 358 70
moment's concern--and the world in general would have too PP III 14 358 70
of all the rest of the world, to wish at least to think PP III 16 369 24
that we are to be the happiest couple in the world. PP III 17 373 10
It will save me a world of trouble and economy. PP III 17 377 39
I am the happiest creature in the world. PP III 18 383 21
Mr. Darcy sends you all the love in the world, that he can PP III 18 383 21
Mary was obliged to mix more with the world, but she could PP III 19 386 5
Georgiana had the highest opinion in the world of PP III 19 387 11
in the world, as there are pretty women to deserve them. MP I 1 3 1
who longed to be out in the world; but what could she do? MP I 1 5 2
in the world to withhold my mite upon such an occasion. MP I 1 6 6
her properly into the world, and ten to one but she has MP I 1 6 6
being the most liberal-minded sister and aunt in the world. MP I 1 8 9
island, as if there were no other island in the world. MP I 2 18 25
than any body in the world except William; her heart was MP I 2 22 35
you came into this house, as any creature in the world." MP I 3 25 12
There is no reason in the world why you should not be MP I 3 26 29
Fanny live with me! the last thing in the world for me MP I 3 28 42
all my peace in this world destroyed, with barely enough MP I 3 29 46
"Those who are showing the world what female manners MP I 5 50 37
Sotherton Court is the noblest old place in the world." MP I 6 53 3
the first favourite in the world, has made me consider MP I 6 57 31
impossible thing in the world, had offended all the MP I 6 58 37
urgent necessity in the world; and when obliged to take up MP I 6 59 43
his being a man of the world or an elder brother, without MP I 7 65 13
I have nothing in the world to say for myself--I knew it MP I 7 68 18
and nothing in the world could be more snug and pleasant." MP I 9 88 24
the greatest bore in the world, and Miss Price has found MP I 9 96 71
a man of the world not to see with the eyes of the world. MP I 10 98 8
"I am afraid I am not quite so much the man of the world MP I 10 98 10
as one finds to be the case with men of the world." MP I 10 98 10
"And for the world you would not get out without the key MP I 10 99 18
nor sorrow in the world; and there certainly would be less MP I 11 113 35
and that nothing in the world could be easier than to find MP I 13 124 13
it is of all parts in the world the most disgusting to me. MP I 14 136 20
I could not act any thing if you were to give me the world. MP I 15 145 46
consequence, bustle and the world, for a wounded spirit. MP II 3 202 25
with the person one feels most agreeable in the world. MP II 4 210 21
"The most interesting in the world," replied her brother--" MP II 5 226 61
it the best aspect in the world--sloping to the south-east. MP II 7 242 23
was such a throat in the world?--or perhaps--looking MP II 8 259 20
Believe me, I have no pleasure in the world superior to MP II 9 262 9
such a woman as he thinks does not exist in the world. MP II 12 293 10
There is not a better girl in the world, and you do not MP II 12 293 11
to Sir Thomas Bertram; that will be enough for the world. MP II 12 293 11
if there is a girl in the world capable of being MP II 12 293 15
The impossibility of not doing every thing in the world to MP II 12 296 30
honour, and dignity in the world to what I shall do?" MP II 12 297 35
of what you ought to have known before all the world. MP II 13 299 5
My uncle, who is the very best man in the world, has MP II 13 299 5
with bringing them up and putting them out in the world! MP II 13 305 24
There was every thing in the world against their being MP II 13 305 26
her materials without knowing what in the world to say! MP II 13 307 30
years longer in the world, without being addressed by a MP III 1 319 39
the connection was still the most desirable in the world. MP III 2 329 12
Let him have all the perfections in the world, I think it MP III 4 353 45
heart among you, than one finds in the world at large. MP III 5 359 12
The world, Mary on something of less philosophic tendency. MP III 5 360 13
whose knowledge of the world made her judgment very MP III 5 361 16
of circumstances occasion in this world of changes. MP III 6 374 27
have pained her mother by alluding to her, for the world.-- MP III 7 386 40
most devoted H. C. in the world. For Henry is in Norfolk; MP III 9 393 1
very worst third in the world--totally different from Lady MP III 10 403 15
She is the only woman in the world whom I could ever think MP III 13 421 2
It is the influence of the fashionable world altogether MP III 13 421 2

'The only woman in the world, whom he could ever think of MP III 13 424 4
had for the world, and which could never be valued enough. MP III 13 425 5
proportion of the female world at least, must feel with MP III 13 425 6
subject in the world for a little medical imposition. MP III 14 429 1
poor young men less in the world; and with a fearless face MP III 14 434 13
to draw the notice of the world, and to excite her MP III 15 438 4
to any one woman in the world, and shame him from MP III 15 438 5
had to announce to the world, a matrimonial fracas in the MP III 15 440 14
leader in the fashionable world, having quitted her MP III 15 440 14
her, that as far as this world alone was concerned, the MP III 15 442 21
This is what the world does. MP III 16 455 18
In this world, the penalty is less equal than could be MP III 17 468 22
years in the world with very little to distress or vex her. E I 1 5 1
It is the greatest amusement in the world! E I 1 12 41
worst predicament in the world for having much of the E I 3 21 4
to make-- cannot be at all beforehand with the world. E I 4 30 20
of useful understanding or knowledge of the world. E I 4 35 44
troublesome office for the world"--brought on the desired E I 6 49 41
"Not for the world," said Emma, smiling graciously, "would E I 7 53 21
of being intimate with you for any thing in the world." E I 7 54 26
recommendations to the world in general, for she is, in E I 8 63 44
for any inducement in the world; and something about a E I 8 68 58
the luckiest woman in the world; for, beyond a doubt, Mr. E I 8 68 58
the rise in the world which must satisfy them." E I 9 75 27
One half of the world cannot understand the pleasures of E I 9 81 77
and common sense of the world as appears at first; for a E I 10 85 19
had only a shilling in the world, she would be very likely E I 10 85 19
most natural thing in the world, or would have been the E I 10 88 33
fortunate woman in the world; and as to slighting Mr. E I 11 95 19
There could hardly be an happier creature in the world, E I 13 108 1
air to produce a very white world in a very short time. E I 13 112 24
was not a creature in the world to whom she spoke with E I 14 117 1
which I imagine to be the most certain thing in the world." E I 14 121 15
the world, for in general every thing does give you cold. E I 15 127 15
You are the worst judge in the world, Mr. Knightley, of E I 18 146 11
does, as well as all the world must know, that he ought to E I 18 147 18
very best method in the world of preserving peace at home E I 18 148 24
appears to me the most desirable arrangement in the world." E II 1 161 30
She knows I would not offend for the world. E II 3 176 44
idea of any thing in the world, full ten minutes, perhaps-- E II 3 178 52
I did so wish myself any where in the world but there.-- E II 3 178 52
and every thing in this world, excepting that trunk and E II 5 186 1
for the fashionable world, if Jane Fairfax could be E II 5 194 43
"My dear sir, upon no account in the world; my father can E II 5 195 46
less of the man of the world in some of his notions, less E II 6 203 42
be the best man in the world if he were left to himself; E II 7 205 2
"No, upon no account in the world. E II 7 210 20
old spinnet in the world, to amuse herself with.-- E II 8 215 16
and thought it the most natural thing in the world. E II 8 219 42
the wretchedest being in the world at a civil falsehood." E II 9 234 32
"No trouble in the world, ma'am," said the obliging Mrs. E II 9 235 39
world, fastening in the rivet of my mother's spectacles.-- E II 9 236 46
have Mr. Knightley know any thing about it for the world! E II 9 239 51
out of the world, and am often astonished at what I hear. E II 11 252 32
in the world if I were not--for a few weeks at least. E II 12 262 39
all the clearness of head in the world, for attraction. E II 13 269 16
advisable to mix in the world in a proper degree, without E II 14 275 30
I honestly said that the world I could give up--parties, E II 14 276 36
Blessed with so many resources within myself, the world E II 14 276 36
superior knowledge of the world, to enliven and improve a E II 15 281 1
who wants to be wiser and wittier than all the world! E II 15 288 39
hand in knowledge of the world, but she would soon shew E II 16 290 3
"But you have not seen so much of the world as I have. E II 17 299 8
a cold sleety April day rush out again into the world!-- E II 17 303 23
have heard of there being such a creature in the world." E II 18 307 23
"Not the least in the world.-- E III 4 338 7
to all the rest of the world, with the gratitude, wonder, E III 4 341 36
the oddest dreams in the world--but if I am questioned E III 5 345 16
for it she never betrayed the least thing in the world. E III 5 346 16
for one another, as any two beings in the world can be. E III 5 350 37
Suckling, the Highbury world were obliged to endure the E III 6 352 1
one married woman in the world whom I can ever allow to E III 6 354 15
as carelessly as she could--"upon no account in the world. E III 7 369 19
a better creature in the world: but you must allow, that E III 7 375 60
is every thing in the world that can make her happy in it. E III 8 382 23
importance in the world, and Jane Fairfax's, struck her; E III 8 384 32
33
her more good than any thing else in the world could do. E III 10 396 42
been known to no being in the world but their two selves." E III 10 399 60
Of such, one may almost say, that 'the world is not E III 10 400 66
and she was ready to give it every bad name in the world. E III 11 408 33
is the last man in the world, who would intentionally give E III 11 411 40
41
Was it new for any thing in this world to be unequal, E III 11 413 48
Mr. Knightley to all the world; let Donwell and Hartfield E III 12 416 1
"Oh! the best nature in the world--a wedding." E III 13 425 5
family sought round the world for a perfect wife for him, E III 13 428 23
While I, to blind the world to our engagement, was E III 14 441 8
For the world would not she have seemed to threaten me.-- E III 14 442 8
Emma would not have smiled for the world, and only said, " E III 16 456 26
could do such a thing by you, of all people in the world! E III 16 458 42
next to his daughters and Mrs. Weston, best in the world. E III 17 465 28
as these, was one of the happiest women in the world. E III 17 468 32
I would not have missed this meeting for the world. E III 18 479 72
luckiest creature in the world, to have created so steady E III 19 482 4
very happiest being in the world herself, had found enough P III 1 4 6
for a few weeks annual enjoyment of the great world. P III 1 7 12
designs of one part of the world from the notice and P III 3 17 4
was the very best preserver of furniture in the world. P III 3 22 24
experience enough of the world to feel, that a more P III 3 24 36
not that any thing in the world, I am sure, would induce P III 5 35 14
creature in the in the world, it would be enough to spoil P III 6 45 9
place, because, all the world knows how easy and P III 6 46 10
It is not that mamma cares about it the least in the world, P III 6 46 10
used to feel alone in the world; and Mr. and Mrs. P III 6 47 13
years longer in the world than her real eight and thirty. P III 6 48 18
affliction, as the most graceful set of limbs in the world. P III 8 68 30
our family, they seem shut out from all the world. P III 12 102 2
than those of any other set of beings in the world. P IV 3 144 20
correct opinions, knowledge of the world, and a warm heart. P IV 4 146 6
simplest process in the world of time upon a head P IV 4 147 7
had lived very much in the world, nor the restrictions of P IV 5 153 7
She had seen too much of the world, to expect sudden or P IV 5 154 9
education in the world," know nothing worth attending to. P IV 5 155 9
There is so little real friendship in the world!--and P IV 5 156 11
her think worse of the world, than she hoped it deserved. P IV 5 156 12
and all names in the world, to be the chosen friend of P IV 5 158 19
in the world, the most unaccountable and absurd! P IV 7 175 5
who is too modest, for the world in general to be aware of P IV 8 187 28
the most agreeable in the world, the person who interests P IV 9 194 16
time, more than all the rest of the world put together." P IV 9 194 16
most probable thing in the world to be wished for by P IV 9 197 36
generous spirit in the world, would have divided his last P IV 9 199 55
When one lives in the world, a man or woman's marrying for P IV 9 201 64
and twenty years in the world, "and have seen none like it. P IV 9 203 72
to take you back into the world immediately, and continual P IV 11 232 19
"Granting your assertion that the world does all this so P IV 11 232 20
letter depended all which this world could do for her! P IV 11 237 41
concerned--and would not stir without her for the world. P IV 11 238 45
She had but two friends in the world to add to his list, P IV 12 251 10
I did not know there was such a place in the world." S 1 369 1
did not know there was such a place in the world.-- S 1 370 1
the properest wife in the world for a man of strong S 2 372 1
their getting out into the world, as much as possible. S 2 374 1
He lives too much in the world to be settled; that is his S 4 382 1
the useless things in the world that cd not be done S 6 390 1
I am not a woman of parade, as all the world knows, & if S 6 393 1
Here have I lived 70 good years in the world & never took S 6 394 1
did the man take who sent him out of the world.-- S 6 394 1
If there are young ladies in the world at her time of life, S 7 395 1
in serving your friends & doing good to all the world.-- S 9 409 1
But my dear Miss Heywood, we are sent into this world to S 9 410 1
The world is pretty much divided between the weak of mind S 9 410 1
"No, my dear Tom, upon no account in the world, shall you S 9 411 1
the simplest thing in the world, by those who have studied S 10 418 1
"The easiest thing in the world--cried Miss Diana Parker S 12 423 1

WORLD'S (2)
that 'the world is not their's, nor the world's law.'" E III 10 400 66
thing of Harville's from the world's end, if he wanted it. P III 8 69 40

WORLDLY (17)
of Udolpho, lost from all worldly concerns of dressing and NA I 7 51 54
be classed by the laws of worldly politeness, to what a NA I 12 92 3
too easily the forms of worldly propriety, he displayed a SS I 10 49 9
be treated as one in all worldly concerns; anxious that SS III 5 293 2
have sacrificed every better feeling to worldly advantage. PP I 22 125 18
rational happiness nor worldly prosperity, could be justly PP III 7 307 51
in a more active and worldly profession, where he would MP I 11 111 30
in the middle state of worldly circumstances, is all that MP II 4 214 41
with all her high and worldly notions of matrimony, would MP II 13 306 26
I was afraid of the bias of those worldly maxims, which MP III 4 351 36
been governed by motives of selfishness and worldly wisdom. MP III 17 461 4
her claims were great to a high worldly establishment?-- E III 11 414 50
In a worldly view, he had nothing to gain by being on P IV 3 140 11
defying public opinion in any point of worldly decorum. P IV 4 146 6
disingenuous, artificial, worldly man, who has never had P IV 9 208 93
defiance even to greater accessions of worldly prosperity. P IV 12 252 12
had been so low in every worldly veiw, as with all her S 3 379 1

WORLDS (3)
"For worlds would not I have had a letter of her's seen by SS III 13 365 17
but I would have given worlds--all the worlds one ever has E II 10 242 17
the worlds one ever has to give--for another half hour." E II 10 242 17

WORMED (1)
him; & unluckily she had wormed out of Manwaring's servant LS 32 302 1

WORN (30)
learning what was mostly worn, and her chaperon was NA I 2 20 8
The wheels have been fairly worn out these ten years at NA I 9 65 28
will last about twenty years after it is fairly worn out. NA I 9 65 30
but her spirits were quite worn down; and, to be silent NA II 14 235 13
Rooms, you know, and I have worn them a great deal since. NA II 14 238 24
what was worn and hackneyed out of all sense and meaning." SS I 18 97 7
So altered--so faded--worn down by acute suffering of SS II 9 207 26
and his civilities were worn out like his information. PP II 4 152 4
ideas were nearly worn out before the tete-a-tete was over. PP III 1 257 66
It has never worn an amiable form to me." MP I 6 60 51
and had the burnt, fagged, worn look of fatigue and a hot MP II 1 178 7
it to; and though she had worn it in that manner once, MP II 8 254 8
And as for this necklace, I do not suppose I have worn it MP II 8 260 22
They must and shall be worn together. MP II 9 262 8
might, Fanny was worn down at last to think every thing an MP II 9 267 22
note to William had worn away, she had been in a state MP II 9 270 40
His therefore must be worn; and having, with delightful MP II 9 271 40
"I am worn out with civility," said he. MP II 10 278 20
subjects limited, and long worn thread-bare in all common MP III 3 341 28
the freshness of its wearer's feelings, must be worn away. MP III 6 368 8
monotony of Lady Bertram's, only worn into fretfulness.)-- MP III 8 392 11
it seemed a relief to her worn mind to be at any certainty; MP III 10 401 9
worn and faded, so comfortless, so slatternly, so shabby. MP III 11 408 2
or time would have worn away much of its ill effect. MP III 17 463 8
Campbell married, the impression may be a little worn off." E II 3 175 43
my dear Jane, that my influence is not entirely worn out. E II 16 296 36
Quite worn out and broken up. P III 8 64 9
have worn out on each side equally, and without violence. P IV 6 172 42
replied Mrs. Smith, gravely, "but it seems worn out now. P IV 9 194 22
manner--tho' more thin & worn by illness & Medecine, more S 10 413 1

WORN-OUT (1)
The worn-out past was sunk in the freshness of what was E II 5 188 8

WORRIED (3)
and she was sometimes worried down by officious condolence SS II 10 215 13
And now he had been so worried by what passed, that as SS III 2 273 16
His aunt worried him by her cares, and Sir Thomas knew not MP III 14 429 2

WORRIES (1)
solicitude, alternately her worries and her comforts. MP III 8 389 4

WORRY (4)
They shall no longer worry others, nor torture myself. SS III 10 347 30
sent off with a parting worry to dress, moved as languidly MP II 9 267 22
Campbell has been here, quite in a worry about you; and MP III 7 378 10
and she was herself in a worry of spirits which would have E II 18 311 36

WORRYING (2)
and as I hate to be worrying and officious, I said no more; MP II 2 189 5
left alone to bear the worrying of Mrs. Norris, who was MP II 9 267 22

WORSE (141)
& disagreable, & now he is grown worse than ever. LS 21 279 1
Mama will never forgive me, & I shall be worse off than LS 24 286 7
make him appear the worse)--and had Frederica possessed LS 24 288 11
& I can hardly tell which would have been worse for her. LS 27 296 1
her; but had nothing worse appeared, that might only have NA II 4 149 1
The longer he stays, the worse it will be for him at last. NA II 4 150 4
her; it had wafted nothing worse than a thick mizzling NA II 5 161 25
"So much the worse!" thought Catherine; such ill-timed NA II 8 187 14
seemed always at hand when least wanted,) much worse!-- NA II 9 194 6
"It contained something worse than any body could suppose!- NA II 10 204 13
Afterwards he got worse, and became quite my shadow. NA II 12 217 2
she hardly supposed there were any thing worse to be told. NA II 13 223 13
"You are too good, I am sure, to think the worse of me for NA II 13 223 13
Oh! worse than cold-hearted! SS I 4 21 14
I hope it is not to say that your sister is worse." SS I 13 63 10
May be his sister is worse at Avignon, and has sent for SS I 14 70 2
still be reserved," said Marianne, "and that is worse." SS I 17 94 45
Their being her relations too made it so much the worse; SS I 21 118 2
once, but I never was very handsome --worse luck for me. SS II 4 163 18
and his spirits were certainly worse than when at Barton. SS II 5 169 12
now before you; expensive, dissipated, and worse than both. SS II 9 210 32
but, what was still worse, must be subject to all the SS II 14 248 6
against him, which must be worse than all--his mother has SS III 1 269 53
she would be glad to compound now for nothing worse.' SS III 5 297 31
except that there was no amendment, did not appear worse. SS III 7 308 5
on the absurdity, and the worse than absurdity, of SS III 8 321 34
Those three or four weeks were worse than all. SS III 8 327 55
inflicted--I hardly know what could have made it worse." SS III 8 330 66
take her along with them in the chaise is worse than all. SS III 13 371 37
offence was unpardonable, but Lucy's was infinitely worse. SS III 13 371 38
think of nothing worse) than marry a man I did not like."-- W 318 2
Mr Watson returned in the evening, not the worse for the W 343 19
is infamous, eliz:; said he, worse than ever it was. W 349 24
As for me, I shall be no worse off without you, than I W 362 32
her sister was worse, and that she could not leave her. PP I 8 40 59
Bennet had not found Miss Bennet worse than she expected. PP I 9 41 2
I can recal nothing worse. PP I 16 80 27
instead! her liveliness had been never worse timed. PP I 17 87 14
you accuse him of nothing worse than of being the son of PP I 18 95 46
worse of her understanding, than I now do of her heart. PP II 1 135 13
Lady Catherine will not think the worse of you for being PP II 6 161 6
and it grew so much worse towards the evening that, added PP II 10 187 41
I dare say he often hears worse things said than I am PP II 16 220 10

At any rate, she cannot grow many degrees worse, without PP II 18 232 20
surprise in her uncle and aunt, as made every thing worse. PP III 2 260 2
but that it was no worse, she had need to be thankful. PP III 7 307 51
awkward enough; but her's she thought was still worse. PP III 13 346 22
any private fortune, and Miss Frances fared yet worse. MP I 1 3 1
and she had nothing worse to endure on the part of Tom, MP I 2 17 22
him, my spirits still worse, all my peace in this world MP I 3 29 46
It is much worse to have girls not out, give themselves MP I 5 50 39
That is worse than any thing--quite disgusting!" MP I 5 50 39
His own forgetfulness of her was worse than any thing MP I 7 74 58
well, and that any alteration must be for the worse. MP I 8 79 23
you find the place altogether worse than you expected?" MP I 10 98 6
why a man should make a worse clergyman for knowing that MP I 11 109 17
It is a great defect of temper, made worse by a very MP I 11 111 29
greater danger of becoming worse in a more active and MP I 11 111 30
could not have died at a worse time; and it is impossible MP I 13 122 4
to be of any use, but I think we could not choose worse." MP I 14 131 3
she would do it worse," was doubtless receiving all the MP I 14 136 21
to something so infinitely worse, to be told that she must MP I 16 150 1
This acting scheme gets worse and worse you see. MP I 16 153 8
the expenses, and what was worse, of the eclat of their MP I 18 164 1
I do not think you will find your woods by any means worse MP II 1 181 16
beds of stones, it was worse than any thing you can MP II 2 189 5
such amusements to nothing worse than a tete-a-tete with MP II 4 210 21
every one; and what is worse, cook has just been telling MP II 4 212 31
almost every thing, is at others worse than nothing. MP II 6 235 18
But, on the contrary, it was no worse than, "I am sorry to MP II 7 250 60
"Then you have had fatigues within doors, which are worse. MP II 9 268 26
herself occasionally called on to endure something worse. MP II 10 273 7
there would be nothing worse to be endured than an half- MP III 5 357 5
which, to say nothing worse, is certainly very ill-bred. MP III 5 361 16
but much worse looking, and with a blackguard character. MP III 5 361 16
to part with Rebecca, I should only get something worse. MP III 7 385 39
family, his habits were worse, and his manners coarser, MP III 8 389 3
they were, would have been worse but for such MP III 9 395 4
creditor to dupe me--and worse than simple to let him give MP III 11 412 20
Would not it be worse than simple? MP III 11 412 20
so very ill-looking as I did, at least one sees many worse. MP III 12 416 2
The prospect for her cousin grew worse and worse. MP III 12 417 4
verdure, was infinitely worse;--but even these incitements MP III 14 432 9
which was so much the worse, as there seemed no chance of MP III 17 465 15
She had not eloped with any worse feelings than those of MP III 17 467 18
She is a flatterer in all her ways; and so much the worse, E I 5 38 15
companion or useful helpmate, he could not do worse. E I 8 61 38
I have read worse charades. E I 9 72 15
sister, she had nothing worse to hear than Isabella's kind E I 12 104 45
altogether than travel forty miles to get into a worse air. E I 12 106 58
Going in dismal weather, to return probably in worse;-- E I 13 113 26
rooms and worse company than they might have had at home." E I 13 113 26
Smith was not better, by no means better, rather worse. E I 13 114 31
And now, poor girl! she was considerably worse from this E II 4 184 10
"So much the better--or so much the worse:--I do not know E II 6 202 35
one nor the other--nothing worse than every day remarks, E II 8 219 43
"It would be a crowd--a sad crowd; and what could be worse E II 11 249 14
an improvement--a very bad plan--much worse than the other. E II 11 251 26
They would catch worse colds at the crown than any where." E II 11 251 26
"Emma," said she, "this paper is worse than I expected. E II 11 253 41
to Enscombe were neither worse nor better than had been E II 13 266 5
"Worse than I had supposed. E II 14 279 52
Worse and worse. E II 14 279 52
In one respect Mrs. Elton grew even worse than she had E II 15 281 3
have power to draw me out, in worse weather than to-day." E II 16 294 22
the mere proposal of going out seemed to make her worse.-- E III 9 390 18
a disagreeable business--but things might be much worse.-- E III 10 393 17
At least, however, I cannot be worse off than I should E III 11 407 26
Why was it so much worse that Harriet should be in love E III 11 408 32
thus-- "very bad--though it might have been worse.-- E III 15 445 14
15

How much worse, had they been obliged to meet! E III 16 451 1
tone of great ill usage,) which made it so much the worse. E III 16 457 40
the building in which N. takes M. for better, for worse." E III 17 463 14
Her connexions may be worse than his. E III 18 473 24
got over, had he not done worse; but he had, as by the P III 1 8 17
grounds, and still worse to anticipate the new hands they P III 5 36 19
I really am very ill--a great deal worse than I ever own." P III 6 44 7
apprehensions were the worse of being vague;--they P III 7 54 4
no revenge, for he was not altered, or not for the worse. P III 7 61 34
and disappointed him; and worse, she had shewn a P III 7 61 36
Now they were as strangers; nay, worse than strangers, for P III 8 64 3
You know how much he wanted money--worse than myself. P III 8 67 23
His cold politeness, his ceremonious grace, were worse P III 8 72 60
No, no; Henrietta might do worse than marry Charles Hayter; P III 9 76 15
for her, and still worse for me; and therefore it is very P III 9 76 16
without sufferings which made her worse than helpless! P III 12 114 59
No symptoms worse than before had appeared. P IV 1 121 2
Elliot's not being the worse for her exertions, and had P IV 1 126 20
years had not altered almost every feature for the worse. P IV 3 141 12
in Bath; and as for the men! they were infinitely worse. P IV 3 142 13
her think worse of the world, than she hoped it deserved. P IV 5 156 12
sore-throats, you "know, are always worse than anybody's." P IV 6 164 8
"We do not like our lodgings here the worse, I can tell P IV 6 170 29
or always suspecting the other of being worse than it was. P IV 7 175 6
He is worse than last year. P IV 9 203 72
moments, that no flagrant open crime could have been worse. P IV 9 210 97
Worse than all! P IV 11 238 47
Elizabeth did nothing worse than look cold and unconcerned. P IV 12 248 1
become considerably worse than before, as soon as the S 1 364 1
She cd see nothing worse in Lady Denham, than the sort of S 6 392 1
reflections--& much worse than all the rest, must have S 11 420 1

WORSHIP (2)
As for Colonel Brandon, she was not only ready to worship SS III 5 293 2
Harriet seemed ready to worship her friend for a sentence E III 11 411 42

WORSHIPPED (1)
deserve to be less worshipped than now; and it really was E III 15 450 38

WORSHIPPING (1)
indeed, with such a worshipping wife, it was hardly E I 11 92 5

WORSHIPS (1)
It is he who sees and worships your merit the strongest, MP III 3 344 41

WORST (50)
worst, where the motives of her conduct have been doubtful. LS 14 264 2
Prepare my dear madam, for the worst. LS 24 291 17
The worst of it is that its weight makes it difficult to NA II 6 165 4
but as an escape from the worst and most irremediable of SS II 7 184 15
resolution, as some of the worst was over; "Colonel SS III 4 289 31
be the worst of all parties; & the others were delighted.-- W 357 28
everybody else Mr. Darcy was condemned as the worst of men. PP II 1 138 31
partly governed by this worst kind of pride, and partly by PP II 10 187 40
account of the real, the worst objections to the match, PP II 13 204 1
A flirt too, in the worst and meanest degree of flirtation; PP II 18 231 18
My father and mother believe the worst, but I cannot think PP III 4 275 5
"Oh, yes!--that, that is the worst of all. PP III 5 284 15
the worst, there is no occasion to look on it as certain. PP III 5 288 37
about law being the worst wilderness of the two, but I MP I 9 94 55
against comedy, and this is comedy in its worst form." MP I 14 136 20
of it, to be rid of the worst object connected with the MP II 2 194 21
But I have long thought Mr. Bertram one of the worst MP II 4 212 30
her own two were the very worst, engrossed her completely. MP III 7 385 38
A quick looking girl of Susan's age was the very worst MP III 10 403 15
Rushworth, was all in her worst line of conduct, and MP III 12 418 4
mother, that the worst consequences might be apprehended. MP III 16 450 9
He called it a bad thing, done in the worst manner, and at MP III 16 452 13
worst manner, and at the worst time; and though Julia was MP III 16 452 13
had taken, as opening the worst probabilities of a MP III 16 452 13
proved to have much the worst of the bargain; for when his E I 2 16 4
Miss Bates stood in the very worst predicament in the E I 3 21 4
I think her the very worst sort of companion that Emma E I 5 38 15
them, and people think little of even the worst weather. E I 13 115 39
That was the worst of all. E I 16 134 1
The first error and the worst lay at her door. E I 16 136 10
You are the worst judge in the world, Mr. Knightley, of E I 18 146 11
She was, besides, which was the worst of all, so cold, so E II 2 169 15
to say, "of all horrid things, leave-taking is the worst." E II 12 259 12
13

going with her, that the worst of the business might be E II 14 270 2
however, to know the worst at once--she hurried on--"and E II 15 287 26
"I have often thought them the worst of the two," replied E II 16 293 21
"Very soon, very soon indeed; that's the worst of it. E III 8 382 27
was persuaded that she must herself have been the worst. E III 12 421 17
all the worst of her sufferings had been unsuspected.-- E III 16 452 8
you had seen her, as I did, when she was at the worst!"-- E III 16 454 17
have saved her from the worst of all her womanly follies-- E III 17 463 15
Mr. Woodhouse could not be soon reconciled; but the worst E III 17 466 30
"You are prepared for the worst, I see--and very bad it is. E III 18 470 12
which often makes the worst part of our suffering, as it P III 2 12 4
"The worst is over!" P III 7 60 26
It is the worst evil of too yielding and indecisive a P III 10 88 26
The worst of Bath was, the number of its plain women. P IV 3 141 13
That's the worst of him." P IV 10 217 20
"Here," said he, "ended the worst of my state; for now I P IV 11 243 70
To say the truth nerves are the worst part of my S 10 415 1

WORSTED (1)
in measuring lengths of worsted for her rug, to see any SS II 7 181 7
8

WORSTING (1)
in the neighbourhood worsting; and the rapid increase of P III 1 6 11

WORTH (149)
you my dearest Susan, Mr De Courcy may be worth having. LS 9 256 1
they are worth reading; some fun and nature in them." NA I 7 49 36
"Now you have given me a security worth having; and I NA I 10 78 41
of whose fidelity and worth she had enjoyed a fortnight's NA I 10 81 61
"The finest place in England--worth going fifty miles at NA I 11 85 23
that it is very well worth while to be tormented for two NA I 14 110 27
it is not worth arguing about, for whatever might pass on NA II 3 145 13
That he should think it worth his while to fancy himself NA II 3 148 29
Had not Miss Morland already seen all that could be worth NA II 8 185 6
the reach of something worth her notice; and felt, as she NA II 8 185 5
It is a power little worth knowing however, since it can NA II 9 196 21
upon it, it is something not at all worth understanding." NA II 14 234 10
new friends you make I hope will be better worth keeping." NA II 14 236 15
"no friend can be better worth keeping than Eleanor." NA II 14 236 16
"Fifteen years! my dear Fanny; her life cannot be worth SS I 2 10 19
felt assured of his worth: and even that quietness of SS I 3 16 13
the admiration of a person who can understand their worth. SS I 3 17 18
You know enough of him to do justice to his solid worth. SS I 4 20 9
"yes, yes, he is very well worth catching, I can tell you, SS I 9 44 23
and he is very well worth setting your cap at, I can tell SS I 9 45 32
"She knows her own worth too well for false shame," SS I 17 94 44
person whose good opinion is so well worth having as yours. SS I 22 128 9
your own feelings, your opinion would not be worth having." SS II 2 150 34
young man in the world worth having; and with your pretty SS II 8 192 3
"More than you think it really and intrinsically worth." SS II 11 225 32
now, will marry a man worth more than five or six hundred SS II 11 227 50
to think his acquaintance worth having; and Mr. Dashwood SS II 11 228 52
that was worth hearing, and his wife had still less. SS II 12 233 18
all out of charity with the modesty and worth of the other. SS II 14 250 12
is his, if he think it worth his acceptance--but that, SS III 3 282 19
neither did she think it worth inquiring into; and SS III 4 286 18
Brandon seems a man of great worth and respectability. SS III 4 290 36
37

it is not worth while to wait two or three months for him. SS III 4 291 51
is worth the trial however, and you shall hear every thing. SS III 8 319 29
by saying, "it is hardly worth while, Mr. Willoughby, for SS III 8 320 30
31

and cheerful society as the only happiness worth a wish. SS III 10 343 8
But there are many works well worth reading, at the park; SS III 10 343 9
which made them all worth hearing, & she only regretted W 335 13
both his own cards--it is worth anything in the world!"-- W 358 28
a most disagreeable, horrid man, not at all worth pleasing. PP I 3 13 20
"Mr. Darcy is not so well worth listening to as his friend, PP I 5 19 9
the younger sisters not worth speaking to, a wish of being PP I 6 21 1
He can be a conversible companion if he thinks it worth PP I 16 82 48
worth of each was eclipsed by Mr. Bingley and Netherfield. PP I 18 103 77
to say that could be worth hearing, and were listened to PP II 4 152 4
Stupid men are the only ones worth knowing, after all." PP II 4 154 19
that it was much better worth looking at in the summer. PP II 6 162 13
cherished opinion of his worth, and which bore so alarming PP II 13 204 2
connected with a little absurdity, are not worth a regret. PP II 18 231 17
The officers will find women better worth their notice. PP II 18 232 20
liberty--which it is not worth while to relate; but his PP III 5 284 14
though we can teach only what is not worth knowing. PP III 12 343 37
think meanly of their sense and worth compared with my own. PP III 16 369 24
that his worth was invaluable; but she checked herself. PP III 16 371 46
could have a little trifle among them, worth their having." MP I 3 30 52
the never failing hope of his arrival was worth much. MP I 4 35 6
and great, as possessing worth, which no one but herself MP I 4 37 8
the Miss Bertrams were worth pleasing, and were ready to MP I 5 44 3
fruit should be so little worth the trouble of gathering." MP I 6 54 10
worth reading, to his sisters, when they are separated. MP I 7 64 10
Dr. Grant doing the honours of it, were worth looking at. MP I 7 65 13
the poor chaplain were not worth looking at--and, in those MP I 9 87 15
How can two sermons a week, even supposing them worth MP I 9 92 46
the only two characters worth playing before I reached MP I 13 122 2
"It is not worth complaining about, but to be sure the MP I 13 122 4
Will not this be worth gaining?" MP I 16 155 16
proof and importance, was worth ages of doubt and anxiety. MP II 1 176 3
"but it is not worth while to bore my father with it now. MP II 1 181 16
"I hope we shall always think the acquaintance worth any MP II 2 190 6
to harden yourself to the idea of being worth looking at.-- MP II 3 198 8
their young inmates really worth visiting; and though MP II 7 238 1
as to whether it were worth while, "because Sir Thomas MP II 7 238 2
for that queen; no, no, a dozen is more than it is worth. MP II 7 243 27
It is not worth minding. MP II 7 249 53
she was going to were worth those she left behind; and MP II 8 256 12
Such a trifle is not worth half so many words." MP II 8 260 22
a part of every woman's worth in the judgment of man that MP II 12 294 16
Henry Crawford had too much sense not to feel the worth of MP II 12 294 16
without fear; there can be no difficulties worth naming. MP II 13 303 15
him a commission for any thing else that is worth having. MP II 13 305 25
to your finding one still better worth listening to.-- MP III 1 314 16
manner was now an object worth attaining; and she felt MP III 1 322 50
knew her to have all the worth that could justify the MP III 2 326 3
Fanny was worth it all; he held her to be worth every MP III 3 336 7
of her not estimating your worth to her brother, quite as MP III 4 351 36
her, whose opinion was worth having; and especially MP III 5 361 16
very few young ladies have any affections worth caring for. MP III 5 363 22
her notions, his worth would be finally wasted on her even MP III 6 367 5
when I have any thing worth writing about; any thing to MP III 6 373 26
"my letter will not be worth your reading, for there will MP III 9 393 1
Fanny understanding the worth of her disposition, and MP III 9 397 8
and treated as the friend best worth attending to. MP III 17 462 4
growing worth, what could be more natural than the change? MP III 17 470 27
very often to recollect something worth their putting in. E I 9 70 5
visit that could be at all worth the purchase; and the E I 13 113 25
some one worth having; I ought not to have attempted more. E I 16 137 11

"And those times are, whenever he thinks it worth his E I 18 146 14
"Oh! as for me, my judgment is worth nothing. E II 3 176 48
49
worth a great deal more than any little exertion it needs." E II 5 190 24
his certainly thinking it worth while to try to please her. E II 5 191 28
She listened, and found it well worth listening to. E II 8 214 13
They were a couple worth looking at. E II 8 230 100
"It is not worth while, Harriet, to give Mrs. Ford the E II 9 235 37
opinion of the instrument will be worth having.'-- E II 9 236 46
couple are not enough to make it worth while to stand up. E II 11 248 7
8
him, it might have been worth while to pause and consider, E II 11 250 19
If the Westons think it worth while to be at all this E II 12 257 3
described--it was not worth while to think about them--and E II 13 267 9
Harriet is worth a hundred such.-- E II 13 269 16
body else; but it was not worth while to attack an error E II 14 273 22
23
think letters are never worth going through the rain for." E II 16 293 16
a mere nothing; it was not worth thinking of;--but if he, E III 1 315 1
every body found so well worth seeing, and she and Mr. E III 6 352 2
aware, it was not worth bringing forward again:--it could E III 6 353 3
"No--it will not be worth while. E III 6 365 70
He said nothing worth hearing--looked without seeing-- E III 7 367 2
whose good opinion is most worth preserving, are not E III 16 459 47
His tender compassion towards oppressed worth can go no E III 17 465 24
right that equal worth can give, to be happy together. E III 17 465 25
No sacrifice on any side worth the name. E III 17 468 31
"It is not now worth a regret," said Emma. E III 18 477 56
contemplation of his worth which this comparison produced. E III 18 480 80
and worth which could bid fairest for her little friend. E III 19 482 4
she could not admit him to be worth thinking of again. P III 1 8 17
for nobody would think it worth their while to observe me, P III 3 17 4
commanders particularly worth attending to--and beg leave P III 3 17 4
and visited again, to make the worth of Lyme understood. P III 11 95 9
of sailors having more worth and warmth than any other set P III 11 99 19
memoirs of characters of worth and suffering, as occurred P III 11 101 24
Such a heart is very little worth having; is it, Lady P IV 2 131 10
being so very well worth seeing, for as he has a taste for P IV 2 131 12
"Family connexions were always worth preserving, good P IV 4 149 12
good company always worth seeking; Lady Dalrymple had P IV 4 149 12
"it was an acquaintance worth having," and when Anne P IV 4 150 15
be worth knowing, always acceptable as acquaintance." P IV 4 151 19
education in the world," know nothing worth attending to. P IV 5 155 9
and if they are intelligent may be well worth listening to. P IV 5 155 10
A sick chamber may often furnish the worth of volumes." P IV 5 156 10
he saw a place on it well worth occupying; when, at that P IV 8 190 47
"Is not this song worth staying for?" said Anne, suddenly P IV 8 190 49
"No!" he replied impressively, "there is nothing worth my P IV 8 190 50
in the case, was not worth enquiry; for there was a P IV 9 192 2
Even the smooth surface of family-union seems worth P IV 9 198 53
Never worth remembering. P IV 10 223 44
Was it unpardonable to think it worth my while to come? P IV 11 243 70
in return for all the worth and all the prompt welcome P IV 12 251 10
Anne was tenderness itself, and she had the full worth of P IV 12 252 12
by her innate worth, on the affections of her patroness.-- S 3 378 1
utmost to send you company worth having; & think we may S 5 387 1

WORTHIES (1)
She was quite one of her worthies--the most amiable, E II 15 284 12

WORTHIEST (1)
is enough to prove him one of the worthiest of men." SS III 9 337 16

WORTHING (1)
like Brighton, or Worthing, or East Bourne--but not to a S 1 368 1

WORTHLESS (7)
of mothers--still condemns Frederica as a worthless girl! LS 17 271 7
had abhorred as the most worthless of men, Willoughby, in SS III 9 333 2
prepossession for that worthless young man!--and without SS III 9 336 14
had quite doted upon the worthless hussey, and was now, by SS III 13 370 37
to their mother, was worthless in their eyes when opposed PP I 7 29 4
on one of the most worthless young men in Great Britain to PP III 8 308 1
more unbecoming, or more worthless, than the uniform of a MP III 6 368 8

WORTHLESSNESS (2)
chapters; in which the worthlessness of lords and NA I 4 34 9
himself that Wickham's worthlessness had not been so well PP III 10 321 2

WORTHY (41)
can be no dissimulation worthy notice, & Miss Vernon shall LS 4 248 2
of being able to make a worthy man completely miserable. LS 14 264 4
worthy than she has yet done, of her mother's tender care. LS 14 265 5
in seeing him still worthy your esteem, still capable of LS 23 285 7
them the family of a most worthy old friend; and, as the NA I 5 36 3
I only wish I were more worthy of him.-- NA I 15 117 6
They are a set of very worthy men. NA II 11 210 6
Such an agreeable, worthy man as he seemed to be! NA II 14 238 26
wish of waiting on their worthy neighbours, that he might NA II 15 243 9
I think him every thing that is worthy and amiable." SS I 4 20 6
from among her sisters as worthy of being the mistress of PP I 17 88 14
my pretensions to please a woman worthy of being pleased." PP III 16 369 24
have parted with you, my Lizzy, to any one less worthy." PP III 17 377 37
I know this to be the truth; and most worthy of you are MP III 4 353 46
who must prove a far more worthy companion than himself; MP III 10 403 15
affections for an object worthy to succeed her in them. MP III 17 470 25
A worthy employment for a young lady's mind! E I 1 12 42
And that excellent Miss Bates!--such thorough worthy E I 12 102 31
Her disposition and abilities were equally worthy of all E II 2 164 6
afforded no young man worthy of giving her independence; E II 2 168 14
Dixon seems a very charming young man, quite worthy of him. E II 3 175 39
Mr. Elton is a most worthy young man--but'---- in short, I E II 3 176 44
But she had believed them to be well meaning, worthy E II 3 179 53
aunt, very worthy people; I have known them all my life. E II 5 194 45
to settle early in life, and to marry, from worthy motives. E II 6 204 43
I know what worthy people they are. E II 7 210 20
The less worthy females were to come in the evening, with E II 8 214 13
She must have delighted the Coles--worthy people, who E II 9 231 1
Who can this be?--very likely the worthy Coles.-- E III 2 323 19
And how did you find my worthy old friend and her daughter? E III 9 385 6
or esteemed so little worthy as a friend: but she had the E III 9 391 21
as infinitely the most worthy of the two--or even the more E III 13 431 38
time, as worthy of your affection, as you think me already. E III 17 464 20
Nothing, but to grow more worthy of him, whose intentions E III 18 475 39
drawn form every poet, every work worthy of being read, some attempt P III 10 84 7
worthy of her brother; "and a very respectable family. P III 10 92 47
charming woman, quite worthy of being known in Camden- P IV 3 141 13
A scheme, worthy of Mrs. Wallis's understanding, by all P IV 9 208 92
He was now esteemed quite worthy to address the daughter P IV 12 248 1
beyond her expectation worthy people--& finally was S 3 378 1
She was felt to be worthy of trust--to be the very S 3 379 1

WOULD-BE (1)
seemed terribly like a would-be lover, and made it some E I 14 118 4

WOUND (22)
duty, could induce me to wound my own feelings by urging a LS 30 301 4
These were thrilling words, and wound up Catherine's NA II 2 140 8
She would not wound the feelings of her sister on any SS I 4 19 5
covered with kisses, her wound bathed with lavender-water, SS I 21 121 10
to speak, lest she might wound Marianne still deeper by SS II 7 184 15
I have no right to wound your feelings by attempting to SS II 9 207 26
no power to wound them, sat pointedly slighted by both. SS II 12 232 16
would receive a deeper wound from the want of importance PP II 10 187 40
the valley, into which the road with some abruptness wound. PP III 1 245 3
"Oh! you do not consider how much we have wound about. MP I 9 94 62
supper, wound up the enjoyments and fatigues of the day. MP III 7 376 5
and wound up her spirits for the six days ensuing. MP III 11 408 4
I do not consider her as meaning to wound my feelings. MP III 16 456 25
After what had passed to wound and alienate the two MP III 17 469 23
Where the wound had been given, there must the cure be E I 17 143 15
round to its object, he wound it all up with astonishment E II 5 192 29
low, "time, my dearest Emma, time will heal the wound.-- E III 13 425 12
13
unsuspicious of being inflicting any peculiar wound. P III 7 60 32
good health since a severe wound which he received two P III 11 94 6
There was no wound, no blood, no visible bruise; but her P III 12 109 33
The Admiral wound it all up summarily by exclaiming, "ay, P IV 1 126 21
22
And with a quivering lip he wound up the whole by adding, " P IV 11 232 15

WOUNDED (12)
to Elinor, as her own wounded heart taught her to think of SS II 12 236 39
40
A heart, wounded like yours can have little inclination W 317 2
situation remained the same, her peace equally wounded. PP II 1 134 3
If I have wounded your sister's feelings, it was PP II 12 199 5
malice, and pour into the wounded bosoms of each other, PP III 5 289 42
her sister's hand, her wounded heart swelled again with MP II 1 175 2
consequence, bustle and the world, for a wounded spirit. MP II 3 202 25
its prime and freshness, wounded by no opposition of MP II 6 235 18
Every feeling of duty, honour, and tenderness was wounded MP III 7 386 43
an interesting mixture of wounded affection and genuine E II 3 179 53
or even wounded, by a circumstance of this sort." P IV 6 173 46
With a heart pierced, wounded, almost broken! P IV 8 183 10

WOUNDING (6)
whatever must be most wounding to her irritable feelings, SS II 3 155 6
He is the most fearful of giving pain, of wounding SS II 13 244 40
for his release without wounding his delicacy, nor how at SS III 13 363 6
was wounding, but was very unlikely to recommend his suit. PP II 11 189 5
own feelings, care not how much I may be wounding your's. PP III 16 365 2
3
"They aimed at wounding more than Harriet," said he. E III 2 330 47

WOUNDS (1)
had been inflicting deeper wounds in almost every sentence. MP III 16 457 30

WRAP (4)
"I beg, Catherine, you will always wrap yourself up very NA I 2 18 2
If it was but a good day with my father, I wd wrap myself W 319 2
The door opened, & displayed Tom Musgrave in the wrap of a W 355 28
'If Miss Taylor undertakes to wrap Miss Emma up, you need E II 11 252 37

WRAPPED (1)
glasses, and wrapped herself up, without opening her lips. E I 13 114 27

WRAPT (8)
connection, and Catherine, wrapt in the contemplation of NA II 15 243 10
The piano-forte, at which Marianne, wrapt up in her own SS II 1 145 23
She sat in silence almost all the way, wrapt in her own SS II 4 160 2
She either sat in gloomy silence, wrapt in such gravity as MP I 17 160 8
amiable and affectionate; wrapt up in her family; a E I 11 92 4
to see that it was cold, and too well wrapt up to feel it. E I 13 112 24
Wrapt up in a cloak of politeness, she seemed determined E II 2 169 15
one but Louisa, or those who were wrapt up in her welfare. P III 12 115 66

WREATH (1)
it was by any such broad wreath of gallantry, she yet E II 13 266 5

WRECK (1)
as ever, amidst the wreck of the good looks of every body P III 1 6 11

WRETCH (2)
a visitor, without thinking him at all a tiresome wretch." E I 8 60 27
I was the most miserable wretch! E III 18 478 66

WRETCHED (59)
who has received so wretched an education would not be a LS 3 247 1
could render probable, and must in the end make wretched. LS 12 261 3
She is extremely young to be sure, has had a wretched LS 18 273 2
I know that Frederica is made wretched by Sir James' LS 23 284 4
When that wretched event takes place, Frederica must LS 24 291 17
Frederica was wretched in the idea of going, & I could not LS 27 296 1
that I shall be quite wretched if he remain here; but LS 31 302 1
I have been quite wretched without you." NA I 8 56 12
these memoirs of the wretched Matilda may fall'--when your NA II 5 160 21
at the concert, but made wretched work of it--it happened NA II 12 217 2
Catherine was too wretched to be fearful. NA II 14 230 1
the same with him now; for he writes in wretched spirits. SS I 22 134 52
and Elinor was then as liberty to think and be wretched. SS I 22 135 56
you believe me to be so, while I see you so wretched!" SS II 7 185 23
I have passed a wretched night in endeavouring to excuse a SS II 7 187 42
I care not who knows that I am wretched. SS II 7 189 52
I must feel--I must be wretched--and they are welcome to SS II 7 190 52
when she considers the wretched and hopeless situation of SS II 9 210 32
irritated than before, she did not see her less wretched. SS II 10 212 1
I cannot picture to myself a more wretched condition. SS III 1 268 50
days of illness, and wretched for some immediate relief, SS III 7 312 18
of making myself contemptible and wretched for ever. SS III 8 321 34
She read what made her wretched. SS III 8 328 61
her for Margaret, & poor Penelope was very wretched--. W 317 2
Darcy, in wretched suspense, could only say something PP III 4 277 11
Wretched, wretched, mistake!" PP III 4 278 18
anguish as she reflected on that wretched business. PP III 4 279 24
was impossible to one so wretched as herself; but she had PP III 4 281 29
And in the wretched state of his own finances, there was a PP III 6 297 12
wretched as is his character, we are forced to rejoice!" PP III 7 304 34
was wretched in the thought of what her sister must endure. PP III 9 315 1
"This is a wretched beginning indeed! PP III 17 372 5
disposing of her, was a wretched reflection, and she sat PP III 17 375 28
unsteadiness; and his happiness under it made her wretched. MP I 17 159 6
there was a smile--which made her blush and feel wretched. MP II 10 274 8
without such wretched feelings as she had formerly known. MP II 11 284 8
and cry over what had passed, with very wretched feelings. MP III 1 320 45
good man must feel, how wretched, and how unpardonable, MP III 1 324 58
She did it with wretched feelings, but it was inevitable. MP III 5 357 5
If we feel for the wretched, enough to do all we can for E I 10 87 30
It was a wretched business, indeed!-- E I 16 134 1
reasonable excuse for not hurrying on the wretched moment. E II 2 165 9
"I have made a most wretched discovery," said he, after a E II 8 221 51
little room; but that was scouted as a wretched suggestion. E II 11 254 45
This wretched note was the finale of Emma's breakfast. E II 12 259 10
It was too wretched!-- E II 12 259 10
to share his feelings, he would not have been so wretched. E II 13 265 4
extremely, made her wretched for a while, and when the E II 13 268 13
"On this point we have been wretched. E III 10 396 43
mortifying; that she was wretched, and should probably E III 11 411 43
have been under wretched alarm every night of his life. E III 19 483 10
I never saw quite so wretched an example of what a sea- P III 3 20 16
As to the wretched party left behind, it could scarcely be P III 12 110 43
She was so wretched, and so vehement, complained so much P III 12 115 65
They were wretched comforters for one another!" P IV 1 122 5
that the wretched state of his affairs was fully known. P IV 9 209 96
They were wretched together. P IV 9 211 101
very little--they have wretched health, as you have heard S 5 385 1
of our own wretched constitutions for any releif.-- S 5 386 1

WRETCHEDEST (1)
the wretchedest being in the world at a civil falsehood." E II 9 234 32

WRETCHEDLY (8)
I am grown wretchedly thin I know; but I will not pain you NA I 15 118 13
You must think wretchedly indeed of Willoughby, if after SS I 15 80 38
When there, though looking most wretchedly, she ate more SS II 8 193 6
So dull, so wretchedly dull!-- SS II 13 243 33
Had I been in love, I could not have been more wretchedly PP II 13 208 8
Wretchedly did he feel, that with all the cost and care of MP III 17 463 9
closest observance; and wretchedly as she had hitherto E III 12 416 2
He had thought her wretchedly altered, and, in the first P III 7 61 36

WRETCHEDNESS (30)
she gave jealousy & wretchedness to his wife, & by her LS 4 248 1
to all the desperate wretchedness of which a last volume NA I 2 19 7
Her own feelings entirely engrossed her; her wretchedness NA I 9 67 33

would have supposed she had any wretchedness about her. NA I 12 92 4
seeking increase of wretchedness in every reflection that SS I 1 7 13
He did not disturb the wretchedness of her mind by ill- SS I 3 16 7
misery of her feelings, by exclamations of wretchedness. SS II 6 177 15
alleviation of her wretchedness, the personal sympathy of SS II 10 214 6
Her wretchedness I could have borne, but her passion--her SS III 8 328 61
They solaced their wretchedness, however, by duets after PP I 8 40 59
pleasure, that will atone for such wretchedness as this! PP III 11 337 55
in such solitary wretchedness; and she made her way to the MP II 11 287 17
There was wretchedness in the idea of its being serious; MP II 13 304 16
she sat in trembling wretchedness, and with a good deal of MP III 1 318 39
and were unhappy too!--it was all wretchedness together. MP III 1 321 46
and arranging every thing there, without wretchedness.-- MP III 6 370 12
last evening at Mansfield Park must still be wretchedness. MP III 6 374 28
"Dear Fanny, you know our present wretchedness. MP III 15 442 23
others only established her superiority in wretchedness. MP III 16 448 2
left in a state of wretchedness, inferior only to what MP III 16 450 10
feelings of shame and wretchedness which Crawford's sister MP III 16 454 18
the disappointment and wretchedness arising from the MP III 17 464 10
and regret to wretchedness--in having so requited MP III 17 468 22
at all the outward wretchedness of the place, and recal E I 10 87 27
saw him coming--his noble look--and my wretchedness before. E III 4 342 38
The wretchedness of a scheme to box hill was in Emma's E III 8 377 1
probably find this day but the beginning of wretchedness. E III 11 411 43
be increasing Emma's wretchedness but the reflection never E III 12 422 20
immediate wretchedness, such uncertain future good.-- P III 4 29 8
or a mind destroyed by wretchedness, and looked so P III 11 100 23

WRETCHES (1)
Tiresome wretches!" E I 8 58 17

WRIGGLES (1)
hard, she starts and wriggles like a young dab chick in P IV 10 218 24

WRIGHT (4)
I should be extremely displeased if Wright were to send us E II 15 283 9
How has Wright done my hair?"--with many other relative E III 2 324 20
And as for Mrs. Hodges, Wright holds her very cheap indeed. E III 16 458 42
She promised Wright a receipt, and never sent it." E III 16 458 42

WRING (1)
must wring her heart, could not be the office of a friend. NA II 9 192 5

WRINKLES (2)
we must make you a few wrinkles, and a little of the MP I 15 146 52
degree, all lines and wrinkles, nine grey hairs of a side, P III 3 19 16

WRIST (2)
too large about the wrist; but Jane is taking them in." E II 9 237 48
tooth, and a clumsy wrist, which he was continually making P III 5 34 12

WRITE (155)
to the Vernons, & when I write to him, it must be under LS 5 250 3
I had intended to write to Reginald myself, as soon as my LS 13 262 1
When I next write, I shall be able I hope to tell you that LS 23 285 8
My dearest friend, I write in the greatest distress; LS 28 297 1
I write only to bid you farewell. LS 34 304 1
Why would you write to me? LS 36 305 1
I charged her to write to me very often, & to remember LS 41 310 4
of two months ceased to write of her absence, & in the LS 42 313 7
& in the course of two more, to write to her at all. LS 42 313 7
for though she could not write sonnets, she brought NA I 1 16 10
ladies do write so much better letters than gentlemen! NA I 3 27 29
a general rule that women write better letters than men, NA I 3 28 34
proper and kind in her to write to Miss Thorpe, and NA I 13 105 40
every particular was deferred till James could write again. NA I 15 122 28
"I will write home directly," said she, "and if they do NA II 2 140 8
Abbey on her lips, she hurried home to write her letter. NA II 2 140 11
What can he write about, but yourself? NA II 3 144 8
Isabella promised so faithfully to write directly." NA II 9 195 20
Pray write to me soon, and direct to my own home. NA II 12 216 2
I would write to him myself, but have mislaid his NA II 12 217 2
"Write to James on her behalf!-- NA II 12 218 3
"You must write to me, Catherine," she cried, "you must NA II 13 228 28
receive a letter from me. I am sure I had better not write. NA II 13 228 29
said, "Oh, Eleanor, I will write to you indeed." NA II 13 229 30
harder for her to write than in addressing Eleanor Tilney. NA II 14 235 14
"But if you write a note to the housekeeper, Mr. Brandon," SS I 13 64 23
"I am not going to write to my mother," replied Marianne SS II 4 160 5
in town, how odd that he should neither come nor write! SS II 4 165 29
"And now," silently conjectured Elinor, "she will write to SS II 5 167 6
relief, Elinor resolved to write the next morning to her SS II 5 171 38
for it, then sat down to write her mother an account of SS II 9 203 10
not to be told, they could do nothing at present but write. SS II 11 230 4
Once Lucy thought to write to him, but then her spirit SS III 2 273 16
They will tell me I should write to the doctor, to get SS III 2 275 22
I write to the doctor, indeed!'" SS III 2 275 22
Should not the Colonel write himself?--sure, he is the SS III 4 286 17
I will not disturb you (seeing her preparing to write.) SS III 4 287 20
and retired to her own room to write letters and sleep. SS III 7 316 27
But whether I should write this apology, or deliver it in SS III 8 323 40
in London would write to them to announce the event, and SS III 12 358 4
"When do you write to Colonel Brandon, ma'am?" was an SS III 12 358 5
And I have promised to write him word who she dances with." W 320 2
"You write uncommonly fast." PP I 10 47 5
I write rather slowly." PP I 10 47 6
"How many letters you must have occasion to write in the PP I 10 47 7
"How can you contrive to write so even?" PP I 10 48 13
give me leave to defer your raptures till I write again?-- PP I 10 48 16
But do you always write such charming long letters to her, PP I 10 48 17
"It is a rule with me, that a person who can write a long PP I 10 48 19
who can write a long letter, with ease, cannot write ill." PP I 10 48 19
her brother--"because he does not write with ease. PP I 10 48 20
of him to write to you at all, and very hypocritical. PP I 13 62 10
He must write his own sermons; and the time that remains PP I 18 101 71
but she could see it and write of it without material pain. PP II 3 149 28
to write to him, and almost promised to answer her letter. PP II 4 151 2
It cannot be done too much; and when I next write to her, PP II 8 173 10
I write without any intention of paining you, or humbling PP II 12 196 4
that is the case, you must write to your mother to beg PP II 14 211 5
6
When Lydia went away, she promised to write very often and PP II 19 238 5
Dearest Lizzy, I hardly know what I would write, but I PP III 4 274 5
He merely added, that he should not write again, till he PP III 5 286 28
when I write to them, and sign my name Lydia Wickham. PP III 5 291 60
I can hardly write for laughing. PP III 5 291 60
to leave London, and promised to write again very soon. PP III 6 295 5
Mr. Gardiner did not write again, till he had received an PP III 6 297 12
as soon as you can, and be careful to write explicitly. PP III 7 303 14
I shall write again as soon as any thing more is PP III 7 303 14
"Oh! my dear father," she cried, "come back, and write PP III 7 303 20
"Let me write for you," said Jane, "if you dislike the PP III 7 303 21
Their father then went to the library to write, and the PP III 7 304 33
I will write to my sister Gardiner about them directly. PP III 7 306 44
I can't write; so I will dictate, and you write for me. PP III 7 306 47
Pray write instantly, and let me understand it--unless it PP III 9 320 33
But I must write no more. PP III 10 325 2
"Write to me very often, my dear." PP III 11 330 5
My sisters may write to me. PP III 11 330 6
Elizabeth, who had a letter to write, went into the PP III 13 346 21
"And if I had not a letter to write myself, I might sit by PP III 18 382 19
but to say the truth, I was too cross to write. PP III 18 382 21
You must write again very soon, and praise him a great PP III 18 382 21
So, if you are not against it, I will write to my poor MP I 1 7 8
It will be readily believed that Mrs. Norris did not write MP I 1 11 19
"But William will write to you, I dare say." MP I 2 16 12
promised he would, but he had told her to write first." MP I 2 16 12
and you may write your letter whenever you choose. MP I 2 16 13
Would it make you happy to write to William?" MP I 2 16 13
Fanny could read, work, and write, but she had been taught MP I 2 18 23
and had charged her to write and invite him to Mansfield MP I 3 33 64
Now, Mr. Bertram, if you write to your brother, I entreat MP I 6 59 41
"If I write, I will say whatever you wish me; but I do not MP I 6 59 42
ever write to him, nor he to you, if it could be helped. MP I 6 59 43
You would not write to each other but upon the most urgent MP I 6 59 43
for William's sake, "they can write long letters." MP I 6 59 44
would not write long letters when you were absent?" MP I 7 64 10
had promised John groom to write to Mrs. Jefferies about MP I 7 73 53
Who could write chat to Sir Thomas? MP II 11 288 24
Pray write to her, if it be only a line." MP II 13 306 28
and of wanting to get away--"I will write directly." MP II 13 306 29
I do not know what I write, but it would be a great favour MP II 13 307 31
I would spell it, read it, write it with any body. MP III 3 343 38
You must write to me. MP III 5 364 32
niece in the evening to write to her soon and often, and MP III 6 373 26
whisper, "and I shall write to you, Fanny, when I have any MP III 6 373 26
'well, Mary, when do you write to Fanny?--is it not time MP III 9 393 1
not it time for you to write to Fanny?' to spur me on. MP III 9 393 1
a long letter from London; write me a pretty one in reply MP III 9 394 1
I know you cannot speak or write a falsehood,--so long MP III 11 411 18
"Certainly; and if he is lazy or negligent, I will write MP III 11 412 28
He makes me write, but I do not know what else is to be MP III 12 415 2
likely, that he would write to her at all events; it would MP III 12 418 5
I found it impossible to write from London, and persuaded MP III 13 420 2
is at a great distance, and I believe I shall write to her. MP III 13 422 2
I shall be able to write much that I could not say, and MP III 13 422 2
I think I shall certainly write. MP III 13 423 2
Oh! write, write. MP III 13 424 4
she must have something to write about, even to her niece, MP III 13 425 6
distressing circumstances, I will write again very soon." MP III 13 426 11
than I deserve--and I write now to beg an immediate answer. MP III 14 433 13
Write to me by return of post, judge of my anxiety, and do MP III 14 434 13
Dear Fanny, write directly, and tell us to come. MP III 14 435 14
has just reached me, and I write, dear Fanny, to warn you MP III 15 437 3
surmise nothing, whisper nothing, till I write again. MP III 15 437 3
He is still able to think and act; and I write, by his MP III 15 442 23
You need not be prompted to write with the appearance of E I 7 52 11
he is attached to her, and can write a tolerable letter." E I 7 54 31
day, to know that her husband could write a good letter." E I 7 54 33
"Why will not you write one yourself for us, Mr. Elton?" E I 9 71 8
to say, to sit down and write a letter, and say just what E I 9 76 35
way; and another, to write verses and charades like this." E I 9 76 35
"Oh! Miss Woodhouse, what a pity that I must not write E I 9 77 39
is no reason why you should not write it into your book." E I 9 77 40
Give me the book, I will write it down, and then there can E I 9 77 42
We admired it so much, that I have ventured to write it E I 9 82 80
He can sit down and write a fine flourishing letter, full E I 18 148 24
who are such a judge, and write so beautifully yourself. E II 1 158 12
Mrs. Goddard; and Emma should write a line, and invite her. E II 7 209 13
Isabella and Emma, I think, do write very much alike. E II 16 297 45
"Isabella and Emma both write beautifully," said Mr. E II 16 297 47
Do not you remember, Mrs. Weston, employing him to write E II 16 298 52
I shall write Mrs. Partridge in a day or two, and shall E II 17 300 10
Still Mrs. Elton insisted on being authorized to write an E III 6 359 37
declared she would not write any such denial yesterday, as E III 8 381 15
"Miss Fairfax was not well enough to write;" and when Mr. E III 9 389 16
"He told me at parting, that he should soon write; and he E III 10 398 53
to be allowed merely to write to Miss Fairfax instead, and E III 12 417 5
My courage rises while I write. E III 14 437 8
Who was so useful to him, who so ready to write his E III 17 466 29
our seeing Mr. Elliot, the next time you write to Bath. P III 12 107 20
to say, "the next time you write to your good father, Miss P IV 1 128 29
"which as you well know, affords little to write about. P IV 6 162 7
Sophy must write, and beg him to come to Bath. P IV 6 173 49
Wentworth said, "we will write the letter we were talking P IV 11 229 2
3
"I can hardly write. P IV 11 237 42
may be propelled to say, write or do, by the sovereign S 7 398 1
I had a few moments indecision;--whether to offer to write S 9 409 1

WRITER (12)
be true, as a celebrated writer has maintained, that no NA I 3 29 52
which proclaimed its writer to be deep in hardened villany. SS II 7 183 14
writer, were she here, would forbid--a dagger to my heart. SS III 8 325 50
To Catherine and Lydia, neither the letter nor its writer PP I 13 64 20
affection of the writer, that could give her any comfort. PP II 1 133 2
feelings towards its writer were at times widely different. PP II 14 212 17
of pleasure from its writer being himself to go away. MP II 9 266 21
reluctance to bring the writer of it and her cousin Edmund MP III 14 435 15
it conveyed very much to the credit of the writer. E I 7 50 4
the writer, and that he must learn to do without her. E II 13 266 6
writer again; but I will not delay you by a long preface.-- E III 14 436 7
her former regard for the writer, and the very strong E III 15 444 1

WRITER'S (1)
she concluded to be its writer's real design, by placing SS III 2 278 31

WRITERS (3)
so common with novel writers, of degrading by their NA I 5 37 4
At this rate, I shall not pity the writers of history any NA I 14 109 24
sentences from the style of our most approved writers.-- S 8 404 1

WRITES (15)
Miss S. writes word that she could not get the young lady LS 16 268 1
the same with him now; for he writes in wretched spirits. SS I 22 134 52
This woman of whom he writes--whoever she be--or any one, SS II 7 189 50
"Very well indeed!--how prettily she writes!--aye, that SS III 2 278 32
"Oh!" cried Miss Bingley, "Charles writes in the most PP I 10 48 22
woman's approbation while he writes with such gallantry." E I 9 82 82
That is what she writes about. E II 1 159 18
Well, now I have just given you a hint of what Jane writes E II 1 162 31
writes one of the best gentlemen's hands I ever saw." E II 16 297 49
Mr. Knightley drily, "writes to a fair lady like Miss E II 16 298 55
So Frank writes word. E II 18 306 11
What a letter the man writes!" E III 15 447 26
You see how delightfully she writes. E III 16 454 13
But I am not afraid of your seeing what he writes." E III 17 464 19
"He writes like a sensible man," replied Emma, when she E III 17 464 20

WRITING (86)
& perhaps may think me negligent for not writing before. LS 19 273 1
of helping myself but by writing to you, for I am LS 21 279 1
writing to you, who I know will enter into all my feelings. LS 22 280 1
it personally in town, ceased writing minutely or often. LS 42 311 1
Writing and accounts she was taught by her father; French NA I 1 14 1
insisted on Catherine's writing by every post, nor exacted NA I 2 19 3
of writing for which ladies are so generally celebrated. NA I 3 27 28
Every body allows that the talent of writing agreeable NA I 3 27 28
in distinguishing the writing than what its ancient date NA II 6 169 12
James had protested against writing to her till his return NA II 10 201 5
little inclination for writing, I think it my duty to tell NA II 10 202 6
7
Frederick's remissness in writing, was free from any real NA II 11 209 5
Lose no time, my dearest, sweetest Catherine, in writing NA II 12 218 2
would lay fifty guineas the letter was of his own writing." SS I 13 65 30
"He cannot bear writing, you know," she continued--"he SS I 20 113 37
"Writing to each other," said Lucy, returning the letter SS I 22 135 54
in writing to her mother, and sat down for that purpose. SS II 4 160 4
"I am writing home, Marianne," said Elinor; "had not you SS II 4 160 4
her that she must then be writing to Willoughby, and the SS II 4 160 5
that Marianne was again writing to Willoughby, for she SS II 5 171 38
hand, directed to Mr. Willoughby in your sister's writing. SS II 5 173 44
command from it, and writing as fast as a continual flow SS II 7 180 1
was that she was writing for the last time to Willoughby. SS II 7 180 4
The hand writing of her mother, never till then unwelcome, SS II 9 202 7
about writing a letter to his steward in the country. SS III 1 259 7

the liberty I take of writing to her; but I know your SS III 2 277 29
30
on its outward leaf her own name in his hand writing.-- SS III 10 342 7
over the pages of her writing!--and I believe I may say SS III 13 365 17
resolved that, instead of writing to Fanny, he should go SS III 13 372 45
Mr. Darcy was writing, and Miss Bingley, seated near him, PP I 10 47 1
"My stile of writing is very different from yours." PP I 10 48 21
proud of your defects in writing, because you consider PP I 10 48 27
garden, or in reading and writing, and looking out of PP II 7 168 1
the next morning, and writing to Jane, while Mrs. Collins PP II 9 177 1
"Since writing the above, dearest Lizzy, something has PP III 4 273 3
He was writing, and, without raising his head, coolly PP III 7 305 39
40
Elizabeth took the letter from his writing table, and they PP III 7 305 43
writing will not comprise what I have to tell you. PP III 10 321 2
you know married women have never much time for writing. PP III 11 330 6
Much as I abominate writing, I would not give up Mr. PP III 15 364 24
evenness of your writing, as another young lady once did. PP III 18 382 19
on her, could not help writing her a much kinder answer PP III 18 383 24
He continued with her the whole time of her writing, to MP I 2 16 20
Sir Thomas has been writing about it, I know." MP I 3 30 55
talking to the steward, writing to the attorney, settling MP I 4 34 1
but I do not at present foresee any occasion for writing." MP I 6 59 42
"Yes, except as to his writing her such short letters. MP I 7 64 10
himself the trouble of writing any thing worth reading, to MP I 7 64 10
a shilling--her writing desk, and her works of charity and MP I 16 151 2
to find her cousin Edmund there writing at the table! MP II 9 261 1
on which Edmund had begun writing to her, as a treasure MP II 9 265 19
was previously engaged in writing for that stupid woman's MP II 12 296 31
she was in the habit of writing for her aunt, and prepared MP II 13 307 30
I have any thing worth writing about; any thing to say, MP III 6 373 26
Miss Crawford's style of writing, lively and affectionate, MP III 7 376 4
would have no motive for writing, strong enough to MP III 7 376 4
of his sister's in writing, for there has been no 'well, MP III 9 393 1
Crawford alone--or, he was too happy for letter writing! MP III 10 399 1
but had had no time for writing; that he thought himself MP III 10 400 8
I have not time for writing much, but it would be out of MP III 12 415 2
of a few years--but I am writing nonsense--were I refused, MP III 13 422 2
Every body at all addicted to letter writing, without MP III 13 425 6
more warm and genuine than her aunt's style of writing. MP III 13 427 12
on its containing little writing, and was persuaded of its MP III 15 437 2
journey, resolved that writing should answer the purpose MP III 17 467 20
attached to me--and his writing such a letter--but as to E I 7 54 30
and is glad to catch at the old writing master's son." E I 8 64 47
her friend were not writing down a declaration of love. E I 9 77 43
September twelvemonth in writing that note, at twelve E I 11 95 19
it is not her time for writing;" and when I immediately E II 1 157 7
Jane, apologise for her writing so short a letter--only E II 1 157 10
That is the reason of her writing out of rule, as we call E II 1 159 18
said her husband) when writing to her nephew two days E II 12 258 7
I have not always known their writing apart." E II 16 297 45
It is like a woman's writing." E II 16 297 50
in writing, and spare no arguments to induce him to come. E III 6 357 31
headach just now, writing all the morning:--such long E III 8 378 8
Wentworth's manner of writing to make you suppose he P IV 6 172 46
No, you would not guess, from his way of writing, that he P IV 6 173 47
turning his back on them all, was engrossed by writing. P IV 11 229 4
towards Captain Wentworth) he is writing about it now." P IV 11 232 15
table where he had been writing, when footsteps were heard P IV 11 236 40
crossing the room to the writing table, and standing with P IV 11 236 40
While supposed to be writing only to Captain Benwick, he P IV 11 237 41
in the West Indies; by writing for her, acting for her, P IV 12 251 11
who were continually writing, inviting & tormenting her, & S 3 378 1

WRITING-DESK (3)

new writing-desk from being thrown out into the street.-- NA II 5 155 4
had my writing-desk, I am sure I could produce a specimen. E II 16 298 52
was locked up in my writing-desk; and I, trusting that I E III 14 442 8

WRITTEN (99)

as her ladyship has now written, I cannot make up my mind, LS 3 247 1
but it seems written with such a determination to think LS 13 262 1
I have now my dear sir, written my real sentiments of Lady LS 14 265 6
the first place actually written to him, to request his LS 22 281 5
letters, that they were written under her mother's LS 42 311 1
"Udolpho was written by Mrs. Radcliff," said Catherine, NA I 7 49 37
that other stupid book, written by that woman they make NA I 7 49 38
written in vain--or perhaps might not have written at all." NA I 14 110 27
sufficed to ascertain written characters; and while she NA II 6 169 11
She thanked him as heartily as if he had written it NA II 10 201 6
I have written to him and my father. NA II 10 202 7
She must think me an idiot, or she could not have written NA II 12 218 4
was not recollected sooner, that I might have written home. NA II 13 225 22
The letter was from this gentleman himself, and written in SS I 4 23 20
whole of his letter was written in so friendly a style as SS I 4 23 20
line of music that he had written out for her, till her SS I 16 83 3
one it is; but that is not written so well as usual.-- SS I 22 134 52
town she would not have written to him, as she did; she SS II 4 165 29
she did; she would have written to Combe Magna; and if he SS II 4 165 29
But if she did, the letter was written and sent away with SS II 5 167 7
know what Willoughby had written, hurried away to their SS II 7 182 12
Her second note, which had been written on the morning SS II 7 187 39
40
of their having been written at all; and she was silently SS II 7 188 43
but what any one would have written in the same situation. SS II 7 188 43
this been known to you, Elinor? has he written to you?" SS III 1 262 14
15
material; and till I have written to Mr. Ferrars, I think SS III 4 286 15
Why Mr. Ferrars was to be written to about it in such a SS III 4 286 16
Tho' they are not written down, I bring your sister's W 339 18
a serious stamp, though written solely for their benefit. PP I 14 69 15
16
to their father, and written with all the solemnity of PP I 23 128 10
Jane had already written a few lines to her sister to PP II 3 147 20
what had been already written; and when it closed, PP II 5 157 10
proved that Jane had not written in spirits, when, instead PP II 10 182 2
which Jane had written to her since her being in Kent. PP II 11 188 1
paper, written quite through, in a very close hand.-- PP II 12 196 3
had not my character required it to be written and read. PP II 12 196 4
Elizabeth was not surprised at it, as Jane had written the PP III 4 273 1
be first attended to; it had been written five days ago. PP III 4 273 2
dated a day later, and written in evident agitation, gave PP III 4 273 2
to make it out, but I hardly know what I have written." PP III 4 274 3
been written a day later than the conclusion of the first. PP III 4 274 4
to London, and Jane has written to beg my uncle's PP III 4 277 15
there were notes to be written to all their friends in PP III 4 281 29
"What a letter is this, to be written at such a moment. PP III 5 292 61
"I have written to Colonel Forster to desire him to find PP III 6 295 6
I have written to Colonel Forster, to inform him of our PP III 8 313 19
that it was written in a dreadful bitterness of spirit." PP III 16 368 22
be satisfied till she had written a long and angry letter MP I 1 4 1
"Yes, when you have written the letter I will take it to MP I 2 16 19
character that ever was written, from Shylock or Richard MP I 13 123 6
conversing in the elegant written language of some MP I 13 125 18
there they had read and written, and talked and laughed, MP I 15 150 1
sent for his hunters and written a few lines of MP II 6 229 1
few hurried happy lines, written as the ship came up MP II 6 232 12
This specimen, written in haste as it was, had not a fault; MP II 9 265 19
that he had actually written home to defer his return, MP II 11 286 16
If he had written to you, there would have been more MP II 11 288 24
must be instantly written, and with only one decided MP II 13 307 30
31
where her heart lived, written with affection, and some MP III 9 393 1
in excuse for not having written to her earlier, "and now MP III 9 393 1
Fanny, "excuse me that I have not written before. MP III 13 420 2
whether Edmund had written to Miss Crawford before this MP III 13 427 12
a few lines from Edmund, written purposely to give her a MP III 14 429 1
that he had written to his new mother on the occasion. E I 2 18 9
letter Mr. Frank Churchill had written to Mrs. Weston? E I 2 18 9
with gentlemen so plainly written as in Mr. Knightley. E I 4 33 34
A better written letter, Harriet, (returning it,) than I E I 7 51 5
and advised its being written directly, which was agreed E I 7 55 35
This letter, however, was written, and sealed, and sent. E I 7 55 36
Miss Nash, head-teacher at Mrs. Goddard's, had written out E I 9 69 4
"Oh no! he had never written, hardly ever, any thing of E I 9 71 9
There can be no doubt of its being written for you and to E I 9 73 18
They are not at all the less written you know, because you E I 9 77 42
Nobody could have written so prettily, but you, Emma." E I 9 78 52
"Yes, papa, it is written out in our second page. E I 9 79 55
I remember it was written from Weymouth, and dated sept. E I 11 96 24
and left for her, written in the very style to touch; a E II 4 184 11
But first of all, there must be an answer written to Mrs. E II 7 209 13
come; Frank had already written to Enscombe to propose E II 11 256 59
all came from her--Mrs. Dixon had written most pressingly. E II 15 285 14
This letter tells us--it is a short letter--written in a E II 18 305 7
stray letter near him, how beautifully Emma had written it. E III 5 347 20
know, to be written to Colonel Campbell, and Mrs. Dixon. E III 8 378 8
But, now that she has written her letters, she says she E III 8 379 8
A note was written to urge it. E III 9 389 16
I, trusting that I had written enough, though but a few E III 14 442 8
influence of his captain, written the only two letters P III 6 51 30
and he had written to "her father by Captain Harville. P IV 6 164 8
and Mr. Musgrove has written "his consent, and Captain P IV 6 165 8
from Harville, written upon the spot, from Uppercross. P IV 6 172 41
Before Mrs. Croft had written, he was arrived; and the P IV 7 174 1
The letter I am looking for, was one written by Mr. Elliot P IV 9 203 70
I cannot produce written proof again, but I can give as P IV 9 204 80
But perhaps you will say, these were all written by men." P IV 11 234 27
where he had leaned and written, her eyes devoured the P IV 11 237 41
42
Of what he had then written, nothing was to be retracted P IV 11 241 61
Laconia, if I had then written to you, would you have P IV 11 247 82
Had he written nothing more, he wd have been Immortal. S 7 397 1
recollection of having written or felt any such thing.-- S 10 412 1

WRONG (139)

I hope this does not proceed from anything wrong, & that I LS 20 278 11
have done something very wrong I know--but you have not an LS 24 286 5
In short Catherine, everything has gone wrong--but it is LS 24 287 9
Perhaps Catherine was wrong in not demanding the cause of NA I 5 36 2
"No, not at all; but if you think it wrong, you had much NA I 8 58 24
wrong in her appearance, she turned away her head. NA I 10 80 59
If I am wrong, I am doing what I believe to be right." NA I 13 100 12
what I thought wrong, I never will be tricked into it." NA I 13 101 22
before, and on a false pretence too, must have been wrong. NA I 13 101 25
hoped you would tell me, if you thought I was doing wrong." NA I 13 104 35
Isabella should be doing wrong, felt greatly relieved by NA I 13 105 41
in order to do what was wrong in itself? if she had been NA I 13 105 41
not mean to say any thing wrong; but it is a nice book, NA I 14 108 15
to believe that Henry Tilney could never be wrong. NA I 14 114 49
"You do acquit me then of any thing wrong?-- NA II 3 146 17
blushed for her friend, and said, "Isabella is wrong. NA II 4 151 13
for he was on the wrong side of five and thirty; but SS I 7 34 6
know when we are acting wrong, and with such a conviction SS I 13 68 72
I am not sensible of having done any thing wrong in SS I 13 68 74
pointing to her daughter) it was wrong in her situation. SS I 19 107 29
"Indeed you wrong me," replied Lucy with great solemnity; " SS II 2 150 32
Oh! my dear mother, you must be wrong in permitting an SS II 4 165 29
I believe I have been wrong in saying so much, but I SS II 5 173 44
"Yes--could that be wrong after all that had passed?-- SS II 7 186 36
right, is there not some reason to fear I may be wrong?" SS II 9 204 18
she felt it to be entirely wrong, formed on mistaken SS II 10 214 6
censure of what was wrong in the other, she thought SS II 10 215 14
carry them away to form wrong judgments of our conduct, SS II 14 248 6
which they know to be wrong, they feel injured by the SS II 14 248 6
"You wrong her exceedingly. SS III 5 296 22
otherwise it would be very wrong to say any thing about it- SS III 5 297 31
"You are very wrong, Mr. Willoughby, very blameable," said SS III 8 329 64
My intentions were not always wrong. SS III 8 329 65
"You are very wrong. SS III 8 332 82
"Or will it be wrong?-- SS III 10 344 15
my own health, as I had felt even at the time to be wrong. SS III 10 345 28
"Your behaviour was certainly very wrong," said she, " SS III 13 368 26
After that, I suppose, I was wrong in remaining so much in SS III 13 368 28
If my opinions are wrong, I must correct them--if they are W 318 2
"Your conjecture is totally wrong, I assure you. PP I 6 27 48
a something about her more wrong and reprehensible, PP I 10 51 46
and thought them very wrong to have so much trouble, and PP I 12 60 6
had they appeared to be wrong, she could no more explain PP I 15 74 12
and often moving wrong without being aware of it, gave her PP I 18 90 4
to prevent it, am I wrong, my dearest Jane, in indulging PP I 21 118 14
without scheming to do wrong, or to make others unhappy, PP II 1 136 17
body acting unnaturally and wrong, and me most unhappy. PP II 1 137 24
She was very wrong in singling me out as she did; I can PP II 3 148 26
that she has been acting wrong, and because I am very sure PP II 3 148 26
"His being so sure of succeeding, was wrong," said she; " PP II 17 224 3
"No--I do not know that you were wrong in saying what you PP II 17 224 7
and the fear of doing wrong, would easily give to those PP III 3 267 3
It was reasonable that he should feel he had been wrong; PP III 10 326 3
to deceive you, but my spirits might often lead me wrong. PP III 16 369 27
the first calculation is wrong, we make a second better; MP I 5 46 23
set people right, but I do see that they are often wrong." MP I 5 50 36
They are given wrong notions from the beginning. MP I 5 50 38
had not a suspicion that I could be doing any thing wrong. MP I 5 51 40
It was very wrong--very indecorous." MP I 7 63 5
It would be very wrong if she did.-- MP I 7 70 29
Fanny, feeling all this to be wrong, could not help making MP I 10 99 21
Nor can I think it wrong that it should. MP I 11 109 17
I hope I should not have been influenced myself in a wrong MP I 11 109 17
to be in the army, and nobody sees any thing wrong in that. MP I 11 109 18
"I think it would be very wrong. MP I 13 125 17
"The innovation, if not wrong as an innovation, will be MP I 13 127 30
not wrong as an innovation, will be wrong as an expense." MP I 13 127 30
Can we be wrong if Mary Crawford feels the same?" MP I 13 129 39
ungenerous, it would be really wrong to expose her to it. MP I 16 154 14
Was he not wrong? MP I 16 156 28
She could not feel that she had done wrong herself, but MP I 17 159 6
her acquiescence in their wrong measures, her countenance MP II 2 188 3
while you do wrong together I can overlook a great deal." MP II 4 211 28
usual luck--for I never do wrong without gaining by it--I MP II 7 241 13
fears she already had, of doing wrong and being looked at. MP II 9 267 22
to her professed opinions, sometimes a tinge of wrong. MP II 9 269 31
It was ill-bred--it was wrong. MP II 11 286 15
tell her uncle that he was wrong--"you are quite mistaken. MP III 1 315 19
He had begun at the wrong end. MP III 3 335 6
Only tell me if I was wrong. MP III 3 342 33
"My uncle thought me wrong, and I knew he had been talking MP III 4 347 15
Maria was wrong, Crawford was wrong, we were all wrong MP III 4 349 26
we were all wrong together; but none so wrong as myself. MP III 4 349 26
She feared she had been doing wrong, saying too much, MP III 4 354 47
the air of a gentleman, and now, I am sure, she was wrong. MP III 5 361 16
Susan saw that much was wrong at home, and wanted to set MP III 9 395 4
That her manner was wrong, however, at times very wrong-- MP III 9 396 6
She hoped it was not wrong; though after a time, Susan's MP III 12 419 8
decency and impudence in wrong; and, last of all, and MP III 16 457 30
to counteract what was wrong in Mrs. Norris, by its MP III 17 463 7
She had taken up a wrong idea, fancying it was a mother E I 4 27 5

never lead any one really wrong; she will make so lasting E I 5 40 22
from allowing,) I should not feel that I had done wrong. E I 8 61 37
were right and her adversary's wrong, as Mr. Knightley. E I 8 67 56
Nothing wrong in him escaped her. E I 11 93 5
She certainly had not been in the wrong, and he would E I 12 98 2
must always arise from my being in the wrong." E I 12 99 5
and that if she were not wrong before, she is now." E I 12 99 10
effects on my side of the argument have yet proved wrong. E I 12 99 11
It was foolish, it was wrong, to take so active part in E I 16 136 10
"Quite wrong, my dear aunt; there is no likeness at all." E II 3 176 45
finding himself debased to the level of a very wrong one. E II 4 181 3
she could observe nothing wrong in his notions, a great E II 7 205 2
one conjectures right, and sometimes one conjectures wrong. E II 10 242 15
If she does wrong, she ought to feel it." E II 10 243 27
You may have done wrong with regard to Mr. Dixon, but this E II 15 284 10
not one in a million, I suppose, actually lost! E II 16 296 42
Mrs. Elton began to think she had been wrong in E II 18 307 17
What you direct in this house cannot be wrong. E III 2 330 45
Does my vain spirit ever tell me I am wrong?" E III 2 330 52
If one leads you wrong, I am sure the other tells you of E III 2 330 53
It was very wrong of me, you know, to keep any E III 4 340 24
We were very wrong before; we will be cautious now.-- E III 4 342 39
I cannot see you acting wrong, without a remonstrance. E III 7 374 56
"I was wrong," he continued, "in talking of its being E III 10 393 17
me in love with him?--very wrong, very wrong indeed." E III 10 396 44
for though he has been wrong in this instance, I have E III 10 397 49
"She thinks herself wrong, then, for having consented to a E III 12 418 7
"Wrong!-- E III 12 419 8
madam,' she continued, 'that I was taught wrong. E III 12 419 8
but he had gone to a wrong place. there was too much E III 13 432 41
of wrong, for that visit might have been sooner paid. E III 14 437 8
to feel that he had been wrong, yet he had been less wrong E III 15 444 1
yet he had been less wrong than she had supposed--and he E III 15 444 1
He knows he is wrong, and has nothing rational to urge.-- E III 15 445 11
that she had done a wrong thing in consenting to the E III 15 446 20
But though I was always doing wrong things, they were very E III 18 477 55
very bad wrong things, and such as did me no service.-- E III 18 477 55
She was persuaded to believe the engagement a wrong thing-- P III 4 27 5
was almost startled by the wrong of one part of the P III 5 34 11
I grant you, it might be wrong to have her so much with me; P III 5 35 14
Mr. and Mrs. Musgrove cannot think it wrong, while I P III 7 57 15
He was only wrong in accepting the attentions--(for P III 10 82 1
shewed something to be wrong; and they had set off P III 12 111 50
I had been grossly wrong, and must abide the consequences." P IV 11 243 65
If I was wrong in yielding to persuasion once, remember P IV 11 244 73
to judge of the right and wrong, I mean with regard to P IV 11 246 79 80
wrong, and to take up a new set of opinions and of hopes. P IV 12 249 3
stand--"there is something wrong here, said he--putting S 1 364 1

WRONG-HEADED (1)
wrong-headed folly, engrafted on an untoward disposition.-- W 361 31

WRONGED (3)
But you,--you above all, above my mother, had been wronged SS III 10 346 28
which had deserted and wronged me, and leaving you, for SS III 10 346 28
to convince you I am wronged, it is not by telling you MP III 3 343 41

WRONGING (1)
brow, she felt secure from all possibility of wronging him. NA II 8 187 13

WRONGS (2)
She could not enter into the wrongs of an economist, but MP I 3 31 60
in spite of all his wrongs towards her, a general MP II 10 276 14

WROTE (83)
out of his head since; he wrote by the same post to LS 13 262 1
I never can sufficiently regret that I wrote to you at all. LS 24 285 1
"No--but I wrote to him. LS 24 286 5
She wrote to Mr De Courcy." LS 24 289 12
When I wrote to you the other day, I was in truth in high LS 25 291 1
You hardly mentioned any thing of her, when you wrote to NA I 7 50 48
She instantly wrote Sir John Middleton her acknowledgment SS I 4 24 20
reward on that person who wrote the ablest defence of your SS I 17 93 29
to her mother; for Willoughby neither came nor wrote. SS II 6 175 1
"Yet you wrote to him?"-- SS II 7 186 35
Willoughby, where was your heart, when you wrote those SS II 7 190 56
at the table where Elinor wrote, watching the advancement SS II 9 203 10
return; he neither returned, nor wrote, nor relieved her." SS II 9 209 30
wit that had procured it, wrote the next morning to Lucy, SS II 14 253 26
post-horses directly, she wrote a few lines to her mother. SS III 7 311 15
Your sister wrote to me again, you know the very next SS III 8 328 61
"I wrote to him, my love, last week, and rather expect to SS III 12 358 6
Mrs. Jennings wrote to tell the wonderful tale, to vent SS III 13 370 37
"I wonder I never mentioned it when I wrote. W 321 2
However, he wrote some verses on her, and very pretty they PP I 9 44 31
the sisters, Elizabeth wrote the next morning to her PP I 12 59 1
She wrote also with great pleasure of her brother's being PP II 1 133 2
She wrote cheerfully, seemed surrounded with comforts, and PP II 3 146 19
in London; and when she wrote again, Elizabeth hoped it PP II 3 147 20
She wrote again when the visit was paid, and she had seen PP II 3 147 23
The letter which she wrote on this occasion to her sister, PP II 3 147 25
these events, Mr. Wickham wrote to inform me that, having PP II 12 200 5
any public exposure, but I wrote to Mr. Wickham, who left PP II 12 202 5
He wrote last week to hurry my return." PP II 14 211 9
"Yes he went on Tuesday as I wrote you word." PP III 5 286 26
He wrote me a few lines on Wednesday, to say that he had PP III 5 286 28
she then intreat him to lose no more time before he wrote. PP III 7 303 19
Mr. Gardiner soon wrote again to his brother. PP III 8 312 18
When Mr. Bennet wrote again to his brother, therefore, he PP III 8 314 22
seizing a sheet of paper, wrote a short letter to her aunt, PP III 9 320 32
"I knew," said he, "that what I wrote must give you pain, PP III 16 368 20
"When I wrote that letter," replied Darcy, "I believed PP III 16 368 22
The feelings of the person who wrote, and the person who PP III 16 368 23
three days of happiness, and immediately wrote as follows. PP III 18 382 20
She wrote even to Jane on the occasion, to express her PP III 18 383 24
wrote to her family on the subject till actually married. MP I 1 4 1
money and baby-linen, and Mrs. Norris wrote the letters. MP I 1 5 3
He wrote with his own hand his love to his cousin William, MP I 2 16 20
He wrote in April, and had strong hopes of settling every MP I 4 40 14
Sir Thomas wrote of it with as much decision as experience MP I 11 107 2
"Oh! if he wrote to his father----- MP II 11 288 24
But if he wrote to his father, no wonder he was concise. MP II 11 288 24
falling forward as she wrote, which she now and then shook MP II 12 296 31
wrote thus, in great trembling both of spirits and hand: MP II 13 307 30 31
Fanny wrote to offer herself; and her mother's answer, MP III 6 371 17
niece's feelings, when she wrote her first letter to her MP III 8 388 1
Her aunt did not neglect her; she wrote again and again; MP III 13 427 12
over her fancy; and she wrote very comfortably about MP III 13 427 12
and alarm; then, she wrote as she might have spoken. MP III 13 427 12
Lady Bertram wrote her daily terrors to her niece, who MP III 13 427 13
alarm him in that quarter, wrote to recommend Sir Thomas's MP III 16 450 8
And he wrote as if he really loved her very much--but she E I 7 50 1
He did speak yesterday--that is, he wrote and was refused." E I 8 60 30
"You saw her answer! you wrote her answer too. E I 8 60 36
and taste; and as Harriet wrote a very pretty hand, it was E I 9 70 4
"He wrote a letter to poor Mrs. Weston, to congratulate E I 11 96 22
countries, and so she wrote a very urgent letter to her E II 1 159 20
in Jane's letter--wrote in Mr. Dixon's name as well as her E II 1 159 20
And I think she wrote us word that he had shewn them some E II 1 160 20
Cole told Mrs. Cole of it, she sat down and wrote to me. E II 3 173 27
very minute directions, or wrote to Broadwood himself. E II 10 241 8
Emma heard that Frank wrote in the highest spirits of this E III 1 317 8
She was told that now he wrote with the greatest E III 1 317 8
You wrote me word of it three months ago." E III 5 344 7
the following morning she wrote again to say, in the most E III 9 390 16
She wrote to her, therefore, kindly, but decisively, to E III 12 416 2
She rose early, and wrote her letter to Harriet; an E III 14 435 5
any thing he wrote, she was sure she was incapable of it.-- E III 14 436 6
with me entirely, and wrote the next day to tell me that E III 14 442 8
You never wrote a truer line." E III 15 446 20
You wrote in the cheerfullest manner, and said you were P III 5 38 32
Mary never wrote to Bath herself; all the toil of keeping P III 12 107 21
He stood his chance for the rest--wrote up for leave of P III 12 108 28
his own means, and at last wrote a very fine letter of P IV 4 149 13
He felt & he wrote & he forgot." S 7 398 1
& wrote to ask the opinion of her friend Mrs Darling.-- S 9 408 1
on the question; she wrote the same day to Fanny Noyce and S 9 408 1
This was the state of the case when I wrote to you;--but S 9 409 1

WROUGHT (1)
The change which a few hours had wrought in the minds and SS III 13 363 6

WRUNG (1)
and Elinor's heart wrung for the feelings of Edward, while SS III 1 268 46

YARD (8)
favourite gown, though it cost but nine shillings a yard." NA I 3 28 35
I gave but five shillings a yard for it, and a true Indian NA I 3 28 38
for some indispensable yard of ribbon which must be bought NA I 14 114 50
without seeing one farm yard, nor walk in the shrubbery MP I 6 58 37
full three quarters of a yard), and was actually forming MP I 14 130 1
I had been looking about me in the poultry yard, and was MP I 15 141 22
The house is by no means bad, and when the yard is removed, MP II 7 242 22
upon some timbers in the yard, or found a seat on board a MP III 10 403 15
YARD-ARM (1)
I would as soon have been run up to the yard-arm. P III 12 108 28
YARDS (18)
Mr. Tilney, within three yards of the place where they sat; NA I 8 53 3
within a few yards of Marianne, when her accident happened. SS I 9 42 8
They were soon within thirty yards of the gentleman. SS I 16 86 20
standing within a few yards of them, in earnest SS II 6 176 3
They were within twenty yards of each other, and so abrupt PP III 1 251 51
but by walking fifty yards from the hall door, she could MP I 7 67 16
"We must have a curtain," said Tom Bertram, "a few yards MP I 13 123 7
carpet work and made many yards of fringe; and she would MP II 1 179 9
I rode fifty yards up the lane between the church and the MP II 7 242 23
She met Miss Crawford within a few yards of the parsonage, MP II 8 257 15
some fifty yards in mutual silence and abstraction. MP III 4 351 35
survey; and walking a few yards forward, while they talked E I 4 31 27
She had not advanced many yards from Mrs. Goddard's door, E I 13 109 6
and I had not got three yards from the door, when he came E II 3 179 52
walk, for you were not six yards from your own door when I E II 16 293 15
16
The iron gates and the front door were not twenty yards E III 3 333 3
hard sand--deep water 10 yards from the shore--no mud--no S 1 369 1
round it, about an hundred yards from the brow of a steep, S 4 384 1
YATES (58)
couple of lovers--all but Yates and Mrs. Grant--and, MP I 12 119 22
The honourable John Yates, this new friend, had not much MP I 13 121 1
be keenly felt, and Mr. Yates could talk of nothing else. MP I 13 121 1
The play had been Lovers' Vows, and Mr. Yates was to have MP I 13 122 2
to make you amends, Yates, I think we must raise a little MP I 13 123 5
"Oh! quite enough," cried Mr. Yates, "with only just a MP I 13 123 8
Maria, Julia, Henry Crawford, and Mr. Yates, were in the MP I 13 125 14
Henry Crawford, and Mr. Yates; on the comic, Tom Bertram, MP I 14 130 3
Here are two capital tragic parts for Yates and Crawford, MP I 14 132 7
Mr. Yates was particularly pleased; he had been sighing MP I 14 132 8
Whichever Mr. Yates did not choose, would perfectly MP I 14 132 8
it, by observing to Mr. Yates, that this was a point in MP I 14 132 8
"Cottager's wife!" cried Mr. Yates. MP I 14 134 13
by Tom Bertram and Mr. Yates walking off together to MP I 14 136 22
Tom, Maria, and Mr. Yates; and Mr. Rushworth stepped MP I 15 138 2
"Yes," cried Mr. Yates.-- MP I 15 139 6
being accompanied by Mr. Yates, and followed soon MP I 15 139 11
"I cannot before Mr. Yates speak what I feel as to this MP I 15 139 11
Mr. Yates, who was trying to make himself agreeable to MP I 15 142 24
Tom, Maria, and Mr. Yates, soon after their being MP I 15 142 25
"Your brother should take the part," said Mr. Yates, in a MP I 15 144 34
and Mr. Crawford, and Mr. Yates, with an urgency which MP I 15 146 53
Mrs. Norris offered to contrive his dress, Mr. Yates MP I 17 158 2
the attentions of Mr. Yates, was talking with forced MP I 17 160 8
did last night with Mr. Yates; and though he and Maria are MP I 17 162 16
She knew that Mr. Yates was in general thought to rant MP I 18 164 2
rant dreadfully, that Mr. Yates was disappointed in Henry MP I 18 164 2
judgment than Tom, more talent and taste than Mr. Yates.-- MP I 18 165 3
Mr. Yates, indeed, exclaimed against his tameness and MP I 18 165 3
Yates is storming away in the dining room. MP I 18 169 21
Mr. Yates might consider it only as a vexatious MP II 1 175 1
Fanny was left with only the Crawfords and Mr. Yates. MP II 1 176 4
The Crawfords were more warm on the subject than Mr. Yates, MP II 1 177 5
at hand; while Mr. Yates considered it only as a temporary MP II 1 177 5
But Mr. Yates, having never been with those who thought MP II 1 177 5
"Then poor Yates is all alone," cried Tom. MP II 1 182 21
At the very moment of Yates perceiving Sir Thomas, and MP II 1 182 22
the well-bred and easy Mr. Yates, making his bow and MP II 1 182 22
Sir Thomas received Mr. Yates with all the appearance of MP II 1 183 23
to an eager appeal of Mr. Yates, as to the happiness of MP II 1 183 24
of a calmer hue; but Mr. Yates, without discernment to MP II 1 184 25
"My friend Yates brought the infection from Ecclesford, MP II 1 184 26
Mr. Yates took the subject from his friend as soon as MP II 1 184 27
Mr. Yates was still talking. MP II 1 185 28
Mr. Yates was beginning now to understand Sir Thomas's MP II 2 191 10
Mr. Yates felt it as acutely as might be supposed. MP II 2 191 10
same table, which made Mr. Yates think it wiser to let him MP II 2 191 10
daughter Julia that Mr. Yates did yet mean to stay a few MP II 2 191 10
Another day or two, and Mr. Yates was gone likewise. MP II 2 194 21
a stranger superior to Mr. Yates must have been irksome; MP II 2 194 21
Mr. Yates had staid to see the destruction of every MP II 2 194 21
"Any Mr. Yates, I presume, is not far off." MP II 5 224 51
"Mr. Yates!-- MP II 5 224 52
Oh! we hear nothing of Mr. Yates. MP II 5 224 52
knows better than to entertain her father with Mr. Yates." MP II 5 224 52
elopement; she is gone to Scotland with Yates. MP III 15 442 23
She was humble and wishing to be forgiven, and Mr. Yates, MP III 17 462 4
it is probable that Mr. Yates would never have succeeded. MP III 17 466 18
YAWN (3)
she replied, vainly endeavouring to hide a great yawn. NA I 2 23 24
of his, she gave a great yawn and said, "how pleasant it PP I 11 55 4
of "Lord, how tired I am!" accompanied by a violent yawn. PP I 18 103 75
YAWNED (1)
She then yawned again, threw aside her book, and cast her PP I 11 55 5
6
YAWNING (1)
Lucas, who had been long yawning at the repetition of PP I 18 100 68
YAWNS (1)
What were the yawns of Lady Bertram? MP II 10 273 5
YE (5)
"Thank ye," cried Thorpe, "but I did not come to Bath to NA I 13 99 7
And you, ye well-known trees!--but you will continue the SS I 5 27 8
to be held on Tuesday Octr Ye 13th, & it was generally W 314 1
'Ye fallen avenues, once more I mourn your fate unmerited.' MP I 6 56 20
Thank ye, the gloves do very well--only a little too large E II 9 237 48
YEAR (183)
rattle perhaps, but a year or two will rectify that, & he LS 20 276 5
She learnt a year, and could not bear it;--and Mrs. NA I 1 14 1
The Skinners were here last year--I wish they were here NA I 2 22 17
better to be here than at home at this dull time of year. NA I 8 54 5
has little variety, and so every body finds out every year. NA I 10 78 45
A bright morning so early in the year, she allowed would NA I 11 82 1
for there is not a soul at Clifton at this time of year. NA I 14 115 50
fifty pounds a year, I should not have a wish unsatisfied. NA II 1 136 48
Mrs. Allen used to take pains, year after year, to make me NA II 7 174 7
year the uncertainty was very great of its continuing so.-- NA II 7 176 17
The pinery had yielded only one hundred in the last year. NA II 7 178 21
But then it was such a dead time of year, no wild-fowl, no NA II 11 209 5
They have half a buck from Northanger twice a year; and I NA II 11 210 6
begun to act about half a year ago, she was sufficiently NA II 11 214 25
A hundred a year would make them all perfectly comfortable. SS I 2 10 16
and over every year, and there is no getting rid of it. SS I 2 10 20
Twice every year these annuities were to be paid; and then SS I 2 11 20
not be sixpence the richer for it at the end of the year. SS I 2 11 23
present, as it is too late in the year for improvements. SS I 6 29 4
spoil her children all the year round, while Sir John's SS I 7 32 1
Why, he is down here every year." SS I 9 43 15
than he knows how to employ, and two new coats every year." SS I 10 51 25
considering the time of year, and that it had rained every SS I 12 62 29
"What can you have to do in town at this time of year?" SS I 13 64 20
a year, and his brother left every thing sadly involved. SS I 14 70 2
six or seven hundred a year; but he lived at an expense to SS I 14 71 4
looks much as it always does at this time of year. SS I 16 87 30
formed, though not till a year after he had quitted as a SS I 22 130 28
a large portion of the year at the houses of her children SS II 3 153 1
of not leaving their mother at that time of year. SS II 3 153 1
At this time of year, and after such a series of rain, we SS II 5 167 3
Two thousand a year without debt or drawback--except the SS II 8 196 22
reached her fourteenth year,) that I removed her from SS II 9 208 28
purchase within this half year; East Kingham Farm, you SS II 11 225 31
"Another year or two may do much towards it," he gravely SS II 11 226 37
and how much she had every year to spend upon herself. SS II 14 249 8
We can ask your sisters some other year, you know; but the SS II 14 253 24
his sisters another year; at the same time, however, slyly SS II 14 253 25
suspecting that another year would make the invitation SS II 14 253 25
just the same by me; for a year or two back, when Martha SS III 2 274 20
Then they will have a child every year! and Lord help 'em! SS III 2 276 28
Every year since my coming of age, or even before, I SS III 8 320 32
that since the first half year of our foolish-- business-- SS III 13 365 17
her in the old rooms at Bath, the year before I married--. W 325 4
"He has about 8 or 900l a year I beleive.-- W 328 8
single man of large fortune; four or five thousand a year. PP I 1 3 14
men of four thousand a year come into the neighbourhood." PP I 1 5 31
after his entrance, of his having ten thousand a year. PP I 3 10 5
estate of two thousand a year, which, unfortunately for PP I 7 28 1
five or six thousand a year, should want one of my girls, PP I 7 29 12
must have occasion to write in the course of the year! PP I 10 47 7
The younger girls formed hopes of coming out a year or two PP I 22 122 3
of year, that she had often great enjoyment out of doors. PP II 7 169 5
to do, which was the more probable from the time of year. PP II 9 180 28
year, and intend to close it with a call at the parsonage. PP II 10 183 4
mine, and within half a year from these events, Mr. PP II 12 200 5
About a year ago, she was taken from school, and an PP II 12 201 5
to feel it most acutely, more I think than last year. PP II 14 210 3
to Hunsford again next year; and Miss de Bourgh exerted PP II 14 214 21
your master much at Pemberley in the course of the year?" PP III 1 248 24
and for the last half year, nay, for a twelvemonth, she PP III 5 283 10
particular, to take him there at this time of year." PP III 10 328 17
that she is uncommonly improved within this year or two. PP III 10 328 22
You forced me into visiting him last year, and promised if PP III 11 332 23
as had flattered them a year ago, every thing, she was PP III 11 337 54
He found her as handsome as she had been last year; as PP III 11 337 56
into Hertfordshire last year, I thought how likely it was PP III 13 348 40
Ten thousand a year! PP III 17 378 43
Ten thousand a year, and very likely more! PP III 17 378 45
felicity with very little less than a thousand a year. MP I 1 3 1
Julia Bertram was only twelve, and Maria but a year older. MP I 2 13 4
William, the eldest, a year older than herself, her MP I 2 15 12
The two families will be meeting every day in the year. MP I 3 27 31
Sir Thomas says you will have six hundred a year." MP I 3 29 49
do rather more--to lay by a little at the end of the year." MP I 3 30 50
These opinions had been hardly canvassed a year, before MP I 3 32 61
Being now in her twenty-first year, Maria Bertram was MP I 4 38 10
twelve thousand a year, he would be a very stupid fellow." MP I 4 40 13
reached her eighteenth year, when the society of the MP I 4 40 15
when one has seen her hardly able to speak the year before. MP I 5 49 32
got into a dreadful scrape last year from the want of them. MP I 5 51 40
"Yes, and I am afraid they will be the last this year. MP I 7 72 44
reigned in it with few interruptions throughout the year. MP I 9 89 30
"Four thousand a year." MP I 12 118 19
Four thousand a year is a pretty estate, and he seems a MP I 12 118 20
is to the family, employing the man all the year round!" MP I 15 142 22
wood so full of pheasants in my life as this year. MP II 1 181 16
of way, allowing for the difference of the time of year." MP II 3 199 14
In that house which she had hardly entered twice a year MP II 4 205 2
mild for the time of year; and venturing sometimes even to MP II 4 208 11
If any body told me a year ago that this place would be my MP II 4 210 17
I can even suppose it pleasant to spend half the year in MP II 4 210 21
expect we shall be all very much at Sotherton another year. MP II 4 210 21
at this time of year, by being up before they can begin?" MP II 4 211 24
She has only to fix on her number of thousands a year, and MP II 4 213 39
walk to a dinner engagement at this time of the year! MP II 5 221 37
apprehend he will not have less than seven hundred a year. MP II 5 226 61
Seven hundred a year is a fine thing for a younger brother; MP II 5 226 61
menus plaisirs were to be limited to seven hundred a year." MP II 5 226 62
will have seven hundred a year, and nothing to do for it." MP II 5 226 63
heart had been yearning to do, through many a past year. MP II 6 233 17
house, above the expenditure of a few hundreds a year. MP II 7 243 27
were now spending from two to three thousand a year in." MP II 7 243 27
or one season of the year: he had set his heart upon MP II 7 246 37
all the holidays of his year might be spent, and he might MP II 7 246 37
"You will divide your year between London and MP II 12 295 25
uncles and aunts pay for them in the course of the year. MP II 13 305 24
every year, to say nothing of what I do for them." MP II 13 305 24
not cold, sir--I never sit here long at this time of year." MP III 1 312 7
a year or two, and sees others made commanders before him? MP III 6 368 8
her mother meant to part with her when her year was up. MP III 7 385 38
"Her year!" cried Mrs. Price; "I am sure I hope I shall be MP III 7 385 39
has staid a year, for that will not be up till November. MP III 7 385 39
and at the season of the year a fine morning so often MP III 10 401 10
Norfolk at all, at this unusual time of year, was given. MP III 10 404 15
and autumn there this year; he felt that it would be so; MP III 10 405 18
fine Sunday throughout the year, always going directly MP III 11 408 4
which he may have laid down for the next quarter of a year. MP III 11 410 16
She who had known him intimately half a year! MP III 12 417 4
Easter came--particularly late this year, as Fanny had MP III 14 430 6
course of the last half year, to be in need of the true MP III 17 469 24
a single evening in the year alone if he did not like it. E I 1 12 41
he has been here a whole year, and has fitted up his house E I 1 13 46
He saw his son every year in London, and was proud of him; E I 2 17 7
Had it taken place only once a year, it would have been a E I 3 20 3
walk, or his short, as the year varied; and since Mrs. E I 4 26 1
where some day next year they were all to drink tea:--a E I 4 27 4
thing; and Mrs. Martin talks of taking a boy another year." E I 4 30 21
Till this year, every long vacation since their marriage E I 11 91 2
field was to bear next year, and to give all such local E I 12 100 16
plan; better time of year; better weather; and that he E I 18 144 2
I have heard her every year of our lives we both began. E II 6 201 27
than Miss Fairfax would have vouchsafed in half a year." E II 6 202 29
but the last year or two had brought them a considerable E II 7 207 6
This had happened the year before. E II 8 221 49
He sends us a sack every year; and certainly there never E II 9 238 51
Larkins let me keep a larger quantity than usual this year. E II 9 238 51
come in their chaise, I think, at that season of the year. E II 14 274 28
be particularly careful, especially at this time of year. E II 16 295 33
the season of the year which one should have chosen for it: E II 18 308 30
A year and a half is the very utmost that they can have E II 18 310 34
"Certainly; you must be sensible that the last half year E II 18 311 44
a weaker state of health than she had been half a year ago. E III 1 317 6
The time of year lightened the evil to him. E III 1 318 13
evening throughout the year, he soon afterwards took a E III 5 351 38
The year will wear away at this rate, and nothing done. E III 6 354 7
Before this time last year I assure you we had had a E III 6 354 7
could be in love with more than three men in one year. E III 15 450 38
time or other--in another year or two, perhaps--it might E III 17 467 30
of baronet, in the first year of Charles ii., with all the P III 1 3 3
4
and expected all the rest of the year; but he never came. P III 1 8 15
Came there about the year --5, I take it. P III 3 23 32
parent living, found a home for half a year, at Monkford. P III 4 26 1
being now too late in the year for such visits to be made P III 6 50 26
he reached his twentieth year; that he had been sent to P III 6 50 28

but be reverted to; the year of their engagement could not P III 8 63 2
and "that was in the year six;" "that happened before I P III 8 63 2
I went to sea in the year six," occurred in the course of P III 8 63 2
Reported fit for home service for a year or two,--and so I P III 8 64 9
fellow, like you, do ashore, for half a year together?-- P III 8 65 14
Bishop in the course of a year or two; and you will please P III 9 76 15
of the last smiles of the year upon the tawny leaves and P III 10 84 7
analogy of the declining year, with declining happiness, P III 10 85 12
time; but I believe about a year before he married Mary. P III 10 89 33
They were come too late in the year for any amusement or P III 11 95 9
They had been a year or two waiting for fortune and P III 11 96 12
present house for half a year, his taste, and his health, P III 11 97 12
She had been at Bath the year before, and Lady Russell had P IV 4 149 12
home, remaining another year at school, had been useful P IV 5 152 2
Mr. Elliot's wife has not been dead much above half a year. P IV 9 196 31
He is worse than last year. P IV 9 203 72
in her eight-and-twentieth year, that she has not lost one P IV 11 243 68
feelings which I had been smarting under year after year. P IV 11 245 74
the very person who had guided you in that year of misery. P IV 11 245 74
Tell me if, when I returned to England in the year eight, P IV 11 247 82
about Brinshore, this last year, to raise that paltry S 1 369 1
had been deterred last year from trying Sanditon on that S 2 372 1
without spending at least 6 weeks by the sea every year.-- S 2 373 1
Excepting two journeys to London in the year, to receive S 2 373 1
what returns it will make her in a year or two. S 3 376 1
she had many thousands a year to bequeath, & three S 3 376 1
encouragement enough this year for a little Crescent to be S 4 380 1
At the same time last year, (late in July) there had not S 4 383 1

YEAR'S (1)
character, which half a year's residence in her family SS I 3 14 3

YEARLY (9)
about four hundred pounds yearly value, was to be resigned NA II 1 135 42
"to have those kind of yearly drains on one's income. SS I 2 11 21
I would not bind myself to allow them any thing yearly. SS I 2 11 22
greater assistance than a yearly allowance, because they SS I 2 11 23
the comfort of making a yearly addition to an income which MP I 1 8 9
in Portsmouth, I hope, but this must not be a yearly visit. MP III 13 423 2
in yearly meetings at Sotherton and Everingham.' MP III 16 456 23
present down to Anne, as had been the usual yearly custom. P III 1 9 19
or the yearly nuisance of its decaying vegetation.-- S 4 380 1

YEARNING (2)
heart had been yearning to do, through many a past year. MP II 6 233 17
truest description of a yearning which she could not MP III 14 431 7

YEARS (316)
me six years ago, & which never succeeded at last. LS 5 249 1
five & twenty, tho' she must in fact be ten years older. LS 6 251 1
I was so much indulged in my infant years that I was never LS 7 253 1
even twelve years becomes in comparison of small account. LS 12 260 2
My years & increasing infirmities make me very desirous my LS 12 261 3
the first fifteen years of her life, that can or will read. LS 17 271 7
little Catherine some years hence on a man, who in LS 20 277 5
to the lakes; & three years ago when I had a fancy for LS 28 298 1
during an union of some years, I cannot forget that the LS 30 300 3
impoverished her for two years, on purpose to secure him, LS 42 313 10
of her due by a woman ten years older than herself. LS 42 313 10
and Catherine, for many years of her life, as plain as any. NA I 1 13 1
the old forlorn spinnet; so, at eight years old she began. NA I 1 14 1
of profligacy at ten years old, she had neither a bad NA I 1 14 1
plain the first fifteen years of her life, than a beauty NA I 1 15 2
only seen her three years before, they would now have NA I 2 24 27
since their respective marriages, and that many years ago. NA I 4 31 2
to know nothing of each other for the last fifteen years. NA I 4 31 2
Miss Thorpe, however, being four years older than Miss NA I 4 33 7
Morland, and at least four years better informed, had a NA I 4 33 7
which had passed twenty years before, be minutely repeated. NA I 4 34 9
The wheels have been fairly worn out these ten years at NA I 9 65 28
will last about twenty years after it is fairly worn out. NA I 9 65 30
though now for many years deserted--the happiness of being NA I 11 88 54
Consider how many years I have had the start of you. NA I 14 107 11
tormented for two or three years of one's life, for the NA I 14 110 27
between two and three years before they could marry, being, NA II 1 135 43
The long, long, endless two years and half that are to NA II 1 136 48
and left deserted for years, and then the family come back NA II 5 158 14
some cousin or kin died in it about twenty years before. NA II 5 158 15
But this was quite an old set, purchased two years ago. NA II 7 175 12
myself about ten years ago, for the benefit of my son. NA II 7 175 15
within the last five years, they were perfect in all that NA II 8 185 5
"She has been dead these nine years." NA II 8 186 10
And nine years, Catherine knew was a trifle of time, NA II 8 186 10
and girl of six and four years old, who expected a brother NA II 14 233 8
of a few years; and then what a pleasure it will be!" NA II 14 236 17
The hope of meeting again in the course of a few years NA II 14 236 18
age, and who for many years of his life, had a constant SS I 1 3 1
But her death, which happened ten years before his own, SS I 1 3 1
son's son, a child of four years old, it was secured, in SS I 1 4 3
children of two or three years old; an imperfect SS I 1 4 3
years, he had received from his niece and her daughters. SS I 1 4 3
hope to live many years, and by living economically, lay SS I 1 4 4
But then if Mrs. Dashwood should live fifteen years, we SS I 2 10 18
"Fifteen years! my dear Fanny; her life cannot be worth SS I 2 10 19
It may be very inconvenient some years to spare a hundred, SS I 2 11 22
It had not been built many years and was in good repair. SS I 6 28 2
fine little boy about six years old, by which means there SS I 6 31 9
years, and on his forlorn condition as an old bachelor. SS I 8 36 2
Mrs. Dashwood, who could not think a man five years SS I 8 37 3
He may live twenty years longer. SS I 8 37 8
A few years however will settle her opinions on the SS I 11 56 11
Seven years would be insufficient to make some people SS I 12 59 4
years; but of Willoughby my judgment has long been formed." SS I 12 59 4
them, at least, twice every summer for the last ten years. SS I 12 62 28
it wanted it very much, when I was there six years ago." SS I 13 67 64
Mrs. Palmer was several years younger than Lady Middleton, SS I 19 106 22
a little girl of three years old, who had not made a noise SS I 21 121 9
"We have been engaged these four years." SS I 22 130 19
"Four years!" SS I 22 130 19
"Our acquaintance, however, is of many years date. SS I 22 130 24
"He was four years with my uncle, who lives at Longstaple, SS I 22 130 28
"Four years you have been engaged," said she with a firm SS I 22 131 34
I have had it above these three years." SS I 22 131 35
I have suffered for Edward's sake these last four years. SS I 22 133 42
but the four succeeding years--years, which if rationally SS II 1 140 2
the four succeeding years--years, which if rationally SS II 1 140 2
We must wait, it may be for many years. SS II 2 147 7
tediousness of the many years of suspense in which it may SS II 2 148 14
have been wanting us to visit them these several years! SS II 2 151 40
spent seven years at a great school in town to some effect. SS II 4 160 3
Ah! poor man! he has been dead these eight years and SS II 4 163 18
Our ages were nearly the same, and from out earliest years SS II 9 205 24
for years, and for the purpose had procured my exchange. SS II 9 206 24
when I heard, about two years afterwards, of her divorce. SS II 9 206 24
"It was nearly three years after this unhappy period SS II 9 207 26
for fourteen years--it is dangerous to handle it at all! SS II 9 208 28
guilty connection, who was then about three years old. SS II 9 208 28
(which happened about five years ago, and which left to me SS II 9 208 28
It is now three years ago, (she had just reached her SS II 9 208 28
years I had every reason to be pleased with her situation. SS II 9 208 28
the gentleman who for many years had had the care of her SS II 12 231 9
done for more than four years, nothing less could be SS III 13 361 1
For many years of her life she had had two sons; but the SS III 14 373 2
attachment, whom, two years before, she had considered too SS III 14 378 15
was not lessened by a ten years enjoyment, had some merit W 315 1
years ago; and very great attention indeed did he pay me. W 316 1
as you were coming home after so many years absence."-- W 317 2
No, tho' I am nine years older than you are, I would not W 320 2
which passed between you & me for the last 14 years." W 321 2
He has been very much in love with her these two years, & W 321 2
since he was 7 years old--but my father reckons us alike." W 324 3
aunt very well about 30 years ago; I am pretty sure I W 325 4
"About 2 years sir." W 325 5
of nature that she should suffer from it many years." W 326 6
her son a fine boy of 10 years old, & Mr Tom Musgrave; who W 329 9
half so handsome as eliz: watson had been ten years ago.-- W 337 17
I have lived here 14 years without being noticed by any of W 348 22
An absence of 14 years had made all her brothers & sisters W 348 23
them with consideration these twenty years at least." PP I 1 5 29
of three and twenty years had been insufficient to make PP I 1 5 34
Mr. Bingley had not been of age two years, when he was PP I 4 16 13
Certain it is, that the living became vacant two years ago, PP I 16 79 27
have not seen her for many years, but I very well remember PP I 16 84 58
however, may live many years longer,) I could not satisfy PP I 19 106 10
as I have already said, may not be for several years. PP I 19 106 10
excited before, how many years longer Mr. Bennet was PP I 22 122 3
Mrs. Gardiner, who was several years younger than Mrs. PP II 2 139 2
About ten or a dozen years ago, before her marriage, she PP II 2 142 19
of Darcy's father, five years before, it was yet in his PP II 2 142 19
You have deprived the best years of his life, of that PP II 11 192 21
man, who had for many years the management of all the PP II 12 199 5
As for myself, it is many, many years since I first began PP II 12 200 5
My excellent father died about five years ago; and his PP II 12 200 5
for about three years I heard little of him; but on the PP II 12 201 5
My sister, who is more than ten years my junior, was left PP II 12 201 5
as the idleness and vice of many years continuance. PP II 13 206 4
endured on a similar occasion, five and twenty years ago. PP II 18 229 3
asked as she has, and more too, for I am two years older." PP II 18 230 13
The town where she had formerly passed some years of her PP II 19 239 7
The children, two girls of six and eight years old, and PP II 19 239 10
at the same time as the other--about eight years ago." PP III 1 247 11
one of miss Darcy, drawn when she was only eight years old. PP III 1 247 20
and I have known him ever since he was four years old." PP III 1 248 30
of an intercourse renewed after many years discontinuance. PP III 1 259 76
him since he was four years old, and whose own manners PP III 2 264 14
a father and mother, both of whom had been dead many years. PP III 6 296 8
If you are a good girl for the next ten years, I will take PP III 6 300 32
advantage, as years of gratitude cannot enough acknowledge. PP III 7 305 36
years after Lydia's birth, had been certain that he would. PP III 8 308 3
Not these two or three years perhaps." PP III 11 330 4
At that instant she felt, that years of happiness could PP III 11 337 54
Yet the misery, for which years of happiness were to offer PP III 11 337 56
Unfortunately an only son, (for many years an only child) PP III 16 369 24
allow in a sister more than ten years younger than himself. PP III 19 388 11
About thirty years ago, Miss Maria Ward of Huntingdon, MP I 1 3 1
Miss Ward, at the end of half a dozen years, found herself MP I 1 3 1
the eleven following years, or at least to make it very MP I 1 4 2
By the end of eleven years, however, Mrs. Price could no MP I 1 4 2
Her eldest was a boy of ten years old, a fine spirited MP I 1 5 2
daughter, a girl now nine years old, of an age to require MP I 1 5 4
seven years hence, and I dare say there would be mischief. MP I 1 7 6
Fanny Price was at this time just ten years old, and MP I 2 12 2
There was in fact but two years between the youngest and MP I 2 13 4
Once, and once only in the course of many years, had she MP I 2 21 34
had his uncle died a few years sooner, it would have been MP I 3 23 2
You have robbed Edmund for ten, twenty, thirty years, MP I 3 23 3
ten, twenty, thirty years, years, perhaps for life, of MP I 3 23 3
He had a wife about fifteen years his junior, but no MP I 3 24 6
You have been five years with us, and my sister always MP I 3 25 9
convince him that the many years which have passed since MP I 3 33 64
to his family, about two years ago, his sister was not out, MP I 5 50 35
Three years ago, the Admiral, my honoured uncle, bought a MP I 6 57 31
of years that he had been absent without tears in her eyes. MP I 6 60 47
An uncle with whom she has been living so many years, and MP I 7 63 4
miss, when you first began, six years ago come next Easter. MP I 7 69 22
in the taste of fifty years back, with shining floors, MP I 9 84 3
lubberly fellow of ten years old you know, who ought to be MP I 15 142 22
within the last three years, when she had quitted them.-- MP I 15 150 1
sketch of a ship sent four years ago from the MP I 16 152 2
agitation than she had been for the last twenty years. MP II 1 179 9
Three years ago, this was nothing but a rough hedgerow MP II 4 208 12
perhaps in another three years we may be forgetting-- MP II 4 208 12
or you should have gone into the army ten years ago." MP II 4 214 44
in having for many years taken in the paper esteemed to MP II 6 232 13
through a period of seven years, and the uncle who had MP II 6 233 14
one he had equipped seven years ago, but a young man of an MP II 6 233 16
and good of their earliest years could be gone over again, MP II 6 234 18
and in the course of seven years had known every variety MP II 6 236 21
his money purchased three years ago, before he knew there MP II 8 259 20
that you may live eighteen years longer in the world, MP III 1 319 39
from her aunt in the course of eight years and a half.-- MP III 2 333 27
in a degree," said Edmund, "from one's earliest years. MP III 3 338 14
twenty, thirty, forty years ago, the larger number, to MP III 3 339 23
inanimate, which so many years growth have confirmed, and MP III 4 347 21
Mrs. Fraser has been my intimate friend for years. MP III 5 359 12
but I have not cared much for her these three years." MP III 5 359 12
would be finally wasted on her even in years of matrimony. MP III 6 367 5
A residence of eight or nine years in the abode of wealth MP III 6 369 10
Price for more than twenty years; and it would be a help MP III 6 372 21
She was interrupted by a fine tall boy of eleven years old, MP III 7 377 7
about eight and nine years old, rushed into it just MP III 7 381 25
into Northamptonshire, who had died a few years afterwards. MP III 7 385 40
being at least as many years as they were his juniors MP III 8 390 8
I was in it two years ago, when it was Lady Lascelles's, MP III 9 394 1
for at least two years, she yet feared that her sister's MP III 9 397 7
as Lady Bertram, and some years her junior, should have an MP III 11 408 2
They have been leading her astray for years. MP III 13 421 2
in the course of a few years--but I am writing nonsense-- MP III 13 422 2
Her friends leading her astray for years! MP III 13 424 4
ever since her being ten years old, her mind in so great a MP III 17 470 27
years in the world with very little to distress or vex her. E I 1 5 1
Sixteen years had Miss Taylor been in Mr. Woodhouses's E I 1 5 3
the affection of sixteen years--how she had taught and how E I 1 6 6
played with her from five years old--how she had devoted E I 1 6 6
of the last seven years, the equal footing and perfect E I 1 6 6
older man in ways than in years; and though everywhere E I 1 7 8
I made the match, you know, four years ago; and to have it E I 1 11 39
Ever since the day (about four years ago) that Miss Taylor E I 1 12 41
for the last four years to bring about this marriage. E I 1 12 42
or twenty years of his life passed cheerfully away. E I 2 16 5
Somebody had placed her, several years back, at Mrs. E I 3 22 8
had lived five-and-twenty years with her; and of their E I 4 27 4
Six years hence, if he could meet with a good sort of E I 4 30 18
"Six years hence! dear Miss Woodhouse, he would be thirty E I 4 30 19
dear Miss Woodhouse, he would be thirty years old!" E I 4 30 19
meaning to read more ever since she was twelve years old. E I 5 37 7
At ten years old, she had the misfortune of being able to E I 5 37 9
It has been so many years my province to give advice, that E I 5 40 24
You do not know it I dare say, but two or three years ago E I 6 43 13
children of three or four years old stand still you know; E I 6 45 21
he was but two years old when he lost his poor mother! E I 11 96 24
I was sixteen years old when you were born." E I 12 99 6
years bring our understandings a good deal nearer?" E I 12 99 7
years, they always are put off when it comes to the point. E I 14 120 11
had first entered not two years ago, to make his way as he E I 16 136 9
deafer than she was two years ago; which is saying a great E II 1 158 14
it really is full two years, you know, since she was here. E II 1 158 14
By birth she belonged to Highbury: and when at three years E II 2 163 3

to overlook, though some years passed away from the death E II 2 163 4
and, before she was nine years old, his daughter's great E II 2 163 4
who could bring only the freshness of a two years absence. E II 2 166 10
which for those two whole years she had been depreciating. E II 2 167 12
and mother had died some years ago, an uncle remained--in E II 4 183 9
it had been built many years ago for a ball-room, and E II 6 197 5
had been settled some years in Highbury, and were very E II 7 207 6
and who have been your neighbours these ten years." E II 7 210 19
a boy of six years old, who knows nothing of the matter?" E II 8 224 67
Do not you remember what Mr. Perry said, so many years ago, E II 11 252 37
it is not your being ten years older than myself which E II 16 294 22
time, by the progress of years," said John Knightley, "I E II 16 294 23
Miss Fairfax, that ten years hence you may have as many E II 16 294 23
Mr. Suckling, who has been eleven years a resident at E II 18 310 34
she might not have many years of existence before her; but E III 1 317 6
two of his daily meals had, for forty years, been crowded. E III 5 347 18
He had not been at Donwell for two years. E III 6 356 30
I shall go abroad for a couple of years--and when I return, E III 7 373 50
Hazel eyes excepted, two years more might make her all E III 7 373 51
poor father twenty-seven years; and now, poor old man, he E III 8 383 29
years, was now spoken of with compassionate allowances. E III 9 387 12
Churchill had been promising a visit the last ten years. E III 9 388 15
She had herself been first with him for many years past. E III 12 415 1
What years of felicity that man, in all human calculation, E III 13 428 23
might be growing older ten years hence--to have his E III 17 461 1
in one of my amiable fits, about ten years ago. E III 17 462 12
for seventeen years; and though not the very happiest P III 1 4 6
Thirteen years had passed away since Lady Elliot's death, P III 1 5 7
A few years before, Anne Elliot had been a very pretty P III 1 6 10
than she was ten years before; and, generally speaking, if P III 1 6 11
had begun to be thirteen years ago; and Sir Walter might P III 1 6 11
Thirteen years had seen her mistress of Kellynch Hall, P III 1 6 12
For thirteen years had she been doing the honours, and P III 1 6 12
felt her approach to the years of danger, and would have P III 1 7 12
an interval of several years, felt with anger by Elizabeth, P III 1 8 17
If he will adopt these regulations, in seven years he will P III 2 12 4
of her having been three years at school there, after her P III 2 14 11
he has been stationed there, I believe, several years." P III 3 21 21
to the gentleman who lived a few years back, at Monkford. P III 3 22 25
know, Sir Walter, some time back, for two or three years. P III 3 23 32
More than seven years were gone since this little history P III 4 28 7
Uppercross was a moderate-sized village, which a few years P III 5 36 20
years longer in the world than her real eight and thirty. P III 6 48 18
abroad had worked its way to Uppercross, two years before. P III 6 50 28
He had been several years at sea, and had, in the course P III 6 51 30
often, puzzling over past years, and at last ascertaining P III 6 52 33
eight years ago,--was a new sort of trial to Anne's nerves. P III 6 52 33
to be feeling less. eight years, almost eight years had P III 7 60 28
almost eight years had passed, since all had been given up. P III 7 60 28
What might not eight years do? P III 7 60 28
feelings eight years may be little more than nothing. P III 7 60 29
No; the years which had destroyed her youth and bloom had P III 7 61 34
"Pretty well, ma'am, in the fifteen years of my marriage; P III 8 70 52
who for more than forty years had been zealously P III 9 78 19
forward child, of two years old, having got the door P III 9 79 28
which he received two years before, and Captain P III 11 94 6
Elliot had not, for many years, been on such terms as to P III 12 106 18
The offence which had been given her father, many years P III 12 107 21
eight years afterwards, be charmed by a Louisa Musgrove. P IV 1 125 13
an interval of so many years, to be well received by them. P IV 3 140 11
years had not altered almost every feature for the worse. P IV 3 141 12
It was now some years since Anne had begun to learn that P IV 4 147 7
it had existed so many years that she could not comprehend P IV 4 147 8
and Miss Hamilton, three years older than herself, but P IV 5 152 2
two years before, had left his affairs dreadfully involved. P IV 5 152 4
Twelve years were gone since they had parted, and each P IV 5 153 6
Twelve years had changed Anne from the blooming, silent, P IV 5 153 6
gentle; and twelve years had transformed the fine-looking, P IV 5 153 6
feeling that eight or nine years should have passed over P IV 7 179 28
I have been acquainted with you by character many years. P IV 8 187 32
He had many years ago received such a description of Miss P IV 8 187 34
partiality of her many years ago, as the Mr. Wentworth, of P IV 8 187 35
"I think you spoke of having known Mr. Elliot many years?" P IV 9 198 45
"I have not seen Mr. Elliot these three years," was Mrs. P IV 9 198 52
till within the last two years of her life, and can answer P IV 9 200 57
to what Mr. Elliot appeared to be some years ago. P IV 9 202 67
and twenty years in the world, "and have seen none like it. P IV 9 203 72
I have shewn you Mr. Elliot, as he was a dozen years ago, P IV 9 204 80
which had been for many years under a sort of P IV 9 210 98
claim it under many years; and that, on the strength of P IV 10 217 20
Eight years and a half is a period!" P IV 10 225 60
"than when you almost broke it eight years and a half ago. P IV 11 237 42
by so many, many years of division and estrangement. P IV 11 240 59
Six years of separation and suffering might have been P IV 11 247 84
I was born, man & boy 57 years, I think I must have known S 1 366 1
Every five years, one hears of some new place or other S 1 368 1
A very few years ago, & it had been a quiet village of no S 2 371 1
happily married 7 years--& had 4 sweet children at home;-- S 2 371 1
lined on their eldest son's coming of age 10 years ago.-- S 2 373 1
at the distance of 40 years, but she had so well nursed & S 3 375 1
After a widowhood of some years, she had been induced to S 3 375 1
After having avoided London for many years, principally on S 3 378 1
within the last 2 years--till our new house was finished.-- S 4 379 1
the course of a very few years;--the growth of my S 4 381 1
Two years ago I happened to be calling on Mrs Sheldon when S 5 386 1
Here have I lived 70 good years in the world & never took S 6 394 1

YEARS' (7)
would during a four years' engagement, your situation SS II 2 147 8
I shall let a seven years' lease of Everingham. MP II 12 295 20
received at the end of about ten years' happy marriage." MP III 4 354 46
and another twenty years' absence, perhaps, begun. MP III 6 373 24
wife died after a three years' marriage, he was rather a E I 2 16 4
"I have still the advantage of you by sixteen years' E I 12 99 10
her arrival, after a two years' interval, she was E II 2 167 12

YEILD (2)
my dear Alicia I yeild to the necessity which parts us. LS 39 307 1
ungrateful that it can hardly be made to yeild a Cabbage.-- S 1 369 1

YEILDING (1)
for a short period, & of yeilding admiration only to her LS 12 261 6

YELLOW (7)
I remember I wore my yellow gown, with my hair done up in NA I 15 118 11
it was Japan, black and yellow Japan of the handsomest NA II 6 168 10
her candle, the yellow had very much the effect of gold. NA II 6 168 10
yellow leaves about them, to jump up and walk for warmth. MP II 4 208 11
There are the yellow curtains that Miss Nash admires so E I 10 83 4
so beautiful, would still never match her yellow pattern. E II 9 235 35
yellow and forlorn than any thing I could have imagined." E II 11 253 41

YEOMANRY (1)
The yeomanry are precisely the order of people with whom I E I 4 29 14

YEOMEN (1)
to those of the yeomen and labourers,--the mansion of the P III 5 36 20

YESTER MORN (1)
the same hour of yester morn, that captian Wentworth had P IV 1 126 20

YESTERDAY (100)
praise, and yesterday he actually said, that he could not LS 8 255 2
He arrived yesterday. LS 20 275 1
She arrived yesterday in pursuit of her husband; but LS 32 302 1
Since we parted yesterday, I have received from LS 34 304 1
Oh! I must tell you, that just after we parted yesterday, NA I 6 41 16
had an account of it in a letter from London yesterday. NA I 14 112 33
I left her and Bath yesterday, never to see either again. NA II 10 202 7
her for what she had been yesterday left to endure. NA II 14 235 14
"Catherine took us quite by surprize yesterday evening," NA II 14 237 21
he chanced to complain yesterday (a very cold damp day) of SS I 8 38 11
I was talking to her yesterday of getting a new grate for SS I 8 39 17
It was not so yesterday, I think. SS II 5 168 9
you the day before yesterday, nor my astonishment at not SS II 7 187 39
40
Till yesterday, I believe, she never doubted his regard; SS II 8 199 40
"I wished very much to call upon you yesterday," said he, " SS II 11 221 9
flattering as Mrs. Ferrars's way of treating me yesterday? SS II 13 239 4
"we spent such a day, Edward, in Harley-Street yesterday! SS II 13 243 32
discovery that took place under our roof yesterday." SS III 1 265 34
Poor Fanny! she was in hysterics all yesterday. SS III 1 265 36
He left her house yesterday, but where he is gone, or SS III 1 268 48
two happy hours with him yesterday afternoon, he would not SS III 2 277 30
I heard it yesterday by chance, and was coming to you on SS III 5 294 8
"He opened his whole heart to me yesterday as we travelled. SS III 9 336 12
It seems but the day before yesterday that I saw them all W 334 13
You will not dine as you did yesterday, for we have W 341 19
is to be imputed to my getting wet through yesterday. PP I 7 31 29
30
"Yes, she called yesterday with her father. PP I 9 44 27
might, the very cold manner of our meeting yesterday.-- PP I 16 77 12
heard of her existence till the day before yesterday." PP I 16 83 54
him that her ladyship was quite well yesterday se'nnight." PP I 18 97 59
I will read it to you--"when my brother left us yesterday, PP I 21 117 10
11
Caroline did not return my visit till yesterday; and not a PP II 3 148 26
tell you of Lady Metcalfe's calling yesterday to thank me? PP II 6 165 32
of manners which she had yesterday witnessed, however PP III 2 263 10
in so amiable a light, which yesterday had produced. PP III 2 265 16
but were not missed till yesterday morning at eight. PP III 4 274 3
Colonel Forster came yesterday, having left Brighton the PP III 4 274 5
we were yesterday informed by a letter from Hertfordshire. PP III 6 296 11
I declare when I got back to Sotherton yesterday, it MP I 6 53 2
"How did you like her yesterday?" MP I 7 63 1
The painter was sent off yesterday, and very little will MP II 2 193 13
with a blush as it was yesterday, there is decided beauty; MP II 6 229 5
I could not tell what she would be at yesterday. MP II 6 230 7
told you what happened to me yesterday in my ride home." MP II 7 240 13
As she walked slowly up stairs she thought of yesterday; MP II 9 267 23
I would not allow myself yesterday to say how delighted, MP II 13 299 5
that--I told him enough yesterday to convince him--he MP III 1 314 17
to me on this subject yesterday--and I told him without MP III 1 314 17
I know he spoke to you yesterday, and (as far as I MP III 1 315 18
I gave him no encouragement yesterday--on the contrary, I MP III 1 315 19
manner of speaking of it yesterday, particularly pleased, MP III 4 351 35
36
home yesterday, and we were glad to see each other again. MP III 9 393 1
but she had not quite enough for the demands of yesterday. MP III 9 393 1
Mansfield, and was to dine, as yesterday, with the Frasers. MP III 10 400 8
We were speaking of it only yesterday, and agreeing how E I 5 36 6
appear to have spoken yesterday, it is not unlikely that E I 8 60 27
"how do you know that Mr. Martin did not speak yesterday?" E I 8 60 28
He did speak yesterday--that is, he wrote and was refused." E I 8 60 30
as he was coming back yesterday from Clayton Park, he had E I 8 68 58
to try his skill, by his manner of declining it yesterday." E I 9 76 29
yesterday, and may not be said and heard again to-morrow. E I 13 113 26
that it did not begin yesterday, and prevent this day's E I 13 115 39
you yesterday he was precisely the the height of Mr. Perry. E II 3 174 39
Miss Woodhouse," said Miss Bates, "four weeks yesterday.-- E II 3 176 44
"I told you yesterday," cried Mr. Weston with exultation, " E II 5 190 24
which she had believed herself to discern in him yesterday. E II 7 205 1
sure! and it was but yesterday I was telling Mr. Cole, I E II 8 215 16
I was saying this to Mr. Cole but yesterday, and he quite E II 8 216 16
Jane came back delighted yesterday. E II 9 237 48
You had, somehow or other, broken bounds yesterday, and E III 7 369 11
"Dating from three o'clock yesterday. E III 7 369 13
"Three o'clock yesterday! E III 7 369 14
(it was the day before yesterday, the very morning we were E III 8 380 15
write any such denial yesterday, as Jane wished her; she E III 8 381 15
yesterday evening it was all settled that Jane should go. E III 8 381 15
Till yesterday, I know he said he was in the dark as to E III 10 397 51
as if they had forgotten the conversation of yesterday.-- E III 12 416 2
of Tuesday afternoon and yesterday morning, but had the E III 14 436 7
made myself intelligible yesterday, this letter will be E III 14 436 8
A few words which dropped from him yesterday spoke his E III 14 438 8
I could not give any connected detail yesterday; but the E III 14 440 8
Mr. Knightley was at Hartfield yesterday, and spoke of it E III 16 456 28
me one word about our dinner at the Pooles yesterday." P III 5 39 35
I was very well yesterday; nothing at all the matter with P III 5 39 37
You saw how hysterical I was yesterday." P III 7 56 10
I was dreadfully alarmed yesterday, but the case is very P III 7 57 14
She took hardly any notice of Charles Hayter yesterday. P III 9 77 16
I wish you had been with us yesterday, for then you might P III 9 77 16
had been in Kellynch yesterday--(the first time since the P IV 1 126 20
"The house was cleared yesterday, except of the little " P IV 6 163 7
a note from Mrs. Croft "yesterday, offering to convey any P IV 6 164 8
His sister had a letter from him yesterday, in which he P IV 6 172 41
"though I came only yesterday, I have equipped myself P IV 7 177 14
who opened the door to you, when you called yesterday?" P IV 9 197 38
"We had your sister's card yesterday, and I understood P IV 11 236 36
and of yesterday and to-day there could scarcely be an end. P IV 11 241 59
Kentish Gazette, only yesterday morng in London--I think S 1 366 1
the day before yesterday--I heard again from Fanny Noyce, S 9 409 1
immediately, we were off yesterday morng at 6--, left S 9 409 1
promised the poor woman yesterday to get something done S 12 423 1

YESTERDAY'S (6)
the other for some particulars of their yesterday's party. NA I 15 116 1
in the course of their yesterday's party, received the NA I 15 117 8
Fanny had hoped, in the course of his yesterday's visit, MP III 1 311 1
an account of the yesterday's party at his friend Cole's, E I 10 88 34
the agreeableness of yesterday's engagement seemed to give E II 9 233 25
He came down by yesterday's coach, and was with me this E III 18 472 20

YEW (3)
go and sit up in an old yew arbour behind the house, you SS II 8 197 22
the canal, and the yew arbour, would all be made over to SS II 10 216 15
old farm house, with the yew trees, because I can never MP II 7 241 13

YIELD (15)
this opposition was to yield,--when Mrs. Ferrars would be SS I 19 102 2
a family party; and the young ladies were obliged to yield. SS I 19 109 40
"To yield readily--easily--to the persuasion of a friend PP I 10 50 35
"To yield without conviction is no compliment to the PP I 10 50 36
often make one readily yield to a request, without waiting PP I 10 50 37
But at last your uncle was forced to yield, and instead of PP III 10 324 2
Mrs. Rushworth being obliged to yield to Lady Bertram's MP I 8 76 4
obliged to yield--no matter--it was all misery now. MP I 16 157 28
of even fond dependence on her good nature, she must yield. MP I 18 172 32
Fanny found herself obliged to yield that she might not be MP II 8 258 17
most used of the two to yield; till a little bustle in the E II 8 226 85
too anxious for securing any thing to like to yield. E II 11 250 23
him with Jane, would yield its proportion of pleasure. E III 18 476 46
if not quite the luckiest, to yield only to herself. E III 19 482 4
The lady could not but yield to such joint entreaties, and P IV 4 145 2

YIELDED (15)
effort, the door suddenly yielded to her hand: her heart NA II 6 168 10
He yielded implicitly, and would fetch his hat and attend NA II 7 177 17
The pinery had yielded only one hundred in the last year. NA II 7 178 21
The lock yielded to her hand, and, luckily, with no sullen NA II 9 193 6
would have yielded the northern and western extremities. NA II 10 200 3
of consent must be yielded, and that once obtained--and NA II 16 249 2
After some opposition, Marianne yielded to her sister's SS II 11 220 1
their endeavours, he had yielded to his brother-in-law's PP III 6 298 13

uncle would never have yielded, if we had not given him	PP III 10 324 2
His good and her bad feelings yielded to love, and such	MP III 6 367 4
He yielded, but it was with agonies, which did not admit	MP III 16 453 16
house in town had yielded greater profits, and fortune in	E II 7 207 6
but on being pressed had yielded; and in the course of	E III 12 418 5
When I yielded, I though it was to duty; but no duty could	P IV 11 244 73
I could think of you only as one who had yielded, who had	P IV 11 245 74
YIELDING (10)	
evident that Jane was yielding to the preference which she	PP I 6 21 1
It is I believe too little yielding--certainly too little	PP I 11 58 28
smallest intention of yielding; but his answers were at	PP II 16 223 26
was of an obliging, yielding temper; and they could not	MP I 2 17 21
and yielding temper would have shrunk from asserting.	MP III 9 395 4
struggle--half a wish of yielding to truths, half a sense	MP III 16 458 30
likely to have a more yielding, complying, mild	E I 18 148 23
It is the worst evil of too yielding and indecisive a	P III 10 88 26
It had been gradually yielding to the better hopes which	P IV 11 241 60
If I was wrong in yielding to persuasion once, remember	P IV 11 244 73
YORK (6)	
I would undertake for five pounds to drive it to York and	NA I 9 65 30
had driven directly to the York hotel, ate some soup, and	NA I 15 116 1
if we were at York, provided she can have her own way.--	PP I 20 113 28
"From Bath, Norfolk, London, York--wherever I may be,"	MP II 2 193 12
of "men's beavers" and "York tan" were bringing down and	E II 6 200 16
was hung last assizes at York, tho' we really <u>have</u> raised	S 12 424 1
YORKSHIRE (7)	
Churchill, of a great Yorkshire family, and Miss Churchill	E I 2 15 2
She questioned him as to the society in Yorkshire-- the	E II 8 221 48
Your Yorkshire friend--your correspondent in Yorkshire;--	E II 16 297 48
"Indeed!--from Yorkshire, I think.	E II 18 305 8
Enscombe is in Yorkshire?"	E II 18 305 8
of the funeral for Yorkshire, was to be to the house of a	E III 9 388 15
They will soon be in Yorkshire.	E III 13 426 13
YOU'LL (2)	
If you'll believe me, I did not once put my foot out of	PP III 9 319 25
You'll do it very well.	MP I 15 146 52
YOUNG (850)	
My young lady accompanies me to town, where I shall	LS 2 246 1
& by her attentions to a young man previously attached to	LS 4 248 1
to one in particular, a young Frederic, whom I take on my	LS 5 250 2
of a lady no longer young, I must for my own part declare	LS 6 251 1
a handsome young man, who promises me some amusement.	LS 7 254 3
to see a young man of Reginald's sense duped by her at all.	LS 8 256 4
I hear the young man well spoken of, & tho' no one can	LS 9 256 1
could prevent a young man's being in love if he chose it.	LS 10 258 2
made Mr Manwaring & a young man engaged to Miss Manwaring	LS 11 259 1
I know that young men in general do not admit of any	LS 12 260 1
Lady Susan, to a young man of his age & high expectations.	LS 13 262 1
Sir James Martin had been drawn in by that young lady to	LS 14 264 4
Miss S. writes word that she could not get the young lady	LS 16 268 1
She is extremely young to be sure, has had a wretched	LS 18 273 2
In the breakfast room we found Lady Susan & a young man of	LS 20 275 2
he appears both to Mr. Vernon & me a very weak young man.	LS 20 276 2
Sir James is a young man of an amiable disposition, &	LS 20 276 5
The folly of the young man, and the confusion of Frederica	LS 20 278 9
into the protection of a young man with whom she had	LS 22 282 6
Young men are often hasty in their resolutions--& not more	LS 23 284 6
to save that ill-fated young man--& I must make myself	LS 25 293 4
have the gout--too old to be agreable, & too young to die.	LS 29 298 1
before, but this happy meeting will make us young again.	LS 40 309 1
task "to teach the young idea how to shoot."	NA I 1 15 6
And that a young woman in love always looks -----"	NA I 1 16 9
at their door--not one young man whose origin was unknown.	NA I 1 16 10
But when a young lady is to be a heroine, the perverseness	NA I 1 16 11
will not befal a young lady in her own village, she must	NA I 1 17 12
as delight in forcing young ladies away to some remote	NA I 2 18 2
Sally, or rather Sarah, (for what young lady of common	NA I 2 19 3
fitted to introduce a young lady into public, being as	NA I 2 20 8
and seeing every thing herself as any young lady could be.	NA I 2 20 8
For some time her young friend felt obliged to her for	NA I 2 21 9
She was now seen by many young men who had not been near	NA I 2 23 27
more obliged to the two young men for this simple praise	NA I 2 24 28
gentlemanlike young man as a partner;--his name was Tilney.	NA I 3 25 2
"I danced with a very agreeable young man, introduced by	NA I 3 27 26
My dear madam, I am not so ignorant of young ladies' ways	NA I 3 27 28
has maintained, that no young lady can be justified in	NA I 3 29 52
be very improper that a young lady should dream of a	NA I 3 29 52
acquaintance for his young charge he was on inquiry	NA I 3 30 52
is Isabella, my eldest; is not she a fine young woman?	NA I 4 32 3
great civility, the eldest young lady observed aloud to	NA I 4 32 4
formed an intimacy with a young man of his own college, of	NA I 4 33 5
intimacy between two young ladies; such as dress, balls,	NA I 4 33 7
Isabella was very sure that he must be a charming young	NA I 5 36 2
the two families, as her young charge and Isabella	NA I 5 36 3
Oh! it is only a novel!" replies the young lady; while she	NA I 5 38 4
Now, had the same young lady been engaged with a volume of	NA I 5 38 4
manner would not disgust a young person of taste; the	NA I 5 38 4
parted yesterday, I saw a young man looking at you so	NA I 6 41 16
Do you know, there are two odious young men who have been	NA I 6 43 33
to watch the proceedings of these alarming young men.	NA I 6 43 34
"One was a very good-looking young man."	NA I 6 43 37
"Only," she added, "perhaps we may overtake the two young	NA I 6 43 40
fast as they could walk, in pursuit of the two young men.	NA I 6 43 44
in the present case) of young men, are not detained on one	NA I 7 44 1
and, on catching the young men's eyes, the horse was	NA I 7 44 3
He was a stout young man of middling height, who, with a	NA I 7 45 5
intended movements of the young ladies; and, on finding	NA I 7 47 18
passed the two offending young men in Milsom-Street, she	NA I 7 47 18
she is just the kind of young woman I could wish to see	NA I 7 50 47
with the scores of other young ladies still sitting down	NA I 8 53 2
and pleasing-looking young woman, who leant on his arm,	NA I 8 53 3
place for young people--and indeed for every body else too.	NA I 8 54 5
increase either the dignity or enjoyment of a young lady.	NA I 8 55 10
the least objection to letting in this young lady by you."	NA I 8 55 10
The young ladies were introduced to each other, Miss	NA I 8 55 10
settled her young charge, returned to her party.	NA I 8 55 10
seemed capable of being young, attractive, and at a ball,	NA I 8 56 11
"Look at that young lady with the white beads round her	NA I 8 56 15
long before he saw him leading a young lady to the dance.	NA I 8 58 31
silence, she added, "he is a very agreeable young man."	NA I 8 58 32
that there is not a more agreeable young man in the world."	NA I 8 58 33
retreat, and she was too young to own herself frightened;	NA I 9 62 10
young man Mrs. Hughes says, and likely to do very well."	NA I 9 69 50
My mother says he is the most delightful young man in the	NA I 10 70 1
Was not the young lady he danced with on Monday a Miss	NA I 10 73 13
Every young lady may feel for my heroine in this critical	NA I 10 74 23
critical moment, for every young lady has at some time or	NA I 10 74 23
but there are hardly three young men in the room besides	NA I 10 78 38
upon my soul!--stout, active,--looks as young as his son.	NA I 12 95 18
Young men and women driving about the country in open	NA I 13 104 31
Do not you think it has an odd appearance, if young ladies	NA I 13 104 33
in them by young men, to whom they are not even related?"	NA I 13 104 33
Young people <u>will</u> be young people, as your good mother	NA I 13 104 36
Young people <u>do not</u> like to be always thwarted."	NA I 13 105 36
But I really thought before, young men despised novels	NA I 14 107 10
a very nice walk, and you are two very nice young ladies.	NA I 14 108 16
young man, unless circumstances are particularly untoward.	NA I 14 111 29
Their conference was put an end to by the anxious young	NA I 15 120 24
in a wish for the young people's happiness, with a remark,	NA I 15 124 48
handsome young man, whom she had never seen before, and	NA II 1 131 15
such a smart young fellow, I saw every eye was upon us."	NA II 1 134 39
When the young ladies next met, they had a far more	NA II 1 135 42
There never was a young woman so beloved as you are by	NA II 1 136 46
what they would be at, young men especially, they are so	NA II 3 146 20
sometimes a thoughtless young man; he has had about a	NA II 4 152 26
Mr. and Mrs. Allen were sorry to lose their young friend,	NA II 5 154 1
The remembrance of Mr. Allen's opinion, respecting young	NA II 5 156 5
But you must be aware that when a young lady is (by	NA II 5 158 15
of disposition in a young lady is a great blessing.--	NA II 7 174 10
But though I may not exactly make converts of you young	NA II 7 176 15
it expedient to give every young man some employment.	NA II 7 176 15
as strongly as one so young could feel it, I did not, I	NA II 7 180 34
spent, on the part of his young guest, in no very	NA II 8 182 1
canvassed by the three young people; and Catherine found,	NA II 11 208 1
surprize, that her two young friends were perfectly agreed	NA II 11 208 1
the number of young dancing people in the neighbourhood.	NA II 11 209 5
I think I can answer for the young ladies making allowance	NA II 11 210 6
and said, "I am come, young ladies, in a very moralizing	NA II 11 210 7
and young men never know their minds two days together.	NA II 12 216 2
I rejoice to say, that the young man whom, of all others,	NA II 12 216 2
"I am sorry for the young people," returned Mrs. Morland; "	NA II 14 234 12
It is always good for young people to be put upon exerting	NA II 14 234 12
for the parents of a young lady of seventeen, just	NA II 14 235 13
much such a subject, about young girls that have been	NA II 15 241 6
she beheld was a young man whom she had never seen before.	NA II 15 241 7
incapable of giving the young people even a decent support.	NA II 15 246 12
the young man on whom the Fullerton estate must devolve.	NA II 15 247 13
"Catherine would make a sad heedless young house-keeper to	NA II 16 249 1
The young people could not be surprized at a decision like	NA II 16 250 3
home, to watch over his young plantations, and extend his	NA II 16 250 3
to a precision the most charming young man in the world.	NA II 16 251 5
the most charming young man in the world is instantly	NA II 16 251 5
The son, a steady respectable young man, was amply	SS I 1 3 2
He was not an ill-disposed young man, unless to be rather	SS I 1 5 7
was very young when he married, and very fond of his wife.	SS I 1 5 7
death--a very comfortable fortune for any young woman."	SS I 2 10 14
gentlemanlike and pleasing young man, who was introduced	SS I 3 15 4
ideas of what a young man's address ought to be, was no	SS I 3 16 13
But yet--he is not the kind of young man--there is a	SS I 3 17 18
the danger attending any young woman who attempted to <u>draw</u>	SS I 4 23 19
it was too long ago for his young cousins to remember <u>him</u>.	SS I 6 30 6
collecting about him more young people than his house	SS I 7 32 2
numerous enough for any young lady who was not suffering	SS I 7 32 2
The Miss Dashwoods were young, pretty, and unaffected.	SS I 7 33 3
room repeated to the young ladies the concern which the	SS I 7 33 4
at being unable to get any smart young men to meet them.	SS I 7 33 4
at the park, but who was neither very young nor very gay.	SS I 7 33 4
woman, he hoped the young ladies would not find it so very	SS I 7 34 4
The young ladies, as well as their mother, were perfectly	SS I 7 34 4
weddings among all the young people of her acquaintance.	SS I 8 36 1
and the vanity of many a young lady by insinuations of her	SS I 8 36 1
of her power over such a young man; and this kind of	SS I 8 36 1
"And what sort of a young man is he?"	SS I 9 43 16
that he is a respectable young man, and one whose	SS I 9 44 24
"That is what I like; that is what a young man ought to be.	SS I 9 45 28
a delight, that any young man of five and twenty must have	SS I 10 47 3
Willoughby was a young man of good abilities, quick	SS I 10 48 7
lively nor young, seemed resolved to undervalue his merits.	SS I 10 50 13
of a strong affection in a young and ardent mind.	SS I 11 54 4
in the prejudices of a young mind, that one is sorry to	SS I 11 56 12
romantic refinements of a young mind are obliged to give	SS I 11 56 17
to give the name of the young man who was Elinor's	SS I 12 61 15
We will not say how near, for fear of shocking the young	SS I 13 66 57
The law was allowed to be genteel enough; many young men,	SS I 19 102 4
and honourable, and a young man of eighteen is not in	SS I 19 103 4
Her husband was a grave looking young man of five or six	SS I 19 106 22
a family party; and the young ladies were obliged to yield.	SS I 19 109 40
they had met with two young ladies, whom Mrs. Jennings had	SS I 21 118 2
The young ladies arrived, their appearance was by no means	SS I 21 119 3
introduction to these young ladies took place, they found	SS I 21 120 6
of screams in the young lady on hearing it, gave them	SS I 21 121 10
to stay behind, the four young ladies were left in a	SS I 21 122 10
not as many genteel young men in Devonshire as Sussex?"	SS I 21 123 27
But perhaps you young ladies may not care about the beaux,	SS I 21 123 28
Now there's Mr. Rose at Exeter, a prodigious smart young	SS I 21 123 28
" twill be a fine thing to have her married so young to be	SS I 21 125 35
very agreeable young man to be sure; I know him very well."	SS I 21 126 39
his mother; but I was too young and loved him too well to	SS I 22 130 28
The young ladies went, and Lady Middleton was happily	SS II 1 143 10
prettiest behaved young men I ever saw; but as for Lucy,	SS II 2 148 22
I shall speak a good word for you to all the young men,	SS II 3 154 2
town; I would have every young woman of your condition in	SS II 3 156 8
fitted up, and the young ladies were immediately put in	SS II 4 160 3
Well, Colonel, I have brought two young ladies with me,	SS II 4 163 18
Aye, it is a fine thing to be young and handsome.	SS II 4 163 18
Well! I was young once, but I never was very handsome --	SS II 4 163 18
between a daughter so young, a man so little known, to be	SS II 4 165 29
at all discompose the feelings of her young companions.	SS II 5 168 11
nearly twenty young people, and to amuse them with a ball.	SS II 5 170 29
conversation with a very fashionable looking young woman.	SS II 6 176 3
on catching the eye of the young lady with whom he had	SS II 6 177 11
saw a young woman so desperately in love in my life!	SS II 7 181 7 8
Whom did I ever hear him talk of as young and attractive	SS II 7 190 58
it is true, he has used a young lady of my acquaintance	SS II 8 192 3
he is not the only young man in the world worth having;	SS II 8 192 3
her young friend's affliction could be increased by noise.	SS II 8 192 4
Well, it don't signify talking, but when a young man, be	SS II 8 194 10
can ever be given up by the young men of this age."	SS II 8 194 10
and you know young people like to be laughed at about them.	SS II 8 195 16
marriage been happy, so young as I then was, a few months	SS II 9 206 24
The consequence of this, upon a mind so young, so lively,	SS II 9 206 24
go to Bath with one of her young friends, who was	SS II 9 208 28
resolved, that while her young friends transacted their's,	SS II 11 220 2
the two young ladies to this formidable mother-in-law.	SS II 12 231 12
something very trying to a young woman who <u>has been</u> a	SS II 12 236 43
revenge on her, "you think young men never <u>stand</u> upon	SS II 13 243 38
the engagements of her young friends; for as she wished to	SS II 14 246 2
congratulated her young friends every night, on having	SS II 14 247 5
perceived among a group of young men, the very he, who had	SS II 14 250 11
But while she wondered at the difference of the two young	SS II 14 250 12
so much pleased with any young women in her life, as she	SS II 14 254 28
report should reach the young ladies under your care as to	SS III 1 258 5
Mr. Edward Ferrars, the very young man I used to joke with	SS III 1 258 7
that she had asked these young women to her house; merely	SS III 1 266 36
Miss Lucy Steele is, I dare say, a very deserving young	SS III 1 267 45
And to have entered into a secret engagement with a young	SS III 1 267 45
"Poor young man!--and what is to become of him?"	SS III 1 268 49
"Poor young man!" cried Mrs. Jennings, "I am sure he	SS III 1 268 51
deserving young woman--have I been rightly informed?--	SS III 3 282 17
attempting to divide, two young people long attached to	SS III 3 282 19
He is not a young man with whom one can be intimately	SS III 3 282 19
"Well, my dear," she cried, "I sent you up the young man.	SS III 4 291 47
are both very agreeable young men, I do not know that one	SS III 5 297 29
marry this young woman, <u>I</u> never will see him again.'	SS III 5 299 35
young brood, she found fresh sources of merriment.	SS III 6 303 10
The rapid decay, the early death of a girl so young, so	SS III 7 313 20
revival, tried to keep her young friend from indulging a	SS III 7 314 22
of my attachment to some young lady in Devonshire, and	SS III 8 328 61
the young lady was, and made her more jealous than ever.	SS III 8 328 61
for that worthless young man!--and without selfishness--	SS III 9 336 14
for the loss of her two young companions; and Colonel	SS III 10 341 5
after you, ma'am, and the young ladies, especially Miss	SS III 11 354 27
She was always a very affable and free-spoken young lady	SS III 11 354 29

very handsome young lady--and she seemed vastly contented." SS III 11 355 44
of the most fortunate young women in the world, as it is. SS III 14 375 9
"A young man of very good fortune, quite independant, & W 315 1
very much attached to a young man of the name of Purvis a W 316 2
for me, if one could be young for ever, but my father W 317 2
"A young man must think of somebody. said eliz:--& why W 321 2
young ladies were carefully recommended to lose no time.-- W 323 3
Mr Sam Watson is a very good sort of young man, & I dare W 324 3
the circumstances of his young guest than had yet reached W 325 4
your officers for captivating the ladies, young or old.-- W 326 5
It is quite as necessary to young ladies in their first."-- W 326 6
"Rather more so, my dear--replied he, because young ladies W 326 6
was long to the two young ladies; & tho' Miss Edwards was W 326 7
the proper security of her young Charges' shoulders & W 327 7
they were accosted by a young man in a morning dress & W 327 7
He came into possession of it, when he was very young, & W 328 8
which seemed to call the young men to their duty, & people W 328 9
who was certainly a genteel, good looking young man.-- W 329 9
Ld Osborne was a very fine young man; but there was an air W 329 10
Miss Carr, & a party of young men were standing engaged in W 330 11
avoid seeming to hear her young companion delightedly W 332 11
other people in a ball room, what are young ladies to do?" W 337 15
or waiting to see how the young lady's inclination lay. W 339 18
It struck me as very becoming in so young a man, but I am W 344 20
The surprise of the young ladies may be imagined. W 344 21
& describe a very odd young lady; but the gratification W 347 22
pounds, there was a young man who wd have thought of her." W 353 26
so far as to say--"the young man who was here last night W 360 29
Netherfield is taken by a young man of large fortune from PP I 1 3 10
it, and live to see many young men of four thousand a year PP I 1 5 31
What say you, Mary? for you are a young lady of deep PP I 2 7 18
He was quite young, wonderfully handsome, extremely PP I 3 9 1
admitted to a sight of the young ladies, of whose beauty PP I 3 9 3
sisters, the husband of the eldest, and another young man. PP I 3 10 4
consequence to young ladies who are slighted by other men. PP I 3 11 13
"He is just what a young man ought to be," said she, " PP I 4 14 2
"He is also handsome," replied Elizabeth, "which a young PP I 4 14 3
The eldest of them, a sensible, intelligent young woman, PP I 5 18 2
One cannot wonder that so very fine a young man, with PP I 5 20 18
"If I were as rich as Mr. Darcy," cried a young Lucas who PP I 5 20 21
"What a charming amusement for young people this is, Mr. PP I 6 25 26
Mr. Darcy, you must allow me to present this young lady to PP I 6 26 38
39
distance for the young ladies, who were usually tempted PP I 7 28 3
my heart; and if a smart young Colonel, with five or six PP I 7 29 12
Elizabeth accepted their company, and the three young PP I 7 32 39
"It is amazing to me," said Bingley, "how young ladies can PP I 8 39 43
"All young ladies accomplished! PP I 8 39 44
I am sure I never heard a young lady spoken of for the PP I 8 39 45
on her, "is one of those young ladies who seek to PP I 8 40 56
"She seems a very pleasant young woman," said Bingley. PP I 9 44 30
Perhaps he thought her too young. PP I 9 44 31
"He seems to be a most conscientious and polite young man, PP I 13 63 13
He was a tall, heavy looking young man of five and twenty. PP I 13 64 21
But I can assure the young ladies that I come prepared to PP I 13 65 25
And what sort of young lady is she? is she handsome?" PP I 14 67 6
"She is a most charming young lady indeed. PP I 14 67 7
which marks the young woman of distinguished birth. PP I 14 67 7
often observed how little young ladies are interested by PP I 14 69 15
16
But I will no longer importune my young cousin." PP I 14 69 16
them that he bore his young cousin no ill will, and should PP I 14 69 17
But the attention of every lady was soon caught by a young PP I 15 72 8
as it should be; for the young man wanted only regimentals PP I 15 72 8
Mr. Denny and Mr. Wickham walked with the young ladies to PP I 15 73 10
to the young ladies who introduced him to her notice. PP I 15 73 11
As no objection was made to the young people's engagement PP I 16 75 1
into insignificance to the young ladies he certainly was PP I 16 76 5
She could have added, "a young man too, like *you*, whose PP I 16 80 36
of a young man of such amiable appearance as Wickham.-- PP I 17 85 1
The two young ladies were summoned from the shrubbery PP I 17 86 9
of this kind, given by a young man of character, to PP I 17 87 13
that young lady, whose bright eyes are also upbraiding me." PP I 18 92 23
and I find that the young man forgot to tell you, among PP I 18 94 45
Mr. Wickham is by no means a respectable young man. PP I 18 95 50
himself mentioning to the young lady who does the honours PP I 18 96 57
decide on what is right than a young lady like yourself." PP I 18 97 61
His being such a charming young man, and so rich, and PP I 18 99 63
Let the other young ladies have time to exhibit." PP I 18 101 69
that he was a remarkably clever, good kind of young man. PP I 18 101 71
and offer to introduce him to any young lady in the room. PP I 18 102 73
where I assure you there are many amiable young women. PP I 19 106 10
"that it is usual with young ladies to reject the PP I 19 107 13
I do assure you that I am not one of those young ladies (PP I 19 107 14
young ladies (if such young ladies there are) who are so PP I 19 107 14
the the peculiar duty of a young man who has been so PP I 20 114 32
influence a young man so totally independent of every one. PP I 21 120 28
for well-educated young women of small fortune, and PP I 22 122 3
We must not expect a lively young man to be always so PP II 1 136 14
young ladies in the country. let Wickham be *your* man. PP II 1 138 27
A young man, such as you describe Mr. Bingley, so easily PP II 2 140 6
of friends will persuade a young man of independent PP II 2 140 7
At his own ball he offended two or three young ladies, by PP II 2 141 9
with regard to this young man will influence her. PP II 2 141 12
he is a most interesting young man; and if he had the PP II 3 144 2
where there is affection, young people are seldom withheld PP II 3 145 7
remarkable charm of the young lady, to whom he was now PP II 3 149 28
They are young in the ways of the world, and not yet open PP II 3 150 29
conviction that handsome young men must have something to PP II 3 150 29
I should be sorry, you know, to think ill of a young man PP II 4 153 18
"Oh! if that is all, I have a very poor opinion of young PP II 4 154 19
I am always glad to get a young person well placed out. PP II 6 165 32
that I recommended another young person, who was merely PP II 6 165 32
Your younger sisters must be very young?" PP II 6 165 34
Perhaps *she* is full young to be much in company. PP II 6 165 35
give your opinion very decidedly for so young a person.-- PP II 6 165 36
I often tell young ladies, that no excellence in music is PP II 8 173 10
than one young lady was sitting down in want of a partner. PP II 8 175 18
Young ladies of her age, are sometimes a little difficult PP II 10 184 19
believing him the kind of young man to get into a scrape PP II 10 185 28
favourite of my father, a young man who had scarcely any PP II 12 196 5
the separation of two young persons, whose affection could PP II 12 196 5
eldest sister, to any other young woman in the country.-- PP II 12 197 5
My father was not only fond of this young man's society, PP II 12 200 5
the observation of a young man of nearly the same age with PP II 12 200 5
at the persuasion of the young man, who, on meeting him PP II 13 205 4
But I am particularly attached to these young men; and PP II 14 210 3
the idea of two young women travelling post by themselves. PP II 14 211 13
Young women should always be properly guarded and attended, PP II 14 211 13
You must send John with the young ladies, Mrs. Collins. PP II 14 212 13
extremely dull to a young lady like yourself; but I hope PP II 15 215 2
It was the second week in may, in which the three young PP II 16 219 1
mismanagement in the education of those two young men. PP II 17 225 15
Well, he is a very undeserving young man--and I do not PP II 17 228 27
the young ladies in the neighbourhood were drooping apace. PP II 18 229 1
This invaluable friend was a very young woman, and very PP II 18 230 11
of lines, crowded with the young and the gay, and dazzling PP II 18 232 22
it was the picture of a young gentleman, the son of her PP III 1 247 9
"Does that young lady know Mr. Darcy?" PP III 1 247 14
"Oh! yes--the handsomest young lady that ever was seen; PP III 1 248 22
Not like the wild young men now-a-days, who think of PP III 1 249 38
only because he does not rattle away like other young men." PP III 1 249 38

such a design against a young woman of Lydia's connections, PP III 4 275 5
It appears to me so very unlikely, that any young man PP III 5 282 1
But she is very young; she has never been taught to think PP III 5 283 10
Every body declared that he was the wickedest young man in PP III 6 294 4
possible, from some of the young man's intimates in the PP III 6 295 6
one of the most worthless young men in Great Britain to be PP III 8 308 1
And there are several of the young men, too, that she PP III 8 313 21
The easy assurance of the young couple, indeed, was enough PP III 9 315 4
young man to resist an opportunity of having a companion. PP III 9 318 19
any young woman of character, to love or confide in him. PP III 10 321 2
well, I suppose, what has been done for the young people. PP III 10 324 2
young lady's whispering to Elizabeth again, he walked away. PP III 12 342 25
and sensible young man, without having a wish beyond it. PP III 12 343 32
Oh! he is the handsomest young man that ever was seen!" PP III 13 349 41
Some-where about the grounds, walking with a young man, PP III 14 352 8
to be prevented by a young woman of inferior birth, of no PP III 14 355 43
The upstart pretensions of a young woman without family, PP III 14 356 50
I expected to find a more reasonable young woman. PP III 14 356 60
I know it all; that the young man's marrying her, was a PP III 14 357 62
Young ladies have great penetration in such matters as PP III 15 362 12
"This young gentleman is blessed in a peculiar way, with PP III 15 362 15
young couple into your house as soon as they were married. PP III 15 363 22
situation, and his expectation of a young olive-branch. PP III 15 364 22
these violent young lovers carry every thing their own way. PP III 17 377 39
quitted the room, "if any young men come for Mary or Kitty, PP III 17 377 40
evenness of your writing, as another young lady once did. PP III 18 382 19
and young men, her father would never consent to her going. PP III 19 385 4
The young people were all at home, and sustained their MP I 2 12 3
and entertaining their young cousin, produced little union. MP I 2 14 7
sort of merriment which a young man of seventeen will MP I 2 17 22
on the introduction of a young man who had recently MP I 4 38 9
He was a heavy young man, with not more than common sense; MP I 4 38 10
address, the young lady was well pleased with her conquest. MP I 4 38 10
declared that of all the young ladies she had ever seen, MP I 4 39 10
appeared precisely the young man to deserve and attach her. MP I 4 39 10
number of balls, the young people justified these opinions, MP I 4 39 11
They were young people of fortune. MP I 4 40 15
habits of a young woman who had been mostly used to London. MP I 4 41 15
a young man and woman of very prepossessing appearance. MP I 4 41 17
"to what any young person says on the subject of marriage. MP I 4 43 25
The young people were pleased with each other from the MP I 5 44 1
while they were the finest young women in the country. MP I 5 44 1
He was, in fact, the most agreeable young man the sisters MP I 5 44 2
good sort of young man, and it is a great match for her." MP I 5 45 13
it so; a talking pretty young woman like Miss Crawford, is MP I 5 47 26
Bertrams were very fine young men, that two such young men MP I 5 47 27
young men, that two such young men were not often seen MP I 5 47 27
rate; he was the sort of young man to be generally liked, MP I 5 47 28
Few young ladies of eighteen could be less called on to MP I 5 48 30
Anderson in your eye, in describing an altered young lady. MP I 5 49 35
a word or a look from the young lady--nothing like a civil MP I 5 50 35
agreeable as I could; the young lady perfectly easy in her MP I 5 51 40
You young ones do not remember much about it, perhaps. MP I 6 54 9
pointed out even to a very young eye what little remained MP I 6 61 56
A young woman, pretty, lively, with a harp as elegant as MP I 7 65 13
from the example of the young ladies at the park, and MP I 7 66 14
party included all the young people but herself, and was MP I 7 70 30
A young party is always provided with a shady lane. MP I 7 70 30
trick for a young person to be always lolling upon a sofa; MP I 7 71 34
should be disengaged; the young ladies did not forget that MP I 8 75 1
happy to have seen the young lady too, Miss Price, who had MP I 8 76 4
to have it so, and the young ladies were in spirits again. MP I 8 80 28
as an amendment; the young ladies neither smiled nor spoke. MP I 9 84 2
The young Mrs. Eleanors and Mrs. Bridgets--starched up MP I 9 87 15
could be done, when the young people, meeting with an MP I 9 89 32
interest it excited in the breast of another young lady. MP I 11 107 4
She has done no more than every young woman would do; MP I 11 108 12
it was while all the other young people were dancing, and MP I 12 116 11
or spendour of many a young lady's first ball, being the MP I 12 117 11
Young folks in their situation should be excused complying MP I 12 117 13
delightful, ma'am, to see young people so properly happy, MP I 12 118 16
steady young man, so I hope Miss Julia will be very happy." MP I 12 118 20
for acting so strong among young people, that he could MP I 13 121 2
Nobody is fonder of the exercise of talent in young people, MP I 13 126 25
I am not the *only* young woman you find, who thinks it very MP I 15 140 12
be one steady head to superintend so many young ones. MP I 15 141 22
Such a forward young lady may well frighten the men." MP I 15 144 32
imagined him a very fine young man, and advised Fanny to MP I 15 147 57
I could name at this moment at least six young men within MP I 15 148 58
A quiet-looking young man. MP I 15 148 59
the help of a young man very slightly known to any of us. MP I 16 153 8
must, arise from a young man's being received in this MP I 16 154 14
cheerfulness to the young people in general, and that did MP I 17 161 9
and useful pursuits of all the young people as for her own. MP II 1 179 9
say, "how do you think the young people have been amusing MP II 1 180 13
young man, who appeared likely to knock him down backwards. MP II 1 182 22
the acquaintance of a young man whom he felt sure of MP II 1 183 23
We bespeak your indulgence, you understand, as young MP II 1 185 28
as a well-judging steady young man, with better notions MP II 1 186 35
The young people have been very inconsiderate in forming MP II 2 188 3
themselves; but they were young, and, excepting Edmund, he MP II 2 188 3
the sort of amiable modest young man who wants a great MP II 2 188 3
No young people's are, I suppose, when those they look up MP II 3 197 3
For so young a woman it is remarkable! MP II 3 198 13
Rushworth was an inferior young man, as ignorant in MP II 3 200 19
Mr. Rushworth was young enough to improve;--Mr. Rushworth MP II 3 201 22
A well-disposed young woman, who did not marry for love, MP II 3 201 22
make way for the fortunate young woman whom her dear son MP II 3 202 28
The plan of the young couple was to proceed after a few MP II 3 203 31
Becoming as she then did, the only young woman in the MP II 4 205 1
must wish to go, since all young people like to be MP II 5 219 18
so much between the two young men about hunting, so much MP II 5 223 48
I shall come on purpose to encourage a young beginner. MP II 5 227 65
are such unconquerable young ladies of eighteen (or one MP II 6 231 11
seven years ago, but a young man of an open, pleasant MP II 6 233 16
He honoured the warm hearted, blunt fondness of the young MP II 6 235 19
the first ardours of her young, unsophisticated mind! MP II 6 235 20
the recitor, to know the young man by his histories; and MP II 6 236 21
Young as he was, William had already seen a great deal. MP II 6 236 21
find the Grants and their young inmates really worth MP II 7 238 1
There was no want of respect in the young man's address; MP II 7 246 37
to give pleasure to the young people in general; and MP II 8 252 1
be tempted to give the young people a dance at Mansfield. MP II 8 252 2
of the notice, to collect young people enough to form MP II 8 253 7
Invitations were sent with dispatch, and many a young lady MP II 8 254 8
beyond the happiness; for young and inexperienced, with MP II 8 254 8
she supposed all the other young ladies would appear in? MP II 8 254 8
to have, by the many young ladies looking forward to the MP II 9 266 22
table the eyes of the two young men assured him, that the MP II 10 272 4
To be placed above so many elegant young women! MP II 10 275 12
Young, pretty, and gentle, however, she had no MP II 10 276 13
the deserted chair of each young man might exercise her MP II 11 282 2
he said he was the finest young man in the room; somebody MP II 11 283 4
"We miss our two young men," was Sir Thomas's observation MP II 11 284 9
To the young lady at least in each family, it brought very MP II 11 285 15
Being the only young person at home, I consider *you* as the MP II 11 287 18
It is the general way; all young men do." MP II 11 287 20
He is a very--a very pleasing young man himself, and I MP II 11 287 22
But it is very foolish to ask questions about any young MP II 11 288 28
it never pardonable in a young man of independent fortune. MP II 12 292 9
the promotion of young price, and inclosing two more, one MP II 13 298 3
"It is amazing," said she, "how much young people cost MP II 13 305 24

and very judiciously, for young people's being brought up MP III 1 312 12
Here is a young man wishing to pay his addresses to you, MP III 1 315 27
Young as you are, and having seen scarcely any one, it is MP III 1 316 31
and would have every young man, with a sufficient income, MP III 1 317 34
in modern days, even in young women, and which in young MP III 1 318 39
young women, and which in young women is offensive and MP III 1 318 39
Crawford exactly what a young, heated fancy imagines to be MP III 1 318 39
Here is a young man of sense, of character, of temper, of MP III 1 319 39
from the personal intreaty of the young man himself. MP III 1 320 44
a knowledge of what had passed between the young people. MP III 2 329 11
an hour's intreaty from a young man like Crawford could MP III 2 329 11
He is a most extraordinary young man, and whatever be the MP III 2 330 14
common character; though, young as you are, and little MP III 2 330 14
It would not be fair to enquire into a young lady's exact MP III 2 331 18
And you must be aware, Fanny, that it is every young MP III 2 333 26
The two young men were the only talkers, but they, MP III 3 339 22
one more effort for the young man before he left Mansfield, MP III 4 345 2
the young man's inclination for paying them were over. MP III 5 356 3
exigeant; and wants a young woman, a beautiful young woman MP III 5 361 16
young woman of five-and-twenty, to be as steady as himself. MP III 5 361 16
looked up to by all the young people of her acquaintance; MP III 5 361 16
who jilted a very nice young man in the blues, for the MP III 5 361 16
the havock he might be making in young ladies' affections. MP III 5 363 22
very few young ladies have any affections worth caring for. MP III 5 363 22
and there are so many young men's claims to be attended to MP III 5 364 29
Experience might have hoped more for any young people, so MP III 6 367 6
of one of those days the young travellers were in a good MP III 6 372 21
half a mind to go with the young people; it would be such MP III 6 372 21
it would be a help to the young people in their journey to MP III 6 372 21
the passage, he exclaimed, "devil take those young dogs! MP III 7 383 30
a very well behaved young man, who came to call for his MP III 7 384 36
some hasty washing of the young tea-maker's, a cup and MP III 7 384 36
I am unwilling to fancy myself neglected for a young one. MP III 9 394 1
the dashing young captains whom you disdain for his sake." MP III 9 394 1
The young ladies who approached her at first with some MP III 9 395 3
, there is scarcely a young lady in the united kingdoms, MP III 10 402 11
interest, while the young people sat down upon some MP III 10 403 15
Tom had gone from London with a party of young men to MP III 13 426 10
the house of one of these young men, to the comforts of MP III 13 426 10
To have such a fine young man cut off in the flower of his MP III 14 434 13
Poor young man!-- MP III 14 434 13
If he is to die, there will be two poor young men less in MP III 14 434 13
in which affairs then stood with the young people. MP III 16 450 9
to the character of any young people, must be the totally MP III 17 463 7
that had there been no young woman in question, had there MP III 17 465 13
had there been no young person of either sex belonging to MP III 17 465 13
Let no one presume to give the feelings of a young woman MP III 17 471 28
possibility of the two young friends finding their mutual MP III 17 471 29
A worthy employment for a young lady's mind! E I 1 12 42
"Mr. Elton is a very pretty young man to be sure, and a E I 1 14 47
a very good young man, and I have a great regard for him. E I 1 14 47
their own, nor any other young creature of equal kindred E I 2 16 4
of him as a very fine young man had made Highbury feel a E I 2 17 7
favourable idea of the young man; and such a pleasing E I 2 18 10
and by Mr. Elton, a young man living alone without liking E I 3 20 2
for a woman neither young, handsome, rich, nor married. E I 3 21 4
and new systems--and where young ladies for enormous pay E I 3 21 5
It was no wonder that a train of twenty young couple now E I 3 22 5
to some young ladies who had been at school there with her. E I 3 23 8
Smith's being exactly the young friend she wanted--exactly E I 4 26 2
man; that there was no young Mrs. Martin, no wife in the E I 4 27 5
A young farmer, whether on horseback or on foot, is the E I 4 29 14
"I have no doubt of his being a very respectable young man. E I 4 29 16
That is too young to settle. E I 4 30 18
meet with a good sort of young woman in the same rank as E I 4 30 18
The young man had been the first admirer, but she trusted E I 4 31 26
he looked like a sensible young man, but his person had no E I 4 31 27
to allow it; but if any young man were to set about E I 4 34 42
On the contrary, I think a young man might be very safely E I 4 34 42
by Emma for driving the young farmer out of Harriet's head. E I 4 34 44
well-meaning, respectable young man, with any deficiency E I 4 35 44
And he was really a very pleasing young man, a young man E I 4 35 45
She is not the superior young woman which Emma's friend E I 5 36 6
I hope, with all my heart, the young man may be a weston E I 5 38 15
the gratitude of her young vanity to a very good purpose, E I 6 42 1
He is an excellent young man, and will suit Harriet E I 6 49 44
"Upon my word," she cried, "the young man is determined E I 7 50 2
I can hardly imagine the young man whom I saw talking with E I 7 51 5
how the young man could have the assurance to ask it. E I 7 54 29
However, I do really think Mr. Martin a very amiable young E I 7 54 30
that Emma believed if the young man had come in her way at E I 7 55 35
whether I thought her too young; in short, whether I E I 8 59 27
He is an excellent young man, both as son and brother. E I 8 59 27
Mr. Martin is a very respectable young man, but I cannot E I 8 61 37
She has been taught nothing useful, and is too young and E I 8 61 38
Nothing so easy as for a young lady to raise her E I 8 64 47
He knows that he is a very handsome young man, and a great E I 8 66 53
of a large family of young ladies that his sisters are E I 8 66 53
He felt the disappointment of the young man, and was E I 8 66 55
The possibility of the young man's coming to Mrs. E I 8 67 56
used to be when he was young--he wondered he could not E I 9 70 5
of his had addressed to a young lady, the object of his E I 9 71 10
I wonder who the friend was--and who could be the young E I 9 72 17
no weather to prevent the young ladies from tolerably E I 10 83 1
"Where is the young man?" said John Knightley. E I 11 95 20
He is but young, and his uncle perhaps-----" E I 11 96 22
"I have no doubt of his being a most amiable young man. E I 11 96 25
and by not being a pretty young woman and a spoiled child. E I 12 99 10
however, is just such another pretty kind of young person. E I 12 104 47
48

own cook at south end, a young woman hired for the time, E I 12 104 50
amiable, pleasing young man undoubtedly, and very much in E I 13 111 13
of that poor young man without the greatest compassion. E I 14 121 17
those views on the young man, of which her own imagination E I 14 122 18
one can hardly conceive a young man's not having it in his E I 14 122 22
A young woman, if she fall into bad hands, may be teazed, E I 14 122 22
one cannot comprehend a young man's being being under such E I 14 122 22
satisfied with persuading her not to accept young Martin. E I 16 137 11
no, I could not endure William Coxe--a pert young lawyer." E I 16 137 11
dependence on seeing the young man had been so much more E I 18 144 2
one could wish, that a young man, brought up by those who E I 18 145 10
Such language for a young man entirely dependent, to use!-- E I 18 147 17
I wish you would try to understand what an amiable young E I 18 148 21
"Your amiable young man is a very weak young man, if this E I 18 148 22
I have not the least idea of his being a weak young man: I E I 18 148 23
No, Emma, your amiable young man can be amiable only in E I 18 149 26
often look upon fine young men, well-bred and agreeable. E I 18 149 29
To take a dislike to a young man, only because he appeared E I 18 150 37
He is a most amiable, charming young man, I believe. E II 1 160 20
He is a most charming young man. E II 1 160 23
officer and most deserving young man; and farther, had E II 2 163 4
It was easy to decide that she was still too young; and E II 2 164 6
could not be unseen by the young woman, nor could her E II 2 165 7
affections of Mr. Dixon, a young man, rich and agreeable, E II 2 165 7
the really accomplished young woman, which she wanted to E II 2 166 11
that Highbury afforded no young man worthy of giving her E II 2 168 14
"She believed he was reckoned a very fine young man." E II 2 169 17
"Did he appear a sensible young man; a young man of E II 2 169 17
whole evening by two such young women; sometimes with E II 3 170 2
is a very pretty sort of young lady, a very pretty and a E II 3 171 12
a very pretty and a very well-behaved young lady indeed. E II 3 171 12
"He is very young to settle," was Mr. Woodhouse's E II 3 174 34

He is the very best young man--but, my dear Jane, if you E II 3 174 39
Miss Hawkins,--I dare say, an excellent young woman. E II 3 175 39
And Mr. Dixon seems a very charming young man, quite E II 3 175 39
Well, I had always rather fancied it would be some young E II 3 176 44
Mr. Elton is a most worthy young man--but'---- in short, I E II 3 176 44
while he lamented that young people would be in such a E II 3 177 51
by the house where a young woman was making up a gown for E II 3 177 52
The young man's conduct, and his sister's, seemed the E II 3 179 53
situations, that a young person, who either marries or E II 4 181 1
now addressing all the young ladies of the place, to whom, E II 4 182 5
without delay, and unattended by any alarming young man. E II 5 186 3
such a very fine young man; you have only had my account E II 5 189 13
a very good looking young man; height, air, address, all E II 5 190 22
indulge in it," said the young man, "though there are not E II 5 190 25
that I was to find a pretty young woman in Mrs. Weston." E II 5 192 30
that you have spoken of her as a pretty young woman." E II 5 192 31
this morning," said the young man; "another day would do E II 5 194 39
40

said Emma, "she is a very elegant young woman." E II 5 194 42
you that you will find her a very agreeable young lady. E II 5 194 45
He argued like a young man very much bent on dancing; and E II 6 198 5
"Ill, very ill--that is, if a young lady can ever be E II 6 199 9
"did you ever hear the young lady we were speaking of, E II 6 201 26
than that "all young people would have their little whims." E II 7 205 1
As Mrs. Weston observed, "all young people would have E II 7 206 3
of such a handsome young man--one who smiled so often and E II 7 206 4
Mr. Knightley, he is not a trifling, silly young man. E II 8 212 3
is more like a young woman's scheme than an elderly man's. E II 8 217 29
a young man who had more retirement at home than he liked. E II 8 221 49
as to its effect on the young lady, as he had E II 8 222 57
While waiting till the other young people could pair E II 8 229 99
Busy as he was, however, the young man was yet able to E II 10 240 2
only to walk with the two young ladies to Hartfield gates, E II 10 246 55
Instances have been known of young people passing many, E II 11 247 1
passed by the two young people in schemes on the subject. E II 11 247 2
"And there will be the two Gilberts, young Cox, my father, E II 11 248 4
A word was put in for a second young Cox; and at last, Mr. E II 11 248 9
That young man (speaking lower) is very thoughtless. E II 11 249 11
Do not tell his father, but that young man is not quite E II 11 249 11
"Ah! sir--but a thoughtless young person will sometimes E II 11 252 31
young people set off together without delay for the crown. E II 11 253 40
Mrs. Weston was afraid of draughts for the young people in E II 11 254 44
No, the young lady, to be sure. E II 11 255 57
The loss of the ball--the loss of the young man--and all E II 12 259 10
young man--and all that the young man might be feeling!-- E II 12 259 10
was time to go;" and the young man, though he might and E II 12 261 35
She was almost sure that for a young woman, a stranger, a E II 14 270 4
"Oh! yes--very--a very pleasing young woman." E II 14 271 8
She does seem a charming young woman, just what he E II 14 272 15
The advantages of Bath to the young are pretty generally E II 14 275 32
would make them the safest model for any young woman." E II 14 278 47
a very pretty sort of young lady; and I dare say she was E II 14 279 54
However, she seems a very obliging, pretty-behaved young E II 14 279 54
"Yes: but a young lady--a bride--I ought to have paid my E II 14 280 56
your sanction to such vanity-baits for poor young ladies." E II 14 280 59
Not merely when a state of warfare with one young lady E II 15 282 4
charming young woman--but not even Jane Fairfax is perfect. E II 15 288 36
Young ladies should take care of themselves.-- E II 16 294 25
Young ladies are delicate plants. E II 16 294 25
"My dear Miss Fairfax, young ladies are very sure to be E II 16 294 27
"Oh! when a gallant young man, like Mr. Frank Churchill," E II 16 298 55
He is generally thought a fine young man, but do not E II 18 309 30
What were nine miles to a young man?-- E III 1 317 10
A very few to-morrows stood between the young people of E III 1 318 12
spend some quiet interval in the young man's company. E III 2 319 2
did she begin, that the young man himself, though by no E III 2 321 14
"A very fine young man indeed, Mr. Weston. E III 2 321 15
I think him a very handsome young man, and his manners are E III 2 321 15
Much better employed talking to the young ladies. E III 2 323 19
A fine young man certainly is Frank Churchill. E III 2 324 21
their rubbers were made up,--so young as he looked!-- E III 2 325 32
whole row of young men who could be compared with him.-- E III 2 326 32
had no partner;--the only young lady sitting down;--and so E III 2 326 33
"Mrs. Gilbert does not mean to dance, but there is a young E III 2 327 37
A young lady who faints, must be recovered; questions must E III 3 333 4
very retired; and when the young ladies had advanced some E III 3 333 5
How the trampers might have behaved, had the young ladies E III 3 333 6
Such an adventure as this,--a fine young man and a lovely E III 3 334 9
young man and a lovely young woman thrown together in such E III 3 334 9
Nothing of the sort had ever occurred before to any young E III 3 335 10
those who talk most, the young and the low; and all the E III 3 336 12
The young ladies of Highbury might have walked again in E III 3 336 13
This gallant young man, who seemed to love without feeling, E III 5 348 23
I am no young lady on her preferment. E III 6 354 14
be something for a young man so much in want of a change. E III 6 365 67
parties--young ladies-- married women-----" E III 7 370 20
that can entertain Miss Woodhouse, or any other young lady. E III 7 372 38
young man's spirits now rose to a pitch almost unpleasant. E III 7 374 54
I suppose, as no young woman before ever met with on first E III 8 379 8
that so much could be given to a young person like Jane." E III 8 382 23
distinguish any one young woman with persevering attention, E III 10 396 44
and accomplished young women in England for your daughter." E III 10 400 68
the unexceptionable young man who would have made her E III 11 413 49
And is he to be rewarded with that sweet young woman?-- E III 13 426 16
He meets with a young woman at a watering-place, gains her E III 13 428 23
gave me the idea of a young woman likely to be attached; E III 14 438 8
Ah! that was the act of a very, very young man, one too E III 15 446 18
very young man, one too young to consider whether the E III 15 446 18
not a word of a certain young physician from Windsor.-- E III 16 454 17
Charming young man!--that is--so very friendly; I mean E III 16 455 20
Here have I been sitting this hour, giving these young E III 16 457 36
young woman might think him rather cool in her praise. E III 17 464 19
care of themselves; the young people will find a way."-- E III 17 467 31
wife; he only hoped "the young lady's pride would now be E III 17 469 36
against any young man who told her he loved her." E III 18 473 25
No objection was raised on the father's side; the young E III 19 482 4
She had, while a very young girl, as soon as she had known P III 1 7 14
He was at that time a very young man, just engaged in the P III 1 8 15
after taking the young man so publicly by the hand: "for P III 1 8 16
them all; and as to her young friend's health, by passing P III 2 14 12
She was a clever young woman, who understood the art of P III 2 15 15
of their personableness when they cease to be quite young." P III 3 20 17
He was, at that time, a remarkably fine young man, with a P III 4 26 1
in an engagement with a young man, who had nothing but P III 4 26 3
Anne Elliot, so young; known to so few, to be snatched off P III 4 27 3
Young and gentle as she was, it might yet have been P III 4 27 5
to change her name, by the young man, who not long P III 4 28 7
but she felt that were any young person, in similar P III 4 29 8
her absence; but she was young, and certainly altogether P III 5 34 12
upon the marriage of the young 'squire, it had received P III 5 36 20
in the old English style, and the young people in the new. P III 5 40 45
were Henrietta and Louisa, young ladies of nineteen and P III 5 40 45
young ladies, living to be fashionable, happy, and merry. P III 5 40 45
for an answer;--or in the young ladies' addition of, "I P III 6 42 1
from Clifton;--a very fine young man; but they could not P III 6 52 33
they parted, that the two young aunts were able so far to P III 7 54 4
young woman who came in his way, excepting Anne Elliot. P III 7 61 38
cried the Admiral, "what stuff these young fellows talk! P III 8 65 12
What should a young fellow, like you, do ashore, for half P III 8 65 14
especially the attention of all the young women could do. P III 8 71 57
were so hospitable, the young so agreeable, that he could P III 9 73 1
a very amiable, pleasing young man, between whom and P III 9 73 4

in the country, the young Hayters would, from their	P	III	9	74	5
daughters, and of all the young men who came near them,	P	III	9	74	9
at the cottage: the young couple there were more disposed	P	III	9	75	9
I do not think any young woman has a right to make a	P	III	9	76	13
conduct in a well-meaning young woman, and a heart to	P	III	9	77	18
accepting must be the word) of two young women at once.	P	III	10	82	1
They had taken out a young dog, who had spoilt their sport,	P	III	10	83	6
It was mere lively chat,--such as any young persons, on an	P	III	10	84	7
Winthrop, however, or its environs--for young men are,	P	III	10	85	13
Upon hearing how long a walk the young people had engaged	P	III	10	90	38
and bring us home one of these young ladies to Kellynch.	P	III	10	92	46
And very nice young ladies they both are; I hardly know	P	III	10	92	46
The young people were all wild to see Lyme.	P	III	11	94	7
of him as an excellent young man and an officer, whom he	P	III	11	96	12
He was evidently a young man of considerable taste in	P	III	11	100	23
and resignation to a young man whom she had never seen	P	III	11	101	26
that being by the sea, always makes him feel young again.	P	III	12	102	2
into the feelings of a young lady as of a young man,--	P	III	12	103	3
of a young lady as of a young man,--though here it was	P	III	12	103	3
some active, respectable young man, as a resident curate,	P	III	12	103	3
be called a young mourner--only last summer, I understand."	P	III	12	108	25
enjoy the sight of a dead young lady, nay, two dead young	P	III	12	111	49
young lady, nay, two dead young ladies, for it proved	P	III	12	111	49
A new sort of way this, for a young fellow to be making	P	IV	1	126	22
is very well, I believe, but he is a very odd young man.	P	IV	2	130	5
He is one of the dullest young men that ever lived.	P	IV	2	132	16
He is not at all a well-bred young man.	P	IV	2	132	16
knowing her but in public, and when very young himself.	P	IV	3	140	11
had adopted, when quite a young man, on the principle of	P	IV	3	144	19
"The notions of a young man of one or two and twenty,"	P	IV	3	144	20
He thought her a most extraordinary young woman; in her	P	IV	5	159	21
Lady Russell saw either less or more than her young friend,	P	IV	5	161	30
She was persuaded that any tolerably pleasing young woman	P	IV	6	167	19
But first of all, you must tell me the name of the young	P	IV	6	170	31
That young lady, you know, that we have all been so	P	IV	6	170	31
I wish young ladies had not such a number of fine	P	IV	6	171	33
turn of all; for this young lady, this same Miss Musgrove,	P	IV	6	171	33
"I thought Captain Benwick a very pleasing young man,"	P	IV	6	171	36
I find, is bespoke by her cousin, the young parson.	P	IV	6	173	49
"A very fine young man indeed!" said Lady Dalrymple.	P	IV	8	188	39
curiosity to know what Mr. Elliot was as a very young man.	P	IV	9	198	51
between the heir and the young lady; and it was impossible	P	IV	9	201	59
I was very young, and associated only with the young, and	P	IV	9	201	64
now, as a young man he had not the smallest value for it.	P	IV	9	202	66
had consented to the young people's wishes, and that their	P	IV	10	217	20
What a blessing to young people to be in such hands!	P	IV	10	218	23
to so much misconduct and misery, both in young and old!	P	IV	10	218	23
starts and wriggles like a young dab chick in the water;	P	IV	10	218	24
she; "but I do believe him to be an excellent young man."	P	IV	10	218	25
hayter, and what the young people had wished, and what I	P	IV	11	230	5
"I would rather have young people settle on a small income	P	IV	11	230	7
I so abominate for young people as a long engagement.	P	IV	11	230	8
It is all very well, I used to say, for young people to be	P	IV	11	231	8
He met with a clever young German artist at the Cape, and	P	IV	11	232	15
When any two young people take it into their heads to	P	IV	12	248	1
gifted in this part of understanding than her young friend.	P	IV	12	249	4
had sacrificed, for the young man's sake, the possibility	P	IV	12	250	8
favourite--for a young & rising Bathing-Place, certainly	S		1	368	1
or three genteel looking young women followed by as many	S		1	370	1
The young ladies approached & said every thing that was	S		1	370	1
it to a something of young renown--and Mr Parker could not	S		2	371	1
Heywood, a very pleasing young woman of two and twenty,	S		2	374	1
and to give the visiting young lady a suitable knowledge	S		3	375	1
into account, those of the young female relation, whom	S		3	377	1
to introduce this young lady, or that young lady as a	S		3	377	1
this young lady, or that young lady as a companion at	S		3	377	1
In ours, it is Sidney; who is a very clever young man,--	S		4	382	1
Such a young man as Sidney, with his neat equipage &	S		4	382	1
a small lawn with a very young plantation round it, about	S		4	384	1
beheld a more lovely, or more interesting young woman.--	S		6	391	1
No, she was a very sober-minded young lady, sufficiently	S		6	391	1
Aye--that young lady smiles I see;--I dare say she thinks	S		6	393	1
Miss D. was a fine young woman, but cold & reserved,	S		7	394	1
If there are young ladies in the world at her time of life,	S		7	395	1
That the young lady at the other end of the bench was	S		7	396	1
My young folks, as I call them sometimes, for I take them	S		7	399	1
For they are very good young people my dear.	S		7	399	1
And poor young man, he needs it bad enough;--for though I	S		7	400	1
He is a very fine young man;--particularly elegant in his	S		7	400	1
A handsome young fellow like him, will go smirking &	S		7	400	1
cried Lady D--and if we cd but get a young heiress to s!	S		7	401	1
Now, if we could get a young heiress to be sent here for	S		7	401	1
Ah! young ladies that have no money are very much to be	S		7	401	1
houses, very fit for a young gentleman & his sister--and	S		7	402	1
library were followed by a young whitby running off with 5	S		8	403	1
Miss Heywood, or any other young woman with any	S		8	405	2
She was his rival in Lady D.'s favour, she was young,	S		8	405	2
Mrs G. meant to go to the sea, for her young people's	S		9	408	1
of a certain Miss Lambe a young lady (probably a neice)	S		9	409	1
no penance to have a fine young woman next to him,	S		10	415	1
The young man's attentions were instantly lost.	S		10	416	1
Miss Lambe too!--a young Westindian of large fortune.--	S		10	419	1
young ladies under her care, to Miss D. P.'s notice.--	S		10	419	1
& comfort of one of the young ladies under her care, a	S		10	419	1
a young W. Indian of large fortune, in delicate health."--	S		10	419	1
The rich Westindians, & the young ladies seminary had all	S		11	420	1
such great girls & young ladies, as wanted either masters	S		11	420	1
The other girls, two Miss Beauforts were just such young	S		11	421	1
In Miss Lambe, here was the very young lady, sickly & rich,	S		11	422	1
of a Tandem, little Mary's young eyes distinguished the	S		12	425	1

YOUNG-LADY-PERFORMERS (1)

were the only young-lady-performers; but soon (within five	E	II	8	229	98

YOUNGER (63)

younger brother's having possession of the family estate.	LS		5	249	1
personal beauty, and the younger ones, by pretending to be	NA	I	4	34	8
On his two younger sisters he then bestowed an equal	NA	I	7	49	43
The younger Miss Thorpes being also dancing, Catherine was	NA	I	8	52	2
in the room; my two younger sisters and their partners.	NA	I	8	59	37
curiosity to be raised in the unprivileged younger sisters.	NA	I	15	120	25
Perhaps it may seem odd, that with only two younger	NA	II	7	176	15
interest were the demands of his younger brother to rest?	NA	II	11	208	1
Fortunately he had a younger brother who was more	SS	I	3	16	6
think a man five years younger than herself, so	SS	I	8	37	3
Colonel Brandon is certainly younger than Mrs. Jennings,	SS	I	8	37	4
my younger sister in spite of all this tumbling down hills.	SS	I	9	44	23
Mrs. Palmer was several years younger than Lady Middleton,	SS	I	19	106	22
John, "than to see his younger brother in possession of an	SS	III	1	269	56
to be intolerable and the younger sisters not worth	PP	I	6	21	1
at the request of her younger sisters, who with some of	PP	I	6	25	24
answer, and forced his younger sister to be civil also,	PP	I	9	45	35
do cure the younger girls of running after the officers.--	PP	I	10	52	55
"As to her younger daughters she could not take upon her	PP	I	15	71	3
The attention of the younger ones was then no longer to be	PP	I	15	72	7
for and talk of, the younger Miss Bennets would have been	PP	I	17	88	15
It was, moreover, such a promising thing for her younger	PP	I	18	99	63
On finding Mrs. Bennet, Elizabeth, and one of the younger	PP	I	19	104	1
					2
The younger girls formed hopes of coming out a year or two	PP	I	22	122	3
addresses to one of her younger girls, and Mary might have	PP	I	22	124	11
Mrs. Gardiner, who was several years younger than Mrs.	PP	II	2	139	2
they were older or younger than herself, whether any of	PP	II	6	163	15
Are any of your younger sisters out, Miss Bennet?"	PP	II	6	165	32
The younger ones out before the elder are married!--	PP	II	6	165	34
Your younger sisters must be very young?"	PP	II	6	165	34
would be very hard upon younger sisters, that they should	PP	II	6	165	35
"With three younger sisters grown up," replied Elizabeth	PP	II	6	166	37
Colonel Fitzwilliam, the younger son of his uncle, Lord ---	PP	II	7	170	7
I speak feelingly. a younger son, you know, must be inured	PP	II	10	183	10
"In my opinion, the younger son of an earl can know very	PP	II	10	183	11
Younger sons cannot marry where they like."	PP	II	10	183	12
pray, what is the usual price of an earl's younger son?	PP	II	10	183	15
younger sisters, and occasionally even by your father.--	PP	II	12	198	5
retailing them all to the younger Miss Lucases; and Lydia,	PP	II	16	222	21
eight years old, and two younger boys, were to be left	PP	II	19	239	10
and younger children would by that means be provided for.	PP	III	8	308	3
Her younger sisters soon began to make interest with her	PP	III	13	349	41
allow in a sister more than ten years younger than himself.	PP	III	19	388	11
Had my daughters been younger than herself, I should have	MP	I	1	10	14
The two girls were more at a loss from being younger and	MP	I	2	12	3
necessary, and the younger brother must help to pay for	MP	I	3	23	2
Though I have no younger sister, I feel for her.	MP	I	5	51	41
actual comparison, of her preferring his younger brother.	MP	I	12	114	1
expense, and being the younger son of a Lord with a	MP	I	13	121	1
representation of younger sons who have little to live on.	MP	II	4	214	45
Seven hundred a year is a fine thing for a younger brother;	MP	II	5	226	61
Thomas had been bringing up no wife for his younger son.	MP	II	10	278	20
had left there not much younger when she went into	MP	III	7	385	40
the best of the three younger ones was gone in him; Tom	MP	III	8	390	8
attaching herself to a younger brother again, was long in	MP	III	17	469	24
at Hartfield, the younger branch of a very ancient family--	E	I	16	136	9
says the orchard was always famous in her younger days.	E	II	9	238	51
have given the idea of her being younger than she was.	P	III	1	6	12
more willing mind in her younger sister; and Lady Russell	P	III	4	28	7
The younger boy, a remarkable stout, forward child, of two	P	III	9	79	28
He is younger than I am; younger in feeling, if not in	P	III	11	97	13
I am; younger in feeling, if not in fact; younger as a man.	P	III	11	97	13
in time to receive their younger children for the	P	IV	2	129	1

YOUNGER-BROTHER-LIKE (1)

so pitiful, so younger-brother-like, that I detest it."	MP	II	4	211	22

YOUNGEST (39)

The two youngest Miss Thorpes were by themselves in the	NA	I	15	116	1
for by all but the two youngest children, a boy and girl	NA	II	14	233	8
the shrewd look of the youngest, to her want of real	SS	I	21	124	32
the indisposition of her youngest daughter; and for this	SS	II	6	175	1
see directly it was the youngest Miss Steele; so I took	SS	III	11	354	27
lately married to--to the youngest--to Miss Lucy Steele."	SS	III	12	360	22
					23
were not often reckoned very like her youngest brother.--	W			324	3
Lydia, my love, though you are the youngest, I dare say Mr.	PP	I	2	8	26
afraid; for though I am the youngest, I'm the tallest."	PP	I	2	8	27
The two youngest of the family, Catherine and Lydia, were	PP	I	7	28	3
as to think our two youngest daughters uncommonly foolish."	PP	I	7	29	11
In Meryton they parted; the two youngest repaired to the	PP	I	7	32	41
Mrs. Bennet, accompanied by her two youngest girls,	PP	I	9	41	1
Upon this signal, the youngest of her daughters put	PP	I	9	45	35
of it was, that the youngest should tax Mr. Bingley with	PP	I	9	45	35
"Yes, my youngest is not sixteen.	PP	II	6	165	35
wild giddiness of his youngest daughters; and her mother,	PP	II	14	213	17
My youngest sister has left all her friends--has eloped;--	PP	III	4	277	11
"She is my youngest girl but one.	PP	III	14	352	8
My youngest of all, is lately married, and my eldest is	PP	III	14	352	8
I am no stranger to the particulars of your youngest	PP	III	14	357	62
There was in fact but two years between the youngest and	MP	I	2	13	4
youngest of the sons, sitting crying on the attic stairs.	MP	I	2	15	9
you shall marry the youngest Miss Bertram, a nice,	MP	I	4	42	19
all my attention to the youngest, who was not out, and had	MP	I	5	51	40
I thought that was always the lot of the youngest, where	MP	I	9	92	42
friend and his friend's youngest sister, he believed he	MP	II	2	191	10
and Betsey, the youngest of the family, about five--both	MP	III	7	377	9
She was the youngest of the two daughters of a most	E	I	1	5	2
children with her--the youngest, a nice little girl about	E	I	12	98	2
orphan, the only child of Mrs. Bates's youngest daughter.	E	II	2	163	1
Miss Hawkins was the youngest of the two daughters of a	E	II	4	183	9
follow but that of a youngest sister, made the book an	P	III	1	7	12
be listened for, when the youngest Miss Musgrove walked in.	P	III	6	50	26
servants to control--the youngest child to banish, and the	P	III	7	53	3
Captain Benwick looked and was the youngest of the three,	P	III	11	97	14
Sir Walter talked of his youngest daughter; "Mr. Elliot	P	IV	3	143	18
to present him to his youngest daughter"--(there was no	P	IV	3	143	18
And our youngest Br--who lives with them, & who is not	S		5	385	1

YOUNKER (1)

Ah! the peace has come too soon for that younker.	P	IV	6	170	29

YOUR'S (32)

Modesty such as your's--but not for the world would I pain	NA	II	2	139	7
I would not speak disrespectfully of a brother of your's,	NA	II	3	145	13
has deserted my brother, and is to marry your's!	NA	II	10	204	19
so ill by our family, she may behave better by your's.	NA	II	10	206	33
not, in our concern for his sufferings, undervalue your's.	NA	II	10	206	38
"And if you would stand by your's, you would not be much	NA	II	12	219	15
he is undoubtedly supported by the same trust in your's.	SS	II	2	147	8
I am sure you will be very comfortable there. "your's, &c.	PP	II	3	149	26
and their father has not so good an income as your's.--	PP	II	6	164	20
be offensive to your's, I can only say that I am sorry.--	PP	II	12	197	5
your's, &c. "Edw. Gardiner."	PP	III	7	303	14
mother.--your's, &c. "E. Gardiner."	PP	III	8	313	19
not so dreadfully racked as your's seems to have been.	PP	III	10	321	2
Your's, very sincerely, "M. Gardiner.	PP	III	10	325	2
own feelings, care not how much I may be wounding your's.	PP	III	16	365	2
					3
I was not in a humour to wait for any opening of your's.	PP	III	18	381	14
"Your's, &c."	PP	III	19	386	7
say, or, at least of your's, would not grow up in this	MP	I	1	6	6
It may hereafter be in my power, or in your's (I hope it	MP	I	3	23	3
Your's sincerely.'	MP	I	6	59	43
it, must be exceedingly painful to such feelings as your's.	MP	I	11	111	29
happier than he goes. your's affectionately, M. C."	MP	II	13	303	15
to a fair sister of your's, a fine girl of fifteen, who	MP	III	12	415	2
tales, but--but--but. your's, affectionately."	MP	III	12	416	2
Your's ever, my dearest Fanny."	MP	III	13	424	2
You will see me early, by the mail. your's, &c."	MP	III	15	443	23
But your's--your regard was new compared with-----	MP	III	15	446	34
up my opinion against your's-- and I am sure I shall not	E	I	4	31	25
dancing would not have agreed with me, after your's."	E	II	8	230	102
name) shall inquire for your's too and bring them to you.	E	II	16	295	34
had not made him ill. "your's ever, "A. W. "	E	III	14	436	7
myself too sure of your's, and of those among your friends	E	III	14	437	8

YOURSELVES (12)

you; but you men think yourselves of such consequence."	NA	I	11	90	63
"Who! why yourselves, and the Careys, and Whitakers to be	SS	I	18	99	20
and I shall be as much benefited by it as yourselves.	SS	II	3	155	8
enough to find yourselves and Mrs. Jennings at home.	SS	II	6	177	9
I suppose you know among yourselves."--	W			344	20
that, to have conducted yourselves so as to avoid any	PP	II	12	198	5
Has it not been industriously circulated by yourselves?	PP	III	14	354	30
so forward and clever yourselves, you should always be	MP	I	2	19	27
tame confidante, that you may not like to do yourselves."	MP	I	13	129	38
Sue--take care of yourselves--keep a sharp look out," he	MP	III	10	403	14
Picture to yourselves my amazement; I shall not easily	P	III	3	20	16
You were a large party in yourselves, and you wanted	P	IV	9	193	12

YOUTH (54)

to bestow them--& all this, without the charm of youth.	LS		4	248	2
having seen one amiable youth who could call forth her	NA	I	1	16	10
done little; but, where youth and diffidence are united,	NA	I	7	50	44
All those things should be allowed for in youth and high	NA	II	3	146	18

Her youth, civil manners and liberal pay, procured her all NA II 14 232 6
but the influence of youth, beauty, and elegance, gave an SS I 9 42 9
considering her sister's youth, and urged the matter SS I 16 85 10
prevent your whole youth from being wasted in discontent. SS I 19 103 7
with that happy ardour of youth which Marianne and her SS II 4 159 1
a man in the bloom of youth, of hope and happiness, saw SS II 8 200 43
He had left the girl whose youth and innocence he had SS II 9 209 30
recovery slow; and with youth, natural strength, and her SS III 10 340 1
the greatest part of our youth was passed together; PP I 16 81 37
as good a right to the pleasures of youth, as the first. PP II 6 165 35
off the companion of my youth, the acknowledged favourite PP II 12 196 5
any attraction beyond youth and a tolerable person; and PP II 18 231 18
Her father captivated by youth and beauty, and and that PP II 19 236 1
of good humour, which youth and beauty generally give, had PP II 19 236 1
Wickham passed all his youth there, you know." PP II 19 240 13
attractions has she beyond youth, health, and good humour, PP III 5 283 8
and in spite of her youth and her manners, she retained PP III 19 387 8
You will allow for the doubts of youth and inexperience. MP I 4 43 23
as any thing pursued by youth and zeal could hold out. MP I 14 130 2
many of the feelings of youth and nature, let her not be MP II 9 265 19
who had been guarded by youth, a youth of mind as lovely MP III 2 326 3
been guarded by youth, a youth of mind as lovely as of MP III 2 326 3
object of their youth--could have had no useful influence MP III 17 463 8
the tyrannic influence of youth on youth, it had not E I 2 16 6
influence of youth on youth, it had not shaken his E I 2 16 6
Her youth had passed without distinction, and her middle E I 3 21 4
who had worked hard in her youth, and now thought herself E I 3 22 5
been the fashion of his youth; but his conviction of E I 3 24 12
What is passable in youth, is detestable in later age. E I 4 33 36
an attachment as her youth and sort of mind admitted. E I 9 69 2
To youth and natural cheerfulness like Emma's, though E I 16 137 13
The youth and cheerfulness of morning are in happy analogy, E I 16 137 13
up with astonishment at the youth and beauty of her person. E II 5 192 29
and the low; and all the youth and servants in the place E III 3 336 12
He had been remarkably handsome in his youth; and, at P III 1 4 5
enjoyment as in her early youth; but now she liked it not. P III 1 7 12
the modest drawing back of youth; and in one of their P III 1 7 14
as it cuts up a man's youth and vigour most horribly; a P III 3 19 16
I have often observed it; they soon lose the look of youth. P III 3 20 17
clouded every enjoyment of youth; and an early loss of P III 4 28 6
She had been forced into prudence in her youth, she P III 4 30 9
No; the years which had destroyed her youth and bloom had P III 7 61 34
and the images of youth and hope, and spring, all gone P III 10 85 12
the bloom and freshness of youth restored by the fine wind P III 12 104 6
was to be blessed with a second spring of youth and beauty. P IV 1 124 10
naturally clear, and only erring in the heyday of youth. P IV 4 147 7
to hold a living for a youth who could not possibly claim P IV 10 217 20
lost one charm of earlier youth: but the value of such P IV 11 243 68
She had not <u>Camilla's</u> youth, & had no intention of having S 6 390 1
Such was the influence of youth & bloom that he began even S 10 415 1

YOUTH-KILLING (1)
state of most wearing, anxious, youth-killing dependance! P III 4 27 3

YOUTHFUL (8)
will, I trust, gradually overcome this youthful attachment. LS 27 297 2
and deference of the youthful female mind, fearful of NA I 7 48 32
exclaiming and conjecturing with youthful ardour.-- NA II 14 234 10
as he appeared to the youthful fancy of her daughter, SS I 8 37 3
The youthful infatuation of nineteen would naturally blind SS II 1 140 2
beings, and enjoying the youthful simplicity which could E I 4 27 4
of youthful expression to the steady eyes of the artist. E I 6 46 24
might be pardoned the youthful infatuation which made her P III 1 4 6

YOUTHS (1)
Such squeamish youths as cannot bear to be connected with PP II 18 231 17

YR (6)
me. Yr most obliged & affec: sister S. Vernon. LS 1 244 1
a short distance of you. Yr most attached S. Vernon. LS 25 294 7
no defying destiny. Yr sincerely attached Alicia. LS 38 307 3
no great distance. Yr affec: mother C. De Courcy. LS 40 309 1
There is not the least likeness in the world; Yr brother's W 324 3
I mention this, in hopes of Yr being drawn out to see W 347 21

YRS (11)
grossly deceived by her at once. Yrs &c. Cath. Vernon. LS 6 252 2
If you can get him away, it will be a good thing. Yrs LS 11 259 2
Her little cousins are all very fond of her. Yrs affec: LS 18 273 3
Adieu my dear madam, Yrs &c. Cath. Vernon. LS 20 279 12
of her injured mother. Yrs affec:ly S. Vernon. LS 22 282 8
I finish as I began, with the warmest congratulations. Yrs LS 23 285 8
is of consequence. Yrs ever, Cath. Vernon. LS 24 291 18
common excuse for losing my temper. Yrs ever, Alicia. LS 28 298 2
I am enchanted with my lodgings. Yrs ever, S. LS 29 299 4
With anxious wishes, Yrs faithfully Alicia. LS 32 303 2
At present it is not very likely. Yrs &c. Cath. Vernon. LS 41 310 5

& (1611)

weeks with you at Churchill, & therefore if quite LS 1 243 1
if quite convenient to you & Mrs Vernon to receive me at LS 1 243 1
stay, but their hospitable & chearful dispositions lead LS 1 243 1
for my present situation & state of mind; & I impatiently LS 1 243 1
situation & state of mind; & I impatiently look forward to LS 1 243 1
that attention which duty & affection equally dictated, & LS 1 244 1
affection equally dictated, & I have but too much reason LS 1 244 1
me. Yr most obliged & affec: sister S. Vernon. LS 1 244 1
only four months a widow, & to be as quiet as possible,--& LS 2 244 1
to be as quiet as possible,--& I have been so; my dear LS 2 244 1
I did not marry him myself, & were he but one degree less LS 2 245 1
in that respect, & that riches only, will not satisfy me. LS 2 245 1
so jealous in short, & so enraged against me, that in the LS 2 245 1
husband stands my friend, & the kindest, most amiable LS 2 245 1
family are at war, & Manwaring scarcely dares speak to me. LS 2 245 1
determined on leaving them, & shall spend I hope a LS 2 245 1
is always given, & I am known to be so intimate with his LS 2 245 1
Charles vernon is my aversion, & I am afraid of his wife. LS 2 246 1
The price is immense, & much beyond what I can ever LS 2 246 1
the Christmas with you; & we are prevented that happiness LS 3 246 1
us almost immediately--& as such a visit is in all LS 3 246 1
as well from the elegant & expensive stile of living there, LS 3 246 1
that no one less amiable & mild than himself could have LS 3 247 1
have overlooked it at all; & tho' as his brother's widow & LS 3 247 1
tho' as his brother's widow & in narrow circumstances it LS 3 247 1
one, her display of Greif, & professions of regret, & LS 3 247 1
& professions of regret, & general resolutions of prudence LS 3 247 1
his heart, & make him really confide in her sincerity. LS 3 247 1
But as for myself, I am still unconvinced; & plausibly as LS 3 247 1
gain any share of my regard; & I shall certainly endeavour LS 3 247 1
of being acquainted with me, & makes very gracious mention LS 3 247 1
separated from her mother; & a girl of sixteen who has LS 3 247 1
Susan, & we shall depend on his joining our party soon. LS 3 247 1
I am glad to hear that my father continues so well, & am, LS 3 247 1
My dear sister I congratulate you & Mr Vernon on being LS 4 248 1
By her behaviour to Mr Manwaring, she gave jealousy & LS 4 248 1
& wretchedness to his wife, & by her attentions to a young LS 4 248 1
have dined with him at Hurst & Wilford)--who is just come LS 4 248 1
the house with her ladyship, & who is therefore well LS 4 248 1
I long to see her, & shall certainly accept your kind LS 4 248 2
at the same time & in the same house the affections of two LS 4 248 2
to bestow them--& all this, without the charm of youth. LS 4 248 2
& according to Mr Smith's account, is equally dull & proud. LS 4 248 2
Where pride & stupidity unite, there can be no LS 4 248 2
dissimulation worthy notice, & Miss Vernon shall be LS 4 248 2
deceit which must be pleasing to witness & detect. LS 4 248 2
I shall be with you very soon, & am your affec. LS 4 249 2
just before I left town, & rejoice to be assured that Mr LS 5 249 1
I arrived here in safety, & have no reason to complain of LS 5 249 1
She is perfectly well bred indeed, & has the air of a LS 5 249 1
is not very surprising--& yet it shews an illiberal & LS 5 249 1
yet it shews an illiberal & vindictive spirit to resent a LS 5 249 1
me six years ago, & which never succeeded at last. LS 5 249 1
at the time of his marriage--& everybody ought to respect LS 5 249 1
we have lived with Charles & kept him single, I should LS 5 249 1
of marrying Miss De Courcy, & the event has justified me. LS 5 249 1
Here are children in abundance, & what benefit could have LS 5 250 1
will never be wanting; & as to money-matters, it has not LS 5 250 1
The house is a good one, the furniture fashionable, & LS 5 250 2
fashionable, & everything announces plenty & elegance. LS 5 250 2
all their names already, & am going to attach myself with LS 5 250 2
I take on my lap & sigh over for his dear uncle's sake. LS 5 250 2
wife & sister, & lamentations on the cruelty of his fate. LS 5 250 3
I passed off the letter as his wife's, to the Vernons, & LS 5 250 3
this dangerous creature, & must give you some description LS 6 250 1
She is delicately fair, with fine grey eyes & dark LS 6 251 1
grey eyes & dark eyelashes; & from her appearance one LS 6 251 1
five & twenty, tho' she must in fact be ten years older. LS 6 251 1
Her address to me was so gentle, frank & even affectionate, LS 6 251 1
me for marrying Mr Vernon, & that we had never met before, LS 6 251 1
of manner with coquetry, & to expect that an impudent LS 6 251 1
is absolutely sweet, & her voice & manner winningly mild. LS 6 251 1
She is clever & agreable, has all that knowledge of the LS 6 251 1
makes conversation easy, & talks very well, with a happy LS 6 251 1
She speaks of her with so much tenderness & anxiety, LS 6 251 1
Langford for Churchill; & if she had not staid three LS 6 252 2
her visit to the Manwarings, & when I recollect on the LS 6 252 2
taking notice of Frederica, & I am grateful for it as a LS 7 252 1
She is a stupid girl, & has nothing to recommend her. LS 7 252 1
I want her to play & sing with some portion of taste, & a LS 7 253 1
as she has my hand & arm, & a tolerable voice. LS 7 253 1
to attend to anything, & consequently am without those LS 7 253 1
in all the language arts & sciences; it is throwing time LS 7 253 1
Grace & manner after all are of the greatest importance. LS 7 253 1
be more than superficial, & I flatter myself that she will LS 7 253 1
You know on what I ground my hope, & it is certainly a LS 7 253 1
I am sure of Sir James at any time, & could make him renew LS 7 253 1
& talk to him about Frederica that he may not forget her. LS 7 253 1
in this affair extremely, & regard it as a very happy LS 7 253 2
it as a very happy mixture of circumspection & tenderness. LS 7 253 2
which her heart revolted; & instead of adopting so harsh a LS 7 253 2
You may well wonder how I contrive to pass my time here--& LS 7 254 3
He is lively & seems clever, & when I have inspired him LS 7 254 3
I have disconcerted him already by my calm reserve; & it LS 7 254 3
& to persuade Reginald that she has scandalously belied me. LS 7 254 3
This project will serve at least to amuse me, & prevent my LS 7 254 3
this dreadful separation from you & all whom I love. LS 7 254 3
He means to send for his horses immediately, & it is LS 8 254 1
an alarm which might seriously affect his health & spirits. LS 8 254 1
of hunting with Mr Vernon, & of course I cannot receive LS 8 255 1
& which Reginald himself was entirely disposed to credit. LS 8 255 1
as of any woman in England, & when he first came it was LS 8 255 1
to delicacy nor respect, & that he felt she would be LS 8 255 1
of pretension, of levity--& she is altogether so LS 8 255 2
no more than was natural; & I did not wonder at his being LS 8 255 2
struck by the gentleness & delicacy of her manners; but LS 8 255 2
of man by such loveliness & such abilities; & when I LS 8 255 2
loveliness & such abilities; & when I lamented in reply LS 8 255 2
to her neglected education & early marriage, & that she LS 8 255 2
marriage, & that she was altogether a wonderful woman. LS 8 255 2
of admiration vexes me; & if I did not know that Reginald LS 8 256 3
on Mr De Courcy's arrival, & advise you by all means to LS 9 256 1
is we know considerable, & I beleive certainly entailed. LS 9 256 1
Sir Reginald is very infirm, & not likely to stand in your LS 9 256 1
I hear the young man well spoken of, & tho' no one can LS 9 256 1
days last week, & called several times in Edward Street. LS 9 256 1
I talked to him about you & your daughter, & he is so from LS 9 257 1
I gave him hopes of Frederica's relenting, & told him a LS 9 257 1
he had been only in joke, & we both laughed heartily at LS 9 257 1
at her disappointment, & in short were very agreable. LS 9 257 1
at present in want of money, & might perhaps till the old LS 10 257 1
I have made him sensible of my power, & can now enjoy the LS 10 257 1
to dislike me, & prejudiced against all my past actions. LS 10 257 1
good opinion of her brother, & conclude that nothing will LS 10 257 1
My conduct has been equally guarded from the first, & I LS 10 258 2
I have subdued him entirely by sentiment & serious LS 10 258 2
& serious conversation, & made him I may venture to say at LS 10 258 2
Let her think & act as she chuses however; I have never LS 10 258 2
Reginald has a good figure, & is not unworthy the praise LS 10 258 3
which put one in good humour with oneself & all the world. LS 10 258 3
to afford me amusement, & to make many of those hours pass LS 10 258 3
law's reserve, & listening to her husband's insipid talk. LS 10 258 3
Your account of Sir James is most satisfactory, & I mean LS 10 258 4
long conversations together, & she has contrived by the LS 11 259 1
He is not at all disposed to leave us, & I have given him LS 11 259 1
all his former ill-opinion, & persuaded him not merely to LS 11 259 1
of having made Mr Manwaring & a young man engaged to Miss LS 11 259 1
well acquainted, & whose character he so heartily despised. LS 11 259 2
for a father's anxiety, & think themselves privileged to LS 12 260 1
to refuse him their confidence & slight his advice. LS 12 260 1
You must be sensible that as an only son & the LS 12 260 1
acquainting your mother & myself or at least without being LS 12 260 1
whole of your family, far & near, must highly reprobate. LS 12 260 1
other men, her extravagance & dissipation were so gross & LS 12 260 2
& dissipation were so gross & notorious, that no one could LS 12 260 2
My years & increasing infirmities make me very desirous my LS 12 261 3
but her family & character must be equally unexceptionable. LS 12 261 3
I can promise you a ready & chearful consent; but it is my LS 12 261 3
She is poor, & may naturally seek an alliance which may be LS 12 261 4
You know your own rights, & that it is out of my power to LS 12 261 4
I honestly tell you my sentiments & intentions. LS 12 261 4
I do not wish to work on your fears, but on your sense & LS 12 261 4
is no secret to your friends, & to warn you against her. LS 12 261 5
woman for a short period, & of yeilding admiration only to LS 12 261 6
only to her beauty & abilities without being blinded by LS 12 261 6
Lady Susan, to a young man of his age & high expectations. LS 13 262 1
our being quite alone now, & very much in need of him to LS 13 262 1
long letter full of it all, & particularly asking for an LS 13 262 1
I say all I can however to satisfy your father, & he is LS 13 263 1
but be the occasion of so much vexation & trouble. LS 13 263 1
as to injure me in your opinion, & give you all this alarm. LS 14 263 1
I know not why she should chuse to make herself & her LS 14 263 1
have never denied her; & equally low must sink my LS 14 263 1
Our difference of age must be an insuperable objection, & LS 14 263 1
dear sir to quiet your mind, & no longer harbour a LS 14 263 1
to my affection for herself & her husband in the length of LS 14 264 2
of Lady Susan's conduct, & removes all the blame which has LS 14 264 3
who living in the world & surrounded with temptation, LS 14 264 3
totally his own invention; & his account of her attaching LS 14 264 4
to pay her some attention, & as he is a man of fortune, it LS 14 264 4
on the catch for a husband, & no one therefore can pity LS 14 264 4
Lady Susan was far from intending such a conquest, & on LS 14 265 4
the truth of this reasoning, & will hereby learn to do LS 14 265 4
governed only by the most honourable & amiable intentions. LS 14 265 5
Her prudence & economy are exemplary, her regard for Mr LS 14 265 5
even to his deserts, & her wish of obtaining my sister's LS 14 265 5
she has not the blind & weak partiality of most mothers, LS 14 265 5
Every person of sense however will know how to value & LS 14 265 5
her well directed affection, & will join me in wishing LS 14 265 5
I admire her abilities, & esteem her character; but if you LS 14 265 6
equally convinced by my full & solemn assurance that your LS 14 265 6
mortify & distress me.-- I am &c. R. De Courcy. LS 14 265 6
My dear mother I return you Reginald's letter, & LS 15 266 1
must come from herself, & I am less disposed to beleive it, LS 15 266 1
He is very severe against me indeed, & yet I hope I have LS 15 266 2
present as she is in real distress, & with too much cause. LS 15 266 2
is a sad thing & of course highly afflicting to Lady Susan. LS 15 266 2
Frederica must be as much as sixteen, & ought to know LS 15 266 3
She has been sadly neglected however, & her mother ought LS 15 266 3
Frederica continue with her, & if he cannot succeed, to LS 15 266 4
of the letter--& is his judgement inferior to mine? LS 15 267 4
to come to Churchill, & justly enough, as it seems a sort LS 15 267 5
But it was impossible to take her any where else, & she is LS 15 267 5
You must support & encourage me--you must urge the LS 15 267 6
Frederica is too shy I think, & too much in awe of me, to LS 16 268 2
Consideration & esteem as surely follow command of LS 16 268 2
Reginald is never easy unless we are by ourselves, & when LS 16 268 2
I like him on the whole very well, he is clever & has a LS 16 268 2
deal to say, but he is sometimes impertinent & troublesome. LS 16 268 2
heard to my disadvantage, & is never satisfied till he LS 16 268 2
he has ascertained the beginning & end of everything. LS 16 268 2
I infinitely prefer the tender & liberal spirit of LS 16 269 3
whatever I do must be right; & look with a degree of LS 16 269 3
contempt on the inquisitive & doubting fancies of that LS 16 269 3
coming into this country, & lodging somewhere near me LS 16 269 3
to themselves & the opinion of the world. S. Vernon. LS 16 269 3
We are therefore prepared for her arrival, & expected them LS 17 269 1
They came while we were at tea, & I never saw any creature LS 17 269 1
Lady Susan who had been shedding tears before & shewing LS 17 269 2
& without betraying the least tenderness of spirit. LS 17 269 2
She hardly spoke to her, & on Frederica's bursting into LS 17 270 2
took her out of the room & did not return for some time; LS 17 270 2
eyes looked very red, & she was as much agitated as before. LS 17 270 2
friend in such distress, & watched her with so much tender LS 17 270 3
This pathetic representation lasted the whole evening, & LS 17 270 3
evening, & so ostentatious & artful a display had entirely LS 17 270 3
She looks perfectly timid, dejected & penitent. LS 17 270 4
so blooming as Lady Susan's--& she has quite the vernon LS 17 270 5
countenance, the oval face & mild dark eyes, & there is LS 17 270 5
oval face & mild dark eyes, & there is peculiar sweetness LS 17 270 5
evil disposition than her's; & from what I now see of the LS 17 270 5
severity of Lady Susan, & the silent dejection of LS 17 270 5
real love for her daughter & has never done her justice, LS 17 270 5
with my neice; she is shy, & I think I can see that some LS 17 270 6
into her dressing room, & Frederica spends great part of LS 17 271 7
proceeded form no justifiable cause, & had no provocation. LS 17 271 7
what Lady Susan has made him & wants to make me beleive, LS 17 271 7
an impatience of restraint, & a desire of escaping from LS 17 271 7
He scarcely dares even allow her to be handsome, & when I LS 17 271 7
& at others that her temper only is in fault. LS 17 271 8
should be to blame, & probably has sometimes judged it LS 17 272 8
her of ill-nature & sometimes to lament her want of sense. LS 17 272 8
deserving of our regard, & when I have communicated a LS 18 272 1
He is certainly very handsome--& yet more--there is an LS 18 272 1
must be highly prepossessing, & I am sure she feels it so. LS 18 272 1
Thoughtful & pensive in general her countenance always LS 18 272 1
says anything amusing; & let the subject be ever so LS 18 272 1
on such a heart as his; & could Frederica's artless LS 18 272 2
has had a wretched education & a dreadful example of LS 18 273 2
to be excellent, & her natural abilities very good. LS 18 273 2
fond of books & spending the cheif of her time in reading. LS 18 273 3
now than she did, & I have her with me as much as possible, LS 18 273 3
& have taken great pains to overcome her timidity. LS 18 273 3
We are very good friends, & tho' she never opens her lips LS 18 273 3
& perhaps may think me negligent for not writing before. LS 19 273 1
the reason of her behaviour, & soon found myself to have LS 19 273 1
of true girlish perverseness & folly, without considering LS 19 273 1
on getting out of the house, & proceeding directly by the LS 19 273 1
to her friends the Clarkes, & had really got as far as the LS 19 273 1
when she was fortunately miss'd, pursued, & overtaken. LS 19 273 1
Frederica Susanna Vernon, & if we consider that it was LS 19 274 2
from keeping the girl; & it seems so extraordinary a peice LS 19 274 2
Her feelings are tolerably lively, & she is so charmingly LS 19 274 2
her being ridiculed & despised by every man who sees her. LS 19 274 2
Artlessness will never do in love matters, & that girl is LS 19 274 3
dearly loves to be first, & to have all the sense & all LS 19 274 3
& to have all the sense & all the wit of the conversation LS 19 274 3
brought forward here, & canvassed by the wise heads of Mr LS 19 275 4
Mr & Mrs Vernon; & I cannot just now afford to go to town. LS 19 275 4
children while they dined, & supposing I should be wanted LS 20 275 1
the nursery soon afterwards & was half way down stairs, LS 20 275 1
as ashes came running up, & rushed by me into her own room. LS 20 275 1
I instantly followed, & asked her what was the matter. LS 20 275 1

"Oh! cried she, he is come, Sir James is come--& what am I	LS	20	275	1
colouring violently, Mama has sent for me, & I must go."	LS	20	275	1
We all three went down altogether, & I saw my brother	LS	20	275	2
In the breakfast room we found Lady Susan & a young man of	LS	20	275	2
love with Frederica, & with full encouragement from mama.	LS	20	276	2
him; and tho' his person & address are very well, he	LS	20	276	2
he appears both to Mr. Vernon & me a very weak young man.	LS	20	276	2
Lady Susan behaved with great attention to her visitor, &	LS	20	276	3
Sir James talked a good deal, & made many civil excuses to	LS	20	276	3
things over and over again, & told Lady Susan three times	LS	20	276	3
He now & then addressed Frederica, but more frequently her	LS	20	276	3
lips; her eyes cast down, & her colour varying every	LS	20	276	3
situation, proposed walking, & we left the two gentlemen	LS	20	276	4
I led her thither accordingly, & as soon as the door was	LS	20	276	5
than by Sir James's arrival, & the suddenness of it	LS	20	276	5
Sir James is a young man of an amiable disposition, &	LS	20	276	5
two will rectify <u>that</u>, & he is in other respects so very	LS	20	276	5
with the greatest pleasure, & am persuaded that you & my	LS	20	276	5
& am persuaded that you & my brother will give the	LS	20	276	5
silent on it so long, & agree with me that such	LS	20	277	5
on a man, who in connection & character is alike	LS	20	277	5
Catherine will be amply provided for, & not like my	LS	20	277	5
in the welfare of herself & her daughter, & then said, "I	LS	20	277	6 7
of herself & her daughter, & then said, "I am not apt to	LS	20	277	6 7
my dear Mrs Vernon, & I never had the convenient talent of	LS	20	277	6 7
foreign to my heart; & therefore I trust you will beleive	LS	20	277	6 7
ever love you as I now do; & I must farther say that your	LS	20	277	6 7
& understand the real affection we feel for each other!	LS	20	278	7
God bless you, for your goodness to me & my girl, &	LS	20	278	7
solemnity of expression! & yet I cannot help suspecting	LS	20	278	8
When Sir James first came, he appeared all astonishment &	LS	20	278	9
entirely engrossed him; & tho' a little private discourse	LS	20	278	9
the liberty of a relation, & concluded by wishing with a	LS	20	278	10
feelings are much as both her uncle & I beleive them to be.	LS	20	278	11
I hope this does not proceed from anything wrong, & that I	LS	20	278	11
the greatest consciousness & embarrassment; but I see	LS	20	278	11
I am very miserable about Sir James Martin, & have no	LS	21	279	1
or aunt on the subject; & this being the case, I am afraid	LS	21	279	1
no better than equivocation, & as if I attended only to	LS	21	279	1
attended only to the letter & not the spirit of mama's	LS	21	279	1
<u>you</u> do not take my part, & persuade her to break it off, I	LS	21	279	1
<u>of</u> taking my part with her, & persuading her to send Sir	LS	21	279	1
I always thought him silly & impertinent & disagreable, &	LS	21	279	1
& disagreable, & now he is grown worse than ever.	LS	21	279	1
My dearest friend, I was never so enraged before, & must	LS	22	280	1
Guess my astonishment & vexation--for as you well know, I	LS	22	280	1
made the best of it however, & told my story with great	LS	22	280	1
civilly to Sir James, & gave her to understand that I was	LS	22	280	1
her affection for Reginald, & from not feeling perfectly	LS	22	280	1
Frederica spontaneously & unnecessarily, & once had said	LS	22	280	1
& once had said something in praise of her person.	LS	22	280	1
& the whole business seemed most comfortably arranged.	LS	22	281	3
Charles vernon or his wife, & they had therefore no	LS	22	281	3
Everything however was going on calmly & quietly; & tho' I	LS	22	281	4
of all my schemes, & that too from a quarter, whence I had	LS	22	281	4
solemnity of countenance, & after some preface informed me	LS	22	281	4
with me on the impropriety & unkindness of allowing Sir	LS	22	281	4
required an explanation, & begged to know by what he was	LS	22	281	4
he was impelled, & by whom commissioned to reprimand me.	LS	22	281	4
a few insolent compliments & illtimed expressions of	LS	22	281	4
herself, Sir James, & me, which gave him great uneasiness.	LS	22	281	4
to request his interference, & that on receiving her	LS	22	281	5
the particulars & assure himself of her real wishes!	LS	22	281	5
her little rebellious heart & indelicate feelings to throw	LS	22	282	6
I am equally confounded at <u>her</u> impudence & <u>his</u> credulity.	LS	22	282	6
be overcome; & I hope I was afterwards sufficiently keen.	LS	22	282	7
At length he left me, as deeply provoked as myself, & he	LS	22	282	7
I may therefore expect it will sooner subside; & perhaps	LS	22	282	7
ever, while mine will be found still fresh & implacable.	LS	22	282	7
tender tale of love in vain, & exposed herself forever to	LS	22	282	8
contempt of the whole world, & the severest resentment of	LS	22	282	8
Our prospect is most delightful; & since matters have now	LS	23	283	1
his complexion was raised, & he spoke with great emotion.	LS	23	283	3
It is a great while since I have seen my father & mother.	LS	23	283	4
& with still greater energy, I must warn you of one thing.	LS	23	283	4
She is a sweet girl, & deserves a better fate.	LS	23	284	4
She is an amiable girl, & has a very superior mind to what	LS	23	284	4
He then left me & ran upstairs.	LS	23	284	5
I concluded of course that she & Reginald had been	LS	23	284	6
had been quarrelling, & looked with anxious curiosity for	LS	23	284	6
perfectly unconcerned, & after chatting on indifferent	LS	23	284	6
Young men are often hasty in their resolutions--& not more	LS	23	284	6
surprised if he were to change his mind at last, & not go."	LS	23	284	6
They must have quarrelled, & about Frederica too.	LS	23	285	7
James is gone, Lady Susan vanquished, & Frederica at peace.	LS	23	285	8
The quarrel between Lady Susan & Reginald is made up, & we	LS	24	285	1
Reginald was all but gone; his horse was ordered, & almost	LS	24	285	1
& sat with him in his room, talking over the whole matter.	LS	24	285	2
I met her on the stairs & saw that she was crying.	LS	24	285	2
he is going, Mr De Courcy is going, & it is all my fault.	LS	24	286	3
the misery I have been in, & mama had ordered me never to	LS	24	286	5
me never to speak to you or my uncle about it,--&--"	LS	24	286	5
was two hours about it--& when my letter was done, I	LS	24	286	5
I met him in the passage, & then as I knew that everything	LS	24	286	5
immediately; I dared not look at him--& ran away directly.	LS	24	286	5
Do you think that your uncle & I should not have espoused	LS	24	286	6
they have had a dreadful quarrel about it, & he is going.	LS	24	286	7
Mama will never forgive me, & I shall be worse off than	LS	24	286	7
She has no right to make you unhappy, & she shall <u>not</u> do	LS	24	287	7
I have entirely misunderstood Lady Susan, & was on the	LS	24	287	9
Reginald was glad to get away, & I went to Lady Susan;	LS	24	287	10
been this morning engaged, & which had ended very much to	LS	24	287	11
This idea struck me at the moment, & I instantly	LS	24	288	11
does justice to herself; her manners are shy & childish.	LS	24	288	11
make my own child miserable, & that I had forbidden her	LS	24	289	12
"His disposition you know is warm, & he came to	LS	24	290	13
I have a real regard for him, & was beyond expression	LS	24	290	13
We were both warm, & of course both to blame.	LS	24	290	13
his intention however, & at the same time began to think	LS	24	290	13
feel a degree of affection, & I own it would have sensibly	LS	24	290	13
wisely & command herself as she ought, she may now be easy.	LS	24	290	13
owed it to my own character; & after this explanation I	LS	24	290	13
Sir James's carriage was at the door, & he, merry as usual,	LS	24	291	15
of her mother's anger, & tho' dreading my brother's	LS	24	291	16
I see how closely she observes him & Lady Susan.	LS	24	291	16
the severest punishment; & your resolution of quitting	LS	25	292	3
& with those lively feelings which I know you to possess.	LS	25	292	3
relations to whom you are so much attached & are so dear.	LS	25	292	3
My remaining here cannot give that pleasure to Mr & Mrs	LS	25	293	3
society must; & my visit has already perhaps been too long.	LS	25	293	3
convenience be hastened; & I make it my particular request	LS	25	293	3
Here I concluded, & I hope you will be satisfied with my	LS	25	293	3
between returning tenderness & the remains of displeasure.	LS	25	293	3
into the utmost submission, & rendered more tractable,	LS	25	293	3
such an instance of pride; & am doubtful whether I ought	LS	25	293	4
our reconciliation, or by marrying & teizing him for ever.	LS	25	293	4
I must punish Frederica, & pretty severely too, for her	LS	25	293	4
receiving it so favourably, & for the rest of his conduct.	LS	25	293	4
insolent triumph of her look & manner since Sir James has	LS	25	293	4
that ill-fated young man--& I must make myself amends for	LS	25	293	4
I have also an idea of being soon in town, & whatever may	LS	25	294	4
my veiws may be directed, & at any rate, I shall there be	LS	25	294	4
be rewarded by your society & a little dissipation for a	LS	25	294	4
my daughter & Sir James, after having so long intended it.	LS	25	294	5
to take her to town, & marry her immediately to Sir James.	LS	25	294	5
was produced, & at best, the honour of victory is doubtful.	LS	25	294	6
matters, my dear Alicia, & let me know whether you can get	LS	25	294	7
I am gratified by your reference, & this is my advice;	LS	26	295	1
& the rest of his family, by making her marry Sir James.	LS	26	295	1
You should think more of yourself, & less of your daughter.	LS	26	295	1
do you credit in the world, & seems precisely in her	LS	26	295	1
misery enough; & come yourself to town, as soon as you can.	LS	26	295	1
Manwaring came to town last week, & has contrived, in	LS	26	295	3
He is absolutely miserable about you, & jealous to such a	LS	26	295	3
for them to meet at present; & yet if you do not allow him	LS	26	295	3
Besides, if you take my advice, & resolve to marry de	LS	26	295	3
Manwaring out of the way, & you only can have influence	LS	26	295	3
& my wishes, he will be laid up with the gout many weeks.	LS	26	295	4
be able to chuse our own society, & have true enjoyment.	LS	26	296	4
in Upper Seymour St, & we may be always together, there or	LS	26	296	4
Mr Johnson was her guardian & I do not in general share	LS	26	296	5
Frederica was wretched in the idea of going, & I could not	LS	27	296	1
I should have feared too for her health, & for everything	LS	27	296	1
& I can hardly tell which would have been worse for her.	LS	27	296	1
be with Reginald--& that would be the greatest evil of all.	LS	27	297	1
Our regular employments, our books & conversation, with	LS	27	297	2
with exercise, the children, & every domestic pleasure in	LS	27	297	2
were soon to be in London, & immediately contrived to have	LS	28	298	1
the Hamiltons to the lakes; & three years ago when I had a	LS	28	298	1
I have received yours, & have engaged the lodgings in	LS	28	298	2
much effect on you, & that de courcy is certainly your own.	LS	28	298	2
Let me hear from you as soon as you arrive, & in	LS	28	298	2
here it all falls upon me--& he bears pain with such	LS	28	298	2
to be formal, ungovernable & to have the gout--too old to	LS	29	298	1
have the gout--too old to be agreable, & too young to die.	LS	29	298	·1
I arrived last night about five, & had scarcely swallowed	LS	29	299	2
contract between his person & manners, & those of Reginald,	LS	29	299	2
his person & manners, & those of Reginald, to the infinite	LS	29	299	2
resolution of marrying him--& tho' this was too idle &	LS	29	299	2
tho' this was too idle & nonsensical an idea to remain	LS	29	299	2
the freedom of my spirit; & if I resolve to wait for that	LS	29	299	3
than the commonest flirtation; & he is tolerably appeased.	LS	29	299	4
I have received your letter; & tho' I do not attempt to	LS	30	299	1
state of our affairs, & every reveiw has served to	LS	30	300	1
in his daughter in law, & I am sometimes quarreling with	LS	30	300	2
I have now been but a few months a widow; & however little	LS	30	300	3
to the censure of the world, & incur what would be still	LS	30	300	3
know, ill fitted to endure; & when to this, may be added	LS	30	300	3
& of insensibility to yours, you will hardly suspect me.	LS	30	301	4
as necessary every where, & whose sensibilities are not of	LS	30	301	4
Tell me that you submit to my arguments, & do not reproach	LS	30	301	5
I must endeavour to seek amusement abroad, & fortunately	LS	30	301	5
You know how sincerely I regard both husband & wife. I	LS	30	301	5
He is devoted to me, heart & soul.	LS	31	302	1
I have told him that I am not quite well, & must be alone--	LS	31	302	1
quite well, & must be alone--& should he call again there	LS	31	302	1
You will not find him a heavy companion, & I allow you to	LS	31	302	1
he remain here; you know my reasons--propriety & so forth.	LS	31	302	1
My dear creature, I am in agonies, & know not what to	LS	32	302	1
Mrs Manwaring had that instant entered the house, & forced	LS	32	302	1
for I was out when both she & Reginald came, or I would	LS	32	302	1
my husband's interference, & before I could be aware of it,	LS	32	302	1
concealed, was known to him; & unluckily she had wormed	LS	32	302	1
in town, & had just watched him to your door herself!	LS	32	302	1
of intending to marry you, & would speak with him alone,	LS	32	303	1
has fretted herself thinner & uglier than ever, is still	LS	32	303	2
is still here, & they have been all closeted together.	LS	32	303	2
I have been under, & the absolute necessity of an	LS	34	304	1
necessity of an immediate & eternal separation from you.	LS	34	304	1
bear a doubtful meaning, & which the ill-nature of the	LS	35	304	1
Come to me immediately, & explain what is at present	LS	35	305	1
misconduct during the life & since the death of Mr Vernon	LS	36	305	1
with the world in general, & gained my entire beleif	LS	36	305	1
has for some time existed, & still continues to exist	LS	36	305	1
to exist between you & the man, whose family you robbed of	LS	36	305	1
Can you, dare you deny it? & all this at the time when I	LS	36	305	1
Far from me be all complaint, & every sigh of regret.	LS	36	305	1
My understanding is at length restored, & teaches me no	LS	36	306	2
I am satisfied--& will trouble you no more when these few	LS	37	306	1
compatible with your veiws, & I rejoice to find that the	LS	37	306	1
act of filial obedience, & I flatter myself with the hope	LS	37	306	1
Be assured that I partake in all your feelings, & do not	LS	38	306	1
for the rest of his life--& you know it is impossible to	LS	38	306	1
But she is still so fond of her husband & frets so much	LS	38	307	2
Miss Manwaring is just come to town to be with her aunt, &	LS	38	307	3
I think as Manwaring, & with such an open, goodhumoured	LS	38	307	3
Mr Johnson & he are the greatest friends in the world.	LS	38	307	3
But I dare say you did all for the best, & there is no	LS	38	307	3
Our friendship cannot be impaired by it; & in happier	LS	39	307	1
For this I shall impatiently wait; & meanwhile can safely	LS	39	307	1
myself & everything about me, than at the present hour.	LS	39	307	1
Your husband I abhor--Reginald I despise--& I am secure of	LS	39	307	1
Manwaring is more devoted to me than ever; & were he at	LS	39	308	1
& am equally determined that Frederica never <u>shall</u>.	LS	39	308	0
				1000
To-morrow I shall fetch her from Churchill, & let Maria	LS	39	308	1
<u>She</u> may whimper, & the Vernons may storm; I regard them	LS	39	308	1
<u>those</u>, to whom I owe no duty, & for whom I feel no respect.	LS	39	308	1
My dear Catherine I have charming news for you, & if I	LS	40	308	1
He has been only an hour in the house, & I have not been	LS	40	308	1
Nothing is wanting but to have you here, & it is our	LS	40	309	1
& entreaty that you would come to us as soon as you can.	LS	40	309	1
I hope nothing will make it inconvenient to Mr Vernon, &	LS	40	309	1
& your dear neice is included of course; I long to see her.	LS	40	309	1
hitherto, without Reginald, & seeing nobody from Churchill;	LS	40	309	1
Frederica runs much in my thoughts, & when Reginald has	LS	40	309	1
him of his heart once more, & I am full of hopes of seeing	LS	40	309	1
Can it be true that they are really separated--& for ever?	LS	41	309	1
we had a most unexpected & unwelcome visit from Lady Susan,	LS	41	309	1
looking all chearfulness & good humour, & seeming more as	LS	41	309	1
chearfulness & good humour, & seeming more as if she were	LS	41	309	1
She staid nearly two hours, was as affectionate & agreable	LS	41	309	1
& agreable as ever, & not a syllable, not a hint was	LS	41	309	1
Your kind invitation is accepted by us with pleasure, & on	LS	41	310	2
& on Thursday next, we & our little ones will be with you.	LS	41	310	2
was to fetch her away; & miserable as it made the poor	LS	41	310	3
I was thoroughly unwilling to let her go, & so was her	LS	41	310	3
was her uncle; & all that could be urged, we <u>did</u> urge.	LS	41	310	3
Her manner, to be sure, was very kind & proper--& Mr	LS	41	310	3
I charged her to write to me very often, & to remember	LS	41	310	4
I took care to see her alone, that I might say all this, &	LS	41	310	4
But I shall not be easy till I can go to town & judge of	LS	41	310	4
between some of the parties & separation between the	LS	42	311	1
intercourse of Mrs Vernon & her neice, for the former soon	LS	42	311	1
her mother's inspection, & therefore deferring all	LS	42	311	1
what had passed between him & Lady Susan to sink the	LS	42	311	2
removed from such a mother, & placed under her own care; &	LS	42	311	2
& placed under her own care; & tho' with little hope of	LS	42	311	2
an early visit to London; & Mr Vernon who, as it must have	LS	42	311	2

Context	Work	Letter	Page	Section
after her arrival in town; & she was met with such an easy	LS	42	311	2
was met with such an easy & chearful affection as made her	LS	42	311	2
She was in excellent spirits, & seemed eager to shew at	LS	42	311	2
sense of their kindness, & her pleasure in their society.	LS	42	311	2
uncomfortable, & confirmed her in the plan of altering it.	LS	42	311	3
that he was not in London; & in all her conversation she	LS	42	311	3
only for the welfare & improvement of her daughter,	LS	42	312	3
growing every day more & more what a parent could desire.	LS	42	312	3
Mrs Vernon surprised & incredulous, knew not what to	LS	42	312	4
knew not what to suspect, & without any change in her own	LS	42	312	4
to part with her daughter; & as, tho' her own plans were	LS	42	312	5
Mrs Vernon however persevered in the offer of it, & tho'	LS	42	312	5
Frederica returned to Churchill with her uncle & aunt, &	LS	42	312	6
a prolongation of her stay, & in the course of two months	LS	42	313	7
& in the course of two more, to write to her at all.	LS	42	313	7
Frederica was therefore fixed in the family of her uncle &	LS	42	313	8
could be talked, flattered & finessed into an affection	LS	42	313	8
all future attachments & detesting the sex, might be	LS	42	313	8
She had nothing against her, but her husband, & her	LS	42	313	9
who coming to town & putting herself to an expence in	LS	42	313	10
on Tuesday Octr Ye 13th, & it was generally expected to be	W		314	1
over as sure of attending, & sanguine hopes were	W		314	1
who lived in the town & kept their coach; the Watsons	W		314	1
3 miles distant, were poor & had no close carriage; & ever	W		314	1
& had no close carriage; & ever since there had been balls	W		314	1
the latter to dress dine & sleep at their house, on every	W		314	1
W.'s children were at home, & one was always necessary as	W		315	1
himself, for he was sickly & had lost his wife, one only	W		315	1
in the neighbourhood; & her eldest sister, whose delight	W		315	1
undertaking to drive her & all her finery in the old chair	W		315	1
thus instructed & cautioned her inexperienc'd sister.--	W		315	1
"I dare say it will be a very good ball, & among so many	W		315	1
but he is a great flirt & never means anything serious."	W		315	1
"A young man of very good fortune, quite independant, &	W		315	1
why it did not take place, & why he is married to another	W		316	2
veiw of gaining him herself, & it ended in his	W		316	2
his visits & soon after marrying somebody else.--	W		316	2
own part--a little company, & a pleasant ball now & then,	W		317	2
& a pleasant ball now & then, would be enough for me, if	W		317	2
us, & it is very bad to grow old & be poor & laughed at.--	W		317	2
attentions from me to her, & whom she was very fond of;	W		317	2
means anything serious, & when he had trifled with her	W		317	2
her for Margaret, & poor Penelope was very wretched--.	W		317	2
the friend she goes to see;--& she has taken a vast deal	W		317	2
him & given up a great deal of time to no purpose as yet.--	W		317	2
"I suspect the Dr to have an attack of the asthma,--& that	W		318	2
She professes to keep her own counsel; she says, & truly	W		318	2
She must have too masculine & bold a temper.--	W		318	2
Poverty is a great evil, but to a woman of education &	W		318	2
I have been at school, Emma, & know what a life they lead;	W		318	2
I have observed it ever since you came home, & I am afraid	W		318	2
"Yes--she has great spirits, & never cares what she says."-	W		318	2
"Yes--especially in company; she is all gentleness &	W		318	2
But she is a little fretful & perverse among ourselves.--	W		318	2
body else, & is always expecting him to come to the point.	W		319	2
I am sure she is mistaken, & that he will no more follow	W		319	2
"No indeed--I dislike & despise him."--	W		319	2
"Dislike & despise Tom Musgrave!	W		319	2
I hope he will come with a large party, & then he will not	W		319	2
Well, we shall see how irresistable Mr Tom Musgrave & I	W		319	2
a good place by the fire, & he never comes till late; & if	W		319	2
& he never comes till late; & if the Osbornes are coming,	W		319	2
coming, he will wait in the passage, & come in with them.--	W		319	2
father, I wd wrap myself up, & James should drive me over,	W		319	2
him; & I should be with you by the time the dancing began."	W		319	2
There, I said you were very refined;--& that's an instance	W		319	2
I am a stranger here, & know nobody but the Edwardses; my	W		320	2
your company than of mine, & I shd most readily return to	W		320	2
readily return to my father; & should not be at all afraid	W		320	2
You are very pretty, & it would be very hard that you	W		320	2
Emma expressed her gratitude, & for a few minutes they	W		320	2
which passed between you & me for the last 14 years."	W		320	2
He has been very much in love with her these two years, &	W		321	2
spare him, & just now it is a sickly time at Guilford--"	W		321	2
"I am afraid not: you know she is an only child, & will	W		321	2
Her father & mother wd never consent to it.	W		321	2
But Mary Edwardes is rather prim & reserved; I do not	W		321	2
"A young man must think of somebody. said eliz:--& why	W		321	2
as Robert, who has got a good wife & six thousand pounds?"	W		321	2
I have been unlucky enough, & I cannot say much for you,	W		321	2
You may see the church tower over the hedge, & the White	W		321	2
thro' the turnpike gate & entered on the pitching of the	W		321	2
of the town--the jumbling & noise of which made farther	W		321	2
to take the right turning, & making only one blunder, in	W		321	2
Mr E. lived in the best house in the street, & the best in	W		322	2
end of the town with a shrubbery & sweep in the country.--	W		322	2
moving--safely arrived;--& by the market clock, we have	W		322	2
we have been only five & thirty minutes coming.--which I	W		322	2
The Edwards' have a noble house you see, & they live quite	W		322	2
all but strangers to her, & tho' her spirits were by no	W		322	3
from any other cause, & increased her sense of the	W		322	3
woman, had a reserved air, & a great deal of formal	W		322	3
deal of formal civility--& the papers, seemed very	W		322	3
being obliged to hurry away--& some very, very languid	W		322	3
Mr Edwards had a much easier, & more communicative air	W		322	3
street, & he came ready to tell what ever might interest.--	W		323	3
evening, they come so late, & go so early;--but great	W		323	3
had supplied him with, & they chatted with greater	W		323	3
moment for dressing arrived, & the young ladies were	W		323	3
Emma was shewn to a very comfortable apartment, & as soon	W		323	3
a modest unpretending mind, & a great wish of obliging--&	W		323	3
& a great wish of obliging--& when they returned to the	W		323	3
which went thro' the winter, & a new cap from the	W		323	3
feelings & more natural smiles than they had taken away.--	W		323	3
however sanctioned--& tho' complacently veiwing her	W		323	3
but a qualified admiration; & Mr E. not less satisfied	W		323	3
The discussion led to more intimate remarks, & Miss	W		323	3
accompany the question, & there seemed something still	W		324	3
Mr Sam Watson is a very good sort of young man, & I dare	W		324	3
There might be resemblance in countenance; & the	W		324	3
& the complexion, & even the features be very unlike."--	W		324	3
He has a long face, & a wide mouth.--	W		324	3
mind of her eldest sister, & sometimes I see a look of	W		324	3
see a look of Miss Penelope--& once or twice there has	W		324	3
"I see the likeness between her & Miss Watson, replied Mr	W		324	3
am very sure there is no resemblance between her & Sam."--	W		324	3
This matter was settled, & they went to dinner.--	W		324	4
he does; & very few people that play a fairer rubber.--	W		325	4
& if he cd but have his health, how much he wd enjoy it."	W		325	4
"I dare say he would sir--& I wish with all my heart he	W		325	4
You had better meet every night, & break up two hours	W		325	4
So far, the subject was very often carried;--but Mr & Mrs	W		325	4
that point; & Mr Edwards now turned to something else.--	W		325	4
become a little of a gossip, & having some curiosity to	W		325	4
Ah! I remember--& she is gone to settle in Ireland.--	W		325	5
a blush on Miss E.'s cheek, & in remembering what	W		326	5
to wonder & waver between his influence & her brother's.--	W		326	5
Emma drew her hand across her eyes--& Mrs Edwards on	W		326	5
to the two young ladies; & tho' Miss Edwards was rather	W		326	6
7 o'clock was some releif--& luckily Mr & Mrs Edwards	W		326	7
some releif--& luckily Mr & Mrs Edwards always drank a	W		326	7
drank a dish extraordinary, & ate an additional muffin	W		326	7
to order hers to the door; & in a very few minutes, the	W		327	7
to the bustle, noise & draughts of air of the broad	W		327	7
her young Charges' shoulders & throats, led the way up the	W		327	7
the ears of her followers, & Miss Edwards on hazarding the	W		327	7
young man in a morning dress & boots, who was standing in	W		327	7
together, passing in & out from the adjoining card-room.--	W		327	8
near neighbours ensued--& as soon as they were all duely	W		327	8
He came into possession of it, when he was very young, &	W		328	8
& mother think it has given him rather an unsettled turn.--	W		328	8
The cold & empty appearance of the room & the demure air	W		328	8
other carriages was heard, & continual accessions of	W		328	8
of portly chaperons, & strings of smartly-dressed girls	W		328	8
were received, with now & then a fresh gentleman straggler,	W		328	8
"I am Capt. Hunter."--& Emma, who could not but watch her	W		328	8
but by no means displeased, & heard an engagement formed	W		328	8
A new face & a very pretty one, could not be slighted--her	W		328	9
from one party to another, & no sooner had the signal been	W		328	9
the young men to their duty, & people the centre of the	W		328	9
height--well made & plump, with an air of healthy vigour.--	W		328	9
a lively eye, a sweet smile, & an open countenance, gave	W		328	9
& expression to make that beauty improve on acquaintance.--	W		328	9
very pleasantly to her; & her feelings perfectly coincided	W		329	9
called general notice, & "the Osbornes are coming, the	W		329	9
After some minutes of extraordinary bustle without, &	W		329	9
a fine boy of 10 years old, & Mr Tom Musgrave; who	W		329	9
Compts of some acquaintance, & she heard Ly. Osborne	W		329	9
Emma looked at them all as they passed--but chiefly & with	W		329	9
50, she was very handsome, & had all the dignity of rank.--	W		329	9
was not fond of women's company, & he never danced.--	W		329	10
amongst the osborne set; & she was immediately struck with	W		330	11
with the fine countenance & animated gestures of the	W		330	11
little woman of 5 or 6 & 30, to a lady who was standing	W		330	11
cried the boy. & we are to dance down every couple."--	W		330	11
On the other side of Emma, Miss Osborne, Miss Carr, & a	W		330	11
in ver lively consultation--& soon afterwards she saw the	W		330	11
I know you will excuse me, & I will certainly dance with	W		330	11
turned again to Miss Carr, & in another minute was led by	W		330	11
crimson'd cheeks, quivering lips, & eyes bent on the floor.	W		330	11
Emma did not think, or reflect;--she felt & acted--.	W		330	11
forwards with an honest & simple thank you Maam was	W		331	11
of unexpected pleasure, & lively gratitude, she turned to	W		331	11
her neighbour with repeated & fervent acknowledgements of	W		331	11
of so great & condescending a kindness to her boy.--	W		331	11
than she felt herself--& Charles being provided with his	W		331	11
provided with his gloves & charged to keep them on, they	W		331	11
It gained her a broad stare from Miss Osborne & Miss Carr	W		331	11
many inquisitive glances; & after a time Ld Osborne	W		331	11
time Ld Osborne himself came & under pretence of talking	W		331	11
had it made both the boy & his mother; the latter of whom	W		331	11
gave him anything to say; & she learnt, by a sort of	W		331	11
that he had two brothers & a sister, that they & their	W		331	11
& a sister, that they & their mama all lived with his	W		331	11
he was very fond of riding, & had a horse of his own given	W		331	11
own given him by Ld Osborne; & that he had been out once	W		331	11
she moved into the Tearoom; & Emma was accordingly on the	W		331	11
to have a little bustle & croud when they thus adjourned	W		332	11
room within the cardroom, & in passing thro' the latter,	W		332	11
Mrs E. & her party were for a few moments hemmed in.	W		332	11
to it spoke to his nephew; & Emma on perceiving herself	W		332	11
of attention both to Ly. O. & him, had just turned away	W		332	11
to enjoy his own thoughts, & gape without restraint.--	W		332	11
Emma--"there's Lord osborne--let you & I go & sit by him.--	W		332	11
"But you may come to Wickstead & see mama, & she can take	W		332	12
There is a monstrous curious stuff'd fox there, & a Badger-	W		333	12
sister leaning on his arm--& no sooner were they within	W		333	13
& they were immediately impelled in opposite directions.--	W		333	13
in Mr H. which suited her--& in a few minutes afterwards,	W		333	13
Tom Musgrave towards him & say, "why do not you dance with	W		333	13
I want to dance with her--& I will come & stand by you."--	W		333	13
my Lord, I'll be introduced & dance with her directly."--	W		333	13
"Aye do--& if you find she does not want much talking to,	W		333	13
not want much talking to, you may introduce me by & bye."--	W		333	13
Away we went--Ld Osborne after him--& Emma lost no time in	W		333	13
without loss of time--& Emma, however she might like to be	W		333	13
He was evidently surprised & discomposed.--	W		334	13
the rules of the assembly--& I am sure it will never be	W		334	13
more fortunate another time--& seeming unwilling to leave	W		334	13
"My eldest sister is the only one at home--& she could not	W		334	13
my negligence wherever I go, & I confess it is a shameful	W		335	13
to receive from her sisters, & gave him probably the novel	W		335	13
& of wishing for more attention than she bestowed.	W		335	13
was required to stand up--& Tom Musgrave's curiosity was	W		335	13
friend carried him the news--& he was continually at	W		335	13
made them all worth hearing, & she only regretted that he	W		335	13
The two dances seemed very short, & she had her partner's	W		335	13
At their conclusion the Osbornes & their train were all on	W		335	13
I shall order a Barrel of oysters, & be famously snug."	W		335	13
"Let us see you soon at the castle; & bring me word how	W		335	13
Emma & Mrs Blake parted as old acquaintance, & Charles	W		335	13
by the hand & wished her "goodbye" at least a dozen times.	W		335	13
From Miss Osborne & Miss Carr she received something like	W		336	13
her a look of complacency--& his Lordship actually came	W		336	13
room, to "beg her pardon", & look in the window seat	W		336	13
his plan to have succeeded, & imagine him mortifying with	W		336	14
unpleasantly, distinguished, & the two dances which	W		336	14
two dances which followed & concluded the ball, were	W		336	14
the tables were prepared, & the neat upper maid was	W		336	14
enjoyed the eveng so much--& Mr Edwards was as warm as	W		336	14
of the fullness, brilliancy & spirit of the meeting. tho'	W		336	14
But he had won 4 rubbers out of 5, & everything went well.	W		336	14
& retrospections which now ensued, over the welcome soup.--	W		336	14
me he was gone to ask you--& I had heard you say two	W		336	14
"Mr Norton, & Mr Styles."	W		337	15
"No--perhaps not--but I remember my dear when you & I did	W		337	15
Mrs E. said no more, & Mary breathed again.--	W		337	15
A great deal of goodhumoured pleasantry followed--& Emma	W		337	15
spirits, her head full of Osbornes, Blakes & Howards.--	W		337	15
on the morng after a ball, & this neighbourly inclination	W		337	16
Many were the eyes, & various the degrees of approbation	W		337	17
Some saw no fault, & some no beauty--.	W		337	17
annihilation of every grace, & others could never be	W		337	17
this succession of company--& Emma was at once astonished	W		338	17
by finding it two o'clock, & considering that she had	W		338	17
to examine the street, & was on the point of asking leave	W		338	17
leave to ring the bell & make enquiries, when the light	W		338	17
Mr Musgrave was shortly afterwards announced;--& mrs	W		338	17
with no unbecoming ease, & continuing to address Emma,	W		338	17
the visitation that day, & that as his road lay quite wide	W		338	18
to employ on the errand, & I was fortunate enough to	W		338	18
intimacy with the proposer--& yet fearful of encroaching	W		339	18
She enquired into the particulars--& then said "we shall	W		339	18
is quite at your service, & Mary will be pleased with the	W		339	18
This was precisely what Emma had longed for; & she	W		339	18
The ladies were silently firm, & the gentleman found	W		340	18
How long did you keep it up, after the Osbornes & I went	W		340	19
There seemed no vacancy anywhere--& everybody danced with	W		340	19
You can imagine nothing more *naive* or *piquante*; & what do	W		340	19
tho' he were *not* a Lord--& perhaps--better bred; more	W		340	19
of pleasing, & shewing himself pleased in a right place.--"	W		340	19
Emma gave him no encouragement, & he was obliged to keep	W		340	19
And now tell me how you like them all, & what I am to say	W		341	19
ourselves, continued eliz: & then we shall lose no time.--	W		341	19

& / &

"You did very right; tho' I wonder at your forbearance, &	W		341	19
I did long to see you, & it was a clever way of getting	W		341	19
him no favour, & I doubt his having any interest with Mary.	W		341	19
She danced twice with Capt. Hunter, & I think shews him in	W		341	19
her disposition, & the circumstances she is placed in.--	W		341	19
She once mentioned Sam, & certainly with a little	W		341	19
Well--now begin, & give me an account of everything as it	W		342	19
Emma obeyed her--& eliz: listened with very little	W		342	19
Why--he is quite one of the great & grand ones;--did not	W		342	19
"His manners are of a kind to give <u>me</u> much more ease &	W		342	19
I allow his person & air to be good--& that his manners to	W		342	19
anxious for distinction, & absolutely contemptible in some	W		342	19
"Aye--that is just like him. & yet this is the man, she	W		342	19
Can you lay your hand on your heart, & say you do not?"--	W		342	19
"Indeed I can, both hands; & spread to their widest extent.	W		343	19
but as playing cards with ly osborne, & looking proud.--	W		343	19
I only hope it will last;--& that he will not come on to	W		343	19
said she, to have things going on in peace & goodhumour.	W		343	19
poor Margt is very snappish, & Penelope owns she had	W		343	19
for the exertion of the day, & consequently pleased with	W		343	19
he had done, & glad to talk of it, over his own fireside.--	W		343	19
spoken of as the preacher, & as having given them an	W		343	20
He reads extremely well, with great propriety & in a very	W		343	20
in a very impressive manner; & at the same time without	W		343	20
do not like the stupid air & artificial inflexions of	W		343	20
very popular & most admired preachers generally have.--	W		343	20
to inspire devotion, & shews a much better taste.--	W		344	20
Mr H. read like a scholar & a gentleman."--	W		344	20
He related the dishes & told what he had ate himself.	W		344	20
to see me amongst them--& I must say that everybody paid	W		344	20
paid me great attention, & seemed to feel for me as an	W		344	20
make me sit near the fire, & as the partridges were pretty	W		344	20
agree with my gouty foot--& Mr Howard walked by me from	W		344	20
from the bottom to the top, & would make me take his arm.--	W		344	20
the parlour with the tray & the knife-case, she was	W		344	21
of a riding-whip cd give--& tho' charged by Miss W. to let	W		344	21
hold the parlour door open for Ld Osborne & Tom Musgrave.--	W		344	21
least, a nobleman & a stranger, was really distressing.--	W		344	21
they were obliged to live; & having in her aunt's family	W		345	21
her from such mortification--& tho' shrinking under a	W		345	21
Osborne near Emma, & the convenient Mr Musgrave in high	W		345	21
more to say for some time, & could only gratify his eye by	W		345	21
for his entertainment--& after hard labour of mind, he	W		345	21
it's being a very fine day, & followed it up with the	W		345	21
all have the inclination, & I fancy Miss Watson--when once	W		345	21
<u>That</u> is a point on which ladies & gentlen have long	W		346	21
<u>He</u> was rewarded by a gracious answer, & a more liberal	W		346	21
Unused to exert himself, & happy in contemplating her, he	W		346	21
who half opening the door & putting in her head, said "	W		346	21
he knew it very well, & such honest simplicity, such	W		346	21
the name of her shoemaker--& concluded with saying, "my	W		347	21
to nothing, the smartest & most fashionable man of the two.	W		347	22
But did not you hear him ask where Miss Penelope & Miss	W		347	22
a very unlikely thing, & describe a very odd young lady;	W		347	22
but did not suit her pride, & she wd rather have known	W		347	22
same privilege of coming, & accompanied his Lordship--but	W		347	22
under immediate pain, & ill disposed to be pleased, he	W		348	22
for half a day, the tranquil & affectionate intercourse of	W		348	23
speedy return of Margaret, & a visit of two or three days	W		348	23
of two or three days from Mr & Mrs Robert Watson, who	W		348	23
to bring her home & wished to see their sister Emma.--	W		348	23
of the sisters at Stanton, & to busy the hours of one of	W		348	23
were considerable, & as eliz: had at all times more good	W		348	23
An absence of 14 years had made all her brothers & sisters	W		348	23
made her dread her return; & the day which brought the	W		348	23
with himself for the same, & for having married the only	W		348	23
that six thousand pounds, & for being now in possession of	W		349	23
where she gave genteel parties, & wore fine Cloathes.--	W		349	23
had a slight, pretty figure, & rather wanted countenance	W		349	23
her manner was all affection & her voice all gentleness;	W		349	23
gentleness; continual smiles & a very slow articulation	W		349	23
Emma scarcely knew how to answer such a proposition--& the	W		349	24
Mrs R. W. eyed her with much familiar curiosity &	W		349	24
at the moment of meeting;--& she cd. not but feel how much	W		349	24
Robert was carelessly kind, as became a prosperous man & a	W		349	24
advance in posting, & pondering over a doubtful halfcrown,	W		349	24
"You are very good--replied her mother--& I assure you it	W		350	24
I was forced to say we were only going to church & promise	W		350	24
bring her without her maid, & I am as particular as ever	W		350	24
it be for months together.--& I am sorry, (with a witty	W		350	24
Perhaps Emma may be tempted to go back with us, & stay	W		350	24
too mixed,--but our parties are very select & good.--	W		350	24
been used to in Shropshire, & setting it as certain that	W		350	24
Emma was quite distress'd by such behaviour;--& she did	W		351	24
when I come to see you--& now I do hope you have not been	W		351	25
"I suppose, said Margt rather quickly to Emma, you & I are	W		351	25
"Oh!--(in a soften'd voice, & rather mortified to find she	W		351	25
<u>me</u> with money, replied Emma, & <u>I</u> am a woman too.--"	W		351	26
<u>was</u> very good to me; & if she has made an imprudent choice,	W		352	26
The most liberal & enlightened minds are always the most	W		352	26
I was her own neice, & he left to herself the power & the	W		352	26
providing for you, to your father, & without the power.--	W		352	26
That's the long & the short of the business.	W		352	26
natural affection among us & breeding you up (I suppose)	W		352	26
robt rather softened--& after a short silence, by way of	W		352	26
You must come to Croydon as well as the rest, & see what	W		353	26
to Robert, who had equally irritated & greived her.--	W		353	26
I think there is powder enough in my hair for my wife &	W		353	26
Mr Marshall & Mr Hemmings change their dress every day of	W		353	26
"Do be satisfied with being fine yourself, & leave your	W		353	26
To put an end to this altercation, & soften the evident	W		353	26
Dinner came, & except when Mrs R. looked at her husband's	W		353	27
head, she continued gay & flippant, chiding Elizth for the	W		353	27
the profusion on the table, & absolutely protesting	W		353	27
"I do beg & entreat that no turkey may be seen today.	W		354	27
"My dear, replied Eliz. the turkey is roasted, & it may	W		354	27
but was prevailed on to come down & drink tea with them.--	W		354	28
Margaret & I have played at cribbage, most nights that we	W		354	28
road, & contained no gentleman's family but the Rector's.--	W		354	28
of the house to the front door, & then within the passage.	W		355	28
The door opened, & displayed Tom Musgrave in the wrap of a	W		355	28
He had been in London & was now on his way home, & he had	W		355	28
at extraordinary seasons; & in the present instance had	W		355	28
the other was thrown open, & he beheld a circle of smart	W		355	28
of visiting round the fire, & Miss Watson sitting at the	W		355	28
He recollected himself, & came forward, delighted to find	W		355	28
such a circle of friends, & blessing his good fortune for	W		355	28
He shook hands with Robert, bowed & smiled to the ladies,	W		355	28
& smiled to the ladies, & did everything very prettily;	W		355	28
to throw off his greatcoat, & drink tea with them.	W		355	28
came avowedly from London, & had left it only 4. hours ago,	W		356	28
report as to public news, & the general opinion of the day	W		356	28
to the less national, & important demands of the women.--	W		356	28
My kind brother & sister brought me home this very morng.--	W		356	28
dreaded the meeting, & at the same time longed for it.--	W		356	28
He hesitated; Margaret was fair herself, & he did not	W		357	28
her; but Miss Osborne & Miss Carr were likewise fair, &	W		357	28
were likewise fair, & his devotion to them carried the day.	W		357	28
for a truly feminine complexion, & she is very fair."--	W		357	28
The ladies were not wanting in civil returns; & Robert	W		357	28
card table being set out, & the fish & counters with a	W		357	28
being set out, & the fish & counters with a tolerably	W		357	28
be the worst of all parties; & the others were delighted.--	W		357	28
Elizth--my sister recommends it, & I fancy we all like it.	W		358	28
ever beheld--such quickness & spirit! he lets nobody dream	W		358	28
She was quite vanquished, & the fashions of Osborne-Castle	W		358	28
Mrs Blake is a nice little good-humoured woman, she & I	W		358	28
& Howard's a very gentleman-like good sort of fellow!--	W		358	28
I fancy you must have a little cheek-glowing now & then	W		358	28
others, to regulate the game & determine some disputable	W		359	28
some disputable point; & his attention was so totally	W		359	28
engaged in the business & afterwards by the course of the	W		359	28
he had been saying before;--& Emma, tho' suffering a good	W		359	28
have felt little interest, & perhaps maintained little	W		359	28
but his presence gave variety & secured good manners.--	W		359	28
& few situations made him appear to greater advantage.	W		359	28
He played with spirit, & had a great deal to say & tho'	W		359	28
the wit of an absent friend; & had a lively way of	W		359	28
The ways, & good jokes of osborne castle were now added to	W		359	28
the oversights of another, & indulged them even with a	W		359	28
was thus agreably occupied; & when Nanny came in with her	W		359	28
The carriage was ordered to the door--& no entreaties for	W		359	28
On finding him determined to go, Margt began to wink & nod	W		359	28
for the following day; & eliz, at last not able to resist	W		359	28
I shoot with Ld Osborne, & therefore must not engage--you	W		360	28
a short time the next morng; & had proceeded so far as to	W		360	29
here last night my dear Emma & returns today, is more	W		360	29
very inapplicable reply, & jumping up, ran away from a	W		360	29
the morning in the kitchen herself directing & scolding.--	W		360	30
After a great deal of indifferent cooking, & anxious	W		360	30
T. Musgrave never came, & Margt was at no pains to conceal	W		360	30
The peace of the party for the remainder of that day, &	W		360	30
the length of Robert & Jane's visit, was continually	W		360	30
invaded by her fretful displeasure, & querulous attacks.--	W		360	30
by <u>them</u>, but Eliz. & the maids cd never do anything right--	W		360	30
cd <u>never</u> do anything right--& Emma, whom she seemed no	W		360	30
above, with her father, & warmly entreated to be his	W		361	30
constant Compn each eveng--& as Eliz. loved company of any	W		361	30
To Emma, the exchange was most acceptable, & delightful.	W		361	30
Her father, if ill, required little more than gentleness &	W		361	30
than gentleness & silence; &, being a man of sense and	W		361	30
of unequal society, & family discord--from the immediate	W		361	31
low-minded conceit, & wrong-headed folly, engrafted on an	W		361	31
their existence; in memory & in prospect, but for the	W		361	31
She was at leisure, she could read & think,--tho' her	W		361	31
nor likely to lessen; & when thought had been freely	W		361	31
in contrasting the past & the present, the employment of	W		361	31
The change in her home society, & stile of life in	W		361	31
From being the first object of hope & solicitude of an	W		361	31
with the care of a parent, & of tenderness to an aunt	W		361	31
from being the life & spirit of a house, where all had	W		361	31
where all had been comfort & elegance, & the expected	W		361	31
had been comfort & elegance, & the expected heiress of an	W		361	31
of domestic comfort, & as little hope of future support.--	W		361	31
She was very much pressed by Robert & Jane to return with	W		362	32
return with them to Croydon, & had some difficulty in	W		362	32
highly of their own kindness & situation, to suppose to	W		362	32
almost every day, & robt & Jane will be very kind to you.--	W		362	32
ways are new to <u>you</u>, & they would vex you more than you	W		362	32
representations--& the visitors departed without her.--	W		362	32
A gentleman & lady travelling from Tunbridge towards that	S	1	363	1
which lies between Hastings & E. Bourne, being induced by	S	1	363	1
to quit the high road, & attempt a very rough lane, were	S	1	363	1
be necessarily their object, & had with most unwilling	S	1	364	1
He had grumbled & shaken his shoulders so much indeed, and	S	1	364	1
so much indeed, and pitied & cut his horses so sharply,	S	1	364	1
The severity of the fall was broken by their slow pace &	S	1	364	1
the narrowness of the lane, & the gentleman having	S	1	364	1
having scrambled out & helped out his companion, they	S	1	364	1
neither of them at first felt more than shaken & bruised.	S	1	364	1
sprained his foot--& soon becoming sensible of it, was	S	1	364	1
remonstrance to the driver & his congratulations to his	S	1	364	1
congratulations to his wife & himself--& sit down on the	S	1	364	1
to his wife & himself--& sit down on the bank, unable to	S	1	364	1
His wife fervently hoped it was--but stood, terrified &	S	1	364	1
to do or suggest anything--& receiving her first real	S	1	364	1
the house they had passed--& the persons who approached,	S	1	364	1
his Haymakers at the time, & three or four of them	S	1	364	1
field, men, women, women & children--not very far off.--	S	1	364	1
that road in a carriage--& ready offers of assistance.	S	1	365	1
His courtesies were received with good-breeding &	S	1	365	1
good-breeding & gratitude & while one or two of the men	S	1	365	1
are extremely obliging sir, & I take you at your word.--	S	1	365	1
Mr H. looked very much astonished--& replied--"what sir!	S	1	365	1
myself from the morning post & the Kentish Gazette, only	S	1	366	1
ever since I was born, man & boy 57 years, I think I must	S	1	366	1
Shepherd lives at one end, & three old women at the other."	S	1	366	1
He took the peices of paper as he spoke--& having looked	S	1	366	1
There are two Willingdens in this country--& your	S	1	366	1
or Willingden Abbots, & lies 7 miles off, on the other	S	1	366	1
Well sir--I dare say it is as you say, & I have made an	S	1	367	1
everything was in the hurry & confusion which always	S	1	367	1
myself with a breif enquiry, & finding we were actually to	S	1	367	1
setting the Carge to rights & turning the horses round,	S	1	367	1
steps into the turnpike road & proceed to Hailsham, & so	S	1	367	1
Hailsham, & so home, without attempting anything farther.--	S	1	367	1
Saline air & immersion will be the very thing.--	S	1	367	1
the ancle had been examined, & some refreshment taken, &	S	1	367	1
& some refreshment taken, & very cordially pressing them	S	1	367	1
common remedies for sprains & bruises--& I will answer for	S	1	367	1
for sprains & bruises--& I will answer for the pleasure it	S	1	367	1
it will give my wife & daughters to be of service to you &	S	1	367	1
service to you & this lady in every way in their power."--	S	1	367	1
of immediate assistance--& consulting his wife in the few	S	1	367	1
us."--turned again to Mr H--& said--"before we accept your	S	1	367	1
your hospitality sir,--& in order to do away with any	S	1	367	1
favourite--for a young & rising Bathing-Place, certainly	S	1	368	1
by nature, & promising to be the most chosen by man."--	S	1	368	1
or other starting up by the sea, & growing the fashion.--	S	1	368	1
the price of provisions & make the poor good for nothing--	S	1	368	1
the demand for every thing, & the sure resort of the very	S	1	368	1
of thorough gentility & character, who are a blessing	S	1	368	1
diffuse comfort & improvement among them of every sort.--	S	1	368	1
Every body's taste & every body's finances may be suited--	S	1	369	1
opinion excessively absurd, & must soon find themselves	S	1	369	1
stagnant marsh, a bleak moor & the constant effluvia of a	S	1	369	1
within 3 miles of the place--& as for the soil--it is so	S	1	369	1
for the soil--it is so cold & ungrateful that it can	S	1	369	1
if you have heard it differently spoken of-----"	S	1	369	1
applied to your leg--& I am sure by your lady's	S	1	370	1
she is quite of my opinion & thinks it a pity to lose any	S	1	370	1
to speak for themselves & their mother. (two or three	S	1	370	1
The young ladies approached & said every thing that was	S	1	370	1
their father's offers; & in an unaffected manner	S	1	370	1
The Heywoods were a thoroughly respectable family, & every	S	2	370	1
kindest & most unpretending manner, to both husband & wife.	S	2	370	1
<u>He</u> was waited on & nursed, & <u>she</u> cheered & comforted with	S	2	371	1
every office of hospitality & friendliness was received as	S	2	371	1
Mr Parker's character & history were soon unfolded.	S	2	371	1
he was very openhearted;--& where he might be himself in	S	2	371	1
A very few years ago, & it had been a quiet village of no	S	2	371	1
advantages in its position & some accidental circumstances	S	2	371	1
having suggested to himself, & the other principal land	S	2	371	1
they had engaged in it, & planned & built, & praised &	S	2	371	1

had engaged in it, & planned & built, & praised & puffed,	S	2	371	1
in it, & planned & built, & praised & puffed, & raised it	S	2	371	1
& planned & built, & praised & puffed, & raised it to a	S	2	371	1
& built, & praised & puffed, & raised it to a something of	S	2	371	1
were that he was about 5 & 30--had been married,--very	S	2	371	1
happily married 7 years--& had 4 sweet children at home;--	S	2	371	1
was of a respectable family, & easy though not large	S	2	371	1
generations had been holding & accumulating before him;--	S	2	371	1
and 2 sisters--all single & all independant--the eldest of	S	2	371	1
materially promote the rise & prosperity of the place--wd	S	2	372	1
Sanditon on that account--& probably very many more--and	S	2	372	1
who were sad invalids, & whom he was very anxious to get	S	2	372	1
of wife, Childn, brothers & sisters--& generally kind-	S	2	372	1
Childn, brothers & sisters--& generally kind-hearted;--	S	2	372	1
husband sometimes needed, & so entirely waiting to be	S	2	372	1
Sanditon was a second wife & 4 children to him--hardly	S	2	372	1
to him--hardly less dear--& certainly more engrossing.--	S	2	372	1
his lottery, his speculation & his Hobby Horse; his	S	2	372	1
his Hobby Horse; his occupation his hope & his futurity.--	S	2	372	1
were as grateful & disinterested, as they were warm.--	S	2	372	1
fortuitous aids of exercise & spirits in a semblance of	S	2	373	1
really in a state of secure & permanent health without	S	2	373	1
The sea air & sea bathing together were nearly infallible,	S	2	373	1
anti-sceptic, anti-bilious & anti-rheumatic.	S	2	373	1
They were healing, softing, relaxing--fortifying & bracing-	S	2	373	1
was the certain corrective;--& where bathing disagreed,	S	2	373	1
Mr & Mrs H-- never left home.	S	2	373	1
Marrying early & having a very numerous family, their	S	2	373	1
small circle; & they were older in habits than in age.--	S	2	373	1
Adventurings were only now & then to visit her neighbours,	S	2	373	1
been new when they married & fresh lined on their eldest	S	2	373	1
share of luxuries & change--enough for them to have	S	2	373	1
indulged in a new carriage & better roads, an occasional	S	2	373	1
month at Tunbridge Wells, & symptoms of the gout and a	S	2	373	1
the maintenance, education & fitting out of 14 children	S	2	373	1
obliged them to be stationary and healthy at Willingden.	S	2	373	1
They never left home, & they had a gratification in saying	S	2	374	1
When Mr & Mrs Parker therefore ceased from soliciting a	S	2	374	1
It was general pleasure & consent.--	S	2	374	1
of the daughters at home, & the one, who under her	S	2	374	1
had been particularly useful & obliging to them; who had	S	2	374	1
to them; who had attended them most, & knew them best.--	S	2	374	1
Charlotte was to go,--with excellent health, to bathe & be	S	2	374	1
of those she went with--& to buy new parasols, new gloves,	S	2	374	1
new parasols, new gloves, & new Broches, for her sisters &	S	2	374	1
new Broches, for her sisters & herself at the library,	S	2	374	1
who asked his advice, & that nothing should ever induce	S	2	374	1
The great lady of Sanditon, was Lady Denham; & in their	S	3	375	1
introduction of Lady Denham & that she was a very rich old	S	3	375	1
was very much looked up to & had a poor cousin living with	S	3	375	1
particulars of her history & her character served to	S	3	375	1
parish of Sanditon, with manor & mansion house made a part.	S	3	375	1
but she had so well nursed & pleased Mr Hollis, that at	S	3	375	1
her everything--all his estates, & all at her disposal.	S	3	375	1
succeeded in removing her & her large income to his own	S	3	375	1
that she had married--& Mr P. acknowledged there being	S	3	376	1
it is not offensive;--& there are moments, there are	S	3	376	1
frame for a woman of 70, & enters into the improvement of	S	3	376	1
admirable--though now & then, a littleness will appear.	S	3	376	1
She cannot look forward quite as I would have her--& takes	S	3	376	1
That is--we think differently, we now & then, see things	S	3	376	1
a year to bequeath, & three distinct sets of people to be	S	3	376	1
she had no doubt been long, & still continued to be, well	S	3	376	1
least in favour & Sir Harry Denham's the most.--	S	3	376	1
expressions of very unwise & unjustifiable resentment at	S	3	377	1
to her from their childhood, & of being always at hand to	S	3	377	1
constantly at Denham Park; & Mr P-- had little doubt, that	S	3	377	1
had little doubt, that he & his sister Miss D-- who lived	S	3	377	1
Miss Denham had a very small provision--& her brother was	S	3	377	1
"He is a warm friend to Sanditon--said Mr Parker--& his	S	3	377	1
As it is, he does what he can--& is running up a tasteful	S	3	377	1
any such addition, and long & often enjoyed the repeated	S	3	377	1
and to secure for herself & her family that share of the	S	3	377	1
Mr Parker spoke warmly of Clara Brereton, & the interest	S	3	378	1
now;--it was solicitude & enjoyment, as she heard her	S	3	378	1
with great good sense, & evidently gaining by her innate	S	3	378	1
Beauty, sweetness, poverty & dependance, do not want the	S	3	378	1
With due exceptions--woman feels for woman very promptly &	S	3	378	1
writing, inviting & tormenting her, & whom she was	S	3	378	1
inviting & tormenting her, & whom she was determined to	S	3	378	1
of such a home, & at the end of three days calling for her	S	3	378	1
another hour in the house, & she was preparing in all the	S	3	378	1
preparing in all the anger & perturbation which a beleif	S	3	378	1
gross imposition there, & an ignorance of where to go for	S	3	378	1
the cousins, the politic & lucky cousins, who seemed	S	3	378	1
at this important moment, & learning her situation,	S	3	378	1
She went; was delighted with her welcome & the hospitality	S	3	378	1
welcome & the hospitality & attention she received from	S	3	378	1
expectation worthy people--& finally was impelled by a	S	3	378	1
of their narrow income & pecuniary difficulties, to invite	S	3	378	1
a neice--, more helpless & more pitiable of course than	S	3	379	1
on an encumbered circle--& one, who had been so low in	S	3	379	1
all her natural endowments & powers, to have been	S	3	379	1
Clara had returned with her--& by her good Sence & merit	S	3	379	1
The six months had long been over--& not a syllable was	S	3	379	1
steady conduct & mild, gentle temper was felt by everybody.	S	3	379	1
& soften Lady D--who wd enlarge her mind & open her hand.--	S	3	379	1
She was as thoroughly amiable as she was lovely--& since	S	3	379	1
house, well fenced & planted, & rich in the garden,	S	4	379	1
well fenced & planted, & rich in the garden, orchard &	S	4	379	1
rich in the garden, orchard & meadows which are the best	S	4	379	1
house where I & all my brothers & sisters were born & bred-	S	4	379	1
where I & all my brothers & sisters were born & bred--&	S	4	379	1
brothers & sisters were born & bred--& where my own 3	S	4	379	1
& sisters were born & bred--& where my own 3 eldest	S	4	379	1
were born--where Mrs P. & I lived till within the last 2	S	4	379	1
He gets a better house by it--& I, a rather better	S	4	380	1
air or veiw, only one mile & 3 qrs from the noblest	S	4	380	1
& the Land's end, & without the smallest advantage from it.	S	4	380	1
However, Waterloo is in reserve--& if we have	S	4	380	1
call it Waterloo Crescent--& the name joined to the form	S	4	380	1
It supplies us, as before, with all the fruit & vegetables	S	4	380	1
fruit & vegetables we want; & we have in fact all the	S	4	380	1
"My dear, we shall have shade enough on the hill & more	S	4	381	1
comfort within doors--& you can get a parasol at Whitby's	S	4	381	1
"Yes indeed, I am sure we do--& I will get Mary a little	S	4	381	1
our house, simply rages & passes on--while down in this	S	4	381	1
that old Stringer & his son have a higher claim.	S	4	381	1
I encouraged him to set up--& am afraid he does not do	S	4	382	1
give him what help we can--& when any vegetables or fruit	S	4	382	1
fruit happen to be wanted--& it will not be amiss to have	S	4	382	1
"Very well my love, that can be easily done--& cook will	S	4	381	2
Andrew now, & says he never brings her what she wants.--	S	4	381	2
He has always said what he chose of & to us, all.	S	4	382	1
He is here & there & every where.	S	4	382	1
Such a young man as Sidney, with his neat equipage &	S	4	382	1
& fashionable air,--you & I Mary, know what effect it	S	4	382	1
it secure us, to the prejudice of E. Bourne & Hastings."--	S	4	382	1
They were now approaching the church & neat village of	S	4	382	1
was covered with the woods & enclosures of Sanditon house	S	4	382	1
to an inconsiderable stream, & formed at its mouth, a 3d	S	4	383	1
with delight to Charlotte, & two or three of the best of	S	4	383	1
up with a white curtain & "lodgings to let"--, and farther	S	4	383	1
to be seen with their books & camp stools--and in turning	S	4	383	1
Such sights & sounds were highly Blissful to Mr P.--	S	4	383	1
Blue shoes, & nankin boots!--	S	4	383	1
house, & saw the top of the house itself among its groves.	S	4	383	1
A little higher up, the modern began; & in crossing the	S	4	384	1
house, a Bellevue Cottage, & a denham place were to be	S	4	384	1
of amused curiosity, & by Mr P. with the eager eye which	S	4	384	1
to dinner--but the sands & the terrace always attracted	S	4	384	1
at his own house, & everywhere out of his house at once.	S	4	384	1
His spirits rose with the very sight of the sea & he cd	S	4	384	1
In this row were the best milliner's shop & the library--a	S	4	384	1
detached from it, the hotel & billiard room--here began	S	4	384	1
the descent to the beach, & to the bathing machines--&	S	4	384	1
& to the bathing machines--& this was therefore the	S	4	384	1
was therefore the favourite spot for beauty & fashion.--	S	4	384	1
were safely set down, & all was happiness & joy between	S	4	384	1
down, & all was happiness & joy between papa & mama &	S	4	384	1
happiness & joy between papa & mama & their children;	S	4	384	1
& joy between papa & mama & their children; while	S	4	384	1
her ample Venetian window, & looking over the	S	4	384	1
buildings, waving linen, & tops of houses, to the sea,	S	4	384	1
to the sea, dancing & sparkling in sunshine & freshness.--	S	4	384	1
I sent him an account of my accident from Willingden, &	S	5	385	1
& are subject to a variety of very serious disorders.--	S	5	385	1
what a day's health is;--& at the same time, they are such	S	5	385	1
such excellent useful women & have so much energy of	S	5	385	1
They have only weaker constitutions & stronger minds than	S	5	385	1
And our youngest Br--who lives with them, & who is not	S	5	385	1
Having run his eye over the letter, he shook his head &	S	5	385	1
will be quite sorry to hear how ill they have been & are.--	S	5	386	1
I like to have my friends acquainted with each other--& I	S	5	386	1
in existence, & therefore must give a good impression."	S	5	386	1
"My dear Tom, we were all much greived at your accident, &	S	5	386	1
Bile & hardly able to crawl from my bed to the sofa.--	S	5	386	1
he was cleaning the carriage & cd hardly limp into the	S	5	386	1
steadily persevered in, (& I rubbed his ancle with my own	S	5	386	1
they can do nothing for us & that we must trust to our own	S	5	386	1
commission with pleasure, & have no doubt of succeeding.--	S	5	387	1
She has accordingly had 3 teeth drawn, & is decidedly	S	5	387	1
more languid than I like--& I fear for his Liver.--	S	5	387	1
Most sincerely do we wish you a good season at Sanditon, &	S	5	387	1
you company worth having; & think we may safely reckon on	S	5	387	1
entertaining in this letter & make us laugh for half an	S	5	387	1
the end house of the terrace,--& extra beds at the hotel.--	S	5	388	1
operation--to every operation--& have such fortitude!--"	S	5	388	1
it too far sometimes--& so do you my love, you know.--	S	5	388	1
they wd leave themselves more alone--& especially Arthur.	S	5	388	1
sickly for any profession--& sit down at 1 & 20, on the	S	5	388	1
early visit to the library, & the library Subscription	S	6	389	1
library Subscription book, & Charlotte was glad to see as	S	6	389	1
see as much, & as quickly as possible, where all was new.	S	6	389	1
inhabited lodging;--here & there a solitary elderly man	S	6	389	1
who was forced to move early & walk for health--but in	S	6	389	1
& tranquillity on the terrace, the cliffs, & the sands.--	S	6	389	1
The shops were deserted--the straw hats & pendant lace	S	6	389	1
fate both within the house & without, and Mrs Whitby at	S	6	389	1
The Lady Denham, Miss Brereton, Mr & Mrs P---- Sir Edw:	S	6	389	1
& Mrs P---- Sir Edw: Denham & Miss Denham, whose names	S	6	389	1
Dr & Mrs Brown--Mr Richard Pratt.--	S	6	389	1
Mrs Davis. & Miss Merryweather.--	S	6	389	1
It was but July however, & August & September were the	S	6	389	1
from Surry & Camberwell, were an ever-ready consolation.--	S	6	389	1
him to every body, & they were fully occupied in their	S	6	390	1
in their various civilities & communications, while	S	6	390	1
all her glossy curls & smart trinkets to wait on her.--	S	6	390	1
that cd not be done without, & among so many pretty	S	6	390	1
so many pretty temptations, & with so much good will for	S	6	390	1
she reflected that at two & twenty there cd be no excuse	S	6	390	1
for her doing otherwise--& that it wd not do for her to be	S	6	390	1
She had not Camilla's youth, & had no intention of having	S	6	390	1
from the drawers of rings & Broches repressed farther	S	6	390	1
farther solicitation & paid for what she bought.--	S	6	390	1
an alteration necessary, Lady Denham & Miss Brereton.--	S	6	390	1
They had been to Trafalgar house, & been directed thence	S	6	390	1
thence to the library, & though Lady D. was a great deal	S	6	390	1
as any thing requiring rest, & talked of going home again	S	6	390	1
be pressed into their house, & obliged to take her tea	S	6	390	1
them, would suit her best,--& therefore the stroll on the	S	6	390	1
No, no, Miss Clara & I will get back to our own tea.--	S	6	390	1
We wanted just to see you & make sure of your being really	S	6	391	1
She went on however towards Trafalgar house & took	S	6	391	1
Lady D. was of middle height, stout, upright & alert in	S	6	391	1
motions, with a shrewd eye, & self-satisfied air--but not	S	6	391	1
an unagreable countenance--& tho' her manner was rather	S	6	391	1
manner was rather downright & abrupt, as of a person who	S	6	391	1
there was a good humour & cordiality about her--a civility	S	6	391	1
about her--a civility & readiness to be acquainted with	S	6	391	1
with Charlotte herself, & a heartiness of welcome towards	S	6	391	1
great delicacy of complexion & soft blue eyes, a sweetly	S	6	391	1
blue eyes, a sweetly modest & yet naturally graceful	S	6	391	1
might be most beautiful & bewitching, in all the numerous	S	6	391	1
Such poverty & dependance joined to such beauty & merit,	S	6	391	1
influenced by them; & while she pleased herself the first	S	6	391	1
in the degree of observance & attention which clara paid.--	S	6	392	1
kindness, on the other grateful & affectionate respect.--	S	6	392	1
present number of Visitants & the chances of a good season.	S	6	392	1
She wanted tp have the place fill faster, & seemed to have	S	6	392	1
A West Indy family & a school.	S	6	392	1
demand for them & such a diffusion of money among us, as	S	6	392	1
Our Butchers & Bakers & Traders in general cannot get rich	S	6	392	1
If they do not gain, our rents must be insecure--& in	S	6	393	1
raised, though--& I shall keep it down as long as I can.--	S	6	393	1
I am not a woman of parade, as all the world knows, & if	S	6	393	1
but some may be consumptive & want Asses milk--& I have	S	6	393	1
milk--& I have two Milch Asses at this present time.--	S	6	393	1
It wd be only encouraging our servants & the poor to fancy	S	6	393	1
There is the sea & the downs & my Milch-Asses--& I have	S	6	393	1
Here have I lived 70 good years in the world & never took	S	6	394	1
very neighbourly, I beleive Miss Clara & I must stay."----	S	6	394	1
them, Sir Edwd Denham & his sister, who having been at	S	7	394	1
on to pay their compliments; & the duty of letter-writing	S	7	394	1
by an introduction to them, & found them, the better half	S	7	394	1
Miss D. was a fine young woman, but cold & reserved,	S	7	394	1
her consequence with pride & her poverty with discontent,	S	7	394	1
her poverty with discontent, & who was immediately gnawed	S	7	394	1
& which their groom was leading about still in her sight.--	S	7	394	1
Sir Edwd was much her superior in air & manner;--certainly	S	7	394	1
address & wish of paying attention & giving pleasure.--	S	7	394	1
He came into the room remarkably well, talked much--& very	S	7	394	1
he chanced to be placed--& she soon perceived that he had	S	7	394	1
gentleness of voice, & a great deal of conversation.	S	7	394	1
Sober-minded as she was, she thought him agreable, & did	S	7	395	1
to go, & persisting in his station & his discourse.--	S	7	395	1
of life, more dull of fancy & more careless of pleasing, I	S	7	395	1
of pleasing, I know them not, & never wish to know them.--	S	7	395	1
which commanded the road & all the paths across the down,	S	7	395	1
across the down, Charlotte & Sir Edw: as they sat, could	S	7	395	1
not but observe Lady D. & Miss B. walking by--& there was	S	7	395	1
D. & Miss B. walking by--& there was instantly a slight	S	7	395	1
her of her halfhour's fever, & placed her in a more	S	7	395	1
"Perhaps there was a good deal in his air & address; and	S	7	395	1

must begin with the terrace, & there, seated on one of the S 7 395 1
one end of the bench, & Sir Edw: & Miss B. at the other.-- S 7 395 1
not have been able to prevent) her air was calm & grave.-- S 7 395 1
Lady D.'s elbow, listening & talking with smiling S 7 396 1
on their all joining & agreeing to walk, & by addressing S 7 396 1
walk, & by addressing his attentions entirely to herself.-- S 7 396 1
of the party & to give her the whole of his conversation. S 7 396 1
He began, in a tone of great taste & feeling, to talk of S 7 396 1
feeling, to talk of the sea & the sea shore--& ran with S 7 396 1
of the sea & the sea shore--& ran with energy through all S 7 396 1
praise of their sublimity, & descriptive of the S 7 396 1
in a calm, it's Gulls & its samphire, & the deep fathoms S 7 396 1
it's Gulls & its samphire, & the deep fathoms of it's S 7 396 1
tempting it in sunshine & overwhelmed by the sudden S 7 396 1
tempest, all were eagerly & fluently touched;--rather S 7 396 1
quotations, & the bewilderment of some of his sentences.-- S 7 396 1
our sensations--"like Angel's visits, few & far between." S 7 397 1
from his character;--& poor Burns's known irregularities, S 7 397 1
He felt & he wrote & he forgot." S 7 398 1
He was all ardour & truth!-- S 7 398 1
His genius & his susceptibilities might lead him into some S 7 398 1
it at all, not very moral--& being moreover by no means S 7 398 1
of some feelings or other, & very much addicted to all the S 7 398 1
clear brain she presumed, & talked a good deal by rote.-- S 7 398 1
of Sir Edw: for one morng, & very gladly accepted Lady D. S 7 398 1
in tearing himself away, & they united their agreeableness-- S 7 398 1
a true great lady, talked & talked only of her own S 7 399 1
only of her own concerns, & Charlotte listened--amused in S 7 399 1
from her was an honour, & communicative, from the S 7 399 1
tone of great satisfaction--& with a look of arch sagacity- S 7 399 1
wants me to invite her & her brother to spend a week with S 7 399 1
this, & her praise of that; but I saw what she was about.-- S 7 399 1
than the simple enquiry of--"Sir Edward & Miss Denham?"-- S 7 399 1
to Monday; and very delighted & thankful they were.-- S 7 399 1
I always take care to know what I am about & who I have to S 7 399 1
I do not think I was ever over-reached in my life; & that S 7 399 1
But (with a bit of a sigh) he is gone, & we must not find S 7 399 1
Nobody could live happier together than us--& he was a S 7 400 1
produce a great impression--& seeing no rapturous S 7 400 1
He only told me, & <u>that</u> but once, that he shd wish his S 7 400 1
"Yes, my dear--& it <u>is</u> not the <u>only</u> kind thing I have done S 7 400 1
the <u>dowager</u> my dear, & he is the <u>heir</u>, things do not stand S 7 400 1
a shrewd glance at her & replying--"yes, yes, he is very S 7 400 1
he is very well to look at--& it is to be hoped that some S 7 400 1
He & I often talk that matter over.-- S 7 400 1
A handsome young fellow like him, will go smirking & S 7 400 1
go smirking & smiling about & paying girls compliments, S 7 400 1
And Sir Edw: is a very steady man in the main, & has got S 7 400 1
& stay at Sanditon house, she will find herself mistaken.-- S 7 401 1
evidence of real penetration & prepared for some fuller S 7 401 1
me in the face at this very moment, numbers 3, 4 & 8. S 7 402 1
fit for a young gentleman & his sister--and so, my dear, S 7 402 1
the dampness of Denham Park, & the good bathing always S 7 402 1
to come & take one of these lodgings for a fortnight.-- S 7 402 1
Charlotte's feelings were divided between amusement & S 7 402 1
indignation had the larger & the increasing share.-- S 7 402 1
She kept her countenance & she kept a civil silence. S 7 402 1
attempting to listen longer, & only conscious that Lady D. S 7 402 1
He has persuaded her to engage in the same speculation--& S 7 402 1
This poor Sir Edward & his sister.--how far nature meant S 7 402 1
We have many leisure hours, & read a great deal.-- S 8 403 1
Such are the works which I peruse with delight, & I hope I S 8 403 1
by the tranquil & morbid virtues of any opposing character. S 8 404 1
capabilities of the heart, & which it cannot impugn the S 8 404 1
His fancy had been early caught by all the impassioned, & S 8 404 1
parts of Richardsons; & such authors as have since S 8 404 1
every opposition of feeling & convenience is concerned, S 8 404 1
part of his literary hours, & formed his character.-- S 8 404 1
the spirit, the sagacity, & the perseverance, of the S 8 404 1
all his absurdities & all his atrocities with Sir Edward. S 8 404 1
With him, such conduct was genius, fire & feeling.-- S 8 404 1
It interested & inflamed him; & he was always more anxious S 8 404 1
more anxious for its success & mourned over its S 8 404 1
He read all the Essays, letters, Tours & criticisms of the S 8 404 1
& criticisms of the day--& with the same ill-luck which S 8 404 1
from lessons of morality, & incentives to vice from the S 8 404 1
he gathered only hard words & involved sentences from the S 8 404 1
he knew himself to possess, & such talents as he did also S 8 405 2
To be generally gallant & assiduous about the fair, to S 8 405 2
with high compliment & Rhapsody on the slightest S 8 405 2
in Lady D.'s favour, she was young, lovely & dependant.-- S 8 405 2
He had very early seen the necessity of the case, & had S 8 405 2
Clara saw through him, & had not the least intention of S 8 405 2
was ill-suited to his purse, & prudence obliged him to S 8 405 2
the quietest sort of ruin & disgrace for the object of his S 8 405 2
as very lately arrived, & by the quantity of Luggage S 9 406 1
Delighted to have such good news for Mr & Mrs P., who had S 9 406 1
to hurry on & get into the house if possible before her. S 9 406 1
was on the steps & had rung, but the door was not opened, S 9 406 1
The ease of the lady, her "how do you do Morgan?--" & S 9 406 1
"How did she come? & with whom?-- S 9 406 1
Miss Diana P. was about 4 & 30, of middling height & S 9 407 1
with an agreable face, & a very animated eye;--her manners S 9 407 1
her brother's in their ease & frankness, though with more S 9 407 1
though with more decision & less mildness in her tone. S 9 407 1
come, & meant to get into lodgings & make some stay."-- S 9 407 1
Susan & Arthur!-- S 9 407 1
This was better & better." S 9 407 1
"And how has Susan born the journey?--& how is Arthur?--& S 9 407 1
how is Arthur?--& why do not we see him here with you?"-- S 9 407 1
Mr Woodcock's assistance--& when I left her she was S 9 407 1
of the Luggage, & helping old Sam uncord the trunks.-- S 9 407 1
coat & sent him off to the terrace, to take us lodgings.-- S 9 407 1
That's right; all right & clean. S 9 407 1
to secure for you--the West Indians, & the seminary.--" S 9 408 1
Here Mr P. drew his chair still nearer to his sister, & S 9 408 1
"yes, yes;--how active & how kind you have been!"-- S 9 408 1
best of the good--prove to be a Mrs Griffiths & her family. S 9 408 1
Only a <u>short</u> chain, you see, between us, & not a link S 9 408 1
& wrote to ask the opinion of her friend Mrs Darling.-- S 9 408 1
Mrs G.'s letter arrived, & was consulted on the question; S 9 408 1
and mentioned it to her--& Fanny all alive for <u>us</u>, S 9 408 1
instantly took up her pen & forwarded the circumstance to S 9 408 1
I answered Fanny's letter by the same post & pressed for S 9 408 1
recommended by Mrs Darling, & that the West-Indians were S 9 408 1
no connections in the place, & no means of ascertaining S 9 409 1
she was particularly careful & scrupulous on all those S 9 409 1
than all the rest--& very delicate health.-- S 9 409 1
& indolent, as wealth & a hot climate are apt to make us. S 9 409 1
left Chichester at the same hour today--& here we are.--" S 9 409 1
Diana, you are unequal'd in serving your friends & doing S 9 409 1
I shall take only one however, & that, but for a week S 9 410 1
& I know what Invalides both you & your sister are." S 9 410 1
useful as possible, & where some degree of strength of S 9 410 1
between the weak of mind & the strong--between those who S 9 410 1
those who can act & those who can not, & it is the bounden S 9 410 1
can act & those who can not, & it is the bounden duty of S 9 410 1
My sister's complaints & mine are happily not often of a S 9 410 1
existence <u>immediately</u>--& as long as we <u>can</u> exert ourselves S 9 410 1
on her own <u>disposition</u>--& after having <u>noticed</u> & caressed S 9 410 1
having noticed & caressed them all,--she prepared to go.-- S 9 410 1
"I will come to you the moment I have dined, said he, & we S 9 410 1
Our dinner is not ordered till six--& by that time I hope S 9 411 1
at the hotel all the eveng, & delighted to see you at any S 9 411 1
done about our own lodgings, & probably the moment dinner S 9 411 1
lodgings or other & be settled after breakfast tomorrow.-- S 9 411 1
Susan never eats I grant you--& just at present <u>I</u> shall S 9 411 1
Camberwell will be here to a certainty, & very soon.-- S 9 411 1
& independant as Mrs G.--can travel & chuse for herself.-- S 9 411 1
intending to make some stay, & without appearing to have S 10 412 1
Disorders & Recoveries so very much out of the common way, S 10 412 1
in want of employment than of actual afflictions & releif. S 10 412 1
The parkers, were no doubt a family of imagination & quick S 10 412 1
the love of distinction & the love of the wonderful.-- S 10 412 1
They had charitable hearts & many amiable feelings--but a S 10 412 1
spirit of restless activity, & the glory of doing more S 10 412 1
Mr & Mrs P. spent a great part of the eveng at the hotel; S 10 413 1
lady whom she had never seen, & who had never employed her. S 10 413 1
being removed into lodgings & all the party continuing S 10 413 1
& sister & herself were entreated to drink tea with them.-- S 10 413 1
They were in one of the terrace houses--& she found them S 10 413 1
open window, but the sopha & the table, & the S 10 413 1
but the sopha & the table, & the establishment in general S 10 413 1
or manner--tho' more thin & worn by illness & Medecine, S 10 413 1
& Medecine, more relaxed in air, & more subdued in voice. S 10 413 1
as incessantly as Diana--& excepting that she sat with S 10 413 1
at home on the mantelpeice,--& made a great many odd faces S 10 413 1
made a great many odd faces & contortions, Charlotte could S 10 413 1
fire, opening the window, & disposing of the drops & the S 10 413 1
of the drops & the salts by means of one or the other. S 10 413 1
to see Mr Arthur Parker; & having fancied him a very puny, S 10 413 1
quite as tall as his brother & a great deal Stouter--broad S 10 413 1
deal Stouter--broad made & Lusty--and with no other look S 10 413 1
the family; principal Mover & actor;--she had been on her S 10 414 1
or their own, & was still the most alert of the three.-- S 10 414 1
two heavy boxes herself, & Arthur had found the air so S 10 414 1
as nimbly as he could,--& boasted much of sitting by the S 10 414 1
not only had she by walking & talking down a thousand S 10 414 1
housemaids, Washer-women & bathing women, that Mrs G. S 10 414 1
to wave her hand & collect them around her for choice.-- S 10 414 1
Mr & Mrs P.-- & Charlotte had seen two post chaises S 10 414 1
were setting off,--a joyful sight--& full of speculation.-- S 10 414 1
The Miss Ps-- & Arthur had also seen something;--they S 10 414 1
removals to look at the sea & the hotel, Charlotte's place S 10 414 1
of his person as a screen, & was very thankful for every S 10 415 1
inch of back & shoulders beyond her preconceived idea. S 10 415 1
Such was the influence of youth & bloom that he began even S 10 415 1
It has always some property that is wholesome & S 10 415 1
She kept her countenance however, & said--"as far as I can S 10 416 1
idea of the efficacy of air & exercise for them:--daily, S 10 416 1
"Oh! I am very fond of exercise myself--he replied--& mean S 10 416 1
I shall be out every morning before breakfast--& take S 10 416 1
the terrace, & you will often see me at Trafalgar house."-- S 10 416 1
It produced a great & immediate change. S 10 416 1
one sort of Herb-Tea & Miss Diana another, & turning S 10 416 1
& Miss Diana another, & turning completely to the fire, S 10 416 1
it to his own satisfaction & toasting some slices of bread, S 10 416 1
of a few broken sentences of self-approbation & success.-- S 10 416 1
as gallant a line as ever, & proved that he had not been S 10 416 1
his earnest invitation to her to take both cocoa & toast.-- S 10 416 1
you get your cocoa stronger & stronger every eveng"--, S 10 417 1
conversation on dry toast, & hear no more of his sisters.-- S 10 417 1
too near the fire at first--& yet, you see, there is not a S 10 417 1
you directly--& afterwards I will spread some for myself.-- S 10 417 1
It irritates & acts like a nutmeg grater.--" S 10 417 1
a great deal too much, & declaring he was not to be S 10 417 1
besides, he only wanted it now for Miss Heywood.-- S 10 417 1
Such a plea must prevail, he got the butter & spread away S 10 417 1
but when her toast was done, & he took his own in hand, S 10 417 1
as much butter as he put on, & then seize an odd moment S 10 417 1
of an indolent temper--& to be determined on having no S 10 418 1
but such as called for warm rooms & good nourishment.-- S 10 418 1
who have studied right sides & green tea scientifically & S 10 418 1
& green tea scientifically & thoroughly understand all the S 10 418 1
This is a letter of recommendation & introduction to me, S 10 419 1
Camberwell--& <u>her</u> name happens to be griffiths too.--" S 10 419 1
rushed into her cheeks, & with much perturbation she added- S 10 419 1
Mrs G.-- from Camberwell, & the three young ladies under S 10 419 1
a respectable introduction--& Mrs C. Dupuis therefore, at S 10 419 1
Mrs G.'s cheif solicitude wd be for the accomodation & S 10 419 1
"Impossible" & "impossible", was repeated over & over S 10 419 1
An accidental resemblance of names & circumstances, S 10 419 1
She must put her shawl over her shoulders, & be running S 10 619 1
the hotel, to investigate the truth & offer her services.-- S 10 419 1
Surry & the family from Camberwell were one & the same.-- S 11 420 1
The rich Westindians, & the young ladies seminary had all S 11 420 1
had wavered as to coming & been unequal to the journey, S 11 420 1
decided, & who was without fears or difficulties.-- S 11 420 1
in the cause by the vigilance & caution of Miss Diana P--. S 11 420 1
<u>Her</u> intimate friends must be officious like herself, & the S 11 420 1
subject had supplied letters & extracts & messages enough S 11 420 1
supplied letters & extracts & messages enough to make S 11 420 1
her immediate reflections--& much worse than all the rest, S 11 420 1
clear-sighted & infallible than she had beleived herself.-- S 11 420 1
There were so many to share in the shame & the blame, that S 11 420 1
Fanny Noyce, Mrs D. dupuis & Mrs C. D's neighbour, there S 11 420 1
receiving such great girls & young ladies, as wanted S 11 420 1
Of these three, & indeed of all, Miss Lambe was beyond S 11 421 1
& precious, as she paid in proportion to her fortune.-- S 11 421 1
She was about 17, half Mulatto, chilly & tender, had a S 11 421 1
best room in the lodgings, & was always of the first S 11 421 1
an upright decided carriage & an assured look;--they were S 11 421 1
were very accomplished & very ignorant, their time being S 11 421 1
as might attract admiration, & those labours & expedients S 11 421 1
admiration, & those labours & expedients of dexterous S 11 421 1
in every change of fashion--& the object of all, was to S 11 421 1
any thing to smallness & retirement, yet having in the S 11 421 1
There, with the hire of a harp for one, & the purchase of S 11 421 1
drawing paper for the other & all the finery they could S 11 421 1
economical, very elegant & very secluded; with the hope on S 11 421 1
Beaufort's side, of praise & celebrity from all who walked S 11 421 1
the sound of her instrument, & on Miss Letitia's, of S 11 421 1
Miss Letitia's, of curiosity & rapture in all who came S 11 421 1
the Trafalgar House-Family, & with the Denhams;--and the S 11 421 1
to be attributed the giddiness & false steps of many.-- S 11 421 1
In Miss Lambe, here was the very young lady, sickly & rich, S 11 422 1
she had been asking for; & she made the acquaintance for S 11 422 1
for Sir Edward's sake, & the sake of her Milch Asses. S 11 422 1
of settling her new friends, & considering that it S 11 422 1
the visitors at Sanditon, & on one side, whatever might be S 11 422 1
many an eye upwards, & made many a Gazer gaze again.-- S 11 422 1
round about, & added two steps to the ascent of the hill. S 11 422 1
& sound her ladyship as to a Subscription for them. S 12 423 1
their distress is very great & I almost promised the poor S 12 423 1
set a Subscription on foot--& therefore the sooner the S 12 423 1
the sooner the better,--& Lady Denham's name at the head S 12 423 1
earnest application to me, & my being willing to promote a S 12 423 1
All said & done, in less time than you have been talking S 12 423 1
& I have undertaken to collect whatever I can for her. S 12 424 1
Lady Denham <u>can</u> give, if she is properly attacked--& I S 12 424 1
of another charity which I & a few more, have very much at S 12 424 1
that I promised to come & keep up her spirits, & go in the S 12 424 1
come & keep up her spirits, & go in the Machine with her S 12 424 1
he will certainly eat & drink more than he ought; --but S 12 424 1

felt all their impropriety & all the certainty of their S 12 425 1
Mrs P. was delighted at this release, & set off very happy S 12 425 1
friend & her little girl, on this walk to Sanditon house.-- S 12 425 1
It was a close, misty morng, & when they reached the brow S 12 425 1
one horse to 4; & just as they were concluding in favour S 12 425 1
distinguished the coachman & she eagerly called out, "T'is S 12 425 1
opposite to them, & they all stopped for a few minutes. S 12 425 1
pleasant among themselves--& it was a very friendly S 12 425 1
meeting between Sidney & his sister in law, who was most S 12 425 1
The rest was common enquiries & remarks, with kind notice S 12 425 1
kind notice of little Mary, & a very well-bred bow & S 12 425 1
Mary, & a very well-bred bow & proper address to Miss S 12 425 1
Sidney Parker was about 7 or 8 & 20, very good-looking, S 12 425 1
decided air of ease & fashion, and a lively countenance.-- S 12 425 1
joy on the occasion, & exulted in the credit which S 12 425 1
approach, between fields, & conducting at the end of a qr S 12 426 1
extensive had all the beauty & respectability which an S 12 426 1
& a curve <u>there</u> threw them to a better distance. S 12 426 1
there were vacant spaces--& through one of these, S 12 426 1
the pales of something white & Womanish in the field on S 12 426 1
Miss B. into her head--& stepping to the pales, she saw S 12 426 1
the pales, she saw indeed--& very decidedly, in spite of S 12 426 1
the outside of the paling & which a narrow path seemed to S 12 426 1
apparently very composedly--& Sir E. D. by her side.-- S 12 426 1
They were sitting so near each other & appeared so closely S 12 426 1
nothing to do but to step back again, & say not a word.-- S 12 426 1
before them--a steep bank & pales never crossed by the S 12 427 1
The house was large & handsome; two servants appeared, to S 12 427 1
& every thing had a suitable air of property & order.-- S 12 427 1
Lady D. valued herself upon her liberal establishment, & S 12 427 1
room, well-proportioned & well-furnished;--tho' it was S 12 427 1
rather originally good & extremely well kept, than new or S 12 427 1
had leisure to look about, & to be told by Mrs P. that the S 12 427 1
stand back in his own house & see the best place by the S 12 427 1

&C (35)

so well, & am, with best love &c., Cath. Vernon. LS 3 247 1
I am &c. Cath. Vernon. LS 8 256 4
of my intentions very soon.-- yours &c. S. Vernon. LS 10 258 4
assurances as to marriage &c., do not set my heart at ease. LS 13 262 1
mortify & distress me.-- I am &c. R. De Courcy. LS 14 265 6
to an higher power. yours ever &c. Cath. Vernon. LS 15 267 8
Adieu my dear madam, Yrs &c. Cath. Vernon. LS 20 279 12
be easy if her daughter were not with her, for masters, &c. LS 41 310 3
pretended only to comfort, &c.; flattering himself however NA II 5 162 27
beware how you give your heart. "believe me," &c. NA II 10 202 7
in writing to him and to me, who ever am, &c. NA II 12 218 2
to see them, and love to Miss Marianne, I am, &c. &c. SS III 2 278 30
most imminent--the Palmers all gone off in a fright, &c.-- SS III 8 330 69
unable to accept the honour of their invitation, &c. PP I 3 9 4
with me. "yours, &c." PP I 7 31 30
I am sure you will be very comfortable there. "your's, &c. PP II 3 149 26
"I am, dear sir, &c. &c, PP III 6 297 11
your's, &c. "Edw. Gardiner." PP III 7 303 14
mother.--your's, &c. "E. Gardiner." PP III 8 313 19
He should be particularly happy at any time, &c. &c.; and PP III 13 344 3
Yours, &c." PP III 18 383 21
"Yours sincerely, &c. PP III 18 383 23
"Your's, &c." PP III 19 386 7
sons--of cousins in love, &c.;--but no sooner had he MP I 1 6 5
they could all see it, &c." but her only offer of exchange MP I 8 81 32
from the Mediterranean, &c.; and the good luck which MP II 6 232 13
your note, I remain, dear Miss Crawford, &c. &c." MP II 13 307 31
I wish you may not repent it. "yours, &c." MP III 15 437 3
You will see me early, by the mail. your's, &c." MP III 15 443 23
Emma would be "very happy to wait on Mrs. Bates, &c." and E II 9 237 47
48
regulations, food, hours, &c.; and their surprise at his P III 8 64 4
cold the day before, &c. &c." which was all as politely P IV 3 143 18
Yours most affecly--&c" S 5 387 1
to mortals given with less of earth in them than heaven" &c S 7 397 1
with almost as many Teapots &c as there were persons in S 10 416 1

&C. (22)

grossly deceived by her at once. Yrs &c. Cath. Vernon. LS 6 252 2
music, singing, drawing &c. will gain a woman some LS 7 253 1
in your opinion of her. I am &c. Regd De Courcy. LS 12 261 6
repeating after her ladyship. I am &c. Cath. Vernon. LS 17 272 8
At present it is not very likely. Yrs &c. Cath. Vernon. LS 41 310 5
of their brothers, &c. which Catherine heard with pleasure, NA I 4 33 6
&c. extorting from him occasional questions and remarks. SS I 16 89 42
china, &c. to supply the place of what was taken away. SS II 11 225 35
their coming to town, &c. which Edward ought to have SS II 13 241 22
to see them, and love to Miss Marianne, I am, &c. &c. SS III 2 278 30
was above with her sister, &c. she urged him so strongly SS III 7 309 5
Kenelworth, Birmingham, &c. are sufficiently known. PP II 19 240 12
"I am, dear sir, &c. &c, PP III 6 297 11
He should be particularly happy at any time, &c. &c.; and PP III 13 344 3
your note, I remain, dear Miss Crawford, &c. &c." MP II 13 307 31
them again on the morrow, &c. and so they parted--Fanny in MP III 10 406 22
her, a quick low pulse, &c. and she was sorry to find from E I 13 109 6
supper; merely sandwiches, &c. set out in the little room; E II 11 254 45
as to modes of agriculture, &c. and Emma received a smile E III 6 361 40
bear any degree of cold, &c. but heat was intolerable--and E III 6 363 53
away in his coat pocket, &c. to have another moment for P III 6 49 25
taken cold the day before, &c. &c." which was all as P IV 3 143 18

Context	Text	Vol.	Ch.	Page	Line
---- (18)					
"And what are you reading, Miss ----?"	NA	I	5	38	4
isabella:-- Bath, April---- my dearest Catherine, I	NA	II	12	216	1
					2
son of his uncle, Lord ---- and to the great surprise of	PP	II	7	170	7
for the town of ---- in Hertfordshire; and, as they drew	PP	II	16	219	1
The carriage was sent to meet them at ----, and they were	PP	III	9	315	1
They were in ---- street.	PP	III	10	322	2
Mr. Bertram set off for ----, and Miss Crawford was	MP	I	6	52	1
he would have taken a ---- not a good temper into it; and	MP	I	11	111	30
To Miss ----.	E	I	9	71	14
"For Miss ----, read Miss Smith.	E	I	9	73	18
Only think of those sweet verses--'to Miss ----.'	E	I	9	74	22
"---- The best of all.	E	I	9	77	42
The marriage of Lieut. Fairfax, of the ---- regiment of	E	II	2	163	2
worthy young man--but'---- in short, I do not think I am	E	II	3	176	44
that period to her at ---- : in short, the full direction	E	III	14	442	8
case, for lady, read ---- mum! a word to the wise.--	E	III	16	454	13
than to any mere Mr. ---- ; a Mr. (save, perhaps, some	P	III	3	24	36
"February 1st, ----. "my dear Anne, "I make no apology	P	IV	6	162	7
----SHIRE (12)					
he was to have a lieutenant's commission in the ----shire.'	PP	I	15	73	11
The officers of the ----shire were in general a very	PP	I	16	76	3
I hope your plans in favour of the ----shire will not be	PP	I	16	78	19
"which was my chief inducement to enter the ----shire.	PP	I	16	79	23
his entrance into the ----shire militia, in which he had	PP	II	13	205	4
this summer, after the ----shire have left Meryton, and	PP	II	16	219	4
Eliza, are not the ----shire militia removed from Meryton?	PP	III	3	269	8
					9
Since the ----shire were first quartered in Meryton,	PP	III	5	283	10
And when I returned home, the ----shire was to leave	PP	III	5	285	16
of his companions in the ----shire, might be able to give	PP	III	6	296	8
from the ----shire, as clearly as Mr. Gardiner could do.	PP	III	8	313	20
the ----shire, and of his being gone into the regulars.	PP	III	11	337	51

1 & 20 (1)
sit down at 1 & 20, on the interest of his own little — S 5 388 1
10GS (1)
on to undraw her purse, would as readily give 10Gs as 5.-- — S 12 424 1
12TH LIGHT DRAGOONS (1)
of the 12th Light Dragoons, (the hope of the nation,) — NA I 14 113 39
14TH (2)
till after the 14th, for we have a party that evening. — MP III 12 417 3
before or after the 14th, was certainly no concern of — MP III 12 418 4
15TH OCTOBER (1)
Hunsford, near Westerham, Kent, 15th October. — PP I 13 62 12
17 (1)
She was about 17, half Mulatto, chilly & tender, had a — S 11 421 1
1800 (1)
by which lady (who died 1800) he has issue Elizabeth, born — P III 1 3 1
1806 (1)
in the summer of 1806; and having no parent living, found — P III 4 26 1
1814 (1)
time, (the summer of 1814,) wearing black ribbons for his — P III 1 8 17
19 (1)
have forgiven the person who kept me from a ball at 19." — W 320 2
190 MILES (1)
"Yes, they are about 190 miles from London. — E II 18 306 9
1ST (3)
kind as to promise to dance the two 1st dances with him."-- — W 330 11
selfishness reflect, 1st, that he had not been half so — MP I 3 24 4
"February 1st, ----. "my dear Anne, "I make no apology — P IV 6 162 7
50 (1)
50, she was very handsome, & had all the dignity of rank.-- — W 329 9
57 (1)
since I was born, man & boy 57 years, I think I must have — S 1 366 1
3D (4)
On the 3d day after the ball, as Nanny at five minutes — W 344 21
I have hardly taken out a gun since the 3d. — MP II 1 181 16
& formed at its mouth, a 3d habitable division, in a small — S 4 383 1
Had there been a 3d carriage, perhaps it might; but it was — S 10 414 1
3DLY (1)
piece of work of it; and 3dly, that the future incumbent, — MP I 3 24 4
4 (9)
But he had won 4 rubbers out of 5, & everything went well. — W 336 14
one thousand pounds in the 4 per cents. which will not be — PP I 19 106 10
married 7 years--& had 4 sweet children at home;--that he — S 2 371 1
Sanditon was a second wife & 4 children to him--hardly — S 2 372 1
me in the face at this very moment, numbers 3, 4 & 8. — S 7 402 1
Miss Diana P. was about 4 & 30, of middling height & — S 9 407 1
It is now only 1/2 past 4.-- — S 9 411 1
talk;--and while the other 4 were cheifly engaged together, — S 10 415 1
Pheaton,--from one horse to 4; & just as they were — S 12 425 1
40 (1)
at the distance of 40 years, but she had so well nursed & — S 3 375 1
20 (4)
of her beauty, and her 20,000l. any one who could satisfy — MP III 17 469 24
a still-born son, nov. 5, 1789; mary, born nov. 20, 1791." — P III 1 3 1
& who is not much above 20, I am sorry to say, is almost — S 5 385 1
Sidney Parker was about 7 or 8 & 20, very good-looking, — S 12 425 1
200L. (1)
did not make more than 200l. per annum, and though it is — SS III 3 282 19
22D (3)
induced him to fix on the 22d, as the most eligible day. — MP II 8 253 7
Portsmouth on the 24th; the 22d would therefore be the — MP II 8 253 7
the 22d herself, as by far the best day for the purpose. — MP II 8 254 7
23D (2)
On the 23d he was going to a friend near Peterborough in — MP II 8 255 10
and my birth-day is the 23d--just a fortnight and a day's — E I 4 30 17
24TH (2)
William was required to be at Portsmouth on the 24th; the — MP II 8 253 7
should dine out, on the 24th of December) had been spent — E I 13 108 5
26TH OF NOVEMBER (1)
We have not met since the 26th of November, when we were — PP III 2 262 8
26TH ULT. (1)
the event of the 26th ult., as you will conclude, — E III 14 440 8
28TH (3)
will come; we cards for her first party on the 28th.-- — MP III 9 394 1
Mr. John Knightley must be in town again on the 28th, and — E I 9 79 63
Weymouth, and dated sept. 28th--and began, 'my dear madam,' — E I 11 96 24
29TH OF SEPTEMBER (1)
She could not think of much else on the 29th of September; — P III 6 48 16
2D (2)
chance of seeing the 2d lieutenant of H. M. S. Thrush, in — MP III 6 368 8
whom her 2d husband had hoped to make a good bargain for.-- — S 3 376 1
2DLY (1)
as some of his friends; 2dly, that his father had made a — MP I 3 24 4
6 (4)
little woman of 5 or 6 & 30, to a lady who was standing — W 330 11
"Gracechurch-Street, Sept. 6. — PP III 10 321 2
without spending at least 6 weeks by the sea every year.-- — S 2 373 1
were off yesterday morng at 6--, left Chichester at the — S 9 409 1
7 (6)
I thought myself sure of you at 7. — LS 33 303 1
since he was 7 years old--but my father reckons us alike." — W 324 3
The entrance of the tea things at 7 o'clock was some — W 326 7
or Willingden Abbots, & lies 7 miles off, on the other — S 1 366 1
happily married 7 years--& had 4 sweet children at home;-- — S 2 371 1
Sidney Parker was about 7 or 8 & 20, very good-looking, — S 12 425 1
7TH OF NOVEMBER (1)
long ago as the 7th of November, (as I am going to read to — E II 1 161 29
8 (7)
At a little before 8, the tomlinsons carriage was heard to — W 327 7
"He has about 8 or 900l a year I beleive.-- — W 328 8
after tea, that he was going home to an 8 o'clock dinner.-- — W 355 28
"For whether he dined at 8 or 9, as he observed, was a — W 356 28
me in the face at this very moment, numbers 3, 4 & 8. — S 7 402 1
, the corner house may be too large for them, but either — S 7 402 1
Sidney Parker was about 7 or 8 & 20, very good-looking, — S 12 425 1
8 OR 9000 L (1)
To find yourself, instead of heiress of 8 or 9000 L, sent — W 352 26
8G (1)
secured a proper house at 8g pr week for Mrs G.--; she had — S 10 414 1
8TH (2)
I once saw Henry the 8th acted.-- — MP III 3 338 13
"He was four-and-twenty the 8th of last June, and my birth- — E I 4 30 17
9 (3)
from the White Hart, to be at osborne castle by 9.--" — W 323 3
will throw off at Stanton wood on Wednesday at 9 o'clock.-- — W 347 21
"For whether he dined at 8 or 9, as he observed, was a — W 356 28
9 OR 10 O'CLOCK (1)
warm last Saturday about 9 or 10 o'clock in the eveng--? — W 358 28

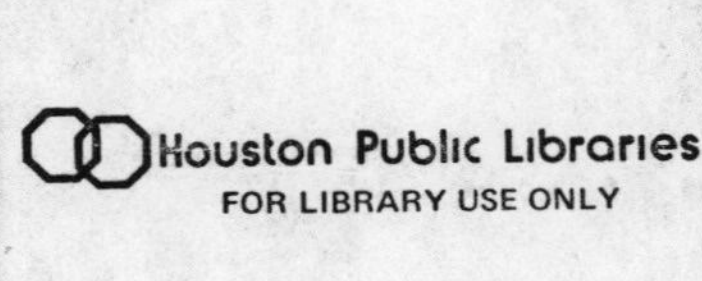
Houston Public Libraries
FOR LIBRARY USE ONLY